SIGNS USED ON THE JACKET

Basilisk or cockatrice, a fabulous reptile hatched from a cock's egg; its breath and look were fatal.

BOTTOM FRONT

Maori hei-tiki, a grotesque amulet representing a fetus, carved from greenstone. These ornaments were kept in memory of dead friends and ancestors.

Balinese tjili, silhouette of a girl with headdress of flowers. Presumably once associated with the "rice mother," now a feminine abstract motif used on temple offerings and altar ornaments.

BACK

Figure in the dance, a Bushman rock painting from Cape Province in South Africa. Painting in this style dates from seventy-five to several thousand years ago.

Animal shape adapted to the geometric style of porcupine-quill embroidery; example of work of the Delaware tribe.

Animal painting on Tiahuanaco beaker (central coast of Peru, pre-Inca).

Woman with conventionalized tulip, an early American appliqué design from a quilt.

The eye that wards off evil, commonly introduced in designs of the Mediterranean area; from a piece of modern Egyptian appliqué work.

Navaho sand painting, from the Shooting Chant. Such paintings are done under the direction of a medicine man and must be completed and destroyed in one day.

Alligator, silhouette, from Nicoya polychrome ware (Costa Rica-Nicaragua area, pre-conquest).

Ironwork inn sign, from the Fox Inn, Huntingdon, England (probably 18th century).

Funk & Wagnalls

STANDARD DICTIONARY

of

FOLKLORE, MYTHOLOGY, AND LEGEND

FUNK & WAGNALLS

STANDARD DICTIONARY OF

FOLKLORE

MYTHOLOGY AND LEGEND

MARIA LEACH, EDITOR JEROME FRIED, ASSOCIATE EDITOR

FUNK & WAGNALLS NEW YORK

CONSULTANTS

Melville J. Herskovits

Alexander H. Krappe

MacEdward Leach

Erminie W. Voegelin

Library of Congress Cataloging in Publication Data

Main entry under title:

Funk & Wagnalls standard dictionary of folklore, mythology, and legend.

   "Key to countries, regions, cultures, culture areas, peoples, tribes, and ethnic groups": p.
   Reissue of the 1949–50 ed. with minor corrections.
   1. Folk-lore—Dictionaries. I. Leach, Maria, ed.
II. Freid, Jerome, ed.
GR35.F82   398'.042   72-78268

Manufactured in the United States of America

ISBN 0-308-40090-9

   3 4 5 6 7 8 9 10

PREFACE
TO THE ONE-VOLUME EDITION

This edition of *Funk & Wagnalls Standard Dictionary of Folklore, Mythology, and Legend* contains several hundred revisions, but it is complete and uncut, except for a few unimportant articles, or parts of articles, which have been replaced by more significant and useful material. The convenience gained by having the whole coverage in one book has long been needed and requested.

The significant feature of this one-volume edition is a key to the 2,405 countries, regions, cultures, culture areas, peoples, tribes, and ethnic groups presented or discussed in the book. Twelve major religions of the world, past and present, have been included in this supplement, because every religion creates its own culture, regardless of geographical place.

MARIA LEACH

PREFACE
TO THE ORIGINAL EDITION

This book is an experiment: an attempt to cut a cross section into the spiritual content of the world, an attempt to gather together in one place several thousand things heretofore scattered in learned journals, memoirs, monographs, manuscripts, rare and out-of-print books, records transcribed by working anthropologists and folklorists in the field,—and in people's heads. Completeness was an end never contemplated. Sir George and Lady Alice Gomme gave up their idea of compiling a folklore dictionary when, at the end of four years, they had filled two large volumes with the children's games of two small islands in the world (Alice B. Gomme: *Traditional Games of England, Scotland, and Ireland*, London, 1894–98). A dictionary of pan-Germanic beliefs and customs, songs, tales, proverbs, riddles was 28 years in the making and runs to four volumes (H. F. Feilberg: *Bidrag til en Ordbog over Jyske Almuesmål*, Copenhagen, 1886–1914); just the superstitions of Germany fill ten volumes (Hans Bachtold-Staubi and Eduard von Hoffman-Krayer: *Handwörterbuch der deutschen Aberglaubens*, Berlin-Leipzig, 1928). The archives of the nations contain folktales, songs, proverbs, riddles that would mount into millions if all totals were added. Completeness can never be an end until there comes an end to spontaneous song and creative symbol, or an end to the grim or humorous "saw" with which the human mind meets its situation.

Here are, however, gathered together a representative sampling of the gods of the world, the folk heroes, culture heroes, tricksters, and numskulls, . . . of the folklore of animals, birds, plants, insects, stones, gems, minerals, stars, . . . dances, ballads, folk songs, . . . festivals and rituals, . . . food customs and their significances, . . . games and children's rimes, riddles, tongue twisters, . . . diviners and "lookmen," witches, witchcraft, omens, magic charms and spells, . . . supernatural impregnations, . . . and the supernatural beings of folk belief and story, such as demons, ogres, fairies, and "little people," guardian spirits, werewolves, vampires, zombies. Here are folktales—and motifs out of folktale, ballad, and song. Here are the kings asleep in the mountain, the belief in the hero, or savior, who will come again, and some hundred other instances of the inextinguishable hope that all that is wrong in the world can somehow be put right, and the ways (magic, prayer, or song) in which men try to put things right. In addition are the general covering regional articles and articles on specific folklore subjects (ballad, dance, riddles, etc.) by specialists in those respective fields.

The book is called a dictionary, in that, as stated above, it can not be exhaustive, and in that it deals with the terminology of a special branch of knowledge.

Many things are included because of their great diffusion, known importance, or fame, others for their uniqueness or obscurity. Often what looks like a nonce occurrence of a motif or practice turns out to be a clue to something huge or widespread but hitherto unguessed, or a touchstone to the philosophy of a culture.

The book belongs to no "school" of folklore, adheres to no "method," advocates no "theory." It has tried to represent all schools, all methods, all theories, and to state their findings and dilemmas. Each contributor has been free to hold to his own convictions, enthusiasms, and skepticisms. All is valid that represents the state and scope of the folklore field today. The twenty-six definitions entered under FOLKLORE in the book represent the varying and controversial points of view of modern folklore scholarship.

The material is not divided into rigid percentages. Out of the many cultures touched upon, Greek and Roman myth and religion have probably been more sparingly treated than any other, because these are the best known, and most voluminously written. Those parts of Greek and Roman culture most inextricably involved in other folklores, however, have been treated with especial care (e.g. Cronus the swallower, the wonder-working Twins, Hercules the strong man, Perseus the dragon slayer). American Indian and Negro (Old and New World) have received somewhat fuller representation because of the new materials which keep piling up and pouring in, and because of the growing wave of interest in these peoples.

Statements of location throughout the book, such as those placing a belief in West Africa, a tale in central Europe, a practice among the Eskimos, etc., do not mean that *all* the people so named throughout the region are involved, but that the term is used *among* and *by* some of the people named, not necessarily a majority, and within the region named. *Hoodoo hand* is not a term common to *all* "southern United States Negroes," for instance, but since the term is used by southern United States Negroes it must be thus identified and located.

In the case of transliteration from non-Roman alphabets, the book has accepted the systems of its contributing specialists. Spellings of Hindu names follow those adopted in the Penzer-Tawney *Ocean of Story*. Irish spellings, for the most part throughout the book, follow the Irish system of showing aspiration of a consonant by the superior dot, rather than by adding *h* to the aspirated consonant (formerly a more common transliteration). In regard to the names from Greek mythology, however, the familiar spelling has been given preference, with the idea that such choice will not confuse the scholar, whereas such transliterations as *Iachkos* (instead of the more widely used *Iacchus*) would not be as acceptable to the general reader. The same preference has been followed with many words from Egyptian and the Semitic languages.

The editor wants to express the deepest gratitude to the four consultants in this work and to all the contributors. Everybody who has been asked to help has gone the second mile with enthusiasm and generosity. Above all I am indebted to my associate editor, Jerome Fried, for advice and knowledge, unfailing support, and persevering work.

MARIA LEACH

CONTENTS

CONTRIBUTORS

BALYS, JONAS (1909–) [JB]
Lithuanian folklorist and ethnologist. Universities of Kaunas, Lithuania, and Graz and Vienna, Austria. Leader of newly founded Lithuanian Folklore Archives, 1935; Dozent of Folklore, University of Vilnius, Lithuania, 1942. Associate member, Lithuanian Academy of Sciences, 1941; later Director of the Institute of Ethnology at the Academy. Assistant for the *Deutsches Volksliedarchiv* (German Folksong Archives), Freiburg i. Br., 1944–45; Associate Professor for Folklore and Ethnology, Baltic or Displaced Persons University, Hamburg, Germany, 1946–47; since Oct. 1948, Instructor in the Eastern European Area, and Researches Assistant to the Dean of the Graduate School, Indiana University. Member, International Commission on Folk Arts and Folklore. Chief published works: *Motiv-Index of Lithuanian Narrative Folklore* (1935); *Donner und Teufel in den Volkserzählungen der baltischen und skandinavischen Völker* (1939); *Lithuanian Folk Legends*, Vol. I (1940); *Hundert Folk Ballads* (1941); *Lithuanian Folk Tales* (1945); "Litauische Hochzeitsbräuche," *Contributions of Baltic University*, No. 9 (1946); "Litauische Fastnachtsbräuche," *Schweizerisches Archiv für Volkskunde*, Bd. 45, pp. 40–69 (1948); *Handbook of Lithuanian Folklore*, 2 vols. (1948); "Die Sagen von den litauischen Feen," *Die Nachbarn*, I (1948).

BARBEAU, MARIUS (1883–1969) [MB]
Anthropologist and folklorist for Canadian government, National Museum of Canada, 1911-1949. Specialist in ethnology and history of Huron-Iroquois, and tribes of northern Rockies and Pacific Coast. Student of French and Indian lore of the frontiers, in connection with American Folklore Society, 1915. President, American Folklore Society, 1917; co-editor, *Journal of American Folklore*, since 1917. Pioneer in French folklore collection. Held professorships at both the universities of Laval and Montreal. Bio-bibliography published by Clarisse Cardin (*Archives de Folklore*, II, 1947): 576 titles to end of 1946.

BASCOM, WILLIAM R. (1912–) [WRB]
Anthropologist. B.A., University of Wisconsin, 1933; M.A., 1936; Ph.D., Northwestern University, 1939. Field work: summer 1935, among Kiowa Indians of Oklahoma; 1937–38, among Yoruba of Nigeria as Fellow of the Social Science Research Council of New York City; summer 1939, among New World Negroes in Georgia and South Carolina; 1942–45, three trips to West Africa as U.S. Government employee in Nigeria and the Gold Coast; 1946, Ponape, Eastern Caroline Islands; summer 1948, Cuba, on grant from The Viking Fund. Assistant Professor in Anthropology, Northwestern University, 1946– . Publications: *The Sociological Role of the Yoruba Cult Group*, Memoir 63, American Anthropological Association; "West and Central Africa," in *Most of the World* (edited by Ralph Linton); "The Sanctions of Ifa Divination," *Journal of the Royal Anthropological Institute*; "The Relationship of Yoruba Folklore to Divining" and "Literary Style in Yoruba Riddles," *Journal of American Folklore*; "The Principle of Seniority in the Social Structure of the Yoruba" and "West Africa and the Complexity of Primitive Culture," *American Anthropologist*; "Ponapean Prestige Economy," *Southwestern Journal of Anthropology*, and other articles.

BOGGS, RALPH STEELE (1901–) [RSB]
Panamerican and Spanish folklore scholar. Ph.B., University of Chicago, 1926; Ph.D., 1930. Instructor, University of Puerto Rico, 1926–28; Professor of Spanish and Folklore, University of North Carolina, from 1929. Director, Folklore Americas, an association of folklorists of the New World; member of many organizations in the field. Bibliography: annual classified and commented Bibliography in the March number of *Southern Folklore Quarterly; Index of Spanish Folktales (FFC #90,* 1930); *Folklore, an Outline for Individual and Group Study* (1929); *Spanish Folktales* (1932); *Leyendas épicas de España* (1935); *Three Golden Oranges and Other Spanish Folktales* (1936); *Outline History of Spanish Literature* (1937); *Bibliografía del folklore mexicano* (1939); *Bibliography of Latin American Folklore* (1940); *Clasificación del Folklore* (1954); *Folklore en los Estados Unidos* (1954); and many articles.

BOTKIN, BENJAMIN ALBERT (1901–) [BAB]
American folklorist. A.B., Harvard University, 1920; A.M.,
Columbia University, 1921; Ph.D., University of Nebraska, 1931. University of Oklahoma faculty, 1921–40. Julius Rosenwald Fellow, 1937–38; resigned from University of Oklahoma to pursue government work, 1940. Folklore editor, Federal Writers' Project, 1938–39; chief editor, Writers' Unit, Library of Congress Project, 1940–41; Associate Fellow in folklore, Library of Congress, 1940–41; Fellow of Library of Congress in folklore since 1941. Chief, Archive of American Folk Song, Library of Congress, 1942–45; resigned to give full time to writing, 1945. President, Oklahoma Folklore Society, 1928–40; President, American Folklore Society, 1944. Co-founder and first chairman, Joint Committee on Folk Arts, WPA, 1938–39. Editor: *Folk-Say, A Regional Miscellany*, 4 vols. (1929–32); *The Southwest Scene* (1931); *A Treasury of American Folklore* (1944); *Lay My Burden Down: A Folk History of Slavery* (1945); *Folk Music of the United States from Records in the Archive of American Folk Song*, Albums VII–X (1945); *A Treasury of New England Folklore* (1947); *A Treasury of Southern Folklore* (1949). Author: *The American Play-Party Song, with a Collection of Oklahoma Texts and Tunes* (doctoral dissertation, University Studies, University of Nebraska) (1937).

BRAKELEY, THERESA C. [TCB]
Writer and editor. B.A., Radcliffe College, 1934. Formerly member of editorial staff, Funk & Wagnalls Company. Writer and editor in book, magazine, advertising fields. Member, American Folklore Society.

ESPINOSA, AURELIO MACEDONIO (1880–1959) [AME]
American Spanish dialectologist and folklorist. B.A., University of Colorado, 1902; M.A., 1904; Ph.D., University of Chicago, 1909. Professor of Modern Languages, University of New Mexico, 1902–10. From 1910, Assistant Professor, Associate Professor, and Professor of Romanic Languages, Stanford University; retired, 1947. Investigator and productive scholar in Spanish dialectology, folklore, and metrics; over 100 articles published in philological and folklore journals in Europe and America in these fields; in addition, eight volumes in Spanish dialectology, folklore, and literature. Among these: *Estudios sobre el español de Nuevo Méjico*, 2 vols. (1930, 1945); *Cuentos populares españoles*, 3 vols. (1946–47); *Historia de la literatura española* (1939). In 1920, collected folklore materials in Spain under auspices of American Folklore Society. Editor, *Hispania*, 1917–26; Associate Editor, *Journal of American Folklore*, 1916–37, and *Language*, 1925–28. President, American Folklore Society, 1923, 1924. 1922, King Alfonso XIII conferred upon him the title of Knight Commander of the Royal Order of Isabel la Católica; 1946, Spanish government conferred the title of Knight of the Grand Cross of Alfonso el Sabio.

FOSTER, GEORGE M. (1913–) [GMF]
American anthropologist. B.S., Northwestern University, 1935; Ph.D., University of California, 1941. Joined Institute of Social Anthropology of the Smithsonian Institution, 1943; taught anthropology at the National School of Anthropology, Mexico City; took students into the field for ethnological studies, primarily among the Tarascan Indians of Michoacan and neighboring mestizo peoples. Director of the Institute of Social Anthropology, Washington, 1946. Research among the Yuki Indians of northern California (1938), Popoluca Indians of Vera Cruz, Mexico (1940 and 1941). Articles on California Indians and folklore, Mexican and Latin American ethnology, linguistics, folklore, primitive economics, etc. Monographs: *A Primitive Mexican Economy* (1942); *A Summary of Yuki Culture* (1944); *Sierra Popoluca Folklore and Beliefs* (1944); *Empire's Children: The People of Tzintzuntzan* (1948); *Sierra Popoluca Speech* (with Mary L. Foster, 1948).

FUNK, CHARLES EARLE (1881–1957) [CEF]
American lexicographer. B.S., University of Colorado, 1904. Co-editor, with Dr. Frank H. Vizetelly, *New Comprehensive Standard Dictionary*; associate editor, *New Standard Encyclopedia* and *New International Yearbooks*, 1931–38. Editor-in-chief of the Funk & Wagnalls Standard Dictionaries and *New International Year Books*, 1938–47; produced *Junior Standard Dictionary* (1940); *New Practical Standard Dictionary* (1946). *New College Standard Dictionary* (1947). Honorary degree of Doctor of Letters, Wittenberg College, Springfield, Ohio, 1936. Author: *What's the Name, Please* (1936); *25,000 Words, Accented, Spelled, and Divided* (with L. A. Leslie, 1932); *A Hog*

on Ice, and Other Curious Expressions (1948); various articles for magazine publication.

GASTER, THEODOR H. (1906–)   [THG]
M.A., University of London, 1936; Ph.D., Columbia University, 1942. Professor of Comparative Religion and Folklore, Asia Institute, New York; Visiting Professor of Comparative Religion, Dropsie College, Philadelphia; Lecturer in Semitic Civilizations, New York University. Formerly: Chief, Hebraic Section, The Library of Congress, Washington, D.C.; Curator, Department of Semitic and Egyptian Antiquities, The Wellcome Museum, London. Hon. Lecturer in Old Testament Archaeology, New College, University of London, 1937. Member of Council, Folk-Lore Society of England, 1937–43. Fellow, Royal Asiatic Society. Visiting Professor of Old Testament, University of Chicago, 1948. Author of numerous studies in religions and civilizations of the Ancient Near East in: *Journal of the Royal Asiatic Society; Journal of the American Oriental Society; Journal of Near Eastern Studies; Folk-Lore; Religions; Review of Religion; Journal of Biblical Literature; Palestine Exploration Quarterly; Iraq; Archiv Orientalni; Studi e Materiali di Storia delle Religioni; Orientalia; Archiv fuer Orientforschung; Jewish Quarterly Review; Expository Times,* etc. Prominent in the interpretation of the recently discovered Canaanite literature of Ras Shamra–Ugarit. His major work, *Thespis: Ritual, Myth and Drama in the Ancient Near East,* was published in 1950.

HARMON, MAMIE (1906–)   [MH]
Artist and editor. B.A., Wesleyan College, 1926; M.A., University of Chicago, 1927. Studied art with Chinese tutors and in Paris, and at the Art Students' League of New York. Lived abroad, 1928–32, and observed at first hand the folk art of a number of countries. During the following decade, became associate editor, The New International Year Books and the Standard Dictionaries, writing on art and art terminology. Prepared a standard textbook in the fine arts, *The Natural Way to Draw* (1941), a posthumous resumé of the teaching methods of Kimon Nicolaides. Particularly interested in symbolism as a practicing artist; also active in graphic arts. Member, American Institute of Graphic Arts.

HERSKOVITS, MELVILLE JEAN (1895–1963)   [MJH]
Anthropologist. Ph.B., University of Chicago, 1920; M.A., Columbia University, 1921; Ph.D., 1923. Professor of Anthropology, Northwestern University, 1935– . Guggenheim Memorial Fellow, 1937–38. Led field expeditions in Dutch Guiana, West Africa, Haïti, Trinidad, Brazil. Member and chairman of various committees on music and anthropology for the Department of State, National Research Council, American Council of Learned Societies. Member, permanent council, International Anthropological Congress. Officer of the Order of Honor and Merit, Haiti. Honorary Fellow, Royal Anthropological Institute; Fellow, American Association for the Advancement of Science (vice president, section H, 1934), Society for Research in Child Development. Member, American Anthropological Association (councilor; president, central section, 1939), American Association of Physical Anthropologists, American Folklore Society (president, 1945), Societé des Africanistes de Paris, International African Institute (member, governing body), International Institute for Afro-American Studies. Editor, *American Anthropologist,* 1949– . Bibliography: *The American Negro—A Study in Racial Crossing* (1928); *The Anthropometry of the American Negro* (1930); *An Outline of Dahomean Religious Beliefs* (with Frances S. Herskovits, 1933); *Rebel Destiny, Among the Bush Negroes of Dutch Guiana* (with F. S. Herskovits, 1934); *Suriname Folklore* (with F. S. Herskovits) *with transcription of Suriname Songs and Musicological Analysis by Dr. M. Kolinski* (1937); *Dahomey, an Ancient West African Kingdom,* 2 vols. (1938); *Acculturation* (1938); *The Economic Life of Primitive Peoples* (1940); *The Myth of the Negro Past* (1941); *Backgrounds of African Art* (1946); *Trinidad Village* (with F. S. Herskovits, 1947); *Man and His Works* (1948); many articles in journals, reviews, collections, etc.

HERZOG, GEORGE (1901–)   [GH]
Primitive and folk music and folklore scholar. Hungarian Academy of Music, Budapest, 1917–19; Hochschule fuer Musik, Berlin, 1920–22; University of Berlin, 1922–24; Columbia University, 1925–29; Ph.D., Columbia University, 1938. Assistant, Phonograph Archives, University of Berlin, 1922–24; Assistant Professor in Anthropology, 1932–35, Yale University, and 1936–48, Columbia University; Professor of Anthropology, Indiana University, 1948– . In charge, 1930–31, University of Chicago expedition to Liberia; 1939, Columbia University field party

for the study of Comanche language and culture. In charge, 1941–48, Archives of Primitive Music, Columbia University. See ARCHIVES OF FOLK AND PRIMITIVE MUSIC, INDIANA UNIVERSITY. His field work includes studies and surveys of Southwestern Indian music (1927), Dakota Indian poetry and music (1928), Maine folk songs (1929), Navaho Indian poetry and music (1929, 1931, 1932), Pima Indian poetry, language, and music (1929, 1933, 1936), Eastern Liberian music, language, poetry, and native cultures (1930–31), the music of the Indian tribes represented at the Chicago World's Fair (1933), Comanche Indian language and music (1939). He has also made various studies of American Indian, African, Micronesian, Siberian music; Hungarian and Jugoslav folk music; Jugoslav epic poetry; Jewish ritual music; American Indian poetry; African drum-signalling. He has collected and recorded some 3,000 primitive and folk melodies. His bibliography, in addition to many articles in journals, includes *Jabo Proverbs from Liberia* (with Charles G. Blooah, 1936); *The Cowtail Switch and Other West African Stories* (with Harold Courlander, 1947); transcriptions of melodies in P. Barry, F. Eckstorm, M. Smith, *British Ballads from Maine* (1929); "Die Musik auf Truk" in A. Kraemer, *Truk* (1933); "Die Musik der Karolinen-Inseln" in A. Eilers, *Westkarolinen,* vol. 2 (1936); "Research in Primitive and Folk Music in the United States—A Survey," *Bulletin 24, American Council of Learned Societies* (1936); transcriptions of melodies in John A. and Alan Lomax, *Negro Folk Songs as Sung by Lead Belly* (1936); "A Comparison of Pueblo and Pima Musical Styles," *JAFL* 49: 283–417; "Etats-Unis d'Amerique" in *Folklore Musical—Musique et Chansons Populaires* (1939); transcription and analysis of Tutelo music in F. G. Speck, *The Tutelo Spirit Adoption Ceremony* (1942).

JAKOBSON, ROMAN, (1896–)   [RJ]
Slavic philologist and folklorist. Lazarev Institute of Oriental Languages, 1914; Universities of Moscow and Petersburg, 1914–16; organized Moscow Linguistic Circle, 1915, chairman to 1920; field work in Russian dialectology and folklore, sponsored by Russian Academy of Sciences, 1915–16; Buslaev Prize, Moscow University, for monograph on the language of northern Russian *byliny,* 1916; research associate to Chair of Russian Language and Literature, Moscow University, 1918; Charles University, Prague, 1920–21; created, with Professor V. Mathesius, Cercle Linguistique de Prague, 1926, vice president to 1939; Prague University, Ph.D., 1930, dissertation: comparative study of Slavic epic decasyllables; created, with N. Trubetzkoy, International Phonological Association, 1930, secretary to World War II; professor, Russian philology and Old Czech literature, Masaryk University, Brno, 1933–39; lectured, Copenhagen, Oslo, Uppsala Universities, 1939–41; Professor, general linguistics and Czechoslovak studies, École Libre des Hautes Études, New York, since 1942; Professor (general linguistics, later Slavic philology), Columbia University, 1943–49; Samuel H. Cross Professor of Slavic Languages and Literatures, Harvard University, since 1949. Member, Norwegian Academy of Sciences; Danish Royal Academy of Sciences; Bohemian Royal Society of Sciences; Finno-Ugric Society (Helsinki). President, International Council of Acta Linguistica (Copenhagen). Principal publications: *Newest Russian Poetry* (1921); *Czech Verse as Compared with Russian* (1925); *Two Old Czech Poems on Death* (1927); *Remarques sur l'évolution phonologique du russe* (1929); *Characteristics of the Eurasian Linguistic Affinity* (1931); *Old Czech Verse* (1934); *Beitrag zur allgemeinen Kasuslehre* (1936); *Description of Mácha's Verse* (1938); *Kindersprache, Aphasie und allgemeine Lautgesetze* (1941); *Wisdom of Ancient Czechs* (1943); *La Geste d'Igor'* (with H. Grégoire and M. Szeftel; 1948); *Russian Epic Studies* (with E. Simmons; 1949).

JAKOBSON, SVATAVA PÍRKOVÁ   [SPJ]
Slavic linguist and folklore scholar. Prague Classical Gymnasium; Collège d'Angoulême, France; Ph.D., Charles University, Prague, 1933. Research Fellow, Social Institute of the City of Prague, 1933–35. Fieldwork in folklore, 1931–33, in Czechoslovakia, and 1935–37, in Bulgaria. Study trips to Poland (1930), Yugoslavia (1930), Rumania (1935), Hungary (1937). Contributor to the folklore sections of *Sociální Problémy* and *Sociologická Revue.* Produced, witn Prof. Ulehla, "The Vanishing World," 1932, an ethnographic sound film devoted to Moravian popular traditions, exhibited both in Europe and America. Studied Scandinavian literature and oral tradition and the organization of Scandinavian ethnographic museums, 1939–41, in Denmark, Norway, and Sweden. École Libre des

Hautes Études, New York, 1942–46, teaching Czech language and literature. Compiled anthology of folk songs of the United Nations for the State Department's world broadcasts, 1943–44. Lecturer in Czech and Slovak language, literature, and oral tradition, Columbia University, 1943– Lecturer of Slavic Languages and Literatures (Oral and Written), Harvard University, 1949– . Lectured on Slavic folklore at Connecticut Academy, 1946; American Folklore Institute, Indiana University, 1946; American Folklore Society, Chicago, 1946; Brooklyn College, 1948. Member, American Folklore Society and Editorial Committee for the Handbook of this Society. After 6 years of intensive field work in Czech and Slovak folklore in America, she established an archive of American Slavic folklore, including manuscript records, wire recordings, a collection of original handwritten and printed song books, diaries, etc.; distributed a questionnaire among American immigrants and natives of Czech and Slovak background and published the results in the *New Yorske Listy*, 1943–45.

JAMESON, RAYMOND DELOY (1895–1959)   [RDJ]
Scholar of Chinese folklore, history, and literature. Studied and lectured at Universities of Wisconsin, Chicago, Montpellier, Florence, Vienna, and London, 1913–25. Employed in several capacities by the Ministry of Education of the National Chinese Government, 1925–38. Administrator of Consultant Services, Library of Congress, Washington, D.C., 1938–42. American National Red Cross, Consulting Historian, 1942–48. Publications: *Three Lectures on Chinese Folklore*, 1932; other publications on social history, history of literature, etc.

JOFFE, NATALIE F.   [NFJ]
Cultural anthropologist. B.A., Barnard College, 1934; Ph.D., Columbia University, 1940. Studied acculturation among Fox Indians of Iowa, 1937; research on food habits of primitive peoples with V. Stefansson, 1938–41; with Committee on Food Habits, National Research Council, 1942–44; researching food habits of selected groups in the United States, in connection with problems of wartime emergency feeding; also worked on group reactions to concentrated emergency foods. Prepared material on food habits of seven cultures and culture areas for Common Council for American Unity. Work on cultural backgrounds of female puberty for seven Western culture groups, 1946; staff of Research in Contemporary Cultures, Columbia University, analyzing culture of East European Jews, 1947– . Author of articles and monographs on foods and food patterns in various magazines and journals.

JONES, LOUIS CLARK (1908–)   [LCJ]
Folklorist, museum director; specialist in New York State folklore, American folk art, folklore of the supernatural. B.A., Hamilton College, 1930; M.A., 1931, Ph.D., Columbia University, 1941. Long Island University, Department of English, 1931–32; Syracuse University, 1933–34; New York State College for Teachers, Albany, 1934–46. Executive Director, New York State Historical Association since 1947, including directorship of The Farmers' Museum. Guggenheim Fellowship, 1946, analysis of folklore of supernatural collected by over 1000 students he had trained. Field work in various parts of New York State; organized Folklore Archive now at Farmers' Museum; a founder of New York Folklore Society; editor of its Quarterly 1945–50. Vice president, American Folklore Society, 1950. Editor, *New York History*; editorial board, *American Heritage*. Author: *Club of the Georgian Rakes* (1941); *Spooks of the Valley* (1948); *Cooperstown* (1949); various articles in folklore and historical publications.

KRAPPE, ALEXANDER HAGGERTY (1894–1947)   [AHK]
International scholar, folklorist, and linguist. Early schooling in England, Holland, Germany; student of Romance languages and medieval history, University of Berlin. A.M., University of Iowa, 1917; Ph.D., University of Chicago, 1919. Assistant Professor, University of Minnesota, 1924–28; Graduate Lecturer, Columbia University, 1926, 1928; private scholar, 1928–1947. Member: (British) Folk-Lore Society (1922), American Folklore Society (1942). Delegate, Folk-Lore Congress, London, 1928. Hon. Fellow, American-Scandinavian Foundation (1930). Corresponding Member, Hispanic Society of America (1930); full Member (1934); awarded the Medal of Arts and Literature of the Society, 1945. Membre correspondant, Société de Correspondance Hispanique, Bordeaux (1940). Membre de l'Institut de Philologie et d'Histoire Orientales et Slaves et Professeur titulaire, Université Libre de Bruxelles (1944). His bibliography includes *The Legend of Roderick* (1923); *Balor with the Evil Eye* (1927); *Études de mythologie et de folklore germaniques* (1928); *The Science of Folk-Lore* (1930); *Mythologie universelle* (1930); *La Genèse des Mythes* (1938). Articles and monographs have appeared in *Folk-Lore, Modern Language Review, Romania, Revue Hispanique, Bulletin Hispanique, Revue Celtique, Revue Archéologique, Revue des études anciennes, Revue des études grecques, Le Moyen Age, Revue des études slaves, Revue de l'histoire des religions, Mercure de France, Nuovi Studi Medievali, Studi e Materiali di Soria delle Religioni, Lares, Rheinisches Museum f. Philologie, Archiv f. d. Studium d. neueren Sprachen, Neuphilologische Mitteilungen, Mitteilungen d. Schlesischen Gesellschaft f. Volkskunde, Neophilologus, Journal of the American Oriental Society, Classical Philology, Speculum, Philological Quarterly, California Folklore Quarterly*, etc.

KURATH, GERTRUDE PROKOSCH (Tula) (1903–)   [GPK]
Dancer and folk dance scholar. B.A., Bryn Mawr College, 1922; M.A., 1928; Yale School of Drama, 1929–30. Professional dance training in several systems: Wigman, Humphrey-Weidman, Mensendieck, Dalcroze, Shawn, Russian ballet, folk dance (particularly English and Morris dancing at Bryn Mawr). Special research in Medieval and Renaissance dance and music and American folk themes, 1932–46. Produced dance dramas to specially composed music: *Hurricane, Francis of Assisi, The Legend of Sleepy Hollow, The Marriage of the Moon*; research on American Indian dances for *Marriage of the Moon*, 1936, and continuously since 1942. Field work in Mexico, 1946; Sauk and Fox Indians, 1945, 1947; Iroquois Indians (Cayuga of Six Nations Reserve, Seneca of Allegany Reservation), 1948. Member, American Folklore Society (on Education Committee), American Anthropological Association, Archaeological Society of New Mexico. Treasurer, Michigan Folklore Society. Her bibliography includes numerous articles on dance theory and comparative study of the dance in journals and reviews.

LEACH, MACEDWARD (d. 1967)   [MEL]
American ballad scholar and collector. B.A., University of Illinois, 1916; M.A., 1917; Ph.D., University of Pennsylvania, 1926. Associate Professor of English, University of Pennsylvania. Secretary-Treasurer since 1941 of American Folklore Society. Since 1948, Liaison Fellow, American Anthropological Association. Member, Medieval Academy of America; Council of Learned Societies. Publications: *Amis and Amiloun*, Early English Text Society (1937); articles in various journals.

LOOMIS, ROGER SHERMAN (1887–1966)   [RSL]
Scholar in Celtic folklore and Arthurian romance. Williams College; Harvard University; B.Litt., New College, Oxford. Since 1920, at Columbia University; Professor of English, 1947– . Special interest in Celtic folklore and literature and their relation to Arthurian romance began in 1923; numerous articles in scholarly journals on the subject since then. Bibliography includes *Celtic Myth and Arthurian Romance* (1927); *Thomas of Britain, The Romance of Tristram and Ysolt*, revised edition (1931); *Arthurian Legends in Medieval Art* (with Laura Hibbard Loomis, 1938); *Arthurian Tradition and Chrétien de Troyes* (1949).

LUOMALA, KATHARINE   [KL]
Anthropologist. B.A., 1931; M.A., 1933; Ph.D., 1936, University of California. Study at Bernice P. Bishop Museum and field work among the Diegueño, 1934; ethnographical summary of Navaho culture and history, 1936–37; research fellowship, American Association of University Women, for study of mythology, 1937–38; Lecturer in Anthropology, University of California, and assistant to A. L. Kroeber in research on art of North and South American Indians, 1941; Yale University Fellow, Bernice P. Bishop Museum, for research in Polynesian anthropology, especially mythology, 1938–40; Assistant Head, Community Analysis Section, War Relocation Authority, 1944–46. At present, Assistant Professor in Anthropology, University of Hawaii (from 1946); Associate in Anthropology, Bernice P. Bishop Museum (from 1941); Associate Editor, Journal of American Folklore (from 1947); Fellow and Council Member, American Anthropological Association; Member, Society for Applied Anthropology, Polynesian Society, American Folklore Society, American Anthropological Association, Anthropological Society of Hawaii, Anthropological Society of Washington, D.C., American Association of University Professors. Her bibliography includes *Maui-of-a-thousand-tricks, His Oceanic and European Biographers* (in press); *The Native Dog of Polynesia in Culture and Myth* (in press); *Maui, Tinirau, and Rupe, Variations on a Polynesian Mythological Theme* (in press), "Missionary Contributions to Polynesian Anthropology"

in *Specialized Studies in Polynesian Anthropology* (1947); *Oceanic, American Indian and African Myths of Snaring the Sun* (1940); "Documentary Research in Polynesian Mythology," *Polynesian Soc., Jour.*, 49: 175–95 (1940); "Notes on the Development of Polynesian Hero Cycles," *Polynesian Soc., Jour.*, 49: 367–374 (1940); "More Notes on Ra'a," *Polynesian Soc., Jour.*, 49 (1940); "A Hero Among Gods," *International Quarterly* (1940); "Ho'opa'apa'a," *California Monthly* (Nov. 1938); *Navaho Life of Yesterday and Today* (1938); "Dreams and Dream Interpretations of the Diegueño Indians of Southern California" (with G. Toffelmeir), *Psychoanalytic Quarterly* 5: 195–225 (1936); publications on applied anthropology relating to the program of the War Relocation Authority, Department of Interior, in regard to American citizens and aliens of Japanese descent; and restricted reports on attitudinal surveys on various subjects in the U.S. for Program Surveys Division, Bureau of Agricultural Economics, U.S. Department of Agriculture.

MACDOUGALD, DUNCAN, JR. (1915–)   [DMD]
Philologist, musicologist. A.B., Princeton University, 1936; Universities of Berlin, Heidelberg, and Paris, Collège de France, Columbia University, 1936–39; former senior fellow (for sociological music research), Rockefeller Foundation. Member, American Anthropological Association, American Musicological Society, American Oriental Society. Bibliography includes: "The Popular Music Industry," *Radio Research* (1941); *The Languages and Press of Africa* (1944); "A Genealogical Classification of the World's Principal Languages" in *Funk & Wagnalls New Standard Dictionary* (1949); *The Kitchen and the Boudoir* (1950); volume one of *A Genealogical Classification of the World's Languages, Dialects and Systems of Writing* (ready for press). Editorial consultant, *The First Four Centuries of Organ Music* (1948), *Folk Dances of the Slavic Nations* (1950), *Songs to Grow On* (1950). Annotator, Program Notes, RCA Victor Red Seal Records, 1947–48; writer of several juvenile record albums.

MÉTRAUX, ALFRED (1902–1963)   [AM]
Anthropologist, ethnologist, and folklorist. Studied in Lausanne, Paris, and Gothemburg, Sweden. Graduate, National School of Oriental Languages, Paris; École des Hautes Études (Sorbonne); Docteur ès lettres, Sorbonne, 1928. Director, Institute of Ethnology, National University of Tucuman, Argentina, 1928–34. Editor, *Revista del Instituto de la Universidad de Tucuman*, the first international anthropological journal in Latin America, 1929– . Headed the French expedition to Easter Island, 1934. Staff member, Bernice P. Bishop Museum, Honolulu, 1935–37; visiting professor, University of California (Berkeley and Los Angeles) and Yale University, 1937–39; in South America, Guggenheim Foundation fellowship, 1939–41. Staff member, Bureau of Ethnology, Smithsonian Institution, for *Handbook of South American Indians*, 1941–43. Assistant Director, Institute of Social Anthropology, Smithsonian Institution, 1943–45; Director of Section Studies and Research, Department of Social Affairs, United Nations, 1946; United Nations Educational, Scientific, and Cultural Organization (UNESCO), 1948. Various anthropological expeditions in South America, mainly in the Argentine, Bolivia, and Paraguay, and many South Seas islands. At present, engaged in a wide anthropological survey of a Haitian valley in connection with UNESCO's pilot project in fundamental education. Many articles in scholarly journals and reviews, e.g. a series on the Uru-Chipaya of the central Andes in the *Journal de la Société des Américanistes de Paris*, 1935–36. Other publications: *La civilisation materielle des Tupi-Guarani* (1928); *The Ethnology of Easter Island* (1939); *L'Ile de Paques* (1942); *The Native Tribes of Eastern Bolivia and Western Matto Grosso* (1942); *Myths and Tales of the Pilaga Indians (Gran Chaco)* (1946).

MISH, JOHN LEON (1909–)   [JLM]
Scholar in Eastern studies. Universities of Breslau (1926–30) and Berlin (1930–34). Ph.D., Berlin, 1934. Then went to Poland, where he was at first Professor of Chinese and Japanese, later Deputy Director, of the School for Oriental Studies, Warsaw; concurrently, Instructor in Japanese, Warsaw University. Chinese Liaison Officer in Bombay for Government of India, 1941; King's Medal for Service in the Cause of Freedom (1946). Acting Chief, Oriental Division, New York Public Library, 1946– . Associate Professor of Japanese Language and History, School for Asiatic Studies, Asia Institute, New York. Publications include *The Conditional Sentence in Classical Chinese* (1936); articles in various periodicals (in this country, the

Saturday Review of Literature and *New York Public Library Bulletin*).

PHILLIPS, WILLIAM JOHN (1895–)   [WJP]
Educator, Pennsylvania Dutch folklorist, lecturer. B.A., 1920; M.A., 1924, Ph.D., 1930, University of Pennsylvania. Instructor, Assistant Professor of English, University of Pennsylvania, 1921–46; Associate Professor, Professor of English, Ursinus College, from 1946. Member, American Folklore Society, Modern Language Association of America.

POTTER, CHARLES FRANCIS (1885–1962)   [CFP]
Lecturer, author, clergyman. B.A., Bucknell University, 1907; M.A., 1916; B.D., Newton Theological Institution, 1913; S.T.M., 1917; Hon. Litt.D., De Landas University, 1940. Minister, Baptist churches, 1908–14; Unitarian churches, 1914–25; Universalist Church of the Divine Paternity, New York, 1927–29. Professor of Comparative Religion, Antioch College, 1925–27. Founder and Leader, First Humanist Society of New York, 1929– ; Founder and First President, Euthanasia Society of America, 1938– . Author of many books and magazine articles on comparative religion, folklore, and folk rimes. Bibliography includes *The Story of Religion, with Special Reference to Atavistic Survivals and Parallel Customs in Ethnic Religions and Modern Cults* (1929); *Humanism, A New Religion; Humanizing Religion; Is That In the Bible? Technique of Happiness; Beyond The Senses; The Preacher and I; Treasury of American Folkrime; Creative Personality.*

SEEGER, CHARLES (LOUIS) (1886–)   [CS]
Musician and musicologist. B.A., Harvard College, 1908. Professor of Music, University of California, 1912–19; lecturer and teacher, Institute of Musical Art and New School for Social Research, New York, 1921–35; Chief, Music Division, Pan American Union, 1941–48; Chief, Division of Music and Visual Arts, Pan American Union, 1948– . Member: Gesellschaft für Vergleichende Musikwissenschaft (vice president and acting president, 1934–35); New York Musicological Society (chairman, 1930–34); American Musicological Society (vice president, 1934–35; president, 1945–46); Société Internationale de Musicologie; American Folklore Society; Southeastern Folklore Society; Music Educators National Conference, Music Teachers National Association; Music Library Association; International Society for General Semantics. Miscellaneous musical compositions. Author: *Harmonic Structure and Elementary Composition* (with E. G. Strickler, 1916); *Folksong, U.S.A.* (with J. A. and Alan Lomax, and Ruth Seeger, 1947); many articles on music, special chapters, etc., in journals, surveys, encyclopedias.

SMITH, MARIAN W. (d. 1961)   [MWS]
Anthropologist, B.A., Barnard College, 1929; M.A., Columbia University, 1934; Ph.D., 1938. Field work: 1935–36, 1938, 1945, among American Indians of Washington and British Columbia; 1941–43 and during trip to India 1948–49, among Sikhs of New York, British Columbia, etc.; 1944–45, during war work, on Japanese culture. Taught anthropology at Barnard College, City College, Brooklyn College, New York University, Vassar College, Columbia University. Editor, American Ethnological Society; Secretary, Section H (Anthropology), American Association for the Advancement of Science; 1st Vice President, American Folklore Society. Books: *The Puyallup-Nisqually; Indians of the Urban Northwest* (in press); *Archaeology of the Columbia-Fraser Region* (in press). Articles and reviews of subjects relating to India, articles, etc., on anthropological subjects, in various journals.

TAYLOR, ARCHER (1890–)   [AT]
Germanic scholar and comparative folklorist. B.A., Swarthmore College, 1909; M.A., University of Pennsylvania, 1910; Ph.D., Harvard University, 1915. Instructor, Assistant Professor, Associate Professor, Washington University, 1915–25; Professor of German Literature, University of Chicago, 1925–39; Professor of Folklore, 1938–39; Professor of German, University of California, 1939– . Editor, *Journal of American Folklore* (1941); editor, *California Folklore Quarterly* (now *Western Folklore*), 1942– . Honorary member, Schweizerische Gesellschaft für Volkskunde; Gustav Adolfs Akademi för Folklivsforskning; Norsk Videnskabers Selskab (Oslo); Finnish Literary Society; Finno-Ugric Society; Finnish Academy of Sciences; Sociedad Folklórica Argentina; Sociedad Folklórica Mejicana; Folklore of Ireland Society; Fellow of the Medieval Academy; Fellow of the Newberry Library. Author: *The Proverb* (1931); *Edward and Sven i Rosengård: a Study in the Dissemination of a Ballad*

(1931); contributor to the *Handwörterbuch des deutschen Aberglaubens* and the *Handwörterbuch des deutschen Märchens; A Collection of Welsh Riddles* (with Vernam E. Hull, 1942); *The Literary Riddle Before 1600* (1948).

THOMPSON, STITH (1885–1970)   [ST]
Educator, author, folktale scholar. B.A., University of Wisconsin, 1909; M.A., University of California, 1912; Ph.D., Harvard University, 1914; Litt.D., University of North Carolina, 1946. Bonnheim Research Fellow from University of California to Harvard University, 1912–14; Professor of English, Colorado College, 1918–20; Associate Professor of English, University of Maine, 1920–21; Professor of English, Indiana University, 1929–39; Professor of English and Folklore, 1939– ; Dean of the Graduate school, 1947– . United States delegate and member of executive committee, International Folklore Congress, Paris, 1937; vice president, International Association for European Ethnology and Folklore Congress, Edinburgh, 1937; technical advisor in folklore to Ministry of Education of Venezuela, 1947; lectures throughout South America; director, Folklore Institute of America, 1947– . Member, American Folklore Society (president 1937–40); Modern Language Association of America; Medieval Academy of America; American Philosophical Society; honorary member, Gustav Adolfs Akademi för Folklivsforskning (Sweden); Société finno-ougrienne (Helsinki); Asociacion Folklorica Argentina; Sociedad Folklorica de Mexico; Folklore of Ireland Society; Sociedade Brasiliera de Folklore; Instituto de Investigaciones Folkloricas de la Universidad de Chile; Servicio de Investigaciones Folkloricas Nacionales (Venezuela); Folklore of the Americas. Author: *European Tales among the North American Indians* (1919); *The Types of the Folktale* (1928); *Tales of the North American Indians* (1929); *British Poets of the Nineteenth Century* (with Curtis H. Page, 1929); *Our Heritage of World Literature* (1938); *English Literature and Its Backgrounds* (with B. D. N. Grebanier, 1939); *Motif-Index of Folk-Literature*, 6 vols. (1932–37); *The Folktale* (1946).

VOEGELIN, ERMINIE W. (1903–)   [EWV]
Anthropologist and folklorist. B.A., University of California (Berkeley), 1923; M.A., 1931; Ph.D., Yale University, 1939. Field work: Tubatulabal (California); Shawnee (Oklahoma); Ojibwa (Michigan and Ontario); Klamath, Modoc, Shasta, Achomawi, Wintun, Maidu (California). Indiana Fellow in

Anthropology, Yale University, 1933–35; Research Associate in Anthropology, University of California (Berkeley), 1935; instructor in anthropology, Indiana University (Folklore Institute), 1943, 1945, 1946, 1947. Review editor, *Journal of American Folklore*, 1940; editor, 1941–46. President, American Folklore Society, 1948; Guggenheim Fellow for study of unwritten literature of native North America, 1948. Executive secretary, American Anthropological Association, 1947– . Fellow, American Anthropological Association; member, American Folklore Society, Indiana Academy of Science, California Folklore Society. Major publications: "Kiowa-Crow Mythological Affiliations," *American Anthropologist* 38 (1931); *Tubatulabal Ethnography*, Anthropological Records 2 (1938); *Culture Element Survey; Northeastern California*, Anthropological Records 10 (1940); *Mortuary Customs of the Shawnee and Other Eastern Woodlands Tribes*, Prehistory Research Series, vol. 2, no. 4 (1944); *Linguistic Map of North American Indians*, American Ethnological Society, Publication No. 21 (with C. F. Voegelin, 1944).

WATERMAN, RICHARD A. (1914–)   [RAW]
Anthropologist. B.A., Santa Barbara College, 1937; M.A., Claremont College, 1941; Ph.D., Northwestern University, 1943. Faculty, Northwestern University, 1943– . His publications include *Folk Songs of Puerto Rico*, Archive of American Folk Song, Library of Congress (1946); "Afro-Bahian Cult Music," *Boletin Latino-Americano de Musica*, Vol. 6 (with M. J. Herskovits, 1947); *Bibliography of Asiatic Musics*, serially published by *Notes* (journal of the Music Library Association) beginning with 2nd Series, Vol. V, No. 1 (Dec., 1947); " 'Hot' Rhythm in Negro Music," *Journal of the American Musicological Society*, Vol. 1, No. 1 (1948).

FRIED, JEROME   [JF]
GOTTLIEB, GERALD   [GG]
HAAS, SALLY PEPPER   [SPH]
HAZEN, JOHN W.   [JWH]
KJÖSTERUD-RANDBY, GUDLAUG   [GKR]
LEACH, MARIA   [ML]
ROTHMAN, JULIUS L.   [JLR]
SMITH, GRACE PARTRIDGE   [GPS]

ABBREVIATIONS

AA *American Anthropologist*
ARW *Archiv für Religionswissenschaft*
BASOR *Bulletin, American Schools of Oriental Research*
BBAE *Bulletin, Bureau of American Ethnology*
CFQ *California Folklore Quarterly*
Child *English and Scottish Popular Ballads*—F. J. Child (1882–98)
DGF *Danmarks gamle Folkeviser*—S. Grundtvig and A. Olrik (1853–1920)
ERE *Encyclopedia of Religion and Ethics*—J. Hastings (1908–27)
FFC *Folklore Fellows Communications*
FUF *Finnisch-Ugrische Forschungen*
GEG Gelehrten Esthnischen Gesellschaft
Grimm *Kinder- und Hausmärchen*—J. and W. Grimm (1812–57)
Jacobs *The Fables of Æsop*—J. Jacobs (1894)
IJAL *International Journal of American Linguistics*
JAFL *Journal of American Folklore*
JAOS *Journal of the American Oriental Society*
MAAA *Memoirs, American Anthropological Association*

MAFLS *Memoirs, American Folklore Society*
MIJAL *Memoirs, International Journal of American Linguistics*
MLN *Modern Language Notes*
MLQ *Modern Language Quarterly*
MLR *Modern Language Review*
MP *Modern Philology*
MSFO *Mémoires de la Société Finno-Ougrienne*
NYFQ *New York Folklore Quarterly*
PMLA *Publications of the Modern Language Association of America*
RBAE *Report, Bureau of American Ethnology*
REJ *Revue des Études Juives*
RHR *Revue de l'Histoire des Religions*
RLC *Revue de Littérature Comparée*
SATF *Société des Anciens Textes Français*
SBWA *Sitzungberichte der Berliner Akademie der Wissenschaften*
SFQ *Southern Folklore Quarterly*
ZDMG *Zeitschrift der Deutschen Morgenländischen Gesellschaft*
☞ Symbol indicating change of author within entry (article)

Numbers of folktale motifs, appearing as letters followed by numbers (e.g. S300–395), refer to Stith Thompson's *Motif-Index of Folk Literature* (1955–58).
Numbers of folktale types, appearing as the word

"Type" followed by a number (e.g. Type 145), refer to *The Types of the Folk-Tale* (1928), a translation and enlargement by Stith Thompson of Antti Aarne's *Verzeichnis der Märchentypen* (1910).

See also pp. xi–xv for contributors' initials.

Funk & Wagnalls

STANDARD DICTIONARY

of

FOLKLORE, MYTHOLOGY, AND LEGEND

These old myth-covering tales—whether we call them
Greek or Aryan or what else—are as the grass that will
grow in any land.

—Fiona Macleod, *Winged Destiny*

A la troisième fontaine. . . Car voilà, il y avait une
troisième fontaine. . .

—Henri Porrat, "Les Trois Fontaines,"
in *Le Trésor des Contes*

A

Aa In Assyrian and Babylonian religion, the consort of Shamash. Compare GULA.

Aalu or **Aaru** One conception of the underworld of ancient Egyptian religion. The fields of Aalu were reached through either 15 or 21 gates, each guarded by a host of evil demons armed with long knives: a concept of Osiris-worship, probably antedating the solar concept outlined in UNDERWORLD. Aalu was a kind of Elysium, where the fields were cultivated for food for the dead apart from the offerings made by their survivors.

Aarne, Antti (1867–1925) Finnish folklorist; docent at Helsingfors for Finnish and Comparative Folklore; specialist in folktale and fable. He was the chief exponent and developer of the geographical-historical approach to folklore research first presented by Kaarle Krohn, and became with him leader of the modern Finnish folklore-study movement. Chief works: *Vergleichende Märchenforschungen*, Helsingfors, 1907, and *Verzeichnis Märchentypen*, published in *FFC* #3, 1910, revised by Stith Thompson and published in #74, 1928, under the title *Types of the Folktale in World Literature*. This became the foundation stone for subsequent folklore scholarship in Europe and America. See FINNISH FOLKLORE.

Aaron The first high priest of the Hebrew people; elder brother of Moses and spokesman for him to his own people and later to Pharaoh (*Ex.* iv, 14 ff.): archetype of the high-priesthood. Aaron's rod was used by him to perform many feats of magic in the attempt to convince Pharaoh to release the Israelites: it was changed into a snake and swallowed the snake-rods of the Egyptian sorcerers; it remained a rod and engulfed the rods of the magicians. Three of the plagues were brought upon the Egyptians by Aaron's hand and rod: the rivers of blood, the frogs, and the lice. In Jewish tradition, Aaron was accompanied by his son Eleazar and by Moses to his last resting-place on Mt. Hor. There, in a cave, he lay down upon a divine couch and died, leaving his vestments and office to Eleazar. The cave entrance was obliterated by God, but when the people murmured that perhaps Moses had killed Aaron in jealousy for his popularity, Aaron was shown to them on the couch, floating in the air. In Moslem legend, Moses and Aaron went up the mountain together, not knowing which was to die. In the cave they found a coffin, which did not fit Moses, but was exactly Aaron's size. Another Moslem story says that the couch of death was found in a house atop the mountain. Moses, knowing that Aaron was to die, suggested that Aaron rest for a while. The couch and Aaron on it were then transported to heaven. In Jewish legend, Aaron is in Paradise, seated beneath the Tree of Life, instructing the priesthood in its duties.

Aaron's rod The rod cast by Aaron before Pharaoh, which became a serpent (*Ex.* vii, 9–15) and which later blossomed (*Num.* xvii, 8): typical of the magic wand of all magicians of all times and all peoples. With it Aaron brought the first three plagues on Egypt. When Pharaoh demanded a sign of Moses and Aaron standing before him, Aaron threw down his rod and it became a serpent. When the magicians of Egypt matched that one, Aaron's rod swallowed the rods of the Egyptians. Later Aaron's rod alone of the twelve rods of the 12 princes of Israel blossomed in the tabernacle and bore ripe almonds, in token of the validity of the priesthood of Aaron and his descendants. One legend states that it was made of sapphire and inscribed with the ten Hebrew initials of the ten plagues; another that it was one of twelve rods which Moses cut from the Tree of Knowledge. Rabbinical legend says this rod was a gift from God to Adam when he was driven out of Eden. It passed from father to son until it came to Joseph, on whose death it was stolen by Jethro, the Egyptian. Jethro planted it in his garden, but could never again pull it out of the earth, until Moses came to that place, read the name of God engraved thereon, and took it up in his hand. Moses received Jethro's daughter in marriage: the traditional reward for the miracle. There are many Christian and Mohammedan modifications of these stories, among them that the rod became part of Christ's cross. The story presents three typical elements of world folklore: the magic wand, the dry rod blossoms, and the sword in the rock.

Aarvak In Norse mythology, one of the horses of the sun; the dawn.

Ababinili The supreme being of the North American Chickasaw Indians: literally, Sitting-Above or Dwelling-Above, or Loak-Ishtō-hoollo-Aba, Great Holy Fire Above. His earthly manifestation is fire, especially the annual sacred fire of the Chickasaws. He is at the same time the sun, and the spirit of fire apart from the sun, giver of warmth, light, and of all plant and animal life.

abandoned children A motif (S300–399) occurring in folktales all over the world, in which one child, often two children, sometimes several, seven, or all the children of a tribe, are either abandoned or driven away. The reasons are either economic and social, such as unfitness to survive, illegitimacy, incestuous parentage, famine or destitution, disease, etc., or various other reasons common to folklore and legend, such as supernatural parentage or birth, fear of the fulfilment of a prophecy, jealousy of a relative, parent, or step-parent, alleged ungratefulness on the part of the child, as well as disobedience or stupidity.

Poverty and lack of food are the most frequent reasons; fear of the fulfilment of a prophecy is next. Invariably, however, the abandoned children flourish and prosper. They are nursed by animals (Romulus and Remus) or fed by birds; animals provide them with magical aid; they are fostered by supernatural beings (Abraham), or picked up by kings and reared at court (Cyrus, Moses, Joseph, Œdipus, Orestes, etc.). And they frequently return to heap succoring coals of fire on the heads of their still starving parents. Perhaps the most popular of all abandoned children stories is *Hansel and Gretel;* the Filipino *Juan and Maria* is very similar.

Children abandoned in time of famine by one or both parents is a frequent motif in North American Indian tales, which almost invariably also include the supernatural animal helper and usually the return of the child or children with aid and forgiveness. In a Gros Ventre story all the children of a certain camp were deserted by the adults; they wandered off and were killed by an old woman, except for one girl and her little brother; a bird in the forest helped the girl perform the hag's tasks; a two-horned animal helped them cross a river and drowned the pursuing hag. When they caught up with their parents, they were deserted again and hung up in a tree. But the little scabby dog (also abandoned) cut them down, gave them the gift of fire, and the three lived together and prospered. The boy killed game for food by a glance, built tents, made clothes, etc., by a glance; the girl told him what to look at! Eventually the starving elders returned, were fed and forgiven, but unfortunately the boy happened to look at them and they all fell dead! The Lipan Apache abandoned children story varies, however, in the motive for abandonment and the tone of the ending. An old woman denies and abandons her own two children to marry a young man. They thrive in the forest, learning first to make and use bow and arrows, subsisting on grasshoppers, then birds, then rabbits, then deer, wearing deerskin clothes, living in deerskin tipis, etc. The story ends with the discovery of the prosperous children by the starving villagers, whom they generously feed. But the boy kills the mother with a club. The charming Cochiti story of the deer who found the abandoned baby and took him home riding on his antlers lacks the conventional ending: because of a broken tabu on the part of the over-eager mother, the little one had to remain a fawn among the deer's fawns forever. See ANIMAL NURSE; DEER BOY; REVERSAL OF FORTUNE.

abandoned wife The theme of a cycle of stories which almost invariably begin with the heroine's having her hands cut off and being abandoned by her family for any of several reasons. She may be abandoned in a boat (S431), left on an island (S433), driven into the forest (S143), thrown into the water (S432), or cast into a pit (S435), but she is always discovered by a king who perceives her true worth and marries her. When her child is born she is again abandoned or cast out, this time by her husband, usually because of the slanders or intrigues of jealous or evil sisters, rivals, in-laws, etc. The common accusation is that the wife has given birth to an animal or monster or that she has murdered her child. She wanders off into the world with or without the child. Here the water of life motif enters in; eventually she comes to a magic lake or well or is given a wonderful drink which restores her to wholeness and beauty. She wins back her husband and the evil ones are punished. In Kashmir and Bengal variants seven queens are blinded

by their husband on the whim of a jealous eighth and cast into a well. The water restores their sight and the usual justice ensues.

This story, most typically known as *The Maiden Without Hands,* is known all over Europe from Lapland to Sicily, Brittany to Russia, with minor variations. It turns up in the Near East, and in India; there are at least six African variants and two North American Indian versions; it is found also in Brazil and Chile. It appears in literary guise as early as 1200 A.D. in England; Chaucer used it in "The Man of Lawes Tale," Gower in *Confessio Amantis.* Variants occur in the *Arabian Nights* and the *Pentamerone,* and it is the theme of a number of South Slavic folk songs.

abandonment Desertion of the aged, the sick, the deformed or crippled, the helpless, or of infants and children by parents, family group, or community: a time-rooted practice among many peoples. Technically abandonment is desertion of the aged and helpless; abandonment of infants to perish is called exposure.

Basic causes for abandonment have always been economic: lack of food or fear of such lack, and the uselessness of the aged to the group, i.e. uselessness to the point of becoming burdensome or encumbering. This holds especially in nomadic cultures. The Arabs either abandoned the old and helpless or buried them alive. The ancient Persians and Armenians left them in the deserts to be devoured by wild beasts. The early Romans hurled everyone over 60 into the Tiber. Certain South African peoples, especially the Bushmen and Hottentots, take their old people into the wilderness and leave them inside a small enclosure with a little food. The enclosure is to protect them from wild beasts. Hunters often come upon human skeletons within these circles of stakes. Many North American Indians left the old, the sick, and the weak behind when the camp moved on (Hudson Bay Eskimos, the Hurons, the Iroquois). The Algonquians abandoned the sick whether old or young; certain California tribes either killed or abandoned the old; the prairie Indians left the old behind with a little food and water; the Utes continued to abandon their aged late into the 19th century. Even our own pioneers of the covered-wagon treks across the plains, as recently as 1849, left the weak or dying beside the trail with a little fire. Melanesians either burn or bury alive their aged parents, and abandon the very ill in haste through fear of the demons by which the delirious are believed to be possessed. Many South American Indian tribes also leave the sick to their fate through fear of the evil spirits which have caused the disease. In fact superstition is almost as potent a factor in abandonment as famine or destitution.

Abandonment and exposure of infants and small children stem from the same causes, plus other economic reasons, such as the dowry that must be paid on a daughter, which makes daughters a liability, as contrasted with the bride-price on marriageable daughters, which makes female infants desirable. In Sarawak where the son-in-law works for the bride's father, girl babies are cherished and boy babies are hung in baskets on a tree and left to die. Other reasons are shame for the deformity, illegitimacy, or incestuous origin of a child, and superstitious fears in regard to the abnormal. In some countries twins and triplets are invariably exposed because they are believed to be unlucky. The strange phenomenon known as Siamese twins still dismays most human minds; *Life* (March 10, 1947) pictures a pair of abandoned Chinese Siamese twins picked up by a childless mother. In India, even until recently, parents were averse to raising a child born on an unlucky day. Concern for perfection of the race caused the ancient Spartans to expose misshapen or unfit infants. The Nilotic Negro mother who has lost one or more children believes that if she leaves the next one in the road at sunrise as an offering to hostile spirits the bad luck will be broken. The natives of central and southeastern Australia have such a prolonged suckling period that any child born before the preceding one is weaned is either killed or abandoned. And when food is scarce the Smith Sound Eskimos expose their newborn to the cold if they already have two children.

Only when the death of the child is definitely desired, as in cases of gripping superstition, is one abandoned or exposed in a place where it is unlikely to be found. The growth of foundling homes in China, France, Cuba, and other parts of the civilized world bears witness to the fact that most infants are abandoned in the hope they will be picked up. Babies left on seats in railroad stations or found in railroad station lockers are examples. Today it is illegal to abandon the aged, ill, helpless, infants, or children; and in some of the United States it is illegal even to abandon a disabled or helpless animal. See ABANDONED CHILDREN; INFANTICIDE.

abandonment on the island A motif (S145) occurring in various types of folktales all over the world, in which the abandoned person always outwits the abandoner and escapes. The motif turns up representatively in the **Ojibwa (western Ontario) tale,** *The Marooned Egg-hunter,* **belonging to the widespread North American Indian cycle of son-in-law test stories.** After having failed to outwit and kill his son-in-law by various ruses, one day Wemicus, the Trickster, proposed that they go to a certain rocky island for gulls' eggs. When the son-in-law was well ashore, the old man pulled off in his canoe and left him there. Undismayed, the young man filled his shirt with eggs and flew home across the lake by means of a pair of gull's wings he took from one of the island gulls. The wife was cooking the eggs and the children playing with the wings when Wemicus got back.

The motif occurs in the stupid ogre cycle. There are Finnish and Russian stories of a hero, about to be abandoned on an island by an ogre, who concealed himself in the ogre's clothing and the ogre himself unwittingly rescued his victim from the island. The type is the Norwegian story of a wife, falsely accused, abandoned by her husband on an island, from which she is rescued and catches up with him just in the nick of time to save him from some terrible fate.

Abbot of Unreason or **Misrule** Scottish term for the Lord of Misrule.

Abbots Bromley Antler or **Horn dance** A men's dance with reindeer horns held near the head, performed only at Abbots Bromley in Staffordshire. The traditional date for its performance, Twelfth Day, has been moved to the Monday after September 4 to coincide with Wakes week. There are six dancers, as in the Morris, three with the great antlers painted white and three with red. The other characters also resemble those of the Morris: there is a Maid Marian, a hobby horse, a fool, also an addi-

tional boy with a bow and arrow. The dance is preceded by a circuit of the farms to bring luck. Finally in one of the farmyards, to an accordion, they "deer"-circle, serpentine, then progress in loop patterns; then at a grunt from the leader, they meet and retire in two lines and cross over. Formerly there were also heys and other figures. The symbolic coloring, deer horns, and formerly ritual characters (man-woman and clown) point to an ancient ritual significance, marking this as one of the few surviving animal dances in Europe. [GPK]

abdominal dance A dance based on certain stylized swinging movements of the *rectus abdominis,* usually performed only by women. In its late development it is called the belly dance, or (in north Africa) *danse du ventre,* but in its most primitive form it involves not only the abdominal muscles, but movements of the entire pelvic region, which are typically known as the "pelvic roll." All over Asia this dance is performed and watched with reverence as symbolic of "the mystery and pain of motherhood." Asiatics maintain that only Occidental misinterpretation could transform it into the pure sex pantomime called the danse du ventre or the burlesque performance of circus side shows called the hootchie-kootchie. The ancient primitive type is performed in the Caroline Islands, in New Guinea, in the Celebes, in the Solomons, and in eastern Polynesia generally, and from coastal north Africa to Loango and Zanzibar. It is danced also among the Canella Indians of the Ge and of northeastern Brazil. It is known to have been performed in certain districts in ancient Greece and was the fine art of the famous dancing girls in old Cadiz (the Gaditanas). Originally it was a fertility dance, with the stimulation of sexual excitement only a secondary object. In primitive cultures the miming of the sexual act and the accentuation of the child-bearing part of the body constitute a sympathetic magic to insure and promote prolificness and the life process.

abduction The capture, carrying off, or detention of a girl or woman with intent to marry or mate: one of the most primitive forms of marriage. The Old Testament book of *Judges* describes the abduction of 400 virgins of Jabesh-gilead for wives for the tribe of Benjamin, who later went to Shiloh during a feast and "took them wives according to their numbers of them that danced, whom they captured." The rape of the Sabine women by the Romans is one of the famous mass abductions of history. Abduction was also a custom among ancient Teutonic peoples; and among certain southern Slavic groups marriage by abduction was practiced well into the 19th century. So deeply rooted in the human mind is the psychology of marriage by capture that many marriage celebrations still include a mock capture of the bride with mock resistance on the part of her relatives. Abduction is the motif, for instance, of an old Scandinavian folk dance, the *Bort-dansingen,* in which both men and women dancers try to steal the bride from her female guardians.

The folktales of the world are full of abductions, especially abductions of a beautiful maiden by a supernatural lover. There are countless stories of gods, centaurs, ogres, giants, dwarfs, whirlwinds (Basuto), fairies, water-spirits, mermen, and animals, who have abducted lovely women through the ages and taken them to live a magical carefree life in their supernatural abodes. The story of Europa and the bull, of Hades and Persephone, are famous and classical examples. The polar bears who abducted the blond Scandinavian maidens proved to be kind and wealthy husbands. Even the fearful Water-Monster of the Chiricahua Apache Indian stories, who caught the young girl when she came to the pool to fill her jug, turned out to be a beautiful young man in his own land and a son-in-law of great benevolence to the girl's people left behind.

Other abduction motifs describe how the Devil carries off faultfinders, scolding women, usurers, and other wicked people. The Hottentot story of the boy abducted by baboons has its modern parallel in the abduction of Mowgli by the Bander-log in Kipling's *Jungle Book*.

Abel The second son of Adam; the first man to die—the victim of the first murder (*Gen.* iv, 2–8). In both Hebrew and Moslem tradition, Cain and Abel had twin sisters, Cain's the prettier of the two. Adam and Eve planned to have the brothers marry each other's sister, but Cain balked. When, in addition, the offering of Abel, the best of his flock, was accepted by God, and the offering of Cain, a poor sheaf and the remainder of a meal, was refused, Cain decided to kill Abel. But since he did not know just what would cause Abel to die, he had to keep throwing stones at his brother, until one struck a fatal blow in the neck. Cain now tried to dispose of the body by hiding it in the earth; of course, God knew it was there and He cursed the earth for accepting the body of Abel. According to other tradition, Cain did not know how to get rid of the corpse and carried it about on his back until he saw one bird burying another.

abiku Evil spirits of the Yoruba of West Africa, especially dangerous to children: omnipresent, always hungry and thirsty, and always seeking to enter the body of some child in order to obtain food and drink. When one finds human habitation, he shares his food with other abiku still unembodied, with the result that the child dies. To rid a child of the abiku the parents offer it food in likely places, and, while it is eating, bell the child, for abiku dislike the sound of bells. Sometimes they rub pepper into small cuts in the child's skin and the abiku depart to escape the pain.

In Dahomean belief, among the people directly west of the Yoruba, an abiku is one of a group of forest spirits, permitted by Mawu, the creator, to enter the womb of a woman, to be born, dwell on earth for a time, die, and be reborn in the same family. When the parents of a child suspect or become convinced that their child is an abiku, they dedicate him to a Vodu (a god) with the intent that the Vodu will protect him from the spirits which will surely come to take him back to the forest. Sometimes they scarify the child's face, either to make him unrecognizable or so ugly that the spirits will not want him. Iron anklets hold such a child to earth; belled bracelets prevent his running away. Abiku is also a generic term for the spirit of all such children.

Abokas The afterworld or home of the dead in the Melanesian mythology of parts of the New Hebrides. It is always believed to be on a nearby island. See AFTERWORLD; MELANESIAN MYTHOLOGY. [KL]

Above Old Man The Creator of the Wiyot Indian mythology, who thought things into existence. His name is Gudatri-Gakwitl, and he remains a living deity today among this almost extinct people. He more nearly ap-proximates the creator of monotheistic thought than any other creator of northwestern California Indian religion.

abracadabra A magic word or formula used in incantations against fevers and inflammations and sometimes against misfortunes. The patient wore an amulet around his neck bearing the inscription

ABRACADABRA
ABRACADABR
ABRACADAB
ABRACADA
ABRACAD
ABRACA
ABRAC
ABRA
ABR
AB
A

The idea was that the disease would gradually disappear just as the inscription gradually dwindled to nothing. The word first occurs in the writings of Severus Sammonicus, a Gnostic physician of the 2nd century. Jewish scholars question that it is of cabalistic origin, but point to a striking parallel, the Talmudic spell against Shabriri, the demon of blindness. A person in danger of becoming blind must say: My mother hath told me to beware of

SHABRIRI
ABRIRI
RIRI
RI

and the demon disappears along with his name. By this token it may be that the word abracadabra was originally the name of some demon, now unrecognizable.

Belief in the magic word is rooted in the ancient belief not only in the identity of the self with its name, but also in the power inherent in names. To speak the name of a supernatural being, sometimes even to know it, gave one the power to invoke that being. In the evolution of magic, however, the manipulation of the words and formulas themselves gradually superseded the importance of the name or the meaning of the word, until the more incomprehensible or fantastic the word, the more power in it. See NAME TABU.

Abraham In the Old Testament, the first of the patriarchs, progenitor of the Hebrews: prototype of absolute and unquestioning faith, the "friend of God" to whom and his numberless seed was promised the land of Canaan. Faith in the face of misfortune and despair is the story. At God's bidding the shepherd Abram migrated from Haran, whence he and his father Teran had come from Ur in Babylonia to a strange land (Canaan) where the famous covenant took place, and he received from God the promise of a son in his old age and the new name Abraham, "father of many nations." At God's bidding too he would have sacrificed Isaac, that "son of promise," but because of his faith God showed him a ram in the bush to be sacrificed instead, and renewed the promise to multiply his seed "as the stars of heaven."

Rabbinical legend adds to this story many stories of Abraham's opposition to Chaldean astrology, stories of his smashing the idols in his father's house because they would neither partake of the sacrificial foods nor answer prayer, and his subsequent mission in the world as spokesman for the one and living God. Rabbinical legend also ascribes to Abraham the towering size of the typical culture hero, along with the discovery of astronomy, invention of better modes of agriculture and seeding, invention of the alphabet, and knowledge of magic. He wore a precious stone around his neck with which he healed the sick.

In Mohammedan legend, the story of Abraham begins with a slaughter of 70,000 male infants to prevent the fulfilment of a prophecy that a boy would be born to rise against Nimrod, king of Babylon, and would break all the idols. Hence Abraham was born in a cave outside the town and on the tenth day abandoned. But the angel Gabriel put the baby's finger into its mouth, milk flowed from the finger, and when the sorrowing mother returned to the cave on the twentieth day, she found a sturdy youth already praising the God who created heaven and earth. The iconoclast stories are many and elaborate, culminating with Nimrod's order to cast Abraham first into prison, later into a fiery furnace. He was fed by Gabriel for one year in prison and drank from the spring which God caused to gush from the walls. He was catapulted into the fire which none could approach and live, but his faith in God caused the fire to cool and become a rose garden. Whereupon all the people believed in the God of Abraham from that moment on. This story is told by Thomas Moore in *Lalla Rookh*. Abraham figures as largely in Mohammedan legend as in Jewish, in that Mohammed claimed to preach, not a new faith, but the "restoration of the religion of Abraham." See ABANDONED CHILDREN; SLAUGHTER OF THE INNOCENTS; TOWER OF BABEL.

absurdity rebukes absurdity The motif (J1530) of an enormous group of stories belonging to the nonsense folklore of the world: usually the sole motif in the story containing it. Typical of these is the story of the man whose foal strayed into a field with two oxen belonging to a neighbor. When he went to bring home his foal, the neighbor claimed it. The case was taken to the king who adjudged the foal to the man who swore it belonged to his two oxen. The next day a man was seen fishing in the road with a huge fishnet. The king went out to question him. It was the rightful owner of the foal, who said, "As easy to catch fish on dry land as for two oxen to produce a foal." Of course justice was given. This story occurs in the German märchen, is well known in all Baltic folklore, and in Spain. Even more famous and ancient is the story (widely current in India, Tibet, Ceylon) of the man who went on a journey leaving a bag of gold dust in another's care. When he returned the friend handed him a bag of sand, saying, "It changed to sand in your absence." Some time later this friend too took a journey and left his small son in the other's keeping. When he returned and asked for his child he was given a lively ape. "He turned into this in your absence," said the friend. As usual the satisfactory exchange was made. This motif is closely related to the *reductio ad absurdum* motif (H952) and the rule must work both ways motif (J1511).

acacia *A. seyal* may be the shittah wood of which the Israelites built the ark of the covenant and the altar of the tabernacle. When Jacob went to Egypt, he planted "cedar trees," and the wood of these was carried into the desert in the exodus. Of the 24 varieties of "cedar,"

only shittim wood could be used, the Lord having foreseen the sin which the Israelites would commit at Shittim (*Num.* xxv), and the use of the wood in building the ark and the altar atoning for the crime. In later rabbinical tradition, it was ruled that this wood could be used only for this purpose and not for ordinary building and furniture making. The thorns of the acacia are supposed to have been in the crown that Christ wore to Golgotha. The wood of the acacia is burned on Buddhist altars, and Hindus use it in preparing their sacrificial fires. In India, it is believed that an evil spirit resides in the acacia, but that he will work evil only if a bed is made from or repaired by acacia wood: such a bed cannot be slept in. Frazer (*Magic Art* II) mentions an acacia in Patagonia in which a spirit abides, and to which the natives make offerings, even of clothing and horses. The ashes or the bark of the babul (*Acacia arabica*) are used in post-operative treatment by certain groups of eunuchs in India. In folktale, the "heart in the acacia flower," taking its name from an incident in the tale of *Anpu and Bata (The Two Brothers)*, is a well-known variant of the separable soul motif.

acatlaxqui The dance of the reed-throwers: a primitive dance of the Otomí Indians of the municipality of Pahuatlán, Puebla, in Santa Catarina Nopochtla, around St. Catherine's Day, November 25, and also in Atla and Tlalcruz, México. The dancers (ten or more young men) dressed in white cotton coats, red knee-pants, wear red bandanas crossed over one shoulder and under the other, conical paper hats with paper ribbons streaming from the points, and sandals which patter on the stone floor. Each carries a strong reed, of about an arm's length, ornamented with feathers, and having about a dozen slender reeds attached to it, the whole so devised as to slide out and arch upwards when the dancers make their cast. The center figure is a boy dressed as a girl, called the Maringuilla, the little Mary. She carries a gourd containing a wooden snake. The dance begins inside the church with the dancers in two rows, changing to one row before the entrance, and later forming a circle around the Maringuilla, while one holds the snake over her head. Finally she is lifted onto a small platform while the dancers circle round her. The climax of the dance is the flinging up of the reeds into an arched dome over her head, and the simultaneous ringing of the church bell and bursting of rockets.

The Otomí Indians are noted for the persistence with which their primitive religious beliefs and observances survive under cover of Catholicism. This dance points not only to their ancient serpent-worship (the serpent god Mixcoatl was theirs), but the boy in girl's dress (always a phallic symbol), the reeds (another phallic symbol), and the centering of the dance around the boy-girl, all suggest some ancient fertility rite whose significance may (or may not be) lost, except for the tradition of pre-Columbian origin. [GPK]

acculturation Although the term has been defined in various ways, in essence acculturation is to be regarded as denoting the study of culture-change in process, where change is induced by contacts between peoples having different ways of life. First employed by J. W. Powell in 1880 in the sense of culture-borrowing, it was largely displaced by the word "diffusion" until the middle of the 1930's. Diffusion studies, which were in essence attempts to reconstruct the unwritten history of peoples by drawing conclusions from the distribution of various cultural traits and complexes, reached their climax by 1925. At this time it became apparent to those engaged in studies among peoples in contact that the diffusionist approach revealed only hypothetical results at best, and could never yield precise conclusions as to the dynamic processes involved in cultural change.

Thus, in the United States especially, there arose the area of research that came to be known as "acculturation studies." In such research the contemporary state of the life of the people is stressed, and the historic facts of its contact with other groups are analyzed to ascertain not alone what had been borrowed, but under what circumstance and ultimately why they had been taken over. More important still, the question became paramount how, in the process of adoption, cultural elements have changed in form or meaning as they are integrated into their new setting. In England, some of the same problems were studied under the general designation of "culture contact research." In 1935, a committee of the Social Science Research Council drew up a *Memorandum for the Study of Acculturation,* influential in focusing research on the study of diffusion in process. The definition of the word acculturation given there, however, stressed the duration and intensity of contact as criteria, and these have been set aside as not being susceptible of satisfactory delimitation. Definition in terms of method —that is, of observation and the use of historic documents in the study of culture-change, rather than historical reconstruction—would seem to be more satisfactory.

It is evident that the concept of acculturation has much significance for the study of folklore; while, conversely, folklore can make important contributions to its study. Because of the manner in which the tale can be broken down into component elements of character, incident, and plot, and because, moreover, literary forms of a people reveal the basic sanctions of their way of life, these aspects of culture afford a uniquely precise instrument in the study of cultural change in process. We need but recall such a form as the nativity myth of the Zuñi Indians where Mary is impregnated by the Sun, Jesus is transmuted into twins, and the tale becomes an explanation of why the mule is sterile, to make the point. For folklorists, the concept acculturation can be used as an effective instrument in unraveling and understanding the way in which the literary kaleidoscope operates to produce the multitude of variations found on any given theme. M. J. HERSKOVITS

Acephali A fabled nation, in Libya, of men without heads: mentioned by Herodotus and Josephus. They have been pictured with the face shown on the chest.

achachila The spirits and demons of the religion of the Aymara Indians of Bolivia. They are believed to live underground in the mountains and are said to send rain, hail, or frost. They appear to human beings in the guise of old men. [AM]

Achan In the Bible (*Josh.* vii), an Israelite of the tribe of Judah who took for himself a part of the spoils of Jericho dedicated to the Lord. His crime was unknown, but after the defeat at Ai, Joshua was instructed by God to discover the transgressor among the Israelites. By lot, Joshua chose the tribe, then the family, then the household, and finally the man, who confessed. Achan, for breaking the tabu on the "devoted thing," was stoned and burned to death, and a heap of stones was raised over his body.

acheri In Indian folklore, the disease-bringing ghost of a little girl which lives on mountain tops but descends to the valleys for nightly revels. The acheri will not molest those who wear red garments, so a scarlet thread is tied around the necks of children to protect them from disease. When children are ill, the acheri is said to have cast her shadow upon them.

Acheron In Greek mythology, the river of woe, one of the five rivers surrounding Hades: sometimes synonymous with Hades itself. In Jewish eschatology, the souls of the dead must cross it or bathe in it before entering paradise. In Christian legend, Acheron (or the Acherusian Lake) flows with waters white as milk and within it stands the City of God. Into it repentant sinners are cast by Michael and then brought by him to the City of God where the righteous dwell.

Achikar, Ahikar, Achiacarus, or **Ahiqar** The wise old counselor of Sennacherib, king of Assyria, who was falsely accused and condemned to death, escaped by hiding, and reappeared in the moment of his king's dire need to save the situation. When he was 60 years old Achikar had 60 wives but no son; he adopted his nephew Nadan, who ungratefully plotted against his uncle and succeeded in getting him condemned to death. No sooner was Achikar reported dead than Pharaoh, king of Egypt, proposed to Sennacherib that he build him a castle suspended between heaven and earth, for which Pharaoh would pay an extravagant tribute, but failing the castle, Sennacherib would pay the same to him. Consternation spread through the land until Achikar stepped out of hiding and revealed himself alive. Sennacherib sent him off at once to Pharaoh as official minister and magician. He easily built the castle in the air, turned out a few ropes of twisted sand, and returned home with Pharaoh's rich tribute for Sennacherib. This story, along with the moralizing precepts of Achikar, is preserved in ancient Syriac, Arabic, Ethiopic, Armenian, and Slavonic writings. It is extant in a 5th century B.C. papyrus manuscript, but is believed to be of Macedonian origin even more ancient. There are Jewish, Turkish, and Rumanian versions of the story. It is mentioned in the *Book of Tobit* and told in detail in *The Thousand and One Nights* (Burton *Supplemental Nights* as "The Say of Haykar the Sage"). It is easily the prototype of an almost world-wide folk motif relating how during a famine the king ordered all the old men in the country to be killed. But one youth hid his old father, who came forth when everything was going wrong, and by his wisdom saved the land.

Achillea The name of a large genus of plants of the thistle family, including yarrow and sneezewort: named for Achilles' spear, or in some traditions, for a plant used by Achilles in curing Telephus.

Achilles The greatest, strongest, most beautiful, and bravest of the Greek heroes in Homer's *Iliad;* son of Peleus and Thetis. While he was an infant his mother dipped him in the Styx, thus making him invulnerable, except in the heel by which she held him. He was educated by the centaur Chiron; and grew to manhood dressed as a girl at the court of Lycomedes, king of Skyros. Here he was discovered by Ulysses and induced to join the Greeks against Troy. Later when Agamemnon was awarded Briseis, a slave-girl to whom Achilles was devoted, Achilles "sulked in his tent" and refused to fight again for Agamemnon. Things were going badly for the Greeks until Patroclus, Achilles' dearest friend, wearing Achilles' armor to terrify the enemy, went forth and routed the Trojans. But Patroclus himself was killed, whereupon the Greeks again fell back, until Achilles came raging out against the enemy to avenge the death of his friend. He rescued the body of Patroclus, killed Hector the next day, and completely defeated the Trojans. Later story says that Paris discovered the secret of his vulnerable heel and killed him with a poisoned arrow.

In pre-Homeric myth, Achilles often appears as a sea god whose temples were built on capes and cliffs along the coasts, where navigators could propitiate him for favorable winds, safe arrivals, etc.

In folklore Achilles is the prototype of the superhuman hero who preferred glory to long life. His story contains four typical world folk motifs: the hero disguised in women's clothes, the vital spot, the magic weapon, the talking horse. See SWORDS; VULNERABLE SPOT; XANTHOS AND BALIOS.

Achilles' spear The wonderful spear or lance of Achilles, which had the power to heal whatever wound it made. Telephus, king of Mysia, was wounded by it in a battle with the Greeks who landed on his shores en route to Troy. The wound would not heal until Telephus, heeding the words of Apollo, "He that wounds shall heal," sought out Achilles among the Greeks encamped before Troy. An ointment containing rust from the spear was applied to the wound and it was healed.

A Cholla mo Run Scottish musical legend of "the piper's warning," embodying the belief that the bagpipe had the power of speech. See BAGPIPE.

açon A type of rattle, usually a calabash containing pebbles or seeds, used in connection with drums and ogan in Haitian vodun rites. The rattle, played by an initiate who is an accomplished singer, establishes a ground rhythm against which the drums work out their more elaborate patterns and, when shaken in prolonged continuous sound, serves to break the beat of one song before the beginning of another. During the singing and dancing the player of the rattle joins the dancers, shaking his instrument high over their heads in short sharp notes, takes the lead in new refrains, and takes solo parts in the characteristic exchange of solo and chorus parts. The açon is prepared for its part in the ceremonies by a baptismal rite along with the drums and the ogan.

aconite Any of a genus (*Aconitum*) of plants of which monkshood is one well-known species. From ancient times in Europe and northern Asia the plant has been recognized as the source of a powerful poison. India especially is noted for its mountain aconites. The Nepal aconite of the Himalayas is probably the most deadly: source of the famous Bikh poison. The Nepalese have been known to use it generously in wells and springs to protect towns and stop advancing armies. Many species are as deadly in local application as when taken internally. All over northern Asia it was used on arrow heads to kill tigers and other game as well as against human enemies. Aconite arrow poison among the Ainus and other peoples of the east Asiatic coast is well known. Aconite arrow, lance-tip, and harpoon poison is equally common among the Kamchadal hunters, especially whalers, to the north of this region, and came to America with the Asiatic culture drift across the Bering Strait from the Kamchatka region, to be widely practiced by the Aleutian and Kodiak whalers.

The Penzer notes to the *Kathā Sarit Sāgara* mention a Neapolitan story of two lovers tricked to their death with this poison. A young girl was persuaded by her unscrupulous father to rub her body with an ointment he had prepared, assuring her it was a love charm to bind her lover to her forever. The girl used the ointment (which contained aconite) and both she and her lover died of it that night. Various preparations from some species, however, are used locally to give relief from neuralgia, or internally as a tonic, febrifuge, or aphrodisiac. Compare POISON DAMSEL.

acorn The fruit of the oak (*Quercus*), a one-seeded nut fixed in a little woody cup. The tree is usually about 20 years old before the acorns appear and they themselves take one, two, or three years to mature. In many species they are edible. In folklore and proverb the acorn is the symbol of prolonged effort preceding perfect achievement. Great oaks from little acorns grow not only expresses the *de minimis maxime* idea, but also implies they were a long time a-growing. The famous German story of the man who said he would pay the devil when he harvested his first crop and then went out and planted acorns is in the tradition. The ancient Celtic druids ate the acorns of their sacred oaks in preparation for prophesying.

The acorn figures little beyond this symbolization among peoples where cereal grains or maize abound. But among peoples who have no corn and where acorns are plentiful, especially among tribes of California Indians, the stories are full of references: Sun's wife was cooking acorn mush for supper (Achomawi); two boys on a journey gathered, cooked, and ate acorns (Wappo); Coyote and his grandmother had a famous argument about how to prepare them (Yurok). The Natchez (southern Mississippi valley), who did have corn, had also a story telling how the animals once had a chief who let each one choose the food he wished to live on. And Squirrel chose acorns. But the Luiseños (southern California coastal tribe), who even as late as 1905 still subsisted largely on acorns and fish, have a myth giving authority for their diet. Wiyot, the first (or last) born of sky and earth, was the guardian of all earthly things and beloved by all of them. Only Frog hated him because she envied his beautiful legs. She spit in the spring from which he drank and in ten months he died. But before he left the earth he taught the people all he knew, gave them their laws and arts, and promised that from his ashes would come their most valuable possession. Out of the ashes grew the oak tree and the acorns were as big as apples. Then the people sent Crow to the big star to find Wiyot. Crow could not find him. Then Hummingbird went and came back with the message: "All birds and animals, eat the seeds of my tree. All men, make flour from the seeds and make cakes from the flour." So with gladness the people took the acorns and made the feast of the acorns. See COYOTE AND THE ACORNS.

acorn dance or **feast** The autumn feast of the Hupa Indians of California, the coast Yuki, and other northwest California tribes: a first-fruit ceremony of these people. A special group of women is appointed to gather, grind, and leach the acorns and make them into a mush. At noon on the feast day the people gather to await the coming of the priest. But they must not look at him as he approaches the feast-ground because he impersonates Yinukatsisdai, the god of vegetation. He builds the ceremonial fire and heats the stones with which to cook the mush. When everyone has eaten, he then burns all the leftovers with prayers that the new crop may not be eaten by rodents. The stones are never used again, and never touched by anyone but the priest, who piles them up in order year by year.

Actæon In Greek mythology, a hunter who was turned into a stag because he saw Artemis bathing, and was killed by his own dogs. This is the prototype of many stories of punishment for breaking the tabu against seeing a goddess nude. Tiresias was blinded by Athena for the same reason. See TRANSFORMATION AS PUNISHMENT.

act of truth Any act or event which takes place immediately following and because of the absolute verity or falsity of a statement or declaration. As a motif the act of truth is widespread and important throughout Sanskritic story and is frequently identical with the chastity test. Typical is the tale of the chaste woman whose story raised the fallen elephant, "King Ratnadhipati and the White Elephant Svetarasmi" in the *Kathā Sarit Sāgara*. The wounded elephant could neither rise nor eat. To the distressed king, in prayer, it was revealed that the elephant would rise if a chaste woman touched it with her hand "but not otherwise." The king called on all his 80,000 wives but the elephant never got up until a servant named Silavati placed her hand upon his side and he got up and began to eat. From the same source comes the story of Rāma and Sītā in which the pregnant Sītā, falsely accused and deserted by Rāma, sought to be tested in a certain lake. "Oh, Mother Earth," she said, "if my mind was never fixed upon anyone but my husband, may I reach the other side of the lake." Whereupon the goddess bore her to the other side. This overlapping of the act of truth with the chastity test turns up again in the Tibetan tale of *Two Brothers*, in the story of the elephant who could not bring forth until a pure woman touched her, and also in the Old Irish *Echtrae Cormaic*, the *Adventure of Cormac*. In this story the marvelous golden cup, which broke in three if three lies were told over it and became whole over three truths, proved to Cormac the chastity of his wife. The act of truth is as common to Irish legend as to Sanskritic.

The act of truth is not always a chastity test. It is invoked to prove the paternity of infants, to turn back forest fires, free captives, counteract poison, cure leprosy, heal wounds, etc. In local legends the imprint of a human hand in a rock is usually attributed to an act of truth. The famous rock near Welsholz, Saxony, still bears the imprint of Count Hoyer's head. Hoyer, a general of Kaiser Henry V, on the eve of the fatal battle of Feb. 11, 1115, boasted that he could not be defeated any more than that rock could show the imprint of his head. The rock softened and took the mark of the head; the battle was lost and Hoyer was killed.

The act of truth was too convenient a testimony for the human mind to relinquish altogether. People cross their hearts and hope to die today if it is not the truth they speak; they swear on the Bible and fear disaster should they lie. "If I am not innocent may I choke on bread and cheese," many a colonial witch declared. See FENDA MARIA.

actionless, all-powerful old woman A supernatural being of the Chemehuevi Indian tribes of California; Hawichyepam Maapuch. She appears as a power rather than as a character in the origin myth of these people. Through her power the waters which first covered the world receded (or dried up) and allowed the two culture heroes (Coyote and Puma) enisled on Charleston Peak to descend and populate the earth. Coyote married a louse from whose eggs the various tribes were born; but the Chemehuevi, the Mohave, and certain other favored southerly tribes were born from Coyote's excrement. The death of Puma at the hands of "eastern enemies" caused unbroken night to come upon the world. But Coyote recovered daylight, and, with the funeral rites which he performed for his brother, instituted the pattern for the funeral rites the Chemehuevi were to follow forever. The actionless, all-powerful old woman is an element also of the Mohave origin myth, as are also the elder brother's death and the establishment of his (and hence the tribal) funeral rites.

Adad or **Hadad** Ancient Assyrian and Babylonian god of storm, wind, and rain. Among the Assyrians he was Adad; among the Amorites he was Addu or Dadu (the same word minus the first syllable) or Adad (minus the last). Very early Amorite settlers took him to Babylonia where his name became synonymous with Ramman, the thunderer. As a storm and wind god he was greatly feared; but as a rain god, giver of waters, he was worshipped and propitiated and regarded as a protector of harvests. He early assumed the role of war god to be invoked as a destroyer of enemies with thunderbolts, whirlwinds, or drought. He plays an important role as a storm god in the Babylonian flood myth and is listed in the second divine triad along with Sin and Shamash, although he is sometimes replaced by Ishtar. His symbol is the thunderbolt; his sacred animal is the bull; his sacred number is 6. His first seat of worship in Babylonia was at Muru in the south. His consort was Sala or Shala.

Hadad was the most important of the ancient gods of northern Syria in the 8th century B.C. There he was worshipped as a god of rain and vegetation and harvest guardian. His name as Adad turns up in Syrian cuneiform about 3000 B.C. In Canaan he was the chief god, worshipped as Martu (the Amorite) and Kur-Gal (the Great Mountain), and probably was baal of Mt. Lebanon. His consort in Palestine was Asherah. In Roman times he was known either as Jupiter Optimus Maximus or Jupiter Damascenus, but in any guise the ancient Syrian Adad can always be identified because he is invariably represented with the bull.

Adam The Hebrew and Biblical word for *man*: name of the first man and progenitor of mankind. He was created in the country of Eden in Babylonia near the confluence of the Euphrates and Tigris rivers. *Adamah* is the Hebrew word for *ground. Genesis* i–iii tells the familiar story of the creation of Adam, of Eve from Adam's rib, her seduction by the serpent into tasting the forbidden fruit, Adam's eating of it also, and the judgment of God upon them for their disobedience: pains of childbirth for the woman, labor and toil for the man, and expulsion from Eden for the two of them, to make their way in a less bountiful environment, where they became the parents of three sons, Cain, Abel, and Seth.

Apocryphal and rabbinical legend enlarge upon the details: Adam was made from red clay from the four regions of the earth (*adom* is the Hebrew word for red); his body reached from earth to heaven (before the fall), and "he was of extreme beauty and sunlike brightness." The *Slavonian Book of Enoch* tells how all the angels bowed before Adam except Satan who in punishment for his rebellion was hurled into the abyss and henceforth became the enemy of man; also, how the angels, full of wonder at Adam's beauty, were about to worship him until God put sleep upon him to show them he was mortal. Adam was meant for immortality but death became his lot when he ate the forbidden fruit, and the animals no longer obeyed him but feared and attacked him. The pseudepigraphic *Secrets of Enoch* contains the poetical description of the creation of Adam from seven (or eight) substances: his flesh from the earth, his bones from rocks, his veins from roots, his blood from water (or dew), his eyes from the light of the sun, his hair from grass, his thoughts from the wind, his spirit from the clouds. Another story says that Adam's soul was created 1000 years before his body. When the time came for the soul to enter the body he refused to exchange heaven for human flesh until Gabriel beguiled him into it with music in a moment of ecstasy. Ever since the soul has been as reluctant to leave the body as it was to enter it.

Mohammedan legend anticipates the evolutionary theory of creation with the story of how Allah sent rains upon the earth to prepare the slime from which to create Adam. Adam's body lay stretched out upon the ground for 160 years before it received the breath of life. When Allah put the breath of life in his nostrils, Adam sneezed and said, "Praise be to Allah."

An Arabian story remarks upon the cleverness of Adam at the moment of expulsion from Eden to remember to grab up an anvil, two hammers, a pair of tongs, and a needle to face the new world with. Adam was cast out of Eden from the Gate of Penitence, Eve from the Gate of Mercy, Iblis from the Gate of Malediction, and the serpent from the Gate of Calamity. Adam landed in Ceylon, Eve at Jiddah, Iblis at Ailah, and the serpent at Isfahan in Persia. Two hundred years went by before Adam and Eve met again at Jebel Arafat, the Mount of Recognition.

These stories are typical of Adam lore in the great body of Jewish and Mohammedan tradition; there are countless others, often identical in incident and import, but with a wealth of ramification. The story of the fall is found among other peoples too. The Prometheus-Pandora myth of the Greeks is built about the same elements; the motifs are almost identical. See LILITH.

Adam and Eve and Pinch Me A catch rime which goes as follows:

> Adam and Eve and Pinch Me
> Went down to the river to bathe.
> Adam and Eve got drownd*ed*,
> And who do you think was saved?

The unwary listener who answers as expected gets pinched.

Adam Bell, Clim of the Clough, and William of Cloudesly An English ballad (Child #116) telling the story of three famous outlaws, all marvels in archery, and how two of them shot up the town of Caerlel to save the third, William of Cloudesly, from being hanged. William had just slipped home from the forest to see his wife and had been caught. The three then forestalled higher justice by going to London and securing the king's grace before he could hear the news. William of Cloudesly is the English William Tell, who shot an apple from his son's head. But the English ballad differs from the European legend in that Cloudesly undertook the shot of his own free will; it was not imposed by the king. The first wonder, too, the splitting of the hazel-rod with "twenty score paces betwene," was done only to make the people marvel. But the two marvels won favor for Cloudesly and his family and his two fellow outlaws with the king forever.

Adam of China The first of China's legendary kings: Fu Hsi.

Adam's apple The prominence made by the thyroid cartilage in the front of the human throat, conspicuous in men: the morsel of forbidden fruit which stuck in Adam's throat (A1319.1).

Adam's Peak A mountain in Ceylon (native name *Samanala*): site of a rock bearing a depression resembling an enormous footprint, and goal of continuous Moslem, Hindu, and Buddhist pilgrimage. In Moslem legend, as the place where an angel showed Adam all the ills of the world, it bears the footprint of Adam. In Buddhist legend, it is the site of the Sripada or Sacred Footstep of Buddha, the imprint of Buddha's last contact with this world. The Hindu Śaivite believes it to be the footprint of Śiva, and a Tamil legend describes how rivers flow from Śiva's foot upon the Peak. Christians worship the spot as the footprint of St. Thomas.

adaox The Tsimshian Indian word for myth, as distinguished from *malesk,* which is either a personal adventure or historical story. Among the Tsimshian a myth is always a story about the past; animals are the characters, speaking and behaving like human beings; many are origin stories (origin of the world, of man, the animals and their individual characteristics, of various features of the present world, etc.). The malesk may contain supernatural incidents and characters, for the supernatural is ever-present in Indian daily life; it may even be weighted with religious significance. But no story is an adaox or myth unless its setting is that early, marvelous period when the world was entirely different from the world of the present day. The Kwakiutl word for myth is *nuyam;* Chinook is *ik!anam;* Thompson Indian is *spetakl.* All three make the same distinction. The Salmon-Eater tribe of southern Alaska have the word *adaorh* which means myth or a *true* story. An adaorh is not only recounted orally, but is illustrated on totem poles and represented in other carvings. The great Haida and Tsimshian epic about Dzelarhons, revealing the migration to America via the Aleutians of the Salmon-Eater tribe is a typical adaorh.

Adapa A mythological Babylonian hero and fisherman of the city of Eridu on the Persian Gulf; son of Ea, god of wisdom, by whom he was given the gift of great knowledge and intelligence. One day while he was fishing, Shutu, the South Wind, upset his boat, and Adapa found himself in "the house of the fish." Enraged, he turned on Shutu and broke her wings. For seven days there was no wind. "Why?" asked Anu, god of heaven, and when told the reason he summoned Adapa to his court. Ea warned his son not to partake of the bread or the water that would be offered to him, with the implication that, if he did so, he would never be permitted to return. Adapa appeared in penitence before Anu and on the intercession of Tammuz and Gishzide was forgiven. Then realizing that Adapa, having beheld the secret heart of heaven and earth, must be made worthy of this knowledge, the gods offered him the bread of life and the water of life, which would have made him immortal like themselves. But Adapa was afraid to take it, believing (as Ea had warned him) that it was the bread and water of death. Thus because of his fear he lost the chance of immortality.

Adapa is construed by some scholars as the hero of the Babylonian fall of man myth; he is likened to Adam, who, having received the gift of knowledge, was denied the gift of eternal life by a jealous god. See FOOD TABU IN THE LAND OF THE DEAD; SEMITIC MYTHOLOGY.

adaro The ghosts of the dead in San Cristoval, Ulawa, and southern Mala island: in Melanesian mythology distinguished from the figona or spirits which were never human. See MELANESIAN MYTHOLOGY. [KL]

adat Customary law, traditions, or traditional customs and practices handed down from generation to generation among Indonesian peoples. The Indonesian explanation for any deeply rooted custom is, "It's adat." [KL]

added equipment The motif of a story told among the Chiricahua, Lipan, and White Mountain Apache Indians, in which Coyote is challenged to tell a lie and get away with it. He admits he can tell a lie so as to be believed, but what he uses for a lie is at home. If some one will lend him a white horse (mule, burro) he will go and get it. He so handles the animal as to make it balk and refuse to budge until it is equipped with a fine saddle, saddle-blanket, then a bridle, then spurs. When all this equipment has been added to the animal, Coyote rides away, and either never returns, or else paints the horse black, returns and sells him to the owner, and escapes with the added equipment when the first rain reveals the trick. One version adds the owner's hat, coat, and boots to the collection before Coyote departs.

This story is of possible European origin, belonging to the widespread stolen goods sold to owner stories (K258), reflecting some variant of the ancient and widespread master thief cycle, or stemming from some one of the numerous tales of lying everywhere so popular. If this is true, the adaptation to Indian life, environment, and thinking, to the sense of humor inherent in Indian character, and to the Indian delight in the trickster has been complete.

Adeborsteine The stork-stones of Pomeranian folk belief, associated with the prevailing German myth that babies are either brought up out of the water by certain water birds (swans or storks) or found by them in rocky mountain caves. Various likely rocky places of this kind were called Adeborsteine, stork-stones; and the infant brought from such a place was a stork-child.

This is one more birth story pointing to the world-wide belief that children are born first of their mother, the earth.

Adibuddha The principal Buddha of Indian Mahāyāna Buddhism, which was developed in the 2nd century in northern India. This theistic form of Buddhism spread throughout central and southeastern Asia to Ceylon and survives today in China and Japan. It superimposes on the various Buddhas (five or six) another over-all Buddha, primary, self-existent, unoriginated, and many-named: an omniscient spiritual being from whom emanate all existing things. He is unseen, yet he is pure light. He is in Nirvana. He is worshipped in temples, not to be invoked with prayer, yet regularly so invoked by Tibetan Buddhist lamas. In the 10th century a new concept was added: by his five acts of thought Ādibuddha produced the five Buddhas of Contemplation (Vairochana, Akṣobhya, Ratnasambhava, Amitābha, Amoghasiddha and sometimes Vajrasattva), creators of the five Bodhisattvas of contemplation, creators in turn of the five worlds of the universe, of which we now inhabit the fourth. In the *Nāmasamgīti*, Mañjuśri is called Ādibuddha, as the personification of that knowledge from which all Buddhas spring. Icons represent him with the sword which destroys ignorance.

Adiri The Kiwai (Melanesian) land of the dead. Life in Adiri is similar to but easier than life on the earth. Originally Adiri was a barren place inhabited by a man (Adíri) and his daughter, Dírivo. Sído, the first man who died, opened the way to Adiri. He then married Dírivo and from his semen came all the different plants which grew in the afterworld. He made fire by rubbing his teeth with wood and then built a house several miles long, in which thenceforth the spirits of the dead resided.

Aditi In Hindu religion, infinity, boundless space, sometimes a purely abstract personification of immensity or infinity, sometimes the mythological personification of the female principle in creation, known variously in the Vedas as the mother of the world, mother of the gods, supporter of the sky, sustainer of the earth, and wife of Vishṇu. In the *Mahābhārata* and *Rāmāyaṇa*, however, she is the mother of Vishṇu. The *Purāṇas* refer to her as the mother of both Vishṇu and Indra. She is constantly identified with various other gods and with nature. In the *Rig-Veda*, Aditi bore eight sons but presented only seven of them to the gods. The eighth she cast away and this was Mārtt-aṇḍa (the sun), her son by the sun. The remaining seven are the Ādityas.

Ādityas In Vedic mythology, the seven sons of Aditi (eight counting Mārtt-aṇḍa): a group of divine abstractions or moral deities. Their names are Mitra (the light of day), Bhaga (good luck, wealth, bounty), Aryaman (comrade, bosom friend), Anśa (bounty), Daksha (dexterity, skill), Varuṇa, and probably Sūrya or Savitri (the sun). Sometimes Indra is substituted for Daksha; and sometimes Savitri and Dhātṛi are added to the list. Varuṇa, their chief, ruler of night, upholder of the moral order, is known as The Āditya. In later Sanskritic writings Āditya is one of the names of the sun, a not surprising development, considering that each name in the list has been that of a sun god at one time or another. In the *Brāhmaṇas*, their number is twelve, an adaptation to interpret each as representing an aspect of the sun during each of the twelve months of the year. The most ancient concept of the Ādityas, however, is the literal one: sons of Aditi, inviolable, eternal beings sustaining and sustained by the eternal celestial light.

Adlet A terrible people believed by the Eskimos to be descended from a red dog. An Eskimo woman who married a red dog had ten children. Five of them were dogs, whom she set adrift in a boat, and five were monsters. The dogs drifted across the big sea, landed safely, and begot the white men. But the monsters begot worse monsters, a cruel, blood-drinking people, called Adlet by the Labrador Eskimos and Erqigdlit by the Eskimos west of Hudson Bay. The story is also known among the Greenland and Baffinland Eskimos.

Adlivun Literally, those beneath us: the underworld of Central Eskimo mythology, where Sedna rules in her big house with the big dog at the door. Sedna has no deerskins in her house because she dislikes the deer. All who disobey her during life must go to Adlivun for one year when they die. Murderers can never leave that place but the others (in Greenland tradition) eventually reach Adliparmiut (literally, those farthest below), a darker, remoter, but not quite so dreadful world, where hunters may still know the joys of hunting whale and walrus, though always enduring terrible storms, winds, snow, and ice. Davis Strait tribes believe that the spirit-dwellers of Adlivun, called tupilaq, return to their villages at times in shabby flapping clothes, as malevolent spirits who cause disease and death. But once the soul reaches Adliparmiut, it experiences comparative peace and need never return. See QUDLIVUN.

Admetus King of Pheres in Thessaly, husband of Alcestis, and once unwitting master of Apollo doing penance for bloodshed as thrall to a mortal. The kindness and the beauty of Admetus soon won the god's admiration and he did much to prosper the fortunes of his master. He discovered that Admetus had only a short span of life allotted to him, but secured the promise that a longer life would be granted if Admetus could find someone to die in his stead. No volunteers rushed forward as substitutes, not servants, comrades, or aged parents. Finally Alcestis offered herself for her husband, and at the appointed hour she died. But Hercules, an unexpected guest on the funeral day, wrestled with Thanatos at the tomb of Alcestis (or with Hades in the lower world) and brought her back to Admetus. This story is a classic example of the interweaving of common folk motifs: death evaded by substitution, and wife dying to postpone her husband's death. In a Japanese analog of the latter, the devoted wife drowns herself to appease the gods and thus prevents them from capsizing her husband's boat.

adolescence ceremonies Among nearly all primitive peoples (North and South American Indians, Australian, Polynesian, Melanesian, and Indonesian, the New Guinea tribes, all Arctic populations, and all African), various ceremonies, often severe and painful, performed for and by young boys and girls at the time of puberty to initiate them into adulthood and its rights, privileges, obligations, and responsibilities. All adolescence ceremonies are initiation rites. Initiation rites, however, are not limited to puberty rites; they usher the individual not only into manhood but into all kinds of secret societies, priesthoods, magic powers and mysteries, and other holinesses, even into death.

Adolescence ceremonies are intended as safeguards against the evils and dangers which threaten a youth or young girl at this time of life. They are considered necessary, not only for the individual but also for the welfare of the tribe. Most ceremonies involve certain purification acts and instruction in or preparation for intercourse with the opposite sex. They usually include a preliminary period of seclusion, sometimes the imposition of complete silence for a period, no contact with the opposite sex, and fasting (total, or from certain foods). The importance of dreams and visions is stressed, for through them the youth discovers the guardian spirit which is to walk with him throughout his life. Severe tests (of pain or endeavor) are imposed to develop strength, hardihood, courage, or endurance. Mutilation, circumcision, sub-incision, flagellation, tooth-filing, knocking out a tooth, flesh-gashing, incision of tribal marks, etc., are regarded either as charms against future evils, as purifications, tests of endurance, or are willingly undergone to develop courage and endurance. Solitary confinement or other isolation, accompanied by terrorizing, also often precede final instruction of the youth by the old men in tribal lore, sexual knowledge, and religious or magical matters. The ritual of death and resurrection is also a common puberty initiation rite, especially among totemic peoples.

Among Malay tribes, the word for adolescence ceremonies is *masokjawi*, literally admission into the Malay people; but they also have another name for it, *chuchi tūboh*, which means purification. Tooth-filing and shaving off the characteristic top-knot of Malay boys are typical features of all Malay adolescence ceremonies. The complete ceremony involves purification rites, tooth-filing or tapping, head-shaving, appeasing certain gods, a huge banquet, and culminates with circumcision, which is performed with the ritual bamboo knife in a little hut. Girls undergo ear-boring, tooth-filing, and the staining of the teeth black. Incision is not common among the Malays except as a feature of Mohammedan conversion.

Among both North and South American Indians adolescence ceremonies for boys are often associated with the initiation rites which admit them to tribal membership or introduce them to the mysteries of various secret societies. North American Indian girls, however, step into womanhood through a complicated pattern of behavior involving seclusion or isolation, food and other tabus, looking and contact tabus, symbolic fertilizing, and symbolic hairdressing. Hopi girls go through a four-day corn-grinding task in the house of an aunt during their ritual which also includes fasting from meat and salt, never scratching the head or body with the hand but only with a certain stick, and remaining in a shaded room until the proper moment to emerge wearing the new hairdress which announces to the public that they are marriageable. The Taos girl also grinds corn for four days, always protected from the sun. Should the sun shine upon her during this period she might bear twins after marriage. This fear is possibly related to an almost world-wide belief in magical impregnation from the sun. She also fasts from salt and "Mexican" food, dons the traditional women's boots; both her dress and hairdress are altered. After this she may join the spring-tide circle dances or join the pilgrimages to Blue Lake. Southern Athapascan, Yuman, and Pima-Papago tribes all emphasize girls' adolescence ceremonies; but Zuñi girls do little more than celebrate their first menstruation by grinding corn for a little feast and assuming the symbolic maturity hairdress. The adolescence ceremony for Chiricahua girls involves a four-night singing ceremony, the whole comprising a prayer for long life. At sunrise on the fifth day the last song is sung to White Painted Woman, the earth mother who symbolizes the female principle. The Mescalero Apaches have a similar adolescence rite for girls symbolizing creation and the seasons, and a long good life throughout all seasons, rooted in faith in the power of the song itself.

Girls among the Thompson Indians of British Columbia fast from bear meat lest they become barren; they pray daily to the Dawn, and record their ritual acts and offerings in paintings on rocks and boulders. Thompson Indian boys also execute rock paintings during their puberty observances to insure long life. Haida girls may not look at the sea lest the motion of the waves cause facial tic, or into fire lest their faces turn red. Their eyes might turn red too if they saw a red salmon.

Seclusion of girls at puberty is an almost world-wide practice among primitive peoples from the Zulus in Africa, who believe that if the sun touches a pubescent girl she will quickly shrivel into haghood or the skeleton state, throughout the Pacific cultures, where the seclusion lasts anywhere from several days to several years, to the Tsetsauts of British Columbia whose girls are made to wear huge fur hats for two years and live in huts apart from others, the Tlingits who confine their daughters at the first sign of menstruation in small huts or cages for a year, and the Alaskan Koniag Eskimos who caged their girls for six months on their hands and knees.

☞ A few of the simpler groups of Middle America, in contrast to the higher cultures of Mexico and Guatemala, observe puberty rites. Among the Cuna of Panama a girl is placed in a special hut at the time of her first menses, while older women pour water over her, bob her hair, and paint her black. Among the Chocó of Panama the girl is secluded, limited in diet, and required to use a special stick to scratch herself. Sumu (Nicaragua) boys undergo fasting, flogging, and scarification to prove that they are ready for marriage. The Lacandon father (Mexico) offers a set of bow and arrows to the gods, in behalf of his son, praying that the boy may become a good hunter. The boy is then allowed to wear a loin cloth and take part in adult rites. A girl's puberty is indicated by her wearing red feathers tied to the back of her hair. [GMF]

☞ The puberty hammocks of southern Brazil and Bolivia are well known. Young girls are sewed into them, suspended from the ceiling, and periodically beaten to discourage the evil believed to be inherent in them at this time. Periods of such suspension vary from four days to four months. Guiana Indian girls are not only suspended from the top of the hut for a month but are subjected to the painful bites of certain large ants.

Seclusion of girls at puberty, typical of world adolescence observances, points to the basic undercurrent fear of the menstruating woman. She is believed to emanate a power dangerous not only to all who might come in contact with her, but also to places, objects, and to herself. The Ticunas of Brazil tear out the hair of young girls at puberty for no other reason than that it is a danger to the girl herself because it must surely contain all the infectious evils that surround her at this time. One remarkable exception to puberty fear, however, occurs among the East African Warundi. On the day of her first menstruation the Warundi girl is led through the house by her grandmother to touch every household object and thus endow it with the special holiness that has come upon her. The basic idea of emanation is here—emanation of mystery and power, feared as potential for evil by most peoples but evoking expectation of good among the Warundi. See BULL-ROARER; INITIATION; MAGICAL IMPREGNATION; PUBERTY DANCES; PUBERTY RITES.

Adon Literally, lord, master: title applied to certain Semitic gods. The root may be seen in Adonai, Adonis, etc. The Adon of Gebal, who became Adonis, may have been Tammuz.

Adonai The plural of Semitic *adon*, lord: in Hebrew religion the most usual substitute for the wonderful, the unutterable, the hidden name of God. In the Masoretic text the word occurs 315 times in juxtaposition with the tetragram YHWH. Originally an appellation of God, the word became a definite title. When the tetragram became too holy for utterance, Adonai was substituted for it, so that as a rule, the name written YHWH receives the points of Adonai and is read Adonai, except where Adonai precedes or succeeds it in the text, when it is read Elohim. The translation of YHWH by the word Lord in the King James and other versions of the Bible is due to this traditional reading aloud of the tetragram as Adonai. In the early period of the Second Temple the name was still in common use; in the beginning of the Hellenistic era the use of it was reserved for the Temple; elsewhere the priests were obliged to use Adonai. Josephus tells the story of how Moses besought God to impart to him the knowledge of His name so that he might be able to invoke Him at the sacred acts; whereupon God communicated his name, hitherto unknown to any man. And the name is not to be used by any man. See AARON'S ROD; NAME TABU.

Adonis The title (from Semitic *adon*, lord) of the Babylonian god Tammuz, misinterpreted, as his cult moved westward, as the name of the god. Thus Tammuz, the young lover of Ishtar (earth-mother goddess) became in Greek mythology Adonis, the beautiful youth beloved by Aphrodite. He was killed by a wild boar while hunting in the mountains. The red anemone sprang from his blood. So great was Aphrodite's grief that the gods arranged to let him spend half of each year on earth with her, and half of each year in the underworld. This story of the dying god and his resurrection, symbolizing the seasonal death and reappearance of vegetation, appears everywhere from western Asia and the Mediterranean regions throughout Europe to the British Isles.

The most ancient and eastern of the Adonis stories is the Syro-Phœnician version in which Myrrha (or Smyrna), daughter of Theias, a king of Assyria, was caused to conceive an incestuous love for her father by Aphrodite, whom she had either refused or neglected to honor. Myrrha contrived to satisfy her passion by taking advantage of the old man's drunkenness in the dark. But he, in his sober anger, would have killed her if she had not fled and sought the protection of the gods. They turned her into a myrrh tree; and from the trunk of a myrrh tree Adonis was born. Most of the stories state that the bark was ripped open by a wild boar and the child came forth. Aphrodite found the infant and, charmed by his loveliness, put him in a little chest and gave him to Persephone to care for. Persephone too became enamored of his beauty and later refused to give him up. So Zeus decreed that Adonis should spend four months of the year with Aphrodite, four with Persephone in Hades, and four he might have for himself. Later he was killed by the boar while hunting. Another variant says that Adonis was brought up by the nymphs, that Aphrodite met him while out hunting and fell in love with him, and that he was killed by a wild boar either sent by, or embodying, the jealous Ares, Aphrodite's previous lover. The judgment of Zeus in allowing him to return to this world for part of every year is the Greek variant of the eastern Tammuz resurrection story.

The trail of the cult is easily followed from Babylonia and Syria through Phœnicia and Cyprus into Greece where Adonis-worship was well established in the 5th century B.C. His worshippers believed that every year Adonis was killed by the boar on the mountain and went to the underworld; every year his goddess-lover left this earth in search of him. While she was absent the earth lay scorched under the sun; no passion, no love existed between male and female; no living thing bloomed or was born. Every year the women of western Asia and Greece mourned the death of Adonis, cast his image into the sea along with the little Gardens of Adonis, sang the beautiful hymn of hope for his return, and seven days later rejoiced for his reappearance on the face of the earth when the red anemone bloomed. In Byblos in Phœnicia the celebration was timed to coincide with the mountain freshets which made the river of Byblos run blood-red into the sea. This was believed to be the blood of Adonis. The appearance of the red anemone in the woods of Syria about the time of Easter symbolized his return. Thus the whole story was dramatized and enacted within the space of about 10 days. Rites at Alexandria were similar. At Argos pigs were sacrificed to Aphrodite to signify her connection with Adonis.

The boar had special significance in the Adonis cult. The boar ripped open the bark of the tree from which Adonis was born; the boar killed the youth in the forest. All the most ancient cults identify the animal that killed the god with the god himself. In one of the most primitive forms of Adonis- (Tammuz-) worship, Adonis himself was the sacred boar, worshipped by a cult of women who believed themselves to be sows. Every year the boar was killed, torn to shreds, and eaten while the women bewailed his death, in a few days celebrating his resurrection with the deification of a new boar.

One 10th century Arabic writer and several more recent scholars have suggested that the Adonis-Tammuz of the eastern Mediterranean peoples is one with the Phœnician corn spirit, deliberately slain, his bones ground up in a mill and scattered to fertilize the fields. In place of the modern corn effigy of the corn spirit, the most ancient rites quite possibly represented the slaughtered god with a human victim whose body was divided into portions, buried at intervals in the field, and regarded as returned to life with the harvest. This lifts the Adonis story out of the realm of pretty death and renewal of vegetation symbolism, and places it not only in the simpler and starker category of hunger and fear of hunger rituals, but pushes it still farther into that symbolism of the god killed *by* man *for* man with the resulting mystery of his resurrection promising life *to* man.

In addition to the fact that Adonis is identified with Tammuz, the death and resurrection motif, linking his myth with various primitive fertility and vegetation symbolisms, relates it also to the stories of Persephone, of Attis (Phrygian), Osiris (Egyptian), Dionysus-Zagreus (Thracian or Cretan), Jesus (Hebrew), Balder (Scandinavian), John Barleycorn (English). His story parallels also that of Old Irish Diarmud, who was beautiful, beloved by women, killed by a wild boar, and given immortality by a god; but the seasonal vegetation symbolism seems to be entirely lacking here. Adonis is associated with the Jesus story pattern in the motifs of god in human form, death and resurrection of the god, and the coincidence of Easter with both rituals, the long period of mourning and fasting, and the moment of joy. See EATING THE GOD; LINUS; MIDSUMMER EVE.

adoration A Haitian Creole song sung (a) after each animal sacrifice at vodun ceremonies, and (b) at the end of the novena in the ritual cycle of the cult of the dead, during the singing of which the officiating priest receives the offerings of money for his services.

adultery In Euro-American cultures, usually extramarital heterosexual intercourse, though a more adequate statement would refer it to sexual intercourse outside of the permitted sexual group. Thus in group marriages as among some Australian tribes each person in the group is generally available to all others though local custom may impose restrictions. Among the Tungusic Manchus the wife of the oldest brother was available to all the younger brothers until the next brother married, when she was expected to restrict her attentions to her husband; but the second brother's wife became available to the other brothers. Among the aboriginal Lolos of China marriage to one sister is considered as giving access to all the others. In Islam and under the Roman Lex Julia intercourse was permitted between the master and slaves and servants, and under English common law a master had access to his female servants. Peoples who regard promiscuity as the proper way of life sometimes consider intercourse outside of certain recognized groups as adulterous though it is considered harmless within the recognized groups. Some African tribes do not consider intercourse with a white man as constituting adultery, though intercourse with other members of the group is so considered. The jus primae noctis which gave the lord of the manor the right to deflower young wives on his estate on the night of their marriage is another case of recognized latitude.

Christian cultures have surrounded adultery with religious, legal and social prohibitions which give it a character not generally known elsewhere. Occidental ethnographers have been affected by this bias, though no doubt unconsciously, and have hypothesized conditions in prehistoric cultures about which by definition nothing can be known with certainty. By starting with one of two opposed hypotheses they prove either that man began by living under conditions of absolute promiscuity where adultery was impossible and "evolved" to a condition where adultery was recognized as horrid or that primitive man lived in a condition of sexual purity which has been contaminated by civilization. Reports about societies which, because they are not European-Christian are inferior, are adduced to support a number of conclusions and must be tabled until adequate testimony can be collected. For example, sexual jealousy, the basis of Euro-American views about adultery, is not a universal and therefore not a "natural"—in the sense of inevitable—component of human cultures. Adultery is of no great importance in many African tribes, among the Tupi of Brazil, the Conebo of the upper Amazon, among the Aleuts, Kamchadals, Gilyaks; peoples of Mongolia, Afghanistan, the Hindu-Kush, Baluchistan, the South Sea Islands, or Australia. Although the attempts of the cultural evolutionists have been discredited on theoretical and practical grounds, attempts to find the origins of European prejudices, superstitions, and beliefs in "primitive" cultures persist. In many communities outside of the restricted Euro-American culture circle wives are not the chattels of their husbands but have had in patriarchal cultures a considerable freedom. Among many communities marriage is so casual an institution that the protection of the family purity is a matter of indifference. Until communities are studied individually and objectively all statements which assert that the institution of the family is the first step in the growth of civilization must be questioned.

An examination of the extreme variations in custom and belief about adultery justifies only a few very general conclusions. Ethnic units living close to each other and having the same or related languages have strongly opposed views about adultery. The Reindeer Koryaks for example are said to be puritans. The virginity of girls must be intact at marriage and after marriage even the suspicion of adultery means death and couples found in adultery must be disemboweled. The consequence is that wives cultivate a sluttish appearance and filthy clothes lest they be thought impure. The Maritime Koryaks however regard the wife's adultery as an honor and, should a child result, thank the father. The Land Dyaks of Borneo are extremely strict. The husband who discovers his wife in adultery must cut off her and her lover's head and if he fails, his wife's brother must perform the execution. Among the Bukat tribes after the husband has executed his wife and her lover his wife's brother must execute him. Neighboring tribes however live in great promiscuity, lend wives, and are indifferent to the purity of the home.

In many communities the severity of laws about adultery is in marked contrast to the customary treatment of it. The crime consists in being found out, when punishments from a small fine to death are legally permissible. Although adultery is a crime against the state in many parts of the United States, the law is seldom invoked. Among many social strata in Europe, America, India, and elsewhere adultery is considered illegal and shameful but husbands even when they know they are cuckolds still stoutly deny the fact. Mohammed's wife 'A'isha was once separated from her husband when they were on an expedition. The next morning she returned to camp in the company of a man. Despite the great scandal the Prophet succumbed to 'A'isha's persuasiveness and announced that it had been revealed to him

that his wife was chaste. The old law that adulterers be stoned to death was changed and thereafter whores and pimps were to be scourged by 100 stripes but those who cast imputations and were unable to produce four witnesses were scourged with 80 stripes. In modern Islam the law permits the death penalty for wives caught *in flagrante* but if the wife swears she is innocent the marriage is dissolved without punishment. In communities where adultery is punished by fines paid to the wronged husband or the husband and wife separately, the institution is a source of profit.

The "unwritten law" which permits a husband to castrate, mutilate, or murder the wife's lover, or even both the wife and the lover is subject to a number of restrictions which seem to derive from the general feeling that sexual jealousy becomes violent if a man is deprived of his customary outlet. Communities such as those of pre-Islamic Java, Burma, Cambodia, Afghanistan, and others consider it bad form or dangerous for a husband to enter the room while the wife is committing adultery because he might do harm to the woman and her lover. In other communities mutilation is treated lightly if it is performed immediately upon discovery. Cutting off a woman's nose is one of the popular customs. The shaving of the heads of women of occupied territories who in the last war consorted with the enemy is a parallel custom if the enemy be considered as outside of the recognized group with whom intercourse is permissible. In some parts of the United States intercourse between white men and Negro women is not regarded as an adulterous union justifying homicide. In most communities which invoke the unwritten law to justify murder or violence, such an act must be impulsive and immediate, often before the avenger leaves the room.

Adultery with the wives of men of exalted rank frequently is treated more severely than adultery with the wives of commoners. In pre-Columbian America men who committed adultery with any of the many wives of the Inca were burned alive with the woman, their relatives executed, and the village was destroyed. In Africa the king of Dahomey had 1,000 wives who were guarded with extraordinary precautions. Another African king who received wives as customary tribute returned them to their people but insisted that they remain chaste. When the king sent agents to investigate, the women in order to maintain their standing denounced several men in each community. The men were fined and the royal income increased. Members of the upper classes in Euro-American culture tend to consider adultery as less reprehensible than members of the lower classes when it is committed with one of their own group. Widows of chiefs in New Caledonia may not remarry but may have lovers at will. Similar customs are reported from the Carolines and Samoa. Samoan chiefs often put their wives aside after a short period. These women are established in a separate building and entertain visiting guests. Though adultery is accepted as customary, elopement with one of these women is a very serious offense.

Many communities regard adultery as commendable or acceptable at special times or for special reasons. Some religious ceremonies which are prepared for by a period of continence are concluded by promiscuous orgies. Temple girls and religious prostitution have been studied in detail. The nuns in medieval convents were at one time available to clerics and others who belonged to acceptable circles. A certain amount of promiscuity has been and in some communities still is connected with beliefs about general fertility. In at least one of the aboriginal tribes of China an itinerant priest is expected to have intercourse once a year with one of the women in each community. If the community prospers the act is thought to have been performed adequately. The community greets the arrival of the priest with festivities and there is no reason to assume that the community regards the priest as a god in disguise. Here folk theology like folk philosophy is less involved than anthropologists of the Occidental Christian tradition imply. Promiscuity in the spring seems to be a biological urge among the Eskimos and others and has been rationalized as necessary to assure the germination of the seeds.

Views and customs about adultery in Occidental Christian communities are complicated by Christian mysticism. Roman views were secular rather than religious. In 285 B.C. a temple was erected to Venus paid for by fines imposed on women for adultery. Cicero says that the cult of Vesta was fostered in order that womankind might feel that it is woman's nature to suffer all forms of chastity. Under the Republic sexual misconduct was brought before a domestic court or family council. The Lex Julia made adultery an offense against the state. After the marriage was dissolved the woman lost half of her dowry and a third of her estate. The wronged husband had 60 days to take action and if he failed to do so action could be taken by any one who wished to. Although the punishments of Lex Julia were considered severe they did not apply to men equally, a situation which Seneca, Plutarch, and others regretted.

Christ's concern was that men should attain a state of mind that made sin abhorrent or impossible. This, as developed by Saint Paul, introduced into the Christian Occident a mystic view of purity which explains such statements as "Adultery is unfaithfulness of a married person to the marriage bed," "defilement of the home," and the like. Customs in the early Christian communities were not uniform. The Law of Constantine condemned adulterous wives to banishment. Justinian abolished the death penalty and if the wife was not taken back within two years she was sent to a nunnery. The Code of Theodoric also decreed death for adultery and the death penalty was abolished in England under Canute. Cæsar's reports on Anglo-Saxon promiscuity are of a general nature. In later England and parts of the United States adultery is the only grounds upon which a divorce can be obtained. Until very recently some Protestant churches would not perform the marriage ceremony for divorced persons. The lives of the troubadours make clear that in the chivalric as well as in both earlier and later periods the laws about adultery were regarded lightly. According to the chivalric code love was not possible between husband and wife and a wife's capacity to draw knights and poets to her husband's party was important in a young couple's ability to improve themselves. One evidence that Percival was an unmannered boor was his embarrassment at being bathed by the young women of the castle.

Current American views about adultery impose rituals and ceremonies as complex as any found among the most "primitive" of "primitive" races. Inasmuch as adultery is prohibited by social, legal, and religious codes married persons impelled to have intercourse with those to whom they are not married must, if they take the codes seriously, find reason to have the marriage dissolved, and as their own adultery is often not an acceptable reason they must adduce the adultery of either the wife or husband who may be innocent or find other cause which courts will find acceptable. They are then permitted, usually after a considerable lapse of time, to marry again. The ritual divorce and remarriage is thought to give purity to an act which would otherwise be considered indecent.

The laws about adultery do not reflect the folk attitude toward it. The reports of anthropologists of the European-Christian tradition show bias, to the point that one recent study contains a warning that the views about adultery being punished with death at some unspecified former time must be accepted with caution and skepticism. Statistics on the incidence of adultery are unsatisfactory though a paging through of the literature on sexual folklore shows that it occurs in all parts of the world and though it is considered reprehensible by many cultures it has enjoyed a considerable popularity in all cultures and at all times.   R. D. JAMESON

advice of helpful animal disregarded The motif (B341) of a group of stories which emphasize the misfortunes and disasters that inevitably befall the hero who does or leaves undone something the friendly animal has enjoined him either to do or not to do. The typical story is that a man meets up with an animal, who, either out of gratitude or admiration, helps him to a marvelous wife, palace, treasure, station in life, or the like. Usually the animal enjoins the hero not to go to a certain place, do or say a certain thing, etc., or asks to be provided with certain daily foods or attentions, etc. Always the hero forgets, wilfully disobeys, or offends by ingratitude, and loses everything, including friendship with the animal.

The advice disregarded motif belongs to the helpful animal cycle of folktales (B300–599). It is closely related to the name tabu motif, and also to the ingratitude punished motif which runs through the Puss-in-Boots cycle. This advice disregarded motif overlaps and fuses markedly with the ingratitude to the animal motif in the North American Indian Zuñi story in which a little flock of turkeys pity a poor, neglected young girl and help her to attend the sacred dance, provide her with suitable garments, jewels, etc., requiring in return only that she not forget or neglect them. She is so popular at the dance that of course she forgets the turkeys. When she suddenly remembers and rushes home, her fine clothes disappear and she is in the same state she was in before. Even the turkeys have gone away.

adykh Among the Buriats, an animal dedicated to a god or ongon. The animal is purified with smoke of burning juniper, sprinkled with wine, and decorated with ribbons of the ongon's color. It is then returned to the herd, never again to be ridden or worked, but is associated with and sacred to the ongon either for a specified time or forever. Animals thus dedicated vary greatly. The adykh may be a horse, a gray ox, a red ox, a raven, a pigeon, even a fish, which of course is henceforth never to be caught. The Mongolian Buddhists took over the custom and the idea, dedicating the animals, not to the primitive ongons, but to their own Buddhist deities. Their word for adykh is *seterty*.

Ægir or **Hlér** A jötunn of Scandinavian mythology, friendly and sociable with the gods: a sea deity. His name is related to the old Gothic *ahwa*, water. He is often referred to as the Norse sea god, but is more properly associated with the sea in its calmer aspects as a stiller of storms. He is not to be blamed, evidently, for the destructions wrought by his terrible wife, Rán.

ægis In Greek mythology, an attribute or part of the accouterment of Zeus and Athena, symbolizing magic power. It protects the wearer, and when shaken terrorizes and puts to flight his enemies. In the *Iliad* it is described as having golden tassels. Zeus not only used it to raise a mighty storm, but loaned it to Apollo to put the Greeks to flight. In the *Odyssey* Athena used it to terrorize the wooers of Penelope. Literally the word means goat-skin. Herodotus describes Athena's ægis as a goat-skin; and as an attribute of Zeus it has been interpreted as the skin of the she-goat Amalthea. It is not surprising to find it also, in Zeus's hands, symbolizing the thundercloud, but this symbolization has deeper and more elemental ramifications, paralleling the ægis with the primitive weather-fleeces which were shaken by the early rain and fertility gods to produce rain. For proof that it was originally a fleece, many point to the fact that Athena wrapped it around her. In art, the ægis of Athena is represented as a kind of cloak fringed with serpents, bearing the Gorgon's head, and draped over her left arm. The shield or breastplate depiction is a much later development.

Æneas In Greek and Roman legend, a Trojan hero, son of Anchises and Aphrodite, founder of Lavinium, and ancestor of Romulus and Remus. While Troy burned Æneas left the city, bearing with him his father, "the wise Anchises," his household gods, and the sacred hearthfire which he kept going all through his seven years of wandering before the wrath of Juno. His voyagings took in Thrace, Delos, Crete, Sicily (where his father died). He was swept by storm upon the coast of Africa, where Dido, queen of Carthage, loved him and sought to hold him back. But Æneas, full of that *pietas* which kept a man true to his fate, continued his wanderings until he landed at the mouth of the Tiber. There he was welcomed by Latinus, king of Latium, married Lavinia, the king's daughter, and founded the revered city named for her, Lavinium, about 17 miles down the river from modern Rome. The *Æneid* ends with the death of Turnus, Æneas's jealous rival for the hand of Lavinia, who waged war against him. Later writers report that he vanished from this earth in a thundercloud and was later worshipped as Jupiter Indiges.

The most significant adventures of Æneas from the point of view of the folklorist are his descent to the underworld to consult the shade of his father, and there being shown the glories of the Rome that was to rise and the Roman people he was destined to father; his plucking of "the pliant shoot of gold," the Golden Bough (evidently mistletoe) from the evergreen oak before the gates of the underworld, to be a potent sign for his entrée into the forbidden places of death; and the forging of his shield by the divine smith. The brief allusion to the well-known folk motif of the deceptive land purchase, "as much as a bull's hide would encircle," is also of note.

Æolus (1) In Greek legend, king of the floating island of Æolia, to whom Zeus entrusted the keeping of the winds. This island is believed perhaps to have been Pantelleria which looms high up in the windy strait between Sicily and Carthage; but is more generally believed to be (as in Homer) the island of Lipara in the Tyrrhenian Sea. When Odysseus landed there Æolus gave him all the winds tied up in a bag except the one wind favorable to his course. The ship was nearing Ithaca when the curiosity of the mariners about the contents of the bag got the better of them; they untied the bag and the winds came forth and drove the ships back to Æolia. But Æolus was provoked and irritated by this stupidity and refused to tie the winds up again. During the eight centuries between Homer and Vergil Æolus developed from guardian of the winds to god of the winds. The *Æneid* so designates him and describes how he kept them in a cave.

(2) A king of Thessaly, legendary ancestor of the Æolian people. He was the son of Hellen and grandson of Deucalion; father of Phrixus and Helle, and many others, including Sisyphus, Alcyone, etc., and the ancestor of Jason.

aeromancy Divination from the air, the winds, or atmospheric conditions: an ancient and widespread technique, still used for, among other things, primitive weather forecasting. In its most exact sense, aeromancy pertains only to divining by a current of air, for example, as it passes over a vessel of water which is uncovered at a proper moment. In medieval writings on divination the term (usually spelled aerimancy) was expanded to include almost all phenomena occurring in the air.

Æsculapius The Roman god of medicine: Latinization of **Asklepios,** Greek god of healing. Apollo (also a god of healing) was his father, his mother (in most versions) the nymph Coronis. One story says he was taken from his mother's womb upon her funeral pyre; another that he was abandoned and suckled by a she-goat. In either case he was given by Apollo into the care of Chiron, the centaur, under whose tutelage he became the most skilled of all physicians. At the peak of his career he restored the dead to life, either Hippolytus for the sake of the mourning Artemis (the commonest story) or some unknown deceased for the sake of the fee. Apollodorus names two men raised from the dead by Æsculapius, attributing the means to the Gorgon's blood which he received from Athena. Blood from the veins on the left side worked bane to men; from veins in the right, salvation. Hades, in alarm for the depopulation of Hades, complained to Zeus. Affronted by the physician's presuming to tamper with the laws of life and death, Zeus hurled Æsculapius into hell with a thunderbolt, but later admitted him among the gods.

Æsculapius had two sons, Podaleinius and Machaon, both surgeons, noticed in the *Iliad* as leaders before Troy; and three daughters, Hygeia (Health), Iaso (Healing), and Panacea (Cure-All), none of any great importance either in cult or story except Hygeia, whose cults were both associated with and existed independently of Æsculapius'.

The cult of Asklepios was widespread through Greece. His temples (Asklepia) were more than temples; they were houses of healing (prototypes of the modern hospital) where the priests of the cult applied their secret knowledge plus religious rites to effect their cures. The most famous temple of Asklepios was in the ancient seaport of Epidaurus. Here the sick came to sleep, to be cured by the priests or by the god directly in their dreams. Only the dying or women in childbirth were denied admittance.

To this temple at Epidaurus the Romans came, seeking deliverance from the pestilence that was sweeping their city in 293 B.C. The serpent (that serpent in whom the god himself was known to abide, *anguem in quo ipsum numen esse constabat*) slipped from the image of the god and followed the Romans through the streets into their ship. At the mouth of the Tiber he left the ship, and the temple to Æsculapius was built on the little island where the serpent went ashore.

The serpent is the symbol of Æsculapius, representing, some say, rejuvenation in the sloughing of his skin; the staff too is his symbol, representing his wanderings from place to place dispensing cures. Both are combined in the caduceus, the staff entwined by the snake, still the symbol of medicine and the medical profession.

Aēshma (Pahlavi *Aēšm*, Persian *Xišm*) In Iranian mythology, a fiend or demon of lust and outrage: aide of Angra Mainyu. Aēshma is the most dreadful of Zoroastrian demons, contriving evil for the creatures of Ahura Mazda. When he is unsuccessful he stirs up strife among the demons themselves. He assails the souls of the dead when they near the Chinvat Bridge. Sraosha is assigned by Ahura Mazda to keep him under control until the final great conflict when Sraosha will destroy Aēshma.

æsir (singular *as*) The Teutonic gods. Odin was chief of them, known frequently as the father of the gods. His sons Thor, Balder, Tyr, Vali, Vidar, Hoder, Bragi, and Hermod, and his brothers Vili and Ve were also æsir. Frigga, Odin's wife, and 18 other goddesses or *ásynjur*, among them Sif, wife of Thor, Nanna, wife of Balder, Iduna, wife of Bragi, etc., also belonged to the group. Loki, the evil one, the mischief-maker, is one of the æsir. Their habitat was Asgard, though each had his own home also. Odin's was the famous Valhalla. They were an organized, judicial community and the council met daily under Yggdrasil. Some sources mention among the æsir the names of Hœnir, Forseti, Oller or Ullr, and Ing, an interesting deity of the East Danes, who disappeared eastward over the sea. Compare VANIR.

Æsop The vague personage whose name is associated with the most famous group of fables in the world. He was born in the Greek island of Samos, in Sardis in Lydia, Mesembria in Thrace, or Coticœum in Phrygia. His birth is thought to have been about 620 B.C., his death about 564 B.C. Herodotus identifies him in Samos about 570 B.C. Further legend says that he was the slave of two different masters in Samos: first Xanthos, then Iadmon, who freed him out of admiration for his wit. Æsop then visited Crœsus at Sardis and Pisistratus at Athens. Plutarch's *Symposium of the Seven Sages* reports that Æsop was a guest at the court of Crœsus along with the seven sages of Greece, and that Crœsus not only said, "The Phrygian has spoken better than all," but even persuaded Æsop to remain in Sardis and execute for him many difficult matters. Later Crœsus sent him to Delphi to distribute a great sum of money among the citizens. Æsop was so disgusted and infuriated with the wrangling that arose among them that he refused to give it. "Unworthy," he called them, and they threw him over a high cliff. Such a plague subsequently swept through their city that they advertised a sum of money to atone for the murder of Æsop. Iadmon, grandson of Iadmon, his former master, went to receive it.

Perhaps the most famous of the many folktales about Æsop are how he told the story of *The Frogs Asking for a King* in the public place in Athens and thus saved Pisistratus from being overthrown by the populace; and how he went to a neighbor's house one day to borrow fire and carried it home in a lantern. The passer-by who asked him what he was looking for with a lantern in the daytime received the answer, "A man who will mind his own business."

Æsop's Fables The famous collection of fables ascribed to Æsop. Although they come to us now in literary form, they are generally conceded to be not only of folk origin, but to have been current among the folk in Greece during Æsop's lifetime. In answer to the theory advanced by Benfey and others that Æsop is innocent of responsibility for them, we have only the certainty that they were linked with his name in Athens, that Herodotus, less than a century after Æsop's death, mentions him with definiteness, that Aristophanes mentions both Æsop and his "drolleries," that Aristotle and Lucian cite Æsop's story of the wisdom of the bull in having horns upon his head instead of on his shoulders, that Socrates versified some of Æsop's fables, and that they were praised, as Æsop's, by Plato.

Concerning their oriental origin, out of the whole number extant (something between 231 and 256) only one fourth can be directly traced to India. Thirteen of them are identified with certain "Stories of the Past" in the *Jatakas,* among them The Wolf and the Lamb, The Ass in Lion's Skin, The Fox and the Raven, The Goose That Lays the Golden Eggs. Among a few obvious parallels to stories in the *Mahābhārata* are The Lion and the Mouse, The Belly and the Members, The Farmer and the Serpent, The Two Pots, and The Cat Turned into Maiden. All the rest are believed to have been folk fables of Greece and are associated with Æsop as preserver, adapter, and hander-on. That some clever mind used and adapted traditional material is strikingly shown in the religious and political applications of the stories.

Many anecdotes exist pointing up such application. The fable of The Wolf and the Crane is said to have been used by a Rabbi ben Hananiah to prevent the Jews from rising against the Romans. Kriloff used them to needle the Russian bureaucracy. And the first translation of Æsop into Chinese was immediately suppressed by sensitive officials who suspected them of local authorship.

Demetrius Phalereus made the first collection of *Æsop's Fables* and "put them in a book" about 300 B.C., which though lost, is said to be the basis for the famous collection by Phædrus, who translated 42 of them into Latin elegiacs in the 1st century A.D. This is usually considered the most celebrated of the collections. Babrius, a Roman poet, versified them in Greek no later than the 2nd century A.D. In the 9th century Ignatius

Diaconus put 53 of them into verse. Maximus Planudes, a 13th century monk, collected 144 of the fables, including certain oriental and Hebraic additions and a life of Æsop, which were published at Milan about 1480 along with Ranuzio's 100 *Fabulæ Æsopicæ*. This was published again in Paris in 1546 with a few additional fables. There was a Heidelberg edition in 1610 containing 136 fables in imitation of the Babrius rendering. These were followed by various collections of more or fewer fables published in Oxford and Leipzig, 1718–1820. All of the fables, 231 to date, were arranged and published by J. G. Schneider at Breslau in 1810. The numbering system for the fables adopted here follows that of Joseph Jacobs' *The Fables of Æsop* (New York, 1894).

aes or **aos side** People of the mounds, or "shee folk": the ancient Irish Tuatha Dé Danann, or people of the goddess Danu, the ancient Irish gods, who took up their abode in the hills and mounds (*side*) of Ireland after their defeat by the Milesians: now the fairies of contemporary Irish folklore. Compare DAOINE SĪDE.

Afrekete A goddess of Dahomey religion; youngest child of Agbê and Naéte of the Sea pantheon, and guardian of the treasures of the sea. She appears also in the role of clever, undisciplined trickster in some of the myths. Afrekete has the reputation of being a great gossip and teller of secrets; those who represent her in the dance hold a finger to their lips. The dance of her possession resembles that of Legba.

African and New World Negro folklore Negro folklore is told today throughout Negro Africa, south of the Sahara, as well as in the regions of North America, the West Indies, and South America where descendants of African slaves are found. Two striking characteristics of this body of tradition—its present wide distribution and its remarkable toughness—can be appreciated only in terms of its history. Surviving the drastic social changes that accompanied the forceful transplanting of African peoples into slavery on a strange continent, Negro folklore has persisted in the New World as a well-defined and basically homogeneous entity regardless of the folklore, culture, and language of the dominant groups, whether English, French, Spanish, Portuguese, Dutch, or American. Many elements from these European groups have been incorporated into the folklore told today by Negroes in the New World; however, as the term Negro folklore is used in this article, it indicates only those items which have African origin.

The wealth of Negro folklore is no less impressive than its persistence. Struck has estimated the number of African folktales at nearly a quarter of a million. Klipple estimates that five thousand different African myths and tales have actually been published, although her bibliography, prepared in 1938, contains references to nine thousand. If publications from the New World are included this number is considerably increased. Yet in reality only a beginning has been made at recording Negro folklore. Among the thousands of tribes in Africa, there is not a single one for which a complete collection of myths and tales has been published. Published collections of more than two hundred tales are almost unheard of, although the number of tales known to single tribes undoubtedly runs into thousands.

Numerically at least, the position is better with respect to proverbs, but some of the largest African collections have not been translated and others are almost certainly incomplete. Doke explicitly denies any claim to the completeness of his well-known collection of 1,695 Lamba proverbs from Northern Rhodesia: "Lamba proverbs seem to be without number. Since putting together the present collection I have gathered another two hundred without any effort on my part; and a further number has been laid aside owing to lack of confirmation. Mulekelela, the Lamba story-teller, supplied me in the first place with more than half of these aphorisms: he has a wonderful mine of this lore, and one day reeled off as many as 250 at a single sitting." The largest collection from a single African tribe is still that of 3,600 Ashanti (Twi) proverbs from the Gold Coast, edited by Christaller in 1895, of which 830 have been translated by Rattray. For the New World, the largest collection is Beckwith's 972 proverbs from Jamaica.

In addition to myths, legends, folktales (märchen) and proverbs, which have received the most attention, there are several other forms of "unwritten literature" in Africa and the New World. The verses or lyrics of songs are, of course, found in great numbers in all Negro cultures, as are riddles. Tongue twisters and praise names also seem to have a wide distribution. A variety of other set verbal formulæ are also widely found in Africa, although they are seldom included in collections of folklore. The Yoruba, for example, distinguish between myths and legends (itan) which they regard as historically true, folktales (alǫ apagbe), riddles (alǫ), proverbs (owe), songs (orin), praise names (orile), curses or incantations (ǫfǫ), and the Ifa divining verses (ęsę).

Folktales Of all Negro folklore, the Uncle Remus stories published by Joel Chandler Harris are probably the most widely known. Animal trickster tales of the same type are common in other parts of the New World and in Africa. In Uncle Remus, Bre'r Rabbit is the outstanding trickster while Hare or Little Hare appears in this role in East Africa and among the Jukun and Angass of Nigeria. Tortoise, who is the primary trickster among the Yoruba, Edo, and Ibo of Nigeria and is found as a trickster of secondary importance in many parts of West Africa and in East Africa, is the primary trickster in Cuba. Spider, the animal trickster in Liberia, Sierra Leone, and the Gold Coast, is known by his Twi name, Anansi, in Jamaica and Dutch Guiana and is referred to as Aunt Nancy by the Gullah of South Carolina.

Because of the fame of Uncle Remus, animal stories have come to be regarded as the typical Negro folktales. The larger published collections, however, indicate the importance of human-trickster, and divine-trickster, and other non-animal tales such as those about Hlakanyana among the Zulu. From West Africa a cycle of Dahomean tales collected by M. and F. Herskovits centers about Yo, described as a "trickster of gross undisciplined appetite." Among the Yoruba, the deity Eshu often appears in tales in a role similar to that of Tortoise, and the part played by Orunmila or Ifa, the deity associated with divination, does not differ markedly.

Tricksters Of the many incidents involving tricksters, several are widely distributed in both Africa and the New World. The trickster feigns illness or fatigue in order to ride a powerful and important animal as if it were his horse. He stations his relatives along the course so that he always appears ahead in a race with a swifter animal. He challenges two giant animals to a tug-of-war, which he arranges so that they pull against each other without knowing it. He escapes death through counter-suggestion, as when Tortoise begs those about to kill him not to throw him in the water. One by one, he devours the children of a larger animal by posing as their nurse or governess. He borrows from a series of animals, arranging his payments so that each animal who comes to collect is killed in turn by a stronger creditor, and tricks the last one into canceling the debt. He pretends to cook himself to feed a guest; his guest dies in trying to imitate him. He induces another animal to throw his food into the water, smear his face with birdlime, jump into a fire, remain in a burning hut, kill his wife or mother, drive a red-hot nail into his head, or cut off his head or leg. The trickster himself, however, is by no means infallible or immune to tricks, as witness the most widely distributed story of this type, Tar Baby.

The difference between the European and African interpretations of the "Tortoise and the Hare" reveals the distinctive characteristics of the African trickster. Where the European Tortoise wins through dogged persistence while his rival sleeps, his African counterpart uses his wits. Clever, shrewd and unscrupulous, in common with tricksters all over the world, in Negro folktales he is invariably the underdog, apparently at the mercy of his larger and stronger associates. The triumph of brain over brawn and of brilliance over steadiness—the reverse of the European grasshopper-ant fable—is the consistent theme of the Negro trickster tale. Its prevalence in the New World has been interpreted as a psychological reaction to slavery, but this explanation does not account for its importance in African folklore.

To Spider, the Temne ascribe the qualities of "cunning, sleeplessness, almost immortality, an unlimited capacity for eating and an equal genius for procuring necessary supplies." Spider, who appears to be the Temne national hero, is shrewd, designing, selfish, and at times vindictive and cruel, while their secondary trickster, Cunnie Rabbit (actually a chevrotain) is intelligent and loveable. As foils for these two, Elephant is enormously strong but lacking in mental acuteness, while Deer is consistently stupid and helpless. It is not difficult to appreciate the psychological satisfaction to audience and narrator that comes from identification with a trickster who symbolizes freedom from physical limitations and moral restraints.

Tales in which the trickster escapes an impossible obligation by posing an equally impossible condition point up and illustrate a traditional right to contest an unjust display of authority, revealing a significant aspect of the attitudes of Africans toward their chiefs. Among the Kru, when Nymo is commanded by the king to weave a mat from rice grains, he asks for an old mat of the same kind to use as a pattern. Among the Ganda, a person ordered by the king to fashion a living human being, requests a thousand loads of charcoal made from human hair and a hundred pots of tears, to use for materials. In Zanzibar when Kibunwasi is challenged by the Sultan to build a very high house in one day, he invites the ruler to ascend a kite-string to see how the work is progressing. When the Sultan asks "How can a man climb a string?" he counters, "How can a man build a high house in a day?" Other examples are encountered in connection with the tests set for prospective sons-in-law. Among the Bulu of the Cameroons, when Tortoise is asked to fetch water in a basket, he asks his future father-in-law for a carrying-strap of smoke.

Non-trickster tales While trickster tales are common and widely known, many folktales do not involve tricksters. A common example is the story in which a vegetable or animal agrees to become the child of a barren woman on condition that its antecedents are never mentioned, and returns to its former shape when the bargain is broken. Similar is the theme of the metamorphosed wife or husband. A number of ogre tales, involving neither tricksters nor animals, conclude with the killing and opening of the ogre and the rescue of the victims he has eaten. In another tale, a person finds a pot that produces food whenever a certain magic password is given and then loses it; when he returns to the place where it was found, he receives a stick and, on pronouncing the password, is severely beaten. A deserving person obtains wealth from a supernatural source, while a jealous imitator receives snakes, wild beasts, and insects. A variant of this theme appears in the Hausa tale where a jealous woman, whose co-wife's dead child has been resurrected, kills her own daughter in the hope that she will be restored in a less ugly form, but gets only half a girl, with one eye, one arm and one leg.

A group of unfinished tales leaves the audience presented with dilemmas. A dilemma tale from the Bura of Nigeria, for example, describes a blind man whose mother, wife, and mother-in-law are also blind. When he finds seven eyes, should he leave his mother-in-law with only one eye and be "ashamed" before her and his wife all his life, or should he deprive his mother? As in the case of Stockton's "The Lady or the Tiger," no solution is suggested.

Tall tales are relatively rare in African literature, but several have been published by Frobenius and Fox, one of which contains the following incident: As a man shot an arrow at an antelope, his companion jumped up, ran to the animal, killed it, skinned it, butchered it, packed it away, caught the arrow in flight, and asked, "Are you trying to shoot a hole in my knapsack?"

In one Hausa tale, a combination of the two types is effected. A chief tells his three sons to mount their horses and prove their skill. The eldest charges at a baobab tree, thrusts his spear through it, and jumps through the hole with his horse. The second lifts his horse up by the bit and jumps over the top of the baobab. The youngest pulls up the baobab tree by the roots and rides up to his father, waving it aloft. The story-teller concludes with "Now I ask you who excelled among them? If you do not know, that is all."

Cycles Negro folktales often occur in cycles. For example, a narrator may begin his tale with a reference to a situation from which the trickster had just extricated himself. The cycles usually involve a central character, such as an animal-trickster, or the Dahomean Yo. Other cycles center about the adventures of twins, orphans, or precocious children.

The existence of cycles may explain the attempts of some students to read into African folktales a consistency and continuity there is no reason to expect. The appearance of one animal in the role of another, or the existence of several tales accounting for the death of the same trickster in different ways, need cause no concern. Among the American Indians, where more variants have been recorded, it has become evident that even within a single tribe a search for the "correct" version of a particular tale is artificial and unrealistic. Junod has shown that this is also true for Africa in his discussion of the sequence of episodes in Thonga folktales, where, "although these form definite cycles, it is rare to hear two narratives follow exactly the same order," and "the tricks of the Hare are sometimes attributed to the Small Toad."

The manner in which a different twist may be given to a story by a slight alteration in a familiar plot comes as no surprise if the folktale is viewed as a form of verbal art, and if the story-teller is credited with something of the creative imagination of the novelist. Variation is disconcerting only if one assumes that the only well-told tale is one memorized and recited word for word. Studies of the art of story-telling that take into account the creative role of the raconteur, such as those which have shown such promise in the field of American Indian folklore, will not be possible for Africa until variants have been systematically recorded and published.

Collections of Negro folktales usually suffer from the suppression, deliberate or unintentional, of non-animal tales regarded as atypical or non-Negro, of variants considered inaccurate, and of "dirty stories." Cronise and Ward, for example, assert that "Evidence was occasionally found of the existence of another class of stories such as the missionary would not care to hear or to record."

Legends Many Negro stories fall into the categories of legend and myth, both of which differ from the folktale in that they are looked upon as historically true. Reminiscences and personal anecdotes often conform so closely to patterns of folklore that they may be considered legends. In the New World there are legends of life in "slavery time," of slave uprisings and suicides, of the emancipation, and of floods, cyclones, famines, and other disasters. In South Africa legends dealing with tribal migrations are numerous, while in West Africa the succession of chiefs, the establishment of ruling houses, the sequence of tribal wars, and accounts of other events are related at length.

Tribal histories of this type are valuable sources of information where written documents are inadequate, and in many cases they contain no more fantasy than our own elementary history textbooks. But while they may refer to actual historical events, these accounts are handed down in the same way as folktales and myths, and in the course of time have assumed the character of folklore. Traditions of this sort cannot be accepted unreservedly as accurate statements of fact. That caution is necessary should be evident from studies of the growth of legends about individuals in Europe or America where historical documentation is available, and from the comparison of American Indian accounts of tribal origin and migration with archeological evidence.

Myths Accounts of the activities of the gods and of the origins of natural phenomena appear to be especially important in West Africa where a large body of mythology has been recorded. There are no comparable collections of myths from the southeastern Bantu, but Werner has been able to demonstrate the existence of mythology throughout Africa, turning to analyses of African religion where the literature on folklore was deficient. The gaps in the literature are understandable, since African myths are regarded as sacred and often esoteric. Frequently, atonement must be offered before a myth may be told. In some tribes the knowledge of a family's totemic myths is believed to give to the knower power of life or death over its members; in such cases an informant's refusal to tell myths to an outsider is not surprising.

In the New World informants may be reluctant to tell myths of African origin because of the fear of ridicule by "progressive" groups or because African cults are proscribed by law. Stories about African deities have survived in recognizable form in Brazil, Haiti, Cuba, and Dutch Guiana, where their African names have been retained. The identification of African deities with Catholic saints, such as the Yoruba thunder god, Shango, with Santa Barbara, is a common phenomenon. From the opposite point of view, the reinterpretation of Christian mythology can be seen in the Sea Island versions of Bible stories collected by Stoney and Shelby.

Explanatory Elements Explanatory elements are common in folktales, myths, and legends, although there is considerable variation from one group to another in their use. For example, etiological tales are common among the Ila but infrequent among the Lamba in East Africa; in West Africa the same is true of the Ashanti as compared to the Hausa. In some tribes it is not considered necessary to state the explanation as explicitly as "That is how the tortoise got his shell," or "Since then the leopard lives in the forest." Similarly, while many Negro tales illustrate the consequences of good and bad behavior, the moral is not always explicitly stated.

Proverbs When the moral precepts of folktales are pointed up, this is usually done by concluding the tale with a proverb which sums up its philosophical implications. The meaning of a proverb, in fact, may be derived from a folktale in which it occurs, and may be explained to a stranger by reciting the folktale at length. Moreover, proverbs may be quoted by characters in folktales in the course of dialog. This leads to proverbs of the following type: "Sandpiper says: An orphan does not have great desires," or "Chicken says: We follow the one who has something."

The foregoing Jabo proverbs illustrate a form of statement typical of Liberia, but found in other parts of Africa and the New World as well. Thus, the Dutch Guiana proverb, "Koni-Koni says: When there is no more land, there remain the holes in the trees." Koni-Koni is "a rabbitlike animal" to be compared with Cunnie Rabbit of Sierra Leone, although the name in both cases is undoubtedly derived from the English "coney." Other typical proverb forms include those which begin "One does not . . ." and "No matter how . . ." and the balanced forms "If . . ., then . . .," "Where . . ., there . . .," "We . . ., but we do not . . ." and their variants.

The piquancy of some proverbs can be appreciated without reference to their cultural context, as in the following Yoruba examples: "One does not set fire to the roof and then go to bed"; "The world is in a bad way when an egg falls and breaks the bowl"; "No matter how sweet the journey, the householder returns home"; "No matter how small the needle, a chicken cannot swallow it"; "The flood spoils the road; it thinks it is renewing it"; "The chicken alights on a rope; the rope doesn't get any rest, and the chicken doesn't get any rest"; "He who runs and hides in the bush is not doing it for nothing; if he is not chasing something, we know that something is chasing him"; "One does not become so mad at his head that he wears his hat on his buttocks."

Riddles Negro riddles are commonly stated in the form of declarative sentences rather than questions; thus, a stranger sometimes does not realize what he is expected to guess. In the following Yoruba riddles, the implied question is "Who is he?": "They cut off his head; they cut off his waist; his stump says he will call the town together." "They tell him to sit beside the fire, he sits beside the fire; they tell him to sit in the sun, he sits in the sun; they tell him to wash, he says, 'Death comes'." In some Yoruba riddles a proper name with no meaning is given to the character whose identity is to be guessed. "I look here; I look there; I don't see my mother, Odere." "Elephant dies, Mangudu eats him; buffalo dies, Mangudu eats him; Mangudu dies, there is no one who wants to eat him." The answers to these four riddles, drum, salt, ear, and cooking pot, might be guessed by strangers. Some riddles, like some proverbs, however, assume a knowledge of Yoruba institutions or artifacts, while others are based on puns and cannot be answered without knowledge of the language.

Verbal formulæ Negroes employ a variety of set verbal formulæ including spells, curses, incantations, blessings, invocations, prayers, greetings, passwords, and the like, which are stable in form and recited verbatim. Some, such as the passwords of the Yoruba Ogboni society or the secret formulæ taught to boys in the East African circumcision and initiation rites, are esoteric. All differ in form of expression from ordinary speech or conversation. They fall, no less than riddles or proverbs, within the more precise definition of folklore as verbal art, which would exclude the religious beliefs and social customs with which they are associated, except in so far as study of these is necessary to understand their meaning and to describe the situations in which they are employed.

Examples of set verbal formulæ are more often to be found in descriptions of African religion and social life than in collections of folklore, and their analysis from a stylistic or literary point of view has been neglected in favor of the social or religious customs in which they are imbedded. A plausible explanation of their neglect by folklorists would seem to be that their translation is often extremely difficult, and that even when individual words or sentences are understood, no coherent meaning may be recognized and the idea expressed may still be obscure. For example, a magical incantation that has no meaning may still work and often, even when an archaic or esoteric meaning is involved in a formula, it need not be understood by the person who recites it. Neither comprehension nor communication of meaning is essential for these forms so long as they are recited accurately and at the appropriate times. By this characteristic the verbal formulæ, like the tongue twisters and praise names, are set completely apart from proverbs, riddles, myths, legends, and folktales in all of which the desire to convey an idea is of primary importance. Tongue twisters are found throughout the area of Negro folklore, but few have been recorded, possibly because they lose effect in translation.

Praise names Praise names, which are known as *kirari* among the Hausa, *orile* among the Yoruba, and *isibongo* among the Zulu, are recited in honor of chiefs, important individuals, sibs, tribes, deities, animals, and inanimate objects. Personal characteristics or individual achievements are recounted in highly stylized form and often in archaic language. A person of exceptional importance among the Yoruba may have a series of praise names, one of which is played to him by the drummers and is referred to as his "drums" (ilu). Not infrequently proverbs are employed as Yoruba praise names, and among the Hausa the kirari of animals are sometimes encountered in dialog in the folktales. The butterfly is addressed in Hausa as "Oh Glistening One, Oh Book of God, Oh Learned One open your book." The lion is "Oh Strong One, Elder Brother of the Forest." The dog's kirari refers to the beatings he receives, to the belief that a prayer will not be heeded if his shadow falls on one who is praying, to his thinness and other characteristics: "Oh Dog, your breakfast is a club, your *fura* a stick, Oh Dog, you spoil a prayer, you are Hyena's perquisite, your ribs are like the plaits in a grass mat, your tail is like a roll of tobacco, your nose is always moist."

Songs Songs, of which words rather than music fall within the realm of folklore (considered as verbal art), are included in many African and New World Negro folktales. The verses of ceremonial songs, used to "call the gods" and for other ritual purposes, have much in common with spells and incantations, and what has been said about them also applies here. A third type of song of great importance in both sections of the Negro world is the topical song of current events used to spread news and gossip, and employed at times in a kind of blackmail. Composed in terms of African versification, these songs, even when created in European tongues as in the case of calypsos of Trinidad, the songs of allusion of Haiti, or the Plenas of Puerto Rico, frequently ignore rime in favor of prosodic rhythms. Many blues songs of the United States fall within the same general category.

Improvised sometimes by amateurs, sometimes by professionals, the topical songs have been known to persist for generations when they commemorate some historic event or when they treat with some incident of lasting interest. Thus, songs referring to battles of the 18th century are still current in Nigeria, just as calypsos were composed in Trinidad deriding certain slave overseers or commemorating the first visits of *The Graf Zeppelin* or *The Duke and Duchess of Kent*. Songs denouncing the infidelity of a sweetheart, or perhaps the injustice of a law-court, are composed constantly, following traditional patterns, and after brief periods of popularity are usually supplanted by others of the same variety.

Spirituals, a widely discussed but relatively unimportant form, are a blend of European and African motifs, deriving their distinctive features from the African musical phrasing they employ. Work songs of the Negro of the New World follow close on African patterns in both words and music. Ring-shouts, common to church parties in the South of the United States, also show African musical and verse structure, as do the Afro-Cuban popular songs.

Consideration of songs has been sketchy in most discussions of Negro folklore and documentary material has only recently become available on phonograph records, notable among which are the albums issued by the

Library of Congress. Yet, to mention only one form, the topical songs are no less important in Negro folklore than are the songs of the troubadours in European literature.

Setting and functions Folklore in published collections can be classified according to form, studied in terms of traditional stylistic devices, and analyzed in terms of the history and diffusion of specific incidents, proverbs, and the like. Recorded texts, however, are only the fleshless, bloodless skeletons of a form of art that is alive and warm. Since they are verbal rather than written, all forms of folklore except some of the secret spells used in black magic, involve both the reactions of the audience and the mode of expression of the speaker. The human, social situations in which folktales are told or in which proverbs are quoted are essential parts of folklore. Related to this is the problem of the functions of the various forms of folklore, the ends they serve, and the uses to which they are put.

Reading folktales is perhaps even less satisfactory than reading a play instead of seeing it. Equivalents of interpretive instructions to the actors are not indicated and stage directions are usually omitted. Moreover, the musical participation of the audience that adds so much to Negro folktales may be impossible to put into words, and is commonly not even indicated. Listeners may reply to direct questions from the story-teller or interject expressions of assent and approval to encourage him. More characteristic, and even more effective, is the response of the audience when they take up the chorus of a song, clapping their hands to beat out the rhythm. To many audiences the songs that stud Negro folktales in both Africa and the New World are more important than the tales themselves. If a Yoruba narrator attempts to cut short a favorite song his audience protests. Each time the song appears he must wait until his audience is ready before he can resume his story. Repetition in Negro folktales, which may strike Europeans or Americans as monotonous, is sometimes explained by the popularity of a melody rather than by any element of the story itself. A good story-teller creates additional occasions for well-liked songs. He lengthens or shortens his tales depending on the reaction of his audience, in the same way that he rearranges familiar plots and characters. For this reason tales heard in their actual setting may be considerably at variance with texts set down while working alone with an informant.

The Negro story-teller combines the art of actor with that of dramatist. From all parts of Africa and the New World have come descriptions of his dramatic timing, his expressiveness, and his virtuosity in acting out the various roles, altering his voice and employing pantomime to mimic each character in turn. In both Africa and the New World, folktales are told at night, heightening the fantasy and adding to the effectiveness of the dramatic techniques employed by the story-teller. Sessions of story-telling commonly begin with riddles before the younger children fall asleep, and on certain nights, when the moon is full or a wake is being held, they may last late into the night. It is widely felt that folktales are the special domain of the spirits of the dead, and that story-telling during the day will be punished.

Although it has long been recognized that folklore is a favorite form of amusement, its other functions have usually been disregarded. Praise names, passwords, curses, incantations, and other set verbal formulæ have nothing to do with amusement. Each has its own function and setting, indicated by its name. The same is true of certain types of songs, such as lullabies, love songs, work and war songs.

Songs, myths, and verbal formulæ may be essential parts of social or religious ceremonies. Myths and legends, as sanctions of custom, are foundations of cultural stability. When a ritual, a social distinction, or an accepted behavior pattern is questioned, there is usually a familiar myth or legend to explain how it originated, a proverb to show its wisdom, or a moral tale which shows, for example, what happens to those who are greedy or who disregard their totemic taboos.

A special, but none the less revealing, example of this is found in the Ifa divining verses of Nigeria, Dahomey, and Cuba. These verses usually begin with phrases interpreted as diviners' praise names. Many of them recount how that individual prospered who made a sacrifice prescribed by the diviner, or how one who refused to sacrifice suffered. These accounts are in a form which, under other circumstances, would be recognized as folktales and myths; here, however, they are incorporated as integral parts of the verses and of the divining ritual itself. The Ifa verses demonstrate that folktales, no less than myths or sacred songs, may be essential parts of religious ceremonies, with a function quite distinct from amusement. Many of the tales, furthermore, are etiological, with explanatory elements of the usual "just so" types based on whether the sacrifices were or were not offered. By reciting tales, many of which have the same moral, the diviner strengthens his client's belief in the efficacy of sacrifice and divination, with well-known facts of nature often cited as proof of the truth of the verses.

Functions of proverbs Negro proverbs constitute one of the most potent factors for individual conformity and cultural continuity. In West Africa proverbs are cited in court trials in much the same way that European lawyers cite cases which serve as legal precedent. Where questions of equity rather than fact are concerned, quoting an especially apt proverb at the appropriate moment may be enough to decide the case.

Proverbs are constantly being used to influence the behavior of others and as instruments of self-control. The Chaga, who say that proverbs "strike like arrows into the heart," resist the suggestions of evil comrades and the temptations of their own desires when a proverb is called to mind. The same proverb that may be used to criticize the actions of an enemy or rival may be quoted by a friend as kindly advice. The proverb of the flood and road cited above can be used either in criticism or ridicule of someone who thinks he is helping but is only making matters worse, or quoted to him as friendly advice to leave the matter alone. That of the chicken and the rope is used to chide a person who has jumped "out of the frying pan into the fire," or as a friendly warning to "Look before you leap."

A typical use of Negro proverbs is for derision or defiance. The Yoruba proverb about the egg and the bowl is used as a warning to a smaller or weaker person who presumes to challenge or criticize those above him, while that of the needle and the chicken is used in defiance of a stronger or more influential person. So characteristic is this use of proverbs that in West Africa the songs of defiance and derision, which are commonly based on similar proverbs, are known as "proverbial songs." The proverb of the needle and the chicken is the basis of a topical song sung by Yoruba women in defiance of senior or stronger co-wives.

A fundamental characteristic of proverbs is that they are almost never applied in their literal sense. Once the usage of a proverb is explained, the appropriateness of the interpretation is apparent, but it may be somewhat different from the association which first comes to the reader's mind. For this reason collections consisting only of lists of proverbs with translations and explanations of their literal meanings are inadequate; yet collections such as those of Herzog and Blooah (Jabo), of Herskovits and Tagbwe (Kru), and of Travélé (Bambara), which analyze the situations to which proverbs apply, have been exceptions.

Most Negro proverbs seem to be applicable to a number of different circumstances, yet each is regarded as most apt for one particular situation. An individual's skill in citing the proverb most appropriate to a particular occasion is recognized by the Yoruba. Their proverbs "An elder cannot see a rat but that it becomes a lizard next time" and "An elder does not finish washing his hands and then say that he will eat some more" are both applicable to a person who cannot make up his mind. Yet the former is regarded as more appropriate for this situation, while the latter is reserved for the person who is too greedy in his demands on younger people.

Unlike folktales and riddles, proverbs are seldom recited; they are quoted in the course of ordinary conversation. Almost never does a discussion lack the spice of proverbs. African college girls on the Gold Coast and in Nigeria are said to carry on metaphorical conversations for hours, using nothing but proverbs, but this may be considered atypical and ostentatious. As collections of folktales are devitalized by the absence of gesture, facial expression, vocal emphasis, and the reaction and participation of the audience, so lists of proverbs suffer by being torn from the context of speech in which they normally occur.

Folklore in education In operating to ensure cultural stability and continuity, folklore is important in the process of transmitting culture through the education of the individual. Myths, legends, and secret formulæ may be a part of the instructions given by a parent to a child or by a priest or chief to an initiate, while other forms of folklore may be learned informally in social situations not specifically directed toward education. Riddles, which are regarded as sharpening a child's wits, also teach lessons which must eventually be learned. In addition to the characteristics of animals, human beings, and other natural objects, they may refer to social distinctions and social etiquette, as the following: "Who drinks with the king?" (Fly). "Who goes down the street past the king's house and does not salute the king?" (Rain water).

The role of Negro folklore in education has been best analyzed by Raum among the Chaga. Stories about monsters are told to the youngest children, with implied threats to those who misbehave. Later, these are gradually replaced by moral tales which indicate such attitudes as diligence and filial piety, and show the consequences of laziness, snobbishness, and rebelliousness. When the Chaga child reaches fourteen, folktales and riddles give way to proverbs. These are employed by parents to epitomize a lesson which they wish to teach their children, and they appear as a didactic device in the instructions given to Chaga boys during the initiation ceremonies. "When a child flies into a rage, when he lies or steals, when he is recalcitrant or violates the code of etiquette, when he makes an ass of himself, when he is cowardly, he hears his actions commented upon in the words of a proverb." The impression made upon the child is frequently so forceful that the conditions under which a particular proverb was first heard can be remembered in adulthood. The importance of folklore in African life, and of proverbs in particular, is perhaps best summarized in the words of one of Raum's informants: "The Chaga have four big possessions: land, cattle, water, and proverbs."

Selected Bibliography:

Africa

Bascom, W. R., "The Relationship of Yoruba Folklore to Divining," *JAFL* 56: 127–131.

Bleek, W. H. I., *Reynard the Fox in South Africa.* London, 1864. (Bushmen)

Callaway, Rev. Canon, *Nursery Tales, Traditions and Histories of the Zulus.* Natal, 1868.

Chatelain, H., *Folk-tales of Angola. MAFLS,* vol. 1, 1894. (Bunda)

Christaller, J. G. (ed.) *Twi Mmbusem Mpensa-Ahansia Mmoaano. A Collection of Three Thousand Six Hundred Tshi Proverbs in use among the Negroes of the Gold Coast speaking the Asante and Fante Languages.* Basel, 1879.

Cronise, F. M. and H. W. Ward, *Cunnie Rabbit, Mr. Spider and the Other Beef.* London, 1903. (Temne)

Doke, C. M., *Lamba Folk-lore. MAFLS,* vol. 20, 1927.

Equilbecq, F. V., *Essai sur la Littérature Merveilleuse des Noires.* Paris, 1913. (French West Africa)

Frobenius, L., *Atlantis: Volksdichtung und Volksmärchen Afrikas.* Jena, 1921–28. Vols. IV–XII. (Congo, Guinea Coast, Western Sudan, Nilotic Sudan)

Frobenius, L., and D. C. Fox, *African Genesis.* New York, 1937.

Gaden, H., *Proverbes et Maximes Peuls et Toucouleurs. Trav. et Mém. de l'Inst. d'Eth.,* vol. 16, 1931.

Gutmann, Bruno, *Volksbuch der Wadschagga.* Leipzig, 1914. (Chaga)

Herskovits, M. J., and S. Tagbwe, "Kru Proverbs," *JAFL* 43: 225–293.

Herzog, G., and C. G. Blooah, *Jabo Proverbs from Liberia.* London, 1936.

Jacottet, E., *The Treasury of Ba-Sutu Lore.* London, 1908.

Junod, H. A., *Chants et Contes des Ba-Ronga.* Lausanne, 1897. (Thonga)

———, *The Life of a South African Tribe* (2nd ed.), 2 vols. London, 1927. (Thonga)

Klipple, M. A., *African Folk Tales with Foreign Analogues.* Unpublished doctoral thesis, Indiana University, 1938.

Lederbogen, W., *Kameruner Märchen.* Berlin, 1901.

Lindblom, G., *Kamba Tales of Animals. Arch. d'Études Orientales,* vol. 20, pt. 1. Uppsala, 1926.

Nassau, A. H., *Where Animals Talk.* Boston, 1912. (French Equatorial Africa)

Rattray, R. S., *Hausa Folklore,* 2 vols. Oxford, 1913.

————, *Ashanti Proverbs*. Oxford, 1916.

————, *Akan-Ashanti Folk-Tales*. Oxford, 1930.

Raum, O. F., *Chaga Childhood*. London, 1940.

Schon, J., *Magana Hausa*. London, 1885.

Smith, F. W., and A. M. Dale, *The Ila-Speaking Peoples of Northern Rhodesia*, 2 vols. London. 1920.

Stayt, H. A., *The Bavenda*. London, 1931.

Struck, B., "Die Afrikanischen Märchen," *Volkerkunde*, Berlin, 1925, p. 35.

Tauxier, L., *Les Noires du Yatenga*. Paris, 1917.

————, *Nègres Gouro et Gagou*. Paris, 1924.

Thomas, N. W., *Anthropological Report on the Ibo-Speaking Peoples of Nigeria*, vol. VI. London, 1914.

Travélé, M., *Proverbes et Contes Bambara*. Paris, 1923.

Tremearne, A. J., *Hausa Superstitions and Customs*. London, 1913.

Weeks, J. H., *Jungle Life and Jungle Stories*. London, 1923. (Belgian Congo)

Werner, A., "African Mythology" in *Mythology of All Races*, vol. 7, pp. 101–448. Boston, 1925.

————, *Myths and Legends of the Bantu*. London, 1933.

New World

Andrade, M. J., *Folklore from the Dominican Republic*. *MAFLS*, vol. 23, 1930.

Beckwith, M., *Jamaica Anansi Stories*. *MAFLS*, vol. 17, 1924.

————, *Jamaica Folk-lore*. *MAFLS*, vol. 21, 1928.

Fortier, A., *Lousiana Folktales*. *MAFLS*, vol. 2, 1895.

Harris, J. C., *Uncle Remus, His Songs and Sayings*. Boston, 1880.

————, *Nights with Uncle Remus*. Boston, 1883.

Herskovits, M. J., and F. S., *Suriname Folklore*. New York, 1936.

Magalhães, B. de, *O Folk-lore no Brasil* (based on tales collected by J. da Silva-Campos). Rio de Janeiro, 1928.

Parsons, E. C., *Folk Tales of Andros Island, Bahamas*. *MAFLS*, vol. 13, 1918.

————, *Folklore of the Sea Islands, South Carolina*. *MAFLS*, vol. 16, 1923.

————, *Folklore of the Antilles, French and English*. *MAFLS*, vol. 25, pts. 1–3, 1933–42.

Stoney, S. G., and G. M. Shelby, *Black Genesis*. New York, 1930.

Sylvain-Comhaire, S., "Creole Tales from Haiti," *JAFL* 50: 207–295; 51: 219–346.

RICHARD A. WATERMAN and WILLIAM R. BASCOM

afrīt, afreet, or **ifrit** In the Koran. an epithet applied to a demon: later construed as the designation of a particularly terrible and dangerous kind of demon, and prevailingly so accepted in Arabian mythology and among all Moslems.

afterbirth The placenta. In the folk belief of nearly all the peoples in the world (civilized and primitive) the afterbirth is closely associated with the soul, life, death, health, character, success, or failure of the person with whom it is born, and is therefore equally tied up with the deeply rooted human belief in the separable or external soul. What becomes of the afterbirth (and with it the umbilical cord and caul) either influences or determines the whole life-story of the child. It is variously believed to embody his own soul-substance or his guardian spirit, to be either his brother, twin, or actual double, or to be so mystically and inseparably connected with

him that its treatment or fate will shape his skills, luck, and fate. Among peoples and cultures from British Columbia to Tierra del Fuego, Iceland, Siberia, Europe, and South Africa, among the peoples of China, Indonesia, the south Pacific, and also among certain North American Indians, the afterbirth is regarded with awe and is either preserved or disposed of according to the belief of the group.

The Kwakiutl Indians of British Columbia present the afterbirth of a boy baby to the ravens, believing that this will endow him with the power to see the future; the afterbirth of a girl baby is buried at high-tide mark to insure her becoming a good clam digger. The Yukaghir peoples of northeastern Siberia have this same reliance on the sympathetic magic involved when they tie up the afterbirth in a reindeer skin and attach to it a miniature bow and arrow, a little wooden knife, and scraps of fur to make a boy a good hunter. A toy woman's knife, thimble, and needle attached to the afterbirth bundle of a girl will make her a skilful worker. A people as far removed from these two groups as the Aymara Indians of Bolivia cover the afterbirth with flowers and bury it along with tiny farm tools for a boy and cooking pots for a girl. All over Europe the people believe that one's fate is tied up with his afterbirth. Great care is taken to prevent its being found and eaten by an animal, or exposed to evil spirits. If an animal should find and eat it, the child would grow up with all the most unattractive qualities (physical or mental) of that animal.

The belief that the afterbirth contains part of the soul-substance of the child is found as far apart as Iceland and Zanzibar, Australia and Sumatra. The Swahilis of Zanzibar bury the afterbirth under the house in which a child is born to insure his loyalty to home. The Karo Bataks (Sumatra) also bury it under the house, believing that it contains the child's true soul. He has another soul for everyday life, but the true soul resides in the afterbirth and must be kept safe. The Bataks of Sumatra also bury their afterbirths under the house, believing they contain the souls of their children. Some of the tribes of Sumatra, however, carefully preserve them with salt and tamarinds and invoke the souls therein, a practice bordering on the guardian-spirit idea. This guardian-spirit idea is shared by the Sumatran Kooboos, who believe the afterbirth contains the guardian spirit that will protect an individual from evil all his life. Sumatran Bataks believe everyone has two guardian spirits: one contained in the germ of conception (called elder brother) and one in the afterbirth (called younger brother). Central Australian tribes also believe the afterbirth contains the child's spirit and hide it safely in the ground. Queensland, Australia, tribes believe that only a certain part of the soul, the cho-i, remains in the afterbirth. They never fail to bury it at once and mark the spot with a cone of twigs so that Anjea may easily find it to make another baby.

Among the Baganda of central Africa the afterbirth is the actual twin or double of the child that is born. It is put in a pot and buried under a plantain tree (evidently *Musa arnoldiana*). It becomes a ghost and goes into the tree, which is carefully guarded lest anyone not kin should make food or drink from it. If this should happen the ghost-twin would go away and the child in the house would follow its twin and die. The king's "twin" is kept in a little temple and a special guardian is appointed, the kimbugwe, to take care of it. He takes it out of its wrappings once a month, allows the moon to shine upon it, rubs it with butter, shows it to the king to assure him of the welfare of his double, and returns it to the safety of the temple. Tribes south of the Uganda also believe the afterbirth is a human being. Certain North American Indians tell vivid stories revealing belief in the afterbirth as twin of the child. In the Creek Indian story of the *Bead-Spitter and Thrown-Away,* the father hides and watches for the secret playmate of his son, who has surprisingly asked for two toy bows with arrows. From his watching place the man sees another boy come from the afterbirth in the bushes (where he himself had thrown it) and play with the other. It is the child's own twin. This development of twin from afterbirth appears also in Wichita, Pawnee, and Cherokee tales. But in the Natchez Indian story, Thrown-Away developed from the discarded umbilical cord.

The Batanga belief of the little ghost in the tree ties up the folklore of the afterbirth with another widespread folk belief, i.e. the birth-tree and its identity with the child for whom it is planted. In Calabar, West Africa, a young palm tree is planted when a child is born and the afterbirth is buried under it. The afterbirth insures the growth of the tree as the growth of the tree insures the growth of the child. This belief and practice prevail in New Zealand and the Molucca Islands, in Pomerania in Prussia, and in other parts of Europe. It is paralleled by the Hupa Indians of California who split in two a young fir tree at the birth of a child, put the afterbirth and umbilical cord inside, and bind the tree together again. The welfare of the child depends thereafter on the fate of the tree.

In ancient Jewish practice various mysterious medicines and charms were made from the ashes of the afterbirth. Mixed with milk they would charm the wasting disease away from a small child; mixed with snapdragons and tied in a little bag around a child's neck, they proved a powerful charm against bewitchment. In China medicinal pills were often made from the placenta. The Peruvian Aymara Indians also value its ashes as a kind of cure for various ills.

The Javanese custom differs from all these. In Java the women place the afterbirth in a little vessel, bedeck it with fruits, flowers, and lighted candles, and set it adrift in the river at night to please the crocodiles. This is either because all afterbirths are crocodiles, brothers and sisters of their human counterparts, or because the crocodiles are inhabited by the ancestors of the people, and one twin is religiously returned to them.

afterworld The abode of the dead; the world after death: a concept of all human mythologies and religions. Sometimes it is situated in gloomy regions under the earth or under the sea, sometimes in a bright sky world; sometimes it is on a nearby, or distant, island, as the Abokas of New Hebrides (Melanesian) mythology, or it is thought to be far across the sea, or sometimes just "in the west."

Many mythologies contain the dual concept of a wonderful abode for the blessed and a grim underworld for the less fortunate. The Central Eskimo, for instance, have Qudlivun, a happy land in the sky full of games and pleasure, Adlivun, an undersea world of discomfort and punishment, and Adliparmiut, an even lower region, which is not quite so terrible as Adlivun, but from which there is no return. Other afterworlds typical of the dual (or multiple) concept are: the Greek Elysium, for heroes and the blessed, originally situated in the western ocean, and Hades, the underworld of shades; the Norse Valhalla, hall of the chosen slain, Bilskirnir, Thor's huge palace where the thralls were entertained as well as their masters in Valhalla, Fensalir, Frigga's palace, where happy married couples were invited to come and stay forever, and Hel, the underground realm of death; and the Christian system of heaven, hell, and purgatory. The Caroline Islands (Micronesian) afterworld includes a sky heaven for those souls who, in the shape of sea birds, manage to reach it, a special region set apart for warriors so that they may go on with their fighting, and a place where earth and heaven meet for women who die in childbirth. But men who hang themselves are shut out altogether, because the gods do not like to see their protruding tongues.

Nai Thombo Thombo is the afterworld of Fijian (Melanesian) belief. Life there follows the pattern of life on earth; but few souls ever reach it because the journey is so beset with perils and frustrations. The soul must carry a whale's tooth, for instance, which has been put into the dead hand. This he must hurl at a certain tree to which he will come. If he misses, he must return to his grave; if he hits it, he may proceed to another place where he awaits the souls of his strangled wives. He cannot continue his journey until they have all caught up with him. (Bachelors are always caught by demons.) The soul with his wives then advances on his journey, fighting demons on every side. If he does not overcome them, they eat him. If he wins, he eventually reaches a mountain place where he is questioned. After the questioning he is either sent back to earth to be deified by his descendants, or he is dumped into the sea: the path to the last place. Nai Thombo Thombo is not only a real place in Fijian belief, but a real road leads to it, through a real town. In this town the people take care to build all doors exactly opposite each other, to make easier the way for the bewildered souls. They are careful, too, to leave no sharp implements lying about which might injure the passing ones.

Tongan and Samoan (Polynesian) mythology has an afterworld named Pulotu, which is either on an island "to the northwest," or under the sea. Samoans believe that the entrance to it is through two round openings in certain rocks on the west end of Savaii island. The big opening is for chiefs, the smaller one for other people. Once through the openings, the souls drop into a pit; at the bottom of the pit runs a river which carries them to Pulotu. There they bathe in the water of life and are young again.

Society Islanders (also Polynesian) believe that the soul is met at death by other souls who conduct it to Po, an underworld of darkness, where it is fed to a god three times and, after the third reshaping, is deified. The people of the Marquesas believe in an upper pleasant world for gods and chiefs, and three lower worlds, one below the other, to which the souls of the dead are consigned according to the number of pigs sacrificed for them. The lowest of these regions is the pleasantest, the top the worst.

The shaman of the Caingang Indians (Brazil) sits

beside the body of one newly dead and instructs the soul how to face the dangers of the journey to the afterworld. The soul must be careful not to take a certain forking path which leads into the web of a giant spider; it must take care to avoid a certain trap which would hurl it into a boiling pot; it must walk warily on a slippery path beside a swamp where a huge crab is waiting. If the soul escape these dangers it will come at last to a western underworld where it is always day; here the aged become young and hunt joyfully in a forest teeming with deer, tapirs, and all kinds of game. Later comes a second death, after which the soul inhabits some insect, usually a mosquito or ant. The death of this insect is the end and obliteration of the soul. Hence the Caingang do not kill insects.

In North American Karok Indian belief, mortals who visit the world of the dead see their departed ones living and dancing just as they did on earth. But the earthly visitor discovers that he has been away from the world a year, when he thought it was a day. Among the Omaha the Milky Way is the path the spirits travel to a sevenfold spirit world. An old man sits by the Milky Way directing the souls of the blessed to a short cut. The souls of the Caribou Eskimo pass into the keeping of Pana, the Woman-Up-There, whose sky heaven is full of holes. The holes are stars; and when anything is spilled Up There it comes through the holes in the shape of rain, snow, hailstones, etc. The dead are reborn in the house of Pana, and brought back to earth with the help of the moon, to live again as human beings, or animals, birds, fish, etc. The nights no moon is visible are the nights the moon is busy helping Pana bring the souls to the world again.

The Dahomean Negro afterworld is said by some to be in the sky, by others to be beneath the earth. But the path to it is so well known that there is a map of it. In Bantu mythology the souls of the dead inhabit an underground region referred to by many of the tribes as Ku-zimu. Earthquakes are believed to be caused by agitation among these underground populations.

agaric A fungus of the mushroom group (order *Agaricales*). The agarics of folklore are the fly agaric (*Amanita muscaria*) whose deadly poison is often used in a decoction for killing flies, and an agaric found growing on birch trees which provides the spunk or touchwood of such sudden and magical combustibility.

The Siberian Koryaks endow this poisonous fungus (the fly agaric) with a spirit or personality. Wapaq they call it and believe the wapaq are powerful guiding spirits for anyone who dares to eat. The myth says Big Raven caught a whale, but could not send it home again because he could not lift the big grass-bag the whale would need for food en route. He cried out to Vahiynin (Existence) and Vahiynin said, "Eat the wapaq." Vahiynin spat upon the earth and there stood the little white plants with the foam of the spittle turning to spots upon their hats. So Big Raven ate the wapaq and suddenly felt so gay and mighty that he easily lifted the big grass-bag for the whale, and the whale went home to the sea. Then when Big Raven saw the whale swimming home he said, "O wapaq, grow on the earth forever," and to his children he said, "Learn whatever the wapaq shall teach." So the Koryak believe today that a person affected with agaric is guided by the wapaq. If

an old man should eat agaric and the wapaq within the agaric should whisper, "You have just been born," that old man would begin to cry like a baby. If the wapaq should say, "Go to the afterworld," then the old man would die.

In Europe, Scotland, Ireland, and various Celtic islands, another kind of agaric (probably *Polyporus officinalis*) which grows on trees is looked upon as having great mysterious powers and properties. The seeming magic of its sudden combustibility is probably the reason for its use in kindling the Beltane fires (the *teine éigin*, the fire from rubbing sticks). Not only is the flare so instantaneous and bright as to seem pure magic, but this wonderful substance is believed also to possess great potency as a charm against witchcraft and various diseases. It was also thought to be able to render poisons impotent.

Agastya or **Agasti** A famous Rishi of India, regarded as the author of certain Vedic hymns: in Hindu mythology, noted for his asceticism, his magical birth from a water-jar into which his two fathers, Mitra and Varuna, had dropped their seed on seeing the nymph, Urvaśī, and his creation by magic of the beautiful Lopāmudrā, whom he married in order to have sons and save himself and his ancestors from destruction. He is celebrated for halting the growth of the Vindhya mountains and for drinking up the ocean. The *Mahābhārata* describes how a certain group of asuras, who were at war with the gods, hid themselves in the ocean and decided to work from there against holy men and Brāhmans and put an end to the world. The gods appealed to Agastya for help, so he drank up the ocean; the asuras were exposed in their hiding place, and killed by the gods. Perhaps the most famous feat of Agastya was his preventing the Vindhya mountains from stopping the course of the sun. Vindhya wanted to be higher than Mount Meru around whose peak the sun and moon revolved. So he began to grow up and up until the gods were afraid he would stop the sun in its course altogether. They begged Agastya to do something to stop the alarming growth. Agastya packed up his belongings and with his family started on a journey into the south. When he came to Vindhya, he asked a boon: that Vindhya cease growing until his return. So Vindhya stopped growing, and is waiting yet, the same height as on that day, for Agastya decided to stay in the south forever. Some stories say he came back; but most people believe he never did because the mountain has not grown an inch. How his miraculous digestion put an end to the indigestible demon ram who expected to kill Agastya from within, is another favorite Hindu story.

After his death Agastya was assigned a place in the heavens and is identified with Canopus. Popular mythology ascribes to him the power of staying monsoons, i.e. controlling the waters of the ocean and restoring the sun to man. He is still living (though invisible) on Agastya's hill in Travancore, and regarded as the patron saint of southern India who was instrumental in the introduction of Hindu literature and religion in that region. See MAHĀBHĀRATA.

agate A variegated quartz or chalcedony having the colors usually in bands, but existing also in solid white, brown, and red, as well as white and black, white and gray, white and red varieties: according to Theocritus named for the river Achates in Sicily where it was first found. Agate relieves thirst if held in the mouth long enough; it reduces fever; and it was once believed to turn the sword of an enemy against himself. It is dedicated to June; symbolizes health and longevity. In Jewish lore the agate was believed to prevent one from stumbling or falling, and was especially prized by horsemen for that reason. In Arabia arrow-shaped amulets made of agate were worn as being good for the blood. The medieval belief that agate was a specific against the bites of scorpions and snakes was somewhat dispelled by Jacques Grevin, a physician of 16th century Paris. He published various writings casting doubt on the efficacy of toadstone and turquoise for detecting poisons, but could not deny that powdered agate *on the tongue* (not worn as an amulet) would cure a poisoned patient. The varieties of agate used by certain North American Indians to make implements and blades are loosely and popularly called *flint*.

agave A plant of the genus *Agave;* especially, the century plant (*Agave americana*), so called because it flowers when it reaches maturity (in ten to thirty years) and then dies, giving rise to the fable that it blooms once in a century. The plant is a native of arid regions in the southern United States and Central America and has long been cultivated in Mexico for its sap, which is fermented. The resulting thin, buttermilk-like liquid is called pulque and is widely consumed in Mexico. A very intoxicating liquor, mezcal or aguardiente de maguey, is distilled from pulque.

The goddess and discoverer of the plant, Mayauel, is represented with four hundred breasts and seated before or on the plant. The agave was regarded by the Nahua people as the Tree of Life and its milk was used by Xolotl to nurse the first man and woman created by the Aztec gods.

Agbe Chief god of the Thunder pantheon (Xevioso) of Dahomey religion. He was entrusted with full charge of world affairs by his mother Sogbo (in this pantheon, synonym for Mawu). In the Sky pantheon Agbe is the son of Mawu and Lisa, but the Xevioso cult identifies him with Lisa. Agbe has the whole sea for his dwelling, but to converse with his mother Agbe goes to that place where the sea and sky meet. Hence the round rising and setting suns are called the eyes of Agbe (Dahomey being so situated that the sun is seen both to rise from and sink into the sea). In spite of his powers in the world, Agbe was not shown how to send rain. He must send water up from the sea to his mother who causes it to fall from the sky as rain upon the earth. Hence when lightning strikes a ship at sea, Agbe has struck it; but lightning on the earth is sent by Mawu (Sogbo) (see Herskovits *Dahomey* II, 151, 156, 159).

The Dahomey Agbe survives in Haiti as Agwe or Agwe Woyo, a god of the Rada division or class of the vodun pantheon. Here too he is god of the sea and has a son and a daughter, Agweto and Agweta. His worship is strong only in coastal communities. In the overlapping of Catholicism in Haiti upon the basic vodun elements, St. Expeditius has been equated with Agwe.

Agdistis Offspring of the seed of Zeus dropped in sleep upon the earth, a hermaphrodite: identified with the Phrygian Earth-Mother, Cybele. The story as told by Pausanias states that the gods abhorred the ab-

normality and severed its male organs. From these grew the almond tree from whose blossom (or fruit) Nana conceived Attis. Later the sight of the beautiful Attis filled Agdistis with such passion, that at the moment of his marriage she drove Attis mad and he castrated himself. The father of the bride in like madness did the same. Attis died of the wound, and Agdistis, grief-stricken and repentant, implored Zeus never to allow the beautiful body of Attis to decompose. This Zeus promised. According to Hesychius, Strabo, Ovid, and many others, Agdistis and Cybele are one and the same. The story explains the practice of the self-emasculation of the priests of the original Attis cults during the orgiastic rituals. It is tied up with the symbolism of the joint male-female potencies in nature, with the motif of the uncorrupted body, and of course with the widespread Adonis-Aphrodite, Osiris-Isis vegetation myths.

ages of man The periods of time into which the life of an individual is considered to be divided. What walks on four legs at morning, two legs at noon, and three legs at evening? The answer to this riddle of the Sphinx: Man (who creeps on all fours in infancy, walks upright in manhood, uses a cane in old age). The division of the life of man into seven stages is said to have been first defined by Hippocrates: infancy, childhood, boyhood, youth, manhood, middle age, old age. This has been reworded by many writers as infancy, childhood, puberty, youth, prime, old age, senility. References to these seven periods are frequent in Midrashic writings. Probably the best known is the following: The child of a year is like a king, adored by all; at two or three he is like a swine, playing in the mire. In the third period he is likened to a kid "which capers hither and thither making glad the hearts of all who look upon it." This third period continues until the individual is about eighteen years old. At twenty he is like a horse, spirited and confiding in the strength of youth. Then comes the fifth stage when he is like an ass, burdened with wife and children, and having to travel backward and forward to bring home sustenance. The sixth stage is not attractive, being that time during which man snatches his bread wherever he finds it, caring for nothing but his own household. In the seventh stage he is like an ape, asking for food and drink and playing like a child, "but a learned man like David is a king, though old."

ages of the world Those periods of the earth's existence between cosmic cataclysms. Both the Jews and Babylonians record their history as before and after the flood. The idea of the deluge is found in most primitive cultures, either past or future, while many North American Indian mythologies derive creation out of a watery chaos. Most Indians of South America record two destructions, water and fire. The Aztecs record four: earth, air, fire, and water, i.e. famine, hurricane, fire, and flood, although the order is not certain.

The Golden, Silver, Bronze, and Iron ages of the ancient classical world are the most widely known. During the Golden Age, ruled by Saturn, man lived to a great age in an abundant Garden of Eden, free from restraint of law or necessity for work. The Silver Age or Age of Jupiter was characterized by licentiousness and voluptuous living. Men refused to worship the gods and were finally destroyed. The Bronze Age of Neptune was a violent period of warfare in which everyone was destroyed by internal strife. And in the Iron Age of Pluto, there was neither justice, law, nor religion left in the world. Hesiod in his *Works and Days* gives a fifth age after the Bronze called the Heroic Age when men strove to do better, but failed.

The ancient Hindus divided their existence into four periods, or yugas, of declining morality. Duration of each successive period diminishes by one fourth, as does man's life span, stature, and virtue. In krita yuga, men were giants and lived in plenty. Neither gods nor demons existed and sacrifices were unknown. This period lasted 4,000 divine years (360 years each) plus dawn and twilight periods, or 1,728,000 years. In the treta yuga, which lasted 1,296,000 years, man's life span declined to 300 years. Vice crept in, but sacrifices were made devoutly. In dvapara yuga vice and disease were rife, ceremonies increased, marriage laws were needed for the first time, and sacrifices were made only with the hope of gain. In the kali yuga religion disappears altogether and the world is given over to sin and strife; and at the end the earth will be destroyed by fire and flood. The cycle, which lasts 4,320,000 years, will not be repeated for a thousand times this period.

The Buddhists also use the four yugas which were later elaborated. Their system consists of four imponderable periods made up of twenty intermediate parts of four yugas each. The first imponderable is a period of destruction, the second of nothingness, and the third of reconstruction. First come sun, moon, and gods; then, in nineteen successive stages, life is distributed, including man who lives to the age of 80,000. When demons appear, reconstruction is completed. In the imponderable of destruction, through increase of vice and disease, man's life declines to ten years by the end of the fourth yuga. In the second intermediate period the yugas are reversed and man improves until he is back at the beginning, and so on for twenty intermediates before the next destruction. Even destructions move in cycles of 64, seven by fire and one by water, etc., until the 64th which is by wind and the worst of the set.

St. Agnes' Eve The night before St. Agnes' festival day, January 21: a time of divination for young unmarried girls. In England and Scotland all kinds of charms, rimes, and special rituals are said and performed by which young girls expect to be shown whom they will marry. "Agnes sweet, Agnes fair / Hither, hither now repair / Bonny Agnes let me see / The lad who is to marry me," is a favorite incantation, said while sprinkling a little grain on the ground. A young girl about to fall asleep will say, "St. Agnes, that's to lovers kind / Come ease the trouble of my mind." But before getting in bed she has put a sprig of thyme in one shoe, a sprig of rosemary in the other, and placed one on each side of her bed. This is sure to bring the hoped-for revelation, i.e. her future husband's face in a dream.

Agni or **Agnis** In Hindu mythology, god or personification of fire: one of the three chief deities of the Vedas (others were the rain god, Vāyu or Indra, and the sun god, Sūrya). Agni represents lightning and the sun as well as earthly fire. In the latter he is always present in every household and is believed to be the giver of immortality who purges from sin, burns away the guilt of the body after death, and carries the immortal part to heaven. As the altar fire he is the god of priests and the priest of gods, the mediator between gods and men.

He was born of the lotus, according to the earlier Vedas, created by Brahmā (*Mahābhārata*), kindled by Bhrigu for the diffusion of fire on earth (*Rig-Veda*) as the son of two pieces of wood which he immediately swallowed. He was one of the eight lokapālas, guardians of the cardinal and intermediate points. He is described as red, with two faces and seven tongues to lick up the butter used in sacrifices, or sometimes with three heads and seven rays, clothed in black, carrying a snake standard and a flaming javelin, and is shown in a chariot drawn by red horses.

In mythology, he betrayed Bhrigu's wife into the hands of a Rākshasa, was cursed by Bhrigu, and condemned forever after to consume everything. Agni rebelled against this and hid himself until both men and gods recognized his indispensability. Then Brahmā assured him that he would devour only in the sense of digesting. He exhausted his vigor by consuming too many oblations, and renewed it by burning the Khāndava forest while Kṛishṇa and Arjuna guarded each end of it so that its inhabitants could not escape and Indra could not stop the proceeding.

In popular belief to poke a fire wounds Agni. He is invoked by lovers to intervene in their affairs, and by men for virility. His worship and ritual have degenerated in modern Hinduism and he has no professed sect, but Agnihotri Brāhmans still perform the fire sacrifice or *agnihotra*. Compare ĀTAR.

Agunua The principal figona of San Cristoval island: a Melanesian creator who, unlike most figona, is represented as a male snake. Agunua created the sea, the land, men, storms, and a woman. When the woman was old, she changed her skin and returned looking young and lovely. Her daughter did not recognize her and would have nothing to do with her. The woman went away again, put on her old skin, and so death came into the world, for men could thenceforth no longer change their skins when they were old.

Rain came to the earth because Agunua was thirsty. Food, too, was given to man when Agunua gave his twin man-brother a yam and told him to plant it in a big garden. The brother cut the yam, put the pieces in a basket, and began to plant them. The basket never emptied and from the crop came all kinds of yams, bananas, almond trees, coconuts, and fruit trees. Then Agunua gave him fire from his own staff and the man cooked the yams. From the burnt ones came the uneatable fruits, from the unbaked pieces came taro and bananas. Finally the figona bore a male child and then produced a girl who knew how to make fire and cook.

Sacrifices are made to Agunua in the form of shell money and by burning a pudding made of yams and almonds. See MELANESIAN MYTHOLOGY.

Ahasuerus (1) A shoemaker of Jerusalem: one of the personalities and names ascribed to the Wandering Jew. Ahasuerus was standing in his doorway to catch a sight of Jesus passing by, weighed down under the cross, on his way to Calvary. Jesus stopped to rest a moment, but the shoemaker in righteous zeal told him to move on. Jesus moved on, but turned to say, "Thou shalt wander without rest until the last day." Ahasuerus followed the crowd and watched the crucifixion. At that moment it came upon him that he must go forth into all lands. He is said to be perpetually wandering over the face of the earth, repentant and longing for the release of death.

(2) In the *Book of Esther,* king of Persia; husband of Vashti and Esther. He has been identified with Xerxes. Ahasuerus was inclined to be swayed by his passion of the moment, or by whoever had his ear, as did Haman. He commanded Queen Vashti to appear before him and his nobles to show her beauty, but the king was drunk and Vashti refused. He therefore degraded her by making her no longer queen and sought among the virgins of his land for a new queen until he discovered Esther, whom he made queen. By Haman's connivance he ordered a slaughter of the Jews in his realm, and when he learned that the Jews were Esther's people, he reversed his orders.

Ahayuta achi   The twin war gods of Zuñi mythology, culture heroes and inventors, hunters, protectors of gamblers, mischief-makers and benefactors, destroyers of monsters, great and adventurous travelers, and lusty rapers. They live inside the mountain and guard the towns, and in this capacity are called the Ones Who Hold The High Places. They are impersonated at the War Society ceremonies and also as kachinas. As kachinas they have to be killed as symbolic of how they themselves learned to be skilful killers. The War Chiefs pray to them at the winter solstice for good crops and long life for the people.

In story they figure usually as two little boys magically begotten by the Sun: sons of the Sun and Waterfall or Dripping Water. They always live with their grandmother, who is usually named Spider Woman. They are always mischievous, always teasing and disobeying the old lady, stealing salt from animals, stealing masks from the kachinas, and always going where the grandmother says not to. This gives rise to many stories of monster slaying, and specifically to the story of their journey to the sky to find their father the Sun.

As culture heroes they gave the people their whole way of life, and designated the directions of the four quarters of the earth. They founded the Curing societies at Zuñi and Sia. The Tewa Twins also made the mountains; among the Hopi they made the water courses, and dug the canyons to drain the water out of the earth that was so soft and muddy before that, that the people sank into it.

As travelers the Twins had many adventures. Masewi (one of them) of Laguna went to the four corners of the world on errands for the underground Mothers. On one escapade the two of them killed the dreaded Chakwena giantess, after Sun revealed to them that the monster kept her heart in her gourd rattle. They always returned triumphant from their journeyings, having killed a monster, saved a village from a man-eating ghost, etc., in justification of their disobedience in going to that place. The Acoma Twins stole the four magic staffs that bring snow, hail, frost, and lightning, from the Direction Chiefs while they were sleeping. When the Chiefs awoke they sent the Water Serpent after the brothers, and in the wake of the Serpent came destroying floods. The people ran up the mountain while the Twins killed the Serpent with arrows of the Sun and saved the village.

The War Twins are prominent through all Pueblo mythology and folktale. At Zuñi they are the Ahayuta achi, War Brothers, War Twins, little war gods, sons of the Sun; at Taos they are the hayunu, the Stone Men, two brothers; at Tewa they are known as the Towae sendo, Little People; the Hopi call them Pü'ükonghoya, little Smiter, and Pa'lüngahoya; the Keres and Jemez call them Masewi and Uyuyewi. One of them is the Slayer-of-Monsters developed so elaborately in Apache and Navaho mythology. In Hopi story the Twins once kindly turned into stone two little children who had been whipped and had run away from home, with the result that the Hopi now never whip their children. The Twins punish inhospitality the same way. Many tales of the War Twins resemble very closely Taos stories of Echo Boy and the Hopi, Tewa, and Cochiti stories of Ash Boys, Fire Boys, Poker Boys, etc., but the Zuñi Ahayuta achi are not truly identified with any of these.

At Zuñi they are closely associated with lightning and with falling stars and comets. The myth of their search for their father in the sky merges into their identification with the Morning Star. When the Franciscans first told the Christ story in the pueblos the people identified Jesus with these two little boys and leaped to the charming analogy between God the Father and God the Son, and Sun and Morning Star. See TWINS.

Ahi   Literally, the snake: another name for Vritra (although sometimes distinct), the cosmic dragon of Vedic mythology, who absorbed the cosmic waters and lay in coils upon the mountains. For this reason he was sometimes called the cloud demon. Indra killed this monster with his thunderbolt, and the precious waters flowed from its riven belly in streams across the land. Sap rose in the trees and warm blood flowed again in human veins. Ahi or Vritra is sometimes otherwise interpreted as the personification of winter (not just the hoarder of rain) whose slaying unlocks the frozen streams.

ahimsā   The Indian doctrine of the sanctity of life, originally set forth in one of the *Upānishads* about the 7th century B.C.: common to all Indian sects ever since. The Brāhman may deprive no creature of its life, not man, beast, worm, nor ant. He may not even pour out water on the ground lest some aquatic organism perish in the dry sand. Jainism gave the idea first place in its tenets. Ahimsā is the first of the five Jainist ascetic vows, and the true Jainist carries its observance to minute and fanatic extremes. He will not kill body vermin; he sweeps the ground before him so as not to tread or sit on any tiny living thing. He will not eat at night lest inadvertently he swallow a gnat. Early Buddhists would not eat meat or fruit, since both contain worms. But present-day Buddhists do not go beyond reason in their observances or diet. Vegetarianism is widespread but not absolute among them. Discussion still goes on as to whether or not the root and strength of ahimsā is the doctrine of the transmigration of souls. Consensus seems to be pointing towards the negative answer. Decent human reaction against the callous non-concern with life of the early sacrifices gave impetus to the idea throughout much Brāhmanic writing.

Ahl at-trab   Supernatural beings inhabiting a world just below the surface of the Sahara desert. In Moslem Tuareg folk belief, these spirits do great damage. They trip camels and they drink the springs dry just before travelers arrive. They are sometimes seen in the shape of whirling pillars of sand during sandstorms.

Ah Puch The Maya god of death: represented in codices as a skeleton or bloated corpse. He was also known as Hunhau, in which manifestation he presided over Mitnal, the ninth and lowest underworld. The modern Maya believe in Yum Cimil, the modern form, who visits the houses of the sick looking for victims. See MULTIPLE HEAVENS, HELLS. [GMF]

Ahriman Pahlavi name for the principle of evil, Angra Mainyu.

Ahti or **Ahto** The Finnish god of water, conceived of in the shape of an old man: helpful to fishermen. His wife is Vellamo. The name Ahti is also used as one of the names of the hero Lemminkäinen. [JB]

ahuizotl In ancient Mexican (Aztec) folklore, a strange animal about the size of a dog that lived in the water. It had hands and feet like a monkey and another hand on the tip of its extraordinarily long tail. It lived in deep waters waiting for human beings to come to the edge, then it reached out the long tail with the hand on the end and dragged the unlucky one into the water. In three days the body was cast upon the shore without eyes, teeth, or nails. These were the only things the ahuizotl wanted. No one dared touch the body but a priest, who attended to having it carried to its final place, a small house surrounded by water. This was because the Tlalocs (rain gods) had chosen that soul for paradise. Flute music was played to him and his relatives were told to rejoice because of this choosing.

The ahuizotl had another ruse for catching people. Sometimes he caused frogs and fish to jump around near his hiding place, so that some hapless fisherman would be tempted to approach near enough to cast his net and so be caught. The ahuizotl would sometimes even sit on the bank and cry like a child to deceive passers-by, and then grab them with the hand on the end of his tail when pity made them curious. Once an old woman caught one in a jug, but the priests made her put it back in the water, because it was subject to the rain gods. It was said that if anyone ever saw the ahuizotl and was not either caught or scared to death, he would die soon anyway.

The creature appears often in the elaborate and intricate carvings of the Aztecs, but the hand on the end of the tail is never shown. The tail is always carefully coiled and the tip kept hidden. The conventional sign for water is always present, either on the back of the animal or in the base of the representation. The most famous carving of the ahuizotl yet known was taken to the Royal Ethnological Museum in Berlin.

Ahura Mazda (Pahlavi *Aūharmazd*, Persian *Ormazd* or *Ormuzd*) Literally, Lord Wisdom: in old Iranian mythology, supreme deity: the principle of good, law, and justice. Ahura Mazda is the spirit of wisdom living in eternal, endless light, the opponent of Angra Mainyu who lives in darkness. The six attributes of Ahura Mazda are the Amesha Spentas or Amshaspands: Vohu Manah (benevolence), Asha Vahishta (perfect order), Khshathra Vairya (good, power), Spentā Ārmaiti (devotion, wisdom), Haurvatāt (health, prosperity), Ameretāt (immortality), and Sraosha (obedience) sometimes included as a seventh to complete the holy number when Ahura Mazda is not included with the group. These were frequently personified but never regarded as distinct persons in the *Gāthās*. In the later *Avesta* they were separated from Ahura Mazda as entities and referred to as gods or archangels who were to aid Ahura Mazda in guiding the world.

Ahura Mazda is constantly regarded as the opponent of Angra Mainyu. According to one myth both sprang from Eternity; according to another, Angra Mainyu was the product of a moment of doubt on the part of Ahura Mazda. Angra Mainyu in the *Gāthās* is pictured as opposing Spentā Mainyu, the Holy Spirit of Ahura Mazda. Later this distinction between the two phases is lost.

In mythology the first man, Gaya Maretan, was born from the sweat of Ahura Mazda who is pictured as a stately, bearded man enclosed in a winged circle, grasping a ring in one hand, the other uplifted as if blessing his followers. He is also depicted as putting on the solid heavens as a garment and covering himself with flames of fire. He has been identified with the Vedic Varuna, Greek Zeus, and Baal Merodach of Babylon. See AMESHA SPENTAS. Compare MARDUK.

Ai apaec The supreme deity of the Mochica people of northern coastal Peru: an anthropomorphized feline god carried over from the ancient cat god of Peru's north coast. He is usually represented in the shape of a wrinkle-faced old man with long fangs and cat whiskers. Many Mochica four-faced pottery vessels, however, verify his anthropomorphic nature in showing the human and feline faces back to back with the god eyes in the cat face. The rich ceramic art of the Mochicas depicts Ai apaec also as farmer, fisherman, hunter, musician, and physician. He presided over human copulation, seeing to it that the act bore fruit. He fought (and always won) against demons, vampires, fish-monsters, dragons, eared serpents. He is depicted also as holding court attended by a lizard for servant and a dog for friend.

Aido Hwedo The great rainbow serpent of Dahomey mythology, who transported Mawu from place to place as she went around creating the universe. Every morning in whatever place they spent the night mountains stood: the piles of excrement left by Aido Hwedo. When the world was finished, they realized that too many things were too big; the earth was too heavy; it was going to topple. So Mawu besought Aido Hwedo to coil himself and lie beneath the earth to bear its weight. Then because Aido Hwedo cannot bear the heat, she caused the sea to be around him for his dwelling place. If he gets uncomfortable and shifts a little, there is an earthquake. As soon as his diet of iron bars under the sea is depleted, Aido Hwedo will begin to swallow his own tail, and on that day the world will fall into the sea.

The rainbow serpent, Aido Wedo, survives in both Surinam and Haitian vodun belief, ritual, and songs of invocation. In Haiti great care is taken never to arouse the jealousy of this deity. When a young couple wish to get married, if either of them is a devotee of Aido Wedo, he or she makes special offerings to allay whatever jealousy or resentment the god might harbor. Parents and relatives also must "instruct" Aido Wedo not to harm or trouble the newlyweds.

Aigamuxa (singular *Aigamuxab*) In Hottentot mythology, a fabulous people with eyes in the back of their feet: comparable to the ogres of European folklore. They eat human beings, ripping them apart with their extraordinarily long teeth. Jackal, the Hottentot trickster, found out where they kept their eyes, strewed tobacco dust where it would get into them, and thus escaped. Most of the Aigamuxa stories resemble ogre stories elsewhere, containing many of the familiar ruses by which clever victims escape the savage but stupid ogres.

A'ikren In the Karok Indian language, he who dwells above: in Karok mythology, the Duck Hawk who lives on top of Sugarloaf Mountain and is guardian spirit to the village of Katimin. It was A'ikren who came to comfort the two maidens weeping for the death of their lovers. He led them through the thick brush to that place where the two youths were; and there the two girls saw their lovers stepping around before the deerskin dance just as they used to do. A'ikren left them there for a year but it seemed like only a day to them. The maidens did not want to go back, but the people gave them a portion of the salmon backbone meat of that place, and showed them how to smear the mouths of the dead with it to revive them. When they returned to earth they showed the people this mystery, so that there was no more death among them for a time. But finally the salmon backbone meat gave out and now people die among the Karoks from time to time. But they do not grieve for their dead as they used to do, because of the knowledge revealed to the two maidens by A'ikren: how the people are dancing in that place just as they used to do on earth.

Ailill mac Matach In Old Irish legend, king of Connacht; husband of Medb; father of Findabair and the seven Manes. He emerges in the *Táin Bó Cuáilgne* as the henpecked husband of Medb, who, however, praised him in the famous pillow-talk anecdote for being brave, without fear, without avarice, not churlish, and second to none in bounty. The pillow-talk quarrel ends with Ailill still stubbornly declaring that Medb has *not* more possessions than himself. In the *Táin Bó Fraech* Ailill's role is that of the wily king and stern father who opposed the marriage of Findabair with Fraech to the point of tricking Fraech to his death, relenting only at the end of the story, when the restored Fraech promised to aid Connacht in the War for the Brown Bull.

Áine In Old Irish mythology, a woman of the *síde* (*ban síde*) of Munster, daughter of Owel, foster son of Manannán and a druid. The ancient story that she was ravished by a king of Munster, whom she killed with magic, survived into the 14th century legend of the fairy Áine and a mortal lover to whom she bore a famous son, Gerald, 4th Earl of Desmond. This Earl Gerald lives today deep in the waters of Loch Gur, reappearing every seven years to ride around the edge of it on a shining white horse. Munster families still claim descent from him. Knockainy, near Loch Gur in Munster, is literally *Cnoc Áine*, the hill of Áine. Reminiscent of Áine in the role of minor earth goddess, associated with love, desire, and fertility, are local tales of how once she planted that whole hill with peas in one night. She is still associated with the fertility observances on the hill on Midsummer Eve. See CELTIC FOLKLORE.

Airávata In Hindu mythology, Indra's elephant: guardian of one of the points of the compass. According to the *Mātaṅgalīlā,* after the sun-bird, Garuḍa, came into existence, Brahmā sang seven holy melodies over the two halves of the eggshell which he held in his hands. The first divine elephant to emerge from the shell in his right hand was Airávata. He was followed by seven more males and then by eight females which emerged from the other half of the shell which Brahmā held in his left hand. These 16 became the ancestors of all elephants and the caryatids of the universe, supporting the world at the four cardinal points and the four intermediate points.

According to the *Mahābhārata,* Airávata, a milk-white elephant, arose from the Churning of the Ocean. The original elephants and their offspring had wings and roamed the sky, until they were cursed by an ascetic whose class they interrupted by settling on the limb of a tree under which he was teaching. From that time on they were doomed to remain on the ground and serve men. White elephants today are believed to be endowed with the magic virtue of producing clouds.

aire Literally, air. Fear of air as a cause of illness is general in Middle America. Evil spirits, unseen, may travel through the air, particularly cold air, and if it is inhaled a person may become sick. Hence, the stereotyped picture of the Mexican Indian on a frosty morning with his blanket drawn up to cover his mouth and nose. [GMF]

Airi In Indian folklore, a bhut of the hills: the ghost of a man killed in hunting, who travels about with a pack of hounds. To meet the Airi presages death. His saliva is so venomous that it wounds anyone on whom it falls. If a man sees an Airi face to face, he will die of fright, but, if he is fortunate enough to survive, he will be shown hidden treasures. Temples to the Airi are placed in solitary regions and he is worshipped for two weeks in the month of Chait (March–April).

Aïssâoua or **Aisāwa** An ecstatic frenzied dance of the Aisāwa (a Mohammedan saintly confraternity) of Biskra, Algeria. It is characterized by superhuman feats of whirling and self-mutilation on the part of the dervishes: cutting the flesh with knives, eating live coals, and other manifestations of the subjugation of the body and "loss of self" in religious ecstasy. [GPK]

Aitvaras The house spirit, in the shape of a flying dragon, of Lithuanian folk belief and legend. He was first mentioned in 1547 and is common throughout the country still today. He brings to his master stolen goods, mostly corn, milk, and coins, and when flying appears all fiery tail. In the house he is like a cock. He can be bought, or brooded from the eggs of a seven-year-old cock. Occasionally, he is just found, and because unrecognized, brought home, or he may be obtained from the devil for the price of one's soul. He must be fed with omelet, and once in the house it is difficult to drive him away. Nevertheless, it is possible to slay him. A young bride, says a well-known legend, who was obliged to grind grain with a hand-mill, found that the basket was always full. Following clever advice, she discovered by the light of a sacred candle a cock vomiting the grains, and she killed him. The mistress of the house became very sad because this "cock" was the cause of all her wealth. The origin and meaning of the word *aitvaras* is unexplained. See AJATAR; PUK. [JB]

aiza One of the most important spirits of Dahomey religion: protector of groups. Aiza differ in kind but never in function; every sib, village, region, compound, and market place has its aiza or guardian spirit and his mound or shrine; and aiza mounds stand also at many important crossroads. The sib aiza is believed to be the spirit of the founder of the sib, and his bones are buried in the mound. To'aiza, protector of a village or region, is the spirit of the founder of that place; xwe'aiza is the spirit of a compound; ax'aiza, of the market place.

Every aiza mound is built over certain specific objects to insure a specific guardianship. For the establishment of an important sib aiza, for instance, sometimes the king permits the sacrifice of one man and one woman, since it is the men and women of the sib the aiza is to protect; for a regional aiza, two men and two women are sacrificed, indicative of a larger group to be protected. A market aiza must be built with the earth from seven well-known markets, and buried in it must be a fragment of each thing bartered or sold in that place: food, crops, cloth, metal, animals, and formerly slaves. The human sacrifices for the establishment of a new market aiza, are sometimes of great number, for the market is a royal institution in Dahomey, and they are believed to be sacrificed for the king himself.

Prayers are made to the ax'aiza for good business and offerings of thanks for good business follow; verbal complaint or abuse and no offerings are given in return for bad business or no business. The mother of twins must bring them to market and "show" them to the ax'aiza with offerings, that they may be recognized as members of the group, and that she herself may become pregnant again. Various cult initiates also are taken to the market shrine when they come out of their prolonged training in the cult house.

Ajatar or **Ajattara** The dragon; an evil female spirit of the woods who suckles snakes and produces diseases; the Devil of the Woods of Finnish folklore. In southern Estonia she is Äi or Äijo or Äijätär, the mother or daughter of the devil. The word is used also as a curse. She is probably a borrowing from the Lithuanian (see AITVARAS). Any explanation connecting these two Finnish words with the Persian or Turkish ones is not convincing (see *FUF* XII, 1912, pp. 150–153). [JB]

Aka-Kanet, Akakanet, or **Algue** In the mythology of the Araucanian Indians of Chile, the power or deity enthroned in the Pleiades who sends fruits and flowers to the earth. Aka-Kanet is similar to Guecubu, the author of evil, perhaps the same deity in a dualistic system.

akalo Sa'a and Ulawa (Solomon Islands) friendly ghost of the dead; also, the soul of a living man. Every person becomes an akalo when he dies and as such is invoked by his own people. The ghosts of chiefs, valiant fighting men, and men who have spiritual power, however, become li'oa. The living catch the ghost of a dead man with a miniature rod and put it into a relic case in a corner of the house which contains the skull, jawbone, tooth, or lock of hair of the deceased. Offerings are placed in these cases when someone is ill and at the first-fruit offering of the yam harvest.

akbi'aruscariča Literally, woman impersonator: a term applied to the clowns of the Crow Indians. They are not organized and not ceremonial, despite certain of their phallic actions. They use mud for their body paint; their cloth masks are smeared with charcoal. They ride the ugliest horses, with ridiculous caparison. They ridicule anything they wish, and perform ridiculous dances, fall down, pretend to die laughing. One of them, dressed as a pregnant woman, used to simulate copulation with a "male" clown. At times they would introduce merriment into the hot dance. [GPK]

Akhtya Chief of the yatus or sorcerers of Zoroastrianism. [MWS]

akonda Literally, I fight: a gbo or magic charm of the Dahomey people, worn around the upper left arm. It gives the wearer strength for work or conflict. It is a circlet of woven raffia to which are attached tough hairs from the neck of the ram known as agbŏ. These are included because the ram is a good fighter. As he fastens the akonda on his arm, the wearer must say, "Akonda, when the ram goes to fight, he does not die in his place." (Herskovits *Dahomey* II, 268)

akpoú Literally, near the pocket: a gbo or magic charm of the Dahomey, carried by travelers to protect them against ghosts. It consists of a slender rod of iron dressed in a skirt. It has one flat pointed end, the other having a cuplike opening. The point is painted with black and white stripes, symbolic of the inherent power of the akpoú to repel evil. This power resides in a certain leaf plastered onto the shaft with kaolin under the skirt. Strong drink is fed to the akpoú through the cup-shaped end to excite its functioning powers. The traveler by night carries an akpoú in one hand. If he meets a ghost he extends the akpoú towards it, and the ghost does him no harm. (Herskovits *Dahomey* II, 266)

Akūpāra In Hindu mythology, the tortoise upon which the earth rests.

āl In Armenian belief, one of a group of demons, half-animal, half-human, male or female, shaggy and bristly, who live in watery or damp places or in the corners of the stable or house: familiar figures in Armenian myths and folktales. Formerly the āl was a demon of disease, now it is a demon of childbirth who also steals seven-months children. It is fiery-eyed with snakelike hair, fingernails of brass, iron teeth, and it carries a pair of iron scissors. The āl is believed to blind unborn children and to cause miscarriage. To keep āls away, women are surrounded with iron weapons and instruments. The king of the āls is chained in an abyss and shrieks continually. Sometimes the devs take over the functions of the āls, stealing human children and leaving changelings in their place. In Afghanistan the āl is a woman about twenty years old with long teeth and nails and feet reversed who feeds on corpses, like the Hindu churel.

Aladdin The hero of the story "Aladdin and the Wonderful Lamp" which appears in most collections as a supplementary tale to the *Arabian Nights Entertainments.*

Aladdin, the ne'er-do-well son of a Chinese tailor, was enticed by a magician from Morocco to enter a cave and obtain a lamp. Before descending into the cave Aladdin was given the magician's signet ring to keep him from hurt and fear. Returning with the lamp Aladdin loaded his pockets with the jewels, which he found growing on trees in the cavern. The magician refused to help him out of the cave, but demanded the lamp. Aladdin would not hand up the lamp, so the magician closed the entrance.

Aladdin, in despair at not being able to get out of his underground prison, chanced to rub the ring given to him by the magician. Immediately the ring's attendant spirit appeared and at Aladdin's request transported him to the earth's surface. He learned the secret of the lamp also by chance (i.e. that rubbing it called up the jinni of the lamp to do the bidding of the possessor of the lamp) and used it henceforth to keep himself and his mother supplied with everything they needed.

Aladdin fell in love with the Sultan's daughter, Lady Badr al-Budur, and won her after meeting (with the aid of the jinni) the excessive demands made by her father, which included building overnight a pavilion containing 24 windows made of precious stones. Meanwhile the Moroccan magician, having discovered that Aladdin had escaped from the cave and was the owner of the lamp, set out to retrieve it. He went up and down the streets crying, "Old lamps for new! who will exchange old lamps for new?" The princess gave him Aladdin's rusty lamp, not knowing its true value. The magician then commanded the jinni of the lamp to transport the pavilion and the princess to Africa. But Aladdin, aided by the jinni of the ring, soon retrieved the lamp through a ruse and killed the magician.

The motifs of a magic object found in an underground room (D845), of a magic wishing lamp (D1470.1.16), as well as of the lamp's loss and recovery and the loss and restoration of the palace (Type 560–568) appear in both Asiatic and European tales. The scene of the magician and Aladdin at the cave, and the transporting of the wazir's son and the princess to Aladdin's house on their wedding night, are believed to be Arabic. The Arabic and several Indian versions also differ from the usual one in that the talisman is recovered by the devices of the hero. In many tales it is obtained from and later recovered by grateful animals. In a Bohemian story the hero saves a dog, cat, and serpent. The father of the serpent gives him an enchanted watch which procures a palace for the hero and the king's daughter as a bride. She, disliking her husband, uses the watch to build herself a palace in the middle of the sea. The dog and cat recover the talisman but drop it into the sea. It is restored by a fish.

Alaghom Naom or **Iztat Ix** In the mythology of the Tzentals of Chiapas, Mexico, the highest of goddesses, responsible for the mental and immaterial part of nature: the mother of wisdom.

alalá A song type of Spanish Galicia, expressing in emotional terms the dreams and longings of farmers, teamsters, herdsmen, mothers rocking their babies, etc., and generally making use of the typical Spanish ballad stanza. The name is derived from the characteristic nonsense syllables found in the early examples of the type.

alan Tinguian (Philippine Islands) spirits, half-human, half-bird, with toes and fingers reversed. They are sometimes mischievous or hostile, but are usually friendly. They are described as hanging, batlike, from trees and as living in the forests. In Tinguian mythology and folktales they appear as the foster mothers of the leading characters and are pictured frequently as living in houses of gold.

Alasita A popular fiesta of the Aymara Indians, held in honor of Ekeko, the good-luck fertility spirit. In Bolivia his image is kept in the people's houses, so that he may preside over all sex activity. Every year the Alasita festival is held in certain places where miniature houses for Ekeko have been built and kept in constant repair. Inside these little houses the people place miniature clay farm animals and implements, household utensils, clothing, etc., as a sign to Ekeko that they desire and need these things all the following year. A market is then pantomimed, during which these tiny objects are bought and sold for potsherds, stones, and other trifles, and given to the children for toys. *Alasita*, an Aymaran word meaning *Buy from me* is constantly uttered by the vendors. Sexual license among the young men and women is a feature. [AM]

albatross A large, web-footed sea bird (genus *Diomedeidæ*) with very long narrow wings and extraordinary powers of flight. Albatrosses are seen great distances from the land, chiefly in the southern oceans and the northern Pacific. Tales about the bird include the belief that it sleeps in the air because its flight appears motionless, and that an albatross hovering about a ship brings continued bad weather. Coleridge's *Ancient Mariner* is based on the more common belief that to kill an albatross brings bad luck.

Alberich In Teutonic legend, the king of the dwarfs who lived in a magnificent subterranean palace studded with gems. Among his possessions were a belt of strength, an invincible sword, the Tarnkappe or cloak of invisibility, and a magic ring. His subjects, the dwarfs, were master craftsmen who produced Odin's ring, Draupnir, Sif's golden hair, and Freya's necklace. They also manufactured the sword Tyrfing which fought by itself. In the *Nibelungenlied* Alberich was the guardian of the Nibelung hoard and gave Siegfried a cloak of invisibility and the sword called Balmung.

Alburz The sacred mountain of old Iranian mythology: the first of the mountains, around which the sun and moon revolved. Light shone out from it and light returned into it, but on the mountain itself there was no dark. Mithra's dwelling was upon it, from which he watched the world. Zoroastrian legend holds that all other mountains grew from the root of Alburz. Alburz was the mountain where dread came upon Tahmurath. Here he was overcome, because of fear only, by the demon Angra Mainyu.

alchemy The immature, empirical, and speculative chemistry characterized by the pursuit of the transmutation of base metals into gold, the search for the alkahest and the philosopher's stone. Alchemy developed from a secret science belonging to the goldsmith's craft into a mysterious science dealing with changes in the organic as well as the metallic world. Its history includes three distinct epochs: the Greek and Egyptian period, the Arabic period of the Middle Ages, and the modern period extending from the 16th century to the present.

In legend, alchemy was founded by Thoth (Hermes), by the fallen angels, or was revealed by God to Moses and Aaron. Historically it is believed to have originated in Egypt from where it spread to Greece and Rome and thence to Arabia. By the second century it had assumed a mystical and magical character; gods, patriarchs, and prophets were pressed into its service, for greatness such as theirs implied a knowledge of all mysteries. Adam, Abraham, and Moses were described as the true authors of alchemistic treatises.

The Arabs carried alchemy to Spain. From there it spread to western Europe through the medium of Latin translations of Arabic-Greek treatises. The fundamental theories of alchemy, developed by the Greeks, were modified and elaborated by the Arabs.

Paracelsus in the 16th century gave alchemy a new goal by suggesting that its object was the preparation of medicines. The discovery in the 20th century of the transmutation of radioactive elements has not produced the gold or silver from base metals sought by the alchemists (except as a laboratory curiosity), but it has made it possible to break down elements or to produce new elements in the laboratory and factory—essentially the goal of the alchemists.

alchera or **alcheringa** The mythical past or "dream time" of Australian mythology; the ancestral totemic ancestors who lived in that time and established the world and customs as they are now; also, any object associated with the totem: a term used especially by the central Australian Aranda (or Arunta). The Murngin of Arnhem Land refer to the mythical past as Bamum when totemic ancestral spirits, the Wongar, lived. Great Western Desert tribes of West and South Australia called the period Tjukur. The Dieri call their ancestors Mura-mura. Other tribes have comparable terms for the mythical past and their totemic ancestors who lived then. See AUSTRALIAN ABORIGINAL MYTHOLOGY. [KL]

Aldebaran (Arabic *Al Dabarān,* the Follower) Originally the name of the Hyades; now the reddish, brightest star, Alpha in the constellation Taurus: the Follower who forever follows the Pleiades. It is also called the Eye of the Bull or the Bull's Eye. The French astronomer, Camille Flammarion, designated it with the Hebrew Aleph and called it God's Eye. One of the most ancient indigenous Arabic names for this star is Al Fanik, the Stallion Camel; another is Al Muhdij, the Female Camel; and the adjacent Hyades were the Little Camels. Aldebaran was worshipped as a bringer of rain by the tribe Misām. The Hindu name, Rohini, Red Deer, is probably from the star's red coloring. Aldebaran, the "Broad Star," is prayed to by Hopi Indian curers. In astrology Aldebaran is regarded as fortunate, and a portent of wealth for those born under it.

alder A tree or shrub (genus *Alnus*) characterized by short-stalked, roundish leaves and pendulous, reddish catkins: distributed throughout the north temperate zone and along the Andes in South America. In Norse mythology the first man and woman were made from an ash and an alder. In Brythonic mythology the alder was associated with Bran. Gwydion guessed Bran's name at the Battle of the Trees from the alder twigs in his hand: "Bran thou art, by the branch thou bearest"; and the answer to an old Taliesin riddle, "Why is the alder purple?" is, "Because Bran wore purple." In the Irish Tree Alphabet the letter F (*fearn*) means alder, and in the Old Irish *Song of the Forest Trees* it is described as "the very battlewitch of woods." In Ireland the felling of an alder was formerly punishable, and is still avoided. It is regarded with such awe probably because when cut the wood turns from white to red. In the *Odyssey* the alder is one of the three trees of resurrection; and Bran's alder too was a symbol of resurrection. The alder is also one of the ancient Irish trees of divination, used especially for diagnosing diseases.

In Newfoundland an infusion of alder buds is recommended for the itch and for rheumatism; and a salve for burns is made with suet and alder bark. Newfoundlanders also hold that mosquitoes breed in young alder buds.

alectryomancy or **alectromancy** Divination from the actions of a cock in a circle: an ancient practice. Grains were placed on the letters of the alphabet traced within the circle. From the order in which the cock picked up the grains, the required word, name, or message was read.

alekoki One of the first standing hulas or olopa of Hawaii. The Hindu influence is apparent in the fluid gestures of hands, wrists, and elbows, with definite expressive symbolism often identical with the mudras of India. The purpose of these hulas is not erotic, but is intended to refresh the grace of the gods. The alekoki is a women's dance. [GPK]

aleuromancy Divination from flour: an ancient practice still more or less in use. Messages, written on slips of paper, are enclosed in balls of flour paste which are distributed at random after being mixed together. One of the epithets of Apollo was Aleuromantes. A modern variant may be found in the "fortune cakes" of the metropolitan Chinese restaurants.

Alexander the Great Alexander III (356–323 B.C.), son of Philip I of Macedon, conqueror of the world from the Nile to the Indus, is the great king-hero of the world. Like all folk heroes from Sargon and Gilgamesh to Paul Bunyan and King Arthur, the Alexander of legend has drawn to himself tales and incidents originally quite independent of actual historical fact, the whole building into one of the great epic structures; in fact, however, Alexander's historical career is more amazing than any of the apocryphal stories about him. An intelligent youth, tutored by none other than Aristotle, Alexander ascended the throne at 20; by magnificent strategy and military tactics, he conquered first the West and then the East; and he was dead at 33.

He claimed descent from Hercules on his father's side, and from Æacus on his mother's. This is confused with his reputedly being the son of Zeus Ammon; Alexander, who fostered the popular belief in his divinity, made it a point to undertake a hazardous expedition to Ammon's temple in the desert when he was in Egypt. His mother, Olympias, was a devotee of the Dionysian mysteries, and thus arose the legend that Alexander was the son of a snake. It is said that the strained relations between Olympias and Philip began when the king found a snake in his wife's bed. A sophisticated version of the story claims the Egyptian magician king Nectanebus as Alexander's father. This Nectanebus had ruled Egypt, protecting his kingdom by means of wax figures of his enemies' forces, which he destroyed at need. Driven from Egypt, he set up as astrologer in Macedonia, and to him came the queen seeking information about an heir to the throne. Nectanebus told her to prepare for a visit from Zeus Ammon, donned a dragon costume to make the nocturnal call himself, and thus sired the future conqueror. Philip, who could count, is said to have been suspicious of these events, and Nectanebus once more dressed as a dragon to allay the king's fears. He came to his end at the hands of Alexander. Once, as he explained astrology to the 12-year-old Alexander, Nectanebus was pushed into a pit, the youth at the same time demanding whether he had foreseen the event in the stars. Several other versions of the progenitors of Alexander are known: the Persians, for example, make him the son of Darius, whom he in fact conquered.

The legendary career of Alexander is filled with hundreds of familiar incidents of folklore. The taming of his black horse Bucephalus by leading him towards the sun when he alone recognized the animal's fear of its own shadow; the meeting with Diogenes, the acid-tongued philosopher, who asked the king of all the world to stand out of his light; the forcing of an involuntary, yet auspicious "Thou art invincible" from the Pythoness at Delphi are familiar anecdotes. Also connected with the Alexander story are the general motifs B552.1, hero carried aloft by two birds (he directed them by means of a bit of liver attached to a spear and held before them), and N135.3.1, he orders a feast, on his dying bed, for those who have not known sorrow, and none come to the feast. This is related to the motif of the cure with the shirt of the happy man (the only happy man that can be found is a beggar with no shirt) or the cure in the house where no death has ever occurred. In Arabic legend, Alexander is a spreader of the True Faith, an iconoclast. He carries a black flag and a white, with which he can make night or day. He wars against the race of Gog and Magog, horrible savage pygmies, and builds a wall of iron and brass to keep them confined. In Arabic legend he is Zu-l-Qarnain, He of the Two Horns, a figure generally conceded to be Alexander, although some say it is a contemporary of Abraham. This horned figure, the horns being those of Jupiter Ammon or of the he-goat or symbolical of the rule of the East and the West, is central in the story of Khidr, the Green One, who became immortal. While Alexander was seeking the Fountain of Life, Khidr, the cook of the expedition (or the king's vizier), went off from the rest of the group to prepare a dried fish for the meal. As he washed the fish in a pool, the fish came to life and swam off. Khidr then drank or bathed in the water and made himself immortal, turning green at the same time. Alexander became jealous when the pool could not be rediscovered and tried to kill the underling. In vain he attempted several methods, and finally threw Khidr into the sea with a stone tied about his neck. Khidr became a sea deity and still lives. This tale appears in a somewhat garbled version in the Koran (*Sura* xviii–The Cave). Familiar to folklore too is the City of Brass Alexander builds in a Persian tale, and so too is his method of obtaining diamonds by tossing meat down into a valley and having eagles carry out the meat with the diamonds adhering to it. In medieval Christian legends, the exploits of Alexander in India include battles with gigantic ants and female cannibals, with six-headed giants, with one-legged dwarfs, with horses with human faces, and with dog-faced people. Also in Christian legend, Alexander tries to storm Paradise, but fails. In a Jewish story, Alexander reaches Paradise and is there instructed in the futility of human endeavor: the eye tries to take in all the universe and yet may be covered by a little bit of earth.

Stories of Alexander are found among nearly all the peoples from India to the Atlantic Ocean. Most of these stem from the *Secretum Secretorum*, a collection of writings said to have been sent from Aristotle to Alexander after the teacher became too old to travel with his pupil. It is here that the famous story of Alexander and the poison damsel appears. This work, coming from the writings of the pseudo-Callisthenes of the 3rd century A.D., was translated into practically every European language, and was the most widely read book of the Middle Ages. It has left its mark on every one of the European literatures; compare the name Alexandrine for the typical 12-syllabled French verse line, the popularity of Alexander (Sandy) as a Scottish name, etc. Throughout the Moslem world, the legends of Iskander are legion. The story of Alexander is used in the *Shāhnāma* of Firdausi. In the Ethiopic version of the story, the Greek gods become the prophets of the Bible, and Alexander is an ascetic saint. In the Syrian stories, Alexander is a Christian. In Moslem tales, he is one of the four great conquerors, with Nimrod, Solomon, and Nebuchadrezzar. In medieval Christian legend, he is not only Christian, but a believer in the Trinity, and one of the Nine Champions. Popularly, Alexander is one of the kings in the pack of cards. Alexander, in other words, from the time that he influenced the myth of Dionysus, by having that god and culture hero's itinerary extended to include India, down to the present day, has been the greatest of all folklore figures over a wider area than any other comparable personage. Remodeled in the shape of the hero desired by the various peoples who interpreted the legend, he remains today historically and traditionally without a peer.

alfar The elves of Teutonic mythology. The *Prose Edda* divides them into two classes: the Liosálfar, the light elves who live in Alfheim, and the Döckálfar, the dark elves who live underground. Frey, the sun god, is lord of Alfheim. Wieland the Smith is often thought of as lord of the earth-dwelling ones, the Döckálfar, because of their confusion with the dwarfs. They are quite distinct from the dwarfs, however. In medieval German legend Ælfrich or Alberich became king of the elves.

The alfar possess great supernatural powers and are often associated with the gods as aids and allies against their enemies. Especially are they associated with Thor and with Holde. Intimations of belief in their divinity are seen in the fact that in earliest times a bull was sometimes sacrificed for them, his blood let flow upon the elf-hill, and his flesh prepared for their feasting. See SVARTALFAR.

alferez In the modern Andean Indian and mestizo communities of Ecuador, Peru, and Bolivia, a person who assumes the financial responsibility for the religious feasts and ceremonies for one year. This heavy burden is taken on only by the wealthiest individuals and they are assisted by relatives and friends. As a symbol of his function the alferez carries a flag, hence his title, which in Spanish means *flag-bearer*. [AM]

Algol A bright white star, Beta in the constellation Perseus: called the Demon, or the Demon Star, from the Arabian Rās al Ghul, the Demon's Head. It was interpreted by Hipparchus and Pliny as the head of Medusa hanging from the belt of the hero. Ptolemy called it "the bright one of those in the Gorgon's head." The ancient Hebrews knew it first as Rōsh ha Sātān, Satan's Head, later as Lilith, Adam's first wife, who has developed into a nocturnal evil spirit. The dark star that revolves around it, periodically dimming its brilliance, lends it the illusion of a baleful winking eye, and gives it the alternate name of Blinking Demon. In astrology Algol has always been interpreted as an evil star and a danger to any one born under it.

Ali Baba A poor wood-gatherer, hero of the story, "Ali Baba and the Forty Thieves," which appears as a supplementary tale to the *Arabian Nights Entertainments.*

Ali Baba, while gathering firewood, saw a band of horsemen stop near a large rock and unload their booty-filled saddlebags. Their leader approached the rock and said, "Open, O Simsim!" and a wide doorway appeared in the rock. After the men had entered, the door closed. Finally the bandits emerged and the leader said, "Shut, O Simsim!" and the door closed. After the men had departed, Ali Baba said the same words. The cave opened; and he discovered on entering a store of silks, brocades, carpets, and heaps of gold and silver coins. He loaded his asses with sacks of gold and returned to town. When Ali Baba's brother, Kasim, discovered Ali Baba's wealth (a gold piece had stuck to wax Kasim's wife hid in the scales that Ali Baba borrowed), he demanded to know where the wood dealer had obtained it, and threatened to report him to the Governor if he would not tell. So Ali Baba was forced to tell and immediately Kasim set out with ten mules. He found the rock and entered. After collecting enough gold and jewels to load his ten mules, he discovered that he had forgotten the words necessary to open the door.

When the robbers returned the next morning, Kasim ran out hoping to escape, but they seized and killed him, and hung his body on the inside of the door. There Ali Baba found it in his search for his missing brother.

After the disappearance of Kasim's body, the bandits realized that someone else knew the secret of the cave. They were able to trace Ali Baba and to enter his house through a ruse. The bandit captain posed as an oil merchant and asked to store his oil jars in the shed. In all the jars but one were hidden the robbers waiting for a signal to appear and kill Ali Baba.

The servant, Morgiana, needing oil to finish her work after the household had retired, went out to the jars. One of the men, hearing footsteps, whispered, "Is it now time for us to come forth?" Morgiana was frightened but replied, "Not yet." Surmising that these must be robbers, she filled a caldron with the oil from the single jar, boiled it, and poured it over the thieves, scalding them to death. In gratitude Ali Baba married Morgiana to his nephew.

The motif of the thieves hidden in oil casks (K312) is found also in Indian, Arabian, Ekoi (African), Estonian, and Finnish stories. In the *Mabinogion,* warriors were concealed in leather sacks hung on pillars in the great house built for Bran when he crossed to Ireland to rescue Branwen. Other familiar motifs in the story are scales borrowed (J1141.6), mountain or rocks open to magic formula, or Open Sesame (D1552.2; N455.3), underground treasure chamber (F721.4), the marked culprit (K415).

alimagba Literally, road not crooked: a gbo or magic charm of the Dahomey people, worn to insure safety on a journey. It is a small carved figure made in the shape of a man, because it is safer for two to journey than for one to travel alone. It is infused with the power to protect by being washed with water containing certain leaves and by having the blood of a newly killed cock poured over it. It is worn on the belt by travelers. The verbal formula associated with alimagba reiterates that this place, that place is not crooked. (Herskovits *Dahomey* II, 280.) Compare AKPOU.

Aljoša Popovič A Russian historical personage figuring in several byliny of the cycle of Vladimir: the unsuccessful aspirer to the hand of the absent Dobrynja's wife; conqueror of the dragon-hero Tugarin (thought to be Tugorhan, an 11th century chief of the Polovcy). He was one of seventy heroes who died at the battle of Kalka, 1224. See DOBRYNJA AND ALJOŠA.

Allah The name for God among Moslems, analogous to the Hebrew Jahweh. The pre-Mohammedan Arabic god Hobal had as his title Al-lahu, meaning "the god," related to the general Semitic term for god, El. As the patron of the Kaaba at Mecca, already supreme, he was maintained in Mohammedan theology as the one god; the others were banished to the realm of the demons. However, the Mohammedan Allah resembles the established monotheistic gods Jahweh and Ahura Mazda much more than he does the primitive Al-lahu. What Mohammed did was to codify, simplify, and establish Allah to his unassailable position. Mohammed's concern was to abolish all gods but Allah, establish his unity, and discourage the perversion of his attributes or "titles" into lesser deities. Mohammed's message was, "There exists no god except the one whom you already call Allah." Allah may be invoked by many titles—99 to be exact—but only by those authorized in the Koran or by Mohammed himself. Allah also has a secret name, the Ism al-A'zam, the "exalted name," said by some to be revealed in the Koran and by others to be known only to saints. Whoever calls upon Allah by this name will realize his dearest hopes. Hence dervishes spend protracted hours seeking it, and many a prospect is lured into joining dervish orders with the hope of discovering it.

all eight balance and all eight swing An American square dance term. Partners face each other and balance by taking four short steps backward and four forward; or they may balance by taking one step sidewise, bringing the feet together first to the right and then to the left, and repeating the same (eight counts). Very skilful dancers sometimes cut a pigeon wing, especially if the balance is followed by a swing. After the balance the gentleman swings his partner (four or eight counts). [GPK]

Allerleirauh Literally, of different kinds of fur: title and heroine of a well-known German version (Grimm #65) of the Catskin story. See CAP o' RUSHES; CINDER-ELLA.

All Fools' Day or **April Fool's Day** April 1: the day on which practical jokes of the salt-in-the-sugarbowl type are commonly practiced. Especially typical is the sending of people on fool's errands. The day is widely celebrated but of obscure origin. The alleged beginnings include the fruitless mission of the dove sent out from the ark by Noah, the adoption of the Gregorian calendar, the Roman feast of Cerealia, the Indian festival of the Huli, the celebration of the vernal equinox, or the uncertainty of the weather at that time of year. Whatever its origin, the celebration of the day came into common custom in the 18th century in England. In Scotland it is called hunting the gowk (cuckoo). In France the person fooled is a *poisson d'avril*. The fooling includes "sleeveless" errands, April Fool candy, rubber mice, the pocketbook on a string, to fool the unsuspecting.

In Mexico All Fools' Day falls on December 28 and centers around the borrowing of objects, if any person is foolish enough to lend, since items borrowed on that day need not be returned. A box of sweets or miniature objects, usually with a poem reminding the lender that he has been fooled, are sent instead. The day is popular in Italy, Spain, Portugal, Sweden, Germany, and Norway. In the latter two it is celebrated on the first and last days of April.

allheal Any of a number of medicinal herbs, referred to also as heal-all in folk medicine. These names are given especially to valerian, self-heal, mistletoe, woundwort, and yarrow.

alligator A large reptile (order *Crocodilia*) found only in the southern United States and in the Yangtze River, China. It has a shorter, blunter snout than the crocodile, and is further differentiated by the fact that its lower molars clamp into pits in the upper, instead of into marginal notches. The reports of early travelers in this country constitute a mine of astonishing misinformation about alligators which might be classified as a whole folklore in itself. The alligator is soundless, for instance, or he roars habitually; he roars only in the spring; he makes a "hideous Noise against bad weather." Seeds from trees fall into the small crevices between his scales, germinate therein during his hibernation in the mud, and sprout in the spring, so that the alligator often resembles a small, wooded, swimming island. William Bartram's *Travels* (1791) describe the alligator thus: "Waters like a cataract descend from his opening jaws. Clouds of smoke issue from his nostrils. The earth trembles with his thunder."

Like the crocodile, the alligator is the object of dread or reverence, propitiation, and worship in those regions where it is found, and plays an important role in folk belief, folktale, and "conjure." An important god of the Chiriqui Indians of Panama is depicted in their ceramic and stone art with human body and legs and alligator head, or sometimes with human torso and an alligator head at each end. Typical are the bulging eyes of the god, mouth open to show the alligator teeth, and (in metal work) often a wire coil symbolizing the recurved snout. The Guaraní Indians of Paraguay have an alligator ferryman who carries souls to the afterworld. In these instances the reference is probably to the closely allied native caiman.

North American Choctaw Indians, especially the river tribes, also venerated the alligator and never killed it. The Chickasaw Indians have an alligator dance (hatcûntcûba' hīla') a night dance with three songs. A Creek Indian folktale tells how Eagle pounced down and broke Alligator's nose in a ball game, Alligator opened his mouth, Turkey grabbed the ball out of it, and the birds won the game. Alligator retains a dent on his nose to this day. An Alabama Indian story, *Rabbit Fools Alligator*, tells how Rabbit, the trickster, tricks Alligator into a field of dry grass and sets fire to it. Another Alabama Indian tale, *Benevolent Alligator*, narrates how Alligator grants a certain man two wishes in gratitude for being carried on the man's back and put in the water.

South Carolina Negro folktale attributes Alligator's scaly skin to his being trapped in a fire by Brer Rabbit. This is almost a direct retelling of a Rhodesian Negro crocodile story. It would be interesting to know if the Alabama Indian tale, *Rabbit Fools Alligator*, is of Negro provenience. An Alabama Negro folktale describes how Rabbit, wishing to cross a swamp, induced Alligator to line up his whole family, "one by one across the swamp," to be counted. On the pretext of counting, Rabbit walked across the swamp on their backs, but the last alligator bit his tail off. This same story is told of the Indonesian crocodile with mousedeer as trickster, and in Japan with the monkey as trickster. A Louisiana story explains why Alligator has no tongue. Alligator, who once could whistle, talk, and bark "just like a dog do now," loaned his tongue to Dog, who wanted to make an impression at a party. But Dog never returned the tongue to Alligator, and that is why Alligator goes for any dog that comes to the bank of the river. Gullah Negroes believe that when the alligator roars he is calling for rain and that rain will come.

alligator teeth In many folklores alligator teeth are believed to be especially efficacious against poison, pain, witches, etc., and are used as potent ingredients in magic and "conjure." Sea Island Negroes will sometimes tie a necklace of alligator teeth around the neck of a teething baby to alleviate the pain. Such a necklace is also a protection against witches. A visiting nocturnal witch, for instance, would have to stop and count every one of the teeth before she could proceed with her evil business, and day would surely come before she counted the last one. In many localities alligator teeth are believed to counteract poison; even the South American Abipon and Mocovi Indians would press a caiman tooth against a snake bite to heal the wound, or wear one (or many) around the neck to avoid being bitten. Alligator teeth are active ingredients also of many a charm, conjure bag, and hoodoo "hand" of southern United States Negroes; they are also known to be an important inclusion in the bags of New Guinea sorcerers.

Allison Gross A popular Scottish ballad (Child #35) in which Allison Gross, the ugliest witch "i the north country" endeavored to seduce a fine young man. Because he repulsed her, she turned him into an ugly worm "to toddle about the tree." But the queen of the fairies, riding by on Hallow-even, broke the spell and changed him back to his "ain proper shape." This is the only known instance, in English or Scottish folklore, of a fairy unspelling the spell of a witch, although numerous ballads are concerned with the spelling and unspelling of evil enchantments.

All Saints, All Saints' Day, All-hallows, or **All hallowmas** November 1: the festival commemorative of all saints and martyrs known or unknown, introduced by Pope Boniface IV in the 7th century probably to supplant the pagan festival of the dead. Originally it was observed on May 13 but was shifted to the November date by Gregory III and has been retained by the Church of England and many Lutheran churches. In the Greek Church it is celebrated on the first Sunday after Pentecost. Most folk customs center around Allhallow Even or Halloween. Compare ALL SOULS.

All Souls or **All Souls' Day**   November 2: a day of commemoration in the Roman Catholic Church on which special intercession is made for the souls of the dead in the belief that those not yet purified sufficiently will be aided by the prayers of the living. The day was instituted as a memorial in 998 by Odilo, Abbot of Cluny, after he was told by a pilgrim returning from the Holy Land about an island on which an opening to the infernal regions permitted travelers to hear the groans of the tormented. By the end of the 13th century the day was almost universally observed. During the Reformation it was abolished in the Church of England, but its tradition and customs survived among Continental Protestants.

Essentially, All Souls is the adaptation of an almost world-wide custom of setting aside a part of the year (usually the last part) for the dead. The Babylonians observed a monthly Feast of All Souls in which sacrifices were made by priests. The Greek commemorative feast of All Souls was held on the last day of the Anthesteria; the Romans celebrated theirs during the Parentalia which fell on Feb. 13–21, the end of the Roman year. The Buddhist Feast of the Dead is celebrated on April 15, the date of the death of Buddha and his attainment of Buddhahood. In China and Japan the festival in honor of the dead is known as the Feast of Lanterns.

In many Catholic countries the belief that the dead return on this day is so strong that food is left on the tables (Tyrol, Italy) and people (France, Italy, Germany) still decorate the graves of their dead.

almanacs   These compilations of calendar and astronomical data (ephemerides) and miscellaneous information, wit, wisdom, and humor, originating in the 2nd century A.D., have taken a variety of forms, including prophetic, farmer's, Christian, patent-medicine, comic, *World* (statistical and encyclopedic) almanacs. The almanac's first link with folklore consisted of astrology, serving as the basis both of predictions and prognostications and of the doctrine of planetary influences in medicine and surgery. Long after people had ceased to take these superstitions seriously, the Man of the Signs (*homo signorum*), or Moon's Man, or the Anatomy—"a figure of a man surmounted by the twelve Signs of the Zodiac, each referred to some part of his body by means of a connecting line or a pointing dagger"—continued to adorn almanacs as a trademark or colophon.

This outmoded lore, however, was gradually replaced by the practical lore of weather, crops, health, cookery, manners, etc., with medical advice, agricultural hints, and recipes, supplementing the usual almanac data on rising and setting of the sun, phases of the moon, eclipses, tides, storms, and holidays. Out of the miscellaneous useful information on postage rates, values of coinage, courts, roads, post offices, military fines, population of towns and countries, etc., developed the almanac of the fact-book type. In another direction, the entertaining lore of popular poetry, anecdotes, jests, enigmas, riddles, maxims, etc., passed into the comic almanac and the keepsake.

Through interleaved jottings of family and local history, observations of weather, records of crops, expenditures, etc., the almanac became a valuable source of social history and "folk history." Through the medium of the allegory and proverb (the former seen especially in *The [Old] Farmer's Almanack* of Robert B. Thomas, established in 1793 and still published, and the latter in *Poor Richard's Almanack*, edited by Ben Franklin from 1732 to 1757) the almanac made important contributions to native American humor and proverbial lore.

Continuing in the jest-book tradition, with the addition of the oral tradition of the fireside and campfire yarn, the comic almanac (probably originating in the burlesque of the serious almanac and its prophetic absurdities) was an important link in the development of native American humor of tall talk and tall tale, as notably in the Crockett almanacs (1835–1856).

Bibliography:

Kittredge, George Lyman, *The Old Farmer and His Almanack*. Boston, 1904.
Rourke, Constance, *Davy Crockett*. New York, 1934.
Dorson, Richard M., *Davey Crockett, American Comic Legend*. New York, 1939.

B. A. BOTKIN

almond   A small tree (*Prunus amygdalus*) native to western Asia, Barbary, and Morocco, but now cultivated widely in the warmer temperate regions.

In the Bible the almond is referred to as the *shaked* or *sheked* meaning "to waken" or "to watch," probably because it is the first tree to flower (January) in Palestine (*Jer.* i, 11, 12). Aaron's rod (*Num.* xvii, 10) was cut from an almond tree. In the story of Tannhäuser Pope Urban exclaimed after hearing the minnesinger's tale, "Guilt like yours can never be forgiven! Before God himself could pardon you, this staff that I hold would grow green and bloom!" Tannhäuser returned to the Hörselberg. Three days later the Pope's staff suddenly put forth almond flowers and leaves. The Pope sent messengers to search for Tannhäuser but he could not be found.

In Greek legend, Phyllis, daughter of the Thracian king Sithon, fell in love with Demophoön, son of Theseus. Demophoön returned to Attica to settle his affairs before the wedding and was delayed so long (according to one story by interest in another maiden) that Phyllis put an end to her life. The gods, as a token of their admiration for her constancy, changed her into an almond tree. When Demophoön finally returned and learned what had happened he fell at the foot of the tree and watered its roots with his tears whereupon it burst into bloom.

In Phrygian cosmogony an almond figured as the father of all things, and in the myth of Attis, Nana conceived him by putting a ripe almond in her bosom, or by eating an almond.

Pliny's *Natural History* states that eating five almonds permits one to drink without experiencing intoxication, but that if foxes eat them they will die unless they find water nearby. In the 16th century pills compounded of almonds, liver, and oil of violet were recommended by Guglielmo Gratarolo to travelers in areas where food and drink were scarce.

The almond is used as a divining rod in Tuscany. Church legend assigns the tree to the Virgin. Moslems regard it as the hope of heaven and use almond paste, mixed with the milk of a mother who has a baby girl, to cure trachoma.

alọ Yoruba term for folktales and also for riddles. The more or less general African synonymity of folktale and riddle carries over also into New World Negro dialect and tradition. In the Sea Islands off South Carolina a tale is a riddle, a riddle is a tale. "How you split de diffunce between riddle an' story?" said one Sea Island narrator, when questioned. "Dere is singin' in a story." (E. C. Parsons: *Folklore of the Sea Islands, MAFLS,* vol. 16, p. xix.) Compare ITAN. See AFRICAN AND NEW WORLD NEGRO FOLKLORE.

Aloadæ In Greek mythology, the giants Ephialtes and Otus, twin sons of Poseidon and either Iphimedeia or the Earth-Mother, who imprisoned Ares in a bronze pot. When they were nine years old the twins, who measured nine cubits in breadth and nine fathoms in height, threatened to do battle with the Olympian gods, planning to pile Mount Pelion upon Mount Olympus and Mount Ossa upon Pelion so that they might reach the heavens. Apollo, however, killed them before they were able to carry out their plan. In the *Iliad* they sought Artemis and Hera in marriage, but Artemis tricked them into killing each other. In some legends the Aloadæ were beneficent beings, founders of cities and rescuers of their mother and sister.

'Alo'alo In the religion of the Tongans of western Polynesia, the god of wind, weather, vegetation, and harvest; son of the sun: the "fanner."

aloes The term as used in the Bible (*Num.* xxiv, 6; *Ps.* xiv, 8; *Prov.* vii, 17; *Cant.* iv, 14; *John* xix, 39) refers to the gum of the *Aloexylon, Aquilaria ovata,* and *Aquilaria agallochum* which are not true aloes. Aloes were used medicinally by the Romans. They were used in the Middle Ages in suffumigations and magic compounds. In the 16th century they were used in medicines. In India aloes are used in the treatment of eye infections, and modern Americans sometimes paint babies' fingers with an extract of aloes to stop finger-sucking or nailbiting. In Egypt an aloe plant is hung over the door of a newly built house to insure long life and success to the occupants and the house. The aloe will live thus for two or three years without water or earth.

alomancy (more properly *halomancy*) An ancient method of divination using salt. From the flames of a fire into which salt has been thrown, the diviner reads the message he seeks. The present-day custom of throwing a pinch of salt from an overturned saltcellar over the left shoulder may be connected with this.

alphabet rimes A mnemonic and usually acrostic device to assist children and other illiterates in learning letters of the alphabet. The idea is at least as old as the 119th Psalm, which consists of 22 eight-verse sections corresponding to the 22 letters of the Hebrew alphabet, with every verse in each section beginning with a word whose first letter is, for instance, in section one, "aleph," section two, "beth," and so on. There are several other acrostic alphabets in the Hebrew scriptures (See *Enc. Rel. & Ethics,* vol. I, p. 75) notably in the well-known description of a virtuous woman in *Proverbs* xxxi, 10–31, in memorizing which the Jewish girl learned both virtue and the alphabet. Chaucer's "*A. B. C.*" (c. 1375), a poem in honor of the Virgin Mary, is the oldest extant alphabet rime in English, but it was taken from a French original, *Pèlerinage*

de la vie humaine, by Guillaume de Deguilleville, written a half-century before.

Two very old alphabet rimes are still repeated by children today. The popular Tom Thumb's Alphabet contains the lines:

> A was an Archer, who shot at a frog;
> B was a Butcher, who had a great dog; . . .
> I was an Innkeeper, who loved to bouse;
> J was a Joiner, who built up a house; . .

Here the age of the rime is betrayed by the riming of "bouse" with "house," whereas we now pronounce and even spell it "booze." Later in the alphabet the use of Tinker, Usurer, and Vintner, to say nothing of "Zany, a poor harmless fool," confirm our suspicion that Tom Thumb's Alphabet is at least 300 years old. Perhaps not quite so old, but of respectable age and well worn by use is the Apple-pie Alphabet, beginning:

> A was an Apple-pie.
> B Bit it.
> C Cut it.
> D Dealt it.
> E Eat it. . . .

The use of "eat" (pron. ett) instead of "ate" for the past tense goes back to colonial days in New England, where they were then using in learning their "A. B. abs" another more pious rime from the *New England Primer* which began with:

> In Adam's fall
> We sinned All,

and ended with:

> Zaccheus he
> Climb up a tree
> His Lord to see.

(And don't let anyone tell you it should be "Did climb a tree" with a long i in climb. It is *short* i for the past tense, for I got it by oral tradition through 12 generations from Elizabethan England.)

The "Peter Piper" who "Pick'd a Peck of Pickl'd Peppers" is the sole stanza now known to our children from a merry alphabet rime popular in England and America in the early 18th century, beginning:
"Andrew Airpump Ask'd his Aunt her Ailment,"
and running through such exciting adventures as that of "Matthew Mendlegs" who "Miss'd a Mangl'd Monkey," and "Needy Noodle" who "Nipp'd a Naybour's Nutmegs."

In 1833 Thackeray composed and illustrated one of these alphabet rimes for "Little Eddy" who until he died in 1915 at the age of 86 could still recite the whole poem beginning:

> Great A; it is an Animal & called an Alligator.
> Its countenance will shew you, that it's of a cruel Natur.

But Col. Edw. Fred'k Chadwick preferred to say the P:

> P is a Pimple—'tis a thing which grows
> Sometimes upon a luckless Parson's nose.
> (*The Thackeray Alphabet,* Harper, 1930.)

Contemporary with Thackeray was Edward Lear, who composed for another little Eddy, who became the 15th Earl of Derby, some of the world's most famous children's rimes, including many alphabet verses. With Lear, A was sometimes an Ape who stole some white tape, or an Ant who seldom stood still, or even an "Absolutely

Abstemious Ass." (*The Complete Nonsense Book*, Dodd Mead, 1934.)

Of the flood of modern alphabet rimes the most interesting are the ones in Lois Lenski's *Alphabet People*, (Harper, 1928) where occupations are featured, as:

> A for Artist in a smock
> With brushes, paints galore;
> She hangs her paintings on the wall
> And then she paints some more.

With these I place the clever *The Jaw-Breaker's Alphabet* by Eunice and Janet Tietjens (A. & C. Boni, 1930) with its intriguing:

> A's for Archaeopteryx
> Of whom perhaps you've heard,
> The up-and-coming reptile
> Who first became a bird.

Nor can we well omit "A Moral Alphabet" in Hilaire Belloc's *Cautionary Verses* (A. A. Knopf, 1941) where:

> A stands for Archibald who told no lies
> And got this lovely volume for a prize.

CHARLES FRANCIS POTTER

Alphabet Song   An occupational song of sailors, giving the names of the parts of a ship in abecedarian order, and forming a sort of catechism for the greenhorn. This is an example of an ancient type of song outlining facts or principles to be memorized, a similar one being sung by woodsmen of the northeastern United States to the same air, cataloging the tools and tricks of the logger's trade.

alphorn   A long wooden trumpet, four to 12 feet long, used in the Alps for centuries to call herds, for signal over long distances, and for sunset rites. The pitch is controlled by lips and breath, rather than by stops, and the few traditional tunes, also sung as *kuhreihen* or *ranz des vaches*, show signs of archaism. The word *lobe* used in some of the songs is of magical significance and probably imitative. The tone is strong, audible for miles, and is believed to prolong the light of day when twilight draws on. The period of dusk was thought to be dangerous for men and herds, and the sounding of the alphorn, or imitation of its tone with the voice, was protection against the dangers of transition. In some areas Christianity has added the singing of the evening prayer as the instrument sounds. Similar sunset practices are observed in Norway, Poland, Rumania, India, South America, and Australia.

alraun   The German name for the mandrake root or for a similar root such as that of bryony used in magic as a substitute. Small good-luck images shaped from these roots are also alrauns; and so is the helpful elf or goblin associated with both. This goblin was one foot high, was kept in a cupboard, and fed on milk and biscuit.

Alsirat, al-Sirāt, or **Al Sirat**   In Moslem religion and legend, the bridge and only way to paradise over the abyss of hell. It is sharper than a sword, narrower than a spider's thread, and beset on either side by briars and hooked thorns. The good traverse it with ease and swiftness; the wicked miss their footing and fall into hell. In later Moslem eschatology the bridge is described as the length of a journey of 3000 years. The righteous pass over it quickly, but less perfect Moslems take longer to traverse it, the length of time required depending upon the degree of sin committed. In the Koran, it is the narrow path or correct way of religion.

Altjira   In the religion and mythology of the Arunta of Australia, the sky-dweller or All-Father who is generally considered to be indifferent to mankind.

alum   In modern Egypt, a charm against the evil eye. A piece about the size of a walnut is placed upon burning coals and left until it has ceased to bubble while the first and last three chapters of the Koran are repeated three times. When the alum is removed from the fire it will have assumed the shape of the person whose malice is feared. It is then pounded and mixed in food fed to a black dog. A piece of alum ornamented with tassels is sometimes attached to a child's cap as a protective amulet.

Negroes of the southern United States use alum to stop bleeding, to cure blindness, and to cure chickens of cholera. Used with bluestone it is believed to cure gonorrhea; boiled with poke root and salt it is used as a liniment for rheumatism. Sucking a ball of alum is believed to be effective in preventing harm from conjuration.

Alvíss   Literally, All-Wise: in the lay of Alvíss in the *Elder Edda*, the underground dwarf who sued for the hand of Thrud, Thor's daughter. Thor was against the match, but said he would not refuse his daughter if Alvíss could answer certain questions. Alvíss, just having run through nine worlds, thought he would know all the answers and consented to answer the questions. So Thor put his 13 questions: what is the name of the world, the sky, the moon, sun, clouds, wind, calm, fire, sea, trees, night, wheat, beer, in all the worlds of the aesir, vanir, giants, elves, and gods. Alvíss knew all this and easily answered. Then Thor revealed his trick: the questions and answers had occupied the night; the sun was already in the room; Alvíss had to hurry off with the light of day or be petrified. This is one of the oldest of the world's riddling suitor-test stories, except in this case the successful riddler did not get the girl.

Amadán   Literally, fool: the fool of the side, or the fairy fool of Irish folklore, whose touch is incurable. Those whom he touches forever after have a crooked jaw or twisted face (facial paralysis) or suffer crippling injury, or else die soon. For this reason the amadán is also often called the *stroke lad*. June is the time one is most in danger from him; June is the month when the Fool is most apt to give his stroke. Lady Gregory says "If you don't say 'The Lord between us and harm' when you meet him, you are done for, forever and always." A young girl who passed by his castle (*bruidean*) one night was crippled forever after. But it is equally well known that he often punishes wrong deeds with his stroke, for once he struck a miser who was mending shoes on Sunday. Amadán Mór is the Great Fool of the fairy host of Irish folktale and poetry. Amadán na bruidne, the fool of the fairy mounds or fairy palaces, is greatly feared.

Amaethon or **Amathaon**   In Brythonic mythology, a son of Dôn mentioned in *Kilhwch and Olwen*, which tells the story of the field impossible to till, tilled by Amaethon. His name is basically Cymric *amaeth*, plowman, and for this reason he is often interpreted as an agricultural god or culture hero. This role is further substantiated by a later story in which he brought back to this world a roebuck and a young dog belonging to Arawn, lord of Annwn, the Otherworld. See BATTLE OF THE TREES.

Amala In Tsimshian mythology, the supporter of the world. The world is flat and circular and turns continually on the end of a long pole which Amala supports on his chest. His predecessor was an old chief who lived on an island in the vast southwest sea. The old chief, ill and dying, heard of Amala's supernatural strength and sent for him to take over the task. Amala came, lay down beside the aged chief, and the old man transferred the pole-of-the-world to Amala's chest. Amala still holds the world on his chest, but when he dies the world will end.

This is the final incident in a long story about Amala or Very Dirty (literally the word means 'smoke hole'), involving, in addition to the Atlas motif, both the youngest son and Cinderella themes in varying degree. Amala or Very Dirty was the youngest of a number of brothers. He slept late, took no part in family activities, was ridiculed, named Dirty, thought weak and worthless, but secretly acquired supernatural strength, performed the impossible, such as pulling up trees and saving his relations from their enemies. He then conquered the big animals, the strong trees, the strong birds, and the big mountain, and was chosen to take care of the world. The story partakes of the Cinderella theme in that Amala slept in the ashes, wore only one ragged deerskin, was disregarded or ridiculed by the rest of the household, was unhappy about his lot, received supernatural aid, astounded one and all with his beauty and prowess, and was eventually chosen to fill a superior position.

There are eight variants of this story among the Tsimshian, Nass, Skidegate, Kaigani, Masset, and Tlingit tribes. The earth on the pole idea is limited to the Tsimshians, Tlingits, Skidegates, and Hares. The white man's influence is suspected, but not assumed, by J. R. Swanton, in the turning of the earth upon the pole idea; but no doubts are cast on the originality of Amala's having a big spoonful of grease for the pole to turn in, or his sustaining his own strength for the task with annual anointings of wild-duck oil.

Amalthæa or **Amalthea** In Greek mythology, the goat who provided milk for the infant Zeus while he was hidden in Crete. One of the horns of Amalthæa, reputedly broken off by Zeus, became the cornucopia or horn of plenty.

Amarāvatī In Indian mythology, the capital of Svarga, Indra's Heaven, situated near Mount Meru. The city has a thousand gates, is decked with the fruits of desire (jewels, objects of vanity and pleasure), and adorned by the Apsarases. There is neither heat nor cold, grief nor despondency: to it come those who do penance or sacrifice, and the warriors who fall in battle.

amasiado A popular term for the type of extra-legal mating found among Brazilian Negroes, this word is derived from the verb *amasiar-se*, which is a synonym for *amancebar-se*, this giving the word *amancebido* the more literary designation for this kind of relationship.

The institution it designates is that found in the lower socio-economic strata of all Afroamerican groups whose patterns of family life have been studied from the ethnological point of view. Terms recorded for its counterparts are as follows, the word in each case being that most often encountered, without indication as to whether it refers to the situation itself, or to the participant: arrimao, (arrimado)—Cuba; companyá—Curaçao; plaçage —Haiti; endamada—Honduras (Black Caribs); keepers— Trinidad; commonlaw (verb, to commonlaw)—United States. All these forms are socially sanctioned, even though, for the woman, they carry less prestige than marriage, as mating in accordance with legal formalities is always termed, in contradistinction to them.

To understand the significance of family groupings of this kind, it is essential that the economic and social position of women be taken fully into account, since this has struck all students of the New World Negro family. The woman's primacy, whether as grandmother, mother, or aunt, contrasts strikingly with patterns of the majority groups among whom the Negro lives. She is the focus of the family group, and, where there is no male head, its provider. She wields authority over its members, and is thus characteristically to be termed the significant parent.

This does not mean that matings of this kind are haphazard. They are always distinguished, by verbal symbol, from transient relationships in the same societies. They are entered into with an assumption of permanence, which they obtain to a degree surprising to outsiders. In Brazil, amasiado matings of lifetime duration are not uncommon, and numerous instances of twenty years' duration and upwards have been recorded. In such cases, the place of the father becomes of increasing importance; and even where a couple separate, his relations with his children may continue warm, and he will in many instances contribute to their support.

This institution is to be referred to the dominant family form of those parts of Africa from which New World Negroes were derived. The nucleus of this system is the woman's hut within the polygynous compound, headed by the common husband, who lives in his own hut where his wives cohabit with him in turn. The continuation of the polygynous household, like that of the wider social groupings of extended family and sib, all male-dominated, was rendered impossible by circumstances of slavery in the New World. This left the nuclear woman-dominated group as the one on which the Negroes could build, since in it were retained not only a traditional form, but the emotional focus that it manifested in Africa.

This would also explain why, though a deviant from legally sanctioned norms, this New World family type is in no way to be considered as an index of the demoralization of those societies where it is formed. No stigma attaches to children born of matings of this sort, nor to those party to it. It is thus to be considered as a mode of adjustment and as a means by which social stability has been retained despite the difficulties of life experienced by Negroes in adjusting to slavery and to various post-slavery regimes. M. J. HERSKOVITS

Amaterasu Omikami The Japanese Sun Goddess: also called Tensho Daijan in Sino-Japanese pronunciation. See JAPANESE FOLKLORE. [JLM]

Ama-tsu-mara In the Shinto religion and mythology of Japan, the cyclopean blacksmith god who, with Ishi-Kori-dome, made the solar mirror which was used in enticing Amaterasu out of the cave in which she had taken refuge.

Amazon In Greek mythology, one of a race of female warriors who lived on the north coast of Asia Minor with their capital, according to Herodotus, at Themiscyra. From there they invaded at various times Thrace, the islands of the Ægean, Greece, Syria, Arabia, Egypt, and Libya. The Amazons were ruled by a queen. To prevent their race from dying out once a year they visited the neighboring Gargareans. Their girl children were brought up and trained in the pursuits of war, riding, hunting, and agriculture. According to some, each girl had her right breast cut off in order to handle arms more freely, from which custom arose the common ancient derivation of the name "a-mazos," without breast. However, since no work of art shows the Amazons without breasts, other etymologies, none quite satisfactory, have been suggested. The boys were sent to the Gargareans, put to death, blinded, or maimed.

Folktales and myths of women warriors are found among the people of India ("Story of King Vikramā-ditya," for example, in which the king dreams of the man-hating Princess Malayavatī), in Arabia, England, Ireland, and among the Makurap of the upper Guaporé River, Brazil. The Makurap believed that a village not far from their territory, called Arapinjatschäküp, was inhabited only by warlike women who kept men at bay.

The Koniag Eskimos of Kodiak Island have several woman-warrior tales, among them one in which a girl was abandoned by parents who were too poor to feed her. An old man came and told her to drink from the river. When her strength had increased the old man (strength-giver) disappeared and the girl became a huntress. There are four footprints on a certain cape of that region which are said to be hers. Later she went to her family's camping place and outshone her brothers who became jealous. They attempted to trick her, took away her arrows, and left her. She gnawed the flippers of a seal until only the nails were left and then used these to shoot otters. She grew very handsome and finally married. While she was hunting at sea a storm came up, so she cut off her female parts and threw them into the sea, calming the waters. See HERCULES.

amber A cloudy or translucent yellowish to brownish fossilized resin of coniferous trees of the Oligocene epoch, found along the coasts of England, of the Baltic Sea, in Sicily, Rumania, Burma, and Yunnan, China. The greatest amber-producing region is in East Prussia.

Amber is second only to the pearl in the antiquity of its use. Strings of rough amber beads were worn even in prehistoric times. The resin was carried down the Elbe and Moldau trade route, through the Rhone valley to the Mediterranean, and to the British Isles. Such trade is believed to have flourished before 2000 B.C. Amber has been found in early Minoan strata in Crete; Homer mentions the flourishing Phœnician amber trade; and Pliny chides Sophocles for his falsehoods concerning it. According to Apollodorus its origin is in poplar trees. The Romans used it for throat infections and to prevent fever.

In Greek legend, amber was a concretion of the tears shed at the death of Meleager by his sisters. In Scandinavian mythology, it was the tears shed by Freya when Odin wandered out into the world. To the Chinese, amber was the soul of the tiger transformed into the mineral after death. They used it as a symbol of courage and attributed medicinal qualities to it. In the Buddhist paradise pure beings have bright yellowish faces and their merit may grow in the shape of diamonds, flowers, amber, etc.

In the Middle Ages amber was worn to ward off croup; and amber necklaces for small children were sold as croup-preventatives throughout Europe as late as the 19th century. It was dissolved and used as a cordial. It prevented epilepsy if placed over the heart, checked paralysis if the spine were anointed with it, and acted as a restorative if one inhaled it. In the 15th and 16th centuries in India it was mixed with food as a medicament.

Moslems include amber beads on their talismanic chains and bracelets, believing them a cure for jaundice. They rub sore eyes with ashes of amber and take it in powdered form internally to strengthen a weak heart or to induce sweating. The Italians use amber amulets against witchcraft. The French of Louisiana still use it to cure croup.

Amber mountains and amber islands were the forerunners of the glass mountains and islands in the folktales of Scandinavia, central and eastern Europe, and the British Isles. The Scandinavian Glaesisvellir was an amber valley-paradise and Glaesir an amber grove at the gates of Valhalla. The word glass, originally meaning "resin" or "amber," was applied to glass when that product was introduced into northern Europe.

Ambrogio and Lietta A popular ballad of northern Italy (from the Piedmont region) in which Ambrogio cruelly and heartlessly compels his wife, Lietta, heavy with child, to travel faster than she is able. This ballad closely parallels the theme of the English *Child Waters*.

ambrosia In Greek and Roman mythology, the food or drink of the gods which made all who partook of it immortal. In Homer, ambrosia was the food of immortality and its accompanying nectar the drink of the gods. Sappho and Anaxandrides spoke of ambrosia as the drink of the gods, nectar as the food. Compare AMRITA; MEAD; SOMA.

Amen or **Amon** An important god of ancient Egypt, almost always worshipped as identical with another god. Amen was probably originally a local god of Thebes and the neighboring Luxor and Karnak and may have been an air god. However, in later religion, he became a god of reproduction, was spoken of as one of the creators of the gods, of mankind, of the universe. As patron of Thebes he became, in the XVIII Dynasty and afterwards, the chief god of Egypt (Amen-Ra), and his priests wielded power greater than that of the pharaohs. He was depicted as a bearded man wearing a cap with two tall plumes, or as a ram. Both the ram and the goose were sacred to him, and at Thebes he was said to be embodied in the ram. As the national god of Egypt, he was incarnate in the Pharaoh. The ruins at Karnak are the remains of his temple. The Greeks identified him with Zeus, and his great oracle was the famous stone in the temple of Jupiter Ammon.

Amenti or **Amentet** In the Osiris cult of Egyptian religion and in mythology, the underworld; literally, the hidden land, located in the west where the sun sets. When the soul entered Amenti, Anubis conducted it into the hall of Osiris where it was judged by the 42 judges; then the heart was weighed against the feather of truth. Those souls which passed the test went on to the fields of Aalu while the others were consigned to torment. The four spirits of Amenti, the tutelaries of the underworld and children of Horus, represented upon the four Canopic vases, were Amset, Hapi, Tuamatef, and Kebhsnauf. Compare BA.

American Anthropological Association Formal interest in anthropology is of long standing in the United States, but it was not until 1879 that an immediate progenitor of the American Anthropological Association was organized. In that year a group of men, mainly ethnologists and doctors of medicine, formed the Anthropological Society of Washington "to encourage the study of the natural history of man, especially with reference to America."

It was not long before the localized interests of this group and others such as the American Ethnological Society in New York (founded in 1842) and the Philadelphia Anthropological Society (later in origin) widened enough to require an organization of greater scope. Thus, in 1882 the American Association for the Advancement of Science created an anthropology section which brought together for the first time in a nationwide structure persons of anthropological interests. In 1899 this anthropology section of the American Association for the Advancement of Science took over the journal *American Anthropologist*, which had been the organ of the Anthropological Society of Washington since 1888, and reestablished it as the *American Anthropologist, New Series*.

The needs of anthropologists and the growing dignity and importance of the science were still in part unfulfilled, however, and as a consequence the first steps toward founding an independent, national organization were taken during the latter part of 1901. Subsequently, an Act of Incorporation for the American Anthropologic(al) Association was recorded on March 26, 1902, in the District of Columbia and a founding meeting was held in Pittsburgh on June 30, 1902.

The purposes of the Association, as quoted from the original constitution, were "to promote the science of Anthropology; to stimulate the efforts of American anthropologists; to coordinate Anthropology with other sciences; to foster local and other societies devoted to Anthropology; to serve a bond of union among American anthropologists and American anthropological organizations present and prospective; and to publish and encourage the publication of matter pertaining to Anthropology." The original constitution has been amended in 1916, 1941, and 1946. The last date saw the institution of major changes with an increased attention to the professional interests of the membership. Thus, to the original aims were added the provisions that the Association shall "take action on behalf of the entire profession and integrate the professional activities of anthropologists in the various special branches of the science; promote the wider recognition and constant improvement of professional standards in anthropology; and act to coordinate activities of members of the Association with those of other organizations concerned with anthropology, and maintain effective liaison with related sciences and their organizations." In the furtherance of these aims, the amended constitution gave increased authorities and discretion concerning professional matters to the executive board of the Association. One of the first acts of the executive board was the establishment in August, 1947, of an Executive Secretariat, with the aid of a grant of $10,660.50 from the Carnegie Corporation

of New York, charged with general responsibilities concerning professional information and public relations. Another measure, designed to enhance the professional interests of the Association, was the creation of two classes of membership, Fellows and Members, with eligibility to the former status restricted to persons who meet certain professional standards. Early in 1948 two further statuses, Foreign Fellows and Liaison Fellows, became effective. At the end of 1970 the Association's membership was about 7,000, including 1,574 Fellows and 46 foreign Fellows.

With regard to the encouragement and organization of research the Association is unique among learned societies in having official representative membership on all three of the major research councils in the United States, i.e. the National Research Council, the Social Science Research Council, and the American Council of Learned Societies, and in addition provides two representatives to the American Association for the Advancement of Science.

Publications of the Association are: the *American Anthropologist*, published 6 times a year (volume 72 in 1970) and the *Memoirs* (101 volumes), superseded in 1969 by the *Anthropological Studies*. These contain many articles and monographs of milestone importance, which have affected the currents of anthropological thought not only in the United States but in other nations as well. A third publication, a mimeographed *News Bulletin*, established in 1947, now the *Newsletter*, reports matters of current interest and importance to the Fellows of the Association. The *American Anthropologist* is also the official organ of the American Ethnological Society, the Anthropological Society of Washington, the Philadelphia Anthropological Society, the Central States Branch of the American Anthropological Association, the Anthropological Society of Hawaii, and the Western States Branch of the American Anthropological Association, all of which are affiliate organizations. In addition, the Association maintains close relations variously through joint membership, reduced annual dues, and an editorial council with all of the above as well as with the Society for American Archaeology, the American Folklore Society, the Linguistic Society of America, the Society for Applied Anthropology, the American Association of Physical Anthropologists, the Inter-American Society for Anthropology and Geography. There are also three annual *Bulletins:* "Annual Report and Directory," "Guide to Departments of Anthropology" (museums added in 1971), and "Preliminary Program and Abstracts" of the annual meeting.

Annual business meetings have been held every year since the Association was founded, with a scientific meeting held in conjunction nearly every year as well. Whenever possible, these meetings are held jointly with various of the affiliated and kindred organizations.

Since 1946 the Association has, through the offices of a special committee, selected the annual recipient of the Viking Fund Medal and Prize in Cultural Anthropology.

American folklore Even without insisting on special American qualities in American folklore, we can now safely assume that there is such a thing as "American folklore" and not "only European (or African, or Far Eastern) folklore on the American continent." [1] The late Alexander Haggerty Krappe's objection to the term

"American folklore" as a "bad misnomer" must be judged in relation to his Old World conception of folklore as synonymous with "survivals" and of the folk as synonymous with the peasantry. In America it is no longer possible to accept his definition of the former as the "sum total of stories, songs, beliefs, and practices which belong to a bygone age and have ceased to have any direct and organic connection with actual life," or of the latter in terms of "purely agricultural regions."

The real trouble, however, lies in the ambiguity of the word folklore, which has the double meaning of the material and its study. It is true (and Krappe may have had this in mind) that there can be no scientific, historical study of American folklore apart from Old World sources. But equally important to the study of American folklore is what happened to the Old World heritage after it was transplanted and took root. Although Krappe rightly insists that the folklorist must be equipped with a "good history of the American 'land-taking,' " he still thinks of this largely in terms of the "ethnical provenance and age of each settlement" and the "shifts of populations." But provenance is only half the story. If folklore is universal in diffusion, it is local in setting. And the study of the local setting takes special importance from the fact that "it is upon the mass of the inarticulate in American society that effects of environment are likely to be most marked." [2]

There is, in other words, such a thing as an indigenous American folk, in terms, as the present writer stated in 1929, of "not one folk but many folk groups— as many as there are regional cultures or racial or occupational groups within a region." [3] As basic to this conception the writer accepted J. Frank Dobie's definition of the folk as "any group of people not cosmopolitan who, independent of academic means, preserve a body of tradition peculiar to themselves." Or, as Martha Warren Beckwith put it in 1931: "The true folk group is one which has preserved a common culture in isolation long enough to allow emotion to color its forms of social expression." [4] She names as isolating factors "geographical conditions," "common language and national heritage," and "occupation," found separately or in conjunction with one another.

From the cultural point of view, there is not only an American folk but also an American study of the folk and its lore. This involves, more than the provenance and distribution of folk songs and tales in the United States, the social and cultural history of folk groups. It is the study not simply of diffusion but of acculturation—"those phenomena which result when groups of individuals having different cultures come into continuous first-hand contact, with subsequent changes in the original cultural patterns of either or both groups." [5] And folklore acculturation studies in turn involve not only local folklore collections, correlated with life histories of and interviews with informants and with field and historical studies of cultural areas and centers and routes of migration, as in the *Linguistic Atlas,* but the whole relation of local and regional history to American social and cultural history and of folklore to the "roots of American culture" in what Constance Rourke calls the"humble influences of place and kinship and common emotion that accumulate through generations to shape and condition a distinctive native consciousness." [6]

Recognition of the cultural diversity of the American folk, as well as of the fact that, for the purposes of collection and study, American folklore is too big to be treated as a whole, led to the following division of the field by the American Folklore Society at the time of its organization in 1888: "(a) Relics of Old English Folklore (ballads, tales, superstitions, dialect, etc.); (b) Lore of Negroes in the Southern States of the Union; (c) Lore of the Indian tribes of North America (myths, tales, etc.); (d) Lore of French Canada, Mexico, etc." [7] With the addition of later immigrant and other nationality groups, these categories still mark the main cultural divisions of American folklore and the division of labor among American folklorists.

Although the study of the lore of foreign-language groups, like that of the American Indian, has been delegated to specialists, it must not be thought that the folk culture of national minorities is entirely cut off from the main body of English-speaking groups. Ghettoes, islands, and "pockets," it is true, make for partial or relative isolation; but linguistic barriers are no obstacle to the diffusion of folklore, which follows the principal cultural routes and areas, with resultant interchange and modification of the folkways and folklore of the various ethnic groups.

The nature and degree of separation and exchange between groups are further affected by social and economic influences, education, and mass communication. Although the forces that make for standardization are diffused through all groups and areas with apparent uniformity, the interplay of cultural norms and variations is complicated by group acceptances and resistances, local attachments and sectional loyalties, and traditional reliance on folk beliefs and practices as an alternate mode of procedure to scientific and institutional forms.

To the forces of survival and contra-acculturative reversion must also be added the forces of revival as intercultural and folk education, folk festivals, etc., seek to promote group self-respect and mutual understanding by showing the essential unity underlying differences, stressing participation in a common culture rather than "contributions," reconciling conflicts between old and new cultural patterns, and generally replacing stereotypes with cultural variations.

As part of this cultural dynamics, the following trends may be distinguished in the development of American folk groups and their lore. Where regional variations are coupled with a distinct ethnic and linguistic stock, in a state of partial or relative cultural isolation, a more or less homogeneous body of regional lore exists in much the same sense that regional lore and regional dialects are found in the Old World. This is true, for example, of the lore of the English-Scotch-Irish mountain whites; the Afro-American lore of the Deep South (Coast, Sea Islands, Delta), and the West Indies; and more particularly the lore of the Pennsylvania Germans, the Louisiana French, and the Spanish-American and Mexican-American groups of the Southwest. Again, where work is related to place, a distinctive occupational lore has grown up about such callings as deep-water sailing, whaling, fishing, canal-boating, steamboating, railroading, lumbering, grazing, and coal- and metal-mining. Regional culture and folkways have further conditioned and fostered the growth of certain regional types of lore, such as the Southern Negro slave songs and prison work songs, white spirituals of the Southern uplands, Shaker songs and dances, and Mormon lore, as well as regional styles of story-telling, singing, square-dancing, square-dance calling, and folk arts and crafts.

With the recent revival of interest in American folkways and regions, scholarly and popular attention has been focused on the lore of such colorful subregions as the Maine coast, the White and Green Mountains, Cape Cod, the Catskills, the Allegheny, Cumberland, Blue Ridge, Great Smoky, and Ozark Mountains, the Tidewater, Florida, the Gulf Coast, the Mississippi Delta, the Bayous of Louisiana, the Great Lakes, the Upper Peninsula of Michigan, the Rockies, and the various Southwest and Northwest areas.

Turning from folk groups to folklore, we note a twofold effect of the twin forces of diffusion and acculturation. On the one hand, the same song or story, in slightly altered form (the product of localization), may turn up in different localities, attached to different individuals, each claiming to be the original. Such is the case with migratory legends and traditions of lovers' leaps, haunts of the devil, witches, ghosts, pirates, and buried treasure. On the other hand, a genuine body of place lore (inseparable and sometimes indistinguishable from regional culture) has grown up about local traditions connected with topographical features, landmarks, flora and fauna, artifacts, population, settlement, foods, architecture, speech, place names, and local attachments and loyalties of all kinds, from social, political, and economic feuds and rivalries to local pride and patriotism generally. Place lore, of course, is mixed with historical traditions, as in the South, where colonial, plantation, Civil War, and Reconstruction days have their respective legends, heroes, and symbols.

If American folklore is, on the whole, closer to history than to mythology, it is because America as a whole is closer to the beginnings of settlement and to the oral and written sources of local history. America is rich, not only in local history (much local historical writing, it is true, being amateurish, antiquarian, and local in spirit) but also in folk history—history from the bottom up, in which the people, as participants or eye-witnesses, are their own historians. And in so far as everyone has in his repertoire an articulate body of family and community tradition he is to that extent his own folklorist as well as a folklore informant.

The combination of history, folklore, and folk history is nowhere seen to better advantage than in old-timers' stories and reminiscences, which not only contain valuable folklore data but also throw valuable light on the backgrounds of folklore and folk groups. Through the combined efforts of old-timers, folklorists, and historians, an extensive literature (much of it in the vernacular) of pioneer folkways and customs has grown up in America. This tells us how people lived in the early days; how they fought wild animals, Indians, drought, fire, flood, cyclones, blizzards, sandstorms, pests, sickness, disease, crime; how they made their own entertainment and how many hands made light work in the social gatherings, merrymakings, and work bees of the frontier; what they ate and what they wore; how they educated themselves and how they worshipped. All this, if closer to folkways than to folklore, is still valid material for the folklorists' study, since folklore properly includes the life of the folk as well as its lore.

The relation of history to legend is also close in America. The mixture of the two has given rise to a large body of unhistorical "historical" traditions (corresponding to "unnatural" natural history) or apocryphal traditions of doubtful exploits of historical characters and "untrustworthy traditions of doubtful events." And in so far as history, with its legends and symbols, selects, transmits, and shapes traditional values and assumptions, it acquires folklore coloring and significance.

The lore of place names is particularly rich in local history and historical traditions. Factual place names arise "either from an immediate circumstance attending the giving of the name, a happening, an object present, a natural feature of the landscape, or from memory association with other places or names." [8] Mythological names originate in assumed or folk etymology which may "sometimes furnish under the guise of fiction useful clues to the real facts." [9] But there are historical and mythological elements in both kinds of place-name stories, as myth has some basis in history or history is touched with fantasy.

The somewhat overstressed predilection of the American folk for extravagant or ludicrous exaggeration, which would seem to be in contradiction to its historical impulse, is related to the proverbial traits of boasting and boosting and the burlesque thereof, and may be explained and reconciled on the ground that in America and American history nothing is usual. In the first place, Americans, living in a land of marvels and being born travelers, have always loved to hear and tell tales (especially travelers' tales) of the marvelous. In the second place, since Americans have always tried to improve on nature, American story-tellers are seldom averse to improving a tale. In this task of "making a good story a little better," folk story-tellers have had the example and assistance of professional historians, from the Mathers, with their habit of glorifying marvels (or "providences") as a means of improving religion, to the latest historian or pseudo-historian who uses legend to heighten the drama and color of history.

In spinning extravagant yarns and lying tales the folk has also had the cooperation of professional story-tellers in the reciprocity of oral and written tradition that exists in America. Thus a long line of Southern and Western humorists, culminating in Mark Twain, converted the yarn and tall tale from oral to literary use, emulating the matter and manner of the oral and natural story-teller. As a result (e.g. in New England), the line between folklore, local history, and local-color writing is sometimes hard to draw. On the one hand, almanacs, newspapers, magazines, chronicles, memoirs, travel accounts, and town and county histories have helped to circulate oral traditions and anecdotes of the smart sayings and doings, the jests and pranks of local characters and old-timers. On the other hand, poets, dramatists, and fiction-writers have made liberal artistic use of local anecdotes and legends.

The fact that American folklore grew up in an age of print has had still other effects on the aesthetics, culture, and science of this lore. It has, according to Paul Engle, resulted in a greater and more successful effort (on the part of untrained, and even unconscious, as well as trained folklorists) "to retain in print those often insubstantial folk sayings, folk customs, folk anecdotes, which are the rich substance of a country's life."

It has also given American folklore more than a touch of the sophisticated and even synthetic. In the case of Paul Bunyan, for example, there is strong evidence of diffusion from above downward, and more than a suspicion that lumber advertising men had as much to do with inventing the logger hero as he had to do with inventing the lumber industry.

Paul Bunyan stories, originating fairly recently in separate anecdotes or jests of the Munchausen and joke-book variety, also illustrate the tendency of anecdotes to escape from print into oral tradition. Short, pithy, funny stories, learned from either source and both in and out of cycles, have always been popular among the folk because easily remembered and quickly told. But the anecdotal, fragmentary character of much American story-telling and the relative scarcity of long, involved tales may indicate that the more highly developed forms of folk story-telling have become a lost art. Certainly, under the influence of commercialized mass media of entertainment and with the general speeding up of modern living, shorter, snappier forms have displaced long-winded tales and ballads.

The anecdote also flourishes in America as a result of the separation of story-telling from mythology and ritual and its survival chiefly as a social pastime growing out of the chat or as a practical device for clinching an argument or illustrating a point. Hence the vogue of the anecdote as a rhetorical form popular with political, after-dinner, and other speakers and the large number of collections preserving oral anecdotes of master story-tellers like Lincoln and continuing in the tradition of exempla and ana.

The typical American form of story-telling, however, is not the anecdote but the yarn, which may be considered the parent type or an elaboration and expansion of the anecdote, depending upon whether one considers the anecdote a vestigial or germinal form. As a long, loose, rambling tale of personal experience, the yarn has its roots in "own stories" and reminiscences of thrilling or improbable adventures. Like the anecdote, the yarn is told "casually, in an offhand way, as if in reference to actual events of common knowledge," and with the utmost solemnity in the face of the most preposterous incidents. Unlike the anecdote, however, the yarn often substitutes anticlimax for climax, building up elaborately to a letdown instead of sacrificing everything to the punch line. The accumulation of circumstantial detail, often digressive and irrelevant, after the fashion of garrulous raconteurs, is also a device for establishing confidence and securing credence.

Although more involved than the anecdote, the yarn still falls short of the highly developed art of the Old World folktale. Two favorite devices of the yarn—the repeated obstacle and the retarded climax—are devices of the fairy or household tale, which survives in the United States chiefly on the childhood level. Thus one of Richard Chase's informants for *The Jack Tales* (1942) confessed that he didn't like to tell stories "unless there are a lot of kids around."

Underlying the art of stringing out the story in a yarn is often the purpose of stringing or taking in the listener. Even where the latter is not having his leg pulled, the favorite theme of anecdotes and yarns (in the universal and perennial folk tradition) is pranks and tricks, hoaxes and deceptions (also seen in animal tales of the trickster type). The "scrapes and 'scapes" of yarns satisfy the taste for marvels and adventures once supplied by fairy tales and tales of ghosts and witches. At the same time they provide an outlet for the "individual competitive aggressiveness" of American society.

In the latter connection one is frequently struck by the antisocial character of much American lore and many American heroes. Just as the myth of the individualism of the pioneer has been revised in the direction of cooperation, as evidenced by neighborhood undertakings like the log-rolling and the barn-raising, so the socially useful folk rituals of cooperative work and play are partly offset by the rough, tough, antisocial humor of the frontier. This ranges from sells, pranks, and practical jokes in the hazing tradition of breaking in the tenderfoot and the greenhorn (snipe hunts and badger fights, fool's errands, circular stories, mythical monsters) to the grim hoaxing and persecution of minorities (Indians, Negroes, Mexicans, and Chinese) by frontier bullies and rogues like Mike Fink and Roy Bean. To the horse sense and cracker-barrel wit of the shrewd Yankee and the suspicious squatter (as in *The Arkansas Traveler*), with its characteristic "reluctant" eloquence, were added the raucous horseplay and horse laughter of the backwoods, where "pretty cute little stunts" and fool doings became crazier as the country became wilder and where the traditional form of expression was reckless and bamboozling tall talk and sky-painting oratory, or making a noise in language. In this way the pioneer let off steam and "laughed it off" or made "terrible faces playfully" at the hazards and hardships of the frontier.

The same raw buffoonery and the same distrust and manhandling of the stranger and the outsider produces, in the direction of verbal rather than practical jokes, the lore of popular reproaches, taunts, and gibes, and local cracks and slams—facetious place names, uncomplimentary nicknames, satirical repartee, and bywords, ribbing anecdotes and jests about Boston, Brooklyn, Arkansas, Missouri, "dam Yankees," Southern pride, California and Florida climate, the "big country" of Texas. Whether based on literary or social stereotypes and myths or on historical traits and rivalries, such as existed in neighborhood feuds, county wars, sectional conflicts, feuds between cattlemen and sheepmen, the parochial, invidious lore of hoax and libel (the seamy side of local tradition and the provincial or neighborhood spirit) reflects the geography of culture, the ruthlessness of frontier and industrial society, and the intolerance of clannishness and chauvinism.

In the folklore of pride and prejudice brags and lies go hand in hand with cracks and slams, since the desire to see what one wants to see, believe what one wants to believe, and make others see and believe as one wants them to leads to extravagant as well as to insulting representations and distortion. Boosting and booming, or exaggerating the advantages of a place, accompany the American myth of a paradise on earth, the dream of a land flowing with milk and honey, the search for God's country. The fairyland of guide books and official puffs is full of the same wonders that one encounters in countless yarns and tall tales—of a climate so healthful that people rarely die, except from accident or old age; of soil so fertile that a man has to cut his way out of cucumber vines that spring up as he plants the seed; of corn that grows so fast that a man who ties his team to a corn stalk finds himself, team, and wagon pushed up into the air so that food has to be shot up to him to keep him from starving to death. On the adverse side, one hears complaints about a climate so dry that people sweat dust or so wet that the pores sprout watercress or a country so poor that it takes nine partridges to holler "Bob White" or that the dogs have to lean against the fence to bark.

The unnatural natural history of queer animal behavior, fearsome critters, and other freaks of nature is related partly to hoaxing and boasting and partly to superstitious awe and dread and the hallucinations inspired by the mysteries and terrors of the wilderness of sea and forest, mountains and deserts, and the violent extremes and contrasts of weather and climate. Here the anthropomorphism of shrewd, benevolent, or malevolent beasts is balanced by the theriomorphism and totemism of the half-horse, half-alligator and the ring-tailed roarer, of tall talk and strong language, with "many terms transferred from animals to men by the hunters of the West." In their brags and war cries, boasters like Davy Crockett refer to themselves as "an entire zoological institute," claiming various animal traits and features to prove their intestinal fortitude and savage destructiveness. In this rampant and raucous animalism is additional evidence of what Lucy Lockwood Hazard calls "the dwindling of the hero" from the godlike to the human and ultimately to the subhuman level under the picaresque, predatory influences of the frontier.

Real and mythical flora and fauna also enter into the symbolism of state flowers, seals, nicknames, emblems, flags, automobile license plates, and the totemism and fetishism of local legendry and mythology, politics, and business. "Look for a Thunderbird Tourist Service," writes Mary Austin of the "Land of Little Rain." "What more competent embodiment of the spirit of service, in a land where for ten thousand years it has been looked for from the corn rows, augury of a fruitful season, the dark-bodied, dun-feathered cloud of the summer rain, wing stretched from mountain to mountain, with arrows of the lightning in its claws." [10] Half-gargoyle, half-Phœnix, the legendary bird of Kansas, the Jayhawk, gives its name and likeness to things Kansan—the bird with the large yellow beak and bright yellow slippers that "flies backward and so doesn't care where he's going, 'but sure wants to know where he's been.' " [11] And in the old hall of the Massachusetts House of Representatives the sacred codfish commemorates the maritime and fishing preeminence of the Bay State.

The same mingling of the primitive and the practical characterizes American folklore as a whole. American popular and legendary heroes are divided between the prosaic, plebeian Yankee virtues of hard work, perseverance, common sense, thrift, faculty or "know-how," and handiness, and the primitive virtues of red-blooded courage, muscle, brawn, brute force, and animal cunning. Because the New England ethos bred strong characters and eccentrics rather than heroic types, the typical American hero is the Western hero—the picaresque type of footloose adventurer, product and symbol of a "society cut loose from its roots" and of a "time of migrations." In the thin and shifting line that separates law-enforcement from law-breaking on the frontier, hero-worship glorifies the good bad man and the bad good man along with the poor boy who makes good.

Yet throughout the galaxy of American heroes—tricksters, showmen, conquerors, saviors—the familiar lineaments of the whittling, tinkering, scheming, prying comic Yankee are seen. As a culture hero he culminates in the comic demigod of the Paul Bunyan type—the superman and the work giant in a world of gadgets, who has the whole country to tinker and whittle with.

The logging fraternity of the generous camp boss and his loyal crew grew out of the fluid, mobile social relations of the frontier, before the tightening of class lines and the sharpening of the struggle between worker and boss. In the same way cowboy songs reflect a society in which the "boss rode with the hands" and "every cowpuncher was a prospective cowman; all that was needed to start a herd was a stout rope and a running iron." [12]

Thus the frontier ideal of a free, resourceful, outdoor, migratory life, self-sufficient and individualistic, is perpetuated in American hero tales and songs, whose heroic age is the age of industrial pioneering and craftsmanship, before the days of mechanization and unionization of labor. The heroes are lusty, blustering strong men and champions, star performers, and master workmen, the "biggest, fastest, and bestest" men on the job. The ballads of the men who built America are the rousing, rhythmic, dramatic, humorous shanties, hollers, and gang work songs of the leader-and-chorus type—last encountered in the Negro prison camps of the South.

In the progression from the comic demigods and roughnecks of the Paul Bunyan-Davy Crockett-Mike Fink breed to the heroes of endurance and duty—Johnny Appleseed, John Henry, Casey Jones, and Joe Magarac—one notes a heightened sense of social responsibility and mission. A similar development of social consciousness results in the sharpened criticism and protest of campaign and revival songs, coal miners' songs of disasters and strikes, wobbly and union songs, and Negro spirituals and freedom songs.

As the folklore of a new, young, and big country, mirroring the rapid changes from rural and agricultural to urban and industrial society, American folklore is a mixture not only of the lore of peoples from all lands and all parts of the country, but of oral and written tradition, of the sophisticated and the primitive, the very new and the very old, the antisocial and the social. In such a country men become heroes within their own lifetime and living story-tellers may encompass within their memories the whole cycle of development of their community and region. And if the genius of this lore has been for realistic anecdote, extravagant yarn, and comic hero legend rather than for sacred hero tale, other worldly myth, and fairy tale, the reason is simple. Americans, like people the world over, sing, yarn, jest, brag, create heroes, and "whistle in the dark," not only about universal themes and motives and in age-old patterns, but also about the experiences that are closest to them and interest them most.

Notes:

1. Alexander Haggerty Krappe, " 'American' Folklore,' *Folk-Say, A Regional Miscellany* (Norman, Okla., 1930), pp. 291–297.
2. Constance McLaughlin Green, "The Value of Local History," *The Cultural Approach to History*, ed. for the Am. Hist. Assn. by Caroline F. Ware (New York, 1940), p. 278.

3. "The Folk in Literature: An Introduction to the New Regionalism," *Folk-Say, A Regional Miscellany* (Norman, Okla., 1929), p. 12.
4. *Folklore in America: Its Scope and Method* (Poughkeepsie, N. Y., 1931), p. 4.
5. "Memorandum for the Study of Acculturation," by Robert Redfield, Ralph Linton, and Melville J. Herskovits, *American Anthropologist*, N. S., vol. 38 (Jan.–March, 1936), no. 1, pp. 149–152.
6. "The Significance of Sections," *The New Republic* (Sept. 20, 1933), p. 149.
7. *Journal of American Folklore*, vol. I (April–June, 1888), no. 1, p. 3.
8. George Philip Krapp, *The English Language in America* (New York, 1925), vol. I, p. 188.
9. Robert L. Ramsay, Foreword to Frederic G. Cassidy's *The Place Names of Dane County, Wisconsin*, Publication of the American Dialect Society, Number 7 (April, 1947), p. 5.
10. *The Land of Journey's Ending* (New York and London, 1924), pp. 443–444.
11. John Gunther, *Inside U. S. A.* (New York and London, 1947), p. 262.
12. Margaret Larkin, *Singing Cowboy* (New York, 1931), p. xi. B. A. BOTKIN

American Folklore Society The American Folklore Society was organized at Cambridge, Massachusetts on January 4, 1888. Its founders were the most important folklore scholars in America: Alcée Fortier, the first president, W. W. Newell, permanent secretary and editor, Franz Boas, F. J. Child, George A. Dorsey, J. Walter Fewkes, Alice Fletcher, Joseph Fortier, Daniel Brinton, T. F. Crane. The list of presidents of the society reads like a head roll of the important folklorists of America: Alcée Fortier 1888, 1894; Francis James Child 1889; Daniel G. Brinton 1890; Otis T. Mason 1891; Frederick Ward Putnam 1892; Horatio Hale 1893; Washington Matthews 1895; John G. Burke 1896; Stewart Culin 1897; Henry Wood 1898; Charles L. Edwards 1899; Franz Boas 1900, 1932, 1935; Frank Russell 1901; George A. Dorsey 1902; Livingston Farrand 1903; George Lyman Kittredge 1904; Alice C. Fletcher 1905; Alfred L. Kroeber 1906; Roland B. Dixon 1907–08; John R. Swanton 1909; H. M. Belden 1910–11; John A. Lomax 1912–13; Pliny Earle Goddard 1914–15; Robert H. Lowie 1916–17; C. Marius Barbeau 1918; Elsie Clews Parsons 1919–20; Frank G. Speck 1921–22; Aurelio M. Espinosa 1923–24; Louise Pound 1925–26; Alfred M. Tozzer 1927–29; Edward Sapir 1930–31; M. W. Beckwith 1933–34; Archer Taylor 1936–37; Stith Thompson 1938–39; I. A. Hallowell 1940–41; H. W. Thompson 1942; G. A. Reichard 1943–44; B. A. Botkin 1944–45; M. J. Herskovits 1945–46; J. M. Carrière 1946–47; E. W. Voegelin 1948–49; Thelma James, 1949–50.

The original proposal in which the object of the Society is stated is as follows: "It is proposed to form a society for the study of Folk-Lore, of which the principal object shall be to establish a Journal, of a scientific character, designed:—

(1) For the collection of the fast-vanishing remains of Folk-Lore in America, namely:
   (a) Relics of Old English Folk-Lore (ballads, tales, superstitions, dialect, etc.).
   (b) Lore of Negroes in the Southern States of the Union.

   (c) Lore of the Indian Tribes of North America (myths, tales, etc.).
   (d) Lore of French Canada, Mexico, etc.
(2) For the study of the general subject, and publication of the results of special studies in this department."

This proposal and the practices that grew out of it mark a major development in the study of folklore. Up to this time folklore as generally studied in Europe had consisted largely in investigation of the *relics* of culture: popular antiquities, and popular literature. The founders of the American Folklore Society, probably because they were in the New World, enlarged the study of folklore to include all categories of culture, not simply literary, and to include in addition the study of "living" folklore as found especially among the American Indians. The American Folklore Society from the beginning inspired the collection and investigation of Negro folklore: literature, music, songs, superstitions, and beliefs. With the American Anthropological Association it also pioneered studies in Indian folklore, considering it most promising, for here "the investigator has to deal with whole nations and as a result the harvest does not consist of scattered gleanings."

From the time of its origin, the American Folklore Society recognized that its function could not be insular, that only by a study of folklore in general could the folklore of any one people be understood and so from the beginning the papers in the Journal were open to general studies of folklore and to studies of the folklore of peoples everywhere in the world. As the Society has developed it has constantly broadened its functions until today a more accurate name would be the American Society of Folklore.

The first number of the Journal appeared in April, 1888, under the editorship of W. W. Newell. Its contents are representative of the publication through the years. T. F. Crane wrote of the diffusion of popular tales, William Newell on voodoo worship and child sacrifice in Haiti, H. Carrington Bolton on counting-out games of children, D. G. Brinton on Lenape conversations; W. M. Beauchamp published a collection of Onondaga tales; Franz Boas presented a detailed study of the songs and dances of the Kwakiutl.

The Journal is now (1971) in its 84th volume. These 84 volumes contain many very important collections and studies from the pens of the major folklorists of America. There exist, for example, in the Journal more than a hundred articles on the ballad in America—a body of material that constitutes a large appendix to the great Child collection. It is unfortunate that no adequate index of the contents of the Journal exists.

In 1906 the Society was incorporated in Massachusetts and a constitution embodying the original proposals was adopted. The Society operated under this constitution until 1946 when the present constitution was adopted.

Early in the history of the Society the Editor and Officers felt the need of a monograph series in addition to the Journal to contain book-length specialized studies in folklore. Accordingly, in 1894 the Memoir Series was inaugurated with the publication of Heli Chatelain's *Folk-Tales of Angola* as volume 1. Now (1971) the Memoir Series is in its 59th volume. These studies are highly diversified, concerning themselves with Japanese peasant songs, fiddle and fife tunes of Pennsylvania, myths and tales of the Gran Chaco of Argentina, Spanish songs and tales, French folklore, studies in Negro and Indian folklore, collections of folklore from specific regions of America, such as Maryland, Iowa, Nova Scotia, plant and animal lore, Filipino folktales. For many years members paid additional dues to secure the Memoirs, but for a while after 1943 the Society followed the policy of giving both the Journal and the Memoirs to all regular dues-paying members.

Every year the Society holds a two- or three-day meeting for transaction of business and the reading and discussion of papers. These meetings are usually arranged to coincide alternately with those of the Modern Language Association and those of the American Anthropological Society.

Throughout its history the American Folklore Society has fostered the establishment of local folklore societies. Some fifty such societies over the United States and Canada have at one time or another been affiliated with the mother society. At the present time ten such societies are closely affiliated with the American Folklore Society through joint membership arrangements. The American Folklore Society is a constituent of the American Council of Learned Societies, and of the International Commission on Folk Arts and Folklore.

At present the Society has a membership of over 2,000, the largest in its history. Dues are $10 a year for individuals, $12 for institutions. All members may buy the *Memoirs* and the *Bibliographical Series* at 30% discount. The 1970–71 officers are: Daniel G. Cowley, President; Don Yoder and Edward D. Ives, Vice Presidents; Kenneth L. Goldstein (Box 13, Logan Hall, University of Pennsylvania, Philadelphia, Pennsylvania), Secretary-Treasurer; Américo Paredes, Editor.

Amesha Spentas (Persian *Amshaspands*) In Zoroastrianism, the attendant ministers of Ahura Mazda; archangels: literally, Immortal Holy Ones. The function of the Amesha Spentas is to aid Ahura Mazda who prefers to act through their ministering hands. They are invisible, immortal, and dwell in Paradise, sitting, according to the *Bundahishn*, before Ahura Mazda (Ormazd) on golden thrones. The guardianship of an element of the universe is assigned to each. Vohu Manah is responsible for the care of useful animals, Asha Vahishta for fire, Khshathra Vairya for metals, Spentā Armaiti for the earth, Haurvatāt for water, and Ameretāt for vegetation. These six are constantly opposed by the six archfiends, Aka Manah, Sauru, Indra, Nāoṅhaitya, Zairicha, and Taurvi, whom they will finally vanquish at the time of the resurrection.

Originally there were six Amesha Spentas in addition to their leader, Ahura Mazda, but some of the angels, among them Sraosha, Ātar, and Gošurvan, were admitted to the group so that the number varied.

The Amesha Spentas receive special worship and are said to descend upon paths of light to the oblation. A special month and day are assigned to each in the pontifical calendar. According to the *Dīnkart* they appeared before King Vīshtāspa and helped Zoroaster convert him. Compare ADITYA; ARCHANGEL.

amethyst A purple or violet gem of the quartz family, known since early times: birthstone of February or Pisces. Its name derives from the Greek word *amethystos,* meaning non-intoxicating, and its principal attribute throughout the ages has been to enable its wearer to drink his fill without becoming intoxicated. Wine drunk from an amethyst cup will not intoxicate. It is supposed to put a sobering check on the passions, control evil thoughts, quicken the intellect, and make a man shrewd in business matters. It protects soldiers, aids hunters, and is extensively worn by sailors, businessmen, lawyers, bishops, and medical men, especially on the third finger of the left hand. Curative powers are ascribed to it both when worn and when taken internally. It is especially effective against headache, toothache, and the gout, and protects its wearer from poison and the plague.

An 18th century French poem tells how Bacchus, angry at neglect, vowed the next mortal he met should be devoured by his lions. This was a maiden on her way to worship at the shrine of Diana who, hearing the maiden's cries, turned her into a beautiful transparent stone. Bacchus, in remorse, poured wine over the stone which accounts for its beautiful color. The Romans valued it as a preventive of intoxication, as a means for access to kings, and as a talisman against spells, hail, and locusts. Among the tribes of the Upper Nile, the rain-makers use the amethyst as a rain stone, plunging one into water and motioning with a cane when rain is desired. In ancient Egypt it was used in amulets and as a gemstone.

The amethyst is mentioned in *Exodus* as one of the stones in the High Priest's breastplate, and in *Revelation* as one of the foundations of the New Jerusalem. St. Valentine is said to have worn an amethyst ring engraved with a Cupid.

Amis and Amiloun A Middle English romance, French in origin, of two perfect friends. Amiloun fights instead of Amis at a combat trial; as punishment, he becomes a leper. Amis kills his two children after dreaming that their blood will cure Amiloun. The leprosy disappears and the children awake as from sleep.

Amitābha, Amita, or **Amida** In Mahāyāna Buddhism, one of the five Buddhas of Contemplation: Infinite Light. Amitābha has practically replaced Śākyamuni, the historical Buddha; he is the embodiment of every divine grace; he is all-wise and all-powerful with the attributes of grace, mercy, and beneficence. The worship of Amitābha emphasizes devotion rather than emulation. As O-mi-to-fo he was the most reverenced and popular of the celestial Buddhas in China. The Jodo sect introduced the doctrine of Sukhāvatī, the Western Paradise of Amitābha, into Japanese Buddhism, where its patron was called Amida. In Sukhāvatī there is neither mental nor bodily pain but only perpetual bliss. With the aid of the Bodhisattvas Avalokita (Kuan-yin) and Mahāsthama (Ta-shih-chih) all who invoke Amitābha's name are brought to salvation. In legend, Amitābha was born spontaneously from a lotus.

Amleth or **Hamlet** In early Danish legend, the son of Horvendil, king of Jutland, and Gerutha. As Saxo Grammaticus tells the story, Horvendil was killed by his brother Feng (or Fengi) who took the throne and married Gerutha. Amleth (which means mad) escaped death at the hands of his uncle by feigning madness. He rode his horse facing the tail, called sand the meal of storms, etc. The young girl sent to test his sanity proved to be a friend and would not betray him. Feng's old counselor then suggested that Amleth be left alone with his mother, while he would hide in the room and witness his conversation and his actions. But Amleth was not deceived; still playing mad he ran his sword through a pile of straw in the room and killed the old man hiding in it.

Feng's next move was to send Amleth to Britain with a letter to Britain's king, directing him to put the bearer to death. The wary Amleth, however, changed the message to read that the king give his daughter in marriage to the "wise youth" who brought this letter, and that the two courtiers with him be put to death. At the feast that night Amleth would not eat. When questioned he replied that the bread was bloody, the water tasted of iron, the meat smelled of human dead, and three times the queen had behaved like a bondwoman. These insults were reported to the king, who instead of being angry, investigated the source of the food. He discovered that the corn for the bread was grown on an old battlefield, that a rusty sword lay in the bottom of the well, that the pigs had broken loose and eaten the unburied corpse of a robber, and it was true that the queen had picked her teeth at table, lifted her skirts when she walked, etc. The king was impressed with the wisdom of this "wise youth," and carried out in full the details of the altered letter.

Amleth then returned to Denmark, killed Feng with Feng's own sword, and was received joyfully as king by his own people. Here is shown the ancient Teutonic (especially Danish) belief, the deep-rooted and almost religious conviction, that all perjurers and traitors must, and inevitably do, die by their own swords.

Later Amleth returned to Britain, where his father-in-law, the king, sworn to avenge the death of his friend Feng, sent Amleth on an errand to Hermutrude, queen of Scotland, again bearing a sealed message instructing his death. But after once seeing Amleth and learning his story, the lady herself altered the letter to read that she must marry the bearer. Amleth was easily convinced that he should take a second wife, and did so. He defeated the king of Britain in battle by the stratagem of placing dead men in upright positions to simulate a huge army. His first wife remained loyal to him, so Amleth, with two wives, returned to Denmark. Later he was killed fighting against Wiglek of Denmark. Hermutrude had vowed she would die with him, but comforted herself by marrying Wiglek.

There is a very old Norse version of this story in which two sons of the murdered king feign madness and avenge their father by setting fire to the hall. Through Saxo Grammaticus the Danish legend became widely known among Germanic peoples. It is, of course, the source of Shakespeare's *Hamlet*. [MEL]

Ammit or **Ammut** In Egyptian mythology, an underworld monster, compounded of the hippopotamus and lion and having a crocodile's jaws. Ammit was stationed at the scales of judgment in the hall of Osiris; those souls whose hearts were found heavy with sins were eaten by her. Compare CERBERUS.

Ammon or **Amon** The Greek and Roman name for the Egyptian god Amen, appearing as Zeus-Ammon and Jupiter-Ammon: when associated with Ra, **Ammon-Ra**, **Ammon Re**, **Amon-Ra**, or **Amon Re**.

amniomancy Divination from the caul occasionally found enveloping the head of a new-born child: gener-

ally European and believed to be originally from the East. The condition of the caul, lax, dry, etc., indicated the future general state of health of the owner.

amorous bite A folktale motif (T467) commonly found in the various poison damsel stories, in which the poison damsel bites her lover on the lip, thus causing her own poisonous saliva to enter his bloodstream, so that he dies. This seems to be associated with the very ancient (Babylonian) and very widespread belief that the spittle of witches is poisonous. See POISON DAMSEL.

amphidromia The festival, held on the fifth day after the birth of a child in Attica, Greece, during which the baby was carried at a running pace around the family hearth. During this celebration friends and relatives brought presents and the women who had assisted at the birth cleansed their hands. This custom has been variously explained as a purification rite, as an initiation rite, or as a rite to ensure fleet-footedness for the child.

amṛita, **amṛta**, or **amṛit** In Hindu mythology, the drink of immortality; the lost water of life produced at the Churning of the Ocean. The name is applied in the Vedas to various things sacrificed, but especially to the soma juice.

Rāhu, an asura, disguised himself as a god and obtained possession of some of the amrita which he drank in order to make himself immortal. Nārāyana (Vishnu) caught him and cut off his head. Rāhu's body became the progenitor of the comets and meteors; his head, immortal because of the amrita he had been able to gulp, chases the sun and moon which betrayed him to Vishṇu, and sometimes swallows them (eclipse). Compare AMBROSIA; MEAD; SOMA.

Amsterdam The oldest of the capstan chanteys, mentioned, though not specifically as a sea song, in *The Rape of Lucrece*, by Thomas Heywood, which was seen in London early in the 17th century. The chantey celebrates the charms of a maid of Amsterdam who was "mistress of her trade," and has become popular as a glee-club song. It is also called *A-Rovin'*, from the words of its refrain.

amulet A material object, usually portable and durable, worn or carried on the person, placed in a house, or on or among one's possessions, to protect the owner from dangers such as death, shipwreck, lightning, attacks by thieves or animals, evil spirits, witchcraft, or the evil eye; to aid him in acquiring luck, wealth, physical strength, magical powers; and to bring success in hunting, trading, battle, or love. The use of amulets is world-wide among almost all peoples, and is familiar to almost all Americans in the form of horseshoes, lucky coins, watch-chain charms, and the rabbit's foot. Amulets are not only worn by men, women, and children, carried in bags or pockets or sewn to clothing, but they are attached to domestic animals, buildings, tools, weapons, placed in fields near growing crops, in storehouses, barns, henneries, and tied to dangerous rocks, bridges, or at the top of passes. They are sometimes used as containers for the soul. Eskimo medicine men, for instance, conjure the soul of a sick child into an amulet to keep it out of harm during the illness.

Amulets are primarily preventive and are to be distinguished from talismans which transmit qualities, from charms which are magic formulas to be sung or recited (also loosely applied to amulets over which charms have been said).

Amulets of common stone chosen either for shape, color, or the importance of the place where found, are worn by the Mongols as a protection against thunder and lightning, by the Jews to prevent miscarriage, in Italy as a protection against witches (madreporite) and for the prevention and cure of snake-bite (serpentine). In the Torres Straits water-worn pebbles are regarded as love charms. In Ireland perforated stones of any kind are hung on cattle byres to prevent malicious fairies from stealing the milk. Stones are worn by the Blackfoot Indians as hunting charms. The Aymara use bezoar stones removed from the stomachs of llamas or vicuñas as amulets. Fragments of stone are carried by childless Japanese.

Amulets of animal parts or substances depend frequently for their efficacy on the sympathetic transference of the characteristics or qualities of the animal from which they are acquired. Greenland Eskimos sew a hawk's head or feet into a boy's clothing to make him a great hunter, the skin from the roof of a bear's mouth to give him strength, and a piece of a fox's head or dried fox dung to give him cunning. The Chickasaw Indians put the foot of a guinea deer into hunting pouches to make themselves successful hunters. Hidatsa girls wear beavers' teeth to make them industrious. The Dogribs carry antler points for success in luring deer or moose within rifle range. The Bororo wear breast ornaments of jaguar and monkey teeth to give them strength and skill.

Plants or parts of plants such as seeds, berries, pieces of wood, and leaves, are world-wide in amuletic use. Vegetable amulets far outnumber all other types in India, where one of the most potent is made of chips from ten different kinds of holy trees glued together and wrapped with gold wire. In Europe peas are thrown into the lap of a bride. Eating the fruit of a tree bearing for the first time, possessing mandrakes, or drinking birch-sap are all supposed to produce fertility. The Greeks used snapdragons and peony tea against sorcery and an olive leaf bearing the name of Athena or an herb grown on the head of a statue tied around the head to cure headache. The Romans used garlic to keep off witches and touched the doorway with a sprig of strawberry plant for the same purpose. The Japanese use fruits, flowers, and vegetables amuletically in their homes and hang garlic at the doors to keep out infectious diseases. Double walnuts and almonds are worn as amulets against the evil eye, witches, headache, and for good luck in Italy. A powerful Chinese amulet to ward off evil spirits is made of peach wood or peach stones; padlocks made from peach kernels are believed to bind children to life when attached to their feet. Many peoples believe that a potato carried in the pocket keeps off harm and cures diseases. The Shoshone Indians use powdered spruce needles to prevent illness. The Apache and Navaho filled and wore buckskin bags with pollen from the cat-tail and other plants to secure peace, prosperity, and happiness. Petrified wood is used in Hopi amulets.

Manufactured amulets are as widespread in use and almost as old as are natural objects. Figurines of gods were buried under the thresholds of Assyrian palaces. Egyptian uzas or sacred eyes made of lapis-lazuli, gold, pottery, or wood, and the uaz or green column usually made of feldspar, as well as the dad and buckle were placed in tombs for amuletic reasons. The Greeks used images of gods and geometric figures as amulets. The Romans attached small metal rattles and bullæ to their children's clothing. In Vedic India rings were used as amulets. The Celts had figures of the horse, bull, and models of a wild boar's tooth; the Mayas used golden frogs arranged singly or in groups, images of lizards, crocodiles, crabs, eagles, gulls, parrots, or monkeys, each provided with a ring for suspension on a cord or chain. Certain Eskimos sometimes wear an image of the object for which they are named. The Lengua use wax images for good luck in hunting. The Iroquois carry miniature canoes to keep from drowning. The Hindus wear lockets containing the image of a god or goddess. And the Japanese use bells and images of deities in addition to the more common written amulets.

Whether or not all ornamental jewelry was originally amuletic is open to question, but jewelry is worn for amuletic purposes in many parts of the world. In India, rings of copper, silver, gold, or iron are worn to repel sorcery. In the Punjab copper rings or earrings are worn to frighten away the sciatica spirit. In southern India an important part of the marriage rite is the tying-on of the lucky thread which is a saffron-colored cord attached to a small pendantlike gold ornament. This is worn around the neck for the same reason the wedding ring is worn in Europe, and because it is believed to bring good luck. The Lapps attach a brass ring to the right arm while transferring a corpse to a coffin and then to the grave to prevent the ghost of the deceased from doing any harm. American Negroes believe a silver ring, a ring inscribed with Chinese characters, or a ring made from a horse-shoe nail to be good luck. Chinese children are protected from harm by jade bracelets or anklets, and Tibetan women wear chatelaines depending from a small silver casket which usually contains an amulet or charm.

The elements included in Jewish written amulets were the names of God and angels, Biblical expressions or phrases, a list of the functions of the amulet, and the name of the person for whom the amulet was designed and that of his mother. Another type of written amulet consisted of a series of figures made of curved and straight lines tipped with circles, interspersed with geometric forms. The Zahlenquadrat or magic square, formed by a series of numbers arranged so that the sum of the numbers in each row, whether added vertically, diagonally, or horizontally, would be the same, was popular among Christian cabalists and adapted by medieval Jews. The mezuzah, originally anti-demonic in character, was given a religious significance by the rabbis who had Bible verses (*Deut.* vi, 4–9; xi, 13–21) inscribed on it as a reminder of the principle of monotheism, but its amuletic properties have always outweighed its religious significance. The Chinese and Moslems use similar strips of paper. The former hang them over doors, on bed curtains, and even wear them in the hair.

Tibetan amulets are frequently pieces of paper inscribed with sentences to Buddha, while those of Ethiopia (which measure from 50 centimeters to two meters in length) contain legends, spells, secret signs, words of power, spells, and legends explaining how they originated. These scrolls are rolled and bound with cord, sewed in a leather case or inserted in a telescoping capsule. Japanese amulets against lightning, dangers while traveling, sickness, burns, and to better one's fortune, are usually roughly printed sacred texts or rude wood-cuts of the divinity appealed to, printed with words explaining the purpose of the amulet, folded, and enclosed in an envelope. These are sold at temples, are not taken out and read, but are renewed annually. Compare FETISH; GBO; GRIGRI; MAGIC OBJECT; TALISMAN. [SPH]

An or **Ana** The Sumerian god of the sky, to whom Nammu, the sea, gave birth. By Ki, the female earth-goddess, An was father of Enlil, god of the air. When earth and sky were separated, An carried off the heavens, Enlil the earth. Enlil superseded An as chief god of the Sumerian pantheon by the 3rd millennium B.C., though An nominally remained chief. The word *an* is ideographically represented by an eight-pointed star which is prefixed to the names of gods; it signifies high or heaven, and may also signify, as here, "god," dingir. Compare ANU; ANUNNAKI.

Anāhita The ancient Iranian Great Mother; the goddess of fertility, especially of fertilizing waters, and specifically of the spring among the stars from which flowed all the rivers of the earth: worshipped from Iran westward to the Ægean and identified with other Great Mothers of the region like Nina, Ishtar, Semiramis, Cybele, Aphrodite. She appears in the pantheon of Mazdaism after Zoroaster and is closely associated with Mithra or Mazda as one of the chief deities of the religion. An entire Yašt or hymn of praise, is given to her in the *Avesta*. She is called there Ardvī Surā Anāhita, the high, powerful, undefiled one. Anāhita was the goddess of reproduction and of the maintenance of good things; she "purified the seed of the male and the womb and the milk of the female." She was called upon by marriageable girls and by women in childbirth; she aided in time of great illness. She is described in the *Avesta* as a beautiful maiden, tall and powerful, wrapped in a gold-embroidered cloak, wearing earrings, necklace, and crown of gold, and adorned with thirty otter skins. Anāhita was also the goddess of war and drove a chariot with four white horses (wind, rain, cloud, hail); she gave victory to a contender. Through the influence of Chaldean star-worship, she became identified with the planet Venus.

In Armenia, as Anāhit, she was the most popular of all the gods. Here she was identified with neither the planet nor the waters of fertility. She had several temples, particularly the great sanctuary at Akilisene, where members of both sexes of the nobility entered her service as slaves, and where the female slaves practiced sacred prostitution.

In Pontus and Cappadocia, and perhaps in Cilicia, she became identified with the goddess Ma. She was probably brought to Sardis in Lydia by Artaxerxes II, and there merged with Cybele. Her noisy and licentious rites occurred in Armenia about the 15th of September.

The Greeks, who also called her Anaitis, the Athena of Ilium, and the Persian Artemis, confounded her with Aphrodite as a fertility goddess, and with Athena as a war goddess. Since the bull was sacred to Anāhita, she became confused with the Greek Artemis Tauropolos in Lydia, Armenia, and Cappadocia. Generally she was known as the mistress of the beasts; sacred herds of white heifers were branded with her mark, a torch, and sacrificed to her along with green branches in Armenia. After the 1st century A.D., her worship as Magna Mater spread

through the Latin world along with that of Mithra.

Anāhita is probably of Semitic origin, perhaps identical with Anath. The temple prostitution practiced by her worshippers and her identification with Nina and Ishtar give support to the view. Herodotus says that the Persians learned from the Assyrians to worship the heavenly Aphrodite "whom they call Mithra," which latter may be a misreading of Anāhita. In inscriptions of the Achæmenian kings of Persia, Mithra and Anāhita are united.

Ananga The bodiless: an epithet of Kāma, Hindu god of love: so called because he was consumed by the fire of Śiva's eye when he interrupted Śiva's devotions with thoughts of Pārvatī.

Anansesem Literally, spider stories: generic title of a class of folktales told by the Akan-speaking peoples of the old Gold Coast, so called whether the spider takes part in the story or not. The Anansesem are told for group entertainment and are definitely distinguished from the myths. They are also known as Nyankonsem, or "words of the sky god."

Once upon a time Kwaku Ananse, the Spider, went to buy the sky god's stories. The price to be paid was very great. Nyame, the sky god, demanded in exchange that Kwaku Ananse bring him the python, the leopard, the fairy, and the hornets. Spider promised all these things and returned home. One by one he tricked the prizes into his possession, and then added his mother to the lot for good measure. The sky god was so amazed that Kwaku Ananse, the Spider, could bring in the price of the stories when very great kings and chiefs had often failed, that he called his chiefs and leaders in for consultation. The verdict was that beginning that day the sky god's stories should henceforth belong to Kwaku Ananse and be called Anansesem, Spider stories, forever. The Paramaribo Negroes of Surinam, South America, give the generic title of Anansi-tori to all their folktales. In Curaçao they are called *cuenta di nansi*.

Anansi The Spider: hero and trickster of an enormous body of West African folktales. Under various names he plays the same outrageous, cunning, and wily role in the folklore of the Gold Coast, the Ivory Coast, Sierra Leone, Liberian, Togo, Dahomean, Hausa, Yoruban, Warri, Fjort, Cameroons, Congo, and Angolan peoples. He is known everywhere in the West Indies and other parts of the New World, and has become almost as familiar to white children through their countless Mammies and Uncle Remuses, as to Negro children.

Among the Hausas the Spider is named Gizõ; the Akan-speaking peoples call him Kwaku Ananse. In Curaçao Anansi has become Nansi. He turns up as Miss Nancy in South Carolina Sea Island folktales, and in Gullah, specifically, as Aunt Nancy. 'Ti Malice is his name in Haiti. He survives as Anansi, however, among the Surinam Negroes, both Paramaribo and Bush, and in Jamaica. In Jamaica the Anansi stories are now told chiefly at wakes and other gatherings for the dead. The Negroes of Trinidad are said to have lost interest in them; but here too they are still told at wakes. The real Anansi perpetuators in Trinidad, however, are the children, who not only know the stories, but know them well, and tell and retell them to each other.

Anansi was originally a creator of the world in Gold Coast mythology, and still plays the role of culture hero in such tales as those in which he steals the sun. In Bantu folklore Spider is definitely associated with the sun. His dominant role, however, throughout Negro folktale everywhere is that of the crafty and cunning trickster who prospers by his wits. He is always duping other animals, to his own profit, and sometimes man, in some modern versions sometimes missionaries. Tiger is frequently the butt of his jokes; but occasionally Anansi falls into his own pit or fails to outwit one or another of his intended victims. He is also somewhat of a magician, being able to appear sometimes as man, sometimes as spider. There are a number of stories in which Anansi turns into a spider at the moment of greatest danger, thus saving himself from some awful retribution, and thus sometimes explaining the origin of spiders. He figures in numerous versions of the tar-baby story, of which several variants account for his flattened body.

The character of the Spider of West African folktale is paralleled by that of Hare and Tortoise in the story cycles of certain Bantu tribes, and by Brer Rabbit in the southern United States. B'Rabby in the Bahamas is the same folktale trickster hero. His name is a byword in West African proverb: "Woe to him who would put his trust in Anansi—a sly, selfish, and greedy fellow" and "The wisdom of the spider is greater than that of all the world put together." One of the most famous of the Anansi stories (Ashanti and Yoruba) is the one about the pot always full of food, found and broken by Anansi's children, and the whip which he got to punish them, which would not stop beating them when they investigated it as they had the pot. See ANANSESEM.

Anansi and the Gum Doll Anansi kept stealing the food out of a man's (or the king's, or another animal's) big field. But the man did not know who it was. So he put a big gum doll out there. When Anansi saw the gum doll he thought it was a real person. "Hello, there," he called out. But the gum doll made no answer. "Answer me or I'll kick you," cried Anansi. The gum doll did not answer. Then Anansi kicked him and his foot stuck. "Let loose or I'll hit you," he cried. The gum doll did not let loose. Then Anansi hit him and his hand stuck. He kicked with the other foot and that stuck; he hit with the other hand and that stuck. Then the man came out to find the thief. And the man beat Anansi until his body was flat as flat (until he got eight legs; until he had the mark of a cross on his back).

This story is especially interesting as being the bare bones of the Anansi-tar-baby combination as told in Africa, with a few of the Surinam variants indicated. The same story is told of Hare in Angola, of Jackal among the Hottentots. For the whole gamut of Anansi-Hare-Rabbit-Tortoise-Jackal substitutions and tar-baby variants, see each of these and also BRER RABBIT; STICK-FAST; TAR BABY.

Anansi Rides Tiger Anansi remarked to the king that he rode Tiger. The king doubted it, so he asked Tiger. Tiger said "No" and went to fetch Anansi to make him take back the words. But Anansi said he could not go now; he was too ill; he could not walk; he could not stand up. But Tiger would not wait; Anansi must come to the king at once and take back that lie—even if Tiger had to carry him there himself! So Anansi consented—just to prove to Tiger that he never said any such thing

in the first place. But Anansi needed a saddle, just to brace his feet, he was so weak, lest he fall off. Tiger was in a hurry; he consented with impatience. Then Anansi needed a bridle, just to hold on to!—and a whip, just to swish the flies away! Tiger did not care, as long as Anansi would come to the king right away and take back the lie. So they arrived at the king's house: Tiger galloping, Anansi in the saddle, plying the whip, pulling on the bridle, and crying to the king to come look—Anansi rides Tiger!

This is the story as told by the Surinam Negroes, both urban and bush. They have another version which ends with the spider living in the king's house forever, as reward for bringing him such a fine horse. In the parallel Sierra Leone story Turtle rides Leopard. Br'er Rabbit rides Br'er Fox or Br'er Wolf in southern U. S. Negro versions.

Anansi-tori The Anansi stories: generic term among the Surinam Negroes for the great body of spider stories transplanted from West Africa. They vary very little in urban and bush versions. These are the same spider trickster folktales known to the Ashanti as Anansesem, and include also the same story of how they came to be so called.

The Paramaribo Negroes include the Anansi-tori as an important feature of their rites for the dead, especially on the eighth night after a death, when the evening begins with hymns and riddling and the stories last till dawn. They are never, never told in the daytime by anyone, lest the dead come and listen and their proximity cause the death of the narrator or his parents. The Saramacca Bush-Negroes tell these stories to the dead during the seven days a body lies in the village death house awaiting burial. Owing to the importance attached to them as entertainment for the dead, the term has become extended to include also the dances for the ancestors and the songs sung during these rites.

Ananta In Hindu mythology, an epithet meaning the infinite, applied to the serpent Śesha and sometimes to Hindu deities, especially to Vishṇu.

Anapel Literally, in the Koryak language, Little Grandmother: the name for the divining stone whereby the Koryak father discovers the name of the dead relative whose soul has just been reborn in his newborn child, and whose name that child must bear. The divining stone is hung on a stick and allowed to swing to and fro of itself while the stick is suspended. The father calls the roll of all dead relations on both sides of the family. When Anapel quickens in her swinging, it is a sign that at that moment has just been mentioned the name of the dead relative whose soul has come to live in the newborn child. Thus the child is named, and the father carries it through the village announcing, "A relative has come," or to this one and that one, "Your father has come" or "Your uncle has come."

Anath or **'Anat** A primitive Semitic (Canaanite) war goddess, the "queen of heaven, mistress of the gods," worshipped widely in the Semitic world, whose cult was in Egypt by the reign of Thothmes III (15th century B.C.) where she became daughter of Rā. She is represented with helmet, shield and spear in right hand, battle-ax or club in left; a late picture shows her seated on a lion. No connection of Anath with the Babylonian Antu has been proved; she may be identical with the

Syro-Phœnician Anhyt and the later Antæus, both Phœnician war goddesses. She was identified in the Hellenistic period with Athena. See SEMITIC MYTHOLOGY.

ancestor worship Veneration (only occasionally actual worship in the religious sense) of ancestral spirits: perhaps the most widespread of all religious forms, always implying animistic belief, and sometimes linked with totemism. The cult of the dead, those observances meant to dispose of the body and attend to the comfort of the spirit of the dead, is based in the belief in souls; ancestor worship considers the effect these not-quite-departed spirits may have on the world of the living and varies its cult observances accordingly. The dead may be malevolent or benevolent, feared or admired, given bribes to keep them from working mischief or gifts to make them happy. The tremendous mass of evidence of ancestor worship indicates that belief in the unfriendly dead is more prevalent than belief in well-wishing spirits, but no conclusion drawn from this, no generalization about the ways of the mind of primitive man, is completely valid. That ancient Greek and other religions seem based in propitiation of the ever-present evil spirits of the dead is balanced by an equally widely distributed belief that the spirits of dead parents and dead chiefs guard those who remain alive. The dead father or chief continues to guide his family or tribe; the stranger or the enemy, or the victim of an accident snatched from life suddenly, still may cause trouble through evilness or envy. Offerings are made, occasionally or at stated intervals, in either case: the evil spirit must be made to feel that he has something to gain by not molesting the people; the good spirit is deserving of the care a grateful people can give him.

Possession by an ancestral spirit may be oracular, or it may be through metempsychosis (or reincarnation). The newly born child may have the spirit of a departed ancestor, thus the naming of children for the revered dead. Thus also the feeling that a family has a larger bond, beyond its immediate descent, in the duty it owes to the dead. In a wider application, the clan, claiming descent from a common ancestor, may heroize or deify the ancestor; and if the clan or tribal myth is such, the ancestor may be the totem animal. There is no way of knowing into what form or shape the ancestral spirit will reappear on earth; it may be in a stone, a mountain, a scorpion, a cat, or any person whatever. See MANISM.

☞ In ancient China, ancestor worship was a well-developed cult in the Chou Dynasty, c. 1000 B.C. In modern China it has religious and civic aspects. Religious: The male head of the family or clan must make periodic sacrifices of ceremonies and food before the tablets and graves of his ancestors, though the more recently dead receive the greater homage. The two souls, the superior soul in heaven and the inferior soul informing the body, are thus nourished until disintegration occurs. If the souls of the ancestors are not sufficiently nourished they become ghosts and create mischief. Civic: The doctrine that proper respect must be paid ancestors, living or dead, was part of the Confucian attempt to restore seemliness in a decadent culture. Parents' natural desire that they be taken care of after death and tales of the wickedness of hungry ghosts are two facets of an attitude which has had such wide social acceptance that it is much more than a doctrine or creed. [RDJ]

ancestral tablets In Chinese and Japanese ancestor worship, wooden tablets inscribed with the names and birth and death dates of the deceased, kept in the ancestral hall of a clan or in a household shrine, to which offerings and prayers are made, and used when sacrifices are to be made at the shrine rather than at the tomb itself: probably derived from the burial of the deceased within the home plot. The tablets are believed to be occupied by the spirits of the deceased when the offerings are made, but after the offerings are completed the spirits depart. The Chinese tablets, traditionally originating during the Chou dynasty (1122–255 B.C.) but finding their source much earlier, are interlocking and fit into a wooden base. The last two characters of the inscription mean "spirit throne," and the very last is left uncompleted until a ceremonial "canonization," when a priest adds the finishing touches to the letter. The tablets are carried in the funeral procession and are kept, following the mourning period, in the ancestral shrine. Among the poorer classes, who cannot afford ancestral halls, the tablets are usually kept in the left rear corner of the living room in the household shrine, being placed there with invocation of Tso Sha Shen Chun, the God of Spirit-Tablet-to-Ancestors. Offerings are made before the tablets in certain days, such as the anniversary of death, and the Ch'ing Ming Festival, some three months after the winter solstice.

In Japanese Buddhism, the *ihai* is a rectangular tablet, rounded at the top and inscribed with name and dates. Offerings are made to it, especially at the Bon festival, when spirits are thought to come into the world. Similar tablets are found in parts of New Guinea. [RDJ]

Anchanchu A terrible demon in the folklore of the modern Aymara Indians. He deceives the unwary with his smiles and friendship and then afflicts them with deadly diseases. He also sucks the blood of his victims during their sleep. The Aymaras believe that his presence is accompanied by whirlwinds, and they avoid rivers and isolated places where he is supposed to reside. [AM]

anchunga Tapirape Indian (central Brazil) term for two kinds of spirits: true spirits (i.e. the disembodied souls of human beings), and malevolent demons. Tapirape shamans often see the true spirits in dreams. A famous shaman and culture hero of Tapirape legend, named Ware, destroyed all the evil anchunga in the south. He set fire to their hair, which was so long that it dragged on the ground behind them. The anchunga to the north, however, are still active.

Ancient Spider The creator of Nauru Island (Micronesian) mythology. See AREOP-ENAP.

Andersen, Hans Christian (1805–1875) Danish poet and story writer, second perhaps only to the Grimms in world-wide reputation as a teller of fairy tales. He was born in southern Denmark, the son of a shoemaker who died in 1816, leaving the boy more or less to his own devices in spending his time. He quit school and, becoming interested in the theater, built his own toy theater, dressed his own puppets, and read every play he could lay his hands on. In 1819, convinced that he had a good voice, he went to Copenhagen and haunted theatrical managers unsuccessfully, getting a reputation for being slightly crazy, and starving slowly. However, some friends he had made, notably Jonas Collin, director of the Royal Theater saw to it that the king, Frederick VI, had the youth sent to grammar school, where he remained until 1827. In 1829 his first success, a satirical fantasy, *A Journey on Foot from Holman's Canal to the East Point of Amager,* was published. After some indifferent pieces, in 1835 *The Improvisor* became a great success, and Andersen an established author. In the same year he published the first of his *Fairy Tales (Eventyr),* and until 1872 they continued to appear, slowly gaining for their author a world-wide fame. He continued writing novels, plays, miscellanies, travel books, as well. In 1872 he injured himself severely, falling out of bed, and died three years later without ever having fully recovered from the effects of the fall. Among Andersen's best known fairy tales, somewhat literary and often tragic and moralizing renderings of well-known types and motifs in the folktale, are: The Ugly Duckling, The Tinder Box, The Red Shoes, The Snow Queen, Big Claus and Little Claus, The Fir Tree, The Emperor's New Clothes, The Fellow Traveler, The Little Mermaid, The Tin Soldier, The Little Match Girl, The Ice Maiden. His stories were first translated into English by Mary Howitt in 1846 and by Caroline Peachey also in 1846.

St. Andrew's cross The saltire or decussate cross, formed like the letter X, common in ancient sculpture, and still to be seen as a symbol (usually white on a blue field) as in the Union Jack of Great Britain. St. Andrew is said to have been crucified on such a cross, but the legend has not been traced back farther than the 14th century, and the cross in the convent of St. Victor at Marseilles, reputed to be his, is an ordinary upright cross exhibited resting on the cross beam and foot. Achaius, king of the Scots, and Hungus, king of the Picts, saw this cross in the heavens before their battle with Athelstan, which they won. They therefore adopted the cross as the national emblem of Scotland.

St. Andrew's Day November 30: the day of the martyrdom of St. Andrew, and the only Apostle's day said to be observed on such an anniversary. It is a day for reunion of Scotsmen residing abroad, and for banquets and feasting by Scotsmen everywhere. There are several local customs in the British Isles on this day, as the carrying of a sheep's head in procession before the Scots (London), a driving out of evil spirits with noise and a ringing back again of good ones with bells (Stratton in Cornwall). On the evening of St. Andrew's Day in Germany [Luther's *Table-Talk*], young maidens strip themselves naked, recite a prayer to St. Andrew, and hope to see "what manner of man it is that shall lead me to the altar." A form of divination is performed on St. Andrew's Day by young Germans, in which little cups of foil representing each of the young people present are floated in a vessel of water and, by their approach to each other and to cups representing priests, establish a sort of marriage and sweetheart divination.

Androcles and the Lion Designation for a type of folktale appearing all over the world and belonging to the great cycle of grateful animal tales. The type takes its name from a story appearing in the *Noctes Atticæ* of Aulus Gellius, but is undoubtedly much older. Androcles, a runaway slave, hides in a cave, into which comes a lion. Instead of attacking him, the lion holds up a paw in which a thorn is sticking. Androcles extracts the thorn. He is recaptured and sentenced to fight a lion in the arena. The lion is the one he has aided and refuses to kill him, with the result that Androcles gains his freedom. The story appears in Æsop, in the *Gesta Romanorum,* etc. The moralizing turn of the tale, goodness for goodness, marks it as being probably of oriental origin. In the *Kathā Sarit Sāgara,* a Brāhman rescues a monkey and in return is given a fruit which makes him immune to old age and disease. A hunter abandoned by his companions, in a Wyandot story, draws a sharp object from a lion's paw and is given many hunting charms.

Andromeda In Greek legend, the daughter of Cepheus, king of Ethiopia. Cassiopeia, her mother, boasted that she was more beautiful than the Nereids, and Poseidon, at the nymphs' request, sent a monster to ravage the country. At the direction of the oracle of Amon, her parents had Andromeda chained to a rock, said to have been at Joppa, as a sacrifice to end the monster's ravages. Flying back from the slaying of the Gorgon, Perseus saw her, fell in love with her at sight, and after a bitter struggle with the monster slew it, either by means of Medusa's head, or with his sword. Cepheus then fulfilled his promise and gave Andromeda in marriage to Perseus. A disappointed suitor, Phineus, burst in on the marriage feast, but Perseus again raised the Gorgon's head and changed Phineus and his followers into stone. The couple later went to live on the island of Seriphos. They had many children, among them Electryon, the father of Alcmene; Alcæus, the father of Amphitryon, and Perses, the ruler after whom the Persians were named. Compare ANDROMEDA THEME.

The constellation Andromeda is hung just north of Cassiopeia, appropriately between Perseus and Pegasus, and safely out of reach of Cetus. The concept of this constellation as the Woman Chained is far older than the classical story. The Maiden Chained was known to the Chaldeans, for instance; and the Babylonian story of Marduk and Tiamat as told in the *Creation Epic* is perhaps the basis for the later Andromeda legend. Almost everywhere and in all times it has had the same designation. The Arabs too interpreted it as Al Mar'ah al Musalsalah (the Woman in Chains), but never showed the human form in their depictions, lest the image demand its soul on the Judgment Day. Instead they showed it as a Seal with a chain around its neck. Alternate names for it among classic Latin writers were Persea, an interpretation of Andromeda as the bride of Perseus, and Cepheis, for her father.

Andromeda theme A principal theme of the dragon-slayer type (#300) of the folktale, in which a maiden about to be sacrificed to a monster is rescued by a hero: spread all over the world, and often combined with other themes of the dragon-slayer type. It is perhaps an elaboration of the very ancient concept of the fight between light and darkness found in the Babylonian Marduk-Tiamat combat, or a reflection of the ancient custom of making human sacrifices to the water gods. Tales containing the theme are found from Central Asia to the Americas. In a French-Canadian story, Ti-Jean kills the monster, cuts out its seven tongues, and confounds a would-be glory-stealer when the latter presents the seven heads as proof of his supposed prowess. A Gipsy tale from the Transylvanian region tells of a hero transformed into a woman who slays the dragon and accepts the princess, forgetting the transformation. He manages, however, to get cursed back into proper form by an apple-guarding monster. Ideas found in close association with the Andromeda theme are the substituted sacrifice, the serpent (monster) guardian, and the helpful animals.

Andvari In Norse mythology, the dwarf from whom Loki stole the Nibelung treasure. Loki slew Otter, one of the sons of the king of the dwarfs, and with Odin and Hœnir was imprisoned by the king. Loki was permitted to go out to get ransom for the gods, as much gold as would cover both sides of Otter's skin, from Andvari. At the waterfall where Andvari dwelt, there was only a salmon, which Loki caught, and which was Andvari. Loki took all the gold, then ripped Andvari's ring from his finger. The dwarf cursed the gold and the ring, which from then brought only ill luck to their possessors. Sometimes Andvari is considered as the king of the dwarfs.

anecdotes Originally, things unpublished or "secret history"; biographical incidents, sayings, and extracts from unpublished writings, used to illustrate traits of character or customs; then illustrative stories generally; also, a universal and rudimentary type of folk and popular literature consisting of a single incident or motif, found separately, in cycles, or as components of longer narratives.

As short, pointed, pithy narratives, anecdotes were an early development of the literature of the people, whether gratifying the popular taste for gossip and scandal or employed for edification or entertainment. Since historical and literary anecdotes satisfy the curiosity of the many concerning the private affairs and thoughts of the few, the taste for ana, or collections of anecdotes relating to a particular person, grew with the vogue of memoirs and biography in the 17th and 18th centuries. Folk or traditional anecdotes appeal to the same taste, applied to fictitious or legendary characters, though, unlike myths and fairy tales, folk anecdotes are often told to be believed or as if they were true.

At the same time, even historical and literary anecdotes have a traditional aspect in that, as waifs and strays, attached to different individuals in different times and places, they are orphans that "glory in a numerous parentage by adoption." In folk and traditional anecdotes the historical and biographical interest is frankly subordinated to the apocryphal. With the loss of historical truth comes a corresponding gain in moral application, as in the great medieval collections of exempla or illustrative stories, such as the *Gesta Romanorum* (where the stories are arbitrarily referred to certain Roman emperors).

Then, as entertainment is substituted for moral instruction or edification, the serious anecdote gives way to the humorous anecdote, and the exemplum to the jest-book or collection of *facetiæ*. But it is the same pointed or proverbial quality of the anecdote that makes it suitable for use either to edify or to amuse. The brevity of the anecdote (sometimes explained on the ground that "The people have less time to sit still and listen to a story than the nobles") is largely inherent in the fact that, in a story with a point, the purpose is to get to the point as quickly as possible. Moreover, as stock or staple incidents or motifs or key stories, which

are widely diffused in time and space, anecdotes are quintessential elements which remain more constant than the plots into which they may be fitted.

As social types and relationships, wise and unwise conduct, rewards and punishments (to use the headings in Stith Thompson's *Motif-Index of Folk-Literature*) constitute the subject matter of a large part of serious anecdotes, so ludicrous mistakes and escapes, eccentricities, lies and exaggerations, deceptions, tricks, and pranks, the smart doings and sayings of clever persons, and retorts and repartee of all kinds make up the bulk of humorous anecdotes and jests. As many literary anecdotes are based on bon mots, word-play, and table talk, so many humorous anecdotes or jests are based on quibbles and repartee; and anecdote generally is related to the riddle, the epigram, and the apothegm. In another direction, there is a close connection between the anecdote or illustrative story and the apolog and parable.

In modern times the exemplum and parable have passed into the practical anecdote, whose purpose is to illustrate or make a point rather than to teach a lesson or adorn a moral. Numerous collections of such practical anecdotes and humorous illustrations have been compiled for the benefit of after-dinner and other speakers. The local anecdote, which is often a localized migratory anecdote, has also become popular in connection with the study of popular antiquities and local history. In the United States the "funny story" (by which, according to Bret Harte, "arguments were clinched, and political principles illustrated") developed, on the literary side, into the short story, and, on the folk and oral side, into the yarn and the tall tale. Almost every community has its local raconteurs and prize story-tellers (corresponding to the literary anecdote-mongers), who are masters of the folk anecdote and the local anecdote. Their repertoire is found in local histories and memoirs and is also the basis of many individual collections (e.g. the anecdotes of Lincoln) supplementing the literature of ana (e.g. the anecdotes about Lincoln). [BAB]

angakok or **angakoq** (plural *angakut*) The shaman, medicine-man, or magician of the Central Eskimo. He is the authority, judge, and teacher of all religious matters. He becomes an angakok by acquiring the protection of the tornait, especially of the tornaq of a bear, by means of a mysterious ceremony witnessed by no one but himself and the specific tornaq involved. The angakok's first and foremost duty is to discover the causes of sickness, death, or misfortune in the village, and by various acts, songs, and incantations to cure the ill and atone for broken tabus, or command how the offender shall atone. Every Eskimo believes in his heart that he must tell the truth when the angakok questions him. And the angakok never ceases to question until he secures the confession of some broken tabu that has undoubtedly caused the disease or disaster. He controls the weather and procures good hunting for the people by intercession with the tornait that control the animals. He has power over the souls of the dead, the dreaded tupilaq. The angakut know a sacred symbolic language used only in their songs and incantations and invocations of the tornait. They invoke the tornait with great shoutings and violence of motion. If a tornaq approaches in answer to the call, the hut shakes, all present believe that the roof is lifted off, and the soul of the angakok (who is now lying motionless in a trance) flies away with it to unknown strange regions where he may propitiate the angry ones. Sometimes he is tied with ropes during this spirit-flight, but when he returns the ropes are always found to be untied. His hardest job of all is to drive away Sedna from the village. This is undertaken only by the most powerful of the angakut and is accomplished at the Feast of Sedna. The angakok is always paid for his services. He is always feared and obeyed; but if he is discovered using his powers to a bad end, he is killed.

Angang The ominousness of an encounter; a form of divination, usually limited to the first person or animal met in going on or returning from a journey, but sometimes including those encountered while journeying: a German term applied by folklorists specifically to this belief throughout northern Europe, although similar beliefs are world-wide. The omen may be lucky, as in encountering a man or a horse, or unlucky (old woman, priest, raven, etc.). There seems to be a relationship between the purpose of the journey and the role of the one encountered. For example, while any such meeting with an old woman, a symbol of barrenness, would be considered unlucky, an encounter with any woman in starting a specifically manly pursuit, like hunting, would be unpropitious. Meeting with an animal is ominous in so far as the animal itself is generally ominous; divination from such encounters sometimes takes on totemic overtones.

angel of death Azrael, the terrible angel of Jewish and Mohammedan belief, who takes the soul from the dying body. Related to belief in the angel of death is the concept of the psychopomp, a being who, like the Greek Hermes and the Araucanian Tempulcague, conducts the soul to its afterworld home or to the judgment place.

angels An order of spiritual beings attendant upon the Deity: the heavenly guardians, ministering spirits, or messengers, or their fallen counterparts. The term must be limited to such beings in monotheistic belief, the subordination in duty and in essence inherent in the definition not being present in polytheistic or animistic religions. Angels, as in Christianity, Judaism, and Islam, often seem to be almost polytheistic deities of natural phenomena and abstract qualities. There have been times, for example, when the cult of angels has become very strong within the framework of Christianity. However, where Zeus may be strong as father, ruler, and despot among his surrounding gods, clearly his rôle is not the supreme one of Jehovah amid the angels. It has been surmised that where some saints and similar personalities preserve local pagan deities in the changed context of a new religion, angels are the survival in a like attempt to satisfy a popular belief in animistic deities while preserving the monotheistic outline. The yazatas, fravashis, and Amesha Spentas of Zoroastrian belief are, most clearly of all angelic beings, simply deposed animistic gods.

In pre-Captivity Hebrew literature, angels, not much further differentiated, are the "sons of God" or the "messengers of God," "the messengers" or the "holy ones." Later, beginning with the book of *Daniel,* certain angels are named and take on distinct personalities, e.g. Michael, Gabriel. Some time previously, there had been attempts to differentiate and rank the various classes of angels—cherubim, seraphim, ḥayyot, ofanim, arelim—but on the whole the Biblical writers accept and do not speculate on the angels. In the centuries between the completion of the Old Testament canon (about 100 B.C.) and that of the Talmud (4th to 6th centuries A.D.), a great angelology arose, diffuse and formless because of the variations in place and time in which the materials came into being, but strongly affecting written tradition. At about the same time as the writing of the Talmud, the supposed writings of Dionysius the Areopagite, who is mentioned (*Acts* xvii, 34) as hearing Paul preach at Mars Hill, set forth the basic structure of the angelology which was to be accepted in the Middle Ages and after [*The Celestial Hierarchy,* ch. 15].

According to the pseudo-Areopagite writings, there are three triads of the celestial hierarchy between God and man. The first and nearest to God includes Seraphim, Cherubim, and Thrones; the second, which receives the reflection of the Divine Presence from the first, comprises Dominions, Virtues, and Powers; the third, the angelic triad, ministering directly to man, includes Principalities, Archangels, and Angels. The term angel is applied to all, though specifically limited to the ninth and lowest class. The names themselves come from earlier writings: seraphim and cherubim from the Old Testament; archangel and angel from later Jewish texts; and the remainder from the New Testament (*Eph.* i, 21; *Col.* i, 16). On this structure there was later piled a mass of cabalistic magical terminology, the names of angels (and demons) to be invoked for personal reasons of gain, of health, etc., with the formulas for calling and controlling each.

The many theological questions concerning angels—their elementary composition, their existence before the Creation, the well-known cliché about their size (how many could stand on a needle point), their duties, aspect, etc.—do not fall within the scope of folklore. Nor properly is the question of their representation in heraldry and art a folkloric subject, except in so far as it is later reflected in popular belief, although the transformation of the angel to resemble the Greek winged victory, and the evolution of the cherubim from the terrible figures placed to guard Eden to the cupidlike winged babies, are inherently interesting. It is rather in their contacts with men that the angels enter the province of folklore. Many of the texts of the Bible, for example, have a later embroidery of angelology in the traditions of the people, although here too it is sometimes difficult to determine the boundary lines among theological, literary, and folk traditions. For example, in Jewish legend, Esther, wishing to accuse Ahasuerus of condemning her people, had her hand directed by an angel to point at Haman; when Haman tried to plead with her while the king walked in the garden, an angel tripped him so that he fell on her bed in an attitude that made Ahasuerus think he was trying to attack Esther (compare *Esther* vii, 5–8). The angel visitors to Abraham find parallels in the visits of the gods and other superhumans in other folktales, e.g. the visit of Zeus and Hermes to Philemon and Baucis in later Greek tradition, and the European story of the three wishes granted first to the good host and then to the bad one.

An Arab story concerns two fallen angels, Harut and Marut, who came to earth, were tempted, and fell. Offered the choice between punishment on earth and punishment hereafter, they chose the former as having a limit. Thus, Harut and Marut hang in a well in Babel where they teach the secrets of magic to men, "Yet no man did these two teach until they had said, 'We are only a temptation. Be not then an unbeliever.'" (*Koran*, Sura ii, 96).

Perhaps the best known of all folktales in which an angel figures is the originally Indian story told in one form by Longfellow about Robert of Sicily (*Tales of a Wayside Inn*). The angel replaces the proud prince who is then thrust out by his own retainers, and who cannot gain recognition until he realizes true humility. With varied incidents, the story has been told of a number of princes, even of Solomon in Jewish tradition, Solomon being tricked by the demon Asmodeus who takes his place for three years, during which Solomon wanders. Finally the true king forces Asmodeus to flee by demanding that he show his foot. Compare AMESHA SPENTAS; ANIMISM; ARCHANGEL; FRAVASHI; POLYTHEISM.

angklung An ancient musical instrument of southeastern Asia and Indonesia, consisting of bamboo pipes set loosely in a frame and tuned so as to produce a chord when shaken. Whole sets of such instruments have been found used together as an orchestra in old Balinese villages. The music accompanies marching. In Java it was used to signal the approach of the ruler and in time of war.

Angler and the Little Fish One of Æsop's fables (Jacobs #53). An Angler once caught a little fish who begged to be thrown back in the river. He was too small, he said, hardly a mouthful, but if the man would throw him back, he would then grow to full size so the man could catch him again to greater profit. "Oh, no," said the man, "I have *got* you now, and there is no certainty that you would not escape me in the future." Present possessions are preferable to future possibilities. A small thing surely possessed is better than a great thing in prospect. See BIRD IN THE HAND.

Angra Mainyu (Old Persian *Drauga*, Pahlavi *Ahriman*) In Iranian mythology: the devil or principle of evil: the opponent of Ahura Mazda. Angra Mainyu arose from the abyss of endless darkness or was the product of a moment of doubt on the part of Ahura Mazda. He is a demon of demons from the beginning, whose sole purpose and choice is to thwart good, and whose greatest satisfaction and victory is achieved when a human soul rebels against Ahura Mazda. He is the source of death, disease, and disorder, and the innovator of all imperfections. At his side is Druj, the female embodiment of evil.

In Zoroastrian mythology and legend, to destroy the faithful he formed the dragon Azhi Dahāka; to destroy the gaokerena, or tree of life, growing in the sea Vourukasha, he created a great lizard. In one myth he slew the primeval ox, Gēush Urvan.

Angra Mainyu is not eternal. At the resurrection he will be annihilated or imprisoned in the earth, since sin will be removed from the world. He does not know his fate, so is unable to devise means to guard himself against it. Compare SATAN.

Angur-boda or **Angrbodha** In Norse mythology, a giantess of Utgard, the worker of calamity, whose name is literally "anguish-boding." She was the mother, by Loki, of the Fenris wolf, the Midgard serpent, and Hel, and by Gymir, of Gerda.

Angus Og or **Óc** Literally, Angus, the Young. In Old Irish mythology one of the Tuatha Dé Danann, son of Dagda and Bóann, queen of the side (the divine race of Ireland) and father of Macha, ancestress of the Red Branch. He is regarded as the god of love and beauty, special deity of youths and maidens, and is sometimes referred to as the Irish Adonis. He was accompanied by four bright birds flying over his head, and seems to have traveled with the pure, cold wind. He was also called Angus of the Brug because he lived with his mother in the Brug na Bóinne, the famous city of the side on the River Boyne.

Angus Og and Caer A story in the Ulster cycle of Old Irish legend: one of the most famous swan-maiden stories in the world. Angus Og fell in love with a young girl who came to him every night for a year in his dreams, but whose name he never succeeded in asking. After her disappearance from the dreams, and a fruitless year's search, Bodb Derg discovered that she was Caer, daughter of Ethal Anbual, one of the side of Connacht. With the help of Ailill, king of Connacht, Ethal Anbual was brought before them. He disclosed that Caer was under a spell and lived year and year about in the shape of swan and maiden alternately. Angus sought Caer in her swan-shape on the lake and was transformed into a swan beside her. The two of them flew, singing unearthly music as they flew, to Angus's home in the Brug na Bóinne.

Anguta Literally, his father: the supreme being of the Central Eskimo, father of Sedna. He created the earth, the sea, and the heavenly bodies. He lives in Adlivun with his daughter, each occupying one side of the big house where no deerskins are, and where the big dog guards the door. He is the one who carries the dead to Adlivun, where the big dog moves aside just enough to let him through with the hapless soul. Here the souls must abide for a year and sleep side by side with Anguta, who pinches them.

Anhanga A forest spirit or demon of the modern Indians and caboclos of the Amazonian basin: formerly a bush spirit of the Tupi tribes of eastern Brazil. He was regarded as a mischievous being who played tricks on travelers and hunters. [AM]

Anher or **Anhouri** A sun and sky god of ancient Egypt, "he who leads heaven." He was the god of several places, Thinis in Upper Egypt particularly claiming to possess his mummy. He appears in human form, carrying a scepter. As a sun god he became identified with Shu, son of Rā. See ANHUR.

Anhur, An-hôret, Anhert, or **Onouris** A war god and god of the dead, local deity of Abydos in Egypt, sometimes shown as a man standing with spear poised. In the period of Greek influence, he became identified with Ares. He is probably identical with Anher.

animal as earth-anchor In the mythology of the Huchnom Indians of California, after the Creator, Taikomol had made two unsuccessful attempts at creation, he at last was able to achieve a fairly stable earth stretching from the north to the east. But the world still swayed, and Taikomol sent a coyote, an elk, and a deer to the northern end to steady it. That did not quite do it, for the animals too floated about. Finally Taikomol had them lie down and the earth thenceforth was still, except for the earthquakes which still occur when the animals stir.

animal children Children in the form of animals, either real animals, transformed human beings, or masquerading gods, born to human mothers: a concept found in the folklore, folktales, and mythology of many peoples all over the world. Often the animal children result from a beast marriage; the ideas are intimately connected. But the principal significance of the animal children theme is rather in the direction of etiology and totemism. Among the etiological stories is one of the Dyaks and Silakans in which a boy and a cobra are twins. The cobra goes off into the forest, advising the mother that if ever any of her children is bitten by a cobra, he must remain in the same place for twenty-four hours. Later the twin meets the cobra in the jungle and cuts off his tail, so all cobras since then have had blunted tails. There is a Belgian story of the origin of the first lizards, which says they are the offspring of a vain girl's intercourse with the devil. The Formosans account for the origin of crabs and fish as the result of a brother-sister marriage. These latter are, in addition to being etiological, part of the generally held belief that illegal intercourse can result only in the birth of monsters, etc. (Twins, for example, are in several cultures unmistakable evidence of adultery.) Such concepts as these reflect some of the feeling of horror or awe attendant on the birth of teratisms, twins, and the like. In the typical totemic legends, twins are born, one the ancestor of the tribe, clan, or group, the other the totemic animal. Thus, the Dogrib Indians tell of a woman who bore six puppies, three remaining dogs, three changing into the human ancestors of the tribe. Sometimes the child is an animal when born, and is transformed into the ancestor later. The tale, in Herodotus, of the lion born to one of Meles's concubines is illustrative. Meles was one of the Heraclid kings of Lydia, and Hercules, his ancestor, has been identified as a development of the lion god, often being pictured as wearing a lion-skin. Among the famous animal children of mythology are the Minotaur, born of Pasiphae's lust for the sacred bull sent by Poseidon; the Fenriswolf and the Midgard-Serpent, born to Angurboda and Loki; and the Celtic seal or fish twins, such as the trout born to Mugain before she gave birth to Aed Slane. Compare ADLET.

animal curers The animal or beast gods of Pueblo Indian religion; certain animals believed to possess great powers for curing disease. The prey animals especially are thus regarded. They are patrons of the curing societies and are impersonated by the shamans in the curing rituals. Among the Keres, for instance, bear, badger, mountain lion, wolf, eagle, shrew are all curing animals; but Bear is the most powerful doctor. Bear and Mountain Lion predominate ritually among the Hopi. At Zuñi Bear and Badger are both prominent. Weasel, rattlesnake, and gopher also occur. All the curing societies function through the animals they impersonate. Chiefs of the Zuñi curing societies have animal names: White Bear, Wildcat, Mountain Lion, etc. During a curing ceremony a thread from a blanket or shawl and a small portion of the prayer-meal offered to the

shaman are placed in a corn husk together and regarded as food and clothing for the animal being invoked.

That animals can both cause and cure disease, especially illnesses caused by fear, is common Zuñi belief. A woman in childbirth will wear a badger's paw, or place one on the bed, because badgers can dig themselves out quickly. Hopi women regard the fat, meat, or skin of the weasel as powerful delivery medicines. The Zuñi also believe that one can make a lifelong friend of an animal by giving it a compulsive gift, i.e. the receipt of the gift compels the animal to reciprocate with friendship or guardianship. In return, for instance, the animal will cure the donor's sores. See ANIMAL GUARDIANS; BADGER MEDICINE; BEAR MEDICINE; BEAST GODS.

animal guardians Certain prey animals regarded as guardians and protectors: a general Pueblo Indian concept. Figurines of animals are carried as guides and protectors in the hunt. Zuñi hunters "feed" their lion figurines just before undertaking a deer hunt; and the little lion image which the individual hunter carries with him is buried in the deer's heart, as reward for the hunter's success, or is dipped into the blood. Details of practice vary among the pueblos. Animal stone images are found on almost all pueblo altars. The family group also usually houses at least one such image as guardian (at Laguna, Hopi, Acoma, and San Juan). Among the Hopi, a traveler carries with him a small animal image and sleeps with it in his pillow so that it may warn him of danger in his dreams. Pueblo doctors also give their patients animal images to protect them against disease-sending witches, and are apt to leave one with a sick man to watch over him. See ANIMAL CURERS; BEAST GODS.

animal languages The languages spoken by animals among themselves: a recurrent motif (B215–217.8) of the folklore and mythology of Europe and Asia and thence in much of the rest of the world, in which the gift of understanding these languages is obtained by a human being who thereupon is able to use it to advantage. Underlying the almost universal use of the theme is the same primitive concept basic to augury: that animals in many ways are wiser than men. The ancient Arabs, for example, believed that eating the heart or liver of a serpent gave the power to read omens from birds.

Among their other accomplishments, animals, especially birds, have unlimited opportunities for discovering secrets simply by being unobserved at important meetings and by being able to travel to places inaccessible to men. The fortunate man who possesses the power of understanding their speech, whether that faculty is acquired as a gift from a god or a grateful animal, by magical means, or by his being born with the gift, has opened to him therefore a storehouse of knowledge not available to other men, and he is able to do extraordinary things.

By far the most common way of acquiring the gift is through a serpent or a dragon, perhaps stemming from the belief that the snake is intermediate between the birds and the beasts. A well-known story of the folktale tradition of Asia and Europe, told specifically of Melampus in Greek legend, attributes the knowledge of the language of the birds to the licking of his ears by snakes. Siegfried or Sigurd, tasting the dragon's blood, understands the language of the birds at once. In other tales, it is the eating of the flesh of a snake, particularly the flesh of a white snake, that gives the power. But in Saxo Grammaticus, Rollo, by eating of a black serpent, learns everything, including the speech of both wild and tame animals. This belief is represented not only as folktale incident, however, for in northern Europe and through Germany and Bohemia, it was believed until fairly recently that partaking of serpents' flesh would bring such knowledge.

In combination with a tabu motif (C425), the animal languages story as it appears in one of the best known tales of Europe and Asia, is: A man, taught the languages by a snake, is forbidden to tell anyone of his gift. When he overhears two animals talking, he laughs. His wife will not desist in her attempts to learn why he has laughed, although he tells her he must not divulge his secret. He is about to tell her and die, when he hears a barnyard conversation about a man keeping order in his own house. He does not tell his wife. Several plants also are believed to give one the gift of understanding animal languages. An Irish belief is that a person wearing a four-leafed shamrock can understand barking dogs.

animal mime   The impersonation of animals to obtain power and aid from their spirits for beneficial, life-sustaining effects on the community. Among primitive peoples, where animal mime is still functional, costumes and motions often show an overwhelming realism. The prime function of animal mime (or dance) is obviously to increase animal life and to lure game animals. Effects of the mime-magic are believed to extend also into vegetable and human life.

Hunting drama is mimed in the antelope dance of the African Yammassoukro, and during the hunting season (November through January) among the Rio Grande Pueblo Indians, as in the dance of the game animals performed at San Juan and San Felipe. This dance was also formerly performed among Plains Buffalo Societies. The Comanche buffalo-hunting dance, the *ta'one*, enacts the hunt with shooting and trapping. Among the Hopi costume and action are highly stylized. In the Yaqui deer dance the hunt-mime itself has become blurred.

Certain animals are associated with fertility and vegetation: the snake and turtle universally, the rain-bearing eagle in the American Southwest, the goat, bull, and horse in Europe and all Latin-American countries. The masks and shaggy "wild men" of European medieval carnival had their origin in pagan spring rites and survive today in the sheepskin-covered *Rautschegetten* of Switzerland and other clown-demons. The dance of the agricultural *tlacololeros* of Guerrero, Mexico, mimes a hunt of the fearful *tecuanes* (tigers, wild beasts). Beneficent influences are exerted by the animal spirits of the California Kuksu-hesi rites, but destructive powers are represented by various fantastic spirit- or demon-animals in certain puberty rites, such as the Máuari of the Venezuelan Maipure Indians. Animal spirits have curative effects on human beings, are curers, or "doctors," as in the old Plains Indian Bear, Buffalo, and other Animal Societies and Iroquois bear and buffalo dances.

Animal representations function as emblems of societies, as among the Plains War societies, or as totems, as in Africa among the Javara of the Upper Volta (stork, crocodile, antelope, etc.), and among the American Northwest Coast Haida and Kwakiutl Indians (raven, wolf, etc.)

Some animal dances have degenerated into mere entertainment, as the highly mimetic monkey dances of the African Ivory Coast (near Odienne) and the Shoshone pony and dog dances. Among some American Indians the mimetic character of the dances has been forgotten and they now survive only as social dances for couples, as the Iroquois fish and coon dances.

On the whole men predominate in animal mime enactments, but they are joined by the women among the Fox, Sauk, and Iroquois Indians. Women monopolized the Blackfoot and Mandan Buffalo Societies, and among the Pueblos, maidens serve as decoys.

Separate articles discuss specific animal dances more fully. See also DANCE: FOLK AND PRIMITIVE. [GPK]

animal nurse   A character of the folklore and mythology of many peoples all over the world: the animal helper (B535) who is foster-parent and nurturer of an abandoned child (or twins), the child being fated to be a hero. The Roman legend of Romulus and Remus, suckled by a she-wolf, is perhaps the best known of the many stories in which an animal nurse appears. Similar tales, in which the animal either suckles or provides food or protection for the abandoned, lost, or kidnapped child, appear in as widespread places as China and Brazil, Ireland and Zanzibar, Canada and India, Greece and Indonesia.

The animal nurse may be one of those creatures, as cow, goat, or mare, which actually provide milk for human nourishment as domestic animals; it may be an animal which resembles these in its milk-giving habits and which might if tamed be used for such purpose, as doe, panther, or bear; it may on the other hand be completely fantastic as an animal nurse, as swan, snake, or buffalo bull, and yet in the tales these latter always manage to provide nourishment for the child. In the Gros Ventre story of the boy adopted by seven buffalo bulls, for example, the bulls confer, decide that since humans eat flesh they must kill buffalo for him, and doing this they keep the child alive. Iamus, abandoned by his mother Evadne, is fed with honey by two serpents, according to a Greek legend told by Pindar. The baby girl of a medieval (perhaps more ancient) story is placed in an egg shell and hatched by serpents. She inherits the serpents' venomousness and, when she strikes Alexander's fancy, is placed in a ring of venom by the suspicious Aristotle as a test, and chokes to death. Ptolemy I (Soter) was supposedly nurtured by an eagle.

There is perhaps in these stories and legends an inkling of underlying totemic meaning, to some extent strengthened by the resemblance of the names of the hero and the animal nurse. For example, Cycnus is fed by a swan, Hippothoos by a mare, Telephus by a deer, Lugaid Mac Con by a dog. In addition, if a hero or king is brought up by an eagle, a lion, or similar "noble" animal, it would seem reasonable to expect that he will partake of that creature's qualities; if this happens to strengthen his claim to throne or worship, so much the better. Therefore, Cybele was nourished by panthers, Atalanta by a she-bear, the Deer Boy of the Tewa Indians by a deer.

The Norse giant Ymir drew milk from the cow Audhumla, whose name means nourisher. Cyrus too was suckled by a cow; Paris by a she-bear; Æsculapius by a bitch or a she-goat; and Ægisthus, Phylacides, and Philandrus were nurtured by she-goats. That the idea has not completely disappeared today is apparent from the occasional Antelope-Boy or Wolf-Girl receiving publicity in the press, or from such as Mowgli or Tarzan in contemporary fiction.

animal paramour The animal lover of a woman or a man: a motif (B610–614) used from earliest times in the folklore and mythology of many peoples in every part of the world. While the idea is somewhat similar in theme to the beast marriage, in stories of animal paramours the transformation theme is not so prominent, or so essential to the sense of the story. Beast marriage tales as a rule are of the märchen type, and depend for their principal effect on the happy ending. Animal paramour stories on the other hand are as often as not etiological or moralistic. The beast husband or wife often turns out to be a prince or a princess; the animal lover usually is slain and the human paramour is punished, although in various totemistic or etiological stories these events may not occur. In the famous aśvamedha, or horse sacrifice, of India, the horse is dead before he copulates with the queen; and in a Lipan Apache story, the dog is killed by the woman's husband, and the woman is scratched to death by the puppies with which she is pregnant. Among the many animal paramours are birds, dogs, bears, horses, bulls, fishes, crocodiles, and snakes. Perhaps the most famous animal paramour is Europa's, Zeus in the form of a bull. A scurrilous tale still alive says that Catherine the Great of Russia kept a specially trained stallion in her stables to satisfy her abnormal sexual appetite. Medical records attest to actual and perhaps frequent cases of bestiality, but the popular tales of women and greyhounds or wolfhounds, and of pet cats and lapdogs, if taken at their frankly exaggerated face value, may be classed as animal paramour stories.

animals The dramatis personæ of folklore and folktale to such tremendous extent that almost *sine qua non*. From the moment man was aware of himself on the face of the earth he recognized his kinship with the animals and called them brothers. Only the so-called "higher" civilizations relegate them to separateness. To early man the animals were different only in shape, not in nature. He witnessed their acuteness and wisdom, in many cases also their superior strength and cunning. He sought to learn in their school; he mimed them in his dances; he admired, loved, feared, and worshipped them, both dead and alive.

To the primitive mind a living animal is open to argument and persuasion, a dead one's spirit to propitiation and appeal. Hand in hand with cognizance of the transience of all physical form goes belief in transformation, the separable soul, and reincarnation.

Thus throughout the folk belief and religions of the world, animals figure as reincarnated ancestors, creators or as aids to a creator, scouts, messengers, and earth-divers (in deluge stories), as guides of souls to afterworlds, messengers of gods, and as gods themselves and hence recipients of worship and objects of cults. They figure as supporters of the world and causers of earthquakes, as swallowers of suns and moons and thus causers of eclipses, as witches' and magicians' familiars and household familiars, weather prophets and weathermakers, as life tokens and doubles, and as such, habitats of individual separable souls. There are friendly and helpful and grateful animals, animal guides (both individual and tribal), animal tricksters, animal culture heroes, tutelary animals, and animal field spirits. The animal or beast marriage, a commonplace of all folklores, gives us innumerable animal husbands, animal wives, animal lovers, animal children, and animal nurses. Animal ancestors are prominent in etiological and totemic myths.

There are animal kings and chiefs, kingdoms, and armies, and animal languages which human beings are sometimes allowed to learn. Animals as baby-bringers include not only the well-known and traditional stork, but the equally well-known and traditional (Malay) lizard who brings the baby and also causes its soul to enter into it.

Many a folktale begins with the statement that "these things happened" long ago when animals could speak like men. But contemporary primitive folk belief does not relegate speaking animals to the past. That animals can (and do) speak is a living and unquestioned fact among North and South American Indians, Australian aborigines, among various African peoples, and in other contemporary primitive societies. Agricultural folk in Europe and America still believe that on Christmas Eve the animals speak together in the barn, only no man dare listen.

animal tale A story having animals as its principal characters: one of the oldest forms, perhaps the oldest, of the folktale, and found everywhere on the globe at all levels of culture. Excluding the animal myth as being essentially religious, three classes of the animal folktale type should be distinguished: the etiological tale, the fable, and the beast epic. The animal tales current in western folklore stem from such sources as the literary fables of India, the *Jātaka*, the medieval and Renaissance embroiderings of collections like *Æsop's Fables* and the Reynard cycle, and the oral tradition of northern Europe (especially of the countries of the Baltic and Russia).

At its simplest, the animal tale is an attempt to explain the form and habits of the several animals, a fruitful source of material for the primitive storyteller. These stories underlie the mythologies of various peoples, as is evidenced by the animal attributes of many gods in their pantheons. In various instances, as with the Great Hare of the eastern North American Indians and the animal-headed gods of Egypt with their dual animals, it is comparatively easy to reconstruct an etiological animal story antedating the stated myth. In other cases, like the wolf attributes of Zeus and Apollo or the lion story behind the Hercules legend, the process may be more difficult. Other etiological tales, like the one telling how the bear lost his tail, have become attached to one or another of the beast epics. One curious explanatory motif is that of the exchange of parts, found in most parts of the world, telling of the trading or lending of eyes, fur, or the like, among animals, and purporting to explain such natural phenomena as the lack of eyes of the blindworm (he loaned his single eye to the nightingale who added it to hers and kept it).

The line between the literary and the folk fable is not easy to determine, since tales from collections like that attributed to Æsop have had wide popular circulation and have been taken from and gone back into the oral traditions of large groups of people. However, the area of contact between the didactic, moralizing fable and folklore is slight, for the animal tale proper is meant essentially to entertain. The hearer is required to suspend belief and see the animal speaking, thinking, and acting like a human being. In fact, in many of the animal tales, like those of the North American Indians or the Anansi stories of Africa and the New World, one is never sure that Coyote (Anansi, Raven) is performing in an animal or a human role.

Those cycles of stories revolving about one central character, usually a trickster, in animal shape, but with a wily and lucidly logical mind, have been called the beast epics. It has been suggested by Krappe that the beast epic "presupposes" both the fable and the epic, and that the beast epic, the Reynard the Fox tales clearly in mind, is a bourgeois caricature of the aristocratic troubadourish epics themselves. The fable as fable, the short animal tale pointed with a stated moral, is not present among the American Indians; and the sophisticated epic type is likewise missing. The probable source of the beast epics is the agglutinative mind of the story-teller, the desire to respond to the "tell us more" of his audience. Where there may have been several tricksters, or a heterogeneous collection of tales about a number of animals, there evolves one long series of stories about the one central character that catches the imagination of teller and audience alike. The migrations of the Bear and Fox story into regions where the bear was not known, and the amusing pointlessness of substituting the wolf for the bear in the etiological story of the tail frozen into the ice (explaining why the bear has no tail in the one instance, explaining nothing about the wolf's tail in the other), show this process of accretion rather clearly. Such tickling tales as the "Well Begun, Half Done, All Gone" in which Reynard steals and eats the food while supposedly reporting on the progress of a christening have traveled to most of Asia, all of Africa, North America (Negro, Spanish, French, Portuguese), and the North American Indians, and in the process the hero of the tale is variously Anansi, Rabbit, Coyote, etc., whichever is the focal animal of the beast epic of the region. There are of course hundreds of such individual tale types, some very widespread, some with only a local circulation. The migration of the very popular Tar-Baby story from India to America, through Africa, through Europe and the Spanish peninsula, has been investigated by Espinosa and others. The relationship of the purely beast type and the ogre (demon) and man tales (northern Europe as against northern France) has been demonstrated by Gerber. The folktales in which animals figure along with human heroes, e.g. Puss in Boots, Dick Whittington, or the helpful animal tales, are either fairy tales or other types not properly animal tales.

animal thief A character of the folklore of many parts of the world, often the trickster: typified by the European Reynard the Fox, the transformer of the North Pacific Coast and eastern Siberia, and the raven and magpie. The thief may be an ant, a swallow, a raven, parrot, wolf, fox, wolverine, or even a cow. In the transformed trickster story told among many of the Indian tribes of British Columbia and Alaska, and the Koryak of Siberia, the trickster, changing himself into a salmon or the like, runs away with the coveted harpoon or fishhook. In a story found among the Lapps, Hottentots,

American Negroes, and the North American Indians, the fox shams death, is picked up and thrown into the fish cart, and tosses the fish off the wagon to his confederates. The trickster's animal is taught to feign death, in a Japanese story, and after the supposed carcass is sold, returns to his master. The trickster who reports to his fellows that the baby's name is Just Begun, Half Done, All Gone while he eats all the stored food is found in Europe, Africa, North America. Sometimes the animal is a professional thief; sometimes he merely seizes the chance to steal. The crow that loses the cheese to the fox is more scorned for not knowing with whom he dealt than pitied. The most familiar of the thieving animal stories is perhaps the tale, based on the penchant of certain species for shining or brightly colored objects, of the bird, often a jackdaw or a magpie, which weaves a ring or a necklace into its nest, causing great trouble to the victim of the theft.

animism The belief in souls; the attribution of spirit or personality to physical objects or phenomena; specifically, the religious philosophy found universally in mankind which peoples the physical universe with spirits found in animals, plants, stones, weapons, meteorological events, etc.: believed by many scholars to be a principal basis of religious thought, either the fundamental religious belief of mankind or a second phase in its development.

Three principal forms of belief are comprised in animism: a) Belief in and worship of the spirits or souls of men and animals, living or dead, especially necrolatry and ancestor worship, the worship of the souls of the dead; b) belief in spirits not definitely connected with physical objects; c) belief in and worship of spirits residing in objects. Objections have been made to the use of the term and the concept of animism. Substitute terms have been suggested for its various aspects: *animatism*, as relating to that phase having to do with spirits residing in objects; *polydæmonism*, to contrast the unranked spirits of the animistic world with the hierarchy of the polytheistic beliefs. That it forms a phase of the "normal" development of religious belief has likewise been criticized. Some have claimed to find in animism traces of a degenerated monotheism. But while a direct chain from animism through theriomorphism, anthropomorphism, polytheism, and monotheism can be demonstrated by scholarly analysis, the existence of animism in such complex societies as the Polynesian seems to indicate that the evolution of one form from another is not a universal occurrence. Animism does not appear as a clear-cut religious system, but is rather a philosophical basis for many systems.

The belief in the "animation of the inanimate" is not limited to the simpler cultures. The man who calls his automobile "she" can be seen throwing his golf club to the ground forcibly because it interfered with his making a good shot. A child will be seen kicking a chair from which the child has fallen. Basically the distinction between what is lifeless and what contains life is never thoroughly made. As d'Alviella points out, science postulates certain unexplainable forces differing principally in context from the mana or orenda or manitou residing in objects. This force, possessed by spirits, good and bad, who reside in the various objects in the world, is something the primitive feels he must reckon with, just as he must reckon with the personality of those men and women with whom he comes in contact. He must tread with care, propitiating where necessary, but if necessary chastising the object, or destroying it and the spirit living in it.

The complexity of the relationship between animism and fetishism, between animism and ancestor worship, between animism and the various other forms of elementary religious belief, cannot be easily unraveled, and leads to what is often confusion in the writings of the several students in the matter of religion. Animism, as used in this book, indicates a belief in the existence of personality in objects. These objects may be in natural form, or they may be manufactured forms.

anito Supernatural beings of Filipino religion: a general term including deities, lesser spirits both benevolent and malicious, and the souls of the dead, in fact, any incorporeal being. The meaning and application vary from tribe to tribe. The most prevailing concept, however, seems to be that the anito are the souls of the dead, with the result that ancestor worship is the prevailing cult. The Filipino fears the anito, but does not exactly worship them; to keep their good will is his chief aim. He will pay their debts and make sacrifices to them. Sacrifice, as practiced in Luzon and Mindanao, is of the most logical kind. If a man would sacrifice a jug of wine to his anito he takes the jug of wine to the spirit house, repeats his prayer of dedication, allows the jug to stand in the place for a certain time, then takes it back home for family consumption, leaving the soul of the wine to the soul of the ancestor. If a Bagobo man would sacrifice his spear, he leaves it in the presence of the anito only long enough for the soul of the spear to pass into the possession of the anito. He then takes the implement back for his own use. The only difference between a spear that has been sacrificed and one that has not been is that the man may never sell or give away or lose the spear whose soul is in the possession of his anito.

Anjea Among the natives of the Pennefeather region in Queensland, Australia, a being who fashions babies from mud and places them in the mother's womb. Anjea is also the guardian of souls, which he takes from buried afterbirths and preserves in various places until they are ready to be used for new persons. While the navel cord is being cut by the grandmother, Anjea's various retreats are recited. The one mentioned as the cord breaks will be the child's hunting grounds by right, and the child is known as being a baby of a pool, rock, etc.

ankh In Egyptian art and mythology, a tau cross having a looped top; the crux ansata: a keylike emblem held in the hand of a god (or of a king) as a symbol of generation or the power of life, and sometimes called the "key of life." Its origin has been variously conjectured to be the winged globe, the phallus, the Egyptian loin-cloth, the sandals painted on the mummy case, etc. The symbol is often depicted as being applied by a god to the nostrils of the dead to restore the breath of life. It is found from Sardinia to Persia, and in somewhat similar form in India and in Central America.

Ankou In the folklore of Brittany, the last person who has died in each parish or district during a year, driver of the spectral cart whose coming to a certain house or place means death. The Ankou is either a tall, haggard figure with long white hair or a skeleton with revolving head who sees everybody everywhere. Two other figures

walk beside the cart, one on each side, to open the gates or doors and lift the dead into it. See CELTIC FOLKLORE.

Anniebelle A work song of American Negroes, used in wood-chopping, spiking steel, loading lumber, and in mining: sung in short phrases punctuated by a grunted sound as the blow of the work falls.

anniversary, wedding See WEDDING ANNIVERSARY.

Annwn or **Annwfn** The Otherworld of Brythonic mythology: literally construed either as "abyss," or as *an*, not, and *dwfn*, the world. It was located either on the face of the earth, under the earth, or over or under the sea; it was a group of fortified islands out to sea, or a great revolving castle surrounded by the sea. It was called Land Over Sea, Land Under Wave, etc., or Caer Sidi (revolving castle). It was a land of delight and beauty without disease or death. Arawn was its lord or king. It shared with other Celtic Elysiums, along with its delights, a magic caldron (either inexhaustible or gifted with some mysterious power of discrimination such as would make it refuse to boil a coward's food), a well of sweet or miraculous water, and various marvelous animals greatly desired by men.

The old *Book of Taliesin* locates Annwn beneath the earth and again identifies it as an island fortress which Arthur visited in his ship Prydwen. In the *Mabinogion* Annwn is the next-door kingdom to the kingdom of Pwyll; and in *Kilhwch and Olwen* it could be reached via Scotland.

Anshar or **Ansar** In Babylonian mythology, the god of the upper world, son of Lachmu and Lachamu, consort of Kishar, and father of Anu, Ea, and Enlil: believed by some to be identical with the Assyrian Ashur. In the creation myth, Anshar commands Anu and Ea to fight Tiamat, but both turn in fear; finally, when Marduk is sent as the avenger of the gods to fight the mother of chaos and slays her, Anshar regains some of his lost power. Anshar was the god of the night sky, particularly personified as the pole star, which was the peak of the mountain of stars, where he danced as a goat, surrounded by his six assistants of the Dipper.

An Spailpin Fánach Literally, *The Itinerant Laborer*, an Irish folk melody which has been sung to countless sets of words, including *The Girl I Left Behind Me*, a vaudeville parody about a golfer's adventures with "the dirty little pill," a ribald drinking song, and a Vermont song *Old England Forty Years Ago*.

Antæus In Greek mythology, a giant living in Libya, the son of Poseidon and Ge. As a wrestler he was invincible as long as he remained in contact with his mother, the Earth, and he compelled all strangers to do battle on condition that, if conquered, they should be put to death. Hercules discovered the source of his power and strangled him while holding him off the earth. The strength received from the earth motif is also found in a Swiss story in which the strength of witches depends upon their touching the earth.

Ant and the Grasshopper (or *Cricket*) The title of one of Æsop's fables (Jacobs #36) in which a grasshopper who had sung happily throughout the summer, went to the ants in the winter and asked for a little of the food which they had put by. "What did you do all summer?" they asked her. When she replied that she had sung all day long, they told her now she could dance for the winter, and turned her away. This fable (Type 249) is included in a group of motifs embodying the idea: in time of plenty provide for want (J711–711.3). Stith Thompson reports at least three North American Indian borrowings of this Asiatic-European story.

antelope In the Congo, antelope horns and skins are used as charms; among the southern U.S. Negroes antelope horns are a favorite place in which to confine spirits.

In the emergence myth of the Lipan Apache Indians, the antelope was one of three monsters, enemies of other animals and of the ancient people, finally overcome by Alligator or (in some versions) by Killer-of-Enemies. Among the Hopi Indians, the antelope is a medicine animal.

In India the wind god, Vayu, is pictured riding on the back of an antelope; in China powdered antelope horn (Ling-yang-koh) is given as a medicine in puerperal cases.

Antero Vipunen A primeval giant: wisest of the heroes of the Finns. He lay asleep under the earth, but was wakened by Väinänöinen, who came seeking to be taught magic words and creative spells, to build his boat. Antero Vipunen immediately swallowed Väinänöinen, who proceeded to prod, and hack, and torture the giant from within. At last Vipunen sang to Väinänöinen all his ancient wisdom (see *Kalevala*, song 17). The Christian-Catholic influence is obvious in the naming of this hero, as the name Antero is derived from St. Andreus and Vipunen means the cross of the same saint (see Harva in *FUF* XXIV, 1937, p. 59–79). [JB]

Anthesteria A three days' festival in honor of Dionysus held annually at Athens from the 11th to the 13th of the month of Anthesterion (February-March). Its object was to celebrate the maturing of the wine stored at the previous vintage and the beginning of spring. The first two days, the Pithoigia (opening of the casks) and Choes (feast of beakers), were considered as ill-omened and required expiatory libations; on those days the souls of the dead walked abroad. On the third day, called Chutroi (feast of pots), a festival of the dead was held.

ant-hill A mound of earth and humus heaped up, grain by grain, by ants while constructing their underground habitat: associated with the idea of fertility and sometimes prominent in snake-worship. In the myths of the Korkus of central India, Mahadeo (Śiva) fashioned two images in the likeness of man and woman from the red earth of an ant-hill; the Dhangars of the same region believe the first sheep and goats came out of an ant-hill, and to stop their destruction of the crops, Śiva created the Dhangars. The Susus of West Africa consider ants' nests the residence of demons. The aboriginal object of worship at Tiruvothyur and Melkote, Mysore, was an ant-hill, the abode of the cobra or naga-snake. The Alur tribe of the upper Nile buries men in ant-hills as regular treatment for insanity, and in South Africa the bodies of children are placed in ant-hills excavated by ant-eaters.

anthropological school Largely as a reaction against the mythological school, which sought to explain folktales as a detritus of Indo-European myth, the anthropological school saw in the folktale the fossil remains of the cultures of the remote past. Folktales, they thought, are best explained in terms of the practices of primitive societies, since often the folktale preserves customs, rituals, beliefs that have long been discarded. The members of the anthropological school—Lang, MacCulloch, Gomme, von der Leyen in folklore, and Tylor and Frazer in general culture—saw proof of this in the fact that the folktales of medieval Europe have close analogs in the folktales of the savages. Andrew Lang, perhaps the most persuasive member of this school, saw the general pattern of development as follows: (1) The original tale, made up of several motifs and originating among "savages" evolves into (2) The popular tale of peasants, which in turn can develop into either (or both) (3) The tale of the semi-realistic hero (e.g. Perseus), or (4) The literary version, such as that of Andersen or Perrault.

While recognizing the fact that tales are frequently diffused from people to people, this school was inclined to explain general resemblances among folktales and especially among folktale motifs by polygenesis. They felt that all men pass through the same stages of development and that consequently they embody the details of their development in essentially the same stories. This group was consequently primarily interested in tracing every element and detail of story and culture back to sources in primitive life. And in this lies the weakness of the school, in failing to recognize differences in cultures and people, cross-influences, inventiveness—in short, in failing to recognize that each tale should be studied as an individual product and studied by the same methods that are used to study a story of conscious art. See COMPARATIVE METHOD; DIFFUSION; HISTORIC-GEOGRAPHIC METHOD; POLYGENESIS. [MEL]

anthropomancy Divination using the entrails of human sacrifices: one of the most ancient and perhaps still widespread means of divining. Most often the victim is a child or a virgin because of the implied purity, but one of the common types in ancient times was the sacrifice of prisoners to foretell the outcome of an imminent battle. The practice has existed only where human sacrifice has been common.

anthropomorphism The ascription of human form or qualities to divine beings, particularly to the gods; the ascription of human characteristics to the powers of nature or to a natural object, animate or inanimate, but especially to animals. The development of the concept of a god often follows a set pattern. The god is thought first to be an animal (theriomorphic state) as Zeus was an eagle, Artemis a deer, etc. Then man begins to endow the god with his physical attributes, so Zeus assumes the physical nature of man (physical anthropomorphic stage). Man also creates lower animals in his image when he endows animals with his attributes and form. Stories abound of animals who marry human beings, live in houses, eat human food, talk, shoot arrows, and exhibit in general the mental and moral traits of man. Anthropomorphism is also applied to the plant world, as the spirit of a tree becomes, by the process of anthropomorphism, a god, or a supernatural being endowed with human characteristics. Osiris, for example, was originally an immanent tree spirit. Man viewed the world through himself and consequently not only endowed the tangible with his qualities but built up the intangible in his own form and endowed it with his inner nature.

Goethe says it succinctly: "Man never knows how anthromorphic he is."

Thus everywhere since the beginning of religious concept, man has projected himself into his gods. Even the animal gods *per se* possessed human reason, and purpose, and eventually acquired the ability to transform themselves into men temporarily. The animal-headed gods of Egypt are projections of this dual concept. The Greek gods in human form who walked and talked on earth typify the inevitable anthropomorphic trend. Xenophanes wrote, in the 6th century B.C., "The gods of the Ethiopians are swarthy and flat-nosed; the gods of the Thracians are fair-haired and blue-eyed." Prayer thus becomes basically a request, as of man to man; sacrifice partakes of the nature of a bargain *(do ut des,* I give that you may give), or a gift. The names of the gods everywhere mirror the man-concept: Father, King of Kings, Lord of Hosts, Above Old Man, Sky Woman, Our Grandmother, etc. Even the concept of an immaterial god, bodiless, completely spiritual, is conceived in terms of the human soul. [MEL]

Antichrist An opponent or enemy of Christ, originally probably the incarnate devil: the archetypal opponent of Christ, expected by early Christians to appear before the end of the world and the second coming of Christ (I *John* ii, 18, 22; II *John* vii). In the New Testament this concept is variously worded as the man of sin (II *Thess.* ii, 3), Belial (II *Cor.* vi, 15). In *Dan.* vii, the beast, the antimessiah of Jewish eschatology. It is believed that the idea of Antichrist had its origin in the Babylonian chaos myths in which Tiamat rebelled against and was defeated by Marduk. Thus the opponent of God often appeared in the form of a terrible dragon. The Antichrist of *Daniel* was a mighty ruler, the leader of huge armies, who would destroy three kings, persecute the saints, rule three and a half years, and devastate the temple of God. In Moslem literature the false messiah (masihu 'd-dajjal) was to overrun the earth mounted on an ass, and rule 40 days, leaving only Mecca and Medina safe.

The historical figure first attributed to Antichrist was the Syrian king Antiochus IV Epiphanes, the persecutor of the Jews. Gradually, the bitter feeling against Rome, that actuated the Jews from 30 to 130 A.D., permitted no other conception than that Rome's ruler would marshal the heathens for the final struggle. Nero filled the ideal of wickedness sufficiently to be considered a worthy Antichrist. This belief spread among the Christians as they suffered from the Roman power and gradually the figure of Antichrist became a type of God-opposing tyrant incarnate now in one and then another historical character.

By the 12th century people saw Antichrist in every national, political, social, or ecclesiastical opponent; the name sounded on all sides in the struggle between Emperor and Pope, between heretics and the church. Even the view that the Pope of Rome was the Antichrist, or his forerunner, was cultivated by the Franciscans, who held to the ideal of poverty, and by Martin Luther. As events in the history of the Middle Ages seemed to indicate the approach of Antichrist, myths concerning him became widespread. Some believed him a devil in a phantom body, others an incarnate demon, others a desperately wicked man acting upon diabolic inspiration. Myths, recorded by Rabanus Maurus, state that the Man-fiend would heal the sick, raise the dead, restore sight to the blind, hearing to the deaf, speech to the dumb; he would raise storms and calm them, remove mountains and make trees flourish or wither at a word in an attempt to pervert and mislead men.

Rumors of the birth of Antichrist circulated so rapidly and caused so much agitation that Henry IV of France issued an edict in 1599 forbidding the mention of the subject. A witch under torture in 1600 acknowledged that she had rocked the infant Antichrist on her knees and that he had claws on his feet and spoke all languages. In an announcement of the birth of Antichrist in 1623 purporting to come from the brothers of the Order of St. John, he is described as a dusky child with ". . . pleasant mouth and eyes, teeth pointed like those of a cat, ears large . . . the said child, incontinent on his birth, walked and talked perfectly well."

Legends of Antichrist reached their height during the Middle Ages and then gradually died out. During World War II Hitler was sometimes referred to as the Antichrist. [SPH]

ants Small social insects found from the arctics to the tropics, in cities, deserts, fields, forests, beaches, and mountains. Because of their numbers and distribution, they play an important part in folklore and social ethnology. The Hebrews considered ants wise (*Prov.* xxx, 24–8); among Hindus black ants are sacred; in Bulgaria and Switzerland they are a bad omen; in Estonia a good omen; in France bad luck follows the destruction of an ant's nest. The Pueblo Indians of North America believe ants are vindictive and cause diseases; disturbing or urinating on an ant-hill will especially anger them. And the diseases caused by ants can be cured only by an Ant Doctor or Ant Society. The Zuñi believe that ants are helpful war insects because their activities obliterate tracks, and therefore the Ant Society has a ritual function in Zuñi war dances. The Hopi Indians believe the first people were ants; the Apaches call the Navahos the ant people, and Taos women are told that they will turn into red ants if they consort with white men. In a myth of the Kariri Indians (Chaco) the red ants cut the tree by which the first people climbed to the sky.

Ants play a part in the religious beliefs of people scattered over the globe. In Dahomey and Porto Novo, West Africa, ants are considered messengers of the serpent god, New Guinea natives believe that a second death after the first is possible, in which case the soul becomes an ant. (See AFTERWORLD.) The Aruntas of Australia believe that the bite of a bulldog ant will kill the power of a medicine man. The Hindus and Jains give food to ants on days associated with the souls of the blessed dead. The Aztecs believed that the black and red ants showed Quetzalcoatl the place of maize. The Shans believe the earth was brought from the depths by a species of white ant.

In China the ant is a symbol of patriotism and virtue as well as of self-interest. In American folklore ants know when it will rain and if there are many ants in summer there will be a cold winter; to dream of ants means prosperity. In Morocco patients are fed ants to overcome lethargy. A tea made from white ants is administered by some American Negroes to prevent whooping cough. Guiana Indians use ants as counter-irritants. The sting of ants is explained in a Tagalog story in which the ant, hearing that the snake had received a gift of poison from God, obtained the same power and then scurried back to earth so quickly that his speed enraged God. So he was deprived of part of his power lest he use it unreasonably. Among the Apalai (South America) the painful bite of black ants is used to drive away the demons brought into the village by strangers. Girls of the Guiana Indians are stung by ants at puberty to make them strong to bear the burden of maternity or as purification. The Mauhes of Brazil force the boys to thrust their arms into sleeves stuffed with ferocious ants again and again until they are able to endure the pain without a sign of emotion. When he has reached that point of endurance, a Mauhe boy is considered a man and can marry.

In Jewish and Mohammedan legend, the ants taught Solomon modesty and humility. In a German story ants carried silk threads to a prisoner who made a rope from them and escaped. In a Chinese transformation story a monkey was changed into an ant.

Anu or **Ana** In Babylonian mythology, the sky god, chief god of the great triad of Anu, Enlil, and Ea: city god of Uruk (Erech), creator of star spirits and the demons of cold, rain, and darkness. Anu was enthroned in heaven on the northern pole. He is the fount of the authority of the gods, the ruler of destiny, and with Bel one of the two great Mesopotamian gods. Compare AN; SEMITIC MYTHOLOGY.

Anubis or **Anpu** In Egyptian religion, the jackal-headed or jackal god, guardian of tombs and patron of embalming, who shared with Thōth the office of conductor of the dead. In the judgment hall of Amenti he weighed the hearts of the dead against the feather of truth and right. In the early Pyramid age Anubis was the god of the underworld, but was replaced in the V Dynasty by Osiris, becoming, with his brother Upuaut, "sons" and attendants. Anubis was identified by the Greeks with Hermes. In Egyptian mythology, Anubis is the son of Nephthys or Isis and Osiris. He embalmed the body of Osiris (in one myth he swallowed his father) until Isis resuscitated it.

Anunnaki or **Ennuki** (1) In Sumerian mythology, the children and followers of An: the dreaded judges of the netherworld.

(2) In Babylonian mythology, deities of the earth (underworld): the star gods who had sunk below the horizon and who pronounced judgment on men as they entered the underworld, determining the conditions of their sojourn there. Compare IGIGI.

ao In Polynesian mythology, the period of light in which man has existed, as contrasted with *po*, the dark time of the spirit world. Ao is also the personification of the daylight and of the world, i.e. the world of the living. The long *Kumulipo* genealogy of Hawaii is divided into two sections, the second of which deals with ao, with the coming of light, the creation of man, and the generations of men. Compare ATUA.

apacheta A cairn: found generally in the high passes of the Peruvian and Bolivian Andes. Native travelers add a stone to the heap, or offer as a sacrifice an eyelash, the coca which they chew, or an old sandal. This observance is supposed to relieve the traveler of his fatigue and to insure the success of his journey. [AM]

Apakura The heroine of a legend of the Marquesas, Samoa, and New Zealand. Apakura (Apekua in the Marquesas version that follows) is one of two children in human form of a chief. Her son is slain when he goes for his bride, the daughter of Hatea-motua, although he gives signs of who he is and the chief's priest warns against killing him. Seeking for revenge, Apakura enlists the aid of one of her brothers, who tries to build a canoe but is balked by the tree Aniani-te-ani, which refuses to be felled. The assistance of a long-armed brother is obtained; he tells where to get the adze to fell the tree, and snatches people, to be sacrificed at the dedication of the boat, from the house of Hatea-motua. Then the champions of Apakura slay the defenders of Hatea-motua, a vine that drags canoes down, seaweed that traps them, and an octopus that eats them. Hatea-motua is killed and Apakura has her revenge. The details of the story vary to some degree through the islands but in outline it is essentially the same story of revenge for lost child.

Apalala In Buddhist legend, a water dragon or serpent who lived at the source of the Swat River. His conversion by Buddha is often depicted in Buddhist art.

Apauk-kyit Lōk In Kachin (Burma) mythology, an old man who was the cause of death. He lived at the time all men were immortal. Nine times he grew old and lost his teeth, but each time he was mysteriously rejuvenated. One day he found a sĕkhai (squirrel?) sleeping. He covered it with clothes and placed it in a basket, then went and hid. Rumor spread that the old man was dead. When the Lord of the Sun heard, he examined the man's sumri (life essence) and found it unchanged. So he sent messengers to investigate the situation. They, while dancing at the funeral feast, covered their feet with honey and touched the clothes, thus drawing them away so that the fraud was discovered. The Lord of the Sun was so angry that he cut off Apauk-kyit Lōk's life connection. Thus death entered the world.

Apepi, Aapep, or **Apophis** In Egyptian mythology and religion, the foe of the sun god: leader of the demons against the sun by whom they were overcome, and hence a symbol of storm and the struggle between light and darkness. He was represented as a crocodile with a hideous face, as a serpent with many coils, or a snake with a human head. The sun (Horus or Rā or Osiris) fought Apepi and his demons throughout the night in his journey from west to east, winning the battle every morning.

Aphrodite In Greek religion, the goddess of love, beauty, and marriage; an influence on the fertility of plants and animals; the epitome of feminine charm: sometimes the protectress of sailors: in Sparta a war goddess. Originally she may have been an oriental nature divinity similar to Ishtar. Under the title Aphrodite Urania, she was identified by the Greeks with the Semitic goddess of the heavens, Astarte, and with the Iranian goddess Anahita. In later Greek literature, influenced by Plato, she became the embodiment of spiritual love, the antithesis of the Athenian Aphrodite Pandemos (personification of earthly or common love). Her cult, in one form or another, was universal in the Mediterranean lands and Aphrodisia (festivals in her honor) were frequent. In Greco-Roman Egypt she was identified with and partially supplanted Hathor. The Romans identified her with Venus.

In Greek mythology she was pictured variously as the lover of Adonis, the mother of Æneas, the wife of Hephæstus, and the lover or consort of Ares. According to Homer she was the daughter of Zeus and Dione. According to Hesiod she arose from the foam of the sea and landed either at Cythera or at Paphos in Cyprus, hence she was sometimes called Cypris, Cytherea, or Aphrodite Anadyomene.

Apis or **Hāp** In Egyptian religion, a sacred bull worshipped from the IV Dynasty to the time of the Emperor Julian. See HAP.

apo A ceremony or rite of the Ashanti of the Gold Coast, West Africa. It is directed towards chiefs and rulers in the belief that those who wield power over others need protection against the resentment of those whom they may have injured. The performance consists of the voicing of all kinds of derision, reproach, and maledictions on the part of the subjects against their chiefs. This is believed to save the souls of the chiefs from the harm which would inevitably result from the ill-will or anger of their subjects. The Ashanti believe that the cumulative power of repressed resentment or anger will harm, even kill, the object of it, and that the ritual expression of it not only protects but saves all concerned. (Herskovits, *Man and His Works,* 59)

apocalypse In Jewish and Christian literature, a revelation of hidden things given by God to one of his chosen saints, or the written account of such a revelation. Characteristic features of apocalyptic literature include revelation of the mysteries and secrets of heaven, explanations of natural phenomena, predictions of impending events, and a picture of heaven and hell. These are often disclosed through a vision or dream, or brought by angels, and embellished with mythological material borrowed from both Jewish early eschatology (Old Testament mythical beings such as Leviathan, Behemoth, Gog and Magog) and the Hindu and Egyptian cosmogonies. Another characteristic of apocalyptic writings is the marked use of the elements of mystery and fantastic imagery—especially the beasts in which the properties of men, birds, reptiles, mammals, or purely imaginary beings are combined in startling and often grotesque manner (*Dan.* vii, 1–8; viii, 3–12).

Apocatequil The culture hero in the mythology of the region of Huamachuco: father of the twin heroes hatched from eggs. See TWINS. [AM]

Apollo One of the most important of the Greek Olympian gods, representing the most complex creation of polytheism; the god of youth and manly beauty, of poetry, music, and the wisdom of the oracles. In his earlier character (he is believed to have been introduced variously from the north, from Asia Minor, and from Egypt), he was the fosterer of flocks, guardian of colonies, villages, and streets. He was also the sovereign god of healing and ceremonial purification in association with Asklepios, who performed the actual healing functions. To Homer he was the sender as well as the stayer of plagues and the giver of sudden death. As Apollo Smintheus, or mouse god, he was either the protector or destroyer of mice (an image of a mouse stood beside the tripod in his temple in the Troad and white mice lived

under the altar). As Phœbus (Phœbus Apollo) he was god of radiance and light, later identified with Helios.

Numerous festivals to Apollo played a major role in Greek life. The most important were the Delphinia, held in May to celebrate the opening of navigation and the influence of the sun in restoring life and warmth to the creatures of the waves, especially the dolphins which were highly esteemed by seafarers; the Thargelia, held in May to propitiate the deity of the sun, to celebrate the ripening of vegetation, and to return thanks for the first-fruit; the Hyacinthia, celebrated in July in Sparta as a fast and feast corresponding to the Thargelia; the Carnea, held in August in Sparta to propitiate the god and as thanksgiving for the vintage; the Daphnephora, held in the spring to celebrate the day of Apollo's coming and believed to have symbolized the year; the Pythia, celebrated every fourth summer to commemorate his victory over the Python.

The oracles of Apollo, particularly that of Delphi, were widely consulted, especially during the Peloponnesian War when the craze for knowledge of the future exceeded even that evidenced during modern wars. The universal recognition of the Apollo cult and the oracle of Apollo increased the importance of the Delphian amphictyony politically.

In Greek mythology, Apollo was the son of Zeus and Leto; twin of Artemis; lover of Psamathe of Argos, Coronis of Thessaly, Clymene, Calliope, and Cyrene; spurned by Daphne and Marpessa; wooed unsuccessfully by the nymph Clytie; and father of Orpheus, Asklepios, and Aristæus. Shortly after his birth he spent a year in the land of the Hyperboreans, then went to Delphi where he slew the Python, sang his song of victory, the Pæan (still synonymous with jubilation and victory), and instituted the Pythian games. He slew Tityus and the children of Niobe and, with Artemis, overthrew the Aloadæ. Phaethon drove Helios' sun chariot on a wild ride across the sky and was killed by Zeus. Asklepios, Apollo's physician-son, restored the dead to life, and paid with his own. Apollo, indignant, killed the Cyclops who wrought the thunderbolt used by Zeus to kill Asklepios, and was sentenced to serve a mortal (King Admetus of Thessaly) as a shepherd for a year. The birth, wanderings, and battle with the Python are sometimes explained as symbolic of the diurnal and annual journeys of the sun. See DELPHIC ORACLE.

Apollodorus An Athenian grammarian of the 2nd century B.C. The *Library,* generally attributed to him, is a principal source of knowledge of Greek mythology and is said to be an abridgment of a lost larger work of the gods. Frazer, following Robert, in his introduction to the *Library,* doubts that the work is by Apollodorus the Grammarian and, from internal evidence, states that the work was written in the 1st or 2nd century A.D.

apotropaism The science and art of preventing or overcoming evils, usually by incantation or a ritual act. Such rituals and incantations are world-wide. Typical are the central European custom of naked women drawing a plowshare around a village at night to drive away an epidemic, and the Japanese custom of offering a white horse, pig, and cock during the seed-time ritual to save the crops from a curse.

Apotropaic remedies include human spittle, blood, human excrements, strong smells such as that of garlic used in southern Europe to combat witches, various plants (vervain, dill, oreganum, rowan, juniper, flax, holly, shamrock, ringwort), noise (the bells of the Jewish high priest and Christian churches originally rung to drive away evil spirits before services, and church bells still rung in parts of Europe to dispel hailstorms), dances (to drive away evil spirits, diseases), miscellaneous objects (blue glass beads used today on camels, bells on horses and cattle, metal suns and moons used on harness, the hex signs on Pennsylvania Dutch barns, and the horseshoe found over many U.S. doors), various gestures, and incantations.

apple A pome fruit and the tree bearing this fruit, widely cultivated in the temperate regions, originally growing wild in Europe and western Asia. The apple tree and its fruit play an important role in classical, Arabian, Teutonic, and Celtic mythology and folklore. The apple as such is not mentioned in the Bible in conjunction with Adam and Eve. Despite the popular conception of the story, the cause of the trouble was the "fruit (unidentified) of the tree which is in the midst of the garden" (*Gen.* iii, 3). The apple mentioned in the *Song of Solomon* (ii, 3, 5; vii, 8; viii, 5) and in *Joel* (i, 12) may be the apricot or the orange (the apples of gold, *Prov.* xxv, 11) which flourished in Asia Minor.

In mythology and folklore the apple is celebrated in numerous functions: as a means to immortality, an emblem of fruitfulness, an offering or a distraction in suitor contests, a cure, a love charm, a test of chastity, a means of divination, a magic object, and according to Voltaire's story of Newton, it was responsible for the discovery of the law of gravity. In Greek mythology, the golden apples of the Hesperides were sought by Hercules for Eurystheus because of their immortality-giving quality. Scandinavian mythology includes the story of the apples of perpetual youth kept by Idhunn in Asgard. The wonderful apple thrown to Conle, son of Conn, by the woman from the Land of the Living, was food and drink to him for a month, and never diminished; but it made him long for the woman and beautiful country of women to which she was enticing him. Gna, messenger of the Scandinavian Frigga, dropped an apple (symbol of fruitfulness) to King Rerir. He and his wife ate it together, with the result that they had a child. In Greek myth the suitor of Atalanta, compelled to race with her, threw down golden apples to distract her, and so won the race and the girl. Frey sent eleven golden apples to Gerda as a marriage offer. The apple is the central tree of heaven in Iroquois Indian mythology. In a Wyandot myth, an apple tree shades the lodge of the Mighty Ruler.

The apple of Prince Ahmed in the *Arabian Nights* cured every disorder. In U.S. Negro folklore, apple-shaped birthmarks can be removed by rubbing them with apples and keeping the person on an apple diet. They are also used in voodoo love charms. The apple is a love charm also in Danish, German, and English folklore. In Danish folktale it serves as a chastity test, fading when the owner is unfaithful. In Ireland, Wales, Scotland, and the Isle of Man apples are used in divination. The custom of dipping for apples or catching one on a string on Halloween is a remnant of druidic divination. The apple is a magic object in Scandinavian, Irish, Icelandic, Teutonic, Breton, English, and Arabian folktales.

It is also the subject of numerous proverbs and sayings: Eat an apple going to bed, Make the doctor beg his bread (now, An apple a day keeps the doctor away), There is small choice in rotten apples, and From the egg to apples (now, From soup to nuts).

April Fool's Day Same as ALL FOOLS' DAY.

Apsaras In Hindu mythology and religion, one of the celestial water nymphs or dancers of Indra's heaven. In the *Atharva-Veda*, the Apsarases were associated with the Gandharvas, and their sphere was extended to include the earth where they haunt several varieties of fig tree in which the music of their cymbals and lutes is heard. According to the *Rāmāyana* they were produced at the Churning of the Ocean (their name signifies "moving in the water"). When they first appeared, neither the gods nor the asuras would have them as wives, so they became promiscuous. They are pictured as beautiful and voluptuous and are offered as the reward for fallen heroes in Indra's paradise.

Apsu In Babylonian religion, the primeval fertile waters; the Deep, home of Ea; the origin of all things in the present orderly universe as opposed to Tiamat, the dragon of watery destruction and chaos. Apsu was slain by Ea-Enki and Mummu was imprisoned in a house built on his body. From the clay of Apsu man was fashioned: this seems to be Sumerian myth, for Kingu's blood serves this purpose in the *Enuma Elish*. In the Babylonian creation myth of the *Enuma Elish,* Apsu is the primeval father who existed before the heavens and earth were made; consort of Tiamat from whom sprang the gods; father of Mummu. See SEMITIC MYTHOLOGY.

àp thmòp (feminine *mī thmòp*) A Cambodian sorcerer: chiefly a practitioner of black magic. The àp thmòp foretells the future, sells amulets and charms, and causes illness by means of incantations or spells. In casting spells on people the sorcerer makes a wax figure and pricks it at the spot where the customer wishes the person to be affected. Compare KRU.

apuku Forest spirits worshiped by the Bush Negroes of Dutch Guiana and held to inhabit the natural clearings found in the bush. These small, powerful beings are much feared, and the places where they are believed to dwell are never used for cultivation or camping grounds. They are to be assigned to the general West African category of "little people," which includes the Ashanti *mmoatia*, the Dahomean *azizan*, and the Yoruban *ijimere*. Whether the Jamaican *pukkumerian* cult is comparable to the apuku cult of Surinam cannot be said, but this has been advanced as a hypothesis to explain the forms of worship found under this designation in Jamaica. [MJH]

Aqhat The central figure of a fragmentary Canaanite death-and-resurrection myth, told in the Ugaritic Ras Shamra texts. Aqhat is the perfect son bestowed upon Daniel by El; the father gives the son a bow made by the divine smith. Anath, the war goddess, covets the bow and tries to buy it from Aqhat. He refuses. She makes a second offer: "Ask for life and I will give thee; for not dying and I will bestow upon thee." He resists this offer too, for "How can a mortal acquire permanence?" She storms at him, runs off to complain to El, and finally conspires to have Yatpan, a killer for hire, murder Aqhat. The mother of vultures, Ṣamal, eats Aqhat's body while (this is conjectural) Anath considers whether she will restore life. Daniel recovers the fat and bones of his son and buries them, while Paghat, Aqhat's sister, gets Yatpan drunk and kills him. The portions relating to Aqhat's resurrection, whether by Daniel from the recovered fat and bones or by Anath, have not yet been found (if the reconstruction of the myth is correct and if they exist). H. L. Ginsberg (*BASOR* 97) draws a parallel between this story and the Biblical tale of Naboth and the vineyard coveted by Jezebel and Ahab (I *Kings* xxi). See SEMITIC MYTHOLOGY.

Aquarius The Water-Carrier: the 11th constellation or sign of the Zodiac, anciently the location of the winter solstice. Astrologers equate Aquarius with cold, rainstorms, floods, and dark.

The ancient Egyptians equated this constellation with Khnum, god of water and creator of men, beneficent bringer of water to their arid land. They believed the Nile overflowed its banks when the Water-Carrier dipped his bucket into it. The Arabs too rejoiced with the rising of Aquarius who brought the warm rains. The Arabs thought of it as the source of all the rivers of the earth; but their representations of it show only the bucket, or sometimes a mule carrying two water jugs.

The Babylonians called it Gu, or Overflowing-Water-Jar, and associated it with their mythical Deluge and their 11th month Shabatu, Curse of Rain. The Akkadians called it Ku-ur-ku, Seat of Flowing Waters. Persians, Hebrews, Syrians, Turks, each had a word for it meaning Water-Bucket.

In Greek mythology, Aquarius was originally identified with Zeus, symbolizing creation and the life-giving power of water. Later, it was said to be Ganymede, cup-bearer of the gods. Other Greek myths identify it with Deucalion, survivor of the Greek Deluge, and with Aristæus, rain-giver to the people of Ceos.

This constellation was the first sign of the old Chinese Zodiac, the Rat, bringer of water. Jesuit influence changed it to Paon Ping, Precious Vase; but it is still the Rat in Central Asia, Cochin China, and Japan. It is also the first sign of the Zodiac in India.

Aquila The Eagle: a constellation of the northern hemisphere, described as flying eastward across the Milky Way. It was interpreted as an eagle alike by the ancient Hebrews, Greeks, and Romans. The Hebrew name for it was Neshr (Eagle, Falcon, or Vulture). The Arabs called it Al 'Okāb, Black Eagle. To the early Turks it was Taushaugjil, or Hunting Eagle. Hindu mythology interprets the three bright stars of Aquila as the three huge footsteps of Vishnu in his stride across the heavens. Altair is the brightest of these three, situated exactly opposite Vega across the Milky Way. To the Chinese the constellation Aquila is thought of as the Draught Oxen, belonging to the Herdsman. For the Chinese story of the celestial Weaving Maid (Vega) and her Herdsman lover (Altair) see CHIH NÜ.

Ara (1) or **Er** In Armenian mythology, the beloved of the Semitic Semiramis who proposed to marry him or hold him as a lover. Ara rejected her and was killed by the forces of the goddess which she led against him. When she could not revive him, she dressed up one of her lovers and pretended that the gods had restored Ara to life. According to Plato Ara was revived when he was about to be laid on the funeral pyre.

(2) A southern constellation: interpreted by Ptolemy

and others as an Altar, a Censer, a Brazier. By the Romans it was variously thought to be the altar of Dionysus, an Incense Burner, a little altar on which incense was burned for the dead, a Hearth, and also occasionally as Vesta, the hearth goddess. In Arabian astronomy it is called Al Mijmarah, the Censer, an adoption from the Greeks. Medieval Biblical scholars and astronomers thought of it as one of the altars of Moses, or as the altar built by Noah after the Flood.

Arabian Nights' Entertainments or the **Thousand and One Nights** A collection of stories written in Arabic and first introduced into Europe in a French translation by Antoine Galland in 1704: literally the *Thousand Nights and a Night*, but generally referred to as *Arabian Nights*. The framework of the story is Persian, but the stories told by Sheherazade are believed to be Arabian, Indian, Egyptian, and Jewish. They include merry tales, fairy tales, rogue stories, stories of buried treasure, etc.

Arachne In Greek mythology, the most skilful weaver of Lydia who challenged Athena to a weaving contest. Athena wove into her web the stories of those who had aroused the anger of the gods, while Arachne chose stories of the errors of the gods. Enraged at the excellence of the work, Athena tore Arachne's web to tatters. Arachne hanged herself in grief and was transformed by Athena into a spider.

àràk In Cambodian belief, one of the good spirits or tutelary guardians of families. The àràk lives in a tree or in the house, and is invoked especially in cases of illness. It seems to be a human ancestor or friend of the family, long dead, who has become its protector. When someone is ill, a kru (shaman) is called in who is able to make the àràk incarnate in himself and with his aid discovers the evil spirit which is torturing the patient. The guilty spirit is then exorcised by the spraying of rice-wine over the patient and by gashing him. A festival is held each year between January and March in honor of the àràks.

Aralu or **Arallu** In Babylonian religion and mythology, the desolate land of no return in the underworld to which the soul descended after death. This was surrounded by seven walls pierced by as many gates and ruled by Nergal and Allatu. The souls "like birds with wings" lived in darkness amidst dust surrounded by evil spirits and demons. There the souls ate dust and clay, and unless they were provided with food and drink by the living, wandered in search of garbage and discarded food.

Aramazd The chief deity of ancient Armenia, who, although supreme, was not exclusive: a corruption of the Persian Ahura Mazda. Aramazd was the creator of heaven and earth, father of gods, especially of Anāhit, Mihr, and Nanē (no consort is named), and the peace-loving giver of prosperity and abundance. He presided over the Navasard (New Year's festival) and made the fields fertile and the vineyards fruitful.

Arawn Lord and king of Annwn, the Brythonic Otherworld. The *Mabinogion* tells the story of how Arawn one time out hunting in this world met up with Pwyll, king of Dyfed, with whom he struck up great friendship. They made a compact to exchange shapes and kingdoms for a year, in order that Pwyll might overcome Havgan, Arawn's rival for the kingship of

Annwn. At the end of that year Pwyll disposed of Havgan with a single blow. Then Pwyll and Arawn met again, exchanged shapes once more, and each returned to his own kingdom, no one but the two of them knowing that either had been absent from his own country. Pwyll discovered that his kingdom had never been ruled with greater wisdom, generosity, and justice than in the year just gone by. Arawn discovered that for a year Pwyll had shown affection to the beautiful queen of Annwn only in public and had withheld himself from her at night. Such faithfulness and honor the two discovered in each other that they were strong friends forever.

Arawn was owner of the magic caldron that Arthur coveted, and all the various marvelous animals ascribed to Celtic Otherworlds. Certain marvelous swine are mentioned, given by Arawn to Pryderi, son of Pwyll. The *Triads* tell of a wonderful bitch and a white roebuck (and in some versions, a lapwing) stolen by Amaethon, son of Dôn, the theft of which caused the Battle of the Trees.

arbutus Any member of a genus (*Arbutus*) of evergreen trees or shrubs whose bark, leaves, and fruit are used in drugs: a common name for the trailing arbutus (*Epigæa repens*), the state flower of Massachusetts. The arbutus was sacred to the Romans and was an attribute of the goddess Cardea, who used it to drive away witches and to protect little children. Ovid speaks of its fruit as the food of man during the Golden Age. Water distilled from the leaves and blossoms of arbutus was considered powerful against the plague and various poisons. The Greeks believed that snakes which fed upon the berries ceased to be venomous.

The arbutus of Algonquian Indian legend is *Epigæa repens*. Peboan, the winter manitou, sat in his lodge, weak and weary, for he had found no game. He called for help and Segun, the summer manitou, clothed in grass and young leaves, walked into the lodge with a message that Peboan's time on earth was ended. The old man gradually disappeared. His furs turned to leaves and his tepee became a tree. Segun took some of these leaves and put them into the ground, breathing upon them. They freshened and changed into the trailing arbutus, the sign to children that summer has come and winter has gone away.

Arcadian hind In Greek legend, the hind (also known as the hind of Cerynea) chased by Hercules for a year and captured as his third labor. The hind, with antlers of gold and hoofs of bronze, was sacred to Artemis and could not be killed. Hercules tired it out by chasing it all over the Peloponnesus (or all over the world). He brought it back to Eurystheus and then released it.

arch A structural member rounded vertically to span an opening. In folk practices arches are used to purify, cure, and to form a barrier against evil spirits, enemies, and diseases. The most familiar use of the arch was that made by the Romans who marched under a triumphal arch after battle. This has been explained as a purificatory measure to rid them of the stain of bloodshed and to impose a barrier between the men and the ghosts of their enemies.

A cure for whooping-cough, boils, or rheumatism (England, Wales, France) was to crawl under an arch formed by a bramble. The popular cure for scrofula (Bulgaria) was to make a patient crawl naked three times through an arch made of vine branches. The Bagandas transfer disease to a plantain tree, carry the tree out to wasteland, and then raise an arch of branches over the path taken, to prevent the return of the disease. A similar custom is practiced in the Cameroons where the spirit of smallpox is drummed out of a village and then the village is enclosed with creeper ropes and the paths arched with bent poles to which are suspended plants, nests of termite ants, and a freshly killed dog.

archangel An angel of highest rank: in Christian legend, one of the seven, in the Koran one of the four chief angels: in Roman Catholic theology a member of the eighth of nine divisions of angels. The names of the archangels vary, although the first four are generally Michael, Gabriel, Raphael, and Uriel. In the apocalyptic *Enoch* (xxi), they are listed as Uriel, Raphael, Raguel, Michael, Sariel, Gabriel, and Jerahmeel. In the Koran the list includes Gabriel, angel of revelations; Michael, the champion who fights the battles of faith; Azrael, the angel of death; and Israfel, who is to sound the trumpet of resurrection.

The dominant role of astrology during the medieval period led to the association of the archangels with the planets and constellations. Various archangels were assigned to the planets by Jewish astrologers, but the preponderance of references seem to assign Raphael to the Sun, Gabriel to the Moon, Aniel to Venus, Michael to Mercury, Kafziel to Saturn, Zadkiel to Jupiter, and Samael to Mars. In medieval Christian thought, derived from the Moslem philosopher Averroes, the Sun was associated with Michael, the Moon with Gabriel, Venus with Anael (Aniel), Mercury with Raphael, Saturn with Cassiel (Kafziel), Jupiter with Sachiel (Zadkiel), and Mars with Samael. The archangels were also bound up with the 12 signs of the Zodiac, new ones being borrowed or invented to make up the required number, and were used by conjurers who employed their names in effecting cures. There are close parallels between the archangels and the seven planetary spirits of Babylonia, the Amesha Spentas of Zoroastrianism, and the Hindu Ādityas.

arch dances Dances which include as a dominant figure the procession of the coupled dancers through an arch formed by others. This arch is an ancient symbol of the green bough, and now survives in the Virginia Reel and London Bridge. Innumerable folk dances of Ireland, England, Scandinavia use this motif, forgetful of its meaning. As final figure of the Provençal farandoule some of its import shimmers through. In Spain and its colonies the arch dance survives as ceremonial in a special elaborated form, namely: each dancer holds a bent half-hoop decorated with flowers. Sometimes these dancers are Basque sword dancers, sometimes they are girls dressed as *pastoras* or shepherdesses. Mexican carnival celebrations feature these flowered arches in the danza de los arcos, danced by men of Tlapalita, Tlaxcala, and by the *pastorcitas* of Taxco, Guerrero. As commonly in Mexican ceremonial dances, it is difficult to assign either native or foreign origin, and only possible to suggest a blend of pagan customs. [GPK]

Archives of Folk and Primitive Music, Indiana University The Archives of Folk and Primitive Music at Indiana University, Department of Anthropology, in charge of Dr. George Herzog, established recently, comprise approximately 10,000 phonograph records with at least 20,000 recordings. Almost all this material consists of private, non-commercial recordings. The bulk is concerned with primitive music. The music of the North American Indian is represented by over 7,000 records; thus the Archives are, in this field, the largest depository in existence. Smaller collections illustrate the native music of South America, Africa, Asia, and the Pacific; the several branches of Oriental music, and the folk music of various nations. Over two thirds of the material was gathered during the era of the phonograph cylinder; much of it is of considerable historical and musicological value and is irreplaceable. The cylinder collections are being recorded on disks in order to improve their quality, to make their contents available for study, and to safeguard the fragile originals. This large collection includes deposits of many private individuals and of various scientific institutions, such as the American Museum of Natural History, the Chicago Museum of Natural History, Columbia University, Yale University, and the University of Chicago.

Especial efforts were made in connection with many of the collections to secure also an exact transcription and linguistic analysis of the song texts so that these can be studied together with the music. There is also extensive information on musical instruments, on the ethnological background, and very detailed bibliographic data.

The primary purpose of the Archives is to function as a study collection and as a depository for the safekeeping of materials pertaining to traditional music. The Archives cooperate with other institutions and with collectors. Publication of occasional albums of records is intended.   George Herzog

Arcturus A golden yellow star, Alpha in the constellation Boötes, but described by Ptolemy as golden-red. It is brilliant and conspicuous in the summer evening sky, so brilliant as to be visible 15 or sometimes 20 minutes before sunset. Arcturus has been known and mentioned variously since earliest times; Hesiod (c. 800 B.C.) was the first to mention that it rises 50 days after the winter solstice. There are indications that it was identified as early as the 15th century B.C. in an Egyptian stellar calendar. It is known to have been the Chaldean Papsukal, Guardian Messenger, and deity of the 10th Chaldean month. The allusions to Arcturus in *Job* ix, 9 and xxxviii, 32 in the King James version are now regarded as mistranslations of references to the Bear. In India this star was called (among other names) Nishtya, or Outcast, perhaps because it lies so far north of the zodiac. To the Arabians it was the Keeper of Heaven, Al Hāris al Samā, probably because it dominated the early evening sky before the other stars were "let out." It has always been regarded as a stormy star, in its rising and setting, for both the sailor and the farmer; but astrologically it portends wealth and fame for anyone born under it. Hippocrates in 460 B.C. assigned to it various influences on the human body, and held that all diseases waxed more critical after the rising of Arcturus.

Ardhanārī In Hindu mythology, Śiva, represented as half-male and half-female, typifying the incarnation of the male and female principles of the world. See ŚAKTI.

Ardvī Surā Anāhita In Iranian mythology, the source of the celestial waters, deified as a goddess of prosperity and fertility: literally, the wet, strong, and spotless one. Ardvī Surā Anāhita is personified as a handsome woman, stronger than horses, wearing shining gold footgear and golden raiment. See ANĀHITA.

areca One of the sacred plants of India. Its nuts are used to adorn the gods and with the betel leaf it enters into every important ceremony of the Brāhmans. Village deities of the Kurumo caste are represented by five areca nuts which are kept in a box. The Indian custom of presenting an areca nut to guests is traditional.

The areca is used by the Melanesians of the southeastern Solomon Islands in black magic, as propitiatory offerings to ghosts, in religious and betrothal ceremonies, and as a sign of mourning. Areca palms are cut down when a chief dies. A spray of areca is held in the hand of an orator at a feast as an emblem of peace. The nuts are given to women to enlist their affection.

The areca nut and betel-chewing are important in many Asiatic and South Pacific folktales. In the Solomon Islands there are many stories of a magic areca palm that lengthened out and carried the man climbing it into the sky.

Areop-Enap In the mythology of Nauru (Micronesia), the Ancient Spider, creator of the sun and the moon. At first only Areop-Enap and the sea existed, but one day Areop-Enap discovered a mussel shell. After much trouble he opened it and crept inside, but it was so dark he could see nothing. He crawled around, felt a small snail, then a larger one. He passed on to the small snail some of his power and made it the moon. By the faint light of the moon, he spied a worm which he set to work separating the upper and lower parts of the shell to make the sky and the earth. This the worm did, and died of exhaustion. The large snail became the sun. The worm-sweat, running into the lower shell, became the sea. From stones, Areop-Enap made men to support the sky, and then traveled about the newly created world. He discovered other beings and learned their names by creating a winged creature from the dirt under his nails. This flying "bird" annoyed the people and they called to each other to kill it. Thus Areop-Enap knew what they were called.

Ares In Greek religion, a god of war representing its brutal and barbaric aspects; the son of Zeus and Hera and the lover or consort of Aphrodite. In Greco-Egyptian religion he was identified with Onouris and, as Ares Mahrem, he was worshipped in Aksum (Ethiopia). The Romans identified him with Mars. He never became a god of great moral or theological importance and his name was used to represent the war power of the enemy which would be overcome by the Greeks with the aid of their gods of civilized warfare, Zeus, Apollo, and Athena. In Greek mythology, the Aloadæ bound and imprisoned him in a metal pot until Hermes was able to rescue him 13 months later. In a Homeric merry tale he was detected by Hephæstus in an amorous intrigue with Aphrodite, caught with her in a net, and exposed to the ridicule of the gods. Sophocles called him the "god unhonored among gods."

Argo or **Argo Navis** The ship Argo: a huge constellation of the southern hemisphere, east of Canis Major: interpreted as the ship in which Jason and his fifty companions sought the Golden Fleece in Colchis. It was placed in the sky by Athena, or Poseidon, to be a guide forever across the southern seas. Another Greek myth identifies it with the first boat ever made, and the one in which Danaus and the Danaides traveled from Egypt to Rhodes. In relatively recent times it has been divided into three smaller constellations: Carina, the Keel; Puppis, the Stern; Vela, the Sail. To the Romans also it was Argo. The Arabian name was Al Sufinah, the Ship. Biblical astronomers called it Noah's Ark.

Canopus, the brilliant star in the rudder of Argo, is called Agastya for a famous Rishi of Hindu tradition, who was a stayer of storms and could control the ocean. See AGASTYA.

Argonauts In Greek mythology, the band of heroes who accompanied Jason on his quest for the Golden Fleece held by Æetes, king of Colchis. After many adventures, Jason and his men reached Colchis in the fifty-oared galley, the Argo. With the help of Medea, the king's daughter, he completed the tasks set by Æetes as the condition of surrendering the Fleece and then returned home to Iolcos taking the Fleece and Medea with him. The name is often applied to adventurous seekers after riches, as for example those taking part in the California gold rush of 1849.

Argus (1) called *Panoptes*. In Greek mythology, the giant with a hundred eyes set by Hera to guard Io during her disguise as a heifer. Hermes beguiled Argus into sleeping and slew him. Hera took his eyes and scattered them as ornaments on the tail of her peacock.

(2) In Greek legend, Odysseus's dog who recognized him on his return from his wanderings.

(3) The builder of the ship Argo, son of Phrixus or of Arestor.

Arianrhod Literally, silver wheel: a goddess of Brythonic mythology famed for her beauty, and assumed to be the daughter of Dôn. In the *Mabinogion,* she is the sister and mistress of Gwydion. She claimed to be a virgin in order to enter the service of Math, but her pretenses were given the lie by certain tests imposed on her by Math and by the birth of her twin boys, Llew Llaw Gyffes and Dylan. Dylan leapt into the sea, but Gwydion saved Llew and reared him carefully. Arianrhod so resented the boy's very existence that she endeavored to thwart his advancement in life at every turn. There is a reef off the Carnarvon coast still called Caer Arianrhod and believed to be the remains of Arianrhod's island castle where Gwydion tricked the relentless mother into bestowing on Llew the arms she intended to withhold.

In early religious belief possibly Arianrhod played the dual role of virgin plus fertility goddess. In late folklore the constellation Corona Borealis became known as Caer Arianrhod.

Aries The Ram: the first constellation or sign of the Zodiac. The very ancient eastern Mediterranean or Mesopotamian myth that the world was created when the sun entered the constellation of the Ram points to human knowledge of the Ram in those distant centuries during which the Ram held the stars of the winter solstice. By the time Hipparchus (2nd century B.C.) began to systematize astronomy and reckoned his year from the "first point of Aries," the Ram then contained the stars of the spring equinox. About 4000 years from now Aries will hold the stars of the summer solstice.

Early mythologies identify the Ram with Zeus, with Amen, the ram god of Egypt, and later with the ram of the Golden Fleece who bore the mistreated children of King Athamas away from Thessaly. In fact Aries is usually depicted as a reclining ram with head turned to observe his golden fleece. The Hebrews, Syrians, Persians, and Turks all had words for this constellation which mean Ram. One of the early Arabic names was Al Kabah al 'Alif, the Tame Ram, later just Al Hamal, the Sheep. In China this constellation was originally the Dog (Heang Low) of the Chinese zodiac, and was later renamed White Sheep (Pih Yang). It is also part of a greater Chinese constellation (involving Taurus and the Gemini) known as the White Tiger. Early church writers (12th–16th centuries) likened Aries to the ram of Abraham found in the bush, or to St. Peter, or to the Lamb of God sacrificed for the world.

In astrology Aries is held to endow with violent temper those born under his sign, and to presage some physical harm that will come to them, sometimes death by hanging.

Arikute or **Ariconte** In the mythology of the Tupi Indians of Brazil, the twin of Tamendonar or Tamanduare. A quarrel between the brothers resulted in the great flood which covered the earth. The two climbed trees on the highest mountains and saved their wives and themselves while all other men perished. From these couples, after the flood, came the Tupinamba and the Tominu who perpetually feuded and warred with each other. See TWINS.

Arioi or **Areoi Society** A Polynesian (specifically Tahiti and the Society Islands) religious association of initiates—comedians and actors—performing traditional plays and dances, joking and satirizing on certain occasions, and having mysteries connected with the god 'Oro. The Arioi were considered divine; Tangaroa or Rongo was father of the first Arioi. The Arioi of the Society Islands were ranged in seven or eight orders, the higher grades partaking of the deference accorded to divinity. The sign of their initiation into the society was tattooing, which as the initiate rose higher in the scale became more and more complex, until in the higher orders, it is said, the tattooing covered nearly the entire body. The lower groups were not permitted to have children, any born to them being killed; an attempt to preserve the child resulted in expulsion from the society. (This custom must be read into the context of a highly overpopulated area in which some form of population control was necessary.)

Members of the Arioi were of both sexes (men seem to have outnumbered women in the proportion of five to one), and the highest rank of the association consisted of a chief of men and a chief of women. The one requirement for entry into the society was inspiration; anyone could become a member, chiefs more easily than commoners and into higher ranks. To the Arioi belonged the most intelligent and the most handsome inhabitants of the island group. After a period of training and learning word for word the traditional chants, the candidate exhibited publicly his achievements. When he was accepted into the society, he took a new name, by which he was thenceforth called.

The society had houses on the various islands of the group. The members of a lodge from one island often made mass voyages, carrying the god of the Paradise of the Arioi, Romatane, in the canoes, to other islands or other places on the same island where they took up residence in these guest houses.

Their ceremonies, being associated with harvest festivals, and depicting such myths as the union of Tangaroa with matter, seem to have shocked the missionaries and other outside viewers, and, in connection with the infanticide they practiced, gave to the Arioi the reputation (reflected in related terms in several of the Polynesian languages) of great immorality. Performances of the society, by the lower grades, with the higher-ranking dignitaries of the society looking on, began with a religious chant or the telling of a myth; then a legend of some hero followed; a comic drama or an erotic word-play and a dance concluded the ceremony. The Arioi Society of the Society Islands died out with the conversion of the members to Christianity, practices such as infanticide being incompatible with the Christian religion. Similar groups existed in other Polynesian islands; unorganized but similar artists were known in the Marquesas, Cook Islands, etc. See 'ORO.

Aristæus In Greek and Roman mythology, the son of Apollo and the nymph Cyrene, guardian of herds, keeper of bees, and protector of the vine and olive. Aristæus desired Eurydice who, trying to escape him, trod on a snake and so met her death. Soon after this the bees died and Aristæus was sent by his mother to Proteus to ask for an explanation. Told that the nymphs were avenging the death of Eurydice, he sacrificed to them and paid funeral honors to Orpheus and Eurydice, and thus restored his bees to life.

Arjuna In Hindu religion and mythology, the third and most prominent of the five Pāṇḍava princes: a son of Indra. According to the *Mahābhārata*, Arjuna, a brave warrior and a famous archer, made a pilgrimage to the Himālayas to propitiate the gods and to obtain celestial weapons for use against the Kauravas. From there he went to Amarāvatī, capital of Indra's heaven, where he improved his knowledge of arms. Indra sent him against the Daityas, whom he vanquished. In the struggle with the Kauravas, Kṛishṇa acted as his charioteer and before the great battle began, recited the *Bhagavad-Gītā* to him. In modern Hinduism Arjuna is of little importance.

ark (1) The cradle made of papyrus, daubed with slime and pitch, in which Moses was hidden by his mother (*Ex.* ii, 2–3).

(2) The vessel built by Noah and occupied by Noah and his family and the animals "two and two" during the Deluge (*Gen.* vi, 14–22). This was a boxlike, three-story structure built of gopher (pine) wood, made water-tight with bitumen, and provided with cells or rooms. It was 300 cubits long, 50 cubits wide, and 30 cubits high. The ark came to rest on Mt. Ararat and after a year its occupants were able to leave it (*Gen.* viii, 13–16). Its fate is uncertain and legends concerning the finding of the ark or pieces of it have persisted throughout history.

In rabbinical literature and legend, the ark was lighted by precious stones which shone by night and were dull by day. The animals walked onto the ark of their own accord or were led on by angels, and Noah was so constantly employed in feeding them that he did not sleep during the year. The giant Og, king of Bashan, was too large to fit into the ark so he rode out the flood on its roof.

In Mohammedan literature and legend, there was a difference of opinion on the dimensions and plan of the ark. Baidawi gave the Biblical dimensions; Al-Tha'labi in his *Kisas al-Anbiyya* said it was built of teakwood and was 80 cubits by 50 cubits by 30 cubits. Each plank of the ark contained the name of a prophet and the body of Adam was carried in the middle to divide the men from the women. Three missing planks were brought from Egypt by Og, son of Anak, the only giant permitted to survive the flood. The ark came to rest on al-Judi and Noah locked it up, giving the key to Shem.

An ark appears in some Deluge legends outside the Bible. In the Babylonian *Epic of Gilgamesh* Ea commanded Utnapishtim to build a ship in the shape of a barge upon which was set a house 120 cubits high, divided into six stories, each with nine rooms. Ziusudra, the Sumerian Noah, built an ark on the advice of Enki, the Sumerian water god. A box or ark was used by the Banar of Cambodia and in some forms of the Greek Deucalion-Deluge legend.

(3) or **ark of the covenant, ark of the testimony,** or **ark of the Lord** In Jewish history, a chest of shittim-wood (*Ex.* xxv, 10–22), 2½ cubits long, 1½ cubits wide, and 1½ cubits high, overlaid inside and out with gold, which supported the mercy seat with its golden cherubs. It was equipped with a gold ring at each corner through which staves of gold-covered shittim wood were inserted to facilitate carrying. It was made by Bezaleel of the tribe of Judah (*Ex.* xxx, 23–26) or by Moses (*Deut.* x, 1–5). The two tables of stone containing the Ten Commandments were placed in it and it was deposited in the most sacred part of the sanctuary.

The ark of the covenant was probably a movable sanctuary and as such was carried when the people moved. In the crossing of the Jordan River the ark preceded the people and was the signal for their advance (*Num.* x, 33; *Josh.* iii, 3, 6). The ark was carried around Jericho before the battle (see CIRCUMAMBULATION) and later was placed in the Temple at Shiloh from which it was removed when the Israelites were defeated at Ebenezer. It was captured by the Philistines in the second battle (I *Sam.* iv, 3–5, 10, 11), but misfortune followed it and they finally returned it to the Israelites after seven months. David had the ark removed to Zion, danced before it, and placed it in a tabernacle (II *Sam.* vi, 15–20; I *Chron.* xvi, 1–3). Later it was placed in the Holy of Holies in Solomon's Temple.

In rabbinical literature and legend, the ark transcended the limitations of space. It leveled the hills before the army of the Israelites and when the Philistines returned it, in a cart drawn by two milch cows without a driver, the beasts took the ark to Bethshemesh and sang a song. When Solomon brought the ark into the Temple, the golden trees in the Temple were filled with moisture and produced abundant fruit. When an idol was placed there, the fruit immediately dried up. The ark was not only a receptacle for the Law, but a protection against the enemies of Israel. Two sparks came from between the two cherubim which killed serpents and scorpions and burned thorns. When the Temple was destroyed, the ark disappeared. Some believed it was taken to Babylonia, others that it was hidden.

In Mohammedan literature and legend, the ark was the sign that God had chosen Saul to be king. According to Al-Tha'labi, the ark was sent down by God from

Paradise with Adam when he fell. In it, cut from a ruby, were figures of all the prophets to come, especially of Mohammed and his first four califs. According to Ibn 'Abbas, a cousin of Mohammed, the ark and the rod of Moses are now lying in the Lake of Tiberias, to be brought forth at the last day. [SPH]

Arkansas Traveler A classic of native American humor and the best-known piece of folklore about the mythical state of "Arkansaw" (not to be confused with Arkansas). A lost and bewildered Traveler on horseback, in quest of lodgings, approaches the log cabin of a fiddling Squatter, who stubbornly evades or pretends to misunderstand his questions. The Traveler, tiring of the comic contest of wits, in which he is "straight man," resorts to the stratagem of offering to play the balance or "turn of the tune" that the Squatter is sawing on his fiddle, and so breaks down the other's resistance and is welcomed with open arms.

Whimsical, quizzical dialogs between a harassed traveler and a crotchety innkeeper are found elsewhere (e.g. "Whimsical Dialogue between an Irish Innkeeper and an Englishman," *Wit and Wisdom*, London, 1853, pp. 28–29). The theme of ingratiation by fiddling occurs also in "A Musical Tennessee Landlord," by "Dresbach" (*Spirit of the Times* XVI [February 13, 1847]: 603). In Yankee humor, as Walter Blair points out (*American Speech* XIV [February, 1939]: 11–22), the roles are usually reversed, the inquisitive native being the questioner. *The Arkansas Traveler* fits into the pattern of frontier hospitality where "strangers were under suspicion until their intentions and character became reasonably clear."

About the medley has grown up the legend of the "Original Arkansas Traveler." According to tradition, Colonel Sandford C. ("Sandy") Faulkner, of Little Rock, was touring the state with four prominent politicians during the campaign of 1840 and became lost in the Boston mountains. On his return the Colonel related the encounter with the Squatter as having taken place under the circumstances described and was thereafter much in demand for his rendition of the dialog and the tune, and was popularly credited with their authorship. This distinction has also been conferred upon the young Arkansas artist, Edward Payson Washbourne (Washburn), who in 1858 painted "The Arkansas Traveler," and in 1860 began the companion picture, "The Turn of the Tune," completed by an unknown artist after Washbourne's death at the age of 28. Both paintings have become almost as familiar as the dialog through the Currier & Ives lithographs (1870).

Two other rival claimants to authorship of the dialog and the tune are José ("Joe") Tosso, the eminent Western violinist, and Mose Case, a guitarist, whose version of the skit was printed in 1862 or 1863. Of the many published and manuscript versions, the one issued by B. S. Alford of Little Rock, in 1876, as "arranged and corrected by Colonel S. C. Faulkner," and based on a lost original printed between 1858 and 1860, is generally accepted as standard. The tune (a jig or hoe-down also known as "The Arkansas Traveler") was first published in 1847 under the title of "The Arkansas Traveler and Rackinsac Waltz," arranged by William Cumming.

Whatever its origin, the dialog is obviously a "synthesis of questions and answers already current" (James R. Masterson, *Tall Tales of Arkansaw*, Boston, 1942, pp.

240, 376). Parallels have been found for most of the jests included, such as the leaky roof which can't be repaired in wet weather and doesn't need repairing in dry weather (perhaps the most celebrated jest in the piece): the fair-and-square tapping of a barrel of whisky through spigots at both ends by husband and wife who pass a single coin back and forth between them in token payment; the assignment of nicknames to cutlery; and the presence of a good road several feet below the mud.

The many-sided entertainment value of "The Arkansas Traveler"—dramatic, musical, humorous—resulted in wide diffusion in print (jestbook, songster, broadside, sheet music) and oral tradition, often in paraphrase or garbled form. There is also evidence of its use as a folk play, such as Thomas Wilson recalls from his boyhood in Salem, Ohio, where it was acted out by wagoners in a tavern barroom (*Ohio Archaeological and Historical Quarterly* VIII [January, 1900]: 296–308). The popularity of the medley in vaudeville (and later on phonograph records) suggested a five-act melodrama, *Kit, the Arkansas Traveler* (originally entitled *Down the Mississippi*), written by Edward Spencer and revised by Thomas B. de Walden, popular for thirty years between 1869 and 1899, whose only relation to the skit, however, is in the title of the hero and the use of the tune. Other instances of the influence of the classic as a household word and as an artistic inspiration are the magazine, *The Arkansaw Traveler*, established in Little Rock, in 1883, by the Arkansas humorist, Opie Read, and P. D. Benham, and David Guion's symphonic composition based on the tune. [BAB]

Arkansas Traveler pattern A traditional American patchwork quilt pattern named for the *Arkansas Traveler*, song and story, probably dating from about the 1850's. Each large square of the design is made up of four smaller squares pieced from seven still smaller scraps. The units are simple, straight-edged, geometrical shapes which allow the thriftiest use of miscellaneous scraps of material and are characteristic of the designs worked out in frontier homes.

armadillo Any burrowing nocturnal mammal of the family *Dasypodidae*, having an armorlike covering of bony plates. Armadillos are common in South and Central America and range as far north as Texas.

The armadillo appears in the folklore and folktale of South American Indian tribes of Bolivia, Brazil, and Guiana. The Mosetene (eastern Bolivia) attached pieces of armadillo liver to a dog as a hunting charm. The Mascoi (Brazil) believe a horned armadillo lives under the ground and the Chamacoco of the Gran Chaco say that this armadillo caused the Flood.

In the myths of the Toba and Pilagá Indians of the Gran Chaco, Armadillo gave the people fruit by planting tasi under an algarroho tree. The tasi wound around the tree and bore fruit. Since then the plants have spread everywhere, supplying men with fruit. These Indians identify two bright stars under Orion as the celestial armadillo who unearthed the first women who fell from the sky and were buried in the ground. He is master of all living armadillos.

arrieros Literally muleteers: a men's group dance of Acopilco and Tenancingo Indians of Mexico. It is an enactment of a native legend about the arrieros. At the end of a day of wandering through the mountains the muleteers relax, dance, eat, play, and go to sleep. They are attacked by bandits, but are rescued by the Lord's miraculous answer to their prayers. The attack and the miracle do not feature in the dance, but the dancers bring their props on adorned burros, play dice, and sit down to a small feast. In white shirts and *calzones*, sashes, and sombreros, they two-step through a variety of longways figures, to an insipid fiddle tune. Two men pretend to sleep on a *petate*. The end is casual and anticlimactic. In Tenancingo the arrieros are flagellants, with sacks on their backs, and alabanzas (songs of praise to the Virgin) on their lips. [GPK]

arrimao or **arrimado** Name for extra-legal, socially sanctioned mating found among Negroes of the lower socio-economic groups in Cuba. See AMASIADO. [MJH]

arrow A weapon shot from a bow; usually a slender shaft with a sharp point or head of stone or metal and feathers or vanes fastened at the butt. The use of the bow and arrow, first appearing in late Paleolithic times, has become world-wide. It is absent only among the Polynesians, Micronesians, and a few African tribes, while the arrow and blowgun are used by the Malays, Melanesians, and South American Indians. Arrows are put to many uses other than warfare and hunting. They are employed in religious rites, in ordeals, as love charms, protective charms, amulets, lucky objects, touchstones, for divination and games, against witchcraft, as a preventive or cure for illness and the evil eye, and as symbols of deities, of lightning, rain, fertility, disease, famine, war, and death.

Cheyenne Indian worship centers in a set of four medicine arrows which the tribe claims to have possessed from the creation of the world. These are exhibited annually and whenever a Cheyenne Indian has been slain by a member of his own tribe in order to cleanse the slayer from his tribesman's blood. These arrows probably are relics of a period when the tribe worshipped a thunder god.

Many North American Indian tribes begin certain religious rituals by shooting an arrow to each of the six directions. The Mexican Quetzalcoatl, in his wind god aspect, carries a thunderbolt in the form of a flint arrowhead. Mixcoatl, as thunder god, carried a bundle of arrows (thunderbolts) in his hand.

South African Bushmen sacrifice arrows to the river or to ancestral spirits residing in rivers. The Ostyaks (Finland) never passed a sacred tree without shooting an arrow at it as a mark of reverence. Arrow offerings are made to the Bagobo (Philippine) god of the hunt, Abog.

Arrows are shot into the air during an eclipse by the Cayapo, Bororo, and Tapuyos (Brazil), and by the Caribs and Arawaks (Guiana) to frighten the sun into shining. The Ojibwas, believing that the sun was being extinguished, shot fire-tipped arrows to rekindle it. The Sencis (Peru) shot burning arrows to drive away the savage beast with which the sun was struggling, and the Indochinese shot arrows at the dragon trying to swallow the sun.

As amulets, arrows or arrow-shaped pendants are hung around the neck in Italy to keep away illness and the evil eye, in Arabia to protect the blood, in France to facilitate childbirth, in Ireland as a protection against elf-shooting, among the Acoma Indians as a protection for children. They are carried by the Malays as lucky objects on which to sharpen their krises and cockspurs and as touchstones for gold, by Zuñi women when venturing out at night, and by Zuñi racers (in their hair) for luck. In Ireland water poured over neolithic celts and arrowheads is given to children to cure the croup. Pliny mentions that sleeping on arrows extracted from a body act as love charms. Kwakiutl women desiring a male child place arrows on a bailer under their beds. A bow and arrow are placed on a baby's chest or an arrow is shot into the afterbirth to make the child a good marksman in the same tribe. Miniature bows and arrows have been introduced by missionaries on Easter Island as toys.

The arrow is associated with the moon, sun, and atmospheric deities in various mythologies. The Libyan goddess Neith, the Greek gods and goddesses of love (Eros), hunting (Artemis), the sun (Helios); and the Centaur Chiron, the Assyrian Ashur and Ishtar, the Etruscan sun god Usil, the Hindu gods of war (Kârttikeya) and love (Kāma) are all depicted with bow and arrow.

The Madras god of iron, Loha Penu, directs the arrows of his followers against the enemy, averting their countershafts; and Ten Geris, Siberian Buriat thunder god, fights evil spirits with a fiery arrow. Śiva destroyed Tripura with his mystic arrow. The Japanese god Susano-wo possessed a life-bow and arrows and a humming arrow with a whistling attachment (known in China during the T'ang Dynasty and used to make birds rise or to frighten enemies).

Not only do arrows appear in the folktales and legends of all the peoples using them, but in many instances they play a major role. An island is created by shooting an arrow (Greek); an arrow speaks, revealing its hiding place (Hawaiian); a magic arrow indicates a lodging for the night (German), a place to build a city (German), a place to seek a bride (English, German, Hawaiian), a place to build a church (Danish), a burial place (English); a magic arrow shakes heaven (Chinese), summons a water spirit (Chinese), and affords transportation (Arabian); is visible to one person alone (numerous tribes of North American Indians, especially in the North Pacific, Mackenzie River, and Northeastern Woodland regions, Siberia, and Asia generally). Magic arrows play an important role in Arabian, Breton, Chinese, Greek, Hawaiian, Hindu, Icelandic, Jamaican, and North American Indian tales.

In a Koryak tale, when Ememqut's wife was abducted by a Kala, Ground Squirrel gave him an arrow which he threw into the fire. This opened a way to the lower world where he found his wife. They returned through the hearth; Ememqut removed the arrow, and the road closed. Ememqut's arrow was also responsible for the impregnation of Fox and Triton. The Koryak believe in arrows with eyes which fly anywhere they are sent without benefit of the bow. In a related Alaskan tale, Raven transforms a bird into an arrow which will fly wherever Raven points. In a Nez Percé Indian tale the trickster, Coyote, changed himself into an arrow.

A familiar feature in Hindu legend is the śabdabhēdī arrow which strikes what is heard. Prithīrāj of Delhi, in the Ālhā folktales, uses an arrow to sew up a sword wound and thus enables the wounded man to continue fighting.

In folktales it is usually the culture hero who discovers and teaches the people how to make arrows. The

Cheyenne Mut-si-i-u-iv and the Cree Wisakedjak, typically, taught their people the art. [SPH]

arrow chain A motif (F53) appearing in folktales of the Plateau and North Pacific Coast Indians, the Tupi Indians of Brazil, the Guarayú (Bolivia), the Jibaro of Ecuador, the Koryak of Siberia, and numerous peoples of Oceania. Typically the hero shoots a large number of arrows into the sky, one after another, so rapidly that they form a chain up which he travels, usually to rescue a friend. In some stories there are descriptions of battles with the sky-people and references to the stealing of fire from the sky.

In the Coos Indian version, the brother of a canoe-maker who was killed by a man of the sky-people, made an arrow chain by which he ascended in order to avenge his brother's death. This he did and then returned to earth bringing his brother's head with him. He put the head back on the body and it became the red-headed woodpecker, the red being the blood of the slain man.

In a Guarayú story, Tamoi (Grandfather) had two sons who shot arrows upward, one into the butt of another, until the chain was formed. Then they climbed the arrow chain until they reached the sky where they became the sun and moon.

In a Banks Islands swan-maiden story, the wife of Qat, a sky-woman whom he had captured by taking her wings, was scolded by his mother. The sky-woman's tears uncovered her wings, which her husband had buried, and she quickly put them on and flew back to the sky. Qat shot arrows into the heavens forming a chain to which a banyan root attached itself. Then he climbed up and recovered his wife, but as he was descending, a man hoeing in the sky struck the banyan root. Qat fell dead and the woman flew back to heaven.

In a Koryak tale the arrow chain is reduced to one arrow sent up to heaven thus making a road leading upward. In an Athapascan version two brothers are carried to the sky by a single arrow. In the Vai tribe of West Africa the arrow chain becomes an arrow bridge.

Artavazd The unfilial son of King Artaxias: an evil power of old Armenian mythology. He resented the numerous sacrifices and suicides at his father's funeral as a depletion of the kingdom he was to inherit. Artaxias cursed him from the grave; and soon after, Artavazd fell from his horse over a precipice of Mount Massis. There he remains in a cave chained by iron fetters. When these are broken, he will emerge and rule over or destroy the world. The noise from a blacksmith's hammer is believed to strengthen his bonds, so smiths still strike their anvils a few blows every day, even on holidays and Sundays to prevent Artavazd from breaking loose.

Artemis In Greek religion, a virgin goddess of nature and the moon; originally a mother deity and goddess (non-Hellenic in character) of lakes, rivers, woods, and wildlife, especially of animals of the chase as the fawn, stag, and boar. From fosterer of wildlife she developed into a goddess of fertility, marriage, and childbirth. In Attica and Arcadia she was identified with Callisto, and honored as mother of the tribe with the name Artemis Calliste or Brauronia. At Sparta she was worshipped as Artemis Orthia, protector of women and children; as Artemis Lochia she was a goddess of childbed, as Artemis Curotrophus the nurse of youths. As Artemis Tauropolus and Treclaria she was an agricultural goddess. Homer

spoke of her as Agrotera, the huntress. Her early association with Hecate resulted in her rule of magic, night, and the moon. In Artemis Parthenos the conception of her virginity crystallized.

First-fruits of the hunter and fisherman were dedicated to her at her shrines or hung on trees; in the worship of Artemis Laphria bears were burnt. To Artemis Brauronia goats were sometimes sacrificed; on other occasions she was worshipped in ceremonies which were probably a survival of initiation customs. Maidens from five to ten years of age danced in saffron robes and were called bears. None could marry before undergoing this rite. Traces of human sacrifice to Artemis are preserved in the myth of Iphigenia.

Before the battle of Marathon the Athenians vowed to sacrifice to Artemis a number of she-goats equal to the number of enemy warriors killed. So many warriors were slain that the vow was necessarily compromised and only 500 were sacrificed every year.

Artemis is represented with a torch, possibly as a moon symbol or a symbol of vegetation. She dwelt on Mt. Taygetus where her herb, artemisia, grew, and her shrine at Lusi was famous as a healing center.

She was equated with Bast in Greco-Egyptian religion and identified with the local goddess, Diana, by the Romans. As Artemis Tauropolos she was confounded with Anāhita. She was the chief goddess of the amphictyony at Ætolia, associated with Apollo at Delphi, and one of the more important of the Olympian deities.

In Greek mythology, Artemis was the daughter of Zeus by Leto, twin of Apollo, and was associated with the nymphs Britomartis and Callisto, and with Iphigenia, Opis, Hecate, Echo, and the Naiads. She was born on the island of Delos to which her mother had fled to escape the wrath of Hera. She was associated with her brother in nearly all his adventures. With him she subdued Tityus and the Python, assisted in the punishment of Niobe, and reputedly transformed Callisto into a bear because she had deserted the huntress-band for Zeus. Her severity is celebrated. She visited the Greek army with a pestilence before the Trojan War and produced a calm to prevent their sailing because Agamemnon had killed a stag sacred to her. When he was about to sacrifice his daughter, Iphigenia, to placate the goddess, Artemis snatched the maiden away, leaving a hind in her place, and made Iphigenia a priestess at her temple in Tauris.

Artemis changed Arethusa into a stream to enable her to escape Alpheus, and Actæon into a stag because he spied her nude while she was bathing. Unknowingly, she shot the hunter Orion. Bewailing her error, she placed him among the stars with his dog Sirius, and with the Pleiades, whom he loved, always flying before him. Her non-Hellenic character is probably attested to by the grotesque part Homer gave her in the battle of the gods. In this contest she opposed Hera who whipped her with her own bow and sent her off the field weeping.

Arthur A British chieftain of the 5th–6th century: central figure of a great cycle of romance. Legend says that he was born at Tintagel Castle in Cornwall, lived at Caerleon, Wales, with his wife Guanhuvara (Guinevere), was leader of the Round Table, hunted the fabulous boar Twrch Trwyth, and fought and slew the Demon Cat of Losanne, conquered many lands, was betrayed by his wife and dearest knight, was **mortally**

wounded at the battle of Camlan, and was taken to Avalon by three fairy queens, whence he will return in the hour of his country's need.

☞ Historically, a victorious battle-leader of the Britons against the Saxons about 500 A.D., of whose life and death nothing more is known. The vast pseudo-historical and romantic literature which grew up about him from the 12th century on reflects folk traditions and mythological concepts.

Nennius, a Welsh cleric, writing about 826, furnishes, besides an untrustworthy account of Arthur's battles, a list of marvels. Two are localized in the neighborhood of the Wye: a stone in which Arthur's hound Cabal had left its footprint during the hunting of the boar Troit; and the grave of Arthur's son Anir, the length of which varied each time it was measured. The Welsh tale of *Kilhwch and Olwen*, composed about 1100, belongs to the general Jason and Medea type and contains much mythical and folktale material. Several personages (Mabon, Modron, Manawyddan, Llwch) are taken over from the Continental Celtic and the Irish pantheon; others are helpful companions, who assist the hero in his impossible tasks, as did the Argonauts and similar figures in modern folktales. There are giants to be slain, vessels of plenty to be sought, and the supernatural boar, mentioned by Nennius, to be hunted from Ireland across South Wales and Cornwall into the sea. The details of the chase show the characteristic interest of Welsh and Irish in accounting for place names. Arthur has become a king and shares in several quests and adventures, but seems to have acquired no supernatural attributes. The same may be said of him as he appears in *The Spoils of Annwn*, a poem probably of the 10th century, raiding the island fortress of the gods in his ship Prydwen, and returning with a magic caldron from which none but the brave could obtain food.

The most famous mythical concept attached to Arthur is that of his immortality and Messianic return to reestablish the Britons in their kingdom, but it is not attested before 1113. In that year certain French canons, having been shown Arthur's seat and oven (probably megaliths) on Dartmoor, came to Bodmin, and a fracas arose between their servants and a Cornishman who insisted that Arthur was still alive. From the same source we learn that Bretons and French quarreled over this question, and from then on the testimony is continuous that, especially in Brittany, the belief in Arthur's survival and return was firmly fixed. Alanus de Insulis (1174–79), in commenting on Merlin's prophecy that Arthur's end would be doubtful, says that anyone who proclaimed in Brittany that Arthur had shared the fate of mortals could not escape stoning. Malory, years later, testifies that some men in many parts of England believed that the king was "had by the will of our Lord Jesu into another place," and would come again and win the holy cross.

The "British hope" represents an old pagan belief that the hero is a god who cannot die, a belief revitalized and prolonged through the centuries by the simple human urge to optimism which in modern times refused to accept the death of Bonaparte and Kitchener. Certainly there was a strong mythological element in the tradition, for every account of Arthur's survival in medieval literature or modern folklore either places him in the world of the immortals or implies his superhuman nature.

Geoffrey of Monmouth in his *History of the Kings of Britain* (c. 1136), drawing on Breton sources, tells us that Arthur was borne to the isle of Avallon to be healed of his wound, and in the *Vita Merlini* (1150) informs us that Arthur lies on a golden bed in an ever-fruitful Isle of Apples, where the inhabitants live to be over a hundred, and where he is tended by the fay Morgan and her sisters. Thus Arthur's abode is the mythical Isle of Women of the Celts, and Morgan le Fay (in many accounts Arthur's sister) is specifically called a goddess by three medieval writers.

The wandering Breton *conteurs* transmitted the legend of Arthur's survival to Sicily, for there we find him dwelling with Morgan according to *Floriant and Florete* and Torrella's *Faula*. The latter poem (1350–81) adds a mythical trait: Arthur remains young since he is fed yearly by the Grail. This equates him with the Maimed King, who is likewise fed by the Grail and whose vital forces are in sympathetic relation to the fertility of his land. Gervase of Tilbury (c. 1211) describes Arthur as living on in a Sicilian palace, his wounds annually reopening—another reflection of Arthur in the role of a vegetation spirit.

Gervase combines the motif of the island abode of Arthur with the widespread concept of the king in the hollow mountain, for it is in the dark depths of Mount Etna that the British king is discovered. The same concept was known to Cæsarius of Heisterbach and the authors of the *Wartburgkrieg* and the *Dispute between a Christian and a Jew*. We find it again in the 19th century attached to many caves in Wales and England and to the Eildon Hills in Scotland. These folktales represent Arthur as lying asleep, surrounded by his knights, awaiting the day when he will issue forth to victory—a blend of the Messianic return motif and a belief in some chthonian deity.

The tradition of Arthur's subterranean dwelling had two strange developments. In Etienne de Rouen's *Draco Normannicus* (1167–68) Arthur is held up to ridicule as ruler over the lower hemisphere, threatening to return to his old domain with a host of antipodean subjects in order to overthrow Henry II. Moreover, since Walter Map (1181) reports a folktale in which the king of a subterranean realm was conceived as a dwarf riding on a goat, we can understand why a mosaic at Otranto (1165) depicts Arthur astride the same bizarre mount.

Long-lived was the belief in the British king as leader of the Wild Hunt, originally the personification of winter and its storms. Gervase and two other 13th century writers assign this role to Arthur, and tell how he and his company of riders may be seen by moonlight in the forests of Britain or Brittany or Savoy; we have a Scottish reference from the 16th century; and at Cadbury Castle, Somerset, and in several parts of France, the belief was still current in the 19th century.

Another folk tradition holds that Arthur lives on in the form of a bird. Cervantes tells us that the English believed that their ancient hero assumed the form of a crow, and an 18th century tourist in Cornwall was rebuked for shooting a raven, which might have been Arthur. The latest testimony from Cornwall takes the bird to be a chough or a puffin. One might surmise that this transformation is related to the fact that Bran, son of Llyr, the euhemerized sea god of the *Mabinogion* and the prototype of the Maimed King, bears a name meaning "crow." Certainly in the *Mabinogion* and Irish sagas we have instances of divine figures taking the shape of birds.

Barring the modern folk traditions of Arthur's survival, the British battle-leader's name lives on almost ·entirely in association with places or natural objects. In Scotland there is the majestic hill called Arthur's Seat; in Wales there are a Craig Arthur near Llangollen and an Arthur's Stone near Swansea; Cornwall boasts Arthur's Hall, Hunting Lodge, and Grave, and Brittany Arthur's Camp. These are but a few of many such names. Well might Tennyson write of

that gray king whose name, a ghost,
Streams like a cloud, man-shaped, from mountain peak,
And cleaves to cairn and cromlech still.

Bibliography:

Chambers, E. K., *Arthur of Britain* (1927), ch. VI, VII.
Snell, F. J., *King Arthur's Country* (1926).
Loomis, Gertrude Schoepperle, "Arthur in Avalon and the Banshee," *Vassar Mediaeval Studies* (1923), 3.
Loomis, R. S., "King Arthur and the Antipodes," *MP* 38: 289.
——, *Arthurian Tradition and Chrétien de Troyes* (1949), ch. III, XXVIII.
Krappe, A. H., "Die Sage vom König im Berge," *Mitteilungen der Schlesischen Gesellschaft für Volkskunde* XXXV (1935), p. 76.

ROGER S. LOOMIS

artificial whale A folktale motif (K922) especially popular among the American Indians of the North Pacific Coast. A hunter returns home and finds his wife and child crying. They have been mistreated by her brothers in his absence. The man proceeds to make many killer whales out of wood—alder wood, red-cedar wood, spruce, hemlock, etc., but all are mere logs when put in the water, until finally he makes some out of yellow-cedar wood (or yew), paints them with white stripes and white bellies, shouts to them to live and swim, and these live and swim, catch red cod, salmon, halibut, etc. So at last he is satisfied.

The next day when the wife's brothers go hunting, the man sends his killer whales to upset their canoes, but with instructions to save the youngest brother, because he alone was kind to the wife and child. The whales do this: the canoes of the brothers are broken, the brothers are drowned, but the canoe of the youngest is conducted safely home. After this satisfactory revenge the man (in a Skidegate version) then names his whales and tells them to depart and go live in various places.

In other versions, a group of animals make an artificial whale in order to kill Thunderbird. A Rivers Inlet variant tells of two culture heroes who make an artificial whale in order to kill Thunderbird, who carries away people. When the whale is finished the people enter it. There are many variants, giving details of how the whale gets stuck in the mud, or does not swim properly until the inmates are taught how to handle it. When the whale appears in front of Thunderbird's house, Thunderbird sends out his children to catch it. All are killed, drowned, have their feet cut off by the inmates near the blowhole, and Thunderbird himself is finally killed.

There is a Koryak story in which the two daughters of Big-Raven make a wooden whale as a means of escaping from the wilderness and finding human habitation. Big-

Raven and his wife took the two girls into the wilderness and left them there. At home the parents ate fat reindeer meat and sent the lean strips to the daughters. At last the two daughters made a wooden whale from a log and put it in a pail of water; in the morning the whale had outgrown the pail. They put it in a small lake; in the morning the whale had outgrown the lake. They put it in a big lake, and in the morning it was bigger than the big lake. So the sisters put the whale in the river, entered into it, and said, "O Spotted Whale, take us to a settlement." The whale swam down the river and out to sea. The story does not tell about their coming to another settlement.

This story contains parallels of two very well-known and widespread motifs: image comes to life (D435.1) and, in the case of the animal's expedition to kill Thunderbird, the Trojan horse motif (K754.1). Of especial interest, however, in North American Indian folklore, is the matter of trial and error in the making of the whale and the final discovery of the appropriate wood to use to insure success. This is but one of numerous stories of the North Pacific region in which the people try various kinds of wood to make canoes, animals, birds, children, etc. that will behave as desired for specific purposes.

arts and crafts The distinction between arts and crafts is one that critics are slow to attempt, particularly in the folk and primitive field where the esthetic is so often a byproduct of the utilitarian. For this reason the two are generally bracketed together, and together they include all those activities and skills where objects are created, produced, or adorned by non- or semi-mechanical methods. If a broader term is desired, covering all the work activities of a people, *arts and industries* may be used; the arts include the creative crafts, and industries cover those which are strictly useful and repetitive together with such other activities as gathering, cultivating, hunting, fishing, and manufacturing.

In this volume, arts and crafts are considered to be a part of folklore. Not all critics adhere to this point of view. However, folk art and folklore are so intertwined that separation is academic. Religion is intricately involved in the graphic and plastic concepts of supernatural beings, the dance with costume and mask, ritual with place of worship and many ritualistic objects, music with the creation and decoration of instruments, custom with the nature of shelter, utensils, implements, weapons, clothing, vehicles, and other possessions. Events and calculations involve pictograph and picture story. In fact, little would be known of extinct cultures but for surviving examples of arts and crafts. Among many peoples of the world these abilities were the gift of the culture hero, and a basic part of their mythology and legend. See PRIMITIVE AND FOLK ART. [MH]

aru In the belief of the people living on Bartle Bay (New Guinea), the shadow of a living human being or the spirit or soul of a dead one. The aru goes to Maraiya, the land of the dead in which there is plenty of food, no illness, but which otherwise resembles the world of the living.

Arunkulta Term for supernatural evil power or an object with such power of the Central Australian Aranda tribe. [KL]

Aruru In Babylonian religion and mythology, a mother goddess associated with Marduk as the creatrix of the seed of mankind; in the *Epic of Gilgamesh*, the creatrix of Eabani (Enkidu). See SEMITIC MYTHOLOGY.

arval, arvel, averil, arfal, arddel, or **arthel** In England and Wales, a funeral repast usually including bread or cakes with ale and wine; the sweet cake served at a funeral repast; also, the funeral ceremonies. The name is sometimes connected, on rather slim evidence, with the Roman Fratres Arvales (the Arval Brethren), a college of 12 priests who annually, at the Arvalia, a May festival, sacrificed to the Dea Dia, thought to be Ceres, the goddess of the fields. While the connection between the spirits of the dead and fertility is not uncommon, no specific evidence is available to show the descent of the British custom from the Roman.

Asa'ase Ashanti-Fanti earth deity, whose worship has been retained among the Negroes of Dutch Guiana, and is also known to the Maroons of Jamaica. In the Gold Coast, the name of the deity is Asase Ya, the female day-name for Thursday being added to the designation. Thursday is the day sacred to this deity. In West Africa, and in the Guiana bush as well, no cultivation is done on that day. [MJH]

asafetida A gum resin, red-brown in color, prepared from certain plants of the fennel family, especially *Ferula assafoetida*, an umbelliferous plant of Afghanistan and Persia. It is acrid, bitter, and strong in odor, due to the presence of organic sulphur compounds. Medically it is administered to stimulate the intestinal and respiratory tracts and the nervous system. It is used as a condiment in India and Persia and as a vegetable. The resin is used for "conjure" and as an amulet among the Negroes of the southern United States and West Indies. A favorite concoction of West Indian witch doctors is made by mixing bones, ashes, grave dirt, and nail parings, with asafetida. Worn around the neck, it is supposed to ward off witches, keep away the spirits of disease, or cure rheumatism. In parts of Europe it is carried in the pocket as a preventative of smallpox.

Asafoche The Ashanti-Fanti term for bands of young fighting men that comprised the units in the tribal armies of preconquest times. There is evidence that certain aspects of the *Asafo* groupings had to do with cooperative work-groups, such as are found in West Africa under the term *dokpwe* (Dahomey) or, in the New World, *combite* (Haiti), though in the Gold Coast these functions were subordinated to military ones. The Asafoche groups still exist, but their ancient authority to punish violators of community property is not recognized by the British. [MJH]

asagwe A type of Haitian vodun dancing, known as the salute to the gods. The manman, the largest of the three vodun drums, signals for this figure to start and sets the distinctive rhythm to which it is performed. The dance figure itself is characterized by sweeping circular movements, dips, and semiprostrations.

Āśāpūrnā, Āśāpūrā, or **Āśāpūri** In Hinduism, an earth or mother goddess: literally, she who fulfills desire. Āśāpūrnā is worshipped by the Chārans and the Hinglāj and as a form of Gaurī by the Rājputs. Her image at Madh in Cutch is a red-painted rock to which an annual sacrifice of seven male buffalos is made.

Asbjörnsen, Peter Christen (1812–1885) A Norwegian author and folklorist; contributor to the study of comparative mythology. Chief works: *Norske Folkeeventyr,* Christiania, 1842, produced in collaboration with Jörgen Moe; *Norske Huldreeventyr og Folksagn,* Christiania, in 2 vols., 1845–48; and a second volume of the *Norske Folkeeventyr,* Christiania, 1871. These books have been translated into English in *Popular Tales from the Norse,* 1859; *Tales from the Fjeld,* 1874, by Sir George W. Dasent, and in *Round the Yule Log,* 1881, by H. L. Braekstad.

Ascension Day The fortieth day after Easter Sunday, on which is commemorated Christ's ascension after his resurrection (*Acts* i, 9). The institution of this celebration is attributed to the Apostles, and some of the customs observed are closely related to the Christian significance of the day while others are pagan in origin.

During the Middle Ages the day was celebrated with a religious procession which symbolized Christ's entry into heaven. In some Roman Catholic churches an image of Christ was raised from the altar through a hole in the roof and a burning straw figure representing Satan was thrown down through the same hole. In Munich until a hundred years ago the expulsion of the devil from the city was enacted on Ascension Day (ceremony of the human scapegoat). The night before, a man, disguised as a devil, was chased through the streets by people dressed as witches and wizards. When he was caught he was ducked in puddles and rolled in dunghills. Finally, the disguise was removed, stuffed, and hung in the tower of the Frauenkirche until the next day when it was burned. Similar ceremonies are said to be observed in Upper Bavaria. In Rouen, France, a prisoner (scapegoat) was released and pardoned on Ascension Day. He confessed his sins and received absolution in the city square. The next day, in the presence of a great assembly, he was reproved for his sins and admonished to give thanks to God, St. Romain, and the canons for his pardon.

In Roman Catholic churches on this day the paschal candle is removed from the altar and extinguished after the Gospel at High Mass, symbolizing Christ's departure from the Apostles.

On this day the English custom of beating the bounds is still performed in some parishes. School children, accompanied by clergymen and parish officers, walk through the parish and the boys are switched with willow wands along the boundary lines to teach them the bounds of their parish. In Exeter, the Lamb is hailed on Ascension morning, as a result of the belief that the figure of a lamb actually appears in the east. In the north of England a smock race is run by girls for the prize of a Holland chemise. Men in the slate quarries of northern Wales believe that if they work on Ascension Day a fatal accident will occur.

In Nottinghamshire, England, it is believed that an egg laid on this day, placed on the roof of a house, will ward off fire, lightning, and other calamities. In Swabia, Germany, wreaths of red and white flowers, hung over the stable doors, served the same purpose. In Denmark, a rowan tree cut on Ascension Day and placed over a door will prevent the entrance of witches.

In northern Germany it is still believed that melons planted on Ascension Day will thrive. In Hildesheim young girls ring the church bells while swinging on the ropes. The girl who is carried highest by the swing of the bell will get the longest flax at harvest time. In Hesse, herbs collected on Ascension Day are considered especially powerful medicinally. The people of Sicily believe in miraculous cures effected on the stroke of midnight preceding Ascension Thursday.

ascent to sky on feather A folktale incident or motif (F61.2) in which the hero travels on a large feather to the sky: found especially in tales among North American Indians of the North Pacific Coast, the Plateau, and Plains areas. The hero either adheres magically to the feather, which draws him to the sky, or he is simply carried on it. In a certain Bella Coola Indian story a little boy watches the hero depart on a large feather which soars and swoops in large circles through the sky. [EWV]

ascent to upper world A world-wide folklore motif (F10-17, F50-68) in which the ascents are made by various means and for many reasons. Sometimes the hero goes to the sky to retrieve a wife or friend, to obtain fire, for revenge on the sky people, to obtain gifts which produce food and riches, because of curiosity, or to catch the sun.

The Indonesians and South American Indians use a vine as a sky rope. Ascents or descents are made in a basket in tales of the North American Indians and in Siberian stories. A ladder appears in the vision of Jacob in which he saw angels ascending and descending a ladder leading from earth to heaven. A Mazovian legend tells about a pilgrim to the Holy Sepulchre who saw a ladder made of bird's feathers. He climbed it for three months and reached the Garden of Paradise. Other instances of the use of a ladder are found in tales of the Cape Verde Islands, Egypt, Gold Coast, and Mongolia.

Ascents are made by a stretching tree in Indonesian, Ekoi, Congo, Cape Verde Islands, Charente (Brazil), and North American Indian tales. In the sun-snaring myth of the Wyandots a strong child climbed a tree which was too short, so he blew upon it and lengthened it until it carried him to the land above the sky. While there he set snares for game, but caught the sun instead. Until the sun was released by a mouse, there was no day on the earth. In the *Kalevala*, Väinämöinen made a fir tree grow till it touched the sky, then Ilmarinen climbed it to get the moon and Great Bear, but was blown off by a magic wind.

In some cases the plant grows to the sky overnight as in the typical Jack and the Beanstalk story. This is found in British, Tuscan, Breton, Flemish, Slavonic (via a giant cabbage), Jamaican, Philippine, and Fijian tales. In the latter a boy, son of the sky king, Tui Langa, stuck his walking stick into the ground and lay down to sleep. In the morning it had become a tree up which he climbed and introduced himself to his father. The arrow chain is another means of heavenly ascent, restricted in its recorded range to northwestern North America, Siberia, part of South America, and Oceania. Mountains reach or stretch to the sky in Australian, Egyptian, German, Ekoi, and Maidu and Ts'ets'aut folktales.

In Chinese, Melanesian, Indonesian, Greenland Eskimo, Koryak, Mongol Turk, and North American Indian tales, a sky window gives admission to the upper world.

Ascent to heaven can also be made by a road (African), a narrow road (Burma, Indochina), a tower, by pursuit of game (Iroquois), or by stretching (Dionysus in a Greek myth). Transportation to or from the upper world sometimes is supplied by a cloud (Greek, Chinese), by a feather or by adhering to a feather (North Pacific, Plateau, Plains Indians), by a bird (Arabian, Ekoi, Seneca), by a god (Rhodesia), on horseback (Siberia, Arabia), on a sheep (India), by thought (Thompson River Indians), on a rainbow, by a ladder of sunbeams (Egypt), by magic (African), by shooting with a magic bow (North American Indian).

Asgard, Asgardhr, or **Asgarth** In Scandinavian mythology, the sacred space reserved for the abode of the gods and goddesses, the æsir and ásynjur, reached only by the bridge Bifrost. In saga, Asgard usually included 12 realms: Valhalla, home of heroes slain in battle; Gladsheim, home of Odin and the chief gods; Valaskialf, the hall of Odin; Vingolf, home of Frigga and the ásynjur; Thrudheim, realm of Thor; Breidablik, home of Balder; Folkvang, the realm of Freya; Ydalir, Uller's damp region; Sokkvabekk, the home of Saga; Landvidi, home of Vidar; Himinbiorg, home of Heimdall; and Forseti's bright palace, Glitnir.

asgardsreid Literally, Asgard's ride or chase: in Teutonic mythology, the wild ride of Odin or Frigga. It is still spoken of as being especially active during the dark, stormy Yule nights.

ash In Scandinavian myth, the world tree was the ash, Yggdrasil; and an ash torn out of the earth by the gods was transformed into Ask, the first man. The ash was regarded with awe in Ireland. "Cruel the ash-tree" is in the Battle of Trees; and today the shadow of an ash is said to blast grass and crops.

In England, where the ash was considered especially potent, children were sometimes passed through a cleft in an ash tree as a cure for rupture or rickets; Scottish Highland children were given the astringent sap of the tree as a medicine and as a protection against witchcraft. In many parts of England warts were transferred to the ash, sometimes by rubbing them with a piece of bacon and then slipping the bacon under the bark of an ash tree, sometimes by saying a charm such as, "Ashen-tree, Ashen-tree, Pray buy these warts of me," while a pin was stuck first into the tree, then into the wart, finally into the tree where it remained.

Ash rods were used in some parts of England for the cure of diseased sheep, cows, and horses. The Shrew Ash, still standing in Richmond Park, is a reminder of the cure for cramp or lameness in cattle. By boring a hole in the ash, inserting a live shrew mouse in the hole and then plugging it up, the disease was transferred to the tree.

Belief in the efficacy of the ash tree against snakes was first mentioned by Pliny, who stated that a snake would not creep over ash leaves and that if a circle were drawn with an ash rod around a snake it would die of starvation. This belief persists in England and the United States and the snake's fear of ash leaves has been extended to a fear of the shadow of the tree.

asherah (plural *asherim*) A sacred pole which stood in close proximity to the massebah and the altar in early Semitic sanctuaries. Originally it was a sacred tree, later it was artificially constructed of wood (I *Kings* xiv, 14, 23; II *Kings* xvii, 10, 16), sometimes in imagelike form (I *Kings* xvi, 13). Such posts were a part of the cultus equipment of the temple of Jahweh in Jerusalem down to the Deuteronomic reformation of Josiah (II *Kings* xxiii, 6).

The Phœnician asherim are represented variously as slender posts surmounted by a crescent moon, curved lines forming a kind of sun disk, or by two sun disks. They are often represented as conventionalized date palms in drawings. In the Hebrew cult the posts were sometimes carved into the semblance of a human form or of its reproductive organs and were often draped. From the asherah was developed the wooden idol.

The asherah was sometimes regarded as a symbol of a deity and gave its name to the god or goddess it symbolized. The Canaanites called their goddess of fertility and prosperity Asherah and the consort of the Syrian god Amurru was an Asherah. Among the Israelites there is some indication of the same transference (*Judges* iii, 7; II *Kings* xxiii, 4). The name also attached itself to the mother goddess in some areas. Krappe believes her to be the great goddess of the Syrians, and the posts either a survival of a dendromorphic stage or, on the analogy of the Roman Terminus, the boundary-markers of the sanctuary area. In Palestine, Asherah's consort was Adad; in Arabia, he was the Minean Wadd.

ashes The residue left after the combustion of a substance such as coal or wood or after the cremation of human or animal bodies or plants. Ashes are used in folk practices to control the weather, in religious rituals, in mourning customs, to fertilize fields, flocks, people, as a badge of humiliation, in divination and exorcism, to prevent sorrow, plague, vermin, lightning, fire, sore eyes, contagious diseases, skin eruptions, swollen glands, also to cure headache, nosebleed, colic, rheumatism, consumption, and in ablutions and amulets.

Because of the qualities attributed to ashes, probably stemming from a belief that they share in the mysterious nature of the fire which produces them, they are used for religious or semireligious purposes in many parts of the world. A purificatory bath of ashes is used by the Lingāyats (India). The Brāhmans rub the body with ashes in preparation for religious ceremonies. Lamas of Tibet model images of Buddha from a mixture of clay and the ashes of a holy man, put them in shrines and perform devotions before them. Hindus use the ashes taken from the fires in honor of Darma Rajah and Draupadī to drive away demons and devils. The Kachins (Burma) propitiate Trikurat, the forest spirit, after a hunt by treading on ashes taken from the house hearth. Aztec priests blackened their faces with ashes before celebrating religious ceremonies. In the Hebrew Red Heifer ritual for purification from defilement by contact with a corpse, ashes from an offering were put into water, and the contaminated person was sprinkled with the mixture. According to the Mishnah, during fast days proclaimed because of drought, the Ark of the Covenant, as well as the people participating in the procession, were sprinkled with ashes. Covering oneself with ashes either served as an expression of self-humiliation or in memory of Abraham who said, "I am but dust and ashes" (*Gen.* xviii, 27). Ashes are used as a symbol of penitence on the first day of Lent in the Catholic Church.

Ashes are scattered in the air to condense clouds and bring rain during droughts (Muyscas, New Granada), to disperse mist (Peru), and to clear the clouded evening sky (Guarayú, Bolivia); they are thrown on the water to bring fair weather (Alacaluf, Tierra del Fuego), thrown into a whirlwind to calm it (Abipón, Chaco, South America), scattered in the fields to prevent hailstorms (Bavaria, Bohemia), used as a talisman against thunder and lightning (France, Bohemia).

In fertility rites the ashes of a sacrificed human being were scattered over the fields (Osiris rites, Egypt; Marimos, Bechuanaland; Khonds, Bengal); the ashes of animals were used to insure the fecundity of flocks and a plentiful milk supply (Romans); those of the Easter fires, frequently mixed with palm ashes in Catholic countries and those of the Midsummer fires (Germany, Switzerland, Ireland) were fed to animals or spread on the fields.

Ashes are used to prevent or cure all types of disease or illness in men and animals. They cure sore eyes (Salee, Morocco; Moslems, North Africa; Mikirs, Assam; Hopi, North America), are considered a remedy for consumption when taken daily by the spoonful moistened with water (Belgium); they prevent skin eruptions and itch (Bosnia, Herzegovina, India, Hopi), heal swollen glands (France), cure headache (Bombay), prevent hair from falling (Berbers, Morocco), stop fever (early England), cure stomach trouble (Miwok), stop nosebleed (Dakotas, Winnebagos), counteract inflammation (Hopi). The ashes of a male infant can be used as a cure (Quechua, South America) for soccahuayra, an illness caused by malignant winds. Ashes are given to cattle to insure them against plague and other ills (Germany, Armenia) and to fatten them (China).

More familiar uses of ashes are those of mourning customs in which they are symbolic of affliction. Many peoples strew themselves with ashes during funerals. The widow of a deceased member of the Arunta tribe smears her torso with white clay and then coats the clay with ashes. The Nahua carry the ashes of honored chiefs as talismans. The Digger Indians mix the ashes of a dead man with pine-tree gum and smear the mixture on the heads of the mourners. To absorb the qualities of the dead a number of South American Indian tribes mixed their ground bones or ashes with food or drink. The Tarianas and Tucanos disinter and cremate a corpse a month after burial, mix the ashes in caxiri and drink the concoction. In Bengal ashes are used to determine into which animal the ghost of a dead man has migrated.

Ashes are used in divination, especially on Hallowe'en (Ireland, Isle of Man, Lancashire), to determine the guardian deity of children (Yucatan), to prevent the sight of ghosts or return of the spirit of a dead person (Mexico, Philippines, northern India), to make a bridegroom subservient to the bride (India). They are blown toward the new moon so that men's strength will increase as the moon increases (Gold Coast). The Kwakiutl Indians rub the ashes of lupin on a child to make it sleep, ashes of cedar to make it strong, ashes of a snail for strong eyes, and the ashes of sallal berries and feathers to keep it quiet.

In the cosmology of the Mocoví the Milky Way is believed to be the ashes of the celestial tree which was burned in early days. The Incas believed that at one time the moon was brighter than the sun and that the sun, in a jealous rage, threw ashes into the moon's face to obscure her brilliance.

In mythology and folktale man was created from ashes (Gilbert Islands, Aztecs), the Milky Way is made of ashes (Bushman), ashes speak (Jamaica), a trespasser (ghost, lover, fairy, etc.) is detected by strewing ashes (Denmark, Germany, Seneca Indians), resuscitation of a cremated man is effected by blowing on the ashes (Bakairi, South America) and by throwing ashes on the funeral pyre (India). People or objects are magically reduced to ashes in Indian, Arabic, and Danish folktale; ashes are used to mark a road or path (Germany, Jamaica, Benga, Ekoi, Gold Coast, American Negro).

Ashes appear in riddles and proverbs: If a stick of tobacco cost six cents and a half, how much would a pipeload come to? Answer, ashes (Barbados); Every man must eat a peck of ashes (or of dirt) before he dies. [SPH]

Ashmedai or **Ashmadai** In Hebrew mythology and legend, the king of the demons who visited heaven every day to learn the fate of human beings. According to the *Haggadah,* Solomon sent Benaiah ben Jehoiadah to capture Ashmedai who knew the whereabouts of the shamir, a worm whose mere touch would cleave rocks. Ashmedai was forced to reveal the worm's whereabouts and then to remain with Solomon until the Temple was completed. One day the king asked the demon wherein the greatness of the demons lay if their king could be kept within bonds by a mortal. Ashmedai replied that if Solomon would remove the chains and lend him the magic ring, he would prove his greatness. As soon as he was released, Ashmedai seized Solomon, flung him out of Jerusalem, and palmed himself off as king. After long wanderings and provided with another magic ring, Solomon regained his throne and the demon fled.

Ashtoreth or **Ashtareth** The name used in the Old Testament for the Semitic mother goddess, Astarte-Ishtar (*Judges* ii, 13; x, 6; I *Sam.* vii, 3; xii, 10).

Ashur (1) or **Ashshur, Ashir, Asshur,** or **Assur** In Assyrian religion and mythology, the chief god: a god of battle. Originally Ashur was the baal of the city of Ashur and probably was a solar deity. As Assyria grew more and more warlike, Ashur's attributes as a war god became more all-absorbing and his cult became the dominant worship of the entire country. His divine city depended upon the location of the royal residence and the king was the sole high priest.

Stories, feats, etc., attributed to Anu, Enlil, and Marduk were gradually transferred to Ashur as the Assyrians subdued the country, so that he came closest in the Assyro-Babylonian religion and mythology to crystallizing the principle of a central single god. He was pictured as an eagle-headed, winged deity, usually with a disk symbol surmounted by the figure of a warrior. He was chief of the Igigi, who fought for Ashur and the king. His consort was Ashuritu, Beltu, or Bēlit. Ishtar sometimes appears as his wife and sometimes as an independent queen united with Ashur in the leadership of the Assyrian people. The theory that he was identical with the Aryo-Indian Asura and the Persian Ahura has not been accepted, but he was almost identical in character with the Jahweh of the early Israelites.

Ashur (2) or **Ashura** In the Mohammedan lunar calendar, the 10th day of Moharram, the first month of the Mohammedan year: the Mohammedan New Year. Among the Berbers of North Africa, this is the day on which bonfires are built so that the people, by leaping over the flames or driving their cattle through them, can purify themselves from evil or prevent their cattle from becoming diseased. Girls who wish to marry wash in water boiled over the bonfire which is sometimes built on the evening before Ashur. Compare BELTANE.

Ash Wednesday The first day of Lent: so called from the ceremonial use of ashes as a symbol of penitence in the Roman Catholic Church. Of the Protestant churches only the Episcopal or Anglican marks the day by a special service and the use of ashes has been discontinued as a "vain show" since shortly after the Reformation. The ashes, used on the heads of the faithful in the Roman Church and made by burning the palms used on the Palm Sunday of the previous year, are placed there with the words, *Memento, homo, quia cinis es; et in cinerem reverteris.* At first ashes were administered only to public penitents who appeared barefoot and in penitential garb before the church door. As the number of penitents grew larger, ashes were administered to the entire congregation.

Ash Wednesday and the three days following originally were not a part of the Lenten period, but were added about 700 A.D. to make the fast days 40 in number (since the Sundays in Lent are not included as fast days) to correspond to the number of days Christ fasted.

Ash Wednesday is the beginning of a period of abstinence, quiet, and penance, in strong contrast to the preceding period of carnival. In Germany the Jack-o'-Lent made its appearance on this day: a ragged, scarecrowlike effigy used to personify Lent. In rural France a personification of good cheer was carried around and money was collected for its funeral as a symbol of the burial of good living during Lent. In Italy, Spain, Germany, Austria, France, and Greece a personification of the carnival was sentenced to death and stoned, burned, or drowned by the peasants on Ash Wednesday or, occasionally, on Shrove Tuesday.

In Germany it is considered bad luck to tie up cattle or sell them on Ash Wednesday. In Hesse, Meinengen, and other districts, people eat pea soup with dried pig ribs on this day. The ribs are then collected and hung in a room until sowing time, when they are inserted in the fields or in the seedbag among the flaxseed as an infallible specific against earthfleas and moles, and to cause the flax to grow tall and well.

Asin In the folklore of the Toba Indians of the Chaco, a character sometimes regarded as a culture hero and creator of palm trees, Barbary figs, and bees, sometimes believed to be a great shaman who plays the role of a miserable and very homely man only displaying his true power after great abuse, and sometimes regarded as the symbol of the humble man who proves his mettle.

asisi or **atiti** In the belief of the Orokaivas of Papua (Melanesia) the shadow or reflection; also the immaterial entity not necessarily visible but identified (especially in dreams) with or substituting for some person. The asisi is not a soul but an immaterial substitute. Animals and inanimate objects also have asisi. The asisi is not synonymous with the sovai, which survives death.

Ask or **Askr** In the *Völuspa,* the first man, created from an ash tree or a block of ash. Odin gave him a soul, Hœnir gave him motion and the senses, Lodur gave him warm blood. In the *Prose Edda,* the three creators are Odin, Vili, and Ve. See EMBLA.

Asking Festival or **Ai-yá-g'ûk** An Alaskan Eskimo festival in which an attempt is made to fulfill the wishes and desires of each member of the community. On a certain day a man chosen by the group carries from house to house a wand, named Ai-yá-g'ûk, from which hang three hollow globe-shaped objects. In each house, when the Ai-yá-g'ûk enters, the head of the house states his own wish, and on learning the wishes of others, gives something that another has asked for. It is wrong to refuse any request made with the Ai-yá-g'ûk. In parts of the Lower Yukon, instead of verbal statement of the wishes being made, images of the things desired are hung on the wand and carried from one member of the community to another, for the fulfilment of individual desires.

Asmodeus or **Asmodæus** In Hebrew mythology and legend, an evil spirit or demon; son of Naamah, sister of Tubal-cain, and Shamdon; he appears first in the apocryphal *Book of Tobit*. Asmodeus fell in love with Sarah, the daughter of Raguel, and tried to prevent her from having a husband by killing each of her seven husbands successively on the nights of their marriage to her. He was rendered harmless when Tobias married her and, at the instance of the angel Raphael, burned the heart and liver of a fish. Asmodeus fled to Egypt where Raphael caught and bound him. In the *Testament of Solomon* he is pictured as the destroyer of matrimonial happiness. Solomon compelled Asmodeus to help in the building of the Temple. Asmodeus was the spirit of lust and anger; he was king, Lilith queen, of the demons.

Asmodeus is Persian in origin and may be identical with the demon Æshma, one of the seven archangels of Persian mythology, and the Zend Æshmo daëva. He is identified with Ashmedai, but the relationship of the two is in dispute. Asmodeus seems to be an evil, destructive spirit while Ashmedai, like the devil in medieval Christian folklore, is no longer the dreaded archfiend, but the degraded object of irony and humor.

asogwe The rattle of the chief priest of any Dahomean cult: used to summon the gods. It could be obtained only from the king, and is an absolute essential for the establishment of a cult-house, whatever the cult. In the days of the monarchy, at the time for the annual taxation of cult-houses, the rattle had to be presented at the ceremony, whether or not the priest himself was able to attend. Its main function, however, is religious; without the asogwe no god can be called. [MJH]

aspen Any of several poplars of Europe and North America with tremulous leaves, especially *Populus tremula* and *P. tremuloides*. The leaf is said in Brittany to tremble because Christ's cross was made of aspen wood, or because at the hour of the Passion the plants and trees of the world trembled and bowed their heads —all except the aspen which asked, "Why should we weep and tremble? We have not sinned!" Before the aspen had ceased speaking it began to tremble and will continue to do so until Judgment Day. In German tradition, during the flight into Egypt, the aspen was cursed by Jesus when it alone, of all the trees in the forest refused to acknowledge Him. At the sound of His voice the aspen began to tremble. Another belief is that the leaves of the aspen were made from women's tongues. According to the doctrine of signatures the aspen is a specific for the ague.

ass A long-eared equine quadruped, smaller than the horse and with shorter mane and tail-hair. The ass appears in folk beliefs and tales wherever it is domesticated, especially in the countries around the Mediterranean Sea. Egyptian tomb pictures of about 2500 B.C. show asses laden with huge saddle bags, others treading out grain on a threshing floor. Both the wild and domestic ass are mentioned in the Bible (*Job* xxiv, 5). The domestic ass was used for riding (*Num.* xxii, 21; *II Kings* iv, 24; *Judges* x, 4; xii, 14), for carrying burdens (*Gen.* xxii, 3; xlii, 26) and for plowing (*Isa.* xxx, 24; *Deut.* xxii, 10).

According to rabbinical literature the ass was created to carry burdens, its blood was a remedy for jaundice, and its bite more dangerous than that of a dog because it might break a bone. A strap made from ass or calf hide was used in judicial scourging. The ass of Abraham when he traveled to the sacrifice of Isaac was declared to be the same animal which later bore Moses' wife and her sons into Egypt (*Ex.* iv, 20) and which is to serve the Messiah (*Zech.* ix, 9). The mother of this ass is the one upon which Balaam rode and which was created at the close of the sixth day of creation.

Greek and Latin writers accused the Jews of ass-worship and later made the same accusation against the Christians. These accusations probably originated in the misconception that the Jews worshipped Dionysus to whom the ass was sacred. The ass was the religious symbol of the Gnostic sect of the Sethinai, and is a traditionally sacred animal because of Christ's entry into Jerusalem upon an ass. The dark stripe running down its back crossed by another at the shoulder was given to it because it carried Christ.

In Greek legend, Midas was asked to judge the better flute player in a contest between Pan and Apollo. He imprudently judged Pan the winner. Apollo, angered, changed the king's ears into those of an ass to indicate his stupidity. Midas and Marsyas were originally probably satyrs or sileni (ass-demons or horse-demons) among the Thraco-Phrygians where the ass was sanctified and sacrificed. The flaying of Marsyas in the story of the contest with Apollo, which paralleled the Pan-Apollo story, may be an etiological explanation of ass sacrifice. In Greco-Roman art Midas and Marsyas became human in form. In Macedonian legend Midas caught one of the sileni in his rose gardens and Apuleius adopted the story saying that eating roses would restore to human form a man changed into an ass.

In Vedic mythology an ass drew the chariot of the Aśvins. Armenians who have unsatisfied claim against someone sacrifice an ass at the grave of an ancestor of the debtor believing that the soul of the ancestor will be transferred to an ass if the claim is not satisfied.

The ass was associated during the Middle Ages with Palm Sunday and Saint Nicholas. An ass was also an essential feature of the Feast of Fools.

The ass was believed to have great curative powers. Early writers advised a man stung by a scorpion to sit on an ass facing the animal's tail or to whisper in its ear, "A scorpion has stung me," and the pain would be transferred to the animal. In England hairs taken from the cross on the animal's back were believed to cure whooping-cough if hung in a bag around the neck of the sufferer. In the Hebrides a child was passed three times over the back and under the belly of an ass in the name of the Blessed Trinity to prevent the same disease. In the Middle Ages fresh asses' dung was squeezed and smeared over the eyes to cure various ailments, and asses' hoofs were bound to a patient's extremities, right on right, left on left, to cure gout. The congealed blood of the animal was used in suffumigations from which the future was foretold. A lotion made from an ass was sprinkled on insane people to cure them.

The ass appears as a leading character in numerous folktales, fairy tales, and fables in Arabia, Belgium, Brittany, Czechoslovakia, Denmark, Egypt, Estonia, Finland, France, French Canada, Germany, Greece, Holland, India, Ireland, Italy, Lapland, Norway, Persia, Philippine Islands, Russia, Spain, Sweden, and among the Hebrews and American Indians. Æsop has 27 fables about the ass, and ass fables appear also in the Talmud, Phædrus, and Bidpai. Many stories are designed to illustrate the stupidity of the animal. The Indian tale in *Kathā Sarit Sāgara* is a good example. A thin ass was covered with a panther's skin by its owner and let loose in a neighbor's corn. People were afraid to drive it away. One day a cultivator saw the animal and, bending down, started to creep away. The ass, thinking him another ass, brayed, giving himself away.

Few animals are referred to in proverbs as frequently as the ass. Among the most popular sayings and proverbs are: To make an ass of oneself (do something foolish); The ass waggeth his ears (applied to those who talk wisely but have little learning); Well, Well! honey is not for the ass's mouth (persuasion will not convince fools); Every ass loves to hear himself bray; *Asinus in unguento* (Latin, ass among perfumes—bull in a china shop); *Asinus ad lyram* (Latin, an ass at the lyre—an awkward fellow); *Asno con oro, alcanzalo todo* (Spanish, an ass laden with gold overtakes everything—a rich fool is thought wise); *Âne chargé de reliques* (French, an ass laden with relics, applied to a person who gives himself airs when he acquires a little authority). [SPH]

Ass, Feast of the A festival popular in northern France during the Middle Ages, held on Jan. 14 to commemorate the flight of Joseph, Mary, and Jesus into Egypt. Originally a girl carrying a baby and seated on an ass was led through the streets to a church where mass was said. The festival degenerated into a farce which in Beauvais fell so low that an ass was led to a table in the church and given food and drink while a burlesqued vesper service was conducted. The people and clergy then danced around the animal imitating its braying. A presentation of farces followed outside the church and the mad affair ended with a midnight mass at the conclusion of which the priest brayed three times. The feast was suppressed by the Church in the 15th century but did not entirely disappear until much later.

Assassin A member of an Oriental sect of fanatics whose religion was a mixture of Mohammedanism and Magianism. The order was founded in Persia at the end of the 11th century by Hasan-ben-Sabbah, and is still represented in India by the Khōjās. Assassins were skeptical of the existence of God and believed that the world of the mind came into existence first, then the soul, finally the rest of creation. At death, man's soul rejoins the universal soul. It is imprisoned in the body only to execute the orders of the imâm and if it quits the body while obeying, it is carried to the upper world. If it disobeys, it falls into darkness.

This belief made the faithful disciples willing to perform any deed without question and without fear. The assassinations for which the sect was famous were committed at first to wipe out its persecutors. Later they were committed for anyone willing to pay for the service. Assassins were trained for assassination. They were taught foreign languages, the ceremonies of foreign religions, and how to adopt and maintain disguises in order to win the confidence of their intended victims. They were widely feared, especially because they struck when and where least expected. The name of the sect is derived from the Arabic *Hashshashin*, hashish-eaters, given to them because it was suspected that they intoxicated themselves with hashish before attacking an enemy. See OLD MAN OF THE MOUNTAIN.

Astarte, Ashtart, or Ashtoreth The mother goddess of Phœnicia; deity of sexual activity, fertility, maternity, and war, erroneously identified as a moon goddess. She is shown with horns in Phœnician art, but these horns were the horns of a cow (fertility) and not those of the moon. In Sumeria the mother goddess was called Inanna, in Armenia Anâhit, in Phrygia Cybele, in Babylonia Ishtar, in the Bible Ashtoreth, and in North Africa Tanith or Dido. In southern Arabia Athtar, a masculine deity, was the result of the bifurcation of Astarte, the feminine half being called Shams. The worship of the masculine Athtar spread to Abyssinia where he was known as Astar. The Biblical Ashtaroth is a plural, like Baalim, and refers to "goddesses" in general, as Baalim does to the heathen gods.

In primitive worship fruits of the earth, newborn animals, and first-born children were sacrificed in order to increase fertility. Astarte was worshipped by the Israelites after the conquest of Canaan (*Judg.* ii, 13; x, 6; I *Sam.* vii, 3; xii, 10). The Philistines also adopted the cult of Astarte. The cult spread from the Phœnicians to the Greeks and Romans, reached Malta and Sicily and the British Isles. This cult seems not to have spread into Syria because of the strength there of Atargatis, the Syrian aspect of the mother goddess. Astarte has been identified with the Egyptian Hathor, Greek Aphrodite, Norse Freya, Irish Danu, and Hindu Indrani—all fertility deities.

The gazelle (at Mecca) and dove (at Eryx) were sacred to her as was the myrtle. At Arbela she was represented as robed in flames, armed with sword and bow. In Assyrian-Babylonian art she is pictured caressing or blessing a child held in her left hand. See ISHTAR.

aster (from Greek *aster*, star) The flower has always been associated with the stars and with astrologers who class it as an herb of Venus.

In Greece the aster, when burnt, would drive away serpents. The Romans used wreaths of the flowers to deck the altars of the gods. In much of Europe and the United States, the aster, like the daisy, is used in love divination. In China a wine made from the fermented stems and leaves of the aster is a delicacy, drunk especially on the ninth day of the ninth moon. Once Fei Ch'ang-fang of the Han dynasty advised a follower to go to the hills to drink aster-scented wine and to fly kites on this day. Upon returning home he found his domestic animals dead and realized that he might have met a similar fate. According to the *Feng Su Chi* the people living in the Li district live to be 120 or 130 years old because they drink water flavored by the asters growing on the surrounding hills.

The Chippewa Indians smoke the dried, powdered root of a variety of aster (*Aster puniceus L.*) to attract game. The smell of the smoke is believed to resemble that of a deer's hoof and deer come toward a hunter when the plant is smoked. See BEAR MEDICINE.

astragalomancy Divination by means of small bones, such as vertebræ: an ancient and almost universal custom. The bones are lettered and drawn from a mixed group haphazardly. The letters give the spelling, anagram, or general clue to the desired message. The use of more generalized forms, such as bone or wood cubes or bone cylinders, is believed by some to have given rise to games of chance.

astrology The science of the stars, anciently equivalent to astronomy, which was known as natural astrology, and used to predict such natural events as eclipses, the date of Easter, and meteorological phenomena. By the 17th century the term became limited to another branch of the study, judicial or mundane astrology, which purports to trace the influence of the heavenly bodies (stars, planets, sun, moon, etc.) on the course and events of human life. This star-divination, or astromancy, attempts to determine, usually by the configuration of the heavens at the time of a crucial event, like birth, the future destiny and general temperament of men. Astrology is one of the most ancient forms of divination, and prevailed among the nations of the East (Egypt, Chaldea, India, China) at the very dawn of history. The Jews became much addicted to it after the Captivity. It spread into the West and to Rome about the beginning of the Christian Era. Astrologers played an important part at Rome, where they were called Chaldeans and "mathematicians"; and though often banished by the Senate and emperors under pain of death and otherwise persecuted, they continued to hold their ground. In Europe, during the Middle Ages, especially in the 14th and 15th centuries, astrology became the master study to which practically all other fields of investigation were correlated and subordinated. With the rise and acceptance of modern astronomy after Galileo and Kepler, astrology fell more and more into discredit in the Western world. Belief in its findings still has many adherents in the West and almost every part of the world.

In its most primitive form, astrology may have arisen from the observable connection between the positions of the stars in the heavens and the seasonal changes on earth. From this to a belief in the causal influence of the stars, not only upon natural phenomena, but also upon man himself, is not a far step. One versed in the lore of stars then becomes helpful to the economic life of the community, and to the personal planning and well-being of the individual. Rulers, down to Hitler, have had their personal astrologers. The astrologer as a diviner eventually uses supplementary means of determination, and we find close connection between astrology on the one hand, and Chinese geomancy, Near Eastern hepatoscopy, Chinese and Japanese tortoise shell divination, and Gipsy palmistry on the other. For example, the names of the mounts of the hand in chiromancy retain their planetary significance, and their prominence is used by the palm-reader to ascertain the supposed temperament of the subject. Aside from the Jewish and Arabic belief that every man has his own personal star in the heavens, astrology holds that the ascendancy of a specific planet at a critical moment determines the personality of the person, as for example the influence of Mercury giving a mercurial temperament; Jupiter, a jovial, etc. By the casting of an exact horoscope in genethliac astrology, the astrologer makes his determination. The methods of horoscope-casting are traditional and the interactions of the various planetary signs have become more or less fixed in meaning.

Belief in astrology is based on the geocentric idea of the universe, since the influence of the heavens is inward upon the earth. When the Copernican theory and modern astronomy took over what had been natural astrology, the basis and hence the validity of judicial astrology was destroyed. Nevertheless, popular magazines on astrology continue to thrive in the fifth decade of the twentieth century, one periodical alone in the United States having a monthly circulation of perhaps a quarter of a million copies. See LAPIDARIES.

asura In early Vedic mythology, the supreme spirit: an epithet meaning god, applied especially to Varuna. In the *Brāhmanas* and *Upanishads* it was used to mean the opposite of demons or enemies of the gods (but not of mankind). The asuras are the descendants of Prajāpati and for a time divided the world with their younger brothers, the gods or suras. But they waged war with the gods frequently until they were slain by Indra with the aid of Vishnu (or by another god). The asuras dwell in the caverns of Mount Meru, below the level of the sea, in the four towns of Shining, Startassel, Deep, and Golden, and they leave their abysses only to battle the inhabitants of Meru.

In the epics, the asuras (the name is here used interchangeably with Dānava and Daitya) are still regarded as foes of the gods, but some of them are spoken of as friends and protégés of the gods. Śukra, descendant of Bhṛigu, is their teacher and guide; their abode, Pātāla, is a magnificent dwelling surpassing heaven in its splendor. In popular story, the asuras are sometimes heroes. When they are pictured as contending with the gods, however, they revert to their Vedic character of demons able to become invisible and to commit deeds of violence. Compare ĀDITYA; NĀGA.

Aśvamedha or **Aśwa-medha** The horse sacrifice, one of the most important and impressive Indian ceremonies of Vedic times. Two hymns for this ceremonial appear in the *Ṛig-Veda*. Horse sacrifices are principal events in both the *Rāmāyana* and the *Mahābhārata*. Originally the sacrifice was perhaps a fertility ritual, in which the king's wives passed the night with the sacrificed horse, the chief wife performing certain specific and formal rites. Later, the ceremony was extended and became a ritual statement of the sovereignty and aspirations of great kings. In the spring, usually, a horse was chosen, symbolically tethered to the post of sacrifice, and then released to roam at will for a year. The horse was followed by a representation of nobles to guard it from harm or defilement. If the horse traveled into the territory of another king, the latter could submit to the invasion and thus tacitly acknowledge the owner of the horse as his superior, or he could fight, as many did. During the period of the wandering of the horse, the population at home took part in ceremonies of celebration and preparation. At the end of the year, the horse returned and was sacrificed in a three-day ceremony, along with a he-goat and, in later forms of the ceremony, with many other animals. The horse was first ornamentally dressed, anointed and adorned, by the three queens of highest rank. Then he was smothered with robes, before and after which act riddles were asked the priests by other priests and the women by the priests. The chief queen performed the ritual act under the robes, thus taking to herself the horse's power of fertility. The horse was then cut up, roasted, and offered to Prajāpati, after which came the ceremony to purify the sacrificer, accompanied by the giving of gifts to the priests.

While vestiges of the earlier fertility ceremony are found in the later ritual, especially in the deliberate obscenity of some of its verbiage, essentially the strength and quickness of the horse was transmitted to the king by this later form of the ceremonial. So virtuous did the king become through the rite that it was believed the completion of a hundred such sacrifices would enable him to overthrow Indra and become the ruler of the gods. There is the additional idea of expiation or atonement in the sacrifice: the Aśvamedha performed by Yudhishṭhira on the advice of Vyāsa in the *Mahābhārata* was meant to atone for the wars he had caused. Brahmā is said to have made ten such sacrifices at the Daśāśmedh Ghāt in Benares, one of the principal places of pilgrimage in that city.

Aśvins or **Aświns** In Vedic mythology, twin cosmic gods variously deities of the dawn, of heaven and earth, of day and night, of the sun and moon, the morning and evening stars, twilight (one half light, the other half dark), or personifications of the two luminous rays supposed to precede the break of day. They are also divine physicians, the sons of Dyaus or of Sūrya (the sun) or Savitṛi (the activity of the sun), by the nymph Sañjñā. They are the horsemen whose golden chariot, drawn by horses, a bird, an ass, or a buffalo, precedes Ushās (the dawn) who is sometimes considered their sister, sometimes their wife. In other parts of the *Ṛig-Veda* their joint wife is Sūrya or they help Soma, the moon, to win Sūrya, and lose one chariot-wheel in the process.

In Brāhman mythology, they are no longer cosmic deities, but physician gods of great kindness and personal beauty, often given the epithets of Nāsatyā and Dasra. In the *Mahābhārata* they rejuvenated Chyavana for which they were given a share of soma. They restored the eyesight of Upamanyu and furnished Vispalā with an iron leg. They were the fathers of the youngest Pāṇḍu princes, Sahadeva and Nakula. In the *Rāmāyaṇa* they fathered the monkeys Dvivida and Mainda. See DIOSCURI; TWINS.

asylum Any place of shelter and refuge where the refugee is inviolate by virtue of the place itself. Among almost all peoples, ancient and contemporary, places sacred to them, and certain personages or objects regarded as sacred afford asylum to the hunted. The right of asylum is the right of a specific place, person, or object to afford such protection because of its inherent holiness. All over the world altars, temples, churches, tombs, the king's house, the king's person, the individual family hearth and home itself were (or are) sacred places where no blood can be spilled. The holy groves of many people protect plants, animals, and criminals alike.

Among some peoples just taking refuge with, or even touching, a woman affords asylum, because of the mysterious power believed to be inherent in the female sex.

Among the ancient Hebrews all altars afforded asylum to all fugitives except murderers. Later the right of asylum was transferred from the local altars to six certain cities, three on either side of Jordan. Even the wild birds were not driven from the altars. "The sparrow hath found her a house and the swallow a nest for herself where she may lay her young, even thine altars, O Lord of hosts" (*Ps.* 84). The Greeks and ancient Syrians also regarded birds nesting in holy places as untouchable. The sparrows of Æsculapius in Athens, for instance, and the pigeons of an early Syrian goddess in Hierapolis are often mentioned.

In ancient Greece all temples and altars were asylums; no person who put himself under the protection of a deity could be taken; no act of violence to remove him from the deity's presence could be enacted, in the belief that the deity would punish violators of the sacred place. Fugitives were usually runaway slaves or criminals fleeing either arrest or trial. Abuses of the privilege of sanctuary became so numerous and extreme that eventually the right of sanctuary was limited only to certain temples. The Romans (under Tiberius) reduced even this number; but statues of Roman emperors and eagles of the legions were asylums. With the Christian era right of asylum was transferred to the churches.

In medieval England a criminal could take refuge in a church, but after 40 days he was starved out. Usually he was given his choice between trial and exile. Henry VIII designated certain cities as places of permanent refuge, each harboring no more than 20 refugees, each of whom wore an identifying badge. Murderers, rapers, highway robbers, and committers of arson were denied sanctuary. In the reign of James I the right of asylum to fugitives from justice was legally abolished but the practice continued well into the reign of George I. In Spain it continued into the 19th century. Even today Portugal grants asylum to alien fugitives who would be killed if delivered up.

Typical of the observance of asylum and its ubiquity are the following: In New Guinea it is believed that the arms and legs will shrivel of anyone who lays hands on a fugitive within a temple. The big tree inhabited by the Samoan god Vave gives refuge even to murderers, although they have eventually to stand trial. In Hawaii, on the other hand, the criminal who takes refuge with the god Keave walks home safely in three days' time with the aura of divinity insuring his immunity from arrest. In Usambara a murderer is safe if he can touch the person of the king; in Madagascar, if he can but see the king. Hence in West Africa criminals are gagged lest they call on the king's name, or knives are pushed through their cheeks to hold down the tongue. The Ashanti slave goes free who flees to the temple and falls upon the fetish. Among the Marutse a criminal escapes punishment if he can evade his pursuers long enough to reach and throw himself upon the king's sacred drums.

Among many primitive peoples the house of a king or chief, priest or magician affords asylum. The coupling of the sanctity of the home with the idea of asylum is widespread in Europe.

The rights of asylum have dwindled in proportion to the spread of civic justice. International law controls the rights of neutral powers to harbor belligerent armies. The time limit for the stay of belligerent ships in neutral harbors is usually 24 hours. In South America embassies, legations and consulates are still regarded as asylums.

ásynjur The goddesses collectively of the ancient Teutonic pantheon. They belong to the æsir and Frigga is the chief among them.

Ataensic Sky Woman, the First Mother of Huron mythology: called Eagentci by the Seneca. She fell to earth from heaven, but was caught on the wings of waterbirds and borne safely to the earth. While this was going on Muskrat dove through the waters to find oeh-da (earth); and this he placed on Turtle's back. Ataensic bore twins, the Doyadano, Good and Evil, and then died. Hahgwehdiyu (Good) shaped the sky with the palm of his hand, and created the sun from his mother's face. Hahgwehdaetgah (Evil) set darkness in the west. Then Hahgwehdiyu made the moon and stars from the breast of Ataensic, to lighten the dark, and gave her body back to the earth. From it sprang all the living ones. In some variants of this myth Ataensic gave birth to a daughter, who became impregnated by the wind and died giving birth to the twins, who were left to the care of their grandmother, Ataensic, or Sky Woman.

Ataguju The creator in the mythology of the Huamachuco Indians of Peru. [AM]

Atahen Literally, man: the first man, and culture hero of the coastal Juaneño Indians of California. See CHINGICHNICH.

Atalanta In Greek (Arcadian) legend, the daughter of Iasus and Clymene, exposed by her father and suckled by a she-bear. She became a famous huntress. She slew the Centaurs who pursued her, participated in the Calydonian hunt, took part in the games in honor of Pelias, and may have gone along with the Argonautic expedition. Her father recognized her and urged her to marry. She agreed on condition that each suitor must contend with her in a foot race, death being the penalty for defeat, her hand the prize. Meilanion won by throwing out three golden apples given to him by Aphrodite. Atalanta stopped to pick them up, permitting her suitor to win. She was the mother of Parthenopæus. She and Meilanion were metamorphosed into lions after displeasing Zeus. In Bœotian legend, she was the daughter of Schœnus, her successful suitor was Hippomenes, and they were metamorphosed into lions by Cybele.

Ātar or **Ātarsh** (Persian *Ādar*) In Iranian mythology, the fire god, son of Ahura Mazda and conqueror of the dragon Azhi Dahāka; chief of the yazatas or Zoroastrian angels. Atar, who is sometimes classed as an archangel or Amesha Spenta, is a personification (imperfect) of fire. In the *Avesta*, five kinds of fire are recognized, the Bahrām, the spark of life in the human body, the fire contained in wood, the fire of lightning, and the fire in heaven.

Atargatis or **Atar** A goddess of fertility worshipped by the Syrians. Fishes and doves were sacred to her, and her temple at Hierapolis, the largest and richest in Syria, included a pond of sacred fish. Lucian, in his treatise, *de Dea Syria*, describes her cult and calls her Hera. In the inner temple at Hierapolis were three golden images, the first that of Atargatis, the others probably Hadad and Attis. The idol of Atargatis had attributes of Hera, Athena, Aphrodite, Rhea, Artemis, Selene, Nemesis, and the Moiræ.

Atargatis has been frequently identified as a local form of the Semitic goddess Ishtar-Astarte. Like Astarte, she was a goddess of fertility and water. Wherever the worship of Astarte went, that of Atargatis seemed to have followed. She is referred to in the Apocrypha (I *Macc.* v, 24; II *Macc.* xii, 26). Her chief temple in Palestine was at Ascalon. In her temple at Carnaim, Judah Maccabeus slew the inhabitants who had fled there for refuge and then burned the temple. Ctesias called her Derceto and the Romans knew her as Dea Syria.

Ate In early Greek mythology, the goddess of mischief, who incited men to crime. She was the daughter of Zeus and Eris, but was driven out of heaven for creating discord among the gods. In later mythology, she became an avenging spirit, somewhat akin to the Erinyes.

Atea Literally, Vast-Expanse, sometimes translated Light: the atmosphere, sky god, and male parent of Polynesian mythology. In the great creation chants of Tahitian, Tuamotuan, Marquesan, and other Polynesian mythology, Atea is described as having been "extended" by means of the pillars which Ta'aroa placed under the vast expanse. At this time Ta'aroa also invoked a great spirit to pervade Atea. Then when Ta'aroa called out "Who is above?" Atea answered "I, Atea, the moving space, the sky-space." In Tuamotuan mythology, Atea was specifically a shapeless being molded into beauty by Vahine Nautahu (Enchantress Woman). His wife was named Fakahotu (in some islands, the Marquesas, for instance, Atanua or Dawn). From their union were born sons and daughters, the gods (handsome offspring), then birds, butterflies, and creeping things (common offspring).

The creation chants describe Atea's long struggle with Tane, in which he is finally killed; but Atea's power (mana) could not die. It still prevails in the islands. The creation chants also tell the circumstances of Atea's and Fakahotu's exchange of sex. All that was masculine in Fakahotu was transferred to Atea; all that was feminine in Atea was transferred to Fakahotu. By this strengthening of the male and female in each, more and mightier gods were born. In the story of the attempt to raise the sky, two gods equipped with wonderful adzes journeyed to Atea, thinking to chip him off and prop him up with rocks. But when they beheld the grandeur of Atea they were afraid; they put the adzes back in the basket and fled. So there are still no artisans who can raise Atea, separate sky from earth.

It is a common practice in the Society Islands to invoke Atea (along with Tane and Ta'aroa) during the first bathing of a newborn royal infant "to render sensitive the skin of the child."

New Zealanders call this deity Rangi, or Sky Father; among the Tuamotuans he is Rangi-Atea. In the Society Islands he is Te Tumu, the Source, and the alternate name of Fakahotu is Papa. In Hawaii Atea is known as Wakea, and his wife is Papa. See VATEA.

Atharva-Veda One of the four collections of hymns, prayers, and liturgical formulæ which constitute the Vedas, the most sacred literature of the Hindus. This is the latest of the Vedas and probably of popular rather than priestly origin. It deals with the hostile powers which the sorcerer seeks to win over by flattery or to drive away by imprecations and has nothing to do with the sacrificial ceremony of the three other Vedas.

The *Atharva-Veda* consists of twenty books containing about 730 hymns. Of these the first six books probably formed the nucleus to which additions were gradually made. Many of its hostile spells are intended as remedies for a number of diseases and are to be used with various herbs. Others are charms invoking the dispellers of demons such as water, fire, and healing plants; charms for the prosperity of the fields and flocks, for harmony, for happiness in love and marriage. Among the hostile spells are imprecations against rivals and spells for the expiation of sins or moral transgressions. Some spells are for use in securing power, victory, or fame for the king.

The *Atharva-Veda,* in conjunction with the *Ŗig-Veda,* is the oldest source of information on early Aryan culture, mythology, and religion. See VEDA.

Athena, Athene, Athenaia, Athana, or **Athenaie** In Greek religion, the goddess of wisdom, of the arts and sciences, and of war; the virgin goddess. As a goddess of wisdom she was the protectress and preserver of the state, of social institutions and of everything which contributes to the strength and prosperity of the state such as agriculture, industry, and inventions. In this role she was the inventor of the plow and rake and the creator of the olive tree. She also taught men to yoke oxen to the plow and how to tame horses with the bridle. She is credited with the invention of numbers, the flute, the chariot, navigation, and nearly every kind of work in which women are employed as well as the arts of shipbuilding, goldsmithing, and shoemaking. She was celebrated with Hephæstus as the patron of the useful and elegant arts. As a war goddess Athena represented prudence and intelligence in contrast to Ares, the personification of brute force and rashness. As the patron goddess of the state she was the protectress of the phratries or clans and played an important part in the development of legal ideas. She was believed to have instituted the court of Areopagus.

Athena may have been a Minoan-Mycenæan goddess adopted by the Aryan invaders of Greece. Attempts have been made to identify her with the lightning and thunder but there is no proof that she was ever a cosmological goddess. In early Hellenic history she was the patron deity of cities, especially of Athens where she was one of the three most highly honored gods, the others being Zeus and Apollo. There as Athene Parthenos she represented the artistic and literary genius of the people. Her temple was the Parthenon on the Acropolis.

With the establishment of the Macedonian Empire, Athena lost her position as goddess of a civic empire but remained the Madonna to whose care Athenian boy-athletes and marriageable girls were dedicated. She was worshipped in all parts of Greece and in Rhodes.

In Greco-Egyptian religion she was worshipped at Sais and at Oxyrhynchus she was identified with the local goddess Thœris (Taurt). At Delphi as Athena Pronaia or Pronoia she was associated with the amphictyonic deities Apollo, Leto, and Artemis.

Her epithets are numerous and attest to the variety of her powers and interests. As Optiletis, Oxyderces, and Ophthalmitis she was gifted with keenness of sight and a powerful intellect. As Athenaia she was the special patron of Athens; as Itonia she was the goddess of Coronea; while at Sparta she was Agoraia, presiding over the popular assemblies. She was also worshipped there as Athena Chalcicecus of the Brazen House. As Areia she was a goddess of war; as Agraulos, an agricultural deity. As Alea she was the light or warmth in Arcadia; while as Apaturia and Phratria she was the goddess of the Athenian clans. The epithets Chalinitis (the bridler), Damasippus (horse-taming), and Hippia refer to her as the goddess of war horses. As Ergane she was the goddess of industry; as Curotrophus, the nurturer of children; as Polias, the goddess of the city; and as Bulia, the goddess of the council. Athena Boarmia, the oxyoker, was worshipped in Bœotia while Athena Hygieia, the health goddess, was associated with Asklepios at Athens. As Nikē or Nikēphoros Athena was the goddess of victory and was represented in statues as holding an image of Nikē in her outstretched hand. As Athena Mechanitis she was the discoverer of devices and as Athena Promachus, the goddess who fights in front. Her poetic epithet of Pallas or Pallas Athene may have resulted from the myth of her slaying the giant Pallas in the battle between the gods and giants.

A trace of totemism is seen in the name Glaucopis, or owl, which may have been worshipped earlier as a god and which, as so often happened, became the companion of the goddess who succeeded it. The epithets Coryphasia (head or summit), Acria (topmost) and Tritogenis (for the nymph of Lake Tritonis) may have been applied to her because of the myths explaining her birth.

Her most celebrated festival was the Panathenæa which featured a torch race and a regatta. Other festivals held in her honor included the Scirophoria with a procession from the Acropolis to the village of Sciron at the height of the summer to entreat the goddess to prevent great heat; the Chalceia or feast of smiths; the Plyntēria and Calluntēria, the feasts of washing and adorning during which her wooden image in the Erechtheum was cleaned and adorned; and the Arrhēphoria or Errēphoria during which two maidens began weaving the new pepla made each year for her statue.

Cows, bulls, and rams were usually sacrificed to Athena. She was represented as a woman of severe beauty carrying a lance, helmet, and shield on which was depicted the Gorgon's head. Her attributes were the owl, serpent, cock, crow, and ægis. The images of her which guarded the heights of Athens, called Palladia, represented her with shield uplifted, brandishing her spear to keep off the foe.

Athena was identified with the Egyptian Isis, the Vedic Ushãs, with the Roman Minerva, and sometimes with the Persian Anãhita.

In Greek mythology, she was the daughter of Zeus, born from his forehead. According to Hesiod, Metis was her mother but Zeus, on the advice of Ge and Uranus, fearing the birth of a son who would be greater than he, tricked Metis into changing herself into a fly and then swallowed her, afterwards giving birth to Athena himself. According to Pindar, Hephæstus split the head of Zeus with his ax and Athena sprang forth. Athena has also been regarded as the daughter of the winged giant Pallas whom she afterwards killed because he attempted to violate her chastity. Another tradition calls her the daughter of Poseidon and the nymph Triton or Tritonis in Libya. She was said to have invented the flute in Libya when Perseus cut off the head of Medusa. Athena imitated on a reed the sound of the wailing of Medusa's sisters and the plaintive sounds of the serpents which surrounded their heads. In the Greek flood legend Zeus commanded Prometheus and Athena to repopulate the earth by fashioning images of mud. Then he bade the winds breathe into the images and make them live.

Athena was prominent in Attic legend as the promoter of agriculture. Her foster son was Erichthonius, the earth god with whom she was honored in the Erechtheum on the Acropolis. According to one story she gave the chest containing Erichthonius (seed-corn) to Agraulos, Herse, and Pandrosos (the dew sisters, signifying the fertilization of the earth by the dew, and sometimes identified with Athena) with instructions not to open it, but Agraulos and Herse opened it and in a maddened frenzy brought on by their deed cast themselves down from the Acropolis. Athena then took charge of the child who lived in her temple. In a contest with Poseidon for the land of Attica, the gods promised the preference to whichever gave the most useful present to the people. Poseidon gave the Athenians the horse (or a salt spring) while Athena produced the olive tree and was adjudged the victor. From her Athens took its name. In the Trojan War the goddess sided with the Greeks. She was the companion of Odysseus and assisted him against the lawless conduct of the suitors. Despite her reputation as a virgin goddess, some traditions describe her as the mother of Apollo and Lychnus by Hephæstus.

Atlantis A legendary island in the Atlantic Ocean, beyond the Pillars of Hercules: first mentioned by Plato in the *Timæus*. Atlantis was a fabulously beautiful and prosperous land, the seat of an empire nine thousand years before Solon. Its inhabitants overran part of Europe and Africa, Athens alone being able to defy them. Because of the impiety of its people, the island was destroyed by an earthquake and inundation. The legend may have existed before Plato and may have sprung from the concept of Homer's Elysium. The possibility that such an island once existed has caused much speculation, resulting in a theory, whose chief exponent is Brasseur de Bourbourg, that pre-Columbian civilizations in America were established by colonists from the lost island.

Atlas In Greek mythology, the god assigned to keep the earth and heaven asunder. According to Hesiod he was the son of Iapetus and Clymene, brother of Menœtius, Epimetheus, and Prometheus. He led the Titans in their contest with Zeus, and his punishment was the bearing of heaven on his head and hands or shoulders forever. In later tradition he was a man metamorphosed into a mountain because he refused Perseus rest and food after the hero had slain Medusa. Perseus held up the Gorgon's head and Atlas was changed into stone, his beard and hair became forests, his bones rocks, his head the summit, and each part increased in mass until he became the mountain which supported the heavens. This mountain was believed to lie on the boundary of the earth. As the world increased in size with each new geographical discovery, the name Atlas was applied to mountains in other places, but the general belief that the true Atlas was in northwestern Africa in the area of the Atlas mountains persisted. The Berbers

regarded these mountains with great reverence and the Libyans regarded Mount Atlas both as a temple and a god.

The idea of a man (or mountain) supporting the world or the heavens is found also in the mythology of Siberia, of the Aztecs who believed that four gods supported the sky at world-quarters, of the Chibcha (Colombia), and among the Mackenzie River, Tlingit, Haida, Wishosk, and Yuki Indians of North America.

Atlas motif A motif (A842) found in a number of ancient and contemporary mythologies in which the earth is supported by a human being. The Greek story of Atlas who bears the world on his shoulders is the classical example. The Tsimshian hero Amala supports the world, not on his shoulders, but on the end of a long pole which revolves in a spoonful of duck grease which he holds on his chest. The Tlingits and certain Athapascan tribes conceive of the earth as being held in place by Hayicanako, the Old Woman Underneath Us. Chibchachum, deity of the Colombian Chibcha Indians, like Atlas, supports the world on his shoulders. If he moves, the earth shakes.

Atli In the *Volsunga Saga*, the name of Attila, king of the Huns, and brother of Brynhild. As atonement for Brynhild's death, Gudrun, sister of the Nibelungs, was promised to Atli in marriage. Unwittingly, Gudrun excited Atli's greed by her descriptions of the life and wealth of the Nibelungs. He invited the Nibelung princes to visit his court and then treacherously killed them. Gunnar and Hogni, the sole survivors, were put to death when they refused to tell the secret hiding place of the Nibelung treasure. Gudrun avenged her brothers' deaths by killing her own and Atli's sons, Erp and Eitel, and then by killing Atli.

ātman In Hindu religion, the inner essence of the soul; also the inner essence of the whole world. According to the *Śatapatha Brāhmaṇa*, "The ātman has for body, the life; for form, the light; for essence space . . . It permeates all the world." The ātman is all-comprehending, self-existent, the eternal thinker. Ātman originally meant "body," then it came to denote Self or Soul, the principle on which the functions of an individual depends. Ātman is the psychical phase of life; brahman, the cosmical. The two are considered identical in the Vedānta philosophical system of the Brāhmans.

Atmu or **Atum, Tem** or **Tum** In Egyptian mythology, one of the aspects of the sun god; the sun at evening. Atmu was the original god, self-created from nothing. In other myths, Atmu was created by the four frogs and four snakes which existed in the primeval chaos of waters. Shu and Tefnut, the first pair of the gods, were created by Atmu by himself, by spitting or by masturbation. He is pictured as a bearded man wearing the double crown of Upper and Lower Egypt.

Atnatu In the belief of the Australian Kaitish, the god who made and named himself and rose into the sky in the distant past; father and benefactor of men, interested in their ritual but not in the moral aspect of their conduct. Before creating the alcheringa, he drove his disobedient sons out of heaven and dropped after them everything now used by the people. Two churinga (bull-roarers) dropped by Atnatu became men who now make wooden bull-roarers, which imitate the sound of

Atnatu's celestial bull-roarer (thunder). Atnatu performs sacred services and punishes mortals who do not sound the bull-roarer at initiation ceremonies.

Aton or **Aten** An Egyptian god of the solar disk: symbolized by the disk with rays ending in human hands. During the reign of Amenhotep IV, this god became officially the one god of Egypt; Amenhotep took the name Ikhnaton, meaning "splendor of Aton"; great temples of the god existed at Thebes and Memphis. This attempt at reducing the power of the priests of Amen failed however, and after they recaptured their original hold on the state religion from Ikhnaton, the worship of Aton died out completely in the land and was never revived. One interesting conjecture holds that Moses was a priest of Aton who was forced to leave Egypt and carried the monotheistic belief into the Arabian desert where it became attached to Jahweh, the principal god of the desert region. Aton was a universal god, the source and embodiment of all, the friend of the oppressed, the comforter of the ailing, the fountain of good.

Atreus In Greek legend, the son of Pelops and Hippodamia; father of Agamemnon and Menelaus; king of Mycenæ. His wife Ærope was seduced by Thyestes, his younger brother, who was consequently banished. Thyestes sent Pleisthenes, Atreus' son, to kill his father by a ruse, but Atreus unwittingly slew his own son. For revenge he killed three sons of Thyestes and served them to their father at a banquet. Thyestes cursed his brother and departed. Later, Atreus was slain by Ægisthus, son of Thyestes.

Attis or **Atys** In Greek and Roman religion, a Phrygian god of vegetation, always worshipped in connection with the Great Mother. Attis was either of Semitic origin or was influenced by Semitic religion. His cult, centralized in Phrygia and Lydia, spread to Greece and finally throughout the Roman Empire.

His worship, characterized by frenzied orgies, was carried to Rome after the worship of Cybele had been adopted by the Romans in 204 B.C. Each year on March 22 a pine tree was cut and brought into the sanctuary of Cybele where it was swathed in woolen bands, decked with violets; an effigy of a young man (Attis) was tied to it. March 24 was known as the Day of Blood, for on this day the ceremonies reached their peak. They were characterized by blood-letting, the barbaric music of flutes and cymbals, and the whirling contortions of the lesser priesthood, who in a frenzy of excitement slashed themselves to bespatter the altar and the sacred tree with their blood. Probably it was on this day that they performed the act of self-emasculation which was an essential part of the cult. On the next day the resurrection of Attis was celebrated in the form of a licentious carnival.

March 26 was a day of repose, and the festival closed on March 27 with a procession bearing the image of the goddess Cybele to the Almo River where the wagon and image were bathed.

According to one legend Attis was the son of Cybele; in another he was the son of Nana, daughter of a river god, who was impregnated by an almond (pomegranate). Attis was loved by the hermaphroditic monster Agdistis, but planned to marry Ia, daughter of Midas. Agdistis struck the wedding party with madness, and

Attis castrated himself under a pine tree. Ia committed suicide. From the blood of Attis sprang the violet, and Zeus allowed the body to remain undecayed, the fingernails to grow, and the little finger to move.

In another legend Attis was put to death because of his love for Cybele, daughter of Meion, king of Phrygia and Lydia. The plague and famine which followed drove the Phrygians to institute the worship of Attis and Cybele. In a Lydian version of the story Attis was killed by a boar.

atua or **otua** In Polynesian belief, a spirit; any supernatural being, whether animistic, ancestral, or human. Some persons were recognized as atua while yet alive, for example priestesses of Pele in Hawaii who embodied the goddess and lived in seclusion on the volcanoes where she manifested herself. Atuas were of great sacredness; among the Maori, mention even of the name of some atuas required many precautions. As in all animistic belief, atuas resided in and displayed themselves in the various natural phenomena: animals, fish, wind, rain, mountains, forests, plants, even in war and songs and dances. The power of a chief derived from the atua of an ancestor of the tribe.

Audhumla or **Audhumbla** In Scandinavian mythology, the monstrous cow, formed in Ginnungagap by the cold from Niflheim and the heat from Muspellsheim. She sustained the first giant, Ymir, with her four streams of milk and herself fed from the salty hoarfrost, licking it into the being, Buri, whose son Bor was the father of the gods Odin, Vili, and Ve.

Augean stables In Greek legend, the stables of Augeas, containing 3000 oxen, which had not been cleaned for 30 years. Hercules' fifth task, set by Eurystheus, was to clean these stables. This was accomplished in the required single day by turning two rivers through them. Augeas then reneged on the pledge of a tenth of his herds to Hercules, exiling his own son Phyleus who had witnessed the feat and sided against him. Later Hercules slew Augeas.

In a New Zealand legend, Rupe, one of the younger Mauis, performed a similar task, cleaning the debris-filled courtyard of Rehua's house.

augurs Members of a priestly class whose duty it is to read and interpret omens, particularly with ceremonial observances. There have been several such groups; the best known were in Mexico, Peru, and Rome. The Roman augurs belonged to one of the four great priestly colleges. They are first recorded in Numa's time, but were much more ancient. Their number varied from three or four in early times to 16 under Julius Cæsar. The augurs had great political power, as they were able to suspend certain public affairs by the unchallengeable declaration of an unfavorable omen. The *lituus* (a bent staff without knots) and the *trabea* (toga with scarlet stripes and purple border) were the insignia of office. The augur, accompanied by a magistrate, marked with his staff a *templum* both on the ground and in the sky at midnight. He then sat in a tent within the templum and watched for signs. Signs in the east, usually on the left, were considered favorable; those on the other hand unfavorable.

augury Divination from the flight or song of birds (ornithomancy), or generally from omens such as lightning, thunder, or the movements of animals, usually under formal, ceremonial conditions (compare AUGURS): a practice both ancient and widespread, from Homeric Greece and ancient India to modern Melanesia and Africa. Strictly speaking, augury should be limited to the observation of auspices (Latin *avis,* bird, and *specia,* view) but commonly it is applied to divination in general, since the Roman augurs themselves used other omens than those from birds. The most usual omen birds are the crow or raven, and the hawk or eagle. Augury may have arisen from the belief that birds, inhabitants of the heavens, partake therefore of the divine; or it may spring from a totemistic linking between the bird or animal and the person affected. The eagle and serpent emblem in Mexico's coat of arms mirrors the legend of the founding of Mexico City in 1325, when a group of Nahuas saw the two on the shores of the lake and accepted this as a good omen for the establishing of the city there.

auki In the religion of the Quechua of Peru, a mountain spirit. It is believed in the Peruvian Andes that mountain peaks are inhabited by these spirits and contain concealed haciendas equipped with herds of livestock guarded by the servants of the aukis. These servants include the vicuñas which are the spirit's llamas, the condors (his chickens) and Ccoa (his cat, the most feared of his servants).

The aukis are called upon by sorcerers to help in curing, and the superior sorcerers (the alto misayoc) converse with the aukis while divining. In Kauri curing is performed by a brujo or curer who enters the sickroom which contains coca, sugar, a bottle of aguardiente, a whip, and 20 centavos. The brujo darkens the room and places a piece of white paper on the floor. He whistles three times and the auki enters through the roof and settles on the paper. Then follows a conversation conducted, with the aid of ventriloquism, between the auki and the brujo in which the cause and treatment of the malady are revealed. The auki then flies out by way of the roof, the brujo consumes the coca, etc., takes the 20 centavos, and leaves.

Auld Lang Syne A song with words set by Robert Burns to an old Scottish folk melody, also known as *The Miller's Wedding* and *The Miller's Daughter.* The Burns setting, widely popular in English-speaking countries, has been adopted as a toast of friendship to be sung as a closing song for social gatherings, and at midnight on New Year's Eve.

aunga In Melanesian belief, the good part or soul-substance of a man, which passes away after death, in contrast with the adaro which is the bad part and remains after death as a ghost.

Aunt Nancy The Spider: corruption of Anansi in Gullah (South Carolina) folktale. See AFRICAN AND NEW WORLD NEGRO FOLKLORE.

Auriga The Charioteer: a large constellation of the northern hemisphere, represented as a young man holding a whip in his right hand and carrying Capella, the Goat, with her Kids in his left arm. It is believed that this concept of the constellation is as old as the ancient peoples of the Euphrates. But the early Arabs thought of it as a Mule, as did also the Turks. Latin writers, Germanicus for instance, identified it with the lame

Ericthonius who needed a chariot to get around. Others identified it with the charioteer of Œnomaus, named Myrtilus, others with Hippolytus; others called it the Charioteer and Rein-holder. Biblical astronomers have likened it to St. Jerome, to the Good Shepherd, and to Jacob deceiving Isaac with "the savoury meat of two good kids."

Aurora Borealis The northern lights: a brilliant radiance visible only at night in the sky of high northern latitudes, usually appearing in streamers varying in color from pale yellow to blood red, sometimes as an arch of light across the heavens. The phenomenon is thought to be electrical but many explanations are given by the peoples of northern countries. The Eskimos and Tlingit Indians believe that it is the spirits of the dead at play and occurs after the death of many people; the Saulteaux Indians say that it is the spirits of the dead dancing. The Mandans explain the Aurora Borealis as an assembly of medicine men and warriors of northern nations boiling their prisoners and enemies in huge pots. The Makah Indians believe the phenomenon is caused by a race of small Indians cooking seal and walrus meat. The Kwakiutl Indians say it is the souls of deceased members of a family dancing for those living or about to die.

The Greeks and Romans were familiar with it: Pliny thought it due to natural causes but would not deny that it might have some connecton with untoward events. The Norse explained it in terms of the light reflected from the shields of the Valkyries while gathering the heroes slain in battle. In an Estonian folktale the Aurora Borealis is explained as a wedding in the sky attended by guests whose sledges and horses emit the radiance. In Scotland the phenomenon is used in predicting weather. If it appears low on the horizon there will be no change; if it is high in the sky stormy weather will follow. The Finns believe it to be the souls of the dead and the Ostyaks say it is the fires kept burning by the god of fish, Yeman'gnyem, to show travelers the way in winter.

austerities In the social, moral, and religious life of primitive people austerities or acts of discipline, self-inflicted or willingly borne, replace the asceticism of more advanced peoples. Austerities may be undergone for magical purposes, to make life more tolerable, to placate the gods, as initiatory ceremonies, or during a period of mourning.

Austerities vary considerably in their extent and nature, ranging from sacrifice involving property or possessions to seclusion for a long or short period of time, exposure to the elements, flagellation, fasting, or abstinence from specific foods, gashing or cutting the body, mutilation of some member of the body, bloodletting, making of scars or cicatrices, amputation, circumcision, subincision, excision, knocking out or filing of teeth, tattooing, and the supreme sacrifice (widows of India) of death. These ordeals must be undergone, usually, without any show of pain, although many of them are so rigorous that death often results.

During adolescence initiation ceremonies, for example, an Indian boy of the Californina tribes of North America was stung with nettles until he could not move, then subjected to the stinging of ants. After this he fasted,

Initiation into the priesthood in early societies is characterized by a severe training involving many austerities. Since the medicine man usually performs his functions while in a state of trance, or ecstasy, it is necessary for him to learn how to induce such conditions. This is frequently done by undergoing austerities. The Greenland angakok trainee induces trances by excessive fasting. The Guiana novitiate fasts, wanders alone in the forest, and drinks tobacco-juice water, to attain a state of delirium. After training the abnormal state is more easily produced, sometimes spontaneously, sometimes by artificial means such as flagellation, fasting, or the use of narcotics.

Australian aboriginal mythology Since the 18th century when the English and Dutch first described Australia, it has seemed to the civilized world a natural history museum of "living fossils," primitive types of animals, plants, and human beings, preserved through isolation and lack of contact with more advanced types either to stimulate development or cause extinction. Smallest of the continents, Australia has less than three million square miles of desert, bush, and grass fringed on the northeast and east by forests of acacia and giant eucalyptus. Archaic types of animals include egg-laying mammals like the duckbill and spiny anteater; marsupials like the kangaroo, bandicoot, wallaby, and wombat; and flightless birds like the emu and cassowary. These and other creatures have leading roles in Australian mythology which describes the origin and nature of peculiarities of animals, plants, and physiographic features, together with their cultural and assumed biological affiliations with human beings. These explanatory tales, R. B. Dixon states (1914), are "as typical, on the whole, for Australia as are the Maui myths for Polynesia, the wise and foolish brothers for Melanesia, or the trickster stories for Indonesia."

Though lacking agriculture, pottery, metallurgy, writing, and domesticated animals (except for the half-domesticated dingo, a disputed member of the genus *Canis*), the aborigines had achieved an adjustment to the inhospitable environment by a seminomadic, food-gathering economy which in 1788, when the British annexed eastern Australia and Tasmania, supported an estimated 300,000 individuals divided into over 300 separate tribes, each with its own dialect, territory, and subdivisions into hordes (Elkin, 1938). The complex social organization and world view counteract the effect of cultural poverty given by the meager material culture. The close spiritual, temporal, and spatial continuity and cohesion of members of a local group with their ancestors and home territory are expressed intellectually in myths told at ceremonies, now popularly called corroborees, where discussion among the men leads to a form fixed as to sequence of events and important details.

Much of Australia, except the extreme south and parts of the east (Knowles, 1937), has a characteristic mythological pattern that concerns the careers of totemic ancestors. Sometimes the ancestors, while possessed of supernormal powers, are human; sometimes they combine human with botanical and zoological qualities. During the mythical past, the "dream time" (called *Alchera* by the Aranda of central Australia, whose terminology has become anthropological *lingua franca*),

they emerged from the ground or a remote direction, often northerly, to wander over the horde's land. At "story places," now sacred spots and totemic centers, near water holes or elsewhere along their "dream path," they created plant and animal species, modified the landscape, and established ceremonies and customs for their descendants to follow. They named places, species, and natural phenomena, and created songs and sacred objects like that called *Churinga* by the Aranda (Spencer and Gillen, 1927), which are used in *Intichiuma*, food-increase rites, or in boys' initiation ceremonies. Before disappearing into the earth or sky or transforming themselves into rocks or creatures, after having tried out different places to settle, they left either their own spirits or spirit children in various incarnations to enter women magically to be reborn.

Illustrating the pattern is the narrative of Great Western Desert tribes (Tindale, 1936; Berndt, 1941) who tell of the Wati Kutjara, "Two Men," of the eternal dream time, who came from the northwest. One was lazy, the other energetic. As each had a species of iguana as a totem they are sometimes called "Men Iguana"; occasionally they assumed iguana disguise and used iguana designs on objects they made. On their "walkabout," the route of which men today follow ceremonially to reenact ancestral deeds ("We must do the same as did Wati Kutjara"), they made water holes, physiographic features, and the ceremonial board comparable to the Churinga, which they hid. They went on, made a bull-roarer, and subincised each other. With a magic boomerang they killed a wanderer who tried to steal their women and turned him into stone (the first death). Later they made ritual headdresses before going out of the territory or into the sky. A sample of the narrative follows . . . "after making a waterhole at Kanba, they proceeded northeastwards to Windalda where they made rock shelters. From Windalda they travelled west to Pinmal where they built an enclosure of cliffs suitable for corralling and spearing kangaroos when they come to water. Then they went north along the low scarp-face to Tjawan where they made trees, the fruit of which they stacked in heaps and made into fruit cakes by pounding them on stone mills. They went back again to Kulardu and here they accidentally left their spears, from which trees, yielding wood fine for spears, sprang up."

Each individual authority knew only portions referring to his horde's land; the total history was assembled from different hordes and tribes in the region. Spiritual and economic factors bind an aborigine to well-defined and respected boundaries. When he goes anywhere that his totemic ancestors have not traveled, he feels himself a transient in dire danger. Mythology makes the land home and tells him how to live in it. To be reborn, he must die in familiar territory so that his spirit will know its path and not wander homeless in totemic form. Mythological history is ritually reenacted to the accompaniment of myths, songs, paintings, and dramatic representations that revitalize the religious and emotional bond between people, land, and ancestors.

Though excluded from many ceremonies women, at least in northwestern tribes (Kaberry, 1939), are specialists on myths sanctioning rites involving the increase of certain plants, and the laws of female totemic ancestors responsible for the origin of birth and related matters. Besides serious myths associated with ritual, tales are told in everyday life for the fun of telling and listening to stories.

References to the mythical past constitute the final word on any debated matter. Adding authority is the name of the principal totemic ancestor, like Baiame of New South Wales, who by earlier writers was regarded as an All-Father, and the rainbow serpent associated with rain and fertility and known over much of the continent, being especially important in the northwest where he is called Kalseru. A moral tone dominates many myths. For example, the Wikmunkan tribe of Cape York Peninsula (McConnel, 1935) tells of the punishment of two male initiates who killed flying fox, tabu to them. The Murngin tribe of Arnhem Land (Warner, 1937) narrates how Bamapama, a trickster hero, committed many asocial acts including incest. His character and adventures recall Coyote of North American Indian mythology. Laughter and ridicule of his behavior express both vicarious enjoyment of tabooed acts and disapproval of "crazy men" like him.

One of the most valuable analyses of style, structure, and function of myth cycles is given by Warner (1937) for the Murngin tribe for the Wawilak and Djunkgao myths and rituals.

Existing regional differences in mythology have scarcely been analyzed; emphasis has been on description of function. The problems of analyzing mythic elements, tracing their distribution, noting their variations, and classifying them are rendered more difficult because mythological characters having the same name or dialectical variants of the same name are rare in Australia, unlike Polynesia. The prominence of certain names in discussions of Australian mythology is rarely due to their wide provenience but to their value as representative characters. For example, though the concept of a rainbow serpent is widely diffused, his name differs from one region to another.

Dixon's distinction, made in 1914, between two major mythological areas paralleling linguistic areas, is valuable now mainly as a springboard for further research which should include the numerous recent collections. Dixon distinguished between a southern and eastern area, on the one hand, and a northern and central, on the other; little had been recorded then in the west. Few tales or incidents are common to both areas, Dixon found, a view which further research would perhaps modify. Many hero myths in the central area are, he stated, known only to limited groups and not even to an entire tribe.

Australians, he pointed out, assume world pre-existence, but have much about the origin of, for example, mankind, fire, death, and natural phenomena. Explanatory myths, common throughout the continent, are obscured in the northern and central area by accounts, absent in the other area, about the careers of totemic ancestors. The south and east, unlike the north and central region, has more or less definite tales of a creator-being and creation together with myths about creation of man. The north either assumes man's pre-existence or narrates an explanation, widely known in Australia and present in Tasmania, about amorphous beings who were fashioned into human shape.

Tindale (1946) distinguished four different strata of myths: (1) simple tales of hunting and food-gathering told in the extreme south and in Tasmania about characters who act like human beings; (2) "man hero" tales, including those about Baiame and Wati Kutjara, of southern Australia from east to west, transitional to (3) myths about totemic ancestors with plant or animal qualities, told in central, northern, and northwestern Australia, and finally, (4) Papuan myths lately diffused into Cape York Peninsula.

The view of Australian aborigines as "living fossils" stems, in part, from their physical type, which, while having some characteristics of each, is neither Caucasian, Mongolian, nor Negro. Though regarded by certain scholars as Neanderthaloid, or otherwise related to precursors of *Homo sapiens*, the aborigines are customarily grouped into a separate racial division, the Australoid, representative of protomodern man.

Comparative mythology has not, at least as yet, shed much light on Australian origins. In the assumed migration from Asia via Indonesia into Australia, Negroid Tasmanians probably preceded Australians, who replaced them on the continent, but not in Tasmania where European settlers have since exterminated them. One theory has Tasmanians by-passing Australia to reach their island. Neither Australians nor Tasmanians (except occasional tribes in Cape York Peninsula) have myths about ancestors and heroes traveling from other parts of Oceania into their present country. Mythology, reflecting the basically similar culture of Australia and Tasmania, includes common elements relating to the origin of fire, the dual heroes or twin myth, the revival of dead people by stinging ants, the belief that characters become stars or constellations, and the myth that two sky-beings, perhaps twins, shaped rudimentary creatures into human beings. Tasmanian fragments of myths recount that two strange men, dwellers in Castor and Pollux, threw fire to human beings. Later the two rescued the bodies of two women slain at a pool by a monster and revived them with stinging ants. Then the four disappeared to become stars.

Melanesian resemblances, to Dixon, are most marked in southern and eastern Australia where occur themes like swan-maiden, spear chain to the sky (continental counterpart of arrow chain), liberation of concealed water, and theft of fire kept in a creature's body. The latter theme, also known to Aranda who tell of a male euro keeping fire in his sexual parts, is familiar to Polynesians and Micronesians. An embryonic being shaped into human form appears in Indonesian and Polynesian myths, where, in Hawaii, Maui himself is the artist. Dixon finds only hints of typically Melanesian tales about wise and foolish brothers in southern Australia. Papuan resemblances to central and northern mythology, Dixon notes, are of a negative sort in the virtual absence of cosmogonic myths and the restriction of many tales to small groups.

To Thomson, certain Cape York hero myths associated with a cult are Papuan in origin but reinterpreted by Australians to fit their totemic-ancestor complex; McConnel's theory (1936) about them is almost exactly opposite. Warner (1932) finds no distinct Malay mythological themes among Murngin visited by Malay voyagers, though beliefs about Malays are incorporated into myths.

The mentality and mythology of the aborigines have been the subject of innumerable theories, including those of Freud, Durkheim, and Lévy-Bruhl, based on the assumption, denied by many scholars, that the aborigines, having the most primitive culture known today, illustrate how early ancestors of all mankind lived and the nature of their intellectual and spiritual concepts.

Many of the following items cited below in order of first reference in the text have bibliographies. R. B. Dixon, "Oceanic" in *Mythology of All Races*, vol. 9 (Boston) 1916; A. P. Elkin, *The Australian Aborigines* (Sydney) 1938; N. Knowles, "Australian Cult Totemism," in *Twenty-fifth Anniversary Studies* (ed. D. S. Davidson), Publ. Phila. Anthrop. Soc., 1937; B. Spencer and F. J. Gillen, *The Arunta*, 2 vols. (London) 1927; N. B. Tindale, "Legend of the Wati Kutjara . . ." *Oceania*, vol. 7, pp. 169–185, 1937; R. M. Berndt, "Tribal migrations and myths . . ." *Oceania*, vol. 12, pp. 1–20, 1941; P. M. Kaberry, *Aboriginal Woman* (London) 1939; U. H. McConnel, "Myths of the Wikmunkan," *Oceania*, vol. 6, pp. 66–93, 1935; vol. 6, pp. 452–477, 1936; W. L. Warner, *A Black Civilization* (New York) 1937; N. B. Tindale, "Australian (aboriginal)" in *Encyclopedia of Literature* (ed. J. Shipley) New York, 1946; Davidson, D. S., "The Relation of Tasmanian and Australian Cultures" in *Twenty-fifth Anniversary Studies*, Publ. Phila, Anthrop. Soc., 1937; D. F. Thomson, "Notes on a Hero Cult from the Gulf of Carpentaria, North Queensland," *Royal Anthrop. Inst. Grt. Brit. and Ireland, Jour.*, vol. 63, pp. 453–537, 1935, and vol. 64, pp. 217–235, 1934; U. H. McConnel, "Totemic Hero Cults in Cape York Peninsula . . ." *Oceania*, vol. 6, pp. 452–477; vol. 7, pp. 69–105, 1936; W. L. Warner, "Malay Influences on the Aboriginal Cultures of Northeastern Arnhem Land," *Oceania*, vol. 2, pp. 476–495, 1932; S. Freud, *Totem and Taboo* (New York) 1924; E. Durkheim, *The Elementary Forms of the Religious Life* (trans. J. W. Swain), London, 1926; L. Lévy-Bruhl, *La Mythologie Primitive* (Paris) 1935; Also see other articles in *Oceania* and *Journals of Royal Anthrop. Inst. of Grt. Brit. and Ireland;* K. L. Parker, *Australian Legendary Tales* (London) 1897; *More Australian Legendary Tales* (London) 1898; W. R. Smith, *Myths and Legends of the Australian Aboriginals* (London) 1930; and A. van Gennep, *Mythes et Légendes d' Australie* (Paris) 1905.

KATHARINE LUOMALA

autograph album rimes Verses, preferably original, were written in personal blankbooks called albums by relatives, acquaintances, and schoolmates of the owners of the albums, asserting undying friendship, conveying good wishes, prophesying a bright future, or merely asking to be remembered forever. The rimes were signed, dated, often decorated elaborately with floral designs and calligraphic flourishes and paraphs, and the residence of the writer usually given.

There was great variety in the size, shape, decoration and binding of the albums, and the type of verse changed greatly with the decades. Every album was different, reflecting the taste and circumstances of the owners.

Autograph albums first appeared in any great numbers in America in the 1820's and 1830's, then increased in popularity slowly until the sentimental seventies and elegant eighties when they were quite the rage. Sporadic revivals of the craze have taken place since, and some stationers report it current now, but of late years it has been increasingly confined to teen-agers and rural romantics. Modern writers of album verse are apt to apologize by tending toward burlesque. The echoes sound mocking.

But students of folklore know that album verse with its ancient and honorable history needs no defense or exculpation. The custom stems directly from the album amicorum and the German Stammbuch, and for four hundred years has been followed by both the mighty and the meek.

It was about the mid-16th century that there suddenly appeared and spread rapidly among university students throughout Europe, first in Germany but soon thereafter in Scotland and England, the custom of carrying about a little leatherbound book called an *album amicorum*. It was not merely a "book of friends" as a superficial translation would indicate. In the lingua franca or conversational Latin of that day, used by scholars of all countries, amicus meant not only a friend in our modern sense of the word, but also was practically synonymous with patronus and socius. That is, in the album amicorum the student would seek to have inscribed the names and approving sentiments of patrons and protectors, companions and comrades, as well as those of his intimate friends. Students traveled widely then, and a book full of recommendations was of great practical value as well as of sentimental and even literary importance. Some of the artistic alba amicorum containing names of note which have survived wear and worm are almost priceless today.

James F. K. Johnstone, F.S.A., Scot., in *The Alba Amicorum of George Strachan, George Craig, and Thomas Cumming* (printed for the Univ. of Aberdeen, 1924), throws some light on an otherwise neglected subject. At a time when Scotch students were traveling all over Europe these three lads' alba cover most of the years between 1599 and 1619. One gets the rare flavor of the times when Johnstone quotes some of the rimes. In 1602 Robert Stuart wrote in Strachan's album the quaint and rather touching couplet:

> Ev'n so thocht fortoun force us to dissiver
> I sall induer your faethfull frind for ever.

And in 1605 J. Hopkyns wrote in Craig's vade mecum:

> Be as thou art my worthie friend,
> A Rock that firm remaines.
> That in the end the Rock of rockes
> May guerdon all thy paines.

Thus early we have a good example of a frequently occurring whimsy common to album writers unto this day who needs must bring in cunningly and usually punningly the name of the owner of the album. (Craig is Scotch for rock; cf. our crag.)

In Germany the album amicorum was more likely to be called a Stammbuch, for, as the name implies, it was more of a family affair. Even today in New York among families of German descent the folk custom persists that all accessible members of the family must be among the first to write in a new autograph album.

Thus we find a century and a half ago the great Goethe himself writing in his young son's Stammbuch the opening inscription which might be roughly translated into English:

> Hand to the patron the book, and hand it to friend and companion;
> Hand to the traveler too, passing swift on his way;

He who with friendly gift, be it word or name,
thee enriches,
Stores up for thee a treasure of noble remembrance
for aye.

In this book Schiller wrote, but when the boy asked Madame de Staël to autograph it, she flung it from her petulantly and said: "I do not like these mortuary tables!" Ladies with less foresight are doubtless responsible for the fact that hardly an album is to be found today without several pages missing.

The extent to which the circulation of these little books was carried may be inferred from the fact that Goethe owned one that had belonged to the Baron de Burkana who in his travels had collected 3,532 entries, expressions of esteem and friendship adorned with "compliments, maxims, epigrams, witticisms, and anecdotes" including contributions from Montesquieu and Voltaire.

The names of Charles Lamb and Leigh Hunt are definitely and often connected with the writing of romantic album verses in England in the first half of the 19th century. Both loudly deplored the vogue of young ladies chasing celebrities to secure not merely their signatures but an original sentimental poem as well, and gratis. Hunt might write for a damsel's album the protesting lines:

Albums are records kept by gentle dames
To show us that their friends can write their names,

and Lamb might growl about:

Those books kept by modern young ladies for show,
Of which their plain Grandmothers nothing did know,

but both poets knew as well as a Hollywood actor the publicity value of a crowd of autograph hunters. In fact, Lamb admitted as much in the preface of a volume of such verses, published in 1830: "I had on my hands sundry copies of verses written for albums . . . I feel little interest in their publication. They are simply advertisement verses."

Among these publicity poems were those written "In the Album of a Clergyman's Lady" in which he compares albums in turn to Gardens of wholesome herbs, Cabinets of curious porcelain, Chapels full of living friends, and Holy Rooms full of spirits of lost loved ones; "In the Album of a French Teacher"; "In the Album of a Very Young Lady"; and "In the Album of Lucy Barker."

Lucy was a young Quakeress, and Lamb took the opportunity to compare her innocence and purity with the spotlessness of her new album. Hundreds of writers since have rung the changes on the etymological derivation of the word album from the Latin adjective meaning "white," but none have matched the first and last stanzas of Lamb's ideal album poem:

Little book, surnamed of white,
Clean as yet, and fair to sight,
Keep thy attribution right . . .
Whitest thoughts in whitest dress,
Candid meanings, best express
Mind of quiet Quakeress.

By the time Lamb was writing in Lucy's album, the custom had spread to America and taken vigorous root. An old man, writing in Chambers Journal for Sat., Aug. 30, 1873, reminisced: "Those who can look back for half a century will remember the rage there was in their youthful days for albums. . . . legion was not a name multitudinous enough for them; literary men crouched under their tyranny; young maidens wielded them as rods of iron . . . Splendid books they were in their day, bound in rich morocco and gold, and often contained contributions from Scott, Moore, Montgomery and Praed; whilst Prout's beautiful sketches adorned their pages side by side with other artists."

The album-writing fad suffered a sea-change in crossing the Atlantic, for while the Montgomery-Hunt-Lamb style florid did obtain for a period in young ladies' seminaries and similar circles, and we do have a Blendena writing in the album of Elizabeth her classmate in Homer Academy in 1834:

Enough has Heaven indulged of joy below
To tempt our tarriance in this loved retreat,
Enough has Heaven indulged of secret woe
To make us languish for a happier scene,

we also note a lighter touch appearing as early as 1836, when Mary wrote in the album of Augusta of Coxsackie, N. Y., the chaste but purposely ambiguous:

I wish you health and happiness
And heavenly grace beside
And if you have *another* wish
That it may be supplied.

Once well started, the album verse burgeoned into many varieties which would have shocked Goethe. Everybody began writing poetry, or verse, or doggerel, using sheer nerve or Yankee ingenuity when talent gave out. One can but admire the originality of the Tillie who in 1856 wrote in the album of Mary Tice of Newburgh, N. Y.,

Ma chere amie Marie
Until life's last sand has run
May thy days flow lightly on
Is wished by Tillie Stevenson.

The emphasis on originality drew protests, of which the following was the most often used:

You ask me for something original:
I scarcely know how to begin,
For there's nothing original in me
Unless it's original sin.

Brief verses became popular, especially among the young men who settled for one like:

If on this page you chance to look,
Just think of the writer and shut the book.

There were several tricky arrangements, such as turning the book upside down and writing merely:

I'm the girl who ruined your book
By writing upside down.

or revolving the book and writing spirally or in concentric circles:

Round is the ring that hath no end;
So is my love to you, my friend.

The last page of the album was much sought, with a mock humility, and was often crowded with several:

Way back here just out of spite
These two lines do I indite.

Way over here at this back end
I inscribe myself your sincere friend.

Faded leaves, usually rose geranium, scent old albums, accompanied by the couplet:

> On this leaf, in memory pressed,
> May my name forever rest.

Pine needles were attached to album leaves and subscribed with the ever popular:

> I pine fir yew:
> I also balsam.

In one century-old album I found a curl of human hair glued gruesomely above this verse:

> This lock of hair I once did ware
> I now commit it to your care:
> And when you view this lock I've braided
> Then think of her whose brow it shaded
> H.P.B.D. June 24, 1840

In other less literal ways the young ladies let down their hair in these albums:

> This is the girl that got a kiss
> And ran to tell her mother:
> That she may live to be an old maid
> And never get another.

> Pray do not be so fickle
> As to love each man you see
> Or you'll get into a pickle
> Before you're twenty-three.

> If you wish to be blessed with Heavenly Joys,
> Think more of God and less of the boys.

> Remember me when at the tub,
> Remember me before you rub,
> If the suds should be too hot,
> Lather away, forget me not!

Boys did not like to write in these albums, but sometimes took the chance to retaliate thus:

> When this you see, remember me,
> And take a little catnip tea

(This is somewhat subtle, for the brew was consolation for old maids.)

> When you get married and have twins,
> Don't come to my house for safety-pins.

> Fall out of the cradle, fall into the river,
> But never never never fall in love.

The masculine revolt revealed itself in another way—writing answers opposite or below trite sayings. Where a feminine hand had written:

> Great oaks from little acorns grow,

there was likely to appear nearby a scrawled reply:

> Great aches from little toe corns grow.

The second line of:

> Remember well and bear in mind
> That a true friend is hard to find

would be crossed out and this line substituted:

> That a jaybird's tail sticks out behind.

I remember that one of my boy cousins hated the rime:

> Early to bed and early to rise
> Makes a man healthy wealthy and wise

and rephrased it in a girl cousin's album:

> Makes a man mad and pulls out his eyes.

And a fellow who had been reproved for his mulish obstinacy in refusing to write in a girl's album finally seized the book and wrote:

> On a mule you find two feet behind;
> Two feet you find before:
> You stand behind before you find
> What the two behind be for.

Just as the valentine, the rimed expression of love, when it became saccharine and stickily sentimental, found its rebuke in the shocking comic valentine, so its sister, the rimed expression of friendship in an album verse, when it became too vulnerable, was sure to be correctively treated by an observant realist.

When I arrange chronologically my collection of several thousand American autograph album rimes, I find I have a rather valuable means of insight into the changing folk life and folk thought from 1820 up to today. Recently I asked the proprietor of a large and long-established New York stationery store if he thought autograph albums were coming in again, and he replied laconically: "They never went out, mister."

CHARLES FRANCIS POTTER

Autolycus In Greek mythology, the son of Hermes, celebrated for his skill as a thief. He built up his flocks by stealing his neighbors' sheep and mingling them with his own, until Sisyphus outwitted him by secretly marking his sheep on the soles of their hooves.

automaton An automatic contrivance in human or animal form which imitates the actions of living things. The use of automata in folktales is almost world-wide. One of the earliest automaton legends tells how the mythical Dædalus invented the bronze man, slain by the Argonauts.

In the Middle Ages the imagination was constantly stirred by attempts to invent automata and perpetual motion machines. In the 11th century Ibn Gabirol created a mechanical servant who would do his bidding when he placed the Divine name in its mouth or on its forehead. The legendary Polish Rabbi, Elijah, created an automaton that grew so big he was forced to destroy it. In the 16th century, Rabbi Löw of Prague created the Golem, who worked on all days of the week as long as a plate inscribed with the Divine Name was kept under its tongue. On Friday evening the plate was removed so that the Sabbath would not be desecrated. One Friday, however, this was forgotten and the automaton fell to bits.

While automata most frequently have human form in folktales, they are sometimes dolls (Hindu, Italian) or animals (Italian, Jewish, Norse, American Indian, Koryak). Human-shaped automata frequently are statues or images able to render judgments (Arabian), indicate a favor to a suppliant (German, English, Spanish, medieval), reveal a crime (Indian), weep (Swiss), or sew (Spanish). They are frequently men wrought of iron in Danish and Asiatic tales. See BRAZEN HEAD.

ava Literally, mother, in the language of the Mordvins: often used for the names of female protecting spirits. For example, *mastor-ava* is the mistress of the Earth; *kov-ava*, the deity of the Moon, *varm-ava*, the mother of wind, *vir-ava*, mistress of the forest, *ved-ava*, the mother of water, *tol-ava*, the guardian of fire, and *kud-ava* is the spirit of the house. The word *ava* is of Turkish-Tartarian origin. Compare AWA. [JB]

Avalokita or **Avalokitesvara** In Mahāyāna Buddhism, the god of mercy or compassion, the Bodhisattva whose face is turned in every direction in order to save everyone; the son of the Buddha Amitābha. In his early development Avalokita was usually depicted with four or seven other bodhisattvas surrounding or below a Buddha. His dwelling place is in the paradise of Amitābha, Sukhāvatī, and at the end of the present age he will appear as the thousandth and last Buddha.

In his later development Avalokita became the national god of Tibet, eclipsing Amitābha. As patron of the Tibetan Church, he is incarnated in the person of the Dalai Lāma. He is represented in icons as human in form with two arms and one head. In one hand he holds a lotus, with the other he makes the gesture of a blessing. When he is identified with Śiva his eyes, faces, and arms are multiplied. In one figure he is represented with 11 heads and 1000 arms.

In China, Avalokita was identified with the personification of the cosmic female energy and evolved into the feminine Kuan-yin.

Avalon In Arthurian legend, the island (first mentioned by Geoffrey of Monmouth, c. 1136) where Arthur's sword Caliburnus (Excalibur) was made and to which Arthur was conveyed for the curing of his wounds after his battle with Mordred. Geoffrey later described it in the *Vita Merlini* as the Isle of Apples, where vegetation flourished, men lived to be over a hundred, and the beautiful Morgan le Fay and her eight sisters dwelt, skilled in the healing arts and in flying through the air. The fullest account of Avalon as an elysian isle is given in the *Gesta Regum Britanniae* (c. 1235). The tradition goes back ultimately to the pagan Celtic concept of an island of fairy women, of which Old Irish voyage-sagas preserve a record. In Welsh we find mention of Ynis Avallach, which meant, somewhat confusingly, either Isle of an Apple-orchard or Isle of Avallach, father of the goddess Modron. The Breton *conteurs* took over the tradition from the Welsh and adopted the form Avalon, perhaps influenced by the name of the famous Burgundian town. Celebrated under this name by the wandering Bretons, the fairy isle became known to Geoffrey, Marie de France, and the French romancers. When the tradition of this mysterious land, whither Arthur had been conveyed, thus returned to Britain, there was speculation as to where Avalon was located. Now the Welsh seem to have equated their mythical Isle of Apples with an equally mythical elysian Isle of Glass, for this explains how Avalon came to be identified with Glastonbury. Before 1136 the Welsh monk Caradoc of Lancarvan asserted (mistakenly) that the name Glastonbury was a translation of Isle of Glass. Later some ingenious person must have argued that since the Isle of Apples was the Isle of Glass and since the Isle of Glass was Glastonbury, ergo Avalon was Glastonbury. This inference was supported by the fact that Glastonbury was almost surrounded by marshes and lay in apple-growing Somerset. But where was Arthur? Since he certainly was not to be found at Glastonbury in the flesh, he must have died, contrary to the belief of the Bretons and Welsh. This the realistic Anglo-Normans were willing enough to believe. So in 1190 or 1191 the monks of Glastonbury professed to have discovered in their cemetery the bones of Arthur and Guinevere, with an identifying inscription, and down to

the dissolution of the monasteries the tomb was to be seen. Thus the Celtic isle of women became firmly fixed among the green marshlands of Somerset, no longer the abode of immortals, but the burial place of a British hero. And so we find that Malory combines both versions of Arthur's end. In one chapter he is borne away in a barge by the weeping queens, presumably to their faery isle; in the next we find him buried by the Archbishop of Canterbury in a chapel near Glastonbury. [RSL]

avalou or **yanvalou** Literally, supplication: one of the vodun dances of Haiti, characterized by violent arm- and shoulder-muscle movements. [GPK]

avatar or **avatara** In Hindu religion and mythology, the incarnation of a deity as a man or animal, especially that of Vishṇu who, according to the *Bhagavad-Gītā*, is reincarnated to defend his rule whenever there is a decline in the law and an increase in iniquity. Vishṇu went through ten incarnations: 1) Matsya or Fish, 2) Kūrma or Tortoise, 3) Varāha or Boar, 4) Narasinha or Man-lion, 5) Vāmana or Dwarf, 6) Paraśurāma or Rāma with an ax, 7) Rāma, the gentle Rāma, hero of the *Rāmāyaṇa*, 8) Kṛishṇa the black, 9) Buddha, and 10) Kalkī, the white horse. The first five avatars were mythological, the next three heroic, the ninth religious, the tenth is yet to come. In the *Bhāgavata Purāṇa* the number of specified incarnations is extended to 22 with the statement that the incarnations of Vishṇu are innumerable.

Avenger's Sword A Danish ballad (DGF 25) celebrating the grim weapon of Scandinavian tradition which "leaps to kill" of itself and sometimes even turns upon its holder. In this ballad it says, "Now lust I for thine own heart's blood. Hadst thou not named me by my name, right now should I have been thy bane." Compare TYRFING. See BALLAD; NAME; SWORDS.

Avesta The sacred book containing the teachings of Zoroaster, now the holy scripture of the Gabars of Iran and the Parsis of India: also the dialect in which it is written. Originally the *Avesta*, according to the *Dinkart*, contained 21 books. These were divided into three groups, the *gāsān* or *Gāthā*, containing spiritual and moral teachings, the *dātīk* containing the laws, and the *hātak-mānsarīk* containing both spiritual and legal matter.

This material was carefully preserved until the invasion of Alexander when the two archetypic copies, one kept at Persepolis and the other at Samarkand, were destroyed. The invasion of Alexander almost destroyed the Zoroastrian faith as well as entailing the loss of many portions of the scriptures. The later invasion by the Moslems and the ensuing religious persecution forced Zoroastrians either to abandon their faith or go into exile, and the texts then extant were burned. A small part of the original text was remembered by the priests, however, and in written form, and this remnant forms the present *Avesta*.

This consists of the *Yasna*, the chief liturgical work which includes the *Gāthās*, the *Vīsparad* containing additions to the *Yasna*, the *Yashts* or hymns to angels and the heroes of ancient Iran, miscellaneous fragments and minor texts, and the *Vendīdād* which contains the account of the creation, a priestly code for purification, directions for treatment of the dog (reverenced by

Zoroastrians), a discussion of the character of the true and the false priest, and a revelation of the destiny of the soul after death.

The *Avesta* was first introduced to Europe when it was deciphered by Anquetil-Duperron and published in 1771 under the title *Zend-Avesta, Ouvrage de Zoroastre.*

Avya The sun and the moon in the cosmological mythology of the Cubeo Indians of southeastern Colombia. Avya is a man who walks across the sky. He makes daylight so that women may work, but gives less light at night (in his moon aspect) so that people may sleep. It is Avya who causes women to menstruate; copulating with Avya at night causes this. During an eclipse of the moon the people say, "Avya is dying." They believe that some evil shaman has caused this illness of Avya, and if ever they discover which shaman did it, the hapless fellow is put to death at once.

awa The word for mother of the Cheremis. It is often used in the names of specific deities; for example, *teleze-awa* is mother of the Moon, *melande-awa,* mother of the Earth, *ketše-awa,* mother of the Sun, *mardež-awa,* mother of the Wind, *wüt-awa* is mother of Water, and *tul-awa* is mother of Fire. Compare AVA. [JB]

awassa A social dance of the Surinam Bush Negroes, often performed as a preliminary to religious rites where spirit-possession occurs. It is danced by men and women, facing each other. In the Gold Coast, this dance is called *awisa,* and is said to have had greater vogue in earlier times. Its derivation is given by the present Ashanti as of Hausa origin. [MJH]

Awl Boy Title and hero of a Tewa Indian folktale in which, at the time of migration of a whole village to another place, a young mother gives birth to a baby boy, then rises and hurries away after her people. The abandoned baby grows miraculously in a number of days, runs around looking for food, and comes by chance into the house where his father lived. A voice calls to him from the rafters. It is Awl, who bids the child take him down and wrap him in cowhide, and promises to help him in the hunt. When the boy hunts, he carries Awl with him, henceforth has marvelous luck, kills many rabbits and deer, and has plenty of meat. From now on the boy is named Awl Boy. Eventually Awl Boy, guided by Awl, goes to seek his people. He finds them in bad circumstances, but easily provides them with an abundance of meat and parrot feathers. And they elect him their chief.

A variant of the story begins with the abandoned baby and his miraculous growth; but it is Corn Mother who speaks to him from the rafter of the house and tells him what to do. She bids him place her in the middle of a basket which is full of corn meal. Then she bids him bring the awl and place him too in a basket and to put a deerskin cover over that basket. In the night, she says, Awl will make him clothes. So the boy places the awl in the basket, covers the basket with deerskin, and then goes to sleep. In the morning he finds shirt and trousers and moccasins of deerskin beside him. He puts them on, and taking with him the Corn Mother and Awl Man, he goes forth into the world. Corn Mother and Awl Man direct him to a place where there are many people. After a series of adventures he eventually comes to his own people, who had nothing but greens to eat. They were thin and miserable and having hard times. The boy orders that the people clean the town and sweep the houses, and when it is done, he walks through the town throwing seeds of corn into every open door. When the people see their houses full of corn, they make the boy their chief.

awl-elbow witches In the folktales of the Ojibwa, Micmac, Cree, and Menominee Indians (Algonquian) old women with sharp awls (sometimes knives) for elbows. The hero of tales in which these villainous characters appear usually avoids them by a ruse, causing them to kill each other by mistake.

Awl Man A spirit of Pueblo Indian religion: personification of the awl (the sharpened stick, bone, or stone used by North American Indians as a perforator in sewing). Awl Man is one of the many tutelary spirits of Pueblo culture who "gives of himself." Just as Corn Mother gives of her flesh for the people, as Clay Mother gives of herself to the potters, or Salt Woman, or the Flint Boys, or the game animals give of themselves, so Awl Man gives of himself to help those who need him. Hodge points to the human faces incised on certain old bone awls as illustrative of this personification. And the common role of Awl Man as benefactor in folktale bears witness to the fundamental animism of pueblo daily thought and act.

Awonawilona In the Zuñi Indian origin myth, the All-Container, who existed before the beginning of being. He made himself into the form of the Sun, "who is our father" and who thus came to be. By his thinking he created the mists that promote growth. His light and warmth resolved the mists into the primeval sea, and the green scums grew and widened. From balls of his cuticle which he threw upon the waters came forth the Earth Mother (Awitelin Ts'ta, Fourfold-Containing Mother Earth) and Sky Father (Apoyan Tachi, All-Covering Father Sky). From these two came all life on the face of the earth. Mother Earth caused the clouds and rains to come; Father Sky showed the stars shining in the palm of his hand as he moved it across the bowl of the sky.

The myth continues in great detail with stories of the emergence of tribes from lower regions, and the distribution of tribes, the origin of death, the lizard hand, brother and sister incest, twin heroes who visit their father the Sun, and other incidents common to many other North American Indians. The parallel development of the details of the Zuñi origin myth with Zuñi ceremonialism is the outstanding point of interest.

ax or **axe** An edged tool for hewing. The history of the ax begins with the Stone Age; it was one of the first if not the first tool produced by man. Originally the head was of stone, then of bronze, and finally of iron and iron alloys. It has varied from a roughly chipped piece of stone to a beautifully ground blade, often half-moon in shape as the battle-axes of the Middle Ages, or double-edged as those found in the excavations of Knossos. It has also had a varied history as a weapon of war, as the symbol of a number of gods, among them the Mexican thunderer Tlaloc, the Semitic Ramman, the Cretan Dionysus, and the Greek Artemis, Apollo, and Athena, as the instrument used in sacrificial killings by early peoples such as the Hittites, as a unit of exchange, and in Crete as the object of a religious cult. The ax, as a symbol of Tlaloc, is a sky support in Mexican mythology. A Mixtec story describes a copper ax on Mount Apoala with the sky resting on its edge. The ax figures in modern folk beliefs, proverbs, divination, and folktales.

The double-headed ax was a cult object in Ægean religion. In excavations at Haghia Triadha in southern Crete a chapel has been uncovered containing axes on pedestals. Two scenes on a sarcophagus found in the same area show the ax being adored. An ax worshipped by a priest in Chaldean garb also appears on an Assyrian agate cylinder. The ax was dedicated to Apollo at Delphi. Axes were found in the cave of Zeus on Mt. Dicte. Small axes or simulacra, often perforated, have been found in prehistoric sanctuaries of Malta, Cyprus, and other Mediterranean lands. On the Continent votive axes sometimes were made of sandstone which could have had no practical purpose. The ax used to slay the ox at the Athenian bouphonia was tried, condemned as guilty of the slaying of the ox, and thrown into the sea. The ax is still regarded as sacred in the Congo, is used as a ceremonial symbol in the Siouan sun dance, and by the Warramunga, Tjingilli, and Walpari tribes (Australia) to strike a tree or stone in order to release the spirit child of a Wingara ancestor into a woman's body.

Negroes of the southern United States believe that carrying an ax through the house on one's shoulder will bring calamity to the inmates, and that to dream of an ax is a sign of danger or death. An ax placed under the bed will cut the pains of an ill person. Both the southern Negroes and the people of Prussia believe the ax beneficial in bad weather. Prussians strike the doorsill with an ax to drive away bad weather, while the Negroes go into the yard and chop up the ground with an ax to "cut de storm in two." Axes are also a preventive of witchcraft. In Prussia, cows taken out for the first time in the spring are made to step over an ax to make them invulnerable to witchcraft and magic. Axiomancy, or ax divination, is performed by driving an ax into wood or casting it into water.

The ax plays a part in the folktales of Finland, Sweden, Denmark, Iceland, Holland, Germany, England, India, Rhodesia, French Canada, the Caribs of South America, and in the Paul Bunyan legends of the United States. [SPH]

Ayar Name of the four brothers who were ancestors of the Inca family and related lineages. They and their four sisters (known collectively as Mama) left their caves to find a fertile country in which to settle. During the journey Ayar-Cachi, who was endowed with supernatural strength, was walled into a cave by his brothers who feared his destructive power. Ayar-oco changed himself into the sacred stone at Huanacauri. Ayar-auca became a protector of the fields. Ayar-manco married his sister Mama occlo, and founded the city of Cuzco where his gold rod disappeared into the ground. He became the first Inca. See PACCARI TAMBO. [AM]

Aymuray Literally, the song of the harvest: name for the month of May in the Inca calendar. It is also the harvest song sung at the end of the Ayriwa.

ayotl A turtle shell used as a friction instrument by pre-Conquest Mexicans, and still played on the Isthmus of Tehuantepec. It was scraped with deer antlers to produce weird and mournful sounds at ceremonies for the death of kings, warriors, or sacrificial victims,

Ayriwa Literally, the dance of the young maize: name for the month of April in the Inca calendar. Under the mask of the Catholic rite for the Commemoration of the Cross on May 3, the Quechua Indians still observe their ancient festival for the beginning of the harvest. They erect a tree laden with fruits and gifts and around it dance the Ayriwa. At the end of the dance the gifts and fruits are shaken out of the tree and divided. The Aymuray, the triumphal song of the harvest, is then sung.

Azazel A supernatural being mentioned in connection with the ritual of the Day of Atonement (*Lev.* xvi, 21–28). On the tenth day of Tishri two goats were brought to the tabernacle, one for Yahweh, the other for Azazel. The goat for Yahweh was slain as a sin-offering for the people; the goat for Azazel (scapegoat) was laden with the sins of the people and led forth into the wilderness. The name Azazel has been interpreted by the Rabbis as the name of the mountain cliff from which the goat was cast down, but modern scholars have accepted the idea that Azazel belongs to the class of se'irim or goatlike demons haunting the desert, to which the Israelites offered sacrifice.

In the *Book of Enoch* Azazel is leader of the rebellious giants in the time preceding the Flood, who taught men the arts of warfare, of making swords, knives, shields, and coats of mail, and women the art of deception by dyeing the hair and painting the face and eyebrows. He also revealed the secrets of witchcraft and led men into wickedness until, at the Lord's command, he was bound by the archangel Raphael and chained to jagged rocks, where he is to remain in darkness until the Day of Judgment when he will be cast into the fire.

In the Cabala Azazel is one of the chief demons. In Mohammedan mythology, he is the chief of the sons of God who married the daughters of men. He may originally have been a Babylonian deity. See IBLIS.

azeman In Surinam Negro belief, a vampire: a woman who changes her human form for animal form at night and goes about drinking human blood. She can be beguiled from her purpose (or caught) by scattered grains and seeds or by a broom. If rice, pepper grains, etc., are scattered in a room, or a broom left in sight, by some inevitable compulsion she must stop and gather and count every grain or count all the straws in the broom, before she can proceed or leave. Thus morning will come before she can finish and she will have to depart, leaving her intended victim unharmed, or sometimes, still counting, she can be caught. Another way to catch the azeman is to sprinkle pepper on the sloughed off skin; it will be too painful to put on again. Still another belief is that vampires cannot cross over a broom, and therefore that a broom propped against or laid across the door will keep her out altogether. Anyone suspected of being an azeman is either killed or expelled from the community. In Haiti the vampire concept has become fused or identified with the legarou or werewolf belief. The Trinidad Negro term for vampire is sukuyan.

Azhi Dahāka or **Dahāk** (Pahlavi *Až-ī Dahāk*, New Persian *Až Dahāk*) In the *Avesta*, a three-headed dragon or serpent who ruled the second millennium of human history, the eighth of creation. In the *Shāhnāmah* he is described as a man with two serpents growing from his shoulders. He was created by Angra Mainyu to destroy the faithful. In the *Būndahishn* his lineage is traced to Angra Mainyu and he is said to have committed incest with the demon Aûṯak, his mother. In legend Azhi Dahāka slew Yima and tried to seize his glory. He was conquered after a reign of a thousand years by Thrāētaona (or Ātār) who bound him on Mount Demāvand. He will break his fetters before the coming of Keresāspa at the end of the world, will destroy a third of mankind as well as water, fire, and vegetation, but will be slain by Keresāspa. Azhi Dahāka seems to personify the thousand years of Iranian oppression by the Babylonian Empire.

aziza The Dahomean "little people" of the forest, conceived as spirits who gave magic and knowledge of the worship of the gods to man. As dwellers in the forest, they are believed to have transmitted the power of magic through the medium of hunters, whose magic the Dahomeans hold to be especially potent. [MJH]

Azrael or **Azrail** In Jewish and Mohammedan mythology, one of the archangels: the terrible angel of death who receives from God the leaves upon which are written the names of those about to die. He is depicted sometimes as a formidable being whose feet rest on the edges of the world while his head reaches into heaven. He is also described as having as many eyes as there are men in the world and one of these closes whenever a being dies. At the end of the world only eight eyes will remain open, one for each of the four throne bearers and the four archangels. Azrael takes the soul from the dying body.

Azrael is said to gather the souls of believers into a white silk cloth and the souls of unbelievers into a rag. These are then sent to heaven or hell. In the folktales of the *Arabian Nights' Entertainments* he is a man of forbidding aspect and horrible presence clad in tattered clothes with an asker's wallet at his neck.

Azuma-uta Literally, songs of the East: popular love songs of the northeast coast of Japan, sung in the 8th century and collected in the *Manyoshu,* an anthology of the period.

B

ba In ancient Egyptian religion, the soul, an actual but invisible entity inhabiting the human body during life, leaving it at death, but not irrevocably: in later representations a bird with a human face and head and preceded by a lamp. It left the tomb and flitted about the cemetery at night, fed with cakes and cared for by the sycamore tree goddess of the cemetery, as contrasted with the ka, which subsisted on foods buried in the tomb, or the kas of buried food. The body had to remain intact so that the ba might return to it. The concept of the ba (still a living belief in Egypt) is thought to be very early, antedating all Osiris and Rā theologies, and is probably rooted in observation of the huge white owls so numerous among the tomb-pits. An ancient belief was that the stars were bas lit by their lamps. See KA.

baal or **ba'al** (feminine *baalat;* plural *baalim*) The generic name for numerous ancient Semitic gods, especially of Syria and Palestine, each usually the local agricultural deity bestowing fertility upon land and flocks. With later theological development we may speak of a god Baal (compare Babylonian Bel), but originally there were as many baalim as sacred places in which they dwelt. There is no direct evidence of baalim separate from physical surroundings, e.g. gods of abstract qualities, the theory being that the baalim developed about the sacred nature of places like springs and oases in the life of an agricultural desert people. The cult of Melkart, the baal of Tyre, reached prominence in Palestine under Ahab and Jezebel and brought forth denunciation from the prophets because of its license, human sacrifice, etc. The word baal has the basic meaning of "master, owner" and still survives, for example in several Yiddish words as "baalboos," "master of the house, home-owner." See ASTARTE; BEL; SEMITIC MYTHOLOGY.

babalawo Yoruban term for a diviner who utilizes the techniques of the Ifa cult. The methods employed by these specialists consist in manipulating palm kernels, the resulting combinations being interpreted in terms of an extended series of verses, which give point and meaning to an appropriate tale or myth which is called upon for a given interpretation. These verses and associated stories, relevant to the system of throwing the kernels at hazard, number thousands, and their mastery calls for intensive training of seven years or more. The cult of Ifa divining spread to Dahomey, where its practitioners are known as bokonon. The word babalawo has persisted in the New World, simplified forms of Ifa divination being known especially well in Brazil and Cuba. [MJH]

Baba Yaga or **Baba Jaga** A female supernatural of Russian folklore. The Baba Yaga seems to be analogous to the South German Berchta. She is a cannibalistic ogress, who steals and cooks her victims; she prefers young children, though she often travels about with Death, who gives her souls to eat. Her abode is a little hut constantly spinning around on fowls' legs in a clearing in the distant forest; this is surrounded by a picket fence topped with skulls. The Baba Yaga rides through the air in an iron kettle stirring up tempests, or in a mortar which she moves by a pestle as she sweeps her traces from the air with a broom. She is a guardian of the fountains of the water of life. Her teeth and breasts of stone are used to tear her victims' flesh. She is often reduplicated in folktale, there being two or three sisters, all called Baba Yaga, all customarily lying in their huts, head to the door, a foot in either corner, and nose touching the ceiling.

Babe, the Blue Ox Paul Bunyan's wonderful ox, his companion and chief assistant in his logging operations. Babe was born white, but turned blue in the Winter of the Blue Snow. The spread between his eyes was 42 ax handles and a plug of chewing tobacco, and he was 93 hands (whether Paul's or not is not known) in height. When Babe ate hay, a crew of men was kept busy picking baling wire from his teeth. Babe loved hotcakes and met his end by swallowing a fresh batch, stove and all. The Blue Ox was so heavy that he sank knee-deep in solid rock when he took a step, thus causing among other things, the formation of the lakes of Michigan and Oregon. Babe hauled in one load entire 640-acre sections of timber. Among Babe's many exploits may be mentioned his pulling of the scoop, or glacier, with which Paul dug Puget Sound; his mighty tug that straightened the twisted river (some say it was a logging road); and his hauling from the ground the dry oil-well that was sawed into post-holes. Some people believe that the Black Hills of South Dakota were heaped by Paul to mark Babe's grave, but this is to be doubted.

babies from cabbages A well-known euphemism popularly used to answer children's premature questions about childbirth: perhaps rooted in the ancient acceptance of trees as immortal spirits capable of giving birth to human beings, as among the ancient Greeks and Irish and in South Africa and Indonesia.

babies from the earth, lakes, or wells In ancient Teutonic belief babies were born first of all from their mother, the earth, before coming to human parents. In token of this they were laid, the moment after birth, upon the ground. Many old German and Scandinavian stories tell of babies being found in hollow trees, which were perhaps regarded as exits from the earth. In southern Germany Frau Holle kept the souls of unborn children safe in the bottom of lakes and wells, which were called in consequence, *Kinderseen*, children's lakes, and *Kinderbrunnen*, children's wells. See ADEBORSTEINE.

Babylon Title of a Scottish ballad (Child #14: "Babylon; or, The Bonnie Banks o Fordie") in which a robber kills two of three sisters for resisting him. The third threatens him with the vengeance of her brother Baby Lon and they thus discover that the robber has killed his own sisters. The theme is found in all branches of Scandinavian balladry.

baby taken from murdered (or dead) mother's womb A folktale motif (T584.2; T612) associated especially with the widespread North American Indian *Lodge-Boy and Thrown-Away* cycle. Five well-known Shoshonean stories contain it, among them *The Wolf and the Geese*, in which Wolf asks the geese to find him a dead woman with a baby. They find two. Wolf takes a baby boy from one and a baby girl from the other. The girl can walk immediately and travels about with Wolf. In the story *Wolf's Son*, Wolf acquires his son by beheading his wife, killing several babies he finds within her begotten by others, and saving his own. Similar is the story of the woman who went to visit Snake and did not return. Her sons went to look for her and found their mother dead and swollen. They opened her abdomen from which came forth two lizards and a snake and finally an Indian baby girl, whom they reared. Typical of the *Lodge-Boy and Thrown-Away* and *Bead-Spitter and Thrown-Away* stories is the pregnant mother murdered in her husband's absence by man or monster who takes living twins (or child and afterbirth) from her body, leaves one behind the curtain, and throws the other away. In the Micmac story of *Ketpusye'genau* the unborn child is taken from the murdered mother's womb and thrown in the brook.

Although this motif turns up in North American

Indian tales everywhere from the northern and southern Atlantic tribes to the northwest Pacific, it is especially associated with the Plains area. It is not limited to North America, however. The Greek Æsculapius was removed from his mother's womb on her funeral pyre; the Yuracare Indians of Bolivia have similar stories; and there is a Melanesian story from the New Hebrides in which a woman is murdered and thrown in a thicket, where her twin boys come forth of themselves.

Bacabs In the mythology of the Mayas of Yucatan, four brothers who were deities of the four directions; upholders of the earth or of the sky; guardians of the waters and bringers of rain: they were personified by animal- and human-headed water-jars. Las Casas describes a Yucatec story of the Trinity in which Bacab is equated with the Son, is scourged and crucified, and arises from the dead. The condensation of the four gods of direction into one person and the connection with the cross which points four ways is, as Alexander shows, an obvious and natural change. Compare TLALOC.

Bacchus Dionysus as the noisy and riotous god of wine: so called by both Greeks and Romans. The Bacchanalia, or orgies connected with the mysteries of Dionysus in Rome, where they were introduced in the 2nd century B.C., seem to have become within a very short period so extremely licentious that they were banned by the Senate in 186 B.C. At first the communicants were only women, but, claiming inspiration of the god himself, one matron transformed the festival into a public scandal: in place of the three days a year of observance, she proclaimed five days every month; men were admitted; the observance was to take place at night rather than in the daytime, etc. After the edict against the Bacchanalia, a milder form of Bacchus worship took place at the Liberalia, Liber being another form of the god. See DIONYSUS; SATYR.

bachelor's-button Any of certain plants (genus *Centaurea*) with button-shaped flowers or heads, such as the cornflower. In England it was customary for a young man to carry one of these flowers in his pocket for a time. If it lived, he would marry his current sweetheart; if it died, it was a sign that he would soon be seeking a new sweetheart.

Bachúe A fertility goddess of the ancient Chibcha Indians of Colombia. She emerged from a lake with a small boy who became her husband when he grew up. She populated the land with her children. After exhorting the people to live in peace, she and her husband were changed into snakes and disappeared into the lake. She is also called Fura-chogue (beneficent female). [AM]

backward speech or **behavior** Saying or doing something in reverse of its normal order: a custom or practice found throughout the world but adapted for different purposes by different peoples. Wherever it is found, imitative magic is probably at its base.

Talking backwards, or saying the opposite of what is meant, is used as a common form of humor among North American Indians, as by the Arapaho Crazy Dancers and several of the Pueblo societies, especially as a typical ceremonial custom. Despite the surface levity, Pueblo clowns are considered as powerful curers in that they recite certain medicinal formulas in reverse order. Among the medieval Jews, the reciting of the opening of *Leviticus,* forwards, then each word backwards, then the whole passage reversed, was thought to be a counter to magic. Among the practices attributed to followers of the Devil in western Europe is the reciting of the Lord's Prayer backwards. The Mass of St. Secaire, in Gascony, features a backward recitation that brings death to the one against whom revenge is desired. Similar beliefs are found among the Arabs and Buddhists. In the *Kathā Sarit Sāgara,* the recitation of a given formula forwards makes a man invisible, while a backward reading permits him to assume whatever shape he desires.

Doing things backwards likewise has a certain power. Ringing the chime backwards as an alarm is such a custom, as is the flying of a flag in reverse as a sign of distress. These probably are based as much on the idea of reversal of fortune as on the noticeable incongruity of the action. In the United States some maintain that a garment accidentally put on in reverse must not be taken off and put on correctly or ill luck will follow. Medieval Jews deliberately reversed their clothing or walked backwards to reverse a suspected charm against them. Throwing things behind one likewise has a certain efficacy in preventing evil, or as in some folktales in slowing up pursuit.

Badb (bŏv) Literally, scald-crow: in Old Irish mythology, an evil spirit delighting in carnage. She incited armies against each other, filled warriors with fury, and is usually interpreted as a war goddess. She was one of three such beings (with Macha and Neman). Badb was the daughter of Ernmas, one of the Tuatha Dé Danann, and either the wife or granddaughter of Nét, as was also Morrigan (later Irish, Morrigu) who plays a parallel or identical role. The Gauls had an analogous figure called Bodua. Badb, the scald-crow, appeared on the battlefield in this form, presaging the death of heroes or appeared in still more hideous guise to warriors about to be defeated. Badb, along with the Morrigu, helped drive the Fomorians out of Ireland. A. H. Krappe interprets the valkyries of the *Njals Saga* as "a transposition in an Icelandic milieu of these Celtic furies."

In later Irish folklore, the word means, in addition to scald-crow, a scolding old hag or witch. Today Badb is sometimes identified with the banshee in function, presaging death to certain families, except that she appears always in the form of a scald-crow.

Badger The first animal sent up to earth through a hole in the sky by the ancestors of the Hopi Indians before their emergence from the underworld. Badger is often connected with doctoring by the Pueblo Indians. In a Tewa tale he is the doctor; at Isleta he is a powerful animal; at Zuñi, a south directional spirit. Among the Micmac Indians of the northeastern United States, Badger is a trickster. [EWV]

In Japanese, badger is *tanuki,* one of several animals of Japanese folklore who possess extraordinary magical powers. He is usually depicted with an enormous bell. [JLM]

Badger medicine The curing power of the Badger: a concept of Hopi and other Pueblo Indian religion. Badger knows about certain plants and roots which he is always digging up out of the ground. Badger as curer originated as a kachina at Oraibi where he appeared carrying his medicines and his buzzard feathers for exorcising. Ever since then the medicine chief of the curing society has always been a Badger clansman. Badger medicine is valued especially as a delivery medicine at Zuñi and Isleta. A badger paw (called Badger Old Woman) is either worn by the woman in childbirth, or it is placed on the bed, or on the ground nearby. This is because the badger digs himself out quickly. Badger fat and the sexual organs of the badger are good medicine for impotent men. See ANIMAL CURERS.

bad man Western "killer" or "gunman": so called because in his law-breaking or law-enforcing capacity he was a "bad man to fool with," or dangerous to oppose. The beginnings of the bad man era are traced to the wave of banditry and depredations after the Mexican War and the bloody Missouri-Kansas border conflict before the Civil War. Homicidal lawlessness reached its height during the feudal cattle wars and sheep and cattle wars of the Great Plains and the gold and silver mining boom of the Southwest and the Black Hills, as well as in the no-man's land of Indian Territory. Notorious haunts of the bad man included the wide-open cowboy capitals and trail-end terminus towns of Denison, Fort Worth, and El Paso, Texas; Albuquerque and Las Vegas, New Mexico; Abilene, Dodge City, and Ellsworth, Kansas; and the "Helldorado" mining towns of Denver, Leadville, and Central City, Colorado; Tombstone, Arizona; and Deadwood, South Dakota.

With popular sympathy on the side of the outlaw as the enemy of the rich, the folk imagination tended to blur and break down the distinction among the three main types of killer or gunman—the homicidal maniac or professional killer who killed in cold blood (Billy the Kid, John Wesley Hardin, the Apache Kid); the more civilized or chivalrous "good bad man" (Jesse James, Sam Bass, Pretty Boy Floyd); and the peace officer who was not above shooting on inadequate provocation and to settle a private feud (Wild Bill Hickok, Wyatt Earp, Luke Short, Bat Masterson). An attempt was however made to distinguish between the gun fighter, who fought fair, and the gunman, who didn't. More or less outside the "killer" class was a peaceable marshal like Bill Tilghman of Oklahoma, who never took a life unless he had to in order to save his own, only (in the end) to be the victim of his own generosity.

In his supreme daring and uncanny skill with weapons as well as in the fact that he killed to avenge a personal wrong, if not always in self-defense, the bad man satisfied the heroic requirements of challenge and ordeal by combat, an even break or a fighting chance. Moreover, he was generally the victim of society or circumstances or a dual personality, split (as in Billy the Kid's case) between a "good-humored, jovial imp" and a "cruel and blood-thirsty fiend." Death through treachery or by walking into a trap conferred martyrdom upon him. Jesse James was shot by "that dirty little coward," Robert Ford, brother of a former accomplice of his, in order to claim the reward. Billy the Kid was trailed to his sweetheart's home and shot in the dark by his erstwhile friend, Sheriff Pat Garrett. Sam Bass was double-crossed by one of his own gang and slain in ambush. Wild Bill was shot in the back, while playing poker in a Deadwood saloon, by Jack McCall—presumably to avenge the slaying of his brother by Wild Bill. (When Bill was picked up, two black aces and black eights fell out of his hand—a combination known thereafter to superstitious gamblers as "The Dead Man's Hand.")

In the popular imagination the bad man was frequently identified with Robin Hood. Of William C. Quantrill (Quantrell), the guerrilla leader, the ballad sings:

Oh, Quantrell's a fighter, a bold-hearted boy,
A brave man or woman he'd never annoy.
He'd take from the wealthy and give to the poor,
For brave men there's never a bolt to his door.

And of Jesse James:

He stole from the rich and he gave to the poor,
He'd a hand and a heart and a brain.

Of Jesse James, Sam Bass, and Rube Burrow is told the story of how the outlaw paid off the poor widow's mortgage and then stole the money back from the mortgage-owner. Pretty Boy Floyd has been described as a "nice, soft-spoken boy, good to his mother."

As a deadshot the bad man added a touch of showmanship by his trick or fancy gunplay or "folklore shooting." According to Frost Woodhull (*Southwestern Lore*, Austin, 1931, pp. 1–14) Henry Starr of Oklahoma liked to ride up and down country lanes cutting barbed wire with his .45, while Wild Bill was fond of shooting knotholes and the O's in saloon signs. Perhaps the most sensational feat ever performed by the latter was his simultaneous killing of two assailants who had entered by opposite doors of a restaurant. Drawing both pistols, "with one he killed the man in front of him, and at the same time with the other gun resting on the opposite shoulder he killed the man behind him, looking through the mirror" over the front door (George D. Hendricks, *The Bad Man of the West,* 1941, p. 96).

The absurdly exaggerated legendary claims of the phenomenal records of gunmen include 30 men killed by Bat Masterson at Dodge City, 21 men by Billy the Kid in his 21 years ("not counting Indians"), and "ten men single-handed" by Wild Bill in the McCanless massacre. Wild Bill had more than his share of miracles. During the Civil War his horse Black Nell, with her "trick of dropping quick," saved his life more than once. In Sam Bass's case, horses figured prominently. Besides the Denton mare, which he matched in all races, he had a horse that carried him down cañon sides "where human foot could not find place, carrying on unfalteringly, and at last, when danger threatened, waking its sleeping master by shaking him"—an adaptation of Swift Nick and Dick Turpin (Charles J. Finger, *Frontier Ballads,* 1927, p. 71). Like the pirates of old, Sam Bass left behind him a folk heritage of buried treasure legends. But none of these miracles could compare with the final touch in the Wild Bill saga. His remains, on being exhumed for reburial, showed evidence of natural embalming.

Survival legends are another folklore attribute of the bad man. Rumors that Billy the Kid was still alive persisted as late as 1926. No less than seventeen persons, according to his granddaughter, have claimed to be the "original Jesse James." From Texas comes the legend that Quantrell, badly wounded but not killed during the Civil War, was for many years a country school teacher in East Texas (akin to the Marshal Ney legend). In Wyoming, tradition has clung to the notion that Tom Horn was cut down alive from the gallows and spirited away.

The bad man lives on not only in folklore and legend but in the Western "thriller," from the Beadle dime novel to the "Western story" magazine and comic book, and the horse opera of movies, radio, and television, where the Lone Ranger's bandit mask symbolizes the enigma of the bad man's personality and reputation.

B. A. BOTKIN

bagpipe A wind instrument important in folk and military music from the Middle Ages to the present, probably of Asiatic origin, but known in the western world since the time of Nero, who was reported to have played it. It consists of one or more reed pipes of either oboe (double reed) or clarinet (single reed) types, inserted into a bladder or windbag which is inflated by mouth or by a bellows attachment to supply air for sounding the pipes. Generally one pipe, the chanter, has finger holes for playing the melody, and the others are drones of fixed tones for accompaniment. Chiefly known now as the national instrument of Scotland, the variety of its types and names in many languages indicates the widespread popularity of the bagpipe (French *cornemuse, musette, chevrette, loure, bignou* or *biniou,* etc.; German *Dudelsack, Sackpfeife;* Italian *cornamusa, piva, piffero, zampogna* [also the name among many Gipsies]; Galician Spanish *gaita;* Russian *volynka;* Irish greatpipe, *píob mór, píob Uilleann,* union-pipes; Tamil *sruti;* Hindustani *masak;* etc.).

As a folk instrument in medieval Europe, the bagpipe served as accompaniment for religious observances, for weddings and funerals, for dances, May games, and impromptu festivities. It was thought to have a peculiar charm for animals, to be beloved by fairies, to be the Devil's instrument, and to have the power of speech.

Processions of the early Irish Christian church moved to the sound of the bagpipe, and its wailing music supported the keen at funerals. Roman Catholic services in Edinburgh, especially outdoor rites, sometimes included bagpipe music as late as the 16th century. In Italy, where Calabrian pipers were noted for their skill, the bagpipe accompanied folk singing before statues of the Virgin and Child in pre-Christmas ceremonies. In Brussels, in 1529, a feast for the Virgin was observed with a masque in which wild beasts danced around a cage where two ape characters played the bagpipes. In England, in 1584, a piper named Cochrane played at the Coventry Mysteries.

For dancing, the bagpipes appeared along with the pibgorn and the pipe and tabor at country dances and Morrises, the piper being a character in the dance. Lincolnshire or Lancashire pipers, both esteemed for virtuosity, were regularly hired by the great English houses to play for the dancing of the common people at Yuletide. Street dancing led by bagpipers became such a disturbance of the peace in 16th century Scotland that laws were passed forbidding the playing of pipes on Sunday and after supper. Wandering pipers of Germany gathered village groups to dance to the dudelsack, and Gipsies of eastern Europe played for weddings, dances, and feasts on the zampogna. The national dances of Hungarians, Bulgarians, and Serbians, as well as sword dances of the Scots and Irish, were traditionally footed to pipe tunes.

Bagpipes also entered into work activities. Hiring of pipers to set the pace for harvest hands in England is recorded, and the rat-catchers of continental European towns, frequently Gipsies, pursued their trade to the drone of the pipes, even as the Pied Piper of Hamelin is supposed to have done in 1284. Shepherds of central Europe and the Near East were believed to be able to draw their flocks in by the alluring strains of their crude goatskin pipes.

The instrument was also thought to be especially attractive to bears, whose heavy dancing steps were directed by Gipsy pipers, and in India and Ceylon a primitive bagpipe has been used for centuries by snake charmers.

Animal players of the instrument are depicted in many medieval sculptures and woodcuts in churches, the favorites being bears, monkeys, and hogs. An Irish version of the song, *Frog Went a-Courting*, brings in a snail bagpiper as one of the wedding guests. Angels, too, are shown puffing gaily on the pipes, though it was more often associated with demons. A 15th century woodcut shows it in the hands of a skeleton figure in a dance of death.

As a military instrument, the pipes were played by the Romans during their colonization of Britain, by French regimental pipers up to the 19th century, and have made the battle music of the Irish and Scottish foot soldier since the Middle Ages. The *piob mór,* war pipe of ancient Ireland, advanced at the head of the kerns against British, French, and Scottish enemies, its wild music bringing terror to the opposition as the pipers played in the thick of the battle. The great Highland pipe of Scotland has served to whip the fighting spirit of Scotsmen in clan feuds, in the Stuart cause, and even in the World War II battle of El Alamein. Scarcely a battle in which the pipes figured is without its legend of a heroic piper who, though wounded or cut off from his regiment, played to his death to hold off defeat.

The position of the piper has varied considerably in legend and history. Though generally not so esteemed by the aristocracy as the harper or minstrel, he often came in for marked royal favor. In ancient Ireland pipers and jugglers were admitted to the king's house and made free of his beer. Both English and Irish nobility often maintained bagpipers on their regular payrolls for the entertainment of their servants and guests. In the 15th century in Scotland, many towns supported hereditary town pipers, who were lodged at public expense and sometimes given a grant of land called "the piper's croft." Vienna, too, had its town pipers, selected from the musicians' guild. In France, during the 17th century, the bagpipe became fashionable at court, the *musette,* a highly decorated bellows pipe, being taken up by the ladies, and a royal piper, Destouches, becoming a court favorite.

So loyal were the household pipers of the Irish and Scots and so effective their music in battle that the English passed laws against them. In Ireland it was made illegal to harbor pipers, story-tellers, and rimers because they acted as spies, and Scottish pipers of the Jacobite period were put to death if captured, their pipes being considered instruments of war.

Stories about bagpipes and pipers are of several types. One type concerns ghosts, changelings, and other evil spirits. Seventeenth century popular belief often made the bagpipe Satan's favorite instrument, the Devil's bellows. Witches were executed on the accusation that they had danced to the Devil's piping. There are Highland tales of ghostly pipes playing at dusk in the lonesome hill passes where some defeat or retreat of the Jacobites took place. One famous Scottish chanter was said to crack as a prophecy of the death of the clan's chief. Another was said to have carried magic powers in battle for the Grants and the MacPhersons.

A second Celtic story type concerns fairies. The green-coated ones in their mounds loved the music of the pipes, played and taught it, and gave special favors to pipers. Many of these stories are of the *Rip Van Winkle* variety, in which a piper is lured away with the fairies, plays for them for what seems a few moments, and returns home to find that years have passed. Sometimes he returns with a magic token, perhaps a new set of pipes, given to him by the fairies and proving the actuality of the experience. Other stories common in many lands tell of shepherds who frighten thieves or wild animals by the playing of their pipes.

On Skye and Mull particularly there is a traditional story pattern dealing with a piper who, with a dog or some friends, enters a cave inhabited by a demon or wild beast. The dog or the friends return without him and the last sound that is heard is the piper's lament for his own fate, often with the words, "Oh, that I had three hands; two for the pipes and one for the sword." On stormy nights the melancholy piping still comes from such caves, it is said.

The message of the pipes is characteristic of many Scottish tales. One such, crediting the instrument with the power of speech, is *A Cholla mo Run*. It tells of a piper who was captured during the absence of his chief from home and held prisoner while an ambush is plotted for the chief's return. When the chief is seen coming, the piper plays him a warning, which he hears and understands. However, the enemy also understands the language of the pipes and the piper is killed.

Bagpipe music includes reels, strathspeys, laments, marches, pibrochs (variations on a theme called the *urlar*), etc. The MacCrimmon "Lament for the McLeod," "The White Cockade," and "Flowers of the Forest" are among the most famous bagpipe tunes. [TCB]

Bahiana Literally, a Bahian woman, but by extension a term used to designate Bahian Negro women who are members of African cult groups. Their distinctive dress, popularized in the motion pictures by Carmen Miranda and others, is a more colorful counterpart of the dress of Negro women in many parts of the New World. The Bahiana of today appears on the street in her traditional dress, most often as a seller of cooked foods, or in processions on festival days; and she is likely to be a woman well into middle age. [MJH]

Bahrām fire or **Berezisavanh** The sacred fire of Iran, which represents the essence of all fires and is made from 16 different kinds of fire: the earthly representative of the divine essence. The Bahrām fire is maintained in the great temples and is fed sandalwood five times a day by a priest. The Bahrām is one of the five sacred fires of Iranian religion. It is the one which shoots up before Ahura Mazda. The other kinds recognized in Iran are Vohu Fryāna (literally, good friend) which keeps the bodies of men and animals warm, Urvāzishta (most delightful) the fire of plants which produces flame by friction, Vāzishta (best-carrying) the lightning, and Spēnishta (most holy) which burns in Paradise. See NAIRYŌSANGHA.

Bahramgor or **Bahram Gur**   Hero-prince of many adventures, probably a Sassanian king of Persia of the 5th century A.D. He is said to be the father of Persian poetry, and is often a character in Indian tales. [MWS]

Baiame   The great totemic ancestor of the Kamilaroi and other tribes in New South Wales, who lived in the mythical past and originated totemism and other customs. He answers invocations for rain and figures in initiation and other ceremonies. He left mementos behind him which include a large stone fish trap on the Barwan River. He had two wives, Cunnembeillee, by whom he had children, and Birrahgnooloo, his favorite, who sends floods on request. The three are now in the sky. Women may not use Baiame's name but call him "Father." The theory of early writers that he was a kind of All-Father, a vague, otiose, spiritual being, now has many critics. See AUSTRALIAN ABORIGINAL MYTHOLOGY.
[KL]

baile de cintas or **baile del cordon**   The Spanish ribbon or Maypole dance, still performed ceremonially by men at fiestas around a flower-decked pole, in Valencia, Castile, Huesca, and Teneriffe and elsewhere in the Canary Islands. In Catalonia it forms part of the Carnival celebrations by both men and girls. In Portugal it celebrates St. John's Day, June 24. The pole is called St. John's pole, and is surmounted by a puppet. The Basque *cinta dantza* is a furious course following the sword dance or *ezpata dantza*.

In Mexico the baile de cintas is often performed as part of a longer sequence, as by the Yaqui *matachini* and Pueblo *negritos* dancers and the *tocotines* of Papantla, Vera Cruz (*voladores*). In Ixmiquilpan, Hidalgo, both men and women participate in special costumes. In Yucatan it forms part of the Carnaval. Both in the Old and New World it is an ancient spring celebration around a sacred budding tree, but has been renamed and recostumed in Mexico. [GPK]

baile de la xisterna   Literally, dance of the well: a Spanish dance of the Island of Majorca, performed especially for the fiesta of San Salvador, August 6. With arms upraised and little forward jumps, termed *mateixa*, the dancers approach the sacred well. They describe a zigzag path typical of many fertility rites. The dance retains much of this ritual significance in its worship of water, well, rain. [GPK]

Bailiff's Daughter of Islington   An English ballad (Child #105) of separated lovers. The bailiff's daughter and the squire's son meet on the road after seven years. When she tells him that his lover is dead, he says he will go "into some far countrey," whereupon she makes herself known. The theme, with roles reversed, is found in Italian, Spanish, Portuguese, and Romaic ballads. The ballad is known in the United States, as for example *The Bailer's Daughter of Ireland Town* (reported from New Jersey) and *The Comely Youth* (Mississippi) where Islington becomes "Hazlingtown."

baingan, baigan, begun, or **bhāṇṭā**   Literally, eggplant: in the folktale, "Baingan Bādshāhzādī," told as "Princess Aubergine" in *Tales of the Punjab* collected by F. A. Steele, Baingan was a princess born from an eggplant and brought up by a poor Brāhman couple. A neighboring queen jealous of her beauty decided to kill her by magic. In trying to discover Baingan's life token, the queen killed her own seven sons. Finally she discovered the token to be the nine-lakh necklace hidden in a box in a bee in a fish. The princess died as soon as the queen obtained the necklace, but she was laid out in the forest by the Brāhman couple who neither buried nor cremated her. There the king found her and daily watched beside the body which was as fresh and beautiful as if alive. After a year, the king found a child beside the body who told him that his mother was alive at night when the queen removed the necklace, but dead in the daytime while the queen wore it. The child got possession of the necklace and the king and princess were married. They buried the malicious queen in a ditch filled with serpents and scorpions.

bajang or **badjang**   In Malay belief, a malignant spirit whose presence foretells disaster and is the cause of illness. The bajang is said to take the form of a polecat and is very dangerous to children. In some areas of the Malay peninsula the bajang is the enslaved spirit of a stillborn child, obtained at midnight by incantations said over the grave. As a familiar it is handed down in a family. It is kept in a bamboo vessel, fed eggs and milk, and sent forth to prey upon victims who are seized by unknown ailments when attacked.

bakemono   Generic term for the goblins of Japanese folklore. [JLM]

bakru   Surinam form of the West African "little people," who are brought into being by practitioners of evil magic. Belief in them is especially strong in Paramaribo, the capital of Dutch Guiana, and other parts of the coastal area. Bakru come in pairs, one male and one female. They are envisaged as the size of children, with large heads, and as half-flesh and half-wood. They are obtained by compact with a worker of evil magic, for the purpose of bringing the owner coveted wealth. The price paid for them is in meeting their exacting demands. In the end, it is believed, the family of the owner is destroyed by the gods and ancestors in punishment for these antisocial acts. [MJH]

Balaam   The last and greatest of the heathen prophets of Biblical tradition (*Num.* xxii–xxiv). Balaam, son of the prophet Beor, was himself prophet of Pethor in Mesopotamia. As a prophet and diviner he was equal to Moses in everything but moral sense. Because he was cruel and tried to destroy a whole nation, God permitted no more heathen prophets. Balaam had, according to rabbinical tradition, one eye and was lame in one foot. By some he is held to have been identical with Laban.

When Balak, king of Moab, became uneasy about the spread of the Israelites into nearby territory, he sent for Balaam. Balaam, to whom as to all heathen prophets the Lord spoke only at night, kept the envoys, and then refused to go with them when forbidden to by God. A further embassy met with better luck, for God permitted th prophet to go if he would repeat God's words when the time came. A Mohammedan story says that the ambassadors bribed Balaam's wife, and that her nagging was the real cause of his going to Balak. On the way, in a narrow path, the Angel of Mercy, invisible to Balaam, descended and stood in the way of his ass.

The ass refused to go on, and Balaam whipped the beast. Three times this happened and the third time the ass spoke, reproaching his master, and then died, since animals could not be permitted to rival men in speech. Here for example the stupidest of beasts, the ass, outargued Balaam, the greatest of prophets. The speaking mouth of the ass was one of the traditional twelve miraculous things created on the sixth day.

balam In Quiché mythology, the *tigre* or jaguar; a supernatural; a magician. The mythical ancestors of the Quiché, associated with the four directions, bore the names Balam-Quitzé (Smiling Tiger), Balam-Agab (Nocturnal Tiger), Iqi-Balam (Moon Tiger), and Mahu-catah (Famous Name), probably a euphemism for a feared Tiger or Sorcerer name. Among the Mayans of present-day Mexico, the balams are magical beings whose special province is the protection of villages and their inhabitants and the cornfields.

balance and swing An American square-dance term. The gentleman places his right arm around the lady's waist and takes her right hand in his left, while she places her left hand on his arm below the shoulder. In this position he swings her to the right about. It is usual for couples to swing completely around twice, though they may swing once. If they are skilful and in the mood for it, they may swing three or four times. See ALL EIGHT BALANCE. [GPK]

Balder or **Baldr** Norse god of light and joy; son of Odin and Frigga, and twin brother of Hodur: one of the most important and the best loved of the æsir. The story of Balder's death from a spear of mistletoe, the only thing that had not promised not to harm him, and thrown by Hodur, the blind, at the instigation of Loki, and of the descents of Odin and of Hermod to the underworld, forms a prominent part of the Norse legend of the approach of Ragnarök. In the Scandinavian tradition, as told by Saxo Grammaticus, Balder is slain by Hodur, who wields a magic sword, in a fight over the beautiful Nanna. Compare ADONIS; DESCENTS TO THE UNDERWORLD; TWINS.

Bali In Hindu mythology, king of the Daityas, son of Virochana, Hiraṇyakaśipu, or Prahlāda. By his devotion he humbled the gods and obtained dominion over the three worlds. Vishṇu appeared to him as Vāmana, the dwarf, and asked for as much land as he could cover in three strides. When the request was granted. Vishṇu stepped over heaven and earth and, out of respect for Bali's goodness, then made a short stride, leaving Bali the underworld. He is also called Mahābali. Compare DECEPTIVE LAND MEASURE.

Bālī or **Bālin** In Hindu mythology, the monkey king of Kishkindhyā, the son of Indra, who was slain by Rāma. Bālī was supposed to have been born from his mother's hair.

balian The general Indonesian term for a medium. The balian communicates with the spirits while in a trance to learn how to protect individuals and the community. He also conducts purification rites, is a diviner, and knows the formulas and charms used to protect the rice granaries and property.

Balitao A Philippine peasant dance in mazurka rhythm, descriptive of work movements, planting, reaping, and winnowing the rice. [GPK]

Balkis The Queen of Sheba: in Abyssinian, Jewish, Mohammedan, and European tradition. The Biblical story states simply that, hearing of Solomon's wisdom, she visited him, found his fame not so great as the fact of his wisdom, and departed (I *Kings* x, 1–13). The kings of Abyssinia, however, trace their line back to Menelik, supposedly the son of Solomon and the Queen of Sheba. In Mohammedan tradition, Solomon requires Balkis or Bilkis to submit to him as overlord and adopt his religion. After testing his wisdom, she accedes and becomes his wife. Both the Arabian and Jewish tradition are much embellished with stories of Solomon's control over birds, animals, and spirits and demons, with which he threatens her. Traditionally, she propounds a series of riddles which he answers without trouble (Ginzberg lists 22).

ballad A form of narrative folk song, developed in the Middle Ages in Europe, to which has been applied very ambiguously the name ballad (Danish *vise*, Spanish *romance*, Russian *bylina*, Ukrainian *dumi*, Serbian *junačke pesme*, etc.). This type of folk song varies considerably with time and place, but certain characteristics remain fairly constant and seemingly fundamental: 1) A ballad is narrative. 2) A ballad is sung. 3) A ballad belongs to the folk in content, style, and designation. 4) A ballad focuses on a single incident. 5) A ballad is impersonal, the action moving of itself by dialog and incident quickly to the end.

A ballad is story. Of the four elements common to all narrative—action, character, setting, and theme—the ballad emphasizes the first. Setting is casual; theme is often implied; characters are usually types and even when more individual are undeveloped, but action carries the interest. The action is usually highly dramatic, often startling and all the more impressive because it is unrelieved. The ballad practices a rigid economy in relating the action; incidents antecedent to the climax are often omitted, as are explanatory and motivating details. The action is usually of a plot sort and the plot often reduced to the moment of climax; that is, of the unstable situation and the resolution which constitutes plot, the ballad often concentrates on the resolution leaving the listener to supply details and antecedent material.

Almost without exception ballads were sung; often they were accompanied by instrumental music. The tunes are traditional and probably as old as the words, but of the two—story and melody—story is basic. Many ballads were sung to a variety of melodies. Unlike lyric songs in which the meaning is not so important and which are consequently subordinated to the music, ballads, in which the contrary situation obtains, always subordinate the melody to the words. More variety exists in ballad music than in ballad form and content, for it ranges from the modal types of the West, based on the Gregorian, to the more florid and ornamental types of Greece, the Balkans, and Russia owing much to Byzantine tradition. Here and there, as for example among the South Slavs, instead of melody the ballad is often accompanied by rhythmical chant, almost recitative. The point is, of course, that the ballad is not simply recited or told, but given interpretation and emotional power by the accompanying melody.

The ballad belongs to the folk, but it is by no means primitive or barbaric; rather it is the product of accomplished and often literary-conscious poets. The folk of the ballad have behind them a long tradition, a tradition partly conditioned and shaped by conscious and lettered culture. The folk are unlettered, rather than illiterate. They are homogeneous, interested in one another, in the dramatic aspects of life. They have a great store of traditional story stuff—märchen and folktale, and a store of folklore, part of which is with them only conventional and half-believed in. So the ballad is likely to be a compound of folklore, legend, and local history. Through the years the folk have their way with the ballad, shaping it, varying it in theme, incident, and style, putting their unmistakable touch upon it.

The last two points may be discussed together. The ballad takes a single incident, as does the short story, brings that into sharp and economical focus. In this respect it is unlike the folktale or epic which develop their stories through a series of incidents episodically. This stripping the story of all excrescences of description, motivation, incidental material, and especially of editorializing, results not only in utter impersonality but in a "gapped" narrative in which the reader gets only the moments of most dramatic action.

The Danish ballad, *Sir Peter's Leman,* is typical. It is very short—twenty-one couplets—but it evokes a dramatic and complex story. Sir Peter and Kirsteen, his sweetheart, are "jesting" with one another as they sit over their meal. "When will you take a wife?" she asks. Sir Peter answers with a joke. Kirsteen comments that when he does take a wife, she will go to the bridal though it "were two hundred miles." (Stanza 6) With no transition, no explanation the ballad plunges into the events of the marriage feast, telling of Kirsteen pouring the wine. (Stanza 7) The bride asks who she is. A serving-maid tells her that Kirsteen is Sir Peter's love. Abruptly the ballad passes to the next scene, the bringing of the bride to bed, Kirsteen bearing the bridal torch.

"The sheets of silk o'er the bed she drew
There lies the swain I loved so true."

The next stanza tells of Kirsteen locking the door and setting the house on fire, so the "bride must burn on the bridegroom's arm."

These three scenes told largely through dialog give us the story. This technique is more common in the Western ballads than in the Eastern, but even in the Russian ballad the story is basically developed by a succession of scenes rather than by alternation of scene and panorama.

In addition to these primary characteristics one should note certain secondary characteristics. Sometimes the ballad was accompanied by dance. Frequently this was so in the Scandinavian countries, but it was rare in England and found only sporadically in other parts of Europe. We cannot think of the ballad as basically a dance song, but must realize that occasionally it was adapted to that purpose. Likewise many ballads contain a refrain—a word, phrase, line or several lines—repeated after each stanza, or sometimes interwoven with the stanza. But the refrain, though common in the English and Germanic ballad is not generally characteristic of ballad. Certain stylistic qualities are fairly constant, such as the use of stereotyped expressions so common to folk poetry in general, the use of repetition of line and incident, of incremental repetition, triad arrangement, climax of relations, and the testament device. These secondary characteristics partly account for the wide variety in the ballad as one passes from one country to another and from one time to another. The constant element in the ballad is the form and the manner of telling a story.

The problem of ballad origins has occupied the attention of folklorists and balladists from the beginning of ballad studies. Much confusion about the matter of origin comes from the failure of the first scholars, such as Herder, Grimm, Gummere, in not making clear the distinction between ballad and folk song in general. They saw in the ballad a continuing tradition from primitive times and consequently applied to ballad conclusions arrived at from a study of primitive folk song in general. And so was born the communal theory, that the folk made the ballads by a kind of communal improvisation, a kind of cooperative composition. Later critics (e.g. Kittredge) accepted this explanation but with modification. Feeling that the folk is too indefinite, too unorganized for such concerted effort, they suggested that ballads were composed by the folk under the direction of a leader who brought the necessary discipline into the composition and who functioned as organizer and selector. But they felt that the folk contributed much of the matter. At the present time, however, most scholars favor out-and-out individual authorship. They point out that the ballad is certainly the product of the late Middle Ages, that it is certainly not a product of a primitive society, that it is a highly artful and rather difficult form, that the music is intimately and fundamentally a part of it. All of this would argue for conscious trained authorship. Minstrels, clerks, clericals, wandering scholars have all been suggested as the professionals who originated and perfected the form. After an individual ballad was composed, then the folk came in. Ballads were oral. The folk took them over. Through the years of singing them the folk modified them, changed them, improved them sometimes, sometimes debased them, but the folk had their way with them, and over the years put their mark upon them. And it is a distinguishing mark and an unmistakable one.

The main body of English and Scottish ballads is to be found in the great collection of F. J. Child (1882–1898). This great work contains 305 separate ballads and many variants divided between England and Scotland. It is sometimes difficult to separate the English from the Scottish, for often some variants of the same ballad are Scottish, others English. One variant of *Edward,* for example, is English, the other Scottish. *The Three Ravens* is English; the *Twa Corbies,* Scottish. In general the English pieces seem more realistic and more sophisticated. Here are the Robin Hood ballads, the larger group of historical ballads, the romantic and sentimental love ballads. The Scottish, on the other hand, are more stark, shorter. Most of the fairy-lore and supernatural ballads are Scottish, as are the short tragic ballads and ballads of the Border. But the ballad passed freely not only between England and Scotland but between the British Isles and Germanic Europe.

The texts of most English and Scottish ballads are 16th, 17th, and 18th centuries. The actual date of composition is in many cases much earlier. The earliest ballad text extant is that of *Judas* found in a 13th century manuscript now in Trinity College, Cambridge. Some of the Robin Hood ballads certainly belong to the 14th century, but probably more of the extant English ballads belong to periods after the 15th century, rather than before. Even though few ballads are as early as the Middle Ages, the ballad as a form of narrative poetry emerged in the medieval period. It is certainly not a part of primitive poetry and consequently is not to be compared with songs and stories of savages. Culturally the ballad everywhere is post-epic.

The best known of all English ballads are the Robin Hood ballads. It matters little whether Robin Hood actually lived or not. The Robin Hood we know is pure folk ballad creation and the only character in English balladry around whom a cycle of ballads has developed, for the English ballad with the exception of *A Gest of Robyn Hode* is short and non-cyclic; that is each ballad tells an individual story and there is no tendency to carry one hero from ballad to ballad, as is so common in other European countries. *A Gest of Robyn Hode* is certainly a literary product. Probably sometime before 1400 a ballad poet combined several ballads concerned with Robin Hood with transitional material of his own, weaving them into this long popular heroic poem of 456 four-line stanzas. Here Robin Hood appears characteristically as a popular hero though an outlaw, for he robs the rich to give to the poor and escapes apprehension by incredible feats of agility and daring. Many of the ballads of Robin Hood and his men of the Lincoln Green appear through the 15th, 16th, and 17th centuries. The best are the earliest; the later Robin Hood ballads show degeneration and even debasement of the character of Robin Hood himself. Late in the tradition Maid Marian drifts into the story from medieval pastoral poetry to add a romantic touch, foreign, of course, to the traditional story. Robin Hood is not the only outlaw in English ballad. Other ballads of this character are *Adam Bell and William of Cloudesly, Johnny o'Cockley's Well, The Outlaw Murry, Sir Andrew Barton (Henry Martyn), Johnie Cock.* This last, an extremely interesting ballad full of old folk belief and custom, relates the heroic death of an outlaw.

The finest of the English and Scottish ballads are the tragic ballads. Most of them are Scottish and most of them are early. Typical are *Sir Patrick Spens, The Twa Sisters, The Cruel Brother, Lord Randal, Edward, Babylon, Leesome Brand, Twa Corbies.* Many of these are widely dispersed over Europe. *Edward,* for example, is found throughout the Scandinavian countries and in Finland; *Lord Randal* as far as Italy.

Particularly charming for their romantic and imaginative character are the fairy and enchantment ballads. Three of the finest are *Thomas Rymer, Tam Lin, Lady Isabel and the Elf-Knight.* The first tells of Thomas Rymer's visit to fairyland; the second of the rescue by his mortal sweetheart of Tam Lin, bespelled and captured by the fairy. *Lady Isabel* is a widely known European ballad; it recounts Lady Isabel's escape from an elf-knight by trickery. Other ballads of this type treat of the fairy mistress (lover) theme, of changelings, fairy nurses, fairy enchantment, fairy forest, fairy music and its bespelling power. Several ballads like *Kemp Owyne* and the *Laily Worm* are concerned with enchantment wrought by mortals, usually stepmothers, and the unspelling by kisses of someone intrepid enough to kiss the victim in her loathly form. Here and there among the ballads is found the semisupernatural character Billy Blin (Blind Barlow, Billy Blind, etc.). He functions as a

household familiar assisting the hero with advice and information. He is cunning and well-versed in counter magic. He seems to belong rather to the dwarf tradition than to the tradition of the fairy. Allied with the fairy and enchantment ballads are those concerned with the dead who return, revenants from the world of the grave. *The Unquiet Grave* is based on the belief that too much weeping over the dead disturbs their rest. *The Wife of Usher's Well* relates the visit of three dead sons to their sorrowing mother. *The Suffolk Miracle,* a widespread European ballad the original of which is probably Greek, is the dramatic story of the dead lover who returns to carry off his sweetheart. It is the source of Bürger's *Lenore.* (See DEAD RIDER.)

Justly famous among English and Scottish ballads are the Border Ballads. These are spirited recitals of border feuds, of cattle raids, and of conflicts between English and Scotch, suggestive of the stuff out of which in earlier culture the epic grew. The most famous are *The Hunting of the Cheviot, The Battle of Otterburn, Johnie Armstrong.* Most of these are realistic and generally literary.

It is interesting that the English ballads have little to do with old Germanic mythology and tradition, nor much concern with Christian legend and theme. There are some few of the latter such as *Judas, St. Stephen and Herod, The Cherry Tree Carol.*

The old ballads were brought to America by the early settlers and even today can be found widespread among the folk of the outlying regions. Such ballads as *Barbara Allen, Lord Lovel, The Cruel Mother, Lord Randal, Lady Isabel, The Gypsie Laddie, The Golden Vanity* are widely found. About one third of the traditional ballads are still sung in America. A few narrative songs more or less in the old ballad form and in old ballad style have been composed in America. *Springfield Mountain, Frankie and Johnny* (or *Albert), John Henry, Jesse James, Casey Jones, The Little Brown Bulls* are typical.

A great stock of fine ballads exists in Danish dating from the 14th century. Like the English they show a variety of themes: historical, supernatural and magical, realistic, stories of the trials and joys of everyday life, love, and blood feuds. Many of them are analogs of the English. The historical ballads, like epic stories, glorify the virtues of bravery, loyalty, and honor in the lives and characters of the national heroes. Some of the best of these concern Stig Hvide who dies valiantly defending the king's standard; King Waldmar and his wife, Sophie, and his mistress, silken-clad Tove; Niels Ebbeson, who rid the country of a foreign oppressor; and the half-dozen ballads dealing with the conflict between Marsk Stig and King Erik. There is a general tendency toward cyclic development among these historical ballads, for they roughly group themselves into the following divisions: 1) Those concerned with Waldmar, his queen, and his mistress. 2) The exploits of Marsk Stig. 3) The cycle of Waldmar II and Dagmar. This is a tendency hardly found in English but common enough in the eastern ballad.

The Danish supernatural ballads generally lack the airiness and grace of the English; they are concerned mostly with trolls, mermaids, mermen, werewolves, magic runes, transformation. In *The Mermaid's Spaeing* a captured mermaid reads the future for the queen. *Agnes and the Merman* is the story of the love between a merman and a mortal girl. *The Lady and the Dwarf King* tells of a mortal lady married to the dwarf king and forced to live with him under the hill (cf. English *Young Akin*). In *Sir Magnus and the Elf-Maid* Sir Magnus cuts the elf-maid to bits when she tempts him; whereupon she turns into "blazing fire." *The Maiden Hind* is the story of a son who forgot his mother's injunction not to kill the little hind; only after it was dead did he discover that he had killed his little sister transformed into a deer. *Young Svejdal* relates the story of Svipdag who released Menglad from the magic mountain. Sir Torré is bespelled in an elf cave, but escapes through the help of the elf queen. *The Lind Worm* (cf. English *Laily Worm*) is the usual transformation story. *The Knight in Bird Dress* gets to his sweetheart by transforming himself into a bird. An unusual ballad is *The Avenging Sword;* the story tells of a magic sword that fights of itself for its owner. Several Danish ballads deal with giants, dragons, and monsters. The best of these are *Vidrick Verland's Son and the Giant Langbane, King Diderick and the Dragon, Child Orm and the Berm Giant, St. George and the Dragon.* Many supernatural and magic elements appear through the whole body of the Danish ballads: tabu, power of runes, informing dreams, magical music, witchcraft, transformation, shape-shifting, werewolves.

The realistic ballads comprise a large and interesting group; in them one can trace the course of the life of the individual from birth to death, so detailed they are. Many of them are love ballads, and many of them tragic. *Ebbe Skammelson* is full of realistic detail concerning wedding customs; it tells of a younger brother winning the older brother's betrothed and the murder of the two by the elder brother on their wedding night. *Svend of Vollerslov* is a story of revenge involving the son of a slain man.

The Danish and Scandinavian ballad in general was frequently accompanied by dance. Olrik states that the dances were originally accompanied by pure lyrics and that the ballads were sung in the hall, but that about 1200 the practice grew up of starting the dance in the accustomed manner with a lyric song and then continuing with a ballad whose substance marked the emotion expressed in the lyric. As time passed the ballad came to be regarded as the conventional accompaniment for dance.

The Danish ballads are generally somber in tone and intense in their recital of action. Their themes are overwhelmingly tragic, with tragic love and blood feuds most common. Only a very few are humorous; none have the light touch of the ballads of the south.

Folk song is richly represented in the West Germanic languages but it is rather lyric than narrative and more local than national. There is no body of general ballad poetry such as that of England and Denmark. Most of the folk poetry is satiric or allegorical; much of it is political. These special types of folk song are usually not in stanzaic form; the ballad pieces usually are. Many of the pure ballads are on historical themes, but they are likely to give general accounts of battle rather than to focus on the exploits of a single hero. The *Battle of Sempach* is typical. Outlaw ballads form another category; characteristic are *Epple von Gailingen, Lindenschmid.* Most of these are concerned with robber barons, a type peculiar to German balladry. The large number of folk songs on religious themes that sprang up after the Reformation

are hardly ballads though many use ballad techniques and story. Most are sung to hymn tunes. As in England some ballads are adapted from old story, epic, and romance. *King Ermanaric's Death* and the ballads celebrating Dietrich are examples. Several Biblical stories are reworked as ballads. The Dutch *Hallewijn* is probably the Holofernes story; the German *Judas* is rather lyrical than narrative (cf. English *Judas*). As usual in ballad collections, stories of the supernatural bulk large. The water sprite is common, as are mermaids and mermen, dwarfs with magical powers, ghosts, revenants, poltergeists, kobolds. The familiar *Pied Piper of Hamelin* is typically German. *The Fiddling Hunchback* is another ballad whose action turns on the theme of the magical power of music. Ballads of the type of the English-American *Froggie Went a-Courtin'* were popular in German. Some of these are parodies of human behavior; others allegories. By the 16th century German ballads had largely degenerated into accounts of horrible crimes, sensational adventure, tavern brawls.

So different are the Russian *byliny* from the ballads we have been discussing that it is a question whether or not they should be admitted into the category of ballad. Some critics (e.g. Entwistle) discuss them as ballads; others (e.g. Chadwick) look upon them rather as heroic literature and so more akin to the epic lay. They do have many ballad characteristics, being short, narrative, somewhat dramatic story songs. But the meter is casual and often determined by the music. Usually each line is marked by a metrical foot. They do not rime, nor are they divided into stanzas. Their subjects are usually the exploits of heroes. Each character or hero may be the central figure in a number of byliny; it is consequently possible to arrange them in cyclic order. Thousands of variants exist, since each singer is accustomed to combine, delete, and add elements at will.

Some organization of this mass of widely diverse material is got by grouping the stories concerned with a particular hero, period, or region. The earliest cycle centers around the heroes Svyatogor, Volga, Mikula; these are the "older" heroes. They are related to Russian history but in a very artificial way; most of their exploits come from folklore. For example, Svyatogor is a giant possessed of great strength. He rides a great omniscient horse which gives him on occasion valuable information. He seems to be basically a folktale hero; many of the stories told of him include general folklore motifs. The most dramatic is the account of his death. Crossing a plain one day, he and his friend Ilya see a coffin bearing the inscription: For the one who can lie in it. Ilya tries but is immediately expelled. When Svyatogor lies in the coffin, the lid clamps down and though Ilya attempts to pry it open with Svyatogor's magic sword, it will not move. Svyatogor's tears flow out forevermore forming a great river. This illustrates the general difference between the Russian ballad and the ballad of western Europe. Here are not realistic stories in which the emphasis is on the story element, but fantastic narratives with the emphasis on the hero, a fabulous and epiclike character. Mikula is a sort of Paul Bunyan of the peasants. His great strength enables him to plow more land, fell more trees than any other peasant. Volga is versed in the language of the birds and animals; he possesses great powers of magic and can transform himself at will into an animal or bird. He is head of a *druzhina* who help him in his exploits against the Turks. In many of these stories the fabulous and supernatural are linked with the historical.

Another and larger cycle is that of Kiev. These stories, now found only in the north, were originally Ukrainian stories and were probably founded on fact. The central figure is Vladimir I (10th century). Most of the stories relate the exploits of his druzhina. Here are mostly stories of adventure, but now and then personal narratives like those more frequently found in ballad appear. The most important characters in this cycle are Dobrynya, Ilya of Murom, Nikitich, Aljoša Popovich, Nastasya, Dyuk Stepanovich, Mikhailo. The latter is the hero of a fantastic story involving many folklore motifs: swan maiden, water of life, petrification. It is impossible here to give more than a suggestion of this material so varied and extensive it is.

The *dumi* of the Ukraine are different, for the Ukraine was subject from the late Middle Ages on to much Western influence. Their ballads are more conventional in form and subject. They rime; many of them are stanzaic. The music is definitely melodic. Their subjects are of a more domestic sort—love, courtship, marriage, faithfulness or lack of it, death. They are more impersonal, less inclined to celebrate great heroes. A number of the dumi are based on historical themes, recounting battles against the Turks and Poles, raiding expeditions that suggest the English and Scottish border. Here too can be found a number of ballads general to all Europe.

The folk poetry of Yugoslavia falls into two somewhat arbitrary groups: the *junačke pesme*, men's songs, and the *ženske pesme*, women's songs. The junačke pesme are heroic and narrative, the ženske pesme, lyric, often love songs. Unlike the men's songs the women's songs were often danced to. The men's songs are distinctly heroic; in fact they represent really an epic urge working itself out in the shorter narrative form. Typical are the story poems telling of the exploits of Marko Kraljević, the famous Yugoslav hero, killed probably in the battle of Rovine, 1394. The ballad of *Marko and Andrija* shows analogical relation to *Edward* and to the *Two Brothers*. In a quarrel Marko drives his sword into his brother's heart. Dying, Andrija begs Marko not to let his mother know what happened. When she asks why the sword is bloody Marko is to say that he has just killed a stag. If she asks for Andrija, Marko is to say that he has been bespelled by a lady and lured to the land of no return. He then tells Marko to call on him by name whenever he needs aid in battle. In *The Marriage of Marko* Marko through the help of his faithful falcon secures as wife one of the *vile* (beautiful supernatural winged maidens). After living with him for several years and bearing him a child, the vila one day gets possession of her wings, which Marko had kept from her, and flies away. But the story, unlike the swan maiden stories, ends by Marko getting the lady back and their living happily ever after. *Marko Kraljević and the Arab King's Daughter* tells the story of Marko's escape from prison by aid of the jailer's daughter who loved him. These stories are the usual compound of physical adventure of an exaggerated sort and folklore. Some seem very like folktales translated into ballad form.

More dramatic and more poetic are the fine stories that form the cycle of Kosovo. These stories were inspired by the battle of Kosovo (1389) in which the Turks defeated the Serbs. Characteristic is the ballad, *The Fall of the Serbian Kingdom*, which describes the battle as a whole, making the defeat of the Serbs inevitable and therefore dramatic and tragic. Many of the ballads in this cycle particularize events of the battle. In *The Death of Jugovici's Mother*, the mother receiving the severed hand of her son dead on the field of battle voices her lament and dies. Simple pathos is found in *The Maiden of Kosovo*. At daybreak the maiden goes out on the battlefield, turns over the bodies of the slain, wipes the blood from their faces, searching for her lover. In this cycle are some of the finest of European ballads.

In Yugoslavia are to be found a goodly number of ballads dealing with religious story, of which the largest group is hagiographic, often with a touch of didacticism. The stories of supernatural characters form a minor group, mostly concerned with dragons and vile. *The Walling of Skadar* has interesting European analogs. Three brothers try to build a wall around the town, but each night the wall is destroyed by a vila. Finally, the vila tells them that they must immure whichever wife brings their dinner on the next day. Two of the brothers warn their wives; consequently the wife of the third is walled up. For a year she suckles her child through a hole in the wall and ever after milk flows from that place.

In Bulgaria most of the ballads are concerned with supernatural characters and themes: samodiva, lamia, dragons, Charontes, fates, snakes, talking birds and animals, bespelling music, magic instruments—the whole of Bulgarian folklore crowds into ballad story. The sun and moon appear as supernatural characters in many of these ballads, as they do in Yugoslavia. Another important type is the love ballad—largely stories of seduction, trickery, and tragic love. *Latin Andro and Maid Marica* tells of the protracted grief of Marica at the death of Andro, and of her being murdered on his grave by her jealous husband. As she lies there, the hands of the two lovers meet beneath the sod. A rose grows from Marica and a stream of cool water flows forever from Andro's side.

The ballad in Yugoslavia and Bulgaria has had vigorous growth from the Middle Ages to the present. In Yugoslavia it is one of the most important of all types of literature. It has played a large part in keeping alive tradition, and solidifying the people against outside forces.

The folk songs of France are largely lyrical. What narrative folk songs do exist are reworked from lyric or borrowed from abroad. The *pastourelle* is typical of the lyric-narrative. It is far removed from the true narrative song like the ballad, for the narrative of the *pastourelle* is generalized, patterned, and subordinate. The best of the French narrative folk songs have drifted in from across the borders or have been simply adapted from literary sources. Typical are: *Belle Hélène*, *The Torch of Love*, *Renaud, the Woman Killer*, *King Loys' Daughter*, *La Belle Barbière*. There is no body of ballads like that of England and Denmark. The same remarks hold generally for Italy, where many of the French songs penetrated as well as those from other countries. *Donna Lombarda* is probably the most famous of Italian ballads. It is the story of Rosamund and her poisoning of her lover. It was first told in the *Historia Langobardorum* and from that became general folk legend. Italy develops more historical ballads than France though most of them are late.

Though other Romance countries show little in the way of organized narrative song material, Spain developed a great body of such songs. They came to be known as *romancero* (a word that traveled to France and Germany to denote a body of short dramatic narrative). These songs, unlike the French and Italian, are basically narrative. They are impersonal and dramatic in the same way that the best of the English are. But unlike the English they tend to be tied to specific history. The Spanish ballad too developed a rigid form, highly conventionalized. There is evidence that they are more intense and less diffuse than they were originally; evidently the folk here as usual deleted excrescences and kept alive only the most dramatic elements. Most of the Spanish ballads are semihistorical. But it is rather the personalities of history that interest the balladists. For example, King Pedro the Cruel appears in several ballads but always personally and only incidentally as king and ruler. But ballads of raids, forays, and battles are also found. Many of these recount conflicts between Moors and Christians. Another category is made up of material from the old epics and epiclike chronicles. The most famous of these are the some 200 ballads of the Cid, and the *Infantes de Lara*. In the ballads the character of the Cid changes from that of a distinguished statesman and warrior as he appears in the old epics to that of a young dashing, devil-may-care hero, a great folk hero of Spain. Dozens of ballads work over the old Carolingian stories, the French *chansons de geste*, and even the romances, but all are made history and most of them Spanish history, for the very essence of the Spanish ballad is credibility and historical value. Even general fictional stories are forced into the pattern of history, like *Count Alarcos, Count Dirlos, Gaiferos*. Among the best ballads of a general sort are *Ramón Berenguer and the German Empress* (cf. English *Sir Aldinger*), *Count Sun* (cf. English *Young Beichan and Susie Pye*), *Doña Arbola* (cf. English *Child Waters*), *Moriana* (cf. Italian *Donna Lombarda*), *Rico Franco* (cf. Dutch *Hallewijn*), *Don Pedro and Doña Alda* (cf. Danish *Elveskud*). Typical of the few ballads that turn largely on folk themes are *Espinelo* which is based on the superstition that assigns multiple fathers to twins, and *Bovalias*, the central feature of which is a light-giving stone. All in all the Spanish ballads in number, forcefulness, and dramatic story are among the most important in Europe. See SPANISH BALLAD.

We have tried to make implicit throughout this article that from the point of view of folklore the ballad richly repays study, for it exhibits not only folk beliefs that are contemporary, but also the fossil remains of the lore of the folk reaching back to remote antiquity. Many of these fossil remains found in the ballad survive, of course, as mere conventions, carried from generation to generation, but valuable to the folklorist for all of that. Not the least interesting aspect of this is the fact that here in the ballad is to be found much material for a history of rationalization.

But the main importance of the ballad is not in furnishing material for folklorists. It is of great intrinsic importance. It is often magnificent poetry with beauty and definitiveness. The felicity of its lines, its moving stories, its suggestiveness and evocations are all of the high order of poetry. It often gives a deep reading of life, concerned as it is so frequently with eternal matters, such as love and death, and presenting these matters with the simplicity and directness of Greek drama. Socially it is important. It is the expression of people when they were close to one another and to the community, a homogeneous and largely classless group living in close integration. It was an expression of their unity and likewise it was a force making for that unity. "Give me the making of the songs of a nation and I care not who makes its laws" has point when nation means such a society. The debt of the literature of record to the ballad is immense, but the extent of it can never be fully determined, for the ballad long ago became a permanent part of our general cultural inheritance.

Bibliography:

Child, F. J., *English and Scottish Popular Ballads*, 5 vols. Boston, 1882–1898.

Gerould, G. H., *The Ballad of Tradition*. Oxford, 1932.

Grundtvig, S., and Olrik, A., *Danmarks gamle Folkeviser*. Copenhagen, 1853–1920.

Olrik, A., *A Book of Danish Ballads*. Princeton, 1939.

Doncieux, G., and Tiersot, J., *Le Romancero populaire de la France*. Paris, 1860.

Durán, A., *Romancero general*. Madrid, 1849–1851.

Rubnikov, P. N., *Pesni*. Moscow, 1909.

Ralston, W. R. S., *The Songs of the Russian People*. London, 1921.

Meier, J., *Deutsche Volkslieder mit ihren Melodien*. Berlin, 1935–1937.

Chadwick, H. M. and N. K., *The Growth of Literature*. Cambridge, 1936.

Entwistle, W. J., *European Balladry*. Oxford, 1939.

Pound, L., *Poetic Origins and the Ballad*. New York, 1921.

MacEdward Leach

ball de la teya Literally, torch dance: a serpentine processional dance performed on the eve of a religious festival, in mountain villages of the province of Lérida, Spain. A bonfire is lit on a neighboring mountain. The people run and leap carrying large branches on their shoulders. These they light and return to the village, dancing exultantly through the streets and around the church. Finally in the plaza the fiery serpent coils and uncoils, contracts and expands, and winds into a spiral —a fusion of fire purification and fertility magic. The most recent bridegroom is the leader. [GPK]

ball del ciri Literally, candle dance: a Catalan dance for couples of men and women, performed at religious festivals. Two couples dance at a time, the first group consisting of married couples, the succeeding ones of unmarried couples. The first two women carry branches of flowers, the others carry lighted candles. In Castelltersol, on the second day of a fiesta, six couples circle with small skips, hand in hand. They execute various figures, as the hey, or a radiation of the women to the center, the men to the periphery. The candles are replaced by flowers in the left hands of the women and by *morratxes*, glass vessels, in their right. During a processional they sprinkle perfume from the morratxes on the spectators—possibly a vestige of ancient rain magic. Renewal symbolism is inherent in the group transference of the dance from married to unmarried dancers. [GPK]

Ballet of the Boll Weevil An American Negro plantation song dating from about 1900 when the boll weevil moved from Mexico into Texas to the destruction of the cotton crops. The field hand's sympathy is with the boll weevil against the white man and stanzas have multiplied as fast as the beetle itself. Since World War II it has been sung as a commentary on the housing shortage, in which the singer, like the boll weevil, is "a-lookin' fur a home."

ball pla A Catalan round dance for couples. The music, in triple time, is in two parts, corresponding to the dance: the *entrada* or entrance, a simple promenade, and the dance proper. A variation is the ballet de deu, literally, dance of God, in a slow austere tempo, with one section separating men and women into two lines which fluctuate forward and backward. Another variant, *bal cerda* from the old region of Cerdana, is in light, quick tempo. After a circular promenade, the couples dance singly with small steps and jumps, the man following the woman at a prescribed distance. Finally couples hold hands for another promenade or a mill. These and other variants of the ball pla are performed at religious festivals and pilgrimages, before the church, in city, or mountains. [GPK]

ball play A man's ball game played with racket and stuffed ball: found in all eastern North American Indian tribes and now adapted, without the original accompanying ritual, as in the modern Canadian lacrosse and Louisiana Creole raquette.

Ball the Jack A dance accompanied by hand-clapping and recitative, the head and feet remaining still and the rest of the body undulating, with a rotation of the hips called "snake hips." American Negroes originated this particular form, which was taken over into minstrel shows, but similar dances are done in the Bahamas and along the Congo. The recitative may be a rhythmic chant similar to children's game rimes, ending with "And I ball the jack on the railroad track." The term derives from railroad slang, meaning to go ahead, go fast, be reckless, risk all, etc. "Ball" is an abbreviation of "highball," the signal to go ahead, which in early railroad practice was a painted metal globe hoisted to the top of a tall pole, and the "jack" was the locomotive. Much of American Negro song and verse contains similar allusions to railroads and trains, which symbolized escape.

balm Any of various aromatic plants of the genus *Melissa*. Taken in wine, balm cured snake and rabid-dog bites and was recommended by Arabian physicians for hypochondria and heart trouble. In an English legend of the Wandering Jew, Ahasuerus knocked one evening at the door of an ill Staffordshire cottager who asked him in and offered him a glass of beer. After finishing the beer, the wanderer asked the cottager from what illness he was suffering. The doctors had given him up, he said. Ahasuerus told him to gather three balm leaves, put them into a cup of small beer and drink it, and to refill the cup as it was emptied and put in fresh balm leaves every fourth day. This he did and was cured within 12 days.

Balor In Old Irish mythology, a king of the giant Fomorians, son of Dot son of Net, and grandfather of Lug. He had only one eye, which killed whatever it looked upon; but luckily it was nearly always closed except on the battlefield. Four men attended him to lift the lid with a handle that passed through the edge. He got such an eye as a child from peeking at his father's druids brewing charms. The fumes of the brew went into the eye and poisoned it, so that nothing forever after could survive its glance.

Balor was among the leaders of the Fomorians at the battle of Mag Tured. That day when Lug and Balor met in battle, Balor cried to the four men "Lift up mine eyelid," and just as the lid was raised, Lug cast a slingstone into it that carried the eye out the back of Balor's head, and killed three times nine of Balor's men behind him.

Balor is among those grandfathers of world mythology whose death at the hand of a grandson was prophesied, who exposed to perish or otherwise disposed of the fatal infant, only to die at the hand of that grandson, always somehow miraculously saved to fulfil the prophecy. The Balor story exemplifies the strong Celtic belief in the evil eye. His story is classified also by Krappe and some others with the Old Year or Winter versus New Year, sun, and spring combats and rituals.

Bamapama The stupid, gay trickster hero of Murngin mythology (Arnhem Land) who is called "crazy man" because he violates many tabus, including those against clan incest. See AUSTRALIAN ABORIGINAL MYTHOLOGY. [KL]

bamboche Haitian term for a dance attended only for recreation: sometimes applied (in Mirebalais) to the vodun dances by those who go merely for social exchange, to watch the performance, or to join only in the huge singing dance-circle which never ceases to move around the tonnelle (the temporary brush construction that shelters the actual vodun performance) during the ceremony. [GPK]

bamboo In India a symbol of friendship and an emblem of the sacred fire, since it is believed that jungle fires are caused by the rubbing together of bamboo stems. Its origin is told in the tale of Murala, a Brāhman girl who, unknowingly was wed to a man of the Sudra caste. When she discovered the deception, she decided to end her life. She prayed to Vishnu and then mounted a funeral pyre. From her ashes grew the bamboo.

In all of southeastern Asia and the East Indies the belief is prevalent that the flowering of the bamboo (which rarely occurs) is the prognostication of approaching famine. In the Philippine Islands bamboo crosses are placed in the fields to aid the growth of crops. Among the Semang of Malaya and many Melanesian tribes bamboo is used in magic. The Aka-Bo of the Andaman Islands believe the first man, Jutpu, was born inside the joint of a big bamboo, came forth, and made his wife from clay of a white ants' nest. The bridge of death of the Kachins of Burma is a slender bamboo under which are rows upon rows of boiling cauldrons which bubble up and engulf the wicked.

The bamboo is connected with the moon, especially in Japan where one of the holy men cut down a bamboo, transformed it into a dragon, and rode to the lunar heaven on its back.

Bamboo Princess The title of a Malay legend. Khatib Malim Seleman, carrying a jungle knife, adze, chisel, and betel-nut scissors, went in pursuit of a beautiful princess. While he was asleep the princess appeared and cooked him food, disappearing at dawn. In the morning Khatib tried to cut open the bamboo under which he had been sleeping and in which the princess had told him he would find her. Finally he succeeded in cutting off the top shoot with his betel-nut scissors and split the bamboo downwards. He took his princess to Bukit Peraja where both disappeared. There they still live, invisible, but if their aid is invoked they will perform anything asked of them and then disappear again.

banana A large plant (genus *Musa*) growing ten to twenty feet high, cultivated in tropical climates for its edible pulpy fruit, which grows in long, usually pendent, clusters. In regions where the banana is indigenous, the banana tree is often the birth tree or life tree of an individual. In the Solomon Islands it is believed that sometimes the soul of a dead man will enter the bananas, and no fruit is eaten from trees believed to be thus inhabited. In New Guinea young banana trees are sometimes whipped with a stick cut from an old and fruitful tree, so that the fruitfulness of the old may pass, via the stick, to the young tree. A Tahitian story explains why the fruit of the *meia* (lowland banana) hangs down instead of standing upright like the fruit of the *fei* (mountain and highland banana): long ago the *meia* were defeated in war by the *fei* and henceforth hung their heads. Polynesian mythology accounts for the origin of many plants as having sprung from the bodies of human beings who died at the time of the Sky-Raising. They recognize the trachea of man in the stem from which the banana flowers hang below the fruit. Trees with cracked bark grew from people with chapped skin; the tender under-bark grew from man's tender inner skin. Among certain Bantu people it is customary to bury the afterbirth of a child under a young banana tree. See AFTERBIRTH.

Banba In Old Irish mythology, a queen of the Tuatha Dé Danann, wife of Mac Cuill, one of the three kings from whom Ith received such a surly welcome in Ireland. The *Book of Invasions* tells how the advancing Milesians met Banba in Sliab Mis and asked her name. She told it, saying it was her name that was the name of that country, and she begged that it might remain the name of it forever. And the Milesians promised it. Later they met up with Fódla, sister of Banba, and had the same conversation and made the same promise. Still later they met Ériu, the third sister, who told the Milesians, "Yours will be this island forever," and she too begged that her name might remain the name of that island. The Milesians promised her that Ériu would be its chief name forever. It is believed that these three queens are fictions created to explain the three ancient poetic names for Ireland.

banjo A musical instrument of the guitar family imported into the United States by Negro slaves from West Africa, where one of its ancestors was called *bania*, and favored by Negro musicians for accompaniment of singing and dancing. It consists of an open drum, covered on one side with parchment, a long neck, and a varying number of strings, and probably derives from Arabian or European types of guitar. Legend says it was invented by Ham in the Ark and thus gives the Negro claim to recognition as a master musician.

Like certain other folk instruments—the bagpipe, the fiddle, the guitar, etc.—the banjo is a favorite of the Devil, who is a virtuoso player and will teach you to play it if you meet him at the crossroads at midnight and give up your soul. This kind of belief was fostered by religious influences, because music and entertainment of the kind that centered around these instruments was not likely to be pious. It kept people out of the churches and led them into evil ways.

Played for dances, hoe-downs, and singing by Negroes, the banjo was taken straight over into minstrel shows and carried its rippling, strongly rhythmic music all over the United States. The five-string type, most popular of all, found special acceptance among the white mountaineers of the South, who developed with it a peculiarly American kind of music, combining Negro, minstrel, and old English dance and ballad elements. Such old-time favorites as *Cindy*, *Dinah Gal* (a nonsense ditty about a wooden leg), *Ida Red* (a bit of foolery about gin), and *Old Dan Tucker* are typical tunes of the banjo picker, and have been sung, danced in square sets, or spun out to shorten the journey by covered wagon, truck, or bus over the length and breadth of the United States. The material of the song could be anything. Even a mine calamity in Kentucky gave rise to a banjo piece, *The Cold Creek March*.

bannik A spirit living in the stove or under the seat in the bathroom: one of the Russian household spirits. A little water in the tub and a bit of soap on the bench are left after a bath for the use of the bannik or any other of the household spirits who might take it into their heads to bathe. Going to the bathroom alone at night or in the evening may be dangerous because of the bannik. Compare DOMOVIK; HOUSEHOLD SPIRITS.

banshee Literally and originally, a woman of the side or fairy folk, in Irish folklore usually appearing as a beautiful woman weeping (and thus foretelling) the death of someone, often a member of a specific family. She is usually associated with the primitive earth goddess of the district which she haunts. (See ÁINE.) The banshee appears either as a beautiful maiden weeping the coming death or as a gruesome hag foretelling it. She is often identified with the Washer Of The Ford, who is seen at a ford washing bloody garments by one about to die. She is also often associated with the White Ladies of other folklores, partly because of her function as a foreteller of death, and partly because of the etymological confusion between *bán*, meaning fair, white-haired, and *ban-*, a prefix meaning woman, or the actual *bean side*, woman of the *side*.

Banya A Gold Coast dance that has been retained by bush and town Negroes of Dutch Guiana. One Surinam form of the dance, the *bakafutu banya* (cross-foot banya) is associated with dancing for the ancestors. [MJH]

banyan An East Indian fig-bearing tree (*Ficus benghalensis*), epiphytic in its early life, which sends down from its branches roots that develop into new trunks, thus producing a thick and shady grove, sometimes of giant proportions. The tree is named from the use of the ground under it as a market place by native banians or merchants. The singular character of the banyan's growth is represented by a Mindoro riddle, "When a tiny infant I was stolen by a night prowler who later dropped me into the arms of a kind woman who took pity upon me, nurturing me from the milk of her own breast. When I became older I loved my foster mother so much that I smothered her with caresses." The prowler is the fruit bat which ate the banyan fruit and dropped the seeds in a tree, usually a palm, where they rooted. The roots eventually embrace and kill the palm.

Tahitian (Polynesian) mythology explains the shadows on the moon as the branches of a huge banyan tree from which Hina-i-aa-i-te-marama (Hina-who-stepped-into-the-moon) took bark to make cloth for the gods. Once while clambering around in the tree she broke off a branch accidentally with her foot. It flew through space to the earth, took root, and became the first banyan tree in the world. Hina's companion in the moon was a wild green parrot (*u'upa*) who lived in the tree and ate its figs. This little bird, at Hina's instigation, scattered a bunch of these little red figs across the earth and from them grew all the Polynesian banyans. Here is a folktale strangely contrary to the natural fact that the banyan propagates by its branches. The Polynesian peoples make a good cloth from the bark of the banyan, and thus Hina is still tutelary deity of the sacred cloth-beaters.

The Hindus call the tree Vaibadha, the breaker, and invoke it when they desire vengeance on their enemies. In Indian mythology, Vishṇu was born under the shade of the banyan. The tree is confused with the Bo-tree and therefore shares its place in heaven. Like the latter it is the Tree of Knowledge. It is also the tree of Indian ascetics and seers. In Indian folklore the tree is a representation of Śiva and anyone who cuts one down will be punished by the annihilation of his family.

baptism Ceremonial purification by immersing, bathing, or sprinkling with water, usually symbolic of acceptance into the community, typically the religious community, and often accompanied, as in the instance of the newborn child, by name-giving: a practice originating in the pre-Christian era and found today among many cultures all over the world. While baptism as a sacrament is most common in Western culture, similar ceremonies without this religious background are widespread. Baptism, essentially, seems to be based on the concept of the removal of the ceremonial uncleanness of the mother and child, and of safeguarding them against the demons and evil spirits to which the ordeal of birth has made them especially susceptible. Water, as a pure, "living" material, is most used, but baptism by saliva, blood (human or sacrificial animal), milk, clay, dirt, and even rum is known. Adult baptism is usually an initiatory rite, as for candidates to the Eleusinian mysteries or for proselytes to Judaism, though sometimes the ceremony is a reaffirmation of faith.

Generally, in Europe, underlying the religious significance of the Christian rite of baptism are more ancient, indigenous beliefs. The idea is that the unbaptized, adult or child, is a pagan, hence subject to pagan influences. In Ireland of the 16th century, for example, the right arm of the male child was left pagan (unbaptized) so that it might strike harder blows. The general belief that the newborn child is endangered by fairies or demons gives rise to numerous customs for safeguarding the child and the mother until baptism and churching. In the Middle Ages it was thought that witches took a toll of unbaptized children on Walpurgis night. The Greeks and the Slavs believe that the Lamia has a cer-

tain power over the unbaptized. An obscure Coptic custom, adapted from Christian baptism but observed by many Copts and Moslems in the Middle Ages, was the baptismal river festival in the Nile on Epiphany Eve which cured all illnesses. Group baptism in rivers in the United States has been well publicized. No matter how cold the water or how raw the weather, United States Primitive Baptists believe baptizing never leads to a cold. Among the Lapps, a second or third or subsequent baptism, with renaming, may be gone through in case of illness to foil the malignant spirit causing the ailment.

Baptism accompanied by naming ceremonies is found in Africa, Malaya, Polynesia, India, and Iran, among the North American Indians, Teutons, Greeks, Lapps, and Celts. In Europe, the circumstances attendant on the naming of the child are accompanied by a number of customary observances and beliefs. The behavior and physical and moral perfection of the godparents, the actions and speech of the officiating clergyman, the occupation of the parents during the ceremony, all have influence on the future development of the child. The actions of the child himself during the baptism are important. Widespread in England is the belief that a child who cries is expelling the devil. On the other hand, in Germany a crying child will not live to grow old.

Among the ancient Teutons, the *vatni ausa* (sprinkling with water) of the infant by the father acknowledged it. After that the child was a member of the community and could not be exposed by the parent. The idea behind this is recognition of the infant as a new person in the social group. The formalized religious overtones and ceremonies, while significant, are perhaps subordinate in origin. It is the first bathing of the new child that is of community importance. In Fiji, the group holds a feast without the child being named at that time, although the name itself is significant in later community life.

baraka The word used by Mohammedans of Morocco for the supernatural energy, or holiness, attached to certain persons or objects. Baraka is a beneficent power, but it also has a distinct element of the perilous in it. It may be transferred, as from a holy person to a place or thing. Baraka is possessed by brides, plants, trees, mountains, the horse and saddle, camels, greyhounds, prayers, rainbows, and other natural phenomena, certain numbers (the odd having more baraka than the even), etc. Compare MANA; TABU.

Barashnūm A Zoroastrian ceremony of purification "the purification of the nine nights": conducted especially to restore purity to those contaminated by contact with the dead. Originally it was performed only for a woman who had given birth to a stillborn child or for a man who had had contact with a corpse; but it is now observed generally by the Parsis of India as a means of securing purity. Every member of the Parsi community must go through the ceremony, which is conducted by the local priest, before the age of 15, and perhaps again later, in order to prepare his soul for its entrance into heaven. If he does not, he cannot cross the Chinvat bridge after death. Trees are felled to prepare a special place suitable for the ceremony. Holes are dug, furrows marked; the one seeking purification walks to each hole, says a prayer, and is sprinkled with water and *gomez* (cow's urine). The ceremony is performed also at the time of a priest's initiation into the priesthood, for the purification of the initiate and for the sake of some person (living or dead) in whose honor he is entering the priesthood. The whole elaborate ritual is described in detail in *Vendîdâd* ix. See BAPTISM; BARSOM.

Barbara Allen The beautiful and cruel maiden in the ballad *Bonny Barbara Allen* (Child #84) who shows no pity or kindness to the young man dying for her love. When she hears the dead-bell ring, she sickens and dies of remorse. Child has only three versions of the originally English and Scotch ballads on the subject, but in America it has become the most widespread of all the transplanted ballads, showing greater geographical range, more tunes, and more text variants than any other ballad. It was first printed in Great Britain in 1740, in the United States in 1830.

Barbarossa Frederick I (1123?–1190), Holy Roman emperor, called Barbarossa (Redbeard) by the Italians: a German national hero. Frederick is the best known of the kings and heroes thought to be asleep in a mountain and waiting to return in time of their country's need. The Kyffhäuser Mountain in Thuringia is Barbarossa's resting place. He sits there at a marble table in a cave with his beard growing either through the table or around it. In a late version, when the beard has encircled the table three times he will awaken. Compare BEARD; KING ASLEEP IN THE MOUNTAIN.

barber The hair-cutter and trimmer and remover of beards, formerly also the phlebotomist and tooth-puller, at all periods since Roman times (5th century B.C.): renowned as town gossip and retailer of news. The barber's reputation for being talkative is a popular stereotype in many parts of the world. Formerly the barber performed the offices of a surgeon, and his art was called a profession, but under Louis XIV in France and George II in England the hairdressers and surgeons were finally separated, although for some time bleeding and tooth extraction were still performed in the barber's shop. In northern England barbers for a time sold books. The row of shaving mugs, each with its owner's name, was a familiar sight in early 20th century barber shops in the United States. In India the barber is still a surgeon and a masseur, also a matchmaker and expert on marriages. The barber's wife is often a midwife. The Eastern barber appears in the *Kātha Sarit Sāgara* in the "Story of Kadaligarbha," and in "The Hunchback's Tale" of the *Thousand Nights and a Night*. The barber in the North European tale of the three skilful brothers manages to shave a running hare. Barbers like Monsieur Beaucaire and Figaro are familiar figures in modern fiction.

barber's pole The striped pole seen in front of barber shops. The red and white stripes on the barber's pole are a survival of the time when the barber was also a surgeon. The white stripe symbolizes the bandage used in the operation of bleeding; the pole itself, the wand grasped by the patient as the vein was opened. Formerly a basin topped the pole to indicate the basin in which the blood was caught. See BARBER.

barghest or **barguest** The specter-hound of Cornwall, known also in northern England. Literally, perhaps it means bear-ghost (*bar geest*) but there is also some argument for its being derived from German *berggeist*, gnome. It appears to people in the form of a bear or a huge dog, and the sight of it usually precedes a death in the family. Traditionally it cannot cross water. In Lancashire it is sometimes called the Shriker, because of the shrieks it lets out when invisible, and sometimes called Trash because it walks with a splashing sound.

bariaua In Tubetube and Wagawaga (Melanesian) folklore, shy, harmless spirits inhabiting the trunks of old trees. They often borrow the sea-going craft of mortals, since they are unable to make them themselves. The bariaua are afraid of being seen by men and run away when approached.

barley A hardy bearded cereal grass or its grain, genus *Hordeum*, of temperate regions, with long leaves, stout awns, and triple spikelets at the joints which distinguish it from wheat. Barley has been cultivated since prehistoric times as a staple food and evidence exists that it was one of the first if not the first cereal cultivated by man. Grains of barley have been found in Egyptian remains dating from the pre-dynastic period and in the pile dwellings of Switzerland. It is mentioned in the Old and New Testaments (*Judges* vii, 13; *Ruth* ii, 17; II *Kings* iv, 42; *John* vi, 9, 13). The meal offering of jealousy (*Num.* v, 15) seems to have been the only use made of barley in the Hebrew ritual. Its use in bread is indicative, however, of poverty.

Indra is called "He who ripens Barley" and the Indians use this cereal when celebrating the birth of a child, at weddings, funerals, and during the rites of the sraddha. Pliny says a boil may be removed by rubbing nine grains of barley around it and then throwing them into the fire. To the herbalists barley was a plant of Saturn, more cooling than wheat, and efficacious in the treatment of fevers, agues, and heats in the stomach. A meal of barley boiled with fleaworts and made into a poultice with honey and oil of lilies, applied warm, will cure swellings under the ears, throat, and neck.

Barley is used in making malt for beer; a Babylonian recipe for beer dates from 2800 B.C. In rune II of the *Kalevala*, Väinämöinen fells the forest to let the barley grow.

Barmecide's feast In "The Barber's Tale of his Sixth Brother" in the *Thousand Nights and a Night*, an imaginary feast served to a beggar by a prince of the house of Barmak. The beggar, falling in with the jest, despite his hunger, pretends to eat the imaginary food from the imaginary dishes. Finally, he pretends to become very drunk from imaginary wine and gives the prince two very real buffets. The phrase has been applied to anything imaginary, illusory, or disappointing.

bar mizvah, bar mitzvah, or **bar mizwah** The Hebrew term for a boy entering his fourteenth year. Until the thirteenth birthday, responsibility in religious matters rests in the father, but after that the bar mizvah assumes the attributes of maturity and takes his own place in the religious community. The ceremony solemnizing the event occurs on the Sabbath following the thirteenth birthday, at which time the youth is called to read a portion of the Law. Customarily the boy then recites a learned oration, and receives presents from the guests. The rite has been a fixed custom only since the 14th century, but various indications, such as *Gen.*

xxxiv, 25, where Levi is called "man" at thirteen, suggest an origin in antiquity.

barnacle goose An Old World goose (*Branta leucopsis*) nesting in the Arctic. During the Middle Ages its then unknown breeding habits gave long life to the legend that the bird was in some way hatched from driftwood or that it originated in shells growing on a seaside tree in some obscure place. The story was repeated as late as 1668 despite its being disproved in the 15th century by Æneas Sylvius. Some disagreement existed among medieval rabbis about the bird, since several forbade eating it on the grounds that it was a shellfish, while others discussed the question of slaughtering it as fowl or eating it unslaughtered as fish. A similar Christian debate was concerned with the edibility of the fowl during Lent.

barn dance A social country dance, often held in a barn, at which square dances, quadrilles, etc., are danced, to the directions of a "caller" and the music of a small band or often of a fiddler. The dance music, forms, and calls are to a great degree traditional, even to the humor of the calls, and occur in all parts of the United States with regional variants.

Barnyard A cumulative song of the mountains of the southern U. S. which enumerates the barnyard animals with imitations of their cries in a manner similar to that of *Old MacDonald Had a Farm.* "I had a cat and the cat pleased me," it says. "Fed my cat under yonder tree. Cat went fiddle-i-fee." The hen went "shimmy-shack" and the duck, the goose, etc., made their particular noises in a long series, each verse adding another.

barrel house A cheap saloon of the period about 1900 during which jazz developed, in which the customers could fill their own glasses from a cask, the drip from the spigot falling into a "gut bucket" on the floor. The term is applied to the kind of music played in such places, and especially to the rough, "dirty" timbre of instrumental tone characteristic of this early jazz.

barrenness In folklore and folktale, barrenness is removed or prevented by the use of blood or charms, by eating or drinking certain substances, by bathing, or by sacrifice, often sacrifice of a child. Certain persons are considered unlucky because of their barrenness, and are an evil omen if encountered. Old women and priests in particular are so regarded in northern Europe. See BELTANE; BLOOD; PROMISED CHILD; TWINS.

Barry, Phillips (1880–1937) Scholar of comparative literature, philology, early Greek music, and the history and theology of New England; scholar and authority on ballads and folk music of New England. He became interested in ballad while studying under Leo Werner at Harvard and began his collection of New England folk music in 1903. He had one of the earliest collections of recordings in the country. Together with Louise Pound, he advanced the theory that the ballad is originated by an individual, and is recreated and changed by each subsequent singer, rather than developed by a group and kept reasonably intact.

In 1930 he founded and edited the *Bulletin of the Folk Song Society of New England.* Besides articles in that publication, he contributed to *The Southern Folklore Quarterly, Journal of American Folklore* and the

Musical Quarterly. Many of these articles are reprinted in *Folk Music in America* (New York, Natl. Serv. Bu. Publ. 1939), put out in his name by the Federal Theater Project of the WPA. He also edited *The Maine Woods Songster* (Cambridge, Mass., 1939) and in collaboration with others, *British Ballads from Maine; The Development of Popular Songs* (New Haven, 1929) and *The New Green Mountain Songster* (New Haven, 1939).

barsom or **baresmān** Originally, a bundle of the cut stems of a plant which cannot now be identified, used in the chief Zoroastrian ceremonies; now, among the Parsis of India, a bundle of wire rods varying in number from 5 to 33, bound together with leaves, and used in sacrificial ceremonies. The Zoroastrians of Persia use bundles of pomegranate, tamarind, or date twigs bound with the bark of the mulberry tree. The barsom is powerful against demons, wizards, and witches. A single offering of barsom is so powerful that the druj is weakened when it is made. The bundle, however, must be removed from a house in which a person or a dog has died and it is a sin to prepare barsom improperly or point it toward the north (the region of demons).

Bartók, Béla (1881–1945) Hungarian composer and folk-music scholar. Educated at the Royal Academy of Music in Budapest, where he studied with János Koessler and István Thomán and where he became professor of piano in 1907, Bartók started his researches into the ancient folk music of Hungary and neighboring countries in 1905. He was particularly concerned with uncovering the indigenous music from the layer of Gipsy music regarded as typically Hungarian until that time, and in the course of collecting joined forces with Zoltán Kodály. Their studies resulted in the publication of *Hungarian Folk Songs for Voice and Piano*, in 1906, followed by Bartók's *Twenty Songs* and *Szekely Ballads*. In all he collected, transcribed, and scientifically classified more than 6,000 songs of Magyar, Rumanian, Slovak, and Transylvanian singers, and extended his field in 1913 to African-Arab music. His monumental work, *Hungarian Folk Music*, appeared in 1924. His investigations also included regional music of Bihar, 1913; Hunyad, 1914; Maramures, 1923; colinde, 1937; and folk instruments and instrumental music. With Kodály he founded the New Hungarian Music Society in 1911. His own compositions, numbering among others an opera, *Prince Bluebeard's Castle*, two ballets, six string quartets, many songs and piano pieces, concerti for piano, violin, and orchestra, make extensive and original use of both melodic and rhythmic material from the folk-music studies which were his signal contribution to comparative musicology.

basers Members of the chorus in American Negro spiritual singing who sing the response after a narrative line from the leader and "spell" him for a breath before his next line. They take up so quickly that the singing has a continuity that gives the effect of never stopping for breath.

basil Any of certain aromatic plants (genus *Ocimum*) of the mint family: so called because it was believed to be an antidote for the basilisk's poison, although its earlier Greek name, *basilikon*, probably derives from its use in some royal ceremony. Basil, paradoxically, in folk belief is both sacred and dedicated to the Evil One, is dear to lovers (Italy) and an emblem of hatred (Greece), the propagator of scorpions and the antidote to their stings. Galen and Dioscorides believed it poisonous; Pliny and the Arabian physicians recommended it; Culpeper thought it poisonous because it would not grow with the poison antidote, rue; Gerard recommended smelling it for the heart and the head. It has been and still is used as a cooking herb.

In India holy basil or tulasī (*O. sanctum*) is sacred to Vishṇu and Lakshmī. It is grown in pots near every Hindu dwelling and temple, is a protection for every part of the body, ensures children to those who desire them, and opens the gates of heaven to the pious.

In Greece and Rome the planting of basil is accompanied by cursing, without which the plant will not flourish. In Persia and Egypt the plant is found in cemeteries. In Moldavia its enchanted flowers will stop a wandering youth and make him love the girl who hands him a sprig. In Africa it is eaten so that one will not feel the sting of scorpions, but in some places smelling the plant breeds scorpions in the brain. Elsewhere the smell of the plant is beneficial to the heart and head and produces cheerfulness. See POT OF BASIL; TULASĪ.

basilisk or **cockatrice** A fabulous reptile of classical and medieval European legend and folktale whose breath and look were fatal. Physical descriptions of the creature differ, but generally the basilisk was thought to be hatched from a cock's egg on which a toad or serpent had sat and which preferably had matured in a dunghill or amidst poisonous materials; the glance of the basilisk was fatal whether it wished to kill or not; its breath was poisonous to all plants and animals; contact with its body split rocks, and killed men (even a horseman using a spear), animals, and plants; and its hissing drove away all other serpents. The basilisk usually had a spotted crest, indicating its kingship among the serpents, and a horrid face, either that of a cock or of a human being. It walked upright and, in some instances, was winged. In heraldry, the cockatrice is depicted as having the head of a cock, wings and feet of a fowl, and barbed serpent's tail. Such was the power of the glance that the basilisk could kill itself by looking in a mirror; human beings of course could not look at the basilisk directly but had to use a mirror. If a man saw the basilisk before it saw him, the basilisk would die. There was also a small weasel-like animal which could kill the basilisk, and from this and the fact that the more or less general words for snake in the Hebrew version of the Bible (e.g. *Isa.* xi, 8) have been translated as "basilisk" and "cockatrice," it is believed that the original of the reptile was either the horned adder of the Sinai peninsula or the hooded cobra of India, the latter fitting well with the common description. Compare DRAGON; POISON DAMSEL.

Basin Street A street in the French Quarter of New Orleans, one of twelve blocks comprising Storyville, the red light district marked off by an alderman named Story. Here jazz had its original hearing. One of the most popular of blues pieces was named for the street, *Basin Street Blues*.

basket dance A ceremonial dance centering the action around a basket carried in the left hand by the dancer. In all cases the bearer is a woman who may strew seeds from the basket, and in all cases it is a vegetation cere-

mony. In the medieval Nürnberg and modern Thracian carnival dances an old woman of the corn (meaning rye) carries a baby doll in a basket. The distant (in space and time) Tarascan *sembradora* sows meal or flower petals. In the basket dance of Cochiti, nine women kneel before nine men and symbolically grind corn on their inverted baskets. In these various instances the symbolism doubtless evolved independently. [GPK]

Basque folklore The Basques, "the oldest people in Europe," have preserved little of their ancient culture. The Romans, the French, and the Spanish have profoundly influenced them away from their old traditions, and Christianity since the 7th century directly and indirectly has forced them into the general pattern demanded by the church. Their language, too, so difficult that even the devil has never been able to learn it, has been a factor in keeping Basque culture from spreading and so surviving as, for example, elements of Breton culture were preserved. The language barrier may account for the fact that folklorists have long neglected these people. Even now records are few and often unscientifically compiled.

The Basques seem not to have had an elaborate mythology. They did believe in a universal god, the Yaun-Goicoa, lord of the universe. He created the three principles of life: Egia, the light of the spirit; Ekhia, the sun, the light of the world; Begia, the eye, the light of the body. There is no evidence of an extensive cosmogony such as that of the Indo-Europeans. In some conflict with the belief in the god creator is the evidence of belief in the mother goddess, the great mother of Pan-Mediterranean culture. The Basques called her Erditse, goddess of maternity. All we know of her in Basque culture comes from an inscription on an altar dedicated to her.

A few explanatory myths survive. The Basques account for themselves more easily than most scholars account for them. In the beginning a great fire-serpent lived under the world. Restless in its sleep, it threw up the Pyrenees mountains as it turned its heavy coils. From its seven gaping jaws flowed forth fire which destroyed all the world, purifying everything; then out of the fire the Basques were born. The Basque explanation of the constellation of the Dipper is somewhat different from the usual story. The first two stars in the cup of the dipper are two oxen stolen by two thieves from a laborer. The next two stars are the two thieves following the oxen. The first star in the handle is the son of the owner, sent to apprehend the thieves; the double star is the daughter and her little dog, sent to find the brother. Then following all is the laborer. God condemned them all to this endless journey because of the curses of the laborer at losing his oxen. Most of the myths have been Christianized with the introduction of the Christian god, of Jesus, and of the saints as characters. The moon is a man with a load of fagots, condemned by God to light the world because he cut the fagots on Sunday.

Though the Basques no longer have a pagan mythology, they do retain belief in a group of supernatural creatures and about them tell many stories. Tartaro is a Cyclops-like creature. He is usually described as a giant having one eye in the middle of his forehead. At other times he appears as a great hunter or shepherd living in the mountains; in one or two stories he is simply a grotesque animal. In most stories he is outwitted by his human opponents and so beaten. The Herren-Surge is a great seven-headed snake. In some stories he must be appeased by offerings of human beings; in others he appears in the role of the conventional dragon. One long story in which he figures is the Basque version of the widespread folktale of the ransomed woman as it appears in the usual version of the *Two Brothers*. The Basa-Jaun and his wife, Basa-Andre, are wild creatures of mountain and wood. Their characters shift considerably from story to story. Often Basa-Jaun is a sort of faun or wood sprite (French *Homme de Bouc*); he is mischievous, not malignant. His wife is often depicted as a sorceress, sitting at the entrance of a mountain cave, combing her long hair, luring men to their doom. In other stories Basa-Jaun is an ogre, and his wife is a witch. And strangely enough she often helps her husband's captives to escape. The Laminak are fairies, probably related to the Celtic little people, for like them the Laminak live underground in beautiful castles. The Lamia in Basque story is a water sprite or mermaid, with none of the malignancy of the conventional lamia of classical mythology. In addition to these rather specific characters, one finds the usual assortment of witches (*astiya*), sorcerers, magicians, and the like. Stories of the witches' Sabbat (Basque *aquelarre*, goat-pasture) abound. Usually they tell of a human being who is an accidental witness to the Sabbat proceedings and who overhears some bit of information by which he can break the spell that the witches or their god, the Devil (in the form of a goat), has placed on their victim. In the religious folktales Christ, St. Peter, Mary appear as beneficent supernatural beings little different from the witches and fairies except that they always work for the good of men. A number of these religious tales are highly moralistic, their terseness and pithiness reminding one of the *Jātakas*. Like the *Jātakas* too are the animal stories. The usual characters are the fox, the wolf, and the ass. Each has his traditional role. Each story is well told by way of sprightly dialog.

One finds among the Basques a goodly store of folk songs. Almost all of the songs are lyrics rather than narratives; in fact, only a very few ballads have been recorded. The lyrics fall into five groups: hymns, carols, love songs, satiric and humorous songs, religious legends. The earliest of the songs, the hymns, are modal, and as one would expect, show close affiliation with church liturgy. The most original of all Basque music is that of the following period when the Basque folk singers began experimenting in the major and minor scales. Most of these songs are love songs of great beauty and charm. The third period of Basque musical development shows the influence of French and Spanish songs. To this period belong the long and tiresome religious legends. The Basques have long been fond of the satirical songs. These carry a weight of social and political protest, and were often as effective as the similar songs in Provençal.

Instrumental folk music was not developed to a degree comparable to that of the vocal. It is composed almost entirely as accompaniment for dance and procession. The instruments generally found are the three-holed flute, the tambourine, and the gaita. Until recent times the violin and accordion, so common in other parts of southern Europe, were not popular with the Basques.

The traditional Basque dances are the round and square figure dances. Among the most interesting are the sword and club dances. In these dances each man fences in intricate dance with his opponent and as the dance becomes faster and faster, the whole dissolves into a general mêlée. Both dances are very old; they memorialize, as some think, the old conflict with the Moors. The masquerades are part dance and part play. They are very elaborate with the participants in fantastic costumes, each representing characters from history and legend. Much of the music which accompanies them is old and traditional. All walks of life from shepherds to lords and ladies—not to mention animals like bears and horses—are represented. The whole is an elaborate Mardi Gras.

There is probably influence back and forth between the masquerades and the folk plays for the plays are widely popular. In spite of the fact that the written versions extend only from the beginning of the 18th century the Basque plays are as old as the Middle Ages in form and tradition, with many elements common to the miracle and mystery plays. Some scholars see a kinship or even influence of Greek drama. The subject-matter of these plays is varied though about half of them are drawn from the romances, chiefly from the cycle of Charlemagne; many are on Biblical subjects, some few on classical subjects (Œdipus, Bacchus); some retell the lives of the saints. The authors of a number of them are known; they are usually teachers, or local scribblers who adapt a chapbook story (most of the romances are still so printed even today) or a Biblical story to the conventional play form for the use of local groups. Once the play is composed successive groups of players are likely to modify and change it in the same way the folk modify and change a ballad. Though manuscript copies survive, the plays are most often carried locally from generation to generation in the memories of the players, father teaching his own part to son.

As we have said, the plays show similarity both to the medieval miracle and mystery plays and to the Greek dramas. Like the earlier plays they are highly stylized in the use of stock characters, in the acting, and in the methods of staging. Usually the play is furnished with a chorus, but the chorus functions differently from that in the Greek plays. Here it is a chorus of Satans whose function is to aid the villain and the forces of evil and to combat the good. This chorus of Satans is dressed in elaborate and colorful costumes and each member carries a ribbon-decorated wand with which the action is controlled. One touch of the wand restores the "dead" or strikes down the "living." The chorus is assigned elaborate songs and dances, and generally it plays a colorful and picturesque part. The "bad" characters are represented as Turks, infidels, demons, and less frequently, Englishmen. They are always garbed in red. The "good" characters are the French and the Christians. They are always blue. The action of the play always depicts the struggle between the bad (aided and abetted by the Satans) and the good, always with the ultimate triumph of the good. The action is very lively, with dancing, singing, gesturing, posturing, and by-play. The lines are delivered in a semichant, completely conventional. The interlocutors advance and retreat on the stage in regular dance formation as they deliver their lines. The good characters move in a dignified and majestic manner always from the right side of the stage; the bad indulge in grotesque steps and gestures always appearing from the left.

The plays are performed on an elevated stage usually situated in the public square. At the four corners of the stage are stationed soldiers in colorful uniforms armed with guns which they fire at appropriate moments. Place is provided on the stage for certain local dignitaries, such as the mayor and priest. The orchestra is located on the stage. It is composed of a tambourine, flute, trumpet, and guitar. The highly conventionalized music marks the changes in action and introduces the characters; a rapid march, for example, indicates the appearance of the Satans, a slow, grave march the appearance of the good characters.

Although the costumes are elaborate with much headdress and decoration, the stage props are few. The actors are drawn from the local folk, and many of the roles are hereditary. Women play some parts, but never are women and men on the stage at the same time. Usually, as in the medieval theater, the female parts are taken by boys. One other custom also common to the early theater is the procession of actors in costume through the village on the morning before the play is acted. These plays of the Basque have long been very popular; now they, like much of the traditional culture of the folk, are fast dying out.

The Basque have a great store of proverbs, conventional sayings, riddles. Many of these are common to most of the people of Europe, but a number are unique among the Basque. Familiar enough are such sayings as: There is no tree without shade; On hard bread the teeth will break; The puppy and the bitch are both dogs. Without fire there is no smoke. In the proverbs original with the Basque one is struck by the cynical tone (or is it just keen observation?). A golden key will unlock any door; Marriage of love, life of sadness; Two sisters make a full house. Mention of foxes, dogs, wolves, chickens, and mules occurs constantly in these proverbs. When you have a wolf for a companion keep a dog by your side; A cheap mule is expensive; The fox having a long tail thinks all animals are like him. As one might expect all aspects of the weather are caught up in proverbial sayings. Red morning, south wind and rain; Wet May, happy year; The year of much snow, happy year.

The riddles, like many riddles of the folk, are usually childish or far-fetched. What looks toward the house when going to the wood and toward the wood when going toward the house? The horns of the goat. A fellow with a neck but no head, arms but no hands? A shirt. These Basque riddles lack the subtlety and poetry of Old English riddles.

The Basques have many folk customs, such as telling the bees when death occurs, the bridal procession through the village at which all the presents are carried and along with them certain tools like the hoe and the spinning reel to symbolize marriage, but these customs are also found, with modifications, generally in Europe. Early accounts of the Basques assert that they practiced the couvade. This seems to have been a characteristic of the pre-Indo-European Pan-Mediterranean culture in general and consequently one would expect it among Basques. At present the custom seems to have died out completely. Modern research has failed to find any practice of it. Common still today though is the institution of

aizoa, the neighbor. A person who lives nearest another on the side of the rising sun is closely integrated with his family by very special ties and duties. He is godfather; he attends at births, marriages, and deaths, performing all necessary duties. It is he, for example, who climbs the roof when a member of the family is dying and removes the tiles so that the soul can escape more easily. He holds the candle over the body of the dead, letting the seven drops of hot wax fall on the naked flesh.

MacEdward Leach

Bast, Bastet, Pasht In Egyptian mythology, goddess of Bubastis represented in two distinct forms: (1) as a lion-headed woman with the solar disk and uræus; (2) as a cat-headed goddess bearing a sistrum, in which form she was called *Pasht.* She was the personification of life and fruitfulness, and was essentially mild, although she has been identified as a war goddess. She is sometimes confounded with Sekhmet and often identified with Mut. The Greeks identified her with Artemis, but this seems to have been simply formal and unconnected with actual worship. People from all parts of Egypt attended her unruly festival. The chief center of the deity was at Bubastis, and the rise of the XXII Dynasty (the Bubastites) helped make her influence more widespread. There were two festivals, the greater and the lesser, Memphis rather than Bubastis perhaps being the scene of the latter.

Bastian, Adolf (1826–1905) German ethnologist. He was born in Bremen, and educated as a physician at Berlin, Heidelberg, Prague, Jena, and Würzburg. As ship's doctor, in 1851–66 he traveled to all continents, amassing a great volume of information. He was professor of ethnology at Berlin and head of the ethnological museum there from 1886. With Virchow and R. von Hartmann he edited the *Zeitschrift für Ethnologie* (1869). He published almost 60 works on various anthropological subjects, more than 80 volumes, among them: *Die Völker der östlichen Asien* (1866–71); *Ethnographische Forschungen* (1871–73); *Der Buddhismus in seiner Psychologie* (1882); *Amerikas Nordwestküste* (1883); *Indonesien* (1884–94); *Der Fetisch an der Küste Guineas* (1884); *Die mikronesischen Kolonien* (1899–1900). Bastian was proponent of the theory that mankind's common psychological basis explained the existence of common folklore materials like tales, games, beliefs, etc.

Bat A humorous character in some Southwestern and Basin North American Indian mythologies. Bat, in the person either of an old man or an old woman, successfully brings down a deity or human being(s) marooned at the top of a high cliff. Humor enters into the tale because of Bat's size, teasing by Bat of the stranded person, or the song sung while transporting the person to earth in a carrying net. See BATS. [EWV]

Batāra Guru or **Bĕtara Guru** The name for Śiva used in the Malay peninsula, Bali, Java, and Sumatra: to the Malayan the all-powerful spirit who held the place of Allāh before the advent of Mohammedanism. Batāra Guru has been identified with Si Raya, the spirit of the sea from low-water mark to mid-ocean, and sometimes with Mambang Tali Harus, the Malay spirit of the mid-currents. In Sumatra belief Batāra Guru created the earth by sending a handful of earth down to his daughter who had leaped from the upper world into the limitless sea. When this was set upon the sea it grew larger. As it increased in size, it shut off the light from the Naga Padoha, a serpent which lived in the sea. The Naga was vexed and gave the land a shove. It floated off. When Batãra Guru saw what had happened, he sent down more earth and a hero who pinned the serpent in an iron block. His squirming, however, made the mountains and valleys and even now causes earthquakes. When the earth was finished Batãra Guru created the animals and plants. Then his daughter, Boru deak parudjar, and the hero begot the first people.

bats Nocturnal flying mammals (order *Chiroptera*), which, in various families comprising more than five hundred species, are of world-wide distribution. The furry body, leatherlike wings, and night-flying habits make of the bat (flittermouse, night puck, bald mouse, leather wing, etc.) a bizarre creature; and when to these characteristics are added occasionally bright color, like tan, white, or orange, such strange features as are possessed by the leaf-nosed and mastiff bats, and the diet of blood of the vampire bats, there obviously exists a popular subject for the folklore of the world. Colloquial expressions like "as blind as a bat" and "bats in the belfry," indicate popular interest, if not a scientific accuracy of folk observation.

The bat's short legs, according to the Chiricahua Apache story of the rescue from the height, result from the inability of the boy who killed the eagles to keep from looking down. Bat, basket, and boy fell; Bat's legs were broken, and remained short. According to a Lipan Apache story, Bat advised Coyote to take the wife of the missing Hawk chief, which so angered the Hawk that he threw Bat into a juniper bush. Since then bats hang head downward, even when asleep, as did that first bat caught in the juniper by his long moccasins. The night-flying of the bat has been explained variously: as the avoidance of creditors (Æsop), as a search for wives who ran away when they saw Bat in the light (Yavapai Indians of Arizona), as dislike of the dazzling light (Philippine Islands). The Chinese say that the bat flies head downward because its brains are so heavy. Among more recent beliefs about the bat may be mentioned the "scientific" idea that the bat in flight was able to avoid obstacles by his sense of smell. As a corollary result of the development of radar, however, it has been discovered that the reflection of sounds above the range of the human ear enable the bat to navigate surely.

Among some tribes of Victoria, the bat is a man's brother, a male sexual totem, as the nightjar owl is of women, and sacred as a totemic animal. Tongans hold bats sacred, perhaps as containing the souls of the dead. In parts of Australia, in Bosnia, in Shropshire, England, bats are respected, probably for similar reasons, and never killed. On the Ivory Coast of West Africa, there is an island inhabited by many large bats which are sacred to the natives of the mainland because they embody the souls of the dead. A murderer among the Guayaki of eastern Brazil fears that the ghost of his victim will return in the shape of a bat. The bat belongs to the ghosts, according to the Kwakiutl of British Columbia, and hunters will not kill them for fear of becoming unlucky in the hunt. The Babylonians believed that ghosts in the form of bats flew through the evening, while a Finnish story pictures the soul as a bat. A great many of the haunted houses, castles, and caves of Europe and the

United States retain a strengthened reputation because of their high bat, hence ghost, populations.

In Ireland, the bat is a symbol of death, and one of its names is *bás dorċa* (blind death). A Queensland variant of the Adam and Eve story says that when the first woman approached the forbidden sacred bat, it flew off, bringing death into the world. A bat coming into the house is an indicator of death in folk beliefs recorded in India, Alabama, and Salzburg.

Although the bat is almost always considered an evil omen, in China and Poland it is a good sign. The war god, Sepi Malosi, of Samoa, embodied in a large bat, flies before the war party when they are to be victorious, and towards the party if they are to meet defeat: a belief reminiscent of the eagle's ominousness in Rome.

It is considered lucky to catch a bat in one's hat, as the familiar popular rime beginning "Bat, bat, come under my hat," would indicate, but this good luck is canceled if the bat brings bedbugs with it. The association of bats with bedbugs sounds a bit improbable, but the belief that bats coming into a house means that the tenants will soon move out may be quite in harmony with it. On the other hand, in Sarajevo, bats coming into a house are a lucky sign, at variance with the common belief that bats bring ill luck or even death when they enter. To the Chinese, the bat signifies long life and happiness, and the symbol of the five bats indicates the five blessings: wealth, health, love of virtue, old age, and a natural death. Long life and excellent eyesight result from eating bat preparations. The Bantu of Natal will not touch the bat, and we find it spoken of in the Bible as one of the unclean birds and as an illustration of horrible things. The natives of Victoria will not eat the bat; and it is tabu as food on Strong Island in the Pacific. During the Middle Ages, it was thought that the bat's tongue and heart were poisons, and that bat's blood was a depilatory, or a preventive to the regrowth of plucked hair. In Macedonia, a bat's bone is carried as a charm, since the bat is considered there the luckiest of animals. A heart cut from a live bat and tied to the right wrist where it cannot be seen brings luck in gambling (Mississippi).

The bat's outstretched wings were used by Killer-of-Enemies, say the Lipan Apache, for the diaphragm of the horse when he made the first horse in the upper world. There is a common custom of nailing a bat up with wings outspread: as a charm to keep locusts away (Arabic), as an amulet (Pliny), as a form of the devil (Sicily). The Kwakiutl use a bat, or the intestines of a bat, as a charm in a child's cradle, believing that the child will then sleep all day like the bats. The Arabs of Iran think that a bat's eye will cure insomnia, but add that the bat should be spared because it is always reading the Koran's first *sura*. The same charm in Bohemia, a bat's eye, makes its carrier invisible. The wings of a bat placed on an anthill would prevent the ants from coming out, according to one medieval writer; the wings are an ingredient in certain gri-gris of more recent times.

Among the British some believe that the flight of the bat indicates fair weather; and in Kentucky, it is thought that a bat lighting on the head will cling there until it thunders. The clouds coming up from the mountains, after the rain, in keeping with an incident in a tale of the Southern Ute, are caused by Bat smoking his hidden tobacco.

The devil often takes the form of a bat, according to a widespread belief. In Sicily, where the bat is thought of as a form of the devil, they sing a song to the bat and either burn it to death or hang it up. In common with other "loathesome" creatures, the bat is thought to bring disease. The story is told of a French physician that he cured a patient suffering from melancholia by making a small incision and releasing a bat he had been holding in a bag. Somewhat along the same way of thought, bats (or frogs) are taken from the mouths of possessed persons in Nigeria. The Bongo of the Sudan call the bat by the same name they give to their witches or spirits, *bitabok*. Bats were thought to be the familiars of witches; the imps of one witch were seen to be intermediate between rats and bats by one 18th century observer. An Alabama Negro belief is that spirits can be spelled into a bat, and that they will then cease to be troublesome.

There is a belief of general European distribution that bats will become so entangled in women's hair that nothing but scissors and haircut can get them free, or, in Cornwall, a bat may so hold on to a person's face that a knife is needed to cut it off again. Almost as widespread is the belief that bats will eat bacon hung in the chimney flue.

The bat is specially invoked by the Lipan Apache to prevent the fall of a running horse, since the task of preventing such falls while the horse is running, as in a race, was given to Bat boy by Killer-of-Enemies when he made the first horse. Bat is a prominent character in Navaho ceremonials.

Chamalkan, the bat, is the chief god of the Cakchiquel Indians of the Pacific coast of Guatemala. The Mayan bat god was Camazotz, who was much dreaded. Sepo Malosi and Taisumale are Samoan bat gods connected with war.

There are many folktales, fables, and myths in which the bat is a principal character: in the Philippines, Africa, North and South America; among the Arabs, Europeans, and Polynesians. The European fable of the bat who joined both sides in a war between the animals and the birds has been shown to be literary and not truly of folk making. But the Creek and the Cherokee have a story in which bat is refused by both sides as being neither animal nor bird, but when tolerated by the animals (he has teeth) he wins the game for them. From a Philippine tale: the bat is the only survivor of the many creatures that went into the composition of the one man living; he flew away and became the ancestor of the bats. In two humorous Bulu stories, bat becomes the strongest of all the animals by getting into champion elephant's ear, flapping his wings, and making the elephant so dizzy that he falls down; and bat gets all the honey by waiting until the animals cut down a honey tree, then crawling into a hollow tree, flapping his wings, and scaring the group away. Och-do-ah, an evil spirit in bat form, who poisoned the spring he guarded from noon to dawn, is prominent in the legend of the origin of the death dance of the New York State Iroquois. Among the Plains, Plateau, and Southwestern Indians of the United States, Bat, sometimes as Old Woman Bat, is the animal rescuer who helps the hero stranded on the high rock or tree to get to the ground in the basket held by a strap of one thread of a spider's web. Another cycle of the Plains and Southwest pictures bat as a trickster-hunter whose two wives discover that he is bringing back parts of himself as food. By a trick they see him, his teeth and pus-filled eyes, and run away. He spies them at a dance, there is a fight, and Bat is badly hurt. The story, with elaborations or omissions, is found among the Ute, Shoshone, Yavapai, Paiute, and other tribes of the region. See VAMPIRE.

Battle of Mag Tured or **Moytura**   The most important story in the Old Irish Mythological Cycle: story of the victory of the Tuatha Dé Danann over the Fomorians. According to earliest accounts there was but one battle of Mag Tured in which the Tuatha Dé Danann overthrew both the Firbolgs and the Fomorians. Later narratives report two battles: the first in what is now county Mayo on the west coast of Connacht against the Firbolgs, the second seven years later in Sligo against the Fomorians.

When the Tuatha Dé Danann first arrived in Ireland on May 1 the first thing they did to make sure of victory was to burn their boats "in order that they themselves should not have them to flee therein from Ireland." When they demanded the kingship from the Firbolgs, they were a long time fighting that battle of Mag Tured, but they won at last and the Firbolgs were slain, 1100 of them, and lay on the plain from Mag Tured to the shore. A few survivors fled to islands in the sea: Aran, Islay, Mann, and Rathlin.

In that battle Nuada, king of the Tuatha Dé, had one arm cut off at the shoulder. A wonderful silver arm was made for him by the physician Diancécht and Credne, the brazier, which was a living arm with movement in every finger. But he could not be king with only one true arm, and the kingship was given to Bres, son of the Fomorian king, Elatha, and a woman of themselves. The minute Bres was king he laid tribute on Ireland and put menial tasks on the champions. Ogma had to carry firewood, for instance, and Dagda was set to digging ditches. The severe exactions and inhospitality of Bres caused great discontent among the Tuatha Dé Danann. When Cairbre, the poet, came to Bres's house and was given a small dark hut without fire or bed and three dry cakes on a small dish, he was not thankful and put a satire on Bres that caused his overthrow.

In seven years the chiefs asked back the kingdom from Bres. He gave it, but went at once to the Fomorians to ask their king, his father, for an army.

"What is the need?" said Elatha.

"My own injustice is the cause," said Bres. "I took their jewels and their food, and now I need an army to take back the kingdom."

"You should not gain it," said the father, "because of the injustice." But he sent Bres on to Balor and to Indech and these mustered a fearful army among the Fomorians to fall upon Ireland.

The second battle of Mag Tured was fought farther to the north in what is now county Sligo, on Samain (Nov. 1). Among the kings and chiefs of the Fomorians were Balor and Bres and Elatha, father of Bres, Goll and Irgoll Loscennlomm, Indech, son of the king, and Octriallach, son of Indech. It was a bad battle. Lug was in front heartening the Tuatha Dé. The slaughter was terrible and dead heroes floated in the river Unsenn. Indech wounded Ogma. Balor killed Nuada, but Lug killed Balor with a sling-stone into his one eye. It went through his head and killed three times nine men behind him. Seven hundred, seven score, and seven men of the Fomorians were killed and counted, and as for the rest that were killed, it were easier to count the stars in the sky. And Luġ and Dagda and Ogma pursued the remnants back to their own place.

So the battle of Mag Tured was won. The dead were cleared from the ground. Baḋb and Morrigan proclaimed the battle and the victory of the Tuatha Dé Danann all over Ireland, to all its fairy hosts, and told the tale to the waters around Ireland and to all the river-mouths.

Battle of Otterburn A border ballad (Child #161) of the Scottish-English warfare of the 14th century. The battle took place on August 19, 1388, when an English force under Harry (Hotspur) and Ralph Percy attacked a Scottish force captained by the Earl of Douglas which was raiding Northumberland. Though outnumbered the Scots routed the English, captured both Percys, but lost the Douglas, who in some versions of the ballad was killed by Hotspur, in others by a boy. The extant tellings of the ballad are much later than the event, but are undoubtedly survivals of ballads composed about 1400. The main version given in Child has been told by an English apologist, and in that version the English among other things are outnumbered and keep the field after the battle. *The Hunting of the Cheviot* probably tells the story of the same battle.

Battle of the Trees Câd Goddeu: a battle of Brythonic mythology fought by Arawn against Amaethon, because of the white roebuck, the whelp, and the lapwing which Amaethon had taken out of Annwn. The *Triads* describe it as one of the "three frivolous battles" of Britain. The *Book of Taliesin* contains the long, disorganized poem, *Câd Goddeu*, which purposes to name the trees in the order of battle.

The battle is also called the Battle of Achren because there was a woman of that name in the battle on the side of Amaethon. Bran fought on the side of Arawn, and no one could overcome Bran without guessing his name; and the same thing was true of Achren. Gwydion, fighting on the side of his brother Amaethon, guessed Bran's name from the alder twigs he carried, and the victory went to Amaethon.

The usual interpretation of the Battle of the Trees is that Gwydion turned the trees into warriors. "Warriors were dismayed/ At renewal of conflicts/ Such as Gwydion made. . . . The alders in the front line/ Began the affray/ Willow and rowan tree . . ." are named next, then holly, oak, gorse, ivy, hazel, fir, "cruel the ash tree," birch, heath, "the long-enduring poplar," and elm. "Strong chieftains were the blackthorn." Whitethorn, broom (anciently used for staves of spears), furze, yew, and elder are also mentioned. The "courtly pine," being "inexperienced in warfare," was not in the battle.

Robert Graves in the *White Goddess* (New York, 1948) has undertaken to sort out and rearrange this long and disorganized and deliberately garbled poem, the *Câd Goddeu,* into a sequence which reveals its ancient meaning. He agrees with the assumption of the Rev. Edward Davies, stated in his *Celtic Researches,* that the Battle of the Trees was not a battle of warriors but a battle of letters of the learned. Graves ties up the Battle of the Trees with all the symbolism of the ancient Celtic Tree Alphabet and the mysteries of the druids (*derwydd* means oak-seer), and seeks to lay bare a complex magic centuries-old and centuries-hidden.

Batu Herem In the belief of the Menek Kaien and Kintak Bong (Malay peninsula), the stone pillar which supports the sky. Part of the pillar (the Lambong) projects above the sky. This is loose and balanced at an angle on the lower part. Four cords run from this part of the pillar to the four quarters of the world and are weighted with stones which hang below the earth's surface. The Batu Herem is said to stand in Kedah which is therefore the center of the earth's surface.

batuque A native Brazilian courtship dance (of African origin) imported via Portugal to Spain in the 18th century. Some writers on the dance do not differentiate it from the lundu. It is described as originally an impassioned dance accompanied by finger-snaps, the girl fluttering on her toes, her partner circling around her with a winding and twisting pattern until the final embrace. It was popular among all classes, including Negroes and mulattoes. By the 20th century it had become modified into a ballroom dance. [GPK]

Bau A principal Sumerian goddess of fertility; the Great Mother; consort of Ningirsu, and with him chief deity of the city of Lagash. The Festival of Bau opened the new year in calendars preceding and contemporary with Sargon's era. As the creatrix she is identified with **Gula,** the Healer, and with **Ma** or the serpent goddess **Nintu.** She seems to be the beneficent aspect of Tiamat, the dragon. Later Bau was absorbed into the personality of the Semitic Ishtar. The Phœnician Baau, mother of the first man, may be a translated form.

Baubo In the Orphic tradition of Greek religion, one of the daughters of Celeus of Eleusis (elsewhere she is called Iambe), who by a jest and by obscene gestures made the grieving Demeter smile. The jesting and the gestures formed part of the Eleusinian rites, and probably the story was invented to explain these after the fact. Baubo is also considered by some the nurse of Demeter, or the nurse of Iacchus who in one of the common versions of the story himself made the gestures at Demeter's sorrow.

bay tree The Grecian laurel (*Laurus nobilis*). To the herbalists the bay was an herb of the sun, under the celestial sign of Leo, and a protection against witches, the devil, thunder and lightning. Its root was used to open obstructions of the liver, spleen, and other inward parts, while the berries were effective against the poison of venomous creatures and the pestilence and were an aid in treating consumption and coughs. According to Albertus Magnus a wolf's tooth wrapped in a bay leaf gathered in August will prevent anyone from speaking an angry word to the wearer. The Greeks made the bay sacred to Apollo who once loved Daphne the daughter of the river god, Peneus. She fled from the god and sought the protection of her father who changed her into a bay tree. Thenceforth Apollo wore bay leaves and a garland or crown of the leaves became the award for victory or excellence. The Romans believed also that a bay tree was never struck by lightning. The withering of a bay was an omen of death.

For pleasant dreams put bay leaves under your pillow. If burning bay leaves crack noisily, good luck will come; it is a bad sign for them to burn without snapping. In Britain the bay was long regarded as a symbol of resurrection, because a withered bay tree will revive from the roots.

Bead-Spitter and Thrown-Away A Creek Indian story. Two young women went in search of Bead-Spitter of whom they had heard, because they wanted some beads. They met up with Rabbit, who claimed to be Bead-Spitter. He tricked them into staying all night, raped one of them, and provided some beads. Upon discovering that the beads were stolen, however, the two girls traveled on and arrived at the house of Turkey-Killer. He was the one. He tested the chastity of the two with a sieve: water ran through the sieve of the one who had slept with Rabbit; the sieve of the other not only held water, but when she was told to sift, the water came through as beads. This one Turkey-Killer married.

One day in his absence the wife was devoured by a monster, who, however, left her abdomen in the house. Turkey-Killer opened it, found a living child inside, threw the afterbirth in the bushes, and reared his son as well as he was able.

Then follows the story of the little wild brother (Thrown-Away), who rose from the afterbirth in the bushes, how he was captured, taken into the house to be reared with his brother, and the sequence of disobediences, adventures, and escapes the two participated in until their mischief-making compelled the father to try to get rid of them. The brothers enlisted the help of various birds as warners of the father's approach and finally killed their father with a horde of bees and wasps. Then with an arrow they rubbed the dead man's buttocks and he flew off in the shape of a crow. "We must be bad boys," the two said and decided to separate. One went east and one west. There are also Alabama and Koasati versions of this story. Another Koasati story (*The Origin of Crow*) belongs to the group, but emphasizes not the miraculous saving of the live baby from the dead mother's womb and the after-birth-as-twin idea, but only the disobedience of the two boys in spying on their father's activities, his turning against them, the killing by bees, and their transformation of him into Crow.

Bead-Spitter plays no spectacular bead-spitting role in any of these Muskogean tales. Hearsay about him is merely the starting point for a series of adventures of the two girls in search of him, or of the two boys born of one of them. But the whole bead-spitting idea is so common among certain North American Indians (the Algonquians, Iroquois, and Muskogeans especially) that their bead-spitters should undoubtedly be numbered among the remarkable spitters of world folklore. Other well-known folk concepts and motifs in this story are dipping water with a sieve as a chastity test, a typical tar-baby trap in one of the brothers' escapades, enemy killed by bees, and the afterbirth as twin.

Bean-curd Gods In Chinese folk belief, three gods invoked by the bean-curd makers and sellers. The chief of these is Huai Nan Tzu because he invented the dish. The other two are Chiao Kuan, and Kuan Yü, the great war god who was a bean-curd seller in his youth.

bean dance An agricultural dance addressed to the spirit of the life-sustaining bean, with similar objectives as the corn dance, but of lesser importance. The Hopi Indian bean-sprouting rite, or *powamu*, is also a puberty rite. The Fox Indian bean dance is a contra for men and women who cross and recross. The Iroquois bean dance, *degondaneshonta*, or hand-in-hand dance, is a slow processional ending with a fast trotting dance or *ga'dášot*. The Iroquois also celebrate a one-day Green Bean Festival in August, with a typical succession of dances: among the Seneca of Tonawanda reservation, for instance, a women's dance, feather dance, ga'dášot, hand-in-hand, and women's dance—a succession common to other festivals which supplicate and give thanks for crops. [GPK]

beans Beans are all colors and most shapes, according to Josh Billings, who was also impressed with the fact that a quart of them "biled two hours" come out a gallon and a half. They are at least as old as Esau, Josh adds, and "there ain't but phew things that can beat a bean climbing a pole."

Beans, of which there are 150 species and unnumbered varieties in the world, play a prominent part in the ritual and folklore of the world. In the ancient Aryan religion they held equal place with honey as food for the dead. Beans were used as ballots by the early Greeks and Romans: white beans signifying yes, black beans, no. The Romans had a festival on June 1 called the Bean Calends because at that time they offered beans to the dead. The Greek bean tabus, as articulated by the Orphics, Pythagoreans, and by Empedocles, probably stem from the doctrine of the immortality and transmigration of the soul through its long discipline of human, animal, and plant existence. A 4th century B.C. writer, however, testifies that Pythagoras himself observed no interdict on beans, but esteemed them highly for their laxative effect. Beans were on the list of those things so ritually sacred that they could not be touched or even named by the Roman *flamen Dialis*. In the old Roman midnight observance that closed the three-day Lemuria (annual entertainment of the dead) the head of the house walked barefoot through all the rooms throwing black beans behind him and saying nine times, "These I give and with these I redeem myself and my family." The ghosts followed close behind him, picked up the beans, and departed, not to return until their appointed time the following year. This ceremony greatly resembles the Japanese New Year's Eve ceremony for driving out demons. The head of the household puts on his richest garments and goes through all the rooms at midnight scattering roasted beans and saying "Out—demons! In —luck!" The association of beans with the dead or with the powers of the afterworld prevails in many ancient and contemporary societies.

The Seneca Indians believe that beans are the special gift of the creator to man and are under the guardianship of one of the De-o-ha-ko, the three daughters of the great Earth Mother. Among the pueblo peoples beans play an important part in the kachina rituals. Kachina initiations follow the color-order of the beans cooked for the kachinas by the families of the initiates. In the ceremony of Whipping the Children the little boys are whipped in the order that the beans have been cooked in their homes: the little boy with the yellow beans gets whipped first, etc. Beans are of such importance to the Hopis, both as foodstuff and symbol, that they speak of their great Powamu ceremony as the Bean Festival when speaking to outsiders. They plant beans in the kivas in preparation for the Powamu. If the beans grow high, it is a good omen; if they break before the night on which they are to be cut, a very bad omen, and the kiva members are whipped by the Whipper for allowing this to happen. This February bean-planting in the kivas is a kind of compulsive magic that influences the summer crop. Every man must go into the kiva in preparation for the Powamu, and must sit up all night. If he falls asleep he is whipped, because his sleep will retard the growth of the beans. At Walpi beans are included with other seeds in the make-up of the Corn Spirit fetish. At Tewa meal ground from a small white bean is used as medicine for neuralgia. At Zuñi a bean is given to a woman in childbirth to swallow, to hasten delivery, because "it slips down quickly."

The Kariaks of the Egyptian Sudan twice a year honor with a meal of beans the wagtail and the snake, in whom they believe dwells the spirit of the grandmother or Mother of Food.

Folktale is full of magic beans: speaking beans which reprove wrong-doers or save fugitives by speaking in their stead, beans that laugh till they split, thus acquiring their characteristic black stripes (very widespread), and the magic beans given to young boys that grow into towering stalks to marvelous upper worlds.

Half a white bean is one of the ingredients of certain New Orleans voodoo charms. Of unidentified but probably European origin are a number of bean beliefs and saws: It is good luck to plant beans on Good Friday. Beans should be planted in the light of the moon. If you dream of beans you have a rich and cruel unknown enemy. If you dream of beans you will have a quarrel. Beans cause bad dreams, and therefore presage misfortune.

bear Early explorers' and travelers' tales about bears of the New World are as tall and fabulous as any of the bear myths or folktales. The writings of various early voyagers maintain that bear cubs are born as unformed shapeless lumps which the mother licks into shape, that bears suck their paws for nourishment while hibernating, and sing *h-m-m-m-m* over the delicacy, thus betraying their hide-outs to hunters. John Bartram, honest Quaker, explains that when a bear catches a cow, he punctures the hide with his tooth, and blows into the hole until the cow swells and dies.

Hunters, woodsmen, and frontier settlers add their marvels to the bear stories. A fisherman in the Maine woods peeked through a knothole and watched a big bear steal his molasses from the cabin shelf, then saw him catch twelve trout and leave six in payment—and the woman who went to milk the cow in the dark and milked a she-bear instead (the woman's starving baby liked the milk)—and the village strong man walking home through the woods in the dark, full of joy and other spirits, "rassled with a big fellow in a fur coat" because he wouldn't get out of the road.

Louisiana Negroes say to dream of fighting a bear portends persecutions; to dream of a running bear means happiness. Ghostly bears have been seen by Georgia Negroes. In Maine when a dog sucked his paws it was said that he had a streak of bear in him. New Brunswick Indians held that a wounded bear would hasten to a boggy place and plug his wound with moss. If bears hibernate early, it portends a hard winter. February 2 is the day for the bear's reemergence; if he comes out of his den and sees his shadow, he will go back to sleep for six more weeks. This weather portent

has been transferred from the bear to the groundhog generally throughout the United States. Years ago in Germany bear's gall applied to an aching tooth was said to cure it. If you meet a bear in the woods fall down and play dead and he will not bother you (see BEAR WHISPERED IN MAN'S EAR). In India bears are believed to be powerful against diseases; children are given a ride on a bear's back to ward off disease, or sometimes one hair from a bear is hung as an amulet around their necks. For why the bear has no tail or a short tail, see BEAR FISHES THROUGH ICE WITH TAIL.

In mythology, folktale, and folk belief the bear figures as god, ancestor, totem, sacred animal, dying god (in the role of food-giver), as guardian spirit, as bear lover, wife, husband, child, as tutelary bestower of medicines and as a curing supernatural spirit, soul-animal, and separable soul.

☞ The bear is a sacred animal among many of the Finno-Ugric peoples. Among the Ob-Ugrian he is the son of *Num-torem*, god of heaven. The ceremonies performed for hunting, slaughtering, and eating the sacred animal are very complicated, because they have to do with the sacrificing of a god. The bear's bones are kept unbroken, and are buried in the same position as in the living animal so that the slain bear may come to life again. The skull of the bear is hung on a tree or a stake. (Karjalainen in *FFC* 63, p. 193–235). See LEIBOLMAI. [JB]

☞ Peculiarly respected, perhaps because of its resemblance to human beings, the bear enters into many North American Indian myths, ceremonies, and beliefs. The tales of *Bear-Woman and Deer-Woman* or *Bear-Woman and the Fawns,* and of *Bear-Woman (Wife* or *Paramour),* are widely known. In several California Indian tribes shamans impersonated bears, or were transformed into bears according to popular belief. Bear was also considered a powerful spirit helper from whom vision seekers obtained supernatural power. Among all circumpolar peoples special rites are undertaken when a bear is killed; a speech of apology is made to the dead bear, who is often addressed as grandfather, and before the flesh is eaten the body, head, or hide is laid out, decorated with beads and cloth; special attention is given to the disposal of the bones. Some of these observances have diffused as far south as the Central Woodlands and Northeastern Algonquians of the United States. [EWV]

beard Sharing with hair much reverential attention, the beard has received plenty of its own. Through many years and in widely separated tribes it has been the sign and symbol of many attributes, including not only the obvious ones of masculinity and strength but also the rather illogically inferred qualities of wisdom, dignity, sanctity, responsibility, nobility, and royalty.

Races of men naturally beardless, like the Mongolians and American Indians, were sometimes erroneously deemed effeminate by their bearded neighbors. According to Herodotus (i, 105) the ancient Greeks decided the beardless Scythian men must be women, suffering this humiliating condition as a punishment by an avenging deity for having plundered the temple of Aphrodite. The Emperor Julian in the introductory paragraphs of his celebrated satire *Misopogon* (Beard-Hater) written in Antioch during the winter of 361–362 taunted the Antiochians about the smooth chins which "so slightly revealed and barely indicated" their manhood. In some Eastern countries a smooth face is deemed to indicate effeminacy; consequently the clergy of the churches in those parts have found it advisable not to shave. By the same token missionaries from Western lands where beards are forbidden to the clergy are, by a special dispensation, permitted to wear them in the East.

Erasmus in his *Adagia* (1523), noting that several classic writers had connected beards with wisdom, such as Lucian's mention of the "learned beard," explains that "As the beard is not completely formed until the age of manhood, it has always been considered an emblem of wisdom." Rather more subtly the author of *Pappe With an Hatchet* wrote in the same century (1589), "Let me stroake my beard thrice like a Germin, before I speak a wise word."

Erasmus might have added that in classic times the philosophers of Greece had proudly worn the beard as a distinctive badge of their learned profession. Alexander the Great (356–323 B.C.) had introduced the custom of shaving, for the alleged reason of thus affording no opportunity for the enemy to seize his soldiers by their beards. The custom then spread from Macedonia throughout the whole Greek world. Aristotle, alone among the philosophers, conformed to his famous pupil's innovation. They retained their beards, rather defiantly, as a distinctive mark, and for centuries after the Macedonian period the Greek word *pogonotrophos,* "man with a beard," meant philosopher.

While the French have a proverb reminding their young men that "Il est temps d'être sage, quand on a la barbe au menton" (It is time to be wise now that you have a beard on your chin), they also have another "La barbe ne fait pas l'homme" (The beard does not make the man), recognizing that physical maturity does not necessarily bring sapience. Thomas D'Urfey was merely versifying the observations of several predecessors when he wrote (1690):

> If Providence did beards devise,
> To prove the wearers of them wise,
> A fulsome Goat would then by Nature
> Excel each other human creature.

In spite of ridicule the beard maintained its position as an emblem of dignity and any assault upon it was regarded as an indignity and highly dangerous, reflected in the common phrase "to beard the lion in his den," that is, to pull his beard. In April, 1587, Sir Francis Drake, returning from his bold raid on the Spanish fleet in the harbor of Cadiz, boasted, "I have singed the Spanish king's beard!" In ancient Israel, according to II *Samuel* x, 4 ff., compelling a man to cut off his beard was tantamount to insult and disgrace. The Israelite wore a full beard and it was never shaved except in case of leprosy (*Leviticus* xiv, 9) or for the deepest mourning (*Jeremiah* xli, 4–7). Even trimming the beard was forbidden (*Leviticus* xix, 27, xxi, 5). When the Ammonites shaved off one half of the beard of each of David's servants, "the men were greatly ashamed: and the king said, Tarry at Jericho until your beards be grown, and then return. And . . . the children of Ammon saw that they stank before David" (II *Samuel* x, 5–6). They knew that they had wounded the pride of the Israelites in the sorest spot, their

beards. The succeeding verses record the bloody vengeance which David wreaked on the Ammonites and their allies for this supreme indignity.

For among Orientals, especially those of certain Semitic strains, the beard is not only a sign of manhood, wisdom, and dignity: it is actually sacred to the point of sanctity. It was sacred enough to swear by, as the Semitic Moslems frequently did. Mohammed kept his beard unshorn and his followers kept theirs uncut in faithful discipleship. Indeed the most devout saved every hair that fell from their beards, adding it to the collection preserved in a small box they carried with them for the purpose. The box was buried with them. It was and still is considered, among orthodox Moslems, that to swear by the beard of the Prophet and their own is as if one swore in the presence of Allah himself.

Various reasons have been alleged for this overanxiety to preserve the integrity of the beard. The *Jewish Encyclopedia* states that Jewish sages agree that the reason is "that God gave man a beard to distinguish him from woman and that it is therefore wrong to antagonize nature." A *Defence of the Beard,* published by James Ward (1769–1859), gave eighteen Scriptural "reasons why man was bound to grow a beard, unless he was indifferent to offending the Creator and good taste." Another (pseudonymous) defender of the beard called it a "Divinely provided chest protector."

These apologia are likely to be deemed mere rationalizing when considered in the light of the well-known anthropological fact that all over the world, among not only primitive tribes but semicivilized as well, it is believed that black magic can work through and by the hair of the victim. Any part of the body, even a single captured hair, is vulnerable to sorcery. It embodies a part of the soul of the man from whose beard it came. He who possesses it has power over the original owner. Among some tribes a captive is kept prisoner by the simple process of the captor cutting off a lock of the captive's hair and keeping it safe. The prisoner is not bound or restrained in any other way.

Like the beard of Mohammed, that of a king was reckoned particularly sacred and important to the whole realm. When Philip V of Spain could not grow a beard, nor Louis XIII of France, their loyal subjects shaved off their own. And "there's such divinity doth hedge a king" that at one time it was thought that three hairs from a French king's beard secured under the wax seal on a document assured the fulfilment of the promises in it.

The ancient kings of Persia, Nineveh, Assyria, and Babylon are depicted with beards. For state occasions Egyptian kings, often naturally smooth-chinned, and at least one queen, Hatshepsut, put on false beards. So did the artists picture Abraham and Adam, and Zeus and Christ and Jehovah himself. It was part of their divinity, according to the belief of the artist. To draw God without a beard would still in some parts be deemed blatant blasphemy.

Legend and folklore have ever found beards of interest. A favorite tale in several versions tells of a sleeping king with a long beard in a mountain cavern. Frederick II (1194–1250), Holy Roman emperor, king of Sicily and Jerusalem, was for a long time after his death believed to be still alive, sitting in a cave in the Kyffhäuser mountain in Thuringia, asleep at a stone table through which his beard had grown. When the fullness of time had come he would wake and restore the Golden Age of Peace to the Empire. The legend was later attached to his grandfather, Frederick I, probably because the elder king had a better beard for the story and was known by it as Frederick Barbarossa.

Even the nursery tales of children preserve the ancient idea of the oath upon the beard:

"Little pig, little pig, let me come in!"
"No, no, by the hair of my chinny, chin, chin!"

CHARLES FRANCIS POTTER

Bear Dance A mimetic dance impersonating the bear, usually performed for curative purposes: among the Indians of North America performed by ceremonial societies. Most realistic were the representations by the Plains-Cree in complete bearskins or masks. Despite the enactment of hunting, the dance was also a prayer for long life. In the Hesi cycle of California tribes the grizzly-bear impersonation is realistic in action and appearance (the Maidu *pano-ng-kasi* and Miwok *uzu-mati*). Members of the Pawnee Bear Society received their curative powers from the sun and danced head down with their palms up to receive the rays. This gesture is also found in the Fox Grizzly-Bear Dance. Among the Fox and Iroquois, women participate as well as men, not in special costume but with a bearlike waddle. The former dance is performed in a straight line; the latter is a trotting progression in an anti-clockwise circle. The Cherokee *yona* progresses like the Iroquois *nyagwai'oeno*, with the same waddling shuffle and vocal antiphony, but it differs by winding into a spiral, and by adding clawing gestures, similar to those of the Fox Indian bear dancers, and by underscoring the antiphony with movement responses. Among the Cherokee this one-time ritual has become secularized to the point of obscene raillery; among the Iroquois and Fox it has preserved its curative aspects, though without healing tricks as in the Ponca *matcogahri*. Hunting functions have fallen by the way along with the loss of this pursuit for sustenance. The same is true among Plains tribes as the Ute, where the bear dance is an annual huge social celebration, with vague reference to the animal. [GPK]

bear fishes through ice with tail A general and very widespread European folktale motif (A2216.1; Type 2) explaining why the bear has no tail (or a short tail). Bear originally had a long tail like the other animals. One winter day he was persuaded by Fox to fish through a hole in the ice with his tail. The tail froze fast in the ice; and when he was attacked and jumped up to escape, it broke off.

This one motif comprises one of the most famous animal stories in Europe, especially in the Baltic countries, so popular as to have migrated into Africa and the Americas, even into some regions where the bear is unknown. It is included in a cycle of animal tales gathered together in the Middle Ages into the famous *Roman de Renart*. Kaarle Krohn's study of these stories, *Bär und Fuchs* (1886), puts their probable origin in northern Germany and holds that they were then (1886) at least 1000 years old. He attributes the transference of the tail-in-the-ice experience from bear (illogically) to wolf to the influence of *Reynard the Fox* (a sophisticated and satirical usage of the original folk material) in which

wolf's wife is tricked by the fox into fishing with her tail through the ice, and is raped by the fox when she cannot pull free.

There are three known African versions of this story and 13 North American Indian tellings. In the African version the tale adapts itself to an iceless portion of the world in that Fox fools Bear merely into using his tail to fish with, and it is bitten off. The story turns up among southern United States Negroes with Rabbit having his tail snapped off through the ice the same way.

Bear Foster Parent Title of a North American Indian myth very widespread among tribes of the Northeast Woodlands area, and known also among the Kutenai Indians of Montana and British Columbia. A lost child is discovered in the woods by a she-bear, adopted and reared with the cubs, taught to eat bear food, and taken into hibernation in the cave when cold weather comes.

One night the old bear wakes up and sings, "Come; the people wish us to help them." This happens at the time the Indians are smoking their pipes and praying for food and well-being. So the she-bear and the cubs leave the cave. When they return they bear arm-loads of pipestems, each representing a prayer. The old bear examines each stem: the true prayers are put in one pile, to be granted; the pipestems of those who mocked the bears are put in another pile. The names of these people are remembered, to be terrified by the bears in the Summer. In the Spring the bears and the boy come out of the cave and wander in warm places until the time comes again for the long winter sleep in the cave.

When the Indians again begin to perform the Bear Ceremony, the old bear hears them, and this time gives the young boy the power also to hear his people singing and dancing. Again the bears go forth and bring back the pipestems, and this time the boy too is taught to "read" them. In the Spring when the bears again emerge from the cave, the boy is sent back to his own people, with messages from the bears to pray only in earnest. The boy's father, who had thought his child was dead, receives him with joy. The boy tells the people how the bears can hear the prayers, can tell the difference between the true and insincere petitions, and "feel like" helping only persons of integrity.

Bear medicine The curing power of the bear: a concept of certain Pueblo and other North American Indian religions. Bear is the most powerful patron of Keresan, Tewan, and Zuñi curing societies. Shamans "call the bear" to come and attend the curing rituals, and Bear comes. When the shaman pulls on the bear-paws and impersonates the bear, he is Bear, and then possesses the curing power of Bear. He can transform himself into a real bear, just as bears can transform themselves into men. When he dies a shaman goes to live with the bears in the spirit world. Bear gave to mankind a particularly potent medicine, the aster root. It is named for Bear (bear root, bear medicine) and is regarded almost as a cure-all. During a curing ceremony the shaman chews the bear root, which induces in him a trancelike condition during which he can "see" the witch who has caused the illness of his patient.

All members of the Chippewa Indian Midewiwin (curing society) are said to "follow the bear path;" i.e. they use the wonderful medicines revealed to them by the bear. The Sioux also value especially the medicines given to mankind by the bear. They regard him as the chief of all healing animals, partly because his claws are so well adapted to digging roots, partly because benevolence from an animal usually considered ill-tempered takes on particular significance. See ANIMAL CURERS; BEAST GODS.

Bear's Ear   Title and hero of an Avar (Caucasian) story belonging to the ancient and widespread Eurasian Bear's Son cycle of folktales and also to the dragon-fight cycle. Bear's Ear is the typical Bear's Son by virtue of the bear's ears and superhuman strength inherited from his bear father. He saves the daughter of an underworld king from a water-hoarding dragon. One day out of every year a maiden is sacrificed to the dragon in return for a flow of waters on that day. Bear's Ear kills the monster and is offered the maiden in marriage. But he refuses the reward, desiring more to return to the upper world. This is one of the tales in the vast dragon-fight cycle in which the hero does not marry the sacrificial maiden.

bearskin quiver comes to life   The motif of a story in the Apache Indian Coyote cycle: told by the Chiricahua, Mescalero, Jicarilla, and White Mountain Apaches. In the Chiricahua version Coyote killed a bear, dried the hide, and was going to make a quiver of it. Someone came along and advised him not to do that or misfortune would befall him. But Coyote went ahead and made the quiver, slung it over his back, and went along, went along. He came to a place where there were many walnuts on the ground. He leaned the quiver against the tree and began to pick up the walnuts. The quiver began to shake; it came to life; it was a bear again. The bear chased Coyote.

Coyote ran and ran. He met Gopher. "Why are you running?" said Gopher. "Bear is after me." "Jump in," said Gopher. So Coyote hid in Gopher's cheek pouch. Bear came along. "What have you got in your mouth?" said Bear. "Teeth," said Gopher. But Bear gave him a good kick and Coyote tumbled out. Bear chased him. Coyote ran and ran, and at last got away.

This story is of special interest for its embodiment of the Chiricahua Apache awe of the bear. They will not eat bear meat, touch or use the hide for fear of being visited with grave and mysterious ills.

Bear's Son   Generic term for and hero of a cycle of folktales (Type 301) very widespread in Europe and Asia. F. Panzer's *Studien zur germanischen Sagengeschichte* reports some 200 variants of the tale in 20 languages, from all over Europe and some regions in Asia. In the most primitive form of the story Bear's Son is: 1) a youth of superhuman strength, son of a bear who has stolen the youth's mother (F611.1.1), or 2) the human son of a woman (abducted by or married to a bear while pregnant by a human husband), born in the bear's cave and having acquired bear characteristics (B635.1). In these versions mother and son usually return to the woman's home and the child is adopted by the human father; the youth often avenges his mother by killing the bear. As told in Germany and Croatia, the child is stolen by a she-bear, and acquires bear-strength and bear-nature from being suckled by the bear. In all instances, however, the boy has bear

characteristics: bear's teeth, or ears, or is hairy. He always possesses the superhuman strength of the bear, and he always performs superhuman feats. He kills monsters; he slays a dragon, always rescuing either a maiden who is being sacrificed to it or a whole city from its depredations.

There are a number of North American Indian stories of the Bear's Son in which a woman wanders too far from a settlement, usually while picking berries, and is lost. She marries a bear in the forest and gives birth to either one or two bear cubs. These she transforms into human shape. Then follows the long sequence of their adventures in which human wit plus bear-strength carries all to success.

In most European tellings, the hero (often a youngest son) acquires before starting on his adventures some wonderful or miraculous weapon, adds to himself a group of extraordinary companions (F601 ff.) with whom he comes to and enters an empty house (G475.1). The owner arrives (a supernatural being of some sort— dwarf, giant, ogre, demon) who maltreats one by one the hero's companions. The hero himself then fights the monster, wounds it, follows it to the underworld (F102.1) (often underwater) by its trail of blood; there he kills it and either rescues a maiden or a princess from a dragon or wins great treasure (N773; R111). By some treachery or desertion on the part of the companions (K1931.2) he is long delayed from returning home. The story often ends with the companions returning home with a number of liberated maidens, and the hero arriving at the last minute to stop the marriage of the youngest one and marry her himself. (N681; L161). This, in outline the German folktale *The Gnome* (Grimm #91), is the typical Bear's Son story.

The superhuman deeds of Beowulf, especially his struggle with Grendel in the mead hall, the pursuit by the trail of blood to the undersea cave, the nine-day underwater battle with Grendel's dam, and the final slaying of the treasure-guarding firedrake, have led many scholars (F. Panzer and others) to fit the Beowulf story into the Bear's Son pattern. Dr. Rhys Carpenter has done the same for the Odysseus legend in Chapter VII of his *Folktale, Fiction and Saga in the Homeric Epics*.

The frequency with which Bear's Son slays dragons associates, inevitably, the Bear's Son with the dragon-slaying cycle, especially in so far as the dragon slayer is of miraculous birth. In later fairy tale many heroes have been identified as Bear's Sons by transference: they perform deeds identified with Bear's Son deeds, or the story pattern follows, or almost follows, the Bear's Son formula. The actual bear origin of the hero is either forgotten, over a period of time and retellings which enhance the adventures *per se*, or as has been suggested by O. L. Olsen in his *Relation of the Hrolfssaga Krake and Biarkarimur to Beowulf*, Chicago, 1916, sophisticated fairy tale has purposely substituted the dragon-slaying for the original (bear) patricide. Grimm's *The Gnome*, classified as belonging to the Bear's Son cycle, excellently illustrates the whole transmorphosis.

bear taken for a cat   The motif (K1728; Type 1161) of a popular European folktale in which a troublesome ogre, bogle, etc., is gotten rid of by the bear of an itinerant bear trainer. The ogre (or bogle) always returns, asking if the big cat is still there, and on being told yes, and that it has three kittens, gives up haunting that place forever. See BOGLE IN THE MILL.

Bear Went Over the Mountain An American humorous song about a bear who went to see what he could see and found nothing but the other side of the mountain. It is one of many texts set to an air dating from the time of the Crusades. See MALBROUGH S'EN VA T'EN GUERRE.

bear whispered in man's ear A general European folktale motif (J1488) found typically in Æsop's fable of *The Travelers and the Bear* or *The Bear in the Wood*. A traveler and his companion (or paid guide) met a bear in the forest. One of them was terrified and climbed a tree, regardless of what might happen to the other. The other traveler fell down, held his breath, and played dead. The bear approached, sniffed his face and ears, and walked away. When the one in the tree climbed down, he said, "What did the bear whisper to you?" "He said never trust a coward." This motif embodies the old belief that a bear will not touch a dead man, and that to lie still and play dead is a sure way to avoid being molested.

Bear Wife or **Bear Woman** Title of a number of North American Indian stories in which a man has a bear for a wife. These are known all over the continent, among the northeastern Algonquians, the Plains tribes, and the Carrier Indians of British Columbia. In a Fort Fraser Carrier Indian tale a young man hunting in the woods meets a young woman who turns out to be a black bear. He kills a grizzly for her who is an enemy to her people, and lives happily with her until salmon-fishing time. Then he takes his wife and returns to his own village. The Bear Wife refuses to help with the communal drying of fish and also refuses to gather berries. When the winter supply of food is all gone, however, she reveals a miraculous underground store of dried salmon and dried berries, so that no one in the village lacks for food all winter.

In the summer when all the families go to the fishing places; there the young husband chances to meet and flirt with a former sweetheart. The Bear Wife knows this and weeps all night. In the morning she and her child change into bears and go away. Sorrowfully the young man follows their tracks, looking for them, but they have disappeared. This story contains the typical disappearance of the offended supernatural wife (or husband).

Bear Woman Title of a North American Indian folktale known to the tribes of the North Pacific Coast, California, the Plateau, Plains, Central Woodlands, and the Southwest. In the typical *Bear Woman* stories a young woman commits adultery with a bear or has a bear lover. Her family discover this and kill the bear, whereupon the girl instantly changes into a bear and attacks the slayers of her lover. Her family (usually a little sister, a little brother, and a number of older brothers) escape by means of the magic obstacle flight. The angry Bear Woman follows them; they discover that she is invulnerable; the one vulnerable spot is revealed to them by a bird; one of the brothers shoots the bear, and she falls dead. In some versions the children are unwilling to return home because all their relatives are dead, so they decide to live in the sky. Thus they become the

Seven Stars (Ursa Major): the little brother is the pole star, the sister is nearest him, and the five brothers follow in order of age.

☞ On the North Pacific Coast the Bear-Woman is a young Indian woman who changes into a bear and has twin cubs. Argillite carvings of the Bear-Woman myth have been produced in recent times on the North Pacific Coast. For a description of these, and discussion of the myth, see Marius Barbeau, "Bear Mother" *JAFL* 59, p. 231 ff. [EWV]

☞ The Chinese give a Bear Woman explanation for the non-Chinese Gold tribe custom (Lower Sungari) of always offering a girl in marriage first to a maternal uncle. The story is the usual one of a young girl abducted by a bear. The child born to them was a daughter. After a number of years the girl's brother discovered her whereabouts, killed the bear, took the woman and her young daughter back home, and married the daughter. Ever since then a marriageable girl is first offered to her maternal uncle. Only if he does not want her can she be married to anyone else. The Chinese say this is because only on the mother's side are the Gold people human; the ancestors of the fathers were bears. The Gold themselves deny this.

Bear-Woman and the Fawns Title of a very widespread California Indian story telling how two fawns escaped from Bear-Woman, who had killed their mother. The Lassik version is more or less representative. Grizzly Bear and Deer were the wives of Chickenhawk. One day by the river Grizzly Bear, pretending to delouse Deer, killed her instead and took the head home to roast. Deer's two children cried out when they recognized their mother's head roasting in the fire, but were told to go and play. As they went, the Deer-mother's hair cried out to them in warning that their lives were in danger. Deer's children and Bear's children were playing together, and the two fawns made a fire and smothered Bear's children with the smoke in a hollow log. They took the meat home and gave it to Bear-Woman. She cooked it and while she was eating it the two fawns taunted her with eating her own children, and ran off. Bear-Woman chased them. The fawns ran and ran; Bear-Woman was after them. They were almost caught. But when they came to a river old Grandfather Crane stretched out his neck and made a bridge for them to cross. The two deer children crossed over and were safe. When Bear-Woman came along and tried to cross over the crane bridge, old Grandfather Crane gave a twist to his neck; she fell off and was carried away by the river.

This story, very prominent among the California Indians, is known also with variations among certain Indians of the Plateau area and the North Pacific tribes. The Shoshoni of the Plains also have a version.

beast epic A cycle of tales having an animal, e.g. Reynard the Fox, as its central character. Compare ANIMAL TALES.

beast gods The animal curers, intercessors, guardians, and companions of Zuñi and other Pueblo Indian religion. Certain birds, in the role of messengers and scouts, are associated with them. They are also regarded as spirits, and they dwell "in the east" in Shipap, or (Zuñi) Shipapolima, the spirit land of the dead; all curing rituals are performed to the east. Specific animals are specifically associated with the six ritual directions, however, differing in the different pueblos: North, mountain lion, oriole; West, bear, bluebird, weasel; South, badger, wildcat, parrot; East, gray wolf, magpie; Zenith, eagle; Nadir, mole, gopher. See ANIMAL CURERS; BADGER MEDICINE; BEAR MEDICINE.

beast marriage A common motif of folktale and ballad found all over the world, in which a human being is married to a beast, in very primitive tales to an actual animal, in later elaborations to a human being doomed to exist in beast form until some woman will love him in the beast-shape. Often the human lover must also burn the sloughed skin of the animal spouse in order to clinch the disenchantment. The stories fall into certain types: those in which the bewitched lover cannot return to human form until some woman's devotion proves stronger than the spell; those in which the lover takes on animal form himself to go a-wooing; those in which a deity assumes animal form and carries off a human bride, and those in which some animal by union with a human being becomes the ancestor of a tribe. There are stories of marriage to a person in animal form, in which one or the other spouse is a beast by day and human by night, involving either a formula for disenchantment or tabus against discovery; and there are stories of marriages to animals in human form, involving tabus against naming or mentioning lest they vanish or depart. The list is endless: marriage to a god in bull form (Greek), to a human being in dog form (Chinese, North American Indian), to a deer (Irish, North American Indian), a seal (Celtic), snake or serpent (Hindu, Indochinese, Basuto, Kaffir, Zulu), fox (Indonesian, North American Indian, Chinese, Japanese), lion (Angolian), bee (Indonesian), crane (Japanese), elephant (Hottentot), vulture (South American Indian), fish or whale (North American Indian). The Eskimo story of Sedna who married a gull (or a dog) is very well known, and is closely related to the Dog Husband stories. The story of the two girls who wished for an eagle and a whale for husbands, got them, and had a hard time escaping is common among the Greenland, Labrador, and West Hudson Bay tribes.

The motif turns up in every country in Europe. Some scholars claim Indian origin for it; others hold that it is too widespread and too scattered for this theory to be reasonable. Mme. de Beaumont's *Beauty and the Beast* and Grimm's *Frog Prince* are famous European versions. A more modern treatment is Keats' *Lamia*. See ANIMAL PARAMOUR; NAME TABU; SWAN MAIDEN.

☞ Tales of beast marriages between men or women and animals are of frequent occurrence in North American Indian mythology. Some of the most widespread are the Fox-wife story of the Eskimo, the Piqued Buffalo Wife story of the Plains and Eastern Woodlands, Splinter-Foot-Girl of the Plains (in which the heroine marries a buffalo bull), Eagle and Whale Husband stories of the Eskimo, Snake Husband and Bear Husband tales of the Plains, Dog Husband of the North Pacific Coast, and Deer Wife of the Plateau. [EWV]

beating the bounds A ceremonial procession about the boundaries of the community with stops at the several landmarks. It was a spring festival, at Easter or on May Day, and in recent times combined religious ceremonies with feasting, drinking and merrymaking. At the landmarks young people were ceremonially whipped "to help them remember" or thrown into the boundary streams for the same purpose. In Cork, Ireland, in the last century, the mayor in robes of ceremony threw a dart into the harbor. The place where it fell marked the limit of municipal authority. The custom is also known from ancient Greece and Rome and also in England, Russia, Norway, and elsewhere in Europe. Similar ceremonies which give people an excuse to get out of doors in the spring are known in most parts of the world. Phallic boundary-markers (the two-headed Janus), together with suggestions advanced by Granet in his studies of ancient China, lead to the possibility that this segment of the complex of spring festivals was at one time connected with fertility rites. Other names for the ceremony are "riding the marches," "riding the fringes," "common riding." [RDJ]

Beauty and the Beast Generic title of a world-wide beast-marriage story of which Mme. Leprince de Beaumont's version is the renowned example. *Beauty and the Beast* belongs to that cycle of beast-marriage stories in which the prince, magically transformed into beast or monster, can be delivered or unspelled only by the love and devotion of a woman.

The heroine is the youngest daughter of a merchant who has lost his fortune. Before setting out on a journey to retrieve his losses, the merchant asks each of his three daughters what he shall bring home. The two elder ask for sumptuous presents; Beauty asks for a rose. The merchant fails to regain his wealth, but on the way home picks a rose in the garden of a wonderful palace where he finds himself mysteriously entertained. The minute he plucks the rose the Beast appears, threatening him with death for the theft, unless he will send back one of his daughters in her stead. Beauty volunteers to go to the Beast. There in his palace, surrounded by luxury and kindness, she realizes that the hideous creature with whom she lives is of a generous and noble nature. Admiration for his character and pity for his plight gradually turn to genuine affection. A number of stock incidents follow: permission to go home to see her dying father, the visit overstayed beyond the promised moment, the mirror as life-token of the Beast which reveals that he is dying, and the magic journey back to the Beast's garden. There Beauty finds him almost dead, but her grief for him and her avowal of love suddenly unspell the terrible enchantment. The beautiful prince is thus liberated from his beast form, and Beauty becomes his queen. The good old father is benefited; the jealous sisters are punished.

There are Basque, Swiss, German, English, Italian, Portuguese, Lithuanian, Magyar, Indian, and Kaffir versions of this story. In the Basque story the beast is a huge serpent, his life-token a ring instead of a mirror. In the Lithuanian story the beast is a white wolf, in the Magyar version, a pig. Perrault's *Riquet à la Houppe* is almost this identical Beauty and the Beast story, but with the sophisticated, unfolkloristic moral attached. Grimm's *Frog Prince* (#1) and the British *The Well At the World's End* both follow the true Beauty and the Beast pattern of disenchantment through love and devotion, as does also the unique Kaffir tale in which the young girl consents to lick the crocodile's face and is rewarded by **having a** handsome prince slowly emerge.

The Scottish ballad *Kemp Owyne* (Child #34) elaborates the same theme in reverse: it is the lady who is transformed into a thing of horror and released by the kisses of her lover. Compare LOATHLY LADY.

Beaver Among several North Pacific Coast, Plateau, and Northern Athabaskan American Indian groups, Beaver is the companion of Porcupine, who tricks his friend and is in turn tricked. Tales of beaver-husband or beaver-wife are popular animal-marriage tales of the Ojibwa and other Central Algonquian Indians. [EWV]

Bédier, (Charles Marie) Joseph (1864–1938) French author and medievalist. He was appointed professor of medieval French language and literature at the Collège de France in 1893 and in the same year won his doctorate with *Les fabliaux*. This work constituted a strong refutation of Theodor Benfey's famous Indianist theory for the origin of the folktale. Bédier's attack did not at once wean away the Indianist disciples, but stimulated stricter scientific approach on the part of such scholars as G. Paris and E. Cosquin. His prose adaptation of *Roman de Tristan et Yseult* was published in 1900; a study, *La formation des légendes épiques*, in 1908; *Les chansons des croisades* in 1909; and a critical edition of *Chanson de Roland* in 1921. In *Les fabliaux* Bédier attacked the intuitive method of Benfey as falling short of ultimate analysis. He said merry tales, particularly, have such simple plots that comparison and analysis of great numbers of variants can have no worthwhile result. Bédier advocated the theory that medieval epic cycles found their development along the routes of pilgrimages.

beech (from Old English *bēce, bōc,* beech or book, from the fact that the early Saxons and other Teutonic peoples wrote their runes on thin beech boards.) The beech, like the ash, is instantly deadly to snakes when they touch its bark.

Jason's Argo was built largely of beech timber; Bacchus drank his wine from beechen bowls, and, according to Lucian, the oracles of Zeus at Dodona were delivered through the medium of the sacred beeches and oaks.

The herbalists held that the hard beech wood, if brought into the house, caused hard travail in childbirth and miserable deaths. The leaves, however, are cool, binding, and were applied to blisters or chewed for chapped lips and painful gums. The water found in the hollow places of decaying beeches will cure scurf, scab, and running tetters. The Catawba Indians make a beech tea from the bark to cure weak back. Mixed with lard the beech tea is used to relieve rheumatism.

bees The ancient belief that bees originate in the dead bodies of cattle (B713) springs from the fact that the skeleton cage of the ribs provides a good natural framework for a wild beehive. "The swarm of bees and honey in the carcass of the lion" (*Judges* xiv, 8) is a case in point, of which Samson made the riddle, "Out of the eater came forth meat, and out of the strong came forth sweetness," which the men of the city could not guess without help. In a German folktale bees were created to provide wax for church candles; in a Breton story they sprang from the tears shed by Christ on the Cross. In Egyptian mythology they came from the tears of the sun god, Rā. In South American Caingang Indian myth they were given to man by their culture hero, Kayurukre.

A bee was the symbol of the Hindu gods Indra, Krishna, and Vishnu, who were called *Madhava,* the nectar-born. The bow-string of Kāma, the Indian god of love, was a string of bees. A bee was the symbol of Artemis at Ephesus; and Melissa (bee) was a title of the priestesses of Demeter, Persephone, and the Great Mother (perhaps Rhea). Bee stings have been regarded as medicinal through the ages. Sufferers from rheumatism, arthritis, and neuritis from early times used to visit beekeepers for treatment: two stings were given as a first dose; later a few more per visit until the patient reported some relief. This belief is more widespread today than ever. An extract from bee stings, called bee venom, was on sale in Europe before World War II, and is now available in the United States (see B. F. Beck, *Bee Venom Therapy,* New York, 1935).

Almost everywhere in Europe and quite generally in rural sections of the United States, people still *tell the bees* when somebody dies in the house. If this is not done they will either leave or die or stop making honey. This is possibly a remnant of an old European belief that bees were messengers to the gods and notified them of mortal deaths. In Ireland not only are the bees told of a death in the family, but crepe is hung on the hive. The Irish tell their secrets to the bees; any new project is also told them in the hopes the bees will prosper it. Bees won't thrive if they are quarreled over. They must not be bought on a Friday. Some people say they must not be bought at all, but bartered for. This is especially true for the first swarm.

It is bad luck to have a swarm of bees come to you of themselves. Even to dream of a swarm lighting on a building portends misfortune. Mississippi Negroes say that to dream of bees in a swarm is a death omen; to dream of being stung means a friend will betray you. If you see them making honey in a dream, you are in for some money. From ancient Greece to modern New England a bee flying into the house means a stranger is coming. It is very lucky to have one fly in and then out; but if one dies in the house, that's bad luck. If you hold a bee in your hand, it won't sting you as long as you hold your breath. In New England and the Maritimes it is said that bees lay by unusually large stores of honey before a hard winter.

The bee in folktale plays the role of God's spy (A33); there are helpful bees (B482), and bees as familiars (G225.1). There are marriages to bees (B655.1), separable souls in bees (E715.3.1), reincarnations as bee (E616.1), and souls in the form of bee (E734.2). A bee identifies a lost princess by alighting on her (H162).

"The old wisdom of the bees"—"the secret knowledge of the bees"—"ask the wild bee for what the druids knew" are frequent phrases of Scottish Highland and island story (see Fiona Macleod, *Winged Destiny,* New York, 1910, p. 38 ff.) See ARISTÆUS; LEMMINKAINEN.

bees produced to rout enemies A motif found in the Koasati Indian *Story of Crow* and the Creek tale of *Bead-Spitter and Thrown-Away,* in which two young boys collect a great quantity of bees, wasps, and hornets and turn them loose upon the warriors whom their father has mustered to punish the pair for their disobediences. The warriors are stung to death.

The idea is far from being limited to North American

Indian folktale. A similar motif (B524.2.1) in which helpful bees sting an approaching army occurs in both Jewish and Japanese legend. The Irish St. Gobnait (6th century) went out to save her district from being invaded by a neighboring chief with a small hive of bees in her hand. The bees swarmed upon the invaders and blinded their eyes. The idea of routing enemies with bees also occurs in Danish, English, and German tales.

beetle Any insect of the order *Coleoptera*, having biting mouth parts and hard horny anterior wings serving as covers for the membranous posterior pair when at rest. The *Coleoptera* are the true beetles, and there are 250,000 known species in the world. Many insects resembling them are so designated, however: the cockroach is often called a "black beetle," for instance.

In general European and United States folk belief, beetles are both deaf and blind, and to kill one brings rain. It is lucky to turn one over on its feet that has fallen on its back. In the Palatinate it is said that this kind deed cures or prevents toothache. If a beetle flies through the house it is an omen of unexpected news. To hear the death-watch beetle (a small wood-boring beetle) in your house means a death in the family. United States southern Negroes say that when its ticking stops whoever is in sickbed will die. Southern Negroes also cure earache by taking the head off of a certain species of wood beetle and dropping into the ear the one drop of blood the insect exudes. Beetles are often included in Negro mojo hands for good luck. In Silesia it is believed that the first cockchafer of the season, caught and sewed up in a little cloth bag, is effective as an amulet against fever.

In Ireland the *darbhdaol* is a species of long black beetle often called the devil's coach horse. Some say that the devil in the form of *darbhdaol* eats the bodies of sinners, and the insect is therefore sometimes construed as the symbol of corruption. If you see one raise its tail it is putting a curse on you. If you accept money from the devil you will find a *darbhdaol* in your hand. Reapers sometimes enclose one in the handle of their tools to give them speed and skill in the work. The *druib* is a large chafer found in Irish bogs and dried pools; if a white or spotted cow happens to swallow one all her hair will fall off the white parts. The *druib* affects no other color.

A huge Beetle is the creator of the world in Lengua (South American Chaco Indian) mythology. From the grains of earth he had left over, Beetle then created man and woman. At first they were joined together, but Beetle separated them, as they are now. Among the modern Toba Indians black beetles are always *pa'yak*, i.e. supernatural spirits.

The Sia Indians of North America have a myth in which Utset, Mother of Indians, gave to Beetle (Ishits) a sack of stars to carry from the underworld to the world above. He made the journey with success, but had become so tired with his load that he bit a tiny hole in the sack to see what was in it. The stars flew out and scattered across the sky. When Utset came up with Beetle she made him blind forever for his disobedience. This is why the Sia say that Beetle has no eyes. There were a few stars left in the bag and these Utset arranged herself: seven in one place (for the Great Bear), three bright ones in a row (in Orion's belt), and seven others in a group (the Pleiades).

In Zuñi Indian mythology it is told that when Coyote (culture hero) marked off certain strips of restricted land between the clans and villages, he buried in each strip a beetle and a poisonous spider, so that whoever disobeyed and tried to cultivate for himself the restricted land would go blind, like beetle, or die of poison. If a Zuñi Indian is struck by lightning he is given a drink of rainwater from that very storm containing black beetle and suet. If he fails to drink it he will "dry up." Or he is given black beetle in a piece of bread. Among the Hopi Indians Beetle is a helpful war spirit; he covers up tracks. Beetles are also brewed in the emetic drink of the Snake war society. See COCKROACH; LADYBUG; SCARAB.

Befana or **St. Befana, la Strega,** or **la Vecchia** An ugly but good-natured old hag who leaves presents in the stockings of children on the eve of the Epiphany, or Twelfth Night, in parts of Italy and Sicily. In Rome and many other Italian cities and towns young and old assemble and make a great noise in her honor with trumpets, tambourines, drums, and tin horns. In other places singers and musicians serenade the houses and rag-doll effigies of Befana are displayed in the windows.

In Christian legend, when the three kings passed on their way to adore the Christ Child, they invited a certain old woman to accompany them, but she said she was too busy cleaning her house. Later, she attempted to follow, but became lost and never saw the Holy Child. Every year she comes looking for him. She visits the children while they sleep and fills their stockings, giving to the good candy and sweetmeats; stones and charcoal are left for the naughty ones.

The name Befana is said to be a corruption of Epiphany, although parts of the legend date from pre-Christian times. In addition to obvious Santa Claus and Ahasuerus analogies, the legend contains also some elements of the practice of expelling demons with noise. Compare BERCHTA; SAINT NICHOLAS.

Béfind In Celtic folklore and mythology, one of the three fairies who are present at the birth of every child, who predict its future and endow it with good or doubtful gifts: literally, white woman. They are cognate with the Roman Parcæ, and in Brittany, as in ancient Rome, a table was spread for them in the birth-room. They are definitely Celtic survivals, however, survivals of ancient Celtic goddess triads, earth mothers or goddesses associated with fertility and love.

In Old Irish mythology, Béfind was specifically a woman of the síde, married to a mortal, Idath, and mother of Fraech. She was sister to Bóann, queen of the side of all Ireland.

Beg The undersea afterworld of Papuan (New Guinea) mythology: a temporary abode for the soul on its way to the blissful final place named Boigu.

Bego Tanutanu Bego the Maker, the younger of two brothers of Mono-Alu (Melanesian) mythology, of whom the older is lazy. Bego shaped the landscape, made the food plants, and otherwise contributed to the life and culture of the Mono-Alu islanders. His wife impounded the sea, but when her grandsons spied on her, she released it, causing a flood. (See G. C. Wheeler, *Mono-Alu Folklore*, London, 1926.) [KL]

begyina ba (plural *begyina mma*)   Literally, in Ashanti, a come-and-stay child: the child (born to parents all of whose former children have died) for whose survival special magical precautions are observed. The loss of all previous children is believed by the Ashantis to be caused by evil spirits, who must now either be out-witted or overcome if the next child is to live. Some-times the begyina ba is given a deceptive name-suffix, usually a slave designation, to lead malicious spirits into believing that this one is not particularly desirable; or sometimes it is even tattooed with the markings of a slave class, for the same reason. Frequently, however, the begyina ba is dedicated to some specific god who is then obliged to protect it. Its hair is not cut short like other children's, but allowed to grow long, and all kinds of protective amulets, bells, etc., are fastened into it. Compare ABIKU; NAME TABU.

beheading bargain   A motif (M221) in which a giant or other supernatural challenger bargains to allow himself to be beheaded tonight providing he be allowed to behead his opponent tomorrow night (or one year from tonight). Many a hero agrees to the bargain, be-heads the challenger (who immediately resumes his head), and shirks presenting himself for decapitation at the appointed time. Only the bravest, truest, most honorable of heroes keep faith, the result always being, of course, that the challenger spares him because of his fearless honor. It usually follows also that the challenger has been in disguise, and reveals his true identity to proclaim the virtue of the hero. Probably the two most famous beheading bargains recorded are the one be-tween Cuchulain and the bachlach and that between Gawain and the Green Knight, the former now consid-ered the source of the latter. See BRICRIU'S FEAST.

behemoth   A huge animal described in *Job* xl, 15, usu-ally thought to be the hippopotamus but by some be-lieved to be the elephant: the plural of *behemah,* beast. According to early and medieval Jewish tradition, as the leviathan was king of the fishes and the ziz the greatest of the birds, so behemoth was the king of the animals. Two of the monsters were created (or only one, a male); however, since a thousand mountains' produce made but one day's food for behemoth (a gloss on *Ps.* 1, 10), and since all the waters of Jordan served the mon-ster for only one swallow, he was provided with no sex-ual desire lest he and his offspring devour the world; he was given a barren tract of land to live in. Behemoth and leviathan will be hunted by, or their fight will serve as a spectacle for, the blessed after the Messiah comes and their flesh will serve as a feast for the chosen at the great banquet. In Moslem tradition, Behemoth is a great fish upon which stood the bull supporting the ruby underlying the world. Compare HADHAYOSH.

bĕisać   In Cambodian belief, the souls of those who have died a violent death. The bĕisać return from the hells (Buddhist) to demand food from the living. They take revenge on those who refuse to appease them by afflicting them with all kinds of evils. Food is left among the brushwood for them. Compare PRĀY.

Bel   The Babylonian form of the title *baal,* lord or master; at first generally applicable to the gods of places, later an appellation of the principal gods, and finally the title, or the name, of the chief god—Enlil or Mar-

duk or Ashur. The Bel of the Old Testament was Marduk. Bel, the god of the earth, was a member of the supreme triad with Anu and Ea. As Bel, he brought on the flood, wishing to destroy the human race: Marduk is not mentioned in the Deluge story. The consort of Bel is Belit, the lady, a general title paralleling that of Bel.

bĕla kampong   An annual ceremony of the Malays of Endau, performed to keep the local spirits happy and to gain their aid in averting misfortune and disease. During the celebration a village is under a tabu. No strangers may enter it nor may the villagers leave, dig, made a loud noise, shoot animals, or pick coconuts.

Bele   A Trinidad Negro social dance and its associated rites for the dead, wherein the ancestors are feted to assure that they will exercise a benevolent surveillance over their descendants. These dances have been held clandestinely in modern times because of official and clerical disapproval, and only upon the insistence of the ancestors, who manifest their desires in dreams, and their displeasure with the failure to hold this ceremony by harassing the family with ill health, or bad harvests, or loss of emploment. [MJH]

Belet   The Menek Kaien (Malay Peninsula) abode of the dead: an island to the northwest of the Malay Pe-ninsula. A soul leaves the body through the big toe and journeys to the sea. After seven days, during which time the soul can revisit its old home, it is escorted (if good) by Mampes across Balan Bacham, the switchbacked bridge which spans the sea. When the soul arrives in Belet it sees the Mapik tree where it meets the souls of those who have died previously. These souls break the limbs of the newcomer and turn his pupils inwards, making him a kemoit or real ghost, after which he can wear the flowers of the Mapik tree and pluck its fruit. The Mapik tree bears all things desirable such as food. At its base are breasts from which the ghosts of little children get their milk.

The wicked are doomed to watch from another place the good enjoying the life in Belet. According to I. Evans the Menek Kaien and Kintak Bong are the only groups among the Semang who have any conception of an existence after death. Compare PULAU BAH.

Belial or **Beliar**   One of the synonyms for Satan or one of the minor devils; principally, the Antichrist: as used in the Old Testament, a modifying genitive signifying worthlessness or recklessness, e.g. "sons of Belial" as in the story of the Benjamite war (*Judg.* xix). Hence, the underworld (Sheol) and the personification of wicked-ness. Belial may perhaps be a modification of the Bab-ylonian Belili, a deity connected with the underworld in the Ishtar-Tammuz story.

Belit   The feminine form of the Babylonian title Bel; hence, the lady, the mistress: an appellation of rank construed as the proper name of the consort of the chief god Bel (or Enlil, Marduk, or Ashur). Hence, Belit is identifiable with Ninlil. Belit was worshipped in Assyria both as the consort of Ashur and as the ancient goddess of Nippur.

bell   A hollow vessel, usually of metal, sounded by being struck by a clapper suspended within or by a separate stick or hammer, and serving among almost all peoples for thousands of years as amulet, fertility charm, summons to a god, prophetic voice, curative agent, or purely musical instrument.

The practice of wearing bells on the person is worldwide and originally had the same purpose everywhere—protection from evil spirits and from bodily harm. Bells of gold were prescribed by God for the hem of the high priest's garment in Israel (*Ex.* xxviii, 35). The sound was to protect him as he came and went from the holy place against the demons that frequent the threshold of sanctuaries. Siberian shamans wear bells for incantations and prophecies, and South American Indians protect themselves in the same way. In medieval Europe, warriors and jousters wore bells on their belts or hems in combat. In Ashanti, mothers tie iron rings and bells on the ankles of an ailing child or a child born after the death of several others to drive off the unfriendly spirits who cause sickness and death. (See BEGYINA BA.) These spirits are believed to dislike both iron and the tinkling of bells and can be lured out of the child's body with food while the amulets are put on. Yaqui Deer Dancers of Mexico also wear belts hung with bells. As the original purpose began to be forgotten in Europe, bells appeared on the dress of fops and on fools' motley.

Animal bells, though now largely thought of as utilitarian devices for finding strayed animals, were also first used to drive off harmful spirits. The most useful creatures of each region—goats, camels, elephants, donkeys, cows, horses, etc.—were guarded by neck bells or bell-strung trappings.

As fertility charms bells have been significant for many agricultural peoples. In China, bells were rung as a call for rain, the largest bell of the country serving for one occasion only—the emperor's prayer for rain. The decoration of the bell consisted of fertility symbols such as the sown field, nipples, and the number 9, identified with renewal. The Nilotic Bari people used bells to bring rain by filling the bowl of the bell with water and sprinkling the earth with it. In Europe, Tyrolean farmers insured a good harvest by ringing bells while circling their fields; and at Brunnen on Lake Lucerne, a Twelfth Night ceremony for ringing out witches also carried a potency for making a full fruit crop. Church bells were appealed to in some European countries at harvest time for the safe gathering of the crops.

Ceremonial bells have rung for religious rites of widely varying beliefs. A large bell from the Assyrian period, about 600 B.C., bears the symbols of the gods Ea, Nergal, and Ninurta. Chinese temple bells are sounded between verses of the Confucian hymn and are equated in a complete cosmological system of harmony with autumn, with the west, with dampness, and with metal. (The Babylonians also correlated pitch and season.) Peruvian aborigines used bells and jingles in addressing their gods. In Egypt, the feast of Osiris opened with bell-ringing, and in India, Java, etc., a hand bell decorated with Śiva's trident, Vishnu's eagle, and other religious symbols was used by Hindu priests during prayer. African Negro priests, as well as Haitian vodun hungans, invoke gods and loa with bells and dancing. Hand bells, considered effective for keeping away the evil ones, are beaten to accompany the Coptic chant. In the Mohammedan paradise, it is said, bells will hang on all the trees to make music for the blessed.

Since the 5th century bells have been associated with sacred rites in Christian churches, and have often been inscribed with religious lines. The passing bell called the faithful to pray for the departing soul and warded off evil spirits who might pounce on the soul; the excommunication proceedings called for "bell, book, and candle," the bell tolling as if the sinner were dead; the "pardon bell" of pre-Reformation England rang before and after services; processions of the church were accompanied by bell-ringing to scare off demons, etc. Saints Patrick, Gall, and Dunstan are all linked with special bells.

Customs and legends surrounding Christian church bells are common to all Europe. Bells were publicly baptized, named, and dedicated to a saint in many communities, with sponsors, baptismal dress, gifts, and sprinkling of holy water. In Lithuania it was the belief that bells would not sound until baptized, that unbaptized bells would give trouble by falling from their steeples or other mischief. After baptism the bells would frighten away sorcerers, witches, and the Devil himself. The souls of the dead were supposed to rise to heaven on bell sounds.

Certain bells were thought to ring of their own accord on occasions of great import. An Aragonese legend tells of a bell in which one of Judas's thirty pieces of silver was cast, which sounded without human assistance before national calamities. The ballad of *Sir Hugh of Lincoln* embodies this belief, relating the unprompted tolling of the bells of Lincoln for his fate.

Bells which have sunk to the bottom of ponds or lakes or have been buried underground (of which every European country traditionally has examples) also ring at solemn times, such as midnight on Christmas Eve. Such bells were generally engulfed as a punishment for some human impiety. One Dutch bell was sunk after being stolen by the Devil.

Some of the self-ringing bells say actual words. Some gratefully sound the names of their donors. One in Denmarks tells of its mate, sunk in the Schliemunde on its way to the bell tower. One rings out words of pity for a lad cruelly slain by the king.

Apart from ringing on their own initiative and talking, other activities and individual properties have been ascribed to bells. All church bells were believed in medieval Europe to make a pilgrimage to Rome to keep Good Friday, and the townspeople stayed indoors so as not to see their flight. No bells rang until they had returned to their steeples. If the local bell missed the excursion, bad luck, poor harvests, etc., might follow. Bells might grow indignant at insults or injuries and take revenge. One bell of singularly sweet tone was ordered by the king to be removed from Sens to Paris. It refused to ring in its new site in spite of all efforts, but on being returned at last to Sens, it burst into joyous sound in the cart that was hauling it. A bell in Zweibrücken was about to be destroyed in 1677 by invaders when it sweated blood.

For centuries all over Europe bells were rung to break the power of advancing thunderstorms, which were believed to be the work of evil spirits of the air. English church records show the payment of fees to bell-ringers for services during tempests, and many bells bear such inscriptions as "Fulgura frango, dissipo ventos," or "Lightning and thunder, I break asunder." The wicked spirits were shamed by the bell-ringing and fled. Norse bells were also often marked with the bent cross, the hammer of Thor, the Thunderer.

It was church bells and hymn-singing, according to legend, that frightened the mountain dwarfs, giants, and trolls away from Sweden, Denmark, and Germany. A ferryman of Holstein got a hatful of gold for ferrying a boatload of emigrating dwarfs across a river when they couldn't endure the bells any longer.

Church bells also overcame witches and were regularly used to drive them out in certain especially witch-troubled seasons. The practice was about the same in various parts of Europe—Germany, France, Switzerland, etc.—whether the occasion was May Day, Twelfth Night, St. Agatha's Eve, or every Friday in March—all the people rang bells and beat pots and pans, the church bells rang, and fires or torches were lighted; with shouting and screaming the witches were routed. A similar custom also held on the coast of Guinea to expel ghosts and witches, and an equivalent ceremony took place when the Emperor Justin II sent ambassadors to the Turks. The shamans chased whatever powers of evil might be attending the meeting with bells and tambourines.

As a curative agent, bells have served in many ways. In time of pestilence they cleared the air of corruption, and were prescribed for that purpose by an English doctor in 1625. St. Mura's bell, in Ireland, could cure any ailment if liquid were drunk from it. An American Negro belief holds that a child can be cured of stuttering by drinking from a bell. In England it was thought that childbirth could be eased by tying the bell rope to the woman's girdle. One particular bell could cure insanity by being placed over the head of the afflicted person.

The prophetic implications of bell-ringing are usually for ill-luck. The Grimm collection has a tale of a household bell which rang to foretell a death in the family. American Negro stories connect bells with death or misfortune; even a ringing in the ear points to death from the direction of the noise.

The use of bells for warnings or summons is more modern, generally, than these other purposes, though the Greeks used their *koda* in this way in military groups; the Romans sounded the *tintinnabulum* for the hours of bathing and of business; and the curfew, signaling the hour for extinguishing fires and lights, was probably introduced into England by William the Conqueror. Bells have also rung for victory, to celebrate Christmas, to warn of the approach of a leper, etc. But for public announcements, heralds or criers were used earlier. Shop bells, now used to bring the proprietor out to his customers, originally guarded the entrance against threshold demons.

Much lore centers around the casting of bells and the mixture of metals required for good tone. Blood was sometimes used, probably deriving from sacrificial customs. For casting the Great Bell of China, it is traditional that the bell-maker's daughter, who had heard of the efficiency of maidens' blood in creating fine bells, threw herself into the metal to save her father from failure with his important commission. There are also many European stories of wicked bell-makers who stole the precious metal contributed for bells and substituted lead. They all met hard fates.

Purely as musical instruments, bells have been used chiefly in the Orient, but English bell-ringers have developed a music of their own, change-ringing, which consists of a progression through the tones of a set of bells. In the Javanese gamelan, the trompong, a set of metal bells arranged in scale in a frame, takes the leading melody. Military bands of the Chou dynasty in China used bells. Malayan and Indian musicians play on sets of resting bells (not suspended or swung in the hand, but set rim upwards on the floor) made of metal or porcelain and struck with a stick. This type of bell has also been used in China and Greece.

Classes of bells and bell-like instruments differing from the definition given here are as follows: *chimes*, sets of tuned bells; *carillons*, sets of bells mechanized with clock works, first made in Flanders in the 13th century; *jingles*, hollow metal balls containing loose beads, pebbles, etc., which are more like rattles. Gongs, which have a dead rim and sounding center, are struck plates, as distinguished from bells, with their sounding rim and dead center.

The origin of bells is not known and even the comparative age of various types is uncertain. Bells of shell, wood, etc., of certain primitive peoples may be imitative of the cast or shaped metal bells of other civilizations.

THERESA C. BRAKELEY

belladonna The deadly nightshade (*Atropa belladonna*), a Europen poisonous plant with reddish, bell-shaped flowers and shining black berries. The plant, according to Plutarch, is the one which produced fatal effects upon the Roman soldiers during their retreat from the Parthians under Mark Antony. Belladonna is used in small doses to allay pain and spasm and is smeared on the eyes to dilate the pupils during medical examinations.

The origin of its name, which is Italian for beautiful lady, is uncertain, but one explanation is its use as an eye beautifier, another that it was used by Leucota, the Italian, to poison beautiful women.

Belle Hélène A folk ballad of France telling the story of a dancing girl who was drowned. She was dancing on a bridge and taken by the water spirits. This ballad is of Scandinavian origin and has Icelandic, German, Lusatian, and Hungarian parallels. See BALLAD; FRENCH FOLKLORE.

Bellerophon or **Bellerophontes** In Greek legend, a Corinthian hero; son of Glaucus (or Poseidon) and Eurymede; grandson of Sisyphus; the master of Pegasus; the slayer of the Chimera: a local Corinthian demigod, perhaps originally identical with the Argive Perseus, perhaps not Greek in origin though adopted as early as the time of Homer. Bellerophon was first named Hipponous, but he slew either his brother or the Corinthian Bellerus and was forced to flee to Tiryns. There he lived for a time at the court of Proetus, king of Argos. Antea (or Sthenobia), the queen, attempted to seduce him and, when he refused her, accused him of making advances himself. Proetus dispatched Bellerophon to Iobates of Lycia, his father-in-law, with a tablet or letter containing secret instructions that Bellerophon was to be killed. Iobates, like Proetus, unwilling to slay a guest out of hand, sent Bellerophon against the Chimera. (See CHIMERA; PEGASUS.) This failing and Bellerophon returning alive, the hero was sent on expeditions against the Solymi and then the Amazons; Bellerophon conquered in both. After slaying the pick of Iobates' warriors who lay in ambush for him, Bellerophon was accepted by Iobates as somewhat more than human, given the king's daughter (Philonoe, Anticlea, or Cassandra) for wife, and presented with a large part of the Lycian kingdom. Bellerophon accomplished his revenge on Antea by taking her for a ride on Pegasus and pitching her off the flying horse to her death. At last, however, his pride led to his downfall, probably when he attempted to fly to the gods on Pegasus. Zeus sent a gadfly to sting the horse and Bellerophon was thrown off to fall to earth, which left him blinded and crippled. The gods' vengeance reached Bellerophon's children, Isandrus, Laodamia, and Hippolochus, all of whom succumbed to an evil fate. Embittered by this turn of fortune, the hero wandered alone through the Aleian plain for the rest of his life, and came to an obscure death. A sanctuary of Bellerophon stood in a cypress grove near Corinth. Compare LETTER OF DEATH; POTIPHAR'S WIFE.

belling the cat A folktale motif (J671.1) in which the mice take counsel together as to how they may get rid of the cat. A clever one among them points out that if a bell were tied to the cat's neck, they all would forever after be forewarned of her approach and whereabouts. A wonderful idea! But, as one grizzled and experienced old mouse adds, Who will put the bell on the cat? This is Æsop's fable (Jacobs #67) in toto, one of the few known to be of true folk origin, and occurring in the folklore of various peoples as far apart as the Estonians, Finns, Italians, and southern United States Negroes. How can mice rid themselves of cats? is also one of the traditional questions asked of travelers on specific quests to other worlds (H1292.10) and the answer is always, Tie a bell on its neck. Belling the cat has long since been synonymous with the proposal of some impossible remedy, or synonymous with the predicament of one who hesitates to risk his own life for the salvation of many.

Bellona (1) The Roman goddess of war; companion (either sister, wife, daughter, or nurse) of Mars. Bellona acted as Mars' charioteer, preparing and driving his chariot, and appearing herself in battle with disheveled hair, a bloody whip in one hand and a torch in the other, to spur the warriors on. She is equated with the Sabine war goddess Nerio. Her temple stood in the Campus Martius and there the senators received foreign ambassadors and Roman generals claiming victories. There too the fetiales declared war for the Roman people, throwing a spear over the pillar (*columna bellica*) before the temple, the precinct being considered foreign territory. Human sacrifices were offered only to her and to Mars.

(2) An Asiatic goddess of war, the Cappadocian Ma, perhaps identical with the Greek Enya of Pontus and Cappadocia, brought to Rome by Sulla to whom she appeared: often confused with the native Italic Bellona. Her priests, the Bellonarii, dressed completely in black, pierced their limbs and either drank the blood or sprinkled it on the assemblage. By confusion, this offering came to be made on March 24, the day of the original Bellona, and the day became known as the *dies sanguinis*. Her day originally was June 3.

Belly and the Members One of Æsop's fables (Jacobs #29). The Members of the Body once complained that they were tired of serving the Belly, who did no work. The Hands thenceforth refused to carry food to the Mouth; the Mouth refused to chew the food for the Belly; the Legs refused to carry the big fat Belly around. It was not long, however, before the Members began to weaken and fail without the sustaining nourishment the Belly provided. And they soon realized that all were mutually and essentially useful. This story belongs to a group of folktales embodying the motif (J461) known as the senseless debate of the mutually useful. The belly and the members (J461.1) is the generic classification for the various tales involving debate between various parts of the body, animal or human, found in Indian folktale, Jewish, Roman as well as Greek, and Italian popular tradition. There is an analogous Nigerian Bantu story.

belly dance A late development of the primitive abdominal dance, limited to movements of the *rectus abdominis*: known as *danse du ventre* in North Africa.

belomancy Divination by the use of arrows: an ancient method used by the Babylonians, Scythians, Slavs, Germans, Arabs, etc. Arrows bearing inscriptions were shot, the distance covered by the arrow determining which inscription was to be read. (Cf. *Ezek*. xxi, 21). One form was like astragalomancy, with lettered arrows. Another technique used three arrows, one marked yes, one no, and one blank. The Gold Coast ordeal with poisoned arrows is another type of belomancy. The casting of arrows in groups so that certain markings appeared face upwards—notches for example, or colored bands—is believed to have developed in course of time into divining sticks and thence into divining cards which were the forerunners of our playing cards.

Beltane (Irish *Bealtaine*) The Celtic May Day (May 1), and the great festival observed on that day: also, the word for the month of May. Beltane begins officially at moonrise on May Day Eve and marks the beginning of the third quarter or second half of the ancient Celtic year. It is believed to be a survival of an early pastoral festival accompanying the first turning of the herds out to wild pasture, all the ritual observances being intended to increase fertility (as also in the Midsummer, or St. John's Eve agricultural celebration). Witches and fairies are said to be abroad in great numbers. Frazer suggests that the prevalence of witches and fairies on Beltane Eve points to a very early female fertility cult. It is bad to be out late on May Eve; it is worse luck to sleep out; and it is said in Ireland yet that whoever is foolhardy enough to join a fairy dance on Beltane Eve will not be set free till Beltane next year. Beltane is still observed in Ireland, the Scottish Highlands, Wales, Brittany, and the Isle of Man, with more or less varying survivals of the ancient practices.

The Beltane rites were intended to increase fertility in the herds, fields, and homes. The one great ritual of the day was the building of the Beltane bonfire. It was kindled either by a spark from flint, or by friction; in fact the Irish term *teine éigin* (fire from rubbing sticks), is sometimes synonymous with the Beltane fire. The people used to dance sunwise around it (see DEISEAL); the cattle were driven through it, or between two fires, to protect them from murrain and other ills; the people crept through it also, to prevent disease, to forestall bad and invite good luck, and to cure barrenness. Contact with the fire was interpreted as symbolic of contact with the life-giving sun. In the Isle of Man rowan branches or twigs were carried deiseal three times round the fire and then taken into the homes and hung over byre doors to avert evil from family and animals alike. In Ireland today the rowan branch is still hung over the house fire on May Day to preserve the fire itself from bewitchment (the house fire being symbolic of the luck of the house). *Idir dá teine lae Bealtaine,* between two Beltane fires, is an Irish saw today meaning "in a dilemma." In early Celtic times the druids kindled the Beltane fires with specific incantations. Later the Christian church took over the Beltane observances; a service was held in the church, followed by a procession to the fields or hills, where the priest kindled the fire.

In the Scottish Highlands the kindling of Beltane fires on the hills and the practice of "burning the witches" continued into the 18th century. The young men would take bits of the fire on their pitchforks and run through the fields yelling "Fire! Fire! Burn the witches!" The fire was scattered through the fields to increase fertility (which it did). The ritual drama of the combat between King Winter and Queen May is still enacted in some parts of the Isle of Man. In some rituals, however, a King and Queen May symbolize the male and female principles of productivity.

Beltane cakes Large round oatmeal or barley cakes made for the Beltane festival. They figure variously in the celebration, but are usually divided into portions, which are drawn by lot and eaten as part of the ritual. Whoever draws the "black bit" (a portion previously blackened with charcoal) is then the devoted person, the sacrificial victim. The sacrifice is now usually mimed by the victim's running or jumping through the fire three times; but the selecting of a victim for sacrifice is believed to be the original object of the Beltane cake and its division by lot.

In the Scottish Highlands the cakes were specially prepared, sprinkled with milk and eggs, and made with a pattern of raised (usually square) lumps or knobs. Each of these was dedicated to some elemental being or animal believed to be the preserver or destroyer of domestic animals. As the group faced the fire, each person broke off one of these knobs, flung it over his shoulder, saying (to the protective elements), "This I give to thee. Preserve my horses." "This I give to thee. Preserve my sheep."—or (to the predatory animals) "This I give to thee, O fox. Spare my lambs." "This I give to thee, O hooded crow. Spare my chicks."

Sometimes the Beltane cakes were rolled down hill (evidently in imitation of the sun's motion, whose continuance thus would be insured). If the cake broke it was a sign that the owner would die within the year; if it arrived whole it was a sign of good luck.

Beltane carline The Beltane hag or old woman: term applied to the person who gets the blackened fragment of the Beltane cake when the pieces are drawn by lot. This person is then said to be devoted or dedicated. The people mime throwing him into the Beltane fire; in some localities they even throw him on the ground and go through the play of quartering him. After he

has been through the fire, the people not only mention him as one dead, but for one year he is treated as if he were not living among them. The whole idea evidently stems from an ancient Celtic human-sacrifice ritual. The primitive victim, however, was a woman, as the epithet carline indicates, pointing perhaps to a primitive female fertility cult.

Benfey, Theodor (1809–1881) German Sanskrit scholar and philologist; born at Noerlen, Hanover, and studied at Göttingen, Munich, Frankfort, and Heidelberg. From 1848 he was a professor at Göttingen, and from 1862 he occupied the chair of Sanskrit and comparative philology there, until the time of his death. Following early essays into the field of literature, he gave himself almost entirely to comparative philology, Sanskrit, and other Oriental languages, and to mythology. Benfey's principal contribution to comparative folklore was a translation of the *Panchatantra* (1859), in whose introductory volume he traces the course of the Indian stories in both Eastern and Western literatures. He was the propounder of the famous Indianist theory, postulating the Indian origin of folktales and their westward migration into Europe. This theory was accepted by folklore scholars until later scholarship pointed up the scientific invalidity of ascribing Indian origin to *all* tales. Benfey wrote a dictionary of Greek roots (1839–1842), a complete grammar of the Sanskrit language (1852), and a Sanskrit-English dictionary (1850).

Benten The only woman among the Seven Gods of Luck of Japanese mythology: patroness of music, eloquence, fine arts, and female beauty. See JAPANESE FOLKLORE. [JLM]

Beowulf The hero and title of an epic poem in the West Saxon dialect of Old English. It was composed c. 700 A.D., and is preserved in a manuscript of c. 1000. The subject matter of the poem is Scandinavian and the setting in and around what is modern Jutland. The hero is a Geat who crosses the sea to help his kinsman Hrothgar, a Dane, against the monsters who are attacking his people. The poem contains three main episodes: Beowulf's fight with Grendel, in which Beowulf in a mighty wrestling match overcomes Grendel by pulling his arm from his body; the fight under the sea between Beowulf and Grendel's mother, in which Beowulf kills the water-troll by use of a magic sword found in her cave; Beowulf's fight with a dragon, in which Beowulf, helped by the young warrior, Wiglaf, kills the marauding dragon, but is mortally wounded.

The story is a compound of folktales and historical legend. There is good evidence that the first two episodes belong to the general Eurasian folktale cycle *The Bear's Son;* the fight with the dragon likewise has many analogs in general folklore. Stories similar to those in *Beowulf* occur in Scandinavian saga. Especially close are the accounts in the *Grettisaga* of Grettir's fight with the troll-wife, and Grettir's fight with the giant in an undersea cave. The *Samsonsaga* contains another analog, the story of the hero, Samson, fighting a troll-wife in a cave behind a waterfall. The general story pattern of the *Hrolfssaga* suggests kinship with *Beowulf* though probably not direct. In this saga Bothvar Biarki performs the same kind of service for Hrolf that Beowulf performs for Hrothgar, i.e. frees the country from a devastating monster. These tales were probably part of the stock of story of all north Germanic peoples, to be used at will. *Beowulf,* like the sagas mentioned above, is the product of folktales deftly fused with historical chronicle. [MEL]

Berchta, Frau Berchta, Berkta, Bertha, or **Brechta,** also **Precht, Percht,** or **Perchta** In German folklore, a little, ragged, disheveled, old woman with stringy hair, bright, beady eyes, a long, hooked nose, and one foot large and flat from working the treadle. Whether as hobgoblin or minor goddess, she is still used as a threat to naughty children and lazy youths in parts of Austria, southern Germany, Switzerland, and Alsace. Unkempt herself, she demands cleanliness and industry in others, especially between Christmas and her feast day, Twelfth Night. She is particularly concerned with the condition of the barns and the women's spinning. Fresh straw should be sprinkled on the threshholds and there should be no flax or wool left on the distaff. She will put a plague on the cattle or do bodily harm to the lazy if all is not to her liking. Yet she is fond of little children and will often steal into a room to rock the cradle if a child is left alone. Sometimes she is seen traveling with a trail of little children following her like a flock of chickens.

On Twelfth Night everyone must eat pancakes for supper (in some sections herring and dumplings). They must leave the remains on the table for Berchta or she will cut open their stomachs, remove the food, and then sew them up again, using a plowshare threaded with chains. In many sections dancers, or berchten, are chosen who go about dancing and jumping up and down. Farmers are careful to provide refreshment for the dancers to insure that they will jump in their fields to drive out evil spirits and insure fertility. The dancers are divided into beautiful and ugly berchten and wear elaborate costumes in some places. This rite is observed on Shrove Tuesday in a few localities. See PERCHTEN.

Berchta, whose north German counterpart is Holde, has been combined and confused with many other mythical and legendary figures in various parts of south Germany, ranging from the benevolent White Lady to a savage witch who carries off her victims and eats them, from a hobgoblin frightening naughty children to the earth goddess Erda. Some say she rides the storm followed by a howling pack like the Wild Huntsman; others claim that she was the mother of Charlemagne. Her children are variously either the souls of dead children or the spirits of the unborn. See EPIPHANY.

Ber Rabbit Rides Ber Wolf Title of a South Carolina Sea Island Negro folktale. There was a big dance-party to which all the animals were invited. Ber Rabbit and Ber Wolf wanted to take the same girl. So Ber Rabbit told the girl Ber Wolf couldn't go because Ber Wolf was his riding-horse. When Ber Wolf heard that he went straight to Ber Rabbit and wanted to know why he had said such a thing. Ber Wolf demanded that Ber Rabbit come along right now and tell the girl it wasn't so. "I'm sick," said Ber Rabbit. "I'll carry you half way," said Ber Wolf. Ber Rabbit thought he couldn't go unless he had a saddle. "Put it on," said Ber Wolf. So Ber Rabbit took the spurs along too; and just as they were about half way, he "lick his spur in Ber Wolf's side" and rode up to the girl's house in style. "Didn't I tell you this was my ridin'-horse?" said Ber Rabbit.

A variant tells how Ber Rabbit tricked Ber Wolf into carrying him to the dance on his back, and how, after the dance, Ber Rabbit tricked Ber Wolf into looking up into a tree, threw dust in his eyes, and rode him home again. See ANANSI RIDES TIGER; BRER RABBIT.

berries in winter A folktale motif (H1023.3) in which the hero or heroine is sent by a jealous and cruel relative to pick berries (fruit, roses) in winter, with the hope and intent that he or she will die on the impossible quest. Probably the best known representative (Type 403) is Grimm's story #13, *The Three Little Men in the Wood,* in which a cruel stepmother one winter day gave her stepdaughter a paper frock and ordered her to go into the woods and pick strawberries, with the injunction not to come back without them. The child wandered through the snow until she came to a little house in the forest where three little men bade her come in and get warm. She shared her meager crust with them, and was handed a broom to sweep the snow from the back door. Under the snow she found the beautiful red berries, and hurried home with her basket full to her stepmother.

This motif is very widespread in Europe, belonging to a larger group of motifs (H1020–1029) comprising tasks contrary to the laws of nature.

The search for berries in winter is also common in the test stories of certain American Indian tribes of the North Pacific coast (Kwakiutl, Comox, Squamish); it has also been found among certain Plateau and Plains tribes. The motif here is generally conceded to be indigenous, and not of European provenience. A jealous father, uncle, or brother of a girl subjects the youth who has married her to a series of tests, among which being sent to pick berries in winter is one. The youth always returns with a wonderful supply to confound the ill-wishing sender. In the Kwakiutl version the son-in-law brings back a basketful of salmonberries, which turns out to be an inexhaustible supply. In the Comox version, a supernatural grandfather helps the young man by whistling the cranberries onto the bare and empty vines. These too prove to be inexhaustible; the father-in-law cannot empty the dish. The Squamish version differs in that the youth produces the salmonberries by magic himself, and Hummingbird, Bumblebee, and Wren fly around them singing, to ripen them. This last incident is closely related to another idea prominent in that region, i.e. that the singing of certain birds (usually the thrush) will sprout and ripen fruit.

There is another group of folktales in which a berries in winter variant (H1023.3.1) appears as one of the innumerable stories containing the reductio ad absurdum motif. A young man given the task of gathering berries in winter finds it impossible to leave home to go in search of them because his father is ill from snake-bite (another impossibility in winter). This is closely related also to the absurdity rebukes absurdity tales.

berserker or **berserkr** Literally, in Old Norse, bear-shirt: savage warriors of Norse mythology capable of assuming, at will, the shape and attributes of bears or wolves. Ordinarily they appear as human beings and are no stronger than other men, but in battle only their eyes are human. They go into savage frenzy, howling, barking, foaming at the mouth and, invulnerable to fire and steel, they sweep their enemies before them.

beryl A mineral family of gems including the sea-green aquamarine and emerald, here used to denote the aquamarine. Known since early times, it was usually designated the birthstone of October or Scorpio. It is a defense against foes in battle and litigation, and is used to detect thieves. It quickens the intellect, cures laziness, yet leaves a man amiable but unconquerable. It promotes the love of married couples. Medicinally it is used extensively for diseases of the eyes and disorders of the throat, jaws, and head, and against spasms and convulsions. Kunz, in *The Curious Lore of Precious Stones*, mentions that engraved with a hoopoe holding a tarragon herb before it, it conferred power to invoke water spirits and to call up the mighty dead for questioning. Engraved with a frog, it promoted friendship and reconciled enemies, and engraved with Poseidon it protected sailors. Some authorities on the Bible claim it was one of the stones of the High Priest's breastplate and one of the foundation stones of the New Jerusalem. It was sometimes used to make crystal balls.

Bes In Egyptian religion, a shaggy-haired dwarf god wearing a lion's skin and having a tail: a foreign god probably imported from Punt or Nubia to the south and east of Egypt. Although an ancient god, the large-headed, short-legged figure did not attain his greatest popularity until the XXVI Dynasty (c. 650 B.C.) and after. The image of Bes was a talisman against evil, whether evil omen or witchcraft, and it appeared more often in the Egyptian home than that of any other god. Bes was a god of dual aspect: he was a sensual god, patron of dance, music, and joyfulness, protector of children and of women in childbirth; and he was also a warlike avenging god. The latter was perhaps his original character, but his quaint physical features gained him such popularity that he acquired the genial aspect that became the more common.

Bessy, Bess, or **Besom-Bet** In northern England, the name of the female impersonator in the Fool Plough ceremonies and processions: a man dressed grotesquely as an old woman. The Bessy is a stock character also in pantomime, mummers' parades, and sword dances, but is especially associated with the Fool Plough.

bestiaries Western European handbooks of natural history with articles on numerous real or imagined animals moralistically interpreted. Although the earliest may have been put together about 200 B.C. they owe much to St. Ambrose's (c. 340–397) *Hexameron* and St. Isidore's (c. 560–636) *Etymology*. In the Middle Ages and later, bestiaries were enormously popular. Copies have been preserved in the Armenian, Syriac, and Ethiopian languages as well as in the languages of western Europe. They have influenced ecclesiastical art and folk speech and have been influenced by them. [RDJ]

betel chewing A widespread and ancient custom of eastern Asia, the East Indies, and Melanesia, of chewing the seed of the areca palm (popularly called the betel nut), wrapped in leaves of the vine *Piper betle* together with a bit of lime and other flavoring ingredients: the "chew" is called in modern India *pān-supārī*.

So prevalent is the habit that it, and the materials chewed, form part of many important ceremonies of the region. For example, throughout the area, betel nuts or leaves are used in puberty ceremonies, marriage ceremonies, and death ceremonies, in courtship, bride bargains, and birth divination, etc. There are more or less rigid tabus connected with the nuts and leaves, their growth, sale, and use. The equipment used by the betel chewers (areca-nut cutters, lime boxes and spatulas, betel bags, spittoons, etc.) is often highly elaborated with native art work. Habitual betel chewing makes the teeth black and eventually rots them, and it stains the saliva red. The Shans say that beasts have white teeth, seemingly differentiating beasts from betel chewers. For a comprehensive survey of the literature and customs of the area connected with betel chewing, see Penzer's "The Romance of Betel Chewing" in Tawney's *The Ocean of Story*, vol. VIII, pp. 237–319.

betony A European herb (genus *Stachys*, formerly *Betonica*) of the mint family. According to Pliny betony was an amulet for houses (xxv, 46) and so antipathetic to snakes that they lash themselves to death when surrounded by it (xxv, 55). Antonius Musa, physician to Augustus Cæsar, wrote a book on the virtues of betony as a preserver of the liver and protector from epidemic diseases and witchcraft.

To the herbalists the betony was an herb of Jupiter, under the sign Aries, which helped jaundice, palsy, gout, and convulsions. Taken in wine it killed worms; mixed with honey it aided childbirth. Dry and hot, it was used for infirmities of the head and eyes, the breast and lungs.

bezoar A concretion, often of lime and magnesium phosphate, formed around foreign substances in the stomach, liver, or intestines of ruminants; occasionally, similar stones found in other parts of the bodies of hedgehogs, porcupines, monkeys, and human beings. It was considered a gem by the ancients of both the Old and New World. Bezoars were first mentioned as a medicine by the Arabs and Persians, and it was not until the end of the 12th century that they were introduced into Europe, where they soon gained high repute. They are universally considered an antidote for poison, whether used internally, placed on the wound, or merely worn as an amulet. The Chinese wear them set in rings which they suck whenever they believe they have been subjected to poison. The Sioux Indian tribes believe that blowing powdered bezoar into the eyes strengthens the sight and the brain. Used with a laxative the bezoar is good for chronic and painful diseases. The Hindus and Persians use it in this manner as a periodic tonic. In Germany and Bohemia it is used internally for toothache. Unlike many medieval remedies, it evidently had some effect, as it caused profuse perspiration, and care had to be exercised in administering it or it would blacken the teeth. Stones from different animals found particular favor with various authorities, but those from the porcupine, monkey, and man are generally considered best. Those of the New World, although often rough on the outside and of drab color, are equally effective, as is a mineral stone of similar composition found in Sicily. By the middle of the 18th century it had become so popular that medicinal bezoar sold for fifty times the price of emerald and a piece the size of a pigeon egg sold for $1,200. The Mongolians claim that it will produce rain. [JWH]

☞ In the New World, bezoar stones, particularly those found in deer, were believed to possess great magical powers to aid hunters, sorcerers, and medicine men. The medicinal properties believed by the Spaniards to be inherent in these stones made them a valued object of search. Some of the New World stones were believed to be superior to those of the Old World. Because of this intense interest, and the resulting monetary exchange value of the stones to Indian finders, this Old World belief seems to have become incorporated into the folklore of nearly all Middle American Indian tribes. [GMF]

bhagat Priests, medicine men, and exorcists of India. [MWS]

Bhagavad-Gītā Literally, the song of the Divine One: a dialog inserted in the sixth book of the Hindu epic, the *Mahābhārata*, in which Krishna, as an incarnation of Nārāyaṇa Vishnu, expounds his philosophical doctrines to Arjuna and reveals himself as the one and only God. One of the most loved and used of Hindu scriptures, the poem is believed to date from the 2nd or 3rd century A.D. It is divided into three sections each containing six chapters. During the war between the Kauravas and the Pāṇḍavas, Krishna agreed to act as charioteer for Arjuna, leader of the Pāṇḍava princes. The latter, disliking the coming slaughter of friends and relatives, asked Krishna for guidance. This beautiful and lofty dialog followed, in which the doctrine of bhakti (faith) and Kharma yoga (action), and the duties of caste are exalted above all other obligations.

Bhairava In Hindu mythology and religion, any one of the eight (or twelve) fearful forms of Śiva: worshiped especially by outcaste groups of India. In this fearful aspect Śiva often rides upon a dog. In his modern character, Bhairava has been identified with the local village deity Bhairon and the characteristics of the two have been merged. Bhairava is worshipped in the agricultural districts of northern and central India as a black dog, a snake-girded drummer, or a red stone.

Bhairon In Indian belief, a local village god, personification of the field-spirit, whose identification with Bhairava has given him the attributes of Śiva. In Benares he serves as the guardian of the temples of Śiva. In Bombay he is represented in a terrifying aspect as Kala Bhairava or Bhairoba armed with a sword or club and carrying a bowl of blood. See GRĀMA-DEVATĀ.

bhangas In Hindu dance, the bends or deviations of the body from the plumb line: abhanga (slightly bent), samabhanga (equally bent) or in equilibrium, atibhanga (greatly bent), and tribhanga (thrice bent). [GPK]

Bhīma or **Bhīma-sena** In the *Mahābhārata*, second of the five Pāṇḍava princes; son of the wind god Vāyu. Bhīma was burly, prodigiously strong, courageous, coarse, and brutal. His appetite was such that he ate half the food of the family. During the first exile of the brothers, Bhīma subdued the asuras and they promised to cease molesting mankind. In the great battle between the Kauravas and the Pāṇḍavas he engaged in combat with Duryodhana. When Bhīma was losing, he struck an unfair blow, smashing Duryod-

hana's thigh. Balarāma was so incensed by the foul attack that he declared Bhīma henceforth should be called Jihma-yodhin, the unfair fighter.

Bhīma is a nationally worshipped hero who may originally have been a Rākshasa. Like Arjuna, Sītā, and many other epic heroes and heroines, he has the marks of an originally divine nature. He is now the chief rain god of the Central Provinces. The Gonds celebrate a festival in his honor close to the time of the monsoon.

Bhīshma Literally, the terrible: in Hindu mythology, the son of King Śāntanu by Gangā. When his father wished to marry the young and beautiful Satyavatī, her parents objected because Bhīshma was heir to the throne and her sons could not inherit the kingdom. Bhīshma agreed never to accept the throne nor to marry and Satyavatī's parents then agreed to the marriage. Her sons by Śāntanu, however, died without children and the children of her son, Pāṇḍu and Dhritarāshtra, born before her marriage to the king, were brought up by Bhīshma who acted as regent of Hastināpura for them and directed the training of their children, the Kauravas and Pāṇḍavas. In the battle between the two groups he sided with the Kauravas and was mortally wounded. His body was so covered with the arrows shot by Arjuna that they held him up when he fell from his chariot. He is the model for modern ascetics who lie on beds studded with nails. He is also revered in India for his filial devotion and a festival is held in his honor during Karttik (November-December).

Bhrigu In Vedic mythology, one of the rishis or seers: the founder of the race of bhrigus and bhargavas. Bhrigu was generated from the heart of Brahmā or from the seed of Prajāpati which had been cast into the fire by the gods. He was, according to the *Aitareya Brāhmaṇa* and the *Mahābhārata*, adopted by Varuṇa. According to the *Purāṇas*, the rishis were undecided about which god to worship, so they sent Bhrigu to test the characters of the gods. Bhrigu found Śiva so much engrossed in his wife and Brahmā in himself that neither would receive the seer. Vishnu was asleep, so the sage angrily kicked him. Vishnu, awakening, stroked the sage's foot and expressed the honor he felt at this method of arousing him. Bhrigu reported Vishnu the most worthy of worship. See AGNI; CHYAVANA.

Bhūmiya or **Khetrpal** (feminine *Bhūmiyā Rānī*) In Northern Indian belief, a local earth god or goddess. The god is worshipped when a marriage takes place, when a child is born, or during the harvest. He sometimes changes sex, becoming identified with the earth mother and, like her, has a malignant aspect, bringing sickness to those who are disrespectful. He is worshipped as a snake by the Dāngīs of the United Provinces. When the Jats establish a new village the first man to die in the community is buried in a special mound, a shrine named for him is erected, and he is deified under his name as the local earth god or Bhūmiya. Local Bhūmiyas are gradually being absorbed into both the Vaishnava and Śaiva systems.

bhūt or **bhūta** In Hindu belief, the general name for a malignant ghost of the dead; the spirit of a man who has died by accident, suicide, or capital punishment. To avoid them people lie on the ground, since bhūts never rest on the earth. They have no shadow, speak with a nasal twang, and are afraid of burning turmeric. [MWS]

bia Songs sung by the Australian Buin people as laments for the dead. The words are the mourning exclamations and cries of relatives at the cremation.

bibliomancy Divination by means of books, or by use of the Bible. This is generally a method in which any book composed of verses may be used as an oracle. In the Middle Ages, the _Æneid_ was used in the _sortes Vergilianæ_; throughout Europe, the Bible, often opened with a golden needle, was employed; and in Moslem countries, the Koran. In essence, the method takes force from the sacred nature of the book employed, and it is allied to sortilegium in its acceptance of the chance factor. A Western European variant was to weigh a suspected person against the Great Bible; a guilty person weighed more than the Book.

biersal In German folklore (Saxony), a kobold who lives down in the cellar and will clean all the jugs and bottles as long as he receives his own jug of beer daily for his trouble.

Bifrost or **Asbru** In Teutonic mythology, the rainbow bridge made of fire, air, and water for the gods' use, arching from the world-tree, Yggdrasil, on earth, Midgard, to Asgard. It was forbidden to Thor because of his heavy tread. It will be destroyed at Ragnarök by the weight of the giant Surtr and his sons.

Big House ceremony A twelve-night ceremony of the Delaware Indians held, at least in modern times, in a rectangular structure known as the Big House. It is held to propitiate the Master of Life (supreme deity) and to ensure for the tribe good health, well-being, and the blessings of the supernatural. Esoteric songs obtained in visions are sung by their owners during the several nights of the ceremony; speeches and prayers are made by ceremonial leaders, and feasting concludes the rites. The interior center and side posts supporting the Big House have carved wooden faces on them. For a detailed account of the construction of the Big House and the ceremony held therein, see F. G. Speck, "A Study of the Delaware Big House Ceremony" (_Publications of the Pennsylvania Historical Commission_, Vol. II, pp. 5–192, 1931). [EWV]

Big Owl A destructive, cannibalistic monster, usually having the form of a large owl, in Apache Indian mythology. The White Mountain Apache picture Big Owl as the evil, blundering son of Sun, who killed all the people and was in turn killed by his brother, the culture hero. Among the Mescalero and Chiricahua Apache he is a wicked giant; in Lipan mythology Big Owl induces the culture hero to marry his daughter, so that he can kill him; in Jicarilla Apache tales Big Owl transfixes his victims with his glance, carries them home in a basket, and eats them. [EWV]

Big-Raven The creator in Koryak mythology: Quikinnaqu.

Big Sea Day An old coastal celebration of New Jersey, formerly celebrated every year on the second Saturday in August. People came to the shore in wagons and buggies prepared to spend the day—whole families out of the woods and pines of southern Jersey. Everyone went

in bathing in the sea, wearing whatever they happened to have on for the day, and dried in the sun. It was also called Farmers' Wash Day, with the tongue-in-cheek implication that New Jersey farmers bathed only once a year. Seagirt was honored with the special celebration of Little Sea Day, the third Saturday in August. This celebration was for those who had to stay home the week before to do the chores. Both celebrations have vanished with the "commercial invasion" of the Jersey coast resorts.

Bile In Old Irish mythology, one of the Milesians, a king of Spain. His name is listed with the 41 Spanish chiefs who accompanied the sons of Mil to Ireland to avenge the death of Ith. Bile's name is listed also with those who were drowned in the druid storm sent by the Tuatha Dé Danann to prevent their landing.

Bile as a king of Spain is interpreted by some scholars as a god of darkness and death, Spain being an overseas Otherworld (specifically, a land of the dead). Recent students, however, prefer to interpret both Bile and Spain more literally. Reinach assumes both a racial and commercial relationship between Ireland and Spain, even in earliest times, either by sea or via Gaul. In fact, botanists and zoologists alike can advance evidence that there was once an unbroken European coastline from Ireland to Spain. Old geographers and chartists assumed the two countries were much closer than they are; and that Ith glimpsed Ireland from his father's tower in Spain bears testimony to this concept.

bili (singular _bile_) The sacred trees of the ancient Celts: early believed to be the habitation of gods or elemental spirits, later associated with kings and belief in the sanctity or godhood of kings. The king's scepter was made from a branch of his own tree, and a branch of his tree was symbolic of the king. It was sacrilege to pluck or fell the king's tree. Evidently the life token or separable soul idea was here involved. In later Celtic romance one often reads of some hero, giant, knight, etc., defending a certain tree from having fruit or a bough taken from it or from being felled. In Ireland today any sacred or historical tree is called a bile, especially one within a fort or growing beside a holy well. Any unusually big or very aged tree, or one oddly shaped is a bile and regarded as sacred. People will pray near it, and sometimes even still make offerings to it.

Biliku, Bilik, or **Puluga** A prominent deity of the Andaman Islands, associated with monsoons, usually the northeast, while Tarai (another deity who may be wife or brother) is associated with the southwest. Both are associated with weather in general and natural phenomena. The term _biliku_ among the northern Andamese means "spider." Lowie (_Primitive Religion_, p. 129 ff.) discusses data collected by Man and Radcliffe-Brown, and denies that evidence points, as Father Schmidt believes, to Biliku as being a "High God." [KL]

Billy Blin A semisupernatural being, a sort of household familiar of English and Scottish popular ballad: also known as Billy Blind, Belly Blin, and Blind Barlow. See FAIRY.

Billy Boy A question-and-answer song detailing the housewifely merits of a possible bride, known in many variants all over Great Britain and widely popular in America. There are many differing versions, which were probably introduced separately by colonists from various sections.

bilwis or **pilwiz** In medieval German literature, an evil, soul-like being with a sickle on his big toe who devastated fields, teased men, and tangled their hair. He was especially active on Walpurgis Night. He was believed to live in trees; and offerings were sometimes left for him to protect children from disease.

bina The name given in the Guianas to the plants used by the Indians as hunting and fishing talismans. Many Indians cultivate them near their huts to have a ready store of them. The binas generally bear some resemblance to a distinctive feature of the animal species on which they are supposed to have an influence. Thus, for instance, the armadillo bina typifies the shape of the small projecting ears of this animal. [AM]

Binnorie One of the variants of *The Twa Sisters* (Child #10), named from its refrain. This ballad embodies the motif of the singing bone: the young girl who was drowned by a jealous older sister tells of her murder through the harp (or occasionally fiddle) made from her bones. Some of the variants of *Binnorie* go into lengthy detail about exactly which parts of her anatomy were used for the parts of the magical instrument which sang her story. The story is repeated half across the world in tales or ballads and may be of Danish or Norwegian origin. It is also known as *The Berkshire Tragedy, The Milldams of Binnorie, Bow Down,* etc. and is one of the few songs found in America which preserves this motif.

birch Any tree or shrub of the genus *Betula* with hard, close-grained wood and outer bark separable in thin layers, common in northern Europe and North America. The birch is widely used in folk medicine and is regarded as a safeguard against wounds, gout, barrenness, caterpillars, the evil eye, and lightning. The Catawba Indians boil the buds of the yellow birch to a syrup, add sulfur, and make a salve for ringworm or sores. In Newfoundland the inside bark of a birch is applied with cod oil to cure frostbite. Culpeper recommended the juice or a distillation of the leaves to break kidney stones and to wash sore mouths.

The Roman fasces with which the lictors cleared the way for the magistrates were made of birch. The books of Numa Pompilius, according to Pliny, were written on birch bark. In Scandinavian mythology the tree was consecrated to Thor and symbolized the return of spring. The birch is especially esteemed by the Russians for whom it is the source of light (torches). It stifles cries (oil of birch is used to lubricate cart wheels), it cleanses (in the Russian steam baths birch branches are used to scourge the body), and it cures, for its sap is used as a cordial in cases of consumption.

Birch branches were used generally in Europe for beating the bounds, and for beating evil spirits out of lunatics. Birch is especially efficacious against evil spirits and for that reason is used in the English country "besom brooms" used for getting rid of witches. The letter B, beth (meaning birch), begins the ancient Irish Tree Alphabet and thus begins the year. In the Scottish ballad *The Wife of Usher's Well* (Child #79) the dead sons return to their mother in the winter time with hats of birch. These were taken from the tree beside the gates of Paradise: a sign (as suggested by Robert Graves in *The White Goddess*) to the living that these ghosts will not haunt the world but wear the birch in token that they will return to their heavenly abode.

The birch is the personification of Estonia to that country's people. The Swedes believe the dwarf birch was once a full-sized tree, but when a rod of it was used to scourge Christ, the tree was doomed to hide its stunted head. In Finland the origin of the birch is attributed to a maiden's tear. In Newfoundland it is unlucky to make birch brooms in May, for they will sweep the family away. The Canadian Dakota burn small pieces of birch bark to keep the Thunders away. When the Thunders see this, they are restrained in their violence.

a bird in the hand is worth two in the bush A familiar proverb, well known, in various wordings, throughout Europe, common in folktale and literature. John Heywood's version, "Better one byrde in hand than ten in the wood," is almost as frequently heard. Better a fowl in the hand nor two flying (Scottish): One bird in the net is better than a hundred flying (Hebrew): Better one 'I have' than two 'I shall haves' (French): A sparrow in the hand is better than a pheasant that flieth by (German): Better one 'take this' than two 'will gives' (Spanish) are all common property. "He is a fool who lets slip a bird in the hand for a bird in the bush," said Plutarch in *Of Garrulity* (1st century A.D.). The most common wording, "A bird in the hand is worth two in the bush," quoted and used so widely (John Bunyan, Cervantes, others) can be traced back to one of the *Idylls* of Theocritus (3rd century B.C.) who thus expressed the quintessence of Æsop's fables of *The Hawk and the Nightingale* and *The Angler and the Little Fish* (6th century B.C.). In one the angler wisely keeps the little fish already caught rather than throw him back in the uncertain hope of catching a bigger fish later. In the other the hungry hawk refuses to release the little nightingale, on the grounds that the little bird he has is worth more to his empty belly than a big bird not yet caught. The bird in the hand occurs also in folktale motif, appearing variously as the bird in the hand, the little fish on the hook, and the sleeping hare which the lion foregoes to follow a shepherd (J321.1; J321.2; J321.3).

bird languages The languages spoken by birds among themselves: prominent in folktale as a medium of warning, advice, prophecy, or aid to those human beings endowed with the gift of understanding them. The gift is variously acquired: either as a reward for befriending some animal or bird, as the gift of a god, or by eating some magical herb. Occasionally the hero is born with the ability to understand the languages of birds, but often it comes suddenly upon one who has eaten of a snake. In Icelandic belief one could acquire the understanding of bird languages by carrying a hawk's tongue under the tongue. Usually overhearing the conversation of a bird with its mate or friends gives the hero the information needed for his successful outcome in the story. The bird languages motif (B215.1) is common in Celtic and in European folktale from Iceland to Arabia, and is equally frequent in Slavic, Hindu, and Hebrew story. Familiar and typical instances of its use occur in Grimm's stories *The White Snake* (#17), *The Three*

Languages (#33), and *Faithful John* (#6). See ANIMAL LANGUAGES; MELAMPUS.

bird-man The most familiar and least complicated of these composite beings are the medieval angels and demons, the fairies, and the Greek Keres (represented as tiny human figures with butterfly wings). Many representations of Egyptian gods embody combinations of human and bird anatomy, for the gods were first birds and animals and only gradually evolved into men. Perhaps the most complicated and fearsome of these creatures is the Gorgon, which had serpent hair, the hideous face of a woman, the wings of a bird, and the body of a lioness with bronze claws. The most frightful of these was Medusa. The important feature of the Hindu Garuda bird is that it is one of the few combinations with the head of a bird. Other features vary with locale (it is known in India, Indochina, China, Japan, etc.). It ranges from a simple bird-headed man on wings to a Japanese variety which has the wings and head of a bird on the torso of a woman and the legs of a crane. She has a white face, red wings, golden body, and the tail of a phœnix. The Egyptian soul was sometimes depicted as a bird with a human head, as was also the Greek Harpy, which befouled everything it touched. The Sirens were similar in form, but had beautiful voices and lured men to their downfall. The Welsh Washer of the Ford (Gwrach y Rhibyn) is a spectral female in black with the wings of a bat. The Furies are another of these combinations.

The Sphinx is a combination of man-bird-beast, that is, the head and chest of a man, wings of a bird, and the body of an animal. In Egypt sphinxes were always male, and had the body of a lion. The Greek female sphinx also had a lioness's body. The Babylonian shedu, the Hebrew shedim, and the Sumerian alad were similar to the Egyptian, and male. They had the bodies of bulls, neatly curled beards, and often wore hats. The female counterpart of the sedu was called lamma or lamassu and could fly. The Syrian female sphinx had wings and resembled the Egyptian. She was probably a representation of Astarte.

bird of truth A bird which reveals the truth and often identifies murderers, traitors, and other wrong-doers: one of the most widespread of folktale motifs (B131–131.6). In one of the typical stick-fast or tar-baby stories of the Fjorts of the French Congo, it is a bird who reveals to Antelope that Rabbit, forbidden by Antelope to drink from his well, has nevertheless been drinking from it every day. In an Angola tale Turtle-dove plays the role of truth-finder in helping Blacksmith discover which of many identical Blackbirds owe him for his hoes.

The famous parrot story, in which a man enjoins his parrot to watch and spy upon his wife's virtue in his absence, is told twice in the *Arabian Nights Entertainments:* on the 5th night in "The Husband and the Parrot," on the 579th night in "The Confectioner, His Wife, and the Parrot." When the man comes home the parrot tells all that she has seen: that the wife has made merry and had a lover night after night. The man righteously punishes the wife. No one can imagine how the man found out, but eventually the woman discovers it was the parrot who told. During the husband's next absence she and her maids counterfeit the noise of a storm so successfully, that the parrot's report of the storm discredits her previous report about the wife. The man now believes both stories were lies and kills the parrot. Later, of course, he discovers that the parrot was a bird of truth. The Scottish ballad of *The Bonny Birdy* (Child #82) partakes of both the bird of truth and speaking bird motifs.

One of the most familiar birds of truth occurs in Grimm's story (#96), *The Three Little Birds,* in which three marvelous children of a king are exposed to perish by the jealous sisters of the queen. They are found and reared by a fisherman and their true identity is eventually revealed to the king by the bird of truth. The bird also reveals that the innocent queen is in prison and that the jealous sisters were the intentional murderers. The story ends with all the satisfactory restorations and punishments.

birds If a bird flies into the house, it is a forerunner of important news. Some people say that it is a sign of death, especially if it cannot get out again; and if it is a white bird it is a sure sign of death. In Alabama, however, a bird flying into the house is considered good luck. If a woodpecker taps on the house, he brings bad news, often news of a death in the family. It is very good luck if a wren builds near the house. When you first hear the whip-poor-will in the spring, you may know that you will be in the same place, doing the same thing, the same day the following year. If you can make a wish when you hear him calling for the first time, that wish will come true.

A rooster crowing in front of the house is announcing company. In Nova Scotia it is said that a rooster crowing at the wrong time of night is announcing a death. Southern Negroes interpret a flock of crows around a house as a bad sign. It is generally believed throughout the United States that to hear an owl hooting is a sign bad luck is coming; to hear a hoot owl is a sign of death. The hoot owl says "Who-o, who-o, who are you?" Barn swallows nesting on a barn bring prosperity, but to destroy their nests brings calamity. Some say it will make the cows give bloody milk.

Peacock feathers are very unlucky; they prevent girls from marrying and babies from being born. It is also a general U.S. folk belief that it is bad to have designs of birds or bird decorations on wedding presents: the happiness of the newlyweds will all the sooner take wing. It is not a good thing to have stuffed birds in the house either. They will fly off with your luck.

In Ireland it is said that the crossbill's beak got twisted from pulling out the nails from the cross during the Crucifixion; and the robin is held sacred because it is believed that its breast is stained with the blood of Christ. Irish fishermen believe that sea gulls embody the souls of the drowned. If the rooks desert a farm bad luck will surely follow. The wagtail is said to have three drops of the devil's blood on his tail, which he cannot shake off. And no Irishman will kill a swan because of the Children of Lir.

bird seizes jewel A folktale motif in which a jewel is carried off by a bird, occurring especially in a group of stories involving the loss and recovery of various magic objects (Types 560–568). The motif in which a bird seizes some jewel (ring, necklace, etc.) or a turban or other headdress containing a jewel, and flies off with it, is found in the *Pañchatantra,* several times in the *Arabian Nights Entertainments,* and also in Hebrew legend. Frequently the theft results in the accusation of some innocent person, who is eventually pardoned when the truth is revealed; or the loser of the jewel follows the bird and is led to distant lands, undergoing many adventures before the jewel is at last brought to light and the story to a happy ending.

Typical of the former is the story of "The Stolen Necklace" told on the 596–597th nights of the famous Thousand and One. A certain woman who had devoted herself to religion was keeper of the bath in the king's palace. One day the queen handed her a precious necklace to keep safe while she went into the bath. The pious woman laid the necklace on the prayer-rug while she prayed. A magpie caught sight of the bright thing, and, unseen by the woman, seized it, and flew off with it, to hide it in a cranny in the palace wall. When the queen came out of the bath and asked for the necklace, it was gone. Neither of them could find it. The king had the woman beaten and questioned over fire, but she continued to deny the theft; at last she was thrown into prison. Some time later the king himself saw the magpie flitting about the corner of the wall and was amazed to see it pulling at a necklace. The bird was caught and the necklace retrieved; the woman was pardoned and set free. The second is represented by motif N352, in which a bird carries off the ring which a young man has removed from the finger of his lover in her sleep. This is related to the accidental separations group of motifs (N310–319) in that the pair are separated in a long series of adventures in their search for it and for each other.

The bird seizes jewel motif occurs also in a medieval French legend, reused with humorous adaptation in "The Jackdaw of Rheims" ballad (in Barham's *Ingoldsby Legends*). A jackdaw flew off with the ring of the archbishop of Rheims. The archbishop cursed the thief, whoever he might be, with such a blasting curse that the jackdaw drooped and failed into a lame, unsightly, bald, and sickly bird. At last the jackdaw revealed the hiding place of the ring; the curse was lifted; he regained his health and fine feathers, and became a devout Christian.

bird-soul The soul in the form of a bird: distinguished from *soul-bird,* a co-existent double of an individual. The bats of Babylonia, flitting in the dusk, were the bird-souls of the dead; when Gormw shot Llew Llaw Gyffes, the latter's soul flew away as an eagle, or bird-soul. But the parrot in the forest, born at the same time as the boy in the hut, whose life is bound up with the life of the boy, is a soul-bird. The distinction is often not clearly drawn by students of folktale and folk belief, and the term is often further confused by being used synonymously with separable or external soul in a bird. See BUSH-SOUL; SEPARABLE SOUL; SOUL-ANIMAL.

Birds' Wedding Title and motif of a very widespread European folk song (B282 ff.; Type 224) describing the marriage of certain birds to other birds and occasionally to other animals; widely known in French, German, Lettish, Wendish, English, Russian, French Canadian, Danish, Czech, Estonian, Walloon, etc., and even in Japanese. Eagles, larks, nightingales, pigeons, woodpeckers intermarry with owls, wrens, robins, sparrows, magpies, wagtails, ravens, quails, cuckoos. In Germany cocks and hens are typical brides and bridegrooms. The nursery story of the wedding of the owl and the cat (B282.4.2) is an example in English. The form is often cumulative, as in the related type of animal marriage of *Frog Went a-Courting.*

Bird That Made Milk An African Negro folktale existing in several variants among the Basuto, Kaffir, Zulu, and Sechuana peoples. In the Basuto version a woman comes into the possession of a wonderful bird that provides the family with milk. She conceals it carefully in the hut, and every evening it fills as many clay vessels with milk as the family requires. The children discover it, however, play with it, fill themselves with milk, and finally lose it in the forest. They try to recover it but fail. Suddenly a violent storm comes upon them, so violent that the trees are uprooted. But an enormous bird comes and covers the children with its wings so that they are not harmed. When the storm is over the bird carries them off, nurtures them carefully, at the proper time even putting them through their puberty rites, and returns them safe and beautiful to their parents after that. The joyful villagers then reward the bird with gifts of cattle. After that there is much visiting back and forth between the bird and the people.

The Kaffir version is especially famous in that it contains the incident of the crocodile who takes one of the runaway children to his underwater home, presses gifts upon him, and bids him bring his sister also. When the girl arrives he beseeches her to lick his face, and as she does so, a handsome man emerges. This is one of the most famous of all Beauty and the Beast variants. Other motifs involved in this story are the animal nurse (B535), speaking bird (B211.9), bird gives shelter with its wings (B538.1).

Bird Whose Wings Made The Wind A Micmac Indian story relating how the people along the shore could not go fishing because of the high winds and fierce storms upon the sea. They became so hungry that they walked along the shores hoping to pick up a fish here and there that might have been cast to land by the waves. One day Gluskabe, the culture hero, looking for fish came upon the cause of their troubles. A big bird stood on a point of land which jutted into the sea flapping his wings and causing all the storms. He called out to the big bird, "O, Grandfather," he called him. He then proceeded to convince the bird that he was cold and took him ashore on his back. Carefully the man stepped from rock to rock until he came to the last one. Then he pretended to stumble, fell, and broke the bird's wing. The kind man immediately set the bone, bound up the wing, and told the old bird to lie still and he would bring him food. Dead calm fell upon the waters. Day in and day out it was calm, until the salt water was covered with scum, and stank. No longer could the fishermen see through the water to spear fish or eels, and were as bad off as before. So they set free the bird, whose wing was now healed, but they explained to him that he must flap his wings gently. They have not had so much trouble since.

This idea of the big bird whose wings made the wind is common to Micmac, Malecite, and Passamaquoddy tribes; it is known among Georgia Negroes, turns up in

Norse and Icelandic mythology, and is one of the motifs in the Babylonian Adapa story. See GLUSKABE.

birthdays Among people with well developed sense of time, birthdays mark the transition from one stage of being to another. Because any change is dangerous, birthdays are the times when good and evil spirits and influences have the opportunity to attack the celebrants who at these times are in peril. The couvade and all the rites of the threshold are two of the many examples of this almost universal tendency in folk thinking. The presence of friends and the expression of good wishes help to protect the celebrant against the unknown pervasive peril. Ceremonies and games at birthdays frequently are a symbolic wiping out of the past and starting anew. The American child who at his birthday blows out all the candles on his cake with one puff is eager to demonstrate his prowess, but the secret wish he makes will be granted only if all the candles can be extinguished at once. Trials of strength and skill on birthdays are demonstrations of progress. Among some tribes puberty ceremonies are initiated on the birthday. Some of the tribes of the Congo and, in North America, the Hupas and Omahas believed that counting was wicked and kept no record of time. Among these groups, birthdays were not marked. This is also true of some of the aboriginal tribes of Australia who have names indicating the generation but no actual reckoning. The exchange of presents and communal eating, except in communities where eating together is dangerous or bad manners, strengthen communal bonds and this is associated with the importance of ingratiating good and evil fairies, godmothers, and wealthy relatives, on their or our birthdays. The Tshi of West Africa sacrifice to their protective spirits on their birthdays by smearing themselves with egg and asking for good luck. The ceremonial observance of weekly or monthly birthdays has been reported from West Africa, Burma, ancient Syria, and elsewhere. The social importance of birthdays increases with the importance of the celebrant: kings, heroes, saints, gods. Because kings are endowed in folk thinking with magical functions in that a good king or president can bring among other things good fortune to the people, that is peace and good crops, the birth of a royal heir is the occasion for great social and mild sexual excitement. In Christian communities the birthdays of martyrs are their death days, when they are born into eternal life.

The date, hour, and place of birth may be the clues to good or bad fortune as determined by the complex computations of astrologers, numerologists, and geomants. Prudential ceremonies either at birth or at stated anniversaries, depending on the system of computation, are good insurance. Memorial services, or sacrifices at tombs or before ancestral tablets, are in some places customary on the birthdays of the deceased. The function is a mixture of natural affection, the desire to keep the deceased at peace and therefore to keep his ghost from troubling the living.

The birthdays which mark the transition from childhood to adolescence, from adolescence to adulthood, the acceptance of the individual into the tribe, community, or church (confirmation day) have ceremonies which are more or less impressive depending on the ethnic complex. In China the birthdays which mark the transition

from one stage of being to another have each special ceremonies. The 60th birthday is an example. Noodles which, being long and numerous, symbolize long life and many years, are part of all birthday ceremonies and a necessary dish on the 60th. Filial sons present gifts and garments with the longevity symbol, and put themselves into debt to buy magnificent coffins for their respected parents, and the parents themselves at this date become members of the older generation. On this 60th birthday and for the next ten years, men are advised to put women from their beds though on their 70th birthday filial sons may present their fathers with a new concubine. Christ's birthday on December 25 was, in the Julian calendar, the date of the winter solstice. Egyptians exhibited images of infants on that day and Syrians and Egyptians who had retired into caves emerged at midnight crying, "The Virgin has brought forth. The light is waxing." [RDJ]

Birth of Cormac or **Geineaṁain Cormaic** Title of an ancient Irish story of the cycle of Conn of the Hundred Battles, contained in the *Book of Ballymote* and the *Yellow Book of Lecan*. When Art son of Conn of the Hundred Battles traveled westward to fight the battle of Mag Mucrama he spent the eve of the battle in the house of a smith, and begot a son on the smith's daughter, Étain. Art told Étain that her son would be king of Ireland, and said to bring the child for fosterage to Lugna Fer Trí. Art was killed in that battle and Étain set out before the child was born so that it might be born in the house of its fosterer. The birth-pains overtook her on the way and she lay in a bed of ferns and gave birth to a boy. The moment the child was born a clap of thunder announced to Lugna that Cormac son of Art was in the world, and he set out to find him.

Étain slept after the birth and her maidservant kept watch. Finally the maid also slept and a she-wolf came and carried off the infant. So when Lugna found Étain she could only weep and say the child was gone, she knew not where or how. One day a man brought news to Lugna of having seen a human child in a wolf's cave crawling among the whelps. They brought the child home and the wolf whelps with him, and he was raised with Lugna's sons. At length Lugna took Cormac to Tara to live in the house of Mac Con, successor to Art. Immediately Cormac proved his true birth with a true judgment. The sheep of a certain woman had eaten the king's woad and Mac Con had taken the sheep as compensation for the woad. "No," said Cormac. "Take the wool of the sheep for the eating of the woad, because both will grow again." And the side of the king's house from which the crooked judgment had been made collapsed. Legend says the Crooked Mound of Tara is named for this.

The people unthroned Mac Con and Cormac was made king. He kept his wolves by him, and Tara prospered while Cormac was king.

birth omen Any unusual happening during the delivery of a child: considered portentous by many peoples. Mesopotamian records contain many statements like: "If a woman has brought forth, and its right ear is small, the house of the man will be destroyed" and "If a woman has brought forth twins for the second time, the country will be destroyed." In general, multiple births are considered to be unlucky; but exceptions are widespread. Marks on the baby's body have significance; on the island of Karpathos near Crete, such marks, however tiny, are called "the fating of the Fates." The month, day of the week, etc., of the birth have significance, being important for the horoscope, and also because certain days are *per se* lucky or unlucky. A difficult delivery is widely taken to be a sign of the mother's infidelity, as were twins in Teutonic belief. Although no direct evidence exists of actual belief or practice, the presence of Roman names like Dentatus and Agrippa, Sextus and Decimus, indicate the importance of birth omens in Europe. Various customs have existed to foretell the future occupation of the newborn; the infant, for example, is shown two objects (e.g. a violin and a purse) and reaches for one. See AFTERBIRTH; ASTROLOGY; CAUL; DIVINATION; TWINS.

birthstone A jewel identified with a particular month of the year (or, more rarely, with a day of the week or a sign of the zodiac): thought to bring good luck when worn by a person whose birthday falls in that month. Lists of these stones vary greatly in detail, from country to country and through the centuries. The tabulation below places the currently accepted stone for each month first, with some of the principal variants following in parentheses:

January—garnet
February—amethyst
March—aquamarine or bloodstone (jasper)
April—diamond (sapphire)
May—emerald (agate, chalcedony, carnelian)
June—pearl or moonstone (chalcedony, agate, emerald)
July—ruby (onyx, carnelian, turquoise)
August—sardonyx or chrysolite (carnelian)
September—sapphire (chrysolite)
October—opal or tourmaline (aquamarine, beryl)
November—topaz
December—turquoise or lapis lazuli (ruby)

birth tree A tree planted at the birth of a child in the belief that its welfare has some mysterious connection with the welfare of the child all its life. If the tree thrives, the child will grow strong and prosper. If the tree withers, is felled, or damaged, the person will sicken, die, or be injured. The planting of birth trees is still widely practiced and believed in by European peasantry, especially in Germany. In certain districts in Switzerland an apple tree is planted for the birth of a boy, a pear tree for the birth of a girl. Sometimes a tree already grown is acclaimed the child's tree at birth, and to establish his union with it, the afterbirth and the umbilical cord are either buried beneath it or bound into a cleft that has been made to receive them. The birth tree is a living practice and belief among the Ainus, the Papuans, the Dyaks of Borneo, the Balinese, the Maoris of New Zealand, in various parts of Africa, and also among certain North American Indians. It occurs as a motif in the folktales of England, France, Germany, Italy, and Russia. There is so indistinguishable a line between birth tree and life token that the birth tree is often called life tree. See AFTERBIRTH; LIFE TOKEN.

birthwort Any plant (genus *Aristolochia*) with stimulant tonic roots, now used principally in aromatic bitters. Hippocrates (5th century B.C.) recommends birthwort in the treatment of women, for pains in the side, and ulcers. Dioscorides (1st century A.D.) first recommended this plant as an aid in birthing and described three species: round-rooted or female with bitter leaves and white flowers; long-rooted or male with heavily scented purple flowers; and *A. clematitis*. Pliny said if taken with beef immediately after conception it assures birth of a male child. Fishermen of Campania used it to kill fish so that they might scoop them from the surface of the water. The property for which it was named, both in Greek and English, that of facilitating birth, was least often mentioned; its principal use was on wounds and as an antidote for poison. It was also believed to drive out demons. This explains its use in hiccough, convulsion, epilepsy, melancholy, and paralysis. Besides being useful in treatment of female ills, it was recommended for all manner of complaints of the teeth, liver, spleen, loins, lungs, and for diseases of the skin.

Bisan (Toba *Boru ni Hapur*) In Malay belief, the spirit of the camphor: a female spirit which assumes the form of a cicada. Not only do the camphor hunters speak a special language, *bahasa kapor,* while in the jungle, but they propitiate the camphor spirit. On the first night of the expedition a white cock is sacrificed and a conversation with the Bisan is recited by the pěnghulu (leader). When seeking camphor men always throw a portion of their food into the jungle for Bisan, who if not properly propitiated, will send the hunters home empty-handed.

Bishamonten The Japanese God of Riches: one of the Seven Gods of Luck. See JAPANESE FOLKLORE. [JLM]

biter bit The motif of a number of folktales in which a cruelty or other misdeed boomerangs back to the originator. Sometimes even an unthinking remark or wish is revisited on the sayer. Typical is a story from the *Jātaka* in which a quail beseeches a wonderful and mighty elephant not to trample on her young. The elephant happens to be the Buddha incarnate, at the head of a herd of 80,000 elephants. He stands over the fledglings and protects them while the herd passes by. But the quail's next encounter is not so fortunate. As a certain single elephant approaches, again she beseeches the mighty one not to trample on her young. This elephant, however, deliberately crushes the young birds with his foot, saying, "What can you do to me?" Whereupon the little mother quail in sequence befriends a crow, a fly, and a frog, who in return for her kindnesses, attack the elephant. The crow picks out his two eyes; the fly lays eggs in the eye-sockets and the maggots feed upon the sore flesh. Then in pain and thirst the elephant hears the frog croak upon the mountain top. Following the sound he climbs the mountain seeking water; the frog croaks again at the foot of the mountain and the elephant falls over the precipice and is killed. Thus was the biter bit.

Biter Bit is the title of a Serbian folktale which begins with an old man's remark that he wished it would please God to send him a hundred sons!—with the result that he eventually finds himself the father of no fewer. It is a long story recounting the old man's search for a hundred wives for his hundred sons, his promise to a giant obstructing the wedding-party to give him what he has forgotten at home, only to discover that this is his eldest son. The next biter bit, however, is the giant. He teaches the young man, thus fallen into his power, many magical skills and transformations, only to be outdone by his pupil in the end, caught, and destroyed.

bitter water Holy water, mixed with dust from the floor of the tabernacle, used to blot out a curse written by the priest after being spoken, and finally swallowed by a woman accused of adultery: a chastity ordeal (*Num.* v, 11–31) of the Hebrews, the only judicial ordeal mentioned in detail in the Bible. The bitter water, containing both the dust of the holy place and the ink of the words of the curse, would, if the woman were guilty of adultery, cause her thigh and her belly, the guilty parts, to rot. In fact, however, the ordeal served as a means of obtaining circumstantial evidence, where the husband had only a jealous suspicion, the guilty woman fearing to go through with the ordeal, the innocent victim of jealousy being absolved by the ritual. The ordeal of bitter water would have no result if the husband too were guilty of adultery; Johanan ben Zakkai (c. 60–70 A.D.) suspended the rite because the number of adulterous husbands had become so great as to make the ordeal pointless. Similar chastity tests are known elsewhere in the world. The Gold Coast ordeal in like circumstances makes use, however, of a really poisonous substance; the threatened results are the same, and women often confess to avoid the consequences of swallowing the drink. See ORDEAL.

Bitter Withy An English carol based on a legend of the childhood of Jesus, in which he goes out to play ball, meets three young aristocrats who refuse to play with the stable-born son of a simple maid, leads them across a bridge of sunbeams from which they fall and are drowned, and is whipped by his mother with a willow switch when he goes home. He curses the willow, saying, "The bitter withy that causes me to smart shall be the very first tree to perish at the heart." Fragments of the tale and of the song have survived in the United States.

black and white sails A folktale motif (Z130.1) in which the color of the sails on an approaching ship indicates good or bad news: one of a group of motifs (Z130–133) involving color symbolism. The classic example occurs in the Greek story of Ægeus. Theseus, returning from the Minotaur adventure, forgot the promise to his father to change the black sails of mourning which carried the young victims to Crete to white sails if he were returning safe; and when the watching father saw the ship returning with black sails still spread, he took the sign to mean his son was dead and threw himself into the sea in sorrow and despair. Another famous use of the black and white sails motif is found in a late version of the Tristram and Iseult story. Tristram, dying in Brittany of a poisoned arrow wound, sent for his old love, Iseult of Ireland. The sign of her coming was to be a white sail on the ship. His wife, Iseult of Brittany, kept watch for the ship, and jealous and fearful of her famous rival, told Tristram that the sail was black. He died of shock and grief.

Black Bear One of the guardian spirits and supernatural powers of Osage Indian religion; also one of certain animals who symbolize strength and courage to the Osage. His name is Wacabe. And he is also their specific symbol of old age and longevity. Black Bear is the subject of many Osage ceremonial songs and wígies connected with the Rite of Vigil. (The wígies are the recited parts of the rituals which relate the traditions of the people.) Certain of the wígies narrate how Black Bear first performed all the symbolic acts used by the Osage in preparation for their supplications to the invisible powers for aid in overcoming their enemies.

These first acts were performed when "The male black bear, he that is without blemish/ Fell to meditating upon himself." He then performed the six sacred acts: plucked and gathered the grasses together into a pile, tore down and broke up branches of the redbud trees and gathered the pieces into a pile, also the gray arrow-shaft tree and the never-dying willow, tore open the hummock with his paws, disclosing the holy soil, and gathered together seven stones in a little pile. Then Black Bear sought and found a cave in which to rest, "the mysterious house of the bear" that excludes the light of day, and there "He put down his haunches/ To rest for a period of seven moons."

The wígie continues with the Black Bear's bestowal of old age and long life upon the little ones (i.e. the people). When the seven moons had passed and Black Bear once again beheld his own body, he said, "Lo, my flesh has sunken to nothing.../ I am a person of whom the little ones should make their bodies/ They should make of me an emblem of old age.../ These my toes that are folded together/ I have made to be the sign of old age/ When the little ones make of me their bodies/ They shall live to see their toes folded together with age, . . ./ They shall be free from all causes of death/ They shall cause themselves to be difficult to overcome by death." The reference to the people making their bodies of the black bear probably means acceptance by them of the black bear as life symbol. The wígie continues with pointing out the wrinkled ankles of the bear as he emerges from his hibernation, the loosened muscles of thigh, abdomen, arm, and chin, the prominent ribs, the scanty hair. It concludes with the poetic description of how the bear moved to the door of his cave and saw the whole land covered with mist, how he heard the sound of the birds and stepped out onto the earth, leaving seven footprints in the soft spring mud. These seven footprints too symbolize certain valorous war deeds of the people. Then the Black Bear came to a place where the sun was warm and "the grass rustled to the tread of his feet," and he stood on the bank of a river where Beaver was already at work. The rest of the wígie is devoted to Beaver's symbolic acts.

Black, Black, Black or *Black Is the Color of My True Love's Hair* A traditional love song of the southern mountains of the United States, sung to several tunes, and characterized by the farewell fidelity theme.

> I love the ground whereon she stands . . .
> I love my love and well she knows
> I love the grass whereon she goes
> If she on earth no more I see
> My life will quickly fade away.

The original has been rearranged by J. Niles in the fashion of a typical Elizabethan love song, but no English original is known. The one line "Black is the color of my true love's hair," found in an old sea song, seems to be unrelated to this American mountain love song.

black drink A decoction made from *Ilex vomitoria*: drunk as an emetic by the Creeks, Chickasaw, and other southeastern Indian tribes of the United States for ceremonial purification. It is also used as a stimulant, and to induce visions. [EWV].

Black Hactcin One of the most powerful of the hactcin or supernaturals of the Jicarilla Apache Indians of the Southwest. Black Hactcin is identified with the East, or with darkness and night. He is the leader of the hactcin in the underworld, the creator of man, birds, and water-beings, who gave animals and birds their way of life. [EWV]

Black Jack David A ballad from southern Illinois, also called *Gypsy Davy*, resembling (and probably a corrupt version of) *The Gypsy Laddie* (Child #200). The Illinois ballad has been confounded to some extent with the game-song *Weevily Wheat*.

Black Tamanous The cannibal spirit who inspired the Cannibal Society of the North Pacific Coast Indians: one of the monsters the Transformer did not kill when ridding the earth of evil beings. [EWV]

blanket divided A European folktale motif (J121) in which a man gives his aging father half of an old blanket (quilt, rug, carpet) to keep him warm. The man's small son appropriates the other half and puts it away. When questioned, the child tells his father that he is saving it for him when he too becomes old. The man, thus unwittingly reproved by his child, is ashamed of his ingratitude.

blarney Cajolery; the gift of a cajoling tongue; also, in verb usage, to cajole, wheedle, flatter: from the Blarney Stone in Blarney Castle in the village of Blarney, County Cork, Ireland, about 4½ miles west of Cork. Whoever kisses this stone will "never want for words;" forever after he possesses the cajoling tongue and the gift of skilful lying without detection. The stone is set in the parapet of Blarney Castle, built by Cormac MacCarthy in the 15th century. The magic in the stone was revealed to Cormac by Clíodna herself. Cormac was worried about a lawsuit. But Clíodna told him, "Kiss the stone you come face to face with in the morning, and the words will pour out of you." So when Cormac woke, he walked forth and kissed the stone; the words came out; he won the lawsuit. Then for fear all Ireland would be kissing it and be troubled with easy speech, he carried it up to the parapet and set it where it is today. To kiss it now, one must climb to the top of the castle and lower himself head down over the edge to reach it. An iron grating safeguards the visitors, but most of them feel safer if someone holds onto each foot while he hangs upside down for the kissing.

Blessing Way A religious ceremony, held for purposes of curing, by the Navaho Indians of the southwestern United States. The Blessing Way is the procedure which the Holy People first followed when they met to create human beings. [EWV]

blind dupe A folktale motif (K333.1; K863; K1081.1; K1081.2; K1081.3) associated especially with North American Indian stories, but prominent also in European, Semitic, and Oceanic legend and mythology. Isaac, blind in his old age, duped by Jacob into bestowing on him the blessing intended for the first-born Esau, is probably one of the best known blind dupes in the legends of the world. The blind Hoder of Teutonic mythology, tricked into killing Balder, is another. This incident of the Balder myth (K863) is in the series of fatal deception motifs (K800–999). Another European usage of the idea is represented in motif K1081.1, in which someone tells a group of blind men that he is giving some money to one of them which he wants divided among them all. He gives it to none. Each one, then, receiving nothing, believes that he is being cheated by one or more of the others and they fight.

The blind dupe occurs in North American Indian tales of the North Pacific Coast, Plateau, MacKenzie, Plains, and Woodlands areas. The Menomini tale of the *Deceived Blind Men* (K1081.2; K1081.3) and the Smith Sound Eskimo story of the *Deceived Blind Man* (K333.1) are both typical.

blinding In both early and advanced stages of culture down to the Middle Ages, infringement of law was punished, at times, by blinding the criminal, putting out one or both eyes. This particular state was indeed a symbol of death. The laws of England at an early period prescribed blinding as a punishment for rape; in Uganda, putting out the eyes of a person is common; among the Iroquois, the adulterer was so treated. Examples of blinding in Biblical times may be mentioned: *Gen.* xix, 11 (the vicious Sodomites stricken); *Jer.* xxxix, 7 (Nebuchadnezzar puts out the eyes of Zedekiah, King of Judah); *Jud.* xvi, 21 (the Philistines blind Samson). In the first case, the plight of the Sodomites appears to be a judgment.

Blinding has been carried out not only as a punishment but from motives of revenge, reprisal, ambition, or jealousy. We find instances of blinding in Greek and Roman mythology: the one-eyed giant, Polyphemus was blinded by Odysseus; Orion was blinded for rape, and Œdipus put out his own eyes in horror at having committed both murder and incest. Blinding is found in the *Arabian Nights* and in other Eastern narratives. It occurs also in the folktale, an example of which may be found in Grimm's *The Two Travelers* (#107). Variants of this type (Type 613) are widespread and are found in Scandinavian countries, Russia, Greece, France, Italy, as well as among Negroes and American Indians. [GPS]

blinding the guard A folktale motif (K621) in which the prisoner or victim by some clever ruse blinds his guard or watcher and escapes. The classical example is Odysseus blinding the one-eyed Cyclops, Polyphemus, and escaping from the cave with his companions under the bellies of the sheep.

The motif occurs in European folktale and among the North American Indians; but its most prevalent occurrence is in the American Negro *Watcher Tricked* stories, versions of which are known in Virginia, North and South Carolina, Georgia, and Jamaica. There are African versions, and a Louisiana Creole version. The St. Helena, S.C., version is typical, in which Bu Wolf is chased by Bu Eagle into a hollow tree; Bu Frog is left to watch the tree while Bu Eagle goes home for his ax; Bu Wolf tricks Bu Frog into looking up, spits tobacco juice in his eyes, and, while Bu Frog runs to the pond to wash his eyes, escapes.

blind man carries lame man A general European folk motif (N886) occurring especally in the strong woman as bride (Type 519) cycle of stories. Typically the bridegroom, unable to cope with the bride on the bridal night (she has sworn to marry no one but her equal in strength) makes an excuse to go outside and sends back in his stead his strong friend and helper, who subdues the bride. Later the woman (usually a princess) discovers the hoax, cuts off the feet of the helper, and drives out her weakling husband. The helper joins up with a blind man. The blind man carries the footless one, and the footless one directs his steps. They journey together until they find the healing water, and are both restored. The helper then returns to his master and reinstates him in his true place. Compare LEGLESS AND BLIND BOYS CURED.

Blind Old Man In the mythology of the Yuma Indians of southern California, the quarreling companion of Kwikumat, the creator. He is not the creator's brother, as in the myths of most Yuman tribes; but he was born at the bottom of the ocean, and was blinded with the salt water as he emerged. See CREATOR BORN AT BOTTOM OF OCEAN.

blind trickster The North American Indian trickster blinded, usually by some trick or blunder of his own. The incident often follows his climbing a tree to stop the creaking of the limbs, getting caught between the limbs, and having to sit in the tree while strangers come along and eat his feast on the ground below. When he finally gets loose there is no food left. So he turns himself into an ant, enters a buffalo skull which he has found, and eats the brains. He transforms himself back into a man, but has forgotten to come out of the skull. His head is stuck in the buffalo skull and he cannot see. In his blindness he feels his way among the trees, asking them how to go, and they direct him. Trickster stories involving the buffalo skull motif (J2131.5.1) and guidance by trees (D1313.4) are common to North American Indians of the Central Woodland, Plains, and Plateau areas.

The Chiricahua Apache Indians have a story about their trickster, Coyote, who got himself a wife without revealing that he was blind, and lost the girl because of his blindness. With her help to guide his aim he had shot a cow; they butchered it; and the girl had put the meat over the fire to cook. She told Coyote to turn the meat over. He could hear it sizzling but he could not find the pieces to turn them. He kept picking up burning coals and dropping them. The girl looked into his face, saw the worms dropping out of the eye-sockets; then she knew that he was blind and ran away. There are also Mescalero and White Mountain Apache and Navaho versions of this story.

Blodenwedd The dawn goddess of Welsh mythology. In the *Mabinogion*, the flower-wife of Llew, created for him by Gwydion and Math, son of Mathonwy, the magician, to circumvent the curse of Arianrhod, who said that Llew should have no wife from any race that peoples the earth. So Gwydion and Math devised for him a wife made from the flowers of the oak and broom and meadowsweet. She was very beautiful, and they named her Blodenwedd, or Flower-Face. But Blodenwedd brought little joy to Llew. She fell in love with a passing hunter (Gronw Pebyr) in Llew's absence, with whom she planned to kill Llew. Llew was invulnerable, but Blodenwedd schemed to discover the one secret means by which his life could be taken. She inveigled Llew into the position which exposed him to her lover, and Gronw killed him. For thus contriving the murder of Llew, Blodenwedd was transformed into an owl to fly by night.

blood Primitive men generally look on blood as being life itself. They see blood flow and the body die and therefore assume that life flows out of the body in a literal sense. Closely allied to this is the belief that the soul or spirit of the being is in his blood, and that when blood escapes the blood-soul escapes too. For these reasons, tabus, superstitions, magical practices, and rituals have grown up in great number in connection with blood. Blood accidentally spilled must be carefully and completely disposed of lest a sorcerer use it to work magic against its owner. It is burned or, when the owner is a king or man of importance, swallowed by underlings kept for that purpose. Malignant spirits, witches, devils, werewolves can be rendered harmless by securing a drop or two of their blood. The blood of human beings and of many animals must not fall on the ground, for it will impregnate the earth with the soul or spirit of the owner, thus making the ground on which it falls dangerous ground. It is believed that the soul of the owner will forever afterwards be there ready to work harm on intruders. For these reasons many people abstain from eating or drinking the blood of animals, lest the spirit of the animal enter into them. The Estonians, some American Indians, and Jews carefully bled food animals so that the eaters would not be contaminated by the animal spirits.

But more commonly the reverse is the practice. Since the blood contains the soul and animus of the owner, and since by the drinking of the blood his spirit and animus becomes a part of the drinker, many people have practiced blood-eating and -drinking to enrich themselves. The blood of a courageous father will be fed to his son to make him courageous too; the blood of a healthy and strong child will be given to a weak and sick one. Men in battle will drink the blood of fallen heroes, friends or foes, to add the store of courage and might of the hero to their own. Some of the Australian aborigines regularly drink the blood of certain of their warriors noted for bravery before they go into battle. And likewise the blood (and flesh) of certain animals is eaten so that the special qualities of those animals may pass to the human beings partaking of it. Norwegian hunters drank of the blood of bears to secure strength; Hottentots drink the blood of lions to ensure bravery, and conversely avoid that of hares lest they acquire timidity. In the Germanic *Kudrun* Hagen slew a fierce animal and drank its blood to become "exceeding strong."

Blood being life can likewise, according to primitive thought, protect or restore life. Blood is consequently widely used by the folk as medicine. Leprosy was generally treated by bathing the person afflicted in blood. Stories of this practice abound from early Egyptian times through the Middle Ages, the most famous of which is the often-told story of Constantine the Great. In folktales generally, blood appears almost as frequently as the Water of Life as the means of restoring the dead. The widespread tales of the *Two Brothers* and *Faithful John* contain accounts of the blood bath used to reanimate men turned to stone and to restore the dead to life. Sigurd became invulnerable by bathing in the dragon's blood. In the Middle Ages blood was also given as a treatment for epilepsy. A 12th century legend describes how the blood of Thomas à Becket, placed on the eyes of a blind woman, restored her sight. Such beliefs in the efficacy of blood are behind European practices of pouring blood into holes bored in graves "to feed the dead" and of revenants slipping in at night to suck the blood of the living.

Since blood contains the life and soul of its owner, it is often an instrument of vengeance. A dead body bleeds in the presence of its murderer, for instance. According to a well-known medieval legend Richard Lion Heart came upon the dead body of his father on the battlefield of Le Mans. As he stood looking at it, it began to bleed. Richard, conscience-stricken and feeling that he had caused his father's death, fled from the place and then organized a crusade to free him from the sin of murder. Stories abound of murderers trying in vain to wash the blood of their victims from their hands, or from their clothes. One of the most dramatic stories of the indelible blood stains is often connected with the Devil. The Devil is cut by broken glass as he escapes from the cathedral at the elevation of the host. His blood drops on the stone windowsill leaving stains that no one can eradicate.

Special fears and consequently tabus have to do with menstrual blood. The belief is general that such blood is caused by the bite of a snake, or lizard, or some other such animal, or by the bite of a malignant spirit. To the primitive mind it is abnormal, and therefore to be doubly feared since it is both abnormal blood and the blood of a woman. It is a common practice to isolate women at these times. Some tribes suspend menstruating women in a cage away from contact with the earth, so that they can contaminate nothing. The calamities that would result from a menstruating woman breaking her seclusion are enough to disrupt the courses of nature itself. Compare the list in Pliny's *Natural History.*

Blood has played a large part in the rituals of most religions. The ritual of drinking the blood of the god is based on the belief that the qualities of the god are so transmitted to the worshipper. The sacredness of the Grail in many of the Grail stories comes from the belief that it once contained the blood of Christ. It is consequently a life-giving vessel.

The most common of all religious rituals is that of sacrifice to the gods and basically every sacrifice is a blood (not flesh) sacrifice. One propitiates the gods by giving the best—the blood of one's first-born. In later stages of society animals are substituted, their blood poured in libations, or allowed to run over the altar of the god. It is significant that often the flesh is eaten by those making the sacrifice. Likewise in many religions the god gives the blood of his son in sacrifice to mankind. And so the blood sacrifice becomes a covenant.

Since blood is so powerful an agent, it is natural that man should use it as a positive instrument in securing closer ties among his kind and in sealing compacts. Broadly speaking, blood covenant is a term applied to any agreement ratified by the use of blood of the contracting parties. This blood may be drunk, eaten mingled with food, smoked, bathed in, mingled together and let flow in the earth. Essential to the covenant is an exchange of blood, so that one party to the contract comes into contact with the blood of the other. In later stages of culture an actual contract may be written in blood or signed in blood. The blood covenant is a much more binding agreement than such temporary covenants as food or salt covenants, for it merges the souls of the contracting parties. To primitive man its validity comes from the fact that neither party can work harm on the other without its reacting on the doer since each through his blood is fused with the other. A common form of blood covenant is that between two or more persons entered into to seal a compact or to bind them in a common cause. The ritual consists in partaking of each other's blood by the contracting parties, or of sharing the blood of a neutral person or animal. The Boumali, for example, seal a peace between two villages by assembling all the inhabitants of each, then killing a slave, dividing the body into two halves, one half for each village, and then each person present eating a bit of the flesh and drinking a bit of the blood. Tertullian records that Catiline and his fellow conspirators mingled their bloods in a cup of wine and drank it as a mutual pledge of unity.

The most common type of blood covenant is blood brotherhood, practiced by virtually all people in some form or other. It owes its necessity to the fact that tribal blood ties (actual kinship) are very strong and that members of a family are bound to protect, and if necessary, avenge one another. One who had no brothers was at a disadvantage. He, therefore, entered into a blood covenant, blood brotherhood, with another like himself needing protection. This covenant made them legal brothers, brothers-in-fact; one married the "brother's" widow (if the tribe had such a custom), inherited his "brother's" property, etc. The rite varies among peoples of the world, but it always involves the exchange of blood. A common Germanic ritual will illustrate. Two men who are to perform the rite make an arch of turf, leaving the ends attached to the earth; then, crawling under the arch, they open the veins in their wrists allowing the bloods to mingle and flow to the earth under the arch; then they crawl out through the arch, born anew from mother earth, forever brothers. Chiefs and leaders took advantage of this rite to secure the utmost in loyalty and service from their followers by entering into a blood covenant with each of them. Such a group had not only a bond with the leader but a common tie among themselves. Out of such groups develop the organized bands of warriors, such as the *comitatus* in Germanic society, and ultimately the Irish Red Branch, the Peers of Charlemagne, the Knights of Prussia, and the Knights of the Round Table.

References:

Strach, H. L., *Der Blutaberglaube.* Munich, 1892.

Hartland, E. S., *Primitive Law.* London, 1924.

Trumbull, H. C., *The Blood Covenant.* Philadelphia, 1898.

Frazer, J. G., *The Golden Bough.*

Crawley, Ernest, *The Mystic Rose.* London, 1902

MacEdward Leach

The folklore of hereditary transmission through the blood is based essentially in the concept of blood-brotherhood, which is extended to include family, nation, and race, with their actual or supposed characteristics. The "Joe Miller" about the Englishman who received a transfusion of blood from a Scotchman and then (and therefore) refused to pay for the transfusion illustrates this common belief that "blood will tell." From such verbal concepts as "blue blood" and "bad blood" a popular belief, influenced by the figurative language, has developed and burgeoned into pseudo-scientific sociological and anthropological theory. The idea that blood transmits skin color, nose shape, hair form, or any other physical characteristic that may be used as a racial determinant has been proved to be pure myth. Yet so deeply is it ingrained in some groups that during World War II the American Red Cross, to avoid the possible psychic injury a wounded white soldier from the South might sustain from getting a transfusion of "Negro blood," segregated the blood obtained from white and Negro donors.

Blood-Clot-Boy A Plains Indian popular tale of a boy miraculously born from a clot of blood that is deposited in a pot or other receptacle. In the numerous versions collected from the Plains tribes the clot of blood is often brought into the lodge by an old man who has been ill-treated by his son-in-law. The boy grows rapidly and, despite the warnings of his aged grandparent, sets out on a series of adventures to avenge the latter. Blood-Clot-Boy is also known among some California Indian tribes; in California versions a boy is born from a clot of blood found by an old woman after her daughter has been killed by a bear. When he grows to manhood Blood-Clot-Boy disobeys his grandmother, goes adventuring and avenges his mother's (or parents') untimely death. [EWV]

blood horns Elk horns in the velvet: eaten as a medicine and tonic by men among the Wulakai of Manchuria. Elk horn in the velvet is believed to be especially potent in cases of weakness, impotence, and sterility. The idea is that the blood of the elk rises into the new young horns at this time, which therefore contain the strength and life-power of the stag (see *JAFL* 46: 283).

blood on the moon An evil omen: the moon's color during a lunar eclipse, when the moon is in the earth's shadow and shining dully by refracted light. Omens such as this are of great import; any celestial phenomenon so extraordinary as an eclipse or a comet is thought to have bearing on many lives. The belief is mirrored often in literature: Horatio speaks in *Hamlet* of "stars with trains of fire and dews of blood" among the other portents of "fierce events" before Cæsar's fall.

bloodstone A stone of green chalcedony containing red spots. It is the birthstone of March or Aries. Its name derives from the color of its spots and hence it is a potent remedy for hemorrhage. An early Christian legend says the spots were caused by the blood of Christ falling on a piece of jasper at the foot of the cross. It is credited with many magical properties. It guards a man from deception, yet whatever he says will be believed. It is a calming influence, removes discord, and assuages the wrath of kings. Before it all bonds

will be broken, all doors opened, and, if necessary, walls will be rent asunder. It will foretell the future, cause rain, thunder, lightning, tempest, and earthquake, and turn the sun red. It preserves the general health of the wearer, cures inflammatory illnesses, and, mixed with a little honey, removes tumors.

Blow the Man Down A halyard chantey known to British and American sailors in two main versions: one chiefly devoted to experiences on ships of the Black Ball Line, the most famous of the packet lines between New York and Liverpool; the other, to adventure ashore on Paradise Street in Liverpool. Negro seamen and dock workers also sang the song, sometimes substituting the phrase "knock a man down," for the words of the title and refrain. In the Bahamas it is still sung by Negro fishermen for "launching" their boats, by which they mean hauling them up on shore in the fall. See CHANTEY.

Bluebeard Title and villain of a very widespread European folktale in which Bluebeard (a king, wealthy merchant, or sorcerer) marries, one after the other, three (or seven) beautiful sisters. He hands his young wife the keys to the castle and departs, saying that she may unlock any door in the place except one certain one. She disobeys, opens the forbidden door, beholds a number of corpses (or a basin of blood). The egg she holds in her hand, which she was told to keep intact, breaks and betrays her disobedience, or the key becomes indelibly bloody. Bluebeard appears and kills her (or chains her in a dungeon to eat only human flesh). The same sequence of events befalls the next sister (or sisters). But the youngest and last, who also disobeys and unlocks the forbidden door, either kills Bluebeard herself with a saber (Basque version), or is saved by a page who kills Bluebeard and marries her (Estonian), or by her cleverness prevents Bluebeard from discovering she has looked into the room, resuscitates the sisters or delivers them from the dungeon, hides them in a sack of "gold" which Bluebeard must carry to her father, then herself dons feathers and escapes, while the brothers sent to rescue her arrive suddenly and murder the murderer. This is Grimm's story *Feather-bird* or *Fitch's Bird*. In the Norwegian version, the murderous husband is a troll; in the Italian, the Devil himself. In a very ancient Greek story he is Death, who devours corpses, and kills the living girls who refuse to eat his fare. In several northern versions, the brothers rescue the sisters with the aid of animals.

The prominent feature of the tale is the tabu motif and the presentation of the horrible fate of those who break a tabu. The happy ending is said by many scholars to be a comparatively recent fairy tale accretion. More specifically, however, it is the forbidden chamber (C611), forbidden door (C611.1) motifs which are important here. Bluebeard motif (S62.1) is the common name given to traditional murderous husband incidents.

Bluejay Creator-Transformer-Trickster of the coastal North American Indian tribes of Washington and Oregon and several inland Plateau groups. Many of the creative deeds and misdeeds credited to Raven by the northern North Pacific coast tribes, and to Mink by British Columbia coastal peoples, are assigned to Bluejay by the tribes farther south. Bluejay's adventures are recounted in long tale-cycles that depict the hero as always anxious to outdo his rivals. Bluejay is also an important character in the winter ceremonies of the Plateau peoples. Among the Jicarilla Apache of the southwestern United States, Bluejay is the hero of a long cycle in which various of his adventures are recounted, and in which he is given the power to ordain a way of life for all the birds and animals. [EWV]

blues A type of sorrow song of the American Negroes ("the po' man's heart disease") which emerged in the South shortly after the Civil War, growing out of the work songs, hollers, and spirituals, and popularized about 1912 by the publication of some of the songs by W. C. Handy. First essentially a vocal music, the blues have spread over into instrumental types, such as boogie-woogie, and into jazz forms far removed from the folk, but are also still being created in a folk manner as songs.

Musically, the blues are distinguished by an 8 or 12 bar structure (16 and 20 bars in later stages), by a strongly antiphonal quality, by the syncopation and polyrhythm characteristic of Negro music, by simple harmonic progressions, and by a slight flatting of the third and seventh intervals of the scale. These latter are the "blue notes." Singers make use of subtle variations of pitch and rhythm, portamento, and a wide range of tone coloration. Certain passages may be hummed or rendered in nonsense syllables called "scat." Instrumental accompaniment (by guitar, piano, or various combinations) improvises melodic and rhythmic patterns to the singer's lead or around a solo instrument, and achieves enormous tonal variety by the use of vibrato, mutes, and ordinarily non-musical instruments such as washboards, jugs, etc.

The poetry of the blues—the tender, ironic, bitter, humorous, or topical expression of a deprived people —tells of "careless love," of the woman who has lost her man or the no-good woman a man can't forget, of the train whistle in the night and the longing to go with it, of floods and cyclones, of jails and chain gangs and levee camps, of lonesome roads, river boats, back alleys, and barrel houses, of hard times and hard work.

The stanza consists typically of a statement repeated one or more times, sometimes with slight variations, and a gnomic comment or response. This construction, both in the words and in the music that is molded to them, relates to the earlier Negro styles of religious and work singing, with their narrative or call lines and responses, and on back to African singing. The "punch" lines, in their frequently proverbial form, hark back to the widespread African use of proverbs in song and story, and the whole song may be of a double-meaning, allusive character close to the African songs of allusion and derision.

The images are graphic ("The gal I love is chocolate to the bone," "You got a handful of gimme, a mouthful of much obliged," "I've got the world in a jug, the stopper's in my hand") and folk beliefs and animal fables enter into the conceptions.

Singing the blues is one way to say what would not be tolerated in speech. Chain-gang bosses, for instance, will ignore comment in song about the work, the food, the misery of prisoners, that would bring swift reprisal if spoken. So long as the picks and hammers keep swinging to the music, the words of the song don't matter, except to those who sing them.

You have to feel blue to sing the blues, Negroes say. "The blues is nothing but a good man feeling bad." "Got dem blues but too damn mean to cry." The blues will help you when you're down in trouble. You sing about what you have on your mind, about what happens to you, or what you wish would happen.

The earliest and simplest of the blues songs were country blues sung by anonymous singers with regional variations in different parts of the South. The best of the singers gradually found larger audiences in the large cities, where the songs began to deal with more sophisticated themes. Then the blues and the singers moved northward, chiefly up the Mississippi River from New Orleans to Chicago, and east and west, the music winning advocates among young white musicians en route, and eventually, with growing acceptance, wide recording and imitation, losing its folk character in some aspects.

The great blues singers have been mostly women—Ma Rainey, "the mother of the blues," Bessie Smith, "the empress of the blues," Trixie Smith, Victoria Spivey, and numerous others—whose singing was accompanied by the instrumental virtuosity of the great jazz players. Among the songs they made popular are *Careless Love, Levee Camp Moan, Empty Bed Blues, Young Woman Blues, Pallet on the Floor, Moonshine Blues, See See Rider,* etc. See JAZZ. [TCB]

Blue-Tail Fly An American Negro minstrel song dating from the 1840's and combining a refrain that is probably authentic Negro folk song ("Jimmie crack corn and I don't care") with ballad verses of a hack song writer of the period. Its theme, behind the gay tune, is the slave's carefree reaction to the death of his master as a "victim of the blue-tail fly."

Blunderbore In English folklore, a giant tricked into killing himself by Jack the Giant-Killer. Jack hid a bag under his vest and stuffed into it so much that the giant was hard put to keep up with his "eating." Then Jack relieved himself by plunging a knife into the bag, releasing the contents. The stupid giant did likewise and died.

Bóann In Old Irish mythology, queen of the Tuatha Dé Danann, the divine race of Ireland, known also as the *side* or people of the hills; wife of Dagda, the Good, and mother of Angus Og. She lived in the great city of the *side*, Bruġ na Bóinne, the City of Bóann. Once Bóann went to look into the marvelous well of water that was in Sid Neċtan. This well had the reputation that no one could look into it (except Neċtan himself or one of his water-carriers) or the two eyes would burst out of his head. Bóann boasted that the well could have no power over her, and she went to it, and not only looked into it but walked round it three times *tuatal,* i.e. counter-sunwise. Three waves rose out of the well and took one eye, one hand, and one thigh from Bóann. In shame she ran toward the sea. But the waters followed her and drowned her at last in the mouth of the river that now bears her name, the river Boyne.

Boar's Head Carol One of various English feasting carols of the 15th century, sung as the festive dish with the boar's head was borne to the banquet. A boar's head carol in the Bodleian Library is the only surviving page of the collection printed in 1521 by Wynkyn de Worde. The form is macaronic, the burden in Latin. See CAROL.

Boas, Franz (1858–1942) German-American anthropologist and ethnologist, who together with his many eminent pupils made a monumental contribution to the study of the North American aborigines, including voluminous folktale collections. He was born in Westphalia, educated at Heidelberg, Bonn, and Kiel (1877–1881), and in 1883–1884, made a scientific journey through Baffin Land. From 1899 until his retirement in 1937, he was professor of anthropology at Columbia University; and from 1901–1905, curator of ethnology at the American Museum of Natural History. The most important of his many journeys of investigation to Mexico, Puerto Rico, and North America, was the Jesup North Pacific Expedition which he planned and whose reports he edited. This expedition revealed interesting connections between north Asiatic and northwest American cultures. Boas' *Indianische Sagen* (1895), one of his most important works, takes up the question whether folklore similarities were due to "psychic unity" or to diffusion. In a brilliant analysis he proves that only the latter theory could explain his British Columbian material. In *Tsimshian Mythology* (1916) he reconstructed the history of the tribe from its lore and created a virtual "tribal autobiography." Boas had an exhaustive knowledge of the tales of the Kwakiutl Indians and another of his notable works was the *Social Organization and Secret Societies of the Kwakiutl Indians* (1897). Other works include *Baffin Land* (1885), *The Central Eskimo* (1888), *Indians of British Columbia* (1888–1892), *The Mind of Primitive Man* (1911), *Kultur und Rasse* (1913), *Anthropology and Modern Life* (1928), and *Race, Language and Culture* (1940).

Boastful Deerslayer Title of one of a distinctive group of moralistic folktales found especially in Estonia, Lithuania, Finland, and other Baltic localities. A man kills a stag. When he is reminded that God was his helper, he denies that the stag is God's gift. He killed it himself, he says, with no help from anyone. While he is making this boastful declaration, the wounded deer gets up and runs off. This story (Type 830) is representative of a number of other Baltic tales based on punishments for scoffing at church teachings (Q225). Analogs are found in Nigerian Bantu folktale in which the tabu against refusing credit to the god is always punished by the god (C53).

Bochica The great culture hero of the ancient Chibcha Indians of Colombia, who came from the east and wandered across their country in the guise of an old bearded man. He instructed their ancestors in the moral laws and taught them the most essential manual arts. Many caves and natural "footprints" are associated with his passing. He has become one of the major gods of the Chibcha pantheon. [AM]

bocor or **bokor** The Haitian Negro term for a practitioner of magic, who is distinguished from other workers with the supernatural by the fact that he has acquired his powers by the purchase of spirits rather than by having had the gods come to him of their own accord or through inheritance. The bocor is outside the vodun hierarchy; unlike vodun priests, his power come primarily from the spirits of the dead he controls as his "messengers." Like the vodun priest, however, he is also a diviner. [MJH]

Bodb (pronounced bōv) In Old Irish mythology, one of the Tuatha Dé Danann, eldest son of the Dagda, and a king of the side, with his headquarters at Sid al Femen in county Tipperary, Munster. He plays an active part throughout the Mythological Cycle. After the battle of Tailtiu, when the Milesians defeated the Tuatha Dé Danann, Bodb was chosen king of the Tuatha Dé for his own great virtues and his sonship to Dagda. It was he who discovered for Angus Og that the sweetheart of his dreams was the swan maiden Caer, and changed Aoife into a demon for her treachery to the children of Lir.

bodhisattva, bodhisat, or **bodhisattwa** In Buddhism, one whose essence is perfect knowledge; title given to those who are believed to be the future Buddhas; one who by the practice of virtues and meditation has arrived at the Bōdhi. The bodhisattvas are usually represented in Indian art as youthful or feminine figures.

body marks Blemishes, moles, dimples, freckles, as distinguished from tattooing, painting, mutilation, are subjects of study by persons learned in astrology, in chiromancy, and in physiognomy. Chaucer, a master of the astrology of his day, reported of the lusty Wife of Bath who was Martial and Venerian, that she was gattoothed, bore the print of St. Venus seal, and the mark of Mars upon her face and in another private place. Christian saints who are very holy have at times been honored by the stigmata, marks identical with the marks of Christ when crucified. In India the interpretation of body marks is known as samudrika. Buddha had 32 lucky and 80 minor marks. The virtuous minister Gunaśarman decided that because the beautiful Sundarī had a mole on her nose, she must also have one on her breast, and therefore would have rival wives. Vararuchi got into trouble because from his knowledge of the arrangement of the auspicious marks in the portrait of the queen he decided she must also have one on her waist and painted it there. English women who have a mole on the upper side of the right temple above the eye will have a good and happy future in marriage. Persians, Arabs, and Western Europeans have thought that moles were signs of great beauty in women. Artificial beauty marks are still popular in some communities. If a man in India have two lines on his forehead he will live for 40 years, if three lines, 75 years, and if four lines, 100 years.

A dimple while smiling means a loose character; a double or broad chin means a strong character; a thin rounded chin or long ears indicate a licentious character or mark a man who wants the love of women. A man with a deep horizontal line at the top of his nose wants to be authoritative. A woman whose little toe overlaps the next or does not touch the ground is morally bad and sexually promiscuous. Among some of the tribes of southern India a curl on the head is lucky, unless it is on the back of the head or near the right temple. Tamil farmers are said to believe that a woman will become a widow if the curl is on her forehead and that the oldest brother of her husband will die if the curl is on the back of her head.

The erotologists of China, India, Peru, and ancient and modern Europe have collected large quantities of lore which is sometimes reduced to a system. In India a woman with a chakrá, flag, umbrella, or lotus on her hand, or with moles on her left breast, is auspicious. Communities which hide the sexual parts are generally agreed that a long nose in a man means a long organ, and that fat men have small organs. In some places a woman with small feet is thought to have small organs, in others small mouths mean small organs. Physical anthropologists have drawn interesting conclusions from their study of the proportions between the several parts of the body, and psychiatrists have studied not only the physical types but also the psychological effects of stigmata, real or imagined. The lore of body marks is contained in many popular rimes such as "Mole on the arm, have a rich farm; mole on the neck, money by the peck." [RDJ]

Bogarodicza One of the earliest of European folk songs, a war song of Poland, recorded in a manuscript dating from the 13th century.

bogey, bogie, or **bogy** A terrifying spirit of English folklore, of uncertain, but probably hobgoblinish, nature: invoked especially to frighten children. It is usually thought of as "it," and as being black. "The Bogey Man will get you," is a common saying. Bogey itself is a 19th century word, but like all analogous terms—bogle, boggart, pooka, puck, etc.—is probably derived from ME. *bogge* or *bugge,* meaning terror and bugbear, and cognate with the Welsh *bwg* (*bug*) meaning ghost or hobgoblin. Analogous beings in other folklores are the German Bumann or Boggelmann, the Irish bocán or púcá (pooka), the Bohemian bubák, etc.

boggart A hobgoblin or ghost; a supernatural being of English folklore, especially of Lancashire and Yorkshire, very mischievous, sly, and annoying: often invoked to frighten children. Threats of being thrown into some black "boggart-hole" are usually enough to silence the expression of any childish woe. The Lancashire and Yorkshire boggart is equivalent to the Scottish bogle and the puck of general English folklore. There is a typical old Lancashire verse which runs: "Stars is shining/ Moon is breët/ Boggard woănt cum oot toneet."

The boggart is full of tricks and devilment, but seldom works serious harm. Sometimes he walks through the rooms at night, twitches the covers off sleeping people, or raps loudly on the door and never comes in or answers. Sometimes he rearranges the furniture so that people who have to get up in the dark bump into it; or sometimes he lays the baby gently on the floor, just to astonish its parents who find it safely sleeping there in the morning. The boggart is often a helpful kind of spirit to have around the house. He has been known to wash the dishes, milk the cows, feed the horses, or even harness them on occasion. But if he is angered in any way, he will break the cups, upset the cream that has been set for butter, or unfasten the cow or horse to let it wander in the night. Nearly every old English house had its own boggart, variously regarded either as a ghost or as the mischievous trick-playing spirit just described. The boggart of Staining Hall (near Blackford) was the uneasy ghost of a murdered Scotchman; the boggart of Hackensall Hall lived

in the shape of a horse who was a willing worker as long as he was catered to. The people even built him a fire to lie by on cold nights, and if he did not get it he complained loudly, or refused to work. But boggarts are less and less frequently seen and heard today; that is because they are afraid of automobiles.

Boggart's Flitting Title of a Lancashire folktale, also well known all over Europe. It is the story of a farmer who was so annoyed and tormented by a boggart who had taken abode in his house, that he decided to pack up his belongings and move with his wife and children to another place. As they were about to drive off, the man explained to a neighbor, Yes, they were flitting because of the boggart who was making life unendurable, only to hear a voice say, from the top of the loaded wagon, "So you see, Georgey, we're flitting." The man gave up; he decided to remain in his old home rather than undergo the old annoyances in a new place.

Colonel Bogie or **Bogey** An imaginary opponent against whom one competes in games and contests in which a score is made. Colonel Bogie always makes what is considered an average or a good score. The Colonel's original game was golf, where his score, as opposed to par (the score made by perfect play of the hole), was a not-impossible mark for players to aim at.

bogle A hobgoblin or ghost; a supernatural being of Scottish folklore: equivalent to the Lancashire and Yorkshire boggart and the puck of general English folklore, and no doubt a close relative of the Icelandic evil spirit, the puki.

Bogle in the Mill Title of a well-known European folktale in which a bogle took abode in a mill, to the great despair of the miller. He poked holes in the bags of grain so that the grain trickled out, and performed numerous other annoying and troublesome tricks. One day a traveling juggler left his bear in the miller's keeping and the miller put the bear in the mill. The bear didn't like the bogle either and treated him so badly that he left the place. Every year the bogle came back and asked the miller, "Is the big brown cat still here?" The answer was always yes and after the miller said the big brown cat had kittens, the bogle disappeared forever.

This story is said to be originally a Scandinavian story —told everywhere in Norway, Sweden, Finland, Estonia, etc.—introduced to the rest of Europe about 1060 along with a white polar bear which was sent as a present from Iceland to King Svein of Denmark. The story is known also as *The Bear Trainer and His Bear* (K1728; Type 1161) a story in which the bear chases the ogre out of the room, and a year later on learning that "the big white cat" is still there, the ogre goes away forever.

bog-myrtle The Irish *roideog* or *roilleog*: also called sweet willow. An infusion from its branch tips makes a yellow dye, and is also used in tanning. It is the "palm" carried on Palm Sunday in many parts of rural Ireland. It must not be used as a switch for cattle because it is said to have been used as a scourge for Jesus.

Bohinavlle Literally, the Nail of the North: the Lappish name for the North Star. This nail is regarded as supporting the sky. The Samoyeds also call the North Star "The nail of the sky," around which the heavens revolve. [JB]

Boigu The afterworld of the Melanesian people of certain eastern islands of Torres Strait, situated on an island; a happy land of feasting and plenty, where no work has to be done. To reach it the soul must travel under the sea to a place named Beg, and from Beg it is led to Boigu by Terer, the first man.

bolero A famous Spanish couple dance from the province of Castile. It is performed in either 2/4 or 3/4 time to the accompaniment of castanets, guitar, and tambourine. The step is slow and gliding: the woman's steps more varied than the man's, both characterized by sideward leg extension. The common pattern is as follows: *paseo* (promenade), *differencia* (step changed), *travesía* (cross-over), *finale*, and *bien parado*. The bolero is a tender but intoxicating love-making dance, more dignified, less impassioned than the fandango. The boleros have wide distribution in Spain, and are especial favorites in Majorca. [GPK]

Bolte, Johannes (1858–1937) the greatest of all students of the folktale in Germany, and perhaps of the world. His early years were spent largely in making comparative notes of 16th century jestbooks of Germany and in collecting the learned articles of Reinhold Köhler, librarian of the Ducal Library at Weimai, together with his own additions, in a work of three volumes, *Kleinere Schriften* (1898–1900). His principal contribution was five volumes of notes on the Grimms' *Household Tales, Anmerkungen zu den Kinder- und Hausmärchen der Brüder Grimm* (1913–1931). These volumes were issued with the cooperation of George Polivka of Prague, but the work was nearly all Bolte's, Polivka contributing the part on the Slavic lands only. Bolte edited the *Zeitschrift des Vereins für Volkskunde* during the latter half of his life and was a great stimulus to German folklore scholarship, being largely responsible for the development of a group of noted folklorists.

bomor A Malay medicine man usually called in to cure human diseases. The name bomor is used interchangeably with pawang, but the latter is the name usually applied to the class of medicine men which practices magic to ensure good crops, locate ore, and for successful jungle clearing. The bomor determines the treatment of ill patients by means of divination. He makes propitiatory offerings of food to the spirits, uses counter-charms, or strokes the patient to drive out the 190 (or 193) evil influences. He also recalls the patient's soul (sĕmangat) which is wandering when a man is ill.

Bon (1) The pre-Buddhist, shamanistic, devil-charming cult of Tibet which persists with Buddhistic externals. It has been suppressed since the introduction of Buddhism, but it still openly professed in much of eastern and southeastern Tibet where the Chinese administration (brought in to protect the people and their religion from Lāmaism) kept out the influence of the lāmas.

In Bon belief there are 18 chief deities of which the most popular are the red and black demons, the snake devil, and the fiery Tiger god. The chief god is gShenrabs Mi-bo, reputedly a deified priest. The Bon priest's attire during special celebrations is a coat of mail armor decorated with flags and a high hat ornamented with flags, tufts of wool, and effigies of human skulls. Ordinarily, he wears red robes. Sacrifices, substituted for the

sacrificial animal of earlier times, include wool and yak hair and images of men and animals made of dough. The sacred symbol is the swastika with the hooks of the cross reversed.

(2) or **Obon** A Japanese festival of Buddhist origin, celebrated in July, in honor of the spirits of the dead, which return on the days of the festival for entertainment, food, etc. In country areas, only the New Year's feast is more important. The festival is sometimes called the Feast of Lanterns. See JAPANESE FOLKLORE.

Bona Dea The ancient Roman goddess of fertility and of chastity; the prophetic sister, wife, or daughter of Faunus and often called Fauna. She was also known as Fatua, Oma, Damia, and identified with Cybele, Maia, Ge, Ops, Semele, Hecate, and others. Her worship was restricted to women, knowledge even of her name being withheld from men. Yearly on May 1 her festival was held at a ruling magistrate's house and was conducted by vestals. The profanation of this ceremony by P. Clodius in 62 B.C. at Cæsar's home was a *cause célèbre* and led eventually to Cicero's exile. Myrtle, men, and wine were forbidden at the ceremony, the wine actually used being called milk and the wine vessel a honey jar. Later etiological tales explain the circumstances of the ceremony. Her father, Faunus, failing to seduce her even after getting her drunk, whipped her with myrtle rods. He finally had his will of her when he transformed himself into a serpent. According to another story, Fauna became so much the drunkard that her husband, Faunus, beat her to death with myrtle, and then deified her. Her ceremony was held at night. There was a grotto in the Aventine dedicated to her. She usually appears as an old woman with pointed ears, holding a serpent. The Marsian Angitia seems to have been the same goddess in a different locale.

bonang Gong chimes characteristic of Javanese orchestras, tuned in octaves and set in a low horizontal frame, the higher octave designated as male, the lower as female. See CHIMES; GONG.

bones (1) The corpse, particularly the bones, which decay last, is the residence of the physical or animal soul as distinguished from the spiritual soul which enters the body either at the moment of birth or at the moment of baptism. The Chinese have elaborate ceremonies to keep the physical soul out of their houses and contentedly in the tomb or sealed up in it. If the animal soul has sufficient vitality, it will animate the skeleton or skull and commit horrid and revolting crimes—cannibalism, rape, etc.—in the countryside. Bones are thus involved in the systems of beliefs about life tokens, separable souls, and the like.

The bone in the European folktale of the *Singing Bone* (Grimm #28) was taken from the corpse of a murdered brother and fashioned into a flute. When played it accused the murderer. When one of the Indian Yakshini played on a lute made of bones and recited a charm, ascetics who heard her grew horns and fell into the fire. The Yakshini then devoured them. Some of the Australian aborigines are said to bury their dead in trees. When only the skeleton remains they take it down, being careful not to touch the bones, and bury it except for the arm bone which after certain ceremonies is broken and buried separately. Australian "bone pointing" probably has other connections. The Ogowe in Africa beat their corpses until all bones are broken and thus make it impossible for the spirit to return and make trouble for the tribe. The driving of a stake through the body of a criminal or witch buried at the crossroads is part of this system of belief.

Cardinal Newman explained that the bones of saints retain a part of the virtue which was once immanent in the saints' bodies. Saints' bones thus become objects of veneration and are thought to possess great power to cure physical and spiritual ills. South Slav burglars are said to throw the bone of a dead man over the roof to put the inmates to sleep. Blackfoot Indians carried a skull to make themselves invisible. The "hand of glory," a dead or hanged man's hand holding a candle made of human fat, insured invisibility in many parts of the world. Ruthenian burglars remove the marrow from a human shinbone, pour tallow in it, light it, and march three times around the house to put the people to sleep or make themselves invisible; or they may make a flute of the human leg bone and play on it. (Earth from a grave sprinkled around the house has the same effect.) An Indian ascetic, protected by a circle made of the yellow powder of bones did magic on a corpse. Similar beliefs are found in many parts of the world. The widows of the Carrier Indians carried the charred bones of their husbands with them. The bone used by the Sicilian girl to make a hole in the wall so that she may become pregnant by exposing herself to the sun is possibly incidental, though some Indian tribes used bone instruments on girls during puberty ceremonies. The fashioning of olisboi out of bone or ivory in China, Japan, Greece, and Rome may be convenience rather than superstition. The communal bonfire ("bone fire"), originally built for destroying corpses and bones by fire, is now usually an expression of general high spirits after victory or delivery from danger and is connected with folklore about bones only by its name. [RDJ]

☞ The use of bones in divination is world-wide. Astragalomancy, divining by means of small bones, like the vertebræ, has given rise to several series of games: board games like pachisi, dice games, jacks, etc. The cracks in or the formation of the shoulderbone of a sacrificed animal (scapulomancy) give Mohammedan diviners clues with which to read the future.

A common belief, going far back into prehistory and perhaps older than modern man (species *Homo sapiens*), is that preservation of the bones is necessary for the resurrection of man. Bones colored with ocher and preserved in their natural order have been found in the remains of prehistoric man. The *Talmud* says that the bone of Luz, one of the bones of the spine, is indestructible, and that from it the body can be recreated at the resurrection. The skeleton is still figured as the ghostly symbol of spirits; the rattle of bones and chains is heard in many haunted places. The skull and crossbones, symbol of piracy and death, is used to indicate poisonous drugs, poisonous wells, and the like. [JF]

(2) A musical instrument consisting of two long, slightly curved sticks of locust wood, held between fingers and shaken so as to strike together with rhythmical clicking sound like that of castanets: used especially among mountain men of the southern United States. Originally two actual bones, of birds or animals, were used in the same way by plantation Negroes in their music-making. [TCB]

bone-throwing An ancient custom, especially in northern Europe, of hurling gnawed bones during a feast. The trick was to catch them in mid-air and throw them back, so that no one was injured. In medieval Icelandic literature, bone-throwing is referred to as the sport of trolls and giants. In Scandinavia it was a custom more ancient than the literature, and functioned both as sport, punishment, and insult. A lawbreaker was seated lowest at the feast, for instance, and all present were allowed to throw bones at him. And the youngest or weakest of the company was always fair target for the bone-throwers. Bothvar biarki in the *Hrolfssaga* not only saves the boy Hott (later Hialti) from beneath a pile of bones, but catches a bone thrown at the youth and hurls it back with such force that it kills the thrower.

bonga The Santal (India) name for an evil spirit who lives in the hills, trees, or rivers. Bongas are usually female and may be married to or have intercourse with human beings. All dead people become bongas except uninitiated children who become bhūts, and women who die in childbirth and are not cremated. These become churels.

The bonga figures in numerous Santal folktales. In one a prince, imprisoned by his father because he refused to marry, found a bonga maiden beside him when he awoke, agreed to marry her, and was released. In another, a bonga rewarded the good deed of a cowherd by giving him the ability to see bongas and to understand the speech of ants as long as he told no one about the gift. His wife cost him the gift by insisting that he tell her.

Bongo A Trinidad Negro dance for the dead. It is performed at wakes, and also at the "forty days" observation after a death. The rhythms are beaten with sticks on a small wooden bench, or against a short pole held by two men, and played by a third. Bongo songs are principally topical; dancers are both men and women, though the dance is performed by no more than two persons at a time. [MJH]

bonito maidens In the belief of the people of Sa'a (Solomon Islands), maidens who live in pools with the bonito fish and bring them out during the bonito fishing season. These maidens are beautiful, adorned with porpoise teeth, shell money, and shell ornaments. They forewarn the shaman of the appearance of the bonito by giving him a bunch of areca nuts while he is asleep. An altar is built for them and the first bonito caught is laid upon it and is ceremonially washed. Then it is carried to the canoe house, incantations are said over it, and it is baked and eaten by the shaman alone. In folktales sons who have lost their father's prized ivory bonito hooks go to the maidens to retrieve them. See MALAOHU BOYS.

Bonny Bee Hom A Scottish ballad (Child #92) involving the separation of lovers. When the ruby-stone his love has given him turns dark and gray in a foreign land, the lover knows that she is dead and he too dies. See LIFE TOKEN. [MEL]

bon-odori-uta Songs of Japanese peasants sung with dancing for the Obon Festival, or Feast of Lanterns. Many are preserved in *Yamagachoju-ka*, a collection of songs compiled in 1771.

boobrie A fabulous water-bird of Scottish Highland folk belief, which haunts lakes and salt wells.

boogie-woogie (1) A type of piano blues first played by the Negro pianist Jimmy Yancey at Chicago rent parties in the early 1920's: popularized about 1936, and later played in various instrumental combinations. It is characterized by a rhythmic ostinato bass, free rhapsodizing of the right hand, and numerous short figures in varied rhythms, and is frequently made up of 12-measure sections. The various patterns are sometimes described as "traveling," "climbing," "walking," etc. The parties were held to enable the tenants of the house or apartment to pay back rent, and guests were expected to make contributions of money, food, or drinks, or to participate in the impromptu entertainment. The sessions often lasted throughout the night, ending with *Five O'Clock Blues.*

(2) A dance to this music, often of a slow, tensed, attitudinized, and despairing character. See BLUES; JAZZ.

book fetishism Belief in the magical qualities of books or written matter: bibliolatry. The connection of books with the wise men of all ages gives them a share of reverence sometimes approximating superstition. The reverential act of kissing or touching a book such as the Bible, for example, suggests the idea of contagious magic. After that act the mouth can speak only truth. Miniature books, written scrolls, or sentences inscribed on strips of paper are also used as amulets.

Book of Ballymote A late 14th century manuscript of the west of Ireland, containing for the most part historical material. It contains one version of the famous story of the *Birth of Cormac* and also the "Adventures of the Sons of Eochu Muigmedón." This last is of especial folkloristic interest in that it contains the motif of the loathly hag transformed to a beautiful woman by the kiss of the courteous young Niall.

Book of Changes or **I Ching** An ancient Chinese classic: one of the nine books included in the Confucian canon. It contains the Eight Trigrams allegedly copied by the legendary ruler of China, Fu Hsi, from the back of a creature which emerged from the Yellow River. These diagrams correspond to the powers of nature. Supplementary material including definitions, observations, and a commentary by Confucius were added. The book is a mixture of speculation and a system of divination.

Book of Death In Hebrew and Christian legend and belief, the book in which are listed the names of the unrighteous together with their evil deeds. Those so listed will be cast into a lake of fire after death.

Book of Destinies or **Tablet of Destinies** The Babylonian book of life in which Marduk's scribe recorded the fate of the living and the decrees of the ruler of the underworld. Compare BOOK OF LIFE.

Book of Leinster or **Lebor Laigen** A 12th century Irish manuscript containing early histories (especially of Leinster), genealogies, sagas, and poetry. It contains a version (probably 8th century) of the great *Táin Bó Cúailgne* or *Cattle Raid of Cooley*, also the *Exile of the Sons of Usnech*, *Melodies of Buchet's House*, *Destruction of Dinn Ríg*, the *Bórama*, and the grim tale of the fifty captives buried alive around the grave of a son, killed in battle, of Eochu Muigmedón, king of Leinster, 358–366. It contains also, among other things, a 6th century *Dinnshencas*, or history of places (i.e. legends explaining place-names) which mentions Cromm Crúach, the great idol on the plain of Mag Sleact to which the ancient Irish sacrificed their children on Samain.

Book of Life The book or muster roll of God in Hebrew and Christian legend which contains the names of His followers. From it the names may be blotted out either to signify death (*Ex.* xxxii, 32, 33) or because of unrighteousness (*Ps.* lxix, 28). This thus becomes the list of those who will be admitted to future blessedness. According to the *Book of Jubilees*, there are two heavenly tablets: a Book of Life for the righteous and a Book of Death for the adversaries of God. According to the Pharisees, God sits in judgment on the first day of each year (Rosh ha-Shanah) with three books open. In one is recorded the fate of the wicked, in another that of the righteous, and in the third that of an intermediate class. This middle class is allowed a respite of ten days till Yom Kippur to repent and become righteous. Hindus, Moslems, and Buddhists share this belief in registers holding the fate of men.

Book of the Dead or **Books of Thoth** In Egyptian religion, the guide for the dead containing formulas, hymns, incantations, and prayers which were believed to secure eternal life for deceased persons, to enable them to escape the dangers and snares besetting their journey to Amenti, to answer the 42 judges, and to secure a triumphant vindication before Osiris. The book was believed to have been transcribed originally in the handwriting of the god Thoth; it was written actually over a period of centuries. Copies of the entire book or of sections of it were inscribed on the sarcophagus or tomb, on the inside of the mummy cases, or on papyrus which was rolled up and placed in the mummy case.

The title, *Book of the Dead*, is erroneous, for Egyptians called the collection the *Chapters of Pert em Hru* or *The Coming Forth By Day*. Many versions of the book have survived. The size and content varied with the wealth of the dead man or of his friends, and papyri varied from a few feet to a hundred-foot roll. Included in the material was information on how to preserve the body from decay or the ravages of certain animals (cockroaches or beetles?), charms against the serpent Apepi and the crocodile which takes the charm from the deceased, and the ritual of the judgment of the dead.

Book of the Dun Cow or **Lebor na hUidre** An early Irish manuscript compiled in part by a monk of Clonmacnoise before 1106. It contains, in addition to the Mythological Cycle and *The Voyage of Maelduin*, for the most part the stories of the Ulster cycle, among them the long humorous story of *Bricriu's Feast* and the famous prose epic *Táin Bó Cúailgne* or *Cattle Raid of Cooley*, the oldest heroic epic of ancient Europe. This is the story which gives the manuscript its name, for the *Táin Bó Cúailgne* is said to have been recited by Fergus Mac Róich (summoned from his grave for the purpose) to Ciarán of Clonmacnoise who wrote it down upon the hide of a dun cow.

book rimes Two distinct sorts of rimes appear on front fly leaves: versified warnings to book-borrowers and thieves, as:

> If this book you steal away,
> What will you say
> On Judgment Day?

or mere identification rimes, often closing with a pious sentiment:

> Marlboro is my dwelling-place;
> America's my nation;
> Henry Dudley is my name,
> And Christ is my salvation.
> or And heaven my expectation.

Book rimes were common in the United States in the 18th and 19th centuries but have lately largely disappeared or been superseded by engraved or printed book plates. [CFP]

Boötes A conspicuous northern constellation, containing the important bright star Arcturus; the Oxdriver, or driver of the Wain; the Herdsman; the Bear Warden, etc.: named wherever it is recognized for its following the constellation of the Great Bear as if guarding or driving it. It has been called for example, the Barking Dog (Arabic) or the Shouter (as of the driver to his oxen or the huntsman of the Bear to his dogs). The stars of Boötes form a long, kite-shaped figure resembling a man, the two faint triangles of stars on either side of Arcturus forming the legs, the wider triangle north of Arcturus being the head and shoulders. In China, the cho-t'i, or attendants of Arcturus (the small triangles), were indicators of the approach of the Spring season and were important in figuring the calendar.

borage An herb (*Borago officinalis*) with bright blue flowers and hairy leaves and stem, used in salads, in making claret-cup, and believed valuable as a febrifuge, demulcent, and diaphoretic. The flowers figured in Tudor and Stuart needlework. In medieval times the leaves and flowers were put into wine to drive away sadness. The plant was also believed to revive the hypochondriac and to inspire courage; according to the old couplet, "I, Borage,/ Bring alwaies courage."

bordón-danza The Basque religious sword dance of Guipuzcoa and Tolosa, performed by a group of men in two facing lines. They wear white shirts and breeches, red sashes and berets. They run through various longways interweavings. They meet, and cross long sticks (which have replaced swords). The accompaniment is usually in the 5/8 time of the zortzico. The dance is most commonly performed on St. John's Day, June 24, thus suggesting a former connection with solstice rites. [GPK]

Boreas In Greek mythology and religion, the north wind; son of Æolus, ruler of the winds, or of Astræus and Eos, the starry night and the dawn. In early Attic legend, Boreas carried off Oreithyia, daughter of Erechtheus after trying unsuccessfully to woo her. Their children were Cleopatra, Calais, and Zetes. The latter two accompanied the Argonautic expedition. Boreas assisted the Athenians in the Persian war by destroying their enemies' ships and aided the Megalopolitans against the Spartans. The Athenians held the Boreasmoi in his honor; a festival was celebrated with sacrifices in Megalopolis; and the Thurians also sacrificed to him as the destroyer of the fleet of Dionysius of Syracuse. He was depicted as a winged, bearded man blowing a conch shell and identified by the Romans with Aquilo.

bori A class of spirits of the Hausas of Nigeria, each one of whom is credited with causing a specific disease, and each of whom has its own name. The cult which centers in the bori involves the summoning of specific ones with drumming and particularized song, and possession by the bori of the summoners during the ritual dances. The dances are intended both to drive out and avert disease. Whenever an individual is stricken with a disease, a summoner of the bori (i.e. medium) is consulted, who puts himself or herself into relation with the spirit (i.e. becomes possessed), and appeases it with offerings or otherwise rids the sick one of it. Sixty-five dancers participate in the communal possession dances, also called bori, which are now absolutely forbidden in northern Nigeria. (See A. J. N. Tremearne, *Ban of the Bori*, London, 1914.)

Born-from-Water Identical with CHILD-OF-THE-WATER.

born with teeth An occurrence variously interpreted as good or bad among the peoples of the world. That a child born with one tooth (occasionally two teeth) will have a wonderful future is the general folk belief in France, Italy, and other Latin countries, and is known to have prevailed from Roman times. The tribune Lucius Sicinius (450 B.C.) carried the epithet Dentatus from the fact that he was born with one or more teeth.

Slavic and Finno-Ugric peoples believe that children born with a tooth will become sorcerers or vampires. Bohemians and Moravians call such a child a *drud,* or (fem.) *drude* or witch. Certain groups of Wends call them *murava;* Kasubians refer to them as *ohyns* or vampires. Often the tooth is immediately pulled out and the child is thus rendered normal and harmless. Hungarian peasants believe that infants born with teeth are *táltos,* changelings, and such children are cruelly mistreated. English babies born with teeth are said to be "hard-bitten" and are always suspect. Most Asiatic peoples regard dentate births as events of evil omen. A number of African peoples are said to destroy at birth any infant born with one tooth or more already formed. Alabama Negroes believe that a child born with teeth will have bad luck all his life.

borrowed feathers A folktale motif (K1041) in which a dupe lets himself be carried aloft by a bird and then is dropped. The motif is found in Danish, Greek, Spanish, Indonesian, Rhodesian, American Negro, and American Indian tales. In a Micmac story the cranes, jealous of Badger, carried him into the air and dropped him, but Badger called himself back, part by part, until he was whole and alive again. In a Nez Percé tale, Coyote was not so fortunate. On a hunting expedition with his brothers-in-law (geese) he was carried on their backs over the river until they reached the middle. There the geese let him go and he had fallen almost to the river when he wished himself a feather and immediately went up again. He was afraid of going too high so wished himself an arrow and dropped down almost to the river. Then he made a mistake, said "To be an arrow," and plummeted into the river.

boträd The abode-tree: an elm or lime tree growing in front of a Swedish homestead and regarded as the abode of the guardian spirit of the family. Not even a splinter was cut from this tree and sacrifices and prayers were offered beside it to ward off evil. Pregnant women embraced it to make delivery easy.

Bo tree, Bodhi tree, or **Bodhidruma** The sacred tree (pipal or *Ficus religiosa*) under which Gautama sat on a couch of grass facing the east until he obtained knowledge and the perfect state. This tree, located in Bodh Gayā, Bīhar, has been sacred to Buddhists for nearly 2400 years. Pilgrims flock to it from all parts of Asia to present their offerings and to pour libations at the foot of it. The tree now standing is regarded as identical with the tree of Buddha. The present tree, however, is probably a direct descendant of the original tree, propagated by seed. King Asoka is supposed to have cut and burned the tree in the 3rd century B.C., but it was miraculously restored from its ashes. He was so overwhelmed that he did not return home. The queen then had it cut down, but it was again restored.

According to one tradition Gautama spent seven weeks under the Bo tree; according to another he spent seven days under this tree, seven days under the Goatherd's Banyan, seven days under the Rājāyatana tree, and then returned to the Banyan. The Bo did not shed its leaves in summer or autumn, but denuded itself and developed an entire new set of leaves on the anniversary of the day Buddha achieved nirvaṇa. The Bo tree is worshipped by Buddhists and Hindus. Today a mud platform is built around the largest pipal in each North India village and there discussions and meetings are held.

A Bo tree in Amirādhapura, Ceylon, grown from a slip of the original sacred tree, is also revered by Buddhists and is believed to be a parable of the universe. Its trunk represents the connection between the invisible and the visible worlds and its vertical branches and roots represent man's striving for perfection.

bottle imp An imp or spirit shut up in a bottle, the bottle or other container often serving as the medium whereby the presence of the confined spirit may be invoked. The bottle imp is common in Arabian folktales and appears also in Estonian, Finnish, Swedish, Swiss, Hebrew, and Philippine tales.

Bought a Cow W. G. Pitts reported (1909) (*JAFL* 26: 128 #18) a folk rime from country whites in Mississippi as:

> Bought a cow of farmer Jones,
> She wasn't nothing but skin and bones;
> Kept her till she was as fine as silk;
> Jumped the fence, and strained her milk.

This is a sort of "pore relation", a deteriorated descendant of an English 17th century rime which had for its second line:

> She was nowt but skin and bones,

which had a concealed double meaning, for the word "nowt" formerly meant cattle (cf. neat's-foot oil) as well as "nought."

It is also obviously related to one of the many old "If I had a . . ." rimes:

> If I had a cow 'n' she give good milk,
> I'd dress her in the finest silk;
> I'd feed her on corn oats and hay
> And milk her forty times a day.
>
> [CFP]

Bouki or **Uncle Bouki** The dupe of the Haitian trickster cycle, who is the foil for the quick, clever 'Ti Malice. The relation between the two characters is essentially that between Brer Wolf and Brer Rabbit in the Uncle Remus tales, both of which series form part of the widespread African and New World Negro series of trickster stories. [MJH]

boundary A limiting or dividing line or mark; also, any object serving to indicate a limit or confine. Boundaries between nations, tribes, or the holdings of individuals are frequently the subject of dispute. To prevent the encroachment of neighbors or neighboring peoples, folk customs have developed and laws have been passed. Natural landmarks such as rivers, trees, boulders, seas, and mountains, and artificial landmarks such as boundary stones, pillars, posts, hedges, walls, or fences have been employed throughout the world. Trespass was and is usually considered a crime. Trespassers were often killed when caught, or punished by mutilation (India), and quarrels were frequently settled at the boundary stones.

Boundary markers or stones were regarded as sacred by many peoples (New Zealand, Brazil, India). Those of the Khonds were sacred to the god of boundaries, Sundi Pennu; those of the Semites were sacred to Nabu, Papu, Ninib, Nusku, and Shamash. Zeus and Hermes were the protectors of Greek boundaries, Jupiter Terminus of Roman landmarks. Thor, Frigga, and Holde were Teutonic boundary deities. Cruel and severe punishments were meted out to those who removed landmarks. Punishments varied from death (New Zealand, early Rome, Aztec Mexico), a curse (Etruria, Babylonia, New Britain, South America), to large fines (late Roman Empire, Wales).

In Scandinavian and Teutonic folk belief, the Jack o'Lantern was the ghost of someone who had violated a landmark. Local legends are full of men condemned to carry the boundary stones which they had moved to increase their holdings in their lifetime. The water from a boundary stream was used with silver to remove the curse of the evil eye.

Bouphonia or **Buphonia** In Greek (Athenian) religion, the sacrifice of an ox at the altar of Zeus on the Acropolis. Oxen were driven around the altar during the festival of Diipoleia, and that ox which nibbled at the cereals on the altar was killed with an ax which was then condemned and thrown into the sea. Meanwhile the flesh was eaten and the hide stuffed with grass, sewn together, and yoked to a plow.

The origin of this sacrifice was the killing of an ox by Sopatrus after the ox had eaten the cereal he was offering as a sacrifice. Seized by remorse, Sopatrus buried the ox and fled to Crete but a famine followed and so the Bouphonia was instituted. The custom, according to Frazer, points to a belief in the ox as a form of the corn spirit or, according to Robertson Smith, to totemism.

bourrée A peasant dance of Auvergne, France: a double file choral dance performed by men and women facing each other. The two lines advance and retreat from each other, and one by one, beginning with the leader and his partner, the dancers exchange places. The bourrée is also danced as a lively couple dance in 3/8 tempo, men with arms raised, women holding their skirts. In Limousin it is a lusty, stamping, jumping, finger-snapping performance. The Languedoc bourrée is in 4/8 time. It was introduced at a court festival for Catherine de Medici in 1565 but was not performed except as a peasant dance until much later. Finally, as a court dance, the bourrée appears as a ballet form. The ballet *pas de bourrée* is a brief grapevine with tiny steps (r. back, l. side, r. forward, reverse) producing a kind of rocking in place; or the grapevine can also be prolonged to a progression from side to side. [GPK]

Bow bells   The bells of St. Mary-le-Bow, in Cheapside, London, within sound of which cockneys are born; hence, the region within London called cockneydom. In the legend of Dick Whittington, it was the Bow bells which he heard say, "Turn again Whittington, Lord Mayor of London."

box   A slow-growing evergreen tree or shrub (genus *Buxus*) highly valued for hedges and for its tough close-grained wood. The use of the wood for musical instruments was mentioned by Pliny, Vergil, and Ovid. *Isaiah* (lx, 13) mentions box as one of the three trees to beautify his place of sanctuary. Box attains exceptional old age.

Why does the box retain its leaves longer than most other trees was one of the wise questions put by the ancient Jewish physician and philosopher, Isaac Israeli, in his Arabic *Universal Diets,* and re-asked by Petrus Hispanus in the 13th century in his inquiry into the occult properties of various plants and animal parts.

In the north of England a basin filled with sprigs of box used to be placed outside the door of a house in which there was a funeral. As the mourners left the house, each would take a sprig of box and later drop it into the grave after the coffin was lowered. In parts of France crosses and wreaths were made of box for Palm Sunday, and kept from year to year, long after they were withered. If an animal sickened during the year, the byre was cleansed and one of these old wreaths or crosses was burned inside the place. This fumigation drove out the disease.

In a Breton folktale the separable soul of a giant is hidden in an ancient box tree in his garden. To kill the giant the hero must cut the root of the tree with one blow of the ax.

Boxwood combs are used in crossroads divination in Japan; running the fingers along the teeth of the comb invites the gods to speak.

box dropping from sky   A motif occurring in the Coeur d'Alene Indian Coyote's-son cycle in which the Spider Women in the sky help Coyote's son drop back to earth in a box. The motif occurs in the typically northwestern Indian story *Coyote Steals His Daughter-in-law.* Coyote coveted one of the wives of his son. He managed to send the son into the sky, and then took for himself the wife named Tern. Coyote's son had many adventures in the sky; he had the beaver girls for his wives, and he had children by the beaver girls. But he was homesick for his earthly wife, Black Swan, and her child. He went to the Spider Women and asked them to help him get back. They put him in a box with a lid and told him how to go. They said the box would stop four times before it got to earth; each time it stopped he must roll around and it would continue to drop; but he must not get out until he heard the wind blowing in the grass. Coyote's son got into the box and all happened as he was told. When he heard

the wind blowing in the grass he got out. He found Black Swan and his child outcasts from the camp. So he returned to the camp and killed everybody. The story ends with the closing formula, "That is the end of the road."

In many variants Coyote's son is marooned on a high rock from which he escapes, or he drops from the sky in a spoon (Sahaptin), or he causes a flood which destroys the faithless wife (Columbia River). But the usual medium for his return is the spiders' rope. And the four pauses of the box in its descent is vivid description of any spider's descent from a high place.

boxi moni   The British Guiana equivalent of the Trinidad cooperative savings device known as 'the 'susu.
                                                                            [MJH]

Boy and the Mantle   An English minstrel ballad (Child #29) with the chastity test motif and in which the Arthurian material is prominent. A boy arrives at the court of King Arthur with a mantle which, he says, will never become a wife who has "done amisse." Only Craddocke's lady could wear it, to the embarrassment of the other court ladies. Then the boy killed a boar and invited each of the knights to carve it, saying that a cuckold's knife could not cut it. Finally he produced a horn of red gold from which a cuckold could not drink. Only Craddocke could carve the boar's head and drink from the horn.

boy judge   The hero of a number of folktales of clever decisions: related to the Solomon cycle, the group of tales of the clever peasant girl, the king and the bishop, the maiden who confounds the king's wisest counselors, and the like. In the type tale of the boy judge, the king overhears the decision of a boy acting as judge in a children's game based on an actual problem the king faces. He summons the boy to court and has him decide the real case. In the *Arabian Nights* the tale of Ali Cogia (Burton, Supp., III: "Ali Khwajah and the Merchant of Baghdad") the problem of the jar of olives and the gold pieces hidden therein is solved by the boy's calling, as judges of the age of the olives, experts who can say that they are fresh olives and not seven-year-old olives. Another Eastern story tells of the deposed vizier who hears children playing a game closely paralleling his own misfortunes. Repeating what he has heard the boy say, he tells the sultan that in return for the goods taken from him he wants back the years sacrificed for them. Cyrus, in a story told by Herodotus, and Jesus, Mohammed, and Charlemagne are all heroes of stories telling of their precocious wisdom in the face of adult dilemmas. The tales are of course related to the game children play, like School or Play House. The game of the boy-Kazi is a favorite of Arab children. The story of the boy judge, along with other tales of so-called "enfants terribles," is known from Mongolia to Arabia and in Europe. Perhaps the best known of all folktales of the boy judge is that of Daniel and Susannah: how the young Daniel questioned each of the two accusers of the innocent but convicted woman and how their testimony, when taken separately, did not agree. Related to this are other stories of adultery exposed or refuted by the cleverness of a child. In a Persian story, the boy discovers that the illness of the king is caused by the adultery of one of his wives. The

Three-Year-Old Child in the *Arabian Nights* who cries prevents, by his explanation, the libertine from having his will of the woman.

božaloshtsh In the belief of the Wends (eastern Germany), the messenger of death: literally, God's plaint. She is a little woman with long hair who cries beneath the window of a person about to die. Compare BANSHEE.

bracken Any large, coarse fern, especially the common brake (*Pteridium quilinum*) common in Europe and North America. It is often called "poor man's soap" because its root stocks will make a lather in water. In Biblical legend Christ was born on a bed of bedstraw and bracken. The bedstraw, proud of the honor, burst into flower and was rewarded with golden instead of white blossoms. The bracken, however, refused to honor Christ and so has been flowerless ever since. In Shropshire, however, it is said that the brake flowers once a year, at midnight on Michaelmas Eve, but that the flower is gone by daybreak.

To the herbalists the plant is under the dominion of Mercury, and is drunk, when boiled in mead, to kill broad and long worms. In Ireland the bracken is a symbol of fecundity. "As prolific as the bracken" is a common saying. A beverage made from the roots is considered good for worms. Tea from the leaves is a soothing application for burns and scalds.

Braes o Yarrow A Scottish Border ballad (Child #214), in which a young man leaves his young wife to go to meet her brother John "upon the braes o Yarrow." There nine armed men awaited him. "Four he killed and five did wound," but a "coward loon came him behind" and pierced him to the heart. The young wife found her true-love lying dead and took her own life beside him. In another, and probably earlier, version, *The Dowy Houms o Yarrow*, she drank the dead man's blood and cursed her old father (who had disapproved of the match) for causing her young lord's death.

Bragi or **Brage** In Norse mythology, the god of poetry and music: one of the original Æsir. Son of Odin and Gunlod, he was born in a stalactite-hung cave, put on board a vessel belonging to the dwarfs, and presented with a magic golden harp. As the boat floated out of the subterranean darkness, Bragi seized the harp and began to sing the song of life. When the vessel reached the shore, he leaped ashore and walked through the forest playing his harp. The flowers bloomed and the trees budded as he played. There he met and wed Ithunn and the two hastened to Asgard where Odin traced runes on Bragi's tongue and decreed that he should compose songs in honor of the heroes received in Valhalla.

Bragi is often pictured as an old man with a long white beard. At Scandinavian feasts a horn consecrated to him was used for drinking while each man made a vow to perform a deed during the succeeding year worthy of immortalization in verse or saga.

Brahmā or **Brahman** The first of the Hindu trinity; the deity of the later Brāhmaṇas who assumes the creator role of the Vedic Prajāpati and Hiraṇyagarbha: the personification of the supreme brahman. Brahmā, in mythology, sprang from the egg created by the supreme first cause. According to the *Rāmāyaṇa* he arose self-existent and, becoming a boar, created the world and raised the earth. According to the *Mahābhārata* he sprang from the navel of Vishṇu or from a lotus growing from the navel of Vishṇu. The Śaivites believe Rudra to be the creator of Brahmā.

Brahmā probably had his origin in speculation rather than in popular cult. The world of Brahmā will endure for 2,160,000,000 years (a day and night of Brahmā) after which the world will be consumed by fire, to be recreated by the god again and again until a hundred years of such days have passed, when the whole universe and the gods themselves will be resolved into the primeval substance.

Brahmā is represented as red in color with four heads (a fifth was burnt off by Śiva when he spoke disrespectfully to the latter) and four arms. He controls a quarter of the universe with each face. He holds in his hands a scepter, or string of beads, or spoon, bow, water-jug, and the Veda. His vehicle is a swan or goose. His consort is Sarasvatī with whom, as the father of men, he had incestuous intercourse. He was the father of Daksha and the four Kumāras, the mind-born sons who remained forever boys. Brahmā is rarely worshipped and is of secondary importance. In a mythological argument between Vishṇu and Brahmā as to who was the creator, Śiva settled the argument by proving himself the supreme force.

Brāhman or **Brāhmin** [masculine, accented on the last syllable] A member of the first of the four castes of Hindus; usually, but not necessarily, a priest. The chief duties of the Brāhman are the study and teaching of the Vedas, the performance of religious ceremonies, and the making of sacrifices. His life is divided into four stages: Brahmachārī, in which he is a religious student; Grihastha, in which he is a householder, married and teaching the Vedas; Vānaprastha, in which he lives as an anchorite after having discharged his duties as a man of the world; Sannyāsī, during which he is a religious mendicant subsisting on alms, heedless of joys or sorrows in his desire for final absorption in the essential principle of the world. The Brāhmans were and still are privileged. They claim divinity on the basis that there are two kinds of gods—the gods and the Brāhmans who have learned the Vedas. Many modern Brāhmans neglect their religious duties and engage in secular occupations. The Brāhman is a popular character in Indian folktales.

Brahmāpura In Hindu mythology, the heaven and city of Brahmā, situated on the summit of Mount Meru.

Bran (1) In Brythonic mythology, a son of Llyr, brother of Manawyddan and Branwen, and legendary king of Britain. He was a huge being, likened in some versions of his story to a kind of sea giant. Traditionally it was Bran who waded across the strait between Great Britain and Ireland and (like Orion in the Ægean) caused the great tides.

The story, as told in the *Mabinogion*, is that Bran was sitting on a great rock on the shore at Harlech, when he saw 13 ships sailing toward Britain from Ireland. It was Matholwch, king of Ireland, coming to ask for the hand of Branwen in marriage. Branwen was given to Matholwch for his wife. The feast was held in tents because no house could contain Bran. One day soon after this Evnissyen (a half-brother to Bran, noted for his envious nature and desire to stir up strife) was walking among the horses and trappings of the Irish, and suddenly in rage he turned and cut off the lips and eyelids and tails of the Irish horses. The creatures were maimed and useless. Matholwch could not understand this insult.

Bran did what he could: he explained that the deed was no one's will but the whim of an ill-natured half-brother; he made up the loss, horse for horse, and added a silver staff as tall as himself and a gold plate as wide as his face. Then lest it seem not enough, Bran gave to Matholwch a caldron of such a nature that if a man be slain today and cast into it, he will come out alive tomorrow, though speechless. This was the caldron of regeneration, given to Bran by a man and woman who came out of a lake in Ireland.

The first year that Branwen was queen in Ireland she was loved and acclaimed, and a son was born to her named Gwern. But in the second year, the minds of the men of Ireland remembered the old insult they had received in her country, and they took vengeance by driving Branwen from Matholwch's bed, turning her to do the cooking, and causing her to receive a blow every day. No man that came to Ireland from Britain was ever allowed to return lest he tell the story. But Branwen took a young starling and reared it in the kneading trough. She taught it to speak and obey her, and explained to the bird how to recognize Bran. At last she wrote "a letter of her woes," fastened it to the starling, and sent the bird to find Bran.

When Bran read the letter he embarked with his hosts and sailed towards Ireland. But Bran's ship lay deep in the water with his weight and could not reach the shores. So he got out and walked on towards Ireland beside the fleet. Watchers were dismayed, and when they described that a mountain was seen coming to Ireland beside the ships, Branwen knew it was her brother Bran.

Messengers from Matholwch met Bran, proposing to build a house for him, who had never had a house, in compensation for the wrongs done to Branwen. Bran accepted the offer and the house was built. It had a hundred pillars in it and on each pillar were hung two long leather bags, with an armed man in each one. Evnissyen saw the bags, felt of each one, and crushed with one hand the head of every man in every bag.

At the feast that was given, the sovereignty of Ireland was conferred on Branwen's son, who passed among the visitors one by one, greeting his uncles, Bran and Manawyddan and many others. All loved him, except Evnissyen, who grabbed him up and threw him in the fire. A terrible fight took place then and many were killed. The Irish renewed their slain by casting them into the caldron of regeneration. And when Evnissyen saw that, he threw himself among the dead, was cast into the caldron with them, stretched himself, and cracked it. Only seven of Bran's people escaped from the place, and Branwen went with them.

Bran bade his companions cut off his head and bury it in the White Hill in London, facing France, so that it might protect the country forever from invasion. So they cut off the head, and the head, the Urdawl Ben, or Noble Head, entertained its guardians for 87 years before it was buried in the White Hill. In its presence time passed in merriment and jest and feasting. But at last it was buried where Bran had said; and it pro-

tected Britain from invasion until Arthur dug it up, preferring rather that the valor of its defenders protect the land. (Belief in the power of a buried head to turn back invaders was a strong and ancient belief. The heads, sometimes the bodies, sometimes sculptured heads of warriors, were buried in certain places for this purpose.)

Bran later became known as a Christian saint, Bendegeit Vran, the Blessed Bran, one of the three kings of Prydein who brought Christianity to the Cymric people, after he had been seven years in Rome as hostage for his son Caradawc (probably the historical Caractacus).

There is a riddle of Taliesin's to which the answer is Bran, embodying both the mythological and legendary aspects of Bran's story, along with the uncertain implication of his position as a sea god: "I was at the court of Dôn before the birth of Gwydion; my head was at the White Hill in the Hall of Cymbeline: it is not known whether my body is flesh or fish."

(2) One of Fionn mac Cumal's wonderful dogs: one of two whelps born of Tuiren, wife of Iollan, a chief of the Fianna. Tuiren was transformed into a bitch by a former sweetheart of Iollan's, a woman of the síde, and given as a present to Fergus Fionnliai, who did not like dogs. Later, after Tuiren was restored to Iollan, Fionn took the two beautiful whelps and named them Bran and Sceolan. They were famous for their wonderful intelligence. Bran was especially beloved by Fionn; she was so swift that she could overtake the flight of wild geese. Bran and Sceolan were the two dogs who conducted the young doe safely through the forest into Fionn's dún, where she was safe from her enchantment and became, in her own shape, Fionn's beloved wife, Sadb. Later she was tricked out of the dún and became a deer again. After that Fionn would allow no dogs to hunt except Bran and Sceolan, who would know her. And it was Bran and Sceolan again who discovered the boy Oisín naked in the forest, and brought him to Fionn, who knew him for his own son, child of Sadb, the deer.

It was Fionn himself who gave Bran her death and never got over grieving it. One day Fionn was hunting and Bran was following a fawn. Fionn heard the fawn cry out in despair that nothing could save her from Bran. "Run through my legs," said Fionn. So the fawn ran through his legs, and as Bran followed Fionn crushed her with his knees. Fionn's grief was terrible because of this. It is believed he could never have done it, except that the quarry must have been his own mother or Oisín's.

brando An Italian folk dance of moderate tempo: orginally a 15th century peasant dance and still performed as such in the province of Bologna. It developed into the court spectacle. It was a chain round, retaining much that was typically primitive choral dance; but in the late 16th century, it became a square, executed in 14 varying figures, by two diagonally facing couples. [GPK]

branle A French 16th and 17th century mimetic couple dance, danced in groups, either in open file or closed circle, and characterized by a typical balancing movement. There were many variants: a different branle for each province, the branle of Poitou, of

Champagne, of Burgundy, etc. The branle of Brittany was a passepied. There was a branle for all ages: *branle gai,* very fast and lively (in sextuple rhythm) for the young; *branle simple,* rather lively, for married couples; *branle double,* with a slow rhythm for the old. There were mimetic branles, such as *branle des hermites, du sabot, des lavandières,* etc. Most of them were in quadruple time. The *branle des oficios,* also mimetic, is claimed to have developed into the volte, which later became the waltz. [GPK]

Bran, son of Febal Hero of the 8th century Irish *The Voyage of Bran and His Adventure.*

Branstock In Teutonic mythology, a mighty oak in the great hall of Volsung's palace which pierced the roof and shaded the building. One day Odin thrust the sword, Gram, into the trunk of the tree, up to the hilt. Only Sigmund was able to withdraw it.

brazen head An oracular head of brass: said to have been made by several of the medieval magicians. The giant Ferragus of Portugal had one which told of the past, present, and future. That of Friar Bacon, which spoke to Bacon's assistant while the master magician slept, and was shattered before he awoke, is the best-known brazen head in English tradition. See SPEAKING HEAD.

Brazen Serpent An image set up by Moses at the command of God, which is said to have healed those who looked upon it. When the weary Israelites, near the close of the desert wanderings, were forced to march around Edom, thus prolonging the journey, they murmured against God and Moses. As a punishment, fiery serpents were sent against them. When they repented, Moses was told to put upon a lofty pole a bronze image of a serpent, so that those who had been bitten might look upon it and live. When he hurled the image on high, it remained floating in the air, so that those who raised their eyes and thought about God were healed. Gradually the people forgot the symbolical meaning and came to worship the snake itself, so Hezekiah found it necessary to destroy it (II *Kings,* xviii, 4). In rabbinical belief, the serpents were considered a punishment for sins of the evil tongue (*Num.* xxi, 5).

bread Many peoples believe bread the gift of the supernatural, and will not eat bread unless an offering has been made. The Jews must sacrifice a portion of the dough as *chalah.* In ancient times it was given to the priest who was ritually clean, who consumed it, but now this is impossible, so instead a portion the size of an olive is removed and burned. On the New Year, the ritual loaf is shaped like a ladder to symbolize man's ascent to heaven. On the Sabbath, the oldest male of the house blesses the Sabbath loaf and the wine, cuts the loaf, and each person present must partake before the Sabbath meal can begin. On Passover, the Jews eat unleavened bread, *matzo,* to commemorate the expulsion of the Jews from Egypt when they did not have time to let the bread rise.

In Northwest India, the first of the grain reaped is mixed with milk and sugar to be eaten by a member of the family, while among the Ainus, the new crop of millet was baked, and worshipped by the old men before anyone else could eat it. Among the Natchez Indians the first sheaves of maize were made into loaves, and offered to the setting sun before they could be eaten. In Peru, the first of the harvest had to be consumed by the Inca and the nobles, who were descendants of the Sun, before they could be eaten by the common people. In Silesia, only the family may eat of a loaf made from the last sheaf. In the Volga River region, when the first bread from a new harvest is baked, the entire village assembles in the house of the oldest inhabitant. They open the eastern door, face it, and pray. Then the bread is cut, each person is given a morsel by the old man, and then all pray. In Lithuania all types of grains were mixed and baked into sacrificial loaves, one for each member of the family.

Bread may also be regarded as the body of the supernatural. In Yorkshire, the clergyman cut the first corn from which he made the communion bread. In Hermland, in Sweden, the last sheaf was ground and baked into a loaf shaped like a little girl which the entire household ate, for it embodied the corn spirit. The Aztecs ate the body of Huitzilopochtli, twice a year, in May and December, in the form of cakes baked in the idol's image. In Spain to avert a storm which threatens the crops, bread is placed in a napkin, and placed on the window ledge facing the direction whence the storm is coming. One says three times: "Lord, let not harm come to thy body." In Rumania long, wheaten loaves, "beautiful like the face of Christ," are baked for weddings, baptisms, festivals, and funerals.

Bread also can cure disease or act as an amulet. In Holland stale bread is placed in the baby's cradle to ward off disease, and in Morocco it is thought that stale bread cures stuttering; in Egypt just licking it cures indigestion. In Belgium, crumbs blessed in church on St. Hubert's Day, November 3rd, were sewn into the pockets of garments to avert rabies. This bread was first eaten by the family, and then fed to the dogs. (St. Hubert is the patron of hunting).

It is sinful to waste bread in many parts of Europe. After her death a wasteful Polish housewife may be heard scrambling around for every crumb of bread that she has dropped in her lifetime, and her soul knows no peace until she has picked it all up. Among other Slavs it is believed that these wasted fragments are weighed against the soul of the culprit, and if they are heavier than he, his soul belongs to Satan. In Transylvania, if bread falls to the ground it is picked up and kissed, for it is sinful to throw it away or step on it. However, it can be thrown into the fire as an offering to the dead. The Russian uses bread and salt as a symbol of friendship, and among the Poles the bride is greeted in her new home by her mother-in-law with bread and salt. The Greeks believe that it is sinful to take two bites of any food in succession without a mouthful of bread between.

Bread symbolizes the home and family in other ways. A Rumanian proverb has it: "The bread of my land though to others hard and bitter, to me is sweet." A Slavic proverb says: "Without bread, even a palace is sad, but with it a pine tree is paradise." To the Italian, bread is all food, the rest is merely accompaniment, and such is his regard for bread, his superlative simile is "as good as bread." To the Spaniard: "All sorrows are less with bread," and for the Dane: "Bread is better than the song of the birds." In many parts of Europe bread baked on Good Friday would never stale. If a woman baked on Good Friday and the five Fridays following, she was particularly blessed. However to the Russians, baking on any Friday was unlucky, and on Good Friday particularly so. To them Good Friday was a vengeful old hag, so jealous that if a woman baked, her hands would be turned to wood. In Scandinavia, if a boy and girl ate from the same loaf, they were bound to fall in love.

Menstruating women were dangerous to the bread for their touch would prevent it from rising. Therefore, they were enjoined from baking it or kneading the dough in eastern Germany, Italy, and southern France.

It is a common belief in England and America that a loaf of bread, weighted with quicksilver, will locate the body of a drowned person. Such a loaf set in the water travels towards the lost body and remains motionless over it. [NFJ]

bread dance A term applied to various Amerindian dances for sustenance: to the Iroquois Spirit-of-the-Food dances, to the Shawnee spring and fall dances, respectively a plea for crops and for plentiful hunting. The Shawnee female deity, Kokumthena, Our Grandmother, is sometimes present and her voice is sometimes heard above the women. The three Iroquois life-sustaining sisters, corn, beans, and squash, are also conceived of as feminine, because the raising and preparation of crops is primarily a woman's occupation. The Shawnee follow the two bread dances with all-night social dances. The Iroquois have a definite sequence, varying with each reservation. [GPK]

break An American square dance term: all drop hands, followed by swing (joint pivot in place). [GPK]

Breathmaker The Seminole Indian culture hero, Hisagita misi, who taught the Indians how to fish and dig wells. He made the Milky Way and the koonti (pumpkin) plant. He is equated with Jesus by modern Seminoles.

Brennan on the Moor or ***Bold Brennan*** An Irish come-all-ye based on the story of the outlaw, Willie Brennan, who was betrayed by a false-hearted woman and hanged for highway robbery in County Cork, 1804.

Brer Rabbit The rabbit (or hare) has played a role in folklore quite out of proportion to its diminutive size and timorousness. Among the traditions that have helped to establish it in the folk mind as a charmed creature may be mentioned the lunar hare (the Eastern equivalent of the Western Man in the Moon), the *Osterhase* or Easter bunny, and the belief in the rabbit's foot as a lucky charm or countercharm against witchcraft. The divinity assigned to the hare in the *Jatakas* or birth-stories of Buddha is somewhat approximated by the role of the Great White Hare as a culture hero among the Algonquians.

The rabbit's trickster role in Negro folklore is anticipated in the *Panchatantra* and the *Hitopadeśa* of India, where the hare outwits the elephant and the lion, and in Burma and Tibet, where it outwits the tiger. In Africa, from which the slave brought Brer Rabbit, the rabbit trickster is general, except on the Slave Coast, where it is replaced by the tortoise, and the Gold Coast, where it is replaced by the spider. See ANANSI; AUNT NANCY. Among the Kaffirs of South Africa the rabbit finds its counterpart in the Tom-Thumb-like Hlakanyana. In Liberia its place is occupied by the chevrotain, a nimble, graceful, fawn-colored creature about eighteen inches long, whose elusiveness and cunning have made it an object of veneration. The confusion of Brer Rabbit with Cunnie (Cunning) Rabbit, another name for the chevrotain, is often cited as reason for the Negro's transference of the cunning of the latter to the former.

The popularity of rabbit trickster tales (including the "Tar Baby" story) among the American Indians, points to Negro-Indian exchange. J. W. Powell and James Mooney lean toward the view that the Indian would have been less likely to accept and transmit Negro tales than the Negro would be to take over Indian tales. Joel Chandler Harris (*Nights with Uncle Remus*, Boston and New York, 1881, p. xxv) supports the opposite theory, and Stith Thompson states (*Tales of the North American Indian*, Cambridge, 1929, p. xxii) that the animal tales so popular among the Southeast Indians have "become so greatly influenced by the 'Uncle Remus' tales as to be at least as Negro as Indian." By the same token, Mary A. Owen's rabbit tales (*Voodoo Tales*, New York, 1893) seem to be as much Indian as they are Negro.

In American Negro folklore the assignment of the trickster role to the rabbit is associated with the Negro's own role in slavery, where cunning and deception ("hitting a straight lick with a crooked stick") were often his only weapons against oppression. This, however, according to M. J. Herskovits, is an "adaptation and reinforcement of the African ways of thoughts," and is in line with the universal tendency on the part of oppressed people to identify themselves with the weaker and triumphant animal in the pitting of brains against brute force and superior strength.

In Harris's versions the tales of Brer Rabbit are closer to literature than to folklore, though it is a tribute to his artistry and his folk-art that they have established themselves as American classics. In this way Uncle Remus has fulfilled the social function of the Negro nurse or house servant as story-teller to his master's children—a role which made possible the slave's retention of African animal tales but which at the same time has conditioned whites to look upon Negroes as mere happy-go-lucky entertainers. While many plantation stereotypes linger in the nostalgic versions of Brer Rabbit and other Negro folktales by Harris and others, including Louise Clark Pyrnelle and Virginia Frazer Boyle, more authentic (and more painfully accurate in their Gullah dialect) versions are to be found in the work of Mrs. A. M. H. Christensen, Ambrose E. Gonzales, and Charles C. Jones, Jr. More recently, as the hero of bed-time stories and animal comics (under such designations as Peter Rabbit), the rabbit has degenerated into a purely comical or whimsical character, along with a host of other small animals, some of whom have taken over the rabbit's role as good-natured rogue and trickster tricked. [BAB]

Bres In Old Irish mythology, the son of Elatha, a king of the Fomorians, and Eri, a woman of the Tuatha Dé Danann; brother to Ogma, and husband of Brigit. He was called Eochaid Bres, Bres the Beautiful, because nothing was more beautiful than he. By the time he was born, he had attained a two weeks' growth; when he was seven, he was as big as a boy fourteen; and so he continued. To Bres the Tuatha Dé Danann gave the kingship of Ireland in the hope that his reign would

ensure peace and good will between the Fomorians and
the Tuatha Dé Danann. But Bres was unworthy, and
only trouble followed. See BATTLE OF MAG TURED.

Brethren Culture heroes of Torres Straits Islands and
Papuan New Guinea mythology: unrelated to the
brothers of the cycles of eastern Melanesia (Haddon,
*Reports of the Cambridge Anthrop. Exped. to Torres
Straits*, vol. 1, Cambridge, 1935). See MELANESIAN MY-
THOLOGY. [KL]

Bricriu Nemtenga Bricriu of the Bitter Tongue; in
Old Irish legend, a warrior and trouble-maker in Ulster.
It was he who incited the first three champions of Ulster
(Loeġaire, Conall, and Cuchulain) to quarrel over the
champion's portion at his famous feast, and instigated
the rivalry of the champions of Ireland for the carving
of MacDatho's pig, which resulted in such wholesale
bloodshed. In the *Táin Bó Flidais* (The Driving of the
Cows of Flidais), however, Bricriu appears in quite
different character. Here he plays the role of poet and
ollam, satirist of bitter but not venomous tongue; he
satirizes Fergus for his broken promises and his seduction of Medḃ, acts as ambassador of Ailill, king of
Connacht, to Ailill, husband of Flidais, and is honored
in every place.

Bricriu's Feast Title of one of the oldest and longest
stories in the Ulster cycle of Old Irish legend and romance. Bricriu Nemtenga made a great feast for Conchobar, king of Ulster, and the Ulster warriors. He built
a huge special house for it, and then traveled to Emain
Macha to invite the king and his chiefs. The chiefs
were unwilling to go, saying the dead would outnumber
the living because of Bricriu's setting one man against
another. But Bricriu said he would do that sooner if
they did not come. So Conchobar and the chiefs of
Ulster went, but they would not let Bricriu himself into
the hall. Bricriu had foreseen that they would take this
precaution, and had already secretly led each of the
three best champions of Ulster (Loeġaire, Conall, and
Cuchulain) to expect the champion's portion. Likewise
he incited the wife of each one to expect precedence
over the others. Tests of valor and prowess among the
three heroes followed, but no satisfactory decision could
be made that anyone would abide by, neither the decision of the Ulstermen themselves, nor of Bricriu, nor
of Medḃ and Ailill whose verdict they sought, until at
last the three went to Cú Roi mac Dairi for judgment.
All three heroes had opportunity to show great courage, keeping watch and guard on Cú Roi's castle. Cú
Roi's judgment was as follows: the champion's portion
always to be Cuchulain's for he was first in valor, and
to his wife precedence before the women of Ulster. But
when the three got back to Emain Macha Cuchulain
did not want the champion's portion, for he loved more
the good will of his companions. Not until another time
was the champion's portion definitely assigned to him—
after the great beheading bargain proposed by the
bachlach who visited Emain Macha nightly. Munremur,
Loeġaire, Conall, all accepted the challenge and beheaded the bachlach, but shirked the appointment to
allow themselves to be beheaded each following night,
when the bachlach returned, whole and headed, each
time. Only Cuchulain kept faith. He beheaded the
bachlach one night and stretched his own neck across
the block to be slain in the next. But the bachlach·

brought the great ax down blunt side first beside him,
proclaiming him not only fearless but true. "The sovereignty of the heroes of Erin to thee from this hour
forth and the champion's portion undisputed," the
bachlach cried and vanished. But later it turned out it
was Cú Roi mac Dairi in disguise, keeping his promise
to give judgment on the heroes of Ulster.

bride A newly married woman, or a woman about
to be married. The state here discussed is from the time
of betrothal up to the time the bride becomes a participant in the wedding ceremony. The bride-elect of
today participates in certain customs which were unknown to primitive brides. Some of these usages, known
at present in America and in other countries, are to a
certain degree similar to those of long ago; but in Africa,
Asia, and Indonesia, and elsewhere, marriage was a business devoid of romance, and so probably was the interim
between betrothal and wedding.

In England and on the Continent, the bride looks
forward to the day of the wedding; certain days are
more favorable than others, Wednesday being the favorite day. Especially important is the weather for the
great day. The belief in this respect is summed up:

> Blest be the bride the sun shines on,
> Curst be the bride the rain falls on.

If married on a rainy day, as many drops, so many tears;
but snow foretells happiness. Another thing that concerns the bride is the initial letter of her future husband's name:

> Change the name and not the letter,
> Change for worse and not for better.

In preparation for the wedding ceremonies, dress is
important. Its color appears to be of first importance
and there are many jingles which prescribe for this occasion. The bride will be unhappy if married in *black*;
bad luck will attend her if married in *green*. "Married
in *white*, you've chosen right." Further, the bride is supposed to wear

> Something old and something new,
> Something borrowed and something blue.

She must not wear pearls as they symbolize tears. She
may decide on the material for her dress by divination,
that is, by skipping a rope and saying, "silk, satin,
calico,..." until there is a miss on the name of the
goods her dress will be made of. She may count buttons
for the same purpose. The veil is an indispensable item.
Some symbolism is attached to the veiling of the bride,
but it is generally thought that the veil is to protect the
bride from the evil eye. The bridal wreath is composed
of different flowers, or vines. In Germany the myrtle
wreath is usual and it has its special symbolism.

Tabus for the bride include the following: the ring
must not be worn before the ceremony, nor must the
wedding dress be put on, and on no account must the
bride make the wedding cake herself or assist in its
making. Lovers may not meet on their wedding day
until the hour and place of the ceremony, nor may the
prospective bride and groom be photographed together.
When leaving the house for the wedding ceremony, she
must be careful to step out with her right foot first and
she must also weep and groan.

Bride favors were tokens given out at certain festivities either before or after the ceremony; they consisted

of topknots or garters, sometimes of other articles, such as small baskets to hang in the house. Loveknots were conspicuous in these favors and the colors used were significant: blue (for constancy), and so on. [GPS]

bride cakes In ancient Rome, *confarreatio*, a round cake of salted meal was baked by the Vestal Virgins for the wedding ceremony. It was carried before the bride as she went to her new home, broken over her head, and she and the groom ate of it as a sacrifice to Jupiter. Then it was given to the guests. In Macedonia an elaborate cake was begun on the Monday before the ceremony, when the bride and her friends sifted the grain; it was kneaded on Wednesday, when a boy with a sword stood at one end of the trough, while a little girl dropped a ring and a coin into it. The dough was left overnight and then divided up among the guests. The person finding the ring returned it to the groom, who ransomed it with a gift. The dough was then baked, was sung and danced to, then broken up and thrown over the heads of the couple. In Norway, coins are placed on a cake, by each guest in the bride's new home, for the couple. In Spain they used a pie instead for collecting the coins—each guest made a slit in the crust, those who danced with the bride paid more. The cake was eaten daily, and when finished another party was held for the same guests. *Karavai* was the Ukrainian wedding cake, in which all present shared, but the older were served before the younger. To avert the evil eye, in Germany, a cake with a silver coin in it was given to the oldest man in the village on the day before a wedding.

Cakes are distributed at weddings for luck or for the poor, as in China where the groom sends meat-filled cakes to his bride's family, who in turn give them to their friends. In Czechoslovakia, the invited guests get cakes before the wedding, and they send food to the couple. In England, the bride's cake used to be a type of cracknel, which were thrown at her and then given to the poor. In later times they were buns, which were piled up, and the couple kissed over them. Tradition has it that a French chef introduced the idea of icing the buns together, and thus when the cake was broken over her head, it fell apart. In England and America it is believed that if an unmarried girl sleeps with a piece of wedding cake under her pillow she will dream of her future husband. Bride cakes in the United States are usually light in color, rather than dark fruit wedding cake, and are cut at the wedding, the bride and groom holding the knife together to make the initial cut. [NFJ]

Brigit Ancient Irish goddess of fire, culture goddess associated with fertility, cattle, and crops, all household arts and smithcraft, poetry, and wisdom; daughter of Dagda. She appears in Gaulish and British inscriptions as Brigindo, Brigantia, Brig. Her personality passed over to the 6th-century SAINT BRIGIT. See BRES; DANU.

Brihaspati or Brahmanaspati In Vedic mythology, an abstract deity, the Purohita (family priest) of the gods; the Lord of Prayer; the heavenly Brāhman, prototype of the earthly Brāhman, and sometimes also the god Brahmā. In Brāhman mythology he is a divine sage, the son of Angiras, progenitor of the family of Agni, with whom he is identified in the *Rig-Veda*. He helped the gods vanquish the asuras. To teach Indra how to rule the world, Brihaspati, as wisdom incarnate, wrote a treatise on government; to teach him the virtues of secular life, he wrote a treatise on married love. An ancient Indian law code bears his name. Brihaspati's wife, Tārā, was carried off by Soma but restored at the command of Brahmā. Brihaspati is represented with seven mouths, sharp horns, a hundred wings, and armed with an ax and a bow. His chariot or car is called Nītighosha and is drawn by eight horses.

Brisingamen In Scandinavian mythology, the magic necklace, emblem of the stars or fruitfulness of the earth, fashioned by the dwarfs in Svartalfaheim and given to Freya on the condition that she would be unfaithful to her husband, Odin. Freya wore the necklace day and night but occasionally was persuaded to lend it. Loki tried to steal it by entering Freya's palace as a fly. Heimdall saw the robbery with his eagle eyes and pursued the thief. As he was about to strike off Loki's head, the god transformed himself into a flame. Heimdall changed himself into a cloud and sent down rain; Loki changed himself into a polar bear; Heimdall also became a bear and a fight ensued. Loki, however, fearful of disaster, changed himself into a seal. He was vanquished by Heimdall in the same guise and forced to surrender the necklace.

broadside ballads Ballads printed in broadside form and hawked by pedlars in the 17th century. These include both traditional (often in debased versions) and non-traditional ballads.

Brocken The highest peak of the Harz mountains, Germany; in North German folklore, the rendezvous for the Sabbat, the festival of witches and the Devil on Walpurgis Night.

Broomfield Hill A Scottish ballad (Child #43) in which a maiden keeps tryst with her lover but preserves her virginity by putting a sleep-spell on him. [MEL]

Broom Goddess In Chinese folk belief, the Goddess of Fine Weather; "the girl who sweeps the weather clear," named Sao Ch'ing Niang. She has her residence on the Broom Star, Sao Chou. During the great rains little girls cut a human figure representing her out of paper and hang it near the gate. In times of great drought she is also invoked to send the rains. [RDJ]

Brother Jonathan or Jonathan Personification of the people of the United States collectively. The origin of the name is uncertain but it is often attributed to Washington's frequent references to Jonathan Trumbull (1710–1785), governor of Connecticut, whose aid and counsel he often sought. Compare JOHN BULL.

brother-sister incest Sexual intercourse between persons having the relationship of brother and sister (i.e. in certain societies between cousins considered to be of such consanguinity as to make them brother and sister in that society's rules of relationship, as well as between children of the same parent or parents): a custom usually considered criminal but in special instances highly desirable. The complex systems of relationship obtaining in many cultures, for example matrilineal predominance over patrilineal, makes determining of permissible spouses a matter of almost as much confusion and tracing of genealogies to the member of the society as to the stranger-investigator. The motif of involuntary incest, brother and sister not knowing of their relationship, met with in widespread folktales, may be a development of this kind of complexity.

The marriage of brother and sister among the royalty and the higher nobility (a custom noted in Egypt, Persia, Peru, Siam, Ceylon, Wales, Burma, Hawaii, Uganda) is not a primitive one, but the result of a highly developed system of caste relationships. So that a member of exalted royalty or aristocracy might find a mate of suitable high estate, it is necessary for the marriage to occur with a brother or sister. In Hawaii, the most sacred of all persons was the child of such parents who in turn were children of a brother-sister marriage. This child was so sacred that a subject might be killed if his shadow crossed the threshold of the hut of the royal child. It is suggested, as well, that marriage of this kind in societies where possessions were inherited in the female line was the only kind calculated to retain the goods of the father in the hands of the brother. The custom of brother-sister marriage is said also to have been a usual one among the people of Egypt, commoners as well as those of higher rank, disappearing only with the appearance of Christianity.

Much more general than the belief that brother-sister marriage is a good thing is the idea that such a relationship is evil or calamitous. From the earlier belief, reflected in *Genesis* xx, where the marriage of Abraham with Sarah, his half-sister, was not frowned upon (in a polygynous patrilineal society where the children of the various wives were brought up separately), Hebrew thought developed to the statements in *Leviticus* xx, 17 and *Deuteronomy* xxvii, 22: "Cursed be he that lieth with his sister, the daughter of his father, or the daughter of his mother." Death or banishment is often required to allay the wrath of the gods and turn it from the society in which the crime has occurred. The Toradjas of Celebes can raise a rainstorm by causing animals to have incestuous relations. But they refrain from human incest because a storm so induced would be a disaster and because the people performing the act would have to be executed. In addition, droughts and other manifestations of the fertilizing deities are ascribed to such conduct, possibly in the belief that a deed like incest is counter to nature and therefore necessarily infertile. This belief is reflected in folktale, where, as in a Chinese tale, the child of brother-sister incest is misshapen (T550.3).

Mythology and folktale repeat these beliefs and customs. The marriages of Zeus and Hera, of Isis and Osiris, of the moon and the sun—all marriages of brother and sister—are not in any way reprehensible, for these are marriages in the upper strata of beings. But similar incest, when it occurs in nondivine pairs, brings trouble. A Persian tale is climaxed by the loss of Paradise by the unhappy couple; it is possible that Adam and Eve may originally have had something of the same background. In the *Kalevala* (runos 35–36), Kullervo seduces his sister without realizing who she is. When he discovers that she is his sister, he is thunderstruck and cannot prevent her from leaping into a stream and drowning herself. He, returning later to the place of the crime, and discovering the grass and flowers withering on the spot, is overcome with remorse and runs upon his sword. Similarly, in the Scottish ballad

Babylon and its Danish parallel *Herr Truels' Daughters,* the death-or-rape of sisters by their brothers is the basis of tragedy.

The motif of brother-sister incest (T415 and its subdivisions) has several variants and embroideries in folktale. In some stories, the lovers renounce their passion when they discover their kinship; in others, a brother and sister discover to their joy that they really are not related. There are tales of the trickster type in which the lecherous brother manages to have intercourse with his sister by one or another subterfuge; others exist where the brother refuses the lecherous sister. Related to the unwitting ravishing of the sister as in the *Kalevala* (T471.1) is the Welsh tale of the brother and sister who commit incest without realizing it (N365.3). The tale of Gregory on the Stone (Type 933; Q541.1) is a European story: The child of incestuous parents becomes pope and receives the confession of his parents. In a Koryak tale, the child is told by the ducks that his parents are brother and sister; in a variant from British Columbia, the son infers the relationship from the fact that the parents look alike. Folktales of brother and sister incest are world-wide, from Germany and Ireland, Persia, Egypt, China, the Philippines, North America.

It is a principal motif of the Philippine myths of the origin of mankind. A brother and a sister are the only people left; they must commit incest if the human race is to survive. The action is condoned. In a Sanpoil story (*JAFL* 46:133) brother and sister are found out by their parents. The father kills the boy; the girl commits suicide on his body. When the father wants to restore them to life, the other chiefs refuse. He in turn refuses when their children die, and thus permanent death comes into the world. An incident in this story, the discovery of the deed by paint transferred from the girl to the boy, is important in a widely told myth of the Pacific Coast Indians of the origin of the sun and the moon. To discover who the lover is who visits her at night, the girl paints her hands. She sees the paint on her brother's back and flees to the sky. He chases her. They become the sun and the moon. This motif of the sun sister and the moon brother (A736.1) occurs in Norse, Lapp, Rumanian, and German stories too.

☞ Among the Eskimo, and a few Mackenzie area and southeastern United States North American Indian groups, brother-sister incest is portrayed in the tale known among the Eskimo as *Sun Sister and Moon Brother.* As an incident in other tales, however, brother-sister incest is mentioned in tales from almost all parts of native North America. [EWV]

Brown, Frank Clyde (1870–1943) American educator and folksong scholar: born in Virginia, educated at the University of Nashville and the University of Chicago, from which he received his Ph.D. degree. He began teaching in 1893 and became professor of English at Trinity College, Durham, N. C. He organized the North Carolina Folklore Society in 1913 and became its treasurer. He was a member of the Folklore Societies of the United States and of England. In 1915 he became editor of *North Carolina Folklore.* Among his writings is *Elkanah Dettle—His Life and Works* (1910).

Brown Girl An Illinois variant of the ballad, *Lord Thomas and Fair Annet* (Child #73), appearing in a MS. belonging to Mrs. Clara Walpert, Belleville, Ill.

(*JAFL* 52:75). This version has nine stanzas, less than half of the D variant of Child's collection which it most closely resembles. It has changed considerably in transmission, since Elender (Elinor) is now the possessor of house and land, and Lord Thomas is her father.

brownie A household spirit of English and Scottish Highland folklore, also of the Shetland and Western Isles, usually thought of as wearing a brown hood and cloak. He attaches himself to families; especially he frequents farmhouses, barns, and byres, and does the chores at night while the people sleep. He helps with the churning or brewing, sweeps the rooms, saves the corn. Some brownies have even been known to assist at childbirth, or to help their masters win at draughts. But if ever they are criticized they will break dishes, spill milk, turn the cows astray, spoil the crops, and work all kinds of small revenges. Special cakes and bowls of milk are set aside for them, but never, never any wages or reward. A kindly woman once made a little cap and coat for the brownie who so faithfully cleaned her pans. He put them on and then was gone forever. In fact to get rid of a troublesome brownie all you have to do is make a new little hood and cloak for him; he will put them on, chanting, "A new cloak, a new hood/ Brownie will do no more good" or "Gie brownie coat, gie brownie sark/ Ye'll get nae mair o' brownie's wark." Compare AITVARAS, BOGGART; BOGLE; DOMOVIK; KAUKAS; NISSE; PARA.

Brug na Bóinne The city of the Boyne; the great city of the Dagda of the Tuatha Dé Danann, the round underground fort (*sid*) on the river Boyne near Stackallen Bridge in Leinster, Ireland. This was the dwelling place of Dagda, of Bóann, his queen, and of their people: later taken over by Angus Og, his son. See SÍDE.

Bruin The bear in *Reynard the Fox;* hence (not capitalized) a bear, in popular allusion.

Brunhild In the *Nibelungenlied,* a legendary queen who vows that he who wins her must first defeat her in hurling a spear and other feats. By the magical aid of Siegfried, King Gunther is successful, but, finding her unmanageable, he again appeals to Siegfried, who beats her and, by taking away her ring and girdle, effectually tames her. Discovering the deceit and trickery of her conquest, she persuades Hagen to avenge her by murdering Siegfried.

Brut, Brute, or **Brutus** Legendary king of Britain and founder of the British race; great-grandson of Æneas of Troy. After inadvertently killing his father, Sylvius, Brut led a remnant of the Trojans to England which was inhabited then only by a few giants. He founded New Troy or Trinovantum (now London) and was the progenitor of the legendary line of kings which included Bladud, Gorboduc, Ferrex, Lud, Porrex, Cymbeline, Vortigern, and Arthur. The legend is told in Nennius's *Historia Britonum* (9th century), in Geoffrey of Monmouth's *Historia Regum Britanniœ* (c. 1135), in Wace's French *Roman de Brut* (c. 1155), and in Layamon's English *Brut* (c. 1200).

Brynhild In the *Volsunga Saga,* a Valkyrie who is thrown into an enchanted sleep by Odin because she had given victory to a younger, handsomer king than the one Odin designated. She is awakened by Sigurd who falls in love with her, but, through the power of a magic drink, he forgets her and marries Gudrun. Later he woos and wins Brynhild for Gunnar, Gudrun's brother. Brynhild learns of the substitution of Sigurd for Gunnar and, enraged, provokes Gunnar to have Sigurd killed, after which she kills herself.

bucca A supernatural being of the folklore of Cornwall: related to the Irish puca, Welsh pwca, English puck. See CELTIC FOLKLORE.

Bucephalus Literally, ox-head; the war-horse of Alexander the Great. Untamed and never before ridden by man, the horse was refused by Philip, Alexander's father, as being too wild; Alexander then mounted, the horse permitted itself to be managed, and an oracle was fulfilled whereby Alexander would inherit the crown of Macedonia.

Buddha Literally, the Enlightened: a deified religious teacher; specifically, Gautama Siddhartha (563?–483? B.C.), the founder of the Buddhist faith; Gautama was born in the Lumbini Grove (Nepāl) near the ancient town of Kapilavastu. His father was a prince of the Sākya clan who ruled a small kingdom in what is now the northeastern part of the United Provinces and the southern part of Nepāl. His mother, Māyā, is said to have conceived him after a dream in which she saw him descending from heaven and entering her womb in the form of a white elephant.

Buddha had many earlier existences which are described in the *Jātaka.* As the time approached for his final birth, earthquakes and miracles occurred and the water of the ocean became sweet. It was prophesied that he would become either a universal monarch (*chakravartin*) or a Buddha enlightened for the salvation of mankind. When the time came, Buddha, while still in the Tuṣita heaven, made the five observations to determine the right family, continent, district, time, and mother in which to be born. At birth his body bore 32 primary and 80 secondary marks; he had a marvelous tongue which could read forth to the world of Brahmā, indicating his greatness; he uttered the shout of victory and took seven steps. At the same moment were born the Bo tree, his future wife, his horse, elephant, and charioteer.

He was raised in luxury and was prevented by his father, who wished him to become a ruler, from seeing the three (or four) sights—a decrepit old man, a diseased man, a dead man, and a religious ascetic. Despite his father's guards, Gautama did see the four sights and, realizing the impermanence of earthly things, at 29 he made the "Great Renunciation." He gave up his kingdom, left his wife and child and departed from the city. The gods made his exit possible in the dead of night by preventing his horse's hoofs from touching the ground and by opening the city gates noiselessly.

In the company of five ascetics, Buddha entered upon a course of discipline under a Bel tree near Gayā. After six years, however, he was convinced that asceticism was not the road to truth, and became a beggar. His companions then deserted him. Later, while he was sitting under the tree of knowledge, the prince of evil, Māra, and his daughters, tried to dissuade him from his purpose, but the stones and darts he and his cohorts threw changed to flowers when they reached Gautama. At sunset the period of temptation was over and Māra was vanquished. The following night Gautama attained Buddhahood, became enlightened, and the serpent-king Muçalinda celebrated his victory by covering him with his hood during the storm which followed.

While Buddha was debating whether or not to teach men the truths he had learned, i.e. that existence involves suffering which is the result of desire, and thus the "suppression of desire will lead to extinction of suffering," Brahmā appeared and reminded him that, unless men were told, they could not obtain salvation. His first converts were two merchants who brought him rice and honey-cakes, and later the five ascetics who had earlier deserted him. He then wandered from place to place for 45 years preaching to all who would listen.

When Buddha realized that he was going to die, he lay down under two Sāla trees which bloomed out of season. He made his last convert, Subhadra, and asked of the assembled monks whether they had any doubts concerning his teaching. Hearing none, he went into a series of trances from which he entered the realm of the infinity of space, then of consciousness, of nothingness, of neither perception or non-perception and non-sensation, finally reaching nirvana. His death was accompanied by signs and portents. His funeral pyre could not be lighted until Kaśyapa had arrived and paid reverence, whereupon the pyre burst into flame spontaneously. Buddha prophesied the decline and disappearance of the religion. When it is no longer honored, the relics will gather under the Bo tree and teach the doctrine to the gods from all the worlds and then will put forth flames and burn up.

There is more than one Buddha and each may have an earthly life, but there is never more than one in the world at any one time. Buddhas come into being at irregular intervals and only when there is a special need for their presence. In the Mahāyāna system of Buddhism there are 300 million śakyamunis (Buddhas).

Buddha is usually represented in art with cropped curly locks seated on or in a lotus symbolizing the essence of enlightenment. The chief Buddhist symbol is the stūpa which is a relic shrine believed to contain a bone or some relic of the Buddha and thus symbolizes him. His shadow and footsteps (Sripada) are found in many parts of Asia. See ADAM'S PEAK.

Buffalo An animal character of many Plains, Southwestern, and Central Woodlands North American Indian tales, an animal being for whom many ceremonies, feasts, and dances are given by Plains and Woodlands tribes: often associated with rain. Tales of visits of human beings to a land under the earth where the buffalo live, tales of buffalo-human marriages and the experiences of the offspring of such, are frequent. Among the Kiowa, Apache, and other tribes, Buffalo and Buffalo Old Woman are well-known myth characters. Several Plains and Woodland tribes have Buffalo-head ceremonies; the Hidatsa of North Dakota offer food and prayers to buffalo skulls placed on an altar when they need rain; the Shawnee dip a buffalo tail in water and shake it gently to produce rain. [EWV]

Buffalo Dance A North American Indian mimetic group dance addressed to the spirit of the buffalo: danced to procure success in the hunt, or good health.

It is confined to American Indian tribes dependent on the buffalo for sustenance. The performers, ornamented with fantastic body-painting, wear also a horned furry headdress, often also the tail. Among the Plains Indian men's societies, the Mandan Buffalo Dance was the most terrifyingly realistic mime of milling herds, whereas the women's White Buffalo Cow society merely stamped in upright posture. The function of this dance, and of the Blackfoot women's Ma'toki (a realistic drama of the hunt) was to lure the herds. Both were associated with the sun dance. From November to January, Rio Grande pueblos still mime the buffalo; at San Felipe and San Ildefonso the buffalo are lured by Buffalo Maidens. The Fox and Iroquois Buffalo societies effect cures, the Fox partly by fire association and charcoal marking. They jump, whirl, butt, bellow, progressing in a circle, the Fox with the sun, the Iroquois contrary. Plains Buffalo societies are mostly extinct. [GPK]

Buffalo Gals One of the favorite American play-party and square-dance songs: a fiddle, fife, and banjo tune, sung in 1844 as a minstrel song, *Lubly Fan*, and changed from town to town to suit the local ladies as *Louisiana Gals, Bowery Gals, Pittsburgh Gals*, etc. A copyrighted swing version appeared in the 1940's and was popular on the radio and juke boxes.

bug or **bog** The word for "god" in all Slavic languages, occurring in numerous compounds, such as Biel-Bog (white or good god), Cherno-Bog (black or bad god), Stribog (god of winds), etc., and used also for the Christian "God."

bugah or **booger dance** Clowned mimicry of the Cherokee Indians. Seven bogeys wear masks of gourd, wood, or pasteboard and shawls and sweaters which are collected from the women. They enact any ludicrous characters they fancy, including white traders, Negroes. or joking relatives; one by one they portray their character with appropriate gestures by a uniform step similar to that of the Iroquois False Face (gagósä)—a heavy jump on both feet. They do everything in a topsy-turvy manner and tease relatives and scare children. In the end everyone joins in the *yona*, the bear round dance.

The name, booger dance (*tsunagadali* in Cherokee), suggests origin in impersonation of the spirits of the dead. At present its chief function appears an outlet for suppressed aversions. [GPK]

bugbear A sort of hobgoblin of English folklore, thought of as being in the form of a bear; literally, a goblin bear: invoked to come and eat naughty children. The meaning has become extended to apply to anything dreaded and feared, especially when needlessly feared. See BOGEY.

Bugios Literally monkeys: clowns or demonic buffoon dancers in grotesque animal masks, associated with the Portuguese *Mouriscada* at Sobrado on St. John's Day. The leader rides into town backwards, sowing flax (which he calls maize); he harrows, then plows with an upside-down yoke. He is not masked and wears gorgeous church vestments. The wild, uncouth Bugios do battle with the sedate Mouriscos until the Bugio leader is captured and led off amid lament. With a *serpe*, or dragon, they recapture him and join the Mouriscos in a final Christian Dança do Santo. Vestiges of fertility and vegetation magic are apparent in the preliminary entry and in the symbolic battle between the destructive (winter) powers and the radiant (summer) powers. As in other Moriscas this is more significant than the Christian veneer. [GPK]

building castle between heaven and earth A folktale motif (H1036) in which the impossible task of building a castle suspended between heaven and earth is imposed either as an alternative for the death of the hero, to secure tribute from the hero's king, or for some other reason beneficial to the imposer of the task. Probably the most famous compliance with this request was that of Achikar, minister and magician to Sennacherib, king of Assyria. He evidently turned the trick with no trouble at all, thus saving his sovereign from having to pay the enormous tribute demanded in lieu of the castle.

Often throughout European folktale the answer of the victim to such a request is, "I will, indeed, if you will supply the materials." That is what Dom Jean said. Dom Jean (hero of a French folktale) was servitor to a king who had incurred the wrath of a neighboring king. Dom Jean not only countered with the poser of demanding the materials but went up the mountain and caught four young eagles, which he secretly trained to fly above his head, each holding one corner of a paper house. When the day came for Dom Jean to produce the castle in the air, he threatened to cut off the head of the demander of the miracle, if the king did not produce the materials for building the castle "in the morning." The materials were not forthcoming, and the frightened king offered Dom Jean his daughter in marriage instead. Dom Jean refused the daughter, but let the old king off for a tribute of gold to his own monarch. Once this was given Dom Jean produced the four young eagles bearing the paper castle in the air. Great was the wonderment at the cleverness of young Dom Jean, who of course went home with the tribute of gold and received as reward the hand of his own king's daughter.

building ceremonies Usage today in the construction of domestic, civil, or religious buildings has little in common with that in ancient and medieval times throughout the world. Our building rites and ceremonies at present are but "pale and attenuated survivals." Phases of the lore on various steps in building construction through many centuries may here be considered briefly:

1 *Site* Early peoples selected sites favorable to their occupation; in medieval times and among backward people of modern Europe, sites were selected by divination of various types among which animal omens were the most common.

2 *Survey and consecration of the land* Marking off the land was a ceremony with domestic, religious, and agricultural connotations. Dido's ruse for the site of Carthage (cutting a bull's hide into slender thongs wherewith to measure the area) finds similarities in legends for the same purpose in Britain, Scandinavia, Siberia, China, Holland, and elsewhere. The land was consecrated after survey by prayers, blessings, and holy water through the medium of priests, medicine-men, and others.

3 *Laying the foundation* Both the day and the hour had to be lucky; local spirits and the earth spirits had to be propitiated; evil spirits had to be driven away and witches' spells had to be averted or destroyed. Ancestral spirits must be placated and new guardian spirits arranged for. Omens of luck must be put in the foundations, such as bread, salt, plants and herbs of a health-giving nature, gold and silver and money. The pot of coins used in the foundation stone is explained by J. Rendel Harris as "ransom money" for the "person that ought to be there." (*Folk-Lore* XV: 441).

4 *Foundation sacrifice* Building sacrifice was practiced in Denmark, Germany, Siam, Japan, Australia, and elsewhere. It was generally believed that no edifice could stand firmly unless it was laid in blood, such was the magical virtue ascribed to this vital fluid (See BLOOD). Accordingly, there existed in both pagan and Christian times the practice of placing in the wall of a house, castle, fortress, or church a human being, frequently a child sold by its mother for this purpose. There exist many affecting legends about such sacrifices. This belief of mural inhumation for stability existed down to the mid-1800's. An earlier method of gaining the desired blood-bath for foundations was that of crushing victims in a pit, used in Borneo and Siam. These practices, it should be mentioned are not merely legendary but are attested by authentic records. Mass hysteria has prevailed in some cases, recorded in Europe as well as elsewhere, from fear of mural burial.

5 *Substitutions for human sacrifice* There was the actual mural sacrifice of animals and the symbolic sacrifice, whereby a fowl—most generally a cock—or animal was killed and its blood let drip into the foundation pit. In England and on the Continent, workmen have found, when dismantling walls of homes and churches, the bones of animals, dolls, coffins, images, and other items which seem to have acted as substitutes for human sacrifice at the foundation rites.

6 *Other ceremonies and customs* Dances were held in Mexico and Central America after raising a building. During or after the construction workmen in Scotland were sometimes given ale, whiskey, bread, and cheese. In early days it was customary to feast workers or to give them some entertainment to which they looked forward. Building in Africa, Asia Minor, in Georgia (United States) was carried on to the accompaniment of music or song. Some of these customs, especially those of dancing and feasting, have been noted in United States pioneer communities. [GPS]

bula The smallest of the trio of vodun ceremonial drums, approximately 18 inches high and 8 inches in diameter. Like the other drums of this group, it must be baptized after it is made. It begins the drum rhythm in the rites, following the ogan and the rattles, and is played with two sticks. Sometimes known also as *bébé* in Haiti, its name in Surinam is *babula*.

Bulfinch, Thomas (1796–1867) American compiler of myths. Son of Charles Bulfinch, eminent architect, he was born at Newton, Mass., and educated at Boston Latin School, Phillips Exeter Academy, and Harvard, where he was graduated in 1814. He held a job as clerk in a bank from 1837 until his death, a position which gave him a living and leisure time to study and write. Among his books were *Hebrew Lyrical History* (1853), *The Age of Fable* (1855), *The Age of Chivalry* (1858), *Legends of Charlemagne* (1863), and *Poetry of the Age* *of Fable* (1863). His best known work is *The Age of Fable*, which attempts with some success to make mythology interesting, and deals with Greek, Roman, Scandinavian, Celtic, and Oriental mythologies. *The Age of Chivalry* tries, but with less success, to do the same thing for Arthurian and early Welsh legends.

bull The cult of the bull is best known from references to it in the Near, Middle, and Far East. The ancient Persians worshipped the Supreme Bull who caused grass to grow and was pure and uncreated. In India, Nandi, Śiva's bull, was the leader of Śiva's attendants. Although ethnographers exaggerate when they assert that there "is not a god in Semitic religions who is not assimilated to, and represented as, a bull," the bull cult competed with Yahweh who at one time was worshipped in the form of a bull. The bull was prominent as an incarnation or attribute of Egyptian gods and kings. In ancient Greece, young men, made temporary kings, sacrificed bulls to Poseidon. The bull is also associated with Dionysus. The Achaian priestesses of earth drank bull's blood before entering their caves to prophesy and Pausanias mentions bull's blood as a test of chastity. The blood and perhaps testicles of bulls were used in the mysteries of Attis and Cybele. Peoples have variously associated the sun, the moon, and the constellation Taurus with the bull; the Hittites associated the bull with thunder, and a similar reference is found in the *Rig-Veda*. The Zulu warriors drank the gall of bulls killed by their warriors with bare hands and the boys ate the flesh.

The use of bulls as draft animals has been associated by ethnographers with the cultural transformation from the stage when women did all the agricultural work to the time when men did it. The best known European references to the sexual prowess of the bull are in the stories of Europa who was seduced by one, and of Pasiphae who herself did the seduction with the help of Dædalus and produced the Minotaur with man's body and bull's head. Attempts have been made to find in this a vestigial sun myth. The ceremonies performed by the king and queen of Knossos masked as bull and cow, and the crane dance, have been adduced in support of this. As will have been noted most of the evidence—except the Zulu ceremony which belongs to a different order of folk-thinking—comes from a period when professional theologians of the era worked popular belief into some sort of religious system. Consequently conclusions drawn by folklorists who did not distinguish the theology of the "we-group" from the theology of the "they-group" are open to question. The word "bull" in the term "Irish bull" is a linguistic accident as it derives from a word probably related to Old French *boule* meaning to trick or confuse. [RDJ]

bull dance An impersonation of the bull: in Europe of the native cattle, in the American Great Plains of the buffalo. In Europe, anciently, from Egypt to Scotland, the blood of the sacrificed bull was believed to imbue the earth with life, and the practice of shedding the bull's blood was preserved in the British Isles as bull-baiting into the 19th century. In Crete the monstrous Minotaur was deified and sacrificed to, and his slaying was reenacted in the Athenian Theseus plays. In Egypt the bull Apis and corn god Osiris, after their death and dismemberment, were resurrected as Osiris-Apis. Such bullfight and resurrection rites have found their way through Spain to Mexico and New Mexico, in the huehuenches of Villa Alta, Oaxaca, in the toreadores of the Sierra de Puebla, in the toro-abuelo (bull-grandfather) fight connected with the San Ildefonso and San Juan matachina. Of independent origin, the bull dance of the Plains Buffalo societies mimed the hunt to insure success. See BUFFALO DANCE. [GPK]

Bullkater Literally, tom-cat: a field spirit of Silesian peasant belief. The reaper who cuts the last sheaf of rye is himself called the Tom-Cat. He is dressed in rye stalks and equipped with a long braided green tail. His function is to chase onlookers with a long stick and beat them when caught. This is to chase away the *old* Bullkater, by whom they are believed to have become possessed while watching the reaping. Compare CAILLEAC; KORNWOLF.

bull-roarer A noise-making instrument of almost world-wide distribution, used by primitive peoples as an important element in magic ceremonies, puberty and initiation rites since Paleolithic times, and still significant in certain tribal rituals of Australia and New Guinea. It consists of a flat oval slab of bone, stone, or wood, tapered toward each end, with a cord or thong threaded through a hole near one end, by which it is whirled over the head to produce a harsh roaring or wailing sound. The magic symbolism of the bull-roarer derives partly from its shape and decoration, partly from its weird and terrifying sound, partly from the variations in size of the instruments.

The shape, interpreted in various ways, represents potency, procreation, fertility. When construed as a fish (often further identified as such by serrated edges and painted or incised scale patterns) it bears the double fertility meaning of the teeming roe and of water. Sometimes it is painted red, the blood color, hence the color of life itself, which may be used on instruments for men only. Among the Diegueños of California, it represented an arrow and carried three notches, denoting the three feathers of the arrow and the practice of swinging it three times to the east as a summons to religious rites. In New Guinea, the bull-roarer is often covered with magic symbols of warning.

The sound of the bull-roarer is the voice of a ghost, an ancestor, a monster, or some powerful spirit, who has power to frighten enemies, to summon the gods and the elements, to convey supernatural warnings, to ward off evil, to insure the wielder's own procreative powers. Sometimes the voice is associated with the wind, which may, by its invocation, be forced to bring rain. In any case, the harsh and strident sound is characteristic of instruments sacred to civilizations and ceremonies in which the men are dominant.

The significance of the size of the instrument has to do with the common conception that greater size is a sign of greater importance and is a male attribute, and with the difference in the sound produced by difference in size. The smaller the oval slab and the faster the swing of the cord, the higher the pitch. The Bukaua and Yabim (or Jabim) tribes of New Guinea think of the small, shrill-voiced bull-roarers as female, the wives of the larger and deeper-toned ones. Large ones are divided into "ruling" and "serving" categories, each named for a respected man of the past, according to their standing in the tribe. These are handed down from generation to generation and the names are used as battle cries. Miniature bull-roarers are worn by the chiefs at certain feasts, and all prominent Yabim tribesmen take bull-roarers with them to the grave.

Throughout Australia and New Guinea, the use of the bull-roarer, wherever it is found, is well defined. Its terror-inspiring roar is heard almost exclusively as an accompaniment to puberty and initiation rites. The details of the ceremonies, the regulation of the conduct of women, and the explanation of the noise differ somewhat from tribe to tribe, but the general pattern is this: The boys are led from the village to shelters in the forest where their circumcision, subincision, and other initiation procedures take place. Women must remain at home, where the voices of the swinging bull-roarers carry to them the sense of unimaginable horror of the events they have been told will go on.

The Bibinga tell women and children that what they hear is the voice of Katajalina, a spirit who lives in an anthill, eats up the novices, and then brings them back to life. The story of a monster who swallows and then disgorges the boys is common to many tribes of this area, including the Yabim, Bukaua, Kai, and Tami of New Guinea, and the name of the instrument is either the word for monster or for ghost ("grandfather" among the Kai). One tribe actually builds a monster-hut for the initiates to stay in, and the bull-roarers are swung in its belly to make it roar.

The Urabunna of central Australia tell the uninitiated that the bull-roarer's sound is the voice of a spirit who changes the lads into initiated men by taking them away, replacing their insides with new material, and returning them. If a woman should see the bull-roarers, the boy related to her would die, along with his mother and sisters.

Boys of the Unmatjera (also central Australia) must sound the bull-roarer after circumcision and subincision until they recover from the operation, lest an evil spirit swoop out of the sky upon them and carry them off.

The secret of the bull-roarer, which is ordinarily hidden from women in men's club houses, in stream beds forbidden to women, or other safe hiding places, is revealed to the initiates under strict vows of silence. One ceremony of this kind involves striking each boy on the forehead and under the chin with the bull-roarer. Others threaten him with his own death as well as that of any woman or child to whom he reveals the secret. The might of the bull-roarer is such that if it should break and a chip strike any one, he would be wounded wherever the bull-roarer had touched him in his next fight. Among some tribes, the touch of the bull-roarer, or even the sight of it, brings instant death to the uninitiated.

The Wonghi, or Wonghibon, tribe of New South Wales, explains the sound of the bull-roarers as that of Thuremlin, or Daramulun, a supernatural being who knocks out one tooth of each novice as a part of his initiation. They allow no uninitiated person to see the bull-roarer under pain of death.

Similar customs prevail through Melanesia and even in Africa, among the Ekoi of South Nigeria and the Nandi of East Africa. The Yoruba, however, permit women to see and handle bull-roarers with impunity, but not to know the source of their sound.

In central Brazil, the Bororo whirl the bull-roarer at mortuary rites, from which women are excluded. The noise is the signal for women to hide to escape the death which would surely overtake them, should they see it.

North American Indian ceremonies making use of the bull-roarer were religious, but most tribes no longer remember the purpose or importance of the instrument, which survives occasionally as a toy. However, the size of the ceremonial bull-roarers indicate that they were used outdoors. Diegueño chiefs used them to summon the people to religious rites and occasionally might use them as a warning in time of danger. The Tusayan Indians used the bull-roarer in their Flute Observance, anointing it with honey; and the Hopi Flute Fraternity whirl it on solemn occasions, from which women are not excluded. The Pomo Indians of California used it during the Thunder Rites at the end of summer rituals.

The origin of the instrument is unknown and it may or may not come from a common source to the widely separated cultures in which it figures. Any device so simple could have been invented many times over. Schoolboys have developed its principle for themselves by slipping a string through the hole in a ruler and swinging it with noisy results. Even infants delight themselves by similar combinations of available objects. The elementary mechanical impulse to put a string through a hole is almost universal.

However that may be, in recent times, like many other magic devices, the bull-roarer has descended in many places, as it has among American Indians of the west coast, to the level of a toy, and in the Malay Peninsula to the practical function of scaring elephants away from plantations.   THERESA C. BRAKELEY

Bumba The name for the Bush Negro love amulet; also (as Ma Bumba), a deity of the winti cult of Negroes of Paramaribo, Dutch Guiana: probably of Congo origin. [MJH]

bundling An old courting custom of Holland, Ireland, Scotland, Wales, etc., which survived in certain parts of the United States, notoriously in New England and especially in Connecticut, and in which lovers or engaged couples, dressed or partly dressed, lay on or in the same bed. It is also said that belated visitors or travelers were sometimes invited to share the bed of the daughter of the house. The custom was naturally the subject of much moralizing and satire; but (to quote *The Rev. Samuel Peters' LL.D. General History of Connecticut*) "I am no advocate of temptation; yet must say, that *bundling* has prevailed 160 years in New England, and, I verily believe, with ten times more chastity than the sitting on a sofa. I had daughters, and speak from near forty years' experience." Although in theory and practice simply a convenience to save fuel or to keep the courting couple from freezing in the intimacy of their single possible private interviewing place, the girl's bedroom—only the principal rooms of the house being heated—, the practice of bundling led occasionally to "natural consequences." Bundling died out in the United States in the early decades of the 19th century, having attained a peak of notoriety during and just before the American Revolution (c. 1750–1780). Bundling probably derived from the older common bed, in which everyone in the household, and the visitors who stayed the night, slept under the same cover. The custom of wife-lending, as for example among the Eskimos, is not the same, despite parallels which have been drawn, but the American traveling-salesman stories are probably related in origin.

bungling host A widespread North American Indian tale of the failure by Trickster to imitate magic methods of procuring food: told in many versions in all of North America except the Arctic, and especially popular on the North Pacific Coast. The tale is also known in Siberia. After seeing his host produce food in various ways (host lets oil drip from his hands; birds produce food by song; animal cuts its hand or feet; animals stab or shoot themselves; wood is transformed into meat; host kills his children for food, etc.), Trickster, when he is host, attempts to do likewise, but fails and often barely escapes death. For detailed analysis of this tale see Franz Boas, *Tsimshian Mythology* (*RBAE* 31, 1916). [EWV]

Bunyip A bellowing water monster of Australian native mythology who lives at the bottom of lakes and water holes into which he draws his human victims. [KL]

al-Buraq or **Al-Borak** Literally, the bright one; the white animal on which Mohammed rode during the mi'raj, or night journey to the seven heavens. Some say it was a horse, some say an ass, but Mohammed said "something in-between." Hence al-Buraq is generally mentioned as a mule, although he had wings and is often pictured as a kind of griffin. See MI'RAJ.

burdock Burdock leaves are used as a fever remedy in New England: the leaves are bandaged, point down, to the patient's wrists and ankles. They thus absorb the fever, which will run out at the points. Missouri Negroes cure colic by hanging a string of burdock around the baby's neck. In Ireland the roots of the great common burdock (*meacan an tataba*) are pounded, boiled, and made into a poultice for ringworm. The poultice is usually prepared on the opposite side of a river from the patient, lest the worm get a whiff of the root and shift to another place.

Buri or **Bure** In Teutonic mythology, the progenitor of the gods. While Ymir slept, his cow, Audhumla, licking the briny ice, uncovered a head. Buri stepped out and immediately produced a son, Borr. The giants, becoming aware of his existence, started a war which lasted until the marriage of Borr and Bestla.

burial From early and primitive efforts to keep the spirit of relative or friend from returning to trouble his survivors the burial customs of mankind show a fairly steady evolution toward the current civilized type of ritual which emphasizes quite the opposite concern—the sorrow of the bereaved that their loved one has left them. It is difficult for modern folk to understand the point of view of the ancients and the remaining primitives, so far have we come from them psychologically and theologically. Yet anthropology and archeology have by now evaluated the evidence of old burial sites and remains, and comparative religion has added its logical inferences, with the result that we

now know that the big idea of burials was to defend the survivors from the very dangerous discontented souls or ghosts of the recently dead.

Suddenly unemployed and quite ill at ease the only partly departed spirits were supposed to sit around, muttering and gibbering, watching the living and wishing they were back among them again. The most unhappy and therefore the most dangerous ghosts are those sulking around because they died young and did not have a chance to enjoy life or because they died childless. These spirits are so envious that they chase the living at night, cause disease and other disturbances, and make it necessary for the medicine man to conduct elaborate and expensive exercises of exorcism.

Some tribes went so far as to anticipate the ghost's release from the living body. Beginning with the moment when it became apparent that a member of the tribe must soon die of his disease or wound, measures were taken to protect the tribe itself from his soon-to-be-released spirit, which, if not properly exorcised by correct burial rites, would come back to wander uneasily about his old "haunts" and trouble the living. So strong and deep-seated was the primitive fear of a corpse and its nearby ghost that the dying person was, among tribes as far apart as Ceylon, Russia, the Philippines, South Africa, and Samaria, removed from the house lest he pollute it by dying within and make necessary its burning.

In certain country parts of Europe where the dying are taken from their beds and laid upon straw or the bare ground, one rationalized explanation is that a man cannot die upon feathers for that is unlucky. Another is that by coming into direct contact with the earth the dying man may more quickly enter the underground realm of the dead. Doubtless, in many cases, he did die sooner, from the exposure. The custom has been defended on that very basis, that by shortening the man's sufferings a favor is done him, a sort of involuntary euthanasia.

But there is no such mercy in the widespread practices of abandonment of the dying and even their burial before death. Tribes in Australia, Central America, Burma, and the Sudan are reliably reported to practice the former, while the latter custom prevails, or did until very recently, in parts of Paraguay, Fiji, and among the Hottentot and Bantu peoples. Among the Yakuts of Siberia, so great was the dread of a corpse in the hut or even in the village that the very old and diseased were given the best seat and the best food at their own funeral feast, then taken out into the forest and buried alive surrounded by food and possessions, including even horses for their trip to the next world—to make sure the ghosts had no excuse for remaining in the vicinity of the village.

Fear of the corpse is reflected in the ceremonial uncleanness acquired by contact with one. The Jews, their scriptures reveal, regarded a corpse as particularly defiling, and whoever touched one was "unclean" for seven days (*Haggai* ii, 13; *Numbers* xix, 11 ff.). On the third and seventh days, purification was required, and on the seventh day, bathing and clothes-washing as well. The purification was an elaborate process and evidently of ancient, perhaps animistic, origin, as the detailed description in *Numbers* xix suggests.

A spotless unblemished red heifer which had never

borne the yoke was killed outside the camp and the blood sprinkled by the priest with his finger before the tabernacle seven times. The heifer was then burned, skin, flesh, blood, and even dung. Cedar wood, hyssop (probably caper bush), and scarlet (cochineal pigment) were flung into the burning. The resultant ash was mixed with running water and then sprinkled from a hyssop switch by a "clean" person upon the defiled one who had touched the corpse. Thus the ghost was driven away by the triply effective combination of fire, water, and aromatic woods and herbs. The hyssop was reckoned a particularly effective agent in exorcising evil spirits and its aspergent properties are recognized even today in the celebration of the mass when the sprinkling of the holy water is accompanied by the Anthem "Purge me with hyssop and I shall be clean" based on Psalm li, 7 (l, 9 in the Vulgate). The same mixture used to purify ceremonially the person who has touched a corpse must also be sprinkled upon the tent in which the man had died, upon all vessels within it and all persons present at the death.

The aspergent solution was also used to purify anyone who had touched a grave, which is why gravemarkers should be white, to warn the living. "Whited sepulchres," to which Jesus compared the Pharisees, "which indeed appear beautiful outward, but are within full of dead men's bones, and of all uncleanness," (*Matthew* xxiii, 27) were whited, not to make them appear beautiful, but to warn passers-by not to touch the grave, lest they too become full of uncleanness and require seven days' purification.

The relatives of the dead man were sometimes considered unclean, and, according to *Hosea* ix, 4, the very food of mourners defiled all who ate it. In fact the custom of wearing distinctive mourning garb probably originated as a warning against contamination by contact with the close relatives of the newly deceased.

The preparation of the body for its final disposition has varied greatly, dependent somewhat upon the method chosen to dispose of it, which in turn depends upon where and how far the soul is supposed to be going. If the journey to the next world is to be long, or if the body is expected to be reanimated after a considerable period of time, or periodically, by the return of the soul or by resurrection to some heaven, it is likely that an attempt at preservation of the body will be made. Oiling, salting, pickling, smoking, drying, stuffing the removed skin, and mummifying by filling the eviscerated body with bitumen and spices, all these methods have been used, the last mentioned with more success than the others, particularly in Egypt, Peru, and the Canary Islands. Howells, in *The Heathens*, in his informative chapter on Souls, Ghosts and Death, reports on several instances of chance mummification, including the accidental tanning of a cellarful of cadavers in the crypt of St. Michan's church in Dublin.

For the preservation of the body for a short period of time, less attention is necessary and is more apt to be expended on beautifying the corpse. Painting the body has occurred frequently, and varies from the masterpieces of the Congo corpse-painters, who are quite uninhibited in their art with rather startling results, to the present-day professional embalmers, who use every cosmetic artifice to restore the bloom of youth to even the elderly face, with results sometimes equally

startling to those who knew the deceased. The murmured admiration by chronic funeral-attenders is in the same class with the louder expressions of the dwellers on the Congo who pay admission to see the art exhibit.

An interesting survival of the ancient anxiety to get rid of the body as soon as possible lest the ghost be encouraged to remain is seen in the quick burials customary among Jews even today—within a few hours if possible, preferably before sundown. Other reasons for the hasty interment are often offered, and few Jews today are aware of the origin of the custom, but the Mosaic code itself is explicit concerning the ceremonial uncleanness of a corpse.

The subject of funerals is covered in another article, but the interment service at the grave falls properly under the subject of burials. And the getting of the body out of the house and safely into the grave or burned has important folklore connotations, for the object is to prevent the ghost from finding the way back to haunt the house. Of course, the safest way is to burn the house, and that was often done in primitive communities. Sometimes the rest of the houses in the village were torn down and the house of the deceased left standing, leaving the ghost in solitary splendor, where he could not hurt anyone. The people of some cultures still take the corpse out of the house through the roof, or a window, or a hole in the wall. The same idea, to fool the ghost, is in mind among the Menomini Indians when the nearest relative sneaks away home from the cemetery "while the soul is still absorbed in its own funeral." (Howells, *op. cit.*, p. 163.) Chinese set off firecrackers on the way back from the grave. In New England, the writer remembers being shocked as a young minister by the race home from the grave which he was assured was an old and honored custom, "no disrespect intended." He thought then that the mourners were in a very unmannerly hurry to get back to the bounteous repast always served at the home after the burying, but he now suspects that, whether they knew it or not, these devout mourners were hastening *from* as much as *to*.

The methods of disposing of the body, the act which is after all and from the beginning the main purpose of the burial, have been many. Cremation is treated in another article, but the other ways, not so rapid nor so final, had their reasons for being, and included interment in graves which might be in consecrated ground or not, interment in huts, tombs, vaults, caves, and catacombs, or in canoes, boats, ships, on rafts, or in rivers or the sea itself. Then there is suspension in the air on burial platforms or in trees as practiced by some American Indians. The Parsees of India, who consider both fire and the earth too sacred to be polluted by a corpse, expose their dead inside towers of silence to which come the birds of the air to leave nothing after an hour or two but the bones, which are gathered twice a year and put into a central dry well where they soon crumble from exposure to the elements. Still a different, though related, form of burial is the secondary or bundle burial practiced by North American Indians in Maine and Wisconsin, and also in parts of Polynesia and Asia, and long ago in Bronze Age Europe. This method varies in the way the flesh is removed from the bones, either by scraping or burying in the earth. The cleaned bones are tied up in a skin, then buried in a pot or in a pile. Frequently when exhumed by scientists they are found to have been smeared with red ocher.

Various incidental practices deserve mention. As to the question of determining who has the right to decide where, when, and how the body shall be buried, the decision was originally left to the tribe through the chief or medicine man. It is now widely accepted in the United States "that the bodies of the dead belong to the surviving relations, in the order of inheritance as property, and that they have the right to dispose of them as such . . ." This would mean that the decisions referred to belong first to husband or wife, children next, and then according to the "nearest relative" order. The wishes of the deceased, if known through a will or otherwise, and the customary practice of the deceased's church or fraternal order, are usually respected. Reburials however are under the court's jurisdiction.

Notice should be taken of the recent great changes in the general attitude of the American public toward burials, which are now commonly conducted with less deep mourning and rather more dignity. Black crape has largely given way to flowers: the mourners are less lugubriously costumed, and the dirt formerly cast at the descending casket to the accompaniment of "Ashes to ashes: dust to dust" has been superseded by flowers. See BARASHNŪM; CREMATION; FUNERAL CUSTOMS; GRAVE; MUMMY. [CFP]

Among most South American Indians, with the exception of those tribes which observe a death vigil, burials take place immediately. The haste shown by most Indians on such occasions is prompted by the fear of the ghost of the deceased. The corpse is usually placed in the grave in a fetal position (i.e. with the arms flexed against the chest and the legs raised against the abdomen).

Many tropical tribes bury their dead in huge jars (Tupinamba, Guarayu, Tucuna, Katawishi, Yumana, Caripuna, etc.), a custom which is also followed by some people of the Andes (northwest of the Argentine, the Manabi, and occasionally by the ancient Peruvians). Among the natives of the Guianas and the Upper Amazon, the corpse is often deposited in a canoe or in an excavated tree-trunk. The Araucanians of Chile placed their dead chiefs in dug-out tree-trunks which rested on heavy forked poles or were wedged in trees.

Funeral chambers in which the corpse was left with his goods are characteristic of the ancient people of Colombia, Ecuador, and Peru. Crude vaults are also prepared for the dead by some tropical tribes (Guahibo, Aruaca, Achagua, Tupinamba, etc.). Burial under cairns is typical for the ancient populations of the southern tip of the continent, particularly for the Tehuelche and Puelche Indians.

Secondary burial, that is, the transfer of the bones of a dead person after an interval of time to a second place of interment was wide-spread east of the Andes. The bones were either placed in a basket or an urn (Guahibo, Carib, Rukuyen, Indians of Marajo, Camacan, Caraja, Otomac, Saliva, Ature, etc.), or were exhumed and reburied (Bororo, Apinaye, Nambikuara), or destroyed by fire or thrown into a river (Piapoco, Omagua, Carib of Venezuela).

Most tribes from the West Indies to the Gran Chaco bury the dead in their own huts, which are then abandoned or set on fire. In many tribes (Witoto, Yagua, Coroado, Iquito, etc.) the family continued to live in the funerary hut and deserted it only when it was overcrowded with graves. When a member of a tribe that practiced house burial died on a journey, a miniature hut or shelter was often built over his grave. [AM]

buried alive Burying a person alive was an ancient punishment. In some cases it was walling-in; in others, it was actual burial in earth. The walling-in method was reserved for monks, nuns, wives of knights, and girls of noble blood to enable them to avoid the shame of a public execution. In Rome, Vestal Virgins who were convicted of immorality were walled up in a subterranean chamber. In Peru, wives of the Sun were buried alive if they were unfaithful; in Mexico and Central America when a great man died, his best loved wives and sometimes his servants were appointed by him or self-elected to be buried alive with him. In China, the custom was of great antiquity, continuing down to comparatively modern times; it was also common in Germany in the 15th century. The usage gradually died out.

In this connection, mention should be made of the lore clustering about persons buried alive while in a cataleptic trance. The legend of "the living dead" appears in ballad, romance, and drama. (Cf. Henri Hauvette *La Morte Vivante*, Paris, 1933.) Folk stories are common on the European continent of persons buried alive while in the cataleptic state and awakened by robbers attempting to open the coffin to steal gems, and the like. Some of these tales are quite recent. [GPS]

burkan Gods or holy ones: an approximate translation of this word of the Gold tribe of the Lower Sungari, Manchuria. It is the collective designation for a number of small human-shaped "god-figures" made of wood and of brass and pewter, strung together on a cord, which shamans of the Gold tribe wear around their necks for specific ceremonies. One of the burkan is called *êchihê*, and perhaps means ancestor; other of the figures are designated as *sarka, ganki, kirinh, bukchunh*. (See O. Lattimore, *The Gold Tribe*, "Fishskin Tatars" of the Lower Sungari, MAAA 40, 1933.)

Burr-Woman An old woman whom the hero of certain North American Indian folktales takes upon his back and who he discovers cannot be dislodged. The motif (G311) turns up among several Plains, Central Woodland, and Iroquois tribes. In a Southern Paiute story told among the Shivwits of southern Utah, the idea takes another turn: Wolf retaliates on Coyote for various tricks and deceptions by causing a load of wood to remain in his arms. Coyote is unable to lay it down; neither can he remove the loaded basket from his back. Compare OLD MAN OF THE SEA.

burying the dead horse A shipboard custom of British sailors celebrating the working-out of the first month's pay. See DEAD HORSE CHANTEY.

bury league A cooperative savings organization of Negroes of United States, whereby sufficient funds are set aside to assure members (and often members of their families as well) adequate burial. Operating in the lower socio-economic levels of Negro society, the popularity of these groupings is evidence of the vitality of the African cult of the dead, wherein the need for proper burial is paramount no matter what sacrifices this entails. [MJH]

Bury Me Not on the Lone Prairie An American cowboy song about a dying boy whose last request was not to be buried in the lonely emptiness of the prairie: remade somewhere in the American West from a favorite song of the East written by a Universalist clergyman in 1839, called *The Burial at Sea* or *The Ocean Burial*. This expressed the same wish in connection with the deep, deep sea. The song is also known as *The Dying Cowboy*, and is often sung to the old ballad air of *Hind Horn*.

Bushido The way of the samurai, or the way of the ideal warrior: the code of the medieval Japanese samurai, epitomized by the Emperor Meiji as "the perpetual code of human relations." It was a strict code of chivalry and honor, physical training, mental and spiritual discipline, and daily behavior. Its precepts stressed loyalty to country, lord, and parents; personal courage, with the fine line drawn between what is brave or merely foolhardy; self-control and self-discipline, to the point of serene endurance of hardship, privation, or death; honor, a vital sense of personal honor, fair play and truthfulness, and passionate fidelity to a promise. Bushido required rigorous training in the military arts, and simplicity, almost severity, of life. Politeness, kindness, benevolence, sympathy were fostered; nothing brutal or underhand was countenanced. "The tenderness of the warrior" was a common phrase. A kind of gaiety grew from this, gaiety as the symbol of spiritual strength, in that any display of sorrow or discontent was both a sign of weakness and selfish inconsiderateness. Alertness of perception was stressed from many angles, not the least being sensitivity and appreciation. To train the young in sensitivity children were told stories or habituated to pictures of the warrior who halted his army so as not to trample a path strewn with the blown petals of the cherry.

bush soul The soul of a human being dwelling in a wild animal in the bush: a West African Negro concept. The Efik (southern Nigeria) word for bush soul is *ukpong*. The ukpong is both the soul within the man, his life, separable but returnable, the soul of the man within the animal, and also the animal itself: leopard, crocodile, hippopotamus, wild pig, etc. If the animal prospers, is lucky, or sickens or dies, the man will undergo the same fate. And if the man dies, his bush-soul animal becomes insensible to danger and is easily caught and killed. Chiefs sometimes have more than one bush soul.

Bush souls can also be inherited and even purchased. The custom of purchase sometimes leads to community trouble, for any man who envies his neighbor's flocks may acquire by purchase from the magician a leopard bush soul to prey upon the sheep and goats of the herder. A bush soul acquired by purchase is usually considered more powerful than one inherited.

If a man's bush soul has been trapped or wounded, the man falls ill. He goes at once to the magician to discover who the offender is. Anyone suspected of wilfully trapping or harming another's bush soul is put to a severe test and tried by tribal law. Conjectures about any development of the hereditary bush soul into totemism are not yet substantiated.

Būshyāstā In Zoroastrian mythology, the yellow demon of lethargy and sloth; the evil genius which causes men to oversleep and to neglect their religious duties.

Bushy Bride Title of a Norwegian folktale in which the false or substituted bride is the principal motif (K1911). A king fell in love with the portrait of a beautiful young girl, and sent her brother (possessor of the portrait) to bring the girl to him, intending to make her his wife. The girl's hideous stepsister managed to put herself in the true bride's place, with the result that the king, when he saw her, was so enraged with her ugliness that he had the brother punished. Three times after this the true bride came to the king's palace and reproached the Bushy Bride for usurping her place. The third time she was held and questioned by the king, who, when he learned the truth, killed the impostor, restored the brother, and married the beautiful young girl. Compare FALSE BRIDE.

busk The Anglicized name for *púskita* (fast) of the Creek Indians of the southeastern United States: an annual, 4–8 day religious ceremony, held during July or August when the crops mature, in an open square ground or dance ground near each Creek town. A new fire is kindled in the middle of the square, and during the course of the busk the male participants drink the *passa* or black drink for ceremonial purification. There is a series of named dances which are performed by men and women on different days of the busk, and a feast is prepared by the women from the newly ripened corn. The women also kindle new fires in their homes, from fire taken from the square ground. Both men and women cleanse themselves during the ceremonies by rubbing ashes on their bodies and plunging into water. Besides the black drink, men also take a decoction made from 15 different plants, which has been prepared by a shaman, and acts as a physic. The busk concludes, on the final night, with the so-called "mad dance." [EWV]

Buso A class of demons greatly feared by the Bagobo, a Malay people of southeastern Mindanao, P.I. They have long bodies, feet, and necks, curly hair, a flat nose and one big yellow or red eye, and two long, pointed teeth. They live in the branches of graveyard trees, or haunt forests and rocks. They never eat living flesh but dig up the buried dead and devour all but the bones. In the beginning of time the Buso were friendly and helpful to men, but since "the great quarrel" they have been man's deadly enemies. The Tigbanua are the worst of the Buso; they crave human flesh all the time, and never rest from trying to change living people into dead ones. The Tagamaling are the best, for they are Buso only half the time, month and month about. In spite of, or perhaps because of, the ever-present fear which the Buso inspire, Bagobo folklore is full of stories in which these evil creatures lose or miss their victims through some clever trick. They are always being made fools of, lied to, or embarrassed. Many of the stories involve the family cat. "The cat is the best animal," they say. "She keeps us from the

Buso." One favorite story tells how the cat consented to let the Buso kill and eat her mistress if only first he would count the hairs on her tail. The Buso started to count, but the tail kept twitching so that the Buso had to start over and over again, and could not finish before morning. When daylight came he had to rush off.

Butcher Boy An English folk song, probably dating from the 17th century, about a girl who hanged herself for the love of a faithless butcher boy. It is, in its variants, extended with many of the wandering stanzas of folk song and has links to numerous other songs. For example, the final stanza is generally the one about "Dig my grave both wide and deep," and "on my breast inscribe a turtle dove," etc., which is also found in *The Alehouse* (known as a student song in this country under the title of *There Is a Tavern in the Town*) and the stanza about the dance-hall or alehouse, etc., in the town where the true love takes another girl on his knee, which also appears in the song *I Know My Love*. It also is sung with stanzas such as "Now I wear my apron high," which are found in the early blues song *Careless Love*. The town in which the tragedy occurred is named as London town, Dublin City, Jersey City, Boston City, Johnson City, etc., to suit the geographical fancy of the singers. Early versions are known as *The Squire's Daughter, The Cruel Father* or *the Deceived Maid, Deep in Love, Must I Be Bound or Must I Go Free, The Brisk Young Lover* (who may have been a sailor), etc.

buttercup One of the various species of crowfoot, (genus *Ranunculus*) with yellow cup-shaped flowers: natives of the north temperate zone in the Old World which have been introduced into America. The common name was given to the flowers either because they were believed to increase the amount of butter given by cows feeding upon them, or because the yellow color of butter was due to them. Irish farmers rub the *cam an ime*, literally, cup of butter, on the udders of their cows on May Day to encourage richness in the milk.

The buttercup, according to the herbalist Culpeper, is an herb of Mars, fiery and hot-spirited, used externally in an ointment to draw a blister. Hung in a linen cloth around the neck of a lunatic, it would cure lunacy. According to Gerard, when mixed with salt and hung on any of the fingers, it would cure toothache. Children hold a buttercup under the chin of a playmate. If the color is reflected, they say, "You like butter."

butterfly It is not surprising that a creature as beautiful as the butterfly should become the object of a mass of folklore and superstition. Belief in the butterfly as the soul of man is general in Europe, Japan, many of the Pacific islands, and among many North American Indian tribes. Some peoples, like the Maori, believe that this butterfly soul returns to earth after death, while others, such as the Finno-Ugric peoples, believe the soul can leave the body while the person is asleep, and in this way they account for dreams. The Serbians look on the butterfly as the soul of a witch, and believe that if they can find her body and turn it around while she is asleep, the soul will not be able to find her mouth to reenter, and the witch will die. Probably this concept of the soul explains why many medieval angels have butterfly wings rather than those of a bird.

The early Greeks sometimes portrayed the soul as a diminutive person with butterfly wings, and later as a butterfly. In south Germany some say the dead are reborn as children who fly about as butterflies (hence the belief that they bring children). In the Solomon Islands the dying man has a choice as to what he will become at death, and often chooses a butterfly. Among the Nagas of Assam the dead are believed to go through a series of transformations in the underworld, and are finally reborn as butterflies. When the butterfly dies, that is the end of the soul forever. In Burma, rice has a butterfly-soul, and a trail of husks and unthreshed rice is very carefully laid from the field to the granary so that the soul may find the grain, otherwise none will grow the following year.

Among some peoples the butterfly is worshipped as a god, often as Creator. One of the tribes of Sumatra claims to be descended from three brothers hatched from eggs laid by a butterfly (their wives were sent down from above fully grown), and in Madagascar and among the Naga tribes of Manipur, some trace their ancestry to a butterfly. A North American Pima Indian myth says that the creator, Chiowotmahki, took the form of a butterfly and flew over the world until he found a suitable place for man. Among some tribes of Mexico it is the symbol of the fertility of the earth. The spirit of Nyikang, the first Shilluk king, who led his people into Egypt, appears to his people as a creature of great beauty, often a butterfly. Samoans believe that if they caught one it would strike them dead.

Not all butterflies are looked on as good. In much of Europe they are tabu. In parts of Scotland, Friesland, and Bosnia, moths are regarded as witches; in Serbia and Westphalia, butterflies are so regarded. In the latter place St. Peter's Day, February 22, is set aside for their expulsion. Children go about knocking on the houses with hammers, reciting rimes and incantations to drive them out of the houses. Elsewhere they are thought to be fairies in disguise, who steal butter and milk.

In the matter of capturing and killing butterflies there is a good bit of disagreement. Among the Magyars it is lucky to catch the first one of the season. In Oldenburg the first one should be caught and allowed to fly through your coat sleeve; in Devon it should be killed; but elsewhere in the west of England it is unlucky to kill it. In Essex the first white one should be caught and its head bitten off, but it should be allowed to fly away. In Somerset and Dorset they kill the moths; in the north of England, the red butterflies; in Pitsligo, the tortoise-shell ones; in Llanidloes, the colored ones; and in the Vosges region of France they should all be caught. In Scotland it is unlucky to kill or keep them, while in Suffolk they should be tenderly entreated, and in the west of Scotland the white ones are fed.

There are many superstitions regarding specific butterflies. Among the Bulgarians a dark one presages sickness. In Brunswick if the first one of the season is white it is an omen of death, if yellow, of birth, and if variegated, of marriage. In Ruthenia, the first one, if white, announces sickness, and health if red. Some say that if the first butterfly is white it will be a rainy summer, if dark, a season of thunderstorms, and if yellow, sunny weather. Among the Celts, to see one fly by night

means death, and in North Hampshire to see three together is a bad omen. Some say that if a butterfly is
put in a gun it is impossible to miss the target. To get
a new dress all a girl need do is to catch a butterfly of
the desired color and crush it between her teeth while
muttering a magic formula.

buttocks watcher In nearly all tales of the hoodwinked dancers Trickster commands his buttocks to
act as watchman for him while he sleeps. His buttocks
speak and warn him that his food is being stolen, but
Trickster ignores the warning. Closely related incidents
to this motif (D1317.1) are those of talking privates, in
which a man is given advice by his genitals, talking
privates which betray unchastity (H451), and Mentula
loquens (D998; D1610.3; H451) in which a man's penis
speaks and can only be silenced by his mother-in-law.
See FECES. [EWV]

buzzard If you wear a buzzard feather behind your
ear, you will never have rheumatism. If you see a lone
buzzard, you will soon see someone unexpected. Make a
wish before the sailing buzzard moves his wings and it
will come true. If you see a buzzard's shadow and not
the buzzard, that is an omen of death. In fact, it is
dangerous to let a buzzard's shadow touch you. Death,
illness, or evil fortune will soon follow.

Kentucky Negroes say that if you look up at a buzzard overhead, or speak to him, he will vomit on you.
But Georgia Negroes throw a kiss to him, make a wish,
and expect it to come true. If a buzzard catches a child
he will pick its eyes out. Georgia Negroes believe that
witches sometimes take the form of buzzards. Maryland
Negroes say

O, Mr. Buzzard, don' fly so high
Yo can't make a livin' aflyin' in de sky.

Many southern Negroes also believe that the buzzard is
a thief-finder. This is the folklore of fact, stemming
from slavery days when a Negro would sometimes cache
a piece of pig meat in his loft. Pork plus heat makes
for such rapid putrefaction that it would be a poor
buzzard who couldn't detect it. Thus the presence of a
buzzard on the roof was a sure giveaway.

Buzzards, because they eat carrion, are associated
with the dead, and are regarded with particular awe
by the Negroes of the southern United States, and
vested with unknowable mystery and power. Buzzard's grease will cure smallpox, for instance. A little
bag containing buzzard feathers is sometimes tied
around a baby's neck to ease the pains of teething. For
fainting or an epileptic fit two wingfeathers from a
buzzard are burned under the nose of the patient. Buzzard feathers are also effective in charms. To drive
someone crazy, Mississippi Negroes pick up the victim's footprints, put them in a gourd along with two
buzzard feathers, and throw the gourd into running
water at midnight. The person will go insane the next
day.

Among many of the North American Pueblo Indians
Buzzard, because he is a scavenger, is regarded as a
purifying and cleansing power. Buzzard feathers are
used in exorcism by all the curers. (See BADGER MEDI-
CINE.) In a Hopi ritual performed to induce the clouds
to send water to the people, a buzzard feather is used
to dip the water from the six directions from the sacred

spring into the gourd which is to be carried to the
altar. Buzzard is the cleanser. Whenever the word
"cleanser" occurs in the ritual songs accompanying the
Hopi cleansing rite, the exorciser scatters the purifying
ashes with his buzzard feather. In the various Pueblo
brushing rites, the shaman brushes away the evil with
a buzzard feather. Buzzard droppings are burned at
Taos to smoke one who has fainted.

The Hopi myth of raising the sun explains how Buzzard got his bald head. At first when the sun stopped
half-way up the sky, two children were sacrificed, whose
spirits helped it along its way somewhat. But it was
still too near and the earth was too hot. Turkey flew
up to raise the sun. The heat burned his head red and
all the feathers fell off; so he came back. Then Buzzard
tried. Buzzard pushed the sun up a little farther. The
sun burned all the feathers off his head but he kept on
trying. Now Buzzard is bald. In southern U.S. Negro
folktale, Brer Rabbit gave a feast. During grace, while
all eyes were shut, he suddenly reached out and ducked
Buzzard's head into a dish of hot hominy. Since then
Buzzard is bald.

Bwebweso In Dobu (Melanesian) belief, the afterworld; the hill of the dead on neighboring Normanby
Island: literally, extinguished. Some spirits do not go
to Bwebweso; for example, the spirits of those slain in
war go to another afterworld, bodies disfigured by
disease live in a swamp at the foot of the mountain
as fish with human heads, and some spirits wander off
to the hill of lice, Koiakutu. The spirit leaves the body
after a few days and arrives at Bwebweso carrying the
betel-nut fee for the warder, Sinebomatu, the Woman
of the Northeast Wind, or Kekewage, her husband. The
fee is paid and, if free from disease scars and sufficiently rotted (a "fresh" spirit cannot pass), the spirit
goes to Bwebweso. The spirits of children whose parents
still are living are cared for by Sinebomatu and Kekewage until one of the parents dies, else the child will
have no guardian in the afterworld. Sometimes, in
sleep or voluntarily (some magicians can do this), the
spirit of a living person visits Bwebweso and talks with
the spirits of the dead. But the visiting spirit must not
eat of the Dokanikani banana in Bwebweso, for if it
does it can never get back to the living world. (Fortune,
Sorcerers of Dobu.) Compare FOOD TABU IN THE LAND
OF THE DEAD.

byliny (singular *bylina*) The narrative poems of Russian oral tradition: also called *stariny* or old songs. The
term bylina probably means "past happenings," and
since about 1860 has been applied to the special genre.
Byliny are slow-moving, descriptive, free in their verse-
forms, unrimed, unstanzaed, the rhythm of the chant
determining the length of line which, though irregular,
tends to even out. They are chanted without accompaniment, but seem at one time to have been sung to the
music of the gusli, a one-stringed, bowed instrument.
Prose versions of some of the byliny exist, recited rather
than sung, preserving the language and figures of the
poems, but without their meter. The subject-matter is
secular; religious poems in similar style are called *stikhi*.
There has been some influence on the byliny from the
West and from the Balkans, but the byliny remain apart
from the general stream of European balladry.

The matter of the Russian byliny is both historical

and legendary, often, and usually, so confused that it is impossible to differentiate between fact and invention. For, rather than being the comparatively bald narrative of the Western ballad, the byliny permit elaboration by the reciter with stock phrases and situations, motifs being transferred from one setting to another regardless of the person or event under discussion. The matter groups itself into cycles (e.g. the Older Heroes, the Kiev cycle, the Novgorod cycle) more or less related to the epic poetry of the Russians; the borderline between the two types is not clear.

The byliny seem to have reached their peak in about the 16th or 17th century after a period of dormancy under the rule of the Tatars (12th–16th centuries). In the time since then the older ballads have gradually disappeared from the centers of their origin in Great Russia and are found today for the most part in the northern fringes of Russia, the Urals, and the Caucasus.

Cabeiri or **Cabiri** In Greek mythology, mysterious deities, worshipped in many parts of the ancient world, of whom little is definitely known. They were perhaps Phœnician in origin, and were worshipped particularly in Samothrace, but also in Asia Minor, Macedonia, and northern and central Greece. The cult became early identified with that of Demeter and Cora, and with Hermes (Cadmilus) and Hephæstus or Hades. The Cabeiri seem to have been guardians against peril, especially that of the sea (like the Dioscuri), and also fertility deities of some kind. Little of the mythology connected with them has survived, although their cult enjoyed its greatest expansion in the period from the peak of the Athenian hegemony to some time after the death of Alexander (5th and 4th centuries B.C.). Cabeiros and his son Casmilos are the principal Cabeiri; the names Axieros, Axiokersos, and Axiokersa were noted as belonging to the Cabeiri by Mnaseas in the 3rd century B.C.

caboclo In the northeastern part of Brazil, this term is applied to cult-groups that worship both African and autochthonous Indian deities, principally Tupi and Guarani. The African worship tends to be preponderantly of the Congo-Angola type, with African deities predominating, but also including certain categories of deified ancestral dead. These caboclo sects may be regarded as related to that aspect of non-Christian New World Negro religion which pays respect to the spirits of the aboriginal inhabitants of the land in which the group lives. In this category of religious life would be the *Ingi winti* of Dutch Guiana, and the *loa créole* of Haiti. [MJH]

Cachimé A deity of the Arecuna and other Indian tribes of the Venezuelan Alto Orinoco: the focus of a strange dance orgy for the well-being of the tribe. His image is kept in a cave and held in fearful veneration. At certain seasons men and women prepare themselves in retreats by complete inebriation. Four priests disguise themselves in animal pelts, feathers, and face paint, and bring the image from the cave. The people perform a circular dance around them. After the ritual return of the image, the priests remove the disguise and bathe ritually. The dance and its deity resemble the more spectacular Mauarí of the Maipure Indians which celebrates puberty rites. [GPK]

cachucha A lively dance of Cadiz and Jerez, Andalusia, characterized by acceleration and intensified excitement. The rapid $\frac{3}{4}$ time is accented by castanets. Leg-swings embellish the footwork. Strictly speaking, it is a couple dance, but can be danced by a woman alone, as on the stage by the once famous Fanny Elssler. This apparently completely secular dance has nevertheless been included as part of the ball de gitanes, a dramatic Carnival dance of Catalonia. Literally, a cachucha is a kind of cap. [GPK]

cactus Any plant of the family Cactaceæ, green, fleshy, with typically leafless joints, very spiny and remarkably drought-resisting. There are more than 100 genera and some 1300 species, including the edible prickly pear, night-blooming cereus, the mescal, etc. Certain ones are usable as forage; some contain powerful narcotics used as stimulants and for ceremonial intoxication among certain Mexican Indians. Cactus in China is called the fairy's hand and is considered unlucky for pregnant women.

The cactus is of special religious significance among American Pueblo Indians. It is one of the plants that "give of themselves" to the people. The Zuñi Cactus Society is a war society functioning also for the control of game and the curing of wounds; it approaches the cactus with a special beaded prayer feather. In the ritual whipping of chiefs being installed, the Cactus Societies of Zuñi and Jemez both use cacti. This gives those who are whipped great power and luck in hunting and gambling. Members of the Hano Cactus Society also whipped each other with cacti to induce bravery and endurance, and to make the ground freeze so their warriors would leave no tracks. At Tewa, Cactus Grandmother is passed from hand to hand with song within the Winter kiva. If she is dropped it portends bad luck. During this "journey" thrice round the circle she becomes smaller and smaller and in the fourth round she finally vanishes and has returned to her own people. When the people go to look, there she is growing in her own place as fresh as ever.

Pieces of cactus are put in the corners of each new Hopi house "to give the house roots." At Acoma during certain kachina activities, men rub themselves against the cactus (carried by others) to attain manliness.

Among the exploits of the Lipan Apache culture hero Killer-of-Enemies and his brother is the incident of making the prickly pear cactus safe to approach and gather. The Chiricahua, Mescalero, and Jicarilla Apache, and also the Navaho, have stories describing the sexual use of cactus.

Cacus A robber giant, son of Vulcan, three-headed and flame-breathing, who lived in a cave on the Aventine where Rome now stands. When Hercules passed that way with the cattle of Geryon, Cacus stole several, dragging them into his cave by their tails backwards. Hercules, thus unable to trace the cattle, was about to go on his way when the lowing of cattle in the cave before which he was driving the remainder of the herd caused him to realize what had happened. He entered the cave and slew Cacus. The legend was an important local story of Rome, Hercules being reputed to have established, with the consent of the then ruler Evander, the ara maximus, or ox market. The Scalæ Caci, however, are on the Palatine. It is thought that Cacus, with his sister Caca, who was worshipped somewhat like Vesta, form a pair of very ancient Roman deities to whom has become attached an originally Greek story. Because Vergil calls Cacus *semi-homo*, Dante made him a centaur, though he placed him apart from the Greek Centaurs.

Cacy taperere or **Sasy-perere** A popular supernatural being in the folklore of the Indians and mestizos of southern Brazil. He is a one-legged dwarf with fiery eyes, a red cap, and a pipe. He enjoys playing tricks on people, such as disturbing, misplacing, or hiding their belongings. [AM]

Cadmus One of the famous culture heroes of ancient Greece; the founder of Bœotian Thebes; introducer of the alphabet from Phœnicia to Greece; inventor of agriculture and bronze work. He was the son of Agenor, king of Phœnicia, and Telephassa, and brother of Europa. When Zeus abducted his sister, Cadmus went in search of her, with instructions from Agenor not to return without her. His quest was futile, and at last he went to the oracle at Delphi, where he was told to abandon the search, to follow a cow marked with a crescent on each side, and to found the city Thebes wherever the cow stopped. When in Bœotia the cow lay down, Cadmus built the Cadmea, later the citadel of Thebes. Preparing to sacrifice the animal, he sent his companions to a spring for water. There they were attacked and slain by a guardian dragon, a son of Ares. Cadmus killed the creature and on Athena's advice sowed the dragon's teeth in the ground. Fully armed warriors sprang up, and Cadmus either threw stones among them to cause them to fight or was warned away by one of them. In any event, they fought until only five were left alive. Because he had slain the dragon, Cadmus had to serve Ares for a long year (eight years) in expiation, at the end of which time he was given the daughter of Ares and Aphrodite, Harmonia, as wife. All the gods of Olympus came to the wedding, and Harmonia received as gifts a peplus worked by Athena and the fatal necklace made by Hephæstus. The children of Cadmus and Harmonia were Semele, Ino, Autonoe, Agave, and Polydorus (Illyrius was born much later); the vengeance of Ares followed these children and their descendants down to the destruction of the line after Œdipus. The ill fortune they met with in Thebes caused Cadmus and Harmonia to leave. He later served as general and king of the Enchelians. At last he and Harmonia were changed into serpents and taken by Zeus to Elysium. Cadmus is reported to have cast mother and child adrift in a chest when he discov-

ered the birth of Dionysus to his daughter Semele. The entire legend of Cadmus has been overlaid with later explanatory incidents and characters, such as Cadmus' brothers Phœnix and Cilix, the founders of Phœnicia and Cilicia when they gave up the search for Europa, herself a similar ancestral character. Cadmus was worshipped in several parts of Greece. Compare CECROPS.

caduceus The magic herald's wand, a sacred rod having power over wealth, prosperity, happiness, and dreams, carried by the messengers of the Greek gods, especially by Hermes in his role as psychopomp. In its earliest form the caduceus appears as a forked rod, the prongs knotted or crossing to form a loop; later, the rod is twined about by two serpents with their heads meeting at the top. The legend states that Hermes discovered two serpents fighting and thrust his rod between them. The caduceus was thus a sign of the settlement of quarrels, carried by heralds and ambassadors (who were immune to attack). It became the symbol of commerce much later. Another legend states that Hermes and Apollo exchanged lyre for wand. Sometimes the caduceus appears winged as the symbol of Hermes. A modified drawing of the caduceus was used in alchemy for the metal mercury, and the same symbol is still used for the planet. The winged caduceus is the insignia of the U.S. Army Medical Corps. Compare ÆSCULAPIUS.

Cæneus In Greek mythology, a Lapith slain by the Centaurs. Originally Cæneus was a woman called Cænis, and was raped by Poseidon. As recompense, she asked that she be changed into a man, for in that form such indignity might not occur, and that she be made invulnerable to wounds: these requests the god granted. The man Cæneus took part in the Argonautic expedition and in the Calydonian boar hunt. Cæneus however set up his spear as a god, would worship only the spear, and ordered the people to worship it. Zeus became angered, and in the fight between the Lapithæ and Centaurs, when Cæneus daringly fought in the open, unafraid of wounds, Zeus caused the Centaurs to drive him into the earth and bury him with fir trees. When he died, he was changed back into a woman, although, in Ovid, Mopsus, the seer, declared a yellow-winged bird seen on the heap of logs to be Cæneus. Compare CHANGE OF SEX.

Cæsarean birth The delivery of a child by section of the abdominal wall and womb of the mother when natural delivery is impossible: so called because Julius Cæsar is said to have been born in this way. The child of a Cæsarean birth is said to possess great strength, and the power to find hidden treasure, and to see spirits. Miraculous birth from a slit under the arm, in the side, or in the thigh is a concept as ancient as the mythologies of the world. See BABY TAKEN FROM MURDERED MOTHER'S WOMB.

Cagn or **Kang** The Creator of Bushman mythology: believed to be manifested sometimes in the form of the mantis (*!kaggen*), sometimes in the form of the caterpillar (*ngo*). He is called Cagn or Kang by the northern Bushmen, Thora by the southern Bushmen. All Bushmen reverence the mantis; all are loath to kill it. Cagn created all things, but he met with so much opposition in this world that he went away. Now the people pray to him for food, saying, "O Cagn, O Cagn, do you not see the hunger of your children?"

Cagn had a wife named Coti, and two sons named Cogaz and Gcwi, who became chiefs and made digging-sticks with sharp stone points and showed the people how to dig with them for roots. But how Cagn himself came into the world no one knows, except the initiated. Cagn had a tooth in which his powers and vital force resided; sometimes he would lend it to a friend who needed extra strength for some exploit. Birds were Cagn's messengers. His daughter married a snake, and the snakes henceforth were called Cagn's people. Cagn himself could take animal form at will, usually that of an eland bull. His wife once gave birth to an eland fawn. Anyone who displeased him had bad luck: baboons were once men, for instance, but were doomed to their present shape for once sneering at Cagn's cleverness. Once the thorns killed Cagn and the ants ate him, but he came to life again. Today no man knows where he is; only the elands know. When Cagn calls in the forest, all the elands run to him. Men have seen this happen.

cailleać Literally, old woman, hag: in Celtic folk-lore, the last sheaf of harvest regarded as the embodi-ment of the corn or field spirit. Personification of the last sheaf as the spirit of the growing grain itself is world-wide, and the treatment of this material represen-tation everywhere testifies to the deep human belief that its safekeeping insures fertility for the following harvest, provided that some portion of it is given to the cattle and horses to eat, and some portion of it strewn in the field or mixed with the seeds for the next crop.

In the neighborhood of Belfast, Ireland, the last sheaf is called the Granny and its personification is achieved not only by thus naming it, but by a special ceremony of cutting it. In certain sections of Scotland it is called the carlin (old woman). In the Scottish Isle of Lewis the old hag or cailleać is dressed up in clothes, her apron turned and tied up and filled with bread, cheese, and a sickle. In Pembrokeshire in Wales, she is carried home by one of the reapers, whose fellows noisily accompany him, drench him with water, and endeavor to snatch the cailleać away. If he gets home safe, he keeps the hag on his farm till the following year. On the day of the first spring plowing, he takes whatever grain remains intact on the hag and feeds it to his plow horse or mixes it with the seed to be planted, both acts serving to insure fertility. In some Scottish districts the reapers hold reaping races; the man who finishes first calls his last sheaf the corn maiden; he who finishes last makes his last sheaf into the cailleać, the hag, or "old corn wife." In some localities, however, the cailleać is passed from farm to farm. The man who finishes his reaping first makes the cailleać and passes her on to his neigh-bor, who hastens to finish and pass her on to the next. The cailleać thus automatically remains for the year with the farmer who was last to finish his harvesting. Nobody wants the old hag, who in this aspect takes on an added symbolism of reproach for procrastination. In the Hebrides the cailleać is still taken at night and placed in the fields of dilatory or lazy farmers.

Cain The first-born son of Adam and Eve; the first murderer; builder of the first city, whose evil offspring invented boundaries, measures, and walls and destroyed

the freedom of men: thought to be a later Hebrew addi-tion to the Biblical narrative to explain the more primi-tive way of life of the Kenites of the Sinai peninsula. The Biblical story is incomplete (e.g. in what way did God accept and reject the offerings of the brothers) and contradictory (e.g. Cain is condemned to wander, yet founds a city). The essence of the tale seems to be blood: Cain's was not an acceptable sacrifice because it was bloodless; the earth becomes infertile because Abel's blood is spilled upon it. There are two principal ver-sions of the story: one, following the Biblical tale, ex-plains the jealousy as that of land-tiller for shepherd. This ancient argument appears in several Mesopotamian tales—Kramer (*Sumerian Mythology*) discusses three. The other, an apocryphal story of Jewish and Moslem lore, bases the quarrel in sexual jealousy. Cain and Abel each had a twin sister, and Adam planned to marry the boys to each other's sister. But Cain's was the prettier and he objected. Not knowing how to kill Abel, he threw stones at him until he hit a vital spot. Then, ignorant of what to do with the body, he watched two ravens fight and saw the victor scratch a hole in the earth to bury the other. God cursed the earth for permitting Abel's body to be hidden. Cain and his sister then were banished to the land of Nod. But first, because of Cain's spoken re-pentance, God marked the sinner to protect him. What mark it was, and whether it was a warning sign or a protective one, etc., are subjects of speculation: some authorities hold that the tribe of Kenites wore a dis-tinguishing mark. Cain was killed by Lamech, whose son, Tubal-Cain, saw Cain from afar, thought that the horned being (the horn was either the mark, or a natural consequence of Cain's father being Sammael-Satan) was an animal, and told his blind father to shoot. The Dioscuric implications of the story of Cain and Abel have been remarked upon by Krappe. Compare the founding of Rome by Romulus and the building of the first city by Cain.

Cain and Abel Title of an American Negro song re-lating the story of the first murder. "Some folks say that Cain killed Abel/ Yes, my Lord!/ He hit him in the head with the leg of a table/ Yes, my Lord!" Similar words are found in the tall-tale song *I Was Born Ten Thousand Years Ago.*

cairn A mound or heap of stones as a marker or memorial. Cairns are used in many parts of the world as place markers. In the passes of the Himalayas, a cairn marks the top of the pass, and offerings are put on the pile by travelers. In Tibet, the traveler adds another stone. The herms, or road-marking busts of Hermes, of Greece probably developed from a similar cairn-as-marker custom. Stones, said to have been placed there by Hermes, protector of travelers, when he cleared the roads, stood at the roadside. The custom was to mark roads by such stones and piles of stone. Offerings of food were placed on these cairns (or later on the herms), ostensibly for the use of travelers, but probably as sacrifices. In medieval Lithuania, scattered among the towns, cairns, or perhaps groups of larger stones, were sacrificial places, altars at which offerings were made and sacrificial blood sprinkled, and the sacrifices distributed among the people.

The use of cairns as burial places is very ancient and world-wide. It is, for example, the typical form of burial of the southernmost Indian tribes of South America. The stones protect both the dead and the living; they guard the corpse against mutilation or desecration, they prevent the spirit from rising and exercising its malignancy against the living. Cairns are thus associated with barrows, dolmens, cromlechs, and the like, as early graves. At such cairns, too, the universal practice is to place another stone on the heap. The custom is still carried on by several peoples, even where the cairn has disappeared and the gravestone has taken its place.

cake customs Certain acts of propitiation, sacrifice, divination, etc.: frequently associated with the annual cycle and taking into account phases of the solar year. Cakes are used in critical aspects of the life cycle and thus are intimately connected with baptisms, weddings, funerals, and rituals for the dead. Often cakes molded into the shape of human beings or animals are conceived of as substitutes for their prototypes. In extreme cases artificial objects may take the place of the food offering.

In ancient Greece, cakes of dough were thrown into a chasm as an offering to Demeter and Persephone, the deities of the harvest. Some of the cakes were eaten by serpents who lived in the abyss. The remnants were removed by women who had been purified ritually, and what was left were taken to the altars of the goddesses. In Egypt often there were images made of dough, in the shape of pigs and other animals, which were sacrificed to Osiris and to the moon. For the dead, often those who were poor used real cakes or those made of stoneware, to be placed in the tomb as food for the dead. In Rome, matrons sacrificed millet cakes to Liber, to Ceres, and to Mater Matuta. To feed the dead, the Hindus placed cakes beside the corpses upon which were piled boiled rice, sugar, and ghi (melted butter). In order to avoid taking life, these people also made models of the persons to be sacrificed in the shape of cakes made of meal and butter. The Veddas of Ceylon also fed the deity Śiva by means of rice cakes, while in Japan, on New Year's Day, two flattened spherical cakes were laid on the shrine—a male cake to the sun, and a female cake to the moon.

Cakes of various shapes were used in Greece as sacrificial and propitiatory offerings, such as those offered to Helios at Delos and Delphi, in the form of arrows or of girls; to Artemis cakes and honey were placed as an offering, and to Zeus in Athens they offered barley cakes in the Eleusinian mysteries. In Athens a twelve-knobbed cake was offered to Cronus every spring (compare BELTANE CAKES), and in a ritual called the "Supper of Hecate," circular cakes, topped with candles were placed at crossroads by the rich at the time of the new or the full moon. In Sweden a cake in the form of a woman was made from the last sheaf to be harvested which was shared by all members of the family. In Estonia, Sweden, and Denmark, the meal from the first sheaf was made into a cake in the form of a boar.

Cakes were given away at the New Year, or used as magical means to drive evil away. In Scotland, on Hogmanay (last day of year), children sang carols from house to house and were given oat cakes. In France, pancakes were made, tossed on a griddle, on New Year's Day to assure good luck and riches. On Candlemas Day, in France, pancakes were also made to assure the rising of the dough in the oven during the rest of the year.

The Lenten season was ushered in by feasting. In Hungary, before King Fat was chased out by King Lean, fat foods and well-shortened cakes were eaten, for King Lean began to reign on Ash Wednesday. On Collop Monday, the day before Shrove Tuesday, in England, one feasted on meats, fats, eggs, and rich cakes. Boys would beg for food on this day and, if refused by a stingy housewife, they could pelt her with broken crockery.

Shrove Tuesday or Mardi Gras is celebrated by eating pancakes, throughout the Christian world. In France, it was said that eating pancakes would preserve the grain from rot. In Bulgaria, on Plow Monday, the day preceding Shrove Tuesday, there was a special ceremony: a man, clad in a goatskin, baked a cake with a coin; he then divided up the cake, and he who received the coin, would prosper—only then could the plowing begin. In Russia, bread or cake, which had been blessed in the church, was placed near or mixed with the seed corn to assure a prosperous harvest.

Begging for materials for Easter cakes takes place during the latter weeks of Lent. In Czechoslovakia, on Caroling Sunday, the Sunday preceding Palm Sunday, the girls would beg for eggs, flour, and spices to be baked into Easter cakes, while in Bulgaria on Palm Sunday a cake called "kula" or "kolack" was made: this cake was decorated with flowers and human features. Bits of these were cast into the water, and she whose morsel floated the furthest would be luckiest during the year. After this all would feast on the loaves.

On Good Friday, Hot Cross buns, a bun which was marked with a cross cut into the dough, or more recently marked with a cross of icing, would be eaten. Eating of these brings good fortune.

In Russia and Poland, a tall cake, rich with eggs, butter, spices and fruit is made. In Russia it is a tall cylinder, called kulich, while in Poland it is ring-shaped and called babka. In Russia this was topped with a mixture of sweetened cheese and sour cream, which was blessed in the church by the priest. The Rumanian Easter cake was studded with cloves to represent the nails of the cross. In Kent, cakes with the figures of twins stamped on them were given to the poor.

Beltane, the Celtic May Day, was celebrated with Beltane cakes, which are considered by some to have been used in selecting a human sacrifice.

Cakes were offered to the dead, or to beggars in the name of the dead. Arval cakes were given to the poor at a wake or a funeral. Halloween cakes often contained a ring and a coin—he who got the coin would prosper. On All Saints' Day, children begged for cakes in the name of the dead or for souls in Purgatory. In Shropshire such cakes were leavened flat buns, while in the Tyrol, godparents would give cakes shaped like animals to their godchildren. These were in the form of horses and hares for the boys, and hens for the girls. They were left overnight on the table for the souls to eat. In Belgium, soul cakes were eaten hot, while saying a prayer for the departed. In Antwerp, this cake was decorated with saffron to symbolize flames. In Saint Kilda, soul cakes were triangular. In Ireland and Scotland they were griddle cakes. The Scottish "dumb bannock" was made by a group of girls: each one traced her initials on the dough, and it was baked

before the fire between eleven and midnight on Halloween. While it was baking each girl kept complete
silence, and turned the cakes once. At midnight a man
was supposed to appear and lay his hands upon the
initials of the chosen one.

Cakes used at Christmas time are varied. In Shropshire they ate cakes embellished with caraway seeds
which were dipped in ale. In Yorkshire, spice cakes or
plum cakes or gingerbread and cheese were served at
this season: "For every Yuletide cake and every cheese
tasted at a neighbor's house, a happy month will be
added to one's life." In Serbia a special cake was broken
over the Yule log; these cakes were theriomorphic, in
the shape of lambs, pigs, and hens. For all members of
the extended family, a cake was baked by a girl, which
had a coin in it for luck. Everybody partook of this at
the Christmas dinner, and portions were kept for
absent members. In Estonia a cake was baked on
Christmas Eve, which stood on the table on New Year's
Day, when some of it was given to the cattle, and the
rest was kept for them until spring. In Slavic countries, on the dawn of Christmas Day, the maidens go
to the river to get water for *chernitza*, a loaf which is
flat and wheel-shaped. Good luck tokens are placed in
it. At noon it is cut by the head of the house, or tossed
over the horn of the oldest ox, and if it breaks, it
means good luck. In some parts of France it is believed
that Christmas cakes will cure illness throughout the
year.

In many places the Christmas season was celebrated
until the 6th of January (Epiphany). In Hertfordshire,
a ring-shaped cake was tossed over the horn of the
oldest ox; then he was toasted in ale, and tickled so
that he would toss the cake for luck. In Silesia, there
is a guardian of spinning, called Frau Perchta. On the
eve of Epiphany she goes about inspecting the distaffs
and spinning wheels and, if she finds flax, she splits
open the bellies of the lazy girls and stuffs them with
flax. In order to have the knife glance off the bellies,
the girls eat pancakes at the evening meal.

In France and in Germany Twelfth Night was
celebrated by a feast in which a cake was featured.
This cake contained a bean or a kernel of corn, and
he who got it was the king. Each member present got
a slice, and a part, usually the first slice was dedicated
to God, to the Virgin, or to charity.

Cakes were also used in exterminating fiends for, in
Macedonia, they were scalded by the frizzling fat in
which pancakes were cooked.   NATALIE F. JOFFE

cakewalk A form of social entertainment, originating
among the Negroes of the southern United States, at
which a cake is given as prize for the very best walking.
Originally, the walk was performed stiff and erect, with
a bucket of water on the head. Whoever walked
"straightest and proudest" and spilled not a drop got
the cake. Later, various fancy and original variations
were introduced. The dance which developed from
these expressive grotesqueries of walking consists usually
of a high prance performed with the arms folded
across the chest, the head thrown well back, and sometimes the whole body arched back.

Calabar bean The ordeal bean of Calabar, Africa:
the highly poisonous seed of an African twining climber (*Physostigma venenosum*) of the bean family. An
extract from it is used for contracting the pupil of the
eye, occasionally for tetanus, epilepsy, and other nervous
disorders. Among the people of Calabar it was used
in a poison ordeal to test for crime, witchcraft, etc. It
contains certain poisonous alkaloids. An infusion of
the bean was made, called ordeal water, and given to
the accused to drink. Sometimes the uncooked bean
was given to him to be swallowed. If he vomited and
survived the ordeal unharmed, he was innocent; if he
was poisoned, he was guilty. The Calabar bean was
also used in what was termed "wager law": each of the
litigants ate half a bean. Whichever one survived, or
was the least affected, was in the right.

calabash tree A tall tropical American tree (*Cres-
centia cujute*) the hard rind of whose gourdlike fruit
is used for dishes, bowls, drinking vessels, containers,
and other utensils, and also musical instruments. Many
of these artifacts are painted both inside and out; many
are gorgeously and elaborately decorated with plant and
animal and symbolic patterns. The Indians of Matto
Grosso, Brazil, use dried calabashes for keeping records;
incidents are inscribed on them in pictographs. Even
demons flee from the unmistakable pictographic charms
inscribed thereon against them. In Hawaii sorcerers
use calabashes to confine the wandering souls of living
people which they have caught. In regions where
Catholicism has superimposed its saints' days observations upon earlier indigenous practices, the calabash
tree itself must be planted on St. John's Day, June 24.
If this precaution is not taken the fruit will fall off
before it ripens. If the tree fails to bear, it is beaten,
also on St. John's Day.

caldron of regeneration In the *Mabinogion*, the wonderful caldron given to Bran by a monstrous man and
woman who came out of a lake in Ireland. This pair
lived first with Matholwch, a king of Ireland, for a
year, but were hated by the people because of their
outrages and molestings. An attempt was made to
roast them alive in an iron house, but they escaped
and fled to Britain, where Bran received them. They
gave to Bran this caldron which restored the slain to
life; and it was this caldron that Bran gave in turn to
Matholwch as a gift of atonement for an insult. It
parallels the miraculous healing spring of the Irish
physician, Diancécht, which also restored the mortally
wounded. It is numbered with the numerous magic
caldrons of Celtic myth and legend: Dagda's (inexhaustible), the caldron of Annwn which would not boil
a coward's food, the caldron of inspiration prepared by
Cerridwen for her son, and others. See BRAN; MAGIC
CALDRON.

calinda, calenda, caleinda, etc. The stick dance or
mock-battle dance of the New World Negroes: adopted
to some extent by the whites of the area. The calenda
songs of Trinidad are also sung at communal labor,
with improvised, topical verses, often sharply and personally satirical, often more seemingly innocent than
they are. There are a variety of traditional refrains.
Lafcadio Hearn, reporting the caleinda from Martinique, stressed the improvisational character of the
verse. Imported into Louisiana from the Antilles, the
calinda originally was a battle dance, performed by
men only, armed with sticks. Stripped to the waist, the
dancers performed their mock fight with bottles of

water balanced on their heads; as soon as the water spilled the dancer was disqualified. The development of the calinda in Louisiana became so orgiastic that it was banned by state law in 1843. Compare CAKEWALK.

Calling the Deer Title of a story in the Coyote cycle of the Coeur d'Alene Indian mythology. Coyote lay starving and wished for food. Suddenly he saw a deer foot lying by the fire. He ate it. This happened four times: first a deer foot appeared, then a shoulder, half a deer, etc. Coyote wondered where this meat came from. The next morning he watched with the blanket half over his eyes. Half a deer dropped beside him. And he saw Woodtick. She begged him not to look; but Coyote said "So it's you—without even a neck!" Woodtick was insulted and went away.

After a while Coyote was starving again. He went to look for Woodtick. After a while he found her, old woman Woodtick in her house. She set the table for two but did not bid Coyote eat; so Coyote could not break the code and eat. Woodtick had wanted him for her husband until he said she had no neck. Finally she let him stay there, so Coyote lived with Woodtick. Woodtick would call out "Deer, come!" and the deer would come running into the house. Woodtick would take two and pierce their ears and the rest would run out. This happened often and they had plenty of meat.

Coyote thought he would be the one to call the deer. So he killed Woodtick. Then Coyote called the deer, and the deer came. But when he tried to pierce their ears, as Woodtick had done, he hurt himself instead. Woodtick's spirit called to the deer to run away. So the deer ran away. The meat that was laid on the rock turned into a deer and ran away; the meat in Coyote's quiver turned into a deer and ran away; the meat he was cooking on the fire ran away; and even the bones he was saving in an old sack ran away in the shape of living deer. Then Coyote threw Woodtick out of the house, because it was all her fault. She went far off and her spirit called away all the deer, and Coyote starved.

This story, especially well known to the Coeur d'Alene, is also of very wide distribution over other areas. It is of especial interest in that it points up Coyote's characteristic greediness, ingratitude, and discourtesy, and develops the unsuccessful imitation motif found also in the widespread bungling host tales.

calling the wind A singing call of the American Negroes of slave times: "Co' win'," repeated three times, followed by a long whistle. This call was used when rice was to be fanned, when a sail hung idle, or when a field was to be burned. It closely resembles a rain invocation of Togoland.

Callisto In Greek mythology, the Arcadian nymph, companion of Artemis, who became the constellation Ursa Major. In the oldest extant version, Callisto was seduced by Zeus masquerading as Artemis. The goddess, discovering Callisto's pregnancy, changed her into a bear. Later, Arcas, Callisto's son, hunted her for violating a place sacred to Zeus, and mother and son were transformed into the asterisms Ursa Major and either Boötes or Ursa Minor. In various other tellings of the myth, it was Zeus himself who changed Callisto into a bear to avoid Hera's suspicions, or Hera caused the change as punishment; Artemis shot Callisto; Zeus disguised himself as Apollo and not as Artemis, etc.

The myth appears to have developed from an Arcadian aspect of Artemis Calliste (Fairest) whose symbolic animal was a she-bear. See URSA MAJOR.

calumet dance A widespread North American Indian ceremony focused in elaborate smoke-offering to the Great Spirit. The particular sacredness of tobacco and the pipe to the American Indian becomes evident in the light of native symbolism. Fire, ashes, smoke are endowed with purifying and life-giving powers; furthermore, the smoke in its ascent may communicate with the Creator and carry messages to Him. By inhaling and then exhaling this smoke, the breath of life, the soul of the smoker arises with it. Similar qualities of communication are attributed to the soaring eagle, who has power over weather, the sun, lightning, rain, and thus over the earth and its bounty. These natural associations must be born in mind in the following summary of the various forms of the calumet dance.

Its cult was most intensive and variegated in the Great Plains, became attenuated in its travel eastward, and is absent in the Southwest. The stem of the calumet is commonly of ashwood, the bowl of Dakota catlinite. The tobacco was originally cultivated as *palani* among the agricultural Pawnee, who also developed the most elaborate ceremonial, the hako.

1) The calumet functions most commonly in ceremonial invocations to the six directions, in introducing peace and friendship pacts, welcoming important personages, rejoicing over a victory. Many tribes, as the Iowa and Plains Cree, featured a smoking ceremony for peace, a circulation of the pipe from warrior to warrior, and a petition for success in war, abundance of fruit and buffalo, and long life. This ceremony often culminated in a dance. Ordinarily there were two pipes, decorated with feathers and hair. These were handed to the dancers by the greatest warrior, who boasted of his great deeds (Iowa, Illinois). Most Plains Military Societies had two special pipe-bearers, who also danced exclusively with the pipes, thus the Oglala *tokala*, *kɑgi-yuha*, *ihoka*, *sotka*, *wic'iska*, the Blackfoot *Catchers* with their black-covered pipes, the Pawnee *Two Lance Society* with their black-banded pipe representing the trachea.

2) **The highly sacred and elaborate** *hako* type of ceremony originated among the Pawnee, and was accepted practically in its original form by the Omaha and Kansa (as *mocu watci*), in somewhat altered form by the Ponca (as *wawa watci*), and by the Crow as their Medicine Pipe dance. *Hakkow* means a breathing mouth of wood, and applies collectively to the sacred paraphernalia used in the hako: the two calumet stems, *raka'katittu*, with dark eagle feathers, representing the female principle, and *rahak'takaru* with white feathers representing the male principle, also a blue-painted ear of corn with eagle down, two squash rattles representing the gift of the earth mother, an oriole nest, etc. The perforated stems were tipped with duck bills and decorated with owl and woodpecker feathers, uniting the birds of the day, night, water, and trees. The hako, which could take place at any season except winter, was a prayer for offspring, plentiful crops, and long life. In the 13th ritual the ceremonial leader, or *ku'rakus*, attached a bowl to the female stem and sent up a smoke invocation for peace and plenty. A child

was painted and anointed: a symbolic connection between the ceremonial groups of "fathers" and "children" and a symbol of progeny. In the 19th ritual two dancers simulated bird flight in concentric circles, waving the calumet in their left hands and the rattle in their right. Thereupon followed gifts and thanksgiving. In the similar ritual of the Iowa the pipes are both considered as male.

3) Eastern derivatives—the Cherokee calumet and Iroquois eagle dance (*gane'gwa'e*) combine, in highly condensed version, elements of the peace pipe ceremony, the hako, and Grass Dance. The pipe stem is simply a wand with an attached eagle-feather fan. Pairs of dancers vibrate these in the left hand and shake a rattle in the right hand, then hop, as eagles feeding on the ground. The dance is for well-being and cure. As in the Grass Dance, the dance is interrupted by interludes of boasting. Give-away features, the gifts, common to all of these dances, have shrunken from horses to small cakes. Possibly the Iroquois received the dance from the Cherokee, who used catlinite pipebowls, or directly from the Plains, or possibly by way of the Meskwakie (Fox). The Meskwakie pipe dance is a challenge dance for pairs of dancers with similar choreography to that of the Iroquois. The Iroquois claim its bestowal from a giant eagle, *Ha'guks*, with power over wilting things. Possibly we have here an amalgamation of an aboriginal eagle dance with the hako concept.

All forms of the calumet dance are doubtless of great antiquity. It was well established in the Great Lakes in the 17th century, as testified by Father Marquette, and in a form then already declined from the great hako. This most complex Pawnee ritual was probably the high point in the development of the calumet dance, rather than its original form, for the obvious function of a pipe, the smoking of it, had already become subsidiary. The Plains smoking ceremonies would appear the most logical inception, with a purpose transcending sociability and brotherhood, a symbolism akin to the incense offering of the Orient. [GPK]

caluşar The Rumanian hobby-horse dance, so pagan that the hobby is excluded from the church. He associates with an assembly resembling the English Morris dancers: a fool, a man-woman, a goat, and a troop of dancers. These are a sworn brotherhood and precede the dance with an initiation which features a horse's head and the sacred number nine. Their round dance and their battle is fiercer than the Morris, formerly even bloody: a realistic enactment of the battle of the seasons. The dance takes place in the midwinter season and on All Souls' Day. [GPK]

Calydonian boar hunt A famous tale of Greek antiquity in which the names of Meleager and Atalanta are most prominent. Œneus of Calydon having omitted a sacrifice to Artemis, the goddess sent a huge boar to ravage his country. His son Meleager invited the great heroes of Greece to join him in hunting the animal—Idas, Castor and Pollux, Admetus, Theseus, Jason, Peleus, Telamon, Nestor, and Atalanta, among others. Atalanta was the first to wound the boar; Meleager killed it and presented the head and hide to Atalanta, with whom he was in love. Traditions vary as to the sequel. According to some, Althea, Meleager's mother,

revenged the slaying of her brothers (killed by Meleager when they tried to take the spoils from Atalanta) by throwing Meleager's life token, an unconsumed brand, on the fire, thus killing him. Another version tells of a battle between the Calydonians and the Curetes over the spoils, with Meleager sulking apart because he was cursed by his mother for killing her brother.

calypso The best-known of the Negro song types of Trinidad, a witty, improvised song in English, dealing with social criticism, personal comment and ridicule, topical subject-matter, etc., sung to tunes derived from European folk or popular sources. Developed originally in connection with carnival dancing (*calipso* or *caliso*) and preserving the African pattern of songs of personal allusion and comment, calypso singing sometimes takes on the aspect of a duel or contest, or "calypso war," with an exchange of such improvised jokes and derisive musical remarks. Titles well-known through recordings are: *Bad Woman, Matilda,* and *Hitler Demands.* Two Tin-Pan-Alley versions of songs of the calypso type which achieved wide popularity in the United States through radio, records, night-club singers, and juke boxes were *Stone Cold Dead in the Market,* first composed about a murder in Port-of-Spain in 1939, and *Rum and Coca Cola.* A distinctive element of the type is the false accent given to the words to make them fit the meter.

Camazotz The Ruler of the Bats or the Death Bat: a Mayan deity greatly feared, powerful and malignant, and worshipped in vampire form. In the *Popol Vuh,* Hunahpu and Xbalanque, on a quest for flowers for the Xibalbans, stop for the night at the house of Camazotz. They are forced to lie prone, and when, during the long night, Hunahpu raises his head, Camazotz tears it off. A turtle takes the place of the head, the real head being stuck up on the ball court by the Xibalbans. The twins however beat the Xibalbans in the last part of the game and recover Hunahpu's head.

Cambric Shirt One of the American ballad versions of *The Elfin Knight* (Child #2), collected both in New England and in the southern mountains, and showing linguistic characteristics of the 17th century. It embodies the theme of the test of love, in which the suitor sets impossible tasks for his true love and she answers with equally impossible tasks for him to fulfil. The refrain, "Parsley, sage, rosemary and thyme," is almost the same as that of the English ballad, *Scarborough Fair.*

camel Among caravan men the slyness, stubbornness, salacity, and wrong-mindedness of camels are accepted facts. In the German language the word is used to designate a large, lumbering, stupid person. In Arabia, however, racing camels are so highly valued that the word "camel" is a term of endearment. The most valued sacrifices the Bedouins can make are camels. Camels with ten offspring were thought of as sacred, could not be mounted or milked, and the tenth offspring was sacrificed and eaten at a feast from which women were excluded. When given to a sanctuary in recognition of success, camels were sacred. Camels were sacrificial animals among the Iranians and were considered unclean by the Hebrews. In India a Vidyādhara, having attempted to rape a beautiful maiden, was punished by being changed into an "ugly" camel. In the animal fables the camel is tricked and eaten by other beasts: crow, lion, panther, jackal. Ghosts in India will not cross the threshold of a house if camel bones are buried under it. [RDJ]

Camelot In Arthurian legend, the seat of Arthur's court and Round Table: variously identified with Caerleon-upon-Usk, Monmouthshire; with Queen's Camel, Somersetshire; Camelford in Cornwall; and said by Malory to be Winchester.

cám kham In Annam, the prohibition post, made of bamboo, placed before the door of a house in which a woman has just borne a child. On top of the post is placed a lighted coal with the burning side turned outward if the child is a girl, inward if it is a boy. The cám kham is put up to prevent women who have borne Con lōn or who have had accidents after a confinement from entering and bringing evil to mother or child.

Camlan In Arthurian legend, the battlefield where King Arthur was killed. The *Annales Cambriæ* for the year 537 mention a battle of Camlan where Arthur and Mordred both were killed. It is thought to be situated perhaps near Camelford in Cornwall; Malory puts it "upon a down beside Salisbury, and not far from the seaside."

camomile A strongly scented bitter herb (genus *Anthemis*) especially the European perennial (*A. nobilis*) whose bitter, aromatic flowers and leaves are used in medicine. The Egyptians so reverenced the camomile as a remedy that they consecrated it to their gods. The Greeks called it *chamaimēlon* or earth-apple because of its smell. The Romans used it to cure snake bites. Culpeper says a decoction of camomile will remove pains and stitches in the side. The flowers, if boiled and drunk, will help to expel aches, pains, and colds. It is still used in many parts of Europe and North America in the form of a tea for a weak stomach or to stop vomiting. In Germany the flowers are called *Heermännchen* and are said to have been soldiers who died accursed for their sins. In Germany camomile is widely used for toothache: roasted and administered in small cloth bags, brewed in vinegar and used as a mouthwash, or the flowers are boiled in milk which is then filtered through saltpeter in a towel, and the liquid held in the mouth so as to submerge the tooth. In Bohemia hot oil of camomile is dropped into the ear beside the painful tooth. In Ireland a tonic tea is made from camomile leaves which is regarded as a remedy for pleurisy.

caña A Spanish couple dance considered to be of Arabic origin: named from the Arabic *gaunia*, song. In Andalusia it has been traditionally accompanied by songs of Moorish quality. In Argentina, the gauchos dance it under the name of *media caña*. An alternate interpretation of this name is the formation of a half circle (called *caña* by Argentine natives) at the end of the dance. [GPK]

canario An exotic couple dance introduced from the Canary Islands to Spain and Portugal, thence to the French court. In the early 16th century it had the reputation of lascivious vitality, and was at times per-

formed at funerals—a function retained from the island of its origin. As a court dance it was still characterized by difficult and rapid footwork, alternating heel-and-toe stamps as in the zapateados. Each couple enacted a pantomime of courtship: after dancing together, the lady stood still while the gentleman retreated from her, approached and retreated again; the same was repeated by the lady. The music was in dotted 3/8 time. The dance continued in fashion until late in the 18th century. [GPK]

cancellation A mild form of youthful fortune-telling whereby a boy will cross out letters in a girl's name identical with those in his own and apply the "she loves me—she loves me not" formula to the remaining letters, to discover if his affection is returned. [CFP]

Cancer The Crab, Lobster, Crayfish, Scarab, etc.: a faint ecliptical constellation, having no star brighter than the fourth magnitude, yet important from ancient times as one of the signs of the zodiac. It contains a nebulous cluster, the Beehive (Manger, Crib, Præsæpe), which the Chaldeans called the Gate of Men, the entrance-way for souls coming from Heaven to inhabit their human bodies (the exit lay in Capricorn, the opposite sign in the zodiac). Cancer was the name given to the constellation because it was here that the summer solstice formerly occurred (now in Gemini), the sun seemingly stopping and then beginning a backwards sidling motion downward through the sky towards the south.

In Greek mythology, the crab nipped Hercules as he fought the Lernean Hydra; Hercules paused only long enough to crush his annoyer and then resumed his fight. Hera, Hercules' enemy, rewarded the crab by placing it among the stars, but it remained crushed and inconspicuous. Another name given the region in the heavens is the Asses: these were the animals which Bacchus and Silenus rode and which frightened the giants away with their braying.

The Beehive, several other stars in Cancer, and one of the stars in Gemini make up the Chinese Shun Show, a zodiacal sign, the Quail's Head, Pheasant, Phœnix, or Red Bird (modern Keu Hea, the Crab), which with Leo and Virgo is the residence of the Southern (Red) Emperor. In astrology, Cancer is one of the watery signs, the House in which the moon was at the creation, the sign governing the breast and stomach and unlucky as such. When the sun is in Cancer, storms are catastrophic and bring famine and locusts. According to Berossus, the end of the world by water will occur when all the planets are in Cancer.

candle Candles have been used from ancient times in rituals, ceremonies, festivals, and processions in both domestic and religious life. In the family, they were used on such occasions as weddings and funerals; in the Church—Roman, Greek, and Anglican—in various ceremonials, especially in those designed to celebrate a particular day. Wax lights had to be used in the Church, for it was the tradition that bees came from Paradise.

There was and is now much figurative and symbolic thought connected with candle usage in the Church. Among the folk, candles and their ways are ominous: they may presage a happy or unhappy marriage by the way they burn; death in the family is forecast if they gutter. Candles are used in divination and in charms, by girls to determine their future husband, and in very many other customs and beliefs current today as well as in the past in the British Isles and various sections of the Continent. [GPS]

☞ If a candle burns blue there is a ghost in the house. If a candle burns dim there is a ghost in the house. If a candle burns blue there will be frost. When the candle flames irregularly, melts a lot of tallow, and burns up too fast, there is said to be a thief in the candle. When a candle gives forth a spark into the air, it means a letter is coming to the one sitting nearest it. It is a general European folk belief that it is unlucky to burn three candles in the same room at once. If a candlewick divides and burns with two flames, it is taken as an omen of death in Germany, but as the sign of a letter in Austria. To dream of a bright-burning candle means you will receive a letter from your love. In Arkansas, a lighted candle placed under a person's house is an aid to the conjurer; likewise a lighted candle is regarded as a protection against spells. In Ireland it is customary to keep twelve candles burning around a dead body before burial. This keeps evil spirits, who cannot enter a circle of fire, from carrying away the dead man's soul.

candle dance A dance in which the performers bear lighted candles. The ball del ciri of Catalonia and the baile de la candela of the Venezuelan Guayuncomo tribe both involve a group of men and women; in the former, the group performs in couples in a consecratory Christian ceremony; in the latter, in separate groups in an orgiastic jumping and circling. The candles are shrunken descendants of the great beeswax candles and torches of the pagan (and contemporary) torch processions. These were (and are) commonly performed for three occasions: most anciently, in a torchlight circling of the fields, when the vitality of the flame was believed to be communicated to the crops; secondly, in candle-bearing wedding processions (reminiscent of the flame-bearing Eros); thirdly, in honorific processionals. The Catalan ball de la teya exemplifies the first function, the Hungarian gyertyás tánc, the second. The Philippine candle dance serves as a dance of selection: a girl chooses a mate while waltzing and manipulating a candle. The Christian Candlemas processionals on February 2 now honor the Virgin, but actually date back to pre-Christian worship. [GPK]

Candlemas A Church festival celebrated on February 2: in the Eastern Church, commemorating the Presentation of Christ in the Temple, in the Western, the Purification of the Virgin Mary. The Armenian Church calls it the Coming of the Son of God into the Temple. The blessing of candles for the altar, for which the day is named, was not an observance associated with this feast until the 11th century A.D.

☞ It is observed generally with candlelight processions. In Europe the custom probably goes back to the ancient torchlight processions for purifying and invigorating fields previous to the sowing season, and to honor or propitiate the various associated spirits, beneficent or harmful. In Mexico, February 2 corresponds to the Aztec New Year, observed with renewed fires and celebration, especially at the end of the periodic nemontemi, the five days of inactivity and sorrow-

ing terminating a cycle of 52 years. The largest festivals are those celebrated at San Juan de los Lagos, Jalisco, for the Virgin, and in Tzintzuntzan, Michoacán, featuring the moros and sembradoras, or sowers. Both festivals retain features of agricultural spring ritual. See CANDLE DANCE. [GPK]

candomblés Religious societies of the Negroes of Bahía, Brazil, originating in Africa, especially among the Yoruba and Ewe peoples. The candomblés still reflect the old mythologies and the original African dances, music, and ritual. They are identified by "nation" and the members speak the old language of the tribe they represent. The candomblés de caboclo are the "new" societies, characterized by indigenous Indian gods, dances, and magic. Each candomblé is headed either by a pae-de-santo or mãe-de-santo, i.e. a father or mother in sainthood. Women predominate in the cults, in that the functions of the cult belong to the women, such as preparing the sacred foods, making ritual garments, tending altars, etc. The men have more often certain honorary or temporary authorities, such as for instance the alabé, who directs the drummers. Edson Carneiro's discussion of the candomblés (JAFL 53: 217 ff.) reports, however, 37 fathers and 30 mothers in sainthood in Bahía, 1933–39. These fathers and mothers in sainthood are the spiritual parents of those initiated into the specific groups, each of whom has "made" his saint, i.e. has learned to receive (become possessed by) a specific deity. The drumming is important; it is a means of communication between the gods and the people. See CABOCLO.

cane of breath and spittle In the Mohave Indian cosmogonic "dream tale" about the beginning of the world, the cane belonging to Mastamho, the younger of two brothers born to Sky and Earth. The cane consisted of Mastamho's own breath and spittle. He thrust the cane into the earth and a great river flowed out of that place. Mastamho then entered into a boat with mankind and traveled from there to the sea. The way Mastamho twisted and tilted and turned the boat or let it go straight caused the shape of the bottom lands and canyons along the river. Then he turned and took the people up the river to the northern part of what became the Mohave country.

cannibalism Man-eating, also known as anthropophagy; the eating of the human body or parts of it, or the drinking of human blood, by human beings. The emotions which cannibalism arouses are powerful. Consequently the cannibal feast needs to be examined both as a social event and as a fact of the imagination. Although no census of the number of persons who are currently cannibals is available, reports from casual observers who are not always disinterested indicate that Christianity and Mother Hubbards are not considered appropriate to cannibal feasts. The social and psychological mechanisms involved in apostasy among the fringe cultures are unexplored areas in a very rich field. Though a large number of people in many parts of the world know of cannibalism as a social event, many more people know of it as a fact of the imagination.

Because it is difficult to observe this custom over a long period of time under controlled circumstances, field studies leave many questions unanswered. People who accept cannibalism as part of their normal way of life are not inclined to discuss it frankly with white ethnographers who disapprove of it and are, or think they are, in hazard. Experience has shown cannibals that outsiders are likely to make more trouble about this dietary habit than about any other tribal or religious custom. Even when cannibals are persuaded that they can speak without fear of reprisal or ridicule, they tend to regard this as part of their own way of life which they have no need to make clear to outsiders, and the outsiders themselves conduct their interviews with a notable and understandable delicacy. Cannibals who have been converted formally or wholly or partly to other customs introduce into the discussion of their past errors, tones and attitudes which distort history and motive. (Discussions between monogamists and polygamists, homo- and heterosexuals, and accounts by reformed drunkards recently returned to respectability display both types of distortion.) Observers who make use of the direct question, however carefully prepared for, and ask "Why do you eat human flesh?" receive a variety of answers of more interest in illuminating the mental processes of the cannibal than in explaining the custom. When, as is frequently the case, they have no clear idea of why they eat human flesh or why the subject should be of any interest to anybody, they courteously present specious answers, tell the outsider whatever comes into their heads, or give free play to a sly sense of humor which, when it appears in the field notes, is difficult to identify. Consequently attempts during the last half century to organize travelers' tales into a systematic account of cannibalism must be taken with reserve: many of the reports are inadequately documented; reports which are otherwise acceptable are insufficient in number and distribution to permit general conclusions; others are distorted by the reporters' own views about primitive society, evolution of culture, totemism, and the like, which, invaluable in their place, have been expanded with imprudent generosity.

Cannibalism has been reported as an accepted or as an occasional custom from all parts of the world. Attempts to confine it to 10° north or south of the equator are misleading. Arctic travelers, ship-wrecked sailors, hunters, and immigrant pioneers, forced to choose between eating a starved comrade and starvation themselves, have preferred to eat the comrade. Human flesh often appears on the markets of famine areas of China. One British merchant was unable to decide whether or not in a famine area he had unwittingly eaten human flesh disguised as stew, though under the circumstances it was possible that he did. This occasional cannibalism must be distinguished from the cannibalism in Chinese *exempla* of filial piety in which children serve their own flesh to starving parents to keep the parents from death. In these instances the starving sailor and the filial son both violate rigid social prohibitions but both find social justification for their transgression.

This occasional cannibalism is not centrally part of folklore. The literature on customary cannibalism is ably reviewed in J. A. MacCulloch's article, "Cannibalism," in Hastings' *Encyclopaedia of Religion and Ethics*. Because the explanations which MacCulloch's sources reported cover most of the reasons imaginable

for eating anything, together with some that are hard to grasp, the article may be taken as comprehensive, though before the conclusions can be accepted the sources need reexamination in the light of more recent reports. In his discussion of prehistoric cannibalism, MacCulloch, at times influenced by the views of the cultural evolutionists, was trapped by a premise. He assumed that as hominids became omnivorous they included meat on their diet and that meant human flesh. He therefore concluded, in opposition to H. Schurtz, that cannibalism was not pathological, a "disease of childhood," but was once universal. He was unwilling to distinguish in primitive society, despite the appeal of the word "omnivorous," between endo- and exo-cannibalism, that is, the eating of relatives as opposed to the eating of outsiders; but because of the inconveniences which would appear if the family systematically ate itself up, MacCulloch conceded that endo-cannibalism might have occurred after the individual was dead anyway or had outlived his usefulness. Anthropologists are not in agreement about the cannibalistic significance of the bones found in the early caves. Openings in the skulls of *Sinanthropus pekinensis* together with some evidence of formal burial, may indicate that these anthropoid brutes liked the taste of human brains, or that they removed the brains for magical purposes, or that they wanted to quiet a ghost, etc. Similarly the custom which is occasionally reported of eating the aged and useless members of the community may or may not be a "survival" from prehuman cultures.

Accounts of cannibalism among prehistoric men are speculative. Accounts of cannibalism in societies which are assumed to be similar to those of prehistoric man are frequently infused with the technical folklore created by the anthropologists themselves. Some students reasonably aver that the prohibition against eating kinsmen, when it occurs, could come only with a growing sense of kinship, on the ground that if the person eaten was not, according to local law or custom, accepted as a "relative" he was obviously not a "relative." Evidence is insufficient to justify the conclusion that a sense of kinship grew from a time when prehistoric men were rugged and lonely individuals. Recent studies in the sociology of contemporary apes are ambiguous and analogies between apes and almost-human brutes are dangerous. Ethnographers commonly accept totemism as a type of social organization which defines, among other things, exact lines of kinship. The former objection in western Europe to marriage with the deceased brother's wife on the grounds of "incest" is an example of the complexity of kinship. MacCulloch observed that "one result of totemism was the tabu against eating the totem animal." Brenda Seligman's discussion of endogamy and exogamy did much to clarify ideas about totemic and other forms of kinship and raised new questions; but the fact about cannibalism which normally had to be accounted for is that some totemic groups do eat their totem animal, which is variously regarded as father or creator of the clan or as part of it, and some do eat their own kin. The reports show great variety in custom. Some tribes eat only enemies, and never eat their totem or kinsmen; others do eat only relatives (Dieri) or fathers do not eat their own children but mothers do. Ethnographers meet the problem with an ingenuity which is refreshing and plausible. For example an exogamic husband can eat his wife without violating the totemic prohibition, because the wife is of a different totem. His daughter who is of his totem is prohibited food. Other relatives, brothers- and sisters-in-law, for example, may be eaten when, according to the complex rules of the particular totemic organization, they are not totemkin, that is for dietary purposes are not regarded as members of the clan and therefore related. The assumption that all members of the social group are equally subject to its privileges and prohibitions is here dangerous. A final and convenient explanation is that relatives are eaten when the totemic prohibitions have lost their force and totemism is in decline.

The distinction between killing for food (the term "gluttony" sometimes used of this situation has implications which are somewhat more than descriptive) and eating men for other reasons is useful. Cannibal hunts and cannibal murder are reported from Australia, New Caledonia, the Marquesas, Samoa, Luzon, among the Ostyaks and Samoyeds, from northern Japan, Burma, Africa, and North and South America, though reports are vague about the conditions of social tension and need which precede the hunts. Scattered tribes have reported that they began eating human flesh during famines and later developed the taste. Others (New Guinea) have said that their women introduced them to cannibalism. Still other reports indicate that cannibalism occurs when, as after a battle, large quantities of human meat are available which might otherwise spoil or when the group works itself into the mood for eating human flesh. The mood of battle which is known to relax other social prohibitions might well be conducive. Two still unpublished reports (Luzon and New Guinea) indicate that the proposed victims were able to divert the mood of the group into other objectives. That singing was in both cases the device used may not have been incidental. Even when cannibalism for food purposes is customary, it is not entirely casual. Communities which are normally undernourished or have a very monotonous diet regard any unusual food as a feast and meat as a special treat to be consumed with ceremony. Thus the etiquette of a cannibal feast is as worthy of study as the etiquette of a British or American Christmas dinner, though the relevance is to the customs of the banquet rather than the proper way of carving and serving a human carcass.

Other explanations of cannibalism may be listed briefly. Thus because food gives strength one can assimilate the strength of a person or animal by eating it or by eating only parts of it: heart, liver, lips, etc. Or one can assimilate the qualities of the person eaten: his courage, skill, or "magical" powers. We still feed red meat to athletes to develop "stamina." These personal qualities, according to some reports, can be acquired by eating only a part of the carcass as symbolic of the whole. The complex symbolism of the Eucharist is here relevant. Another motive favored by those who are impressed by "animism" is that the cannibal acquires power over the soul of the person eaten. The soul of the person consumed becomes bound to the consumer and thus subservient to him and his clan. Some of the ritual connected with blood convenants which involve the drinking of blood—before battle, at times of ethnic

crisis, or in initiation ceremonies—have the object of assimilating the individual by consuming part of him. Chinese physicians of the old school teach that each of the parts of the human body has specific therapeutic values (human blood, gall); human semen has been prescribed as a tonic for old men as animal ovarian extract has been prescribed in the Occident.

A philanthropic explanation of cannibalism appears too frequently in literature to be ignored. In this group of explanations, mentioned in Herodotus and reported from all continents, the bodies of the aged are eaten to keep their souls from becoming weak or to be sure that they have proper burial. Other related reasons are to keep the souls and qualities of the aged in the clan or to keep their remains from being desecrated by enemies who might use them for magical purposes. Somewhat similar to this is the cannibalism which derives from what MacCulloch calls morbid affection. When a female member of one of the coast tribes of north-central Australia died, her body was eaten by the male "kin" and by all the other males who had had sexual intercourse with her. Some of the South Australian tribes are said to have eaten the body of the dear departed in order to assuage their grief. At moments when they were overwhelmed by sorrow they comforted themselves by chewing on a juicy piece of the dead body. Deirdre lapped the blood of Naoise after he was slain. The cannibalistic phrases used to children ("Good enough to eat," "I'm going to eat you") and similar phrases used among lovers lead into the unexplored obscurities of oral erotism.

Religious cannibalism, which involves the eating of human beings who were sacrificed to the god, involves another set of explanations which is supported by evidence and logic of sufficient force to be examined with care. One of these is that human beings are sacrificed to the god because human flesh is the best possible food and therefore suitable for the feast of a god. Another motif (ancient Greece, Crete, and elsewhere) is that the human sacrifice is eaten as a representative of the god in order that the congregation might become literally "one with god." Accounts of gods who consume their own worshippers have been devised by theologians and need not be examined at this point.

The eating of criminals is and has been customary in a number of societies, though here the word "criminal" needs careful definition. When the criminal as a member of the "they-group" is potentially dangerous, his spirit is absorbed when his body is eaten. The qualities required to become an enemy of society awaken in some clansmen a deplorable admiration. These qualities can be made a part of the group if the person having them is eaten. Religious motifs are involved when the stranger, who is possibly an enemy or a god in disguise, is sacrificed and eaten in order to assure the prosperity or salvation of the group.

Social and political cannibalism appeared in the coronation ceremonies in Africa and the Sandwich Islands or in the blood-drinking ceremonies of initiation and brotherhood rites. This sort of cannibalism may be total or symbolic in that only a part of the body may be eaten as a symbol of the whole, or only a part may be eaten to acquire desired characteristics. The breakfast of champions in the Sandwich Islands was the eye of an enemy, which the king ate on the morning of his coronation. Several of the motifs already cited are involved in social and political cannibalism.

Cannibalistic magic is part of the witch cult in many parts of the world: India, Africa, South Australia, Christian Europe, and elsewhere. The eating of human flesh is part of the initiation of witches, who after eating are thrown into frenzy and are incapable of normal human emotions. Participants in the Greek mysteries became "enthused," in the sense of infused with divinity, when they ate the body of Dionysus. The theological accounts of the Christian Eucharist deserve special study in this connection. The generally reliable account of the Cambridge expedition to the Torres Straits reported that sorcerers ate the flesh of corpses or mixed the flesh of corpses with their food when they were about to practice their art. The consequence was that they became violent and, when angered, committed murder. Too little is known of the steps taken to induce the shamanist trance except to note that cannibalism in this instance promoted the consumer to an unhuman or superhuman state.

Cannibalism is a motif in many myths, legends, and folktales: Odysseus and the Cyclops, Tantalus and Pelops. In such folktales as *Hänsel und Gretel* and *Jack the Giant-Killer* and their many analogs, the hero outwits a cannibalistic witch or ogre. In *Van den Machandelboom* and *Die Kinder in Hungersnot*, a parent either eats the children or threatens to. Other tales are about a parent who sent the child to be killed, but must have the heart or liver returned, or about the mother who sent a child prepared as a stew to its father, or about husbands and wives who trick each other into eating their lovers similarly disguised. Students who sought to find in folktales remnants of forgotten history and custom saw in these cannibalistic motifs "survivals" from early stages of culture.

A few other aspects of cannibalism need to be mentioned. In some Australian tribes only special parts of the body were served to the women, either because these were the least tasty or because women and men were not supposed to eat the same foods. In 1920 Detzner reported that among the inland tribes of New Guinea, women left alone with prisoners whom the men had decided to spare often killed and ate them, and a less trustworthy source reported that Fiji women during battle rushed upon fallen enemies and drank their blood. The elements of sexual distrust and satire found in folktales and folk belief about cannibal wives, dentate vagina, poison damsel are not entirely unknown in the fantasies of the modern Occidentals.

If the available literature on cannibalism makes anything clear, it is that the evidence is insufficient to support a single and simple explanation of a custom, which is known either by direct experience or through imagination to the peoples of all parts of the world. If one could demonstrate the major premise it would be logical to concur that cannibalism became universal when the later hominids became omnivorous. The further assumption that an early cannibalistic *Homo sapiens* evolved from cannibalism into dietary specialization is weak, particularly in view of the comment by a cultural evolutionist that the "worst forms of cannibalism do not occur among the lowest races." When evolutionists, survivalists, and originists assert that cannibalism in folktales and märchen is a survival from primitive times, one may well inquire whether the grave historians in the nursery are interested in these episodes because of their interest in the past of the race, or whether they interpret the episodes in terms of other interests. When better field studies are available and when our knowledge of the processes of human imagination has been greatly extended, the place of cannibalism as an event in society and an event in the mind will be better understood. For the present, although no explanation can be accepted as entirely satisfactory, all must be examined as suggestive, partial, or possible. R. D. JAMESON

Cannibals Cannibal deities, monsters, giants, human beings, birds, or animals are frequently characters in North American Indian and Eskimo mythology and belief. Tales of the Cannibal Bird occur throughout the Basin. The giant with a basket who packs off children to eat is well known in the Southwest (see BIG OWL), as are other cannibal monsters and deities—giant eagles, buffalo, and the antelope who kills with his eyes. In the Northeast persons who eat human flesh become cannibal giants (windigo); in the Central Woodlands cannibal boys are associated with the Shawnee female creator. The Eskimo have many tales of weird cannibal monsters. Among the Southern Okanagon of Washington a cannibal is the guardian of flint. On the North Pacific Coast the belief in cannibals still persists; although the world was rid of many of them soon after it was formed, some still survive. The Kwakiutl of Vancouver Island had a cannibal society (see BLACK TAMANOUS) which met each year during the winter ceremonial season. Initiates and members of the society were required to eat human flesh as part of the rites. Tales of man-eating cannibals are also prevalent among the northeastern North American Indian tribes. In an Ojibwa myth, Trickster is captured by a cannibal, but saved by a weasel whom he persuades to jump into the cannibal's body and bite the heart string. In other cannibal tales of the Micmac, Passamaquoddy, Malecite, Montagnais-Naskapi, Cree, Ojibwa and Menomini, cannibal giants are tamed by a woman who calls the giant "father" and treats him with kindness; they are beguiled by shamans; or they are easily overcome by reason of their stupidity, by any one of several actors.
[EWV]

cante fable A narrative form in which a story is told partly in song: common in folktales of many languages and many countries. The song sections, usually in dialogue, are the most important or emotionally charged elements of the story, containing magical utterances, witty or wise replies to questions, riddles, sayings of poets, musicians, birds, or animals, wishes or calls, etc. The prose narrative explains or sets the scene for the song, which may be repeated, with or without change, in the course of the tale. Examples are found in the Grimm collections, in *The Thousand and One Nights*, in the *Panchatantra*, in old Irish romances and Scandinavian sagas, in British folktales, among the Negroes of Africa, the West Indies, and the United States, in scattered and fragmentary form among the white population of the United States, etc.

Traditional English ballads, as found among Negroes of the West Indies and the United States, tend to fall into the cante fable form. Several such versions of *The Maid Freed from the Gallows* (Child #95) and *Little*

Musgrave (Child #81) are known. Occasionally the English material has been so reworked as to fit into the pattern of Anansi stories. American Negro singers, such as Leadbelly, will even cast a fairly recent Negro ballad, *Frankie and Albert,* or an early jazz piece, *The Rock Island Line,* in the form of a running narrative with snatches of song interwoven.

Survivals among white singers of the United States show a special fondness for the humorous tale, especially of the deceived husband variety, *Our Good Man* (Child #274) having been preserved in cante fable style among soldiers, sailors, hillbilly singers, etc.

Some scholars have put forth the hypothesis that the cante fable is the ancient forerunner of both the ballad and the folktale, pointing out the elliptical quality of the narrative thread in ballads as possibly resulting from the omission of the spoken part of the story. This controversial suggestion has not met with wide acceptance. However, the survival of many puzzling bits of song and of many tales with interspersed rimes is noted as the vestige of cante fables whose stories or tunes have been forgotten.

cante hondo or **jondo** Literally, deep song: a type of sorrow song of Andalusia, preserved and developed by Gipsy singers and somewhat similar in mood and subject matter to the blues. It includes tragic love songs and plaints, prison songs, and forge songs, sung in long undulating notes, possibly related to the cantillation of Sephardic Jews, and is accompanied by guitar-playing of a dramatic and intense character. See FLAMENCO.

Canute or **Cnut** (994?–1035) A Danish king; king also of England from 1017. Holinshed's *Chronicles* tells the story of his sitting on the shore and commanding the rising tide to come no farther. The tide continued to roll in and the king was soaked. He did this, it is said, to reproach certain flattering adherents, to whom he pointed out that Canute, the Great, could not even prevent the little waves from advancing up the beach.

Cá ōng or **Cá voi** (feminine *bà ngu'*) The Annamese name for the dolphin, which is revered especially by the maritime population: in English, Mister Fish. The Cá ōng is believed to rescue shipwrecked sailors by carrying them on his back and the discovery of the body of a dolphin at sea is considered good luck. The body is hauled ashore and buried with a special ceremony. After three months and ten days the body is exhumed and the bones are laid in a sanctuary, thus ensuring the prosperity of the village. The dolphin has a real cult among these fishing villages, and communities without a dolphin tomb are considered unfortunate. Sometimes they are given one by a village possessing several. Usually, after a dolphin has been buried, there is a supernatural manifestation in the village. The spirit of the dolphin declares, through a possessed inhabitant, whether it is male or female, so that it may be properly addressed.

Capac raimi The initiation ceremony of adolescents belonging to the royal lineages of the Inca. This feast was held every year in December near Huanacauri. It combined magico-religious features and virility tests. Dances and sacrifices were accompanied by ritual flagellations and races. The young men were given their first weapons and breechclouts. The climax of the feast was the perforation of their ears to receive the heavy earplugs distinctive of the Inca family. Some of the rites observed, such as the eating of sacred bread, were directly connected with worship of the Sun God. [AM]

Capella The Little She-Goat; a white star, Alpha in the constellation Auriga. The three small stars just beneath it are called the Kids, usually pictured as two kids resting on the arm of the Charioteer. Capella and the Kids are called the Shepherd's Stars alike by the early Arabs and the South American Quechua Indians. In fact Arabian shepherds prayed to this "rainy star" to fertilize their pastures. The Arabs also called it Al Rākib, the Driver, because it was conspicuous in their northern sky and followed the rising of the Pleiades, which they thought of as herds being driven ahead of it. Temples of Ptah in ancient Egypt were oriented to the setting of this star, named Ptah, for this god. To the Akkadians Capella was the Messenger of Light, herald of spring and a new year. In Assyria it was called I-ku, the Leader, for the same reason. In India it was named Brahmā Ridaya, the Heart of Brahmā. Capella was sometimes also designated by Latin writers as Amalthea, for the she-goat who fostered the infant Zeus in Crete, and sometimes Cornu copiæ, the Horn of Plenty, which the child broke off. In astrology Capella is the bringer of wealth or military fame to one born under it.

caper A dance term suggested by the grotesque, playful leap of the goat or *cabra*. It is a term used for the hitchkick in morris dancing. In the 16th century this jump was called *capriol*. The fictitious pupil of Arbeau's *Orchésographie* goes by that name. In ballet terminology it is a *cabriole*. [GPK]

cap of invisibility One of the magic objects of folktale, conferring upon its wearer the power of seeing and not being seen: a motif found in myth and folktale in many parts of the world. In Greek legend, it is the cap of Hades forged for him by Cyclops, and worn by Hermes and Perseus. In the mythology of northern Europe, it is the Tarnhut, confounded to some degree with the Tarnkappe or cloak of invisibility, which belonged to Alberich and was worn by Siegfried. The cap of invisibility, in märchen, is often stolen or "borrowed" by the hero from giants, or brothers who have inherited it, who are quarreling over the division of a group of magic objects: the hat of invisibility, the seven-league boots, the inexhaustible pot, or other similar things. The motif is found in North American Indian tales of the Plains, Woodlands, and Southwest.

Cap o' Rushes Title of an English version of a very widespread European folktale in which the heroine, banished by her father for protesting that she loves him as dearly as bread (or meat) loves salt, goes through a series of hardships, serves as a nameless scullion clad in a cloak and hood of rushes, attends a dance three times in her own fine clothes and escapes unrecognized, finally reveals herself to the young son of her master (pining for love of her since the dance) by means of a ring which she drops in his gruel, marries him, and serves a wedding feast at which every dish is unsalted. The father is present at this feast and recognizes at last the true value of his daughter's love.

This story is known in Europe from Greece, Italy, and Spain to Germany, Belgium, Scandinavia, and the British Isles. *Loving Like Salt, Value of Salt,* and *Blear-Eye* are variant Italian titles, the last from the heroine's disguise as an old woman. It is known as *Ass-Skin* in Corsica, as *Little Dirty-Skin* and *Slut-Sweeps-the-Oven* in Belgium; in France it appears as *The Turkey Girl* (from the heroine's menial task); it is called *Salt and Bread* in Sweden. There are innumerable others. There are also Arabian and Indian variants.

Cap o' Rushes belongs to a large group of folktales based on the value of salt. The love like salt motif (H592.1), the humble (or rough) disguise (K1815), the disguise as menial (K1816) motifs are usually prominent. The flight of the heroine in humble or rough disguise and her menial position link the Cap o' Rushes story with the Catskin cycle; the motif involving the three-fold flight from the ball (R221) links it with the Cinderella cycle. The identification by ring (H94) or other token is fairly frequent. Grimm #179, entitled *The Goose-Girl at the Well,* is a well-known German version.

Capricorn The Horned Goat or Ibex, the Sea Goat: a zodiacal constellation recognized at least as early as the 2nd millennium B.C. and probably much earlier, although it is second in faintness only to Cancer among the constellations of the zodiac. The Persian, Turkish, Syrian, Arabic, Hindu names all mean goat. Chaldean astronomy placed it in the "Sea," that group of constellations said to represent the warriors of Tiamat; the goat has the tail of a fish. In Greek myth, this is explained as the result of the fright of either Pan or Bacchus at the appearance of Typhon: he leaped into the water as he transformed himself into animal shape; the upper part of the body became a goat, the lower a fish. The Egyptians connected the constellation with the yearly Nile inundation, and figured it as a fish or a mirror. The Aztecs pictured it as a horned fish, connected with Cipactli.

It was the Chaldean Gate of the Gods, the entrance through which souls passed into heaven, as they had come to earth through the Gate of Men in Cancer. In astrology, Capricorn is part of the earthly triad; it is the place of the creation of Saturn (with Aquarius); it governed the thighs and knees; it was generally unpropitious but, under certain conditions, sometimes of good influence. The sun enters the astrological sign on December 22. Roman legend said that Numa Pompilius began the calendar when the sun was midway in Capricorn after the winter solstice.

Captain Kidd A long forecastle song of the come-all-ye type, relating in the first person the misdeeds of William Kidd of piratical fame, known to sailor singers for unknown reasons as Robert. There is a homiletic turn to the narrative, with a warning to all those who see him die not to follow his example and fall in with bad companions. In style and form the song closely resembles the drinking song *Samuel Hall,* the confession of a more unregenerate sinner.

Captain Wedderburn's Courtship A Scottish popular ballad (Child #46) in which the suitor test of out-riddling the maiden is the main motif. Captain Wedderburn, "a servant to the king," meets the laird of Bristol's (or Earl of Rosslyn's) daughter walking alone

in the woods. The minute he lays eyes on her he is determined to take her "to his ain bed and lay her next the wall." He lifts her to his horse and takes her home. But the lady will not consent to get into the bed until the ardent suitor has answered first three, then six, then four more riddles. Among these are the famous cherry without a stone, chicken without a bone riddles, the sparrow's horn riddle, and "the priest unborn" to marry them. Captain Wedderburn answers all 13 posers without batting an eye. The cherry in blossom has no stone, the chicken in the shell has no bone, the sparrow has a horn in every claw and two for his beak, the priest waiting at the door was never born "for a wild boar bored his mother's side, he out of it did fa'." So the maiden "maun lye in his bed" but she refused to lie next the wall in one version, while another indicates that she did. Compare ALVÍSS.

capturing the moon An observance performed at midnight during the Chinese Moon Festival, Chung Chiu. It consists in catching the full moon's reflection in a basin of water.

Caragabi The culture hero of the Choco Indians of western Colombia, born from the saliva of the high god Tatzitzete. He created the ancestors of the Choco and established sibs and families to prevent incest. He placed the sun, the moon, the light and stars in the sky and caused the tree of life to be felled. He wandered through the world giving food plants to mankind; and after transforming many men into animals he retired to the sky. But he is expected to return after the destruction of the world by fire. Many stories deal with the continuous mutual challenge and conflict between Caragabi and his powerful rival Tutruica to prove their power. [AM]

carbuncle A red garnet cut *en cabochon* (i.e. convex but not faceted); anciently, any gem of brilliant fire and deep red color, usually a garnet or ruby. The Bible mentions it among the stones of the High Priest's breastplate and in Christian tradition it was symbolic of Christ's sacrifice. According to the Koran it illuminates the fourth heaven. An early tale claims it also lighted Noah's Ark. In early Spanish astrology it represented the sun. Among the Arabs and in India it was believed to protect a soldier in battle, and in Greece it guarded children from drowning. As an amulet it is a potent force against poison, plague, bad dreams, evil thoughts, and incontinence. It stimulates the heart, but care must be exercised lest it arouse anger or passion and cause apoplexy, and while it cures melancholy and sadness, it leads to sleeplessness. Loss of luster is a sign of impending disaster. See RUBY.

Cardea The ancient Roman goddess of the door-hinges, protectress of little children against the attacks of vampire-witches. She obtained the office from Janus in exchange for her personal favors.

careado A longways couple dance of the Asturias region in northwest Spain. During the first part the torso sways from side to side, while the arms are relaxed at the sides; during the second part the arms are raised to play castanets and the feet execute simple cross-steps. The dancers accompany themselves by song. *Carear* means to place face to face. [GPK]

Careless Love One of the earliest of the blues songs, a lonesome tune set to a favorite blues theme, tragic love. Perhaps originated by white singers of the American south, but equally popular among Negroes, it has acquired many stanzas and developed many variants. See BLUES; BUTCHER BOY.

Carmenta or **Carmentis** The ancient Italian goddess of prophecy, singing the future and the past, and of healing; protectress of women in childbirth: said to have been called originally, in Arcadia, Nicostrate, but also named as chief of the Camenæ. By Hermes she became the mother of Evander, and following him to Italy changed the Greek alphabet into that used by the Romans. Her Roman temple stood between Tiber and the Capitoline. The Carmentalia, in her honor, was celebrated on January 11th and 15th, at which time her protection was asked for children born during the year. One of the gates of Rome bore her name.

Carna or **Carnea** The ancient Roman goddess of physical health: sometimes confused, as by Ovid, with Cardea. She presided over the vital internal organs. Her festival on June 1st was instituted by Brutus and was called *fabriaræ calendæ* from the beans and bacon then offered to the goddess. Carna seems to have been an underworld goddess originally.

carnation The perennial, herbaceous, fragrant flower of any of the many cultivated varieties of the pink family (genus *Dianthus*), especially the clove pink or scarlet carnation (*D. caryophyllus*). The carnation has been cultivated for more than 2000 years and is mentioned frequently in folktale and legends. It first appeared on earth when Christ was born, or it sprang from the tears of Mary, the mother of Jesus, shed on her way to Calvary.

The carnation was used as a substitute for the expensive cloves of India to spice wine and ale in Elizabethan times, hence its name Sop-in-wine. The early name Gilliflower (Gyllofer, Gilofre) is a corruption of the Latin Caryophyllum or clove. The flower, which is under the dominion of Jupiter, was said to have medicinal properties, especially effective against pestilential fevers. A well-known remedy for toothache all over Europe and the United States is oil of cloves (*oleum caryophylli*). It is reported that the seeds are used to fill cavities in Bohemia, Croatia, Dalmatia, and Slovakia.

In Korea the *Dianthus sinensis* is used in divination. A cluster of three flowers on a single stem is worn in the hair. If the top flower dries first the last years of one's life will be difficult. If the bottom pink dries, the wearer will have misfortunes in youth. If all dry together the wearer's lot will be sad indeed.

Carnea One of the important festivals of ancient Sparta, observed in many parts of the Peloponnesus, in Cyrene, Magna Græcia, etc.: held in honor of Apollo Carneius, the ram god of flocks and herds and of fertility in general. It was also a military festival. The ceremony may have been an older festival in honor of a supposed Carneus, taken over and identified with Apollo by the Dorians. It was held in the month of Carneus (August), and traditionally was instituted in 676 B.C. No military operations were held during the period, and it is said that the main army of the Spartans would have been at Thermopylæ rather than the small guard

of Leonidas' men had not the festival prevented their movement.

carnelian A transparent red chalcedony, known since early times, and often used for seals because it left a clean impression. In Egypt it was called "blood of Isis" and was placed on the throats of the dead as a buckle or tie. It is also found in Iron Age burial mounds in Japan. In Burma it parallels the Chinese use of jade. Mohammed wore a carnelian ring, and among Moslems it preserves tranquillity in the midst of turmoil and keeps the wearer happy and blessed. Among the Arabs it is a remedy for loose teeth. In Australia it is a potent charm of the medicine man against all disease. It cures tumors and respiratory diseases, strengthens the voice, and stops bleeding. It restrains anger and imparts dignity, but also gives courage in battle. It counteracts the effects of sorcery and drives away evil spirits and dreams. It is even proof against injury from falling houses and walls. It was probably one of the stones in the High Priest's breastplate mentioned in *Exodus* and was formerly much used as a birthstone for August. It was sometimes confused with the ruby.

Carnival A boisterous communal celebration dating back to the Middle Ages and still observed in most of Europe and in the Americas. It features masquerades, floats, torch processions, dances, fireworks, noise-making, and tomfoolery which often reaches a point of nuisance and licentiousness. The festival season formerly began at the winter solstice or on Twelfth Night, that is (in far northern countries) at the first signs of returning spring; it now comes to a climax on the last three days before Ash Wednesday.

The etymology is uncertain. Carnival is explained as being derived from *carne vale,* or flesh farewell (Latin *caro, carnis,* flesh, and *vale,* farewell), a name befitting the last days of fleshly unrestraint before Lent; or as derived from *carrus navalis,* cart of the sea, a boat-shaped vehicle on wheels used in the processions of Dionysus (later in other festival processions) and from which all kinds of satirical songs were sung.

Carnival may have had its source in the Roman *Bacchanalia, Lupercalia,* or *Saturnalia,* or in the ship-cart pageant for the Germanic Nerthus or Hertha, earth mother and goddess of fertility. Often the cart carried a plow instead of an image of the Earth Mother. In the 14th and 15th centuries the Carnival attained its full glory in Europe, especially in the Nürnberg *Fastnacht* and *Fastnachtsspiele,* and in Italy, in Nice, Venice, Naples, Florence. Obscene songs, *cante carnascialeschi,* were developed into an art by Lorenzo de Medici.

Carnival is identified with the primitive ceremonies for the expulsion of death, winter, and demons harmful to the coming crops. That was the purpose of the noise-making, the *Lärmumzüge,* noisy processionals with songs, bull-roarers, drums, bells, fools' whips. The fool's whip or slapstick is the direct descendant of the *Lebensrute* (life-rod), the rod of life, which transfers fertility. Vegetation magic also lies behind the ducking, sprinkling, fire-throwing, charcoal-blackening, leaping, in the obscenities above all, and in all the special disguises and enactments. Elaborate medieval ceremonies married the shaggy wild men to the wild women, who were accompanied by a train of animal masks, the *maisnée herlekin* (originally troop of the dead), the *Holzleut,* wood folk, dressed in foliage or moss, and the old woman of the corn with baby and basket. The *Metzgersprung* of Nürnberg was a leaping serpentine dance of the butchers' guild, perhaps dating back to animal sacrifice. Their associated *Schembartläufer* (runners with bearded masks), with lances and male and female masks, also ran in a serpentine and threw fire and ashes. *Scheme* is a Middle High German word for mask or apparition.

The Schemen still run in Innsbruck during *Fasching* or Carnival: a mad train of *Scheller*, female *Roller Spritzer* (sprinklers), *Kübele Maien* (water squirters), *Hexen* (witches), and other demons. In Switzerland the *Rautschegetten* cavort in black sheepskins. These demons have their counterpart in the *kalogheroi* of the Thracian Carnival, which obviously dates back to the *orgia* of Dionysus Dithyrambus. The elegant faction had its counterpart in the Munich *Schäfflertanz*, a traditional longways dance with hoops, discontinued in 1928. The battle of the forces of summer and winter, preserved in its original meaning in the Isle of Man, became confused with Christian symbols in the battles of the Moors and Christians elsewhere. Matrimonial and resurrection dramas were enacted by the Morris groups, the English Mummers, the Basque *masacaradas*, the Majorcan *cociés*. Later on these performances were frequently advanced from their original pre-Lenten date to May Day, Corpus Christi, or other festivals.

However, in Spain and its colonies, particularly in Mexico, these battle mimes remain a gala feature of Carnival. In Spain was added the interment of the King of Evil (*el entierro del Rey del Mal Humor*), also quadrilles or solos performed by *diablos* and *muertes* (impersonations of death). Catalonians have a Maypole dance for both sexes.

In Mexico the Carnival flourishes with a dazzling array of dances: not only moros, diablos, and muertes taken over from Spanish Carnival, and dances transferred from Corpus Christi and Saint's Days, such as the *arcos* and *pastoras*, danced with flowered arches, but above all innumerable native dance survivals and native post-Columbian inventions. In the pueblos of central Mexico, Carnival is a religious fiesta, an objective for votive pilgrimages. The European importations, so interwoven with native qualities, suggest amalgamation with existing rites. Carnival corresponds to the second month of the Aztec calendar, Tlacaxipehualiztli, dedicated to the worship of Xipe Totec, god of agriculture. The costumes, whether embroidered silk or shabby cottons, the masks, whether of wood or buckram, are always distinctive and original. The *teponaztle* (Aztec drum) accompanies a European type of flute and tabor. Native and European steps, Christian and pagan verbal allusions all blend. Dialog usually accompanies the *moros y cristianos* plays and their related *Santiagos* of Mexico, Guerrero, Puebla, and Vera Cruz Sierras, and the similar *tastoanes* of Jalisco. Medieval morality plays live on in a new form in *Las Tres Potencias* of Guerrero. An original drama is enacted for five days in Huexotzingo, Puebla, showing how the bandit, Augustin Lorenzo, was captured by magnificent bands of soldiers —*zapadores*, Apaches, *zacapoaxtles*, Zouavos, and *serranos* (clowns). The Tlaxcalans and distant Huichols each enact a bull fight; the natives of Zaachila, Oaxaca, put on a burlesque battle between the priests and devils.

The Tlaxcalans have invented *los catrines, los paraguas* (a quadrille of French type), *los casquetes* (helmets) —all dances in medieval garb—and *los cihuames* (from Aztec *cihuatl*, woman), the only woman's dance, which uses a kerchief for mask.

Native survivals are the *huehuenches* of Mexico, *chinelos* of Morelos, *tecuanes* of Guerrero. The great concheros dances, though not confined to Carnival, are most numerous at that time.

Carnival has not found its way into the more primitive northern tribes. But elsewhere, on the two coasts to the south, the big cities celebrate Carnival sometimes for weeks in advance, with fantastic masked parades and with *carros alegóricos* (fancy balls with a queen or *reina*), notably in Oaxaca City, Vera Cruz, Guadalajara, Tepic, Mazatlán, Cuilacán. Here the ceremonials are replaced by *zapateados* and *jarabes*, ballroom dances, and the flute and tabor by *mariachi, marimba*, and brass band.

Yucatan's capital, Mérida, celebrates Carnival with a certain ceremonialism, in *cintas, paulitos, negritos*, and native *xtoles*. Trinidad combines ostentation with *moros* dances, and native calypso singing. A semiceremonial longways dance is called *carnevalesca* in Argentina.

The famous Carnival of Rio de Janeiro, the Mardi Gras of New Orleans, and the Cuban *comparsas* are modernized, in subject matter for the floats, in the dances (*frevo, maxixe, conga*, etc.), and are more rowdy and meaningless than the corresponding survivals in large cities of Europe. See FASTNACHT; RODS OF LIFE. [GPK]

carol A traditional song type in English, originally unrestricted in subject matter, composed in a fixed stanza form throughout, and having a burden, but for centuries associated with the Christian celebration of Christmas and including almost any kind of Christmas song. To a lesser extent it also includes songs to the Virgin and various saints, stories of the Epiphany, the Annunciation, the baptism of Christ, the Eucharist, the Passion, and the round of the seasons. In the popular sense, the carol corresponds approximately to the French *noël*, the German *Weihnachtslied*, the Greek *kálanta*, the Rumanian *colinde*, certain examples of the Spanish *villancico*, etc., though the international influences are obscure. Like *ballad*, the word has its source in dancing (Old French *carole*, Latin *choraula*, Greek *choraules, choros*) and in its earliest forms the song probably accompanied a round dance, the burden being sung by the dancers as they circled, the stanzas by a leader.

Developing contemporaneously with the dramatic spectacles of the mystery plays, the religious carol marks the passage of devotional observance from the formality of the Church and the Latin tongue into the marketplace and the vernacular. This change, however, was not, in all likelihood "by popular request," nor because of any desire on the part of the masses to usurp the functions of the churchmen, but the result of a deliberate popularization by the clergy to combat the "licentiousness" of the pre-Christian song-and-dance festivals that had survived to upset the decorum of their parishes. The mendicant friars all over Europe, and particularly the Franciscans, campaigned with religious songs in the vernacular and humanized the stories of the saints, turning to their own uses the tunes that pleased the public ear. Their success is demonstrated by the way in which carol-singing took hold and went its way among the people.

Carols, in the popular acceptance of the term, are cast in many forms: ballads (*The Cherry Tree Carol*, for example); lullabies of the women of Bethlehem (*The Coventry Carol*); macaronics, with lines of Latin interwoven (*In Dulce Jubilo*); cumulative and numeral songs (*The Twelve Days of Christmas* and *The Joys of Mary*); wassails, or toasts, and feasting songs (*The Boar's Head*); question-and-answer songs (*The Seven Virgins*); celebrations of nature, etc.

One type common all over Europe is the call to the neighbors to wake and visit the lovely baby born in a cow's stall. In these carols the Holy Family have been made in the image of the people who sang—Mary crying out in labor, the Infant shivering on his pallet of straw, old Joseph, tired, anxious, bewildered, and a bit grumpy. Overflowing with solicitude and neighborly good-will, each visitor, according to his trade and his lot, brings the gift most suitable to the situation of the three destitute strangers stranded in a barn. Shepherds in a Besançon bagpipe carol offer sheep-milk and water heated in a pan and a lambskin to wrap the baby. A carol from Holland, the dairy land, provides new milk, butter, and junket. A Czech contribution is a fur coat for the baby to cut the chill of a December night. Others list a lamb to play with, a ball, a shepherd's pipe, cheese, eggs, stumps of vines to warm and soften the makeshift cradle. The spirit of all such carols is caught in an American Negro lament, *Po' Little Jesus:* "Didn't have no cradle./ Wasn't that a pity and a shame!/"

Many of the songs detail the hardships of the pilgrimage to visit the Child, and, in doing so, reveal the people who sang almost as clearly as their selection of gifts. *The Gouty Carol*, from Provence, for instance, tells of an old man with the gout who hobbles painfully in the rear of the train of visitors. A Burgundian song mentions among the pilgrims, taxers and lenders and poor men in the rich men's grip.

As compared with the number of these poems of peasant interest, there are few carols bearing the marks of royal and courtly tradition, though here and there the images and symbols of chivalry appear. Mary is likened to a rose, a queen, a bird. She and Joseph are titled "Sir Joseph and his fair lady." The absence of the trappings appropriate for a newborn king and god is carefully explained.

The ballad group of carols draws its narrative material from a number of sources outside of Holy Writ, notably the Apocrypha. The *Gospel of Pseudo-Matthew* furnishes the story of the crop sown and reaped the same day in *King Pharaoh*, a carol widely spread by Gipsies, in which also appears the legend of the cooked cock that crowed. This cock crows also in *The Carol of St. Stephen* and *The Carnal and the Crane*. *The Cherry Tree Carol*, in which the tree bows to allow Mary to pick cherries, is also drawn from *Pseudo-Matthew;* though it also bears a near relationship to a story in the *Kalevala*.

The wassails are of pre-Christian origin, taking their name from the words of the toast (Old English *waes hael*, be whole) and preserving a secular, if not pagan character. One of them carries a line which may refer to the Danish invasions of England. Another is said to have been sung not only during the Christmas and New Year's festivities, but also in the custom of "wassailing the apple trees" on Epiphany Eve to assure good crops. This procedure was ended with a lusty blast on a cow's horn. Traditionally the wassail songs were sung by merrymakers carrying a huge bowl bedecked with wreaths and ribbons, or by waits begging for a handout from the holiday feasts at the great houses. Generally they closed with good luck wishes for the house, the master thereof, and all his herds and crops in the coming year.

The Greek *kálanta* (compare Latin *kalenda*, and Rumanian *colinde*) have been sung into the 20th century in much the same way on New Year's Eve. Caroling children carried lanterns and a paper ship in a house-to-house procession singing good wishes for the New Year and begging for money. The ship custom seems to be connected with a ship full of fruitful objects traditionally carried through Athens and Smyrna on the feast of Dionysus.

The subject of a large group of Greek carols is St. Basil, especially in relation to four themes: 1) the staff that budded, an Apocryphal story of the saint's boyhood; 2) love songs interwoven with the above; 3) the golden tree, the legend that where Christ trod a tree of gold grows (an idea ancient in Greek literature), and 4) the miraculous crop, in which the saint's oxen were blessed by Christ and his land brought forth an amazing abundance. The Greek equivalent of waits cry the blessings of St. Basil on the wheat, barley, and children of the house, saying, "May your kids and lambs be female, your children, boys."

The nature carols in English, though many took on various Christian aspects, also preserved pagan greetings to the change of seasons and pre-Christian symbolism. The numerous "holly and ivy" carols, possibly first sung to dancing by men and women, embody ancient fertility rites, holly representing the male and dominant principle, ivy, the female. Yet some versions of these songs mingle the Christian and pagan elements in such carefree style as this: "The holly bears a prickle/ As sharp as any thorn/ and Mary bore sweet Jesus Christ/ On Christmas Day in the morn."

The characteristic burden of strict English carol form stands at the head of the song and is repeated after each stanza, though it is usually completely separate from the sense of the song as conveyed by the stanzas, a fact which explains why many carols have lost their original burdens and why some burdens serve for several carols. The most common type of burden is a couplet, though quatrains and even longer forms occur. The link with the stanza is generally a rime with the tail rime of the stanza. Most of the burdens are older than the verses they accompany, having been adopted without change from the old folk-dance carols and applied to the religious songs, even when the clergy composed the latter. Some are Latin maxims and tags from various church services. The lullabies have a string of soothing sounds, such as "lully, lullay," as burdens. Some burdens exhort the singers, as formerly the round dancers, to sing, rejoice, be merry. Some (though few in English) imitate instrumental sounds, as "tyrly, tyrlow." Others are moralizing proverbs.

The great period of folk-carol composition in England was the 15th century, coinciding to a great extent with ballad-making, but carol-singing flourished until the Puritan Parliament abolished Christmas observance in 1647 and forbade any form of celebration. English carols went underground to be preserved only in folk memory, in manuscripts such as the *Commonplace Book* of Richard Hill (a grocer's apprentice whose jottings of records, recipes, poems, and romances from the early 16th century proved a gold mine to later researchers) and by the fly-by-night printers of broadsides. When new carols were composed after this hiatus, the beef and pudding and groaning board provided a good deal of the inspiration. Many of the early carols were not recovered until 19th century research, coupled with the uninterrupted popularity of similar songs on the continent of Europe, restored them to sufficient respectability for church use. Some of the early ones, infrequently recovered in England, have been found in the woods of New England and the mountains of the American South. See individual titles and song types.

THERESA C. BRAKELEY

carole or **carola** (from *carolla*, crown or wreath) A round dance and song for couples, which spread in the 12th century from Spain to Norway. It was a kind of processional march, turning right to left and beating one foot against the other. Originally it was a dance-song particular to May; later it was a feature of fairs, saints' day festivals, midnight vigils, Christmas. The symbol of fertility was retained in the object carried by the choral leader: a May branch, a bunch of flowers, a torch. The term is now associated specifically with choral Christmas songs. Compare CAROL. [GPK]

carrizo A social couple dance of the Maipure Indians of Venezuela. Three musicians play six-reed pan-pipes of native timbre, but the quasi-waltz step suggests mestizo origin. The couples, arms entwined, circle the musicians two by two. They follow the changes in the music, plaintive or vivacious. In the end the circle breaks up into a confusion equal to that of ballroom dances. [GPK]

carrot A long reddish-yellow edible root of the plant *Daucus carota*. In New Hampshire it is said that if a carrot is allowed to go to seed, someone in the family will die before the year is over. Formerly it was a common saying in England and the United States that carrots would relieve asthma if eaten in large enough quantities. This fact and the belief that carrots aid eyesight has now been substantiated by the discovery that certain forms of carotene, the pigment principle of carrots (and certain other plant and animal substances) promote the formation in the body of vitamin A, beneficial in cases of night blindness and lowered resistance to infections.

carrying water in a sieve A folktale motif (H1023.2), used as task, punishment, or means of escape: found in folktales of ancient Greece, modern Africa, Polynesia, Indonesia, Europe, and North America. The classical example is the story of the Danaides' punishment. They were doomed in the afterworld to attempt to fill a leaky vessel with broken jars. Similar is the incident in *Master Pfreim* (Grimm #178; Type 801) in which the complaining cobbler sees the angels drawing water into a leaky bucket and causing the rain. *The Grave-Mound* (Grimm #195) tells how the Devil fails to fill the sole-less shoe of the soldier, a task very similar to that of filling the sieve. Not everyone entrusted with the task fails, however; in ballad this is one of the things a chaste woman does; a pious child can accomplish the same thing. Sometimes the intended victim thinks a bit: the vessel is repaired or the holes in the sieve are stopped—with moss, with gum, with clay.

Monkey, in an Angola tale, refuses to try to dip water with a fish-trap and thus gets the better of Leopard. He is therefore able to avenge the death of Antelope, who *was* tricked by Leopard into trying. In an Indonesian tale from Halmahera, the husband of Sunrise sends his sister-in-law to bring water in a punctured bamboo. While she is delayed at the stream, he and Sunrise escape from her unwanted company. The delaying action occurs also in a Tahitian story; Tuture runs away from his cannibal mother while she tries to fill the pierced gourds. Compare BEAD-SPITTER AND THROWN-AWAY.

cartomancy Divination, or fortune-telling, by means of cards, especially playing cards: popularly one of the methods preferred by the Gipsy fortune-tellers, and the basis of the belief that the Gipsies imported playing cards into Europe. The suits and individual cards have traditional meanings and values, e.g. the ace of spades means death. Special cards and packs of cards are occasionally used.

Casey Jones John Luther Jones, American railroad hero, engineer of the Illinois Central's famous "Cannonball," noted for his skill, daring, and resourcefulness. He died in a train wreck in 1900, and was found with one hand still on the whistle and the other on the airbrake lever. Wallace Saunders, his Negro enginewiper and close friend, created the original of the famous American ballad, *Casey Jones*. Later, the words and music, given a chorus and framed in the style of a vaudeville song by Siebert and Newton, attained wide popularity.

Cassandra (1) or **Alexandra** The most beautiful of the daughters of Priam and Hecuba; the prophetess of the Trojan legend whose foresight was doomed to go unheeded. She and her brother Helenus slept as children in the temple of Apollo; they were found there in the morning, wound about with snakes which by licking their ears gave them the gift of prophecy and of understanding the languages of the animals. Cassandra again slept in the temple when she was a young woman. Apollo tried to ravish her and was repulsed. Unable to revoke his gift of prophecy, he caused her sayings to go unbelieved. According to another story she reneged on the bargain she had made with him and he thus punished her. It was Cassandra who recognized in the shepherd Paris the princely son of Priam; she recognized the wooden horse for what it was: again and again she predicted what later happened, yet no one believed her. She was in fact considered demented by the Trojans, Priam even confining her for a time. At the fall of Troy, she was torn from the sanctuary of Athena by Ajax the Lesser, perhaps even raped on the spot, and in the division of prisoners fell to the lot of Agamemnon. She was killed with him by Clytemnestra, and their children, Teledamus and Pelops, were slain by Ægisthus. Her tomb was either at Amyclæ or at Mycenæ. Compare ANIMAL LANGUAGES.

(2) The daughter of Iobates. See BELLEROPHON.

cassava or **manioc** An edible tuber from which bread is made by the Indians of South America. See MANIOC.

cassia A bark similar to cinnamon, and thought by the ancients to be an inferior grade. Chinese religious legend describes a cassia tree as the world-tree or tree of life, growing to incredible height in Paradise, far up the Hoang-Ho river. Whoever ate of its fruit lived forever. Compare MOON TREE; PEACH.

Cassiopeia, Cassiope, or **Cassiepeia** (1) In Greek mythology, the wife of Cepheus, mother of Andromeda. She praised her own or her daugher's beauty as being greater than that of the Nereids and brought upon her country the sea monster slain by Perseus. A constellation in the northern sky is named for her. See ANDROMEDA.

(2) A W-shaped, five-star constellation lying in the Milky Way exactly opposite the Great Bear, the north star lying equidistant between them. It is often called Cassiopeia's Chair and sometimes the Celestial W. Greek astronomers of the 5th century B.C. spoke of this constellation as She of the Throne. The ancient Egyptian *Book of the Dead* calls it the Leg. To the Arabians it looked like a Hand, each of the five stars representing a bright finger-tip stained with henna. They also called it Al Dhāt al Kursiyy, the Lady in the Chair. Latin writers knew it both as Cassiopeia and as Mulier Sedis, Woman of the Chair. To the early Celts it was Llys Dôn, Don's House. Religious astronomers of the 17th century identified the constellation with Mary Magdalene or with Bathsheba on her throne.

castanets Paired hollow clappers of wood clicked together rhythmically between thumb and forefinger of dancers. Known in ancient Egypt, but probably Greek imports there, in Rome, and in Greece, where they were used by Dionysian dancers, castanets may be a Phœnician contribution, for they are still used in the sections colonized by Phœnicians in Spain, southern Italy, and the Balearic Islands. Castanets have been used to provide rhythm for many dances of strong excitation—the tarantella dance mania of the 18th century—the moresque choral dance, the sarabande, and the fandango. The term is derived from Latin *castanea*, chestnut, from the appearance of the instrument.

cast down A country dance term: the dancer or dancers turn outward and move backward along the set. [GPK]

cast off A country dance term: the dancer or dancers turn outward and dance outside the set. [GPK]

Castores Roman name of the Dioscuri: from Castor, who seems to have been the first of the twins to be worshipped by the Romans.

Castrén, Matthias Alexander (1813–1852?) Swedish-Finnish ethnologist and philologist, and collector of Finnish ballads and legends. He was born in Finland, but all his books are in Swedish. In 1838 he and a fellow student, Dr. Ehrström, traveled in Lapland; then he alone traveled in Karelia; in 1841, with Elias Lönnrot he made a three-year journey to Obdorsk, Siberia; later he explored the entire Government of Siberia adding to the store of folklore knowledge. In 1850 he was appointed to the new chair of Finnish Language and Literature at the University of Helsingfors and the following year became the chancellor of the University. The first outline of a Finno-Ugrian mythology was made by Castrén in a lecture in Finnish and published in Swedish and German (the latter called *Nordische Reisen und Forschungen,* 1853). Castrén is considered to be the founder of Ural-Altaic philology. Among his books are *Reseminnen från åren 1845–44* (sic), *Föreläsningar i Finsk mythologi, Reseberättelser och bref åren 1845–49, Ethnologiska föreläsningar över altaiska folken,* and *Smärre avhandlingar och akademiska dissertationer.* He translated the great Finnish epic *Kalevala* into Swedish.

cast up A country dance term: the dancer or dancers turn outward and move forward along the set. [GPK]

Caswallan In the *Mabinogion,* a son of Beli. He conquered Britain while Bran was in Ireland righting the wrongs of Branwen. Caswallan threw around Caradawc, Bran's son, the Veil of Illusion, so that all Caradawc could see was the sword slaying his people right and left, but never the wielder of the sword. In the *Triads* Caswallan is mentioned as a war king, and historically he is uncertainly associated with a certain chief named Cassivellaunus, who opposed Cæsar. J. A. MacCulloch's study of their legends reports them confusedly mingled.

catching a man's breath A folktale motif (H1023.13; Type 1176) occurring in a huge group of stories centering around the impossible or absurd task: especially popular in Baltic countries. Catching a man's breath and tying a knot in it belongs specifically in the category of tasks contrary to the nature of the objects involved (H1023). These often occur in that widespread group of tales about the man who sells his soul to the devil but eventually saves himself by some ruse, such as imposing the impossible task on the devil. Bringing berries in winter, carrying water in a sieve, mending the jug, skinning the stone, etc., all belong to the group.

catch tale A story told in such a manner as to trick the listener into asking a certain question or making a certain remark to which the teller gives such a ridiculous or obvious answer as to make the listener the butt of the joke. The "Just Like Me'" formula is a fair example. The story-teller enjoins the listener to say "Just like me" after every statement of his story. The story ends with the words, "And I saw a little monkey," to which the listener either inadvertently says, "Just like me" or is quick-witted enough to reply, "Just like you." Most catch tales and catch rimes are primarily children's joke pastimes. But no complete study of the type and no extensive collection has yet been made. See ADAM AND EVE AND PINCH ME; TONGUE TWISTERS.

caterpillar The larva of the butterfly or moth: of widespread occurrence. The caterpillar's origin, in Rumania, is thought to be from the Devil's tears; the Bantu believe the souls of the dead take this form. In Switzerland and elsewhere, it is said tree spirits are responsible for the caterpillar and that they send them to creep into man's brain to make him mad or ill-humored, or that they send them to the fields to annoy the folk. The appearance of these wormlike creatures may well have suggested the superstition that they were made by witches with the Devil's help. One name applied to them in Germany and thereabouts is *Teufelskatze* (Devil's cat). In Pennsylvania, a black caterpillar indicates a hard winter; in France, the temperature is judged by its ways. Folk medicine attributes some virtue to the caterpillar: in antiquity, the cabbage caterpillar was used with oil for rubbing after the bite of a venomous serpent; in England, to carry a caterpillar about was an aid in fevers; it was also prescribed for toothache. [GPS]

Cathbad In Old Irish legend, the chief druid of Ulster in the reign of Conchobar: in some legends the father of Conchobar. Cathbad was one of the tutors of Cuchulain. It was Cathbad who prophesied at the birth of Deirdre that because of her "more blood will be shed than ever was shed in Ireland since time began. Great heroes will lose their lives because of her."

St. Catherine's Day November 25, anniversary of the martyrdom of St. Catherine of Alexandria about 307. From medieval times to the 18th century it was observed in England and Europe as a holiday by wheelwrights, haberdashers, and lace-makers, of whom she is the patron saint: still observed by spinsters, milliners, and dressmakers especially in France.

One of the ancient trade guilds of London, the Gild of Haberdashers, was referred to as the guild of St. Catherine the Virgin. The members of this guild celebrated the day by closing up shop and marching in processions.

Girls were wont to fast on St. Catherine's Day, hoping thus to obtain a good husband. On this day virgins went to church to offer up a special prayer:

A husband, St. Catherine;
A handsome husband, St. Catherine;
A rich one, St. Catherine;
A nice one, St. Catherine;
And soon, St. Catherine.

Merrymaking was engaged in on that day, particularly in the textile districts. This included processions and begging for apples and beer, chiefly by roistering children. Such merrymaking was called Catherning or Caterning, and the bowl used for begging was called a Catherine bowl. Children employed at spinning in the workhouses of Northampton and elsewhere paraded in the streets, dressed in white, headed by one of the tallest girls designated by them as Queen and wearing a crown.

In Paris and throughout France, St. Catherine's Day is still observed by unmarried women under 25 years old, especially by those employed in the millinery and dressmaking establishments, which close for the day. The merrymaking takes the form of gay processions in the streets, the girls walking arm in arm, wearing "Catherine bonnets"—fantastic confections of paper and ribbon which they themselves have made. Before the merrymaking, they have attended church, and have renewed the crown on the head of the saint's statue there.

"Coiffer Sainte Catherine," to wear St. Catherine's bonnet, is a common saying in France, and signifies, for a woman, to live and die in celibacy. The saying is that at 25 an unmarried girl puts the first pin into her St. Catherine bonnet; at 30 she puts in the second; at 35 the bonnet is finished.

Miraculous wells exist in the environs of Edinburgh and Aberdeen, called St. Katherine's wells, to which resort people afflicted with tumors, skin trouble, and stone in the bladder, which illnesses the waters are reputed to cure.

The Catalans have a weather rime for Catherine's Day:

Santa Catarina	Saint Catherine's Day
o molt freda	expect much cold
o molt humida	or much dampness

The olive growers have another rime:

Avans det Santa Catarina	Before St. Catherine's,
no cullos la uliva	don't harvest olives

An old English euphemism refers to the menopause as "turning St. Catherine's corner."

los Catrines A burlesque on the bourgeois (catrines) during Carnival festivities at Santa Ana Chiautempan, Tlaxcala, Mexico. Some of the men dress as women, covering their faces with a kerchief. Others wear double-breasted or swallowtail suits, neckties, and grotesque pink masks. They carry umbrellas throughout their cavortings. [GPK]

cats Never kick a cat, or you'll get rheumatism. Never drown one or the Devil will get you. Cats have nine lives, but if you take even one, the cat will haunt you, send bad luck, or work some other vengeance. These three adjurations, gleaned by N. N. Puckett (*Folk Beliefs of the Southern Negro*, Chapel Hill, 1926) represent in Negro belief the very widespread European and African belief that it is bad luck to kill or mistreat a cat. The concept is rooted perhaps in those ancient religions in which the cat was a sacred animal: retribution always befalls anyone who harms the sacred animal. Belief in the benefits to be acquired from eating the sacred animal survive in such old-wives' remedies (Alabama Negro) as black-cat broth to cure consumption.

Seeing a black cat is usually a bad omen in Germany, the British Isles, and the United States. It is especially bad for a black cat to cross one's path. But it is lucky to own one. Southern U. S. Negroes believe that black cats are powerful hoodoo; they cause bad luck, misery, disease, and death. A black cat is a witch; it is a witch's familiar; it is the Devil; it is a "haunt" from the dead: all beliefs of European origin enhanced with Negro intensity and flavor. Cats can see ghosts. Cats' eyes are used in certain southern Negro voodoo charms; so is cat hair, especially the whiskers.

When the cat washes her face, it is a sign of rain, or a sign of good weather, or that company is coming; especially if she washes her face in the parlor, company is coming. That cats always wash themselves facing the wind is keen folk observation, not necessarily a wind-direction omen. In Maine they say if a cat looks out the window it is looking for rain. A common New England saying is that you can tell the time of day from the size of a cat's pupils. In the Maritimes a cat's pupils are nearly closed at low tide, wide open at high tide.

Welsh sailors say if the ship's cat mews constantly it portends a difficult voyage. If the ship's cat is playful, sailors expect a gale of wind astern. Any uncooperative person can raise adverse winds by confining the ship's cat under a pot. In rural England they say that a kitten born in May will never make a mouser; instead it is apt to bring home glow-worms! In Sussex they say a May kitten is apt to grow up melancholy. Some people say it is good luck to sleep with a cat; others that cats suck the breath of sleepers. In some parts of Europe it is thought that cats prey on corpses. If a cat jumps over a corpse, that corpse will become a vampire, and the funeral is stopped until the cat is caught and killed. In some parts of France where the cat was believed to be the Devil, cats were burned in Shrove Tuesday and Easter bonfires.

Beliefs in the cat as fertility charm are indicated in such practices as those of Transylvania farmers: about a month after a wedding a cat is brought into the house in a cradle and rocked in the presence of the newlyweds. In Bohemia a cat is sometimes buried in a field of grain: a practice related to the belief in the cat as field spirit. See BULLKATER.

In Indonesia among the various Malay peoples it is believed that bathing a cat will bring rain. See AI APAEC; BAST; BELLING THE CAT; CCOA; KING OF THE CATS; PUSS IN BOOTS.

cat's cradle The European and American form of string figures: a two-player, four-handed game, played with a loop of string, and consisting of a very few figures which evolve one from the other: perhaps a slim remainder of a once greater number. Cat's cradle has none of the ritual connotations of string figures elsewhere, as for example among the Eskimos, and compared with the elaborate and varied figures reported from some peoples, e.g. the Australian aborigines, it is simply a childish diversion with a meager repertoire of figures. See STRING FIGURES.

catseye A gemstone, usually chrysoberyl or quartz, which shows a line of light across the dome when cut *en cabochon*. On the theory that like affects like, it was universally used for diseases of the eyes and to ward off the evil eye. The Assyrians carried this theory a step further and claimed that it made the wearer invisible to his enemies. In Ceylon it is a charm against witchcraft and considered to be the abode of genii. It is reputed to relieve croup and asthma, to cure chronic diseases and to put color into the cheeks. It gives pleasure to the mind, relieves the soul of melancholy, and protects its wearer from financial ruin. It is held in high esteem in China and India.

Catskin Designation of a cycle of European folktales partaking of many Cinderella and Cap o' Rushes elements. The story usually begins with the flight of the heroine from marriage with an incestuous father. She wanders in disguise in a mantle made of many kinds of fur (*Allerleirauh*, Grimm #65), or a cloak of mouse-skin or louse-skin (Russian, Slavonic), of catskin (Irish, English), pigskin (Italian, Sicilian, Finnish), ass-skin (French, Spanish, Basque), wooden dress or sheath, (Greek, Italian, Portuguese, Swedish), crow-skin (Swedish), old-woman skin, boy's clothes, rags and tatters (various), bear transformation (in the *Pentamerone*) etc., etc. She takes a menial position in the ménage of a king: goose-girl, turkey-girl, kitchen or scullery maid, swineherd, shepherdess, stable-boy. She is always discovered by the young prince, sometimes at a ball which she attends clad in her own original (or magic) garments. But she escapes unrecognized, only to reveal herself, when he sickens with love for the unknown one, by a recognition token in his food (her ring, or presents which he has given her at the ball). The story ends with a happy marriage, and sometimes with the punishment of the father.

This story is known everywhere in Europe and in Asia Minor. It turns up in Dixon's *Ancient Poems, Ballads, and Songs of the Peasantry of England* (1857) entitled "The Wandering Young Gentlewoman, or Catskin."

cat's only trick Climbing a tree: a folktale motif (J1662; Type 105). Æsop's fable about the cat and the fox (Jacobs #38) tells the story. The Fox remarked to the Cat that no matter what the danger, he had 100 tricks by which to save himself. The Cat said she had only one; if that should fail she would be lost. Just then a pack of hounds burst upon them. The Cat dashed up a tree. The Fox tried one after another of his tricks but was caught by the hounds at last.

This story is well known all over Europe from Greece and Sicily to Lapland. There are Arabian variants. There is an analogous Angola folktale about Partridge and Turtle who were discussing how to escape when fire should come across the land. Partridge said Turtle would be burnt because he could not fly away. When the fire was coming Turtle crawled into a big anthill. Partridge ran and began to fly; but the fire was faster and Partridge was burnt. When the fire passed on Turtle crawled out of the anthill. "Partridge is burnt," said Turtle.

cattle The veneration of cattle belongs to a pastoral stage of society. In ancient times they were revered in Egypt as well as in India and this attitude toward cattle is characteristic of the modern Hindu and most of the pastoral tribes of Africa. Wherever people depended upon cattle to furnish them sustenance, the animals were carefully guarded to promote their health and fertility. In sickness they were well tended, and great grief was expressed at the death or theft of one. Not only was the herd as a group venerated, but individual cattle were treated in some cases like divinities. In early times, special attention was bestowed on the leader of the herd.

In comparatively modern times—in Germany, Spain, central and eastern Europe, Greece, Scotland, and elsewhere—special customs were carried out to make the cattle fruitful: they were frequently driven through fire, sometimes beaten for health and good luck as well as to promote fertility and the multiplication of the herd.

Various means have been used to protect cattle from disease (sprigs of mullein), from wolves, witches, evil spirits, and the like (charms, such as boughs of mountain ash hung in the cow-house or at the stable door). Zulus use charms to recover strayed cattle.

Portions of the body of cattle were early used in folk medicine, a practice not yet outmoded. Cattle figure in sagas, folktales, and sayings of Rome, Finland, Russia, Greece, and other countries. One of the most interesting beliefs about cattle is that they acquire the gift of speech on Christmas Eve. Cattle "calls" are of interest. None appear to be recorded from early pastoral society, but modern ones may be mentioned, viz.: "Sukey, Sukey!" "Co-boss, Co-boss!" (common in the United States) and "Co-o-o-p!" (Come up!) in dialectical English. There are many others. [GPS]

Cattle Raid of Cooley The War for the Brown Bull of Cuailgne: Táin Bó Cuailgne.

cat washes face before eating A European folktale motif (K562; Type 122B), existing usually as a single anecdote. A captured rat persuades the cat to wash her face before eating. While she is busily washing it, the rat escapes. This anecdote, especially familiar in the Baltic regions is known to have five variants in African Negro folktale. It belongs to a vast group of stories in which escape by subterfuge is the main motif (K500–699); and explains why today the cat eats first and washes afterwards. The sheep who persuades the wolf to sing, thus summoning the dogs is a type parallel (Type 122C).

caul A covering or membrane; specifically, the membrane sometimes enveloping the head and face of a newly born child, or, occasionally, the fatty tissues around the liver.

In Biblical usage, the word means most often, in connection with sacrificial regulations, "the caul that is above the liver" (*Ex.* xxix, 13), i.e. the diaphragm. Compare *Lev.* iii, iv, vii, viii, ix.

Generally, in folklore, the caul or "veil" is part of the amnion which, for any of several reasons, remains attached to the child when it is born. This is distinctly an omen of good luck, and has been so considered since at least the time of the Romans. The caul, preserved as a talisman, is a protective against drowning. The French proverbial expression "être né coiffé" is used to characterize those having persistent good fortune. The possessor of a caul obtains from it several magical and medicinal virtues. He can see ghosts and talk to them; even if deaf, he can hear the spirits talk. The caul itself is an amulet partaking of the ideas of the genius and life token. Among the Negroes of Louisiana, it is believed that the owner dies if the caul is torn. As a corollary, a limp caul indicates that the owner is ill, while a firm, crisp caul means that he is in good health. Another American Negro belief, adopted from the English, is that the person born with a caul can tell fortunes. The caul itself is a magic instrument quite apart from its connection with the original possessor. It is widely believed to be a protection against demons, particularly (in Jewish tradition) against storm demons. Hence, the caul is among sailors a valuable protection against drowning. Cauls could be and were bought and sold for high prices. "I was born with a caul, which was advertised for sale, in the newspapers, at the low price," says David Copperfield, ch. i, "of fifteen guineas." Compare AMNIOMANCY.

cave painting Painting on the walls of caves: a term used primarily in reference to the prehistoric mural art found in the caves of southern France (Dordogne), and northern and western Spain (in the Pyrenees), although paintings are found in caves and rock shelters in other parts of the world, notably Australia and North Africa. Rock pictures, both painted and engraved, have a world-wide distribution.

Probably the most exciting moment in art history occurred in 1879 when a lawyer, Marcelino de Sautuola, exploring a little-known cave near Santander, Spain, came upon the first prehistoric paintings known to modern man: a magnificent panorama of animals of 20,000 years ago, some long extinct. Other explorations and discoveries followed, but the Altamira cave remained the outstanding example, until two schoolboys hunting rabbits stumbled upon the French cave of Lascaux near Montignac in 1940.

This art began in Upper Paleolithic times and extended presumably from 20,000 to 10,000 B.C. later work often being superimposed on that which preceded. (Two epochs, Aurignacian and Magdalenian, are distinguished.) It is remarkable for its portrayal of animals (bison, mammoth, rhinoceros, deer, wild boar, ancient cow, horse, ibex, bear, elephant) vividly realized with regard to both line, bulk, and movement. Some are as much as 18 feet long. The colors, in some cases perfectly preserved in the dry sealed caves, include earth red and yellow, a green from oxide of manganese, black from charred bone or carbon. Incised line is used, or sometimes later imposed. Human figures occur, but less frequently and with far less realism or conviction. The sticklike male with conspicuous penis appears, as in other rock pictures.

The artists were hunters and the scenes depicted are those of the hunt; to what extent they were real scenes and to what extent designed to bring good hunting is a matter of conjecture. One figure in the Cave of the Three Brothers is interpreted as a sorcerer in a dance, wearing a mask. In a scene from the Lascaux cave showing a fallen hunter and wounded bison, the hunter has the head of a bird, a similar bird on a stick beside him might have totemic significance. The animals are so accurate as to be readily identifiable. One however —a spotted beast with two rectilinear horns like the single horn of the mythical unicorn—is the only candidate, so far, for the category of "mythical beast."

Cave art includes some sculpture, though not so much. Two clay bisons from a cavern in the Arière, the Tuc d'Audoubert, are beautiful examples. [MH]

Ccoa The evil cat spirit of the Quechua Indians of South America who fear him intensely. The Ccoa is the servant of the aukis, perhaps following their orders, perhaps acting on his own initiative. He is cat-like in form, about two feet long with a foot-long tail, and gray with darker stripes lengthwise on his body. The head is larger in proportion than an ordinary cat's head; the eyes are phosphorescent, and from eyes and ears there runs a stream of hail.

☞ He is responsible for hail and lightning, which he uses to ruin crops and kill people. Sorcerers derive their power from him and are his devoted servants. This cat demon must be propitiated with offerings of magical products to keep his anger from constantly being aroused. Many of the attributes of Ccoa are those of Santiago, who in modern folklore has taken the place of the ancient thunder and lightning god, Illapa. [AM]

Cecrops The snake-tailed, autochthonous founder of Athens: a misty figure about whom little is known, whose cult centered on the Acropolis and was early replaced by that of Erechtheus. He may have been of Thracian origin. When Poseidon and Athena disputed for possession of Attica, the sea god made a well but Athena called Cecrops to witness her planting of an olive tree. Cecrops could give evidence only of what he had seen done and the verdict was for Athena. He is a culture hero, having instituted marriage, a new form of bloodless sacrifice, the burial of the dead, the division of Attica into twelve communities, writing, etc. Later tradition gave him three daughters—Agraulos, Herse, Pandrosus—the goddesses of the Acropolis, but originally he had neither parents nor offspring.

Celtic folklore The regions which for the purposes of this article are called Celtic may be divided into three groups: 1) The Goidelic, including Ireland, the Isle of Man, and the western highlands and islands of Scotland. In language, race, and tradition these form a homogeneous block. 2) The insular Brythonic, including Wales and Cornwall, where also we find kindred peoples with a somewhat similar history. 3) The Continental Brythonic, that is, Brittany. Though racially akin to the Welsh and Cornish, the Bretons have had a very different history and enjoy a distinct culture.

In all these regions the collecting of folktales and the recording of customs and beliefs have been carried on from the second half of the 19th century down to the present day. Far and away the most scientific work has been done in Ireland under the guidance of the Folklore of Ireland Society, the Irish Folklore Institute, and the Irish Folklore Commission. In Wales the beginnings of an exhaustive study have been undertaken by the Commission on Welsh Calendar Customs of the National Museum of Wales.

It was natural that among the peoples of the so-called Celtic fringe, remote from great urban centers and also remote (except in the South Wales coal fields and in the neighborhood of Belfast) from industrial concentrations, the lore of the folk should have persisted from generation to generation with great tenacity. In regions where urban forms of entertainment were unavailable, scientific agriculture was unknown, scientific knowledge unattainable, and books were scarce, the people inevitably retained their old seasonal festivals, explained the phenomena of nature as did their ancestors of a millennium ago, retold the timeless stories, and lived and died by a creed which blended relics of paganism with Christianity. Needless to say, much of Celtic folklore is of a piece with the folklore of the rest of Europe.

The most remarkable distinction to be found in the study of this body of material is the amazing abundance and variety of Irish folktales. Over half a million pages of story taken down from the lips of peasants and their entertainers in the last two decades or so are in the files of the Irish Folklore Commission. This peculiar state of affairs is attributable to two factors: first, the bringing down of the culture of the Irish noble and scholarly classes to the common people as a result of the confiscation of estates by the English; and second, the persistence of the professional story-teller, the shanachie (*seancaide, seanchaidhthe*), to this very day in western Ireland.[1] Sagas which had been told in medieval times in the palaces of kings were now heard in whitewashed cottages; and hedge schoolmasters passed on what they had read in books. The shanachie of the present day preserves and embellishes this traditional lore; he may have a stock of fifty to two hundred tales; he takes a pride in his art, and has a social position of prestige. These conditions have not been matched elsewhere in the Celtic fringe, though in Cornwall as late as 1829 there were professional "droll-tellers," who enjoyed the hospitality of the cottages and taverns,

and fiddled, sang ballads, purveyed news, and related brief tales of hauntings, piskies, giants, and so forth.[2] It may justly be claimed that Ireland has the finest body of folklore in the world.

The subject of Celtic folklore will be treated under two main heads: 1) Folktales; 2) Beliefs and Customs.

FOLKTALES

Goidelic Several of the tales still current in Ireland are descended from the oldest strata of mythological and heroic fiction. The story of Balor and his prophesied death at the hands of his grandson Lug (essentially the same as that of Acrisius and Perseus) must go back to a pagan Ireland.[3] Another saga of undoubted antiquity tells of the rivalry of Curoi and Cuchulain over the captive maiden Blathnat, Curoi's abduction of the maiden, her betrayal of Curoi, either by revealing the secret of his external soul to Cuchulain, or by giving the latter the sword by which alone Curoi could be slain. Both methods are combined in *The Barestripping Hangman* from Argyllshire,[4] but simpler variants have been recorded in Mayo as the tale of *Donald Doolwee and his Delilah*,[5] in Donegal as *The Hung-up Naked Man*,[6] and in South Uist (Hebrides) as *The Lay of Melodious Sorrow*.[7] Old sagas relating how Cuchulain got his name (Hound of Culann), was trained by the woman warrior Scathach, killed his own son incognito in combat, and surpassed his rivals Conall and Loegaire for the champion's portion, are (or were recently) reflected in oral tradition, though one may suspect some bookish influence. The tragic story of Deirdre and the sons of Usnach, and the uncanny adventures of Nera in the Cave of Cruachan [8] also survive to this day.

More common than these narratives of the Mythological and Ulster cycles throughout Ireland and Gaelic Scotland are tales of the Fenian or Ossianic cycle. Noteworthy are versions of the birth and boyhood of Finn, his thumb of knowledge, the elopement of his wife Grainne with Diarmaid, the love of Oisin (Ossian), Finn's son, for the fairy princess from the Land of Youth, and of his Rip Van Winkle return. There are also many conglomerate tales, made of stock motifs, which have been attached to Finn and his heroes. Moreover, in the course of centuries the old native traditions have been contaminated. For instance, the Great Fool story, repeatedly collected in Goidelic territory since the early 18th century, is evidently based on the ancient sagas of Finn and the Clan Morna, but the episode of the *gruagach* (wizard-warrior) and his white, red-eared hound seems to have been caught up from an Arthurian romance.[9]

Definitely medieval in origin but not indigenous to Ireland are certain tales: an analog to Chaucer's *Friar's Tale* of the Devil and the summoner; the hermit and the angel; the wolf's tail frozen in the ice; the cooked cock's crowing as a token of Christ's resurrection.[10] Of still later derivation are stories inspired by the witch mania of the 17th century, and in modern times a number of international plots, such as Puss in Boots and Rumpelstiltskin, seem to have passed from print into oral circulation.

There are a vast quantity of long yarns of which no account can be given except that they are strung together out of familiar motifs: the male Cinderella; the widow's youngest son; the grateful dead; the quest for magic swords or inexhaustible vessels or the giant's daughter; impossible tasks; helpful animals and skilful companions; journeys to lands under springs and lakes, or beyond the seas, and so forth. There are also shorter anecdotic narratives, related usually of specific persons and places. An inebriate peasant finds himself in a palace of the fairies; a husband rescues his lost wife from a cavalcade of the dead.[11] In many places throughout the British Isles we find a local legend of a chief and his warriors, sleeping in a cave or hollow hill and awaiting the day when they will wake and come forth in the hour of need. In Ireland it is Earl Gerald who sleeps with his troopers in a cavern under the castle of Mullaghmast; in Argyllshire it is Finn and his men; in Wales it is either King Arthur, as at Craig-y-Ddinas in Glamorgan, or Owen Lawgoch, one of the last chieftains to fight the English, as in Cardiganshire.[12] In several instances this theme is combined with that of the robbery from fairyland, the visitor to the cave attempting to carry off treasure and being badly beaten.

Insular Brythonic Wales, though possessing a rich fairy-lore (of which more will be said under the heading of Beliefs and Customs), has preserved few elaborate stories. One, a special form of the fairy mistress theme is found in Map's *De Nugis Curialium* (1182 A.D.) and is still attached to many lakes throughout the principality.[13] A peasant lad woos a coy lake-maiden and induces her to wed him, but she imposes the condition that he must never strike her with iron. She brings with her many cattle from her watery home, and her husband prospers exceedingly, until by accident he breaks the tabu. She promptly returns to the lake, calling her cows after her. A number of Welsh families claim descent from one or another of these Undines. The most famous version of the romance localizes it at Llyn y Fan Fach in Brecknockshire, and says that the fairy after her departure used to revisit her sons and teach them the lore of healing herbs, so that they and their descendants achieved renown as physicians. Moreover, the belief persisted well into the 19th century that the water fay herself used to appear on the first Sunday in August, and thousands of country folk used to flock up to the mountain on that day to see what they could see.

Cornwall possesses little but the anecdotic tale of belated travelers who find themselves in fairy palaces, see there departed friends or sweethearts, are warned not to eat the food, and so forth. Stories of changelings and of human midwives who attend on fairy mothers are also known. We learn of a farmer's boy who joined a throng of tiny men one night, and was whisked with them through the air successively to Portallow Green, to Seaton Beach, to the King of France's cellar, and back again. When the boy's story was challenged, he was able to produce a rich silver goblet from the King of France's cellar as proof of his veracity.

Continental Brythonic Brittany has its share of these anecdotic types of fairy tale, but also a rich body of more ancient and varied narratives. An analog of the Irish story of Blathnat's betraying the secret of her husband's external soul is attached to the Breton Bluebeard, Comorre. In other tales we find motifs familiar to the Arthurian scholar: the serpent maiden disenchanted by a kiss; the black and white sails; an empty castle where a table is spread with viands, or

where the hero is served by invisible attendants; taking a piece of a shroud from a cemetery; a hermit uncle who counsels the hero; the dragon-slayer and the false claimant. The precise significance of these Arthurian parallels, though some are doubtless fortuitous, has been recently studied.[14] Certain traditions regarding the amorous sirens known as Morgan or Morganes or the cave fairies called Margot la Fée seem quite definitely to be survivals of medieval legends of Morgain le Fée. To the same early period must go back a not uncommon tale of a peasant girl wedded to a splendid stranger, who was both the Sun and Death personified, and taken by him through a cavern to his shining castle; for the same concepts and roughly the same pattern are found (contaminated by the Orpheus myth) in the Breton lai of *Sir Orfeo*.[15]

A legend circulating as early as the 16th century and variously localized is that of the submerged city of Ker-Ys. The beautiful and lascivious daughter of King Gralon, named Ahes or Dahut, stole from her father the keys of the sluice-gates and gave them to her lover, who let in the waters of the sea. Her father then sought to escape the flood on horseback, with Ahes on the crupper behind him. St. Guénolé, the king's confessor accompanied them, and finally, when the waters threatened to engulf them, bade the king cast off the she-devil who had caused the mischief. At these words Ahes fell with a shriek into the waves and disappeared. Her father reached dry land, but Ahes still haunts the seas in the form of a lovely siren, luring fishermen to their doom.

A people as piously Catholic as the Bretons recount many legends of the saints. St. Anne was a Breton duchess who, turned out of doors by a cruel husband, was wafted in an angel-guided vessel to Jerusalem, there gave birth to the Virgin Mary, brought her up in the ways of piety, and then returned to her native soil. Of St. Eloi the widespread legend is told that he was working at his forge when a stranger, seemingly a blacksmith, entered. The saint grew suddenly weary and gladly accepted the stranger's offer to shoe a horse. One after another the substitute smith cut off the horses' legs, affixed a horseshoe to each, and replaced the legs, while the animal stood quietly during the operation. Astounded at this miracle, St. Eloi questioned the stranger and learned that He was Christ himself. Another familiar hagiological pattern occurs in the story of the wolf which devoured the ox used by St. Hervé in plowing. The saint preached so eloquent a sermon that the wild beast, in atonement for its crime, begged to be allowed to serve in the ox's stead and thereafter faithfully drew the plow.

FOLK BELIEFS AND CUSTOMS

Goidelic Until modern times Ireland kept many practices which were rooted in heathenism. In the 5th century St. Patrick alluded to the adoration of the sun as prevalent among his contemporaries, and as late as 1844 flowers used to be deposited at the altar of the sun on Mount Callan (County Clare) the first Sunday in August. In the 18th century it appears that bulls and rams were slaughtered on this spot.[16] The date was called Crom Dubh's Sunday, and was observed not only here but in many parts of the country with pilgrimages and games. In 1844 Crom was said to be a god, and later tradition from Mayo declared that "bad as he was, it was he that was giving the people the light of day, the darkness of night, and the change of seasons." Presumably then Crom Dubh, venerated in the 19th century, is identical with Crom Cruach, the chief idol of Erin, which was overthrown by St. Patrick 1400 years before.[17]

The pagan festival of Lughnasadh, which seems to mean the wedding of Lug, the sun god, and to commemorate his marriage with Eriu, the incarnation of Ireland, was held also on the first Sunday in August.[18] The place was Teltown in Meath, and even in modern times young men and women used to resort thither to arrange trial marriages, which, if they turned out badly, could be broken by the pair's resorting to the same spot a year later, turning back to back, and walking away from each other. The ceremonies were brought to an end by the clergy, but the phrase, "a Teltown marriage," is still applied to irregular unions.

The celebration of May Day or May Eve with bonfires in which a horse's skull was burned or by the decoration of a May bush with candles seems to be a relic of the pagan feast of Beltaine, which ushered in the summer. Six months later on November Eve, the beginning of winter (Samhain) was the occasion for the lighting of bonfires and for processions from house to house to solicit contributions of coin and food. In County Cork the procession was led by a man called the "White Mare" (Lair Bhan), wearing a white robe and carrying a rude representation of a horse's head.[19] On this same eve the peat fires in the cottages were put out, to be lighted afresh the following morning. The fairies and the spirits of the dead were supposed to be abroad, food was set out to propitiate them, and churchyards were carefully avoided.

Another practice linked to the immemorial past is the cult of springs throughout Ireland. In many places the peasants still resort to these holy wells, pass round them sunwise (deiseal) on their hands and knees, and leave pins or buttons in the water or hang rags on thornbushes nearby. Doubtless these rites and offerings reflect an ancient cult of the divinities of the spring, but they have been adapted to the Christian faith by naming the wells after the saints and addressing prayers to them. The waters are generally credited with healing virtues.

The belief in fairies is by no means extinct. They dwell under the hills, in prehistoric barrows or earthen forts, or near some solitary thornbush. To cut down such a bush was sure to bring some calamity. The association with barrows (side) has given the fairies the name of daoine side or in English "shee folk," and their size is responsible for the name daoine beaga, "little folk." They may ride to hunt, or stir up an eddy of dust, or engage in battles, or steal babies, or milk cows, or prevent butter from forming in the churn.

In Connaught the king of the fairies is Finbheara (pronounced Finvarra), while in Munster there are three fairy queens. Cliodna (pronounced Cleena) used to lead the revels within a great rock near Mallow on May Eve, and was reputed to carry off good-looking young men from fairs held in the neighborhood. Áine and her fays throng the slopes of Knockainy (County Limerick) on Midsummer Eve. The country folk of the neighborhood at this same time used to go round the hill, carrying lighted wisps, to a certain little mound, and then proceed down to the village to visit the meadows and cattle. Once, when some girls lingered behind, Áine appeared to them and asked them to leave the hill to the fairy folk. She is said to be the mother of Earl Gerald, who sleeps under the castle of Mullaghmast. The third of these fairy queens was Aoibhill (pronounced Eevil), and all three were regarded as beneficent beings who warded off disease from the sick.

But these and other female fairies also assume the uncanny role of a banshee (bean side, fairy woman), whose warning wails are heard on the approach of calamity to the chief of some clan. Aoibhill is the banshee of the Dalcassians of North Munster, Cliodna of the MacCarthys and other families of South Munster. Though rarely visible, the banshee may appear as a beautiful, pale young woman, with floating hair. The warning fairy may also take the gruesome form of the Washer of the Ford, a woman usually seen washing the bloody clothing and armor of those who spy her and who are about to be killed.[20] The antiquity of this concept is vouched for by the fact that the Irish goddess, the Morrigan, is described, in a poem ascribed to the 8th century, as washing spoils and entrails. There was current recently in County Clare the belief that Richard de Clare, the Norman leader of the 12th century, had met a horrible beldame, washing armor and rich robes "till the red gore churned in her hands," and had been warned by her of the destruction of his host.

There are several other types of supernatural creature familiar to the Irish peasant. There is the leprechaun (probably luchorpan, little body), a solitary dwarfish shoemaker, gaily dressed in old-fashioned clothes. If a person can catch him, he can be forced to give up his treasure, but he will vanish if one takes one's eyes off him for an instant.

There are mermaids who, like the Welsh lake ladies, marry mortal husbands, bear them children, but return to their subaqueous homes. The puca is a sprite of the most variable forms and functions. He may appear as a bull, a horse, a goat, an ass, or a combination of several animal shapes. He may, like Milton's "drudging goblin," good-naturedly do the housework while the family sleeps, or he may snatch the nocturnal wayfarer, take him for an involuntary ride on his back, and at cockcrow throw him off into a pool. This latter prank seems to relate him to the water horse, which is supposed to emerge from a lake and which, if set to a menial task, will drag a mortal back into and under the waters. Still another supernatural animal of popular tradition is the Glas Ghaibhneach (pronounced Gainach) or Glas Ghaibhleann (pronounced Gavlen), that is, the gray cow of Goibniu, who was the Wayland or Vulcan of the Irish pantheon, and also the provider of an inexhaustible feast. The animal is said to have presented herself before every house in Ireland, giving to each a plentiful supply of milk gratis, but, offended by the avarice of a woman who kept some of the milk for sale, she plunged into the sea and made for Scotland or Wales.

It is impossible to list the infinite number of Irish beliefs about ghosts, corpses, days and seasons, natural phenomena, animals and plants, as well as the countless minor rituals, customs, and games, and we will turn to the Isle of Man.

The Manx preserved into the 19th century not only

the usual beliefs about fairies but also two remarkable relics of the cult of Manannan, the Irish sea god. On Midsummer eve the people of the neighborhood used to carry green meadow grass to the top of Barule in payment of rent to Mannan-beg-mac-y-Leir. The grandfather of a woman living in 1910 used to pray to the same divinity for a blessing on his boat and a good catch;[21] and he could hardly have been the only one to do so. There was a belief that Mannan was a great magician who could create an illusory fleet out of peashells and sticks, to discourage an invasion of the island. As in Ireland there was also a cult of springs, with the usual accompaniment of offerings and reported cures. The Manx counterpart of the water horse was called *glashtyn*, and that of the *puca* was well known as *fenodyree*. The latter, too, was sometimes a faithful drudge and, if rewarded with clothing, was ungrateful enough to depart.

May Day was called *Laa Boaldyn* (Day of Beltaine) and was elaborately celebrated. The evening before, people climbed the mountains to set fire to the gorse and scare away the fairies; on May morning there was a great blowing of horns for the same purpose, and flowers were placed over the doors to ward off malignant influences. In the 18th century most of the parishes witnessed a procession to the common, and a sham battle, in which the May Queen's forces of young men engaged those of the Queen of Winter, represented by a man in woman's clothes, loaded with furs and woolen wraps. After the fray the men and maids of the winter party repaired to a barn to divert themselves, while the May Queen's party remained to dance and feast on the green. This was, of course, a seasonal rite whose origin is lost in the mists of time. Ancient also was another custom—the hunting of the wren on the day before or the day after Christmas. Every wren that could be found was killed, and the corpse of one was carried from door to door, its feathers were exchanged for coins, and finally the carcass was solemnly buried. This hostility to wrens was accounted for by a legend that a malign fairy, who enticed men into the sea, had assumed this disguise.

In the highlands and islands of Scotland vestiges of animal and human sacrifice persisted into the 19th century. In South Uist about 1875 an old Gael was observed furtively killing a lamb on a knoll at sunrise.[22] Near Callander on May Day boys used to cut a round trench in the turf, make a fire in the midst, draw bits of cake, which they had baked, out of a bonnet blindfolded, and whoever got a piece which had been blackened was supposed to be sacrificed and had to leap through the flames three times. In the Hebrides St. Michael's Eve was the occasion for circuiting the graveyard sunwise and for a dance in which the death and resurrection of the year were symbolized by a woman.

The Washer of the Ford of Celtic Scotland is sometimes known under the generic name of *ban nighechain* (little washerwoman) or *nigheag na h-ath* (little washer of the ford), and is described as a little woman with red webbed feet, washing clothes of battle after dark at a ford. Or she may bear the name of the Irish goddess Badb. The banshee is known as the *caoineag* (wailing woman), is seldom seen, but often heard in the hills and glens, by lakes or running water. Other supernatural beings are the *tarbh uisge* (water bull) and the

each uisge (water horse). The latter assumes human shape, woos maidens, and can be recognized only by the water weeds in his hair.

Insular Brythonic In Wales visiting of springs for healing, throwing pins into them, and tying rags on adjacent bushes were rites practiced in modern times but are now extinct. We have record from the 19th century of a ritual combat between the forces of Summer and Winter, very similar to that observed on the Isle of Man. The congregating of the country folk at the Llyn y Fan Fach on the first Sunday in August has already been mentioned. A most curious custom, observed mainly in South Wales, bears a marked resemblance to that of the White Mare in County Cork.[23] It belongs to the Christmas and New Year season and goes under the name of *Y March* (the horse) or *Y Warsel* (the Wassail) or *Mari Lwyd*, which may mean either "Gray Mare" or "Holy Mary." The principal figure of the party was a man carrying a horse's skull (or a wooden imitation) and draped with a sheet. The celebrants went from house to house, sometimes engaging in a poetic contest with the inmates, and receiving from them money-gifts or drink in a wassail bowl.

The belief in fairies was strong throughout the principality. The general name was *tylwyth teg* (fair people); sometimes the diminutive ones are called *ellyllon*, and the females *y mamau* (the mothers), a title which links them to the pagan Celtic deities, the *Matres*. These people live in lakes or streams or in hollows of the hills. Associated with them are the usual traditions of moonlight dance, the supernatural passage of time, the stealing of children, and the substitution of changelings.

There are special varieties of the fairy folk. An invisible island off the coast of Pembrokeshire is inhabited by the *Plant Rhys Ddwfn* (children of Deep Rhys), who are midgets in size but assume human form to visit the market towns on the mainland and do their shopping. There is a *coblyn* or Knocker, whose tappings are heard in the mines. The Washer of the Ford seems to be represented by the *Gwrach y Rhibyn* (Hag of the ?),[24] a spectral female in black with batlike wings, who was to be seen plashing the water of a pool and whose shriek foretold misfortune or death. The *pwca* is obviously the same being as the Irish *puca;* he may be a willing drudge or a mischievous poltergeist or a will-o'-the-wisp.

Until recent times belief in the Wild Hunt flourished throughout the principality, though with marked variation in detail. Sometimes the master of the hunt is robed in gray and rides a gray horse; sometimes he is the Devil and his mount is black with fiery eyes. The hounds are called *Cwn Annwn* (hounds of fairyland or hell) or *Cwn Mamau* (hounds of the mothers). Sometimes they are described as white with red ears; sometimes they are followed by a cavalcade of doomed souls. The phantom chase is usually heard or seen in midwinter and is accompanied by a howling wind. It seems to be, as elsewhere in Europe, a storm myth and its antiquity is suggested by its appearance in the mabinogi of *Pwyll* (c. 1060).

Two of the supernatural animals of Irish folklore are known also to the Welsh. There is the *ceffyl-dwr* (water horse), which rises above pools and waterfalls and may be caught and mounted, but, after a wild flight through the air, throws its rider to the earth. There is also the

Fuwch Frech (brindled cow). When anyone was in want of milk, she would fill the biggest pails; but once a wicked hag milked her dry, and the animal left the country. According to another version, an avaricious farmer was about to slaughter the marvelous cow, when his arm was paralyzed and a fairy figure appeared, calling the cow and all her progeny; and the fairy and cow all disappeared into a lake.

Cornwall, a generation or more ago, retained many of its old beliefs and practices. The fairies were generally called the little people or piskies, dwelt among megalithic monuments on the moors, danced in rings, thrashed the grain by night, employed human midwives, exchanged their own for human babies, led belated travelers astray. The sea strand near Newlyn was haunted by a dangerous sprite called Bucca (evidently the same as the Welsh *pwca*), who had to be propitiated by an offering of fish; and the mines were haunted by knockers, who warned the miners of danger. Boulders and other rock formations were attributed to the giants.

The Wild Hunt went under the name of the Devil and his Dandy Dogs. A wayfarer on the moors on a windy night might be pursued and overtaken by the yelping, fire-snorting pack and their horned and tailed master, which could only be put to flight by prayer. The demon hounds are also said to pursue a certain steward named Tregeagle, who died in 1655, after acquiring a wicked reputation for all manner of crimes. Tregeagle himself can also be heard moaning and cursing, as he tries to empty Dosmary Pool with a leaking limpet shell or to bind a truss of sand. The soul of King Arthur enjoys a happier fate, for it inhabits the body of a chough or puffin, and bad luck would follow the Cornishman who killed a chough.

Cornwall could boast many holy wells with curative virtues, chief of them St. Madron's well near Penzance. It was resorted to particularly in May when its oracular waters were supposed to indicate by bubbles the number of years before a maiden's marriage. Sickly children and invalids were plunged into it; others drank the water and then lay on the ground all night; pieces torn from the patients' clothing were hung on a thorn tree overhanging the spring. At several towns Furry Day was observed early in May with the gathering of hawthorn branches and with dancing in the streets and in and out of the houses. At Helston, on May 8 the Furry festival has been held in very recent years; and the story goes that it was instituted to celebrate a fight between St. Michael and Satan.

Continental Brythonic In Brittany belief in fairies of various kinds, though moribund, is still feebly alive. Along the coast of eastern Brittany the female fairies go by the name of *bonnes dames* or *nos bonnes mères les fées*, recalling the ancient Celtic cult of *Matres* and the Welsh *mamau*. The sirens of the western seaboard and islands were known as Morgan or Mari Morgan, and had male counterparts. There were also the ghostly *cannered noz* (washerwomen of the night), who were supposed to be washing their shrouds as a penance and could be heard about midnight beating their linen on the banks of pools or streams. The male dwarfs were usually called *corrigans* and were the subject of the usual superstitions: they guarded treasure, helped in the housework, danced on moonlight nights among the menhirs and dolmens, led travelers astray with a torch,

could transform themselves into black horses or goats. A mortal who found himself in the midst of a corrigan dance was likely to hear them repeating in chorus "Monday, Tuesday, Wednesday," and if he could complete the list would win their favor. A child suspected of being a changeling was called "Little Corrigan."

More powerful and persistent is the group of Breton beliefs about death and the dead. The hoot of an owl, the croak of a raven, or even the chatter of a magpie is an omen of death. The sight of a phantom funeral prognosticates a real one. When the soul leaves the body, it may be seen issuing from the mouth in the form of a gnat or fly. Its destination, according to one witness, is the land of the Setting Sun [25]—a concept which parallels the identification of the personified Sun with personified Death in the folktale mentioned above. But the home of the dead may also be underground, inside a hollow hill, or under the sea. At any rate, the dead constantly return to their earthly haunts, and stories of revenants seen in broad daylight are common. Especially on Hallowe'en are the spirits abroad, and the living are expected to prepare a feast for them. As evidence of their ghostly presence stools and plates have been heard to move.

The personification of Death, known as the Ankou, is a living reality to the Breton peasant. He is a gaunt or skeletonlike figure bearing a sword, scythe, or lance with which he strikes down his victims. The creaking of the cart in which he rides may be heard in the dead of night, even though the rider and the cart may be invisible. According to one tradition, the home where Ankou rests after his nightly labors is a palace, brilliantly lighted by candles, of which the entrance is a pit in the Bois de Huëlgoat.

Megaliths abound throughout the country and are naturally responsible for many rites and etiological tales. Aphrodisiac rites were enacted at certain menhirs. Girls would rub their naked bodies against one of these stones, and then pick a husband from among the eligible young men who congregated in the neighborhood. If a wife was sterile, she and her husband at the full of the moon would strip naked beside a menhir; he would chase the woman around it until he caught her and then cohabit with her at its foot. Pregnant women used to rub themselves against a statue called the Venus of Quinipily in order to ease their labor. The imposing stone alignments of Carnac are explained as pagan soldiers miraculously turned to stone by St. Cornély, while another legend attributes their erection to dwarfs. Elsewhere we find a petrified hunting party and a marriage procession. Near Trébuerden is a dolmen reputed to be the tomb of King Arthur.

One of the most remarkable of Breton practices is one reported from the year 1845. After a prolonged drought all the inhabitants of Concoret formed a procession with banners and a crucifix at the head, marched to the spring of Baranton, and prayed for rain. This is palpably a Christianized form of the custom reported by Wace in his *Roman de Rou* (c. 1170) that huntsmen in the forest of Brecheliant were able to produce rain by pouring water from this spring on a stone block nearby.

The folklore of the Celtic fringe naturally contains much that belongs to the common heritage of the Indo-European peoples. Indeed, a little may have been borrowed from or influenced by the Scandinavian settlers in Ireland and the coasts of Scotland. The Bretons may have preserved traces of an older Armorican culture. Then there has been the impact of the English and the French. But the comparative (though far from complete) isolation of the humbler Celtic-speaking classes from the races from the East has left them with a distinctive tradition, so that even today it is possible to point to customs and tales which have survived a millennium and more on Celtic ground.

Footnotes:

1. K. Jackson, in *Folk-Lore* XLVII (1936): 264–71; S. Thompson, *The Folktale* (New York, 1946), pp. 454 f.
2. R. Hunt, *Romances of the West of England,* 3rd ed. (London, 1896), pp. 26–28.
3. W. J. Gruffydd, *Math Vab Mathonwy* (Cardiff, 1928), pp. 64–87.
4. *Folk and Hero Tales,* ed. J. MacDougall (London, 1891), pp. 76–112.
5. C. Otway, *Sketches in Erris and Tyrawley* (Dublin, 1843).
6. E. C. Quiggin, *A Dialect of Donegal* (Cambridge, 1906), pp. 201 ff.
7. *Miscellany Presented to K. Meyer* (Halle, 1912), pp. 26–33.
8. *Essays and Studies Presented to Prof. Eoin Mac-Neill,* ed. John Ryan (Dublin, 1940), pp. 522–34.
9. *Modern Philology* XLII (1945): 197–211.
10. R. Gibbings, *Lovely is the Lee* (New York, 1945), pp. 79 f.
11. *Ibid.,* pp. 201 f. Cf. Rhys, *Celtic Folklore* (Oxford, 1901), I, pp. 239 f., 248 f.; *Modern Language Notes* LI (1936): 28–30.
12. E. S. Hartland, *Science of Folklore* (New York, n.d.), pp. 207–11. Rhys, *op. cit.,* II, pp. 458–68, 481–84.
13. Rhys, *op. cit.,* I, pp. 2–130. *Speculum* XX (1945): 195–97. Hartland, *op. cit.,* pp. 274–78, 301–07, 325–30.
14. R. S. Loomis, in *Annales de Bretagne,* 1949 or 1950.
15. *Revue Celtique* II (1873–75): 289–320. Luzel, *Contes Populaires de Basse-Bretagne,* I, pp. 3–65.
16. *Proc. Roy. Irish Acad.,* ser. 2, Pol. Let., I: 265–72.
17. *Ibid.* XXXVI (1922): 23–67.
18. *Folk-Lore* XXXI: 120. Rhys, *Lectures on the Origin and Growth of Religion,* 2nd ed. (London, 1892), pp. 409–19.
19. Wood-Martin, *Traces of the Elder Faiths in Ireland,* II, p. 268.
20. G. Schoepperle, in *Journal of English and Germanic Philology* XVIII (1919): 1–7. *Aberystwyth Studies* IV (1922): 108 f.
21. Wentz, *Fairy-Faith in Celtic Countries,* p. 118.
22. Fiona MacLeod, *Washer of the Ford* (New York, 1896), p. 7.
23. I. C. Peate, in *Man* 35 (May–June, 1943): 53–58.
24. Rhys, *Celtic Folklore,* II, p. 453 n.
25. F. J. Snell, *King Arthur's Country* (London, New York, 1926), p. 66.

Bibliography:

Bealoideas, *The Journal of the Folklore of Ireland Society.* Dublin, 1927–date. (Most of the contributions are in Irish, but are accompanied by English summaries.)

Campbell, J. F., *Popular Tales of the West Highlands.* Edinburgh, 1860–62.

Curtin, Jeremiah, *Hero-Tales of Ireland.* London, 1894.

——, *Myths and Folklore of Ireland.* Boston, 1890.

Henderson, George, *Survivals in Belief among the Celts.* Glasgow, 1911. (Mainly concerned with Celtic Scotland.)

Hull, Eleanor, *Folklore of the British Isles.* London, 1928.

Hunt, Robert, *Popular Romances of the West of England, or the Drolls, Traditions, and Superstitions of Old Cornwall,* 3rd ed. London, 1896.

Jones, T. Gwynn, *Welsh Folklore and Folk-custom.* London, 1930.

Kennedy, Patrick, *Legendary Fictions of the Irish Celts.* London, 1866.

Le Braz, Anatole, *La Légende de la Mort chez les Bretons Armoricains,* 3rd ed. Paris, 1912.

Luzel, F. M., *Contes Populaires de Basse-Bretagne.* Paris, 1887.

Moore, A. W., *The Folklore of the Isle of Man.* London, 1891.

Ó Súilleabháin, Seán, *A Handbook of Irish Folklore.* Dublin, 1942. (A very full survey of every kind of tale, belief, and custom, in the form of a questionnaire for collectors.)

Owen, Elias, *Welsh Folk-lore, a Collection of the Folktales and Legends of Northern Wales.* Oswestry and Wrexham, 1896.

Rhys, John, *Celtic Folklore, Welsh and Manx.* Oxford, 1901.

Sébillot, Paul, *Le Folklore de France.* Paris, 1905.

——, *Légendes Locales de la Haute Bretagne,* Nantes, 1899.

——, *Contes Populaires de la Haute Bretagne,* Paris, 1880–82.

Spence, Lewis, *Legends and Romances of Brittany.* New York, n.d.

Trevelyan, Marie, *Folklore and Folk-stories of Wales.* London, 1909.

Van Gennep, Arnold, *Manuel de Folklore Français Contemporain,* Vols. 3 & 4. Paris, 1937–8. (An elaborate bibliography of French folklore in all its branches, and subdivided by districts. See Bretagne.)

Wentz, W. Y. Evans, *The Fairy Faith in Celtic Countries.* London, New York, 1911.

Wilde, Francesca Speranza, Lady, *Ancient Legends, Mystic Charms, and Superstitions of Ireland.* London, 1888.

——, *Ancient Cures, Charms, and Usages of Ireland.* London, 1890.

Wood-Martin, W. G., *Traces of the Elder Faiths in Ireland.* London, New York, 1902.

Yeats, William Butler, *Irish Fairy and Folk Tales.* New York, n.d.

                                                    ROGER S. LOOMIS

Centaurs In Greek mythology, a race of Thessalian monsters, half man, half horse: originally perhaps simply the wild horsemen of Thessaly, noted for their riding ability. The Centaurs seem to have been of two kinds: the wise and friendly companions of the Greek heroes, like Chiron and Pholus; and the wild, lawless, violent beasts who were conquered and destroyed by Hercules and the Lapithæ. The latter species were the offspring of Ixion and Nephele, Nephele being a cloud substituted when Ixion attacked Hera, or the children of Centaurus, the offspring of this union, and mares. Another myth says that the Centaurs arose from the semen of Zeus spilled in his passion for Aphrodite. The Centaurs had names suggestive of trees or mountains and are somewhat similar, as forest and mountain spirits, to the Sileni and the Satyrs. They have been compared to the Hindu Gandharvas, but as there is correlation neither in characteristics nor in name the connection is now discredited. The Centaurs in later times were pictured as being ridden by Erotes or as drawing the car of Dionysus. Their earliest form is that of a man's full body with the body and hind legs of a horse attached at the waist; later, the horse's body, with all four legs, was surmounted by the head and torso of a man. The Babylonian sign for the constellation Sagittarius was, as early as the 11th century B.C., a Centaur. Compare KIMPURUSHAS; LAPITHÆ.

centipede In China the immortal or shape-shifting centipede is one of the protagonists in a battle between shape-shifters. During combat one of the warriors changed into a centipede in a black cloud and vomited forth a stupefying fog. He was overcome by the hero in the shape of a five-colored cock who flew into the cloud and pecked the centipede to pieces. With the scorpion, snake, lizard, and toad, the centipede is one of the "five venoms" in China, and is painted on cakes on the Double Fifth (fifth day of the Fifth Moon). A mixture of spirits of wine and phosphorus rubbed on the heads of infants on this day will protect them against the five venoms. In an Indian tale a king who suffered from "centipedes in his head" was given similar treatment.

There is a West African folktale which features a helpful centipede. The word centipede is said to be tabu in Java and among Malayan tin-miners. In Tahiti the two indigenous centipedes are regarded as shadows of the medicine gods, and are never disturbed or killed. If one can be induced to crawl over a sick person, that person will surely recover. [RDJ]

Cephalus In Greek mythology, the name of two men almost inextricably confused: one, the son of Hermes and Herse, became father of Phaethon by Eos; the other, son of Deion of Phocis and Diomede, was grandfather of Laertes, and husband of Procris (Procne), the daughter of Cecrops or Erechtheus. Eos was attracted to the latter, and when he rejected her advances revenged herself by causing him to doubt the fidelity of Procris. Cephalus disguised himself and with the aid of gifts managed to seduce his wife, then disclosed his identity. Procris fled to Crete, where she was received by Minos. There she obtained from Minos the perfect hunting dog and the spear that never missed, after drugging him when they slept in the same bed, to avoid being poisoned by the loathsome insects and reptiles that bit and killed the women with whom Minos had intercourse. Dressed as a youth, she returned to Cephalus and in turn was able to confound him when she accepted her love in return for the dog and the spear. The two then became reconciled, but Procris remained jealous of the attentions of Eos and often spied upon Cephalus as he hunted. One day, hearing him call on the evening breeze (*aura*) to cool him and

thinking he called another woman, she moved in the bushes from which she was spying, and quickly Cephalus hurled the infallible spear, killing her. The hound was lost in Thebes when, assisting Amphitryon, Cephalus loosed it at an uncatchable fox. Zeus solved the dilemma by turning fox and dog into stone. Cephalus, to atone for the killing of Procris, exiled himself to the island later called Cephalonia, and there threw himself into the sea.

Among the motifs woven into this story are K1813 and K1814—the disguised husband (disguised wife) wooing and winning the love of the spouse; K675—sleeping potion given to man who is to pass the night with a girl; D1653.1.2—the unerring spear, or D1084—the magic spear; N322.2—husband unwittingly kills eavesdropping wife; and Q301—jealousy punished. For several of these motifs, the tale of Cephalus and Procris is the type tale in which the motif appears.

Cerberus In classical mythology, the doglike monster who served as guardian of the portals of Hades; the janitor of the underworld home. Cerberus was the offspring of Typhon and Echidna and lived in a den on the infernal side of Styx, where he prevented the shades from leaving the underworld and greeted, sometimes in friendly manner, sometimes snarling, the souls ferried by Charon. The dead were therefore provided with honey-cakes to feed Cerberus as they passed, the traditional "sop to Cerberus." His form and name, not described in Homer where he is simply the dog of Hades, are gradual developments: Hesiod, first to use his name, described him as having fifty heads. The three-headed form, with dragon's tail and neck and back bristling with serpents' heads, was not fixed until the time of the Roman poets. Cerberus figures in the many classical stories of descents to the underworld, principally in the harrowing of hell performed as the twelfth and most daring of the labors of Hercules. Granted permission to take the monster if he could without weapons, Hercules seized the dog's heads and though bitten by its tail carried it to Eurystheus. This is the only exploit of Hercules specifically mentioned in Homer, who adds that Hercules threatened even the god of the underworld with his arrow.

Other watchdogs of hell or of death have been compared to Cerberus. The Vedic dogs of Yama, Syama the black and Sabala the spotted, were either guardians of Yama's realm against those who tried to enter or psychopomps sent to find and guide the dead. The wolves of Odin, Geri and Freki, ran through the land when war raged. The Egyptian Ammit was a monster guarding the underworld which had the trunk and legs of a hippopotamus and the head of a crocodile.

Cercopes In Greek legend, a race of apelike but human pigmies. Following their thievish bent, they tried to steal the weapons of Hercules. He caught them and tied them upside down on a pole, whereupon they discovered that he was the black-rumped man their mother had warned them of. Their jesting at his hairiness, however, pleased Hercules so that he released them. They were finally transformed to apes or stones by Zeus for trying to trick him.

ceremonial drinking A recent observance, with many elements borrowed from Catholic ritual, of various Southwestern North American Indian groups. In native

North America north of Mexico fermented beverages of any sort were unknown to all tribes in aboriginal times, but ceremonial drinking of *sahuaro* and maize wine, to induce rain and for the general good of the crops, is now a practice among various Yuman tribes, the Pima, and the Yaqui, all of whom live near the Mexico–United States border. The *sahuaro* ceremony is held before the rainy season; *sahuaro* syrup is mixed with water in large ollas or clay pots in a ceremonial house; the ollas are set in a circle, and while the syrup ferments the watchers smoke ritually, perform rain-making rites, and dance a circle dance each night. If no rites such as these are held, men sing during the ritual drinking of the wine by the shaman, singers, and people in general. When maize wine is made the drink is carried about the village during a procession and various Mexican dances, pascola, deer, and matachin, are performed during the ceremony. Catholic and native elements of ritual are curiously blended in these recently adopted drinking ceremonies.

For the drinking of a non-intoxicating drink, as an emetic, see BLACK DRINK. Various tribes in central and southern California also drank a decoction made from the pounded roots of jimsonweed (*Datura meteloides*) in order to induce visions in which they received supernatural power. This drink was administered to youths by elderly persons, more or less ceremonially; emphasis was laid, however, on the dangerous nature of the drink. Persons taking it fell into a stupor and had to be carefully watched; they were obliged to abstain from food and water for a certain number of days before and after drinking jimsonweed. [EWV]

Ceres The ancient Italian goddess of growing grain and of harvests: identified with Demeter. In her honor the spring Cerealia was held at Rome. Her cult was one of the oldest plebeian cults of Rome.

Chac The Maya rain god, the equivalent of the Aztec Tlaloc. By extension he was also a god of the wind, thunder, lightning, of fertility, and of agriculture. He was at the same time one god and four gods in one, each of whom was associated with the four cardinal directions, and each of whom had his distinctive color: red, east; black, west; white, north; yellow, south. Chac was benevolent, the friend of man. To the Maya farmer he was even more important than Itzamna, for through him, one had food, and hence, life. [GMF]

cha-cha A gourd rattle used to accompany Haitian vodun dancing. The name is onomatopoetic and is also occasionally given as *kwa-kwa*.

chacona A Spanish couple dance of the 16th century: the musical form is in slow triple time—a basso ostinato with variations. Of nebulous heritage, it was formerly an exotic, sensuous, theatrical dance much like the sarabanda. It was transformed by the French into a social dance to conclude a ball, with a characteristic multiple form in contrast with the binary or ternary form of other dances. All took part in the first figure, then a couple danced between the lines, next came the ensemble, then another couple variation, and so on up to eight variations or couplets. This intrinsically rondo form later became, in the hands of musicians, the highly developed theme with variations that resembles the equally notable passacaglia. [GPK]

chacs or **chaacs** In Mayan mythology, minor gods of rain and plenty: probably subordinate to Chac, the rain god, as the Aztec tlalocs were subordinate to Tlaloc. Like the bacabs, the chacs were associated with the four directions. A spring festival was held in which the bacabs and the chacs were jointly worshipped. Also, in March, the hearts of the different species of wild animals were sacrificed to the chacs and to Itzamna at a festival designed to bring the rain for good crops. The four men chosen to assist the priests at the festivals were called chacs.

Modern Mayan mythology, under the influence of Christianity, makes of the chacs (one of the kinds of *yuntzilob* or lords) little bearded men, some of whom live in the sixth of the seven heavens, smoking and tossing away their cigarette butts, which become the shooting stars. The chacs are of varying rank, each kind with specific rain duties, e.g. those causing steady rain and those causing quick, heavy storms. They act under orders from Jesucristo, riding on horses through the air and scattering rain from their calabash containers.

chain tale A folktale based on a characteristic series of numbers, objects, characters, days of the week, events, etc., in specific relation. Cumulative tales are chain tales, but there are many distinctive chain tales which are not cumulative. Typical is the story of the origin of chess (Z21.1): a chain tale involving numbers in geometric progression. The inventor of chess asked in payment one grain of wheat for the first square, two for the second square, four for the third, eight for the fourth, etc., etc. But the king could not pay the great amount. The *Carol of the Twelve Numbers* belongs in this category also. Another story (Z21.3), similar to the children's game *The Farmer Takes a Wife*, tells how the rich farmer paid his servant: the first year he gave him a hen, the second year a cock, the third a goose; goat, cow, horse, etc., continued the series until finally the young man was given the farmer's daughter for wife and inherited the farm. Still others are the familiar nursery rime: Solomon Grundy/ Born on a Monday/ Christened on Tuesday/ Married on Wednesday/——Buried on Sunday (Z21.4.1.3); and the exasperating story about the house that burned (Z23.1). The house is burned down.—That is bad.—That is not bad at all; my wife burned it down.—That is good.—That is not good,—etc., etc. The listener never hits on the right answer. Very famous is the possibilities chain:—I hope I am not called to go to war.—Do not be alarmed. There are two possibilities: either war will break out, or it won't. If it doesn't, no cause for alarm; if it does, there are two possibilities: either they take you or they don't. If they don't, no cause for alarm; if they do, there are two possibilities: either you get combatant or noncombatant duty. If noncombatant, no cause for alarm; if combatant, there are two possibilities: etc.

The chain tale is always amusing and often childish, but the device is also occasionally used for a more pretentious narrative. One such is the story of the "The Ambitious Chaṇḍāla Maiden" in the *Kathā Sarit Sāgara*. A certain young Chaṇḍāla maiden had decided to marry the highest of all sovereigns. So one day she followed the procession of the king, intending to attract his notice and marry him. A hermit stood by the way. The king got down from his elephant and bowed at the holy man's feet. So the hermit is greater than the king, she thought, and followed the hermit. The hermit entered the temple and bowed before Śiva, so the maiden decided to marry the god. Just then a dog ran in and lifted his leg against the pedestal of the image. So the dog is greater than Śiva, thought the girl, and followed the dog. The dog ran into the house of a young Chaṇḍāla and rolled with joy and love at the young man's feet. So the Chaṇḍāla maiden married the Chaṇḍāla youth, convinced that her caste was the best of all.

Chakal Lele   A primitive dance of Papua miming the swift actions of a hunter after his prey. [GPK]

chalcedony   A translucent waxy gem of the quartz family but never found in crystalline form; it is usually a smoky blue, but may be cloudy white or yellowish. Blue chalcedony is sometimes confused with sapphire in ancient works and under the name of leucachate it was sacred to Diana. California Indians picked up bits of this stone for amulets. The Egyptians used it for their scarab seals. It was credited with driving away phantoms and visions in the night and banishing sadness. It secures public favor, gives victory, and protects the wearer from shipwreck and at times of political revolution. It is mentioned as one of the foundation stones of the new Jerusalem in the Apocalypse. White chalcedony is worn by Italian mothers to increase the supply of milk. See CARNELIAN.

Chalchihuitlicue   The lady of the jade green skirts; the Aztec underworld goddess of flowing water; wife or sister of Tlaloc, the rain god, with whom she jointly held rule over the waters. She was worshipped in connection with the tlalocs, the assistant rain gods, whose sister she was sometimes said to be. Maize and serpents were associated with her. She was both a cleansing goddess and an angry wrecker who drowned sailors; at the first bath of the newborn child Chalchihuitlicue was invoked. She presided over the sun of one of the mythological cosmogonic periods, and it was during this period that maize first was used on earth. Later, the son of Quetzalcoatl and Chalchihuitlicue was immolated in the making of the sun we now see in the heavens. The goddess is depicted bearing a tasseled white and blue headband and a blue neckband.

Chameleon   A sacred character of West African mythology. In Dahomey, he is associated with Lisa, the sun god, since in the tales, it is recounted how this animal brought fire to man from the sun. [MJH]

☞ Chameleon is also a prominent character in the origin of death stories of East African mythology. In a Duruma myth, when man first appeared on the earth, the animals consulted together in regard to his fate. Lizard wished all men would die. Chameleon said he wished they could live forever. They ran a race: whoever won would make the decision. Lizard won, so the fate of man is to die. Now Chameleon goes slowly and silently on his way, wishing he could have prevented death.

In a Yao (Mozambique) myth it was Chameleon who first discovered man (a man and a woman) in his fishtrap. Everybody was greatly puzzled over the new creatures; but when Chameleon showed his catch to Mulungu (a sky deity), Mulungu said, "Put them down on the earth and they will grow." This was done. All the animals watched to see what man would do. Man made fire; he killed the animals and ate them; at last the bush caught fire and all the creatures had to run. Mulungu went into the sky to live. Thus the gods were driven off the face of the earth by the cruelty of man.

In the Nyasaland death myth, God gave messages to Lizard and Chameleon to take to man. Chameleon was to tell the people that when they died, they would return. Lizard was to tell them that when they died it was the end. Lizard got there first and said, "When men die, that is the end." In a little while came Chameleon. He said, "When men die, they will return." The people did not know which one to believe. But today they kill Chameleon with tobacco juice whenever they see him, because he came too late with good news. Lizard is also hated, because of the news he brought, and he runs for his life whenever he sees a man.

champion's light   The light of battle seen over the heads or radiating from the faces of warriors during battle. The ancient Irish *lón láit*, literally, light of battle, was customarily seen blazing from Cuchulain's forehead and face during the rage and frenzy of the fight. The classic example is the light over the head of Achilles, which Athena kindled and caused to blaze fiercely during the retrieve of the body of Patroclus from the Trojans. Compare ILLUMINATING BEAUTY.

champion's portion   In early Celtic times, the choicest portion of a feast, assigned to the bravest warrior there. Often it was given without question to the hero of the moment, unanimously beloved and acclaimed; often it was contested instantly, and the assignment decided by a fight in the feast hall. The story of *Bricriu's Feast* recounts the famous and prolonged contest between Loeġaire, Conall, and Cuchulain for the champion's portion at the feasts of Ulster.

chaneques, chanekos, or **chanes**   Dwarflike peoples of supernatural qualities: believed in throughout Mexico and Central America. In parts of Mexico they are known by the term chaneque, or its variants. Sometimes good, sometimes bad, they frequently steal the souls of human beings, thus causing illness or death. In Guerrero, Mexico, they can be frightened away by tobacco smoke. Among the Popoluca (Veracruz, Mexico) they are "masters" of game to whom hunters make offerings and burn incense to obtain supernatural approval of their expedition. See MEXICAN AND CENTRAL AMERICAN INDIAN FOLKLORE; SOUL LOSS. [GMF]

changeling   An ill-favored, deformed, huge-headed, or imbecilic child, believed to be the offspring of fairies (in the British Isles, France, Italy), of underground dwarfs or gnomes (in Germany, Scandinavia, and among Slavic peoples), or of a witch or demon (in various parts of the world), and supposed to have been substituted by them for a normal or beautiful one stolen away in infancy while unguarded or before baptism. The changeling belief stems from one still more ancient: that infants are peculiarly liable to demoniacal attack until after certain purificatory rites.

The best way to get rid of a changeling is to make it laugh if possible (in the British Isles, Brittany,

France, Germany). The mother who broke an egg in two and set water to boil in each half had great success. The watching changeling said, "I'm fifteen hundred years in this world and never saw that before"; he burst out laughing, and instantly the true child was in its place. This story of the eggshells (either boiling water in the two halves or brewing the shells of twelve eggs in a pot) is told from Germany, France, Brittany, Ireland, and Wales, to Japan. There are occasional other stories (English) of how exceeding loving care bestowed upon a changeling will so gratify the supernatural mother that she will bring the human baby back to the human mother and give both good luck forever. In Brittany, Wales, and France, there are stories of a human mother who was advised to whip the changeling child in order to get her own child back. She did so; the changeling wailed; and "one came crying, 'Do not beat him. I have not done yours any harm,'" and the exchange was made.

change of sex A folktale motif (D10), appearing in stories all over the world, in which a man becomes a woman, or a woman becomes a man. The most famous tale of the change of sex is that of Tiresias who saw snakes coupling and not only was changed into a woman but afterwards was transformed back into a man. The motif appears often in Greek myth and legend, for example in the story of Cæneus. The myth of Callisto seduced by Zeus in the shape of Artemis is akin to this theme. Related also are other transformation motifs, principally those of the beast marriage, the disguised suitor, and the use of magical objects. Change of sex occurs often in Persian and Indian tales and is accomplished through the medium of magic pills or plants, or by exchange with some supernatural being. For example, in the *Mahābhārata*, the girl Śikhaṇḍin is brought up as a boy, marries as a man, and is contemplating suicide when a Yaksha offers to trade sexes with her and leave her a man. This she does, and is overjoyed to discover that the Yaksha has been condemned to remain a woman until the death of the transformed man. The magic well or magic caldron which changes the sex of one entering it appears in Arabic stories. In a Koryak myth, Big Raven, the ancestor of the Koryaks, transforms himself into a woman by cutting off his sexual organs. After a while his wife, Miti, comes to the camp where he is living. She is masquerading as a man and eventually wins Big Raven as her bride. When they lie down together, however, they are at a loss. But by and by Big Raven's organs, which he has kept, migrate to their rightful place, and in the morning wife and husband leave the hut as they formerly were. Apparent change of sex, by dressing as man or woman, is likewise a widespread motif. The change of clothes of the sexes still occurs at certain holidays in European culture, as for example the Halloween, Christmas, and (in the United States) Thanksgiving Day masquerades. This switching of roles was formerly resorted to as a counter to the evil eye and may have developed the concept utilized in the folktale. Certain instances in medical records, however, indicate that an actual change of sex occasionally takes place, and given an occurrence as abnormal as this, in a simpler society the story-telling mind would naturally incorporate the example into the folktales.

Chang Fei One of the Gods of Butchers in Chinese folklore and legend: a composite god (i.e. represented by parts of two animals into which he was transformed). He is eight feet tall with a panther's head, a swallow's chin, and voice of thunder. Originally he was a butcher: butcher to Kuan Kung, with whom he got into a fight, and to Liu Pei, who separated them. The date of the oath of friendship and brotherhood taken by these three is given as 191 A.D. They are often referred to as China's "Three Musketeers," three military heroes who swore allegiance in an effort to unify their land. Later Chang Fei again became a meat-seller. But in the temple of Kuan Kung, Chang Fei is numbered among the 24 assessors of that deity, one of 24 heroes deserving gratitude for service to their country. [RDJ]

Chang-hko In Káchin (Burma) mythology, the woman who was saved (alone or with her brother Pawpaw) in a boat during the great flood. She and Pawpaw took nine cocks and nine needles with them. After days of storm they threw overboard one cock and one needle but the cock did not crow and the needle was not heard striking the bottom. This was repeated until the ninth day when the cock crowed and the needle could be heard, a sign that the flood had subsided.

After leaving the boat the two wandered around until they came to the cave of two nats (all nats survived the flood) who invited them to stay. Chang-hko soon had a child which the she-nat watched while the parents worked. Whenever the baby cried, the nat threatened to cut it to pieces at a place where nine roads met. Finally she did just that, scattering the pieces over the country but reserving some which she made into a curry. Then she put a block of wood into the cradle. When Chang-hko discovered what had happened, she ran out to the crossroads crying for her child. The great nat offered to make her the mother of all the nations of men. Immediately from each road sprang men—all the races—and Chang-hko claimed them all as her children. But they scoffed at her. In her anger she cried, "If you will not own me as your mother, then I will live upon you." And even today men must "eat to the nats" by giving them offerings.

Chang Hsien In Chinese folk belief, one of the patrons of child-bearing women: invoked especially for male issue and easy childbirth. He is depicted as a white-faced, long-bearded man with a small boy by his side. He holds a bow and arrow and shoots at the Heavenly Dog, T'ien Kou Hsing, the Dog Star, who is greatly feared by pregnant women. [RDJ]

Changing Woman The beneficent, ever-beautiful female deity of the Navaho and closely related Apache Indian tribes of the southwestern United States. Changing Woman is the mother of the two Apache culture heroes, Killer-of-Enemies and Child-of-the-Water. Her name derives from the fact that she can change at will from baby to girl to woman to old woman, and back again; also, she is the changing moon. [EWV]

Chang Kuo or **Chang Kuo Lao** (*Lao*, old) One of the Eight Immortals of Taoist lore, said to have lived in the 7th and 8th centuries: the typical old man. It is reported that he died about 746, but when his followers opened the tomb, it was empty. He was born old and is a great traveler. He rides thousands of miles a day on his white donkey, which, the journey finished, he folds up like a piece of paper. He rides facing the tail and carries sometimes a phœnix feather, sometimes a peach of immortality, and sometimes a cylindrical musical instrument. He was always an expert conjurer, everywhere noted for necromancy. His image offering a child to a newly married couple is often placed in bridal chambers. [RDJ]

Channukah The Jewish Festival of Lights. See HANUKKAH.

chanson de geste Literally, song of deeds; Old French epic, usually consisting of thousands of lines, dealing with history and legend, for example the heroic feats of great men such as Roland, Charlemagne, Huon de Bordeaux, etc., written in assonant verse divided into thought sequences of varying length, called *laisses,* and sung to a brief, litanylike melody repeated for each line. The most famous example is the 11th century *Chanson de Roland.* Some, such as *Gormond et Isembard* and the *Chanson de Willame,* had burdens of a ballad type. Chansons de geste formed a part of the repertoire of the wandering jongleurs of the 10th and 11th centuries.

chanson de la mal mariée A type of French and Provençal song devoted to the faithless young wife of a cruel or impotent old man. Often with the connivance of servants or neighbors, she takes a series of lovers and defies the old man's wrath.

chanson de romance A love song; specifically such a song sung by a girl in payment of a forfeit at a Haitian Negro wake, when games are played to amuse the dead.

chant A monophonic style of singing or recitative in free rhythm, used as a heightened speech form or speech-song for the delivery of sacred texts, ritual formulas, or magical incantations in many cultures. The term is applied to such widely differing styles as the liturgical music of the Christian, Buddhist and Confucian religions; the cantillation of the Jews; the Indian cantillation or Vedic chant; the battle songs of various tribes; the complex ceremonial song cycles of such American Indian tribes as the Navahos; the incantations of shamans or special singers of numerous primitive peoples for curing, placating the supernatural, accompanying birth, puberty, and funeral rites; the singsong of children's counting-out rimes, jeering songs, jump-rope and ball-bouncing rimes, etc. The Christian chants include the four great Western divisions, Ambrosian, Mozarabic, Gallican, and Gregorian, the Eastern forms, Byzantine, Syrian, and Armenian, and the Coptic and Ethiopian chants of northern Africa. Both Greek and Jewish influences are preserved in the melodies, but local folk dances distinguish each type. From the tropes and sequences of the Gregorian chant, originally devised to aid in memorizing complicated melismatas by suiting a syllable to each note, grew religious folk song in the vernacular and religious folk drama. Formulas of the Byzantine chant, which made use of free poetry for its texts rather than the psalm texts of the Western chants, are still preserved in the colinde of Rumania. The Coptic chant is sung chiefly by blind singers, who are considered the only people of sufficient spiritual and un-

worldly character to sing the sacred melodies, and the transmission of the form is thus entirely oral. It has developed, beyond the liturgy, a body of religious folk songs for festivals and other public occasions. The Ethiopian chant is sung by priests who maintain a strong volume to the point of exhaustion; dancing, hand-clapping, and drum-beating on the part of the congregation contribute to the attainment of an ecstatic state. This procedure is similar to that of the shout of American Negroes.

Jewish cantillation consists of melodic formulas intoned with Biblical texts, the musical elements having been transmitted orally until the 16th century. Oriental Jews sing without instrumental accompaniment, though in ancient times, accompaniment was always used. The unfixed melodies of their style are believed to have some part in the development of cante flamenco.

The Vedic chant is developed around a three-tone melody with high-pitched stresses on vowel sounds. High, middle, and low tones are accompanied by raising, leveling, and lowering of the head as an aid to correct placing of the tones, and notes are located by a system of finger-counting.

Julius Cæsar recorded his observation of the battle chants of the Gauls, which were sung to the brandishing and clashing of weapons, as they invoked the help of their gods for champions at single combat and raised the cry of victory. Unrimed, alliterative chants were sung by the Milesians as they approached Ireland, calling on the magic of nature to assist them.

It is a common belief among primitive peoples that a special chant is taught to the singer by a supernatural being and that the song is then his inalienable property until passed on to successor or heir. Cosmogonic, genealogical, and mythological subjects form a considerable body of primitive chant, aside from the spells and curing formulas of the medicine men. Dancing may accompany the singing. [TCB]

☞ The popular English name for the curing rituals of the Navaho Indians of the American Southwest is chants. Elaborate origin myths, in which it is narrated how a deity or supernatural being performed the chant for the first time, are attached to the many Navaho chants which exist; during the course of a chant the famous earth- or sand-paintings of the Navaho are made as part of the curing ceremony. Chants last several days and nights; the chanter and his helpers must be paid, and oftentimes large groups of Navaho assemble from far and wide to witness the ceremony; food must be provided for these visitors. Certain Navaho are well known for their knowledge of the long texts of various Navaho chants. These texts or songs, which are chanted rather than sung must be repeated letter-perfect, else the entire chant is invalidated. No man should sing a chant more than three times a year; if he sings it oftener he will be stricken with the same disease which is cured by the chant. Grave errors in the singing of a chant may also be followed by disease; of Washington Matthews, who early learned and recorded the Night Chant, used for curing paralysis, it was said by the Navaho after Matthews was himself stricken with paralysis, that he must have learned the chant badly, and gotten its songs mixed up. [EWV]

chantey or **shanty** A strongly rhythmical work song of sailors, generally with a solo passage sung by the leader, or chanteyman, and a refrain roared in chorus by all hands to coincide with the concerted effort of the task. To the hard-fisted officers who mastered the square-riggers on which chanteying reached its peak, as well as to the singing men on the deck, these songs were as important in the working of the vessels as the straining ropes and the bellying canvas at the masts. For every kind of back-breaking job aboard ship there was a song to pace the work. Three main types of chanteys became traditional for the three main kinds of labor: (1) Short-haul or short-drag chanteys, used when only a few lusty pulls were required, as in boarding tacks and sheets or "sweating up" a halyard. These were the earliest and simplest songs, barely removed from the shouted work cries commonly heard as long ago as the 15th century on the Venetian galleys. The oldest short-drag chantey known is *Haul on the Bowline,* dating from the time of Henry VIII. (2) Halyard chanteys, timed to the massed pull and relaxed interval of long hauls, such as hoisting sail, catting the anchor, and occasionally pumping. In this class are *Whiskey, Johnny, Blow, Boys, Blow, Blow the Man Down,* and *Reuben Ranzo.* (3) Windlass or capstan chanteys, sung to the heavy processional beat of sea boots around the capstan when hoisting anchor or warping the ship into the dock, and the type generally carried over into the most gruelling toil of the seaman's life, pumping ship. The first and last duty of the voyage required the strength of every man's back at the capstan bars, and some of the finest of the chanteys grew up around its turn-post. Favorite capstan chanties were *Sally Brown, Shenandoah, Rio Grande, Amsterdam* or *A-Rovin',* the oldest of them all, and *Stormalong.*

The chanteyman, selected or self-appointed, not for his musical talent but for his seamanship, stood erect at the leading part of the rope, while the rest "tailed on" in crouching position behind him. It was his responsibility to choose the right song for the job, to set the pitch and tempo, and to improvise stanzas, if the usual ones were finished before the work was done. He might sing through the chorus once at the beginning to be sure that the men knew his version. Choruses were fairly well standardized and known to forecastle hands everywhere, but the chanteyman exercised considerable freedom in his rendition of the solo parts, altering names and places to fit the circumstances. Irishmen were especially esteemed as chanteymen, but in the late days of sail American Negroes became famous as the greatest ever to throw a song to the gale. (Harmonizing in the chorus was never heard except among Negro crews.) It was a moment of relief for many a hard-pressed mate when the first strong voice lifted a working song to whip a sullen, drunken, disorganized crew of polyglots into action at the beginning of a voyage.

Sung without accompaniment to airs borrowed from ancient ballads, music-hall ditties, or any contagious melody heard on shore, these frequently ribald songs of unknown date and authorship followed sailors all over the world, gathering stanzas and new tunes and losing their roots as they went. They celebrated the sprees ashore, the girls and drinks of every port and every continent. They gibed at the harsh mates and masters of every well-known packet line in a way that would not have been tolerated in speech. They lauded the proud and beautiful ships and damned the "hard case" ones, deriding the food and the quarters and bemoaning the hard life of the sailor. Men of every race serenaded certain salt-water heroes and heroines, notably Sally Brown, the lady of easy virtue, Reuben Ranzo, the inept seaman who became a captain, and Stormalong, the sailor's sailor.

British seafarers were responsible for the bulk of the chantey repertoire up until the 19th century, when the American clippers challenged the merchant fleets of the world, driving their lean, full-sailed ships to unbroken speed records. Then American chanteys, drawing their inspiration from pioneer songs, railroad and wagon-train songs, lumbermen's come-all-ye's, and Negro work chants with an early touch of the blues, were heard in the China tea ports, the Alaska fur anchorages, on the Liverpool packet runs, and howling around the Horn to California gold-rush towns.

The competition of steam at first only contributed to the richness of the chantey, because the sailing skippers drove their crews to the point of exhaustion to save the trade for the square-riggers, and only with singing could the last effort be exacted.

The latest chanteys of all came from the nitrate ports of Peru and Chile, where, even up to World War I, ships of all nations swapped songs, creating hybrids such as *Slav Ho,* and *Bangidero,* in which a tune from one country was matched to meaningless sounds in imitation of the poorly understood language of another.

The origin of the word is disputed. First mention of it occurred in 1869, under the spelling *shanty. Chantey* first appeared in 1884. Some authorities argue that the derivation is from shanty, a shack, and was due to the lumbermen who often left their shanties to ship for a voyage in off seasons. However, it seems most probable that the word comes from the French imperative, *chantez,* sing. Compare FORECASTLE SONG. [TCB]

Chanticleer A name for the cock and chiefly used as a proper name, but often without the capital. Chanticleer is the name of the cock in the *Roman de Reynart,* a medieval beast epic or fable. [GPS]

chaos In Hesiodic mythology, the pre-existing empty space, filled with clouds and darkness, which evolved Erebus, Night, Tartarus, and Eros. All things, men, and gods arose from this goddess, Chaos. In the later Orphic belief, Chaos, Night, and Erebus existed at the beginning. By the time of Ovid, Chaos had evolved from the Hesiodic nothingness into a confused mass from which all things were created by harmonizing the various parts. The word was applied also to the underworld. Compare TIAMAT.

Chao San Niang Goddess of the Wig Makers in Chinese folk belief. Chao San Niang was the wife of a scholar, one of the first members of the Academy. While he was away receiving honors and performing his duties at court, she and his parents suffered great hardship and want. Chao San gave the parents whatever food she could get and she herself lived on chaff and husks. When the old people saw this, they insisted that the three of them share equally whatever food there was, but they died as a result. Chao San Niang had no money to buy coffins, so she sold her long, beautiful hair, her only wealth. When the time came for the husband to return home, Chao San was in great distress, because she could not face him with a shaven head. But she managed to find enough hair to make herself a wig. Today she is regarded as the patroness of the wig trade. [RDJ]

Chapayekas Literally, long slender noses; the ritual clowns of the Mayo-Yaqui of Sonora, Mexico, carried over into Yaqui settlements of Arizona. During Lent they form a masked police group and rule absolutely from Ash Wednesday to Easter Saturday. Membership in the group is by vow taken because of a sickness. Together with the unmasked "soldiers of Rome" they constitute the Fariseo society, with Pilato as their head.

They wear plaid shawls, deer-hoof belts, and often cocoon rattles (*teneboim*) like the Mazo and Pascolas. They strike an ornate machete in their left hand against a lance (Mayo) or stick (Yaqui) in their right, as they caper. The name-giving masks are of goat or wild pig skin with patches of hair remaining as beards, and with long ears and noses or snouts, and among the Mayo, with huge horns, which among the Yaqui have dwindled to crescent stubs. Some clowns, called *viejos*, wear old coats and canes. Masked, ritual silence is preserved, and communication is by sign language only.

The Chapayekas are supposedly incarnations of the Devil; yet they police the people, guard the image of Christ, bury the dead, and carry rosaries in their mouths. All action is in reverse, ludicrous, and often obscene. During Easter processions and church services they cavort to weird music of fiddle, fife, and drum. A typical step consists of three stamp-brushes and a stamp. At noon on Easter Saturday they shed all evil by rushing out of the church and burning all paraphernalia except masks and deer-hoof belts. Members of the Chapayekas group are buried in their masks. These vestiges of primitive ritual are probably related to the Tarahumara *chapeones*, and to pueblo clowns such as the Taos *k'apio*, mingling fertility, animal, and death ritual. [GPK]

Charites (Latin *Gratiæ*) In Greek mythology, daughters of Zeus and Eurynome (though the several authors and various religious rites give them differing parentage); personifications of grace, loveliness, and charm: originally goddesses of vegetation who developed into deities attendant upon and subordinate to the principal gods of the pantheon. Traditionally, they are three: Euphrosyne (mirth), Thalia (abundance), and Aglaia (splendor). They symbolize the Greek ideal of the mean between license and restraint. Charis (the singlar form of the word) is mentioned in Homer as the wife of Hephæstus, but so is Aphrodite, and perhaps the two are identical; the Charites often appear as attendants of Aphrodite. Originally the Charites may have been two: Cleta and Phaenna were the Spartan Charites; Auxo and Hegemone the Athenian. The Athenian youth made his oath to defend the city by Auxo, Hegemone, and Agraulos (daughter of Cecrops). Their rites at Orchomenos (the Charitesia) were best known, and they were worshiped at Messene, Athens, and in other places. They formed no part of the Roman religion. Earlier representations show the Charities clothed; later they appear naked and with arms linked in a graceful circle, two facing forwards and one backwards. Their attributes are the myrtle, the rose, and musical instruments.

charivari (American *shivaree*) A French marriage-baiting custom dating from the Middle Ages. Originally common after all weddings, then directed at unpopular or unequal matches as a form of public censure, the charivari became so licentious and violent as to be prohibited by the Church, surviving only in rural districts. Similar customs have existed all over Europe under different names. Introduced into America by the French of Canada and Louisiana, where the name was corrupted into shivaree, the custom fitted into the frontier and backwoods pattern of rough horseplay and wild sports, especially in the South and the Middle West.

The constant element in the shivaree has been the noisy mock-serenade produced by a discordant din of noise-making instruments and rustic and domestic implements—horns, cowbells, kettles, dishpans, boilers, tin plates—tick-tacks on screens and windows, rattling of sticks on picket fences, and firing of guns (a Colonial custom preserved in the Southern "running up" of the bridegroom). After the privacy of the bridal chamber has been invaded and while the couple's attention is distracted, they are subjected to all kinds of annoying pranks, such as hiding their clothes, tying the bedclothes in knots, and placing cracker crumbs, hair clippings, and even live toads in the bed. More recently the couple may be captured and separated and driven about town in a hilarious procession of honking cars, with tin cans tied behind. Other pranks include handcuffing the groom, tying him to a tree, forcing the couple to dress in "tacky" clothes, and trundling them in a wheelbarrow.

Certain survivals may be noted in the customs of the shivaree, e.g. the noise may once have been intended to drive away evil spirits, and Old World customs of consecration and divination, such as sewing the bride up in a sheet or hanging a bell under the bed, may be preserved in the bedroom pranks. The treat exacted from the bridal couple in the form of drinks, cigars, candy, ice-cream, etc., may be a survival of the practice of purchasing peace by ransom.

The convivial and social features of the shivaree have gradually been taken over by more agreeable and harmless functions, such as parties, bridal showers, and "open house," while the honeymoon and the motor car together have provided first a convenient escape and then a substitute. [BAB]

Charlemagne (742?–814) Charles the Great, or Charles I, king of the Franks, who reestablished the "Roman" Empire. Some 200 years after his death he became the central figure in a cycle of chansons de geste or popular romances about the adventures of one or more of his 12 peers, the "matter of France." Best known of these, and possibly the first, is the *Chanson de Roland* which tells of a disastrous rear-guard action led by Roland and his best friend Oliver against the Moors at Roncesvalles. These metrical novels, produced for the entertainment of a sophisticated court and as social and political propaganda, were rewritten frequently between the 11th and 16th centuries. Though the Carolingian cycle contains a number of motifs from popular folklore, that, for example, the king will rise from the dead when his people need help, it is less dependent on this sort of episode than is the Arthurian cycle which influenced it. Research in the 20th century has gone far to invalidate the romantic hope that in the Carolingian cycle one might observe the operations of the memory of "ein dichtendes Volk" which made men into myths because they were historically important. [RDJ]

Charleston An angular ballroom dance for partners who dance face to face but not in a ballroom embrace. The feet fly alternately forward and back; at each step the toes and knees turn in and the arms swing in opposition. It is named after Charleston, South Carolina, where Negroes working on the docks invented these step combinations and entertained the passengers of the steamers. In 1925 it was crystallized into a ballroom dance, and in 1926 became popular in Europe. [GPK]

Charlie Chaplin rimes It was inevitable that the children should adopt into their lore the quaint figure of the movie comedian. There are many verses about him, especially among the skipping-rope rimes, of which the most popular is:

> Charlie Chaplin sat on a pin.
> How many inches did it go in?
> One, two, three,—(until the jumper misses)

But a close rival, with many variants, is:

> Charlie Chaplin went to France
> To teach the ladies how to dance,
> And this is what he taught them,—
> First the heel, and then the toe,
> Skip and a hop and away you go.
> Salute to the king, bow to the queen,
> And turn your back on the Kaiserine.

Sometimes the rime begins:

> One, two, three, four,
> Charlie Chaplin went to war,

and then it is the nurses whom he teaches to dance. Sometimes he teaches elephants to dance: he can do anything. Once:

> He pulled the trigger,
> And shot a nigger,
> And that was the end of the war.

In World War II the ending of the France-dance rime became:

> Salute to the captain, bow to the queen,
> And turn your back on the old submarine,

and, strangely, in Utah, the last line became:

> Stick up your nose to the crippled old king.
> [CFP]

charming of game Among North American Indians, the recitation of charms and short formulas by persons gifted with supernatural power, to attract game: a fairly widespread practice. Intensive use of this method of securing game has been noted for several Paiute groups of Nevada. [EWV]

charms Practically every magical rite is accompanied in South America by chants to which the Indians assign great powers. No man can claim the title of shaman unless he knows a great many charms. The importance of magical chants as a means of averting impending dangers may be exemplified by the behavior of the Apapocuva-Guarani who, at the slightest difficulty or just because they feel tired or depressed, resort to chanting. According to the Ona of Tierra del Fuego, the magic chants known to their ancestors had the power of bringing whales to the shore. The Shipaya Indians of the Xingu River believe that a charm could assume a human form in order to accomplish the wish that caused its expression. Certain charms could go in the guise of a man to an enemy village and kill every one they met.

Shamans use charms and incantations to combat evil influences, to expel diseases, destroy their enemies, summon spirits, and endow objects with supernatural powers. Ordinary people, as a rule, also know charms to ensure good luck and ward off dangers. The Taulipang, a Carib tribe of the Guianas, classify charms into two categories: those which ensure the success of a cure or of an enterprise, and those intended to cause damage. Each charm is validated by a myth explaining its origin, and by reciting its past successes. See AMULETS; FETISH; GBO; TALISMAN; WITCHCRAFT. [AM]

Charon In Greek mythology, the son of Erebus and Nox; an old, dirty man who ferried the shades of the dead over the Styx to the realm of Hades. He would carry only the properly buried dead, and these paid him with a coin placed in their mouths at their burial. This custom of putting a coin in the corpse's mouth still existed in Greece until recent times. Charon is probably a later figure formed from an earlier popular god of death. See COIN OF THE DEAD.

Charos or **Charontas** In modern Greek folklore, the Angel of Death, a figure of terror who rides a horse and carries off the dead. He is probably a modernized survival of a very ancient god of death whose literary development led to the Stygian ferryman Charon.

Charun An ancient Etruscan god of death who carried a hammer with which he finished off his victims. He was a companion of Mars on the battlefield.

Charybdis In Greek legend, a monster, the whirlpool she formed, and the rock cliff under which she lived, facing Scylla from the Sicilian side of the Straits of Messina. The rock was lower than Scylla's cliff and was topped by a fig tree. Three times a day Charybdis sucked in the sea water, and three times a day she vomited it forth as a whirlpool. Both Ulysses and the Argonauts sailed through the straits safely. In later literature, Charybdis was supposed to have robbed Hercules and then to have been cast into the sea by Zeus. The expression "to fall into Scylla while avoiding Charybdis" seems first to have been used in the 12th century A.D. Compare SYMPLEGADES.

chastity In primitive societies wide variation exists in sex customs. In many societies, e.g. the Bahuana, Kaffir, Maori, Nagas, sexual intercourse is common and unrestrained among children up to the age of puberty. At puberty boys and girls are segregated, initiated into adulthood, and prepared for marriage. After marriage strict chastity is required of the wife with severe penalties, such as death or slavery, for violation. In many other societies chastity means virginity from birth until the time of marriage; this is invariably true when a bride price is paid by the husband. But in no early society is chastity required for moral reasons. Rather it is based on practical considerations, such as the necessity of having a recognized provider for children. Chastity does not, therefore, mean refraining from sexual intercourse outside the marriage tie, but rather refraining from sexual intercourse with another without the husband's wish, permission, or sanction. The wife is the huband's property. If she surreptitiously takes a lover, she and the lover are violating a property right and for this reason both are severely punished. Many societies practice wife hospitality, exchange of wives, priest rights, and other such customs in which the husband willingly gives his wife to another. The point to be emphasized is that primitive peoples do not look on sexual intercourse as immoral or "bad" in itself; it is the circumstances attending it that are important. Among certain native tribes of Australia and many other peoples a girl at puberty must submit to the perforation of the hymen by a man appointed for that purpose. Then for several days she freely has intercourse with many men of the tribe. The purpose seems to be to make her "safe" for the husband-to-be. Yet the same girl, should she seek out a man, would be universally condemned and punished. See ADULTERY. [MEL]

chastity sword The two-edged sword, or the "naked sword" laid between a man and a woman sleeping together to preserve their chastity. See SEPARATING SWORD.

chastity test A test applied to women to ascertain whether or not they have been faithful to husbands or lovers. Many forms of testing are found in folklore and legend; they are generally connected with the ordeal. The test by fire is the most common. The suspected woman was forced to thrust her arm into boiling water, or boiling lead (Isolde), or in a flame, or forced to walk barefoot over red-hot plowshares (Queen Matilda), etc. If she was burned, she was believed to be guilty; if unscathed, innocent. In the test by water she was thrown into a body of water; if she sank, she was guilty; if she floated, innocent. According to legend, Vergil, in his role as necromancer, constructed a huge brass serpent as a sort of mechanical chastity-tester. A suspected woman could be tested by forcing her to place her arm in the creature's mouth. If she was guilty, the animal would close its jaws and hold her arm fast. Other tests are associated with personal objects usually given to the person tested by the spouse or lover. Typical of these chastity tokens are a shirt which remains white as long as its wearer is faithful (King Horn), a ring that will pinch or even cut off the finger of the faithless wearer, a sword that will rust if the owner's fidelity is blemished. The chastity token is certainly a development of the life token. See ACT OF TRUTH; LIFE TOKEN. [MEL]

Chelm A town near Lublin, Poland, the inhabitants of which were the traditional superlative fools of European Jewish lore. Compare GOTHAM.

Ch'êng Huang In Chinese folklore, god of the Ramparts, City Walls, Moats, and Ditches: also known as a Spiritual Magistrate of the People. This god and his attendants exercise in the spiritual world functions similar to those exercised by the civil governors in the terrestrial world. They are in constant communication with Yen Lo, Judge of Hell, and report evil deeds to him. They also communicate with Shang Ti, the Supreme Being, from whom their power derives. They are also believed to have power over diseases and evil spirits.

The worship of Ch'êng Huang dates from the ancient days when all towns were surrounded with mud walls or ramparts, which in turn were surrounded by the water-filled excavations from which the earth for them had been dug. The *Book of Rites* reports that one of the successors of the legendary Huang Ti instituted sacrifices in honor of certain "Eight Spirits," among them inventors of dikes and mud walls, and Ch'êng Huang, and of whom one may have been god of the city or community. Another sacrifice, dated 513 B.C., shows that the gods of the city gates also received honor.

Ch'êng Huang's cult has maintained the great popularity it achieved in the Sung dynasty (960–1127 A.D.) during the dominance of the Taoists. Consequently the lore is shot through with rationalizations, borrowings, euhemerisms, and the like. In large cities the temple is an imposing edifice containing quarters for Ch'êng Huang, his Lady, and his attendants. It also contains depictions of the courts of Hell and the tortures which are to be met in each. Chief among Ch'êng Huang's attendants are two secretaries, Ox-Head and Horse-Face, and two constables, Mr. White and Mr. Black. A whole system of Ch'êng Huangs developed and many of them bear the names of persons important in local legend. Ceremonies and iconography show great local variation. In former times there were periodic celebrations and splendid processions during which Ch'êng Huang was brought out of the temple and carried through the streets to inspect the city. [RDJ]

Cheng Wu Guardian of the North: a Taoist Worthy representing a mixed cult. His temple is visited during the Lantern Festival, the middle of the First Moon. Here scenes from his life are painted on colored transparencies. After his conversion to The Way, Cheng Wu left the court. During a mood of discouragement with the difficulties of The Way, he decided to return to the world. He met an old woman grinding an iron bar into a needle and decided that persistence will accomplish anything. Because his body tormented him, he cut himself open and removed his five vital organs, which became savage beasts and created unhappiness among the people. He then turned them all into musical instruments. The knife and scabbard Cheng Wu used to disembowel himself became a youth and a maiden. The maiden, Cheng Wu's daughter, hates marriage and tries to spoil young brides. In this she is assisted by the spirit, Hsiung Shen, who is so ugly that when he sees himself in a mirror he runs ten thousand li. This group, which contains other unpleasant creatures, of whom one helps people into the noose when they hang themselves, and another is helpful in crawling into small holes, is involved in the festivals of life and death. The Supreme Lord of Heaven appointed Cheng Wu Guardian of the North, with residence at the North Pole. [RDJ]

Cheremissian or **Marian folklore** The Cheremis are a Finno-Ugric group (about 413,000 in 1920) living between the central Volga and Vyatka, in the Gouvernments of Vyatka, Kazan, N. Novgorod, and Kostroma. The highest God of the Cheremis is *Kugo-jumo* (compare JUMALA), a manlike being, living in the sky. Like the people on the earth, he practices agriculture and has many excellent cattle; he even keeps bees. In the prayers he appears as a worldly ruler with a large train of lesser deities, to whom sacrifices are also made. The word *jumo* means the heaven, sky, or the weather. *Kürdertše-jumo* is Thundergod, and *Wolgeṅdže-jumo* is Lightning-god. The word for soul is *ört*. Not only man has a soul, but also objects and all manifestations of nature. The evil spirit of the Cheremis is *wodež;* and there are many of them: *wüt-wodež—*the spirit of the water; *kude-wodež—*the spirit of the house; *tul-wodež—* the spirit of fire. The creator of all the evil on the earth is *Shajtan* (derived from Satan), a demon common also to the Mordvins. Other spirits are *ia* or *ija—*devil. The water spirit is usually called *wüt-ia* or *wüt-oza.* His daughter is called *wüt-ian üder;* she is a beautiful sea maiden and can be married to a man. The water spirits are very dangerous at noon; this time is forbidden for bathing or fishing. *Kugo-jen,* the tall man, is an evil spirit. In case of disease a sacrifice must be made to him. The good one is *Puirše,* Creator and protecting spirit. Many deities of nature are named in combination with the word for mother (see AWA).

The Cheremis have many feasts. The great feast in the month of May is *Shürem.* It takes three days, and the Devil is driven out with noise and blowing on horns (*MSFO* 59: 29–30). Another great feast, *Küso,* involving numerous sacrifices, is celebrated at the end of June (*MSFO* 78: 185 ff.) Important feasts are consecrated to the dead. *Nelle parjam* or *nelleše* is the feast for the dead, observed 40 days after burial. Till this day the dead one is fed at home, but after this feast he definitely leaves the living relatives. Another feast of the dead is *tošte-mari.* This is a general feast observed the week before Easter and Whitsuntide, for all the dead. At this time all the dead leave their graves and walk in the villages. It is also called *sorta ket' še—*the day of the candle—or *sorta pairam—*the feast of the candle (*FFC* 61: 37).

The sacrificial priest is *kart.* The oldest or most capable is "great kart," the others being "small kart." *Kudo* is a separated corner within a Cheremisian hut, the dwelling of the "kudo-spirit" (Compare KUALA of the Votjaks).

The most important works on Cheremissian folklore and mythology are:

Beke, Ö., *Tscheremissische Texte zur Religion und Volkskunde.* Oslo, 1931. (Folk beliefs and customs, superstitions, proverbs, riddles, etc.)

———, *Tscheremissische Märchen, Sagen und Erzählungen.* Helsinki, 1938. *MSFO* 76.

———, "Texte zur Religion der Osttscheremissen," *Anthropos* 29, 1939.

Berdnikov, V. M., and E. A. Tudorovska, *Poetika Mariiskich narodnich pesen (Poetics of the Mari Folk Songs).* Joskar-Ola, 1945.

Holmberg, U., *Die Religion der Tscheremissen.* Helsinki, 1926. *FFC* 61.

Paasonen, H., and P. Siro, *Tscheremissische Texte.* Helsinki, 1939. *MSFO* 78. (Tales, songs, prayers, magic formulas, proverbs, riddles, notes on religion and cultus).

Wichmann, Y., *Volksdichtung und Volksbräuche der Tscheremissen.* Helsinki, 1931. *MSFO* 59.

JONAS BALYS

cherkesska A saber dance of the northern Caucasus, performed by men. It is fierce and virile, with leaps and turns. At present it is an exhibition dance, but may formerly have shared the vegetation symbolism of all leap and sword dances. It does not, however, enact a battle; similar to the Arabian *danse du sabre,* it is a solo display of dexterity in manipulating the weapons.
[GPK]

cherry The fruit of any of certain trees (genus *Prunus*) of the rose family: a small round or heart-shaped drupe enclosing a small pit. All parts of the tree have been used in folk medicine. Negroes of the southern United States give a cold tea made from cherry bark (in some localities taken from the north side of the tree) to stop post-natal and menstrual hemorrhage. It is general U.S. folksay that a cherry tree will sprout in the stomach of a child who swallows a cherry stone, or that it is unlucky to dream of a cherry branch. In Ontario it is said that a strict cherry diet will cure allergies. A lock of a child's hair is sometimes put in the trunk of a cherry tree to cure his asthma. In Newfoundland a tonic drink is made from cherry bark. Certain North American Indians used cherry roots to decoct a remedy for syphilis. Cherry gum dissolved in wine is still used to relieve coughs, and is also considered an excellent tonic. In Switzerland the first fruit of a cherry tree is given to a young mother to eat, preferably one who has just had her first child. This insures an abundance of fruit in the orchard. In some parts of France the cherry orchards are wassailed as the apple orchards are in England.

Cherry Tree Carol An English ballad carol (Child #54) based on Apocryphal material from the *Gospel of Pseudo-Matthew* xx, and other sources, telling the story of a miracle performed by Christ before his birth. Mary and Joseph walked through an orchard or garden where cherry trees grew. Mary asked Joseph to pick her a cherry and, when he refused roughly, the unborn Child in her womb bade the tree bow down to give his mother fruit. The tree obeyed, to Joseph's chagrin. The first mention of the story in English was in the Coventry Mystery of the 15th century, though it was not a carol in that reference. The varying sets of words that have survived, both in England and in the United States, are of later date. In a number of American versions the Child goes on to foretell the date of his birth: "On the 6th of January/ My birthday will be/ When the stars in the elements/ Shall tremble with glee." This day, Old Christmas, has been celebrated even in recent years in mountain sections of Kentucky. Other European songs on the same story vary as to the fruit concerned, according to the favorite fruits of the country—date, fig, apple, etc. The last runo of the *Kalevala* relates a similar tale of Marjatta, a maiden who went to milk the cows and passed a tree with a scarlet berry. The tree invited her to gather the fruit, which was so far out of reach that she had to knock it down with a stick. At her command the berry jumped into her lap and then into her mouth. She became the mother of Ilmori, the Air. See CAROL.

chestnut In many places chestnuts are believed to have curative powers. In Germany they are carried in the pocket as a charm against backache, in the United States against rheumatism, but in England they must be begged or borrowed to be effective in these ways. They were formerly considered good for the blood, but eating too many would thicken it and cause headaches. Chestnut leaves boiled in water, with honey and glycerine added, will cure asthma and chest complaints. In

Tuscany they are the appointed food for St. Simon's Day, in Piedmont for All Saints' Eve, and some are always left on the table for the souls of the poor dead.

Chhalla A ritual libation of the Aymara Indians of Bolivia. Small cups (always in ritual number) are lined up on a blanket; in each of them the priest (yatiri) places different substances: mica, feathers, silver and golden paper, flour, incense, alcohol, and maize beer. The proper combining of these substances is part of the traditional ritual of the popular religion. The contents of the cups are thrown to the wind as offerings to the spirits and deities. [AM]

Chiang Tzŭ-ya The God of Fishermen of Chinese folk belief: another name is Chiang T'ai Kung. His legend says that he lived from about 1210–1120 B.C., began life as a humble fisherman, and became a general and adviser of generals during the establishment of the Chou Dynasty. He is worshipped as the god of fishermen and is said to have fished with a "straight hook and a grain of rice for bait" until he was 80 years old, at which ripe age he became Prime Minister under Wu Wang. [RDJ]

Chiapanecas Literally, girls of Chiapas; a mestizo dance of the state of Chiapas, Mexico, usually performed by women. Alternating Austrian waltz and Indian shuffle steps, the dancers swirl their full skirts and clap their hands at a given moment in the music. Thus it is also called the "handclapping dance," and the audience joins in the clapping. Two lines of girls, or girls and boys, form a V after their entrance, cross over and circle. As a couple performance in Mexico City, it has been elaborated with pirouettes and leg swings. The gay Ländler tune to which it is danced probably dates from the brief rule of Maximilian and Carlotta.
[GPK]

Chibcha-chum An ancient tutelary deity of the Bacatá region of Colombia: referred to as god of earthquakes in Chibcha mythology. Once he tried to flood the valley of Bogotá, but was thwarted by Bochica, who created the big waterfall of Funza Bacatá to divert the waters. Chibcha-chum either fled or was driven underground, where he still supports the world on his shoulders. [AM]

Chicomecoatl Literally, seven snakes; Aztec goddess, sometimes called the "goddess of nourishment"; the female counterpart of the maize god Cinteotl, their symbol being an ear of corn. She is occasionally called Xilonen.

Chie The goddess of sensual pleasure in the Chibcha religion. Bochica is said to have turned her into an owl or the moon. [AM]

Chief In many North American Indian mythologies it is assumed that each animal species has a chief who speaks for the species, and to whom animals and human beings are accountable. This belief is especially strong among the Eastern Woodlands and Southeastern groups.
[EWV]

Chih Nü The celestial Weaving Maid of Chinese mythology and legend; heroine of a star myth that occurs in many versions, e.g. in China, Korea, Japan. Chih Nü is generally identified with the constellation called Lyra in the West or with Vega, its principal star; her lover, the Cowherd, is Aquila, or Capricorn, or the star

Altair. The Weaving Maid was an immortal who was banished to earth. She fell in love with an oxherd. When, her banishment having come to an end, she returned to Heaven, her herd-boy lover tried to follow her but was stopped at the Milky Way.

Another form of the story belongs to the world-wide swan-maiden type: The Weaving Maid spent her time in Heaven weaving clothes for the gods. Once she and her sister descended to earth to bathe in an earthly stream. A cowherd was told by a magic cow to steal the garments of the loveliest maiden. This he did. Consequently the Weaving Maid was not able to return to Heaven and the looms of the gods were idle while she was living happily on earth with her lover. She was recalled to Heaven. The cowherd, wrapped in the skin of his magic cow, followed but was stopped at the Milky Way. The Jade Emperor of Heaven decreed that the two might meet once a year if the night is clear and the magpies make a bridge with their wings.

The festival is observed on the Seventh Night of the Seventh Moon, when the lovers meet. The legend has obvious connections with the spider legends, Arachne, etc.

chikuli A Mexican cactus worn in the belt for luck by the Indians of the regions where it is found, and sometimes for aid in hunting.

Child, Francis James (1825–1896) American philologist and distinguished ballad scholar. His first collection of *English and Scottish Ballads* appeared in eight volumes (1857–1858). His final collection, *The English and Scottish Popular Ballads*, first appeared in ten parts (1882–1898), later in five volumes, and is still the standard ballad authority and reference. Graduated at Harvard in 1846, he was professor there from 1851 to the year of his death, holding the chair of English Literature from 1876. He accumulated at the University one of the largest folklore collections in the world and by his influence made Harvard the main center of folklore study in the United States. The famous *English and Scottish Popular Ballads* (1882–1898 ed.) was reissued in facsimile reprint (5 volumes in 3) in 1956.

child abducted by cannibal A folktale motif (G400ff.) especially popular among the Indians of the North Pacific Coast. Typical is the story of a group of children beguiled by chewing gum into the basket of a giantess, who made off with them. Several escaped from the basket but not all (sometimes all but one). The hero is a young boy suddenly born from the mucus of his mother's nose (T542.1) who grew to miraculous wit and strength in four days. He went forth to search for his brothers and sisters (or sister), found the Cannibal giantess's cave, and the dried bodies of children in it. He hid in a tree by the river but was discovered by the Cannibal by his reflection in the water (R351). She asked him how he became so beautiful. The boy explained that he had had to endure great pain to become so beautiful. The Cannibal giantess besought him to give her the same treatment, but the boy taunted her with being unable to endure it. She agreed to submit to the treatment (i.e. have her head pressed between two stones [K1013], or be beheaded, etc.). She came back to life at once, but he killed her again and this time broke the spell. He then resuscitated the children (or child) in the cave and led them all safely home. [EWV]

childbirth The many peculiar practices incidental to the birth of a child, various and widespread as they are, arise, for the most part, from only three main fears: 1) fear of blood-tabu contamination, 2) fear of the unknown spirit-sources of life, and 3) fear for the child's welfare, immediate and future. These three overlap greatly at times.

The primitive tabus associated with woman, particularly throughout the reproductive period of her life, become temporarily attached to the infant and also to all persons and objects intimately connected with the birth.

It would seem that the respect for and fear of blood which is so general in early cultures is increased and magnified when the blood is that of childbirth or menstruation, perhaps because the reason for these natural biological processes was so vaguely if at all understood. Blood plus mystery was of old and still is an unbeatable combination for arousing human curiosity and interest. From the dawn of history until today there have been whole races and religions asserting that there is some mysterious wonder-working power in the blood.

The documents included in the Hebrew scriptures bear ample evidence of the fear of contact with menstrual and parturient blood (*Isaiah* xxx, 22; *Leviticus* xv, 19–33 and xii, 2–8) and the persistence of those same birth tabus is to be seen today in civilized Christian countries where in some orthodox communions women must still be "churched" to purify them after childbirth (see CHURCHING OF WOMEN).

The tabu atmosphere surrounding the arrival of the baby accounts for the various required actions of the father of the infant, including not only the widespread custom of couvade but also in many cultures his expected absence from the scene, and usually that of all other men as well. The preference of many women, especially in rural districts, for the attendance of a female midwife instead of a male obstetrical expert is probably a survival of this custom, as is the traditional vigorous shooing of all men from the vicinity by the women. On the other hand, among some tribes all relatives, including the men, flock to the birth; and in other tribes the husband is expected to assist or even acts as midwife.

In the Marquesas Islands the husband is even required to have sexual relations with his wife as she bathes immediately after the birth. This might seem to be the very antithesis of respect for the birth-blood tabu, but is probably also inspired by a recognition of the terrible power of the tabu and the desire to counteract and terminate it by heroic measures, antidotal in character, like the couvade.

Correlative with the absence of the husband is a similar device, the return of the pregnant woman to her mother's house until after the delivery of the child. The custom is common in Africa and India, especially for the birth of the first child, which, among the Basuto, traditionally belongs to the maternal grandparents. According to very old accounts, Gautama Siddhartha the Buddha was born in the Lumbini Grove when his mother was overtaken by her pains on the way to her mother's house. It may be that the custom of the husband's absenting himself is a substitute for and a survival of the presumably older matriarchial culture.

Still further evidence of the birth tabu is the usage in widely separated regions where the woman gives birth in seclusion. It may be behind the maternal grandmother-to-be's hut (South African Herero), in the forest (British Columbia), on the shore of a river (la Plata), or in a little shed, as formerly in Japan. In Russian Smolensk the birth is in the barn. Where circumstances, such as severe winter cold, make birth in the house necessary, it must be behind a screen or curtain. On the west coast of India one tribe secures the needed seclusion for the woman in the hut by having the other inmates leave for five days.

These various methods may be explained by all concerned as due to the woman's desire for privacy, but the original motivation was undoubtedly the protection of the relatives and neighbors, especially the men, from the dangerous powers of the life force infesting the place of birth at the time—powers resident and manifest particularly in the blood.

The contamination of birth, like that of death, extended to objects in the house. Fishing-nets and gamecocks in the Philippines, bows and arrows in Brazil, and the cuttings of plants in New Britain are removed from the house because otherwise they would all be unlucky. In New South Wales among certain tribes every dish used by the pregnant and parturient woman is carefully destroyed.

It would appear that the newborn child is dangerous even to himself, for if he looks in a mirror, he is said in some country sections to be very likely to contract rickets.

The birth practices inspired by fear for the child's welfare begin long before its arrival. Parsons reports (*Pueblo Indian Religion* i, 91) that a Sia woman would not run a sewing machine during her pregnancy lest the umbilical cord get sympathetically tangled, and the Isletan women avoided the flickering moving-pictures lest their children become betwitched. Likewise, on the positive side, ancient Mexican women are reported to have worn shells of the sea-snail that their expected children might creep forth from the womb as easily as the snail from his shell.

Women with more pretense of civilization have been known to indulge during pregnancy in similar sympathetic magic, either positive or negative, much to the irritation of the attending scientific-minded obstetrician and the disturbance of his program of prenatal care. Belief is common that looking upon a rabbit as it eats will cause a woman's child to have a harelip, and a trip to the zoo is likely to have untold consequences.

In some parts of China great care is taken to have everything auspicious as the birth-pains start. Incense is burned before the ancestral tablets; red candles for joy are lighted in the birth-chamber; all conversation must be cheerful, all ill-omened words carefully avoided. See section *Birth* in CHINESE FOLKLORE. When the child does arrive, the precautions taken all over the world to ensure good luck are multitudinous and varied enough to occupy several volumes. See AFTERBIRTH; AMULETS; CAUL; BAPTISM; CIRCUMCISION; UMBILICAL CORD; etc.

In *Ezekiel* xvi, 4 we have, by negation, a good description of the Hebrew birth practices in the 6th century B.C.: "And as for thy nativity, in the day thou wast born thy navel was not cut, neither wast thou washed in water to supple thee; thou wast not salted at all, nor swaddled at all."

In other countries newborn infants were rubbed with oil, or raw eggs, or alum, or sulfur, or a mixture of other substances. In every instance, some practical hygienic, sanitary, or therapeutic purpose is today alleged, by very ingenious rationalizations, but the origin of the custom is either obviously or inferentially to be found in the desire to protect the child from evil influences and spirits (supposed to be particularly apt to haunt the vicinity of births) by some beneficent insulation through the use of evil-repelling sacred emulsions or powders. The oil is "sacred oil" as in modern Greece, or the water is "holy water" as in many Christian lands.

The first clothing of the infant is important. In parts of China the newborn is dressed in robes resembling those of a Buddhist monk, to fool the evil spirits. The cumbersome and otherwise unexplainable long gowns in which helpless infants were nearly smothered until a generation ago in England and the United States probably had their origin in some such idea of disguising the child as an adult. The custom in Kent of putting a boy's nightshirt on a baby girl, and vice versa, is supposed to be in order to make her or him attractive to the opposite sex when grown, but appears to be another disguise mechanism.

The day of the week on which the child is born was once thought to be of importance, especially in Scotland, England, and parts of the United States. But the popular rimes disagreed sadly as to which days were auspicious. While all versions said:

> Monday's child is fair of face; and
> Tuesday's child is full of grace,

there, for a while, the unanimity ended. Wednesday's child was full of woe in England, sour and sad in Georgia, but loving and giving in New England. Thursday's, in the same regions respectively, had far to go, was merry and glad, or must work for his living, while Friday's was loving and giving, full of sin, or full of woe. Saturday's had to work hard for his living in England, was pure within in Georgia, and had far to go in New England. But Sunday's child, how favored! The old jingle must have started in Scotland, where a bairn born on a Sabbath was deemed most highly lucky and, significantly, safe from the malice of evil spirits. So we find the rimes in England and New England chiming together:

> But the child that is born on the Sabbath-day
> Is blithe and bonny and good and gay.

Georgia's version is even more pious, ending:

> To heaven its steps shall tend away.

In parts of rural England many quaint and evidently very old customs survive, such as laying the newborn first in the arms of a maiden, covering a boy with his mother's petticoat or a girl with her father's pants, and taking the child to the top of the house before it is carried out of doors.

The various fears connected with childbirth and the customs deriving therefrom disappear suddenly in a few weeks, after the mother, father, child, and house have been ceremonially cleaned and accepted back again into the community.   CHARLES FRANCIS POTTER

☞ Certain post-natal observances and tabus among the Indians of Middle America should be mentioned. Usually the mother rests for a week or ten days after a birth. In areas where the temescal sweat bath is used, she bathes on successive days and is cleansed. In parts of central and southern Mexico the NAGUAL or TONAL is discovered by placing ashes around the cradle of the child to note the tracks of the animal which comes to visit its new charge. Newborn babes may have the *mollera* "set," i.e. the midwife pushes up on the hard palate to prevent illness. Copal incense, perhaps mixed with tobacco, may be placed in a tiny bag around the neck or wrist of the infant as an amulet to prevent illness. A seed, *ojo de venado* (deer's eye) is also widely used in this way.

Most Indian children eventually are baptized by a priest. Among the Tarahumara (northwest Mexico) a curing ceremony takes place, three days after the birth of a boy, and four after the birth of a girl, at which the officiating medicine man burns incense and describes crosses with burning pine-pitch torches. Friends of the family avoid admiring the new child unrestrainedly lest they be accused of involuntarily exercising the evil eye.

Food tabus for some time for the mother are common, though there is little unity from one tribe to another. To illustrate, the Tarahumara mother does not eat squash or apples for several weeks. No explanation for this practice is given. See COUVADE; MEXICAN and CENTRAL AMERICAN INDIAN folklore; UMBILICAL CORD. [GMF]

Child-Born-in-Jug (Pot) A miraculous-birth tale, occurring among some Great Basin and Southwestern North American Indian groups. [EWV]

Childermas The name in England of Holy Innocents' Day, commemorating Herod's slaughter of the children: observed on December 28 (December 29, Old Style, in the Greek Church). The day is considered unlucky; any undertaking begun on this day is doomed to failure. Among its many local names is Cross Day in Ireland, and there are several local legends emphasizing the day's unpropitiousness. In the British Isles it was the custom in various places for parents to whip their children before the children got out of bed, that they might better remember the significance of the day. This later degenerated into a widespread custom of the early risers beating the lie-abeds.

Child-of-the-Water Culture hero of Apache and Navaho mythology. Among some Apache groups Child-of-the-Water is the chief culture hero who slew monsters and other enemies of mankind; he is attended by a subordinate, a younger brother, relative, or friend, known as Killer-of-Enemies. In other Apache groups the positions of these two are reversed, with Child-of-the-Water a lesser character than his companion. In several Apache mythologies the two heroes are sons of Changing Woman. Child-of-the-Water has become identified by the Apache with Jesus. [EWV]

Children of Lir One of the Three Sorrows of Storytelling of Old Irish mythology and legend: *Oidead Clainne Lir*, the Tragedy (or Sorrowful Fate) of the Children of Lir. Lir, lord of the sea, one of the ancient gods (see LEAR), had four children by his first wife, Aeb, daughter of Bodb: Fionguala, a daughter, Aed or Hugh, and Conn and Fiachra (twin sons).

These children were turned into swans by their jealous stepmother, Aoife, also a daughter of Bodb. Fionguala begged Aoife for a limit on the curse and Aoife said "till a woman of the south be joined to a man of the north." Because Fionguala had asked for the limit to be said, and Aoife had said it, neither Lir nor Bodb nor any magic of the Tuatha Dé Danann could undo the curse, until the children of Lir had spent 300 years on Lake Derryvaragh, and 300 years on the Mull of Cantyre (the Straits of Moyle, between Ireland and Scotland), and 300 years in the open Atlantic near Erris and Inishglory, off the stormy western shores of Mayo. But Bodb changed Aoife into a demon forever because of the evil thing she had done. Lir and Bodb came to see them on Lake Derryvaragh and discovered that the beautiful swans still had their human speech and possessed the wonderful gift of music which only the Tuatha Dé Danann knew.

The swans lived in peace on Lake Derryvaragh for 300 years. The next 300 years on the Straits of Moyle were bitter cold and stormy, and the swans were granted no respite of land or shelter. Off the coasts of Erris too, in the last 300 years, they suffered cruel hardships. The night the sea froze solid from Erris to Achil was the most terrible of all.

They remained in Inishglory till the time the hermit Mo Caemóc came to that place; and for the first time the swans heard matin bells. They then sang their own unearthly lovely song. Mo Caemóc heard it and sought them, and found them and cherished them, and they were happy while they stayed with him.

Soon Deoc, daughter of Munster's king, was married to Lairgrén, king of Connacht. Thus a woman of the south was joined to a man of the north. The enchantment on the children of Lir was ended when Lairgrén grabbed the swans to take them for a gift to Deoc. The swan-shape fell off them under his violent hands, and all he saw was four ancient withered human beings, about to die. Mo Caemóc baptized them as fast as he could, and buried the four in one grave.

For centuries in Ireland no man would kill a swan because of the sorrowful story of the children of Lir; and the people of Ireland are loath to kill swans to this day for the same reason.

children's songs The oldest and most widely diffused of folk songs, showing great similarity both as to melody and to subject-matter all over the world and preserving the vestiges of ancient ceremonies and beliefs. They include the game songs, counting-out rimes, mocking songs, begging songs, divinations, historical verse, and mnemonic rimes sung or chanted by children themselves, and the lullabies, chin-choppers, finger and toe enumerations, knee-dandling rimes, etc., sung to children by adults.

Game songs still played and sung today carry survivals of foundation sacrifice, the belief of the Devil's enmity to bridges, the war between saints and devils, as in *London Bridge,* which has counterparts in many languages. They preserve the May-Day courting customs and the Druid's tree, as in *The Mulberry Bush;* the washing and burial of the dead, as in *Green Gravel* and *We've Come to See Miss Jenny Jones;* the handkerchief morrises, as in various drop-the-handkerchief games, and many other beliefs and practices. They also vicariously put the child into a place in the adult world by

dramatizing the work and social functions of men and women—washing, ironing, planting, selecting a mate, etc., as in *The Farmer in the Dell, Go In and Out the Windows, Oats, Peas, Beans and Barley Grow,* and *Here Come Three Dukes A-Riding.*

Many songs or chanted rimes accompany ball-bouncing, rope-skipping, etc. These tend, while preserving from generation to generation a basic pattern, to adjust themselves to the times. For example, a rope-skipping chant of World War I vintage said, "Cinderella/ Dressed in yellow/ Went down town to buy an umbrella/ She walked so slow/ She met her beau/ And he took her to a ten-cent show." Ten-cent shows having become unknown in 1949, the rime now goes, "Cinderella/ Dressed in yellow/ Went down town to buy some mustard/ On the way her girdle busted/ How many people were disgusted?" Derisive chants once devoted to Kaiser Bill easily made the shift to Hitler. Shipyard strikes, comic-book characters, and movie heroes have entered the picture; and a consciousness of race prejudice has eradicated some of the phrases known to earlier generations, possibly with the censorship of parents and teachers. *Eeny, meeny, miny, mo,* for instance, now often says "Catch a bunny (or baby or monkey) by the toe," instead of "nigger."

Begging songs (*chansons de quête*) are those sung at Christmas, New Year's, etc., in a house to house canvass for a handout in return for good wishes. Some, such as *Here We Come A-Wassailing* are still sung by carollers.

It has been observed that the one- and two-tone babble songs of infants repeat the patterns of the earliest known and most primitive forms of music. Such jeering tunes as are sung to words of the character of "I know a secret," or "Cry, baby, cry/ Put your finger in your eye," etc., are almost identical the world over. See CAROL; CHANT; COUNTING-OUT RIMES; GAMES; LULLABIES; SKIP-ROPE RIMES. [TCB]

Child Waters A popular English ballad (Child #63) found in the Percy manuscript, in which the test of endurance of a woman's love is the main theme. Faire Ellen, pregnant with Child Waters' child, runs barefoot as a page beside the horse of her heartless lover. Child Waters will not ease the pace, compels her to swim a river, humiliates her in the feast-hall where they arrive, sends her into the town to hire the fairest lady she can find to be his bedfellow, and compels her to rise before dawn to feed the horse. In the stable Faire Ellen gives birth to her child. When Child Waters comes to the stable door he overhears her singing a lullaby to the baby and wishing she were dead. His heart softens at last, and he promises Faire Ellen marriage and churching both in one day. *Burd Ellen* is the title of the Scottish version of this ballad. The Piedmontese ballad, *Ambrogio and Lietta,* closely parallels the theme.

chilena A Mexican mestizo couple dance of Guererro and coastal Oaxaca: derived from the Chilean cueca, and characterized by kerchief play. [GPK]

Chi Lung Wang The Fire-Engine Dragon King: in Chinese popular belief, a carry-over from the worship of Lung Wang, the Dragon King who beneficently supplies the earth with water and rains. Chi Lung Wang is invoked to facilitate the use of the hand-pumps of Chinese town and village fire-fighting mechanisms.

Chimera In Greek legend, a fire-breathing monster with the head of a lion, the body of a goat, and the tail of a serpent, or, according to Hesiod, with the heads of these three animals. The Chimera was the daughter of Typhon and Echidna. When she ravaged the Lycian country, Iobates sent Bellerophon against her. That hero, from the back of Pegasus, slew the monster. The name has come to be applied to any fantastic or horrible creation of the imagination, and also to a grafted hybrid plant of mixed characteristics.

chimerat A term proposed by the famous Swedish folklorist, C. W. von Sydow, as an international term for the type of folktale variously called märchen, conte populaire, fairy tale, household tale. The term was approved by the Premier Congrès International de Folklore which met in Paris in 1938, but has not yet received wide usage or acclaim.

chimes Tuned sets of bells, gongs, or stones struck with a stick or hammer. Known in the Far East from earliest sources, suspended, L-shaped stone chimes (Chinese *pien ching*) were played for formal public and religious occasions, and for private entertainment. Similar sonorous stones are also found in Annamese temples, in Venezuela, on Chios, and in the Christian churches in Ethiopia. Sounding stones are also used in the ceremonial rite of preparing kava, a drink, in Polynesia, where maidens chop the ingredients on tuned stones. Metal chimes, used both in the East and the West, for musical purposes, for religious accompaniments, and on down to dinner chimes, are a development from these stones. See BELL; GONG.

ch'in One of the two main types of long zither, the original stringed instrument of China, distinguished from the other type, the *shê*, by having frets and by its smaller size: played exclusively by scholars and sages for small, select audiences. It is integrated in the cosmic system with south, summer, and silk. The player washed his hands and burned incense before taking up his instrument, and the ancestral spirits were believed to attend the delicate wailing music of its silk strings. It is often erroneously described as a lute. The Japanese name for it is *koto*.

Chin Chia One of several patrons of Chinese literature, known as the "Gentleman in Golden Armor." He punishes wicked scholars, and waves a flag before the homes of families whose descendants will attain high honor in the Imperial Examinations. See WÊN CHIANG. [RDJ]

Chinelos Carnival dancers of Morelos, Mexico, especially famed in Tepoztlan. Formerly they were disguised as Negroes. Nowadays they wear long loose embroidered satin gowns, fantastic hats topped with ostrich plumes, and amazing masks with horn-shaped black beards. Despite their encumbrances, they jump, skip, and clown. In Cuautla they are modernized to the point of wearing their regular trousers, which show in telltale fashion, and of concealing, in the ornaments of their crowns, flashlights which they blink on and off. Their ceremonial origin is lost in obscurity. [GPK]

Chinese folklore Folklore in China is a vital and living force. Whereas elsewhere the student of folklore is frequently embarrassed by lack of data, in China he meets a richness of custom, belief, and ritual which is made more complex by geographical variations and an extraordinarily long and complete written record. Any observations of Chinese folklore in one area can be contradicted by observations in other regions; and conclusions about the folklore of one period of Chinese history need to be checked against conclusions of other periods. In view of the incomplete state of our present knowledge, all conclusions must be tentative.

In general characteristics Chinese folklore is identical with the folklore of other peoples. Before the 5th century B.C. it had stratified into the lore of the aristocrats and the lore of the populace although social revolution and the passing of feudalism tended to confuse these distinctions. Chinese folklore has been modified by the rise of philosophical schools, the migration of religious systems, and the tides of politics, but its essential outlines come generally from the large, complex, and as yet only partially known corpus of beliefs and practices characteristic of all eastern Asia. This corpus with its modifications is very clearly preserved in China today (1949). It can therefore be referred to as "Chinese folklore." Because the Chinese nation is composed of several cultures and many racial strains, the separate contributions made by the predecessors and ancestors of the present inhabitants of China cannot be identified; because the record is continuous it frequently anticipates the western records in its accounts of practices and beliefs. This sort of anticipation has no connections with the "origins" of the practices. Similarly, Occidental students preoccupied with stellar myths, diffusionism, or other attempts to codify imagination have tried to force Chinese beliefs into patterns they prefer. Attempts to explain Chinese folklore, like attempts to explain its origins, are no part of these notes. The capacity of the Chinese to absorb alien customs and beliefs and the ubiquity of folkloristic habits of thought serve as warnings against hasty generalization at the same time that they call for further collection and study of a comparative nature.

Difficulties in the study of Chinese folklore are created by: (a) the long period through which it extends; (b) the size and indefiniteness of the territory in which it exists; (c) the mixture of cultures constituting the Chinese nation and (d) borrowing and lending as between these races; (e) the existence of a scholarly class with great power and prestige; (f) the priestly class which has reworked and rationalized the material. Two further difficulties are: (g) the Chinese written language (the medium through which the history of folklore must be approached) is the property of scholars and thus may be taken as distorting the material it has recorded. Finally, (h) the extensive collections made by missionaries eager to demonstrate the evil effects of the superstitions of others or by ardent ethnographers attempting to impose European systems on Chinese data, though enormously valuable, are incomplete and fail to demonstrate the remarkable variation of custom and belief in the several parts of China.

Pre-History and Early History The Chinese nation as it is known today seems to have had its beginnings in the provinces west of the Shantung peninsula, the regions drained by the Yellow river. Here a belt of early culture stretched from a point several hundred miles inland from the sea through the modern provinces of Shantung, Hopei, Honan, Shansi, Shensi, and Kansu toward the indefinite western border of modern China. In this territory, the Shang Dynasty (c. 1500 to 1100 B.C.) reached a high degree of sophistication. Their bronzes are of a "late" type—no early bronzes have as yet been found in China; their divination was by means of ideographs scratched on bone or tortoise shell; their religious system did not differ greatly from systems today still current among the peasant class. Their arts and crafts and manners were highly developed to a point which compares favorably with the more degenerate moments in our classical renaissance or our contemporary civilization. Though early references to "aboriginals" or non-Chinese tribes which still exist in isolated cultural pockets must be treated carefully, scholars are generally agreed that the peoples of the Shang as well as those of some later dynasties were immigrants into the rich and fruitful valley of the Yellow River.

Sources of information for these early periods are not satisfactory. The first classical Chinese histories produced in the Chou Dynasty (c. 1100 to 221 B.C.) were mostly if not entirely destroyed in the Ch'in Dynasty (221–206 B.C.). They were rewritten from various sources by the reformers of the Han Dynasty (206 B.C. to 221 A.D.) with such additions and deletions as seemed useful. Consequently the validity of these histories is subject to serious debate unless confirmed by archeological findings.

The most useful of these early accounts was compiled by the learned and critical Han historian, Ssu-ma Ch'ien. According to this scholar the first rulers of the universe were the 12 Emperors of Heaven who reigned 198,000 years; the 11 Emperors of Earth who reigned 198,000 years (18,000 years each); the 9 Emperors of Mankind, 45,000 years, and the 16 Sovereigns about whom nothing is known. These were followed by the culture heroes, inventors of the arts and crafts, Fu Hsi and Shên Nung, who had serpent bodies and human heads. Shên Nung was the first tiller of the soil, Huang Ti was human. He taught the savage peoples under him the forms of government, crafts, manners, and the proper sacrifices to the gods, mountains, and streams. Yü founded the Hsia Dynasty (c. 2205 to c. 1557 B.C.) which, though recognized by Ssu-ma Ch'ien, is possibly pre-Chinese. Yü spent 13 years regulating the floods which covered the entire country. Because his devotion to duty was so great that during this time he never entered his house, though he passed close enough to hear the cries of his children, he has been revered as the perfect civil servant.

Early Beliefs and Customs Because of the capacity in China for folkloristic agglutination which has preserved very early beliefs into modern times, comments on primitive customs must be taken as highly generalized accounts. The following elements were undoubtedly early in origin: "yin-yang," divination, *wu* cults, the priest kings with their cults of heaven, earth, soil, and grain, and ancestor worship.

Yin-yang, though later elaborated by the Taoists, derives from the basic concept in Chinese culture that balance is the law of existence. The symbol of this belief is a circle bisected by a sine curve. However this symbol may have been interpreted in primitive times, it came at an early date to represent the opposition in balance of the positive and negative forces of the universe; male-female; heaven-earth. The principles thus symbolized became an important part of Lamaism in which the portrayal of sexual union represented the highest balance of which mankind was capable, opposition in unity. The attribution of male (yang) and female (yin) characters not only to heaven and earth but to the parts of the human body is important in Taoism, geomancy, and folk medicine. The maintenance of balance and harmony is found also in divination of auspicious or inauspicious days for new undertakings in that any new act which deviates from the customary on the yang side or the yin side must be undertaken only when the forces of nature are favorable to the restoration of the balance. The maintenance of balance induces serenity and has had much to do with the preservation of the rites and sacrifices.

Divination in the Shang Dynasty was part of the aristocratic cult. Ideographs were scratched on bones and tortoise shell and treated with heat. Priests interpreted the cracks which subsequently appeared. The questions put had to do most frequently with the proper days for sacrifices, journeys, wars. The ideographs were similar to the current "characters," though of a much earlier form, and in many cases were sufficiently removed from the primitive "pictographs" to justify the conclusion that the peoples who used them had a culture requiring the use of non-pictorial abstractions. The fact that millions of Chinese still consider the written character as sacred and to be preserved from all defilement, and the traditional and present position in China of the learned scholars suggests that knowledge of the written character and knowledge of how to interpret the oracle bones were the secret lore of the priests.

The *wu* priests undoubtedly operated in both the aristocratic and the popular cults. Their learning was transmitted through their colleges. Their ritual which included trance states, singing, and dancing is thought by some Chinese scholars to have contributed to the development of the Chinese theater. Mediumistic practices were important. Many of their rites were similar to those of the shamans recently observed in Mongolia, Siberia, and elsewhere.

Yin-yang, divination, and the professional *wu* priests were part of the agrarian Shang culture. The patriarchal Chous (c. 1000 B.C.) introduced king-priests, worship of the male ancestors, and an astral religion.

The priest kings had as their most important duty the pacification of T'ien or Heaven, personified as Shang Ti, of Earth or Ti, a flat surface opposed to T'ien. T'ien was yang (male) and Ti was yin (female). Hou T'u was the God of the Fields, Shê the God of Soil, and Hou Chi the God of Millet. Only the Emperor as Son of Heaven could perform the ceremonies to Heaven. At various times he also sacrificed to the Lords of Earth and Millet—possibly an example of the agglutination of Shang (agrarian) and Chou (nomadic) traditions; the lesser kings and aristocrats performed the lesser ceremonies for their specific areas. The sacrifice to Heaven was performed on the first day of the agricultural year which in the lunar calendar and in the basin of the Yellow River marks the coming of Spring. At this time Imperial calendars were issued which for the next year controlled the days of planting, harvest, and other domestic activities. Grain from the imperial granaries was distributed. The green and yellow garments worn at this time by the Emperor, the Son of Heaven, are interesting though insufficient evidence that he represented an earlier "corn king."

Ancestor worship, of great importance in modern times and connected with the fertility cults, was highly developed in the earliest records. The cult generally maintains that man has two souls: the animal soul, *p'o*, is created at the moment of conception; the spirit soul, *hun*, enters the body when a child is born. The physical soul, p'o, follows the dead body to its tomb, is nourished by the sacrifices of descendants, and is dissipated as the body disintegrates. If the p'o should escape and find other means of nourishing itself it becomes a *kuei* (ghost or demon) and creates untold mischief. The spiritual soul, hun, if it escape the earth spirit which devours it and the Heavenly Wolf which guards the gate of Shang Ti, ascends to the palace of Heaven Himself and is there sustained by the sacrifices of descendants, replies to their divinations, and intercedes for them. If, because of the extinction of a clan, the sacrifices cease, both the p'o and the hun become hungry, miserable, and malicious demons. The attempts made by some scholars to identify these cults, which exercise considerable authority among contemporary Chinese, with primitive fertility cults are incomplete. Nevertheless it is possible that the tablets before which the sacrifices are placed in the ancestral temples have a phallic origin which has since been forgotten.

Sacrifices followed patterns known in other cultures. In early times the soul of the aristocrat was probably followed by the souls of his wives and retainers sacrificed for that purpose. In modern times papier-mâché figures are burned at the grave to perform the same function. The God of the Yellow River in ancient times claimed each year a beautiful maiden as his bride. After a period of feasting the girl was dressed in ceremonial clothes, put on a marriage bed in a boat, and launched in the river. In modern times the hesitation in some provinces to rescue drowning persons is attributed to an unwillingness to deprive the River of his sacrifice.

Homage was also paid to the spirits of rivers and mountains. Any action which might upset the rhythm of balanced living, the crossing of rivers or mountains, the formation of great or small alliances, the taking of journeys, the transition from one age to another, requires rituals. The mass of these rituals transmitted from antiquity is very great. The weight which modern Chinese give them varies with the character of the individual and the society in which he lives.

The Rationalists Instead of destroying ancient beliefs and customs the rationalists—philosophers, historians, and theologians—of the Chou Dynasty preserved and reinterpreted them. During the Chou Dynasty, scholars who inherited that part of the learning of the professional priests of the Shang Dynasty that had to do with reading and writing attained power at the courts of emperors and kings. With the disintegration of the Empire, the dissolution of manners and morals, and the rise of the "hundreds schools" many opposing tendencies appeared.

One was represented by Confucian philosophers, another by Taoists. The Confucianists maintained that the Chinese must return to the practices of the wise rulers of earlier times. The consequence was research into the past and codification of legends and rituals in the Five Classics of the Confucian canon. These are: *I Ching*, the Book of Changes, largely devoted to the arts of divination, particularly the "P'a Kua," eight trigrams; *Shu Ching*, Book of History; *Li Chi* and *Chou Li*, Books of Rites; *Shih Chin*, Book of Poetry; and *History of Lu*. The first four of these were at one time thought to have been written by Confucius but now authorship of only one, *History of Lu*, is tentatively ascribed to him. All four of these repositories of early Chinese folklore have two characteristics in common, in addition to the fact that the restorations of the Han scholars have preserved texts of dubious authenticity. First, having been compiled originally in a period of rationalization induced by rapid and disconcerting social changes, they represent at best the views of Chinese antiquarians of the 5th century B.C. who were concerned with the regeneration of their people. Second, though the Confucian school has enjoyed great popularity in China during the last 2000 years, the authority ascribed to the ancient beliefs has been subject to the sorts of distortion seen in other countries. Allegorization, moralization, euhemerism, and the like have modified the beliefs. Among 450,000,-000 Chinese the tendency to behave as though in accordance with Confucian teaching cannot be ascribed entirely to the influence of the Great Master. The Confucian doctrines seem to have been an answer to an ethnic need, the formulation of a doctrine which crystallized an important quality in the ethos of the peoples of that part of the world. For the folklorist who has the patience to interpret them and for the comparatist who can free himself from preconceptions, the Five Classics are a rich and untended field.

A second philosophical school made more important contributions to the preservation of Chinese folklore than the Confucianism to which it is opposed. The Taoists representing an antinomianism opposed to the rationalism of the Confucianists are thought to have derived from a philosopher who, if he had much influence on them, lived more than a century before Confucius. The Taoist cult as it has existed with many ups and downs during the last 2000 years is a huge repository of popular belief and superstition. Though the Taoist canon has been catalogued it still awaits systematic study. The Taoists sought the Tao (pronounced Dow) or Way. This is the balance between the individual and the complex and ever-changing forces of the external world, physical, human, and supernatural, to the end that having attained complete harmony, immortality will result. Taoists studied physiology with the thought that proper exercises at proper times would correct an excess of the yin element over the yang or vice versa. Elaborate physical exercises became rituals to conserve energy and induce serenity. In chemistry while searching for the philosopher's stone of immortality they discovered or exploited gunpowder and other inventions. Divination was important in anticipating factors in the universe which were favorable or unfavorable, and talismans attracted good and warded off evil. The rites associated with the passage from one phase of life to another, birth, adolescence, marriage, death, were collected and performed with many variations in the several parts of China.

Several distinctions must be made when thinking about Chinese Taoism and Confucianism. These two philosophical systems must be distinguished from the popular cults which bear their names. Though the Confucian cult is somewhat battered by the impact of Occidental ideas along the coast and by the great revolutions through which China is passing, its rituals are still preserved in the interior, and Confucian proverbs and legends are known to all Chinese. Though Chinese scholars now have to devote to their own study of Occidental science the time their fathers spent in the study of the Confucian classics, they are Confucian by principle. Similarly the organization of the Taoists with a central "pope" and thousands of convents of priests and nuns who devoted their lives to the attainment of The Way has disintegrated. The temples now are likely to be filled with priests ignorant of the complex lore of their discipline, mumbling words and performing rituals to forgotten gods.

A third powerful influence in Chinese folklore is Buddhism. Though Confucianism and Taoism can be seen to have derived from customs and beliefs generally characteristic of eastern Asia, Buddhism, which in its popular form had a line of descent alien to China, was an importation which the peoples of China accepted. The Bodhisattvas became Pusas (Gods) and the Chinese peasant neither knows nor cares whether the god to whom he brings sacrifices of incense or gifts is Buddhist or Taoist. He is interested only in whether that god is able to avert the evil or achieve the good which for that moment is needed.

A reading of Chinese folklore shows evidence of many other importations which have become part of the corpus of belief and practice. Important contributions came from the lamaist north and the Tantrist south, as well as from hundreds of tribes which have wandered in and out of the territory now known as China, and have been absorbed in whole or in part to contribute to the complex phenomena known as Chinese culture. It is not without significance that Marco Polo's image is found in many temples and that Chinese students coming to modern universities in China have been known to "pacify the god of the machine" before beginning their experiments.

General Structure of Chinese Folklore An examination of the customs and beliefs of any region of China in any period is apt to find implicit in them one or more parts of a general structure. Although in our present state of ignorance the quantity of material is imposing and parts of the data contradict each other, the general structure does tend to emerge.

The universe is governed by Shang Ti, thought of as the Supreme Ruler or Heaven, or Yü Huang, the Jade Emperor, the highest of all things, physical or spiritual. The Taoists teach that government is carried on through an elaborate bureaucracy of Spirits and Powers who report to the Supreme Being and carry out his mandates. In some regions the attributes of Yü Huang are similar to those of the Buddhist divinity Indra, and some authorities assert that Yü Huang was invented by Taoists who were competing with the Buddhists during periods of Buddhist popularity.

Government by the Supreme Power is carried on through many bureaus of which three groups may be taken as typical. The gods of the cities control life in the villages and towns; the gods of place control life in the country; and the Kitchen God controls life in the home. The many Ch'eng Huang, Gods of the Cities and Villages, report to Shang Ti on the problems and trouble-makers of their administration much as the mandarins and village elders report to their own higher administrative offices. The Gods of Place or Locality, the T'u Ti, whose temples are scattered in the fields, are for the peasant a direct approach to Heaven. Acknowledgment is made to them in moments of crisis, fear, hope, gratification. Events in the household are noted by Tsao Chün or Tsao Wang, the Kitchen God, who reports once a year on the behavior of each family.

The nether world contains 10 courts, each ruled by a king and subdivided into 16 wards. Most important of these courts is the Fifth, controlled by King Yen Lo. The 10 courts of Hell and their wards together with the tortures inflicted in each are depicted in the temples of the City Gods, the Ch'eng Huang. Heaven punishes serious crimes by the Thunder God, Lei Kung. Lei Kung has a bird's head and claws and holds a hammer and drum, or a string of drums and a chisel. Although some authorities assert that there is only one Thunder God and explain the tardiness of divine punishment by the fact that one god cannot be in every place at once, others report that Lei Kung is President of a Ministry of Thunder with emissaries to carry out his orders which are frequently received through official channels. If the person whom Lei Kung is to destroy dies before he arrives, he will destroy the tomb with thunder. It is significant that persons guilty of great crimes can be protected by persons of great virtue.

Heaven decrees the moment of death. At this moment Yen Lo, Prince of the Fifth Court of Hell and judge of the lower regions dispatches his officers. The soul is judged according to the Book of Destiny which contains a record of his acts in this and in all previous existences. Buddhist ideas dominate the traditions of those who are concerned about these matters. The 128 hot hells, the 8 cold hells, the 8 dark hells, and the 84,000 other hells of Buddhist lore are modified and improved upon in several parts of China. The rationalist Confucian tradition has little to do with this aspect of folklore and the Taoists have attempted to introduce some simplification. The judges of Hell who are instructed by the government officials of the human world treat them, their human colleagues, with considerable respect. All power, whether in Hell, on Earth, or in Heaven derives from the Supreme Power.

At the moment of death one or more officers from Hell display their warrant and make the arrest. Several roads lead to Hell. One of them passes through a cave in the western province of Szechuan. Another route is through a dust cloud which blinds the soul. In any case, the journey is painless and often the soul is astonished at its whereabouts. The souls of persons who come to a premature death or souls which for one reason or another are not able to follow the normal course become malicious demons. The souls of persons who commit suicide haunt the place where the deed was done and attempt to make others commit suicide. If they are successful they will reincarnate themselves in the suicide's body. When people are murdered, their souls, too, haunt the place of the crime and inflict punishment.

Demons, spirits, ghosts constitute an important part of the population of China. In addition to errant souls one may meet other demons, spirits, fairies, gods. Until adequate comparative studies have been made, Chinese terminology translated into Occidental terminology will continue to cause confusion. It is clear that all things are informed by one or more spirits, *hsien*. The lore of the hsien is particularly complex. The ideograph is a combination of the symbol for "man" and the symbol for "mountain." The term is variously translated as "spirit," "demon," "fairy." These ubiquitous spirits can become invisible or can manifest themselves in the form of friends or relatives. It is frequently difficult to know whether the woman in the house who has begun to act strangely is the wife of one's bosom as one had supposed or a hsien who has taken her place. Thus the beggar at the door, the prostitute, the stranger in the street may be simple human beings or they may be demons in human form plotting schemes which are certainly malicious and probably wicked.

The two souls of man may mingle with the throng of demons, spirits, ghosts, and at times can be distinguished only by specialists. The rational Confucianists assert that the superior soul is dissipated after death; some Taoists teach that it resides in Hell, and the Buddhists that it is reincarnated. Despite differences in dogma, belief in reincarnation is common. The superior "hun" sometimes takes possession of the body of a human being or animal recently deceased. A soul which has left its body may return to it if the body has not decomposed and if another soul has not already taken possession. Thus among the Chinese the idea of the resurrection of the dead is not particularly extraordinary, a fact which, according to a Jesuit deeply learned in these matters, "ne prouve pas grand'chose." A "hun" may take possession of the body of any creature whose own "hun" is for one reason or another elsewhere. In these cases it speaks through the man's mouth and is difficult to identify except that the individual is seen to behave in extraordinary ways. The inferior "p'o" informs the physical body and after death, i.e. the final departure of the "hun," preserves it until, its strength having been exhausted, the body decays. When the inferior soul is very strong it makes the body commit terrible crimes, kill and devour others, violate women. If these physical souls have great physical stamina they may cling to skeletons and commit the most horrible outrages. In addition to these superior and inferior souls, each part of the body has its own spirit or coteries of spirits.

During sleep the superior soul leaves the body and goes about its own affairs which become the substance of dreams. Sometimes on its wanderings the superior soul is frightened or captured and is not able to find its body again. Sometimes the inferior souls appear to behave rationally and because the superior souls seem to have the same appearance as the human creature in costume and feature, the individual seems to be in two places at once. Some people are able to send their souls out to report events in distant places.

The souls of men, animals, and things enjoy the pleasures and vices enjoyed by living human beings. At times these pleasures are innocent, though the fox spirits, the hu hsien, are libidinous and great drunkards. At times the spirits show kindnesses to human beings to reward them for kindnesses rendered the spirits—when, for example, they were hiding from the Thunder God. At other times they make use of human beings to increase their own power.

Geomancy, divination, fortune-telling, astrology are complex sciences. The purpose of each is to discover fortunate and unfortunate influences. Houses, tombs, and palaces should face the south and should be located properly near the veins of strength so that they may absorb the yang (male) influences which produce strength. They should be protected at the back by high mounds or trees which screen off the yin (female) influences from the north. By attracting errant spirits, pagodas in the neighborhood protect the household from evil or discomfort. In houses haunted by ghosts and other spirits shrines must be built in the proper places to pacify and nourish and keep the haunts generally good-natured. The diviners and fortune-tellers make use of the devices common in other places: trances, cards, dice, and the random choice of symbolic objects. They and the astrologers who study destiny in terms of the year, day, and hour of birth are much concerned about maintaining the balance of forces. Thus the great movable feasts of birth, marriage, and burial, together with many other activities, sowing and harvesting, the eating of certain foods at certain times, even sexual intercourse, will have good or evil consequences if performed at the right time and place.

The Chinese Calendar A brief review of the Chinese calendar may illustrate the scope of Chinese folklore. Although the Chinese year is frequently referred to as the moon year and the calendar as the lunar calendar, it is in fact a combination of lunar and solar calendars. It has 12 months, "moons," the solar cycle; and each moon has 28 days, the lunar cycle. Intercalation of extra moons makes the cycle come out right. The years are grouped in cycles of 12 each and each of them has the name of an animal. These are similar to the symbols on the Greco-Chaldean zodiac. The 28 days of the lunar month also have names and each is auspicious or inauspicious for human action. In Chinese reckoning the year is further divided into 24 two-week periods of 15 days each. These are the joints and breaths of the year and serve as accurate dividers of the seasons. Finally the days are divided into twelve periods, each two hours long. These periods also have the names of animals and each is either yin or yang. Thus before undertaking any action it is important to know the influences which govern the hour, the day, and the year.

The festivals of the seasons are observed in China with many regional variations. The First Moon, the beginning of Spring, is everywhere filled with ceremony. All work is supposed to cease during the first days of this moon and the period is generally one of renewing relations with family, friends, and deceased ancestors and of taking precautions that the new year will bring good fortune, i.e. money and babies. During this time the household gods and the spirits of the ancestors return to the home and are received with ceremonious offerings of food and drink. On the Third Day of the First Moon, the Chinese sacrifice to Tsai Shên, the God of Wealth. The early part of the month is a period of friendship, rejoicing, and new resolutions.

The mistress of the house purifies it by carrying a pan filled with steaming vinegar into each room. Exorcists break the spell of bad luck if the family has been unfortunate. Each of the first ten days has a special significance. The first is the birthday of fowls, the second of dogs, the third of pigs, and so forth. The public bath houses reopen on the fourth, the day of ducks. On the sixth, the day of horses, one should visit relations; and on the seventh, the birthday of mankind, one should remain at home and eat red beans, 7 for the man and 14 for the woman, to protect oneself against sickness. Li Ch'un, the beginning of Spring, is a movable feast which usually falls about the seventh to the tenth days of the First Moon. It once was celebrated with processions and the sacrifice of an ox or water buffalo. The Feast of the Lanterns, on the 15th day of the First Moon is vaguely associated with prosperity and longevity. Offerings are made to all the stars on the 18th day, and on the 19th the household should retire early because that is the rats' wedding night. This is also the day the Gods visit the Supreme Being, married daughters visit their parents. Near the end of the month the great fairs open in the large towns.

The Second Moon is a period of homage to the Sun God and the Earth Gods. The 19th is the birthday of one of the most popular of all Chinese divinities, Kuan Yin, who in Buddhist lore was Avalokitesvara, Lord of Love and Compassion, born of Buddha's tears of pity for the suffering world. As the cult moved into China, Avalokitesvara became transformed from a male into a female deity. In China Kuan Yin is the compassionate goddess. Although many theories have been advanced to explain the place of Kuan Yin in Chinese folklore, it is possible that this comparatively recent divinity has usurped the functions of the other matriarchal cults. The birthdays of Confucius and Lao Tze also occur in the Second Moon.

The Spring festival, Ch'ing Ming, is movable and occurs 106 days after the winter solstice. This usually is near the beginning of the Third Moon. Granet has given reason to believe that in early times this was the occasion of orgiastic fertility ceremonies. At this time too homage is paid at the graves of ancestors, an assurance that the line of descent is unbroken. Other festivals of the Third Moon are the birthday of Hsi Wang Mu, the Mother of the Western Heavens, pilgrimages to several of the temples, and reverence to the literary worthies.

The Fourth Moon is the Summer moon and the eighth day is the birthday of Gautama, the historical founder of Buddhism. In this month too ceremonies honor the Eight Immortals or saints of the Taoist cults. These, once human beings, achieved immortality through disciplines discovered by the Taoists. The Eight Immortals are a happy, fun-loving crew whose antics are the subject of many tales. They travel on clouds, set fire to the ocean, get disgustingly drunk in low dives, and dance over the fields of China and into the gates of Heaven itself.

The Dragon Boat Festival is the principal festival of the Fifth Moon. It is connected with the propitiation of the water spirits. In this, the pestilential moon, rites are performed in honor of the Gods of Medicine and of Exorcism. The 13th day is sacred to Kuan Ti, the God of War.

The rainy season in central China appears in the Sixth Moon when homage is paid to Lung Wang, the King of Dragons. A paper or cloth effigy of the dragon is carried through the streets with a dozen or more coolies acting as bearers. When the rains are late, various expedients are tried to bring them on. The Great Bell near Peking booms all the day. Elsewhere the image of Lung Wang is brought from the temple to view the parched fields. This is also the moon of Ma Wang, Protector of Horses, Niu Wang, Guardian of Cattle, Lu Pan, Patron of Carpenters.

The Seventh, the Moon of the Hungry Ghosts, is the Autumn moon. The festival is similar to the Occidental festival of All Souls' Day and lasts from the 15th to the 30th of the month. On this day food is prepared for the ghosts who have no descendants to care for them, and therefore are always hungry. Lotus-flower lamps are carried through the streets, or at dusk candles are stuck into tiny boats and floated down the streams.

The harvest occurs in the Eighth Moon and is celebrated by theatricals, troupes of entertainers, and stilt-walkers. The Harvest Festival on the 15th of the Eighth Moon is the Moon's Birthday. The 9th Day of the Ninth Moon is the day for mounting the hills and flying kites. The 25th of the Ninth is the birthday of one of the famous City Gods, the Cheng Huang.

The Tenth or "Kindly Moon" opens with the festival of the dead. The Eleventh, the "White Moon," the month of the Winter solstice, is the appropriate time for sacrifices to the ancestors and for weddings. The Twelfth or "Bitter Moon" marks the beginning of preparations for the New Year. On the 20th the houses are cleaned. On the 23rd the Kitchen God, his lips smeared with honey so that he will speak no evil, is burned and begins his ascent to Heaven where he will report on the behavior of the family during the year. By midnight of the last day of the year all debts must be paid. The Gate Gods who protect the house against evil spirits are pasted on the doors.

The Festivals of Life The ceremonies attendant on the transition from one state of being to another have, like most folkloristic data, a dual significance: some of them are obviously superstitious, sometimes admittedly so and sometimes denied; at other times they are social ceremonies which relieve emotional strain and give the participants a sense of increased social security. In China the use of posters and pious maxims pasted on the walls are at the same time the expression of hope and the substitute for prayer. It may be noted in passing that students of Occidental lore face a similar problem with the "God Bless our Home" captions in many American houses. Similarly social gatherings at moments of transition, such as birthdays, confirmations, engagement parties, are in one sense clearly social and in another a realization that danger attends these moments when an accustomed phase of being is exchanged for a new one.

Birth Most of China is patrilocal. Not only is the line carried through the male, but the head of the house performs as priest the ceremonies for the ancestors of the group. Male offspring are therefore necessary to assure peace for the ancestral manes and, it may be, their success in the political intrigues they undertake in Heaven. Conversely a powerful ancestor can be of great assistance to those of his descendants still living on the earth. Many sorts of ceremonies are thought to help in getting a male heir. Kuan Yin, whose cult resembles in some respects that of the Great Mother, is potent. In some temples the hopeful parent puts gifts of baby shoes before her image; in others a shoe is stolen from the temple and replaced by a better one when the child is born. Elsewhere images of male infants are stolen and taken to bed. The Daughter of the God of the Sacred Mountain, T'ai Shan, and her attendants are invoked. The attendants are the Lady of Posterity, the Lady of Fecundity, the Lady who Activates Birth, the Lady who Brings the Child. Kuei Hsing, one of the Gods of Literature, receives attention perhaps because scholarship is the road to success in China, although Kuei Hsing's iconography indicates that he was at one time master of other powers. Images of the Unicorn and other beneficent forces receive honor. Pilgrimages to the shrines of local deities, some of them with phallic significance, are useful in producing male offspring. The act of procreation may be attended by ceremonies and precautions. The Taoists have examined not only the year, the moon, the day, and the hours favorable to the procreation of male infants, but have also described the coital positions and other details of procedure most likely to be rewarded by success. These computations are complicated by the year, day, moon, hour when each parent was born. Households which produce only females can break the spell by giving a boy's name to the next girl to be born, or the mother may carry on her chest a small gold knife to frighten the female spirit about to enter her body. The knife will also frighten mischievous demons who plague pregnant women. Attempts to divine the sex of the unborn child differ little from those practiced elsewhere. Talismans to hasten delivery are sometimes pasted on the body of the pregnant woman or burned, mixed with tea, and swallowed. A small mirror is carried as a protection because demons are frightened at the sight of their own faces. When several male children have died in infancy, the next to be born receives a girl's name and is dressed in girl's clothes. This will deceive the evil spirits. On the 15th day of the Eighth Moon, the Moon Goddess' birthday, friends may steal a melon from a neighbor, dress it in baby clothes, and present it to the couple. The theft must be secret. The gift is followed by a feast. The many seeds in the melon are associated with potency. On this same night women do not empty their chamber pots. Neighbors steal them in the hope of having children.

Before delivery a red candle lighted in the bedroom frightens away homeless ghosts who may attempt to dispute possession of the child's body with its own proper spirit. In order not to offend the Lady who Brings the Child, dirty water must be disposed of carefully, poured into a pit, and covered. Persons known to be evil must be kept at a distance during childbirth. On the third day after birth, a cock, here as elsewhere potent in frightening devils and ghosts, is brought into the room. The mother or, if she is too ill, the midwife pays homage. The cock is then sacrificed. On this day the infant is ceremonially bathed, thanks are given to the Lady who Brings Children, and the child's horoscope is cast. During the first month the mother may not enter the houses of neighbors. At the end of the month the child's head is shaved and he is carried in

ceremonial processions in order, according to some authorities, to protect him against fear but more likely for the pleasure of showing him off to the village. The child's cap is decorated with many amulets. In some places earrings are attached, one for a male and two for a female, or nose rings are used to tie the child to life. Circles of cinnabar, the magic drug, are painted on the child's face to deter evil spirits.

From birth through maturity to death men pass through many dangerous ages. Each period of growth is attended by ceremonies which show a realization that the process of growing up and dying is beset with difficulties. Study of the remedies for the diseases of childhood leads into a fascinating field too complex even to be surveyed at this point. In central China children who keep their parents awake all night are pacified when a notice is tacked to the wall asking passers-by to read it and help the parents get a good night's sleep. One of the most pathetic customs in a country of pathos is "calling back the soul." When an infant has died the mother frequently wanders through the streets holding out its clothes and calling gently, "Where are you playing? Come back home," or "What has frightened you? Come back home," or simply, "Small son, come home."

Marriage After the marriage broker has made tentative arrangements between the families of two young people, the families exchange pieces of paper containing eight characters: two for the year, two for the month, two for the day, and two for the hour of birth. The fortuneteller then decides whether the marriage is possible. Women born under the sign of the Tiger for example are always dangerous though men born under this sign have special qualities. Gifts are exchanged. If after three days no inauspicious event has occurred, the contract is sealed and the ceremonies continue. The choice of wedding gifts is important. Fruits containing many seeds are propitious. Several days before the wedding the costumes are purified by being passed over flames (the male element). After this they may not be touched by woman (the female element), particularly a pregnant woman or one in mourning, as these conditions strengthen the female influence. The day of the marriage is chosen by persons deeply learned in the complex lore of divination, but must always be during the waxing, never during the waning moon. If the bride dies before the ceremony the groom may be given a pair of her slippers. He burns incense before them, not because they contain her soul, as the Jesuits assert, but because they have an obscure phallicism. The bride is well supplied with amulets. One of them is a purse in the form of a lotus which is sometimes thought to protect her against the slanders of her mother-in-law. The bride makes the trip from her father's to her husband's home in a sealed sedan chair. At this moment she is imbued with female (yin) force and this powerful virginity must be protected against any male (yang) influence. The bride is carried over the threshold. After many ceremonies, now mostly regarded as merely social, the couple prostrate themselves before the tablets of the groom's ancestors. This act fixes the marriage. They then enter the nuptial chamber where the bride remains for an entire day. The male members of the family and close friends are permitted to come into this room and to subject the young woman to the most indecent conversation imaginable. The girl's behavior during this ordeal is carefully noted by the groom, his mother, and friends.

Death and Burial The disposition, the repose, and the happy journey of the soul are matters of great importance to the family. The dying man is placed on another bed and carried outside so that the household bed will not be haunted. His pillow is taken away from him and destroyed and his burial costume is put on. This is as formal and ceremonial a costume as the family can afford. After death the family takes a lantern, a papier-mâché sedan chair, symbolic money, and symbolic food, and accompanies the soul to the shrine of the local God of Place, T'u Ti. After three days and more ceremonies the soul is accompanied by the family and T'u Ti from this shrine to the shrine of the local God of the District, who in turn will accompany it to the shrine of the City God, who will introduce it to the Judge of Hell. The good offices of each of these gods are assured by the offering of gifts, known to the Occident as "bribes." The tablet of the deceased is set up in the ancestral temple, and the date of burial is chosen by the fortune-tellers as the place is chosen by the geomancers. Before the body is taken for burial crowds of priests and professional mourners create a terrific uproar. The funeral processions are often very elaborate and are designed both to keep the physical soul attached to the body, for an errant soul is a great nuisance, and to make the journey of the superior soul pleasant and profitable. Paper concubines, servants, money, food, sedan chairs are provided for his comfort. In modern China paper automobiles and airplanes replace the sedan chairs. A white rooster rides on the catafalque. At the tomb the gifts for the soul are protected from thieving spirits by circles marked with chalk. Ceremonies for the repose of the soul, sometimes very elaborate, may be continued for years. The oldest son as the family priest, must at regular intervals perform ceremonies before the ancestral tablets.

General No general outline of a folklore as alive and protean today as it was a thousand years ago can give an adequate sense of the quality of Chinese popular beliefs and customs. The attempts of the Taoists, deeply learned in the popular beliefs of their part of the world, to sort them out into systems have been baffled by the capacity of the Chinese to create new gods, to accept strange gods as Westerners accept patent medicines because they are supposed to be helpful in this or that situation, and to create legends. The myths and legends of the Greeks and Romans can be studied because so few have been preserved for us; the myths and legends of the Chinese have not been studied in a systematic sense because there are too many of them. The thousands of major and minor deities who constitute the bureaucracies of Heaven and Hell, the hundreds of stellar deities, the Bodhisattvas, the arhats, the lohans, and the many others referred to by the populace as spirits or gods or Pusas, not to mention the tens of thousands of shape-shifting foxes, and other shape-shifting animals, plants, and stones, constitute an enormous population of which no census has been taken. In Chinese legends the localization of a floating tale on the person of a known historical figure for reasons which are obscure is a common practice which distorts the folkloristic meanings of the legend itself. The Chi-

nese folktale follows the little known laws of that type of imagination as seen in other countries. All of the themes listed in the current directories are to be found in China and some of them were recorded several hundred years before they appeared in writing in Europe.

A final difficulty in accounting for Chinese folklore is the difficulty which besets all students of folklore, namely these traditions, beliefs, and practices are created and preserved to assure the mental health of communities and individuals and thus are projections of human fears and aspirations. They therefore involve social mechanisms which Western scientists, preoccupied with physical nature and indifferent to human nature, have had little time to study.

Bibliographical notes: Doré, le Père Henri, *Recherches sur les Superstitions en Chine,* 14 vols., Shanghai, 1911–1919, is the great treasury from which all Western students of Chinese folklore draw shamelessly. Doré's attempt to learn all he could about Chinese folklore in order to demonstrate that Chinese religious beliefs were inferior to his own frequently got him into tight spots. His wide reading of Chinese sources and his scholarly conscience compensate for lack of objectivity. The volumes need an index; but because the pagination is erratic and the structure of the volumes is *ad hoc* rather than logical, indexing is difficult. Doré's one volume conspectus, *Manuel des Superstitions Chinoises,* Chang-Hai, 1926, is useful. E. T. C. Werner's *A Dictionary of Chinese Mythology,* Shanghai, 1932, is for the most part an alphabetical list of the data contained in Doré, though Werner added much from his own wide reading. His *Myths and Legends of China,* London, 1922, is verbose and opinionated. J. J. M. de Groot, *The Religious System of China,* 6 vols., Leyden, 1892–1910, does for the Protestants what Doré did for the Catholics. De Groot was a very distinguished Sinolog and his book contains valuable material. Because China has no "religious system" and its many cults are complex and interrelated, de Groot's initial confusion is often communicated to the reader. Juliet Bredon and Igor Mitrophanov's *The Moon Year,* Shanghai, 1927, and Bredon's *Peking,* Shanghai, 1931, contain much sound material though in the "pretty-pretty, quaint-quaint" style. In Le Père L. Wieger's *Folk-lore Chinois Moderne,* Hsien hsien, 1909, literal translations of Chinese texts for all periods enable the reader to form his own conclusions. As the Chinese text is included, the unlearned Westerner can decide what sort of "god," "demon," "spirit," "fairy," "immortal," the Chinese character "hsien" may be referring to in any given context. (De Groot's *Religious Systems* also contains the Chinese texts.) R. D. Jameson's *Three Lectures on Chinese Folklore,* Peking, 1932, though centrally concerned with popular narrative contains a bibliography. Western Sinologs working in the Confucian tradition have been more concerned with the Classics, the Official Histories, and with the application of "Western historical method" to Chinese data than with folklore. Thus the several thousand volumes which Chinese scholars of the last 2000 years have written about their own folklore cry for attention. These contain dictionaries, summaries, treatises. Until the data in these have been summarized and organized all discussions of Chinese folklore must remain on the unsatisfactory level of broad generalization found in these notes.   R. D. JAMESON

Chinese folktales Chinese folktales deserve special mention because the collections are so much more rich in variety and extensive in historical time than the collections of other peoples. In China all fiction is regarded as merely popular and not worthy the attention of serious men. Consequently until recently the distinction has not been made between popular and other tales and all collections of stories are rich in folktale material. All of the themes and most of the variants listed in the handbooks of the *Märchenforscher* are known in China. At times complete versions were published in China hundreds of years before they were published in Europe. Thus Des Perrier's story of Pernette in *Nouvelles Récréations*, 1558, the first European version of one of the complete Cinderellas, was anticipated in China by 700 years in Tuan Ch'eng Shih's *Yu Yang Tsa Tsu*, published in the middle of the T'ang Dynasty. In other instances it is possible to observe in China the transformation of an historical episode through successive tales, novels, and plays into one of the popular themes of Occidental folktale. Thus an incident in the history of the Sung Dynasty was changed through successive tellings until it became a clear example of the Occidental theme of the persecuted queen. In another series of tales Chinese versions and Occidental versions exist together and though the Chinese tell one version more frequently than the other, both versions are known. In the story of the shape-shifting fox most common in China, a student retires to a secluded temple to prepare for his official examinations. He meets and loves a beautiful strange girl who by her sexual prowess reduces him to the point of death. Sometimes she leaves because she feels compassion for him. Sometimes she is unmasked and driven away. Most frequently she leaves because having exhausted his vital essence she has no more to gain from him. In another series of tales a farmer finds his house cleaned and his dinner on the stove each night when he returns from the fields. One day he hides and sees a fox enter his house, shed its skin, and become a beautiful woman. He steals the skin and makes the woman his wife. Many years later she finds her fox skin, becomes a fox again, and deserts the farmer. An "Index of Chinese Folk-Themes" still in manuscript contains several thousand variants of this sort. The following contributions by Wolfram Eberhard are invaluable: *Chinese Fairy Tales and Folk Tales*, 1937; *Typen Chinesischer Volksmärchen*, FFC, 1937; *Volksmärchen aus Südost China*, 1941. [RDJ]

Chingichnich A deity of the American Indian tribes of southern California (Juaneño, Luiseño, Gabrieleño, Chumash, Diegueño): known as Kwawar among the Juaneño, and as the Creator of the Gabrieleño. Among the Luiseño Chingichnich is the god who ordained the sacred practices of the initiation rites, and who dictates the conduct of daily life. He is the chief figure in a pantheon which includes four brothers who are connected with the earthquake. The chief ceremony which Chingichnich instituted was the initiation ceremony of jimsonweed-drinking; among tribes to the north of those mentioned above, Chingichnich is not recognized as a deity, but it is said that jimsonweed was once a man who told the people he would die and be changed into a plant, and that they must drink a decoction made from his roots, for health and to obtain visions. [EWV]

Ch'ing Ming Pure Brightness: a Chinese Spring festival which falls 106 days after the Winter solstice, usually early in April. It has obvious though somewhat obscure connections with fertility in the home and in the field. On this day people visit the graves of their ancestors in the fields and tidy them up. Willow wands and chaplets are customary. Ch'ing Ming is also the official day for planting trees, Arbor Day, and is one of the few customs carried over from Imperial China and sponsored by the Republic. In the T'ang Dynasty the children of courtiers made fires on this day by rubbing willow sticks together in the Imperial courtyard. Marcel Granet's stimulating study of the Spring festival in ancient China (*Fêtes et Chansons Anciennes de la Chine*, Paris, 1919) has not been followed by competent examinations of this seasonal festival in later periods. [RDJ]

Ch'in-Kuang Lord of the first of the ten Taoist hells. He receives all souls and decides what body the soul must next inhabit in order to atone for its sins and acquire merit. Ch'in-Kuang thus controls the span of human life. Souls are dispatched quickly if their good deeds balance their evil ones. Wicked souls are forced to see in a mirror all the evil they have done. Persons who have taken their own lives to bring grief to an enemy, rather than because of loyalty to a prince, filial piety, or preservation of chastity, are returned to earth where they wander as hungry and homeless ghosts until the person they have harmed has recovered. Lazy priests, who have taken money but have not read the prayers they promised, are put into a dark room lighted only by a tiny lamp which is always going out, and are forced to read the prayers they have omitted. [RDJ]

Chinūn Way Shun In Kachin (Burma) belief, the nat who existed before the formation of the world and who created the other important nats (Chitōn, Mu, Sinlap, Ponphyoi, Mbōn, Wăwn, Jān, and Shitta). After their creation Chinūn Way Shun made a pumpkin and called upon these nats. Each added something to it. Chitōn gave legs, Mu eyes, etc., and thus the first man, Shingrawa or Ningkwawnwa, came into existence. Under the name Ka, Chinūn is the spirit of tilth or the nat of the earth.

Chinvatperetu or **Chinvat Bridge** The Parsi bridge of death which stretches from the Peak of Judgment to Alburz; the Bridge of the Decider. This is a many-sided beam with edges which vary from the thinness of a razor blade to the thickness of 27 reeds. When souls of the righteous arrive, the beam turns to a wide side; when the souls of the wicked appear, the bridge becomes thin and sharp, to make their passing painful or impossible. This bridge is the prototype of the Moslem bridge, al-Sirāt.

Chiotikos A modern Greek dance for two girls or a couple: so named for the island of its origin, Chios. The steps are similar to the balances and grapevine of the Greek open rounds; but the two dancers are either face to face with hand-hold, or they pass each other, or turn under each others' upraised arms. The arch motif suggests that the dance may have the same significance as the traditional Greek arch dances, i.e. vernal rite. [GPK]

Chiron or **Cheiron** In Greek mythology, a Centaur, son of Cronus and Philyra, the Oceanid; the wisest of the Centaurs and friend and tutor of many of the Greek heroes. Cronus, to escape Rhea's jealousy, transformed Philyra or himself into a horse. The nymph's labor in bringing forth Chiron proved so terrible that she was changed into a linden tree. The young Chiron was tutored by Apollo and Artemis, and had great knowledge of music and medicine. Among his pupils were Hercules, Æsculapius, Jason, Peleus, Achilles, Theseus, Nestor, Meleager, and the Dioscuri. Chiron was immortal, but in the fight at the cave of Pholus he was accidentally wounded in the knee by one of the poisoned arrows of Hercules. Knowing by his medicine that the wound was incurable, Chiron tried to die and could not. Prometheus however offered to take upon himself Chiron's immortality and the Centaur was transformed into the constellation Centaurus.

Chisholm Trail An American cowboy song running to some hundreds of stanzas with varying refrains, sung to any of five or six tunes, to tell the story of the hardships met on the long cattle drive from San Antonio, Texas, to the grasslands of Montana and the Dakotas, and the celebrations at the end of the journey. One of the most widely sung of cowboy songs, this has had improvised additions to suit the complaints of nearly every man who ever rode the trail. The refrains are mostly imitative of the Indian war whoops used when driving cattle.

Chitragupta In Hindu belief, the recorder of the vices and the virtues of men; the judge who sends men to heaven or hell. Compare THOTH.

Ch'iu Shê The Autumn-Snake Charm of the Chinese Taoist cult: a magical charm used by Taoist priests and nuns for exorcising certain very serious illnesses.

The paper charm represents him as a twice-coiled, banded and spotted snake with a human hatted head. There are also Spring-, Summer-, and Winter-Snake charms, the Female-Snake charm, the One- to Five-Colored-Snake charms, and the One- to Nine-Headed-Snake charms, each a powerful exorcising charm for a specific disease, and each represented by its own paper image.

chlevnik In Russia, a spirit of the cattle shed; one of the species of domovik or household spirit. The chlevnik's good will is necessary for successful cattle-raising, and the owner must select the right location for the shed and accede to the chlevnik's preferences in the color of the cattle. An offering is made to the spirit when a new animal is brought to the farm, else the chlevnik may harm the beast. In some regions, they try to drive the chlevnik out by beating on the walls or making other attempts to frighten it, or the chlevnik may be asked to leave more quietly.

cho-i In the folklore of primitive Queensland peoples, that part of a child's spirit or soul-substance which remains in the afterbirth and from which Anjea makes another baby.

Ch'o-je or **Ch'o-kyoṅ** A group of chief sorcerers of Tibet, believed to be incarnations of the rGyal-po or king fiends, one of the eight classes of indigenous gods. The necromancer-in-ordinary to the Tibetan government (Nä-ch'un) is the highest of these sorcerers.

chorten or **mch'od-r-ten** Literally, receptacle for offerings; a Tibetan funeral monument, usually a solid con-ical masonry structure similar to the Indian stūpa, erected over the remains of Grand Lāmas and in memory of canonized saints: the Tibetan name for the funeral monument erected over the relics of Buddha or his saints. Chortens are favorite objects of pilgrimage and worship by circumambulation. Miniature chortens are carried by itinerant priests from village to village for exhibition, and others, inscribed with sacred sentences, are consecrated by priests and sold as amulets or as votive objects. Compare STŪPA.

Christmas The Mass of Christ; the Christian festival of the Nativity, the physical birth of Jesus Christ, occurring on December 25: in some places, e.g. Armenia, celebrated on January 6, which elsewhere is the festival of Epiphany, the baptism or spiritual birth of Jesus. The festival of Christ's birth was in the early days of Christianity celebrated on various days in December, January, and March, but in the 5th century it became set, in the Western Church, at its present day. Correspondence of the Christian festival with the close of the Roman observances of the Saturnalia (December 17–24) and the *natalis invicti solis*, the Mithraic observance of the birth of the sun, has often been remarked upon and is not an accidental phenomenon. The members of the early church were recruited from among the pagans, and by the establishment of a festival at this time the energy and attention of the proselytes could be focused thus in a Christian festival. There were, within the Church, criticisms of the observance on the grounds of its resembling pagan rites, of its being sun-worship (the Armenians called the Roman Church members idolaters as well, because of the identification of Christmas with the date of the birth of the sun), and, as late as 1644, during the Puritan ascendancy, the English Parliament forbade observance of the festival. The date of the birth of Christ was said to be December 25, A.D. 1, variously called a Wednesday or a Friday, but actually a Sunday.

December 25 is close enough to the winter solstice for other pagan winter festivals besides the Saturnalia which celebrate the turn of the year to have become absorbed in it. The Yule feast of northern Europe, a solstice observance celebrating the lengthening of the day with the return of the sun and concerning itself principally with the spirits of the dead, became adapted to Christmas, and many Christmas customs of today and of the past are those of the Yule season. The Angli, according to Bede, observed December 25 as their New Year's festival; the eve, *modranecht* or mother night, seems to have been a vigil connected with fertility rites. The Wild Hunt (Asgardsreid) was heard in the storms of the winter season, and Frey especially, the god of fertility, was worshipped then.

There are thus two separate traditions meeting with the Christian story of the Christ child. One, more serious than the other, comes from the Yule celebration, which was essentially a feast of the dark ancestral spirits; the second, in happier and lighter mood, stems from the Saturnalia, with its freedom, its leveling of rank and age, its making light of tradition.

Principal popular custom centers in Christmas Eve, the night before Christmas, but most of the observances are not official; they are custom, outside the Church, and "holy" only by association. Then it is that the Midnight Mass is attended. Specifically only the adoration of

the Child in the crib is peculiar to the Christmas ceremony; all other parts of Christmas service and observances, the fasting, the vigil, etc., are common to the other
festivals of the Catholic Church in so far as ritual observance is concerned. The crèche, or representation of
the birth of Christ, with the Holy Family and the ox and
the ass, is said to have been brought into the church itself
by St. Francis. The Christmas story of the travelers overtaken by night and forced to stay among the animals in
the stable, the Child in the manger, the worship of the
Child by the Three Magi led to Bethlehem by the light
of the star, is represented in this crèche, a model often
fashioned in great detail.

Christmas Eve is the night when St. Nicholas comes;
Santa Claus, with his reindeer and sleigh, carries his bag
of gifts down the chimney and fills the stockings of good
children with toys and sweets; the Bonhomme Noël
leaves gifts for French children on the hearth, or his
companion Père Fouettard leaves bundles of switches
for the bad ones. Sometimes it is the child Jesus, le petit
Noël, who brings the gifts. However, the giving of gifts
on Christmas is primarily a northern custom; elsewhere
the gifts (French étrennes, Latin strenæ) are made on
New Year's Day.

The Christmas tree seems a comparatively recent
development, a German custom spreading elsewhere in
the past century and a half, and is perhaps a parallel
to the May-tree, which is of much older tradition. On
Christmas Eve the tree is decorated with tinsel and
lights; beneath or on the branches of the tree are the
gifts for the children and the rest of the family; atop
the tree is the star of Bethlehem or a heralding angel.
The lights on the tree are perhaps a reflection of the
Jewish Hanukkah (the Feast of Lights) which occurs at
this season, for the houses of the Holy Land must have
been lit with them when Jesus was born. However, the
general import of winter solstice festivals everywhere is
that of light and lights, and correspondence of the
Christmas tree and the Hanukkah menorah is probably
incidental. The evergreen tree (sometimes a branch
only) is kept through the festival season and is not discarded until after Twelfth Night. The Yule log too is
burned, and the mistletoe hung up during the Christmas season. The Yule log, a huge piece of wood, is in
some places burned a little during each of the twelve
days of the season. Elsewhere some of it is kept to light
the fire of the next Yule log the following Christmas.
In parts of France it is believed that a piece of the Yule
log, if kept safe during the year, will protect the house
against fire and lightning, will insure bountiful crops,
and enable the cattle to bear their young easily. The
mistletoe, connected with the magic oak of the Celtic
lands, is suspended. Traditionally the girl who stands
under it may be kissed by a boy of the company willy-
nilly, usually the former.

There are countless other traditional Christmas games
and amusements. Christmastide is the time of the costumed mummers and carolers, of the snapdragons and
the apples and nuts on strings or at the end of swinging beams, of the waits, of Hogmanay, and of the Lord
of Misrule. This latter (called in his Scottish version the
Abbot of Unreason until the office was abolished in
1555) was the master of the revels during the whole
season from All Hallows to Twelfth Night. He arranged
the entertainments, he inflicted the penalties he ad-

judged fit, he was the spirit of anarchy. In him was embodied the spirit of the Feast of Fools that prevailed at
the Saturnalia, when all were equals, servants and
masters, slaves and freemen, the spirit of the revolution
that comes with the changing of the year.

Christmas was the time for gifts from tradesmen to
their patrons, the time when servants and underlings
partook of the good things their masters had during the
year. In Russia, the peasants, singing outside the houses
of the lords, were given gifts. The overturning of the
usual course of nature extends to the animals as well.
On Christmas Eve the cattle spoke and kneeled in
honor of the Saviour. But listening to them, or attempting to overhear what was said, was dangerous and oftentimes fatal.

Christmas food is in keeping with the festivity of the
occasion. Special Christmas dishes are as many as the
various localities. The roast pig with the apple or lemon
or orange in its mouth is related to the *julgalti*, the pig
offered to Frey to induce the fertility of the coming
year. In Bohemia, as early as the 15th century, the distributing of apple slices and the baking of white bread
were Christmas customs having some relationship to the
fertility of the coming year.

In keeping with the northern observance of the season
as a period when the spirits of the dead returned, many
of the Christmas customs have to do with receiving
those guests. The house is cleaned and everything is
prepared for Christmas before the family leaves for
church. Then, while the house is unoccupied, the
spirits come and inspect what has been done. They partake of the meal; in northern Sweden, a special table is
spread for them. In northern Germany, it is the Virgin
Mary and her attendant angels who come to eat of the
food. This careful maintenance of good relations with
the ancestral and other spirits is necessary for obtaining
a good year.

Many legends center about Christmas, the great
happy holiday of Christianity. The story of the Glastonbury thorn, brought by Joseph of Arimathea to England, where it flowered every Christmas, is among the
most famous. The revelry of the period is pictured in
the story, told of the court of Charles VI of France, of
the king and his courtiers who dressed in tow and
tar to make believe that they were bears. They were
chained together, and in the drunken rout someone applied a torch to discover who the masqueraders were.
The king escaped alive, but some of the nobles were
burned to death.

Special popular beliefs are widely connected with the
season. A white Christmas presages a prosperous year
to follow; a green, or hot, or cloudy Christmas will fill
the churchyard. An English belief is that the sun shining through the fruit trees on Christmas Day will bring
much fruit. The sound of angels singing will be heard
by one sitting under a pine tree on Christmas Eve, but
death will soon follow, as it will to the one overhearing
the cattle speak at midnight or before dawn. The person born on Christmas Day is able to see spirits, according to a widespread belief.

Christ's-thorn A shrub of Palestine of the buckthorn
family (*Paliurus spina-christi*) with long, sharp thorns:
so called from the belief that Christ's crown of thorns was
made of it. It is so common a shrub throughout Judea

that certain Biblical botanists have said no other similar plant would have been so available. In Ireland the white-thorn is said to be the thorn from which Christ's crown was made.

chrysanthemum From the Greek, golden flower. In Japan the 16-petaled chrysanthemum was the emblem of the Mikado. It has been the national flower of Japan since the 14th century and there is a national festival to the golden variety. In the Far East it is the symbol of purity, perfection, and long life. In Korea the roots are boiled and used for a headache remedy. In Nai Myang, China, there is a spring in a bank of chrysanthemums and this water will enable one to live for a hundred years. Legend says that Keu Tze Tung fled to the Valley of the Chrysanthemum when he accidentally offended the emperor. Here he drank the dew from the petals of this flower and became immortal. The Buddhists, expanding this story, claim he was given a text to write on the petals, and this text gave the dew its power.

chthonic deities The underworld deities, as contrasted with the heavenly deities. Worship of the chthonic deities was an important part of Greek religion, based on propitiation, and requiring, for example, that the entire sacrifice be offered to the god. It is believed that the chthonic gods were originally the ancestral spirits, and that they represented the ghosts of the departed. The correspondence between the form of many chthonic deities, who appeared as snakes in one aspect or another, and the form of the ancestral spirits, which were often conceived of as being tomb-snakes, makes this identification likely. Many of the Olympic gods had their chthonic aspects, e.g. Hermes Chthonius, Zeus Chthonius, and while these Olympic gods were not worshipped with the same trepidation as the wholly chthonic deities, these aspects were combined with other forms of their worship. One example of the fear in which these spirits were held lies in the fact that they usually were nameless, and were called by some euphemism.

Ch'uang Kung and Ch'uang Mu or **P'o** Gods of the Bed in Chinese folk belief; specifically, the Lord of the Bed and the Mother of the Bed. They are propitiated to preserve the bedchamber from quarrels, but their particular function is to insure pregnancy. The Lady of the Bed is fond of wine; the Lord of the Bed prefers tea. They are propitiated with wine, tea, and cakes before the images, and the images are turned to face the bed, while the couple, with clasped hands kowtow three times before the bed. [RDJ]

Chuan Lun King of the tenth of the Taoist hells. Here souls who have expiated their crimes and are to be reincarnated pass over one of six bridges. The Spirit of the Wind then takes them to the Tower of Forgetfulness and gives them a drink which makes them forget their previous existence. [RDJ]

Ch'u Chiang King of the second of the Taoist hells, the hell of thieves and murderers. It consists of a large lake of ice. Ch'u Chiang is honored on the first day of the Third Moon. [RDJ]

Ch'ü Hsieh Yüan The Ministry of Exorcism of the Taoist cult, whose function is to expel demons from houses and otherwise control them. The lore of this ministry has been rationalized by its practitioners until

the ministry has developed into a complicated bureau with seven chief ministers, each entitled Great Heavenly Prince. The most important of these is Chung K'uei, the Great Spiritual Chaser of Demons for the Whole Empire. [RDJ]

Chuku The supreme deity of the Ibo of the Calabar District, eastern Nigeria. *Chi-uku*, literally the great Chi, is the best-known variant of a number of variants of Chi, of which *Chineke* (*chi-na-eke*, the creator) may be taken as an example. [MJH]

chullpas The mummified corpses of the ancestors of the Aymara Indians of South America, about which they tell many fabulous stories. The rectangular funerary structures in which the ancient Aymara buried their dead are also called chullpas. [AM]

Chung Ch'iu The Chinese Harvest or Mid-Autumn Festival; the Festival of the Moon, celebrated on the 15th day of the Eighth Moon by feasts and theatrical performances. The moon represents the female principle, as the sun represents the male; consequently men never make obeisance to the moon. But women and children especially make offerings. Moon cakes, circular in shape, are offered. In some places they are eaten immediately after the festival; elsewhere they are kept until the New Year. Watermelons cut in lotus shape are also appropriate. Effigies of the rabbit and the three-legged toad who can be seen in the moon are common. The rabbit spends his time with mortar and pestle preparing the pill of immortality. Although sufficient evidence exists in the rich records of China to warrant a full-dress study of the seasonal festivals (Spring, Summer, and Autumn) the data has not been brought together in practicable form. [RDJ]

Chung K'uei In Chinese Taoist lore, the "Great Spiritual Chaser of Demons for the Whole Empire": a beneficent and powerful expeller of demons. He is worshipped on the 15th of every month with offerings, and his ma-chung, or paper image, is also burned at this time. His legend is that he was canonized by one of the T'ang Emperors (618–907 A.D.) for freeing the emperor from the red demon of emptiness and desolation. Chung K'uei is one of the seven officials in the Taoist Ministry of Exorcisms. He is especially honored in the Fifth Moon, known as the pestilential, the evil, or the wicked moon. Compare CH'Ü HSIEH YÜAN. [RDJ]

Chu'ngu In Annamese belief, the original owners of the land whose descendants are no longer living; autochthones. The Chu'ngu are jealous of those who now possess their land, so during the first three months of every year each landowner must make a sacrifice to them. Whenever evil befalls a farmer's cattle or crops, it is attributed to the Chu'ngu who are then appeased by sacrifices. To insure protection from them the land is bought from the spirits by the payment of imitation money.

Chu-nhà In Annamese belief, the house guardian who resides in the lime jug. Every household possesses such a jug in which the lime used in preparing betel pellets is stored. If it is broken, it forbodes the death of a member of the family and the broken pieces are carefully placed on or under the trees near a pagoda in order to propitiate its resident, who then takes up residence in the new jug.

churching of women The custom of reading an appointed service when a woman comes to church after a confinement to render thanks to God for her safe delivery and return to health. In England, a mother never crosses the threshold until she has been "churched"; in Scotland, she never sets to work until she has been "kirked." There are certain other tabus for mothers after childbirth in the British Isles but once they have been churched these are removed and women are then free to go about, make visits, and so on. Purification ceremonies for women on this particular occasion were carried out by priest or mediator with lustrations, prayers, or blessings in France, Germany, Italy, Austria; among Negroes and American Indians. Churching is a remnant of the old Mosaic Law (*Lev.* xii) which prescribed purification after any so-called defilement; it is also an echo of the release from more primitive tabus after childbirth with their strenuous requirements. [GPS]

churel In modern Indian belief, the malignant ghost of a woman who dies in childbirth or in a state of ceremonial impurity: originally the ghost of a low-caste person. The churel usually has reversed feet, no mouth and haunts filthy places. Sometimes, in the form of a beautiful young woman, she captures young men and keeps them in her power until they are gray-haired, old men. Spells, propitiation, and exorcism are used to rid an area of such a spirit and the body of a low-caste person is buried face downward to hinder its escape.

churinga or **tjuringa** The Australian Aranda (or Arunta) term for a ceremonial object of much sacredness used in rites of many tribes, where, however, it has different names. A churinga may be a polished stone or piece of wood engraved with the group totem design. When it has a hole in it through which a string is passed, it is called a bull-roarer. Women are told the whizzing sound made by swinging it is the voice of spirits. Sacred objects are kept in caves or rock shelters dangerous for women and the uninitiated boys to come near. A churinga has marvelous properties for healing wounds, especially those caused during circumcision and subincision, and for giving courage and power. [KL]

churning The process by which butter is made, i.e. beating or otherwise agitating cream until the oily globules separate from the other parts. In general European folk belief, sometimes the butter will not come because it is bewitched or because it has been stolen by witches or fairies. In some parts of rural England when the butter refuses to come, a hot horseshoe is dropped into the churn. This is believed to unspell the bewitchment. In some places a horseshoe (or ass shoe) is nailed to the bottom of the churn. In Ireland it is said that a bit of burning turf placed under the churn will keep the fairies from stealing the butter. Even more potent against supernatural theft is a churn handle or crosspiece made of quicken wood, or rowan. But if no rowan went into the manufacture of the churn, women will tie a branch of it around the churn or on the handle for the same reason. In some parts of Ireland it is said that this branch must be cut on May Eve. If a stranger enters the house while the churning is going on, he (or she) must lend a hand to the dash for a moment or the butter will be "abstracted." It is especially good luck to churn before sunrise on a May morning.

Churning of the Ocean In later Hindu mythology, a joint project on the part of the gods and asuras (demons) to recover the Elixir of Immortality, amṛita, lost at the time of the Deluge. When the gods appealed to Vishṇu for renewal of strength he told them to cease temporarily from their eternal war with the asuras for dominion of the world, to join forces with them, collect all plants of all kinds in the world, throw them into the cosmic Milky Ocean, and churn the ocean to recover the precious drink. For this work they were to use Mt. Mandara for a churning-stick and coil the serpent Vāsuki around it for a rope. All this the gods and asuras did, and churned together for a thousand years. Out of the waters rose a number of things of diverse personification and symbolism: first, the Cow, Surabhi, the cow of plenty; then Varuṇī, goddess of wine; Pārijāta, the wonderful coral tree that perfumed the world; then the Apsarases, celestial nymphs a thousand-fold, next rose from the churning; then the moon (see SOMA), and the powerful and terrible poison, said to be twin-liquor to amṛita; next emerged Śrī or Lakshmī, goddess of beauty, bearing a lotus. Last of all came Dhanwantari, physician to the gods, bearing the amṛita in a milk-white bowl. Among other things mentioned as emerging at the Churning of the Ocean are kaustubha, the marvelous jewel worn by Vishṇu (or Krishna), and Airāvata, the milk-white elephant taken by Indra. The story of the Churning of the Ocean is told in the *Mahābhārata*, the *Rāmāyana*, and the *Purānas*.

Chu Yi One of the patrons of Chinese literature: popularly known as Mr. Redcoat. An immortal princess fell in love with him and took him to heaven to live with her. He returned to earth because he preferred studying the classics and becoming an imperial minister to a life of connubial bliss in heaven. [RDJ]

Chyavana In Hindu mythology, a sage who was shriveled with age, the son of Bhṛigu. The Aśvins tried to seduce his young wife, Sukanyā, who remained faithful to her husband and taunted the two horsemen with being incomplete. She promised to explain the taunt if they would make her husband young. This they did by telling him to bathe in a certain pond. She in turn explained that they were incomplete because they were excluded from the gods' sacrifice. Chyavana compelled the gods to permit the Aśvins participation in the soma ceremonial by creating a fearful demon, Mada, who threatened to devour Indra unless he agreed.

CIAP The International Commission on Folk Arts and Folklore is an international institute for ethnological and folklore research. It was founded in 1928 under the auspices of the League of Nations on the occasion of the first International Congress of Folk Arts and Folklore held in Prague. Its statutes were revised during the 3rd General Assembly which CIAP held in Paris in 1947. Its aim is the comparative study of the life and customs of peoples and its field extends to ethnology and folklore. It proposes to promote studies and coordinate research on a world scale. Its principal object is to bring out the concordance of the essential aspirations of Man, in spite of the peculiar features of each culture.

CIAP is composed of members and associates elected by the General Assembly by co-option in view of their competence in the relevant field of CIAP's activity. National committees or societies contribute in each country to the accomplishment of CIAP's program. CIAP has at the present moment some thousand members.

The governing bodies of the CIAP are the General Assembly, the Governing Board, the Secretary-General. The Governing Board meets, in principle, every year, and the General Assembly every three years. The Governing Board of the CIAP is composed as far as possible of representatives of every nationality. At the present moment (March, 1949) 62 nationalities are represented. The CIAP has one President, and six Vice-Presidents, who are, to some extent, the representatives of the different continents.

The CIAP is a foundation member of the International Council for Philosophy and Humanistic Studies, created in 1948 under the auspices of UNESCO, which contributes to the financing of this work. The fact of belonging to this Council in no way diminishes its autonomy or scientific independence. Within the Council CIAP represents ethnology and folklore studies.

CIAP's scientific work is divided into ten Sections: 1) Bibliography. 2) Theory, Methodology, Terminology. 3) Museums, Collections, Archives, Libraries, Information centers. 4) Habitation, Work, Technology. 5) Society, Religion, Law. 6) Literature. 7) Dramatic arts and games. 8) Plastic and decorative arts, Costume. 9) Music and Dance. 10) Exhibitions, public performances and festivals, workers' spare time. This division has been made purely for convenience in work and is not intended to be rigid and watertight.

Beside the work of the Sections the CIAP organizes international studies conferences or small expert meetings for the study of particular points on its program. For the year 1949–50, for example, the following meetings are on the program: Expert Conference on the methods and techniques to be applied in folklore and ethnological research. An international study course on methodology and the drawing up of a textbook. A meeting to draw up a dictionary in several languages of ethnological and folklore terminology. An expert committee to make a series of films based on ethnology and folklore and intended to stress the concordance of the essential aspirations of Man. These films will be of a scientific nature but will also be designed to interest the general public. An International Studies Conference on Rural Architecture and the Role of Peasant Tradition in the Reconstruction of War-Devastated Countries. An expert committee on the publication of a collection of textbooks of different national folklores, having the same tables of contents in order to stress the relationship of the traditional cultures of different peoples. Etc. etc. The 4th General Assembly and the 15th Session of the Governing Board.

CIAP's organs of expression are: *CIAP Information* which comes out according to the needs of the moment, sometimes several times a month. *LAOS*, a journal not appearing at regular intervals, devoted to comparative ethnology and folklore. The first number will appear in the course of 1949. *LAOS* replaces the reviews *Recherche* and *Mouseion* (with the latter's monthly supplement) which were both published until the end of 1946 in collaboration with the former International Museums Office. The last volume of *Recherche* (1946) was devoted to a comparative study on Primitivism and Classicism. The collection of *Mouseion* includes 58 volumes. In this publication are to be found more particularly descriptions of collections dealing with ethnology and folk art. CIAP has taken over the publication of the *Volkskundliche Bibliographie;* three volumes, dealing with the years 1939, 1940 and 1941 will appear during 1949. This publication will in future contain a translation in English or French of the titles of works which hitherto were given only in German. Among CIAP's scientific works we further indicate the following: Folk Arts, 2 vols.; Musical Folklore, 2 vols.; Folk Arts and Workers' Leisure; The Museology of Ethnological Collections; The Significance, Aims and Museum Technique of Collections of Musical Instruments; Why and How is Folk Music Collected; Manual of Museology; International Museums Directory; Chilean Folklore; Peruvian Traditions; Art, Life and Nature in Japan, etc. In *CIAP Information* for 1948 there have been a series of studies on ethnological and folklore research in different countries.

The title of the CIAP is an abbreviation of the French title: Commission Internationale des Arts et Traditions Populaires. The temporary headquarters of the CIAP is: Palais de Chaillot, Paris XVIe, France. The Secretary General is E. Foundoukidis.

E. FOUNDOUKIDIS, Secretary General

čifte tel An abdominal dance of Turkey, the old Caucasian Turkish provinces, Azerbaijan, Anatolia, Baku: also known in Persia. It is ordinarily danced by one woman in a circle of women, or by a single man for a group of men. The abdominal muscles are not stressed as much as in the *danse du ventre*. The quivering motion extends to the shoulders and upraised arms and horizontal jerking of the head (the Hindu *sundari*). Footwork is subordinate. Members of the upper classes have become reluctant to perform this dance, even though it is not performed in the nude as is the danse du ventre. The name means literally "curls of the bangs of the forehead." [GPK]

Cin-an-ev Wolf culture-hero and trickster of the Ute Indians. [EWV]

Cinderella Title of the best known folktale in the world (Type 510A), found nearly everywhere in the world from Alaska to South Africa, from Europe to Indonesia and South America; more than 500 versions of the tale are known in Europe alone. Its place of origin is unknown, but probably it is an originally Oriental story. It has been carried by Europeans to Indonesia and the Philippines, and to North and South America. The earliest known version happens to be Chinese, from the 9th century A.D.; its European history begins some time before its appearance in Perrault and Basile. The story as told by Perrault has had very wide circulation, yet it contains many familiar elements not basically essential to the Cinderella story and it omits several important motifs (e.g. the help of the dead mother, Cinderella as turkey or goose girl) found in variants of the tale elsewhere in the world.

Essentially the Cinderella story, as differentiated from its sister tales *Catskin, Cap o'Rushes,* and *One Eye, Two Eyes, Three Eyes,* is that of the ash-girl (German Aschenputtel and Aschenbrödl, French Cendrillon, Italian Cenerentola, etc.) who, with the aid of an animal or her dead mother, appears at the dance, festival, or in later versions at church, disguised as a grand lady, wins the admiration of the prince, is discovered by the ring or slipper test, and marries the prince.

Perrault's telling of the story begins with the cruel stepmother and the wicked stepsisters, contrasting with them the meek and good Cinderella, forced to do the drudgery of the household and to wait upon the women. Cinderella is so good she does not fail to do her best in dressing her stepsisters when they go off to the grand ball. But when they leave, she begins to weep in despair. Her godmother, who is a fairy, appears in order to help her. Perrault here does not follow the more common incident of the world story, for elsewhere it is Cinderella's mother, as a domestic animal—cow, goat, etc. (Kaffir, Finnish, Celtic, Portuguese, French, etc.)—, as a tree growing from the mother's grave, or by means of an animal sent by the mother, who helps the girl. The fairy godmother is rarely found in the story. Cinderella then, in Perrault's version, goes to the ball in the pumpkin-coach, with mouse-horses, rat-coachmen, and lizard-footmen. Her fine dress and beauty strike the prince to such a degree that he cannot leave her side. At a quarter of twelve she departs hurriedly, for when midnight strikes her finery will disappear. The next night she comes back to the ball, and this time she forgets. The clock strikes twelve as she flees, and only a little ash-girl is seen to leave the palace grounds. But, she has dropped her slipper. Other versions introduce a threefold visit to the ball or festival or church. The use of the witching hour of midnight is Perrault's; so too is the glass slipper. In the Chinese version above mentioned, it is a golden slipper; sometimes it is a ring (compare *Cap o'Rushes* and *Catskin*). Whether Perrault's "pantoufle de verre" was originally a "pantoufle de vair" (fur) is a question that has aroused some interest, but it is quite unessential to the basic elements of the story. The prince, determined to find her, sends throughout the kingdom for the one whom the glass slipper will fit; Cinderella's is the only foot it will go on; she produces the slipper's mate, forgives her sisters, and marries the prince. There are numerous versions in which the dénouement is not as happy for the stepsisters and the stepmother.

Cinderella was the subject of the first detailed study of a folktale ever made, that by Marian Cox in 1892. Miss Cox's work shows the story appearing in combination with other tale types, disguised, often distorted, with elements omitted, yet clearly still the Cinderella story. The Zuñi tale (outlined by Stith Thompson in *The Folktale*, pp. 127–128), for example, has been completely adapted to Zuñi culture. The heroine is an abused turkey girl who gets her fine clothes from the turkeys. But she stays too long at the dance and the turkeys take the finery away. See AMALA; DIRTY BOY; UNPROMISING HERO.

Cindy American folk song and banjo or fiddle tune played for square dances and reels. It has a rollicking chorus and numerous stanzas devoted to the charms and complexities of a backwoods girl.

cinnamon The aromatic inner bark of a tree of the laurel family, used as a spice. It was first mentioned in the writings of the Chinese in 2700 B.C. Used by the Jews and Arabs as a perfume it was one of the earliest items of trade in the East. The Jews used it in the anointing oil in their temples. The Arabian priests had the sole right to gather the bark, and the first bundle was dedicated to the Sun. In early times it ranked in value with gold and frankincense. It was said to make an excellent tonic for the system and developed immunity to disease. In early times cassia was thought to be an inferior quality of cinnamon, and they were used interchangeably. Cassia was used in the embalming fluid of the Egyptians.

Cīrapé "Younger brother" and companion of Old Man Coyote, the trickster of the Crow Indians of Montana. Cīrapé accompanies Old Man Coyote on his wanderings and shares in many of his adventures. [EWV]

Circe In Greek mythology, a sorceress, usually the daughter of Helios and the Oceanid Perse, and sister of Æetes, king of Colchis. She murdered her husband and was exiled to the island of Æaea where she delved into the secrets of magic, surrounding herself with wild beasts which she transformed from men. Ulysses' crew, when they were cast up on her island, were likewise transformed by her magic cup into swine, but the hero himself, protected by the herb moly from the effects of the drink, and informed of her actions by Eurylochus who had escaped the change, forced her to return his men to their proper shapes. Her wiles nevertheless caused him to remain with her a year, during which time he became the father of Telegonus. Before he left, she advised him how to interview Tiresias in Hades, and on his return from the underworld pointed out the dangers he would meet in his journey. Homer calls Circe the fair-haired goddess. Either Circe or the Witch of Endor may claim the distinction of being the most famous of all witches.

Circe motif A motif (G263.1), related to the large group of transformation motifs, in which the lovers of a sorceress are turned by her into swine or other animals: the tales embodying this idea are found from western Europe to Mongolia. Krappe states that the motif spread from the Near East, originating in the Babylonian myth of Ishtar who slew her lovers when she was sated with them (like many another goddess or god or king of myth or history). The dulling of the point of the original myth (actual death to transformation into beasts) is typical of the change to popular tale from myth.

circular tale A variety of the endless tale: also called *prose round*. It is characterized by suddenly beginning again as it reaches the climax. See ENDLESS TALE.

circumambulation The ceremonial walking around an object, site, or person with the right hand towards it, either as a religious ceremony, act of reverence, or magical practice: also called the sunwise turn, holy round, etc., the Brāhman *pradakṣiṇa*. It brings good luck, fends off evil, cures diseases, blots out sins, and is also sometimes regarded as a kind of cosmic magic to insure the continuation of the sun in its course and with it the benefits of the solar cycle: crops, animals, human progeny, warmth, life itself. It is an ancient and widespread practice occurring and functioning variously in a number of cultures.

In India, Tibet, China, Japan, galleries or walls are

still found around Buddhist shrines so that pilgrims may make the holy rounds. Hindus and Mohammedans circumambulate the tombs of saints, believing that the act wipes out sins. The Kaaba at Mecca is an object of circumambulation; so is the Holy Sepulchre at Jerusalem for Oriental Christians. The Roman Catholic Stations of the Cross are also always done sunwise. Circumambulation of religious objects, shrines, etc., propitiates the god or other spirit associated with it, or imparts to the circumambulator some aura of its sanctity or power, and protects both from evil. Many North American Indians perform their rituals sunwise. The Navaho and others associate anti-sunwise motion with curses and witchcraft. The circuits of the great Midewiwin ceremony are performed sunwise. Eskimos, Lapps, and the peoples of northern Siberia all possess sunwise ceremonials. And certain Carib Indians perform their initiation ceremony dances sunwise.

Circumambulation of the dead or of the grave is an ancient practice found from the Central Eskimo, Lapps, Buriats, to India, throughout Europe and the British Isles, and in British Guiana. Achilles made the war chariots circle the body of Patroclus three times (*Iliad*, xxiii). The Argonauts circled the body of Mopsus, the seer, three times when they buried him. In Ireland a corpse is still carried sunwise around the graveyard before burial; the graveyard is always approached sunwise (see DEISEAL). The Koryaks speed the souls of slain bears into the sun by carrying the stuffed bearskin in ceremonial sunwise circuit.

The magical power for good inherent in the act of circumambulation is seen in such practices as the turning of boats sunwise by fisherman of the Orkneys and Shetlands, Iceland, and Ireland before undertaking a trip, and the encircling of the sacred pipul tree by barren Brāhman women to induce pregnancy. The famous fire charm of northern Europe was the sunwise circumambulation performed with the proper incantations. European balladry celebrates many a brave "fire-rider" who was burned to death with his horse before he could complete the required number of circuits.

Brāhman and Buddhist marriage ceremonies include the circumambulation by the couple of hearth or housepole. In early Roman marriage ceremonies they circled the family altar. In rural Europe and the British Isles they circumambulate the house or the church. In some parts of Scotland today family and friends will circle sunwise around someone who is going on a journey, to give him luck. Opler, in *Dirty Boy* (*MAAA* 52: 36) notes that Jicarilla Apache on the raid customarily skirt enemy camps sunwise. The Japanese believe that to advance against an enemy anti-sunwise is defying heaven. In all Celtic countries the ill encircle holy wells to be cured. The Estonian father will run around the church while his child is being baptized to make it a good runner. Moslems stir their food and pass their dishes sunwise. In China and Japan a cup of tea is given one complete sunwise turn, sip by sip, between the first sip and the last.

Circumambulation occurs in folktale for the undoing of evil spells (D787), for transformation by encircling three (or four) times (D563), the acquiring of magic power by circumambulation (D1791). See AMPHIDROMIA; DEISEAL; JERICHO; ROUND DANCES; SWASTIKA; TUATAL; WITHERSHINS.

circumcision The operation removing all or some portion of the prepuce or foreskin, the skin covering the glans of the penis: an almost universal custom all over the world except in Europe and non-Semitic Asia. An analogous operation is often performed on women, the clitoris and sometimes the labia being removed. Male circumcision is sometimes attended in Australia by the companion operation of subincision, the slitting of the urethra the length of the penis; and in Jewish ritual circumcision by the tearing of the mucous membrane covering the glans. The knife used is often of stone, leading some to believe that the custom originated in the stone age, before metal was worked and used by man.

The cutting of the prepuce may be only symbolic, as among the Chams of Indo-China; it may be simply a gash or cut in the prepuce, as in the Americas and parts of the Pacific; or it may be the total excision of the prepuce, the common meaning of the word. Literally, the word means "a cutting around," and perhaps it should be limited to the complete operation, but the sacrifice or test implied in the cutting of the organ of generation is so widespread that any similar operation on penis or vulva must be included in a discussion of circumcision.

Wherever it occurs, circumcision is a form of initiation. Most commonly it takes place at or before puberty; universally it precedes marriage. Many theories have been advanced explaining the reason for circumcision: it is a sacrifice to the goddess of fertility; it is a test of the ability to withstand pain; it is a mark of social distinction, setting the circumcised apart from and above the uncircumcised; it avoids the danger inherent in sexual intercourse by sacrificing a part for the whole; it is a sanitary measure; it has even been said, without evidence, that it is meant to increase sexual pleasure by making the penis less sensitive. While many of these theories hold true for one or a limited number of peoples, none answers the question fully.

However, the ritual which surrounds circumcision (e.g. Jewish, Australian, African) and its inclusion in initiation rites of some sort; the rejection of the uncircumcised from the (circumcised) group (e.g. the Masai will not permit the uncircumcised to handle iron, the term "uncircumcised" is an insult among the Arabs, etc.); the insistence that circumcision makes a man of a child, intercourse and marriage not being safe before circumcision; the inclusion of the naming rite in the circumcision ceremony—these, while of scattered occurrence, all indicate that circumcision is basically an initiation ceremony.

Who is circumcised (males, females, both; the higher classes, as among the Aztecs, or everyone but the highest class, as in Tonga), the timing of the operation (from the age of a week or so to an age immediately preceding marriage), the identity of the operator (father, uncle, father-in-law; priest, doctor, special official), what instruments are used and what they are made of, and other similar questions are too complex to be entered into here, and are of more interest to the anthropologist or the student of sociologic institutions than to the folklorist. Even the universality of several of the statements may be dubious: within recorded times the custom has been seen to be adopted and discarded by several peoples; the Zulu king, Chaka, abolished it in the 19th century, and though of recent introduction among the central Bantu it is dying out among them.

It is of interest to the folklorist to note that myths or tales about circumcision are rare, so rare that even origin tales do not often occur. The Arunta creation myth does relate in detail the story of the origin of circumcision and subincision, which forms an important part of the Alcheringa myth. The Biblical reference to circumcision as the mark of the covenant between the Israelites and Yahweh is well known. Members of the same age group, circumcised together, are sometimes as close as blood brothers among the Kaffirs, the Bechuanas, the Papuans. A seat is left for Elijah at the Jewish circumcision. Some legendary persons (Adam, Moses, Zerubbabel) were born circumcised. But apart from the types which these myths, customs, and beliefs represent—and they are few in number—the folklore of circumcision does not exist, perhaps because it has been absorbed in religious ritual, perhaps because of the tremendous tabu that must lie over a subject so closely related to the generative power and the mysterious sacrifice of manhood to attain manhood. Students of psychoanalysis applying their techniques to anthropology have professed to see in circumcision a reflection of the unconscious castration-fear complex, but this too is only tangentially related to folklore.

Cirein Crôin In Scottish Highland folklore, the sea serpent, believed to be the largest of all living creatures. Seven whales were an easy meal for him.

ciriwanu A self-accompanied dance of the Aymara Indian men of Bolivia: probably so named for the Chiriguano tribe. Dressed in a white skirt and ostrich-feather crown, each dancer holds in his left hand an enormous pan-pipe and a drum; in his right hand he manipulates a drum stick. [GPK]

Ciuateteo or **Ciuapipiltin** In Aztec belief, certain female spirits (literally "noble women") who had died in childbirth (or in their first childbirth) or who had been warriors. Their patroness was Cihuacoatl, the serpent woman, probably an aspect of Coatlicue. The Ciuateteo lived in the western sky, through which, from the time it reached the meridian, they carried the sun to deliver it to the lords of the underworld. From this connection with the underworld they probably derived their dangerous character. Sometimes they flew out of the west as eagles, bringing epilepsy to children and lust to men. At certain times they scared people on the roads. From the corpse of such a woman, the stupefying thieves' candle (hand of glory) might be made, hence great precautions, in the form of armed guards and the like, had to be taken against the body being stolen or mutilated. Under Spanish influence, the ciuateteo has developed into La Llorona, the weeping woman of folktale, who wanders through the streets seeking her lost children.

cláirseac An Irish harp, especially a festival harp of ancient times.

Clementine A late popular American ballad dealing with the drowning of a forty-niner's daughter.

Clerk Saunders A Scottish popular ballad (Child #69) in which Clerk Saunders induces his true love,

May Margaret, to take him to her bed, to his undoing. She opens the latch with Clerk Saunders' sword, so that she may swear her hand did not let him in; she blindfolds her eyes in order to say she has not seen him; she carries him to the bed, in order to say he has not crossed her floor. But after the true lovers are sound asleep, May Margaret's seven brothers appear at the foot of the bed, discussing whether or not to kill Clerk Saunders. The consensus is not to part the beautiful and loving pair. Only the seventh brother (sometimes the eldest) is unmoved; he draws his sword and runs it through Clerk Saunders. The ballad ends with May Margaret's grief and refusal to be comforted for the man she was going to marry. There is a version in the David Herd manuscript running to 41 stanzas: the story as here told plus the incident in *Sweet William's Ghost* (Child #77), i.e. May Margaret is not left to live on uncomforted; she follows her lover's ghost to the graveside and dies with grief beside it. Sir Walter Scott first presented *Clerk Saunders* to the reading public in his *Minstrelsy of the Scottish Border*.

cliff-ogre The incident of a monster kicking people over a cliff so that they may be eaten by her brood, occurs in many North American Indian tales over the continent, as also in early Greek story (G321). [EWV]

climax of relations In folklore, ballad, and legend, the introducing of the relatives of the protagonist in the order of their importance to him and to the resolution of the action. This is a familiar motif in a number of ballads and folk songs stressing the fact that the condemned one's sweetheart (or wife or husband) is more merciful than blood relations. The English ballad *The Maid Freed from the Gallows* (Child #95) typically illustrates the sequence of refusals to ransom the condemned girl: father, mother, brother, sister, all arrive in this sequence; all refuse ransom—"For I am come to see you hanged"—until the girl's true-love arrives, who has come to see her saved. The American Negro version of this ballad, *The Gallows Pole*, names papa, brother, sister, sweetheart.

Many Negro jail songs also follow the climax of relations: "My mama don't write to me, poor me"—working up to the sweetheart's line, which is always the punch line, whether the sweetheart has written or not. A number of Negro spirituals also use the device—"My mama has gone to the Other Side," etc.—working up to the singer himself.

In the English ballad *Lord Randal* (Child #12) a sequence of bequests is the vehicle for the climax of relations: "What do you leave to your mother, Lord Randal, my son?"—then to sister, brother, and true-love, who, in sharp contrast with the first three affectionate bequests, is consigned to hell-fire for poisoning her lover. In the English and Scottish versions of *Edward* (Child #13) it is the mother who caps the climax of relations and is left with the bitter curse of the son to whom she has given murderous counsel.

Clíodna (pronounced *Cleena*) In Old Irish mythology, daughter of Gebann, chief druid to Manannán mac Lir, lord of the sea. Clíodna of the Fair Hair had still not given her love to any man when Ciaban (pronounced Keevan) came to Manannán's house. The way Ciaban came was this: he was sent away from Fionn's country because of his charm for women and the jealousy of the men of the Fianna. He left Ireland in a curragh with two strange men; and a storm rose around them of such mountainous waves and din that Ciaɓan wished himself on land. A rider on a gray horse rose out of the sea and brought him out of danger. Ciaɓan was carried with the rider to Tir Tairngaire, the Land of Promise, where stood the city of Manannán.

A great feast was going on there at the time and the famous entertainers were doing their tricks. One of the tricks was to throw nine straight willow rods into the rafters of the house and catch them coming down, but standing on one leg and with one hand behind the back. The tricksters used to persuade strangers to try the trick just to see them fail. So one of them handed Ciaɓan the nine rods and Ciaɓan did the trick. Clíodna loved Ciaɓan from that moment and went away with him the next morning. They went in a curragh to a place on the south shore of Ireland. Ciaɓan pulled up the curragh on the strand and went on shore, seeking a deer in the thicket for their food. He left Clíodna waiting in the curragh with Iuchna, a musician of Manannán's who was with them. Iuchna played such music that Clíodna slept, and a huge wave rolled over the curragh and drowned her and swept her away. The surge of that place is still called Tonn Clíodna, Clíodna's Wave.

In later folklore, Clíodna is regarded as one of the three fairy queens of Munster, active in May Day celebrations and seducer of young men at fairs. She is also believed to be the special banshee of certain families in the south of Munster.

Clootie A Scottish name for the devil: from *cloot,* meaning one division of a cleft hoof. *Old Cloots* is a variant of the epithet. *Clootie's Croft* is a piece of land left untilled (or found untillable) by the villagers, as a gift to the devil.

Cloud People or **Shiwanna** Among the Pueblo Indians, spirits with whom the dead are associated. The Cloud beings live in the four or six regions of the universe and are associated with the colors of these regions; or, they may live in towns on the shores of the encircling ocean, or in the mountains, below a spring or lake. Clouds, and the dead as clouds, are represented as kachina and impersonated by masked dancers in Pueblo kachina ceremonies. [EWV]

Clouston, William Alexander (1843–1896) Scotch journalist and writer born in the Orkneys of an old Norse family. Most of his writing was devoted to Oriental fiction and to folklore, and his principal work from the folklore point of view was *The Book of Noodles: Stories of Simpletons, or Fools and Their Follies,* which was published in London in 1880, and appeared in a popular edition in 1903. Among his other works are an edition of *Arabian Poetry for English Readers* (1881); *A Persian Romance* (1883); *The Book of Sindibad, From the Persian and Arabic,* edited by Clouston (1884); *Popular Tales and Fictions: Their Migrations and Transformations* (1887); *A Group of Eastern Romances and Stories from the Persian, Tamil and Urdu* (1889); *Book of Wise Sayings, Selected Largely from Eastern Sources* (1893); *Flowers from a Persian Garden* (1894); and *Hieroglyphic Bibles, Their Origin and History.*

clover Any of several species of plants (genus *Trifolium*). Farmers consider clover a sign of good soil. Because of its triple leaf it is regarded as a symbol of the Trinity, and a proof against spells and witchcraft. The druids also had a high regard for clover as a charm against evil. Pliny mentioned that when the leaves of the clover tremble and stand up it is a sign of a coming storm, a belief still held today. Also it is said that the leaves are rough before a storm. In Newfoundland an infusion of clover is used for bathing skin diseases.

Four-leafed clovers are generally considered lucky in Europe and North America, but they must not be given away. Some believe they give clairvoyance and the ability to see things as they are, or to see the fairies, elves, trolls, etc. They are protection against the Devil and his minions. Some say that one possessing a four-leafed clover will see his or her love within a short time. This is especially true of girls: they will marry the next man they see. They say in Newfoundland that wherever you see a four-leafed clover, a foal was born. Some believe the possession of one should be kept secret for it to be effective, others that it should be placed in the left shoe; in Silesia it should be sewn inside the clothes. Five-leafed clovers are bad luck if found and kept, but it is good luck to both parties to give them away. In some places to find a five-leafed clover indicates that you will soon be sick.

clown medicine The curing power of the clown: a religious concept among many North American Indians, especially among the Pueblo and Iroquois and certain California Indians. In the pueblos clowns are believed to have great powers of eyesight. San Juan and Hano pueblo clowns can even see the kachina in their distant places. For this reason clown medicine is believed to sharpen eyesight. The Jicarilla Apache clown wears a bandoleer of bread. From this he tears off a piece, chews it, and then transfers it to the mouth of his patient. The Jicarilla Apache believe that contact with human or animal excrement will cause sieges of vomiting. To cure vomiting the Jicarilla clown administers a herbal medicine mixed into white clay with the excrement of a dog or child. Thus public clowning with voidings is probably basically related to this curing magic. Ashes of dog voidings constitute a good stomach medicine. Many diverse clown groups possess medicaments for sick stomach. The Black Eyes (clowns of Taos) are regarded as especially good baby doctors. Zuñi clowns, the Ne'wekwe, or Gluttons, will eat anything (green fruit, peach stones, sticks, pebbles, ashes, urine, voidings, small live animals, etc.) in token of their power to cure anything. Hano clowns also possess this "medicine."

clowns Ludicrous characters, who commonly use backward speech or indulge in contrary behavior and scatological practices are, quite generally, among the actors in many Plains, Southwestern, Great Basin, and California Indian ceremonies. In the Plains and Southwest clowns are often organized into societies; they are frequently masked when they perform, and wear elaborate costumes. A great deal of license in ridiculing the sacred and vested authority is allowed the clown; in at least one California tribe it was he who could talk against and depose a chief. Notable among Pueblo clowns are the **Koshare** or **Delight Makers** of the Hopi, and the Koyemshi, the masked kachina clowns of the Zuñi. Clowning in the pueblos consists of gluttony, eating or drinking filth, drenching or being drenched with urine or water, begging, burlesquing, satirizing, distributing prizes or food, playing games, and so forth. Members of Pueblo clowning societies inspire a certain amount of fear among the people; since they are licensed to do what they please they can be punitive. Furthermore, they are generally supposed to practice witchcraft. In the Eastern Woodlands and especially among the Iroquois and neighboring tribes, the Shuck Faces who accompanied the False Faces on their rounds to rid villages of sickness, acted somewhat as clowns, amusing and frightening the people. [EWV]

Among various North American Indians, clowns are impersonators of chthonic beings with identical farcical attributes, which in the course of time have become their distinguishing features. By identification with the spirits of the dead, animals, fire, and other natural forces, clowns possess magical powers for curing, for weather control, and fertility, and have complete license of action. Their reversed action and speech are characteristic of the contrary behavior associated with ceremonies for the dead, but are specifically the mark of clown humor. Fire ordeals (heyoka) and ash scattering (by the gagósä of the Iroquois and the no-hahluigak of the California Pomo) exhibit their supernatural curative powers; female impersonations and obscene mime serve phallic purposes (see AKBI'ARUSCARIČA; KOSHARE). They also may police or completely control dances at certain times (chapayekas, chapeones).

They impersonate the supernatural by means of various types of disguise: wooden, hide, or cloth masks, or paint, or female clothes. The Iroquois False Faces, or gagósä, as wind and disease spirits, wear black or red wooden masks with distorted features. Wooden masks representing goats or old men are worn by the Mayo-Yaqui pascola, the Tarahumara chapeones, the Isleta k'apio, and the Acoma and Laguna chapio. Hide masks with long ears, horns, and long thin noses cover the heads of the Mayo-Yaqui chapayekas, the Papago djidjur, Apache ł'ibáhi, and the tsabiyo of San Juan, Alcalde, Cochiti, Santa Ana, and Jemez. Again, the Bûngi windigokan cut eyeholes in sack masks; the koshare and Yahgan kina clowns paint their faces with black and white stripes and tie their hair in a poke; the Zuñi mudheads use mud. The Iroquois Husk Faces (gadjisa'), dressed as women, possess fertility magic for increase of crops and babies.

These North American clown types find their counterparts throughout the world in the totemic animals of the African Javara, in the theriomorphic Carnival kalogheroi of Thrace, descended from the Dionysian daimones; in the Portuguese bugios, the Swiss Rautschegetten and Ueberlingen Zottler, descended from the wild men of the medieval Carnival; in the horned sooty devil; and in the female Schemen and the Bessy of the English Morris and Fool Plough. The ancient costume of shaggy fur may today be represented only by tatters (as worn by the Zottler and Mexican viejo), or may be replaced by foliage (Leafy Fool, or Jack-in-the-Green of medieval England). Various other paraphernalia have life-giving properties: furry caps and tails, swords or sticks, whips (serpents), agricultural implements, water

sprinklers, flowers, gourd rattles, bells, and other demon-frightening noise-makers.

Today the ghostly origin of the clown tends to fade into obscurity. The South German Perchten, though still ceremonial demons, have lost their ancient meaning as the followers of Berchta or Frau Holle, custodian of the dead. The European Carnival train of animal masks, following the medieval wild men—the maisnée Herlekin—no longer represents das wilde Heer, the wild horde of the dead, but has ended on the stage as Harlequin, a semipathetic entertainer. And the springtime expulsion of death and resurrection of the ancestors have degenerated into Carnival and Halloween pranks. See DANCE: FOLK AND PRIMITIVE. [GPK]

clúracán A diminutive old-man fairy of Ireland, traditionally believed to inhabit wine cellars. He takes care that the beer barrels or wine casks are not left running, and for reward he is always given his supper. In County Cork the clúracán is often associated with the leprechaun, but this is because of his dwarfish, aged appearance, and the fact that he too knows the whereabouts of hidden treasure.

coal This fuel which we take for granted as a part of our civilization today has been in use in the Western world for a relatively short time. The mention of coal in such early works as the Bible usually refers to wood charcoal. Coal was known to the Chinese as early as 1000 B.C. as ice charcoal, but was still in limited use at the time of Marco Polo. Aristotle's pupil, Theophrastus, mentions it in his work on stones as being occasionally used by smiths. There are indications that it was used in scattered places in Britain by the Roman soldiers, but although there were exposed seams of coal in existence in Italy at that time, its use was not carried back with the legions on their return. In England and parts of Germany, hard coal has been used to make trinkets since medieval times. There is record of crystal balls and a "Devil's mirror" made of polished cannel coal. This coal was used occasionally in England for architectural carvings and panels and for a church floor.

Its use as a fuel did not begin until the 12th century and then only by a few industries and by the very poor who could not afford any other fuel. People disliked the smoke which it made (and still makes) in English fireplaces and for a time its use was banned by law. It was known to the alchemists of the Middle Ages who were familiar with some of its many byproducts.

The Venerable Bede mentions that when burned coal drove out snakes, but in this instance it was burned as a fumigant rather than a fuel. In parts of England today it is carried in the pocket for luck and it is often carried by burglars, perhaps originally to give invisibility. Irish prisoners sometimes carry it at their trials to give them luck "with the authorities." In Knollingly, Yorkshire, it is the first thing brought into the house in the New Year. In some places Jews put a piece in a child's pocket to ward off the evil eye.

Coatlicue Literally, the lady of the serpent skirt; in Aztec mythology, the magically impregnated mother of Huitzilopochtli; an earth-serpent deity; one of the wives of Mixcoatl, the Cloud Serpent of the Milky Way. She is of especially horrible aspect: her skirt is of snakes, her necklace of hearts and hands supports a skull pendant; her hands and feet are clawed; her breasts are flabby. She feeds on the corpses of human beings; and she is called Tonantzin, our mother, or Tlazolteotl, the devourer of filth. In the myth, as Coatlicue swept one day, she picked up on her broom a ball of feathers and put it in her bodice. From this she became impregnated. Her daughter egged on her sons to kill their mother for her supposed crime, but the child within her womb told Coatlicue to have no fear. When the brothers arrived, the child, Huitzilopochtli, the Aztec war god, sprang into the world fully armed and slew the sister and most of the brothers.

cobra Any of several venomous snakes (genus *Naja*) of India and Africa which can dilate their necks into a hood. The cobra, as a symbol of the life force that motivates birth and rebirth, is adored in northern India and it is never knowingly killed. If one is accidentally slain its body is cremated with the same rites as those used for a man. Childless women worship the snake on the fifth of each month for a period of a year or of three years with offerings of flowers, water, and milk. In Coorg it is believed that the cobra lives a thousand years. In its middle life its body begins to shrink and to brighten until it shines like silver. When it is only a foot long it shines like gold, and finally it shrinks to the size of a finger. Then it dies and a serpent stone is left. Anyone stepping on the spot where the cobra died will be the victim of an incurable skin disease.

The cobra, as a supernatural being, plays an important part in Indian folktales and mythology. The marking on its hood is believed to be the footprint of Krishṇa, and Devī is frequently represented with the serpent.

cobzar An itinerant musician of Rumanian villages, who sings and improvises to his fiddle or guitar. Many of the songs of the cobzar are legends of ancient times or apocryphal stories of Old and New Testament.

cociés or **cosiers** A Majorcan ceremonial dance centered around a hobby horse. The actors consist of a *dama*, a man-woman with fan and kerchief, two demons with horns and cloven feet, and six boys in white with ribbons and elaborate floral hats. They dance figures similar to the English Morris, cross-overs and heys, periodically during the processionals of Corpus Christi and the Assumption. All except the devils also dance in the church at Alaró and Montiurí. The accompanying instruments are a chirimía or bagpipe, tamborino, and flaviol. The dance is considered of the same type as the Moriscas in the rest of Europe, a pagan vegetation rite in Christian garb. [GPK]

cock The cock's origin was probably India, although the Greeks called it "the Persian bird." In these countries it was venerated and it was a desecration to put such fowls to death, both in India and in Russia. As announcer of the dawn, the cock was sacred to Helios, the sun god; it was sometimes called the "son of Mars," on account of its fighting abilities and its pugnacity; it was also dedicated to Mercury and often associated with the chthonic gods. The Romans offered the comb of the bird to the Lares. The cock was a bird *par excellence* for sacrifice; it was offered to the sun in Mexico and it was conspicuous for its substitution for human sacrifice in building ceremonies and for other symbolic uses of its blood.

In Rome, the cock was used in auguries; in Germany and Hungary, it was a weather prophet; "hence," says an authority, "its effigy on buildings, but its place on church-spires is said to owe its place because of Peter's denial of Christ and as a reminder to Christians not to do likewise." In the mantic capacity of this bird, its crowing frequently forecast victory in war.

As a symbol of fertility, the cock played a part in marriage ceremonies among the southern Slavs and in Hungary when the bridegroom carried a cock or its image in the marriage procession. Cock-decoration of the roof of a house is another example of the bird as life-bringer.

Many omens are referred to the cock: in Wales, it is lucky to own a white cock; its crowing in the daytime announces the visit of a friend; if it crows about midnight, it is a death omen. If the cock is black, it becomes a bird of evil; an offering of a black cock appeases the devil (Hungary). It is used in black magic and in folk medicine: it is used in cases of tuberculosis (Morocco); applied to the skin to take the poison from a snake bite; a stone from the cock's stomach was supposed to inspire the one who swallowed it with strength and courage (Scotland).

The cock appears as a character in the folktale. An outstanding example may be cited in Grimm's *The Bremen Town-Musicians* (#27), versions of which are widespread—from Scandinavian countries to the Old World in India and elsewhere. He is the principal in the story, "The Cock that Wished to Become Pope" (Thomas Frederick Crane, *Italian Popular Tales* (New York, 1885), pp. 272–274, after Gonzenbach). Further examples are in the simpler cumulative tales where the cock is one in a "chain." (Cf. Benjamin Thorpe, *Yule-Tide Stories* (London 1892), "The Cock and the Hen in the Nut Wood," pp. 333–335, after Asbjörnsen). The 12th century *Roman de Renart*, built on still earlier models, has served as pattern for stories of the wiles of the fox in many countries toward various creatures, including the cock. [GPS]

Cockaigne A land of pleasure, wealth, and luxury: wholly imaginary. The name has been applied to London ("cockneydom") and also to Paris. In this fabled land, all sorts of strange things happen; roast pigs run along the street with knife and fork stuck in their backs, streets are paved with pastry, houses made of barley sugar, a kettle on a mountain of cheese is boiling macaroni and dumplings which later roll down to the waiting gourmands. This topsy-turvy land is celebrated in poem and story, especially in the Middle Ages. Grimm's tale, *The Story of Schlauraffenland* (#158) and *The Ditmars Tale of Wonders* (#159) give some idea of the extravaganzas of the "lying tale." [GPS]

cockcrow The shrill crow of the cock which announces the rising of the sun is one of this bird's characteristics. It has been variously referred to in literature as "trumpet of the morn" (Shakespeare), "shrill clarion" (Gray), and in other similar descriptive phrases. When the cock ceases to crow, it is believed that the Day of Judgment will be at hand.

Fairly universal is the superstition that ghosts, witches, evil spirits, or whatever roams abroad at night are obliged to vanish at cockcrow; even the Devil takes flight. In this connection, the colors ascribed to the cock are significant. When the *white* cock crows, little attention is paid to it; the crow of the *red* cock is a warning; but at the *black* cock's crow all frequenters of the night quickly disappear. Many tales and ballads illustrate such beliefs. Sometimes the *white* cock is lacking and sometimes a *gray* cock is substituted for the *red*.

It is pointed out that memorable incidents which have happened at cockcrow in the past tend to stimulate superstitions of this hour. The Nativity and the Resurrection occurred near this time and it was at cockcrow that Jesus said that Peter would deny him (*Mat.* xxvi, 34; *Mark* xiv, 30; *Luke* xxii, 34). [GPS]

cockroach This representative of the family Blattidæ has an ancient tradition, since it existed in great numbers and varieties in the Carboniferous epoch and earlier. Fossils have been found in Silurian sandstone. Folktale puts its origin in Finland (*FFC* VIII:122, #125). But it is indigenous to all parts of the world except the polar regions, and there are 2250 species on the face of the earth. In general it thrives in a warm, humid environment. Many of the tropical species are brilliant green, yellow, orange, or variegated. The flying Malaysian roach, often called the Australian cockroach, has traveled the world in ships and often turns up unexpectedly in urban kitchens. The death's-head roach, named for its markings, of Florida, Mexico, the West Indies, and Central America, attains a length of 2½ inches. With its nocturnal habits and its appetite for both animal and vegetable food, nothing is safe from it. People of the Chaco keep their cotton garments in pottery jars sealed with clay to avoid their being devoured by the native cockroaches. Names given to the cockroach in Germany and France, such as *Bäcker*, *bête à pain*, suggest some of its habits.

In Russia and in France the cockroach is looked upon as a protecting spirit; its presence in the house is lucky. It portends bad luck if "the roach" leaves. In many sections of Europe and the United States methods are various for getting rid of roaches, such as sweeping them out on Good Friday or impaling one on a pin as warning for the lot. Enclosing one in a box and presenting it to a corpse, or taking one to a neighbor's house are other Continental methods.

The name "black beetle" often applied to the cockroach is incorrect entomologically, but is in keeping with many associations of the cockroach with the devil or witches. In Ireland it is thought sometimes that witches in the shape of cockroaches come to plague farmers. The Irish always kill a cockroach because it is said to have revealed the hiding place of Jesus.

The cockroach has entered folktale, although instances are infrequent compared with stories about other insects. Four cockroach stories have been reported from Jamaica in Martha Beckwith's *Jamaica Anansi Stories, MAFLS* 17. A story from Antigua, entitled *Why Fowl Catch Cockroach,* tells how Cockroach, who is always playing and singing, meets a tragic end suggestive of the fable of the *Ant and the Grasshopper.*

In folk medicine the cockroach was used in the treatment of urinary disorders, for worms in children, for epilepsy, and various other ills. To catch a witch Mississippi Negroes lay a large jar or bottle in the hearth ashes overnight. If there is a cockroach in it in the morning, that's the witch. She will die whatever death is meted out to the cockroach.

cock's step In Ireland, *coiscéim coilig,* a cock's step, is a term used to mean a short or imperceptible interval. The increase in the length of a day, when the days first begin to lengthen, for instance, is but a cock's step.

coco macaque A magic stick found among Haitian Negroes that walks by itself. The owner can send it on errands, especially punitive errands. If he hits an enemy with it, the man will die before morning.

coconut One of the most widely cultivated trees in the world: said to have originated in Ceylon. One story says that it sprang from the head of a slain monster, another that the king's astrologer named a certain day as auspicious for planting, and that anything planted on that day would grow into a tree beneficial to mankind. The king planted the astrologer's head. The Chinese say that when the prince of Yue was beheaded, his head caught in the branch of a palm, and became a coconut. In India it is said to have been created by the sage Sisvamitra, who was a great thinker.

In some parts of India, coconut palms must be planted by Brāhmans because they are free from evil. In other parts there is a belief, when a tree is planted, that one of the family will die when it puts forth leaves again, and another when the first blossoms appear. In Malabar when a boy is born, his parents plant five coconut trees, enough to support him. In Mindoro if you look up when you are planting, the tree will grow very tall before it will bear, but if you comb your hair, the tree will be full of nuts. If a tree is not fruitful, it may be made so by planting a certain vine at its base.

In Nariyal in western India there is a Coconut Day, when coconuts and flowers are thrown into the sea to propitiate the sea and as a thank offering. The Parsees break a coconut on the threshold as an act of welcome to a near relative, or a bride and groom.

Among the Fijians, if a coconut is spun near a sick man, he will die if it falls to the west, but if it falls to the east he will recover. Among the Sengalese they say that a coconut will not fall on anyone unless he has displeased the divine powers. On Mindoro they claim that the nuts will yield more oil if the oil-making takes place at high tide.

Cocoyomes An unknown ancient people: said by the Tarahumare Indians of Mexico to have been (1) their ancient enemies, (2) their ancestors, (3) the first people in the world. The Cocoyomes lived in caves, were cannibals, and supplemented their diet with agave. Because of their wickedness, the sun came down and burned them up. The few survivors who fled and took refuge in caves at Zapuri were exterminated by the Tarahumare.

Codrus In Greek legend, the last king of Athens. In a war between the Dorians and the Athenians, the Delphic oracle declared that that side would win whose king died. Codrus then disguised himself as a peasant, entered the Dorian camp, and picked a quarrel with some soldiers. The Dorians gave up the hopeless war when they found who it was that had been killed, and returned home. Since this action on the part of Codrus could never be surpassed by any future king, the Athenians abolished the kingship and appointed Medon, the son of Codrus, archon for life.

Cõ-hon In Annamese belief, the souls of those who have died a violent death on land or at sea and who have not had proper burial. There are millions of Cõ-hon which hide in the shade of shrubs and trees, attacking passers-by at night or causing misfortunes to those who forget them. Businessmen, especially, try to gain their favor. Small wooden temples or stone altars at the feet of trees are erected for them, and offerings of imitation gold or silver, paper shoes, and rice are made to them.

coin of the dead The custom of placing "a penny piece on each eye" of the newly deceased was not confined to Dickens' England (*Martin Chuzzlewit*, ch. xix). Today in New England, where the half-dollar is the proper coin, the purpose is alleged to be to keep the eyelids closed as rigor mortis sets in, lest the open eyes become fixed in an unseemly stare. Judging from many parallel examples, however, the practice is a partial or token survival of the ancient custom of burying all a man's valuables with him in order that he might not return as a ghost and haunt his home vicinity.

By classical times that custom had already been simplified by placing a coin under the corpse's tongue or between the teeth, and rationalized by calling it "Charon's obol," the fee to the underworld deity for ferrying the soul of the deceased over the Acheron or the Styx to the realm of the dead. The custom was supposed (because of a passage in Diodorus Siculus) to have been borrowed from the Egyptians, but the Egyptians probably had no coinage at the indicated time, and Charon himself is very likely a revised and refined edition of the earlier Etruscan deity Charun, depicted on sarcophagi as a half-human, half-animal monster, holding high a threatening hammer as he tears the dead man from the bosom of his family.

The convention of using corpse coins is widespread. The Juma River tribesmen of South America think of the rainbow as the mouth of a great snake through which the soul enters heaven. To pay the toll a coin is placed in the mouth of the cadaver or, if the family is poor, a fig may be substituted. The substitution idea is general. The Pahari people of North India use either coins or other small articles of value. The Japanese, for ferry fee across the Sandzunogawa River, formerly put six pieces of money in the dead man's little traveling bag, but now thriftily substitute a paper with a picture of even more than six coins. The European Franks of the Middle Ages used thin silver imitation money; the Chinese permit pearls and other valuables in place of coins; the Balinese sometimes put a gold ring on the tongue.

Special sympathetic magic inheres in corpse coins. Frazer (*Golden Bough* i, 149) reports that a Serb or Bulgarian woman, looking for variety in love, will wash in wine or water the copper coins from a dead man's eyes and give her husband the solution to drink that he may be rendered as blind to her adventures as the corpse. [CFP]

colinde The Christmas carol of Rumania and Macedonia, chiefly in blank verse. The best known is *White Flowers*. See BARTÓK; CAROL.

collahualla or **collahuaya**; sometimes **kollawallas** Hereditary herbalists and magicians of the provinces of Caupolican and Munecas in Bolivia. They represent a special subgroup within the Aymara nation. For many centuries medical arts have passed from father to child in most families of this tribe. The collahuaya were already known as ambulant and skilful practitioners at the time of the Conquest, and they seem to have formed a specialized caste by the time of the Inca empire and perhaps earlier.

The collahuaya constantly travel in the Andean region from Colombia to Argentina. Not many years ago they went as far as Buenos Aires. They may be recognized by their special costume and by the bags in which they carry their herbs. With the money received for their drugs, they bought mules which they resold at a high profit in Bolivia. The collahuaya also trade in various kinds of amulets and talismans. Most of their drugs come from the Yunga region where they go to supply themselves before starting on their long journeys. [AM]

collasiri Specialized magicians and medicine men among modern Aymara Indians. They are bone-setters and expert diagnosticians. One of their favorite methods of identifying the origin of an ailment is to examine the viscera of an animal which has been put into contact with the patient. They also practice various other forms of divination to ascertain the nature of the diseases. One of their usual cures consists in transferring magically the disease to an animal or object. [AM]

colors Everyday speech is full of color, from such expressions as "Was my face red!" to the metaphoric "That's white of you" and the symbolic "He's got a yellow streak down his back." Similar to this colloquial form of expression is the color cliché of literature, well established in folk forms like the ballad and folktale: hair black as raven's plumage, lips red as rubies, skin white as milk or ivory or snow. Not only the catalog of the charms of fair ladies but many other things have typical colors: the violent red-headed person, the black (or red) Devil or imp, the black-cat or black-dog familiar of the witch, the white ghost, pink elephants, purple patches in literature, and red hazes swimming before the eyes. The symbolism of color directs traffic on the highways—red to stop, green to go—and signals approaching storms to shipping.

Among the Pueblo Indians of the United States, color symbolism has been systematized perhaps to a greater degree than anywhere else in the world. Each of the six directions has its color: east is white, north is yellow (sometimes blue or black), west is blue (or yellow), south is red (or blue or buff), above and below are variegated or black. These colors vary from tribe to tribe, but ascription of color to compass direction appears everywhere in the pueblos. The colors and compass points have their specific gods and animals and birds. The Zuñi name for Dr. Kroeber, says Parsons, is Oriole, because he came to Zuñi from the north wearing khaki clothes; and yellow is the color of north, oriole the bird of north. The many-colored kinds of corn too are associated with the directions of the compass; in the mythology, the Corn Girls are of the specified colors.

It is not alone in the pueblos of the Southwest that this type of color symbolism is found. The Cherokee associate abstract qualities as well as direction to the colors: red is east and success, blue is north and trouble, black is west and death, white is south and happiness.

Cherokee places of refuge were called white towns, peaceful islands in time of trouble. In Mexico and Ireland, in China and Vedic India colors were assigned to the directions. Modern Europe too has its symbolism of color for qualities: white is purity, black is death, red is passion, green is life. The Western Church uses colors as symbols not only of qualities but also of days and periods. Violet is the color of the Lenten season; black of Good Friday, etc.

Color in costume is also significant. Mourning dress in Europe is generally black; but in imperial Rome and in modern China white symbolizes mourning. It has been suggested that black is worn to echo the emptiness of death; and that white, the color of purity, will ward off the jealous spirit attempting to return to its former place in the world. Similar theory equates red with the blood of war, anger, and passion; blue with the sky and the sacredness of the heavens; green with growth, etc. But so many exceptions may be noted that any such generalization is dangerous. In India black and red and yellow are all protective against spirits, which do not like these colors. Red and purple are potent in Japanese magic. The Yezidis of the Caucasus and Armenia cannot stand blue and their worst imprecation is "May you die in blue garments." Green is disliked by some peoples, perhaps because it is the color of pus and corruption, but in Islam it is the color borne by the descendants of Mohammed. The "blue-blooded" aristocracy of Europe is born to wear the purple. But in Malaya the blood of kings is white, and the purple of the ancient world was more often a shade of crimson than it was a purple (thus the fame of the Tyrian purple dye).

Flags and coats of arms have symbolic colors. The flags of Moslem countries show green; the flag of revolution is red with the dawn of a new day; the pirate's flag was black as death. The colors of the Stars and Stripes were early officially defined: white for purity and innocence; red for hardiness and valor; blue for vigilance, perseverance, and justice. Colors also have their significance in games. White and black always vie in chess, and in chess problems white always is "to move and win." The White Sox, the Red Sox, the Browns, and the Reds play major-league baseball; the Crimson of Harvard and the Blue of Yale meet on the football field, as the Blue and Light Blue of Oxford and Cambridge row against each other.

Color plays an important part in the relationship of men socially. Race, color, or previous condition of servitude are singled out in the 15th amendment to the Constitution of the United States. The "black" race is no more black than the "white" race is white, yet those are the color terms commonly in use, though the one is brown rather than black and the other pink rather than white. Colors, a striking feature of what we see, are often not discriminated clearly. Not because they are color-blind, but because they have no use for a finer distinction, some primitive peoples see no more than three or four colors in the world around them. They have no terms for many of the colors other peoples see. But the artist sees many more than the average person does, and beyond the limits of the range of human sight lie the many rich colors of dreams and fairyland.

☞ Ancient Maya and Aztec legends are replete with references to the symbolism of color. Colors most frequently mentioned are yellow, red, white, and black, the colors of the main types of maize grown. Each cardinal direction was associated with a particular deity who helped support the sky, and who was also symbolized by one of these colors. This basic theme of color symbolism seems to have pervaded all of Middle America. Modern myths from as far south as the Cuna Indians of Panama speak of colored mists, winds, or directions. [GMF]

coltsfoot A low perennial herb of the composite family (*Tussilago farfara*) bearing yellow flowers. The dried leaves of this plant, burnt and inhaled for lung infections, is a remedy so old as to have been known to Pliny; it still bears the popular name "coughwort." In Ireland the coltsfoot, *sponnc*, is used for tinder, sometimes as a substitute for tobacco, and is said to be "good for many ills." Soldiers in Europe during World War II are known to have smoked it as a substitute for tobacco. In Bavaria a soothing poultice is made of coltsfoot leaves to relieve toothache; the white-ribbed surface of the leaves is placed against the cheek.

columbine A herbaceous plant (genus *Aquilegia*) with flowers of five petals: named from Latin *columba*, dove, from the remembrance of the flowers to a group of doves. It was once called lion's herb from the belief that lions fed on it, and merely rubbing the hands with the leaves imparted courage and daring. It was an herb of Venus, and also an emblem of folly and the deserted lover. A concoction made from the leaves was considered a cure for jaundice, sore mouth, and sore throat.

combite A cooperative agricultural work organization of Haiti: the Mirebalais form of the more general Société Congo. Whenever anyone needs help in the fields, he calls a combite, any day but a Tuesday or a Sunday. Tuesdays are reserved for work in one's own fields; Sundays are rest days. Combite gatherings are occasions of great fun and social merriment. The hard work involved is offset by the emotional stimulus of the rhythmical working together, the social contacts, the gossipy combite songs, and the big feast when the work is over.

The workers line up in long lines with their hoes, with the drummer in front of them. The work is accompanied by drum and lambi (conch-shell horns) which set the rhythm, and the songs of the simidor (song leader) who is among the workers. The rhythm of the drum is the rhythm of the work, and the rhythm first set is maintained throughout, with the result that an enormous amount of work is accomplished with marvelous speed. The women of the household that called the combite prepare the food for the evening feast. Shirkers are ridiculed, i.e. those who came late, ostensibly for the feast, or those who dawdled and fell out of the rhythm of the work. Etiquette demands that they too be fed at the feast, but they always receive small portions. Those who worked hardest are given heaping dishes, and sometimes a hard worker will discover that he has bitten down on a piece of money hidden in his food. See DOKPWE.

combite songs Songs sung by Haitian agricultural work groups, or combites, to set a rhythm for the hoes. They are strongly melodic in character and generally follow the pattern of a theme stated by the leader, the simidor, with a chorus in unison by the rest of the workers. The simidor improvises on any subject of current interest, often gossip about a neighbor, sly digs at the hospitality of the household for which the work is being done, ridicule of a slacker, or the juicy details of the latest scandal. Songs of ridicule and derision are dreaded, and with reason, for the simidor is a wit and often a cruel one. Though the words are in the mixed French and Negro dialect of Haiti, the custom of such singing is rooted in Africa, where for centuries the ancestors of these work groups have used their songs to pace their labor and to keep every person in his place.

come-all-ye A type of narrative song, street ballad, or "vulgar" ballad, beloved of English, Irish, and American singers, so called from the characteristic opening phrase ("Come all ye loyal Union men," it may say, or "all you sons of freedom," or "all you jolly sailors," etc.) and devoted to the careers, loves, and adventures of working people—lumbermen, sailors, carpenters, miners, maidservants. It differs from the earlier classic ballad in metric pattern and rime scheme, being in double common meter, often with syllables crowded between accents (the "accordion line"). "You have to mash some of the words together to make it come out," singers explain. It also differs from the classic ballad in narrative technique, running as a continuous, journalistic account, sometimes in the first person, with names, places, dates, weather conditions carefully detailed, with very little dialogue, and often with a pointed moral. The singing style, too, is unlike ballad-singing. The singer identifies himself emotionally with his story, and especially in the northeastern United States makes use of the dramatic *rubato-parlando* recitative manner, with the final word spoken rather than sung.

Such songs appeared widely in England in the late 17th century, peddled in the streets and country byways by itinerant broadside venders, singers and beggars, and in Ireland in the 18th and 19th centuries, when the English language was taking hold among the people. *Van Dieman's Land* and *The Girl I Left Behind Me* are examples of the type. Many of them have refrains from the Gaelic ("shule aroon," for instance) some so corrupted as to appear to be nonsense.

In America this ballad style, especially as sung to old Irish airs by Irish immigrant workingmen, became the most popular and was the model for the native balladry of the shanty boys, the railroaders, the miners and cowboys, etc. A typical career ballad such as *The Sailors' Come-All-Ye* builds up the heroism, cleverness, and stamina required for the particular calling and warns the girls against the men of any other rival trade. Other types tell of the death of heroes of the group (*The Jam on Gerry's Rocks*), of bold bad men (*Sam Bass* and the Irish *Brennan on the Moor*), of jamborees, and practical jokes, and the drinking capacity of the men.

The term "come-all-ye" is applied indiscriminately by the singers to all sorts of folk song, including survivals of ancient ballads such as *Lady Isabel and the Elf Knight, Lord Randal,* and *Our Good Man,* several of which have been recast by Irish and American singers to a style more like the street songs. [TCB]

comet Not only in antiquity, but through the centuries among all people, comets have aroused in man a feeling of terror and foreboding. These mysterious visitors in the heavens have been thought to be connected with war, famine, the plague, the downfall of kings and monarchs, the end of the world, universal suffering, ill-luck, and sickness. Outstanding examples of the fear excited in the minds of the people are the incidents connected with the appearance and reappearance of Halley's comet. In 218 this comet preceded the death of Emperor Macrinus, in 451 that of Attila. In 1066 it was regarded as a "warning" against the Norman Conquest and is depicted in the Bayeaux tapestry.

In the Tyrol, the comet, if white, may bring luck and peace and a change in the affairs of men. The comet may herald a divinity; the Star of Bethlehem is sometimes said to have been a comet. Early conceptions of the comet saw in it a dragon or a serpent. Throughout the world when these heavenly visitants appeared, the rites of protection against them were prayers, bell-ringing, fasting, and so on. [GPS]

comics Cartoons or illustrations in a panel or a series of boxes arranged in a single strip or block, with speech generally enclosed in a balloon pointing to the speaker's mouth, used to tell a complete story or part of a story, amusing or exciting, about a continuing cast of characters. As a form of mass entertainment and mass communication developed in the 1890s by yellow journalism under the guise of "giving the public what it wants" and to build circulation, the comics have become a profitable and powerful American institution and industry that has spread throughout the world. By dealing with noncontroversial subjects, stressing humor, sentiment, and action, and building up a strong, attractive, central personality, the comics appeal to the widest possible audience. Like other subliterary forms, the dime novel and the pulps, the comics depict a world of adventure, mystery, and love, in which, however, fun, fantasy, and action take the place of success.

The comics use familiar folk themes and motifs (e.g. the bad boy, the henpecked husband, the helpless clown, the bungler, the feuding cat and mouse, Cinderella, the little man who is always kicked around but gets his in the end), draw upon the folklore of American life (the he-man, the racing fan, the hill-billy), and transmute these universal and local elements into a gallery of folk characters that take their place beside the heroes of fairy tale, mythology, and fable.

Beginning as "funnies" (the Sunday color comics or "funny papers" antedating the daily across-the-page strip in black and white), with a strong appeal to children, the comics at first largely employed child and animal characters: James Swinnerton's *Little Bears and Tigers* (1892), R. F. Outcault's *Yellow Kid* (1896) and *Buster Brown* (1902), Rudolph Dirks' *Katzenjammer Kids* (1897), Swinnerton's *Little Jimmy* (1905), and George Herriman's *Krazy Kat* (1910). Turning to sports, business, and family life in such strips as Bud Fisher's *Mutt and Jeff* (1907), *Hall Room Boys* (1910), Harry Hershfield's *Abie the Agent,* and George McManus' *Bringing Up Father* (1913), the comics gradually became more adult, serious, and "straight" in content. In 1929, with the advent of Tarzan and Buck Rogers, cartoon gave way to illustration and humor to suspense—a change confirmed with the coming of the comic book in 1933. (See Coulton Waugh, *The Comics,* New York, 1947).

Many later strips—*Moon Mullins, Smoky Stover, Silly*

Milly, Peter Piltdown, Oaky Doaks, and *Sad Sack*—continue in the slapstick and clowning tradition of earlier successes, from F. Opper's *Happy Hooligan* (1899) to Segar's *Popeye* (1929). But recent successes tend away from gags and laughs toward action-packed adventure and romance of the illustrated story type, from the more realistic Joe Palooka, Mickey Finn, Don Winslow, and Terry, to the romantic Tarzan and Prince Valiant, the interplanetary Buck Rogers and Flash Gordon, and the supernatural Superman, Mandrake the Magician, Phantom, Wonder Woman, and Batman. In the same illustrated-story genre are the westerns (King of the Royal Mounted, The Lone Ranger, and Red Ryder), the detectives (Dick Tracy). Two strips competing for first place, *Blondie* and *Li'l Abner,* are in the earlier tradition of humor and sentiment, while Barnaby, Henry, Smitty, Nancy, and Little Lulu inherit the mantle of Skippy, Skeezix, Skinnay, Dotty Dimples, and Little Mary Mixup.

The same division of labor between humor and adventure, cartoon and illustration, is also seen in the comic book, where the favorite animal screen characters (Mickey Mouse, Donald Duck, Bugs Bunny, Porky Pig, Woody Woodpecker, and Andy Panda) still delight tiny tots and appease solicitous mothers, while crime, teenage problems, love, westerns, and interplanetary adventure compete with the pulps, true confession magazines, and soap opera for the adolescent and adult audience. On the screen the animated cartoon (especially in the hands of Walt Disney) adheres more closely to the original "funnies" formula, recreates fairy tales (*Three Little Pigs, Snow White and the Seven Dwarfs*), and draws upon American folklore (Uncle Remus, Johnny Appleseed, Pecos Bill).

At the same time the powerful potentialities of the comic books (which have created an entirely separate industry with its own problems of editorial policy and public criticism and control) for educational and propaganda purposes have enlisted the attention of educators and psychiatrists (both as advisers and critics) as well as of advertising agencies and promotion departments of the great industrial corporations. The cultural impact of the comics may be gauged by the fact that in Crystal City, Texas, in the heart of the spinach-growing section, a monument has been erected to Popeye; and Sadie Hawkins Day is celebrated by some 40,000 groups over the country.

To American folk humor and speech the comics have contributed a wealth of gags, slang, and proverbial expressions—Mutt and Jeff's fall guy, good thing, piker; Popeye's goon, I yam what I yam; Rube Goldberg's I'm the guy, Ike and Mike they look alike; Barney Google's heebie-jeebies; Tad Dorgan's applesauce, 23 skidoo, cake-eater, dumb Dora, dumbbell, nobody home, you said it, the cat's pajamas, Quick Watson, the needle— and the vocabulary of violence, pow, zowie, socko, bam. To folklore too belong the "changeling personality" or transformations of Clark Kent to Superman, with the magic amulet that enables Tiny Tim to assume minute or normal size, and the magic formula, "Schazam," that changes a crippled newsboy into Captain Marvel, Jr. Alley Oop's time-machine and Buck Rogers' space ship are typical of the comics' inventions, in the Jules Verne– H. G. Wells tradition. In 1939 Buck Rogers mentioned

"atomic bombs." Even more miraculous is the ham-shaped creature, the Shmoo, which lays eggs, gives creamery butter and Grade-A milk, dies of sheer joy when looked at hungrily, tastes like chicken when fried, like steak when broiled, like pork chops when roasted, and multiplies so fast that it always keeps a half dozen ahead of you. In prolificness, versatility, and inexhaustible abundance the Shmoo is a true symbol of the comics.

B. A. BOTKIN

commonlaw A term used in the United States, especially in verb form (*to commonlaw*), by Negroes of lower socio-economic strata to denote the act of living in an extra-legal, but socially sanctioned mating of the type found in various New World Negro societies. See AMASIADO. [MJH]

Common Mother In a few South American Indian tribes, the highest deity. The Kaggaba Indians of Colombia describe her as the "mother of all human races, of the world, of the animals, fruits, trees, rivers, thunders, the Milky Way, songs, demons, sacred objects, and sanctuaries." Her sons were the ancestors of mankind. The most powerful spirit of the Chamacoco Indians was also a woman who controlled the world and sent rain. The Yaruro have a goddess from whom "everything sprang." [AM]

compadrazgo Throughout Middle America, the reciprocal relationships which arise through the taking of godparents: Spanish in origin. However, its importance is so great as to suggest that it takes the place of some type of pre-Conquest formalized friendship organization. It is found equally among the most remote Indians and in large cities among mestizos. Two types of relationships are set up: (1) between godparents and godchildren, and (2) between godparents and the parents of their godchildren. The latter address each other as *compadre* or *comadre,* "co-father" or "co-mother," or by Indian equivalents. Godparents are taken particularly at baptism, confirmation, and marriage, but they may be taken on many other occasions, such as fiestas and the like. One can have *compadres* and *comadres* without having godchildren. Sometimes, for example, at the completion of a new home, a housewarming ceremony is held in which the owner and his wife take *compadres* of the house, which in a sense functions itself in the place of a godchild. [GMF]

Compair Bouki Comrade Bouki: Louisiana Negro designation for the Bouki of Haitian folktale. What animal Bouki represents in the Louisiana stories is not indicated. The name seems to have been accepted without question or knowledge of its meaning. Dr. Alcée Fortier in *Louisiana Folk-Tales, MAFLS* 2, p. 94, says that Bouki is a Wolof word for hyena. Charles L. Edwards in *Bahama Songs and Stories, MAFLS* 3, suggests that if the B'Bouki of Bahama Negro folktale is from *bouc,* goat, the story-tellers do not know it, an assumption entirely borne out by a Bahama story in which B'Goat, B'Bouki, and B'Rabby all start out together to go fishing. See BOUKI.

Compair Lapin Comrade Rabbit: Louisiana Negro name for Brer Rabbit.

companyá A type of extra-legal mating found among the Negroes of Curaçao. See AMASIADO.

comparative method A system of study of folklore material used generally by the anthropological school, based on the general observation that culture develops evolutionarily and that consequently each people passes through the same general stages of development, but not at the same rate. It is valid, the proponents of this method hold, to study a backward culture to explain the more puzzling elements in a more advanced culture. For example, they hold that the common uncle-nephew relation in the stories of the Middle Ages can be explained by the belief that these people once had a matriarchial system of society in which, of course, a man's nearest relative was his sister's son. See ANTHROPOLOGICAL SCHOOL. [MEL]

Comparetti, Domenico Pietro Antonio (1835–1927?) Italian philologist, known especially for his studies in epigraphy, papyrology, and dialect, and as a student of Romance philology and of medieval culture. He was born in Rome and died in Florence. In 1859 he was appointed professor of Greek at the University in Pisa. With Alessandro d'Ancona he edited a collection of Italian national songs and stories, *Conti e racconti del popolo italiano* (nine volumes, 1870–1891?). Many of these were collected and written down for the first time, by Comparetti. In *Il Kalevala o la poesia tradizionale dei Finni* (1891), translated in English in 1898 by I. M. Anderton, Comparetti discusses whether an epic can be composed by the interweaving of national songs, as in the *Kalevala*. Comparetti decides against it and applies his conclusion to the problem of Homer. The same question is dealt with in his treatise *La commissione omerica di Pisistrato* (1881). Comparetti's researches concerning the Book of Sindibad have been translated and printed in the *Proceedings* of the Folklore Society.

complaint An old type of folk poem or song arising from funeral customs in which the dead were propitiated by eulogies and lamentations. The Scottish coronach and Irish keen are survivals.

complainte A term favored by many scholars for the come-all-ye type of ballad in French and for the women's chanson de toile, including pastourelles, chansons de mal mariées, reverdies, etc.

compressible objects A folktale motif (D491 ff.) in which objects become large or small according to the need, convenience, or will of the hero. Giants and ogres (or the Devil) contract to normal size; pigmies and dwarfs become giants (as the ocean thumbling in the *Kalevala* who shot to hero stature and felled the oak for Väinämöinen), or diminish in order to enter bottles (or the nostrils of ogres or cannibals, as in a Zulu folktale). There are compressible canoes in Iroquois folktale, compressible ships in old Scandinavian legend, reducible and expandable animals, game, food, kettles, etc., throughout general Eurasian and American folktale, to say nothing of the white mule of Chang-kuo Lao, which could be folded up like paper and put in his wallet.

Comus In late Roman mythology, the god of revelry, drunkenness, and mirth: a winged youth, overflowing with health, a companion of Dionysus. He and Momus had charge of entertaining the Olympians. He is represented crowned with roses, dressed in white, and bearing a torch.

Con A major deity of the coastal people of ancient Peru. He was conceived of as a boneless being that moved swiftly across the air. In his rapid and sinuous wanderings, he changed the surface of the earth, leveling some mountains and turning plains into summits. He created men and women and gave them all kinds of food plants. Because of some offense on the part of his creatures, he dried up the land and prevented the fall of rain. Then came Pachacamac who, like Con, was the Sun's son. He changed Con's men into wild cats and created new people to whom he gave all the things owned by their descendants. [AM]

Conall Céarneaċ Conall the Victorious; in Old Irish legend one of the three first champions of Ulster (with Cuchulain and Loeġaire Buadaċ), and cousin of Cuchulain. Conall with Loeġaire Buadaċ was one of the companions of Cuchulain on his journey to the land of Scáthac, until they were turned back by enchantments and Cuchulain went on alone. Conall was also one of the three champions of Ulster who contended for the champion's portion at Bricriu's feast.

concha A primitive lutelike instrument of Mexico, having five double strings and a body of armadillo shell: literally, shell. It is played in simple chords of self-accompaniment by the dancers during the concheros' ceremonies and is regarded not as background but as an integral part of the dance. Its origin is obscure. The dance which it accompanies is partly of pre-Columbian origin. The way of playing differs from the European, but since lutes were unknown on the American continent before the Conquest, the concha may be a later adaptation of some ancient Aztec instrument.

los Concheros Literally, the concha players; members of votive dance societies, especially widespread among the Aztec Indians, the Otomí, Matlacinco, and Chichimeca of the Mexican states of México, Querétaro, and Guanajuato. Both primitive and Christian elements are fused in their specific dance, a Danza de Promesa, whose function is the fulfilling of a vow. There is no explanation of any other meaning. The huge multicolored, beaded, feather headdresses (typically Aztec) and fringed costumes follow pre-Columbian tradition; the banners which lead the preliminary processionals depict Christian symbols, usually Christ Crucified between two sorrowing Marys. The Holy Cross is worshipped in the recurring step of the dance, called *la cruz*, the cross. But in secret rites the cross is worshipped as the four winds. In San Miguel de Allende, very ancient personifications accompany the dancers: Oxomoco and Xipactonatl, the Nahua ancestors of the gods and creators of mankind, also a pair of sortílegos (masked sorcerers), a ragged viejo (old man), a horned clown-devil, and two transvestite Malinches.

The Concheros march to the church in a group with their banner-bearer. An alabanza (religious praise-song) begins the performance. The leader starts the first tune on his concha; the others join. They punctuate with native stampings their phrases of springy European jigs, skips, rockings, pas de basques. The incisive beat of the hard-soled sandals (huarachas) keeps perfect time with the typical rhythmic chords of their self-accompaniment on the conchas. Each dancer dances for himself, in his own place, to his own accompaniment. The strenuous performance continues at intervals all day.

At Carnival the Concheros share fiestas with other ceremonial groups. In San Miguel de Allende, on St. Michael's day (September 29), they commemorate in spectacular array the raising of the Holy Cross on Sangremal. The memorable battle of Sangremal is enacted by los Rayados, taking the parts of both the Chichimecas and the conquering Christians. The ancient indigenous symbols and this battle mime suggest an original function similar to that of the European Moriscas, i.e. vegetation rites. But the missionaries have instilled into the minds of the Indians a confused notion that the dance represents the joy of the Indians at being conquered for the realm of Christ. Although transfered to a newer Deity the ancient ritualism survives in the dance in an intense, aloof fervor of mien and gesture. [GPK]

Conchobar mac Nessa In Old Irish legend, king of Ulster about the beginning of the Christian era; uncle and fosterer of Cuchulain. Fergus was king before him, whose wife Nessa persuaded him to give up the throne to her son Conchobar. Some say Conchobar was the son of Cathbad the druid. His seat was at Emain Macha; the ruins of the great fort can still be seen near Armagh. It was Conchobar who spared Deirdre at her birth against the advice of Cathbad, and said he would have her for wife himself when she was grown. Conchobar did have her for wife himself for one year, after his betrayal of the three sons of Usnech. But Deirdre killed herself. For this betrayal Conchobar was doomed to see all of his sons die ahead of him. A later legend says that Conchobar died the day that Christ was crucified, in a fit of overexertion in proof of what he would do to save Christ if he were near that place.

Concordia The Roman goddess of peace and harmony: identified with the Greek Aphrodite Pandemos and with the deified Harmonia. Concordia had several temples in Rome, one on the Capitoline dating from the reestablishment of concord between the patricians and plebs and erected by Camillus in 367 B.C. As Concordia Augusta, she presided over the peace of the imperial household. Offerings were made to her on the birthdays of the emperors. Her symbols were the herald's staff entwined by serpents, and two clasped hands. She was represented as a matronly figure, bearing the cornucopia in her left hand, and an olive branch in her right.

confession Catharsis by the recital of some transgression involving an uncleanness affecting an individual or his group: a religious custom found all over the world from the Eskimos to the Bechuana in Africa, from the Tupinamba in South America to the Bataks of Sumatra, and from the most ancient times in Babylonia and Egypt to the present day. Confession is sometimes direct, as by a worshipper to his god; sometimes the confessor must have the mediation of a priest (shaman, etc.); sometimes confession is made before the group assembled. Penance or sacrifice is often entailed, though sometimes simple admission of guilt effects the purification or salvation. As contrasted with positive confession of sins committed, the ancient Egyptians had a Negative Confession denying specific sins,

those sins not in the canon being ignored. Among the Eskimos, as reported by Rasmussen, a public confession takes place after a certain degree of inspiration has occurred; revival meetings in the United States are reminiscent of this "intoxication of delight" of the Eskimos. The transgression of moral or divine law is sometimes manifested by storms, earthquakes, or the like, and requires the guilty person to stand forth and confess. Personal damnation such as that undergone by the unconfessed sinner of Christianity may infect those with whom he comes in contact. Confession is therefore a necessity to the community lest it suffer blight or other disaster through divine anger, just as confession is necessary to the man ill and like to die because of his sin.

The confessional and its secrets are favorite themes of medieval European folktale. Since sincere repentance, even at the moment of death, might save the soul of the sinner from eternal damnation, tales of miraculous opportunities for the dying to confess occur: the unshriven are brought back from death that they may confess (V23.1); death is held back that a soul may be saved (V251); the dumb obtain the power of speech that they may confess (V23.2). The anticlerical motifs of the priest who hears the confession of and gives absolution to his own paramour and of the priest who discloses confessional secrets appear in various tales. Confession runs like a theme through a collection like Boccaccio's *Decameron*. Typical is the tale of the clever woman (3rd day, 3rd story) who informs her lover when and how to come to her by "confessing" to the friar that he has made advances to her. The friar in turn chides the young man, who has done nothing of the sort, and thus acts unwittingly as the go-between until his services are no longer required.

☞ The confession of "sins," that is to say of ritual and magical transgressions, was widely practiced among the ancient Peruvians. It was compulsory in case of illness and before certain feasts. At first confessions were made in public, but later they became secret. Certain hideous crimes were reported only to the supreme priest or to his immediate assistants. After enumerating his sins, the penitent bathed in a river to purify himself. To placate the offended supernaturals, he observed several penances, such as continence, fasts, or periods of complete isolation. Confession still plays an important part in the religious life of the Kaggaba and Ijca Indians of Colombia. It is also reported among a few tribes of the Amazonian lowlands, in particular among the ancient Tupinamba. Tabu violations were confided to shamans in order to avert greater evils. [AM]

conflicting brothers One of the major recurrent themes of Melanesian mythology, in which the culture hero is hampered in his beneficent, creative, or tutelary activities by one or more lazy, stupid, or sometimes antagonistic brothers. Qat in the Banks Islands, Tagaro in the Banks and New Hebrides, Warohunuga in the Solomons, To Karvuvu and To Kabinana in New Britain are popular examples. R. B. Dixon in the *Mythology of All Races*, vol. 9, "Oceanic," discusses these at length. See MELANESIAN MYTHOLOGY. [KL]

Confucius (551–478 B.C.) Chinese sage, philosopher, and moralist. See KUNG FU TZE.

confusion of tongues A widespread motif of mythology and folktale (A1333) explaining why the peoples of the world speak different languages. In practically all mythologies all the people once spoke but one language and all could understand each other. Usually in punishment either for some impudence, disobedience, or broken tabu the separation of languages is visited upon them and they cannot understand each other.

The story is very widespread among North American Indians of the West and is also known among the northeastern Algonquians and among the Iroquois. Entirely apart from the Tower of Babel idea (which has found its way into North American Indian folktale) the separation of languages occurs variously. Sometimes it occurs casually without specific reason: the Chemetunne (Oregon) creator, for instance, merely "told the man" that he, his wife, and their children would speak different languages and be progenitors of the different tribes. In a Shoshonean myth Coyote did the wrong thing by opening the creator's sack in his absence; the people rushed out of the sack all shouting in different languages, and were therefore destined to fight and kill one another. Another Shoshonean story says that Cõtsipamã-pot, the old woman who made the earth, caused all the tribes to speak different languages.

From Siberia to Indochina, in the Pacific, and in Africa there are explanatory myths for the difference of languages. Frazer's study of the Tower of Babel turns up a number of world myths unconnected with the Biblical story. Diversity of language is accounted for among the East African WaSamia, for instance, by the fact that once the people, crazed with famine, wandered jabbering in all directions. A hill tribe of Assam tells how the people once attacked a huge python to rescue the king's daughter, but as they struck the first blows, they were suddenly beset with confusion of tongues, and separated, each to become ancestor of a different tribe. Another Assam tale describes how three grandsons of a certain chief suddenly began to speak different languages while chasing a rat, and so great was their misunderstanding that the rat got away. The three boys parted and founded different tribes. A South Australian people were punished with confusion of tongues by an old woman named Wurruri, who used to walk among them and scatter their night fires with her stick. When she died the people rejoiced, divided, and devoured her body. Those who ate the different parts henceforth spoke different languages. (See Frazer, *Folklore in the Old Testament*, vol. 1, pp. 384 ff.)

The actual instability of some tribal languages from generation to generation is explained by a number of scholars as resulting from strict adherence to specific tabus, not from broken tabus. Among many primitive peoples, for instance, tabus against speaking the names of the dead cause many words to be dropped from a language, especially as innumerable personal names are also common nouns. See TOWER OF BABEL.

Conga A category of Haitian vodun deities, associated with the rada group in the organization of the vodun pantheon. [MJH]

Congo Among New World Negroes, the word Congo has been preserved as one of the most distinctive cultural retentions contributed by the many natives of this large area of Africa who were brought to the New World. Cult-groups termed Congo-Angola are found in Brazil; there are Congo spirits (*loa Congo*) among the vodun deities of Haiti; and the Place Congo in New Orleans was the center of African dancing. In such context, the name derives as much from the Kingdom of Kongo, near the mouth of the Congo River, as it does from the river itself (called until the mid-18th century the Zaire) or from the present African territory of that name. [MJH]

conjuration, conjurer, conjah, etc. Terms used by Negroes of the United States for the process of working magic, the worker of magic, and magic itself. In its varied forms, conjuration, like magic practices among New World Negroes everywhere, shows a high degree of purity of retention of Africanisms that indicate it to have been one of the most tenacious of African carry-overs. This is to be accounted for by the personal, uninstitutionalized forms taken by magic, and the ease with which it can be done even under the most repressive circumstances. Also of significance here is the conviction which the African magic carried to those who came into contact with it, often to whites as well as Negroes. [MJH]

Conla In Old Irish legend, the son of Cuchulain and Aoife. When the boy was grown she sent him to Ireland to find his father, but under *geis* not to tell his name to a single warrior. When he arrived he met and bested every warrior who went to meet him. His request to be met by two warriors, so that he could tell his name, was refused "for the honor of Ulster," because in Ulster two warriors never went out against one. He was killed by Cuchulain, his own father, before Cuchulain knew his name.

Con lõn In Annamese belief, spirits which appear in short successive incarnations; literally, entering life. The Con lõn are premature or stillborn children and a series of miscarriages occuring to one woman are believed to be reincarnations of the same spirit. A woman who has produced one or more Con lõn is believed contagious. No one will touch her or mention her. To prevent a reappearance of the Con lõn a dog is killed and buried under the bed of a woman who is about to be confined. See CÁM KHAM.

Con ma dãu In Annamese belief, the spirits of people who have died of smallpox: the cause of all serious cases of this disease. Victims are isolated by the Annamese, not for hygienic reasons but for fear of the Con ma dãu which are residing in their bodies.

Connla's Well In Old Irish mythology, a well under the sea (in the Land of Youth or Promise). Over it hung nine hazel trees, which leaved, flowered, and bore fruit all at once. These were the hazels of wisdom and knowledge and inspiration, the wisdom being concentrated in the nuts. The nuts dropped into the well and the salmon swimming in it ate the nuts. One could tell how many nuts a salmon had eaten by counting the spots on its body. Whoever drank of the water of this well, or ate of the nuts, or of those salmon would be endowed with miraculous wisdom and poetic inspiration. It is told how Sinend, a granddaughter of Lir, went to this well seeking wisdom, but the waters were unwilling to give it and rose up and drowned her, and washed her body to the shores of the river

Shannon. The Shannon is named for her: Irish, *Sionnain*. One of the *Dinnshenchas* mentions a beautiful fountain near Tipperary which is called Connla's Well.

Magic wisdom acquired from drinking of a certain well (D1811.1.2) is a common motif in Irish story, as is also the inevitable punishment following on a woman's disrespect of or intrusion on a magical or sacred well.

Conquista Literally, the Conquest; a mimetic battle dance of Mexico and Ecuador, related to the Morisca. In Mexico it enacts the conquest and conversion of Moctezuma by Cortes, aided by his mistress, Malinche. It is performed on saints' days from Nayarit to Chiapas, especially in Jalisco, Guerrero, and Oaxaca. Usually the native dialog, which alternates with the dance, is in Spanish; sometimes it is in obsolete and unintelligible Náhuatl, as the manuscript of San Cristobal. Here as in Oaxaca, the drama is entitled *un Cuarno* or *Cuaderno*. The elaborate version in Culiacán, Oaxaca, is called *Danza de las Plumas*. The Indians perform waltz, mazurka, and polka steps in quadrille formations. Their gorgeous high feathered headdresses contrast vividly with the drab blue soldier suits of Cortes' followers. In Jalisco the Spaniards are often represented as selfless soldiers of the Cross. [GPK]

Consentes Dii The twelve major Etruscan (and Roman) gods, six male and six female, who formed the council of Jupiter: often confounded with the twelve principal gods of Greece. Only Juno, Minerva, Summanus, Vulcan, Saturn, and Mars are known to have been among them; there is no agreement concerning the names of the others.

Constantine and Arete or **The Dead Brother's Return** A Greek traditional ballad, stemming from the ancient balladry of Asia Minor current when Hellenic civilization reached as far as the Euphrates. It features the dead rider motif: the demands of his mother compelled Constantine to return from the grave and fetch home his sister, Arete, from a distant land. Arete had married a foreign lover against her mother's will; the mother had finally consented to the match only because of Constantine's promise that he would go and bring her back when necessary, whatever the circumstances. Plague fell on the city; Arete's nine brothers all died; the mother sickened and called for her daughter. The dead Constantine, true to his promise, rode to the foreign country and brought his sister to the mother's bedside. But the girl and mother both died from the terror of the experience.

The Albanian *Constantine, the Dead Voyager,* the Rumanian *Voichita,* Bulgarian *Lazar and Petkana,* and the Serbian *Jovo and His Sister* are all separate (from each other) developments of this ballad. The English *Suffolk Miracle* (Child #272) is also a direct descendant from the Greek ballad, having been brought in by seafarers in the 18th century. See DEAD RIDER.

Consus An ancient Roman god, originally an agricultural deity, variously conceived of as the god of good counsel, of secret deliberations, of the stored harvest, of the underworld. There were two Consualia, festivals of Consus, one on August 21, another on December 15. At the August festival, among other countrylike amusements, there were horse-racing and racing of chariots drawn by mules. This connection with horses made

later writers identify Consus with Neptune (Poseidon Hippios), but there is no real parallel between the two. Ops was the consort of Consus.

The altar of Consus stood in the Circus Maximus and it was from the races at the Consualia that the horse-racing at the Circus arose. The games were believed founded by Romulus, and the famous rape of the Sabine women occurred at the first of these celebrations.

Contes de ma Mère l'Oye "Tales of Mother Goose," a collection of fairy tales by Charles Perrault published in 1697 as *Histoires ou Contes du Tems Passé avec des Moralités,* and then credited to Perrault d'Armancour, Perrault's ten-year-old son. These tales, written by Perrault, were collected from his contributions to the *Recueil de pieces curieuses et nouvelles,* a periodical published at The Hague from 1694 on. Among the prose tales thus reprinted in the *Histoires* were: The Sleeping Beauty (La Belle au Bois Dormant), Little Red Riding Hood (Le Petit Chaperon Rouge), Bluebeard (La Barbe Bleue), Puss in Boots (Le Maistre Chat ou Le Chat Botté), and Cinderella (Cendrillon, ou la petite pantoufle de verre). The popular name *Contes de ma Mère l'Oye* appears on a placard in the frontispiece of the *Histoires* as a subtitle. Perrault's stories are considered the telling *par excellence* of the French fairy tale.

contests Contests of many varieties are repeatedly mentioned in North American Indian myths, and serve either as self-contained incidents in tales, or as the central element and *raison d'être* for a tale. This plethora of contest material reflects, in a general way, the popularity of games of skill and chance among American Indians. The contests mentioned in tales may however be of quite a different order from those indulged in for stakes by actual men and women. Some of the contests described in tales which coincide with actual practices are: shooting, jumping, and wrestling matches, climbing a smooth pole, racing, ball games, diving, gambling, shinny, and sweating contests. More imaginative ones are: backscratching contest, contest for daylight, contests to keep awake, to spit up more fat than one's opponent, to eat more than one's opponent, to walk on water, and contests between heat and cold, sun and wind, etc. Many of the contests which reflect actual practices are won by deception in the tales, and the winner is often Trickster. Contests which involve the use of magical power are less likely to contain any elements of deception. [EWV]

Con-tinh In Annamese belief, the malevolent spirits of maidens who have died prematurely. The Con-tinh hide in old trees and laugh weirdly, rob passers-by of their souls and drive them insane. They also take vengeance on those who cut their trees, so the Annamese often persuade Christians to strike the first blow when they are forced to cut such a tree.

contradance Literally, dance of opposition; a dance performed by many couples face to face, line facing line, in square or longways. It developed in the 17th century and reached its height of popularity in the 18th century, only to give way to the waltz in the romantic era. The principle of this dance form is, however, by no means an innovation of the 17th century, but involves the principle of sexual attraction, approach, separation, and uniting, multiplied into communal participation. Such dances are very ancient and still exist among primitive peoples.

European peasantry and bourgeois society developed the contradance to its highest possible complexity. The corresponding country dances of England, numbering some 900 in 1728, and intensely popular to this day, explore every form of crossover and interweaving, with numbers of participants varying from four to an indefinite number. Sometimes each couple in succession leads through the figures, sometimes alternate couples, sometimes the whole group performs simultaneously.

The elaborate Spanish contradanza includes quadrille and longways types. The Italian cuntradanza is usually danced in longways form. There are variants in every province, as the *cuntradanza muntanaera* of Bologna, which ends with a grand right and left. The German and Scandinavian Kontra is usually a quadrille, often having unique figures. The *Föhringer Kontra* contains circling, swinging of partners, and a wheelbarrow step of the boy pushing the girl backwards. Offsprings of the French contredanse were the cotillon and quadrille, which developed into the American square dance. [GPK]

contradanza In Spain and Latin America, a figure dance for eight, sixteen, or thirty-two couples, corresponding to the French contredanse and the English country dance. The contradanza includes almost every possible kind of group pattern: *cruz* (crossover), *esquinas* (corners), *cadenas* (heys), *latigazos* (whips), *molinillos* (mills), *caracol* (snails), etc.

The contradanza *cuadrada* is performed by four couples in square formation, as indicated by the name. The contradanza *de dos parejos* involves two couples face to face. The contradanza *larga* (long) is performed in longways formation.

These same formations occur in less complete array in ritual dances for men, especially in sword dances. But the contradanza proper is a social dance, which displaced the minuet in the 18th century. The music is in duple time, in phrases of eight regular measures. [GPK]

Con trăm nu'ó'c In Annamese belief, a fabulous water buffalo. Anyone who possesses a hair of the Con trăm nu'ó'c and holds it in his hand can cross a river dryshod.

contrapás A Catalan round dance for men and young women, holding hands in alternation, the woman to the right of her partner. It is related to the Greek sirtos, Rumanian sarba, and Serbian kolo, and particularly resembles the Catalan national dance, the sardana. It is as popular in the streets and plazas of the cities as in rural districts. In the province of Gerona the progression of the *empurdanés* (named after Ampurdán) is predominantly to the left; that of the *selvatá* (after Selva), to the right. At times the *cap* and *cua* (head and tail), who direct the steps, break their hold and convert the closed round into an open round. The grapevine-type steps, called punts, are of two kinds. The first part of the dance consists of *curts* (shorts) with two steps to each side, the second part of *llarcs* (longs) with four steps each way, usually dwindling to combinations of two and three at the end of a section,

to fit the irregular phrasing of the music. The *trencats* are rapid, bouncing elaborations. The *camadas* and *girats* are high kicks and turns by men at the end of a phrase. As a climax the men may hoist the ladies into the air, a figure called *lo salt*, the leap.

The music of the special ensemble, the *cobla*, was originally scored for a *cornemusa* or bagpipe, also called *criatura verde* (green creature) because of its green color, a one-man drum and flaviol, and a cornet. Nowadays the ten musicians play the drum-flaviol, four woodwinds, four brass winds, and a double bass. The tunes, new and old, are original and in a Mixolydian mode. The tunes for the *llarcs* are livelier than for the *curts*.

A chant precedes the dance, commemorating the Passion of Our Lord, possibly at one time a joyful pæan. A century ago the contrapás was still part of the liturgical drama enacted in the church or atrium; today, though secularized, it retains much of its ceremonial absorption. Its origin is probably a pre-Christian rite adapted to ecclesiastical purposes. [GPK]

controversies Controversial arguments between two characters usually revolve, in North American Indian tales, around such questions as whether people shall stay dead after they die; whether life shall be easy or difficult; whether childbirth shall be easy or hard; how long day and night, or the seasons will last. Generally two animals, one of them Trickster, argue these matters out; usually the proponent for the negative or more disagreeable side wins. Occasionally a certain poetic justice manifests itself when the winner of the controversy is himself distressed, as in the tale of the origin of death, in which Coyote argues that people shall die and stay dead, but later when his own child dies regrets his decision. [EWV]

conundrums The petty and more trifling riddles, especially those containing puns, are commonly termed conundrums. They are usually based upon a single point of fanciful resemblance, often forced, between objects or persons, or upon a play on words, stated in brief question and answer form; whereas riddles *per se* are apt to be longer, more complex in imagery, and more pretentiously literary in structure, frequently in rime.

Punning questions were widely known, of course, long before the word conundrum was used to designate them, and have always been common, particularly in the folklore of the illiterate and semi-literate. Many of them depend upon oral presentation for their force, and lose it when written.

Radio and video programs today repeat "wheezes," "gags," and "screams" (so named colloquially from the effect supposedly induced in the listener) which are merely revamped conundrums from the minstrel and vaudeville shows of the 19th century, conundrums which had already suffered several previous incarnations. A few samples are sufficient:

> Why is the letter K like a pig's tail?
> Because it is the end of pork.
>
> Why is it easier to read in October?
> Because then the leaves turn themselves.
>
> Why is no one hungry in the Sahara Desert?
> Because of the sand which is there.

The fact that for centuries many people had no book but the Bible led to the growth and wide circulation of a number of Biblical conundrums. (The writer has collected 155 from correspondents who got them by word of mouth from older folk and had usually never seen them written.) Some of these Biblical conundrums are atrocious puns, and several must needs abide in the oral tradition. There was evidently seldom if ever any conscious irreverence in their use, however, but rather an attitude of friendly familiarity with the Bible characters. The following are representative:

At what time of day was Adam created?
A little before Eve.

When was salt meat introduced into the navy?
When Noah took Ham into the ark.

Who was the best wrestler in the Bible?
Jonah, because even the whale couldn't hold him after he got him down.

How do we know Moses wore a wig?
Because sometimes he was seen with Aaron, and sometimes without.

It may be noted that this last conundrum and the previously given Sahara Desert one illustrate the essentially oral character of these trick questions. See RIDDLES.
[CFP]

cooked cock crows The motif (E528.2.1) of a Christian legend very widespread in western Ireland. A group of soldiers, set to guard the tomb of Christ, were sitting on the ground around their fire. They were boiling a cock in the pot for their morning meal. And they were troubled in their minds, for it was said that Christ would rise from the dead and walk out of the tomb. One of them, however, believed no foolish tales; he declared Christ would not rise, "no more than the cock in the pot." Whereupon the cock jumped out of the pot and crowed, and at daybreak Christ rose and came out to them. Certain variants put the fatal words in the mouth of Judas's wife, to comfort her husband who was worried lest Christ should rise. The incident occurs also in European, English, and Scottish balladry and carol. See CAROL.

copal The native Middle American incense, used in pre-Conquest times, and widely used today in many ceremonies, both Christian and pagan. It is a gum secreted from trees of the genus *Elaphrium*. [GMF]

copeo A popular couple dance from the island of Majorca, performed by one couple alone or by many. The woman leads, dictating the various vigorous movements, jumps, turns, etc. The man may imitate her or improvise. [GPK]

Cophetua Hero of an English ballad, *Cophetua and the Beggar Maid*, found in the Percy manuscript; a traditional African king and misogynist, who fell in love with a beggar maid whom he happened to see. They were married and lived uneventfully. The girl's name was Penelophon. The story is referred to by both Shakespeare and Jonson, and it is the subject of Tennyson's poem, *The Beggar Maid*.

copper This metal, which is sometimes found in pure state, has been known to man since a very early age. Unlike pure gold, copper was suitable for use as a tool or weapon, and so among early peoples it was often more highly prized. It was in use in the world long before the discovery of iron. In Asia it was the metal of the Queen of Heaven (Astarte, etc.); astrologers and alchemists assigned it to Venus; it was sacred to the Fire God and the Seven Gods of Babylonia and Assyria; North Pacific Coast Indians and several other groups assigned it to the Sun; in India and parts of North America it was a sacred metal used principally for ornaments and sacrificial instruments; the Indians of the Lake Superior region regarded the lumps of copper they found as divinities or as the gift of gods that dwelt beneath the water.

In India, especially in the Punjab, copper earrings were worn to ward off the demons of sciatica, and in Europe in the Middle Ages it was believed that copper wire bound about the waist would relieve rheumatism. In some places there is a custom of placing copper on a corpse (in Ireland, pennies on the eyes; in Dharwar, 21 engraved pieces). Among the Swahili a Balderlike myth tells of a chief who could be killed only by a copper needle driven through his navel. Pliny mentions that in Arcadia the yew tree is fatal to anyone sleeping under it unless a copper nail is driven into the tree. As late as the middle of the 18th century the Spaniards believed that copper grew in the ground, and that if a mine was left alone, it would become productive again.

Coquena The supernatural protector of the vicuñas in the Quechua folklore of the Puna de Atacama. He is a little man dressed in white who travels at night driving large herds of vicuña. He punishes those who wantonly destroy these animals. [AM]

Cora The Maiden, a name of Persephone. In some variants of the Persephone legend, Cora becomes mother, without there being a father, of Corybas, the ancestor of the Corybantes. See PERSEPHONE.

coral A calcareous treelike structure formed by colonies of marine skeletons, and used as a gem. While usually red in color, it may be white, pink, yellow, blue, brown, or black. It has been highly valued as an amulet everywhere it occurs and a list of its properties reads like a catalog of the ills suffered by mankind from the mind, the body, and the elements. It is so desirable that in Africa human sacrifice is offered to induce it to remain and reproduce. The Chinese and Hindus use it to adorn their gods. It guards those who wear it from fascination, bewitchment, and lunacy. Pure red coral is effective against evil eye, demons, and furies; in Italy where conditions are worse, witches, wizards, incubi, succubi, and phantasmata were added to the list. Brown coral is not so used, however; the evil spirits like that. Hung in the house coral prevents discord, disharmony, envy, and evil influences; hung on the bedpost it prevents nightmare, terror in the night, and night sweats; carried about the person it guards against feuds, guile, scorn, etc. In the Middle Ages it was a must in every pharmacy, and moreover care had to be used in its preparation. Coral ground in a brass mortar was very dangerous to the patient, only marble could be used. It was used medicinally in various forms as a charm, amulet, or talisman; by rubbing the affected part, internally as a powder, in solution, or as a tincture in alcohol. In any event, administered according to the whim of the doctor, it checks hemorrhages, cures diseases of the eyes, stomach complaint, plague, poison, teething troubles, disorders of the spleen, whooping cough, sore feet, diseased gums, gout, blood-spitting, epilepsy; it also fortifies the heart, and relieves indigestion. Sewed up in a dog-collar with a flint arrowhead, it cures rabies (in the dog). Bound with a sealskin to the masthead of a vessel, it averts wind and tempest, and is generally effective against thunder, lightning, storm, whirlwind, and hail. In India it is supposed to ward off the evil effects of the strong sun. The ancient Persians thought that genuine coral smelled of seawater; the Hindus claimed that it tasted both sweet and sour. It is tied on fruit trees to insure fruitfulness. Yellow coral is the gem of everlasting life in Arabia. White coral is used in Italy to increase the supply of milk. Dancers, especially in the ballet, still carry it for luck.

Cordão A Brazilian carnival dancing group. The cordões of Rio de Janeiro, Bahia, and Recife are famous for the elaborateness of their costuming and the excellence of their singing and dancing. The name derives from the fact that, in the crowded streets of carnival time, it was necessary for some members of the group to keep onlookers away from their fellows by a rope held taut, thus affording room for the performance. [MJH]

Cormac Connlonges In Old Irish legend, son of Conchobar, king of Ulster. He went into voluntary exile in Connacht in protest against the treacherous killing of the sons of Usnech, because he had been one of the sureties. Conchobar, on his deathbed, sent for Cormac to come and take the kingship of Ulster after him. Cormac started on the journey; but one night on the way he was murdered by a band of Connachtmen on their way home from raiding Ulster. This fulfilled the curse that Cathbad, the druid, put on Conchobar after the slaying of Usnech's three sons: that none of Conchobar's line should have the kingship after him forever.

Cormac Mac Airt Cormac, son of Art son of Conn of the Hundred Battles: most famous of the ancient Irish kings, now thought to be an authentic historical king. He ruled in Tara for forty years (probably 227–266) and Tara prospered under his hand. Cormac is famous for his true and generous judgments and has been likened to Solomon for wisdom. It was during the reign of Cormac that Fionn Mac Cumhal and the Fianna walked and talked and intermarried with the ancient gods and performed the marvels that made them famous. See BIRTH OF CORMAC.

Cormac's cup The wonderful golden cup given to Cormac Mac Airt by Manannán Mac Lir in the Land of the Living. If three lies were spoken over it, it would break in three; three truths told made it whole again. Cormac used it during his kingship to distinguish falsehood from truth in Ireland. But when Cormac died the cup vanished, just as Manannán Mac Lir had said. See ACT OF TRUTH; ECHTRAE CORMAIC.

corn or **maize** A pre-Columbian staple cultivated food plant of the American Indians of the Southwest, Southeast, and Eastern Woodlands, and of the village tribes of the Plains, including the Mandan, Hidatsa, and Arikara on the upper Missouri River. Corn enters widely into the mythology and religious practices of all these tribes. The plant is usually personified either as

Corn Mother(s) or Corn Maidens. The Hopi corn god of the underworld is however a male personage, Muy-'ingwa; the Keresan underworld corn deity is Iyatiku, Corn Mother. Among the Iroquois of New York state, Corn, Beans, and Squash are referred to as the three sisters, always mentioned together. Origin myths concerned with the disappearance of Corn person and her return, are told among all the maize-growing tribes. Various parts of the plant are used ritually, especially in the Southwest: corn husks, pollen, silk, smut, etc., as well as whole ears, kernels, and prepared corn meal. Major ceremonies are often held prior to corn-planting and after the harvest, especially among the tribes of the eastern United States. [EWV]

On Mindoro (P. I.) if you laugh while planting corn there will be space between the kernels. Corn should be planted as soon as the hardwood leaves are as large as a squirrel's (or mouse's) ear, or when you see the first bobolink or oriole. The Negroes of South Carolina say that it should be planted during the light of the moon. Others say that if it is planted when the sign of the zodiac points to the bowels, it will rot, and if planted when the sign is at the head, it will grow tall and slender, with few ears. One of the traditional corn-planting rimes goes, as each kernel is planted,

> One for the cut worm
> One for the crow
> One for the blackbird
> And three to grow.

Warts will go away if you take a kernel for each wart and throw them over the left shoulder into a river or bayou, or if you bury them too deep for them to sprout. [JWH]

corn dance An American Indian ceremonial dance series addressed to the powers which control the germination and growth of maize; thus it includes prayers for rain, and thanks for harvest. It is naturally confined to those American Indians dependent on maize for sustenance; it is performed from the Andean tribes to the Iroquois, and has reached a most elaborate development in the desert country of the Rio Grande pueblos.

The Aztecs performed innumerable seasonal rites with human sacrifice, serpentine dances, and skirmishes by priestesses, for the agricultural deities, for the corn deities, the male Cinteotl (son of Xipe Totec), Chicomecoatl (seven serpent), Xilonen (goddess of young corn), and Tonantzin (mother of gods, now identified with the Virgin Mary but formerly conceived of in three aspects: Coatlicue, Cihuacoatl, and Tlazolteotl). The spring festivals for Xipe, during Tlacaxipehualiztli, approximately coincide with Carnival. They featured the *ayacachpixolo* or rattle-strewing ceremony, a mimetic seed strewing with a stick rattle or *chicahuaztli*. The festivals for Cinteotl and Chicomecoatl, during the month of Huey Tozoztli (in April), correspond to Easter. These corn rites survive in the Mexican Carnival and Easter fiestas, but without the ancient features. Only the Tarascans preserve a corn-sowing dance in the now mestizo *sembradora* or sowing dance.

The Tarahumara and Huichols still carry on their ancient rain ceremonies for the sprouting seeds. As the Huichol equate corn, deer, and *hikuli*, their híkuli dances are also addressed to agricultural powers.

The famous Green Corn Dance of the Pueblo Indians has fragments of major ceremonies, now enacted secretly in the kivas. They perform many beautiful dances for the crops, rainbow, rain cloud, basket, snake, yellow corn, the corn maidens, harvest; but the *tablitas*, or saints' day dances, are the most spectacular. These are so called because of the high tablet crowns worn by the women. The tablitas in San Felipe (May 1) and Santo Domingo (August 4) are the best preserved; in marginal Taos these festivals are degenerating. They are apparently addressed to the image of the patron saint, but this is a purely superficial concession to Catholicism. The traditional dance begins with the entrance of the *koshare*, the impersonators of ancestral spirits (clowns outside the dance). Then follows a defense of the crops from invaders. Finally the men and women of the summer and winter kivas alternate until sundown in a mass dance. An impressive men's chorus drums and chants in shifting rhythms. The shuffling women tag slightly behind the trotting men in a huge double circle, long double lines, or small circlings for one or two couples.

The Corn Dance is built on similar patterns among the Shawnee, Cherokee, Creek, Yuchi, and Iroquois Indians. Among the Cherokee-Shawnee in Oklahoma the Green Corn Dance is still celebrated as one of the bread dances, a thanksgiving for crops, and is a form of worship of Our Grandmother. Among the eastern Cherokee and the Creek it has died out as a vegetation rite, and survives among the former as a curative ceremony, including animal and "social" dances, and divination. These follow the peculiar serpentine and spiral course of typical Cherokee dance with planting gestures.

The Iroquois Green Corn Festival (*ahdake'wäo*) lasts four days in early September and includes various rites of thanksgiving: the Great Feather Dance (*ostowégowa*), women's *tǫwisas*, and many social dances, including the corn dance proper (*onéontóenǫ*). This is addressed to the spirit of corn, the most important of the three life-sustaining sisters, corn, beans, and squash. It progresses in a circle or serpentine. In contrast with the male-dominated dances of hunting cultures, these corn dances feature women as prominent actors, both in the dance and in the underlying mythology. [GPK]

cornflower Any flower growing in grainfields; especially the bachelor's-button or bluebottle (*Centaurea cyanus*). In Greek legend the youth Cyanus worshipped Chloris (Flora) and spent his time gathering flowers for her altars. When he died the goddess gave his name to this plant or transformed him into it. The Centaur Chiron cured the wound made with an arrow dipped in the blood of the Hydra by covering it with the flowers of the *Centaurea* and thus gave it its name and its reputation for great healing properties.

The cornflower was burned to drive away serpents according to Lucian. In Russian legend the plant is known as Basilek. A young man of this name was enticed by the nymph Russalka into the fields and there transformed into the cornflower. In Jamaica the flower is boiled with the leaves of the "Gungo pea" and used as a gargle or with alum to cure toothache. The cornflower is also called bluecap, bluebonnet, bluet, and hurtsickle. The last name is used because it turns the edges of the reapers' sickles.

corn from body of slain person A folktale motif (A2611.1) explaining the origin of corn, especially typical of North American Indian mythology. The Abnaki myth is representative, in which a beautiful golden-haired woman appeared to a lonely and hungry man.

She would not let him approach her, but instructed him to burn a patch of ground and drag her body across the burned patch, promising that if he would do this, she would be with him forever. The man did as he was told. When he saw the lovely hair of the woman shining between the leaves of the plant that grew up where her body had touched the ground, he understood that she was keeping her promise in the gift of the corn. The Cherokees have a version of this story in which Sélu (Corn) instructs her child and his little "wild brother" (who intend to kill her) to drag her body over the ground and corn will come up. Further details of this tale explain why corn grows in spots instead of all over, and why the Cherokees work their corn crops only twice. In the Huron origin myth corn sprang from the breast of the dead mother of the twin culture heroes. The story varies little in the many eastern Indian versions. Longfellow's *Hiawatha* tells the tale with little change. It is also known in many variants in the West and among certain South American Indians where maize is known. The gift of food to the people from the body of a slain food-goddess occurs also in Babylonian and Japanese mythology (A1420.1).

corns Aching corns are a sign of rain in all countries. In Ireland applications of hot ivy-leaves or houseleek are said to relieve painful corns. An early English folk device for extracting corns was to steep a pearl button in lemon juice until dissolved, then to place a piece of lemon soaked in this liquor upon the corn every day until the corn could be easily extracted. Another English prescription says to steal a small piece of beef and bury it. As the meat rots, the corn will diminish. Both of these remedies have traveled as far as Mississippi where they are recommended by the Negroes of that section. Another southern U.S. Negro corn cure is to rub a kernel of corn on the toe-corn and feed it to an old rooster.

cornucopia or **cornu copiæ** In classical mythology, the horn of abundance, always filled with fruit and self-replenishing according to the wishes of its possessor. It is an attribute of many deities, such as Flora, Concordia, Plutus. The horn itself was broken from the goat Amalthea which nourished the infant Zeus; or, by some accounts, was torn from Achelous by Hercules. The never-empty horn is related to the self-setting table of folktale.

Corona Borealis The Northern Crown: a bright circle of stars lying between Boötes and Hercules: variously interpreted in different mythologies as the Wreath (early Greek), the Crown of Ariadne (later Greek), al Fakkah, the dish (Arabian), the Woomera or boomerang (Australian), Caer Arianrhod, the House of Arianrhod (Brythonic), twelve dancing star maidens, of whom one was the wife of White Hawk or Arcturus (North American Shawnee Indian), the cave into which the Great Bear entered in his flight from the world up the northern sky (also North American Indian), the Crown of Thorns (Christian).

coronach A type of song of lamentation composed by Scottish bards and sung or chanted at funeral ceremonies of clan heads or other important persons. The words eulogized the dead and brought forth bursts of wailing from the women of the clan. See COMPLAINT.

corpse bleeds in presence of murderer A very old folk belief, especially in England, Ireland, and Scotland, occurring as motif (D1318.5;2) in the popular ballads of Scandinavia, England, and Scotland. The motif appears typically in *Young Riedan*, a variant of *Young Hunting* (Child #68):

> White, white waur his wounds washen,
>   As white as ony lawn;
> But sune's the traitor stude afore,
>   Then oot the red blude sprang.

The belief that the wound of a dead man would open and bleed at the approach of or at the touch of his murderer was often put to the test in ordeals to detect the criminal. The belief is also fairly general in the United States, especially among some groups of southern Negroes, who claim that blood will flow even from the dry bones of a dead man in the presence of his murderer. Alabama Negroes say that the intestines of the dead will grumble and be heard when the murderer approaches the corpse. In Mississippi it is said that dried bloodstains at the scene of a murder will moisten and stain the murderer's feet if he walks in the place.

corpse light A phosphorescent light seen over marshes, etc.: called variously ignis fatuus, jack o' lantern, corposant, and by other names. The mysterious phenomenon of strange lights seen at different places and at different times in the British Isles and elsewhere has been explained as caused by, possibly, an atmospheric condition or gaseous emanation from the ground. These lights are seen in the air and near the earth, in the house and out-of-doors, on the lake or on the sea, sometimes white, red, or blue. They are fickle and erratic; they recede if a person approaches them, then reappear behind.

A light of this sort betokens death. Sometimes the light goes from the churchyard to the house of a person sick or near death; sometimes one is seen on the breast of a dying person; often, it appears on the rooftop signifying a death in the family of the house over which it hovers. Many stories are related of the appearance of these lights in connection with the death omen. In this capacity and in their elusive wanderings they parallel the ignis fatuus. Compare FETCH CANDLE. [GPS]

Corpus Christi Literally, body of Christ (in German, *Fronleichnam*); a Catholic holiday dedicated to the body of Christ in the form of the Host. It is a movable feast occurring on the Thursday after Trinity Sunday and commemorating the institution of the Eucharist. In 1246 it was officially instituted following a vision of the nun Juliana in the diocese of Liège. Juliana saw in her vision a full moon representing the Church, and one black spot on the moon which represented the lack of a feast honoring the Eucharist. The feast was extended to the entire world in 1264. Though of such recent origin, it has become one of the most splendid of Catholic celebrations, especially in Spain, Portugal, and Provence. Its stupendous processionals follow the Host-bearing clergy; yet they include figures that date back

to paganism. There are fantastic cardboard masks of *gigantes,* giants, *enanos,* dwarfs, *águilas,* eagles, *serpes,* dragons, *tarascos,* or floats, on a great water serpent. Formerly, as at Penafiel and Oporto, Portugal, there were processionals, dances of professional guilds, and mystery and miracle plays performed by the various guilds. A Provençal celebration of the feast of Corpus Christi features a parade of the saints, with St. Simeon carrying a basket of eggs.

Special traditional features were the symbolic battles of the Moors and Christians, and the sacred plays called *autos sacramentales* representing Biblical and allegorical subjects. Some of these survive. In Seville Cathedral, and until recently in Toledo, the famous dance of the *seises* is performed on Corpus Christi as well as on other holidays. In Majorca the related *cociés* dance in the processional as well as before and in the church, at Alaró and Montuirí. Mexico also has splendid processionals in the cities. In the remote pueblos of the Sierras de Puebla and Veracruz, the *Moros* battle with the *Cristianos* or *Santiagos.* The most elaborate celebration of the indigenous *voladores* or Flying Pole dance at Papantla, Veracruz, takes place on Corpus Christi. Native *quetzales* and imported *moros* and *negritos* participate. The Tarascans of Michoacán celebrate with mock markets and a harvest processional.

In Europe and the New World Corpus Christi probably corresponded with and was grafted onto an old harvest festival. It coincides with the Inca winter solstice, Inti raimi, and with the Aztec seventh month, Tecuilhuitontli, for Huixtocihuatl, older sister of the tlalocs or rain gods. [GPK]

corranda A North Catalan couple dance, popular on both slopes of the Pyrenees. In the *corrandas bajas* (low corrandas), the couples, arm in arm, skip and jump through the streets. In the *corrandas altas* (high corrandas), two or four couples dance in a square. The men jump with a high hitchcick, the *camada rodona.* Sometimes they enact a pursuit of their lady. Sometimes all join in a kind of contrapas. As a finale the four men lift the four ladies to form a human pyramid; sometimes the man sustains his lady, sitting on his hand, in the air above his head. The name derives from the running steps, advancing and retreating. The term corranda is also applied to a song of four verses. See COUPLE DANCE; LIFT DANCE. [GPK]

corri-corri A Spanish dance from the province of Asturias, danced especially on St. John's Day by six women with one man in pursuit. This running dance with its flight and pursuit motif of sexual mating is reminiscent of the fertility rites associated with St. Johns' Day. [GPK]

corrido A characteristic ballad type of Mexico, derived from the Spanish *romance,* but set in quatrains and sung to melodies which repeat certain phrases over and over. The narrative deals with tragedies of love, with calamities, fights, revolution, with heroes, strong men, and outlaws. Even ballads from literary sources are often quickly taken over and reshaped into corridos by illiterate singers.

corrigan In the folklore of Brittany, a female fairy: said to have been one of the ancient druidesses, and therefore malicious towards Christian priests. She is fond of pretty human children, and usually gets the blame for all changeling substitutions.

corroboree The Australian East Coast native term for ceremonies: now applied by Australian whites to any native ceremony, dance, or gathering. See AUSTRALIAN ABORIGINAL MYTHOLOGY. [KL]

Cosquin, Emmanuel (1841–1921) French scholar and follower of Benfey. The Grimms encouraged him to collect folktales, and his principal work, *Contes populaires de Lorraine*, is generally considered to be the representative French collection, holding a similar position in France to that of the Grimms' *Household Tales* in Germany. Like Benfey he considered India the reservoir of old tales, but he qualified that theory in two respects: he disagreed with Benfey as to the importance of the Mongols as disseminators of the Indian stories over Europe, and he did not believe that every folktale everywhere was of Indian provenience, though many were. He admitted that the Egyptian tales antedated those of India. Cosquin, Gaston Paris, and Gédéon Huet were the three principal representatives in France of the literary school of folklorists, originated by Benfey. Cosquin's numerous special studies have been gathered into two volumes, *Études folkloriques* (1922) and *Les contes indiens et l'occident* (1922).

cotton It was grown and used for cloth in India in early times, and spread from there to the East. After the conquests of Alexander it began to be known in Greece and the West. Now it is grown principally in the United States, India, and Egypt. The Khonds always plant cotton immediately on moving to a new settlement. In the Punjab, just as the bolls begin to burst, they select the largest plant in the field and sprinkle buttermilk and rice-water on it and offer prayers that the others may be as large and strong. Before the women begin to pick, they circle the field eating rice-milk. The first mouthful they spit on the field from the west. They exchange the first cotton picked for its weight in salt, which they keep in the house during the picking and pray over it. The Negroes of South Carolina claim dew on the cotton produces plant lice. A piece of cotton stuck to a dress indicates a letter, and the shape of the cotton shows the initial of the person from whom the letter will come. The bark of the cotton root was used by the American slaves as a stimulant, and was credited with causing abortion.

Cotys or **Cotytto** The Thracian Great Mother goddess, whose festival, the Cotyttia, was notorious in later classical times for its licentiousness, being like that of the Phrygian Cybele. The worship of Cotys spread throughout Greece and Italy, among other places to Athens and Corinth. Her worship was celebrated at night on hills.

coulin Ancient folk tunes and airs of Ireland, said to be *ceol síde*, fairy music, learned by Irish harpers who overheard the playing of the harpers of the síde.

counting-out rimes To determine who shall be "It" and chase the rest or take some other unwanted part in a game, children have universally and from time immemorial used various sortilegic devices usually requiring the recitation of magic rimes. When rimes are used the process generally begins with a self-appointed leader standing in front of the other children and reciting the verse, during which he points to each player in turn, one child to a word or syllable, until the end.

The player upon whom the last word (usually "buck" or "out") falls is out of the counting, which is continued until but one player is left, who is automatically and undeniably "It." Adult observers have noted that the dictum is obeyed with more alacrity than the average child obeys a parent's command. If any child refuses, or is even reluctant, he is ostracized by the others until he learns to accept his fate when the lot falls on him.

The practice is called counting-out or telling-out in America and England, and chapping-out or titting-out in Scotland. On the Continent, the child who is It is called in Germany the Wolf, and, correspondingly, in France, the Loup, a nomenclature which may derive from the deep racial fear of the animal. In Japan the child chosen by counting out is called Oni, that is, the devil or evil spirit; in the Malagasy tribe of Madagascar he is the Boka or leper; and in Hawaii the Pupule or crazy one.

There is a rich field for research in anthropology, lexicography, comparative religion, and folklore in the rather neglected game-rimes of children of the world. At this moment millions of children in playgrounds and farmyards, schoolyards and alleys are saying these verses. The writer in a brief period has collected over 2000 different counting-out rimes from forty states and thirty foreign lands in many different languages. You can tell them at a glance from other kinds of child-rimes, for they have a characteristic rhythm and are full of quaint word-fossils worn smooth by much repetition. They are strangely alike and practically interchangeable, forming a sort of international language of their own. Say one in any tongue to an American playgroup and they will adopt it and adapt it to their vocal organs immediately, as they have already done to many rimes brought here by immigrants.

Counting-out rimes resemble another favorite of children, the tongue twisters, for both seem at first hearing to be mere gibberish, but the very real difference between them is that the latter are deliberately contrived or accidentally discovered to be difficult to say, whereas the former have been smoothed down by frequent and rapid repetition until they almost say themselves. In such a rime, for instance, as the twenty-one type, which ends with the word "twenty-one" and originally contained that number of stressed syllables, we find that an early form:

> One-ery, two-ery, six and seven,
> Holy bone, crack-a-bone, ten and eleven;
> Spit, spot, it must be done,
> Twiddle-um, twaddle-um, twenty-one,

is so changed by use that six and seven becomes ziggery, zan; Holy bone is known in such variants as Hollowbone, Hallabone, Arrabone, Halibo, Halibut, Alibo, and even Alibi; and the third line becomes Spin, span, muskidan.

In other counting-out rimes, or to use the old oral tradition word for them, rimbles (see EENY, MEENY, MINY, MO), we have interesting changes from

> One is all, two is all, six is all, seven,
> Bobtail dominicker, little poll ram;
> Harum, squarum, Virgin Marum,
> Sinctum, sanctum, buck!

to the obviously related but distant cousin:

> One erzoll, two erzoll, zickerzoll zan,
> Bobtail vinegar, tickle and tan;
> Harum, scarum, merchant marum,
> Stingelum, stangelum, stuck!

The dominicker is in variants from Georgia, Tennessee, and Colorado, and the vinegar from Delaware, Indiana, New York, and several other northern states, while the second line became in Philadelphia:

> Baptist minister, good Irish man.

Considering the many words with Latin endings and religious connotations in these variants, it is likely that the Georgia dominicker rooster was probably originally nearer the old prayer form so frequently occurring in such rimes as this one from North Carolina:

> Haley, maley, tipsy tee,
> Harley, barley, Dominee;
> Hotchy, potchy, cotchy, notchy,
> Hom, pom, tuskee.

This rimble serves well to illustrate how in changed but recognizable sounds the children have unconsciously preserved old church chants and holy phrases, for we know from other variants of this particular jingle that not only is Dominee obviously of church origin, but also that Haley Maley is Hail, Mary, and that Hotchy potchy, which also occurs as Ochre, poker; Oka, poka; Hocca, proach; and Otcha, potcha; is definitely from Hocus pocus, which in turn is from the *hoc est corpus* phrase of the mass.

The age of these rimes which have come down by the schoolyard grapevine is discussed in the article on Eeny, meeny, miny, mo, the best known one. Let it be added here, just to show the rich fossil bed which awaits folklore explorers in this particular field, that the writer has identified in these rimbles such fascinating old word relics as:

Passwords of the wide-roaming freemasons of the Middle Ages,
"Juggles" from the jongleurs of Provence,
Sanskrit sacred syllables and mantras,
Secret magic formulas for telling fortunes,
Irish filid (poet-wizard) death-rimes and druid exorcisms,
Bible characters and popular saints' names,
Prayers, paternosters black and white,
Cymric shepherd's score numerals,
Romany charms and patter.

Following are a few representative rimbles:

> Onery, twoery, tickery, tabery,
> Alabo, cackabo, tennery, labery,
> Hustadang, bangalang,
> Humpty Dumpty is ninety-nine,
> And one's a hundred.

> Onery, oery, ickery Ann,
> Phillisy, phollisy, Nicholas John,
> Quevy, quavy, English Navy,
> Stinkelum, stankelum, buck!

The two above were, according to a correspondent, current in Indiana about 1910. The Phillisy, phollisy, Nicholas John line occurs in many variants, and sounds suspiciously like the Pharos and Colossus at Rhodes, always of considerable interest to freemasons. It is worth noting that Masons from six different states sent versions of this particular rime to a collector of children's rimes in the 80's, although Masons of today appear to know nothing about its ever having been in the Masonic ritual.

An old English rimble, popular in many similar forms in Nova Scotia and New England, runs musically:

> Intra, mintra, cutra, corn,
> Apple-seed and apple-thorn;
> Wire, brier, limber lock,
> Three geese in a flock
> Sit and sing by a spring,
> One flew east and one flew west,
> And one flew over the cuckoo's nest,
> Crying, one, two, three,
> Out goes he.

In their wanderings these three geese become Three wires in a clock (Yorkshire, England) and even Five mice on a rock (Florida).

A more modern counting-out rime which has been sent the writer from all English-speaking countries and is apparently quite popular is:

> A bee, a bee, a Bumble bee
> Stung a man upon the knee,
> Stung a pig upon the snout,
> I'll be dogged if you ain't out!

But, more popular and rivalling even Eeny, meeny, is:

> Monkey, monkey, bottle of beer,
> How many monkeys are there here?
> One, two, three, Out goes he!

See TONGUE TWISTERS.   CHARLES FRANCIS POTTER

Country Maid and Her Milk Pail One of Æsop's fables (Jacobs #77) in which a Country Maid planned to turn the proceeds of her can of milk first into eggs, then chickens, and finally into a new gown in which she would flirt at the next year's fair. Carried away by her thoughts she tossed her head and dropped the pail. Moral: Don't count your chickens until they are hatched.

couple dance Any mimetic courtship dance: performed usually by a man and a woman, sometimes by two men, one in women's clothes. The usual pattern is the wooing dance of the man around his lady. The most ancient form, still performed in Asia, even into the Caucasus, and in Mexico, in which the woman dances in one place while the man dances or dances and sings around her, has gradually developed everywhere into the traditional courtship pantomime in which both partners perform the steps and enact the sequence of flirtation or enticement, pursuit, retreat, and final love embrace or conquest.

A few of the most famous contemporary couple dances of this pattern are: the *cueca* of Chile and its Peruvian analog, the *marinera*, the Mexican *chilena*, the Spanish *bolero*, *fandango*, and *jota*, the Venetian *furlana*, the Hungarian *friss*, the Russian *lezghinka*, the Moravian *rozěk*, the Colombian *cumbia* and *guabina*, and the Balinese *djoged*.

The original function and intent of the couple dance was not mere representation of sexual mating, however, but through the pantomime of sexual mating to invoke fertility upon crops, animals, and the tribe or community. The appearance of a man dressed as a woman is always a phallic symbol in primitive and folk dance, and for this reason the couple (or fertility) dance performed by two men, one in woman's clothes, is often prominent among many primitive peoples. [GPK]

couvade A birth custom, found in many parts of the world, requiring certain abstentions by the father of a newly born child, and typically observed by the lying-in of the father. Protection of the child from injurious acts of the father seems to be the underlying reason for the couvade; certain food and drink, hunting or working, may be too much for the child to survive, and since the child is part of the father, the father must guard against certain customary actions which might prove injurious. Since so much of his activity is circumscribed, the father repairs to the couch or hammock as the safest place under the circumstances. The mother, on the other hand, returns to her daily round as soon as possible. The custom is widespread in South America, from the tropical tribes to the Yahgan in the far south; it is found among the Ainus, in Assam and Borneo, in Africa, India, and China. It is mentioned among the Celts and the Basques, but the only reliable reports of it in Europe are from among the Corsicans and the Albanians. According to Tylor, the custom is found among peoples whose matrilineal system is changing to patrilineal. During the period of transition, the father, by means of the couvade, asserts his rights in the child. Another theory holds that the child has been separated from the father and that both are weak and in need of care and nursing. Whatever be the reasoning, the couvade period stretches sometimes for weeks, as among the Indians of Guiana; sometimes it lasts only until the mother is ceremoniously purified after birth, a week, as among the Ainus, more or less. The couvade may also be suspected in less striking action on the part of the father than the going to bed: abstentions from certain foods or actions may be considered milder forms of the birth tabu so bizarrely exemplified by the couvade.

☞ The word couvade has been applied in South America to customs which are somewhat different from the European couvade, which is a symbolic lying-in of the father after childbirth. In practically all South American tribes, with the exception of the people of the Andean region, both parents refrain from performing certain activities and eating certain foods before and after the birth of a child.

The avoidance of food is based on the belief that some unfavorable characteristics of an animal or a plant may be transmitted magically to the infant. The activities which are tabooed are those which may render childbirth difficult.

There exists also a strong belief in the mystic relationship between a newly born baby and his father. The father must therefore give up for a short period all violent activities which can endanger the life of his offspring. He must refrain from hunting, fishing, swimming, handling cutting instruments, etc. The fact that most fathers in the tropical area spend this idle time in their hammocks should not be construed as a mock confinement. It is the normal behavior of any Indian who has nothing to do. These tabus end generally when the baby's navel cord falls off. Among the Guiana Indians, if the father of a newly born child has to travel, he is obliged to take great precautions lest the soul of the child that follows him suffer any harm. For instance, he will clearly mark the path for the child and avoid getting near rivers where bad spirits lurk.

The couvade is still observed by most Indian tribes of the Guianas and by many members of the Tupi Guarani family. [AM]

☞ This custom is not widespread in Middle America, and where it is found, it probably represents a survival from earlier cultural strata. Among the Tarahumara of northern Mexico and the Cuna of Panama, the father does not work for three days following the birth of a child. Among the Sumu and Moskito of Nicaragua the father refrains from hard work for several days following the birth of a child, and avoids certain foods, especially salt and chiles. [GMF]

Coventry Carol An English lullaby carol originally sung in the Pageant of the Shearmen and Tailors at Coventry. In the play, it was sung by the women of Bethlehem to their children just before the troops of Herod appeared on the scene to kill them. The melody as sung in 1591 has been preserved, and the text survives as reworked and written down by Robert Croo in 1534. The song has been recovered from folk singers in both England and the United States. It has the characteristic crooning burden, "lully, lulla," of numerous lullaby carols. See CAROL.

cow Although cows are still sacred in India these animals were once of considerable importance in the theology of the Egyptian and Greco-Roman peoples. Ethnologers have found traces of this importance in some customs of comparatively recent times. Authorities differ as to whether the worship of the cow in India originated in historic or in prehistoric times.

The Indian myth is that Prithu, a culture hero, wished to recover edible plants for his subjects. He attacked the earth which assumed the shape of a cow and fled through the heavenly regions. Finally she yielded and promised to fecundate the earth with milk. "Having made Svāyambhuva Manu, the calf, he milked the Earth and received the milk in his own hands." The antecedents of this myth are obscure. N. M. Penzer's summary is in brief that the Vedic Indians ate the flesh of the ox, sheep, and goat, though because of their value oxen were slaughtered only on festival occasions such as great entertainments and wedding festivals. The *Rig-Veda* has several allusions to the mystic relation between the cow and the earth. The prohibition against killing or molesting cows became general only after the general views of transmigration had been formulated. Though the offer in some of the early sutras to kill a cow for an honored guest is thought to have been merely a polite formula and the guest was supposed to refuse in formal language, it may be a survival from an earlier period. By the time of the *Mahābhārata* the sacredness of the cow was fully recognized: its great purity, the merit acquired by gifts of cows. The five products of the cow, milk, curds, clarified butter, urine, and cow dung, are also pure and are used in the purification ceremonies.

The cow cult of Egypt is possibly older than the cow cult of India. Egyptian princesses were assimilated to cows and when one died her body was buried in a cow-shaped sarcophagus. Apis, the bull, represented Osiris. During the first days after a new bull had been installed in the temple the women stood before him and according to Greek reporters lifted their clothes to expose their sexual parts, a fact which in view of the general visibility afforded by the costume of the Egyptian upper classes may be of some ritualistic importance. In Thebes, Hathor was the cow-form of Isis and was served by Egyptian princesses who were buried with sacred bulls, a custom which some have interpreted as a symbolic marriage. The discovery of a mummified bull's phallus in one of the tombs might strengthen this view, particularly if the object is correctly described or it might lead to other explanations.

Pausanias, the Greek archeologist of the 2nd century A.D., did little to clarify the confusions about cow-worship and the symbolism of cows which have been transmitted by sophisticated writers of highly civilized periods of Greece and Rome. Thus Pausanias identified an image in Io's temple at Thalamai with the cow goddess Pasiphae. Io who aroused the desires of Zeus was transformed into a heifer. She is said to be one of the components or aliases of Demeter and is scarcely distinguished from the cow goddess Europa, who according to Moschus was seduced by Zeus after Zeus had transformed himself into a bull. Pasiphae by entering an artificial cow had intercourse with the bull of Minoa.

The words of the bride at Roman weddings have been rendered, "Where thou art the Bull, I am the Cow." A similar formula has been reported from the heroic literature of the Celts, and Briffault quotes authorities about fertility ceremonies among the Kurds. Here the priest announced to the congregation that he was the Great Bull and a woman recently married replied that she was the Young Cow. At this point lights were lowered and the congregation indulged in promiscuous sexual intercourse. [RDJ]

Cowboy's Lament An American cowboy ballad of the fate of a "young cowboy who done wrong" on the trail of wine, women, and cards, and who is dying of a shot in the breast. A favorite of the cowpunchers, and set in almost any town of the West, according to the loyalty of the singer, it is drawn from an Irish song, *The Unfortunate Rake*, current about 1790, which was the lament of a dissolute soldier dying of syphilis and requesting a military funeral. The drums and the fifes were preserved in the cowboy version. Another song from the same source, *The Maiden's Lament*, was sung in both England and the United States.

cowboy songs Work and recreational songs of the American cowhand, made up of bits and scraps of older ballads and come-all-ye's, music-hall and minstrel ditties, and mingling the lyric singing style of the South (from which many cowboys came) with the true-speaking workingmen's songs of the Northwest, and a touch of Spanish influence from over the southwestern border as well as a trace of Indian warwhoops in the refrains. They deal with the hard and dangerous life on the cattle range (*The Horse Wrangler, The Night Herding Song,* etc.), with violent death in cattle stampedes (*When the Work's All Done Next Fall*) or from "lead poisoning" or gunshot (*The Cowboy's Lament*), with the heroes of their kind who generally died saving someone in a stampede, with their unrequited love and their faithless sweethearts back home, with tall tales and

boasting and practical jokes on the greenhorns, and occasionally with religion (*The Great Round-up*).

cowslip A wildflower of the primrose family sometimes called palsy- or Peter-wort. It was used in all manner of folk remedies, especially for palsy. It was recommended that the leaves be put in wounds. The roots if crushed and strained, made excellent nose-drops for purifying the brain and curing migraine. The odor of the flowers calmed the heart and nerves and strengthened the brain. Either wine made from the flowers or an infusion in milk at bedtime cured insomnia. The flowers mixed with linseed oil are good for burns. This plant is also good for skin blemishes and wrinkles, and for cramps, convulsions, and muscular disorders. It is sometimes made into tea, or used as a pot herb.

Cox, John Harrington (1863–1945) American educator, philologist, and folklorist. After studying under Kittredge at Harvard, he became, in 1902, professor of English philology at West Virginia University, where he fostered an interest in early narrative poetry, among other things founding the Beowulf Club. In 1925, he published *Folk-Songs of the South,* a development of his dissertation at Harvard. This work, edited by Cox, was a collection made under the auspices of the West Virginia Folklore Society of which he was the organizer. Among the other works of Professor Cox are *Traditional Ballads, Mainly from West Virginia* (1939); *Folk-Songs, Mainly from West Virginia* (1939).

Cox, Marian Emily Roalfe (1860–1916) Folklore scholar. Her *Cinderella,* published in London in 1893, is a massive study of a single folktale cycle. It is a detailed, comparative and analytical presentation of 318 *Cinderella* variants, with reference also to their diffusion.

Coyote Trickster par excellence of the Great Basin, Plains, central Californian, and some Plateau and Southwestern North American Indian groups; also, for the majority of these tribes, creator or culture hero. Usually, as a trickster, Coyote is accompanied by a companion—very often by Wolf, less frequently by Wildcat, Fox, Rabbit, Porcupine, Badger, or some other animal. Both Coyote and his companion are presented as behaving and talking like human beings; sometimes they are represented as looking like men, at other times, like animals. Coyote's activities as a trickster-culture hero almost always belong to the pre-human mythical age, when animals lived and talked as people. Some groups, however, depict Coyote as a trickster whose existence and foolhardy escapades continue to the present time. The dual character of Coyote—as the culture hero who releases impounded game, imparts knowledge of arts and crafts, secures fire or daylight or the sun, etc., and as a bullying, licentious, greedy, erotic, fumbling dupe, —is hard for Indian narrators of tales to resolve, and is frequently commented upon by them. Trickster Coyote stories may form the bulk of some groups' repertory of tales (as in the Basin), or only a small part of the total repertory (as among some Southwestern groups). Among the Navaho of the Southwest, Coyote as a Holy Being is referred to by one name; as Trickster by another, "Trotting Coyote." Many Coyote trickster stories are of the short, single-incident variety; such short discrete tales may however be strung together into what amounts to loosely knit cycles. In longer Coyote trickster tales the action in one incident often depends on previous action, and furthers that of succeeding incidents. Trickster stories are often erotic or obscene. They can be counted upon to arouse general amusement, but they are also often told to point a moral. Children, or human beings in general, should *not* behave as Coyote behaves in the stories. Some of the most widespread Coyote trickster stories, which may also be told of different tricksters of other regions of North America, are: *Coyote Steals* or *Marries his Mother-in-Law* (*Daughter,* or *Daughter-in-Law*), *Coyote and Porcupine, Coyote and Wildcat, Dancing Ducks, Dancing Bulrushes.* [EWV]

Coyote and the Acorns One day Coyote went visiting and the people fed him sour acorns. He liked them so much that he asked how they were prepared. The people answered, "Put water on them, press them down hard, and in two days, look." That sounded so easy that Coyote would not believe them. "There must be another way," he said. And he pestered them with questions until in anger they said, "All right! You load a canoe with acorns, tip it over and drown them. Then walk along the river bank and pick them up." Coyote was gleeful. He had the secret at last.

So he ran home to tell his grandmother. Sour acorns? Of course! "You damp them and press them," she said. "Oh, no! You drown them!" said Coyote. He took all his grandmother's acorns to the river and dumped them. That was certainly an angry old woman. Then Coyote walked along the river bank, but of course he never found a one. He got hungrier and hungrier because his grandmother would not feed him. "Go eat all those acorns of yours," she would say. Of course one day he smelled and found the acorns his grandmother was boiling. She declared it was excrement, but he knew the difference and ate them, so of course he did not starve.

In addition to having significance as a story of Yurok acorn culture, this story also belongs to the extensive Coyote Trickster cycle with Coyote as numskull.

coyote dance A ceremonial dance of the Yaqui and Mayo Indians (Cáhitas) of southern Arizona and Mexico; the go'imye'e: performed for the death of all soldiers, pueblo officials, and matachini chiefs, and at certain specific fiestas. Although definitely a soldiers' dance, performed by soldiers for soldiers, it does not seem to have any significance of war. It is a feature of the special soldiers' fiestas: Guadalupe, Dec. 12, and the Fiesta de la Cruz, and the great Yaqui national fiesta, Santa Isobel, on July 4. It is also danced in the churches on the day before Easter.

It is performed by three men to the accompaniment of a kind of water drum. Each wears the head and hide of a coyote, the head held in place on the dancer's head by a headband crested with eagle, hawk, or buzzard feathers, the hide swinging loosely down his back. Cocoon rattles are also worn. He holds a bow in his left hand which he strikes with a piece of incised cane of a certain length. The step is slow, stamped with the flat of the foot, and performed in crouching position. The dancers advance and retreat from the drum, hour after hour, all night, and finish just at dawn. An irregular, very complicated rhythm-beat signifies the retreat; a rapid, regular rhythm-beat signifies the advance. All the motions of the dancers mime the coyote; they toss their heads, look swiftly over their shoulders, etc. The

drum, which he holds in his hands. The dance is always watched from beginning to end by the pueblo officials. Just as dawn is about to break a plate of meat is placed in front of each of the three dancers, halfway between him and the drum. Each man picks it up in his teeth and delivers it to the drum.

Coyote and Porcupine Title of a North American Indian folktale popular among the Plains, Plateau, and some California and Southwestern groups. The tale falls usually into two parts: (1) Porcupine kills a buffalo by climbing into his paunch (or killing him with a knife) as he is being carried across a stream by the buffalo (K952.1); (2) Coyote cheats Porcupine out of the buffalo meat in a jumping contest (K17). They agree that whichever one jumps over the buffalo carcass shall have all the meat, the other none. Coyote jumps over; Porcupine cannot. Porcupine gets even for this by killing Coyote's child (or children) and in some versions by killing the whole family. [EWV]

crab The natives of the island of Nias have a myth of origin in which the first men, having descended from the moon, became mortal because they ate bananas instead of crabs which shed their skins and hence would have made them immortal. In Manipur crabs in a pot of water can make rain. In New Caledonia a goddess in the form of a giant land crab hates married people, and causes elephantiasis; little crabs are her messengers. She lives in a tree in a special grove, and offerings of food are hung on the tree for her. In Tahiti crabs are regarded as the shadows of local gods. The sea hermit-crab is a god himself, and to eat him under the wrong circumstances causes swollen glands, or even death. A Tahitian legendary hero once escaped from his pursuers on the back of a fresh-water crab; hence the fresh-water crab is held to be the shadow of the god of fugitives.

Bahama Negroes pour water from the claw of a crab into the earhole to cure earache. The famous Gullah Jack (conjure-man of the 1882 South Carolina Vesey Insurrection) made himself and others invulnerable by means of a crab claw held in the mouth. It is no good to go crabbing on a moonlight night: that is the one time when crabs are "poor," i.e. not meaty. [RDJ]

cracks and slams Popular reproaches, traditional taunts and insults, local witticisms, and wisecracks belonging to the general class of aggressive humor and social criticism in folklore. In folk speech, terms of disparagement outnumber terms of approbation and deal most frequently with such subjects as personal appearance, mental gifts or capacities (or their lack), intoxication, and the countryman or rustic (Marie Gladys Hayden, *Dialect Notes*, Vol. IV, Pt. III, 1915, pp. 194–223). Even more interesting to the folklorist than terms applied to individuals are those applied to a group, place, class, occupation, etc., which are expressive of group attitudes and regional folkways. For slurs and insults aimed at ethnic groups A. A. Roback (*Dictionary of International Slurs*, 1944) coined the term *ethnophaulism.* Earlier terms for proverbial local witticisms and reproaches are *blason populaire* and *Ortsneckereien.*

As the American equivalent of the latter terms, the term "local cracks and slams" was first employed by B. A. Botkin in *A Treasury of American Folklore* (1944,

p. 317) to denote "terms, phrases, sayings, allusions, rhymes, songs, and jokes that poke fun at a particular locality or group." Local gibes and taunts in the United States are related to the "geography of culture" or ethnocentrism as reflected in provincialism, sectionalism, and localism, and are an integral part of place lore and local-color humor. They range from uncomplimentary or derisive nicknames for cities, states, and regions and their inhabitants (e.g. Beaneater for Bostonian, Puke for Missourian, Sucker for Illinoisan, Bluenose for Nova Scotian or New Brunswicker) to legends (Nantucket was known as "The Devil's Ash Heap" from the Indian tradition that it was formed by the giant Maushope's emptying his pipe after smoking), jingles ("Cohasset for beauty, Hingham for pride; If not for its herring, Weymouth had died"), and bywords ("A rib was taken off Billerica to make Bedford").

As applied to extreme types of country (dry, wet, hilly, flat), cracks and slams are the product of "boosting in reverse" and "laughing it off." Although many local cracks and slams have their origin in actual economic and political feuds and rivalries, such as divide North and South, East and West, others are associated with regional and ethnic stereotypes (the close-mouthed or scheming Yankee, the feuding, moonshining Kentucky mountaineer, the wild and woolly Westerner, the "dumb" Irishman, the frugal Scotchman). In still other cases, the popular reproach is simply a localization of an old joke or migratory tradition, as in drolleries of the Gothamite type, which regard the inhabitants of a certain village or region as outrageous fools.   B. A. BOTKIN

crane In China the crane, much used in decorative art, is a symbol of longevity, though fragmentary reports from Confucian historians indicate that members of what appears to have been a crane cult came to a bad end (in the Chou and later Han Dynasties). Greek farmers began their autumn plowing with the southern migrations of the cranes. The crane dance, which Plutarch reported as associated with the Cretan labyrinth, is thought by some to have been part of a solar mythology. In folktales from Russia, Sicily, India, a crane is the animal guide who leads a younger brother into many adventures. In another series of tales the sly crane tricks the fish in a pond by offering to transport them to a spot where there are no fishermen, and eats them while pretending to save them. Not only is the slyness of cranes featured in North American Indian tales, but Old Grandfather Crane can usually be depended upon to help fugitives across rivers (by stretching out his long leg for a bridge) and to dump their pursuers into the water. Alabama Negroes believe that if a crane circles three times over the house, some one in the family will die soon. [RDJ]

Crane, Thomas Frederick (1844–1927) Teacher, scholar, and author, pioneer in the United States in folklore study as well as in that of medieval literature. He pointed out to Americans the work of European scholars in these fields. Crane was born in New York City, was graduated at Princeton University in 1864 and received his degrees of Doctor of Philosophy and Doctor of Letters there. He was admitted to the bar in 1866, but became assistant professor of Spanish and German at Cornell University when it was opened in 1868, was

Professor of Romance languages from 1882 to his retirement in 1909. He was a member of the board of editors of *Journal of American Folklore* at its beginning. Among Crane's works are *The Exempla, or Illustrative Stories from the Sermones Vulgares of Jacques de Vitry* (1890); *Medieval Sermons—Books and Stories* (1883); *Medieval Sermons—Books and Stories and Their Study since 1883* (1917); *Italian Popular Tales* (1885); and a carefully edited edition of *Liber Miraculis Sanctæ Dei Genitricis Mariæ, Published at Vienna, 1731, by B. Pez* (1925).

cranes of Ibycus A motif of legend and folktale (N271.3) of ancient Greece based on the idea that "murder will out" and "the sun brings all to light." Ibycus, a poet of Rhegium, who lived about 550 B.C., was waylaid and slain by robbers near Corinth. As he died, he called on some cranes flying overhead for vengeance. Soon after, one of the murderers, at the theater in Corinth, saw the cranes flying by, and cried involuntarily, "Behold the avengers of Ibycus!" Immediate investigation brought the crime to light and the killers were punished. The exclamation of the murderer became a proverbial expression. Similar stories are common in the oral tradition of Europe from Spain to Russia.

creaking limbs In the North American trickster tales of the Central Woodland, Plains, and Plateau areas, the cause of one of the absurd predicaments into which the trickster gets himself. He hears two trees scraping their branches together in the wind. Out of sympathy he climbs the tree to see if he can help them and gets caught between them, while passers-by eat his food on the ground below. See BLIND TRICKSTER.

creation True creation myths in which something is created out of nothing are rare among the North American Indians and non-existent among the Eskimo. Only among the Zuñi, a Pueblo group of the Southwest, among certain southern California tribes and perhaps one or two of northern California, and in the Eastern Woodlands, are anything like true creation stories recorded. For an outline of the Zuñi myth see AWONAWILONA. References to a "Master of Life" (Delaware), "Great God" (Shawnee), or "Great Spirit" in the Eastern Woodlands are to a supreme deity or high god who is assigned the role of creator; however this being is usually an otiose deity and does not enter into the mythology. There is always doubt whether such a being represents a native concept or a borrowing from Christianity in post-Columbian times. Origin myths do however abound among the North American Indians and to a much lesser degree among the Eskimo; such myths explain the origin of the world, of people, of animals, of death, of social groups, customs, arts and crafts.

Interest in origins varies however, from very little interest among the Eskimo, the Mackenzie, and the Great Basin tribes, to great interest in the Plains and Eastern Woodlands; evidence of this interest is shown in the number of features accounted for. The Eskimo, for example, account only for the origin of sea animals (see SEDNA), and the Great Basin tribes only for the origin of the earth, human beings, a few customs; whereas the Plains and Eastern Woodlands tribes have origin myths not only for the earth, people, animals, but also for tribal divisions, for clans, for ceremonies, cultivated plants, religious bundles, and so forth.

The most widely distributed of all North American Indian origin myths is that accounting for the creation of the world from a few grains of sand or a bit of mud which an animal brings up from the primeval waters or after a world flood, and which the culture hero then enlarges into the earth. This particular tale of earth-diving is told from California through the Great Basin, Plains, and Eastern Woodlands to the Atlantic Coast, either in simple or elaborated form. On the North Pacific Coast and among the present-day western Eskimo, the transformation of the earth to its present state commands more interest than the actual creation of the world. The origin of human beings is not so widely accounted for; when explained at all, they are said to have been made from sticks, mud, feathers, cuticle, but in many North American Indian mythologies people are simply existent, or appear, their origin being left unexplained. The origin of tribal divisons or of clans and gentes is of concern in the Southwest, and in the Eastern Woodlands; in the Plains where sacred bundles were so numerous, each bundle had an origin myth attached to it and when the bundle was sold the myth was considered part of the sale.

The culture hero is responsible for the origin of many phenomena, for the fact that death must be final, for menstruation. Origins of celestial phenomena, the sun, moon, certain constellations receive consider-able attention, especially among certain Plains tribes. The Star Husband tale, however, is not restricted to this region. Explanatory elements within tales or attached to the end of tales point out the origin of animal characteristics. Quite restricted in distribution are such origin stories as those of wailing (Apache), or of the division of labor between the sexes (Tübatul-abal). For creation myths of other areas of the world, see specific entries. [EWV]

creator In North American Indian mythology, crea-tion of the earth and mankind is generally attributed to a character who combines the attributes of creator with those of a culture-hero-trickster-transformer. In a few tribes, however, such as some Pacific Coast, Cali-fornia, and Pueblo groups, and among certain Eastern Woodlands Algonquians a creator, or supreme being, is referred to in the mythology. Such a creator or high god is generally an otiose deity, and many of the details involved in bringing the world to its present order are relegated to more active subordinate deities. The presence of a "high god concept" among some of the most primitive North American tribes has been used to support the thesis that monotheism is a primary concept in the history of religion. [EWV]

creator born at bottom of ocean A concept typical of the origin myth of the Yuman tribes of southern Cali-fornia. In the beginning two brothers were born at the bottom of the ocean: one the creator of life and mankind, Tuchaipa (Chakumat, Chaipa-Komat, or Mayoha among the Diegueño; Kwikumat among the Yuma; Matavilya among the Mohave); the other his opponent and causer of death, Kokomat or Yokomatis (Blind Old Man among the Yuma). The younger brother was blinded by the salt water as he emerged.

The creator fashioned mankind out of clay; the brother imitated him, but his creatures turned out web-footed, and from them are descended all the web-footed birds of the earth. The creator offended his daughter, Frog, and she killed him by swallowing his excrement. The consequent mourning of the people for his death and the whole dying god concept is one of the most dominant (and probably indigenous) themes in all Yuman mythology.

Creator's Grandmother The grandmother of the creator or culture hero, casually mentioned and taken for granted in certain North American Indian mytholo-gies, especially in Micmac and other Eastern Woodland Indian tales. When Glooscap first appeared among the Micmacs, for instance, his grandmother was with him. Among the Shawnee of this region the grandmother assumes a leading role in the mythology as well as in the religious observances, overshadowing her grandson, Habotchkilawetha. The culture hero's grandmother also figures in the myths of the northern California Shasta (she helps Coyote make the first snowshoes, directs the packing and storing of meat, etc.) and also in the tales of northern California Hupa and Wintun Indians. [EWV]

cremation The burning of the dead. Cremation, which destroys the corpse, may be contrasted with dis-posal of the dead by burial and its more or less elabo-rate techniques of preserving the body as long as possible. When they can be shown to have developed successively in the same culture they may be evidence that views of death and afterlife have undergone a profound revolution, or they may be diffusions from immigrant cultures. Funerary evidence in the form of funeral mounds and bone-fires (bonfires) from south Russia to the Scandinavian peninsula shows the spread of the custom. The Greeks of the Homeric period are thought by some to have introduced the custom into the eastern Mediterranean. Cremation is customary among the Hindus, some tribes in Siberia and North America, northern tribes of South America, and in the Bismarck Archipelago. Tribes with no fixed abode sometimes cremate their dead to protect the corpses from molestation by enemies who might work magic on them. This is an explanation given by the Mexican Cocopa Indians. Natives of East Africa cremate their dead to free the ghosts and enable them to enter the society of spirits. A potent reason for cremation is to get quit of the ghost, at times thought of as the animal spirit and distinguished from the spiritual soul. The burning of witches with consequent destruction of their powers is common in many communities. Elsewhere, as among the natives near Tanganyika, cremation kept the bones from coming to life after the bodies had decom-posed. Fire worshippers have special views about enter-ing the new life through fire. [RDJ]

Cretan bull In Greek legend, the bull, thought to be Pasiphae's, sent by Poseidon as a sacrifice but kept by Minos for its beauty and captured by Hercules as the seventh of his labors. After the hero released the bull, it settled at Marathon, first wandering over all of Greece.

cricket The cricket was much esteemed in antiquity and it is said that our modern superstition concerning it and our attitudes toward it have probably been transmitted to us from ancient times. The common house-cricket has a very wide distribution in the Old World, but nothing is known as to its original habitat. Some of the widespread beliefs about this representative of the *Gryllidæ* may be mentioned:

1. *As bringer of good or bad luck* It is good to have a cricket in the house; if it leaves the chimney it is a fatal sign; if you kill it, it is a breach of hospitality; it is dangerous to imitate the chirp of the cricket; it will eat your clothes if you kill it; in Silesia, the cricket's cry indicates ill-luck, the presence of a dead person in the house, or a theft committed. In Ireland, if a cricket is heard chirping on Christmas Eve, he is called "the king of all luck."

2. *As prognosticator* The cricket forecasts rain, death, or the approach of an absent lover.

3. *As a nostrum in folk medicine* In antiquity, the cricket was used as a cure for asthma (Pliny, *Hist. Nat.* XXX: 49: the prescription was 20 insects in sweet wine); powdered crickets were used in certain ills. The Cherokee Indians believed that a tea brewed from crickets would make them good singers like that insect.

4. *As personification of the house-spirit* It is in this capacity that the cricket is usually thought of in the United States and in England. The well-known story by Charles Dickens, *The Cricket on the Hearth*, expresses this relation of cricket to hearth and home in a simple but effective pattern. [GPS]

St. Crispin's Day October 25, anniversary of the translation of the relics of St. Crispin and St. Crispinian from Soissons to Rome in the 9th century. In Westphalia, the festival day is June 20, anniversary of an earlier translation of the brother saints' relics there by Charlemagne.

In both France and England, until the end of the 18th century, the day was an occasion for processions, feasting, and merrymaking on the part of the shoemakers' guilds. In England, the day coincides with the anniversary of the Battle of Agincourt, and has therefore a double significance.

At Soissons, at Rogations, the St. Crispin processions are still held and still pause before a certain house in the Rue de la Congrégation, the site of a chapel, St. Crépin-le-Petit, which once stood there. At Bourges similar celebrations took place in olden times, and master-cobblers who absented themselves from the ceremonies were fined a pound of wax to be delivered to the chapel. At Moncontour the day was celebrated until 1870 by a procession of shoemakers who walked two by two from the tavern to the church, where holy bread was distributed to them. The bread was used at the banquet at the tavern subsequently.

A song is still sung by French children which recalls these processions and celebrations, and which runs something as follows:

> Aujourd'hui
> les cordonniers, bien mises,
> vont visiter le Saint-Crépin
> qui, lui,
> travaillait en bras-de-chemise.

Today the shoemakers, all dressed up, pay a visit to Saint Crispin, who himself worked in his shirt sleeves!

A Provençal legend accounts for the number of cripples and hunchbacks practicing the craft of shoe-making. St. Crispin was so pleased by the first celebrations in his honor that he asked God to reward the shoemakers by giving them a glimpse of Heaven. The request was granted; St. Crispin lowered a long ladder; but only the prideful dared to climb it. When they reached Paradise, the festival of St. Peter was being celebrated, and the *Sursum corda* was being sung. St. Paul, in charge of the heavenly gates, being deaf, mistook the words for a command to cut the cord—in Provençal, *Zou sus la cordo!*—which he did. The shoemakers tumbled to earth, and many of them were crippled.

In Tanby, Wales, on St. Crispin's Eve the saint's effigy was suspended from a steeple by the carpenters. Next day it was cut down and carried through the streets by the shoemakers. They stopped at the door of each guild member, where a mock will and testament of St. Crispin was read aloud, and a portion of the effigy's dress, bequeathed to the inmate, was cut off and left behind. When nothing was left but the stuffing, that was rolled into a ball and thrown to the crowd to be kicked around. On St. Clement's Day the shoemakers avenged St. Crispin by making an effigy of a carpenter, which was given the same treatment.

Crockett, Davy Backwoods hero of history, legend, and folktale. With the motto, "Be always sure you're right, then go ahead," David Crockett (1786–1836), Tennessee born and bred, rose to fame as hunter and Indian fighter, "coonskin congressman" and backwoods humorist. In Congress he was determined to "wear no man's collar" (that is, Jackson's) and to represent the interests of small farmers and new settlers (having been one of them himself) when they were threatened by speculators. In 1835, having stood defeat in two elections, this irrepressible champion of lost causes went to Texas and was one of six survivors of the Alamo to be shot at the command of Santa Ana, March 6, 1836.

Crockett's personal popularity rested not only on his good sense and courage but also on his backwoods picturesqueness of action and speech, uncouth and salty, half natural, half assumed—qualities that lent themselves easily to ridicule and to exploitation by the Jackson and anti-Jackson forces. Provoked by the inaccuracies and gibes in the anonymous *Sketches and Eccentricities of Col. David Crockett of West Tennessee* (1833), some of the best stories in which were his own, he wrote, or had a hand in writing, *Narrative of the Life of David Crockett, of the State of Tennessee* (1834) and *An Account of Col. Crockett's Tour to the North and Down East* (1835).

The legend that he himself thus helped to create and perpetuate—of the homespun oracle and the rustic clown—soon passed into myth. He himself boasted that he was so ugly that his grin could bring a coon down from a tree (once he grinned the bark off a knot which he had mistaken for a coon), and claimed that in less than a year he killed 105 bears. And in 1835, when the people fearfully awaited Halley's Comet, they said that Crockett was going to mount the highest peak in the Allegheny mountains and wring the fiery tail off the comet to save the world from death and destruction.

After his death he continued to grow in legendary stature until the comic backwoodsman had won out over the homely statesman, and horseplay triumphed over horse sense. In the "Crockett" almanacs (1835–1856) he became a giant and a superman performing impossible feats in a "backwoods fairyland," along with other bullies and boasters, such as Mike Fink and Ben Hardin (named for the Kentucky congressman).

As in the case of Paul Bunyan, Crockett's character merged with that of other heroes, some of the same stories being told about John Sevier and Andrew Jackson. He and his tall tales, tall talk, and practical jokes, real, legendary, or fictional, served as the inspiration of much of the humor of the old Southwest in the 1830's and '40's, including the character of Col. Nimrod Wildfire in James K. Paulding's play *The Lion of the West* (1831). Folk memories of Crockett linger in hunting yarns told in Tennessee and Arkansas. And he started a long line of politicians who tell stories to get votes.

Perhaps he will be remembered most for his coonskin trick, his encounter with a sensible coon, and his morning hunt. During the campaign of 1827, finding himself without cash or credit and obliged to stand treat to his thirsty constituents at a stump-speaking, he went out and shot a coon and traded the skin for a quart of rum. Every time the Yankee rum vendor threw the skin under the bar, Crockett surreptitiously pulled it through the cracks between the supporting logs, so that before the day was over he had managed to buy ten quarts of rum with the same coonskin. The joke won him the election.

The sensible coon, recognizing Crockett, gave himself up without a struggle, for he considered himself shot. And when Crockett, charmed by the compliment, patted him on the head, saying, "I hope I may be shot myself before I hurt a hair of your head," the coon calmly walked off—"not doubting your word a bit, d'ye see, but lest you should kinder happen to change your mind."

One cold January morning, when the daybreak froze fast as it was trying to dawn, the earth froze fast in its axis, and the sun got jammed between two cakes of ice, Crockett unfroze them with hot oil squeezed from a fresh twenty-pound bear that he had picked up on the road. Then, as the sun came up, "I lit my pipe by the blaze o' his topknot, shouldered my bear, an' walked home, introducin' the people to fresh daylight with a piece of sunrise in my pocket, with which I cooked my bear steaks, an' enjoyed one o' the best breakfasts I had tasted for some time." [BAB]

crocodile The Egyptians regularly fed the crocodiles of the god Souchos who was a crocodile himself. At one period in Egypt crocodiles were thought of as oracles and were embalmed when dead. The custom of ordeal by crocodiles has been used as a motif (H224) in Arabian folktale (i.e. judgment depended upon whether the accused was eaten or rejected by the crocodiles). In some parts of Africa crocodiles are the homes of dead ancestors. In West Africa a person attacked by a crocodile is believed to be the victim of the vengeance of someone he has harmed, now incarnate in the crocodile. He who kills a crocodile becomes a crocodile. The Basutos believe that crocodiles can sieze a man's shadow and drag him into their pool. The regular feeding of crocodiles in some parts of West Africa may be for religious reasons, though

one observer has remarked that a well-fed crocodile is a better neighbor than a hungry one. "The strength of the crocodile is in the water," says a South African Vandau proverb. Some Bantu tribes banish a man who has been splashed by a crocodile. The peoples of Borneo, Sumatra, and the Philippines treat crocodiles with great respect. The numerous popular tales from the Pacific about women who have had crocodiles as lovers belong to the large cycle of tales about women with serpent lovers to be examined elsewhere. See AFTERBIRTH; ALLIGATOR; NAME TABU. [RDJ]

Crocodile The villain of a folktale told by the Vandau people of Portuguese South Africa. One day a big crocodile arrived in the river; it killed sheep, cattle, herders, travelers. The people feared it greatly, but did not know how to kill it. One day the king called a meeting of his chiefs and people to discuss how they might rid themselves of Crocodile. Fox came to the meeting. Fox jumped up on a log and said to the king, "O King, I am small, but wisdom surpasses bravery. Why do you wait for your enemy to grow strong? What do I do? I eat crocodiles while they are still in the eggs. Get rid of your enemy before he is stronger than you."

Crocodile and Hen Title of a Fjort Negro folktale: classified as a legal story. A little fat hen went daily to the river bank to pick up food. Crocodile saw her, was about to eat her, when the little hen cried out, "O brother, don't." Crocodile was troubled in his mind. Why did she call him brother? But he gave up puzzling, and decided to eat the hen. Next day little fat Hen was on the river bank picking up food. Crocodile was going to eat her. Hen cried out, "O brother, don't." And Crocodile turned away. Was he her brother? Crocodile decided to go ask Nzambi (Mother Earth, the creator). On the way, he met Mbambi, the big lizard, and told him his dilemma. "Don't you know," said the lizard, "that all who lay eggs are brothers?—Duck, Hen, you, me?"

crocodile tears Simulated or pretended weeping; hypocritical grief: from the tale of ancient travelers that the crocodile weeps over those he devours.

Crœsus The last king of Lydia, 6th century B.C.: proverbial as the richest of all men, superseding in this the mythical Tantalus. Solon the wise came to Crœsus' court and told the king that no man might be considered happy until he finished his life happily. When Sardis, the capital of Lydia, fell to Cyrus, and Crœsus was condemned to be burned to death, he remembered Solon's words and repeated his name three times. Cyrus overheard and was told the story by Crœsus. He ordered the fire put out, but no one could extinguish it. Crœsus, already in pain from the heat of the blaze, prayed in tears to Apollo, and a rainstorm arose to quench the pyre. The two kings became friends, and after the death of Cyrus, Crœsus remained at the court of Cambyses, the son and successor of Cyrus. For the wanton shooting of the son of Prexaspes, Crœsus rebuked Cambyses, then fled from his anger and was hidden by some of the courtiers. Cambyses recovered from his rage and when Crœsus made his reappearance greeted him warmly. At the same time, however, he ordered those courtiers who had aided Crœsus killed,

Cromm Crúac A huge idol which stood on the plain of Mag Sleact (the plain of adoration or prostrations) in County Cavan, in Ulster, near the present village of Ballymagauran: also called *ríg-iodal h-Eireann*, the king idol of Ireland. "Around him were twelve idols made of stone but he was of gold" and to him the early Irish sacrificed one third of their children on Samain (Nov. 1) in return for "milk and corn" and the good weather which insured the fertility of cattle and crops. The idol and the sacrifices are mentioned in the 6th century *Dinnsenchas* in the *Book of Leinster*. Cromm Crúac was held in horror for his terrible exactions; it was dangerous even to worship him, for the worshippers themselves often perished in the act of worship. A pre-Christian king named Tigernmus is said to have introduced the worship of Cromm Crúac to Ireland and to have been destroyed himself with three fourths of his people one Samain night during the prostrations.

The twelve lesser idols encircling the golden image have led to the assumption that Cromm Crúac was a solar deity; certainly he was a fertility god. But he has not been identified with any ancient Irish god. Dagda, in his agricultural aspect, has been suggested for this role, but no identity can be substantiated.

The *Dinnshenchas* names the idol Cromm Crúac (bloody crescent or bloody bent one); it is referred to as Cenn Crúaic (bloody head) in the *Tripartite Life of Patrick*. Legend says that Patrick cursed and destroyed it. The *Dinnshenchas* story tells how Patrick preached to the people on Mag Sleact against the burning of milk-cows and their first-born progeny.

Cromm Dub's Sunday In Irish folklore, the first Sunday in August: anniversary of the destruction of the famous idol known as Cromm Dub. On this date flowers were still offered at his place on Mt. Callan in County Clare, as late as the mid-19th century. For this reason the day is also called Garland Sunday. The flower offerings were reminiscent of a time when more bloody sacrifices were prepared. Compare CROMM CRÚAC. See CELTIC FOLKLORE.

crónán Literally, humming; in Irish folk song, a kind of humming, often a chorus, probably imitative of the drone of a bagpipe. Crónán is the Irish word for the drone of the bagpipe, and also for the purring of a cat. The song *Ballinderry* has a crónán burden of three notes running throughout. This kind of singing is often done for children, for cows at milking, and for plow horses. It demands considerable stamina to produce the long, continuous sound.

Crónán snagac was the difficult slow humming demanded of the poet Senchán by Marbán, Guaire's swineherd, during the great visitation of the poets to Guaire. Senchán had promised any form of minstrelsy desired. But the crónán snagac was so exhausting (and Marbán would not let them stop) that the 27 hummers in the group fell prostrate. Senchán himself "raised his beard in the air" and hummed the crónán snagac till one of his eyes burst out. Not till then would Marbán give him respite.

Cronus In Greek mythology, the youngest of the Titans, son of Uranus and Ge, and father by Rhea of Hestia, Demeter, Hera, Hades, Poseidon, and Zeus: probably a pre-Hellenic diety, superseded, as outlined in the myth, by the cult of Zeus and the Olympians. Cronus, together with the other children of Uranus, was imprisoned in the body of his mother, the earth. She induced him to repay this jealousy by dethroning his father; and after castrating Uranus with a sickle and tossing the severed member into the sea, Cronus became ruler of the universe. During his reign, happiness and peace made the time a Golden Age. But Cronus was warned by his parents that one of his own children would supplant him and as his sons were born he swallowed them. At the time Zeus, his youngest, was born, he was given a stone to swallow instead of the infant, and Zeus was taken away to be reared by the Curetes in secret. At last, with the aid of the Titans (excepting Themis and Prometheus), Zeus overthrew Cronus and obtained the regency. Some commentators say Cronus was imprisoned in Tartarus; Plutarch places him on a far-western island, near Britain, where he sleeps with his followers, the Cyclopes and the Hecatoncheires, guarded by Briareus.

The only important festival of Cronus in classical times was the Cronia, celebrated as a typical harvest festival with class distinctions abolished, in Athens, Rhodes, and Thebes. Cronus was represented holding a curved object, perhaps the reaping-hook, the castration of Uranus being an explanatory story. The Greeks identified him with such foreign gods as Moloch; the Romans with their own Saturn. The name was in later times etymologically linked to Chronos, time, but there is no justification for this linkage.

The swallow story so prominent in the myth is not mentioned in Homer and may be a later addition. A youngest son theme may be traced in the succession of Cronus and Zeus to the rule of the universe, the same sort of sequence found in the mythology of other lands of the Mediterranean ancient world.

cross The term "cross" has been applied to many symbols. The *Encyclopoedia Heraldica* is said to list 385 different varieties. Although specialists are not in agreement on the terms used to designate them, the following list may be found useful: In the Greek cross a vertical line is bisected by a horizontal line of equal length. In the Latin cross the lower part of the vertical is longer than the upper part and the two lines are often not of equal length. In the tau cross the horizontal line runs across, not through, the top of the vertical. The looped or handled cross has a circle above the horizontal line. St. Andrew's cross is in the form of an X. The Maltese forms have four triangles joined at their apex. The gammate or swastika has lines running at right angles to and at the ends of the four lines of the Greek cross. The archiepiscopal cross is a Latin cross with two horizontal lines; the papal cross has three horizontals. These general types have many subtypes, each with a different name. Thus if in the swastika the horizontal line runs toward the left of the top of the vertical it is called by some a "sauvastika." The swastika has also been called the "gammate" cross because it is formed by joining four gammas together, or the "fylfot," presumably because it was used to fill the foot or base of a figured window. Crosses are further distinguished by their functions in ritual, such as the altar cross, the processional cross. For the last thousand years Christians have designated the Latin cross with the image of Christ on it, the crucifix.

The importance of the cross in Christian cultures and the lore which Christians attach to it as a symbol of death and resurrection have led many people to investigate crosses in non-Christian cultures and to formulate views about them. The central questions in this as in other inquiries about the habits of thought and feeling of human beings living in social groups in many parts of the world are: What, in fact, is the symbol to be studied? Which groups know or use the symbol? What meanings do they attach to it? What is its value, function, and importance in their community?

The statement that "the use of the cross as a religious symbol in pre-Christian times and among many non-Christian peoples may probably be regarded as almost universal and in many cases was connected with some form of nature worship," though both obscure and misleading, is representative of the sorts of confusion to be guarded against. Confusion is increased by the statement of another authority that the "swastica or gammate cross is the most primitive form of the symbol and always had a symbolico-religious sense." Definitions are in order. Although the swastika is a complex symbol of which the cross is a part, it may, for purposes of analysis, be included in the group of symbols designated by the term "cross." The author of the statement does not make it clear whether the word "primitive" is to mean that the swastika is the first form of the cross to appear on the surface of the earth, i.e. first in time, or whether, though different cultures began their use of crosses at different times, the first cross they made was the swastika which they later simplified into a simple cross. In this case the word "primitive" would refer to something about "first in terms of 'cultural evolution'" and subtly commit the reader to views about the nature of social groups. Speculation on these questions of origin which has occupied many excellent scholars is diverting but inasmuch as the answers are lost in the miasmas of prehistory the speculation is futile.

The symbolico-religious meanings which cultures in the several parts of the world have attached to crosses in their 385 or more complex forms have been elaborated further by modern students of crosses. Thus ethnologers have suggested that the form of cross, the looped cross (see ANKH), found frequently on ancient Egyptian artifacts symbolized variously, and depending on the ethnologer, a nilometer, a key to a canal lock, a loin cloth, a phallus, a uterus, etc., and thus from the things symbolized derived a religious or magic value. Clearly accounts of the cross and its meaning present semantic problems of considerable complexity.

The simplicity of a symbol formed by the intersection of two lines makes it useful for a number of separate purposes and thus gives it a number of separate meanings. Thus the cross in the margin of an American husband's shopping list may mean either that the article must under no circumstances be forgotten, and thus has a symbolico-social meaning, or that the article has been purchased, and thus has a symbolico-historical meaning. Crosses used by newspapers to mark the spot where an event occurred, usually of the Maltese, Greek, or St. Andrew's variety, have an adverbial function indicating position where. Geographers use lines formed

by crosses to indicate boundaries and economists to compare one set of values with others. The cross an illiterate John Doe uses as his mark has a socio-legal meaning. When the point of intersection is important the cross is useful to indicate exact location. When the direction in which the arms point is important, the cross is used to indicate directions, particularly directions of the winds, as in weather-vanes. To this practical meaning of a cross as wind-pointer other meanings have been added. It then becomes a "wind-symbol" and may be used to call up winds when they are needed. Lines radiating from the point of intersection may symbolize the sun. Thus students of the cross in non-Christian cultures have seen in it symbols of the wind, the storm, therefore the rains, the sun, and fertility. That these values have been associated with the cross in some cultures is incontestable; but the exact relation to each other of these symbolic values must be determined by an examination of each culture and ritual.

The crosses used by meteorologists to determine the speed of the winds might be called wind symbols but have practical values far removed from Christian dogma. The market crosses in European towns are probably of Christian origin and legends have been attached to them as the places where miracles were performed or saints martyred but they are principally useful as place-markers: the social center of community life, the geographical center of the village, the center of municipal authority. The use of crosses as decorations on Bronze Age artifacts and elsewhere raises similar questions and leads to the confused problem of the relations between esthetic and religious values and functions.

Crosses have been found on the artifacts of most known cultures. The difficulties of interpreting the Egyptian cross have been mentioned. The Phœnicians and other Semitic peoples are said to have added magical powers and associated this cross with Astarte as the Greeks associated crosses with Aphrodite, the Ephesian Artemis, and others. The Elamite and Sumerian cultures used crosses. The Assyrian kings wore crosses as pendants.

In the Near East Schliemann turned up crosses in his excavations on the site of Troy. A cross on the pubic region of a female figure from this site, like crosses painted or tattooed on the pubic regions of women of other cultures, may be decoration, a defense against the entry of devils into the vagina, or it may serve other purposes. Plato in a somewhat Pythagorean mood says the soul of the world was created in the form of a cross, and Saint Jerome in a platonic mood says the cross is the form of the world in its four directions. Pre-Christian crosses have been found in Europe as far north as Sweden and the Irish crosses may well have the combination of Christian and pagan meanings characteristic of peripheral cultures. The hammer of the Gaulish Thor was a cross which destroyed by storm, and after storm produced fecundity. Phallic symbols in Greece, Rome, and Japan are sometimes in the form of inverted tau crosses though some students of sexual folklore tend to draw from this fact the extreme view that inverted tau crosses are always sexual symbols.

In India the swastika, which was one of the body marks of the Lord Buddha, is thought to be a good symbol as the sauvastika is bad, but it has other associations such as an apparatus for making fire, "a symbol for the living flame whose mother is the Goddess Māyā, personification of the productive power," as well as the sun, the lightning, the storm. The spread of Buddhism is said to have brought this form of cross into many parts of Asia. In China long before Buddhism, crosses of one sort or another were radicals which either alone or combined with other strokes formed the pictograms which later became the Chinese ideographs. From the earliest times Chinese etymologists have used great ingenuity in rationalizing these and some have thought them connected with the directions, the soil, fertility, etc.

The cross is known in Africa. The women of the Hottentots keep wooden crosses above them during confinement, and because moon ceremonies are important among these peoples such crosses are thought to be moon symbols. The Maori of New Zealand wore greenstone crosses as amulets or decorations. Crosses are on the statues of Easter Island and on the sacred stones of eastern New Guinea. Crosses were widely used in North and South America, Mexico, and Central America. In North America on trees, crosses marked the limits of camps. The Athapascans used crosses in their sacrifices to the new moon. Certain Indians of California showed the Great Mother with her limbs extended on the form of a cross.

Early explorers of Mexico were astonished to find that there the cross had an unquestionable religious significance. In one form the cross is surmounted by a large bird (turkey? parrot?) and on another in the form of a tree the worshipper seems to be offering sacrifice. By anticipating the diffusionist theory of cultural growth these adventurers decided that it had been introduced by Saint Thomas or by Spaniards driven across the sea by the Moors. The Mexican cross carried by the Aztec goddess of the rains is now thought to have been associated with the sun or wind. When in the form of a tree with its roots in the water it is called the "tree of life." Crosses have been found in the shell mounds of New Mexico and among the pictographs of the Dakotas.

The history of the cross as a religious symbol among Christians is obscure. It became important as a symbol for Christianity in the 4th or 5th century; the crucifix bearing the image of the crucified Christ appeared in the 8th, and the cult of the cross was epidemic in the 13th century. Each of these moments in the movements of Christian thought and feeling should be taken as approximate. Each occurred at a time when the complex of Christianity was undergoing rapid change and for each the antecedents whether immediate or remote are obscure.

Punishment by crucifixion was a Roman custom applied usually to slaves or to non-Romans and is associated with the custom of tying victims to a stake or tree and allowing them to die of hunger and thirst. Though this punishment is known to savages of all cultures including the modern Euro-American, the term "arbor infelix" was a useful foil to the term "arbor vitæ" after the cross had become a symbol of resurrection and human salvation. In the 3rd century Saint Clement of Alexandria called the cross the sign of Christ, and Tertullian at about the same time

referred to Christians as *crucis religiosi*. In this century too the monogram of Christ was devised. It was the first two letters of Iesus Xristi and was written ☧. The author of the article in the *Catholic Encyclopaedia* asserts without further explanation that the early Christians did not openly worship the cross because the pagans worshipped cruciform objects, and that the sign of the cross, first made over the forehead and later over the whole body, was a secret sign by which Christians identified themselves to each other.

The vision of Christ and the cross attributed to Saint Constantine, the first Christian Roman emperor, in the beginning of the 4th century together with the command to conquer with this sign marks the beginning of another moment in the thought and feeling about the cross. St. Helena, Constantine's 80-year-old mother, undertook to excavate Christ's tomb near which it was later said the Jews had buried the true cross in order to keep relic-hunters from defacing it and profiting from the miracles it could produce. Only a few Jews knew the site. One of them, Judas, later called Cyriacus, identified it. Three crosses were found and none knew which was the true cross until, when taken to the bedside of a dying old woman, one of them restored her to health. Fragments of this object, thought to be the true cross, produced miracles. Even nails from it had great power. It was housed in the Basilica Saint Constantinus over the site of "Christ's tomb," was destroyed by the infidels, and in Christian legend is said to have reappeared in many places. Large numbers of chips of wood thought to be taken from the true cross and reverently worshipped in many places has led to the assertion that the cross can miraculously reproduce itself. Eusebius, a contemporary of St. Helena, does not mention her discovery of the true cross. The feasts of special adoration of the cross are on Good Friday and on September 18, anniversary of the date when the Basilica Saint Constantinus was dedicated. At this period people began to build churches in the form of crosses.

The crucifix or the Roman cross containing the image of the crucified Christ became popular in the 7th and 8th centuries when it took its place with other images as an object of worship. This worship is explained by the view that veneration paid to a symbol is transferred to the thing symbolized.

Although Bede in the 7th century reported that Saint Augustine of England carried a processional cross, the altar cross appeared in the 13th century, a period of considerable religious tension when Jacobus de Voragine by his *Golden Legend* greatly stimulated the growth of Christian folklore. In this period too, an elaborate account of the history of the cross reported that Seth got the Tree of Life from the Garden of Eden and planted it over Adam's grave. Wood from this tree served many purposes until finally it was made into the cross on which Christ was crucified.

The miracles attributed to the cross are innumerable but generally have to do with physical or spiritual salvation. Thus the cross will frighten away devils and protect against evil. A cross surreptitiously introduced into contracts with Satan will make the contract void. A cross grasped or venerated at the moment of damnation may save the soul or at the moment of death may restore life and health.   R. D. JAMESON

☞ The cross is sometimes the symbol of the four heavenly directions. The Tarahumara Indians of Sonora and Chihuahua, Mexico, in whom the ancient religion is strong, still use the traditional directional crosses in their ceremonial patios. The Concheros pray to the four directions. The sorcerer in the Negritos dance of the Sierra de Puebla invokes the four winds. This already deep-rooted religious significance of the cross facilitated adoption of the Christian symbol. [GPK]

cross-eyes It is bad luck to meet a cross-eyed person. It is good luck to meet a cross-eyed person of the opposite sex. To avert the bad luck in wait for you from meeting a cross-eyed person, spit through your fingers, but do not let him see you do it. If you are a fisherman you must spit in your hat. One way to keep a cross-eyed person from injuring you, is to outstare him. This is quite easy to do. You will lose at cards if you play with a cross-eyed partner. There is no available information as to whether a cross-eyed person ever wins.

Negroes in some sections of the southern United States say it is bad luck to meet a cross-eyed woman. If you meet one in the morning, things will "get crossed" all day. If you meet one on a Monday morning, you can expect a bad week. Never look one in the eye, they advise. They also warn against letting a baby look into a mirror before he is a year old, lest he become cross-eyed. If he does, however, the bad result can be averted by rubbing blood from a black chicken on the back of his neck. For a rabbit foot to be really effective as a luck charm, it must be the left hind foot of a graveyard rabbit killed by a cross-eyed Negro at midnight.

crossroads The place where two or more roads intersect. Something sinister about crossroads has made such conjunction of highways a matter of interest for superstitions, beliefs, and customs connected with this particular spot. Crossroads superstition was prevalent generally through Europe, in India, Japan, Greece, among the Mongols and the American Indians. Here were to be found demons, evil spirits, ghosts and witches, sprites, kobolds, and fairies. It was the burial place of suicides and murderers, a dump-heap for parricides, and a rendezvous for witches who frequently used this uncanny place for their Sabbat revels. Anything might plainly happen here. People feared and avoided this meeting of the ways.

Divinities were sometimes associated with the crossroads, perhaps to repel or neutralize the evil influences attached to the locality. In Greek mythology, both Hermes and Hecate were connected with the crossroads. Such ceremonies were practiced at this spot as sacrifice, offerings, divination, and many magic rites. [GPS]

Crow The crow enters into the mythology of North American Indians to some extent, but is by no means mentioned as frequently as is Eagle, and has not the definite character of the greedy and voracious Raven, trickster of the northern North Pacific Coast tribes. Among the Chipewyan of eastern Canada, Crow is the trickster, and references to Crow as a character occur in various Southwestern, Plains Indian, and other tales. Originally white, Crow turned black when he ate snakes' eyes (Kiowa and other tribes). Pueblo groups refer to crows as chickens. The Crow-Water society of the northern Plains Blackfoot was a ceremonial organization for men and women, membership in which enabled persons to become wealthy and to cure the sick. Another northern Plains group, a Siouan-speaking tribe, is now known as the Crow Indians; this is a translation through French *gens des corbeaux* for their own name for themselves, *Absa'roke,* which means crow, sparrow hawk, or bird people. Among the Navaho of the Southwest, missionaries are humorously referred to as crows, because of their black garments. [EWV]

Cruel Brother A Scottish popular ballad (Child #11) in which the main theme is the revenge of a brother whose consent has not been asked to his sister's marriage. The young suitor asked the consent of parents and sisters, but forgot to ask brother John. It was the brother, however, who set the bride on her horse to go to her new home, and as she leaned to kiss him goodbye he stabbed her to the heart. As the journey progressed the lady grew paler and weaker, until she could go no further. The ballad ends with the incremental repetition of bequests, to mother, sisters, brother John, brother John's wife, and sometimes brother John's bairns. This hardly seems like the climax of relations motif, with brother John's wife and bairns following as anticlimax to the gallows-tree bequeathed to brother John. But Phillips Barry has made a suggestion (*JAFL* 28:300) that ill-will on the part of John's wife toward the young bride motivated the murder.

Some of the Scottish manuscripts give the title of this ballad as *The Bride's Testament.* It was extremely popular both in Scotland and the west of England, and is known to have been current in Ireland in 1860. Compare EDWARD; LORD RANDAL.

cruit Irish word for harp, especially the ancient bardic instrument. *Síod-cruit* is the fairy harp, the harp of the side.

csárdás or **czárdás** A Hungarian couple dance, consisting of a slow and a quick part. In the peasant version the slow *lassan* consists of two-steps with heel-click in ballroom position, and of turns shoulder to shoulder; the fast *gyors* consists of vertical jumps and jump-hops. The citified version has acquired technical labels. In the slow *lassú* the two-step and click are called *andalgó;* the turn, *páros forgó;* the *bokázó* is a triple heel-click for the man and a twisting heel-change for the woman. The fast *friss* introduces the *ingó,* a side-to-side balance, the *kis harang,* a coupé or cutting step, two varieties of forward leaps (the *cifra* and *tétováző*), a toe-heel hop (the *csillag*), and a number of more complex steps. The style is characterized by flexibility in the knees, emphatic stamping, heel-clicking, in-and-out foot twists, a proud bearing, elegant in the women, martial in the men. [GPK]

Cuailgne (pronounced Cooley) An ancient hilly district in County Louth in Ulster, Ireland: scene of the famous táin, or cattle raid, led by Medb and Ailill of Connacht to steal the famous Brown Bull of Cuailgne. The district was defended by Cuchulain alone while the Ulstermen were in their weakness. See TÁIN BÓ CUAILGNE.

Cucaracha, La The Cockroach; a Mexican revolutionary song with innumerable stanzas, some devoted to Villa, Zapata, and Carranza, some consisting of proverbial or epigrammatic statements about women, love, etc., which are older than the song. The chorus, from which the title is derived, says that the cockroach can't go on his way because he has no marihuana to smoke. Various explanations have been offered for the significance of the cockroach: that it may also be an old maid, a pet name for a dancer, a nickname for Carranza, etc. The song has achieved considerable popularity across the border in the United States, becoming a radio and juke-box favorite in the early 1940's.

Cuchulain Hero of the Ulster cycle of Old Irish epic and romance: said to have lived about the first century A.D. He was the son of Dechtire, sister of Conchobar, king of Ulster, by whom he was fostered. Luġ of the Tuatha Dé Danann was his father. Cuchulain was of extraordinary beauty, growth, and achievement. At the age of seven he ran away and sought training with Conchobar at Emain Macha, and was tutored by Ulster's seven greatest heroes and poets. He was called Setanta until he was 12, when he earned the name Cuchulain, the Hound of Culann. The boy was attacked by the fierce hound of Culann, the smith, killed it, and then served as watch and guard for Culann until a pup "just as good" could be reared to take its place. Among other boyhood deeds, he killed the three sons of Nechtan before their own dún: three huge brothers whom no Ulsterman had ever challenged and come away alive. He wooed and won Emer, daughter of Forgall the Wily, who contrived to send Cuchulain alone to the Isle of Skye to take training under Scathać. Forgall believed that Cuchulain would either perish on the journey or be killed by Scathać herself, who hated strangers. But Cuchulain won his way to the woman warrior's presence, took her training, and endeared himself to her by his skill and courage.

Cuchulain is hero of the *Táin bó Cuailgne,* the *Cattle Raid of Cuailgne,* called the War for the Brown Bull. Queen Meďb of Connacht coveted the famous Brown Bull of Cuailgne, and while the Ulstermen were in their weakness (see EMAIN MACHA) raided Ulster with her hosts to take it. Cuchulain alone was immune to the curse of Macha, because his parentage was half supernatural. Single-handed he held off Meďb's forces, killing them from ambush, sometimes at the rate of twenty a day, and finally, by agreement with Meďb, meeting one warrior a day in single combat, during which time Meďb agreed to halt her advance. (See FERDIAD; FINDABAIR.) Meďb finally captured the bull, but in the end Conchobar and the Ulster warriors rallied to Cuchulain's aid and drove the forces of Connacht out of Ulster.

Some years later Cuchulain met his death in one famous battle against all Ireland. In vengeance Meďb had gathered together the sons of three kings whom Cuchulain had killed. Three satirists among the hosts tricked Cuchulain out of the three spears he carried; and when he gave up the famous Gae Bulg, he was killed himself. Cuchulain's charioteer, Loeg, was killed in that battle; so was the Gray of Macha, the wonderful horse that loved Cuchulain and fought off his enemies with his hooves. The story of this last fight against odds, Cuchulain's last stand tied to a pillar-post so that he would die standing up, the fear of each king's son to approach him, until finally a raven lighted on his head to take the eyes, thus proving he was dead, is probably the most stirring story in all west European literature. See BRICRIU'S FEAST; CONLA; SATIRE; TÁIN BÓ CUAILGNE.

cucking-stool A chair in which disorderly, and especially scolding, women or cheating shopkeepers were exposed and sometimes immersed for punishment by public derision: often confused with ducking-stool and sometimes called choking-stool. The original idea was evidently to punish by the embarrassment of being seen publicly on a stool intended for private use, since the cucking-stool was made to resemble a close-stool and since, more particularly, the word "cuck" meant to defecate. The ducking of the prisoner, chair and all, in a stagnant pond, was a later refinement. The "coking-stole" was in use in Cornwall in the 13th century and is frequently referred to in English literature thereafter until the 18th. The latest recorded punishment thereby was in Leominster in 1809. The practice was confined largely to England until, in the 17th century, in the form of the ducking-stool, it was adopted by the American colonies, where it seems to have served more as a warning than as an engine of punishment. [CFP]

cuckoo Any member of the family *Cuculidæ* of birds. The *Cuculus canorus,* "messenger of Spring," is familiar in Britain and in nearly all the Old World; one American species ranges roughly from Canada and the Great Plains to Argentina.

The cry of the cuckoo as it returns every year about the same time is greeted everywhere with excitement. In Germany, peasants roll on the grass for joy and their greeting is not *"Wie geht's!"* but *"Der Kuckuck hat gerufen!"* It is then that if they have money in their pocket, they turn it over for this will ensure them plenty in the future and general good luck. In the British Isles on this occasion, workmen stop work for a time to enjoy "cuckoo-ale."

No bird is ascribed more oracular ability; it prophesies the hour of the day, the number of years of life, how long a maid will remain unmarried, and so on. It is looked to as a love-oracle, the sight and sound of the cuckoo being a good omen for marriage. It will be recalled that the Indian god, Indra, took the form of a cuckoo in his love adventures as did the Greek Zeus. From its well-known habits, e.g. laying its eggs in other birds' nests for them to hatch, it is in ill repute as an adulterer (the English word "cuckold" is derived from *cuculus*) and is connected with phallic symbolism. Further, it is said that ghosts and the Devil can assume the form of the cuckoo. An insane person, one who is "batty" or has "bats in his belfry," is also "cuckoo," perhaps in reference to the traditional cuckoo clock which always is out of order and tweets at the wrong time, etc.

In folk-literature, the apolog, "The Cockoo and the Nightingale" is well-known; tales of the stupid ogre in which the cuckoo appears are found in Norway, Finland, Sweden, Greece and the Cape Verde Islands (Type 1029). An amusing English tale recounts the effort of the Wise Men of Gotham to enjoy perpetual spring by "hedging in" the cuckoo (William A. Clouston, *The Book of Noodles,* London, 1888, pp. 26–27).

cueca or **zamacueca** A courting dance of the Chilean Indians and mestizos, more individualistic and violent than many analogous European couple dances. There is much coquettish play with kerchiefs, approach, flight, beckoning, pursuit, escape, and final love conquest. This dance is distinctive in that the man whose lady retreats from him must be quick enough to turn his back on her at the same moment. If he is not as quick as she, he is ridiculed by the audience. The music for this dance (guitar, tambourine, and harp) begins softly and tenderly, and increases to passionate intensity. [GPK]

Cult of the Friendly Dead One of the oldest strata of belief among Ceylon Veddas. It includes a cult of the spirits of recent ancestors (Nae Yaku) who, if well treated, will care for their survivors with kindness, and of spirits (yaku) of certain heroic Veddas, long dead, of whom the most important is Kande Yake. Kande before death was Kande Wanniya, the great hunter. Associated with his spirit, which is invoked for hunting success, is that of his younger brother, Bilindi, whom Kande killed in a fit of temper. Both are now invoked with other Nae Yaku by a shaman through whom they accept food offerings and communicate hunting advice.

Later strata of belief, originating among the Tamils and Sinhalese, concern foreign spirits naturalized among the Veddas. Some of these have been made into friendly spirits like the Nae Yaku while others have remained hostile and occasionally influence adversely the interpretation of the Friendly Dead. See YAKA. [KL]

culture hero In the mythology, folklore, and legend of any people, a character (human or animal, prehistoric or not) regarded as the giver of a culture to its people. All good and useful things are either given by him, invented, originated, or taught by him: the foods, arts, devices, and usages of a people. The typical culture hero steals or liberates the sun, fire, or summer for his people, regulates the winds, originates corn, acorns, beans, and other foods, marks the animals and plants with their characteristic marks, determines the courses of rivers, teaches men to plant and plow, hunt, hold their ceremonies with efficacious songs and dances, invents alphabets, gives to men their medicines and magic, and usually sometime before the world becomes as it is now, he goes away into the west to await a certain time appointed for his return.

☞ The culture hero is a familiar figure in nearly all North American Indian mythologies, often identical with the trickster (also Coyote) and transformer, and also with the creator. In the majority of cases the culture-hero-transformer-trickster is an animal or bird (Raven, Mink, or Bluejay: North Pacific Coast; Coyote: California, Great Basin, Southwest, Plains; Hare: Eastern Woodlands; Rabbit: Southeast); in a few instances he is apparently human in form (Gluskabe: northeastern United States; Child-of-the-Water, and Killer-of-Enemies: Apache groups of the Southwest; White Man: Blackfoot; and Sendeh: Kiowa of the Plains). Among the deeds beneficial to mankind which the culture hero performs are: securing daylight for the people, releasing impounded water and game, teaching useful arts and crafts, instituting ceremonies, ridding the world of dangerous monsters. The culture hero is pictured as living on earth during the mythical age, or before the advent of human beings, and retiring to a region above the earth after humans appear; sometimes this region is located in the west. He will return at need. The culture hero generally has a companion who travels about with him and shares in his beneficent deeds, as well as in his antics as trickster. [EWV]

☞ The prominent character of South American Indian mythology is the culture hero who is often also the Creator or the first Ancestor. His great deeds and adventures follow, in the Fuegian Indian myth, almost the identical pattern of those of the highly civilized Indians of the Andes.

After creating the world and man, the culture hero wanders up and down the tribal territory performing great miracles. He is a transformer *par excellence* and takes special delight in changing the shape of things and in turning people into animals or vice versa. Many features of the landscape are explained by some of the metamorphoses he performed. He is always regarded as a benefactor of mankind, to whom he often gave food plants, the basic arts and crafts, and the religious and social laws. The culture hero is also father of the Twins, who, like him, are great transformers and benefactors of mankind. Therefore it is not always easy to distinguish between the role of the Twins and that of their father.

Once he has performed his task the culture hero departs toward the west, to the end of the world where he takes his abode among the dead. He waits there for the time when he will return to destroy the universe he has made.

The culture hero of the Toba was a hawk (*Polyborus plancus*) a wise and generous being who helped them in their struggle against cruel monsters. One of the best known South American culture heroes is Bochica who was worshipped by the ancient Chibcha of Colombia. [AM]

cumin A plant of the carrot family whose seeds are used as a condiment in the East. It symbolized meanness and cupidity in Greece. In Germany and Italy it is put in the bread to keep the wood spirits from stealing it. In Italy it is fed to fowl to tame them and make them content with their homes. It was believed good for stopping hemorrhage. As a poultice it is effective against boils, swellings, pleurisy, and the stitch. In a broth it is good for chest colds. Pliny mentions that it makes the countenance pallid, and that if it is fed to lovers, they will remain faithful.

cumulative song A type of folk song common in many languages, both ancient and modern, and in many parts of the world, consisting generally of a statement to which each stanza adds a new element and every refrain is the enumeration of all the elements from the last to the first. Most of these songs are sung purely for fun and go to rollicking tunes. An example is the familiar carol, *The Twelve Days of Christmas*, which lists day by day the gifts "my true love sent to me," ending in the twelfth refrain with "Twelve drummers drumming/ Eleven pipers piping/ Ten lords a-leaping/ Nine ladies dancing/ Eight maids a-milking/ Seven swans a-swimming/ Six geese a-laying/ Five gold rings/ Four calling birds/ Three French hens/ Two turtle doves/ And a partridge in a pear tree." Others well-known in English are *The Tree in the Valley*, or *The Green Grass Growing All Around* ("The nest was on the twig/ And the twig was on the branch/ And the branch was on the tree/ And the tree was away down in the valley, oh") and the very similar song *There's a Hole in the Bottom* *of the Sea.* One of the most widely distributed songs of this type is *The Twelve Apostles* (also called *The Ten Commandments* and *The Dilly Song*) which has been sung in many tongues, including Hebrew. *Alouette,* a French example, turns up in group-singing almost anywhere to this day. In Mexico they sing *La Rana,* a ditty about a frog singing under the water, which runs somewhat like the nursery tale about the pig that wouldn't get over the stile, involving bull, water, fire, stick, dog, cat, mouse, etc., all to quiet the frog.

cumulative story A type of folktale found among all peoples, primitive and sophisticated, ancient and modern, having many forms and variations, but everywhere usually evincing an animistic attitude. Most of the tales take for granted that all things (human, animal, vegetable, and inanimate) are equally possessed of intelligence, emotion, and reason. The more sophisticated the group, however, the nearer the story has degenerated into nursery tale or trivial jingle.

The action, characters, names, speeches, or whatever is the feature of the accumulation, builds up to an impasse or a climax, and often, but not always goes through the list again in reverse in order to resolve the plot. This is the pattern of the well-known *Old Woman and her Pig* (Z41). The pig would not go under the fence (or over the stile). In despair of getting home before dark, the old woman appealed to a dog to bite the pig; but "dog won't bite pig, stick won't beat dog, fire won't burn stick, water won't quench fire, ox won't drink water, butcher won't kill ox, rope won't hang butcher, rat won't gnaw rope, cat won't kill rat," until finally the cat is given some milk and attacks the rat, "the rat begins to gnaw the rope, the rope begins to hang the butcher, the butcher begins to kill the ox, the ox begins to drink the water, etc., each object doing as requested until the dog bites the pig, the pig goes under the fence, and the old woman gets home before dark.

Among cumulative stories which do not reverse the accumulation are found the general European tale of the pancake which runs away as soon as it is made (Z31.3.1). A series of animals try to stop its flight, but cannot, until at last the fox catches and eats it. See CHAIN TALE; FORMULA TALE; HORSESHOE NAIL.

čunč'a or **chuncho** A longways dance of the Aymara Indians of Bolivia, performed by men and women in long lines, dancing in unison. They wear huge feather headdresses and carry bows and arrows. The men's trousers are decorated with many feathers, and their jackets with festoons of gray-black beans called čunča or čunču. Their faces are masked by strings of beads, beans, and ancient silver coins. Three flutes and three drums accompany the dance. The dance is said to imitate the Chuncho Indians of the Montaña. [GPK]

Cupid and Psyche A classical beast-marriage folktale (Type 425A) told by Apuleius in the *Metamorphoses* (*The Golden Ass*), and perhaps the only example in Latin literature of such only slightly embellished folktale telling: undoubtedly a much earlier Greek story retold in Latin. The story of Cupid and Psyche is very similar to the tales of Melusina, Beauty and the Beast, Urvaśī and Purūravas, and other familiar examples of the beast marriage, nuptial tabu tale. In *Cupid and Psyche,* however, the emphasis is distinctly on the breaking of the tabu, whereas emphasis in the others

is on the beast form and the transformation from beast into human being; *Cupid and Psyche* is relatively uncomplicated with other great folktale themes, as for example the swan maiden incident in *Urvaśī and Purūravas.*

In Apuleius, this "pleasant old wives' tale" is recited by an old woman in the thieves' den. Psyche's beauty had aroused such adoration that the worship of Venus all but disappeared. The goddess asked Cupid, her son, to cause Psyche to fall in love with some loathsome old man, but Cupid fell in love with the girl himself. Since Psyche's two sisters had married well, although they were not so beautiful as she, the anger of the gods against her was suspected. Her father sent to the oracle of Apollo at Miletus, which replied that her destined husband was a dragon (serpent) who would receive her corpse from a high hill. From the hill Psyche was carried by zephyrs to a secluded valley containing a wonderful palace. There, at night, her husband came, and eventually she grew to love this unseen being. She contradicted herself in describing her husband to her sisters, and they, jealous, aroused her fear that he was really a monster. One night, in disobedience to the tabu, she lit a lamp. But nervously, she spilled a drop of hot oil on the sleeping Cupid, no dragon but a handsome youth, and he awoke. The tabu broken, he flew off. Psyche realized how great was her loss and searched through the world for him. But neither Ceres nor Juno, at whose temples she made offerings, dared help, knowing of Venus' wrath. At last Psyche approached the temple of Venus and was seized by one of the servants of the goddess. Venus arrived and struck and reviled the girl, though Psyche was pregnant with Cupid's child. Venus set her three tasks: to separate a mixed heap of grain (the ants did this for Psyche); to gather fleece from a flock of wild sheep (she picked it from reeds the flock went through); and to collect some water from the waterfall source of the Styx (an eagle dipped some up while flying above it). Finally Venus sent Psyche to Hades to bring back a container with some of Proserpina's beauty in it. Psyche made the perilous journey, giving Charon and Cerberus their due, but when she returned above ground curiosity again got the better of her and she opened the container. Inside had been sleep, which spread over Psyche. Cupid in the meanwhile had escaped from the imprisonment in which Venus had been keeping him, and he discovered Psyche sleeping. He wiped the sleep from her, replaced it in the container, and sent her on to Venus. Then he obtained Jupiter's consent to the marriage, Psyche was made immortal, and the wrath of Venus was appeased, since Psyche was now her son's equal and no longer a mortal being.

Familiar motifs abound in this tale. Central to the story is C32.1, the tabu against looking at the supernatural husband. C32, offending the supernatural husband in some way, is found in such tales as Grimm's #88, *The Singing, Soaring Lark,* where the wife permits light to fall on her husband. Parallel are the broken tabu against looking at the wife in the tale of Melusina, and the broken tabu against being seen unclothed by the supernatural wife in *Urvaśī and Purūravas.* Examples can be multiplied. The search for the lost husband and the tasks assigned by Venus are both in threes: she goes to three goddesses, and she accomplishes three tasks successfully. The sorting of the grain by ants (H1091.1) is found for example in many stories of the grateful animals and, in the form of gathering scattered grain, in widespread tales (e.g. the British North Borneo [Indonesia] story of Serungal, in which the grateful ants refill the basket with rice spilled from it all over the field). The incident of the dripping lamp (C916.1) is repeated in *The Three Black Princesses* (Grimm #137), where the hero deliberately drops wax from a holy candle on the faces of the sleeping princesses.

In the Aarne-Thompson study of folktale types, *Cupid and Psyche* is a specific form of the more general tale of the search for the lost husband, containing most of the incidents (in its widespread occurrence if not in Apuleius' version) of the latter story. Sometimes the monster is monster by day and man by night. The girl (or her father) promises herself to the monster in return for a favor. The bride removes the enchantment by a kiss and destroys the animal skin. But this is done too soon, or she tells her sisters or otherwise breaks the nuptial tabu (here by looking at him), and is forced to search for him until she wears out a pair of iron shoes. She gets help from various agencies—an old woman, the wind and the stars. Finally she climbs the glass mountain and, in exchange for jewels that she has, is permitted to sit for three nights in her husband's bedroom. On the last night he awakens and they are joyfully reunited.

Such a tale is *Bull-of-all-the-Land* of Jamaica. King Henry is bull by day, but man at night. His wife burns his bull clothes and he leaves her. She accomplishes the task of washing his shirt, is cheated of recognition of the feat by another woman, and at last calls King Henry Bull-of-all-the-Land, a name of his that only she knows.

curandero Literally, one who cures; a Spanish term generally used in Middle America to designate the medicine man. The feminine form, *curandera*, is used for women. [GMF]

cures The lore of cures leads into the complexities of folk medicine, a science which is the personal property of witch doctors, barbers, shamans, priests, physicians, and surgeons, who in each *Kulturkreis* tend to form corporations which compete with each other and establish conditions under which new members are to be admitted. Folk medicine and folk pharmacopeia are centrally concerned with cures. Their structures are determined by the social, economic, and theological structures of the communities which evolve them. The people of the United States, for example, accept many superstitions about cures and healing if they are disguised. The specific which is "nature" spelled backwards is not presented as something opposed to "nature" but makes use of a device, well known in most of the popular materia medicas, which involves the reversal of natural (in the sense of customary) acts. This is connected with another set of appeals for specifics that contain "no harsh chemicals" and work the easy, that is to say the natural and good, way. Another set of specifics in folk medicine is made acceptable by the phrases "statistics show . . ." or "science has proved . . ." or "prescribed by many . . ." doctors or hospitals.

The folklore of vitamins is another rich field for the study of American superstitions about cures and healing. Among communities which are not scientific in the American sense, cures consist in transferring the illness to inanimate objects. An example of this is that warts can be transferred to a stone, to animals, to other human beings, sometimes even to the doctor himself, or in ritualistic performances at times and places which are usually inconvenient, the eating of substances which are not commonly part of the community diet and are often disgusting, distasteful, or hard to get.

Folk ideas about healing, cures, and health are contained in innumerable proverbs and saws: One should eat spinach for iron; sulfur will cleanse the blood in the spring; health will be acquired by going to bed early and getting up early. Sometimes these proverbial instructions work in two directions at the same time. Thus it is argued that "Feed a cold and starve a fever" means that it is proper to feed a cold and proper to starve a fever, or conversely that if you feed a cold you will have a fever to starve. Cures for jaundice touch on a number of salient beliefs in "unscientific" communities. The ancient Hindus are said to have banished yellow jaundice to the yellow sun. Plutarch cured it by looking at a stone curlew with yellow eyes. The modern Greeks are said to put a piece of yellow gold into a jug of wine, expose the wine to the stars for three nights, and then drink the wine at the rate of three glasses a day. Reports from all parts of the world indicate that cures have been effected by the intervention of saints or gods or by faith, prayer, or meditation. [RDJ]

The cures performed by shamans from the Guianas to Tierra del Fuego consist essentially in massaging, blowing, and sucking the patients. These operations are often preceded, north of the Amazon, by consultations with spirits. The shaman puts himself into a state of trance and then flies to the land of the spirits to ask their advice or to fight against the witch who caused the illness.

The climax of each cure is however the energetic and often brutal sucking of that region of the body in which the dart or the stone causing the disease is supposed to have lodged. After a while the shaman extracts the pathogenic object and destroys it. This treatment is usually followed by strict fasting on the part of the patient and his family, and by the administration of various drugs. If the patient's soul has been kidnapped, the shaman sends his own soul to discover its whereabouts and to fight against the spirit or the witch who keeps it in captivity. [AM]

Curetes In Greek mythology, a group of demigods associated with the Cretan Zeus Curos, the boy-Zeus, and sometimes confused with the Corybantes. The infant Zeus was brought to them to care for and to hide from the jealous Cronus. With the clashing of arms in their war dance, they drowned the infant's cries so that Cronus could not hear him. They may originally have been Cretan youths associated with the celebration of the infant Zeus in a cult manifestation.

Cú Roi In Old Irish legend a great wizard of the south of Ireland to whom the three champions of Ulster (Conall, Loegaire, and Cuchulain) went seeking judgment between them. Cú Roi gave the judgment to Cuchulain as first of the heroes of Ireland but the cause was not settled until after the famous beheading bargain between the bachlach (Cú Roi in disguise) and Cuchulain, in which the latter was proved to be the greatest in bravery and integrity of the heroes of Ireland. See BRICRIU'S FEAST; CHAMPION'S PORTION.

curse A malediction; the wishing of evil upon a person; also, the effect of such wishing, and, loosely, any persistent evil. Cursing is practiced by almost every people in the world. A curse invokes a power—divine, demonic, or magical—against which the person cursed has no defense, unless he in some manner propitiates the power or brings to bear against it a stronger power. The curse is dangerous; it must alight, even if after seven years (Irish); it may affect later generations (Greek, Hebrew), or, if laid upon an ancestor, all the relations of the person cursed (Maori). It may however return on the head of the curser, or if sufficiently strong injure both curser and victim, or anyone who hears it. Some curses, a father's or the curse of the dying, are more potent than others; some are intended to affect only the belongings of the accursed, or they may make him ill, or kill him and perhaps damn him to hell forever, depending not only on the strength of the formula used but also on the counterspells of the one cursed. The curse may be a formula with symbol or image accompanying it, and be part of a ritual to secure the death or illness of someone or some group. Curses are thus a kind of spoken magic, spells of evil wished upon others. With the loss of belief in the efficacy of magic, curses become either blasphemy—the fruitless and irreverent invocation of the gods—or a meaningless ritual unless performed by the divine being himself, since man cannot force his will upon the gods.

Curupira A famous demon in the mythology of the Tupi-Guarani tribes of the Brazilian coast, who has become very important in the folklore of the caboclos (mestizos) of modern Brazil. Curupira is a small demon who walks with upturned feet. As the protector of game animals he is often generous toward those who propitiate him with gifts, but he punishes severely those who show disrespect. Strange noises in the forest are attributed to him. [AM]

Cwn Annwn The dogs or hounds of Annwn; in Brythonic mythology, a pack of snow-white, red-eared spectral hounds which sometimes took part in the kidnappings and raids occasionally made on this world by the inhabitants of Annwn. They are associated in Wales with the sound of migrating wild geese, and are said to be leading the souls of the damned to hell. In England, they are called the Gabriel Hounds or Ratchets, sometimes the Yell Hounds. The hunter who rides with them is Gwyn, or Bran, or Arthur, sometimes Gabriel, sometimes Herne the Hunter.

Cybele The Great Mother of Phrygia; the Anatolian name of the ancient Mediterranean mother goddess; goddess of mountains and forests, of the earth, of reproduction. (Compare ISHTAR; ISIS; MA.) Cybele was identified by the Greeks with Rhea as the wife of Cronus and mother of Zeus; the Romans equated her with Ops. Her cult was brought to Rome in 204 B.C. during the wars against Carthage; it spread throughout the Empire as one of the more important Oriental cults, and existed in Gaul as late as the time of Martin of Tours, the goddess there being known as Berecynthia. Cybele, Magna Mater, appeared in Rome as a black meteoric stone (set as the face of a silver statue); her temple was on the Palatine. Attis, her lover or son, was the human being linked with her, as Tammuz was with Ishtar, etc. The myth of the self-castration of Attis explained the eunuchized priests of the goddess. A wild orgiastic celebration marked the Cybele festival at the Spring equinox. Among the attributes of Cybele were the diadem of towers (she was the founder of cities), the cypress or pine, the lion, and cymbals. See EUNUCH.

Cyclops (plural *Cyclops* or *Cyclopes*) In Greek mythology, one of a race of giants with one eye in the middle of their foreheads. In Homer, they are wild cannibalistic shepherds, uncivilized, caring nothing for the gods or for men. Their chief is Polyphemus, in whose cave Ulysses and his men were imprisoned. In Hesiod, the Cyclopes are Titanic sons of Uranus and Ge, storm gods, three in number—Arges (the Shiner), Steropes (the Lightning), Brontes (the Thunder)—who were thrown into Tartarus by both Uranus and Cronus and released by Zeus to help him in the battle against Cronus. In gratitude they gave him his thunderbolts and the lightning. They were killed by Apollo for giving Zeus the thunderbolt with which he killed Æsculapius. In later tradition, the Cyclopes were the assistants of Hephæstus at his forges under Etna and other volcanoes, helping him make the arms, armor, and metal ornaments of the gods. Their number was increased, new names were added to the old, e.g. Pyracmon, Acamas. Later still, the full circle from Homeric savagery was completed and they were said to have been the builders of the great fortifications of Argos, Tiryns, Mycenæ, who lived in Thrace under their king Cyclops.

The Cyclopes are thought to have been a development of certain Pelasgian quarriers who wore a lantern on the forehead, but this euhemeristic explanation is not quite satisfactory. One-eyed giants are no rarity in folklore. In myths of Bulgaria, Croatia, and Slovenia, there is a variety of div which has only one eye and dwells in caves. The one-eyed giant is found in Welsh and Irish folktale; for example, the Surly One of Lachlann who guards the quicken-tree and is slain by Diarmuid in his flight with Grainne has one eye; the Ainu also have a one-eyed giant. The ascription of prehistoric walls to the Cyclopes finds parallels in the Riesenmauer or Teufelsmauer of Germany, which perhaps are the remnants of Roman walls, but huge ruins in many parts of the world are always "built by giants."

Cygnus The Swan; a spectacular constellation "in full flight" in the Milky Way: also called the Northern Cross. It is named from the Greek myth of the boy Cycnus, friend of Phaethon, who dove and dove into the river Po trying to retrieve the remnants of his comrade's body. He was transformed by the gods into a celestial swan (Cygnus) as a reward for his devotion. Cygnus is also associated with the myth of Zeus incarnate as the swan who visited and wooed Leda.

But the designation of this constellation is much more ancient than the Greek myths. Possibly our Cygnus, it is thought, is the constellation known as Urakhga among the Arabs, prototype of Sindbad the Sailor's Roc. Early Christians saw it as the cross of Christ, Christi Crux. Today it is as often called the Northern Cross as Cygnus. In China it is sometimes interpreted as one of the magpies which form the bridge across the Celestial River so that Chih Nü may make her annual visit to her lover.

cymbals Paired concave metal plates, with or without rims, sounded by being struck together: used to accompany dancing, dramatic performances, religious ceremonies, prophecy, military processions, etc. They may be held one in each hand, or, in small sizes, clapped together by two fingers of one hand in the manner of castanets. Probably originating in central or western Asia, they were carried east and west by Turkic peoples, noted for their metalworking skill.

Two different sounds are distinguished in many cultures: tinkling and clashing, the former associated with indoor religious or chamber music or dancing, the latter generally with more exciting outdoor rites and processions. There are also two main methods of striking the cymbals with special significance. In Tibet, for example, one type of cymbals is held horizontally and clashed together with a vertical motion in the worship of celestial gods; a second type is held vertically and clapped together with a horizontal motion for earthly divinities. Similar distinctions in playing are noted in ancient Assyria and in kinds of cymbals used in Java and in medieval Europe.

In Israel of the time of David and Solomon, cymbals were a part of the ritual accompaniment for such occasions as the installation of the ark of the covenant, the consecration of the Temple, daily services in the Temple, and prophecies of the priests.

Cymbals were introduced into Greece along with the worship of various western Asiatic goddesses, such as the Phrygian Cybele, whose cult included rites of self-emasculation as a sacrifice for fertility. The clashing metallic music of these ceremonies whipped the participants into an ecstatic state. The feasts of Dionysus took on a similar orgiastic character, and cymbals played a part in the Cretan ceremony of the death and resurrection of this god. Cymbals were also adopted for use in the Greek theater, where they were regarded as effeminate, as are many other types of clappers elsewhere traditionally used by women.

In Rome, cymbals played an important part in the spring festival of Attis, the lover or son of Cybele, and in the march of the eunuch priests of the cult. The self-emasculation, death, and resurrection of Attis were dramatized by a wholesale castration of priests and by a secret sacrament in which the novice ate from a drum and drank from a cymbal, instruments associated with Attis.

China adopted cymbals, probably from Turkestan, early in the Middle Ages, and for centuries they have served in temples there. Examples found in Mongolian temples are unusually large.

Invading Huns may have carried cymbals to India about the 5th century A.D. The instrument has become associated in Hindu mythology with the sirenlike Kinnaras, with Rāvaṇa, king of the demons of night, and even with Vishṇu, who clashes cymbals to the dance of the death goddess, Bhadrakālī, and Īśvara the Destroyer.

The marionette or shadow plays of Burma are performed to tinkling music in which cymbals figure prominently, and Balinese orchestras include a number of cymbalists, whose instruments, onomatopoetically named *tjeng-tjeng*, produce an elaborate polyrhythm.

Both Ethiopian and Coptic churches use cymbals, blind singers of the Coptic chant accompanying themselves. The instrument was used by dancers in ancient Egypt also, where it was imported from Greece.

Origen, a father of the early Christian Church, gave symbolic interpretations to the instruments used in the services of his time (3rd century A.D.), and to him the cymbals represented "the eager soul enamored of Christ." In England, a 12th century writer, Ailred, complained of the noise of cymbals in church, where, he said, the simple folk stood bewildered.

Europe first saw cymbals in the hands of invading Avars and Huns, and later associated them with the battle music of Turkish janissaries, so that even now cymbals are used in musical composition to give a barbaric, oriental, or "Turkish" atmosphere. [TCB]

Cynthia In classical mythology, a name of Artemis, from Mount Cynthus on the island of Delos, where she was born; hence, the moon. Apollo who also was born there is sometimes called Cynthius. There are on Mount Cynthus the remains of a temple to Zeus Cynthus and Athena Cynthia.

cypress An evergreen tree of southern Europe, western Asia, and the southern United States. It is the emblem of generation, death, the immortal soul, and woe. The island of Cyprus was named for this tree and the early inhabitants worshipped it as a personification of the goddess Beroth. The Greeks and Romans assigned it to the god of the underworld, the Fates, and the Furies. In the *Zend-Avesta* it was sacred because Ormazd's word was first carved on it. According to Parsi tradition Zoroaster planted a cypress, so they are planted at the gates of Zoroastrian temples. According to Ovid it was sacred to Apollo. It is revered by the Chinese because its roots grow in the form of a seated man.

The Athenians used cypress wood for the coffins of heroes and it was used by the Egyptians for mummy cases. From it were made Cupid's darts, Jove's scepter, the club of Hercules, the pillars of Solomon's temple, and the cross of Christ.

If a man ate the seeds for a long time he was sure to become strong, healthy, and young, and it sharpened his senses. The fruit is good for dysentery, diarrhea, and will stop blood-spitting, bleeding of the gums, and will tighten loose teeth.

There are many stories as to its origin: it is one of the three seeds given to Seth by an angel to plant under Adam's tongue after he had died; Zoroaster brought a shoot from Heaven; in other places it is believed to be any one of various people who were turned into trees by the gods.

D

Dã The serpent deity of Dahomey, West Africa: symbol of all that is dã, i.e. living and sinuous, and thus by extension, of fortune, which is conceptualized as sinuous, in the sense that it slips away and is, therefore, treacherous. Everything that has life has the quality of dã, the roots of a tree, the umbilical cord of animal and human forms being examples of this. Compare DAM-BALLA; DANGBÈ. [MJH]

Da or **Dab-lha** The enemy-defeating god who sits on the right shoulder of every Tibetan: the greatest of the familiars by whose worship enemies are overcome. The Da is clothed in golden mail, flies through the clouds on a white horse, and carries in his left hand a blue-bladed, flame-bordered spear with two eyes. He is accompanied by a black dog, a black bear, and a man-monkey. From his shoulders spring a lion and a tiger.

da-cha or **dar-lch'og** The Tibetan luck or prayer flag: inscribed with pious sentences, prayers, and charms, and flown above every Lāmaist settlement as a luck-commanding talisman. The prayer flags are printed on unglazed, tough paper and sold by the lāmas. The planting of such flags confers merit on the planter and benefits the entire countryside. There are four types of flags: the Lung-rta or airy horse, the Chö-pén, the Gyal-tsan dsemo, and the gLañ-po stob-rgyas.

The airy horse or Lung-rta is four to six inches long with the figure of a horse in the center surrounded by text. It is hung on ridges of houses and near dwellings. One for each member of a household is flown on the third day of each lunar month. The Lung-rta is also sometimes hung on the branch of a tree or on a bridge, and a little flour, grain, flesh, and beer are offered to the local god at the same time. The Chö-pén is eight to ten inches long and narrow in width. It contains only texts and is fastened to twigs or bridges or planted on sticks on the tops of hills. The Gyal-tsan dsemo is similar to the Lung-rta, but contains more holy texts and usually includes the eight glorious symbols (the Golden Fish, Umbrella, Conch-shell Trumpet, Lucky Diagram, Victorious Banner, Vase, Lotus, and Wheel). It promotes power, health, and wealth. The gLañ-po stob-rgyas is the vast flag pasted to the walls of houses or worn folded up as a charm and is planted at speci-fied times whenever anyone is unhappy or troubled by demons.

Dactyls In Greek mythology, fabulous smiths who dwelt on Mount Ida in Phrygia or in Crete: often con-fused with the Curetes, Corybantes, Cabeiri, Telchines. Their number is indefinite: five, ten, fifty-two, one hundred; six giants and their five sisters, or 32 ma-gicians and 20 countermagicians; their names are just as vague. Perhaps originally there were three: Celmus, Damnameneus, Acmon. They were connected with the worship of Rhea in Phrygia. The Dactyls discovered iron and the means of working it; they were magicians, the inventors of the Ephesian incantations. Their names

had a certain potency, being uttered as magical words when people were suddenly frightened.

daddy-long-legs or **grandaddy-long-legs** A long and slender-legged, insect-eating arachnid of the order Phalangidæ: in some sections of America, called strad-dlebug, in England called harvestman. In England har-vesters take care not to injure one. If one is killed, there will be a poor harvest, or one of the reapers will be in-jured. In England and America generally, the belief is that killing a daddy-long-legs causes the cows to go dry. It is also quite general folk belief that a daddy-long-legs will point out lost cattle. They say "Grandaddy, gran-daddy, which way did my old cows go?" at the same time holding it by one or more legs. In answer Gran-daddy lifts up one or more legs and that is the direction to go to find the cattle. Another rime goes: Grandfather gray/ tell me right away/ Where the cows are/ Or I'll kill you./ In New England children wish on a daddy-long-legs for good luck. In the Ozarks, they say the daddy-long-legs deposits its eggs on bats which hatch out into bedbugs. Some say that the odor of the Gran-daddy when trodden upon is similar to that of a bed-bug. [GPS]

Dædala The name of certain festivals in ancient Bœotia. The explanatory myth says that Hera and Zeus once quarreled and Hera fled in a huff to Eubœa. Zeus was unable to get her to come back and decided to trick her. He dressed a carved oak-trunk as a bride and had the news spread that he would remarry. As the proces-sion with the mock bride passed Mt. Cithæron, Hera descended in fury, ripping the clothes from the statue. She was so pleased at the deception that the two were reconciled.

Every six years or so, the people of Platæa went to an ancient oak grove where, by means of food snatched by ravens, they would decide which trees to fell for images. These dædala were then carried in a cart to the river Asopus and back to Platæa. This Little Dædala was succeeded every sixty years by the Great Dædala. Then all Bœotia joined in the celebration; all fourteen images collected during the minor festivals were apportioned to the different cities; the images were transported to the top of Mt. Cithæron where they were burned on a carefully constructed altar along with sacrifices to Zeus and Hera.

Dædalus The cunning great craftsman of the my-thology of Greece, especially that of Athens and Crete, the first artist and sculptor, a descendant of Hephæstus. His nephew Talus (sometimes called Calos or Perdix) was his first pupil, and in time surpassed his master, inventing the saw and the potter's wheel. The jealous Dædalus threw him from the Acropolis, or tossed him into the sea. Condemned to death for the crime by the Areopagus, Dædalus fled to the court of Minos in Crete. There he constructed the cow-disguise for Pasiphae and built the Labyrinth for the Minotaur. Because of his complicity in this affair, or because he helped Theseus escape from the maze, he was imprisoned in it with his son Icarus. Escaping, perhaps with Pasiphae's aid, he found all shipping barred to him by Minos' order. With wax, he fashioned wings for himself and the boy, and although Icarus fell to his death Dædalus escaped to Italy and then to Sicily, where he was entertained by Cocalus. The pursuing Minos was killed by Cocalus and his daughters.

Throughout the Mediterranean lands, many buildings and works of art were attributed to Dædalus. The name Dædala was given to a type of gilded wooden statuary, colored and draped; his name was applied to a whole period of early Greek art. Compare JEALOUS CRAFTSMAN AND HIS APPRENTICE.

Daemon Lover A variant title, e.g. used by Scott, for the ballad *James Harris*.

daēva (1) In Hinduism and Buddhism, a dēva; a divine being.

(2) In Zoroastrianism, a demon, personification of sin, distress, and disease: etymologically identical with the Sanskrit *dēva* but diametrically opposite in meaning. The daēvas are the seed of darkness created by Angra Mainyu from evil thought to war against mankind and good. They are usually bodiless but can appear in human form and lurk about ready to pounce upon anyone who comes under their power. The daēvas abound in the vicinity of dakhmahs and haunt foul places. They are especially numerous in the Alburz chain and south of the Caspian Sea. Their number is infinite but they equal the number of divine forces created by Ahura Mazda. Zoroaster's mission was to banish the daēvas. They hid beneath the earth at his birth, but later returned. Their leader is Angra Mainyu whose six archfiends command the legions of daēvas. The modern Persian name for them is dīv.

daffodil, Lent lily, or **goose leek** A plant (genus *Narcissus*) having solitary yellow flowers. Pliny and others wrote that the asphodel, whose name has been corrupted into daffodil, grew on the banks of Acheron, delighting the spirits of the dead. It was also said to cover the Elysian Fields which may account for the practice of planting daffodils on graves. There is the childhood jingle common to English-speaking countries:

Daffadowndilly has come to town
In a yellow petticoat and a green gown.

In Maine they say that if you point at a daffodil it will not bloom. On the Isle of Man daffodils are called goose leeks, and it is considered unlucky to bring them into the house until the goslings are hatched. In Wales they say that if you find the first bloom of the season, you will have more gold than silver that year.

dagäę'óenǫ The chicken dance of the Iroquois Indians; a social dance. At the end of each song the singer crows like a cock. The step formation and music are as for the *gędjǫ̧enǫ*, the fish dance, with a few added special features. The women line up in the beginning, join in the singing, and each chooses a male partner. They dance in single, not in double couples. [GPK]

Dagda The "good god" of Old Irish mythology; chief of the Tuatha Dé Danann; father of Angus Og and Brigit. He possessed an inexhaustible caldron, which came from the mythical city of Murias and was counted as one of the treasures of the Tuatha Dé Danann. He also had two marvelous swine (one always cooking, one always living), and ever-laden fruit trees.

He is said to be named for his prowess: he boasted that he alone would perform all the wonders which the druids were promising that the Tuatha Dé were to work against the Fomorians. "Thou art *dag dae,* the good hand," they said to him. But J. A. MacCulloch states that the name more likely means good god. He is also referred to as creator and great father.

In the Battle of Mag Tured the Dagda killed uncountable numbers of the Fomorians. Wherever his spear trailed on the ground a deep ditch was marked. After the Battle of Mag Tured the Fomorians took captive the harper of the Dagda. Luġ, Dagda, and Ogma went after them into their camp. When they entered the building, Dagda saw his harp hanging on the wall, invoked it, and it flew into his hand and killed nine Fomorians as it passed. He then played "the three strains," i.e. the strain of Sorrowing, the strain of Laughter, and of Sleep. The last put the Fomorians to sleep, and the Dagda, with Luġ and Ogma, passed out unchallenged. After this he divided up the hills and mounds (*side*) of Ireland among the Tuatha Dé Danann. His own síd was the Bruġ na Boinne, later taken over by his son Angus Og. Later myth says that the Dagda died, that Bodb Dearg divided the side among them, and that Manannán gave them immortality.

MacCulloch states that Dagda is probably an early agricultural deity, since he is known to have had power over corn and milk, and suggests that possibly he was some local form of Cromm Crúaċ, to whom sacrifices were made in return for corn and milk.

Dagon The so-called "fish god" of the Philistines and Phœnicians. Dagan of Babylonia and Assyria, although no definite connection with Dagon has been shown, is believed to be the same god of agriculture, brought to both areas by the Amorites. Popularly Dagon is thought to have been human in form from the waist up, and fish from the waist down; the tradition stems from the derivation of the name from the word for *fish* by St. Jerome and medieval Jewish scholars. Little or no evidence supports this conception; no early representation of a fish god carries Dagon's name, and those mermanlike figures which have been preserved are probably depictions of Ea, the water god. More probable is the derivation of Dagon from the word for *corn*, making of him an earth god more or less identifiable with Bel; his name occurs in context where Bel's often appears, e.g. in connection with Anu.

Dagowe The variant of Dangbe heard in coastal Dahomey, West Africa and, in the New World, in Dutch Guiana and certain localities of Haiti. [MJH]

Dähnhardt, Oskar (1870–1915) German teacher and mythologist. His *Natursagen* (four volumes, 1907–1912) is a very complete collection of animal tales with commentary and discussion. It contains a good treatment of legends based on the Old Testament, some of which may still be heard in contemporary oral tales. Dähnhardt was rector of the Nikolaischule in Leipzig from 1910. Among his books are *Heimatklänge aus deutschen Gauen* (1910), *Deutsches Märchenbuch* (1914), *Naturgeschichtliche Volksmärchen* (1912), and *Schwänke aus aller Welt* (1908).

dahut A traditional hunting quarry in France—sometimes a bird, sometimes an animal—in either case the medium for a practical joke played on an unsuspecting person. The practice is also observed in North Africa. Dahut hunting is comparable to our American snipe hunt, in which the tenderfoot is primed with wonderful tales of the hunt, given a sack to gather in the game while his companions beat the bush, and then left literally holding the bag until he finally sees he has been tricked after hours of waiting. In the standard version of the hunt, the butt of the joke is told that the snipe is attracted by light, and is stationed with bag and lantern in a lonely place at night. His companions then go off to beat the bush, they say, and frighten the snipe towards the light. Instead they go home quietly to bed, while the "sucker" waits in momentary expectation of bagging a snipe.

daina (plural: Latvian *dainas;* Lithuanian *dainos*) The word for "song" to the Latvians and Lithuanians. The word is probably cognate with Vedic Sanskrit *dhénā* or Celtic *daena;* "to sing" is in Sanskrit *diyati,* and in Lithuanian *dainuoti.* (Compare S.G. Oliphant in *JAOS* 32 (1912): 393–413.) Another name for every serious song was *dziesma* (Latvian) or *giesmè* (Lithuanian), plural *dziesmas* and *giesmès* respectively. By *giesmè* the Lithuanians meant the rare old contrapuntal secular dancing and work songs. Among the Dzūkai of southern Lithuania all serious singing is still called *giesmè.* In modern Lithuanian literature the secular song is always called *daina,* and the term *giesmè* is used for religious hymns. The new, long Latvian folk songs of balladic or epic nature are called *singes* (compare German *singen,* to sing).

The daina, Lithuanian and Latvian folk song, is the most important creation of their folklore. The songs of each country are, however, distinct in their form and content and also melody; therefore they must be treated separately. Only the mythological songs and ballads show any considerable similarity; the great mass of other songs are quite different. [JB]

Daire mac Fiachna In Old Irish legend, a chief of Ulster; owner of the Brown Bull of Cuailgne. Daire really caused the War for the Brown Bull. After promising to lend the bull to Queen Medb of Connacht for a year, he refused him to the messengers who came to lead him to Medb. The reason was that one of them, drunk at the feast, had been overheard to say that Daire was a fool to lend Medb the bull since Medb would take it by force if he refused her. So Daire refused, and Medb and her hosts advanced into Ulster to take it. See CUCHULAIN.

daisy Either of two plants, the ox-eye daisy (*Chrysanthemum leucanthemum*) which grows wild in America and parts of Europe, and the smaller English daisy (*Bellis perennis*) which grows wild in Europe: from Old English *dæges ege,* day's eye, because it closes at night.

The ox-eye daisy is sacred to St. John and is used in decoration for Midsummer's Night ceremonies. It is also sacred to Mary Magdalene and is said to have sprung from her tears. It was used as a cure for ulcers, lunacy, and wounds of the chest. The Slovaks used them as a cure for toothache. The North American Mohegan Indians made a wine of the flowers for a spring tonic.

The English daisy is sacred to St. Margaret of Antioch, probably by association with the name of the flower in French, marguerite. It was used as a cure for severe pains such as gout and rheumatism. The juice of the leaves and roots was taken through the nose to cure migraine and to clear the head.

An emblem of fidelity, the daisy is often used in love divination. Children pluck the petals from the daisy, repeating, "She loves me, she loves me not," or "This year, next year, sometime, never," which tells when marriage will come. In England a girl plucks a handful of grass with her eyes closed. The number of daisies in the bunch tells when she will be married. It is considered lucky to step on the first one of the season, but it is unlucky to uproot them, or the children in the house will not prosper. It was believed that if daisies were fed to a puppy in milk, it would not grow large, and a nursing child should not touch one lest it stunt his growth.

Daitya In Hindu mythology, an asura descended from Diti and Kaśyapa, the grandson of Brahmā. The name is used interchangeably with asura. Compare DĀNAVA.

Dajoji In Iroquois Indian mythology, Panther, the west wind. He was called by Ga-oh into the sky to fight the storms. Dajoji the Panther is strong enough to fell forests, support the whirlwind, whip up the waves of the sea, and control tempests. Even the sun hides his face when he hears the snarl of Dajoji in the night.

Daksha In Vedic mythology, an Āditya: as both the son and father of Aditi, the male principle or creative force. In the *Brāhmaṇas,* Daksha is identified with the creator Prajāpati: according to the *Mahābhārata,* he sprang from the right thumb of Brahmā. His daughters numbered 24, 50, or 60. Ten of these he gave to Dharma, 13 to Kaśyapa, 27 to Soma, and one married Śiva. The wives of Kaśyapa and Dharma became the mothers of gods, men, demons, and all living things; the wives of Soma became the Nakṣatras.

The story of Daksha's sacrifice appears frequently in Hindu literature. In the *Mahābhārata,* the gods decided to perform a sacrifice and Daksha undertook the duty. The gods apportioned the sacrifice but, not knowing Śiva, omitted a share for him. Śiva, enraged, shot through the sacrifice which then took refuge in heaven. Then he broke the teeth of Pūshan and the arms of Savitṛi, and tore out Bhaga's eyes. The ṛishis and gods propitiated him and gave him a share of the sacrifice, whereupon he restored the three whom he had injured in his wrath. According to the *Purāṇas,* the sacrifice was instituted by the gods to Vishṇu, but Śiva was not invited. Śiva's wife, Umā, urged her husband to show his power. A catastrophe followed in which the gods and demigods were struck with arrows or run through with swords. Only when Daksha propitiated the deity was peace restored.

Dalai Lāma (Tibetan r*Gya*-m*tsho*) The highest ranking monk of Tibet, believed to be an incarnation of Bodhisattva Padmapāṇi (Avalokita) whose spirit passes into a child at the death of each Dalai Lāma. The identity of the child, who must be born at least 49 days after the demise of the former chief monk, is determined by divination. The child thus chosen is made a novice at the age of four, and when he is seven or eight he becomes a monk and the titular head of Lāmaism.

The first Dalai Lāma was Ṅag-dbaṅ-blo-bzaṅ rGya-mts'o who was given his title by the emperor of China. He made his counselor, the abbot of Tāshi-lhunpo monastery, second in power as the Tāshi Lāma who is the incarnation of Amitābha.

dalang The Balinese story-teller: narrator of the story, impersonator of the characters, and manipulator of the puppets in the famous shadow plays. He also chants the stories enacted in the legong.

Damballa or **Damballa Wedo** The powerful serpent deity of the Rada pantheon of Haitian vodun gods. This being is much beloved by the Haitians, but is held greatly in awe. He is identified, by the process of syncretism, with St. Patrick, and is especially worshipped on Thursdays. He forms the rainbow which is regarded as an *arc d'alliance* between him and Aida Wedo, his wife. [MJH]

Dame Lombarde A French-Canadian *complainte* with a historical basis: almost unique for antiquity in folk song. It is the story of Rosmonde, wife of a Lombard king, and later of one of his officers. She attempted to poison her second husband at Ravenna in 573, but was forced to share with him the wine she had poisoned with snake venom. The song followed an unusual route in its travels, going from Italy up through France, and finally reaching French Canada in two separate versions brought by the early settlers.

Damon and Pythias In classical folktale, two friends of Syracuse. When the tyrant Dionysius I condemned Pythias (or Phintias) to death, Damon offered himself as hostage while his friend went to his home to settle his affairs before death. Just as the time expired, Pythias returned and released his friend from the pledge. Dionysius, struck by this loyalty, pardoned Pythias and asked to be made one of their friendship. There are retellings of the story in which the roles of the friends are reversed.

Danae In Greek mythology, the mother of Perseus; a daughter of Acrisius of Argos, to whom an oracle foretold that his daughter would give birth to a son who would kill Acrisius. The king shut her up in a brazen tower where Zeus, who took a fancy to the maiden, visited her as or in a shower of gold. When Acrisius discovered Danae and the newborn Perseus, he had them placed in a chest and cast out to sea. The chest floated to Seriphos where its occupants were rescued by Dictys, the brother of Polydectes, king of the island. Later, Polydectes became so pressing in his suit to Danae that she fled to a sacred altar, where he besieged her until Perseus turned him to stone with Medusa's head. In Latin legend, Danae came to Latium and was one of the ancestors of Turnus. See PERSEUS.

Danaus In Greek mythology, the father of the fifty Danaides. Danaus was a son of Belus, king of Egypt, and Anchinoe, and twin of Ægyptus. He fled to Argos, the home of his ancestress Io, with his daughters and became king there. But the fifty sons of Ægyptus followed and Danaus was forced to permit his daughters to marry them. However, he gave each of his daughters a knife and told them to kill their husbands on the wedding night. All obeyed except one, Hypermnestra, who spared her lover Lynceus. (Amymone and Berbyce are, in other tradition, said to have refrained also.) Lynceus then slew Danaus and his daughters and became king of Argos: this is the more common story; but Pindar says that Danaus offered the girls as wives to those winning in the races. Amymone was the mother of Nauplius by Poseidon, so that others besides Hypermnestra must have been spared by Lynceus. The daughters were condemned in Hades to fill a sieve or bottomless jar with water from broken pitchers, probably in an effort to obtain sufficient water for a purifying bath.

Dānava In Hindu mythology, an asura descended from Dānu and Kaśyapa, the grandson of Brahmā. The name is used interchangeably with asura.

dança do Genebrés A Portuguese ceremonial dance for men, performed at the *romaria* or pilgrimage of Na. Sra. dos Altos Ceus at Lousa (Beira Baixa). It resembles the dança do Rei David in the self-accompaniment on stringed instruments, but retains more characteristics of the Mouriscada, in the tall mauresque shakos, and the unsheathing of a sword by the leader. Two men dressed as girls dance between the two lines of dancers (evidence of ancient fertility symbolism). [GPK]

dance: folk and primitive Folk dance is communal reaction in movement patterns to life's crucial cycles. Its true magico-religious function concerns preservation of the individual and the race. Natural cultures dance from the cradle to the grave; mechanized society, for sociability and diversion.

Ritual tends towards crystallization and secularization. Yet even European peasant dances retain vestiges of their symbolism. In Iberia and Latin America dance remains a vital festal expression; the American Indian clings to many of his traditional rituals. In Africa and Haiti life and dance are integrated. Native tribes throughout the world celebrate in dance the cycles of man's life and of the seasons.

The same dance may serve all occasions, as the *Rutuburi* of the Tarahumara Indians in Chihuahua, Mexico. Or a special dance may have a circumscribed function, as the *Deer Dance* of the Pueblo Indians of New Mexico. Rarely are purposes in special compartments. Fecundity of human, animal, and plant, impersonations, demon exorcism, cure, and death, all blend into one concept. The conflict of the seasons becomes a battle mime, identified with the resurrection of all things living and divine. Enigmatic symbol of this fusion is the sacred clown, priestlike among aborigines, but banished to the circus in the modern world.

These universal functions of folk dance vary according to climate, geographical conditions, and temperament. Despite identity of certain steps and formations, every continent, nation, tribe has its distinctive style. Trade and conquest transfer small elements or entire rites which often blend with native practices, thus uniting distant cultures.

The following bald statements list examples of 1)

Universality of Purpose, 2) Racial Personality, 3) Acculturation, 4) Comparative Choreography. Detailed descriptions are distributed through the dictionary.

I. Purposes of Dance Rites
Puberty Initiation

South Seas—Samoa, Formosa, Andaman Islands, New Guinea; Fiji Islanders *Ruku-Ruku.*
Africa—Dapangos, Bagos: circumcision, men's and boys' secret societies.
South America—Incas: *huarachicoy* rites.
Bolivia: Aymara maturity rites.
Argentina: Puelche and Tehuelche girls' puberty.
East Brazil: Fulnio girls' puberty.
Archipelago: Yahgan boys and girls.
Chaco: Mataco, Toba, Lengua, Choroti *Kausima* rite—women and boys dramatize attack and defeat of evil spirits.
    Chamacoco *Anapösö*—resembles *Kina* and *Klóketen* rites.
Venezuela: Maipure *Máuari*—similar to Mataco, etc.
Arizona—Papago *Wakita.*
Apache *Crown Dance*—gahe.
California—all tribes.

Courtship

The innumerable dances of sexual selection and attraction will be listed according to countries. Though commonly regarded as *the* folk dance, actually they form only one category.

The drama of love varies from pursuit and capture to rejection; from Hungary's emphatic arrogance to Scandinavia's demureness; from the frank obscenities of primitive tribes to the cool proximity of square dances. Sometimes men or women display prowess and allurements separately. Usually both sexes mingle in simple rounds, complex figure dances, or embrace.

Children's games retain courtship play—*Here Come Three Dukes a-Riding, Here We Come Up the Green Grass.* Fan and kerchief feature skilfully, the former in Japan, Burma, Spain, the latter in Algiers, the Philippines, Malay Peninsula, Russia, Spain, Bohemia, England, Peru, Chile, Mexico.

Friendship

Australia—aborigines—*Molonga* corroboree.
Polynesia—Maori *Haka,* welcoming dance to visitors.
Denmark—*Dance of Fellowship.*
Sweden—*Nigarepolskan.*
Bohemia—Minet.
Mexico—Canacuas—welcome to guest.
American Indian—Sauk and Fox *Friendship Dance,* Chippewa and Menominee *Drum Presentation Ceremony. Give Away Dances.*

Weddings

General social dancing at weddings is a common practice.
    Special dances are: Jewish *Broyges Tanz,* Yugoslav *Scatovač,* Polish *Wesele U Witosa,* Swiss *Lauterbach,* Valencian *Ball de Casament,* Basque *Purrusalda,* Norwegian *Kyndeldans* (Torch Dance), Mexican *Xochipitzahua* (a Huastec Huapango).
    Hungary's many wedding dances include: *Bride's Dance* (Mennyasszony Tánc), *Cook's Dance* (Szakacss-zonyok Tánc), *Turks' Dance* (Törökös Tánc), *Dawnjire Dance* (Hajnaltüz Tánc).
    German bride and groom mime farm labors.
    The Oraons of India precede a wedding by a *Wedding of the Dead,* a *Wedding of Earth Mother and Sun God,* and a *War Dance.*

Occupations

Work dances are functional, magico-mimetic, or recreative. The African Dahomean Dokpwe achieves efficient rhythmic unison in cooperative work, as also its descendants, the Haitian Combite and Société Congo, and similar work to drum and song in the Virgin Islands, Jamaica, and some of the Sea Islands off the Georgia coast. Among the Colombian Paéz-Moquex work is ceremonially performed.

Many mimetic work dances portray cultivation of the fields, sowing, harvesting. Medieval guilds mimed each of their professions in festive processions, some still preserved in European folk dances.
Japan, Philippines, Madagascar—rice-planting (Philippine *Balitao*).
South America—Colonial Quechua of Arequipa—wool-cutters with shears.
Europe—Spain: *La Filada* (women spinning).
    Portugal: *Dança dos alfaiates* (tailors), *dos ferreiros* (smiths). *Llaço dos oficios* from *Dança dos Paulitos.*
    Germany: *Webertanz* (weavers), Nürnberg *Metzgertanz* (butchers), Munich *Schäfflertanz* (coopers), *Schneidertanz* (tailors).
    France: old *Branle des Hermites, Branle des Lavandières* (laundresses).
    Hungary: *Szénagyüjtéskor* (hay-making).
    Denmark: *Shoemaker's Dance, Linen, Tinker's Dance, Washing the Clothes.*
    Sweden: singing games—*Vafna Vadna* (weaving), *Skorda Linet* (Reap Flax).
    England: *Cobbler's Jig, Sailor's Hornpipe.*
Mexico—Tlaxcala: *Jarabe Tlaxcalteco* (making of atole).
    Jalisco: *Las Espuelas* (horseback-riding).

Vegetation

The growth of crops, mainstay of life, is furthered by invoking benevolent powers and warding off spirits of destruction. The orgiastic festivals often attending these rites also serve the propagation of the race.
Planting and Growth
Africa—Nilotic Lango: *Bell Dance* for rain.
Ecuador—Inca: *Wayara* to influence Frost, Air, Water, Sun.
Mexico: Festivals for Xilonen, Cinteotl, etc., of ancient Aztecs.
    Voladores, Quetzales of Puebla, Veracruz, Hidalgo, Guatemala.
    Tlacololeros of Guerrero.
    Las Sembradoras (with baskets) of Michoacán.
    Rain Dances of Huichol and Tarahumara Indians.
U. S. Indians—Papago *Wiikita.*
    All Pueblos: *Kachina* for health of crops and tribe.
    Hopi: *Powamu* (Bean Planting). Alternate *Flute* and *Snake-Antelope Ceremonies*
    Zuñi: Ceremonial *Kokochi.*
    San Felipe, Santo Domingo, Acoma, Taos, etc.: *Green Corn* or *Saint's Day,* alias *Tablita Dance.*
    Cochiti: *Basket Dance.*

Santa Clara: *Rainbow Dance, Race of the Rain Clouds.*
Santo Domingo: *K'aiyak'ayet.*
Shawnee: *Bread Dance.*
Iroquois: *Planting Festival, Thunder rite.*
Europe—Poland: *Zasiali Gorale* (sowing of rye and oats).
Germany: *Springtanz.* Games—*Alle Vögel Sind schon da; Dornröschen; Im Sommer, im Sommer.*
France: medieval *Carole, Espringale;* modern *Les Saisons* of Dauphiné; *La Chouade* of Gascony (oats).
England: *Bean Setting* of Morris. Games—*Oranges and Lemons, Oats and Beans and Barley Grow.*

Harvest

India—Mundas: *Sohorai Festival,* after *Lashua* or *Karam* dances.
Palestine: wine-treading dances, *Lag B'Omer* for harvest, ancient *Feast of Tabernacles.*
Europe
Russia: *Polyanka, Moldavanetz, Bulba Dance* (potato).
Lithuania: *Ruguciai* (rye), *Kubilas* (The Tub), *Aguenele* (poppy).
Finland: *Harvest Dance* with scythes and rakes.
Ireland: *Port an Fogmair* (harvest jig).
Greece, Hungary, Italy, Portugal, France: wine-treading dances.
South America—Peru: *Ayriwa* of Quechua.
Venezuela: *Tura* of Churuguara.
U. S. Indians
Iroquois: *Strawberry, Raspberry, Green Bean Festivals.*
Fox, Delaware: *Bean Dance.*
Creek: *Busk Festival.*
Shawnee, Delaware, Cherokee, Yuchi, Iroquois: *Green Corn Festival.*

Astronomical Dances

Sun, moon, stars are objects of worship both among agricultural and nomadic races, as in
the *Moon Dance* at the North African Feast of Ramadan,
the *Astronomical Dance* of the Egyptians,
the *Sun Dance* of the Incas, still performed in Bolivia,
the Arizona Papago *Ciwiltkona,*
the Plains Indians *Sun Dance,* with its curative and heroic aspects,
the *Sun Dance* of the Dené and Salish of Canada.

In their *Eclipse Dance* the Dené tried to restore the light of the sun. The sun's course, by determining the seasons, influences human activity: hunting in the winter, agriculture in the summer. Many rites celebrate solstice and equinox. For instance:

Solstice

Winter (return of sun)	*Summer* (sun turns north again)
Inca *Inti raimi* (June 21).	*Capac raimi* (December 21).
Keres *Hanyiko* (December 21).	*Hanyikikya* (June 21).
Scandinavian *Jul.*	*Midsomervaka*
	Pagan vestige—*Johannisfeuer, Foguerinha de São João,* St. *Ivan's Fire* (Hungary), *Bonfire Dance* (Ireland).
Christian *Christmas, Epiphany Pastorales* Mummer's Plays	Christian *Corpus Christi.*

Other ecclesiastical festivals have been identified with pagan ones—Carnival coincides with the pagan expulsion of Winter; Easter and May Day, with further rituals of seasonal resurrection, corresponding to the Egyptian *Osiris rite* and Greek *Orgia* of Dionysus Dithyrambus. Holy Cross, May 3, corresponds with the Quechua *Ayriwa,* harvest fiesta.
Voladores fly most often at Corpus Christi and around the Autumn equinox.
Moriscas take place most frequently at Carnival and Corpus Christi.

Hunting

Hunting dances achieve hypnotic power and propitiate the spirit of the animal by 1) imitation; 2) hunting mime—usually both.
India—*Jadura* Festivals of Mundas; *Arrow Dance* of Veddas of Ceylon.
Africa—Yammasoukro *Antelope Dance,* with two sacred hunters.
South America—Aymara fertility rite with mime of vicuña hunt.
Mexico—Tantoyuca, Veracruz *Hunters' Dance.*
Huichol, Mayo-Yaqui *Deer Dance,* the latter (*Maso*) with *Coyote* and *Pascolas.*
Indians of United States—Yuma *Deer Dance.*
Pueblos of New Mexico, Plains *Buffalo, Deer Dance, Bow and Arrow Dance.*
Onondaga *Da Ga Yak.*
Miwok *Kalea* (Bow and Arrow Dance).
Yurok *White Deerskin.*
Eskimos—Baffin Land, and Chukchee women and shaman release seals.
Alaska Tigara *Nalukutuk* (whale hunt feast).

Animal Mime

In addition to their function in hunting, animal impersonations have a demonic role:
1) in fertility and vegetation rites:
Africa—Ongaladougon *Thunder Dance.*
South America—Puberty Rites.
California—*Kuksu-Hesi* rites: Maidu, Pomo, etc.
Europe—*Bugios,* associated with Portuguese *Mouriscada.*
Schiechenperchten associated with Salzburg *Schönperchten* (ugly and beautiful Perchten, respectively).
Carnivalesque *Wild Men.*
Mexico—Guerrero *Tecuanes* (tigers) associated with *Tlacololeros* (planters).
Visionudos of Huixquilucan, Mexico, Carnival: snake symbol carried by *Malinche,* man-woman.
U.S.—*Snake Dance* of Shoshonean Hopi, Comanche, and Ottawa with live snakes; of Fox, Sauk, Cherokee in figuration (now social).
Eagle: Zuñi, Tesuque (and other pueblos), Comanche, Fox, Cherokee; Iroquois *Ganegwa'e.*
Turtle: Isleta, Maidu.
Goat, Cock, Bull are fertility symbols from the Greek ancient *Komos* to Yaqui *Pascola,* from Santal *Cock Dance* to Portuguese and Keresan *Rooster Pull,* from the horned *Dionysus Zagreus* to the Mexican Mixtec *Pachecos* (cowboys) with two men-women, Puebla *Toreadores,* and Tewa *Matachines.*
The horse as hobby horse has appeared since the

Middle Ages in May Day and Carnival festivities, and still in connection with *Moriscas*.

2) In totemic worship—Australian aboriginal emu, kangaroo, frog, opossum; Kwakiutl wolf, etc.

3) For cure—Fox, Iroquois *Bear*, *Buffalo*; Plains *Buffalo*; Huichol *Deer*. The Bear has power from the sun and transfers it to the Plains shaman.

4) As emblem of Indian war society (not always mimetic)—notably Kit Fox, Badger, Little Dogs, Big Dogs; less often Bear, Buffalo.

5) As symbol of divine spirit—Haiti.

> *Damballa Wedo* (snake), *Chebo* (tiger), *Agasu* (panther); Haitian *loa* of vodun cults; Mashacalí *parrot dance* and Apinayé, Sherente, Northern Cayapó *great anteater masquerades* (eastern Brazil).

Their nature depends on habitat: Nigerian ogorodo bird; Tibetan tiger, lion, roc, monkey, stag; Siberian Chukchee raven, seal, wolf, fox; Mexican tiger (jaguar), quetzal bird; San Felipe Pueblo elk, antelope, mountain sheep; Plains buffalo, prairie chicken, bear, crow, coyote; Miwok, Meskwakie grizzly bear; Kiowa, Sauk, Menominee owl; Makah (Neah Bay, Wash.) elk, goose, raven, wolf, snipe, raccoon; Iroquois, Cherokee, Creek, Yuchi duck, pigeon, coon, bear, buffalo, otter; Onondaga partridge.

Many American Indian animal dances have become social dances. See these.

Battle Mime and Moriscas

The war dance in preparation for battle and in celebration of victory serves to

1) strengthen communal bonds;

2) aid sexual selection by display of prowess;

3) symbolically connect with agricultural rites. Primitive tribes still perform them with spear, shield, and sword, or bow and arrow; the American Indian until recently functionally, now mostly as social dance. European sword and stick dances mingle Christian and pagan symbolism with a heredity from the Greek pyrrhic and the Roman Salii. Sometimes swords are bent into hoops and form bowers, or are interplaited, or grasped hilt and point.

Men or matured boys—mimetic—

Massed effect of multiple lines—

Africa—*War Dances* of Johannesburg, KonKumba, Dapangos.

Bali—*Baris Dance* with spears.

Two opposing lines—

Eastern Archipelago—Headhunters.

Formosa—Nagas in Assam.

Africa—Shilluks of the White Nile, Nessoué near Abomey.

Venezuela—Pariagoto (comic).

Amazon River—Parintintins, Itogapuks.

Peru—Inca *Cachua*.

Two opponents

Borneo—Dyak *War Dance*.

Philippines—Bontoc and Igorot *War Dance*.

Solo

Borneo—Dusun youth in war mimicry.

African Baloki.

American Indian mimed feats in

> War Dances—Navaho *N'Dah*, Iroquois *Wasáse*, Kiowa *Shield and War Dance*, Chippewa *Toma-*

hawk Dance, Sauk, Fox *War Dance*, Osage *Charcoal Dance* (obsolete).

Men and Women—not mimetic—

Polynesia—Maori *Peru Peru*.

Indian Scalp Dances—Paraguay Chaco: Toba

U.S. Papago, Zuñi, Mandan, Plains Cree, Teton-Sioux, Blackfoot, Chippewa, etc.

Victory Dance—Bûngi, Fox (Meskwakie), Sauk.

Women only—

Hindu, Kush, Kaffirs; Sioux, formerly, during men's absence.

Borneo Dusun priestess' *Victory Dance*.

Kwakiutl solo *War Dance*, British Columbia; Pawnee *Scalp Dance*.

African Bassari girls' *Stick Dance*.

Non-functional brandishing of weapons

India—Coorg *Sword* and *Stick Dances*.

Arabia, Turkey—*Danse du Sabre*.

Russia—*Lezginka*, Georgian *Dagger Dance*, Ukrainian *Zaporotchez* for four men.

Denmark—*Stick Dance*.

Isle of Man—*Dirk Dance*.

Stick duel dances

Spain—*Paloteo, Torneo*, Basque *Stick Dance*.

Italy—*Bal de Baston*.

Portugal—*Dança dos Paulitos*.

Lithuania—*Mikita*.

Hungary—*Kun Verbunkos* (no weapons).

Dance between two crossed swords or sticks on ground

Hungary—*Kanász Tánc*.

Catalonia—*L'Hereu Riera*.

Finland—*Skin Kompasse*.

England—*Bacca Pipes; Broadswords*.

Scotland—*Gilly Callum* (sword and scabbard): Argyllshire and Lochaber.

Moriscas and sword dances

Dalmatia—*Moreška*.

Rumania—*Joc de Călușari* (literally horse play). ⎫
Austria—*Perchtentanz*. ⎬ pagan vestiges
 ⎭

Italy—*Mattacino* and *Moresche*. ⎫ developed into
France—Renaissance *Matachins* or ⎬ entremets and
 Bouffons. Bacchu Ber. ⎭ court masques

England—*Morris, Sword Dance;* ⎫
 Shetland Island *Sword Dance*. ⎪
Germany—Renaissance *Maruschka-* ⎬ with interplaiting
 tanz; Überlingen *Schwertles-* ⎪
 tanz. ⎪
Basque Provinces—*Zamalzain, Bordon Dantza, Ezpata Dantza*. ⎭

Portugal—*Mouriscadas, Dança do Rei David*.

Spain—*Matachini, Los Moros y Cristianos, Los Seises* of Seville Cathedral (related).

Majorca—*Els Cosiers, Ball de Cavalets*.

Trinidad and Guatemala—*Baile de los Moros*.

Mexico—Plateau: *Santiagos, Moros y Cristianos*.

> Puebla and Veracruz: *Moros, Santiaguitos, Negritos, Zacapoaxtles;* related *Acatlaxqui* and *Toreadores*.

> Oaxaca, Jalisco: *Las Plumas, La Conquista*.

> Michoacán, Jalisco: *Moros, Negros, Morisma, Los Machetes, Conquista*.

Cora, Tarahumara, Mayo-Yaqui: *Matachini*.

New Mexico Pueblos—

Santo Domingo, San Ildefonso, San Juan, Alcalde, Bernalillo *Matachines*.

Santo Domingo *Santiago* and *Bocayanyi* and *Sandaro*.

Santa Ana *Konyisats*.

Texas and California—*Matachines*.

These enigmatic *Sword Dances* are often performed by men's sworn societies. Their actions and accessories point to an ancient fertility rite attended by sacrifice. The *Perchtentanz* is an obvious vestige of a pagan Germanic cult of Perchta and her wild horde (*Wildes Heer*), related to the Herlequin or Arlequino of the theater. In *Los Moros* the Christians, headed by Santiago on a hobby horse, vanquish the Moors—symbol of victory of Summer over Winter, Good over Evil. In England Santiago was St. George, the Dragon Killer, later on Robin Hood. True *Moriscas* are accompanied by a fool, a man dressed as woman, an animal (dragon or bull) which is killed and resurrected. In the *Txonkórinka* of the Basque *Sword Dance* the Captain is hoisted up inert in a sublimation of Death. Mexican *Moros* enact a battle, but the *Matachini* have no battle mime, except in the oppositional choreography and the plumed trident (former sword). They have a *Malinche*. Pueblo *Matachines* retain the bullfight. Dialog in native dialect often accompanies the drama.

Survivals in children's games

Roman Soldiers, The Rovers, King of the Barbarees, Le Roi de France, Marlborough.

Morisca survivals

In Spain, Portugal, and the Balkans the *Morisca* has retained its ceremonial function, though its precise meaning is forgotten. In Germany, Austria, Rumania, even its pagan originals are preserved. In the New World this importation by Spanish friars fused for a second time with native ritual into solemn, ambiguous observances.

On the other hand, the Renaissance *Matachin* of France was a buffoon; the *Morris* of England, the *Mattacino* of Italy developed into secular entertainment and court masque. The *Morris* has become an exhibition for solo or group. Since its discovery in remote villages it has been featured in gymnasium classes and Elizabethan pageants without an inkling of its import.

Cure

1) By exorcism or frightening away of demons and evil spirits—

Sacred Clown-Demons (see chart).

South America—Incas *Sitowa*; Mataco, Toba (Chaco) *Jumping Dance*.

U.S. Indians—Navaho *yeibichai* night ceremony; Shoshoni *Naroya*; Yurok *Jumping Dance*.

Shamanistic trance dances of Siberia, especially Yakuts, and of American Indians.

2) Psychotherapy by artificial hysteria or gymnastics—

Africa—Yoruba *Bori*, possession cult of 'iskoki spirit-worship; India-Bathinga, Kolamthullal, Nayars of Malabar self-curing dances.

China—*Cong Fu Cult*.

Europe—*Dance Mania* of Middle Ages; *St. Vitus' Dance; Dance against Plague*; Italian *Tarantelle* against the bite of the tarantula.

American Indian visionary cults—Huichol, Plains Indians *Peyote*; Potawatomi, Menominee, Winnebago, etc., *Midewiwin Medicine Society*.

3) Cure derived from animals—

American Indian—*Deer*: Huichol, Zuñi, Yuma, Maidu. *Buffalo*: Pawnee, Iowa, Fox, Iroquois. *Bear*: Pawnee (power derived from sun), Iroquois.

4) With the purifying aid of fire or charcoal—

American Indian—Osage *Charcoal Dance*; Pawnee *Iruska*; Fox *Buffalo Head Dance, Thunder Dance*; Iroquois *False Face Dance*.

Death

	FUNERALS	MEMORIALS	CULT OF DEAD —ANCESTOR WORSHIP
Samoa	*Otahite Wake*		
New Ireland		Five-day Memorial	
Borneo	Kayan *Departure of Spirit*		
Japan			*Bon Odori*
China	Yao Ceremonials		
Egypt, Greece	Funeral Dances		
Africa	Boloki Wake		Whydah *Ghost Dance*
Haiti	Wakes		
E. Brazil			Mashacalí Impersonation of Dead
Tarahumara		*Rutuburi, Pascola*	
Yaqui		*Maso, Pascolas, Matachini*	
Maidu Yuma Mohave	*Cremation Ceremony*	*Karok*	
Plains Indians			*Ghost Dance* —reunion with dead
Chippewa		*Restoration of Mourners*	
Kansa		*Brave Man's Dance*	
Kwakiutl, Salish			*Totemic Dances*

Middle Ages

	FUNERALS	MEMORIALS	CULT OF DEAD
Spain, Mexico	*Jota* (at wakes)		*Dance of Death, La Muerte, Ball de la Mort*
Italy	*Baraban, Lucia*		
Hungary	*Gyás Tánc*		
Scotland	*Reel* (at wakes)		
Ireland	*Jig* (at wakes)		
Games	*Lott ist Tod, Old Roger is Dead, Jenny Jones*		

Everywhere merrymaking to please or appease spirit, or dispel fear.

Memorials to dispatch ghost thoroughly into other-world.

Ecstatic Dance

1) Mystic trance, curative or sadistic, induced by drumming or whirling; magic powers, immunity to pain of self-mutilation by fire or swords—
Siberia—Shaman's *Epileptic Dance,* especially Chukchee, Yakuts, Ostiak, Koryak; *Hysterical Dance* by Kam of Altai-Iran; *Angakok* of Eskimo.
Gilbert Islands—*Epileptic Dances.*
Bali—*Sanghyang* and *Kris Dances.*
Moslem World, China through Turkey and Syrian Tripoli—Whirling Dervishes of 30 Islamic sects; Bektashi (Beggars); Rufai (Howling); Sadi (Fire Eaters); Mevlevi (Mystics).
Africa—North: Algeria *Aïssâoua.*
Ivory and Gold Coast: *M'Deup,* sorcerer-spotting dance.
Always superhuman acrobatic feats, whirling, leaping, distortion, climbing, crawling, writhing, falling; at times rigidity at climax.

2) Mystic communion with divine forces, induced by narcotic or intoxicant; spirit leaves body, which is entered by demon, spirit of ancestor, or animal; often sublime visions and escape to better existence—
Ancient Greece—*Orgia* by Mænads in worship of Dionysus.
Aztec and South Mexican—*Teonanacatl* Cult.
Huichol, Tarahumara: *Hikuli Dance* (Peyote).
U.S. Indian—*Peyote Dance* (not acrobatic, but rigidity), especially Quapaw, Kiowa, Arapaho, Cheyenne, Ute, Pawnee, Kickapoo, Sioux, Caddo, Iowa, Winnebago, Menominee: brought from Mexico.
Without narcotic—
Hausa—Bori cult.
Haiti, Brazil—Vodun cult, mounting by loa (Legba, Gedé, Damballa, etc.).
U.S. Indian—*Sun Dance:* Great Plains, e.g. Arapaho, Gros Ventre, Crow, Ute, Bûngi, etc.
Ghost Dance: Arapaho, Cheyenne, Shoshone, Pawnee, Dakota, Iowa.
Dream Dance: Potawatomi, Menominee, Chippewa, etc. (variant of *Grass Dance*).
Crazy Dance: Omaha, Arapaho.
American religious sects—Jumpers of New England (origin in Wales); Shakers of New Lebanon, N. Y. (origin in Manchester, England)—shake evil out of hands; Church of Holy Spirit and Holy Rollers of Southern states.

Clowns

Enact supernaturals or spirits of dead. Antinatural and obscene action, speech in reverse, often falsetto. Usually wear demon or animal masks of wood or leather, with long noses, beards, horns or hair pokes; or smear faces with soot, mud, or black and white stripes. Often wear shaggy coat or tatters, or carry desiccated animal or tail; or dress like women. Bells, rattles, whips, bull bladders, often wooden lances and swords, or sticks.

Sometimes enact battles or mock travesties. May police or scout. Associated with fire, black magic, weather control. Powers to promote rain, cure, fertility.

Medieval Carnival Clowns suggest origin in pagan evil spirits, shaggy Dionysiac *Daimones,* unruly phallic *Kómos,* the *Wildes Heer;* and developments such as:

Wild Men
Altvater became
  Überlingen *Hänsele, Zottler*
  Tyrol *Huttlerläufer*
  Pinzgau *Tresterer*

  became Mexican *Mal Viejo*
  Abuelo

Schemen became *Casquetes* of Ocotoxco, Mexico

Schiechenperchten related to French *Harlequin*
Bugios maisnée *Herlekin* Italian *Arlequino*

Devil of Middle Ages obviously became Mexican *Diablo*

Basque *Noirs* are related to *Arap* and other Fools with black faces, Mexican *Negros*

Certain Indian Clowns are probably indigenous and interrelated: Yaqui *Pascolas* and *Chapayekas;* Papago *Novico;* Pueblo *Koshare, Black Eye K'apio;* Hopi *Natacka,* Iroquois *gagǫsä,* etc.
Non-sacred Clowns: Wolof *Griots,* Burma *Loobyets,* Persia *Mutrub* and *Batcha,* Quechua *Sijilla,* medieval Court *Buffoon,* Tlaxcala (Mexico) *Catrines.*
Semi-profane Clowns of ritual origin: Mayo-Yaqui *Pascolas,* Crow *Akbi'aruscarica* of Grass Dance. Animal mime: Japanese *Heron Dance,* Borneo *Macaque monkey* and *hornbill,* Africa *monkey mime* near Odienné, South America Macusi *tiger.*

Ceremonial Clowns

Country	Dance	Demon	Animal	Phallic	Cure	Death Ancestor	Bells	Rattles	Mask	Other Properties
New Guinea	*Imigi* of Papuans	x	—	x	—	x	—	—	x	—
Ceylon	*Devil Dance*	x	x	—	x	—	—	—	x	horns
Tibet	*Devil Dance*	x	x	—	x	—	—	—	x	horns
	Acharyas	—	—	x	x	x	—	—	x	—
India	*Bhringi*	—	—	—	—	x	—	—	x	—
Europe										
Thrace	*Kalogheros* of Carnival	x	x	x	—	x	x	—	x	shaggy, soot
Portugal	*Bugios*	x	x	x	—	—	x	—	x	tatters, battle, agricultural implements

Ceremonial Clowns (*cont.*)

Country	Dance	Demon	Animal	Phallic	Cure	Death Ancestor	Bells	Rattles	Mask	Other Properties
Pinzgau	*Tresterer*	x	x	x	–	x	–	–	x	–
Salzburg	*Schiechen- perchten*	x	x	x	–	x	–	–	x	battle, tatters
Nürnberg	*Schembartläufer*	–	–	x	–	x	x	–	x	foliage, run, fire, ashes, soot
Tyrol	*Huttlerläufer*	–	–	x	–	–	x	–	x	tatters, run
	Zottler	–	–	x	–	–	x	–	x	tatters, run
England	*Morris Fool*	–	skin	–	–	–	x	–	–	soot on face
	Tommy of Sword Dance	–	skin	–	–	–	x	–	–	–
General	*Wild Men* (medieval)	x	x	x	–	x	x	–	x	whip, stick, shaggy
	Carnival	Devil	x	Fool	–	Death	x	–	x	Fool—pointed cap

South and Central America

Country	Dance	Demon	Animal	Phallic	Cure	Death Ancestor	Bells	Rattles	Mask	Other Properties
Chile	*Carnaval*	Diablo	x	Buffon	–	Muerte	x	–	x	
	Yahgan *Kina* rite	–	–	–	–	x	x	–	stripes	poked head-dress
Bolivia										
Aymará	*Ačačila* (*Čoqela*)	–	associated with vicuña	x	–	x	x	–	x	hunt, sticks
Mexico	*Tecuanes*	x	x	–	–	–	–	–	x	hunted
Tarascan	*Viejitos*	–	–	–	–	x	–	–	x	cane
Tarahumara	*Chapeones*	–	skin	–	–	x	–	–	x	whip, bladder
Yaqui	*Chapayekas*	x	skin	x	–	–	–	x Deer-hoofs	x	strike sticks, long nose
	Pascolas	x	x	x	–	–	–	x Deer-hoofs	x	hunt, poke on head

U.S. Indians

Country	Dance	Demon	Animal	Phallic	Cure	Death Ancestor	Bells	Rattles	Mask	Other Properties
Apache	*łibáhi*	x	–	x	x	–	–	x	x	–
Papago	*Novico*	–	–	–	x	x	–	x	x	feathers
	Djidjur	x	–	x	–	–	–	x	x	horns
Navaho	*Tonenile*	–	–	x	–	–	–	x	x	water sprinkler
Hopi	*Natacka, Tümas*	x	–	–	–	–	–	x	x	whip
Zuñi	*Mudheads*	–	–	x	x	x	–	x	x	associated with rain
	Ne'wekwe	–	–	x	x	–	–	x	x	associated with rain
	Koyemshi	–	–	x	–	x	–	x	x	rain
Pueblo	*K'apio chifunin* in Koshare	–	–	x	x	x	–	x	stripes	rain, war, poked headdress
	Te'en (Abuelo)	–	–	–	–	x	–	–	–	whip, battle
Pawnee	*Iruska*	–	–	x	–	–	–	x	x	fire power, whip
Oglala	*Heyoka*	–	x	–	x	–	–	x	–	associated with war
Bûngi	*Windigokan*	–	–	x	x	–	–	x	x	tatters, war
Iroquois	*Gagǫsä*	x	x	–	x	–	–	x	x	fire, ashes, nose
	Gadjisa'	x	–	x	–	–	–	–	x	corn

Fusion of Concepts

Aboriginal

Country	Dance	Animal	Demon	Hunt	Phallic	Vegetation	Cure	Battle	Death	Resurrection
India	Oraon *Wedding*	–	x	–	x	–	–	x	x	–
Africa										
Yammasoukro	*Antelope Dance*	x	–	x	–	–	–	–	x	–
Ongaladougon	*Thunder Dance*	x	x	–	x	x	–	–	–	–
Dahomey	*Adahun*	–	x	–	–	x	–	x	–	–
South America										
Venezuela	*Puberty Rites*									
Mucuchi	*Chirasté*									
Maipure	*Máuari*	x	x	–	x	x	–	x	x	–
Arecuna	*Cachimé*									
Bolivia										
Aymara	*Čoqela*	x	–	x	Ačačila	x	–	x	x	–
Chaco										
Terenos	*Rhea Feathers*	x	–	–	–	x	–	x	–	–
Mexico										
Guerrero	*Tlacololeros*	x	x	x	–	x	x	x	x	–
U.S. Indians										
Papago	*Wükita*	–	x	–	–	x	x	x	–	–
Pueblo	*Kachina*	–	x	–	x	x	x	x	x	–
and	*Eagle Dance*	x	–	–	–	x	–	–	–	–
	Snake Dance	x	–	–	x	x	–	–	–	–
Plains	*Buffalo Dance*	x	–	x	–	–	x	–	–	–
and	*Sun Dance*	x	–	–	–	x	x	–	–	–
Yaqui	*Deer Dance*	x	–	x	–	x	x	–	x	–

Moriscas

Country	Dance	Animal	Demon	Hunt	Phallic	Vegetation	Cure	Battle	Death	Resurrection
Europe										
Dalmatia	*Moreška*	x	x	–	x	x	–	x	x	x
Rumania	*Joc de Calušari*	x	x	–	x	x	–	x	x	x
Spain	*Moriscas*	–	x	–	x	x	–	x	x	x
Basque	*Ezpata Dantza*	–	–	–	–	x	–	x	x	x
Portugal	*Mouriscadas*	x	x	–	x	x	–	x	x	x
France	*Bacchu-Ber*	–	–	–	–	x	–	x	x	x
Germany	*Schwertlestanz*	–	–	–	⌐	x	–	x	x	x
Shetland Is.	*Sword Dance*	–	–	–	–	x	–	x	x	x
England	*Morris Dance*	x	x	–	x	x	–	x	x	x
Mexico										
Morelos Mexico	*Moros y Cristianos*	x	Viejo	–	–	–	–	x	x	x
Puebla Vera Cruz	*Santiagos*	x	x	–	Malinche	x	–	x	x	x
Yaqui Tarahumara	*Matachini*	–	–	–	x	x	–	–	–	x
New Mexico	*Matachines*	x	x	–	x	–	–	x	x	x

II. Areas of Racial Dance

Africa

African Negro dance, particularly of the Gold Coast and Ivory Coast, is the dancer's dance, incredibly acrobatic and rhythmically infallible. It has no temporal structure, but often fine group counterpoint and solo virtuosity. It serves a religious purpose for many occasions—circumcision, hunt, burial, war.

The Dahomean vodun are the antecedents of the Haitian *vaudou* cult. The most beautiful dances are:

Xevioso, of Thunder pantheon: 1) *Dance of Legba*, 2) the *Gobahun*, 3) the *Adahun*, Thunder Dance.

Nessoué, the River, highly descriptive and complex. *Sagbata*, epileptic dance.

Dā, the Snake.

Lisa, chief deity.

The *Vegetation Dance* of Ongaladougon combines communal circular dance; grotesque Old Men's Dance; a sowing mime by four young girls; realistic mime of animals' copulation. Animal masks and *Animal Mime*, especially that of the Javara, simulate every detailed trait of Monkey, Antelope being hunted, and every conceivable native beast.

Acrobatic Dances include: 1) groups of men flinging about young girls or boys: 2) sacred jumping dances, e.g. of Yammasoukro; 3) women professionals, e.g. of the Dioula; 4) men's savage, yet controlled solos—leaps, spins, somersaults, back bends—in perfect time with the music.

Despite the obscenity of certain symbolic dances, there are no erotic couple dances, and few social dances, like those of the Wolofs, similar to our ballroom dances, notably the *Goumbé*.

African Dance Colonies

African slave trade has colored the dance the full length of the East Coast Americas, in the *vodun* cults of Haiti, Cuba, Brazil, and in the ballroom.

Haiti is dominated by deities descended from the theology and ceremonialism of West Africa, especially from that of Dahomey and Yorubas of Nigeria. In the vodun rites, spirits or *loas* mount "servants" and goad them to frantic dances of possession, which take on characteristic patterns. Meanwhile onlookers circle a central pole or po'teau in the *Bamboche*.

Social dances of African descent include *Pinyique, Pastorelle, Ciyé, Chica, Ti Crip, Mangouline, Zesse, Raboto, Martinique, Mascaron, Malfini, Huba;* the stiff *Méringue* is of European descent.

Haitian movements are forthright, strong, sweeping, and acrobatic.

Ballroom dances from Cuba: *Rumba, Conga, Danzón.*

Brazil: *Maxixe, Zamba, Batuque*, etc.

U. S.: *Jitterbug* and *Boogie Woogie, Juba, Cakewalk.*

Despite their syncopated rhythms, certain aspects of these dances are not African—the idea of the couple dance, the often infinitesimal movements. *Juba* and acrobatic *Boogie* are more truly African.

Other aspects: Work songs and dances of Haiti and the southern United States; religious revivals and ecstatic dances of Church of the Holy Spirit and Holy Rollers.

Asia

The dance culture of Asia, while distinctive as compared with other continents, exhibits great contrasts—

1) between the upper sophisticated castes of India and China and the primitive tribes of the mountains and islands.

2) between the vast, sparsely populated areas of Siberia with their paucity of dances and the wealth and variety of the Archipelago and tiny Pacific Islands.

It is nonetheless possible to distinguish large areas, all of them except Siberia under the influence of India.

Siberia

The shamanistic trance dances of the Chukchee, Yakuts, Ostyaks, and Koryaks, near the Bering Straits, aim at communion with demonic spirits, animals, and ancestors, for cure, rain, and in celebration of a successful hunt, seal or whale catch. To insure good hunting women may circle around the frenzied shaman, and the whole community join in orgiastic celebration. The shaman corresponds to the Eskimo *Angakok*, the *Kam* of Altai-Iran, the *Dervish* of Islam, and the American Indian *Medicine Man*, with similar powers.

Central Asia (Iran—Turkestan) combines the Siberian shaman complex with the fierce courtship and sword dances of the Caucasus and the technique of arm gesture and neck motion (*sundari*) of India.

India

At its apex the Hindu *Temple Dance* was one of the noblest and most gracious of rituals, by priestesses or Devadasis. In the *Alarippu* and the still extant *Tillana*, for instance, intricate footbeats, *Laghu*, accompany bends, *Bhangas*, and symbolic sinuous hand movements, *Mudras*. Dances represent the five incarnations of Siva, the love of Krishna and Radha. Today the religious dance is decadent, the Devadasis are lasciviously graceful courtesans.

The secular entertainers on streets and in palaces—the *Nautch* dancers—are obese and vulgar, though boy performers exhibit more vitality than women.

The little explored rites of aboriginal tribes continue to exist alongside the folk and religious dances of the Aryan upper castes: hunting dances of the Veddas of Ceylon, totemic mimes of the southern Dravidians, wedding celebrations of the southern Todas, and agricultural festivals of the eastern Mongoloid Mundas, Santals, Oraons, and northern agricultural Aryan peasantry. These last, as well as the *Kummi* and *Kolattam* folk dances of the south, have the elegance of gesture and foot-beat so characteristic of the famous temple and theater dances.

The Badagas still dance on live coals as a ritualistic trick. The Coorgs skip in circular *Sword Dances* and tremble in possession by Kālī. Brahmin priests dance the *Kathak*.

Southern India has witnessed a recent renaissance in the Kathakālī School of Dance. Within ancient traditions new dances are created, such as the *Lasyanatana*. Competent exponents tour the Occident in exotic and eloquent programs.

Tibet and Ceylon: Devil Dances

These powerful and original demon impersonations retain much of their aboriginal function of exorcism. In Tibet they are enacted by the Lāmas of Buddhist monasteries. Frightful animal masks represent evil spirits. All are grotesquely virtuoso, the legendary *Black Hat Dance* of Tibet consisting of highly controlled turning leaps in ingenious choreography. The *Acharyas* are dwarfs in a travesty of a weird old man and woman. Function is ritualistic.

China

Chinese dance is dying of old age, even in the theater, though this was revitalized by Mei Lan-Fang. The Cong Fu Cult, founded perhaps in the 3rd millennium B.C., is still being taught by priest physicians; it is a mystic healing cult of gymnastics. Twice a year priests dance in Confucian temples.

The Yao peoples of Yao province celebrate weddings, funerals, and other events with dance and ceremony. The Nau people of Kwangsi province have some folk dances, such as *The Mute and the Cripple*. The Lolos of southwest Yunnan skip in circles in their native villages. There is no true social dancing.

Yet the role of China is important as source of the *Bugaku*, the Japanese religious dance, introduced some 2000 years ago.

Japan

Japan represents one of the high points of Oriental dance in:

1) The religious *Kágura* of Shinto priestesses, derived from the divine dance of Ume-no-utsame to recall the Sun Goddess Amaterasu. The popularization of the *Kágura* founded the Kabuki, popular theater.

2) The classic Nō drama blended 800 years ago the existing popular songs with original dances, and is now mimed in the old tradition. It is derived from the trivial *Saru-gaku* or monkey mime and the *Den-gaku* or acrobatic dance developed by Buddhist priests. As in ancient Greece and in Burma, only men perform this aristocratic form of theater. A comic interlude between the melancholy Nō episodes is the *Kyōgen*.

3) The popular *Odori* is as old as the race. Outstanding are the *Uta-gaki, Genroku Hanani* (Cherry Blossom), *Honen-odori, Saibara;* the *Bon-odori,* a welcome to the dead by peasants; the *Tanabata-odori* by children; the *Gebon-odori* by merchants of Wakayama. The professional *Odori* dancer is the Geisha.

The *Ondo,* derived from the Odori, is danced as a social dance in the Japanese street festivals of San Francisco and Salt Lake City. The highly mimetic Japanese dance has a wide range of expression in stylized gestures, with a back-tilted posture and turned-up toes. As in all Oriental dance its precision results from long, arduous training.

Burma

The *Pwe* is a gay, rhythmically exciting festival. Professional girls and Loobyets or clowns dance the ordinary *Pwe* with acrobatic crouches and extreme arm curvatures. Village boys and girls dance the spectacular *Yein Pwe* at country and religious festivals.

Cambodia

Women mime fragile and aristocratic dance dramas, with a filigree of intricate steps and stylized gestures.

Malay Peninsula

Indonesia, from Malaya to Java, superimposes a cosmopolitan culture on an aboriginal substratum. Primitive puberty rites, the "gamber," tiger worship, and other animal dances of the Jakun and Sakai of Semang, recall similar rites of Madagascar and the South American Chaco. Shamanistic magic and cure dances relate to Siberia, the *main dabus* or fanatical sword dance to Islamic and North African exhibitions. There are Chinese and native operas and womens' dances of Japanese quality, and finally special Malayan-Balinese trance and *djoged* dances.

Bali

The *Djojeo* and *Legong*—curiously jerky and precise social dances—are for children. The *Kabyar* is a series of angular arm gestures for men in a seated position. The *Redjang* is a slow religious procession; the *Kris,* Dagger Dance, and *Sanghyang,* Trance Dance, are inspired by mystic possession.

Java

In the Javanese *Slendang* the sinuous arm movements are derived from India. The *Wayang Wong* is derived from the Javanese shadow-puppet play; human actors portray legends from the Hindu *Mahābhārata.* Men portray women. True folk types include *Nautch* by boys at fairs; *folk dances* of western Dutch Java; the

Bodjeje of religious origin, slow and controlled, or acrobatic, by boys and girls.

South Pacific

The expressive, symbolic arm and hand movements of the Gilbert Islands, Tahiti, Samoa, Hawaii are largely offspring of the *Mudras* of India. The Samoan *Marara,* Tahitian *Orare,* Hawaiian *Noho* or seated *Hula* by the Ho'o-pa group, and standing *Hulas, Alekoki* and *Ho'ohenokeia,* by the Olopa group are sublimations of courtship and mystic sensuousness.

Elaborate gestures prevail throughout the South Pacific. In Hawaii they serve as a symbolic code; in the rest of Polynesia and Melanesia they usually imitate daily actions realistically, with elegance on Easter Island, with violence in the Tuamotos, the Marquesas, and in the Maori and Samoan war dances. Both the seated and standing dances are usually stationary, with emphasis on hip, arm, and hand jerking or undulating; but war dancers of Samoa, Uvea, and Futuna leap about in drill-like maneuvers, and boys and girls of Rarotonga pair up in a round dance.

Australia

The declining aboriginal dances of Australia show several cultural levels of the most primitive nomadic hunters' dances: phallic, puberty, totemic, and hunting animal dances. There are the phallic *Caaro* dance of Wachandi men in the west, the totemic circle dances of the central Aranda, the realistic animal dances of the north and the southeastern Kurnai, the Kurnai boys' initiations, and the individual pan-Australian *Corroboree* for hunt, war, or greeting.

Philippine Islands

Despite the proximity of Japan, Indonesia, and the South Pacific islands, the Philippines resemble none. The war, wedding, courtship, head-hunting ensembles of the Igorots, Bontocs, Ifugaos, Kalinga, and Apayaos have a virile elegance. The Mohammedans, or Moros, have developed an excellent manly standard of mimetic performance, as the bee-hunting dance. The mestizo couple *bailes* of the Christian Filipinos derive mostly from Spain; only a few, as the *Balitao,* are reminiscent of native harvest festivals.

North Africa and Arabia

Outposts of Indian style to the west are the degenerate Arabian dances of the café, the *Chethat-al-Maharma,* and the related woman's *Danse du Ventre* of Tunis, Algiers, Egypt. Most Arabian dances extol feminine charm. Their posture stories are not set by tradition as in India, but are subject to individual creation.

Spain

Indirectly, by way of the Moors, Spain owes much of its eloquent though not symbolic gestures to India, as well as to the equally Asiatic Gipsies. In Latin-American dances of Spanish heritage this sinuousness is lost and only footwork retained. Otherwise India might be said to extend its influence around the world.

Asia Minor and the Balkans

These form an intermediate culture area between East and West.

Turkey ties up with the Orient in the vibrating head, arm, and torso movements of the women's *Çifte Tel,* with the wild Caucasian men's dance in the *Zeybek*, and with Palestine, the Balkans, and the coast of the Mediterranean in the open round for men and women, the *Yallï* (for girls alone, the *Trata*).

In the popular *Horra* of Palestine men and women similarly hold hands in a circle. Individualistic ancient dances have been recently revived: the *Sher*, *Sivchu*, *Pam Achat*.

The peasants of Armenia, Greece, the Balkans progress in closed circles, more often in semicircles or serpentine, with elegant steps and small, rhythmic jerks of head and shoulders. Men and women, placed *ad lib.*, hold hands, sometimes with kerchiefs, or link elbows or place arms on shoulders. The leader crouches, leaps, pirouettes, very like the famous Cossack dancer. The Rumanian *Hora* is more languorous than the emphatic Hebrew *Horra* or precise Serbian *Kolo* (circle).

These open rounds, or *Link Dances*, perhaps originated in Greece, from the *Choros*. The varied steps include hops, heelbrushes, grapevine on a foundation of a "double" right, a "simple" left. A special version is the *Chiotikos* for two women with intertwined arms, and the *Zabakelos* for one man with castanets. The traditional *Romaiika (Zyganos* and *Choros)* commemorates the suicidal Suliot women.

In the geographically arranged chart below, it will be seen that these dances extend horizontally across southern Europe to Catalonia. On the other hand, in a northerly direction, Asia Minor blends with the Caucasus.

European National Dances

Russia

This vast assembly of contrasting tribes, with its expanding boundaries, possesses the wild couple dances and fierce sword dances of Caucasian tribes; the acrobatically vigorous Cossack dances of Don and Ukraine; on its outskirts, the Carpathian, Lithuanian, Latvian, and Polish dances.

Ukrainian and Carpathian couples lift their knees high in cross polka and pas de basque, crouch, leap, stamp, fling their arms wide. Lithuanian, Latvian, Polish couples combine Slavic stamp and arm swing with ballroom steps and with the circular progression of the ancient round.

A new creation, *Yablochko*, the Russian Sailor's dance, follows the peasant tradition of solo interpolated into group activity; the *Orlitza* and other city products follow the ballroom trend.

Central Europe

Such fairly recent semi-peasant couples' rounds extend into central Europe, side by side with the vestiges of old religious rites. Each country displays a special kind of vigor. In Hungary the women are aloof and the men impetuous as in the Caucasus. Magyar and Czech dancers click their heels, twist their feet, the Bohemians with more leaning of the body and head.

Peasants of Germany and Austria shake the ground in boisterous gaiety, clap and leap in the famous *Schuhplattler*. Several Austrian country dances resemble west Slavic rounds: *Schwefelhölzl, Buamaschlag, Der Paschade Flugsummi*. But there is no grouping in the lusty *Drehtanz*, ancestor of the sentimental *Waltz*.

There is much variety in the relationship of partners.

In Czechoslovakia, for instance, partners can progress in anti-clockwise circle:

1) Face to face in double circle: *Maleni, Paterka, Javornik, Tancuj*.
2) Parallel, hands joined: *Černa Venka, Káčă*.
3) Girls backwards in single circle: *Trojky, Šáteček, Kdyš Jsem*, with kerchief.
4) One circles round the other: *Vrtěná*.

Holds are particularly varied in Bohemia, Scandinavia, above all Finland.

The Bohemian *Tancuj* is a closed face-to-face position, left shoulders touching, elbows horizontal.

Finland has hand grasps, single and double; arm grasps, hand above elbow; arm hooks; cross grasps, in back or front; holds at waist level or above the head; the Wormsö grasp with right hand round partner's waist, left hand on right shoulder.

The waist-shoulder grasp (man holds girl's waist, she his shoulders) is Hungarian. Partners are swapped in the *Strašak, Greifpolka, Wechselbayrische*, and Finnish *Old One from Laucka*.

Scandinavia

Scandinavia has preserved a few ceremonials, but observes festivals mostly with native versions of central European folk dances. The *Rounds* of the Norwegian Faroe Islands still enact interminable 11th century ballads, with a step resembling the *Branle*. Norway has revived them. Finland has adopted the *Sigurdsvaket* and others.

The special legacy of Sweden are its singing games. In general, Scandinavians favor gay and harmless pantomime, of flirtation (*Firtur*), rivalry (*Vingakersdans*), or mock fight (*Oxdansen, Degnedansen*). There has been much give-and-take in quadrille formations between Denmark, the British Isles, and France.

British Isles

English *Country Dances*, Irish and Scotch *Reels* (2/4) and *Jigs* (6/8) are the most ingenious group dances of Europe, numerically and geometrically, particularly in the Irish "cross overs" and "loops" and the English "heys." The floor patterns are executed with simple, though not monotonous, steps, an easy, erect carriage, light hand hold, arm movements motivated by the joining of hands. The solo *Jigs* and *Hornpipes*, on the other hand, exhibit dazzling footwork on one spot, toe-touchings, beats, turns, arms raised, or one hand on hip. The Scottish *Highland Fling* excels in concise energy and crispness.

There is little pantomime. The picturesque English titles are only song titles: "The Catching of Flees," "The Friar and the Nun." The Scottish *Cailleach an Dundain* does enact resurrection of a woman by a man. The *Sailor's Hornpipe* is a chantey in movement. The Irish *Waves of Tory* suggests the motion of waves. *Sword* and *Morris Dances* suggest their original combat mime.

The *Country Dance* has found its way to Holland in *Anna van Duinen* and *Drickusman*, to Sweden in the *Klappdans*, Bohemia in the *Judentans*, Portugal in *O Pretinho (Strip the Willow)*. Its fate in America will receive special discussion.

Southwest Europe: France, Iberia, Italy

France is the home country of the *Contre Danse* and *Cotillon*, which merged into the *Quadrille*. France and

England both claim the origin of this art form. Spain and Italy have taken them over. In fact, the *Seguidillas* are quadrilles.

Court dances of the Middle Ages and Renaissance originated in all of these countries, and were interchanged and propagated. Taken from the peasantry or from foreign lands, they have returned to their point of origin. Most of the regional dances of France descended from the old *Ronde, Branle, Bourrée, Gavotte.*

Italy dances these as well as borrowings from Spain. It is devoted to sentimental fragments of pantomime, with sighs and coquetry (*Bal d'l'Ahi*) and much exaggeration. These regional dances, as well as those of Spain, require special listing.

Besides its national dances, Spain shows great variety of style—from the simple folk type with sharp footwork of Aragon to the arrogant voluptuousness, hand and arm allurement of Andalusia, but with rhythmic complexity throughout. Portugal has the same equality of sexes in its gay folk dances. But Basque men overshadow the modest women with their tremendous leaps.

Court Dances

France	France	Italy	Germany
Estampie	(cont.)	Paduana	Medieval Firlefanz,
Carole	Gavotte	Saltarello	Hoppelvogel,
Baleries	Passepied	Triori	Krummereihen
Reverdie	Musette	Barriera	Quaternaria
Branle	Boccane	Piva	Allemanda
Basse Danse	Tambourin	Trescona	Volta
Gaillarde	Ecossaise	Rebeca	(from France)
Tordion		Colascione	became
Courante	*Spain*	Passamezzo	Drehtanz
(from Italy)	Pavana	Corrente	became
Rondeau	Sarabanda		Waltz
Volte	Chacona		
Bourrée	Passacalle		
Minuet	Villanesca		

Exotic Dances

Spain: Zambra, Zarabanda, Leyla from Arabia; Furlana from Friul; Canario, Tajaraste, Serinoque from Canary Islands; Rigodon from Martinique; Zambapaolo from West Indies; Habañera from Africa by way of Cuba; Guaracha from Cuba; Tango from Argentina.

Portugal: Guineo from Guinea; Batuque, Machicha, Lundum, Frevo from Africa through Brazil.

Italian Regional Dances

Various provinces have a typical dance: Lombardina of Lombardy, Bergamesca of Bergamo, Romana of Rome, Siciliana of Sicily, etc. Of special interest are:
Bologna: Ruggir, Baraban, Bal d'l'Ahi, Vetta d'Or, Girometta, Ballo della Catena.
Campagna: La Ciociara, Tarantella, Saltarello Neapolitano.
Sardinia: Douro Douro.

Spanish Regional Dances

Basque Provinces: Guipuzcoanas (S.), Aurresku, Atzesku, Zortziko, Muchikuok, Pasamanos, Arin Arin, Biribilketa. Carrica Dantza,

Asturias: Pasiegas (S.), Giraldilla, Pollos, Perlindango, Pandero, Careado, Saltón, Pericote, Corri Corri, Danza Prima.
Castile: Seguidillas, Bolero, Fandango, Zangano.
Galicia: Gallegada (S.), Muiniera, Serranilla.
Aragon-Navarra: Jota.
Catalonia: Sardana, Farandola, Filada, Contrapás, Ball Pla, Bolangera, Nyacras, Corranda, Eixada, Pila, Morrata, Ball de la Teya.
Valencia: Valenciana (S.), Xaquera Vella, Paradetes, Tarara, Jota.
Mallorca: Seguidillas, Copeo, Baile de la Xisterna.
Murcia: Murciana (F.), Parranda, Zangano.
Andalusia: Seguiriyas (S.), Sevillanas (S.), Malagueña (F.), Rondeña (F.), Granadina (F.), Jaleo, Panderos, Polo, Zapateado, Zorongo, Cachucha, Jarabe Gitano, Vito, Paso Doble.
   Cuadro Flamenco: Por Soleares (women), Farruca (men), Bulerias, Alegrías.
Many provinces have a classic *Seguidillas* (S.), but only southern Spain has the Flamenco tradition, *Fandango* (F.), and *Gitano* from the gipsy.

III. Dance Acculturation in the New World

For religious dance acculturation in the New World, see RITUAL DANCES.

Regional Dances (Bailes Regionales)

South America
Venezuela—*Joropo.*
Brazil—Gaucho *Chacarera;* ballroom *Batuque; Machicha, Frevo, Samba;* Negro influence: vodun *Macumba.*
Uruguay—Gaucho *Pericón.*
Paraguay—*Guató.*
Argentina—*Gato, Palito, Huella, Firmeza, Zamba; Media Cana;* ballroom *Tango;* English *Country Dance.*
Chile—*Cueca* or *Zamacueca.*
Peru—*Cashua, Huaynu* of Inca origin.
Ecuador—*Huaino, Sanjuanito* of Inca origin; *Fandango, Pasacalle* of Spanish origin; *Marinera,* similar to *Cueca.*
Colombia—Coast: *Porro, Cumbia, Gaita, Bullerengue, Paseo Vallenato.* Interior: *Bambuco, Pasillo, Guabina, Torbellino, Fandango, Pasacalle.*
Panama—*Tamborito.*
All these are uniformly a love play of meeting and pursuit, coquetry, and conquest, varying from the sombre *Sanjuanito,* headstrong *Cueca,* to lusty *Pericón.* Much use of the kerchief, like a lasso in *Pericón,* in joint grasp in *Guabina.* Occasionally in ballroom position, as in the stamping waltzlike *Joropo.*
Mexico
Yucatán—*Tunkul, Jarana Yucateca, Bomba Yucateca.*
Chiapas—*Las Chiapanescas, Jarabe Chiapas, Cachito.*
Oaxaca—*Chande, Pandería, Chilena* (Cueca), *Son* (Cuba), "*Djezz hawt,*" *Polka; Zandunga, Tortuga, Llorona* of Tehuantepec, Juchitán, Salina Cruz; *Jarabe Mixteco, Jarabe Yalalteco.*
Veracruz—*Huapangos,* especially *La Bamba; Danzón.* (Cuba); "*Djezz hawt.*"
Puebla—*Huapangos.*
Tlaxcala—*Jarabe Tlaxcalteco.*
Michoacán—*Jarabe Michoacano, Jarabe de la Botella, Las Sembradoras, Canacuas, Iguiris.*

European Social Folk Dances: Geographical Distribution

THIS TABLE IS TO BE READ LIKE A MAP, NORTHWEST IN THE UPPER LEFT, ETC. IT DOES NOT INCLUDE
DANCES ELSEWHERE DISCUSSED AND TABULATED, BUT REPEATS CERTAIN WIDELY DISTRIBUTED FORMS, TO
EMPHASIZE THEIR SPREAD. AN * PRECEDING THE NAME OF A DANCE DENOTES THAT THE DANCE IS NATIVE
TO THE PLACE THERE INDICATED.

SCOTLAND
Couple
Cailleach an Dudain
Scotch Polka
Solos
Sword Dance
Highland Fling
Hornpipe
Shean Treuse
Group
Strathspey
Reel o'Tulloch
Petronella
*Highland
Schottische
IRELAND
Solo
Hornpipe
*Jig
Group
Round (Donegal)
Longways
*(Antrim Reel)
Quadrille
(Fairy Reel)
PORTUGAL
Jogos de Roda
Country Dances
O Pretinho
Tirana
Pae de Ladrao
from ALGARVE
Coridinho
ESTREMADURA
Bailarico
DOURO
Rusga
Rabelo
ALL PROVINCES
Furlana
Verdegaio
Vira
Chamarita
*Folía
Gota
Fandango
SPAIN
Furlana
*Gitana
Schotish, Vals
*Jota
*Fandango
Galope
Folía
Cutilio
Cuadrillas
Contradanza Larga

NORWAY
Rounds
*Faroe Ballads
Gangar
Springar
Halling
Reels
Seksril
Sekstur
Kadriljs
Couples
Polka
Schottische
ENGLAND
Solo
*Hornpipe
Country Dances
Rounds
Newcastle
Longways
Sir Roger
Quadrilles
Strip the Willow
FRANCE
BRETAGNE
Branle
Gavotte
Triori
Dérobée
Jabadao
LIMOUSIN
Promenade
Lou Panliran
BRESSE
Branle Carré
Rigodon
DAUPHINÉ
Rondes Fermées
Rondes Ouvertes
MANOSQUE
Bravade
AUVERGNE
Bourrée
ROUSSILLON
Bails
Montagnardes
L'Entaillisade
Valse
Jota
Fandango
Lanciers
*Cotillon
*Quadrilles
*Contre Danse

SWEDEN
Singing Games
Rounds
Quadrilles
(Klappdans)
Couples
*Varsovienne
Swedish Schottische
Polka
DENMARK
Rounds
Kontras
Quadrilles
French Reel
Couples
Polka
Rainlander
Hopsa
Polonaise
Waltz
(Hukgestok)
GERMANY
Bayrische Polka
Quadrilles
Föhringer Kontra
Windmüller
Kegelquadrille
Rounds
Peasant Reigen
Couples
Langaus
Schwabentanz
Polkas—slow
Rheinländer
Polkas—fast
Greifpolka
Wechselbayrische
Galop
Rutscher
Dreher
Schuhplattler
AUSTRIA
Ländler
Steirer
Gedrehte Allemande
*Walzer
ITALY
Polesana
Giga
Galletta
Spagnoletto
Friulana
Gitana
Cotillon
Quadriglia
Cuntradanza

FINLAND
Rounds—
from Faroes
Longways
Quadrilles
Polka
Galop
POLAND
Couples
Komarinskaia
Orlitza
Kujawiak
Krakowiak
*Mazurka
*Polka
*Polonaise
*Rejdovak
Obertas
Imported
Walc Kaszubski
Wengierka
CZECHOSLOVAKIA
Couples—Rounds
*Polka
MORAVIA
Malení
Káča
Kam Ty Jedeš
Paterka
Sateček
Trojky
Longways
Ja Ked Sajanöska
Quadrille
Kanafaska
SLOVAK
Tancuj
Černa Venka
Janko
Vrtčná
CZECH
Kuzelka
Kdyš Jsem
Strašak
Reel
Motovidlo
(Chytavá)
HUNGARY
*Vengerka
Czárdás
Magyar Kettös
Magyar Keringö
Körmagyar
*Galop
Men
Sapka Tánc (Cap)
Campos Tánc
(Shepherd)
Csapacsolás
(clapping)

RUSSIA
Couples
Komarinskaia
Orlitza
Alexandrovska
Korobotchka
Oyda
LATVIA
Country Dances
Ackups
Sudmalinas
Jandalins
LITHUANIA
Couples
Suktinis
Klumpakojis
Kriputis
Dzuku
Kepurine
Kubilas
Kalvelis
Noriu Miego
Vengerka
Two lines
Našlys
Quadrille
Jonkelis
UKRAINE
Couples
Zbojecki
Kolomaika
Hrechaniki
Kinn Kuzi
Four men
Zaborotchez
COSSACKS
Hopak
Trepak
Krissachok
CARPATHIANS
Tatra
Czarkes
CAUCASUS
DAGHESTAN
Lezginka
Cherkesska
Tatarotchka
GEORGIA
Kundur Strogoi
Turkish Dances
AZERBAIJAN
Turkish Dances
ERIWAN
Armenian Dances
ANATOLIA
TURKEY
Solo
Çifte Tel
Zeybek

N
↑

European Social Folk Dances: Geographical Distribution (*cont.*)

(*Link Dances*)	(*Link Dances*)	(*Link Dances*)	(*Link Dances*)	(*Link Dances*)
SPAIN	FRANCE	ITALY	HUNGARY	TURKEY
BASQUE PROVINCES	ROUSSILLON	Douro Douro	Gyertyás Tánc	Yalli
Aurresku	Barbantane	YUGOSLAVIA	Sor Tánc	Trata
Soka Dantza	BAYONNE	Sockako Kolo	GREECE	ARMENIA
Zortziko	Pamperuque	DALMATIA	Chasapikos	Hoynar
CATALONIA	BÉARN	Kolo	Tsamikos	Hellene
Sardana	Branlou Bach	Deljaniček	Syrtos	Lepolele
Farandola	GASCOGNE	RUMANIA	Kritikos	PALESTINE
N	Rondes Ouvertes	Hora	Kalamatianos	Horra
	PROVENCE and	Maricara	(*Non-Link*)	(*Non-Link*)
	LANGUEDOC	Sarba Jancului	*Two girls*	Contras
	*Farandole	Braul	Chiotikos	Sher
		Ca la Breaza	*One man*	Sivchu
		Ratchenitza	Zabekelos	Pam Achat

Jalisco—*Jarabe Tapatío, Jarabe de la Botella, Las Espuelas.*

Nayarit—*Mitote* of Cora, Tepehuanes, Aztecs.

Chihuahua—*Jarabe Chihuahuano.*

Metropolitan—*Paso Doble* and other Spanish forms; *La Cucaracha, Jesucita, La Raspa.*

Southwestern United States

Mexican origin—*Jarabe Tapatío, Michoacano, Zandunga, Las Espuelas, El Vaquero, Chiapanecas, La Cucaracha, Jesucita, La Raspa.*

Colonial Spanish—*La Mestiza, El Palomo y la Paloma, El Jilote, La Camila, El Taleán.*

South American origin—*La Chilena* (Chilean, from Cueca), *La Cuna* (Argentina).

European origin—*Las Cuadrillas, Polka Cruzada, Galope, Varsoviana, Vals de la Escoba* (Broom), *Vals de los Paños* (Kerchiefs), *El Chote* (Schottische).

Philippines

Native with Spanish veneer—*Balitao, Tinikling, Candle Dance; Kakawati, Bulaklahan* (Flower Dances), *Boa* (Coconut).

Spanish Mestizo—*Surtida, Cariñosa* (Waltzes); *Rigaudon; Salacot* (Hat Dance).

Ballroom Dances from Latin America

Tango Argentine (by way of Paris), *Machicha* (Tango Brasilienne, also much expurgated) *Conga, Danzón, Son, Rumba, Zamba, Frevo.*

In the *Bailes Regionales* (regional couple dances) identification of native and foreign traits is fairly simple:

Native: Posture: straight back or stooped, man's hand cupped behind his back in Mexico; bent knees; impassive face; lowered eyes; shuffle, back pull; reticence. No castanets.

Spanish: *Zapateado* steps and variants, much of the music and costume, olé shouts.

Austrian: *Waltz* step and tunes (Chiapanecas, Candle Dance).

Polish: *Mazurka* step and music (Jarabe Tapatío).

Bohemian: *Polka* step (Jarabe Michoacano).

Russian: *Komarinskaia* step and music (Jarabe Tapatío), possibly crouches (Concheros).

Proportions vary from the thoroughly European *Jarabe Tapatío* of the charro and ranchero, and the haughty mestizo *Zandunga*, to the native *Canacuas.*

Negro influence is slight except on the Atlantic sea border: in the *Huapangos* of Veracruz and Tamaulipas, Mexico. In the West Indies and Brazil it outweighs the native Indian constituents.

In the cities the same partner dances are popular as in Europe and the United States (*Polka, Waltz,* etc.), and even in the villages a stiff version of jazz and the *Beer Barrel Polka* are making inroads: commonly called "*piezas.*" These embrace-dances contrast with the aloof contactless partner dances. Occasionally a perfect hybrid results. Few *bailes* are clearly indigenous: *Mitote, Huaino.*

American Indian Social Dances

The United States Indian has with one exception adopted only dances from other tribes. These he clearly recognizes as imported. *Squaw Dances* were always social. *Animal, War, Victory Dances,* and the *Grass Dance* have recently become secularized.

Native

Blackfoot *Horseback, Kissing, Begging.*

Shoshone *Peqowa Noqan, Banda Noqai, Biepungo Noqai (Lame), Waipe Noqa* (women).

Ute *Bear, Turkey, Lame, Dragging Feet, Round.*

Comanche *Horse, Dog, Love.*

Sioux *Hoop, Kahomini, Hatąka, Hahepi Wačipi, Begging.*

Kansa *Heluk Watci, Dali Watci* (women).

Kiowa *Snake, Rabbit, Owl, Brush.*

Shawnee *Deer, Quail, Fish, Leaf, Alligator, Drunken, Stomp.*

Sauk *Owl, Rabbit, Snake, Grapevine, Gourd, War, Victory, Two-step, Stomp.*

Fox *Swan, Snake, Mesquakie, War, Victory, Friendship, Stomp.*

Menominee *Rabbit, Partridge, Frog, Owl. Crawfish, Sunfish, Begging, Friendship, Forty-nine.*

Winnebago *Swan, Fish, Snake.*

Iroquois *Fish, Coon, Robin, Pigeon, Duck, Garters, Fishing, Marriage, Stomp.*

Cherokee *Ant, Raccoon, Partridge, Pheasant, Pigeon, Snake, Friendship, Stomp, Wood Gathering.*

Yuchi *Horse, Buffalo, Rabbit, Chicken, Duck, Buzzard, Leaf, Fish, Drunken.*

Creek *Buffalo, Horse, Rabbit, Duck, Chicken, Buzzard, Screech Owl, Alligator.*

Adopted

Fox *Snake* (from Shawnee).
Iroquois *Snake* (from Cherokee).
Yuchi *Leaf* (from Shawnee).

Widespread: Sioux *Grass Dance:* Blackfoot, Piegan, Gros Ventre, Crow, Omaha, Yankton to Chippewa, Winnebago.
Naslo'han Wacipi: Shuffling Feet: Teton Sioux, Assiniboin, Oglala, Cheyenne, etc.
Squaw Dance: Plains and Eastern Woodlands, including Wampanoag.
Feather Dance: Plains and Eastern Woodlands (still ritualistic among Navahos and Iroquois).

Social Dances of the United States

Ballroom dances are based largely on the One Step and Two Step.
From Europe—*Cancan, Chahut, Galop, Mazurek, Polka, Schottische, Varsouvienne, Waltz, Yale.*
Original—*Cakewalk, Fox Trot, Turkey Trot, Bunny Hug, Grizzly Bear, Shimmy, Boston* (from *Waltz*), *Charleston, Black Bottom, Castle Walk, Eight Step, Hoosier Hop, Lindy Hop, Big Apple, Trucking, Susie Q., Jitterbug, Jersey Bounce:* man swings and pivots woman.
Boogie Woogie: Mooch, Sand, Duck Walk, Camel Walk, Rochester, Fish Tail: partners dance separate.
Jitterbug and *Boogie* have from the Negro their flatfooted, grotesque abandon, hip and shoulder movement, and frequent acrobatics.

Rounds and Longways

In the West, *rounds* and *longways* are virtually nonexistent, except for old-fashioned ballroom dances loosely termed "rounds." In New England, however, the hybrid *Sicilian Circle* type is popular, and so are *"Contrys"* in two lines. Some of these are direct borrowings: *Petronella* from Scotland; *Pop Goes the Weasel* from England. Some are descendants: the *Virginia Reel* from *Sir Roger de Coverley* and *Kinkkaliepakko. Lanciers* and *Virginia Reel* are now confined to formal social affairs. *"Contrys"* and *squares* feature in the increasingly popular barn dances of summer resorter and New England rustic; circular *Kentucky Running Sets* pervade the South.

Square Dances

The development of the Square Dance is probably as follows:

Contre Danse Cotillon	Quadrille Country Dance	Kentucky Running Set	New England Quadrille Cowboy Square Dance

The Middle West partakes of qualities of both **East** and **West**.
Following are some distinctions between countries:
England: Formations set to music; couples numbered clockwise.

Walking, running, skipping, sliding, "simple," "double," "turn single."
Five parts, no visiting all round, at most adjacent couple.
Usually start with "double" forward to center and back; many forms of "hey," often as finish.
Longways preferred.
Great decorum.
Ireland: More steps, including jig and reel.
All formations found in America, including mill (wheel), crossovers.
Usually four parts, starting and ending with promenade.
Wealth of "heys"—half, whole, single, double, by couples, for three, in line, in circle, square chain.
Denmark: Honors, circle, swing, mill.
Gaiety.
Various grasps; boys lift girls.
Kentucky: Gliding, shuffling run or clog, hand-clapping.
Start circle, swing. Birdie in the cage, Ladies in the center, Lady round the lady, figure eight. End promenade, Grand right and left.
New England: Set formations, couples numbered crosswise.
Shuffling run and chassé (sashay).
Start honors, circle, swing. Includes ladies' chain.
End promenade or grand right and left and swing.
Lately the freer Cowboy dance has reinfluenced New England, which now has calls and looser coordination of figures and music.
The "Singing Quadrille" may be the origin of the prompter's calls.
West: Steps correspond only to musical phrasing.
Waltz and polka sometimes replace shuffling run.
Couples and figures counted anticlockwise.
Three parts, everybody being visited all around.
Honors, balance and swing, circle. All formations, including mill.
Ladies' chain only for four. Many forms of grapevine twist.
Picturesque calls—"Dive for the oyster," etc.
Gaiety, Spanish swagger.
Boys lift girls off ground.

IV. Comparative Choreography

Patterns

Circle and straight line constitute the fundamental elements of floor patterns. The figures all doubtless have their origin in vegetation symbolism, now forgotten in the elaborate quadrille.
Circle—round a sacred pole or object, following or opposing the sun's course. Interpretation of direction needs further evidence. Rites of death and penitence reverse into "widdershins" circuit, but so do social rounds at times.
Open Round (Serpentine, Zigzag, Spiral)—One released pair of hands converts the *Closed Round (Ronde Fermée)* into an *Open Round (Ronde Ouverte)* or *Link Dance.* Yet the former grows into the *Quadrille* by way of the *Branle Carré* and *Tambourin;* the latter opens into an arc or serpentine, or rolls into a spiral. Serpentine and zigzag mime the serpent, emblem of fertility.
Serpentine: Aztec *Dance for Chicomecoatl* (Seven Serpent); Arikara *Women's Dance; Pyrrhic Dance* of

Patterns

Circle

Country	Dance	Single Sunwise	Counter	Double	Multiple	To Center	Hey	
India	Dance of Todas	–	x	–	–	–	–	
	Coorg Sword Dance	–	x	–	–	–	–	
New Caledonia	Pilu Pilu	–	–	–	x	–	–	
Ecuador	Cachua	x	–	–	–	–	–	
Inca	—	–	–	–	–	–	–	
Venezuela								
Maipure	Marieyé	–	x	–	–	–	–	
	Baile de Cintas	–	x	–	–	–	x	Maypole
Otomaco	Gamo	–	–	–	x	–	–	
Mexico								
Aztec (old)	Quetzalcoatl Dance	–	–	–	x	–	–	
(modern)	Concheros	x	x	–	–	x	–	
Tarahumara	Rutuburi	–	x	–	–	–	–	
Huastecos	Matlanchines	x	–	x	–	x	x	Arch
Cora	Mitote	–	x	–	–	–	–	
Tarascan	Sembradoras	–	x	x	–	–	x	Maypole
Otomí	Volador	x	–	–	–	–	x	Maypole
Totonac	Volador	x	–	–	–	–	x	Maypole
U.S. Indians								
Yuma	Akil	–	–	Opposite	x	–	–	
Pueblo	Tablita	x	–	–	x	–	–	
Zuñi	Scalp Dance	–	x	–	–	–	–	Pole center
Shoshoni	Naroya	x	–	–	–	–	–	
Gros Ventre	Minataree	–	–	x	–	x	–	Fire center
S. Ute	Round Dance	x	–	–	–	–	–	
Sauk	Owl	x	–	x	–	x	–	
Fox	Shawnee Dance	–	x	–	–	x	–	
	Victory Dance	x	x	–	–	–	–	
Plains	Scalp Dance	–	–	x	–	–	–	Pole
	War Dances	–	x	–	–	–	–	
Iroquois	False Face	–	x	–	–	–	–	
Europe								
Basque	Cinta Dantza	–	–	–	–	x	x	Maypole
Catalonia	Bal del Ciri	–	x	–	–	x	–	
	Sardana	–	x	–	x	–	–	
Asturias	Perlindango	–	x	–	–	–	–	
	Danza Prima	–	x	–	–	–	–	Maypole
	Baile del Cordón	–	x	–	–	–	x	Maypole
Portugal	Chamarita	–	x	–	–	–	–	
Italy	Douro Douro	x	x	–	–	–	–	
	Galletta	–	–	–	–	–	x	
	Ballo della Catena	–	x	–	–	–	x	
France	Branle	x	–	–	–	de Malte	–	
	Filles du Village	x	x	–	–	–	–	
	Rondes Fermées	x	x	–	–	–	–	
	Treilles	–	–	–	–	–	x	
Switzerland	Weggis Dance	–	x	Parallel	–	x	–	
Germany	Reigen	x	x	x	–	–	–	
	Bändertanz	x	x	–	–	–	x	Maypole
Hungary	Mécs, Mécs	x	x	–	–	–	–	
	Szabad Péntek	x	–	–	–	–	–	Center figure
Czech	Kdyš Jsem	–	–	–	–	–	–	
Moravia	Czibulenka	–	–	x	–	–	–	
	Káča	–	–	x	–	x	x	
	Tancuj	–	–	x	–	–	–	

Patterns *(continued)*

Circle (continued)

Country	Dance	Single Sunwise	Counter	Double	Multiple	To Center	Hey
Slovak	Vrtěná	–	–	x	–	–	–
Lithuania	Kalvelis	x	x	x	–	x	–
Finland	Stigare	x	–	–	–	–	–
	Tantoli	–	–	x	–	–	–
Sweden	Bleking	–	x	x	–	–	–
Norway	Faroe Rounds	x	–	–	–	–	–
Denmark	Firtur	–	x	–	Mill	–	–
England	Newcastle	x	x	–	x	x	–
	Peascods	x	x	–	–	x	–
	Sellenger's Round	x	x	–	x	–	x	Maypole
Ireland	Donegal Round	x	x	–	–	–	x
	Piper's Dance	x	x	x	x	x	x
	Bonfire Dance	x	x	–	–	x	–
	Seisir-Dheag (Quadrille structure)	x	x	–	Multiple	x	x

Longways

Country	Dance	Meet	Parallel	Down center	Cross	Cast off	Serpent	Dos-à-dos	Mill	Circle	Corners	Arch	Hey
Australia	Molonga	x	–	–	x	–	–	–	–	–	–	–	–
Venezuela	Yapuraro	x	–	–	x	–	–	–	–	x	–	–	–
Mexico													
Puebla	Quetzales	–	x	–	x	–	x	–	–	–	x	–	–
	Toreadores	–	–	–	x	–	x	–	–	x	x	–	–
	Negros	–	x	x	x	–	x	–	–	–	–	–	x
	Santiaguitos	x	x	x	x	x	x	x	–	x	–	–	for 2
Michoacán	Negritos	–	–	–	x	x	x	–	–	x	–	–	–
México	Arrieros	–	x	–	–	x	x	–	–	x	–	–	–
	Moros	x	–	–	x	x	–	–	–	x	–	–	–
Sonora	Matachini	x	x	–	x	x	x	x	–	x	–	–	–
Europe													
Spain	Los Seises	x	x	x	x	x	x	x	–	–	x	x	x
	Contradanza	x	x	–	x	–	x	–	x	x	–	x	x
Basque	Ezpata Dantza	x	–	–	x	x	x	–	x	x	x	x	x
Portugal	Mouriscada	x	x	–	x	x	–	–	–	–	–	x	–
France	Bourrée	x	–	–	x	–	–	–	–	x	–	–	–
	Contre	x	–	–	x	x	x	–	x	x	–	x	x
Ireland	Cor Aentrium	x	–	x	x	–	–	–	x	–	–	–	–
	Bridge of Athlone	x	x	x	–	x	–	–	–	–	–	x	–
	Rinnce Fada	–	–	x	–	x	–	–	x	–	–	–	–
	Harvest Jig	x	–	–	x	–	–	–	x	x	–	–	–
	Gates of Derry	x	–	x	–	–	–	–	x	–	–	x	–
England	Morris	x	x	x	x	x	x	x	–	x	x	x	x
	Black Nag	x	x	x	x	–	–	x	–	–	x	–	x
	Trenchmore	x	x	–	–	x	–	–	–	–	x	x	–
	Pick up Sticks	–	–	x	x	–	–	–	–	–	–	–	x
	Nonesuch	–	–	x	–	–	–	–	–	–	–	–	x
	Sir Roger de Coverley	x	–	–	–	–	–	x	–	–	x	–	x

Longways (continued)

Country	Dance	Meet	Parallel	Down center	Cross	Cast off	Serpent	Dos-à-dos	Mill	Circle	Corners	Arch	Hey
Finland	Harvest Dance	–	–	x	x	x	–	–	–	–	–	–	x
	Kinkkaliepakko	–	–	x	–	–	x	–	–	–	x	–	–
U.S.													
New England	Virginia Reel	x	–	x	–	x	x	x	–	–	x	x	–
	Lady of the Lake	–	–	x	x	x	–	–	–	–	–	–	–
	Green Mountain Jig	–	x	x	–	x	–	–	–	–	–	–	–
	Irish Hornpipe	–	–	x	–	–	–	–	x	–	–	–	x
Southwest	Vals de los Paños	x	–	–	x	–	–	–	–	–	–	–	x
and Mexico (mestizo)	La Bamba	x	x	x	x	x	–	x	–	–	x	–	–

Quadrilles and Squares

Country	Dance	Forward-Back	Circle	Mill	Cross	Divide [a]	Arch	Hook [b]	Promenade	Swing	Hey
France	Tambourin	–	x	–	x	–	x	x	x	x	x
	Lanciers	x	x	x	–	–	x	x	x	x	x
Germany	Föhringer Kontra	–	x	–	–	–	–	–	–	x	x
	Schneidertanz	–	x	–	–	x	x	–	–	x	x
Denmark	Contra and Quadrille of Slagelse	–	x	x	–	–	–	–	–	x	x
	Linen Dance	–	x	x	x	x	–	–	–	x	–
	Oxcow	–	x	x	x	–	x	x	–	–	x
Finland	Pellinge Quadrille	x	–	–	x	–	–	–	x	–	x
	Räisälä Sappo	x	x	x	–	–	–	x	–	–	–
England	Chelsea Reach	x	x	x	–	–	–	–	–	–	x
	Oranges and Lemons	x	x	–	–	–	–	x	–	–	x
	Hunsdon House	x	x	x	–	–	–	–	–	–	x
	Dull Sir John	–	–	–	x	x	–	x	–	–	x
Ireland	Fionnala	x	x	x	x	–	x	x	x	x	x
	Cor Achtair	x	x	–	x	–	–	–	x	x	x
U.S.											
New England	Plain Quadrille	x	x	x	–	–	–	–	x	x	x
	Portland Fancy (also Longway)	–	x	x	x	–	–	–	x	–	x
West	Divide Ring and For'd Up Six	x	x	–	–	x	–	–	x	x	x
	Old Arkansaw	–	x	–	–	–	–	–	x	x	x
	Inside Arch and Outside Under	–	x	–	–	–	x	–	x	x	x
	Butterfly Whirl	–	–	x	–	–	–	–	x	x	x
	Star by the Right	–	x	x	x	–	–	–	x	x	x
New Mexico	Las Cuadrillas	–	x	–	x	–	x	–	–	x	–
	Polka Cruzada	–	–	x	x	–	–	–	–	x	–
	El Taleán	–	x	x	–	–	–	–	–	–	x

a Divide: a couple walks across and separates, passing between either the opposite or side couples.
b Hook: a pivot with linked elbows.
  American Soldiers' Joy and Sicilian Circle combine a four-hand reel with a round.
  America, Denmark, and Ireland also have, respectively, the grapevine twist, knot, and loop.

Greek Klephts; Catalan *Ball de la Teya* (flame). Link dances of Mediterranean (see EUROPEAN NATIONAL DANCES above). Sauk and Fox *Snake Dance;* Sauk *Grapevine;* Cherokee *Snake, Pigeon, Ant;* Kwakiutl *Children's Dance.* Mexican children's *A la Vibora.*

Zigzag: Imerina of Madagascar *Puberty Dance;* Gran Chaco *Ghost Dance;* Chippewa *Bean Dance;* Santa Ana Pueblo *Histiyani Aiyadots;* Italy *Lo Zigo Zago;* France *Villanelle, Beaujoyeux;* Majorca *Ball de la Xisterna* (girls).

Stationary Line or Lines—Yurok *Jumping Dance,* Maidu *Turtle,* Pueblo *Kachina,* Fox *Thunder,* Bohemia *Kačer.*

Multipe Lines—African *War Dances,* Maori *Peru Peru;* massed effects: Plains *Buffalo;* Irish *Harvest Time Jig* (three lines), *Siege of Ennis* (many lines of four, very spectacular).

Two Opposing Lines—Joining or conflict of two forces, male and female, summer and winter, light and dark, etc. Characteristic of battle dances, especially when associated with vegetation. Play of sexes in longways.

Hey—Combination of two lines and serpentine, fructifying interplaiting of natural forces, also in plaited swords. English *Maypole Dances* are vestiges of double circuits around a sacred tree, as also the Spanish *Baile de Cintas* or *del Cordón,* spread to Venezuela and to Mexico, where, however, it may also be indigenous. The Basque *Ezpata Dantza* and Yaqui *Matachini* often wind a maypole, as part of the Pyrrhic *Morisca* rite.

Arch—The green bough or leafy bower. Spain, Portugal, Mexico *Arcos.* Basque *Arkuxtxikiak.* German *Schäfflertanz* (whole hoops).

Games: Hungary *Green Branch, Green Leaf;* Germany *Die Goldene Brücke;* England *Oranges and Lemons, London Bridge, Needle's Eye;* Mexico *Santo Domingo, Amadrus Señores, Melón y Sandía.*

Numerical Variety

The couple and the eight person quadrille or longways are the most common forms. But numbers are varied, up to the "as many as will" formation.

Three: Moravia *Trojky;* France *Écossaise Triolet;* Italy *Galletta;* Denmark *Crested Hen, Peat Dance, Three Men's Reel;* Sweden *Vingakersdans;* Norway *Krossardans, Mountain March;* Scotland *Reel of Three;* Ireland *Galway Reel, Cor na Gaillimhe;* Argentina *Palito.*

Four: (Two Couples): Denmark *Kydholm Dance, Little Man in a Fix;* Scotland *Reel O'Tulloch, Foursome Reel;* Ireland *Fourhand Reel, Fionala, Humors of Brandon;* England *Parson's Farewell, Saint Martin's, Althea, Heartsease.*

Five: Denmark *Five Dance.*

Six: Denmark *Six Dance, Figure Eight, Pear Waltz, Triangle, Seksril;* England (best) *Black Nag, Grimstock, Adson's Saraband, Morris;* Ireland *Spinning Wheel, Cor Seisir* (Fairy Reel).

Nine (Three one sex, six other): Denmark *Tinker's Dance;* Finland *Holola Polka, Nine Persons' Post.*

Ten: Finland *Ten Persons' Polka.*

Twelve (eight boys, four girls): Finland *Post Dance* (six couples), *Harvest Dance;* Ireland *Piper's Dance* (ingenious), *Twelve Hand Reel.*

Sixteen (double quadrille): Finland *Pellinge Quadrille, Kontra, Osterbinsk Four Corners;* Ireland *Cor Seisir Dheag* (break up into four small circles).

Variation in Style

Despite the universality of certain choreographic elements, each people has its own technique, expressive of its character and way of life. Japan and Java use arms and hands with a turned-out stance; North Africa, vibration of the breast and flanks; Negro Africa, sweeping acrobatics, with swayed back; Europe and the American Indian, a straight back, much use of feet and legs with knees forward; India and its sphere of influence, the entire body, knees out in Asia, in Spain, forward, with a swayed back.

Beyond such generalization, the bounding aboriginal Santal of India contrasts with the hip-swaying Nautch girl; the erect and straight-kneed Morris dancer with the stealthily advancing, relaxed yet pulsating Plains Indian. The gentle horizontal glide of the Otomí Indian is very different from the powerful impact and rebound of the dynamic Yaqui.

Equally varying is the role of the woman, on an equal footing with the man in northern Europe, even eclipsing him in Andalusia; but in the Caucasus, Bavaria, Catalonia, the island of Ibiza, among American Indians, slowly revolving, retreating, shuffling, during the vehement gyrations of the man.

These contrasts differentiate dances which on analysis may have the same patterns, steps, and structural devices.

Steps

Human imagination has devised in the folk dance every step within physical possibility. Virtually no step is universal property—even the common stamp step does not occur among the Kwakiutl. The two step spreads through Europe and the Americas, but Mexicans accent it with a heelbrush. Again, few steps are unique—the Spanish "vuelta quebrada" (renversé), the Magyar heelclick practically (except the Mexican toreadores). Many steps are typical of certain nationalities, but do not occur in others.

"Double to side": *Branle,* Faroe Islands *Rounds,* Otomí *Santiaguitos.*

Pas de Basque: Basque, Russia, Hungary, Scotland *Sword,* Mexico *Concheros.*

Heeltoe Rock: Hungary *Bokázó,* Scotland *Highland Fling,* Mexico *Concheros, Jarabe Tapatío.*

Pat-step: American Indian, *Boogie* (the latter with hip action).

Step-heel-toe-heel: India, Yaqui *Deer, Boogie.*

Toe-touching: *Hornpipe, Jig, Concheros, Jarabe Tapatío.*

Turning Leap: Santals, Tibetan *Devil Dance,* Slavic Dances.

Skip: Impulse down and up among Coorgs of India, up and forward in England, with forward pull in Russia, with back pull among American Indians.

Acrobatics

Some feats of strength serve to exhibit prowess; others, as the leap, to further the growth of crops. Or they result from trance-induced loss of inhibitions.

Crouch: Borneo Kayans; Persians, Burma *Pwe;* Tibet *Skeleton Dance;* Russian *Cossack;* Serbian *Kolo* (leader); Greece leader; Spain *Charrada;* Scotland *Hornpipe;* Switzerland *Hocketanz;* Gran Chaco girls of Pilaga; Mexican Aztecs, modern *Concheros;* Apache gahe; Kiowa *Squat Dance.*

Leap: Maori *Peru Peru;* Africa *War Dances;* Eastern Archipelago *War Dance;* Russia "Prisjadka"; Hungary *Szolo;* leader of *Link Dances; Seven Jumps* (Germany, Holland, Denmark); Basque *Zaspi Jausiak* (seven jumps), *Aurresku;* Bavaria *Schuhplattler;* Norway *Halling,* Midsummer Fire Leaps.

Kick: *Aurresku; Sardana; Halling;* Brittany *Triori* (women); Catalonia *Camada Redona* (man's leg over girl's head), also Sweden *Daldans;* Mexico *Jarabe Tapatio.*

Lift Girl: Moravia *Rozek, Kanafaska;* Naples *Saltarella;* Spain *Jota al Aire, Sardana* (Corranda Alta); France *Branle de l'Official;* Denmark *Firtur;* American *Cowboy Dances.* African dancers also throw girls about.

Special Feats: Stilt-dancing of Cameroon; Oaxaca (*Zanco*), formerly Aztecs.

Hammock Dance, Sierra Leone, Africa.

Blanket Tossing Dance, Eskimos of Baffin Bay.

Human Pyramids of Spanish *Mojiganga* and ancient Aztecs.

Spiral descent from pole of Mexican *Volador.*

Structure

Rhythmic Patterns

Rarely do steps follow musical rhythms to the letter, the self-accompanied *Concheros* being an exception. A regular beat is the rule. The Negro dance and Boogie may syncopate. Spanish heels, castanets, finger-snapping, handclapping form complex counter-rhythms. The accent may recur every second, third, or fourth beat, rarely at irregular intervals; on the second beat of the measure (*Sarabanda, Mazurka*); the last beat of a phrase (Russia); or be absent (*Square Dance*). Counter-accents occur in 2/4 against 3/4 of *Guabina* and *Llorona,* and in the Yaqui *Matachini,* with a 15-measure phrase against 16 of the music. Spaniard and American Indian often suddenly change tempo and meter.

Common rhythmic units are two short and a long (*Two Step, Zamba, Rumba*), three steps and a skip (*Polka*) or tap ("*double*") or brush (*Quetzales*) or kick (*Conga*); iambic long and short (*jig, slide, galop*).

Form

1) Crescendo: Increase of intensity to the saturation point is typical of "primitive" dancing: Africa, often the American Indian. This is the most rudimentary form.

2) The development of dominant themes into a structure is a sophisticated device, as in the Tibetan *Black Hat Dance.*

3) Stretto (the contraction of rhythmic units): *Siebenschritt* of central Europe: 7 steps forward and back, 3 each side, turn.

4) Two-part phrase: Finland *Ålands Flicka;* Sweden *Bleking, Tantoli;* Germany *Herr Schmidt;* Austria *Strohschneider;* Bohemia *Komarno;* Lithuania *Noriu Miego;* Mexico *La Raspa:* forward alternation of heels, then hook and swing.

5) Binary form of slow and fast: *Zyganos* and *Chorós, Mazurek* and *Obertas, Lassu* and *Gyors* (Hungary), *Schwabentanz* and *Dreher, Pavana* and *Gaillarda, Gangar* and *Springar.*

6) Thematic alternation: *Minuet, Rondeau,* Fox Indian *Bean Dance.*

7) Medley of figures: *Jarabe Tapatio, Jarabe Michoacano.*

8) Logical succession of figures: Three part *Square Dance,* Four part *Irish Reel* (Opening, Body, Figures, Finish), Five part *Country Dance, Lanciers* (La Dorset, Victoria, Les Moulinets, Les Visites, Les Lanciers).

9) Grouping of dances into a kind of suite, involving dramatic climax:

Surtida (Birgoire, Camantugol, Tambururay, Haplin, Ligui, Voluntario, Incoy, Estrella, Salpumpati): courtship drama.

Morris (Laudnum Bunches, Bean Setting, Rigs o'Marlow, Shepherd's Hey, Constant Billy): vegetation conflict.

Ezpata Dantza (Yoakundia, Zortzikoa, Ezpata Zokua, Makil Aundiak, Banakoa, Binakoa, Txonkórinka): apotheosis of combat.

Such elaboration leads on the one hand to the orchestral suite, on the other into the mimed drama.

Survival and Revival

In many parts of the world traditional rustic dances are being accepted whole-heartedly in urban areas. Folk dance societies have sprung up like mushrooms, starting with the English Esperance Girls' Working Club. Valuable collecting and teaching has been accomplished by the Danish Society for the Promotion of Folk Dancing, the National School of Irish Dancing, the Jugendbewegung, the shortlived Mexican School of Indigenous Dance; in the United States by the Country Dance Society, City Folk Dance Society, Community Folk Dance Center of New York, Youth Hostels, Civic Centers, recreation programs in parks; internationally by the Y.M.C.A., Y.W.C.A., Y.M.H.A.; during World War II the U.S.O.

In America groups from many countries practice at international centers or special headquarters. Native traditions have been upheld in various colonies: Slavs, Germans, and Irish in Pennsylvania; French in Canada and Louisiana; Scandinavians in Minnesota, Iowa, North Dakota, and Seattle, Wash.; Spaniards and Mexicans in California, New Mexico, and Texas.

A larger public is reached by folk festivals, such as the National Folk Festival, formerly held in Washington, D.C., now in St. Louis, Mo., the Mountain Folk Festival of Asheville, N.C.; the programs of the Berea Mountain School, Ky.; the Summer Dance Camp in Buzzards Bay, Mass.; the Monadnock Folkways Summer School, N.H.; also the more professional series at museums, especially the American Museum of Natural History in New York, and at the Ethnologic Dance Center. Also, white friends of the Indians are arranging increasingly numerous powwows at convenient centers. Except in the New Mexico pueblos, the Indians themselves are becoming less averse to white visitors to their local powwows.

In Latin America gala gatherings convenience the tourist: near Lima, Peru, the *Fiesta of Amancaes;* in Bolivia the *Fiesta of Copabacabana;* in Masaya, Nicaragua, the *Fiesta of San Geronimo;* in Guatemala the *Fiesta of Chichicastenango;* near Oaxaca, Mexico, the *Guelaguetza* (*Fiesta del Cerro*). But besides these, the ancient religious celebrations continue, without regard for spectator value, as sacred pilgrimages, even at great accessible fairs: Guadalupe, Remedios, Amecameca, Tepalzingo, Papantla, San Juan de los Lagos, San Miguel de Allende in Mexico.

Creative Aspects of Folk Dance

Communal dance is growing into new forms, largely due to the ingenuity of creative leaders.

1) New combinations on old models, especially *Cowboy Squares* and *Lumberjack Stags*.

2) American *Play Party Games:* formed on frontier of Tennessee, Iowa, Nebraska, Missouri, Texas. Country people play games with words, tunes, dance figures, dramatic action, jingles, ballads, popular songs, calls—all with a medley of realism and nonsensical antics.

3) Children's *Singing Games:* new versions of these remnants of ancient ritual.

4) Improvisatory *Flamenco* performances.

5) Improvisatory *Jitterbug* and *Boogie Woogie:* hypnotic American folk dance.

6) Improvisation and original step combinations: Sioux *Kahomini*, Fox *Snake* and *Eagle Dance*, other American Indian dances.

Ritual may remain immutable for centuries. But changing circumstances, mixture of races and religions bring innovations. The Pawnee *Iruska* (Fire Dance) grew out of the Dakota-Ojibwa *Heyoka* and Omaha-Osage *Crow-belt*, and developed into the Arikara *Hot Dance* and Plains *Grass Dance*, now secularized, thence into the Central Algonquian *Dream Dance*, mingled with Christian ideology. Recently recovered Palestine has renovated its ancient heritage. Peru has instituted a flashy modern vintage *Fiesta de la Vendimia* in March, near San José de Surco. Contemporary events intrude into the masquerade of the one-time sacred *Carnival* and *Mardi Gras*.

Eventually *Komos, Kágura, Morisca, Cuadro Flamenco, Barn Dance, War Dance* and *Fiesta* accumulate spectators, interpolate the spoken word, and end up as theatrical spectacle, elaborate and meaningless in proportion to the disappearance of practical value.

GERTRUDE PROKOSCH KURATH

Dancers An American Indian name for the constellation commonly known as the Pleiades: so named for the constant twinkling of its stars. Explanatory myths about the Dancers occur especially among the North American Cherokees, Caddos, Micmacs, and Iroquois. These people also perform dances in imitation and memory of their lost dancers. An Onondaga story tells of a group of children dancing in the woods, warned by the chief to stop, and refused food by their parents because they would not stay home to eat. One day as they danced they began to rise and whirl through the air. The parents ran out of the houses with food, calling to them to come back. But the children danced higher and higher, and now dance forever in the sky. In a Seneca variant the eleven sons of a hunter were beguiled at night into joining the dance of the sky spirits. Once dancing, they could not cease dancing and were carried into the sky. Finally the Moon, pitying their fatigue, changed them into a group of fixed stars and put them in charge of the New Year festival, to dance over the council house for three days at that time. In a Blackfoot (Algonquian) story the dancers were seven young men

who danced around a field of sacred grain all night to guard it. For other Pleiades origin stories, see PLEIADES.

dance with reeds A motif found in the Coyote cycle of all Apache Indian folktale. The Chiricahua Apache version is typical: After Coyote was blinded, he was going along, and walked into a bunch of reeds in a swampy place. The reeds were blowing and swaying in the wind; so Coyote yelled and danced with the reeds all night. In the morning he climbed out of the reeds and came to a camp. The Lipan Apache story is the same, except that Coyote is not blind, and he personifies the reeds as reed-girls. Compare DANCING BULRUSHES.

dancing bulrushes The motif of a number of North American Indian trickster stories of the Plains and Lake regions in which the trickster sees the bulrushes waving and dancing in the wind and dances with them until he is exhausted. Compare DANCE WITH REEDS.

dandelion (from French *dent de lion*, lion's tooth). In Maryland, when the dandelions do not open in the morning, it will rain. When there is no wind, yet the down flies off the stalk, it will also rain. In England an infusion of the roots is used as a blood purifier and spring tonic; it is also good for the liver and rheumatism. Wine made from the flowers is generally believed to be a tonic. In Ireland dandelion is regarded as a tonic and remedy for heart disease. The juice of the stalks rubbed on warts drives them away. In Silesia dandelions gathered on St. John's (Midsummer) Eve possess enhanced medicinal properties and the power of keeping off witches.

There is much children's lore connected with the dandelion. Blowing the seed-heads will tell the time: as many puffs as it takes to blow them all away is what o'clock it is. If a child can blow all the seeds away in three puffs, his mother does not want him; if some remain, he had better run home. How much your sweetheart is thinking of you can be told by the amount of down remaining after one puff. Picking a dandelion, or wearing one, makes a child wet its bed (the dandelion is sometimes called piss-a-bed).

Dandoo The title often used in America for *The Wife Wrapt in Wether's Skin* (Child #277): so named from the nonsense syllables of the refrain.

Dangbe The snake *tauhwĭyŏ* (ancestor) or sib founder and deity of a famous old Dahomean family: still worshipped in Dahomey, especially at Whydah. Dangbe is Dã, but distinguished from Dã in that Dangbe is serpent life *per se*, while Dã is the living quality or essence in all things living and sinuous. There are cult houses and shrines for Dangbe in Dahomey. One of the most conspicuous elements of the West African Dangbe cult is the practice of distinterring the skulls of the dead to serve as altar receptacles for offerings to the deified ancestors (*tovodų*). Sib members are ritually called Dangbevi, i.e. children of the snake Dangbe. Dangbesi, literally Dangbe-wife, is the term applied to initiated cult devotees. See DAGOWE.

Danu or **Dana** (genitive *Danann*) In Old Irish mythology, the mother of the gods, the Tuatha Dé Danann or people of the goddess Danu. She has been the subject of much speculation, interpreted variously: 1) as Anu, the goddess of plenty mentioned in Cormac's *Glossary* and for whom are named the Paps of Anu, two mountains in Kerry; 2) as Brigit, daughter of Dagda, and thus mother of Brían, Iuchair, and Iucharbar, called the three sons of Danu (this MacCulloch thinks is through confusion with the word *dán*, meaning art, knowledge, poetry, of which Brigit was patron); 3) as some possible, still earlier earth mother or underworld fertility deity who mothered the gods; and 4) tentatively, as ancestor of the Black Annis of Leicestershire who required human victims. Danu is identified with the Dôn of Brythonic mythology.

danza A Spanish term for dance. It refers to special couple dances in several Latin American countries, danced in modern ballroom position. The music is in duple time, in Puerto Rico with a syncopated accompaniment, in Mexico with a tango rhythm. In the 15th, 16th, and 17th centuries the term danza was used for Spanish court dances in distinction from *bailes* or popular dances. It is also applied to religious dances. [GPK]

danzón An amplification of the Spanish word for dance: a couple dance of African origin, popular in Cuba and Veracruz, Mexico. Modern instruments—brass and woodwind and a *güiro* or notched gourd—burst into exuberant, primitive rhythms. With an expression of almost religious solemnity, the dancers betray a subtle undercurrent of eroticism in their small one and two steps. [GPK]

daoine maite Literally, the good people: the fairies of contemporary Irish folklore.

daoine side Literally, the people of the mounds: the tall divine folk of Old Irish mythology, the Tuatha Dé Danann. See AES SÍDE.

Daramulum In Australian mythology, the son or deputy of Baiame to whom he is sometimes troublesome. Also, he is the chief totemic ancestor of the Yuin tribe. The name occurs among tribes of New South Wales. [KL]

Dardanus The mythical ancestor of the Trojans; son of Zeus and Electra. He was an Arcadian who married Chryse and received as dowry the Palladium given to Chryse by Athena. Having killed his brother, Dardanus fled to Samothrace, and from there during the flood crossed to the Troad on a raft or a blown-up hide. There he married Batea, daughter of Teucer, and succeeded him on the throne. He was thus the ancestor of Æneas, and as son of one of Hera's rivals caused her to side against the Trojans, his descendants, in the war at Troy.

Daśaratha In Hindu mythology, the childless king of Ayodhyā who performed the horse sacrifice (Aśvamedha) after which four sons were born to his three wives. According to the *Rāmāyaṇa*, Vishṇu gave Daśaratha a bowl of nectar which he divided among his wives. He gave Kauśalyā half and the other two each a quarter. Thus Rāma, son of Kauśalyā, shared half the nature of Vishṇu, while the others shared in proportion to the amounts of the nectar their mothers had drunk.

Dasent, Sir George Webbe (1817–1896) Englishman and Scandinavian scholar, assistant editor of the *Times* (1845–1870). He published translations of Norse tales, *Popular Tales from the Norse* (1858) and *Tales from*

the Fjeld (1896). Among his excellent translations are Asbjörnsen's *Hen who went to Dovrefjeld to save the World* and *Cock who fell into the Brewing-Vat*, examples of the cumulative tale.

date Among the ancient Egyptians, the Sumerians, and the Taoists of China the date palm was considered the tree of life, and among the Taoists, also the symbol of offspring. The Hindus thought the tree possessed intelligence and was only one step removed from the animal kingdom. The genus name of this tree is *Phoenix*, from an ancient belief that if the tree falls from age or is burnt, it will grow again greener than ever. In some places Mary is reputed to have given birth to Jesus under a date palm, and a new mother must eat three dates. The root boiled and mixed with flour makes a poultice for swellings and is used to regulate the bowels. The wood is used for building, the leaves are woven into numerous articles, the juice of the tree is used in making palm wine. The fruit is the staple food of many peoples, the seeds are ground into an oil, and one species produces a sugar. See TREE OF LIFE.

datu The Moro (Philippine Islands) name for a chief. The word datu is used generally in the Philippine Islands for a chief and in Sumatra for a shaman, who frequently is also a chief. Among the Bagobo the datu holds his position because of his personal wisdom and bravery and, of primary importance, with the consent of the spirits. (Among the Bataks of Sumatra originally there were no priests, but after the introduction of Hinduism a kind of priesthood was instituted. These datu are priests according to Loeb in so far as they hand down the main part of the Hindu ritual and learning.) As datus their duties actually resemble those of the shaman. The datu is a physician who practices curing magic. He is also a clairvoyant and a weather-maker. He conducts public ceremonies, summons the spirits in a secret language, and determines the propitious time for war-making.

datugad Literally, in Irish, a color or dye; coloring. The word is often applied to the magical power some people seem to have in always being dealt the best cards in a card game, i.e. the "coloring" of the cards.

David King of Israel about 1000 B.C.; father of Solomon: perhaps the greatest hero of Hebrew tradition in all respects. David possesses many of the attributes of the folk hero: his parentage was high but obscured; he was a despised youngest son; he served as a shepherd; he was the slayer of giants and beasts; his weapons were magical; he was a great musician; his principal failing was caused by his love of women; his son rebelled against him, etc. His story is told in I and II *Samuel*, I *Kings*, and I *Chronicles*; he is also said to be the author of many of the *Psalms*. Under David, the Kingdom of Israel achieved eminence among its neighbors (in a weak period of Egyptian dominance of the region), an eminence exceeded only by the glory of the kingdom under Solomon.

Jesse, David's father, took a liking to one of his slave girls. But Nazbat, the lawful wife of Jesse, disguised herself as the slave girl, and thus David was conceived. When David was born, however, his mother let it be thought that he was the son of the slave. A legend states that the child was destined to live only 3 hours, but when at the Creation God permitted Adam to see the future inhabitants of the world, Adam had presented seventy of his allotted thousand years to David. In fact, some say, the world and all upon it were created only that David might one day live. For David is to be reborn as Messiah, though some tradition holds that one of David's descendants will be the Redeemer. The claim that Jesus was the Messiah rested very strongly in his descent from David; the genealogy is emphasized by the Gospels.

As a young man, David was Jesse's shepherd, living the solitary life of the flock-tender. Several of his adventures in the desert are traditional. He slew with his hands four lions and three bears. Once, thinking it was a hill, he climbed up the side of the monstrous animal, the reem. When it stood up, David was lifted far above the earth. In his prayer for help, he vowed to build a temple as high as the reem's horns if he were permitted to descend. (The building of the temple was accomplished by David's son, Solomon.) Therefore God sent a lion, before which king of the beasts the reem bowed down. Then, as in all good hunters' tales, as David got off the horns of the reem, a deer appeared, the lion chased it, and David escaped unharmed.

At the age of 28, David was anointed somewhat secretly by Samuel as the successor of Saul. It was then that his mother revealed that he was not a slave's son. He came to the court, and there, arousing the jealousy of other courtiers, he became the butt of much of Saul's morose ill-humor. After David had killed Goliath with the sling and pebble (three or five speaking pebbles had offered themselves to David and became one when he fought), Saul became more convinced than ever that David was fated to succeed him. David had to flee into the desert, where he and his band, a sort of Robin Hood's crew, became marauders on the outskirts of Saul's kingdom. Once as David hid in a cave Saul almost discovered him, but a spider spun its web across the cave's entrance and Saul went on convinced that the cave was undisturbed.

Eventually David became king. His son Absalom, one of the joys of David's life, rebelled against him and was killed when the uprising was put down. The lament of David is one of the most poignant speeches ever written. David sent Uriah the Hittite to his death in order that the will of God that David and Bathsheba marry be fulfilled. A famine, one of the ten greatest ever to occur, desolated the land. It was finally discovered that the cause of the famine was the burial of Saul and Jonathan outside the land. When the bodies were reinterred in the lands of the tribe of Benjamin, the famine ceased.

David knew that he would die on the Sabbath, and, despite his pleas that it be some other day, it was so. Knowing that the Angel of Death could not take him while he studied the Law, David spent the Sabbaths deeply immersed in study. But the Angel of Death one Sabbath caused a noise in the garden, and David arose from the Book to find out what had happened. While thus distracted from his studies, he was vulnerable, and as he walked down the steps into the garden, they collapsed. David's body fell into the garden in the full sun. As it was the Sabbath, the body might not be moved. Therefore Solomon called great eagles which with their wings shaded the body and kept it cool.

David's tomb in Jerusalem, his capital city, was the scene of several miracles. A Moslem notable once accidentally dropped his sword into the tomb. Four of his followers went down to retrieve it, and all four were brought up dead. It was then announced that the Jews of the city would be made to restore the sword under threat of dire punishment. After a three-day fast, the beadle of the synagogue was chosen by lot to descend. He was hauled up, much shaken, but with the sword. He said later that within the tomb an old man had appeared and handed him the weapon.

On the day of judgment, David will recite the benediction over the wine at the great feast for the elect. God will pass the cup to Abraham, who will pass it on, for he is the progenitor of the Ishmaelites. Isaac too will pass the cup, for Esau's children destroyed the Temple. Jacob will pass the cup, for he violated the law by being married to two sisters at the same time. Moses, who was not permitted to enter the Holy Land, and Joshua, who was not fit to be the father of a son, will similarly refuse the honor. But David, the sweet singer, will say the blessing.

Davy Jones In sailors' lingo, the spirit or personification of the sea; **Davy Jones's locker** is the bottom of the sea. To go to Davy Jones's locker is a common phrase meaning to be drowned at sea, or to die and be buried at sea.

Dayan In Indian belief, a witch who frequents burning grounds and cemeteries, drinks blood, casts the evil eye on children, and knows the **dāyan kā mantar** or charm for destroying life: a name derived from Dākinī, the female demon. Among the Oraons a woman who desires the power of a Dayan goes to a cave wearing only a girdle of broken twigs taken from a broom. There for a year she learns spells and, during each seance, drops a stone in a hole. If at the end of the time the hole is full, she has the ability to take away or restore life; if it is only partly full, she has the ability only to take away life.

day-names Gold Coast (West Africa) designations for human beings (and sometimes supernatural beings) given in accordance with the day of the week on which a person of one sex or the other is born. They are found in those parts of the New World where the Negroes are predominantly of Fanti-Ashanti derivation—Dutch Guiana, Jamaica, and the southeastern coast of the United States. Versions from Jamaica and Dutch Guiana (Surinam) can be given here:

| | Jamaica | | Surinam | |
	Male	Female	Male	Female
Sunday	Quashe	Quasheba	Kwasi	(A)Kwasiba
Monday	Cudjo	Juba	Kodjo	Ajuba
Tuesday	Cubena	Beneba	Kwabena	Abena
Wednesday	Quaco	Cooba	Kwaku	Akuba
Thursday	Quao	Abba	Yao	Yaba (Yawa)
Friday	Cuffee	Feeba	Kofi	Afi
Saturday	Quamina	Mimba	Kwamina	Amba

The derivation of such American Negro names as Quashee, Cuffee, and Codjo is apparent from this list. The tradition of giving day-names apparently persisted in the United States after the African names themselves had disappeared, as witness the names

"Thursday" or "Saturday" borne by men living in the Sea Islands off South Carolina and Georgia. [MJH]

day of the dead In some communities a special calendrical day on which it is proper to do honor to the dead, though the ceremonies of the day of the dead are conditioned by the views the community holds about death and about the ceremonies needed for purification and protection. Frequently these ceremonies are determined as much by the hope that the ghosts will be kept from troubling the living as by affection for the departed. The custom is further complicated by the readiness with which communities accept alien customs for protection. In China, for example, important ceremonies are performed in Spring, Summer and Autumn (the second, seventh, and tenth moons). These ceremonies are to give ease and comfort to man's two principal souls: the spiritual soul which in heaven will, it is hoped, exercise political pressure in favor of its descendants on earth; and the animal soul, which if it has great vitality, might still animate the corpse or skeleton or parts of it and cause terrible trouble among the living.

The elaborate Hindu śrāddhas (rituals for the ancestors) contain elements found in several parts of the world. They last for ten days when the ghost receives food to help it obtain liberation from the ten different hells it must visit. On the first of the new autumn moon the head of each Hindu family performs ceremonies for the dead of the last three generations. Additional ceremonies are performed on the anniversary of the day of death. Reports from all continents indicate that ceremonies occur which might be called (a) general, for the souls of all the dead such as All Souls Eve in Christian countries, or the Feast of the Hungry Ghosts in China; or (b) particular, for immediate ancestors, heroes, and the like. Other ceremonies for classes of dead fall between these general and particular ceremonies and belong to the special days on the calendars. Among these are memorial days for those who died in battle, those who died at sea, those who died in great disasters. In this connection it is proper to note that the souls of persons who died by violence are more restless and dangerous to the living than the souls of those who died "naturally." [RDJ]

dayong A Kayan (North Borneo) medium whose duties include that of doctor (but not midwife), soul-catcher, magician, and conductor of important ceremonies. The dayong is frequently a woman. In soul-catching she sends her own soul in search of the lost one which is causing its owner misfortune by its absence. When she finds it, she entices it back to the body of its owner and then places palm-leaf wristlets sprinkled with blood on the patient's wrists to make certain that the soul will stay where it belongs. The dayong directs funeral ceremonies, keeps a fire burning to guard against the evil spirits which crowd around after a death, and chants instructions to the spirit of the dead person. She also entices unfriendly spirits onto a small raft loaded with food and gifts and sends the craft away with the spirits aboard, thus ridding the village of these beings though only temporarily.

Dead Horse Chantey A chantey sung on American ships at the halyards or capstan, and on British ships to accompany the celebration of "burying the dead horse." The dead horse represented the first month's work on the ship, for which wages had been paid in advance and spent ashore. When the debt was worked out, a dummy horse of rags and straw was dragged around the deck and thrown overboard, to the tune of the chantey. The chantey is also called *Poor Old Man.*

dead man's hand In the American West, the poker hand of aces and eights has been known thus for three-quarters of a century. The famous scout of the plains, Wild Bill Hickok (J. B. Hickok of Cheyenne, Wyoming) was shot at Deadwood in the Black Hills on August 2, 1876, while playing a game of poker. The assassin was Jack McCall and the weapon a .45-caliber Colt. When the body was removed from the saloon where the murder took place, it was noticed that the dead man's fingers were tightly clenched upon the cards he had held and that the hand contained two pair, aces and eights. [GPS]

dead rider The motif (E215) of a cycle of traditional European ballads in which a dead man returns and takes with him on his horse some dearly loved person—wife, child, or sweetheart. In some versions the living rider does not know the other is dead; often the living narrowly escapes being taken into the grave with him. In the Greek ballad *Constantine and Arete* or *The Dead Brother's Return,* Constantine returns from the dead to bring his sister, Arete, to their dying mother's bedside. During the ride Arete learns that her brother is dead when she hears the birds in the trees commenting on the wonder that a dead man rides with a living girl behind him. Frequently a dead lover abducts his betrothed and carries her with him to the grave. Sometimes she is saved from going into the grave by a cock's crowing; but she almost always dies the next day. The dead rider motif is found in Icelandic, Danish, German, Bulgarian, Rumanian, Greek, Albanian, Serbian, Czech, and English balladry, and turns up also in an Araucanian legend. Hungarian Gipsy ballads also use the theme. The English ballad, *The Suffolk Miracle* (Child #272) on which Burger's *Lenore* is based, is an undramatic version of this grim story. *Sweet William's Ghost* (Child #77) belongs to the general group.

dead shoes Shoes provided for the dead because of the long journey they must make to the afterworld: a very ancient custom, surviving quite generally in Europe to relatively modern times. The ancient Teutonic and Scandinavian Helskô (or *Todenschuh*) were bound to the feet of the dead to ease the rough going of their journey along the Hell way. The traditional Scottish ballad, *The Lyke-Wake Dirge,* presents an old belief prevalent on the border that to give new shoes to a poor man in life guarantees that at death an old man will meet you with the shoes in his hand, so that you need not walk unshod over the stones and thorns in the path.

Southern United States Negroes do not put shoes on their dead for burial, and mourners must not wear new shoes to a funeral lest the dead be envious and try to get them: a strange combination of contradiction and verification of the belief that the dead need shoes.

dead smell bad The reason why the California Huchnom Indian creator, Taikomol, gave up the idea of resurrection of the dead. After Taikomol had created the earth for the third time, built a dance house, and made human beings, he gave to them the *hulk'ilal wok,* or dance of the dead. During the dance, one of the people did something wrong, and sickened and died. Taikomol buried him, but assured the man that he might come back in the morning. So in the morning the dead man walked back into the dance house. All the people said to each other that that one who came back smelled very bad. They could not stand it and were sick. So Taikomol gave up the idea of allowing the dead to return.

death Nearly all North American Indian tribes offer some explanation of the origin of death. The most widespread tale is that of an early controversy between two characters, either animal or human. One character wants people to die and be revived, the other wants death to be permanent. The second character wins the controversy; often, a little later a close relative of his, such as a son, dies and the parent wishes the decision reversed. His opponent reminds him, however, that he himself has already decided the matter. [EWV]

Surprising unity of death belief is found over the entire Middle American area. The underlying theme is that the soul on its way to the afterworld is confronted by dangers and difficulties which must be overcome. The soul of the ancient Aztec had to pass between clashing rocks; among the modern Miskito of Nicaragua trees clash together to catch the unwary traveler. Among the Popoluca of Veracruz in Mexico a whip woven of seven strings, the tribal sacred number, is placed in the hands of the corpse to permit it to drive dangerous animals from the path to the hereafter. In Tehuantepec the corpse is provided with thick sandals, since the path to the hereafter is filled with thorns and brambles. It is commonly believed that dogs, often red, must help the souls of their masters across a body of water which lies between them and paradise. For this reason, Indians almost never kill dogs, even though they may permit them to starve. In other cases, as among the Cuna of Panama, the soul of the dead traverses the water in a canoe. Christian influence is reflected in the frequent modern explanation that the water is the River Jordan. Rare is the Tarahumara custom of destroying or abandoning the house of an adult after his death. See AFTERWORLD; DEAD SHOES. [GMF]

death baby A New England popular name for a species of fungus (genus *Ithyphallus*). Its appearance in the yard of a house is said to portend a death in the family, and it is destroyed as soon as sighted.

death coach In Irish folklore, the spectral vehicle whose stopping at the door of a house means that someone in that house will die the next day. It is driven by a headless driver and drawn by black (sometimes headless) horses, and therefore often called the "headless coach." If it is seen passing through a village street, it must not be stopped; it must not be stopped before a house door either, for only in that place where it stops does it mean someone will die tomorrow. There are occasional stories that the banshee rides the death coach, or that sometimes it travels through the air. It is certain that a fallen bridge is no trouble to it; it crosses easily. Compare ANKOU.

death dance A dance or dance drama enacted by a group for the spirits of the departed or personifications of Death. Of the many underlying concepts, the following are the most prominent:

1) Release or exorcism of the spirit, motivated by fear of its malignant potentialities. American Indians often perform a series of funerary and anniversary rites. The California Luiseño banished the spirit from his familiar haunts with the *tuvish* and *chuchamish* (which resemble wakes), and in memorials for all the dead of the year or several years with the *yunish matackish* (which imitates the dead), with the *tauchanish* (which involves burning of images made of rush), with the *notush,* and with the *ashwut maknash,* or eagle-killing for chiefs. Similar to the *tauchanish* is the *keruk* of the Diegueño and *ka'aruka* of the Yuma; the images are danced to a shelter (*keruk*) and burned with stacks of gifts for the other world. The Tarahumara Indians of Chihuahua dance the *rutuburi* and *matachini* and a death dance around the belongings, during a third-week fiesta; after a year they dance the *yumari* and *pascol.* The Yaqui of Sonora hold a fiesta and dance the *pascol* at the wake of a child; the *matachini* dance in honor of a member of their society; the *chapayekas* for anyone dying during Lent. A second wake or *velación* finally releases the *hiepsi* or spirit; this novena occurs after three days among the Yaqui, after the proper eight days among the Mayo. Among the Cáhita (Mayo-Yaqui) Indians ghosts are not feared as in California.

2) Catholicism has introduced the appellation of *angelitos* in the case of the death of children. This motif of cheer and consolation pervades the Spanish wakes for children. "Están con los angeles"—they are with the angels, they say. The *jota* and *canario* are danced on these occasions. Consolation is probably mingled with vague early concepts in the dancing of the *jig* at Irish and Scottish wakes, and of the *baraban, lucia,* and *mattacino* of dirges in Sicily and Tuscany.

3) Memorial rites may also have a curative function, as the Iroquois *'ohgiwe,* the women's chant for the dead.

4) Communion with the dead, paramount in ancestor-worshipping cultures. Usually identification is effected by means of masks, as in the ghost dance with mask and shroud enacted by African Wydah and Yoruba tribes, the Brazilian Machacali and Caingang and in ancient times the Roman *archimimus.* Sometimes this communion is mystical, without impersonation, as in the Plains *Ghost Dance.* This however is not mortuary, and so deserves separate treatment.

5) Propitiation of the spirit, especially of enemies slain in battle. In the Plains scalp dances, California Yuki head dance, sentiments of triumph mingle with those of fear.

6) Personification of the concept of Death, preeminently in the medieval European *Dance of Death.* This is best known through frescoes and woodcuts, but has foundation in prolonged dance mimes. The grotesque skeleton of Death capers in turn with sinners of all classes and ages, cardinal, child, and laborer: an expression of the medieval horror of death, its *memento mori.* In Catalonia skeleton impersonations still cavort during religious holidays, notably Carnaval and Semana Santa (Holy Week): called the *danza macabra* or *ball*

de la mort, in Ampurdán a quadrille of skeletons carrying a scythe, clock, and banner. In Mexican carnivals *la muerte* is a horrid clown.

7) Fusion of the concept of death and of resurrection, the eternal cycle of life, is prevalent in pagan religions. Thus *la muerte,* apparently Christian, expresses the Aztec attitude typified by Coatlicue, goddess of maize and death. During the Middle Ages funeral dances enacted death and resurrection by a kiss. In the Hungarian *Gyás Tánc* one of the dancers performs this gruesome mime at funerals. The Bororo funeral ceremony is also a boys' puberty rite. The erotic *canario* celebrates a Spanish wake. In Europe and the Americas orgiastic rejoicing commonly follows the mourning, to produce life out of death.

A peculiarity of death rites is the reversal of directions and symbols, probably to mislead evil spirits. [GPK]

death feigned to meet paramour In North American Indian mythology, the tale of a woman who feigns death and is "buried" in order to marry her paramour, is told among Plateau and North Pacific Coast tribes generally, but has also been recorded for at least one Eastern Woodlands group, the Shawnee. The guilty woman marries her lover and lives happily for a time, but eventually is recognized and killed. [EWV]

death postponed by substitution A motif of folktale and myth in which one person's death can be postponed if a willing substitute can be found (D1855.2; T211.1; T211.1.1). Probably the most famous use of this motif is in the Greek story of Admetus and Alcestis. Another folktale, fairly well known in Europe (Type 612; motif E165), is about a man who resuscitates his dead wife by prayer, agreeing to give up half (or twenty years) of his own remaining time in exchange.

death prophesied The motif of a large number of European and Asian folktales (M341ff.) in which someone's death is prophesied in detail: at what age, on what day or hour of the day, by what instrument (hanging, drowning, fire, poison, lightning, a certain sword, a spindle wound, bite of a stone lion, or at the hands of someone of a certain name), at what place, etc. Every extreme of precaution is always taken to prevent the fulfilment of the prophecy (the sword is sunk in the sea, every spindle in the kingdom is destroyed, for instance, or the fatal child is exposed to perish, etc.) but the death prophesied inevitably comes to pass. Compare JASON; LITTLE BRIAR ROSE; TWO BROTHERS.

death tick or **death watch** The tapping or ticking noise made by a small wood-boring insect (family Anobiidæ), called the death watch beetle. In general European and United States folk belief to hear it means there will be a death in the family. To hear it tick *only three times* is especially fatal in Lancashire belief. See BEETLE.

débat A song type in which a question-and-answer contest or an argument takes place: literally, French for debate. Examples in English are *Riddles Wisely Expounded; Inter Diabolus et Virgo* (Child #1a); and *The Farmer and the Shanty Boy,* an American song in which two girls argue out the merits of men of each calling as husbands. The type started with a homiletic purpose but developed secular forms.

Deceived Blind Man A Smith Sound Eskimo folktale containing both the blind dupe motif (K333.1) and the healing water motif (B512). A blind boy's (or youth's) mother helped him aim his arrow at a bear. The arrow hit its mark; the bear was killed. But the woman told the boy that he had missed, and cooked and ate the meat herself. The sister, however, secretly gave half of her share to her brother. Thus he knew how his mother had tricked him. One day a great loon came to him, dived with him into a pond again and again until his sight was not only restored but as keen as the loon's own. After that he was not duped again. This story and *Deceived Blind Men* have about the same distribution.

Deceived Blind Men A Menomini Indian Trickster story in which the Trickster (Raccoon in this instance) comes upon two blind men living together who possess plentiful food. They have a system of lines rigged up by which they are guided back and forth to the edge of the lake. Raccoon is hungry and decides to steal their food. He changes the lines about, so that the next time one of the blind men goes for water, he is led into a tangle of bushes. By the time the other one investigates, the Trickster has changed them back again. Thus the second one brings back the water, and the two sit down to eat, facing each other with a bowl of meat between them. They divide the food evenly; each has six pieces of meat. While each of them is munching his first piece, Raccoon reaches out and takes four pieces from the bowl. Soon one of the blind men discovers there are only two pieces left, and accuses his companion of gobbling more than his share. Thus falsely accused, the other naturally suspects the first, and an angry quarrel ensues. In the midst of the argument Raccoon taps each on the face. Whereupon, each thinking the other has hit him, the two old men fall into a blind scrambling fight and upset the food. Raccoon grabs the last two pieces of meat and runs off. But the two blind men hear him laugh as he runs, stop fighting, and trust each other once more.

This story, containing two of the blind dupe motifs (K1081.2; K1081.3), is known among the Indians of the North Pacific Coast and the Plateau and Central Woodland regions. It is found only occasionally on the Plains and among the Iroquois. There is a California Shoshonean (Paviotso) version in which Eagle as Trickster steals the food from between the pair while they are feeding each other. This story, however, as in many other variants, ends with the Trickster restoring the sight of the blind men (or women).

deception by lousing A folktale motif (K874) very widespread among North American Indians, in which by lousing or pretended lousing of the ogre or other villain of the story, the hero escapes his fate. In a Lummi Indian (Washington) tale, for instance, a woman pretends to louse her cruel husband, then holds him tight by the hair while her relatives kill him to avenge her wrongs. There are many stories in which the lousing is demanded by the ogre (father-in-law, etc.) with the intent that the very large, dangerous vermin in his hair will kill the hero (K611.1). The hero deceives the ogre, however, by cracking berries (usually cranberries) in his teeth, and thus escaping the fate intended for him. Or the lousing is merely required as

a test of courtesy or obedience (G466). Often the lousing is volunteered in order to put the ogre to sleep and effect an escape (D1962.2). This last is a general European, African, and Jamaican Negro, as well as American Indian incident. Many a folktale ogre has happily snoozed off while being deloused and waked to find his captives flown.

There is a seemingly pointless and malicious Indonesian story about an ape who pretends to louse a heron and pulls out all his feathers instead (K874.1) so that the heron cannot fly. Another heron avenges his friend by beguiling the ape to sea in a boat made of leaves, pecks a hole in it, and flies off, leaving the ape to drown.

deceptive bargains The motif of an extensive cycle of world folktales (K100–299) including many clever, dishonest, and tricky transactions: the sale of objects falsely claimed to be magic, for instance, such as the soup stone which needs only meat and vegetables added (K112.2), the gold-dropping horse (K111), the Jamaican soup-making pot (K112.2.1), etc.; the sale of worthless animals and objects—what the seller meant when he said the horse would not walk over trees is revealed to the buyer when the horse refuses to cross a bridge (K134.1); deceptive divisions—A gets the corn, B gets the chaff (K171.2), A shears the sheep, B shears the pigs (K171.5); the deceptive land measure (K185 ff.). Other deceptive bargains involve cheating the Devil out of the soul he has been promised (K210 ff.), withholding sacrifices or offerings promised to gods or saints after the need or danger is over (K231.3 ff.), failing to pay for things ordered, selling stolen property to the owner, exchanging new lamps for old (see ALADDIN), counting out pay into a container with a hole in it (K275), etc. See MASTER THIEF.

deceptive land measure A motif (K185) belonging to the deceptive bargain cycle (K100–299) of world folktale. The classic example is the story of Dido's arrival on the coast of North Africa (from Tyre) where she bought as much land as the hide of a bull would cover. The thin strips into which she cut and stretched the hide were enough to measure off the circumference of the space on which she built the citadel of Carthage. Deceptive land purchase stories appear everywhere from Turkey, across Europe, and North America, to Indonesia. The deceptive measure, however, varies: the purchaser bargains for as much land as a bull, ox, or horse-hide will measure (Turkish, Finno-Ugric, Greek, general European, Icelandic, North American Indian), as much land as Vishṇu can lie on (Hindu), as a shawl will cover (the huge shawl being prepared beforehand in Java, Brigit's miraculous cloak spreading of itself in Ireland), as can be plowed in a certain time (Scandinavian), or as can be shadowed by a certain tree, the piece of land being bought just before sunset (Indonesian).

The North American Wyandot Indians have a story describing the coming of the white man to their neighbors the Delawares on the shores of the Atlantic. The white men needed land and proposed to buy as much as a cow's hide would measure. The Delawares agreed, believing that a people who could live crowded together in a little ship would need only a comparable strip of land. The newcomers, however, cut and stretched the hide into threadlike strips which measured off a large area. Wyandot comment to the end of this story is: "This is the way the white man does." The Delawares and Shawnee also tell the same story.

Dechtire In Old Irish legend, the sister of Conchobar, king of Ulster; mother of Cuchulain by Luġ. In the form of a mayfly Luġ fell into her cup of wine on the night of her wedding to Sualtim, an Ulster chieftain, thus causing the supernatural impregnation. Luġ whisked her away that night to his own abode and she was not heard of again until she sent for Conchobar to announce the birth of her son.

decoration Usually, that part of an artist's work which embellishes or ornaments, presumably without being essential to the functioning shape of the whole; by connotation we are likely to assume that it is added purely for the sake of beauty or pleasure, that it is not utilitarian. It covers a good deal of the same territory as design, but the existence of a distinction is revealed by the fact that the phrase *decoration and design* is often used. In the case of a chair with a stenciled pattern, for example, the design of the chair includes both the shape of the chair and the added pattern. If the word decoration is used, however, it is clear that one is referring to the stenciled pattern, for decoration conveys the idea of an embellishment that is added to, is an extension of, the basic piece of work.

Thus, it seems useful, in folk art, to refer to decoration as such when one wishes to analyze it as a separate process in the construction of an object, e.g. for the painting as distinct from the folding of a box, the incising as distinct from the coiling of a dish, the carving as distinct from the hewing of a post. But it would not be accurate to assume that its purpose is primarily to embellish, that it is non-utilitarian, for embellishment is seldom the whole purpose in primitive art (or so we believe) and it is a secondary purpose in much of folk decoration. The sampler, while it was hung on the wall as a decoration, was executed to demonstrate or develop the skill of the needleworker. The figurehead is the vessel's presiding spirit. The quilt was a covering designed to utilize scraps. And it is only when these reasons are forgotten that the work can be said to be purely decorative in purpose. The embroidery on the priest's robe conveys the symbols of his office. The flourishes on a birth certificate mark its importance. The ceremonial vessel might be a cooking pot but for the pattern derived from the deity. In short, embellishment and utility develop hand in hand, and the function and quality of the so-called decoration merge with that of the object as a whole.

Any object (art or not) may be said to be "decorative" if it happens to fit in with the beholder's taste as to what is pleasing or ornamental. Any object may be put to a decorative use and decoration may be added to almost anything. This does not mean that it necessarily falls in the category of decoration in the art sense.

Ornament is another word used to mean a decorative pattern, but since it has specific uses of its own, it might as well be reserved for them. It is a term widely used in architecture. It is the word commonly used for objects of personal adornment and for a variety of small objects used to embellish a house, a Christmas tree, a harness or wagon, etc. Compare DESIGN. [MH]

Dedari Tundjung Biru Literally, possession by Blue Lotus: a temple dance of Bali. Blue Lotus is a heavenly goddess of Bali impersonated by the child temple-dancers. In a kind of charmed sleep the dancer becomes possessed by this spirit. She trembles all over; she sways from right to left, faster and faster; her head rolls loosely from side to side. At last when the full personality of Blue Lotus is in possession of her, she gathers strength and attacks the forces of evil and illness. At last she falls exhausted and unconscious. This dance borders on the convulsive type; self-will has departed from the body, and the dancer, in profound religious experience, is in the hands of the god.

Deer A popular character in the mythology of many western tribes of native North America, but also not unknown as a character in other parts of the continent. Deer in some tales is referred to as a male being, in others as a mother, sister, or wife of some other animal character. The tale of *Bear Woman and Deer Woman* is widespread in western North America. Another rather widespread tale is that of the marriage of a human being to a deer wife; the wife is finally offended (as animal wives often are in North American Indian tales) by remarks concerning her eating habits. She leaves her human husband after bearing him a son. There are numerous other American Indian tales in which Deer figures as a prominent, if not a leading character. Deer rarely, if ever, appears as a trickster, however. [EWV]

Deer Boy An abandoned baby story of the Tewa (and other Pueblo) Indians. This lacks the heartless parent motif of the typical abandoned children tales. A young girl out hunting rabbits with the boys and girls of her village fell behind and gave birth to a baby. She did not know what to do with it so she left it lying in the grass and went on after the hunters; but she was very unhappy. Nearby lived "a woman who was a deer" who found the infant, took him home, and raised him among her own fawns. The child grew strong and swift playing and racing with the fawns. One day a hunter observed his footprints among the deer tracks, and went home and told his people. The Deer woman prepared the child for being caught, and told him how to recognize his own father and mother and what to say to them. The hunters came; the child was taken with affection and joy. The conditions on which he could return to his human family were that he remain unseen in a room for four days. The conditions were carefully observed. But the mother could not wait; she peeked. The child took on deer-form and ran north to join his Deer mother, who led him with his deer brothers west to Comp'ing or Snow Mountain (now San Francisco Mountain).

deer dance A North American Indian mimetic dance for securing benefits from the spirit of the deer. Among the Papago the powers are thought of as baneful as well as beneficial; in the Southwest, however, they are generally considered benevolent. To obtain power over the animal in the hunt, and to appease its spirit, is the function of the realistic Yaqui Deer Dance, the *Maso*, performed together with the Pascola and Coyote dances at household and church fiestas, throughout Easter Sunday and night. The rebounding footwork, the posture, the nervous turn of the head are expressive of the deer at play and eluding pursuit. Between dances the Maso engages in horseplay with the pascolas. In contrast with this solo dance, the Deer Dance of San Juan and San Felipe pueblos is enacted by 18 men impersonating deer decoyed in from the hills by a virgin. In the end they all run away again, except four, who are symbolically hunted and killed. The Tepehuane of Durango enacted a realistic pursuit of the deer with bows and arrows, for mutiplication not only of deer but of crops, particularly corn. The Huichol Deer Dance is identified with the *hikuli* or peyote dance, and with rain and fertility. As part of the Papago harvest festival (*wiikita*) the deer worked magic over the crops. The Hopi Deer Dance is a prayer for rain. The California Yurok White Deer Dance induces bountiful wild crops. The Zuñi Deer Dance is performed for cure. The Piegan Blacktailed Deer cult enacted impersonation for curing sickness as well as to facilitate capture.

Head and hide, deer-hoof and claw belts or bells, and tails form common accessories. Costume and motions show every degree of realism: in Taos, among the Yaqui and Tepehuane the dancer wears an actual deer head; in San Ildefonso, only the antlers. Sticks in the hands simulate four-footedness. In San Juan he wears a yucca headgear. Among the Hopi there is complete stylization in mask and costume and loss of mimetic suggestion. In the Yuma Deer Dance men wear deer heads, but they simply stamp in a sidewise circle, around an inner circle of women.

As a rarity in Europe, the Abbots Bromley antler dance blends Morris character with six performers carrying deer heads. [GPK]

degánodǫt'óenǫ The Iroquois Indian alligator dance, a social dance still popular among the Cayuga of the Six Nations, but condemned by the Seneca because of the contact between men and women. It is called their swing dance, for, alone among Iroquois dances, the woman dances to the right of the man, elbows linked. With a shuffle of the *ga'dášot* type they progress in this double file around the room, then in the middle of the song they pivot to the right, with the woman as axis. With each new song the woman moves on to a new partner, in the manner of the fickle Iroquois woman in real life. [GPK]

degwiyágǫ́'óenǫ The Iroquois buffalo dance, a round dance performed only by members of a restricted medicine society. The fundamental step is a side stomp, with men in the lead and women in arrears. The individual performers whirl, butt each other, and imitate the buffalo's roar. It is one of the few Iroquois mimetic dances, purely ceremonial in function, and confined to the midwinter ceremonials. The music is as archaic as the choreography; the song, accompanied by the water drum, is confined to short phrases and limited themes. The dance is supposed to cure pains, caused by the buffalo, in the shoulder and neck which make the sufferer hunch up into the semblance of the buffalo. The society must meet at least once a year. [GPK]

Deianira In Greek legend, the wife of Hercules and by him the mother of Œneus and Althæa, whose jealousy of Iole led to Hercules' death. Deianira had been loved by both Hercules and Achelous, and after a combat in which the river-god assumed many shapes by transformation and in which he was beaten by

Hercules, she married the hero. Some years after this, at the fording of a river, the centaur Nessus attempted to rape Deianira, but was shot by Hercules with a poisoned arrow. As he died, the centaur told Deianira to steep his shirt in the blood and, if ever she feared losing Hercules to another woman, to use the shirt as a charm to retain his love. This she later did, when she suspected Hercules' infatuation for Iole, thus causing his death. When she heard the news, she killed herself. Compare TRANSFORMATION COMBAT.

Deirdre The heroine of the Irish legend, *Longes Mac Nusnig* (*The Exile of the Sons of Usnech*), also known as *The Tragical History of the Sons of Usnech*, and as one of the great Three Sorrows of Storytelling. The story is an *aithid*, or elopement story, a common story type among the Celts. The Deirdre story exists in several versions rather different in detail. The story is found in the *Book of Leinster* and the *Yellow Book of Lecan*. The following outline is largely drawn from the oldest manuscript account, in the *Book of Leinster* (12th century). It is one of the *réim sceala*, or prologs, to the *Táin Bó Cuailgne*.

During a feast which Fedlimid is giving to Conchobar, king of Ulster, Fedlimid's wife gives birth to a girl-child. Cathbad the Druid at once prophesies that the child will be the ruin of Ireland and the destruction of the Red Branch (the king's body of warriors), and adds that she should be called Deirdre (troubler). All the warriors insist that she be put to death but the king intercedes and orders that she be sent to one of his forest strongholds and fostered there away from men by a nurse, a forester, and Levarcham, the king's "confidence woman." And he announces to all that Deirdre shall be his wife.

So she lives until she is grown. One day the forester kills a calf and the red blood runs out on the snow and a raven comes and drinks the blood. Deirdre, seeing this, says to Levarcham that she would have a husband whose hair is black as the raven, whose cheeks are as red as the blood, and whose body is as white as the snow. Levarcham remarks that such a one is Naoise, one of the sons of Usnech, and nephew of Conchobar. At Deirdre's request she invites Naoise to come to the castle. Deirdre tells Naoise that she loves him and persuades him to elope with her to Scotland. Naoise's brothers, Ainle and Ardan, go with them.

For many years they live in the forest completely happy. But Conchobar still covets Deirdre and finally sends Fergus, one of the great heroes of Ireland, to fetch them home under a safe-conduct. Though Deirdre fears treachery, Naoise and his brothers decide to return with Fergus. Sorrowfully Deirdre consents and singing her famous song, *Farewell to Alba*, joins them in the boat. When they land, Conchobar by a ruse separates Fergus from the sons of Usnech, whom he quarters in the house of the Red Branch. There Levarcham warns them of the treachery of the king, and there the king's men attack them. The sons of Usnech and Fergus' sons, who remained with them, fight desperately but are finally conquered by spells cast upon them by Cathbad. The sons of Usnech are taken and beheaded. "Then comes Deirdre to where the children of Usnech lie and Deirdre dishevels her hair and begins to drink Naoise's blood and the color of burning embers comes

into her cheeks." She sings the lament for the death of the brothers and after that she throws herself into Naoise's grave and gives him three kisses and dies.

Other accounts tell the end differently saying that Deirdre is taken by Conchobar and that after a year Conchobar tires of her and gives her to one Eogan, and that Deirdre then jumps from Eogan's chariot and dashes out her brains on the stones. And common is the statement that Conchobar had two yew stakes driven into the graves of Deirdre and Naoise and that the stakes grew into trees which twined themselves together above the graves.

As a result of the king's perfidy many of his best warriors desert him and go over to Ailill and Medb, king and queen of Connacht, and fight against him in the *Táin Bó Cuailgne, The Cattle Raid of Cuailgne*, called the War for the Brown Bull, and so help bring about the fulfilment of the prophecy uttered at Deirdre's birth.

In Irish this story is preserved in the *Book of Leinster* and in manuscripts in the Advocates Library in Edinburgh; it is also found in oral tradition in Scotland and in Ireland. English translations were made by O'Flanagan and published in the *Transactions of the Gaelic Society*, and by Eleanor Hull (*Cuchullin Saga*). The most important writers in English who have made use of the story in poem, novel, and drama are James Macpherson, James Stephens, John Millington Synge, George William Russell (AE), Lady Gregory, William Butler Yeats, William Sharp. [MEL]

deiseal Literally (Irish), a turning to the right: a sunwise turn; the ancient Celtic circumambulation or "holy round" around certain sacred stones, wells, trees, fires, etc. It imitates the circuit of the sun and is rooted in the primitive belief that to imitate the sun strengthens the sun's continuance and is beneficial and cathartic to earthly beings. The deiseal brings good luck, wards off evil, and propitiates certain elemental powers. Dancers around the Beltane fires danced deiseal, for instance. Coals from the midsummer fires are carried deiseal three times around the house, or around the sheaf. When Medb set out to war against Ulster her charioteer made one deiseal (or sunwise turn) first to counteract the evil that was prophesied. In modern Ireland certain wells are still approached deiseal or sunwise; boats are turned thus when being maneuvered into the sea; a lighted sod is sometimes carried three times around the churn before churning, for luck with the butter; funerals take care to approach the graveyards deiseal or sunwise; and the grave is thus circled before the dead are buried. As an interjection deiseal means "May it go right!": said in the Aran Islands when one sneezes or chokes on a morsel. See CIRCUMAMBULATION; TUATAL.

Dekanawida An Iroquois Indian hero of the 15th century: one of the founders of the Iroquois confederacy. He possessed great *orenda*, i.e. supernatural powers of wisdom, prophecy, and strength against opposition. His story follows the true mythological hero pattern of miraculous birth and rapid growth. He was born of a virgin mother, who, before his birth, received omens that through him misfortune would come upon her people (the Hurons). Three times therefore she tried to drown the infant through a hole in the ice, and three times woke up the next morning with the child safe in her arms. Dekanawida attained manhood in a few years and set out on his journey to the south. As life token he left an otter skin hanging by the tail in his mother's lodge, which would vomit blood should he die by violence. Many constitutional principles and laws of the confederation are attributed to Dekanawida. His chieftainship was by merit, not heredity; and he could forbid the appointment of a successor on the grounds that his work was done: no one could follow after to organize the five Iroquois tribes into a confederacy. The name itself means "two river-currents flowing together." (See *BAEB* 30: 383.) See HIAWATHA.

Delphic oracle The most famous oracle of the classical world; a shrine of Apollo in Phocis on the southern slope of Mount Parnassus. The Delphic oracle of Apollo was the ultimate authority of ancient Greece. Originally it was called Pytho, and Apollo was said to have slain Python, the dragon guarding a shrine of the Earth Mother there, and to have taken the place for himself. As a dolphin he led a group of sailors to land near the spot and made them his priests. Within the temple precinct was the omphalos, or navel, the center of the earth, where two eagles let loose by Zeus at the ends of the earth met.

The oracle itself was delivered by a priestess, the Pythia or Pythoness, originally a maiden, but in later years a woman of over fifty. After bathing in and drinking the waters of the Castalian spring, she was seated on a tripod over an opening in the ground and was said to become intoxicated by vapors emitted from the earth. There is no basis for believing that these vapors actually existed, nor in the story of the discovery of the spot by goats intoxicated by the vapors. The Pythia in her trancelike state uttered words which were noted and turned into hexameter verses by the priests.

The Delphic oracle is prominent in Greek folktale, mythology, and legend, appearing again and again in such tales as those of Orestes, of the Argonauts, of Hercules, of Codrus.

Delphinus The Dolphin: a small constellation of the northern hemisphere, lying on the edge of the Milky Way just east of Aquila. The four bright stars form a miniature diamond, which is the body of the Dolphin, with a fifth representing the tail. It is often now called Job's Coffin.

The early Greeks regarded this constellation as their Sacred Fish. Ovid named it Amphitrite, on the grounds that the dolphin on which Poseidon rode persuaded her to marry the sea god. Another story tells how Arion, the harpist, returning from Sicily to Corinth, was threatened by the crew of the ship, who desired the treasures on board. Arion promised to throw himself into the sea on condition that he be allowed to play once more. The crew agreed to this; and a school of dolphins beside the ship were so charmed with the power of the music that one of them took Arion upon his back as he fell into the sea, and sped with him to Corinth. For this the gods put the dolphin in the sky.

Early Hindu astronomers had a constellation Simshumāra, later Zizumara, Porpoise, of which there is some confusion between Draco and Delphinus. Arabic astronomy reports several names: Al Ka'ūd, the Riding Camel, Al Salīb, the Cross, believed to be the cross of Christ raised into heaven, with the tail star identified as the pillar of the cross. Later Arabian astronomy took the Greek interpretation and called it Dulfim, Dolphin, an animal which they believed followed ships to rescue drowning sailors.

deluge or **flood** A world cataclysm during which the earth was inundated or submerged by water: a concept found in almost every mythology in the world. The exceptions are Egypt and Japan; and deluge stories are only occasional in Africa. The fact itself finds no place in the geological history of the earth, neither in the light of the structure of the earth itself, or in that of zoological or botanical evidence.

Early folklorists liked to assume that the world distribution of the myth was evidence either of the flood itself, or of man's descent from a people who experienced it, or of some numerous local catastrophes which gave rise to the story. A local flood would be easily mythicized into a world deluge. The appearance, however, of divergent flood theories sometimes even within the same mythology has given such assumptions pause. Sometimes a flood destroys a world already made and the people in it; sometimes creation itself begins with the primeval water.

The bare bones of the most usual deluge story are as follows: The gods (or a god) decide to send a deluge on the world, usually as punishment for some act, broken tabu, the killing of an animal, etc. (in a Tsimshian myth the deluge comes because the people have mistreated a trout), but sometimes for no reason. Certain human beings are warned, or it comes without warning. If warned, the people construct some kind of vessel (raft, ark, ship, Big Canoe, or the like), or find other means of escape (climbing a mountain or tree, growing tree, floating island, calabash or coconut shell, a turtle's back, crab's cave, etc.). Sometimes they also save certain things essential to a way of life, such as food, rarely domestic animals. The deluge comes (rain, huge wave, a container broken or opened, a monster's belly punctured, etc.). Bird or rodent scouts are often sent out, but this is not universal. When the deluge is over the survivors find themselves on a mountain or an island; sometimes they offer a sacrifice (not universal), and then repeople the earth, recreate animals, etc., by some miraculous means. See ARK; DEUCALION; EARTH DIVER; FLOOD; MANU; NOAH; PRIMEVAL WATER; YIMA.

☛ Extremely widespread as an incident in North American mythology is the account of the deluge. Hundreds of North American accounts of the origin of the world either picture the world as once covered with primeval waters, or suddenly covered by a flood. Some tribes account for the flood as caused by the tears of a jealous suitor or deserted husband, or from water which escaped from the punctured belly of a large monster. Escape from the flood by certain characters is effected by climbing a tree which grows up and up into the sky, or by clinging to the sky, etc. It seems probable, from its wide distribution, that the deluge tale of the North American Indians is native to the New World and is not an adaptation of the Old World Biblical tale. The latter is also told by many American Indian groups (often the native tale and the Biblical one will be told by the same tribe) but certain incidents (such as Noah and the ark) are nearly always included in the Biblical version and make it easily recognizable. [EWV]

☞ The myth of the deluge is almost universal in South America. As a rule it is described as a local disaster which overcame the ancestors of the tribe a short time after creation.

Various causes are given for it. In Inca mythology it was provoked by the supreme god, Viracocha, who was dissatisfied with the first men and decided to destroy them. Likewise the god Chibchachum inundated the plain of Bogota to punish the Chibcha Indians for some offense. The primitive Yahgan of Tierra del Fuego say that Moon sent the deluge in revenge for the beating she received when men discovered the secret of the initiation rites. The ancient inhabitants of the region of Quito in Ecuador, the Jivaro and Murato Indians, link the deluge with the killing of a supernatural boa. The Bororo believe that it was brought about by a water spirit who had been wounded.

Various Guiana tribes (Ackawoi, Wapishiana, Taulipang, Taruma, Carib, etc.) explain the deluge or flood as an aftermath of the felling of the Tree of Life. The Cashinawa held the Men-of-the-Sky responsible for the disaster which they unleashed when they cut some huge trees of the upper world. A Caraja tradition reports that the deluge came when a mysterious man from the underworld broke gourds full of water. According to the Ipurina, the deluge was brought about by the overflowing of a kettle located in the sun. The Araucanians say that the deluge resulted from the rivalry of two monstrous serpents, Kaikai and Trentren, who caused the waters to rise in order to show their power. The violation of a menstrual tabu is the reason given by the Toba for the flood which once destroyed their tribe.

The deluge is produced either by excessive rains (Inca, Canari, Yaruro, Tupinamba, Tembe) or by a sudden overflowing of water (Canichana, Yagua, Witoto, Jivaro, Mura, Tupinamba, Bororo), or by the swelling of the sea (Canari, Araucanians).

According to most tribes, the highest summits of their respective countries were the sites to which the people fled when the waters were coming. In the Andean region (Choco, Canari, Jivaro, Guajiro, Araucanians) certain mountains grew higher and higher as the waters rose. In many tropical tribes the survivors climbed tall palm trees.

The ark motif is rare in South America, and where found seems to be of European origin. However, it may be indigenous among the Macushi, the Island Caribs, the Yagua, and the Apinayé. In a version common to the Chiriguano, Guarayu, and Chane, the only survivors of the flood were a little boy and girl who had been placed in a calabash. The Caingang version offers an interesting element because of its North American parallels. When the survivors of the deluge were about to die of starvation, a water bird flew to them with a basket of soil. The birds, with the help of ducks, recreated the earth.

According to the Macushi the only survivor of the flood repeopled the earth by throwing stones behind him. The same motif occurs among the Tamanak. In the Inca, Guanca, and Aymara versions, the survivors found shelter in sealed caves. Later they emerged to spread across the world.

The Taino myth of the origin of the sea may well be interpreted as a deluge story. Four mythical brothers caused a mass of water to fill the earth when they broke a magic calabash. [AM]

Demeter In ancient Greek mythology and religion, an earth goddess; specifically, the goddess of the fruitfulness of the earth, perhaps personified in the seedgrain (as opposed to the new grain which her daughter Persephone symbolized); hence, the goddess of nature, of marriage, of women, of harmony, of health: a chthonic deity in Sparta and Argolis, she may have had some original, but now obscured, connection with the Great Mother fertility goddess of the Near East, or may be a native goddess of Crete. Demeter is most important as one of the central characters in the Eleusinian mysteries and in the myth of Persephone forming their central episode. The worship of Demeter, while best known in the Eleusinian worship, is not by any means limited to that locale but spread all over the ancient world; the rape of Persephone, for example, was reputed to have taken place in the mythical Nysa in Asia and in the equally mythical island west of Spain in the Atlantic. Essentially Demeter and Persephone are two aspects of the corn goddess, and were called in Greece the "Great Goddesses" or simply the "Two Goddesses" as at Eleusis.

Demeter was the daughter of Cronus and Rhea, and thus the sister of Zeus and Poseidon. She was swallowed by her father and later disgorged. By Zeus she became the mother of Persephone (and of Dionysus in some stories); by Poseidon she was mother of the horse Arion and a goddess called at Phigalia Despoena (or the Mistress, seemingly a synonym for Persephone as queen of the underworld) and of hidden name elsewhere.

After the rape of Persephone, Demeter donned black mourning clothes and, taking two torches lit at Mt. Etna, searched nine days for her daughter. On the tenth day she met Hecate who had overheard the cries of the maiden, and together they went to Helios, who had witnessed the abduction and who told the story to the seekers. Angered at the deception of Zeus, who had promised Persephone to Hades without telling Demeter, the goddess avoided Olympus and its companionship, wandering on earth and accepting the position of nurse to the son of Celeus. Crops failed; nothing grew; and the gods were deprived of their sacrifices. Demeter stubbornly refused to listen to representations from the gods unless she were permitted to see Persephone. At last Hermes came to Hades, who agreed to release the maiden. However, before she left, Persephone ate part of a pomegranate in the underworld, and thus was forced to spend a third (or a half) of every year with Hades as his consort. The partaking of the food of the gods or fairies is a familiar one in mythology and folklore: compare the Babylonian myth of Adapa and the more recent tale of Rip Van Winkle.

Demeter then agreed to rejoin the company of the gods, but before leaving earth she instructed her companions among men, Triptolemus, Diocles, Eumolpus, and Celeus, in her mysteries and worship, and left with them the gift of agriculture. This is the underlying story of the Eleusinian mysteries, the climax arriving when the priest and priestess of Demeter descended to an obscure place where the priestess, as the goddess Brimo, brought forth an ear of corn which the priest displayed to the communicants.

Other myths concerning the goddess are those of her union with Iasion in a thrice-plowed field (the *hieros gamos*), and her connection with Poseidon. During her wandering, Poseidon saw her and made advances. She,

Demeter Erinys, the raging Demeter, to avoid him, transformed herself into a mare, whereupon he became a stallion, and as a result of their intercourse the magical horse Arion was born. There was also a daughter, of unknown name. At Phigalia this daughter was called Despoena, and here Demeter was figured as a black, horse-headed goddess. In this, and in Demeter's identification with her symbolic animal, the pig, there is indicated the union of the fertility personifications, Dionysus the horse god and Demeter the corn goddess, in a ceremony which, like the Iasion story, is a dramatization of more ancient fertility ceremonies. Demeter also cursed Erysichthon who cut down trees from a grove sacred to her by making him always hungry. As a result, he was forced to sell his daughter Mestia, in order to obtain food, but she by her ability to shift shapes always returned to him.

Demeter was worshipped from Crete to Attica, from Asia to Italy. Principal among the festivals at which she was honored were the Thesmophoria and the Eleusinia. Pigs, cows, bulls, fruit, and honey cakes were offered to her; she was patroness of all fruits, excepting only beans, which were forbidden the Eleusinians. Demeter is always depicted as being fully dressed, sometimes riding in a chariot drawn by horses or, attesting to her chthonic nature, by dragons. She is not identifiable with Ge, who assisted Hades in the abduction of Persephone, despite the supposed derivation of her name as from Ge Metre, or Earth Mother. More likely the name is derived from *deai,* a form of the Greek word for barley.

The Romans identified Demeter with Ceres, who may have been an Etruscan goddess whose name only remains, or who may have been a form of Cora, the Maiden, Demeter's daughter.

demon An ambiguous term applied to almost any spirit, especially to an evil spirit. See SPIRITS.

demon dances Masked impersonations of supernatural powers, performed to secure their intervention in cures or for their exorcism. Ordinarily the demon is conceived as malignant; but he is not necessarily so, and was not originally so. The Greek *daimones* were intermediary deities responsible for ill or good fate, ill or good health of animal or vegetable life. The spirits of the dead came to join their company. Medieval superstitions came to conceive of the *daimones* as evil beings and to equate them with their ancient pagan deities, in contrast with the beneficent Christian God. They were vague and fearful, whereas the Devil assumed a concrete and largely humorous character.

Demon dances are particularly prominent in primitive puberty ceremonials, as the *Máuari* of the Venezuelan Maipure. In the Chaco, Mataco, and Toba, Choroti, Lengua, and Ashluslay puberty rites for girls, boys impersonate animal and bird demons and the women ward them off. The Iroquois gagósä, the Apache gahe, and the California Kuksu rites impersonate demons, the first two for cure, the last for prosperity, especially of crops. The Kuksu animal spirits are not approached with fear, any more than the *daimones* of the Dionysian cult. The Dahomean masked vodun dancers and the self-curative maskless Haitian vodun dancers work themselves into a frenzy of often destructive behavior. Particularly among the Apache and California Indian tribes there is danger attached to the impersonation, madness or illness resulting from a misstep. But power for himself and the tribe attends a successful impersonation. [GPK]

dentlé A notched stick scraped with a strip of bamboo to provide rhythmic accompaniment to secular dances of Haitian Negroes. It belongs to a class of musical instruments found among primitive peoples from paleolithic times, but has recently been largely replaced in Haiti by the kitchen grater, called *grage.* See SCRAPER.

deo Originally, any one of the 33 great divinities of Hinduism.

Deohako In Seneca Indian mythology, the collective name for the three daughters of the Earth Mother, spirits and guardians of the corn, beans, and squash. Each is conceived of as clad in the leaves of her own special protegée. At first they were all planted together in one hill. One time, however, Onatah (Corn) wandered from her place in search of dew. Hahgwehdaetgah (the evil one) caught her, took her underground, and sent such blighting winds across the fields that Bean and Squash fled also. Finally Sun reached forth to find and bring her back. But now Onatah stands alone in the field, enduring drought or rain, never wandering to seek relief. Now she never leaves the field until the maize is ripe. At planting time she calls her crows to come eat the grubs that would destroy her roots.

Derby Ram An English lying song or "tall tale" about a ram of colossal size, with a refrain devoted to assertions of the truth of the story. A sea-going version sung on American ships equipped the ram with spyglasses, sextant, and all the trappings of a navigator.

descents to underworld The motif of numerous stories occurring in the mythology and folklore of every people in the world, ancient and contemporary: symbolic of the human wish that death can be overcome and that the dead may return. Invariably the descent is made to rescue someone either abducted to the land of the dead, or rightfully dead; to find the answer to a question or discover a secret from the ruler of the afterworld; to ask a favor, or to seize some treasure. Occasionally curiosity only motivates the journey. The success of the quest to the land of the dead is always contingent on the observance of some tabu: not to eat or drink, not to look back, or touch, speak, etc. To partake of the food of the dead (or of fairyland in later folklore) prevents the visitor from ever returning to the land of the living.

Among the most famous descent stories are the Greek myths of Demeter and Persephone, Orpheus and Eurydice, Hercules' labor of bringing Cerberus up from Hades; the Babylonian story of Ishtar's descent to rescue Tammuz; the Norse myth of Hermod's journey to bring back Balder. In North American Indian mythology, there is one interesting and widely distributed parallel to the Orpheus story, occurring in about 40 versions, three of which end with success, and thought to be indigenous. There are similar tales in Hindu, Chinese, and Japanese writings, and in Ainu, Maori, Melanesian, etc. mythology. Descents to Hell are common also in early Christian literature. See ÆNEAS; AFTERWORLDS; ASCENTS TO UPPER WORLD; FOOD TABU IN LAND OF DEAD.

design The term *folk design* usually applies to the decorative patterns characteristic of folk arts and crafts, but this is a limited use of a term which, in its general sense, is almost as broad as art itself. Design in the art field has to do, basically, with plan or arrangement or organization. It overlaps to some extent with *form*, but while form is thought of as the shape or quality of shape that results from the plan, design is the plan itself. It is, in the general sense, the planning aspect of any work of art, involving either the creation or combining of elements; often it signifies creation as opposed to execution, as in the design for a costume or a piece of furniture.

In the more limited sense, designs may retain this idea of plan; the patterns for making lace, the cartoons used as a guide in tapestry are designs. But by extension designs may be thought of as the executed patterns themselves rather than the quality or act of arranging them; the planning or creative aspect may be far in the past or not under consideration.

Such patterns or designs may be classified according to their range from the abstract to the literal. There are:

(1) Completely abstract designs which comprise an arrangement of lines, shapes, colors, not consciously based on an object or concrete idea. This type of design, in folk and primitive art, is prevailingly *geometric* —the so-called *free shape*, which is neither geometric nor representational, being less common.

(2) Partially abstract designs in which the subject, while present, is not literally depicted but rearranged, with the natural contours of objects reduced or adjusted to a pattern. Since such patterns tend to crystallize by repetition and are recognized by general agreement (by convention) as a substitute for the thing, the term *conventionalized design* is used. The degree of rearrangement varies from the slightly to the highly conventionalized. In the latter case (as in Arapaho bead embroidery, where a person is represented by a diamond shape, a butterfly by a double triangle) the design might be viewed as completely abstract unless its source or subject happened to be known. In the process of conventionalizing, geometric shapes are frequently but not necessarily used.

(3) Representational designs, in which the subject is depicted, i.e. more or less faithfully copied, rather than conventionalized. When the design is completely representational it becomes like a picture—the literal bunch of grapes on the bottom of a fruit dish, the ship tattooed on a sailor's chest. In such cases, the word *decoration* is to be preferred since the basic meaning of design (plan or arrangement) suggests some degree of abstraction or conventionalizing. However, design and decoration overlap to such extent that they are loosely interchangeable.

Any design (whether conventionalized or purely abstract) is called *geometric* nowadays if it is based on arrangements of straight and curved lines or geometric figures such as the square, circle, triangle, rectangle, etc., and such formal shapes as spiral, cross, radial, arabesque, interlaced lines. However, it is not to be thought of as derived from a knowledge of geometry or mathematics or the use of mechanical tools. The term geometric is applied to the ancient Pueblo symbol enclosing a crude rectangle within a crude rectangle, as well as to the Chinese yang and yin, which is a mathematically exact division of the circle, and to the Pennsylvania German barn symbols, usually executed with a compass.

The occurrence of geometric design is virtually universal from prehistoric times to the present day. Familiar examples, the checkerboard, meander, zigzag, arrow, line and dot patterns, and many others, occur in similar form in many parts of the world. It is interesting to speculate why this should be so. Obviously certain techniques result in an emphasis on either straight or curved lines; weaving and folding produce the former, coiling the latter, for example. There is also without doubt a common association of contrasting ideas with these contrasting shapes. The female is associated with the curved or round, male with the square or straight, even in prehistoric cave art. The round of the sun and moon is opposed to the straight line of the horizon, the triangle of tree or mountain or tent. It is also possible that in folk art as well as in sophisticated art, the precision of geometric shapes suggests itself as a way of making order or "art" out of the profuse shapes of nature.

The process of conventionalizing subjects for purposes of design is often thought of as one of simplification and this is often true, for example in the suggestion of a wing by a few parallel lines, as in Nazca pottery, or the depiction of a man in simple cross-stitch or knitting patterns; but sometimes the designs, as in Mayan or Haida or Buddhist art, seem more complex than a literal depiction would be. Convention in design is a matter of rearrangement rather than mere simplification, and the reasons and methods for accomplishing it are innumerable. One can only suggest: the adaptation of the subject to the design area (as in the depiction of the tree of life to a round plate), or to the over-all shape as in scarification which follows body contours; the limitations of the medium (in weaving, all depictions, even that of the sun, must become angular); the exaggeration of certain elements like the beak of Raven, or the teeth of Beaver, and the omission or reduction of others; simplification, as seen in the triangular nose and zigzag teeth of the Halloween pumpkin, or elaboration for its own sake, as in the spirals of New Zealand carving or the finials of medieval illuminated letters; the influence of adjacent elements in the design, as in the zigzag of the border added to an animal motif; development of the counter (negative area of the design) at the expense of the depiction; the effect of prolonged copying, slurring, or speeding-up of execution, change or loss of the original idea; the repeating of elements within the design or the fusing of various elements; the injection of abstract ideas such as fertility in a visual symbol.

Designs may be analyzed, also, with regard to their construction. They may comprise a single figure, a band or bands, repeated figures or over-all patterns. Bands are a common form of decoration for even the simplest objects. They emphasize the rim of vessels (marginal designs), the edges or bulges of innumerable useful objects. Bands may be composed of straight lines, wavy lines (scallops) or repeated rows of dots, parallel lines, arrow points or chevrons, crosses, lozenges, S-shapes, etc. The repeated figures in the band are often linked so as to form such familiar continuous patterns as the zigzag, double zigzag, scroll, meander or key pattern, and stairstep pattern. The figures are multiplied or alternated, like the egg and dart, triangle and dot.

A design element may be repeated, not only to form a band, but in a variety of ways. Often it is doubled, especially with the two sides in reverse, producing the bilateral symmetry common in many art cultures.

(Sometimes only part of the design is doubled, like the Austrian eagle with two heads and a single tail.) It may be repeated in three parts (the trefoil) or in four parts (a Carolingian belt buckle or the mouth of a Congo mask exemplify the circle bisected by a cross, in which the four resulting areas show repeated elements) or as many times as it is desired to subdivide or cover a given area. Often a design is repeated in concentric fashion— a simple rectangle within rectangle or the more complex hawk, holding a hawk, in a Tsimshian headdress.

The more important aspect of design, from a cultural point of view, has to do not so much with its construction as with its significance. It is sometimes argued that all folk art, and especially all primitive art, has meaning, that there is no such thing as purely abstract design. Such assumptions present difficulties, for the impulses behind a piece of work and even behind the evolution of complete art forms are not always known. The parallel bars scratched along the sides of a prehistoric arrowhead may have been symbolic of its flight or purely decorative. As designs are repeated thousands of times, meaning is forgotten and they are used in a completely abstract way, whatever their original purpose. Nevertheless, appropriateness is a factor in any study of design—Mother Goose characters are suitable for the nursery wall, mating birds for the Turkish harem. Much of design is connotative, much definitely symbolic. An excellent example of the latter may be found in the analysis of design in DRUM. (See SYMBOLISM.)

Motif and pattern, as well as decoration and ornament, are words that are often used interchangeably with design, and since the whole subject covers such a vast range, it would be convenient if these terms could be made to apply to different aspects of it. Actually, there is some basis for such distinctions. *Motif* or *motive* in folklore, outside of art, is used in connection with a concept or an incident. Therefore, it would be logical in folk art to use the word for a design or group of designs in which some meaning or symbolism or prevailing detail is involved. Phœnix, dragon, thunderbird, frog, tulip, acanthus, eye, cloud, sun supply the motif for a number of designs adapted to different shapes, sizes, materials, or objects.

Pattern suggests something that is copied, imitated, or repeated. And since most designs are repeated or made from a pattern, the words have become almost synonymous. But pattern is the suitable word, particularly, for two aspects of design: (1) for the model or sketch which is to be copied, as a dress pattern or a stencil pattern; (2) for the kind of design which is characterized by a repeated element, like lace and weaving patterns. (The individual unit of such a pattern is usually called a *figure*.) Compare DECORATION.   MAMIE HARMON

despised boy The hero of a number of Apache Indian folktales, who never washed and was so lazy that the people thought he was no good. The Chiricahua version begins with the statement that the boy slept all day. Actually the boy was out all night and came home every morning at daybreak. One day when his people had no food, the boy went out, weaponless, ran down a deer, and brought it home. So at last the people realized that all his life the boy had spent the nights learning to be a swift runner. He was not lazy at all.

The Lipan and Mescalero Apache also tell this story, and there is a Navaho version. Usually the stories begin with the statement that the lazy, dirty, and despised boy lives with his grandmother. He eventually proves his worth to the people by performing marvelous running feats and showing great courage. The Jicarilla Apache version of the story, *Dirty Boy*, is based on this theme, but is a long, elaborate and detailed narrative dealing with the hero's horse-raiding expeditions, encounters with enemies, etc. See AMALA; DIRTY BOY.

deswadę́yǫ́ or **changing-a-rib** The continuation of the *iyondátha*, the Iroquois women's curing rite. The dance and general character of the songs is the same, with a whole series of like tunes and new words. At one point, however, before the dance begins, there is a bantering back and forth between the men and women in song. These refer to the legend of a confirmed bachelor who was fooled into marrying a frog woman and who brought back the songs from her people. [GPK]

detective story A story in which a culprit is detected by some clever means: related to the tales of the clever maiden and the riddles, to tales of clever judicial decisions, etc. The story of Susanna and the Elders, in which Daniel questions Susanna's accusers separately and then refutes the accusation by comparing the contradictory evidence, is paralleled (though in a reverse direction) in the Arabian story of the parrot and the adulterous wife. The parrot's testimony is thoroughly discredited (although it is true) when he describes a storm, faked by the wife, that the husband knows did not occur. Solomon is the hero not only of riddling tales, but of several detective stories too. He decides the famous case of the two mothers by threatening to cut the baby in two: the real mother is at once apparent. He discovers what the Queen of Sheba's legs look like by sitting in a glass house: she thinks he sits in water and raises her skirts as she approaches.

Abhaya, minister to King Śreṇika, in an Indian story, discovers who has stolen the mangoes from the king's garden. He attends a meeting of the lowest characters in the city and tells them a story. A wife must perform an obligation, but is stopped by a gardener, some robbers, and a Rākshasa who wish to lie with her. She promises to return if they permit her to do what she has promised to do first. Her husband lets her go back to them, but each in turn, as he hears the story, leaves her unmolested. Abhaya then asks the group who has been most magnanimous in the story. Only the mango-stealer votes for the robbers, and Abhaya thus recognizes the identity of the culprit.

determination of seasons Tales narrating how the number and length of the seasons were determined are told by nearly all North American Indian tribes. Often such tales are told as a dispute between two characters, one of whom wants summer to be year-long. In other forms of the tale a council of animals decides the number and length of the seasons. The majority of such tales are set in the pre-human animal period when the earth was still being formed and ways of life determined. [EWV]

Deucalion In Greek mythology, the survivor of the flood and ancestor of the human race; son of Prometheus and Clymene (or Pandora); king of Phthia in

Thessaly; husband of Pyrrha. For their piety, Prometheus warned the couple of the flood caused by Zeus to destroy mankind, and on his advice they built a ship with which they rode out the nine days' flood. The ship came to rest on Parnassus (other places mentioned are Athos, Etna, Othrys) where they descended and asked at the sanctuary of Themis how to restore the human race. The answer was, perhaps carried to them by a messenger of Zeus, "Cover your heads and throw the bones of your mother behind you." Taking the latter to mean stones, the bones of the Mother Earth, they did so. From the stones thrown by Deucalion there sprang up men; from those by Pyrrha, women. They descended from the mountain top and Deucalion built a house at Opus where he became the first king of that city. By Pyrrha he was father of Hellen, Amphictyon, Idomeneus, and other children. Compare DELUGE.

dev In Armenian belief, a gigantic male or female spirit, harmful, but also often believed to be foolish and harmless. The dev sometimes has one eye, sometimes more and they are as large as earthen bowls. Devs often possess seven heads and are so strong that they can toss large rocks great distances. They live in caverns and thick forests. Devs can appear as human beings, as serpents, or (in dreams) as wild beasts. Insanity, fainting, itching, sneezing are signs of their presence. Cutting the air with a stick or sword will protect against them.

deva (1) In Hinduism and Buddhism, a god or divine being: literally, a shining one of the Vedas. There are 33 Hindu devas, eleven for each of the three worlds.

(2) In Zoroastrianism, a demon or daēva.

dēvadāsi Literally, slaves of the gods: a caste of dancers and courtesans connected with some Hindu temples, especially in the Deccan and Madras. Their duties include fanning the idol, singing and dancing before the god when he is carried in procession, sweeping and purifying the temple floor by washing it with cow-dung and water. They receive a small salary for the religious duties performed and supplement this by selling their favors. They are usually married to the god or to a sword with a special rite. Until recently they were better educated than married women.

devak In Bombay, the Deccan, and the Bombay Presidency, a guardian deity: an animal, tree, or trade implement considered the ancestor or head of the house. The devak is treated with respect and worshipped chiefly at the time of marriage or upon entering a new house. Frequently people with the same devak cannot marry, suggesting a totemistic origin.

Devatā In Hindu mythology, a god: a term generally applied to the inferior gods.

Devī or **Mahādevī** In Hindu mythology and religion, the great goddess, consort of Śiva, and daughter of Himavat: the mother goddess worshipped by the śāktas and the female principle or energy of Śiva. In the latter form she has two aspects: one mild under which she is known as Gaurī (the yellow), Pārvatī (the mountaineer), Umā (light), Jaganmātā (mother of the world); the other, in which she is most frequently worshipped, the terrible. In her terrible aspects she is Chandī (fierce), Bhairavī (terrible), Durgā (inaccessible), and Kālī (the black). On the one hand she is represented as adorned

with jewels, with abundant food, and beautiful; on the other hand she is represented in hideous aspects usually with the symbols of death (the noose, iron hook, rosary, and the textbook of prayer).

The worship of Devī reached its height during the period of the Tantras. Apparently at the end of the Vedic period or later several goddesses were acknowledged as wives of Rudra-Śiva, while other goddesses were worshipped by different classes of people in different parts of India. Gradually these goddesses were coalesced into one great goddess who, however, has never completely superseded the local grāma-devatā or matris. These, in many cases, are considered a manifestation or incarnation of Devī and as such are promoted above the other members of their rank. As Śakti she is worshipped by the Vāmāchārīs or left-handed śaktis with licentious rites as the active female principle. Modern orthodox Hinduism, however, denies any connection between the grāma-devatā or earth goddesses and the Hindu deities.

As Durgā, the inaccessible, she is a yellow woman riding on a tiger who guards her devotees from distress, is the refuge for the shipwrecked and those lost in the wilds or attacked by evil men. She is worshipped especially in Bengal. As Kālī she is black, dripping blood, adorned with skulls and human heads, and regarded as the protectress against the evil spirits which haunt desolate places, and against wild beasts. In some places she is the goddess of bird-catchers. As Vindhyavāsinī Devī is worshipped in the Vindhyas with bloody sacrifices. Her other epithets include Mahā-māyā (illusion), Dakshajā (born of Daksha), Ambikā (mother), Anantā (everlasting), Satī (virtuous), Dakshiṇā (right-handed), Kotarī (naked), Bhūta-nāyakī (spirit leader). Her emblems include the bow and arrow, bowl, goad, hook, ladle, noose, prayer-book, rosary, and the sword.

In Hindu mythology, she is the unconquerable, sublime warrior-maid, produced from the combined wraths of all the gods in council when Mahiṣāsura, the colossal buffalo monster, threatened to undo the world. The indignant divinities poured out their energy as fires which rushed together and assumed the shape of the goddess. Provided with the weapons of the gods, riding on a lion, the goddess roped the monster with a noose. The beast escaped in a lion transformation. This the goddess beheaded but again the asura escaped in the form of a hero, and again as an elephant. The goddess finally killed him after he had returned to his buffalo form.

According to the *Upānishads,* she was the daughter of Himavat. She was sometimes connected with the ṛishis as the daughter of Daksha (according to the Purāṇas) and abandoned her bodily existence when her husband was slighted in Daksha's sacrifice. She was the mother of Skanda and Kumāra.

Devil The archfiend; the evil principle and the enemy of mankind of Judeo-Christian belief. See SATAN.

devil Term frequently used for demon, imp, or other evil spirits. See DEMON; SPIRITS.

devil dance A form of exorcism, said to be allied to the shamanism of northern Asia, prevalent in southern India and appearing also in Ceylon, northern India, Tibet, etc. It is usually employed to entice the demon from the body of a sick person into the body of the dancer, whose frenzied actions while possessed are said to attenuate and dissipate the power of the infecting demon. Devil dancing is found in the demonic Bon cult of Tibet. Compare POSSESSION.

☞ Devil dances and devil beating ceremonials found in various places in China may be a lamaist importation. Data is incomplete. In lamaist temples priests disguised as gods and devils attack each other in mock combat. The date is variable. [RDJ]

☞ A representation of a malignant supernatural power or devil, usually in a horror-inspiring mask, performed with grotesque and often obscene gestures. As all demon dances, these are intended to propitiate the evil spirits, and to effect cures or good crops. The devil dances of Tibet and Ceylon are curative. Actually, they are demon dances addressed to powers held in fearful veneration. The Apache devil dance, so-called, represents really the Gahe mountain supernaturals and is essentially beneficial.

The classical Devil, that is, he of medieval tale, miracle play, and carnival, the Diablo, Lucifer, Satanas of Spain, by no means inspires unmitigated horror. On the contrary, his character is tinged with considerable humor, even good nature, and he may even be regarded with a certain affection, as shown by the German tales of "gute, dumme Teufel"—good, dumb Devil. His physical attributes are capricious, not only his bounds and capers, but his cloven hoof, tail, horns. He is red, or green, or more often sooty; he is accompanied by fireworks, or manipulates an agricultural tool, a pitchfork. In the Majorcan *Cociés* he plays the part of the fool. In Catalonia he appears in numerous guises in the *ball de diables*. The diablo of the Mexican carnaval is certainly borrowed from Spain, an addition to clown figures that represent native deities.

The various attributes of the various devils of the devil dances and particularly the undercurrent of affection he inspires would lend support to the theory of his origin in some agricultural deity, half mischievous and half beneficient. But of course he is evil in the eyes of the clergy. [GPK]

devil's bedstead The four of clubs, an unlucky card. A bet made on a hand containing the "four-poster" will not win.

devil's promenade A Comanche Indian festival, July 3–6 inclusive, held jointly with the Kiowa and Creek tribes. It consists of games, game dances, and social dances for men and women. The latter are performed in a circle, first counterclockwise, then, for the walk-off, clockwise. The step is a side progression with a straight-bend motion of the knee. The bear hug is a step for couples performed with a crossing step similar to the *pas de bourrée*. [GPK]

Devil's riddle The theme of a type of folktale especially characteristic of Scandinavian and Baltic peoples, in which a man, promised to the Devil, saves himself by solving either three or seven riddles posed by the Devil. The riddles and answers follow three patterns: identification of the true nature of the Devil's many possessions (i.e. the Devil's horse is a he-goat, his spoon a whale's rib, his wineglass a horse's hoof, etc.), answering unanswerable questions (How far is it from heaven to earth? The Devil knows for he has fallen the distance, or One step, for my grandfather has one foot in

the grave and one in heaven. What is harder than stone? Death), or explaining the symbolic meanings of certain numbers. Many of the stories describe how the man learned the answers: overhearing by some ruse the Devil's conversation with a friend, or being aided by the Devil's grandmother; other tales leave the answers to the man's own unexpected but solid wit.

dewatsihása'ǫ An Iroquois Indian social dance; the garter dance. Its form is fairly elaborate, combining features of the *ga'dášot* and *gędjóenǫ* types. The music shares the tonality and melodic antiphony of the former, in addition to self-accompaniment by two dance leaders with horn rattles. The structure is an extended ternary, with modulation in B, some songs repeating A four times and B three times. This corresponds to the choreographic development, the first part being identical with the *ga'dášot*. But during the remaining repetitions the dancers, who are arranged in couples, cross over the recross as in the fish dance. This always happens during B to a vibration of the rattles. The step throughout is a stomp. [GPK]

deyodasǫ́dayǫ The Iroquois Indian dark dance, performed in complete darkness as a curative rite. For hours the dancers stamp in place, the women at times joining the men in the singing, to both drum and rattle. Its legend deals with the little people (*djǫgäǫ*) and a good hunter who chased a supernatural beast and slew him, and returned with his flesh as medicine. The ceremony is always private, performed in the home of the patient. [GPK]

deyǫdanäśǫta The Iroquois Indian hand-in-hand dance, performed in an antisunwise round by men and women in alternation, with hands linked among the Cayuga but not among the Seneca. It is a slow processional with the stomp step, accompanied by a horn rattle in the hand of the leader and by well-developed songs in major tonality. The second part develops at length the rhythmic motif of the first. Sometimes there are four repetitions of the entire song. A fast *ga'dášot* is always appended to the dance proper. Its meaning is enigmatic. Some informants identify this dance with the bean dance, one of the spirits-of-the-food dances. It is part of the regular ceremonial sequence among the Tonawanda Seneca. Other informants trace it back to a dance of victory and unity after the repulsion of an invader. [GPK]

deyǫgenyótges Literally, cousin dance: the Seneca choose-a-partner dance, a social entertainment. It is of the *gędjóenǫ* or fish dance type in every respect, but has the unique feature of the women leading off with a *ga'dášot* round and each choosing her partner for the rest of the cycle. [GPK]

Dharma In Hindu mythology and religion, the sage who married 10 (or 13) daughters of Daksha; a personification of law and justice; judge of the dead. His children were personifications of religious rites and virtues. In the *Mahābhārata* he was the father of Yudhishthira, the chief of the Pāṇḍavas. In Bengal, Dharma is worshipped as a supreme god by some lower castes. Compare ADHARMA.

Dharmapālas Literally, Protectors of Religion: in Buddhism, especially that of Tibet, fierce, mispro-

portioned beings with broad heads, huge teeth, protruding tongues, and a third eye in the forehead. In
Tibet they are the demon generals who execute the will
of the Yi-dam or tutelaries. They are of the fiercest
fiend type and the females are metamorphoses of Kālī.
The chief Dharmapālas are Hayagrīva and Devī. Their
Tibetan name is *Ch'os-skyoṅ.*

Dhartī Māī, Dhartī, Dhartī Mātā, or **Bhūdevī** In
Hinduism, the earth goddess who upholds human,
animal, and vegetable life: the "Mother who supports."
Dhartī Māī is present everywhere in the ground. She is
worshipped by the Bhuiyās with the sacrifice of goats,
pigs, and fowls. The Chamārs of Madras Presidency
worship her by digging up five spadefuls of earth, taking them home, and placing them in the courtyard
before a marriage ceremony takes place. As a village
goddess she is often worshipped as a pile of stones or
as a pot. Pious Hindus say a prayer to her upon awak-
ing in the morning.

Dhātri In Vedic mythology, a deity, the maker or
creator who promotes generation, presides over domestic life, and preserves health. He is an abstract deity
usually considered either an agent or an attribute. In
later mythology he appears as one of the Ādityas and
is identified with Prajāpati or Brahmā as the creator.

Dhol or **Dhaul** In Indian folktales, the white cow
which supports the earth on its horns.

Dhruva In Hindu mythology, the pole star. Dhruva,
according to the Purāṇas, was the son of Uttānapāda
by his second wife. His brother, Uttama, received all
his father's attention, so Dhruva decided to attain virtue
by venerating Vishṇu. As a reward that god elevated
him to the position of pole star.

diamond The adamant of the ancients: highly valued,
although many were actually other clear, brilliant stones.
It is only within the past century that the full fire and
sparkle of the stone has been released by newer types
of faceting. It is doubtful if the diamond of the High
Priest's breastplate could have been genuine for at that
time it was not possible to engrave this hard stone,
and the cost of a diamond of that size would have been
prohibitive. As is natural for a stone of such beauty and
value, the diamond possessed most of the virtues
ascribed to all other gems, but while up to the Renaissance most other stones were believed to be beneficial,
this was not true of the diamond. In Persia it was considered a source of sin and sorrow and an invention of
evil. In the 16th century Jerome Cardan explains that
it makes its wearer unhappy because its brilliance
irritates the soul as an excess of sun irritates the eye.
It was believed that a good diamond could lose its
virtue through the sin of the owner. There was also a
widespread belief that the spirit of the diamond resented being sold, and it then lost its virtue. It must be
given in love and friendship. Among the Hindus, poor
diamonds were considered worse than none at all as
they caused jaundice, pleurisy, leprosy, lameness, and
all manner of misfortunes. It was generally believed
that the diamond was poison if swallowed.

There would be many more fine diamonds in the
world today, except for the belief that these stones
could not be broken by a hammer and anvil, but only

with goats' blood. There were many other superstitions
connected with this gem, such as the belief that it could
only be found at night, and that it grew a cubit every
two or three years when left under the soil. Many
believed that diamonds were thunderbolts, and it was
said that a magnet would not pick up iron in the
presence of a diamond.

In India there were four castes of diamonds: the first
gave good fortune, the second, success, the third prevented old age, and the highest gave power, wealth,
friends, and luck. To give a diamond to a shrine was
to be assured of eternal life. They also made a decoction of diamond which gave longevity, beauty, strength,
happiness, and virility.

In the Middle Ages the adamant would make the
wearer proof against poison, plague, and pestilence. It
cured diseases of the bladder, leprosy, insanity, nightmares, and insomnia, but produced somnambulism. It
gave strength, courage and victory and used in the
magic arts, it made its possessor indomitable. Many
held that it made the wearer invisible. It was emblem
of the sun and of innocence, and was capable of producing a state of spiritual ecstasy. It protected ladies
from incubi, which has been suggested by some cynics
as the origin of the custom of removing rings before
retiring.

De Boot, an authority of gems in the middle of the
17th century, was inclined to be skeptical as to some
of the properties of the diamond (and other stones) and
performed some tests himself. He was willing to
believe that diamonds would repel poison, pestilence,
witchcraft, madness, and terrors in the night. However,
he doubted its efficacy as a test for adultery.

Diana See ARTEMIS; HIPPOLYTUS; KING OF THE WOOD;
ORESTES.

Diancécht In Old Irish mythology, a clever physician
of the Tuatha Dé Danann. He had a powerful healing
spring in which he restored every man who was mortally
wounded at the Battle of Mag Tured, unless his head
was cut off. It was he who made the wonderful silver
arm for Nuada, which was so like a living arm that
every finger had the gift of motion. Diancécht was
invoked in charms even into the 8th Christian century.

didī A gbo or magic charm of the Negroes of Dahomey,
used by hunters to protect them against lions: named
for the seed of the didī tree, because this seed never
bursts. The didī contains a piece of lion's skin which
serves the twofold purpose of repelling the lion and
imparting lion's strength to the user. (Herskovits
Dahomey II, 275)

Dido In classical legend, a Phœnician goddess, whose
name was taken by Elissa, daughter of Belus of Tyre,
and founder of Carthage: the story is told with some
changes in Virgil's *Æneid.* She was married to her rich
uncle Acerbas (or Sichæus) who was killed by her
brother Pygmalion. With the treasures of her husband
she fled to Africa where she purchased from Hiarbas,
the king of Mauretania, as much land as could be enclosed with the hide of a bull. She cut the hide into
the thinnest strips possible and on the land thus bought
she built the fortress Byrsa, around which Carthage
grew up. Hiarbas, growing fearful of her power, de-

manded that she marry him, threatening war if she did not. Since the Carthaginians wished her to marry, she, who had vowed eternal fidelity to her dead husband, pretended to accede to the demands. But first she built a huge funeral pile, with the excuse that she wanted to make an expiatory sacrifice to the spirit of Acerbas. Then, before the people, she stabbed herself, and was burned on the pyre. She was afterwards considered a divinity at Carthage. In the Vergilian story, she killed herself when Æneas deserted her to go on to his promised home in Italy.

diffusion theory The theory that similarity of stories and story elements among different countries is due to their spread, i.e. their diffusion, from a common center. It was widely held, for example, that many of the stories, especially the fairy tales of Europe, originated in India and migrated westward from there. The diffusion theory is opposed to the theory of polygenesis which holds that very similar stories may originate independently in different parts of the world since man was often confronted by similar conditions of environment. At present folklorists see truth in both theories and insist that neither can be the sole explanation of story similarity, and that consequently each story must be studied independently.

Certain criteria are important in determining whether a given story is the product of diffusion or has arisen independently. General plot similarity is not an indication of diffusion; on the other hand, irrelevant details in common are. For example, stories of child sacrifice would arise independently, but the child sacrifice stories that tell of the children being restored and found the next day playing with an apple (France and England), an orange (Italy), a round sunbeam (Celtic), etc., must come from a common source, since they have gratuitous and irrelevant details in common. Common stylistic features like the figures of speech in the Deirdre story in which Deirdre describes the man she would have for husband as having hair black as the raven, cheeks as red as the blood the raven is drinking, and body as white as the snow into which the blood is flowing, would indicate diffusion of that incident if not the whole story. There are other stylistic criteria, many of them subjective, like the "Celtic magic" that stamps a Celtic story. The same whimsical or haphazard arrangement of motifs in similar stories from different countries would suggest diffusion. Often historical, topographical, or linguistic data are helpful. Finally, a study of all known variants of a story by the geographical-historical method can fix the place of origin and determine whether the story was a drifting one or one of independent origin.

Stories, like culture in general, are diffused by many different agencies: conquest resulting in prisoners, slaves, hostages; trade; exogamous marriages; migration of peoples; fugitives; shipwrecked sailors; proselyting religions like Mohammedanism and Christianity; itinerant entertainers; seepage across borders. The Gipsies and the Jews have been important in spreading stories from east to west. [MEL]

digging sings Songs sung by Negro field workers in Jamaica. The words are in English or the local dialect, "deep" English, and are somewhat religious in character. They are sung particularly for spring farm work.

dill An old world annual of the parsley family (*genus Anethum*) with pungent seeds: used as a condiment and medicinally. In some parts of the world, it was abhorrent to witches, but elsewhere it was freely used in their own witch-brews. It was in general use to relieve flatulence, colic, and obesity. In Prussia the steam from an infusion of dill was inhaled to stop a toothache. In England, boiled in wine, its fumes were inhaled to halt yexing (hiccup), and the ashes of the seeds were used in cases of scalding and on venereal infections.

Dinewan The personified emu, who plays a leading role as chief of birds in New South Wales mythology, particularly in that of the Eualayhi (Ualayi) tribe, where his loss of wings is attributed to the trick played on him by Goomblegubbon, the Bustard, who was jealous of his speed. In revenge the emu got the bustard to destroy all but two of his twelve youngsters so that they would grow as large as emus. Now emus are wingless and bustards lay only two eggs. [KL]

Dingbelle A female of the gremlin family, operating only on the ground. These creatures, first discovered by the Canadian Wids (Women's Division), fouled up typing, flipped on public-address systems in the middle of personal conversations, and during off-duty hours were apt to toss pictures of handsome Wing Commanders out of the Wid's kit bag while she was entertaining her LAC boy-friend or vice versa. Dingbelle is not to be confused with Fifinella.

Dinnshenchas The *History of Places* (Irish *dinn-seancas*, topography, especially of famous places): a group of Old Irish local legends in prose and verse, explaining the names of famous rivers, fords, lakes, hills, other places, in Ireland. It exists in the 12th century Rawlinson manuscript, now in Bodleian Library, Oxford University, and in the *Book of Leinster*.

Dione In Greek mythology, a vague figure, undoubtedly an earth goddess, the most ancient consort of Zeus: she bears approximately the same relationship in characteristics and etymology to Zeus as Juno does to Jupiter. She is associated with Zeus at Dodona, being seated alongside him, but with the rise of the Delphic oracle and the decline of Dodona, she lost importance and was supplanted by Hera as Zeus' wife. In the *Iliad* she is the mother by Zeus of Aphrodite (who is called Dione herself); as time passed she became a lesser personage, in Hesiod an Oceanid, a nymph of Dodona in Pherecydes, an Atlantid or a Titanid in Hyginus. She was thus in later mythology variously the nurse or the mother of Dionysus or the mother of Pelops and Niobe.

Dionysus The Greek god of the vine; originally a god of vegetation, he kept his office over fruit trees and the grape: because of his prominence in Orphic religion, at one time he was the most popular of the gods. Dionysus is probably Phrygian in origin, the corresponding Phrygian god being Diounsis, although a Thracian origin is often supposed. However, his mother Semele seems obviously to be the Phrygian Zemelo, an earth goddess. His cult observance was one of death and dismemberment and resurrection, which caused identification of the god by the Greeks with the Egyptian Osiris. The Roman Liber or Bacchus was also identified with Dionysus.

In mythology, Dionysus was the son of Zeus and Semele. When Semele died because of her foolhardiness in the sixth or seventh month of her pregnancy, Zeus saved the infant from her ashes and kept him in his thigh until the full nine-month term had expired. The epithet Dithyrambos, derived from the song of the Dionysian followers, was said to have evolved from this "double entrance" into life. When the child was reborn from the thigh, Zeus entrusted him to Hermes, who gave Dionysus to Ino and Athamas to rear. They brought him up as a girl, until the jealous Hera drove them mad, whereupon Zeus transformed Dionysus into a kid. In cult observance, it was often a goat which was rent alive by the followers of the god, either because of this myth or because the goat nibbled at the shoots of the vine. From the chorus of goats voicing the dithyramb in the festivals arose Greek tragedy, such at least being the current belief regarding the derivation of the word *tragedy* from *tragōidia*, goat song.

Ino and Athamas being insane, Hermes escorted Dionysus to the Nysan nymphs, the Hyades, who brought him up. A series of myths exist concerning Dionysus' travels through Asia Minor, Egypt, and India, in which regions he taught the use of the vine and into which his worship spread. These stories tell of the refusal of a ruler or other person to accept Dionysus' divinity, and of the punishment visited on the ruler or his people by the god, for example the tearing to pieces of Pentheus by women. The *Seventh Homeric Hymn* tells of the kidnapping of the god by pirates, and how he covered the decks and masts with ivy, driving the crew mad so that they leaped into the sea to become dolphins. In another myth, Dionysus sought to descend to Hades to bring Semele to the abode of the gods, but he did not know the way. Prosymnus or Polymnus or Hypolipnus offered to point out the route in exchange for a curious gift. When Dionysus returned, he discovered that his guide had died in the meanwhile, but he kept his promise by carving the promised thing from a fig tree and placing it on the grave. Hades would not release Semele unless he also had a gift in exchange from Dionysus, this time the thing he loved best. So Dionysus presented him with the myrtle, because ivy, the grape vine, and myrtle were associated with him. Among the attributes of Dionysus were the thyrsus, a wand tipped with a pine cone (apparently a phallic symbol), the grape vine, myrtle, and ivy, and the panther.

The original general office of Dionysus as a god of fertility, underlying a portion of the myths and remaining to some degree in the observances, did not carry over prominently in Greece, for there were other gods presiding over fertility. However, the rites connected with wine, the riotous singing procession of sileni, satyrs, bassarides, bacchantes, took root in Greece and became extremely popular. Dionysus was honored at four Attic festivals: the Dionysia, the Lenæa, the Oschophoria, the Anthesteria. He held a position at Delphi perhaps equal to that of Apollo. Thebes was said to be his place of birth. He was a bringer of civilization, a culture hero, in Crete.

Dioscuri Literally, sons of Zeus; Castor and Pollux (Greek Polydeuces), the Spartan twins of Greek mythology and legend; sons of Tyndareus and Leda in Homer, although other tradition says that the two boys and Helen were born from one egg or that Pollux and Helen were children of Zeus and immortal while Castor was mortal. They figure in three principal adventures:

(1) The rescue of Helen from Athens after Theseus abducted her. While Theseus was away from Attica, the brothers invaded the land. There they were told by Academus, a native of Attica, that Helen was being kept by Theseus' mother, Æthra, at Aphidnæ. They took the town, rescued their sister, and carried off Æthra. Academus thereafter was honored by the Spartans, who refrained from invading his land, outside Athens, whenever they waged war in Attica.

(2) The Argonautic expedition. Pollux, who was a great boxer, killed Amycus of the Bebrycians, a son of Poseidon, with his fists in single combat. The twins are also said to have taken part in the Calydonian boar hunt some time before the voyage of the Argo.

(3) The fight with the Apharetidæ. The Dioscuri had run off with Hilaira and Phœbe, the betrothed of their cousins Idas and Lynceus. According to some, the fight arose directly from this; others say that it began over the division of a herd of cattle. During the fight, Idas killed Castor and Pollux slew Lynceus. Pollux, the immortal twin, begged Zeus, who had slain Idas with a bolt, to be allowed to share his brother's fate. As a result, the brothers, either together or alternately, lived one day in the earth and the next among the gods of Olympus. They are also said to have been placed among the stars, the constellation Gemini, the Twins, being their asterism.

Castor and Pollux were worshipped as divine not only in Sparta but in other parts of Greece, Sicily, and Italy. They were protecting deities of sailors, of travelers, of the laws of hospitality, of oaths. Either as a result of their connection with Zeus, the god of thunder, or through their association with Poseidon, the sea and horse god, they are horsemen, riding on white steeds, presiding over the public games. They were the inventors of the war dance, hence protectors of the dance and likewise of poets.

In Rome, they were worshipped in early times, Castor seemingly first, for the twins were known as the Castores. For their assistance to the Romans at the battle at Lake Regillus, a temple was erected to them in the Forum opposite the temple of Vesta. The equites, whose patrons they were, annually on July 15, the anniversary of the founding of this temple, rode in procession through the streets of the city past the temple. Weights and measures were tested here, in keeping with the role of the twins as guardians of honesty, which is also attested to by the popular oaths, used by women, *mecastor* and *edipol*. In 168 B.C. the Castores announced the capture of the Macedonian King Perseus to Publius Vatinius on the very day that the capture occurred. Vatinius was, however, thrown into jail for announcing this, but was released and given a grant of land when word arrived that the capture was a fact.

The relationship of the Dioscuri to other twins in Indo-European mythology and to heavenly twins the world over has been discussed by A. H. Krappe (*Mythologie universelle*, ch. IV). He traces the development of the investigation since its exposition by Harris early in the 20th century. The springboard for the study has been the similarities found among the Aśvins of Vedic tradition, the twins of several northern European mythologies, and the Spartan Dioscuri. Some ten general similarities of the heavenly twins are blocked out, and the mass of accumulated information is brought to bear to support these "postulates." In brief, Krappe's premises are: (1) All dioscuric pairs are twins, expressly or otherwise. If specific mention of the facts is omitted in the texts we have, one of three reasons may be the cause: either there has been inadvertent omission, or the facts were too well known to require repetition, or some special reason required that the fact be hidden. (2) The basis of belief in twin gods lies in the ominousness generally given by primitive people to the birth of twins. Such births may be an evil omen, requiring the persecution of one or both of the twins and sometimes the mother as well; or the births may be an omen of fertility and riches. (3) The universality of these beliefs make it impossible to confine them to origin among any one people or in any single culture. (4) Less often but still rather generally, the twins are children of the sky or thunder god. (5) Similarly widespread is the elevation of the twins to the heavens and their identification with the stars, for example with the morning and evening star(s) or with a constellation like Gemini. (6) The persecution of the twins and their mother leads to their being avengers of mother, sister, betrothed, or wife. (7) Such twins are usually indistinguishable one from another because of their physical resemblance. But where it was important to make the distinction, there was a decided lack of resemblance. (8) The twins, following the general human custom in such cases, bear one generic name. (9) Since no other cause seems so obvious, the birth of twins had to be the result of the mother's adultery, a justification of the ill-treatment she underwent. (10) The twins also had animal aspects, generally of horses or birds, especially of sea birds. Hence, they were often believed to have been hatched from an egg.

The conclusions drawn from this series necessarily deny the theory of the Indo-European origin of all cases of heavenly twins: (1) None of the ten "postulates" is peculiar to any linguistic or ethnographic group. (2) The belief is so ancient that the Indo-Europeans knew it both before and after their separation. (3) The Indo-Europeans carried their beliefs concerning dioscuri into lands which also had their own beliefs on the matter, and it is now impossible to say whether or not we are dealing with an Indo-European belief or with an indigenous belief. (4) Every locality had its pair of heavenly twins, making it an absurdity to associate all such pairs with an Indo-European prototype.

The examples cited by Krappe are drawn for the most part from Harris and Frazer and cover all parts of the world from South Africa and Ecuador to Java and North America, and all periods ranging from the ancient Babylonian through the classical Greek and the medieval European (evidencing certain twin pairs of saints) to the modern.

Dipper The popular English name for the northern constellation commonly known as URSA MAJOR or the GREAT BEAR: so called from its shape.

directional spirits Many North American Indian tribes identify their deities and powerful spirits with the directions, but nowhere on the continent is this identificaton of spirits with directions emphasized quite so strongly as in the American Southwest. Among the Pueblos and other groups in this area, six directions are often recognized: the four cardinal ones and zenith and nadir. With each of these is associated a color, a chief of the direction, and many other spirits. [ewv]

dirge songs Songs sung over dead bears by Indians of the Gitksan and Niskae tribes of the Skeena and Nass rivers. The songs were taught to Peesunt by her husband, Bear, to be sung over his body after his death. Compare MOURNING SONGS.

Dirty Boy A myth-character of the Jicarilla Apache Indians of the American Southwest, whose exploits as a runner, warrior, and leader are told in a Jicarilla Apache myth notable for its great length: one version recorded in English by Morris Edward Opler runs to 40,000 words or 75 printed pages (Morris Edward Opler, *Dirty Boy: A Jicarilla Tale of Raid and War. MAAA* 52, 1938). The story of Dirty Boy is also known to other Apache groups beside the Jicarilla. Briefly, it is concerned with the tale of "a dirty and apparently lazy young man who lives with his grandmother, who trains himself and hunts secretly at night, and who finally becomes a noted runner, warrior, and leader" (Opler, p. 3). The version of the tale published by Opler is particularly rich in cultural details of Jicarilla Apache concepts of raid, war, relationships between human beings, and status. A wealth of factual material concerning Jicarilla dress, dwellings, economy, weapons, hunting, campcraft, and domestic life is introduced. See DESPISED BOY. [ewv]

Dis In Roman mythology, Pluto, the god of the underworld. Dis is probably the same as Dives, the Rich, a translation of the name Pluto. The cult of Dis and Proserpina was established in Rome in 249 B.C. The name was also applied to the underworld itself. See HADES; ORCUS; PLUTO.

Disappointed Fisher Title of a European folktale (Type 832) having the punishment of child murder (plus greed) for its motif (Q553.5). A fisherman and his wife had always caught three fishes every day for themselves and their child; but one day they killed the child in order to have more to eat for themselves. After that they caught only two fishes every day.

disdainful woman or **man** Tales of the disdainful girl or man who refuses to marry any suitor, and her or his subsequent humbling experiences, are popular among certain North American Indian tribes, namely those of the North Pacific Coast, the interior Plateau region, the western part of the Mackenzie Yukon region, and among some Plains tribes. [ewv]

diseases Plagues were anciently looked upon as visitations of God's wrath upon a people. Syphilis especially, until very recently, was thought to be divine punishment for promiscuity. Cotton Mather of colonial Boston called disease "the whip of God for the sins of man" and held also that the sins of the fathers caused infant ills. Martin Luther made a great advance when he acquitted both God and man as cause and declared diseases were "naught but the Devil's work." Everywhere before the advance of medical science, and today in many places, diseases are believed to be caused by God, or gods, by demons and evil spirits, by object intrusion and other forms of witchcraft, by the air or other mysterious causes, or to be the consequences of broken tabus. See AIRE; CURES; EPILEPSY; MEDICINE.

↪ One of the main causes of illness in Middle America is believed to be the intrusion of small animate objects, such as spiders, worms, and the like, in the body of a witchcraft victim. Unlike the common pattern in North America, inanimate disease objects are rarely, if ever, used. See MEXICAN AND CENTRAL AMERICAN INDIAN FOLKLORE. [GMF]

↪ Diseases among South American Indians are rarely assigned to natural causes. Most of them are attributed either to a mysterious missile which enters the body of the sick person or to loss of the soul, which has been kidnapped or has left the body for some other reason. The theory of the intrusion of some pathogenic object in the patient's body is by far the most common. The material cause of the illness is described as a dart, or a piece of quartz, shot by a spirit or a sorcerer. The magic virus may also be some nondescript substance; or the pathogenic object may even be a spirit that has taken on material shape after entering the victim's body. The belief in the harmful effects of the loss of the soul is widespread among the Indians of the Andean region, but is also shared by many tropical tribes. Spirits and sorcerers are generally held responsible for the kidnapping of the soul, but the accident may occur as the result of sudden fright.

The ancient Peruvians and some modern tribes of South America, such as the Araucanians and the Chaco Indians, believe that epidemics or misfortune can be driven away like real foes. They perform ceremonies during which, after purifying themselves, they charge their invisible enemies, the evil spirits, and threaten them with their weapons. The great *situa* feast, celebrated in the Inca empire, had as main purpose the cleansing of cities and villages of all ills. [AM]

dittany An herb of the rue family originally found on Mt. Dicte in Crete, hence its name (*Dictamnus origanoides*). The *Encyclopedia of Bartholomew Angelicus* attributes knowledge of this herb to the hind "for she eateth this herb that she may calve easier and sooner; and if she be hurt with an arrow she seeketh this herb and eateth it, which putteth the iron out of the wound." Wild goats also knew of this herb, and it cured Godfrey (in Tasso's *Jerusalem Delivered*). The root applied in salves eased sciatica; the juice in wine cured the bites of snakes and other poisonous animals. It is a hot herb under the sign of Venus and is also sacred to Diana. It is sometimes called gas plant because it exudes a volatile oil in hot weather which is inflammable.

For toothache the Slovaks fumigate with bastard dittany, a species of horehound. The root of this plant is also used for epilepsy, hysteria, and worms. American dittany (*Cunila origanoides*) belongs to the mint family and was employed by the Indians as a stimulant, a nerve tonic, and in intermittent fevers.

dive for the oyster An American square dance figure. The first couple dives under the raised arms of the second couple; second couple the same; then the first couple dives and passes through and around, all holding hands the while. [GPK]

divide-the-ring An American square dance figure. One couple advances through the center and between the opposite couple, thus dividing the ring. [GPK]

divination The act or art of knowing or foretelling the unknown, whether future or distant in space: a practice of the greatest antiquity, performed everywhere in the world, by peoples in every cultural status, and utilizing almost every conceivable instrument or phenomenon as an indicator. Divination is a form of sympathetic magic; the status or action of the divining medium is determined by the future or far-off event, and vice versa; both the indicator and the event are in some form of logical harmony; each is the cause or the reflection of the other. Thus, dreams, when interpreted correctly, foretell the future, if not by picturing it directly then by symbolic constants. Sometimes the meaning of the dream is clear; sometimes it is obscured by the complexity of the symbolic events which occur in it. Therefore, to interpret dreams, or to read the augury of the flight of birds, or to explain the markings of the shoulderbone or the liver of the sacrifice, or to determine the precise configuration of the stars and planets at a given moment and thus their meaning, a class of diviners (shamans, priests, augurs, astrologers, doctors, bokónộs, lukumans, etc.) has existed from early times. These diviners, as the augurs in Rome, often have been men of great influence in their communities, for an action that the portents show will be of unlucky termination can be stopped by them for the community's welfare. Abuses of this power have been frequent; even the great oracle of Apollo at Delphi was not entirely above suspicion. With the rise of the great religious systems these practices have been condemned as partaking of magic. Nevertheless, they continue: astrology and various forms of marriage divination have flourished under Christianity; geomancy is popular in Arabic Islam; gematria, letter and number symbolism, was significant in Jewish scholasticism. "Superstition" generally concerns itself with omens: the black cat, the twitching eyelid, the dropped spoon—all minor events foretelling some future event, good, bad, or indifferent. Yet even where such practices are recognized as magical relics, few would care to risk a breach of etiquette by refusing to say "God bless you" or "Gesundheit" at a sudden sneeze—formulas that recognize the danger of the soul's escape during a sneeze, or the entrance of a demon—both the sneeze and the saying being symbols of some greater event.

As the word itself indicates, divination is the act of determining the will of the gods, and in several of its forms approaches animistic belief, e.g. the gods as the spirits of the dead, the soul of the sleeper in the land of the dead, etc. Oneiromancy, divination by dreams, presupposes basically the soul's communion with the knowing spirits. Shamanism or other types of possessive divination rely for their effect on the voice of the god or spirit speaking through the human medium. In more direct fashion, necromancy is the conversing of a person in full possession of his conscious faculties (the dreamer is unconscious, the shaman is deliriously or otherwise possessed) with the spirits of the dead. Augury depends on the widely held belief that birds and animals are closer to the gods than human beings or that they incorporate the departed spirits. Ordeals, lot-casting, and other means of divination are based on the assumption that the gods interfere with the actions of people or objects as indicators of their good or ill will.

The oracle at Delphi, traditionally the great classical oracle, must originally have been a place of augury, connected with serpent-divination. Even when the method changed, and the possessed or intoxicated priestess of Apollo uttered her cryptic phrases, the name of Pythoness was kept. There are, thus, certain places suitable for divination, potent regardless of the means used. High places are such in early Semitic belief, and so are sacred groves and springs. The time of day (e.g. midnight, the break of dawn) or the season of the year (e.g. the solstices) is often important: Halloween and Christmas, times when the spirits have returned to earth, are such days; night is the time when the future husband appears in a dream to the maiden on St. Agnes' Eve.

Most divination is systematized. The Chinese use a complex system of diagrammatic symbols; the Arabs have a standardized method of reading the points marked on the ground; there were regularly recognized meanings for the markings on the liver of the sacrifice in Babylonia; judicial astrology maintained distinct meanings for the various relationships of the stars, planets, signs, etc.; there was system behind the readings of omens by the Roman and Aztec augurs—these are patterns, and are prepared for by the diviner beforehand. But much divination is from accidental signs: if the ear burns, someone is speaking of you (good or evil depending on which ear); if twins are born, some calamity is impending; if a person trips, if he sneezes, if he breaks a mirror, if he meets a priest or an old or cross-eyed woman first thing in the morning, he has an omen of an event to occur. Here, despite the lack of ordered arrangement of omens and signs, the same primitive logic is still at work: a lesser event is connected with a greater, causally. Things happen in chains; deaths follow each other in threes; three-on-a-match is unlucky; what you are doing at midnight on New Year's Eve determines what you will do for the remainder of the year. From such beliefs stems the idea that all signs are indicators of the future, and when the sign is obscure or ambiguous the trained reader of omens, the diviner, is necessary to trace the chain, to tell what indication the peal of thunder, the number on the dice, the figure of the wax in water, gives of the further action of the spirits or gods.

Apart from oganized systems and accidental occurrences are the isolated popular forms of personal divination. The petals of the daisy tell if "she loves me" and the florets, tossed into the air and caught on the back of the hand, tell the number of one's children-to-be. The wishbone of the fowl and the candles of the birthday cake, the wedding cake under the pillow and the bride's bouquet are instruments to determine the future course of events. Often a rime is recited as the divining is performed, but in general such incantation is of a lesser, perhaps degenerated ritual than the more formal and priestly kinds of divination. Yet tea-leaf reading and palmistry and cartomancy are but median forms of the reading of omens. On the one hand lie the "signs and portents," the augurs and the other mighty diviners, priests, and shamans; on the other lie the little "superstitions" that tell of good or bad luck.

☞ A variety of techniques are known in Middle America. The most widespread consists (and consisted before the Conquest) in throwing grains of colored maize or beans on the ground, and interpreting the question from the position in which they fall. Other methods may be used to determine causes of illness. Feeling the pulse for strength indicates whether the soul has left the body, which, if so, results in sickness. An egg may be rubbed over the body of the patient, broken open, and examined, to determine whether the evil eye or some other cause has made the patient ill (see EGG CURING).

The Popoluca of Veracruz (Mexico) divine by throwing small balls of copal incense in a pot of water, and depending on whether they float or sink, the question is answered affirmatively or negatively. The Zapotecs of Mitla, Oaxaca (Mexico), kill a fowl over a cross drawn on the ground to determine whether a sick person will recover. If the fowl expires with its head to the east, the answer is affirmative. The Chorti diviner (Guatemala) asks questions of a spirit which lives in his right calf, first chewing tobacco and rubbing the saliva on his skin. A twitching of the calf muscles means an affirmative answer to direct questions. [GMF]

djägowa'óenǫ An Iroquois Indian social dance, the pigeon dance. The choreography could be attributed to the coupling habits of the pigeon, for men and women circle against the sun in pairs. The step is the *ga'ddsot* type. There is no development in the dance formations, yet the songs have a wide range and ingenious treatment of the rhythmic theme. The only accompaniment is provided by the two leaders with horn rattles. [GPK]

Djambu Baros The Batak (Sumatra) tree of life which grows in the topmost heaven. On each leaf of the Djambu Baros is written a word such as wealth, fruitfulness, etc. The tondi (soul) must obtain one of these before it can depart for the earth, since the longevity and fortunes of each unborn child depend upon what the tondi is able to obtain for its future being.

djoéga'óenǫ The Iroquois coon dance, of the *gędjóenǫ* or fish dance type. It is somewhat slower than the fish dance, and is preceded by a stomp round dance in moderate tempo. At the end of each song the dancers and singers whoop in imitation of the coon. Otherwise it is like the fish dance. [GPK]

djoged A Balinese dance performed by a professional girl dancer and any man whom she "entices" out of the audience. Steps follow the pattern of the legong, but the djoged is the world-wide courtship dance of flirtation, pursuit, and retreat, ending with the man's attempt to get near enough to the girl to enact the Balinese "kiss." This means getting his face near enough to hers to smell her perfume and feel the warmth from her skin. As the dance proceeds and emotion intensifies, one by one other men from the audience cut in on the performers and continue the eternal pursuit.

Sometimes the djoged is performed by a boy in girl's clothes; when this is the case the dance is called *gandrung*. At a gandrung performance there is even greater rivalry among the men in the audience, participation becomes intense and violent and fights sometimes occur. The djoged in both its aspects is forbidden in Tenganan.

djǫwiyaik'óenǫ An Iroquois social dance; the robin dance. It may at one time have been a ritual bird impersonation, but retains only very faint mimetic suggestion in little hops at the end of each musical section. Its choreography is archaic, a circular side-shuffle against the sun, men in the lead, segregated from the women—a procedure typical of animal medicine rites. The songs, to horn rattle accompaniment, have most original syncopated rhythms, which the best dancers follow in variants on the fundamental step, in two-steps and stamps. A threefold cry opens each song, announces its repetition and its end. During the cries in the middle of the dance the rattle vibrates and the dancers face about with small hops, repeat the dance with backs to the center, and face the center again on the terminal cries. [GPK]

Djunkgao The Australian Murngin myth cycle and the rituals associated with the career of the Djunkgao sisters, who on their travels named the clan countries and animals and made totem wells with their yam sticks. After the younger sister had been incestuously raped, they lost their totems to the men so that they became ordinary women. They are associated with movements of ocean tides and rainy season floods. [KL]

Dobrýnja and Aljoša Title of a Russian bylina depicting vividly the Kiev background and narrating several exploits of the hero Dobrýnja: of especial folkloristic interest for its relation to the German Noble Moringer theme. This is the old Odysseus and Penelope story: the story of the hero who departs on the morning after his wedding for distant lands and some great adventure (usually the wars, in this instance the extermination of a great dragon). He bids his newly wedded bride await his return for seven years. She waits the whole appointed time and longer, but Dobrýnja overstays the tryst, and she is forced into a new and unwelcome marriage with Aljoša Popovič. Dobrýnja returns in disguise, arriving just in time to drop his ring into the cup that traditionally goes the rounds of the wedding feast, and Aljoša is dismissed with dispatch. See NOBLE MORINGER. Compare HIND HORN. [MEL]

Dobrýnja Kikitich or **Dobrýnaya Nikitich** A Russian historical personage, noted for great courtesy; central figure and hero of several byliny of the cycle of Vladimir; killer of a terrible dragon (or serpent) with twelve tails. He killed the dove of the witch Marina, who in turn transformed him into a bull. He was also the hero of several encounters with the Tatars. Dobrýnja was blood brother of Aljoša Popovič, who tried unsuccessfully to betray him and steal his wife. Legend says that he was eventually conquered by a warrior giantess; historically he was killed at the battle of Kalka in 1224. See DOBRÝNJA AND ALJOŠA. [MEL]

Dõc Cu'ó'c In Annamese belief, the longitudinally half-bodied good spirit who stands on his single leg and brandishes an ax over his head with his single hand. Dõc Cu'ó'c is as swift as lightning and can see evil spirits from afar. He protects the country and its inhabitants, cures diseases, and sends good or bad weather. His ritual contains formulas which are written on paper or shells and are used as charms against toothache, nightmares, barrenness, and ghosts. Figures of paper, straw, or wood are made by the priests of his temple which are sent to wreak vengeance upon men or animals.

docey-doe The Western square dance form of *dos-à-dos*, back to back. [GPK]

Doctor Knowall A folktale (Type 1641), known in all parts of Europe and Asia, in some parts of Africa and the New World, and most familiar in the Grimm version (#98) from which it is named. Crabb, a peasant, dresses like a doctor and begins to act like a savant. A nobleman, having lost some money, asks Crabb to recover it. Crabb and his wife go to the castle where they sit down to a meal. Crabb, alias Doctor Knowall, nudges his wife as the fine dishes are passed, and says, "That's the first," "That's the second," etc. The guilty servants who carry the dishes are terrified, thinking he means them. So when Crabb, asked to guess what is in a covered dish, cries, "Alas, poor Crabb," they are sure he knows, for crabs are in the dish, and the servants call him out of the room and confess. He reveals the hiding place of the money to the lord, protecting the servants, and is rewarded by both servants and nobleman.

The story of "The Brāhman Hariśarman" in the *Ocean of Story* contains an incident missing in the German tale but found elsewhere in variants often enough to be included in the type tale. Hariśarman steals a horse, hides it, and pretends to hidden knowledge to locate it. Sometimes the missing animal is found inadvertently because the sham doctor gives a laxative to the searcher: when the laxative takes effect the horse (or other animal) is found in the bushes. Often the stolen horse is followed by stolen cow, pig, etc., all to build up the reputation of the "doctor."

The tale is a balancing parallel to the wise maiden-riddle answerer type. The maiden is really clever; Doctor Knowall is an ignoramus who succeeds despite himself, despite his blurting and blundering. There is some indication that the story, known in about 400 versions, is an originally Eastern tale, and spread from the Indian region eastward to the Philippines and westward to Europe and Africa. The two Philippine variants, collected and discussed by Fansler (*MAFLS* 12: 1–10), about Suan and his luck, seem to have been influenced to some degree by European sources, but the tales are basically cognate with, rather than derivatives of, the European tales.

Big John the Conqueror (Kennedy, *Palmetto Country*) is a recent southern U. S. Negro Doctor Knowall. He sees the diamond ring accidentally thrown out by the mistress and swallowed by the turkey. (In most of the tales, the recovered ring is fed to the fowl to cover the identity of the real thieves.) So Big John is able to tell where the ring is and strengthen his reputation as a "fortune teller." Then, as in Oriental versions, his master bets everything he owns on John's being able to tell what is beneath an overturned wash-boiler. John scratches his head and sighs, "You got the old coon." Of course, an old coon is under the boiler. The punning on two meanings of the same word is a theme running through all the incidents of the story. The doctor's name is Crab or Cricket or Rat (and a crab or cricket or rat is in the jar or covered platter); or he says in disgust, "Oh, filth!" (and filth is the hidden object); or he complains, "O tongue, see what trouble you have caused yourself" (and Tongue is the name of the thief). The basis of the story thus seems to be success through misunderstanding.

Dodona   The oak or beech grove in Epirus where the oldest of the oracles of ancient Greece, that of Zeus, was situated. According to the legend, Zeus gave two pigeons to his daughter Thebe, which were endowed with human speech. One flew to Libya where the temple of Amen was founded, and one to Dodona. The oracle was founded by the Pelasgians. From the rustling of the leaves of the trees, or from the sounds of the spring which gushed from the roots of the sacred oak, priests (later priestesses of advanced age) gave the words of the god to men. These priests were called Selli or Helli. The sound of the wind in the oaks was accentuated by the hanging of vessels of brass in the trees. The importance of the oracle of Zeus at Dodona became secondary to that of Apollo at Delphi only within historical times.

dog   The dog, the only domesticated animal which the North American Indians possessed prior to the arrival of Europeans, figures as a character in various North American Indian tales. The best known and most widespread American Indian dog tale is that of the *Dog Husband*. A girl has an unknown lover who is a dog by day and a man by night. The girl gives birth to puppies, and is deserted by her tribe. Crow helps her by hiding fire for her. The girl destroys her children's dog skins, thus changing them into human beings; her sons succeed as hunters, and when Crow visits the family, Crow is given meat. The girl's tribesmen are starving; when they discover through Crow that she has meat they gladly return to her. This tale is told, in approximately the above form, by many Eskimo, Mackenzie, Plateau, and Plains tribes; it is also known in Siberia. The incident of a girl's lover being a dog (or other animal) by day, and a man at night, occurs as a part of other stories than that of Dog Husband, in all parts of North America.

Other stories in which the dog figures as a central character are the tale of the talking dog who informs a husband of his wife's infidelity, and the Eastern Woodlands origin account in which the dog pleads that he may be man's companion on this earth. The Shawnee, an Eastern Woodlands tribe, picture their female deity, Our Grandmother, as an old woman who is always accompanied by a small dog. The picture of the old woman bending over a cooking pot, with her dog by her side, is to be seen on the face of the full moon. Among the Southern Utes, a western tribe of the Great Basin, a few stories are told of dogs who, in the prehuman age, "were once people and lived in a village."

The dog was honored by various ceremonies among North American Indians, and dog flesh was eaten by the Iroquois and several Algonquian tribes of the Central and Eastern Woodlands ceremonially. Other tribes on the American continent ate dog as a flesh food, or in times of famine. [EWV]

Dog   Hero of a folktale of the Fjort tribes of West Africa (i.e. the coastal provinces north of the Congo River) in which a young man could marry certain beau-tiful young girls only if he could find out their names.

The parents of two beautiful daughters had decided not to ask for rich presents when their daughters were asked in marriage, but to require the suitors to find out their names. A neighboring prince named Nsassi came and asked for the girls. "Guess their names and you shall have them." Nsassi's little dog was with him, heard everything that was said, and watched his master walk away grieving for the girls. So the little dog hung around, here and there, all day, listening. He heard the father say "Lunga! Lenga! Come here." He ran as fast as he could to tell Nsassi the names, but on his way he forgot them. He went back. "Lunga! Lenga! Give the little dog some food," said the father. The little dog ate and ran as fast as he could to tell his master the names. Again he forgot. He went back. "Lunga! Lenga! Give the little dog food and water." The little dog ate and drank, and ran home and told Nsassi the names.

Nsassi was very happy. He and the little dog set out to go claim the girls. But on the way they both forgot the names. So the little dog went on alone, again heard the names, ran home fast thinking of nothing else, told his master, both ran fast to the village of the girls. Then Nsassi asked for Lunga and Lenga for his wives and received them.

dògai   In the western islands of Torres Straits (Melanesia), female mischief-making spirits, easily outwitted. The dògai wear a woman's dress and ornaments, have hideous features, long, skinny legs, and huge ears, one of which is used as a bed and the other to cover the dògai. Dògai are sometimes able to personify beautiful women and in this guise deceive human beings. In folktale they transform themselves into animals, trees, constellations, or rocks, play tricks, and sometimes kill boys or girls. Consequently naughty children are threatened with the dògai.

dogheaded people   A group of beast-man beings, the *koerakoonlased* of Estonian folklore, similar to the Centaurs of the Greeks. They were half man and half dog, vertically, with one hand and foot like a man's, the other hand and foot like a dog's, or the whole body was a man's body with the head of a dog, with one big eye in the middle of the forehead. Their reasoning was a mixture of human and dog sense and they could run on all fours. The Dogheads lived on the end of the world and were constantly attacking, murdering, and robbing human beings. The latter were unable to defend their homes. Only the smell of the rhamnus shrub drove the Dogheads away. The Dogheads overpowered people, bit and murdered them, ate them, and feasted their children with human flesh. Women and children were taken as captives, fattened, and later slaughtered for fresh meat.

Similar stories are known to the Latvians, but appear only occasionally among the Lithuanians. The idea of dogheaded beings may have originated from real robbers, using the pelts of dogs for masking. Another explanation suggests that they may be reminiscent of the sanitary personnel during the time of a pest epidemic, who carried out the corpses of the dead, took sick people to quarantine, gathered and destroyed infected clothes, etc., and who wore special clothes and often very dreadful masks. The concept may also be a survival of traditions about cannibals and "savage people," as the dogheaded beings are called in Lithuania. The Estonians, seeing in 1854 the Bashkirs, Kalmuks, and Cossacks with the Russian army, considered them as the dogheaded people. Byzantine influence (via Russia) is also possible. (M. J. Eisen, *Estnische Mythologie*, pp. 202–06) [JB]

Dog in the Manger Title of one of Æsop's fables (Jacobs #40) in which the dog, lying in a manger full of hay, snarled and bit at the horse (or ox) when he came and tried to eat. This fable comprises the widespread European motif (W156): the common phrase *dog in the manger* having become a by-word for the selfish person who begrudges to others even what he cannot use himself.

dogwood Two types of dogwood have been known since early times. Red dogwood or dogberry, houndstree, pricke-timber, gater tree (*Cornus sanguinea*) grew and was named from the practice of bathing dogs in a decoction of the berries or bark to cure them of mange. The berries yielded an oil used in lamps, and the wood made a superior charcoal for the manufacture of gunpowder. Cornel tree or cornelian-cherry (*C. mas*) was cultivated for its highly prized edible berries. Galen, a 2nd century Greek physician, claimed that the leaves, when laid in deep green wounds, were an effective cure, but not for small wounds in tender flesh.

Flowering dogwood (*Cynoxylon florida*), the most common American variety, was used by Indian tribes of the eastern United States as medicine. The Nanticoke Indians tell of a grasping chief with four beautiful daughters. Many braves sought these attractive maidens but the chief said they would go to the braves who brought the richest gifts. Soon his lodge was piled high with furs and other articles of value, but the gods were angered with the chief for his greed, and they turned him into a gnarled tree. His daughters are the four white bracts, and the flowers are the gifts.

The Indians of the eastern United States made a decoction of the bark which they gave to warriors fevered with battle wounds. The colonists used this medicine for malaria with good results, and today we know that it contains the active principle of quinine. This knowledge was particularly valuable to the Confederacy during the Civil War when the blockade cut them off from South American sources of quinine. Today it is used principally as a stimulant to the appetite. The Catawbas say the raw berries are good for chills. In Newfoundland and among some North American Indian tribes children are passed through the limbs of the dogwood to make them immune to children's diseases, and as a cure for rupture. Those cured in this way are supposed to feel acute pain when dogwood sticks are burned in the fire. In Tennessee they say that if you chew dogwood you will lose your sweetheart, but in the southern mountains they make an essence of the bark, a few drops of which in a tumbler of whisky is considered very salubrious. Red osier (*C. stolonifera*), the inner bark of which was used as part of the Indian kinnikinnick (tobacco mixture), was very highly thought of. Rough dogwood or real-arrow tree (*C. asperfolia*) was used by the Dakota and Pawnee Indians for the shafts of arrows, and by the Chippewa to lure muskrats and as a remedy for sore eyes.

dokpwe Dahomean term for a cooperative men's work society of the kind widely spread in West Africa and in the New World. Basically, the principle is that of the American frontier "bee," whereby the beneficiary of group labor pays no money for the services rendered him, but must provide food for the group. New World forms reported are the *combite* in Haiti, and the *gayap* of Trinidad. In Dahomey, the dokpwe also functions importantly in the rites of death, its chief, or *dokpwegân*, being in charge of funerals in the district where he exercises control over the men in directing their group labor. [MJH]

doll A small figure made from various materials to resemble a baby, boy, girl, man, woman: often for a child to play with, but used in many cultures for various other purposes. The doll for play is known among almost all people and is of great antiquity in its use as child entertainment and companionship. It was known in Egypt as early as 1900 B.C., among the Greeks, Romans, Japanese, and the East Indians. Dolls have been found in graves in Europe and elsewhere, where from various indications they were used as playthings. In ancient times dolls were made of clay, wax, or dough; they are still sometimes made of wood and painted. In America, even a corncob dressed in a bit of cloth often served for a doll for the frontier child. Throughout a succession of periods in which rag dolls, wax dolls, china dolls, were made, to the plastic dolls of today, great ingenuity has been used, even to the making of unique dolls out of shells, nuts, and other unusual things.

Dolls are significant in the folklore of the Chinese as fertility charms: a woman who desires a child carries a doll on her back in the hope of becoming a mother. Similar doll customs obtain in Russia, France, Sweden, and elsewhere. The dolls on our American wedding cakes, ostensibly bride and groom, probably are a carryover of this symbolism, as is the cake itself.

As a charm, the doll is effective. In general European practice a doll was often given to a sick child to serve as a scapegoat, i.e. for letting the disease go out of the child into the doll. Such uses are known also in Borneo and the Celebes. The doll is used in love oracles. To deceive witches or fairies, a doll is often put in the cradle so that no changeling may be foisted on the parents. In the Middle Ages, dolls were used in the practice of magic, a use later transferred to America wherever the practice of "black magic" occurred. (See ENVOÛTEMENT). As a charm against bombers in Paris, and before that in 1919 as a protection against influenza, people carried about with them dolls representing a man and a woman.

Of great interest is the doll as vegetation *dæmon*. All over the British Isles and on the Continent, it was the custom to make a doll out of the last sheaf harvested. The doll was called the "Old Woman" or the "Maiden," the former referring to the yield just past and the latter to the following hoped-for harvest. In Scotland, this image was called the carline or Old Woman (see CAILLEAĊ). In Germany it was called variously, Bride, Oats-Bride, or Wheat-Bride; in Bulgaria its name is Corn-Queen or Corn-Mother. In most localities the doll is taken, sometimes with pomp and ceremony, to a certain farmhouse and fastened on the wall. For the Doll Festival of Japan, see JAPANESE FOLKLORE. [GPS]

Dō-maṅ or **mDo-maṅ gzun bsdus** A collection of mystic formulas, culled from the *Dō* of the Tibetan

Kāh-gyur, used as potent charms by laymen, and by the lāmas as incantations in the treatment of disease and ill-fortune. All literate laymen possess pocket editions of this collection, since the mere act of reading it is believed to ward off misfortune and disease.

domare dansen Literally, judgment dance; an ancient Swedish folk dance for men and women circling around a central figure with a lighted candle. The meaning is lost but probably refers to the life inherent in the purifying flame, resurrection symbolism reinterpreted in terms of the Christian Day of Judgment. [GPK]

domovik or **domovoj** The one in the house: a Russian household spirit, ancestral and usually the founder of the family, who watches over and protects the inhabitants of the house, taking care that all is in order: probably the inheritor of many observances of the early snake-ancestor cults. The domovik lives behind the stove; he likes fire, and one of his punishments when the family displeases him is to burn down the house. When the family moves, brands of the old fire are carried to the new home, and the domovik is welcomed there as the new fire is lit. He is an old, gray-bearded man, looking very much like the living head of the family. His correct name is never used; he is called "he" or "himself" or "grandfather" (Ded). Some of the supper is left out over night for the domovik, who bustles about in the dark, always busy, guarding against the intrusion of strange and hostile spirits. Sometimes someone brushes against the domovik in the dark: if the person is hairy, he will have good luck; if his hands are smooth, the domovik will bring trouble. There are several kinds of domoviks: the chlevnik, or barn spirit; the ovinnik, or kitchen spirit; the bannik, or bathroom spirit. Every house has them.

Dôn In Brythonic mythology, especially in *Math, Son of Mathonwy*, the sister of Math, mother of Gwydion, Gilvaethwy, Govannon, Eneyd, Arianrhod, and in *Kilhwch*, also of Amaethon. The constellation Cassiopeia was called Llys Dôn, Dôn's House. She is interpreted as a goddess of fertility and identified with the Danu of Old Irish mythology.

Donar The old German god of thunder, corresponding to the Norse Thor.

door A hinged or sliding frame used for closing or opening an entrance or an exit, usually made of wood, but frequently of iron, bronze, or other substances. Whether used in houses, temples, churches, or gates, doors play a large part in ritual and belief over a wide area. The door is a protection from everything that threatens from the outside. Not only the door itself partakes of a sacred character, but all the parts of the doorway: lintel, doorposts, and threshold.

Various ritual acts are carried out at the threshold, such as sacrifices to propitiate guardian or household spirits. Charms and prayers are recited at this spot; the reverence paid to it extends from taking off shoes before entering the building (Chinese, Moslem, etc.) to kissing the threshold. The husband carries his new bride over it. It is dangerous to sit or linger on the threshold; stumbling on it is especially dangerous when starting on a journey (Germany, Scottish Highlands); sneezing was an unlucky omen if it happened on the threshold; and such was the importance of the threshold

that it was often forbidden to tread upon it. The threshold was a superior place for sacrifice and occasionally for burial.

Altars were erected near the door in Greece and Rome, as well as in Assyria, Asia Minor, Mexico, and Polynesia (for Hebrew belief compare *Ex.* xxxiii, 9; *Deut.* xxxi, 15; *Ezek.* ix, 3). Souls were believed in ancient India to dwell under the threshold; in general, persons buried there became guardian spirits. In some cases, special deities became protectors; for example, Janus, the Roman god, was guardian of the door and his image was placed there. As protecting devices salt and pebbles were used. Many ideas connected with the door are also pertinent to the gate. Sacrifices were made here also, as was burial.

Gates and doors are mentioned in myth and legend—of the otherworld, of Heaven, Paradise, Hades, Tartarus—and most of these have guardians and special qualifications for entry. The tabooed door is frequent in folktales. Its metaphorical use is common: compare the Biblical, "I am the door" (*John* x, 9). [GPS]

☞ In rather general European and American folk belief it is unlucky to leave the doors open when going out of a house. One should always leave a house by the same door by which he entered. If a new doorway is cut in a house someone in the family will die; to this southern Negroes add the warning, especially if the old one is closed over.

In Ireland, Scotland, and the north of England especially, all the doors in the house were opened when someone was dying to ease the passage of the soul, and it was wrong to stand or kneel between the dying one and any door. The opening of all doors to ease and quicken childbirth is a common practice among Indonesian peoples.

The power of the door is seen in various southern United States Negro beliefs: A sure way to keep your lover's love is to bury some of his hair under your doorstep. A person's footprint, taken up, tied in a cloth, and put over the door will bring that person to your door. Hair cut from the tip of a dog's (or cat's) tail and buried under the doorstep will keep the animal from straying. The idea of the door as a symbol of entrance to another world is suggested by the Maryland Negro belief that to see a ghost, all you have to do is to look steadily past the edge of a door, or door-frame, in such a way as to see just past the edge. If you persevere in the steady gaze, and keep looking just past the edge, you will see a ghost.

door signs Objects placed on or above a door as the most obvious position to attract attention: used, in general, to ward off danger, to protect from witches and evil spirits, to bring good luck or to avert ill. Such signs have been known from antiquity. In *Exodus*, we read of the blood of the lamb sprinkled upon lintel and door posts to indicate the homes of the Israelites, so the Lord would pass them by when He smote the Egyptians. In Greek mythology, Antenor, the Trojan elder, was advised to hang a panther skin outside on his door to indicate to the Greeks that they were not to sack his house.

The Christian cross has been used on the door in many countries; the swastika is popular in the East as a door sign. Sacred plants and flowers are sometimes placed on the door. The hand, painted in vermilion with fingers extended, is believed to have repelling qualities, especially against the evil eye. It is used in different forms on doors and walls in Tripoli, Tunis, Algiers, Morocco, Syria, Egypt, and Turkey, often dipped in ox-blood before affixing it into position. The Tower of Justice in the Alhambra is pictured with a hand sculptured on the Tower.

In Scotland, sex symbols appear on doors and in a number of cases, on churches, pictured on the archway of the door. In North Africa, people are more realistic and actually hang up the genitalia of animals over the house door entrance. In this connection, the horseshoe should be mentioned. The horseshoe appears over barn doors in America and occasionally over house doors. Signs made by the hobo on house, doorstep, or fence by various markings designate to the next comer what food homes offer to the knight of the road. [GPS]

dor-je or **rDo-rje** (Sanskrit *vajra*) Tibetan symbol of the thunderbolt, a part of the equipment of every monk: used for exorcising and driving away evil spirits. The original dor-je fell from Indra's heaven to a spot near Lhasa. Imitations are made in bronze or other metals.

dosu In the twin cult of West African and New World Negroes, the dosu is the child born after twins. This was also one of the "strong" names of Akaba, king of Dahomey, who reigned from about 1680 to 1708. [MJH]

double A 15th century dance step: three steps (left, right, left, right closes). [GPK]

dove Any of various birds (family Columbidæ) including the domesticated pigeon and especially the wild doves, turtle dove, mourning dove, etc. The dove is said to have originated in Mesopotamia; or, it came out of Noah's Ark. That the dove is of divine origin is an idea popularized in numerous etiological stories about certain animals being created by God, others by the Devil. The Devil can transform himself into any bird except the dove, for instance. God as a dove is mentioned in *Matthew* iii, 16; and His spirit as a Holy Dove descended on the Virgin at her Annunciation. As a symbol of purity, the white dove is used in all Christian art and parable.

The dove was sacred to certain ancient divinities of love and fertility (Ishtar and Aphrodite, for example) and offerings and sacrifices of doves were made to them. In many lands the dove is used in divination and love charms. Even the phrase "billing and cooing," descriptive of lovers, suggests not only the bird's habits but is reminiscent of its early erotic symbolism. Missouri Negroes, for instance, swallow a raw dove's heart, point down, to inspire love in a beloved. A courtship rime is reported, also from Missouri (Puckett, *Folk Beliefs of the Southern Negro*, p. 77) which goes: Is you a flyin' lark or a settin' dove?/ I'se a flyin' lark, my honey love. The settin' dove is a woman already married or permanently attached; the flyin' lark is still free.

That the constant sound of the mourning dove predicts rain is quite general folk belief through the southern United States. A white dove flying over a person means good luck. But Welsh miners fear to see a dove fly over the pithead of a coal mine. It is historical fact that hundreds of miners have refused to enter the pits on a day on which someone has seen a dove fly over the

adits. To dream of doves means happiness. Three wishes made on hearing the first dove of the season will surely come true. The turtle dove protects from death, lightning, and fire. But the constant sound of a mourning dove around the house presages a death in the family within a few days. This omen, say Mississippi Negroes, can be counteracted by tying a knot in each corner of your apron. This not only drives the dove away, but ties the souls of the inmates to the house.

The dead are often reincarnated in the form of a dove. And those about to die sometimes see doves coming to carry their souls to heaven. (See BIRD SOUL.) In fact, the dove is frequently regarded as an omen of coming death. In France, when a sick person craves pigeon to eat, he is considered near death. In England, too, the dove is a death omen, especially if one settles on the roof. Those die a lingering death who die on pillow or bed of dove or pigeon feathers.

Dove's blood has been considered efficacious from antiquity. Blood from the right wing was used for sore eyes, warts, and stomach ills. Its droppings were used for sore eyes, colic, and swellings. Its flesh was eaten raw as a remedy for fevers and epilepsy. The magic power of its blood was seen in the old hunting custom of smearing bullets with it. In France the blood of a dove is used in poultices mixed with wine. For headache and especially for insanity the bird was cut open and applied to the head or side of the patient.

The dove figures in folktale all over the world. Dove is a popular character in Central California and Great Basin American Indian tales of the prehuman era. No particular plot is associated with Dove as a main character, however. (Compare DZŌÁVITS.) There are stories explaining why dove lays only two eggs (A2247.4; A2486.3) balanced against her pride and concern for her large brood (U81.1). There is a tale about her proverbial lack of foresight in nest-building (J16) and another about how thrush teaches dove to build a nest (A2271.1). There are tales about doves transformed into people (D354) and of people transformed into doves (D154.1), reincarnation as dove (E613.6), soul as dove (E732.1), revenant as dove (E423.3.1), etc. See ATARGATIS.

"dozens" Songs of derision used extensively by Negro troops of World War II. The allusions of the "dozens" are sexual, using as a theme parents and parentage, and as a vehicle of spoken and sung banter in rimed and unrimed form. A medium of release through abuse, which affords much opportunity for improvisation, and for which there is no retaliation permitted except a response in wittier and more telling form, this song-type is in the direct tradition of the many other kinds of "songs of allusion" found among African and New World Negroes. [MJH]

dracæna A shrub or tree of the lily family (genus *Dracæna* or *Cordyline*) which grows in tropical climates. In the Solomon Islands the first dracæna is said to have grown from the grave of Pau Tangalu, the sea spirit. It is planted around altars and is grown among their magic plants. It is used in many of the ceremonies of these peoples as well as those of Polynesia. Lime and ginger wrapped in a dracæna leaf and laid in the path of an intended victim will cause his sickness and death. A leaf buried in a village will cause the inhabitants to fight among themselves. Spirits causing sickness can be made to flee with a leaf of this plant. These leaves are used in divination of the weather, of the cause of illness, and for the discovery of the innocence or guilt of those suspected of adultery. In the Celebes the sick are beaten with dracæna leaves, for, since the plant grows readily when cut down, it is considered to have a strong soul.

In the Canary Islands during the past century there was a dracæna tree known to have existed since 1402, and considered one of the oldest inhabitants of the earth. In England the imported resinous gum of the dracæna, dragon's blood (so called for its bright red color), was burned by young girls and estranged wives, while reciting incantations, to restore their loves.

Draco The Dragon: a circumpolar constellation of the northern sky, identified variously with the Babylonian ocean-dragon deity, Tiamat, with the snake hurled by Athena into the sky, whose tail lies coiled between the two Bears, and whose head lies under the foot of Hercules, or with the terrible dragon of Thebes killed by Cadmus, whose teeth he sowed. Later astronomers called it the Old Serpent who tempted Eve. The early Hindu constellation which they called Crocodile or Porpoise may have been Draco, may have been Delphinus. The Persian Azhdehā, Man-eating Serpent, was Draco. And it is probably the "crooked serpent" mentioned by Job. Arabic astronomers named it Al Shujā', the Snake. In Norse mythology it was the Midgard serpent hurled into outer darkness by Odin.

Four thousand years ago the yellow star Thuban, in the tail of Draco, was the pole star, to whose perpetual visibility the slanting shaft in the Great Pyramid of Khufu at Gizeh was oriented. Draco was a much longer and more serpentine constellation in Chaldean configuration than it seems now, encoiling both Bears.

dragon A mythical creature found in the lore of all peoples of the Old World and many of the New. All dragons have as an anatomical basis a snake or crocodile body covered with scales, the forelegs and head of a lion, eagle, or hawk. Many have wings. The physical characteristics vary with the location so that almost any combination of animals, such as the elephant-dragon of India, or the stag-dragon of China, may appear. Usually the dragon breathes fire, emits a thunderous sound, guards a treasure, lives in a cave, or in a lake, or in a stream, or in the clouds. Usually he is associated with water in some manner. Compare with this the serpents and chthonic deities in the form of snakes associated with the earth. In later folktale and myth, the distinction between water-dragon (e.g. that of the Andromeda story) and the earth-snake (e.g. the Python of Delphi or the Midgard Serpent) is not clearly made. The dragons of all countries must be propitiated by human sacrifice, commonly of a virgin princess.

The story of the dragon-slayer is, consequently, likewise common. Such stories relate how the hero killed the dragon, cutting off its head or heads and removing the tongues; as a reward he is given the princess as his wife. The sowing of the dragon's teeth, from which spring the founders of the city, occurs in Greek mythology. The famous dragon-slayer of British legend is St. George, though King Arthur, son of Uther Pendragon (dragon's head), is also a dragon-slayer. Dragon tales blend with tales of giants and ogres with several heads

who breathe fire; the same motifs, rescue of a people and a princess, cutting off of heads, cave dwellings, and the like, are common to both types of story. In Christian legend, the dragon is the Devil or the servant of the Devil; the leathery webbed feet and pointed tail are characteristic of both. Apocalyptic literature abounds with symbolic dragons, while the apocryphal *Bel and the Dragon* relates the tale of Daniel's slaying of the dragon.

The dragon is associated with the gods by all people; early in the history of each culture it is identified with a specific god. Tiamat, for example, is the dragon goddess of Babylonia, the antagonist in the first dragon myth in history. Considerable evidence exists to prove that the dragon myth was assembled first in Babylonia of elements from Egyptian mythology and thence spread largely by diffusion eastward through India to China where its development has been manifold, and westward through Greece to the people of Europe. Close relation exists between the dragon myth and the cult of the Mother Goddess; this relationship explains the persistence of stories of human sacrifice, concern with thunder and cloud, and with treasure. It explains, too, the virtue of slaying the dragon, i.e. the slayer is protecting mankind from the malignancy of the god. But not all dragons are malignant; some, especially in China, are beneficent, but even they had to be courted by gifts and petitions. The dragon is a prominent character of the mumming parade on the Chinese New Year; dragon kites are flown. [MEL; JF]

Dragon cult In China, a subject of many studies in which learned people have made fantastic suggestions. In the 4th millenium B.C. a dragon delivered the eight mystic trigrams, the Pa Kua, to a legendary emperor. In the legendary Hsia dynasty (c. 2205 to 1557 B.C.) dragons were associated with ancestor worship and fertility. One of the kings collected foam from the mouths of two ancestors who appeared at his palace in the form of dragons. He put the foam in a box. No one in succeeding generations dared open the box. At the end of the reign of the tenth king of the Chou dynasty (c. 1100 to 221 B.C.) the box was opened. The foam spread through the palace. The king made his wives appear naked before it. It became a black lizard and entered the women's apartments. An extraordinary pregnancy occurred. A dragon was the symbol of the emperor; it appeared on the Chinese flag; it represents the essence of yang, the male element. The scholars of the Chou dynasty who collected dragon lore were impressed by its importance but were vague in their interpretations. A Sung emperor in 1110 A.D. divided all dragons into five families: Blue Spirit Dragons, very compassionate kings; Red Spirit Dragons, kings of lakes; Yellow Spirit Dragons, kings who receive vows favorably; White Spirit Dragons, virtuous pure kings; Black Spirit Dragons, kings of mysterious lakes. Another classification: Spirit Dragons are those which rise to Heaven; Earthly Dragons are those hidden in the earth who protect treasure. A number of other classifications are known. Dragons are associated with pools. Carp may be dragons in disguise. Chinese dragon lore has been modified by the Hindu lore of nagas, rakshas, etc. [RDJ]

dragon-fight or **dragon-slaying theme** It was inevitable that the concept of the dragon should beget stories of the slayer of the dragon. Such stories are numerous and widespread. Best known is the dragon sacrifice story known all over the world. The central episode deals with a youth who, when he discovers a maiden (or princess) about to be sacrificed to a dragon, kills the monster, cuts off its heads (usually seven), extracts the tongues, and goes his way, telling the girl that he would see the world before marrying her. He returns (often after seven years) to find the princess about to be married to an imposter who claims that he is the one who killed the dragon. The hero shows up the impostor, proves his own identity by producing the tongues and matching them up with the proper heads, and so marries the princess.

Allied to this story, or to the concept behind it, are the numerous dragon-slayer stories with local heroes as protagonists, heroes usually famous in other legends and myths. It would seem that the slaying of the dragon has been added to their stock of exploits to enhance their stature as heroes. Some of the most famous of these dragon-slayers are: Perseus, Marduk, Hercules, Apollo, Siegfried, St. Michael, St. George, Beowulf, Arthur, and Tristan. See BEAR'S EAR; BEAR'S SON; DRAGON. [MEL]

dragonfly A predatory insect (order *Odonata*) having a slender body, and four finely veined wings, huge eyes, and strong jaws. It feeds on flies and mosquitoes, and for this reason is sometimes called a mosquito hawk. Dragonflies are said to have been sent by Satan to cause mischief in the world. They are often called Devil's-darning-needles. Children are told that if they tell lies the Devil's-darning-needle will sew up their mouths; it is even likely to sew up nose and ears and go right on through the head. It will also sew up the mouths of scolding women and cursing men, and has the whimsical habit of sewing together the toes of anyone it finds sleeping uncovered. It is said that dragonflies can tell good children from bad: when a good boy goes fishing, the dragonfly will settle on the bank of the stream where he is apt to find the best luck. But if it lights on the fishing-pole, the fish will not bite. It is very bad luck to kill one. That dragonflies can sting is a fairly widespread misconception. Dragonflies are sometimes called "snake feeders" and "snake doctors" from the quite general belief that they feed and minister to snakes. In the southern United States the "snake doctor" is even able to revive a dead snake. [GPS]

☞ Among Zuñi Indians the dragonfly is regarded as possessing supernatural powers and it is tabu to kill one. The Somaikoli (Dragonfly) Society of Zuñi cures sore eyes, convulsions, and cramps. The kachina masks have small eyes, and it is dangerous for a pregnant woman to look at one, lest her child have sore eyes. The Zuñi association of awl and moccasin-making with Dragonfly kachina is suggestive of the general sewing superstition connected with the dragonfly.

dragon's blood The blood of a dragon, when obtainable, has many marvelous properties. A bath of dragon's blood restores the petrified to life. Siegfried was made invulnerable by bathing in dragon's blood. Eating a dragon's heart, or drinking its heart-blood, bestows immeasurable courage on the drinker, or else enables him to understand animal languages. In a Danish folktale (Type 305) only the blood from a dragon's heart can cure a certain king (D1500.1.9.3). The hero obtains the blood, overcomes an imposter, and is rewarded by marrying the king's daughter. See BLOOD; DRACÆNA.

Draupadī In Hindu mythology, the wife of the five Pāṇḍu princes. At the svayaṃvara, marriage by choice, at which suitors vied with each other, Arjuna outshone the others in archery and received the garland from Draupadī. When the brothers returned home, however, their mother told them to share their acquisition, so Draupadī became their common wife, spending two days at a time in the house of each.

When the oldest brother, Yudhishthira, gambled with his cousins the Kauravas, at Hastināpura, he lost his kingdom, the freedom of the brothers, and that of their wife. She was mistreated by the Kauravas, Duryodhana and Duhṣāsana, the latter tearing off her clothes. Kṛishṇa, however, restored the clothes as rapidly as they were torn off. The enraged brothers were restrained by Yudhishthira, but Bhīma vowed that he would drink the blood of Duhṣāsana and smash the thigh of Duryodhana, which vows he finally fulfilled. The Pāṇḍus and Draupadī were exiled for 12 years. The 13th year was spent incognito in the service of the king of Virāta, where Draupadī's beauty attracted the queen's brother, Kīchaka. Bhīma, aroused by Draupadī, fought Kīchaka and so mangled him that his bones and flesh were rolled into a ball. The murder was attributed to the Gandharvas who were believed to guard Draupadī and she was condemned to death, but was rescued by Bhīma.

dream books Popular books which interpret all sorts of dreams. A dream treatise published in 1601, *A Treatise of the Interpretation of Sundry Dreams*, may have been a forerunner of various modern dream books much sought after by youngsters, adolescents, and others anxious to know the meaning of their dreams. One extract from its pages reads, "The sick person to dream that he married a maiden, signifieth death to ensue. But good it is unto him which beginneth a new business, for that it shall come into a good purpose." Other items are in the same formal language. The prophecies in modern dream books are quite otherwise—short and snappy: Dream of a cat—bad luck; dream of a neighbor—warning of gossip. [GPS]

dreams Among many peoples, dreams, the mysterious adventures of the soul during sleep, are looked upon as communion with the spirits, both the spirits of the dead and the wandering spirits of other men and women. Hence occurrences in dreams are portentous, for they indicate the will of the powerful dead and may therefore be used to foretell the future. And, since dreams are often not logical in their development, certain standards of interpretation must be placed upon the symbolism of the dream, not only by Freud and his followers, but by the dream interpreters of more primitive civilizations, the shamans and witch doctors, the old wives and the soothsayers. Losing a tooth means a death in the family; the seven fat and the seven lean kine mean seven years of plenty and seven of famine; the river flowing from a king's daughter causes the king to desire his grandson's (Cyrus') death. See DREAM BOOKS; GUARDIAN SPIRITS; INCUBUS; MYSTERIOUS, HOLY, AND POWERFUL; NIGHTMARE; SUCCUBUS.

☞ A basic theme which appears to spread over all Middle America is that dreams foretell the future, that they are among the most reliable of omens. Impending death or misfortune is the most common sign. To cite a few examples, they are presaged by dreams of meat in abundance, dreams of water or drowning, dreams of fire burning one's body, dreams of lizards and serpents, dreams of being married, dreams of the loss of a hat or other personal property, or of the loss of a tooth. Aside from the content of a dream the mere act of dreaming may be dangerous, since many peoples believe the soul leaves the body during this period and wanders about. If something happens to the soul, the sleeper may not awaken. Conversely, sleepers often are not rudely awakened, for fear they may be dreaming and their souls will not have time to return. See DREAM SOUL; SOUL LOSS. [GMF]

dream soul   One of the multiple souls of man: a West African Negro concept, surviving also in the New World. In Dahomey men have four souls, of varying quality, importance, and function; women and children have only three. Among the Ewe and Tshi-speaking peoples of West Africa the dream soul sleeps while a man is awake; when the man sleeps it leaves his body, via the dream, and goes forth to associate with the dream souls of others. As the man wakes, the dream soul returns. The great danger is dream-interruption or sudden awakening, lest the dream soul not have time to return. If it gets shut out the man will sicken, and unless it can be recovered, he will die. Only the sorcerer or witch-doctor knows how to find a lost dream soul or conjure it back into a man's body.

dream time   The mythological past of Australian mythology: variously termed by the various tribes. See ALCHERA; AUSTRALIAN ABORIGINAL MYTHOLOGY.

drilbu   A Tibetan prayer-bell rung by the lāmas to attract the attention of good spirits and to drive off evil ones.

drinking the moon   A folktale motif (J1791.1; Type 1335) in which a numskull sees a cow drinking from a pool in which the moon is reflected. A big cloud drifts across the moon and blots out the reflection. The man, now seeing only darkness in the pool, believes the cow has swallowed the moon, and splits her open in order to save it. This is a very ancient tale, belonging to the great body of noodle stories popular all over the world. One of the most famous uses of the motif is known through an ancient Spanish writer who tells how a group of town worthies once imprisoned an ass for drinking the moon. Observers, who saw the moon in the water disappear when a huge cloud obliterated its reflection, were aghast at the idea of their town having no moon. And the ass was condemned to be cut open that the moon might be restored.

drolls or **drolleries**   Humorous stories of semisophisticated folk type, the humor growing largely out of the antics of dim-witted characters or grotesque and exaggerated situations. Unlike the fable they point no moral; unlike the fabliaux they are seldom satiric or coarse. They resemble the tall tale in humor and exaggeration, but in form are usually shorter, with focus on a single situation, and the main character in the droll story is the butt of the humor. They are humorously odd, prankish, farcical. Some of the best known in English are: *Mr. Vinegar, The History of Tom Thumb, The Three Sillies, The Wise Fools of Gotham.* See ÆSOP'S FABLES; NOODLES. [MEL]

druid   One of a class of priests, teachers, diviners, and magicians of ancient Celtic (perhaps pre-Celtic) religion. They possessed all supernatural and human wisdom. They were physicians, historians, mathematicians, astronomers. Their rank was next to the king, but their decisions were final in all matters. Their enormous learning was never written down and the mysteries of their cult remain mysteries. They functioned at all rituals of naming, burial, and sacrifice. Old Irish texts mention the druids in connection with the terrible human sacrifices associated with Beltane and Cromm Crúać and also Tara.

They could cause illness, sleep, or death, raise storms and mists, and draw the *airbe druad,* druids' hedge or fence, around an army (by simultaneous incantation and circumambulation) which could not be crossed. As healers they are associated especially with mistletoe and the ritual of gathering it. With the persecution and extinction of the druids, the mantle of druid magic fell upon and enhanced the glamour of the Celtic saints. See ACORN; FAET FIADA; MISTLETOE; OAK.

druǰ (Persian *drauga*)   In the Avesta, a female spirit of deceit and treachery; one of a group of demons created by Angra Mainyu to counteract the good created by Ahura Mazda. The druǰ is the opponent of the Amesha Spenta, Asha Vahishta. In later belief, the term was applied to many demons including the daēvas, kavi, yātus, and the pairikās. Angra Mainyu is also commonly known as Druǰ, or Deception.

druǰ Nasu or **Nasu**   In Zoroastrianism, the corpse-demon or spirit of contamination; the best-known of the druǰes. Druǰ Nasu, in the shape of a fly, takes possession of dead bodies and spreads their contagion. It can be expelled from bodies only by means of the gaze of a dog (sagdīd). It is removed from those who have contact with the dead by means of the Barashnūm ceremony of purification.

drum   The most widespread, sacred, and ritually significant of all musical instruments: a hollow frame or vessel with one or two openings covered by a stretched skin and sounded by beating with the hands or with sticks; also, the slit-drum (a log hollowed through a narrow groove and stamped, rammed or beaten with a stick), and certain other percussion instruments lacking the skin head, such as the water drum and the stamped pit. Drums date from neolithic times and have served all over the world for accompaniment to religious ceremonies, dancing, singing, marching, and communal work, for the exorcism of evil spirits and expulsion of scapegoats and evil-doers, for divination, for the induction of a state of possession suitable for communication with the gods and supernatural forces, as a means of signaling, and especially as a fertility charm. Their absence in a given area, as among some Indian tribes of modern Brazil, the early Greeks and European peoples, is the oddity rather than the rule. As a matter of historical record, works of art in Mesopotamia dating from 3000 B.C. show a wide range of drums in use, and sculptured reliefs of India show their importance there at least 2000 years ago.

The origin of the instrument is unknown, though various cultures have legends of drum creation. The Fjort story credits the invention to a bird, Nchonzo nkila, which beat the ground with its drum-shaped tail. Even Nzambi, the Earth Mother, was not allowed to deprive the creator of its ownership. Many Pacific and South American peoples believe that the slit-drum was the invention of a water divinity, whose functions it serves. Whatever the origin, a particular type of frame drum probably spread over Asia and Europe from the Near East, and the slit-drum of many South American tribes extending to its northernmost use in California is of the Pacific type.

The rounded, hollow shape, just as it does in many household vessels, earth pits, etc., carries to the mind of primitive man a female connotation, hence, cohabitation, fertility, water, rain, grain, moon—all closely linked ideas. The original shape was probably cylindrical, the form of a log, and the original material, wood, for these were the earliest manifestations of man's work. In this shape, the slit-drum of Pacific and American cultures, with its hollow body and narrow slit rammed with a pole, is completely mimetic of the sex act. Bulging barrel, kettle, cup, bowl, and goblet shapes, now executed in wood or metal, probably followed the introduction of pottery drums, which evolved in very early times and strengthened the female symbolism of shape, material, and use. Archaic barrel drums of Japan and China were filled with rice or rice hulls, and in other parts of Asia, as well as among North American Ojibwas and Crees, grain-filled drums were used.

The meanings and the sex applications become enormously complicated with acculturation and the multiplication of types of drums, beating instruments, and uses. For example, small frame drums with the skin stretched on a shallow hoop have been almost exclusively the instruments of women in Semitic lands, where they accompany singing and dancing and rites of the moon. Greek and Roman followers of the cults of Dionysus and Cybele used them, as did Egyptian dancing girls of the 18th century B.C. Yet the Egyptian god Bes, attendant at childbirths, is sometimes shown playing this instrument. Furthermore, this drum closely resembles the shaman's drum widespread in Asia. It is differentiated sharply in that, like women's drums generally, it is played with the bare hands, while the shaman's drum is struck with a stick, horn, or bone.

The whole problem of the drumstick has its own symbolism. Probably the most archaic types of drums were all beaten with the bare hands, and many continue to be so played, by both men and women. The use of a stick or tubular implement, which is symbolic of the phallus, contributes the fertilizing agent to the conception of the female instrument, and is consistently reserved for men in most societies. A Koryak rain-making legend tells of attaching a woman's vulva to the frame of a drum and beating with a penis for the stick. East African coronation drums must be beaten only with a human tibia, a phallic symbol. (Today we still refer to the leg bones of fowl as drumsticks.) The large hanging drum of Japan, tsuri daiko, is played with two leather-knobbed sticks, the right designated as male, the left, female.

With this double implication of fertility, therefore, the tabus and restrictions on the use of drums vary considerably from place to place. Chaco Indians use their drums, as they do rattles, to help girls through their first menstrual period and to speed the ripening of algarroba pods. In some African tribes, drumming marks the rites of circumcision. In southeastern Asia, they are beaten for the funerals of men only. The entire usefulness of a drum may be destroyed among certain Pacific island peoples if a woman sees it in the process of construction, but in the New Hebrides women play the slit-drum, which is sounded at the rising of the new moon. The Wahinda of East Africa consider it courting death for men to look at a drum. They will carry it only at night, and even the sultan is safe from the danger of the sight of it only at the time of the new moon.

As against the sexual connotation of the drum in primitive usage, Origen, the early Christian Church father of Alexandria, considered the tympanon, drum of his period, a symbol of the destruction of lust and the great Eastern civilizations extend the symbolism to more abstract concepts. Śiva, in his dancing manifestation, has the attribute of a small hourglass-shaped drum which stands for sound, communication, revelation, incantation, and magic. The Chinese system of cosmic coordination matches drums with north, winter, water, and skin.

The making of drums involves numerous magical practices and beliefs. Lapp drums are made of wood selected for the favorable direction of the grain. The Melanesian drum-makers climb the tree selected for the body of the drum and complete the whole drum before descending. The Babylonian lilis, worshipped and played in lamentation for the darkness of the moon, was covered with the hide of a special black bull, sacrificed in the temple of Ea, god of music and wisdom. The great honor of his fate was carefully explained in incantations sung to the bull before his ritual slaying.

The earliest membranes for drums were probably the skins of fish, snakes, and lizards (water animals), and only later, possibly when drumsticks began to be used, were game animals, cattle, sheep, and goats used. For the huge log war drums of Africa, some tribes consider skins of wild beasts most suitable. Human skin flayed from their captives or slain enemies was sometimes used for the ancient Peruvian huancar, the belief being that the use of a part of his body gave possession of the enemy's strength and vigor and would strike terror to his companions.

Attaching the skin to the frame with nails had a special significance, both for the barrel drums of the Far East and the huehuetl of Aztec Mexico, nails bearing a protective virtue then, as today, in many cultures. Also the inclusion of various objects inside the drum has been thought to add to its powers. Small bits of crystal or obsidian from a volcano are used in the shaman's drum of the Araucanians for curing effect, with amulets, skulls, shells, etc., being used elsewhere. Therefore it can be dangerous to take a casual glance into a drum.

The elaborate formula observed in making the trio of Haitian vodun drums of today is characteristic of such activities. The maker, before cutting the selected tree, offers invocations, lights a candle, and sprinkles cornmeal around the roots. He breaks an egg against the trunk, rubs it well over the bark, and offers a libation of rum. Rum is also poured into the hollow of the drum after it is scraped out. It is also poured at the threshold of his house and out toward his cornfield. The first peg hole for attaching the skin is marked and called the mother (*manman*), and there the first peg must be driven in, the first attachment of the skin must be made, the lacing first knotted, and the tuning begun. Before any skins are put on, all three drums must be aligned in the sun, rum is poured before each, and the maker, calling on the Father, the Son, and the Holy Ghost, lights a candle on each mother peg. The drums are not played until they have been baptized, for which they are dressed in apronlike christening garments by a set of godparents, with prayers and offerings of meal and pouring of water.

The largest of these drums is called the *manman*, the next the *seconde*, and the smallest *bula* or *bebe*, and they are named and endowed with a soul or spirit, the *huntór*. This naming ceremony is paralleled in Sumerian custom thousands of years B.C., in which the balag drum of the god Ea received a proper name and dates were counted from the time of its dedication.

The distinction of size in this vodun practice is paralleled elsewhere. In the New Hebrides, the largest of a group of slit-drums is also called the mother. It is common in primitive societies for the largest drums to have the greatest magical power and to be dedicated to the most important divinities, while smaller ones take on lesser spirits, serve for more ordinary utilitarian purposes, or even descend in time to the level of toys. The two largest drums of the Shango cult of the West Indies speak to St. Michael (Catholic identification of Ogun) and John the Baptist (Shango). Sometimes the original or older type of drum of an area retains its function for solemn ceremonies, while the later importations serve for lighter, secular entertainment. Indians of the Sierra Nevada of South America do their religious dances to a large, single-headed wooden drum, and use a double-headed European type of instrument for secular dancing. The Miskito tribe of the Caribbean lowlands play a goblet-shaped drum for funerals and memorial rites, and use the European type for signaling and less important ceremonies.

Special dress for drums is not unique in Haiti either. Among others, the *huehuetl*, still used by the Huichols of Mexico, has a holiday garb for festivals; the *sahibnahabat* (master drum) of India, a pair of huge silver kettledrums mounted on an elephant for processions, wears a long drapery; the Japanese *da daiko*, a spool-shaped instrument used for great occasions in the bugaku orchestra, is enthroned on a tasseled and draped platform.

More integral forms of decoration of drums include carving, painting, and the attachment of various objects to the frame, nearly always with the purpose of furthering the powers of the instrument. Some of the most ancient log drums, which stood upright or aslant on the ground for playing, were given feet or toothlike appendages to be driven into the earth. The foot, a phallic symbol in itself, was often carved in Malaya and among the African Bakunda (a Bantu tribe) to resemble human legs and feet. In other areas

the foot was conventionalized into a decorative stand. Many slit-drums, such as the Aztec *teponaxtli*, represent complete human or animal bodies—pumas, jaguars, alligators—with the powers of these creatures. Some, as among the Uitoto of Colombia, have a woman's head at one end, and that of an alligator (creature of water) at the other. The dragon and the phœnix, each with its own life associations, appear often on Japanese and Chinese drums, and tongues of flame may be carved above the frame. The Assiniboin of North America used the drum itself on a painted drumhead, and surrounded it by symbols of the rainbow, clouds, and sunshine, while on the other side appeared a star with colors and symbols for night, twilight, and sunshine.

Signs and figures painted with blood or alder-bark juice on the head of a type of Lapp drum were used for divination. A collection of small rings on the head were kept in motion as the drum was beaten, and according to the signs on which they came to rest the shaman made predictions.

The use of rattles or jingles attached to the drum adds to the special powers of those instruments.

The sound of a drum, and certain drum rhythms have their own meanings. West Indian Negroes believe that the drum will remain voiceless until an invocation calls the spirit into it, and each supernatural being of the vodun group, as in the parent African tradition, appears in answer to his own particular drum beat. The voice of the drum is the speech of the god. Chaco Indians distinguish certain traditional rhythms as "the beat of the jaguar," "the beat of the vulture," etc., and the Sumerian *balag*, mentioned above, spoke with "the bull's voice," and like the Lapp drum, was used for divination. When drums are used for rain-making, the sound is thought of as thunder.

Sometimes the drum is used to modify the human voice, give it a non-human, ventriloquistic sound more suitable to incantation. The Chukchee shamans of northeastern Siberia speak into the drum for this effect, and in the Yaqui Coyote dance of Mexico, an old man drummer sings into a hole in the side of his drum as he beats with muffled stick.

Actual language can be conveyed by drums. The Ashanti and other West African tribes, as well as some American and Oceanic peoples, by the use of definite intervals and rhythms in beating their log drums, can so imitate the speech melody of their languages as to convey messages in words and be understood over long distances. This telegraphic use of drums probably antedates more conventionalized signals for fire, assembly, flood, and the transmission of military orders, just as the huge slit-drums of primitive tribes are earlier than the small portable type now used in Malaya by watchmen.

Many methods are used for tuning and changing the timbre of drums, and for both musical and magic purposes the different tones have been desired. Islamic music distinguishes carefully between muffled beats, achieved by wetting the skin, and clear beats, struck from a heated skin. The Siberian shaman may achieve the same effects by heating his drumhead at his fire or moistening it with urine. Tightening or loosening the lacings of the skin may produce difference of tone. An African side-drum was called "the hypocrite" because of the many different tones that could be produced by pressure of the arm under which it was held, and its sound is said to have survived in the Negro humming called "moaning."

When the hand is the striking instrument, the tone may be changed by using the flat of the hand, the fingers, or the base of the thumb. African, West Indian, and Asiatic drummers produce intricate variations by the manipulations of their flying hands and fingers.

Some drums are sounded not by beating at all but by friction. Resin or grit is used on the fingers and rubbed over the head, or a vibrating cord or stick on the membrane produces a continuous rumbling sound. This, in a different way from the ramming or beating of drums, also symbolizes cohabitation and is used at initiation ceremonies of both boys and girls in Togoland. Europe also has its friction drums, now chiefly toys, but probably dating back to fertility ceremonies.

One tuning method for drumheads, the application of a paste to the center of the skin, originated in sacrifices and offerings to the drum. Though the primary significance of this practice is now largely forgotten and only the achievement of two different tones from the areas with and without the paste is intended, the custom originated in smearing the blood of enemies or sacrificial animals on war drums to bring strength in battle, good fortune to the armies. Later, any red-colored substance served the same purpose, and still later the offerings changed to agricultural symbols of abundance, such as rice, meal, saffron, etc. In India some barrel drums are treated with a different paste for each head, so that greater tonal range is obtained. However, Chamar women of southern India paint five cinnabar spots on the drumhead before a ceremony for Mother Earth, and the Haitian vodun drums are still treated with alcohol and flour before a service, not so much for the tonal changes as an offering to the spirit of the drum.

A part of the Mexican Coyote dance previously mentioned includes the offering of meat to the drum. Dancers carry it in their teeth from the plates where it is laid out to the drum. An allotment of meal was regularly provided for the Sumerian drum *a-lal;* the Aztec slit-drum was also the recipient of sacrifices and offerings; and novices of the cult of Attis in Rome ate a sacramental meal from a drum in a secret re-enacting of the death and resurrection of the god.

Certain drums are assigned special houses, guardians, and properties. The sacred jar drums (*bajbín*) of the Chamulas and Tzotzils of Mexico are brought out only at carnival times, in the interim being cared for by two attendants. Every week or two incense is burned before the drums, which rest on a table in the house of one of the guardians. The day before a carnival they are given a drink of brandy, are washed with hot water and camomile, and fitted with new lacings, while one attendant waves a banner in the four sacred directions, the other, in ceremonial headdress dances through the washing, and fireworks are set off. Only after such attentions can the drums be carried to the church door for the carnival dancing.

The African Bayankole maintain a dome-shaped drum house for their two greatest drums, which are served by a woman known as "the wife of the drums."

Her duties are to attend to the milk and butter-making from the herd of cattle owned by the drums, to offer milk to the drums daily, and to keep house for them. Another woman is charged with keeping the fire in the drum house to the temperature preferred by the drums. At the birth of a son or on any occasion for rejoicing, the prominent men of the tribe bring cattle or beer as offerings to the drums. No one may kill one of the dedicated herd except on order of the chief, and the meat is presented to the drums before it can be eaten by the guardians. Hides from the cattle are used to repair the drums, and the butter made from their milk is smeared on the drumheads.

So powerful and holy are the drums in East African society that the drumyard provides sanctuary for criminals and other fugitives as the church did in European tradition. (See ASYLUM.)

In contrast to this idea, drums have also served as the instrument of execution, expulsion, and disgrace. Thieves have been drummed to their hanging; the roll of the military drum in European armies beats a cheat or a disgraced officer out of camp and out of the regiment; and drumfire prefaces the volley of the firing squad when a spy or traitor stands with his back to the wall. In China, human scapegoats, selected as the embodiment of pestilence, have been driven from their villages to the beating of drums that the community might be restored to health. In Burma, cholera epidemics have been broken up by creating a din to frighten away the disease demons, drums adding their sound to the uproar. And on the island of Boru, day-long beating of drums and gongs preceded the departure of a boatload of evil spirits driven out to sea with all the troubles of the community.

Singing, dancing, and drums are almost inseparable in folk customs. Some American Indians have no concept of song without the undercurrent of the drum. Street singers in Egypt today are accompanied only by the drums they carry. The Ethiopian chant is set to drums and hand-clapping. The wedding songs of modern Jews of Yemen are sung to drumming and dancing, much as Jewish singing was done before the Temple at Jerusalem was built. Singhalese, Hausa, and Eskimo—all have their drum songs.

Among the dances dependent on drum rhythm are the healing dances of shamans in Sumatra, in South America, and in Siberia; the whirling dance of dervishes in Cairo; the convulsive dancing of vodun and Shango, and their distant connections in West Africa; the classical bugaku dances and Nō performances in Japan; the prancing of the Morris dancers in England, with their characteristic pipe and tabor accompaniment; the frenzied tarantella of Italy, with its tambourines; the sword dances of medieval Europe, and the jazz of America. Negro slaves, transported from Africa to America without any of the ceremonial objects basic to their lives, improvised drums of barrels, nail kegs, and boxes slapped with the bare hands in order to preserve some vestige of their background. When forbidden to drum, as they were in Louisiana in 1740, they pounded the wooden floors of their shacks with their feet in the intricate drummed and shuffled rhythms essential to their religious ceremonies.

The greatest use of drums for purely musical purposes perhaps is Asiatic. There the drums assume a melodic as well as rhythmic function in the orchestra in a manner not known in the West until the modern experimental art music of the 1920's. In Burma, where the chief outlet for orchestras is the accompaniment of the *pwe* shadow plays, a full drum chime is characteristic. It consists of as many as twenty-four tuned drums, arranged in a circle around the player who plays with his hands in an extraordinary display of virtuosity. The Javanese and Balinese gamelans also feature drums to guide the changing tempi for the choir of gong instruments, and in India the drums frequently outnumber all the other instruments in an orchestra or band.

On the strictly practical level of everyday use, drums have served to set the pace for communal work groups such as the combite and gayap, and for the strokes of rowers in Egypt. American slang holds an indication of the application of showmanship to business in the term "drummer" for salesman, and the phrase "drumming up business." They bring to mind the picture of the ballyhoo of the medicine-show, the sales-talk from the tailboard of a wagon, and the straggling parade behind one bass drum painted boldly with the name of a nostrum.

Finally, drums have boomed as a battle rally on every continent, and have stood as the talisman of victory and the symbol of royal and military might in many cultures, with the attendant sacrificial and signaling meanings previously discussed. The traditions surrounding the military drums of European and American armies are of comparatively modern origin. The importance of the military drum grew up as the foot-soldier superseded the armored and mounted knight as a tactical element in war. Then the drum and the cross-fife came into their own to set the time for the marching feet of the mercenaries. Kettledrums (English *naker*, French *nacaire*), introduced from Arab countries after the Crusades, joined the armies, and kettle-drummers of the 15th and 16th centuries were trained to perform with affected and exaggerated pomp and gesture, still seen in the antics of present-day drum majors and majorettes. The much-admired clash and clang of Turkish Janizary music set the style for European military bands, and Swiss soldiers marched to the roar of some of the largest drums ever made, copied from Near Eastern models. The drum was paired with fife or bugle as the visual and aural motif of war, of military glitter and discipline. Swift trials on the battlefield were held around a great drum serving as table or desk for the judge, and the term "drumhead court-martial" spoke of summary justice. Heroic drummer-boys, as the youngest lads officially attached to an army, provided appealing figures for tales of defeat turned to victory. While mechanized warfare, vehicle-transported troops, and electrical and radio communication have taken from the drums their serious function in war, their appearance in parades still brings out the motor impulses of marchers and spectators that are the secret of the power of the drums in all societies, perhaps an extension of the same motor impulses displayed in the drumming activities of animals. — THERESA C. BRAKELEY

Drunken Sailor A short-haul chantey of late vintage, called the "runaway song," because the crew ran down the deck with the rope as they sang in chorus, hauling a light sail aloft. This could have been done only with the greater deck space of the large ships in the late days of sail. The song details the measures used on ships for sobering up a drunken sailor "early in the morning." It is also called *Early in the Morning*, pronounced with a long i sound for early (earl-eye).

Dryad or **Hamadryad** (plural *Dryads* or *Dryades*) In Greek mythology, a nymph inhabiting a tree, properly an oak tree, who died when the tree died, or, less commonly, moved to another tree. Compare NYMPHS.

drying the candle A European folktale motif (J2122) occurring in the vast cycle of stories known as numskull or noodle tales, in which a candle, having gotten wet, is placed on the stove to dry, with the natural result (unforeseen by the numskull).

dry rod blossoms A well-known European motif (F791.1; Type 756): a dry branch (rod, staff) puts forth flowers, green leaves, or fruit in token of the forgiveness of a sinner, the innocence of someone accused (E131. 0.5.1), or as some other sign. Aaron's rod blossomed as a sign of the selection of Aaron and his descendants for the priesthood. Tannhäuser's dry staff blossomed to disprove the judgment that he could no more be forgiven than the dry staff could bloom. Joseph won the Virgin Mary in a suitor-contest in which the reward was given to the one whose staff bloomed (H331.3). The most widespread folktale using the motif, Type 756B (probably of medieval western European origin, but known in some 209 versions in Ireland, Lithuania, Poland, Russia, Siberia, Germany, Bohemia, Spain), tells of a boy sold to the Devil. He starts out for Hell to retrieve the contract, is guided by a robber, in Hell sees the red-hot chair reserved for his guide, and describes it to him. The robber does penance till his dry staff blossoms or bears fruit (Q521.1) in token of his forgiveness. "When a dry branch sprouts" is one of the by-words for the never concept (Z61).

dual creators Twin or elder and younger brother creators: a concept found in many mythologies of the world. The Hindu Aśvins are probably the most ancient of the world's mythological brother-hero gods. The two-fold creator-transformer-culture-hero is common to all American Indian mythologies. One of the pair is good; one is bad. One is benevolent and constructive; the other either wilfully destroys or stupidly hinders the creative acts of the other, or sometimes clumsily imitates him, bringing forth, however, usually grotesqueries or mistakes. See DIOSCURI; TWINS.

Dúc Bà, Dúc Thánh Bà, or **Bà-Dú'c Chúa** In Annamese belief, the Three Mothers who represent the Spirit of the Forests, the Spirit of the Air, and the Spirit of the Waters. In Tonkinese pagodas the principal room contains the statues of Buddhas, but the second room contains statues of these spirits and their servant tigers, the quan. In legend the Dúc Bà were assigned, one to each region, by the Emperor of Jade, Ngoc Hoàng. The Dúc Bà are worshipped locally as the spirits of feminine trees and in the pagodas on the first and fifteenth of each month, chiefly by women.

duck dance A North American Indian mimetic dance portraying realistically or symbolically the duck, usually to effect their multiplication. The Kutchin wave their arms realistically, the Iroquois merely cry "quack,

quack." The *twę'óenǫ*, a double circle, has become a social dance, with women passing under the arches formed by the men's joined arms, and then caught between couples. The duck dance, or *waima*, forms part of the *hesi* cycle of the Patwin and Maidu Indians of California. Men calling "hat-hat" are joined by impersonations of the spirits of plenty. A completely secular boogie-woogie step, the duck walk, suggests the waddling gait in a curious hips-displacement. [GPK]

bDud   A Tibetan demon, usually male, black in color, and the malignant ghost of a persecutor of Lāmaism. The bDud is one of a large group of demons which belong to the eight classes of *yul-lha* or indigenous country gods. It can only be appeased by the sacrifice of a pig. In the *Kesar Saga* the bDud possesses great treasure, a girl kept in an iron cage, and lives in a castle in the north near a well of milk and nectar.

Dudugera   In a Wagawaga (New Guinea) folktale, the leg-child who became the sun; son of a woman and a fish. A Wagawaga woman, who was weeding her garden near the beach, saw a large fish playing in the surf. She went into the sea and played with the fish each day and, as they played, the fish nuzzled her thigh. Finally her thigh began to swell and ache. When her father cut into it a baby boy burst forth.

Dudugera, as his mother called him, grew up in the village and played with the other boys until one day, while they were throwing spears at trees, he threw his at his companions. Frightened that Dudugera might be punished by the villagers, his mother decided to send him back to his father. They went down to the beach; the big fish came swimming up and carried the child off in his mouth. Before he left, Dudugera told his mother that she and her relatives should move their gardens into the shadow of a great overhanging rock, for he would climb via a pandanus into the sky and all the people, trees, and plants would die.

As Dudugera had prophesied, everything dried up because of the heat from the sun which never ceased during each day to send its merciless heat down to the earth. Finally, Dudugera's mother threw lime into the face of the sun as it came up one morning. Since then clouds appear to relieve the heat and men are able to live.

Dug-from-Ground   Title and hero of a California Indian tale of a woman who digs up a root which turns into a child. When grown the child goes on adventures; he climbs a stretching tree and ascends to the sky, where he kills a deer. Other of the child's adventures are in the form of tests: shinny contest, eating test, heat test, shooting contest, etc. [EWV]

dukun   An Indonesian (Menangkabau, Sumatra) medium whose duties include soul-catching, the practice of magic, and healing by means of simple remedies. The dukun is either male or female and is respected because of his knowledge of curing and of magic formulas which are chiefly Moslem in origin. He, like the Dayong, frequently cures by bringing back the soul when it wanders.

dulcimer   A stringed instrument of the zither family, having a varying number of strings and either struck with two sticks or hammers or plucked. Of Near Eastern origin, the instrument was carried to Europe through Spain by Arabs, who also passed it along to Jews in Africa; to eastern Europe through Turkey; and later to the Far East. The *cimbalon* of Hungarian Gipsies is the chief remainder in Europe. In the mountains of the southern United States, a three-stringed home-made zither is called a dulcimer. It is plucked or brushed with a turkey feather or goose quill, and a stick or reed called the "noter" is moved across the frets to make the melody. It is used to accompany the singing of lonesome tunes, lullabies, ballads, and hymns.

dumi   A type of Ukrainian folksong and ballad, usually with couplet rime in lines of free length. The subject-matter is comparatively modern history, topical to some extent; the style is prosaic, wordy and pedestrian in many cases; the supernatural does not occur. The accompanying music is played on the twenty-stringed lute, the kobza. See BALLAD.

dún   A fortified enclosure within which the ancient Irish kings and nobles dwelt. It was encircled by two or more earthen walls or mounds called ráth. Within the enclosure were a number of wooden buildings: the king's or chief's house, the houses of his chiefs, the feast hall, the guest lodges, etc. Before the dún or ráth was the faitĉe, or lawn, a wide green field used to practice feats, or in some cases perhaps used for pasture. Emain Macha, the residence of Conchobar, in Ulster, and Ráth Cruachan, the residence of Medb and Ailill in Connacht, were typical of these ancient strongholds. The remains of Cuchulain's dún, Dún Delgan, can still be seen today in County Louth, near Dundalk, to which place it gives its name. See RÁTH.

Dund or **Dhûndh**   In popular Indian belief, a headless, handless, footless ghost who rides about with his head tied to the pommel of his saddle. At night he calls outside houses to the people within. It is dangerous to answer; anyone who does will die or go mad.

Durgā   In Hindu mythology and religion, a malignant form of Devī, the inaccessible, represented as a yellow woman riding a tiger.

Dvalin   (1) In Teutonic mythology, the dwarf who invented runes. When Loki cut off the hair of Sif (Thor's wife) as a prank, all the gods were so exasperated with him that he persuaded Dvalin to make a beautiful golden wig to take its place, and also the spear, Gungnir, for Odin, and the ship, Skidbladnir, for Frey, as peace offerings.

(2) In Teutonic mythology, one of the four stags who grazed on the tree Yggdrasil.

dvergar   The dwarfs of Scandinavian mythology: formed by the gods from maggots in the flesh of the giant Ymir. Less powerful than the gods, the dvergar were more intelligent than men. They had dark skin, long beards, green eyes, powerful stocky bodies, short legs, and crow's feet. They possessed caps and cloaks to make them invisible at will. They could not come out in the daylight, lest they be turned to stone by the light. They lived underground, where they mined gold and other metals which they fashioned into beautiful jewelry, wonderful swords, and other magical objects. They were fabulously wealthy, and when captured by mortals, would pay large ransoms for their liberty.

Dvīpa or Dwīpa In Hindu mythology, one of the insular continents, usually seven in number, which stretch out from Mount Meru and which are separated by circumambient oceans. They are Jambu, Plaksha, Śalmala, Kuśa, Krauncha, Sāka, Pushkara. In the *Mahābhārata* four Dvīpas are named: Bhadrāśva, Ketumāla, Jambu-dvīpa, and Uttara Kuru. See LOKĀLOKA.

dwarf Dwarfs are renowned in European tradition as members of a separate community, usually a kingdom with a king of its own. They were underground supernatural beings; they lived in the mountains, in hills and caves, sometimes in rivers, or near a spring. Their dwellings were described as splendid palaces. A dwarf was full-grown at three years of age and a graybeard at seven. Some of their characteristics are indicated by the names given to them: Little Gray Man, Flat-foot, Goosefoot, etc.

Dwarfs have faces like men, but with wrinkled, leathery skin, wide mouths, thick heads, long beards. They are either flat-footed, goose- or duck-footed, or have their feet on backwards. Hence their gait is uncertain and wobbly. They dress in gray or green and wear little red caps with a long tapering point. By virtue of either the cloak or the cap, they can become invisible. German folktale especially presents them as ugly, or covered with moss, big-headed, or humpbacked, or stooped over, long-bearded and gray-bearded. Sometimes they nod at people and seem eager to tell something. Sometimes they are toads by day and dwarfs by night. In the *Elder Edda* the dwarf Alvíss turned to stone at sunrise.

Dwarfs love feasting and dancing, usually at full moon, to light and joyous music. Otherwise they are busy at their forges in the mountains. If clouds and mists are seen over dwarf holes, people say the dwarfs are cooking or forging. They are marvelous smiths and workers in all kinds of metals; their women excel in weaving and spinning. Traditionally the dwarfs taught men to bake, smith, and tailor.

Dwarfs can see into the future and are good weather prophets. They give good advice, and are helpful both in the house and in the field. Although they often tease both children and adults, they also often give them rich presents. In fact any gift from a dwarf is apt to turn to gold in your hand. Thievery is one of their bad habits; so is the kidnapping of women and children. If they plunder the larder, the housewife marks a cross in her dough or strews salt about. For helping in the field, people reward them with little pieces of cake or tidbits placed on the plow. On the whole dwarfs adjust themselves fairly well to the outside world; but if anyone offends them, they take a rude revenge.

There exists a rich and varied folk literature about dwarfs. Perhaps the most famous dwarfs in European folktale are the seven dwarfs in the story of *Snow White* (Grimm #53), whose popularity has been extended through Walt Disney's animated moving picture. *Bibliography:* Hanns Bächtold-Stäubli, *Handwörterbuch des deutschen Aberglaubens,* Berlin & Leipzig, 1927–42; Alexander H. Krappe, "Antipodes," *MLN* 59 (Nov., 1944), pp. 441–47: a discussion of Celtic and Germanic dwarfs as chthonic beings, divine ancestors, and a new interpretation of the word *Antipodes;* Stith Thompson, *Motif-Index of Folk-Literature,* Helsinki, 1935. [GPS]

☞ A native belief in dwarfs is practically universal among the North American Indians and the Eskimo. Scattered references to dwarfs occur in American Indian myths and tales, but with no great frequency except among the Eskimo. The existence of dwarfs, however, is taken quite for granted. Among such tribes as the Coeur d'Alene of the Plateau, the Tübatulabal of east-central California, and the Paiute of the Great Basin, dwarfs are described as small supernatural mischief-makers who frighten people, but rarely do real harm. Some live in springs or rivers, others on land. The Cherokees of North Carolina believe there are four kinds of dwarfs; some are good, some evil. To see them causes, or is a sign of, death. The Cayuga, an Iroquois tribe, believe in twin dwarfs, a male and female, who hunt with slings and stones; the neighboring Seneca also believe in dwarfs or "little people." The Shawnee of the Eastern Woodlands, and the Cherokee refer to the Thunders as powerful male dwarfs. Eskimo tales of dwarfs (*JAFL* 51:149) present them as harmless or benevolent land or water creatures who sometimes help hunters. The Kodiak tell of two hunters in a kayak, caught in thick fog, who met another kayak containing two small men. As soon as they took them into their own kayak the fog cleared. They took the little men home and cared for them secretly and forever after had good luck. The Baffin Land Eskimo believe in a dwarf people who live in the sea; human beings have tried, but unsuccessfully, to fish these dwarfs out of the ocean. See AZIZA; BERRIES IN WINTER; DVERGAR. [EWV]

Dyaus In Vedic religion and mythology, the sky god; the elemental supreme spirit of the primitive Aryans, usually mentioned with Mother Earth as Dyāvāprithivī with whom he shares the offerings of soma in the ritual. He was the sky father whose offspring included Ushās, the Aśvins, Agni, Parjanya, Sūrya, the Ādityas, the Maruts, Indra, and the Angirases.

Dyaus was only slightly anthropomorphized: usually represented as a bull who bellowed downward or as a black horse. His worship was little more than the direct adoration of the sky. In his fatherly aspects he resembled Zeus, but differed from him in that he had no sovereignty over other gods or the world. Varuṇa represents this phase of the Aryan sky god and as his importance in Indian mythology increased, that of Dyaus became evanescent. See DYĀVĀPRITHIVĪ; VARUṆA.

Dyāvāpṛithivī In Vedic mythology, heaven and earth as one deity, regarded as so closely united that they are more frequently invoked together than as Dyaus (sky) and Pṛithivī (earth).

The primitive Aryan invaders of India believed that the universe included only the earth and sky and compared the two to two bowls turned toward each other. Dyāvāpṛithivī, as the union of the male and female principles, was regarded as the universal parents of both gods and men. Sometimes the earth and sky are spoken of as having been themselves created. Speculation on the priority of their creation led to the conclusion, in the *Śatapatha Brāhmaṇa,* that the earth was created first.

Dying Californian An American religious ballad, giving in the first person the dying words and wishes of a 'forty-niner. It has been sung as a hymn among various religious groups all over the United States. It was published in Boston by Ditson in 1855.

Dying Cowboy Variant title for *Bury Me Not on the Lone Prairie.*

Dylan In Brythonic mythology, one of the remarkable twins born to Arianrod after her failure to pass the test of virginity imposed on her by Math, son of Mathonwy; twin brother of Llew Llaw Gyffes: interpreted either as a local sea god or equated with the waves of the sea. The *Mabinogion* states that as soon as he was born, Dylan plunged "and swam as well as the best fish, and for this reason he was called Dylan Eil Ton, Son of the Wave." When he was killed by his uncle, Govannon, the smith, the waves rose to avenge him; and over his grave they "make a sullen sound." The voice of the tide when it turns and roars up into the Conway River is called the dying cry of Dylan. Rhys's interpretation of Dylan as darkness and his brother Llew as light makes of the whole a solar myth that is not substantiated. Dylan's death was loudly lamented, not desired, as would be the case if he represented dark and gloomy winter in contrast to Llew as spring and sun.

Dzelarhons A mythical character of the North Pacific Coast Indians of North America. The niece of Githawn, or Salmon-Eater, she came with six canoe-loads of people out of the sea, and was betrothed to Ka'iti, chief of the Grizzlies. Among the Athabaskan-speaking tribes in the Northwest she is also known as Copper Woman or Volcano Woman, and among the Haida groups as Frog Woman, Copper Frog, or Dzelarhons (Barbeau, *Alaska Beckons*). According to Barbeau, the story of Dzelarhons belongs to the migration tale of the Salmon-Eater tribe to America, via the Aleutian Islands. Boas gives Dzilaogans (Djilaguns) as the name of the Haida for their ancestors. [EWV]

Dzōávits A huge ogre of Shoshonean Indian folktale who stole Dove's two children. With the help of Eagle, Dove rescued the children, and then Eagle gave Dove some tallow from an animal he had killed, also its paunch and some feathers. Dzōávits began to pursue them. They crossed a river via the crane bridge (i.e. Crane stretched out his leg to make a bridge for them to cross it), but Crane delayed Dzōávits by dumping him in the middle of the river. They were helped again by Chickadee, and again by Weasel, who dug an underground passage for them, but delayed Dzōávits by sending him down the wrong hole. When Dzōávits began to catch up again, Dove threw down the tallow Eagle had given her; it became a deep gulch and delayed the ogre a long time. When he drew close again, Dove threw down the paunch; it became a steep cliff which Dzōávits could not climb. The next time Dzōávits was catching up with them, Dove threw down the feathers; they became a thick and covering fog, and the ogre lost track of them for a long time. But at last they heard him behind them again. Badger saved Dove and her children this time. He dug a hole for them to hide in and another hole nearby. When Dzōávits came he asked where Dove was. Badger said "In the hole"; but when Dzōávits wanted to go in after them, Badger turned him into the wrong hole, threw hot rocks in on him, and plugged up the hole. Then Dove and her children could come out and go home. See OBSTACLE FLIGHT.

Džokhk or **Džoxǩ** The underworld of Armenian mythology; an abyss beneath the earth, permeated by the dense smoke from innumerable fires. The souls there wear iron shoes and are tormented by the vermin in their mouths. They are tortured by devils who burn them with red-hot iron staffs. The only exit from Džokhk is the bridge Maze which joins Paradise and Hell. This, however, breaks easily under the weight of sins, drops the souls into the fiery stream beneath, where their torment is renewed.

Ea or **Enki** The god of the waters of Sumerian and Babylonian mythology; one of the supreme triad with Anu and Enlil. Ea was the creator of mankind; the god who gave man his arts, crafts, and sciences; the protector and healer of men. As the god of the deep and of the waters of the earth, Ea was a fructifying god. He was the lord of wisdom, hence the guardian and aid against demons, and was invoked in exorcisms. In these spells, and in the creation myth, Ea principally appears. He later developed into a fish god, half fish, half goat. See ADAPA; NINKI; OANNES.

eać uisge The water horse of Irish folklore, a water spirit usually regarded as malicious towards men: analogous with the kelpie. It is not to be confused with the beautiful lake-dwelling supernatural horses such as Cuchulain captured and trained and which returned into their mountain pool upon receiving mortal wounds during Cuchulain's last fight. Compare NISSE.

Eabani Companion to the Babylonian Gilgamesh.

Eagentci Old-Woman or the Ancient-Bodied; the first mother of Seneca Indian mythology. See ATAENSIC.

Eagle One of the two chiefs of the animal characters in many Central Californian Indian tales, and a prominent character in tales of neighboring Great Basin tribes. Sometimes Eagle is identified with the Thunderbirds. On the North Pacific Coast the Eagle (Na'as) group of the Tlingit was one of the most powerful Tlingit clans. Eagle as an eponymous clan animal is not limited to this area, however. An Eagle dance, in which the bird's motions are simulated, was probably widespread in eastern North America.

Live eagles were shot or trapped and ceremonially killed in California and on the Plains. Eagle feathers and eagle down were widely used by nearly all American Indian tribes for ceremonial costumes, headdresses, and ceremonial objects, such as prayer sticks, pipes, wands, and so forth. [EWV]

eagle As king of birds, the emblem of royalty. The American eagle (genus *Haliætus*) is the national emblem of the United States.

In Greek mythology the eagle is associated with Zeus and lightning and hence could not be struck by lightning. For this reason eagle wings were often buried in the growing fields to protect the crop from destruction by storm. In the *Rig-Veda* the sacred soma was brought to man by an eagle. In the Avesta an eagle lives in the mythical all-healing tree. Everywhere the eagle is noted for swiftness, the marvelous height to which it soars, its inaccessible nests, its keenness of vision, and its longevity. Job mentions the eagle on her crag "and her eyes behold afar off" (*Job* xxxix, 29). In Persian legend the simurg sometimes plays the eagle's role, as does the roc in the *Arabian Nights*.

It is bad luck today to kill an eagle among the Samoyeds, the Bosnians, certain North American Indians (especially the Osage), and in Maine. The first Buriat shaman was the son of an eagle and a Buriat woman, and is regarded as especially powerful against evil spells. The Ostyaks not only revere the eagle, but revere even the tree in which an eagle nests. There is an eagle cult among certain Australian peoples, but in New Guinea the people believe that planting bananas in sight of an eagle-hawk will put a blight on the crop.

In folktale, fable, and ballad the eagle plays a prominent role as helpful or warning bird. Eagle was the warning bird in the Pima Indian deluge story. Well known are the fables in which the eagle saves a man's life by upsetting a cup containing poison which he was about to drink, or snatches the hat off a man's head to lure him away from a wall about to fall (B521.2.1). In the *Kalevala* (Runo 7) Väinämöinen was rescued out of the ocean by an eagle who carried him to the borders of Pohjola. In a Chiricahua Apache Indian folktale (Opler, *MAFLS* 37, p. 91) a young boy climbs to an eagle's nest and brings home one of the young eaglets. He is warned against it by the people, but persists in befriending it. It flies by his side wherever he goes, catches rabbits and other game for him. The warning against it reveals the Chiricahua belief that because eagles eat snakes, mere contact with an eagle will cause sickness.

eagle dance   A mimetic dance expressive of the eagle's soaring flight. Because of its disappearance beyond the clouds, North American Indians associate the eagle with powers beyond the clouds, particularly with powers governing thunder and rain—hence often he is identified as Thunderbird. Early in the spring in Tesuque, Jemez, and other pueblos, the eagle dance takes place: two dancers, representing male and female, approach and circle in difficult crouching, hopping, and swaying motions. Their extended arms hold wings of large eagle feathers; a feather cap projects over their faces in a yellow beak. In the Comanche eagle dance (*kanani kiyake*) a special dancer imitates the eagle. This goes back to the legend of the young son of a chieftain, who died and was later turned into the first eagle, as answer to his father's prayers to the Creator. The former Iowa eagle dance was equally mimetic, but the dancers carried an eagle-feather fan in their left hands; they were associated with war societies and interpolated boasting tales between dances. The Iroquois eagle dance or *ganegwa'e* also features a feathered fan and includes anecdotes, but it is mimetic only in a crouching hop. Two lines of dancers lunge face to face vibrating a feathered rattle in their right hands and holding a wand in their left. The dance resembles the Midwest

and Plains calumet dance and Cherokee *tsugi'dali*. It invokes tribal prosperity.

Eagle feathers not only stand for martial success in Sioux war-bonnets. As ornaments, in fans or brushes, in Pawnee, Yuchi, Delaware, Iroquois ceremonies, they exert purificatory and invocative power. [GPK]

Eaglehawk and Crow   Names of two moieties in several Southern Australian tribes: subject of J. Mathew's theory (in *Eaglehawk and Crow*) that the ancestors of each moiety were of different racial origin. Bunjil (Pundjel) is an eaglehawk and Waang is a crow (Howitt, *Native Tribes*, p. 126). (Also see Durkheim, *Elementary Forms of the Religious Life;* N. W. Thomas, *Kinship and Marriage in Australia*, p. 53 ff.) [KL]

ear   A tingling or throbbing of the right ear in northern Europe is said to be a good sign. Hindu literature has similar references with the addition that among women, the left ear is involved. In the Indian science of physical signs, men with long ears are certain to be licentious. Elsewhere, ears close to the head indicate a stingy nature. Ear ornaments when not for simple decoration are part of the large number of amulets which protect the openings of the body against morbid influences, spirits, powers, etc. When the temple prostitutes of Madras became too old for service they ceremonially unhooked their ear pendants and walked away without looking back. The pendants were later returned to them. In some Hindu stories thieves were punished by having their ears cut off. In others a faithless wife had her ears cut off, though in the Middle and Far East amputation of the nose is the more common punishment for infidelity. [RDJ]

Earl Brand   The Scottish-English version (Child #7) of a ballad of general North European distribution: known in Denmark as *Ribold and Guldborg*, in Sweden as *Hillebrand* or *Redevold*, in Norway as *Rikeball and Veneros*, in Scotland also as *The Douglas Tragedy*, and in the United States as *The Seven Sleepers, The Seven Brothers*, or *Sweet William*. The story seems to derive from the second lay of Helgi in the *Poetic Edda* and has some connection with Hildebrand, of whose name Earl Brand seems to be a modification. The central element of the story is the stealing of a bride, with the subsequent chase by the girl's father, brothers, or servants. Earl Brand fights them off, is wounded (and in bending over a stream he stains the water with his blood), and dies after he reaches his home with his bride. A very essential element of the Continental versions of the story is curiously left out of the English-Scottish and American versions: the motif of the name tabu. As Ribold turns to fight, he warns the girl not to call his name, but she, seeing her brothers dying, calls on him to spare the last, and he is mortally wounded. For some reason, only the barest hint of this appears in one of the versions of *Earl Brand* collected by Child. The American transformations of the story suppose it to have occurred recently.

earth   Worship of the earth, typically as the Earth-Mother, is probably as widespread as any kind of worship in the world. Its origins lie perhaps in the magical nature of planting and growth: crops do fail and a ceremonial approach to the placing of seed in the ground is indicated. The earth as receiver of the seed must be propitiated; hence, Earth becomes personified and deified. Almost universally the earth, as bringer-forth of the fruits, is regarded as female, the mother goddess; and there arises the myth of the Earth-Mother and the Sky-Father. This bountiful female deity also takes into herself the dead, and, as beliefs from North America, West Africa, Mongolia, etc., indicate, this too is a kind of planting ceremony, for the spirit of the dead may enter a woman's body and be reborn. In this aspect, the earth is a rather forbidding deity, and the earth concept includes the idea of an underworld where dead spirits live. (See CHTHONIC DEITIES.)

Of the origin and nature of the earth itself, many and varied myths are told. Earth here is matter and is not personified. It may be made from nothing; it may be fished out from the bottom of the universal waters; it may be the body of a dead god or monster. Earth may rest on an animal or person, or be held up by deities placed at its four corners; thus arise earthquake myths, for when the animal moves or the deities shift position the earth shakes.

☞ The concept of the earth as personified mother to all mankind is widespread in North American Indian mythology. In certain creation stories, such as that of the Zuñi Indians, Earth definitely figures as the mother, and Sky as the father, from whose union man was born. Other American Indian tribes, although lacking such a definite conceptualization of Earth Mother in their myths, refer by allusion in speeches, prayers and formulas to "our mother, the earth." This metaphor is especially common among the agricultural tribes of the eastern United States. The earth as mother is also referred to in the myths of certain Plateau and North Pacific Coast groups. [EWV]

☞ The earth was regarded as a major deity by the ancient Peruvians who called her Pachamama (Mother Earth). The Jivaro, who have received many Andean influences, also worship an Earth spirit who protects the crops. The earth does not seem to have been deified outside of the Andean region. [AM]

☞ As part of the ancient imperial cult of China, the Emperor prostrated himself before five mounds of earth, representing the five directions, i.e. four points of the compass and the center. The Emperor sacrificed an ox; tributary chiefs sacrificed sheep. [RDJ]

Earth In the mythology of the Kato Indians of California, the earth is conceived of as a huge horned animal eternally wallowing southward through the primeval waters. Nagaicho, the traveler-creator of the Kato, was standing on its head directing it, until it finally stopped in its present position. In the mythology of the Yurok Indians of California and many other North American Indian tribes, the earth is believed to be floating in water, and is sometimes referred to as Earth-island.

earth diver In North American Indian myths of the origin of the world, the culture hero has a succession of animals dive into the primeval waters, or flood waters, to secure bits of mud or sand from which the earth is to be formed. Various animals, birds, and aquatic creatures are sent down into the waters that cover the earth. One after another animal fails; the last one succeeds, however, and floats to the surface, half dead, with a little dirt or sand in his claws. Sometimes it is Muskrat, sometimes Beaver, Hell-diver, Crawfish, Mink who succeeds, after various other animals have failed, in bringing up the tiny bit of mud which is then put on the surface of the water and magically expands to become the world of the present time. See CREATION. [EWV]

Earthmaker The supreme deity of the Winnebago Indians of the Great Lakes region; Creator, Great Spirit, and source of all good, who coexists with the evil Herecgunina. Earthmaker created the earth and human beings, and a specific number (five or eight) "great spirits" to free the world of giants and evil. Among these are Trickster, Turtle, Bladder, Hare, also Sun, Red Horn. Some myths state that the Twins were the last "great spirits" created by Earthmaker. Each one of these spirits was given control over something: life itself, victory in war, other blessings. The Winnebago believe that all who strictly observe the doctrines of their Medicine Dance will go to Earthmaker when they die and be allowed to choose whether or not they wish to return to this life, and if so, in what form.

earthquakes Earthquakes are commonly thought to occur when the god or hero who supports the earth changes his position or his hold on it. In Timor when a giant shifts the earth from shoulder to shoulder the natives shout to him not to drop it. The Manichæans thought that this happened once every thirty years. In the Indian archipelago a grandparent was thought to hold the earth and shake it now and again to see whether his descendants were still alive. The Burmese Shans thought that a great fish slept under the earth with its tail in its mouth. Sometimes it woke, bit the tail, and was in great pain. In eastern Peru the creator came down from heaven to see whether his creatures were still alive and caused an earthquake. The natives then shouted, "Here I am." In Africa an earthquake is the voice of god to which the natives reply or it is the movement of an underground god. In the Celebes the natives pluck handfuls of grass which is the god's hair to make him stop, and in Samoa the god was warned to stop before he shook the earth to pieces. The Fiji Islanders made sacrifices so that the earth god would turn over gently. Elsewhere earthquakes were thought to be portents of coming events or punishments for the wicked actions of men. See AMALA. [RDJ]

earwig In the United States the term earwig is popularly applied to a certain small centipede (not to the true earwig), an insect of the family Forficulidæ. It is the little centipede (genus *Geophilus*) which is said to crawl into people's ears and eat their brains out. If one does get into your ear, lie down on the ground with the ear against some newly turned-up soil, and the earwig will run out again.

Easter The Christian festival commemorating the resurrection of Christ, synchronized with the Jewish Pesach, and blended since the earliest days of Christianity with pagan European rites for the renewed season. In all countries Easter falls on the Sunday after the first full moon on or following March 21. It is preceded by a period of riotous vegetation rites (see CARNIVAL) and by a period of abstinence, Lent (in Spain *cuaresma*, in Germany *Lenz*, in central Italy *Quaresima*), and by the special rites of Holy Week.

In Mexico fiestas never cease. The concheros, moros, and other groups continue their pilgrimages, on the first Thursday to Tecalpulco, Guerrero, the third weekend to a great fair in Tepalcingo, Morelos, the fourth Sunday to Acopilco, México.

Palm Sunday is in all Catholic countries an occasion for the blessing of palms. Then festivities cease until Maundy Thursday. The three days before Easter Sunday are given over to processionals, masses, and Passion Plays. In Catalonia and central Mexico the figure of death (la muerte) looms large in the processionals. The Passion Plays of Spain receive original and deeply moving interpretations in Mexico, most impressively so in Ixtapalapa, México; Tzintzuntzan, Michoacán; Oxchuc, Chiapas; and among the Yaqui of Sonora and Arizona. Here the chapayakas and pilatos dance and join in the processions to the Stations of the Cross. On Easter Saturday through the night all dancers, sacred and pagan—matachini, deer dancers, coyotes, pascolas—dance till the fiesta de Gloria.

Everywhere Easter Sunday is welcomed with rejoicing, singing, candle processionals, flowers in abundance, and ringing of church bells. Many pagan customs survive, such as the lighting of new fires at dawn, among the Maya as well as in Europe, for cure, renewed life, and protection of the crops. The German Osterwasser (Easter water) is water dipped against the stream and imbued with curative properties. Ostermärchen are told in order to produce laughter (risus paschalis). The Easter lamb is perennially sacrificed. Children roll pasch eggs in England. Everywhere they hunt the many-colored Easter eggs, brought by the Easter rabbit. This is not mere child's play, but the vestige of a fertility rite, the eggs and the rabbit both symbolizing fertility. Furthermore, the rabbit was the escort of the Germanic goddess Ostara who gave the name to the festival by way of the German Ostern.

Flowers in profusion ornament altars and church façades. This floral association is expressed in the Spanish term pascua de flores. [GPK]

☞ That the sun dances as it rises on Easter morning is quite common folk belief in the British Isles, and people rise early and go to the hilltops to see it. Georgia Negroes say "the sun shouts" on Easter morning.

The children's game of "nicking" Easter eggs is common in the world from Egypt to England, and is also fairly general in the United States, especially among southern Negroes. Two children, each with an Easter egg in his hand, will knock the two eggs together; the one whose egg cracks the least under the treatment appropriates the other's egg.

Easter smacks The German Schmeckostern: the beatings given to each other on Easter Monday and Tuesday by men and women in parts of Germany and Austria to bring them good luck, protect them from vermin, and keep them young and healthy and "green." The custom is observed, by other names, in most Slavic countries. The men beat the women on Easter Monday, the women beat the men on Easter Tuesday. In Croatia the beatings take place on the way home from church on Good Friday. The beatings are commonly given with birch branches, especially branches just sprouted, or sometimes with cherry, or with a willow switch. The new young life inherent in the sprouting branch is thus be-

stowed upon the one beaten with it. In Bohemia vine branches are used, and the women make presents of red Easter eggs to their beaters. These are saved for afternoon egg-rolling. In some sections these beatings are given on Holy Innocents' Day, December 28. See RODS OF LIFE.

eating the god The custom of eating the body of a god is known in many communities although the mystery of the Christian sacrament of communion has made it difficult for ethnographers and theologians to see other customs elsewhere with sufficient objectivity to present satisfactory accounts of the profound human impulses involved in consuming the very body and very blood of God. Frazer's account is elaborate and his parallels are suggestive. The ceremonial eating of the first-fruits, or the ceremonial eating of bread made from the last sheaf, are connected with the belief that the god (often referred to as the "corn god") resides in the first or the last fruits and must be eaten to assure continued crops, that is, his and our immortality. Frazer connects the ceremonial eating of the cereal itself, even when not baked into a loaf or shaped into human form, with the eating of the god. In Yorkshire a clergyman cut the first corn and made it into communion bread. Peasants in the Volga region ate new cornbread handed them by the priest and prayed. In the Celebes the priest collected the first rice, ground it into meal and gave it to the villagers. They harvested the rest of the cereal only after all had partaken. Similar customs have been reported from India and Indochina. Among the Ashanti and the Zulu an orgy followed the celebration.

The North American Creek Indians began such a ceremony by cleaning their houses and clothes. They fasted for two nights and one day and purged themselves so that the old food would not mingle in their stomachs with the new food. They built a new fire with the thought that the new fire would burn out their old sins. They then ate ceremonially the grain and, by it, the corn spirit. Twice a year the pre-Columbian Aztecs ceremonially ate bread which, having been consecrated, became the very body of God, and taught that sacramental food was contaminated when it touched other food. The Ainus of northern Japan and Kamchatka eat the bear god (the bear is either considered as god himself or as a divine messenger to the other gods) in a ceremony which is more striking than Frazer's report of the ceremonial eating of the Ainu millet. Here a bear cub is captured once a year and becomes the pet of the village. As it grows older it is caged beside the house of the chief where it is fed delicacies and is made much of. In the spring the god is murdered with expressions of devotion and great feeling. The blood is drunk and the flesh is eaten.

The ceremonial eating of the very body and blood of Christ, which is essential in the sacrament of the Christian Eucharist, involves theological discussions which lead beyond the scope of this note. In his First Epistle to the Corinthians, Paul reminded the congregation of the seriousness of the custom and repeated to them Christ's clear words about it. Tertullian, Cyprian, and Augustine held in effect that the bread and blood as symbols were not the signs of an absent reality but were in some sense what they symbolized and possessed the effect of the reality. In the 8th century, John of

Damascus held that the eucharistic body was identical with that born of Mary. A modern view, summarized in the *Catholic Encyclopedia* is "The Body and Blood of the God-man are truly, really and substantially present for the nourishment of our souls." Obviously the eating of the very body of the very god involves complex human impulses which are no less impressive among pagans than they are among Christians. [RDJ]

eating the heart Eating the heart to endow the consumer with the qualities of the original owner has been reported from many parts of the world. Thus the Ashanti of Africa who killed Sir Charles M'Carthy in 1843 are reported to have eaten his heart to acquire his courage. A similar custom is said to be popular among the Basutos. In West Africa a king's heart was, according to some reports, eaten by his successor. Other peoples believe that eating the heart of a lion, leopard, wolf, or bear gives courage, or that the heart of a jackal or hare induces timidity, or that a snake's heart gives the gift of languages. [RDJ]

eating the sacred animal A custom observed among several ethnic groups, though social attitudes toward this custom show great diversity. Some totemic groups eat their totem animal, considered as a member of the clan or its founder, either customarily or ceremonially. In some cannibal communities the sacrifice to the god, having acquired a degree of sanctity, is eaten, or the sacrifice is considered a representative of the god, as in the Ainu bear ceremony. Other parallels are the eating of the first-fruits and the Christian Eucharist. Thus the phrase "eating the sacred animal" requires careful scrutiny to fix the quality of sacredness attributed to the animal in the community described. Before eating the bear and drinking its raw blood the Ainu reach a state of emotional exaltation not customarily found among Christians who partake of the Holy Communion, yet the position of the bear in the social and religious organization of the Ainu is vastly different from the position of Christ in the Euro-American religious structure. See EATING THE GOD; TOTEMISM. [RDJ]

eating together Although communal eating is a custom followed in many parts of the world, it is subject to innumerable variations and special ceremonies. The sense of well-being and general emotional exhilaration which follows a good meal, and the transformation of inert food into vitality, or conversely the sickness and death which sometimes follow a meal, make the taking of food an important and hazardous custom. Consequently the taking of food, like other actions with which man passes from one state of being to another, is surrounded by large numbers of precautions to protect against possible danger.

Eating together is one of these precautions which is of particular importance on special days: weddings, birthdays, funerals, days of religious ceremony, birthdays or death days of the gods or heroes. On these days the feast is connected with strong emotions produced by the ceremony and is, at times, preceded by a fast. In some communities eating together is prudent protection against an enemy, who is thus restrained from poisoning food which he himself will share, or against working magic on it. The belief that persons become to some extent part of the social unit, as clansmen, brothers, or

allies, after they have shared food or "broken bread" involves a complex etiquette in some parts of the world, particularly the Near East.

In Europe and America a different degree of social acceptance is involved in having a "business lunch with a man" or "having dinner at the house." To eat food at banquets in honor of, or with, local or national heroes is to participate in a magical rite still only vaguely understood. It involves at least temporary membership in the social group, and thus a share not only in the virtue of the group but in the virtue of the person honored. The grace before meat whether in formal or family meals which consecrates the meat "to our use and us to Thy service" is a recognition of the hazards of eating and an attempt to get the beneficent forces on our side. In communities which are generally undernourished or subsist on monotonous diets, the party meal which at times supplies needed and unaccustomed elements of diet, has other functions in addition to those listed here. In some strict communities all food is shared with the entire group and the portion of the hunter and his family limited by custom. In the United States where food is plentiful, and standing in the community is determined in part by the food served and by the way it is served, and where, moreover, people from many parts of the world constitute the acting social units, the amount of time given to the preparation and serving of party food requires special examination. The fact that Thanksgiving and Christmas dinners have in the United States become orgies of communal gluttony is due in part to the fact that food is plentiful and in part to obscure, old rigid, sexual and orgiastic prohibitions.

Yet eating together is subject to many local prohibitions. In some places people surround eating with precautions of secrecy because they fear that evil may enter their mouths as they take food. Elsewhere the taking of food in public is an indecency. Men and women, particularly pregnant or menstruating women, often eat separately. In the Far East, prostitutes and sing-song girls, though they may sit beside their customers at feasts, do not normally eat with them. In some communities men and women have special food prohibitions. Elsewhere children and adults do not eat together; members of different social classes though they occupy the same quarters eat separately, as in the armed forces. Or again, adolescent males and adolescent females eat communally but in separate places and of special foods. [RDJ]

Ebisu One of the Japanese Seven Gods of Luck; the God of Fishing, Food, and Honest Dealing. See JAPANESE FOLKLORE. [JLM]

Echidna In Greek mythology, the monster, half woman, half serpent, daughter of Chrysaor and Callirrhoe and sister of Geryon, who was mother by Typhon of many of the monsters of mythology and legend: the Chimera, Othrus, the Sphinx, Cerberus, Scylla, the Lernean Hydra, the dragons of the Hesperides and of Colchis, the Nemean lion, the eagle which ate Prometheus' liver. She is perhaps of Oriental origin; she dwelt underground beneath Arima. Hercules was bargained into sleeping with her as he returned with the oxen of Geryon, and she bore three sons from the union, one of whom, Scythes, was capable of bending the bow of Hercules and became king of the Scythians. Echidna was finally slain by Argus Panoptes.

Echo In late Greek and Roman mythology, an oread pursued fruitlessly by Pan. He drove the shepherds in the neighborhood mad and they tore Echo to pieces, scattering her parts, each of which retained the power to speak; or else they tore her until only the voice was left. Another story, told by Ovid, is that Echo was detailed to occupy Hera with chatter while Zeus sported with the nymphs. Annoyed, Hera condemned her to be able to speak only when spoken to. While thus afflicted, she fell in love with Narcissus and faded away to bones and voice, the bones being changed to stones.

Echtrae Conli Literally, the adventure of Conle: the oldest of the adventure stories of ancient Irish tradition. Conle was the son of Conn of the Hundred Battles, king of Ireland in the 3rd century. One day as Conle walked with his father on a hill, he saw a woman in rich garments beside him, who described to him the wonders of the Land of the Living, and promised him beauty and love forever without old age, if he would go with her there. Conn bade the druids sing against the woman's voice, so that Conle would not be tempted. So the woman went away, but she threw an apple to Conle; and Conle ate no food but the apple for a month. At the end of the month the woman returned with more words about the country which delights the mind of anyone who goes there. Conle was torn between love for his own people and longing for the woman and the things she promised. But in the end he leaped into the ship of glass with her, and sailed away in that crystal coracle, never to return. See ECHTRAI.

Echtrae Cormaic or the *Adventure of Cormac* Title of an Old Irish story contained in the *Book of Ballymote,* the *Yellow Book of Lecan,* and the *Book of Fermoy.* One day at sunrise when Cormac Mac Airt, king of Ireland, was walking on the rampart at Tara, he saw coming towards him a warrior who carried a branch with three golden apples. The branch, when shaken, made a music so marvelous that even the ill and wounded would sleep when they heard it. After their greeting and words of friendship, Cormac asked for the branch. The strange warrior gave it, asking in return only the promise of three wishes, and Cormac promised. In a year the warrior came and asked for Ailbe, the daughter of Cormac, and Cormac gave her. In a month he came and asked for Cairpre, the son of Cormac, and Cormac let Cairpre go. The third time he asked for Eithne, the wife of Cormac, and Cormac pursued them, but was lost in a magic mist that fell on the plain. After many sights and adventures Cormac came at last to a castle where he was generously entertained by a handsome warrior. Stories were told while the pig for the feast was cooking. It was a pig that would not cook unless a true thing were told for each quarter. It fell to Cormac to tell the fourth story, and he told how first his daughter, then his son, and his wife had been taken from him. Then the host sang a song and Cormac slept. When he woke fifty warriors sat at the feast and also his wife and son and daughter. A gold cup was handed to the host and Cormac was amazed at the beauty of the carving on it. But its greatest wonder was yet to be shown: for it was a cup of truth. The warrior told three

lies and the cup broke in three. Then he told Cormac that Eithne had lain with no man since she left Tara, nor had Ailbe, and Cairpre had lain with no woman. And for these three sayings the cup was whole. Then the warrior made himself known to Cormac: he was Manannán Mac Lir, and he had brought them all into the Land of the Living. He let Cormac keep the branch and the cup for his lifetime, but he said after Cormac they would not be seen in Ireland again. The next morning Cormac and Eithne and Ailbe and Cairpre woke again in Tara. Cormac used the cup to judge false from true in Ireland after that, but when Cormac died it vanished. See ACT OF TRUTH.

echtrai Literally, expeditions, adventures, also stories and wonders: a group of early Irish stories in which a journey to the Otherworld (Land of Promise, Land of the Living, Island of Women, Many-Colored Land, Land of the Young) is the main theme. The echtrai are to be distinguished from the imrama, voyages, in which the wonders of the voyage itself are the main theme. Most of the echtrai follow a traditional pattern of enticement of the hero by a beautiful woman enumerating the marvels of a marvelous land (...a place without grief, without death, without old age,...there are treasures of every color, listening to music, and drinking of wine,...happiness and laughter, pleasant company without strife...) or by a wonderful warrior who either invites or otherwise brings the hero to the Land of the Living.

The Otherworld is usually situated either in the western ocean, or is reached across a plain on which the hero is lost in a magic mist. The wonderful Otherworld warrior usually turns out to be one of the Tuatha Dé Danann, the divine race of ancient Ireland: sometimes Manannán, sometimes Lug, etc. Either the hero never returns, as in the *Echtrae Conli,* or returns bearing magic gifts and greater wisdom, as in the *Echtrai Cormaic,* or he vanishes in a whiff of ashes when his foot touches the earth, in testimony that he has been gone 300 years, as in the case of one of the companions of Bran in the *Voyage and Adventure of Bran, Son of Febal.* Compare IMRAMA.

eclipses Eclipses are misfortunes which must be corrected. Folk explanations of them show a general similarity; methods of correction differ. The account in the Edda that the sun in eclipse is being pursued by a monster which must be driven off is typical. The Lettish peasants believed that the sun and moon were being devoured during an eclipse. The view among the Buriats was that Alka, a monster, swallowed the sun or moon but, because the gods had cut him in two only the head remained and the objects soon reappeared. The Altaic Tatars thought the cause was a vampire who lived on a star. In India, the Asura, Svarbhānu, eclipsed the sun, or Rahu, a demon, swallowed Soma, the moon. Among the Buddhists Sakyamuni is said to have commanded Rahu to leave the moon in peace. The Armenians, in a variant of a Persian belief, explained that two dark bodies, the offspring of a primeval ox, got between the sun and the moon. In northern North American groups, an eclipse occurred when the sun or moon took their child in their arms. On the northwest coast, the eclipse appeared when the sun dropped its torch. The

Alaskan Tlingits thought eclipses occurred when the female moon visited her husband the sun. The Cherokees, however, thought the moon was male and the sun was female. Among the Eskimos the sun and moon are brother and sister who commit incest during an eclipse. The Tahitians also explained that sun and moon had sexual intercourse during an eclipse. The tribes of the Pampas thought that the eclipsed moon was darkened by her own blood drawn by savage dogs. In Yucatan the day of an eclipse, particularly a solar eclipse, was a day of great national peril, and the Orinoco Indians promised to lead better lives. Although Thucydides' account of the lunar eclipse before the battle of Syracuse had a political purpose it is significant that the period of waiting for the evil effects to be dissipated was thrice nine days or a lunar month.

In an attempt to check the misfortune, the Ojibwas shot lighted arrows to keep the sun from being extinguished; but the arrows shot by the Peruvian Indians were to frighten the beast attacking the sun. The Guarayú Indians of Bolivia shoot arrows at the celestial Jaguar attacking the moon, shouting as the burning missiles fly towards the sky. The uproar made by Chinese peasants has a similar purpose. The Orinocans buried fire during a lunar eclipse to keep some fire hidden. The Kamchatkans brought fire from their huts and offered prayers. The Babylonians offered incantations. The Mexicans sacrificed humpbacks and dwarfs. The Chileatins of northwest America held sunwise circular processions until the eclipse was over and the kings of Egypt walked ceremonially (and sunwise) around the temple. The nubile girls kept in seclusion in Cambodia, were allowed to emerge only during eclipses when they paid homage to the monster who was eating the sun or moon. The Indians of the lower Yukon believed that an unclean emanation descended during an eclipse and to avoid sickness the women turned their pots and dishes bottoms up. The Swabian peasants would not sow, mow, or gather fruit during an eclipse. The Bavarians and Thuringians shared this belief and added that eclipses on Wednesday were particularly bad. See CIRCUMAMBULATION. [RDJ]

☞ Eclipses of both the sun and the moon occasioned energetic responses among many North American Indian tribes. A popular theory was that some mythological being, such as Coyote, a bird, a dog, Frog, Lizard, Rattlesnake, etc., was eating the sun or moon. In many tribes noise was made to frighten the aggressor and bring back the sun or moon to life; dogs were made to squeal by twisting their ears or beating them; people shouted, struck a plank or canoe, shot arrows into the air, turned over vessels, or threw out food and water. Men who knew how to make certain medicines went to the mountains to do so; babies were taken outside and made to howl, or a formula was recited so that they would grow quickly, as the moon grew coming out of an eclipse. [EWV]

☞ The general Middle American belief, which is a part of a wider complex found in all the Americas, is that the sun or moon is fighting with the earth, or that one or the other is being devoured by a celestial animal, usually the jaguar. In either case, it is a critical period for mankind, for if light is lost, life is lost. Hence, man does what he can to prevent this tragedy. The Sumu of Nicaragua shoot arrows at the heavenly body, build great fires, and beat drums in an attempt to frighten off the jaguar. Shouting and otherwise making noise probably is the most widespread activity which accompanies an eclipse. Many groups believe that a pregnant woman who gazes at an eclipse will give birth to a hare-lipped child. This probably is closely related to the ancient Aztec belief that a rabbit is visible on the face of the moon. [GMF]

☞ It is a general belief among South American Indians that eclipses are caused by some supernatural feline, as a rule a jaguar, that attacks the Moon or the Sun (Yuracare, Chiriguano, Mojo, Chiquito, Guarani, Incas, etc.). According to the Vilela, lunar eclipses occurred whenever a gigantic bat (a bird according to the Bakairi) covered the moon with its wings. The Cavina say that partial eclipses are the result of ants gnawing the moon. [AM]

Edward A Scottish-English ballad (Child #13) known also in Swedish and Danish, and in Finnish from the Swedish: probably of Scottish origin. It is regarded by many as the finest of the English ballads. Of the three versions collected by Child, the earliest calls the son Davie, but the ballad is best known in Percy's version, which was at one time suspect because of the antiqued spellings. The tale is barely outlined in a series of related questions: the answers, at first evasive, become at the end precise in a very terrible manner. The dialog is between mother and son. She asks where the blood on his sword comes from, and refuses the answers hawk's blood and steed's blood. He admits he has killed his father. He says he will sail away, leaving his wife and children the world to roam in. "And what wul ye leive to your ain mither deir?" "The curse of hell frae me sall ye beir." The implication of the mother in the killing is sudden and unexpected, and it has been lost from American variants, like *The Cruel Brother*.

eel Much thought seems to have been given to the origin of the eel. Most persistent is the belief that they grow from horsehair in water or that they all spawn in the Mediterranean Sea. The 4th century *Hexæmeron* of Basil holds that eels are generated by mud alone. Others claim they are generated from their own saliva. Some Philippine tribes believe them to be the souls of the dead, but in Madagascar they are considered the souls of the dregs of the population. A Japanese legend says eels are dragons in disguise, which suck the blood from the legs of horses who enter the water. Many peoples believe that eels, like snakes, do not die until sundown. In the Ozark Mountains they say a fried eel left alone will become raw again. In some parts of the United States eels are believed to have a taste for human flesh and there are tales of fishermen who have caught truckloads of eels with human bait. In many parts of the world eels are tabu, or believed to be poison.

In New Zealand the head of the spiny eel is eaten for toothache. In Bengal, the skin of an eel is wound round the leg to prevent cramp; elsewhere eelskins are wound around affected parts to cure various aches. An eelskin wound around the head will surely make the hair grow. Cherokee Indian ball players anoint themselves with eel fat to make themselves hard to hold. The fat is also used in a healing ointment, and in parts of Europe anointing a person with **eel-fat** ointment enables him to see fairies and other supernatural beings. To cure a man of drunkenness, skin a live eel and dip the skin in his drink. Another authority says put a live eel in the drink. This is prescribed on the theory that a man who takes a drink large enough to float a live eel needs to be cured.

Eels are sometimes found as guardian spirits of wells and magic springs. G. L. Gomme, in his *Ethnology in Folklore,* reports a sacred well in County Kerry, Ireland, called Tober Monachan. Those who sought its powers would be given the sight of a salmon and an eel, its guardian spirits, if their petition was to be granted.

The eel figures variously in folktale. There are etiological stories of his origin and why he has no tongue. He figures as paramour (Maori folktale); and men are transformed to eels in Polynesian, Melanesian, and Indonesian story (D173). In the general European story of the fearless hero who went out in the world to learn what fear is (Type 326), nothing frightened him, not sleeping under a gallows nor in a graveyard, not fighting ghostly cats, nor being shaved by a ghost, nor playing cards with the dead. But he was scared out of his wits the night his wife put eels down his back while he was asleep (H1441.1).

eeny, meeny, miny, mo An inquiry conducted among 2000 Massachusetts grammar-school children in 1899 discovered that all but five of them knew one or more counting-out rimes, that the group knew 183 different ones, but that the most popular by far (91%) was:

> Eeny, meeny, miny, mo,
> Catch a nigger by the toe;
> If he hollers let him go,
> Eeny, meeny, miny, mo.

There is no doubt that this version was the most frequently used one at that time in New England and upstate New York, or that it was for a time the dominant rendering throughout the northern states, but it is not the oldest, and there are many variants which give us interesting clues to the history of the rime and to the characteristic evolution of counting-out rimes in general.

The writer remembers that in Massachusetts, only a short time before the survey mentioned above, his mother tried to get the children of the neighborhood to substitute the word "feller" for "nigger" in the rime, but it was too early.

During World War II the children of New York City were patriotically shouting:

> Eeny, meeny, miny, mo,
> Catch old Tojo by the toe;
> If he hollers make him say,
> I surrender, U. S. A.

When the war ended, however, they quickly went back to former versions, and continued the trend away from "nigger" to such variants as "baby," "rooster," "black cat," and "rabbit." In New York City, at any rate, it is distinctly bad form in juvenile circles nowadays to exhibit any form of race discrimination.

How did the word "nigger" get into eeny, meeny, miny, mo in the first place? We have clues in the variants.

Strangely, most adults who learned the rime in childhood now know only one version and almost resent hearing of others. Deep in their subconscious is the "correct" one they learned in infancy. In Nebraska, for instance, it usually was:

> Eeny, meeny, miny, mo,
> Catch a nigger by the toe;
> Ev'ry time the nigger hollers,
> Make him pay you fifty dollars.

In Iowa and Illinois in the Eighties it ended:

> If he hollers, make him pay
> Twenty dollars ev'ry day.

At the same period in Connecticut children were chanting a local variant:

> Eeny, meeny, miny, mum,
> Catch a nigger by the thumb;
> If he hollers send him hum,
> Eeny, meeny, miny, mum.

It is apparent that these various indicated ways of treating the "nigger" are the children's reaction to or interpretation of their parents' conversation when the Fugitive Slave Law of 1850 was being debated. Negro slaves were escaping by the underground railroad through the northern states to Canada. In northern New England and New York the inhabitants were all for letting him go on his flight north. In Connecticut, some, at least, were for sending him back "hum," but in the Midwest and along the Mason and Dixon line others were for making him pay twenty or even fifty dollars toll.

This theory explains the third and fourth lines of the jingle, but leaves the second, and especially the first, unaccounted for. Here is a suggestion as to the origin of the second line. In French Canada the children are still using an eeny meeny which their parents brought from France long ago. They count out by starting with the rime:

> Meeny, meeny, miny, mo,
> Cache ton poing derrière ton dos...

Then, having accordingly "hid his hand behind his back," the counter-out demands of the player on whom has fallen the word "dos" that he guess how many fingers are closed in the hidden palm. If the answer is, say, four, then the fourth player counted is "out."

Now, since the French word *cache* (hide) sounds like the English word catch, and *dos* (back) is easily heard as toe, and since, moreover, it was in the north New England and York states that the first eeny meenies containing the phrase "Catch a nigger by the toe" appeared, it is entirely possible that the Yankee children were simply trying to do their best to make some sense out of the sounds they heard.

We have also to consider the possibility of an Indian or half-breed intermediary, just as the very word Yankee is explained by some folk etymologists as an attempt of the Indians to pronounce the French word for English, *Anglais.*

It is interesting in this connection, and somewhat corroborative of the above suggestion, that the New England oral tradition word for counting-out rime is rimble, easily derived from the French word for it, *rimaille,* since the latter has the liquid l and the former has the short i.

As for the origin of the first line, Eeny, meeny, miny, mo, we must go much further back. The early versions used in the United States had no reference to Negroes and the first line was slightly different:

Eeny, meeny, mony, my,
Huskalony, bony, stry,
Farewell, brown hat,
Kippety, we wah wat.

This version came straight by oral tradition in a family still living near Taunton, Mass., from a Quaker lady ancestress who was born there in 1780. In New York City, the related variant in 1815 was:

Ana, mana, mona, Mike;
Barcelona, bona, strike;
Care, ware, frow, frack;
Hallico, wallico, wee wo wack.

Three years later in Philadelphia they used:

Eeny, meeny, mony, Mike,
Butter, lather, bony, strike;
Hair, bit, frost, neck,
Hallico, wallico, we wo wah wum wack!

All three of these, since they are known to have been used at the very time when mothers and nurses were using the dread name of "Bony" (parte) to scare children into obedience, illustrate the propensity of children to weave into their play-rimes references to much-discussed current events. And all three are plainly derived from an older one evidently brought over from Cornwall, England, since English scholars reported it still current there a century ago. Its correspondence with the American derivatives is more apparent when recited than when read:

Eena, meena, mona, mite,
Basca, lora, hora, bite,
Hugga, bucca, bau;
Eggs, butter, cheese, bread,
Stick, stock, stone dead—O-U-T!

Here is one of the oldest known rimbles—perhaps not as old as Hickory, dickory, dock, but quite respectably ancient—betraying its age by the word-fossils so thickly sprinkled through it. Mixed with the English words are Latin, Cornish, and Cymric (Old Welsh).

We are back in Druid times, about the first century B.C., when we chant some of these words. It was in 61 B.C., so Tacitus tells us, that the Roman conqueror Suetonius commanded the holy Druid groves of the sacred isle of *Mona* (now Anglesea) cut down to end the bloody rites of Druidism. To get to that island, even today, from North Wales, you must cross the *Menai* Strait. *Hora* and *lora* are Latin for hour and binding-straps, and *bucca* was Cornish for hobgoblin or evil spirit.

Julius Cæsar tells us that the Druids were much concerned with divination by magic rimes, charms, and spells which were never put in written form.

Of course, we have only etymological evidence coupled with historical coincidence, and we are inferring from a long stretch of oral tradition, but it is certainly possible that our common eeny, meeny, miny, mo is a descendant of an ancient magic rime-charm used in Druid times to choose the human victims to be ferried across the Menai Strait to the isle of Mona to meet a horrible fate under the Golden Bough of the sacred mistletoe amid the holy oaks.

Since one known method of Druid sacrifice was to burn victims alive in wicker cages, perhaps the words in our last-quoted counting-out rime reflect the scene when the man chosen by this sacred lot of the magic rime was told his *hora* had come and was bound by the *lora* inside the *stick* and *stock* wicker cage or huge *basca* (basket) and burned until he was *stone dead*.

We still have the *eggs, butter, cheese,* and *bread* to account for, and might well consider them comparatively modern additions or incorporations by the children from other play-rimes, were it not for the fact known to anthropologists and students of comparative religion that for many centuries (no one really knows how many) these four have been deemed powerful magic foods. Significantly enough, they are still employed in incantations in rural midsummer festivals still celebrated in former Druid regions, according to Sir James Frazer's *Golden Bough.*

The remaining word eeny is probably also from the same land and period, for it occurs in the very ancient Anglo-Cymric "shepherd's score" by which West of England shepherds count their sheep and Cornish fishermen their mackerel, even to this day, again illustrating the persistence of oral tradition. This "shepherd's score," taught to the present writer as "Indian Counting" by his mother, was used in Indiana about 1875 as a counting-out rime in a version beginning:

Eeny, teeny, ether, fether, fip.

There are many other variants of eeny meeny still used in the United States. One class or type which did not mention the Negro ran:

Eeny, meeny, tipsy, tee,
Delia, dahlia, dominee;
Hatcha, patcha, dominatcha,
IIi, pon, tuss. O-U-T!

Recently movie-wise children have changed the third line to honor their hero thus:

Eechy, peachy Don Ameche.

Somewhat similar is another type often reported from the South and West (Tennessee, Louisiana, Indiana, Missouri, Colorado):

Eeny, meeny, miny, mo,
Cracka, feeny, finy, fo;
Oppa, noocha, poppa, toocha,
Rick, stick, ban, Joe.

In Washington, D.C., and vicinity the children are likely to add to almost any eeny meeny:

O-U-T spells
Out goes he ..
Right in the middle of
The dark blue sea.

Regarding this termination, H. C. Bolton of the Smithsonian Institution once wrote, "the significance of the allusion we have not divined." The children knew their Bible, if he didn't, for what could be plainer than the reference to an early counting-out when "the lot fell on Jonah" to be "It" and, according to *Jonah* i, 15, "So they took up Jonah, and cast him forth into the sea." See COUNTING-OUT RIMES; SHEPHERD'S SCORE.

CHARLES FRANCIS POTTER

egbere A category of Yoruban "little people" of the forest. See APUKU. [MJH]

egg curing A common medical treatment, probably European in origin though widespread among Middle American Indians. It consists of rubbing the nude body of the patient with an uncooked egg. If the purpose is diagnostic, the egg is broken and its form examined. The shape it assumes, any unusual color, or the form of the fertilized spot will indicate the nature of the illness, and the curer then knows how to proceed. If the purpose is therapeutic, usually to relieve fever, the egg is buried in a stream to dissipate the heat it has drawn from the sufferer's body. This treatment, generally known as *curar con blanquillos,* often is used to treat illness resulting from the evil eye. [GMF]

eggs Eggs have long been considered to have symbolic properties, either as representing the earth, life itself, or the seat of the soul. In the folklore of most of Europe, the strength or the life of supernatural beings could be destroyed only if an egg, usually hidden in the body of one or more animals, in some inaccessible place, was broken. Such separable soul tales have been reported from Italy, Iceland, Ireland, Bohemia, Brittany, and Lapland.

Eggs also figure prominently in fertility rites, both human and agricultural. In 17th century France, a bride upon entering her new home had to break an egg to ensure her fecundity. Among the Germans and Slavs, a mixture of eggs, bread, and flour was smeared on the plow on the Thursday before Easter, so that the coming harvest would be rich. In order to protect the poultry from harm, various devices were used: the Mískito Indians of Honduras and Nicaragua saved their egg shells; in Czechoslovakia, on Shrove Tuesday, a man dressed in straw went around the village, and each woman took some of his costume to place in the hens' nests; in Auvergne, on the first Sunday in Lent, fires were kindled in the fields, from which torches were lit, and the ashes from these torches were put into the nests; in Brunswick, eggs were begged on Whitsuntide, and refusal meant that the hens would not lay.

Eggs are also used in sacrifice, particularly to the dead, and as survivals of tree-worship. The Maori buried their dead with a moa's egg held in one hand; the Khassia of Assam placed an egg in the navel of the corpse. The Romans placed eggs in the graves as did many of the Slavic peoples. The Jews of eastern Galicia ate eggs upon returning from a burial.

In the Harz mountains, on Midsummer Eve, fir trees were decorated with flowers and red and yellow eggs, while the people danced around them. In Moravia, on the third Sunday before Easter, a tree decorated with flowers and dyed eggshells was carried from door to door by the girls of the village; and on May Day, in Alsace, trees were carried about, while eggs were collected. In Sweden, they sold in the market place maypoles which were decorated with leaves, flowers, colored paper, and gilt egg shells.

Oomancy (divination by eggs) is widespread. The most common form was to let the albumen drop into water, and from the shapes it assumed the future was foretold. In England this was done on New Year's Eve, in Spain on Midsummer Eve, in Scotland on Halloween.

The use of eggs at Easter is universal in the Western world. In the United States it is common to give children decorated eggs, which may be real or made of candy. Children are told that they are "brought by the Easter Bunny." In many parts of the world egg-tapping takes place, and the person whose egg cracks first is the loser. (See EASTER.) In Old Russia, eggs were most beautifully decorated, and among the wealthy, eggs of semiprecious stones were prized gifts. Egg-rolling, which survives in the United States as an annual custom on the White House lawn on Easter Monday, has counterparts in the Old World. In northern Bohemia, boys rolled red eggs downhill on Easter Monday, and he whose egg rolled fastest won all the others.

The Romans carefully destroyed the shells of eggs which they had eaten, so that they could not be harmed by magic which might be worked upon them. [NFJ]

☞ Southern United States Negroes have a great stock of egg lore. If you put eggs in your parents' bed, for instance, they will quarrel. To remove a baby's birthmark, rub the mark every morning for nine mornings with a fresh hen's egg and bury the egg under the doorstep. Goiter can be removed the same way. Dreams about eggs have a variety of meanings. To dream of eggs means good luck, or riches, or a wedding. To dream of broken eggs portends a lovers' quarrel, or sometimes that the quarrel itself will "break" and reconciliation follow. To dream of unbroken eggs means a quarrel just as often, in England and the United States. To dream of a lapful of eggs betokens riches.

Marks put on eggs under a setting hen will be seen later on the chicks. Eggs from a guinea nest are taken out with a spoon, because a guinea hen will leave her nest if a human being touches it: a general European as well as southern Negro belief. The old belief, common in the British Isles, that to set a hen in May is useless because all the chicks will die, is also general in the southern United States. Another egg-setting belief is that eggs set in the nest by a woman will hatch out all pullets; to carry them to the nest in a man's hat will result in a hatch of cocks. See WORLD EGG.

Egil (1) In Teutonic mythology, a peasant with whom Thor several times left his goats and chariot. Once seeing that the household had no food, Thor bade them kill his goats and eat the flesh, only to be sure to throw the bones back into the skins. But Loki persuaded Thialfi, son of Egil, to break one of the bones and eat the marrow. Thus when Thor wished to reanimate the goats, struck the skins with his hammer, and the goats sprang into being, one was discovered to be lame. To atone for this, Egil gave to Thor his son, Thialfi, and his daughter, Roskova, for bondservants.

(2) In the "Song of Volund" of the *Elder Edda,* Egil and his two brothers, Slagfin and Volund, once came upon three Valkyries bathing. They stole the swan garb which the maidens had laid aside, and were thus able to force them to remain in human form and become their wives. At the end of nine years, however, the women regained their swan shifts and departed. Compare BEAST MARRIAGE. See SWAN MAIDEN.

Egun (Egúngún) A Yoruban secret society, based on the cult of the dead. In the New World, the name and the cult have been retained in Brazil and Cuba, though many of the distinctive features that characterize the African secret society, especially in its public rituals, have been lost. [MJH]

Ehlaumel The creator in the mythology of the California Coast Yuki Indians. He is Thunder, and has superseded in importance the "one who travels alone," the traveler-creator of the Kato. See EARTH; NAGAICHO.

Eileithyia In Greek mythology, the goddess of childbirth: early either an independent goddess later identified with Hera or an aspect of Hera worshipped independently; she became nearly identical with Artemis in the protection of the very young and of women in childbed. There seem to have been two Eileithyias originally, one presiding over easy births, one prolonging birth pains, but these functions were later said to be the manifestations of the pleasure or anger of the same goddess. Eileithyia was displeased by unchastity and by frequent childbearing. She it was who sat outside Alcmene's chamber with her legs held together delaying the birth of Hercules. Eileithyia may have been Cretan in origin.

eingsaung nat The Burman and Talaing house guardian; a benevolent nat; Min Măgayē of the Thirty-seven Nats. The Burman eingsaung nat resides in the south post of the house. This is decorated with leaves and corpses are placed beside it. The Talaings hang a coconut in the southeast corner of the house to obtain the protection of the house nat.

Einheriar or **Einherjar** In Teutonic mythology, the slain warriors who were Odin's guests in Valhalla. They were served by the Valkyries, and feasted on the inexhaustible boar, which came to life again after each meal. They spent their time in fighting, but were healed again by mealtime.

Eira, Eir, or **Eyra** In Teutonic mythology, the goddess of healing. She was Frigga's attendant and taught healing to women (the only ones to practice medicine among the early nations of the North). She appears relatively late, replacing Thor and Odin as healers.

eisteddfod A periodic assembly of Welsh bards, held to conduct examinations and competitions in poetry, prose compositions, and music, at which qualified candidates were admitted to the highly esteemed and trained bardic profession. Begun probably sometime before the 12th century, recognized in the time of Queen Elizabeth as an institution of authority, the eisteddfod (literally, session) lost its prestige during the 17th century and suffered a lapse of about 150 years until its revival in the early 19th century. Since then it has become once more a national institution in Wales and a center for the revival of Welsh folklore and traditions. Musical and literary competitions are still the order of business. The meetings may be on a national or local scale and some have even been held among people of Welsh descent in the United States. See PENILLION.

eixida Literally, exit: a Catalan longways dance for men and women. In spite of the name, the dance does not serve either as exit or finale. The step is a right and left balance. The first couple leads off, then dances face to face with the second couple, then leads off to the foot of the column. The routine repeats for each couple in turn. [GPK]

Ekeko, Eq'eq'o, or **Ekako** An ancient deity of the Aymara Indians, the good-luck fertility spirit, still popular with the modern Indian and mestizo population of Bolivia. His feast, the Alasita, formerly celebrated about the time of the summer solstice, now takes place on January 24, and coincides with the mock selling of miniature pots. Ekeko is represented by comic images of a fat little man covered with toy household utensils. These images are kept in houses as good-luck fertility tokens. [AM]

ekerā In the religion of the Gallas of Ethiopia, the afterworld. Life after death is lived there as a shadow-like existence.

elder A shrub (genus *Sambucus*) with white flowers and purple-black or red berries. In Bohemia men tip their hats to the elder, but in some Christian countries this tree has evil associations because it is supposed to be the tree on which Judas hanged himself, and whose wood was used for the Cross. This is also given as the reason why the wood stinks. On the Scottish border and in Wales it is said that the dwarf elder only grows on ground which has been soaked in blood. Elder wood is never used in shipbuilding or in fires. A cradle of this wood would cause a child to pine away and to be pinched by the fairies. In Germany an elder branch brought into the house brings ghosts; in England it brings the Devil; however, in Scotland elder is hung over the doors and windows to keep evil spirits out. In parts of the United States burning an elder stick in the fire on Christmas Eve will reveal all the witches, sorcerers, and practitioners of the evil arts in the neighborhood. In the Tyrol also an elder stick cut on St. John's Eve will detect witchcraft. Lightning will not strike an elder bush.

In one form or another the elder was thought capable of curing most of the ills of mankind. The North American Mohegan Indians made the bark into a tea. When the bark is scraped upward it is an emetic, and when scraped downward, a laxative. The same tribe gave elderflower tea to infants for colic. In other parts of America elder tea is used for headache, a laxative, and a diuretic. Both elderberry and elderflower are used to make a tonic wine. In Bohemia and Denmark the fresh juice is drunk for toothache caused by a cold. A salve made of the flowers and bark is used by southern United States Negroes for the bites of the red bug and harvest tick. Elsewhere this salve is used for gout, burns, swellings, and tumors. The leaves are used to keep flies and ants out of the house, and in poultices for inflammations. The fruit is a good cure for dropsy, rheumatism, and swollen limbs; the seeds are taken for dropsy and to reduce. Two elder sticks carried in the pocket will keep the thighs from chafing while riding a horse. An elderberry in the pocket prevents ivy poisoning. In Ireland a necklace of nine elder twigs or berries is a cure for epilepsy. Southern United States Negroes make an elder necklace for teething babies. Warts rubbed with a green elder stick will disappear if the stick is buried in the mud to rot. In Bavaria if a fever patient sticks an elder twig in the ground in silence the fever will go away; anyone who removes the stick will catch the fever. In the 17th century a piece of elder between two knots was cut from the tree where the sun never shone to cure erysipelas. If a boy is beaten with an elder switch it will stunt his growth. In Massachusetts elder pulp was carried in a bag around the neck to cure rheumatism. The Slavs cure fever by pulling three elder shoots to the ground while the patient crawls through the arch. Elder was also good for deafness, faintness, strangulation, sore throat, ravings, snake and dog bites, insomnia, melancholy, and hypochondria. See ELLE WOMAN.

Elderberry Bush The cause of mankind's fate to die early, in North American Tsimshian Indian mythology. Stone and Elderberry Bush were quarreling (at a place up Nass River): each wished to be the first to give birth. Stone said if she gave birth first, people would live a long time, but if Elderberry Bush gave birth first, people would have to die soon, as Elderberry Bush herself had to die. Giant came along and heard this, touched Elderberry Bush, and told her to give birth first. So Elderberry Bush gave birth to her child. This is why people do not live very long in this world, and why elderberry bushes grow on graves. Raven (Txämsem) does not enter into this (Nass) variant of the story except as having been there and having heard and seen it happen, but other versions present Raven as the one who bade Elderberry Bush give birth first, and add that if Stone had given birth first, not only would men not have to die, but their skin would have been like their fingernails all over. Tlingit versions of the cause of death story explain that if Raven had made men out of rock instead of leaves (or grass) men would not ever die.

Elfin Knight A Scottish ballad (Child #2) very widespread in Europe and Asia, having for its central theme the motif of the countertask (H591). The knight agrees to be the girl's husband if she will make him a shirt without cut or hem or thread. She in turn says she will deliver the shirt when he delivers grain from an acre plowed with a horn and sacked in a glove. The dénouement of the parting of the lovers seems to be added from some other source than an original form of the ballad. The title too, the elfin-ness of the knight, plays no essential part in the story.

elk Elk as an animal character appears in tales of various North American Indian tribes of the Great Basin, Plains, and elsewhere. One tale is especially notable for its recurrence; it concerns the giant elk which is vanquished by a human hero (often a young boy, sometimes the Twins) with the help of a mouse, rat, mole, or other rodent ally. The Apache, among whom this tale is popular, assign the feat of killing the giant elk to their culture hero, Killer-of-Enemies (or Child-of-the-Water). Tales of Elk husband, or wife, are also of quite frequent occurrence in North America, especially on the Plains. Elk teeth as costume ornaments for women's fancy dresses are highly valued and were much used by Plains Indians. In the origin legends of the Oto, it was Elk who gave the people fire and started them to building villages. [EWV]

Elle Woman The spirit of the elder tree in Danish folk belief; the *Hyldemoer,* or elder mother. No Danish woman would break off a sprig of elder (whether for brew or other purpose) without first invoking or apologizing to the spirit of the tree. No Danish child would injure the branches in any way. Hans Christian Andersen's story entitled *The Elder Tree Mother,* in which the Elder Mother presides over the lives of the people in the house, but takes no part in the action of the story, bears out the belief in the spirit of the tree.

elm A shade tree (genus *Ulmus*) of America, Europe, and Asia. According to Teutonic mythology an elm, given soul by Odin, senses by Hoenir, and blood and warmth by Lodur, became the first woman, Embla. In Finno-Ugric mythology the elms were the mothers of Ut, goddess of fire. In England the elm was once known as elven, and was associated with the elves. Formerly it was the custom to deck the cathedral and close at Lichfield with elm boughs on Ascension Day. When the leaves of the elm are as large as a mouse's ear it is time to plant barley; when the leaves begin to fall out of season it is a sign of a murrain among the cattle. In Devon it is said that lightning will not strike an elm.

Elm leaves are used in poultices for swellings, and the leaves tied on a green wound with strips of bark will heal them. The inner bark is used in skin and venereal infections. The wood of the elm was sometimes used for a soft snuff.

Slippery elm (*U. fulva* or *rubra*) is sometimes used in a cough medicine and as a demulcent. The bark when boiled down makes a jelly which is very nutritious where a bland diet is needed. It was also used in the treatment of syphilis.

St. Elmo's fire or **light** The corposant; a globular or flame-shaped light (an electric brush or glow) sometimes seen at night on the masthead, ends of yard-arms, etc., of ships at sea in stormy or threatening weather. Pliny's *Natural History* describes the phenomenon as appearing not only on masts, spars, etc., but sometimes on men's heads. It is called St. Elmo's fire or light for the patron saint of Mediterranean sailors. This St. Elmo was either the Dominican Pedro Gonzalez of Astorga (1190–1246) who preached to sailors, or the 3rd century St. Erasmus, also patron of sailors. The word corposant is a corruption of Italian or Portuguese *corpo santo,* holy body: early Mediterranean sailors believed it to be the actual presence of their guardian come to warn them. Two of these lights appearing simultaneously are often called Castor and Pollux. Two mean that the ship will have good weather; one alone portends storm.

In Brittany this light is thought to be a lost soul and is prayed for. In Greece it is regarded as an omen of shipwreck and bad luck, and it can only be dispelled by the yells of a pig. German sailors believe it is the soul of a dead comrade with a message: good weather, if the light rises, bad if it lowers.

Elysium In Greek mythology, the fields on the banks of the river Oceanus in the farthest west where the blessed dwell. In Homer, the inhabitants of this fair land without snow or cold or rain are not shades, but heroes like Menelaus, who have been translated without dying. They live there under the rule of Rhadamanthus. In Hesiod, the same land is the Isles of the Blessed and is ruled by Cronus with Rhadamanthus dispensing justice from his side. Roman mythology makes the Elysian Fields part of the underworld, to which the shades are sent by the three judges, Rhadamanthus, Minos, and Æacus. Compare HADES; UNDERWORLD.

Ema Votive offerings in Japan in the shape of a picture of a horse. [JLM]

Emain Macha The capital of ancient Ulster; the seat of Conchobar: now Navan Fort near Armagh. The usual story is that Emain Macha, literally the twins of Macha, was named for the twins borne by Macha at the moment she won the race against the king's horses at that place. Because of her husband's thoughtless boast that his wife was swifter than the horses, she was sent for and made to run, in spite of her plea that she was about to give birth to a child. Because of the king's cruel refusal to wait, and his insistence that she run, she invoked upon the Ulstermen "the weakness of a woman in childbirth" to come upon them in their every hour of peril and need.

Embla, Emla, or **Emola** In Teutonic mythology, the first woman, who, according to the *Völuspá*, was created from an elm tree. Odin gave her life and a soul, Hœnir, reason and motion, and Lodur gave her warm blood and a fair complexion. In the *Prose Edda* she was created from a block of elm wood by Odin, Vili, and Ve.

emerald A clear bright green variety of beryl which throughout the ages has competed with the diamond both in beauty and value. Like the diamond, not all the emeralds of history have been genuine, and also like the diamond, many fabulously valuable stones have been destroyed by ignorant people who tested them by beating them on anvils and stones. The Bible mentions the emerald as one of the foundation stones of the New Jerusalem and one of the gems in the breastplate of the High Priest. The first Mohammedan heaven was of emerald, and in India, to give an idol one of these stones assured its knowledge of the soul and eternal life. In classic legend emeralds were said to have been brought from the nests of griffons.

Engravers kept emeralds on their benches and looked at them to relieve eyestrain. They were of highest importance to early pharmacies: they were suspended over affected parts, held in the mouth, powdered and used internally, or merely worn to secure the desired effect. Like most gems they were effective against snakebite and poisons, and against demoniacal possessions of all kinds. They cured hot pestilence, gastric disorders, and dysentery. They stanched bleeding and were both cure and preventative for epilepsy, leprosy, and the plague. The Hindus prescribed looking at them as a laxative and stimulant for the appetite.

As amulets they were without parallel. An emerald worn on the finger would burn at the approach of poison, and would liquefy the eyes of serpents who merely looked at it. They were carried by travelers for good fortune, and could calm storms at sea. They foreshadowed future events, revealed the truth, and helped men recover what they had lost. They strengthened the memory, quickened the intelligence, and made their possessor an eloquent speaker. They conferred riches, joy, strength, and health. The emerald was an emblem of success in love, and as an emblem of eternal life, it was placed on the limbs of the dead.

emergence myth Among many American Indian tribes of the southwestern and southeastern United States, and among the Huron-Iroquois of the Great Lakes region, the first human beings are believed to have emerged from an underworld, from a hole in the ground (southwest and southeast), or from a cave (Huron-Iroquois). The myths relating their experiences during and after the emergence into the upper world are often long and detailed. The southwestern tribes (Pueblo, Navaho and several Apache groups) are concerned with what happened during the actual emergence, and locate the spot where this occurred. The southeastern Creeks and other groups are more concerned with the migration account of their wanderings after their emergence. Generally speaking, tribes which tell as their origin story the emergence myth do not account for the origin of the earth by the primeval water (or flood-earth-diving myth), although a few southwestern groups of Apache combine these two origin myths. The Huron-Iroquois myth of the emergence of people from a cave is aberrant to the origin myth common to other Iroquoian tribes of the Great Lakes region. [EWV]

Emma The ruler of the underworld of Japanese Buddhism. [JLM]

Emperor and Abbot Title of a folktale, better known in English through the ballad *King John and the Bishop*. It has been found in every ethnic group of which the collection of folktales has been adequately surveyed. The story belongs to the large cycle in which a person of humble birth saves his life, gets a reward, or saves the life of a superior by answering three or more difficult questions. In this story the king will execute the bishop unless within three days the bishop can answer such questions as the following: How high is heaven? How much is a golden plow worth? How much am I worth? A miller, shepherd, or peasant answers the questions to the king's satisfaction. Other titles in the cycle are *The Clever Peasant Girl, The Son of the King and the Smith, The King and the Peasant's Son*.

This story is of particular interest to students of the folktale because of extensive and elaborate studies that have been made of it within the last quarter-century. Walter Anderson's *Kaiser und Abt* appeared in *FF Communications* No. 54 in 1924. In 1928 Jan DeVries published in the same series *Die Märchen von klugen Rätsellösern*. In 1929 Albert Wesselski studied *Der Knabenkönig und das kluge Mädchen*. The special importance of Anderson's study is that it applies to the study of the folktale the historic-geographic method which was developed by the Finnish school. By this method scholars attempt to collect all known variants of a tale, and by analyzing places and times of incidence, to formulate conclusions as to the place of origin and the extent and periods of diffusion. Anderson's conclusion is that the story may have originated in some Jewish community, possibly in Egypt, perhaps about the 7th century after Christ. DeVries believes that the cycle belongs to the legend of Solomon; Wesselski attaches it to the legend of Cyrus and thinks it is not connected with the literature of India.

The contribution of these brilliant studies of the Emperor and Abbot formula is to show the extraordinary care with which modern scholars approach the study of folktales. The general weakness of the historic-geographic method is in its use and interpretation of statistics and more seriously in our ignorance of large areas on the folktale map. Thus when several variants of the formula currently told in China have been brought into the picture new conclusions about the distribution and origin of *The Emperor and the Abbot* may have to be formulated. [RDJ]

Enceladus In Greek mythology, one of the giants who warred against Zeus; son of Uranus and Ge, conceived when the blood of the mutilated Uranus fell upon earth. Enceladus is a partly human figure with serpents in place of feet. During the battle, Athena threw the island of Sicily at him; he was either killed by Zeus or imprisoned under Etna. The earthquakes in the region near Etna are caused by his struggles to free himself. Compare GIGANTES.

endama A type of extra-legal mating found among the Black Caribs of Honduras. See AMASIADO.

endless tale A type of formulistic folktale, especially of eastern Europe, in which a certain incident or set of words is repeated so often as to become unbearable to the listeners. Typical is the story relating how hundreds of sheep were carried across a stream one by one, or how a mountain was moved one grain of sand at a time. It is an endless tale because no listener ever heard the end. One variety of the endless tale is the circular tale or prose round. This is just as often brief as long-winded. It sustains great interest up to a certain point but gets nowhere, the wording being such as to suddenly start over again at the beginning. Typical of these is the tale that begins, "It was a dark and stormy night. The robbers were sitting around the fire"—One of their absent members rides up on horseback, dismounts and joins them at the fire. "Tell us a story," says one of the robbers to the newcomer. And again it begins, "It was a dark and stormy night. The robbers were sitting around their fire"—ad infinitum.

end of world The end of the world is envisaged by some North American Indian tribes as resulting from a world-fire (central Algonquian) or from a huge battle (northeastern Algonquian). Other Algonquians of the Great Lakes region believe that the culture hero and founder of the Grand Medicine Society, Nanabush, will return to this earth from his present abode in the west, before the end of the world. [EWV]

☞ A favorite theme of South American mythology is the destruction of the world by a great fire, caused by the fall of the sun (Mocovi), by a fragment of the moon when it was attacked by Jaguar (Toba), by a spark fallen from the sky (Cashinawa), by demons (Yuracare), by the trickster (Chiriguano), or by the culture hero. The Mataco blame the cataclysm on the Men of Fire who had been insulted by a bird. In most versions a few persons survived the disaster and repopulated the earth. According to the Mataco of the Gran Chaco, vegetation was restored to the world by a little bird who found ashes of the algarrobo tree and beat her drum until a huge tree grew. The Apapocuva-Guarani regard the great fire as one of the first cataclysms which will take place when the Creator removes one of the props supporting the earth.

The tradition of the destruction of the world by a spell of very cold weather occurs in Tierra del Fuego and in the Chaco. The Yahgan say that an angered bird caused snow to fall and ice to form. The melting of the ice sheet was followed by a big flood. The Toba and Mataco Indians speak of sleet and cold spell sent by the culture hero to exterminate most of mankind. [AM]

Enemy Way A Navaho Indian curing ceremony for victims of witchcraft: also known as the *Square dance*. Like all Navaho chants, the Enemy Way has a long origin legend detailing procedure for the chant; this origin myth has been recorded by Father Berard Haile (*Origin Legend of the Navaho Enemy Way*, Yale University Publications in Anthropology, No. 17, Yale University Press, 1938). [EWV]

Enlil The earth, air, and storm god of Sumerian mythology; one of the prime triad with An and Enki. He was patron of Nippur, where his temple was called E-kur, the mountain house; Enlil himself was known as the Great Mountain. He was lord of the spirits of the earth and of the air, the ghosts and demons. In the original version of the *Enuma Elish*, Enlil may have been the hero; indications in the later Babylonian and Assyrian versions are that a storm god acted such a role, but Enlil is not named. He is thus the original conqueror of Tiamat; later, all Enlil's attributes and deeds were ascribed to Bel and Marduk. See BEL; MARDUK; NINLIL; SEMITIC MYTHOLOGY.

Enuma Elish The creation epic of Babylonia and Assyria: so called from its opening words, meaning "When above," viz. "When a sky above had not been mentioned." See SEMITIC MYTHOLOGY.

envoûtement That form of sympathetic magic working through an image or other representation of the person the magician wishes to influence, usually to injure: a practice as ancient as Egypt and Assyria and still found from Ceylon to the United States, Europe to Africa, South America to Siberia. The word comes from Old French *vout*, image, from Latin *vultus*, face. Commonly an image, often of wax or wood, is made more or less resembling the person to be harmed; the inclusion in the statuette of bits of hair, fingernails, etc., of the intended victim is sometimes considered a necessity. While the proper spells are recited, the operator thrusts pins, nails, or splinters into the image, aiming at the spots where the vital organs might lie, or pinches it or strikes it, melts it in the fire or drowns it in a basin or river, or otherwise works some harm to the image. The human counterpart of the figure will then feel pain in the organs through which the pins have been pushed, or will die suddenly or waste away, become very ill or go insane. This practice, with variations due to time and place (e.g. photographs may be used, as among some southern United States Negroes), is remarkably consistent throughout the world and through the ages. It serves not only as a form of maleficent magic, but is also perhaps the most effective means of counteracting magic; the identity of the sorcerer once determined, his image may be made and treated in a like manner to cause his death or illness, or to paralyze his ability to cause harm.

Eos The Greek winged goddess of dawn: equivalent to the Roman Aurora. She was the daughter of Hyperion and Theia or Euryphassa, or of the Titan Pallas; sister of Helios and Selene; lover of many handsome men, whom she carried off. Because of an affair with Ares, Eos was caused by Aphrodite to be constantly in love with someone, and Orion, Cephalus, Tithonus were some among many. She lived with Tithonus and asked Zeus that he be made immortal, but neglected to ask for eternal youth for him. After he had shriveled and lost his voice, she transformed him into a cricket. She was mother by Tithonus of Memnon and because of his death at the hands of Achilles she weeps the nightly dew. She rises from Tithonus' bed at the end of night and in her chariot drawn by two horses travels to the heavens from the river Oceanus to announce the arrival of the sun.

epilepsy A chronic nervous affection characterized by sudden loss of consciousness, sometimes accompanied by paroxysmic seizures, or "fits," of varying intensity and duration: often called the falling sickness because the patient usually falls down when seized by an attack. The disease was formerly believed to be the actual seizure of the person by some supernatural agent, demon, or the like; and in classic times epilepsy was universally honored as being "oracle-possession." The Hindus believed epilepsy was the manifestation of possession by demons, and there were certain Vedic rituals for exorcising them. *Ben nefilim* is the common name for the Jewish demon of epilepsy. The New Testament casting out of devils (*Matt.* viii, 16: they brought unto him many that were possessed with devils and he cast out the spirits) is thought to refer to ridding the afflicted of some such being. Among the Berbers the sacrifice of a cock is believed to appease the spirit which has caused the seizure, to ensure riddance of it, and hence the cure. The Aymara Indians of Bolivia today believe that epilepsy is caused by "being looked upon by a spirit."

Among many early and contemporary primitive peoples epilepsy is a welcome visitation. Persons thus seized are revered for their contact with the supernatural, and shamans, priests, diviners, etc., are often chosen from among the epileptics.

Wearing coins of various kinds was considered good against epilepsy in the Middle Ages, especially coins marked with a cross. A ring made of silver from a Communion offertory was particularly effective. In the 14th century shavings of rhinoceros horn mixed with human blood was thought to be good remedy. Salt of coral was almost universally valued. This was prepared by dissolving coral in vinegar and distilling the liquid. Salt of pearl (similarly prepared) was thought highly of in the 16th century. This was recommended as "a most noble cordial for convulsions and falling sickness, for it purifies and keeps the body sound, comforts the brain, memory, and heart."

In Germany the blood of a she-ass will cure epilepsy, or the blood of someone who has been executed, or (in the Tyrol) the hot blood of a weasel is sometimes recommended. The rural English and general Celtic cure for epilepsy is a decoction of mistletoe. The efficacy of mistletoe is also known in Germany, Sweden, and Holland. In Sweden the epileptic carries with him always a knife with a mistletoe handle. In Germany the mistletoe necklace is effective. The great virtue in mistletoe against the falling sickness lies in the fact that mistletoe is not rooted in the earth. It grows high overhead and has therefore the power to keep one from falling to the earth.

One of the Irish names for epilepsy is *galar Poil* or *tinneas Poil*, the disease of Paul, since Paul is known to have been an epileptic. There are various Irish cures.

One is to wear a necklace made of nine cut pieces of an elder twig. Another is to heat a church key red hot and lay it on the patient's head. Water from a holy well is good, or three drops of sow's milk. Another remedy is to cross running water before sunrise and then bathe in it, or to twist a thread around an iron, or an iron nail, and bury it in the earth. See POSSESSION.

Epiphany (from Greek *epiphaneia*, apparition) A feast observed January 6th, celebrated in the gnostic Christian church as the date for the baptism, thus rebirth, of Christ. Later it became identified with the coming of the three Wise Men or Kings. Generally it is known as Twelfth Night, because of its dating in relation to Christmas. In Europe in general it is a special occasion for observance of surviving pagan winter solstice celebrations, encouragements to the rebirth of the New Year, the beginning of the carnival season. In Germany and Austria destructive spirits are exorcised by noisy bands masked as Perchten and other fantastic figures. In Portugal it is a special occasion for mouriscadas and stick dances, as the elaborate *paulitos* in Noguirinha. In England it was originally the date for the appearance of the Abbots Bromley antler dancers. By coincidence, it is also the date for a number of animal dances of the Pueblo Indians, specifically, the Deer dances at Taos and Santa Ana in the natural hunting season. Mexico's greatest pilgrimage, that of the Aztecs and Otomí to the miraculous Christ of Chalma, occurs on this date. Throughout central Mexico fiestas feature the adoration of the Magi, pastorelas with children dressed as shepherds and shepherdesses, concheros troops, and nacimientos of Biblical and historical scenes. See BEFANA. [GPK]

Epona A pre-Roman Gaulic divinity, goddess of horses, guardian and protectress of horses, asses, mules, and of all who had to do with them: the only Celtic deity to be included in the Roman pantheon. The fact that the Celtic horse-troops fought with the Roman armies spread and popularized the horse-goddess cult widely over the continent. Widespread monuments depict her as riding on a horse, feeding colts, or surrounded by horses. She is often found on the same monument with the Matres (the Celtic mother-goddesses), a fact which marks her perhaps as also a fertility goddess. There is some conjecture that Epona may have been one of the Matres with the special province of the fecundity of horses, growth and well-being of foals, etc.

erawng möt k'rak or **wang ün kēng** Forked sticks, seven to ten feet high, which are planted in rows in front of the Wild Wa (Burma) houses. Each stick is a record of a buffalo sacrificed to the spirits by the owner of the house. In front of some houses are rows of these representing entire herds of buffalo. The heads and horns are piled at one end of the house as proof of the sacrifices. The sticks are usually weathered but sometimes they are painted black and red.

The Chins erect an upright post on which they record the number of sacrificed buffaloes by means of slanting black lines. The Theinbaws plant posts in slanted fashion forming rows of x's to record the same thing.

Erdélyi, János (1814–1868) Hungarian writer and philosopher famous for his collections of Hungarian folk songs, folktales, and proverbs. His collection of Magyar poems and folktales, *Magyar Népköltési*, was published in three volumes (1846–1848); his *A Nép Koltészete népdalok, népmesék és közmondások*, containing three hundred national songs, 19 folktales, and 7,362 proverbs, was published the year after his death.

eré Of Yoruban derivation, this word in the candomblé cults of Bahia, Brazil, and the Shango sect of Trinidad, British West Indies, denotes the childlike beings that take charge of the individual undergoing initiation, and succeed the deity "in the head" of a possessed cult-initiate. In its second role, the eré functions as a kind of half-state between full possession and the resumption of customary personality status. It thus constitutes a psychological mechanism for cushioning the shock of passage from the possession experience into normal life. The eré are conceived as childlike beings, and, when "in a state of eré," as this is termed in Brazil, the devotee behaves like a child-being, usually, though not always, gay and mischievous, playing children's games, eating incessantly, and at times caricaturing the dancing of the gods. Though it is clear that the New World concept is to be related to the broad West African category belief comprised in the "little people," the exact relationship to the various beings found in this category as found among the various West African peoples has not yet been explored. [MJH]

Erebus In Greek mythology, Darkness, a son of Chaos; father of Hemera (Day) and Æther (Upper Air) by Nyx (Night). In Homer, Erebus is the place of darkness under the earth, with its entrance in the farthest west in the land of the Cimmerians, which the shades go through on their way to Hades. In Orphic belief, Erebus existed from the very beginning of things.

Erechtheus A legendary king of Athens: often inextricably confounded with his grandfather or grandson Erichthonius. He is in some way identifiable with Poseidon, one of whose names was Poseidon Erechtheus. In the principal legend concerning Erechtheus, however, Poseidon is his enemy. The oracle at Delphi told Erechtheus that he would not win a war he was fighting against Eumolpus of Thrace and the Eleusinians unless he sacrificed one of his daughters. This Erechtheus did, which act so enraged Poseidon, for by it Erechtheus killed Eumolpus, Poseidon's son, that either he, or Zeus at his request, destroyed Erechtheus and his house. Variants of the legend say that his two elder daughters offered themselves for the sacrifice; that it was his youngest daughter who was killed; that after the sacrifice all his daughters committed suicide.

Erichthonius In Greek legend, an early king of Athens. He was the son of Hephæstus and Ge, somewhat inadvertently, for when Hephæstus struggled with Athena in an attempt to end her maidenhood, she defended herself with her spear, and Hephæstus' seed fell upon Ge, the earth. After Erichthonius was born, Athena put him into a chest and gave Pandrosos, the daughter of Cecrops, charge of it, with instructions not to look in. But Herse and Agraulos, her sisters, did, and were driven mad by what they saw there. According to some, a serpent was in the chest, put there by Athena to guard the infant; others say that the child himself, like

Cecrops, was serpent-footed. Athena then took the child under her own care within her precinct at Athens, and in due time he grew up to become king. Erichthonius is credited with introducing the worship of Athena and the Panathenæa, and with building the temple to her on the Acropolis. He, and not Cecrops, is said to have decided in Athena's favor over Poseidon's claims for possession of Athens. He was the inventor of the chariot or of the four-horse chariot, according to some because he wanted to hide his feet; he was placed among the stars as the Charioteer. See AURIGA; PANDION.

Erinyes (singular *Erinys*) In Greek mythology, the angry and avenging deities who pursued evil-doers and carried out the effects of curses: feared by gods and men, and called in Latin Furiæ or Diræ (the Avengers). They were perhaps originally ancestral spirits, or angry ghosts of the murdered, who maintained the morality of mankind; or they may have developed from an earth goddess similar to Ge: one of the epithets of Demeter in Arcadia was Erinys. Several genealogies are given, the Hesiodic stating that they were born of Ge from the drops of blood falling on her when Uranus was mutilated. Being older than Zeus, they did not serve him, but acted independently. Later tradition makes them three in number: Alecto (the persevering anger), Tisiphone (the blood avenger), Megæra (the jealous). They dwell in the underworld and return to earth to enforce curses and punish antisocial acts, particularly crimes against relations such as the murder of relatives or disobedience to parents. They are the embodiment of impersonal justice, the reason underlying a crime not coming into account at all, the act alone being their concern. Expiation for the crime causes them to desist from pursuit. Thus, the slaying of his mother, by Orestes, despite the moral duty he had to perform, caused the Erinyes to hound him until he was acquitted by the Areopagus. They were thenceforth known as the Eumenides (the kindly), and had a sanctuary at the foot of the Areopagus in Athens. They were likewise called the Semnæ (the venerable ones). Yearly, there was a festival of the Erinyes at which offerings of milk and honey in water were made. Though Æschylus made them appear like Gorgons, their later usual form was that of grave, winged maidens, dressed as huntresses, who could be distinguished by their carrying scourges, sickles, or torches. There seems to be no basis for identifying them with the Indian Saranyu. Compare DEMETER; EUPHEMISM; KERES; MOIRÆ.

Eris In Greek mythology, the goddess of discord, or more properly of emulation: the Roman Discordia. The insatiable sister of Ares, she evoked war and disharmony, remaining on the battlefield and gloating over the bodies of the slain after all the other gods had left. Eris threw the apple of discord among the gods at a feast, usually described as the wedding feast of Peleus and Thetis, saying "Let the fairest have it." The ensuing argument was decided by Paris. (See PARIS.) Hesiod mentions also a good Eris, the goddess of honorable competition.

Ériu In Old Irish mythology, a queen of the Tuatha Dé Danann, third of the three met by the Milesians in their invasion of Ireland, and to whom they promised that her name would be the chief name of Ireland forever. The familiar Erin is the dative case of Ériu. The coronation feast of the early Irish kings was called *fleð baindsi* (literally wedding feast), because it was believed that the inauguration ceremony symbolized the marriage of the king to this ancient eponymous queen. See BANBA; FODLA; ITH.

Eros In Greek mythology, the god of love: similar in some respects to the Roman Amor or Cupid. Eros, not in Homer, was originally the god of love between friends, a beautiful youth, one of the first of the gods, in Hesiod coming from Chaos with Tartarus and Ge. Various parentages were later assigned to him, especially those making him son of Aphrodite by Zeus, Hermes, or Ares; and with time he degenerated into the wanton and cruel winged boy, armed with arrows, from whom not even the gods were safe. He carried torches which no one could safely touch. Later additions to the myth include also the covering of his eyes; two kinds of arrows, golden ones which brought love, and leaden ones bringing aversion; and the multiplication of the god into a number of Erotes. There was also distinguished a brother of Eros, Anteros, the god of returned love, who punished the refusal to reciprocate on the part of the loved one. Eros was worshipped at Thespiæ in Bœotia and at Parion in Mysia. Compare CUPID AND PSYCHE.

Erymanthian boar In Greek legend, the boar caught by Hercules as the fourth of his labors. He chased it into deep snow and then carried it struggling back to Eurystheus, who, when he saw the pair coming, hid in fear in a bronze jar. During the chase of the boar occurred Hercules' visit to Pholus and its tragic consequences.

eskänye The old-time women's shuffle dance of the Iroquois Indians: a homage to the food spirits, the three life-sustaining sisters. Thus it is one of the bread dances and associated with certain dance sequences (see BREAD DANCE). In the great Seneca festivals, Midwinter and Green Corn, it is inserted between two performances of the great feather dance. The women progress to the right, facing the center of a circle, with a sideward saw step, shuttling the heels and toes alternately in and out. Expert dancers swing their arms from side to side with bent elbows, and execute occasional quarter-turns. The latter songs of the cycle recite the cycle of the germination, growth, and fruition of the crops, and describe the climbing of the beans around the corn stalks. The melodies, to drum and rattle background, have a tremendous range and freedom of thematic treatment which contradict the dance's traditional antiquity. [GPK]

espringale or **Springtanz** A European round dance for couples, popular, especially at the time of the Minnesingers, in the 14th century. It was a carole with little leaps and hops and, like the carole, was associated with verdure. The verses of the choral leader invoked nature; the chorus responded with a refrain, imitating instruments as the bagpipe, flute, drum, rebec, and psaltery, or yodelling or rolling the tongue. [GPK]

estampie or **istampida** A European stamping dance for men and women, with an accent on every third beat: a popular round dance from the 12th to the 15th century, in slow 4/4, 3/4, or 6/8 measure, associated in the 14th century with the fast *saltarello*. Of the accompanying songs the 12th century *Kalenda Maya* is the most famous. [GPK]

Estonian folklore The folklore collections of the Estonian people are among the most numerous in the world. The richness of folkloristic records depends on the degree of civilization of the people and on the intensity of the collecting activity, because with the advance of civilization the folk traditions usually disappear. Both conditions were favorable in Estonia from the folkloristic point of view and today the small Estonian people have about 711,000 written pages of folklore material.

The Estonian people were for many centuries enslaved by the German barons and all their cultural life was dominated by Germans. Nevertheless a few educated Germans, so-called Estophiles, showed interest in the common people, their language, history, and culture; and in 1838 was founded the *Estonian Learned Society* (GEG) in Tartu (Dorpat), later, 1842, the *Estonian Literature Society* in Tallinn (Reval). Both societies had their publications, in German of course, in which many important articles on Estonian folklore were printed, especially in *Verhandlungen der GEG,* and in the journal *Inland* (1836–1863). Thus the first works on Estonian folklore were done and published by Germans, mostly pastors, and in the German language.

The first book of great folkloristic importance dealing with the superstitions and customs of the Estonians was *Der einfältigen Esthen abergläubische Gebräuche, Weisen und Gewohnheiten* by J. W. Boecler (Reval, 1685; 2nd edition by F. R. Kreutzwald, St. Petersburg, 1854). The Russian Academy of Sciences also showed interest in Estonian linguistics and F. J. Weidemann (1805–1887), member of the Academy, published not only an Estonian-German Dictionary, but also a large book about the life of the Estonian people, *Aus dem inneren und äusseren Leben der Esthen* (St. Petersburg, 1876). Some material in this work is of doubtful origin and belongs to the numerous falsifications which grew up as the Estonian national awakening was started and as the "young Estonian" movement used folklore as one of their means.

The founder of the Estonian Learned Society, F. R. Faelmann (1798–1850), fabricated some deities and splendid myths (see ESTONIAN MYTHOLOGY). He was eager to furnish a substitute for the national epos. This task was accomplished by F. R. Kreutzwald (1803–1882) and the Estonians were delighted with him (see KALEVIPOEG). Kreutzwald also published a collection of folktales in the literary style of this time, translated into German by F. Löwe (*Esthnische Märchen,* 2 vols., 1869 and 1881). Another similar collection of Estonian tales and legends was published by H. Jannsen (*Märchen und Sagen des estnischen Volkes,* 2 vols., 1881 and 1888). Both editors were greatly influenced by the Grimm brothers and others who stylized folk tradition. A publication of folk songs, *Esthnische Volkslieder* (2 vols., Reval, 1850–1852), was arranged by A. H. Neus (1795–1876) and published by the Estonian Literature Society. The editor used the manuscripts of many earlier and contemporary collectors, and this work was for many years the most important reference book for Estonian folk song, particularly because of German translations. It is regrettable that some songs were stylized too much or were completed by their collectors, and that even more falsifications penetrated into another work, *Mythische und magische Lieder der Esthen* (St. Petersburg, 1854), edited by Neus together with Kreutzwald.

All the above-mentioned works (even if they are not exemplary in the eyes of folklorists of today, in that they contain too many personal supplements made by the collectors), caused a widespread national movement by the Estonians. Estonians were delighted with the traditions of their folk. The gathering of folklore was regarded not as an amusement of rich people, but as a national task in which the whole people took pride. The Estonians themselves came to the work. The Rev. Dr. Jakob Hurt (1839–1907) started a very well organized collecting of folklore throughout the whole country. He had, we can say, a modern conception of the folklore method; he gave good instructions to the collectors and was able to stop the falsificators. The results were astonishing. To his appeal in the press answered hundreds of volunteers from all classes of the people. Practically every house and smallest cabin in the country was visited by a folklore collector, with the result that Hurt's collections reached 124,000 written pages. This period of folklore-gathering activity has been called "the age of folk goods." Hurt also planned the publishing of a big collection of folk songs, a *Monumenta Estoniae antiquae*, but because of lack of money only two volumes appeared: *Vana Kannel* (The Old Harp, 1875 and 1886). At the end of his laborious life he published a very well arranged collection of songs of the Setus (*Setukeste laulud*, 3 vols., 1904–1907), which remains today an unsurpassed work on Estonian folklore. The most important colleague of Hurt was M. Veske (1843–1890), who published a good anthology of Estonian songs (*Eesti rahvalaulud*, 2 vols., 1879–1883).

Another clergyman, M. J. Eisen (1857–1934), started simultaneously with Hurt the gathering of folklore. He obtained 90,000 written pages, mostly tales and legends. He became famous as the author of about 200 popular books, written with the use of narrative folklore. Some of his collaborators, inspired by his example, also imposed a literary style on their collected folktales. One must, therefore, watch for falsifications when using the collection of Eisen. In the free Estonian state, Eisen became professor of folklore, and his studies on Estonian mythology (4 vols., 1919–1926) are of real scientific value. He confessed frankly what were his own creations in his popular editions.

Among the more recent collections a very important one was made by Samuel Sommer who gathered about 124,000 pages from the Setus, mostly folksongs.

The first Estonian holding a Ph.D. in folklore, O. Kallas (1868–1947), organized the recording of folk melodies. His collection contains more than 20,000 pages. A good anthology of the melodies of folk songs with introduction and summary in German, was published by H. Tempere (*Eesti rahvaviiside*, Tartu, 1935).

From the German scholars of the last few decades, those who paid attention to Estonian folklore were very few. The friend of the Estonians, L. von Schroeder, published an important study on Estonian wedding customs (*Die Hochzeitsgebräuche der Esten,* 1888) and another on Estonian gods and elves of German origin (1906).

Another well-known German folklorist, Walter Anderson (born 1885), was for many years acting as professor of folklore at the University of Tartu in independent Estonia He collected about 59,000 pages, mostly children's songs and verses, and published several important studies.

In 1927 the independent Estonian state founded the Estonian Folklore Archives (*Eesti Rahvaluule Archiiv*), which was directed by Dr. Oskar Loorits. There were placed all the earlier collections of Hurt, Eisen, and others, and the new ones, gathered during a period of 15 years under the skilled guidance of Loorits, reached 252,000 pages. Thus on January 1, 1941, Estonian folklore collections numbered 711,573 pages in all. This is a gigantic monument of culture for a small people. The Archives published many studies in its series *Eesti Rahvaluule Archiivi Toimetused*, and separately. Folklore publications became so numerous that folklore bibliography each year covered many printed pages, published in *Jahresbericht der estnischen Philologie und Geschichte*, with German translations of the titles. The author of many of the most important works of this period is O. Loorits.

There must be mentioned a giant plan to publish Estonian folk songs along with all the recorded variants for each song. Only two volumes have been published so far, containing 18 epic songs with hundreds of variants (*Eesti rahvalaulud*, 1926 and 1932, with summaries in German). The work ceased because it was going too slowly, was too expensive, and was of real importance for only a small number of specialists, who could easily find the material in the Archives.

The most important part of Estonian folklore is the folk songs. It must be emphasized that the old songs differ from the new ones, which were created at the beginning of the 19th century under the influence of religious hymns. The old songs have neither rime nor stanza, the rhythm is calm and reserved, the verses are mostly trochaic, sometimes with dactylic-trochaic interferences. Alliteration and assonance, and the repetition of the same contents in other words, or parallelism of the thought, are the most typical traits of the old songs. The epic elements are not so developed as in the Finnish runes and the lyrical mood is predominant. The Estonian songs have been referred to as "women's lyrics." O. Kallas gave the following characteristics of Estonian songs: "The majority of the collected runes...treat the manifestations and happenings of peasant-life, and the revelations of the human heart. They lead the listeners through the whole life story of the Estonian, from cradle to funeral bier. Particularly numerous are the wedding-songs; deepest in sentiment the orphan-songs, as in general all songs of elegiac nature. Love-songs...are conspicuous by their relative rarity. In Estonia such songs are overshadowed by the other varieties....The Estonian is sober in this as in other respects—a calm rational reflecting spirit—and thus in the field of lore he is no dreamer, no knight of romance, but a realist and a naturalist. As a result, Estonian songs of this description deal mostly with married love and fidelity or with sensual erotics. Characteristic of the Setus are their dirges, which are entirely missing among the other Estonians" (*Folk-Lore* 34: 111).

For studies on narrative folklore the Estonian material is of great importance because in this country the Russian and German waves of folktales come together. A type-index of Estonian tales and legends was published by A. Aarne (*FFC* 25, 1918). The west European repertoire is most important. Animal tales are not numerous. On the other hand, the number of magic tales is very great. A large part of the legends are closely allied to similar products elsewhere of Christian influence from both churches, Roman and Greek. Numerous myths tell about the origin of the world, the creation of man, animals, and plants and their peculiarities (*Ursprungssagen*). Despite the difficult conditions of life a very great number of humorous jokes were created or adopted. The legends, particularly local legends, often have historical reminiscence. Two collections of legends were published in German by F. Bienemann (*Livländisches Sagenbuch*, Reval 1887) and by C. von Stern (*Estnische Volkssagen*, Riga, 1935). Some of them contain valuable mythological data, e.g. about the dead, the Devil, house and water spirits, giants, hidden treasures, etc. A peculiarity of Estonian legend is the half man and half dog people. (See DOGHEADED PEOPLE.)

About other kinds of Estonian folklore O. Kallas says: "Of special interest are the proverbs...They offer a pithy, apt and graphic quintessence of popular wit and wisdom and are a keen character study in animated colours; a complete code of popular ethics and knowledge of life in pocket size...The material collected concerning ceremonies and customs, children's games and popular sports is so comprehensive that a whole gallery of pictures of Estonian popular life could be derived from it." (*Op. cit.*, pp. 112–113.)

References:

Kallas, Oscar, "Übersicht über das Sammeln estnischer Runen" in *FUF* II, 1902, p. 8–41.

Kallas, O. T., "Estonian Folklore" in *Folk-Lore* XXXIV, p. 100–116. London, 1923.

Loorits, Oskar, *Estnische Volksdichtung und Mythologie.* Tartu, 1932.

———, "Estonian Folklore of Today" in *Acta Ethnologica* I, p. 34–52. Copenhagen, 1936.   JONAS BALYS

Estonian mythology It is a very difficult task to separate genuine Estonian mythological beliefs from the influences and borrowings of all kinds from abroad. The foreign influence, especially from the Germans, is very great. The ideas of the Catholic Church are sometimes closely mixed with earlier traditions. The infiltration from Sweden and Russia is also obvious. Much confusion was made by the Estonian patriots in the time of the national awakening in the first half of the 19th century. They created for themselves an Estonian Olympus with the names of gods borrowed from the Finns. Ganander's *Mythologia Fennica* was translated in 1821 into German and published, and the Estophiles supposed that the same gods were known to the Estonians, but had only been forgotten. In 1841 F. R. Fählmann fabricated the gods Vanemuine, Ilmarine, Lämmeküne, and one year earlier had created the famous myth, "Koit ja Hämarik" (The Dawn and Evening Glow). Other fabrications: the god Turis was created by K. J. Peterson; M. J. Eisen produced "Kôu ja Pikkar" (Thunder and Lightning). It was not correct to graft the Finnish gods on to the Estonian (even though both peoples are near relatives), and it is not justifiable to create a complicated myth out of a bare name found in the folk traditions.

No wonder that Estonian scholars have different opinions on this complicated matter. Dr. Oskar Loorits made this statement: "I have designated *Animism* and *Manism* as the basic conception of Estonian religious life. Even *Shamanism* is known in a strongly degenerate form, whereas *Polytheism* in the Estonian folk beliefs cannot be seriously mentioned...The modern doctrine about primeval *Monotheism* and the idea about one supreme god cannot be confirmed by Estonian folk tradition...The Estonian folk-religion is rather of *Pantheistic* pattern and it is possible to speak about a kind of *Dynamism*...Thinking in magic terms survives today with great vitality..." (*Grundzüge*, Vol. I, p. 10–11).

We do not have a comprehensive description or presentation of Estonian mythology from some centuries in the past; the best source remains the Estonian folklore of recent days, which, it is true, is often very conservative. The statement of Loorits is based on just this material. It is possible that in older times, as the Estonians were not so much influenced by the religious beliefs of their neighbors and by the Christian doctrine, their mythology had also other traits. Indeed the chroniclers have given us a few statements. For example, in *Chronica Livonica* in 1220 is mentioned the god Tharapita. The philologists explain that probably the heathen warriors yelled "Taara avita!" (Taara help us) before the battle with the Christian knights. The Taara may have been a god of heaven and thunder like Thor of the Scandinavians. The other Finno-Ugric stocks also have gods of heaven called by similar names (cf. Vogulian **Tõrem**, Ostyakian **Tūrem**, Lappish **Turms**, etc.). However it remains an unsolved problem whether here we have a borrowed Scandinavian Thor or a genuine Estonian deity.

The word *jumal* has many meanings and may be a name for heaven and the gods in general. Names like Vanataat (the old man), Taevataat (the old man of the heaven), or Vanaisa (the old father), occurring in popular sayings, do not sufficiently prove any belief in a personal highest god of heaven. There may also be some influence of the Christian God.

The thunder has many names. Uku (the old man) is a borrowing from the Finns (see UKKO). The common Estonian word for thunder is *pikker* or *pikne* (the long one); it means the lightning also. In the North thunder is called *kõu*, meaning the thunderclap in general, probably an old borrowing from Lithuanian *kaukas* (see *FUF* XII: 186–194 and *ERE* VI:23). In the East thunder is called *äike* (the big or old one, grandfather). So the names are many, but there is lacking any evidence that thunder was imagined as a personal god and not only as a manifestation of nature. Nevertheless, the thunder was an object of worship, and sacrifices were offered to him. A prayer was written down by Gutsleff in 1644 from the "heathen priest" to the Pikker and says: "Dear Pikker! We are offering you a bull, two-horned, four-footed, for the sake of the plowing and the sowing, stalks of brass, ears of gold. Push elsewhere the black clouds, over the great swamp, the high forest, the wide plain; air of mead, rains of honey to our plowmen, sowers! Holy Pikker, look after our fields: fine straw beneath, fine ears above, fine grain within!" Pikker also gives rain and fertility like the thunder god of other peoples. Prayers for sending the clouds to the forests and deserts during thunderstorms is known also among Lithuanians.

Estonian nature spirits are very numerous. The common name of the spirits is haldjas (see HALTIA of the Finns). The household spirit is majahaldjas or koduhaldjas, the protector of the house and court. Such a protecting spirit is probably the soul of the first owner of the house. He takes care of the house for the good inhabitants, but must not be offended, and victuals and drinks must be offered to him (compare Finnish TONTTU). The worship of house-serpents is also mentioned from the 17th century, and has survived until recently.

The prevalence of numerous water deities shows very great German influence (see NÄKK). They are imagined in human shape, male and female, and often the same spirit has many names. Not so much developed is the worship of fire and trees. The sacred oak and linden were mentioned by Russow in 1578. Estonians habitually call the nature spirits "mothers" and "fathers," e.g. mother of the sea, mother of the field, father of the cattle, father of the forest, etc.

Estonians also have various idols formed by the hand of man. Seventeenth century sources frequently mention the Metsik, which at the time of New Year and Shrove Tuesday was formed from straw in the shape of a man or woman and put on a tree or fence. The idol was to protect the cattle against wild beasts and also to promote the fertility of the crops. A similar idol is known today to the Setus in the south of Estonia (see PEKO). A third idol was Tõnn from the west. The name is derived from St. Antony. He was formed as a doll from cloth and wax and preserved in a bushel basket in the corn house. He was offered the first-fruits of all kinds of products. There are also deities of fertility. Common are the maidens of the corn-field, called viljaneitsi, and the wolf of the rye.

Very popular in Estonia are the demons of fortune. Such a demon can be bought or made by man and vivified with the help of the Devil. Frequently the man must promise his soul to the Devil, but usually he is able to cheat the Devil and save his soul. The demon brings the owner all kinds of goods, products of milk, grain, and even gold. He has the shape of an animal, usually appearing as a cock, cat, or toad. He is called kratt in the west, tont in the east, puuk in the south and on the Isle of Saaremaa. Another shape of the same demon is like a fiery flying dragon, called in the west tulihänd (the tail of fire), and in the south pisuhänd (the tail of spark). All the demons of this kind came to Estonia from Germany and Sweden, not only their names but also their shapes, their nature, and their legends (compare L. Shroeder, *Germanische Elben und Götter beim Estenvolke*. Wien, 1906, p. 14–61). A magician can himself fly in the form of a demon to steal goods from his neighbors.

Perhaps the most interesting Estonian beliefs are those concerning the dead. Many of the Estonian beliefs are more or less connected with the dead. The deceased man continues his life as before, except that now he is living in the grave. The word kalm means both the grave and the dead. The collective living place of the dead is called Hiiela, a sacred grove where the dead were buried, and Toonela (compare TUONELA of the

Finns). The "old Tooni," master of this realm, functions like a father of a numerous family. There are also houses, fields, and roads in the afterworld, as on the earth. Sometimes the name Manala (under the earth) is also used. It is populated by the dwarfs. The invisible soul of the man is mardus or marras. If one sees it, the man will be dead soon. The dead are often helpful to the living, but they must not be offended. They must be offered victuals during the burial and later when they return home on certain days in the autumn. The bathroom was heated for the souls. Food was also laid on the graves. In early times the living relatives feasted together with the departed on the graves. This custom is known today among the Setus, and in 1428 it was mentioned that the Estonians liked to feast in the churchyards together with their dead. There was no fear and hostility between living and dead. On the contrary, they formed together a close family, guided by love and mutual help. As a result of Christian-Germanic influence, the dead later came to be represented by a revengeful demon (*kodukäija*).

The Devil has many names, old and new, of heathen and Christian origin. For example he is called vanapagan (the old heathen, a name also used for a giant); vanapois (the old boy); äio (grandfather); kurat (the left or bad side); and juudas (dark). The hard struggle between the old and the new religion, between enslaved folk and foreign clergy produced such names for the Devil as säks (a German); poostel (from apostle); and kolmik (from trinity). The beggar is called sant (from *sanctus*); muuk (from monk) is the name for a robber. The Devil of the legends is often helpful to the poor Estonian farmer in the struggle with his oppressor, the German baron.

The priest or magician is called nõid, the old name for shaman (see NOIDE of the Lapps). There were good and bad magicians. The good ones, who were helpful to man by protecting him, healing diseases, and forecasting the future, were called tark (the wise). Their power depended upon knowledge about the origin and nature of evil spirits, for only when they possessed this power could they control them.

The variety of Estonian folk beliefs is very great, a mixture of mythological ideas of many cultural areas. They come from the old Finno-Ugric background, and there are borrowings from the Goths, Germans, Swedes, Latvians, and Russians. The Catholic period has left more traces than recent Protestantism. The oldest survivals are preserved by the Setus in the southeast of Estonia in so-called Setumaa. Folk medicine and the magic practices of daily life are of German origin.

References:

Eisen, M. J., *Estnische Mythologie*. Leipzig, 1925.

Loorits, O., *Estnische Volksdichtung und Mythologie* Tartu, 1932.

———, *Grundzüge des estnischen Volksglaubens*. Vol. I. Lund, 1949.

JONAS BALYS

Estsanatlehi The Woman Who Changes: an important female deity of the Navaho Indians of the Southwest. See CHANGING WOMAN. [EWV]

ethnocentrism The ethnocentric viewpoint is tellingly illustrated in many North American Indian origin myths. In the Eastern Woodlands each one of many tribes claims to have been created at "the heart of the world"; each claims to have been created first, with other tribes created as an afterthought, or semiaccidentally, or by less important deities. The Jicarilla Apache of the Southwest say that one tribe only—their own—existed when the world was new. Ethnocentrism is also pronounced in mythical material on the confusion of tongues. In most of this material it is assumed or stated that the language of the tribe to which the narrator of the myth belongs was the language which originally was spoken universally. [EWV]

ethnochoreography The scientific study of ethnic dances in all their choreographic aspects (steps, formations, rhythms) as related to their cultural significance, religious function or symbolism, or social place. Comparative choreography is the juxtaposition and interpretation of salient elements in dance forms. [Word coined and defined by Gertrude Kurath]

Etzel The German name for Attila the Hun who, according to the *Nibelungenlied,* married Kriemhild, sister of Gunther, king of Burgundy, after the death of Siegfried. He took no part in Kriemhild's plots for revenge against her brothers, but treated the Burgundians as noble guests, and tried to reconcile his wife and her brothers until all were slain. Compare ATLI.

Eugpamolak Manobo, Manama, or **Kalayágan** The Bagobo (Philippine Islands) chief spirit and creator who lives in the sky and watches the doings of men. He is served by many spirits who exact punishment from the people when they do not make the proper offerings. Eugpamolak Manobo is invited to all Bagobo ceremonies, but he refuses bloody sacrifices and does not give favors.

euhemerism The theory that myths are simply explanations of historical events and that the gods were once men who for their deeds became important and after death were worshipped: advanced by Euhemerus, a writer in Macedonia, about 316 B.C., in his *Sacred History* (*Hierā Anagraphē*). The idea does not seem to be entirely original with Euhemerus, it forms a part of the general rationalism of the period, but his statement of it became best known. Zeus, for example, was pictured as a king of Crete whose conquests caused him to be worshipped. Euhemerus was considered an atheist by his contemporaries, and his theories were adopted by Christian writers to prove that the classical gods were not at all divine. The theory has been discarded as a fully explanatory method, but it is still utilized to some extent.

Eumenides See ERINYES.

eunuch A castrated man, often one emasculated before puberty. (The question of female castration is only incidental to the discussion.) The word eunuch may be derived from the Greek words meaning "bed guardian," or, according to Gray, from a Hebrew word meaning "experienced, tried," in reference to the positions of trust they held. Eunuchs were variously classified: those born so, those made so by men, those emasculated by themselves (*Matt.* xix, 12)—this was the distinction later made by the rabbis; also, a distinction was made as between Negro and white eunuchs or between those with no genitals at all and those lacking

the testicles; the Romans distinguished among *castrati* (no genitals), *spadones* (no testicles), and *thlibii* (crushed testicles), and perhaps *thlasiæ* (spermatic cord cut); in the East the *sandali* had no organs, another class had no penis, and a third class had no testicles, or had bruised, burned, or torn testicles. English still preserves the various concepts among its associated words: capon, from Latin *capo,* strike, crush; castrate, from Latin *castro,* cut; spay, from Greek *spaõ,* draw, drag.

The origin of the eunuch is lost in the ages. Probably the custom of castrating men developed from the castration of animals, a usage resorted to to make the animals docile and strong (e.g. horses) or to fatten them for tastier food (e.g. fowl). Human castration seems to have begun in Mesopotamia. Ammianus Marcellinus attributed the practice to the legendary Semiramis, to whose personality almost any kind of sexual legend has been attracted. Castration and the eunuch have been known in Assyria, Israel, Ethiopia, Egypt, Persia, India, China, Greece, Rome, and various parts of the Western world in contact with the East and its peoples. (The African castration customs reported do not seem to be eunuchizing, but have different aims. For example, the former Hottentot custom of cutting off the left testicle was meant to prevent the birth of twins, an event of ill-omen.)

The priests of several ancient Near Eastern goddesses of fertility were eunuchs. The Artemis of Ephesus, the Astarte of Hierapolis in Syria, the Asian Hecate, and Cybele and Attis had an emasculated priesthood. The Galli, priests of Attis, castrated themselves, probably on the third day of their Spring festival, the Day of Blood, March 24. Caught up by the frenzy of the older priests who cut their skins and whirled about splashing blood all over the crowds, the novices slashed off their members and threw them against the image of Cybele. These were later buried in places sacred to the goddess, perhaps as a sacrifice to this goddess of fruitfulness. See, for example, the story of Agdistis, from whose severed organs sprang the fruit that impregnated Nana, and the associated story of Attis who was self-mutilated and bled to death under a pine-tree. Self-mutilation occurred among the Pavayā caste of India who served the goddess Bahucharajī, but the novice had first to prove that he was impotent before he would be considered for admission to the caste: the custom was abolished in 1880, thereby dooming its members, according to them, to future lives of impotence. Castrations such as these have myths to explain them, but in these instances the myths are undoubtedly etiological, *pourquoi* stories explaining the reason for an established ritual. The sky-earth separation myth, however, seems genuinely cosmogonic; Uranus and Cronus both were castrated in the mythology of Greece; a parallel myth from Polynesia, and the Egyptian myth, of the separation of sky and earth indicates that this is a naturally occurring explanation: the sky-father can be separated from the earth-mother only by severing the connecting member.

Generally in Rome and in Europe, the eunuch could not become a priest, since perfect and unblemished bodies were a requirement for the office. Some early Christians, following Origen, who misinterpreted *Matt.* xix, 12 and castrated himself, believed castration necessary, but the Council of Nicea forbade the priesthood to such persons. The Russian sect of Skoptzy surreptitiously practiced castration.

Like capons, geldings, and oxen, eunuchs have had their special uses. "The barbarians value eunuchs more than others," says Herodotus (VIII: 105), "since they regard them as more trustworthy." As the common derivation indicates, they have been used since ancient times as guards, chamberlains, especially of the women's quarters. The reason is obvious: a eunuch, even if subject to temptation, can do nothing to harm the physical virtue of the inmates of the harem. This is especially true if the castration has occurred before puberty; after puberty, provided that only the testicles are removed or crushed, the erectile power of the penis disappears after a time (a year to 18 months). It is said that Roman matrons used recently castrated youths for sexual gratification in view of the absence of fear of possible pregnancy. Despite the prohibition of Mohammed, the castration of young boys for the slave trade in Moslem countries continued in Africa until recently. It is said that the mortality rate made the price of these eunuchs very high. As chamberlains then, the eunuchs were in important positions of trust, able to become skilled in intrigue and to rise rapidly, given sufficient determination and ambition. Logically, a person with whom the wives of king or noble could be trusted might be entrusted with other confidential matters. Eunuchs became great officers of state in China, Persia, India, and the Byzantine Empire. Narses, for example, was a great general under Justinian, and Agha Mohammed, in 1795–98, overthrew the Zends in Persia, though both were eunuchs, hence popularly incomplete men. Potiphar, the master of the Biblical Joseph, was a eunuch, which perhaps explains his wife's trouble.

In India, eunuchs were the lowest of all classes. Throughout the world that knew them, eunuchs were despised and feared by the people, perhaps with reason, for many tales and much history emphasize the malign nature of the eunuch. There is however no basis of fact in the equally popular belief that eunuchs are devoid of sexual passion. Burton states that almost all eunuchs are married and manage to satisfy their wives, though he indicates that their own gratification is incomplete and must be guarded against by the wife lest it be expended in biting or other physical injury. A medical report cited by Bergen Evans states that 10 of 23 castration cases later acquired gonorrhea—at the very least an indication of willing spirit. The story of Abelard is a further indication that desire does not die with the loss of sexual organs. The castration of females among the Australians is said to be performed to prevent their having children by the men of hostile tribes, but the women act as prostitutes within their own tribes and the statement that they feel no pleasure may be discounted.

Castration as punishment has its most famous example in Abelard. Usually rape, seduction, adultery, and the like crimes are the ones entailing such injury. The Egyptians and the Indians made eunuchs of adulterers; a law of Alfred the Great established castration as the penalty for a servant who raped a female servant. In India, a Brāhman who violated his teacher's wife was permitted to choose, among other punishments, the right of castrating himself and walking to the southwest (the direction of destruction) carrying his genitals until he fell dead. An ancient Frisian law stated castration as the penalty for a temple robber; in India it was suffered by one urinating on a person of higher caste; in China, whereas all the older male members of the family of a traitor were killed, the young boys were castrated and made servants.

Castration destroys to some extent the secondary sexual characteristics. The beard and body hair tend to disappear, pigmentation of the skin becomes less, fat accumulates, the joints become more apparent. Eunuchs are also taller than average and have a more noticeable bony structure. The voice loses its masculinity and becomes flat. In boys, the voice remains high; for many years sopranos in the Sistine choir were eunuchs, despite edicts of the Church against castration. As late as the 19th century, where women were forbidden the stage, male sopranos for the Italian opera were provided by castration. Compare TRANSVESTITES.

euphemism "Speak of the Devil and he appears," so if you do not wish him to come you must refer to him by another name, a euphemism. If you are in Scotland, you call him Clootie or Auld Hornie; in Germany, Meister Peter; in the Shetlands, da black tief; in England, Old Nick; in New England, the Deuce or The Old Boy Himself.

Theoretically, he will not know you are referring to him. The idea in the use of euphemisms is to flatter and thus propitiate, or speak enigmatically or metaphorically and thus deceive the Devil, or other evil spirits, or powerful animals you wish to avoid or not to offend, or clever ones you wish to trap, or disease and death you desire to overlook you, or kings and even gods with whom you must deal.

Take the lion, for instance. The Algerian Arabs refer to him respectfully as Mr. John Johnson, the Angolans as Sir, and the South African Bechuanas as the boy with the beard. Depending on where you live, the euphemism grandfather may mean the bear, the tiger, the elephant, or the alligator. Don't use his right name, for even if he doesn't catch you, you'll become sick. The Lapps often call the bear the old man with the fur coat, and the Sioux say water-person for beaver.

In Mombasa you must call smallpox grains of corn, but the Dyaks say jungle-leaves. In China a coffin is boards of old age. Death is widely called a sleep. To die in South Africa is to go home; in the United States it may be to go West, cash in, kick the bucket, or pass away.

Formerly in Siam, Burma, China, and Korea, the king or ruling monarch's real name must never be known or mentioned lest harm come to him from an evil person thus getting control or power over him. Only complimentary titles could be used, under threat of severe penalties.

The name of the Hebrew god, supposed to be Yahweh, was prohibited from utterance, but vowels of another name, Adonai, my Lord, were used to make the hybrid word Jehovah, a euphemism which was safe to pronounce.

In the United States in Christian circles you must not

take the name of God or Christ in vain, but you can usually employ without being criticized the popular euphemisms Gad, Gosh, Gee, Cripes, or Christmas. Even pious old ladies ejaculate Laws-a-massy or Oh, Good Lord! without being struck dead. See NAME TABU.

CHARLES FRANCIS POTTER

Europa In Greek mythology, the daughter of Agenor, king of Tyre and Phœnicia, or, in Homer, daughter of Phœnix. With cosmetics belonging to Hera, she made herself pleasing to Zeus. He, hiding among cattle disguised as a bull, acted so gentle that she climbed on his back. Zeus immediately fled to the sea, and swam off to Crete where he took her to the Dictean cave where he had been brought up. There she bore to him Minos and Rhadamanthus (and, some add, Sarpedon). Later, she married Asterius, but there were no children from the union. According to some accounts, she was also the mother of the Minotaur, and of Evander.

European folklore The spiritual development of mankind having been fundamentally uniform, though by no means unilinear, all over the globe, it is largely for practical reasons that the domain of folklore is divided geographically, by continents. Furthermore, when we speak of the folklore of Europe, the latter term must not be understood in an administrative sense. Caucasia belongs administratively, to European Russia; but its folklore (like its languages) is non-European and inseparable from Iran. On the other hand, certain Near-Eastern countries (Anatolia, Armenia, and Syria) are not really Asiatic but Mediterranean, i.e. European. Their folklore must therefore be considered in any comprehensive treatment of European folklore.

Since the fall of the Roman Empire Europe has never been a political entity; but culturally and historically no other continent has shown as much unity, nay uniformity, as Europe. It is therefore to be expected that European folklore should show an analogous picture of great uniformity throughout the continent. The reasons therefor are sufficiently patent. What we call European civilization is merely the result of the radiation of the ancient Mediterranean culture, developed in the Mediterranean basin from 3000 B.C. at the latest. This radiation occurred in a northerly and northeasterly direction, extending beyond the Baltic (Krappe, *Scandinavian Studies*, XVI, 1941, pp. 165–84) and as far east as the Urals. The strength and the effect of this radiation grew weaker with the distance from the radiation center, a fact which alone accounts for the gradation of culture (German *Kulturgefälle*) noticeable as one moves east and northeast from the Atlantic and the Mediterranean (K. Krohn, *Die folkloristische Arbeitsmethode*, Oslo, 1926, p. 13). This gradation largely explains local differences in folklore which, in the outlying posts (Ireland, Iceland, Scandinavia, Finland, Russia), is apt to reveal more archaic features than could be found, for example, in France or Germany.

The most practical mode of approach would therefore be a survey of the field of folklore types, with special mention of local peculiarities. A detailed discussion must naturally be left to the articles dealing with the various folklore types.

Fairy tale There are current, in Europe, about 500 known fairy tale types, each of which has its own individual plot and virtually all of which are found not only over the whole continent or over large portions of it, but also in Asia and North Africa. A good number of them have been carried to the New World by European settlers. The origin and the history of the diffusion of most of these types are still unknown, though the researches of Kaarle Krohn and his school have definitely shown the Indian origin of some fifty tale types. (Compare K. Krohn, *FFC* 96, 1931).

The most archaic variants are not found, as has sometimes been supposed, in Russia, but in Ireland and the Western Isles of Scotland (Krappe, *Calif. Folklore Quart.*, V, 1946, p. 216). The explanation for this is that Russia has in all ages been a country traversed by the highroads of commerce from the Black Sea to the Baltic, whereas Ireland, the Hebrides, and Iceland have been largely untouched by the great currents of civilization. As a result, archaic features which were promptly suppressed or replaced by more modern ones elsewhere, were preserved in these outlying regions. Similarly, many types widely current on the continent (including Russia) are absent from these islands, a striking parallel, incidentally, to certain zoogeographical facts: many bird species known all over the continent and even in Britain are not known to exist in Ireland, the Western Isles, and, *a fortiori*, in Iceland.

Variants of individual fairy tale types ordinarily show so few local peculiarities that, were a given variant translated into a "neutral" language, say, Esperanto, only an expert folklorist could detect, and that not always, the country of its origin. By far the best clues are furnished by the prevailing demonology. Thus the troll is peculiar to Scandinavia and Iceland, the Baba Yaga to Russia, the nereid to modern Greece, the Orco to Italy, the vila to Yugoslavia, etc. The supernatural being that has given its name to the tale type (*fairy*) is obviously of French origin (*fée*); so is the German *Fee*, the Spanish *hada*, and, very probably, the Italian *fata*. Since in northwestern France, and there alone, fairies occur commonly in local traditions (in which they can be of either sex) and are part of living belief, it is a fair presumption that the whole fairy mythology (as it has been called) originated in Brittany and western Normandy. Its diffusion over England, western Germany, Italy, and northern Spain is a striking pendant to the diffusion of the Arthurian fairy lore in the Middle Ages. The French *fée*, in spite of the Latin etymology of the name ($<$L. *fata*, plural of *fatum*), is not Latin at all, but the creation of the Celtic inhabitants of that region of France, the exact equivalent of the Irish *side* (Paul Sébillot, *Contes populaires de la Haute-Bretagne*, Paris, 1880–81; W. Y. E. Wentz, *The Fairy-Faith in Celtic Countries*, London, 1911).

Tales of vampirism (see VAMPIRE) point to Slavonic Europe, at least when we are dealing with modern variants. For medieval texts this conclusion would not be justified, since the belief in the vampire or living corpse was once even more widely spread than it is now (C. N. Gould, *Scand. Studies and Notes*, IX, 1926, pp. 167–201).

Some Irish stories show a strange affinity with archaic Mediterranean traditions. For example the Phineus episode, with the motif of loathsome animals which befoul a king's table at mealtime, appears in several Irish variants of the same märchen type on which the

Argonaut story itself is based, but in a form more archaic than is found in any of the extant Greek texts. (Krappe, *Folk-Lore*, XXXVI, 1925, pp. 314 f.) The myth of Adonis must have reached Ireland in pre-Christian times. (Krappe, *Folk-Lore*, XLVII, 1936, pp. 347–61). The whole subject, however, is still very imperfectly known.

In many fairy tale variants an archaic and pagan demonology has been replaced by a medieval Catholic one, the leading characters being Our Lady, the Devil, and some of the Apostles, chiefly St. Peter. These Christian features are most prominent in countries which have remained Catholic to this day (Spain, Italy, Austria, and the Catholic cantons of Switzerland), the only exception being Ireland, where St. Patrick occurs only in tales which betray all too clearly their monkish and bookish origin. The Devil has kept his prominence even in Protestant countries; the Virgin and the saints have not. In Russia it is sometimes possible to follow the different stages of this Christianization process. Thus St. Prascovia in a Christian variant will play the part, which in a more archaic one, falls to St. Pyatnitsa (Yugoslavian St. Petka), "St. Friday," who has taken the place of Siva (Lithuanian Seeva), the pagan Slavonic goddess of love. On the whole, however, the survival of pagan divinities in fairy tales is very rare: the Greek Charos, a very ancient god of death, much older than his literary offshoot, the classical ferryman Charon (A. B. Cook, *Zeus*, II, 641 [exhaustive bibliography]), the Italian Orco (<L. Orcus), and Dame Holle (Grimm #24). The Teutonic Woden [Odin, Othin] appears to have survived, converted, of course, into the Devil, in a story of Anglo-Saxon origin, which was translated into French in the 12th century and subsequently became current on the European continent, reaching even to Spain (Krappe, *Arch. Roman.*, VII, 1924, pp. 470–77).

If traces of pagan mythology are rare in European fairy tales, the witch superstition has left its ugly mark on many of them, chiefly on German and Scottish variants (H. Vordemfelde, *Festschrift f. E. Mogk,* pp. 558 ff.), a fact easily explainable by the virulence of the superstition in the two countries (C. K. Sharpe, *An Historical Account of the Belief of Witchcraft in Scotland*, London, 1884). Witches are least prominent in southern European and Hungarian variants. In the last named country this is doubtless connected with the absence of witch legislation in the national code (King Kalman [1095–1114 A.D.]: De strigis vero, quæ non sunt, nulla quæstio fiat).

In certain Mediterranean countries (Greece, Italy, southern France) claims for a survival of ancient myths have sometimes been advanced (B. Schmidt, *Griechische Märchen, Sagen und Volkslieder*, Leipzig, 1877, pp. 6 ff.). The facts themselves are certain; but, whether we are dealing with genuinely popular survivals is another question: in these countries the classical tradition never really died; a fair degree of literacy was maintained even during the Dark Ages, and the role of the Greek schoolmaster must not be underestimated.

The classical tradition is, however, by no means the only tradition known to have affected the folktales of the Balkans and of many other European countries. The *Arabian Nights*, translated into French by Galland, in 1704, and subsequently into all European languages

(V. Chauvin, *Bibliographie*, IV, 1 ff.) soon became widely known throughout the Continent, and two of Grimm's tales (#116 and 142) reveal this Oriental inspiration. How great this influence was in other European countries can only be surmised, since a comprehensive study of this problem is still outstanding.

Unlike the Near East, Europe seems never to have had professional tellers of fairy tales: the professional entertainers of the Middle Ages preferred poetry to prose, and the Icelandic sagamen cultivated genres laying claim to historicity. Thus the 19th-century collectors of fairy tales drew entirely on amateurs, women and men of the country populations. Again, while in other continents, e.g. Africa, the telling of stories is limited to certain times of the day, being forbidden at others, and while in the Near East it is frequently avoided, on the plea that it brings "bad luck," no such tabus are known in Europe; if they once existed there (a thing by no means unlikely) they must have disappeared long ago. The preferred season is, however, winter and the preferred occasion the spinning-party in the village spinning-room. These were suppressed, in Central Europe, by meddlesome authorities, but still continue in Russia (*Mélusine*, III, 1886–87, col. 391 ff. and 445 ff.; D. Zelenin, *Russische (Ostslavische) Volkskunde,* 1927, p. 338).

Merry tale The number of merry tales current in Europe is legion. A number of types have convincingly been shown to be of Oriental origin. (G. Paris, *Les Contes orientaux dans la littérature française*, Paris, 1875, reprinted in *La poésie du moyen âge*, 1885, II, pp. 75–108). Joseph Bédier's objections, in his book *Les Fabliaux* (1st ed., 1893; 3rd ed., 1925) merely prove that the conditions required for a successful tracing of a merry tale type to its origin are not always present. For a list of some merry tales successfully traced, see K. Voretzsch, *Einführung in das Studium der altfranzösischen Literatur*, 3rd ed., 1925, p. 446. Quite a number of merry tales presuppose very elementary human relationships and to that extent are not peculiar to Europe. Other types have died out in countries where the underlying conditions have ceased to exist. Thus medieval Europe delighted in tales showing the *mores* of the clergy in a peculiar light. The advent of Protestantism and the abolition of clerical celibacy put an end to these stories all over northern and the larger part of central Europe. In Russia, where this celibacy never existed, tales of this type are virtually unknown. In Protestant Europe, it is true, the minister promptly took over the role of the priest as the chief butt of popular and jocular tales; but it is usually his deficiency in learning or his avidity for worldly goods that is criticized.

Animal tale The animal tale, virtually always explanatory in character, is probably the most widely spread folktale type and at the same time the most elementary type of fiction known. It is found in the four non-European continents even more commonly than in Europe, where it has lost ground with the spread of scientific knowledge, no doubt because of its lack of sophistication. The country richest in animal tales is Russia and its border lands: Finland, Rumania, Bulgaria, etc. There can, however, be little doubt that the same tales were once known also in the rest of

Europe. They are important because they are one of the sources that fed the medieval beast epic. (Collections of animal tales: O. Dännhardt, *Natursagen*, Leipzig, 1907–12; Moses Gaster, *Rumanian Bird and Beast Stories*, London, 1915; S. F. Marian, *Insectele*, Bucharest, 1903; Adolph Gerber, *Great Russian Animal Tales*, *PMLA*, VI, Baltimore, 1891.) A famous episode of the beast epic, the story of the wolf being inveigled by the fox to catch a fish by putting its tail into a pond about to freeze and losing it in the process, originated in an animal tale explaining how the bear lost its tail in this manner. As the bear disappeared from central and western Europe much earlier than the wolf, the story, once it reached regions where the bear was no longer known, put the wolf in its place, oblivious of the fact that it was thereby losing its point. (Compare K. Krohn, *Bär (Wolf) und Fuchs*, Helsingfors, 1891.)

Edifying stories and exempla Medieval Catholicism delighted in telling marvelous stories about Our Lady and the saints. Many of them are of clerical, i.e. "learned" origin. Others hark back to paganism, Our Lady having merely taken the place of some pagan goddess. The most famous of the latter is, probably, the story of the *Young Man Betrothed to a Statue* (*PMLA*, XXXIV, 1919, pp. 523–79; Gédéon Huet, *La légende de la statue de Vénus*, *RHR*, LXVIII, 1913, pp. 193–217). Most of these stories are now represented only in historical variants (A. Mussafia, *Studien zu den mittelalterlichen Marienlegenden*, in *SBWA*, vols. 113, 115, 119, 1886–89). Protestantism and the Counter-Reformation were equally hostile to these stories. The only country in which they still enjoy a certain vogue is Spain (Krappe, *Hisp. Rev.*, I, 1933, pp. 340–43; XIV, 1946, pp. 164–67). In Russia, the Byzantine origin and bookish features of this story type are equally striking; the extent of their oral diffusion is still largely unknown (L. Calmann, *Altrussische Heiligenlegenden*, Munich, 1922).

The medieval *exemplum* is not, strictly speaking, a folktale type. A product of medieval Catholicism, these illustrative stories were used to enliven the sermons of priests and friars. Nor were the rabbis slow in recognizing the usefulness of the device (Moses Gaster, *The Exempla of the Rabbis*, London-Leipzig, 1924). After the Reformation, Lutheran ministers kept up the custom, and thus we have some German and Swedish Protestant collections of exempla. Calvinism rejected them from the outset, preferring instead the appointment of special officials armed with pokers to keep the congregation from falling asleep during the sermon. Many of these stories have no folklore status but are tales and anecdotes taken from the classical writers, chiefly Cicero, Seneca, and Valerius Maximus. Others relate historical events culled in chroniclers such as Bede. A considerable number, however, are bits of oral folklore heard and reproduced by priests or wandering friars. (Collections: T. F. Crane, *The Exempla or Illustrative Stories from the sermones vulgares of Jacques de Vitry*, London, 1890; Nicole Bozon, *Les contes moralisés*, ed. L. T. Smith and Paul Meyer, Paris, 1889, *SATF*. On the type compare T. F. Crane, *Proc. Amer. Philos. Soc.*, XXI, 1883–84, pp. 49–78; LVI, 1917, pp. 369–402; Krappe, *Bul. Hisp.* XXXIX, 1937, pp. 1–54).

Local legend There is a wealth of material available which suffers only from one drawback: while central and western Europe are extremely well represented, there is little printed information on southern and eastern Europe. Spain and Russia have virtually no collections whatever, though from historical texts it is easy to see that both countries are as rich in local legends as any other. The subtypes (historical and pseudo-historical traditions, ghost stories, stories of stone-hurling or stone-carrying giants, the Devil's pact, in which the Evil One is outwitted in the end, traditions about dwarfs, about nixes, dragons, etc.) are virtually ubiquitous. They have obviously a common basis: features of the European landscape (huge boulders scattered over the plain gave rise to stone-hurling giants), the Church's Devil lore (the oldest Devil's pact variant is the clerical tale of Theophilus), a prehistoric ancestor cult, the doctrine of Purgatory, etc. The banshee is by no means peculiar to Ireland and Gaelic Scotland but is found all over France and central Europe, though under different names. The vampire is in the main limited to the Balkans and Slavonic Europe (which includes the part of Germany east of the river Elbe); but it is found also in Iceland. The traditions of the Wild Hunt are current in central Europe, Scandinavia, France, and northern Spain; but they are known to have existed in ancient Greece and even in India (Krappe, *Mitt. d. Schles. Ges. f. Volksk.*, XXX, 1929, pp. 96–100). We are here evidently with a piece of ancient European lore which emigrants carried with them into the Balkans and to India. Much the same seems to be true of the traditions concerning wild animals endowed with supernatural power: the Nemean Lion and the Calydonian Boar are known from antiquity; but they are also found in western and northern Europe, and are known, in Norse, as *stefnisvargas* (compare W. A. Craigie, *Scandivanian Folk-Lore*, London, 1896, pp. 369 ff.). Quite unexplainable is the isolated occurrence of some story type in widely separated countries. Thus we find the story of the knight or soldier who falls into a dragon pit, lives on the moisture oozing out of the walls, and finally saves himself by sitting down on the dragon's tail as the animal leaves the pit, localized in the Alps (Grimm, *Deutsche Sagen*, #217) and in Prussian Poland, but forming part also of a *lygisaga* (Ake Lagerholm, *Drei Lygisǫgur*, Halle, 1927, pp. lxxiii f., lxxix) and in the Spanish *Crónica general* (compare R. Menéndez Pidal, *Revista de Archivos*, XIV, 1901, p. 880). Since the same tale forms part of the *Gesta Romanorum* (ed. Oesterly, #114), one might be tempted to derive all these variants from a written source. Unfortunately, the theme also occurs in Sajjid Batthâl (*Fahrten*, übers. v. H. Ethé, 1871, II, p. 94) and in China (R. Wilhelm, *Chinesische Volksmärchen*, Jena, 1921, p. 14). And what is one to say of the famous story of a dragon killed by a bull raised expressly for this purpose, a tale found in the Alps (P. Sébillot, *Le Folk-Lore de France*, I, pp. 242 f.) and in Norway (Craigie, *op. cit.*, p. 260). Of special interest are the supernatural beings occurring in local legends. The belief in giants seems to have arisen out of a desire to explain phenomena otherwise unexplainable: large boulders and giant structures such as Roman arenas and aqueducts (cf. the "Cyclopean" walls in Greece). The Irish *side* (pronounced shee), the French *fées* (of either sex), the German dwarfs and "unterirdische," the English and Scandinavian elves, Norwegian *huldre*, are the divinized ancestors (Krappe, *Science of Folk-Lore*, pp. 87 ff.) The nixes of northern Europe correspond to the ancient Greek naiads, the various forms of tree spirits to Greek dryads (W. Mannhardt, *Der Baumkultus*, Berlin, 1904). The "Wild Women" of the Tyrolese Alps, like the Yugoslav *vilas* are to all appearances the creations of the ancient pre-Roman (Thraco-Illyrian?) populations, as are other demonic beings known in this region (Krappe, *Herrig's Archiv.*, 163, 1933, pp. 161–71). The institutions presupposed by the local legends are medieval feudalism and the medieval church: the wicked landlord and the lecherous priest, taken in the end by the Devil, are favorite themes. Even French local legends invariably reflect the state of affairs prior to 1789. Reminiscences of conditions antedating the Christianization of the continent are virtually non-existent, which means that these traditions are in the main medieval products. If the pre-Christian demonology has survived to the extent it has, this merely proves that Christianity merely overlaid, but did not destroy, the older faith.

Migratory legend Strictly speaking every fairy tale and most merry and animal tales are "migratory," nor are local legends necessarily stationary; but for practical reasons we designate as migratory legend (German *Wandersage*) any story not belonging to the above groups but known to have spread from a diffusion center, presumably its origin. Theoretically it might be supposed that such a tale may have sprung up anywhere and spread in any direction. Such is, however, not the case. The diffusion of stories is known to follow certain culture currents (German *Kulturströmungen*), which in Europe have succeeded one another presumably from the beginning of history (H. Schöffler, *Max Foerster Festsch.*, pp. 329–41). The oldest and most important of these currents is the Mediterranean one, emanating from imperial, later from papal, Rome. Its carriers were largely clerics and pilgrims (who were in fact the "tourists" of the Middle Ages). Hence the classical (and pseudo-classical), the "bookish" flavor of virtually all these stories. To them belongs the theme of the *Young Man Betrothed to a Statue* mentioned above, and the tales forming part of the cycle of Vergil the Necromancer (Krappe, *Speculum*, X, 1935, pp. 111–16). Closely connected with this Mediterranean current is the Oriental current, which may be divided into a pre-Islamic and a post-Islamic one. The diffusion centers of the former were Syria and Iran. Christianity having originated in Syria, the propagandists of the early Church carried west a vast amount of legendary material, e.g. the legends of Saint Alexis (A. Amiaud, *La légende syriaque de S. Alexis l'homme de Dieu*, Paris, 1889; Th. Nöldeke, *ZDMG*, LIII, 1899, pp. 256 ff.), of the Seven Sleepers (J. de Goeje, *De legende der Zevenslapers van Efeze*, Amsterdam, 1900; B. Heller, *REJ*, XLIX, 1904, pp. 190–230; A. Allgeier, *Oriens Christianus*, 1916, pp. 1–43 and 1917–18, pp. 33–87), of St. Gregory (Krappe, *Moyen Age*, XLVI, 1936, pp. 161–77), of the Saints Kosmas and Damien (L. Deubner, *Kosmas und Damien*, 1907), etc. The diffusion of Iranian themes is probably connected with the active intercourse between the Christian clergy of the Sassanid Empire and Byzantium. It is significant that this migration of Iranian stories (except through an Arabic medium)

ceases after the destruction of the Sassanid Empire (compare Krappe, *Moyen Age*, XXXVIII, 1928, pp. 190–207; XLIV, 1934, pp. 252–57). The post-Islamic period begins with the conquest of Syria by the Crusaders (i.e. about 1100 A.D.). It is attributable to the superior art of story-telling peculiar to the Orientals and the rich Iranian and Indian lore which had by that time reached the Near East. Because of the preponderance of French knights in the crusading armies, and the Lorraine origin of the first dynasty of the Kingdom of Jerusalem, most of these Oriental themes were carried to Europe by story-tellers of French or Belgian nationality. There is reason to believe that the tradition of the Knight of the Swan received its present form by the elaboration of a well-known Oriental theme. To the same movement is due the migration west of Byzantine material. The most notable of these themes is probably that of King Solomon and his unfaithful wife which, from Byzantium, radiated in two directions: (1) to France and thence to central Europe (Krappe, *JAFL*, LIX, 1946, pp. 309–14), (2) to Russia (A. Wesselofsky, *Salomo i Kitovras* [in Russian], St. Petersburg, 1872).

The founding of the Carolingian Empire (800 A.D.) marks the rise of the second culture current emanating in Belgium, the home of the Carolingian dynasty. Diffused in the forms of French poetic texts (*chansons de geste*) and clerical Latin prose versions, the Carolingian legend reached every part of Europe, including Scandinavia, Spain, and Germany. In Russia the epic cycle of Vladimir the Great of Kiev was modeled after it.

Coeval with the beginning of the post-Islamic Oriental current is that of the third, due largely to the Norman conquest of England (1066). It consists of Celtic (Welsh and Irish) materials and is closely connected with Arthurian legend. Its diffusion centers were Brittany and (subsequently) the British Isles. The whole fairy mythology is due to this current: prior to it the very word *fée* (in the modern sense) was unknown in Europe. An outstanding migratory legend belonging to this current is the story of Tannhäuser (Krappe, *Mitt. d. Schles. Ges. f. Volksk.*, XXXVI, 1937, pp. 106–32; *Mercure de France*, t. 284, 1938, pp. 257–75).

The great Spanish culture current, which set in with the reign of Charles V (1519 A.D.) and the Anglo-American one which starts with the opening of the 18th century, have left no traces in European folklore, not even in Belgium (Spanish until 1714) and Hanover (British until 1837), proof conclusive that the creative period of European folklore properly ends with the Middle Ages: after 1500 Folklore is replaced by Literature.

Prose saga The prose saga, in Europe, is the product of the Norwegian people and reached its apogee in Iceland. There is no trace of its existence anywhere else in Europe: its function is there taken by the Latin (in Spain the Spanish) prose of the chroniclers.

Proverb Proverbs are a spontaneous product of non-literary peoples and classes; they are apt to fall into abeyance with the progress of literacy. This explains why the proverb lore of non-European continents is so much richer than that of Europe, and why countries largely illiterate, such as Spain and (until recently) Russia, abound in proverbs as compared with other regions of the continent.

Folk Song and Ballad At the opening of the Middle Ages and down to about 1100 there existed, in various parts of the continent, isolated forms of epic-lyric poetry, notably in Iceland, Wales, Anglo-Saxon England, and the Teutonic lands of continental Europe. Of these some specimens have come down (Eddic song and epic lay). They disappear about 1100, making room for a wholly different type (with many subtypes), originating in southern France and differing from its predecessors mainly in that (1) it is based on rime, (2) is sung according to a more or less "catchy" tune, and (3) has a dance rhythm. All modern European folk songs, from the Faroe Islands to the Black Sea and from Portugal to Sweden are of this second type. Only sporadically, in relatively isolated corners, do we find older types which have kept alive, though always more or less affected by the second, the "French" type, the best example being the Lithuanian *daina*. The subject can be treated exhaustively only in connection with folk music and folk dance.

The term *ballad* is really a misnomer: the original type denoted by the word *ballata* was a purely lyric song with dance rhythm. The European ballad (Spanish *romance*, Russian *bylina*) appears to have sprung up about 1100 A.D., alike in this to the "French" type of folk song, with which it shares many features. There are, in Europe, four main bodies of ballad themes: (1) the Latin cycle (France, Cataluña, part of Castile, Portugal, and northern Italy); (2) the Teutonic cycle (Britain, Germany, Netherlands, Scandinavia including the Faroe Islands and Iceland, and parts of Bohemia and Poland); (3) Castile; and (4) the Balkans and Russia. The Latin and Teutonic cycles are closely connected, and a number of Scandinavian ballad themes are found in France, particularly in Brittany and Normandy. Within the Teutonic cycle there seems to be a closer connection between the British Isles on the one hand and the Scandinavian countries on the other. Central and southern Italy stand outside the ballad development. (On the whole subject compare W. J. Entwistle, *European Balladry*, Oxford, 1939, and the article BALLAD).

Charms, Nursery Rimes, Riddles Charms are based on the universal, though quite erroneous, belief in the power of the spoken word, a belief which found a forceful expression in as late an author as the English poet Gower (Krappe, *RLC*, XII, 1932, pp. 821–23). This folklore type is therefore one of the oldest mankind has known. A debate has been going on between the school of A. Bastian and the Diffusionists as to whether charms rose spontaneously and independently everywhere, or whether they spread from a common diffusion center, generally identified with Egypt. The difficulty of the problem can best be gauged from the fact that the Old High German *Merseburg charm* has a striking analog in the *Atharvaveda* and thus very probably goes back to the as yet undivided Aryan people. But this would not necessarily refute the diffusionist claims, since the civilization of Egypt is considerably older still. In view of the universality of this type, polygenesis is virtually certain; but this does not preclude the diffusion of certain charms from a radiation center such as Egypt, the less so because more "learned" and hence more "effective" forms are pretty certain to have crowded out, time and again, more rudimentary and unsophisticated ones. (For bibliography compare Krappe, *The Science of Folk-Lore*, 1930, p. 202.)

The subject of nursery rimes is as yet relatively unexplored: certain areas (Germany, Scotland, Scandinavia, Spain) are unusually well represented by good collections, while others (Russia and the Balkans) are blanks. Certain themes, such as *London Bridge*, are well known on the continent; the "June bug rhyme" (German *Maikäfer, fliege*, French *Hanneton, vole*) are known over a considerable part of the continent. They know linguistic frontiers as little as do other folklore types.

In the case of the riddle a rather large-looming bookish element must be reckoned with: quite a considerable number of these riddles have been preserved in Latin form, the work of medieval clerics. (Compare A. Aarne, *FFC*, 26–28, 1918.)

Custom and belief The distinctive feature of European culture as compared with the native cultures of the other continents is the profound and unparalleled social revolution which the continent has undergone since 1688, which led to the overthrow of a centuries-old feudalism and the end of which is not yet in sight. The study of custom and belief is therefore properly speaking a study of survivals. These may be roughly divided into two groups: (1) the purely indigenous items, i.e. such as go back to the neolithic age. They comprise the great mass of agricultural beliefs and practices which are, of course, as old as agriculture itself; (2) later adjuncts of a learned or bookish character, invariably of Mediterranean or Oriental origin, connected with certain relatively recent branches of agriculture such as beekeeping, horticulture, the nurture of the silkworm, further, mining and metallurgy, popular medicine, star lore, etc. The line is not always easy to draw. If, for example, most of the famous Pythagorean "tabus" turn up again among the central and north European peasantry (F. Boehm, *De Symbolis Pythagoreis*, diss., Berlin, 1905; Burnet, *Early Greek Philosophy*, 3rd ed., p. 96), we may be quite sure that the reason must not be sought in any familiarity of the peasants with Pythagoras: it was the philosopher who drew on folklore. The same holds true for much that is found in Pliny's *Natural History*. But here the problem becomes more complex: Pliny was widely known throughout the Middle Ages, and the clerics are certain to have spread some of his lore among the people. This is particularly true for items of plant and animal lore. To an even larger extent the bestiaries, all derived, more or less indirectly, from the *Physiologus*, were responsible for the diffusion of a vast amount of animal lore utterly foreign to Europe. Peasants who had never seen a lion, not even in a zoo, knew a good deal (though most of it of doubtful authenticity) of the animal, and the unicorn was as familiar to them as if they could have seen it in a zoo.

Wholly learned, i.e. imported from the Semitic Orient, is the time-reckoning of historical times and the calendar. The ancient Europeans had no calendar properly speaking, and this primitive stage has been preserved, down to modern times, among the Finno-Ugrian peoples (M. P. Nilsson, *Primitive Time-Reckoning*, Lund, 1920 [*Skrifter udgivna av humanistiska Vetenskabssaufundet i Lund*]). The same holds true, to a very large extent, of numerology, in particular the sexagesimal system of counting.

Of the non-bookish survivals, virtually every one of

them can be matched by items still forming part of the *living* belief and practice observed among the semicivilized of the four non-European continents. This fact explains the inseparability of folklore and ethnography. By the same token it is clear that there is nothing peculiarly European about these items: they are universal in the true sense of the term.

The Meaning of Folklore for European Culture The emphasis laid, in the above account, on the "survival" character of European folklore may lead to the erroneous impression that the social revolution referred to has somehow relegated folklore to a subordinate position. The fact is that European literature, art, and music are alike unthinkable without this folklore base. Without laying undue stress on the fact that the whole of medieval letters from King Alfred to Chaucer and Shakespeare and from Pope Gregory the Great to Boccaccio, Molière, and La Fontaine is essentially folklore, let us remark that the same holds true, to a lesser degree, for modern writers and artists: Walter Scott, Charles Dickens, Thomas Hardy, Pushkin, Ibsen, Hauptmann, Maeterlinck, and E. A. Poe (who was an American only by a freak accident); all have drawn on the vast body of European folklore. Schubert's work is largely based on folk melodies, as is that of Rimsky-Korsakov and Edvard Grieg. Even Richard Wagner appreciated the magic of the old folk themes such as the *Flying Dutchman, Lohengrin,* and *Tannhäuser.* Nor have the societies whose program called for the most radical changing of the old order failed in any way to appreciate the tiue function of folklore. Russia, since 1918, has shown more zeal than many another government in collecting the vast treasures of oral folklore within her borders, and the only criticism that can justly be addressed to her is her failure to make these materials accessible to the outside world.   ALEXANDER H. KRAPPE

European tales in North American Indian mythology Scores of European tales, or incidents from such, have become incorporated in modern folktale and mythology of the North American Indians. Among such tales are those of the Seven-Headed Dragon, John the Bear, Enchanted Horse, Little Poucet, The White Cat, Cinderella, the Treaty of the Oxhide Strip, and many others, as well as the Biblical tales of the flood, tower of Babel, Adam and Eve, and so forth. Sometimes these borrowed tales are told with little change or adaptation; in other instances they are so modified and so recast in native setting that they are scarcely recognizable as importations. References to European articles of dress and food, European-type dwellings and churches, the horse, automobile, and so forth, may be retained in the tales, or native articles substituted for them. Through Spanish and French raconteurs, the tribes of the northeastern United States and eastern Canada, of the western Plateau region, and of the southwest, learned many European tales quite early; also, early missionaries on the eastern Atlantic seaboard narrated Biblical tales which then spread rapidly among the tribes of the eastern United States. [EWV]

Eurystheus In Greek legend, the son of Sthenelus and Menippe; the taskmaster of Hercules in his twelve labors. Zeus having declared that the next child of the line of Perseus to be born on earth would receive the rulership of his fellows, meaning by this his son Her-

cules, Hera circumvented him by causing Alcmene to be delayed in her delivery, with the result that Eurystheus, a descendant of Perseus, became king of Tiryns. After the death of Hercules, Eurystheus was either slain by Hyllus or was captured and put to death on Alcmene's orders. Compare HERCULES.

Evadne (1) In Greek legend, the daughter of Iphis and wife of Capaneus. When her husband was killed at the siege of Thebes, Evadne threw herself on his funeral pyre: the act is unique in Greek legend, and somewhat doubtful, since the bodies of persons slain by lightning were not burned but buried where they fell.

(2) In Greek mythology, a daughter of Poseidon and mother by Apollo of Iamus whom she exposed out of shame. Compare ABANDONED CHILDREN; IAMUS.

Evander In Roman legend, a son of Hermes and a nymph of Arcadia, Themis or Nicostrate (Roman Carmenta or Tiburtis), who came from Arcadia some sixty years before the Trojan War and founded a colony at the foot of the Palatine hill: the name may mean "good man" or "strong man" and seems to be (*Evandros*) a translation of the Italian Faunus. The whole story of Evander may have resulted from an attempt to link the Roman Lupercalia, which Evander was said to have founded, with the Arcadian Lycæa, a festival of Pan as the Lupercalia was of Faunus. Evander was a giver of mild laws, and he taught the arts of peace and social life, especially writing. He sided with Æneas against the Rutuli and the Latins.

evil eye (*mal de ojo* in Spanish) This belief is nearly universal among Middle American Indians. Some persons, unwittingly, may produce malevolent effects by looking fixedly at children, or by admiring them with too much enthusiasm, or by touching them. American ethnologists have found it sound practice not to show too much interest in small children, and above all, not to touch them until they (the ethnologists) are well known to the parents. Because of the similarity to European evil-eye beliefs it seems probable that this is an introduced European trait. See OVERLOOKING. [GMF]

Excalibur or **Caliburnus** King Arthur's sword: probably from Irish, *Caladbolg,* the famous sword of Fergus in the *Táin bó Cuailgne,* forged in fairyland. Geoffrey of Monmouth says that it was made in Avalon; Malory that the sword was given to Arthur by Vivian of the land of the fairy. The first mention of the sword in the stone motif in connection with Arthur occurs in Robert de Boron's *Merlin* (12th century). Arthur succeeds after other knights have failed in drawing the sword from the anvil (stone) and so establishing his right to the kingdom. The episode that occurs in the story when Arthur is wounded in his battle with Modred, of the sword thrown into the lake and received by a hand appearing above the water, seems to be an invention of the author of *Mort Artu,* where it first appears. [MEL]

excrements swallowed The cause of the death of Kukitat, the malfeasant of Serrano (Shoshonean) Indian mythology. Kukitat was so quarrelsome and obstructive, desiring men to have eyes in the back of their heads, for instance, webbed feet, etc., that Pakrokitat, the creator, finally left this earth and went to dwell in the afterworld. Left to himself, Kukitat made so much trouble in the world that the inhabitants decided to get rid of him. Frog did this by hiding in the ocean and swallowing Kukitat's excrements. This story is dominant in both Shoshonean and Yuman mythology, whether told of creator, culture hero, or obstructive brother, and embodies both the dying god concept and belief in the power obtained over another by possession or use of his voidings. See DUAL CREATORS.

explanatory elements Explanatory elements in the great corpus of American Indian mythology could probably be numbered by the thousands. Such elements are generally concerned with natural phenomena of every sort: the origin or shape of a lake, the location of a large boulder, the existence of a spring at a certain spot, the markings on the moon; or with the physical characteristics of animals and human beings: the black tip on the coyote's tail, the snub nose of the wildcat, the flat tail of the beaver, the shyness of the fox. These explanations are, however, incidental to the myths rather than integral parts of them, since they are not used consistently as part of particular tales, and are interchangeable in various versions of the same tale, or in different tales. All tribes insert explanatory elements into at least some of their tales, but the Plateau peoples make perhaps the most extensive use of them. Myths of the Coeur d'Alene and the Southern Okanagon, for example, are loaded with explanations for natural features of the landscape and the characteristics of animate and inanimate objects. The Jicarilla Apache and other Southwestern Apache groups insert explanatory elements into their myths, for abstract qualities such as jealousy and curiosity, for ceremonial usages, for social customs, for physical states such as sleepiness, and even for laughter. [EWV]

exposure of famous persons in infancy The exposure of the hero, culture hero, or god in infancy has come to be regarded as one of the identifying marks of the true hero of folktale, myth, and legend (along with supernatural conception, precocious growth, etc.). Whether the infant is exposed for economic reasons, or reasons of illegitimacy, incestuous parentage, supernatural parentage, deformity, or to avoid the fulfilment of a prophecy, he is inevitably saved in some wonderful way, grows to beauty and heroic stature, attains wealth or power, and returns to take his rightful position in the world, to rescue or avenge someone, or fulfil a prophecy.

The Greek Peleas and Neleus, exposed twin sons of Tyro, were saved and suckled, one by a mare, the other by a bitch, and when grown rescued their mother from her cruel stepmother. Ægisthus, child of incest, was exposed by his parents, suckled by a goat, and lived to carry on the feud of his father. The illegitimate Telephus survived exposure twice, first by his mother on Mt. Parthenion, where he was suckled by a doe, and second being set adrift with her in a chest. The chest stranded in Asia Minor, and Telephus eventually became king of Mysia. The infant Perseus, son of Danaë and Zeus in the shower of gold, because of a prophecy that his mother would bear a son who would kill his grandfather, was set adrift with her in a boat. They were rescued and cared for by the king of the island of Seriphos. Later, after many adventures, Perseus killed his grandfather accidentally by a discus throw. Paris was exposed because of a dream of his mother, was suckled by a she-bear, and lived to abduct the fair Helen. The girl Atalanta was exposed because her father wanted a son, was found and nursed by a she-bear. Iamus, son of Evadne and Apollo, was exposed by his mother, nurtured by "two gray-eyed snakes," and was eventually found by his own grandfather.

The Hebrew Moses, set adrift in a rush basket, was found by Pharaoh's daughter and raised at the court of the king. The Japanese Hiruko, first-born of Izanagi and Izanami, was set adrift in a reed basket on the ocean because at the age of three he still could not walk. In later folklore he is identified with Ebisu, god of fishermen, and one of the gods of luck. See ANIMAL NURSE; BIRTH OF CORMAC; FATAL CHILDREN; TWINS.

external soul The concept (among primitive peoples and recurrent in folktale and folklore generally all over the world) that the soul can reside apart from the body, for safekeeping or other reasons. The more usual term is SEPARABLE SOUL. See BIRD SOUL; BUSH SOUL; LIFE TOKEN.

eyebrows meeting Although this is a sign of beauty in some communities, in others it is a sign that the person is a werewolf, vampire, or witch. The belief has been reported from south Russia, Greece, Bohemia, Germany, Denmark, Iceland, and India.

In England and China, the man whose eyebrows meet is lucky; the girl with meeting eyebrows, depending on the country she lives in, will have a happy marriage or none at all, or make a bad wife. [RDJ]

Eye-juggler Among the North American Indians, title of a tale of frequent occurrence in which the trickster is given the power to throw his eyes into the air and replace them; but he must not do this beyond a specified number of times. Being trickster, of course he throws them once too often and loses them; often he obtains animal eyes as substitutes. [EWV]

The motif of the man or animal who juggles with his eyes and then puts them back in their sockets, which is well known among North American Indians, was recorded only once in South America, among the Taulipang. The jaguar is induced by a crab to project his eyes. A fish swallows them. [AM]

F

Fá (Yoruban *Ifa*) In Dahomean thought, the personification of "the writings of Mawu" (the creator); hence, the personification of Fate. The term is also applied to the divining system employed by specialists of the Yoruba and adjacent peoples of West Africa, based on the permutations and combinations of double and single marks resulting from manipulating sixteen palmkernels. Derived from the Yoruban center of Ife, it is the "official" form of divining, used as one of a large number of other types which are like those widely spread in West Africa. It requires many years of intensive training to learn the thousands of tales and verses associated with the various combinations of marks on which the answers to questions brought by clients for solution are based. These specialists, called *bokonon* by the Dahomeans, or *babalawos* by the Yoruba, are important figures in the religious, social, and economic life of these people, and played a great political role in preConquest times. Because of its highly institutionalized character, the Fá cult has survived in simplified form in the New World chiefly among the Negroes of Brazil and Cuba. But other forms of divination are present everywhere. [MJH]

fable An animal tale with a moral; a short tale in which animals appear as characters, talking and acting like human beings, though usually keeping their animal traits, and having as its purpose the pointing of a moral. The fable consequently has two parts: the narrative which exemplifies the moral, and the statement of the moral often appended in the form of a proverb. The fable is a development of the animal tale, one of the earliest forms of the folktale. The animal tale in its general and earliest form is usually an explanatory story (why crows are black; why the rabbit has a short tail). The fable uses the animal tale not to explain animal characteristics, or behavior, but to inculcate a moral lesson for human beings, or to satirize the conduct of human beings. Consequently the fable is not a folk composition, but a product of sophisticated culture, though it may draw freely on folk material for its story element. And once composed a fable may be taken over by the folk and become stock oral tradition.

The oldest fables that have survived in any number are those of Greece and India; at present the best belief is that neither originated the type, but that it was Semitic in origin, spreading from the Semites east to India and west to Greece and Rome. The oldest collections existing today are those connected with the name of Æsop (fl. 600 B.C.). Æsop was a slave in Ionia, perhaps of Semitic ancestry. His fables from the beginning probably circulated orally, for there is no evidence of a written version before the 4th century (Demetrius of Phalerum). From this time many collections have been made with constant shift in the content as new fables have been added, especially from Oriental sources, and others discarded. The oldest Oriental collections are the *Panchatantra*. A portion of the *Panchatantra* in the

Middle Ages became the *Fables of Bidpai,* which from Persian through Arabic came to Latin and thence to the vernacular languages of Europe. In the Middle Ages the fable stories became a part of floating tradition, widely used in sermon stories and in the exempla books. The fable has its place in modern literature. In English Chaucer, Henryson, Lydgate, Dryden, and Gay have all successfully told the old stories. France has the greatest of all modern writers of fable in La Fontaine. Lessing, in Germany, is the author of an excellent collection of fables and also of a valuable monograph on the history and literary value of the fable.

Some of the most famous fables are: The Country Mouse and the City Mouse; Wren Elected as King of the Birds; Crane Pulls Bone from Wolf's Throat; Fox and the Grapes; Chanticleer and the Fox; Mouse Frees Lion by Gnawing Net.

The fable owes more to the animal tale than form and content. Its compression, pithiness, and dramatic nature must likewise be a carry-over from the earlier type. Characterization and character types in the fables are also frequently directly derived from the animal tale. For example, the animal tale had already established the fox as sly, the wolf as greedy, the lion as courageous and dignified. [MEL]

Fables of Bidpai The name under which the collection of beast fables from the *Panchatantra* became known in Europe. The collection was ascribed to Bidpa or Bidbah, a scholar at the court of an Indian prince who produced it in order to reform an evil king. The French *Fables de Pilpay* is a translation of the *Kalilah wa Dimnah,* the Arabic version of the Pahlavi *Panchatantra.*

fabliau A short narrative in verse of a humorous, satiric, or burlesque character, written in a gay and rollicking style. It flourished in France from the 12th to the 14th century. From France the type spread to other parts of Europe. Some few fabliaux, notably *Dame Siriz,* are found in English. Several of Chaucer's *Canterbury Tales* told by the "lewd sots" are fabliaux; some of the fabliau stories are caught up in the English ballads. The satire in the fabliaux is directed mainly against women, the clergy, and marriage. The fabliaux are usually products of sophisticated writers, basing their stories on contemporary life and manners; yet occasionally they rework stories drawn from folklore and floating legend. [MEL]

As a type of song the fabliaux were designed purely for entertainment. They dealt chiefly with the stock situations and characters of the marital triangle—the gullible husband, the scheming, faithless wife, and the popinjay lover. A typical story is that of *The Dog in the Closet,* of Oriental origin, in which the husband is gulled by the substitution of a dog for the lover locked in the closet. [TCB]

Face of Glory The lion face of Kīrttimukha, which survived his self-consumption: worshipped in Hindu religion as a symbol of protective wrath.

fado The typical song of Portuguese cities, combining both folk and popular elements, dealing with love, unkind fate, nostalgia, despair, the careers of notorious men and women, and sung to the music of two guitars, one for rhythm and the other for melody and accompanying figures. The origin of the type is unknown, its relationship to the peasant folk song of Portugal unclear. Similarities are pointed out to songs of Moorish origin, to sailor songs, and to certain peasant songs sung on St. John's Eve. Earlier music types, the *lundum* and the *modinha*, both song and dance tunes, are cited as ancestors of the fado. The word fado was first used in Portugal in the 1830's, but was known earlier in Brazil, and the songs show some indications of African derivation, whether directly from the trading areas of the African coast or indirectly from Brazil. The fado singer makes use of certain mannerisms and variations of timbre not unlike those used in the blues—a rough, throaty tone, a free and flexible rhythm above the measured accompaniment, and an intimate, often emotional style. There are fados about fados, as there are blues about the blues. The form is a living one, adding new verses all the time, even though the tunes are old—older than any of the words. A favorite subject is the loves and scandals of Severa, the most famous of the *fadistas* (fado singers). University students have adopted the songs and made of them a more lyric expression.

faet fiaḋa Literally, the appearance of a wild animal: the magic power or spell used by the ancient Irish Tuatha Dé Danann and the early druids to make themselves invisible. It was given by Manannán to the Tuatha Dé Danann after their defeats by the Milesians. There is a story included in the Old Irish Mythological cycle in which Eithne, a foster daughter of Angus, lost the faeṫ fiaḋa. When one Finnbarr insulted her, an angel suddenly became her guardian spirit, and after that she lost kinship with the Tuatha Dé Danann and the power of the faeṫ fiaḋa, either to become invisible herself or to see others who were.

The mantle of this power later fell upon the early Irish Christian saints, and it is still mentioned as a living thing in the Gaelic West Highlands. Patrick used the power to turn himself and his companion, Benen, into wild deer on their way to Tara to spread the Christian faith. Enemies lay in wait to stop them, but all they saw pass was a deer with a fawn. Patrick's famous hymn, *The Deer's Cry*, sung to effect the safe passing was a survival of the old faeṫ fiaḋa.

Fafnir or **Fafner** In Teutonic mythology, son of the dwarf king, Hreidmar; brother of Otter and Regin. When Odin, Hœnir, and Loki paid their ransom for killing Otter, Fafnir killed his father for the gold, refusing to share it with Regin. He removed the treasure to Gnitaheid, but it gave him no joy, and he became a wingless dragon from brooding. Regin persuaded Sigurd to slay Fafnir, which he did by digging a trench, and thrusting his sword into the dragon's heart as it passed overhead. But when he learned that Regin intended to kill him, he killed Regin too, and kept the gold, thus carrying on the curse of Andvari. In Wagner's *Ring of the Nibelung,* Mime and Alberich are the brothers, plotting Fafnir's death.

Fair Annie A Scottish ballad (Child #62), known in Danish, Swedish, Dutch, and German versions, and English: the ballads may come from a Low German original, stemming from the same source as Marie de France's *Lai del Fresne (The Lay of the Ash-tree),* all of which tell essentially the same story. The ballad is also known in English as *Burd Helen, Lady Jane,* etc. In the Child A text, Fair Annie, the mother of his seven sons, is told by Lord Thomas that he will have another woman as his wife, for Fair Annie has no lands and his bride-to-be is rich. Fair Annie volunteers to be hostess at the reception and feast. She does so well that the new bride takes a liking to her. When the newlyweds retire, Annie lies on her lonely couch weeping, and the bride comes out to speak with her. The two discover that they are sisters; Annie is a long-ago-abducted lady and not a housekeeper as the bride thought her. The bride leaves for home a maiden.

Fair Charlotte The most popular title of the American ballad YOUNG CHARLOTTE.

Fair Flower of Northumberland An English-Scottish border ballad (Child #9), used by Thomas Deloney in his novel, *Jack of Newberie* (1597), and of which portions correspond to portions of other northern European ballads. The story is that of the ungrateful knight. This knight, freed from his prison by the daughter of his jailer, takes her with him through peril and hardship, promising to marry her when they are safe. But once he is assured of his freedom he abandons her, laughing in her face and telling her he already has a wife and family.

Fair Helen of Kirkconnell Title of a ballad collected in Scott's *Border Minstrelsy,* included in Vol. II of the first edition of Child's *English and Scottish Popular Ballads* (1858), but dropped by Child in the third edition (one of 115 ballads so excluded) because he considered it a lyric without narrative content. The ballad is the lament of a lover for his Helen, who died to save him. Though he has hunted down his foe and "hacked him in pieces sma'," still he is unhappy and will be until he rejoins his Helen.

Fair Janet Title of a Scottish popular ballad (Child #64) in which Janet gives birth to her lover's child just preceding the marriage with an old French lord forced upon her by her father. Willie, the lover, hastens to carry his newborn son to his mother, who takes the child from his arms with love and speeds him back to comfort Janet. Janet is rushed into dressing for the wedding despite her pleas of illness and pain. Gowned in red she rides a white horse to the church, having chosen Willie to lead it through the town for her. At the celebration Janet refuses to dance with all who ask her, including the old French lord, until Willie asks "Bride, will ye dance wi me?/ "Aye, by my soth, and that I will/ Gin my back should break in three." Janet danced through the dance with her lover "but thrice" and fell dead at Willie's feet. The next day they were buried, one in Marie's kirk, "The tither in Marie's quire./ Out of the tane there grew a birk,/ And the tither a bonny brier." Child points to parallels of this ballad in Scandinavian, German, and Breton balladry.

Fair Margaret and Sweet William Title of an English and Scottish popular ballad (Child #74) in which William loves Margaret but marries another. Margaret sees from her window the bridal train en route to the church. "She went out from her bower alive/ But never so more came there." In the dead of night came "Margaret's grimly ghost/ And stood at William's feet." She asks him how he likes his bed and the new brown bride. "Better I like that fair lady/ That stands at my bed feet." In the morning William runs to Margaret's home, kisses the fair corpse in the winding sheet, and dies beside her. "Fair Margaret died for pure true love,/ Sweet William died for sorrow." They were buried in the chancels of the church, Margaret in the lower, William in the higher. "Out of her breast there sprung a rose/ And out of his a brier."

This was an extremely popular broadside ballad in England in the 17th century. It appears also in *Percy's Reliques* in the 18th century, and the famous lines about the grimly ghost were quoted in Beaumont and Fletcher's *Knight of the Burning Pestle*. It is the source of David Mallet's ornate *William and Margaret* (c. 1724).

fairy A term loosely used to denote a type of supernatural being, usually invisible, sometimes benevolent and helpful, sometimes evil and dangerous, sometimes just mischievous and whimsical, dwelling on the earth in close contact with man. The word *fairy* from Late Latin *fata* from Latin *fatum* (fate) meant in Middle English 1) enchantment; 2) a land where enchanted beings dwelt; 3) the collective inhabitants of such a land: these latter should properly be called *fays* (compare French *fée*).

The creatures referred to as fays, fées, fairies in Romance languages and English are by no means confined to West European culture. Under one name or another they are found all over the world; they are more frequently met with in Europe and Asia, less frequently met with in America and Africa. The fairy concept seems to belong to a rather advanced stage of culture.

The fairy has the same general characteristics wherever he is found. He is usually diminutive, often very small but sometimes pygmylike. He can become invisible at will, often by putting on a magical cap. He usually lives underground in a burrow or under a hill, or in a heap of stones. Usually he is clothed in green; sometimes his skin and hair are green. White is also associated with fairies, and frequently solitary fairies are clothed in brown or gray. Fairies are rarely harmful; even when they abduct children they do not harm them. If fairies are mistreated, they retaliate by burning houses, despoiling crops. They delight in playing pranks: milking cows in the fields, soiling clothes on the line, appropriating food, curdling milk. But they are helpful too, for they often take food and money to the poor, give toys to children, work countermagic to break spells laid by witches.

Many theories have been advanced to account for the origin of the concept of the fairy. According to one, the fairy concept grows out of folk memories of the original inhabitants of a country conquered by the present people. Remnants of the conquered people would linger on in mountain and cave preying on their conquerors.

They would necessarily have to operate at night and in a furtive manner, all of which might lead to their being exaggerated into the strange and supernatural. A second theory holds that fairies are discarded gods or heroes reduced in stature and importance as an old set of gods gives way to a new. So Queen Medb, a heroine of Irish epic, in a later age becomes a queen of fairyland. A third theory holds that the fairy are a personification of the old primitive spirits of nature. Primitive man believed that every object was endowed with a spiritual nature as well as a physical. A tree spirit, according to this theory, in a later age would be anthropomorphized into a dryad, a water spirit into an undine, the spirit of a hill into the *side* dwelling in the *sid* or hill. A fourth theory accounts for fairies as spirits of the dead, or as the dead themselves, on the grounds that fairies are commonly found underground, often in a barrow, that they must rush back to their habitations at cockcrow (as must revenants and ghosts), that a mortal eating their food cannot return to the mortal world, that fairylands resemble the abode of the dead as pictured by many people, that to get to the abode of the fairies (and the dead) one must sometimes cross a river. With the probable exception of the first, these theories may explain varying aspects of the fairy and of fairyland. No one of them is sufficient to account for all.

Fairies may be divided into two large groups: 1) Those belonging to the fairy "race" or "nation" living in fairyland in an organized society of their own. Such groups are the people of the *side*, i.e. people of the hills, in Ireland, the dwarfs of the Germanic countries. 2) The individual fairies associated with a place, or occupation, or household, such as the undine, a fairy who lives in a spring or stream, or the leprechaun, who is a shoemaker.

Fairyland, populated in great numbers, is like the land of the dead. It is ruled over by a king and queen, but generally the queen is dominant. In fairyland there is no death, no age, no sickness, no ugliness. Time is, as it is to the dead, non-existent. A mortal in Ireland taken to fairyland passes 900 years thinking it but one night. Frequently the fairy come out of fairyland to wander the earth and mingle in the affairs of men. Their social organization is, of course, like that of man. They live in fairy houses, furnished lavishly with gold and silver. They eat great banquets of rich and delicious food. Much time is spent in music and dancing. Although there is no death in fairyland there is evidently birth, for stories abound of fairy children, of fairy-search for mortal women to nurse them, of abductions of mortal midwives to attend fairy births. The fairies have two domestic animals, the horse and the dog. Often they ride in procession on their white horses, whose manes are braided and hung with silver bells that tinkle as they move. And the fairy dogs run alongside. Fairyland and the life of the fairies is in general an untheological heaven.

The second group of fairies, made up of individuals, is much more varied in nature and behavior. One of the most important of these is the household familiar, such as the Billy Blin of the Scottish ballads. The household familiar (dwarf, kobold, nis, brownie, billy) attaches himself to a human household. He often sleeps on the hearth and comes and goes by way of the chimney. He is generally helpful, though playful and mischievous. He reveals the binding spell and how to break it when the lady of the house cannot deliver her child; he protects the master against deception on the part of his wife; he makes butter come in the churn, and the brew to work, the dough to rise. He also often sweeps the floor, washes the dishes, and lays the fire. But he must be treated kindly, favored with a bowl or cup of milk set out on a stone, and the household must put up with his prankish ways. He is about the size of a year-old child, but often has the face of an old man with a long beard, and usually wears a jaunty little cap. He may well owe his origin to the old belief in ancestral gods.

Other fairies of the second type are associated with particular places. The salamander (fairy) lives in fire, the undine in water, the buccas in mines. Others are associated with trees, air, cairns, shoemaking, tinsmithing, blacksmithing. There is, as one would expect, much more variation in personality and action of the individual fairies. Stories about them are, consequently, varied, ranging from the poetic and dramatic like the story of *Undine* to the slapstick anecdotes of brownies and nixies.

Most fairylore and fairy story has to do with the relations of fairies to mortals. The common types are: 1) Fairies assist mortals; 2) Fairies harm mortals; 3) Fairies abduct mortals for special purposes; 4) Changelings; 5) Mortal visits to fairyland; 6) Fairy mistress or lover.

Among all people accounts abound of fairies assisting human beings in a wide variety of ways. We have seen above that the household familiar is a very helpful fellow in the house. But fairies also help in the field with planting, threshing, wood-cutting, and the like. A Jutland peasant, trying in vain to free his horse stuck in the mud, suddenly is surrounded by fairy folk who easily free the animal. In France a fairy rescues a lady whose jealous husband had imprisoned her. Often fairies give gifts of gold, of vessels that always remain full of food, or of grain, gifts of cheese that never diminishes no matter how much is eaten, or of beautiful finely woven gossamer cloth.

Stories likewise abound of fairies harming man. Constantly they appropriate growing crops: grain, peas, beans (often out of sheer prankishness they shell the beans on the vine leaving the pods intact). They milk animals in the field, ride horses at night in the pasture. In the house they blow out the candles, knock pans off the shelves, roll up the mats on the floor, send gusts of smoke down the chimney, prevent bread from rising. In the mines they pelt workmen with pebbles as they work. Sometimes the antics are just exuberance of spirits, but often they are by way of punishing a mortal for harm done to one of them, or for churlishness. To punish such a one the fairy fastens himself on the household and nothing can dislodge him. There are many stories like the German one in which a man decides to move to free himself from an obnoxious fairy only to discover as he is about to drive away that the little fellow had hidden himself in the churn and so was also blithely on his way to the new dwelling. (See BOGGART'S FLITTING.)

Fairies often abduct mortals, either conveying them bodily to fairyland or by bespelling them and luring them there. Many believe that the fairies must pay a yearly tribute to the lords of hell by sending some of their number there each year. For this purpose they are thought to abduct mortals, especially children. Tam Lin, a mortal abducted by the fairies in the Scotch ballad, was to be so sacrificed but his sweetheart succeeded in rescuing him. This belief may be due to the legend that fairies are the pre-Adamite inhabitants of the earth or that they are fallen angels. (Compare too the common European story that fairies are the descendants of children of Adam and of Eve by malignant spirits before they cohabited with one another.) Women, too, are abducted, especially mothers with small children, for human milk is much prized by the fairy. Midwives are abducted temporarily to help the fairy mothers at time of childbirth. Sometimes they are blindfolded and led to the fairy realm and after their work is done led blindfolded away. Always they are handsomely rewarded.

There are many dramatic accounts of mortals visiting fairyland by accident or by invitation of the fairy folk. Thomas the Rymer went with the queen of the fairies over the river to fairyland and, abstaining from eating any food, he was able to return again to Huntly Bank. There exist many analogs to the Scotch story of the two boys who one night saw a light shining from a crevice in the rocks. On looking in they saw a large company of fairies dancing. One brother went in and joined the throng. When he had not returned in a year, his brother, placing a cross made of mountain ash in his shirt, went into the hill where he found his brother still dancing away. Protected by the charm he was able to bring his brother safely out; the brother thought that he had been dancing but a few minutes. Frequently found are accounts of mortals lured away by fairy music. Hearing the sweet, insistent music of the fairy musicians, they must follow it even against their wills often to fairyland itself. Occasionally a fairy invites a mortal to visit the land under the hill. A Germanic tale tells of a peasant who was so favored. During the tour of the fairy region, he noticed crocks overturned on the shelves. Asking why they were kept so, he was told that they imprisoned souls of drowned human beings. Usually a mortal going to fairyland had to have his eyes anointed by fairy ointment before he could see anything; occasionally his host forgot to remove the ointment before he returned and so forever after he could see the fairies wherever they might be.

The most dramatic and poetic of all fairy stories are the fairy-mistress or lover stories. Such stories of the union of a mortal and a fairy are part of the general story pattern of the love of a mortal and a supernatural being. These stories follow a fixed pattern: 1) A mortal loves a supernatural being; 2) the supernatural being consents to marry the mortal subject to one condition, for example, he must not see her at certain times; 3) he breaks the tabu and loses her; 4) he then tries to recover her and sometimes succeeds. A Germanic story tells of a young man who fell in love with a water fairy. She agreed to become his wife but told him that should he strike her, she would disappear forever. They lived very happily for many years until one day he threw a clod of earth at the horse and accidentally struck his wife. Instantly she disappeared never to be seen again. The German story of the *Knight of Staufenburg,* the lais of *Launfal* and of *Graelent,* the story of Oisín and the queen of fairyland, *Melusina, Sir Orfeo* are a few of the finest of the fairy-mistress stories in European literature.

In the fairy-mistress stories we often meet the complication of the mortal wedded to a fairy, finally wishing to return to earth, being permitted to do so, only to discover that he had been in fairyland a long, long time and that as soon as he returned the weight of his years fell upon him. Such stories usually end with the hero becoming an old man, and disintegrating into a pile of dust. Western Europe saw in the classical Orpheus story a close analog to the fairy-lover theme and made that story over into the charming romance *Sir Orfeo* in which Heurodys is carried away by a fairy lover. Sir Orfeo, the mortal husband, disguised as a harper, penetrates into fairyland and succeeds in securing her return.

Many fairy stories and legends have to do with changelings. Newborn infants are often snatched away and fairy babies left in their places. Several explanations are given: one that the fairy folk want their children suckled by mortal women, another that they are seeking mortal children to sacrifice to the lords of hell. (Such stories are probably nothing other than explanatory stories to account for the abnormal appearance or abnormal behavior of the human child by saying that it was a changeling). Usually the fairy child sooner or later rejoins its own folk in fairyland. A typical tale is the mid-European story of the family who rushed out one night to the stable to see why the animals were making a disturbance. When they returned they found their baby gone and an ill-formed, big-headed, lustily howling brat in its place. The mother tried to care for the changeling but it scratched her and bit her breasts and caused so much confusion that finally the people of the house put it in the oven. Whereupon the fairy mother appeared, put down the mortal child, alive and well, and snatched up her own with the words: "I've treated your child better than you have treated mine." All sorts of methods were used to keep children from being abducted by the fairy. Certain objects, scissors, knives, or nails, plants like rowan and garlic, charms like the cross, the Bible, or holy water placed near the child were believed to be effective. A few stories tell of changelings growing up among mortals; usually they are deformed in some way, but always they are beautiful of face; often they are endowed with some extraordinary ability, such as being able to see in the dark or being able to make the strange, seductive fairy music.

The fairy concept in English comes as a blending of the Germanic dwarf-elf type and the Celtic people of the hills, the *síde.* The household familiar in English has a Germanic background; the idea of the communal fairies is Celtic. The fairy tradition in English literature really begins with the translation of the French romance of *Huon of Bordeaux* in late medieval times and with the fairy lore in the Arthurian stories. It was from the romance, however, that the concept of an organized fairy world came in with the introduction of Oberon (Germanic Alberich), Cephalonia of the Isles, and all the magic background of fairyland. From this tradition came the fairies of Spenser and Shakespeare.

MacEdward Leach

fairy food The food of fairyland is usually described as exotic and delicious; wonderful feasts were held there; but the only human foods mentioned in the early descriptions were apples or wine. General is the belief that a mortal who partakes of the food of fairyland can never return to his earthly home. Even today in Celtic countries there are stories of children enticed into the fairy mounds who have been saved just in the nick of time from eating the dainties offered them, by a woman who followed them. But there are also contemporary Irish stories of certain people, who, having partaken of a bit of mouse-soup within the fairy hill, were forever after gifted with the power to see the fairies.

It is now generally conceded that fairies eat and drink much the same as human beings. They are known to eat berries and nuts, known to sow crops, engage in haymaking, plowing, harvesting, etc., known to beg, borrow, or steal milk, butter, flour, meal, corn, and whisky. A little food is often left out in the kitchen for them overnight, and sometimes a little tobacco. But the food must have no salt in it. Fairies hate salt. In Brittany a table is spread in the birthroom for the fairies who always attend a human birth. There are many well-known stories of a fairy woman coming to a human neighbor to borrow butter for a wedding or butter to hèal a burned child. Whatever they borrow is always paid back. A refusal is also always paid back with malice and often fatal results.

Fairies are especially fond of milk. In Ireland the first drops of milk from a cow are let fall on the ground for the fairies. Any milk left undrunk outdoors, as by workers in the fields or people picnicking, is also poured on the ground for the fairies; and no milk accidentally spilled should ever be begrudged them. Fairies often milk the farmers' cows, and it is said that the one chosen to be milked by fairies is always free from disease. Some people even leave one cow of a herd unmilked for their use. Others, however, sometimes attribute the sudden death or gradual sickening of a cow to its being milked by the fairies. Fairies have been known to steal cows, or to make off with the best cow at a fair.

fairy rings or **circles** Dark green circles in the turf of meadow, lawn, or field, caused by a certain fungus (*Marasmius oreades*). Some say they are caused by a foal being born on the spot; but they are popularly believed to be the dancing-places of the fairies. Often they are surrounded by a ring of mushrooms. It is very wrong to interfere with such a place in any way, on pain of being struck blind or lame.

fairy tale When the writer in English attempts to translate the German *Märchen* or the Swedish *saga,* he has usually resorted to the term "fairy tale." In many ways this is an unfortunate word since not more than a small number of such stories have to do with fairies. As a matter of fact, most tales about fairies are actually traditions and relate real beliefs. Nevertheless, the term is well established and widely accepted.

A considerable number of the tales in Grimm's collection are fairy tales of this kind. Such stories as *Snow White, Cinderella, Cupid and Psyche,* and the *Black and White Bride* illustrate their characteristic qualities. These stories are usually located in a never-

never land where all kinds of supernatural events occur. The characters are usually not named, but are referred to as a certain "king and queen" and "the youngest daughter." Sometimes very common names such as Jack and Mary Ann may be used, but there is no thought of identifying the characters any further. The fairy tale is full of commonplace expressions and motifs which tend to be used in other tales and to be a part of the general style of the story-teller.

There is a difference in the style of fairy tales from country to country even when the same series of motifs is used. But these differences are much less striking than the common style used in tales of this kind everywhere.

Just where and how this peculiar fairy-tale style developed has never been determined. Something of it is found as far back as the Egyptian collection which comes to us from the thirteenth century before Christ, and reflections of this style are found in such literary reworkings of fairy tales as the Apocryphal *Book of Tobit* and the *Cupid and Psyche* of Apuleius. It has been suggested that this style is a part of the Indo-European heritage, but it is found in the tales of many non-European peoples, so that such a position is hard to establish.

Tales in many ways analogous to the European and Asiatic fairy tales are found among primitive peoples, and many of the Western fairy tales have been borrowed by other parts of the world. Comparative study of these tales, therefore, takes the investigator outside the orbit of the particular fairy-tale style and shows that the style is not a necessary part of the tradition.

The European fairy tales have been classified and the collections of them from many countries have been thoroughly listed. It is customary to include not only such fairy tales as several already mentioned, but also anonymous anecdotes, and cumulative tales such as the *House that Jack Built*. The animal tales are also a part of these classifications.

Students of the fairy tale have interested themselves in several aspects: (a) the origin and dissemination of particular tales (see HISTORIC-GEOGRAPHIC METHOD); (b) the style of fairy tales according to the country or state of society where they are told; and (c) the part that fairy tales play among the people where they are told.

In the past many writers have also interested themselves in such questions as what do fairy tales mean, and what is the relation of fairy tales and myths, but these questions seem so intangible that most modern scholars have ceased to attempt an answer.

STITH THOMPSON

fairy wind The *síde gaoite* or *gaot síde* of Irish folklore, or *séideán síde*, the fairy blast: a sudden blast or gust of wind, or whirlwind, believed to be caused by the fairies. Sometimes it is said to be caused by the passing of the fairy host; sometimes they are said to be *in* it; sometimes it is just the stir caused by fairies at work. A little whirl of wind in the hayfield is often said to be the fairies helping with the work. When this happens the farmers believe it is a sign of good weather for the haying. Sometimes the sudden gust of fairy wind and a darkening of the sky accompanies the passing of a soul out of this world. The fairy wind is often greatly feared, for such winds sometimes cause harm to people or cattle, such as injuries to the eye, making them fall, etc.; sometimes people say, "Oh, they are coming for me!" People seeking to dig up fairy treasure are often stopped by a terrific gale of wind. There is a famous story about a musician who learned to play the fairy music. Once when he was so bold as to play some of the tunes at a country dance, he was whisked away suddenly by a blast of fairy wind. It is well known that a fairy blast will lift the roof off a house when certain doors are opened, the opening of which is known to inconvenience the fairies.

Faithful John Title and hero of a well known European folktale (Grimm #6), the most familiar usage of the famous Eurasian faithful servitor motif (P361 ff.; Type 615). An old king on his death bed entrusts his young son to a tried and faithful servant, warning him not to let the prince enter a certain locked room or see the portrait therein, lest perils befall. The prince eventually does see the portait, falls in love with the princess depicted, and despite warning and dissuasion determines to seek her. Faithful John arranges for the journey and embarks with the prince in a fine ship laden with golden objects. In the strange country he beguiles the princess on board with golden trinkets and, while she is admiring the treasure cargo, sets sail for home. The prince declares his love and the girl easily consents to be his bride.

As the ship sails home, Faithful John overhears three ravens discussing the perils to befall the prince: a horse which will fly away with him, a gorgeous (but poisoned) bridal robe, a snake to kill the bride in the bridal bed (or she will swoon and not recover unless three drops of blood are taken from her breast). Moreover, whoever learns these perils and tells them will be turned to stone from head to foot.

All happens as the birds predict: the beautiful horse meets the ship, but Faithful John kills it before the prince can mount; the gorgeous robe is offered, but Faithful John snatches and burns it. These two acts the young prince accepts with blind confidence, but when Faithful John bends over the princess in bed to kill the snake (or endeavors to take three drops of blood from her breast when she swoons) his act is misunderstood, and he is condemned to death for betraying his master. At the moment of execution Faithful John tells the whole story and is turned to stone. The broken-hearted King and Queen keep the statue in the palace for years, until one day they learn that the blood of their two children will restore the faithful servant. Gladly they sacrifice the children, and smear the statue with their blood; Faithful John comes to life, claps the two heads back on the children, who continue their play as if uninterrupted.

The faithful servitor motif is common all over Europe, and is thought to have migrated westward from India some 2000 years ago. It occurs in the *Kathā Sarit Sāgara* in the "Story of the Brāhman Vīravara," who sacrificed his son to save the life of his king (P361.3). The motif occurs also in various European stories, including the tale of the devoted Henry who bound his heart with iron bands (F875) to keep it from breaking when his master was bewitched (see FROG PRINCE) and of the servant who sent his own child to the executioner to save the hero (K512.2.2). It is almost always tied up with the belief in the healing and life-giving powers of blood, and is closely related to the OLD DOG and TWO FRIENDS motifs. See PETRIFACTION; TWO BROTHERS.

faixes Literally, sashes: a Spanish religious dance of Malda, province of Lérida, performed in honor of San Macario on January 2. All the dancers (at least 24 in number) are married men. While executing various longways figures in front of the church, each holds a sash in his right hand. During the processional entry into the church they are joined by these sashes in a long line; during their exit they dip under them one by one. In the plaza they continue their figure dance. [GPK]

Fakir and his Jar of Butter One of the tales of the *Arabian Nights* (Burton ix: 40 f.) illustrating the air-castles motif (J2060 f.) or counting one's chickens before they are hatched (Type 1430). The fakir raises his staff in anger during the dream-story he is inventing and smashes the jar of butter that formed the foundation of his imaginary fortunes. The story is also told in "The Barber's Tale of his Fifth Brother" (*ibid*. i: 335 ff.) where the smashed material is glassware.

fallen angels Both Mohammedan and Hebraic tradition contain certain angels fallen from grace. The Mohammedan angels, Hārūt and Mārūt, were impatient with sinful man, so the Lord placed them on earth in human form for a time. The temptations were too much for them, and they succumbed and were banished from Heaven. They remained on earth and taught man witchcraft and astrology. In *Genesis* vi, 4, the sons of God (angels) lusted after the daughters of man and two hundred of them banded together on Mt. Hermon and descended to earth where they begat giants (demons). Some claim these demons were captured and chained in the bowels of the earth and God sent the Deluge to finish them. Others believe they are still loose in the world. Another story says that some of the angels, through pride, refused to pay honor to Adam who was wrought in the image of God, and were banished.

Much Christian dogma refuses to accept the intermarriage of spirits (angels) and man, but it was often accepted in popular belief. While Hebraic tradition links fallen angels with their demonology, more common Christian belief links them with the fairies, elves, etc. During medieval times it was believed that the angels remained where they fell, some in the upper air, others in the lower air, some on the earth, some in the water, or below the earth, and in caves and catacombs. Or they fell into the sky, the earth, the water, the woods, and Hell. Many claim fallen angels were not entirely evil. The angel Oliver was just in his judgments, and while the majority preferred Hell, some angels would do anything in their power to regain their places in Heaven. They are variously identified as Satan, Lucifer, Belial, the Devil, Semjâzâ, Azâzêl, Samael, and Mastêmâ.

fall from tree toilet The motif of a number of Apache Indian folktales (Chiricahua, Mescalero, and Jicarilla) typical of Apache humor and love of the practical joke. It consists merely of getting the dupe to venture too far out towards the end of a limb so that he falls to the ground. The Chiricahua story of how Goldfinch

gets rid of Coyote is typical. One day Coyote climbs a tree and finds Goldfinch sitting on her nest. He exclaims how beautiful the nest is, but where is the toilet? Goldfinch points out a little branch on the end of a long limb. When Coyote walks out there to see, the branch will not hold and he falls to the ground. Thus Goldfinch is rid of him.

false beauty doctor A world-wide folktale motif, well known in the Baltic countries, in Africa, in Indonesia, and especially common among North American Indians: closely related to the false curing and false strengthening incidents (Types 1134, 1136). The hero or heroine (sometimes the trickster) pretends to make the villain of the story (monster, giant, ogre, witch, etc.) or the dupe beautiful (K1013) or strong (K1012) with the result that the deceived one is injured or killed.

Typical is the North American Kutenai Indian story in which a young girl is about to be killed by a giant. The giant asks how he can become as beautiful as she is. She tells him that to become so he must be baked in an oven. He submits to the treatment and is roasted to death. In a Tsimshian Indian story Mink abducts a woman and takes her to live with him in his den. In the spring he sees the Indians on the river in their canoes and admires the white bone ornaments in their ears and noses. The woman encourages Mink to let her perforate his ears so that he too may wear the ornaments which signify high rank. She drives a spruce branch through his ears into the ground, and while he is thus helplessly pinned she kills him. In an Alaska Eskimo story a jealous wife "beautifies" the three girls whom her husband admires by thrusting their heads in boiling oil.

A Sia Indian folktale tells how Coyote admires the spots on Deer's fawns, and asks how she made her children so beautiful. Deer says she did it with cedar fire: every time a spark struck one of the children it made a spot. Coyote runs home, puts his children in a cave in front of which he builds a cedar fire. The children cry out with the heat, but Coyote tells them to wait a little, they will soon be beautiful. When the fire burns out he finds his children dead. See CHILD ABDUCTED BY CANNIBAL.

False Faces Eastern North American term for (a) Eastern Woodlands Indian carved wooden masks, (b) the performers who wore these masks in a ceremony the function of which was to protect against sickness. Among the Iroquois tribes a definite False Face Society existed; the Shawnee, Delaware, and possibly other Algonquian tribes gave False Face performances, but participants in such were not organized in a society. False Face performers were men who dressed in a bearskin suit, wore wooden masks, used a cane and carried tortoise-shell rattles. They did not speak, and were accompanied on their round of the houses in a village by the Shuck Faces—i.e. male clowns who wore masks made of braided corn husks. These clowns escorted the False Faces, and collected offerings of tobacco for them. The False Face performers, as part of their cleansing observances, smeared dung on their hands and stroked or shook hands with the inmates of the houses they visited. The appearance of False Faces and Shuck Faces in a village, or following a dance, while appreciated by adults as protection of the village against disease, terrified children and dogs. The Iroquois, notable for their wooden masks of many varieties, carved their false-face masks from the living tree, roughing out the face and then chopping it in a block from the tree to finish it. Thus the tree was never killed. The masks themselves were oval-shaped with narrow slits for eye-holes. Only men who were ritually clean could perform in the False Face ceremony; if not "clean" at the time a performer would see fully clothed persons as nude. [EWV]

false or **substituted bride** A very widespread folktale motif (K1911 ff.) in which a beautiful young bride-to-be is ousted by an ugly or treacherous impostor who foists herself off on the unsuspecting husband.

In some versions the servant girl who accompanies the bride gets rid of her en route to the wedding, throws her in a river or pushes her into a well (where she thrives in the care of an underworld queen until the right moment for vindication and retribution arrives). Sometimes a stepsister, often with the connivance of the stepmother, ousts the bride of a prince or king, gets rid of her in some fashion (such as transforming her into an animal, throwing her into a river, or reducing her to menial station), and marries the king herself. Sometimes the substitution is not effected until the girl gives birth to her first child, when both are disposed of, and the ugly stepsister takes on the beautiful wife's role, with no questions asked. The substitution is always eventually revealed, either by an animal, an old woman, frequently by a song, sometimes by the mother's repeated return to suckle her child, or to sleep with her husband. In all cases the true bride (and/or her child) comes into her own and the treacherous impostor is killed.

MacCulloch in his *Childhood of Fiction* cites a Basuto story in which a young girl, en route to her sister's village to become co-wife to her sister's husband, has been warned by her mother not to look back. She cannot resist the temptation, does look back, and sees a witch who effects an exchange of garments with her. When they arrive at the village the witch passes herself off as the girl and marries the husband. The girl is sent daily into the fields where she sings over and over the story of her betrayal and sorrow. An old woman, overhearing, brings the husband to listen. He kills the witch and marries the girl. The witch keeps returning to pester the girl, in the form of a pumpkin, a thistle, a pumpkin seed, etc. Finally the pumpkin seed bites the baby, the husband grinds it to bits, and burns it up.

In a Bushman story the wife of a certain chief is changed into a lioness by Hyena via the medium of poisoned ants' eggs. Hyena then goes into the house in the role of wife. Several times the younger sister takes the woman's child out into the reeds to be suckled by its mother, until at last the mother warns her not to bring the child again, because she feels the lion's nature becoming dominant. The Hyena impostor is recognized but escapes. In leaving, however, she steps in the fire and burns her foot. This is why Hyena limps today.

In a Jamaica Negro story the wife, who is traveling the world seeking a lost husband, reveals to a laundry-woman how to wash out the three indelible drops of blood from his shirt. The man has said that he will marry the woman who can wash out the stains. The wife is the only one who knows how, or who knows the man's true name. The laundrywoman claims the marriage for washing out the blood. In the night the man hears his true wife singing in the next room, singing "Return to me" and singing the true, unknown name of her husband. The man "jumped right up and married the woman." See Beckwith, *Jamaica Anansi Stories, MAFLS* xvii, pp. 130, 266.

The false or substituted bride is one of the most widespread of all folktale motifs. There are Portuguese, Spanish, Greek, Hebrew, Magyar, Indian, and Indonesian. It is common all over Africa, found in Swahili, Kaffir, Fjort, Basuto, Bushman, and Zulu stories. One of the most famous of the false bride stories is the Norwegian *Bushy Bride*. There are Lappish and North American Indian variants. It occurs in the *Ocean of Story*, in Basile's *Pentamerone*, and is the basic theme in Grimm's *Three Little Men in the Wood* (#13), and *The White Bride and Black* (#135).

familiar Specifically, an animal or bird associated with a witch or wizard as attendant, servant, or messenger: usually believed to embody a spirit (often a demon) and frequently also believed to be, especially in primitive cultures, the soul-animal or double of the witch or wizard. In general European belief, however, the familiar is *not* the witch or wizard, but servant and attendant pure and simple. (See SHAPE-SHIFTING).

In Elizabethan England it was popularly believed that demons, incarnate as certain animals, attended and served witches, and also that witches could and did metamorphose themselves into similar animal forms for depredations upon and persecutions of innocent persons. Inevitably whatever befell the witch-animal (injury or death) befell the witch. The black cat of the English and colonial witch is probably the most famous of popular familiars. In Europe and America dogs, hares, insects, toads, etc., are as commonplace in the role of familiar as cats. Flies are familiars in Lapp, Finnish, and Norwegian folklore. In the New Hebrides the sea snake will be the faithful familiar of one who has intercourse with it. Malay witches have familiars, incarnate as owl or badger, whose injury or death also results in like repercussions on the owner. Zulu sorcerers are said to have familiars (*umkovu*) which are reactivated corpses. To acquire one of these the sorcerer must dig up a dead body, run a hot needle up the forehead, and slit the tongue. The umkovu are sent on errands at night. They cause long grass to entangle the feet of night travelers, and "go about shrieking." If they call one's name, it is peril to answer, for this subjugates the answerer to their will and he becomes one of them. To see an umkovu presages death. Witches among the Basuto have familiars called *obe* in the shape of tremendous animals.

The familiar is also often conceived of as an attendant spirit instead of an animal. In Arabian folk belief, every magician or wizard has a *tabi* (literally, follower) who reveals to him hidden knowledge. Certain North American Indian medicine-men, in the midst of their mystical religious experiences, hear their familiar spirits speak with actual voice, giving warning or advice. The Malay pawangs, or medicine-men, have hereditary familiar spirits who continue from generation to generation to act as intermediaries between them and evil spirits.

In many specific instances familiars are called sendings. In Siberia two contending shamans will send forth their familiars, or yekeelas, to vie with each other instead of undertaking combat themselves. If one of the yekeelas is killed, his shaman dies. Among certain Eskimos the shaman is represented by a tupilaq, not a living animal familiar, but an artificial seal which he has made. In southeastern Australia the sorcerer's familiar is apt to be a lizard whom he sends forth to work specific injuries; in New Guinea sorcerers send out snakes and crocodiles on killing missions; among the Yorubas the owl is the sorcerer's familiar, also sent on evil errands. In all these instances, if any hurt befalls the familiar or sending, the same hurt befalls the sender.

The ancient Jewish familiar known as the ôb, however, was neither an animal or spirit which represented the witch or soothsayer (i.e. not life token or double) nor an attendant spirit which obeyed his word. The ôb was evidently some material object made purely for purposes of divination, or else some natural object which became possessed by a prophetic spirit. The witch of Endor had an ôb, for instance. The concept of familiar as attendant spirit came into Jewish belief much later along with the development of demonology and the idea of the subjugation of spirits to human service. See BUSH-SOUL; NAGUAL; SENDING.

fandango A Spanish courtship dance especially of the provinces of Castile and Andalusia. It developed from the gitano, and retains the fiery voluptuousness of the Gipsy dance. The gestures of the dancers reveal every shade of allurement. The dance is performed to the guitar, the music in delirious rhythms, in ⅜ or ¾ time, with the castanets and heels in vibrating counteraccents. The interpolated songs have the minor tonality of Moorish music, but the dance itself is gay. The audience is drawn into enthusiastic participation, among upper classes as well as among the Gipsies. Local variants are *rondeña, malagueña, granadinas, murcianas*. The gestures are less sinuous in other regions—Majorca, Catalonia, and Asturias. The fandango is popular in coastal Colombia, Ecuador, Brazil, and the Philippines as a ballroom dance. The origin is probably not colonial, but Ibero-Moorish. [GPK]

fandanguillo An Andalusian dance for one woman. She hardly moves from the spot, but quivers in her whole body as her heels beat out *taconeos* and her hands manipulate castanets, her face expressionless and eyes fixed and staring. In a dramatic movement she opens her arms wide, takes three large steps, and continues the dance in a kneeling position. Her concluding erect posture and toss of the head are haughty and provocative. The name means small fandango, but its concentrated introversion contrasts with the gay enthusiasm of the typical fandango. The fandanguillo is a subtype of the flamenco dances. [GPK]

fantine A class of well-disposed little people inhabiting the valleys of Vaud province in southeastern Switzerland. When properly treated they bring favorable seasons and good crops. They make little bells so that the cattle will not be lost in the woods.

farandoule An open round dance of Provençal peasants. Its formations suggest origin in a pre-Christian vegetation rite. The leader (often at the same time the flutist) guides a long chain of men and women, linked alternately by their hands, in serpentine courses; then the leading man and woman form an arch and the remaining dancers run through. The step is the buoyant run characteristic of springtime running and leaping dances.

The farandola of Catalonia is almost identical with the farandoule. It is often dedicated to saints, being performed on the town's saint's day. Documents prove its existence as far back as the 14th century. In Catalonia it has taken over some sardana characteristics. The various forms of this dance tie up with the Mediterranean series of open rounds, through Tuscany and Sicily, the Balkans and Greece to the Near East. [GPK]

Faroe step A step used in the round dances of the Faroe Islands which are accompanied by sung ballads, and adopted also in Norway and Finland: a survival from the 11th century. It is a reversal of the branle step: double left, simple right. [GPK]

fasting Voluntary abstinence from food, partial or total, or sometimes from specific foods, sometimes also from drink, for religious reasons, penitential self-mortification, or other reasons. Among almost all peoples fasting is one method of making direct contact with the supernatural, by means of the visions and hallucinations which prolonged fasting induces. It has been regarded everywhere as a form of personal sacrifice and propitiation to the gods, or a god, and as a means of purification before (or after) certain important activities, such as warfare, hunting, fishing, initiation rites, and other religious ceremonies. Everywhere fasting is recognized as a door to mystical experience and revelation.

In early Babylonia and Assyria whole communities sometimes fasted to ward off a threatened evil, and individuals among those peoples sought the favor or forgiveness of their gods by fasting. It is the practice among the Maoris of New Zealand for the women, and others who remain at home, to fast for the welfare and success of the warriors while they are away. In Fiji it is customary for a man to fast until a vow of revenge is fulfilled. The severe fasting prescribed by the Hindu Yoga ascetic philosophy secures marvelous powers for its practitioners.

In medieval Europe prolonged fasting was a symbol of sanctity, either sanctity to be acquired by the fasting, or a token of sanctity inherent if one could survive it. There is a famous story about the 13th century Fasting Nun of Leicester who retained health and rosiness in spite of eating nothing for seven years except the communion every Sunday. G. L. Kittredge cites, however, a specific lack of sanctity in the origin of a many-day fast inflicted by a Salem witch on Mercy Short of Boston.

☞ Among the North American Indians fasting was widely practiced, both by individuals alone, or by groups of males. Of all fasts, that by youths (and sometimes also by young girls) at puberty to obtain a vision is the most characteristic, but fasting was by no means limited to this one occasion. Warriors frequently fasted before setting out on raids, hunters likewise. In some ceremonies, such as the Plains Indian Sun Dance, the chief participants in the ceremony fasted for several days while the dance was being held. Initiation into religious societies also often entailed fasting prior to, or during, the initiation ceremonies.

Fasting often meant abstaining from water as well as food. Continence was observed during fasting periods, and males when fasting often left their homes to escape any possible contamination from menstruating or pregnant women. Reasons assigned for fasting were: 1) to attain ritual cleanliness; this applies especially to fasting prior to or after war activities, religious ceremonies, hunting expeditions; 2) to render oneself pitiful in the eyes of the supernaturals, so that they will give the faster instruction, songs, and some of their own power.

Absolute fasting was in many cases practiced only by men; limited fasting, during which only small quantities of food and water were taken, was practiced by males and females alike; females usually observed such fasting at the time of menstruation, and both men and women observed it after the death of a spouse or child.

[EWV]

fasting against a person A legal procedure practiced in ancient Ireland whereby a person could compel a stronger, or a superior, person to grant a request, yield a point, pay a debt, etc. The petitioner would sit fasting at the house-door of the petitioned, and not eat until that which was required was granted or paid. Continued refusal on the part of the petitioned would bring upon his head guilt for the death by starvation of the petitioner. This kind of fasting was recognized as one of the legal "distresses" of ancient Ireland. Fasting against a person for these reasons was also a common practice in India. The long fasts of Gandhi to gain a point were the same thing. And the fasting of modern prisoners in their cells belongs to the same psychology.

Belief in fasting "upon" a person was strong in England as late as the 16th century. A certain Mabel Brigge was hired by another woman to fast upon a certain man, ostensibly to effect the return of stolen money, but actually to effect his death. Mabel was executed in 1538 for causing the death of a man by fasting. He stumbled and broke his neck before her fast was over. This kind of fasting was called the Black Fast and was believed in as a potent spell. It was abolished by the church before the end of the century.

Fastnacht or **Fasenacht** In the Germanic countries, the festival just preceding Lent; literally, Fast Eve or Lenten Eve: called Fasching in Bavaria and Austria. The festival is analogous to the Carnival of the Romance countries. Popularly in Germany, the term is believed to derive from *fasen, faseln,* to talk nonsense, and the featuring of the Fastnacht plays on this day more or less substantiates the claim. The Fastnacht plays developed out of the burlesque songs and antics of the masqueraders who followed the ancient Teutonic ship-wagon processions, greatly tempered in Christian times to churchly subjects. For a detailed description of the variations in the celebration of Fastnacht throughout the Black Forest, see "Fastnacht in the Black Forest," by Conrad Taeuber, *JAFL* 46: 69–76. See CARNIVAL.

Fastnachtsbär The Fastnacht Bear or Shrovetide Bear: a man or boy clothed in straw and wound with ropes, led from house to house with music on Fastnacht or Shrove Tuesday in parts of Germany, Bohemia, Moravia, etc. In some districts he wears a bear's mask or is clad in skins to enhance the realism. He enters every dwelling and dances with all the girls and women of the household, and is given food, drink, and money. The money is spent later in the evening by him and his companions for ale and merrymaking. There exists a fairly general belief in central Europe that one must dance on Shrove Tuesday (Fastnacht) to insure fertility and growth of all the crops. In some districts the women pluck bits of straw from the Fastnachtsbär to put in their poultry nests and thus insure a plentiful supply of eggs. Compare OATS-GOAT.

fatal children Those children out of myth and legend of whom it was prophesied either before birth or at the hour of birth that they would kill or overthrow a grandparent, parent, or other relative, or some king. These children were always abandoned as infants to perish, were always saved (by an animal, a supernatural being, a herdsman, fisherman, forester, or other humble person, or by an itinerant king, a maternal-minded queen, etc.), grew up unknown, beautiful, strong, and brave, and always fulfilled the prophecy (which was usually unknown to themselves).

Among the famous fatal children of the world were the Greek Œdipus, of whom the oracle said that he would kill his father. He was disposed of, raised by a shepherd and later by a queen of Corinth, eventually returned to Thebes, and unknowingly killed his father, Laius. In Persian legend Astyages, king of Media, dreamed that his daughter gave birth to a deluge which flooded Asia, and exposed the infant Cyrus at birth. Cyrus was found and cared for by a herdsman (or a bitch), and at the appointed time killed his grandfather, Astyages. The ancient Irish Luġ, of whom it was prophesied that he would kill his grandfather, did kill Balor at the battle of Mag Tured. Deirdre, who because of her beauty, was destined to cause the death of heroes, was secluded in a forest hide-out under the care of women, and became the most unwilling cause of the treacherous fight in which were slain the three sons of Usnech, the sons of Fergus, and great numbers of the Red Branch warriors of Ireland. See ABANDONED CHILDREN; EXPOSURE OF FAMOUS PERSONS IN INFANCY.

fatal gifts Gifts sent to enemies who accept them as though they came from friends. This device is so well known to criminologists of all ages and areas that a complete analysis of its place in folk thought would be monotonous and voluminous. Only a few examples can be mentioned. When Hercules and his wife Deianira were fording a stream, Nessus the Centaur offered to carry Deianira while Hercules walked. Nessus then attempted to abduct the woman but was fatally shot by a poisoned arrow from Hercules' bow. Before he died he urged Deianira to take some of his blood, which would be a charm to preserve Hercules' love. Later when Hercules became enamored of another woman, Deianira gave him a shirt steeped in the blood of Nessus which, as soon as it was warmed by Hercules' body, caused his death. Allegorization is seen in the story of one of Vulcan's revenges. In order to punish Venus for infidelity he made a robe dyed in crimes. All who wore it became wicked. Jason, having brought his wife Medea, the barbarian and sorceress, back to civilized Greece, fell in love with Glauce. Medea sent her successful rival a wedding robe which burned her to death. The poisoned rings of the Borgias were, according to popular tradition, always fatal. Other gifts do not kill immediately but bring their owners to a bad end. Such are the necklace of Harmonia, the collar of Arsinoe. Opals bring bad luck. Other gifts are benign as gifts, but fatal if sold. The fatal emerald from the forehead of the great Buddha is a favorite theme among readers of the pulp magazines. [RDJ]

fatal imitation A folktale motif (J2401) in which the imitation of some admirable or successful act ends in disaster for the imitator. There is the stupid ogre who stabs himself, for instance, in imitation of the hero who has merely stabbed a concealed bag of blood (G524). There is Æsop's fable (Jacobs #202) about the ass who tried to greet his master with the same jumping and fawning affection he had seen the dog bestow, only to be harshly beaten off (J2413.1). There is the story about the man who could not sell his cow until he said she was with calf, and wondered why the same plan did not work when he tried to marry off his daughter (J2427).

The motif is very common throughout African, Surinam, and United States Negro folktale. Typical are the South Carolina Sea Island stories in which Ber Rabbit, having seen Ber Rooster with only one foot and no head at night, yet walking on two legs and a head as usual in the morning, asks him why this is. Ber Rooster explains that this is the way he rests. Ber Rabbit decides to try it, tells his wife to cut off his head and three legs, and of course is killed. See BUNGLING HOST; FALSE BEAUTY DOCTOR.

fatalism The feeling that some final pattern determines the occurrence of important human events. In the popular thought of all peoples the feeling tends to be vague. Theologians, fortune-tellers, astrologers in all parts of the world have given it a fictive reality under such terms as destiny, fate, or Fata, to be distinguished abstrusely from fortune, Fortuna, or luck, or karma. The body of knowledge represented by each of these terms has many subdivisions which are accepted or rejected according to the sociotheological traditions of the several communities. The special sciences themselves which involve the books of destiny, the laws of karma, and the conjunction of stellar or other influences at the moment, hour, or day of birth are the property of learned persons, whether clothed in the elaborate robes of the great universities or naked in Africa and the South Sea Islands. While these pursue their occult studies the peoples of the world will continue to believe that you won't die until your time comes, that bomb or arrow didn't have my name on it, I was warned not to take that boat, or it was fated that we should meet. [RDJ]

fatal look A death-dealing glance. The folklore of the fatal look needs to be distinguished from the folklore of the evil eye. Whereas the evil eye brings pain and misfortune with, at times, ultimate death and works over a period of time, the fatal look kills instantly. (Compare the colloquialism "If looks could kill.") A further distinction must be made between creatures like Medusa or a god, who when looked upon, cause death, and creatures who cause death by looking. Classic examples of this motif occur in Indian stories in which a man destroyed a tree with an angry look and restored it

with a kind one, or a beautiful maiden struck the king with a poisonous look from a distance. Isis, in Egypt, embracing the dead body of Osiris, killed a person who spied on her with a look. Snakes are thought to poison the air with their eyes and the snakes of Turkestan are reported by Arabs to have killed with a glance. These views were distributed in Europe through the Alexander Cycle. Shakespeare mentioned the "death darting eye of a cockatrice," which is a serpent hatched by a reptile from a cock's egg. Pliny and Heliodorus reported that a basilisk was a snake with a cock's head and a fatal glance. See ABANDONED CHILDREN. [RDJ]

☞ Belief in the evil eye, comparable to the European beliefs, apparently did not exist among North American Indians in aboriginal times, nor has it gained much prevalence at present. However, in the mythology of many western North American tribes we do find mention of monsters or other creatures who can kill persons by looking at them. [EWV]

Fata Morgana The fairy Morgan: in Carlovingian romance the lake-dwelling enchantress overcome by Orlando; lover of Ogier. See MORGAN LE FAY. The mirages in the Strait of Messina are attributed to her enchantments, and are named for her, Fata Morgana.

Fates The three Roman goddesses who determined the fate of every human: a development of the idea of the *fatum* or spoken word of Jupiter which could not be altered. The Fata Scribendi wrote the destiny of the child at birth: this may be a goddess or goddesses. Since the Fates performed their duties at birth, they were identified with the Parcæ. See MOIRÆ; NORNS.

Father Time The personification of time: an old white-bearded man carrying a scythe and often an hourglass. The figure is probably a descendant of the classical depiction of Cronus (Saturn), also identified with time, who carried a sickle or reaping book. The scythe Father Time bears is the symbol of his power to destroy: all falls like the grain before him. The hourglass is the sign of the constant and unstoppable flow of the years. The wings sometimes seen on Father Time are emblematic of his rapidity. Father Time is the Old Year who passes on the burden to the baby New Year at the stroke of the new year's first minute. He sometimes is also Death, who cuts down those who die.

fatigué Among Negroes of Trinidad, a term applied to songs and the method of singing of calypso style. To "sing on people" in a teasing or derisive way, as was done at carnivals in older times, was "to fatigué."

Fatima (1) In the story of *Bluebeard*, the last of the wives, whose curiosity resulted in the uncovering of Bluebeard's crimes.

(2) In the story of Aladdin, the holy woman slain by the necromancer, brother of the magician, who, dressed in Fatima's clothes, insinuates himself into Aladdin's household. When he asks that an impossible task be performed, the jinni of the lamp discloses the masquerade to Aladdin, who thereupon kills the necromancer.

(3) The daughter of Mohammed (606?–632), one of the four "perfect women." Traditionally she is virginal, one of her titles being the "bright-blooming" or one who has never menstruated; she however actually bore three sons to Ali. Her grave is unknown, mysterious.

faun See FAUNUS; PAN; SATYR.

Faunus In Roman mythology, a woodland deity: one of the most ancient Italic deities, originally probably an agricultural and shepherd god, later identified with the Arcadian Pan and having many of Pan's characteristics. Faunus was an oracular god, sending his prophecies in the sounds of the forests and by dreams to those clothed in the skins of sacrificial lambs and sleeping in his precincts: he was in this aspect known as Fatuus. As the fertility god of shepherds and crops, Faunus was equated with Inuus and Lupercus, the latter identification being made because of the supposed similarity between the Lupercalia and the Lycæa and the identification of Evander and Faunus. There were two Faunalia each year, one on December 15 and one on February 13, at which goats were sacrificed, there were libations of wine and milk, and country games and customs were generally practiced. In legend, Faunus was an early Latin king, the son of Picus and father of Latinus by Marica, who brought to the Latins religion and the arts of agriculture. Numa was supposed to have caught him, as Midas captured Silenus, by getting him and Picus drunk with wine. Like Pan, Faunus had goat's feet and horns, and from his various manifestations became pluralized into the Fauni or fauns, which resemble greatly the Greek Satyrs as spirits of the country. There was also a female counterpart of Faunus, Fauna or Faula. He is also either father or husband of Bona Dea.

Faust The type of the medieval European magician and student of the black arts. The Doctor Faustus we know was undoubtedly drawn originally from the Dr. George—later Johannes—Faust who was born in Swabia about 1480 and died in Syaufen in 1538 or 1539. To the life story of this real Faust there became attached, by popular and literary accretion, stories of the time, often of much earlier origin, about the great traditional magicians—Albertus Magnus, Paracelsus, Simon Magus, and others. Faust thus became the most notorious of those charlatan magicians (*scholastici vagantes*) who traveled from town to town, fair to fair, court to court during the period of the Renaissance's greatest gullibility, and who despite their quackery displayed or stimulated that interest in pseudo-scientific studies which led to the growth of modern science.

As with all such magicians, Faust was thought to be in league with the Devil, who accompanied him, according to Melancthon, as a long-haired dog with red eyes. Faust having turned from the traditional studies of the scholar (medicine, law, philosophy, religion: in Marlowe) in search of something more satisfying to his ambition evoked the Devil by conjuration. In return for the promise of a period, usually 24 years, of free living, he signed a bond with his blood deeding his soul to Satan. This, the devil's pact, is a recurrent theme throughout the period of active belief in witchcraft and devilry. Faust did not, however, derive real satisfaction from this contract; several times he reached almost to honest repentance, but never quite accomplished it; and at the expiration of the term of the bond he was carried off reluctant to Hell. Among the exploits widely attributed to Faust during his career are the fetching of grapes in winter, the ride on an inanimate object (bundle of hay, beer barrel, etc.), the baiting while invisible of the Pope

and his cardinals, and the calling up of various shades of classical antiquity.

Popular belief in devils and the whole atmosphere of the Faust legend was quite real. During a performance of Marlowe's play in the early 17th century, an extra devil, not of the regular stage company and reeking of brimstone (which latter gave him away), was discovered on stage, seemingly called up by Edward Alleyn's incantations in the role of Faust. Tradition (dating from the late 17th century, but based on earlier, similar legend) maintains that Alleyn, the original Faustus of the Elizabethan stage, thereupon quit the acting profession for good and founded Dulwich College on the estate he had bought with money made from acting and managing.

The Faust legend in 400 years has grown in philosophical content and, though the change is principally a literary one, it has echoes in popular tradition. In such popular works as the *Historia von Dr. Johann Fausten*, the first book in which the Faust story is collected, published in Frankfurt a. M. in 1587, and its English version of 1592, Faust is almost wholly the charlatan wonder-worker. With Marlowe's *The Tragical History of Doctor Faustus* (1589–1592), Faust becomes also the seeker after physical and intellectual satisfaction, who fails because his mortal pride is too inbred for him to recant his sins. In Goethe's two-part work (1808 and 1833) Faust the magician is almost entirely replaced by Faust the philosopher and student, and the dominant religious Protestant tone of the earlier story is superseded by one of searching cynicism. Even the "moral" of the story, earlier one of complete retribution for the pact with the Devil, is restated and turned about to the end that good and evil become relative rather than absolute. It is this "literary" Goethean Faust, as opposed to the popular creation, who is alluded to more often in the literature of the 19th and 20th centuries, e.g. Spengler's characterization of Western European civilization as "Faustian." The Gretchen episode of Goethe, absent in the earlier versions, used also by Gounod in his opera, has become, along with the pact with the Devil, the essence of the modern Faust story.

féar gortaċ Literally, in Irish, hungry grass: a kind of mountain grass that causes extreme hunger in whoever treads on it. One should carry food—whoever expects to pass over a place where it grows. Even swallowing one oat grain will cure the famishment thus caused. There is a place near Omeath, Ireland, famous for a strong growth of this grass between two cairns. No one from the environs will go near it without bread in the pocket, for if one falls down on the *féar gortaċ* he cannot rise until he eats. It is believed to grow where a dead body touches the ground; or some say it springs up where a meal has been eaten and no scrap or crumb left.

fear of the abnormal Any departure from the normal arouses the attention, causes apprehension, and, if not immediately and easily explainable, usually results in fear. Fear of the abnormal, including fear of the novel, the strange, the alien, the queer, the enormous, the monstrous, and the occult, accounts for many social and religious practices and folk customs.

The fear of anything beyond the normal range of day-by-day experience is characteristic of mankind. It tends to diminish with civilization as objects or conditions formerly not understood, and therefore dreaded or worshipped, come within the scope of expanding scientific knowledge, but the fear lessens only gradually, and superstition, the common term for this fear of the unknown, usually remains.

Children at play resent and persecute the abnormal and the non-conforming child, just as a brood of white chickens will pick to death the lone black one. The newborn child exhibits his first fears at the unfamiliar face and the unexpected sound. He is apt to yell with fright at his own mother the first time he sees her with a hat on. And the nurse who feeds his inherent fears with a diet of bogey and ghost stories, together with primitive dread of hell and the devil, is unwittingly laying a foundation in the child's mind for what psychiatrists will later call phobias and common people "the horrors."

The folk mind automatically associates anything abnormal with the supernatural, from the birth of a child with the amnion (caul) covering its head to an eclipse of the moon, and from phosphorescence (will-o'-the-wisp) in the meadow to hunchbacks and albinos. Sorcerers and shamans capitalize on fear of the abnormal by encouraging and magnifying it. Misshapen demons, so common in old religious literature, are a device to utilize fear of the grotesque to scare the uneducated into being good. Until recently it was easy to persuade a community that disease in cows and pigs was the evil work of some poor old woman crippled with lordosis.

Because bodily deformities, disfigurements, and chronic skin diseases have in primitive societies often been attributed to malign supernatural agencies, persons thus impaired were prohibited from serving in the most sacred rites of religion. An interesting passage in *Leviticus* xxi, 16–24 confirms this:

"For whatsoever man he be that hath a blemish, he shall not approach [the altar]: a blind man, or a lame, or he that hath a flat nose, or anything superfluous, or a man that is brokenfooted, or brokenhanded, or crookbackt, or a dwarf, or that hath a blemish in his eye, or be scurvy, or scabbed, or hath his stones broken...he shall not go in unto the vail, nor come nigh unto the altar, because he hath a blemish; that he profane not my sanctuaries:..."

The fear of enormous and misshapen beings characterizes the folklore of the entire Mediterranean region, including the Hebrew Behemoth, Leviathan, and Rahab, the Babylonian Tiamat, the Phoenician Molech, the Cretan Minotaur, Egyptian and Greek Sphinxes the Gorgons, the animal-headed gods of Egypt and Phæstos, the Armenian-Zoroastrian devs, druÿes, jatuks, pairikas, hambarus, visaps, and nhangs, as well as the apocalyptic monstrosities of Ezekiel, Daniel, and the various Christian and Gnostic apocalypses.

Fear of monsters (*dysmorphophobia*) is found also in the old Teutonic legends of Brusi, and Grettir, the female fiend who ate eleven merchants, in the stories of Bunyip of the Australian tribes, of the apelike demons of Tibet, and the dog-tailed devil-men of Fiji.

The origin of belief in monsters has been traced to actual oral tradition from times when now extinct huge animals roamed the earth, to the finding of fossil bones of such enormous and queerly shaped beasts, to night terror dreams, to belief that sexual congress between human beings and animals or demons or gods would produce monstrosities (for instance, the story in *Gen.* vi, 4 about how "the sons of God came in unto the daughters of men" with gigantic consequences), to deformities assumed by warriors who used masks and horns to terrify their enemies, and to huge stone ruins of former civilizations. Most likely, however, vivid imaginations fed by dreams and shadows account for most such legends.

Quaint lore of a milder sort, but still evidencing fear of the abnormal, persists in the traditional reverence for the hunchbacks who, among the Bolivian Indians, are said to carry "titulos" (important documents) in their humps. People in many lands touch the hump for luck, and Savonarola believed that hunchbacks have higher than average intellects. Idiots, perhaps because they mutter unintelligible sounds, share this reputation for secret wisdom.

Abnormal mental manifestations such as trances, delirium, seerism, and clairvoyance likewise inspired fear and led to such drastic social retaliations as the Mosaic law in *Lev.* xx, 27, commanding the stoning to death of mediums and wizards, and the well-known law in *Ex.* xxii, 18, "Thou shalt not suffer a witch to live." But related mental phenomena, such as prophecy and the gift of tongues (*glossolalia*), are quite inconsistently regarded at times as evidence of the presence of a good or holy spirit (*Acts of the Apostles,* ii).

The persistent and world-wide belief in the power of the evil eye is but another form of the fear of the abnormal. The death-dealing glance was supposedly possessed not only by the hunchbacked and cross-eyed but also by women who alternated abnormal beauty with monstrously horrible appearance, notably the Gorgons, Circe, and the Sirens, and the daughters of Mara in the Buddhistic mythology. Quite logically the protection against the evil eye and the glance of death is almost universally the making of the sign of life, i.e. exposing the genitals, either by wearing amulets displaying the *fascinum* or by making the *fico* (fig) with the thumb between the first and second fingers. The Christian sign of the cross and the Jewish *mezuzah* are popularly believed to ward off the baleful effects of the evil eye.

CHARLES FRANCIS POTTER

fearsome critters Fabulous and mythical animals, birds, reptiles, fish, and insects (more humorous than terrible) of the American frontier, wilderness, and backwoods, figuring in hoaxes and tall tales to prank tenderfeet, from which they have been attracted into the Paul Bunyan saga. "Apocryphal zoology" is a development of 1) the lore of fanciful traits of animals and erroneous nature observations belonging to "unnatural natural history" from Pliny, the *Physiologus*, and the Bestiaries, to myths of the sea serpent and hoop snake; 2) giant, hybrid, and fantastic monsters of mythology, and 3) fictitious and symbolic creatures of art and heraldry.

One of the earliest American contributions to this playful lore of impossible creatures is to be found in Rev. Samuel Peters' *General History of Connecticut*, 1781, with its descriptions of the whappernocker, the cuba, the dew-mink, and the humility. ("The humility is so called because it speaks the word humility, and seldom mounts high in the air....It...has an eye more piercing than the falcon, and the swiftness of an eagle;

hence it can never be shot for it sees the sparks of fire even before it enkindles the powder, and by the extreme rapidity of its flight gets out of reach in an instant.") Another early and widespread fearsome critter is the variously spelled guyascutus, of which two types may be distinguished: 1) the prock, sidehill dodger, or gwinter —an animal with legs on one side of its body shorter than those on the other in order to enable it to keep its balance while feeding on the side of a steep mountain; and 2) a hoax dating from pre-Civil War days, in which country people pay to see a carefully guarded specimen of a much-advertised monster, only to be routed when the manager rushes on stage and yells, "The guyascutus is loose!"

A list of fearsome critters includes: albotritch, argopelter, augerino, axhandle hound, ball-tailed cat, bedcat, billdad, cactus cat, camp chipmunk, Central American whintosser, club-tailed glyptodont, Columbia River sand squink, come-at-a-body, cougar fish, dingball (ding-maul, plunkus), dismal sauger, dungavenhooter, fibbertigibbet, flitterick, Funeral Mountain terrashot, gazerium, giddy (gillygalloo, whiffenpoof) fish, goofang, goofus bird, gumberoo, guyascutus (godaphro, gwinter, lunkus, sidehill dodger, gouger, or sauger, sideswiper, mountain stem-winder, prock, rackabore), hangdown, happy auger, harpy-hag, hidebehind, hodag, hugag, hymapom hog bear, jayhawk, kankagee, kickle (hickle) snifter, leprocaun, log gar, lucive (lucivee, *loupcervier*), luferlang, milamo bird, moskitto, mountain rabbit, mugwump, philamaloo (filla-ma-loo, phillyloo) bird, pigwiggen, pinnacle grouse, ratchet owl, roperite, rum(p)tifusel, rubberado, sandhill perch, santer, screbonil, slide-rock bolter, sliver cat, snipe, snoligoster, snow snake, snow wasset, snydae, splinter cat, squonk, swamp auger, teakettler, tote-road shagamaw, treesqueak, tripodero, upland trout, wampus cat, wapaloosie, whangdoodle, whiffenpuff, whifflepoof(fle), whirligig fish, whirling wimpus, wiggle-whiffit, will-am-alone, windigo, and wunk.

Some fearsome critters are designed to scare greenhorns or tourists (e.g. the agropelter, which throws chunks of wood at passing lumbermen). Others are merely preposterous (e.g. the rubberado or bouncing porcupine, which gives resiliency to anything eating its flesh). Still others are horrible examples of creatures adapted to their environment (e.g. the snow snake, a deadly, pink-eyed, white-bodied serpent invisible to its prey) or hostile to it (e.g. the augerino, a malevolent subterranean denizen of Colorado whose sole mission in life is to let water out of irrigation ditches).

The linguistic inventions of this animal mythology are a fascinating study in humorous nomenclature. (William T. Cox, *Fearsome Creatures of the Lumberwoods*, 1910; George Philip Krapp, *The English Language in America*, 1925, Vol. I, pp. 109–113; Charles Brown, *Paul Bunyan Natural History*, 1935; H. H. Tryon, *Fearsome Critters*, 1939; H. L. Mencken, *The American Language: Supplement I*, 1945, pp. 245–252.   B. A. BOTKIN

feasting Feasts, ranging from the extremely simple feast of the first game killed by a youth, to the ostentatious, elaborate, and often wasteful potlatch feasts of North Pacific Coast noblemen, were given by the North American Indians as part of almost all gatherings, whether of a religious, social, political, or economic na-

ture. Often a feast concluded a major ceremony, as the Busk or Big House ceremonies, but family and minor ceremonies often consist largely of the feast itself, preceded by a formal or informal prayer. Except in rare instances women prepare the food for feasts; often, however, men serve it. At the present time many tribes attempt to use for their feasts native foods, such as Indian or squaw corn, and wild game (even if only squirrels, where once deer were used), although in daily life non-native foodstuffs are now used more than native ones. See FIRST-FRUITS. [EWV]

Feast of Age or **Feast of Goibniu** One of the three gifts of Manannán to the Tuatha Dé Danann of Old Irish mythology after their defeat at the hands of the Milesians. When Manannán came to advise them, he sent them into the hills and mounds of Ireland to dwell forever and gave them three wonderful gifts: the faei fiada, which gave them the power to become invisible, the Feast of Age at which Goibniu served his ale that kept old age from touching them, and the Pigs of Manannán, which served them for food and whose hordes were inexhaustible.

Feast of Fools A festival of the Middle Ages and earlier in Europe, in principle related to the Roman Festa Stultorum and Saturnalia, and occurring some time in the period about Christmas and New Year's, in which the classes of the lower clergy and officials each, on its own day, presided in burlesqued ceremonials: a type of clowning holiday in which, because it was a holiday and therefore out of the normal course of things, a reversal of normal procedures occurred. The Feast of Fools is the name applied most often to that festival occurring on January 14, and it has therefore been confused with the Feast of the Ass, also celebrated on that date. January 1, the Circumcision, was the day the priests held sway, as for example the choirboys did on Innocents' Day.

The class to whom the day belonged nominated, in France and Italy, a bishop and archbishop of fools. These officers were "ordained" in a burlesqued ceremony and then presented to the people. During the course of the day, the participants in the revels masked (masks were in common use from 1200 to 1445), dressed in women's clothes, danced in the choir, sang obscene songs. At the altar they played dice, or ate puddings, cakes, and sausages there. They burned old shoes in the censers and censed the holy books and places with the vile smoke. Then, in carts, they went in procession through the streets, singing bawdy verses and indulging in obscene postures and gestures. This revelry eventually died out in the 16th century, after earlier ineffective prohibitions, in the general tightening of the Catholic Church in face of the Reformation.

Some have tried to associate the Feast of Fools with April Fools' Day as a vernal equinox celebration, but the change of the year's beginning from March or April to January occurred long after the Feast of Fools was observed. Compare also the Abbot of Unreason, the Lord of Misrule, and that group of entertaining major domos presiding over the late autumn and early winter festivals.

Febold Feboldson Synthetic and talltale inventorhero of the Great Plains, in the person of "an indomitable Swedish pioneer who could surmount any difficulty."

In 1927 or 1928 Don Holmes, of the Gothenburg (Nebraska) *Times,* picked up the character from Wayne T. Carroll, a lumber dealer, who wrote a weekly newspaper column under the name of Watt Tell. Another Gothenburg resident and occasional contributor to the *Times,* Paul R. Beath, is responsible for giving Febold wider circulation and more or less definitive form. According to Beath (*Febold Feboldson, Tall Tales from the Great Plains,* Lincoln, 1948, p. viii), the only historical link in the cycle is Febold's great-nephew, Bergstrom Stromberg, probably based on Olof Bergstrom, a Swedish pioneer who is reputed to have founded Stromsburg and Gothenburg, Nebraska, and who was the hero of many local anecdotes and yarns. The emergence of the Febold cycle from local tradition and newspaper humor illustrates the process by which migratory tall tales and jests in the Paul Bunyan tradition become attached to individual heroes and adapted to regional conditions—in this case, those of the treeless prairie and the hardships and hazards of plains pioneering, such as "tornadoes, hostile Indians, drouths, extreme heat and cold, unsavory politicians, and floods." The result is a mingling of familiar tall tale motifs and creatures (e.g. monster mosquitoes that drill through an iron boiler only to have their stingers clinched inside, the health-giving prairie wind that revives a corpse on its way to the graveyard, cutting and selling frozen postholes, the mugwump bird, the hoop snake, the dismal sauger, the snollygoster, the hodag) with some new variations and inventions (e.g. hitching an eagle-bee to a plow and plowing a beeline for a boundary between Kansas and Nebraska and the saga of the Dirtyleg Indians).

[BAB]

feces Concern with excrement is evident in a great many North American Indian tales, and human excrement was used in certain ceremonies by Eastern Woodlands and Southwestern tribes. In trickster tales especially, trickster's excrements often advise him, or warn him of impending danger; in other tales trickster eats certain foods which physic him, or is suddenly frightened and voids. In a Penobscot tale of northeastern North America the culture hero, Gluskabe, does everything a powerful baby he is trying to win over does, but is defeated in his purpose when the baby eats his own excrement. The Southern Okanagon of Washington personalize feces, and in several Northeastern myths a fecal lake is mentioned. In ceremonies human excrement is handled and pretense at least is made of eating it by clowns in Southwestern Pueblo Indian dances. In the False Face and Shuck Face performances of the Eastern Woodlands the performers smeared human or animal excrement over their hands, and then stroked or shook hands with onlookers whom they were protecting from disease. A great many other specific references to excrement in myths, and instances of the actual use of excrement in ceremonies could be cited; the reaction to all of these by Indians themselves is that the mention or use of excrement makes for a humorous situation. [EWV]

female rain In many Southwestern, Plains, and Eastern Woodlands North American Indian tribes, soft gentle rain is referred to metaphorically in tales and prayers as "female rain"; hard, pelting rain is spoken of as "male rain." [EWV]

Fenda Maria Literally, Lady Maria: title and heroine of an African Negro (Angola) folktale. Fenda Maria desired greatly to unbewitch and marry the beautiful young Ngana (Lord) Vidiji Milanda, who lay sleeping on the bank of a river far away. To do this she had to walk eight days through the forest "where goes the child of Bird, the child of Man is not to be seen therein," and to waken him she must weep ten plus two jugs full of tears. When Fenda Maria had filled ten plus one jugs full of tears, she gave up one jugful in payment for a young slave girl who was being sold by some passers-by. She continued to weep, and when she had filled ten plus one and a half jugs, she told the slave to weep a little, because her eyes were tired and she must sleep. But she told the girl to call her as soon as the jug was nearly full, so that she might waken the beautiful young Vidiji Milanda. The girl disobeyed, however, filled the jug full, and when Vidiji Milanda awoke and said, "Embrace me, my wife," she did not undeceive him. Fenda Maria thus became slave to her own slave, who thenceforth called herself Fenda Maria, and the real Fenda Maria was called Kamaria.

One day before setting out on a journey to Portugal, Vidiji Milanda asked all his slaves to name what presents they wanted him to bring them. Most of them wanted earrings or beads, but Kamaria asked for a self-lighting lamp, a self-sharpening razor, self-cutting scissors, and a truth-telling stone. Vidiji Milanda had to go to many places before he found all these strange gifts. But he did find them and brought them home to the slave-girl Kamaria.

In the night Kamaria struck her magic calabash on the floor, dressed herself in the rich garments that spilled out of it, told her story to these four remarkable gifts, and bade them destroy her if her tale was not the truth. The lamp lighted itself, the razor sharpened itself, the scissors cut, and the stone of truth pounded on the floor, but none of them harmed Kamaria. An old woman saw and overheard this performance for three nights. On the fourth she brought Vidiji Milanda secretly to watch. When he heard the story and saw the acts of truth, he cried out, "Embrace me, my wife." The pair then fainted away out of pure joy. The impostor was put in a barrel of tar which was set on fire. The little white bone that remained was used to make the white smear with which Fenda Maria and Vidiji Milanda smeared themselves. The smearing of the body with the burned flesh or bones of an enemy is a widespread African practice said to prevent the inimical ghost from taking vengeance. The Ki-mbundu text of this story with translation is in Heli Chatelain's *Folktales of Angola, MAFLS* i, pp. 29 ff. See ACT OF TRUTH; FALSE or SUBSTITUTED BRIDE.

Feng Shui Chinese geomancy.

fennel An herb of the parsley family (*Fœniculum vulgare*). Pliny lists it among the remedies discovered by the animals: the serpent eats it when he sheds his skin to renew his youth and to improve his eyesight. All parts of the plant are used to improve the sight, cure poison, reduce excess flesh, and to increase the milk supply of nursing mothers and wet-nurses. It was used in the rites of Adonis, and is a symbol for flattery. The leaves were used for crowning victors in games. "Sow fennel—sow trouble" is an old saying. See MAYWEED.

Fenris or **Fenris wolf** In Teutonic mythology, a huge wolf, son of Loki and Angur-boda whom the gods attempted to fetter. He easily broke two strong chains, but mistrusted the magic silken cord, Gleipnir. He insisted that Tyr place a hand in his mouth during the tying, and when he found himself securely bound, he bit the hand off. The cord will hold until Ragnarök, when he will join Loki, devour Odin, and in turn be rent asunder by Vidar.

Fensalir or **Fensal** In Teutonic mythology, the magnificent mansion of Frigga to which she invited all married couples who had led virtuous lives on earth to enjoy each others' company forever.

Ferdiad In Old Irish legend, friend and sworn brother of Cuchulain, beguiled by Medb to fight against Cuchulain in the War for the Brown Bull. The story of the reluctant three-day combat between the friends, the inevitable, gradual mounting of their anger, the final killing of Ferdiad by Cuchulain, and Cuchulain's immediate grief is one of the most moving and famous stories in the world.

Fergus mac Roich In Old Irish legend, a warrior of the Red Branch, one of the greatest heroes of Ulster in the reign of Conchobar, and one of the tutors of Cuchulain. He left the court of Conchobar and went into exile in Connacht because he could not countenance the treacherous killing of the three sons of Usnech. See DEIRDRE.

fern Any of the flowerless, seedless plants (class *Filicineæ*) reproducing by spores. In Germany a concoction of the male shield fern cures toothache. The root of this fern, dug when the sun is in the sign Leo and hidden in the room, will cause any sorcerers present to turn pale and leave the room. If dug at the full of the moon, steeped in water, and sprinkled on cattle it will keep them from bewitchment. Royal fern is soothing if laid on wounds, bruises, or rupture. They say in Cornwall that biting off the first fern seen in Spring will keep one free from toothache all year. In Northumberland it is unlucky to bring maidenhair fern into the house. In other parts of the country it is used for colds and lung complaints. The Mohegan Indians steep sweet fern in water and apply it to ivy poisoning and use a jelly from the root as a remedy for lung complaints. Moon fern is believed to be so magnetic that it will pull the shoes off the feet of horses and cattle. In the Vosges Mountains the ashes of ferns cut and burned on July 30 (feast of St. Abdon, patron of hygiene) kept away insects and unwanted guests. In Ireland they say St. Patrick put a curse on the fern, yet it is the emblem of fruitfulness, a substitute for tea, and is used as a remedy for burns and scalding. In Wales wearing a fern will cause one to lose his way and be followed by snakes. A fern growing in a tree is a cure for stomach-ache.

fern seed The reproductive spores of the fern, anciently called seeds, and the subject of varied and widespread magic lore. All beliefs regarding the magical properties of fern seed are rooted in sympathetic magic pure and simple. Those who believed that fern seeds were invisible also believed that fern seed would render invisible anyone who carried or ate them. Those who believed that fern seed bloomed with a rare golden blos-som only on Midsummer Eve, also believed that they would lead the finder or possessor to golden treasure. As late as 1870 the Lancashire peasantry believed that fern seed "gathered on the Holy Bible" would render invisible anyone courageous enough to swallow it. In Elizabethan England it had to be gathered on Midsummer Eve to be efficacious. Later anyone caught gathering it was suspected of witchcraft.

In Bohemian belief fern seed blooms only on Midsummer (St. John's) Eve with a golden bloom. If the finder will climb a mountain that night with the precious blossom in his hand, he will either find gold or have it revealed to him in a vision. Many Bohemians sprinkle fern seed in with their savings to keep the hoard from decreasing. In Russia also the golden flower must be picked at midnight on Midsummer Eve. Then if it is thrown into the air it will land over buried treasure.

A whole new variety of fern seed superstitions exists among the Georgia Negroes. Some believe that if you walk with it in your shoe the spirits will follow you; others sprinkle it about their homes to keep out ghosts.

Fescennine Pertaining to a kind of verse recited at Roman weddings in ancient times: said to have been originally a form of obscene, ridiculing verse of harvest festivals, and originating at Fescennia in Etruria. Licentious banter of this sort, never taken very seriously by those it is aimed at, is a common occurrence at festal occasions when inducing fertility is desired, and is a world-wide custom.

Festivals of the Dead (Chinese) Ceremonies (having many local variations) whose general function is to show the spirits that their descendants on earth still respect and venerate them, and to supply them with the necessities of life after death, i.e. food, clothes, servants, money. In China responsibility for the welfare of deceased ancestors is the responsibility of the oldest surviving male member of the family, who, as priest, is responsible for the observation of the domestic rites. Major ceremonies are performed in the Spring (Ch'ing Ming), on the 15th of the Seventh Moon, and on the first of the Tenth Moon. Because the dead are buried in the fields, these times, when the families "sweep the graves" and repair the tumuli, are occasions for picnics. In the Tenth Moon winter clothes are sent to the dead together with gifts of symbolic money. The Seventh Moon, the Feast of Hungry Ghosts, is the time when the Buddhist hells also open their gates and ghosts roam through the country. [RDJ]

fetch In Irish and north of England folklore, the apparition of a living person; one's spirit-double, identical in appearance, even to details of dress. A fetch can be seen usually only by persons with second sight. It is most commonly seen, however, by a special friend or near relative just before or at the moment of death of the original. If it is seen in the morning it is thought to presage longevity for the original; its appearance at night means he is about to die or has just died. The fetch usually comes walking along easily and casually and disappears across the fields or through a gap in a hedge. If it seems to be agitated or distressed, a violent death is known to be in store for the original. One's fetch is even occasionally seen by oneself.

fetch-candle or **fetch-light** In Irish and north of England folklore, a supernatural light like the small flame of a candle seen moving along through the air at night: believed not only to presage the death of the one who sees it, but believed also to pass across his vision between his home and his grave. In some localities it is believed to be accompanying some ghostly funeral, and to be visible only as a death warning to the beholder or as sign of the death of someone he loves. In south Hampshire it is said to go out when the soul of the dying departs. Compare CORPSE CANDLE.

fetish, fetichism These words are derived from the Portuguese *feitiço*, "a thing made," which was applied by the early travelers of this nation to African charms, religious figures, and the like. They are indiscriminately and incorrectly employed by non-scientific writers to denote African religion. Strictly and properly speaking, however, fetish should be used only for a magic charm, and fetichism for the beliefs in magic associated with such charms. They are not to be employed in speaking of entire religious systems, nor of carved or other representations of power sources, such as deities or local spirits. [MJH]

Fialar or **Fjalar** In Teutonic mythology (1) The dwarf who, with Galar, killed the great teacher, Kvaser. They made a drink from his blood and honey which made anyone who drank it a poet.

(2) A cock who crows to announce Ragnarök. He also signifies fire; hence the Norse expression, "the red cock is crowing over the house," means that it is on fire. Sometimes the phrase is used to mean that the sun is rising.

Fianna The organized band of warriors of Fionn MacCumal, Irish chieftain of the 2nd and 3rd centuries: usually termed Fianna Eireann, the Fenians of Ireland.

fidchell An ancient Irish board game whose rules of play are uncertain: often called chess in translations, but on slim evidence. The fidchell board and pieces, often highly ornamented, are mentioned many times in Old Irish literature. Diarmuid, for example, throws berries from the quicken tree to indicate moves to Oisín. This enables Oisín to beat Fionn, who is the better player, and thus betrays Diarmuid's presence in the tree to Fionn.

fiddlin' tunes The traditional melodies played on the violin by folk musicians of the American frontier and still current in rural and isolated communities, in the hillbilly style, and in the folk dance revival. They are chiefly dance tunes, many of them derived from English, Scottish, and Irish airs, and include reels, jigs, hornpipes, hoedowns, jumps, quadrilles, etc. The repertoire is extensive and the titles are indicative of the background and speech of the people who danced to them. *Cripple Creek, Turkey in the Straw, Fire in the Mountain, Sugar in the Gourd, Hell among the Yearlings, Chicken Reel, Possum up a Gum Stump, Irish Washerwoman, Arkansas Traveler, Buffalo Gals*—these are among the favorites. The instruments on which they have been performed might be "store-bought," mail-order, or home-made. The players, some of whom have achieved amazing virtuosity, are largely self-taught and play only by ear, holding their fiddles in various posi-

tions of their own choice—in the lap, between the knees, against the upper arm, etc. Open strings are sometimes used as drones, producing a sound similar to the bagpipe, and continuous double-stopping is occasionally facilitated by whittling the bridge to a flatter shape. Though most of the tunes are in a major mode, the Dorian and Mixolydian occur with some frequency, and certain habits of raising or lowering the fourth and seventh degrees of the scale show a character of musical archaism.

Field of Reeds In Egyptian Osirian religion, the afterworld below the western horizon. This region of perpetual springtime, ruled over by Osiris, was reached by the souls of the dead in a magical boat. Farming the fields was the principal work of the shades, and in the fields grew great harvests, the grain reaching high above the head. Compare AALU; ELYSIUM.

field spirit A spirit of vegetation, seen in grain fields when the wind blows through the stalks; personification of the growing crops: often referred to as *corn spirit*. Field spirits are conceived of in both animal and human form. The field spirit flees from one swathe to another before the mowers or reapers and is believed to be embodied or inherent in the last sheaf cut. He who cuts the last sheaf has captured the spirit. The sheaf then is shaped into a figure representing its inhabitant and presented to the owner of the field, who preserves it carefully until the next spring's planting. Typical of the field spirits of European peasant lore are the German Bullkaters, Haferbocks, Kornwolves, and Roggerhunds. See CAILLEAĊ; ESTONIAN MYTHOLOGY; HARVEST DOLL.

Fifinella A female of the Gremlin family who tickled fighter pilots and bombardiers just as their sights were lined up for a good run. Compare DINGBELLE.

fig Because Mohammed swore by it, the fig, like the date, is sacred; it is intelligent, is but a step removed from the animal kingdom, and is called the fruit of Heaven. In England Palm Sunday was sometimes called Fig Sunday because of Jesus' desire to eat figs on the way from Bethany. Among the Hebrews the fig tree was associated with the vine as a symbol of peace and plenty. Among the Romans it was sacred and the milk of the wild fig tree was sacrificed to Juno Caprotina. The emperor was associated with Dionysus in the artificial fertilization of the fig tree. In central Africa the Timbukas build little huts for the spirits of their ancestors in the shade of these trees which are sacred. In Italy and parts of Africa, the fig tree is the spiritual husband of barren women. They are anointed with the milky sap and tied to the tree. The fig tree is sacred also to the Buddhists because the Gautama found wisdom under the pipul tree (*F. religiosa*). Among many peoples the fig tree is known as either the tree of life or of knowledge.

Either ripe or dried, the fig is a staple article of diet in many parts of the world. In Greece the non-intoxicating milky juice of the tree is given to babies, and is also widely used as a medicine. In Louisiana this milk is used to cure ringworm and to remove warts; among the Hindus it is given to relieve toothache. The Hindus use the bark for a tonic and as a cure for diabetes. In Franconia a dried fig is kept in the mouth to ease toothache, while in Styria and Swabia figs are first cooked in milk for the same purpose. In Bavaria the same remedy is used for ulcerated gums. Heated and split open figs are placed on gumboils to draw them. Boiled in barley water they are used in pulmonary complaints. The juice of figs mixed with hog-grease is used to cure the bites of mad dogs. A sirup of the leaves or green fruit is used for hoarseness, coughs, and all diseases of the lungs and chest. A decoction of the leaves is a remedy for scrofula, running sores, and scabs.

In Timor a fig tree is planted at the time of the sealing of a blood covenant. It is dangerous to lie down in the shade of a fig tree as this is a favorite haunt of spirits. The fig leaves worn by Adam and Eve to cover their nakedness were used because they were the largest leaf growing in Palestine rather than for any symbolic reason. However, in legend, the fig tree, because it was the tree from which the pair ate was the only tree which would permit them to use its leaves to cover themselves. Louisiana Negroes say that if you fall out of a fig tree, you will never get well. They also believe that if fig trees are planted on land which has not been paid for, the land will never be paid for.

In folktale there are magic figs which cause a magic sleep (D981.5) or cause horns to grow on people (D1375.1.1.5.). The rain of figs, like the rain of sausages or fishes (J1151.1.3) is the motif for the story in which an old woman convinces her son that it has actually rained figs, so that when he confesses in court that he killed a man on the night it rained figs, he is let off as a nitwit. An Estonian folktale explains that once the fig tree sheltered Jesus from the rain, and has been evergreen ever since (A2711.4).

(2) A gesture of contempt, known in Italy, France, Germany, Holland, England, etc., and consisting of placing the thumb between the index and middle fingers; biting the thumb is likewise often called "making a fig." The first of these gestures is held by some to be a sign-symbol of the vulva, and is used, as for example in Italy, as both an insulting gesture and a counter to the evil eye (a wish for good luck): one etymological theory holds that the expression originated in an Italian word meaning both the fruit and the pudendum muliebre, thus making of the gesture a punning symbol. The more common legend connected with the origin of the expression is however quite different, if less credible. In the 12th century, the Milanese revolted against Frederick Barbarossa, and expelled the empress, his wife, from their city mounted backwards on a mule. When Frederick retook Milan, he assembled its inhabitants and, under threat of instant execution if they refused, made each of them remove with his teeth a fig stuck in the rear end of a mule. According to this theory of its origin, the gesture began as a sign of contempt for the Milanese. See GESTURES.

fighting of the friends In west of Ireland folk belief, the battle, which takes place around the house where a person is dying, between his friends and his enemies among the dead. The enemies are variously the powers of evil, the fallen angels, or the fairies or síde, and are referred to as "they" or the Others. In Irish folklore, as elsewhere, the fairies and the dead are often indistinguishably confused. One's friends and relatives among the dead fight for him against those Others, and the noise around the house is a great clamor, heard by everyone, but few people are gifted to see it. The battle is either to save the departed soul from the powers of evil, or to save it for this life against the Others who would steal it away.

Lady Augusta Gregory tells the story of a woman who lay ill. Every day for three days she told her child to bake a cake; three times the child baked the cake and three times it vanished. An old man came to the door; it was the child's grandfather (who was dead). He took the three cakes, he said, for he was watching the house for three nights and needed them. There was a terrible fight on the third night, he said, and "they" would have carried the mother away, except that he kept his shoulder to the door and prevented them. After that the mother got well. They say you should not grieve too much if some loved person dies ahead of you. It is a good thing to have some one out there fighting for you when your own hour comes.

This fighting of the friends at the hour of death is found also in the folklore of the Aran Islands.

figona or **higona** The San Cristoval (Melanesia) name for spirits in female snake form which, unlike the adaro, usually are not thought of as the ghosts of men. Figona do not always have form. Those residing in rocks, trees, and pools are never seen. The figona receiving real worship and sacrifice, however, always have a serpent incarnation but can take the form of a stone. The chief figona is Agunua who is "all of them." The Arosi name is hi'ona and that used on Florida Island is vigona. In Bauro the figona may be a ghost of the dead.

filial piety Filial piety, necessary to preserve order in the community, is the most generally praised of Chinese virtues. Innumerable exempla encourage Chinese in this virtue. For example, a son should cut off part of his body to nourish a starving parent. A daughter should nourish her feeble parents with milk from her breasts. Wife and children should starve rather than deprive parents of a bit of rice. One man had wooden images made of his deceased parents which he visited every day. One day the wife stuck a needle into them. When the filial son returned and found the images in tears, he divorced his wife. [RDJ]

Fimbulwinter or **Fimbal winter** In Teutonic mythology, the terrible period of cold preceding Ragnarök. There will be three seasons of winter without a break, followed by three more during which the crimes of man will increase.

Findabair In Old Irish legend, daughter of Medb and Ailill, queen and king of Connacht; beloved of Fraech. Her love and marriage with Fraech was thwarted by her father, who feared the enmity of rival kings. Findabair was extraordinarily beautiful, and was promised in marriage to every hero who would undertake to fight Cuchulain in the War for the Brown Bull. Some say she died of humiliation, and some say she died of heartbreak, after Fraech was killed by Cuchulain.

fingernails The folklore of the fingernails covers beliefs and usages as varied as putting them in love charms, or prognosticating the number of one's friends or foes from the white spots on them, to their use in witchcraft and conjure.

In the British Isles and quite generally through the United States, it is said that a baby will become a thief if its nails are cut before it is a year old. For this reason mothers bite their babies' nails off, for the first time at least.

White spots on the thumb nail mean that you will receive a gift; on the forefinger they indicate the number of your friends, on the middle finger the number of your foes. White spots on the ring finger mean you will receive a letter or your lover is coming. White spots on the little finger mean a journey to go.

That cutting the fingernails strengthens eyesight is a common saying. If you cut them during a waning moon they will not grow back too fast. Cutting them on a Friday either cures or causes toothache. Southern U.S. Negroes say that to dream of cutting them portends a disappointment. To cut the nails on Monday brings news, on Tuesday, new shoes. Cutting them on Wednesday compels you to travel, on Thursday, more shoes or an illness. Cutting the fingernails on Friday brings you either money or a toothache. By cutting them on Saturday you will make sure of seeing your lover on Sunday. But if you cut them on Sunday, bad luck will follow you, you will get into a fight, or see blood before morning, and the Devil will get you in the end.

Fingernails comprise potent and compulsive ingredients of various southern United States Negro conjure tricks. Soak your nail parings in wine, for instance, and this wine served to the one you love will win a return of affection. A dead man's fingernails buried in a little bag under your enemy's doorstep will give him the ague until you take the bag away. The parings of a person's nails sprinkled in a path where he is sure to step over them will put that person in your power for either good or ill.

☞ Many peoples in all parts of the world save the parings of fingernails and the clippings of hair lest they fall into the hands of enemies who can work witchcraft with them. The Seneca Indians are said to have thrown them over the cliffs for the Little People. The markings of the fingernails, the half moons at the base, shape, scars, etc., belong to the art of palmistry. The Indian erotologists report that fingernails should be without spots and lines, clean, bright, convex, hard, and unbroken. While making love, lovers use their fingernails to scratch designs on the bodies of their mistresses. These designs are placed on or near the breast, on the waist, or on the sexual parts. [RDJ]

fingers The folklore of the fingers varies from the rather well-known practice of keeping the fingers crossed while passing a graveyard to the reverence of finger bones as sacred relics and the complex practice of finger mutilation among many primitive peoples. Among the Benga of West Africa, for instance, the first joints of the fingers of dead ancestors are kept (along with the fingernails and a wisp of hair) in a little bag; new finger joints and nails are added as more members of a family die off, and the collection is handed down from generation to generation as sacred relics with which the souls of the dead are associated. Finger bones of chiefs and heroes are likewise preserved and venerated in village shrines in the Solomon Islands.

The practice of finger mutilation or amputation for religious or magical reasons, for sacrifice to or propitia-

tion of gods, for the cure, success, or other benefit to near relatives, or for some benefit to the one giving up the finger, or as a symbol of mourning is known among many primitive peoples. Finger mutilation or amputation as a sign of grief or as propitiation to the dead occurs at many mourning ceremonies. In the Fiji Islands, for instance, it is reported that the death of a certain chief called for the sacrifice of 100 fingers. A child's finger, or one joint thereof, was sometimes cut off for a father. Hottentot women are said to give up a finger joint for the death of a husband. In the Tonga Islands the people cut off a little-finger joint as a sacrifice to some deity or to effect the recovery of a sick relation. This practice for these reasons is also known in some of the Fiji Islands and on Futuna of the New Hebrides.

Sir J. G. Frazer in his *Folklore in the Old Testament* cites the testimony of several early scholars that among the Hottentots and Bushmen the little-finger joint of a newborn child is often sacrificed to prolong its life, especially if previous children of the parents have died. Some Australian coastal tribes are said to amputate the finger-joints of female infants and throw them into the sea so that the girls may become successful fisherwomen.

In European folklore, quite generally in the United States, and commonly among southern U.S. Negroes, to keep the fingers crossed while passing a graveyard protects one from whatever evil might otherwise befall. To keep the fingers crossed while lying is a child's trick. The idea is that to do so "crosses out" the wickedness of lying or protects the soul against the Devil's seizing it in the moment of sin. In England it is said that if you tie a string around your little finger when you go to town, you will receive a gift. Southern Negroes say that pointing your finger at a fruit tree will make the fruit fall to the ground. Locking the fingers together and pulling hard will not only stop an owl from hooting, but will stop your enemy from defecating. Never point at a grave. To do so will either cause your own death to hurry upon you, or the ghost will rise from the grave and chase you, or your finger will rot off. Holding up the hand with fingers spread, and crying "Fingers," or "Fins," is a call for temporary truce or surrender by a player in children's games.

Southern Negroes call the index finger the "dog finger" or the "conjure finger" and say that one must never touch a wound with it or something terrible will happen. This no doubt reflects an old general European belief that the index finger was poisonous and a wound touched with it would never heal. Other fairly general beliefs are that if your joints crack when your fingers are pulled, someone (you know who) dearly loves you. Also to point your finger at a whip-poor-will when you hear him call (a death omen) will counteract that omen. Two fingers spread and pointed up made the magic (i.e. morale-building) V for Victory in World War II.

In folktale and legend the fingers of saints give off light and fire (F552.2), children are sometimes nourished by their own fingers (T611.1), as was Abraham, and an unusual number of fingers (F552.1) is sometimes the mark of the extraordinary hero. Some old accounts of Cuchulain describe him as having seven fingers on each hand. See MNEMONICS.

☞ Although the lore of fingers is properly part of the systematic doctrines of chiromants, fingers enter folklore in other ways. The astrologers describe the fingers as follows: thumb, Venus; index, Jove; middle, Saturn; ring, Sol; little, Mercury. Other names for the fingers are thuma; towcher, foreman, pointer, scitefinger; long-man, long finger; lech-man, medical finger, ring finger, gold finger, digitus annularis; little man, little finger, ear finger. The ring finger is thought to have a direct connection with the heart. If dipped in even a little poison the effect would be felt immediately. This is clearly associated with the folklore of the wedding ring. In India five whorls at the tips of five fingers mean that a man will become a princeling and ten whorls mean he will become a sovereign. Sir George Grierson has reported a general belief from eastern Hindustan that the Water of Life is in the little finger and if we knew how to get it we would become immortal. Grown people in all parts of the world like to play games with the fingers and toes of babies. "This little pig went to market" and "Master thumb is first to come" are well known examples. [RDJ]

Finnbeara King of the fairies of Connacht, Ireland. There are many current stories about him: that he cured a sick woman once, accepted food from her, but refused salt; that he repaid the smith who was not afraid to shoe his three-legged horse with a pound note delivered by a puff of wind. He brings good crops to the region by his presence in Cnoc Meada; but the people expect a lean year if Finnbeara is off somewhere else.

Finn (Fionn) or **Fenian cycle** A body of Irish heroic and romantic tales, dealing with the exploits of Fionn MacCumal, his warriors, called the Fianna, his son Oisín, and his grandson Oscar. Fionn was in the height of his fame and splendor during the 3rd century A.D. The tales exist in manuscripts dating from the 12th to the 17th century in Middle and Modern Irish; but a few of the texts occur in Old and early Middle Irish. The action takes place mostly in Leinster and Munster. Fionn's greatest rival, Goll Mac Morna, is usually identified with Connacht. The whole flavor of the material is one of splendid pagan valor and generosity —generosity both of hand and temper. The tales appear for the most part in characteristic ballad form, interspersed with a number in prose form, of which *The Pursuit of Diarmuid and Gráinne* is famous.

The parentage of Fionn and his feud with Goll Mac Morna are set forth in an 11th century manuscript describing the battle of Cnucha. *The Boyhood Deeds of Fionn*, extolling the wisdom of Fionn as a young boy, perhaps dates from the 12th century but is most popularly presented in a 15th century text. *Oisín in the Land of Youth*, describing the visit of Fionn's son, Oisín, to the typical Celtic fairyland has captured the imagination of poets from Michael Comyn, whose 18th century version is the most common one presented, to William Butler Yeats's *Wanderings of Oisin*. The most famous of all the stories in the Finn Cycle is the long 8000-line story called *The Colloquy of the Old Men (Acallam na Senórec)*. This is one of the earlier texts, composed about 1200 A.D., serving as a kind of frame story for a number of heroic tales and placename explanations. It is the story of the meeting of Oisín and Caoilte, 150 years after the death of Fionn,

with St. Patrick, and the extolling of pagan versus Christian virtues and character.

Finnish folklore The Finnish people possess a great wealth of all kinds of folk literature. Fortunately, this was to a large extent recorded and published rather early. Since the middle of the 19th century the Finns have produced a series of distinguished scholars in the field of folklore, who have materially advanced the science of folklore, and their significance has extended far beyond the boundaries of their country. For the cultivation of the sentiment of nationality of the Finnish people their folk literature has been extraordinarily important, and their whole cultural life up to the present time has been permeated and nourished by their folk traditions.

The First Steps The first folklore book in Finland, a collection of proverbs, was published in the year 1702 by a clergyman, H. Florinus. The first magic song or rune, that for exorcising the bear, had already been published in 1675, and in the year 1733 five other such magic songs were issued by G. Maxenius. Twenty magic runes found in the records of the law courts of the 17th century were published by R. Hertzberg in 1889. H. G. Porthan (1739–1804) issued between 1766 and 1778 five volumes of his work *De Poesi Fennica,* in which he made a thorough study of the meter of the Finnish folk songs. Christian Ganander published in 1789 his *Mythologia Fennica;* it was also he who published the first two Finnish animal tales (1784) and the first collection of Finnish riddles (1783). Z. Topelius (1781–1831), on his trips about the country as physician, had the opportunity of becoming acquainted with the untold wealth of folk songs in Österbotten. During his long illness he prepared and published a collection of folk songs in five parts (1822–1831) which contained 80 old and 20 new folk songs. This was the final result of many years of work and of the great help he had received from a host of friends.

The Finnish Literary Society Founded in the year 1831 by young teachers in the university, the Finnish Literary Society has carried out an extensive program: to spread the knowledge of the native country and its fortunes, to further the development of the Finnish tongue into a cultivated language, and to publish literature in the native speech for the use of both the educated class and the masses of the people. Although their activities had many sides—among other things they issued the translations of Shakespeare's plays— nevertheless it is well known that the principal reason for their foundation was to furnish help to Elias Lönnrot so that he might issue his collection of Finnish folklore. This society thus became the earliest folklore society in the world. The society published as early as 1836 an appeal to the country people, urging them to collect and to send in folklore materials. From year to year it gave scholarships to young students, sending them into all parts of the land to collect folklore, and in this respect achieved great success, especially during the years 1846 to 1849. The society received help from organized student groups and from Finnish nationalists. It became a center for the aspirations for a Finnish national culture. All important works in the fields of Finnish language, literature, and folklore have been prepared under the direction of this society from its beginning down to the present day. In the year 1840 it began the editing of the Finnish scientific-philological journal, *Suomi*, which is still appearing. In the series of books, *Suomalaisen Kirjallisuuden Seuran Toimituksia* (Publications of the Finnish Literary Society), there have appeared up to the year 1946, 230 volumes among which are found a great many works on folklore. The most significant step made by the society was the publication of the national epic, *Kalevala*, which had been brought together by Lönnrot—1st ed., 1835, new and expanded edition, 1849. This work has had a tremendous influence on the development of Finnish culture. In the year 1850 the Tsarist Russian regime forbade any other books in the Finnish language to be published except those dealing purely with religion and farming. The society was not allowed to accept as members any students, artisans, or farmers. Women were also excluded. Fortunately the publication of folklore collections was permitted to proceed, and the society made use of this right. For example, from 1852 to 1866 they published in four volumes the folktales of the Finnish people, which had been collected by Eero Salmelainen.

In 1878 the society adopted a program worked out by E. Aspelin which had as its purpose the systematic collection of all kinds of folklore materials. In the same year (which also witnessed the founding of the English Folk-Lore Society) the society was given official recognition by the state and was granted yearly subventions. In addition, in the year 1884 a commission from the society was formed for the exclusive purpose of promoting folklore research. A large library was brought together for which Lönnrot alone contributed 2,500 volumes, and a beautiful building for the seat of the society was erected at the expense of the entire nation in 1890. Among those who have assisted with its work and have written down folklore material and presented it to the society, there are numbered many humble officials, teachers in the public schools, educated peasants, and artisans. Their recordings are frequently of very high value. To their efforts should be added the results of trained investigators, scholars supported by the society, and other students. The rich folklore collection of the society, which today numbers about one and a quarter million items, is the work of the entire people and is a sign of their national sentiment. The last great effort, which took place in 1935 on the one hundredth anniversary of the publication of the *Kalevala*, brought into the society 133,000 new folklore records. Work continued, and the society keeps on preparing its books of instruction and questionnaires for the organization of the work of the large number of collaborators throughout the entire country.

The arrangement and the publication of the collected materials has proceeded very far. More than to anything else, attention has been given to the old runes. There now exists a completed work of 33 large volumes with about 85,000 variants under the title *Suomen kansan vanhat runot* (The Old Runes of the Finnish People), 1908–1945. The folk melodies were also published under the title *Suomen kansan sävelmiä*, five volumes, 1896–1945. A significant part of folk beliefs concerning hunting, fishing, farming, and raising live stock was published in a work entitled *Suomen kansan*

muinaisia taikoja (The Old Magic Practices of the Finns), I–II, 1891–1892, by M. Waronen; and III–IV, by A. V. Rantasalo, 1912–1934.

The still unpublished material in the society's collections has been copied carefully from the original onto sheets which have been classified according to subject-matter. The work has progressed; in the year 1947 the society possessed a collection of such sheets extending to 275,000 numbers. Among them were: mythical legends, 75,000; historical and local traditions, 20,000; etiological legends, 10,000; folk music, 20,000; customs, seasonal practices, and proverbs, 100,000. The folk melodies were formerly recorded on cylinders, but now are recorded on phonographic discs.

The material of the society has been made much more useful because of the many extensive catalogs which have been published, such as those of Aarne for folktales and traditions (1911–1920), of S. Haltsonen and E. A. Tunkelo for ethnographical descriptions (1938).

In addition to its collections the society possesses the copies of the extensive collection of Estonian folklore made by Hurt and Eisen, consisting of about 60,000 folklore items.

References:

K. Krohn, "Histoire du traditionnisme en Finlande," *La Tradition*, t. IV. Paris, 1890.

———, *Les collections folk-loristes de la Société de Littérature finnoise*. Helsingfors, 1891.

———, *La Société de Littérature finnoise, 1831–1931*. Helsinki, 1931.

———, "Geschichte und Bedeutung volkskundlicher Arbeit in Finland," *Nordische Volkskundeforschung*. Leipzig, 1927.

J. Hautala, "The Folklore Collections of the Finnish Literature Society," *Studia Fennica* V, Helsinki, 1947, pp. 197–202.

The Great Collectors and Scholars That Finland became by the end of the 19th century in many respects the center of interest for folklorists of all parts of the world was not only because of its rich heritage of folklore tradition. By the middle of the 19th century, it was also achieving deserved fame for the thorough and stimulating work of its folklore scholars. For a century now investigators in an unbroken series have given leadership in studies of folklore, not only in Finland itself but also in the rest of the world. Whether all scholars agree or not with the conclusions of that school, no one can ignore the remarkable work of international cooperation and the rigorous techniques for folkloristic study which have come from the initiative and efforts of the so-called "Finnish School." Several of the men responsible for this remarkable development deserve special attention.

Lönnrot, Elias (1802–1884) The most important collector and publisher of Finnish folklore, Elias Lönnrot, was author and editor of the national epic, *Kalevala* (first edition 1835). As a student in medicine in the year 1827 he published his study, *De Väinämöine priscorum Fennorum numine* (the second half of which was lost by fire when the Academy of Turku was burned). Thus early he showed his interest in the material of the *Kalevala*. His first collecting trip to Karelia and Savolax was undertaken in 1828. As early as 1829 he began the issue of lyric folk songs in a collection called *Kantele,* and by 1831 four parts of this collection had appeared. When he published his dissertation on *The Magic Medicine of the Finns* in 1832 he was appointed physician for the community of Kajana. This was a piece of good fortune since the neighborhood was located at the boundary of the government of Archangel at the precise place where the finest and longest of the epic songs were still preserved. His collecting field trips were given financial support by the Finnish Literary Society, already discussed. He became the first secretary of the society.

In arranging his material he grouped the various epic songs in cycles about the chief heroes. By 1833 he had brought together such a cycle consisting of the runes about Väinämöinen (*Runokokous Väinämöisesta*) and containing 16 songs with about 5,000 lines. The next year this collection was expanded and given the name *Kalevala.* In 1835 the work was published by the Finnish Literary Society, but only in an edition of 500 copies. The next year he received from the society 1,000 rubles and made a long journey as far as Lapland. This time in addition to the runes, of which he had already recorded 2,100, he also collected some 5,000 proverbs, 1,200 riddles, and 50 folktales from the tradition of the people. After that he devoted himself to the arranging and editing of the material he had collected.

Soon there followed various extensive works on Finnish folklore: *Kanteletar* (1840), a collection of about 600 old lyric songs (of this a revised edition appeared posthumously in 1887); *The Proverbs of the Finns* (1842) with about 7,000 proverbs; *The Riddles of the Finns* (1844), consisting of 1,648 Finnish and 135 Estonian riddles; the new edition of 1851 was much expanded.

He now set himself to a very great task, to prepare a new edition of the *Kalevala* which would take advantage of all the newly collected material. He found, however, that it was necessary to undertake still further collections in the field. A young student, Daniel Europaeus, spent the entire years 1845–1848 traveling about for this purpose. He recorded some 2,800 variants of runes, most of them hitherto unknown. Lönnrot now began working on the final form of the *Kalevala.* The new edition was not only greater in extent, with 50 songs and 22,800 lines, but from the esthetic point of view was a fully rounded work, essentially a part of popular tradition but nevertheless shaped by a single hand, a work of the man who understood better than anyone else the spirit and creative art of his people. The new or present edition of the *Kalevala* appeared in 1849. It must be recognized that Lönnrot in many places improved the loose structure of the individual runes in unity, and also that in the general frame of the epic he inserted songs omitted by the people. He also brought in a number of interpolations from other songs, so as to make the structure of his poem more complete. Finally he arranged the runes in such an order as to bring out more clearly the inner unity of the epic. In all these respects, however, he was only acting in the same manner as the folk singer himself would do in the same circumstances. Lönnrot himself said, "Because I am sure that not one of the rune-singers could surpass me in the knowledge of the runes, I used my right to put together the songs as it seemed

best." Later the people themselves added some details in the same manner as Lönnrot had, a good indication of his proper feeling for Finnish folk poetry. According to the investigations of A. R. Niemi, only five to six percent of the lines of the *Kalevala* are not taken directly from the lips of the people. It is fortunate also that it can be seen that Lönnrot himself had not the slightest gift as a poet. If he had had, he would have exercised too great a personal influence on the structure of the *Kalevala.* As to his literary taste, it was largely the product of his classical education (on this point see J. Krohn in *Zeitschrift für Völkerpsychologie und Sprachwissenschaft,* v. 18, pp. 67 ff.).

In 1853 he was appointed professor and from then on devoted himself to purely linguistic research. From 1862 to 1880 he worked on a great Finnish-Swedish dictionary. His last contribution to folklore was *The Magic Runes of the Finnish People* (1880).

Among his students Lönnrot produced an able group of young folklorists, among them Julius Krohn, next to be discussed. Seldom has any scholar been so valued and honored by his people as Lönnrot has been by the Finns.

Reference: Anttila, A., *Elias Lönnrot,* Helsinki, 1931.

Krohn, Julius (1835–1888) In 1862 Julius Krohn was appointed Docent for Finnish Language and Literature in the University of Helsinki. His fame rests upon his development of the historic-geographic method (see HISTORIC-GEOGRAPHIC METHOD) for the investigation for the songs of the *Kalevala.* He himself wrote in 1884 concerning the special character of his new method: "Before I reach any final conclusions, I arrange the various versions in chronological and geographical order; for I have discovered that it is only in this way that it is possible to distinguish between the original elements and those which have been added later." His son Kaarle remarks, "The fact that the geographic method of folklore investigation arose in Finland is a result of the unusual richness and variety of the materials of folk song, which is found here for the use of the investigator." Julius Krohn's principal works are *The Genetic Explanation of the Kalevala,* 2 vols. 1884–1885, and *Kalevalan toisinnot* (The Variants of the Kalevala), 1888, and after his death the following works, edited by his son Kaarle: *The History of Finnish Literature* (1897) and *Investigations concerning the Kanteletar* (1900–1902). The results of his investigation of the *Kalevala* were also introduced to German scholars in Veckenstedt's *Zeitschrift für Volkskunde* v. II (1892) and Steinthal's *Zeitschrift für Völkerpsychologie und Sprachwissenschaft* v. XVIII (1880). At the end he had come to the conclusion that the runes about origins contained legendary material, whereas the hero songs had a historical basis, although earlier both of these types had been considered to be truly mythical.

Reference: Krohn, Kaarle, *Die Folkloristische Arbeitsmethode,* Oslo, 1926, pp. 1–16.

Krohn, Kaarle (1863–1933) Kaarle Krohn was appointed in 1888 as Docent of Finnish and Comparative Folklore in the University of Helsinki. Thus sixty years ago the Finnish University became the first in the world to establish a chair of Folklore. While he was still a student in 1881, he collected folktales and later, from January, 1884, to July, 1885, with subvention from the Finnish Literary Society, he traveled to Olonetz and

Wärmland and brought back with him some 18,000 folklore items, among which were about 8,000 folktales. It was also with the folktale that he began his scholarly productions: *Bär (Wolf) und Fuchs, eine nordische Tiermärchenkette* (1889), and *Mann und Fuchs, drei vergleichende Märchenstudien* (1891). Later he developed and advanced the historic-geographic method of folklore investigation and published his final statement of this in *Die folkloristische Arbeitsmethode* (Oslo, 1926). In the latter part of his life he turned to the investigation of the *Kalevala*, and his principal work is *Kalevalastudien* (1924–28), *FFC* 53, 67, 71–2, 75–6. The results of this work are expressed in the following manner by Uno Harva: "The epic songs collected in the *Kalevala* refer to historical happenings; the figures which played a part were heroes of a past age; the geographical background is a landscape of southwestern Finland with its old population centers. The period of development of these old historical songs goes back into the dawn of Finnish history. Earlier Krohn had held for a mythical or legendary background of the songs, but now he was convinced of their historical nature." (*FFC* 112, p. 15 f.). Kaarle Krohn showed a lively interest in mythology, as evidenced by his *Skandinavisk mytologi* (Uppsala, 1922); his *Magische Ursprungsrunen der Finnen (FFC* 52, 1924); and his *Zur finnischen Mythologie (FFC* 104, 1932). Along with Axel Olrik he founded in 1907 the Folklore Fellows (Folkloristische Forscherbund, Féderation des Folkloristes, etc.), an international association generally known by the initials FF. The membership of the association consisted of members of folklore societies in various lands, and other folklore scholars who undertook the duty of aiding comparative folklorists throughout the world with the furnishing of material from their own countries which was difficult to obtain. Up to his death he was the editor in chief of the well known series *FF Communications*. Of this series he issued more than 100 numbers, and since his death the work has continued under the auspices of the Finnish Academy of Sciences and with the collaboration of scholars from the Old and New Worlds.

As an original scholar in the fields of the epic song and of the folktale, Kaarle Krohn deserves a very high place. His greatest contributions to folklore study came, however, from his extraordinary ability as an organizer and coordinator of the efforts of other scholars. During an entire generation he conducted an extensive program of study of the folktale and related subjects in which he secured the collaboration of scholars in all parts of the world. Helsinki became the Mecca for young folklorists, who went there to profit by weeks or months of association and stimulus which came from his sympathetic and ever kindly encouragement. By 1890 he had conceived of a large plan of international folklore research, which would be based upon as large a body of material as possible. Such a plan involved classification and cataloging of material from manuscripts, archives, and other sources, the perfection of a method of investigation, and the promotion of as many of these investigations as possible. Finally he hoped to make a synthesis of the results of these investigations. Fortunately, at the end of his life he completed his synthesis and published it as *Uebersicht über einige Resultate der Märchenforschung (FFC* 96, 1931).

Aarne, Antti (1867–1925) Of Finnish folklorists it was Aarne who developed furthest the historic-geographic method of folktale investigation. The first works, *Vergleichende Märchenforschungen* (1908) and *Die Zaubergaben* (1911) received prompt recognition. In 1913 he enunciated the theoretical principles underlying this method in his *Leitfaden der vergleichenden Märchenforschung (FFC* 13). He then began a series of detailed and thorough studies of individual folktales: *Die Tiere auf der Wanderschaft (FFC* 11, 1913); *Der tiersprachkundige Mann und seine neugierige Frau (FFC* 15, 1914); *Schwänke über schwerhörige Menschen (FFC* 20, 1914); *Der Mann aus dem Paradiese (FFC* 22, 1915); *Der reiche Mann und sein Schwiegersohn (FFC* 23, 1916); and *Die magische Flucht (FFC* 92, 1930). He also investigated two folk songs, *Das estnisch-ingermanländische Maie-Lied (FFC* 47) and *Das Lied von Angeln der Jungfrau Vallamos (FFC* 48). For these studies Aarne assembled an astonishing amount of material necessitating several extensive foreign trips so that he might visit the most important libraries and archives.

Earlier in his scholarly work he had observed that the proper investigation of a folktale, because of the wealth of material and the difficulty of assembling the necessary literature, was an extremely difficult undertaking. It was his ambition to overcome these difficulties for himself and also to be helpful in this respect to all other scholars. With the collaboration of several other scholars in his field he brought to a successful conclusion a very important idea. He constructed a *Verzeichnis der Märchentypen (FFC* 3, 1910) in which he classified all of the well-known folktales in European tradition and gave to each of these types a standard number by which it could always be exactly designated. This type-index proved to be a very great aid to all investigators of the tale, and later it was considerably expanded by Stith Thompson (*FFC* 74, 1928). By this system of type-index, Aarne catalogued all the Finnish folktales (*FFC* 5 and 33) and also the Estonian tales and legends (*FFC* 25). In 1912 he also issued a type-index of Finnish origin legends (*FFC* 8). Since 1910 a large number of folktale catalogs of various people have been issued with arrangement according to Aarne's system.

On the bibliographical side Aarne prepared in 1913 a very valuable *Übersicht der Märchenliteratur (FFC* 14).

Aarne was convinced that the folktale as such did not have any value as an aid toward the study of mythology or other subjects outside its own field. He insisted that the folktale could not be of any use for such studies until its own history had been determined through a comparative investigation. Aarne's monographic studies, according to the opinion of Kaarle Krohn (*FFC* 64, pp. 22 ff.) "have shown that the idea that the only permanent parts of a folktale were the separate motifs is an error, and these studies of Aarne have demonstrated that every single folktale has its particular plot and its own unified composition. . . . As far as many of the folktales are concerned he was the first who was able to show in detail that Benfey's theory of their origin in India was correct. But at the same time he showed that there are other tales belonging to the same general group which undoubtedly had their origin in western Europe during the Middle Ages.

He threw much light on the wandering of folktales from the Orient toward the West and on the development of local forms. He moved up the time of origin of the folktales from an indefinite antiquity to a definite historical period." Aarne also used the historic-geographic method for the investigation of riddles in his *Vergleichende Rätselforschungen (FFC 26–8, 1918–20)*. In these pioneer riddle studies he was able to demonstrate an Oriental cultural influence extending into the Western countries.

Although Aarne never had good health and although it was not until 1922 that his financial situation improved, when he received his post as extraordinary Professor, and therefore spent much time and strength as a teacher in the lower schools, the amount of his scholarly accomplishments was incredible. The products of his research are outstanding through the remarkable richness of the material which he used, through the clarity of his presentation, and through the great care he took before arriving at conclusions.

Reference: Krohn, Kaarle, *Antti Aarne, FFC* 64, 1926.

Chief Aspects of Finnish Folklore: The Finnish runes
The folk poetry of the Finns is characterized by a great number of epic songs or runes (Finnish *runo*). The Finns used the latter word to include folk songs, heroic poetry, and popular ballads in the ancient Finnish meter. A differentiation is made between the heroic and the magic runes. The former tell about the deeds of legendary heroes, Väinämöinen, Ilmarinen, Lemminkäinen, etc.; the latter are used for cures and other magic. Metrically the Finnish runes are trochaic tetrameter without strophic divisions. The rules for the construction of this verse are complicated and consist of much alliteration and parallelism. Something of the general spirit, though not of the detailed structure, is found in Longfellow's imitation of this verse form in his *Hiawatha*. In that poem he followed the general pattern not only of the Finnish meter but also of the general epic style.

Heroic Poetry and the Kalevala The famous Finnish heroic epic, the *Kalevala,* is the chief product of the folk poetry of the nation. The Finnish heroes have their own peculiar characteristics. Their fighting takes place not so much with swords as with words: Through the singing of magic runes the enemy is placed in all kinds of difficult situations and under enchantments. The latter in turn tries to free himself through his own knowledge of magic runes and to defeat his opponent. It is a conflict of singers and enchanters. The greatest singer of all is the old, wise Väinämöinen.

The Cycle of Väinämöinen A good idea of the nature of the Finnish epic poetry may be obtained from a short review of the songs about *Väinämöinen*. We know that at first Lönnrot intended to speak of his famous work as a collection of runes about Väinämöinen and only later changed the name to *Kalevala,* i.e. the home or country of the hero Kaleva. At any rate Väinämöinen is certainly the chief hero of the poem.

We first hear about the birth of Väinämöinen and the creation of the world from a broken egg which a duck has laid on the knee of Ilmatar, his mother. As a culture hero Väinämöinen fells trees and sows barley (Runes 1 and 2). On a journey Väinämöinen meets another hero, the Lappish singer and magician, Joukahainen. When their sledges meet in the narrow road,

they begin to quarrel and fight with each other, using their knowledge of the magic runes. Finally young Joukahainen is defeated by the old and wise Väinämöinen, and must promise his sister Aino in marriage to Väinämöinen (Rune 3). Väinämöinen meets Aino, the promised maiden, in the wood but he is unsuccessful in his courtship because the young girl rather than marry an old man drowns herself in the sea (Rune 4). Väinämöinen falls to bitter weeping and tries to fish her out of the sea. He catches a fish which is the transformed Aino, but he does not guess what it is and the escaped sea maiden laughs him to scorn. Väinämöinen grieves deeply but his mother from her tomb advises him to go to the Northland and find another daughter of the Suomi, more beautiful and more worthy than Aino (Rune 5).

Väinämöinen mounts a steed and begins his journey northward to Pohjola, but the evil Joukahainen prepares revenge. In spite of the warning of his mother, Joukahainen shoots at Väinämöinen and the third arrow strikes Väinämöinen's steed. Thereupon the hero falls upon the water and a mighty storm wind bears him far away from land, where he is compelled to swim six full years in the ocean (Rune 6). He swims only six days and nights through the waters of the deepest sea. Then there comes a giant bird from far off Pohjola which takes Väinämöinen on its back, and bears him to the distant shores of the Northland where he is left alone. The hero is badly injured and weeps for three days. Louhi, the mistress of Pohjola, recognizes that this is the weeping of a bearded hero. She goes to see Väinämöinen, inquires his name, takes the helpless hero in her boat, and rows to the dwellings of Pohjola. There she gives him warmth, shelter, and food, and he soon recovers.

Väinämöinen is eager to go home. Louhi asks him to forge for her the Sampo, the wonderful thing which produces plenty of all sorts of good things: this to be the reward for her help and hospitality. She also promises to give him her daughter. Väinämöinen answers that he himself cannot forge the Sampo but he will send Ilmarinen, who will forge it. Louhi then replies, "To him alone will I give my daughter." Thereupon Väinämöinen goes home (Rune 7).

The daughter of Pohjola sits upon the rainbow weaving webs of golden texture. On his journey home Väinämöinen sees the charming maiden and invites her to come into his snowsledge. The maiden answers that the life of a married woman is very hard. Väinämöinen now performs several difficult tasks imposed upon him by the maiden. The last of these is to make a ship from the splinters of a spindle. Attempting this work he lets the axe fall and cuts his knee. He now begins the magic incantations, such as those about the origin of iron, and thus attempts to stop the bleeding from his wound. His knowledge is insufficient and he must seek the aid of a magician (Runes 8 and 9). Väinämöinen begins to build a vessel. Sampsa Pellervoinen goes to find the proper wood for the vessel and chooses an oak tree. Now Väinämöinen begins to build his vessel by means of singing magic songs, but, alas, three words are wanting. Väinamöinen journeys to Tuonela (the home of the dead) in order to find the ancient wisdom, but he does not succeed and escapes from Tuonela only with great difficulty (Rune 15). A shepherd comes to meet him and says that he can find the words of wisdom in the mouth of the wise giant, Antero Vipunen. Väinämöinen troubles and awakens the giant from the dead; the giant swallows him and finds the morsel the sweetest of all meals. The hero builds a boat through his magic knowledge and establishes a smithy, rows about, and forges inside the body of the giant. The hero says that he is ready to stop the torment if Vipunen will teach him the lost words of wisdom. Old Vipunen opens his store of knowledge and for three days sings the magic songs of wisdom about the origin of things.

Having accomplished his purpose, Väinämöinen leaves the great stomach of the giant and goes home. He finishes the magic-built vessel, and the voyage to Pohjola for the beautiful maiden of the rainbow can be started (Rune 17). On the return from Pohjola the pair come to a waterfall and the boat is caught fast on the back of a great pike. The fish is caught and the front part cooked and eaten. From the jaws of the pike Väinämöinen makes a "kantele," the popular harp-like Finnish instrument. Several of the party attempt in vain to play. Finally Väinämöinen plays on the kantele and all living beings of the earth, the air, and the water hasten to the spot to listen. All of these weep and Väinämöinen also weeps, his tears dropping into the sea and changing into beautiful blue pearls (Rune 41). In a struggle in the lake Väinämöinen loses his kantele and cannot find it. He makes a new one of birchwood and on this he plays and also delights all creatures (Rune 44).

The mistress of Pohjola sends terrible diseases. These Väinämöinen heals by his powerful incantations and magic unguents (Rune 45). The mistress of Pohjola sends a bear to destroy the herds of Kalevala. Väinämöinen kills the bear and a great feast is held (Rune 46). When the moon and the sun descend to listen to the playing, the mistress of Pohjola succeeds in capturing them, hides them in a mountain, and steals fire from the homes of Kalevala (Rune 47). Väinämöinen discovers by divination that the moon and the sun are hidden in the mountain of Pohjola and after heroic adventures he succeeds in releasing them from their prison (Rune 49).

The last rune, 50, gives us a well-built picture of the change from the era of paganism to the era of Christianity. The virgin Marjatta swallows a cranberry and gives birth to a boy. Väinämöinen comes to inquire into the matter and advises that the ill-omened boy should be put to death. But the child reproaches him for his unjust sentence. The boy is baptized as the king of Karelia. At this Väinämöinen is grievously offended and leaves the country, but first he declares that he will come again and will be useful to his people. He sails away in a copper boat to a sphere between earth and heaven, but he leaves behind him as a parting gift his kantele and his powerful songs.

Construction of the Kalevala Although the people like to bring together all kinds of characteristics and deeds around the figure of a beloved hero which originally were entirely foreign to his character, nevertheless they themselves do not construct a fully rounded and unified epic poem. The Finnish heroic songs are grouped around the old, wise Väinämöinen and the principal narrative subject is the stealing of the magic mill, the "sampo." The hand of Lönnrot, however, was necessary to transform these single songs and their cycles into a *Kalevala*. According to the opinion of Kaarle Krohn, the songs of the *Kalevala* were composed in western Finland, where they were no longer to be found in the end of the last century, but were still preserved in Karelia and among the Orthodox Finns. Karelia and the neighborhood of the governments of Archangel and Olonetz are to be considered as refuges in which the folk tradition was not formed, but rather has only been retained for a long time. Place names, among other things, indicate western Finland as the place of origin of the runes. Moreover, Kaarle Krohn came to the conclusion that the epic runes had been composed in historic times, that they reflect historic occurrences, reworked indeed according to the laws of the structure of the folk epic so that the historic reality remains hardly recognizable. He conjectures for example, that the journey of the Finnish hero to Pohjola after the sampo shows a reminiscence of the crusade of the Finns to the rich island of Gottland. See SAMPO.

As in all folk poetry, we find in the *Kalevala* many motifs which are also known among other people. Especially from three peoples have come many motifs of the Finnish runes: Scandinavians, Russians, and Lithuanians. The Scandinavian and Lithuanian influence took place in heathen times, but the Russian contribution did not begin before the 14th to 16th centuries and was intensified much later, around the year 1700. The Scandinavian current flowed through western Finland and Estonia, and then spread over the whole country. The Lithuanian influence is to be detected in Estonia, Ingermanland, and the whole of eastern Finland. The Russian influence penetrated into Ingermanland, into the eastern part of Karelia, and later into the governments of Olonetz and Archangel.

Although the Finns have borrowed many motifs from their neighbors, and have repaid them with many of their own, it is noteworthy that the Finns have preserved these in much purer and more original form than the folk from whom they have received them. This fact is of great importance for comparative folklore and clears up many obscure points in Scandinavian, Russian, and Lithuanian mythology. Of course, there are also some purely Finnish myths, such as the creation of the world by a bird. The borrowed material likewise has been so reworked and elaborated by the Finns that what they have produced is essentially new.

Magic runes As shown in the studies of Lönnrot (1880) and Kaarle Krohn (1924) the Finnish magic runes were of two kinds. Runes of one of these types depend upon some particular situation or story taken from the Bible. These are the more recent of the two, and have been borrowed from Sweden. The other type of rune gives an account of the origin of sickness or of other things, such as fire, iron, etc., and is used to remove the appropriate evil. This second kind of magic rune is older and is of real Finnish origin. We do not find exact parallels to these anywhere else. The more highly developed magic runes which are mixed with elements taken from the epic songs are to be found in the eastern part of Finland. On the other hand, in the western part of the country magic runes are shorter and more primitive.

Reference: For a discussion in English see J. Abercromby, "The Magic Songs of the Finns," *Folk-Lore*, I, 17–46, 331–48; II 31–49 (London, 1890–1891).

Lyric Songs Of less importance in the history of Finnish tradition than either the epic songs or the magic runes are the folk lyrics which appear in modern metrical form. Among these the marriage songs occupy an especially important place. A selection of lyric songs was early published by Lönnrot under the name, *Kantelatar* (1st ed. 1840; 2nd ed. 1887). A German translation of these were made by H. Paul, the translator of *Kalevala*.

The ballads (see Erich Kunze, *Finnische Volksballaden*, Jena, 1943) belong largely to international tradition. They are mostly borrowed from Sweden from the 17th century onward. Frequently, however, they have retained original traits which are no longer to be found among the Swedes. The ballad of the *Cruel Brother*, for example, displays a more natural and more original form than in England itself (Child, *English and Scottish Ballads*, #13).

Among the original Finnish ballads appears the legend of St. Henry, who converted the Finns to Christianity. The ballad concerning the killing of Elina, one of the longest of the Finnish ballads, extending to more than 400 lines, is based on a historical circumstance. In eastern Finland we find a lengthy song concerning the Creator (*Luojan virsi*). The Orthodox Finns also possess laments which they use both for marriages and for funerals. These apparently were borrowed from the Russians.

Folktales and Legends The Finnish collectors of folklore have been more interested in the epic songs than in folktales and legends. Lönnrot recorded only about 80 folktales. The proper taking down of the tales demands a longer preparation on the part of the collector. It was not possible to make successful recordings of tales until Finnish shorthand had been properly developed. It was also true that folktales were not very much valued since it seemed clear that many of them were no more than free translations from the Russian.

As early as 1838–39 the Finnish Literary Society sent M. A. Castrén on an expedition especially to collect folktales. He hoped that he would find in the tales and legends of the people fragments of ancient myths in prose and that these fragments would clarify many obscure points in the songs of the *Kalevala*. He was soon disillusioned, since almost immediately he recognized the Russian influence and came to believe that there was nothing original to be found. Nevertheless, rather early four volumes of Finnish folktales were issued by E. Salmelainen (*Suomen kansan satuja ja tarinoita*, 1852, 1854, 1863, and 1866). This collection did not contain a single legend or tradition. Another collection of Finnish folktales, *Suomalaisia kansansatuja*, was edited by Kaarle Krohn and appeared in 1866 and 1893.

Important for the progress of collecting folktales in Finland was the expedition of Kaarle Krohn in the year 1884–85. By the use of shorthand he recorded over 8,000 folktales from the people and began his leadership in the scientific investigation of the popular tale. (For some details on this development see discussion of Kaarle Krohn and Antti Aarne in this article.)

The wealth and variety of Finnish folktales is due to the fact that in Finland two quite different cultural influences in the field of folklore came into contact, the

western European and the eastern European. The folktales from the West came from Scandinavia, those from the East from northern Russia. Both streams mingled and also received from the Finns their own characteristic modifications. Moreover, these Finnish folktales have retained many original traits which have long ago disappeared both in Scandinavia and in Russia. In the animal tales, which also appear sometimes in verse, and in the folktales concerning the stupid ogre the Western character is most important. On the other hand, in tales concerning kings and princesses the Eastern influence is predominant. Jests about stupid people and fools are very popular, and many communities use these for making sport of each other. In Österbotten they are particularly fond of telling tales about the foolishness of people from Savolax.

The collecting and publishing of mythical legends was long neglected. Not until 1935 was this area seriously cultivated. But now the Finnish Literary Society has important plans for future investigations. It has transcribed on cards some 75,000 legends and elaborated a classification for legends. This classification is divided into 15 headings and each heading into subdivisions. The work is in the hands of Lauri Simonsurri (see *Studia Fennica*, vol. V, pp. 103–25). As an example of his work, he has just published a collection of about 900 legends, *Myytillisia tarinoita* (Mythical Legends, Helsinki, 1947).

A good monograph concerning house demons of the Finns is the work of the well-known folklorist, Martti Haavio, *Suomalaiset kodinhaltiat* (Finnish Household Fairies), Porvoo, 1942.

Important for the comparative investigation of legends are those collected from the Swedes who are living in Finland, and published as *Finlands svenska folkdiktning* (1931).

It is interesting to note that the Finnish saints' legends which they received from western Europe have now found refuge among the Karelians. The Finns who became Protestant no longer retain an interest in these legends, but the Orthodox Karelians still keep telling and enjoying them. Oriental legends have also found their way to the borders of Finland (see Haavio, "Über orientalische Legenden und Mythen in Grenz-Karelien und Aunus," *Studia Fennica*, vol. II, 1–53, Helsinki, 1936).

References:
Schreck, E., *Finnische Märchen*, Weimar, 1887.
Löwis of Menar, A. von, *Finnische und Estnische Volksmärchen*. Jena, 1922.

Proverbs and Riddles Proverbs, which the Finnish people are very fond of using in daily life, were the earliest form of folklore to receive the attention of the educated classes. The first collection, by H. Florinus, appeared in the year 1701 and was the earliest of all books on folklore in the Finnish language. This was followed after many years by the collections of Judén (1818), Gottlund (1832), and Lönnrot (1842). Even later ones have been issued by E. Aspelin and W. Forsman. Proverbs have likewise been composed in the old Finnish meters and often they have two or more parallel stanzas. In respect to their content, they differ markedly, according to the period of their composition. They express very clearly the ideas and character of the Finnish people. Especially in Savolax the people like to enrich their daily speech with proverbs.

The riddles likewise are always composed in metrical form and they usually consist of two or more stanzas. The first Finnish riddles were published as examples of the ancient Finnish meter in the first grammar of the Finnish language written by Eskil Petræus (1649). The first actual collections of riddles were those of Ganander (1783) and Lönnrot (1844, 2nd ed. 1851). The most recent collection and the best arranged is that of M. Haavio and J. Hautala, *Suomen kansan arvoituskirja* (The Book of Finnish Popular Riddles, Porvoo, 1946). From the collections of the Finnish Literary Society, which now contain about 50,000 riddles, the authors have chosen and edited 3,500.

Other Kinds of Folk Literature The folk plays of the Finns were first published by Porthan. As for games and dances, A. H. Reinholm (1819–1893) left a large collection at his death. In these the Swedish influence is very strong.

The first scholarly collection of folk melodies, edited by R. Cajanus and A. Borenius, was published in 1888 by the Finnish Literary Society. Recently the great collection, *Suomen kansan sävelmiä* (5 vol., 1896–1945), has been completed. Concerning folk music, Armas Launis and Ilmari Krohn have made very valuable investigations.

The most important collector of superstitions and beliefs was a village blacksmith from Cajana, Heikki Meriläinen. The publication of superstitions which early begun by Porthan and E. Lencqvist (*De superstitutione veterum Fennorum theoretica et practica,* 1782), has been carried on in recent years by M. Waronen (1891–1892) and by A. V. Rantasalo (1912–1934). In their beliefs and superstitions, the Finns have been most influenced by the western Europeans.

Concerning the religious practices of the Finnish peoples, there have appeared several large volumes in the series *Suomen suvun uskonnot* (Religion of the Finnish Tribes) by K. F. Karjalainen, Kaarle Krohn, and Uno Harva-Holmberg. These have appeared also in German in *FFC.* Harva-Holmberg is certainly the best-informed scholar today in the field of folk beliefs for all the Finno-Ugric peoples.

References:
The Kalevala, The Epic Poem of Finland, into English by J. M. Crawford, 2 vols. New York, 1st ed., 1888, 2nd ed., 1891.
Comparetti, D., *The Traditional Poetry of the Finns.* London, 1898. (Mostly out of date.)
Launis, Armas, *Über Art, Entstehung und Verbreitung der estnisch-finnischen Runenmelodien.* Helsinki, 1913, *MSFO* XXXI.
Kalevala. The Land of Heroes, translated by W. F. Kirby, 2 vols. 1st ed. 1907; 3rd ed., London, 1925.
Krohn, Kaarle, *Kalevalastudien,* I–VI, Helsinki, 1924–1928.
Salminen, Väinö, *Suomalaisten muinaisrunojen historia* (History of the Old Finnish Poetry), Publication of the Finnish Literary Society, vol. 198. Helsinki, 1934.
Haavio, Martti, *Suomalaisen muinaisrunouden maailma* (The World of the Ancient Finnish Poetry). Porvoo, 1935.
Nordische Rundschau, Kiel, 1935. (Articles by M.

Haavio, U. Harva, H. Jensen: for the hundredth anniversary of the *Kalevala.*)
Loorits, Oskar, "The Spirit of the Kalevala," *Baltic Countries,* vol. II, pp. 64–66, Torun, 1936.
Krompecher, Bertalan, "Die Entstehung des Kalevala," *Studia Fennica,* vol. IV, pp. 5–47, Helsinki, 1940.
Meuli, Karl, *Kalevala, Altfinnische Volks- und Heldenlieder.* Basel, 1940.
Meyer, Rudolf, *Das Geisteserbe Finnlands,* Der Finnische Mythos und das Volksepos "Kalevala." Basel, 1940.   STITH THOMPSON and JONAS BALYS

Finno-Ugric peoples The Finno-Ugric family consists of several groups: 1) The Ugric group consisting of the Magyars, Ostyaks, and the Voguls, the last two peoples forming the Ob-Ugric stock; 2) The Permian group: Votjaks and Ziryens; 3) The Volga group: Cheremis and Mordvins; 4) The Lapps; 5) The Baltic Finns: Vepse, Votic, Livs, Ingrelians, Estonians, and Finns.

The Finno-Ugric peoples belong to the Uralic stock, and their old homeland was in the regions beside the middle of the Volga River. The philologists and ethnologists mention several ages as the Finno-Ugric tribes separated themselves from the common stock. The oldest is the Uralic Age, up to 3000–4000 B.C., when the Finno-Ugric and Samoyede tribes were living together. The following is the Finno-Ugric Age, until the Voguls, Ostyaks, and Magyars were separated. Then followed the Permic Age, until the Votjaks and Ziryens were separated; and finally the Volga Age, as long as the Cheremis and Mordvins were living together with the Baltic Finns. The latter, also the ancestors of the Finns, Estonians, Livs, and other smaller units, reached the shore of the Baltic in about 1200 B.C. The Finns went to their modern homeland from Estonia. The Baltic Finns, at first the Livs, came into contact with the later-arriving Indo-European tribes of the Balts, also ancestors of the Lithuanians and Latvians, and many exchanges occurred in the language and other cultural elements, folklore included.

Some of these peoples are very small in number: Livs and Votic, number scarcely 1,000 of each, Ingrelians about 13,000, and Vepse, 26,000. Nevertheless, many of the Finno-Ugric peoples have great riches of folklore and a well-developed mythology. The influence from their neighbors, Scandinavians and Russians, is important. The worship of water deities is well developed among all Finno-Ugric peoples. We find also such interesting religious phenomena as worship of the bear, shamanism, and often a very clear belief in a god of heaven as the supreme deity. The Finno-Ugrians—excepting the Hungarians, Estonians, and Finns—are now living as primitive stocks, mostly as fishers, hunters, reindeer herders, and primitive planters. Their Christianity is only superficial, therefore their indigenous rich folklore and mythology are especially attractive and important for the ethnologist.

Literature:
H. Paasonen, *Über die urspünglichen Seelenvorstellungen bei den finnisch-ugrischen Völkern.* Helsinki, 1909.
U. Holmberg, *Finno-Ugric, Siberian,* vol. IV in *The Mythology of All Races,* edited by MacCulloch. Boston, 1927.

R. Indreko, *Origin and Area of Settlement of the Finno-Ugrian Peoples.* Heidelberg, 1948.

K. F. Karjalainen, *Die Religion der Jugravölker*, 3 vols. Helsinki, 1921–27. FFC 41, 44, 63.   [JB]

fiofio A concept of Surinam Negro belief: an insect engendered by surface friendliness, exchange of gifts, etc., between persons, one or both of whom harbor unspoken enmity or resentment. Fiofio causes illness and eventual death, at least death of the soul, of those who veil their enmity in a show of friendship. An open fight is recommended as a healthful thing. Salvation from the sure death caused by fiofio can be attained with the help of a diviner, who ascertains the hidden cause of the resentment. Then a public ceremony called *puru mofo* (literally, withdraw from the mouth) is performed to purify the minds of those involved and to remove the resentment. (See Herskovits, *Suriname Folklore,* pp. 42, 53, 745; *Man and His Works,* pp. 59–60).

Fionn MacCumal Hero of the Finn or Fenian cycle of Old Irish legend and romance, a chieftain of the 3rd century; leader of the Fianna, and like them noted for enormous stature, extraordinary strength and skill. Fionn himself was famed for generosity and wisdom. Fionn's story begins with his birth and secret nurturing in the forest and his boyhood wonder deeds (once he threw a huge stone over a house, ran through the house and caught it on his finger as it fell). He was named by the poet Finegas in whose service wisdom filled him from eating the salmon that fed on the nuts of the nine hazels of wisdom. He organized the Fianna for the High King at Tara, fought great battles, and had many adventures of the hunt, encounters with giants and hags, and experienced and overcame various enchantments. His first love was Sadb, who was transformed into a deer; their child, Oisín, was discovered in the forest by the dog, Bran.

The story of Fionn's pursuit of his friend and kinsman, Diarmuid, and Gráinne, his promised wife, the final overtaking, and Diarmuid's death in the forest because in the end Fionn could not bring himself to carry water to Diarmuid is one of the most moving and humanizing of the stories about Fionn. The Fianna were finally overcome in the battle of Gabra, in which Oscar, Fionn's grandson, was killed. Fionn never wept tears in his life except for the death of Oscar, and for Bran. Fionn is said to be sleeping now in a cave in the hills of Ireland, surrounded by his big men. When next the Fenian chant is heard, they will all rise again. See BRAN (2); OISÍN.

fir In ancient Greece the fir was sacred to Artemis; a branch tipped with cones and twined with ivy was carried by some of the Dionysian revelers in her honor. Some say the Trojan Horse was built of silver fir. And this wood was used for symbolic reasons in the ceiling of Solomon's temple. The staff of Bacchus was tipped with a fir cone. Legend says that Attis (Atys) was turned into a fir tree by Cybele as he was about to commit suicide. She sat mourning under the tree until Zeus promised that the tree should be evergreen. The Phrygian myths claim that Attis was metamorphosed by Cybele while dying of a wound inflicted by Zeus's boar, or by a Phrygian king in combat. There are indications that the silver fir is as old a birth tree as the palm, especially in the north of Europe. The *ailm* of the Old Irish tree

alphabet would seem to have been a silver fir, rather than the elm, which it became at a later date. This tree whose day was the first of the new year (the extra day of the winter solstice) was female, the tree of birth, sister to *Idho*, the yew of death. There is an Anglo-Roman altar dedicated to the Mothers which has a representation of the fir on it.

Among the Votjaks of Finland the fir tree is sacred and certain branches are regarded as family gods to which sacrifices are made. These people place a fir branch on a shelf in the house and offer sacrifices of bread, meat, and drink. When a house is being built, a small fir tree is set up under the house and a cloth spread before it on which sacrifices are laid out. After a funeral the Finnish Votjaks beat each other with fir branches while returning from the cemetery, to deter the spirits from following them home.

Among the Ostyaks of Siberia, the fir tree is represented by a fir pole to which sacrifices are made. Fir boughs are also used as flagellants at Christmas among many Northern peoples. One of the probable reasons for the popularity of the fir as a Christmas tree is its association with the winter solstice as well as its evergreen nature. Fir or beech logs are most commonly used for Yule logs. Among the Germans it is unlucky to have an odd number of candles on the Christmas tree and among most peoples it is necessary to remove the tree before Twelfth Night or Epiphany. Decorations must also be removed from the church before Candlemas, or misfortune will follow; any leaf or twig remaining in a pew signifies the death of one of the occupants. Death of the master or mistress will follow where a fir tree has been struck by lightning. Pliny looked on the fir as a funereal tree. In Bavaria, poachers seek out a fir tree before dawn on St. John's morn and eat the seeds of a cone growing straight up to make themselves invisible.

In Germany the fir tree is said to cure gout. In some parts a knot is tied in one of the branches; in others the patient goes to a fir tree after sundown on three successive Fridays and, by reciting a magic rime, transfers his gout to the tree, which will wither and die. Turpentine or balsam from the leaves and tips is used for scurvy and troubles of the lungs and breast. Fir balsam is used on wounds and ulcers, and in Newfoundland, for chapped hands. The inside bark is beaten to a pulp and used as a poultice on boils. The Chippewa Indians use it to cure headache.

Firbolg Literally, men of the bags, from Irish *fir*, men, and *bolg*, bag: a mythical, pre-Celtic people of Ireland, defeated first by the Fomorians and later run out by the Tuatha Dé Danann. They settled in Greece, were enslaved and made to carry earth from the valleys to the bare hills, made leather bags to carry it in, later made boats out of the bags, and escaped to Ireland. After their defeat at the battle of Mag Tured they took refuge in the islands of Aran, Islay, Man, and Rathlin.

fire Fire, one of the "elements" of the ancients, has been called the greatest invention of mankind. There are some who would question the "invention" of fire, claiming that man must have obtained fire from natural conflagrations, from forest or prairie fires, from volcanic eruptions, from lightning-fired trees. But the coincidence of the first evidences of both flint-shaping and fire-taming is too great to be ignored, and a relationship between the two must be supposed. Man, primitive or late, would obviously notice the resemblance of the flint sparks to the sparks given off by burning logs or to lightning flashes. And then control of this element, as of other things in the world about him, would become man's accomplished goal in a relatively short time.

The mythology of the origin of fire, however, gives no clue to this. From the constant occurrence of wood-friction to produce fire in the myths and in ritual, it might be supposed that this was the original method. Throughout the world, from South America to Australia, Africa to Europe, Asia to North America, the myths indicate that the original fire of mankind, stolen usually from the gods or from some other previous owner, was hidden in the trees or in a specific tree, and that ever since man has had to rub this wood to produce fire. The general Polynesian myth, for example, is typified in the Maori myth of Maui, who went to his grandmother, Mahuika, the goddess of fire, to obtain it. She produced so much fire, from her fingers and toes, that everything began to burn. The rain put out the fires, but still it remained in some of the trees, from which mankind ever since has been able to get fire. The Tembe of Brazil tell how an old man stole the fire from the vultures and put it in the trees. Sometimes, as among the Basongo-Meno of the Congo and some of the Kiwai in New Guinea, there exists a tradition that fire was discovered by accident, while drilling or sawing.

Two other motifs appear in the fire mythology often enough to be of interest. Among certain North American Indian tribes, fire is stolen and passed from animal to animal in a relay that finally outraces the owner of the fire. In the Pacific, e.g. the Wagawaga of New Guinea's Milne Bay area, the owner of fire is an old woman who keeps the flame in her vagina, producing it as she needs it, and hiding it from everyone else. The same concept occurs in the fire myth of the Tarumas of southeast British Guiana. The chain of reasoning that transfers the fire from the slot in the wood rubbed vigorously with a stick to the female genitals is a natural anthropomorphism, and the parallelism is as obvious as in the other etiological tale of the fire in the trees.

It is not surprising either to discover that in Europe the oak and its associated mistletoe are involved in the fire mythology, oak being a hard wood suitable for fire-making. Though later Greek mythology makes Hephæstus the guardian of the fires of the earth, the myth of the culture hero Prometheus indicates that Zeus, god of heaven and of the oak, was the possessor of the first fire. Prometheus stole this fire in a stalk of fennel (*en nartheki krypsas:* Apollodorus) and was punished for his deed by being chained while a vulture ate eternally at his liver. Diodorus Siculus says that Prometheus invented the fire-sticks, an accomplishment elsewhere attributed to Hermes. It is also curious to note that the gods of the smithy-fires, Hephæstus, Wayland, etc., are crippled, Hephæstus for example as the result of a fall from heaven. Perhaps these were originally the fire-bringers, the thieves who took the fire of the sun and brought it to earth. Perhaps they were chased by a bolt of lightning from the sky god, like that of the Andaman Creator who, angered by a bird, threw a burning log at

it and missed, the log falling to earth and bringing fire.

The fire gods are not only gods of the sun fire, lightning, earth (volcanic) fire. There are gods of the hearth fire, of the sacred altar fire, of the forest fire and the wildfire of the prairies. Hestia, Agni, Helios, Girru, Luġ: the list of fire gods might be made interminable, through almost every pantheon in the world.

Fire's use in magic is likewise widespread. Basically, fire is the purifying element (see the fires of Hell, for example), and throughout magical practice and religious usage, fire is ritually used to cleanse persons and animals and things. The Beltane and Midsummer fires of Europe have their purifying uses; need fires are built specifically to burn clean threatened animals and men. Among the Huichol Indians, the men and women, to purify themselves during expeditions to collect the cactus of the god of fire, tied knots in strings, a knot for each lover, and burned the string in a fire, thus purifying themselves. A Tartar khan of the Middle Ages received visitors or gifts only after they had passed between two fires. Demeter burned the mortality from Demophoon in a fire; and similarly the dross is burned from all substances by fires on altars or in alchemists' laboratories.

Among the Armenians, when a member of the family sets up his own household, he takes fire from the old home with which to build his new fire. So among the ancient Greeks: a colony's fire was lighted with fire taken from the public hearth of the mother city. The sacred hearth fires of the homes of Greece and Rome were paralleled by a community hearth fire. The undying fire of Rome was guarded by the Vestal Virgins; and even to this day eternal fires are kept burning to the sacred patriotic dead. The Olympic games of 1948 in London officially began with the lighting of the torch by fire brought from Olympia, Greece, by overland runners and warship. The symbolism of the torch passed "from falling hands" to other stronger hands is familiar. Fire thus becomes a mark of the continuing of civilization, passed on from generation to generation, the living element going on magically though its fuel is eaten up.

This phœnixlike character of fire, reborn anew from its recurring ashes, makes it one of the most mysterious of all substances. Fire glows within jewels of Indian folktale; it dances puzzlingly as the sign of spirits or gods over marshes and from the masts of ships; it glows in the wake of boats in tropic seas; it burns blue in the presence of spirits; it vomits from the mouth of the firedrake; it burns the bush which is not consumed. The sun burns plants to a crisp, and it brings life; lightning destroys a huge tree in a flash. In Australia and New Britain, among the Telugus and the Arabs, a heavy downpour may be stopped by quenching a fire with water. The sun is swallowed during an eclipse: the Sencis of Peru shot burning arrows into the sky to chase the devouring animal away. The Ojibwas of North America also shot arrows at the eclipsed sun, but their arrows were meant to rekindle the fire.

Brynhild slept within a ring of fire until some hero braved the flames to awaken her. The mistletoe protected homes against fire, especially against lightning, and it had the power of putting out fire. Destruction of towns in war was not complete until fire was applied and the buildings burned to the ground: God destroyed Sodom and Gomorrah with fire.

Everywhere in the world, when sacred fire is needed, it is made fresh and not taken from existing fires; often the old fires must all have been extinguished before the new fire is built. Nevertheless, as Crawley points out, primitive man seldom makes fire; usually there is some fire nearby from which he can obtain a brand.

It is perhaps in folktale that the myriad uses of, and beliefs about, fire are best illustrated. The hog's snout is rounded and incomplete because God had to go to a fire and interrupt the work of creation (A2286.1.1); passing through fire is used as a chastity test (H412.4) and as a suitor's task (H331.1.5); animals breathe fire (B742) or put out the executioner's fire and save the hero (B526.1). There are mountains, valleys, cities, castles, thrones, trees of fire in Arabian and Hindu tales. In a Sicilian story a swan maiden transforms herself into fire in an attempt to escape capture (D285). Just as Gawain's strength waxed and waned with the height of the sun in the heavens, so in a Spanish folktale the princess becomes more or less mad with the height of the fire (D2065.4), or she becomes sicker as the fire blazes and gets well when it goes out (D2064.2). In Malayan and Indonesian folktale, fire shows that a beautiful woman is present (D1061.1), as in the Philippine story where Ini-init discovered from afar the presence of Aponibolinayen in his house because it appeared to be blazing. The many motifs listed in the *Motif-Index* under "fire" serve to emphasize that man's civilization is based on a fire-complex that pervades practically every aspect of his life.

☞ Among American Indian tribes of the eastern United States fire is referred to as "Our Grandfather, Fire." The smoke is believed, by such tribes as the Shawnee, Fox, and other Central Algonquians, to carry the words of prayers up to the supreme deity. Before offering prayers small quantities of tobacco are sprinkled on the fire and the tobacco also ascends in the smoke as an offering to the deity, thus serving to validate the prayer.

How fire was first acquired is accounted for in the mythology of almost every North American Indian tribe. In the western part of the continent fire is usually said to have been stolen, often by an animal or a number of animals; it is said to have been hidden under the thief's wing, or in the tip of his tail, and transported thus, or passed on from one animal to another in a relay race. Other beliefs about fire are that a perpetual fire burns beneath the man-made mounds in the southern United States. The Natchez, a southern tribe, are said to have built their mounds in order to maintain a perpetual fire on them. Many new fire rites are held by tribes in the agricultural areas of native North America. [EWV]

☞ In the mythology of most South American tribes, man owes the possession of fire to some culture hero or to some benevolent animal, who stole it from some other animal or from some monster who refused to part with it. Generally the first attempts to steal the fire were unsuccessful until the hero used some clever stratagem. The acquirer of the fire then gave it to mankind or enclosed it in the wood from which Indians make their fire drill. [EWV]

Some Tupi-Guarani Indians say that one of the divine Twins stole fire from the vultures, after having lured these elusive birds by pretending to be a rotting corpse. A frog who swallowed some embers is the fire-giver of the Guarayu and Chane Indians. In the Chaco, a small rodent is either the jealous master of the fire or the hero who took it away from Jaguar. This feline is often described as the original owner of fire. In some Guiana tribes fire is said to have been produced by an old woman whenever she spat or defecated. The mythical Twins induced her to relinquish it. [AM]

firedrake A type of dragon found usually in Germanic and Celtic folklore. It lives in a cave, where it guards a great treasure. It protects itself by exhaling fire. Beowulf's final and fatal exploit was the killing of a firedrake. [MEL]

fire gods Chinese folklore about fire shows wide regional variations. Ceremonies in Canton on the 22nd of the Sixth Moon were once very elaborate with processions, temporary altars, public prayers. On the Spring festival of Pure Brightness (Ch'ing Ming) ceremonial fires were once rekindled in the courtyard of the Imperial Palace. The Ministry of Fire is composed of a President and five stellar divinities. Chou Yang, a legendary emperor, taught his people to use fire to drive out snakes and wild animals, to keep enemies at a distance, and to forge metals. Huo Shêng, a priest who changed himself into a giant during one of the legendary battles near the beginning of the Chou Dynasty, was also a flame-thrower. Many devices were used to insure houses and shops against fire. Wood-prints of men and women in the act of intercourse pasted on the kitchen wall will prevent fire. One rationalization is that the fire god, being prudish, will avoid houses where such acts are in progress. Another rationalization is that because the yin and yang are at those times in balance, fire, a powerful yang element, cannot gain the ascendency. Because the householder cannot be assured that the harmonizing act is being perpetually performed, pictures are used. [RDJ]

first and last buried In many places it is believed that there is a penalty imposed upon the spirit of the first corpse interred in a new graveyard. It is reported from the Hesse and Westphalia districts of Germany that such a spirit is condemned to wander about eternally, never finding rest. In parts of England and Scotland it is held that the Devil will claim the first body buried in a new cemetery. This belief has been so strongly held that it has proved difficult to get graveyards started. In Scotland the problem was solved in one instance by interring the body of an unidentified tramp, and in Devon the spell was circumvented by the burial of a servant who was a stranger to the district.

In parts of Scotland, Ireland, and Brittany the belief prevails that the last buried in any cemetery must take no rest, guarding all the graves until the next one comes. From County Cork was reported the belief that the last buried has the task of carrying water to wet the lips of souls in purgatory. This may reflect the story in *Luke* xvi, 19–31 where the rich man in hell begs Abraham to send the recently deceased Lazarus "that he may dip the tip of his finger in water, and cool my tongue." [CFP]

first foot Superstitions connected with the symbolism of the first foot to cross the threshold on New Year's (sometimes Christmas or other days) are known to peoples from China to Ireland and belong to the cycle of beliefs, still imperfectly understood, connected with the significance of emerging from one state of existence into another. Thus in northern England it is unlucky to leave the house on the first day of the New Year until someone has come in. The first foot of the New Year to enter one's house brings either good or bad luck. In Scotland the first person to enter a house on New Year's Day got a kiss from the person who opened the door. In Yorkshire the first foot on Christmas Day was given money, gingerbread, or cheese. Although customs in China differ, the Chinese are in agreement that the first person to enter brings either good or bad luck. In many parts of the world girls perform ceremonies at odd times with the thought that the first person to enter the house or the room, or to be met at church, will show them something about their future husbands: tall, short, wealthy, poor, etc. [RDJ]

first-fruits Specifically, the first of an agricultural crop or vintage, but generally including the firstlings of domestic animals or of animals of the hunt or of fish in a catch; by extension, the feast or ceremony at which the first-fruits were eaten or sacrificed. The concepts underlying first-fruits ceremonies are principally two: 1) The part is representative of the whole; and 2) danger is inherent in new things. Because of this danger, from spirits dwelling in the grain, from the jealous dead, from the gods to whom all belongs, etc., some propitiatory gesture must be made. Therefore, before partaking, the tabu must be removed by giving up a fair share to the gods or spirits, or by indicating to them, by a ceremonial approach, that the food is a necessity and that their gift to man will not be wasted. First-fruits ceremonies thus are of two kinds, sometimes combined: sacrifice or feast. The sacrifice may be by burning, or by offering on an altar, by making formal presentation to the chief or priest, or as a token, offering the spirit of the food to the spirit. Feasts may be approached by a fasting period, by the taking of purgatives, by the use of new fire, etc. Frazer maintained that first-fruit ceremonies were communions, the partaking of the body of the god, a provocative but unnecessary hypothesis.

☞ Ceremonial preparation and eating of the first fruit or vegetable products gathered, or in the case of some West Coast tribes of the first salmon killed, is a widespread rite among North American Indians. In western North America several tribes prepared the first acorns gathered as a mush which everyone in the tribe tasted; after this was done, all could gather acorns and use them. The same was done for the first salmon, which was prepared and eaten by a priest among certain Northwest California and Oregon tribes. In the Eastern Woodlands strawberries and other wild berries were gathered and eaten after a dance festival; afterwards all persons could gather and eat the various kinds of berries. Corn, among the eastern agricultural tribes, was treated in much the same way. The Green Corn dance, so widespread in the Eastern Woodlands and Southeast, was probably essentially a first-fruits rite. Compare BUSK.

[EWV]

☞ In Mexico and other parts of Middle America, quite common is the custom of offering first-fruits to deities before partaking. The Huichol of Mexico have one of the most elaborate ceremonies. Both the new corn and the people must be purified and "baptized" before the corn can be eaten. This is done by each family or group of families in front of a home altar on which is placed an image or picture of the Virgin Mary. The Tarahumara have a similar celebration. Several families join together for an all-night fiesta at which they place roasting ears on a family altar, roast them ceremonially, smoke the maize with copal, and then eat it. Among the Popoluca of Veracruz a man and his wife go to the cornfield before sunrise, burn copal incense, cut seven roasting ears, return home and make tamales, and eat them at midnight of the same day. Only then can maize be eaten from that harvest in a profane manner. [GMF]

first is best A motif especially prominent in the chain tale in which the action completes a circle to return to its starting point. In a tale in the *Ocean of Story*, an ascetic transforms a mouse into a maiden. When she grows up he wishes to marry her to a great husband. So he calls the sun, but the cloud can hide the sun. And the wind can drive the cloud, and the mountain can resist the wind, and the mouse can dig holes in the mountain. Therefore, the ascetic changes the girl back into a mouse and gives her to the male mouse. This form must not be confused with the chain tale in which the action begins over and over endlessly when the starting point is again reached; in this type of the tale, the action is completed when the first of the characters reappears on the scene. See CHAIN TALE.

fish Conflicts and confusions in the reports about the fish-lore of various peoples point to the need of a new examination of this and other beliefs in terms of the ethnic atmosphere in which they occur. The Syrians regarded fish as holy, not to be eaten. The Bechuana and certain other Bantu tribes do not eat fish. In parts of India fish are said to be the favorite food of ghosts. Cornish fairies hate the smell of fish. Fish are oracles in Wales, tabu as food among some African tribes, forbidden to pregnant women in Serbia, and recommended in the Talmud. The Tasmanians do not eat fish that have scales.

Attempts to establish the existence of a fish cult in the eastern Mediterranean are inconclusive although the Syrian form of the Semitic goddess Derceto was a fish, and her dying and resurrecting son Tammuz (or Adonis) was associated with the fish, though again the data is inconclusive. The fish early became a Christian symbol: Christ fed the multitude with five loaves and two fishes (*Mark* vi, 38), and He made His disciples "fishers of men" (*Matt.* iv, 19). The Greek word for fish is *ichthos*, and the symbol may have been adopted as a pun on the words *Iesos Christos Theou Uios Soter*, Jesus Christ, Son of God, Saviour, a confessional formula. The Carib view that fish are always young and that men who lived on fish never grew old, together with local legends in many parts of the world about 100-year old fish in temple and other pools are suggestive.

Communities dependent on fish as articles of diet or commerce have special ceremonies. Many western Europeans spit on the hook to ensure a catch. In the south of

France the priest blesses the sea in a ceremony which in one or another form is found in other places. In Alaska the first fish of the season is specially honored. During the fishing season the Queen Charlotte Islanders banish one man of the tribe to the mountains. He may not light a fire or communicate with other members of the tribe. In New Caledonia the fishing season is opened by sacrifices to ancestors. When the men enter the water the women put out all but one of the fires, perform a dance and maintain silence until the men return. Fish totems have been reported from South Africa, Alaska, and North America. The Ottawa Indians believed that the souls of the dead entered fishes.

The orphaned Cinderella in a very early Chinese version of that tale is helped by a fish in much the same way as the northern European girl is helped by a tree growing from her mother's grave and the Anglo-French heroine is helped by a fairy godmother: all probably mother-surrogates. In Greenland the eating of certain fish is said to have made women and even men pregnant. Virgins in Brazil, Samoa, and India have been fertilized by gifts of fishes. If the husband of a childless woman ate a fish from the "Children's Sea" on the south coast of Java he would have offspring. Shape-shifters in the form of fishes have given fabulous gifts to fishermen for setting them free. See ATARGATIS. [RDJ]

fish dance A mimetic dance suggesting the motions of a fish. Menominee and Yuchi Indian fish dancers wave their arms like fins, the former with a dragging forward step simulating the tail. The Iroquois fish dance or *gẹdjoenọ* contains no mimetic gestures. The passing and repassing of partners is claimed to resemble the path of fish in the water, but the resemblance is vague. Only the Yuchi retain any vestige of ceremonial propitiation and thanksgiving to the spirits of this source of food supply. [GPK]

Fisher King In Chrétien de Troyes' *Perceval* and in later Grail stories, the lord of the Grail castle; possessor of the Grail, the bleeding lance, and the silver plate. Wounded by a spear thrust through his thighs, his only solace was in fishing. He can be healed only through the help of the Grail-seeker and when he is healed the waste land which surrounds his castle will become productive again. In Robert de Boron's *Joseph*, Bron is referred to as the Rich Fisher, though there is no account of his fishing literally as there is in *Perceval*. Nor does he possess a bleeding lance or a plate; he is simply the custodian of the Grail. The epithet fisher applied to him may derive from Christ's statement, "I shall make ye fishers of men." [MEL]

Five Brothers In Puget Sound mythology, a Snohomish story of five brothers, four of whom were tricked by the vengeful fifth into following an artificial seal far out through the straits and north through the open sea. It was foggy and the brothers were lost. They drifted to a land where the people were very tiny but powerful men. The brothers grew hungry; they had nothing to eat, so they stole halibut from the canoe of one of the dwarfs while he was diving for more. But the little man discovered the theft and the thieves and was so powerful that he easily threw them into his canoe and took them home. The mouths of these people were so small that they ate only the maggots from the halibut which they allowed to rot. So they permitted the four

Snohomish brothers to camp beside them and cook the halibut for themselves.

On the fifth day occurred the famous battle between the dwarfs and the ducks and cranes who came to attack them annually. The ducks and cranes killed the dwarfs in great numbers. The Snohomish defended the little people, and after they had killed many of the birds one observant duck said, "These are real Indians. Let's get away from here." So the ducks and cranes flew away, and the Snohomish revived the dwarfs by extracting the sharp-pointed feathers which the birds had shot into them.

That evening the dwarfs did not like the idea of the Snohomish eating the dead ducks, so they sent them away. On the way home the four brothers became so tired that they changed themselves into killer-whales in order to travel faster. They did not really want to be killer-whales, but in this condition they found that food was plentiful and travel easy. They returned home, took revenge on the fifth brother who had gotten them into all this, by leading him astray after red salmonberries until he died. Then they went out to sea and became killer-whales forever.

There are four known versions of this story, all starting with the wooden seal and the compulsory voyage into northern waters of either four or two brothers. All but one deal with the battle with the ducks. In a Puyallup-Klallam version, the brothers are captured by an Eskimo for stealing his fish and taken to Alaska. Ducks descend upon and kill the Eskimos. The brothers rescue them by pulling out the feather-spears and are therefore set free.

Five Gods of the House In Chinese folk belief, the five shên, or spirits of specific objects, who preside in every household. They are popularly known as Mên (or Mên Shên), gods of the door who keep watch and ward against evil spirits; Hu, god of the windows; Ching Chu'an, boy-spirit of the well; Chung Liu, god of the eaves; and Tsao Chün, lord of the kitchen stove, who presides over and observes the welfare and conduct of the whole house. See KITCHEN GODS. [RDJ]

flagellation Ceremonial whipping, whether symbolic or real, used to drive out evil spirits, to test the endurance of the celebrant during puberty or manhood ceremonies, or for the sexual stimulation of either the persons whipping or the persons being whipped. At times all three factors are potent. The lamas of Mongolia, Tibet, and North China, and priests and monks elsewhere, wear masks and engage in symbolic whippings in their devil dances. American Indians used whipping to test the endurance of their adolescent males. Stoicism during whipping is part of the lore of small boys in all parts of the world. Actual flagellation for the purpose of attaining salvation became epidemic in Europe in the 10th and 14th centuries and was associated with the willingness to endure pain for or at the hands of the beloved object. The sexual psychopaths have been subjects of a large body of literature about schoolmasters or schoolmistresses. Flagellation as part of social and religious orgies has been reported in numerous connections and needs further study in folklore. [RDJ]

flamen (plural *flamens* or *flamines*) In ancient Roman religion, one of a group of twelve to fifteen priests each serving a specific god. The flamen Dialis (Jupiter), flamen Martialis (Mars), flamen Quirinalis (Quirinus) were Majores, and always patricians; the others were Minores chosen from the plebeians. The flamen Dialis was one of the great officials of the state and had many restrictions and privileges attending the office. He married once, could not be divorced, and had to resign if his wife died. He could not touch horse, flour, dog, she-goat, beans, raw meat. He was prohibited from making oaths, wearing any but plain rings, having knots anywhere in his clothing. In public he always had to wear the apex, a special conical headdress wrapped with a strip of white wool; so forceful was this regulation that if the apex fell off during a sacrifice the flamen resigned his office.

flamenco An intensely erotic song and couple or solo dance of Andalusian Gipsies. The word *flamenco* may mean a Spanish soldier returned from Flanders, a vagabond on a par with Gipsies, or it may mean the flame-colored flamingo bird which lives in swamplands of southern Europe, northern Africa, and India. Neither interpretation is entirely plausible. The dance, the *cuadro flamenco*, contrasts with the ceremonial rounds and gay folk contras of northern Spain in its sensuous intoxication of gesture and counterrhythms of music, footbeats, castanets, and hand-clapping. Dancer and spectators are a unit, performers emerging from the crowd spontaneously and amid cheering. The cante flamenco, like the cante jondo (deep song), with guitar, wails in Oriental minor tonalities. Music and dance have local variants: Rondeñas, Malagueñas, Murcianas, Granadinas, Preteneras, Bulerias, Farrucas, Fandanguillos, Alegrías, Sevillanas, and others. All of them blend virtuoso footwork with undulating arm and torso motion, Oriental in their sinuousness. [GPK]

flax An annual plant (genus *Linum*) with stems about two feet high and blue flowers, and an inner bark which yields the flax of commerce. The mucilaginous seeds are called flaxseed or linseed. In Teutonic countries Holda is said to have introduced flax. It was in common use during the time of Charlemagne, who gave a subsidy to every farmer planting a certain area in flax. Linen cloth was so highly prized that even the angels of the Old Testament were clothed in it. Among the Hebrews it was unlawful to mix linen with other materials in cloth.

Many rites were performed to make the flax grow long and plentiful: jumping over Midsummer's Night fires, ringing church bells on Ascension Day, and running about in the fields on Senseless Thursday (the last Thursday of Carnival). In Yorkshire a man should sit on the bag three times and then face to the east before sowing to ensure a good crop. A few stolen seeds mixed in the bag was believed to help. In Bohemia, while flax belongs to Holda on six days, it belongs to the Devil on Saturday. Dire consequences befell those who had anything to do with it on Saturday, whether picking a flower or weaving cloth. In Estonia there is a household spirit, flax mother, who lives in the linen press and looks after flax. Witches cannot stand the sight of the flowers which are therefore often grown in door yards to prevent their approach. They were also tied to the horns of cattle for the same reason. But the witches used the seeds in their brews and would make a pact

with a farmer not to molest him for a year in return for a handful of the seeds gathered in the dark of the moon.

From the belief that it represents vigorous growth and life, flax was often used in medicine. In Bavaria sickly children were placed in the fields and flaxseed sprinkled over them so that they too would thrive. In Brandenburg persons afflicted with giddiness were advised to run naked three times around the flax field. This made the flax giddy, thus the patient was cured. The idea of flax absorbing ills was also known in Italy. A man who had a headache from working in the hot sun placed a ball of linen tow on a yellow plate and balanced this on his head. The pain, mistaking the plate for the sun, passed upwards and became caught in the tow which was immediately burned. In Ireland three pieces of tow applied to the skin will cure a stitch in the side. Flaxseed tea is very generally used as a cure for rheumatism and as a purgative. Flaxseed poultices are still recognized as beneficial for inflammation. For toothache, the Swabians sleep on a pillow of flaxseed. In Bohemia a girl wishing to become beautiful dances in flax leaves when she is exactly seventeen years old, unless her birthday falls on a Saturday when the flax belongs to the Devil.

flea According to Danish legend the flea was sent to pester mankind as a punishment for laziness. A Flemish tale claims they were created to give women work. However this may be, they have been living on the blood of mankind for many thousands of years in spite of the best efforts of alchemists, scientists, and exterminators. The ancient Egyptians, in the *Book of Cleopatra*, recommended anointing someone, presumably a slave, with ass's milk and all the fleas in the house would gather on him. This method is used in a modified form today in the United States where a sheep is brought into the house for the same purpose. A soldier from Mississippi told of using a goat in this manner, but his father objected, and made him sell the goat. However, after two days the goat had fulfilled its purpose and he remarked that fleas must have been bringing a good price, as he made three dollars on the transaction. Another ancient remedy appeared in the *Geoponica*, the only formal treatise on Greek agriculture. It advised a person in a flea-infested locality to cry, "ouch! ouch!" and the fleas would not bite. This is no longer effective. The use described in the old animal tale of the fox who backed slowly into the water with a piece of moss in his mouth, sounds more effective. All the fleas walked down his nose onto the moss; then he opened his mouth and said, "ahhh," while the fleas floated down the river. Pliny avers that if, on hearing the first cuckoo of spring, you gather up the earth under your right foot and sprinkle it in the bed and around the house, you will not be troubled with fleas all year. In England they recommend airing the bed before Easter. In other parts of England it is believed that fleas return from winter quarters on the first of March, and if the windows are kept closed and the doorstep swept on that day, you are rid of them for the year. Those who neglect this precaution may rid themselves of fleas by jumping over the Midsummer's Night fire. In the United States, splinters from a tree struck by lightning will drive them out of the house. When snow falls in May, if a little is melted in the fireplace, or if a dirty dish cloth is burned when you hear the first thunder in March, the fleas will be driven out of the house. The Irish drive fleas out with spearmint or foxglove. Southern U.S. Negroes use chinaberry leaves to get rid of them. In England it is believed that when fleas thirst for blood, it is a sign of rain. In Silesia it is considered good luck to be bitten on the hand, since there is a chance that the flea will go elsewhere, which is not the case if the flea is inside the shirt. In Germany and Austria to be bitten on the hand is a sign that you will be kissed. It is quite general belief that fleas desert one who is about to die. [JWH]

Fleeing Pancake Title and motif (Z31.3.1) of a general European cumulative tale, especially popular in Scandinavia. In America it is a popular nursery story under the title of the GINGERBREAD BOY.

Flight of the Chiefs The name of the ancient kingdom where lived the ancestors of the modern inhabitants of Bua province, Vanua Levu, Fiji: a legendary realm during whose existence a Fijian Golden Age held sway. Then, the inhabitants knew everything; they even played the card games that their descendants later learned from the white men; they were able to talk with the ancestral spirits, so good, so accurate were their religious and social usages. But at last Flight of the Chiefs broke up over the ambition of its chiefs, and the various villages with their selfish jealousies grew up. Tip of the Single Feather was the great hero of Flight of the Chiefs, invincible, huge, the son of The Eldest, who was chief of the kingdom. Many great men lived in those days, warriors and magicians: Curve of the Whale Tooth, a great warrior; Fog of the Path, who could bring up a fog to muddle enemies; and other such mighty men.

The Flight of the Chiefs is the title given by B.H. Quain to his collection of Fijian epic poetry, tales, and stories collected in the 1930's at The Place of Pandanus (Namuavoivoi) in Bua province. These traditional poems were composed by Velema, an old man who had heard the stories from his predecessors and who had the gift of composing. These poems, traditional though they are, are recomposed, from what the poet remembers, in each generation. He was a magician, whose war club and ax, passed down through his mother's family, gave him the ability to make these *Sere Dina*, true songs. From Solomoni, less gifted and not as highly regarded as an artist as Velema by his fellow Fijians, Quain obtained some of the epic tales, prose recitals of material originally heard by Solomoni as poetry. And whereas Velema obtained much of his information from the ancestors, Solomoni could not commune with them. The study gives an insight into the transmission of traditional lore in a non-literary society.

flint An opaque quartz, flint was widely used during the Stone Age because the manner in which it chips made it possible to secure a sharper, more permanent edge on the various implements needed by primitive man in his daily tasks. It was one of the first items of commerce. Conversion from the age of stone to the age of metal was a gradual process, accomplished at different times by different peoples. We have been able to observe it in recent times in the case of many of the tribes of the North American Indians. Even after stone implements ceased to be used in everyday life, they were often preserved in ceremonials because of tabus associated with metals, especially because iron is believed to be abhorrent to various classes of spirits, and because of the general inflexibility of religious practices. For instance, flint knives were used by the Jews for circumcision long after they were not in general use.

Throughout Europe, Asia, Polynesia in fact in almost all parts of the world where their use had been forgotten, the flint arrowheads and axes turned up by the farmer's plow are considered to have fallen from the sky, are often thought to be thunderbolts, and are called thunderstones. It was not until travelers returned from far places where these implements were in actual use that their origin was known. Even then these travelers' tales received little popular credence. In Scandinavia thunderstones were frequently worshipped as family gods who kept off spells and witchcraft. Beer was poured over them as an offering and they were sometimes anointed with butter. In Switzerland the owner of a thunderstone whirls it, on the end of a thong, three times round his head, and throws it at the door of his dwelling at the approach of a storm to prevent lightning from striking the house. In Italy they are hung around children's necks to protect them from illness and to ward off the evil eye. In Roman times they were sewn inside dog-collars along with a little piece of coral to keep the dogs from going mad. In Sweden they are protection from elves. In the French Alps they protect sheep, while elsewhere in France they ease childbirth. In Burma they are used as a cure and preventative for appendicitis. In Japan they cure boils and ulcers. In Malay and Sumatra they are used to sharpen the kris, are considered very lucky objects, and are credited with being touchstones for gold. Among the Slavs they cure warts on man and beast, and during Passion Week they have the property to reveal hidden treasure.

In the British Isles, however, some idea of their original use is retained and they are often referred to as elf-shot, fairy-shot, or elf-arrows, and are said to have been shot by the fairies at a person or animal to bewitch them. On the other hand, they are thought, for the most part, to protect the possessor from these little people. The presence of flint instruments found in British cinerary urns of the Roman era is explained by two theories: 1) they were used by the mourners to lacerate themselves; 2) flints (like all fire-producing stones) are potent magic for preventing the return of the dead. In Ireland flint stones are soaked in water to make a medicine which is good for man or beast. Mounted in silver they are worn as protection against elf-shot. They are sometimes called adder stone, which is probably as much a corruption of arrow stone as from the resemblance to a serpent's tongue. In North Carolina and Alabama there is a belief that flint stones placed in the fire will keep hawks from molesting the chickens, a belief which probably stems from the European idea that elf-shot protect domestic animals. In Brazil flint is used as a divining stone for gold, treasure, and water.

The flint was an object of veneration by most American Indian tribes. According to the Pawnee origin myth, stone weapons and implements were given to man by the Morning Star. Among the Quiché of Guatemala, there is a myth that a flint fell from the sky and broke into 1,600 pieces, each of which became a god. Tohil, the god who gave them fire, is still represented as a flint. This myth provides a parallel to the almost universal belief in the thunderstone, and reminds us that Jupiter was once worshipped in the form of a flint stone. The Cherokee shaman invokes the flint when he is about to scarify a patient prior to applying his medicine. Among the Pueblos we have the Flint Societies which, in most tribes, were primarily concerned with weather and witchcraft, but sometimes had to do with war and medicine.

Flood The term commonly used for the Biblical deluge (*Gen.* vi–ix): subject of a great body of etiological and humorous folklore. The duration of the rain that caused the Flood was 40 days and 40 nights. Forty is generally used among the peoples of the Near East to indicate some fairly considerable round number. Compare for example the 40 years of wandering in the wilderness, the Koranic statement that a man reaches his maturity at 40, the Persian name "forty-foot" for the animal called by us the centipede, etc. Mt. Ararat in Armenia is the supposed final resting place of the ark; recently, expeditions have been planned to discover its remains on the mountain's slopes. The story of the Flood ends with the beautiful etiological myth of the rainbow: it is God's reminder to Himself of His covenant with living things that no further destruction of all life by water is to occur. Typical motifs attached to the Flood story are the escape from the deluge in the ark (A1021), the saving of the animals in pairs (A1021.1), the griffons balking at entering the ark and now extinct (A2232.4), bird scouts sent out to ascertain the receding of the waters (A1021.2), the ark finally coming to rest on a mountain (A1022). Other folklore incidents include the Devil's entrance into the ark in the form of a mouse, his gnawing a hole in the bottom of the ark, and the lion's sneezing forth a cat to devour the mouse (A1811.2), or Noah's inadvertent curse letting the Devil in (C12.5.1), or the Devil getting in by walking in the shadow of Noah's wife (G303.23.1). The snake on board stops a leak with his tail (A2145.2), or the dog stops the leak with his nose, causing dogs' noses to be foreverafter cold and wet, or Noah's wife stops the leak with her elbow, thus causing women's elbows to be forever cold. Or, Noah himself, when the leak grew still larger, sat on the leak, which explains why a man always stands with his back to the fire. Noah tried to exclude flies from the ark, but admitted them as a lesser evil than the Devil who threatened to come on board if the flies did not (A2031.2). Many local legends all over the world explain exceptionally rocky places as the spots where Noah dumped his ballast. See DELUGE; NOAH.

flute One of the earliest and most widely used of all musical instruments, especially significant in fertility, courtship, and funeral ceremonies; a wind instrument consisting of a tube or pipe in which a column of air vibrates to produce sound when the player blows across the thin edge of a hole at the end or side. This acoustic principle distinguishes flutes from other instruments classified as pipes (oboes, clarinets, etc., which

have vibrating reeds). All, however, by association with their shape and in their use, have a similar symbolism and similar magical properties. Dating from paleolithic times, the earliest flutes were made of bone and had only one tone. The addition of finger holes for playing a melody appears in neolithic flutes.

The flute family includes numerous forms, differentiated by position and construction of the mouth-hole, by method of playing, and by shape. Vertical, or end-blown, flutes have the mouth-hole at the end. Transverse or cross flutes have a side mouth-hole and the upper end is closed. In many flutes of the Orient, South America, Africa, etc., the mouth-hole is notched to a sharper edge. Whistle flutes have the mouth-hole partly blocked to form a very narrow passage through which air is blown over the edge of another hole at the side to set up the necessary vibration. Variations from the common tubular shape include globular flutes (often elaborated into bird, fish, flower, human, and animal forms), an ax-shaped flute used by the Chaké of the northeastern Andes, which has a lateral air duct at right angles to the pipe, and a sausage-shaped instrument found among the Maori and in Peru. A series of one-note flutes played in combination and either tied or molded together constitutes the instrument known as the pan-pipes. Other combinations are double flutes, as used in northern India and among some American Indians, and triple flutes found in Tibet, as well as frequent pairings of separate instruments for certain ceremonies. Such pairs are commonly thought of as male and female wherever they are found—in Melanesia, among the Bantu in Africa, the Sierra Nevada tribes of South America, etc. Variations from the ordinary method of playing include blowing from the nostrils instead of the mouth (nose flutes); using only one hand for the flute while playing another instrument with the other, as with the pipe or galoubet (one-handed flute); and hanging the instrument for the wind to sound (Æolian flute), as is done in parts of Melanesia.

In primitive societies the flute, because of the characteristic tubular shape of the bone, reed, bamboo cane, etc., from which it is so often made, has a phallic symbolism and magic influence over procreation, fertility, and the renewal of life. Hence it is played at initiation and circumcision ceremonies, accompanies dances of courtship and fertility, sounds at funerals and sacrifices, and serenades reluctant maidens. It is also sometimes buried with the dead as a charm for new life, worn or carried as an amulet, and played, as by the shaman of the Chaco Indians, for curing purposes.

The Bukaua and Jabim tribes of northern New Guinea use the flute along with the bull-roarer in connection with circumcision. Boys make flutes of two kinds, called husband and wife, which are played during the rites and for a period of about three months of seclusion afterwards. Women may neither see nor hear the instruments. The ceremony is a dramatization of death and rebirth, the novices supposedly being swallowed and disgorged by a mythical monster. Among the Monumbo people the name of the flute (*murup*) is also borne by a mythical forest monster and by a mask used in the rites of initiation, and the sound of the flute is identified with the monster's cry. The flutes are carefully concealed in the men's lodges and are played also for the burial of male dead and after the erection of a chief's house. The instruments are credited with having souls and receive prayers, sacrifices, and special consecration. They can bring fair weather, protect travelers, give warnings through dreams. Each clan has its own flutes, and at certain feasts the clan head's wife is admitted to the men's enclosure, where the flutes are kept, for the purpose of cohabitation with each man present.

The Sentani of New Guinea have a story of flute origin directly connected with another symbol of rebirth, the cassowary, which in Melanesian belief is equivalent to the classical phœnix. A man was gathering fruit in a tree and tossing it down for his wife, when a piece fell, splitting a bamboo cane and frightening the wife away with the noise. From the split cane emerged a cassowary, making a buzzing sound. The man hurried to tell his friends of the occurrence and to discuss the usefulness of a noise so frightening to women. They all cut pieces of bamboo and tried to imitate the sound. Thus they invented flutes.

Bone and clay flutes were the only melodic instruments of pre-Cortesian Central America and were especially associated with human sacrifice. Each year a victim was selected for the feast of the Aztec god, Tezcatlipoca, was dressed as the god, honored and worshipped for a whole year, given four consorts named for goddesses, and trained in the art of playing the flute. Wherever he went he played his flutes to the adulation of the populace, and when the day came for his death, he broke a flute at each step of the pyramid on the way to the sacrificial altar. The next victim, chosen for the following year, then took his place as the reborn god.

Flutes are found with the bodies in ancient tombs of many races, placed there as a charm for the resurrection of the dead. The instrument is sacred to the Babylonian Tammuz, husband of Ishtar, who killed him and restored him to life. When Tammuz played on his flute of sacred lapis lazuli, the dead arose. Even among a people such as the Toda of India, who neither make nor play flutes themselves, the dead are given flutes obtained from another tribe to assure them rebirth.

The flute was also used for funeral music by the ancient Hebrews and is still used along the northern coast of Africa by Arab peoples to play a dirge melody originally sung as a death lament. However, the funeral instruments of the Greeks and Romans, the *aulos* and the *tibia*, frequently called flutes in translation, and bearing the same connotations as mortuary flutes of other peoples, were actually oboe-type instruments, having the double-reed construction.

As an accompaniment for dancing, the flute retains its phallic, procreative significance, being used especially for animal, harvest, and love dances. Men of the Siusi of Brazil blow the cross flute while dancing a circle dance of courtship with female partners. Among the Sierra Nevada tribes of South America, the men play the flute for dancing of the women, though the sexes do not dance together. The zarabanda, a small Guatemalan flute, may have given its name to the sarabande, a dance originally of sexual pantomime. The vertical

flute has traveled all over the world in Gipsy caravans. It is paired with the drum for the whirling dances of Mevlevi dervishes. The small, one-handed flute called the pipe, played together with the tabor, furnishes the characteristic music for the English Morris dance; and its Provençal counterpart, the galoubet, plays, with a tambourine, for a religious pageant in which, on Christmas night, a lamb symbolizing the Christ Child is paraded through the village of des Baux and carried to the altar of the church.

North American Indians (Chippewa, Cheyenne, Yuman, others) have used the flute for wooing, believing the sound of the instrument particularly persuasive. Special flutes might be given even greater aphrodisiac charm by the invocation of the medicine-man. The Chippewa warrior might also use the flute to signal the approach of enemies without arousing their suspicions. The flute is the chief accompaniment to the song ceremonials of the Pueblo Indians in connection with rain-making, the manufacture and consecration of sacred objects, communication with spirits of the afterworld, and a dramatization of tribal migrations. As in many other cultures, the flute of various tribes is believed to have been the gift or invention of a god. The Chitimacha of Louisiana tell how the supreme deity, disguised as a traveler, came upon a boy who sat wishing he could draw music from a piece of cane, and the god, pleased by a gift of deer meat, taught the lad to hollow the cane, burn finger holes in it, and play upon it.

The Cuna Indians of Panama still make flutes of bird bones, which are strung in sets and worn as necklaces. Girls of the tribe may be subjected to a test of virginity at the time of initiation by wrapping two cane flutes in a leaf and giving them to the performer. If they have changed position when he unwraps them, she is not a virgin.

The flute is thought to have a special attraction for certain animals and aspects of nature, and is the traditional instrument of shepherds. In Mesopotamia, India, Palestine, Egypt, and Arabia, shepherds have for centuries played a long end-blown flute, sometimes with a whistle mouthpiece. There is a Kurdish story of a poor shepherd who fell in love with the daughter of the wealthy man whose flocks he tended. The father objected to the marriage but said that he would consent if the shepherd could keep his flock of 500 sheep from drinking for three days. The shepherd accepted the condition and sat on the hillside, playing the most enchanting tunes he knew whenever the sheep went toward the spring. Each time, the sheep recognized the music as their call and followed him away from the water. The shepherd won his bride and thereafter he and his descendants were known as the masters of the flute.

In India, the cross flute is associated with the god, Kṛishṇa, who, when hidden by shepherds to save his life, assumed the guise of a cowherd and piped in pastoral style to charm the animals and spirits of nature. His instrument is one of those believed suitable for the entertainment of the gods and is thought of as suspended in the celestial regions and played upon by supernatural musicians.

The power of the instrument is related even more

closely to animals in the globular type known almost all over the world. Probably this shape developed originally from coconut shells or other hard fruit shells and was later imitated in clay and modeled like birds and animals whose call resembled the flute notes. These shapes undoubtedly added some of the magical attributes of the various creatures to those of the flute itself. However, even in ancient times such instruments became toys, and today their offspring, a warbling canary with a whistle in its mouth, a water container under its feet, and a mouthpiece in the tail, can often be bought at dime stores and carnivals.

The ancient globular flute of China, the *hsüan,* was said to have been molded on eggs and was equated in the cosmic scheme of equivalents with the southeast direction, the summer-to-autumn season, the earth, and the clay of which it was made.

In general, the material of flutes is less important symbolically than the shape, but the use of some type of bone in flutes on every continent carries with it the phallic implications of the bone—whether it be bird, deer, llama, pig's foot, or human arm or leg. Human bones have been used in New Zealand, in Guiana, in Venezuela, and elsewhere. The victims were generally slain enemies or sacrificed slaves, and the use of a part of their bodies endows the instrument and the player with a part of their strength, virility, or influence. The Ruthenians were said to have used a human leg-bone to make a flute that had the power to reduce all within earshot to somnolence.

Flutes of almost every type have been played with the breath of the nostrils, rather than the mouth, since prehistoric times in various parts of India, Indonesia, Borneo, Polynesia, Melanesia, by the Bechuana in Africa, the Botocudo and Caingang in South America, and even in Europe. An accidental discovery of the method has been suggested for Hindu wearers of the nose-ring, which, if broken, might emit a whistle. Another theory of origin is that it would be tabu for a Brahmin to touch with his lips the instrument made by a low-caste man. Sachs cites the widespread belief that the breath of the nostrils contains the soul and the practices of guarding such breath and utilizing it for magical purposes. (The exclamation, "Gesundheit," when a person sneezes, is a survival of such ideas.) Therefore the powers of the flute may be increased by the particular magic of this breath.

In Europe, where the pipe, the flageolet, the recorder, and other types of vertical flute have been popular in various periods both for folk and art music, the cross flute has been used in much more limited ways. The folk music of Rumania, Yugoslavia, Hungary, etc., where Gipsy transmission and influence has been particularly strong, is often played on the cross flute, and Switzerland and Austria have a tradition of cross flute playing, but otherwise it has appeared chiefly as a military instrument. The fife, from the end of the Crusades to the present, has been paired with the drum for marching.

In America, some folk musicians still play the fife, in the Pennsylvania hills, for example, where its lively tunes are similar to those played by country fiddlers.

As an instrument for the solitary musician, the flute is particularly loved by Indians of South and Central America. Among the Colombia Indians, every man

plays the flute, which he makes of cane, and carries with him as he wanders over the hills, playing mournful airs. The Coras of Mexico, also, all make and play flutes, especially for the annual festivities of Holy Week. See ATHENA.   THERESA C. BRAKELEY

Flying Dutchman The best known of the phantom ships. Similar ships are known in several parts of the world, and the rash oath motif appears not only in these ship tales but in such literary versions of the story of the eternally doomed as Austin's *Peter Rugg.* The *Flying Dutchman* is the name commonly given to the ghostly ship seen in bad weather off the Cape of Good Hope, Africa. The ship is seen beating against the wind, trying to round the Cape; is often hailed, and sometimes boarded. The captain of the ship, a stubborn man, vowed that he would round the Cape during a heavy storm, or be damned (E511.1.3; compare C41: tabu, offending water spirit). Other versions of the legend make the captain guilty of cruelty, or have him thus damned because of a pact with the Devil (E511.1.2 and E511.1.3). Traditionally also, the crew is a crew of dead men, who stand to their tasks unmoving, and will not answer questioning (E511.2.1). (Compare Coleridge's *The Ancient Mariner.*)

The Baltic has its phantom ship, the *Carmilhan;* the legend connected with it is very like the *Flying Dutchman's.* There is a phantom ship of the Gulf of Finland, mentioned by Frazer in the *Golden Bough,* a Finnish ship, undoubtedly, because it overhauls other ships with sails full set in the teeth of the wind, and notoriously the Finns are wizards. Compare PHANTOM SHIP.

Fodla In Old Irish mythology, one of the three queens of the Tuatha Dé Danann encountered by the Milesians during their advance into Ireland, whose name is used as a poetic name for Ireland. See BANBA.

Foggy, Foggy Dew A plaintive song known to English, Irish, and American singers, telling of the one romantic misstep of a weaver, who began and ended as a bachelor, with a blue-eyed son to help him at his trade and to remind him of the pretty maid he protected from the "foggy, foggy dew." The haunting tune is claimed as an Irish harp melody, the weaver has been identified as both English and Scottish, but the song now knows no nationality, being a favorite wherever English folk songs are sung.

Folía (French *Folies d'Espagne*) An ancient Italian *basso ostinato* melody descended from a large group of such tunes associated with the 14th century bassadanza, but applied from the mid-16th century to the frenzied fertility dance, the folía, and set to verses. The connection of dance and tune is obscure and controversial, involving the fusing elements of a dissolving courtly tradition and a rising popular movement.

folía Literally, madness: a Portuguese carnival fertility dance which became a couple dance in Spain, France, and Italy. In its original form it owed its name to the insane din, furious tempo, and lunatic actions of the large crowd of participants. Some carried masked boys on their shoulders; others, dressed as women, whirled and played castanets—clearly a vestige of ancient transvestite fertility symbolism. In Spain the folía was danced as a solo or couple dance with castanets, to the accompaniment of flutes. The movements had become graceful and changeable, alternately pensive and impassioned, always sensuous. The music, in triple time, has a characteristic *basso ostinato,* or ground bass. The French social dance and stage dance by that name are distorted versions. [GPK]

folk etymology or **popular etymology** Plausible but usually incorrect analysis by untrained folk of a word whose meaning, or spelling, or sound is not clear, resulting in the transformation of the word into one more intelligible. French *surloin* (*sur,* above) becomes by folk-etymology *sirloin.* Old English *angnail* (*ang,* painful) becomes *hangnail. Sweetard* (*ard,* a suffix, meaning having the qualities of) becomes *sweetheart.* Old French *assets,* singular in number, is taken into English as a plural and a new singular *asset* coined. There exists a tendency today to turn *asparagus* into *sparrow grass* and to use *gingerly* as if it meant smartly.   [MEL]

folklore Folklore comprises traditional creations of peoples, primitive and civilized. These are achieved by using sounds and words in metric form and prose, and include also folk beliefs or superstitions, customs and performances, dances and plays. Moreover, folklore is not a science about a folk, but the traditional folk-science and folk-poetry.   JONAS BALYS

☞ Whenever a lullaby is sung to a child; whenever a ditty, a riddle, a tongue-twister, or a counting-out rime is used in the nursery or at school;

Whenever sayings, proverbs, fables, noodle-stories, folktales, reminiscences of the fireside are retold;

Whenever, out of habit or inclination, the folk indulge in songs and dances, in ancient games, in merrymaking, to mark the passing of the year or the usual festivities;

Whenever a mother shows her daughter how to sew, knit, spin, weave, embroider, make a coverlet, braid a sash, bake an old-fashioned pie;

Whenever a farmer on the ancestral plot trains his son in the ways long familiar, or shows him how to read the moon and the winds to forecast the weather at sowing or harvest time;

Whenever a village craftsman—carpenter, carver, shoemaker, cooper, blacksmith, builder of wooden ships—trains his apprentice in the use of tools, shows him how to cut a mortise and peg in a tenon, how to raise a frame house or a barn, how to string a snowshoe, how to carve a shovel, how to shoe a horse or shear a sheep;

Whenever in many callings the knowledge, experience, wisdom, skill, the habits and practices of the past are handed down by example or spoken word, by the older to the new generations, without reference to book, print, or schoolteacher;

Then we have folklore in its own perennial domain, at work as ever, alive and shifting, always apt to grasp and assimilate new elements on its way. It is old-fashioned, gray- or white-headed perhaps, fast receding from its former strongholds under the impact of modern progress and industry; it is the born opponent of the serial number, the stamped product, and the patented standard.

Men of learning have in the last century or so gathered, classified, and studied a vast body of materials appertaining to folk tradition. They are called folk-lorists. According to their aptitudes and preferences they have specialized in various aspects of their chosen field, some in folktales or folk songs, others in handicrafts, others in dances and games, still others in beliefs and customs. Their tendency so far has been to restrict rather than to let their research expand all the way to its natural scope.

Much still remains to be undertaken in the study of our folk arts and crafts. And even our working definition of folklore itself should be broadened to embrace the forms of habitation, carving, statuary, metal work—iron, pewter, brass, silver, gold—weaving customs, and ancient domestic arts. Even written documents and materials from our archives may belong as much to folklore as to history, for instance, those bearing on the activities of the old guilds, on the pursuits of workshops, and on the traditional schools of manual training. And the door remains wide open to the comparative study of the folklore harvest taken as a whole and in its branches, for it all forms part of the culture of man from the remote past to the present.
      MARIUS BARBEAU

☞ In anthropological usage, the term folklore has come to mean myths, legends, folktales, proverbs, riddles, verse, and a variety of other forms of artistic expression whose medium is the spoken word. Thus, folklore can be defined as verbal art. Anthropologists recognize that an important group of individuals known as folklorists are interested in customs, beliefs, arts and crafts, dress, house types, and food recipes; but in their own studies of the aboriginal peoples of various parts of the world, these diverse items are treated under the accepted headings of material culture, graphic and plastic arts, technology and economics, social and political organization, and religion, and all are subsumed under the general term culture. There is, however, an important part of culture which does not fall under any of these convenient headings, and which is classed separately as folklore. Folklore in all its forms, thus defined, is obviously related to literature, which is written; but folklore may never be written even in a literate society, and it may exist in societies which have no form of writing. Like literature, folklore is an art form related to music, the dance, and the graphic and plastic arts, but different in the medium of expression which is employed.   WILLIAM R. BASCOM

☞ In a purely oral culture everything is folklore. In modern society what distinguishes folklore from the rest of culture is the preponderance of the handed-down over the learned element and the prepotency that the popular imagination derives from and gives to custom and tradition. The transference of oral tradition to writing and print does not destroy its validity as folklore but rather, while freezing or fixing its form, helps to keep it alive and to diffuse it among those to whom it is not native or fundamental. For the folk memory forgets as much as it retains and restricts and corrupts as much as it transmits and improves. In the reciprocity of oral and written tradition and the flux of cultural change and exchange, revival plays as important a part as survival, popularization is as essential as scholarship, and the final responsibility rests upon the accumulative and collective taste and judgment of the many rather than the few. In this process of creative remembrance, which is tantamount to the genius of a people, the great collections of folk literature are the product of the collaboration of countless folk singers, folksayers, collectors, scholars, religious teachers, and professional artists and interpreters of the arts with the inarticulate folk—Sandburg's "laboring many"; of the "scholar's learning about the folk" with the folk's own learning.

Within the realm of the handed-down, several classes and levels of folklore and folk idiom may be distinguished, and each species or individual item must be judged in relation to its history and function in its own social and cultural setting, since folklore originates and spreads in many different ways and forms. The great bulk and central core of folklore consists not so much in folk songs and stories (although these are more obvious in their appeal as colorful and characteristic) as in the customs and beliefs attending the "periods of emotional stress in the life of an individual in relation to the group—birth, graduation, coming of age, marriage, burial" (Martha Warren Beckwith, *Folklore in America*, 1931, p. 5), which the educated and sophisticated share with the uneducated and naive. Another considerable and important phase of folklore is made up of the mass delusions and hallucinations of myths, especially in the presence of the "wonders of the invisible world," and the apocrypha of hero-worship, with its legends of doubtful exploits of historical personages and "untrustworthy traditions of doubtful events." Both aspects of folk fantasy have their popular counterpart in the prejudices, stereotypes, irrational beliefs, and daydreams inspired or encouraged by commercial and academic forms of mass communication and mass organization of thought.

As folklore approaches the level of the literate and literary, it tends to become more elaborate and self-conscious in expression, to shape about itself a formal tradition with prestige value, and to become absorbed into the main stream of culture. As it approaches the level of the illiterate and subliterary, folklore constitutes a basic part of our oral culture, in the proverbial folk-say and accumulated mother wit of generations that bind man to man and people to people with traditional phrases and symbols. Folklore thus takes root in the "humble influences of place and kinship," of shared experience and wisdom, and has its flower and fruition in those works of art in which the individual artist succeeds in identifying himself with a folk tradition and giving it universal form and significance. On both levels—folk culture or folk art—folklore derives its integrity and survival value from a direct response to and participation in group experience, and the fusion of the individual and the common sense. B. A. BOTKIN

☞ Folklore, or popular knowledge, is the accumulated store of what mankind has experienced, learned, and practiced across the ages as popular and traditional knowledge, as distinguished from so-called scientific knowledge. The distinction between the two is not always definite. The materials of folklore are for the most part the materials of social anthropology that have been collected from the barbarous and "uncivilized" regions of the world, as well as from the rural and illiterate peoples of the "civilized" countries. These materials have been obtained from the anthropological data of history or have been collected by anthropologists and folklorists in modern times. Specifically, folklore consists of the beliefs, customs, superstitions, proverbs, riddles, songs, myths, legends, tales, ritualistic ceremonies, magic, witchcraft, and all other manifestations and practices of primitive and illiterate peoples and of the "common" people of civilized society. Folklore has very deep roots and its traces are ever present even among peoples that have reached a high state of culture. Folklore may be said to be a true and direct expression of the mind of "primitive" man.

The science of folklore is that branch of human knowledge that collects, classifies, and studies in a scientific manner the materials of folklore in order to interpret the life and culture of peoples across the ages. It is one of the social sciences that studies and interprets the history of civilization. Folklore perpetuates the patterns of culture, and through its study we can often explain the motifs and the meaning of culture. The science of folklore, therefore, contributes in a great measure to the history and interpretation of human life.

AURELIO M. ESPINOSA

☞ A survey of materials published as folklore indicates that the subject is pretty much what one wants to make of it. I favor a conservative definition. Without attempting a formal statement, to me the term "folklore" is most meaningful when applied to the unwritten literary manifestations of all peoples, literate or otherwise. Stories, certainly, whether myths, legends, folktales, or anecdotes, are of primary importance. I would also add riddles, rimes, proverbs, folk songs, as well as folk beliefs and superstitions of almost all kinds. Regardless of how they are presented, these materials are folklore. Beyond this point one finds materials which may be treated in folkloristic fashion—games, cat's-cradle, ceremonies, witchcraft, to illustrate—but which in themselves do not, as I see it, necessarily constitute folklore. Outside the central literary core, folklore is best defined in terms of treatment rather than in terms of inherent nature.   GEORGE M. FOSTER

☞ Folklore is that part of a people's culture which is preserved, consciously or unconsciously, in beliefs and practices, customs and observances of general currency; in myths, legends, and tales of common acceptance; and in arts and crafts which express the temper and genius of a group rather than of an individual. Because it is a repository of popular traditions and an integral element of the popular "climate," folklore serves as a constant source and frame of reference for more formal literature and art; but it is distinct therefrom in that it is essentially of the people, by the people, and for the people.   THEODOR H. GASTER

☞ Folklore might be defined—not as applying to certain branches of lore rather than others, nor to certain kinds of people rather than others—but in terms of the ways in which it is acquired, used, and transmitted.

It is true that certain subjects (like ballad) are more associated in our minds with folklore than others, but there is nothing in the basic meaning of lore which suggests that any subject is excluded.

It is also true that certain cultures or groups have a more prevailing folklore than others. But every group and every member of it is a compound of elements that are folk and not folk; it is the proportion that varies. With sufficient search one could no doubt discover an atomic scientist who would refuse to walk under a ladder. With sufficient acquaintance we detect unique qualities in highly typical examples of folk products.

Folklore then may crop up in any subject, any group or individual, any time, any place. It might be thought of as comprising that information, those skills, concepts, products, etc., which one acquires almost inevitably *by virtue of the circumstances to which he is born*. It is not so much deliberately sought (like learning) as absorbed. It is not deliberately invented; rather it develops. It is present in the environment, is accepted, used, transformed, transmitted, or forgotten, without arbitrary impetus from individual minds. There may be deliberate efforts to combat it, as in the Westernization trends in China, or to revive and preserve it, but these are extraneous to *what it is*.

What was once a branch of learning, like astrology, may become folklore. What was once folklore, like the swastika motif, may be taken over and used or exploited in a non-folk manner. An individual work of art, like the Statue of Liberty, may become a group symbol, or a group symbol, like an African mask, may go into the painting of Picasso. These things are folklore, so long as they are acquired, used, and transmitted *in the manner of folklore*. When they cease to be, or before they are, used in that way they are not.

The nature of its development prevents the setting of any rigid limits to folklore. It is most clearcut where the group is most a unit, with cohesion and continuity. Anything which tends to break down the cohesion of a group—communications, diversity of knowledge, specialization, etc.—tends to scatter its folklore. But we are not justified in thinking, because it then becomes more elusive, that it ceases to exist or evolve. Nor can we think of groups simply in the traditional racial or geographic terms; they may be based on occupation, age, sex, economics, education, interest, etc., and in a complicated society new groupings are constantly presenting themselves.

The "group characteristics" which result from the accumulated nature of folklore, and by which we attempt to recognize and label it, are not to be thought of as opposed to individuality. Folklore is something which the individual has in common with his fellows, just as all have eyes and hands and speech. It is not contrary to himself as an individual but a part of his equipment. It makes possible—perhaps it might be defined as that which constitutes—his rapport with his particular segment of mankind.   M. HARMON

Originally the study of cultural curiosities, and held to be the survivals of an earlier period in the history of "civilized" literate peoples, folklore has come more and more to denote the study of the unwritten literature of any group, whether having writing or being without it. This development followed naturally upon the refinement of ethnographic method, which yielded continuously deeper insights into the nature and functioning of human culture, and revealed the defects of the older comparative approach, on which the concept of cultural survival was based. It became clear that the customs of living "primitive" folk could not properly be equated with those of the actual historic predecessors of Western European nations. In other words, "primitive man," wherever found, is not a contemporary ancestor. In Europe, recognition of this fact resulted in the development of the study of peasant cultures and other manifestations of earlier custom as a

discipline separate from folklore. This newer orientation, by defining more critically its field and approach, has freed folklorists for the study of popular literary forms, among peoples everywhere, whether they have a written language or not. This analysis is to be carried on, moreover, not only in the study of plot and incident, or to recover the place of origin and original form of the tales, but also to the end that these popular forms be considered in terms of the criteria, concepts, and problems of any living literature.

MELVILLE J. HERSKOVITS

Folklore in the specific sense, which is the usual one in the United States, embraces those literary and intellectual phases of culture which are perpetuated primarily by oral tradition: myths, tales, folk song, and other forms of oral traditional literature; folk speech and dialect as the medium of these materials; folk music and folk dancing because of their intimate relation to folk song; also customs, beliefs, and "folk science." Folklore thus exists in the city as well as in the countryside, and within groups that cut across such a division, but by preference it has been that of the countryside.

A wider meaning, of "folk life," more familiar in Europe and Latin America, covers the entire culture of a "folk" group, usually a rural group whose mode of life is rather different from that of its urban counterpart. Such a wide expansion of meaning, stemming from a special "folk" concept, has not been applied in the study of "primitive" or preliterate societies where the anthropologist's background in social science and linguistics appears indispensable for the study of native cultures as a whole, and also for a fruitful evaluation of the function and history of oral folklore.

The division of interest and of labor, suggested by these distinctions, has followed the different inclinations and methods of the student of culture and of society—whether anthropologist, rural sociologist, or social psychologist—and of the folklorist as a literary scholar. No doubt both can only gain by greater familiarity with each other's methods, points of view, knowledge, and insights.   GEORGE HERZOG

Folklore is a branch of cultural ethnology. The data of folklore are the myths, legends, traditions, narratives, superstitions, religions, rituals, customs, dances, and explanations of nature and man, acceptable to individual ethnic groups in each part of the world at any historical moment. Because these are all structures of the human imagination and frequently operate most powerfully when the groups or the individuals who constitute them are experiencing moments of crisis, the data of folklore are immediate and potent evidence of the nature of man when man is defining his fears and aspirations and searching for a security which always eludes him. Folklorists whose business it is to study folklore frequently become infected and find that instead of studying folklore they are in fact making it.

The methods of the study of folklore are: 1) collection of the data as they actually occur without, if possible, the intrusion of the folklorist's own mythopœia, a primitive impulse which creates folklore; 2) a comparison of the data to determine what are the similarities and differences of these phenomena in the several ethnic groups; 3) an examination of the beliefs implicit in the data; 4) of the social and psychological impulses which produce them, and 5) the functions folklore performs for the individuals and the social groups through which they operate.

Though persons concerned with folklore in our present period of Occidental culture are known as folklorists, they have been called at other times mountebanks, priests, poets, mystics, medicine-men, scholars. A general purpose of all these people whether they are producing an epic poem or editing the Pentateuch or an encyclopedia of folklore is to put their data together in such a way that they will make sense. The sorts of sense folklorists attempt to derive are various: Many are determined to prove that their social group is superior to others because their superstitions being generally accepted by their group are sound doctrine, whereas superstitions not accepted by the "we-group" are wicked, or at best quaint, heterodoxy. In this way and many others, the pleasure we get for example from the repetition of "family jokes," the folklore of each group tends to strengthen the group and to bring a sense of security and therefore superiority to the members of it.

Modern times have brought a new apology for an old impulse. The "scientific" folklorists search frenetically for origins and fill their pages with discussions of "original" dawn myths, stellar myths, totemism, diffusionism, and other pretentious explanations of an incomplete logic. Instead of having only one meaning, each fact in folklore has many meanings, even for the people of the group who most fanatically accept it. Until this semantic complexity has been grasped and a suitable grammar of discourse has been constructed to accommodate it, folklorists will continue to toy with the skirts of a great mystery. In the meantime the humanists, undismayed by a terminology which implies but does not present a scientific approach, will continue to meditate on the sorts of gaiety and terror which the peoples of all times and places record in the human structures known as folklore.   R. D. JAMESON

 Folklore is the science of traditional popular beliefs, tales, superstitions, rimes, all dealing preeminently with the supernatural, and picturization of these beliefs in festive customs, games, mime, song, dance. It is essentially a communal product, handed down from generation to generation, and committed to writing by trained investigators.

The domains of folklore arouse debate. Its narrowest definition confines it to the shadowy remnants of ancient religious rites still incorporated in the lives of illiterates and rustics. More broadly it includes secular legends and songs, tales figmented from fact, superstitions of recent origin, and fragments persisting among sophisticated urban residents.

Folktale is distinguished from mythological tale by attenuation of religious significance, from fairy tale by the still extant (however vague) faith in veracity and efficacity. Likewise, by the current loss of function, folk dance and folk music are distinguished from ritual forms by their anonymous heritage and from revival and individual composition by folk style.

                               GERTRUDE P. KURATH

 Folklore is the generic term to designate the customs, beliefs, traditions, tales, magical practices, proverbs, songs, etc.; in short the accumulated knowledge of a homogeneous unsophisticated people, tied together

not only by common physical bonds, but also by emotional ones which color their every expression, giving it unity and individual distinction. All aspects of folklore, probably originally the product of individuals, are taken by the folk and put through a process of re-creation, which through constant variation and repetition become a group product.   MACEDWARD LEACH

 The term folklore as used today is ambiguous. The context in which it appears reveals whether the user is referring to all the unwritten narratives of primitive people and thereby drawing a line between the literature of primitive and civilized peoples; or to a poorly defined category of stories vaguely distinguished from mythology (an equally ambiguous term) by being of less serious content and significance to their primitive narrators. A connotation which adds to the confusion is a hang-over from the earlier European use of the word folklore to cover peasant customs, beliefs, and narratives—the anthropology of peasants.

                               KATHARINE LUOMALA

 The entire body of ancient popular beliefs, customs, and traditions, which have survived among the less educated elements of civilized societies until today. It thus includes fairy tales, myths, and legends, superstitions, festival rites, traditional games, folk songs, popular sayings, arts, crafts, folk dances, and the like.

                               JOHN L. MISH

 Folklore is a lively fossil which refuses to die. It is a precipitate of the scientific and cultural lag of centuries and millennia of human experience.

In early times change was slower and less frequent, so earlier customs and beliefs had longer to form and to become deeply entrenched in the racial unconscious. These primitive patterns and mandalas, ripened and mellowed like hand-rubbed woods, have persisted beneath the hasty veneers of later civilizations, to surprise us with their beauty when we chance to uncover them. Beauty they have because they were formed slowly close to nature herself, and reflect her symmetry and simplicity. So, in a sense, folklore is how we used to do it and wish we could now. Hence, folklore is always the delight of children because it is the poetic wisdom of the childhood of the race. It is also the pleasure of the old who are wise enough to renew their youth by rebaptism in the eternal simplicities in completing the circle of life.

There is also, beside the juvenile, a strong feminine element in folklore, because its origin antedates the emergence of reason and belongs in the instinctive and intuitional areas. It is irrational and highly imaginative: much of it truly is termed "old wives' tales." Women have always been the savers and conservators of beliefs, rites, superstitions, rituals, and customs.

So folklore develops as the traditional, and usually oral, explanation of the origins and early history of man, as distinct from history, which is the factual record in writing.

The word folklore is used both for the body of tradition and the science of studying it. Folklore is the survival within a people's later stages of culture of the beliefs, stories, customs, rites and other techniques of adjustment to the world and the supernatural, which were used in previous stages, but the word also designates the scientific study of those survivals by later more sophisticated persons whose own adjustment patterns make the survivals seem quaint, irrational, and superstitious, but also sometimes fascinating and nostalgically desirable. The experienced folklorist is never patronizing toward primitive patterns of life-adjustment.

CHARLES FRANCIS POTTER

☞ It is usual to define folklore either literally as the lore of the folk or, more descriptively, in terms of an oral literary tradition. The first of these is a good broad definition including belief, superstition, and religious practice, as well as myths and tales. But it suffers from the difficulty which arises whenever any attempt is made to define "the folk." It is doubtful that the uneducated or illiterate can be considered apart from other persons, and the hypothesis which establishes the existence of such a folk identity would be almost impossible to validate. Modern interest in folk music and folk dancing has done much, however, toward perpetuating this definition. The second definition relies upon a distinction between an oral and a truly literary tradition represented in such productions as novels, poetry, and holy books. Many folklore analyses have been dependent upon oral materials gathered in societies with a written literary tradition, but a definition resting upon this contrast between the oral and the written fails utterly to meet conditions found among American Indian and other societies formerly without the art of writing.

In order to avoid the pitfalls into which either of these types of definition carry us, it seems wisest to define folklore simply as the study of verbal materials in all their varieties. Technical linguistics, music, the dance, and the graphic and pictorial arts would thus become closely related but essentially separate fields of investigation.

A brief discussion of the three schools of folklore active at the present time will help to illustrate the kinds of problem to which the folklorist devotes himself.

1) The Indic school has been most strongly influenced by the studies of Maurice Bloomfield. The members of this school began as Sanskrit scholars. They are both linguists and humanists. Their study of Sanskrit sources led directly to consideration of folklore, and some of our most valuable examinations of the continuity of motifs in time and space, and of shifts in meaning of phrase and incident, have come from these men. In addition, their work with native Indian scholars taught an appreciation of oral materials not usually to be found in the approach of the historian. Though relatively few in number and little known by the average folklorist, their work is extremely important to our understanding of folklore.

2) The anthropological school has worked largely, to date, in the American Indian field and owes its major emphases to Franz Boas. Its members are social scientists and are interested as much in linguistics as are the scholars of the Indic school. They, too, have insisted that if language materials are to be fully understood they must be most accurately recorded and most minutely studied. There is no substitute for texts and linguistic analyses. Faced, however, with the American Indian situation the emphasis has somewhat shifted. Whereas the Indic school worked in a continuous tradition of written language, the Americanist had to deal with unwritten and unrecorded languages which were not only mutually unintelligible but also belonged to entirely different language stocks. Other cultural aspects differed as markedly, and the Americanist was forced to a consideration of basic differences. Upon his recognition of such cultural difference, he developed an approach which has since been fruitfully applied in other world areas as well. His attention has been directed toward an intensive analysis of culture patterns existing contemporaneously in the world today. Folklore has served as an excellent tool in this analysis; it has been used to investigate, and to illustrate, differences more intimate than formal and more psychological than linguistic. In recent years, although the anthropological school has not lost sight of changes occurring in folklore over space and time, it has tended to examine bodies of folklore with an eye for their uniqueness.

3) The Aarne-Thompson school of folklore differs from the other two in that its methods have derived primarily from a study of European folktales. It works in a purely humanistic atmosphere, and is impressed by the existence of an oral tradition which stands apart from the written or sophisticated like a parallel growth. Members of this school have been particularly interested in the collection and classification of folklore materials and have emphasized the importance of obtaining numerous variants of a tale. Their influence has been widely felt in both the United States and abroad, and has today in the United States become associated with the field of intercultural relations.   MARIAN W. SMITH

☞ Folklore consists of materials that are handed on traditionally from generation to generation without a reliable ascription to an inventor or author. Although proverbs, ballads, and other items of folklore are often credited to a particular person, this is itself a stylistic peculiarity of the genre, and the individual's claims are ordinarily dubious in the extreme. If they are capable of proof, we find that the material has suffered alteration or adaptation in the process of transmission. This "communal recreation" proceeds characteristically according to associative rather than logical ways of thinking. The materials handed on traditionally may be physical objects, ideas, or words. The folklore of physical objects includes the shapes and uses of tools, costumes, and the forms of villages and houses. The folklore of gestures and games occupies a position intermediate between the folklore of physical objects and the folklore of ideas. Typical ideas transmitted as folklore are manifested in the customs associated with birth, marriage, and death, with the lesser events of life, with remedies for illnesses and wounds, with agriculture, the trades, and the professions, and with religious life, notably with Christmas, Easter, and other holy days or saints' days. Verbal folklore includes words considered for their own sake and words occurring as connected discourse. Typical words that the folklorist studies without special regard for their use in connected discourse are place names, personal names (both family and Christian names), and nicknames. Folklore in the form of connected discourse includes tales of various kinds (märchen, jests, legends, cumulative tales, exempla, fables, etiological tales), ballads, lyric folk song, children's songs, charms, proverbs, and riddles. The study of folklore consists in the collection, classification, and interpretation of these traditional materials. Classification involves interpretation to some extent. Interpretation seeks to discover the origin, meaning, use, and history of these materials, to state and explain their dissemination, and to describe their stylistic peculiarities. ARCHER TAYLOR

🖙 Although the word folklore is more than a century old, no exact agreement has ever been reached as to its meaning. The common idea present in all folklore is that of tradition, something handed down from one person to another and preserved either by memory or practice rather than written record. It involves the dances, songs, tales, legends, and traditions, the beliefs and superstitions, and the proverbial sayings of peoples everywhere. It also includes studies of customs, of traditional agricultural and domestic practices, types of buildings and utensils, and traditional aspects of social organization; but for these latter aspects there seems to be a general agreement to consider them, when found in a primitive or preliterate society, as a part of ethnology rather than folklore. This latter division of labor is largely a matter of convenience and is not universally accepted. At least among literate peoples all the subjects mentioned above are considered as folklore, since all of them are truly traditional. STITH THOMPSON

🖙 Among American-trained anthropologists concerned with the cultures of preliterate peoples, the term folklore customarily has been used to refer to the various genres of orally transmitted prose and verse forms existent in primitive groups. Such forms include myths and tales, jests and anecdotes, dramas and dramatic dialogs, prayers and formulas, speeches, puns, riddles, proverbs, and song and chant texts.

This limitation of the term to designate one part only of any preliterate culture contrasts sharply with the customary usage of the same term by students of Euro-American, European, and other folk and peasant cultures. In folk cultures a large part, but only a part, of the total culture is transmitted orally; all such orally transmitted material is generally regarded by humanists as folklore. In this extended sense, then, folklore encompasses not only all traditional prose and verse material, but all traditionally learned arts and handicrafts and a vast body of social and religious beliefs and customs, subsumed by the anthropologists under the general term ethnography.

The educated layman's usage of the word folklore lies between the anthropologist's and the humanist's. This or that fact or theory, transmitted orally or in popular sources, as well as traditional prose and verse material, is folklore. Instead of using the outmoded term superstition, the layman is now more apt to refer to a folkloristic belief.

There is at present a noticeable tendency among cultural anthropologists to use unwritten literature, or primitive literature, or literary forms, to designate material which, even a decade ago, would have been called folklore. With more and more attention being paid by humanists to the study of the traditional in folk cultures, it may well be that the new terms for the anthropologists' relatively restricted materials will gain currency, and ethnography continue in use by anthropologists as practically synonymous with the humanists' use of the term folklore. ERMINIE W. VOEGELIN

🖙 Folklore is that art form, comprising various types of stories, proverbs, sayings, spells, songs, incantations, and other formulas, which employs spoken language as its medium. RICHARD A. WATERMAN

folklore and mythology The term folklore was coined in 1846 by the English antiquarian William John Thoms to take the place of the awkward term popular antiquities. The word has since been adopted by virtually all continental European languages. As currently used, it has two acceptations, viz. 1) the mass of the unrecorded traditions of the people as they appear in popular (i.e. non-literary) fiction, custom and belief, magic, and ritual, and 2) the science which proposes to study these materials.

The science of folklore is an historical science, historical because it seeks to throw light on man's past; a science because it endeavors to attain this goal, not by speculation or deduction from some *a priori* principle, but by the inductive method used in all scientific research.

The scope of folklore is to reconstruct the spiritual history of man, not as represented by the outstanding works of poets, artists, and thinkers, but as exemplified by the more or less inarticulate voices of the "folk." In this task it draws on documents which are partly historical, i.e. culled from chroniclers, poets, law codes, etc., whenever they reflect folkways as opposed to literary, artistic, and learned modes of thought, and partly oral, i.e. collected, roughly, within the last century and a half by professional or semiprofessional folklorists. In the evaluation and interpretation of these documents our science largely avails itself of the comparative method.

The term folklore and the definition given above clearly imply the coexistence of two traditions, a literary and artistic one on the one hand, a folk or popular tradition on the other. This condition is fulfilled only among societies of a certain cultural level. Semicivilized people (savages, barbarians) lack the former of the two. In their case it is therefore inadmissible to speak of folklore. The collection and interpretation of their traditions, which are by definition oral, is the task of the sciences of ethnography and ethnology (anthropology) respectively. Since the comparative method must by definition largely draw on ethnographic data, it follows that folklore and ethnology (anthropology) are virtually inseparable.

An analogous connection exists between folklore and ethnology (anthropology) on the one hand and prehistory (archeology) on the other. Since all civilizations are known to have arisen in prehistoric times out of conditions of savagery and barbarism, the documents brought to light by prehistoric science are in many instances elucidated by beliefs and customs which have lingered on among the folk or are still believed in and practiced by semicivilized people. The fire drill is perhaps the most outstanding example of the survival of a primitive mode of fire-making in folk-ritual.

The science of folklore is eminently valuable in the interpretation of historical documents, chiefly those bearing on the ancient Orient, which include, of course, the Old Testament.

The science of folklore is no less valuable in the interpretation of historical documents forming part of the classical literatures. Many customs and rites described by Homer, Vergil, Theocritus, etc., are elucidated by analogous customs and rites still practiced by the European peasantry. (Compare W. Mannhardt, *Antike Wald- und Feld-kulte*, Berlin, 1905; E. Samter, *Volkskunde im altsprachlichen Unterricht*. I. Teil: *Homer*, Berlin, 1923.) For the same reason folklore is an auxiliary in textual criticism and text interpretation, whence its usefulness to the various philologies (Classical, Semitic, Vedic, Teutonic, Celtic, etc.).

Certain branches of folklore have repeatedly been acclaimed as the forerunners of the modern natural sciences, both pure and applied. This has been notably true for magic, viewed in this light by Sir James G. Frazer. The justification of this claim however is rather doubtful. On the other hand, folk medicine or popular medicine is unquestionably a direct forerunner of medical science. While most of the assumptions underlying folk medicine are based on unproven *a priori* hypotheses, and while it frequently sees causal connections where there are none, many house remedies, forming part of the popular pharmacopœia, are ultimately derived from sound observations and, in some cases, from the results of experimentations, however rudimentary. Nor should it be forgotten that scientific, like popular, medicine is still largely empiric.

In many cases folklore materials, chiefly in the field of the local legend, receive significant illustrations from observations in the realm of psychical research and abnormal psychology, two fields the exploration of which is still in its infancy. This is notably true of various forms of divination, dreams, second sight, second hearing, levitation, telepathy, and similar phenomena.

Even more intimate is the connection of folklore and religion, more particularly the so-called natural, i.e. non-dogmatic, non-revealed, and usually but imperfectly organized, religions of the semicivilized and of classical antiquity, but to a certain extent also the great monotheistic religions (Judaism, Christianity, Islam, Hinduism, and Buddhism). This connection may be of either one of two kinds: 1) A religious system, grown out of a set of popular beliefs (folklore materials), gradually sloughed them off, relegating them to the realm of superstition, retaining only its philosophical and, chiefly, ethical content. This is essentially true of Protestantism and the more puritanical sects of Islam, e.g. the Wahabites. 2) A religion, in its origin purely ethical (such as Pauline Christianity) may subsequently absorb a vast amount of folklore material, so as to end up, for example, in medieval Catholicism. In virtually all known religions a constant strife has been known to be going on between those desirous of reducing the folklore element to the very minimum, considering it incompatible with their concept of true religion, and those others claiming that, while a religion thus purged of the popular element may serve well enough the needs of select spirits, the educated, it will never satisfy the people.

In the non-revealed, non-dogmatic religions of the semicivilized and of classical antiquity the folklore materials referred to usually take the form of myths. A myth (from Greek *mythos*, word, speech) is an explanatory or etiological (from Greek *aitia*, cause) tale trying to account for all sorts of phenomena (now explained by modern science), and, since the agents held responsible for these phenomena are believed to be certain Powers (gods or demons), connected with these Powers. The total of these myths constitute a mythology. Thus we have a Hellenic, a Semitic, an Iranian, nay even an Oceanic mythology. Since these phenomena are not necessarily predicated upon a polytheistic religion, monotheism, too, may have its myths: the Old Testament is full of them. (Compare Sir James G. Frazer, *Folk-lore in the Old Testament*, London, 1918; H. Gunkel, *Das Märchen im Alten Testament*, Tübingen, 1921.) The various mythologies therefore constitute a very important branch of folklore. Since in particular the Hellenic mythology pervades literary works of classical antiquity, a first-hand acquaintance with the classical literatures is an indispensable condition for the student of folklore.

While it is true, as stated above, that all civilized peoples have two traditions, the popular and the literary or learned, it must not be supposed that the two are flowing side by side, as it were in water-tight pipes. The very opposite is true: there is a constant intermingling, and exchanges go on all the time, folklore materials being absorbed by poets and artists, while learned materials, book lore, penetrate to the masses, undergoing various changes and modifications in the process.

This fact has given rise to a controversy of some importance. One school, led by Hans Naumann, proclaims that the people properly speaking never create anything but can only re-create, adopting and modifying materials discarded by their betters. Thus the folk costumes and folk dances of the European peasants are in the main old-fashioned costumes worn by nobles and burghers centuries previously, and society dances once danced by knights and ladies. (Compare H. Naumann, *Primitive Gemeinschaftkultur*, Jena, 1921.) The older school, founded by J. G. Herder and the Brothers Grimm, had claimed that the creative people form the basis, making possible the individualistic art of poets and creative artists.

In the extreme form given it by Naumann the theory is manifestly absurd. On that score, semicivilized classless societies (e.g. most of the Indian tribes of the eastern and central United States and Canada) would be devoid of traditions, a supposition far from true; but it must be admitted that societies with more or less developed class system (e.g. the European, Polynesian, and that of the tribes of Oregon, Washington, and British Columbia) can boast of a considerably richer lore. The presence of social strata would thus seem to enrich the spiritual heritage of a given community, while social equalitarianism is apt to lead to a leveling down and to the production of uniform types.

A class system invariably involves a give and take Thus the feudal society of southern France merely developed the lyric poetry flourishing among the peasants from pre-Roman times into artistic productions, thus creating the troubadour lyric. These types (*pastourelle, aubade, sérénade, chansons de la mal mariée*, etc.) were in turn transmitted to the masses and can even now be heard in village fairs, barn dances, etc. (Compare A. Jeanroy, *Les origines de la poésie lyrique en France au moyen âge*, Paris, 1925; C. R. Baskervill, "English Songs

on the Night Visit," in *PMLA* XXXVI (1921), pp. 565
ff.; A. H. Krappe, *Science of Folk-Lore,* London, 1930,
pp. 153 ff.).

The diffusion of folklore materials is not limited to
an exchange between the various social strata of one
and the same society; it is known to have traveled and
to travel still over vast areas of the globe's surface, thus
presenting one of the most difficult but also most fascinating problems of folklore. In this diffusion folklore
materials are to all appearances less handicapped by
linguistic barriers than is literary material. The common fairy-tale types are known virtually over the whole
Eastern hemisphere including Indonesia and parts of
Oceania, while the French and Spanish-Portuguese
colonists carried them to the New World. The ordinary
types of local legends are found over the entire European continent, and the very term migratory tale tells
its own story. What is more surprising is the ease
with which folk songs and ballads cross linguistic
frontiers: ballads known to be of Scandinavian origin
are found in France and even in Spain, and virtually
all Balkan languages, though differing widely in grammatical structure and prosody, show much the same
ballad types. This phenonemon necessarily presupposes
the existence of bilingual individuals gifted, in spite of
their anonymity, with considerable poetic talent.

In the case of types of folk-literature showing a fairly
complex structure or plot (fairy tales, local and animal
tales, merry tale, folk song, and ballad) it is clear that
the vast majority of them can have arisen only once, in
one place, at one time, and it is the task of the folklorist
to determine that place and that time for each story
type. This is done by a judicious application of the geo-
graphic-historical method, first developed by the Finnish scholar Julius Krohn in his *Kalevala* studies and
continued and extended by his son Kaarle Krohn.
(See FINNISH FOLKLORE.) The dependability of the result largely rests on the number of variants available
for a given story type and on their character, i.e. on
the fact whether some of these variants are attested
at a relatively early time, by historical documents, or
whether they are exclusively oral, i.e. collected from the
mouth of the peasants in the course of the 19th century
or later.

On the respective importance of the historical and the
oral variants, a controversy arose between Kaarle Krohn
and the Bohemian scholar Albert Wesselski. The former
claimed a greater independent value for the oral variants, while the latter was inclined to attribute more
importance to the historical ones. For Wesselski's view
this much must be admitted: If an historical variant
happens to be more widely known, if, for example, it
occurs in the Bible (e.g. the story of Joseph and his
brothers), or if it is represented by a great play (e.g.
The Merchant of Venice) or a poem read and memorized in schools, etc., there is a great probability of
such an historical variant affecting the oral ones, at
least in the regions where the historical ones enjoy
popularity or wide currency. Such a literary contamination of oral variants must therefore be taken into consideration in the evaluation of the materials. Thus the
stories of Perrault's *Contes de ma Mère l'Oye* have been
shown to have influenced the oral folklore of Germany
(compare H. V. Velten in *Germanic Review*, V, 1930, pp.
1–18). Oral variants thus affected are then of extremely

doubtful value in the task of tracing the history of a
story type. Bearing in mind these reservations, we may
claim, however, that by the criteria of internal logic and
structural development the archetype reconstructed
from a large number of variants stands much closer to
the archetype of the story than do the historical variants, no matter how old they may be. (Compare A. H.
Krappe in *MLQ* IV, 1943, p. 272.) This means that the
pure folklore tradition is more conservative than the
literary-artistic tradition. (Wesselski's views are set
forth in the preface of his book *Märchen des Mittelalters*, Berlin, 1925, and in *Sudetendeutsche Zeitsch. f.
Volksk.*, 1929, 1. Beiheft, pp. 44–5. K. Krohn replied in
FFC 96 (1931), pp. 9 ff.)

In his emphasis on the historical variants of folktales Wesselski had been preceded by the Orientalist,
Th. Benfey, the German translator of the *Panchatantra*,
and one of the founders of our science. Benfey paid
relatively little attention to the oral variants of folktales but depended on literary texts and internal criteria
for tracing the history of a story type. He observed, for
example, that the presence, in a tale, of certain Buddhist features, e.g. the peculiar view taken of animals,
points to the Indian origin of the type (compare A.
Aarne, *Vergleichende Märchenforschungen*, Helsingfors, 1907, pp. 3–82). Benfey was prone to postulate an
Indian origin for most fairy tales. This was an exaggeration; but it must be admitted that subsequent research
has borne him out in many instances (Krohn, *FFC* 96).

Benfey's school (to which belonged such illustrious
scholars as Gaston Paris and Emmanuel Cosquin) was
rudely attacked by Joseph Bédier, who in his *Fabliaux*
(1st ed., 1893; 3rd ed., 1925) denied the possibility of
tracing a folktale to its country of origin and of reconstructing its chronology. He did make out a case
for the extreme difficulty of tracing such a history for
many merry tales of extremely simple structure and
presupposing most elementary human relationships.
Such tales may even be supposed to have been invented
more than once, independently, in more than one place
(polygenesis). But for all stories of more complex structures Bédier's scepticism is to be rejected.

In the same work Bédier made a claim which is no
better substantiated by the known facts. He asserted
that stories embodying beliefs and practices peculiar to
ethnical or religious groups are not readily received by
groups to whom such beliefs and practices are foreign.
This is not so. We have already seen that tales reflecting a peculiarly Buddhist attitude toward animals have
frequently been freely taken over by non-Buddhist
groups. Stories based upon the typically Iranian tenet
of divine dualism are similarly known as far west as
Brittany (Krappe, *MLN* 58 (1943), pp. 515–19) and as
far east as the North American Indians of the Pacific
Coast (O. Dähnhardt, *Natursagen*, I). For the diffusion
of a tale it is sufficient that it be a good story, holding
the interest of the listener, and that it be easily understood and reproduced. The fact that it may embody
doctrines by no means held by those who take it over
is of no importance.

Tales of this character, which are known as migratory
tales, properly speaking, and myths are for this reason
much easier to trace to their places of origin. Similarly,
in the case of animal tales and fables, zoogeographical
data frequently furnish a welcome clue. Thus the role

of King Noble, the Lion, in the medieval beast epic and in the fable, militates most strongly against the theory of a European origin of the story types in question.

The possibility of polygenesis must be admitted for many proverbs based on universal or nearly universal institutions, habits, customs, etc., though even here diffusion is by no means excluded. In many cases a closer linguistic analysis will throw light on the subject. Thus the well-known proverb *Ora est labora* cannot go back into Latin antiquity because the verb *orare*, when used in a religious sense (which is by no means always the case), is not used thus absolutely but requires an object and means to entreat, request, pray someone for something, etc. Its absolute use, as in the proverb, is not found until after the Christianization of the Empire. In fact, the proverb originated with the Benedictine monks. This example shows at the same time the utter necessity for a sound linguistic equipment of the folklorist, and it is no accident that most, and the most successful, students of folklore have come from the ranks of the philologists, both classical and modern.

A far more complex problem is presented by the well-nigh universal occurrence of relatively simple, nay rudimentary, folklore materials such as games, dances, rites, beliefs, institutions, etc., such as belief in Powers (the chief root of religion), fear of the dead, rites of aversion, the blood covenant, the awe inspired by multiple births. There are three different explanations available, viz. 1) they may be the common heritage of our species handed down from a time when this species lived in a narrowly circumscribed area and diffused, subsequently, with the diffusion of man over the earth's surface; 2) they may have originated subsequently and independently from a psychological basis common to all mankind; and 3) they may have been diffused from a diffusion-center in a given period more or less recent. The second of these explanations was propounded by a German anthropologist, Adolf Bastian. The third is now preferred by some quite prominent anthropologists: G. Elliot Smith, W. H. R. Rivers, F. Graebner, and others. The first explanation has thus far received least consideration, no doubt because it requires far more data on the mores of the apes, man's nearest relations, than we actually possess. None of the three explanations is, however, ruled out *a priori*, and the main question merely is which one of them is the more likely to explain any given phenomenon.

The answer to this question therefore necessarily depends upon the nature of the material. A good deal of what is now known as moon lore, i.e. beliefs and practices connected with the lunar phases (appearance of the new moon, lunar eclipses, etc.) is probably explainable on the assumption that the nightly star attracted man's attention from the very earliest times.

At the other end of the scale are materials manifestly derived from the one or the other of the great civilizations some of which (e.g. the Egyptian) go back 10,000 years and even more. Egypt and Mesopotamia formed gigantic diffusion-centers for the domestication of plants and animals with the mass of folklore material attached to them.

Explainable by Bastian's *Völkergedanke* are, probably, certain ingrained fears, more particularly the fear

of the abnormal, such as multiple births, albinism, the smith's craft, further certain widely spread institutions such as finger mutilation, the blood covenant, etc. But it cannot be emphasized too strongly that the whole subject is still very much in flux and that all doctrinaire theories such as those defended by the extreme diffusionists are to be rejected.

Man being by definition a gregarious or social animal (this is the correct translation of Aristotle's *zōon politikon*), all folklore materials represent social phenomena. They are the possession of social groups, not of individuals. Whence it follows that a given folklore may die with the death of the social group that has given rise to it and cultivated it. Thus the folklore of the ancient American peoples (Aztecs, Mayas, Peruvians) is as dead as are their languages and cultures. The ruthless destruction of Irish culture by Cromwell's vandals necessarily spelled the loss, largely irretrievable, of vast treasures of Irish folklore (compare Daniel Corkery, *The Hidden Ireland,* Dublin, 1925), and the ill-advised efforts of 19th century missionaries in the South Seas has had similar effects. English folklore is much poorer than Scottish and Irish because the industrial revolution led to the shifting, i.e. the uprooting, of entire populations, which left the land for the big centers of population, and the destruction of social groups thus encompassed resulted in the loss of their traditions.

The same phenomenon, that is, the growing industrialization of continental Europe in the course of the last century and the threatened loss of the traditional lore, led to the efforts put forward by friends of the past to collect these traditions ere it be too late, and this consideration has given our science the fine impetus which made it one of the foremost disciplines in European historical research and in the university curricula. This leads us naturally to present a sketch of the history of the science of folklore.

Like every science, folklore had to begin with the collection and classification of the material, and to do this effectively, it had to gain consciousness of itself. This happened twice in the history of Western civilization, first in Hellenistic times, when after the death of Alexander two or three generations of scholars, mostly connected with the great *Mousaion* of Alexandria, drew up repertoires of Greek and Near Eastern lore as it had been transmitted by poets and chroniclers. Their object was, however, mostly to utilize these materials, not so much for purposes of historical investigation as to clear up and explain allusions in the ancient poets, chiefly Homer and the lyrics, or to work them up in poetic form as fit subjects for literary composition. (Compare E. Rohde, *Der griechische Roman und seine Vorläufer,* 1st ed., 1867; 3rd ed., 1914.) This labor was not wasted, since without it we should not possess the materials stored up in Ovid's *Metamorphoses,* in the compilations of Parthenius of Nicæa and Antoninus Liberalis, to say nothing of the vast literature of the *scholia.*

It was different with the Hellenic mythology. By the time of Alexander's expedition the enlightened classes had completely lost faith in the traditional religion and taken refuge in various philosophical systems. This left open the question of how the traditional religion and the myths told about the gods had arisen in the first place. Two theories were put forward to account for them, and neither one of the two can be said to be completely dead even now. They are: 1) the euhemerist theory, called after its supposed originator, Euhemerus (flourished about 300 B.C.)—in reality there were euhemerists long before Euhemerus—which sees in the gods dead kings and in their myths the distortion of historical facts. Thus the story of the Phœnician Cadmus, who left his home town, Sidon, to found Thebes in Bœotia and to marry Harmonia, was declared to reflect the flight of one Cadmus, cook of the king of Sidon, with Harmonia, the king's favorite flute girl. Hardly less absurd is the euhemerist interpretation of the rape of Proserpine: Proserpine, a daughter of Ceres, a Sicilian lady, was abducted by Pluto, a rich but somewhat unscrupulous farmer. Punishment overtook him, however, as he tried to cross a bog in his chariot: he was swallowed up with his fair prize. 2) The allegorical method, on the other hand, saw in the high gods personifications of celestial and other phenomena: Poseidon stood for water, Hera for air, Hephaistos-Vulcan for fire, etc. The earliest defenders of this theory were the poet Epicharmus (6th century B.C.) and Theagenus of Rhegium (5th century B.C.). This method was justly ridiculed by Plato (*Phaedrus*, 229 C ff.); but it lived on down into modern times, when Francis Bacon still saw fit to apply it (in his essay *The Wisdom of the Ancients*) and Max Müller merely remodeled it. (On the euhemerist theory see G. Boissier, *La religion romaine d'Auguste aux Antonius*, 1909, pp. 122 ff.; on the allegorical theory see P. Wendland, *Die hellenistisch-römische Kultur*, 1912, p. 112. For a critical evaluation of both see also A. H. Krappe, *Mythologie Universelle*, 1930, pp. 19 ff.)

There is some evidence to show that classical antiquity did evolve a sounder view on the origin of the traditional religion than would appear from this survey. Eusebius of Cæsarea (*Praep. avang.*, II. 5), in refuting the allegorical school, drew attention to the fact that myths belong to a period of savagery, when men were as yet devoid of moral ideas and lived like beasts. Subsequently, being loath to give up the heritage of their ancestors, the Greeks retained these stories but reinterpreted them, to remove the stigma of savagery. Eusebius is not likely to have made this discovery by himself. In all probability he drew on some Hellenic philosopher of the school of Epicurus.

Throughout the Middle Ages and even in the Renaissance the euhemerist and allegorical schools reigned supreme. It was only early in the 18th century that the mode of approach adumbrated by Eusebius was rediscovered by the Jesuit father Joseph-François Lafitau (1681–1746), a French missionary in Canada and author of a work entitled *Moeurs des Sauvages Américains comparées aux moeurs des Premiers Temps* (Paris, 1724). In this book the striking similarity between the customs, manners, and religious ceremonies of the Canadian aborigines on the one hand, the Greeks of Homer and the Hebrews of Moses on the other were pointed out. The same reasonings were taken up and continued by Voltaire, in the introduction to his *Essai sur les moeurs*, by Fontenelle in his essay *De l'origine des fables* (see G. Hervé in *Revue de l'Ecole d'Anthropologie de Paris* XIX (1909), pp. 388 ff.), and by the President Charles des Brosses (1709–1777). Des Brosses was the direct source and inspiration of the Scottish

man of letters and scholar, Andrew Lang, the founder of scientific mythology.

Unlike his 18th century precursors, Lang did not have to fall back exclusively on ethnological material, a procedure not free from objections, since to many it seemed incongruous to explain the myths of Hellas and Rome by the lucubrations of savages. For meanwhile the science of folklore had come into being. It began with the collection of folklore materials by scholars, men of letters, and highly intelligent amateurs: Bishop Percy and Sir Walter Scott in Britain, Svend Grundtvig in Denmark, the Brothers Grimm in Germany, Giambattista Basile in Italy, and Charles Perrault in France. The first to use these materials in the manner in which Lafitau and his successors had used anthropological data, namely for purposes of comparison, was the German Mennonite Wilhelm Mannhardt, whose lifework was continued, in Britain, by the Scottish scholar, Sir James Frazer, the leading historical folklorist of the present century. Frazer was not only a brilliant classical philologist, the learned commentator of Pausanias, Apollodorus, and Ovid, but also a highly competent jurist, a fact which accounts for the excellent scholarship shown in his studies of human institutions. If Krohn's historico-geographical method is indispensable in the tracing of the diffusion of folklore material, Mannhardt's and Frazer's comparative method is best adapted for research in origins.

There is one domain which, thus far, has been relatively neglected, namely the psychological side of folklore. It had the misfortune of being discredited, at the outset, by the ill-supported and wholly unsound fancies of Freud and his pseudo-science, represented by the surrealists. But the prejudice thus created, with reason, by their absurdities and aberrations must not blind us to the importance of the psychological processes underlying many of the phenomena and factors of folklore. This is particularly true of folk-memory, which would seem to constitute the very basis of our science, but also for the strange coincidence between certain traditional stories and phenomena brought to light by psychical research. (Compare Alfred Lehmann, *Aberglaube und Zauberei*, übers. v. D. Petersen, Stuttgart, 1925.) This branch of folklore is still in its infancy, and closer cooperation of classical psychology and historical folklore is, at the present time, urgent desideratum. *General bibliography:* For a general survey of the field: A. H. Krappe, *The Science of Folk-Lore*, London, 1930; for the historico-geographical method: K. Krohn, *Die folkloristische Arbeitsmethode*, Oslo, 1926; for the comparative method: W. Mannhardt, *Wald- und Feldkulte*, 1st ed., 1875–77; 2nd ed. 1904–05; *Mythologische Forschungen* (1884); Sir James G. Frazer, *The Golden Bough*, 4th ed., 1935; *Psyche's Task* (1913); *The Belief in Immortality and the Worship of the Dead* (1913–24); *The Worship of Nature* (1926); *Myths of the Origin of Fire* (1930); *Garnered Sheaves* (1931); *The Fear of the Dead in Primitive Religion* (1933–36); *Aftermath* (1936). On the history of classical mythology: O. Gruppe, *Geschichte der klassischen Mythologie und Religionsgeschichte* (1921).   ALEXANDER H. KRAPPE

Folklore Section of the Library of Congress The Folklore Section of the Library of Congress was established by an administrative order of the Librarian of Congress,

Dr. Luther H. Evans, on August 22, 1946, exactly 100 years after the coinage of the word folklore by William John Thoms, a fitting recognition by the Library of Congress of the broadened activities of folklorists in the United States. The Library of Congress' first interest in the preservation of oral materials in the field of folklore began in 1928 when Robert W. Gordon was appointed as Curator of the Archive of American Folk Song. Gordon's scholarly direction was important in shaping the course of the Archive which was subsequently to be under the administration of John A. Lomax and his son Alan (1933–42), Dr. Benjamin A. Botkin (1942–45), and Dr. Duncan B. M. Emrich (1945–). Through their efforts and those of well-known collectors whose work has been associated with the Archive of American Folk Song, the collections grew until in 1949 individual songs, fiddle tunes, banjo tunes, and other pieces reflecting the music of the people numbered more than 50,000 on more than 10,000 different cylinders, discs, and tape recordings. Initially, both Gordon and the Lomaxes made necessary field trips for the collection of the recordings, but as interest in the subject grew in the United States and as recording machines became readily available, field trips were discontinued by the Library staff. Now the collection of records is made by the Library of Congress in cooperation with universities, colleges, foundations, and other scholarly organizations to which the Library of Congress makes equipment available on loan. The Library of Congress has recently encouraged the establishment of regional archives in each state in order that scholars may have locally available the material in their own region. These archives are normally housed in the collections of the state university and have come into being at such institutions as the University of Arizona, University of California at Los Angeles, Occidental College, Murray State College, University of Utah, University of Wisconsin, Wayne University, and the University of Michigan. Only in very exceptional cases is the recording equipment of the Library loaned to individuals who are not connected with institutions. From its collections the Library of Congress has published 22 albums containing 107 records representative of the best material from the recordings. These include albums of Anglo-American songs and ballads, Negro work songs, spirituals, Indian ceremonial chants, and albums of folk music from Latin American countries. They are available to the general public and may be purchased from the Recording Laboratory of the Library of Congress. A catalog describing the series is available upon request at a cost of ten cents.

Important collectors who have cooperated with the Library of Congress in increasing its record collections include Helen Creighton, Austin Fife, Wayland D. Hand, Arthur L. Campa, Sidney Robertson Cowell, Frances Densmore, William N. Fenton, Levette J. Davidson, Frances Gillmor, Melville J. Herskovits, Herbert Halpert, Thelma James, Louis C. Jones, George Pullen Jackson, George Korson, Margot Mayo, Alton C. Morris, Artus Moser, Vance Randolph, J. D. Robb, Charles Seeger, and Henrietta Yurchenco.

The Archive has broadened its activities in recent years and effected exchange agreements with comparable institutions throughout the world, including the Cecil Sharp House in London, the Musée de l'Homme, the Musée des Arts et Traditions Populaires, and the Phonothèque Nationale in Paris, and other institutions in Europe as well as in Latin America and the United States.

The increased interest in the broader aspects of folklore as distinct from folk song are reflected also in exchange agreements which have been realized. These are being effectively carried out through the medium of the International Commission on Folk Arts and Folklore with offices in Paris and the International Folk Music Council with offices in London.

The collections in the field of folklore have also been increased with the addition to the Folklore Section of the WPA manuscript collections.

DUNCAN B. M. EMRICH

folk medicine See CURES; DISEASES; EGG CURING; FORMULAS; MEDICINE, and various individual articles on specific diseases, as EPILEPSY, LEPROSY, etc.

folk-say Coined in 1928 as the title of an annual collection (1929–32) of folklore and folk and regional literature by its editor, B. A. Botkin, the term has been defined by him (*American Speech* VI, 1931, pp. 404–06) to mean "folklore as literature," with the emphasis on the "oral, linguistic, and story-telling (whether in tale or ballad) aspects of folklore and its living as well as its anachronistic phases." Thus conceived, "not as a substitute for 'folklore,' but as an extension of it, to supplement the older term with one possessing wider and fresher connotations, not fixed by academic usage," the word has become specialized in three senses: 1) "as told by" accounts, including reminiscences, old-timers' stories, folk history, etc.—what the folk have to say about themselves, in their own words (see B. A. Botkin, "Folklore as a Neglected Source of Social History," *The Cultural Approach to History*, edited by Caroline F. Ware, 1940, pp. 309–15); 2) the creative use of folk materials, especially as developed in the folklore work of the Federal Writers' Project under Botkin's national direction (see Donald Ogden Stewart, *Fighting Words*, 1940, pp. 7–14); and 3) proverbial, colloquial, idiomatic, and figurative phrases, sayings, and bywords (by confusion of folk-say with folk-saying). In his introduction to *The American Imagination at Work* (1947) Ben C. Clough uses folk-say and book-say as antonyms. [BAB]

folk song See SONG: FOLK SONG AND MUSIC OF FOLK SONG.

folktale The term folktale as used in English is very inclusive. No attempt has ever been made to define it exactly, but it has been left as a general word referring to all kinds of traditional narrative. It applies to such diverse forms as the creative myths of primitive peoples, the elaborate frame-stories of the *Arabian Nights*, the adventures of Uncle Remus, Puss in Boots, and Cupid and Psyche. Such a wide definition is a great convenience in English, since it frequently avoids the necessity of making decisions and often of entering into long debates as to the exact narrative *genre* to which a particular story may belong.

It will be seen that the characteristic feature of the folktale is the fact that it is traditional. It is handed down from one person to another, and there is no virtue in originality. This tradition may be purely oral. The tale is heard and is repeated as it is remembered, with or without additions or changes made by the new teller. Sometimes the tradition may be literary, as when a story keeps being told by one author after another. Many of the tales now current among the peoples of Europe appeared in writing in the collections of exempla used as illustrations by medieval priests. These collections repeated each other through the centuries and may have gone back to oral sources or the inventiveness of some literary author. In any case they became traditional, and the student of folktales is interested in them. Not all scholars would agree to speak of these literary tales as folktales, but the weight of usage tends to include them.

If we use this broad definition for the folktale, we shall find that it is as nearly universal as any form of human literary expression. As more and more of the primitive peoples of the world are studied, we see that men everywhere and in all types of culture have told tales. Though there is a difference in the emphasis and in the proportion of folktales in particular groups, many of the principal forms are practically universal. It is possible with considerable success to make comparative studies not only of the themes of folktales but also of the narrative techniques among peoples of very diverse cultures, from the simple Australian aborigine to the peasant of modern Europe and even the professional story-teller of the bazaars of Cairo.

Forms of the folktale It is convenient to use certain terms in connection with the folktale to differentiate some of the forms in which the tales appear. It must be understood, however, that these differentiations are rather loose and that they vary to some extent from country to country and from one cultural group to another. Usually the teller of tales is not much concerned with such distinctions. Certainly the primitive tale teller would not recognize any such categories as we might set up. On the other hand, folklorists in Europe have come to use such terms as *Märchen, Sagen,* legends, traditions, fables, animal tales, myths, and the like, with some degree of definiteness.

Legends and Traditions Some authors have tried to distinguish between the terms legend and tradition, but an examination of the literature shows that usage in English is utterly confused. There is no word corresponding to the German *Sagen.* Writers in English have, therefore, usually resorted to the combined form, legends and traditions. There is some agreement to include under these headings several distinct catagories of narrative: a) explanatory legends having to do with creation or with origins; b) stories concerned with supernatural creatures such as fairies, dwarfs, and ghosts; and c) legends about historic or pseudo-historic characters such as the Pied Piper of Hamelin or Lady Godiva. A legend or tradition is always told as a fact and is presumably believed by the teller. But though it may be connected with a definite time and place, it may well change such details and still remain an object of belief.

Fairy Tales The German *Märchen* is frequently translated "fairy tale" in English. It is nearly always fictional in intent and thus differs from the legend or tradition. See FAIRY TALE.

Animal Tales Nearly all peoples tell short anecdotes about the adventures of animals. These are, most of them, anthropomorphized so that the animal actually has human characteristics. Good examples are the Uncle Remus cycle from Georgia. See ANIMAL TALE.

Fables When the animal tale has a definite moral, usually expressed at the end of the story, it is known as a fable. Most fables belong to the literary tradition, although they frequently become a part of folklore. See FABLE.

Myths There is little agreement in the use of the term myth. But it certainly can be considered as one branch of the folktale. It concerns the world as it was in some past age before the present conditions were established. It treats creations and origins, and therefore may be identical with creation and origin legends. When it handles adventures of the gods, it may well be identical with the fairy tale. Many divergent theories as to the nature of the myth have been held in the past. All of them contain a grain of truth but none give entire satisfaction.

References:
F. von der Leyen, *Das Märchen,* 3rd ed. Leipzig, 1925.
G. Huet, *Les Contes Populaires.* Paris, 1923.
S. Thompson, *The Folktale.* New York, 1946.

STITH THOMPSON

Fomorian (from Irish *fomór,* giant, pirate) One of a mythical, prehistoric people who raided and pillaged Ireland from the sea: defeated and slaughtered, except for a handful, by the Tuatha Dé Danann at the Battle of Mag Tured. They are sometimes mythologically associated with the powers of nature which challenge man: winter, storm, fog, crop-blight, disease. See FIRBOLG.

fontomfrom drums The talking drums of the Ashanti people of West Africa. They are male and female and are dressed in rich garments. Their specific function is to drum out proverbs: each individual drummer drums a whole saying on his own drum. Seventy-seven of the proverbs are known, drummed, and recognized via the drum medium at Mampon (see R.S. Rattray, *Religion and Art in Ashanti,* London, 1927, pp. 286 ff.).

food superstitions Most widespread in Middle America is the idea of categories of food known as "hot" or "cold," or "fresh" or "irritating," which have nothing to do with the actual temperatures of the foods, or even the presence or absence of spices. To the Maya of Chan Kom, Yucatán, wild turkey, rice, boiled eggs, pork, squash, papaya, and limes are "cold," while coffee, beef, honey, and pinole are "hot." The Tarascans of Tzintzuntzan, Michoacán, in Mexico, consider unboiled atole, pork, bass, milk, tamales, pears, oranges, and peaches to be "fresh," while rice, potatoes, bananas, mangoes, chocolate, wheat, chickens, beef, and boiled atole are "irritating." A third intermediate category is often found. In some cases this is comprised of foods with no distinctive qualities, and in other cases hot and cold foods may be mixed to form an intermediate meal. Among some peoples hot and cold foods must not be eaten at the same meal. [GMF]

food tabu in the land of the dead The proscription against eating or drinking anything in the land of the dead on pain of being detained there forever. By partaking of food or drink in the land of the dead, the partaker becomes kin to or one with the dwellers in that land and is unable ever to leave them or return to the land of the living. The classical story of Persephone, abducted by Hades and doomed to return to Hades periodically for eating one small pomegranate seed, is perhaps the most famous example of the underworld food tabu motif (C211.2).

This motif is not only of classical antiquity but represents a living and widespread belief among contemporary primitive peoples. It turns up in the ancient epics of the world and has filtered into folk and fairy tales, songs, and ballads all over Europe. There are late Jewish usages of the idea and it is conspicuous also in Danish, Swabian, Lapp, Swedish, Manx, and Scottish tradition.

The *Kalevala* reveals how Väinämöinen journeyed to Tuonela in search of certain magic words but had sense enough to refuse the seething tankard of beer that was urged upon him.

The people of New Caledonia believe that when a man dies and arrives in the spirit land, he is given a great welcome and offered a feast of bananas. If he eats he can never return; if he refuses he stands some chance of getting back to the land of the living. The Melanesians warn any living man who would visit Panoi, their underworld, to touch no food in that place or he will be forced to remain there. There is also a New Zealand Maori story, containing the food tabu in the land of the dead motif, about a young girl who died for love. Her lover begged the gods to let him visit her in Reinga, the underworld. They consented but warned him to eat nothing that might be offered him. The tabu against eating in the other world motif (C211) is common also among the Haida, Tsimshian, Kwakiutl, Pawnee, and Cherokee North American Indians. Analogous are many stories, especially of Tlingit, Tsimshian, and Kwakiutl tribes, about people who have drowned and been carried off by the land otters. Those who eat the food of the otters can never return. Two White Mountain Apache boys out hunting birds came to where the ga' ns were living underground. Food was offered them and they ate. When they returned home food was offered them as usual but they could not eat, because they had eaten where the ga' ns lived.

The same tabu holds in the fairylands of the world (C211.1): one must not eat fairy food or he cannot go home again. The food of the gods in the Celtic otherworld confers immortality, not death, upon the partaker; but the same rule holds that it binds the mortal to the god and he cannot return to his human habitation. Once Conle had tasted the apple thrown to him by the fairy woman, he was irrevocably compelled to follow her to that wonderful otherworld from which he never returned. Apples and rowanberries especially are mentioned as conferring a quality of beauty which old age could not dim. The rule works in reverse also. There is a Scandinavian story about a girl from elfland who had to eat earthly food in order to remain with her earthly lover (C661). And in Tonga (Polynesian) mythology also, the eating of mortal food was fatal to beings from the afterworld. Compare ADAPA.

Fool Plough, Fond Plough, or **Fond Pleaf** In England, especially in the northern and eastern parts, an agricultural festival (sometimes a pageant), observed usually the Monday after Epiphany (Plough Monday) before plowing is begun, or sometimes observed at the end of Lent to celebrate the termination of plowing. Young farm workers dressed in white shirts or nightshirts drag a decorated plow through the countryside, from village to village. In the north of England the Fool Plough goes about accompanied by a number of sword dancers and musicians. The Bessy, a man in grotesque woman's clothing, and the fool, dressed either in skins or wearing a fur cap and tail, go from door to door soliciting money. At one time the money was collected to buy candles to burn on local altars; now it is openly intended to provide food and drink for celebration and merrymaking. In Northumberland every time the Bessy receives a contribution, a gun is fired; if she is refused, the men plow up the path or dunghill.

In eastern Yorkshire on Plough Monday or Twelfth Day (January 6) the farm youths go from town to town dragging the plow from which the plowshare has been removed. When they stop to solicit they perform an antic dance around the personalized implement. Each group is said to be headed by "Mab and his wife," the usual clown and man in female garb, with blackened faces.

footprint The mark of the foot left in the earth, or in ashes, sand, etc.: widely believed to be one of the body impressions by which magic can be worked on a person. Certain Australian aborigines believe that they can lame an enemy by putting sharp stones or broken glass in his footprints. In Burma and northern India sores on the feet are often attributed to interference with one's footprints on the part of an enemy or witch. Many African peoples take care to obliterate their footprints for this reason; and insects which scurry back and forth and blot out the tracks of hunters and warriors are especially revered by many primitive peoples. Hunters among the Zulus, Hottentots, and some West African tribes put charms in the tracks of their quarry to prevent the animal from getting too far ahead. Some North American Indians also did this. So identified with the personality of man or beast is his footprint in early belief that the Seneca Indians say the bear knows when someone looks at his track.

In Bohemia, to lame a man the earth of his footprint is put in a kettle along with a nail, a needle, and some broken glass and allowed to boil till the kettle cracks. The man will be lame for the rest of his life. In Lithuania it is said that if the dust of your footprint is buried in a graveyard, you will sicken and die. In Estonia merely to measure the track with a stick and to bury that much of the stick has the same results.

Some southern United States Negroes today believe that if you tie up the earth or sand of a person's footprints in a little red flannel bag, and carry the bag with you, that person will be compelled to follow you. This is used especially as a love charm. Zuñi Indian women also sometimes keep the soil of their husbands' footprints where they sleep, to keep the husbands faithful.

Many peoples believe they can catch the footprints of supernaturals in strewn ashes. The visitations of the returned dead or the identity of guardian animals or spirits, or of troublesome demons, are often ascertained and revealed by their footprints left in strewn ashes. On St. Mark's Eve in rural England ashes were formerly sifted on the hearth; whosoever footprint was seen in it in the morning would die within the year.

In Ireland if the fairy host rushes past you on All Hallows Eve, take up the dust from under your feet and throw it after them, and they will be compelled to give back any human being they are keeping among them.

In folktale there are magic footprints (D1294), transformations from stepping in footprints (D578), transformations to animal form by drinking from an animal's track (D555.1). Footprint as life token occurs in Icelandic saga (E761.1.3.1): if it filled with earth, the hero was sick, if with water, he was drowned; if it filled with blood, it meant he was killed in battle. Local legend everywhere in the world identifies marks on rocks, cliffs, mountains as the footprints of gods, demons, and other supernaturals. See ADAM'S PEAK.

forbidden fruit or **tree** A concept known to all Occidental cultures through the passages in *Genesis* which describe the planting of trees of all varieties in the Garden of Eden and the prohibition against eating the fruit of the Tree of Knowledge of Good and Evil. The theological lore about these trees is extensive with a general agreement that Adam was expelled from the Garden lest, having come to a knowledge of good and evil, he might eat of the tree of life also and become, like God, immortal. Theologians are not in agreement as to whether these trees belonged to the apple, the citrus, or to other genera. The symbolism of the forbidden fruit (forbidden tree) has entered extensively into the folklore of Occidental peoples and has become part of the lore of unique forbidden foods, rooms, questions, and general tabu, of which it is undoubtedly a special form. [RDJ]

☞ There is a Bantu forbidden tree story (known in some six or seven variants from the Basutos to the Begas in the Cameroons) in which the fruit of a certain tree can be eaten only by those who learn the name of the fruit and only with the permission of the owner. The weight of the tabu and the consequences of breaking it do not seem to be pointed up, however. The story begins with messengers being sent to ask the name of the tree. In a Suto version, Lion sends the animals to find out the name of the tree from Koko (literally, Grandmother, and as has been suggested, probably some tribal ancestress). Koko tells them the name and they travel homeward, repeating it lest they forget, fall into an anthill, and do forget. Lion himself goes and asks, also forgets. Tortoise goes, falls into the ant-hill, but remembers anyway. In resentment for Tortoise's success, Lion orders him to be buried. Then the animals proceed to eat and enjoy the fruit, leaving, however, the top branch intact (in some versions evidently a stipulation). In the night, Tortoise digs himself out, eats the fruit on the top branch, and goes back into the hole. The next day Koko comes in anger to the animals, asking who ate the forbidden fruit. Tortoise escapes punishment by reminding one and all that he has been buried.

In some variants the owner of the tree is a god, or the tree is the god incarnate. Some tribal versions give Tortoise the role of messenger; sometimes it is Hare, sometimes Monkey. In the Benga version Python is in charge of the tree; Rat is the first messenger, Tortoise the last and successful one. In this case Tortoise succeeds where the others have failed because his mother has warned him not to eat or drink en route. So when finally he gets back and his canoe overturns on the beach, he is still saying over and over, "Bojabi, bojabi" (the name of the fruit), when the others pull him ashore.

The folktale motif of the forbidden tree (C621) in which the fruit of any tree but one may be eaten is extremely widespread and turns up variously in general European folklore, in the Eddas, in Semitic, Siberian, Latin-American, and also in Indonesian folktale.

forecastle song A leisure song of sailors, sung in the dog-watches in the evening, often accompanied by mouth organ, jew's harp, fiddle, or accordion, and chosen from ballads, music-hall songs, popular or sentimental songs of home. The chanteys, being work songs, were not heard at ships' concerts. On the clipper ships songs of patriotic exploits and battles at sea were favorites, often rousing considerable partisan spirit when Britishers and Yankees in the crew refought the Wars of the Revolution and 1812 with *The Stately Southerner* (*The Yankee Man of War* or *The Ranger*), *Ye Parliament of England*, and *The Constitution and the Guerrière*. Come-all-ye's of all trades took on sea-going trappings to suit the sailors' interests, cotton-picking, lumbering, railroading, soldiering, prison and mining complaints all adding to the song wealth of whalers, fishermen, and "packet rats." Such songs as *Barnacle Bill the Sailor* (known to forecastle hands as *Abel* or *Abram Brown*) and *Bell-Bottomed Trousers*, which have found a new audience over the radio, were popular long ago with seamen, in versions not acceptable for the air. *The Golden Vanity*, in many of its variants, *High Barbaree*, garbled but still spirited, *Blow Ye Winds of Morning*, as uninhibited as the whalers who sang it, were among the ancient British ballads that went to sea, and *The Little Mohee* (*The Lass of Mohea*), as sung by the Pacific whalers made the "fair Indian lass" a "pretty Kanaka" from Hawaii. Men at sea still sing, and while the radio and the ship's movies provide most of their songs, many of the old airs and verses survive, and the new ones are tailored and trimmed to the taste of the twentieth century mariners. *Venezuela*, sung as a forecastle song in the movie, *The Long Voyage Home*, achieved some degree of popularity on land, being often requested from the shouting audiences at folk song concerts in the 1940's.

forget-me-not A small herb (genus *Myosotis*) with tiny blue, rose, or white flowers, sometimes called mouse-ear because of the shape of the leaves.

Forget-me-nots are said to cure the bites of serpents and mad dogs. They are used as a poultice for sore eyes; boiled in milk and water they are a cure for dysentery. In Siberia they are used in the treatment of syphilis. Steel tempered in the juice of these plants is said to be so hard that it will cut stone without being dulled. At one time it was customary to give forget-me-nots to anyone starting on a journey on Feb. 29, and later they were exchanged among friends on that day.

formulas Among the Cherokee Indians, charms or prayers written by the shamans for their own use, but also sometimes recited by the individual requiring them. The sacred formulas of the Cherokees pertain to every phase of their daily life. There are love formulas, curing formulas, childbirth formulas (i.e. to expedite delivery), formulas for luck in hunting and fishing and with crops, and for finding lost articles. No luck follows the hunter or fisher who forgets the sacred formula. There are weather formulas, formulas for protection against evil, and for killing people. There are even formulas for weakening the other side in a ball game.

Most of the formulas begin with the word "Listen" and are written in two parts: 1) a set of practical directions for the use of herbs or other materials; 2) an invocation to specific supernatural forces to bring the desired result. Very often a formula *states as already true* that which it is designed to bring about. "No one is ever lonely with me. Your soul has come into the very center of my soul, never to turn away," is part of one of the most beautiful and most widely published of the Cherokee love charms. Formulas intended to make a rival unattractive and lonesome sometimes result in a social isolation so great that no one will speak, joke, or dance with him.

The disease formulas are next in importance and number to the love charms. They are not all curing formulas, however. Sometimes a man's parents or his best friend will send a disease to him merely to test his endurance or to teach him counterspells. These are called "ordeal diseases." The childbirth formulas are "to make children jump down."

The Hupa Indians of California also possess a vast number of medicine formulas. To cure the sick the shaman recites a long story of some mythical person who went to the end of the world and found the cure for just such a disease as the patient now suffers. The sacred ceremonial curing chants and dances of the Navaho, which have undergone no alteration or omission of either word or gesture since their beginning, might be classified as sacred formulas, although the word is not currently applied to them.

formula tale Any folktale following a certain traditional pattern and in which the plot is secondary to that pattern. Cumulative tales, catch tales, endless tales, circular tales or prose rounds, and unfinished tales are all formula tales. There is also a type which avoids the use of pronouns, and another type which always ends with a question (usually in regard to the awarding of a prize equally deserved by several contestants). This last is of three kinds: either it ends with an unusually clever and inevitable answer, or the problem is posed and the answer left to the audience, or else it falls into a more purely formulistic class such as the typical cumulative story which also ends with a question, as "Once there was a woman; the woman had a son; the son had red breeches; the breeches had black buttons," etc., etc., ending with "Shall I tell it again?" Most formula tales are told in the spirit of pure fun, and some of them are definitely play-game tales.

Forseti or **Forsete** In Teutonic mythology, the son of Balder (light) and Nanna (purity). He was the wisest and most eloquent of the æsir and was made god of justice. No one ever found fault with his decisions. He lived in the radiant palace, Glitnir. Helgoland was once known as Forseti's land because he helped a council of Frisians who had met there to codify their laws.

Fortuna The Roman goddess of fortune and good luck: identified with the more obscure Greek Tyche. Most often she is represented standing on a globe or ball (later a wheel), indicating the mutability of her favors, and with a cornucopia in one hand from which she strews luck with the other. However, she had many other aspects and attributes: she appears with a rudder, guiding the world's affairs; as *Fortuna virginensis,* she protected newly married women; as *Fortuna virilis,* she preserved their beauty so that they pleased their husbands; as *Fors Fortuna,* she was the goddess of luck. Fortuna is often veiled or blindfolded. Her shrines at Antium and Præneste were oracular; the latter is one of her more ancient cult centers, where she was worshipped as *Primigenia,* the oldest daughter of Jupiter, the goddess of destiny. The wheel of fortune, symbolizing the precariousness of things in this life, was a favorite classical allusion of writers of the later Middle Ages.

Forty-Seven Ronin The forty-seven retainers or followers of Asano, heroes of *The Loyal League of Forty-Seven Ronin* or *Chushingura,* a famous Japanese puppet play, based on a historical incident, and first presented in 1748. The *daimyo* Asano was insulted in the Shogun's court by Kira, another nobleman, in 1701. Asano drew his sword, an act of impiety within the sacred precinct, for which he had to commit hara-kiri. His fortune was confiscated and his family declared extinct. The forty-seven Ronin, or retainers, were apportioned to other nobles, but swore to avenge their dead master. After two years of adventuring, they caught up with Kira and assassinated him, thus fulfilling the demands of Bushido, the code of honor. But they had transgressed the civil law and so, after placing the enemy's head on Asano's grave, all forty-seven disemboweled themselves. The Buddhist temple in Tokyo where they are buried is still a popular shrine. The story and characters are the subject of many Japanese paintings.

fox The lore of the fox has taken so many different and distinct directions in the folklore of the world that the data is most readily presented as independent streams which can be brought together only after more elaborate discussion than is possible here. The lore of the British Hunt Clubs, for example, is only remotely connected with the medieval beast epic centered about Reynard the Fox. This in turn has slight connections with lycanthropy (woman into fox) and other European shape-shifting. To this must be added the rich and apparently inexhaustible lore of the Chinese and Japanese shape-shifting foxes (usually, fox into woman). Tales of European and Oriental shape-shifting foxes are parallel to tales of other shape-shifters—Krappe suggests weasels, though the list might be considerably enlarged—and these are undoubtedly parallel to the tales of succubi, incubi, and poison damsels.

The British Hunt Clubs have developed a very special vocabulary which describes the etiquette and procedure of the hunt, and they have a large store of tales about the cunning of the fox in flight as well as about the habits of the fox.

The Epic of Reynard is a series of tales and poems which appeared in Europe about the 11th century A.D.

and reached the height of their popularity in the 14th and 15th centuries. This collection, written by unknown authors, was intended largely for the amusement of the middle and lower classes as the courtly epics were written for the chivalric classes. It satirizes the habits, customs, and prejudices of the churchmen, knights, and lawyers. In the early poems of the cycle, Reynard was called into court to defend himself for his several crimes. This cycle is connected with the literary fables about foxes such as Æsop's Fables and with the lore of the hunters.

The Europeans as well as the Chinese and Japanese have many stories about human beings who at the full of the moon or under conditions of emotional strain either imagine that they are wolves or foxes or actually become wolves or foxes and run about fields and graves. Robert Burton calls this "Lycanthropia, which Avicenna calls Cucubuth, others Lupinam insaniam or Wolf-madness." A classic parallel to this was the classic Greek cult of Zeus Lykaios. The assumption in a large number of these European tales is that the normal state of the creature is human and that the shift in shape and nature is a reversion, a curse, or a form of insanity. The preponderance of evidence in the Chinese tales—if preponderance be taken as the number of stories, variety of incident, or frequency of repetition—is that the nature of the creature was originally fox, though similar formulæ are used for cats, dogs, weasels, even trees, and that these creatures by the exercise of discipline acquired the power to assume human form.

Although the disciplines necessary to acquire the power of shifting shape are, in their very generalized form, late formulations, they can be traced back to very ancient sources, the great corpus of Chinese lore. This is still preserved in part in Chinese popular Taoism. The theory was already corrupt in the T'ang dynasty (618–907 A.D.) but can be traced in the writings of the Han scholars (206 B.C.–221 A.D.) as well as in the *Book of Odes* and the *Book of Rites* of the Feudal Age (1100–221 B.C.). Thus the theory of how foxes or other creatures acquire power to shift shape is part of the Chinese ethos.

Two methods of shape-shifting are available: first, by the study of the classics, and second, by sexual trickery. The first, known as the legal method, is open to all, and shape-shifting foxes on interrogation often express amazement that human beings with so many advantages so seldom make use of it, for ultimately the study of the classics leads to immortality. The general view of the Chinese philosophers that the purpose of study is to produce "sageliness within and kingliness without" is, when translated into popular terms, that study produces elevation, saintliness, or power. Thus foxes who study the classics acquire first the power to become human beings, then immortals, finally gods. Many stories are told about human beings who have surprised groups of young foxes in a circle about an old white fox who is expounding the classics. The motif of the "fox school" is also known in European hunting lore. Some of the Chinese stories conclude with the statement that the teacher, when he assumes human form, is a tutor or a well-known scholar in the village. The difficulty about the legal method of acquiring power to shift shape is that it is arduous and requires a long time, as well as more concentration than most foxes are capable of.

Most stories are about foxes who have acquired shape-shifting power by the illegal method. This method is based on an important tenet in Chinese erotology, namely that in sexual intercourse the person who experiences the orgasm first loses a unit of life essence and if the partner can restrain orgasm this unit is absorbed. Thus foxes who can assume human form, if at first only briefly, can by seducing other human beings steal life essence and add it to their own. The formulæ for this sort of tale range from the simple to the complex. Examples are: A student who retired to a tumble-down cottage or deserted temple to prepare for the state examinations was visited at dusk by a beautiful maiden who became his mistress. Her erotic skill was such that the student became consumptive and finally died. Variations include the student who desired a fox mistress and announced his desires at dusk in a graveyard or before a deserted temple. At times the shape-shifters sincerely love their human paramours, help them with their studies, care in filial fashion for their parents after death; but they seldom are reported to return the life essence they have stolen. Occasionally the parents or friends become aware of the situation in time and call in either a shaman or a Taoist official specially trained in fox exorcism and drive the thief away.

Stories of fox reward and fox revenge are numerous, though Chinese authorities are inclined to believe that stories of fox reward are spurious. Inasmuch as foxes can become invisible and hear everything that is said and read everything that is written, the wise scholar will tell only flattering stories about foxes and keep silent about their wickedness. However many stories are told about hunters or farmers who have been rewarded for freeing foxes from traps or saving their lives when they were being hunted. A popular theme is of the fox and the scholar. Foxes who acquire power by sexual trickery are criminals and subject to death by a blast from the Thunder God. Scholars are by definition upright men possessed of great power whom the Thunder God will not harm. Consequently during thunder storms, foxes either in human or in fox form seek the protection of scholars. The rewards are of many varieties: fame, prosperity, success in the examinations. Because foxes are great thieves and can be invisible, they keep the money chests filled and complications ensue when a neighbor having marked his wealth finds it in the possession of a friend. At times this discovery is engineered by the fox who is offended by some careless comment by its patron.

More stories are told about fox revenge than about fox reward. Fox revenge is often carefully fitted to the offense. A hunter was bitten by a fox when taking it out of a trap to kill it. He shouted, "Defile your mother," which is a common Chinese obscenity, but the fox escaped. When the hunter returned home he found his mother in the embraces of a young man who when attacked changed into a fox and escaped, calling back, "I have done to you what you threatened to do to me." A mandarin who was very fond of his wife took a beautiful maiden to bed while he was on an official journey. After a time he became suspicious that his companion was a fox. He drove her away with curses. When he returned he found a hundred women in his Yamen identical with his wife in every respect: speech, bearing, bodily marks. The many ingenious attempts to separate the true wife from the spurious ones belong in the cycle of the Judgment of Solomon.

Foxes and their numerous families, whether they have acquired power by legal or illegal methods, often take up their residence in deserted buildings, attics, or barns of family compounds. When human children annoy them by being noisy or throwing bricks at them or using impudent language the foxes retaliate by themselves throwing bricks or destroying curios or creating uproar. Other fox families are said to live quietly and respectably, exchange gifts with their hosts on formal occasions, and, when their children become as obstreperous as human children sometimes do, they offer apologies and make amends.

In general the shape-shifting foxes of China are said to be mischievous, tricky, and libidinous. They are very fond of wine and are often discovered because when drunk they assume their true fox form. They most frequently assume the shape of human females if they use the illegal method, though in some instances they become males and steal the essence of human females. Some of the revenge and reward stories are for harm or kindness done in previous existences. In one instance a fox caught *in flagrante* with a human female justified himself by saying that the woman had been his wife in an earlier existence. They had been killed before their time. She had been incarnated as a woman and he as a fox. Having studied to acquire power he had been permitted to visit the woman a stipulated number of times that their destiny might be fulfilled.

Another cycle of fox tales, not so widespread as the cycle just summarized, is of the poor man living alone who came home at night to find his house in order and his dinner on the fire. He discovered that every morning a fox came to his hut, shed her skin, and became a woman. He stole the skin. They lived happily and prosperously for many years until the woman discovered the skin, put it on, and ran away. Stith Thompson has reported variants of this story from North America, Greenland, Labrador. W. Jochelson has a somewhat corrupt version from among the Koryak on the shores of the Bering Sea. Oral variants have been collected from several parts of China and an early 19th century version was reported by a Chinese official visiting on Okinawa which was at that time part of Chinese territory. This fact again raises the question of the origin and diffusion of Chinese tales, which cannot be answered until the dark spots on the folklorists' map have been filled in by better collections than are now available.

Japan has a rich store of tales about shape-shifting foxes. The lore in Japan has been formalized by the Shinto priests until it is a recognized part of the cult. In China too, many of the stories have been modified by the priestly traditions though Chinese scholars have little respect for the Taoist priests, witches, fortune-tellers, and when they are feeling like scholars keep these stories in their proper place as part of the lore of the folk. Alexander Krappe is undoubtedly right when he asserts in an exploratory article, which is excellent in despite of a number of errors, that many of the Japanese tales came from China ("Far Eastern Fox Lore," *California Folklore Quarterly*, April, 1944). The parallels between these Chinese-Japanese tales and stories about succubi and incubi, fatal brides, other shape-shifters, and persons suffering from lycanthropy will, when they are straightened out, form a fascinating section in comparative folklore. [RDJ]

🐾 Fox in Japanese is *kitsune;* the magical animal par excellence of Japanese folklore, said to be able to bewitch people, and assume human shape. All foxes are believed to be malicious, except the Inari fox, the messenger of the Harvest God.   [JLM]

🐾 Fox as a male animal character plays a fairly prominent role in trickster and other tales in western North American Indian mythology. In many instances Fox is trickster's companion; at times he deceives Coyote and eats the food which Coyote has procured for himself. Among the Eskimo the most notable tale about Fox is that of Fox-Woman; this tale has Siberian parallels. The story concerns a man who comes home each night to find that his house has been put in order by a mysterious housekeeper. He hides near home one day and sees a fox enter his house; upon going inside he discovers a beautiful woman whom he marries. One day he enquires what causes the musky odor which he notices about the house; his wife admits that she gives forth the odor, immediately takes off her handsome skin clothing and resumes her foxskin, and quietly slips away from the house, never to return. See OFFENDED SUPERNATURAL WIFE (or HUSBAND). [EWV]

Fox and the Crane   The title of one of Æsop's fables in which the Fox invites the Crane to a meal and serves him soup in a flat dish. The Fox laps it up easily but the Crane cannot eat. The Crane then invites the Fox to return the visit and serves him his food in a long-necked bottle. Moral: Turn about is fair play. This is the subject of a widespread European motif, inappropriate entertainment repaid (J1565), fox and crane invite each other (J1565.1; Type 60) of which there are also one African and three North American Indian retellings known.

Fox and the Grapes   One of Æsop's fables (Jacobs #31), in which a hungry Fox, after trying in vain to reach some grapes hanging on a vine, walks away saying to himself that they were sour anyway. Moral: It is easy to belittle what you cannot get. The aptness of this fable has caused the expression "sour grapes" to become a by-word reference in colloquial English for anyone trying to rationalize a failure by belittling the end he strove for. The most modern retelling of the fable is the cryptic "The Mookse and The Gripes" episode in James Joyce's *Finnegan's Wake* (1939), p. 152 ff.

Fox and the Raven   Title of one of Æsop's fables (Jacobs #8) in which a Raven sitting in a tree with a piece of cheese, is flattered by a Fox who admires her wings and talons. "But," says he, "that such a bird should be lacking a voice!" The Raven, pleased by such flattery, opens her mouth to caw and drops the cheese, which the Fox promptly eats. Moral: A flatterer is no friend. This is a common European folktale motif (K334.1; Type 57).

foxglove   Any plant of a genus (*Digitalis*) of the figwort family: from Old English *foxes-glōfa*, literally foxes' gloves. The term fox-bells is associated with a northern European story telling how at one time foxes' brushes were a potent amulet against the Devil, and the foxes were hunted constantly. They appealed to their gods for help, who put these bells all through the fields so that they might ring and warn the foxes when the hunters were abroad. When the danger was over, the bells lost their sound. There is another story in which these flowers were given for gloves to the foxes by the fairies, to wear while stalking through bird roosts and chicken coops at night. They would make them less noisy.

There is a folk or popular etymology explaining the word foxglove as folk's glove because they are said to be worn by various classes of the little people commonly called folk. The Irish names, for instance, are *lus na mban side*, plant of the fairy women, *méirini púca*, puca or fairy fingers, *méaracán síde*, fairy thimble, etc. Translation of the Welsh term is goblin's gloves; in Yorkshire they are called witches' thimbles. In parts of Scotland they were called dead man's bells. If you heard them ring you were not long for this world. In France they are called *gants de bergère*, shepherdesses' gloves, *gants de Notre Dame*, gloves of Our Lady, *doigt de La Vierge*, Virgin's finger.

In classical Greece and Rome the juice of the foxglove was used to ease the pain of sprains and bruises. In Italy today the leaves are bruised and bound to wounds. It was early known to be a poison, and in Europe it was used only externally until the 18th century, when it began to be recommended for fevers, insanity, and diseases of the heart. It was also found to be "available" for the King's Evil. The Indian tribes of New England knew it as a heart stimulant before this fact was known in Europe. In Ireland foxglove is used to stimulate weak heart, banish fleas, and reduce lumps.

fox persuaded to talk A general European folktale motif (K561.1; Type 6) in which a fox has grabbed a cock and is running off with it, followed by the hue and cry of the people, "The fox has stolen our cock." The cock says to the fox, "Tell them I am yours not theirs." When the fox opens his mouth to speak the cock escapes into a tree. This incident of escape by persuading the captor to talk (K561) is very widespread, with varying details as to captor, captive, and dialog. The fox in the bear's mouth asks the direction of the wind, for instance, and escapes when answered. Jamaica Negroes have an Anansi story called *Grace Before Meat* (see Beckwith *Jamaica Anansi Stories*, MAFLS XVII, 239) in which Anansi and Monkey, traveling together, come upon a tiger in a pit. While Monkey sends his tail down the hole to help Tiger out, Anansi climbs into a tree. When Tiger comes up out of the hole he grabs Monkey and is going to eat him. But Anansi advises him first to clap his hands with joy. Tiger does so and Monkey escapes.

The old woman who is being carried to the sky up a tree in a bag in her husband's teeth, to see the wonders of the upper world foolishly asks if it is much farther. "Not much farther," says the husband; the bag falls to the ground and the old woman is smashed to bits (J2133.5.1). This is in Clouston's *Book of Noodles*.

Fragarach In Old Irish mythology, the terrible and wonderful sword called the Answerer, which Luġ brought with him from the Land of the Living. It could cut through any armor.

frame story A story forming a frame in which other stories are told; a narrative permitting the introduction of several (often many) other stories, unrelated to and having no effect on the frame story itself. The technique is to give a group of unrelated tales an over-all unity and dramatic meaning by making them part of a common situation. Chaucer's *Canterbury Tales* are all related to the frame of the pilgrimage, Boccaccio's *Decameron* to the situation growing out of the plague. The technique is Oriental and probably Indian, where such technique is found from an early period and is developed to fantastic complexities as in the *Panchatantra*.

[MEL]

Frankie and Albert (or *Frankie and Johnnie*) An American popular ballad dealing with a "sporting woman" who shot her man for "doing her wrong." The song dates from the latter half of the 19th century and still has living claimants to the role of Frankie, none of whom can be authenticated. One of these is a Frankie Baker, of Portland, Oregon, who shot Allen Britt under circumstances resembling those of the song in 1899. However, the song is said to have been known many years before that incident. It has hundreds of variants, in blues style, in mountain style, in backwoods and bayou settings, and even in the cante fable manner. The heroine is variously known as Frankie, Sadie, Josie, etc., and the man as Albert, Johnnie, etc. The other woman has more aliases than either of the principals, being Nellie Bly, Alice Fly, Alkali, Ella Fry, etc. It is likely that the story originated on the Atlantic coast and traveled west to develop its many Mississippi versions. It is sung widely by both Negroes and whites and is popular among students, who generally sing it under the title of *Frankie and Johnnie*.

Frau Hütt Subject of a medieval local legend of the Tyrol, built around a certain rock which resembles a woman. The rock is said to be Frau Hütt, a woman of that locality who was turned to stone for wasting food.

Frau Welt The name given to the female supernatural paramour or fairy mistress of general European folk belief by medieval clerics; according to them, the Devil.

fravashi (Pahlavi *fravāhar*; Persian *farvar*) In the Avesta, one of a group of angels with whose aid Ahura Mazda made the plants grow and give offspring; in Zoroastrian belief, one of the guardians of human and divine beings whose name is explained as meaning protection or confession of faith; an ancestral spirit. A fravashi is one of a mighty army of spirits which exists in heaven before the birth of a man, protects him during his life, and is united to his soul at death. The fravashis war against evil and promote the good in the world. According to A. V. Jackson belief in them may date from pre-Zoroastrian times.

Incense is burned in honor of the fravashis and those who fulfill their duties to these guardians will have their houses filled with good things. They are worshipped especially on the 19th of each month and during the last ten days of the year. In the Avesta the *Fravardin Yasht* is devoted to their glorification.

In Armenia the fravashis are also worshipped. They are believed to live near the tombs and houses of their kinsmen and are commemorated on Saturdays and before the great festivals. Compare MANES; PITRIS.

Frazer, Sir James George (1854–1941) Scottish anthropologist. He was born at Glasgow, educated at Glasgow and Cambridge universities, was elected fellow of Trinity College (Cambridge) in 1879, called to the bar in the same year, and became professor of anthropology at the University of Liverpool in 1907. He was knighted in 1914. His principal work, on which his fame rests, was *The Golden Bough* (1890), reissued in 12 volumes under various titles between 1911 and 1915. An abridgment in one volume appeared in 1922, and a supplement, *Aftermath,* in 1936. *The Golden Bough* is an extensive study of ancient cults and folklore and comprises a vast amount of anthropological research. While remarkable as a collection of data, the work's conclusions are now often considered somewhat dubious, in the light of more recent and more factual investigations. Frazer assumes that all peoples have gone through the same stages of cultural development and that they all react and express themselves similarly; also, that in later stages there may be survivals of earlier stages. Frazer's two theories overlook the consideration that each people has its own historical development and its own culture. Among Frazer's many works are: *Totemism* (1887), *Adonis, Attis, Osiris, Studies in the History of Oriental Religion* (1906, later included in *The Golden Bough*), *Questions on the Customs, Beliefs, and Languages of Savages* (1907), *Totemism and Exogamy* (1910), *The Belief in Immortality and the Worship of the Dead* (three volumes, 1913, 1922, 1924), *Folklore in the Old Testament* (1918), *The Worship of Nature* (1926), *Myths of the Origin of Fire* (1930), and *The Fear of the Dead in Primitive Religion* (three vols., 1933, 1934, 1936).

French folklore Folklore has thrived for countless generations in the rich home soil of France, where immigrant peoples encountered and mingled with the natives of ancient Gaul. Very early it began to find its way abroad, first from the *provinces du Midi* (or *Oc*) to Poitou on the lower Loire river, to the *provinces d'Oïl* in the north, and at times the reverse. Then from France it traveled far and wide, across the Pyrenees into Spain, the Alps into Italy, the English Channel into England, and the Atlantic into North America. In almost every century it was enriched with elements brought in by peaceful or warlike invaders: Romans, Goths, Normans, Scandinavians, Saracens, Bretons, Germans, and British. In a rather recent period of expansion, it embarked with fishers, whalers, and adventurers, and landed with them at many ports of call, there to take root and flourish. It also escorted into the New World a horde of colonists, missionaries and teachers, *coureurs-de-bois* and *voyageurs,* and fur traders. Like a tree firmly set in the ground, it spread its branches over a huge field, and shot its winged seeds onto the four winds. Fluid and ethereal, it met with no obstacle across its path, no fast frontier anywhere within reach. On foreign soil, after blending with its like of other extractions, it gave rise to new brands on the borderlands, as it did among the North American Indians.

The legend of Gargantua, the blundering giant of folk extraction immortalized by François Rabelais in his *Pantagruel* (from 1533 on), enjoyed popularity among the people of Poitou and Normandy. So it must have done, in French America as well, at an early date. For the adventurers of the fur trade carried it to the Great Lakes. Point Gargantua in the neighborhood of Grand Portage, according to Bigsby,[1] was "a prominent ...feature on the east side of Lake Superior..., and the River Gargantua issues at the bottom of a small bay beset with isles contiguous to the point."

Folktales The folktales of the Middle Ages, known in France under the name of *Romans de la Table Ronde,* and in England under that of *Arthurian* or *Round Table legends,* entered America along with the earliest settlers. They have stayed there ever since, and nowadays are retold in the basin of the St. Lawrence, at Old Mines (*Vieilles Mines*), Missouri, and around the *bayous* of Louisiana. Not only do they survive among French Canadians and Americans, but also among the Indians that have come under their sway. This belated growth, two or three centuries old, was exposed by Stith Thompson, in his *European Tales among the North American Indians.*[2] Here are analyzed a number of such tales as "The Seven-headed Dragon," "John the Bear," "Little Poucet," "The White Cat," "Cinderella," "Jack the Trickster," "The Master Thief." From old France they and a number of others passed on to many North American natives from the Atlantic to the North Pacific Coast and down the Missouri and Mississippi, with the French immigrants, settlers, voyageurs, and half-breeds. "By far the greatest contribution" [of European tales among the American Indians] Thompson writes, "has been made by the French, in Canada, and to some extent, in Louisiana" (p. 456). "The two or three centuries' contact with the French in Canada has been the most powerful influence; it has introduced the largest number of different tales to the natives" (p. 321).

Folk Songs Folk songs, although less ancient than folktales, have come down in part from the late Middle Ages and the Renaissance. Their sources often are much older than their recorded versions. Like folktales but less freely because of their set form, they moved back and forth, up and down rivers, along highways, over hills and across mountains; they sailed across the seas to islands such as Jamaica, San Domingo, to Brazil. Of this there are sundry examples, for instance *Seven Years at Sea.*

No other sailors' chantey compares with it for historical interest. It tells of a sailing ship seven years at sea. Starving, the sailors decide to draw lots and cut a set of straws. Whoever pulled out the shortest would be feasted upon for the relief of the others. The captain drew the shortest, but dodged his fate only because Ti'-Jean, the page boy, climbed the rigging and burst into singing, "Courage, I see land fore, right, and left, resplendent Babylon town, three doves, and the loveliest maidens three. If ever I land, the youngest I'll take home with me."[3] Scholars have compiled a number of French and Scandinavian versions. Mila discussed nine Catalan versions for Spain. Puymaigre, in his study "A Nau Cathrinetta," spoke of four distinct Portuguese forms. Doncieux' *Romancéro,* in 1904, contains a survey of its migrations; it lists over 26 French versions, more than 11 for Spain and Portugal, 6 in the Breton language, 4 for Scandinavia. The English *Folk Song Journal* has brought to light some British records. This chantey also exists in Switzerland. Nowhere is it as familiar as in

French Canada, where more than 20 versions have been recorded. Its peregrinations, as summed up by Doncieux, all point to its cradle on the seacoast of Brittany and Anjou; this is still its main center of distribution.

From the coast of western France, the mariners carried *Seven Years at Sea* to the shores of Provence and Gascony, then to Catalonia in Spain. The Catalan version was adapted in Portuguese, in the guise of *A Nau Cathrinetta*. This was the name of a famous 16th century ship, the pride of Portugal in her day. Portuguese writers hailed this chantey as of fantastic import, nothing less than the embryo of the maritime epic of their nation. Thackeray adapted it into an amusing rime entitled "Little Billee," where figure three sailors from Bristol—Jim, Jack and Bill, the cabin-boy. Bill, in the topmost sail, beholds Jerusalem, Madagascar, North and South America, the British fleet at anchor, and Admiral Napier, K.C.B. Another English parody appeared in *The Academy*, XXVI, 1884. And this song has since lapsed into a familiar studio parody in Paris. Under this form a sailor is actually devoured by the captain. In due time a funeral is held, and an inscription is graven on the captain's stomach.

Of a different type is the famous tale of *Pyramus and Thisbe*, well over two thousand years old, and familiar to Shakespeare, who uses it in his *Midsummer Night's Dream*. It was already well known in Europe. We find it in the Roman poet, Ovid, who wrote on the ancient lovers of Babylon. Their misfortunes and suicide, in a desert haunted by a lioness, were recounted just before the Christian era. This tragic tale journeyed to Rome all the way from Asia Minor. Then it started on a new trek through the centuries to France and Great Britain. At one time, in Normandy, it was embodied in a semi-narrative and lyric lay of Anglo-Norman expression.[4] The producers of broadsheets and imagery, in the 15th century, exhumed it. Very soon they printed it in verse form, along with the legends of *Alexis, Le Juif errant, Geneviève de Brabant, Damon et Henriette, Saint Nicolas, Julien*...The calendars, in the latter part of the 16th century, embodied *Pyramus*. In the form of a song of 250 lines, bearing the imprint of Pellerin (of Epinal) and of other image-makers, it entered the Lower St. Lawrence, during the past two hundred years. Now it is remembered by Canadian folk-singers, one of whom, in 1916, bore the name of Louis L'Aveugle, a blind itinerant of the Saguenay River.[5]

The story of *Saint Alexis* was nearly as old in its inception; it became as widely traveled. A 4th century fiction from Asia Minor, it has retained the name of Edessa as its starting point. From Edessa, Alexis in the end landed at the port of Ostia near Rome, where he died in sanctity. His story started out on a long devious way, in script or verbally, towards France and Canada. Its exotic theme—the desertion of the bride by the bridegroom for mystic reasons, the life of a pauper in strange lands afar, and the final refuge in his father's castle, where he died, unrecognized and despised, under the stairway—retained its appeal on foreign soil during more than a millenium. In France, it was embodied in one of the three earliest scripts in the *lingua vulgaris* of the 11th century. Resurrected later by the broadsheet makers, it awakened to a new life. Now partly lost in France, it is still recited along the St. Lawrence. It was recorded there several times in recent years, particularly from the folk-singer Louis L'Aveugle of the Saguenay.

Another sample from the dim past is the song of *Dame Lombarde*.[6] As its name indicates, it originated in northern Italy, in the 8th century, and eventually crossed the Alps, northwards. Almost wholly unrecorded in French literature, it followed the 17th century colonists into Canada, and came to light, in no less than 12 versions, all of them recorded at this late day below Quebec city. In a weird affair of poisoning, the tale is told of a Lombard king having incurred the hatred of his wife Rosmonde, who avenged the death of her father. She gave him a wine potion containing venom from a serpent's head crushed between golden plates.

Not quite so ancient, the *complainte* of *La vieille magicienne* (The Old Witch) dates back to 1290.[7] It tells of the profanation of the Host. At the demand of a Jewish pawnbroker, a woman had redeemed with a sacred wafer her garments and jewels, only to see him led to the scaffold on the heights of Paris. On the way, he was consumed by a stroke of lightning. Confiscated, the pawnbroker's property passed to the hands of the guild of joiners called "La Confrérie des Menuisiers de Madame Sainte Anne," and was placed in the care of the religious order of the Carmes mitigés, and its church, Les Billettes, was maintained until the French Revolution. The episodes of this tradition, during the Middle Ages, were illustrated in famous tapestries, and some of the details came down to us in two folk songs, now apparently forgotten in France, but recovered in French Canada.

Not a few folk songs, in the repertory of both France and French America, go back to the Middle Ages, among them *La Passion de Notre-Seigneur, Le petit pauvre et le mauvais riche* or Dives—the Lazarus parable, *Le docteur qui vend son âme au Démon* (Dr. Faustus selling his soul to the devil for renewed life and fortunes—the famous Theophilian legend), *Les danseurs châtiés* (The Impious Dancers chastized—their fate was to dance until their death), *Dessur le pont de Londres* or the disobedient young dancers drawn to their death by drowning when London Bridge collapsed —possibly a 13th century event, *Les ecoliers de Pontoise* (the three young Paris scholars hanged at Pontoise during the reign of St. Louis, and whose deaths were wantonly avenged by an elder brother at the Court of France), and a number of others. Some of these ancient songs have been analyzed by the scholars of several countries; they are *Le roi Renaud,* a Breton and French form of the *Elf King* or the *Vise de Sieur Olaf* of Scandinavia; *La porcheronne* or *Germaine*—the Crusader returning home after a prolonged absence, to find his faithful wife persecuted by his own mother; *La marâtre* or the orphan children ill-treated by their stepmother; they went back to the grave of their mother, who nursed them miraculously; *La fille du roi de France* cast into a dungeon to languish, because she refused to renounce her love; *Le flambeau d'amour,* a princess gives a signal from a tower to her lover; he tries to swim a river and dies by drowning. This last tale is an echo of another story of tragic love, of the classical legend of *Héro et Léandre,* and reminds us of an episode in *Tristan et Isolde.*

The wealth of this epic lore is hardly equalled in

other continental countries. The medieval France of the Crusades erected Gothic cathedrals, wove glorious tapestries, and blossomed forth in countless songs and romances. Yet, strange to say, the best field nowadays in which to find whatever is left of the oral literature of the Middle Ages, is no longer France itself, but the colony founded by France in the New World. Huge collections of ancient tales, legends, and songs are now being recorded in Acadia and French Canada. These oral traditions have in the past century fallen into oblivion or decay in their original homeland.

The *littérature courtoise* of medieval France chiefly centers in its Troubadour poems and songs. Thousands of these have been recovered from archives and compiled by the medievalists of European countries. A unique class in this literature consists of pastourelles or shepherd songs, in which the golden age of chivalry excelled. Women enjoyed no social standing in the Orient and in classical antiquity. This attitude was reversed as soon as the northern European countries, France in the lead, spoke for themselves through art and literature. Gallantry became a mark of refinement; a *chevalier* courted a *grande dame* and placed her upon a pedestal, there to burn poetic incense. These effusions might have become stilted, had not the lover strayed away at times from the staid paths of convention. Pining love led to devious adventures, away from castle or mansion, into Arcadian fields or on pastoral hills. Fond of an escapade or seeking relief in lyrical outbursts, courtly seekers of *faciles amours* at times met with shame and rebuke. In the earlier stages of this literature, they were greeted by shepherdesses still unspoilt and happy. But abuse, at the hands of decrepit or trifling philanderers, set the countryside on its guard. Flageolet tunes or lofty echoes changed to the barking of shepherd dogs are the tricks familiar among a rustic folk. The range of this genre encompasses several centuries, mostly from the 12th to the 14th century. After it had seemingly arisen in Provence and Languedoc, in "Le Midi" which had come under the influence of Latin culture, it spread northward across the Loire River, firmly established itself in the whole of France, and spread to the neighboring countries—Britain, Germany, and beyond, as if from a radiating center.

The *littérature courtoise* held the foreground for many a day in the heart of western and northern Europe. Whether the *pastourelle* or shepherd song is at bottom a folk or a literary creation—scholars still disagree about it—matters little. It has furnished the national repertory with a hoard of genuine folk songs. These are matchless for their beauty. Their lyrical derivatives have branched off into wide expanses: love lyrics of all types, in which feathered messengers—the nightingale, the lark—at times are dispatched a long way to deliver a message; or pining lovers vent their chagrin in solace; or surfeited passion turns back and jeers recklessly. There we enter the by-paths of frivolity if not obscenity, and we encounter the *maumariés* or ludicrous pairs in ill-fated wedlock. The pastourelle and love song in the French collections exceed in numbers, if not in quality, all other kinds. In the compilations of the homeland, they are richly represented, although they have suffered, in melodic content, the blight of age and neglect. Canada has saved a good part of this treasure from oblivion. Hun-

dreds of records now preserved at the National Museum of Canada, the Library of Congress, and elsewhere, stand as witnesses of their cultural import and of their unexpected preservation away from the original centers of their diffusion.

Historical songs to which dates and contexts may be attached, are not a few. Among them we find *Le mariage anglais* or the wedding of an unwilling French princess to a young English king (possibly dating back to 1490, if not earlier in the same century); and several songs bearing on a similar subject—a prince of one nation courting or marrying a princess of another, as *Je ne suis pas si vilaine* or *Passant par la Lorraine;* this last seems to go back to Anne de Bretagne, who married the king of France in 1491. In the *Petit tambour* a prince hides his royal identity when asking for the hand of a princess. *Le prince d'Orange* is a mockery on the traditional enemy of France, the prince of this name who died in 1507. *Le roi Eugène,* as a political song, is a *lèse-majesté* against Francis I; it was composed presumably in 1526, during the imprisonment of the king of France at Madrid. In *Les trois roses empoisonnées* or the poisoned bouquet, a jealous queen in reclusion sends to her rival at court the subtle poison that causes her death; it misrepresents an episode (1599) in the lives of Henri IV of France and Gabriel d'Estrées; other episodes in the same lives were illustrated in Gobelin tapestries. In *La trahison du maréchal Biron,* a once valiant marshal of France is shown up as a traitor who has sold his country to the king of Spain; Biron was condemned to death in 1602. And in *Cartouche et Mandrin* (18th century), a debate takes place in the pre-revolution decades in France, between two famous criminals. Most of these historical songs, well known at one time in France, were better preserved in the folklore of North America than in that of the motherland. During the past 30 years, their variants and versions of the same variants in Canada have been recorded in substantial numbers.

Drinking or bacchic songs, mnemonic ditties, rigmaroles (*rengaines* or *randonnées*), often are almost ageless; they are numerous. How many remained in France before they were cast aside, no one can tell for sure. In Canada alone, six or seven hundred drinking songs have already been rescued and classified. They extol the healing virtues of wine, even in a country too cold easily to grow grapes. The rigmaroles count from 60 to 100 in the least; they belong to the type of song illustrated by *Old King Cole* in England. The main titles in this list are *Le premier jour de mai, que donnerai-je à m'amie?* (The first of May, what shall I give to my sweetheart?); *La Perdriole; Dis-moi pourquoi un—un seul Dieu* (Who is one?—God), a mnemonic ditty meant to recall the mysteries of religion, once familiar in Celtic lore, where it referred to mystic beliefs; and other rigmaroles enjoying a great vogue, particularly in Canada, such as *Alouette!, Mon Merle,* and *Si j'avais les beaux souliers que ma mignonne m'a donnés* (If I still had the fine slippers my sweetheart gave me) . . .

Hundreds, perhaps one or two thousand folk songs, fall into other groups: *complaintes* or come-all-ye's, canticles or *cantilènes,* workaday songs, dances and game tunes, lullabies, ranging from the remote past to the last few hundred years: *A la claire fontaine;*

Vole, mon cœur, vole!; Les trois beaux canards; A Bordeaux, beau port de mer; La courte paille; Derrière chez nous, yat un champ de pois; M'en revenant de la jolie Rochelle; Voici le printemps; Les trois dames de Paris; La fille du roi d'Espagne; Les Prisons de Nantes; J'ai cueilli là belle rose; Bonhomme, que sais-tu donc faire?; Ramenez vos moutons du champ!

Folk Dances The last titles above are of roundelays or "danses rondes". The size of this lot in the French repertory is by no means small. Folklorists are inclined to call dance-songs many compositions that were not necessarily, or may never have been, meant for dancing. In Canada, where singing has continued to this day, some of those songs are considered *chansons de métiers* or workaday songs; or they were canoe or paddling songs of the voyageurs or the lumberjacks.

Folk dances in France and Canada used to lay more emphasis than in English-speaking countries upon dramatic and pantomimic themes; most of them consisted of tunes with refrains; the refrain was usually burdened with meaningless words or syllables accompanying quick dance steps or a pantomime of the type of *Laliptitou*, or *Folderol domdadl*. Many "rondes" or roundelays belong to the important group of *Le pont d'Avignon, Les trois Allemandes, Savez-vous planter des choux? Promenons-nous dans le bois* or *Le loup, Dans la ville de Rouen, Bien travailler, c'est s'amuser* . . . These roundelays follow in the trail of simpler game songs and play-parties for nursery and school, of the type of *The Mulberry Bush* and *London Bridge*. They are *Le lever de la reine, Le petit homme dans la lune, Le cuisinier, Le rat,* and such in great numbers and variety. Even at this late day, the French-speaking folk, young or old, on the lower St. Lawrence, still gambol and frolic to the tunes of *La boulangère, Marion danse, Laquelle marierons-nous? J'ai tant d'enfants à marier, Dans ma main droite je tiens le rosier, Si mon moine voulait danser* . . .

A list of 250 titles compiled by Rabelais, in his *Pantagruel,*[8] confirms the presumption that the prevailing dances in his time—the first part of the 16th century—were of the tune with refrain, and of the pantomime, types. There we read the names, among many others, of dances which even now seem familiar, and probably could be identified, had Rabelais been more explicit, for instance: *Si j'ai mon joli temps perdu, La gaillarde, La frisque, Catherine, Curé, venez donc, La péronnelle, La belle Françoise, L'Allemande, Frère Pierre, La tisserande, La pavane* . . . To this information, Rabelais added: "Fut par la reyne commencé ung blansle double, auquel tous et falotz et lanternes ensemble dansèrent" (The queen headed a *branle* or a set wherein merrily joined carriers of torches and lanterns). "Les autres aux divers sons des bouzines dansarent diversement" (The others stepped forth together to the gay tunes of flutes and rustic oboes). What is more, some revelers were seen dancing "aux chansons de Poictou, dictes par un fallot de Saint-Messant, or ung grand baislant de Partenay le Vieil" (to the tunes of Poitou, as sung by a jester from St. Messant, and a tall sleepy-head from Partenay the Old). This last locality reminds one of another dance song—of later France: *Dans Parthenay*, still familiar in Quebec under the caption of *C'est dans Paris yat une brune* . . . *Maluron malurette* . . .[9]

France and Brittany also possessed dances of the *gigue* or jig and reel varieties, no less than square and round dances, so characteristic across the English Channel, particularly among the folk of Scotland and Ireland, and brought into the New World at an early date, along with fiddle and bagpipes. The frontier between them is as elusive as their genesis. Typical jig and reel tunes are found in the old Mahé collection of Brittany, published by Mlle. E. de Schoultz-Adaïevsky, in "Airs de danse du Morbihan" (*Mélusine* vi: 100–105). The *bourrées* and *branles* of provincial France, revived in present-day festivals, belong as group dances to the same class as the square "sets" of England and North America. Their similarities made it easy for the *voyageurs, canotiers,* and *habitants* of French Canada, Louisiana, including the *métis* or half-breed population of the Northwest, to exchange or adapt features from their neighbors, who often shared the same revelries. In mixed parties, all would join in dancing Canadian *lanciers, cotillons, quadrilles.* Some of the dances were called *La belle Catherine, Les foins, La frégate, La plongeuse, La bistingue, Le salut des dames.* The dancers would also welcome other features from the Orkney Islanders, from Celtic partners in the fur trade, and from later comers in the 1830's. These contributions were Scottish reels and jigs, some of them named *The Moneymusk, Turkey in the Straw, The Devil's Dream, The Brandy* (perhaps from the French dance of the Middle Ages known as *Branle-gai*) . . . From this medley have emerged the famed *Red River* jig of the Northwest, and, in the eastern settlements, *Le mistigri, La grondeuse, Reel McDonald,* and some *Arlepapes* (Hornpipe tunes).[10]

Legends, Rimes, Sayings, Beliefs, Customs, Folk Naming, Observances. Such tales as *Petit Jean, Jean de l'Ours, Jean Sotte,* developed or flourished. Little Jack's cunning and trickery, in these stories, more than made up for his puny size and the scorn of his elders for him; they were bullies or dullards. From them no doubt issued the forest hero Paul Bunyan and his Blue Ox, of the lumber camps in Wisconsin, Michigan, and Maine. There the Quebec lumberjacks once lavished their youth, industry, and inexhaustible Gallic lore. Folk and fairy tales, legends, rimes and ditties, sayings and proverbs reflecting the wisdom of the past, nicknames or *blasons populaires* embodying the names given by the folk to localities and people, beliefs pejoratively termed superstitions, observances religious or otherwise, practices, devices, folk recipes and medicines, yarns and tall personalities, and customs of all sorts, were too formless and elusive to subsist apart from their social environment. Never fully recorded or encompassed, they none the less were extensively sampled by folklorists as well as by observers, first among them Paul Sébillot, in his voluminous *Folklore de France* (1904–07), which is a misnomer. This monumental work deals chiefly with his own special field—Brittany. His range of observation is plainly circumscribed in his *Coutumes et traditions populaires de la Haute-Bretagne* (1882); it includes folktales, legends, beliefs, superstitions, medicinal and magic practices. A somewhat broader outlook prevails in his *Bibliographie des ouvrages français où se trouvent réunies en quantités notables les principales matières du folklore* (1887). Periodicals in this domain are heavy containers of folklore miscellanea in the process of being collected, sifted out, and published. The outstanding among them are *Almanach des Traditions populaires* (3 vols., 1882–84), succeeded by *Annuaire de la Société des Traditions populaires,* under the editorship of Sébillot (1886–94); *Mélusine,* founded by Henri Gaidoz and Eugène Rolland (irregularly published from 1877 to 1912, 11 issues in all); *Revue des Traditions populaires . . .* (32 vols., 1886–1918); *La Tradition . . .* (21 vols., 1887–1907); *Revue du Traditionnisme . . . ,* founded by Beaurepaire-Froment (15 vols., 1898–1914); and others.

An aspect of folk traditions in which a few French masters—foremost among them Sébillot and Van Gennep—have excelled is called *folklore calendaire* or folk beliefs and practices that mark the progress of life through its various stages from birth to burial, or the passing of the year with its feasts and celebrations. Arnold Van Gennep has devoted to it the first two volumes of his monumental *Manuel de Folklore français contemporain* (1943); and Soeur Marie-Ursule, under the guidance of Professor Luc Lacourcière, at Université Laval, Quebec, has followed a similar plan in most of her thesis, "Le Folklore des Lavalois" (in a forthcoming number of *Les Archives de Folklore*). Nearly one half of his *Manuel,* consisting of four heavy tomes (1937–43), is the most extensive bibliography (vols. 3 and 4) of the whole subject ever attempted. It is all but final in parts, in its search for every possible written source, but not for raw materials, this only within France.

Van Gennep's estimate of the attainments of his science in so far as he has surveyed them, is worth quoting: "In the past two hundred years," he has written in French, "other sciences have developed to the point where they now can rely not only on *Manuels* and *Précis* (treatises), but also on great encyclopedias, detailed bibliographies, and even on periodicals" (*Manuel* I: lx). But folklore remains puny among established sciences. On this point, he has written further: "Until recently folklorists have experienced the greatest possible difficulties in publishing their materials" (p. viii). "Folklore, in the past hundred years, had no chance of being studied methodically, and of ever being brought to its many culminative points" (p. vi). "Most of the casual collectors have looked down upon their folklore work as a pastime, somewhat ridiculous, inferior in quality, not deserving much consideration. They have accepted the rank of mere subordinates to the hidebound historians, who until recently despised the study of living documents (*mœurs vivantes*) 11 (p. vi). "To the present day, not a single university chair of folklore has been established in France. This failure is one of the causes for the scientific weakness of the country in this field" (p. viii). "It is incorrect to state, as is often done, that French folklore is very poor" (p. vii), for "hardly one twentieth of the territory in France has been yet systematically explored for its folklore" (p. v).

The seeming poverty of French traditions, which Van Gennep deplores, is also due to other causes. These are cultural and historical. Cultural they are, in so far as the high or academic learning for many centuries has been imbued with a Latin bias. This bias was the outcome of the conquest of ancient Gaul by Cæsar, which imposed upon France a language at first foreign

to itself, and a drastic change in its culture. The folk vernacular, originally Celtic, was cast away as unworthy of survival. Even the "Bas-Latin" introduced after the 4th century of our era, was branded as *lingua vulgaris,* and *vilain* was the term accepted for it. The sway of the Roman Empire, under ever-changing forms, has remained undiminished. France of all European countries is, historically, the one where aristocracy—class aristocracy, and the aristocracy of art and learning—has reached its peak and maintained its hold longest, after its political symbols had given way to other standards, some of them deceptive.

Folklore is the endowment of the people at large, mostly of the illiterate mass. Like the vernaculars embodying its contents, it was destined to obscurity from the first. Only of late years has it dared to raise its humble head. Immense though its latent powers and diversity, it has not as yet awakened fully to the knowledge of its own stature. For it possesses all the unwritten and uncodified activities and lore of a people within the national borders and from the immemorial past. Its storehouse is human memory, the most retentive of all archives; its shop, that of manual arts and crafts, where masters have trained apprentices at all times; and its momentum covers manners and customs, ingrained habit and behavior, in a vast cultural stream beyond the control of the few that boast of authority and high learning.

Manual Arts Historical causes for the alleged poverty of French folklore as it has been recorded, lie in the restrictions arbitrarily imposed upon its scope. These restrictions in the main have been twofold; they have tended to exclude the traditional arts and crafts, and have almost completely ignored the patrimony of ancient France in the New World. The natural extension of French folklore in America as a whole goes back to the 17th century, when the fleur de lis held sway over vast territories from their starting points on the St. Lawrence almost as far as the Rockies and the Gulf of Mexico.

Antiquarians and curio collectors at first were interested only in the vestiges of classical and medieval archeology within their province. They could not encompass the arts and crafts as a whole. Because of a great bulk and diversity, these cultural activities of the past far surpassed their comprehension. They consisted of building and architecture; metal work including iron, pewter, gold, and silver; weaving, embroidery, lace-work, and tapestry-making; tailoring and costume; pottery, leather-tooling; sculpture, statuary, gilding, the making of stained-glass windows; illumination and engraving; and to some extent mural painting. As for the collection of folk songs, tales, legends, and customs, these traditions called for keen observation and a treatment familiar to trained folklorists. Left to other hands, particularly to professional historians or literary writers, they all fell far short of their deserts. As a rule they were dismissed as trivial or secondary, whereas they had been of prime importance in the existence of the nation, ever since the Gothic period and the northern Renaissance. Because of this oversight, we may look in vain for substantial monographs and manuals on most of the subject of craftsmanship. Valuable, at times noteworthy efforts even at the hands of *historiens de l'art,* have failed to do full justice to a country where industry and skill for a millennium have often been unsurpasesd. Of them all, only architecture, carving, statuary, and iron work have figured prominently in print and in albums. Tapestries, stained-glass windows, which contain much of the oral lore of the land, have enjoyed their share; also cabinet-making, pottery, fashions in costuming. Gold and silver smithing and metal crafts were not entirely overlooked. But a great deal has vanished before it was recorded.

Almost neglected have been the guilds and corporations, which were social bodies of great cultural import, after the 12th century, and have produced an untold harvest of masterpieces. A few amateurish books on "tour de France" for apprentices, bearing on the *Confrérie des maîtres menuisiers de Madame Sainte Anne*, and some technical treatises for the use of schools, are all that come to mind. Countless master craftsmen in architecture, carving, and masonry. for instance, lie forsaken in their nameless graves. Their accomplishments to us remain mostly anonymous within the walls of their sublime Gothic temples which for a time swayed the allegiance of western Europe. The guilds have been well studied, in France, only from the point of view of sociology and institutions (see Martin Saint-Léon's book).

In Van Gennep's *Bibliographie méthodique* they are only in part dealt with, under the caption of "Arts populaires." Reduced to a minimum here, only three subjects are listed. Previously they had been the object of many publications, as on ceramics, paper-making, costume and accessories.[12] The apparent reason for dismissing the major arts is that they have stayed in splendid isolation as if by the common consent. They had withdrawn almost beyond reach, as the medieval guilds or corporations were suppressed by the French Revolution. Yet some of them were later revived; their customs until recently survived, like the "tour de France" for apprentices in joinery and woodwork. Fortunately, as Van Gennep points out, the *Encyclopédie ou Dictionnaire raisonné des sciences, des arts et des métiers . . .* , Paris, 1751–80 (35 vols.), of Didérot and d'Alembert, contains a systematic study of "les techniques manufacturières, les procédés de pêche, les petits métiers, l'organisation artisanale" (the technique of manufactures, the processes of fishery, the small trades, the organization of crafts).[13] "From that moment," concludes this dean of French folklorists, "the true descriptive method had been found." But unfortunately it was not systematically followed at large.

An unforeseen expansion of the arts and crafts of old France was discovered on the shores of the St. Lawrence River in recent years. These activities had taken root there as early as the second part of the 17th century. An independent guild of joiners and wood carvers was established in Quebec under the same name as of the parent body in Paris (*Confrérie des maîtres menuisiers de Madame Sainte Anne*).[14] A school of arts and crafts was established by Mgr. de Laval, first Bishop of New France, at Cap-Tourmente near Quebec. The cloistered convent of the Ursuline nuns in Quebec, founded in 1639, was devoted to the teaching of French and the practice of "a thousand and one small crafts" (*mille petites adresses*). The *Confrérie de Sainte Anne* of Paris was not the only one whose representatives migrated very early to the New World. For at the annual procession of Fête-Dieu in Quebec, in the summer of 1646, 6 organized crafts were represented by a delegate bearing a symbolic torch, and two years later, in 1648, their number rose to 12. These delegates were turner, joiner, shoemaker, cooper, locksmith, armorer, carpenter, mason, cutler, baker, wheelwright, and nailer. Craftsmen of various callings, after their settlement in the colony, practiced their art, established families, and in most cases handed down their name, and often their trade, through 11 or 12 generations. The guild of *Sainte Anne* remained in existence for more than 200 years, until 1855 and possibly later, and the training of apprentices by masters survived in many parts of French Canada almost to the present day. The manual arts of later Canada are close derivatives of French fountainheads, with allowances for creative adaptation to new demands, materials, and surroundings.

The flower of feminine crafts entered New France as early as 1639, along with the founders of the Ursulines in Quebec and Three Rivers, and, less than a hundred years later, in Louisiana. Not only did these pioneers contribute much to the evangelization of the natives, but they trained Indian girls in the handicrafts with a great perseverance. Their cultural influence, felt immediately after their landing at Quebec and their establishment down the Mississippi, has since spread from their cloisters to almost every point on the American continent. A few years after their foundation, the number of native seminarists in their care rose to fair numbers; they included Huron-Wyandot, Iroquois, and Algonquian children. Mère Marie de l'Incarnation, the founder, was happy to write home: "They sing with us in unison, they quickly learn all that we want to teach them, and are most supple in our hands. Born though they were in the wilderness, they can easily be cast in the very mold of the daughters of France." Of all the teachings of the Ursulines and other nuns who soon imitated them, the most enduring in their material effects and repercussions were those in the arts and handicrafts—sewing and embroidery in particular. Many women, native or white, over North America still owe a debt of gratitude to those educators who, long ago, initiated their ancesters into what was then called the science of crafts (*la science des ouvrages*), also to read, write, play the viola, and "a thousand other small accomplishments" (*mille autres petites adresses*). The programme of training, as mapped out from the first, included "good French manners, housekeeping, needlework, drawing, painting, music, some notions of architecture and other fine arts" (*arts d'agrément*).

Several minor crafts eventually provided the nuns with a much-needed income, for instance, the making of birch-bark boxes and dishes, fine leather work, bookbinding, also the manufacture of artificial flowers, wax fruit, hair pictures, and painting. The making of birch-bark and "incense" boxes became, for the nuns in various centers, quite remunerative at one time. The bark was sewn with *watap* (spruce roots), and the outer surface was decorated with dyed porcupine quills or moose hair, much like the bark work now made in a derivative way by the Micmacs and other Indians in the

Eastern Woodlands and far beyond. Our museums now house abundant collections of Indian decorated garments and utensils; their inception goes back to such early teachings. Of all these collections, the most ancient and significant is that which was made in the 18th century for the Dauphin de France and now belongs to the Musée de l'Homme, in Paris. This set plainly exposes the French origin of native floral and geometrical designs upon garments or leather, or cloth, or upon bark; and evidence of such designs, besides, is entirely wanting in the prehistory of America.15

The Science of Folklore From Its Beginnings Folklore as a science developed only slowly. Like Cinderella it languished for a long time in obscurity. The activities of the Académie celtique, early in the 19th century, opened a back door to folk traditions. Why a Breton academy should take the lead in this field is easy to surmise. The French Revolution and its deceptive catchwords on the Rights of Man had failed to root out aristocratic prejudices. The *vilain* of old provincial France remained as ever unworthy of attention or scrutiny. But under an exotic Breton caption a lead unwittingly was found. The first "questionnaires" for research began to find their way into the hands of sundry collectors, most of them mere amateurs. The best traditionists of France for two or three generations were mostly Bretons: de la Villemarqué (c. 1840), Luzel, and later, Gaidoz, Sébillot, Lebraz . . .

The romantic conception of folklore in Germany then infiltrated France with the belief that the folk in a crowd can spontaneously do works of art in the form of tales, legends, songs. Napoléon III, emperor of France in the mid-forties of the last century, became acquainted, during a visit across the Rhine, with the achievements of the brothers Grimm. He conceived a plan to be directed by Jean-Jacques Ampère, in 1852, of collecting folk songs through the teachers, *préfets de communes,* and parish priests, in all the schools in the state. This country-wide investigation produced a mass of mixed materials, which puzzled public opinion. The results were eventually cataloged and filed as "Fonds français, Nos 3338–3343," in six large volumes, at the Bibliothèque nationale, Paris.

Later in the last century, the collectors of oral literature reluctantly accepted the term of folklore for their science; it had been invented and first published, in 1846, by William J. Thoms, in England, and was destined to universality. In vain did the French writers try to enforce their preference for *traditions populaires* and hold on to it until after 1900, as they did in such titles as *Revue des Traditions populaires,* and *Congrès des Traditions populaires de 1900.* They called themselves *traditionnistes* instead of folklorists. But folklore as a caption prevailed in the end.

From 1855 on, the stimulus came largely from the medievalists, particularly Gaston Paris, through their *Revue des Langues romanes, Romania,* and *Revue celtique.* Folktales and folk songs, during this period, gained much headway; they found capable exponents in E. Cosquin, Eugène Rolland, Anatole Loquin, George Doncieux, Julien Tiersot, and more recently Van Gennep, Patrice Coirault . . .

The *vilain* misconception of aristocratic France is a diehard. It has persisted to this day, and so far it has blocked official recognition at the university. Not a single chair of folklore exists in all of France, and the chief folklorists are still unsupported free-lance workers. Leadership in this field has been taken in 1944 by Université Laval, Quebec, where a chair of folklore was established, the first of its kind in the French language. This move is significant, as French folklore in its oral forms—folk songs, folktales, and legends—on the whole is better preserved in the New World than in the Old.

Everywhere in French-speaking settlements and colonies, it has thrived undisturbed, comparatively isolated and independent, during the past three centuries. "One feels," a French critic recently has written of Canadian folk songs, "that this music which originated in our land long ago has been saved all the while under a protective blanket of snow." The study of French folklore in Canada and in the United States, in the past thirty years, has brought about the recording of a huge body of materials in a surprisingly good state of preservation. Among them we find nearly 11,000 versions of folk songs; of these 6,000 were recorded on the phonograph or in writing; as well as several hundred folktales and legends. In these island-like survivals, the memory of the illiterate folk often has preserved valuable heirlooms which, through wear and tear, have long since vanished in the motherland.

A significant aspect of the French occupation in North America has taken shape in folk naming (*blason populaire*). This cultural development, partly linguistic and partly folkloric, consists of conferring on people appropriate geographical family and personal names, coined according to obvious features and circumstances. On the maps of our continent, many such names still commemorate the early discoveries or the passage of the *voyageurs* and *coureurs-de-bois,* from the Atlantic to the Pacific, and down the Mississippi. Nicknaming or the giving of new names in order to distinguish the individuals, when family names become useless through multiplicity, has occurred in so many places that it has given rise to folkloric studies that are singularly colorful. They disclose a genius for verbal expression and portraiture that has been lost wherever school standards have established uniformity.

Surveys at first centered in or around the National Museum of Canada, encouraged by the editors of *The Journal of American Folklore,* have recently expanded into the activities of the "Archives de Folklore" at Université Laval, Quebec. These activities have forced open a new phase in French folklore taken as a whole. For this science can no longer, as in the past, confine itself only to the motherland. It must acknowledge its own expansion outside, in the former North American colonies. These colonies have not ceased, after the severance of political ties, to preserve and develop a vital patrimony of cultural traditions.

As initial instalments in the proof of the import of this branch of French folklore stand a series of Canadian numbers in *The Journal of American Folklore* since 1916, and several publications outside, among them: *Tales from the French Folk-lore of Missouri,* by Joseph-Médard Carrière (1937); 16 *European Tales among the North American Indians . . . ,* by Stith

Thompson; [17] the author's *Quebec, where ancient France lingers* (1936), and *Romancero du Canada* (1937); the recently published *Les Archives de Folklore,* I, II, and III; and many other publications: the number of these is now growing at a rapid pace.

The oldest folk songs, in their inception and development, may go back to the 12th or 13th century. But we arrive at their dates of origin only through comparative work. The 15th century yields to us the earliest written records about them. Interesting though they are, these records remain fragmentary; at the time when they were made, they were not meant to be exact transcriptions, but only curiosities which captured the fancy of the readers; they were adapted to current literary mannerisms. Among a few compilations, we find *Vaux de Vire d'Olivier Basselin et de Jean Le Houx* (c. 1670). Of the songs contained there, according to Van Gennep, more than one third are folk songs.[18] Not many songs were picked up until 1828, in an anonymous *Choix de Chansons* (Van Gennep *Manuel* IV: 771). Van Gennep lists, among other items: 1934, *Divers: Musique et chansons populaires* (769); 1843, Dumersan et Colet: *Chants et chansons populaires de France* (771); MSS Bibliothèque nationale, 1852–1876; 1883, Eugène Rolland's outstanding *Recueil de Chansons populaires* in six volumes (773), mostly from the MSS B.N.; and many others, nearly all after 1860.

Better preserved though similar folk songs were in North America, they were not recorded at the time. Yet by a peculiar turn of chance, some of them have come to our knowledge. The *voyageur* and *coureur-de-bois* songs from the St. Lawrence, the Great Lakes, Louisiana, Rivière-Rouge, and the Columbia River, were becoming famous, and so they have remained from the early 19th century.

Thomas Moore, the Irish poet who composed "The Canadian Boat Song," after he had, in 1803, journeyed down the St. Lawrence to Montreal, extolled them in glowing terms: "Our voyageurs had good voices and sang perfectly in tune together . . . I remember when we entered at sunset upon one of the beautiful lakes into which the River so grandly and unexpectedly opens, I heard this simple air with a pleasure which the finest compositions of the finest masters have never given me." Another chronicler later wrote: "There is no wilderness which the little French fiddle has not visited. The Indians recognized it as part of the furniture of every fur trader's camp . . . The gay voyageurs sang to their heart's delight and seemed determined not to give way to care . . . Scottish melodies then alternated with French tunes, and French gaiety would spread as if by magic to robust Highlanders." Baird, in his *Recollections,* adds, "The voyage was enlivened by the merry songs of the light-hearted and ever-happy Canadian crew." M. de la Rochefoucault, a French nobleman visiting Upper Canada early in the same century, was fascinated by the same canoe songs. They gave him "the pleasant illusion of being in Provincial France." And he added, "In all the canoe journeys undertaken by Canadians, songs follow the paddle, beginning as soon as it is picked up and ending when it is dropped." In the remote region of Oregon, a French diplomat—Duflos de Mofras—had a similar experience, in 1844, "Often times, in our journeys

along the Columbia River, our heart was quickened when our canoemen, even under rain and wind, enlivened those distant shores with their chants so reminiscent of old France." [19]

Before any folklorist in France had made a complete first-hand record of a set of folk songs, at least two Englishmen in North America tried their hand at the work. Captain George Back, when engaged on an Arctic expedition to the Coppermine River, in 1823, noted down voyageur songs among the canoemen employed by the Hudson's Bay Company. These tunes later appeared in London under the title of *Canadian Airs.*[20] In his preface, Captain Back explains, "The Airs . . . are sung by the Canadians as they paddle down the Rivers, sotto voce and in a subdued tone as they near the Rapids, but with a burst of Exultation when the Peril is over."

Edward Ermatinger (1797–1876), a few years later— about 1830—wrote down the tunes and words of 11 typical voyageur songs, perhaps the earliest unadulterated set of French folk songs recorded anywhere. His manuscript recently came to light at Portland, Oregon, and in 1943 was presented to the Dominion Archives of Canada.

The French folk songs of North America for the first time made their full entry into printed literature only in 1863, through *Les chants populaires du Canada,* by Larue—40 examples with commentary.[21] Two years later, in 1865, appeared Ernest Gagnon's *Chansons populaires du Canada,* containing about 100 numbers with texts, melodies, and explanations. This last collection, a Canadian classic, until 1916 was supposed to have drained the folk repertory. No other effort was attempted in this field, with the lone exception of Dr. Prevost's, which passed almost unnoticed.

New discoveries on a large scale, in 1916, reopened research in Canadian folk songs. From that moment the work has proceeded in earnest. About 11,000 texts of folk songs and over 6,000 melodies mostly recorded on the phonograph are now embodied in the collections of the National Museum of Canada; a few hundred of them have been duplicated in the Library of Congress. A number of publications,[22] in the past 25 years, have inaugurated the immense task of presentation. Here in substance we find what may be the largest body of folk songs, and folktales, not only of France, but of any country. For a very recent review of the work in this field, see Joseph M. Carrière's *The Present State of French Folklore in North America* (1946).[23] The collection of folk songs in Louisiana meanwhile has gone ahead. Their principal exponent is Irene Therese Whitfield, in her *Louisiana French Folk Songs* (Baton Rouge, 1939).

Folktales and legends for many years have been gathered and classified by mythographers in Europe and America. They passed under the aegis of science only after the brothers Grimm, in Germany, gave them a new life, in print. Some of them had been utilized many centuries before. Poets and romancers, during the Middle Ages, often found their inspiration in the living lore of their time, just as their contemporaries the troubadours and minstrels paraphrased in long poems the simple but pithy songs of the people.

Marie de France, in the 13th century, candidly admitted at the forefront of her *Chièvrefeuil*, where she gave the story of Tristram de Cornouailles, that: "Plusor le m'ont conté et dict/ Et je l'ai trové en escrit/ De Tristram et de la roïne/ De lor amor qui tant fut fine/ Dont ils orent mainte dolor/ Puis en morurent en un jor" (Not a few have told and rehearsed it/ Besides, I have found it in writing/ That Tristan and the queen/ Of their love which was so deep/ That they suffered great pains/ And one day because of it met their fate). (See Joseph Bédier, *Les Fabliaux*, Paris, 1895.)

Folktales once more found their way among the literati when Charles Perrault published *Les Contes de ma Mère l'Oye*, in 1697, under the pen name of Perrault Darmancour. Among these tales are found "Petit Poucet," "Chaperon rouge," "Le chat botté," and "Cendrillon." [Mme. Félix-Faure Goyau, *Choix de Contes de Fées*, introduction. "Il avait peur de ses confrères, les académiciens. Que diraient-ils lorsqu'ils sauraient un des leurs occupé à de pareilles niaiseries" (p. xii).] Imitators, mostly among women, followed his example, the best among them the baronne d'Aulnoy (1698). In all this derivative literature, the traditional stories served as a pretext to "belles-lettres" according to the artificial tastes of the period; they were rearranged, developed, and pampered, yet became household familiars.

Only with Carnoy in *Littérature orale de la Picardie* (1883), and with Cosquin, in *Contes populaires de Lorraine* (1886), did ancient folktales become objectively scientific. Their systematic study, the analysis of their contexts, the classification and arrangement of their episodes, have reached their apex with the mythographers A. Aarne (1908), Bolte and Polívka (1913–) in Europe, and, in the United States, Stith Thompson.24 Folktales and legends in North America, like folk songs, have remained alive to this day, as a folk endowment, whereas in France, both are said to have lapsed into oblivion. In the lumber camps of the North Shore of the Gulf of St. Lawrence, for instance, tellers of folktales are still—or were until very recently—engaged to entertain the workers during the evenings. Their repertory is vast and well preserved as of old.

Alcée Fortier, in his *Louisiana Folk-tales* (1895),25 took the lead in recording Creole tales. The author of this article, at the request of Dr. Franz Boas, in 1915, went extensively into the field of French folktales within Canada. About eight numbers of *The Journal of American Folklore*, since 1916, have included from 150 to 200 texts. As many more are awaiting publication, while others are being gathered and published elsewhere. Joseph-Médard Carrière 26 has issued a considerable set from the ancient Canadian colony of Old Mines, Missouri, now on the verge of disappearing; the new generation no longer keeps the language that embodies them. Carrière has recently published an extensive bibliography.23

The expansion of ancient French lore among the Indians of the North American continent, although fully grasped for many years, has now become the object of a special study. Professor Stith Thompson in several comparative studies from 1919 on, has put down side by side the French folktales of France, of Canada and the United States, and their adaptations by the Indians. Transformed by the natives, they form part of their own aboriginal traditions. Yet they belong to the borderlands of French folklore as introduced in North America by the fishers, the *voyageurs* and *coureurs-de-bois*, and the colonists of the 17th century.

Bibliography

1: John J. Bigsby, *The Shoe and Canoe or Pictures of Travel in the Canadas*, Vols. I, II. London, 1850.

2: Stith Thompson, "European Tales among the North American Indians, a study in the migration of folktales," *Colorado College Publications*, Central Series. Nos. 100 and 101. Language series, Vol. II, No. 34. Pp. 319–471. 1919.

3: Marius Barbeau and Edward Sapir, *Folk Songs of French Canada*. Yale University Press, 1925. Pp. 125–132.

4: André Mary, *La Chambre des Dames*. Paris, Gallimard, 1943. P. 379. "Un monument curieux de la rhétorique courtoise appliquée à la manière antique."

5: Marius Barbeau, *Alouette!* Collection Humanitas, 1946. Thérien Frères, Montréal, 1946. Pp. 195–210.

6: Marius Barbeau, *Folk-Songs of Old Quebec*. National Museum of Canada, Bull. 75. Pp. 15–27.

7: Marius Barbeau and Luc Lacourcière, "Confrérie des Menuisiers de Madame Sainte Anne," *Les Archives de Folklore*. Editions Fides, Montréal, 1946. Pp. 72–96.

8: François Rabelais, *Les œuvres de François Rabelais*, éditions de Pierre Jannet. Tome VII. Pp. 237–244. The "énumération des danses" was omitted from the final script of Rabelais' *Pantagruel*, but embodied only in *Les navigations de Panurge*, in the chapter called "Comment furent les dames Lanternes servies à souper" (How the ladies from La Rochelle were served their supper) to the tune of "vezes bouzines et cornemuses sonnant harmonieusement"—bagpipes . . . ringing harmoniously.

9: Marius Barbeau, *Alouette!* See 5 above. Pp. 41–43.

10: (M. Barbeau) *Veillées du bon vieux temps* à la Bibliothèque Saint-Sulpice de Montréal, le 18 mars et 24 avril 1919. G. Ducharme, libraire-éditeur, Montréal, 1920. Pp. 83–94.

11: Arnold Van Gennep, *Manuel de Folklore français contemporain*. Paris, Editions Auguste Picard. 4 volumes, 1937, 1938, 1943.

12: *Ibid.*, Vol. IV: "Arts populaires." Pp. 939–1012.

13: *Ibid.*, Vol. III. P. 127.

14: Marius Barbeau, "La confrérie de Sainte Anne" (*Mémoires de la Société royale du Canada*, 1945, published in 1946. Pp. 1–18), and "Confrérie des Menuisiers de Madame Sainte Anne," Marius Barbeau and Luc Lacourcière (*Les Archives de Folklore*, Publications de l'Université Laval, Editions Fides, Montréal, 1946. Pp. 72–96).

15: Marius Barbeau, *Quebec where ancient France lingers*, Macmillan Company of Canada, Toronto, 1936. Pp. 19–40. "The Arts of French Canada, 1613–1870": *Loan Exhibition, The Detroit Institute of Arts*, 1946. Pp. 1–52. *Saintes artisanes, II, Les Brodeuses*, 116 pp.; *III, Mille petites adresses*, 157 pp., plus illustrations; Fides, Montréal, 1944, 1946.

16: Joseph-Médard Carrière, "Tales from the French Folk-lore of Missouri," in *Northwestern University Studies in the Humanities*, No. 1. Pp. 1–354.

17: See No. 2, above.

18: See No. 11, above. Pp. 800.

19: *Chansons of Old French Canada,* Preface by C. Marius Barbeau, Château Frontenac, Quebec, 1920. Pp. iii, iv. And *Quebec where ancient France lingers* (see No. 15 above. Pp. 95–104).

20: *Canadian Airs Collected by Captain George Back, R.N. during the Arctic Expedition under Captain Sir John Franklin, with Symphonies and Accompaniments by Edward Knight jun' The Words by G. Soane...and J. B. Planche, Esq*. London, Published by J. Green, 33 Soho Sq*ʳᵉ*. c. 1823.

21: F.-A.-H. Larue, in *Le Foyer Canadien* I, 1863. Pp. 320–384.

22: See Bibliography of Canadian folk songs in M. Barbeau's *Folk-Songs of Old Quebec,* National Museum of Canada, Bull. 75, 1935. Pp. 71, 72. To this bibliography may be added later publications, the more substantial M. Barbeau's *Romancero populaire du Canada,* Beauchemin, Montreal, and The Macmillan Co. of Canada, Toronto, 1937, 255 pp.; and *Alouette!* Collection Humanitas, Editions Lumen, Montreal, 1946, 216 pp.

23: J.-M. Carrière, *Encyclopedia of Literature* (Philosophical Library, New York, 1946). Vol. I. Pp. 134–138. And "The Present State of French Folklore Studies in North America," a paper read at the annual meeting of the Southeastern Folklore Society held in Birmingham, Alabama, on November 28, 1946. Reprint from *Southern Folklore Quarterly,* Vol. X, No. 4, Dec. 1946. Pp. 219–226.

24: Stith Thompson, See No. 2 above. Bibliography, Pp. 460–468.

25: Alcée Fortier, "Louisiana Folk-tales," *Memoirs of the American Folklore Society* II. Boston, 1895.

26: Joseph-Médard Carrière, See No. 16 above.

MARIUS BARBEAU

French harp Term for harmonica in mountain sections of the southern United States.

frevo A Brazilian solo dance performed in the streets during carnival processions, with acrobatic steps and jumps done on one spot when the procession halts. [GPK]

Frey or **Freyr** In Teutonic mythology, son of Niord and Nerthus (or Skadi); god of sunshine and rain, peace, prosperity, and fruitfulness, and the patron of married couples, horses, and horsemen. He came to Asgard as a hostage after the war between the æsir and the vanir. He was given the realm of Alfheim for his home. The dwarfs gave him the golden bristled boar, Gullin-bursti, to draw his chariot and the ship, Skidbladnir, personification of the clouds, which could travel on land, sea, and air, and could be folded into his pocket when not in use. He also possessed the horse, Blodug-hofi, which would dash through fire and water, and a wonderful sword which would fight by itself, but this he gave to his servant for winning him Gerda's hand. Thus he was weaponless for the last battle.

Once, when looking out over the earth, he saw the lovely Gerda in Jotunheim. He became like a lovesick mortal until his servant, Skirnir, undertook to woo the giantess in his name. At first he had no success, but by threatening to make her an old maid with his spells, he prevailed.

Frey was worshipped extensively by the ancient peoples, and especially on the winter solstice, because thereafter the days become longer and the sun stronger. Boars' flesh was served and a flaming wheel, representing the sun, was rolled down a mountain into the sea. Some customs survived well into the Christian era, such as presenting a ham or flitch of bacon to the most happily married couple in the community. Others, such as the Yule Log and boars' head at Christmas, still survive. Legend says that Frey returned to earth as Fridleef I, king of Denmark (40 B.C.).

Freya, Freia, Freyja, Fri, or **Fria** In Teutonic mythology, the beautiful, blue-eyed, blond goddess of love, beauty, and fecundity: in Germany identified with Frigga. She is the daughter of the Van or sea goddess, Niord, and Nerthus or Skald, hence as goddess of the Vanas, known as Vanbride or Vanadis. Other epithets of Freya are Gefn, Horn, Mardel, Skialf, Syr, Thrung. She was not always pleasure-loving, but, as Valfreya, led the Valkyries to the battlefields where she claimed half of the slain. These she entertained at Folkvang, the others went to Odin in Valhalla.

She married Odur, the sunshine, and had two beautiful daughters, Hnoss and Gersemi. When Odur wandered she was sorrowful and wept; the tears formed drops of gold in the stones, and drops of amber in the sea. She lived in the mansion Sessrymnir in her realm of Folkvang. She possessed a falcon garb which enabled her to fly, and the beautiful necklace, Brisingamen.

The early Christians declared her a witch and banished her to the mountains where her demon train still dance on Valpurgisnacht.

Friar Rush In medieval German folklore, Brüder Rausch is the Devil dressed as friar. He plays the role of servant in monasteries in order to confuse, tempt, and seduce the monks. He makes them make mistakes and forget the Psalter. Friar Rush as mischief-maker is the subject of motif F470.0.1. He and his pranks became a popular subject for the English chapbooks in the 16th century. He is described in *Gammer Gurton's Needle* as having a cow's tail, cloven feet, and hooked nails. In later English folklore his anticlerical role becomes somewhat dimmed and he is sometimes mentioned simply as "the friar" who is occasionally found in cellars turning on the wine-taps. Sir Walter Scott (in *Marmion*) confused Friar Rush with the friar's lantern, or will-o'-the-wisp.

Friar Tuck In the Robin Hood legend, the jolly priest who proves more than once, to the discomfiture of his victims, that he is as much a manly man as any of the greenwood band. His fat figure and brawny arm are pleasantly alluded to in several of the Robin Hood adventures of balladry.

Friday An unlucky day in general European folk belief. The reason for this is that Christ was crucified on a Friday. It is bad to get born on a Friday or get married on a Friday. It is bad luck to take a new job on a Friday, cut one's nails on a Friday, or visit the sick on a Friday. If you turn your bed on a Friday, you will not sleep. Sailors are loath to begin a voyage on a Friday; and criminals expect a hard sentence if they are unlucky enough to be tried on a Friday. "Wet Friday, wet Sunday," is a common saying in general weather lore. In Irish folk belief it is good to die on a Friday, be buried on Saturday, and get prayed for on Sunday.

☞ Friday is the day of the Nordic goddess Frigga. For the Moslems, Friday is a holy day when all must attend mosque and hear the address. Early Christians regarded Friday (and Wednesday) as half-fasts but the Syrian Christians fasted from sunrise to sunset and the Nestorians treated it as Sunday. The term "Black Friday" is a late coinage in England. "Friday face" in 17th century English slang was a sad or moody expression. [RDJ]

Frigga, Frigg, Frija, or **Fri** In Teutonic mythology, the second and principal wife of Odin; goddess of the clouds and sky, of married love, and housewives. She is variously said to be the daughter of Fiorgyn and Jörd or of Jörd and Odin, whom she later married. She is the mother of Balder and Hoder, Hermod, and usually Tyr. Certain ancient poems state that Frigga and Odin had seven sons who founded the seven Saxon kingdoms in England. Frigga is represented as tall and stately, clad in long white robes, but as sky goddess the robes could change from shining white to dark. A bunch of keys (symbol of housewifery) always hung from her girdle.

Although permitted to share the throne with Odin, Frigga spent most of her time in her own house, Fensalir, spinning golden thread or weaving varicolored clouds. Through her eleven handmaidens or will-doers (Fulla, Hlin, Gna, Lofn, Vjofn, Syn, Gefjon, Snotra, Eira, Vara, Vor) she attended to the well-being of mortals, smoothing the paths of lovers, presiding over married love, spreading knowledge, and administering justice. Fulla may also be Frigga's sister: the Germanic Frija, for instance, had a sister Volla (Fulla in Norse) interpreted as a bringer of wealth. Frigga's name (Frigg, Fri) survives in Friday.

In Germany Frigga was identified with or became confused with Freya, but no such confusion or identity took place in Scandinavian or Icelandic mythology. Freya is one of the vanir, while Frigga is always one of the æsir. In later German folklore Frigga is paralleled by Holde (Hulda, Frau Holle), and others.

Frithiof, Fridthjof, or **Fridjof** Hero of the 14th century Icelandic *Frithiof Saga* and Tegner's beautiful modern Swedish poem. He was the son of Thorsten and Ingeborg and playmate of the kings Halfdan and Helge and their sister, Ingeborg, with whom he later fell in love. Her brothers, however, would not permit her to marry a commoner, and betrothed her to King Sigurd Ring. Frithiof took the dragon ship, Ellida, and the sword, Angurvadel, which he inherited from his father, and set out on a voyage of piracy, eventually arriving at the court of King Sigurd. When the old king died, he betrothed his wife, Ingeborg, to Frithiof and entrusted him with raising his son.

Frodi or **Frothi** A legendary king of Denmark; son of Fridleif or Frithleif who was believed to be an incarnation of Frey. Frodi's reign was peaceful and prosperous and he is known in legend and saga as Peace Frodi. He possessed the two magic millstones called Grotti, and the two Swedish giant maidens, Menia and Fenia, who ground out gold and peace and prosperity for Frodi. In the *Grottasongr* or Quern Song (in Snorri Sturluson's *Edda*) when Frodi's greed would not let the giant maidens rest, they changed their song and ground out warriors and disasters for Frodi and his kin. The Quern Song mentions the story of the fratricide, how Frodi killed his own brother Halfdan to secure the kingdom, and prophesies Frodi's death at the hands of "Yrsa's son" (who is Halfdan's grandson) and the extinction of his race because of this child of incest. The invasion of the Viking Mylsingr is the result of the grinding out of warriors against Frodi.

In *Beowulf* and in earlier Danish legend it is Halfdan who kills Frodi. In the Quern Song Frodi kills Halfdan. In other Icelandic and in Norwegian saga, Frodi kills his brother Halfdan, whose two sons eventually avenge their father. These two boys (Hroar and Helgi) escape their uncle by feigning madness à la the ancient Jutish Amleth, set fire to the castle, and Frodi is suffocated with smoke in an underground passage. They parallel the numerous other hero brothers of the world, who are exposed or expelled or escape (like Romulus and Remus or the two sons of Duncan murdered by Macbeth) only to return and take back their kingdoms.

The confusion and identification of two Danish kings named Frodi, the mythical Peace Frodi and the medieval Frodi the Peaceful, and the intermingling of their legends is discussed in Axel Olrik's *Heroic Legends of Denmark*, New York, 1919, pp. 446 ff. The legend of the embalming of Frodi's body and the periodic carrying of it through the kingdom to insure the continuance of the prosperity which his presence in life had secured for the people, undoubtedly belongs to the later king.

Frog He Would A-Wooing Go See FROG WENT A-COURTING.

Frog Mourning Song A dirge sung by the descendants of the Githawn or Salmon-Eater tribe of the Alaskan coast, originally sung to destroy the young men of the tribe in punishment for their wilfulness in killing Frog Woman's frogs, as related in the Salmon-Eater epic of migration. The spirit frog of the legend is a cultural heritage from Asia and is the attribute of Dzelarhons, niece of Githawn, head of the clan. Dzelarhons is also known as Copper Woman, Frog Woman, and Volcano Woman, for her gift of metal to the tribe, her spirit frogs, and her personification of fire in the destruction of the people.

Frog Prince or *Frog King* A folktale (Type 440) belonging to the beast marriage cycle, and with varying details found in India, Hungary, Norway, Germany, and the British Isles: similar tales, of the transformation of a water-guarding reptile or amphibian, are found all over the world (e.g. the Kaffir tale of *The Bird That Made Milk* where the crocodile becomes a man again when the devoted girl licks his face).

The Frog Prince (Grimm #1, subtitled *Iron Henry*) combines this story with the story of the faithful servant. The youngest of three princesses drops her golden ball into a well. The frog retrieves it after she promises to be his companion and playmate, to eat with him and sleep with him. But when she has the ball again, off she runs, ignoring the frog's calls. The next night, as the court is at dinner, a knocking is heard at the door. The princess answers, and when she sees who it is, shuts the door in the frog's face. Her father insists that she let the frog in and live up to her promise. So she sits unwillingly next to the frog, and manages to force herself to eat from the same plate, and even carries the frog upstairs at arm's length. But when he wants to get into bed with her, she flings him against the wall. Instead of a frog tumbling to the ground, a prince stands there; and then she is glad to keep her promise. In the morning, the prince's carriage arrives with the faithful servant. As they drive away, the three iron bands with which Faithful Henry had had his heart encircled to keep it from breaking at the absence of the prince snap one by one.

Sometimes the youngest princess is instead a step-daughter, as in the English *The Well at the World's End*. In this tale, the girl must bring water in a sieve; the frog tells her how to smear it with clay. At the climax, she cuts off the frog's head, and it is trans-formed into a handsome prince. Other means leading to the transformation are: simply sleeping in the girl's bed; being kissed; and (the idea typically appears in swan-maiden stories) burning the frog's skin. See BEAST MARRIAGE; BEAUTY AND THE BEAST.

Frogs Asking for a King　One of Æsop's fables. The Frogs prayed to Zeus to appoint a king over them. So Zeus threw a Log into the pond, which made such a great splash that the frogs were overawed at their king and kept a respectful distance. In time, however, they became so bold as even to climb upon his back and bask in the sun. At last they grew dissatisfied with so slug-gish and uninteresting a monarch, and besought Zeus for a more active king. So Zeus sent them a Stork, who set about devouring the frogs as fast as he was able. Again they prayed to Zeus. But he was weary with their discontent and refused them, pointing out that their plight was only the result of not letting well enough alone.

Legend has it that Æsop told this story to the mob in Athens who were seeking to dethrone Pisistratus, and thus prevented the act of violence. It comprises the gen-eral European folktale motif J643.1.

Frog Went a-Courting　The common American title of one of the best-loved and most widely known of all folk songs in English. The first literary mention of the tale of the frog who wooed a mouse occurs in Wedderburn's (or Inglis' or Lyndsay's) *Complaynt of Scotland* (1548). In 1580 it was entered in ballad form in the Register of the London Company of Stationers under the title of *A Moste Strange Weddinge of the Frogge and the Mouse*. The oldest extant musical version is in Ravens-croft's *Melismata* (#20) (1611). Innumerable variants occur in oral tradition all over the United States among both Negro and white singers, and in England, Ireland, Scotland, and Wales. Each region has added local color to its versions, the variation appearing especially in the favorite refrains. Many of the Scottish texts have a "cuddy alone" burden, which in the southern United States has changed to "Kitty alone." Some English texts have a "kimo" burden, which has been picked up in American Negro tradition and found its way into min-strel shows in two burlesques, "Keemo Kimo" and "Kitty Kimo." A humming refrain is also common in American versions. Both Irish and American texts elab-orate on the wedding guests; in the Irish, a snail with a bagpipe enters; in the American, a black snake and a Negro man figure. The wedding feast also has its local variations. In some southern American variants "two green beans and a black-eyed pea," are served. In about

1809 an English stage version was created with humor-ous modern additions, including an opera hat for the gentleman frog, and the burden "Heigh ho, says Row-ley" made its appearance. American Negro children have amalgamated the tale with various other game and hand-clapping rimes of the "Hambone" and "Ball the Jack" types and white children have converted it to a Mickey Mouse framework with a trace of Western thriller plot. In earlier days it took its place with the play-party songs. The airs to which it is sung vary widely, and its titles include the usual Mother Goose one, *The Frog He Would a-Wooing Go, Mister Frog Went a-Courting, The Frog's Courting, The Mouse's Courting Song*. The story is typed as an elaboration of the birds' wedding. See BIRDS' WEDDING; MICKEY MOUSE.

Frozen Girl　One of the variant titles of the American ballad, *Fair Charlotte*.

Fudo　The Japanese God of Wisdom. See JAPANESE FOLKLORE. [JLM]

Fu Hsi, Shên Nung, Huang Ti　Three great leg-endary emperors and culture heroes of China. Fu Hsi instituted marriage rites, because his sister reported to him that men and women were living together indis-criminately without law and that this was degrading to the morals of the people. Fu Hsi then prohibited mar-riage between persons with the same family name and instituted the system of go-betweens, presents, and cere-monies. His legend is that he was the offspring of a miraculous conception; and he is often referred to as Adam of China. Shên Nung, called the patron of agri-culture, succeeded him. He invented the plow, about 2700 B.C., taught the people how to till the soil, dis-covered how to plant seeds and the medicinal properties of certain herbs. He is still honored twice a year in Chekiang province. Huang Ti was the first uniter of China, and his wife, Lei Tsu, was the first to domesti-cate wild silkworms. [RDJ]

Fulla　In Teutonic mythology, an attendant or sister of Frigga whose beautiful, long, golden hair represented the golden grain. She acted as lady's maid and con-fidant. She is the same as VOLLA.

funeral customs and beliefs　The idea of defending or protecting the survivors which prevails in and deter-mines the character of burials (see BURIAL) also domi-nates, in more or less concealed and disguised fashion, the attendant funeral customs and beliefs.

The wearing of black by the mourners, the pall-bearers, and the undertaker and his assistants was originally intended to make those nearest the corpse inconspicuous and thereby protect them from the ghost and any other spirits hovering near on this occasion so dangerous to the living. Even when so protected by black garments, the mourners must not let the sun shine on them; window shades must be kept drawn and even the curtains in the funeral carriages are carefully pulled down. In the border counties between England and Scotland it is believed that if the sun shines brightly on the face of a mourner at a funeral, he will be the next to die.

In the ancient funeral ceremonies of the Sacs and Fox (North American Indians) every relative of the deceased was careful to throw into the grave some article of food or clothing. It need not be an article of much value—even a piece of faded cloth would do. But if anyone failed to throw in something, he was in danger. The ghost of the deceased might return and claim the forgotten gift. If you threw something into the grave, it laid the ghost. The same idea was probably back of the widespread custom of casting soil, clay, dust, or ashes into the grave long before the Christian funeral ceremony included the "ashes to ashes, dust to dust" phrase.

Among southern United States Negroes Dr. Puckett reports that in some localities the body is placed on a cooling-board, under which is carefully put a plateful of salt and ashes. It is supposed that ashes absorb the disease from the body, and at the funeral these ashes are carried to the grave and thrown in at the recital of the committal service. The idea seems to be that even the ashes, in which the disease (or the evil spirit causing it) may have hidden, must be buried with the body.

The Negroes are quite frank about the purpose of wearing black, and are not so apt to use the euphemism common among whites that it is worn "out of respect for the dead." One Negro said plainly to an investigator that wearing black is intended to keep the ghost from bothering you. In Georgia when deaths are of unusual number in a family, a bit of black ribbon is fastened to everything alive that enters that house, even dogs and chickens. White people in these communities smile at the idea of canines and poultry in mourning, but that is not the idea. The black is not grief for the dead, but protection of all living from the contagion of death.

If you would understand funeral customs, you must know the primitive lore of the folk—the ancient wisdom which is aware that all the dead envy the living. You therefore must not wear anything new to a funeral if you are one of the family, especially not new shoes. It is dangerous to excite the envy of the newly dead. Sack-cloth and ashes were worn of old for the same reason and mourners went barefoot. (See DEAD SHOES.)

It is the same idea of being very careful not to offend the dead in any way nor to put any obstacle in the way of a proper and orderly disposition of the body which leads to the observance of customs otherwise difficult to explain. For instance, it is very bad luck in England, in Africa, or in Georgia, to meet a funeral procession face to face. Southern Negroes, in such a case, turn right about face and look steadily in the direction in which the procession is going. If they are in an automobile, they will stop the car and turn completely about in their seats until the funeral party has passed. On the Scottish border, the person meeting a funeral procession must, unless he wishes to die soon, promptly take off his hat, turn and walk along with the mourners. If the bearers are actually carrying the body, he must take the place of one of them for a short distance. After rendering that assistance, he bows to all the mourners, and is free to resume his own direction.

In parts of England it is believed that there will be another death in the family if a hearse has to be turned in the opposite direction after the coffin is placed in it. The corpse must always be taken from the house feet first; otherwise, looking back, it would beckon one of the family to follow it in death. There must be no stopping of the hearse, once it starts for the cemetery: all gates must be already open. Even in crowded city traffic, where this funeral custom cannot always be strictly observed, the funeral has the right of way over other traffic.

In all these instances and many other similar ones, the idea appears to be that it is bad luck to have any interruption or delay which would afford a dissatisfied ghost, reluctant to leave this world, an opportunity to work any mischief before the body is safely put in what is hoped will be its last resting place.

The "eulogy" pronounced at the funeral services, usually by the clergyman but occasionally by the "best friend," is a practice consonant with the underlying principle of the entire proceedings—do nothing to offend the ghost of the deceased, which is popularly supposed to remain in the vicinity until the body is buried, and sometimes for three days thereafter. The overflattering nature of the eulogy, which upon some occasions is carried so far as to bear little resemblance to the actual character of the person, and which therefore gives a flavor of insincerity to the entire obsequies, is a survival in modern funerals of the primitive fear of the displeasure of the ghost.   CHARLES FRANCIS POTTER

Funzi or **Mfuzi** The mythical blacksmith of the Fjort people of Africa. He appears in Fjort mythology subsequent to the stories about the gift of fire which the Fjort received from a river deity. As soon as they had fire Funzi appeared and taught the people how to work in iron and copper. He is credited with making the lightning also. The Funzi marriage rite (one of several marriage rites of the Fjort) is marked by the gift of one of a pair of copper bracelets from the young man to the girl; the other he wears himself.

Furies See ERINYES.

furlana A violent, impassioned couple dance of Venice, performed by one or two couples in 6/8 time: still a living dance well into the 19th century.

Furrina or **Furina** An ancient Roman goddess, whose festival, the Furrinalia, continued to be observed on July 25 in later Roman times and who had a priest, the flamen Furrinalis, despite the fact that her nature had been forgotten. She was perhaps a spirit of the darkness. In the grove of Furrina, C. Gracchus ordered his slave to kill him.

furze, gorse, or **whin** A spiny evergreen shrub (*Ulex europæus*). The name derives from "fires" which these bushes resemble when alight with their bright yellow flowers. Because of its almost continuous flowering, the Scotch say: "When the whin gangs out o'bloom, will be the end of Em'burgh toun," and in Northumberland they say that when the gorse is out of bloom, kissing is out of season. Quite generally in England it is thought that to bring gorse into the house is to invite death. In Ireland furze bushes are burned on May and Midsummer Eve to protect the cattle and crops. The Irish make a wonderful yellow dye from the flowers. They speak of Gaelic furze, a light, tufty variety; they call the coarser, paler-flowered kind "foreign" or French furze. Still another species of the hills called *aiteann Muire*, or blessed furze, is worn on the person to help in finding lost property, and prevent stumbling. The seeds are used medicinally for internal diseases, and for obstructions of the liver and spleen.

Fu Shên The Chinese God of Happiness. He has several legends. One of them states that a 6th century A.D. emperor had a liking for little men, and required that large numbers of them be sent to his court as servants. A certain local judge issued a memorandum stating that little men were also subjects of the Empire and had the same rights and privileges as others. This memorandum so touched the heart of the emperor that he withdrew his levy. The people therefore regarded the now famous judge as the God of Happiness. His image appears frequently on festive occsasions. [RDJ]

fylgja Literally, following spirit: a tutelary spirit of Norwegian folklore, regarded either as a person's double, his own soul, or interpreted as his guardian spirit. As guardian, the fylgja comes to one in his dreams with warnings, advice, or exhortation. As double or soul it is conceived of in animal form, and in this aspect merges with the separable soul concept. Fylgjas are hereditary beings; upon his death, a man's fylgja passes to another member of his family, generation after generation. To see one's own fylgja, except in a dream, means imminent death.

Gabriel In Hebrew, Christian, and Moslem belief, one of the archangels: in *Daniel* and *Luke,* the messenger of God; in Christian tradition, the angel of mercy, in Jewish the angel of judgment; in Moslem tradition the Holy Spirit and revealer to Mohammed of the Koran. Gabriel was sent to bring the glad news to the Virgin Mary at the Annunciation; he will blow the trumpet at the Last Judgment. The Moslems believe Gabriel to be their national protector, as do the Jews, who place Gabriel, along with Michael, Raphael, and Uriel, the protectors of the Jews, within the veil surrounding God's throne. Gabriel is the angel of truth, punishing all who deviate from righteousness; he is the Divine instrument of punishment, carrying the sword of justice. He is made of fire, and is especially entrusted with the office of angel of death for the Holy Land. Sometimes in medieval Jewish angelology, Gabriel is associated with the moon, less often with the planet Mars.

Gabriel's hounds, Gabriel hounds, Gabblerachet, or **Gabbleracket** Wild Hunt of England that makes itself known by a noise in the upper air: explained as the honking or whistling of wild geese, swans, or plovers passing in the night. The passage of the hounds, which are thought to be the souls of unbaptized infants wandering between Heaven and earth, is a death omen.

Gad A Semitic (Canaanite, Phœnician, etc.) deity of fortune: the name literally is "fortune" or "luck."

ga'dášot Literally, standing quiver: the Iroquois Indian stomp or trotting dance, formerly a warriors', now a spirit-of-the-food dance. It opens the evenings of social dances, and regularly constitutes part of the ceremonial cycles—among the Cayuga of Six Nations as the second of four. (See BREAD DANCE.) The step, which is a shuffling forward trot, is used in some dozen dances classified by the Indians as the *ga'dášot* type. The progression of the *ga'dášot* is the usual anticlockwise circle, among the Seneca with men and women alternating in a single line, among the Cayuga with men in the lead and women bringing up the rear. The songs are unaccompanied antiphony between the leader and men's chorus. They are in ternary form, with the middle part shifting to a higher key and the dancers simultaneously swinging into a side shuffle, or, toward the end of the series of songs, staggering toward the center and out again. The effect is cumulative, from a unison start with a small group of men to a large animated mixed line of some hundred dancers. [GPK]

gadjísa' The Husk Face maskers or Bushy Heads of Iroquois Indian curing ceremonials, associated with and following upon the dances of the *gagósä* or False Faces. They wear masks of braided corn husks which automatically associate them with agricultural supernaturals. Some of them represent women who speak of their crying babies at home. Their leader is called O'nis'desǫs, long-ears-of-corn; another one, Osaída'waanę's, large-purple-lima-beans; and the "women" also have names of plant association. They dance in a stiff-legged straddle, to monotone syncopated songs. They use a wooden paddle instead of turtle rattle, and in their fast dance, circle around their staves.

The Husk Faces act as heralds and messengers to the False Faces in the rite of house-purging and beg for tobacco. On the fifth night of the midwinter festival among the Coldspring Seneca they cavort simultaneously with the False Faces and with social dances. At one time their men and women execute a social round dance and the Husk Face "women" have an *ęskänye,* or old time women's dance.

The gadjísa', or Husk Faces, have no language. Their legend is that they come from somewhere in the East from a place of many stumps, *'tgahuntgänǫhǫ,* which is a rocky gorge, and must return there. This suggests a memorial of derival of horticulture from another tribe. [GPK]

Gae Bulg Literally, notched spear: in Old Irish legend, the wonderful spear of Cuchulain. The notches were such as to cause the greatest injury when the spear was being extracted. It was made from the bones of a great sea-monster that died in a fight on shore with another of its kind. It was given to Cuchulain by Aiofe the woman-warrior of Alba, who was the mother of his only son. And it was with the Gae Bulg Cuchulain killed that son, Connla, not knowing it was his own son before him. It was with the Gae Bulg Cuchulain killed his loved friend Ferdiad in the War for the Brown Bull. And in the last fight Cuchulain fought, it was the Gae Bulg he hurled at the satirist who demanded it of him; but Cuchulain got his own death soon after without it.

Ga-gaah The Crow of Iroquoian mythology; one of the most magical and sagacious of all creatures. When he came from the sunland to earth he brought safely in his ear a grain of corn which Hahgwehdiyu planted in the body of the earth. This was the first corn, which sustained and gave life to the Indian. Thus because corn is the gift of Crow to man, Crow especially has the right to hover over the fields, to eat the young grubs which endanger the tender shoots, and claim the first share.

gagates A mysterious gem known to the ancients: said by Pliny to be indigenous to a river named Gages in Lycia. Galen, however, looked for this river and could not find it. An Old French pick-up of the Latin *gagates* passed over into English as *jet*. R. Holme in 1688, however, said there were two kinds, "one russet in color, the other black." It was later, and erroneously, confused with the word *agate*.

Epiphanius (315–403) ascribed to gagates the power to drive away serpents. By the 12th century the power had become extended to the expulsion of demons. The 11th century Bishop Marbod recommended gagates as an amulet against dropsy, in dilution as a preventive for loose teeth and as a remedy for indigestion and constipation, and as a dispeller of illusions. He also recommended it "in fumigation" for epilepsy and to drive out demons. From the 11th to the 18th centuries it was constantly reported as kindling or burning in water, and olive oil was recommended to stop the burns caused by it.

gagósä The False Face dancing society of the Iroquois Indians. They wear black or red wooden masks with distorted features, crooked noses. They represent disease, wind, or animal spirits, supernaturals with power for cure. They meet at the longhouse in the fall and the spring and also during the midwinter ceremonials. They march from house to house exorcising disease, and join in the longhouse ceremonials on the third day (Cayuga) or fourth and fifth days and fifth night (Seneca). They are assisted in the treatment of the patients by the *gadjisa'*, or Husk Faces.

There is a definite sequence to their ceremony: 1) The marching song to the homes or to the longhouse, called *ganǫhwai'wi* or *ganoiowi'*, or the distraught mind. This quiets the wind spirits and resembles the ashes-stirring rite of the midwinter festival. 2) The dance of the common faces or hunchbacks, Seneca *hadigǫsóska'a* or Cayuga *hadui'géha'*. They knock at the doors, enter with turtle rattles and staves, and caper about with grotesque flatfooted hops and hip motions. They take hot ashes out of the stove and blow and rub them into the patients' hair and strew them about all over the floor. 3) Picking-out-partners or thumbs-up dance, *däadinyota'* (they two face each other). The first part is for the doorkeepers, thereupon for two False Faces with two matrons of the society, opposite the patient. 4) The general round dance for all, *deyǫsi'dǫdihas*, literally, they move one foot after another, similar to the *ga'dǎšot*. The two doorkeepers, *hadu'i'*, clear off the benches with their rattles to make all dance. 5) The conductor of the ceremony addresses the assembly either after the marching song or, among the Onondaga, before the round dance. The *gadjisa'* or Husk Faces herald and join the False Faces in a grand pellmell.

The singers straddle a bench, pounding it with turtle rattles, and sing hoarse dissonant tunes with insistent beat, interpolated with moans and roars of the animal spirits. It is an amazing and spectacular ceremony. [GPK]

gahe Supernatural beings inhabiting the interiors of mountains, in the mythology of the Chiricahua and Mescalero Apache Indians, and called by them the *Mountain People:* impersonated by the masked dancers, and equatable to the White Mountain Apache *ga'n*, Jicarilla Apache *hactcin*, Lipan Apache *hactci*, and Pueblo *kachinas*. The gahe have great power for driving away disease, and often can be heard dancing and drumming within the mountains. Some of them paint and cover their faces for the dancing, and these are the ones on which the Chiricahuas pattern the masks for their masked dancers. But no one has power to create a mask unless he has actually seen the gahe. Each of the Chiricahua gahe is associated with a different color and symbolizes a different direction. There is the Great Black Gahe of the east, the Great Blue Gahe of the south, the Great Yellow Gahe of the west, the Great White Gahe of the north. Many others follow in the procession of the dance. Last comes the Gray One, the Clown, probably the most beloved of them all, and believed to be the most powerful too when any serious work is involved. They worship the ceremonial fire which they approach from each of the four directions, beginning with the east. The gahe have great curing power. They can give sight to the blind and restore missing arms or legs. And they nearly always answer the prayers of the people.

Once at the foot of the Chuchillo Mountains a band of Chiricahua Apaches were attacked by Mexican cavalry. Many Apache men, women, and children were killed from a distance by the Mexican guns. But one man and one woman got away. They prayed to the gahe in the mountain as they ran. And the gahe came forth and drove the Mexicans into a cave in the rocks with their swords and then closed up the cave. Now there is a pile of Mexican cavalry boots outside the cave, but the soldiers never got out. The Chiricahuas say the gahe always have real swords.

☞ Apache crown dancers, functioning at curing rites and adolescence ceremonies for the White Painted Woman and pubescent girl. They represent mountain spirits associated with the guardianship of game animals. Their only sound is the spirit call, "hoo-hoo-hoo." They represent the cardinal points in the number of four to a set, and in all ritual approaches. Their spectacular costume includes high pointed horns or crowns with face-covering black hoods, skirts with pendants, body-paint in symbolic designs, eagle-feather decorations, and a pointed stick in either hand to impart endurance. It is dangerous for them to make a mistake or to be touched. The shaman sings special songs during the ritual painting and for each type of dance step—the free step, which is rigid and terse, and the high step, the strenuous broad squat with vehement forward leg flings. They dance around the fire in front of the ceremonial puberty structure all night long for four nights. Pay and ceremonial obligation stimulate this endurance test. [GPK]

Galahad In the Vulgate Cycle of the Arthurian story, the son of Lancelot and Elaine. By passing the test of the Perilous Seat and successfully drawing the sword from the floating stone, Galahad qualifies as "the best knight in the world." Galahad replaces Perceval as the Grail Seeker and is the only one of Arthur's knights who is fully successful in that quest. He is successful because he is a pure and maiden knight. [MEL]

Galatea (1) In Greek mythology, one of the Nereids. Polyphemus loved her, but she in turn loved Acis. Polyphemus caught the lovers together and crushed his rival beneath a rock. Galatea then changed Acis into a river, or, in another version, married Polyphemus. In still another story, she wept so long over the death of Acis that she became a fountain.

(2) In Greek legend, the wife of Lamprus. Her husband ordered her to kill her child if it were a girl, so she brought up her daughter as a son, calling the girl Leucippus. When the deception could no longer be maintained, Galatea and Leucippus fled to the temple of Leto. Galatea prayed to the goddess that the girl might become a boy—and it so occurred. The Phaestians thus worshipped Leto Phytia (the creator) and celebrated, in honor of the event, the ecdysia, or putting off (of female attire by the transformed youth).

(3) In pseudo-classical mythology, the ivory statue created by Pygmalion, with which he fell in love, and which was transformed into a woman. There does not seem to be any basis in classical legend or folktale for ascribing this name to the statue, since it is in extant ancient versions nameless.

Galaxy The Milky Way: so named because it resembles a trail of milk across the sky (from Greek *gala*, milk).

gambling The act of risking or wagering something of value upon a chance. This form of pastime is found all over the world, e.g. among Indians of North and South America, among the Chinese and Siamese, and in India. Finds in excavations testify to the popularity of gambling in games of chance from earliest antiquity. In India, dicing was said to have been carried to an extreme, not merely to divine the future but as part of a ritual. Dicing was a popular pastime in England, indulged in by Queen Elizabeth who, it is recorded, had her dice "treated" that she might always be sure of winning. Slaves in Mexico sold themselves so that they might have money for gambling. Gambling is perhaps an offshoot of divination; it might be called a cousin, in that the will of the gods determines the fortunate winner. Like divining, gambling has utilized every conceivable happening within the human environment; modern Europeans have been known to bet on the color of the next cow appearing to the right of a railroad train; automobile license-plate poker is often played in the United States. Huge wagers, up to and including everything a man owns—wife not excepted—, have been made. There are great national lotteries in many countries; almost every people has its favorite gambling game or situation. The dividing line between gambling and business, the so-called "risk money," is often so important a factor in economy that an unlucky turn of events will bankrupt companies and cause national depressions. The professional gambler, sometimes dishonest, sometimes scrupulously honest but with great knowledge of the game he played and its odds, was (and still is) a familiar figure in frontier life, in the American West, and on the Mississippi packets. Such cosmopolitan centers as Macao in China

or Monte Carlo derive a great part of their income from gambling; fan-tan, roulette, and various banking card games are notorious as gamblers' games. The conquering gambler is a popular motif of many North American Indian myths and folktales. See GAMES.

gamelan Malay word for the characteristic orchestra of Bali, Burma, and Java. The collection of instruments, rather than the performers, constitutes the orchestra, which is owned by a village or a court. The instruments include numerous gongs, gong chimes (see BONANG; REJONG), cymbals, drums and drum chimes, xylophones, wooden clappers, bamboo rattles, and sometimes a flute, the combination differing for the purpose of the performance. The orchestras play for temple feasts, for marionette plays and other dramas, for exhibitions of dancing girls, for marching, for cremations, and for various ritual dances. The music is based on a pentatonic scale, of which there are three distinct types in use, and the rhythm is swift and interwoven on several levels, accented by deep gong tones. The musicians play entirely from memory, experienced players teaching new members of the orchestra.

games Much emphasis is placed in various studies on the games of children, for games play an often predominating role in the budget of time of a child; childhood is game-time *par excellence*. Nevertheless, the games of adults are as important in the over-all study of the subject, and, when correlated with other aspects of the study of human society, more important. Such monumental works as Lady Gomme's investigation of the children's games of Great Britain, Scotland, and Ireland, in two volumes for this small albeit important section of the world, and Newell's *Games and Songs of American Children*, serve only to emphasize the tremendous sweep of the subject, for in neither of these works are the games of grown-ups examined, and in neither is the work complete in regard to variants, the interrelationship of allied games, and foreign forms of the games under discussion. Such a task was of course beyond the resources of either writer, the evidence being incomplete and the space being limited; above all their aims were quite different, collection rather than comparison *per se* being the end in view. However, these works, the chief studies in the folklore of games, may serve the reader as illustrations of the scope of the subject.

It is possible that many other cultures, primitive and complex, have neither the quantity nor intricacy shown by the games of England and the United States. (It should be noted here that this discussion will limit itself primarily to games known to most of its readers. Exotic forms are as a rule the games that we play, played elsewhere with variations and cross-mixtures.)

It is difficult to believe, as investigator after investigator into the way of life of other peoples seem to indicate, that only one or two pastimes of children, often not games at all but simple play, like doll-play, form the extent of the game-life of any group. Even more discouraging are statements like "No games have been recorded" or "The children do not play many games." Conceivably, there is on the face of the globe an occasional, rare culture in which no games are played, in which all the time of all the members of the community from the youngest to the oldest is taken up with the more vital problems of sustaining life, propitiating the spirits, and such immediate necessities. Admitting this as a possibility, and granting that some primitive groups of men live constantly in the precarious balance between life on a minimum basis and extinction on the morrow, in more than one instance the investigator's lack of interest, because his emphasis is directed elsewhere, results in such a finding, or lack of finding. For, given so simple an instrument as a piece of string, men, Eskimos and Australians, Papuans and North American Indians and Africans, have developed a form of play, or instruction, or art, or religious activity, or game, called by some Cat's Cradle, but more generally called String Figures, which in its complexity and universal interest yields to few other forms of human activity. One field worker, investigating where others had met defeat in trying to approach the members of a group, and who succeeded by trading string-figure information, suggests it as a more efficacious tool than any conceivable Esperanto might be. Games may serve in more ways than one as a convenient key to the way of life of a people.

But it is the doll, or the hopscotch diagram, or the ball, not the casual piece of string or the few odd pebbles, that catches the eye of the field investigator when his attention is centered on other matters. Unless he be definitely attracted to games, it is quite possible that he will overlook games that do not require special materials. Moreover, as sometimes it is true, games are mysterious matters, closely linked with religious beliefs or customs like the sexual distinctions, and may thus be ignored completely in an investigation because glossed over or even avoided by the one being questioned.

The problem is further complicated by a lack of agreement in definition. Generally speaking, any form of amusement or pastime is a game. What is serious and essential activity in one context may in another place and time be nothing more than sport. The hunter on a tiger-shoot in India, to whom the quarry is only a large and dangerous target on which to test his accuracy with a rifle, is indulging in sport; to the inhabitant of the nearby village the killing of the man-eating tiger is something quite different. The fox-hunters in red coats riding to hounds are, by different means and for different ends, doing the same as the chicken farmer who lies in wait with his shotgun for the thieving fox. The same cowboy who ropes a calf and throws and ties it for branding may later perform the same act at an inter-ranch contest of skill or at a large regional rodeo. Thus it is too with fishing and running, with shooting the rifle or the bow and arrow, with horse-racing and corn-shucking: many of the sports and games played by men are simply a change in context of an activity closely concerned with the plain facts of daily living of some other men. And games derive not only from the economic, as they may be called, aspects of life. Many are developments of other things men do in everyday living. For example, religion and religious ceremonies have led to ball games and such games as London Bridge and The Farmer Takes a Wife. Educational activities are paralleled in the simple imitative Play-School of our five- and six-year-olds, and in the pseudo-war games of Chess and

Lead Soldiers. Almost anything that man does he also plays at, and in fact the game is often the training ground where he learns, as child, youth, and adult, to acquire an ease and facility which become useful when he comes to practice the activity itself.

We cannot then define game only as pastime or sport or amusement, for the dividing line between game and serious pursuit must be sharper if it is to be discussed with any degree of ease or profit. To begin with, a game must be a social activity; more than one must play. A baby fingering its toes; a child, all alone, mothering its doll; a boy tossing pebbles at a tree; a huntsman practicing with bow and arrow by shooting at a stick are all engaged in activities which form the basis for games but which of themselves are not games. The extra ingredients in each case are another person and the concept of dramatic struggle and climax. Let a mother play with the baby and have her recite, as she or the baby touches each toe, "This little pig went to market," and the social situation necessary to a game is met. Add another child to be the father of the doll and the universal Play-House game is present. If another boy happens along, the pebble-throwing becomes a contest to see who can score the most hits in a given number of throws. Draw a line, measure a distance, set up a wand, and stand several archers on the mark, and a game, or sport, or contest, exists. In every instance what was energy directed towards performing an action for its own sake becomes energy applied to a dramatic end.

Essentially that is what a game is, a drama. There are games in which no winner or loser emerges. Such are round games like Drop the Handkerchief and Tag and The Old Witch. In the first two, ephemeral contests take place, one of the group against another of the group or against the whole group. In the last, the game is repetition of a formula by each of the participants and includes a mock struggle and what amounts to a plot in which the witch loses the game.

But in most games there are a winner and a loser. The winner may be one of several in a game, as in Marbles; he may be one of the two players in the game, as in Chess; there may be several winners and losers, each playing independently, as in Poker or other similar gambling games; or the winner or loser may be a group, as in Baseball or most team games. But success or failure, and the action that leads up to them, are the essential ingredients of a game as they are of the drama. Vaguely (and almost indefinably), a game is a plot worked out by the players during its course of action.

Games also have another peculiar set of circumstances attached to them that differentiate them from the "essential" pursuits of life or from practice for those activities. No game is possible without rules, either explicit or tacitly understood by the players. These rules may consist simply of a general understanding of the aims of the game and of an agreement among the players that some arbiter exists to whom appeal may be made in case of disagreement. In this the game differs from the vital pursuits of life.

It does not matter where the hunter stands to shoot his arrow at the deer; his purpose is to kill the deer, to obtain food, and the only rule essential to his being successful is that the deer not escape alive. The words chosen by the suitor in proposing marriage need be those that obtain the acceptance of the maiden; the exact formula does not exist, really. The thief shot down by the policeman may, if he can, shoot the officer and escape. But, in games, there are rules to prevent such actions. The toe must not cross the line in shooting at the target, and sometimes the winner will not have hit the mark but will have been the one who has come closest. No variation is permissible in the formula used by the suitor in marriage games; the rime to be used is handed down as from Sinai. After the robber is shot by the cop, bang! he cannot get up again unless certain conditions are met; "You can't do that; you're dead" is an inexorable verdict, and until some recognized resuscitating action takes place, the "dead" player's place is on the ground and *hors de combat.*

Rules are of course flexible and subject to amendment at the will of the players—if they agree to the change. A game, with only its general outline the same, will have variants in which, from city to city and from country to country, the specific rules to fit its various complexities will be different enough to make identification by a student of games difficult. But basic to the play of any game is the unexpressed admission that those rules which are accepted will be followed by all the players. "La buona fede è l'onestá sono condizioni necessarie in ogni buon giocatore." (G. Pitré, quoted by F. Rodriguez Marín.) Without these qualities (thus again setting games apart from many other activities where success is more important than morality) most games would be impossible. If Peter decides to lie low after "it" calls "I spy Peter," the game loses its point. If, despite the penalties exacted for the fault, a bridge player persists in reneging through a series of hands, the game becomes so chaotic that play becomes next to impossible. The effect on a quiet afternoon's game of a child who insists on taking the "doctor's" pulse is disruptive. In the drama that is played out in any game, the parts must be kept to; improvisation is admissible where necessary, but the very nature of most games frowns on such anarchic action. Most boys would much prefer playing One or Two O' Cat to participating in a ball game where two or three of the players are common to both sides. The climax is not as clearcut; the sharpness of deciding winners and losers is blunted; the satisfaction derivable from having played through a game is dissipated.

A game then may be defined as a form of play in which two or more participants vie, either as individuals or as groups or teams, under the limitations of rules either tacitly or explicitly understood by the contestants, for the purpose of determining which is the better or best at the particular form of play; a game is a dramatic play contest. This is true whether the game be rope-skipping or baseball, boxing or puss-in-the-corner, charades or "Last one in stinks." The term games, thus, as used here, does not include dances in which everyone performs simply to trace a pattern, or for simple physical action, or the like, because there is no contest involved; social dancing and ritual dancing alike are not included. Nor is drama a game, for the outcome of the contest, while existing in the plot, is not a matter of doubt; it is preordained by the nature of the activity. It is much to be regretted that such play activity as children's games of the type of The Old Witch and The Farmer in the Dell have traditionally been classified as games. While the transmission of such pastimes, and the situations in which they are played, resemble greatly those of actual games, in truth they are not games but juvenile folk-drama. Certain traditional festival games, ball games between married and unmarried women, in which the married women always win, though forerunners of games, cannot be considered games because of the absence of contest: the fruitful married women must win over the barren single ones. It is to be doubted, also, that many of the field sports, like hunting and fishing, are games; the stake of the loser is much too great, and the understanding of, or adherence to, the rules set up by the hunter on the part of the quarry is not present.

The classification of games has been the subject of many students, and there are almost as many ways of considering the subject as there are writers on the matter. Games may be discussed according to the season in which they are played; according to the places where they are played; according to the number of players involved; according to the sex or age of the participants, etc. The investigations of Stewart Culin into the games of the North American Indians and the peoples of the Orient led him to divide games into two main classes: games of dexterity and games of chance; the latter subdivided into games of pure chance and guessing games. Wood and Goddard define three principal types: showdown games, in which each player performs without interference; playing games, in which interference from others occurs; and a play-then-showdown group. Variations within games and hybrids of games belonging to different groups make necessary such straddling classes as Wood and Goddard's third. A striking example of the mixture of two games is seen in the game of London Bridge. This game, as described by Newell, reaches its climax in a tug-of-war between two teams chosen during the previous course of the game. Lady Gomme, in her discussion of the forms of the game in the British Isles, expresses surprise at his emphasis on the tug-of-war, she finding nowhere in the several variants collected by her any such hauling contest between parties. She concludes that in America the game was consolidated with some form of the arch-tug-of-war game, like Oranges and Lemons, to which London Bridge is very similar, and which does have a choosing of sides and a pulling finale like that of the American London Bridge. Yet, despite what seems a radical difference in the aim of the game, the name is London Bridge on both sides of the Atlantic, and undoubtedly is the same game whichever the variant. While instances like this do not upset larger classes, such as those mentioned above, in the long run an attempt to establish a complete, overall classification must break down. The method is useful in tracing similarities between games, but it must not be taken as an absolute method of studying games.

There are two classes of games, however, which make a helpful dichotomy in a historical study of games. Certain games, such as top-spinning, marbles, dice, chess, must be played with specialized equipment. These games are quite distinct, though not sharply so, from those which require no special tools but are played either without accessories or with such materials as pebbles, sticks, and the like, obtainable at random from the surroundings. It is obvious that the former class will leave, as relics for the archeologist to discover, its paraphernalia in the remains of its vanished culture. It therefore becomes easier to trace the history of such a game as chess than it is to track down the origins and diffusion trails of games like hopscotch. Sometimes the task of tracing the origins of games is made easier by literary remains, or by works of art, describing or depicting a game so similar to one we know that a connection is facilitated. Thus, we know from a mural painting in the palace at Knossos that bull-baiting was a sport indulged in by the ancient Cretans more than 3,000 years ago, evidence further strengthened by the picturing of the same sport on vases and other remains of the period. Whether a direct link exists with the modern Spanish bullfight with its up-to-date methods of maddening the bull by exploding bits of gunpowder under its skin, or with the modern American rodeo sport of twisting a steer's neck until he falls to the ground, or whether the modern sports are independent developments of a sport occurring in sections of the world where cattle exist and men demand dangerous amusement, the information about the Cretan practice exists and indicates a possible starting point for an investigation. Pieces resembling chessmen found in Mesopotamia, millennia old, dice from ancient Egyptian tombs, help to link, if not the games themselves and their actual play, the men who played and play the games.

The half-dozen games discussed below have been chosen as types, not of kinds or classes of games, but of what might be termed the ways of games. Johnny-on-the-pony, the only not specifically adult game of the group, is a European game that has come down to us through the centuries in a clear line from the classical world. Chess is a game with cousins in all parts of the world, but specifically a single game with its own distinct characteristics and played by many peoples. Mancala is a game so limited in its geographical distribution that one is tempted to call it the racial game of the Negro; it is at any rate a game peculiarly identifiable with the continent of Africa. Playing cards illustrate the use of equipment for several kinds of games, and for purposes allied with a quasi-religious function, i.e. divination; they are a sophisticated form of the use of special, significant, and manufactured material for several purposes. Dice, developing from natural objects, are found in their most essential as well as in artificial forms, and are used in much the same way in every part of the world, and at every epoch.

Among the games of New York City boys played by the light of street lamps is one called Johnny-on-the-pony. Two teams of equal numbers are chosen. One team are the jumpers, the other the ponies. One of the ponies bends his head against the stomach of one of his teammates who stands with his back to a wall; the next teammate bends, placing his head against the buttocks of the first player and grasping his thighs, forming the beginning of a chain which stretches from the wall until the entire team is in line, all bending forward. Then the other team, one by one, leaps onto the backs of the ponies, jumping high and landing as vigorously as possible in an attempt to break down the line of stooping boys. When all the jumpers are on the backs of the ponies, they chant

Johnny on the pony, one, two, three,
Johnny on the pony, one, two, three,
Johnny on the pony, one, two, three,
     All off.

If the line of ponies has not broken and precipitated the entire mass of boys to the ground in screaming confusion, or if the jumpers have piled up so that they form an unstable pyramid that topples as the ponies sway back and forth to the rhythm of the chant, the ponies become the jumpers. If the line of ponies breaks, it must re-form and permit the jumpers to try again until the ponies are successful in withstanding the assault and become jumpers in their turn.

This game, one among many that seem to stem from a youthful exuberance and desire for a rough game involving bodily contact, is a local form of a game known in many parts of Europe. It is played in several other ways and under several other names in Britain. The French game of the Bear (l'Ours) combines a form of mimic bull-baiting in the ring with the leaping characteristic of the game in question. Forms of the game in combination with other games are known. It is however best known as How Many Horns Has the Buck? in which the leaper holds up a number of fingers and forces the player he bestrides to guess correctly or undergo another leap. In this form, we are indebted to Petronius Arbiter (Satyricon) for the information, the game was played in ancient Rome, with very much the same sort of question as is now used. The Latin question, "Bucca, bucca, quot sunt hic?" is phrased today, "Buck, buck, how many horns do I hold up?" The relationship of this game to the traditional riding of children on their fathers' backs is perhaps more apparent than traceable. It resembles too a form of leapfrog, a game known to have been played in classical Greece.

On the other hand, one of the popular games played in ancient Greece, a game which had houses devoted to its play, and which has now disappeared, was the Cottabus, an adult game imported into Greece from Sicily and originally a method of divination. The object of the game in its various forms was to throw wine from a cup through the air into another container without spilling any during the cast. This game, despite its extreme popularity, which was perhaps as great as that of Bingo in the present-day United States, is no longer played, except perhaps by some few scattered antiquarians in the manner of craftsmen interested in the techniques of making chipped flints like those of the neolithic men. What reason lies behind the survival of the one game and the disappearance of the other? The answer lies perhaps in the seemingly innate conservatism of children. For the one game is a child's game and the other an adult game, and by comparison with what we know of other survivals in children's games where an underlying adult custom or ceremony has long disappeared, a hint perhaps of the nature of the transmission of folklore may be obtained.

The origin of the game of chess seems to be hidden

by the curtain of unmeasurable antiquity. Actually, no definite reference is known before the 7th century A.D., but by then chess had already spread from India to Persia. Chessmen, or pieces that apparently belong to a game like chess, have been found in the ruins of Mesopotamian Tepe Gawra, dating some 4,000 years B.C. But, of course, not all games called chess are the game played today under that name. Checkers or draughts is played with flat pieces of equal value on a checkered board; nine men's morris may be played with flat men or with pegs; the Japanese *go* is played with counters on a surface of intersecting lines; the Irish fidchell was some sort of board game: all, under circumstances where the method of play was forgotten and the equipment alone remained, might be called chess by someone unearthing the materials.

Chess, the game as we know it, however, is a highly specialized game, defined as one in which no element of chance exists, in which pieces of various powers move on a checkered board. The object of the game is to attack and immobilize the chief piece of the opponent. In this, combined with its maintaining a theoretical equality of opportunity between the players, skill alone determining the outcome, chess is unique among games. Its origin is obscure and beclouded with folklore, mythology, and nonsense. Solomon, the Greek Palamedes, Hermes are among the many names mentioned as its inventor. It is said to have originated among the Babylonians, the Jews, the Irish, the Chinese, and among others, the Araucanians. It has been identified as being a derivative of games so obviously not chess as the Roman latrunculi.

There have been competent and careful scholars, like Murray, who, investigating the history and development of chess, have arrived at more or less definite conclusions based less on theoretical guesswork than on factual resemblances. Chess, which Murray calls "the national game of Asia," seems to have started in India as chaturanga, the four angas, or components of the army. From India, it went to Persia, thence to the Arabs as shatranj. Among the Arabs, in the 10th century, is found the first book devoted to the game. Its author, Masudi, speaks of it as a game some hundreds of years old. Within the hundred years following the date of Masudi's book, chess came to Europe, in essence the same game as the one played today, but differing almost completely in detail, such as the setting up of the pieces, and their powers and moves. It is only within the past hundred and fifty years that chess has become more or less stabilized in the form we now play.

Chess may be said to have almost world-wide scope. It is played in Mongolia and in Argentina, in the United States and in Russia. It is played not only over-the-board in European coffeehouses and in chess clubs and on park benches, but by mail between continents, and by telegraph and radio. In the United States alone, 4,000–10,000 devotees carry on contests lasting months, and often a year or more, by postal card. The notation of the game, in the several languages and systems, is readable by practically every player.

Chess has its own folklore. There are tales told of every master player, apocryphal and difficult to trace, as are most anecdotes. Alongside the written code of laws of the game, certain customs have the force of law. For example, the choice of colors by one player from the two hidden pawns in his opponent's fists and the habit of resigning a game, before one is checkmated, by upsetting the king are covered by two widespread but unwritten rules. As with players of many games, chess players have idiosyncrasies approaching superstition.

Another game of skill, known by almost as many names as there are tribes to play it, might well be called the continental game of Africa, although it is played in Arabia, India, Indonesia, and many other places to which Arab traders have carried it. This game, investigated by Culin under its Syrian name of Mancala, is called, for example, Chanka in Ceylon, Madji or Adji by the Dahomeans, Kale by the Fan, and Wa-wee in the West Indies. Generally, the game consists of placing counters in containers or hollows in a board before each of the two players and then moving the counters (pebbles, beans, etc.) in turn about the board, capturing the pieces in the space to which the last piece was played and in those preceding or opposite it whenever the number of pieces in the last-played hole is two (or another arbitrary number). Were dice added to the game, as they sometimes are (e.g. the Egyptian Arabic Seegà), it would resemble to some degree backgammon. Primarily it is a game of skill; it is occasionally played according to rules which permit a knowledge of mathematical rules to enable a player to determine in advance whether he will win or lose, as in the puzzle-trick of taking an odd or an even number from a pile of sticks or pebbles; sometimes the toss of dice adds a greater element of chance to the game.

Culin, and Andrée before him, maintained that the game originated in Arabia and was carried through the continent of Africa to the Atlantic. Schweinfurth held that the game was of central African origin, and that it traveled from the interior to the edges of the continent, where the Arabs picked it up and transmitted it further to those places with which they had contact. In the absence of other, definite proof of either theory, the important note to be made is that the game is played all over the African continent, eastward to the Pacific and westward to the New World, carried to the latter probably by Negro slaves, to the former by Arab traders. According to Herskovits, the game is found in the New World from Louisiana to the Guianas, and is, throughout the area, a rather ceremonial game, connected with the idea of death, and as such not a gambling game. He traces the back-country game of Dutch Guiana as perhaps coming from Dahomey; the game played on the coast seems to come from the Gold Coast. Among the customs he records among the Saramacca of the upper Surinam River connected with the game of Adji is the belief that a board must be made by a man who has lost a wife or one who is old; the board has a connection with the spirits of the dead, there is something dangerous about it. To be a good board, the *adjiboto*, the *adji* boat, so called from its shape, must be rough-hewn and become smooth and polished by the fingers of the players.

There are two games, or more properly groups of games, played with two specialized kinds of equipment, which may truly be said to have world-wide distribution: dice and playing cards. Few places on the face of the globe that have been visited by the exploring or colonizing European have not seen the transplanting of both the "Devil's picture-book" and the "galloping dominoes," for dice and cards, by their nature, lend themselves to the kind of games which rely for their thrill on chance and gambling.

The latter concomitant of games has been only lightly touched upon here because it is not essentially an element of games, but so closely is it associated with the subject that something must be said about it. Where the child or the adolescent finds justification in the physical enjoyment or the training, the social or the prestige elements, of playing in games, the adult, in many societies, seeks to place on the firm basis of permanent acquisition some tangible reason for playing. In societies where money or goods is the measure of the stature of the man, he will attempt, even in his play, to make further additions to his store of wealth. With some games, those, like Wari mentioned above, having a more or less ceremonial nature, gambling is not possible, but in most games, whether of chance or of skill, "a leetle side bet" not only adds to the spice of the game, but often becomes the reason for playing it. In many ways, this is a translation into concentrated action of the dramatic element of games as repetition of the serious pursuits of life. To risk wealth representing a month's, a year's, even a lifetime's work on the turn of a card, a throw of the dice, the speed of a horse, or the agility of an athlete, crowds sufficient drama into the moment of decision to repay the risk of property.

Whether it be fanciful or not, whether it be folklore, fiction, or fact, the story of the man who risks all on the chance of a game is well known. The legends of suicides at the gambling houses of Monte Carlo are only one case in point. There are many reports of missionaries, travelers, and others who knew the North American Indian of the desperate passion for gambling that led some men to wager horse and lodge and wife in a game of dice, and, losing, to revenge themselves by war or feud, thus placing in the scales their own and others' lives. Many accounts tell of whole American Indian villages becoming destitute as a result of unfortunate wagers made against another village in some game. State lotteries, organized "bingo" games, manuals on the laws of chance and the odds in roulette and dice, all attest to an almost universal fever among the men of our time to turn to physical use, to goods and money, the tension and the knowledge of a game, to add to the drama by making it real in terms of real living values. Gambling attaches itself to games rather easily because of their high emotional tension, just as it does to commodity and stock markets, elections, and the other more immediate and dramatic concerns of daily life.

As has been said, playing cards and dice are used in the great gambling games. By their nature they lend themselves to play where the element of chance, the knowledge of the laws of the odds, are paramount. Even in so skilled a card game as bridge, knowledge of the most probable distribution of the cards and of the most probable direction in which to take a successful

finesse distinguishes the better bridge player from the good or the mediocre. Knowing that drawing to two pair leaves the hand less chance of improvement than discarding one pair and drawing to the other in order to make three of a kind is something that many poker players never learn. Whether to bet against or with the thrower in dice depends on knowing the chances of his making a "point": good in the case of 8 or 6, bad if he must throw a 10 or 4. The skilled gambler is, then, as is the skilled player in such games, more or less the mathematician, solving an equation in one unknown on the spur of the moment by assigning an arbitrary and personal value to the chance factor.

The place of origin of our playing cards is open to debate. Some students, e.g. Wilkinson, make a strong argument for their origin in Chinese playing cards, which in turn seem to stem from the divining arrows used by many of the peoples of Asia and North America. Certainly there seems to be a connection between our cards and the Chinese type. However, no direct connection has been shown.

Chinese cards are long and narrow, resembling in many ways the sticks or feathered ends of arrows from which they are believed to derive. The playing sticks, classified by Culin with the playing cards, used by the North American Indians, are of similar shape. The playing cards of India, on the other hand, are round. In both Hindu and Chinese cards, there is division into suits, and into ranked variety within the suits. It has been suggested by Culin that these East Indian cards are derived from play equipment similar to that of the playing disks of the North American Indians. The latter were, however, more akin to dice in their use (they were counted according to the faces turned up in a throw of the series of disks) than they were to cards. A combination of motifs is nevertheless not beyond the bounds of possibility, and some lost game of India may have developed, through an Indian acquaintance with Chinese cards and card games, into a game played with round cards. It might be suggested that tradition holds us to a rectangular card; a round card might be more easily handled and would last longer than the oblong one. But card games are no different from other games, and tradition's weighty hand is turned against change.

At some early point in their history, cards arise from divinatory practices. The idea that they were divided into suits on this divining basis, usually into four suits corresponding to the four directions of the compass, is most appealing. Their use, since their introduction into Europe, has always been, concurrently with their use in competitive games and save for a brief lapse some centuries ago, in fortune-telling, as a means of seeing the future. Cartomancy is an old and well-established study in Europe and in its derivative and allied cultures. On this ground the Gipsies have been "accused" of having imported cards into Europe, since Gipsies are notoriously the palmists and tea-leaf readers, the card readers and phrenologists *sine qua non*. And, working back from this hypothesis, there have been studies tracing the "Book of Thoth" or other such fantastic names for the pack of cards to the Egyptians (which is what the Gipsies' name derives from), whose country, or supposed country, as the most ancient known to Europeans of past centuries, was naturally thought to be the home of the original, and unhappily lost or hidden, mysteries of the human spirit. But the theory that the Gipsies brought cards to Europe is dubious at best. The first playing cards, it is true, are noted on the continent at about the time that the Gipsies arrived from their Eastern lands. Cards, as a game device, would be among the very first things transmitted from one people to another; if anything were to be handed by the Gipsies to their European neighbors, the most likely of all would be playing cards, if that were one of the Gipsies' peculiar possessions. Nevertheless, contact between the Gipsies and the peoples they lived among, for one reason or another, was never close enough for cards to have passed easily from the one group to the other.

Cards have been known in Europe for at least 500 years, the tarot deck being known in France, the Low Countries, Germany, and Italy in about 1350. Willshire places the earliest definite date at 1392. The very earliest of Italian cards were what are known as tarocchi or tarots, cards including a group called attuti or atouts bearing such names as the Pope, the Lovers, the Sun, the Devil, the Tower. Combined with these in the deck were the suit cards, comprising the numbered cards and court or coat cards. The early games played with the tarot deck were all for two players.

Like chess, playing cards have their invention myth; it is said that they were made to amuse the mad Charles VI of France. There was no early standardization of the number of cards in a deck, nor is there today. Our standard pack contains 52 cards, but various games are played with a 32–card pack, or 48, or 53, etc. Some Mexican decks have 104 cards; it is said that in India a deck of 120 cards is used. Our suits of clubs, spades, hearts, and diamonds were once cups and coins, batons and swords (and still are in some countries like Italy and Spain), but our modern suits have developed a traditional symbolism of their own, especially as used in fortune-telling. Hearts relate to love; clubs to knowledge (or as resembling the clover-leaf, to fertility); diamonds, as is quite natural, to wealth; and spades to death and the grave. The court cards too have their names, and have often been printed with the faces of the persons they are supposed to represent. For example, the French names for the four kings were traditionally Charlemagne (hearts), Alexander (clubs), Cæsar (diamonds), and David (spades). Similarly with the queens, and with the knaves, the latter being called for the great knights of legend, e.g. Hector, Lancelot, Ogier the Dane.

In cards, as in all games, tradition maintains a hold not to be shaken, not even by well-thought-out schemes of persons seeking to improve certain of the games. A fifth suit, often suggested, and which probably would result in the development of new and interesting games, has never been kindly received by card players. The very cards themselves, as printed today, are of traditional design; the costumes worn by the royalty on the court cards is early Tudor, although some of the trappings, e.g. the crowns, are of later date.

The deck of cards, as we know it, and with the evidence of the atouts of the "Egyptian book," is probably a development of two types of cards used in two kinds of games. The numbered cards, aside from their arrangement in suits, may go back to some form of game resembling dominoes, with matching of numbers or building up of a series as its basis. The court cards and the tarots may be essentially the descendants of instructional material, of pedagogic cards or of cards used in divining what lay in store for the user of the cards. Michelangelo is said to have invented a Florentine form of the game of cards, using a complete deck of tarots, to instruct children in arithmetic. History, traditional belief, and legend may well be the instructional use of the non-series cards in the deck, as evidenced by the names given to the court cards and by the names of the atouts.

Whereas the origin of playing cards is conjectural at best, there is more solid ground for determining the origin of dice. The beginnings are preserved in one of our popular terms for the implements, the "bones," a term used whether the dice be of ivory, plastic compound, or cubes of sugar. More clearly than is the case with cards, dice may be seen to be originally almost universal instruments for divination, by casting the vertebræ or knucklebones of animals. Where this form of divination is practiced, the fall of the bones with the long spur up, or the short spur up, or in any of the other possible ways, or, where more than one bone is thrown, the various casts in combination, is read by the diviner according to a preconceived plan. What more natural than to turn this form of determining the wishes of the deities into a type of gaming, with the lucky person the one who draws the best omen? In time the bone itself had figures drawn on it; instead of the fall of the spines, the appearance of a painted or incised character became the determining factor. The simple dice games of the North American Indians were played for the most part with pebbles having one face painted and the other left natural or plain, or with pieces of wood flat on one side (marked or unmarked) and with the natural curve of the twig on the other. The distinction between "lot" games, represented by these implements, and "dice" games, seems to be an artificial one, because the two forms of casting to determine a number are essentially the same. In a set of such dice there may be several varieties, or one with special marking. Where number divination is a developed study, the faces of the dice, or bones, may be numbered. Thus we have dice from ancient Egypt more closely resembling ours than the almost contemporary American Indian dice.

Dice may further be used in determining which of certain positions in a chart is to be chosen for divining purposes. One may move pieces to different positions in divining, or make a contest of the moves as in the Indian game of pachisi, the Korean nyout, the European backgammon, the Egyptian seegà. Or one may determine what part of a standard chart, such as the Chinese sixty-four hexagrams or the eight diagrams, is to be read against a standard interpretation. Dice thus become a tool for the determining of a further objective, and may be part of, or all of, the equipment necessary for a game.

The usual things that come to mind when games are spoken of in folklore context are the games of children or the play-party games of some of the "backwoods" sections of our country, the rope-skipping and other games and rimes of children or the traditional play songs. For several reasons these categories have been avoided. First, the much-repeated statement that children are the most conservative creatures on earth seems to be true, and as a truth it leads to a dilemma. Do children play games because the games are traditional or are the games traditional because children play them? And if both, or either, whence the changes that occur in games? This is of course a statement of the chicken-and-egg paradox. Second, there has been overanalysis of children's games. There may be point in proving that London Bridge is an ancient bridge-sacrifice rite, transferred to the child's world by his imitation of his elders, and, upon the disappearance of the rite itself from the adult world, remaining in a vacuum in the play world, and thus changing through the centuries. Interesting, yes; but this is a scholarly hypothesis deriving from what is itself a scholarly game; it has nothing to do with the "why" of the popularity of London Bridge among children. No child plays that particular game today in imitation of his elders' bridge sacrifices; no child makes the connection between the game and bridge sacrifices. No child has heard of bridge sacrifices, unless we subscribe to some theory of a racial consciousness. Though some of the variants of London Bridge do indicate a bridge-sacrifice ceremony as the basis of the game, these are the oldest rimes in theory only. There is no way of dating the comparative age of those particular verses as against the so-called more modern verses of thievery and jail except by deduction, at best a process to be handled charily in the face of inductive evidence. The child of today plays London Bridge because children of the generation preceding his played it, and because he is a Tory. The rope-skipping rimes using the name of Charlie Chaplin are still used in 1949 by six-year-olds who have never seen a Chaplin picture, and who would not recognize the name out of the rime context. The name used in this rime may change with the passing of a few more years; it may change to another popular name, or be garbled into something unrecognizable as a name, or it may remain Charlie Chaplin. But no one will claim, in 200 years, it is to be hoped, that because of historical research it has been decided that the children of that day are reenacting a comedy scene from some early Chaplin picture. They will not be, any more than our children are portraying bridge sacrifice or a Chinvat Bridge ritual. Third, adults have an influence on the games children play. How much of the transmission of the games is through half-forgotten rules and ways of play taught, deliberately fostered in children, by adults long past the games age themselves? How many of the "children's games" are games played in the schools as "quaint survivals" or efficacious methods of keeping a group of children occupied for a half-hour of supervised, recess play? The problem of differentiating between the games taught to children by adults and the games passed on directly from one generation of children to the next is not one to be lightly attempted.

It seems that any of the problems commonly met with in the investigation of children's games may be as easily solved in a sketch of adult games. The principal questions are the two asked in most folklore investigation: what is the significance of variants; and what is the general connection of games to the remainder of the corpus of human activity?

As with belief, folktale, folk song, ballad, or any of the other subject-subdivisions of folklore, games show a related series of variants that study can attempt to map. Similar problems to those found in the other studies

appear here. Which are the lines of transmission? How does a game travel from one country to another, from one century to another, and how does it change in transition? Do games have a geographical starting place; is there one center of diffusion from which a particular game is spread to other places and other times? Do parallel customs give rise to similar games without actual cultural contact transplanting the games? These questions are more or less rhetorical.

Tylor has studied the Indian game of pachisi and compared it with the Aztec patolli, to discover what seems to be a close correlation. This type of lot-game does not seem to have reached Europe, but rather to have spread eastward from India. On the other hand, the later dice-and-board games, related to the "lot" games but specifically using dice rather than lots for determining moves (e.g. backgammon and the various forms of the Game of Goose), spread all over the world, "so that an Icelander could easily play backgammon with a Japanese on an ancient Roman board." Chess, too, and mancala seem to have definite centers of origin, disputed in detail but not in theory. But the more general games, dice and cards, seem to have arisen not in one place or from one source, but in several places, in the presence of certain similar materials and traditions. Given a highly specialized game, therefore, we may perhaps be able to trace its place of origin; even so widespread and common an instrument as the kite has been placed in eastern or central Asia. But to find a place of origin for the top or the ball or the doll, or the general "board game," is something few would dare to attempt. These latter seem to be so related to the universal activities of man that they cannot be limited to one time or culture or place.

Aside from the universals, the problem arises of the means and direction of travel of the remaining games. First appearances of games, where they can be noted, in Europe indicate the lines attaching some games to their place of origin. Chess coming into Europe carried by the Moslems, playing cards being imported by the Gipsies or the home-coming Crusaders, mancala showing an affinity for those countries outside Africa where the Arabs did their trading and to which slaves were brought, demonstrate that games travel the main routes of historical migration of other cultural materials. So likewise does the spread of European colonization bring European games to other peoples.

An instance in point is the spread of the kite. Yrjö Hirn in his study on the instrument has shown that the first mention of the kite in the European area was in England in 1634. The evidence of ancient Greek art, an illustration of what seems to be a kite flying on the end of a string, he shows to be most probably a bull-roarer, because no literary evidence places the kite in Europe after Greek times before the 17th century mention of it. Chadwick shows that, on the other hand, the kite was very popular in Polynesia much earlier than the 17th century, in fact that the art of kite-making and kite-flying began to deteriorate in Polynesia about 750. Taken in conjunction with other evidence of migrations, the conclusion is that the traditional home of the kite in China must be very near to the real one, that the kite was invented somewhere in the territory we now know as China, and went from there eastward to Polynesia during the first millennium of the Christian era, and, later, with the increased contact between European and Eastern cultures, was carried to Europe from China.

Migration alone, however, does not tell the tale. The process of adaptation of a game, once it has been transplanted, in the new milieu is also important. Just as in folk song, where place names which mean nothing to the singer are changed to some other more meaningful form, games too are given a significance more in keeping with their new homes. The earliest American verion of London Bridge, from *Mother Goose's Melodies* about 1786, tells that "Charleston Bridge is broken down." We have already noted the combinations of games, in this same London Bridge, for example, combination in America of the English form of that game with the English game of Oranges and Lemons. In New York City, the adaptation of baseball to the city streets as stickball has made a game almost as distinct as baseball is from one o'cat. The variations of I Spy or Hide and Seek are perhaps as many as the localities in which they are played.

The tendency towards change may be as strong as the conservative tendency in games. Against the traditional nonsense rimes of children, Onery Twoery and Ibbity Bibbity Sibbety San and Eeny Meeny Miny Mo, that seem to go on through the years and from place to place with so little change that they can be recognized quite easily, against the traditionalism of the royalty of the chess pieces and the court cards, must be placed the inventiveness, the desire for new things and thrills, the dramatic instinct that leads people to play games. That is what makes for the invention of a game like cribbage by Sir John Suckling, that is what causes a jaded group of chess players to adopt the Japanese *go* in the United States, that is what starts a mah jong fad or the sudden sweep of gin rummy, that is what causes the adoption of topical characters in children's rimes. The outlines of many games remain the same; the detail varies from place to place, from group to group, from year to year.

The local variations in what apparently is the same game may be due to their basis in what are called vestigials by Corrado Gini. This concept may be contrasted with the theories of diffusion and of autonomous evolution. Gini distinguishes between origin and development. The elements of a game, as of many other customs, the very basis of the activity originates in one place and is diffused. On this small germ, on this vestigial fragment is developed the complex game, by a process resembling autonomous evolution. Thus a game implement, like a top, may be the invention of a specific place or time, and may be carried to other places in the course of time, but the games played with the top will be local developments. As a middle ground combining the other principal theories of the transmission of games, this is a quite satisfactory statement. It permits greatly varying games being recognized as the same game where the diffusion theory fails to account for such variation. It permits resemblances that the universal and parallel development theory does not account for. An index of game elements similar to the Thompson folktale motif-index would be a most helpful adjunct to a systematic study of games.

Games are of course not isolated phenomena. They are conditioned by all the other aspects of the society in which they are played. Just as one cannot study the religious life of a people without knowing something of its economic life, its political life, and its art forms, so one cannot thoroughly study a game without knowing something of the societies in which its variants are found. The relationship of our modern ball games to early religious customs, to fertility rites, to the priesthood has been brilliantly demonstrated by Henderson. The underlying connection of the baseball game with ceremonies ensuring that a sufficient crop would be obtained is no concern of 80,000 followers of the game crowding into a modern stadium to see a struggle between the representatives of two cities, but there is reason to suspect that the emotions evoked may be essentially the same as those that hailed the victory of light or summer over darkness or winter in the outcome of a primitive form of ball play. The inherent drama of games is thus linked with the kind of activity we set apart as drama, which itself began as an expanded form of liturgical exercise in Europe, and which was a form of religious expression in ancient Greece. Enough has already been said about the connection of children's games with primitive religious customs, with sacrifices, with planting ceremonies, with marriage rites, with belief in witches and supernatural beings.

Games are more than a reflection of other activities of life; they are in their own right a part of the way of life of a people. It might even be said, in view of the great emphasis placed upon games and sports in the United States today, that games form the distinctive feature of modern American life. But it will take time and discerning historians to determine the validity of such a statement. If it be true that a religion cannot be studied by a believer, or that a custom cannot be adequately measured until it is decadent and relegated to the limbo of superstition, then the historian of the games of the United States is yet to be born. There may be good reason for the petering out of the study of games that made so great a part of folklore study in the last decade of the 19th and the first decade of the 20th century.

JEROME FRIED

Gammer Grethel Frau Katerīna Viehmännin, a peasant wife in the Hesse-Kassel district, from whose lips the brothers Grimm took down a large number of the märchen in their exhaustive collections. Her name is given to certain of the collections, as narrator; her portrait, sketched by M. Ludwig Grimm, appears as frontispiece in one of his brother's later collections of popular tales credited to her telling.

ga'n White Mountain Apache supernatural beings who live in mountains and caves and underground worlds: impersonated by the masked dancers in various religious ceremonials. Long ago the ga'n lived on this earth the same as people. But they did not like sickness and death, so they went off in search of a world where no disease could come and where eternal life was the lot of all. They are especially venerated as being associated with agriculture and crops. Compare GAHE; HACTCIN; KACHINA.

Gaṇas In Hindu mythology, the servants of the gods; any of the nine classes of inferior deities who are attendant upon Śiva. They are commanded by Gaṇeśa or Nandi and live on Kailāsa. The classes of deities included among the Gaṇas are the Ādityas, Vasus, Viśwedevas, Anilas, Tushitas, Ābhāsvaras, Rudras, Sādhyas, and Mahārājikas.

Gandarewa In the Avesta, a monster of the deep; a fiend with golden heels whose body was in the water and whose head was in the sky, unlike his counterpart, the Indian Gandharva, who lived usually in the sky. Gandarewa was the guardian of the haoma and a dragon eager to destroy the good in the world. He was slain by Keresāspa after a battle in the sea which lasted nine days and nights. In the *Shāhnāmah,* Gandarewa appears as Kundrav.

Gandharva (1) In Vedic mythology, originally a solitary being, the measurer of space, the sun steed, sometimes identified with the rainbow, and the guard of the soma, who is mentioned three times in the *Rig-Veda* in the plural. In the *Brāhmanas,* the Gandharvas are a group of beings who, with the Apsarases, preside over fertility. They dwell in the sky or atmosphere, are skilled in medicine, and have a mystic power over women. Accounts of their origin vary. In some they were born from Brahmā, in another they were the off-spring of Kaśyapa. Their leaders are Viśvāvasu and Tumburu.

The Gandharvas are described in the *Atharva-veda* as shaggy, half-animal beings. Elsewhere they are called beautiful, wind-haired, with brilliant weapons and fragrant garments. In the epics they play lutes and sing at the banquets of the gods. They are also explained as spirits of the wind, the rainbow, the rising sun, the moon, the clouds, and of the soma. There seems to be no more justification for these views than for their identification, in defiance of philology, with the Greek Centaurs.

(2) In the *Mahābhārata,* a race of hill dwellers.

Gandreid The Wild Hunt of Norwegian folklore: literally, spirits' ride. Belief in it still persists in many sections: the survival of an ancient feast of the dead commemorates all who died during the previous year and comes during the Epiphany. The wilder the rush of spirits, the better the crops in the ensuing year. Whatever fields they fly over will bear especially well.

ganegwa'e The striking-a-fan or eagle dance of the Iroquois Indians. It is unlike the Southwest eagle dance in the virtual lack of mimetic action and in its primarily curative intent. The eagle, *ha'guks,* has power to restore life to wilting things and to charm animals for hunt. During the introductory songs, to water drum and horn rattle, someone presents a drum to the first singer, then a horn rattle to the first singer's helper, then a small rattle and fan to each dancer. Each following dance song is interrupted by a speech and small gift, usually money or cakes. The dancers face the bench of singers (Cayuga) or line up in two lines vis-à-vis (Seneca) and in a lunging position shake their rattles and try to pick up a small object with their teeth. To an interesting stretto drumbeat pattern, they hop forward or backward in a crouching position. The songs, some atonal, some pentatonic, are thus in two contrasting parts, the first rhapsodic, the second clearcut. The *ganegwa'e* is probably related to the calumet dance of the Cherokee and Plains Indians, the grass dance, and the Pawnee Hako. Common features are the give-away and one-time boasting speech, the former bustle or crow-belt and the calumet, now a feathered fan. [GPK]

ganéo'ǫ The Iroquois Indian drum dance: a dance of thanksgiving to the Creator, Hahgwehdiyu, for crops,

good health, and other benefits. It recurs in all the major seasonal festivals of all longhouses, usually as climax to the several days of ceremonial procedure. The traditional songs, which number over 100, are accompanied by the water drum. The middle section of the ceremonial is chanted solemnly in monotone rhythms, with interpolated prayers by one of the faithkeepers, addressed to all of creation, from inanimate elements and humblest creatures to supernaturals and the Creator himself. The dancers, men in the lead, circle against the sun, the men with a double thump of each heel, the women with the *ęskänye* step. The best dancers become inspired to angular gestures with the arms and torso. [GPK]

Ganeśa, Ganesha, or **Ganapati** Literally, lord of the hosts: in Hindu mythology and religion, the god of wisdom, prudence, and learning, and the remover of obstacles; leader of the troops of inferior deities; son of Śiva and Pārvatī (Devī) or of the scurf of Pārvatī's body. He is represented as a pot-bellied fat man of yellow or red color, with four hands and a one-tusked elephant head, sometimes riding on a rat or attended by one. He is worshipped in the Deccan and often depicted in Śaivite shrines. The rat vehicle and elephant head symbolize his power to vanquish every obstacle whether it be by trampling the jungle or by entering a granary.

Many of the myths about him account for his head. According to one his proud mother showed him off to Śiva whose glance burnt the child's head to ashes. Brahmā advised her to replace it with the first head she could find. According to another myth, Śiva struck off Ganeśa's head when his son opposed his entrance to Pārvatī's bath and then replaced it with that of an elephant to placate his wife. The loss of one tusk is explained by the legend in which Rāma went to visit Śiva who was sleeping. Ganeśa opposed his entrance and Rāma threw his ax at him. Recognizing his father's ax, Ganeśa permitted it to sever one of his tusks as he waited to receive it.

Ganeśa's importance as a god is first acknowledged in the Purānas. His association with the rat suggests a humble origin, but this has been discounted by some scholars who considered Ganeśa of hieratic origin. As a result of the consequent belief in the sacredness of rats, their extermination became a difficult problem. Compare SARASVATĪ.

Gangā or **Gangā Māī** In Hindu mythology and religion, the sacred Ganges: personified as a goddess of abundance, health, and prowess. The Ganges is the most holy river in modern Hindu belief. Temples have been raised along the river banks and her water is in demand for sacrifice and as a viaticum. Its full efficacy is obtained by bathing in it during the full moon or eclipses. The ashes of the dead are cast into the river to wash away the sins of the dead one and to secure his rebirth in the celestial realm.

In the *Purānas,* the heavenly Ganges flows from the toe of Vishnu. It was brought from heaven, according to a myth told in the epics and in the *Bhāgavata Purāna,* after Agastya swallowed the ocean. King Bhagīratha then devoted himself for a thousand years to fierce penances. Brahmā, pleased with his asceticism, promised to grant him a wish and the king requested that the heavenly river **Gangā** descend to earth. Brahmā agreed but advised the saint to win the grace of Śiva, since he alone could prevent the weight of the river from cleaving the earth. After practicing further austerities, he got Śiva to acquiesce and to catch the impact of the torrent on his head, his snarled hair delaying the current which eventually descended to the Himālayas and thence through the plains to the sea.

Gangā as a goddess is the eldest daughter of Himavat, the sister of Umā, and mother of Bhīshma and Kartikeya (Skanda). Her vehicle is a sea monster.

gangar The slow, sunwise walking circuit performed by men and women, characteristic of Norwegian folk dancing. See CIRCUMAMBULATION. [GPK]

Ganymede or **Ganymedes** In classical mythology, the cupbearer of Zeus. Ganymede was originally a mortal, the son of Tros and Callirrhoe, and the most beautiful of boys. He was carried off, by the gods or by Zeus in the form of an eagle or by an eagle sent by Zeus, and in exchange his father was presented with a pair of divine horses or with a golden vine. Later mythology placed him among the stars as Aquarius and made him the presiding spirit of the fertilizing fountains of the Nile. In later mythology, likewise, the story degenerates into a tale of pederasty, and the name Ganymede—usually in the form *catamite*—becomes typical of the boy kept for homosexual purposes. In Crete, where pederasty attained great refinement, Minos replaced Zeus as the ravisher.

Ga-oh The spirit of the winds of Seneca (Iroquois) Indian mythology. He lives in the northern (in some versions, western) sky, and controls the four winds, and therefore the seasons. These are constrained at the entrance to his dwelling: the Bear (Ya-o-gah, the north wind), the Panther (Dajoji, the west wind), the Moose (Oyandone, the east wind), and the Fawn (Ne-a-go, the south wind). Ga-oh is a benevolent spirit, concerned with the welfare of men on earth.

garde or **guard** The magic charm used by the Negroes of Haiti and Trinidad to ward off evil. In Haiti, it belongs to the same general category as the *arrêt* and *drogue*, employed for similar ends by the Haitians in contrast to the *wanga*. In Haiti, the guard, as the magical device that brings security is called, is contrasted to the "trick," which gives power that enables an individual to pursue ends of personal aggrandizement. [MJH]

Garden of Eden The place of the creation of man (*Gen.* ii, 8), specially planted by God with all the good, food-giving trees and the two trees of life and of the knowledge of good and evil. There Adam lived an idyllic life for the few hours between his creation and the time he ate of the forbidden tree and was expelled. The concept of the earthly Paradise was probably borrowed by the Hebrews from the Persians, with later modification by Greek tradition. The Garden of Eden, in some of the later mystical Jewish writings, is the earthly counterpart of the heavenly Paradise. No living person is permitted to view the Garden (a seraph armed with a flaming sword guards the gate), although it is said the Rabbi Joshua ben Levi tricked the Angel of Death into letting him sit on the wall to see his future place in Paradise, and then leaped into the Garden carrying the Angel's sword. He was permitted to stay after he had surrendered the sword.

Gardsvor Literally, house guardian: in Scandinavian folklore, a household spirit, usually conceived of in the form of a little man, and still believed by many to be a manifestation of the soul of some ancestor.

garlic Sometimes called stinkweed, this species of onion (genus *Allium*) is found in most parts of the world and, because of its pungent odor, is widely credited with antiseptic qualities which scientists say it does not possess. It is especially recommended in time of plague. It is widely credited with the power to drive away evil, whether demons, witches, vampires, or the evil eye, and is hung in houses and around the neck for this purpose. While this holds true in most of India, there are parts of the country where the presence of evil spirits may be detected by the smell of garlic in the air. The idea that a magnet lost its power in the presence of, or when rubbed with, garlic was mentioned by Pliny and was carefully repeated through the ages until Sir Thomas Browne placed it among his *Vulgar Errors*.

Roman soldiers ate garlic in the belief that it gave courage in battle. Bullfighters of the Aymara Indians of Bolivia carry a piece on their persons into the ring, believing that if the bull smells it he will not charge. It was placed at crossroads for Hecate and was also carried by travelers to protect them from her. Besides being universally respected as an antiseptic and preventive of disease, used as an amulet, liniment, salve, philter, or inhalant, it is also considered a potent cure for all diseases of man and beast, except those of the eyes, head, and kidneys. Aristotle mentioned garlic as a cure for hydrophobia and a spring tonic. The Berbers grind garlic and bake it in bread to cure a common cold and use the plant as an aid to conception. It was also recommended for those who had to drink water they suspected of being unsafe to prevent infection.

Garm or **Garmr** In Teutonic mythology, the bloodstained watchdog who guarded Hel's gate and lived in Gnipa-cave. Anyone who had given bread to the poor could appease him with Hel cake. At Ragnarök he will break loose, slay Tyr, and be killed by Tyr.

Garuḍa In Hindu mythology, folklore, and religion, a form of the sun; the vehicle of Vishṇu, represented as a supernatural being, half man, half bird, with a golden body, white face, and red wings. He is king of the birds and was born as the son of Kaśyapa and Vinatā or at the beginning of time from the eggshell which, in the hands of Brahmā, then produced the divine elephants.

Garuḍa is the implacable enemy of the serpents. According to the myth in the *Mahābhārata,* his mother quarreled with her co-wife, Kadrū, the mother of the serpents, and was enslaved. To free Vinatā and himself, Garuḍa defeated the gods, extinguished the fire which surrounded the amṛita, penetrated the whirling wheel, slew the snake guards, and carried off the sacred amṛita; then Vishṇu made Garuḍa immortal and chose him as his vehicle. Indra recovered the amṛita but his thunderbolt was smashed in the fray.

As the relentless annihilator of snakes, Garuḍa possesses magic power against the effects of poison. Persons suffering from snakebite at Puri, Orissa, embrace a Garuḍa pillar in the temple.

Wings are ordinarily not an attribute of Indian celestial beings which either float through space or are carried by vehicles. Garuḍa's however, were so powerful that he could stay the rotation of the three worlds with the wind from their motion. See AIRĀVATA; VISHṆU.

gasgaíǫdadǫ́ The Seneca Indian social dance (called *ganusdágeka* by the Cayuga) the shake-the-bush or naked dance in English. The reason for the name is unknown. It is unique in that the women start the dance first with a choral song, then with an open round in two columns. Pairs of men then are inserted. The odd couples go backward; at a repetition of the music the even couples pass through between them, thus becoming the backwards dancing leaders. The step is of the *ga'dášot* type, embellished with low kicks *ad lib.*, but the couple-swapping resembles the *gẹdjóenǫ* type. The songs, to drum and horn rattle, are well developed and introduce new thematic materials in the second theme. [GPK]

gashädǫdádǫ The Seneca term for the Iroquois gourd or squash dance (literally, shake-a-pumpkin or shake-a-jug): a social dance of the *ga'dášot* type. The corresponding Cayuga *katchätondátǫ* or *niošawäonǫ* is regularly the fourth of the ceremonial spirit-of-the-food or bread dances. The choreography and music are of archaic ritual type, in a counterclockwise circle, men in the lead, women at the tail. The songs, to drum and horn rattle, have a limited range and thematic development, and terminate with a long monotone antiphony between the dance leader and men's chorus. The regular *ga'dášot* is always added to the dance sequence. [GPK]

Gaster, Moses (1856–1939) folklorist, Hebraist, and Rumanian scholar. He was born in Bucharest and received his education there and at Leipzig, Germany. In 1881 he was appointed lecturer in Rumanian literature and language at the University of Bucharest, but four years later was expelled from the country for agitating on behalf of Jews. Proceeding to England, he served in 1886 and again in 1891 as Ilchester lecturer in Græco-Slavonic languages at the University of Oxford. From 1887 until 1919 he was chief rabbi of the Sephardic communities in England. Gaster's published works range over a wide field of interest and include studies on such diversified subjects as Rumanian and Jewish literature, comparative literature and folklore, Bible and Apocrypha, Gipsy lore and the culture of the Samaritans. His *Folk-Literature of Rumania* (*Literatura Populara Romana*), published in 1883, brought him European recognition, and in 1891 there appeared his monumental *Chrestomatie Romana*, still regarded as a classic. He was a pioneer in the comparative study of folktales and a ranking authority on Gipsies. His works include *Græco-Slavonic Literature* (1887), *The Sword of Moses* (1896), *The Chronicles of Jerahmeel* (1899), *Rumanian Bird and Beast Stories* (1915), *The Exempla of the Rabbis* (1924), *The Samaritans* (1925), a translation of the famous Judæo-German *Maaseh Book* (1934), and *Anton Pann: Povestea Vorbii* (1936). Gaster's collected essays were republished under the title of *Studies and Texts in Magic, Medieval Romance, Hebrew Apocrypha and Samaritan Archaeology* (three volumes, 1925–1928). A bibliography of his writings is contained in *Occident and Orient: Gaster Anniversary Volume* (1936).

gātanan, gâtanan Literally, a story, a story: formula with which the Hausa story-teller always begins his tale. His audience always answers "Ta je, ta kōmō"—Let it go, let it come.

gato An Argentine gaucho flirtatious couple dance, known also in Chile, Peru, and Paraguay. It is performed in two styles: one called the *kururu* is a simple walk accompanied by song; the *siriri* is more lively and bouncing. After a particularly arduous and skilful zapateado, the couple pause, turn, and recite verses to each other, typically a proposal on the part of the man and pert refusal on the part of the woman. [GPK]

Gaurī In Hindu mythology and religion, an epithet of Devī in her mild form as the yellow or brilliant one: sometimes an epithet for Varuṇānī, wife of Varuṇa.

Gawain The "perfect knight" of Arthurian legend; nephew of King Arthur. He appears in the earliest sources, and in Malory has certain characteristics of the Celtic solar deity. He is best known in literature through the Middle English *Gawain and the Green Knight*.

It has long been realized that Gawain had mythical antecedents: 1) We are repeatedly told in the romances that his strength waxed till midday and waned thereafter. 2) Several of his adventures are derived from those of the Irish hero Cuchulainn, who possessed marked solar traits, including a diadem of golden hair. 3) Gawain's father Loth has been traced back through Welsh Lluch to the Irish god Luġ, Cuchulainn's father, on whom there used to be a red color from sunset till morning—a trait suggested by the sun as it dips to the horizon and rises from it. The Irish prototype of Gawain, then, is the solar Cuchulainn. Since Irish myth did not reach the French except by way of Wales and Brittany, we should expect to find in Welsh literature an intermediate figure between Cuchulainn and Gawain, and this seems to be Gwri Gwallt-euryn, "of the Golden Hair," so called because his hair was yellow as gold. Gwri's history strongly resembles Gawain's. Both were born under circumstances which brought shame to their mothers; both were discovered as foundlings, swaddled in a rich cloth, and their high birth was recognized; both were baptized, one as Gwri Gwallt-euryn, the other as Gauvain or Walwanius; both after a precocious boyhood in care of foster parents were transferred to the charge of a second foster father; both became warriors of Arthur (note that Gware of the Golden Hair is one of Arthur's household in *Kilhwch*). Much other evidence supports the view that Gwri was the immediate original of Gawain. Gwalchmai is simply a name substituted by the Welsh when they became acquainted with a French form of Gawain, Galvain, which itself goes back through the earliest recorded form, Galvagin, to a Welsh epithet Gwallt-advwyn, meaning "of the Splendid Hair." Thus Gawain's name originated in the gleaming rays of the sun.

Bibliography:
J. L. Weston, *Legend of Sir Gawain* (1897).
R. S. Loomis, *Celtic Myth and Arthurian Romance* (1927), pp. 39–49.
——*Arthurian Tradition and Chrétien de Troyes* (1949), index *sub* Gawain. [RSL]

Gawain and the Green Knight A 14th century English romance by the author of *The Pearl*, the central episode of which is the folklore motif of the exchange of blows. A Green Knight challenges Arthur's knights to a contest in which he will submit to decapitation provided that he be given the right to deliver a blow in return one year later. Gawain accepts the challenge, and cuts off the Green Knight's head. The Green Knight picks up the head and, bidding Gawain come to his castle in one year to fulfil his part of the compact, rides away. During the course of the year Gawain arrives at the castle of the Green Knight, though he does not recognize his host as the Green Knight. The lady of the castle tests his loyalty and virtue, but Gawain remains true to his knightly vows except that he retains the lady's gift of a magic girdle, which will keep him from harm, instead of delivering it to his host as he had promised. When the Green Knight reveals himself and demands that Gawain fulfil his part of the compact, Gawain submits. The Green Knight gives Gawain a light wound and then explains that the whole plan was a test of Arthur's knights instigated by Morgan le Fay, and that he had given Gawain the wound because he had kept the girdle. [MEL]

Gaya In Hindu mythology, an asura whose accumulated merit as a worshipper of Vishnu alarmed the gods. Granted purity by the deities, he soon cleared the universe of its inhabitants, since everyone touching him was purified and went to Brahmā's heaven. Finally it was agreed by Gaya and the gods that one spot should be set aside as a place (Gayā-psetra) in which the sins of any who resorted to it would be washed away. Upon this legend rests the holiness of the town of Gayā in Bihar Province.

Gaya Maretan (Pahlavi *Gayōmart*) In Iranian cosmological mythology, the first man whose body was born from the sweat of Ahura Mazda. His spirit lived during the same period of 3000 years in which that of the primeval ox lived, then Ahura Mazda made him corporeal. He was tall, white, and radiant. When he appeared the demon-infested earth was dark and the creatures of evil were battling with the stars. The demons attacked Gaya but he withstood them and lived for 30 years. At the end of that time the fiend, Jahi, persuaded Angra Mainyu to poison the body of Gaya and to inflict him with hunger and disease. When Gaya died his body became brass and his limbs gold, iron, silver, lead, tin, mercury, and adamant. Spentā Ārmaiti preserved his seed, which was gold, and after 40 years the first human pair came from it. These were Māshya and Māshyoi who grew at first as a stem with fifteen leaves and later were separated.

According to the *Shāhnāmah* Gaya Maretan was the first king of the Iranians who reigned for 30 years. His son was Sīyākmak; his grandson was Hoshang. Sīyākmak was slain in a battle with the wicked king, Angra Mainyu, and Hōshang, who then succeeded Gaya Maretan, became the first lawgiver of the Iranians.

gayap songs The equivalent in Trinidad of the combite songs of Haiti. The communal work group, the *gayap*, is spurred on in its efforts by singing, the beat set by a drum. Compare COMBITE.

gbo The Dahomean (Fōn) word for magic charm. In Dahomey, the charm is the objective and operating manifestation of that aspect of the total religious belief system comprised in the category of magic. The power behind the charm is held to derive in part from certain of the gods, in part from other supernatural beings. Though all priests are practitioners of magic, there are specialists in manipulating these powers that give magic its force. Gbo may be both good and bad, and though the categories of benevolent and malevolent charms are known, this is often a matter of emphasis, since magic that helps the one who controls it may harm another person; or may be used for good in one situation and evil in another. Dahomean gbo are classified as to form and function. Six categories under the former heading have been recorded, and eighteen under the latter. It is to be doubted, however, if this list is complete. See AKONDA; AKPOU; ALIMAGBA; DIDI; NUDIDA; YEGBOGBA. [MJH]

Ge or **Gæa** In Greek mythology, the earth goddess; the personification of the earth; the goddess of the land and the things produced by it: later supplanted by other, more specifically fertility goddesses. Ge was born of Chaos, and was the first of the heavenly beings. From her came Uranus, the heavens, and Pontus, the sea. Mating with Uranus, she produced many offspring, and, jealous of the rights of these children, made the sickle with which Cronus castrated Uranus. As an earth goddess, Ge was also an underworld deity. The Delphic oracle, at which was located the pit which was the world's navel, first belonged to her; at Olympia in very early times she had another oracle. Her cult was widespread in Greece; in Rome, as Tellus or Terra, she was likewise worshipped as a chthonic deity.

Geb, Keb, Qeb, or **Seb** In Egyptian mythology, the earth god; son of (or parent of) Shu and Tefnut; husband of Nut and father of Osiris and the other deities of the Osirian group: Horus, Seth, Isis, Nephthys. He is represented as a goose, or as a bearded man with a goose on his head, the goose being the hieroglyphic symbol of the god. In the Egyptian cosmographic myth, Shu, the air, separates Geb and Nut, earth and sky: the personation of the earth as male, the sky as female, is unusual, the reverse being the common case.

gedjóenọ The Iroquois Indian fish dance (termed *kaiọwa* by the Cayuga of the Six Nations' Reserve). Its typical step is an alternate out-and-in twist of the feet, twice or three times successively with each foot, superficially resembling the Charleston, but certainly not influenced by it. The fish dance is an old and formerly ceremonial dance, though now classified as a social dance. The women sometimes use the same twisting step as in the ritual *ẹskänye*. The choreography is also distinctive: the progression is generally in an anticlockw̱se single circle, but danced by couples. Men enter in pairs, then pairs of women are inserted. Each song has a short part A and a longer B. A is a warming-up step-pat; B is the fish step with an even drumbeat. When A returns, the drum vibrates and the partners change places. In B they resume the fish step. The tempo, already vivacious, speeds up in the course of each song. This pattern is characteristic of five dances, grouped by the Indians as *gedjóenọkạ*—in the manner of the fish dance. The interchange is said to suggest the passing of couples of fish in the water. [GPK]

gee In American cowboy square dances, the term for right. [GPK]

Gefjon or **Gefjun** In Teutonic mythology, Frigga's attendant; goddess of agriculture. She presided over all who died virgins, making them happy forever. She married a giant and had four sons. Once she asked King Gylfi for some land of her own. He was amused and granted her all she could plow around in a day and night. Changing her four sons into oxen, she plowed a great area, which her oxen dragged into the sea, where it is now the Danish island of Seeland. Its shape corresponds exactly to the Swedish lake Malar. She later married Odin's son, Skiold, and founded the royal Danish race of Skioldungs.

Gêge One of the three major "orthodox" African cult-groups of Bahia, Brazil. The Gêge are derived from the Dahomey and Mahi peoples of French West Africa, and are known for their intransigence in the maintenance of traditional values, the excellence of the ritual dancing by their cult-members, and the meticulousness with which the African prescriptions of worship are observed. Because of this insistence on orthodoxy, which exacts an initiation of more than a year as against the requirements of four to six months seclusion by the other African cults, the Gêge group has declined in numbers, but continues to hold the deep respect of cult-members of all affiliations. The designation comes from the Yoruban term for the Fõn-speaking (Dahomean) peoples, and means The many, or The numerous ones. [MJH]

Gehenna (Hebrew *Gehinnom*) The valley of Hinnom, near Jerusalem, where the city's refuse was thrown and burned; hence, hell-fire and hell itself; the place of future torment of the wicked. It is said that sacrifices of children to Moloch were performed in the valley, and that therefore the place was later turned into an offal-dump. A later explanation states that one of the gates to Gehenna, the burning afterworld, stood in the valley, and that thus the name of hell was applied to the valley.

Gekka-o The Japanese god of marriage, who binds the feet of lovers with a red silk thread. [JLM]

gematria A cabalistic, cryptographic method of interpreting passages of the Hebrew Scriptures by substituting numerical values for the alphabetic meaning of the letters (each Hebrew letter being also a digit or number). Thus two words whose numbers added to the same sum might be interchanged to give a new reading of a passage. Thus, for example, the angel Metatron was equated with Shaddai the Creator, since both names added to 314. Several methods of determining such numerical values were used besides simple addition, the mathematical process eventually becoming quite complicated. Gematria also partakes of the Pythagorean belief in the virtue and power of certain numbers. The word itself may be a derivative of the Greek *gramma*, letter, by metathesis (compare English *gramarye*, magic).

Gemini A Latin name of the Dioscuri, Castor and Pollux: name given to the constellation including the stars Castor and Pollux, and to the sign of the zodiac entered by the sun on May 21.

The two stars, Castor (alpha Gemini) and Pollux (beta Gemini), have been recognized as a pair since the earliest times, possibly as long ago as 6000 B.C. in Mesopotamia. In many places they have been identified with the mythical Twins—the younger and the elder Horus in Egypt, Romulus and Remus in Rome, etc.—or with balancing principles, as the yang and yin in China. In Australia they were the Young Men and the Pleiades the Young Girls; in Africa, the Bushmen called them the Young Women, wives of Eland. The two stars form the heads of the Twins (Italian *Gemelli*, German *Zwillinge*, etc.) and their feet bathe in the Milky Way. Gemini is the third sign of the zodiac, immediately preceding Cancer and the summer solstice.

gems or **jewels** Precious and semiprecious stones. Besides serving as personal adornment or a tangible mark of wealth, at various times among various peoples, gems have served as gods, guardians, healing agents, amulets, talismans, charms, and divining agents. Some beliefs in the magic powers of gems sprang from color affinities, while some peoples believe that there is no inherent virtue in the stones themselves, but rather in the carving or words engraved on them, or in their combination and arrangements. In India gems were most valued in traditional combinations such as the *navaratna* (ruby, pearl, coral, emerald, topaz, diamond, sapphire, cat's eye, and amethyst) or the five-gem *pañcharatna* (gold, amethyst, diamond, emerald, and pearl). The Hindus believe that only perfect gems have virtues and that inferior gems are a source of misfortune and unhappiness. Some students of the attributes of gems say that those from tropical climates are more effective. In 315 B.C. Theophrastus advanced the theory that gems were male and female and reproduced in the ground. If smaller ones were left in the ground they would grow and multiply. In spite of the fact that skepticism began to creep in toward the end of the Middle Ages, as with Pedro Garcia, Bishop of Ussellus, who remarked in 1490 that, "In modern times many gems lack the virtues ascribed to them," many of these same virtues are still currently believed in.

The animal with a luminous jewel in its head (B72.2.3) is a commonplace of folktale, as is the serpent with the jewel in its head (B108.2). Folktale is full of magic jewels (D1071), jewels as recognition tokens (H93), extraordinary jewels formed from tears (D1454.4.2), and jewels containing the separable soul (E711.3). There are also jewel-spitting heroes and heroines, jewel-dropping horses, and jewel-bearing trees. See individual gem-stones; LAPIDARIES.

genius (plural *genii*) In Roman religion, a protecting spirit: essentially an indigenous Roman belief comparable to the late Greek concept of the dæmon and to the later Christian belief in the guardian angel. The genius came into existence with the man to whose life he was bound and basically was a spirit of generation: the female counterpart was called a Juno. The genius directed a man's life towards good ends; evil actions cheated the genius. There were genii of the family, the city, the state, the people, etc. To the public genius of Rome sacrifices were offered on October 8. Place genii are usually figured as serpents, although the (personal) genii are often winged youths carrying cornucopias and drinking cups. The plural *genii* (singular *genie*) is also applied to the *jinn* of Arabic belief. Compare LARES; NUMINA; PENATES.

genna Literally, forbidden: among the Nāgas of India, communal rites by means of which all events of social importance such as the birth of a child or a domestic animal, name-giving, ear-piercing, hair-cutting, marriage, or death, are celebrated. They are accompanied by special food tabus and characterized by a temporary disturbance of the normal social relationships. The social importance of any event can be judged by the social unit affected and by the intensity and duration of the genna. Birth, hair-cutting, and ear-piercing affect only the household, other events such as an earthquake would involve the entire village. The genna involves a social group such as the household, the clan, the village, an age or sex group, and is characterized by a nervous exaltation. Breaking genna causes disaster or death. Compare TABU.

gentian Any of a large genus (*Gentiana*) of plants. According to Pliny this plant was named for Gentius, king of Illyria (180 B.C.), who was the first to discover its virtues as a simple. A Christian legend tells of Ladislaus, king of Hungary, who shot an arrow into the air with a prayer that it would lead him to a cure for the plague which was raging among his people. When he found the arrow it had lodged in a gentian plant. Gentian is still used as a medicine. The Swiss mix it with wine to relieve the fatigue of travel, and they use the bitter root in making beer and a liqueur. When mixed in wine it removes aches and colds which have lodged in the joints. The Indians of New England used the root for the stomach, both as a stimulant to the appetite and an aid to digestion. It is also used in cases of intermittent fevers and as an antidote for poisons.

geomancy Divining by means of earth or sand: an ancient and widespread custom, still very much alive in China and among the Arabs. The Arabs' method is to read the points made at random in the sand; the joining of these points, or the pattern they form, gives the required meaning or message. Pebbles or grains of sand on paper, hence ink or pencil marks, are read in much the same way.

Chinese geomancy, or Feng Shui, is the art of locating tombs, cities, and houses auspiciously. In early times the tortoise shell oracles were consulted. During the Tsin Dynasty (265–316 A.D.) however the principles of Feng Shui were collected by Kuo P'o who, after devoting his life to drink and women, composed a magic book with which he was successful in seducing a woman in the service of one of his friends. Two schools developed: the first, which has lost its popularity, deduces the laws of consonance and dissonance from the five great stars and the Eight Trigrams or Pa Kua; the second studies the relations between the tombs, cities, and houses and the surrounding landscape. Mountains, hills, water courses, springs, groves, and neighboring buildings can be useful either in channeling the male yang influences or in deflecting them. The pronouncements of the doctors of Feng Shui are the cause of innumerable unhappy and expensive quarrels. [RDJ]

geranium Any plant of the genera *Geranium* or *Pelargonium*. Geranium comes from the Greek word for crane and the plant is occasionally called crane's bill from the shape of the fruit or seed pod. There is a Moslem legend that it was once a common mallow, but one day Mohammed hung his shirt on the plant to dry, and when he removed it, the plant had developed gaily colored flowers and a spicy aroma. In Massachusetts it is believed that snakes will not go near places where wild geraniums grow and that a geranium in the window will keep the flies out of the house. The root of the geranium is used by the Romany as a remedy for infant diarrhea, for internal bleeding, and for kidney troubles. It is used by certain North American Indians as a cure for dysentery, cholera, gonorrhea, and as a gargle for sore mouth and throat.

Gerda, Gerdr, Gerth, or **Gerthr** In Teutonic mythology, one of the jötnar, daughter of the frost giant Gymir and Angurboda, whose beauty attracted Frey from afar. He despaired of winning her, however, as the jötnar (giants) were his enemies. His servant, Skirnir, seeing his master lovesick, offered to plead for him with Gerda, in return for his magic sword. Frey consented to the bargain, so Skirnir borrowed the horse, Blodughofi, and went to seek Gerda in her fire-encircled bower. When he reached her he offered her twelve golden apples and the magic ring, Draupnir, which she refused, saying she had gold enough of her own. Skirnir then threatened her with his sword, but could not influence her at all until he began cutting runes in a stick which would have made her suitorless forever. She then promised to meet Frey in the grove of Buri in nine days. As one of the frost giantesses, Gerda symbolizes the Winter maiden wooed by Spring; the nine days correspond to the nine northern Winter months. Her union with Frey is interpreted as the surrender of frost to Spring.

Germanic folklore Folklore comprises things, acts, beliefs, words, and lyric, didactic, or narrative themes transmitted and shaped by tradition. The investigation of the origin, meaning, dissemination, and form or style of these traditional materials comprises the study of folklore. The extent to which they are the immemorial possession of the folk or have descended from higher levels of culture is often an insoluble question. Germanic folklore is noteworthy for an abundance of carefully recorded facts and for excellent investigations of the problems associated with them.

Specifically Germanic qualities in folklore are very difficult, if not impossible, to isolate. Although traditional materials of all kinds—houses, tales, or riddles—exhibit characteristic varieties that are limited to particular areas, these varieties yield no safe basis for generalizations about racial peculiarities. Concepts like the vampire, which is Slavic in origin; the notion of second sight, which is almost exclusively limited to Scotland, Ireland, Wales, and northwestern Germany; or the swan maiden, an idea which seems to be typically Germanic, can be recognized as regionally limited only after long research. Like all instances of the *argumentum ex silentio*, any definition of a theme that involves the assertion that it does not appear in certain places is very risky. Although some proverbs are no doubt Germanic, such a book as Champion, *Racial Proverbs*, rests upon an unproved and unprovable assumption. Some scholars have maintained that long-suffering heroines are characteristically Germanic, but this would be hard to prove. Nor does it seem to be possible to show that particular forms of folklore are Germanic, although specific stylistic details may be. Beliefs concerning plants and animals found only in Germanic countries are obviously Germanic folklore. Like the mistletoe and the oak, the rowan or mountain-ash is an object of special interest in Germanic countries. The horse has been associated with ancient practices and superstitions, and these may go back ultimately to the ceremonial eating of horseflesh by heathen Germanic peoples. Although these and other specific beliefs can be identified as Germanic, such endeavors do not lead to useful generalizations. In brief, folklore is international, and with the increasing collection of evidence we see that fact more and more clearly.

Literature: General treatises are available only in German; see W. Pessler, *Handbuch der deutschen Volkskunde* (Potsdam, n.d. [1936–38]); Adolf Spamer, *Die deutsche Volkskunde* (Berlin, 1935).

Records of Germanic folklore The materials of Germanic folklore are of the most varied kinds and extend from the oldest archeological remains of the Germanic peoples down to our own times. The crushed skulls in prehistoric burials may imply fear of the "living corpse," and a small hole found in stone coffins of a later date may imply a belief in an aerial soul. Stonehenge and the ancient carvings on rocks in southern Sweden are yet to be fully interpreted. Split vertebræ in children's graves represent oxen which ancient children, like those in remote Swiss valleys today, used as toys. In the oldest words and the first written records we find folklore. Place names, which often retain ideas older than the use of writing, reveal religious beliefs and cults of varying degrees of antiquity and show what gods were worshipped and where their cults were most popular. They show, for example, that the Scandinavian god Ullr, about whom we can learn very little, was important and that Balder had no cult. Historians, geographers, and travelers—Cæsar, Tacitus, Strabo, and early Christian missionaries—record Germanic stories and customs. The *Elder Edda* (a collection of short, highly sophisticated poems composed between the 8th and 11th centuries in Norway, Iceland, and even Greenland) and the more complicated Old Norse scaldic verse from the 9th century on, contain myths and heroic stories. In the *Younger Edda* written in the first half of the 13th century Snorri Sturluson collected and arranged these myths for the use of poets. These literary texts contain much folklore. The *Elder Edda,* for example, tells of the return of the dead from the grave and the raising of a corpse to foretell the future. In all the Germanic lands monks wrote charms and incantations on the margins and flyleaves of manuscripts, jotted down collections of proverbs, and included words with folklore associations in glosses and vocabularies.

Medieval Germanic literature, which is most abundant in England and Germany, contains many bits of folklore. Such poets as Der Stricker, Chaucer, and others retold folktales, and didactic writers collected proverbs as examples of moral advice and for use in schools. The German folk epic (*Volksepos*), with a misleading name that goes too far in suggesting a relationship to the folk and oral tradition, is actually a rewriting of Germanic heroic lore in an intentionally archaic style for a courtly audience. Its themes go back

through a long history of previous literary versions to tales concerning chiefly the kings and heroes of the age of migrations. The story of Siegfried, which we have in the *Elder Edda* and the *Nibelungenlied,* is a typical example of the genre. It preserves a confused mass of heroic traditions dating from the 5th century and earlier about men of such different ages and countries as Siegfried, a hero of the lower Rhine, the Burgundians of the middle Rhine, the Hunnish invader Attila, and the Ostrogothic Dietrich. In Scandinavia the Nibelungen story exists in combination with the Odinic religion and the Viking culture. Such mingling of unrelated materials of different ages and tribes is characteristic of the folk epic. The earliest historical figure in these epics is Ermanarich, king of the Ostrogoths in the 3rd century. Later figures are the Merovingian Wolfdietrich of the 5th century, the Arian Theodoric, emperor of the Goths in Italy in the 6th century, about whom a large cycle of epics developed, and the medieval dukes, Ernst of Swabia and Henry the Lion of Brunswick. In the 13th century the stories of Theodoric or Dietrich of Bern (Verona), as he was called, were carried to the Tyrol, where they became entangled with local legends of dwarfs and the Rosengarten, which may be connected with pre-Christian ideas of life after death. The authors of folk epics eliminated matters that were too fabulous for courtly ears: the *Nibelungenlied* contains no mention of Siegfried's fight with the dragon and the horny skin that he got from bathing in its blood.

After the Middle Ages we find records of folklore in chapbooks, folk songs, books of charms, dream books, witchcraft trials, and the discussion associated with them, and literary references to stories, proverbs, and customs. A few men collected folklore for its ethnographical value and antiquarian interest, especially at the time of the 17th century revival of the Germanic past, but the quantity of material thus saved is small.

In the second half of the 18th century the discovery of Ossian and the publication of Bishop Percy's *Reliques* drew attention to folklore. Goethe collected folk songs in Alsace and, in *Faust,* described the assembling of witches on the Brocken on Walpurgis Night. Around 1800 the Romanticists, who were especially interested in songs and tales, began to collect and interpret folklore. About the middle of the 19th century F. W. L. Schwartz pointed out the important distinction between higher and lower mythology, and thus directed attention to a new class of materials. The higher mythology, which consists in the myths and the cult of the gods, has been destroyed by Christian missionaries. The lower mythology, consisting of stories of dwarfs, kobolds, Tommy Knockers, water, tree, or house spirits, spirits in the growing crops (*Gerstenalte* and *Roggenhund*), and giants, has survived the coming of Christianity and lives on in modern tales and practices. Wilhelm Mannhardt interpreted the dryads, satyrs, and water or field spirits of classical mythology by comparisons with similar creatures in Germanic folklore, and, in his *Golden Bough,* J. G. Frazer extended the comparisons to the folklore of the entire world.

The folklore of former ages survives in modern tradition, and new folklore comes into being. The songs of

Tin-pan Alley gain popular currency and suffer the changes characteristic of oral transmission. "Lili Marlene" sweeps the German armies and crosses the battle lines. Sayings like "Kilroy was here" and the German "Hier wohnt Bertie" become commonplaces.

Folklore of things Museums like the open-air collection of houses and other buildings (even a church), domestic tools, and costumes at Skansen (a park near Stockholm) and the village of Dearborn, Michigan, have assembled the folklore of man-made things. The Bucks County Historical Society at Doylestown, Pa., has a good collection of tools belonging to various trades, many of them no longer practiced. Tradition preserves such curious relics as the barber's pole, the barber's basin in Germany, the ivy wreath used to advertise a wine shop, and the cigar-store Indian.

Except in certain fields, investigations concerned with the folklore of things are rare. Studies in the shapes of German villages have shown that the spiral city-plan of Leipzig is Slavic and the longitudinal plan of northern German villages is Germanic. Regional forms of German houses have been identified. The traditional kinds of fences have been collected. Studies in the history of domestic tools like Nils Lid's history of the ski are rare and often lead over into the history of inventions.

Costume The special dress worn in various regions, by particular groups, or on special occasions belongs to the folklore of things. Folk-costume is usually the survival of an earlier fashion that has been elsewhere discarded, as for example the buttons on the back of a man's dress-coat that are said to be the relics of buttons intended to hold up the tails when riding on horseback.

Literature: J. R. Planché, *A Cyclopaedia or Dictionary of Dress* (London, 1876–79).

Plants and Animals Many traditions about plants and animals reflect imperfect observations like the notion that the mole is blind. Others retain old beliefs like the tradition that a bear-cub is born as a shapeless mass of flesh and is licked into shape by the mother. Some are auguries like the forecasting of weather by a goosebone or from the appearance of the woodchuck's shadow on February 2. More general auguries are drawn from the flight of birds or the behavior of domestic animals. For customs concerned with plants and animals and for explanatory stories about them see below.

Folk medicine Traditional remedies rest on many kinds of observation of nature. Some, like the use of quinine or digitalis, employ essential qualities that were recognized long before being isolated by modern science. Some employ materials conspicuous for their disgusting qualities. Others involve the concept of sympathetic magic: a red string tied about a wound stops the flow of blood; a sickly child passed through a cleft in a tree is born again; a plant with a leaf or root shaped like some part of the human body yields a remedy for ailments of that part. A tradition of Egyptian medicine, which employed such unusual materials as the powder of a unicorn's horn or of mummy, came to the Romans after becoming the property of the folk and survives in some German medical recipes.

Literature: W. G. Black, *Folk-Medicine* (London, 1883); J. G. Bourke, *Scatalogic Rites of All Nations*

(Washington, 1891); O. von Hovorka and A. Kronfeld, *Vergleichende Volksmedizin* (Stuttgart, 1908–09); I. Reichborn-Kjennerud, *Vår gamle trolldomsmedisin*, I (Oslo, 1928), II (1933), III (1940), IV (1943).

The folklore of acts, ideas or beliefs, and connected discourse, which are subjects usually treated independently, is surveyed in dictionary form in H. F. Feilberg, *Bidrag til en ordbog over jyske almuesmål* (Copenhagen, 1886–1914), which lists under the appropriate Danish word its occurrence in superstitions, customs, songs, tales, and selected proverbs and riddles in all the Germanic languages.

Our knowledge of traditional acts, which have not been adequately collected or studied, is rather unsatisfactory. Many traditional acts take the form of customs associated with special events like marriage. Gestures often have a symbolic meaning. Crossing the legs is an act that suggests a hindrance or stopping in various symbolic connections. The origin of the Shanghai gesture of thumb to nose is uncertain. The sign of the fig (thumb thrust between the first and second fingers) is not Germanic. In the Middle Ages and the Renaissance men were more demonstrative than today and employed gestures freely. Samuel Butler's *Hudibras* abounds in them. The cinema may encourage the preservation and perhaps also the development of gestures. In Germanic folklore studies like Andrea de Jorio, *La mimica degli antichi nel gestire napoletano* (Naples, 1832), are rare.

Literature: R. S. Boggs, "Gebärde," *Handwörterbuch des deutschen Märchens*, II: 318–22.

Symbolic acts with juridical meaning are often preserved as folklore. The Germanic taking of a person under a cloak is an adoption rite. Various rites are associated with the notion of blood-brotherhood. Symbolic acts are frequently associated with punishment. A criminal is seated on a broad stone before execution or kisses the rod with which he has been whipped. Infidelity is punished by the Skimmington ride. There are excellent investigations of both capital and lesser punishments like exposure in a boat, rolling in a nail-studded barrel, and the cucking stool.

Literature: Jacob Grimm, *Deutsche Rechtsaltertümer* (4th ed., Leipzig, 1899); Karl von Amira, "Die germanischen Todesstrafen," *Abhandlungen der Bayerischen Akademie der Wissenschaften* XXXI (1922); William Andrews, *Bygone Punishments* (London, 1899); John W. Spargo, *Judicial Folklore in England Illustrated by the Cucking-Stool* (Durham, N. C., 1944).

Games involve the display of skill, depend upon chance, or dramatize events and ceremonies of adult life. The last category includes possible recollections of ancient rituals like well-worship, divination, marriage ceremonies, or border warfare. Games exist in five forms: the actors may divide into two lines, form a circle, perform individually the parts of a little play, raise an arch through which others pass, or wind and unwind in serpentine fashion.

Literature: Alice B. Gomme, *The Traditional Games of England, Scotland, and Ireland* (London 1894–98); E. L. Rochholz, *Alemannisches Kinderlied und Kinderspiel* (Leipzig, 1857), with mythological interpretations; F. M. Böhme, *Deutsches Kinderlied und Kinderspiel* (Leipzig, 1897), a rich collection with abundant historical and comparative notes; Johann

Lewalter and George Schläger, *Deutsches Kinderlied und Kinderspiel in Kassel* (Kassel, 1911), with exhaustive notes; S. T. Thyregod *Danmarks sanglege* (Copenhagen, 1931), with musical texts, pictures, and references to English and German parallels. *Discussion:* Henry Bett, *The Games of Children* (London, 1929); Yrjö Hirn, *Barnlek* (Helsingfors, 1916).

Customs Customs are associated with the course of human life, especially with birth, marriage, and death, with domestic activities, and with seasons and particular days. They take the form of symbolic acts or definite traditional procedures.

Customs associated with birth, marriage, and death often retain traces of pre-Christian thought. After a death in a family, the bees are told of the event or a mirror is turned to the wall. Samter points out a striking similarity in the customs associated with birth, marriage, and death and explains it by the idea of rituals signifying a transition from one status to another. Customs may involve animistic thinking which ascribes life to inanimate objects or human powers to animals. Some trace such ideas to the spirits of the dead who survive near their graves as creatures living in the ground or trees. Other customs and stories are explained by the notion of the living corpse. This idea that a mysterious and terrifying life continues in a dead body expresses itself in breaking the skull or bones of a dead man and in deserting or burning a house where death has occurred. Cremation, which is explained in a later rationalization as setting free an aerial soul, probably also arose from the fear of the living corpse and the need to destroy it. Dwarfs and demons appear in shapes that suggest a corpse: they are silent, shrunken, aged, stiff, and discolored. Sympathetic magic, which uses an analogy between two things or events, is often present in customs. Crops are planted when the moon is waxing in order that they may grow better. Customs and superstitions associated with them have a position intermediate between the folklore of acts and the folklore of words. The words explaining such a symbolic or superstitious act as throwing spilt salt over one's shoulder or knocking on wood are not necessarily traditional, although the idea is. Many customs and superstitions have bases in fact: the discovery of a drowned man's body sunk in a stream by floating a loaf of bread on the water utilizes the fact that the loaf also follows the course of the current.

Special customs and beliefs are connected with the seasons and many individual days. Those associated with the seasons are, for the most part, concerned with planting or harvesting crops. The customs belonging to such days as New Year's Day, Valentine's Day, All Fools' Day, Easter, St. John's Day, Lady Day, Hallowe'en, and Christmas may be either pre-Christian or Christian in origin. They have reference to many affairs of domestic and social life. The groundhog's shadow on Groundhog Day and the weather on St. Swithin's Day forecast the weather to be expected. The old idea that March 25 is the beginning of the year is retained in the customs and stories of St. Mark's Day. The fires of St. John's Day represent partially Christianized ritual, and many practices belonging to the days before and after Christmas mingle heathendom and Christianity inextricably.

Literature: Handwörterbuch des deutschen Aberglaubens; John Brand, *Observations on Popular Antiquities,* ed. Henry Ellis (London, 1842); Ernst Samter, *Geburt, Hochzeit und Tod* (Leipzig, 1911); T. F. T. Dyer, *British Popular Customs* (London, 1876). Useful miscellaneous material in W. Hone, *Everyday Book, Table Book, Year Book* (London, 1826–27); and R. Chambers, *The Book of Days:* a miscellany of popular antiquities in connection with the calendar (London, 1862–64). Encyclopedic treatment in Paul Sartori, *Sitte und Brauch* (Leipzig, 1910–14).

Folklore of words The folklore of words apart from connected discourse is found chiefly in names. Place names, which are most actively studied, reveal fashions of name-giving that disclose the history of migrations, the making of settlements, and the practice of heathen cults. In Scandinavia, the names of rivers and, in Germany, the names of fields have been separately collected and studied.

Literature: Publications of the English Place-Name Society. Journals: *Namn och Bygd; Zeitschrift für Ortsnamenforschung. Discussion:* B. M. Olsen, *Farms and Fanes of Ancient Norway* (Oslo, 1928).

Collections of family names are available for all the Germanic languages. Some are merely lists, others give etymologies or tell when and where the names have been used. Since names are easily borrowed and are not completely subject to the rules of linguistic developments applicable to common nouns, etymologies are very risky unless supported by abundant historical evidence. The use of family names arose in the late Middle Ages, and those now in use show the manner of life prevailing at the time. The so-called imperative names formed like Shakespeare by compounding a verb and a noun abound in Germany and are found in smaller numbers in other Germanic countries. Since they probably contain, in most instances, a sentence like, "I shake a spear," which was characteristically used by the original bearer of the name or was applied to him, they are better known as sentence-names. Collections of family names and treatises on them are too numerous to mention here.

Many Christian names like Grete, Hans, George, and their derivatives like G. I. Joe, have popular associations that belong to folklore. Although the original meaning of Margareta was very honorable, the contraction Grete had unpleasant associations in Reformation Germany that may be connected with the choice of the name Gretchen in Goethe's *Faust*. These associations, which belong to folklore, are more often felt than listed in formal manner. The use of certain Christian names, especially those of saints, reveals cultural and folklore currents. The originally English Oswald was, for example, carried to Germany by early missionaries and spread from the monasteries in western Germany to Austria, where it is perhaps more popular now than in other regions. The Swiss scholar E. A. Stückelberger has studied such dynamic traditions in Christian names.

Adequate collections of nicknames, especially collections giving the necessary historical information about age, use, and connotation, are lacking. Leonard Bloomfield has suggested orally that many nicknames referred originally to instruments having various uses and were not corruptions of the names with which they are now associated. The name of the instrument has been transferred to the person as a nickname. In other words, the *bob* of *plumb-bob* and the *jack* of *bootjack* may be the original meanings of the nicknames of Robert and John. Many nicknames have become obsolete and many have special connotations.

Literature: A. R. Frey, *Sobriquets and Nicknames* (London, 1888).

As the lack of a good English equivalent of the French *blason populaire* indicates, this concept, which is allied to the nickname, is not clearly isolated in English use. Examples are nevertheless abundant in Germanic folklore. Certain names or adjectives are traditionally used with particular places or peoples like Merry England, the mad Irish. The origin and history of such phrases are often difficult to discover.

Plant and animal names often preserve superstitious beliefs. The word *bear* is not Indo-European, but is a substitute for the animal's original name, which was akin to the Latin *ursus*. The use of such a substitute probably reflects an ancient hunter's tabu against mentioning the creature. Allusions to heathen gods in plant names (less often in animal names) do not necessarily go back to heathendom. They may be deliberate archaizing of Christian names and may be derived from a post-Renaissance interest in heathen antiquities.

Literature: Van Wijk, *A Dictionary of Plant Names* (The Hague, 1912–16).

Names of sickness often contain echoes of superstitious ideas or allusions to traditional themes like St. Vitus' Dance for epilepsy.

Literature: Max Höfler, *Deutsches Krankheitsnamenbuch* (Munich, 1889).

Calls to animals Calls to animals are traditional. The words for summoning, frightening away, or guiding animals vary from region to region and according to the kind of animal. Cats, dogs, cows, and chickens are spoken to in different ways. The terms *Gee!*, *Haw!*, and *Whoa!* are not in universal use in English and have different meanings in different places. Every well-behaved parrot knows "Polly wants a cracker."

Literature: H. C. Bolton, "The Language used in talking to Domestic Animals," *American Anthropologist,* X (1897): 65–90; 97–143.

Oaths, greetings, exclamations, toasts, funerary inscriptions, and other conventional formulas have a place between the folklore of individual words and the folklore of connected discourse. Except for collections of epitaphs, which are usually the object of sentimental and curious interest rather than of study as tradition, little has been done to collect or discuss these formulas. Such references to the suffering of Christ on the Cross as *Zounds!* and *Zooks!* belong to a fashion of swearing that became obsolete about the end of the 17th century. B. J. Whiting has collected examples of oaths taken on someone's soul.

Literature: Julian Sharman, *A Cursory History of Swearing* (London, 1884); Robert Graves, *Lars Porsena or the Future of Swearing and Improper Language* (London, rev. ed. 1936); B. J. Whiting, " 'By my Fader Soule'," *Jour. of English and German Philology,* XLVIV (1945): 1–8. *Epitaphs:* William Andrews, *Curious Epitaphs* (London, 1899); W. H. Beable, *Epitaphs: Graveyard Humor and Elegy* (London, [1925]).

Folklore in connected discourse can be conveniently divided into verse and prose, and verse in turn, into children's songs and folk songs. Children's songs exist in many imperfectly recognized categories that cannot always be separated from games. Arranged according to the age of the child, children's songs comprise lullabies, rimes to count the fingers and toes (*This little pig went to market*) or the features of the face (chinchopper rimes), dandling rimes (*Here we go to Banbury Cross*), mocking rimes (*Georgie Porgie, pudding and pie*), counting-out rimes (*Eenie Meenie Minie Mo*), divinations (*One I love, two I love . . .*), skip-rope rimes, rimes for the days of the week or the letters of the alphabet, and many others. The origin and history of these types and of the individual songs are very obscure. A very curious and important feature of Germanic folklore is the development in English of a canon, which is not too strictly defined, of children's rimes in the collection called *Mother Goose.* Although the contents of this collection vary from edition to edition, there is a generally recognized core of texts. With some obvious exceptions, the interpretations of Mother Goose rimes as allusions to events and figures in English history is dubious.

Literature: See *Games* above. *General collections of English children's songs:* J. O. Halliwell, *Nursery Rhymes of England* (5th ed., London, 1886); *Gammer Gurton's Garland* (London, 1810, repr. 1866); G. F. Northall, *English Folk-Rhymes* (London, 1892). *Prayers:* F. Ohrt, *Gamle danske folkebonner* (Copenhagen, 1928), including English parallels. *Counting out rimes:* H. C. Bolton, *The Counting-Out Rhymes of Children* (London, 1888). *General treatises:* Lina Eckenstein, *Comparative Studies in Nursery Rhymes* (London, 1906); Henry Bett, *Nursery Rhymes and Tales* (New York, 1924). *Mother Goose:* W. A. Wheeler, *The Original Mother Goose's Melody* (Boston, 1892); Katherine Thomas, *The Real Personages of Mother Goose* (Boston, 1930); D. E. Marvin, *Historic Child Rhymes* (Norwell, Mass., 1930).

Folk song Folk song falls into the categories of lyric and narrative songs, which are both characterized by traditional words, situations, themes, and music. Comparatively little English lyric song has been collected. The German Schnaderhüpfel, a quatrain consisting of two distichs, of which the first describes a scene in nature and the second a mood, is current in southern Germany and has parallels in Scandinavia and also outside of Germanic territory. Singers often engage in contests of matching these quatrains.

Literature: W. D. Hand, *The Schnaderhüpfel: an Alpine folk lyric* (Diss., Chicago, 1936).

Ballad The ballad, a narrative song in stanzas, often with a refrain, told in an objective, lyrical manner, apparently arose in the late Middle Ages. It is restricted in its currency to western Europe. In form and subject-matter it differs from Spanish romances and eastern European (Greek or Russian) narrative song. Although the earliest recorded ballads deal with religious subjects, this fact does not necessarily demonstrate a clerical origin of genre. Some ballads have Germanic heroic legends as themes, others are related to medieval romances, and others tell of border warfare or other historical events. Scholars have hotly disputed the extent to which the folk has created and shaped the ballad.

Literature: Collections: F. J. Child, *English and Scottish Popular Ballads* (Boston, 1882–98); L. Erk and F. M. Böhme, *Deutscher Liederhort* (Leipzig, 1893–94); John Meyer, *Deutsche Volkslieder* (Berlin, 1935–); N. F. S. Grundtvig, *Danmarks gamle Folkeviser* (Copenhagen, 1853–). *Journals: Journal of the English Folk-Dance and Folk-Song Society; Das deutsche Volkslied; Jahrbuch des deutschen Volkslieds. Discussion:* G. H. Gerould, *The Ballad of Tradition;* W. J. Entwistle, *European Balladry* (Oxford, 1939); Louise Pound, *Poetic Origins and the Ballad* (New York, 1921).

Songs which can be ascribed to known authors and those which exhibit a very humble literary craftsmanship often use the conventions belonging to the ballads. Circulated as broadsides by wandering singers they often give the details of a recent notorious event, especially the execution of a criminal or the circumstances of a disaster. They stand on the fringe of folklore.

Literature: Collections: Publications of the Ballad Society; Hyder E. Rollins, *The Pepys Ballads* (Cambridge, Mass., 1929–32); Rochus von Liliencron, *Die Historischen Lieder der Deutschen* (Leipzig, 1865–69).

Folktales Folktales are of many kinds and can best be separated according to the intentions of the teller. Tales are told to amuse, to impart moral lessons, to explain the origins and shapes of natural objects including plants and animals, to inform the hearer about a historical or supernatural event. Some minor varieties are told for the sake of their forms rather than their contents.

The fairy tale, which does not necessarily include a fairy among the actors and is therefore better called a *märchen,* is the most important variety of tale told for amusement. It has a conventional form, consisting of introductory and concluding formulas and a biography of the hero that ends with his happy marriage. The incidents often occur in a threefold repetition that exhibits slight variations in the three stages. They usually involve magic or supernatural elements. The examples, like Puss in Boots, Cinderella, The Two Brothers, or Faithful John, often have an international distribution. Berendsohn suggests that there is an older type having two actors in which the threefold repetition is less characteristic.

Jests Jests, which ordinarily consist of a single incident, can be best classified according to their themes. The noodle story (The Wise Men of Gotham, Schildbürgers), the stories of the literal execution of commands (Eulenspiegel), and tall tales (Münchhausen) often group themselves about a single actor. In similar fashion, stories about witchcraft have gathered about Dr. Faustus. Tales about priests and married couples and stories with realistic emphasis are often closely connected with Italian novelle.

Fables Tales conveying a moral lesson are represented by the fable, a form that does not seem to have enjoyed much traditional currency among Germanic peoples.

Etiological tales Etiological tales explain why the bear has no tail or why the aspen continually shakes (Judas hanged himself on it). They apparently belong to a very ancient cultural level, but their number has been increased by narratives based on incidents drawn from Christian history like the story of the baker's daughter who refused to give bread to Christ and hid under a trough, which she must henceforth carry on her back.

Literature: Oskar Dähnhardt, *Natursagen* (Leipzig, 1907–12).

Sagen Tales partaking of the nature of history are called Sagen or local and historical legends. They constitute a characteristic and very abundant variety of Germanic

folklore. The subject-matter includes on the one hand stories of the Devil, water sprites, forest women, giants, dwarfs, cobolds, ghosts, and other supernatural creatures in their relations to men, and on the other hand stories about historical figures. The legend of the Wild Hunt, a ghostly company that races across the sky at various seasons in all Germanic countries, is one of the most impressive Germanic legends. It occurs in an ennobled form in the myth of the ride of the Valkyries. The previously mentioned ideas of animism and the living corpses are frequently found in these legends. The stories about historical figures (Charlemagne and the ring of Fastrada, Martin Luther throwing the inkwell at the Devil, Frederick the Great and the miller of Sans Souci) exhibit the alterations of fact and the additions of fancy that characterize folklore.

Saints' legends belong more to international tradition than to Germanic folklore.

Certain folktales are more interesting for their form than for their contents. The cantefable, which mingles verse and narrative, is rather poorly represented in Germanic folklore. Formula tales appear in the cumulative type of The House that Jack Built and The Old Woman and Her Pig, the circular type represented by rounds, and the endless tale.

Literature: Stith Thompson, *The Folktale* (New York, 1946); J. Bolte and G. Polívka, *Anmerkungen zu den Kinder- und Hausmärchen* (Leipzig, 1913–32), especially volumes IV and V.

Riddles The loosely used term riddle includes many varieties of verbal puzzles. In a strict sense, a riddle is a comparison of two unrelated things like the equating of an egg to a man in Humpty-Dumpty. Its wit lies in the aptness of the comparison and the disclosure that the hearer has misapprehended its meaning. Obscene implications are frequent in riddles. Riddles are often in verse. Other varieties of puzzles are the shrewd or witty question, which calls for information about a Biblical figure (Who was not born and yet died?—Adam), the answer to an arithmetical problem (If a hen and a half lays an egg and a half in a day and a half, how many hens will lay a dozen eggs?), and the explanation of a complicated family relationship, or some other fact. There are also whimsical or humorous versions of such questions: "What did Samson die of?—Fallen arches." The conundrum depends upon a pun: "Why is a cherry like a book?—Because it is red." Another variety of puzzle asks, "What is the difference between . . . and . . . ?" A few questions offering a choice between something apparently attractive and something apparently disgusting are reported in English, and more occur in other Germanic languages. The apparently disgusting object turns out to be the better choice. Narrative elements appear in the neck-riddle, which is a puzzle set by a man who gains his freedom or his life by setting an insoluble puzzle. Since he chooses to describe a situation known only to himself, no one can guess his meaning. An example is "On Ilo I walk, on Ilo I stand, Ilo I hold fast in my hand.—The man has made shoes and gloves of the skin of his dog Ilo." The story or puzzle of the burning barn uses incomprehensible words to describe an event, usually the burning of a barn or the driving of a goat from a cabbage patch. It may be ultimately related to tabus on words that a particular person must not utter.

Literature: Archer Taylor, *A Bibliography of Riddles* (Helsinki, 1939). *Discussion:* Robert Petsch, *Das deutsche Volksrätsel* (Strassburg, 1917); Kenneth Jackson and E. Wilson, "The Barn is Burning," *Folk-Lore* XLVII (1936): 190–202.

Charms Charms are formulas used to cure sickness, heal a wound, restore stolen property, or effect other beneficial or harmful results. They consist of an act alone or of an act and traditional formulas. The act may involve the principle of sympathetic magic. The words, which are often in verse, employ various conventions, especially the notion of counting down to zero, whereupon the wart is commanded to vanish as the numbers have vanished, or the comparison to an event, which is usually chosen from Christian history, as for example the comparison of the stopping of the River Jordan when Christ was baptized to the desired result, the halting of a hemorrhage.

Literature: F. Gredon, "The Anglo-Saxon Charms," *Journal of American Folklore* XXII (1909): 105–237; T. O. Cockayne, *Leechdoms, Wort-Cunning, and Starcraft of Early England* (London, 1864–66); Ferdinand Ohrt, *Danmarks trylleformler* (Copenhagen, 1917–21); Emmanuel Linderholm, *Signelser ock besvärjelser från medeltid ock nytid* (Stockholm, 1927–40). *Discussion:* Oskar Ebermann, *Blut- und Wundsegen* (Berlin, 1902); F. Ohrt, *Trylleord* (Copenhagen, 1922). For individual charms see the *Handwörterbuch des deutschen Aberglaubens*.

Proverbs Proverbs are aphoristic sayings that enjoy traditional currency. They may be statements of fact like "All's well that ends well" or descriptions of scenes like "New brooms sweep clean" that are used in a transferred moral application to a particular situation. Although proverbs are often credited to a particular inventor like Solomon, their origins are almost always obscure and ascriptions are very unreliable. Some statements of fact that do not involve a moral application have become proverbial, especially forecasts of the weather (Mackerel sky, mackerel sky, never long wet and never long dry) and formulations of the law (Two words to a bargain). A curious proverbial variety called the Wellerism couples an assertion with an identification of the speaker and often adds a suggestion of the scene as in " 'Everyone to his taste,' said the farmer and kissed the cow." An investigation of Wellerisms current in southern Sweden has traced many of them to actual recent events, but many Wellerisms must be explained in other ways. Some proverbs are rimed, and many exhibit a characteristic structural parallelism. Proverbial phrases are usually confused with proverbs, but should be regarded as a separate variety of traditional speech. They lack the complete rigidity of a proverb and may vary according to tense and person. They frequently contain a reference to a custom, belief, or the details of a human activity. Examples are "to have an ace in the hole," "to be left at the post," or "to put on the screws."

Literature: Collections: G. L. Apperson, *English Proverbs and Proverbial Sayings* (London, 1929); W. G. Smith, *The Oxford Book of English Proverbs* (Oxford, 1935); K. F. W. Wander, *Deutsches Sprichwörter-Lexikon* (Leipzig, 1867–80); Samuel Singer, *Sprichwörter des Mittelalters*, I (Berne, 1944), II (1946), III (1946), with invaluable references to medieval versions. F. A. Stoett, *Nederlandsche spreekwoorden* (4th ed., Zutphen, 1923–

25), contains abundant English and German comparative material. *Discussion and Bibliography:* Wilfred Bonser and T. A. Stephens, *Proverb Literature* (London, 1930); Friedrich Seiler, *Deutsche Sprichwörterkunde* (Munich, 1922) and *Das deutsche Sprichwort* (Strassburg, 1918); Archer Taylor, *The Proverb* (Cambridge, Mass., 1930).   ARCHER TAYLOR

Geryon's oxen In Greek legend, the superb red cattle of the three-headed (or three-bodied) monster Geryon, which Hercules brought back to Eurystheus from the island of Erytheia in the farthest west as the tenth of his labors. Geryon was king of the island (perhaps the same as Hesperia, and at any rate west of Spain) and herded his cattle with those of Hades. Hercules, building the Pillars of Hercules, became overheated by the sun and, angered, shot arrows at Helios. Amused, or perhaps frightened (for the arrows were poisoned), the sun gave him his golden cup in which he sailed to the island. To take the cattle Hercules had to kill Geryon's dog Orthrus, his herdsman Eurytion, and Geryon himself. Many incidents famous locally in Spain, France, and Italy occurred on his voyage and return in the golden cup of the sun, especially the setting up of the Pillars of Hercules and the slaying of Cacus at Rome. The cattle were finally sacrificed to Hera by Eurystheus.

gestures Folklore is not limited to writing or speech for its transmission or preservation. Since gestures are motions made or positions assumed to convey or emphasize an idea or an emotion, it is natural that certain easily made and useful gestures become stereotyped and are passed down within cultures and from tribe to tribe for many generations.

In gestures particularly, however, the use of identical signs in two or more tribes which have had communication does not necessarily imply borrowing, for the signs which can be made by the human body and its parts are obviously limited, and neural response patterns are bound to be similar among all races.

Moreover, since some primitive gestures probably antedated both writing and speech and were employed when members of different-language tribes first met, they persist as important auxiliary communication devices, especially in such hybrid languages as pidgin English, lingua franca, sabir, beche-de-mer, Yiddish, Canuck, Swahili, and Romany. A similar intermixture of words and gestures is observable in many of the game rimes recited and acted by children—dramatized rimes which form a sort of international language of their own. (See EENY, MEENY, MINY, MO.)

Interesting and ingenious action-languages, composed entirely of gestures, have developed in societies and groups where oral or written communication was tabu, impossible, or unwise.

Among the Warramunga of central Australia, silence is a form of mourning required for a year or two of all female relatives of a deceased male, even to remote collateral degrees of consanguinity, with the result that a majority of the tribal women are usually condemned to keep silent. Consequently, the women have become remarkably proficient in a unique gesture language built upon elbow positions and motions with some assistance from the arms and hands.

Frazer, who cites this (*Folklore in the Old Testament* III: 71 ff.) and other instances of the imposition of silence upon widows in such separated regions as British

Columbia, California, the Congo, and Madagascar, infers from the fact that the Hebrew word for widow is *almanah*—silent one—that a similar tabu anciently obtained among the Israelites. He has etymology, parallels in comparative folklore, and the frequent use of gesture by Jewish women, to strengthen his theory. But the oldest literary and historical evidence indicates that the "silent ones" did not confine the expression of their grief to sign language, but "lifted up their voices and wept."

The Warramunga widows perfected what was really a parallel system to the wigwagging of Boy Scouts and sailors and the semaphores of railroads, two modern gesture languages.

One thinks immediately, of course, of the sign languages of the American Indians and the several systems used by deaf-mutes. A closer parallel to the Warramunga women's language of silence, because it is also the result of a religious tabu, is the method of gesture communication used by Cistercian and Benedictine monks. (See *The Language of Gesture* by Macdonald Critchley, N.Y., 1939.)

Related to the more developed gesture languages and similarly connected usually with religion either directly or indirectly were the formalized stage gestures of the ancient dramas of India, Greece, Rome, and China. These included postures as well as motional gestures and have their counterpart in the meticulously observed attitudes of worship depicted on Sumerian seals of the 4th millenium B.C., as well as the formalized obeisances of submission on bas-reliefs of ancient Egypt, Babylonia, and Assyria. The many *asanas*, or postures, of Hindu yoga are little known in the Western world, but for the *padmasana*, the Buddha pose of the interlocked feet with soles uppermost, which conveys even to the uninitiated the idea of complete composure.

Parallel are the many postures, gestures, and signs used in the ceremonies and devotions of the various branches of the Christian church, especially the Greek and Roman Catholic divisions. There are several "reverences" of which the best known are the genuflections of the Latins before the Blessed Sacrament and the metanies of the Byzantine Catholics in the same presence.

Genuflections of the ordinary sort are a quick bending of the right knee until it touches the floor, and are made by both laity and clergy upon many stated occasions. The double genuflection consists of kneeling upon both knees, bowing the head, and then rising to one's feet: it is made only before the exposed Blessed Sacrament.

Metanies (from the Greek *metanoia*, repentance) are bowings of three carefully differentiated depths: the "salutation" which simply inclines the head and shoulders, the lesser metany which is a bow low enough to permit the right hand to descend to the level of the knees, and the greater metany which is a complete prostration requiring considerable physical agility and suppleness since the forehead, hands and feet must touch the floor, but no other part of the body. (See *A Catholic Dictionary*, Attwater, 1941, p. 339.)

Ordinands, candidates for ordination as deacons, priests, and bishops, must prostrate themselves until flat on the ground, or kneel with the head touching the ground.

Kissing, as a gesture, has had a long evolution in Christianity from the early church where it was customary to "greet all the brethren with a holy kiss," through the period when it was correct (as it still is in the Eastern Church) to kiss the newly baptized and the celebrants of the Eucharist, until later when men could kiss only men and women only women, and finally when only the clergy exchange ceremonial kisses and the people are permitted to kiss the osculatorium—a relic or cross carried to them for the purpose. There are many other liturgical and extra-liturgical kisses applied to the altar, the gospels, the paten, the cruets, palms, candles, rings, the hands of celebrants, and the foot and knee of the pope.

Moslems have for centuries kissed the sacred Kaaba stone at Mecca. Idols of the gods were kissed by early Greeks and Romans. The toe of St. Peter's statue has been worn down by Roman Christian kisses.

Baptism has been a practically universal gesture in many religions and throughout human history for the removal of the tabus surrounding birth, including the second birth of conversion or initiation.

Originally a part of baptism, the making of the sign of the cross was intended to seal the Christian in baptism and to protect him from demons and witches. In early Christian times it was simply performed by drawing an imaginary cross on the forehead with the forefinger. It was later varied by using the thumb dipped in oil or holy water. Today the person who "crosses himself" usually does so by holding together the finger tips and thumb of the right hand and with them touching the forehead, breast, left shoulder, and right shoulder in that order while repeating, "In the name of the Father and of the Son and of the Holy Ghost." Eastern Christians use only the thumb and first two fingers and make the sign from right to left.

Less obviously religious but with connotations of protective magic are the other crosses, such as crossing fingers indicating mental reservations, crossing the Gipsy's palm with silver to learn your future, and the "cross-my-heart-hope-to-die" gesture of the children, a sacred affirmation which may antedate Christianity.

Critchley reports 150 signs and gestures collected from American school children, but few of them have any great significance for students of folklore, such as scratching or shaking the head.

The cocksnook or snook, thumbing the nose in insult, is widespread and has many variations. Sometimes the fingers are vibrated; again, the second hand is added, either side by side or tandem, to double the insult; in rare cases the ears are similarly thumbed. There may easily have originally been an idea of negating or counteracting bad magic.

The fig, or fico, made by putting the thumb between the index and middle fingers, or even by inserting the thumb in the mouth, is closely related to the cocksnook in popular usage as an insult or sign of contempt, and is of undoubted religious origin, for it is still used in some cultures as a means of warding off the evil eye. It has obvious phallic connotations and perhaps phallic origination. It is significant that it is sometimes used to intimate cuckoldry.

The making of the sign of the horns by extending the first and fourth fingers while retaining the second and third in the palm also indicates cuckoldry: yet it, too, is said to counteract the evil eye.

Spitting and pointing are important gestures in primitive and juvenile groups. Puckett reports that some southern U. S. Negroes believe pointing at a grave will result in your getting the finger cut off, or a ghost will chase you, or you will die, but these dire effects can be avoided if you quickly spit on your fingers. In Yorkshire you shouldn't point at the stars.

Scraping the left forefinger with the right is a sign of shame for the person at whom the left one is pointed, and is evidently based on the almost universal idea that the left hand is really "sinister."

The holding aloft of the boxing victor's hand and the "pollice verso" thumb down for the vanquished gladiator doubtless originally had celestial and infernal significance. See MIME.   CHARLES FRANCIS POTTER

Gēush Urvan, Gōshūrūn, or **Gōshūrvan** In Iranian cosmological mythology, the soul of the primeval bull which contained the germs of the animal species and of useful plants; the fifth creation and the sole-created animate being. Gēush Urvan is usually described as a bull, sometimes as a female. The bull was slain by Angra Mainyu after living 3,000 years according to the *Bundahishn*. In another legend, it was slain by Mithra who plunged his hunting knife into its flank. From its limbs grew 12 kinds of medicinal plants and 55 species of grain. From the seminal energy of the bull came a cow and a bull followed by 282 pairs of animals. Gēush Urvan, its soul or travashi, went to heaven as the guardian of·animals. Compare AUDHUMLA; YMIR.

ghost A disembodied spirit. The term is usually applied to the human soul after death, and is used interchangeably with such words as phantom, specter, shade, spook, apparition, revenant. See REVENANT.

ghost dance A dance of communication with the spirits of the dead. As a masked impersonation it is discussed under DEATH DANCE and CLOWNS. As a mystic communion it usually arises in times of stress. This form at times normally develops in ancient tribal ceremonies, as the Bon Odori, the invitation to the dead in a Japanese dance (Shinto), or the Blackfoot Indian dance for the spirits of the dead. But the successive messianic cults of the American West, culminating in the ghost dance religion, were an escape from the intolerable circumstances, cultural disintegration, and starvation due to the avidity of the white man.

Several revivals preceded the great ghost dance: a southern wave about 1800, started by the Shawnee prophet, Tenskwatawa, and adopted by southern tribes, the Cherokee, the Creeks, as well as the Kickapoo and Miami; on Puget Sound, the dream cult of Smohalla, chief of the Wanapûm; and in 1881 the Indian Shaker church started by Squaxin, John Slocum or Squsacht-un, with its admixture of Catholic ritual. Before 1870 Tävito, a Paiute of Nevada, initiated a ghost dance wave which affected the adjacent tribes of California and filtered into the Hesi cult. Living conditions were at the proper stage of disintegration among the Modoc, Shasta, Karok and Tolowa; less so among the Yurok, Pomo, Wintun, and valley Maidu. The new religion was distinguished (among the Pomo), as·*maru he*, from an ancient ghost religion, *hintil he; boli* or human spirits, were distinct from *saltu*, the ancient divinities.

About 1889 the son of Tävito, Jack Wilson or Wovoka (the Cutter), had a revelation during a fever and an eclipse of the sun. Like his predecessors he foretold a regeneration of the earth, reunion with the beloved dead, a life of aboriginal happiness without disease, misery, or white men. He preached good will, denounced lying, fighting, or destructive mourning customs. What/with the virtual extermination of the buffalo and the prevalence of whisky, the prairie tribes sought salvation in this doctrine and in the dance that brought anticipation of the blessed state and visions of the deceased. It spread first to the nearby Bannock and Shoshoni tribes of Nevada and Wyoming, then to the most receptive Arapaho and other Oklahoma tribes, the Kiowa Apache, Cheyenne, and Pawnee, then to the Sioux of Dakota. Less affected were the Ute and Comanche, still less the Walapai, Havasupai, Mohave and Navaho, not at all the stable Pueblo Indians. Woodland tribes were little affected, except indirectly through the grass dance and dream dance.

All ages—men, women and children—joined. After a purificatory sweat bath and ceremonial painting with sacred red ocher, increasingly larger circles sang without drum, and shuffled left with a dragging step. Each song completed a circuit. Fingers were intertwined, and released only in trance. Hypnotists in the center watched for the first trembling; they waved a feather or kerchief before the subject's eyes crying "hu-hu-hu," till she or he staggered into the center. A spasmodic dance ended in rigidity and final collapse. Strictly, four nights every six weeks were devoted to these ceremonies.

In each tribe native mythology and customs varied the pattern. The Yurok removed planking from graves. The Paiute, who called it *nänigükwa* or "dance in a circle," did not practice the trance hypnotism. The Sioux, who called it *wana'ghi wa'chipi* or "spirit dance," wore a special ghost dance shirt. They introduced an element of hostility against white men into this peaceable religion. Ample provocation and interference with the religion led to disasters as the massacre of Wounded Knee. The Sioux were the last tribe to adhere.

Among all tribes except the Sioux the effects were beneficial. Though disappointment followed non-fulfilment, the teachings and the psychotherapy brought temporary improvement. [GPK]

ghoul (Arabic *ghul*; feminine *ghulah*) A demonic being that feeds on human bodies, either corpses stolen from graves or young children. Ghouls inhabit lonely places, especially graveyards: the Arabic ghul of the wasteland seems to be a personification of the terror of the desert. The ghoul may be compared with other cannibalistic vampirelike creatures: the Lilith, Lamia, Yogini, Baba Yaga, etc. Generally the whole of the Moslem world, from India to Africa, knows the ghoul.

giants References to giants are frequent in Eskimo and North American Indian mythologies. Giants may be either human, or animal, or bird in form; usually, but not always, they are males, and almost always they are cannibalistically inclined. The pre-Eskimo Tornit of Central Eskimo mythology were giants; Big Owl of the Southwestern United States is either a huge cannibal bird or a giant humanlike creature. The tale of a giant bird (roc) who carries a boy to a cliff is widespread in North America, as are also the tales of the giant Thunderbirds and of the giant monster who sucks in his victims. Test tales, widespread in native North America, contain references to giants of several descriptions. In the Eastern Woodlands the Shawnee female deity has four giant "boys" who can smell human beings from afar. On the North Pacific Coast, tales of cannibal giants are especially popular. In one such, a giantess who abducts children is killed, but because her soul is outside her body, she revives; the fugitives however escape. In another cannibal giant tale of the North Pacific Coast and Plains the cannibal is burned; the ashes become mosquitoes. [EWV]

According to a famous legend heard by the Spaniards in Ecuador, a race of giants landed in a distant past near Santa Elena. These giants bored a deep well into the hard rock. After killing their women and those of the Indians, they resorted to sodomy, thus arousing the wrath of the gods who destroyed them with lightning. Fossil bones abundant in that neighborhood were attributed to them. [AM]

la gielosia An Italian dance for four couples with mime of jealousy. The folk dance goes back to court *ballo* of the 16th century, a lively dance with hops. The first gentleman dances successively with the lady of the other couples in the row; between changes the group dances *tempi di piva tedesca* with parading for the ladies and turns and jumps for the men. The motif of partner change, a commonplace in European folk dances, has its counterpart in aboriginal dances of the Dinka on the Nile and in the North American Iroquois Indian Alligator dance. It may relate to the licentious exchanges during post-ceremonial feasts. [GPK]

Gigantes In Greek mythology, a race of giants sprung from Earth (Ge) when the blood of the mutilated Uranus fell on her: probably a group of early deities or of inhabitants of Greece, like the Cyclopes, of which the myth is a recollection. The Gigantes were monstrous, huge creatures, with serpents for feet: this is post-Homeric, Homer apparently looking on them as a savage race of men. The Gigantes were induced by Ge to attack the Olympians with rocks and brands made of whole trees. According to what the Olympians were told, the Gigantes were invincible so long as they were able to use a certain herb, and even without the herb could not be defeated unless a mortal aided the gods. There were also individual difficulties to overcome, as for example the giant Alcyoneus being unslayable on his native land. Ge obtained possession of the herb, but Zeus countered by ordering Eos and Helios not to shine and took the herb in the darkness. Then, with the aid of Hercules, the Olympians defeated the giants, burying them in various places in the earth. Alcyoneus was slain by Hercules after the hero dragged him to another land than his own. The Gigantes thus seem to be a sort of earth-spirits, responsible for such phenomena as earthquakes and volcanoes, with which latter they are especially associated. Compare ALOADÆ; CYCLOPS; GIANTS; MONSTERS; RAKSHASAS; TITANS; TYPHON.

Gilgamesh The great hero of Sumerian and Babylonian epic poetry: precursor of Hercules and other folk heroes. See SEMITIC MYTHOLOGY.

Gilles de Laval, Marshal of Retz (1404–1440) One of the persons thought to have been the "original" villain in Perrault's version of *Bluebeard*. Another candidate is Commore the Cursed, also a Breton chief, in this case of the 6th century. Stories about Gilles de Retz,

who led an adventurous life, was associated with Joan of Arc in her battles and coronation, and got involved with the alchemists, still persist in Brittany. Objections to the identification are that the fantasies of young women who think they are married to cruel monsters with designs on their lives are recorded in hundreds of folktales and in the records of most psychiatrists. Large black men with blue beards are generally thought to be virile, seductive, and dangerous to women. The particular objection to Gilles de Retz as the villain is that he had only one wife who survived him and that he was scandalously fond of torturing young boys. [RDJ]

Gimokodan The Bagobo (Philippine Islands) afterworld which lies below the earth. Gimokodan is divided into two sections, one red for those killed in combat, the other like the upperworld but with everything reversed. At the entrance to Gimokodan is the Black River where the gimokod (spirit) bathes in order to forget its former life. There, also, is a giant female covered with nipples who suckles the spirits of infants. After the spirits have entered Gimokodan they move about as they did on earth, but only during the hours of darkness. When the afterworld grows light, each spirit makes a boat-shaped dish for itself from the leaves of a tree and is dissolved into a liquid in it. When darkness returns the spirit resumes its form and activities. Compare BELET.

Ginem A Bagobo (Philippine Islands) ceremony held in December to thank the spirits for success in domestic affairs and war, to drive off the buso, to ward off illness, and to gratify the spirits so that they will favor the people in the future. Formerly the Bagobo went on a skull raid before the Ginem and the spoils were tied to ceremonial poles and dedicated to Mandarangan and Darago. Today offerings such as clothes and knives are made and the spirits are asked, in return, to grant a good harvest and health. Then the poles, now used without skulls, are decorated, carried into the datu's house, and a chicken is sacrificed. Each maganí (a person who has killed two or more persons) then confesses his warlike deeds. A feast, dancing, and songs follow until dawn. In the areas where this ceremony lasts longer than one day the celebration on the succeeding days consists primarily of feasting.

ginger The pungent, spicy rootstock of a tropical plant (*Zingiber officinale*). This spice has been cultivated in the East since time immemorial and is now also grown in the American tropics. Probably indigenous to China, ginger is used throughout the world as a spice. It is chewed as an aid to digestion and a cure for flatulence, and in many places to relieve toothache. In Russia a little ginger is sprinkled in warm rum and a piece of cotton soaked in the mixture is placed in the tooth. In Melanesia it is used to win the affection of women. In the Philippines it drives out the evil spirits which cause disease. If a fisherman chews ginger and spits on his bait, catfish will flock to his hook.

Wild ginger or Indian ginger (*Asarum canadense*) North American Indians believed would when cooked with spoiled meat prevent ptomaine poisoning. They also used the root to cure sore mouth and earache.

Gingerbread Boy or ***Man*** The American title of a general European cumulative tale commonly known as the *Fleeing Pancake* (Z31.3.1; Type 2025). A woman makes a gingerbread boy who springs up and runs away. Various animals, one after the other, try to stop him, until at last the fox catches him and eats him up. The defiances uttered by the Gingerbread Boy to the pursuing animals build up into the cumulative formula. To the dog he says, "I ran away from an old woman, and I can run away from you, I can!" By the time he meets up with the fox, a whole series of pursuers has accumulated: "I ran away from an old woman, a dog, and a cat, and a mouse, and a hen, and I can run away from you, I can!" Whereupon the fox swallows him at one gulp.

Ginnungagap (1) In Teutonic mythology, the fathomless abyss between Niflheim and Muspellheim. The cold winds from the abyss turned the streams into blocks of ice which made an incessant thundering as they fell into the chasm. Sparks from Surtr's sword in Muspellheim fell on the ice and made steam which turned into layer on layer of hoarfrost and in time filled it up. Eventually this mass received life, becoming the giant, Ymir. When Ymir was slain, Odin, Vili, and Ve threw the body into the chasm where his body became the earth and his blood the sea.
(2) The name given to the sea between Greenland and America in the 11th century.

ginseng An herb (genus *Panax*) native to North America and China. This plant is highly valued as medicine in China, Japan, India, and among some tribes of the North American Indians because of the resemblance of its root to the figure of a man. It has sometimes been confused by European writers with the mandrake because of this resemblance, but it has none of the narcotic effect of the mandrake. It is held in highest esteem in China and commands a high price even today. At one time the Chinese and Tartars fought for possession of the countryside where it grew and one Tartar king is said to have erected a wooden palisade around an entire province to protect his supply. This root was the property of the emperor of China. Those engaged in gathering it were required to furnish 2⅔ pounds to the emperor free, and for all they collected in excess of this amount, he paid them an equal weight in silver, which was about a quarter of its market value.
During the early days of the China Trade in New England, shipmasters did a thriving business in American ginseng. This was considered inferior to the Chinese variety, but still commanded a considerable price. In Korea cultivated ginseng is considered worthless, but it was grown by a government monopoly for export. They prized the wild variety, however, and believed that only those who led a pure life could find it, and even to look on the root gave strength and vigor.
In China ginseng is the elixir of life and a cure for all of the ills of mankind. It is also taken regularly by those in perfect health who can afford it, to give them strength and vigor, long life, and clear judgment. The root is powdered and taken in tea or wine. In Japan it gives longevity. In India it is a cure for malaria. Among the Indians of North America ginseng was prescribed for the stomach, flux, menses, sore gums, and sometimes as a love medicine. Bowker's *The Indian Vegetable Family Instructor* (1836) mentions that the dry root grated in hot water is good for stomach-ache

caused by wind. In some parts of Indiana the leaves are smoked by persons suffering from asthma.

gip An English country dance term. It is an exchange of partners who continually face either toward the center or away from it as they describe a circle. [GPK]

Gipsy folklore There is more folklore *about* Gipsies than there is Gipsy folklore. For instance, they were formerly believed to be Egyptians, hence the name Gypsy or Gipsy. But because they call themselves Romany, the folklore of the Gipsies is discussed under ROMANY FOLKLORE.

Gírle Guairle The name of a fairy woman of Irish folklore who took on the task of spinning and weaving some flax for a mortal woman on condition that she remember her name. She told the woman her name was Gírle Guairle, but the woman forgot it, and was in great dread of the penalty. One day beside a fairy ráth she overheard a voice singing:

> If yon woman knew my name to be
> Gírle Guairle
> I would have neither frieze nor canvas.

When the time came, and the fairy woman came with the completed work, the woman greeted her with the words, "Welcome and health to Gírle Guairle." So the fairy had to give her the finished cloth, and then went off in a rage. See NAME TABU; RUMPELSTILTSKIN.

girls' puberty rites See ADOLESCENCE CEREMONIES.

Girru The Babylonian fire god; son of Anu and of Ea: the name is a form of the Sumerian *Gibil*. Girru was a god of metalwork, of the purifying element of fire which destroyed evil. He was identified with the fire in heaven, with the fires in the earth, with the sacrificial altar fire: as god of the latter, he became the intermediary between gods and men, hence the messenger of Bel. Compare HEPHÆSTUS.

gitano Literally, in Spanish, gipsy: an erotic couple dance of the Gipsies of southern Spain. These Gipsies came originally from northern India by way of Egypt and brought with them their heritage of eloquent arm movement and impassioned mournful song. Groups gather spontaneously in the streets of the Gipsy barrios or precincts, or in taverns. As in the flamenco, performer and spectators are drawn into communal enthusiasm, the audience participating with swaying, hand-clapping, and shouts of *olé*. [GPK]

Gizō The Spider of Hausa folklore; trickster-hero of many animal stories. Gizō is said to be the national hero of the Hausas; noted for his bravado and cunning, his sleeplessness, his rapacious appetite, and his ability to escape the consequences of his own tricks by his wits. He can outwit the lion, the hyena, the jackal, hippopotamus, elephant, the snake, and sometimes man. The praying mantis (kōki) is considered his wife. See ANANSI.

Glas Ġaiḃleann Literally, a gray, white-loined cow: in Old Irish mythology, the wonderful cow that gave an inexhaustible supply of milk. She was owned by a famous smith of Ireland, some say Goibniu, some say another, and some say Cian owned her. Anyway, the smith was making swords for Cian, who guarded the cow, and Cian was inside watching the making of the swords, that day Balor came off his island to the mainland and stole the cow. He took her off to Tor Mór, now Tory Island off the coast of Donegal. Cian in disguise went after him to win back the Glas Gaibleann. That night he slept with Ethne, the young daughter of Balor, who loved him and gave him the halter of the cow. And Cian took the Glas Gaibleann back to the smith. Lug was the child born to Ethne from that night's love.

The Glas Gaibleann still walks in Ireland. *Port na Glaise,* harbor of the Gray Cow, is the name given to any richly fertile pasture, from the belief that if the Gray Cow slept in it, she gave some of her own abundance to the grass. "The Gray Cow slept there," is often said of a fine field. And it is well known that a strange cow often comes to stay with a poor family, giving abundant milk and many calves, until some fool strikes her or milks her into a leaky bucket. Then she disappears as suddenly as she came. Nobody knows for sure if it is the same one, but she is called either Glas Gaibleann, the gray white-loined cow, or sometimes the Cow of the Smith.

glass mountain In folktale, the mountain of glass at the end of the world, near the otherworld: a motif (F751) appearing in tales from eastern and central Europe, the British Isles, and Scandinavia. A. H. Krappe (*MLQ* 8: 139–145) held that the glass mountain, a folktale representation of the land of the dead, was originally the amber mountain, the coincidence of the places of appearance of the motif with the old amber routes, and the apparent identification of the land of the dead with the Frisian archipelago, supporting his argument. In later folktales, the glass mountain is one of the tests a suitor, often the dragon-slayer, must surmount in order to win the princess (Types 425 and 530; H331.1.1; H1114). The glass mountain appears also in tales of the lost wife or husband, and here more nearly is related to the land of the dead (compare the Orpheus story). Witches, ogres, swan maidens, and other supernatural beings live on the mountain in still other tales. Quite clearly, it early was a land of the dead, later transformed by story-tellers into a magical place where the princess, for safety, voluntarily or by her father, was placed, and which the hero, using animal claws or thrusting bones into the glass as a ladder, climbed to win her.

Gluskabe or **Glooscap** Culture hero of the Abnaki Indians of the Northeastern Woodlands: sometimes identified with Nanabozho, perhaps erroneously so. The consistently altruistic character and human appearance of Gluskabe distinguish him from the culture heroes of other North American Indian groups. None of the crude buffoonery associated with many North American culture heroes attaches to him; in myths where Gluskabe and Turtle appear together it is Turtle who is frequently the butt for humor. One of Gluskabe's first deeds was to avenge the death of his mother, who had been wilfully killed by Wolf, Gluskabe's younger twin brother. Later Gluskabe is abandoned by jealous neighbors, and his housemates are kidnapped; he rides a whale, overcomes difficulties, and rescues his housemates. After overcoming Jug-Woman, and surviving a trip through dangerous underground rapids, he rescues a friend from Snake, chases a giant beaver which gets away, reduces the size of dangerous beasts, breaks the

windbird's wing to regulate the wind, and kills Frog Monster, thereby releasing impounded water. In the end Gluskabe retires from the world, but will return at need like most culture heroes. He answers requests for eternal life by turning suppliants into trees or stones, but grants more moderate requests made of him by human beings. [EWV]

gnome One of a species of deformed and dwarfish underground beings, whose element is the earth itself, and whose function is usually said to be guarding hidden treasure and quarries. Jewish cabalistic tradition locates them in the very center of the earth. The word was popularized by Paracelsus; in his usage it designated a group of beings who could swim through solid earth as fish swim through water.

goat Among the Greeks and Romans the lore of the goat is various. A goat was the prize in the cult of Hera, was prohibited in the cult of Athena, but a goat was sacrificed once a year on the Athenian Acropolis. A worshipper of the Brauronian Artemis called a goat his daughter and sacrificed it once a year. Five hundred goats were sacrificed in thanksgiving for the victory at Marathon. Aphrodite rode a goat and the animal was sacred to her. Goats were sacrificed at the Roman Lupercalia. Dionysus assumed the form of a goat, and Pan, the fauns, and satyrs have goat (or goatlike) bodies.

In Christian Europe goats are thought to have been familiars of witches or of the Devil who comb their beards once a day. The lechery of the goat is part of European proverbial lore. In some places goats are bringers of fertility. They are bride-gifts in Bulgaria and are connected with marriage in South Africa and the Vosges. Ritual intercourse between women and goats is indicated in Semitic and Latin areas. Goats cause eclipses in Burma by eating the sun or moon. Among Jews goats were sacrificial animals. The Americanism, "to get his goat," means to reduce a man to frustration and rage. Goat is a frequent character in Negro folktale. Among the Hausa, for instance, he can outwit both Lion and Hyena. The Yoruba have a legal story in which Goat outwits Leopard. [RDJ]

goat dance An impersonation of the he-goat demon, invested with a special repulsive fascination, a predisposition to mischief and licentiousness, and a great phallic potency. This creature evidently originated in Thrace, in the cloven-hoofed Dionysian satyrs and sileni with attached phalloi. The Greek tragedy developed from the *tragōidia,* or sacrificial goat-song, the lewd, satiric *sikinnis* from satyr-plays. Their violent dances were trotting and brutish rather than insane as those of the mænads. Goat impersonations reappear in medieval morality plays as devils, in Carnivals as goat-demons, particularly recognizable in the modern Thracian *kalogheroi.* In the New World goat masks are probably a Catholic remodeling of native woodland deities. But Indian fantasy has re-created unique clown-demons in the black-faced *macho cabrillo* or he-goat of the Yaqui *Pascola* and Guerrero *Tecuanes.* [GPK]

goat that flagged the train Subject of a favorite American barbershop quartet song, entitled *The Goat,* sung to the same tune as the drinking song, *When I Die,* in close harmony and with echo imitation. The text tells of a goat that ate three red shirts off the clothes-line, was tied by his owner to a railroad track, but saved himself as the train came along by coughing up the shirts and flagging the train.

gobadán The little sandpiper of the Irish shores. There is an Irish proverb to the effect that the gobadán cannot attend to the two ebb tides (i.e. cannot work both night and day).

goblin A household spirit who plays the same role in French folklore as the Scotch and English brownies, bogles, and boggarts, the German kobolds, etc. He is very helpful around the house but also of capricious and erratic temper, mischievous and prankish, given to rapping on walls and doors, moving furniture in the night, breaking dishes, banging pots and pans around, snatching bedclothes off sleepers, etc. Food is left out for the goblin, and often doors are left open for him, just as for all household spirits of this kind in other parts of Europe. Goblins frequent homes where the wine is plentiful and the children pretty. They bring the children dainty tidbits but also punish them when they disobey their mothers. They are fond of horses and often ride them in the night, but also often tangle their manes. The recommended way to get rid of a goblin (if he becomes more of a nuisance than a help) is to sprinkle flaxseed on the floor. He is such a good housekeeper that he will be obliged to pick it up, but after a while he will get tired and go away.

God The Supreme Being of monotheistic religion, especially the Creator, the omniscient pervasive Spirit of the universe, and the Ruler of all creation of Hebrew and Christian belief. The use of Elohim (a plural form) in parts of the Old Testament, and Adonai (Lord), suggest a development from polytheism to monotheistic belief among the ancient Hebrews. Yahweh, as the Old Testament deity, was also the God of the New Testament, and Christianity recognized in this Being a triune personality: the Father, the Son, and the Holy Ghost. See ALLAH; YAHWEH; JESUS.

god-eyes The eyes of a god, specifically as depicted in some special way in ritual art representations. The eye of the Egyptian god Horus had a separate existence and bestowed wonderful gifts on mankind, such as oil, milk, wine, honey. The sun and moon comprised the two eyes of the god Rā. But of striking interest are the eyes of certain primitive gods whose whole facial distortions and superlatives of good and evil often reveal what man thinks and expects of his supernaturals. The faces of certain Alaskan Eskimo deities, for instance, and those of most North Pacific Coast Indians betray a concept of the terror-striking supernatural combined with the grotesque, funny, and almost human fellow. The Huichol Indians of Mexico make symbolic god-eyes by weaving varicolored yarns across small square bamboo frames which are then fastened diagonally on bamboo sticks. These, the eyes of the god, are placed on the altar when a prayer is made, so that the eyes of the god may look on the supplication. They are used especially in prayers for male offspring and good health. The Tepecanos of Mexico have similar prayer sticks called *chimal*. Both are associated with the netted squash-blossom design of the Pueblo Indians which are also associated with male infants. See AI APAEC.

Godiva (Lady Godiva) Wife of Leofric, earl of Mercia, about 1040 A.D., who rode naked through the streets of Coventry. The legend is that her husband, lord of Coventry, had imposed severe taxes which caused great suffering among the people. He promised to repeal the taxes if his wife would exhibit herself. She was protected by her long hair and an edict that all shutters must be closed during the ride. One man who violated this edict became known as Peeping Tom. Between the 13th and the 17th centuries the ride was reenacted several times a decade. The legend is associated with motifs from general folklore. Thus Pliny reported that the druidic priestesses danced naked for religious reasons. In communities where nudity is not the way of life, rituals performed in the nude bring rain, cure sterility, or are part of the tumescent phase of orgiastic practices. A number of Chinese stories report that some devils are so prudish that they are frightened away by an exhibition of the nude body. The modern nudist movement gives expression to obscure folk impulses not unconnected with ceremonial nakedness. Parades of naked men and women, the nudism of several religious sects, as well as individual exhibitions have been reported in recent times as a device to protest against civil or social injustice. A notable example of this is Saint Francis of Assisi, who on being rebuked by the bishop, snatched off his clothes and walked naked into the streets. Godiva's ride would seem to be more closely allied to this pattern than to the druid priestesses. [RDJ]

gods The deities, or beings who are worshipped, of the religions of mankind. Gods are of more than human powers, either specifically over one aspect of existence or over a more extensive area. They may rule such provinces as the sky, the earth, the waters, thunder; or such abstractions as luck, fertility, beauty, war; in any case, their power over such phenomena makes it necessary to invoke them and to propitiate, threaten, or to explain matters to them. The gods may be thought of as human in form, or animal in form (partly or wholly)—theriomorphic—, or as trees—dendromorphic—, or simply as invisible powers of no specific form. Some scholars believe that gods were once localized in individual objects or phenomena and later consolidated related areas to develop into high gods and eventually into monotheistic Creators and Fathers; others hold that monotheism was a much earlier stage of religion than this theory would indicate. See ANIMISM; ANTHROPOMORPHISM; MONOTHEISM; POLYTHEISM.

Gog and Magog (1) In *Ezekiel,* Gog is prince of Meshech and Tubal; one of the enemies of Israel. In *Revelation,* and later apocalyptic literature, Gog and Magog are aides of Satan the Antichrist. In both references, Magog seems to be a geographical term, a land taking its name from its prince, Gog. A. H. Sayce identifies Gog with Gyges; hence Magog would be Lydia.

(2) The names given to two 14-foot statues in London's Guildhall. It was said that they were the survivors of a race of giants descended from the daughters of Diocletian, and wiped out by Brut. The two captive giants were carried to the royal palace in chains, the palace standing where the Guildhall was later located. They are known to have been there during the reign

of Henry V, were destroyed in the Great Fire, rebuilt in 1708, and again destroyed in the Blitz in World War II.

Gohei Pieces of paper used as charms in temples and houses (Shinto). [JLM]

Goibniu The divine smith of Old Irish mythology, who with Creidne, the brazier, made spears and arms for the Tuatha Dé Danann. Literally, his name means forger. He was a famous magician, and served the brew of immortality at the feasts. His Brythonic counterpart is Govannon. See FEAST OF AGE.

gold Neolithic remains are rich in golden ornaments. Gold has been consistently the most highly prized of metals through the ages, though others, because of their scarcity, have surpassed it in price. Since gold was so highly valued, it early became associated with religion. It was used to make idols, as tribute, and as offerings to the gods. In India the *Rig-Veda* says the giver of gold receives a life of light and glory; the fifth Mohammedan Heaven was of gold. Vessels of gold are common to all religions. The druids used a golden sickle to gather their sacred mistletoe; in the Middle Ages herbalists emulated them by using golden instruments to gather their herbs.

Aristotle believed gold was to be found principally in rivers which ran to the south, as were also the noblest pearls. Others believed gold was begotten by the sun and that the heat of the underground veins slowly burned everything they came in contact with, turning those substances into gold. In the East Indies and Central America gold is believed to have a soul and many tabus are observed in taking it. In Central America it is gathered after prayer and fasting. In Sumatra, tin, ivory, and other materials may not be carried into a mine, lest the spirit of gold flee. Often mining is done in complete silence. The Dyaks of Borneo believe the soul of the gold seeks revenge on those who mine it. In Malaya they believe a golden roe deer owns the gold and can give or withhold it. They also believe the soul of gold departs when it is taken from the ground. In India it was believed that the griffins mined gold with their beaks and the people fought them to collect the gold.

Fighting with griffins was an easier method of obtaining gold than some dreamed up by the alchemists. Some alchemists, like the 18th century German Semler, believed they had succeeded in transmuting the base metals only to find that some kind-hearted assistant had smuggled a little gold leaf into the crucible to please his master. In spite of their fantastic theories and frantic efforts, the alchemists slowly and laboriously laid the groundwork for present-day chemistry. Any high school boy would laugh at the theory that gold was composed of copper and red sulfur, or quicksilver and sulfur, or that it was really quicksilver under the influence of the sun. Obtaining a golden goose, catching a leprechaun, or finding the pot at the end of the rainbow are as yet more practical means than transmutation for obtaining gold.

In early medical practice, gold was a potent curative force. The Chinese believed gold leaf the most perfect form of matter; an unguent containing it was the most powerful remedy of Chinese medicine as it gave renewed life to the human body. Among Western peoples potable gold (gold dissolved in acid) was a panacea. Astrological healers claimed that gold fused under certain signs would cure appendicitis. Others believed a suitable verse inscribed on gold would cure the patient. Its freedom from rust was one of the principles on which physicians based their theories of gold as a preservative charm. That rubbing a sty nine times with a golden wedding ring will cure it is a belief which persists. See ALCHEMY.

Golden Bough The title of Sir James G. Frazer's comparative "Study in Magic and Religion," published in two volumes in 1890 and expanded to a monumental 12 volumes in 1911–15. The Golden Bough is the mistletoe, connected with Balder, Æneas, etc. Beginning with the ritual surrounding the reign of the priest-king of Diana in the grove near Nemi, Frazer explains many ancient customs and beliefs related to magic, agriculture, kingship, divinity, tree-worship, tabus, totemism, rain, fire, etc., bringing to bear on his argument a tremendous mass of material from ancient and primitive cultures. The titles of the books included in *The Golden Bough* are: *The Magic Art and the Evolution of Kings* (2 vol.); *Taboo and the Perils of the Soul; The Dying God; Adonis, Attis, Osiris: Studies in Oriental Religion* (2 vol.); *Spirits of the Corn and of the Wild* (2 vol.); *The Scapegoat; Balder the Beautiful* (2 vol.); and *The Golden Bough, Bibliography and General Index.* In 1936, *Aftermath, a Supplement to the Golden Bough,* included the results of some of Frazer's study since 1915.

Golden Fleece In Greek legend, the fleece of the ram on which Phrixus and Helle escaped, and which hung in the grove at Colchis. See ARGONAUTS; JASON; MEDEA.

goldenrod A widely distributed North American herb (genus *Solidago*) with erect stalks carrying small heads of yellow flowers, sometimes in clusters. It is the state flower of Alabama, Kentucky, and Nebraska. Some say that where goldenrod grows there is treasure buried, and if it appears near a house where it has not been planted, the inmates will have unexpected good fortune. The stalks are sometimes used in divining water. In New Hampshire they say that if a gall from a goldenrod stalk be carried by a person suffering from rheumatism, he will be free from the pain as long as the grub in the gall is alive. Among the Chippewa Indians it was a cure for pains in the chest, fever, ulcers, boils, convulsions, sore mouth, diseases of the lungs, kidneys, and women's diseases. In Ontario it is used in a cure for hay fever. Elsewhere it is considered good for wounds and bruises, both internal and external. The flowers make a lotion which is soothing for bee stings. In some parts of the United States goldenrod was formerly used as a substitute for tea.

golden rule The rule of life given in *Matt.* vii, 12: Whatsoever ye would that men should do to you, do ye also unto them. Compare SILVER RULE.

Golden Vanity A variant title, from popular tradition, of the broadside ballad *The Sweet Trinity* (Child #286). The title is the name of the British ship whose cabin-boy swims to a French galley and sinks it by drilling holes with an auger. *The Golden Vanity* (Child's B version) varies from *The Sweet Trinity* in that the cabin-boy, rather than accepting the captain's refusal to give him a promised reward, threatens to sink the British ship in the same way and is hauled aboard where they "proved unto him far better than their word."

golem Anything incomplete or not fully formed, like an embryo, a needle without an eye, a woman who has not conceived: a Hebrew word used in *Ps.* cxxxix, 16 to mean "embryo." Adam, created from the dust, was thus a golem until the soul was given to him. In medieval Jewish legend, the golem was an automaton servant attributed to the great rabbis and wonder-workers, probably as a development of the stories of magic about Vergil the Necromancer, who had such an unhuman servant.

The most famous of all the golems was that of Rabbi Löw of Prague in the late 16th century. The rabbi used the golem as his weekday servant, but on Friday afternoons he removed the charm motivating it so that it might rest on the Sabbath. Once, when he forgot to do this, he had to chase the golem until he caught it just in front of the synagogue. There he removed the charm and the golem crumbled into dust. A group of tales about this golem exists, some concerned with the golem's championing of wronged Jews. The golem of Elijah of Chelm was the subject of debate by that rabbi's grandson: Was the golem capable of being the tenth and necessary man for a minyan (the quorum needed for prayer)? A golem of Rabbi Jaffe in Russian Poland was created to light fires and perform other duties not permissible to Jews on the Sabbath. But it exceeded its orders one day and burned up practically everything.

The golem was motivated by a charm, a Shem, or paper inscribed with one of the names of God. This charm was placed in the mouth or inserted in the head of the inert mass, which thereafter could move about and obey commands until the Shem was removed.

Goliath A Philistine giant of Gath, six cubits and a span (more than ten feet) tall; the champion of the Philistine army arrayed against Saul (I *Sam.* xvii). Goliath was slain by David, the shepherd lad, who slung a stone against the armored warrior and thus killed him in single combat. According to Jewish tradition, Goliath fell forward on his face, because this made it easier for David to cut off his head, and because thus the image of Dagon on Goliath's breastplate was shamed. With the help of Uriah, David removed the armor of the fallen giant, David promising Uriah, a Hittite, a Hebrew wife. For this rash promise, God made Bathsheba, David's destined wife, the wife of Uriah. Goliath's brothers, when David fled from Saul and sought refuge with the king of the Philistines, tried to have him executed, but King Ahish refused on the grounds that the combat had been open and equal.

Gomme, Lady Alice Bertha (1852?–1938) Collector of rimes and games, the wife of George Laurence Gomme, to whom she was married in 1875. She was noted as an able collector of nursery rimes, folk games, and singing games which she brought together in the excellent, annotated *The Traditional Games of England, Scotland, and Ireland* (1894–1898). Other works include *Children's Singing Games* (1894), in collaboration with C. J. Sharp; a collection of *Games for Parlour and Playground* (1898); and with her husband, *British Folklore, Folk Songs, and Singing Games.*

Gomme, Sir (George) Laurence (1853–1916) English archeologist and a founder of the Folklore Society in England. His wife was Lady Alice Bertha (Merck) Gomme. He was knighted in 1911. He was at various times editor of *Archæological Review, Folklore Journal,* and *Antiquary.* In his *Folklore as an Historical Science* (1908) he attempts to prove the theory, originated by the Grimms, that folklore material may be used to establish historical facts, a theory which is no longer held. Gomme had a very profound knowledge of the past and current history of London, and his book, *The Making of London* (1912), is a classic in that field. Among other works are: *Primitive Folk-Moots* (1880), *Folklore Relics of Early Village Life* (1883), *Chapbooks and Folklore Tracts* (1885), and *Ethnology in Folklore* (1892).

gong The chief musical instrument of southeastern Asia; a more or less convex bronze plate, sometimes with a central boss, and with a narrow vertical rim, sounded by striking the center with a stick. While gongs differ from clapperless bells in that the sounding part of the gong is the center, rather than the rim, the uses and magical properties of the instrument are similar to those of bells. Gongs accompany religious ceremonies, drive out evil spirits, rout the demons of disease. In China, when a child had convulsions, a gong was beaten to summon its spirit into one of its garments, which could then be laid beside the child, safe from the demons who had lured it out of the body. Bathing from a gong is also believed to be curative. The winds respond to the voice of the gong and come at its call. Ownership of gongs, because of their magic power and actual cost, enhances social position and influence. Gongs may even serve as a medium of exchange. Drinking from a gong after taking an oath has a binding significance equivalent to swearing upon a sword or upon the Bible. Such is the respect in which certain gongs are held that they may be given names appropriate to their sound and significance.

Gongs are recorded in China from the 6th century and have been known in India and throughout the Malay Archipelago since the 7th and 9th centuries respectively. The oldest type is shallow and without the boss. Male and female distinctions are made in gongs, as in many other instruments, the deep bosses being regarded as male, and shallower ones, female. Sets of gongs played as chimes are characteristic of Javanese and Balinese orchestras which play for dancing, singing, and dramatic performances, and each set has a double range of tones designated as male and female.

As a signaling instrument gongs are played in a system of communication comparable to the African drum language. See BONANG; GAMELAN; REJONG.

goose An important bird in the mythology and folklore of the world from earliest times. The hero of the Finno-Ugric flood is said to have traveled in the form of a goose. The Goose god of the Siberian Ostyaks is one of their three high gods. Geb (Seb), the Egyptian god of the earth, was goose-headed. There were sacred geese in the Greek temples. And the sacred geese in the Roman temple of Juno saved Rome from invasion in the 4th century B.C. Livy tells the story about how the

Gauls sent scouts ahead of them into the city by night. They climbed the Capitol hill in silence but were loudly proclaimed by the cackling of the geese in the temple, were taken and killed, and the citizens were forewarned. Because of this a golden goose was carried annually in procession to the Capitol in honor of the birds.

In China a pair of geese is often given as a wedding present to a newly married couple, because geese are said to be faithful to each other. In the Middle Ages in Europe geese were often thought to be the familiars of witches and to serve as steeds for them to the Sabbat. The North American Mandan Indians formerly performed a goose dance at the time for the southern migration of wild geese. The ceremony was intended to make the geese remember the plentiful food of the region and was a supplication for their return in the Spring.

The medieval belief that the barnacle goose was hatched out of barnacles is a living belief today in Donegal, Ireland, where its flesh is eaten, the same as fish, on Fridays. In the English shires the goose is still a feature of the Michaelmas quarter-rent day, September 29. In Herefordshire "one goose fit for a lord's dinner" was part of every farmer's land rent, due on that day. The "goose with ten toes" as the goose *intentos* claimed by Lancashire landlords on every 16th Sunday after Pentecost or Trinity. This did not always fall on Michaelmas. In Denmark, the similar goose feast comes about St. Martin's Day, November 11.

In Maryland rural people sometimes say that the cackling of geese foretells rain. In New Brunswick and Nova Scotia wild geese flying low are thought to indicate rain. If it thunders on Sunday new-set goose eggs will not hatch. In East Prussia it used to be considered bad for the geese for the housewife to spin on St. Matthew's Day, September 27.

In folktale the goose plays more roles than can be enumerated. The alarm spread by cackling geese is the incident comprising motif B521.3.2. A goose dives for a reflected star in the night, thinking it a shiny fish (J1791.8). Geese proclaim the beauty of the disguised goose-girl (K1816.5.1). A piece of land measured by the flight of a goose (K185.3) in which a man spreads the goose's wings and carries it over a large area (the domestic goose cannot fly far without lighting) is the motif of a French deceptive land measure folktale. See GOOSE GOD; GOOSE THAT LAID THE GOLDEN EGG.

The wild goose is an important symbol in Hindu mythology. Brahmā is depicted as riding on a magnificent gander, which is thus the manifestation on the animal plane of the god's creative principle, and a symbol of freedom through spiritual purity. The epithet "gander" or "highest gander" indicates the rank of Hindu ascetic, monk, teacher and saint.

The cosmic gander (the divine presence in the universe) reveals itself through a song, which is thought of as the breathing of the supreme being, the rhythm of inhaling and exhaling. This song has the sound of the word for gander, *haṁsa*, the two syllables of which mean "I" and "this" or, when heard in reverse, "this" and "I". When the Indian yogī controls his breath through exercises, the "inner gander" is manifested through the repetition of its name, *haṁsa, haṁsa*.

A typical Hindu duality of thought, embracing simultaneously the earthbound and the divine, is apparently present in the concept. The twofold nature of the gander, at home on water, earth, or in the air, makes it a logical symbol, according to Zimmer, for "the divine essence, which, though embodied in, and abiding with, the individual, yet remains forever free from, and unconcerned with, the events of individual life."

Goose, Game of A dice-and-board game, perhaps as old as ancient Greece, revived in the 17th and 18th centuries in Europe, modifications still remaining among the most popular of games. The board is inscribed or printed with a spiral or oval diagram having a starting point and a goal (marked with a goose in the French game of the 18th century). The players throw dice in turn to determine the number of squares or compartments they may move their counters towards the goal. A number of the compartments are special, requiring the player to go back three spaces, lose a turn with the dice, begin all over again, etc. The Game of Goose is thus similar to pachisi and related four-directions derivatives of divination. Adaptations of the game in the 19th and 20th centuries have been numerous, attempts at pedagogical instruction being superimposed in geographical tours and the like. The basic idea has appeared in game after game capitalizing on the latest fads and heroes. See GAMES.

goose god One of the three great gods of the Ostyaks of northwestern Siberia; protector of birds, especially of the Ob River. He lives in the mountains in a special nest made of furs and skins, which is the charge and care of a particular shaman. His images are made of copper, goose-shaped. Rich garments are sacrificed to him, which he wears. The goose is reverenced among the Ostyaks as possessing specific supernatural powers. The geese which appear every Spring out of the sky to settle on the rivers are believed to come from the sleeves of Tomam (the Ostyak mother goddess). The feathers which she shakes out of her sleeves every Spring become geese as they settle earthward.

goose that laid the golden egg The stories about the goose that laid the golden egg and was killed by its foolish and avaricious owner (D876), and the golden goose are known in all parts of the world. In western Europe, although the individual feathers of the golden goose bring wealth, greedy persons find that they are unable to pull their hands away from the bird (D2171.3.1), and by further elaboration the owner thus brings all the thieves to the king, makes the sad princess laugh, and is rewarded (H341.1). This is Grimm's story of the *Golden Goose* (#64). In an Indian version, the wife of a Brāhman tears the golden feathers out all at once and they become valueless. By the law of substitution other animals such as an ass, ram, or bull take the place of the goose. In the story of the Golden Fleece, for example, this substitution may be observed. Similarly geese are sometimes substituted in the swan maiden cycle of shapeshifters. [RDJ]

Gordius In Greek legend, the father of Midas, and king of Phrygia. During a period of stress in the country, an oracle foretold that the king who would end the trouble would appear in a wagon. Gordius, a peasant, soon after drove into town and was recognized by the assembly as king. His wagon, with its yoke and pole fastened by a knot of bark, was dedicated by Gordius to Zeus on the acropolis at Gordium. The oracle stated that he who untied the knot would rule over all Asia. When the conquering Alexander came to Gordium and was told the story, he drew his sword and cut through the knot, himself claiming application of the legend. The whole story is poorly authenticated.

Gorgons In Greek mythology, three hideous maidens, later represented as beautiful, but characteristically terrifying, with serpents in place of hair, golden wings, claws of bronze, and glaring eyes. In Homer, only one Gorgon is spoken of, a monster of the underworld whose head adorned the ægis of Zeus. In Hesiod, these daughters of Phorcys and Ceto were three: Stheno (the Mighty), Euryale (the Wide-springer), Medusa (the Queen), and because of later legend, the latter is meant when Gorgon is used in the singular. These sisters, of whom Medusa alone was mortal, lived in the farthest west, near Night and the Hesperides; later, their residence was located in Libya. In Attic legend, the Gorgon was a monster brought forth by Ge to aid the giants against the gods and slain by Athena, who placed the Gorgon's head beneath the agora. This legend is confused with the one of Perseus, who is said to have performed the burial instead of giving the head to Athena for her shield. A representation of the head of the Gorgon, called Gorgoneion, was placed on city walls and the shields and breastplates of soldiers as protection; when worn as an amulet, it protected against the evil eye. The Gorgons have been considered the personifications of the nightmare; the paralyzing effect of the head and the meaning of the name Euryale contributing to this hypothesis. Compare ÆGIS.

Gotham A village in Nottinghamshire, England, whose inhabitants during the later Middle Ages acquired the reputation of being born fools. According to a legend, the people deliberately drew down upon themselves this reputation in the 13th century. King John was to pass through the town, and either because the expense of entertaining him would prove too great or because they feared losing some of their good lands as public roads (a customary procedure where the king's troops had passed), the townsmen began doing foolish things to discourage the king from the visit. They drowned an eel in the pond, trapped a bird by building a hedge about it, and performed similar nonsensicalities, with the result that the king would have none of them. This apocryphal story explains the epithet "wise men (or fools) of Gotham," but is undoubtedly a fabrication. Elsewhere, as in the Chelm of Jewish noodle stories, the traditional fools are facetiously called sages, and this is the case with Gotham.

The earliest extant copy of the *Merie Tales of the Mad Men of Gotam* was printed in 1630, but editions dating to 1560 or earlier are referred to by contemporaries. As with similar chapbooks, this was a storehouse of traditional tales, some traceable to India, about fools, and all attributed to the people of Gotham. For example, the tale of the 12 Gothamites who went fishing and feared that one of them had been drowned because in counting each forgot to count himself, is known in Russia, Scotland, India, and Iceland. See NOODLES; PENT CUCKOO.

Götterdämmerung The twilight of the gods: German name for Ragnarök, the day of the great battle between the gods of the Teutonic pantheon and the forces of evil, which will usher in a new regime. In Wagner's opera, *Götterdämmerung*, last in the *Ring of the Nibelung*, it signifies the end of the rule of the gods and the beginning of the rule of love.

gowk storm In Scottish, Irish, and British provincial folksay, a spring storm believed to arrive with the gowk or cuckoo (in April). Consequently, any misfortune, turbulent but brief, is often referred to as a gowk storm. *Cuac* is the Irish word for cuckoo; the Old English is *geac*.

Graces The Gratiæ of Roman mythology: identified with the Greek Charites. See CHARITES.

Grææ In Greek mythology, the three "old women," sisters of the Gorgons whom they protected. Hesiod names only two, but later a third was added, the names being Pemphredo or Pephredo, Enyo, Deino. The sisters had gray hair from birth, the shape of swans, and one eye and one tooth among them. These latter they borrowed according to need, passing them back and forth. Perseus slipped among them, stole the eye, and thus was able to kill Medusa and escape the eyeless sisters with the cap of darkness. Some versions say that he returned the eye and tooth in exchange for the magic cap, shoes, and wallet.

Grail In medieval legend and romance, the **Holy Grail,** or **Sangreal,** was the dish used by Jesus at the Last Supper; it was preserved by Joseph of Arimathea, who received some of Christ's blood into it at the Crucifixion, and brought it to Britain, after which it disappeared because of the impurity of its guardians. Many knights went in quest of it. Galahad, Perceval, and Bors only were chaste enough in thought, word, and deed, ever to catch sight of it. The story is best known through Malory's *Book of Arthur,* Tennyson's *Idylls of the King,* and Wagner's opera *Parsifal.*

☞ The legends of the Grail are among the most widespread of the Arthurian cycle, existing in French, English, German, Norse, Dutch, Italian, Spanish, Portuguese, Welsh, and Irish versions. The extant French texts or lost French romances are the sources of all the others, including the Welsh and Irish. The most famous medieval versions are Chrétien de Troyes's *Perceval* or the *Conte del Graal* (c. 1180), which is the earliest extant; Wolfram von Eschenbach's *Parzival* (c. 1205), Wagner's chief source; the *Queste del St. Graal* (c. 1210); and Malory's condensation of the last in his *Book of King Arthur,* erroneously entitled *Morte d'Arthur* (1469).

The Grail legend is extraordinarily confused and perplexing. The French word *graal* means a rather deep platter and is correctly equated with *escuele* and with Welsh *dyscyl*. But Robert de Boron seems to think of it as a chalice and Wolfram as a stone, on which the names of the guardian knights are inscribed. The custodian of the Grail is variously called Bron, Pelles, Amfortas, or Joseph of Arimathea. The hero who achieves the quest may be Perceval, Gawain, or Galahad. He may, like Gawain, be notorious for his amours, or, like Galahad, a virgin. In view of these and other inconsistencies it is not surprising that scholars have spent as many vain years following various clues to the mystery of the Grail as did the knights of the Round Table in the quest of it. Almost every year a new hypothesis is propounded.

Today the most widely held theories of the origin of the legend are three: the Christian, the ritual, and the Celtic. The first, which regards the phantasmagoric narrative as a deliberate concoction by Chrétien or some contemporary cleric about a eucharistic vessel, can be dismissed on the ground that in the earliest and many later versions the vessel is borne by a beautiful maiden, not by a priest, and the question which Perceval is supposed to ask, "Whom does one serve with the Grail?" has no conceivable relation to sacramental mysteries. If this was designed as a holy adventure, nothing could be more uncanonical or fatuous.

Jessie Weston put forward the plausible theory that the basis of the legend was a pagan fertility cult. The Maimed King was a sort of Adonis, whose sterilizing wound brought desolation on the land. The Grail and the bleeding spear were sexual symbols, the question test an initiation rite. As to the Waste Land, the theory is supported by the specific evidence of the texts, but the rest must be abandoned, both because no ritual of the sort can be cited from any country of Western Europe, and because Grail, spear, question, and many other features can be more adequately explained on the Celtic hypothesis.

This third view has the advantage of antecedent probability since the Grail stories form a part of the Arthurian cycle. Once grant that we are dealing with a highly conglomerate body of fiction, the product of generations of Irish, Welsh, and Breton reciters and of later French men of letters, and we can not only understand the gross disharmonies of the tradition, but also account for nearly every feature. It is impossible in limited space to offer proof for the following statements but the evidence may be found in the bibliography.

An Irish tale, *The Prophetic Ecstasy of the Phantom* (before 1056), tells how a king of Ireland met the sun god Luġ, was invited to his palace, found Luġ already arrived there before him, and was served with huge portions of meat by a crowned damsel, the divine personification of Ireland. She supplied the king with drink, asking Luġ, "Whom shall this cup be given to?" Not only is this sequence of events dimly recognizable in Perceval's visit to the Grail castle, not only is the question echoed in the meaningless question test, but also Luġ's lightning spear is the prototype of the bleeding lance, and Ireland personified is one of the prototypes of the Grail bearer, for both these stately damsels assume elsewhere a hideous shape. From Irish sagas too we get examples of kings (Nuada; Conn of the Hundred Battles) whose maiming or whose union with an evil woman brought calamity on their realms, as in the case of Wolfram's Amfortas.

In the Welsh stage of the tradition Luġ was supplanted as host by the sea god Bran, who like Chrétien's Fisher King was wounded in the foot by a spear in battle; the drinking vessel gave place to a platter of plenty, "the *Dysgl* of Rhydderch; whatever food was wished thereon was instantly obtained." There is every probability that this dish was one of the magic possessions of Bran, who was famous for his hospitality and whose followers, as they feasted for 80 years, never grew older. Certain it is that one French romancer calls the Grail King Bron, three others declare that the Grail supplied whatever viands one desired, and still another describes twelve knights feasting in the Grail castle who,

though over a hundred years old, seemed to be only 40. Wolfram, too, says that whatever a man held his hand out for in front of the Grail, he found ready, warm dishes or cold, flesh of wild or tame; and that if one looked upon the talisman for two hundred years, yet no sign of age but gray hair would appear. Moreover Bran possessed a horn of plenty; "the drink and the food that one asked one received in it when one desired." This reappears in Arthurian romance as a *cor beneit*, blessed horn, and in corrupt form as the name of the Grail castle, Corbenic or Cambenoyt. Mistaken for the *tresbenoit corps* of Christ, the mass wafer, it was also responsible for the many eucharistic associations which gathered about the Grail.

Other Welsh elements contributed to the legend. Kilhwch's arrival and reception at Arthur's court parallels the account of Perceval's at the same court, as narrated by Chrétien de Troyes some 80 years later. Kilhwch's adventures include the quest for several magic vessels—a cup, a dish, a horn, a caldron—and though no precise connection can be made, we seem to have foreshadowed here the quest theme of the French romances.

Essentially, then, the Grail legend represents the interweaving of a score of strands from Irish and Welsh myth and fable. W. P. Ker was right in asserting: "Everything in the poets that is most enthralling through the mere charm of wonder, from the land of the Golden Fleece to that of the Holy Grail, is more or less nearly related to mythology."

Bibliography:

J. D. Bruce, *Evolution of Arthurian Romance to 1300* (1923, 1927).

R. S. Loomis, "Irish Origin of the Grail Legend," *Speculum* VIII (1933): 415.

——, *Arthurian Tradition and Chrétien de Troyes* (1949).

H. Newstead, *Bran the Blessed in Arthurian Romance* (1939).

A. Nutt, *Studies on the Legend of the Holy Grail* (1888).

——, *The Legends of the Holy Grail* (1902).

ROGER S. LOOMIS

Gráinne In the Finn cycle of Irish heroic story and romance, the daughter of Cormac mac Art, promised wife of Fionn MacCumal. She fell in love with Diarmuid of the love spots. Once she had seen him she could not quench her love, and persuaded him (though he was unwilling) to elope with her. After the famous pursuit and Diarmuid's tragic death, Gráinne loathed the sight of Fionn. But Fionn wooed her with gentleness until finally she became his wife. She was mocked for her "heart of woman that changes like water." Gráinne typifies the glamorous, tragic, passionate, and realistically human Irish heroine. Deirdre and Gráinne are the two contrasting heroines of Old Irish literature.

grāma-devatā The guardian village gods of India. Among the jungle tribes these deities are the tribal gods of mountain or forest. The worship of the grāma-devatā is animistic and dates from pre-Aryan times. Beliefs about them are vague, but generally they are considered spirits of good and bad and the cause of all unusual events. The object of their worship is propitiation, since they are beings of uncertain temper and of various functions. In some places they are the smallpox or cholera goddesses.

Their shrines are often only a pile of stones under a tree, a boundary stone, or a little brick building containing a rough figure of the deity, or sometimes a rude stone platform under a tree, bearing a pile of stones or an iron spear representing the deity. Frequently there is no permanent shrine and a temporary one is erected for a festival. In this a clay image, stone pillar, or roughly carved figure is placed. A small, portable, metal image or a brass or earthenware pot filled with water and decorated with margosa leaves is sometimes used in festival processions.

The priests or pūjārīs are usually drawn from the lower castes because the aboriginal inhabitants are believed better able to deal with these godlings. There is no uniformity in their worship. Daily, weekly, or annual offerings are made. These include rice, flowers, fruit, incense, camphor, milk, spirituous liquor, goats, and pigeons.

The grāma-devatā are primarily female, and symbolize the facts of village life. They are often identified with the Earth Mother or with the Mothers whose worship prevails in western India. In Mysore they are called Amma (plural Ammanavaru), Māramma, or Māriamma. In Orissa they are gramdevatī or thakurānī. In the north they are also called gānv-devī, gānv-devatā, dih, and dihwār.

Local worship includes an enormous miscellany of village deities and Brāhman gods. In areas where Brāhman influence is strong, an attempt is made to connect these gods with Śiva and Vishṇu as avataras and in many places this absorption is almost complete. The best known among the grāma-devatā include Āiyānar, Bhairon, Gaṅśām Deo, Hanumān, Māriamma.

Gram In the *Volsunga Saga*, a magic sword which insured victory in battle. Odin thrust it into the Branstock oak in Volsung's hall and Volsung's son Sigmund alone could withdraw it. It never failed Sigmund until Odin broke it during the battle with the Hundings. His wife, Hiordis, saved the pieces and later gave them to their son, Sigurd, who had them reforged by Regin and used it to slay the dragon, Fafnir.

Grandfather The culture hero of the Cariri Indians of eastern Brazil, sent to earth to help the people by Touppart, the Cariri supreme deity. One day Grandfather was taking care of the children while the adults were off hunting. He changed them into peccaries and took them all into the sky with him up a tree, which he bade the ants cut down. The Cariri tried to reerect the tree, but could not; the children tried to descend by means of a rope made of their girdles, but it was too short and they fell. Grandfather remained in the sky, but sent the people the gift of tobacco, to which they still make offerings.

Grandfather is the one who gave the Cariri enough women. In the beginning there was only one woman for the whole lot. The men begged Grandfather for more. He sent them hunting, cut up the one woman into as many pieces as there were men, and gave each man a piece to hang in his hut. The next time the men came home from hunting, each found a fine wife cooking food in his hut. See WOMEN.

grandmother's funeral In the United States, the traditional excuse for not going to work in order to attend the baseball game: said to be the standard excuse of the office boy to his employer, especially on the opening day of the baseball season in April.

grand right and left An American square dance term. Partners face each other, join right hands, and walk past each other, thus bringing each face to face with another lady or gentleman with whom each joins left hands in passing. They proceed half way around, giving right and left hands alternately, and then promenade to places. [GPK]

grapevine twist An American square dance figure. The leader guides the whole line of eight dancers in a series of loops between couples and around. [GPK]

grass dance A strenuous social dance performed by men's societies of the North American Plains Indians. It evidently originated in the Pawnee *iruska*, and thus goes back to the Dakota *heyoka* and Omaha-Osage crow-belt. It has lost the fire symbolism of the *iruska*. The Crow Indian hot dance is like the grass dance and has also lost the exhibitions of immunity to fire, characteristic of the Arikara hot dance. The grass dance has retained many elements, such as feasting on dog meat, the crow-belts or bustles, roach headdresses, pipes. There is a whistle-bearer, and a whip-bearer for urging lagging dancers, sometimes a sword-bearer. It added the boasting and the give-away features of the Calumet ceremony, such as giving horses and blankets to the poor and old, formerly also, as bravado, a throwing away of wives.

A bunch of grass at the belt is the special emblem of the grass dancers. Members of the several societies dance in turn, singly or in pairs, exhibiting their full agility in bends and jumps accompanied by cries. The singers in the center beat a large drum. The grass dance became widely adopted, notably by the Sarsi, Blackfoot, Gros Ventre, Assiniboin, Crow, Arikara, Hidatsa, Arapaho, Pawnee, Omaha, Iowa, Ponca, Kansa, Dakota, Menomini, and Potawatomi Indians. Among the Chippewa and Winnebago it is an intrusive dance during the dream dance. Its spread preceded the ghost dance by several decades, and was motivated similarly by economic conditions and as an outlet for energies in times of distress. Its fine songs serve as a further attraction. Among the tribes that have retained it, it has lost its ceremonial features, and is an occasion for display and merriment. [GPK]

grateful dead The motif (E341 ff.; Types 505–508) of a very widespread group of folktales, which typically begin with the hero, as he starts on a journey, coming upon a group of people ill-treating or refusing to bury the corpse of a dead man who had died before paying his debts. The hero gives his last penny, either to pay the man's debts or to give him decent burial, and goes on his way. Within a few hours a traveling companion joins him (occasionally in the form of a horse or other animal, but usually in human form), who aids him in some impossible task (or a series of tasks and adventures), gets him a fortune, saves his life, marries him to a princess, etc. Sometimes the companion helps the hero on the condition that they divide all winnings. Sometimes this proves to be half the princess, or a first-born child. But he relents and relinquishes his half when the other is about to fulfil the promise. The story ends with the companion's disclosing himself as the man whose corpse the other had befriended. (See Gerould, *Grateful Dead,* Folklore Society, 1908). See Tobit.

grave and **graveyard** Primitive peoples are apt to consider the grave as the home of the departed and try to make it comfortable. Huts are often erected above the grave (South America, Philippines, New Guinea, East Central Africa) or underground chambers are provided (West Africa, ancient Crete). To the grave today relatives bring flowers, and in some cultures food and drink (Russia and China).

The shape of the grave and of the mound, barrow, or tomb above it varied. It might be shallow or deep, fenced against wild animals or leveled to hide it from cannibals, ghouls, and marauders. In the grave the body might be left sitting, squatting, or prone on side or back. The direction in which it was faced or headed was important and varied greatly—Moslems toward Mecca, Christian Europeans toward the West, migrant tribes toward the homeland of their ancestors. Solomon Islanders were always buried with their feet turned inland.

Gravestones, earlier considered shrines to the ghost, are now mere markers, but vary from large and elaborate stones to small wooden signs. Inscriptions and epitaphs defy death, hope for immortality, and usually praise the deceased. Graveposts (American Indians) may be upright or prone and are rudely carved and dressed to resemble the dead man.

Urns, now pots for growing plants, once served as burial receptacles for bones and ashes, as in many burials in the very old (900–400 B.C.) Hallstatt, Austria, burying ground. Willow, cypress, and yew trees are thought appropriate for graveyards. The willow's pendent branches express sorrow; the upright conical cypress, hope; the yew's evergreen leaves, eternal life. In China for centuries cypress and pine have been planted on graves to strengthen the souls of the departed.

Graves are sacred ground, not to be carelessly trodden. Graveyards are to be avoided at night when ghosts may stroll.

The word cemetery, now preferred euphemistically to graveyard, means literally sleeping chamber, and was first used of the catacombs of Rome, then of the consecrated ground around a church, now of any graveyard.

Certain sects controlling cemeteries exclude persons of another faith or no faith, also murderers and suicides. Poor persons buried at civil expense are interred in an undesirable section called the potter's field, after the land bought "to bury strangers in" allegedly with the blood moncy of Judas (*Matt.* xxvii, 7), although some scholars hold that the name of this cemetery, Aceldama or Field of Blood (*Acts* i, 19), is a Christian corruption of Akeldamach, Field of Sleep. See BURIAL; CAIRN; CREMATION; FUNERAL.   CHARLES FRANCIS POTTER

Gray Goose An American Negro ballad, probably of pre-Civil War origin, preserved as a work song among convicts of the Texas State Penitentiary. It is one of the few animal ballads of America and shows the West African pattern of the animal that outwits or outlasts its enemies. The goose survives shooting, cooking, and sawing, and finally flaps off honking with a string of goslings behind it. The refrain, "Lawd, Lawd, Lawd," is sung by the chorus when it serves as a gang song.

Great Bear The constellation usually known as Ursa Major, the Big Dipper, Charles's Wain, etc.: subject of etiological myth and folktale among almost every people, ancient and contemporary, on whom it shines.

In the cold fierce winter a big bear used to devour the game of the Iroquois Indians. The hunters could not catch it; always, just as they came upon it, it would disappear and leave no track. No one ever got close enough to shoot an arrow. One night three brothers in a certain village dreamed that they found the bear. In the morning they took the three dreams for a sign and set out secretly to search for him with their little dog, Jiyeh. Often they saw the bear, but it always vanished in the snow leaving no trail. They did not stop to rest, either night or day, but always kept following the bear or its shadow through ice and snow and pitiless winds, until they came to the edge of the world where it touches the northern sky. There they stood and looked. They saw the icy mists and white clouds and the bear running through the snow on the mountains. So they climbed the paths into the cold north sky. Finally they saw the bear ahead of them, shouldering his way through the clouds and weaving a great invisible net as he traveled. At last they saw him crawl under the curved arch of a cave to rest. They had him at last, they thought. They meant to capture him asleep in the cave. But the bear heard them. He woke from his sleep, rose up with the net in his paws, gathered the hunters into it, and flung them into the sky. There they are yet with their little dog, forever following the great bear of the north who forever escapes.

The four stars in the bowl of the dipper comprise the bear; the three stars in the handle are the brothers, the perpetual hunters. The Iroquois also see the little dog following them. The arch of Corona Borealis shows the mouth of the cave the bear crawled into to rest.

This story of the bear and the hunters is known, with certain definite variations, among North American Indians from the Alaskan Eskimos to the Arizona pueblos, among the Sioux of the Plains, the Nova Scotia Micmacs, and the North Pacific tribes. See URSA MAJOR.

Great Mother The fertility goddess of Anatolia, known by various names throughout the region, and best known as Cybele. She was the source of life, and as such was identified with the nature, earth, and fertility goddesses of surrounding cultures, e.g. of Crete, Egypt.

Great Spirit The erroneous notion that among the Indians of North America there existed a general belief in an overruling deity, the "Great Spirit," is a popular fallacy of the 19th century which still persists to some degree. Although the concept of a supreme deity, either otiose or active, may have been aboriginal for some tribes, actually all groups recognized a number of supernatural beings and attributed power to a variety of animate and inanimate objects. Supernatural power for success in war, hunting, gambling, curing, witchcraft, oratory, and other pursuits could be obtained from a host of beings. Even though prayers might be addressed to one deity in particular in such major annual ceremonies as the Sun dance, the Big

House, or the busk (and even this was not always the case), no tribe can be said to have concentrated on the worship and propitiation of a single high god. [EWV]

Great Tellings Long pseudo-historical narratives of the Mohave Indians; specifically, migration myths and war tales. The Mohave word for them is *ich-kanava*. There is no clear central theme; their great emphasis is on geographical detail, place names, the long marches, and the settlements, interwoven with infinite detail of food, itinerary, and the thoughts of the characters. A complete and uninterrupted recital of one of these narratives would take more than 24 hours. They are believed to have been revealed in dreams.

Green Corn dance A corn-ripening celebration held by American Indians at the time of the edibility of the first green corn, thus a specialized form of corn dance. It adds, to the thanksgiving motive of a harvest dance, a supplication for the continued prosperity of the plants. The Cherokee *se'lu* and Iroquois *oneont'oenǫ* are specific short corn dances that constitute part of the longer all-day sequences of the respective green corn ceremonials, *agohundi* and *ahdake'wäo*. The *agohundi* and Creek *busk* included the administering of medicine to avoid sickness from the eating of the unripe corn. This curative feature has superseded the original function among these two tribes, though other agricultural tribes, as the Iroquois, Delaware, and Pueblos, have adhered to the original significance. See CORN DANCE. [GPK]

Greensleeves An English love song of the Elizabethan period, mentioned by Shakespeare and by Beaumont and Fletcher; it is in Playford's *The Dancing Master* (1686) and in *The Beggars' Opera*. The bass of the melody is the *Passamezzo antico*, an Italian basso ostinato tune of the 16th and 17th century group of such tunes. The melody has been used for a number of other settings both folk and non-folk. A waits' New Year's carol dating from a black-letter collection of 1642 is among these.

Gregory, Lady Augusta, née Persse (1859–1932) Irish folklore student and playwright, wife of Sir William Gregory. She helped found the Irish National Theatre Society, and became director of the Abbey Theatre at Dublin. Her *Our Irish Theatre* (1914) is the story of this movement and theater. Her somewhat free renderings of the ancient Irish legends are, as a result of her poetic gift and sure choice of language, perhaps the most readable expositions of the stories. Among her works are: *Cuchulain of Muirthemne* (1902), *Gods and Fighting Men* (1904), *A Book of Saints and Wonders* (1907), *The Kiltartan History Book* (1909), *Seven Short Plays* (1909), *Irish Folk History Plays* (1912), *The Kiltartan Poetry Book* (1919), *Visions and Beliefs in the West of Ireland* (1920), *Three Last Plays* (1928), *Coole* (1931).

gremlin Any airborne supernatural being (spirit, demon, imp) whose function is to cause pilots and aircrew (especially military) trouble and inconvenience. So far as is known, these little people first began taking to the air during World War I, particularly among the RAF. However, it was 1922 before anyone dared mention their name. According to a letter to *Time* (Sept. 28, 1943) from a member of the British Air Commission, who prefers to remain anonymous for reasons of per-

sonal security, on a routine RAF flight in that year, the pilot called the weather station at Le Bourget field, Paris, for a weather report and was warned, "Gremlins sur la manche." The warning did not make sense, but when his radio went out shortly thereafter he realized its implications. Some people say that the name derives from Old English *gremian*, to vex.

There is little agreement as to their description among those who have seen these little people. In *Punch* (Nov. 11, 1942), an article entitled "Gremlins, Aircrews, for the use of" says: "The standard Gremlin stands about twenty inches high and weighs some seventeen pounds in still air. In appearance it is rather like a North American Jack rabbit crossed with a bull terrier ...(has) large ears which are usually covered with a rudimentary growth of hair, the facial expression being reminiscent of an A.C.2 who has just been advised that his 48–hour pass has been cancelled." W. E. Woosnam-Jones's article (*Spectator*, Jan. 1, 1943) says: "They stand about a foot high when in a fully materialized condition, and are usually clad in green breeches and red jackets, ornamented with neat ruffles. They always wear spats and top hats, although the Fleet Air Arm reports a marine species with web feet and fins on their heels. Oddly enough gremlins have no wings and always fly as passengers." *The New York Times Magazine* (Apr. 11, 1943) mentions "The six-inch tall Gremlins with horns and black leather suction boots..."

However, all airmen, both flight and ground personnel, are agreed that the gremlins possess prodigious strength, a high degree of technical proficiency, and a working knowledge of aerodynamics, advanced mechanical engineering, and meteorology of a very high order. Of them, the motto, "The difficult we do immediately, the impossible takes us a little longer," is indeed a reality. For instance, the article from *Punch* mentioned above tells of gremlins having bodily inverted a Sunderland bomber on patrol over the Bay of Biscay, and the navigator's gremlin which "is a mover of mountains, islands, aircraft-carriers (and)...under extreme conditions it will reshuffle all the stars in the heavens." Woosnam-Jones claims that gremlins have placed the runways of every training airport in Britain on hydraulic lifts, and just as the pupil-pilot is about to make a perfect three-point landing, the duty gremlin pulls a lever either raising or lowering the runway as much as ten feet.

Heretofore, the gremlin has been looked on as a new phenomenon, a product of the machine age—the age of the air. This is undoubtedly an error. After three years of experience, observation, study, and thought on the part of the author, it appears that gremlins comprise a rather cosmopolitan citizen army of spirits. Whether banded together by loss of their homes through war damage, or merely from a natural curiosity concerning airplanes, they continue to prod man and keep him alert, as they have done in the past. Some gremlins are technicians who have been imparting knowledge to man since the beginning of the world; these are probably recruited from the ranks of fallen angels who admittedly know more of the workings of the universe than man will ever learn. Others are craftsmen and artisans such as the dwarfs who provided the knights of the Middle Ages with wondrous steel blades, helmets, and weapons. Some have special knowledge of a particular element, such as the upper and lower air (and here we might mention the spandule which is a gremlin found only above 10,000 ft.). Lastly there is the rank and file of demons and imps who drink up fuel, bore holes in airplane wings and other parts, jab gunners and bombardiers just as they have their sights lined up, and the like. This theory was not arrived at exactly by logic: The author was examining a parted cable which bore obvious tooth marks in spite of the fact that the break occurred in a most inaccessible part of the plane, when he heard a gruff voice inquiring, "How many times must you be told to obey orders and not tackle jobs you aren't qualified for?—This is how it should be done," whereupon another cable parted with a musical twang. The voice was obviously "big brass" and a flashlight beam revealed an awed gremlin surveying the neat new break as a rear-end suggestive of an Inspector-General passed from sight. It was a neater job.

In spite of all that has been written, not all the activities of gremlins are destructive. Many times gremlins have banded together to assist a pilot fly home in a small percentage of the plane he was issued only a few hours before. [JWH]

griffin See GRYPS.

grigri The term for magic charms used by French writers, applied especially to those of West Africa. All reservations entered on the use of the word *fetish* apply in equal measure to employing this term in meaningful description. [MJH]

Grimhild (1) According to the *Sigurd* and *Volsunga Sagas*, the wife of Giuki, king of the Nibelungs and mother of Gunnar, Gudrun, and Hogni. She was an accomplished sorceress and continually brewed potions to make others carry out her wishes, as when she gave Sigurd the drink of forgetfulness, which made him forget Brynhild and marry her daughter, Gudrun.

(2) According to Wagner's *Ring of the Nibelung*, the mother of Gunther and Gutrune by king Giuki, and of Hagen, by the dwarf, Alberich. She was sometimes confused with Kriemhild.

Grimm, Jakob Ludwig Karl (1785–1863) and his brother **Wilhelm Karl** (1786–1859), German philologists and mythologists, the founders of scientific folklore study. The brothers were close companions throughout their lives, living together even after the semi-invalid Wilhelm married in 1825. They collaborated mainly on *Kinder- und Hausmärchen* (vol. I, 1812; vol. II, 1815; translated into English in 1884 as *Household Tales*, but popularly known as "Grimm's Fairy Tales"); *Deutsche Sagen* (1816–1818); and *Deutsches Wörterbuch* (vol. I, 1854); but they published many other works separately or in collaboration. In the *Household Tales*, the Grimms not only produced a remarkable collection of the disappearing folklore of their people, but created a great literary masterpiece, important to the history of the German language and possessing few rivals in other countries.

Jakob Grimm in his *Deutsche Mythologie* (1835) laid the scientific basis for folklore research and won the name of father of folklore science. In his *Rechtsaltertümer* (1828), a study of old Teutonic laws, he discussed a kind of proverb which constitutes the body of popular law in non-literate societies. Jakob Grimm's great and exhaustive work *Deutsche Grammatik* (1819–1837), con-

taining his formulation of Grimm's Law (of the consonant changes in the Indo-European languages evolving to the Germanic languages), is generally considered as having laid the foundation of German philology. The work of Wilhelm Grimm, in revising the tales in the light of a growing knowledge of popular language and of variants of the stories, continued through enlarged and improved editions of the collection until 1857. Wilhelm's essay "On the Nature of Folk Tales" appeared in the second edition in 1819. In 1822 the brothers published a volume of commentary and comparative study of the tales, which formed the third volume of their folktale study.

The final statement of the Grimms' theories of folklore study was made by Wilhelm in 1856. The two chief ideas were: 1) that those tales which closely resemble each other were undoubtedly derived from a common Indo-European ancestry; and 2) the tales are brokendown myths and can be understood only through an understanding of the myths from which they derive. These two main theories are no longer accepted. But two others, made merely as suggestions and not developed further by Wilhelm Grimm, have been worked out and adopted by later scholars. These suggestions were: 1) that situations existed which were "so simple and natural that they reappear everywhere"; and 2) that peoples borrowed folklore materials from one another. These two principles were to become basic in the science of folklore.

Grottasongr The Grotti Song or Quern Song, preserved in the *Prose Edda* of Snorri Sturluson. See FRODI.

groundhog or **woodchuck** A marmot (*Marmota monax*); the American species is known either as groundhog or woodchuck. The animal is associated with Candlemas Day (February 2). On that day, the weather is a most important affair, for on that date depends the good or bad luck for sowing and planting according to omens. If the groundhog comes out of his hole on February 2 and sees his shadow, he will go back in and stay six more weeks. So if the day is sunny, winter will continue and the result will be bad crops; if it is cloudy, the groundhog will see no shadow, and the reverse will be true. These notions prevail on the Continent and in England and are nowhere more popular than in the United States. Here the groundhog or woodchuck is the prognosticating animal; in Germany, it is the badger; previously in Europe and the United States, it was the bear.

In Missouri, Groundhog Day was officially established as February 2 by Act of the Missouri Legislature. However, in Arkansas and in Missouri and elsewhere, a hot controversy arose between individuals and in the press disputing this date. Old-timers cling to February 14 as the proper time for sowing and planting. To them, this date is Groundhog Day and not the usually accepted February 2.

The groundhog appears in some animal tales, for example in the Cherokee story, "Origin of the Groundhog's Dance" (James Mooney, *Myths of the Cherokee*, p. 279). It is essentially a *pourquoi* tale, but suggests the cleverness of the groundhog. In New England very many stories center about the woodchuck. [GPS]

grues Shocking quatrains of a gruesome nature are gleefully recited by adolescents and occasionally used as fillers by newspapers and cheaper magazines and joke-books. They are concerned with the horrible fate or bloody misadventures of some enfant terrible, and run in popularity cycles with a current juvenile hero, Little Willie or Little Bertie. Robert Louis Stevenson is alleged to have named them "grues" which is credible, since in Scotland the noun "grue" means a fit of shivering. One of many variants widely circulated in the United States runs:

> Little Willie on the track
> Didn't hear the engine's squeal:
> Now the engine's coming back,
> Scraping Willie off the wheel.

Another evidently of English origin is:

> Prigged her mother's pickled peaches,
> Dotty did, and died with screeches:
> Heed this touching tale! It teaches
> Mothers shouldn't pickle peaches.

Short gruesome anecdotes of a similar character but done in prose have recently had considerable circulation in such cycles as the Little Moron tales and the Little Audrey stories. [CFP]

Grundtvig, Nikolai Frederik Severin (1783–1872) Danish theologian, historian, student of Icelandic and Anglo-Saxon, and poet; father of the folklorist Svend Hersleb Grundtvig. The elder Grundtvig was given the titular rank of bishop in 1861. Grundtvig had some influence on the educational development in his country, establishing schools in which the national poetry and like studies formed a part of the curriculum. He has been called the Danish Carlyle. Among his works are: *On the Songs in the Edda; Northern Mythology* (1808); *Decline of the Heroic Life in the North* (1809–1811); *The Rhyme of Roskilde;* a collection of religious poems called *Songs for the Danish Church* (sic) (1837–1841); and an anthology of early Scandinavian verse (1838).

Grundtvig, Svend Hersleb (1824–1883) Danish philologist and collector of Danish and Scandinavian folklore, was a son of Bishop N. Grundtvig. The son collected seven volumes of old folk songs, published as *Danmarks gamle Folkeviser* (1853–1912), their publication being continued by Axel Olrik after Grundtvig's death. He published a collection of Danish sagas, *Danske Sagn* (1854–1861), and three volumes of folktales, *Danske Folkeæventyr, efter utrykte Kilder* (1876, 1878, and 1884). From 1869 to his death Grundtvig was professor of Scandinavian philology at the University of Copenhagen.

Gryps or **Gryphus** In Greek mythology, a griffin; a monster with the head and wings of an eagle, the body of a lion, and sometimes the tail of a serpent, dwelling in the country between the Hyperboreans and the one-eyed Arimaspians. The griffins were enemies of horses and were constantly at war with the Arimaspians who tried to capture the gold guarded by the griffins. The chariot of the sun (sometimes that of Zeus and of Nemesis also) was drawn by griffins. The idea of these creatures probably was brought from the East, perhaps from Indo-Iranian mythology. Wherever they appear in legend the griffins are always guardians of mines and treasure, as for example Scythian and Indian gold.

Gu An important god of Dahomey Negro religion; god of metal and war; son of Mawu and Lisa. At birth his body was solid stone from which projected a sharp metal blade. He was sent into the world to help man cope with his environment. He gave man tools and implements, taught him their uses and manufacture (i.e. iron-working). He is conceived of as a power rather than as an animal or anthropomorphic deity; for instance, Gu was the tool in Mawu's hand when she created man, the sharp tool which shaped him.

guabina A couple dance of the interior of Colombia, characterized by a step-hop in 2/4 time against the 3/4 tempo of the guitars. Holding a kerchief between them, the dancers circle around a hat, advance, recede. [GPK]

guardian spirits Guardian spirits are a projection of the belief that the things people want are hard to get and are protected by a spirit or god or power which will be helpful if approached properly but can become dangerous and is frequently unfriendly. In China each plot of earth has its guardian, sometimes assisted by a wife and now and again by a servant. These are the generalized guardians of place propitiated by peasants in moments of great or small crisis. They are important in getting good crops and they conduct the soul of the farmer within a few hours after death to the next higher official in the divine bureaucracy.

Hidden treasures, like the gold of the Nibelungs, are guarded by dragons, gods, ghosts, spirits, demons, or other powers. Mountains, streams, marshes, forests, and seas have each its own guardian, which must be propitiated before a stranger is permitted to penetrate. Each individual also has his genius or guardian spirit. Some peoples have thought of these as two spirits, a good and a bad, associated with the "spiritual soul" and the "physical soul." When these two are not in accord they lead people to do things which are pleasant but wrong. [RDJ]

🖙 Throughout North America, Indians of almost every tribe sought to acquire supernatural spirit teachers, or guardian spirits, who through songs and advice, bestowed supernatural gifts for war, hunting, gambling, curing, oratory, and other pursuits upon the human being fortunate enough to establish contact with them. In many Indian tribes young boys nearing puberty were sent out, naked and without food, to fast and try to acquire a guardian spirit who would bestow power upon them through dreams and visions. Vision-questing took different forms among the different tribes; in some, youths were told to spend anywhere from two to four days in the woods, alone, or in a little perch in the trees; in other tribes they were made to dive in bottomless pools to acquire a guardian spirit. Some tribes allowed vision-questing during the winter only, others, at any time of the year. Girls, during their first menses, when they were isolated and semi-fasting in a hut built for that purpose, were also likely to acquire a guardian spirit. Such spirit might also appear to a child or youth or even to adults in dreams; young people, especially, were closely asked about their dreams by older relatives. At times a guardian spirit might appear, even though no fasting had been undertaken; the spirit was quite likely to have the shape of an animal, or snake, or bird, and later change into human form. It might give a song, and later return to see that the human being had learned the song properly, or to teach him or her additional songs. Usually the power gained through instruction from a guardian spirit was not used until a person was nearing middle age, and often the source of power had to be kept a secret, or the power itself would be invalidated. A person could usually have more than one guardian spirit, if he were so blessed by the supernaturals. In many tribes the shamans, during curing ceremonies, called on their guardian spirits to come and help them; these would appear as animals, advise the shaman of the cause or seat of the illness, and otherwise help him; they would be summoned for this purpose through songs which the shaman had previously learned from them. The acquisition of a guardian spirit or spirits was probably one of the most important of all events in an Indian's life, and until he acquired one through fasting or dreams, he was always constantly urged to try and do so by close relatives. To refuse power from a guardian spirit on the grounds that the spirit knew only evil was extremely dangerous, but was sometimes done.

[EWV]

☞ The concept of the guardian spirit is not as developed among South American Indians as it is in North America. The relationship between a man and a spirit is limited to the shamans. The Guiana and Amazonian *pagé* have at their service one or several spirits who help them in their profession. The ancient Charrua of Uruguay, however, seem to have had toward guardian spirits an attitude very similar to that of the North American Indians. The young men of the Charrua went into the wilderness and exposed themselves to severe hardships until they had a vision of a spirit who became their protector through life. The Island Caribs also established a close association with spirits who were their special guardians. It is still a debatable question whether the *wauki* (*guauqui*) or "mystical brother" of the Inca emperors were guardian spirits or not. [AM]

Guatavita, Lake of   A lake in Colombia famous for the ceremonies of the gilded man (El Dorado). Every year the chief of the region, gilded with gold dust, and accompanied by his noblemen, went on a raft to the middle of the lake to make offerings to a snake god.

[AM]

Gudrun (1) In the *Volsunga Saga*, the daughter of Grimhild and Giuki, king of the Nibelungs. She married Sigurd, after her mother had brewed a magic potion for him which made him forget Brynhild, his betrothed. Her brother, Guttorm, killed Sigurd to obtain the Nibelung gold. Later Gudrun married Atli, king of the Huns and Brynhild's brother. He also coveted the gold. He invited her brothers to visit him, and then treacherously attacked them. Gudrun fought with her brothers in the fight, but all of them were killed. In revenge, she slew her two sons by Atli, fed their hearts to him, and then killed him also.

(2) In the *Gudrun Lied*, a 13th century German epic, the daughter of Hilde and Hettel, king of Hegelingen. She was very beautiful and had three suitors: Siegfried, king of the Moorland; Hartmut, a prince of Normandy; and Herwig of Zeeland. Herwig made war against Hettel and won his consent to marry his daughter at the end of a year. Learning of this, Siegfried attacked Herwig's lands, to draw him off. But while Herwig and Hettel joined forces to attack Siegfried, Hartmut kid-

napped Gudrun. Whereupon Herwig, Hettel, and Siegfried were then unified and set off together to rescue her. Gudrun was captive in Hartmut's castle for 13 years, and because of her persistent refusal to marry him, his mother made the most menial of servants of her. She was finally rescued by Herwig and her brother Ortwin.

Guinevere   In Arthurian legend, Arthur's queen, lover of Lancelot. She figures variously in medieval romance: Geoffrey of Monmouth presents her as Guenhuvara, ward of Cador of Cornwall, but of Roman descent; as Wenhaver in Layamon's *Brut* she is blood kin to Cador; in the 13th century *Arthour and Merlin* she appears as Gvenour, daughter of Leodegran of Carohaise. Geoffrey of Monmouth's Guenhuvara was left in the care of Mordred, Arthur's nephew, while Arthur was warring on the Continent. At Rome Arthur learned that Mordred had taken both the kingdom and the queen. Malory's 15th century *Book of Arthur* develops the love story of Lancelot and Guinevere in fullest detail to the moment of their betrayal to the king. Guinevere was sentenced to be burned at the stake, was rescued by Lancelot, was later restored to Arthur, during his subsequent wars, took the veil, and was eventually buried with him (legend says at Glastonbury).

☞ Guinevere may have been a historical person or a creature of myth. In Welsh literature she is called Gwenhwyvar, which, except for the first element meaning "white," is of uncertain origin. The story of her abduction by Melvas, King of the Summer Land, told by Caradoc of Lancarvan before 1136, and the story of her abduction by Meleagant, told by Chrétien de Troyes about 1170, seem to show that she had inherited the role of a Celtic Persephone. Her rescue by Lancelot and his four combats with Meleagant probably reflect the struggle for the possession of a vegetation maiden by the rival forces of winter and summer.

Bibliography:

T. P. Cross, W. A. Nitze, *Lancelot and Guenevere* (1930).

R. S. Loomis, *Arthurian Tradition and Chrétien de Troyes* (1949), index *sub* Guenievre. [RSL]

guitar   A flat-bodied stringed instrument plucked with the fingers, descended from the lute, which originated in the Orient and reached Europe with the Moors at about the period of the Crusades. It is the characteristic instrument for accompanying much of the folk song and dance of Spain and Italy, of the Gipsies, of Latin America, and of North American folk singers of the southern mountains and the western plains. Related popular instruments of the lute family include the Russian balalaika, the Hawaiian ukulele, and the Japanese samisen, all used to accompany folk and popular dancing and singing.

A connection between the guitar and witches and devils has been made in many areas. Tuscan witch songs include one about a witch who was changed into a guitar called La Magdalena, which was not restored to human likeness until after the passage of a century, when a wizard musician played upon it. Among American Negroes, playing the guitar is a part of the procedure in making a bargain with the Devil. Preparations include filing the nails, arming oneself with a bone of a black cat, and playing the guitar at the crossroads at midnight. The approach of the Devil is announced by music which draws near to the player and accompanies his guitar. He must continue playing without looking up while the Satanic visitor exchanges instruments with him, clips his nails to the raw quick, and then withdraws. Thereafter, the Faustlike character has complete mastery of the guitar and is endowed with the gift of invisibility and other supernatural powers, for which he has given his afterlife to the Devil.

The guitar furnishes the chief accompaniment for flamenco music, for the bolero, and the South American *chacarera*, the *son* of Mexico and South America, the Portuguese *fado*, the cowboy and lumberjack songs of North America, the ballads, lonesome tunes, and country blues of the southern Appalachians, etc.

Gula In Babylonian mythology, the goddess of healing, a creative goddess, and a preserver of life; in later myth, daughter of Anu; consort of Ningirsu (Ninib), and associated with Shamash in invocations. She controlled death, being able to restore life, and diseases; hence, she is sometimes a destroying goddess, using disease to kill. Her feast was late in April. Compare BAU.

Gum Baby See TAR BABY.

gumbo-ya-ya Literally, everybody talks at once: term (equivalent to contemporary American yateta-yat-yat) applied in derision to the traditional "spend-the-day" gatherings of Creole women, where gossip was the main course served. *Gumbo-Ya-Ya* is the title given by the Louisiana WPA Writers' Project to a compilation of Louisiana folklore studies including Creole, Cajun, and Negro material.

Gummere, Francis Barton (1855–1919) American educator and philologist, and a specialist in traditional ballad. Son of Samuel James Gummere, president of Haverford College, he was graduated at Haverford at the age of 17. He tried clerking, then law, but finally settled on teaching, which was the chief profession in his family history. At Harvard he became a pupil of Francis James Child. Later he studied at the universities at Strasbourg, Berlin, Leipzig, and Freiburg. In the field of popular ballad study he is mainly known for a theory of the "communal origin" of the English and Scottish ballads, a theory which goes back to Jakob Grimm, but which Gummere developed further. Among his works are: *Germanic Origins* (1892), *Old English Ballads* (1894), *The Beginnings of Poetry* (1901), *The Popular Ballad* (1907), *The Oldest English Epic* (1909), and the chapter on ballads in the *Cambridge History of English Literature* (volume II, 1908).

Gungnir In Teutonic mythology, Odin's infallible spear, on which oaths were taken.

Gunnar According to the *Volsunga* and *Sigurd Sagas*, the son of Grimhild and Giuki, king of the Nibelungs, and brother of Gudrun, Hogni, and Guttorm. When Sigurd came to live with them, they became fast friends. After Gunnar became king, Grimhild suggested Brynhild as a suitable queen. Because Gunnar could not ride through the ring of fire, however, Sigurd, who had been drugged into forgetfulness of his betrothal to Brynhild, assumed Gunnar's form and wooed her. After their marriage, Brynhild recognized Sigurd, and Gunnar became jealous, but refused to kill him, as they had

sworn brotherhood. After Sigurd's death, all was explained, and when Brynhild killed herself, Gunnar allowed her to be burned on Sigurd's funeral pyre. Atli claimed Gudrun as atonement for the death of his sister, Brynhild. When Atli heard of the Nibelung gold he laid plans to acquire it, and invited Gunnar and his court to visit him. Gunnar accepted, in spite of warnings, but consented to hide the gold in the Rhine. They were treacherously attacked, and after an epic struggle, were all slain, including Gunnar who refused to reveal the hiding place of the gold. Compare GUNTHER.

Gunther (1) According to the *Nibelungenlied*, king of Burgundy and brother of Gernot, Geisler, and Kriemhild. He was a noble warrior with whom Siegfried was allied. When Gunther went to woo Brunhild, he was appalled at the feats of strength demanded of him to win her hand, but Siegfried, in his invisible cloak helped him to succeed. On their wedding night, Brunhild, who was beginning to suspect trickery, bound Gunther in her girdle and hung him on a clothes peg for the night. The next night Siegfried again put on his cloak and gave her such a thorough beating that she never regained her great strength, and, believing that it was Gunther, remained a faithful wife until her death. Gunther took no part in the murder of Siegfried, and mourned his loss. After Kriemhild's marriage to Etzel, he went to visit them, was forced to defend himself against her plotting, and was finally beheaded on her order.

(2) According to Wagner's *Ring of the Nibelung*, king of the Gibichungs, brother of Gutrune and half-brother of Hagen. When Siegfried came offering friendship or combat, he welcomed him to the court. Hagen wished Gunther to marry Brunhilde, and to this end, gave Siegfried a potion to make him forget Brunhilde and marry Gutrune. This was so successful that Siegfried offered to assume Gunther's form and woo Brunhilde for him. Gunther became suspicious when Brunhilde recognized Siegfried after their marriage and allowed Hagen to kill him, repenting too late. Gunther was killed by Hagen in combat for the possession of Siegfried's ring. Compare GUNNAR.

Gunuko One of the principal deities of the Nupe of Northern Nigeria, who has been retained in the New World, where he figures in the African cults of Brazil. [MJH]

guru or **gosāin** In India, a spiritual leader or teacher. Among the members of the Vallabhāchārya sect of Vaishnavism, the guru is supremely important, the mediator between God and the sinner. Any who malign a guru are struck dumb and become serpents. The gurus, who are of the line of Vallabha, follow and reenact Kṛishṇa's early adventures with the gopis.

Gusi cult A religious cult of the Dusun of Borneo, characterized by the worship of Chinese green porcelain jars, regarded as sacred. Old jars (chiefly Chinese) are regarded as valuable by many of the peoples in Borneo and the Philippine Islands, but the Dusun believe that certain of them are inhabited by spirits and are thus sacred. A type of jar called *gusi* is especially reverenced. These are pot-bellied in shape, greenish-brown in color, and often have a finely crackled glaze. The gusi are so highly valued that as much as two to three thousand dollars is paid for a single one. Gusi are kept in a specially enclosed area in Dusun homes and offerings are made to them in cases of illness and annually at the festival of Mengahau. The spirits inhabiting them are those of ancestors: beneficent when well treated, evilly disposed if ignored.

In both Borneo and the Philippine Islands jar burial was apparently common at one time and porcelain jars were imported from China for this purpose. The Spanish cut off the trade in an effort to divert the wealth of the Philippines to their own uses. Consequently jars increased in value until a man's wealth came to be reckoned by the number of jars he owned. These were handed down from one generation to another and tales gathered around them concerning their origins and powers. References to them abound in the folktales of the region. In the interior of Luzon, Mindanao, and Palawan, tribes still reckon the bride price wholly or partly in these jars and one of them is considered payment in full in place of a head when settling feuds.

gusla The characteristic instrument of southern Slavic folk music; a primitive one- or two-stringed fiddle played with a crude, often home-made bow, and held against the thigh. It is played by itinerant musicians called *guslari*, who use it for accompanying long heroic ballads or extemporized songs.

gut bucket The receptacle catching the drip from the cask in a barrel house: term applied to the type of early jazz and to the musical timbre characteristic of music played in saloons of the period during which jazz developed.

Gutrune In Wagner's *Ring of the Nibelung*, Gunther's sister, whom Siegfried is persuaded to marry instead of his betrothed, Brunhilde. This is accomplished by a magic potion of forgetfulness which Hagen gives him. In the main, Wagner's story follows the *Volsunga Saga*, rather than the *Nibelungenlied*. Compare GUDRUN; KRIEMHILD.

Gwau Meo In Mala (Solomon Islands) folklore, the culture hero son of the sun worshipped as a ghost: literally, red-head. Red-haired Gwau Meo arrived as an immigrant at Mala in an outrigger canoe with a group of followers. The band settled inland and populated the island.

Gwydion In Brythonic mythology, a son of Dôn, brother of Amaethon and Govannon, brother and lover of Arianrhod, and by her father of Dylan and Llew Llaw Gyffes. Gwydion is interpreted as a Brythonic culture hero—bringer of gifts from the gods to man. This construction stems from the story of Gwydion's theft of the swine of Pryderi, who is interpreted as an otherworld god of earlier mythology. MacCulloch suggests that Gwydion is a later anthropomorphism of some ancient swine god, all the more so because a swine was one of the temporary shapes into which Math transformed him for helping Gilvaethwy abduct Math's virgin footholder, Goewin. Gwydion was a powerful magician, and is credited with originating April Fool's Day, from the fact that it was on April 1 he conjured up the armies to fool Arianrhod into bestowing arms on Llew Llaw Gyffes. It was Gwydion who helped Math create Blodenwedd, the flower-wife, for Llew. The Milky Way is conceived of as the track made by Gwydion seeking Llew after his treacherous death.

gyertyás tánc The Hungarian candle dance. On the evening following a wedding the guests follow the best man, bride, and groom in a long line, little fingers linked. A candle is held in the remaining fingers of the right hand. With a balancing step the line progresses slowly to the left in circular and serpentine formations. Thus it falls into the tradition of open rounds or link dances (former fertility rites) that extend all along the Mediterranean from Catalonia to Palestine. The symbolism is emphasized by the bearing of the matrimonial candles. See CANDLE DANCE. [GPK]

Gyges (1) or **Gyes** In Greek mythology, one of the Hecatoncheires, the hundred-handed giants.

(2) The first king of the third dynasty of Lydia (reigned 716–678 B.C.) who dethroned Candaules. In Plato (*Rep.* II, 359) the shepherd Gyges discovered a brazen horse in a chasm, and a body within the horse. He took from the body a ring which had the power of making him invisible. With its aid he entered the queen's chamber, there murdered the king, and took the crown for himself. In Herodotus (I, 8–13) is found the better known story. King Candaules induces Gyges despite the latter's reluctance, to enter the bedchamber so that he may appreciate the queen's naked beauty. She spies him and next day offers him the choice of the crown or instant death. Gyges was proverbial for his riches and made many presents to the Delphic oracle.

Gypsy Laddie A Scottish-English ballad (Child #200) telling of the elopement of the lord's wife with the Gipsy Johnny Faa. The spell the Gipsy casts is so strong that she refuses to return to her husband, though with the Gipsy she must sleep in the barn. The ballad reflects some of the feeling against Gipsies in early 17th century Scotland, Gipsies being banned from that kingdom in 1609. Several American versions, often garbled (compare BLACK JACK DAVID), are known.

habañera   A Cuban dance of African origin, slow and voluptuous and with a characteristic rhythm in 2/4 time. From Cuba it went to Spain, thence to Brazil, Haiti, and all Spanish America. The tango is its off-spring. In Brazil it is popular in both forms. As a dance for several couples it is called *contradanza criolla*, of which the music is in 6/8 time, in two parts of eight measures each. [GPK]

Habdalah, Havdalah, Abdalah, or **Abdalta**   Literally, separation, distinction: in Hebrew religion, the prayers and benedictions recited to mark the division of times of different holiness; specifically, the Sabbath-closing ceremony, when benedictions are said over wine, spices, and a freshly kindled light, and a longer benediction is said in order to emphasize the distinction: originally a synagogue ceremony, later performed in the home.

In rabbinical law, no work might be performed after a holy day until Habdalah benedictions had been recited. Such blessings were said over wine or some other beverage, excluding water. The spices (myrtle is prescribed as one) are meant to solace the Sabbath's oversoul, which grieves at the passing of a holy day.

The light, according to some, had to be newly kindled from wood or stone friction. The candle has to have multiple wicks, two as a minimum: this derives from the plural form "lights" in the benediction. According to Jose ben Halafta, by the beginning of the first Sabbath fire was as yet uncreated. Man became wise at the close of the Sabbath, took two stones, and recited the benediction over the fire he thus made. The benediction over fire is not part of Habdalah observance after those festivals when light is permitted, and is thus probably a rekindling ceremony. It is customary to examine the fingernails during the fire benediction, to see the fire reflected in the winecup or on the nails. Among the reasons given are that the nails, constantly growing, symbolize the wish for the growing prosperity of the week to come, and that the blood, emblem of life, may be seen through the fingers. It is also said that one looks at the fingernails for, even should one forget to kindle the post-Sabbath fire, the starlight reflected by the nails would be a reminder. The curing water from Miriam's well may be drawn at the time of Habdalah; at this time Elijah the prophet appears also.

Among the Jews of Russia, Galicia, and Baden, a girl drinking of the Habdalah wine will grow a mustache. Sprinkling the wine on the tablecloth brings good luck. In Kiev, where distilled spirits replaces the wine, the liquor remaining after the service is spilled into a pan and lighted with the Habdalah candle. Good luck ensues if it is burned away completely; some pass their fingers through the flame, putting them into the pockets to bring a full week. If the Habdalah candle burns to the end, one's sons-in-law will be meritorious. Compare FIRE.

Hachiman   The Japanese God of War, originally the deified Emperor Ojin (4th century A.D.). [JLM]

hactcin   The Apache Indian term for supernatural beings, personifications of the power of objects and natural forces; the creators of Earth and Sky, or the children of the Black Sky and Earth. Among the Jicarilla Apache the term is *hactcin;* Lipan Apache, *hactci;* Navaho, *hactce;* Mescalero Apache, *gahe;* White Mountain Apache, *ga'n.* The *hactcin* or *ga'n* are a class of supernatural beings comparable to the Pueblo kachinas, and like the kachinas are represented in Apache ceremonies by masked dancers. See GAHE. [EWV]

haddock   In Christian legend, the fish of St. Peter, so called because the two black spots near the gills are said to perpetuate the finger and thumb prints of Peter when he took the tribute money out of its mouth. It is also sometimes called the Lord's fish, in the belief that these same two spots are imprints of the thumb and finger of Christ from the moment when he grasped and broke the two fish to feed the multitude. Both stories are common in the British Isles.

New England and Prince Edward Island fishermen, however, claim the spots are the Devil's finger marks, and that the black lines along the haddock's sides were made by the Devil's fingers as the fish slipped away. In Scotland it is thought unlucky to burn haddock bones, because once a haddock warned a fisherman that he would be a stranger to any pot on any hearth where haddock bones were ever burned.

Hades, Aides, Aidoneus, Pluteus, or **Pluton**   In Greek mythology, the god and ruler of the underworld: Hades or Aides being his name (originally poetical) as ruler over the shades; Pluton, the more popular name and the one used in the mysteries and in ordinary reference, indicating his role as the wealth-giving god of the earth. Pluton was the son of Cronus and Rhea, and after his father's overthrow he and his brothers Zeus and Poseidon cast lots for the dominion of the parts of the universe. Zeus won the sky, Poseidon the water, Hades the "darkness of night" of the underworld and the earth; the surface of the earth and Olympus were under the dominion of all three.

The principal myth concerning Hades is the rape of Persephone, though he appears in many other myths and legends, e.g. that of Hercules. As king of the underworld and its ghosts, Pluto is not at all synonymous with the Devil or Satan of Judeo-Christian belief. He is not an enemy of mankind, not a tempter, but rather a neutral, inexorably just ruler, whose realm includes a place of torment (Tartarus) and a paradise (Elysium) as well. He was disliked by mortals, hence the several euphemisms like Polydectes (the gatherer of many) and Pluton (the god of wealth). He had a helmet of invisibility given to him by the Cyclopes. On the island of Erytheia and in the lower world he possessed large herds of oxen. His worship as Hades existed principally at Elis, where his enclosure and temple were opened once a year; there was minor worship of the god throughout Greece and Italy.

In Rome, Pluto became as well Dis pater (Dis being equivalent to Dives, the rich) or Orcus, the latter being a slaying god or angel of death, Dis the ruler of the dead.

Hades was represented as a more dismal, graver Zeus, carrying the key to the gates of the underworld or the staff with which he drove the shades to his realm, and accompanied by Cerberus. As Pluto, his agricultural aspect, he appears with the pronged fork and cornucopia. Sacrifices to him were black, and were made with faces turned away; the cypress and narcissus were sacred to him; he was invoked by striking the earth with the hands.

The name Pluton or Pluto is of later origin, first being used in the fifth century B.C.; earlier he was nameless; in Homer, he is only Aides. With the popular use of Pluto as his name, Hades became attached to the house and the kingdom over which he ruled. There were two traditions regarding its location: one placed it in the farthest west; one had it underground. A later synthesis made the entrance to the underground Hades in the west, although there were local traditions about other entrances, as for example an entrance near Sparta. At the founding of new cities, the Etruscans would dig a hole, supposed to lead to the underworld, and, at a stated time each year, would remove the covering stone to permit the ghosts to rise. In Hades, later tradition places both Tartarus and the Elysian fields. Hades was surrounded by the five waters or rivers: Styx (the Hateful), Acheron (the Woeful), Pyriphlegethon (the Fiery), Cocytus (the Wailing), and Lethe (Forgetfulness). Across Styx, the shades of the dead (only of those actually buried, however) were ferried by Charon, passed Cerberus at the gate which was opened only to those entering and only in the instance of Eurydice ever opened to permit a ghost to return to the realm of light, were judged by Minos, Rhadamanthus, and Æacus, and sometimes Hades himself, and assigned either to Tartarus or to Elysium. See AFTERWORLD; UNDERWORLD.

Hadhayōsh or **Hadhayaōsh** (Pahlavi *Sarsaok*) In Iranian mythology, the ox upon whose back men traversed the sea Vourukasha in primeval times: literally, ever pure. At the resurrection the drink of immortality will be prepared from a mixture of the fat of Hadhayosh and white haoma.

hadi'hi'duus The singing rite of the Iroquois medicine-men's society, corresponding to the Menominee and Chippewa *midewiwin*. Membership is by dream or cure. All meetings are held in secret at the home of the patient. There used to be magic tricks as a feature. Today there are throwing songs, sung during the throwing of sharp points (*gai'dǫn*) at the patient, then introductory songs of the medicine-man, then songs by twos for the round dance or *ganǫyague*. These refer to the animal tutelaries of the members. The dance is a side shuffle to the right, facing the center of the circle. The songs, many of them captivating, reveal their antiquity in the narrow range of tones and scant melodic material. They are accompanied by squashshell or large gourd rattles (*onyasa' gasta'węsä*) as is

common among many Indian medicine societies. The *hadi'hi'duus* are associated with the Little Water Medicine society and follow upon the treatment by that group. [GPK]

hadiwanyásoenǫ The Iroquois marriage dance, one of the few performed in a straight line. With a step-pat the bride and groom progress side by side across the room, then face about and return. It is now known only to older people. [GPK]

hadj or **hajj** The pilgrimage to Mecca required of every free Moslem at least once in his life; those who have made the journey are called by the title *hadji*. Among the Koranic statutes concerning the pilgrimage are laws describing the pilgrim's habit, the clipping or shaving of his hair, the trip to Mount Arafat near Mecca, and the circumambulation of the Kaaba.

hadudo or **xadudo** One of the two major categories of Dahomean marriage forms. The meaning of the word "taking a friend into custody" (literally, friend-keep) describes it as one form of those matings wherein the ritualized payments are not made to the family of the girl, and the man's obligation to the woman's parents are at a minimum. In consequence, the children of matches of this type remain under the control of the mother and her family. This dual division of marriage types is of great significance for an understanding of the forms of New World Negro mating, since it gives an institutional basis in aboriginal tradition for the forms of common-law marriage found everywhere among the lower socioeconomic strata of New World Negro societies. See AMASIADO. [MJH]

Haferbock A field spirit of German folklore: literally, the oat goat.

hag An ugly or malicious old woman, believed to be in league with the Devil or the dead; a witch or sorceress; a she-devil. Occasionally a hag is young and beautiful in appearance, but still a witch or she-devil. The "secret, black, and midnight hags" whom Macbeth questioned were ancient females in league with the dead. The word comes from Old English *hægtes*, witch, Middle English *hagge* or *hegge*, akin to German *hexe*, witch.

Hags are said to "ride" people at night; especially do they like to ride handsome young men. They press upon one's stomach or chest, causing great discomfort and nightmares. *Hag-ridden* means distressed by nightmares, or victimized by hallucinations of having been literally ridden. There are countless stories of hags riding people, like horses, in the night, and traveling so far and so fast that the person wakes in the morning not only unrested but exhausted. If this goes on long enough, the victim will weaken and die. Mississippi Negroes prescribe sleeping with a fork under the pillow to keep from being ridden.

In Irish folklore the hags (*cailleaća*) are women ancient, wise, of extraordinary eyesight and supernatural powers. The term for this reason is sometimes also applied to the ancient fairy queens like Áine and Clíodna. The Hag of Beare and the Hag of the Cats (*Cailleać na gCat*), who was fed by her cats, are among the many famous individual Irish hags. Almost all the Celtic hags were mythological cairn and mountain builders.

The extraordinary longevity of hags is attested by an Irish folktale about a hag found sitting by a mountainous pile of bones. They were the bones of animals she had eaten, one of which she had killed each year of her life. Sometimes hags fight each other; at such times the air is full of stones and rocks, and it is wise to stay indoors. The Irish say that sometimes a hag will come into a house where spinning (or some such work) is going on late at night, and will help with the work. Hags are said to be prevalent on the nights of the Beltane and Midsummer bonfires.

For the horrible hag who is transformed into a beautiful woman by the act of love, see LOATHLY LADY; for the harvest hag, see CAILLEAĊ; FIELD SPIRITS; HARVEST DOLL. See also INCUBUS; WITCH.

Hagbard (or **Hagbart**) **and Signe** Title of a Danish ballad recounting the tragic story of the irresistible love of Hagbard and Signe. The legend, based on an epic now lost, is found in Saxo Grammaticus in both prose and verse forms. Hagbard, betrothed to Signe, was hanged by his father (King Sigar) before the eyes of his love, and Signe in despair set fire to her bower and followed Hagbard into death. Haki, the Viking king, and brother of Hagbard, "came running up from the sea" and killed Sigar in revenge. Hagbard and Signe are sometimes called the Romeo and Juliet of the North, or the Tristan and Iseult of the North. The legend, in both prose and ballad forms, contains the famous motif of the hero disguised as a woman entering the chamber of his beloved, and the symbolic idealization of loyal love in Signe's death.

Hagen (1) According to the *Nibelungenlied,* Gunther's uncle. He urged Gunther to welcome Siegfried, and when war threatened, he persuaded Siegfried to help. When Siegfried's wife, Kriemhild, and Gunther's wife, Brunhild, quarreled, however, he sided with Brunhild, and promised to avenge her. He persuaded Kriemhild to sew a cross over Siegfried's vulnerable spot under pretense of protecting him, and killed him. When Kriemhild began giving away Siegfried's gold, Hagen stole it and hid it in the Rhine. He advised Gunther against allowing her to marry Etzel, as this would give her a means to be revenged, and against visiting Etzel's court after they were married, but she accompanied him and fought valiantly against the treacherous attacks of Kriemhild's followers until only he and Gunther were left. She had her brother, Gunther, beheaded and brought the head to Hagen, demanding that he tell her the hiding-place of the gold, but he only laughed at her, whereupon Kriemhild caught up Siegfried's sword and beheaded Hagen too in front of the court.

(2) According to Wagner's *Ring of the Nibelung* the son of Grimhild and Alberich, and half-brother to Gunther and Gutrune. He was charged by his father with recovering the Ring for the dwarfs. He plotted against Siegfried and finally killed him. He also killed Gunther in a dispute over the Ring and was about to take it from Siegfried's lifeless finger when the arm shot up accusingly and frightened him. When the Rhine Maidens recovered the Ring, he pursued them, and was drowned.

(3) According to the 11th century German poem, *Gudrun,* the son of King Sigeband, who at the age of seven was carried off by a griffon. Hagen escaped and took refuge in a cave where he found three little girls who had also escaped from the griffons. He provided for them for several years by slipping out while the griffons were away and killing small game with a little bow and arrow he had made. One day the body of a slain warrior was washed ashore, and Hagen took the armor and weapons and slew the griffons. Then the children signaled a passing ship, only to find that it belonged to one of his father's enemies. In a berserker rage Hagen threw thirty of the warriors overboard, and frightened the others into taking them to his home. As his father died, he became king and married Hilde, one of the maidens. They had a daughter, also named Hilde, who was very beautiful, and he was loath to part with her. Hettel carried her off by stealth, but Hagen overtook them and they fought. Both of them were wounded, and in the end he consented to the marriage as Hettel had proved himself a brave warrior.

haggis Sheep's heart, liver, onions, suet, oatmeal, boiled in its stomach: Scots traditional holiday dish.

Hag of Beare (*Cailleaċ Ḃéara*) A famous hag of Irish and Scottish folklore. Her name is reported as Dirri or Digdi. She is associated especially with Dingle in West Kerry and is sometimes also called the Old Woman of Dingle. She is called the Hag of Beare because she had fifty foster children on the Island of Beare off the west coast of Ireland in Bantry Bay.

Her many lovers, her great age, and her renewal of youth are the features of her story. There is a West Connacht proverb which says: "Three great ages: the age of the yew tree, the age of the eagle, and the age of the Old Woman of Beare." All the books say "she had her youth seven times over and every man she lived with died of old age." There is a lost story about her great love for Fothad Canainne, one of the Fianna. When questioned about her age she would say she saw yon mountain when it was a lake, or such and such a lake "when it was a small round well." In Donegal there are stories about reckoning her age by counting the bones of the beeves she had killed, one each year of her life. This story is also told in Donegal about Áine.

The great wisdom of the Hag of Beare is pithily summed up in the words: "She never brought mud from this puddle to the other puddle.—She never ate food but when she was hungry." Once in a boat in freezing weather she saved her sons from freezing to death by making them bail water first in then out of the boat to keep warm.

Like the ancient Irish goddess Brigit, who later became identified with the abbess of Kildare, the Hag of Beare too is subject of the transition from goddess or semideity into nun. The word itself, *cailleaċ,* means veiled woman and lends itself to the double interpretation of hooded hag or veiled nun. For a hundred years the Hag of Beare wore the veil that Cummine (of the monastery of Clonfert) blessed on her head, and after that old age came upon her. Probably she is best known today because of the beautiful poem, *The Lament of the Old Woman of Beare,* translated by Kuno Meyer out of a 10th century manuscript and included in his small volume of *Ancient Irish Poetry* (London, 1911). It begins: "Ebb-tide to me as of the sea." It is a realistic grieving for lost youth and beauty: ". . . Every acorn has to drop./ After feasting by shining candles/ To be in the gloom of a prayer house./ . . . Gray is the hair that grows through my skin/" are snatches that give the flavor of it.

The Hag of Beare is noted in rural Ireland for participating in farm activities, mowing contests, etc. She is credited with imparting the knowledge that the best flails have a hazel handle (*colpán cuill*) and a holly striker (*buail teán cuilinn*). There are stories about how she used to hire helpers for half a year, stipulating that they would receive no pay unless they could keep up with her in the work. None could ever keep up with the Hag, and many a fine young man she killed with the work, or put to death because he could not keep up. In the story of Big Donag MacManus and the Hag of Beare is mentioned the *darbdaol* (chafer) in the handle of the Hag's reaping hook which enabled her to outdo all others. Big Donag caught onto this, pulled the handle off the tool, the chafer fell out and ran off in the stubble. See BEETLE.

Many place names in Ireland are associated with the Cailleac Béara. She leaped from many a mountain top to another with an apronful of rocks, which would spill and cause some natural formation credited to her. Many a huge rock is her bed or chair; many a cairn is her grave. In Scotland too she figures as legendary place-maker. The Hebrides were formed from loose rocks which fell from her apron. She is also responsible for the Isle of Mull. The whirlpool of the Corry-vrecken between Jura and Scorva is also attributed to her; the one spot especially where the waters "boil up white" is called the Cailleac.

For further lore and legend about the Hag of Beare, see Eleanor Hull, "Legends and Traditions of the Cailleac Béara," *Folk-Lore* 38: 225 ff.

Hahgwehdiyu The Good Creator of Iroquoian mythology; son of Ataensic, or Sky Woman, and twin brother to Hahgwehdaetgah, the spirit of evil. Hahgwehdiyu shaped the sky with the palm of his hand, put his dead mother's face in the sky to be the sun, set the moon and stars in their places, gave to the earth the body of his mother, so that now Mother Earth is the source of all life. He created the rivers and the valleys and put forests upon the hills. He brought the animals and the birds from the land of the sun to inhabit the earth, and he planted the first corn, which was the gift of the crow. But Hahgwehdaetgah, the dark and evil twin, was forever striving to destroy what his brother wrought, brewing earthquakes and hurricanes to beset the world, and ushering in the West to darken the sun. Finally they challenged each other to combat, the winner to rule the earth. Their weapons were the huge thorns of the giant crab-apple tree, sharp as arrows. They fought for many days; but Hahgwehdiyu won, and banished his brother to the pit under the earth, or the underworld. See GA-GAAH; TWINS.

hair gray before beard A folktale motif (H771) classed with the huge group of riddles asked to test cleverness. A man, who is asked why his hair turned gray before his beard, answers that it is twenty years older.

hair of the dog that bit you A folktale motif (D2161.4.10.3), one of a large group dealing with magic cures and magic healing powers, and representing a general widespread belief that a disease or wound can be cured by the same thing (or person) that caused it (D2161.4.10). The classic example occurs in the story of Telephus whose wound would not heal until the same spear (see ACHILLES' SPEAR) that gave the wound was brought to heal it.

Quite generally throughout the United States and Canada it is said that a hair of the dog that bit you, applied to the wound, will cure it. In Newfoundland it is the liver of the dog that did the biting which must be applied to the bitten place. In some parts of rural England it is believed that fat simmered from the snake that bit you will cure snake-bite.

United States southern Negroes say "it takes dog to cure dog": not only is some of the hair of the dog that bit you taken and tied against the bite, but an oyster is applied to the cut from an oyster shell, and a drink of whisky is given to cure the effects of excessive drinking.

The phrase *a hair of the dog that bit you*, used to mean a small drink of whisky to cure a hangover, has been traced in English as far back as John Heywood's *Proverbes*, first printed in 1546: "I pray thee let me and my fellow have/ A haire of the dog that bit us last night." Compare IPHICLUS.

Haitsi-aibab or **Heitsi-eibib** A culture-hero—transformer of the Hottentots, child of a magical birth and killer of the monster called Thrower-Down (Gā-gorib). Gā-gorib used to sit on the edge of a great pit and dare passers-by to throw stones at him. The stone always flew back and killed the thrower, who then fell into the pit. When Haitsi-aibab heard about his, he went to see. But he refused to throw a stone at Gā-gorib, until he diverted the monster's gaze; then he aimed under the ear, and the stone which hit Gā-gorib under the ear killed him and tumbled him into his own hole. The people lived in safety forever after.

In another version of the story reported by W. H. I. Bleek (*Reynard the Fox in South Africa or Hottentot Fables and Tales,* London, 1864) the two had a prolonged struggle and chase round and round the perilous rim of the pit, striking and shoving and yelling "Push the Haitsi-aibab down!"; "Push the Gā-gorib down!" Haitsi-aibab at last fell into the hole; but he prayed it to hold him up, and the hole pushed him up a little way. The third time he asked to be held up, it ejected him altogether. So the chase began again and the pushing in and getting out were repeated until at last Haitsi-aibab pushed Gā-gorib in, and "he came not out." This same story is also told with the Hottentot deity Tsūi Goab for hero, or with the Hottentot trickster Jackal for hero. The frequency of the cairns in South Africa identified as Haitsi-aibab's graves is explained by stories of his multiple deaths and resurrections. Frazer relates that travelers passing these cairns, in the narrow passes of the mountains, add another stone and say, "Give us plenty of cattle."

hajnaltüz tánc Literally, dawnfire dance: a Hungarian women's dance performed the morning after a wedding. It is still danced at Kazar in Nograd County. The girls and bride dance around a fire of straw and the bride jumps through to be thoroughly smoked, i.e. symbolically purified. A fire jump by any other girl signifies her intended marriage in the course of the year. [GPK]

Hako ceremony An important ceremony of the Pawnee Indians of the eastern Plains region of North America. The ceremony itself is called *skari* (*ska*, hand, and *ri*, many) by the Pawnee; Hako, literally, a breathing mouth of wood, is a comprehensive term used to designate all the articles which belong to the ceremony. The first group of participants, 20–100 people, was called the Fathers. Members of this group were all related to the leader (usually a chief) who had initiated the ceremony, and who was called Father. The second group, called the Children, was composed of relatives of a man whom the Father chose to receive the visiting Children; the leader of the second group was referred to as the Son. A third important person was a man, selected by the Father, who knew all the rites and songs of the Hako, and who took charge of the ceremony from beginning to end. Sacred objects used in the ceremony were two feathered sticks, an ear of white corn (Mother Corn), plum-tree sticks, the feathers, wings, etc., of several species of birds, two wooden bowls, and several other objects. Each article had a general symbolism, as well as a special significance peculiar to the Hako. The Hako could be given at any time of the year except in the winter, when all things are asleep; the rites were a prayer for children to increase the tribe, and also a prayer that the Pawnee as a group might enjoy long life, plenty, and peace.

The Hako consisted of two parts, in some twenty phases. First was the preparation; this included making the ritual objects, invitation to the Son, entrance of the Hako party to the village, consecration of the earth lodge where the rites were held. A delegation from the village of the adoption Fathers traveled to the village of the prospective Children and formally adopted the chosen man in a special ceremonial structure. Rituals preceded the departure, continued during the journey, and climaxed in the adoption, the anointing of a child, and an eagle dance by two expert young men. The rites ended with a dance and reception of gifts and a ceremony of blessing a little child, of presenting all the sacred objects (Hako) to the Son leader, and giving thanks to the Children. Second was the Hako ceremony itself, which lasted six days and consisted of a long round of songs, prayers, and ritual actions. The tobacco invocations and eagle dance focused around two calumet stems with eagle feathers, representing the male and female principles. As in the simpler and earlier Plains calumet ceremonies, these pipes symbolized friendship. Their connection with fertility was emphasized by other paraphernalia—ears of corn, an oriole nest, squash-shell rattles, symbolizing the breast of the Earth Mother. Incidental rituals in a Hako ceremony were comforting the child, prayer to avert storms, prayer for the gift of children, and changing a man's name. The Hako may be considered not the origin but the apex of the calumet dance complex. The corresponding eagle dances, distributed among Eastern tribes, are of brief duration and of limited, partly hazy significance. For a detailed study of the Hako ceremony, see *The Hako: A Pawnee Ceremony*, by Alice C. Fletcher, *RBAE* 22: 5–368. Compare CALUMET DANCE; EAGLE DANCE; GANEGWA'E. [EWV;GPK]

halak, hala, or **bĕlian** The Semang (Malay Negrito) and Sakai name for the shaman: Malayan *orang*. The halak is an ordinary man who, when not performing cures or conducting special ceremonies, hunts, gathers food, and lives like the others. When he is consulted by the Semang about the illness of a member of the group, he diagnoses the ailment by means of a magic crystal. He treats the patient directly by applying cooling leaves or giving herb tea, or indirectly by sending his assistant to dig up a nearby shrub and disentangle its roots. When this is completed, the trouble will vanish.

When a special ceremony is necessary for a cure, a hut (*panoh*) of palm leaves is erected and the halak, possessed by a chinoi, chants inside it, while the people gathered outside repeat the lines of the song. This is followed by sounds of body-slapping, grunting, and wailing from the hut.

Among the Sakai this performance is accompanied by the playing of bamboo stampers and the people outside sing and dance themselves into a frenzy. The affair will last until the patient is better or dies.

The Semang and the Sungkai Sakai also believe the halak, who learns his calling usually from his father, can change into a tiger. See PAWANG.

halcyon days A period of calm weather which exists during the seven days preceding and the seven days following the shortest day of the year: so called from a nautical tradition that the halcyon, or kingfisher, builds her nest on the water and that in spite of the violent weather prevalent at this time, the gods grant a respite from all storms while she hatches and rears her young.

haldā'wit Term for those who practice witchcraft among the North American Tshimshian Indians: distinguished from the shamans. The haldā'wit work their bewitchments by means of a piece of a corpse which they keep hidden in a box. They cause varying degrees of illness and disease by means of this box and its contents, and sometimes the death of their enemies. After a death which he has caused, the haldā'wit must circumambulate the house in which the dead body lies and must crawl sunwise also around the grave, disguised in the skin of some animal. If he does not, he will die soon himself. Sometimes if he does, he dies sooner, because the relatives of the dead keep careful watch over the grave to catch anyone possibly performing this circumambulation. If the haldā'wit is caught he is killed. Anyone caught by a group of haldā'wit spying on their activities is compelled to become one of them or die at once at their hands.

haldde The spirit of nature of the Lapps, derived from Finnish *haltia*. The word is often found in combination, as for example: *mära-halddo*—the spirit of the sea, *čacce-haldde*—the spirit of the water. (Compare *Čacce-olmai*—the man of the water, and *saivo-neita*—the sea-maiden.) All the names emphasize the importance of water deities to the Lapps. Compare HALTIA. [JB]

Halfchick The central character of a European folktale (Type 715; K481), known in several variants: the Demi-Coq of French, and the Mediopollo of Spanish folktale. The tale is known in India, Russia, Finland, Estonia, and western Europe, excepting Germany, the British Isles, and Czechoslovakia. The western European versions seem to be of Castilian provenience. In its original form, as reconstructed by R. S. Boggs (*The*

Halfchick Tale in Spain and France; FFC 111), the story is as follows:

Halfchick, a half-grown runt of a chicken, comes across some money while scratching in the manure pile. He starts off to buy some grain from the king. He comes to a river, discusses his errand, and the river decides to accompany Halfchick. The river is hidden in Halfchick's anus. So too with a wolf, and a fox. The king, who wants the money and doesn't want to give grain for it, invites Halfchick to stay overnight, putting him in with his chickens. He thinks the chickens will kill the puny creature. But Halfchick lets the fox out and in the morning all the king's chickens are dead. The next night Halfchick is put in with the horses, and the wolf is let out. On the third night, Halfchick is put in the oven. Out comes the river; out goes the fire. The palace is flooded. The king gives up and sends Halfchick away with the grain and with the money.

The five significant episodes in the tale are the origin of Halfchick, his purpose in making the journey, his helpers (animal and otherwise) and the things they do, the place in which he hides them, and his victory. Though the earliest known reference to the tale is French (1759), it seems to have originated in Castile, spread to the Spanish coast, from there to Brittany and America (Boggs discusses five Spanish American and two American Indian variants), from Brittany eastward and southward in France. Indicative of the change occurring in the variants, and of the essential elements remaining constants, is the Cochiti (New Mexico Indian) tale of Half Rooster (R. Benedict, *Tales of the Cochiti Indians, BBAE* 98, pp. 182–184). Half Rooster complains to the king that his spoon has been stolen. The king is afraid of the big rooster and tries to have him killed. But hidden in Half Rooster's anus are Lion, who kills the wild horses, Bear, who kills the bulls, Wolf, who kills the mules, Grinding Stone, who smashes the santus and pictures in the church, Fire, who melts the ice they pack around Half Rooster to freeze him, and Water, who quenches the fire they build to burn him. The king "took him to his house and he lived with him forever."

Of two literary versions examined by Boggs, that of Fernán Caballero was reprinted by Andrew Lang in *The Green Fairy Book* and became a familiar selection in school readers of the United States. Halfchick here is half a chick who travels, against the advice of his mother, to see the king in hope of finding a court surgeon to cure him. But Halfchick refuses to help river, wind, and fire. At the court, he is thrown into a pot by the cooks and boiled to a worthless lump. He is tossed away. The wind whips him to the top of a tower where he becomes a weathercock, at the mercy of wind, rain, and sun.

half-horse, half-alligator A frontiersman; a Mississippi or Kentucky River boatman: a term braggingly self-imposed to imply strength, bravado, and invincibility. He was a man of marvelous exploits, marvelous strength and spirit, absolutely fearless, full of antics and horseplay, noise, roar, and brag. He could "wade the Mississippi, leap the Ohio," and perform many like feats.

half right and left and half promenade An American square dance term. Two couples cross to each other's places as in right and left through (8 counts); partners then cross hands with the right above the left, walk back to their own places, each couple keeping to the right in passing. When in their own places, without releasing hands, the gentleman turns his partner round into her place on his right (8 counts). [GPK]

Hallewijn or ***Heer Halowyn*** The title of a Dutch ballad, deriving from the Apocryphal tale of Judith and Holofernes (whence Hallewijn), known in all parts of Europe from Italy to Scandinavia, Hungary to England: probably composed not earlier than the 15th century. The ballad, as derived from its ancient source, shows the closest correspondence to the original in the Netherlands version, for only in that ballad does the heroine tell Hallewijn's mother that she is carrying the head and then bring the head to her father's hall. All Biblical reference is however lost. In the ballad, the girl is lured from her castle by the music of the knight. He threatens to kill her as he has her sisters. In the various versions, she kills him, or she is killed and avenged by her brothers, or she is rescued by the brothers.

In the German versions, the knight is Ullinger, Ulrich, etc., and the girl is killed and avenged or she escapes. The Hungarian *Molnár Anna* is an offshoot of the German. The English *Lady Isabel and the Elf-Knight* or *May Collin* (Child #4) has preserved in some versions the supernatural character of the knight, a mischievous, malevolent nature added as the ballad migrated through Scandinavia. In France Renaud is the killer; in Italy the ballad is known as *Monferrina*; in Spain and Portugal it is *Rico Franco*. The death of the girl is avenged by her three brothers in the Czech ballad *The Murderer*. The ballad is said to be very popular in Poland. Taken all in all, the *Hallewijn* ballads may be the most widespread in Europe.

Halloween or **Hallowe'en** All Hallows Eve; the eve of All Saints Day. See ALL SAINTS DAY.

haltia The protecting spirit of the Finns. The word is derived from the Gothic *hallita*, to rule over, and is often found in combination, as for example: *kodinhaltia*, a household fairy; *vedenhaltia*, a spirit of the water; and *metsänhaltia*, forest ruler. Every forest possesses such a ruler. Sometimes the metsänhaltia is in the form of an old man with gray beard and with a coat of lichens. He can stretch his body so high that his head will reach the level of the highest tree. The *metshaldijas* is known among the North Estonians. His cry in the forest is an evil omen, perhaps of death. The most important spirit of this kind is the Finnish *talonhaltija*, the guardian of the home, sometimes representing the person who first died in the house. Besides the spirits of the dwelling-house, there are guardian spirits of each kind of house also: guardian spirits of the bathing-house, the granary, the stable, and others. [JB]

hamadryad In Greek mythology, a tree nymph; a dryad; specifically, an oak-tree nymph as contrasted with a fruit-tree nymph. Later, scholarly contrast was made between dryad and hamadryad, the dryad being simply a tree nymph, the hamadryad being one whose life was in the tree and who died with it, but this distinction was not made by the people. Compare NYMPH.

Haman The villain of the Biblical story of Esther; the close adviser of King Ahasuerus, whose machinations against the Jews of Persia led to his downfall. Haman hated the Jews, Mordecai especially, and induced the king to order the slaughter of the Jews of the kingdom. But Queen Esther, Mordecai's cousin, demonstrated to the king the evilness of Haman, who then was hanged on the gallows 50 cubits high that he had ordered prepared especially for Mordecai. The story is elaborated in Jewish tradition; for example, Haman is an ex-barber and not only must lead Mordecai through the streets on the king's horse (he had thought this honor was to be his), but has to trim Mordecai's beard as a further sign of his subservience. At the reading of the *Megillah*, the book of *Esther*, in the synagogues on the festival of Purim, it is customary to drown out the name of Haman when it occurs, with the sound of rattles and other noisemakers.

Ham Bone An American Negro hand-patting rhythm accompanied by a rimed chant which embodies in its several variants a number of children's rimes and scraps of song texts. The rhythm is made by clapping the hands and slapping shoulders, chest, thighs, and buttocks. The words begin with such phrases as: "Ham bone, ham bone, pat 'em on the shoulder. Gimme a pretty gal; show you how to hold her"; or "Ham bone, ham bone, where you been? All around the world and back again." Then bits of the *Frog's Courting Song*, or the lullaby *Hush Little Baby* ("momma's gonna buy you a billy goat") or various game chants are woven into the rhythm. Compare BALL THE JACK; JUBA.

hamsa or **hansa** In Hindu mythology, the cosmic gander; the vehicle of Brahmā, hence also an animal mask of the creative principle, and also an epithet applied to modern ascetics and teacher-saints who have obtained freedom from rebirth through their spirituality. The hamsa symbolizes the divine essence which abides in the individual but remains free, immortal, and omniscient, and which manifests itself to the Indian yogi in the sound of inhaling (*ham*), and of exhaling (*sa*). At the same time, *sa'ham* (literally, this I), the sound in reverse, asserts the divine nature of the man who breathes. See GOOSE.

Han Chung-li One of the Eight Immortals of Chinese mythology. He was a friend and teacher of Lü Tung-pin and engaged with him in many drunken parties. He has many legends and is sometimes presented as a Taoist priest, as a warrior, or as a beggar taking the pill of immortality. He frequently carries a peach of immortality. [RDJ]

handfasting or **handfesting** A term used to refer to betrothal ceremonies in some parts of Scotland, Denmark, and elsewhere. In this instance betrothal has most of the sanctions of marriage. The formalization of betrothal by communal celebrations and festivities is known in many parts of the world as one of the steps in the marriage ritual, though the amount of sexual intimacy permitted to betrothed couples varies with the cultural complex of the community. Handfasting refers more particularly to a trial marriage, dissolved at the end of the year if either party is dissatisfied. Granet has shown that the ancient Chinese entered into arrangements of this sort during the Spring festival, and that

if the union was fruitful it remained as a marriage. Similar customs exist in several parts of the world in which marriage as we know it is customary. In India it is known as gandharva marriage. Cohabitation without further ceremony is accepted in communities which are visited only rarely by itinerant priests. This custom is also connected with the common-law marriage of English common law. The attempt to explain handfasting by the penetration into England of a Roman custom has little weight. Compare BUNDLING. [RDJ]

hand of glory A charm made from the dried or pickled hand of a dead man, preferably a criminal hanged on the gallows, and conferring invisibility on the owner, or rendering those to whom it is presented motionless: a western European, specifically northern English, belief, but with variants scattered throughout Europe and the Mediterranean lands and in parts of the East and the Americas.

Many of the beliefs about the hand of glory are explained by its etymology. It is undoubtedly a derivative of the French *main de gloire* or *mandragore,* mandragora, the mandrake. (Compare MANDRAKE.) This would explain the specific reference to the hanged man, as the mandrake is known to be found under gallows, the growth germinating from the seed of the dead man.

Ordinarily, the hand is used holding a candle made also from the fat of a hanged man, but sometimes the fingers of the hand itself are burned. The flame of these fingers can be extinguished only by milk. The finger of a newborn or unborn child was believed to be a very efficient form of candle, and it is reported that in 17th century Germany pregnant women were sometimes murdered by thieves to obtain these fingers. To be absolutely certain that everyone in the house to be entered is asleep, the thief lights as many fingers as there are inhabitants. If one of the fingers, specifically the thumb, does not light, the indication is that someone has remained awake. The efficacy of the burning finger is so great that the thief can place it on a table and go about his work safe in the certainty that he will not be interfered with by an awakening.

Similar to the practices surrounding the hand of glory is the use for making unconscious of certain other materials connected with the dead. For example, in Mexico, the stolen left forearm of a woman who has died in her first childbed renders the inhabitants of a house unconscious, "as if dead," if it is beaten on the ground before the house. A human shin bone filled with tallow serves the Ruthenian burglar in like manner. All these practices are of course based on the principles of sympathetic magic.

hands Although the general interpretation of hands belongs to the complex science of palmistry, hands appear in folklore and folk custom in other ways. The use of hands in sign language is highly developed in the alphabet of the deaf and dumb. In occupied territories during World War II the extended thumb and first finger meant "V for Victory." The ceremonial clasping of the worshippers' own hands at appropriate moments is important in the rituals of some Buddhist, Lamaist, Christian, and other sects. Placing thumb between the index and middle fingers, probably a phallic gesture, wards off the evil eye in China, Italy, and elsewhere; and the thumb to the nose is a derisive and insulting gesture in most parts of the known world. When a hand with five fingers extended appeared in the Ganges, it meant, "What cannot five united men effect?" It disappeared when two fingers were displayed meaning, "Two men can accomplish anything." This use of hands and sign language in fraternal or other secret societies requires further study. In an Indian version of the Achilles heel motif, the king's vital spot is in his left hand. In the Orient people dispel evil spirits by waving their hands around their heads. Many peoples cut off the right hands of thieves. The Moslems consider the left hand as unclean, but the Chinese consider that the left hand is on the yang or male side of the body. See FINGERS; GESTURES. [RDJ]

handsel A gift at the beginning of the day, the year, or the enterprise: from Old English *handselen,* hand gift, giving into the hand. It brings luck to a bargain. In some communities the first customer of the day receives a small gift, or the first man at the bar is given a free drink. The gift of a cent thrown into a new purse will insure the purse's owner against the purse's ever being empty. [RDJ]

Handsel Monday The day when gifts are distributed to children and local functionaries in Scotland: corresponding to Boxing Day in England or Christmas Eve in some parts of Germany and the United States. It is a social rather than a religious festival though it may be the occasion of religious ceremonies. [RDJ]

hanging The act of putting a person to death by suspending him by the neck from some support. This punishment seems not to have been used by the Jews, only slightly by the Romans, and infrequently by the Greeks. It was practiced in the steppes on the border of Europe and Asia, in middle and northern Europe, and in North America where it was introduced from England. In the 18th and early 19th centuries, hanging was inflicted even for petty crimes; at best, it did not have the ignominy attached to it that it had later.

It is suggested that hanging was perhaps of ritual origin and that it had on this account sacrificial and religious connotations. As a sacrifice that had been blessed and consecrated and offered to the gods, the clothes of the person hanged, the gallows, rope, nail, and all the paraphernalia used had magical power.

Punishment by hanging is a frequent theme in English and Scottish ballads, and this matter has been intensively studied by scholars. All over central Europe a severe storm meant that someone had hanged himself. It is general European belief that one whose eyebrows meet will die on the gallows. Southern U. S. Negroes say that dogs are afraid to approach a tree on which a man has been hanged. [GPS]

Han Hsiang-tzǔ One of the Eight Immortals of Chinese folk belief. Han is the immortal youth who loved flowers and produced plants with poems written on their leaves in letters of gold. He is portrayed with a basket of flowers or a jade flute. He is said to have been a pupil of Lü Tung-pin and is the patron of musicians.
[RDJ]

Hansel and Gretel A popular German folktale (Type 327A), appearing in the Grimm collection (#15): the title is sometimes applied inaccurately to *Brother and Sister* (Grimm #11), which has some similar elements but is not an ogre story. *Hansel and Gretel* is known throughout Europe, especially northern Europe, thence eastward to India and Japan, all over Africa, among the West Indian Negroes and the North American Indians, in the islands of the Pacific. It is not clear whether the non-European versions are of independent invention or are derivatives of the European tale.

The story belongs to the children and the ogre type, in which the ogre is burned to death in his own fire. Hansel and Gretel, children of a poor woodcutter, are abandoned in the woods after their stepmother convinces their father that there is not enough food for all. But Hansel has overheard the parents talking and, pretending to look back at the cock on the roof of the hut, has left a trail of pebbles. The moonlight on the pebbles shows the children the way back to the hut. The stepmother locks the door that night and Hansel, unable to get more pebbles, has to leave a trail of breadcrumbs the next day. After night falls, the children discover that their path is gone; the birds have eaten the crumbs. After wandering through the forest, they come across a gingerbread-and-sugar house. They break off bits of the house to eat and out comes an old wicked witch. She locks Hansel in a stable (or cage) and begins to fatten him, for her little house is a trap with which she catches children to eat. Gretel obtains a bone for her brother, and when the nearsighted witch tells him to stick out a finger so that she can tell if he is fat enough to eat, Hansel puts the bone through the bars for her to squeeze. At last, impatient, she tells Gretel to build up the fire; she is going to cook Hansel. But, when the witch tells Gretel to crawl into the oven to see if it is hot enough, Gretel says she doesn't know how. The witch demonstrates, and Gretel slams the oven door on her. Filling their pockets with the jewels within the house, the children travel back through the woods, ride across a wide water on a duck's back, and discover when they reach home that the stepmother has died. Father and children are now in comfortable circumstances because of the jewels.

The essential part of the story is the episode of the child-eating witch. But the cruel stepmother (S31), the abandoned children (S300), the disappearing trail of bread or peas (R135), the gingerbread house (F771.1.10) are characteristic of the Hansel and Gretel story. In a version from Jamaica (Beckwith, *Jamaica Anansi Stories. MAFLS* XVII, pp. 146–147), the stepmother has disappeared from the tale as has the trail of bread. Instead the witch, disguised as a bird, directs the children to the hut. From that point, the story follows the same course as the German tale. The cannibal ogre who falls into his own trap (G512.3.2) is known in Hungarian, Portuguese, Lapp, Norwegian, Indian, Persian, Kaffir stories; this is of course a reflection of the stupid ogre deceived by the hero's supposed ignorance (G526).

Han Shih The Chinese festival of cold food; the day before Ch'ing Ming, the Spring Festival of Pure Brightness, occurring late in the Second or early in the Third Moon. On this festival all fires were extinguished and only cold foods were eaten. The fires were rekindled on Ch'ing Ming. [RDJ]

Hanswurst The vulgar and low-comedy attendant of the smooth hero in folk comedy in Europe is given the name of a popular dish: Dutch, Pickle Herring; Italian, Macaroni; French, Jean Potage; German, Hanswurst; English, Jack Pudding. [RDJ]

hantu Generic name for the ghosts and evil spirits of Malay belief. There are many varieties of hantu, among them the storm demon, *hantu ribut;* the deep-forest demon, *hantu rimba;* the grave demon, *hantu kubor;* and the tiger demon, *hantu bĕlian.*

Hanukkah The Jewish Feast of the Maccabees or Feast of Dedication, an eight-day festival occurring on the 25th of Kislev (December): known also as the Festival of Lights or Feast of Illumination. According to a Talmudic legend, after the destruction of the Temple by Antiochus Epiphanes, when the priests reentered the sanctuary only one small cruse of unpolluted oil was found, and it lasted the eight days until a new supply of sacred oil could be obtained. The feast was instituted in 165 B.C. by the Maccabees and the elders of Israel to celebrate the dedication of the altar, previously defiled by Antiochus. However, Hanukkah occurs at the time of an ancient pagan festival and of what was a more ancient Jewish winter solstice observance.

The Hanukkah lamp, lit at this season, gives the festival its popular name, the Festival of Lights. The Shammaite or older tradition lit all eight lights on the lamp on the first night and reduced the number by one on each following night; the Hillelites lit one light the first night and increased by one each succeeding night. There are traditionally as many lamps as there are entrances to the house. The light is intended to illuminate the house outside and is not meant for general lighting; reading by this light is forbidden.

Hanumān In Hindu mythology and religion, the monkey god, son of Vāyu and the monkey nymph Añjanā. Hanumān was the ally of Rāma in his battle with Rāvaṇa and helped him regain Sītā whom Rāvaṇa had carried off. During one of the battles with the demon, the Rākshasas greased his tail and set it on fire, but he swung around and burned their capital city, Lankā. He collected medicinal herbs to restore the wounded and killed the demon Kālanemi. Rāma rewarded him with the gift of perpetual life and youth. He is represented in monkey form with a yellow complexion and an endless tail.

In modern Hinduism, Hanumān is worshiped as a village deity. Originally he may have represented the genius of the monsoon. He is worshiped by women who desire children and by wrestlers. Apes are still considered sacred in India and weddings of apes are occasionally performed as a religious service. See GRĀMA-DEVATĀ. Compare BHAIRON.

haoma The plant of life and of Indo-Iranian sacrifice; also, the drink prepared from it which gives strength to men and gods: the equivalent of the Indian soma. Haoma gave the gods immortality and men the gift of spiritual life. It gave children to women and husbands to girls. The plant received its healing power from Vohu Manah. When deified, it was the son of Ahura Mazda.

Its supra-terrestrial form, the white haoma, was identified with the gaokerena tree. The actual plant, the yellow haoma, is said to grow on the summits of mountains from which it is brought by the birds of heaven. A haoma plant contained the fravashi of Zoroaster whose father, a priest, absorbed it and thus produced Zoroaster.

Haoshyangha, Hōshang, or **Húshang** According to the *Avesta,*, the first ruler and a member of the first royal house of Persia: said to have ruled over the daēvas. According to the *Bündahishn* he was the grandson of Sīyākmak and the great grandson of Gaya Maretan. He was the first lawgiver and the culture hero who introduced the use of fire and metals. In early Iranian myths, he performed a sacrifice on the top of the great iron mountain, Hara Berezaiti, and obtained divine protection and the kingly glory (khvarenanh). The demons fled to the darkness after he had slain two thirds of their number.

According to the *Shāhnāmah* he invented blacksmithing and the making of tools such as axes and saws, and taught men how to irrigate land. On a mountain top he struck with a stone a dragon whose smoke was bedimming the world, and thus caused fire (lightning) to appear. That night he held the feast of Sadah. He domesticated animals (sheep, asses, oxen) and ordered the destruction of beasts of prey. He was succeeded by Takhma Urupi (Tahmūrath), the son of Vīvanghvant (according to the Avesta), or by his son (according to Firdausī).

Hāp, Hāpi, or **Apis** Literally, the hidden: in ancient Egyptian religion, the sacred bull of Memphis, symbol and incarnation of Ptah-Osiris. This bull was the offspring of a virgin cow who had been impregnated by lightning or a moonbeam. In death it was known in Ptolemaic times as the powerful god Serapis (Osiris-Apis); in the Memphite Serapeum, uncovered in 1851, 64 mummified bulls were found. The bull was chosen by its special markings, and succeeded to its post of honor after the death of the preceding Hāp. Those who inhaled its breath became thereby able to prophesy. It is conjectural whether the calf worshiped by the Israelites in the desert during the exodus from Egypt was identical with, or an image of, this bull. See BULL.

Hapiñuñu Female spirits of the Quechua and Aymara Indians of South America. They are said to fly about at night and catch people with their long hanging breasts. [AM]

happy hunting ground A popular term for the hereafter in references by whites to American Indian concepts of life after death. That the Indians believed in a hereafter is well attested, but their own descriptions of the activities which go on in such a land seldom include references to hunting. In the land of the dead all is quiet in the daytime, when the dead are invisible; at night, however, fires are kindled and the dead devote themselves to dancing, gambling, and other social activities. The culture hero, or a notable deity, or a "chief," presides over the land of the dead, and the spirits live under his direction much as people do on earth. The Blackfoot, a northern Plains tribe, believe that the land of the dead is located in some sand dunes to the north of them, and that it is good to die and go there while in the prime of life because the dead are not rejuvenated, but live on in the hereafter at the same age they were when they died, and subject to the same infirmities. Other tribes also localize their land of the dead: the Valley Maidu of California say that their dead go to the Marysville Buttes, visible in Maidu territory, for example. But for the great majority of tribes the land of the dead is merely "across an ocean" in the West (most frequently) or the South, East, or North. Mortals visit the land of the dead occasionally; the Orpheus tale, which is widespread over North America, recounts the visit of one or more men in search of a dead relative to the land of the dead, and the return of these mortals to earth. Accounts of visits by human beings who "die" temporarily and go to the hereafter, and then return to life, usually with a prophecy of some sort, also often contain descriptions of the land. Among some Eastern Woodlands tribes the path to the land of the dead contains obstacles difficult to negotiate, and some spirits fail to reach the hereafter; this may or may not be a native concept. No idea of punishment after death for misdeeds during life, or any concept of heaven and hell, seems to have existed in native North America, although several Eastern tribes have now taken over the idea of punishment and reward after death. See AFTERWORLD.[EWV]

Hapy or Hapi   (1) In Egyptian religion and mythology, one of the four sons of Horus who dwelt in Amenti; a mummiform spirit with the head of a dog or a cynocephalus ape, who protected the embalmed lungs of the dead preserved in the second Canopic jar.

(2) The god of the Nile; an obese bearded man with the breasts of a woman; the Greek Nilus. Both the great stomach and the breasts are symbols of the fertility of this water god; the lotus or the papyrus carried on his head, and the water he poured from vases are likewise fertility symbols. Sometimes the god is dual: as the red god of the lower Nile he wears the papyrus; as the blue god of the upper river, he wears the lotus. Hapy was worshipped especially at the annual inundation; the mysterious resurrection of the life-bringing river caused him to be identified even in early times with Osiris.

Hare   The Hare, Great Hare, or White Hare is a character who, among several Algonquian tribes of eastern North America, is credited with forming the earth, and ordering and enlarging it. A curious identification of the Great Hare and a humanlike culture-hero-trickster, Nanabozho, occurs in specific tribes such as the Ojibwa and Menomini. In these groups the culture hero first appears as a hare, and as Hare, is the chief actor in many of the definitely trickster tales. Among the Potawatomi White Hare (Wabosso, Maker of White) is one of four brothers, Nanabozho being the first-born of the four. Wabosso, seeing the sunlight, went north, assumed the form of a White Hare, and became a powerful magician. To Nanabozho, however, and not to White Hare is given the credit by the Potawatomi of instituting the Midewiwin or Grand Medicine Society. The Ojibwa of the present time, in recounting culture-hero and trickster tales, identify Hare with Nanabozho, but can offer no explanation for this identification. [EWV]

Hare and the Tortoise   Title of one of Æsop's fables (Jacobs #68) in which the Hare and the Tortoise run a race. Sure of winning, the Hare lies down and takes a nap before he reaches the goal, oversleeps, and is passed by the persevering Tortoise, who thus wins the race. This incident (and its moral) comprises the motif (K11.3) of the story as it has spread all over Europe. It is known among the Ainu and in other parts of eastern Asia, and is common also throughout Indonesia.

It is a popular story among almost all peoples of Africa, from whom it has passed into the possession of New World Negroes. The Negro versions, almost universally stress the superior wit of the weaker participant; Tortoise is portrayed in the role of Trickster who wins by his wits instead of by plodding. The Ibo people of Nigeria tell how Frog wins the race against Deer; Turtle beats Antelope among the Bulus.

South Carolina Sea Island Negroes tell this story about Hare and Cootah, and have a version also about the race between Race-Horse and Cootah, who wins by planting his relatives, one at every mile along the course and one at the end post, or about Mr. Deer and Mr. Terrapin, who wins by the same ruse and remarks at the end, "I kin head you off with sense." In two Bahama Negro stories the race is between Lobster and Conch, or between Horse and Conch, and the prize is to marry the king's daughter. These stories combine both patterns: Conch is smart enough to plant his relays, but both Lobster and Horse are oversure and foolish enough to stop and feed en route. Thus Conch with his one foot wins over Horse with his four, and Lobster with his ten. There are also Apache, Cherokee, and Ojibwa Indian versions of the tale.

Harmonia's necklace   In Greek mythology and legend, the unlucky necklace made by Hephæstus and given to Harmonia by Cadmus of Thebes as a wedding gift. It was inherited by Polynices and given to Eriphyle so that she might persuade her husband Amphiaraus to join the expedition against Thebes. After bringing misfortune to other owners, it was dedicated by Amphoterus and Acarnan to Athena Pronaia at Delphi. Even then the misfortunes did not cease, for it was stolen from the temple by Phayallus for his mistress, whose death occurred when her son went mad and burned the house down with her and her treasures inside.

harp   A plucked stringed instrument, the only one in which the strings extend vertically from the soundboard instead of paralleling it; in many civilizations since antiquity the most highly honored of instruments both for religious and secular musical ceremonies. The earliest harps were bow-shaped, the resonator forming a continuation of the arc, and were derived from the primitive musical bow. Such harps were played in Sumer before 3000 B.C., and have been found on an archaic Greek figurine, on relics of ancient Egypt and the earliest known civilization of India, in Africa and Java. Later harps were angular, the resonator set at an angle to the neck. Instruments of this form were seen in Mesopotamia about 2000 B.C., were introduced into Egypt and Greece from Asia and into the Far East from Turkestan in the 4th century. They spread among the Arab peoples from Persia in the Middle Ages. The angular harp known in northern and northwestern Europe before 1000 A.D. is of disputed provenience. All ancient harps lacked the fore-pillar, which forms the third side of the generally triangular frame of most instruments since the Middle Ages. The number of strings varied greatly and may have been more important for the significance of the number than for musical effect—for example, five, for protection from harm; seven, for sanctification.

In Egypt, as in Sumer, the harp was the chief and most treasured instrument. Numerous forms were played, varying in size from a 7-foot type played standing, to a small portable type carried against the shoulder. Certain examples were provided with a leg or foot to be rested on the ground as the seated player touched the strings. Ornamentation was elaborate and symbolic, with painted and mosaic designs, often involving the lotus, sphinx-head carvings, and shapes associated with Isis or Osiris. That the instrument served a religious function is indicated by the fact that the players depicted in the tomb of Rameses III are priests. In the Old Kingdom, players were always men, to whose use the large standing harp continued to be restricted, but women in later eras played the smaller harps.

In Greece, the harp (*magadis* or *pektis*) was considered a dreamy, intimate instrument suited to women, and the accomplishments of the hetæræ included playing it, though other women did not scorn it.

The translation of Hebrew terms for musical instruments has for centuries confused the knowledge of music in Biblical times. Probably the *nevel,* a triangular stringed instrument used for marching, was the harp of the ancient Jews, and the *kinnor,* generally translated as harp, was a lyre, played for light entertainment and pastime by harlots and by shepherds. It was this instrument that was played and, according to legend, invented by David, the shepherd king. However, the so-called harp of David persists in story, in art works, and on down to the Negro spiritual, *Little David, play on your harp.*

In India, the traditional inventor of the harp was Narada, a semi-divine sage and astronomer. The archaic harp of India was probably called *vīnā,* though the name is now applied to a type of zither and has been used for other instruments.

The history of the harp in Europe is complicated by the ambiguity among chroniclers of the 8th to 14th centuries in the use of the words *chrotta* (ML), *crot* or *cruit* (Irish), and *rotta* (on the Continent), which are variously interpreted as harp or lyre, and by the difficult evidence of the worn representations of a stringed instrument on Irish stone crosses of the 8th and 9th centuries, also cited as either harp or lyre. The confusion is further confounded by the Welsh term *crwth,* equivalent to Irish *cruit,* which may have been the ancient harp of the bards but in more recent times refers to a bowed instrument influenced by the violin, and by the Scandinavian *harpa,* which was probably a lyre, plucked in its earliest form and later bowed. National pride has occasionally subverted scholarship in the controversy. Regardless of etymology or construction, the instrument is fixed in the mind of the folk as a harp, and is so conceived in their stories and songs.

Gaulish bards chanted to the accompaniment of the plucked strings and their instrument appears on Gaulish coins. The highly trained and revered bards of the Welsh and Irish peoples improvised their lyric, epic, and satirical poetry to its music, long before the Roman Conquest. Psalms and hymns were accompanied by the cruit in the hands of early Irish churchmen. In Anglo-Saxon England, scops and gleemen carried their wel-

come in their harps. Thus, in the guise of a harper, Alfred the Great entered the camp of the Danes on the Isle of Athelney. Irish minstrels with their wire-strung harps were famous on the Continent in the early Middle Ages, and Saxon harpers were known in France in the 13th century.

The harp was the favored instrument of royalty and nobility, believed to have strong powers over its listeners, and to dispel the spirits of evil. In Welsh custom there were three types of harp (*telyn*)—the king's, the bard's, and the gentleman's. Every important family owned a fine harp. The *Leges Wallicæ* listed three necessities for a man's home—a virtuous wife, a cushion for his chair, and a well-tuned harp. The harp was sacred to the free and might not be handled by slaves. The well-to-do Anglo-Saxon also owned and played a harp, which could not be taken from him for payment of debt or punishment.

In Ireland, where the festival harp (*cláirseaċ*) has become the national emblem, harp stories and traditions abound. The legend of the origin of the harp is that a woman walking on the beach came across the skeleton of a whale with the wind singing so sweetly through its sinews that she was lulled to sleep. Her husband, finding her so, observed the principle of the enchanting sound and made a harp to imitate it. It is also an Irish belief that the Milesians brought a harper with them to the island.

In both Ireland and Wales the fairy folk were believed to be expert harpists, and their music, seldom audible to the ears of men, was irresistible but ominous.

Even the tuning key of famous Irish harps was an object of value, often jeweled or otherwise ornamented, and theft or sequestration of the key was almost as strictly condemned as if it were the harp itself.

Like bagpipers, Irish harpers were outlawed as spies and spreaders of sedition in certain periods of history. Queen Elizabeth, while maintaining an Irish harper at court and sanctioning the appearance of Welsh harpers at an Eisteddfod, enacted laws against the passage of such musicians into disturbed areas. The Cromwellians systematically destroyed Irish harps. During the Jacobite period, harpers attended the Stuarts.

In German folktale the harp is one of the instruments connected with the motif of the singing bone and is used in certain versions of *The Twa Sisters* (Child #10), in which the harp, strung with the hair of the drowned girl, sings the murderer's guilt. Another story expresses the compulsive power of the harp. Horaut the Dane, a minstrel, could play so that not only the guests in the hall but the furniture and tableware danced madly.

The widespread conception that angels in heaven play the harp may derive from the *Book of Revelation,* which says that harps will sound in the New Jerusalem. Chaucer's Pardoner, however, labelled the instrument as the Devil's.

The collection of Welsh and Irish harp tunes has amassed some thousands of airs, many of them still familiar. Much of this music was saved from extinction by the revival of the Eisteddfod, the Granard Festivals in Ireland in the 18th century, and particularly the great Belfast Harp Meeting of 1792, at which Edward Bunting began to note down the tunes of the aged blind harper Denis Hampson and others. Many of the airs used by Thomas Moore are those collected by Bunting, including *Let Erin Remember* (*The Little*

Bold Fox), *The Harp That Once Through Tara's Halls* (*Molly My Treasure*), and *The Minstrel Boy*. The *Foggy Dew* is believed to have been originally a harp tune, as is *Robin Adair*, said to be composed under the title of *Eileen Aroon* by a famous Irish harper named O'Daly.

The Æolian harp, sounded by the wind, harks back to David's kinnor, which sang over his bed in the night breezes. The 10th century Archbishop of Canterbury, St. Dunstan, who was a harper, experimented with wind-blown harps and found himself under suspicion of practicing magic. However, early in the 19th century romantic spirits found delight in such instruments in their gardens, parks, and homes.

Harps among primitive peoples are either of the musical bow type or European derivatives introduced after contact with conquerors. Bamboo bow-shaped harps are found in Borneo, Malaya, and Africa, and are often associated with women's ceremonies. The Wahehe of Africa have a harp story similar to those of the singing-bone motif. Among the Indians of Central and South America small wooden harps, possibly surviving from a Spanish type, are still in use. The Cáhita call theirs *arpa;* the musical bow is called *arpita.* The Yaqui use harps to accompany pascola and deer dancers. The oldest of the pascolas addresses the harp while he inserts a ceremonial stick into its holes, telling it the names of all the animals in the woods. Masks are not worn when the harp and violin accompany the dancing, as they are for dances to the indigenous drum and flute. Probably the use of harp and violin was begun under missionary influence, and a difference is observed in handling them.

A very primitive form of the harp is used in central Africa, where the sound box is a bark-covered pit, and the frame a limber stick stuck into the ground beside it, with a string bending it toward the bark surface. The string is plucked to sound the instrument. As in the case of most primitive instruments, the cycle of development is from such large, earth-bound forms to smaller and more portable types. Compare LYRE.

THERESA C. BRAKELEY

Harpalyce (1) In Greek legend, the daughter of Harpalycus, reared on the milk of mares and cows after her mother died and trained by her father in the manly arts. Partaking of the virtue of the milk she drank, she was too swift for horses to overtake. After she turned brigand when her father died, she had to be trapped in a snare by shepherds, who then killed her.

(2) In Greek legend, an Athenian maiden who died for love of Iphicles. In her honor a song contest was held in Athens.

Harpies In Greek mythology, rapacious wind goddesses commonly depicted as repulsively ugly: usually considered to be personifications of the storm winds, but indicating to some degree a possible origin in ghost belief. They are sometimes confused with the Erinyes and, because of their form, with the Sirens. Homer mentions only one Harpy, Podarge, the mother by Zeus of the magical horses Balios and Xanthos. Hesiod names two, Aello and Ocypete, fair-haired daughters of Thaumas and the Oceanid Electra. Later tradition makes them hideous creatures, birds with hags' faces, clawed talons, hanging breasts, and bears' ears. Poseidon, in some myths, is their father or their lover. They caused the sudden disappearance of the daughters of Pandareus,

and gave them to the Erinyes as servants. The best-known story in which they appear is that of Phineus.

Harpocrates In later Greek and Roman religion, the Egyptian god Horus as a child; the god of silence. In his aspect as an infant, Horus was depicted by the Egyptians with his finger in his mouth, a childish attitude by convention, but mistaken by the Hellenistic Greeks who took the pose to indicate that the god commanded silence, finger to lips. Harpocrates was a very popular god from the XXVI Egyptian Dynasty through the late Roman Empire, and was perhaps figured more often in homes and temples than any other Egyptian god of the period. See HORUS.

Harris, James Rendel (1852–1941) English philologist, paleographer, and Biblical scholar, educated at Cambridge University. Harris was a professor at Johns Hopkins University (1882–85), at Haverford College (1886–92), lecturer at Cambridge University (1893–1903), professor of Theology at the University of Leyden (1903–04), and later lecturer at Oberlin College. He received many honorary degrees from universities in various countries. Harris traveled in the East a great deal, searching for manuscripts. He is important in the field of folklore mainly for calling attention to a great number of significant similarities in the patterns of folktales. Among Harris' writings are: *Picus Who Is Also Zeus* (Cambridge, Bulletin John Rylands Library, 1916), *The Dioscuri in the Christian Legends* (1903), *The Cult of the Heavenly Twins* (1906), *Boanerges* (1913), and *The Ascent of Olympus* (1917).

Harris, Joel Chandler (1848–1908) American writer. He was born in Georgia, practiced law, and later became a journalist. The Uncle Remus stories, on which his fame rests, first appeared in the Atlanta *Constitution,* with which newspaper he was connected from 1876 until 1900. His best-known book, *Uncle Remus, His Songs and His Sayings: the Folklore of the Old Plantation,* was published in 1880. He also wrote *Nights with Uncle Remus* (1883), *Mingo and Other Sketches* (1883), and *Brer Rabbit.* His Atlanta, Ga., home is now an Uncle Remus Memorial.

Hartland, Edwin Sidney (1848–1927) British writer and folklore scholar, son of a Congregational minister. He became a county court registrar in 1869 and rose to a similar position in high court, which he held to 1924. His *The Science of Fairy Tales* (1891) is considered important in the folklore field. It includes an able treatment of the story of Lady Godiva. His great work, *The Legend of Perseus* (3 volumes, 1894–96), is a comparative study of folktales from all over the world, as well as of numerous beliefs and customs. Hartland was chairman of the Folk Tale Section of the International Folklore Congress in London in 1891, president of the British Folklore Society in 1899, Frazer Lecturer at Oxford University in 1922, and received the Huxley Medal in 1923. Among other writings are: *English Fairy and Other Folk Tales* (1890), *Notes on Cinderella* (International Folklore Congress, Chicago, 1893), *Primitive Paternity* (1910), *Ritual and Belief* (1914), *Primitive Society* (1921), *Primitive Law* (1924), and his editing of Walter Map's *De Nugis Curialium.*

Hārūn al-Rashīd (c. 765–809) Harun the Orthodox, the famed Caliph of Bagdad of the *Arabian Nights.* His reign was a brilliant one; his court overflowed with poets, musicians, sages, and practitioners of the arts. Charlemagne and Hārūn made gifts to each other as the respective masters of the Occident and Orient. The nocturnal wanderings of Hārūn and his vizier, incognito in the streets of Bagdad, are a traditional source of tale and anecdote in the Arab world. His reputation as a devout and just ruler is a popular one; history reveals him as a much more petty person.

haruspices In ancient Rome, a class of diviners from omens, specifically from the entrails of slaughtered animals. As a class they did not have the position or dignity of the augurs, who were important officers of the state. The haruspices were said to be practitioners of an Etruscan art, and drew their predictions not only from the sacrificial animals (which had to be of spotless purity) but also from portents of all kinds, as for example lightning. There was in later Roman times a college of haruspices, which had however no official status.

Hārūt and Mārūt In the Koran and in Moslem tradition, two fallen angels. They descended to earth to test their powers to resist temptation and succumbed to the charms of the daughters of men. Given the choice between eternal damnation hereafter and a limited punishment on earth now, they chose the latter. They hang head downward in a well in Babylon, teaching magic and such arts to men, but only after fair warning to the men of the troubles to which they may look forward. Hārūt and Mārūt may have entered Moslem legend from the Iranian Haurvatat and Ameretat, of the Persian Amshaspands, who were probably the successors in Iranian mythology of the Aśvins.

harvest dances Communal dance celebrations of a successful harvest are observed by agricultural peoples the world over, from the Sohorai of the East Indian Mundas to the Ayriwa of the Peruvian Quechua Indians. Often there is a series of festivities, from the first-fruits to the final harvest and storing, which often coincides with the first deer hunt, as in the Papago wiikita.

The nature of the fruits depends upon the climate: the South American Mataco and Chorotí Indians center their rituals around the algarroba harvest, Indians from the Andes to the Iroquois around maize. Mediterranean peoples rejoice over the vintage, Lithuanians over the maturing of the rye. The Iroquois have a typical succession, from June to early November, of feasts for the spirit of the strawberry, raspberry, bean, green corn, and ripe corn, and a final thanksgiving for all crops, with prayer for continued prosperity. This sequence used to be spread throughout the Southeastern tribes.

The date depends not only on the nature of the produce, but on geographical location as well. Maize ripens among the Mexicans in June, among the Iroquois in September; hence, the ancient Aztec festival for Xilónen, goddess of young corn and beans, fell in June; Iroquois Green Corn feasts fall on Labor Day or thereabouts. Similarly, the Peruvian vintage *fiesta de la vendimia* comes in March instead of September.

The dances, usually open to all, take many forms, but two recur with special frequency—the human chain formed by linked hands, following a leader in serpentine formation, as in the Iroquois and Delaware green bean dance, the Venezuelan Cumanagoto harvest dance, and the ancient Aztec dances for Xilónen and for Cinteotl, god of maize; secondly, actual or symbolic skirmishes, during the Aztec festival for Cinteotl during the 11th month, Ochpaniztli, by priestesses with flowing branches, during the Creek busk by two parties of warriors, in the Meskwakie bean dance as simple opposition (crossovers) between men and women. Both types are common in vegetation rites.

Ceremonial procedures include, besides invocations, secular and religious dances, also the offering of firstfruits, sometimes human sacrifice, and in some cases the use of emetics and purificatory bathing. They always conclude with a feast on the proffered fruits, in fact to the point of gorging on food and drink while there is plenty.

The religious significance may include propitiation and thanksgiving to all supernatural powers, not only to the food spirits; thus peace between the people and the spirits. In many instances this meaning has been retained. In Europe it has been submerged in an alien religion or has given way to simple merrymaking. Pagan harvest festivals have been identified with church holidays both in Europe and Latin America: Corpus Christi, St. John's Day, St. Matthew's Day, the feast for the dead (Halloween). In the United States Thanksgiving Day is a staid relic of these orgies. See BREAD DANCE; BUSK; CORN DANCE; GREEN CORN DANCE; SERPENTINE; STICK DANCE; SWORD DANCE. [GPK]

harvest doll The last sheaf of the harvest, dressed in a woman's dress and decked with ribbons, regarded as the embodiment of the spirit of the crop: often in northern England called the harvest queen, also kern baby, i.e. "corn doll." In Northumberland this puppet is attached to a long pole and carried home by the harvesters and set up in the barn. In some communities it goes home on the last load. In some communities the harvest queen is a fairly small and carefully fashioned image; in others it is heavy and grotesque. In parts of Germany especially, it is thought the heavier the better.

In Scotland we find the harvest maiden or the hag— the Old Wife or the Old Woman (see CAILLEAĊ). In Wales too she is the Hag or *wrach*. In Brittany she is called the Mother Sheaf.

In Germany it is the Corn Mother or Harvest Mother or Old Woman who inhabits the last sheaf (sometimes even the Old Man). In Holstein the puppet is carried home in the last wagonload of the crop and drenched with water, as often also in England and Scotland. In parts of Prussia the last sheaf is the Grandmother, dressed in a woman's dress and decked with flowers. In Denmark the harvest doll is more specifically named, as Rye Woman, Old Barley Woman, etc. In Poland the last sheaf is made into a puppet called Baba, or Grandmother; and in some localities the woman who binds the last sheaf is herself called the Baba, is dressed in the sheaf, is carried home in the last wagon and drenched with water, and treated as all representations of the grain spirit are treated.

Gradually, almost everywhere, the ancient belief in the last sheaf as the spirit of growing grain incarnate has given way to its use as a mere emblem of abundance. In some places these observances have passed away altogether; in some places they still survive. See KORNMUTTER; KORNWOLF.

Harvest Home An old harvest celebration still observed in some parts of rural England, participated in by one and all who have helped with the harvest, and observed on the last day of bringing the harvest home. It was frequently also called the Ingathering or Inning, and in Scotland was known as the Kern.

The last load of rye, beans, or other crop is decked with ribbons, flowers, or green boughs, and accompanied by men, women, and children all singing and shouting. The Harvest Home song, sung en route, goes something like this:

> Harvest home! Harvest home!
> We've plowed, we've sowed,
> We've reaped, we've mowed,
> And brought safe home
> Every load.

The Harvest Queen (see HARVEST DOLL) is either carried home on the wagon or is carried high on a pole by one of the harvesters. The load as it enters the farm gate is often met with a volley of apples, and the Harvest Queen and the reaper carrying her are drenched with buckets of water. At the feast which ends the day the head reaper is crowned with a garland and the evening continues with eating, drinking, and all kinds of merrymaking, dance, and song. This is but one of the harvest thanksgiving celebrations observed all over the world. See CAILLEAĊ; SAMAIN.

Hasan of Bassorah Title and hero of one of the tales of the *Arabian Nights;* a story belonging to the worldwide swan-maiden cycle and compounded with the quest for the lost bride. The long journey of Hasan to the islands of Wak Wak, during which he overcomes many perils by both his own and his helpers' wisdom and ingenuity, forms the core of the story; but aside from the colorful descriptions of the various lands and the contrived drawing out of the plot, there is little interest or use of folklore materials. In the beginning of the long tale, however, a considerable group of common folktale motifs appears.

Hasan the wastrel is enticed by a Persian alchemist to go to the top of a steep mountain for the purpose of obtaining materials for the touchstone that will change base metal into gold. During their voyage to the land of the mountain a storm at sea is allayed by Bahram's, the alchemist's, ceasing to maltreat Hasan. After an eight days' journey from the coast they come to the mountain. Hasan permits himself to be sewn into a skin and a roc carries him to the peak. But when he throws down the magic wood, Bahram flees.

Hasan throws himself into the sea, the only way to escape from the mountain; he is washed ashore and finds himself at the palace of seven princesses of the Jann, enemies of the alchemist. He is adopted as their brother, and when Bahram returns the following year with another victim Hasan slays the Persian. The princesses leave on a visit, giving Hasan the freedom of the palace and its keys. Of course, there is one door he must not open. Eventually he does open the forbidden door, climbs the stairs, and comes out on the roof. From this height he spies on ten bird-maidens, and falls in love with their chief. The maidens put on their bird-robes again and fly away. Hasan begins to waste away in his helpless love, but on the advice of the youngest of the seven sisters, when they return, he

waits for the new moon, when the bird-maidens come back. He steals the garment of the maiden of his choice, she being left behind when the others fly away. He marries this princess, for she is the daughter of a sovereign of the Jann.

Hasan hides the bird-garment, returns with his wife to visit his mother. After three years, when they have two sons, Hasan leaves his wife to see his "sisters" again, warning his mother not to reveal the hiding-place of the garment or to permit his wife to leave the house. But the princess goes to the bath, seemingly a harmless occupation; there she is admired by all and is called before the caliph's wife, who wishes to see the beauty everyone is talking of. The princess convinces the caliph's wife that she would appear much more beautiful if she had her feather dress. Hasan's mother is ordered to produce the shirt, and the wife flies away with the children as soon as she gets her hands on the garment. As she departs, she tells the mother that she is going to the islands of Wak, where Hasan may come to claim her if he can. With the aid of his "sisters," their uncle, and a chain of friends, Hasan eventually recovers his bride in the Amazonlike land of Wak Wak, stealing to attain his end a cap of invisibility, and a staff to summon the Jinn. These he later gives to his helpers, after he has returned the seven years' distance to his home.

The many motifs in this tale mark it as a late fabrication. The accidental obtaining of the magic cap and rod, although parallels to the duping of original boy-owners of such magical objects exist in other folktales, has no integral connection with the plot. Among the several motifs the following are notable: voyage to inaccessible place carried by huge bird (B31.1) (wrapping in animal's skin or flesh); the forbidden chamber (C611); the swan maidens (D361.1); flight to magic land (D531; Type 400); the island of women (F112); cap of invisibility (D1361.15); magic staff (D1421.1).

Hasapiko A modern Greek folk dance performed by men and women in no set order, holding shoulders in a line moving in anticlockwise circle, as in the *kolo* and the *hora*. The chief step is a hopping double and simple, also a sort of grapevine. The leader often crouches and turns. [GPK]

hashish or **hasheesh** An intoxicating preparation of the tops and sprouts of Indian hemp (*Cannabis sativa*), chewed, smoked, or drunk: known also as *bang* (Persian), *bhang* (Indian), *fasükh* (Moroccan), *dakhá* (South African). The celebrated Assassins of the years of the Crusades were addicted to hashish, from which their name derives. It affects the senses so as to cause delirium: heat is not felt and events are exaggerated. It is used for example by Eastern men to slow the orgasm and thus to prolong coition. Penzer, following a suggestion of Gibb, believed that the magical passage of time in Oriental stories, where a long time seems to have passed in only a few minutes, may be a reflection of the hashish experience.

Hathor Literally, either the house above or the house of Horus: an Egyptian cosmic goddess, often represented as a cow with the solar disk and plumes between her horns, or as a woman with cow's horns between which was the solar disk: identified principally with Isis, but also identified with many other earlier goddesses of

Egypt. As the sky goddess she was queen of heaven, creatrix, a Great Mother. She became identified with Ishtar-Astarte, the cow and moon goddess of fertility of Mesopotamia, and was perhaps originally identical with her. An early version of the Osiris myth equates Isis with Hathor: Horus beheaded Isis and the missing head was replaced by that of a cow. As with all the cosmic-fertility goddesses of the Fertile Crescent, the confusion of the crescent-shaped horns with the moon symbol makes it impossible to say whether the original province of the goddess was cosmic (moon) or fertility (cow's horns).

Hathor, the goddess of fertility, was also the female principle, the patroness of women and of marriage. She was likewise goddess of love and mirth, of social pleasures, of beauty. The moon goddess, she was a deity of death, a tree spirit of the sycamore groves near the necropolises; she gave nourishment to the soul (ba) of the departed. In mythology, she fed Horus, and the pharaoh, who was the embodiment of Horus.

The seven Hathors were deities of fate, appearing at the cradle and casting lots to determine the course of the future life of the infant. In this role they appear, for example, in the folktale of the Egyptian Empire, *The Enchanted Prince*.

Hatim Ta'i A famous and generous Arab chief whose exploits are told and retold in Persia and India, especially in Bengal. [MWS]

Hatto The name of two archbishops of Mainz, Germany (891–913 and 968–970). The legend of the mouse-tower of Bingen, a building standing on an island in the middle of the Rhine, is told of both. During a famine, Hatto's granary was full, but he would not distribute the grain to the people. At last he was forced to take notice of their muttering. He announced that on a given day his barn would be thrown open to all. When the barn was filled, he had the doors locked and set fire to the building, burning the starving crowd inside. Immediately a vast army of mice appeared and began to converge on the bishop, who fled before them to take refuge in the mouse-tower. But to no avail; the mice entered and ate him to death. This is a local form of the widespread northern European tale of the mouse-tower: the mice are apparently the avenging souls of those killed by the bishop; the mouse-tower (*Mäuseturm*), as Krappe points out, is undoubtedly a *Mautturm* (customs tower) to which the legend has been attracted. See MOUSE-TOWER.

Hatuibwari or **Hasibwari** The supreme being of Arosi (Melanesia), represented as a winged serpent with a human head containing four teeth and four eyes. He is male but has breasts from which he feeds all created things. Hatuibwari lives on sacred hills. In legend he came from the sky and created a woman from red clay and the heat of the sun. From her rib he made the first man. According to Fox this legend is not the product of the introduction of Christianity into the area.

Haul on the Bowline The oldest of the short-haul chanteys, going back at least to the time of Henry VIII. After 1500 the bowline was no longer important in working a ship, but the song remained to serve in the hauling of other lines. The title words were always sung uniformly, but the others were varied as the chanteyman chose, often slyly giving navigation hints to inexperienced officers.

haunted house A house, tenanted or untenanted, which is frequented by ghosts, specters, phantoms, and the like. In the British Isles, haunted houses and castles are common and the "goings on" of their nocturnal company have given rise to many and varied traditional tales. Castles in Scandinavia are likewise haunted. In short, wherever or whenever the dead return, they haunt their former homes. Although Clough says, "America needs more and better haunted houses," there is no dearth of them in the United States from Maine to California and from Texas to Minnesota. [GPS]

Havgan In Brythonic mythology, the opponent of Arawn, king of Annwn, for the sovereignty of that wonderful land. Havgan could be overcome only by a single blow, a second would revive him. Pwyll, fighting in behalf of Arawn, gave him his mortal wound. Havgan begged for another, to end his suffering, but Pwyll refused to give it. Thus Havgan was killed and Annwn was saved for Arawn.

Havmand The merman of Danish folklore, usually bearded and very handsome. He lives in the sea or inhabits rocky cliffs along the shore. He is usually regarded as a friendly being, unlike many other Teutonic water spirits, such as the nix, Hakenmann, the Icelandic Skrimsl, etc. But the *Havfrue*, the mermaid of Danish folklore, has a dual nature. She is very beautiful, sometimes friendly, but sometimes also predatory and seductive. Fishermen who see her through the sea mists expect stormy weather to follow. Sometimes she comes piteously shivering to their fires to seduce them into accompanying her. She takes home the unfound bodies of the drowned.

haw In American cowboy square dances, the term for left. [GPK]

Hawk and the Nightingale A fable ascribed to Æsop, but told by Hesiod in his *Works and Days* in the 8th century B.C.: said to be the earliest known of the Greek fables. A Nightingale, caught by a hungry Hawk, begged to be let go, pleading his tininess. But the Hawk replied that the little bird he had was better for his hunger than a big bird yet to be caught. See BIRD IN THE HAND.

hawthorn A thorny, spring-flowering shrub of the rose family (genus *Cratægus*) with white or pink flowers and small pome fruits or haws, sometimes called white thorn to distinguish it from the blackthorn. In ancient Greece it was used for the marriage torch and girls wore crowns of hawthorn at weddings. In Rome it was a potent charm against witchcraft and sorcery, and the leaves were put in the cradles of newborn babies. In Christian legend it formed the Crown of Thorns and was therefore considered to have many miraculous powers. A sprig of hawthorn was proof against storms at sea, lightning ashore; and in the house it was proof against spirits and ghosts. But in Ireland and parts of England bringing it into the house was considered unlucky, and in some localities it even brought death. The staff of Joseph of Arimathea which sprouted when thrust into the ground was also believed to have been hawthorn. According to Teutonic legend it was believed to have sprung from lightning and it was often used for funeral pyres.

Among the Celtic peoples it was unlucky, if not fatal, to cut down these shrubs, as in the case of Tim Mac-Dougal who reluctantly accepted some much needed money to cut down a bush. The next morning his baby was stolen and the following day his wife ran off with the money. When the baby's clothes were returned, he knew that the little people were displeased, so he took shoots of the bush he had destroyed and planted them in a circle around a wild thyme bed. The next day he found that they had grown, and in the center he found his baby. In Ireland hawthorns are believed to be frequented by fairies, and are therefore sometimes called "gentle bushes." To cut one down brings death upon the cattle or the children, and loss of memory to the feller. Their scent is sometimes said to have the sweet, enchanting scent of death. The boughs are fastened to the outside of barns on May Day to keep out evil spirits and ensure plenty of milk during the summer.

In England, before the calendar reform, hawthorn was used to decorate the doors on May Day and in Northamptonshire a hawthorn branch was placed in the ground before the house of the prettiest girl of the village. The crown of Richard III was found in a hawthorn bush at Bosworth, and was later placed on the head of Henry VII. Thereafter Henry adopted the thorn as his device.

A distilled water made from the thorns was said to draw out thorns and splinters from the flesh. The flowers steeped in wine and distilled are good for pleurisy, stomach and all internal pains. The powdered berries in wine are a good tonic and a cure for dropsy and the stone. The hawthorn is the state flower of Missouri.

hay (1) In most of Great Britain, France, Germany, Bohemia, Spain, India, and the United States, it is considered good luck to see a load of hay approaching. Many believe that if you make a wish and do not look at the load again, the wish will be granted, but if the hay is baled you may have to wait until the bales are opened. Not to wish on a load of hay is bad luck. However, in some parts of England, it is unlucky to meet a load of hay in a country lane and you must spit on the load to regain your luck. Crossed scythes are frequently left on the top of the rick to prevent spontaneous combustion. In parts of England, feeding cattle a little stolen hay on Christmas Eve will make them prosper during the year. Some Northumberland churches are strewn with hay in the summer. There is a belief that to add hay flowers to your bath will cure toothache.

(2) or **hey** An old English country dance: a serpentine figure performed in a circle (same as grand right and left). The straight hay is the same, executed in a straight line; the straight hay for three is a figure 8 featuring the intertwining of three dancers. [GPK]

Hayagrīva Literally, horse-neck, or great wrath king: in Tibet a Dharmapāla with a horse's head growing from his hair; first of the eight dreadful gods called *Drag-gshhed*. To the Mongols Hayagrīva was the protector of horses. His Tibetan name is *r*Ta-*m*grin. In Hinduism, Hayagrīva is a Daitya who, according to

one legend, stole the Veda as it slipped out of Brahmā's mouth while he was asleep. In another legend, Vishṇu assumed this form to recover the Veda which two Daityas had carried off.

Hayicanako The Old Woman Underneath Us; the supporter of the earth in the mythology of the Tlingit Indians and certain Athapascan tribes. Either she supports it herself or tends a post made of a beaver leg, on which the earth is standing. When the earth shakes it is a sign that the old woman is hungry, and the people throw grease in the fire, which melts and runs down to her. See ATLAS MOTIF.

Hayk The national epic hero of Armenia; a handsome giant with a strong arm who led his people from the plain of Shinar and the tyranny of Bel to the cold but free mountains of Armenia where he conquered the native Urartians. Later he met the forces of Bel and defeated them by arranging his smaller forces in a triangle. His symbols are the bow and triangular arrow. He is the eponymous hero of the Armenians who call themselves the Hay and their country Hayastan.

hazel A bushy shrub or small tree (genus *Corylus*) yielding an edible nut. In Celtic legend, especially Irish, this is the tree of knowledge. The salmon in Connla's well ate the nuts of this tree and was the wisest of beings. The druid who fostered Fionn MacCuṁal told the young Fionn to cook a salmon from a certain deep pool in the River Boyne, but forbade him to taste it. While turning the fish, Fionn burnt his thumb and put it in his mouth. Thus he received the gift of inspiration, for this was the salmon which had eaten the nuts which fell into the pool from the nine hazels of wisdom. The hazel was the ninth tree in the Old Irish tree alphabet and symbol of the ninth month (Aug. 6 to Sept. 2). It represented all knowledge of the arts and sciences; and a hazel wand was carried by the heralds as a badge of office. In Fenian legend the dripping hazel was an evil tree without leaves, dripping poisonous milk, and the home of vultures. This tree represented the evil, destructive uses of knowledge.

Hazel twigs and forks are the most universally popular divining rods. In some localities, however, these rods must be cut on St. John's Eve or Night. In addition to this, in Brandenburg one must approach the tree in darkness, walking backwards, and cut the fork silently, while reaching between the legs. In Berlin they say a divining rod is only good for seven years, and must be cut by an innocent child of the true faith on St. John's Night. Before the 17th century hazel rods were used for discovering thieves and murderers as well as water and treasure. To test a divining rod, hold it in water: it should squeal like a pig.

In Prussia they say that if you cannot catch a thief, beat a piece of his clothing with a hazel switch and he will fall sick. In Wales hazel twigs are woven into a wishing cap which will grant the wearer's desire. Also, a shipmaster who wears such a cap will weather any storm. In France, hazel rods are used for "beating the bounds." A hazel breastband on a harness will protect a horse from fairy bewitchment and evil spirits. In Ireland the cattle are driven through the Beltane and Midsummer fires and their backs singed with hazel wands to protect them from fairies. These rods are very powerful for driving the cattle during the year.

The hazel is the tree of Thor and in the dominion of Mercury. The kernels of hazel nuts mixed with mead and honied water are good for an old cough; mixed with pepper they clear the head. In England, a double hazel nut carried in the pocket prevents toothache. A cross fashioned from the wood and laid on a snake bite, while reciting a diminishing rime, will draw out the poison. Binding the legs and feet of a horse, who has over-eaten, with hazel rods and reciting a formula in his right ear will relieve him. See WITCH HAZEL.

heart's-ease One or more of the *Persicariæ,* some species of which are so called because of heart-shaped markings on the leaves: believed to yield a substance beneficial in heart disorders. See PANSY; PERSICARY; VIOLET.

heart saved from cremation A motif in the mythology of the Yuman and Shoshonean Indians of southern California, in which the death of the creator or culture hero is caused by poisoning or by Frog swallowing his excrements. Great was the mourning for the god; great was the mourning that death had come upon mankind. The people prepared to cremate the body of their god, but Coyote coveted the heart. The people tried to circumvent his plans, but Coyote leapt onto the pyre at the last minute, tore out the heart, and ate it. The Juaneño Indians (Shoshonean) long retained a mourning ceremony which dramatized this myth. When an initiate among the Juaneño died a certain ritual was enacted by one called the *ano* (coyote) or the *takwe* (eater), who cut a piece of flesh from the dead man's shoulder and ate it. The hearts (i.e. souls) of the dead whose flesh was thus ritually eaten by the *ano* or *takwe* were "saved" to fly into the sky and become stars. The Pomo Indians performed a similar ritual.

heaven The afterworld in the sky where the souls of the blessed live in company with divine beings. Heaven is the term applied also to the region of the sky where the afterworld is located; in some cosmographies there are several discrete heavens, varying in excellence or in suitability for the various human occupations. See AFTERWORLD; ASGARD; ELYSIUM; PARADISE; VALHALLA.

heb-sed A jubilee festival of the ancient Egyptian pharaohs, during which the king renewed his vigor by magical means and transferred it to the earth: believed to be a substitute for an earlier ceremony at which the enfeebled king was murdered. During the ceremony, the pharaoh ran a prescribed course while carrying a flail, a doubly meaningful ritual of fertility. The coronation was repeated, and the lotus and papyrus, emblems of the two kingdoms, were entwined about a stake. The existence of two tombs for some of the Egyptian kings has led to the conjecture that a symbolic killing of the pharaoh may have occurred at the heb-sed.

Hecate In Greek mythology, an underworld divinity of triple aspect: perhaps a Thracian goddess, perhaps Hellenic in origin. She is not mentioned in Homer, but in Hesiod her powers are already very great: she bestows wealth and success, good luck and advice, is powerful in earth, sea, and heaven. Apart from her eminence in her own cult, flourishing principally in Asia Minor, she appeared as companion and cousin of

Artemis. The best known of several genealogies made her the daughter of Perses and Asteria; as a Titan, she alone kept her powers under the rule of Zeus, having helped him against the Gigantes.

By a transference common in mythology, she became, as a goddess of plenty, an infernal deity, terrible in aspect and often snakelike, the queen of ghosts and mistress of black magic, the keeper of the keys of Hades. She and Helios alone witnessed the rape of Persephone, and Hecate was sent by Zeus to find her, accompanying Demeter with a torch. When Persephone was found, Hecate remained as her companion. She thus became ruler of the shades of the departed, dispatched phantoms and the like from the underworld at night. Hecate wandered about in the dark, accompanied by the souls of the dead and by her hell-hounds. Dogs howled at night when they heard this company approach.

Hecate was to antiquity the great goddess of magic, more important than her daughter Circe. Second as a magician was the Hermes Chthonius later confused with Hermes Trismegistus. The greatest of the magical incantations of antiquity are connected with Hecate. She haunted the vicinity of crossroads, and became the divinity of roads. Triple statues of Hecate Trioditis (Roman *Trivia*) were set up at places where roads crossed, facing in the several directions. Similar statues were erected before houses to keep out the evil spirits. Such representations were believed to be oracular. Food was set out before them at the end of every month (Hecate's suppers), and at night she appeared to taste of it. Dogs and honey and black ewe-lambs were sacrificed to her.

A further evolution made Hecate, already a goddess of plenty and of the night, become the moon goddess: this is considered by some to have been her original aspect. Hecate was represented as carrying a torch and a scourge; sometimes her three heads would be those of a dog, a horse, and a lion; sometimes the triple aspect would be named for Selene, Artemis, and Hecate. She was identified variously with Demeter, Rhea (or Cybele or Brimo), Artemis, Persephone; her worship was connected with that of the Cabeiri and the Curetes and with Apollo and the Muses, and had as its principal locations Samothrace, Ægina, Argos, and Athens. Compare BERCHTA; HERMES; HOLDE; JANUS; MONSTERS; PADMAPANI; RUDRA; ŚIVA.

hedgehog A small, nocturnal, insectivorous mammal of the Old World (family Erinaceidæ), with back and sides covered with stout spines. An early English writer calls it "hedgidog"; Shakespeare names it "hedge-pig" (*Macbeth*). The peculiar noise this animal makes, something between snoring and breathing hard, has given rise to ominous superstitions regarding it, namely that there might be ghosts or evil spirits about when the uncanny sound is heard.

In Morocco, the pounded and roasted liver of the hedgehog is given to school boys to make them remember their lessons; a jawbone is hung around a child's neck to protect it from the evil eye. Hedgehog blood is good for warts, the gall for deafness, and the fumes of its burnt bristles are good for both man and beast. In England, the left eye of the hedgehog fried in oil was a remedy for insomnia in the 17th century.

Popular belief in England says that the hedgehog

carries off apples on its spines; the same belief, but about grapes, is mentioned in two anonymous epigrams in a Greek anthology. English farmers used to believe that hedgehogs milked the cows at night, and hence used to kill them for no other reason. To eat the flesh of hedgehogs was forbidden among the peoples of Madagascar, especially to their warriors, lest they too curl up in fright when attacked.

In folktales there are helpful hedgehogs (B434), hedgehogs as revenants (E423.2.4) and hedgehogs as animal spouses (B641.4). [GPS]

Hedley kow A supernatural being of British folklore noted for its antics and annoying tricks. Often it assumes the shape of a truss of straw. When someone tries to pick this up, to stow it away, it becomes heavier and heavier and heavier, until the hapless carrier has to lay it down to rest. Then suddenly it shuffles away and a peal of laughter is heard.

heiau Hawaiian temples built of lava. These are rarely dedicated to a particular divinity; any god can be invoked in them. They are usually oblong in shape, formed by walls of rock lava which enclose the altar, the house of the priests, and the anu or place of oracles. All heiau and sacred groves are protected by tabu.

Heimdall or **Heimdallr** In Teutonic mythology, god of the early sun, hence of dawn and light. In a late Eddaic account he was the son of Odin and nine giant sisters, born on the horizon, nurtured on the strength of the earth, the moisture of the sea, and the warmth of the sun. He was guardian of the heavenly bridge Bifrost. He could see a hundred miles by night as well as by day, and his hearing was such that he could hear the grass grow. One night he was disturbed by a stealthy noise, and looking across to Folkvang, he saw Loki in the guise of a fly, tiptoeing in Freya's bedroom to steal her necklace Brisingamen.

Once when Heimdall visited the earth, he entered three homes: a hovel by the seacoast, a thrifty farmhouse, and a castle. In each after his visit, a son was born. The first, named Thrall, was dark-skinned and thickset; the second, Karl, was blue-eyed and sturdy; the third, Jarl, was a slender handsome boy. From these three sons were descended the serfs, husbandmen, and aristocrats of the Northern peoples.

Heimdall lived in a castle, Himinbiorg, at the highest point of Bifrost. He wore shining white armor and carried a flashing sword and the famous horn, Giallerhorn, with which he will summon all to the last battle of the world at Ragnarök. He also went under the name of Gullintani, Hallinskide, and Riger.

Heinzelmännchen In German folk belief, friendly dwarfs or elves who come in the night to work for people whom they like, or to whom they are indebted.

hei-tiki A grotesque amulet representing a fetus, worn by the Maori to ward off attacks by the envious spirits of stillborn children, who dislike the living because they themselves have never had a chance to live. Literally it means "tied-on tiki." See TIKI.

Hel or **Hela** In Teutonic mythology (1) The grim, fierce goddess, half black and half white, who ruled over all who died of disease or old age. She was the daughter of Loki and Angur-boda, banished by Odin into Niflheim to rule over the worlds of the dead.

(2) Sometimes known as Niflheim, Niflhel: the realm of nine worlds under the roots of Yggdrasil which was reserved for those who died of disease or old age. Not until Christian times did it become the realm of the damned. It was ruled by the goddess Hel and guarded by the dog, Garm. The name is literally "hollow place," and corresponds more to the Greek Hades than to the Christian Hell, in that it is primarily an otherworld rather than a place of punishment and misery.

Helen In Greek legend and mythology, the most beautiful of women; daughter of Zeus and Leda and sister of the Dioscuri. Originally Helen was perhaps a tree goddess; like her brothers, she was a patron of sailors to whom she appeared as St. Elmo's fire, an evil omen. Whether her deification preceded or followed the legend is a matter still debated.

When a young girl, Helen was abducted by Theseus and then rescued by her brothers when Theseus left her to visit the underworld. The Dioscuri also carried off Æthra, the mother of Theseus, to be Helen's handmaid. Still later, Helen was wooed by the great kings of Greece, and she chose Menelaus, or was given to him by her putative father Tyndareus. To Menelaus she bore Hermione.

After some years of married life as the wife of the king of Sparta, Helen was induced by Paris (with Aphrodite's help) to flee with him to Troy. One version of the story says that they stopped at Egypt on the way, where Proteus hid the real Helen in a cave and sent a shade in her shape on to Troy with Paris. When Troy fell, she was reunited with Menelaus (who stopped at Egypt on his way back to Sparta, thus permitting the resubstitution to be made). She is said to have survived him, to have been driven out by his sons, and to have been killed by hanging by Polyxo in Rhodes.

In the writings of the Renaissance and after, Helen became the type of classical beauty. Marlowe's Doctor Faustus, thirsting for beauty not of this world, called up the shade of Helen from the underworld; the Faust of Goethe had a son Euphorion by Helen.

Helenus In Greek legend, a Trojan soothsayer, son of Priam and Hecuba. He and Cassandra, when children, obtained the gift of prophecy when their ears were licked by serpents. Helenus is a warrior in Homer. He deserted to the Greeks, because of the sacrilegious slaying of Achilles by Paris, or because Odysseus captured him and caused him to foretell the manner of the fall of Troy (by the arrows of Hercules), or because he lost Helen to Deiphobus after Paris died, or simply because he so desired. After the war ended, he became king of Epirus, married Hector's widow, Andromache, and was later buried at Argos.

Heliogabalus or **Elagabalus** A sun god of Emesa in ancient Syria. According to Herodian, a Syrian historian of the Roman emperors, the god was worshipped in the form of a conical black stone. The Roman emperor who reigned from 218–222 A.D. adopted the name, he having been a priest of the god.

Helios In Greek mythology, the sun or the sun god: often confused in later classical times with Apollo. Helios was the son of Hyperion and Theia or Euryphaessa, the brother of Selene and Eos. His consort was Perse or Perseis, by whom he was father of Æetes and Circe. Among his numerous mistresses were Clymene, Clytie, Leucothoe, and Rhode. Helios was all-seeing as god of the sun, and this faculty causes the confusion with Apollo. Helios saw the rape of Persephone; he knew of the adultery of Aphrodite and Ares.

However, Apollo never is pictured in Greek myth as a charioteer, while Helios usually drives the four-horse team of the chariot of the sun through the heavens. The palace of Helios was in the east, from which he drove the sun westward to dip into the stream of Ocean at night, there to rest and bathe after his day's labor, and to be carried back on the stream through the night to his palace in the cup fashioned by Hephæstus. On the island of Trinacria, Helios had seven herds of oxen and seven of sheep, each a herd of fifty head which never increased or decreased. These herds were kept by his daughter, either Phaetusa or Lampetia. When these cattle were attacked by Ulysses' men, Helios was notified by Lampetia; he complained to Zeus who slew all the crew but Ulysses with a bolt. Later myth gave him flocks on Erytheia as well, and wherever Helios was worshipped flocks were sacred to him.

His principal place of worship was at Rhodes, where the famous Colossus (a representation of him) stood. There was however little established worship, although the god was often invoked as the all-seeing. The cock was especially sacred to him, as was honey, and as were also white boars, bulls, lambs, rams, and horses. He was called Sol by the Romans, and often simply Titan. Compare GERYON'S CATTLE; HERCULES; PHAETHON.

heliotrope (1) An herb (genus *Heliotropium*) with small white or purplish flowers. In Greek times heliotrope denoted any flower which followed the sun. Greek legend says the water nymph Clytie was in love with the sun god, Helios, and she sat on a river bank for nine days and nights without food or water, watching his chariot, until the gods took pity on her and changed her into a heliotrope. That is why it is a symbol of eternal love. The common heliotrope was brought from Peru to France in 1736, where it became known as the love flower. From there it came to the American colonies. Among the Border folk it was said to make invisible anyone who walked with a piece in his shoe; but the magic formula for this has been lost.

According to Pliny the heliotrope is not plucked when used medicinally, but tied in knots with a prayer that the patient might recover to untie them. Pliny also said that a scorpion touched by a sprig of heliotrope would die and would not enter a place which had been circumscribed by a sprig of this plant. This belief was based on the resemblance of heliotrope seeds to a scorpion.

(2) Same as BLOODSTONE.

hell The afterworld, usually underground but often placed on earth in some far-off region to the west or north, and inhabited by the souls of the dead; especially, the place where souls are punished for their transgressions on earth as contrasted with heaven. The Greek Hades included the Elysian Fields, a sort of heaven, and did not encompass the concept of punishment. However, the underworld of Egyptian belief included the court of Osiris where souls found lacking were swallowed by the infernal hippopotamus. The hells of world-wide belief are peopled not only by the spirits of the departed, but also by demons, ruled over by a god of the underworld, who aid in the punishment of the soul. It is noteworthy that generally the hells of cold lands are regions of eternal ice, and that the hells of more southerly areas are places of everlasting fire. See AFTERWORLD; HADES; HEL; NIFLHEIM.

Helle In Greek legend, the sister of Phrixus; daughter of Athamas and his first wife Nephele. Ino, their stepmother, hated the children and plotted to get rid of them. She induced the women of the country to roast the seed for the next corn-crop and bribed the messenger who was subsequently sent to Delphi to discover the reason for the crop failure. The false message ordered sister and brother sacrificed, but at the last moment a ram with golden fleece, the gift of Hermes, was sent by Nephele to save them. Off they flew on it, but between Sigeum and the Chersonesus Helle fell into the sea. The place where she fell was afterwards called the sea of Helle or Hellespont. A variant of the legend says that Poseidon rescued her and that she later bore him Paion or Edonus.

Hellespont The Sea of Helle; ancient name of the Dardanelles, the strait connecting the Ægean Sea and the Sea of Marmora: so called because Helle fell there while escaping on the ram with the golden fleece.

Helskô Literally, hell shoes: in early Teutonic practice, shoes bound to the feet of the dead to travel Helveg, the long troublesome road to Hel. This custom is still prevalent in parts of Scandinavia. See DEAD SHOES.

hemlock (1) Poison hemlock (*Conium maculatum*), a poisonous biennial of the parsley family with a hollow, spotted stem and white lacy flowers which give off a noxious odor when bruised. It is found in the United States, throughout Europe and temperate Asia. This plant is believed to be identical with the Greek *kōneion* and a decoction of it was used to execute criminals. It may have been the hemlock which Socrates drank. Plants grown in the full sun and in hot climates are considered most virulent. It is poisonous to cows, but it is said that horses, goats, and sheep are not affected. It has been used sparingly as a medicine since early times. Pliny calls it a cure for drunkenness and recommends it for the liver, scrofula, ulcers, and glandular swellings. It has also been used for rheumatism, neuralgia, whooping-cough, syphilis, and tetanus. Given with opium it was used to quiet convulsions. Culpeper recommends that the bruised leaves be laid on the brow for inflamed and swollen eyes and says that pure wine is the best antidote if too much is taken.

(2) Water hemlock or cowbane (genus *Cicuta*) is also poisonous. Some authorities claim this plant, not the above, was used by the Greeks. It was sometimes used to induce temporary paralysis of the hierophant and priestess in Eleusinian rites.

(3) Another plant called hemlock is the ground hemlock, American yew, or moose grass (*Taxus canadensis*). Many Indian tribes of the northern United States and Canada make a tea from the quills of this plant which they drink for colds and rheumatism, but this was never popular with the white settlers. In British Columbia the medicine-man makes a ring of hemlock boughs

and passes the tribe through it when they are threatened by an epidemic. Several tribes use the bark for sore gums, upset stomach, and dysentery.

hen The female of the common domestic fowl, also of any other kind of bird. Like the cock, the hen acts as a weather prophet. It is an earnest of fertility, as it is thrown into the bride's lap among the southern Slavs in marriage or prebridal ceremonies. It has long been closely associated with connubial bliss; the crowing of a hen even in antiquity was ominous of marital quarrels.

Great moment has been attached to the cackling of the hen; with married people, it is a sign of wifely authority. The crowing of a hen has given rise to the famous jingles:

> Whistling girls and crowing hens,
> Always come to some bad end.

> Whistling maid and a crowing hen,
> Neither fit for God or men.

But the feminist has changed all this and the counter jingle runs:

> Whistling girls and hens that crow,
> Make their way wherever they go.

If a hen runs into the house, someone is coming visiting. If a red hen crows, there will be a fire; if a black one crows, something will be stolen. If hens go to roost early, there will be good weather. A white hen denotes good luck. Hen's blood is used in charms and a black hen's head with a charm can harm an enemy. The blood, liver, fat, gizzard, and other parts of the hen are used in folk medicine. In some cases, a hen is split open alive and applied to the body (cases of peritonitis in the Middle West in the 1890's and earlier).

The hen appears in many folktales: in formula tales ("The Death of the Little Hen"); in tales of magic ("Jack and the Beanstalk"), and in others of the same or other types. The hen and chickens are emblematical of God's providence. [GPS]

Henry, Mellinger Edward (1873–1946) collector of folk songs. A teacher in New Jersey high schools, Mr. Henry became interested in folk songs while on vacation in the southern mountains in 1925. His subsequent study and collection in the Appalachian highlands brought about a thousand songs and ballads to general knowledge. As a contribution to more formal scholarship Henry published in 1937 the *Bibliography of American Folk-Songs*. His other publications include *Songs Sung in the Southern Appalachians* (1934); *Folk Songs of the Southern Highlands* (1938); and numerous articles on American folk song in the *Journal of American Folklore*.

Henry Martyn An English ballad (Child #250) of a Scots pirate: probably a derivative of *Sir Andrew Barton* (Child #167). In the A version, Martyn is killed, as in #167, but in the E version (*Andrew Bartin*), collected in the United States, he remains, after sinking merchantman and warship, master of the seas.

henweh The Kintak Bong and Menek Kaien (Malay Peninsula) name for the dire events following a disastrous storm. The Lenggong Negritos call this *henwoie*. Storms, which are especially severe and frequent in the Malay Peninsula, are accompanied by floods caused by rain and the rising of water from under the earth. The

Negritos believe the storms, and especially their after-events of putrefaction and rising water, are due to such acts as copying the notes of certain birds or having sexual intercourse in the camp. The rising waters are sent by the grandmothers, Yak Lepeh, Yak Manoid, and Yak Takel, who live under the earth, as punishment for such misdeeds. Compare TERLAIN.

Hephæstus The Greek god of fire, especially of volcanic fire, and specifically god of the fire of the smith's forge: usually considered to be of Oriental origin, coming to Greece through Lycia and Asia Minor as a god of volcanic regions. His cult was observed in Lemnos from Homeric times; it, with rival claims for several other volcanic islands and places, was supposed to be his favorite place, in token of which the Lemnian priests of Hephæstus could cure snakebite. The soil of Lemnos stopped hemorrhage, cured insanity, healed snakebite. In Attica, and in Athens, his worship attained some prominence: Erichthonius was his son; Athenian hearths had statuettes of Hephæstus before them; he and Athena were considered the donors of the arts of civilization. At the Hephæstia there was a race with torches; the Chalceia, honoring jointly Athena and Hephæstus, recorded the invention of bronze-working by the god.

Hephæstus was the son of Hera, but whether of Zeus as well traditions vary. The later legends say Hera produced him from her thigh to equal Zeus' feat in giving birth to Athena, but the contradiction saying Hephæstus cleft the forehead of Zeus that Athena might emerge is not explained. Hephæstus, making inquiries among the gods concerning his mysterious parentage, was put off with vague answers. He therefore built a golden throne for Hera, which trapped her when she sat in it and from which she would not release her until she told him of his parents.

Within the Homeric writings there are two distinct versions of how Hephæstus was thrown from heaven. One says that Zeus threw him when he took Hera's part in a quarrel; the other that Hera herself dropped him in disgust at his congenital lameness. Later legend makes the two falls a sequential part of the story. Thetis and Eurynome rescued him after Hera dropped him because of his delicate health, and they taught him metalwork. He made the magic chair in revenge for Hera's cruelty. Then, when Zeus tossed him to earth, he fell on Lemnos and became lame.

He later returned to Olympus wearing artificial supports and aroused great gusts of laughter from the gods. On Olympus he set up a workshop, fashioning self-pumping bellows, or perhaps automatons which worked the bellows in obedience to his orders. Later, his smithies were said to be beneath volcanoes; the Cyclopes were his assistants. There are several stories of automatic objects made by Hephæstus in which he seems to parallel the wonder-working of Dædalus. Hephæstus is similar too to Prometheus as the bringer of useful fire to man.

His wife was Charis or Aphrodite, or Aglaia. A familiar myth tells how he trapped with a net Aphrodite and Ares in adulterous union and held them up to the scorn of the gods. The union of the god of fire, the fertilizing element carried in the race at the Hephæstia, with the goddess of springtime and love is understandable despite their mythological physical incongruity.

Hephæstus and his mythology find parallels in other

parts of the world. The Romans identified him with Vulcan, though Vulcan is simply the god of volcanic fire and has no connection with the artificer's fire. Wieland the smith, Ilmarinen, and Dædalus all made magical objects at their smithies. Agni was footless and Wieland was lame. Compare MAHUIKA; MAUI; PANDORA.

Heqet, Heqt, Hak, or **Heka** In ancient Egyptian religion and mythology, a frog-headed goddess, associated both with the tomb and with resurrection and birth. She was the consort of Khnum, and in one form of the Horus myth the mother of Horus. The frog symbol of the birth goddess appears elsewhere, e.g. the Aztec goddess Chalchihuitlicue. The Egyptians believed that the frogs which appeared in the silt after the annual Nile inundation were generated from the mud and the fertilizing river, hence the symbol of the frog for Heqet.

Hera In Greek mythology, the sister and consort of Zeus; later, the queen of heaven, but not queen of the gods; the only married goddess of Olympus, whose marriage to Zeus (*hieros gamos*) formed the important incident of her worship: probably originally a cow goddess of fertility, native to Greece. Hera, as were all the gods, was subordinate to Zeus, whom she had to obey, but she took this with bad grace, being of quarrelsome and stubborn character. Zeus, when he discovered that beating her was of no avail, once chained her and suspended her in the clouds until she agreed to submit. As a result, she turned to intrigue, even borrowing the girdle of Aphrodite to arouse his passion. Hera was by nature (and with sufficient reason) jealous, and had constantly to be on the alert to prevent Zeus' amours, or to punish his accomplices, after the fact. Thus, she was hostile to Hercules; she was an enemy of the Trojans because of the judgment of Paris against her.

Hera was essentially the goddess of women. Her three principal aspects therefore are as maiden (Parthenos), as matron (Teleia), as widow (Chera). The goddess of childbirth, Eileithyia, was identified with her, though usually she is considered to be the mother of Eileithyia. The principal seat of her worship was at Argos; she was prominently worshipped at Mycenæ, Sparta, and Samos. Compare DÆDALA; JUNO.

Herakhty, Harakhte, or **Horakhte** In Egyptian religion and mythology, Horus of the Horizon; Horus as the rising or setting sun, figured as a falcon: often, as Rā-Herakhty, identified with the sun god Rā. Horakhte was worshipped at Heliopolis alongside Rā-Atum.

herb An aromatic plant used for medicine, seasoning, and for its perfume. Much herb lore lies in the realm of magic and is said to have been originally revealed to some chosen person by one of the gods in ancient times— given to Adam by God in the Garden of Eden, taught to man by the fallen angels of the Mohammedans, shown to a healer by a god or culture hero, revealed in a vision by one of the Christian saints, or revealed through divination as by shooting an arrow into the air as in the case of King Ladislaus of Hungary, who, with a prayer that he might find a cure for the plague which was raging in his country, found the gentian.

Much of this lore was, and still is, handed down by word of mouth from generation to generation. But there is a considerable amount of herb lore which was first set down before the Christian era (as well as some found in the earliest known inscriptions). This formed the nucleus for scientific medicine. Only a small part of this early written lore is accepted in present-day scientific medicine, but much of it is in current use as folk medicine throughout the world among all classes of people.

This written lore has been modified as it was passed down through the ages, partly through errors in copying old texts, partly through confusion as to the actual plant in question, or to the errors incident to translating their names from one language into another, and partly through observation, although frequently properties of a plant are passed on even though the writer admits that he himself has found them to be ineffective or harmful. Although much of this lore has been passed down through the ages by scholars with little or no understanding of botany or medicine except as expounded in books as fact by the ancients, and by many doctors and practitioners of the healing arts who were little better, there have been periods when a truly critical, scientific attitude has been applied to it.

In Roman times some of the emperors had botanists in all parts of the empire gathering herbs to be sent back to the capital. These men were alert to find new herbs and cures, and for the most part checked these cures against actual cases before passing them on to the emperor. This was also the case with the Spanish explorations in the New World. The king sent out several botanical expeditions which obtained considerable knowledge from the natives. During the later Middle Ages and the Renaissance there was a genuine effort among physicians to check these properties with actual experiments and although they were not entirely successful, they discarded much of the valueless or dangerous.

Herb lore is common to all peoples of the world, but there is little agreement among them as to the properties of the various herbs. Often the powers of a given herb are diametrically opposite in different cultures. An herb which among one people is a sure cure for any and all types of poisoning, among others may be used as a poison, while still a third group believe it to be a cure for poison because it is one itself. Often the properties ascribed to an herb are the result of sympathetic magic. The mandrake and ginseng root are cures for all the ills of mankind among many peoples because of their resemblance to the figure of a man. Color also plays an important role in the ascription of curative properties, yellow being an effective agent in the cure of jaundice, while red is considered a sure cure for diseases of the blood, heart, etc. Some herbals rely heavily on astrology and the plants of various zodiacal signs are supposed to cure ailments of the corresponding parts of the body. Where herbal lore is closely tied up with witchcraft and demonology, evil smell and taste are called into play for the exorcism of the demons which cause disease. In some localities and during some periods of Christianity, each disease was the especial province of a certain saint and the herbs sacred to that saint were, therefore, sovereign remedies for that ailment, mental or physical.

In many widely scattered parts of the world there is definite ritual to be observed in the growing, harvesting, and use of herbs. To be effective an herb must often be grown in a certain location, or in conjunction with other herbs. Certain seasons or days (and nights) were specified for the gathering of herbs: often Midsummer's Eve. Ascension Day, or the dark of the moon. Among the

Mohegan Indians of North America it was expressly forbidden to gather herbs during the Dog Days. Many authorities claim that herbs lose their virtue if touched by iron. The Celtic druids are said to have used a golden sickle in gathering mistletoe. Incantations were frequently used when gathering, preparing, and using these preparations. There was one school of thought that held that the only virtue was in simples, or preparations consisting of a single herb; others believed that it was only in certain combinations that any results could be expected.

Some herbs and herb preparations are taken internally, others are applied externally as lotions and unguents, or in the case of wounds the herb is simply laid on the cut. With other herbs smelling their fragrance is sufficient, and they may be hung around the house or carried about the person. Still others are carried as charms or amulets. [JWH]

Hercules or **Herakles (Heracles)** [Herakles, the Greek form of the name, is preferred in present-day scholarship. The Latin form Hercules is, however, the usual literary usage and has been adopted here because of its greater familiarity to most readers. The impropriety of the use of the Latin name in discussing the Labors (of Greek tradition) is no greater than that of the use of the Greek form Herakles in speaking of a local Roman myth like that of Cacus; the gain in accuracy that might be made by adopting a shifting spelling, as for instance in the voyage and return on the adventure of Geryon's cattle, would be lost in the confusion of the reader. Here, as throughout the book, the more or most familiar form of the name in English reference has been preferred above the "exact" transcription from other languages and alphabets.] Hercules was the great hero of the Greeks, perhaps, as Rose suggests, a minor lord of Tiryns, subject to the king at Mycenæ, about whose feats a whole cycle of legend was collected. He seems also to have attracted to him some of the mythology of Asia Minor connected with the lion god of the region, as witness his lionskin costume and club. Physically he was very strong, perhaps not large in size, although the large size of the stadium at Olympia, said to have been paced off by Hercules, made some ancient scholars believe him to be quite tall. Some said that another Hercules, one of the Idæan Dactyls, founded the Olympic games. Hercules possessed great powers of endurance, was brave, at times almost to the point of foolhardiness. He was noted for his good humor and, as correlatives, for his tremendous appetite both for food and for women. He was not the comic Hercules some dramatists pictured by magnifying these appetites; nor was he the stoical dare-all dramatized by others. Hercules was the hero *par excellence* not only of Greek legend and folklore, but generally the type of the hero throughout European countries in which classical tradition was strong, the pattern of a man to which many other folk heroes were and are fitted.

Amphitryon, in the course of regaining the favor of Alcmene, his wife, was absent in a war against the Teleboans when Zeus became enamored of Alcmene. On the night that Amphitryon was to return home, Zeus visited Alcmene in the guise of her husband, and by making the night of triple length begot Hercules. Later the same night Amphitryon returned in fact and Her-

cules' twin, Iphicles, was conceived. Hera, of course, was enraged at Zeus' adventure and became the life-long enemy of Hercules. She, by obtaining a promise from Zeus when he was off guard, cheated Hercules of the sovereignty he was to have had, and Eurystheus, born just before Hercules, became king of Tiryns.

While yet in the cradle with his twin, Hercules strangled two serpents, sent either by Hera to kill the child or by Amphitryon to determine which of the infants was his son and which the demigod. The child and youth Hercules had the very best of teachers in the manly arts: Eurytus for archery, Autolycus for wrestling, Pollux (Polydeuces) for boxing and fencing, Linus for music. The latter Hercules killed with his lyre when the teacher tried to punish him. Hercules was then sent to guard the cattle of Amphitryon on Mt. Cithæron where, at the age of 18, he slew his first lion.

On a visit to the court of Thespius, who wished to reward him for killing the lion, Hercules slept, either on successive nights or in one night, with the king's fifty daughters, or with forty-nine of the fifty in seven nights. Each bore a son, the first and the last bearing twins, which offspring of the hero later colonized Sardinia. Hercules returned to Thebes, meeting some messengers from Erginus of Orchomenus coming to collect an annual tribute. He attacked them, tying their noses and ears, which he cut off, about their necks; in the ensuing war, he defeated the army of Orchomenus and made them pay Thebes double the annual tribute they had been collecting. Creon, the Theban king, rewarded Hercules with the hand of Megara, his daughter.

The two lived happily for some years until by Hera's malevolence Hercules went mad and killed Megara, their three sons, and two of Iphicles' children. Hercules exiled himself as punishment and went to Delphi to ask Apollo where to settle. There he was told to serve Eurystheus for twelve years, and was promised that if he performed the tasks set for him he would become immortal. At Delphi also he was for the first time called Hercules, having until that time been known as Alcides, after his grandfather. The twelve labors of Hercules, accomplished on the orders of Eurystheus, were fixed in legend as early as the 5th century B.C. These, known in Greek as *athloi* (contests, prizes, the Labors) and so named by Homer's time, involved: The Nemean lion, the Lernean hydra, the Erymanthian boar, the Arcadian hind, the Stymphalian birds, the Augean stables, the Cretan bull, the horses of Diomedes, Hippolyta's girdle, Geryon's oxen, Cerberus, and the apples of the Hesperides. Authorities differ as to the order in which the labors were performed. See the various entries in alphabetical place for descriptions of the feats.

Hercules, his penance done, married Deianira after a transformation combat with the river god Achelous, in the course of which one of the horns of the god was broken off and, according to Ovid, made into the cornucopia, or, according to Pherecydes, traded back to Achelous for the horn of Amalthea. Hercules and his new wife came to a river in flood where the centaur Nessus offered to help Deianira across. When he was well out in the stream and thought he was safe from Hercules, Nessus tried to violate Deianira, but Hercules killed him with one of his poisoned arrows. See SHIRT OF NESSUS.

Among the many campaigns carried on by Hercules

was one against Eurytus of Œchalia, waged that he might carry off Iole. He had won her hand in a contest, but her father and brothers refused to give the girl up to him, remembering the fate of Megara and her children. To make matters worse, Hercules had in a fit of rage thrown one of Iole's brothers, Iphitus, from the walls of Tiryns. It was for this crime that Apollo, through the Delphic oracle, made him serve as a slave for a year at the court of Omphale, queen of Lydia. Hercules did not accept the punishment without a struggle; he seized the tripod and attempted to overthrow the oracle. But Zeus tossed a bolt into the midst of the fight and Hercules submitted. He traded roles with Omphale, she bearing the club and the lionskin, he doing women's work. At last, Deianira, fearing that she had lost Hercules to Iole, and remembering the instructions of Nessus, sent the hero the fatal shirt. The pain of his wounds drove Hercules to Mt. Œta where he was placed on the funeral pyre. He was taken up onto Olympus and there married Hebe after making his peace with Hera.

The Greek Hercules, whose labors and exploits begin in the northern Peloponnesus and then extend to Crete, to the Black Sea, to the ocean in the far west, and even to Hades, was combined in later legend with a local Roman hero of the same name, whose exploits are connected with Italian places. It may however be true that the Greek Hercules drew to him legends at first connected with other names and that thus the saga attained its new growth in Italy. Many of the stories are variants of tales told of other heroes; the nine-headed hydra is for example very similar to the seven-headed dragon of the dragon-slayer cycle, the time-serving Hercules is paralleled by the Biblical Jacob, etc.

Hermæ or **herms** (singular *Herm*) In ancient Greece, squared pillars of stone, narrower at the base than at the top, surmounted by a head of Hermes (or some other deity) and with a phallus on the shaft of the column: a development of the more ancient representation of the gods as a mound of stones or an unhewn monolith. Hermæ stood before houses, where they were worshipped by women as bringing fertility, on street corners and roads, carrying there street directions and moral precepts, in front of temples, in libraries and gymnasia. Probably as a survival of the custom of every passer-by placing another stone on the pile of stones representing the god, the Hermæ were decorated with offerings of dried figs and the like and flower garlands. In Rome, the Hermæ were identified with the termini, or boundary markers, and were utilized in more functional ways, such as supporting the barriers in the Circus Maximus. The mutilation of the Hermæ of Athens during the Peloponnesian Wars just as the expedition to Sicily was about to start threw the city into such an uproar that the commencement of the campaign was almost put off, and the implication of Alcibiades in the mysterious sacrilege eventually caused his removal as leader of the expedition. Compare CAIRN.

Hermaphroditus In Greek mythology, a god combining male and female in one body: of Oriental origin. Originally perhaps there was Aphroditus, the male form of Aphrodite, represented as a Herm, or phallic statue. Later, after the common myth developed, Hermaphroditus was depicted as having the upper body of a woman and the lower parts of a man. He is said to have been the son of Hermes and Aphrodite, a beautiful youth, with whom Salmacis, the nymph of the Carian fountain, fell in love. He refused her but was persuaded to bathe in the spring. She then prayed to the gods to be united with him forever; he prayed that bathers in the spring might become hermaphrodites too. Both prayers were granted.

Hermes The messenger of the Olympian gods in Greek mythology; an Arcadian fertility god who acquired varied functions as his worship spread through Greece: identified by the Romans with Mercury, their god of commerce. The characteristic early representations of Hermes are in the form of herms, simple stone pillars topped by a head and with a phallus extended from the front. These stood as signposts on the roads, before the doors of houses, etc., and were believed to have the power of making women fertile. Hermes, the herald of the gods, was also god of roads, guardian of travelers, god of communication and of commerce. He was a wealth-giving god as a fertility deity, and a luck-dispensing god. Thus he became the god of thieves, in an unmoral paralleling of commerce and thievery as bringing quick riches. In connection with these, Hermes was the god of dice; a shepherd's god; the protector of sacrificial beasts. As the herald and messenger, Hermes was the psychopomp, the conductor of the souls of the dead to Hades; he was as well the bringer of dreams, the donor of restful sleep who could withhold his gift. He was the god of eloquence, of social ease, of cunning, fraud, and perjury. His functions were so varied that some classical writers thought that there were several gods of the name.

Hermes was the son of Zeus and Maia; born in the morning, he wandered from the cave of his birth at noon, discovered a tortoise, killed it, strung the shell with reeds, and invented the lyre. That same evening, he sneaked out to Pieria and stole the cows from Apollo's herd there, making them walk backward and plaiting special shoes for himself to confuse the trail. Then he sacrificed two of the cattle to the 12 gods and crept into his cradle contentedly. Apollo discovered the cattle missing in the morning and, with the aid of the testimony of a shepherd who had seen Hermes with the cattle but who could not quite believe what he had seen, accused the day-old baby of the theft. To which both Hermes and Maia shrugged their shoulders. Apollo appealed to Zeus, who sensed an untruth in the denial of the child and ordered the cattle returned. But Hermes played the lyre for Apollo, who was so enchanted that he let Hermes keep the remainder of the herd. The two became friends, and in many ways the duties and character of each resemble the other's. It was Apollo who gave Hermes the golden shepherd's staff which became the caduceus; from Apollo Hermes learned the art of the dice; through him he became protector of flocks. To the extent only that chance could aid in prophecy did Apollo permit Hermes power in that activity. True prophecy remained Apollo's province.

Hermes performed many useful services for the gods: he tied Ixion to the wheel and Prometheus to Mt. Caucasus; he aided in the rescue of Dionysus from the flames which consumed Semele; he led the three goddesses to the spot where Paris judged them; he sold Hercules into slavery to Queen Omphale; he slew Argus Panoptes. Hermes wore the broad-brimmed hat of the traveler (sometimes the hat is small and winged); he carried the magic wand that closed the eyes of the dying (later the wand was combined with the herald's staff, the latter being wound with ribbons which became the serpents of the caduceus); his sandals of gold were winged or at least capable of carrying him great distances; sometimes he carried a traveler's purse. The number 4, the palm tree, and the tortoise were sacred to him; sacrifices included honey, cakes, and lambs among other things appropriate to a fertility god of both pasture and underworld.

Hermod In Teutonic mythology, son of Odin and Frigga, swift messenger of the gods who welcomed the heroes to Valhalla. At the time of the tragic death of Balder, Odin sent Hermod to Hel to sue for Balder's release. On Odin's wonderful horse Sleipnir, he rode nine days and nights, until on the tenth he crossed the Giallar-bridge, which trembled under the hoofs of Odin's horse. At last he came to the gates of Hel and made the famous leap over the walls which brought him into the region of the dead. On he traveled to the banquet hall of Hel where he found Balder and Nanna already there before him. Hermod stated the purpose of his coming and plead the whole night through, but Hel said nothing until at last she said Balder might go back if everything in the world shed tears for his return. Hermod went back to the gods with the answer, and all nature wept and every living creature wept save one old hag in a cave, named Thok. She would not shed a tear, saying it was no sorrow to her if Balder stayed with Hel forever. Thok is usually interpreted as Loki in disguise. See DESCENTS TO UNDERWORLD. Compare ADONIS.

Herne, The Hunter mentioned in the *Merry Wives of Windsor* has only a vague legend in England; but obviously belongs to the large community of spectral hunters. Such a hunter was known in the German Black Forest, in the French Fontainebleau (identified with St. Hubert); and in England, Herne the Hunter paced around the old oak in Windsor Forest. [RDJ]

Hero and Leander In a famous tale of classical antiquity, two lovers who lived in towns opposite each other on the Hellespont. Hero was a priestess of Aphrodite at Sestos with whom Leander, an inhabitant of Abydos, fell in love after he saw her at a festival of Aphrodite. Her dedication as priestess made their marriage impossible, but nightly Leander swam the Hellespont to meet her secretly. One night he was drowned in a storm when the lamp she lit to guide him was blown out and he lost his direction. In the morning Hero found his body on the shore and leaped into the sea, drowning herself. The story is told by Musæus (4th or 5th century A.D.) but earlier references are found in the works of Ovid, Statius, and Virgil.

Herodias In the New Testament narrative, the wife of Herod Antipas. As Herodias had formerly been the wife of Philip, the brother of Antipas, John the Baptist rebuked Antipas for his "adultery," and aroused the ire of Herodias. On the birthday of Herod Antipas, Salome (the name is not given in the Biblical story), the daughter of Herodias, danced before the assemblage so well

that Herod promised her, rather without thinking, anything she desired. The girl went to her mother for advice on what to ask, and then demanded the head of John, at that time a prisoner of Herod. Herod, unable to retreat from his promise, had John beheaded, although previously he had feared the consequences of such an act because of John's popularity. The head was then brought in and presented to Salome on a salver. The story has been much used in music, art, and literature. It is an example of the irrevocable king's promise motif (M203) of folktale, bearing some resemblance to the hasty oath theme illustrated in the story of Jephthah.

In the Middle Ages, in Germany, Herodias was one of the women (see Hecate, etc.) who was said to lead the Wild Hunt.

Herus Literally, the name *Jesus*, as understood by the Apache Indians from their first Spanish contacts. According to Chiricahua Apache folktale a man named Herus came among the Apache and gave them a book. He told the people to keep the book forever, but when he died, they burnt it, according to their own ancient and honored custom of burning the belongings of the dead. And after that they had many misfortunes.

Herus was not identified with Jesus, however, whom the Chiricahua identify with their own hero Child-of-the-Water, but merely the man who gave them the book. M. E. Opler points out that the Chiricahua Herus stories are probably residual from the days of misfortune when the Chiricahua suffered captivity at the hands of the white men in the Indian Wars, and the efforts on their part to induce the Indians to revere the Bible. (See M. E. Opler, *Myths and Tales of the Chiricahua Apache Indians*, MAFLS 37: 96–97.)

Heshwash ceremony The "hiding" ceremony of the California Yokuts Indians; a public performance in which large numbers of shamans from the various tribes come together to vie in bewitching one another. They try to inject magic poisons and disease-carrying objects into each other. Rain, bear, and snake shamans do not take part. Suggestion is the power behind the whole performance. The men strike at each other with their baskets. If the one who is struck cannot extract the magic object which has entered into him (sometimes he can) he must pay his opponent to extract it for him. The Heshwash ceremony is a popular "show." It occupies two nights: a short exhibition on the first night, but the performance lasts the whole of the second. Shaman contests are known also among the Yuki and Maidu.

Hesi An important ceremony and dance in the Kuksu secret society of the North American Indian tribes in central California. Among the Valley Maidu, Hesi was the most important of all Kuksu ceremonies, and in the Hesi ceremony certain personages of subsidiary rank wore the "big head" headdress that in other groups is associated with Kuksu impersonators. The Hesi ceremonies are postulated to have been a later development, which was superimposed by the Valley Maidu and the Patwin tribes on the older, more widespread Kuksu base. The Hesi of the Patwin lasts four days; modern "ghost dance" rites have been added to it. These latter observances are connected with worship of the spirits of the dead; the rites center about a pole wrapped with different colored cloths, which is erected in front of the dance house. [EWV]

Hesiod A Greek (Bœotian) didactic poet of the 8th century B.C. to whom are ascribed the *Works and Days* and the *Theogony* among several other works. He first systematized, in the latter work, the cosmogonic and theogonic myths of the Greeks. The *Works and Days*, which incorporates a religious calendar, has several episodes, e.g. the description of Pandora's creation, which rise above the general prosaic level of the writing. Included also in the work is the earliest known Greek fable, *The Hawk and the Nightingale*. Hesiod's work is an important source for our knowledge of the life and beliefs of the Greeks following the Homeric period.

Hesione In Greek mythology, daughter of Laomedon, king of Troy. Poseidon and Apollo had been enlisted by Laomedon to build the walls of Troy. When Laomedon refused to pay for their help, Poseidon sent a sea monster to ravage the land. To remove this plague on the country, Laomedon had to sacrifice Hesione to the monster: the details of her being chained to a rock, etc., are probably later additions due to confusion of the story with that of Andromeda. Hercules happened along, struck a bargain with Laomedon to rescue the daughter in exchange for Laomedon's horses, was swallowed by the beast and slew him from inside. Again, however, Laomedon backed down on the bargain, and Hercules was forced to raise an army and take the city. Hesione was given as a slave to Telamon, who had fought bravely in the battle. By him she became mother of Teucer. When Priam sent an envoy to obtain her release, the Greeks refused, thus adding fuel to the ill-feeling that was to blaze forth in the Trojan war.

Hesperides In Greek legend and mythology, maidens who guarded the golden apples given by Ge to Hera when she married Zeus. The maidens were seven, or four, or three in number, usually three—Aegle, Erytheia, and Hesperesthusa—daughters of Erebus and Nox (or of Atlas and Hesperis, or Phorcys and Ceto). The tree on which the apples grew was in the western Gardens of Ocean (or where the Hyperboreans dwelt) and was guarded by the dragon Ladon who never slept. Hercules, in the eleventh of his labors, slew the dragon or put it to sleep and so gained the apples. In another version of the story, Hercules assumed the burden of Atlas, who himself got the apples and refused to give them up or to take the skies on his shoulders again. Hercules tricked the giant, however, asking the slow-witted giant to resume the burden for a moment while he got a pad for his shoulders, and returned with the apples to Eurystheus, who gave them to Hercules as a gift. The hero dedicated them to Athena, who returned them to the garden. The apples dropped by Hippomenes in his race with Atalanta were said to have been given to him by Aphrodite who got them from the garden of the Hesperides. Compare TREE OF LIFE.

Hestia In Greek mythology, the goddess of the hearth; one of the twelve great gods: identified by the Romans with Vesta, whose counterpart she was. Hestia was the eldest of the children of Cronus and Rhea, wooed by Poseidon and Apollo but choosing to remain eternally a virgin. As goddess of the hearth and its fire, she partook of all sacrifices and protected domestic life and virtue. The fires of the public hearths were sacred to her and it was from these fires that colonists carried the flame of the home city to new shores. The first-fruits, year-old cows, oil, and wine were sacred to her.

Hethúska Society A society of the Omaha Indians, organized to perpetuate the memory of brave deeds in the history of the tribe, to stimulate heroism, and to belittle the fear of death. The society acted as arbiter and judge as to whether a warrior and his deed were worthy of perpetuation in song. The warrior songs of this society point to the transience of man on the earth, and emphasize the triviality of personal death in the face of the unchanging earth, mountains, and rivers.

hex Wizard, witch, to bewitch; witchcraft: a term of German origin found in many sections of the United States today especially among the Pennsylvania Dutch. A hex can be either a man or woman, but usually it is a man; and a hex can be either amateur or professional; i.e. anyone can work hex spells but certain individuals are recognized as professionally competent. These are often referred to as hex doctors and their ministrations are usually supposed to result in good. They are visited by their clients to get "medicine" to cure ills, to control the forces of nature, to nullify spells put on them by their enemies, in short, to bring about any desideratum. Some of the hex doctors are famous and are visited yearly by hundreds of people. Two of the most celebrated of the past are Joseph H. Hageman and John G. Hohman. Hageman's libel suit against the *Philadelphia North American* in 1903 resulted in one of the most colorful and dramatic of the many hex trials.

The professional hex doctor works through the use of stock magic formulas, some of which are very ancient, deriving generally from two main sources: Gipsy magic and medieval church formulas and ritual. This material is largely found in two books possessed by all hex doctors, the *Seventh Book of Moses* and *The Long Hidden Friend*. This last is a compilation by Hohman done as early as 1819. It is a practical handbook for the practice of hexerei or witchcraft. It contains 187 recipes, spells, and charms covering every aspect of life. Some idea of its nature can be had from the following:

119. Against witches—for Beasts write it on the stall—for Human Beings Write it on the Bedsteads.

Trotter head I pray thee my house and my Court, I pray thee my horse-and-cow-stall, I pray thee my bedstead, that thou shed not thy consolations on me; be they on another house till thou goest over all mountains, countest all the sticks in the hedges and goest over all waters. So come the happy day again to my house, in the name of the Father and of the Son and the Holy Ghost.

121. To Quench Fire without Water

Write the following order of letters on the side of a plate and throw it into the fire:

```
S A T O R
A R E P O
T E N E T
O P E R A
R O T A S
```

Hex stories abound among the Pennsylvania Dutch in Pennsylvania and in other parts of the country. They follow the pattern of witch stories in general. Typical is the following from the country north of Reading, Pennsylvania. One summer the horses and cattle belonging to the people on a certain farm in the neighborhood began to waste away and to die. The farmer finally consulted a hex doctor in Lancaster, who told him that the animals were bewitched and that to break the spell he should take hair from the manes and tails of the animals, place it in a container filled with the animals' urine and bury the whole under the stable. They did this and the animals recovered. But soon the farmer himself became ill. When they consulted the hex doctor a second time, he described in detail the person who was bewitching the farmer; from the description they recognized him at once as a near neighbor. The hex doctor instructed the wife to make a "doll" and fill it with the sweepings from the house and then to draw on it with charcoal the likeness of the neighbor. When it was completed she was to stick the effigy with pins, calling it by the neighbor's name and wishing that he might die. She did as instructed; the neighbor died the same day, and the husband recovered.

The barn symbols so common still today among the Pennsylvania Dutch are often referred to as "hex signs." They are said to protect the animals from the working of spells and especially from the evil eye.

The belief in hexes and hexerei is still widespread. Many aspects of life are still governed by it. So awesome is it that the word *hex* is generally avoided even by those who disclaim belief in it. Further proof of the wide practice of hexerei and the seriousness with which it is taken is found in the fact that hardly a year goes by without cases of bewitching, of accusation of hex murder and the like being taken to the courts. The latest case to come to the courts in Pennsylvania was in 1949 in Lehigh County.   MacEdward Leach

Hexateuch The first six books of the Bible.

hey See HAY (2).

heyoka Ceremonial dancing clowns of the Dakota Sioux. Among the Oglala and Santee in particular the heyoka was a dream cult, in obedience to a vision of lightning or the Thunder-bird. This at times involved fearful obligations, to the point of killing. The actions and dancing emulated "Haoka, the anti-natural god," in backward speech and behavior contrary to usual and expected norms. The clowns were dressed in breechcloths, with white powder and a bladder to simulate baldness; formerly they half-shaved their hair. They carried rattles of dew-claws on a stick.

They were said to represent giants or small men, and in dance they variously rose to full height or crouched. At times, following a vision, they took part in the Santee elk dance.

The *heyoka wozepi* (from *woze*, dip out) immersed their arms in scalding water and pulled out pieces of dog meat boiled for a ceremonial feast. This "heyoka trick" was shared by the related societies of the Omaha *hethuska*, Iowa and Ponca *helocka*, Kansa *helucka*, Pawnee *iruska*, and the Mandan-Hidatsa-Arikara *hot dance*. All used the same grass to protect their arms from the heat of coals or hot water which they handled. However, the heyoka lacked the ceremonial organization of the other societies, and the grass dance features of the helocka and hot dance. See HOT DANCE. [GPK]

Hiawatha The hereditary name (from *Haionhwa'tha*, he makes rivers) of one of the chieftainships in the Tortoise clan of the Mohawk Indians of eastern New York; also, the actual name of an Iroquois Indian who had much to do with the establishment of the famous League of the Iroquois; also, the title of a well-known poem by Henry Wadsworth Longfellow.

Iroquois tradition makes Hiawatha a prophet who probably lived about 1570 A.D., the disciple and active colleague of Dekanawida, founder of the League. Together Hiawatha and Dekanawida brought about the confederation of the five Iroquois tribes, and introduced major intra-tribal reforms one of which was a stringent regulation against the blood feud. Henry Rowe Schoolcraft confused Hiawatha with the Ojibwa culture hero Nanabozho and in his Algic Researches attributed the deeds of the Ojibwa deity to the Iroquois historical figure. Longfellow based his poem on Schoolcraft's material, which of course was purely Algonquian, not Iroquoian. As a result Longfellow's poetic composition, which bears the name of a great Iroquoian reformer and statesman, contains no single fact or fiction relating to him, but is throughout full of Algonquian terms and legendary material. [EWV]

hieros gamos Literally, holy or sacred marriage: the representation, originally perhaps always with human actors, but later sometimes with symbolical substitution for one or both participants, of the marriage of the gods. Specifically the term is best applied to the marriage of Zeus and Hera as symbolized, for example, at the Platæan Dædala. However, marriages between a god or goddess and a human being are likewise sacred unions, the most familiar being that of Demeter and Iasion in the thrice-plowed field. As the term is used by Krappe, the sacred marriage was a fertility ceremony, a fertility-bringing union of an earth-mother, e.g. Semele, Demeter Chthonia, Persephone, Maia, with a sky or rain power. But Farnell (*En. Brit.*, 11th ed., *s.v.* "mystery" and "Zeus") thinks that the ceremony was simply a parallel, auspicious in nature, of marriage among the gods and marriage among human beings. As examples of the more general *theogamy*, Frazer brings in evidence marriage of the gods to their priestesses in Babylonia, Egypt, Athens, Eleusis, Platæa, and Sweden. He describes an annual festival among the Oraons of Bengal in which the fertilizing marriage of the Sun and the Earth goddess is paralleled by human orgiastic ceremonies. The demon lover of folktale may be a development of the belief underlying the sacred marriage.

Highland fling A solo dance or duet of the Scottish Highlanders, characterized by repeated hops and turns on one foot while the free foot beats the ankle. It was originally a dance of victory after a battle. Its distinctive execution calls for sharp crispness coupled with ease. The arms are semi-extended to a precise position at head level; the free toe touches the ankle in a prescribed position. The pivots are clean and swift. [GPK]

Hiisi The evil spirit of the Finns. He lives in the woods, and is an ugly and beardless fellow. He has lopsided eyes without eyelids and is dressed as a scoundrel. The same name is also used for Devil. Hiisi was probably formerly considered the guardian spirit of the sacrificial grove; he was called the son of Kaleva and believed to be a giant of ancient times. [JB]

Hikuleo In the mythology of the Tonga Islands, god of the afterworld who dwelt in Pulotu, the homeland of the dead, in the west. In many Tonga myths Hikuleo plays the same role as Tangaloa in other parts of Polynesia. He fishes up islands, specifically Kao and Tufa islands, north of Tonga. Kao and Tufa are said to have risen up from stones thrown down by Hikuleo. In daily life, Hikuleo is thought to be incarnate in many living things. He is represented in Tongan temples by carved wooden images. On Samoa, where his name is Si'uleo, only one carved image has been identified. See Peter H. Buck: *Vikings of the Pacific*, Chicago, 1959, pp. 299, 301.

hikuli (1) The mescal button.
(2) Same as PEYOTE DANCE.

Hilili A scalp-taking or war kachina of Keresan provenience, adopted first by the Hopi Indians and taken over by the Zuñi about 1892. His dance mask is turquoise and white, bearded, with a snake painted over each eye. Originally Hilili had a flint knife on top of his mask, but its significance was never revealed by the first owners of Hilili kachina, and the Zuñi society substituted instead a duck's head plus sun, moon, and star designs. Further acculturation is evidenced by the cartridges, now substituted for arrowpoints, on Hilili's bandoleer, symbolizing the number of scalps taken. Hilili is said to be a very dangerous kachina, and the Zuñi have enhanced his power by giving the dance leader a stuffed snake (a Zuñi symbol of war). See E. C. Parsons: *Pueblo Indian Religion*, Chicago, 1939, 519n, 1105, 1106.

hill-billy A mountaineer, especially of the southern United States. Hill-billy music is a compound of genuine folk elements with some of the more sentimental aspects of popular music and has had considerable acceptance as radio entertainment. It preserves, in somewhat burlesqued style, the ancient, heady vocal production of ballad-singing, the rhythms of the square dance and the hoedown, and the most common folk instruments of America—banjo, fiddle, guitar. The verses stress the vernacular to the point of parody.

Himavat In Hindu mythology, the personification of the Himālaya mountains; father of Ganga and Umā.

Hind Etin The Scottish version (Child #41) of a Germanic ballad in which a king's daughter is periodically beguiled by a dwarf or hill man, Hind Etin, to live with him in secret in a hill or wood. She bears him seven sons, but when she reveals her secret to her parents, she dies. The Scottish ballad is a rationalization of the supernatural story. [MEL]

Hind Horn The title and hero of a Scottish popular ballad (Child #17), related to the *Horn* romances of the 13th century and after. The exact relationship of the ballad to the romances is not clear, since intermediate material probably has been lost, but W. R. Nelles (*JAFL* 22: 42–62) surmises a lost ballad as being the common source of both *Hind Horn* and parts of the 14th century romance *Horn Childe and Maiden Rimnild*. So many of the motifs appearing in *Hind Horn* are common apparatus in ballads of the period that *Hind Horn* is often erroneously identified with other ballads having a similar story. For example, the lover returning in the nick of time to regain his mistress as she is about to be married to another is a motif common to several ballads

In essence, *Hind Horn* is the story of a ring, a type of chastity index given to Hind Horn by his love. "When this ring grows pale and wan,/ You may know by it my love is gane." He returns to his own land from foreign shores when the ring fades, meets an old beggar-man who tells him of the girl's approaching marriage: the festivities are already in progress. Horn and the beggar exchange clothes, and in disguise Horn "When he came to the king's gate,/ He sought a drink for Hind Horn's sake./ The bride came down with a glass of wine,/ When he drank out the glass, and dropt in the ring." She recognizes him and offers to go with him even as the beggar she thinks he is, and all ends happily. See NOBLE MORINGER.

Hinky Dinky Parlez-Vous Alternate title of the World War I soldier song, *Mademoiselle from Armentières*.

Hiordis or **Hjordis** According to the *Volsunga Saga*, the daughter of Eglimi, King of the Islands, who was Sigmund's third wife. She had also been courted by the Hunding Lygni, who was so enraged at his rejection that he came after her and slew all of the Volsungs including Sigmund. With his dying breath, Sigmund bade her keep the pieces of his sword Gram for their unborn son. She escaped from the battlefield, and was protected by the Viking Elf, who later married her, and raised Sigmund's son Sigurd.

hippocampus A fabled sea-animal of classical myth resembling a horse, but with the hind parts of a fish or dragon. The chariot of Poseidon was drawn by hippocampi.

Hippocrene Literally, the fountain of the horse; a spring on Mt. Helicon, in Bœotia, sacred to the Muses, like its companion spring Aganippe, and supposed to have welled forth from the mark of Pegasus' hoof. The spring and its waters are commonly alluded to as giving poetic inspiration.

Hippolyta's girdle In Greek legend, the girdle of the queen of the Amazons taken by Hercules as the ninth of his labors. Hercules beat the Amazon warriors in battle and either slew Hippolyta, taking the girdle from her body, or captured Melanippa, the Amazon general, and ransomed her for the girdle.

Hippolytus In Greek mythology, the son of Theseus and his Amazon wife, Hippolyta or Antiope. Theseus later married Phædra who made advances to her stepson but was repulsed. According to some versions of the story, Phædra committed suicide, leaving a note accusing Hippolytus of the crime she herself desired. Theseus cursed his son and asked Poseidon, his father, to punish the supposed culprit. One day, as Hippolytus drove his chariot near the water's edge, a bull came out of the sea, sent by Poseidon, and frightened the horses. They bolted and dragged Hippolytus to death. In some variants of the legend, Theseus then discovered the plot; and Phædra committed suicide after the death of Hippolytus. Artemis, whose favorite Hippolytus was, induced Æsculapius, by means of a large fee, to revive the youth, for which presumption Zeus killed Æsculapius. In Italian myth, Diana transported Hippolytus to the grove at Aricia where she (Artemis-Diana) placed him under the protection of Egeria and changed his name to Virbius.

Hiraṇyagarbha In Hindu cosmogonic mythology, the golden egg from which the universe came. In one variant of the myth, the waters existed first. They produced the golden egg by tapas (the process of producing intense physical heat) and from this egg was born the creator Prajāpati who, after a year, spoke three words, "Bhūh," "Bhuvah," and "Svar." These became the earth, the atmosphere, and the sky. The golden egg, in spiritualized form, persists in popular Indian belief. In another myth, Hiraṇyagarbha was Brahmā, the first male, formed in a golden egg by the supreme first cause. After a year, he divided the egg into two parts by thought and formed the heaven and earth from the two halves, placing the sky between.

Hisagita-imisi Literally, preserver of breath: the supreme deity of the Creek Indians. He is also called Ibofanga, the One Sitting Above. He is closely related to the sun, but he is not the sun. He is represented on earth by the busk ceremonial fire. Compare ABABINILI.

historic-geographic method The historic-geographic, or so-called Finnish method of folklore investigation, was developed during the last half of the 19th century by Julius and Kaarle Krohn (see discussion of these under FINNISH FOLKLORE), father and son, but has received its principal practical applications more recently. In his study of the songs which formed a basis for the *Kalevala,* Julius Krohn analyzed them into their component elements and studied the distribution of these elements. It was Kaarle Krohn who first made systematic use of this method for investigation of the folktale. Since his pioneer studies and formulation of principles in the 1880's, scholars have usually spoken of this kind of analytical study as the Finnish method, although many of the best exemplifications of its use have come from outside that country. It has been applied to various folklore genres—legends, games, riddles, and ballads—but most of all to folktales.

The basic assumption is that each tale (or other folklore item) has had its own history and must be investigated independently. General conclusions as to the origin and migration of all or great groups of tales must await the accumulation of monographic treatments of many story-types. During most of the 19th century various scholars had attempted on theoretical grounds and without a thorough study of the tales themselves to answer at once such questions as "Where did our folktales come from?" or "What do folktales mean?" The historic-geographic method is not at all concerned with the latter question and with the first only as a possible distant goal.

For the individual tale, the investigator using the method is interested in (a) establishing an approximation to an original form which will sufficiently account for all the available variants; (b) determining as nearly as may be the age and place of origin; (c) tracing the vicissitudes of the story through time and place, the course of its wanderings, and the modifications it has undergone.

To use this method it is necessary that one have available a relatively large number of versions of a folklore item and also that the item be susceptible of analysis into a series of details.

Arranging his oral versions in geographical and his written ones in historical order with convenient abbreviations for ready reference, the student establishes an invariable sequence for his analytical treatment. He next chooses details which he finds have received varied treatment in these versions. He now makes a study of each of these, arranging in order all versions handling the detail in the various ways, as well as those entirely omitting it. He now makes a percentage count of the various treatments.

When all details have thus been studied he may find certain treatments so predominant that he may feel confident of their belonging to the original type. Usually, however, the evidence is more ambiguous. By a careful study of certain handlings of details different from the predominant one he works out local affiliations and may establish regional subtypes (e.g. Mediterranean, Baltic, Scandinavian, Hispanic). It is from these subtypes that he usually proceeds to posit a general archetype, much as the linguist may take a pre-Germanic, pre-Celtic, and pre-Slavic word and establish a theoretical Indo-European form which will explain them all.

These subtypes and the archetype are hypothetical constructions designed to explain the available versions of the folklore item over its whole area of dissemination and within certain regions.

From this point in his study the investigator endeavors to determine how his versions and groups of versions are related to these types he has established. It is in this interpretation of data that he runs his greatest risk, for he must consider all pertinent facts of history and geography, the natural modifications of tradition and the circumstances of these modifications, the mutual relations of written and oral tradition, of slow and almost imperceptible dissemination, and of rapid transmission by emigration or travel.

No reader of the studies accomplished by this school will be entirely satisfied with the results. The complexity of the many problems of interpretation just mentioned presents many pitfalls and some of the investigators have ignored these. Opponents of the method have attacked it primarily on the ground that it undervalues literary treatments; that it disregards the role of the active bearer of tradition; and that it does not give sufficient attention to the relation of linguistic affiliation, especially in the history of tales.

The best practitioners of the method, such as Walter Anderson, have been aware of these problems and have furnished model studies. The method is being continually improved, so as to make use of the undoubtedly valuable analytical procedure, and to meet the just criticisms of those who have felt dubious about the interpretation of data.

Several important questions in folklore are not touched by the historic-geographic method. It does not go behind a theoretically original tale to account for its origin, nor does it attempt stylistic studies or the relation of an individual version to its social background. Within its own field, however—the history of an item of folklore—it has developed a rigorous analytical method which, whatever may be the weakness in a given interpretation, must certainly form the basis for all serious studies of the dissemination of complex items of folklore.

References:
Aarne, Antti, *Leitfaden der vergleichenden Märchenforschungen, FF Communications* No. 13.

Krohn, Kaarle, *Die folkloristische Arbeitsmethode*. Oslo, 1926.

Thompson, Stith, *The Folktale*. New York, 1946.

Wesselski, Albert, *Versuch einer Theorie des Märchens*. Reichenberg, 1931.

Anderson, Walter, *Zu Albert Wesselskis Angriffen auf die finnische folkloristische Arbeitsmethode*. Tartu, 1935.

STITH THOMPSON

Hiyoyoa Wagawaga (New Guinea) land of the dead which lies under the sea near Maivara on Milne Bay. Hiyoyoa resembles the upper world. There Tumudurere lives with his wife and children and directs the spirits of the dead, telling them where to make their gardens.

hkaung-beit-set Charmed or consecrated objects inserted under the skin by the Burmese: bits of gold, silver, lead, precious stones, pebbles, and pieces of tortoise shell or horn inscribed with incantations. If they are cut out, the charm is broken. The hkaung-beit-set are inserted in cheeks, chest, arms, and thighs, sometimes in large numbers, to procure invulnerability. Yunnan muleteers also conceal precious stones and coins under the skin as a precaution against robbers.

Hkum Yeng The village guardian of the Wild Wa of Burma. The Wa live in terror of this nat and post the spoils of their head-hunting expeditions in order to propitiate him. See NAT; TAK-KENG.

hlonipa A Zulu term meaning to respect or reverence: applied to the non-use of names of revered people or animals, and also to the avoidance of contact with tabued objects or people. To the Zulu woman, for instance, her husband's name is hlonipa; so are those of his parents. A mother-in-law is hlonipa to a son-in-law; they must avoid each other. The name of the king is sacred and powerful and fraught with danger, and therefore hlonipa to all. See NAME TABU.

hmawsayā The Burmese exorcist who restores bewitched persons to health. The hmawsayā obtains his qualifications by drinking water mixed with the ashes of scrolls containing mystic figures and cabalistic squares, by being tattooed with magic squares, incantations, or the figures of nats, or by taking a special internal medicine. In treating the ill, the hmawsayā commands the offending disease-causing nat to reveal its wishes. Occasionally a threat is sufficient, but frequently stronger measures are necessary and pungent substances are rubbed into the patient's eyes and he is beaten. When the spirit is ousted the patient is cured and feels no ill effects from the treatment.

Hobal, Hubal, or **Hobal Hubal** The name of a pre-Mohammedan god, patron of Mecca. Hobal was figured in the form of a human image, said to have been brought from Syria, which stood over the hollow in which offerings of precious materials were stored within the Kaaba. Along with the other idols, the image was destroyed by Mohammed in 630, and it is said that when Hobal fell, Mohammed cried, "Truth hath come and falsehood hath vanished." The idol is however not mentioned by name in the Koran. Some say that Hobal was the real name of Al-lahu, the chief of the gods of pre-Islamic times, who became the one god of Islam, and it is also said that weekly sacrifices of children were made to him on the stone in the Kaaba.

Hodening An English Christmas celebration. In Kent a man covered by a horse blanket and masked as a horse was led from house to house followed by other maskers ringing bells and singing carols. The group received small gifts of food, money, or drink. See MARI LWYD. [RDJ]

Hoder or **Hodur** In Teutonic mythology, one of the æsir, the blind son of Odin and Frigga, twin brother of Balder, and his innocent slayer; god of darkness. One day the gods were amusing themselves throwing weapons at Balder, whom nothing on earth would harm. But Loki had discovered the exception: the mistletoe was the one thing in the world which had not vowed never to harm Balder. So Loki fashioned a dart of mistletoe and wilily suggested that Hoder throw it. Thus the blind Hoder joined the sport, threw the fatal mistletoe, and killed the beloved Balder. Hoder was killed by Vali. At the rebirth of the world after Ragnarök he and Balder will return, reconciled.

Hodmimir's Forest In Teutonic mythology, the forest which Surtr's flaming sword cannot destroy at Ragnarök. Here Lif and Lifthraser will seek refuge and sleep through the destruction of the earth, only awakening when the earth is green and verdant again to found a new race of man.

Hœnir In Teutonic mythology, one of the æsir, and one of the three creators of Ask and Embla, the first man and woman. Hœnir gave them reason and motion, and, according to some, the senses. After the war between the æsir and the vanir, he was exchanged with Niord and went to live in Vanaheim.

Hogmanay or **Cake Day** In Scotland and the north of England, the last day of the year, when children, sometimes masked and sometimes singing songs, went about soliciting oat cakes. The day is also known in Old French as *aguillan-neuf* or *au-guy-l'an-neuf*, an occasion for distributing gifts. Cotgrave's suggestion that Hogmanay is a survival from the times when druids on the last day of the year gathered mistletoe attributes to popular custom more historical continuity than one has reason to expect. [RDJ]

Hogni In the *Volsunga* and *Sigurd Sagas*, the brother of Gunnar, Guttorm, and Gudrun. Brynhild asked him to avenge her by killing Sigurd. Hogni refused because he and Sigurd were blood brothers, but he persuaded Guttorm to do the murder. He hid the Nibelung gold in the Rhine, and only he and Gunnar knew its resting place. He advised Gunnar against visiting Atli, but accompanied him, and was killed for refusing to tell the hiding place. Compare HAGEN.

hogs can see the wind A folk belief of southern Ireland, also found among the Negroes of the southern United States, and in the Bahamas. Any human being who will suck milk from a sow will have the gift of seeing the wind forever after.

hohobi (plural *hohovi*) The Dahomean (Fŏn) word for twin. In the New World, the designation has been retained by the Negroes of Dutch Guiana. In the twin-cult of Dahomey and Western Nigeria, twins are both prized and feared, since they are believed to represent and control supernatural forces that can work benefit or harm. For this reason, they are treated with special attention and, where African rituals are followed in the New World, their birth and stages of development are marked by elaborate rites. It should be noted that the attitude toward twins in Dahomey and Western Nigeria contrasts with that held farther east along the Guinea coast, where the power of twins is so feared that they are done away with at birth. This custom has not been retained in New World Negro cultures. See DOSU. [MJH]

Ho Hsien-ku One of the Eight Immortals of Chinese mythology. Ho, the only woman member of the band, attained immortality by eating mother-of-pearl given her by a ghost. Her iconography contains a peach given her by Lü Tung-pin, a lotus blossom, and a reed organ. She is often shown drinking wine or floating on colored clouds. [RDJ]

Holde, Holle, Hulda, Hulle, or **Holl** A Germanic goddess, especially of the Suevi, Hessians, and Thuringians, appearing in many manifestations. Early she was a sky goddess, often to be seen riding on the wind. Snow was said to be feathers from her bed, detached as she was making it up. Often in her wild rides through the sky she is accompanied by a procession of witchlike creatures. Women suspected of witchcraft were said to "ride with Holde." To her realm in the sky went the souls of unbaptized babies. Holde is also associated with lake and stream. At noon she can often be seen, a beautiful white lady, bathing in the lake, and as she is observed she disappears under the water. To reach her dwelling one must dive down a well. Holde is also a maternal deity and goddess of the hearth. She presides over spinning and especially the cultivation of flax. In this manifestation she is helpful and kind.

Her most common terrestrial manifestation is as the leader of the "furious host" or "furious or wild hunt." The furious host is made up of a group of specters, most of whom are children and babies who died unbaptized. With loud cries and wild rush they tear through the countryside on their uncontrolled rides following Holde like a valkyrie at their head. Wherever this procession passes, the fields will bear double the usual harvest that year. Holde is thus connected by some, as a chthonic deity, with the Greek Persephone, the Roman Bona Dea, etc. Holde as leader of the wild hunt is identified with Dame Gauden and with Perchta, both leaders of the furious host. Stories of Holde as leader of the furious host account for her association with the Venusberg legend. The Hörselberg is said to be Holde's Court and there the wild rides terminate. Characteristic is the story of old man Eckehart who is caught up in the ride of the furious host and carried into Holde's Court, there to abide until the day of judgment. Holle is associated with the legend of Barbarossa, the sleeping king in the mountain, and the Kyffhäuser Mountain.

At present Holde has degenerated into a folk bogey, an ugly old woman with long nose and thick hair, sometimes seen in the forest leading a flock of sheep or goats. Peasant mothers frighten their children into good behavior by telling them Holde will "get" them if they are not good. See WILD HUNT. [MEL]

☛ Grimm's tale, *Mother Holle* (#24), belongs to the world-wide kind and unkind (or courteous and discourteous) motif (Q2; Types 361, 403 II, 431, etc.).

The industrious sister drops her shuttle into the well and is forced by the stepmother to go after it. In the land at the bottom of the well, she prevents the bread from burning and shakes the ripe apples from the tree. Then she becomes a servant of Mother Holle, shaking the beds until the feathers (snow) fly. At last, homesick, she takes her leave of the old lady—who in the story is more a kind witch than the sky and fertility goddess Holde—and is showered with gold as she steps back into the real world. The envious and lazy elder sister quickly goes down the well, passes by the pleading bread in the oven and the apples on the tree, and sleeps in the morning when she should be shaking out the bedclothes. Mother Holle dismisses her, and the lazy girl is showered with pitch which never comes off, instead of the gold she expects.

holding down the hat The motif (K1252; Type 1528) of a general Eurasian folktale in which a man traveling along a road sees another approaching on horseback. Immediately he puts his hat over some horse droppings in the road and holds it down tight by the brim. When the man on horseback arrives and inquires what he is guarding under the hat, the man explains that it is a beautiful rare bird; if the stranger will lend him the horse he will go fetch a cage, that is, if the stranger will hold down the hat until he gets back. The man on the horse agrees, carefully holds down the hat, while the other makes off with the horse (and does not return). After waiting and waiting the stranger finds only dung under the hat.

In Java this story is found with Mouse-deer as trickster, Tiger as dupe. Mouse-deer sees Tiger coming and is afraid, so he begins to fan a pile of steaming dung with a large leaf. Tiger's curiosity is aroused. Mouse-deer explains that he is guarding this food, which belongs to the king, from flies. Tiger is hungry and finally succeeds in persuading Mouse-deer to betray his trust, only to discover how he has been duped when Mouse-deer is out of sight. In Annam, Cambodia, the Kangean Islands, and Sunda Island tales, Ape is thus duped by Tortoise.

There are various North American Indian tellings of this story, reported especially among the various Apache tribes, and among Mexican Indians, and thought to be of European provenience. The dupe is tricked into holding up the rock, holding up the sky, holding up the cliff, etc., while the trickster escapes. In this form the tale is also well known in Africa among the Kaffirs, Basutos, Hottentots, also in the Cape Verde Islands, and was retold by the Uncle Remuses of Georgia.

Holi, Hoolee, or **Hohlee** A vernal fire-festival known in northern India as the Holi, Phāg, or Phaguā, in the Deccan and western India as the Shimgā or Hutāshana. The festival is celebrated before the full moon of Phālguna (February-March) when the most important crops of the Spring harvest are almost ripe, and is intended to promote fertility and reinvigorate the year. It lasts from three to twenty days and begins with the lighting of a fire by the individual householder, the village headman, or by a Brāhman. The participants walk around the fire or, in some cases, walk or are driven through the flames. During the second day dust and colored water are flung on the spectators. There are also characteristic ritual dramas in which the women battle with the men to prevent them from climbing a pole to obtain a sugar ball placed at the top (among the Gonds), or from uprooting a branch (among the Bhīls).

The festival varies in length, depending upon the region in which it is celebrated, and in the ceremonies observed, but most Holi celebrations end with a procession in which a man, usually dressed as a bridegroom, is carried or rides through the streets followed by a singing, dancing crowd. In central and southern India a mystery play is performed to commemorate the death of Kāmadeva. Divination is also practiced by observing the direction in which the smoke of the Holi fire blows. The ashes are valued as a charm against ill-luck, evil spirits, and the evil eye, and as a cure for scorpion stings.

The Holi rites have little or no connection with orthodox Hinduism. They have been explained by numerous legends: according to one the Holi fire is lighted on the day Śiva's wrath reduced Kāma to ashes.

holle kreish A naming ceremony for girl babies practiced by certain German Jews: an adaptation of a similar Germanic rite. When the child is a month old, on the Sabbath of the first visit to the synagogue of the mother after the birth (compare CHURCHING OF WOMEN), preadolescent children attend a party at the house. They surround the cradle, raise it three times, and call, "Holle! Holle! What shall the child's name be?" and the girl's name (her vernacular and not her Hebrew name) is cried out. The Holle so invoked is the German Holde who brings babies and snatches unbaptized children. The circle about the child and the naming—a substitute for baptism—protect the girl from Holde's malevolence. At one time boys were thus named, but circumcision and naming of the boy at that time made holle kreish superfluous. (*Jewish Encyclopedia* VI: 443a) See HOLDE.

holler A freely improvised song of the American Negro at work, particularly at a solitary task in the open, often without words, but also embodying the thoughts of the moment in relation to the work, the weather, the mule, or his feelings. The soaring humming or chanted words are broken at random by muttered comment, or commands to the animal. To the singer these hollers are just a way to get on with the work and to keep himself company. Sometimes one man's holler will be taken up by one or more others, fields away, and tossed back and forth with variations. But it is a nonce creation. It has no title, and is probably never repeated, at least not as first sung. The Archive of American Folksong of the Library of Congress has a number of recordings of Negro hollers made on the scene. But this is probably the only way any holler survives its original and unique impulse and expression.

holly An evergreen tree or shrub (genus *Ilex*) with thorny leaves, white flowers, and red berries. The use of holly in religious ceremonies is of considerable antiquity; probably its use as Christmas decoration was adapted by early Roman Christians from the Roman Saturnalia. Christian legend says the Cross was made of holly wood and as punishment it is now a scrub tree

with thorny leaves and berries representing drops of the blood of Christ. Another legend says that holly was used to make the Crown of Thorns, and the berries which were yellow became red from the blood of Christ.

In Wales taking holly into the house before Christmas Eve leads to family quarrels, and it is unlucky to leave the decorations up after New Year's or Twelfth Night. Some say that holly left after Twelfth Night will bring a misfortune for each leaf and branch remaining. But if a piece of holly from the church decorations is kept in the house it will bring good luck throughout the year. In Louisiana berries from the Christmas holly are kept for luck during the year. Domestic animals thrive if a piece of holly is hung where they can see it on Christmas Eve.

In Wales taking holly into a friend's house will cause death, as will picking holly in blossom. In Germany it is unlucky to step on the berries. Holly picked on Christmas is protection against witches and evil spirits. In some localities little lighted candles are placed on holly leaves and floated on water. If they float it is a sign that the project that the person has in mind at the time will prosper, but if they sink it is as well to abandon it. Plentiful holly berries is a sign of a severe winter. In English Shrovetide dances there are often a holly-boy and an ivy-girl among the dancers. Holly is said to be male and to personify the steadfast and holy.

Medicinally the berries are said to be more active than the leaves and are recommended for colic, intermittent fever, rheumatism, smallpox, gout, and asthma. A fomentation of the bark and leaves is good for broken bones and dislocations. Several North American Indian tribes use holly leaf tea for measles. Some tribes use holly as a ceremonial purgative. In Derbyshire holly branches are used as flagellants to cure chilblains. An old English remedy for worms prescribes that a holly leaf and the top of a sage plant be placed in water; when the patient yawns over the dish, the worms drop out of his mouth.

Holly and the Ivy An English traditional carol, sung not only for the Nativity but also during Lent and in the autumn. It is one of a number of carols in which the holly and ivy carry over a pre-Christian symbolism of male and female principles and which were probably first sung to accompany dancing of men and women. The blossom and berry and leaf of the holly are likened to the lily, to the blood of Christ, etc., the thorn to the crown of thorns.

hollyhock A tall biennial herb (*Althæa rosea*) of the mallow family, with large flowers of numerous shades. It was a native of China, Syria, Turkey, and Greece and was growing in England as early as 1573. It is sometimes called the Damascus rose. It was grown in China for the bees. The leaves are sometimes used for a blue dye and children make dolls from its blossoms.

The leaves of the hollyhock are effective against the sting of a scorpion, bee, wasp, and similar insects. If they are bruised in oil and used as an ointment, insects will not bite. The flowers steeped in water are good for weak stomach and women's complaints if drunk in season. When fried in sheep tallow they relieve gout. Culpeper says that this plant is used mostly in gargles for swollen glands but that the root powdered or boiled in wine "prevents miscarriage, helps ruptures, dissolves coagulated blood from falls, blows, etc., and kills worms in children."

Holofernes In the apocryphal book of *Judith*, the leader of the forces of Nebuchadnezzar, king of the Assyrians, against the regions west of Assyria. He was slain by Judith, and the Jews were thus able to turn back the Assyrian host. In European balladry Holofernes has become Hallewijn, principal character in a large group of ballads spread throughout Europe.

Homer The ancient Greek poet traditionally credited with composing the *Iliad* and the *Odyssey*: believed to have lived in the 9th century B.C., though some place him as early as the 12th century. The modern concept is that the works of Homer are the result of the accretion of years of various poets' composition, and that instead of one poet, Homer is a name applicable to a group, not necessarily of the same place or time. Among the many theories concerning the poet is one claiming that Homer was a woman, this conclusion arising, as do the others, from textual "evidence."

homiletic ballad A narrative song type of didactic or admonitory character, generally in the first person, relating the sins and repentance of a misspent life, and warning all listeners to avoid the mistakes of the sinner. American examples are numerous, including *Wicked Polly*, the tale of a bad girl who went to hell, and *Awful! Awful! Awful!*, which provides a similar fate for a youth who trifled his time away.

honors right and honors left An American square dance term: each man bows first to the lady on his right (his partner) and then to the lady on his left, the ladies reciprocating. [GPK]

Honsu One of a pair of mythical twins, the other being Honsi, who figure in the twin *enfants terribles* category of Dahomean folktales. In these stories, the magical exploits of these twins is always the point of a given tale. [MJH]

hoodoo A category of magic in the beliefs found among Negroes of southern United States. This is to be differentiated from "medicine," which is the knowledge of herbs, roots, etc. The two forms of manipulation of power are carried on by different persons, distinguishable in dress and manner. The hoodoo-man is thus, in southern United States, the practitioner of magic, like the obia-man of the West Indies. The derivation of the word is a matter of speculation, though most students hold that it comes from the Haitian *vodun*, that in turn comes from the identical Dahomean (Fŏn) word that means deity. The meaning found in customary American speech, whereby hoodoo signifies bad luck, is an extension of Negro usage. [MJH]

hoodoo hand A term commonly used by southern United States Negroes for their magic charms, mojos, and tricks or tricken bags. Hoodoo hands have several functions: the love hand will bring your beloved to you; the curing hand will heal disease or unspell evil spells (sometimes the same thing). The killing hand will kill or get rid of your enemy for you. Various hoodoo hands are just luck charms and will "bring things to you" if worn or carried constantly and cared for properly. They not only bring the loved one to you, but hold your possessions and your health close, attract gifts, and give you good luck in gambling. Typical good luck ingredients are a rabbit's foot, fish scales or a fish eye, a beetle, some snakeskin, or a thumb-size dried-up turtle. A twining herb locally known as the "devil's shoestring" ties things to you. Red flannel is also very potent.

Various hoodoo hands used against enemies do not necessarily kill, but cause pain, illness, or weakness, or bad luck. Such hands contain needles and pins, red pepper, graveyard soil, and usually bits of hair and fingernails or footprint dust of the person to be conjured. Small bits raveled from a rope that has hanged a man are especially prized for inclusion in a hoodoo hand.

hoop-and-pole game A widely distributed game among the North American Indians, existing in a great variety of forms and usually associated with the ideas of fertility and generation. A hoop, often covered with a network, is rolled along the ground and shot at with arrows or lances. The count is determined by the way in which the lances fall with reference to the hoop. The game was played by men and boys, not by women. It was especially popular among the Plains tribes, although by no means limited to these groups, and was often played ceremonially, as well as merely for amusement. [EWV]

hoop dance A dance of skill performed by one man, consisting of complex steps in and out of huge hoops. He dances with from one to four hoops, sometimes passing them over his head and across his body. The dance originated among the Sioux Indians and was adopted by the Pueblo Indians. The most famous are the hoop dance of Standing Rock, North Dakota, of the Umatilla, of Taos, and of Santa Ana, where two hoop dancers in green join the buffalo dancers. As an added flourish the hoops may be on fire. [GPK]

hoopoe A long-billed bird (*Upupa epops*) of Europe, Asia, and Africa, about the size of a thrush, with an erectile crest and russet and black plumage. The hoopoe's habits are said to be filthy: it nests in its own droppings and eats insects and worms from dunghills. A Rumanian story explains that the hoopoe would not be satisfied with the food God originally granted it, demanded and obtained better and better food, until God would put up with its demands no longer and condemned it to live by scavenging in dunghills. It is one of the unclean birds mentioned in *Lev.* xi, 19, and *Deut.* xiv, 18 (translated "lapwing" in the Authorized Version). In England, it was formerly a harbinger of evil, but is seldom seen there. In Sweden, it is a bird of war, helmeted and bright with color. The springwort, the magic herb that opens all doors and locks, is said by the Swabians to be brought by the hoopoe. The Arabs call it the doctor bird; the Turks, from its crest resembling that formerly worn by couriers, called it the messenger bird.

Solomon crowned the hoopoe for its wisdom in refusing to pay homage to women. Its walking habit, head down and crest opening and closing as it searches for food, led to the belief, still held by the Arabs, that it is looking for springs and wells: this information it passes on to people. Some hold that the cuckoo and hoopoe are respectively male and female of the same species.

The Bittern and the Hoopoe (Grimm #173) explains the cries of the two birds, formerly herdsmen. The cry of the hoopoe is to its weak, starved cattle: "Up, up, up!" A Rumanian parallel to the story of the greedy fisherman's wife ends with her transformation into a hoopoe. In ancient Greek myth Tereus was transformed into a hoopoe. The original of the Garuḍa bird of Hindu mythology is said to be the hoopoe.

hoop snake Either of two harmless snakes of the southeastern United States (*Abastor erythrogrammus* or *Farancia abacura*): believed by some to take its tail in its mouth and roll like a hoop. *Farancia abacura*, the red-bellied snake, is also thought to be the stinging snake which stings with its tail because it has a sharp spine there which it sometimes uses as a weapon.

hootchie-kootchie A cheapened version of the North African belly dance, which is already a decadent manifestation of fertility ritualism. At the Chicago World's Fair in 1893 the hootchie-kootchie was introduced to Americans in the Tunisian booths. It touched off the spark of release from the artificial and sentimental social repressions of the late 19th century with its nostalgic naughtiness, and spread to burlesque shows dedicated to these repressions. See ABDOMINAL DANCE.
[GPK]

hops A perennial climbing herb (*Humulus lupulus*) used in making beer. But at the time of Henry VIII in England, petitions were circulated to forbid the use of hops in ale and beers because they spoiled the taste. At one time it was customary in the hopfields of Kent for anyone visiting them for the first time to contribute "foot money" lest the luck should leave the fields. Bergen reports a belief in Chestertown, Maryland, that the hop vines peep out of the ground at midnight on the "old Christmas."

Hops were first used in medicine as a stomatic and to induce sleep. A decoction of the tops of the plants was used as a blood purifier, in venereal diseases, and in all diseases of the skin. Hop blossoms were believed to have a slight narcotic and sedative effect and were used in pillows for mania and restlessness. These pillows are also used for toothache, earache, and neuralgia. The blossoms are brewed in a tea to soothe the nerves and as a cure for neuralgia. The Bohemians fill cavities in their teeth with an oil of hops; the Magyars mix privet and hops in wine for toothache. The Dakota Indians of North America use the lower part of the root as medicine and the Shinnecock Indians used the hop pillow, heated, as an application for pneumonia.

hora A folk dance of Rumania and Palestine, similar to the kolo of Serbia, more languid in Rumania, more incisive and stamping in Palestine. [GPK]

Horæ (singular *Hora*) In Greek mythology, the goddesses of the seasons and the order of nature; later, of justice and order. They are mentioned in Homer, but first named in Hesiod: Eunomia, Dice, Irene. Their original number was two (though later usually three are three), as for example at Athens where Thallo and Carpo were worshipped from earliest times, Thallo being mentioned in the Ephebic oath. They are connected with the Charites, act as the ministers of Zeus or of Hera, are beneficent goddesses of the weather and donors of the good of the Spring and Autumn seasons.

Horatii In Roman legend, three Roman champions who fought the three Curiatii, representing the Latins in the reign of Tullus Hostilius during the war between Rome and Alba. Of the two sets of brothers, only one of the Horatii survived the fight. He, on returning home, was greeted by his sister, who, seeing him wearing the garment of her betrothed, one of the Curiatii, wept. In a fit of patriotism, he killed her and was condemned to death. But he appealed to the people, was acquitted, and purified himself by passing under a beam. All the elements of the story are calculated, each explaining some circumstance in Rome that needed legendary background. For example, a beam, the *tigillum sororium,* and an altar of Juno Sororia (actually the Juno of growth) were both under the care of the Horatia gens, and were easily explainable in terms of the legend and a reading of *soror* as sister.

horehound or **hoarhound** A whitish, bitter, perennial herb of the mint family (genus *Marrubium*). It is a time-honored remedy for diseases of the chest, and was used in this connection in a tea at least as early as the 9th century. Today it is still widely used either in a tea or in a candy. Horehound coughdrops are considered especially effective. At one time it was also prescribed for cramps in the stomach and for those who had swallowed poison or been bitten by serpents or mad dogs. Mixed with wine and honey, horehound helps to clear the eyesight. In the 18th century it was also used as a snuff. Stinking horehound (*Ballota vulgare*) pounded with salt was especially good for bites of mad dogs.

horn A wind instrument originally made of the curved horn of an animal, later of metal, blown either from the narrow end or from the side, and used by both primitive and more advanced peoples for signaling, for expulsion of witches, ghosts, and the demons of sickness, for new moon and sunset ceremonies, for frightening off the monster that eats the moon at eclipse, etc. It is not always differentiated from the trumpet, and in primitive concepts carries with it many of the same tabus and customs. The sound has magical powers, the crescent shape of certain horns is significant in moon rites, and the attributes of the animal from which the instrument is taken may influence its powers.

In ancient Mesopotamia, ox horns, some richly adorned with gold and jewels, were used in religious observances connected with bull-worship. In Europe, horns were the first musical instruments of the Teutonic tribes and have been especially associated with hunters, warriors, herdsmen, and watchmen. Heimdall, the watchman of the Norse gods, has the Giallarhorn, with which he sounds the alarm for the gods when Surtr attacks. Robin Hood and Roland both used horn signals. In Africa, ivory horns of elephant tusks are the jealously guarded possessions of tribal chiefs. Similar horns, called oliphants, imported into Europe through Byzantium in the Middle Ages, and also respected as princely instruments, may have originated in Africa. The Jewish ram's horn, *shofar*, which serves its religious purpose under conditions of modern civilization in almost its original form and method, preserves much of the primitive lore of the horn, and the alphorn, actually a type of trumpet still heard in the mountains of Switzerland, as its counterparts are in Asia, South

America, and Australia, retains the meaning of the sunset ritual.

horning A serenade of harsh, discordant music; a charivari.

hornpipe An English and Scottish solo dance of the clog and shuffle variety: so called because originally danced to the old hornpipe. It became popular on shipboard because it took so little space. Amusing sailors' pantomime synchronizes with the typical Scotch toeing, hopping, and rocking. For "Haul in the anchor" the arms reach right forward and haul back over the left shoulder. For "Hoist the sail" the right hand pulls up and down, then the left. For "Hitch trousers" the right hand grasps the trousers in front, the left hand in back (but palm out), with an inimitable forward and backward rock. This is then reversed. [GPK]

Horny or **Old Horny** A provincial English and Scottish euphemism for the Devil.

horse The domesticated horse is probably of Indo-European origin, spreading during the Indo-European invasions of the 2nd millennium B.C. throughout the Near East and Europe. Although only the Celtic Epona and the divine horses of Diomedes in Thracian myth retain the horse form among divinities, many gods and goddesses, demigods and heroes retain a close connection with the animal. As Krappe indicates (*Mythologie universelle*, pp. 67 ff.), the Twins of Indo-European mythologies show a possible origin as caballiform divinities. The Aśvins (literally horse owners) were the offspring of the mare Saranyu, and may originally have been colts. Castor, one of the Dioscuri, was a horse-tamer and, throughout Homeric literature, the Spartan twins were renowned horsemen. The British legendary Hengist and Horsa retain in one of the names a clear reminder of their mythological origin. Demeter, the Greek fertility goddess, sometimes appeared as having a horse's head; among others Poseidon, Athena, Aphrodite, Cronus had horse aspects. In addition, many gods, Helios, Thor, etc., drove chariots drawn by horses. The horse was associated with thunder, which was the sound of the celestial horse's hoofs or the rumbling of the chariot, while the lightning was the whip which sped the horses on their way. Spanish children used to cry at the sound of thunder, "There goes Santiago's horse." Often the Wild Hunt was thought to be the sound of horses in the sky. Pegasus, the winged horse of poetry, originally was the carrier of the thunder and lightning of Zeus. As a result of the connection of the horse with both the thunder (sky) god and fertility, horses, especially white horses, were a favorite and highly acceptable sacrifice.

The horse is one of the principal fertility symbols. As the field spirit he runs across the tops of the grain with the wind. Compare AśVAMEDHA; ATHENA; OAT-STALLION; OCTOBER HORSE.

Formerly in Europe a horse was sometimes buried alive to prevent the death or theft of the others. In Yorkshire they say to save the others it is enough to bury a dead horse whole.

It is lucky to dream of horses (India, Great Britain, United States). Almost everywhere it is lucky to see a white horse. If you see a white horse you will soon see a red-headed girl (and vice versa). Wish on the first white horse you see on New Year's and the wish will come true. But it is considered unlucky for a bridal pair to drive behind two white horses; and in northern Canada you will die within the year if you watch a span of whites out of sight. It is lucky to meet a piebald horse, usually lucky to wish on one.

Horses can see ghosts; sometimes horses are ghosts. These folk concepts turn up in folktale as motifs E421.1.2 and E423.1.3. Horses also occur in folktale as born from eggs (B19.3), as paramours (B611.3). There are magic horses (B181 ff.), speaking horses (B211.3), truth-speaking horses (B133), helpful horses (B401). Horses are tried and executed for crimes (B272.2.1; B275.1.1). The Devil appears in the form of a horse (G303.3.3.5); so do witches (G211.1). That horses know the road in the dark is no fairy tale but the motif occurs as B151.

Horse and the Stag The title of one of Æsop's fables (Jacobs #33) in which a Horse, anxious to punish a Stag who had damaged his pasture, asked a Man to help. The Man said he would if the Horse would agree to be saddled and take the bit in his mouth. The Horse complied, but then the Man would not release him, and the Horse has been subject to man ever since. This incident comprises the general European folktale motif K192.

horse chestnut or **buckeye** Though the nuts are thought inedible, man has found numerous uses for them. They are carried in the pocket as a preventive for rheumatism, roasted and used as a substitute for coffee, powdered and used for soap; fermented they yield an alcohol and an acetone. Fed to horses they cure coughs and improve shortness of breath, and placed in the water they were used to stupefy fish. The flowers may be dried and used in place of hops for making beer. A decoction of the bark is used as a nerve tonic and as a cure for intermittent fevers. The leaves powdered and made into a snuff are good for catarrh and head colds.

horse dance Ritual riding on a live horse or hobbyhorse. Young men ride live horses on the eve of St. Michael on the Isle of Iona around a stone cross, each one with any lass except his wife mounted behind him; at the grave of the goddess Talltiu in Taillten, Ireland, they race to give the chthonic spirits an access of vigor for crop production. The North American Blackfoot Indians for a time gave an equestrian display—a horse dance on symbolically ornamented steeds—to arouse martial courage. The Comanche Indians still perform such a riding dance. The Shoshoni assume the identity of a pony in an entertaining mimetic dance called the *pooke* which expresses the importance of the horse in Plains society, for hunt and for prestige.

More commonly elsewhere the mount is a contraption of wood, cloth, hair, which the rider manipulates in a realistic manner. Either the conception is that of a separate man and beast, as the hobbyhorse of Athens, or of identity of man and beast, as the ghostlike Mari Lwyd (Gray Mare) of Glamorganshire, and the hobby of Padstow, Cornwall. The rider is in a trancelike state in the Balinese *sanghyang djanar* (horse dance). The Balinese horse consists of a head and tail on a bamboo cane and it prances and whinnies like its Spanish, French, and English counterparts—the hobby of the Majorcan

Cosiers, the French Basque *mascaradas* and of the English *morris* and Abbots Bromley Antler dance. In Rumania, the *călușar* recalls the morris horse in its actions and in its association with a pyrrhic dance, a fool and a man-woman. Spain has given Mexico its counterpart in Santiago, who leads the Christians in the battle of the *Moros y Cristianos.* In the valley of Mexico and in the mountains of Puebla and Veracruz the saint gallops on a wooden creature believed to be magically endowed with life. In the New Mexico pueblos, saints' impersonations, called *maiyanyi,* always ride a hobby, as Santiago and Boshaiyanyi in Santa Ana. They are "Indian spirits" possessed with *iyanyi,* beneficent supernatural power, communicated by contact and by the act of impersonation. Strangely enough, this last, most hybrid horse ritual, suggests most clearly the aboriginal meaning and harks back to ancient life-giving horse sacrifices. [GPK]

horse learns to live without food A general European folktale motif (J1914) in which, just as a man has habituated his horse to living without food, it dies. This belongs to a group of anecdotes (Type 1682) of which the point is the stupidity of the man who disregards the laws of nature.

horse-radish A coarse, tall, garden herb of the mustard family (*Amoracia lapathifolia*) used as a condiment. At the Jewish Passover Seder, the horse-radish signifies the bitterness of the house of bondage. Medicinally, horse-radish was used in the treatment of paralysis, chronic rheumatism, epilepsy, dropsy, and hoarseness. Scraped it was applied to the tooth in cases of toothache in Russia; in North America, either the scraped horse-radish (as in northern Ohio) or the leaves (as with the Mohegan Indians) was applied to the cheek as a poultice for toothache. The Negroes of some parts of the southern United States rub horse-radish on the forehead for headache.

horseshoe An archlike frame of iron or other metal fitted to a horse's hoof as protection, or a symbol of similar shape. Among the Greeks and Romans, this use was almost unknown, though vase-paintings show some signs of it. About the earliest instance of the iron horseshoe is the one discovered in England in the 17th century in the grave of Childeric (died 491 A.D.).

The origin of the horseshoe-shaped symbol is suggested as being from the rite of the Passover, the blood sprinkled on lintel and doorposts forming the chief points of an arch. Its two-horned shape is related to the shape of the moon, the crescent moon's "horns" (compare the luck-bringing qualities assigned to animal horns in amulets and talismans, to horses' heads or merely to horns placed on a roof as repellent to the evil eye, such customs being prevalent in Germany, Spain, Arabia, and elsewhere); or the horseshoe's possible origin is in serpent-worship and in religious symbolism in Egypt and Assyria pertaining to this reptilian form.

The magic of the horseshoe may be noted obviously in its manufacture from iron, since iron is a repellent to witches, evil spirits, fairies, and other beings which work harm to man. Horseshoes are placed in chimneys, on the doors of stables, dwellings, and churches; and if not on the door, on the threshold. Tylor says in speaking of such use in England, "Half the stable doors in England still show the horseshoe." In London, many of the West End houses have one on the door and there are plenty of churches which use this talisman or have used it. The Devil cannot enter any building that has a horseshoe over the door. Its use as a good luck charm is common in the United States and luck is enhanced by the chance finding of a horseshoe. In Hungary, it is said that the people mark a horseshoe with black chalk on their stable doors. The horseshoe as a luck bringer is not confined to land, but is efficacious at sea as well. Lord Nelson is said to have had a horseshoe nailed to the mast of his ship *Victory.*

The position of the horseshoe, wherever it may be placed, is important. As a protective charm, it should be placed with the convex side up. As a luck charm the horns should point up so the luck will not "run out." It should always be placed outside, above the door, not inside. A Pennsylvania custom places the horseshoe outside but with the prongs pointing inside so the luck will be spilled inward.

Sexual symbolism is attached to the horseshoe. In Mexico ornate stones in this form have been classed as fertility symbols by their discoverers; in Aztec manuscripts, symbols like the horseshoe relate to agricultural abundance. Similar charms with probable similar meanings have been found in the Cahokia (Illinois) mounds.

The horseshoe is found in popular ballad and often in the folktale in Germany, Lapland, Norway, Bavaria, and elsewhere. In such stories, a smith and the Devil are frequent characters. [GPS]

Horseshoe Nail Title of a cumulative folktale (Z45) characterized by the interdependence of the objects mentioned in the story, and the sequence of disasters which follow on neglect to replace one missing nail from the horse's shoe (N258).

> For want of a nail the shoe was lost;
> For want of a shoe the horse was lost;
> For want of a horse the man was lost;
> For want of a man the battle was lost;
> And all for the want of a horseshoe nail.

Grimm's version of this story (#184) is longer and more elaborate, starting with the merchant who had only six more miles to go to reach home and thought the nail would not matter for so short a distance, and ending with his struggling home late at night carrying his trunk on his back.

horses of Diomedes In Greek legend, the flesh-eating horses of the king of the Thracian Bistonians taken by Hercules, with or without help, as the eighth of his labors. By feeding Diomedes to the horses, Hercules tamed them and brought them to Argos where they were dedicated to Hera.

Horus, Hor, or **Har** Literally, he who is above: an ancient Egyptian solar deity who combined two or more originally separate gods, who were sometimes even in later times still recognized as separate personages. The solar Horus, often called the Egyptian Apollo, was a brother of Osiris, Isis, and Set. This was the falcon-headed god, sometimes depicted simply as a falcon, of Upper Egypt, perhaps the most ancient god of the Egyptian pantheon, and identical with Rā. He appeared as Herakhty, Horus of the Horizon, the rising and setting sun; as Horus the Elder, the Greek Haroeris; as the Horus whose representation was the winged solar disk that protected temples from evil and was carved above their doors.

Horus the Child, or Harpocrates, was the son of Osiris and Isis, the sun reborn each morning from the waters and carried on the lotus flower. Rā was the midday sun and Atum the setting sun, but this is a later attempt to justify the plurality of sun gods, as is the explanation of Osiris as the sun of the underworld and Horus the sun god of the sky. This younger Horus is sometimes figured as a man with a falcon head, but more often he is the child with finger in mouth or suckling and carried by Isis or Hathor. In myth, he was the avenger of his father Osiris, slaying Set. In the struggle he lost an eye which, after he ascended his father's throne and was affirmed in the office by an assemblage of the gods, Thoth replaced. Horus also saw to it that Osiris was properly buried. This Horus was the type of the dutiful son; the eye was the symbol of sacrifice, of duty to the gods and to the ancestors.

The pharaohs always had a Horus name, their first title, written with the falcon symbol. Horus was especially the protector of the Northern Kingdom.

hospitality The folk ceremonies connected with hospitality, though infinitely complex in detail, are connected with the admission of strangers into the we-group and the rights which persons thus admitted may be expected to enjoy. In some communities the stranger at the gate may be accepted or rejected according to local rules. Among the nomadic Arabs and some but not all other nomads, a man who touches the tent rope must be defended to the death. In agrarian cultures groups cut off from all social intercourse except what they themselves can supply offer strangers of appropriate class unlimited food, lodging, drink, and entertainment. The acceptance of the strangers is indicated by the offering and partaking of food in common, though the foods considered appropriate are determined by the traditions of the community and within the community the traditions of the social class involved: bread and salt in some communities, tea in China, cakes or cakes and sherry in some classes in Britain and America. To buy a man a drink in public places in Europe and America involves only limited acceptance, though to refuse to drink with a man in such places indicates definite antagonism.

The simplest form of acceptance is shaking the stranger's hand, though other communities use other gestures. The sharing of communal food involves principles similar to those involved in the ceremony of blood brotherhood, which is sometimes the sign of acceptance. Both ceremonies clearly involve the principle of communion with the idea that "as your blood is in my veins and your food is in my stomach we are therefore united."

Occidental ethnographers devote much space to discussions of "hospitality prostitution," a custom which requires that the host offer his wife, wives, or women to the guest. This custom would be remarkable only in communities where monogamous chastity was a practical ideal. The lavish hospitality usually of a sexual nature offered in the United States to a prospective customer is a parallel custom. The host's women are usually not involved. That sexual hospitality is evidence of the low status of women in communities where it is customary also needs to be questioned. In some parts of Mongolia, for example, it is considered one of the per-

quisites of women to participate if they can in the festivities occasioned by the arrival of a guest. The belief that a stranger may be a god in disguise and that a child resulting from the union of the stranger and the women of the community has been mentioned elsewhere. [RDJ]

hot dance A ceremonial of the Plains Indians, featuring the *heyoka* or hot-water trick: the immersion of the arms in scalding water for purposes of exhibiting antinatural powers. The participants would pull out and serve pieces of dog meat boiled ceremonially, or just splash each other, claiming that the water was cold. The Arikara hot dancers, *kawen'ho*, wore headdresses of deer tails and turkey feathers, and patterns of body paint. To drum and gourd-rattle accompaniment, they crouched low in their dance, like the *heyoka*. The Mandan and Hidatsa took this society over from the Arikara, and evidently transmitted it to the Crow Indians.

The Crow hot dance, *ba'tawé disúe*, corresponds to the grass dance of the Omaha and other tribes, in the ceremonial array of officers, in the paraphernalia of whips, two pipes, "crows" or feather-bustles, war bonnets, in the give-away and boasting features, and in the strenuous individual dancing. The Crow modified the *heyoka* trick by handling the hot meat with cranesticks, and turned the whole procedure into a more social occasion than the similar but strictly ritual IRUSKA and HEYOKA. [GPK]

Hotei The most popular of the Japanese Seven Gods of Luck, represented as a very fat man. See JAPANESE FOLKLORE. [JLM]

Hou Chi The Chinese God of Millet. Like other elements in the Imperial Cults he is the subject of much controversy. A battle of footnotes has been waged as to whether the term should be translated "Prince Millet" or "He Who Rules Millet." Ceremonies to Hou Chi were part of the imperial and at times part of the aristocratic cults. [RDJ]

hourglass drum A drum that is sharply narrowed between the two openings. Such drums are generally small, the largest being a Korean type about three feet in length. Some, such as the *damaru* of India, combine with the clapper feature. Others, such as the Japanese *tsuzumi*, make use of the protruding ring under the skin to form a spool shape. See DRUM.

houri or **huri** or **haura** In Moslem belief (compare *Sura* lv, 56–78 of the Koran), one of the eternal virgins who live in Paradise with the blessed. They are all of perfect beauty, dark-eyed, and untouched by man or jinn. Every Moslem who attains Heaven is allotted 72 houris. The Persian Magi also peopled their Paradise with huran, similar nymph-like companions.

House Carpenter The most common version surviving in America of *James Harris* or *The Daemon Lover* (Child #243). It relates the fate of the wife of a house carpenter who deserts her baby and runs off to sea with a lover, and is an example of the disappearance of supernatural elements in most of the traditional ballads transplanted to the New World.

household spirits Supernatural beings of general European folklore, who frequent homes and farms: often helpful, often mischievous and tricky, sometimes malicious. See AITVARAS; BANNIK; BILLY BLIN; BOGGART; BOGLE; BROWNIE; DOMOVIC; FAIRY; GOBLIN; KAUKAS; KOBOLD; PARA.

house inscription A legend or record inscribed on a house or building: of wide occurrence in the East. Sacred formulas or texts from various sources are placed usually near the entrance. This custom appears in Egypt, Babylonia, Greece, India, and China.

In the United States, inscriptions are frequently incised on public buildings such as museums, art galleries, and sometimes on homes. This custom, in general, would seem to stem from early ideas of repelling evil and inviting luck. However, at the present day, it appears to be a dedicatory gesture, especially on churches. In the home, the inscription is frequently above the hearth on the fire-board, reminiscent of primitive rites in the household and the sanctity of the hearth-fire. An inscription on a fan-light of the entrance door to a home in the eastern Ozarks has been noted ("God Bless our Home"). There are, no doubt, other examples. [GPS]

house leek or **Jove's Beard** A garden plant (*Sempervivum tectorum*) with pink flowers and thick fleshy leaves, which grows on walls and roofs. Charlemagne passed a law that these plants should be grown on the roof of every dwelling. Among the Celtic peoples it is considered good luck to have house leeks growing on the roof. They protect the building from fire, lightning, witches, and evil spirits, and the inhabitants from fever. But in some places they are said to attract lightning, unless grown in company with the common leek. The juice of this plant removes warts and corns and soothes skin which has been scalded, burnt, stung by nettles or bees. At one time it was recommended for the hot ague, gout, and sore eyes. Compare LEEK.

house snake The genius of the Roman house who foretold the destiny of the family. Among Teutons the house snakes embodied the souls of the dead ancestors and watched over children. In Greece and Russia a snake coming into the house is regarded as a good omen. The people believe that they have received a guardian spirit who will "watch over his own." In Armenia also the house snake brings good luck and is treated with kindness. If one leaves, it is a sign that trouble and sorrow will fall on the household. If one suddenly arrives in the night he is given the hospitality offered to strangers, and fed immediately lest he depart. Almost everywhere the house snake is fed with milk. Similar practices and beliefs have been reported from among the Letts, White Russians, Poles, Lithuanians, Greeks. See SNAKE. [RDJ]

House that Jack Built The best known of the cumulative stories (Z44, Type 2035). It begins with the statement: "This is the house that Jack built." And the final formula is: "This is the farmer that sowed the corn that fed the cock that crowed in the morn, that waked the priest all shaven and shorn, that married the man all tattered and torn, that kissed the maiden all forlorn, that milked the cow with the crumpled horn, that tossed the dog, that worried the cat, that caught the rat, that ate the malt that lay in the house that Jack built."

Hou T'u The Chinese God of Earth or Soil; Sovereign Earth. Chinese folklorists and ritualists, like many others, have been confused by the interlocked meanings of "earth," "land," "soil," "fields." The people generally pay honor to the local gods of place whose temples, very simply constructed, are in the fields and whose power extends over small and particular, though not carefully defined, areas. These gods and their consorts are the familiar and intimate gods of the people. Hou T'u was also part of the imperial cult. [RDJ]

hovatu-koiari In Orokaiva (Papua) belief, the spirit of a stillborn or aborted child. It is a foot high with a long tail, which drags as it walks and which is thrown over the shoulder when it sits down. The hovatu-koiari lives in the sago swamps and can be heard sometimes singing a plaintive song while scraping sago.

Hrdlička, Aleš (1869–1943) American anthropologist, who gave his support to the theory that the American Indians are Asiatic by origin. Born in Bohemia, he came to the United States as a young man. He took part in expeditions sponsored by the American Museum of Natural History between 1899 and 1903; was on the staff of the United States National Museum at Washington, D.C., from 1903; and curator of the division of physical anthropology there, 1910–43. He founded the *American Journal of Physical Anthropology* and was its editor from 1918. Besides his work on the origins of the American Indian, he is known also for an anthropological survey of Alaska and for studies in anthropometry and in the evolution of man.

Hrolf Kraki The most famous king of the Danes in the heroic age, called Hrothulf in *Beowulf*: the generous, almost superhuman hero of the *Hrolfssaga,* celebrated also in the *Biarkamal*. His gifts of rings, swords, helmets, estates are made much of; he strewed gold on the plains of Fyfe on the journey to Upsala. Northern legend tells of his berserkers, the twelve warriors pledged to his service; their deeds occupy more of the material than Hrolf's own tragic figure from the first call to battle to his death in the gates of Leire Castle in Zealand, the old seat of the kings. Hrolf had a wonderful hawk, Habrok, who was once caged with thirty Swedish hawks that they might kill him, but killed them all. Hrolf's wonderful dog Garm killed the magic boar sent against him by an enemy. The twelve berserkers and the marvelous sword named Skǫfnung are other attributes of Hrolf which identify him as the typical folk-hero king.

Hrungnir One of the famous giants of Teutonic mythology. One day on Gullfaxi Hrungnir challenged Odin to a race on Sleipnir. Riding neck and neck, he did not notice the direction Odin had taken until he suddenly found himself entering the gates of the gods. But the Æsir would not take vengeance on their ancient enemy thus tricked in sport. They feasted him instead until the drunken Hrungnir boasted he would return and conquer Asgard and carry off its beautiful women. Still the gods ignored the tipsy braggart, until Thor entered, overheard the boast, and challenged Hrungnir to battle. Three days later Thor and Hrungnir met for combat. Hrungnir caught the blow of Thor's hammer on his stone club, which was shattered into bits, thus supplying the whole earth with flint chips forever. But one piece sank into Thor's forehead, and as he fell, his hammer cracked Hrungnir's head so that he fell dead beside him,

hsien and **shên** Chinese terms which have been variously translated as referring to gods, immortals, fairies, spirits, saints, genii, heroes, ascetics, powers. Although both Taoists and Christian missionaries have attempted to fix the meanings of these terms, common usage is still uncertain. The unlearned in China frequently meet creatures that behave in extraordinary ways and therefore (whether they be gods, fairies, or spirits), need to be treated with circumspection. Many Christian missionaries use the term shên to refer to their God, which they refer to as "the true God." [RDJ]

Hsi Shih In Chinese folk belief, the patroness of merchants of face creams and perfumes. She was the daughter of a butcher and became a royal concubine. When she was presented to the emperor, she smelled so sweet that the odor could be noticed for ten li. [RDJ]

Hsi Wang Mu The consort of Tung Wang Kung, formed from the yin principle of the purely female: object of a widespread cult in China. She is the Lady or Mother of the Western Heaven. Her palace in the K'un Lun mountains of western Turkestan is protected by a wall a thousand li long built of precious stones and protected by jade towers. The right wing, on the shore of the magic brook of the kingfishers, is the residence of the male immortals. The left wing is the residence of the female immortals who are divided into seven categories according to the color of their costumes: red, blue, black, violet, yellow, green, and natural. Insurgent princes have from time to time reestablished the cult of Hsi Wang Mu and given it imperial favor. On her birthday, 1st to 3rd of the Third Moon, all the gods visit her. She gives them a great feast: bear palms, monkey lips, dragon liver, and phœnix marrow. The peaches in her garden, female phallic symbols, confer immortality. Chinese women frequently do honor to Hsi Wang Mu on their 50th birthday.

Hsi Wang Mu is also called Chin Mu. *Chin* may be rendered as Gold or Precious or Excellent, and *Mu* as Mother, Lady, Woman. Other names in the several styles of romanization now current are: Hou, Ho, Yang, Hui, Wang Chin.

Although her consort, Tung Wang Kung, Lord of the West, was formed of the essence of yang (male) as Hsi Wang Mu was formed of the essence of yin (female), he is incidental to the cult. Hsi Wang Mu had many children. The absence of much discussion about their paternity, the fact that all but one of those known to me are female, gives the sense, which is by no means a conclusion, that the cult of Hsi Wang Mu has to do with matriarchy, either the sort of matriarchal culture still extant in parts of China, or the matriarchal fantasies inevitable in such social structures as China where, except along the coast, the women control all domestic affairs within the compound.

The only male child known is the ninth son, Hiuensieou, whose title is Chên Jen. The fourth daughter, Hua Lin, is also known as Yong chên, or Nan Chi Fu Jen (Wife of the God of Longevity), or vulgarly, Ch'ou Hsing Lao T'ou Tze (The Old Head of the Star of Longevity). The 13th daughter is Mei Lan or Chung Lin, title, Yu Ying Fu Jen (*Dame de la Beauté droite*) with residence on Mount Tsang Lang. The 20th daughter is Ching Wo or Yu Yin with the honorific, Lady of the Star Tse Wei. Her residence is on Yuen-lung Moun-

tain. The 23rd daughter, Yao Chi, honorific, Lady of the Flowered Clouds, gave the Emperor Yu the formula for evoking demons and spirits. The youngest daughter is Wan, honorific, Lady of the Jade Flower. She was the wife of King Tai Chen. When she plays a stringed instrument the birds gather to listen to her melodies. She rides a white dragon.

The feminine character of the cult is further seen in the gems, jades, and precious woods from which Shên I, a sun god, built her palace, also in the feminine interest in parties, and the collations served to the immortals when they visit her on her birthday, and in the interest in clothes. The kingfisher creek is a pretty touch. The peaches of immortality which grow in her garden and the peach which is part of her iconography are female phalloi.

Hsi Wang Mu is first mentioned in *Mu Tien Tzu Chuan* (Eitel, E. J., tr., *China Review* XVII, 1888–89, pp. 223–240, 247–258) a courtly romance of the pre-Christian Chou period which recounts the travels into the west of Prince Mu. The dating of this romance is most uncertain, though some scholars place it in the 10th century B.C. Western sinologues have presented views. Doré (*Variétés*, No. 44, pp. 486 ff.) tentatively suggests Babylon as the place involved. Charles Gardner (*Chinese Traditional Historiography*, Harvard Press, 1938, pp. 45–46) calls the character in the Prince Mu romance a "male chieftain of the western frontier" and is in agreement with W. P. Yetts (*Catalogue of the Eumorphopolous Collection, Bronzes, II*, London, 1930, p. 49). Paul Pelliot attempted to identify Hsi Wang Mu with an ancient female mythological personage (*T'oung Pao, Archives Concernant l'Histoire, les Langues, la Géographie, l'Ethnographie et les Arts de l'Asie Orientale*, Leiden, XXVIII, 1930, p. 392); Henri Maspéro suggested an ancient goddess of epidemics (*La Chine Antique*, Paris, 1927); A. Forke tried the Queen of Sheba ("Mu Wang und die Königen von Saba," *Mitteilungen des Seminars für Orientalische Sprachen*, Berlin, VII, 1904, pp. 117–172, reviewed by Edouard Huber in *Bulletin de l'Ecole Francaise d'Extrême Orient*, Hanoi, IV, 1904, pp. 1127–1131). H. S. Giles noted parallels with Juno in the palace above the clouds, peaches and apples, phœnix and peacock ("Who was Hsi Wang Mu?" in *Adversaria Sinica*, Shanghai, 1914). Popularizers of Chinese folklore, Bredon and others, have fun with the Gardens of the Hesperides, the Buddhist Heaven in the West, the Celtic Western Isles, etc.

The centers of the cult may be the west of China proper, or among aboriginal tribes still in China which still retain some of the customs from a matriarchal or a sororal-polygynal culture. In the 5th century B.C. the King of Yueh, having been successful in war, built on his return to his capital in modern Chekiang an altar to Hsi Wang Mu to the west of the city, and there offered sacrifices for happiness and long life. In 3 B.C. during the dynasty of the Former Han, and a great famine, rebels in modern Shantung invoked Hsi Wang Mu. An account is in Leon Wieger's *Textes Historiques*, I, p. 695.

Generalizations: Hsi Wang Mu is generally known in China. The centers of the cult may have been in west China or central Asia, though the cult has certainly received further development in China proper. Identifications of Hsi Wang Mu with Juno, the Queen of Sheba, or various primitive goddesses are scholarly folklore in which similarity of fantasy has been confused with identity of origin. Any one of these identifications may possibly be sound; probability, however, must await further analysis, particularly a study of the folklore of the matriarchal societies in Yunnan and central Asia, and a study of the structure of women's cults in other parts of the world.   R. D. JAMESON

huaca Sacred: among the ancient Incas, a word applied to everything supernatural or sacred. It designated gods, demons, spirits, and also the sites and temples where they were worshipped. Among the modern Quechua and Aymara Indians of Peru, it designates all household fetishes, mummified ancestors and their graves, certain sacred animals, gods, images of gods, and their temples. Anything supernatural or smacking of the supernatural is huaca: an egg with two yolks, or twins, or an albino, crossed eyes, harelip, etc. Unusual and inexplicable objects introduced by the Spaniards were also huaca, like glass goblets, sealing wax, etc.

huakanki The love amulets of Bolivia. They are carved in alabaster and usually represent an embraced couple or sometimes a phallus. [AM]

Huanacauri A rock on a hill near the Cuzco which was the most famous fetish of the Inca family. It represents the petrified brother of the first Inca, Manco capac. Before he turned to stone he proclaimed himself protector of the dynasty. The puberty rites of the young boys of the Inca family were celebrated around this fetish. [AM]

huapango (from Aztec *cuah-panco,* wood-over-place) A Mexican mestizo couple dance, of the Huasteca region and on the east coast from Tamaulipas to Veracruz. Footwork resounds on a wooden platform, in the typical rhythm of one-two-three-hold, beating once with the heel and twice with the toe. Skilful dancers perform complex *zapateados* and sometimes tie a knot in a kerchief with their feet during the *Bamba.*

The gay *sones,* usually in quadruple time, are played on ensembles of violins, guitars, jaranas, and harps. The characteristic rhythm is produced by striking the hand on the guitar for the last note of each measure.

In San Luis Potosí a special wedding huapango, *Xochipitzahua* (flower sprinkling) is sung, and bride and groom lead the couples in a circle. At the end flowers and incense are offered at an altar.

In the Sierra Norte de Puebla the huapango is an ingenuous couple dance performed in two face-to-face lines. It employs the simplest zapateado of one forward and two back, or a step-step-step-brush from side to side, the girls holding their full skirts and the boys bowing with their hands cupped behind their backs. The changeable rhythms are played on fiddle and guitar and often sung. This may continue all night during a fiesta. [GPK]

Huasa mallcu The supernatural guardian of the vicuña in Bolivia. He protects his herds by making them invisible to hunters. The Aymara Indians say also that he carries goods on the back of his animals and he may reward men who are friendly to him. He is represented by a small image attached at the end of a pole. He receives offerings during feasts officially celebrated in honor of some Catholic saint. [AM]

Huathicuri A mythical character of the Huarochiri Indians (Peru) who had the power of understanding the language of animals. From a fox he learned the cause of the mysterious illness of a powerful chief, married the chief's daughter, but was compelled to enter into several contests with the girl's sister, who was a powerful magician. One contest was in building a house. Huathicuri won because he was helped by the animals. He finally transformed his undesirable sister-in-law into a deer. [AM]

Huehuenches (from Aztec, *huehuetl,* old, old) A men's ceremonial dance of Morelos and Oaxaca, Mexico. In Villa Alta, Oaxaca, it is most colorful and humorous. The dancers, in bright costumes and feather-decked hats, play at bullfighting with a papier-mâché bull. This feature, certainly of Spanish provenience, suggests relationship of this dance with other fights between old men as *viejos* or *abuelos,* and *toros,* which are spread as far as the *Matachini* dance of the New Mexico pueblos. The Huehues of the state of Guerrero enact a drama of hunting a tiger, with ingenuous jokes. Other characters include a hunter, a doctor, a he-goat, a deer, and a dog. [GPK]

huehuetl Literally, old-old: an ancient Aztec drum made of a single hollowed-out log, set upright. The top is covered with skin and generally struck with the bare hands; the bottom is either cut to form wide feet or rests on a three-legged stand. The originals were elaborately carved. The same type of drum, though cruder and less finely decorated, is still made and played in the same manner by primitive Mexican tribes such as the Huichols, who use it only to accompany songs to their own gods, their Christian ceremonies being accompanied by stringed instruments. Similar drums are found in Polynesia, Melanesia, and parts of Africa. See DRUM.

Huet, Gédéon Busken (1860–1921) Dutch-French philologist and historian, son of the Dutch writer, Conrad Busken Huet. He went to Batavia with his father and then to Paris in 1880 to go to school. With Emmanuel Cosquin and Gaston Paris he was one of Benfey's literary school of folklorists in France. His chief work was *Les contes populaires* (1922). He edited Doon de la Roche's *Chanson de Geste* (1921), issued various of his father's works, and wrote numerous studies, such as *Légende de Charlemagne bâtard, Pélérinage de Charlemagne,* and *Légende des énervés de Jumèges.*

Hueyuku The Mansion of the Sun; the afterworld of the Caribs of the Antilles, a paradise of bliss and plenty.

hu hsien The shape-shifting foxes of Chinese folklore. The term is variously translated as fox-spirit, fox-fairy, or divine fox. By various means these creatures attain the power of assuming various forms or of becoming invisible. Although all things, animate and inanimate, can shift shape, foxes have unusual abilities. When they become youths or maidens the hu hsien have remarkable sexual gifts and are able to steal the vital essence of human beings who fall in love with them. In consequence these human beings become tubercular and die while the hu hsien, having increased their own vital essence by theft from their victims, proceed to seduce others. Hu hsien love to drink wine. When intoxicated or frightened they resume their true form.

Because all scholars, being scholars, are virtuous, the

hu hsien frequently seek the protection of scholars when being attacked by the Thunder God who tries to punish them for their wicked tricks. The stories that hu hsien can show gratitude and help scholars, who have protected them, to attain high honor are not to be trusted. The hu hsien, being invisible, know everything that is being written about them and scholars are afraid to write the truth lest the hu hsien take revenge. [RDJ]

Huitzilopochtli The tribal war god of the Aztecs; the most important of all gods of Tenochtitlan, modern Mexico City, and the most important in all Mexico at the time of the Conquest. According to legend he accompanied the Aztecs in their wanderings before the founding of Tenochtitlan, where subsequently his great temple became the chief religious structure of the Aztecs. He was believed to be the sun, the young warrior who was born each day, who won a victory over the stars of night, and who was then carried to the zenith by the souls of dead warriors where he was taken over by the souls of all women who had died in childbirth, to be taken to the west where he fell and died, again to be reborn in the morning. To triumph, the sun had to be strong and vigorous, and if mankind were to continue, the sun's continued victories were essential. Therefore, mankind had to feed the sun which, however, disdained common foods, nourishing itself on the blood of humans. Hence, the bloody human sacrifice of the Aztecs was believed by them to be necessary to continue the world, and each Aztec was, above all, a warrior whose duty it was to take prisoners to be sacrificed to Huitzilopochtli. [GMF]

hula An ancient religious dance of Hawaii and the Easter Islands. The hulas are from the gods—*noke akua mai*—handed down from the beginning of the world. They are graded in sanctity according to profundities. The most holy speak of the depth within ourselves as well as the world and treat of gods and kings. Those of the lesser order deal with love and nature, the play of divine power into our world. Those of the third order are frankly sexual and comic, yet there are divine potencies at play. Ancient hulas are danced out of doors or in *halau*, the hula hall, the temple to Laka, goddess of flowers. The hula priest is called the *kumu*. The company consists of two great groups, the *ho'opa*, literally, the steadfast ones (the mature men and women, marking time on the larger instruments in a seated or kneeling position) and the *olopa*, literally, the agile ones (the younger men and women in a standing position). There are dances performed by either group alone, by men only, women only, or by mixed sexes, and by both groups. There are slow solemn dances and vivid dances with quick transitions from gentle to vigorous.

Though seemingly erotic because of the hip-swaying and sinuous arm movements, the hulas are not couple dances nor primarily erotic, except for those of the third order. The hip-swaying results from the special manner of transferring the weight from one foot to the other in the rather static footwork. The gestures all have a very definite mimetic or symbolic import like the Hindu *mudras,* from which they are descended. The horizontal swaying is enhanced by the typical grass skirts of the women. The ornaments are made of flowers or of dog-teeth which encircle the ankles. The music consists of song, accompanied by large wooden drums,

rattles of half gourds, covered with fishskin, conch-shell trumpets, and wooden whistles. Some hulas keep time to a rhythmic monotone chant.

The purpose is far removed from the vulgarization seen in so-called hulas on American stages. The true hula is not for entertainment, but communicates the god principle. [GPK]

hulk'ilal wok The dance of the dead in the ritual of the California Huchnom Indians. *Hulk'ilal* means spirits of the dead; *wok* means dance. It was given to the people by their creator Taikomol in the beginning of the world, and he admonished them to perpetuate it in order to have health, good living, and long life. The dancers who impersonate the hulk'ilal wear no masks. Their faces and bodies are marked with stripes of black and white paint, and they tie flowers in their hair. No women, children, or uninitiated boys may enter the dance house during the hulk'ilal wok. Uninitiated boys, about 12–13 years old, spend 6–7 months in the dance house (Fall to Spring) undergoing strict discipline, learning the tribal creation myths and songs, and all the sacred mysteries of this ritual before they are permitted to attend. See TAIKOMOL WOK.

Hummingbird A minor character in American Indian folktale and mythology. The northern Paiute Indians say that Hummingbird once filled his pants full of seeds and started on a journey to see what was beyond the sun. He ate only one seed a day, but had to turn back because his food gave out. He didn't see anything. In eastern Brazil, Hummingbird is the character who hoarded water so that the people had none at all until the Caingang and Botocudo Indians released it.

☞ Since pre-Conquest times the hummingbird has been considered by many Middle American peoples to have supernatural powers. Today it is esteemed by many as a love charm. A dead hummingbird may be worn around the neck in a little bag, to give the wearer the power to attract members of the opposite sex, or it may be dried and a little powder dropped into the drink of the person whose love is desired. [GMF]

humor (North American Indian) Popular notions of the Indian as stolid and unsmiling may still have currency, but are far from actuality, as the reports of many ethnographers and travelers attest. That Indians can be dignified and serious when they consider the occasion demands is true, but repartee, jests, and laughter not only have their place in day to day living, but even during the performance of religious ceremonies. In any Indian group, as in any white group, there are likely to be individuals whose reputation for witty remarks, or for the ability to tell humorous stories, is a matter of general recognition throughout the tribe.

Humor in American Indian tales is expressed through situation, by means of linguistic devices, and, less often, by character. Humorous situations result from cultural incongruities, from obscene actions and emphasis on bodily functions, violations of cultural tabus, from the introduction of modern elements in a mythical setting, and other such devices. Linguistic devices for introducing humor in tales include the introduction of foreign words or sentences, often mispronounced, in myths; use of morphological devices, onomatopoeia, etc. In nearly all tribes the attributes of the trickster are such that mere mention of him causes smiles, but other characters, especially small ones, are often also portrayed as humorous beings.

Clowns who amuse onlookers by their backward speech, audacious remarks, and oftentimes obscene behaviour are regular performers in certain Southwestern, Plains, California, and Eastern Woodlands ceremonies. Their antics and untoward remarks excite merriment and laughter which relieves the tensity of dramatic and serious ceremonies. In the Southwestern pueblo of Keres these clowns or "delight-makers" (*Koshare*) are organized into a society which performs comedies in pantomime in the intervals between public dances given to induce rain. [EWV]

hungan Haitian term for priest of the *vodun* cult, derived from the Fōn of Dahomey. Its literal meaning is deity-chief, *hun* in Fōn being a synonym for *vodun*, deity, and *gã* signifying chief. [MJH]

hunsi The northern Dahomean word for cult-initiate, that has been carried over into Haitian usage. Its literal Fōn meaning is deity-wife—*hu*, deity; *si*, wife. In Haiti, the word denotes any devotee of an African deity. [MJH]

hunsi kanzo A term employed in Haiti to denote a *vodun* cult-initiate who has passed through the ordeal of fire, which consists of dipping the bare hand into a cooking-pot containing boiling corn meal. This is the climax of ritual preparation, and is concluded by stepping on burning coals, or into a blazing, open fire. To be *hunsi kanzo* indicates that one has reached a higher rank in the vodun cult than the *hunsi*. In Fōn, the word *zo* signifies fire. [MJH]

hunting magic Many of the simpler peoples in Middle America propitiate spirits before setting out upon the chase. This appears to be related to the widespread belief that the more important game animals have their "masters," supernatural beings who usually live under mountains where they gather their animals at night, just as domestic animals are brought into enclosures. Hunters must request permission of these "masters," usually by burning incense and saying prayers, if they wish to have luck in their venture. A moral against wanton destruction of game is associated with this belief. A common story tells of a hunter who wounds but does not kill many animals; he goes into a trance, awakes, and finds himself under the mountains in the abode of the "masters," where he sees all of the animals he has wounded. He is told he may not return home until he has cured them, and that henceforth he must be careful in his hunting, killing only that which is needed for food.

Among some tribes a youth does not eat of the first animal or bird of each species which he kills, believing that if he breaks the tabu he will never again kill members of that species. [GMF]

Hunting of the Cheviot or ***Chevy Chase*** An English-Scottish border ballad (Child #162) probably relating the same story as that of *The Battle of Otterburn*, but more romanticized and less accurate, though taking neither side, than the latter. It is a later ballad than *The Battle of Otterburn*, but the A version of *The Hunting of the Cheviot* in Child is earlier than any extant version of *Otterburn*. This is the ballad referred to by Sir Philip Sidney in 1559 in his *Apologie for Poetrie*, and is considered one of the finest ballads in English.

The Percy, Earl of Northumberland, vows to hunt in the Cheviot Hills, country of the Scottish Douglas, for three days. On the first day, he and his 1500 archers kill a hundred harts, but soon after noon they are met by the Douglas, who has promised to drive them out, and 2000 of his men. Douglas, trying to avoid great bloodshed, offers to fight the Percy man to man, and Percy agrees. But an English squire objects to standing by while his chief fights, and the two groups clash. Douglas and Percy meet on the field, battle with each other, and are forced to pause for breath. During the rest, the Douglas is killed by an English arrow; Percy is run through by a Scottish knight. The fight continues until the moon is up: 55 of the Scots and 73 (or 53) of the English alone survive.

hurdy-gurdy (1) A medieval fiddle-like instrument operated mechanically by a crank-turned wheel which rubbed the strings and a set of rods which stopped the strings to play a melody. It originally was very large and required two men to play it. It was used to accompany singing in monasteries and schools. Later made smaller and portable, it became a favorite of the folk and eventually a beggars' instrument played at fairs and markets on the street.

(2) The crank-turned street organ of modern times, so called by association with the medieval instrument. The appearance of the hurdy-gurdy in the streets of New York, London, etc., is one of the first signs of Spring. The sound of the hurdy-gurdy brings children from the tenements pouring out of doorways and alleys to dance around it until the player tires. Two men usually form its crew, one to draw the cart and to crank the instrument, the other to pass up and down the street, hat in hand, collecting pennies from listeners and picking up the newspaper-wrapped coins thrown from apartment windows.

Hwegbadja Second king of the Aladahonu dynasty of Dahomey, who reigned from about 1650 to 1680. He is credited, in Dahomean tradition, wherein he plays mythical role of culture hero, with having consolidated the conquest of the plateau of Abomey, with having instituted the *dokpwe*, and with having instituted the custom of burying the dead, wherefore at every Dahomean funeral a cloth is given in his honor. [MJH]

hyacinth (1) A bulbous plant of the lily family (genus *Hyacinthus*) with a spikelike cluster of flowers. According to one Greek legend Zephyrus and Apollo both loved a youth, Hyacinthus, who cared only for Apollo. One day, Zephyrus killed him out of jealousy, and Apollo turned his blood into a flower, the hyacinth. Another Greek legend says the flower was formed by Apollo from the blood of Ajax when he killed himself. In any event there is a considerable amount of disagreement as to whether the plant the Greeks referred to as hyacinth was an iris, larkspur, gladiolus, turkshead lily, or hyacinth. The wild hyacinth is a native of the Levant, was first cultivated by the Dutch, and was introduced to England in the 16th century. Culpeper says it is of a styptic nature and its virtues are little known. The English used to mash the roots in white wine to hinder the growth of hair.

(2) A transparent red, brown, or orange variety of zircon, but anciently blue to violet: confused with the jacinth and sapphire. Placed on live coals, it extin-

guishes them without injury to itself. It is an aid to childbirth and drives away phantoms.

Hyde, Douglas (1860–1949) known in Ireland as *An Craoibin Aoibinn*, the Excellent (or Delightful) Branch: Irish folklorist, poet, and statesman, born in County Roscommon, the youngest son of a clergyman. He was educated at Trinity College, Dublin, where he got his D.Litt. in 1906. He founded the Gaelic League for the preservation of the Irish language and was its first president (1893–1915), was president also of the Irish Texts Society, and became professor of modern Irish at the National University of Ireland (1909–32). He was a member of the Irish Senate (1909–19) and served as president of Ireland (1938–45). His *Mediaeval Tales from the Irish* (1899) was the first collection of folktales in Irish. Among his other works are: *Beside the Fire* (London, 1890), *Love Songs of Connacht* (Dublin, 1893), *Three Sorrows of Story-Telling* (1895), *Story of Early Irish Literature* (1897), *Literary History of Ireland* (1899), *An Sgeuluide Gaoðalac* (1898–1901), *Lad of the Ferule*, being volume 1 of the publications of the Irish Texts Society (1899), *Religious Songs of Connacht* (Dublin, 1906), *Legends of Saints and Sinners* (Dublin, 1915).

Hygeia or **Hygieia** The Greek goddess of health, worshipped in connection with Æsculapius and deemed to be his daughter, or, as in later Orphic writings, his wife. Originally the guardian of physical health, she later became the goddess of mental health, and eventually a protectress against various kinds of danger, a development she shared with Æsculapius. Hygeia was represented as a kind maiden in a long robe feeding a serpent from a dish.

Hyginus, Gaius Julius (died 17 A.D.) Latin author. A Spaniard, he was appointed head of the Palatine Library by Augustus, but is said to have become so poor when old that he was supported by friends. Of his many works, on biography, agriculture, Vergil, etc., only fragments survive. The two works traditionally attributed to him, *Fabularum Liber* and *De Astronomia*, are held to be by other hands. Both works are drawn from Greek sources: the former, about 300 short mythological sketches, contains a genealogy of the gods and makes use of Greek plays now lost; the latter is a compendium of star myths and an astronomical text.

Hylas In Greek legend, the page of Hercules on the Argonautic expedition: probably, from the legend and the circumstances it explains, originally a minor vegetation deity. Hercules having broken an oar, the Argo put in on the coast of Mysia, and Hylas was sent to find water. He did locate a spring, but the naiads inhabiting it decided, because of Hylas' beauty, to keep him for themselves and dragged him into the water. When he did not return, Hercules set out to find him, and the Argo sailed without the hero. The angry Hercules enlisted the aid of the inhabitants of the region in the search, and annually thereafter at Prusa a festival took place in which the people patrolled the mountains calling for Hylas by name.

Hymen or **Hymenæus** In Greek mythology, the personification of the marriage song: the myths all seem to be attempts to explain the use of the name in the refrain. In one story he was a youth who was killed on his wedding day when the house collapsed, and thus he was invoked to appease his ghost. In other stories he rescued a group of women from pirates and was honored by having marriage songs named for him. In Orphic belief, Hymen was one of those brought back to life by Æsculapius.

Hyperboreans In Greek mythology, a race living in the far north "beyond the north wind," who were connected with the worship of Apollo: probably a reminiscence of some tribe or tribes along the amber routes who worshipped one of the gods later developed into Apollo. Herodotus does mention the Hyperboreans sending offerings to Delos.

Hyrieus In Greek mythology, a Bœotian king; father of Orion; son of Poseidon. He was king of Hyria (or Uria), and had no children. Once Zeus, Poseidon, and Hermes visited him, and in return granted him a wish. He of course asked for a son. The three gods then stood around an oxhide and urinated on it and told the king to bury it in the earth for ten months. The child born from the ground at the end of that time was called, after the act which brought him birth, Urion (later changed to Orion). Hyrieus was also possessor of a treasure which was stolen by Agamedes through a hole in the treasury wall: a story similar to that of the treasure of Rhampsinitus.

Iacchus The principal god of the Eleusinian mysteries; the third member, with Demeter and Cora (Persephone), of the mystic triad: often called the Phrygian Bacchus to distinguish him from the Theban Bacchus, Dionysus, but nevertheless the two are often confounded. Iacchus was the son of Demeter and Zeus and the brother of Persephone; hence, he is sometimes called Corus, the male Cora. He is also occasionally called the son of Persephone, and confused with Zagreus; or he is the husband of Demeter: or he is the son of Dionysus; or he is equated with Dionysus himself. This confusion of tradition exists because Iacchus had no mythology apart from the mysteries, about which information is often untrustworthy because of the disinclination of the initiates to make knowledge of the cult general.

On the sixth day of the Eleusinian festival, the statue of Iacchus was carried in a riotous procession to Eleusis, the initiates dancing and singing the *Iacchus*, the song named for him. Herodotus reports that just before the battle of Salamis the Greek allies of Xerxes saw a cloud of dust as from thousands of people and heard the chorus of the *Iacchus* swelling from it; they thus sensed their impending defeat. Liber is probably identical with the Eleusinian Iacchus.

Iambe In Greek mythology, a woman of Thrace, daughter of Pan and Echo. A slave maiden in the house of Celeus, she by her obscene jesting and gestures made the grieving Demeter smile when the goddess was on her search for Persephone. It was said that iambic poetry was named for Iambe either because the dances with which she amused Demeter were in iambic meter or because she hanged herself in remorse for the actions. See BAUBO.

Iasion or **Iasius** In Greek mythology, the father of Pluto or Plutus. He lay with Demeter in a thrice-plowed grain field and begot thereby the son whose name signifies wealth. The myth is probably an explanatory survival of an old Corn-Mother rite practiced in very early times in Greece. The parentage and the later career and death of Iasion vary in the several myths built up around him. He may have been originally a consort of the pre-Hellenic goddess of agriculture; the myth may have been adapted and incorporated when the identification of the Corn-Mother with Demeter was made. See HIEROS GAMOS.

Íbáhi "Long nose," "gray one," "white painted": the clown associated with the gahe, or Apache crown dancers. His enactment is purely voluntary and he furnishes his own outfit. He wears a long-eared, long-nosed mask of scraped rawhide, a gee string, and white body paint. He serves as messenger for the gahe and as fun-maker, preserving speechlessness during all absurd actions. Though it is not dangerous to touch him, he has more power than the other masked dancers during curing rites. [GPK]

ibeji The Yoruban term for twins, the equivalent of the Dahomean *hohovi*. The word has survived in the New World, retaining its aboriginal significance in Brazil and Cuba. The *ibeji* figures, carved of wood by the Yorubans and also found in Dahomey, represent the spirits of twins, and are a famous category of African art objects. [MJH]

Iberogun The culture hero of the Cuna Indians of Panama. He taught people what to eat, how to prepare it, how to build houses, how to brew maize beer, how to mold gold, how to celebrate girls' puberty, and a number of other things which are part of the modern culture of the Cuna. [GMF]

Iblis or **Eblis** In Moslem belief, the chief of the spirits of evil; the prince of darkness. Originally he was a great angel, called Azazil or al-Haris. But when God commanded the angels to bow before Adam he refused, arguing that a being made of fire as he was could not prostrate himself before a thing of clay. He was condemned to death, but obtained a stay of sentence until the day of the final judgment. He is called Al-Jann, the father of the Jinn, who commands them; he is the chief of the shaitans, the evil spirits. Each man is born with seven of Iblis' aides, and only two angels: thus the influence held over men by this parallel to the Judeo-Christian Satan. Iblis inhabits waste and unclean places, ruins and tombs. His food is the sacrifices made to idols. Mohammed, according to tradition, said Iblis lived principally at the bath, frequented the marketplaces and crossroads. His food was everything eaten without the blessing of the name of God; his drink was intoxicating liquor of any kind. Musical instruments were his muezzins; poetry was his Koran; the marks made in geomancy were his alphabet. And women were his traps.

Icarius In Greek mythology, a native of Attica who played host to Dionysus. In return for his hospitality, the god taught Icarius the art of the vine. Icarius shared his wine with his neighbors who, getting drunk, thought that they were poisoned and killed Icarius. His daughter Erigone (Spring-born) or Aletis (Wanderer) and his dog Mæra finally found his body where the shepherds had buried it. She hung herself, whereupon the three were placed by Zeus or Poseidon among the stars, he as Arcturus or Boötes, she as the Virgin, and the dog as Canis Minor. A drought or a suicidal mania among young women was sent by Dionysus to afflict the Athenians and was alleviated only by the institution of a festival in honor of the father and daughter.

Icarus In Greek mythology, the son of Dædalus. He was warned by his father not to fly too close to the sun when the two were escaping from Crete with the wings Dædalus had contrived. But Icarus flew too high, the heat of the sun melted the wax which held the wings together, and he fell to his death in the Icarian Sea, called so after him. Hercules was said to have found the body when it was washed ashore and to have buried it.

ich-kanava Literally, great tellings: the long migration myths and war tales of the Mohave Indians.

Idomeneus In Greek legend, the chief of the Cretans before the walls of Troy. On his way back from the siege, his ship was caught in a storm and he made an oath to sacrifice to Poseidon the first thing he encountered on landing safely. As in the case of Jephthah and other makers of hasty oaths, this was his own son. As a result, either because he fulfilled his vow or because he tried to and did not succeed, a plague struck Crete and Idomeneus was exiled.

Idun, Idhunn, Ithunn, or **Ithun** In Teutonic mythology, the goddess of Spring who possessed the golden apples of eternal youth. She married Bragi, god of poetry, and went to live in Asgard. She kept the gods young with the apples which the dwarfs and giants coveted. The giant Thiassi persuaded Loki to lure her out of Asgard, and carried her off to his realm. When the gods learned of Loki's treachery, they commanded him to get her back. Loki borrowed Freya's falcon garb, changed Idun into a nut, and carried her back in his beak. Another saga says that she fell out of Yggdrasil into Hel.

Ifa The Yoruban term for the divining cult, held to have come from the Nigerian town of Ife. See FA. [MJH]

ifrit (feminine *ifritah*) See AFRIT.

I Gave My Love a Cherry An American love song, a survival of *Captain Wedderburn's Courtship* (Child #46) of which only the riddle and answer part remains in oral tradition.

Igigi In Babylonian mythology, the spirits appearing as the stars of heaven above the horizon: the Anunnaki were the spirits of the stars below the horizon. The Igigi were the assistants of the chief of the gods, Anu, Marduk, etc., invoked before battles, and fighting for Babylon in just causes.

Ikanam The creator of the Chinook Indians of the lower Columbia River region of Oregon and Washington. See ITALAPAS. [EWV]

ik!anam Chinook term for myth, or a story about the early world that was entirely different from today's world. See ADAOX.

Ikxareyavs The *dramatis personæ* of Karok Indian mythology, now existing as animals, birds, plants, rocks, and ceremonies. They were the Indians who inhabited the Karok country along the Klamath River before the Karok came, and are believed to have departed only a very short time ago. Long Snake was once one of them; so was Bluejay, Spring Salmon, Redfish, Coyote, Lizard, and others. The Karok cling faithfully to the laws and precepts of the Ikxareyavs. All their myths are stories about the Ikxareyavs and *pikváhahirak,* the mythic times, or the days of the Ikxareyavs.

ila The word for dread among the Bechuana peoples of central South Africa: their equivalent for the concept of tabu. The Zulu form *zila* is a verb form meaning to abstain from. For instance, to the Bakatla tribe or clan, i.e. "they of the monkey," the monkey is *ila;* they neither harm nor eat it. Among those whose totem is the crocodile, the crocodile is *ila.* Compare HLONIPA.

Ila or Ida In Vedic mythology, a sacrificial goddess, personification of the oblation of butter and milk as well as praise: sometimes considered a goddess of the earth. According to the *Brāhmaṇas,* after the Deluge Manu went down with Ila from the northern mountains where his ship had come to rest and renewed the human race. According to the *Purāṇas* she was the wife of Buddha and mother of Purūravas. In another legend Ila was the son of Manu but incurred the wrath of Pārvatī and was changed into a woman. After listening to the supplications of Ila's friends, Śiva and Pārvatī agreed that Ila should alternate monthly as male and female.

illa The generic name for all kinds of amulets and talismans among the Incas and their modern descendants. These amulets are stones or plants of unusual shape, bezoar stones, or good luck objects. The prosperity of sheep or llama was also associated with one particular animal that was regarded as the illa of the herd. [AM]

illuminating beauty A motif (F574.1) of numerous folktales in which a woman's beauty is luminous or so great as to shine in a dark place. The "Story of Mṛigānkadatta" in the *Kathā Sarit Sāgara* tells how that prince on his wedding night discovered that the beauty of his bride lit up the room so that no lamps were needed. And the "Story of Somaprabhā" from the same source describes how her beauty illumined the room the minute she was born, and how her face outshone the moon the night her husband discovered she was divine, not human. The motif appears to be especially characteristic of Indian folktale, but has numerous other Asiatic (including Siberian) and European parallels. Balder's beauty was said to shine. The luminous face was a sure sign of royalty in ancient Celtic belief.

Ilmarinen (1) God of wind and good weather (*ilma*) of the Finns "giving calm and bad weather, and fur-

thering travelers (sailors)," according to Agricola. (See Harva in *FUF* XXIX, 1946, pp. 89–104).

(2) One of the heroes of the *Kalevala* (see songs 10, 18–19, 37–38, 49), the eternal smith. He forged the sky, Sun and Moon, and the famous Sampo, even a golden wife for himself. He was a good friend to Väinämöinen and they often went on adventures together. [JB]

Ilmatar A Finnish goddess: Daughter of the Air. She is the creator of the world and the mother of Väinämöinen (see *Kalevala,* songs 1–2). Sometimes she is called Luonnotar, Daughter of Creation. See FINNISH FOLKLORE. [JB]

ilu Literally, drums: term for the praise-name of an African Yoruba chief as drummed out on his drums. See AFRICAN AND NEW WORLD NEGRO FOLKLORE.

Imilozi Literally, whistlers: ancestral spirits of Zulu religion and folklore, who whistle as they speak. That ghosts communicate by whistling is a fairly widespread belief.

immortality Exemption from death or oblivion; eternal life: a widespread belief concerning the human soul which is held to continue for eternity in an afterworld (heaven, hell, paradise, etc.) or on earth as another human being or an animal (metempsychosis, etc.). The practice of burial among the prehistoric forerunners of modern man has led to the conjecture that man's belief in immortality is as old as the species: preservation of the body so that the soul may have a dwelling-place. Egyptian mummification, statues of ancestors or great heroes throughout the world, sacred trees and tombs or other dwelling-places of ancestors all testify to this belief. In Europe, the ancestral spirits developed into gnomes and fairies and eventually into gods; elsewhere in the world the immortal spirits of the ancestors are more obviously apparent. The ancestral spirit never dies as long as descendants live upon earth; so too a god never dies while he has a worshipper. These beliefs vary according to the belief held, in time and place, concerning the soul and the afterworld. See WATER OF LIFE.

☞ Immortality in China is not attained only after death, in which case death is merely a transition from one phase of being to another. Death can be dispensed with. Immortality can be attained by eating the pill of immortality or the elixir of life or strengthening one's essence by exercises. The Taoist teaching about breathing and other exercises has not been studied. Two of the most common exercises for attaining immortality are the "proper" and the "criminal." The proper method is to observe all the virtues, study the classics, and exercise self-discipline. This is the long and hard way which many people lack the power to follow. The criminal way involves occult erotic practices. In brief the principle assumes that a part of one's life is discharged at the moment of orgasm. If orgasms occur simultaneously between persons of equal strength, neither loses. Shape-shifters however steal vital essence by assuming the shapes of maidens or youths and seducing human beings. They induce a high degree of erotic power, until in the course of time the lover or mistress having exhausted his vital essence becomes tubercular and dies, while the shape-shifter having absorbed his vital essence in addition to his own becomes ever more powerful and lovely. These criminal practices are frequently punished by the Thunder God, who is more powerful than the Immortals. [RDJ]

☞ Some North American Indian tribes, as for example the Shawnee of the Eastern Woodlands, attribute much longer lives to the first people who lived before the deluge than is now enjoyed by the present inhabitants of the world. Whether or not this is an idea borrowed from Europeans is not clear. To their deities the Indians attribute immortality, and the idea of a life after death for humans, and also for animals, is of course current throughout North America. Very widespread, especially in eastern North America, is the myth in which human beings request eternal, or merely very long, life. Such an immoderate request is usually made to the culture hero, and the latter's answer is to turn the supplicant into a stone or a cedar tree. [EWV]

Imperial Cults of China   Rites of worship performed by the Emperor. In his capacity of priest-king, the Emperor of China was charged with maintaining balance among the forces of nature. Not only was it essential for him to perform proper ceremonies at appropriate times according to rituals elaborated by the Board of Rites, but failure in the proper performance of these functions produced national disasters. Conversely national disasters, when they occurred, were immediate proof that Heaven had withdrawn its mandate. Floods, crop failures, military defeat, famines, or high prices proved that the Emperor was no longer acceptable to Heaven and therefore should be put aside. The Great Sacrifices were those to Heaven, Earth, Imperial Ancestors, Gods of Land and Millet, Confucius, and the Protectors of the Dynasty. The Medium and Small Sacrifices were to the Sun and Moon, Agriculture, Silk Weaving, Mountains, Rivers, and Great Men. The Great Sacrifices were performed under the open sky. The relation between the Imperial Cults and Taoism, Confucianism, and the "religious systems of China" raises questions too complicated to be examined here. [RDJ]

impossibilities   The theme of a large body of folktales stressing the absurd, impossible, or contrary to nature. Often the victim of the impossible task counters with another impossibility: when told to build a castle between heaven and earth, he asks for the materials; if told to make a rope of sand, asks for the pattern (H1021.1.1); if challenged to hatch boiled eggs (H1023.-1.1) counters with the request that the other sow cooked corn and harvest the crop. The story of the mice that ate the iron balance (thought to be of Buddhist origin) appears in its first literary form in the *Jatakas*. The classical Greeks and Romans had a byword meaning Nowhere: *where mice eat iron*. See ABSURDITY REBUKES ABSURDITY; BERRIES IN WINTER; BUILDING CASTLE BETWEEN HEAVEN AND EARTH; CATCHING A MAN'S BREATH; HORSE LEARNS TO LIVE WITHOUT FOOD; NEVER; NOODLES; QUESTS; TASKS.

imrama   Literally, voyages: a class of Old Irish stories in which the voyage itself provides the main interest. Those now extant in manuscripts are *The Voyage of Bran and His Adventure* (about the 8th century), *Imram Curaig Mael Duin* or *Voyage of the Coracle of Maelduin*, (11th, 14th, 16th centuries), *Voyage of the Ui Corra*, *Voyage of the Coracle of Snédgus and Mac Ríagla*, and the *Voyage of Brandon*.

The voyages are prompted usually either by revenge, as in the case of Maelduin, or pure love of travel, or desire to find the Happy Isles. The voyagers visit innumerable islands ("thrice fifty isles" in the case of Bran) inhabited by supernatural or otherwise marvelous men, women, birds, or animals. The voyagers land here and there, or are not allowed to land; they see strange things, are told strange things, and inevitably learn new wisdom. They always eventually arrive at an island more beautiful and marvelous than the others, whose description reveals that some Christian concept of heaven has been superimposed on or adapted to the ancient Celtic visualization of the Otherworld. Sometimes the voyagers return home to tell the tale; sometimes they fall away in a whiff of dust the minute a foot is set to shore, as if they had been dead 200 years.

The flavor of the primitive Celtic Otherworld is strong in the Voyages of Bran and Maelduin: the Isle of Laughter or Joy is in both; the Isle (or land) of Women is in both. Music, feasts, drinking, lusty health, splendor are part of the visioned quest, promised, sought, found. "A beautiful game they play, sitting at the luxurious wine, Men and women under a bush, without reproach—." And the distant isle promised to Bran was "without grief, without sorrow, without death, without any sickness or age."

The Christian tone becomes stronger, however, in the Snédgus and Mac Ríagla travels. In the *Voyage of Brandon* the final elysian isle is definitely the Christian heaven. Compare ECHTRAI.

Inanna or **Nina**   The Sumerian mother goddess; queen of heaven: later identified with Ishtar. She was the patroness of Nineveh. Her descent to the underworld is the subject of a Sumerian poem. See ISHTAR.

Inapertwa or **Inapatua**   In Australian Aranda (Arunta) mythology, rudimentary creatures from which two Numbakulla, or self-existing sky deities, made animals, plants, and birds, which they then fashioned into human beings. Thus, each individual belongs to the totem the name of which is that of the plant or animal from which he was transformed. The Numbakulla themselves then became lizards. [KL]

Inari   The Rice or Harvest God of Japan. [JLM]

Inconstant Lover   An American folk song; one of the ancestors of *Old Smoky*. It includes stanzas with the words "meeting's a comfort and parting's a grief,"—etc., recognized in phrases of *The Cuckoo* or *The Wagoner's Lad*, and of some texts of *Old Smoky*.

incremental repetition   Term applied by Gummere to one of the narrative techniques of the ballad: that each succeeding stanza is constructed as a substantial repetition of the one before, with the addition of one new element or fact in the plot. This device was of mnemonic importance in the oral transmission of the ballad stories. The question and answer stanzas, as used in *Barbara Allen* and *My Man John* constitute one typical form of incremental repetition, as does also the CLIMAX OF RELATIONS.

incubus (plural *incubi*)   The demon lover; in medieval European folk belief, an evil spirit in the shape of a man (more generally either in male or female shape, though the latter is specifically the *succubus*) who came in the night as a lover to women, and often sired a child. Into this concept of the incubus were poured all the earlier beliefs of supernatural lovers: misshapen children or twins were the offspring of these demons; their human mistresses were witches, or died of exhaustion as the result of their lovers' attentions; the incubi were handsome and virile, with such drawbacks as cloven feet and evil smell, etc. Elves and trolls, ancestral spirits and fauns, pilosi, dusii, and such wild deities and spirits combined with the tempting, malicious, shape-shifting Devil in popular belief to bring forth the incubus. The witch, of course, desired such a lover; but the innocent maiden, plagued by his advances, could protect herself with St. Johnswort and vervain and dill. The incubus was the nightmare as well, riding his victims in the dark. Merlin was the son of an incubus, and the entire race of Huns was popularly thought to be the offspring of forest spirits and female magicians. The demon lover motif is expressed in innumerable folktales and in such ballads as *Lady Isabel and the Elf-Knight* (Child #4) and *The Daemon Lover* (Child #243). Parallels to the incubi have existed all over the world since ancient times: the Greek Ephialtes and Satyrs, the Celtic dusii, the Hindu bhūts, the Arabic jinn, the Samoan hotua poro, among others.

Indian and Persian folklore and mythology India and Persia are distant lands. According to our notions, they are romantic lands, languorous and mysterious. Unfortunately, much of the mystery rests on lack of knowledge, for the modern folklore of these regions has yet to be collected. Yet some information is available and when all is said and done India and Persia are still lands of wonder. The characters of their folklore inhabit a kind of border land of miraculous reality.

The difficulty in obtaining a true picture of Indian and Persian folklore lies not in eradicating romance and mystery but in expanding our concepts to include so much else beside. The really strange part is the combination of the familiar and the everyday with the wondrous. In this article, therefore, it may be well to give the familiar aspects of Indian and Persian folklore before the wondrous or miraculous aspects, and then to turn to the rich literary tradition and to a consideration of the living folklore, especially of India. *Familiar aspects* Both India and Persia spring from the Indo-European tradition which was also parent to the civilizations of Greece and Rome, Europe, and modern America. Although the archeological and historical record goes back many centuries farther, the Indo-European linguistic tradition is well established for the second millennium before Christ. At that time Sanskrit was being used in India and a closely allied tongue, Avesta, was common in Iran.

The ancient kingdom of Iran covered the modern countries of Iraq and Iran, the territory once included in Media, Bactria, and Persia. It was first conquered by Alexander the Great in the 4th century before Christ and later submerged by wave upon wave of Mohammedan conquerors speaking forms of Arabic. Nevertheless, the Sanskrit roots of the language were retained in Pahlavi which was the precursor of modern Persian.

Sanskrit also remained strong in both the written and spoken languages of India. Hindustani has today many Sanskrit words and, despite its predominantly Mohammedan and Arabic background, Urdu likewise contains examples of both Persian and Sanskrit. Other languages of India show similar mixture of recent Indo-European tongues with the basic Sanskrit, and even the Dravidian languages, which are not Indo-European in origin, have been widely influenced by this vigorous Indo-European tradition.

Due to this common linguistic heritage the familiarity of Indian and Persian terms in folklore is sometimes startling. *Thag*, a thief and kidnapper, is clearly our *thug*; and the Arabic *ghul* used throughout India appears in Persian as *ghol* and is the same in meaning as our *ghoul*. Sometimes apparently similar words must be used with caution because of changes in meaning. Thus *pari, piri*, or *feri* is certainly our *fairy*, but she is no fingerling. She is an enchantress, human in size, in beauty, and in desire.

The familiarity does not rest solely upon language. In contrast with folklores which stem from thoroughly different cultural streams, such as those of the North American Indians, we feel at home in many of the stories of India and Persia because of similarities in our ways of life. There is talk of milk and bread, of gold and jewels, of farmers and wicked stepmothers, of heroines who are both beautiful and good. We, too, feel that the good should be rewarded and the evil punished. Yet we are equally aware that this does not always happen. So, in story, we tell of girls who marry princes, beggars who become kings, fools who have good fortune, and sons of wealth who lose their inheritance.

Many of the familiar aspects in these stories go back to the general stream of Indo-European cultural life. We come from the same historical past and our institutions have developed from the same ancient sources of civilization. It is small wonder that many of the same plots which occur scattered through European folklore collections turn up in both Persia and India. Not only were the sources of Indo-European life the same for us all but within the last millennium there has been frequent contact of one sort or another between the people of the West and these sections of the East. *Miraculous aspects* On the other hand, there is a haze of the unreal about the folklore of Persia and India. The staid, talking animals which play such a role in Grimm's tales and in African animal stories have their cycles here too. There are many earthy stories of daily routine told in a simple, sober style. But the favorite tales deal with fabulous beings in a magical world. Ogres and jinn, fairies and snake queens abound. Creatures and objects grow small or large, fly through the air, change form or become invisible, in rapid and often bewildering succession.

Two features of this magical myth world call for consideration. First, it is in part a world which goes back to an early religious setting. Both the dominant Hinduism and Mohammedanism of today have retained traces of earlier beliefs and, in spreading over greater areas and over greater numbers of people, have also absorbed local beliefs and deities. Many of these now find expression in folklore. Early magical beliefs are often said to have been similarly absorbed and retained at a folklore level. Some of these simple magical elements are shared by European folklore, but we have nowhere today the elaborate world of miracle easily accepted in Indian and Persian myth.

Because simple elements of magical belief can be shown to have a long history, it has often been postulated that the magical world of 20th century India represents an early stage in religious development. This postulate has never been satisfactorily demonstrated. On the contrary, non-magical elements of folklore can be shown to have as great antiquity as magical elements. Large blocks of population in India today, blocks numbering millions of persons, use magic and miracle, as we do, only as symbols or literary devices. It is not at all clear that the unreal world referred to in Indian and Persian folklore is due to an early religious setting, or that it exists because of such a setting.

The religious heritage of the Indo-European tradition has always held a strong other-worldly emphasis. All of us who share in that heritage have tended, at times of stress and under certain difficult circumstances, to take refuge in an other-world of happy fulfilment. The thought of such a world has buoyed up our faith in the everyday world and has been incorporated in various of our theologies. But the magic world of Indian and Persian folklore is not an other-world in this sense. It is a this-world. It is a place where people and jinn live together, where things do change form, and men can walk on water.

The second factor of this myth world which calls for consideration, therefore, arises out of the very fact that it is not necessarily tied with the recognized religions. In working with Indian story-tellers, it becomes clear that some among them actually conceive of themselves as living in such a world. The variation from one group to another is great, but in many cases persons do think of the real world as peculiarly insecure and unstable. A dog may be only a dog, but it may also be a transformed human or semihuman being. One can never be positive which it is. Objects can, and do, disappear by magical means. Poisons may be made healthful and the laws of nature may be reversed at any time. Myth elements are readily exchanged from the realm of story to the realm of nature, thus posing for the folklorist an anomalous situation in which some of his richest material comes from accounts of everyday happenings. Reality itself is miraculous.

The literary tradition The exchange which occurs in parts of these regions between narrative elements and interpretations of reality is paralleled by an exchange between the literary and oral traditions. When Sanskrit scholars have distinguished between oral and literary tales in their studies of Indian mythology, the distinction has rested upon form. The substance or content is known to have been indistinguishable. In both India and Persia, written mythological accounts go back in a continuous record for over 3000 years. Both traditions seem to have stemmed from a single source which was probably oral, and both have enjoyed a constant cross-fertilization between oral and written accounts.

The early Sanskrit tradition was formulated largely in terms of a basic conflict between the myriad forces of good and evil. After creation, the holy and the evil ones joined in battle and man shared the conflict or played his part in the final outcome. The core of Iranian religion, and its development in Zoroastrianism, lay in this conflict and in the colorful mythology which attended it. Perhaps the most typical story, told under various guises, dealt with the hero of light who conquered the monster or dragon of darkness and evil. The Sanskrit tradition also reflects a high degree of organization, with authority resting in the hands of hereditary kings. Courts were sumptuous and shifts in religion and politics were often staged, in both fact and mythology, as rebellions against this kingly authority. Such a schismatic movement, started in Zoroastrianism by Mani in the 3rd century A.D., spread across the known world from China to Britain and was particularly powerful among soldiers of the Roman Empire where it vied with early Christianity. Although the basic conflict between good and evil, light and darkness, is expressed in some form wherever there are Indo-European traditions, the concept reached its full vigor in Iran.

In India, the Vedas and the epics mirrored the same conflict. The earliest record of Indian mythology is contained in the *Rigveda* or "Hymn Veda." This, with the *Samaveda* (Chant Veda), the *Yajurveda* (Formula Veda), the *Atharvaveda* (Veda of the Atharvan priests), and the *Brāhmaṇas* or explanatory prose texts attached to them, date in the first and second millennium before Christ. The *Upanishads* or philosophical treatises and the *Aranyakas* or sylvan treatises attached to the *Brāhmaṇas* are somewhat later. The great epics are generally dated in the four centuries bridging the beginning of the Christian era. The *Bhagavadgita* is still probably the best loved portion of the *Mahābhārata* but the tales of the hero Rāma, in the form of the *Rāmāyana* composed by Tulsi Das in the late 16th century, run it a close second. The accounts of Hindu mythology found in the *Purāṇas* do not differ greatly from epic mythology. Although the oldest date from about 600 B.C. they are still an active literary form, thus bringing down to the present day the miraculous deeds of gods and heroes.

The scriptures of religious sects carry variants of the same mythology, and secular or semisecular stories closely paralleling the religious occur in such works as the *Jaimini Bharata,* and the *Gulistan* of Persia. The similarities are marked between these and the popular oral epics of the last century. Some heroes such as Rama of India and Rustam of Persia may be traced directly to their mythological prototypes but other heroes such as Rasalu of the Punjab and Hatim T'ai of Bengal cannot be so derived, despite the fact that so many like adventures are told of them. Indeed, it is fairly certain that the Rasalu tales go back to a Scythian or non-Aryan king of the first centuries A.D. and that Hatim T'ai is an Arab chief whose exploits are told over and over in Persia as well as in India. Real heroes blended into the mythological background, and the epic tradition has been kept constantly alive, fed with fresh materials from historic events.

On the other hand, purely magical elements, many of them secular in tradition, flourished throughout the Mohammedan world. Great encyclopedias of magic were compiled and elements of magic were incorporated in the epic tradition, for instance in the *Bakhtyar Nama,* a Persian romance of the Sinbad type. Their influence has been pervasive. Love stories are as old as mythology in the Sanskrit tradition. They have been affected by the same forces as the mythology and have been popular in literature and folktale. The great Persian epic, *Shāhnāmah*, by the 11th century poet Firdausi, and *Rasa Lila*, the modern Indian story of Radha's love for Kṛishṇa, are less well known in the West than the more corrupt *Arabian Nights*. In all of them, there has been that constant cross-fertilization between oral and written accounts which makes it so impossible to distinguish between literary and verbal traditions.

The literary traditions of Persia and India are tied to their Indo-European origins. Yet there may also have been cross-fertilization, especially in central and southern India, with Dravidian and other non-Indo-European sources which lacked writing. The pattern of Æsop's animal stories can be found in Sanskrit in both Persian and Indian literature. *Panchatantra* tales are told all over India. Peoples of other languages also tell animal stories. Collections of these must be made by the outsider and their history can only be reconstructed by intricate comparative methods. Most of this work remains to be done. Yet the rich oral traditions of the pre-Aryan-speaking Indians have certainly maintained themselves outside of the Indo-European tradition. The two have been neighbors for centuries. It seems fairly clear that there must also have been an exchange between traditions of Sanskrit origin and traditions from other linguistic and cultural backgrounds.

Folklore of modern India If we are constantly surprised by a strange mixture of the familiar and the miraculous in Indian folklore, we are equally surprised by its vitality. Too often folklore is collected in out of the way corners as a kind of heritage from a dying past. It gains an antiquarian aura which is quite false. Folklore may have its springs in the past. But it may also represent common emotional and intellectual responses on the part of a population which are either so immediate as not yet to have found written expression or so unlike the accepted literary forms as not to be written down. Much of the folklore of India has such a quality.

People who cannot write are not necessarily inarticulate. For many hundreds of years Indians have gathered to listen to holy men and teachers tell the stories of the books. They have learned complex forms of expression. Many, even outside of the groups of professional story-tellers, poets and singers, are highly articulate. If this is true of the past, it is supremely true of India today. In a land where newspapers are scarce, news of economic and political events finds expression in song or story. Old forms and old symbols serve new ends. An animal story or a parable may receive a new twist which reflects a shift in evaluation almost too subtle to be caught. Or a timely expression of public opinion may be repeated and passed from village to village only to disappear completely when its interest is over.

India may be largely illiterate but it is definitely articulate. Love stories, fairy stories, animal stories, parables, and tales of the gods are used as media for expressing new feelings and thoughts which must be assimilated to the old traditions and ways of life. Hero tales may follow an ancient pattern while they tell the trials of real men in a shifting political and economic scene. They are, as always, among the most popular of oral accounts. Though India is in transition, its long literary and oral heritage shows no signs of abating.

MARIAN W. SMITH

indigestion Disordered digestion; dyspepsia. In general folk belief indigestion can be cured by wearing a piece of red coral. In Newfoundland the plant called Labrador tea (*Ledum latifolium*) is used to quiet the stomach. The Negroes of the southern United States recommend wearing a penny around the neck to stave off indigestion, but offer also a number of very efficacious folk remedies, such as drinking hot water, or hot water containing ten drops of turpentine, taking a hot bath, etc. Vomiting will stop, they say, if the patient's medicine glass is turned upside down under the bed. For dyspepsia they recommend eating a little of the inner lining of the gizzard of a chicken or other domestic fowl, on the grounds that a tissue which can cope so easily with pebbles, sand, and bits of trash will surely aid human digestive inability.

The 11th century Bishop Marbod in his *Liber lapidum* (describing 60 stones) prescribes gagates diluted with water as a remedy for indigestion and constipation (see GAGATES). Tomasso Gianinni, philosopher of the 17th century, ascribed the melancholy of great men to indigestion instead of to the influence of the planets Mercury and Saturn, as then (and sometimes now) thought.

Indigetes (singular *Indiges*) The gods and heroes who had lived as mortals at Rome and were invoked and worshipped as the protectors of the state; especially, the descendants of Æneas. They are often associated with the gods, e.g. Mars, Vesta, Venus, who had a part in founding Rome, and are mentioned in connection with the Lares and Penates. In this respect, such personages as Janus, Evander, Hercules, Romulus were considered aspects of the supreme god.

Indo-European or **mythological theory** An explanation of the origin and meaning of folktales, first advanced by Jakob Grimm, augmented and amplified by Max Müller, Sir George Cox, Angelo de Gubernatis, and others. According to this theory folktales are the detritus of Indo-European myth and can best be understood by being studied in relation to myth. This theory is now largely discredited through the work of Andrew Lang and others, who have pointed out that many common folktales are by no means the exclusive property of the Indo-Europeans and that folktales generally reflect varying stages of culture and sophistication. See ANTHROPOLOGICAL SCHOOL; COMPARATIVE METHOD; DIFFUSION; FOLKLORE AND MYTHOLOGY; HISTORIC-GEOGRAPHIC METHOD. [MEL]

Indonesian (Malaysian) mythology With the East Indies, Americans, since school days, have a peculiarly sentimental, neighborly bond despite their distance from the Western Hemisphere. To this moist, tropical, and densely populated region Christopher Columbus was en route when he discovered America. He had been inspired by gossip about Marco Polo's stories of gold in abundance "to a degree scarcely credible," sweet-scented trees like sandalwood and camphor, and "pepper, nutmegs, spikenard, galangal, cubebs, cloves, and all other valuable spices and drugs." World War II made names of Indonesian islands, their inhabitants (over 40 million or 800 per square mile in Java alone), their rubber, spices and sugar, and political upheavals (independence for the Philippines and a United States of Indonesia in the south) familiar even to newspaper headline readers. Additional information increases the fabulous quality of the area. The oral literature of its most primitive tribes fascinates because well-known themes occur in exotic settings. The same tales that Uncle Remus told are among the most popular household stories among Indonesians, including the Borneo "wild men" who tell them in their pile dwellings, which are long enough to house a village and all its human skull trophies. Occasionally the characters are unfamiliar animals like, for example, Cousins Longtailed Monkey and Mouse-deer (an antelope-like creature less than a foot high).

The island area extending across the South Pacific from the Asiatic coast to New Guinea has been variously named and subdivided. Precedent exists, however, for applying the terms Indonesia or Malaysia to the region that encompasses the Philippines, the string of islands from Sumatra to Timor, which often is called the East Indies, to Borneo and Celebes, and, near New Guinea, many small archipelagoes labeled the Moluccas. Because the aboriginal Formosans speak Malayo-Polynesian dialects like nearly all islanders to the south, have a related culture, and belong to the same race, their island is included in Malaysia. Indonesian cultural affiliations with the mainland are indicated by the Southeast Asia Institute listing 16 regions from Assam eastward through Indonesia as constituting the Southeast Asia area (Heine-Geldern). In mythology and folk literature, the continuity between Indonesia and the southeastern part of the mainland is striking. India, because of its size, is a separate culture area, but no sharp break exists between its culture, including mythology, and that of the southeast which for centuries has been the recipient of the cultural richness of its great subcontinental neighbor.

Indonesia is the only South Pacific island area in which written literature has, since at least the beginning of the Christian era, greatly influenced the mythology. To the ancient, oral substratum of myths, folktales, and beliefs often reminiscent of Polynesia, Melanesia, and Micronesia, whose first inhabitants passed through Indonesia, there have been added strata of written literature from Asia and Europe. Cross-fertilization has occurred, so that today, as for a long time in the past, myths of primitive Indonesian tribes, distant from centers of higher culture, have details from the written literature which has diffused to them orally. And, similarly, local beliefs of ancient, primitive origin, have been incorporated into Indonesian versions of stories from the *Kathā Sarit Sāgara, Mahābhārata, Rāmāyana, Panchatantra, Jatakas,* and the *Arabian Nights,* to name but a few of the alien literary works. Parts of them had, of course, a folkloristic origin in lands from which traders and colonists introduced them into the South Pacific.

One of the earliest known homelands of the human race, as the bones of *Pithecanthropus erectus* of Java testify, Indonesia has been the crossroads of many different races and cultures. Some of them still persist in modified form. The Negritos, of unknown origin, were perhaps the first among surviving groups to arrive.

Later immigrants forced them into the interior of the Philippines, Malay Peninsula, and New Guinea, but by-passed them in the Andaman Islands, the only place where they have not lost their language and adopted Malayo-Polynesian dialects. Veddoids, related to Caucasians, were in turn pushed back to remote regions and now live in Ceylon, Celebes, and, in mixed form, in other islands. At some time, too, those peoples who settled Australia, Melanesia, Polynesia, and Micronesia, passed through Indonesia. Oceanic Negroid relatives of Melanesians occur, much mixed, in the Moluccas. The first Malays are called Proto-Malays to distinguish them from later relatives, the Deutero-Malays, who like them belong to the Mongoloid race. Proto-Malays clung to homes in islands off the main line of travel while Deutero-Malays claimed the coasts of major islands where, in the historic period, they came into direct contact with Hindus, Arabs, and Europeans.

To some extent, the prehistoric groups—Negritos, Veddoids, Proto-Malays, and Deutero-Malays—are distinguishable as to culture. Except for the hunters and gatherers among non-agricultural Negritos and Veddoids, Indonesians raise rice, for the most part, or maize and sago. Chickens and water buffalos are their principal domesticated animals; pigs are found only in non-Mohammedanized villages. Smaller animals find shelter under grotesque-roofed pile dwellings or village halls often used as men's clubhouses. Bamboo and rattan serve innumerable daily uses. Clothing includes either woven sarongs or tapa wrap-arounds. Whether nominally Mohammedans as very many are, Christians, or members of other alien sects, Indonesians maintain old beliefs in nature spirits, magic, and, most of all, ghosts of ancestors around whom cults with shamanistic practices exist. The amount of Hindu, Arabic, or European influence in mythology and folk literature depends largely on how close a tribe is to coastal areas reached by early foreign arrivals.

The application of Peer Gynt's metaphor of the onion with its many layers to the various racial and cultural strata of Indonesia is a useful academic device, if one remembers that a stew or compote is more descriptive of existing conditions. Certainly that is true of mythology, much as one may, in the present state of research in a complex area, hopefully grasp at what seem distinctive traits of each cultural layer.

The first, outstanding, literary influence of foreign, civilized origin came with Brahman and Buddhist colonizers from India. In the early centuries of the Christian era, they established great, conflicting kingdoms like, for example, Srivijaja, Malayau, Mataram, and Madjapahit, in Sumatra and Java. Often the authority of these kingdoms extended to nearby islands, parts of the Malay Peninsula, and even into Indo-China. This is not surprising since they controlled trade routes connecting the Pacific and Indian Oceans. Science, literature, and art, all frequent servants of religion, flourished, but did not long remain mere copies of Hindu forms. Buddhist-built Borobodur of Java, one of the great religious structures, preserves in statues and bas-reliefs the religious and mythological pantheon of India by depicting scenes from Buddha's incarnations. Kawi, a fusion of Sanskrit and Javanese, became the written medium through which Hindu epics, popularized in puppet shows and dramas with living actors, reached the people. It symbolizes the union of Hindu and native cultures which, increasingly, acquired an Indonesian coloring. The Malayo-Polynesian dialects were enriched by terms for Hindu spiritual, intellectual, and emotional concepts (Kroeber; Winstedt).

As Hindu control waned, Holy Wars of Mohammedans from southwestern Asia and India won for Allah not only followers but political power that reached a peak in the 15th century. Indonesian language and literature, except in lengthy, sentimental romances, were relatively little affected by Arabs. Bali, which remained Hindu, is today called a "museum piece" because it preserves, with Indonesian interpretations, the religion and culture of the Hindus, especially the Brahmans (Cole, 1945). Local Malayan nature spirits and Hindu deities like Indra, Śiva, and Ganeśa, together with cults for the honored, ancestral dead now unite in the totality of Balinese religion.

Following Mohammedans into Malaysia were Christians from the Netherlands, Spain, England, Portugal, and the United States. Chinese have been in and out of the area as long as any outsiders. Early Europeans exploring interior jungles rarely express surprise in their diaries at meeting, at a remote but strategic confluence of rivers, a solitary Chinese engaged in flourishing trade with head-hunting natives. Porcelain jars that Chinese used in trade became symbols of wealth and as sacred objects, the centers of cults (Cole and Laufer; Rutter; Ling Roth). Myths often mention the magical power of the jars and their ability to speak. Any self-respecting hero of a mythical romance in the Philippine Tinguian tribe can magically increase the number of jars ninefold or eighteenfold to win the girl of his choice (Cole, 1915).

Indonesia, not only in religion and mythology but in the rest of its culture as well, is like a much used blotter on which scrawled lines that criss-cross and often cover each other cannot always be deciphered even when held to the mirror of history. The complexity of the literature often leads scholars to attempt to distinguish the prehistoric, oral lore from introduced elements of the historic period and discuss them separately. For example, Dixon (1916) analyzed the mythology of the primitive tribes after trying to subtract whatever was identifiable as Indian or Islamic in origin. Winstedt (1940) dealt mainly with Hindu and Islamic phases of the written literature of the more advanced Indonesians. He included a chapter on mythology and gave specific examples of alien additions to native riddles, proverbs, fables, farces, and romances which circulate orally. He also described alien sources of themes in Indonesian masked dances, shadow plays, poetry, law codes, histories, and legends.

Dixon found that primitive tribes, predominantly Proto-Malay in type, like, for example, the Igorot, Ifugao, and Tinguian of the Philippines, had almost no real cosmogonic tales, the pre-existence of the world being usually assumed. Many myths tell about floods destroying the world which then was reconstructed. Igorot, for instance, narrate that the principal member of their pantheon, Lumawig, created mankind by laying out reeds in pairs which became human couples, each with a different language. Lumawig's sons caused a flood over the earth, leaving only a brother and sister alive, whom Lumawig ordered to marry though they objected. They repopulated the world, and Lumawig taught them customs and arts still practiced (Jenks, 1905).

A widespread Indonesian concept is that over a primeval sea stretched multiple heavens where lived gods who threw down rocks and other material from which to fashion the earth. Sometimes they went to live on rocks exposed in the sea. Birds commonly are their assistants. Dixon regards the concept as genetically related to western and central Polynesian cosmogonic myths which are later in origin than those of marginal Polynesia. Indonesian relationships with the area immediately to its east are with the Melanesian rather than the Papuan inhabitants. Indonesians generally credit the origin of human beings to creative acts by gods or miraculous origins from plants, trees, and eggs. Formosans, for example, are like the Andamanese, Japanese, and Filipino Tagalog, in narrating that mankind originated from a bamboo joint. Sumatran tribes, like those of other islands affected by Hindu and Arab contact, have themes similar to those in primitive tribes but tell them in far more elaborate style and add motifs of continental origin.

Indonesians tell many heroic romances, some of them in meter which Filipinos call corridos, and less sophisticated tales about supernatural heroes and heroines. All have a familiar ring to readers of the Arabian Nights and Hindu epics. Greatest of mythical heroes among the Borneo Dyaks is Klieng, who was found in a knot of a tree by his foster parent. Myths tell of Klieng's devotion to war, travel, and pleasure, and of his ability to transform himself into anything in the natural or supernatural world. To chant the story of his greatest deed, a war raid on the skies, requires a whole evening. The kana, or chant, of his adventures involves, according to collectors (Ling Roth), a perpetual play of alliteration and rime.

Leading characters in Tinguian tales of "the first times" include the couple Aponitolau and Aponibolinayen and their relatives. The prefix Aponi- is a term of address meaning Sir (or Madam) which is followed by the given name. The son of Sir Tolau and Madam Bolinayen was Kanag who had a magical origin similar to that of many heroes in his tribe. He was born when an itching spot on his mother's little finger was pricked. He courted a girl whose mother demanded that a spirit-house be filled nine times with jars, and golden beads be strung on a spider web surrounding the town.

Many popular tales are about the animal kingdom. Mouse-deer, tortoise, ape, tiger, and crocodile are a few of the actors who, dignified by titles and relationship terms from native vocabulary, function in a society and environment patterned after that of the narrator. Basic plots, of which Tar Baby is one, concern the triumph of a slow or weak but clever creature over his strong but slow-witted oppressor. Certain adventures came into Indonesia with the Panchatantra, Jatakas, and other written Indian collections. Others, according to Dixon, are local inventions, either original or patterned after Hindu models, while some that have diffused eastward may belong to an old stratum between the Negrito and Malay. Many themes in the animal-kingdom fables have spread back and forth over the world both by written and oral transmission. Aarne analyzed a tale, popular in Indonesia, about wandering animals and objects, showing how a simple story (of which the Bremen Town Musicians is a familiar European variant) has diffused over the world and assumed various forms.

In addition to cosmogonic myths, heroic romances, fables, and explanatory myths, a type of narrative called *diam* by Tinguians and *pengap* by Dyaks forms part of the mythology. A *diam* or *pengap* is a myth recited as a formula at a ceremony to invoke supernatural beings, who are characters in the myths and perform successfully acts which the human beings hope to imitate.

Among interesting studies of Indonesian lore is that by Fansler who points out world-wide parallels in his collection of Filipino tales. Cole (1915) has shown how Tinguian myths reflect the culture of the people. Radcliffe-Brown has discussed the significance of the myths of the Negrito Andaman Islanders as an expression of Andamanese social values.

References in the text are cited below; many include extensive bibliographies of mythological collections. R. Heine-Geldern, "Research on southeast Asia: problems and suggestions," Southeast Asia Institute (New York), n.d.; F.-C. Cole and B. Laufer, "Chinese pottery in the Philippines," *Field Mus. Nat. Hist., Publ.*, vol. 12, 1912; O. Rutter, *The Pagans of North Borneo* (London), 1929; H. Ling Roth, *The Natives of Sarawak and British North Borneo* (London), 1896; F.-C. Cole, "Traditions of the Tinguian," *Field Mus. Nat. Hist. Publ.*, vol. 14, 1915; and *The Peoples of Malaysia* (New York), 1945; R. B. Dixon, "Oceanic" in *Mythology of all races*, vol. 9 (Boston), 1916; R. O. Winstedt, "A history of Malay literature," *Malayan Branch Royal Asiatic Soc.*, vol. 17, 1940; A. E. Jenks, "The Bontoc Igorot," *Ethnol. Surv.*, vol. 1 (Manila), 1905; A. Aarne, "Die tiere auf der wanderschaft," *Folklore Fellows Commun.*, No. 11 (Hamina), 1913; Radcliffe-Brown, *The Andaman Islanders* (Cambridge), 1933; D. Fansler, "Filipino popular tales," *MAFLS*, vol. 12, 1921; A. L. Kroeber, *Peoples of the Philippines* (New York), 1928.

Other leading works include J. de Vries, *Volksverhalen uit Oost-Indie* (Zutphen) 1925–28; and Bezemer, *Volksdichtung aus Indonesien* (Haag), 1904. Dixon lists most of the journals publishing Indonesian myths.

KATHARINE LUOMALA

Indra (1) In Vedic mythology, the god of the atmosphere who governs the weather and dispenses rain; son of Dyaus or of Tvashtri and a cow or Nishtigri. His place as one of the greatest of the gods was won by slaying Vritra, the dragon of drought, thus releasing the withheld waters and generating the sun and the dawn. He is also the chief aid of the Aryans in their struggles against the Dasyus. He was feared as the ruler of storms, lightning, and thunder, but reverenced as the cause of fertility and bestower of rain. See AHI.

In later mythology Indra is still god of the atmosphere and the ruler of Svarga (Indra's heaven), but his position is inferior to that in the Vedas. He battled with the Suras against the Asuras after the Churning of the Ocean but only with the aid of Vishnu could he gain victory for the gods. Indra was then given the rule of the three worlds; the golden age followed in which, seated on Airāvata, he gazed over the contented world. But he fell into evil ways and finally slew Viśvarūpa, son of Tvashtri, who created Vritra to avenge his son. The gods tried to make peace and Vritra agreed to a reconciliation if he were promised immunity from Indra in wet and dry, from sword or javelin, wood or stone, during the day and the night. Indra, however, slew the monster despite the promise of the gods, meeting him at twilight at the junction of wet and dry on the seashore, slaying him with the thunderbolt and the foam of the sea. Then he fled to a remote lake and lived hidden in a lotus stalk. Drought followed and Vishnu finally promised Indra that he could regain his place by performing a horse sacrifice.

Many instances of adultery and incontinence are recorded in the later mythology of Indra. According to the *Mahābhārata* he tried to seduce Ahalyā, wife of Gautama, and as punishment became covered with a thousand marks or eyes. In the *Rāmāyana* Indra was defeated by Rāvana and carried off to Lankā (Ceylon). The gods had to sue for his release and grant Rāvana immortality.

According to the *Brāhmanas* he cut off the wings of the mountains because they were troublesome. In the epics he took part in human battles and placed the rainbow in the sky as a sign of his presence.

As a rain god Indra later absorbed the name Parjanya (a Vedic rain god) but in modern Hinduism receives no real worship as such. In Benares he has been superseded by Dalbhyeśvara.

Indra is depicted as red or gold in color with arms of enormous length, riding in a golden car drawn by two (sometimes 1100 or 10,000) ruddy horses. His weapons are the thunderbolt (a hundred-jointed, thousand-pointed instrument), the bow (rainbow) and arrows, a hook, net, and spear. He is a gigantic eater and drinker of soma which he stole from Tvashtri after he and the whole warrior race were excluded from it by the gods. His capital is Amarāvatī, his elephant Airāvata, and his horse is Uchchhaiḥśravas which came forth at the Churning of the Ocean.

Indra is not worshipped directly, although a festival is held in his honor. His fall from first rank is explained as having been caused by priests of the Brāhmana period who were rivals of the warrior class. As the god of conquest, Indra was the special god of this caste and thus undesirable in the eyes of the Brāhman caste, who were at the moment consolidating their position in Indian society. Indra has been identified with Thor and Tritā.

(2) (Pahlavi *indar* or *andar*, Persian *andar*) In Zoroastrianism, one of the six archfiends; aide of Angra Mainyu. According to the *Dinkart*, the spirit of apostasy who deceives men concerning their mode of life. Indra is the adversary of Asha Vahishta. [SPH]

industrial lore Occupational lore generally, including that of the crafts and trades, but more particularly the lore of manual, mechanized, and organized labor. Industrial lore first entered into the history of American folklore by way of the lore of handskills (folk arts and crafts), cooperative labor (raisings, log-rollings, quiltings), community activities (markets, auctions, fairs), occupational types and traditional callings (miller, cobbler, tailor, tinker, innkeeper, peddler, sailor, fisherman, miner, doctor, lawyer, clergyman), singing at work, street cries, signboards, trade jargon, and slogans. In New England the development of manufactures, commerce, lumbering, fishing, and shipping gave rise to the lore of Yankee peddlers (tin, woodenware, and clock), clockmakers, storekeepers, hucksters, sailors, skippers, fishermen, whalemen, and lumberjacks, and of Yankee inventions and Yankee notions. In the economic development of the South and the West, a rich body of occupational customs, beliefs, songs, stories, and lingos grew up around the great staples (cotton, tobacco, sugar, corn, wheat, hogs, cattle, sheep, lumber, turpentine, coal, oil, gold, silver, copper and iron ore, steel, furs, fruit) and the epic of freighting, canalling, flatboating, railroading, steamboating, Great Lakes shipping, mining, logging, ranching, and trail-driving.

The great American hero-types of the frontier (the trapper, the fur-trader, the buffalo-hunter, the miner, the logger, and the cowboy) were the product of the pioneering and craft period of industry, just as the so-called industrial heroes (Old Stormalong, Paul Bunyan, Pecos Bill, Gib Morgan) were industrial pioneers rather than industrialists. They belong to the days of wilderness-clearing and land-taking, of wooden ships and iron men, before the timber beast became a timber mechanic and when the boss worked side by side with the hand—the star-performers and hell-raisers who paved the way for the machine but (as in John Henry's contest with the steam-drill) represent man's last stand against it.

In the tightening of class lines and the sharpening of industrial conflict that accompany the mechanization, centralization, and unionization of industry, a new type of hero emerges. He is heralded by Joe Magarac, the Slav hero of the Monongahela Valley steel mills, who made rails by squeezing the hot steel through his fingers—four rails from each hand—and jumped into a furnace to make better steel, recalling memories of foundation sacrifice rites and stories of men who have fallen into vats of molten steel and been buried with the metal. In some versions Joe Magarac is the class-conscious worker who believes that the mills belong to the men rather than the men to the mills.

A typical hero of organized labor is Joe Hill (Joseph Hillstrom), a western migratory worker and I.W.W. organizer of Swedish birth, who wrote some of the most stirring militant workers' songs such as "The Preacher and the Slave," a version of "Hallelujah, I'm a Bum," and a parody of "Casey Jones" (in which Casey is a scab on the S.P. line, who dies and goes to heaven, where he keeps on scabbing until the Angels' Union, Number 23, throws him into hell). He was executed in Salt Lake City, November 19, 1915, on an alleged murder charge, his last words being: "The cause I stand for means more than any human life—much more than mine. Let 'er go!"

The bulk of industrial lore consists of esoteric sayings, jokes, and anecdotes that go the rounds of the workers; initiation ceremonials and practical jokes in which new hands are sent in search of impossible objects; and tall tales of rivalries between old and new hands, piece workers and day workers, hand workers and machine workers, and backward (in the union sense) and advanced workers. A favorite butt of satire in Midwest auto plants is the worker from the sticks (True Blue Highpockets) "who sells his labor at a minimum and sets a pace in getting out the work" (*New Masses*, Vol. LIX, April 23, 1946, p. 14). At the same time there is a survival of the frontier-hero tradition of the hand-craftsman, strong man, or tough customer like the Demon Bricksetter from Williamson County ("I'm a man as is work-brickle. I'm a man as can't say quit. When I lay a-holt, I'm like a turtle and I don't let loose till it thunders") or Slappy Hooper, the world's biggest, fastest, and bestest sign-painter, who feels like giving up because "they don't want big sign-painting

and they don't want true-to-life sign painting, and he has to do one or the other or both or nothing at all" (*A Treasury of American Folklore*, 1944, pp. 532, 550).

A distinctive, if elusive, part of contemporary industrial lore is the metropolitan lore of New York City and Chicago collected by the Federal Writers' Project in 1938 and on file in the Library of Congress—a hard-boiled, hard-hitting lore of gags, wisecracks, and trade jargon with a sharpened sense of economic struggle and competition—of taxi drivers, sandhogs, structural steel workers, plasterers, longshoremen, marine telegraph operators, and workers in the needle trades, packing plants, department stores, restaurants, and hospitals.

B. A. BOTKIN

inexhaustible food, drink, object, etc. A widespread folktale motif (D1652 ff.) in which food, drink, or treasure keeps magically renewing itself, or the object containing it is mysteriously and continuously replenished. The motif is known all over Europe, is especially prominent in Celtic mythology and folktale (the Dagda had one boar always on the spit, and one alive, for instance), is known also in Japan and China, in all the Pacific cultures, and among the North American Indians.

The classical examples are the horn of plenty and the flowing wine and rich viands in the story of Philemon and Baucis and their hospitality to the gods. *Exodus* xvi describes the manna which the Hebrews gathered every morning in the wilderness: "he that gathered much had nothing over, and he that gathered little had no lack" (D1031.1.1). *Mark* vi describes the related miracle of the loaves and fishes (D1032.1).

In folktale the inexhaustible purse, bag, chest furnish money (D1451 ff.), magic tables, pots, caldrons, pitchers, etc., supply food and drink (D1472.1.7 ff.). In Europe we find inexhaustible bread, cake, cheese (D1652.1.1 ff.), in Indonesia inexhaustible rice (D1652.1.3), inexhaustible apples and cows with never-failing milk supply in Irish folklore (D1652.1.7; D1652.3).

☞ The inexhaustible food supply is an incident in many North American Indian tales, widespread over the entire continent. Sometimes food is contained in a cup or kettle; sometimes it takes the form of a nut or bone that can never be consumed. Oftentimes a small quantity of inexhaustible food is set before a hungry visitor(s); the person thinks to himself that the quantity is minute, but finds to his surprise that he can never finish it. His unspoken thoughts on the matter are frequently divined and answered aloud by his host. See BERRIES IN WINTER. [EWV]

infanticide Killing children at or shortly after birth for reasons of convenience, economy, fear, shame, or religion: formerly frequent and lawful, and still obtaining in some primitive cultures. When it occurs, sporadically and abnormally, among the more complex cultures, it is most frequently due to the shame of the unmarried mother.

The economic motivation of infanticide is most clearly seen in the South Sea islands where circumscribed area and limited food supply have for centuries made some method of population control obligatory. Sir James Frazer states that the Polynesians seem regularly to have killed two thirds of their offspring. His figures were corroborated for Tahiti by the Rev.

J. M. Orsmond during the first half of the 19th century. His manuscripts, edited and supplemented by his granddaughter, Miss Teuira Henry, and published by the Bernice P. Bishop Museum (*Ancient Tahiti*, 1928), furnish the best picture we have of this primitive society before it was influenced by contact with continental cultures.

The first missionaries found that *more* than two thirds of the children were destroyed "generally before seeing the light of day. Sometimes in drawing their first breath they were throttled to death, being called *tamari'i 'u'umi hia* (children throttled)."

While the original reason for infanticide in the islands was primarily economic, certain other reasons were given to the missionaries by the natives, and evidently accepted as true. Mr. Orsmond and his granddaughter give as the chief reasons for infanticide, "to keep the abyss wide between the royal family and commonalty, and for the regulation of the *arioi* society."

The lowest of the eight orders of the arioi had only small tatau (tattoo) marks in the hollow of the knees, and their children were not permitted to live. "If any saved their babes they were dismissed in disgrace from the society." But parents of the highest order, covered with tatau marks until they were black from the groin down, must not kill their children, since they were considered descendants of gods, and would inherit the royal titles of their parents. Candidates for admission to the lowest order must have no children and solemnly pledged infanticide if offspring came.

In spite of economic and societal requirements, the Tahitian infant did have a possible chance of escaping annihilation. Since infanticide was a family affair among the lower orders, with near relatives of both sides of the family attending the birth, and since the paternal relatives might urge that the child be killed while the maternal group wished to save it, there might be contention. If the quarrel lasted long enough for the child to draw breath and open its eyes, it was allowed to live, because it had its own *iho* (personality) and could not be doomed to *puaru* (child destruction).

Infanticide in India was likewise due to overpopulation and recurrent famine, but just as the Tahitians rationalized the custom into a support of a caste system so the Hindu people sometimes justified their throwing of infants into rivers as a religious sacrifice to a crocodile god. A more humane Indian infanticide was accomplished by allowing the child to nurse from its mother's breast which had been anointed with datura or opium.

Even more drastic than the Polynesian two-thirds annihilation of the newborn was the practice of the Jagas, a West African Angola tribe, where all children without exception were killed, but for a different reason. The Jagas were always fighters, marauders on the march, and mothers carrying infants were highly undesirable hindrances to speed. One would expect that the tribe itself would soon disappear, but it was kept to full strength by the simple expedient of adopting the adolescent children of the parents whom the Jagas had surprised, overcome, and eaten.

In the Chaco Mbaya women killed all their children except the one they thought would be the last one. If another one came, it was killed. Naturally, since the Mbaya adopted no children, the nation dwindled, and the branch in which the women were most assiduous in the practice completely disappeared.

In several East African tribes, according to reports from Father Picarda of the Catholic Missions in the 1880's, two thirds of the newborn were killed, since only those born in certain unusual presentations were saved.

There are many tribes where infanticide, although not generally practiced, is permissible in certain instances and under recognized circumstances. Among the Guiana Indians of South America, in one tribe or another, three situations justify killing the child: if it is a female, or a cripple, or one of twins.

On the Orinoco a woman who bears twins is thereby dishonored and is likely to be called a rat by the other women. Among the Salivas on the west bank of the Orinoco if a woman bore a child and was aware that another was about to come, she would conceal the fact in spite of great pain and bury it secretly lest her neighbors torment her and her husband be angry with her. Because he could not possibly believe that more than one of the twins was his own, he would consider her disloyal to him. In many tribes, it is the second twin that is killed, unless one is male and the other female. In that case, the female is doomed. This practice of killing girl babies, which often prevails even where there is no choice of twins, is defended by the mothers themselves who say that they do not wish the girl to grow up and suffer as they have, being women. In those tribes where the husbands treat their wives better, there is less murdering of female infants.

Among these Guiana Indians the methods used are breaking the neck, pressing on the breastbone, cutting the umbilical cord so near the navel that it cannot be tied and the infant bleeds to death, exposure, and a method regarded by the natives as so humane that they call it a word meaning "without hurting it at all." The process is simply burying the child alive. Many South American Indians kill without hesitation children who are born hunchbacked, lame, dwarfed, crippled, malformed, or with a harelip.

Among Chaco groups, twins are usually killed, either buried alive or exposed by the tribal shaman, since their birth is a bad omen. The killing is rationalized on the theory that no woman can possibly nurse two children. An unmarried girl kills her child without hesitation. If a woman has a bad dream just before childbirth, she may kill the child, and if a mother dies in parturition, the child is buried alive with her. Among these seminomads, many children are a burden.

Another and rather unusual cause of infanticide obtains among several Chaco tribes. It is the custom for a woman there to refrain from sexual intercourse with her husband during her nursing period, and since it is also the practice to nurse children for 3 or 4 years, she often chooses to kill the child rather than lose her husband. In 1870 a Jesuit reported of one Chaco tribe that they recognized four reasons for infanticide: scarcity of food, any suspicion of illegitimacy, too many children already, or if the parents were on a journey.

From 19th century Chaco to 6th century Arabia is a long jump, but infanticide is the common link. Mohammed is credited with having abolished the practice in Arabia where female infants were frequently destroyed before his reforms. In the Koran, *Sura* xvii, 33, we read, "Kill not your children for fear of want." *Sura* xvi, 60, 61 reflects an Arab father's dilemma at the birth of a daughter, describing how "dark shadows settle on his face" as he ponders, "shall he keep it with disgrace or bury it in the dust?" *Sura* lxxxi pictures vividly the day of judgment "when the sun shall be folded up" and many other things happen including "And when the female child that had been buried alive shall be asked for what crime she was put to death."

Mohammed's reform was not completely successful for it is said that the only occasion when his successor Othman, the cruel third caliph, ever shed a tear was when he was burying alive his little daughter and she reached up her tiny hand and brushed the grave dust from his beard. But Zaid, Mohammed's adopted son, who was said to have had Christian parents, is reported to have offered to support any girl children whom their fathers spared.

Among the many reasons not already given alleged for infanticide, whether actual reasons or rationalized, are discovered the following: killing of deformed children among the Salivas and Manaos because deformity was thought to be caused by demons; abandonment or burial alive of one half the children of Paraguay tribes if deformed, posthumous, or if either parent dies at the time of the child's birth. Any of these kinds of bad luck evidently justified or even required the killing of the infant; similarly bad luck would follow the Brazilian Tapirape parents if they kept more than three children or more than two of the same sex; in eastern Bolivia a baby was buried alive with its mother if she died in childbirth because a baby could be nursed only by its own mother; and in some Polynesian tribes if a child resembled its father too much, it was killed because of the belief that whoever the child resembled would die.

Among Chinese who believe in reincarnation, the killing of girl infants is defended on the ground that it gives them a chance to be reborn as males. In Africa and some South Sea islands where babies are suckled for long periods, the second child is sometimes killed if it arrives before the first has been weaned. In a way this practice parallels that in ancient Greece where infants were exposed in order to keep up the living standards for previous children. In Sparta the deformed newborn were exposed for the good of the state, and at one period Roman law, for the same reason, strictly forbade the rearing of deformed children.

However plausible are the alleged economic and other reasons for killing the malformed newborn, it is likely that fear of the abnormal was and is a large part of the motivation. To attribute eugenic policies to primitive societies is to forget how very difficult it is even in advanced cultures to secure recognition of the principles of eugenics.

Exposure or abandonment of infants, callous as it may seem, really presents an advance in the treatment of unwanted children. Instead of killing the infant outright and immediately, the parents gave it a faint chance of survival. It might be picked up by a stranger before it died of hunger, thirst, or cold or was killed by wild animals. The theme runs through many an old folktale and emerges into world literature. See ABANDONED

CHILDREN; EXPOSURE OF FAMOUS PERSONS IN INFANCY. The Œdipus legend, minus any Christian accretions, is still a folktale in Greece.

The core of the Œdipus exposure story probably goes back to Mycenæan-Minoan times, as recent discoveries indicate, or it may be even earlier. It has been edited and polished by ten thousand tellings until it reflects the deep psychological conflicts felt in families since the family was established. It has lived because it dramatizes man's repugnance at infanticide and the father-hatred thus inspired. And the folktale has rounded out its cycle by becoming in our day appropriated by psychology to denominate a mental complex.

Religious infanticide, especially the killing of the first-born, is apparently in nearly all cases a substitutionary human sacrifice. Cases are recorded among the aborigines of Victoria, Australia, the American Indian tribes of northwestern Canada and some parts of the United States, and in China, Africa, and Russia. It is, however, best known historically to have been common among the peoples of the eastern Mediterranean region and particularly among the Canaanites (Phœnicians), the Sepharvites, Moabites, Israelites, and Carthaginians. And in many instances the bodies of the children were burnt as sacrifices to the various tribal gods.

In some cases, as apparently in that of Abraham's interrupted sacrifice of his son Isaac (*Gen.* xxii), the child was killed before the body was burned, but Diodorus Siculus (xx, 14) tells of the Carthaginian custom of placing the child in the huge hands of a great idol from which it slid off into a fire below. The god variously named Melkarth, Milcom, Moloch, and Melech, with combined forms, was widely worshipped, even by the Israelites at times, for Solomon built an altar to Molech (I *Kings* xi, 7) and Manasseh sacrificed his son, by making him "pass through the fire" (II *Kings* xxi, 6), as did King Ahaz (II *Kings* xvi, 3). All through the 7th century B.C. this practice flourished. It was suppressed by Josiah but was revived by Jehoiakim and persisted until the Babylonian captivity. Even in northern Babylonia the burning alive of infants, as a sacrifice to the Melech group of gods, spread, for "the Sepharvites burnt their children in fire to Adrammelech and Anammelech, the gods of Sepharvaim" (II *Kings* xvii, 31).

Excavations in the Canaanite levels of all the mounds explored by archeologists have revealed jars in large numbers containing the bones of newborn infants, buried under house corners and thresholds and beneath the floors of the sacred high places. With them were small jars formerly containing food and drink. The bones were not charred, and so the babes had not been sacrificed to Molech, but probably to the mother goddess, the giver of children.

Sir James Frazer (*Golden Bough*, vol. iv, pp. 168–176) goes so far as to trace the origin of the Hebrew Passover directly to the sacrifice of first-born infants which he considers to have been an article of the ancient Semitic religion, and bases his argument on *Exodus* xiii, 2, 15; *Micah* vi, 7; and *Numbers* xviii, 15. It is evident from those passages that anciently these child sacrifices may have been made to Yahweh before they were, under Phœnician influence, made to Molech.

CHARLES FRANCIS POTTER

Inferi In classical mythology, the beings living in the earth, especially the gods of the lower world, and more often the shades of the departed: distinguished from the Superi or the Olympians living above the earth, and from the mortals living on the earth. The word thus was construed as including all the inhabitants of the underworld.

Ing A mythical Teutonic hero, mentioned as follows in the Anglo-Saxon *Rune Song:*

Ing was first mid the East Danes
seen of men   until he fared forth eastward (or thereafter)
over the sea.

He has been interpreted as the historic progenitor of certain tribes along the North Sea known as Ingvæons; the Anglo-Saxon *Beowulf* mentions the Danes as *Ingwine.* These five runic lines are pregnant with legendary implication; they serve as nucleus for the regional legend that a progenitor arrives mysteriously in a ship out of the unknown, tarries to establish a ruling race, and departs just as suddenly and mysteriously over the sea.

There is some dispute regarding the transcription of the word *est,* eastward. Some scholars prefer to interpret it as *eft,* thereafter, assuming that Ing fared forth thereafter over the sea to become the progenitor of the Anglo-Saxons. Nothing like this is mentioned, however, in the *Rune Song.*

The Ing legend is considered by some as the most ancient of all clues to the death-journey or journey to the Otherworld myths, which, spreading among the Danes, was superseded by the famous Scyld legends, and traveling southward along the Rhine, became one with the swan-knight story. Possibility of some relationship with the basic myths behind the Celtic imrama has been considered. See ÆSIR.

initiation The ceremonial transition from one state of being into another; the rites, tests, ordeals, etc., imposed or willingly undergone to effect and symbolize this transition—from puberty to maturity, from non-membership to membership into tribe, religious cult, or secret society, into a priesthood, into the knowledge of magic powers, or into a state of special holiness. The initiation rites which mark the passage from adolescence to maturity are often identical with those of induction into tribe or cult or secret society. The ordeals requiring courage and endurance (fasting, filing or knocking out of teeth, ear-, nose-, or lip-piercing, incisions, scarification, circumcision, subincision, etc.) and the terrorizing test the worthiness of the initiate to partake of the privileges of his new status, and are accompanied by instruction regarding his new responsibilities, disclosure of secrets, tribal lore, and investiture with marks, regalia, and insignia. In most societies initiation precludes further association with non-initiates, often includes the ritual drama of death and rebirth to new status and fuller personality, education in sexual relationships, permission to marry, and to join in warfare. See ADOLESCENCE CEREMONIES; AUSTERITIES; BAPTISM; BAR MITZVAH; BULL-ROARER; CAPAC RAIMI; OVENS OF YOUTH; PUBERTY DANCES; PUBERTY RITES.

☞ The transition from puberty to adulthood was marked in South America by ceremonies and ordeals which varied considerably in different tribes.

In the Guianas and the Amazon regions, stress was put on the occasion when a boy had his lip or his ears perforated to wear an ornament reserved to adults. The same symbolic significance was attached to the revelation of the secrets known only to males, for instance the true nature of the masked dancers or of the sounds of the sacred trumpets (Cobeuo, Tucano, Mojo, etc.). A boy is considered an adult among the Caribs and Arawaks of the Guiana when he has undergone with firmness the ordeal of the ant bites and of flagellations.

Initiation rites have, among the eastern Ge, a complexity unequalled elsewhere. They last for several years or are repeated at intervals of ten years. Periods of seclusion, relay races, perforation of ears and lips, display of ornaments, ritual meals are among the many salient features of these cycles. The Sherente require the novices to remain three years in the bush without returning to the village. During this period of isolation, it is forbidden to quarrel, to sing, to laugh, or to talk in a loud voice.

Among the Bororo, a boy who reaches puberty receives a penis sheath and is initiated into the secrets of the bull-roarers and other masculine rites.

The initiation rites of the Chamacoco Indians in the Chaco follows a pattern which is found also in Tierra del Fuego among the Ona, Yahgan, and Alakaluf. The boys are taken into the bush, where under the supervision of their elders they prepare themselves for their future responsibilities by hard work and tests of endurance. They must also listen to the old men who teach them the tribal lore. At the end of the initiation they learn that the spirits whom as children they had greatly feared are only masked men. The spirit impersonators perform dances near the camp to terrify the women and remind them of their subjection to men. For similar rites among the Fuegian Indians, see KINA and KLOKETEN.

The *huarachicoy* feast of the Incas of Peru was also an initiation ceremony for the boys of Inca lineage. It lasted a whole month during which there were pilgrimages to sanctuaries and idols, in particular to the sacred rock, Huanacauri; dances and sacrifices in honor of the gods, and tests of strength and endurance. Finally the boys had their ears pierced for the insertion of special ornaments. Henceforth they were regarded as full-fledged adults.   ALFRED MÉTRAUX

☞ Boys' initiation ceremonies are very important throughout Melanesia and New Guinea. They often include the belief that the boy is swallowed by a monster and is reborn, and that the bull-roarer is the voice of the spirits. Names of ceremonies and precise practices vary from island to island and from tribe to tribe. See MELANESIAN MYTHOLOGY. [KL]

Innocento' Day or **Holy Innocents' Day** The day commemorating the slaughter of the innocents (December 28), called Childermas in England. In France and England, the Boy Bishop had charge of the celebrations.

Ino In Greek mythology and legend, the nurse of Dionysus and the cruel stepmother of Phrixus and Helle. Driven mad by Hera for her bringing up of Dionysus, Ino disappeared and was thought dead by her husband Athamas. Athamas remarried and had two children by Themisto, his new wife. But Ino reappeared and aroused Themisto's jealousy. The latter plotted with the nurse of her two children and the two children of Ino to dress her children in white and Ino's in black, probably in order for murderers to make them out clearly in the dark. But, some say, Ino herself was the nurse and reversed the colors. With her children dead, Themisto committed suicide. Ino, in her turn, plotted against the children of Athamas by his first wife. She bribed the messengers from Delphi to say that the cause of a famine which Ino herself had induced could be removed only by the sacrifice of Phrixus and Helle. The flight of the two children on the golden-fleeced ram led eventually to the expedition of the Argonauts. At last Hera made Athamas and Ino so mad that he killed Learchus and she leaped from a cliff into the sea with Melicertes, her other son. Dionysus however would not let her die, and she was transformed into the sea goddess Leucothea.

insane root A member of the mandragora, mandrake, or "love apple" family and therefore associated with the cult of Aphrodite. The mandrake is greatly prized for medicinal, aphrodisiac, and other purposes. Because of the bifurcated root it is either male or female. One account is that it grows only under a gallows and originates in the juices from a hanged man's body. It will cure barrenness, act as a love charm, make the wearer invisible, or reveal hidden treasures. Although it is grown commercially in Korea, in western Europe it was gathered with stealth and under conditions of considerable hazard. The gatherer circled the plant but did not touch it. The tail of a dog starved for three days was tied to the plant. When the dog was shown food he uprooted the plant which uttered a fatal scream. The dog died and the gatherer would either die or go mad too if he did not cover his ears. The effects of mandragora are mildly narcotic and anesthetic. See MANDRAKE. [RDJ]

Intaphernes' wife In a story told by Herodotus (Book III), the wife of one of the seven conspirators against the usurpers of Cambyses' throne. Darius, the king, ordered that they be admitted to his presence unannounced at any time save when he was in bed with a woman. Intaphernes, on one such occasion, not believing the king's guards, struck off their noses and ears for refusing him admittance. The king heard of his insolence, discovered by interviewing all seven of the privileged ones that the incident was not a result of a conspiratorial collusion, and arrested Intaphernes, his children, and his near family. Intaphernes' wife stood outside the palace gate lamenting, and the king took pity on her. He offered her the life of any one of the family and was astonished when she chose her brother rather than husband or child. Her reasoning, that she might marry again and have children, that her parents were dead, that therefore she could not have another brother, so struck him that he ordered not only her brother but her eldest son saved. But all the rest were killed.

in the way In Irish folk belief, obstructing some passage or violating some place preempted by the síde or fairies. If a farmer builds his byre across a fairy path, the cattle in it die until it is removed. Many is the house, built unwittingly in some such spot, that never has luck. The people in it die, or it burns down, or perhaps the roof won't stay on it, or what's mended in the day gets pulled off at night. Sometimes the síde will knock on the walls all night. And at last, either because of bad luck or discouragement or specific warning the people abandon it, and the síde have free traffic. Occasionally all goes well if the human inhabitants are willing not to use a certain door in their house. Lady Gregory tells of a family enjoined to keep their back door closed. All human traffic had to go in and out the front. If they tried opening the back, a blast of wind would come in—enough to lift the roof off the house from inside. One woman was warned that her house was in the way, and was politely asked to move. But she did not know what the words *in the way* meant, so she stayed on, and all her seven children died, one by one. Another woman wondered why she could no longer make butter from the milk she set in her milk pans; but later she discovered she had been putting the pans to air and dry across a fairy path.

Getting in the way is a thing that often happens in Ireland, they say. The only way to tell whether a house is going to be in the way or not is to place four sticks upright in the ground where the four corners of the house will be, and the sticks will be knocked down in the night if the fairies object.

Inti raimi The feast of the winter solstice celebrated by the Inca in June. It was characterized by its solemnity and the lavish display of gold and silver paraphernalia. The ceremony opened with an homage to the Sun rendered by the Emperor, his family, and the provincial chiefs. After this the Emperor made a libation to the Sun and drank chicha with his relatives. With the Inca leading the procession, everyone went to the Sun temple where the members of the imperial lineage made offerings of precious vessels and images to the Sun God. Omens were read in the entrails of a black llama which was sacrificed to the Sun. A great holocaust of llamas and banquets ended the feast. [AM]

intitchiuma or **intijiuma** The Australian Aranda (Arunta) rites performed to increase totemic plants and animals and thus to insure a good food supply. There is ritual eating of the species following the ceremonies, which dramatically depict events which occurred during the dream time. Other tribes have comparable rites under different names. See AUSTRALIAN ABORIGINAL MYTHOLOGY. [KL]

invisibility The state of being unseeable; specifically, the condition of being invisible, not because of being hidden behind something but because of some factor blinding a possible viewer to one's presence; in folklore, a circumstance induced by various magic objects enabling the possessor to overhear, to spy, to win fights, etc., without being seen: a motif (D1361) of folktale found all over the world. Most commonly the magic object rendering the person invisible at will is a cap, a cloak, a ring, a stone, but other more exotic materials, like fern seed, a serpent's crown, the heart of an unborn child, are similarly useful. In the Thompson index of folktale motifs, some 28 magic objects are listed which render persons invisible, not including the chemicals of H. G. Wells' *Invisible Man*. These objects usually are grouped with other magic objects: shoes that enable the wearer to travel great distances instantly, caps of wisdom, inexhaustible purses, unerring swords, rings to summon up the spirits. Some beings, gods and ghosts and angels, need no such paraphernalia to appear and disappear, but dwarfs and men must have some talisman to do the trick.

The central European story of the Danced-Out Shoes (Type 306), known from the Lapps to the Greeks, is the best-known of the märchen employing the motif. The hero dons the cloak of invisibility, follows the princess (or princesses) to where she dances all night, and thus solves the mystery of why the shoes are worn through each morning. In one version of the Slaying of Monsters myth of the Chiricahua Apache, Child-of-the-Water gets a cloak from Lizard which makes him invisible and permits him to approach the monster Buffalo. The ring of Gyges, in the tale told by Plato, permits him to enter unseen into the queen's bedroom. The Welsh Owen Glendower is reputed to have had a stone which could make him invisible; the stone was obtained from a pet raven of the Earl of Arundel. In Eastern stories, an ointment applied to the eyes serves the purpose. In the *Ocean of Story*, Gunaśarman pretends to be a messenger of the gods and by using the magic collyrium to appear and disappear to Vikramaśakti induces the king to make peace. A Finnish-Swedish tale (Type 576) utilizes magic drops of invisibility. King Arthur had a cloak of invisibility, Hades a hat, Discordia a ring. Fern seed is, not only in folktale but also in folk belief, capable of making its owner invisible. So too is heliotrope, but whether this means the plant or the stone is not definite. Spells may be recited to attain invisibility; in an Indian story, reciting the spell forwards makes one invisible, reciting it backwards enables one to take any shape desired. The "black cat bone," in an American Negro belief derived from the European belief in the ominousness of black cats, is useful principally to make its owner invisible, though the charm has other uses. See HAND OF GLORY.

inyana The Zulu diviner, in touch with the *itongo*, or ancestral spirits. From them he learns his magical incantations in couplet form.

Io (1) In Greek mythology, the daughter of Inachus of Argos; a priestess of Hera originally called Callirrhoe or Callithyia. She was loved by Zeus and changed by him into a white heifer to avoid the jealous spying of Hera. Hera nevertheless became suspicious and asked for the animal as a gift, which Zeus was forced to grant. Hera set Argus Panoptes to guard Io in her grove at Mycenæ. Zeus guided Hermes to the spot, and the latter was able to kill Argus by playing his eyes shut one by one. Hera then sent a gadfly to torment Io. The unhappy heifer crossed the Ionian Sea (named for her) and the Bosporus (literally ox-ford), finally settling in Egypt, where she resumed her human form and gave birth to Epaphus (so called because Io was impregnated by the touch of Zeus' hand, an ancient explanation of the name as meaning "he of the touch"). The later Greeks identified Io with Isis, and Io does seem originally to have been a moon goddess. The various elements of the legend can be explained on this basis, e.g. the eyes of Argus being the stars of the sky, etc.

(2) The Maori supreme deity, probably limited only to one or two North Island tribes and perhaps a post-European development inspired by the Bible: important because of disputes over its age and distribution. There is no evidence of Io's presence in other islands. Stimson's claim that Tuamotuan Kiho was identical with Io was criticized by Emory in bitter battle. [KL]

Iphicles In Greek legend, the twin brother of Hercules; the son of Amphitryon, as Hercules was of Zeus: born the night after Hercules. That Iphicles was not the god's son was determined when Hera, or Amphitryon, put snakes in the cradle; he ran from them, Hercules strangled them. The half-brothers were companions on several occasions, but the chief importance of Iphicles lies in this early distinguishing between the two. The story is an embodiment of the belief that there was something supernatural about twins, that one of them necessarily was not the son of the mother's husband. Compare DIOSCURI; TWINS.

Iphiclus In Greek legend, a son of Phylacus. He was impotent and Phylacus made it a condition of Melampus the seer's obtaining certain of his cattle that the cause be determined. Melampus discovered that Iphiclus had stuck a sacrificial knife in an oak, and prescribed as a cure the drinking for ten days of a potion containing the scrapings of rust from the knife. Like similar sympathetic cures (compare the curing of wounds by touching them with the weapon causing the injury), it worked, and Iphiclus became the father of Podarces and Protesilaus. See ACHILLES' SPEAR.

Iphigenia In Greek legend, the daughter of Agamemnon and Clytemnestra, sacrificed at Aulis to Artemis: probably originally a form of Artemis herself as the name, meaning "mighty born," would indicate, although the name is an appropriate one for a princess. Agamemnon had given offense to the goddess by killing a stag sacred to her and by boasting afterwards that Artemis herself could have done no better, or by failing to fulfil a promised sacrifice. Artemis then caused the Greek fleet, en route to Troy, to be becalmed at Aulis. Calchas the soothsayer proclaimed that only the sacrifice of Iphigenia could lift the calm. The girl was sent for, the pretext being that she would be married to Achilles. When she was about to be sacrificed Artemis substituted for her a hind, a she-bear, a bull, or an old woman. Iphigenia was transported in a cloud by the goddess to Tauris, in the modern Crimea, where she became a priestess of Artemis.

At Tauris it was Iphigenia's duty to assist at the sacrifice to the goddess of all strangers entering the country. Orestes, Iphigenia's brother, came to Tauris to take the image of Artemis from there to Attica and was recognized by Iphigenia. They fled together. In Delphi, Electra encountered Iphigenia, and hearing that her brother had been slain was prepared to avenge this deed on Iphigenia when Orestes arrived and there was mutual recognition. The stolen image was placed in the temple of Artemis at Brauron, where Iphigenia became a priestess and died some years later. Offerings of clothing, specifically of those dying in childbirth, were offered to her there.

There are several local variants of details of the story, principally concerned with observance of the cult of Artemis. For example, in Brauron, near Marathon in Attica, where Orestes and Iphigenia carried the image of Artemis, she is called the daughter of the national hero Theseus. Some versions of the story say that she did not die, but was made immortal and was married to Achilles, was transformed into the goddess Hecate, etc.

Iris In Greek mythology, the goddess of the rainbow, with which she was sometimes identified, but which more often was her road as she went on an errand. Iris was the daughter of Thaumas and Electra and sister of the Harpies; in the *Iliad* she is the messenger of the gods, much as Hermes is in the *Odyssey*. Specifically, she was Hera's messenger, and carried the herald's staff and a pitcher in which was water with which perjurers were put to sleep. As the rainbow goddess, she was the joiner and conciliator who restored the peace of nature. Compare BIFROST.

Iro A costume representing a five-toed chicken of Yoruba mythology, associated with the creation of the world. The phrase "tying Iro" means that the costumes are "untied" after each festival in which Iro takes part, and have to be sewed together anew every year. "Tying Iro" also means donning this costume and taking part in the Iro ceremony. Iro is "tied" and dances at five different festivals during the year, each time impersonated by a chief's son. For the participation of Iro in these five festivals, see William R. Bascom, *The Sociological Role of the Yoruba Cult-Group, MAAA* 63, p. 30 ff.

iron This metal enters into the folklore of most peoples either in religious tabus or as a charm against supernaturals and sorcery. Since iron is not found in a pure state except in the case of meteorites, it has come into use comparatively recently. The first iron implements come from about the 3rd millennium B.C. in Mesopotamia. Commodore Perry in his explorations among the Eskimos found them using bits of a three-ton meteorite which they called "the woman" and which they had reduced to about half of its original size. Mississippi Indians are also known to have used meteorite. The Spaniards found a few knives of iron among the Aztecs which were prized above gold and which they said came from heaven. The Egyptians called iron the "marvel from heaven," and the Babylonians, "heaven fire." Many Europeans call iron pyrites thunderbolts and say that they protect from lightning.

In most cases the tabu against the use of iron in religious ceremonies springs from the tendency to cling to traditional usages rather than to any conception of iron as a base metal. Tools of iron could not be carried inside Greek temples; they were not used in the construction of Hebrew altars; and the sacred Pons Sublicius in Rome was built without the use of iron or bronze. Roman priests were not permitted to shave with iron razors; iron was not allowed to touch the body of the king of Korea; and the archon of Platæa was forbidden to touch it.

In India, genii and evil spirits fear iron in any form. Hindu women wear iron bracelets as wedding bands regardless of caste. In China, even dragons fear iron and the Chinese sometimes throw a piece of iron into dragon pools to irritate them when they need rain. The power of iron to drive off and keep out evil spirits and supernatural beings of all kinds is almost universal. In some places even the sound of iron puts them to rout. Throughout Europe iron is one of the most potent charms against witchcraft. Sometimes it will even keep a witch out of the neighborhood, yet both witches and sorcerers use iron vessels and instruments in the preparation of their brews. It will also ward off fairies and all manner of little men, except the Teutonic dwarfs who are the finest ironworkers in the world. A sword

or a piece of armor made by them was the prized possession of many a knight. In Scotland a piece of iron is put in all food in a house of death to drive death from the house. In many places it is proof against ghosts, but this is not universal, as a number of hardy ghosts spend their nights dragging heavy chains around old castles in many parts of Europe. In Burma a piece of iron is placed beside the body of a stillborn child with the adjuration that the soul may not return until the iron is as soft as down. In parts of India iron is under the protection of the forest god and it is necessary to keep on the good side of him or he will move the iron ore around. In the Celebes it is necessary to have the image of the god of iron in the smithy or the soul of the iron will depart during the forging and it will become brittle and unworkable.

In parts of Ireland iron is sacred metal and thieves will not steal it. The Dorns, a robber tribe of northern India, will expel any member using an iron instrument in his profession. Hindus believe that the use of iron in buildings is conducive to epidemics. In Burma iron pyrites are a charm against crocodiles. Many people believe that it is bad luck to make a gift of an iron instrument. Some claim it is unlucky to put iron to the ground on Good Friday. Early scientists held that the presence of a magnet robbed iron of its weight and that it lifted itself. When a Scottish fisherman swears, it is customary to call out "Cold iron!" while grasping the nearest piece of iron. Iron is frequently used to protect newborn children in Europe and India. In Scotland it is necessary to remove every piece of iron from the person when kindling a need fire. Iron is generally believed to give a person strength. In Italy pyrites preserve the eyes; in Germany the fumes from hot iron on which oil has been poured is a cure for toothache. In Scotland healing stones are kept in an iron box to keep them from the fairies. It is bad luck to bring old iron into the house. An iron nail is sometimes driven into the ground where an epileptic has fallen in a seizure, thus pinning the demon to the ground.

Iruska A Pawnee Indian religious dance, meaning "the fire is in me": now become a social dance. As fusion of Dakota and Omaha ideas, the Pawnee developed this trick, fire-handling, half-clown cult. It corresponds to the Crazy Dancers of the Arapaho, the Fire Dance of Iowa, Cheyenne, Gros Ventre, and the Arikara Hot Dance. The Omaha developed it into the Grass Dance which spread to Osage, Oto, Dakota, and Iowa and through these to the entire Great Plains. The Potawatomi modified it into the Dream Dance of the Great Lakes tribes. [GPK]

I Saw Three Ships An English traditional carol sung all over England in one version or another and set to various tunes, one being a close relative of *Mulberry Bush*. It tells of the arrival by ship on Christmas morning of Sir Joseph and his lady. Another title is *Sunny Bank*.

Ishtar The great goddess of Babylonian and Assyrian mythology and religion: identified with the Sumerian Inanna or Nina, the Phœnician Astarte, the Ashtoreth of the Bible, etc.: a composite deity including the characteristics of many goddesses of the pantheon, absorbed into the character of Ishtar in the course of the centuries. Ishtar had two principal aspects: she was the compassionate mother goddess and she was the lustful goddess of sex and war. As the mother goddess, sometimes depicted suckling a child, she ruled over the earth's fertility and was invoked as mankind's helper, the deliverer from sickness and evil. In myth, she consented to the flood and then wished she had not. Her rule over the fertility of the earth is linked also to her role as goddess of sexual passion. The story of Ishtar and Tammuz is essentially one of overpowering desire, desire so great as to send the goddess through great perils and indignities to rescue her lover from the underworld. As in the Greek myth of Persephone, while Ishtar was below the earth, crops failed, nothing grew. To Ishtar also are attached many stories of lovers taken and killed when the goddess was sated. This myth may be an extension of the fertility practice of the sacred marriage (hieros gamos) in Mesopotamia. The man mating with the goddess (or her priestess) in the fields may have been killed at the end of each year's ceremony and a new one chosen to take his place at the coming rite. Ishtar was likewise a war deity and a goddess of the hunt. She was associated with the planet Venus. Ishtar was also an underworld deity—in this being somewhat confused with Allatu—and she thus appears, as the merciless evil goddess of hell, in the Gilgamesh epic, in which she gets no more respect from the author than does Aphrodite in the Homeric poems.

In mythology, she is the daughter of Anu, the sky god, or of Sin, the moon god, and appears in the second triad with Sin and Shamash. Her mythology is however confused by her identification with many other female goddesses, such identification causing her name to become a generic term for "goddess."

Her cult observance was connected with the Tammuz myth; it is conjectured that the story of Esther in the Bible may be a reminiscence of this cult. Principal seats of Ishtar-worship were Uruk, Akkad, Nineveh, Arbela, Sippar. At Uruk, the oldest seat of worship of the goddess, temple prostitution occurred. Sacred to Ishtar were the lion and perhaps the dove.

Isis The Mother Goddess of Egyptian religion and mythology: depicted as a woman, often as suckling the child Horus seated on her lap; sometimes represented with the solar disk and cow's horns, and then identified with Hathor; in Ptolemaic times, when equated with Taurt, pictured as a hippopotamus. Isis was the sister and wife of Osiris (originally like all the deities in the Osiris myth an independent goddess). She ruled over Egypt while Osiris traveled abroad as a culture hero, spreading discoveries made by Isis. When Osiris was murdered by Set, she searched the land for the 14 parts into which his body had been cut, collecting those parts she could find and burying them. An earth goddess and a devoted mother and wife, she was the goddess of fertility and the type of the faithful wife. She was the patroness of sailors, Stella Maris, and goddess of medicine. From the hieroglyph of her name, resembling a throne, it is believed that she was originally the personification of the throne, from which arose, "was born," the king.

Isis, the Thousand-Named, was the mother of Horus, who was conceived after the death of Osiris, his father. In addition to her close connection with these two sun gods, she appears in a myth concerning Rā. Isis, a mortal magician, wished to become a god. To accomplish this, she obtained some of the spittle of Rā and fashioned a snake of earth and spittle, leaving it in his path. Rā was bitten by the snake, and, in agony, called for help. When Isis told him that he must reveal his real name, his secret name, he tried to deceive her with other names, but in vain: the pain continued until he told her his hidden name. With this knowledge, hence power, Isis attained to godhood. In another myth, the head of Isis was cut off by Horus in his struggle with Set and was replaced with a cow's head by Thoth. This seems to be a late rationalizing development, explaining literally the symbolic head and paralleling the myth of Horus' own decapitation.

The chief centers of Isis-worship were Abydos and Busiris. The Greeks identified her with Athena and Demeter, and in later times her worship spread throughout the Greek and Roman worlds. In the period of the Roman Empire, the cult of Isis was one of the more prominent of the important foreign-goddess cults.

Island of the Blest St. Brendan's Island, that island "before the gates of Paradise where is no day or night": sought and found by Brendan on his famous seven-year voyage into the western Atlantic in the 6th century. This was the happy Otherworld of early Celtic belief (land of apples, blossoms, feasts, music and lovely women, where wailing or treachery was unknown) stripped of its pagan delights and practically identical with the Christian Heaven. St. Brendan's Island was literally believed in by Spanish and Portuguese navigators well into the 16th century. The last voyage undertaken in quest of it was in 1721. That the Land of Promise he discovered was America was a legend, long and ardently believed in Clonfert. The island called I Brasil, the lost island of the Arans, is still popularly said in Kerry to have been St. Brendan's Island. See IMRAMA.

islands of the blessed In the belief of many peoples of the world, the paradise to which the good are assigned after death: often located in the west near where the sun sets. Specifically, the Islands of the Blessed of Greek mythology lay somewhere in the western Ocean and were ruled over by Cronus. Later the islands were more or less confused with Elysium, which was perhaps a more ancient paradise in Greece. The Isle of Avalon of Arthurian legend is similar in nature, as are many of the Isles of Women of folktale. The mythical island of Atlantis and the various islands discovered in the Atlantic and Pacific and never found again are more recent elaborations of the same theme.

Isolt, Isolde, Yseut, or **Essylt** Two women bear the name of Isolt in the romance of *Tristan and Isolt*. The most important is Isolt of Ireland, the heroine of the story. She and Tristan drink the love potion and then undergo the terrible vicissitudes of love and separation, until, unable to remain near Isolt, Tristan crosses the sea to France where he meets the second Isolt, Isolt of the White Hands, sister of his best friend. At the friend's suggestion Tristan finally marries Isolt of the White Hands.

Such reduplication of character is common in folklore and in romance. There are numerous examples: typical are those in *The Golden Tree and the Silver Tree, King Horn, Bevis of Hampton, Guy of Warwick,*

Freisne. In the folktale there was nothing incongruous in a hero's being given a woman as a reward at the end of each exploit. In more sophisticated literature such incidents were rationalized in various ways: marrying one of the women to a friend of the hero, causing the hero to refuse the second woman (or repudiate the first), sending one of the women to a nunnery, dropping the incident entirely. In the medieval *Tristan* Tristan's "sin" in marrying Isolt of the White Hands is against courtly love and so the impressive conclusion in which the legal wife confronts the sweetheart is especially dramatic. See TRISTAN. [MEL]

Italapas Coyote: culture hero of Chinook mythology and creator of the Chinook world. While waiting in the trees for the waters to subside, Italapas threw some sand into the surf which became land. He helped Ikanam, the Creator, make the first men, and then taught them how to catch salmon, and all their other arts, and told them their tabus. Italapas is radically different from Coyote of California Indian mythology, where he is a more or less obstructive foil for the Creator. Blue-Jay plays this mischievous, clever role in the Chinook story.

itan The name used by the Yoruba people for myths, traditions, or histories. They are regarded as historically true and are often quoted by the old men to settle a difficult point in a discussion of ritual or politics. They are also recited by the diviners as a part of the Ifa verses. See AFRICAN AND NEW WORLD NEGRO FOLKLORE.

Ith In Old Irish mythology, son of Bregan of Spain; uncle of Mil, and the first of the Milesians to visit Ireland. One day from Bregan's Tower Ith saw "a lofty island far away" and was filled with a longing to visit it. His brothers tried to hinder him but he was determined and set forth in a ship with his people. The *Book of Invasions* says "their adventures on sea are not related." But Ith's conversation with the three kings of Ireland (Mac Cuill, Mac Cecht, and Mac Greine) is related, and the story of how they killed him in resentment for "the testimony of praise he gave their island." Ith's people took his body back to Spain in the ship, and the sons of Mil saw fit to go to Ireland to avenge him. This is the beginning of the story of the conquest of Ireland by the Milesians.

ithyphallic A term often loosely used to mean "phallic," but specifically meaning "with erect penis": used of certain images and statues connected with phallic worship, in which the sexual organs are extremely prominent or exaggerated. The word is applied to such representations as those of Legba of the Ewe who is depicted squatting and peering at his magnified penis (or vulva, in the rare instances when Legba is conceived of as female). Ithyphallic is used to refer to the phallic staves carried in the processions of Bacchus, and to the meter of the verses recited in those processions. Ithyphallic representations occur all over the world, in amulets, on temples, etc. See PHALLISM.

Itiwana Literally, the middle place: the middle of the world in Zuñi Indian cosmogony. Itiwana is an underlake town to which the Zuñi dead return, instead of having to return all the way to the mythological place of emergence of the Zuñi people.

In the Zuñi origin myth, as the people journeyed on the face of the earth looking for a place to settle, they came to a lake and crossed it. The first ones to cross lost all their children in the lake and grieved for them bitterly. A brother and sister, ahead of the group, had indulged in an incestuous mating while waiting for the others to catch up, and were thereby transformed into supernaturals. These two taught the people who followed how to keep from losing their children in the lake; they made singing and dancing for the lost ones, and opened a road to the middle of the lake so that the parents might visit and behold their children. The children told their parents not to grieve for them. They were happy to stay in Itiwana, they said. They would never have to take the long journey back to the place of emergence; and henceforth all the dead would come and stay in Itiwana. (See Parsons, "Origin Myth of Zuni," *JAFL* 36: 135 ff.) The kachinas associated with Itiwana visit the villages from time to time. They are impersonated during the masked kachina dances to promote rain and fertility.

Itzamna The chief deity of the Maya pantheon, the Lord of the Heavens and the Lord of Day and of Night. He is represented in codices as an old man with toothless jaws, sunken cheeks, and a Roman nose. He was considered benevolent, always the friend of man, and his aid was invoked throughout the year at ceremonies as the god of medicine, as the sun god, to avert calamities, and so forth. [GMF]

ivy Ivy was sacred to the Egyptians. In Greece it was used to crown victors in sports, although the exact species is in doubt. In Greek it was called *cissos* after a dancing girl who, at a feast of the gods, danced with such joy and abandon before Dionysus that she fell dead at his feet. The god was so moved by her performance that he turned her body into the ivy which entwines and embraces anything near it. Dionysus is said to have developed from the ivy as Zeus from the oak. Because ivy is dedicated to Dionysus, it is said to prevent drunkenness. It is hung over the entrances to English taverns to indicate that good wine is served within. In China ivy is associated with the mother goddess. In Christian lore its evergreen quality symbolizes the immortality of the soul.

If ivy will not grow on a grave it signifies the soul is not happy in the other world. If it grows profusely on the grave of a young maiden it means that she died of love. Its clinging qualities make it a symbol of constancy. Ballad and folktale are full of ivy which grows and intertwines from the graves of two lovers.

Ivy is considered to be female and a symbol of fertility or unpredictability. In the Shrovetide dances in England there are frequently an ivy-girl and a holly-boy among the dancers. In County Leitrim, Ireland, if young lads gathered ten ivy leaves in silence on Halloween, threw one away, and placed the other nine under the pillow, they would dream of love and marriage. In Wales they say when old ivy dies or falls away from the house, the owner will meet with financial reverses and lose the house. Usually it is lucky to have it on the house, but in some places it is unlucky to plant ivy. It is generally unlucky to make a gift of ivy: it will break up friendships. In Maine they say that those who keep it in the house will always be poor. A green ivy leaf placed in water in a covered dish after dark on New Year's Eve and left until Twelfth Night will tell the future. If the leaf is spotted near the stem, it is a sign of sickness, if spotted all over, of death, but if it is fresh and green it signifies good health throughout the year.

Like most plants used in folk medicine, ivy was an antidote for poison at one time or another. The leaves are used for dressing wounds, burns, ulcers, and to reduce swollen glands. In Ireland they are applied to ease the pain of corns. Water in which the leaves have been steeped is soothing to the eyes. The tender twigs boiled in butter make a good sunburn ointment. The powdered berries are effective against jaundice, the plague, burns, scalds, and will heal green wounds. If children drink from cups of ivy wood they will be cured of whooping cough. Ivy is also useful in curing the itch and in delousing. In some places it is used as a depilatory; in others it is used to dye the hair. For a toothache, take a pomegranate shell, put in some ground ivy berries, on this pour oil of rose, and heat. This should be poured into the ear opposite to the aching tooth.

I'wai The crocodile totemic culture hero of the Koko Ya'o tribe, Cape York Peninsula, Australia. He was the leading figure among the ancestors who lived "in the beginning at first," a phrase often opening a myth about the prehuman period. [KL]

Ixion In Greek mythology, a treacherous Thessalian: his name is derived by A. B. Cook from the Greek word for mistletoe, and Ixion is made an aspect of the sun moving through the heavens. Ixion married Dia, and when his father-in-law came to collect the promised bride-price, Ixion caused him to fall into a pit of burning coals. For this the gods drove him mad, until Zeus took pity on him, cured and purified him, and invited him to dinner on Olympus. There Ixion tried to violate Hera, but a cloud (Nephele) was substituted for the goddess. From this union the race of Centaurs sprang. As punishment for his crime Ixion was condemned to be bound by Hermes to a winged or fiery wheel which rolls eternally through the air or the lower regions. The punishment of Ixion was, as were those of Tantalus and Sisyphus, famous in the ancient world.

iyondátha An Iroquois women's curing society and dance. Its songs are sung by men with the women an octave higher, to the accompaniment of large gourd rattles. The songs are in defective pentatonic scales, with simple repetitious themes. The women alone shuffle to the right in a centralized round dance. Membership in the society is by dream or cure of some respiratory ailment. Thus the ceremony has many features in common with the men's *hadi'hiduus*, though the music is less archaic. At the end of the song cycle the sponsor makes gifts of cloth and is herself wrapped up. Thereupon follows the *deswadéyǫ'* rite. [GPK]

Izanagi and Izanami The Heavenly Pair who created Japan from drops of brine. [JLM]

Iztat Ix See ALAGHOM NAOM.

J

jabado A French dance for four couples. The first part, in fast duple time, is a clockwise round like the branle, closed by the linking of little fingers. The step is the variant of the branle used in the Breton gavottes, as the *gavotte de Pont-Avon,* a progression left with three steps and a leg swing, a balance right back and again forward. The second part places the couples in quadrille formation, without, however, the elaborate interchanges. While the men balance toward the center of the circle and out, the women balance out and then turn to the next man on the left, thus gradually moving around the circle in the clockwise direction typical of French round dances. [GPK]

jabme-akka The old woman of the dead in the religion of the Lapps. She rules over *jabme-aimo,* the home or realm of the dead. Among the sacrifices to the *jabme-akka* black animals are mentioned, especially the cat and the cock. Kaarle Krohn compares both *jabme-aimo* and *jabme-akka* to the Scandinavian concept of hell, both in sense of place and in sense of the being who rules the place. In Christian times *jabme-aimo* took on the meaning of a transitional stage whence the souls of the dead were directed to a good or bad future existence, according to each man's merit. Ideas of the *jabme-akka* then become mingled with the concept of the Virgin Mary. See Uno Holmberg, *Lappalaisten Uskonto (The Religion of the Lapps),* Porvoo, 1915, p. 25 (in Finnish).

The word *jabme* means dead one, corpse; *aimo, ajmo,* or *aibmo* means land, place, home, world. The different spellings are dialectical. [JB]

jácara A traditional Spanish couple dance, performed with many turns and half-turns, without actual contact: considered by certain 17th century writers on the dance to be merely another phase of the exotic sarabande. [GPK]

jacinth A red transparent gem of the zircon family, used by the Italians as the birthstone for January: often confused with red feldspar and carnelian. It may have been one of the stones in the breastplate of the High Priest (*Exodus* xxviii, xxxix). It is a potent amulet and during the Middle Ages it was recommended for every pharmacy. It was much used by travelers, for it protects against the plague, wounds, and injury. It is good for the heart, dispels sadness, induces sleep, and averts lightning. It insures a favorable response to petitions, augments riches, and induces prudence in the conduct of one's affairs.

jack Mississippi Negro term for a conjure or hoodoo hand or trick wrapped in red flannel. Sometimes it consists of a piece of loaded cane wrapped in red flannel and is used for divination. A piece of red cloth shaped like a finger and stuffed with dirt and coal dust and containing a silver dime will keep the owner from getting lost. Jacks are usually classified among the good or beneficial charms or tricks, and have to be made with the greatest care. Often an incantation invoking the presence and the help of God is recited during the making. (See Puckett, *Folk Beliefs of the Southern Negro,* Chapel Hill, 1926.)

Jack a Kent A character of local renown in the folklore of Herefordshire; a clever trickster who outwits the Devil. J. W. Ashton ("Jack a Kent," *JAFL* 47: 362–368) traces the development of this folk figure from a Welsh parish priest in Kentchurch, Hereford, in the early fifteenth century, who wrote poetical and theological works. Because this parson was under the sponsorship of the Scudamores, a principal local family related to Owen Glendower, it was said that John, the priest, was none other than Glendower the great magician himself. Through confusion with John of Kent, the earlier miracle-working abbot, Parson John became another Faustus-like magician in the popular mind. In Anthony Munday's play *John a Kent and John a Cumber* (c. 1595), the priest is a worker of white magic to forward the interests of two pairs of lovers, defeating the efforts of the Scottish magician to keep them apart. In Leather's *Folk-Lore of Herefordshire* (1912), Jack a Kent has been transformed from the poet and the white magician into a wise lad, another of the Jacks of English folklore, who outsmarts the Devil in several episodes. He is the hero of the familiar above-ground and below-ground crops story; he bargains to get the curly-tailed pigs and sees to it that their tails are kinked by feeding them beans and driving them through water; he agrees to leave the Devil his body whether it be buried inside or outside the church, and arranges to be buried in the wall of the church. Ashton's study shows clearly the development of the local legend of the hero from a minor historical character with attraction of the general attributes of the folk type to the real person. Compare DECEPTIVE BARGAINS.

jackal Among the Egyptians the jackal was associated with Anubis and guided the dead to their otherworld destination. In India the howling of jackals is a sign of approaching misfortune; especially is the howling of a jackal heard on the left an evil omen. He has some of the attributes of the western European fox in the animal tales and fables of the Near, Middle, and Far East. [RDJ]

☞ In Asiatic folktale, jackal provides for the lion; he scares up game, which the lion kills and eats, and receives what is left as reward. In stories from northern India he is sometimes termed "minister to the king," i.e. to the lion. From the legend that he does not kill his own food has arisen the legend of his cowardice. Jackal's heart must never be eaten, for instance, in the belief of peoples indigenous to the regions where the jackal abounds. To eat jackal's heart will make a child grow up a coward, and cause inordinate timidity even in a grown warrior. In northern Africa jackal's gall is regarded as aphrodisiac and is used in a special love ointment by both sexes. In Hausa Negro folktale Jackal plays the role of sagacious judge and is called "O Learned One of the Forest." The Bushmen say that Jackal goes around behaving the way he does "because he is Jackal." Jackal is the beloved trickster of Hottentot folklore. See AIGAMUXA; ANANSI AND THE GUM DOLL.

Jack and the Beanstalk   Title of an English folktale, popular especially in the British Isles and the United States as a nursery story. Jack, the foolish son of a poor widow, was sent to town to sell the cow. He sold her to a butcher for a handful of colored beans which delighted his eye. When he arrived home with the beans, the discouraged mother tossed them into the yard, where by the next morning they had grown into a marvelous tree that reached the sky. Jack climbed it and found himself in a strange land where he was directed to a giant's castle. The giant's tender-hearted wife hid him under a bowl to save him from her husband, who soon came stamping home, crying, Fee-fi-fo-fum/ I smell the blood of an Englishman/ Be he live or be he dead/ I'll grind his bones to make my bread. The giantess pacified the giant, however, by giving him a big supper. The giant then called for his little red hen, who immediately laid a neat golden egg. All this Jack watched from his hiding place, and when the giant was asleep he crept out, stole the hen, slid down the beanstalk, and got safe home. The next day he climbed up again; all happened as before; this time he stole the giant's bags of gold. The third night he stole the giant's golden harp, which, however, cried out to the giant, who heard it, woke up, and chased him. Jack had a good start, slid down the beanstalk, then chopped it down before the giant could get to earth. The giant fell and was killed, and Jack and his mother lived in comfort ever after.

This story belongs to the famous Jack tale cycle, known in Great Britain, Ireland, Western Scottish Highlands, Australia, Canada, etc., in the United States among the whites and Negroes, and existing also in numerous European parallels in Scandinavia, the Baltic countries, Russia, Czechoslovakia, etc. In many European versions the beanstalk does not appear. It is of especial interest for a series of motifs common to folktales almost everywhere: the foolish bargain (J2080 ff.) with which the story opens, the magic object acquired because of the foolish bargain (D837), the plant which grows to the sky (F54.2; Types 852,555), the widespread fee-fi-fo-fum motif (G84), and hero hidden by ogre's wife (G532), the series of thefts from the giant or ogre (G610; Type 328), magic object stolen from the ogre's house (D838.2), the magic speaking object (D1610 ff.) summoning the giant (D1421.4 ff).

The U.S. southern mountain white (Blue Ridge) version follows this pattern, with the difference that Jack steals successively a rifle-gun, a skinnin' knife, and a coverlet tricked out with golden (or china) bells. After his escape, Jack walks along the felled bean tree to see how far the giant got, and finds him about a half mile away from home. He walks on to where the giant's house

has fallen, finds that the dishes are all broken, but he and his mother save a lot of them. In the Ozark version Jack's granny sweeps up a bean and tells him to plant it. The story is told by Jamaica Negroes (M. W. Beckwith, *Jamaica Anansi Stories, MAFLS* 17: 149) and by Andros Island Negroes under the title *Jack Bean* (E. C. Parsons, *Folk-Tales of Andros Island, Bahamas, MAFLS* 13: 133).

jack bean   A climbing bean (genus *Canavalia*) having lilac or purple and white flowers. It is often seen in Negro gardens in the West Indies and parts of the southern United States climbing poles higher than any of the other poles in the garden. It is called the overlook, i.e. it is believed to act as watch and guard for the garden.

Jack Hall   An English folk song sung to the air known as *Kidd's Lament* and similar in stanza to that song. According to Cecil Sharp, the Jack Hall ditty must have been written early in the 18th century, since Jack Hall, its hero, who had been sold to a chimneysweep for a guinea, was executed for burglary at Tyburn in 1701. It is, except in detail, the same song as *Samuel Hall*, which purports to be the song sung on the scaffold by Samuel Hall, an 18th century murderer.

Jack in the Green   A May Day pageant mummer of medieval England, especially associated with the chimneysweeps' May Day festival. One of the sweeps, encased in a framework about 6–10 feet high made of lath and hoops and entirely covered with green holly boughs and ivy topped with flowers and ribbons, danced at the head of a line of chimneysweeps who advanced and capered and sang through the town, collecting pennies. They were accompanied by a fiddling fool and two other performers in red and yellow, with tin whistle, black-encircled eyes, etc.

J. G. Frazer (*Magic Art* ii: 80 ff.) regards Jack in the Green as a relic of European tree worship, along with the Swiss Whitsuntide Basket (another leaf-enclosed boy), the similar Württemberg *Latzman*, the numerous European May kings and queens, the Hanoverian Leaf King, Thüringen Little Leaf Man, etc. The Green George of the Russians, Slovenes, and other eastern European Slavs (a boy decked in branches and flowers who goes about the cornfields on St. George's Day) is perhaps closer to the actual tree-spirit personification. Green George is definitely identified with a birch tree by Carinthian and Transylvanian farmers. Green George, the principal spring observance of Rumanian and Transylvanian Gipsies, is represented by a young willow tree, decked with flowers and set up in the center of the group for one day. The following day Green George is represented by a human double, a boy clad in branches, leaves, and flowers, who is the center of various activities; in the evening Green George is a leaf-clad puppet which is thrown into a running stream. See CLOWNS.

jack-in-the-pulpit   An American herb (*Arisæma triphyllum*) of the arum family, growing from a turnip-shaped bulb or corm, with a spike of flowers enclosed in a greenish-purple spathe: often also called *Indian turnip*. It was called Jug Woman's baby by the Penobscot Indians and regarded as poisonous. Jack-in-the-pulpit was used by certain North American Indians, specifically the Fox Indians or Meskwaki of Wisconsin, the Plains Potawatomi, etc., as a diagnostic medicine. The inner seed, dropped into a cup of water, would float four times clockwise around the cup as a sign the patient would get well; if it sank before the fourth round, he would die. The Meskwaki used to chop up the root and mix it with meat, and leave it out for their enemies, during their wars with the Sioux. Many a Sioux died in an agony of pain and cramp a few hours after eating the mixture. From this property the Meskwaki called the plant *tcîka'- tape,* bad sick. White settlers of the Middle West adopted the use of the dried corm, in minute doses, as a remedy for bronchitis, asthma, colic, and rheumatism. Powdered and mixed with molasses, it is occasionally still given to children as a vermifuge. The intensely acrid juice of the corm was sometimes mixed with lard and used to treat ringworm.

Jack Ketch The hangman, headsman, or public executioner: called so from John Ketch (died 1686), who executed some prominent prisoners under James II. There were ballads including his name, and by 1702 the hangman in the Punch and Judy shows was called by his name.

jack-o'-lantern The phosphorescent light frequently seen moving in the air over marshy places; the corposant or will-o'-the-wisp that retreats from those who try to reach or follow it. It is the proverbial misleader of belated travelers who fall into swamps and marshes or ponds and are drowned. It is also often called *ignis fatuus,* foolish fire: the implication being that only a fool would follow it, and that the light is foolish to flee from a fool. In Lancashire folk speech, it is called either Jack-o'-lantern or Peg-o'-lantern, according to the local concept of its sex. The jack-o'-lantern of German folklore, especially in Lower Saxony, is the *Dickepoten.* This is often the soul of someone condemned thus to wander for having moved or disregarded a boundary mark. In Ireland the phenomenon is variously known as *teine sionniič,* fox fire; *teine side,* fairy fire; *Seán na gealaiġe,* Jack of the bright light; *Liam na lasóige,* William with the little flame, etc.; it is commonly believed to be the wandering soul of one who has been refused entrance into both heaven and hell. He often terrifies night travelers; sometimes he warns them. He is famous for leading them astray, but has been known to direct those in trouble. See BOUNDARY; CORPSE LIGHT; LIEKKIÖ.

Jack o'Lent A ridiculous figure of a man made of straw and old clothes, drawn through the streets at the beginning of Lent and the object of hilarity and contempt. In the end it was burned or shot. Jack o'Lent belongs among the orgiastic spring festivals. Here the connection between Jack o'Lent and Judas Iscariot is psychological rather than historical. See ASH WEDNESDAY. [RDJ]

Jack tales A cycle of folk tales, found in the British Isles and the United States, taking its name from the hero, Jack: parallels from the European continent use the equivalent name—Juan, Jean, Hans, etc. Jack is not the dull moral prince of the fairy tale, but rather the folk hero, sharp, gaining his ends unscrupulously or even immorally, often through luck rather than virtue, often too lazy to work at ordinary pursuits. He is a trickster, or he is the clever youngest son, or he is the unpromising hero, but always he is destined to turn events to his own account rather than having them

shaped in his favor. The Jack stories of the Upper Thompson Indians (*JAFL* 29: 313) are "white man's stories," and some of the tellers distinguish Jack the trickster, Jack the hero, Jack the bear, etc.

The best known of the Jack tales are *Jack and the Beanstalk* and *Jack the Giant-Killer;* in the first Jack kills the victim of his robberies (though sometimes the giant too is a robber), in the second he plays on his victims' slow-wittedness. Richard Chase, in *The Jack Tales* (1943), retells a group of these stories discovered in North Carolina, still told by the descendants of Council Harmon (1803–1896). Some of the tales had been reported earlier, e.g. a Jack version of Type 130—*The Animals in Night Quarters;* Grimm's *Bremen Town Musicians* (#27)—in *JAFL* 1 from Massachusetts, but Chase demonstrated the existence in the United States of the cycle. Herbert Halpert's notes to these tales indicate their connection with the general European cycle.

Jack the Giant-Killer An English folktale, one of the best known of the Jack tales, in which the hero, in loosely connected episodes, kills a number of giants and is rewarded: the story, Type 328—The Boy Steals the Giant's Treasure—in many variants is concerned with the taking of various magical objects from the giants, and makes use of the same motifs as Type 1640—The Valiant Tailor. Basically it is the same story as *Jack and the Beanstalk,* belonging to the stupid-ogre group of tales. Though Jack is sometimes associated with the Arthurian story and is given a seat at the Round Table as a reward for his prowess, the common version of the story has him simply a brave youth who digs a pit and then lures the giant Cormoran into it. He chops off the giant's head and is presented with a sword or a belt by the grateful people or the king. Out to kill Blunderbore, Jack is captured by the giant and put in a dungeon. But the window of his cell overlooks the courtyard, so Jack, when Blunderbore and another giant (though sometimes Blunderbore is two-headed) stand beneath the window, drops a noose around their necks and chokes them to death. He visits a Welsh giant who owns a cloak of invisibility, a cap of wisdom, shoes of swiftness (seven-league boots), and an irresistible sword. At night Jack puts a log or some sticks of wood in his bed and the giant clubs to death what he thinks is Jack. At the breakfast table, Jack complains of flea bites during the night; he empties his porridge into a bag concealed beneath his coat. Then he challenges the giant to eat more than he does (Type 1088: Eating Contest), slitting the bag open when it is full. The giant tries to relieve the stuffy feeling the same way and kills himself. Using the invisibility coat and the swift shoes, Jack traps another giant onto a drawbridge, raises it, and drowns the giant in the moat. After these principal adventures, Jack encounters other giants, and in this main version, and in the variants, many other incidents occur: Jack squeezes water from a stone that is really a piece of cheese (Type 1060); he blows a trumpet that levels a giant's castle; he locks up the giant for "safety" after frightening him with tales of an approaching army (in Type 328); he throws stones at two giants who first accuse and then kill each other; he challenges the giant to a strength test and avoids his part of the contest by boasting; he tricks the giant's wife into the oven (as Gretel does the witch— Type 1121). The story of *Jack the Giant-Killer* is found in the New World, where the English brought it. One of the Jack tales of North Carolina, "Jack in the Giants' Newground," puts Jack to work for the king to keep the giants from trespassing. When the king tells Jack to see what he can do about the monsters, Jack tackles the problem by saying modestly, "I may not kill all of 'em today, but I'll get a start anyhow."

Jacob One of the Hebrew patriarchs; under the name given him by God (*Gen.* xxxii) the eponym of Israel; father of the founders of the twelve tribes. Albright suggests that his era was some time about the 18th century B.C. Jacob, grandson of Abraham and son of Isaac and Rebecca, was the twin of Esau. Even in the womb the twins fought: when Rebecca passed a pagan place of worship, Esau moved; when she passed a House of the Lord or a place of learning, Jacob stirred; Esau granted Jacob the afterworld that he might possess the things of this world; Esau would not give way when the twins were to be born, so rather than cause Rebecca's death Jacob permitted Esau to be born first, and Jacob held Esau's heel as they came from the womb. Before their birth God had foretold to Rebecca that the older should serve the younger. Esau was born hairy, with all his teeth, red as blood, and marked with the sign of the serpent; Sammael was his protecting angel. After Esau was born, with all the dirt and blood of labor, Jacob came forth, clean, sweet, marked with the sign of the covenant; Michael was his guardian. Because Esau looked so strange, Isaac put off his circumcision, and in the end Esau was never circumcised. Esau became a hunter; he slew Nimrod and took the magnificent clothing that aided Nimrod in the hunt. Jacob was a shepherd and a student.

On the day that Abraham died, Jacob prepared a mourning dish of lentil pottage. When Esau returned from his hunting—and other evil deeds—he demanded the dish. So, for the pottage, some money, and the marvelous sword of Methuselah, Esau sold to Jacob the birthright that was his as the elder of the brothers. (In this Joseph Jacobs sees a last remaining trace of an ancient custom of ultimogeniture, misunderstood by the editor of the passage.) Helped by Rebecca, Jacob, disguised with the skins of lambs on his hands and forearms so that his blind father might think him the hairy Esau, received Isaac's blessings. Then, fearing the wrath of the warlike Esau, Jacob fled to Haran, to his uncle Laban.

On the journey to Haran, Jacob met with five miracles. At Mount Moriah, the sun set, though it was only midday, because there the Temple was to be built and God wanted Jacob to spend the night on the spot. So Jacob gathered twelve stones to rest upon. These twelve stones, symbolizing the twelve tribes, had formed part of the famous altars of the times before Jacob: the altar upon which Adam sacrificed, Abel's altar, Noah's altar, and the altar to which Isaac has been bound by Abraham. The stones became one, as the twelve tribes were to be one, and the stone was a soft pillow. Also, the whole of Palestine folded up during the night and rested beneath Jacob's head. As he slept he dreamed of the ladder ascending to heaven. See JACOB'S LADDER. When he awoke, the stone sank into the earth to be the keystone of the world, the rock on which the Temple was founded, the stone on which is engraved the Ineffable Name.

(Compare OMPHALOS.) Then Jacob once again set foot on the path to Haran, and was there instantly. Before the well at Haran, he met Rachel, his cousin, and in the strength of his instant love for her he rolled the stone from the well, something that had hitherto required the work of all the shepherds of the neighborhood. The fifth miracle of the twenty-four hours occurred when the water in the well rose to the brim and required no hauling up.

Jacob labored for Laban seven years to win Rachel, and Laban tricked him by marrying him to Leah. So Jacob worked seven more years and escaped with Rachel. They took with them Laban's household god, and that part of the flocks, granted to Jacob by Laban, that by the magical use of peeled stakes had become "ring-straked, speckled, and grisled." Later, as he was about to meet Esau again—a ticklish situation—Jacob wrestled with an angel, some say with Sammael, some say with Michael, some say it was with God himself, but neither could win. At last the adversary touched Jacob in the hollow of the thigh, laming him, and prevailed. Then Jacob's name was changed to Israel, because he "strove with God." Jacob tried to discover his opponent's name, that he might some time invoke him, but the Being put off the question and gave Jacob his blessing. Jacob lived many years, lived to see his son Joseph regent of Egypt; he went with his sons to live in the land of Goshen in Egypt; he dedicated his son Levi and his descendants to the service of the Lord; and at last he died and was buried beside Leah in the cave of Machpelah. But even here Esau tried to interfere, claiming his own place in the tomb that he had sold to Jacob. Joseph sent for the agreement the twin brothers had made, but one of Jacob's grandsons, the deaf Hushim, son of Dan, mistook the argument and with a club knocked Esau's head from his shoulders. The head rolled into the tomb into the lap of Isaac, and they permitted it to remain. See BLIND DUPE; DIOSCURI; HERCULES; MANDRAKE.

Jacob's ladder The ladder described in *Gen.* xxviii, 12, reaching from earth to heaven, on which Jacob saw in a dream angels ascending and descending. He saw angels in the guise of the princes of Babylon, Media, Greece, and Edom go up a symbolic number of steps and come down, the king of Edom alone not descending. Jacob did not himself aspire to climb the ladder, though a picture of him adorned the Throne of Glory. In Poland and elsewhere in Europe, it is believed that the heavens part on Christmas night to reveal Jacob's ladder with its angels coming and going between earth and heaven. Compare ASCENT TO UPPER WORLD.

Jacques de Vitry (1178–1240)   French prelate, preacher, and historian, born at Vitry-sur-Seine. He studied at the University of Paris, was ordained, and about 1210 became a curé. One of the most zealous preachers of the crusade against the Albigenses, he even took part in some crusades and was present at the siege of Damietta in 1218; from then on he took an active part in Eastern affairs. His letters, and, in lesser degree, also his sermons, are important studies of customs and manners (mores). The collection *Sermone Feriales et Communes* (1229–1240) contains 104 exempla which constitute one of the most important collections of the type. He is believed to have originated many of the exempla himself with which he adorned his sermons. The best known of these is the tale of the Devil and the Lady. His stay in Palestine (1216–1227) is said to have influenced his exempla, but recent scholarship minimizes this influence. De Vitry's history of the Crusades, *Historia Orientalis*, is valued as a source book, the companion volume, *Historia Occidentalis*, as a criticism of European mores. In 1230 he became cardinal-bishop of Tusculum, later was sent on missions to France and Germany, and in 1239 was named Latin Patriarch of Jerusalem.

jade A tough, durable, siliceous mineral also known as nephrite, jadeite, or chloromelanite, depending on its color and composition. Jade is usually thought of as a deep green, but is common in a wide range of colors from black through brown, red, lavender, blue, green, yellow, and white, and occasionally flecked with gold or vermilion. It is generally associated with China, where it is the most highly prized of minerals, but is found and valued elsewhere. Although very tough, it is readily worked and was used in prehistoric times for the manufacture of weapons, implements, and utensils throughout the Orient, central Europe, Ireland, Mexico, and Alaska.

In Mexico, Egypt, and China, jade was placed in the mouth of the corpse to represent the heart when this organ was buried separately; in China it was sometimes used to cover the eyes, ears, nose, and mouth, and as weights on burial robes. Jade, though a mineral, possesses *yang*, the vital masculine principle, to a great degree; thus it serves to revitalize the spirit of the dead. The blue varieties of jade especially are connected with the heavens, and with the souls of those dwelling there. When struck gently, jade produces a rich resonant lingering tone. Prayer stones or gongs, which were in early use in China, have been found in scattered places throughout Africa and among the Hopi Indians of the United States, being used in a similar manner. In Mexico jade was used principally in religious ceremonials and a jade knife was frequently used for human sacrifice. In New Caledonia a small jade cleaver was used for preparing the meat for cannibal feasts, but is now merely the symbol of the chief's authority. The Maori of New Zealand wear grotesque human figurines of jade (*heitikis*) around their necks and these are passed on from generation to generation. Here, no women dare approach the jade-cutters. In the Loyalty Islands it is very highly prized and the people will trade their daughters for objects of jade.

From early times it has been a luck stone in China and its virtues have spread until it is today one of the most universally regarded amulets. Lord Rosebery and Lord Rothschild are both said to have carried jade amulets when their horses won the "Derby." Members of a certain Mohammedan sect carry flat amulets of jade to protect them from annoyance and injury. In China, Burma, and India white jade amulets of various shapes have particular efficacy in specific situations: the Chinese believe any piece of jade rubbed in the hand while making an important decision or embarking on a new venture will impart luck to the undertaking. Chinese emperors communed with Heaven through a pierced disk of white jade.

Its medicinal virtues have been extolled in the Orient from early times, but they seem to have reached Europe principally through the Spanish conquerers of Mexico, who called it the "colic stone." In China they tell of a fountain of jade wine flowing over jade rocks in the Isles of the Blest, which is a specific against all the ills of the flesh; because of its *yang*, it prolongs life, imparts immortality, and if taken in sufficient quantities prevents the body from decay after death. It brings youth, health, children, victory, power, wisdom, and immortality. If this wine cannot be obtained, however, finely powdered jade in water will serve almost as well. Powdered jade will strengthen the lungs, the heart, and the voice. Jade, rice, and dew boiled in a copper vessel purifies the blood, strengthens the muscles, hardens the bones, and calms the mind. If taken consistently, it makes the person impervious to heat and cold, hunger and thirst. But, while jade brings good health, when it becomes dull and lusterless it is a sign of impending death or misfortune. In Burma, India, and Tibet, jade is a cure for heart palpitations, will deflect lightning, and when thrown into water, will bring mist, rain, or snow. Throughout the Orient, a jade cup will crack in the presence of poison. Among the Indians of Mexico it was considered good for the kidneys and effective in all internal disorders. There also it imparted strength and longevity when taken internally. In Great Britain women wore a jade belt to cure rectal stones, and in Scotland there have been several famous jade curative touchstones. In China jade has been called the solidified essence of pure mountain water. [JWH]

Jade (or **Pearly**) **Emperor** Yü Huang Shang Ti, Supreme Ruler of the Taoist Heaven and the universe: chief Taoist deity. His palace is the "fathomless, immaculate jade palace" situated in the constellation Ta Wei (Ursa Major). He is regarded as the giver of life, the vitalizing power of earth, judge, forgiver, and savior of mankind. His birthday festival is observed on the 8th day of the first month, when peasants journey to his temple to present candles and make offerings of fruits and incense. See *General Structure of Chinese Folklore* in CHINESE FOLKLORE; YÜ HUANG.

Jagannātha or **Juggernaut** In Hindu mythology and religion, a form of Kṛiṣhṇa: literally, lord of the world. Kṛiṣhṇa was killed by a hunter; when his bones were found and placed in a box. Vishṇu directed King Indradyumna to make an image (Jagganātha) and to place the bones inside. A certain Viśvakarman agreed to make the image, but was interrupted by the impatient king after 15 days and refused to finish the hands and feet. Hence Jagannātha has neither.

Jagannātha is worshipped in parts of India, especially at Puri, Orissa, where the two festivals held annually in his honor attract multitudes of pilgrims: he is sometimes called Puri from this, his principal seat of worship. During the first of these (Snānayātra) the image is bathed; during the second (Rathayātra) the image, accompanied by images of Subhadrā and Balarāma, is drawn on a car in a procession, giving rise to the story that devotees cast themselves under the wheels. Actually, however, the spilling of blood is considered a defilement.

jaguar A large leopardlike mammal (*Felis onca*) of wooded regions from Texas to Patagonia, figuring largely in South American Indian mythology, shamanism, and folk belief. The curing shaman of the Cariban Taulipáng invokes the jaguar to cure swellings caused by eating deer meat, because the jaguar himself lives on deer meat. The jaguar is a favorite familiar of shamans; the shaman can even turn himself into a jaguar; in fact, the were-jaguar belief is common throughout many South American Indian tribes. See JAGUAR-MAN.

Eclipses are caused by a huge supernatural jaguar who attacks the sun and moon (Abipón, Camacan, Chiquito, Chiriguano, Guarani, Incas, Mataco, Mocoví, Mojo, Toba, Vilela, Yuracare). The Cayapó, Timbira, and Sherente tribes of eastern Brazil have a story about a boy abandoned in a tree who was rescued by a benevolent jaguar and given the gift of fire to take to mankind.

In Caingang mythology, the twin culture heroes, Kamé and Kayurukré, created jaguars out of ashes and coals, but later decided to do away with them. They induced all the jaguars to get on a tree trunk which was lying in a river; Kamé was to push the log off into the swift current, but some of the jaguars grabbed hold of the bank and roared. Kamé was terrified and ran away. Thus the jaguars came ashore and still exist today.

In Bororo Indian mythology (Brazil) Jaguar marries a chief's daughter, warns her against his mother, who is a caterpillar. The old mother finally makes the young wife laugh, however, while Jaguar is away, and she dies laughing. Jaguar returns, removes twin boys from his wife's abdomen, and burns up the caterpillar-hag. See END OF WORLD; EYE-JUGGLER; FIRE.

jaguar dance A dance of the Western Bororo Indians of eastern Brazil; a dance of appeasement and propitiation of the spirit of a slain jaguar, performed by a hunter who has just killed a jaguar. Dressed in the skin of the slain animal and wearing necklaces of jaguar claws and teeth, he dances and leaps in imitation of the animal and is believed to be possessed by its spirit. The dance is accompanied by the wailing of women, lamenting the death of the jaguar.

jaguar-man The South American werewolf. In South America where there are no wolves, the jaguar takes his place. It is a common belief in the Amazon region that sorcerers wander by night as jaguars to attack their victims. It is not always clear, however, whether the belief is that the sorcerer transforms himself into a jaguar or whether he sends forth his soul to incite and lead some actual jaguar against his victims. The belief in jaguar-men was especially strong among the ancient Æbipón. In Paraguay this superstition is still shared by Indians and mestizos alike. [AM]

Jahi (Pahlavi *jeh* or *jah*) The harlot-demon of the *Avesta*, a malicious female fiend: personification of adultery and whoredom. Eredaṭfedhri, the virgin, is invoked to defeat the evil introduced into the world by Jahi. In the *Bundahishn*, Jahi is the personification of sin.

Jalandhara In Hindu mythology, a titan king who, after accumulating great powers as a result of practicing extraordinary austerities, defeated the gods of the created spheres, established a tyrannical, wicked, and selfish government, and then sent Rāhu to challenge Śiva to give up his beautiful bride, Śakti, recently reborn as Pārvatī. Śiva countered this incredible challenge by letting fly from between his eyebrows a terrific burst of power which materialized as a lion-headed demon with emaciated, hungry body and irresistible strength (Kīrttimukha). Rāhu took refuge in the Almighty, Śiva himself, and the monster was then forced to feed upon itself.

Jalang In Semang (Malay Negrito) belief, the wife of Tak Pern, the Supreme Being; daughter of Yak Lepeh, one of the three grandmothers who live under the earth and guard the roots of the stone which supports the heavens. According to the Kintak Bong, Jalang was Tak Pern's sister. See BATU HEREM.

jaljoginī In Indian folk belief, especially in the Punjab, a disease-causing spirit which occupies streams and wells, and casts spells on children and women.

jalpari In Indian folk belief, especially in the Punjab, a water spirit who compels men to cohabit with her, or kills them when she catches them. She can be conciliated by offerings of flowers or a lamb on the banks of the river in which she lives.

Jambū-dvipa or **Jambu-dwīpa** Literally, the rose-apple island: India; in Hindu cosmogonic mythology, one of the seven continents or islands of the world with Mount Meru at its center.

James Harris The title of a ballad (Child #243) of comparatively recent date: known also as *The Daemon Lover* and *The House Carpenter*. The wife of the carpenter, after seven years, is visited by her lost lover, who persuades her to leave husband and children to go with him in his ship. The ship sinks, or she jumps or is thrown overboard, and she drowns. Child gives eight variants of this rather unspectacular (despite its *Daemon Lover* title) ballad, and it has been reported from several localities in the United States.

Jam on Gerry's Rock An American come-all-ye of the northeast woodlands, telling of the death of a young lumberman, Munroe, in a log jam. It is probably based on fact but so far the clues to the actual location and incident have not established whether a Gerry's Rock in the East Branch of the Penobscot River or some other place was the scene of the accident or whether the drowning of two men nearby in the 1860's gave rise to the story. It has been a favorite of woodsmen all over the northern lumbering areas of the United States and Canada, has been found in Wisconsin, Michigan, North Dakota, and has been adopted in Scotland, one of the few songs to reverse the usual direction of transmission. It is generally sung to a set of an Irish air, in rubato-parlando style, without accompaniment, and with the last words spoken.

Jamshīd The Persian name for Yima: in Iranian mythology, the first man, who became sovereign of the abode of the blessed. Jamshīd, as Persian culture hero, appears in the *Shāhnāmah*.

Jan A beneficent nat of the sun of Kachin folklore, worshipped by the chief at a ceremony called *nat sut ai*. Food and drink are offered and the chief begs protection from this nat (and from Shitta, nat of the moon, who is worshipped at the same time) for the whole village.

Janus In Roman mythology, the two-faced god of beginnings, of doorways and entrances: a pre-Latin divinity, who with his feminine counterpart Jana may have been the highest (sun and moon) gods of the pre-Italian inhabitants of the country. When the Latins arrived, with Jupiter and Juno, Janus and Jana (which are variant forms of the names Dianus and Diana) became secondary in importance to them, though Janus always did keep the preeminence of being first invoked before all other gods in important undertakings. Several theories are argued concerning his origin: as god of light and day; god of doorways; god of the heavenly vault; triple-oak god, etc. Some believe doorways (*janua*) were named for him; some that he took his name from doors. Traditionally, the worship of Janus was begun by Romulus; his temple, by Numa. This temple, in which stood the double-faced statue of Janus, was at the northeast end of the Forum, and was an arch facing east and west. It stood open in war, closed in peace: it was closed only four times before the Christian era.

The Agonia, on January 9, was in Janus' honor, as were also the beginnings of every day, month and year. The New Year's Day presents of the Romans included coppers with two-faced Janus on one side, and a ship on the other. Every action, occupation, undertaking, though sanction came from Jupiter, depended on its beginning being blessed by Janus. As Consivius he presided over the beginning of human life. Here, and at the worship of both at the kalends by their priest and priestess, he seems in some manner connected with Juno. His priest, the Rex Sacrorum, was the religious representative of the king as head of the state. Janus was the inventor of agriculture, of civil laws, of religious worship, of coinage; he was protector of shipping and trade.

Early representations of Janus show him as a two-headed god; later, four-faced statues appeared. He originally carried the porter's staff in his right hand and the key or keys in his left; later representations show him indicating 300 with his right hand and 65 (the remainder of the days of the year) with his left. Offerings to Janus were barley, incense, wine, and cakes called Januæ. See CARDEA.

Japanese folklore *I. Mythology—Shinto* a) *Cosmogony* According to the *Kojiki*, the oldest Japanese book, written in 712 A.D., the history of the world begins with the birth of seven deities, who arise and pass away in the "plain of high heaven." After them, five couples of deities were born, the last of whom, Izanagi and Izanami, were ordered by their peers to consolidate the earth, which heretofore had been a chaos of muddy water. Equipped with a jeweled spear, Izanagi and Izanami stood on the "floating bridge of heaven" (probably the rainbow) and dipped the weapon in the brine below. When they drew it up again, a bit of brine which had stuck to the shaft dropped down and congealed, thus forming the island of Onogoro.

The divine couple then descended to this island and built a house, where they begot a child. However, as the first words during their union had been spoken by the Izanami, the woman—which was against the divine ritual—, this child, Hiruko, turned out to be a misfit and was abandoned in a boat of reeds. Their second child, the island of Awa, was not reckoned among their progeny, either. At last, having learnt the cause of these failures from their fellow gods, Izanagi and Izanami amended their words—this time Izanagi speaking first— and thus gave birth to the eight main islands of Japan.

b) *Theogony* Then they proceeded to beget many more deities, until Izanami died during the birth of her last child, the God of Fire. More deities then sprang from her decomposing body, and more again from the unhappy father's tears. Wroth at his consort's death, Izanagi cut off the head of the God of Fire, and more divine beings were born from the victim's blood and limbs.

Meanwhile, Izanami had gone to the underworld, from where Izanagi wanted her to return. She told him to wait, but his patience gave out, and he entered Hades before being called by his spouse. He found her a hideous, rotten heap, and precipitately fled from the underworld, pursued by the Furies whom the offended Izanami had sent after him. Eventually he managed to escape, and blocked the entrance to the underworld with a huge rock.

Outside again, Izanagi felt compelled to wash off the impurity of the underworld, and more deities were born from his limbs while he bathed in a river, as well as from his clothes. Thus Susa-no-wo, the God of Wind, sprang from his nose: from his right eye came the God of the Moon, and from his left eye, Amaterasu Omikami, the Sun Goddess, the principal deity of Japan and direct ancestor of the Imperial House.

The *Nihongi*, written in 720 in Chinese, gives a slightly different version of these myths; but as it appears to be far more influenced by purely Chinese ideas than the *Kojiki*, only the older version of the story is given here.

c) *The Sun Goddess and her impetuous brother* As Susa-no-wo refused to obey his father Izanagi, he was banished. Before departing, however, he wanted to say farewell to his sister, the Sun Goddess, and therefore ascended to heaven. His sister, distrustful of his intentions, asked Susa-no-wo to prove his good faith to her. He offered to bring forth male deities by a miracle; if they should turn out to be female, he would be insincere. Susa-no-wo then produced five gods from a string of jewels which his sister had given him, while Amaterasu broke her brother's sword in three pieces and, crunching these in her mouth, spat out three goddesses. These eight deities became the ancestors of the highest Japanese nobility.

Exulting over his success, Susa-no-wo then fell to committing various acts of mischief, and finally scared his sister, the Sun Goddess, badly by throwing a flayed horse through the roof of her weaving-hall. Amaterasu thereupon retired to a rock-cave, and thus deprived the whole world of light.

All the gods were in despair. At length they hit upon a stratagem, and, by arousing Amaterasu's curiosity by a comic dance and a mirror, lured her from her cave.

Susa-no-wo was punished with a fine and other penalties, and expelled from heaven. Before he finally left the upper regions, he killed the Goddess of Food, whose limbs turned into the seeds of useful plants.

Then follows a cycle of myths connected with Susa-no-o, which seemed to have originated independently and were subsequently woven into the unified scheme of a national mythology. Suffice it to say here that Susa-no-o's descendants are represented as ruling over the province of Izumo before the reign of Japan's legendary first emperor.

d) *The conquest and organization of the earth by Amaterasu* After the pacification of the celestial realm, the Sun Goddess turned to the earth, i.e. the islands of Japan, and after three abortive attempts to establish her rule there—these failures being due to the messengers chosen—her grandson Ninigi was sent down with eight companions to assume power on earth. The descendants of Susa-no-wo in Izumo had already consented to recognize Amaterasu's authority. Ninigi descended to Kyushu and married a beautiful girl there. He had with him the three sacred insignia of imperial power, given to him by Amaterasu: the mirror, Kagami, which had lured the young Sun Goddess from her cave, the sword found by Susa-no-wo in a serpent's belly, and the jewel Yasaka.

Ninigi had three sons, one of whom married the daughter of the Sea God and by her became the father of a boy. This boy, when grown up, in his turn married his mother's younger sister, and thus became the father of Prince Toyomikenu, canonized as Jimmu Tenno, the first emperor of Japan, who is said to have ascended the throne in 660 B.C. Before his final triumph, however, he had to fight his way from Kyushu to Yamato, an ancient district on Honshu, the main island; Yamato thus became the first name of the new state.

II. Mythology—Buddhist Buddhism, introduced from Korea in the 5th and 6th centuries, offered the Japanese, among other things, the promise of a future life beyond the grave, together with paradise and hell. Furthermore, it introduced great numbers of new deities, many of whom were soon surrounded with legends of their own. The final triumph of Buddhism came when all Shinto gods were declared to be reincarnations of Buddhist deities.

Among the countless figures of Buddhist mythology in Japan two at least have to be mentioned separately, namely Jizo and Kwannon. Many tales and legends have been woven around the central figures of both Jizo and Kwannon.

Jizo, according to popular belief, is the great protector of all sufferers, and particularly of little children, whom he looks after even in the underworld. Moreover, he has the power of leading sinners from hell to paradise.

Kwannon, originally a Bodhisattva (i.e. a future Buddha), and therefore of male sex, had already become a woman in Chinese popular iconography, and is now generally known as the "Goddess of Mercy." She is extremely popular in Japan, and may be considered, to a certain extent, the emotional equivalent of the Madonna in Catholic countries.

Under the influence of both Indian and Chinese ideas Japan also evolved a rich demonology. These *oni,* as they are called in Japanese, play an important part in fairy tales, in legends, and on the stage.

III. Popular narratives Japan is truly rich in native fairy tales, many of them very beautiful. Among those known to every child are:

1. The story of Urashima Taro, the Japanese Rip van Winkle, who married the Sea King's daughter and stayed away from his home for three hundred years. When he came back and saw that everything had changed, he inadvertently opened a bottle which his wife had forbidden him to open, and while his life-spirit escaped from the bottle, Taro himself shriveled up and died.

2. The story of Momotaro, who was found as a baby sitting in a large peach (*momo*) and adopted by the old couple who had found him. After growing up, he went to Onigashima ("Devils' Island") and forced the demons to hand over their treasures to him. Eventually he returned in triumph, accompanied by his three animal friends, a dog, a monkey, and a pheasant.

3. The story of Kintaro, whose real name was Sakata no Kintoki. He grew up in a forest, and became a boy of

prodigious strength. Ultimately he joined the celebrated warrior Minamoto Yorimitsu (11th century), with whom he performed many memorable exploits, amply embellished by the imagination of later ages.

4. The story of the Mirror of Matsuyama, which tells of a girl who imagined that she saw her dead mother's face in a mirror, without realizing that it was her own countenance, and thus became a model of filial piety. This tale is told during the Girls' Festival.

5. The story of the Bamboo-Cutter and the Moon-Child, which tells of a divine being who was sent down from the moon to earth as a punishment, and grew up in a poor woodcutter's house. After refusing many suitors, even the Emperor himself, she was taken back to the moon again at the appointed time.

In many fairy tales, leading parts are played by animals, as is the case in other cultures, too; but two animals have quite a folklore to themselves in Japan, namely the fox and the badger. Fox stories came to Japan probably from China, and soon became part and parcel of popular beliefs. The fox is a mysterious being, mostly of a malicious nature, lives to a great age, and can assume human shape, particularly that of a beautiful woman. Foxes are dangerous, because they bewitch people, and "fox fire" is the Japanese name of the will-o'-the-wisp. The only kind foxes are the messengers of Inari, the God of Rice, who is himself sometimes confused with a fox.

The badger is credited with similar attributes, and badger stories generally resemble those told of foxes.

IV. Festival lore Apart from her national holidays, established by law, Japan has a number of traditional festivals, which go back to very ancient times, and often originated in China. Those still observed include, first of all, the "Five Festivals" (*gosekku*):

1. *Nanakusa* (Seven Grasses) on January 7th, when a stew made of rice gruel and seven fresh herbs is eaten ceremoniously; the superstitious believe that diseases can thus be warded off during the following year.

2. *Hinamatsuri* (Girls' Festival) on March 3rd. Its main feature is the display of heirloom dolls in the *tokonoma* or alcove of every house where there are daughters in the family. The dolls represent a medieval Japanese emperor and empress with their court. A feast is spread before them on miniature dishes, and the girls are told stories about exemplary Japanese women.

3. *Tango no sekku* (Boys' Festival) on May 5th, celebrated by all families with sons under seven years of age. From a tall pole in the garden a giant paper carp floats in the air—a symbol of strength and virility, since that fish climbs steep waterfalls on its mating journey. The *tokonoma* or alcove is decorated with dolls representing ancient warriors and heroes of popular tales, as well as miniature weapons.

4. *Tanabata* (Weaver's Festival) on July 7th, of ancient Chinese origin, and commemorating the beautiful legend of the star "Weaver" (Vega), who may meet her lover, the star Altair, only once a year in the Milky Way. On this day Japanese doors are decorated with appropriate poems, written on strips of colored paper. Girls' schools hold special exhibitions of their students' handicrafts.

5. *Choyo* (Chrysanthemum Festival) on September 9th, which in modern times is celebrated mostly by staging exhibitions of chrysanthemums.

The most popular festival is New Year, celebrated

for three whole days. As only children observe their individual birthdays, New Year is also the collective birthday of all adults, from which the years of one's age are reckoned. People visit shrines and temples, prepare and eat special food, pay off their debts, and observe the "first dream." This latter custom consists of putting a picture of the *takarabune* under one's pillow before going to bed on January 3; what one dreams that night is deemed prophetic. It is best to see Mount Fuji in one's dream.

The Japanese equivalent of All Souls' Day is *Obon*, celebrated between July 13th and 16th. It is usually called the "Feast of Lanterns" in Western descriptions. The spirits of the dead are believed to come home once a year during these three days, and have to be suitably entertained with food and such other things as they enjoyed while alive. Special lights burn at the gates to point the way to the spirits, and Buddhist bonzes go from house to house to conduct services for the dead.

Another popular festival is *Setsubun* on February 3rd, when the destiny for the next year of one's life is determined. In the evening of this day, people take one bean for each year of their age, and throw these beans all over the floor, shouting: "In with good luck, out with the demons!"

V. Marriage and funeral customs A traditional Japanese marriage requires the services of a matchmaker or go-between, who deals with the parents only. Even today it is still the exception in Japan for two young people to fall in love with each other and get married; as a rule, marriages are arranged by the parents.

The go-between first arranges a meeting of the parties concerned and their parents—called *miai*—usually in a restaurant or similar public place. If this proves successful, the *yuino,* or engagement gifts, are exchanged. These consisted originally of silk, rice wine, cloth, and the like; but nowadays their place is frequently taken by money, which is sent by the bridegroom to the bride. She then returns part of it to him. This concludes the formal betrothal.

The marriage ceremony itself, for which no religious rite is essential or even customary, is very simple. After the bride's trousseau has been sent to the bridegroom's house, the bride herself proceeds there in the evening of the wedding day, dressed in a special kimono and wearing a triangular hood on her hair (called the "horn-cover," to conceal the "horns of jealousy"). The bridal pair then perform the *sansan-kudo* ceremony, which consists in exchanging ceremonial cups of sake (rice wine) nine times. The official introduction of the newly wedded couple to each other's parents concludes the marriage ceremony.

Funerals were the special domain of the Buddhist clergy for many centuries; nowadays Shinto priests conduct funeral services as well. Both cremation and burial are customary. Buddhists, when choosing the latter, usually place the corpse in the coffin in a squatting position. Prayers are said over the grave, and the ancestral tablet of the deceased is added to the family shrine.

The period of mourning varies greatly, according to the degree of relationship—from 30 days to 13 months. The color of mourning is white, as in China.

VI. Various beliefs The belief that certain times, locations, and objects bring good or bad luck may be said to be the most prevalent superstition among the Japanese. As it exists today, this belief goes back to the Chinese pseudo-science of *fêng-shui*, a mixture of magic, astrology, and geomancy. Thus, for instance, according to one's daily horoscope, one must not move in certain directions—people born under such and such a sign of the zodiac must avoid going south on Thursdays. The same rule applies to whole periods; persons born in the year of the Rabbit (sign of the Chinese zodiac) cannot expect good luck on the day of the Tiger. As the last example shows, the logic behind this reasoning is delightfully simple.

Northeast is always an unlucky direction, because demons are believed to enter from there.

As each individual has his own fortune or destiny, so also buildings. When, therefore, a misfortune befalls a house, it is blamed on the bad luck of the structure, or sometimes on its bad location.

People whose occupations involve great risks are prone to consult fortune-tellers on every occasion. They will also wear talismans or amulets (*ofuda*) usually in the shape of a slip of paper, stamped with the seal of a temple.

The ages of 19, 33, 42, and 47 are believed to be unlucky years, because the pronunciation of these figures in Japanese is open to several interpretations (e.g. 42, if pronounced *shi-ni*, literally "four-two," also means "death").

Fortune-telling is especially important at a betrothal, to ascertain the compatibility of the engaged couple's destinies. Any girl born in a year designated by the zodiacal sign "Fire-Horse" has a poor chance of finding a husband, because she is believed to "burn" her spouse, i.e. to cause his death.

Many Japanese, to counteract these manifold evil influences, have the dates of all important events in their lives fixed by the *ekisha*, the professional astrologer and fortune-teller.

Even ordinary social life has been invaded by such beliefs. When invited to dinner, for instance, a Japanese will always eat at least two bowls of rice, because one bowl would mean an offering to the spirit of a dead person.

Many peculiar customs are connected with illness. When someone suffers from a skin disease, he may put on a large straw hat and then dip into a river, lake, or the sea until the hat floats; the disease will be carried away with the hat.

Under the influence of Shinto, impurity is considered unlucky; this may partially explain the scrupulous cleanliness of the average Japanese. For ritual purification salt is used.

As a parallel to the medieval "abracadabra" the Japanese, too, use magic formulæ which are now meaningless; e.g. the word *aburaunkensowaka*, said when meeting a snake.

VII. Dances The Japanese differentiate between two main kinds of dancing, *mai* or classical dance, and *odori* or popular dance. Classical dancing is characterized by its stately, slow movements, in contrast to the livelier *odori*. A special variety of classical dancing is the *bugaku*, or court dance, introduced originally from China and Korea. There are 160 different *bugaku*, each representing an ancient event in India, China, Korea, or Tibet.

The art of dancing is traditionally derived from the

kagura dance, said to have been performed by the goddess Uzume when she endeavored to lure the Sun Goddess from her cave. The *kagura* dance is still performed at certain temples and shrines.

The *odori* are still a characteristic feature of rural districts. The best known dance of this class is performed during the "Lantern Festival" (*Obon*) in July, when both men and women form a circle and dance on the village common to the accompaniment of flutes and drums, singing ballads or love songs.

VIII. Music and songs The three main instruments in Japan are known as the *sankyoku;* they are the *samisen, koto,* and *shakuhachi.* The first is a kind of three-stringed guitar, played with a large plectrum; the *koto* is a more resonant lute with thirteen strings, and the *shakuhachi* is a bamboo flute. Other popular instruments include the drum and *biwa,* a lyre with four strings.

Japanese music owes much to the music of China and Korea, though it has been developed on independent lines, just as everything else the Japanese introduced from abroad.

Space forbids dealing here even cursorily with the vast field of Japanese folk songs. Suffice it to say that the Japanese are exceedingly fond of singing, and have an inexhaustible stock of folk tunes. See MIN-YO.

IX. Proverbs As with all other peoples, the accumulated wisdom of ages is expressed also by the Japanese in the form of terse proverbs. Given the similarity of human nature everywhere, most of these are similar in meaning, even if not always in form, to their Western counterparts.

Here are a few specimens, culled at random: The devil in one's heart reproaches himself (i.e. a guilty conscience needs no accuser). An ill-smelling being does not know its own smell. A bee to a weeping face (i.e. misfortunes never come singly). It is dark at the foot of a lighthouse (i.e. the darkest hour comes before the dawn). Know another's pain by pinching yourself. The man who steals money is hanged; the man who steals a kingdom becomes king.

Bibliography:

Bush, Lewis, and Kagami, Y., *Japanalia.* London, 1938.

Chamberlain, Basil Hall, *Things Japanese.* London, 1939.

"The Kojiki," translated by B.H. Chamberlain, in the *Transactions of the Asiatic Society of Japan,* vol. 10, supplement. Yokohama, 1882.

de Visser, M.W., "The Fox and Badger in Japanese Folklore," in *Transactions of the Asiatic Society of Japan,* vol. 36.

Erskine, William H., *Japanese Festival and Calendar Lore.* Tokyo, 1933.

Griffis, William Elliot, *Japan in History, Folklore and Art.* Boston, 1905.

Hearn, Lafcadio, *Glimpses of Unfamiliar Japan.* Boston, 1894.

——, *Kokoro.* Boston, 1898.

——, *The Romance of the Milky Way.* Boston, 1905.

Mackenzie, Donald A., *Myths of China and Japan.* London, 1923.

Mason, Joseph W.T., *The Spirit of Shinto Mythology.* Tokyo, 1939.

JOHN L. MISH

jarabe A Mexican mestizo couple dance, also adopted in New Mexico and California. Jarabe means "sweet sirup" and expresses the saccharine, flirtatious quality. Many Mexican states have special jarabes, all using the Spanish *zapateado* as foundation step; but in place of playing castanets the girls manipulate their skirts and the boys cup their hands behind their backs. They smile at each other.

The *jarabe tapatío,* or Mexican Hat Dance, is considered the national dance. *Tapatío* refers especially to Jalisco, but the dance appears on all cabaret programs and is taught in all schools. The Spanish heritage has become well mixed with Polish, Russian, and Austrian traits. The nine melodies with descriptive names are in different rhythms: the jarabe is in 6/8; *El Borrachito* (the little drunk) staggers to a 3/4 mazurka; *La Paloma* (the dove) in 2/4 time gives the dance its turning point, for the girl dances in the brim of the hat, the boy in pursuit. The final triumphant *Diana* uses the vigorous steps and duple rhythm of the *Komarinskaia.*

In the *jarabe de la botella* of Jalisco, the couple take turns dancing over a bottle of tequila. The less ostentatious *jarabe michoacano* features waltz and polka steps, thus a shift from triple to quadruple time. The entertaining *jarabe tlaxcalteco* enacts mime of tortilla-making. There is also a *jarabe mixteco, jarabe chiapas,* etc.

Jarabes are sometimes danced ceremoniously at weddings and by children at funerals. Jarabe steps are used in the ceremonial *morisma* or *machetes,* a knife dance of Michoacán, related to Moriscas. In Oaxaca the jarabe tunes or *sones* are termed *fandangos.* The French and Spanish *jota* or the Andalusian *jarabe gitano* sired the Mexican jarabe. [GPK]

jarana Literally, noisy diversion. (1) A mestizo couple dance of Yucatán, also appropriately called *La Mestiza.* The men, in spotless white trousers and shirts, hold their hands cupped behind their backs; the women, in filmy embroidered *huipil,* ribboned headdress, and high-heeled shoes, lightly lift their skirts. The two lines, face to face, execute waltz and *zapateado* steps, with pull backs and foot brushes. As the two lines cross over, all curve their arms upward, snap their fingers in Spanish style. Nonetheless, the downcast eyes and impassive mien retain an Indian reserve. Though the jarana is a secular dance and popular in large cities (even at Riveroll's in Mexico City), it has ritual associations in Yucatán villages. At all religious fiestas, as well as weddings, dedications, and welcomes to guests, it is danced before the chapel, four times during the fiesta, and with the same ceremonials as the *vaquería.* A *torito* concludes it, or witty interpolations, called *bombas.* [GPK]

(2) A small stringed instrument, a form of ukelele, which gives its name to a type of music and to the characteristic folk dance of Yucatán. It is also used by the leader of the Michoacán comic fiesta dance, *Los Viejitos,* and in the *huapangos.*

(3) A gay tune without words played by jaranas, brass instruments, drums, and sometimes gourds, to accompany the folk dances of Yucatán. See VAQUERÍA. [TCB]

los jardineros Literally, the gardeners: a group dance of valley pueblos in Oaxaca, Mexico. The name is justified chiefly by the wreaths of flowers carried aloft by the dancers. With smirking masks and mincing burlesque of polkas, mazurkas, and waltzes, they take off the superficial extravagances of courtly life. The elegant evolutions of European longways are mimicked by a line of men in short trousers and gay silk shirts, and women-disguised men in short dresses, cloth hair, and heavy oxfords. This ridiculous little performance is probably of recent origin, likely from the ephemeral reign of the Austrian Maximilian and Carlotta; yet it may have a vague association with the more serious *arcos* and other arch dances of pagan vegetation rites. [GPK]

jar-drum A pottery vessel, sometimes partly filled with water or grain, made into a drum by stretching a skin across its mouth, and used in the rituals of many peoples. The Mexican *bajbin* of the Chamulas and Tzotzils is reserved exclusively for carnival times and is treated with the respect and ceremony characteristic of drum customs the world over. Two attendants are appointed for the care of the *bajbin* between carnivals, their duties being to guard the drums in one of their homes, to offer incense and veneration before them at regular intervals, and to prepare them for their public appearances. This preparation consists of washing with hot water and camomile, changing the cords of the drumheads, offering ceremonial brandy to the drums, dancing around the drum table and shooting off fireworks. On carnival days the *bajbin* accompanies dancing close to the church doors.

Jason In Greek legend, the hero who led the Argonauts to Colchis and back to Greece. He was the son of Æson, rightful heir to the throne of Iolcos. However, Pelias, the stepbrother of Æson, usurped the throne and Jason was sent by his mother to be brought up in safety by Chiron the Centaur. Pelias was told by an oracle that he would be killed by one of the Æolidæ, his and Jason's family line, and also to beware of a man with one sandal. Leaving Chiron after years of study, Jason came to a swollen stream and there helped an old woman across, losing a sandal in the fording. The woman, when they reached the other side, revealed herself as Hera, and her aid and Athena's were later of great help to Jason. Jason entered Iolcos wearing the one sandal, was recognized by Pelias, and was warmly greeted. But Pelias, fearing for both throne and life, induced Jason to set forth to recover the Golden Fleece carried off by Phrixus. See ARGONAUTS.

On his return from Colchis with Medea, and after Medea had boiled Pelias to death, Jason was driven from Iolcos by Acastus, the son of Pelias. He and Medea went to Corinth where Jason threw over Medea, the barbarian princess, for Glauce, Creon's daughter. After Medea's escape from the Corinthians, Jason remained seeking to avenge the deaths of Creon and Glauce, and childless now lived out his days in that city. One day, seated in the shadow of the *Argo*, he was struck by a piece of the rotting ship that fell and killed him.

jasper An impure opaque variety of red, green, black, or mottled quartz used by the ancients as a gem as well as for vases and statues. The Indians of California picked it up on the beaches and carried it as amulets. It is mentioned as one of the stones of the High Priest's breastplate (*Exodus* xxviii, 20) and some authorities claim as many as three other stones were also different colored jasper. It was highly thought of by medieval physicians

and recommended for every pharmacy. It was said to quicken thought and action, and at the same time to ensure caution and avoidance of needless risk. Hildegard of Bingen (12th-century nun), in her *Subtleties of Diverse Creatures*, advised women to hold a piece of jasper in the hand during childbirth to guard against the evil that could come to mother and child from demons of the air.

Red jasper was sometimes used by the Egyptians in place of carnelian as the "Blood of Isis" and as the "Buckle of Isis" on the throat of the dead. It was especially fine for young girls, giving them grace and beauty and curing their diseases. Medicinally it was used, for the most part because of its color affinity, to stop hemorrhage, strengthen the pulse, and to check the flux. In modern Italy it makes the wearer invisible. It was sometimes used as the birthstone of March.

Green jasper (*jasper viridis*) was often used in place of jade by the Chinese in the mouth of the dead. Medicinally it was very effective, whether used in place of the emerald, or in its own right. It aided the stomach and spleen by contact, and was worn over the kidneys to prevent retention of urine. In Elizabethan England it was called the "spleen-stone." It also drove away evil spirits and cured fevers, dropsy, and epilepsy, and prevented snakebite. A piece of this stone, inserted under the skin of an epileptic by a surgeon, was known to have prevented seizures for three years, after which time it fell out. It was worn by physicians to aid them in their diagnoses.

Black jasper was formerly used as an aid to the capture of cities and fleets, but today is rarely used except by Italian farmers as a protection from lightning. Mottled jasper was used to prevent drowning or death on or near the water.

Jātaka or **Stories of the Buddha's Former Births** One of the oldest and most important collections of folktales extant; a collection of 547 stories, translated from the Pali; see edition of E.B. Cowell, vols. I–VI, Cambridge, 1895–1907. The *Jātaka* consists of a collection of *gāthās* arranged in 22 sections, according to the number of stanzas forming a *jātaka*, the jātakas of each section progressively containing an additional gāthā. Thus those in the first section contain one stanza, those in the fifth, five, etc. These gāthās are embedded in a prose commentary, which consists of a story of the present explaining why the Buddha is telling the tale of the past, followed by the jātaka (the gāthās) or story of the past, a commentary on the gāthās, and an integration of the two parts. All but the gāthās are considered the work of one author. It is the jātakas which contain the folklore. They include fables, märchen, moral tales, maxims, and legends. More than half the stories are not of Buddhist origin and are found in other Indian collections such as the *Panchatantra* or the *Kathā Sarit Sāgara;* many of the stories, e.g. *The Wolf and the Crane, The Ass in the Lion's Skin,* and others appear in Western literature, especially in *Æsop's Fables.* To the orthodox Buddhist, however, the *Jātakas,* which are part of the Buddhist sacred writings, are autobiographical accounts of Gautama Buddha. See FABLE.

Jatayu or **Jatayus** In the *Rāmāyana,* king of the vultures, son of Garuda; an ally of Rāma in his battle against Rāvana to prevent the abduction of Sītā. He was mortally wounded by Rāvaṇa but was able to tell Rāma what had become of Sītā before dying. In the *Purāṇas* he caught and saved Daśaratha when, searching for Sītā, he was hurled from heaven by śani.

Javerzaharses In Armenian belief, female spirits, invisible and endowed with certain knowledge: literally, the perpetual brides. They can neither learn anything new nor forget anything. They love weddings and singing, are believed mortal, and are interested in the toilette, marriage, and childbirth.

jawbone Bleached and polished jawbone of horse, mule, etc., rubbed with a key or other metallic scraper to produce a rhythmic click: used by American Negroes in slavery times as a musical instrument and probably derived from the African custom of rubbing a notched stick for rhythmic accompaniment to music and religious rites.

jazz A word of disputed and uncertain etymology applied to the instrumental dance music originated by American Negroes in New Orleans toward the close of the 19th century. A number of later derived music forms such as Tin Pan Alley ballads, swing, "symphonic jazz," etc., have also been called jazz, but being composed on paper, arranged and rehearsed note by note, they have little or no relation to folk music. The original jazz, however, is definitely rooted in folk and primitive music, synthesizing in a new form the inherited musical patterns of the African west coast, the urban and rural Negro folk song of the southern United States, and elements of ragtime and blues, combined with some thematic material of European derivation.

Basically it is a group improvisation integrated by rhythm. The chief characteristics, as they are preserved in phonograph recordings and are still played by the bands devoted to "hot jazz," are a duple meter—2/4 or 4/4 time—rarely giving way to triple meters; syncopation and ostinato figures on the off-beat; the use of "blue notes" (see BLUES) and pentatonic or hexatonic scales; the subordination of melody to rhythm; pitch variations similar to those in blues singing; and a vocalized style of instrumental tone production.

The formative period of jazz began when band instruments of European type first became easily available to Negroes. That happened with the breaking up of Confederate military bands after the Civil War and the appearance of drums, cornets, trumpets, trombones, clarinets, and tubas in pawnshops and second-hand stores. Gradually, over a period of 20 years, musical groups of varying size and shifting membership were drawn together around these instruments to practice and eventually play for lodge functions, funerals, parades, Mardi Gras, and dances, and in time to become a feature of New Orleans life. Their repertory included ragtimes, minstrel songs, cakewalks, popular songs, and marches. (*High Society* and *Panama* became marching classics, and the favorite piece for the return from a funeral was *Oh, Didn't He Ramble*.) A band would advertise its skill and the events for which it performed by circulating through the streets in wagons and playing. When rival wagonloads met, a duel of sound took place until one was blasted into defeat. Everywhere the wagons were trailed by an admiring and imitative straggling of small boys serving an apprenticeship that was to produce some of the greatest players of jazz.

The instrument most admired was the cornet, and the cornetist who could blow his rival off the street was accorded the title of "King"—"King" Bolden, "King" Oliver, etc. Among the great New Orleans cornetists and trumpeters are also included Bunk Johnson, Freddie Keppard, and Louis Armstrong.

The early jazz men developed an instrumental technique of their own. Generally self-taught and lacking music-school ideas of purity of tone, they played their instruments as their people had sung, imitating on their horns the wailing, growling, shouting, moaning, laughing, and sobbing tones of the human voice. Their music was closely related to the traditional ways of singing and to the insistent, interweaving rhythms to which Negroes in Africa and in America had danced, worked, and worshipped. Drums and tubas beat out the rhythms formerly carried by stamping feet, clapping hands, and log drums. The trombones, cornets, and trumpets sang out like the voices in the African chant or in the spiritual, in solo statement and chorus response, or in collective improvisation with constant variation on several melodic, rhythmic, and tonal levels. The effect was contrapuntal, rather than harmonic.

Chief patrons of the music makers came to be the "houses" of Storyville, the New Orleans red-light district, where the new music came indoors, changed from a marching to a dancing character, and really crystallized as a music type. More intimate instruments, such as the plucked string bass, banjo, and guitar entered the rhythm section of the band, displacing the tuba. The number of players worked down to a fairly characteristic group of four to seven. And the style of a few Storyville pianists such as Clarence Williams and Jelly Roll Morton made itself felt in the combination. Non-Negro influences included melodic inspiration for theme and variation from current popular song and from French and Italian dances and operas. (*Tiger Rag*, for instance, was evolved by Jelly Roll Morton from a French quadrille.) Clarinet players of Creole background contributed their polished and fluid French-schooled technique to the instrumental complex. And from the Caribbean islands through the port of New Orleans came an already acculturated, secondary African strain with Spanish rhythmic coloration.

At the same time there were jazz bands composed largely of white performers who played in two different ways—the rapid and nervous style of the Original Dixieland Jazz Band and the more even line and tempo of the New Orleans Rhythm Kings.

The legal measures putting Storyville out of business in 1917 provided the impetus for a general northward movement of jazz. From the brothels of New Orleans it went to the speakeasies of Chicago, still sponsored and given a hearing by underworld operators. Nearly all of the Negro virtuosi of jazz were heard there at one time or another, and, though jazz was primarily instrumental music for dancing, the great blues singers sang to their playing. However, the frenetic style which came to be known as Chicago jazz, and the lighter pattern of Kansas City jazz, followed the lines of the New Orleans white bands, even though many of the best-known white players deeply admired and imitated the Negro "kings." The development from there on to the large complement of players, the "name bands" and "symphonic bands" of the 1930's, departed almost completely from folk paths, except insofar as old themes were echoed and the trance mood was sought. The idea of playing in a state of possession relates back to similar states evoked in Negro dancing for religious rites, but in the late periods of jazz it was sometimes induced by marijuana rather than emotional ecstasy.

The underworld connections of jazz, its association with the drug and liquor traffic, and with a release from inhibitions, made it the center of considerable social controversy in the '20's. Jazz was denounced from the pulpit and deplored in the press. Its musical character was little understood and was largely overlooked in the excitement over its moral implications. However, its idiom was seriously studied by art musicians and is strongly influential in much of the concert-hall music of today. The works of Ravel, Stravinsky, Debussy, Hindemith, Copland, Bernstein, and many others have made use of jazz rhythms and blues themes.

Among the secondary folkloristic products of jazz may be mentioned the development of a jargon, "jive talk," combining hundreds of terms for instruments, playing styles, characteristics of performers, etc., with a semi-secret vocabulary referring to the drugs, the places of entertainment, the dives, jails, purveyors of contraband, etc., and the controversies of race with which so many jazz players became familiar. Much of this vocabulary is the equivalent of earlier thieves' cant. Another product of jazz has been noted just recently—the return to the source, by which music now appearing as urban folk song in cities in Africa shows the influence of American Negro jazz. [TCB]

☞ By its very nature jazz is dance music and is performed by jazz bands as such. Yet it is becoming increasingly popular as concert performance, with the tantalizing and curiously frustrating effect of a passive reaction to its intoxications. Ultimately its origin in Negro rhythms is ritualistic and at its best it retains a frenetic ritualism. Negro slaves brought the intricate and ecstatic rhythms of African tribal cults to the southern plantations and there adjusted them to white religion and harmonies in the spirituals, and in virtuoso individualistic dances, such as *juba, cakewalk,* and *clog. Buck and wing* has been adopted in sophisticated circles, and tap is almost entirely an exhibition form. The songs accompanying these exuberant outbursts are also highly syncopated, and they have communicated this quality to folk songs of southern whites and inculcated the dancing of the Kentucky running-set with off-beats of instruments and footwork.

The Music. At the turn of the century ragtime appeared in Louisiana as the progenitor of true jazz, the name referring to the torn rhythms. In 1915 it created a sensation in Chicago, and has since then swept not only this continent, but most of the globe. In the hands of Negro musicians it was and still is an improvisatory and ecstatic heterophony of instruments. (Many orchestras play under narcotic influence.) A jazz band consists of a piano, percussion instruments—various drums, tambourines, gongs, lately also Cuban rattles and *guiro* (notched stick)—a large glittering collection of brass winds, notably saxophones, trumpets, trombones; clarinets; fewer strings, such as a bass violin played by plucking and striking, perhaps a steel guitar, banjo, more rarely violins. A full jazz symphony orchestra adds cornets, tubas, euphonium, fiddles, celesta, and other instruments. Various gadgets and technical devices eke out every conceivable tone-quality: moans, quavers, screeches. The complex percussion on a strong duple beat sets the pace, and becomes increasingly erratic. The other instruments alternate or synchronize in paroxysms of rhythm and harmony. The early jazz produced amazing cacophony. This became more subdued during the 30's (the "swing" period), but reappears in "re-bop," returning to the harsh, fierce outbursts.

One might speak of four types of jazz composition and performance: 1) Popular dance music for actual execution. This includes the creations of W. C. Handy (*St. Louis Blues*), Duke Ellington (*Black and Tan Fantasy,* etc.) and Harry James (*Trumpet Blues*), and the transitory derivative "jazz classics" of Tommy Dorsey (*Minuet in Jazz*) and Ray Noble (*Comanche War Dance*). W. C. Handy popularized the mournful mood of the blues. 2) Musical comedy music of George Gershwin, Jerome Kern, Irving Berlin, etc. This was of course written for theatrical dance performance. 3) Symphonic jazz, introduced by Paul Whiteman in Gershwin's *Rhapsody in Blue,* Ferde Grofé's *Metropolis,* etc., and Robert Russell Bennett's *Sights and Sounds;* and streamlined in Stan Kenton's strident dissonances. This is intended for listening, but has been utilized by concert dancers. 4) Sophisticated concert jazz, on a level with the best classical music: John Powell's *Negro Rhapsody* and *Jazz Age,* Gershwin's *Concerto in F,* Gruenberg's *Jazzberries,* Leonard Bernstein's *Fancy Free,* J. Alden Carpenter's *Skyscrapers,* William Grant Still's *Afro-American Symphony* —some composed for ballets, some as instrumental music. Europe has caught the fever, with some fine results in a more serious vein, notably the New Music of Reginald Forsythe, an English Negro (*Lullaby, Two Hymns to Darkness*); Stravinsky's Bach-jazz blends (*L'Histoire du Soldat*), Debussy, Tansman, Hindemith, and others.

The Dance. All jazz dancing finds its incipience in the musical beat, sometimes bearing the same name as the music, or—as usually in the ballroom—reacting to the newest tunes with any steps that seem fitting to the dancers. In the ballroom the jazz dance is exceedingly individualistic, and rarely draws several couples into one formation. On the same floor the same tune may accompany the most conservative one-step and the most extreme boogie-woogie. In the half century (1900–1950) these steps have come into being in the following sequence, by decades—

(1) The simple and sedate two-step and one-step, which vary their walking with zigzag, turns, serpentines, etc. The shoulder-opposition of the one-step was in Germany distorted and gave the dance the ill name of *Schieber.* The foxtrot, which varies the walk with *chassé* on turns.

(2) Eight step, Castle Walk, turkey trot, Boston (from waltz), etc., all still proper in manner.

(3) In an outburst of postwar danceomania—the shimmy, bunny hug, grizzly bear (in a dead clinch), Hoosier hop, and the jitterbug or jive variants, which amalgamated into the Lindy, black bottom, Charleston, shag, and Lindy hop. Jitterbugs let their arms and legs fly in angular frenzy; with twisting feet they meet, separate, swing about; they jump, fall, and in Negro Harlem and the West Indies, contort in abandoned acrobatics.

(4) Jitterbugging continues and boogie-woogie arises:

a combination of round dance and individual improvisation incorporated in the Big Apple (now extinct); trucking, Susie-Q, Jersey bounce, etc.

(5) Boogie-woogie and its subvariants, mooch, sand, duck-walk, camel-walk, Rochester, fish-tail, Detroit jump, etc. All of these steps return to deepest Africa in the insistent flat-footed emphasis, the sway-back posture, bent or overstretched knee, the full use of the entire body in motions at one moment barely perceptible, in the next daringly acrobatic. Couples may dance in a trance-like embrace, or at a distance, yet electrically united. The man may *mooch,* jerking his pelvis forward and back, while the woman sinks and rises with flexed, shivering knees. The fundamental boogie step, in ballroom position, is a double side-step (to r.) and toe-heel accent (l., r.) The fast boogie, in promenade position, uses a pat-step, with half and full turns under the arch of joined hands, winding, unwinding, and crossing, all at breakneck speed. These steps follow the main beats of the music, but good dancers may syncopate, or stamp out a veritable counterpoint against the already complex musical rhythms, snapping their fingers in a further complementary rhythm. Boogie and jitterbug, the truest forms of jazz, are here to stay.

Jazz is, first of all, a Negro creation, secondly, an adoption (and frequently virtuoso adoption) by American whites. Born in the rural South, it has grown to maturity in the metropolis of the North, but is returning to metamorphose southern folk music into steel guitar ragtime. In most foreign countries it is ill at ease, stiff, and self-conscious, notably in Europe and Mexico. In the Orient it is still in bad repute, but is making gradual, relentless headway. In Mexico it frequently presents the incongruous picture of expert playing on marimbas and a puppetlike execution of "djezz hawt." Only around Veracruz the admixture of Negro blood has produced the erotic *danzón.* The syncopated, sensuous ballroom contributions by Latin American countries (*rumba, samba, tango*) are related to jazz, but are not jazz. However, in the West Indies, the Jamaican *jive* and *mento* vie with Harlem boogie in an apotheosis of erotic dance-realization.

Transference to the stage—as often occurs with these—may render them more artistic and may underscore the ritualistic essence; but such crystallization cools the fever of the spontaneous dance possession. [GPK]

jealous craftsman and his apprentice The theme of several folktales, principally European, in which the pupil surpasses his master, who preserves his rank as best of his kind by getting rid of the apprentice. The classical Greek story is of Dædalus and his nephew Perdix (or Talos or Calos). Dædalus, who invented carpentry, taught Perdix what he knew. But one day Perdix picked up a fish's backbone and cut through a sliver of wood, thus inventing the saw. Seeing that his pupil's imagination would lead him to greater things, Dædalus threw Perdix (who is also credited with the chisel and the compasses) from the Athenian Acropolis. Zeus transformed the youth into the partridge (*perdix*) before he was smashed on the rocks below. Similar stories have been told of artists, sculptors, magicians, etc., etc. The pupil whose work is precocious is dismissed by the master. These stories are similar in theme to the story of the death of Æsculapius, killed because he brought the dead back to life and thus overstepped his bounds. The jinn imprisoned because they give away the secret of what will imprison them, and the ogre who tells where his external soul is, are related in concept. Miach, son of Diancecht, the ancient Irish physician, healed Nuada more quickly than his father thought consonant with good. So Diancecht killed his son, whose curing was evil, and then destroyed knowledge of the properties of the herbs that grew from Miach's body. The theme has its converse too, best exemplified in the story of the master magician Merlin, trapped into eternal imprisonment by his own pupil.

Jean-Jeudi Nickname of the bridegroom of the Beauce region in northern France who has been foolish enough to allow himself to be married on a Thursday. The nickname implies that he has an unfaithful wife. Thursday weddings are avoided for this reason.

Jean Sot or **Foolish John** The typical numskull of the world-wide noodle stories as found in the French folktales of Louisiana. Calvin Caudel (*SFQ* 12: 151 ff.) has made an analytical study of four Louisiana Jean Sot or Foolish John tales with reference to types and motifs, diffusion, and variants. Foolish John typically misunderstands his instructions (shoots the cow instead of milking her), or takes them literally (throws the dog, named Parsley or Percy, into the soup instead of parsley as his mother told him [J2462.1]; or puts baby clothes on the chickens he was told to dress for dinner). He burns his grandmother up trying to warm her, greases the dry cracked edges of a mud-hole with butter or lard out of pity (J1871), gets his head or hands stuck in the porridge pot, wraps up the stove, or a tree, to warm it (J1873.3), takes with him the door he was told to guard (K1413), and sometimes ends up possessor of a fortune stolen by two robbers whom he has unwittingly put to flight.

Jehovah Lord; God; the God of Jewish and Christian religion: often contrasted with Yahweh, the earlier concept of God among the more primitive Hebrews. See YAHWEH.

Jellon Grame A Scottish ballad (Child #90) of a cruel lover: also known as *Hind Henry*. Child collected four versions and a variant of the story. His A and B versions differ essentially in the original situation, but tell the same story. Jellon Grame sends for Lillie Flower, his mistress. She comes to meet him in the woods and he kills her with his sword. But he saves their child that lays "weltring in her blude," and gives it to three times three nurses to rear. When the child is grown to a boy, Jellon Grame shows him the spot where he killed the mother, and the boy puts an arrow into him. The *Hind Henry* variant contains two incidents missing from the A version which are of general folkloric interest. The child saved from the dead mother, like many a folk hero, is extremely precocious; he grows rapidly and learns quickly. And, when he walks in the forest with his mother's killer (he is the son of May Margerie and Brown Robin, not Hind Henry),

> "O how is this," the youth cried out,
> "If it to you is known,
> How all this wood is growing grass
> And on that small spot grows none?"

The infertility of places where a foul and treacherous deed has been done is common in folklore. Compare in the *Kalevala* the barrenness of the spot where Kullervo seduces his sister.

Jenny Jones Most common American title of a children's game song, sung usually to the same melody as *Mulberry Bush,* and preserving vestiges of ancient funeral customs. Players sing, "We've come to see Miss Jenny Jones, and how is she today?" One answers, often in spoken tones, "She's washing (ironing, etc)." Finally the answer is that she is dead. Then the questions deal with colors to be worn for the funeral (blue for constancy, green for grief, yellow for gladness, etc.) until purple is accepted as suitable for mourners. The game becomes a chase when the ghost arises to disperse the visitors. *Jenny Jones* is a corruption of the Scottish *Jenny, My Jo* (jo meaning sweetheart). In France it is *Jeanne, ma joie.*

This song is similar in substance to another singing-game survival of grave rites, *Green Gravel,* in which the washing and burial of the dead are described, and a turning back after the funeral is accompanied by hand-clapping to ward off the spirits of evil. There is also mention of a letter from the dead, symbolizing communication after death. The song survives in England and in the United States. See MOURNING SONGS.

Jephthah In *Judges* xi-xii, the son of Gilead and a harlot. When his father's legitimate sons were grown, they threw Jephthah out; but when the Ammonites invaded their territory, the sons called Jephthah back to lead them. This he did on condition that he should be their chief after the war as well. Jephthah vowed that if he were successful he would sacrifice the first thing that came forth to meet him when he returned home. And it was his only child, his virgin daughter. (See JEPHTHAH'S VOW.) He fulfilled his oath; in the times following, the women of Israel observed four days each year in memory of his daughter. The sacrifice was thought to have taken place at the winter solstice, and in the belief that wells were unfit to use during the solstices and equinoxes, it was said that the blood of Jephthah's daughter poisoned the water at this time. Later the Gileadites fought with and defeated the Ephraimites. Whenever they captured one whom they thought to be an Ephraimite they made him say "Shibboleth," which the Ephraimites could say only as "Sibboleth." Thus friends and enemies were separated, and the enemies were killed.

The Biblical story, according to Pierre Gordon in *Sex and Religion,* reflects several customs in Hebrew context that are found in other Mediterranean cultures. Jephthah, for example, was probably the child of a sacred prostitute, became an outcast and robber chief, and was called upon, as a knowing fighter, in time of need. The two months spent by the daughter in the mountains bewailing her virginity were probably part of the typical seclusion custom of the puberty rite, and the four-day observance by the women were the three days and one more of the initiation ceremony. Parallels to the myth of Persephone are obvious. In Shechem the daughter was actually called Kore, Persephone's name as the maiden. The two traditions, Greek and Hebrew, do not reproduce each other exactly but they show sufficient similarity to indicate similar rites underlying both legends.

Jephthah's vow A folktale motif (S241), found in stories all over the world, in which the fulfilment of the rash promise of the father, "the first thing he meets at home," entails giving up his child: so called from the Biblical story of Jephthah's daughter (*Judges* xi). A whole group of motifs (S240 ff.: children unwittingly promised) utilize a similar idea: what is promised is the first thing over the bridge—evaded by driving the dog over first and so outwitting the Devil (S241.1); or "what you have at home," a child born in the father's absence (S242); the father promises "Nix Naught Nothing," but this synonymic empty promise comes to something when he arrives to find a new child so named (S243). A Fjort (Africa) story embodies S245: what is born on your farm. Two women agree that the owner of the farm owns whatever is born on her land. One gives birth to a child on the farm of the other; the owner of the farm claims, and gets, the child. Similar to the *Frog Prince* story is S247, in which the father promises his daughter to her rescuer, not knowing that the rescuer is a dog: this is in a Chinese tale. The promise made to get out of danger (S222) as in *Beauty and the Beast* and *Hans My Hedgehog,* both transformation stories, often involves giving up a daughter. Also like these are the stories in which a child is promised to a mermaid, a giant, a monster, the Devil, etc., in return for some gift. None of these fairy tales use the motif as pointedly as the Biblical story does, where the daughter is actually sacrificed, but Andrew Lang saw in the Jephthah vow "a moral warning against rash vows, combined with a reminiscence of human sacrifice." Thus, undoubtedly, the appearance in the Middle Ages of the Devil in the story, to whom the child is promised. In a French-Canadian tale, "Le Diable et la Bougie" (*JAFL* 29:110), the fisherman promises a stranger whatever will appear. Since this is always his little black dog, he readily exchanges the promise for the ability to make a good catch of fish. But it is his little son who appears. When the stranger (the Devil, of course) comes for the child, the fisherman's wife bargains. The Devil agrees not to take the boy until the candle goes out. Whereupon the fisherman's wife blows it out: it did not go out, she put it out. A tale of Spanish provenience, reported from Zuñi by Boas, uses the same idea: the woodchopper must sell his son to the catfish; he thought it would be his little dog. Compare HERODIAS; IPHIGENIA.

Jericho The first city conquered by the Israelites under Joshua in the Promised Land. Seven priests bearing seven ram's-horn trumpets preceded the Ark in marching about the wall of the besieged city. On the first day, they circumambulated the city once, on the second day twice, and so on, until on the seventh day they marched around the city seven times. Then, at a blast on the trumpets and a shout from the people, the wall fell flat and the city was taken. See ACHAN.

Jersey Devil A famous phantom of the southern Jersey shore, born variously at Leeds' Point, at Pleasantville, at Estelleville, and other villages: also called *Leeds' Devil.* It was said to be the offspring (sex unknown) of an old woman who had so many children that she said if she had another she hoped it would be a devil—and it was. The supposition is that the woman actually gave birth to a monstrosity, which she kept out of sight in a shuttered room, and that the mystery of the birth plus her expressed wish gave form to the story. The Jersey Devil was no fiction, however, up and down the shore. Its footprints were often seen, its cries often heard; if shades were left undrawn at night, it would come and look in people's windows; it was seen sporting in the surf with mermaids, or sitting gibbering on chimneys. An old woman in her eighties in 1947 reported that she was once chased by it. The newspapers reported its activities constantly; it is still occasionally mentioned by the press. See H. C. Beck's "Jersey Devil and Other Legends of the Jersey Shore," *NYFQ* 3:202.

'Jesha Name of an Afrobrazilian cult group in the city of Bahia. At present it is one of the lesser groupings, being overshadowed by the larger Ketu and Gêge cults. It derives from the Yoruban town of Ilesha, Nigeria, whose people bear the designation Ijesha. [MJH]

Jesse James Most famous of the American "bad-man" ballads, written, according to one of the stanzas, by Billy Gashade, whose identity is unknown, and relating outstanding episodes of the Missouri outlaw's career. Jesse James was born in Clay County, Mo., of a family of Confederate sympathies, fought with Quantrell's guerrillas, and, with his brother Frank and a band of men, committed numerous daring bank robberies and train hold-ups. The stories of his deeds fall into a familiar folk pattern of robbing the rich to give to the poor. His death and betrayal by a member of his own gang completes the legend fittingly. He was shot for a $10,000 reward by Robert Ford on April 2, 1882, in St. Joseph, Mo., where he was living under the name of Howard. The song was composed shortly thereafter and has taken its place as a favorite all over the United States.

Jessie polka A version of the polka as danced in the Middle Western United States. Partners progress counterclockwise in skating position: left heel forward, tilting body back, right toe back; tilting forward, right heel forward; left heel forward and to ankle; four two-steps.
[GPK]

jestbooks Collections of short, pointed stories, usually noodle stories pointed at a disliked class (e.g. scholars) and often interlarded with indecent jokes. A collection of Greek jests, attributed to Hierocles (5th century A.D.), probably dates from the 9th century. During the later Middle Ages and the Renaissance, many collections of facetiæ, Latin and others, were made. Jestbooks were among the first books printed; the famous *Liber Facetiarum* of Poggio Bracciolini of Florence appeared in 1470, from which other collections in Italy, Germany, France, and England drew their inspiration—and material. Aretino in Italy, Rabelais and his followers in France, Bebel and Pauli in Germany follow. In England, Walter Map's *De Nugis Curialium* of the 12th century, though not a jestbook, was filled with anecdotal and sometimes pointed material. The heyday of the jestbook was the period from 1500 to 1700. Collections were attached, for selling purposes, to the names of famous jesters: *Merry Tales of Skelton* (1566?), *The Jests of Scoggin* (1626), *Tarlton's Jests*, books purporting to derive from Peele or Hobson or Mother Bunche, tales of Gotham, the Pasquil stories, the *Hundred Merry Tales*,

all fall within the period. Perhaps the best known today, through reputation, is the collection by Mottley made in the 18th century and attributed to Joe Miller. Jest collections continue to be popular today; any news-stand sells jestbooks claiming to contain "1000 New Jokes," or "1000 Jokes about . . ." what have you. Dialect joke books still sell steadily; and in 1949 a book of jokes about doctors and their patients sold at $2.95. The jokes in the modern jestbook are as old as the stories in Hierocles' *Asteia*. There we find the story of the farmer who complains that just as he has taught his horse to live without food, it died. There too is the story of the sleeper who awoke from a vivid dream that he had stepped on a nail and hurt himself. "Of course," his companion said. "What can you expect when you go to bed without shoes on?" The Little Moron stories current in the United States in the 1940's used these and many other jokes popular in Europe during the past millenium or so.

Jesus Folklore attached to the Jesus story is nearly all explicatory or expatiatory of his precocious infancy or of the dramatic last days of his life. Exceptions are the hog and haddock stories based on motifs (A2287 ff.) that Jesus caused certain characteristics to appear in animals. Finns explain the short snout of the hog, and northwestern Europeans the vestigial toes on the back of the animal's forelegs, as the effects of the presence of the evil spirits driven into the quadruped's ancestors by Jesus (*Matt.* viii, 28–34; *Mark* v, 1–20; *Luke* viii, 26–40). Similarly, the two black spots near the gills of the haddock are said to be marks of the thumb and finger of Jesus as he held and broke the two fishes of the lad's luncheon to feed the 5,000 (*Matt.* xiv, 15–21; *Mark* vi, 35–44; *Luke* ix, 12–17), but other lore attributes the spots variously to St. Peter or the Devil.

The infancy narratives of the apocryphal gospels and other extracanonical books show how soon legend, folklore, and myth began encrusting the story of Jesus. Indeed, radical higher criticism makes the whole story a myth, merely another version of the legend of the sun god, born as a babe at the winter solstice and resurrected at the vernal equinox. Even comparatively conservative Biblical scholars incline to admit that folk beliefs had already been added to historical facts in the Jesus narrative prior to its recording in the accepted gospels.

Particularly the stories of the "wise men from the east" and the marvelous moving star they saw (*Matt.* ii), and of the shepherds and the "heavenly host" of angel singers they heard (*Luke* ii), together with the various visions, dreams, and apparitions of angels, all bear the authentic marks of folklore, paralleling the infancy narratives of the founders of other faiths.

The story of the jealous king (Herod) seeking vainly to kill the child of destiny is, of course, a stock first-act situation in the dramatic folk histories of many others than Sargon, Moses, and Œdipus. Frazer, in *Folklore in the Old Testament*, ii, 437–455, gives ten others. Even the story of the virgin birth of Jesus is by no means unique in the history of religions, for, coupled with the corollary god-father divine parent concept, virgin mothers are alleged to have given birth to no less than thirty saviors, heroes, or founders of religions from Adonis to Zoroaster.

It is of interest to students of folklore that when the synoptic gospels are arranged chronologically in the order of their composition, the first, *Mark*, written about a generation (25–30 years) after the death of Jesus, has no infancy narratives, no mention of a virgin birth, and no record of post-resurrection appearances of Jesus. But these stories all appear in *Luke* and *Matthew*, written barely another generation later. It is also of interest to note that some unknown editor later (probably in the 2nd century A.D.) added a typical folklore section at the end of *Mark* (xvi, 9–20) which appears in the King James and Rheims versions, but has been excised from modern versions since it does not appear in the oldest Greek, Syriac, Armenian, or Ethiopic manuscripts.

The accretionary process of constant expansion and addition of legend and lore continues when we pass to the later Christian apocrypha and pseudepigrapha, on through the church fathers, ante-Nicene, Nicene, and post-Nicene. The stories about Jesus and Mary become more and more miraculous and wildly incredible in the apocrypha of the Eastern Church, especially in Ethiopian Geez and Coptic manuscripts. Most of the extant Coptic fragments are of the 5th century or later, but probably contain stories and quotations from earlier books. They are rich in folklore. Collections are available in French by E. Revillout and P. Lacau, and in English by Forbes Robinson, *Coptic Apocryphal Gospels*. Summaries of and quotations from Coptic and many other apocryphal gospels, acts, epistles, and apocalypses are given in M. R. James, *The Apocryphal New Testament*.

The flavor of Coptic folklore about Jesus may be tasted in the following sample, condensing the Ethiopic *Book of the Cock*, which is read on Maundy Thursday in the Abyssinian Church. The wife of Simon the Pharisee (*Luke* vii, 36–50) served Jesus with a cock cut up and placed in a lordly dish. First Jesus blessed bread and gave it to Judas, who went out, Satan having entered into him. Jesus touched the cock to life, endowed it with speech, and bade it follow Judas and return and report. When the cock returned, it wept bitterly and so did the disciples when it told how Judas had gone home first, where his wife urged him to betray Jesus, then to the temple where he arranged with a rough man, "Paul of Tarsus," to deliver Jesus into his hands. When the cock ended his report, Jesus dismissed it to fly into the sky for a thousand years.

The colorful exaggerations of the East were later matched in the West in the medieval sacred legend collections, the tales of the troubadours and jongleurs of Provence, and the mystery and miracle plays of England and the Continent. We can give here but one of the many outflowerings of this rich field of Jesus folklore, an illustration of how great a plant may grow from one tiny seed. The *Harrowing of Hell* appeared about the end of the 13th century in England, the first drama in our tongue, done in dialog form with alliteration and rime. It tells of Jesus going down into hell to rescue the souls of the just, a task rendered easy by the flight of the gatekeeper. Now, this story is taken straight from the apocryphal book known as *Acts of Pilate* or *The Gospel of Nicodemus*, the second part of which, called *The Descent into Hell*, probably dates from the 5th century. This book in turn is obviously based on and is an expansion of the passage in *Matthew* (xxvii, 50–54) which is palpably a late folklore addition unknown to either *Mark* or *Luke*, relating that at the death of Jesus there

was an earthquake, and the graves were opened, "and many bodies of the saints which slept arose, and came out of the graves after his resurrection, and went into the holy city, and appeared unto many." In the *Acts of Pilate* it is related that two of these resurrected saints, Karinus and Leucius, wrote down what Jesus had done when he descended into hell after his crucifixion, then returned to their sepulchers, leaving their manuscripts with Annas and Caiaphas to be read to the people.

Naturally, the accretions of addition and expansion have increased in number and variety whenever zealous missionaries have brought the Jesus story to folk of other cultures. Consequently, since this process has been going on for 19 centuries after Paul began his missionary journeys, and since of late the acculturation has been accelerated by more rapid means of communication and quicker transportation of both missionaries and bibles, the folklore of the Jesus story, if properly collected and classified, would occupy many scholars for decades and fill a score of volumes.

Take for example the simple motif (B250) of the effect of the sacred nativity upon the animal world. In the canonical gospels, no animals are actually mentioned as being present, but their presence was easily inferred— sheep from the mention of shepherds, an ox from mention of a manger, camels which bore the wise men from the east, and an ass which would be the natural means of transportation for Mary "great with child" from Nazareth to Bethlehem and for the new mother and babe on the flight into Egypt.

The ox and the ass were likely to be worked into the nativity story anyway sooner or later to fulfill two ancient Jewish prophecies. *Isaiah* (i, 3) had written "The ox knoweth his owner, and the ass his master's crib," and the Vulgate version by Jerome had a rendering from *Habbakuk*, "He shall lie down between the ox and the ass." So we find a Coptic Life of the Virgin relating that when Joseph returned with a midwife, the child was already born and the ox and the ass were protecting him. The *Gospel of Pseudo-Matthew* has the ox and ass adoring the child. This belief has spread throughout the world and many Christmas crèches show these two animals with their foreknees bowed in reverent worship.

Throughout Europe in general it is avowed that the cows speak to one another at Christmastide; the Breton peasants attribute this miraculous vocal power to all domestic animals at midnight Christmas Eve. In parts of England it is said that on Christmas morn, the rooster's usual "Cock-a-doodle-doo" becomes "Christus natus est!"

The Middle Ages knew another version of the ox and ass legend. The latter was said to have brayed loudly for joy at the birth of the Christchild, while the phlegmatic ox remained silent. The ass, which had come from Nazareth in Galilee of the Gentiles, was considered symbolic of the Gentiles, while the Bethlehem ox represented the Jews. Since, also, the ass was alleged to have borne Jesus as a child into Egypt, and as a man on his triumphal entry into Jerusalem, there arose from all these notions and associations, in the not always logical fashion of folk custom, a very popular, somewhat sacrilegious and somewhat anti-Semitic festival, honoring the ass. See Ass, FEAST OF THE.

Other legends were not so hard on the ox, allowing him also to accompany the Holy Family into Egypt and picturing him patiently pulling a wagon piled with the baggage of the refugees from Herod's wrath.

By a sort of poetic justice, the relative approbation of the animals is reversed in the acculturized modern version of the nativity reported from Guatemala by Sol Tax (*JAFL* 62, 125 f.). The Chichicastenango Indians have it that Jesus was born in a stable (*un rancho*) on a cold snowy night and the newborn stiffened as if dead. Herdsmen brought in cows and sheep whose breath warmed and revived the child. But the mules and horses coming in did not believe the infant to be God, so instead of breathing on him, they belched in his face. So Jesus blessed the cows and sheep but punished the mules and horses by decreeing that they would always be beasts of burden and never have the privilege of being eaten by man.

At the other end of the Jesus story, attached to various incidents of the passion week, we find such a wealth of folklore, legend, and myth that a few samples must suffice.

There is the Breton story that bees originated from the tears of Christ on the cross, paralleling the old Egyptian legend that they came from the tears of Rā. The carnation pink is said to have sprung from the tears Mother Mary shed on her way to Calvary, but its first appearance is also alleged to have taken place at the time of Jesus' birth, his incarnation.

Many are the examples of the motif (A2721.2.1) that certain trees were cursed for serving as Christ's cross. Crosses on some trees and blood-colored sap in others are thus explained. Throughout northwestern Europe it is said that aspen leaves tremble because all the trees but the aspen refused to be made into the cross. The holly was once a great tree until, say others, it was used to make the cross: since then it has become much stunted and its berries like drops of blood. The crown of thorns was made of holly, which explains why its formerly yellow berries are now red. The birch, too, was a large tree, but is now dwarfed since its birch rods were used to scourge Jesus. But in Ireland it is the bog myrtle or sweet willow that they say was used to beat Christ and must therefore not be used to switch cattle. Yet the English carol *Bitter Withy* has Jesus cursing the willow to be the first tree that shall perish at the heart because his mother used it for his punishment.

The Chichicastenango Indians believe that the Jews made Jesus cut down the tree for his own cross. He struck one blow with the ax and a great chip flew off into the water and became a fish, which is why we eat fish during Holy Week.

One folk belief which is pure poetry will not let the cross of the crucifixion be dead wood. English medieval art of the latter 14th century, in wood and stone carvings, in paintings and stained glass windows, persistently depicts Christ crucified on a huge lily plant. In the Roman catacombs have been found a number of "foliage crosses," which have been interpreted as thus camouflaged to conceal their Christian meaning. But since other symbols plainly indicated that these graves were Christian, the entwined crosses probably thus early proclaimed the faith that the cross signifies not death but eternal life and foretells the lilies of the coming Easter. See ACCULTURATION; ADONIS; AHAYUTA ACHI; CHERRY TREE CAROL; DATE; FIG; HERUS.

CHARLES FRANCIS POTTER

Jesus (in Afroamerican belief) The worship of Jesus Christ is accepted by most New World Negroes (except the non-Christian Bush Negroes of Dutch Guiana), though the reinterpretations of Jesus differ from one region to another, and especially between those countries which are Catholic and Protestant. In Protestant areas, Jesus comes to hold a primary position among the powers of the Universe, as is evident in the character of worship in "shouting" churches of the United States and the West Indies. In Catholic countries Jesus, as one of a large group of spiritual beings, may be identified with an existing cult, as in Brazil, where the syncretism is with *Oshala*. In Haiti, on the other hand, Jesus is differentiated from the saints who are identified with the *loa* of the vodun cult, and is conceived as sharing, with God and the Holy Ghost, the task of ruling the Universe. [MJH]

Jewa-Jewa Among some of the tribes of the Malay Peninsula, a being who lives in heaven and intercedes with the Creator, the One God, on behalf of man: a form of the Malay-Sanskrit *deva-deva*. The magician prays to Jewa-Jewa for aid, and the soul of the magician gets medicine from him. Sometimes Jewa-Jewa is not appeased by the fumes of the incense and the incantations and refuses to intercede with the Creator to give the medicine.

jewel in snake's head A magic object of folk belief, folktale, and mythology; a stone found not only in the heads of serpents, but also in the heads of dragons, toads, dogs, swallows, etc. Sotacus, an early Greek writer, mentions the stone in the dragon's head. Pliny says that while there is a stone in the serpent's head, the serpent must be alive when the head is cut off or the stone will have no virtue. The value of such a stone was great; many charms and much magic could be accomplished through it. The stone in the swallow's head, specifically, was an irresistible love charm. Often the stone is a carbuncle; often it shines by its own light. Many prescriptions are given for obtaining it; Philostratus claims that in India the dragon is put to sleep by incantation and magical golden runes inscribed on a scarlet cloak. But to protect itself, the snake has developed a most efficacious means: it puts one ear to the ground and sticks its tail in the other. The origin of this, as of many other wonder tales, is probably India, from where the idea spread to Europe and to the East. The jewel-bearing snake appears in Malaya and Indonesia. In southeast Borneo, the primeval great serpent is said to have worn a jewel set in a golden crown. See BEZOAR; QUIRIN.

jewels from spittle A folktale motif (D1454.3) probably of Indian origin, very widespread in Europe. It belongs to the larger concept of magic spittle (D1001), i.e. curing spittle, speaking spittle, etc. The gift of spitting gold or jewels is often bestowed on a hero or heroine by some supernatural character or power in reward for kindness or obedience. It is frequent in the kind and unkind cycle of stories.

In the story of "The Cooked Child" in the *Kātha Sarit Sāgara* (see *Ocean of Story* viii:59, 59 n. 3), the narrator unwillingly ate two grains of rice from the pot in which the child of an ascetic had been boiled, and thereafter gold sprang up wherever he spat. In a Tibetan story not only does the hero spit gold but his companion spits turquoises. In a Swedish tale gold rings drop from the heroine's mouth, in its Norwegian variant, gold coins; in a Portuguese parallel pearls fall from her mouth. In a Finnish story the hero, after eating a certain bird, spits gold. Russian folktale has many jewel-spitting heroes, gold-dropping horses. A silver-dropping horse occurs in Votjak story. Roses also often fall from the mouth of the hero in Indian, Arabian, and eastern European folktale. The hero who "laughs roses" is frequent in German tales.

☞ A good many North American Indian tales from all parts of the continent contain the incident of jewels produced by magical means: from spittle (D1001; D1454.3), from excrements (D1454.5) or, more rarely, from tears (D1004; D1454.4). Often the jewels from spittle motif occurs in the cycle of imposter stories about the man or trickster who boasts of his magic power to spit gold or treasure in order to gain a wife. See BEAD-SPITTER AND THROWN-AWAY. [EWV]

Jew in the Thorns Title of one of Grimms' märchen (#110) and given to tale Type 592. A youth leaves service after three years with three pennies, his total pay. These he gives to a poor man, who grants him three wonderful things: a fiddle that makes everyone dance, a bow that never misses, and the power to make everyone do as he tells them. He meets a Jew on the road who asks him to shoot a bird. When the bird falls in a thornbush, the Jew goes to get it, and the youth begins to play on his fiddle, causing the Jew to be all scratched up. Later, the boy is sentenced to hang for theft, asks permission to play, and forces everyone to dance until he is freed. Sometimes the Jew is replaced by that other traditional butt of humor, the monk; sometimes it is a giant who is forced to dance until he cries quits. Often the central theme of the story appears together with other tale types; some thirteen are mentioned in Aarne-Thompson *The Types of the Folktale.* The story appears throughout northern and central Europe, down to Greece. In a Jamaica version of the tale, it is Anansi whose fiddle makes the irresistible music. The story has the earmarks of being connected with one of the medieval tricksters originally: from all indications, probably it was an Eulenspiegel tale at first, in the course of time exchanging Till's villain, the monk, for the Jew. The compulsive music has its parallels in Oberon's horn and in the pipe of the Pied Piper. Similar magical instruments cause not only people, but tables, chairs, etc., to dance, as Orpheus' music made the trees and mountains move.

Jew's Daughter An alternative title, and perhaps a more common one, for the English ballad *Sir Hugh* (Child #155): Child lists 21 versions and additional fragments of the ballad. The story is the famous tale of Hugh of Lincoln, told by Chaucer in the "Prioress' Tale," referred to by Marlowe, etc. Hugh of Lincoln, like William of Norwich and many other little boys of the Middle Ages, was said to have been killed by a Jew for ritual purposes and his body thrown into a well. In the *Annals of Waverley,* the body was rejected by a running stream and by the earth. The well was filled with light and a sweet odor; the body, when it was drawn out of the well, showed the stigmata. Touching the bier cured a blind woman. Matthew Paris, writing during the same period, says that the body was found by the mother. At any rate, eighteen Jews were hanged for the crime. An Anglo-French ballad of the time tells the story, but the first English ballads date from the 18th century.

Hugh of Lincoln, The Jewis Daughter, The Jew's Daughter (Percy) tell the same story. Hugh, playing ball, kicks the ball into the Jew's garden. He asks the Jew's daughter for the ball, and she entices him into the house with an apple, despite his misgivings. Inside, she stretches him out on a table and cuts his throat, or stabs him to the heart, with a knife. The ballad is detailed about the flowing of the thick blood, then the thin, then the heart's blood. She rolls the body in lead and drops it into the well. All the other children come home, but not Hugh. His mother goes out looking for him, and at last he speaks to her from the well. (Whether the blood was supposed to be used in the preparation of matzos, or used for marking the doorposts on Passover, or formed part of some cabalistic ceremony is not stated, but the coincidence of dropping a bloodless Christian cadaver into the well and the known predelection of Jews for poisoning wells undoubtedly added just that touch necessary for the story to be thoroughly accepted in the later Middle Ages.)

In the United States, where the ballad was carried from England and Ireland, it seems to be most often called *The Jew's Garden,* though Child includes a New York variant *Little Larry Hughes and the Duke's Daughter* (Hugh and the Jook's daughter retaining their identities). Elsewhere they are anonymous; the recurrent motifs of the rainy day and the tempting of the child with apple, gold ring, and red cherry appear in several variants. In Mississippi, an old woman remembered the ballad as one she used to be put to bed with.

There are several versions of the song found in America. The Jewish aspect of the story, however, has been lost in a number of the American texts, which refer to the lady as a "duke's daughter," or by no name or identification at all. The town of Lincoln has, by corruption of the phrase "it doth rain in merry Lincoln," become "Mirry-land toune," "Maitland town," and "American corn." In some of the versions the boy asks that he be buried with a prayer book at his head and a Bible at his feet.

jew's harp Probably a corruption of *jaw's harp*: an ancient musical instrument consisting of a frame in loop, notch, horseshoe, or rod shape, with a free vibrating tongue attached by one end to the frame. It is held in the player's jaws by the frame, the tongue being either plucked with a finger or jerked by a cord. The oval cavity forms the sound box and the tone is varied by changing the shape of the cavity. Originally of bamboo, with the tongue separated partially by slits, the instrument has also been made of metal since the 12th century, when it was mentioned and shown in a Chinese book. It is known in southeastern Asia, in Polynesia, Melanesia, Siberia, northern Europe, etc., occurs in excavations from neolithic times, and has been valued for its intimate quality. Nowadays it can be purchased in dime stores and is most frequently a toy. Since its sound is small, it has seldom accompanied activities of large groups, serving to pass the time for the solitary wanderer or itinerant worker and for the entertainment of small gatherings. In the Alps of Savoy it is played to accompany the dancing of a monkey.

jhoting In Hindu belief, the ghost of a low-caste Hindu who has died dissatisfied. He remains in his own house, or in a well or river. In the Deccan he is the spirit of a dead, unmarried youth, who lives in cemeteries or trees and personifies absent husbands. He leads wayfarers astray and waylays postmen who are safe only as long as they hold onto their bags.

Jibona Yoruban term, employed in the Afrobrazilian cults of Bahia, for the sponsor and "tutor" of a cult-member, during her ritual seclusion as a novitiate. [MJH]

jig 1) An intricate solo dance, with repeated hops on one foot, while the free foot points patterns in the air, heel and toe, front, side, or back. It is most popular in Ireland and Scotland. In England the Morris Jig is a virtuoso solo in contrast with the usual group Morris, as also the Bacca Pipes Jig, performed over two crossed pipes, as in the Scotch sword dance.

2) A figure dance for couples in 6/8 time, performed either in longways or quadrille, as the Irish Harvest Time Jig, with twice as many men lined up as women. In the 17th century Kemp's Jig, a man and two women describe patterns forward, back, and turning, and end with a kiss. The fast and furious rhythm consists of groups of three notes, in 3/8, 6/8, 9/8, or 12/8 time, though English jigs were sometimes in duple time in the 16th and 17th century. It corresponds to the French *gigue*, which features in musical suites, and the Spanish and Italian *giga*. This last is probably the earliest; Italian *giga* means instrument or limb and refers to the instrument of accompaniment. It never was a court dance, and has preserved its vitality to this day. [GPK]

Jiggs strip George McManus's pioneering husband-and wife comic strip introduced in 1913 and still going strong. *Bringing Up Father* has become proverbial for trying in vain to make a "gentleman" out of a "boor." Maggie and Jiggs are a newly rich working-class couple battling for mastery. Most of the humor concerns Jiggs' attempts to escape from her and her fashionable friends' clutches and remain true to himself and his old cronies. Jiggs reading his newspaper in solid shirt-sleeved, slippered comfort or gloating amidst the stolen pleasures of Dinty Moore's saloon, wearing incongruous silk hat, cane, and spats, has become a familiar symbol of the American lowbrow and philistine. Ugly, brooding Maggie, with her arms akimbo, her fancy clothes and absurd hats, her original topknot now replaced with a marcel, is a horrible example of the embattled social climber and culture vulture. In her machinations and Jiggs' henpecked maneuvers, social comedy and satire are superimposed upon slapstick. A touch of elegance is added when Maggie hurtles expensive vases at Jiggs instead of clouting him with the usual rolling-pin. The minor characters—the husband-hunting daughter Rosie and the fortune-hunting titled fops, Dinty Moore and his gang, Jiggs' pretty secretary—fill in the picture and help to fix the reader's sympathy on the side of honest, if vulgar, humanity, as against shallow vulgarians striving to keep up with the Joneses. Translated into a dozen languages, *Bringing Up Father* has also been a favorite of tent-show audiences (Winifred Johnston, *Folk-Say*, 1930). [BAB]

Jimmu Tenno Legendary first emperor of Japan, 660 B.C. See JAPANESE FOLKLORE.

jimsonweed A tall, coarse, evil-smelling, very poisonous annual weed (*Datura stramonium*) of the nightshade family: also known as *datura*. The American name is a corruption of Jamestown weed from its first being observed in Jamestown, Va. Beverly in his *History of Virginia* reports that "it was gathered very young for a boiled salad, by some soldiers sent thither to quell the rebellion of Bacon; and some of them ate plentifully of it, the effect of which was very pleasant comedy, for they turned natural fools on it for several days . . ." After eleven days they recovered, however, without any recollection of what had happened. In India datura was sometimes given to a rival prince to make him appear inept and unfit to rule; in fact throughout the East it was used to stupefy people in order to rob them. The *Arabian Nights* mentions datura as the "insane herb."

Among the Mayan Indians of Mexico it is used externally on wounds and on abscesses to draw out the pus, but the Mayans never used it as an intoxicant. Among the Catawba Indians the leaves are used externally on swellings and internally in fevers and for healing bone fractures. In Ohio it is used in an ointment for horses. Bathing the eyes with an infusion of the weed is said to change their color. In a poultice jimsonweed cures headache and rheumatism, and in fact is used to allay most nagging pains. It is said to be used by the courtesans of India and Turkey as an aphrodisiac, but in the United States its effects are believed to be just the opposite. Smoking the weed is believed to be beneficial to asthma sufferers. [JWH]

☞ In the boys' initiation rites of various tribes of southern California American Indians, a decoction of the narcotic drug contained in the roots of jimsonweed is drunk to induce a stupor in which visions are obtained. The boys to be initiated are first made to fast, and then, in several tribes, the drink is prepared ritually, to the accompaniment of singing, and given to each boy in a quantity judged suitable for him. As the effects of the drink begin to manifest themselves, each boy is taken in charge by a man, and helped to a ceremonial enclosure, where the boy remains in a stupor for several days or hours. During the period of stupefaction the initiate dreams dreams and sees visions, usually of an animal from whom he learns a song which he keeps as his own. Fasting, first absolute, then modified, is observed by the initiates, who are closely watched by their guardians since the drug is a dangerous one. Compare BLACK DRINK. See CHINGICHNICH. [EWV]

jinni (plural *jinn*; feminine *jinniyah*) In Arabic tradition, a devil or demon with great miraculous power. There are five kinds of jinn: jann, jinn, shaitan, ifrit, and marid, but these are seldom distinguished in translation. [MWS]

☞ In earliest concept, the jinn were probably malicious nature demons, living in deserted or impure places, often in animal shape. Islam adopted these spirits, admitting a possible dualism in the jinn, some good, some evil. They still retain an animal characteristic, whether paw, or hoof, or tail. Solomon, when he first saw the jinn, was horrified by their appearance; nevertheless, he went on to become their master, and could command them at will. They are usually invisible, but can appear in any shape, human or animal. One favorite form is the snake, but other obnoxious creatures —beetles, toads, scorpions—may be jinn. One family of Mecca were so plagued by the jinn that they went into the desert and began killing all the insects and reptiles they could find. The jinn were so depleted in number that they eventually called a truce. Often the jinn resemble goats; their relationship in concept to the satyrs is obvious, but not fully explicable as a parallel. Of the five classes, the jann are the least powerful, the jinn are mostly evil but sometimes good, the shaitans are imps or devils, the ifrits are terrible and evil, and the marids the most powerful and most evil. The chief of all the jinn is Iblis, the prince of evil. The good jinn are often in the form of household serpents (still common among the Galla of East Africa and Ethiopia). In form and to some degree in substance, these jinn resemble the Roman genii. The spelling *genii* (singular *genie*) for jinni is adopted from the French *génie*. The confusion of the plural form of the Roman word *genius* with the plural *genii* of the French-derived word and the subsequent confounding of both with the singular *jinni* leads to misuse of the various forms. The Persian devas, the divs, rakshasas, yakshas, etc., of Hindu lore, all resemble the jinn somewhat. The Moroccan form of the word—jnun —applies to a demon usually in the form of a toad. Thus, in Morocco, toads are not killed but requested to leave the house, politely. See Qaf.

jitsuki-uta Work songs of Japanese villagers sung at communal labor of pounding the earth to prepare for building foundations. They are lead by a male soloist and have a refrain sung by the chorus of workers, usually women, who pull the ropes that raise and drop a heavy wooden pounder. Some of the songs invoke good luck for the building; some are narrative. They are also called *dotsuki*.

jitterbug A modern dance of free angular style, rhythmically intoxicating: performed to specialized swing music. Partners improvise the succession of toe-heel steps in ballroom position, either with right hands grasped, or without contact. In the fundamental step the man swings the girl out, across, and in pivot turns; but he may, if the pair are expert dancers, throw her over his shoulder or on the ground. Though not entirely African in quality, jitterbug is most skilfully performed in New York's Negro Harlem. [GPK]

jiva In Jainism, the soul or the life principle within matter: innumerable in the universe, indestructible, forever forming matter and working *within* the material form. In Jainism the goal of every religious man is to free the jiva from matter; this is attempted through lifelong observance of certain rules and vows—an ideal of inaction to avoid involvement with matter. At the moment of death, the jiva of a devout (i.e. successful) Jain is liberated into *Kaivalya* or perfect isolation, to exist forever, self-contained and aware.

Jizo A Japanese bodhisattva, commonly regarded as the patron of small children, travelers, pregnant women, and persons suffering from toothache. [JLM]

Job's tears A hardy annual tropical grass (*Coix lacryma-jobi*) named for its tear-shaped pearly white seeds, which are often sold for beads and used in necklaces, bracelets, etc. The grass is native to India, is cultivated in China, and serves as a cereal food generally through eastern and southern Asia and the Philippines. Yunga-yung, one of the deities of the Ifugaos of Luzon, P.I., is noted for giving a charm to the people which consists of Job's tears and a plant called *konúpa* (a wall-covering plant); this charm makes the living invisible to a group of evil spirits known as *Bumugi*, the Spitters, who plague the souls of the newly dead, trying to trick them into some remark or admission that will endanger their living kin.

Job's tears are included in the bead bracelets worn by Moslem wives, and are believed to keep a husband fond. Powdered and slipped into his drink they will have the same effect. Sometimes also they are stealthily given to a rival, but in vinegar, for this will make her unattractive to the husband. In Persia Job's tears are said to possess a power great enough to offset almost any magic.

In coastal New England, especially Maine and Massachusetts, a necklace made of Job's tears was formerly thought to cure sore throat and diphtheria and to "absorb humors." In northern Ohio such a necklace was said to cure goiter.

Jocasta In Greek legend, the wife of Laius; mother and wife of Œdipus: called Epicaste in Homer. She hanged herself when she learned that Œdipus, to whom she had been married for many years, was her son.

Joe Magarac Steel-mill Paul Bunyan and John Henry. In Hungarian and Slovak *magarac* means jackass, and a "Joe Magarac," translated freely, means one who just "eatit and workit same lak jackass donkey." Joe Magarac first appeared at the big party that Steve Mestrovich gave for his pretty daughter, Mary. Determined that she should marry "only strongest mans what ever lived," Steve announced that the one who could lift the heaviest weight would be the lucky man. The winner was a seven-foot giant who said that his name was Joe Magarac and that he was born inside an ore mountain. When he pulled off his shirt, the people saw that he was a man of steel—"steel hands, steel body, steel everything." But, having no time for marriage, he withdrew in favor of Pete Pussick and went to work both day and night shifts in the steel mill, taking five big meals a day at Mrs. Horkey's boardinghouse.

He made rails by squeezing hot steel through his fingers—four rails from each hand. And he made so many rails that the roller-boss said they would have to shut down from Thursday night till Monday morning. On Monday the melter-boss found Joe sitting in a ladle with the hot steel boiling up around his neck. Sick of shutdowns and having heard the big boss say that he wanted the best steel to build a new mill, Joe had decided to offer himself for that purpose. In the contest between himself and ore, to see which could make the better steel, Joe won.

If Joe's saga recalls memories of foundation sacrifice rites and stories of men who have fallen into vats of molten steel and been buried with the metal, it also suggests to class-conscious steel workers the symbolism that the mills belong to the men who make the steel rather than the men to the mills. [BAB]

Joe Miller An old, worn-out joke. Joseph or Josias Miller (1684–1738) was an actor with the Drury Lane company after 1709 and played such comic roles as Trinculo in *The Tempest* and the First Gravedigger in *Hamlet*. The year after Miller's death, John Mottley (1692–1750), a government clerk who had written some successful plays, published *Joe Miller's Jests, or The Wit's Vade Mecum*, a jestbook containing but three stories connected with Joe Miller. The Miller name was attached to the book in the same spirit that had led compilers of the 16th century to use the names of such famous wits as Skelton, Scogan, and Tarlton. Since 1739, however, any jestbook, any collection of stale jokes, any over-used story has been known as a Joe Miller.

Joe-pye weed Either of two tall American herbs (*Eupatorium maculatum* and *E. purpureum*) having whorled leaves and pale purple flowers: often called *gravel root* because the root was formerly much used as a remedy for kidney- and gallstones. The Iroquois Indians were familiar with its properties as a remedy for kidney disorders. The Chippewa Indians made a tea from the dried leaves and flowers of *E. maculatum* to produce sweating. They also used a warm decoction of the root as a wash for stiff joints; often some was put in the bath of a fretful child to quiet it. The Meskwaki Indians regarded it as a love medicine. If a young man would hold some in his mouth while talking to a young woman, or while wooing, the success of the conversation would be assured.

John or **Old John** The clever slave who matches wits with Old Massa and generally wins, though, even when he loses, he has or draws a laugh. The slave's weapon of laughter is symbolized by Old John's tricks, which he shares with Brer Rabbit, and especially the tricks of appeasing or fooling the white man by clever remarks or "bright sayings" and by playing dumb. While the slave found sly humor useful as part of the technique of defense or offense in slavery's "state of perpetual war," John stories are typical trickster and noodle tales, and employ many traditional motifs. Most of them concern the evasions and stratagems by which the slave circumvented the restrictions of plantation etiquette and other social controls, forestalling punishment, gaining small immunities and rewards, and even winning freedom. The pattern is continued in the jokes which Negroes tell "on" whites, disguising the Negro's irony as simplicity, just as in jokes told by southern whites "on" Negroes the "simple" Negro is made to appear "smart" or "uppity." In the best of the John stories John and Massa stand in much the same relation to each other as Brer Rabbit and Brer Fox, each serving as a foil for the other's cunning.

According to Zora Neale Hurston (*The American Mercury* 57:450–458), Old John was originally High John de Conquer, sharing his name and magic with the root of the marsh St. John's-wort, a folk cure-all and charm against rattlesnake bites, ghosts, witches, and nightmares. In his art of "hitting a straight lick with a crooked stick," of "making a way out of no-way," John de Conquer had a weapon more powerful than magic, while he found solace in song and laughter. John sometimes appears as Big John, Jack, and under a variety of common slave names.

Favorite themes of John stories are concealing a stolen pig (variants of the Mak story), telling fortunes (John saves his reputation and life and is rewarded when, in desperation, he says, "Well, you got de ole coon at last," and so inadvertently guesses what is under the pot), swapping dreams or lies, praying under the tree, mistaking voices in the graveyard for those of God and the Devil counting souls. In the comic contest of wits, fooling master alternates with catching John, turning the tables with the "trickster tricked," while an occasional double ending satisfies both parties.

In "Massa's Gone to Philly-Me-York," Old Massa, pretending to go on a trip, returns suddenly in disguise and interrupts a feast in the Big House, only to be told to go out in the kitchen where he belongs. When John is threatened with hanging as the ringleader, he begs for permission to pray under a tree, where a concealed crony strikes matches at John's petition for lightning to strike Massa. Massa runs and set John free.

The "running" ending seems to have a particular fascination. When Massa, disguised as the Lord, comes to take John to Heaven, in answer to the latter's prayer, John, after putting off the inevitable as long as possible, asks the "Lord" to stand back in order to dim the radiance of his countenance, and rushes past him, while John's wife comforts their weeping children with: "You know de Lawd can't outrun yo' pappy—specially when he's barefooted at dat." In "God an' de Devil in de Cemetery," John pushes Massa to the cemetery gate in his wheel chair to prove that he has overheard God and the Devil dividing up souls (actually two men counting out their shares of corn). At the remark, "Now, we'll go git dem two at de gate," Jack lights for home, only to find that Massa has beaten him there in his wheel chair and is sitting by the fire, smoking a cigar.   B. A. BOTKIN

John Barleycorn English and Scottish personification of barley as the grain from which intoxicating liquors are made; hence, personification of intoxicating liquors. Murray's *New English Dictionary* cites in 1620 "a pleasant new ballad about the murther of John Barleycorn."

Sir James Frazer entertains the thought (*Adonis, Attis, Osiris:* p. 189) that John Barleycorn parallels the legion of European vegetation spirits represented by a human victim killed for the sake of fertilization and resurrection of the crops. Burns' poem *John Barleycorn* (1786) could hardly suggest this, since stanza by stanza it merely presents the planting and reaping of the barley, the wagon-loading, threshing, etc., until "a miller used him worst of all / For he crushed him 'tween two stones." The figure continues to the drinking of John Barleycorn's heart's blood, to the mounting joy of all partakers. A. H. Krappe discredits the assumption of human-sacrifice vegetation ritual (*Science of Folklore:* 325), preferring to suppose that if any ritual beyond the natural sequence of reaping, grinding etc., was performed that "the real John Barleycorn perhaps in the shape of the last sheaf" was the only victim. In the United States with the enactment of the prohibition amendment, many brewery or community groups enacted the play of burying John Barleycorn.

John Bull Personification of England, of the English people, and of the typical Englishman, especially with regard to his heaviness and obstinacy: from a character in John Arbuthnot's *History of John Bull* (1712)—"an honest, plain-dealing fellow, choleric, bold, . . . a boon companion, loving his bottle and his diversion." He is depicted as a stout little man in traditional 18th century costume; modern political cartoons, often show a waistcoat made from the British flag.

John Canoe A Christmas dance of the Negroes of the British West Indies. Among these people, the word is usually associated with the name of the buzzard, its derivation most often being indicated as a corruption of the English "carrion Crow." The probability that this is correct is heightened when one hears the West Indian Negro pronounce this term. There is, however, a woman's dance in the Gold Coast, West Africa, called *nyonkro,* in which there are dancing and sexual extravaganza in word play, mimicry, and ridicule, this latter being especially characteristic of the John Canoe dances. [MJH]

john-dory A small marine foodfish (*Zeus faber* or *Z. australis*) of the European Atlantic, the Mediterranean, and Australian seas: also called *Peter's fish,* because it is said to be the one from whose mouth Peter took the coin to pay the temple tax, the spots on either side of its mouth being the marks of his thumb and finger. The name is said to come from the yellow color (*dorée,* gilded, or *jaune dorée,* golden yellow) of the fish, or through humorous allusion to a French privateer in a 17th century popular ballad (Child #284). Compare HADDOCK.

John Hardy An American "bad-man" ballad about the crime and death of John Hardy, a West Virginia Negro employee of the Shawnee Coal Company, who murdered a man in a gambling quarrel, was pursued by the law, and was caught and hanged at Welch, MacDowell County, W. Va., on January 19, 1894.

John Henry Title and hero of an American Negro ballad celebrating the Herculean Negro hero who pitted his strength against a machine and "died with his hammer in his hand." The story originated during the drilling of the Big Bend Tunnel of the Chesapeake and Ohio Railroad through the rough hills of West Virginia about 1873. The hero's description, given by those who claimed to know him, varies from white to black and from average size to giant. He outdrove a steam-drill with his hammer and steel in the story, but actually he died in a cave-in. There were songs about his strength, and about his prowess with the women of the shanty towns, before the contest with the machine. The whole story carries a double symbolism of potency, based on the standard joke of the sweating, half-clad Negro laborers who sat in the tunnel with the steel bit between their legs while the hammer wielders drove it into the rock. The legend of John Henry traveled through all the work camps of the South, gathering new details to make the hero a rival to Paul Bunyan, Pecos Bill, etc. In Kentucky, he became a white man. On the Mississippi, he was the strongest of the roustabouts. The airs to which the song is sung derive probably from a Scotch tune, and are played on the banjo, the guitar, etc., at folk festivals today.

Johnie Armstrong A Scottish ballad (Child #169) of the treachery of James V of Scotland. Johnny Armstrong, who died about 1530, was called before the king in peace, and then executed. "The execution was probably as summary as the arrest was perfidious." The ballad, of which three versions are known, tells how the king writes in his own hand for Johnny Armstrong to come to see him. Johnny is proud of the honor and traps out his eight score followers to fit the occasion. Before the king he asks the usual pardon, but the king refuses to grant the pardon and orders that he be hanged on the morrow. Johnny turns to his men and says over his left shoulder,

> "Asking grace of a graceless face—
> Why there's none for you nor me."

He whips out his sword and just misses cutting off the nimble king's head. He and his men fight the king's men, but they cannot prevail against the weight of numbers of all of Edinburgh. Johnny is struck from behind, and bids his men go on fighting, saying

> "I will lay me down for to bleed a while,
> Then I'le rise and fight with you again."

But he and his men die, and only a little messenger gets away to tell the sad story to the lady.

Johnie Cock A Scottish ballad (Child #114) about a poacher, Johnny o Cockslee's Well. Johnie is being looked for by the foresters. His mother tries to keep him home, but he goes out and makes his kill. Then, sated with the blood of the deer, he sleeps. An old palmer sees him sleeping and tells the foresters. They sneak up on him and cut off his leg (or hit him with several arrows). Johnie Cock awakes and reproaches them:

> "The wildest wolf in aw this wood
> Wad not ha done so by me;
> She'd ha wet her foot ith wan water,
> And sprinkled it oer my brae,
> And if that wad not ha wakend me,
> She wad ha gone and let me be."

But Johnie is not beaten and kills all the foresters but one. Child lists thirteen versions of the ballad.

Johnny Appleseed John Chapman (1774–1845), eccentric, itinerant pioneer nurseryman and colporteur, enshrined in historical, literary, and folk tradition as the American St. Francis and "voice in the wilderness." Beginning in the 1790's, he worked his way west from his native Massachusetts to the Pennsylvania-Ohio-Indiana frontier, planting apple nurseries, spreading "news right fresh from heaven," befriending and winning the respect of settlers and Indians alike, as a mediary and "medicine man." His apple seeds and seedlings, exchanged for food, cast-off clothing, and other articles or for frontier currency, took care of his simple needs, while the profits went into copies of Swedenborg's works, which he separated into parts for wider and cheaper distribution.

Generally pictured as a barefoot, bearded, kindly hermit and tramp, with a tin mushpot or pasteboard peaked cap on his head and a tow-linen coffee sack on his back, he left a trail of legends and anecdotes, folk memories and public memorials, orchards and monuments, not only throughout the Middle West but from coast to coast. He has been celebrated in drama, poetry, fiction, and biography as a saint in action, and memorialized by New Church and horticultural societies as a missionary extraordinary and the patron saint of pomology. As a savior among frontier wastrels, the archetype of "endurance that was voluntary and of action that was creative and not sanguinary," he occupies a unique place in the pantheon of folk heroes—the poetic symbol of spiritual pioneering, of self-abnegation combined with service, of plain living and high thinking.

He is said to have proved his fortitude in enduring pain by sticking pins and needles into his flesh, and his love of every living thing by extinguishing a campfire to keep mosquitoes from burning themselves in it, and by sleeping out in the snow rather than oust a mother bear and her cubs from the hollow log they had pre-empted. Other typical scenes and exploits in the Apple-seed saga include floating down the Ohio River in two canoes lashed together and containing apple seed salvaged from Pittsburgh cider presses, and saving the people of Mansfield from Indian massacre by running 26 miles to Mt. Vernon for help and returning in 24 hours. Among the oddly assorted memorials to his name are a "Johnny Appleseed apple," "Johnny weed" (the annoying dog fennel, which he planted along with other medicinal herbs), and "Johnny Appleseed Week" (the last week in September, celebrated in Ohio since 1941).

B. A. Botkin

St. John's Eve Same as Midsummer Eve.

John the Bear The hero of a number of European tales, or tales of European origin, in the Bear's Son cycle; also, a title often applied to several tale types (e.g. Type 301—The Three Stolen Princesses; Type 650—Strong John) in which the hero is a bear's son. The hero's name is always the same: Juan el Oso, Juan del Oso, Ivanko the Bear's Son. Because of the name of the hero, he is often identified with Jack, the central character of the Jack tales. For example, Teit, in "European Tales from the Upper Thompson Indians" (*JAFL* 29:313), speaking of stories of Jack, says, "One of these Jacks was also a grizzly bear." See European tales in North American Indian mythology; French folklore.

joiku The most ancient folk tunes of Finland, chiefly laments, in recitative, making use of alliteration, repetition, and variable rhythm. They are also found among some Laplanders.

joking relationship and kinship tabus Many primitive peoples observe certain customs which forbid meeting or speaking or other activities between persons of specified relationships, such as parents-in-law, sister-in-law, brother-in-law, sister, first cousin, etc. The extent to which this avoidance is carried varies from never being permitted to be in the presence of specified relatives, even after death, to merely prohibition or tabu against using their personal names or specified words. Customs of avoidance apply primarily to persons of opposite sex who are forbidden to mate by tribal regulations. Sex relations, however, are not the only factor, since kinship tabus are also found between members of the same sex, as wife and mother-in-law, husband and father-in-law.

The commonest kinship tabus are between parents-in-law and sons- and daughters-in-law. That between mother-in-law and son-in-law is found in Africa, the Americas, Australia, Melanesia, Polynesia, and Siberia. This type varies from addressing the mother-in-law with an appropriate term of relationship to the custom among the Lango Negroes of sending word ahead when a man plans to pass through a village in which his mother-in-law lives in order to insure her not getting in his way or sight. In the Banks Islands a man cannot walk along the beach which has been traversed by his mother-in-law until her footprints have been washed away by the tide.

Brother-sister avoidance, frequently explained as a means of preventing incest, feuds, or to preserve status, is found among the Navahos and the Melanesians. Among the Santals (Bengal) the wife of a younger brother can never remain alone with her husband's older brother. On Leper's Island, New Hebrides, boys reach-ing their teens leave home or move into the men's house. They can visit their mothers, but must never eat with their sisters.

Among many of the North American Indians a so-called joking relationship exists between certain relatives, which is sharply distinguished from the respect or avoidance relationships which exist between other relatives. A man shows respect, usually, to his sister and to his mother; in many tribes he has actually to avoid any speech or contact with his mother-in-law. To his sisters-in-law, however, and in some tribes to his wife's sister's daughters, he can make teasing or even obscene remarks, and it is normally expected that a tease relationship, at least, be maintained between them. The same holds true in many instances for a woman and her brothers-in-law and her brother's brother's sons. The joking relationship has been postulated as having originated between persons of the opposite sex who were potential mates; often a man was obligated to marry his wife's sister, either during the lifetime of the wife or after her death (sororate), and a woman who was widowed was expected to marry her husband's brother, or in some instances, his son. The joking relationship is nearly always to be found between persons of opposite sex who are related in a certain way; however, members of one clan group sometimes indulged in something of a joking or "belittling" relationship with members of other clans. Clan or gens joking relationships have not been so widely noted as the joking relationship between relatives, which is by no means confined to North America; among the Shawnee of the Eastern Woodlands, however, the gens joking relationship is as emphasized at the present time as is the one between relatives. [EWV]

Kinship tabus are rare in Middle America as compared to North and South America. The mother-in-law tabu has been noted among several remote groups. Among the Sumu of Nicaragua, for example, the groom must not speak to, or even look at, his mother-in-law. She must live in a special room in the hut, and when either one approaches home, he or she must give warning to the other. If they accidentally meet on the trail, she covers her head with a cloth. If the son-in-law purposely looks at the woman, or fails to give the proper warning, this is considered a deliberate insult for which she is entitled to receive compensation. Among the Tarahumara of northwest Mexico a man and his wife's sister enjoy a "joking-relationship" which permits a degree of obscene joking, play, and other liberties normally not condoned between members of the opposite sex. [GMF]

Jonah A Hebrew prophet; the same son of the widow of Zarephath who was raised from the dead by Elijah. While fleeing from the injunction of the Lord to preach in Nineveh, on board ship from Joppa to Tarshish, he was the cause of a storm that imperiled the ship. They discovered by lot that Jonah and his disobedience had angered God and, after trying other remedies to still the sea, they cast him into the water. The storm ceased immediately, but Jonah was swallowed by a great fish. This fish was about to die; its destiny was to be swallowed by Leviathan. But Leviathan fled before the sign of the covenant borne by Jonah, and did not eat the fish. In gratitude, the fish swam with Jonah to all the places he had wanted to see: the source of the ocean, the place where the Israelites had crossed the sea, etc. And Jonah was comfortable within the fish, for its stomach was large and within it there was a huge diamond that gave light. Therefore God sent another fish, whose insides were very uncomfortable with thousands of little fish, and Jonah was transferred. He then agreed to go to Nineveh and the fish vomited him forth to dry land. Jonah preached well in Nineveh and the city repented its evil ways; but soon the city forgot and was swallowed by the earth. Jonah did not die but was taken alive to Paradise. See SWALLOW STORY.

Jonathan Like the word Yankee, which displaced it, "Jonathan" began as the name of the typical New England countryman, a stock comic figure on the stage and in jest books, and became a nickname of the American people and symbol of the typical American. Like Yankee, too (originally a Dutch term for freebooter which the New York Dutch transferred to their shrewd Connecticut neighbors), Jonathan was a term of derision applied by British soldiers and Tories to Americans during the Revolution. By 1787, when Jonathan first became popular on the stage as the humorous or comic Yankee of Royall Tyler's *The Contrast,* the character had acquired overtones of upstanding simplicity and honesty in contrast to European worldliness and in addition to the raw, bumptious, inquisitive greenness of "Yankee Doodle."

Governor Jonathan Trumbull of Connecticut is generally credited with being the original Brother Jonathan and the proverbial embodiment of Jonathan's practical and common-sense virtues. After Washington had taken command of the Continental army, he placed great reliance on Trumbull's judgment and was heard to remark on at least one occasion, "We must consult Brother Jonathan on the subject," the phrase becoming a byword (Bartlett's *Dictionary of Americanisms,* 1859 ed., p. 50).

From Jonathan is also derived Jonathanism, meaning a Yankeeism or Americanism. [BAB]

jongleur A strolling performer of the Middle Ages whose repertoire included juggling, acrobatics, singing, and playing of instruments for casual entertainment. While the troubadour composed and performed in courtly style, the jongleur was the purveyor of popular song, dance, and tale, and may be credited with much of the transmission of such lore throughout Europe, as well as with the composition of some songs, and the reduction of troubadour works to popular form. The jongleurs' function was taken over to some extent by Gipsies who came into Europe, many as itinerant entertainers, as the wandering minstrel was beginning to disappear.

Jörd, Jördh, or **Fiorgyn** In Teutonic mythology, a giantess, wife of Odin and mother of Thor: personification of the primitive, unpopulated, and uncultivated earth. See FRIGGA.

Jordan flute A type of shepherd's pipe still played in the mountains of Israel. It goes back to the *hālīl* of Biblical times, actually an oboe, which was played at funerals and in Passover and other ceremonies of the Second Temple. During the war for Israel's independence, players of the Jordan flute mingled the new fighting songs of the Jewish armies and guerrilla fighters with the ancient and plaintive folk songs of their hills.

Jormungandr or **Iörmungandr** In Teutonic mythology, the Midgard Serpent, son of Loki and Angurboda, brother of Fenris and Hel. Odin, fearing that the monster would cause trouble, threw him into the sea while he was young. He grew until he encircled the earth and could bite his own tail. It is his writhing which causes tempests. Thor tried several times to kill him, but will not succeed until Ragnarök.

joropo The Venezuelan national dance; a fast waltz for a couple. The routine consists of four main figures: in ballroom position, an emphatic waltz turn, stamping on the first beat of each measure; a combination of *zapateado* and scissors, face to face; alternate turning under the partner's upraised arms; stamping *zapateado,* holding hands, and in turn thrusting forward the right and the left shoulder on the stamp of the right and left foot. The joropo is entirely an urban, colonial product, Spanish with a strong flavor of Austrian Ländler. [GPK]

José-Lizorio A Mexican "vulgar" ballad of recent origin, making use of bits and scraps of more ancient material. It is the story of a mother's curse which brings death to her son.

Joseph Hero of one of the great Biblical stories; son of Jacob and Rachel; his father's favorite son. Jacob's gift of a coat of many colors to the boy was the last straw to Joseph's jealous brothers, over whom Joseph lorded it, especially repeating to them his dreams of becoming greater than any of them. So they cast him into a pit, sold him to slave traders en route to Egypt, instead of killing him as they had planned, tore and bloodied the coat, and told Jacob they had found it in the desert and feared that Joseph had been killed and eaten by animals. The traders sold Joseph to Potiphar, a great officer of Pharaoh. Joseph became overseer of Potiphar's house, but fell afoul of the lust of Potiphar's wife. For his refusal of her, she accused him of an attempt on her virtue. Joseph was thrown into prison, where his ability to interpret dreams led him to foretell that the king's baker would die and the king's butler would live. And so it happened to these two, his fellow prisoners. Thus, two years later, when Pharaoh dreamed of the seven fat and the seven lean kine, the butler remembered Joseph. Joseph's interpretation of the dream, with its warning of famine, caused the king to make him the second person in the land. When the predicted famine occurred after seven years of plenty, Joseph had stored up enough grain to sell to those in need. The dearth was widespread, and Jacob's sons, the brothers of Joseph, came to Egypt to buy food. Joseph recognized them and laid a trap. First, he demanded that they return and bring back Benjamin, who had been left behind with Jacob. Then he put the money they had paid him into their sacks. When they returned with Benjamin, Joseph again did the same thing, but in Benjamin's sack he hid his own silver drinking and divining cup, knowing that when he arrested Benjamin for stealing it Jacob would surely come to Egypt. Judah, the eldest of the brothers, pleaded with Joseph, saying that if they returned to their father without the youth—his father's favorite since the loss of Joseph—Jacob would die of grief. Joseph was unable to contain himself and revealed his identity to his brothers. Then Jacob was sent for, and Jacob and all his tribe came to Egypt and settled in Goshen.

This story, told in *Gen.* xxxix to the end of the book, is an illustration of Type 930, the prophecy that the poor boy will become rich or great. It contains, among its familiar folktale motifs: L425, dream of future greatness causes banishment; K1931.4, hero thrown into pit combined with K2211, the treacherous brother; K512.1, the compassionate executioner and the bloody coat (perhaps more familiar in its *Snow White* variant—K512.2—with the substituted heart); K2111, Potiphar's wife; and H151.4, the cup in the sack.

Joseph is the most important Hebrew figure in the Koran. *Sura* xii, the Chapter of Yūsuf, tells much the same story as the Biblical account, and is one of the most popular tales of the East. Especially is the incident of Potiphar's wife prominent in love poetry. It has been retold in several love songs, in Persian, Turki, and other languages of the Near East. It has even been said that Mohammed warned against women reading or hearing the Koranic account, for fear of its effects on their chastity. Here the name of the Egyptian is Kitfeer and the wife is Zuleika. This childless couple adopted Joseph, but his beauty inflamed Zuleika's desire. She laid hands on him and in escaping he left part of his shirt in her hands. She accused him immediately, but an alert relative of hers (tradition says a baby still in the cradle) pointed out that the shirt was torn from behind, proving that he was escaping. (Compare BOY JUDGE; DETECTIVE STORY.) Zuleika, to still the gossip about her, invited all the women of the city to a banquet, gave each of them a knife, and then brought Joseph before them. Every one cut her hand, paying attention to Joseph rather than to the meat she was supposed to be cutting, and Zuleika repeated once more her desire, now understood by all. Joseph was sent to jail, for a time, until the whole incident should be forgotten. The story follows the Biblical outline, with several variations. Joseph, for example, sends his shirt to Jacob, and when the shirt is thrown in the old blind man's face he recovers his sight. The non-Biblical elements of the story in the Koran have been traced to sources in Jewish apocryphal accounts, to Talmudic tradition, and to Jewish Biblical legends told elsewhere.

Joseph Lieber A German Christmas carol of which both words and music have been preserved in a manuscript of about 1500 at Leipzig University. It was first sung as a part of a mystery play performed around a crib in church.

Joseph of Arimathea According to the account in the Gospels, the one who received and buried the body of Christ. The story is more detailed in Biblical tradition. Joseph, after securing permission from Pilate, took down the body of Christ from the cross, prepared it for burial, and placed it in a tomb which he sealed with a stone. Various accounts mention him as a member of the Sanhedrin, as a friend of Pilate, as a soldier in Pilate's employ, as a secret follower of Jesus. The *Evangelium Nicodemi* expands the story telling of Joseph being imprisoned for what he had done, of Jesus appearing before him in prison, and explaining the symbolism of the ritual of the burial. One sentence of this account is interesting in connection with the Grail story: ". . . the vessel in which you put my blood when you received it from my body will be called the Chalice . . ."

In the Middle Ages the accounts of Joseph of Arimathea become assimilated with other material and expanded into the Grail story and the whole made finally a part of Arthurian legend. Robert de Boron composed in the late 12th century a long romance, *Joseph*, based on the Christian traditions of Joseph of Arimathea and elements from general folklore. This is a detailed account of Joseph, his service to Christ, his wanderings with his relatives and followers, the appearance of the Grail as they reenacted the Last Supper, and finally the transfer of the Grail from Joseph to Bron, referred to as the Rich Fisher. The whole story is distinctly Christian and symbolic. This story combined by subsequent writers with the account of the Grail in Chrétien de Troyes' *Perceval* becomes the source of Grail stories as they appear in the Cyclic romances, and in Malory, Wagner, and Tennyson.

The traditions that connect Joseph with Glastonbury, telling of his founding a church there, planting a tree, the hawthorn, which blooms at Christmas, are late, and probably local additions to the legend. See FISHER KING; GRAIL. [MEL]

Joshua The leader of the Israelites in their conquest of Canaan; the *Book of Joshua*, continuing as it does the story of the first five books of the Bible, has sometimes been considered to form, with the Pentateuch, the Hexateuch. Legend had added to the somewhat vague picture of the Hebrew general. He was swallowed by a whale as an infant and spit out on a distant shore. Kind people raised him, and when he grew to somewhat stupid manhood he followed the trade of public hangman. It thus fell to his lot to hang his father and marry his mother, who was part of his hangman's fee. But as he was about to have intercourse with her, her breasts began spouting milk. Joshua realized that this was a sign that something was wrong. He investigated and discovered the story of his parentage. (There may or may not be Greek influence in this extra-Biblical legend; the resemblance to the story of Œdipus is strong; but abandonment, parricide, and incest are often the lot of folk heroes.)

Though considered a fool, Joshua rose to be Moses' lieutenant, following his master closely and learning by heart all his lessons. As Moses lay dying, he asked Joshua if there were anything he could explain. Joshua replied that, since he knew all that Moses had said, there was nothing that could be added. For this proud answer, God immediately made Joshua forget many points of the law. Then, when the people came to him for guidance in interpretation of the Law, Joshua could not answer. God refused to help; He had given the Law to man, and it was man's to interpret: the Torah itself was revealed, not the reading of it. But to still what might be a revolt against the leader, God ordered an immediate entry into Canaan. The waters of Jordan parted, rose to a height of 300 miles, and while the Ark remained in the bed of the river the Israelites crossed on dry land. Jericho, the first city across Jordan, fell after the Ark and the priests had circumambulated its walls on each of seven days. Eventually the Israelites made themselves possessors of the land (see ACHAN; JERICHO). A battle was fought against the Amorites on a Friday. Seeing that the Sabbath would arrive before the battle ended, and knowing that his army would stop fighting at sundown because of the Sabbath, Joshua commanded the sun, moon, and stars to stand still, using the Name in his invocation. The sun was minded not to do so, being older than man and also fearing that no one would sing the Lord's praises when it was still; but it did, for 36 hours, and the Israelites won the battle. When the fighting was all ended, Joshua divided the land among the tribes by lot. Joshua planted along the boundaries between the portions a plant that could not be eradicated; the furrows of the plow might cross where it was planted, yet the plant would grow amid the grain and still show clearly where the boundary was.

jota A Spanish folk dance, especially of the old region and kingdom of Aragon: believed to have sprung from the *canario*. It is a courtship dance performed by a man and a woman, whose castanets and footwork effect a rapid and complex counterpoint. It is sometimes classified as a lift dance because of the spectacular finish. See DEATH DANCE. [GPK]

jötunn (plural *jötnar;* feminine *gygr*) In Teutonic mythology, a giant. The jötnar were personifications of the inimical forces of nature; their home was Jötunheim to the northeast of Asgard. Some of the giants were normal except for size, some were huge demoniacal beings like the eight-headed Starkadr, while others were monsters as the Midgard Serpent, Jörmungandr.

They can be divided roughly into fire, air, water, and earth giants. Among the fire giants was Surtr with his flaming sword, who guarded Muspellheim and will destroy the world at Ragnarök and overcome Frey. The air or frost giants, the Hrim-thursar were Kari (tempest) and his three sons, Beli (storm), Thiassi (ice) with his daughter, Skadi (winter), and Thrym (frost), lord of the Thursar, whose children were Johul (glacier), Frosti (cold), Snoer (snow), and Drifta (snowdrift). The water giants were descendants of Ægir or Hler and Rán. Among their children were Mimir, Gymir, Grendel, and the nine wave maidens, the mothers of Heimdall. The earth or mountain giants were *bergbui* (mountain dwellers), *bergjarl* (lord of the mountains) and the *bergriser* (cliff giants). Others were identified with particular mountains, as Senjemand, who became so irate at the beautiful giant maiden, Juternajesta, for refusing his suit that he shot a great stone arrow at her. Her lover, Torge, threw his hat in the way and started after Senjemand, who mounted his horse to flee, but the rays of the rising sun caught him and he turned to stone. Today on the island of Senjen one can still see the giant on horseback, Torge's hat with the hole in it, and the arrow, a huge stone obelisk.

The giant Ymir was the first being in the universe. His body, rolled into the abyss by the gods, became the earth and his blood the sea. At that time all of the early giants were drowned in his blood except Bergelmir and his wife, who escaped in a boat. Fornjotnr is sometimes identified with Ymir. Of his three sons, Ægir or Hler produced the sea giants, Kari, the storm and frost giants, and Loki fathered Jörmungandr, Fenris, and Hel.

The giants were not always unfriendly to the gods. Ægir, for instance, gave a banquet in his coral palace to cheer them after the death of Balder. It is difficult to establish clearly whether Loki was of the æsir or jötnar, because he turns up in the company of each group. He is listed with the æsir, but he is also a giant. Several of the gods married giantesses and produced beneficial offspring. Thor, the most relentless destroyer of giants, married the giantess Iarnsaxa (iron-stone) who bore him two sons, Magni (strength) and Modi (courage). See HRUNGNIR.

journey to otherworld An incident of folktale, myth, and legend (motifs F0–199) found in all parts of the world. The otherworld may be heaven or hell, an extraterrestrial paradise or a mysterious land at the bottom of a well or of the sea, across the mountains, on a distant island, etc. The incident attaches itself readily to tale cycles involving quests, e.g. the swan maiden tales in which the husband must journey to the otherworld to recover his vanished wife. In several tale types, however, it forms an even more integral part of the pattern. For example, in Friends in Life and Death (Type 470), two friends vow never to be parted (compare ORPHEUS). One dies and the living friend invites him to return for a visit on Christmas (or a living man invites a churchyard skull to dinner). Then the living travels to the otherworld with the dead. Wonderful sights are seen on the journey, but the living returns to this world. Here he finds that countless years have passed seemingly overnight: this is often the case with otherworld travelers. Everyone he knew is dead and this world has changed almost as magically as the otherworld. He dies the next day and is reunited with his friend. See AFTERWORLD; A'IKREN; ARROW CHAIN; ASCENT TO SKY ON FEATHER; ASCENT TO UPPER WORLD; DESCENTS TO UNDERWORLD; DIONYSUS; ECHTRAE CORMAIC; ECHTRAI; FOOD TABU IN THE LAND OF THE DEAD; HOLDE; ING; JACK AND THE BEANSTALK; JOURNEY TO THE LAND OF THE GRANDFATHER; OTHERWORLD; UNDERWORLD.

☞ "True" stories of the visits of living persons who have gone into a trance for a few days and visited the afterworld, often obtaining instructions from the deity in charge of this region for the good of their fellow men, are of frequent occurrence in North American Indian mythologies from many different parts of the continent. The experiences of such persons usually take the following form: he or she "dies," seemingly, and is prepared and laid out for burial. Before burial occurs, however, the subject evinces signs of life, and when he wakens, tells the people of his experiences in the afterworld and the new dance, ceremony, or instructions that have been given to him by the deity in the afterworld. Accounts of such visits to the afterworld are not to be confused with the same sort of visit made by mortals in search of a dead spouse, and detailed in the widely distributed North American Orpheus myth. [EWV]

journey to the land of the Grandfather The journey of the soul to the land of the dead in the west, ruled over by Tamoi (Grandfather), culture hero and mythical ancestor of the Guarayú Indians of Bolivia.

After burial the soul was confronted with two paths, one wide and easy, the other narrow, obstructed, and beset with dangers. The hard one was the right one to choose. First, the soul had to cross a wide river; the ferryman was a native cayman who would not carry the soul across unless he could accompany the cayman chant with his bamboo stamping tube (a significant musical instrument of the Guarayú). A stamping tube was always buried with the dead for this usage. Then there was a second river which could be crossed only if the soul succeeded in jumping on a tree trunk which kept rushing violently from bank to bank. If the poor soul fell off, he was devoured by palometa fish. Next he came to the home of Izoï-tamoi (Grandfather of Worms) who became smaller and smaller if the traveler was a good soul, bigger and bigger, if his life had been evil. Izoi-tamoi split in half the evil ones.

Once past this place, the soul had to walk through a darkened land by the light of a little burning straw, which faithful relatives always placed in the grave with their dead. Then he came to the ceiba tree, full of humming birds; here he gathered feathers to offer to Tamoi for his headdress. The next danger was Itacaru, two rocks which clashed together in the path. If the soul knew what to say, they would hold back and let him pass. Then he was examined by a gallinazo bird for the perforated lips and ears which every Guarayú must possess in order to reach the happy land. Should he lack these, the bird would lead him astray. Then he had to be tickled by a monkey, and not laugh, and pass the magic speaking tree, and not listen. When at last he arrived in a pleasant lane of flowering trees and singing birds, he knew he had reached the land of the Grandfather. Here he was welcomed, washed in a youth-restoring bath, and lived happily ever after, pursuing activities identical with those of this world. (See Métraux, "Native Tribes of Eastern Bolivia and Western Matto Grosso," *BAEB* 134:105 ff.) See AFTERWORLD.

Jove Jupiter: the genitive form of the name, and specifically in this form, the sky god.

Jovo and His Sister A Serbian popular ballad featuring the dead rider motif. It is a descendant of the Greek *Constantine and Arete*.

Joys of Mary An English carol enumerating the joys of the mother of Christ during the life of her child. The number varies—five, seven, twelve, etc.—but all reflect the folk character of the concept, the admiration of a peasant mother for a son who could read, perform miracles, take his place with the mighty. It is typical of the humanization of the saints which took place in the carols. See CAROL.

Juan and Maria A Filipino (Pampangan) tale embodying the abandoned children, animal helper, and reversal of fortune motifs. Two children, Juan and Maria, driven into the forest because there was rice for two in the house, not four, were adopted by a kind old woman in the woods. By the magical help of a black deer and a fighting cock hatched from an egg which Maria found, Juan eventually became king of the country and Maria married a wandering prince. They succored their wretched parents and forgave them their cruelty. This story unquestionably springs from a metrical romance, *The Life of the Brother and Sister, Juan and Maria, in the Kingdom of Spain*, which just as unquestionably springs from European folktale material. But the divergences of this Pampangan story from the metrical romance, which are as striking as the similarities, serve as an excellent example of what happens to folk fiction in the circuit from folktale to literary treatment back to folk adoption and development. See D. S. Fansler, *Filipino Popular Tales, MAFLS* 12, pp. 295 ff.

juba A name used by New World Negroes for various types of dance, and for the song, recitative, or handclapping setting the rhythm for a dance. 1) The name in some of the West Indian islands for the *bele* type of dance. See BELE.

2) In Haiti, a dance of African origin, first known as a work dance, accompanied by a single drum (tambour), which is straddled by the performer and struck with hands and heel of foot, and by the clicking of sticks on a sounding board wielded by another player. The name is used interchangeably with *Martinique*, however, which is a dance for the dead, like the *bele*.

3) A secular slave dance of Negroes in Louisiana and elsewhere in the southern United States. The hand-clapping rhythms and rigmaroles were developed to furnish accompaniment for this third type. The hands clap together and slap knees and thighs, with rapid crossing and patting. The rhymes are recited to the clapping and are of this order: "Juba dis and Juba dat/ Juba killed de yellow cat/ To make his wife a Sunday hat?/ Juba!" Another one quoted by W. C. Handy says, "Juba jump and Juba sing/ Juba cut dat pigeon's wing/ Juba kick off Juba's shoe/ Juba dance dat Jubal Jew/ Juba whirl dat foot about/ Juba blow dat candle out/ Juba circle, raise de latch/ Juba do dat long dog scratch." See HAM BONE.

Judas The oldest extant English ballad (Child #23): taken from a 13th century manuscript. This ballad, which may have originated in France, is the only evidence before the 14th century of the existence of the English ballad. Its uniqueness is paralleled by the story it tells, for here Judas has an evil sister who causes his downfall. Jesus gives Judas 30 pieces of silver to buy bread. But he meets with his sister and she steals the money. Judas then sells Jesus to "the riche Ieu that heiste Pilatus" for the sum. When Christ tells the "postles" that he has been betrayed, Peter says he will fight though Pilate come with ten thousand knights.

"Still thou be, Peter, wel I the i-cnowe;
Thou wolt fur-sake me thrien ar the coc him crowe."

Judas Iscariot The great traitor of Christian tradition; the disciple of Jesus who betrayed him with a kiss for the price of thirty pieces of silver. Contradictions or silence in the Biblical accounts of Judas have led to varying explanations of his acts. For example, a DeQuincey essay maintains that Judas thus attempted to place Jesus in a situation where his identity as Messiah would be unmistakably shown. The more common idea is that he was under the influence of Satan, or that he was angered by the waste of money on the oil with which Mary Magdalene washed Jesus' feet when the money might have been used by him for other purposes. The usual popular story of Judas holds that before his birth his mother dreamed that he would be a parricide, commit incest, and kill God. The infant, of the tribe of Reuben, was placed in a chest and set adrift. He was cast ashore, was found and brought up by the king of the foreign country. At that court he led an evil life, killed the king's son, and escaped to Judea. There he entered Pilate's service, and, like all fatal children, fulfilled the terrible prophecy. Since the only one who could save him was Jesus Christ, he joined the followers of Christ and became a disciple. He is always the last of the apostles and, his surname indicating "man of Kerioth," the only non-Galilean in the group. Jesus knew Judas' history, yet he made him treasurer of the group. When Judas identified his Master with a kiss, he accepted the thirty pieces of silver and then hanged himself on a branch of the Judas tree (*Cercis siliquastrum*), perhaps as De-Quincey says because Jesus did not display his powers, perhaps to seek his Master in the afterworld to gain his pardon. Traditionally Judas bought with the money the potter's field, Aceldama, and died there, falling to the ground and bursting open (*Acts* i, 18–19). Elsewhere in the Biblical story, it is said that he cast the blood-money into the Temple treasury, but that the priests took it out and bought the burial ground with it. Some tradition says that Judas did not commit suicide but was later killed horribly by a chariot. Dante places Judas in the deepest, darkest part of Hell, between the teeth of Satan, where he is eternally chewed. An old legend, used by Matthew Arnold in "St. Brandan," has it that because Judas was once kind to a leper in Joppa, he is permitted out of Hell each year for an hour.

In parts of central Europe, particularly Germany, an image of Judas is burned in the Easter bonfire; even though this custom has disappeared in places, Frazer says, the fires are still called "the burning of Judas." The straw effigy of Judas burned on Easter Saturday was consumed in a communal fire; the ashes or remains were planted on May Day as a preventive against blight. In upper Bavaria, to prevent hailstorms, the men and boys (women were excluded) raced to light the "Judas" fire with fire brought from the holy candle in the church. The winner was given Easter eggs by the women on Easter Sunday. In Corfu, on Easter Eve, Judas is stoned symbolically by all the people, who throw crockery from their houses into the streets. In Spain, Portugal, and Latin America, Good Friday or Easter Saturday is a time of execution of Judas. Effigies are burnt or blown up with gunpowder, or, as in Mexico City, they are filled with candies, coins, etc., and torn apart by the crowds when the bells signal noon. The Judas candle of the churches at Easter time is a huge wooden stick shaped like a candle, placed in the middle holder of the seven-branched candelabrum, and on which are hung wax figures of Judas; the Paschal candle is placed at the top of the Judas candle. The coincidence of the "Judas sacrifice" and the lighting of new fires at Easter time leads Frazer to believe that a much older pagan spring fertility rite lies behind these Christian-in-context customs. In keeping with his reputation, Judas is traditionally pictured as a redhead. Among southern U.S. Negroes, the evil eye sometimes is called the Judas eye. See JACK O' LENT.

Judas tree Any of a genus of trees (*Cercis*), as *C. siliquastrum*, a European species, or the redbud (*C. canadensis*) with profuse red-purple flowers, of the middle and western United States. The name is derived from the tradition that Judas Iscariot hanged himself from this tree. This tradition also attaches itself to many dwarf trees which are said to have once been tall and straight, but became stunted and gnarled for allowing their wood to be used for the Cross of Christ. Judas is usually said to have hanged himself from a tree of the same species. The dogwood, the elder, the ash, the dwarf birch, the fig tree which Jesus cursed and made barren, and many others are mentioned locally in this connection.

Judge Lynch Personification of lynch-law, the trial and punishment of individuals outside the process of the law, whether without trial or by an extemporary, self-appointed group. Severe, often fatal, floggings, tarring and feathering, rail-riding were originally associated with the system. Now the term in the United States is a synonym for mob hysteria resulting in murder, and especially the hanging and burning of the victim by a mob. Compared with this lawless and chaotic method of exacting "justice," the vigilante spirit makes some semblance of adhering to the law, since its enforcers consider themselves as arms of the law (as opposed to lynchers who think that they enforce justice in the face of the law); members of the pick-up posse of the West actually were sworn in as assistant and temporary officers of the peace; organizations like the Ku Klux Klan moved in opposition to the law but formed a sort of legalistic judicial entity within but not part of the state. Rough summary punishment and destruction of individuals, however, is limited to no country and no people, but takes over in any set-up where the law is either too weak or its officers too numerically insufficient to keep control. Compare, for instance, ROY BEAN.

Lynch-law in the United States is usually conceded to be so named from Col. Charles Lynch (1736–1796), a Virginia planter and judge, famous for his prosecution of Tories during the Revolutionary War, though Capt. William Lynch (1742–1820), of Virginia and South Carolina, also has his supporters as the original. Of each of these Virginia Judge Lynches it is said that he found it difficult to punish wrongdoers because rescue parties of Loyalists or British soldiers would free them while they were being sent to Williamsburg, the official judicial center. He therefore set up an illegal court, and by legal methods punished the criminals; after the war, the legislature legalized the proceedings. But in Galway, Ireland, they will point out to you a "writing" on the wall of the old jail, which testifies that in 1493 Judge Lynch tried, condemned, and hanged his own son for murder. Here evidently Judge Lynch personifies not so much extra-legal trial and mob murder as the depersonalization, inexorableness, and inhumanity of the law itself.

Judgment of God In the Middle Ages, the settling of a dispute by single combat or by ordeal. The referral of difficult decisions to ordeals or chance is customary in all parts of the world. [RDJ]

judgment of Paris In Greek legend, the choice made by the shepherd Paris among Aphrodite, Hera, and Athena. His awarding the apple to Aphrodite, thus choosing love, led to his abduction of Helen and the consequent Trojan War.

Juggernaut Same as JAGANNĀTHA.

juju The spirit dwelling within a made object or fetish, in the belief of the Ibo of the lower Niger. The term is applied generically to the ghosts and evil spirits of Southern Nigeria. In English writing juju is interpreted as being identical with the terms *fetish* and *grisgris*. [MJH]

jujube Any of a genus (*Zizyphus*) of Old World trees or shrubs. *Z. jujuba* may have been the lotus tree of the Lotophagi or lotus eaters (*Odyssey* xi) which made men lose all memory and desire for home, preferring a life of dreamy forgetfulness (D 1365.1.1; F 111.3). Richard Burton, however, prefers to believe that the men of the *Odyssey* were the victims of *hashish* or *bhang*. *Z. jujuba* is also the *Sidrat* or Tree of Paradise of the Koran which grows on the highest point of the seventh heaven on the right hand of the throne of God. Each leaf is inscribed with the name of a human being. On the 15th day of Ramadan the tree is shaken, and the leaves which fall contain the names of those who will die during the ensuing year. Water in which the leaves have been steeped is used for bathing a corpse. In Chinese mythology, the "Jujube of 1000 (or 10,000) Years," The Tree of Life, is the date palm. See LOTUS.

juke or **jook** Term used among American Negroes of Gullah strain for a house dealing in liquor and frequented by "bad" women. It is current slang for places of entertainment featuring coin-operated music boxes (*juke joints*), for the phonograph machines provided there (*juke boxes*), and for the casual, loose-jointed style of dancing done to such music (*juking around*). Conjecture as to the origin of the word ranges through derivations from a West African word *dzug*, meaning to behave improperly; an Old French and falconry term *jouk*, meaning to roost; a Scottish word, meaning to duck or swerve or hide suddenly. The latter word, *jouk*, may, through its suggestion of agile body movement, ultimately describe the dance style.

Jumala The Finnish word for God. It is mentioned for the first time in the year 1026 and is now in use for the Christian God. Jumala may have been an old Finnish god of heaven, but later became the abstract term for God in general.

jumby Generic term, used by the Negroes of the Caribbean islands, for "spirit," usually the ghost of a dead person. In Surinam, the Bush Negroes worship a deity named Dyombi, associated with the silk-cotton tree, and derived from the term for Dahomean spirits who dwell in the forest and, in the folklore, are associated with hunters who conquered the mythical thirty-horned giants. A synonym for *jumby* heard in the British West Indies, is *duppy;* it is also possible that the Haitian word *zombi* is related to it. [MJH]

Jumpers Members of an 18th century Methodist sect in England, and especially in Wales: so called because of the violent contortions to which their religious ecstasy subjected them. Manifestations of this kind which sweep whole groups, communities, or sections, are now classified as "psychological epidemics" and are being studied. The early 19th century 'jerkers' of Ohio, Kentucky, and other parts of the southern United States were so named for the same kind of violent and involuntary manifestations. It is still not uncommon to see "jerkers" at revival meetings or among certain sects, especially in the South. Compare POSSESSION.

jumping dance English term for one of the two special ceremonial dances of the Yurok and Hupa Indians of northern California. The Yurok *wonikulego* (they leap up) recurs at every festival. It is a simple line dance with the following simple steps: 1) Raise the right hand with a dancing basket, swing down, bending the knees so the fingers touch the ground, then jump half a foot into the air. 2) Stamp as the basket descends on the beat of the music, then jump on the off-beat. The Hupa *tunchitdilya* (autumn dance) is the October performance; the *haichitdilya* (winter dance) is the winter per-

formance, ten days in the hut and ten days outdoors. The costume consists of a buckskin headband with woodpecker scalps and a stick topped with a plume. Each ceremony starts with a long formula, and progresses from village to village. There is an increasing crowd of dancers and of successive leaps, culminating in as many as forty leaps. The display of wealth is reminiscent of the potlatch customs of the northwest coast. The jumping dance is associated with the deerskin dance. Both serve to drive away sickness and to aid in the increase of salmon, the chief source of food. [GPK]

jump-up or **calypso jump** A social dance of Trinidad: a recent fad. It is equally popular in the orgiastic Carnival celebrations and in more sophisticated gatherings at clubs. Any good calypso song can start the dancers in the canter step which carries them all over the floor. One couple starts in promenade position; one couple after another hitches on till a merry line, dozens wide, may be moving around the room. In the Carnival dances, enthusiastic dancers break away from the line and jump up, often in high leaps. [GPK]

junačke pesme Men's folk songs or ballads of Yugoslavia: heroic and narrative. See BALLAD.

juniper Any of the evergreen pinaceous shrubs (genus *Juniperus*) whose berries are used in making gin; also, a leafless shrub (genus *Retama*) mentioned in the Bible; occasionally, the American larch, tamarack, or hackmatack (genus *Larix*). In Iceland it is believed that the juniper and the rowan cannot grow together because they generate too much heat, one or the other will die. If branches of both are taken into a house, the house will burn down. If rowan wood is used in building a boat, it will sink unless a piece of juniper is used also. In Wales one who cuts down a juniper bush will die within the year. In some places a branch of juniper preserves the stables from demons and lightning; elsewhere, especially in Aberdeenshire and among the Czechs, the stables are fumigated with burning juniper.

The oil of the berries is used as a cure for toothache and diseases of the gums. The ashes of the wood cure dropsy, scurvy, palsies, and falling sickness. The Hopi Indians eat the boiled greens for sour stomach, constipation, earache, and sore throat. The berries, leaves, and bark are variously used in Europe and by the Indians of North America to cure snakebite, the plague, colds, shortness of breath, colic in any form, chronic rheumatism, chlorosis, venereal diseases, and to strengthen the optic nerve.

In Newfoundland the larch is called juniper and since its branches are said to always point towards Christ (the East) it guides men in the woods. They say that you will always find water under this tree. Bears and wolves fear it, hence hunters surround their game with it.

Juniper Tree Title of a European folktale (Grimm #47; Type 720) in which a stepmother kills her husband's little son and serves his flesh in meat pie to her husband. The father, unknowing, eats heartily of the dish and throws the bones under the table. The little sister gathers up the bones in a white kerchief and lays them in the juniper tree in the house yard. A beautiful bird rises from the bones and flies away singing. His song tells the story: "My mother killed me/ My father ate me/ My little sister gathered together my bones/ In a white silk kerchief/ And laid them under the juniper tree." The bird sings this song to a goldsmith and is rewarded with a golden chain; he sings it to a shoemaker and receives a pair of little red shoes; he sings to the miller's men who are hewing a new millstone and receives the great stone as reward. Then he flies home to the juniper tree and sings again his sorrowful story. The father hears it, runs out of the house to listen, and the bird drops the golden chain around his neck. The little girl runs out to listen and receives the pretty red shoes. At last the stepmother alone in the house cannot bear the song any longer and runs out; the bird drops the millstone on her head and that is the end of her. When the father and little sister look to see what has happened, the cruel stepmother is dead and the little boy stands before them safe and well.

In the Magyar version of this story, outlined by MacCulloch in his *Childhood of Fiction*, p. 296, it is a mother who kills her own child, stews him, and sends a portion of the stew to her husband plowing in the field. The little sister hides the bones in a hollow tree. They are transformed into a bird, who sings his telltale song here and there, receives as gifts a cloak, a stick, and a millstone. The little sister receives the cloak; the father gets the stick to support his failing steps; the cruel mother is killed by the millstone. There are Scottish, English, French, Scandinavian versions of this story. See SINGING BONE.

Juno In Roman mythology and religion, the female counterpart of Jupiter; the queen of heaven; the protectress of women: identified with Hera. Juno, under some of her aspects, accompanied every woman throughout life from birth to death; she was thus a kind of ministering spirit, and Junos were spoken of for women as genii were for men. One of Juno's especial concerns as a goddess of fertility was childbirth, and *Juno Lucina* (bringer of light) was invoked at that time. For a week after a birth there was a table laid for her in the home. The Matronalia, on March 1, was celebrated by matrons in her honor. Juno also protected marriage and its sanctity; hence, a marriage in the month of June (thought to be originally called Junonis) was most auspicious. As a result of Juno's hatred for illicit sexual pleasures, a law of Numa decreed that no prostitute might touch her altar under penalty of sacrificing a female lamb to the goddess.

Juno was also a sky goddess, parallel in some ways to Jupiter, although as *Juno Regina* she seldom hurled bolts. She was the goddess of the moon; the kalends (time of the new moon) were under her protection, and this seems to link her rather more closely with Janus than with Jupiter.

She presided over all human doings, both private and public. As *Moneta*, she gave counsel; her temple on the Capitol contained the mint. *Juno Sospita* developed from the rescuer of imperiled women to the guardian of the state. The bird of Juno was the peacock. Compare EILEITHYIA; GENIUS; HERA; JUPITER.

juoigen The sacred chant of the Lapps: a magical incantation or prayer used to attract the spirits of dead ancestors, whom the Lapps worship and invoke and propitiate. The spirits ignore the daily speech of men, but they will heed extraordinary sounds or words. For this reason the juoigen is couched in a vocabulary outside the scope of normal everyday usage. No translation of it has ever been vouchsafed to an outsider, but it is taught to every male Lapp, almost in infancy. It loses its efficacy if the chanter is not letter-perfect or if he forgets even one word.

Jupiter or **Iuppiter** In Roman mythology and religion, the sky god; the god of atmospheric and celestial phenomena; hence, the chief god of the pantheon: identified in the later Greco-Roman synthesis with Zeus, and acquiring many of the characteristics and myths of the Greek god. The earliest forms of the name were *Diovis pater, Diespiter, Diovis*: all the names seem to stem from a root meaning "light." As the god of lightning, he was anciently represented as a flint, which strikes sparks, and which Jupiter is often represented as carrying. The oath *per Jovem lapidem jurare* was used in the making of treaties, grass from the temple precincts and the flint (*lapis silex*) being parts of the equipment. Places struck by lightning were sacred to him and protected by walls. Many of the epithets of Jupiter stem from his activities as causer of the phenomena of the air: *Jupiter Pluvius*, or *Tonans*, or *Fulgurator*, or *Elicius*.

Jupiter was the guardian of honor from the very beginning, being protector of oaths, treaties, marriage: as *Fides* or *Dius Fidius*, he saw to it that these social bonds were kept. The Tarpeian rock, on the Capitol, where his temple stood, was the place from which traitors were flung. *Jupiter Optimus Maximus* protected the city from this pinnacle. The temple to the "best and greatest" of the gods on the Capitol was built towards the end of the monarchy, and Juno and Minerva were associated with him there under the Greco-Etruscan influence. His ties with Juno, apart from this influence, are very slender. The anniversary of the dedication of the temple, September 13, became a date about which the Roman games centered. To the temple generals came in triumph to celebrate with sacrifices. *Jupiter Stator* prevented flight in battle, and Romulus was said to have invoked him successfully in a battle against the Sabines.

Jupiter determined human affairs, and with Janus, the instituter of things, Jupiter was invoked in all undertakings. He sent prodigies and omens, for example the flight of birds which were known as Jupiter's messengers. He was early the protector of the vineyards and the harvest, and as in his celestial aspect presided over seasonal change. The beginnings of periods of time were sacred to him and sacrifices were made at such times in his honor. The ides of every month (the time of the full moon) were dedicated to him.

His priest was the flamen dialis. Jupiter was identified with Zeus and with Amen as the Romans became acquainted with the religions of other lands. Almost all of the personalized, familial stories of Jupiter are simple transplantations of Greek myths of Zeus. However, the association of *Jupiter Feretrius* with the sacred oak on the Capitol, though resembling the parallel Zeus-oak relationship, is more ancient than Greek influence; the temple of Jupiter Feretrius probably was Rome's most ancient. The name *Jove,* often used synonymously with Jupiter, is the genitive of the name, being perhaps closer to the root-original than is Jupiter, and when used nominatively refers to Jupiter as the sky god.

Juruwin or **Jurua** Andaman Islands evil spirit of the sea: one of a group of invisible beings (sometimes described as white) which live in the sea with their wives and children. They eat fish, devour the bodies of drowned men, and sometimes attack fishermen with invisible spears which cause cramps or sudden illness. Juruwin is the South Andaman term; Jurua is used in the northern part of the islands. See LAU.

Juskaha or **Djuskaha** Seneca Indian culture hero; the second of twin boys, Othagwenda (Flint) and Juskaha (Sapling), born to the young woman magically impregnated by West Wind. Flint was hated by his grandmother and cast out of the lodge soon after birth, but his brother Juskaha found him in a hollow tree and brought him back. After they were grown the boys separated, to increase the size of their earth-island. Later each inspected the other's work. Othagwenda had made a giant mosquito which Juskaha rubbed down to a small size; he also modified other of his brother's troublesome creations so they would not harm man. Othagwenda, on the other hand, spoiled many of the good things Juskaha had made. The inspection of each other's work resulted in the twins' quarreling and the death of Othagwenda. See ATAENSIC; DUAL CREATORS. [EWV]

jus prima noctis or **droit de seigneur** The right of the lords of manor to take the virginities of all girls in their territory on the girls' wedding nights. Catholic authorities and some others are vehement in their assertion that this is a fable of modern date "of which not the slightest trace is found in the laws, histories, or literature of any country in Europe." A passage from the Old Irish *Book of Leinster*, however, says that fathers with marriageable daughters took them first to pass the night with King Conchobar, which has led to the report that Conchobar had the virginity of every maid in Ulster. A number of peripheral facts throw light on the subject. The rupture of the hymen marks an important transition

and hymeneal blood is dangerous. The ceremony should therefore be performed only by persons endowed with virtue: priest, noble, stranger. Some peoples are said to regard the children from these unions as their only legitimate offspring and that these children inherit the divinity, magic, or virtue of their fathers. Some peoples require nubile maidens to engage in prostitution and in this way, incidentally, help to pay for the cost of the wedding. In Cambodia the defloration has been compared with the ceremony of confirmation in occidental countries. The folklore of the *jus prima noctis* is clearly a special case of the folklore of virginity. [RDJ]

Just Like Me A catch tale in which the listener is enjoined to say "Just like me" at every pause of the narrator: "I went up one flight of stairs" / "Just like me" / "I went up two flights of stairs" / "Just like me" / . . . / . . . / . . . / "I went into a little room"/ "Just like me" / . . . / . . . / "I saw a little monkey" / "Just like me"—or "you" according to the alertness of the listener. See ADAM AND EVE AND PINCH ME.

Juturna or **Diuturna** In Roman mythology, a nymph, the personification of healing springs and wells: associated with the Lacus Juturnæ near the temple of Vesta in Rome. In Virgil, she is the sister of Turnus, given immortality by Jupiter in return for her virginity. She was also called the wife of Janus and mother of Fontus. On January 11, the Juturnalia was celebrated in her honor by workmen on aqueducts and wells; at the Volcanalia, August 23, she was celebrated, along with Volcanus and the Nymphs, as a protectress against fire.

Juventas An early Roman goddess of youth: identified with Hebe. The temple of Juventas on the Capitol was more ancient than that of Jupiter; another temple stood in the Circus Maximus.

K

ka In ancient Egyptian religion, an active aspect of the personality; an entity associated with the physical body (born at the same time, as a kind of twin), protecting and motivating the person: somewhat akin to the Roman conception of the genius. The ka dwelt in the body and in images, and survived in its home, the tomb. The ka retained consciousness after death and went before into the afterworld to prepare the way for the dead person. Elaborate funeral offerings were made to it and a kind of deification, an equation with the idea of godship, developed. Certain Egyptian kings had many kas; and in this sense the ka was a double or alter ego or guardian spirit. Animals and objects were also believed to possess this spiritual double; the ka of the person ate the kas of the offerings left in the tomb. In later thought, the ka, though separate, became conceived of also as the human indwelling soul. See BA; WRAITH.

Ka 1) Literally, who: the unknown god of Hinduism; an abstraction and deification of the interrogative pronoun by the authors of the various *Brāhmaṇas*. In the *Kaushitaki, Śatapatha, Tāndya,* and *Taittirīya Brāhmaṇas,* Ka is identified with Prajāpati. Thus later, in the

Purāṇas, Ka has developed into a supreme deity; and in the *Mahābhārata* he is identified with Daksha, the creator.

2) The name of Chinūn Way Shun (primordial creator of all nats, in Kachin [Burmese] belief) in his aspect of the spirit of tilth. He receives special sacrifice and invocation to send a good harvest at the general prayer-place (*natsin*) outside each village before sowing time. The chief, *tumsa* (exorcist), and *kyāng-jong* (butcher) are the only members of the community permitted to be present at this ceremony. Following the sacrifice the *tumsa* determines which household shall sow first. After they have sown, two days must elapse, then offerings of eggs and liquor are made and the community sowing begins. In Karen belief, Ka controls forests, streams, and houses, and causes illness.

Kaaba Literally, the cube or cube building: the sacred shrine of Islam at Mecca, standing in the courtyard of the great mosque, and containing as part of its walls the Hajaru 'l-Aswad, the black stone. The Kaaba, about 30 feet high, was first erected by Adam, destroyed and rebuilt several times, and finally cleared of its idols by

Mohammed when he conquered Mecca. The black stone, probably a meteorite and much older than Islam, is an irregular oval about seven inches in diameter, and set in gold at the southeast corner of the Kaaba. When Abraham and Ishmael, in obedience to God's command, rebuilt the Kaaba, they dug down to the foundation laid by Adam. But only three stones were at hand to mark the corners. Ishmael went off to search for another stone, and met the angel Gabriel, who gave him the black stone. Mohammed said that the stone originally was white, but that pilgrims touching it had turned it black with their sins. When the Kaaba was being built in Mohammed's youth, a dispute arose among the various tribes about who was to put the black stone in place in the wall. They agreed to let the first person to enter the gate arbitrate. Mohammed was the man; he had the stone placed on a cloth and raised to the correct level; then he set it in place himself. The Kaaba and its stone is the focal point of Islamic worship. Towards it Moslems face in prayer; once in his life the Moslem makes his pilgrimage to Mecca. The stone, touched or kissed during the circuit of the Kaaba, will on the Judgment Day have eyes to recognize those who have kissed it, and its tongue will sing Allah's glory. The Kaaba was the place where the Arab tribes kept their idols; Mohammed destroyed the idols, but made the shrine, through the pilgrimage, a point of unity among the tribes. See HADJ; HOBAL.

Kabandha In Hindu mythology, a huge, hairy, headless Rākshasa, with a mouth in the middle of his belly and one big eye in his breast. His terrible deformity was the result of a previous quarrel with Indra, who pushed his head down into his body; another story says it was caused by the curse of a sage. Kabandha was killed and burned by Rāma. From the fire emerged Gandharva (Kabandha's original form before deformity) who advised Rāma in the war against Rāvaṇa.

Kabīr (1450?–1518?) A religious leader of the 15th century in the Punjab: hero of many popular parables and moral tales today. A famous banyan tree near Broach is said to have sprung from the tooth-twig of Kabīr. [MWS]

Kaboniyan or **Kabonian** Tinguian (Philippine Islands) deity or culture hero, sometimes placed above Kadaklan, sometimes identified with him, but holding a much stronger place in the affections of the Tinguian people. He gave the people sugarcane and rice, taught them to plant and reap, showed them their ceremonies, and how to foil the evil spirits. He also taught them the words of the sacred magic formulas (*dīams*) used in their rites and ceremonies.

Kaboniyan lives in the sky or in a cave near Patok, from which come the talking jars and the gongs used in dances. In Tinguian mythology he married a Tinguian woman in the first times. He also entered the body of a woman and taught her how to cure illness.

kabuki A form of Japanese drama based on dancing and singing, completely fanciful and decorative in content and presentation. Kabuki was created three and a half centuries ago by an actress-dancer, Okuni Izumo. It was at that time a type of primitive dance, *Nembutsu Odori*, or prayer dance. For a time it was performed entirely by female dancers, or geishas, but has now, together with other features of the great classic Nō drama, adopted the convention of performance entirely by male actors. Female parts are taken by special actors, called *onnagata*.

The form of the stage and the various techniques are highly conventionalized and peculiar to the kabuki. Many features betray their origin in puppet plays (*mahuronmono*). In fact, many of the best dramas have been taken over from the puppet play, which originated in the 17th century (*ningyō-joruri*, the telling of a story by a chanter).

A characteristic feature of the kabuki stage is the "flower way" (*hanamachi*), a passage leading to the stage through the left section of the theater, an important asset in the creation of the mood. The *kurogo* (prompter) also adds to this unreality. Dressed in black (*kuro* means black) he frequently stands behind the chief actors. He is assisted by a stage helper, or *koken*, who, however, shows his face. Other devices are the revolving stage, the *chobo* (ancient music) played from the *geza* (music box), and the frequent background sound of the *ki* (wooden clappers).

Artistic unreality is emphasized by expressive postures, called *mie*, underscored by the *ki*. Dumb show (*dammari*) also makes extensive use of stylized gesture, in grotesque, colorful, and nonsensical scenes. *Mitiyuki* and *tatimawari* also portray stylized scenes of love and sword play; *monogatari* depends for its effect largely on posturing. All of this dance-type action is performed to musical accompaniment.

Of the original eighteen best kabuki plays ten are still performed; the most famous are *Sukeroku* and *Kanjinchō*. In the first the hero Sukeroku stands for the people's rights against the tyrant samurai, Okyu. The *jidaimono* are plays with historical backgrounds, or puppet-play origin, and *sewamono* and *kizewamono* are genre plays. Many of them contain scenes of violence, of death, of suicide (*seppuku* or *hara-kiri*), of murder, of sword play, of the inspection of a severed head, and of vendetta.

Symbolism is the keynote of kabuki. The scenery, too, contributes to this, and the splendid make-up of the actors. The actor's face, while not masked, is painted with decorative yet expressive patterns. Even scenes of tragedy and horror contribute to the beauty and the esthetic effect of this form of traditional drama. [GPK]

kabyar or **kebiyar** A Balinese sitting dance performed by one man. He never rises from the floor; the legs are not used; the dance involves the use of torso muscles, arms, and hands, and emphasizes facial expression. It is performed to full Balinese orchestra and interprets with utmost sensitivity all the nuances of the moods of the music. This is a modern dance, introduced to Balinese audiences by a young man named Mario, who made it and himself famous. The dancer must have, first of all an expressive face, and sensitivity and intensity of personality, plus superlative technical training. Since Mario's time few dancers have been found equal to the kabyar, but occasionally there is one.

kácǎ "Kitty": a Bohemian waltz-type couple dance, performed in a double counterclockwise circle. Holding inside hands, the dancers swing their arms freely as they turn from and towards each other. In the second part all circulate in a grand right and left, with a waltz pivot on each meeting of new partners. Finally a double chain weaves in and out, in a grand right and left by couples,

The title refers to the words of the accompanying song: "Red and blue violet, where did you find it? . . ." Refrain: "Run away, Kitty, run away, while the old cat is chasing you." The words do not, however, call forth mimetic actions. [GPK]

Kachawharr A dance-song of the Diegueño Indians of Southern California, performed at Jacumba. It is performed at sunset, accompanied by the rhythmic rubbing of a stick over a basket, and dramatizing a religious story of two gods, brothers, who arose out of the ground near a hot spring at Jacumba. As told in the chant and acted out by the dance, the events include the building of a house, the coming of rain, the harvesting of tobacco, seeking mates, games of forfeit at the end of which one brother is killed, the entrance of Coyote, the departure of the dead brother as a bird and of the other to join the Maricopa Indians.

Kaches Literally, the brave ones: a group of spirits of Armenian belief. The Kaches were incorporeal beings who lived in stony places, waged wars, hunted, stole grain and wine, and tortured men. They have been superseded in modern belief by the devs.

kachina A term applied by the Hopi and other Pueblo Indians of the American Southwest to supernatural beings, the mythical ancestors of the present human beings, who revisit the earth for half of every year during the winter months, and then retire to the spirit world for the rest of the year. The arrival and departure of these beings, of which there are a host, are the cause for dramatic ceremonies among the Pueblo peoples. While on earth the kachinas are impersonated by male dancers wearing masks (these latter are also referred to as kachinas), who perform in many of the Pueblo dances. It is a fundamental Zuñi belief that kachinas when killed become deer.

The term *kachina* is also used for the small wooden dolls, painted and decorated to represent individual kachinas, which adults carve and give to children during the season when the kachinas are above ground. In some pueblos the children are led to believe that it is the kachina spirits who will whip boys at the boys' initiation rites—actually, of course, a male impersonator of the kachinas does this.

The literature of the Pueblo kachinas is large. See Elsie Clews Parsons, *Pueblo Indian Religion*, 2 vols. (1939); Jesse Walter Fewkes, *Tusayan Kachinas, RBAE* 15 (1897), and *Hopi Kachinas, RBAE* 21 (1903). [EWV]

☞ In ancient times the kachinas used to come to the pueblos in person in the same guise now worn by the dancers. They brought rain, corn, and melons. When they ceased coming they gave the people their masks, so that now men can impersonate them, or be identified with them by wearing the masks. The *koshare* and *kurena* used to accompany them, looking like the dancers of today.

The transforming masks are completely unrealistic. They are made of rawhide, mostly in "inverted bucket" shape, covering the head; a few are dome-shaped or cover only in front of the face. There are dozens of types of designs, each with a specific name and symbolism. Triangular or round eyes predominate, and black and green coloring. Many have horsehair beards, and spruce or wildcat fur collars. Some have snouts and one or two ears. Many are crowned with an arc of eagle feathers, or

with stylized horns (antelope and deer kachinas), or occasionally painted with rainbow symbols. They are in a word, reminiscent of the Navaho *yebechai* masks. This extreme conventionalization is a Hopi characteristic. The rest of the costume also suggests Hopi provenience, the kilts and fringed belts, with accessories of animal fur and spruce. *Manas* or maiden kachinas, impersonated by men, wear white half-masks, hair-whorls in Hopi style, black wool dresses, and goat-hair bangs.

All mature men and boys belong to the kachina societies, which correspond to the two moiety kivas—turquoise and squash. San Felipe alone has a third group, *ya'ctsa.* Initiation is accompanied by ordeals of whipping, etc., at Acoma and Zuñi, but not at San Felipe. The initiated are called *si'cti,* "those who know" (i.e. that the kachina are men).

For each dance event there are four preparatory days spent in retreat, preparing initiates and paraphernalia, and painting masks and practicing dances. On the fifth day all emerge into the plaza, the medicine men in the lead. They line up in two groups, the line dancers in a file, and the side dancers attending specific line dancers. The former all wear identical masks, the latter different kinds. Maiden kachinas line up behind the men, near the wall. The leader starts the step, shaking his rattle—a stamp and knee raise, stamp and heel raise, incessantly repeated. Shaking rattles and singing their own accompaniment, the kachinas prance in unison never moving from the spot, except for an about-face on signal. They dance in sunwise circuit at all four walls of the plaza, four times in the morning, four times in the afternoon. They give away corn and melons and seeds to the spectators, and sometimes kachina dolls. They receive aspersions of meal and water from the medicine men. They return to the spirit land and give their masks back to the spirits.

In most pueblos they appear at various times all the year round, to produce rain or snow and insure the growth of crops. At Hopi they go away in July at the Niman ceremony and are replaced during the summer by the Snake-Antelope or Flute societies. They officiate at the February *powamu* ceremony. In Zuñi they are prominent in the *kokochi* at summer solstice and in the dance series by the summer and winter kivas. They are most spectacularly welcomed in the advent of the kachina or *shalako* ceremony. Along the Rio Grande they dance sporadically, in the deer dance of Santa Ana for rain, in September or October for harvest.

The masked dances are not open to visitors. But unmasked dances, which can be witnessed, have the same form. These "good" kachina or "dark" kachina dances are commonly held in the early spring. At Taos, Isleta, and the Tewa pueblos, they are termed Turtle Dances. At Isleta they also form part of the Spruce ceremony. They often dance in connection with curing ceremonies. In fact, some of the masks have special curative attributes, particularly the Long Horns with their bearlike tread and call. The koshare and kurena accompany them in turn. At times the kachinas take part in the horseplay of these clowns. At Zuñi during intermission the *koyemshi* clowns hold forth. At Acoma a special drama is enacted, an attack of fructifying blows called *shuracha,* made realistic by the wearing of blood-filled bladders.

The kachina are entirely beneficent spirits and are regarded with affection, in contrast with the much-feared koshare. The uninitiated, including most women and all children, firmly believe that the dancers are the actual spirits. The impersonators believe in their divine identification, though no element of trance enters into this highly ritualized institution. [GPK]

Kadaklan The greatest of the Tinguian (Philippine Islands) deities. Kadaklan lives in the sky, and created the earth, moon, stars, and sun. By his wife, Agemem, he had two sons, Adám and Balujen, whose duty it is to see that Kadaklan's commands are obeyed. His dog, Kimat, is the lightning, which also sees that his desires are fulfilled, for Kimat will bite a house, tree, or field whenever Kadaklan desires that a special ceremony be performed. During storms Kadaklan amuses himself with his drum, the thunder. He is held in great esteem by the Tinguians, but is not personalized, has little hold on their affections.

Kaddish The Jewish prayer for the dead, recited by male mourners twice a day for a year; also, a male child who will recite the Kaddish for a deceased parent. The prayer, specifically called the Mourner's or Orphan's Kaddish to distinguish it from the use of the prayer at other times, is in Aramaic with the exception of the closing phrase. The Kaddish is said at the burial, and after that for eleven months. This period was originally twelve months, the period traditionally that a soul spent in Gehenna, but it was thought to show a lack of respect for the parent to admit that the full term in Gehenna was necessary, and the period was lessened to eleven months. The Kaddish is also repeated every year on the anniversary of the death of the parent, the Jahrzeit.

Kadrū In Hindu mythology, one of the thirteen daughters of Daksha who were married to Kaśyapa; the mother of the 1000 Nāgas (serpents) whom she bore in order to people the valley of the Kashmir. See GARUDA.

kagami The Japanese word for "mirror": an object often mentioned in Japanese mythology and fairy tales; also, one of the "Three Imperial Jewels," the regalia of Japan. See JAPANESE FOLKLORE. [JLM]

kagura An ancient Japanese dance form of the Shinto religion; one of the forms of *mai,* slow dance. At Shinto shrines priests enact the myth of the sun goddess Amaterasu, who was recalled from a cave by the dancing goddess Ume-no-utsume. More commonly the dancers are very young priestesses. They dance sedately in brilliant white to their own accompaniment on a kind of sistrum and to *koto* playing by an elder priestess. *Mikagura* is (or was) the ceremony performed before the Imperial sanctuary at harvest festivals or on accession to the throne. Sometimes the dancers are masked. When not masked they are termed *sumen.* The kagura introduced the Japanese custom of manipulating props while dancing. These ritual objects are called *torimono.*

In country festivals a joyous note is introduced in the music of the *daikagura* and *sato kagura.* The instruments are a flute and large drum, perhaps also brass and wooden clappers of the kind used in the *kabuki.* According to the number of musical pieces furnishing the accompaniment, the kagura is termed the sevenfold, twelve-fold, twenty-five-fold, and seventy-five-fold kagura. [GPK]

Kāh-gyur, Kāng-gyur,* or *Kanjur The scriptures of Lāmaism. The name means "translated commandment" and is thus used because the books were translated from Sanskrit or (sometimes) from Chinese. It is divided into three parts (corresponding to the Tripitaka of the southern Buddhists): the *Dul-va* or Discipline, the *Dō* or Sermons, and the *Ch'os-non-pa* or Metaphysics. These are believed to be antidotes for the three original sins: lust, ill-will, stupidity. The *Kāh-gyur,* together with its commentaries, the *Tän-gyur,* is worshipped with incense and the burning of lamps. Even fragments of books or manuscripts containing holy words are treasured and it is profane for anyone to throw on the ground even a fragment of holy writ. See DŌ-MAN.

Kaiānians or **Kayānians** In Iranian mythology, a dynasty of legendary kings, originally not followers of Zoroaster: probably the ruling families of various Iranian tribes. The first king of the dynasty was Kavi Kavāta who is said to have been abandoned on Mount Alburz. There Rustam went to find and make him the Iranian sovereign. His successor was Kavi Usan (Kai Kāūs) to whose wonderful ox disputes over the boundary between Iran and Turan were referred. The greatest of the Kaiānians was Kai Khusrau or Haosravah who waged war on the Turanians. The last of the dynasty was Vishtaspa or Gushtasp who was converted by Zoroaster. The legends of these rulers were coordinated by the poet Firdausī in the epic *Shāhnāmah.*

kakamora Melanesian supernatural beings of Guadalcanal and San Cristoval. They vary in height from six inches to five feet, have long, sharp nails, straight hair, are as strong as three or four men, wander in the forest, live in holes, caves, and banyan trees. They have a king and queen, are usually harmless, but are fond of deluding children. Sometimes they kill and eat men. They fear anything white. Stories are told of the capture of the kakamora, indicative that they are now extinct as far as Melanesian belief is concerned. On San Cristoval they are called *pwaronga* or *kakangora.*

kakko A small cylinder drum of Japan, set on a low stand for playing. It is characteristic of the "left music" of Japan, that derived from Chinese and Indian influences, as differentiated from the "right music" of Manchurian and Korean influences, a distinction dating from the 9th century.

Kāla The Black One: in Hindu mythology, time; male counterpart of Kālī, a form of Śiva as creator of the universe, and also its destroyer (death), for he draws it in and swallows it. The universe is born again after each destruction, but the wise who understand all things attain union with the creator and are not reborn.

kalalōa In Kulaman (Philippine Islands) belief, the soul which is the cause of success or failure. The kalalōa are conceived as two in number, one on the right side and one on the left. At death the right kalalōa goes to the sky; the left kalalōa goes to Kīlot, the underworld. Illness is due to evil spirits or to the desire of the kalalōa to leave its abode.

Kālanemi In the *Rāmāyaṇa* a Rākshasa, uncle of Rāvaṇa. He attempted to kill Hanumān. To Hanumān, however, the true nature and purpose of Kālanemi was revealed by a crocodile maiden whom he disenchanted; whereupon he seized Kālanemi by the feet and hurled him to Lankā so that he fell at the feet of his co-conspirator, Rāvaṇa.

kalau (singular *kala*) Generic term for all the evil spirits and powers of Koryak folk belief: among the Paren also termed *kalak* or *kamak,* among the Reindeer Koryak *ñe′nveticñin* or *ñi′nvit.* They are often thought of as terrible cannibals, more often just as supernatural killers. They are sent to this world by the supreme being to torment wrong-doers, or to cause disease and death and thus test the strength of the incantations of the people against disease and death. The underground kalau come out of the earth and cause headaches by knocking people in the head; they bite people and thus cause swellings, or cause sores by pinching pieces of flesh out of them. Earth-dwelling kalau cause diseases by merely breathing among the people with their poisonous breath. Sometimes these kalau are visible in animal shape; sometimes they look like people with pointed heads. Big-Raven is forever at war with them. There are numerous myths relating how Big-Raven gets the best of the kalau. See Waldemar Jochelson, *The Koryak* (vol. vi, part 1, p. 27 ff., *Publications of the Jesup North Pacific Expedition,* Leiden and New York, 1905).

Kaleva The great national hero of Finnish and Estonian folk poetry. Many attempts have been made to explain the origin and meaning of the word. M. A. Castrén considered it as synonymous with "hero" in general. A. Schiefner, and later Julius Krohn, paid attention to the similarity of the Finnish Kaleva with the name of the Russian hero Kolyvan and Kolyvanovitch, son of Kolyvan. The inhabitants of Iceland called the State of Novogrod Kylfingaland and the privileged class of that state were called Kolbjagi. The Finnish philologists, Alqvist and Setälä, derived the name from the Lithuanian word *kalvis,* smith, with evolution to "strong man, giant, hero." Kaarle Krohn, like Schiefner, thought that Kaleva or Kalevi was a proper name of some hero with a real historical background in regard to time and place. The Russian name for Tallinn in about the year 1223 was Kolyvań and there also were other towns with the same name in Russia. Kaleva is also a culture hero, the cultivator of the ground, but not a giant of the tales. He is the earliest hero of the Finnish and Estonian people; however in the folk poetry of today, it is not Kaleva acting, but his descendants. Therefore, *Kalevala* means the home or land of the hero Kaleva, which is Finland. E. Lönnrot chose this name for the title of his compilation of the old epic songs in 1835. See FINNISH FOLKLORE. [JB]

Kalevipoeg The son of Kalevi, the chief hero of Estonian tradition. He is a very strong man, a giant or culture hero, friendly to man. The epic *Kalevipoeg* is a creation of F. R. Kreutzwald, published in 1857–1861 with a German translation, containing 20 songs with 19,000 verses in all. Kreutzwald followed the example of Lönnrot's compilation of the *Kalevala.* But Kreutzwald did not have enough basic material, since there are few heroic folk songs in Estonia, and he was forced to use many prose legends about a traditional strong youth. His creation is therefore not to be considered as original Estonian folk epic. Nevertheless the influence of his work on Estonian culture has been very great.

References: W. F. Kirby, *The Hero of Estonia.* 2 vols., London, 1895. Aug. Annist, *F. R. Kreutzwald's 'Kalevipoeg.'* 2 vols., Tartu, 1934 and 1936 (with summary in German). [JB]

Kālī The Black One (feminine of Kāla): the supreme mother goddess of India; consort of Śiva: also known as Chandi, Durgā, Pārvatī, Satī, Umā. As Kālī she is the mother goddess in destructive aspect, devouring the life she has produced. The power of Kālī abides in every woman. She is usually depicted with four arms. As life-giving mother, she is depicted with a golden ladle in her right hand, the bowl of abundant food in her left. In a famous hymn Kālī says "Whosoever eats food, eats food by me" (H. Zimmer, *Myths and Symbols in Indian Art and Civilization,* New York, 1946, p. 212). In her dual aspect she holds the symbols both of death and immortality: the noose to strangle her victims, the iron hook to drag them in, the rosary, and the prayer book. She is sometimes pictured as a horrible, hungry hag who feeds upon the entrails of her victims.

In some Tantra texts she stands in a boat floating on an ocean of blood, drinking from a skull the lifeblood of the children she brings forth and eats back. In another Tantric depiction Kālī is shown black as death with a necklace of heads; in her two right hands she holds the sword and the scissors of physical death; in her two left hands, the food-full bowl and the lotus of generation. She is strangely beloved in India as the beautiful, horrible, wonderful, life-giving, life-taking Mother. For the first European translation of the *Kālikā Purāṇa* containing the life story of Kālī, see H. Zimmer, *The King and the Corpse,* New York, 1948, p. 240 ff. See DEVĪ.

Kāliya In Hindu mythology, the five-headed king of the serpents who lived in the river Yamunā (Jumnā) and emerged to lay waste the surrounding country. Kṛishṇa, while a child living with the cowherds, one day climbed a tree and dived into the serpent's pool. The splash from the pool set fire to the tree. Kāliya and his bejeweled serpent army challenged Kṛishṇa, encoiled, and almost overcame him. But Kṛishṇa, remembering his own divine essence, loosed himself easily, placed his foot upon Kāliya, and danced on the serpent's head until his power was broken. He banished Kāliya to the ocean, but promised that the Garuḍa bird (enemy of serpents) should not destroy him.

Kalki or **Kalkin** Literally, the white horse: in Hindu mythology, tenth and last incarnation of Vishṇu, which will appear at the end of the present age of the world (*kali yuga*). In this avatar Vishṇu will destroy the wicked and restore purity. See AGES OF THE WORLD; KŪRMA; MATSYA; YUGA.

kalogheroi Phallic dance of Thrace and its two chief characters: performed on the last Monday in Carnival. They wear goatskins as headdresses, the horns removed and stuffed with hay. One of the kalogheroi carries a wooden phallus, the other a toy bow. The one with the phallus chases and is married to a boy impersonating a girl (*koritsi*). He is then shot by the one with the bow; there is mourning over his body; he is buried; and he rises again. Throughout the rite the church procedure is parodied. Associated with this obvious fertility-inducing drama are other customs tending to the same effect: plowing, making a house-to-house collection, etc. See GOAT DANCE.

Kalojan or **Caloian** A clay image of a young man figuring in a Rumanian ceremony occurring on the Monday before Assumption: the name is a corruption of *kalos Joannes* which in turn is a rendering of *kalos Adonis*, beautiful Adonis. The figure is put into a coffin by girls and covered with flowers and sweet-smelling herbs. He is buried ceremonially. At dawn of the third day, the group returns to the grave and digs up the coffin, weeping and calling for rain or singing to him that his mother is weeping for him. The figure is then taken to a running stream or a well and thrown in; sometimes it is broken up before being consigned to the water. The entire company then go to an inn where, over their cups, they tell each other that Kalojan is not dead but is risen from the grave. The ceremony is plainly a fertility and rain-making rite. The throwing of the figure into the water is reminiscent of the flowery Gardens of Adonis, which contained a figure of the god; the breaking of the figure makes the Kalojan resemble a transplanted Osiris; the weeping of the women for rain is paralleled in *Ezekiel* viii, 14: "and, behold, there sat women weeping for Tammuz." See ADONIS; JACK IN THE GREEN.

Kalou-Vu The "root gods" of Fiji, i.e. the original gods, perhaps originally deified Fijian ancestors, or possibly (as suggested by several scholars) Polynesian gods superimposed on the pantheon of these invaded people. Chief among the Kalou-Vu is Ndengei (definitely pure Fijian), creator in serpent form, whose shiftings and turnings in his mountain cave cause earthquakes. Ndengei was worshipped with enormous quantities of first-fruits, crops, pigs, turtles, etc. The priest went alone into the cave to present the prayer of the people. If the prayer was for abundant crops the priest emerged from the cave with a yam in token of the answer "Yes"; if the prayer was for rain, he came out drenched and dripping; if the people besought victory, Ndengei gave the priest a flaming brand to take out to them. Ndengei's son, Rokomautu, is sometimes interpreted as creator; among other things, he gave the people fire.

The long myth sagas of the Fijians recount the adventures of Ndengei's two grand-nephews, who will some day return and bring the people an era of abundance and all good. The first Europeans to visit Fiji were at first thought to be the descendants of these twin culture heroes. Others among the Kalou-Vu are Ndauthina, fire god, and god of seafarers and fishermen, a malicious, trick-playing god, except towards fishermen, whom he protects and betters. Ratu-mai-mbulu, god of the land of the dead, is also a serpent-shaped, cave-dwelling god. He makes the sap run in the trees and crops to sprout. During his special month, the people are quiet; they do not beat the drums, dance, sing, or fight, in order not to disturb or distract Ratu-mai-mbulu. The shark god, variously named among the various tribes, is conceived as a benevolent god who tows home upset canoes, helps in sea-fights, etc. His flesh is tabu to his worshippers. See MELANESIAN MYTHOLOGY.

Kalseru The name, in northwestern Australia, of the rainbow serpent associated with rain and fertility. The rainbow serpent is known over most of Australia, but the name differs from tribe to tribe. See AUSTRALIAN ABORIGINAL MYTHOLOGY.

kaluk The generic name for spirits among the Buddhist Talaing people of Burma: same as NAT.

Kalu Kumāra Yaka A Sinhalese demon who prevents conception, delays childbirth, and causes puerperal fever. Originally he was a saintly Buddhist sage (*arhat*) with the power of traveling through the air. While traveling he saw and fell in love with a beautiful princess. Immediately he lost his superhuman powers and died, becoming the demon, Kalu Kumāra Yaka.

Kalunga Name of the god of the sea in the pantheon of African deities worshipped in the Congo-Angola cult of Bahia, Brazil. [MJH]

kalvelis The Little Smith: a Lithuanian couple dance with bits of occupational mime. Partners may form two lines or a single circle. If danced in a circle, the dance begins with a round to the right, and then to the left with seven polkas and three stamps. The hammer and anvil of the blacksmith are suggested by hand-claps, as in *Peas Porridge Hot*. The phrase is concluded by partners pivoting with hooked elbows. In the second part, performed in a circle, girls move center and out, then boys do likewise, always with the typical polka step. [GPK]

Kāma Desire: the god of love of Hindu mythology; in the *Rig-Veda* called the first-born of the Mind. He was a beautiful young god, carrying a flower-bow with flower-string and five flower shafts (Exciter of Desire, Inflamer, Infatuator, Parcher, Carrier of Death); or sometimes he is depicted with a bow of sugarcane, the bowstring of bees, the arrows tipped with flowers, and riding on a parrot. Kāma holds the mastery over every human being and even the gods are "disordered" when the spell of love touches them. Thus is insured the perpetual creation of the world, which is never finished.

The most famous of the myths of Kāma is the one in which Brahmā, the Creator, is himself held in the spell of love at sight of Dawn, the beautiful woman produced also out of his own meditation, and is ridiculed by Śiva. Śiva's laughter at Bramhā's plight, i.e. filled with desire for his own daughter, shocked the Creator out of his passion and he "let the image of the woman go." Although freed of his passion, he was angered by the ridicule, and cursed Kāma, saying on the day Kāma should let loose his shaft at Śiva, he would be reduced to ashes by one glance from Śiva's middle eye.

Later, after Kāma was united in joy with the beautiful Rati, daughter of Daksha, Brahmā induced him to go and "unsettle" Śiva for the good of the universe, to create the mood of love in that solitary god, lest the perpetual creation of the universe cease. This Kāma did; and the woman produced to be the object of Śiva's desire was the great Mother of the World herself. When Brahmā called upon her, she rose from her cosmic dream and consented to enrapture Śiva. Thus the Great Mother (who, incarnate as Lakshmī, was wife of Vishnu) consented to be reborn as daughter to Daksha and was named Satī. When the time came and Satī was presented to Śiva, Kāma let fly his arrow, and Śiva shouted "Be my wife!" In the story in which Brahmā's curse is fulfilled, and Kāma is burned to ashes by the glance of Śiva, the curse is mitigated by Kāma's rebirth.

In various texts Kāma was the son of Dharma and Śraddha, the son of Lakshmī, or produced from the urgic meditation of Brahmā, the Creator; born from water; or self-existent, "unborn." In the *Purāṇas*, his wife is Rati, Delight, his son Aniruddha, his daughter Trisha. See HOLI.

Kāmadhenu, Kamdhain, Kamdhenu, Nandinī, or **Surabhi** In Hindu mythology, the cow of plenty produced at the Churning of the Ocean; the fountain of milk which granted its possessor, the sage Vaśishṭa, all things he desired. Among the wonders produced by Kāmadhenu was a host of warriors who fought against Arjuna.

Kami In Shinto, a god or similar spiritual being. [JLM]

kampós tánc Literally, shepherd's dance: a Hungarian men's dance performed with a shepherd's hat and the ornate and cherished crook. The dancer manipulates the crook while executing *pas de basque* leaps and leg-swings with upturned toes. During one step the hands are clapped under the raised leg. It may be performed purely for amusement, but is probably an ancient leap dance for the welfare of the flock. [GPK]

Kaṃsa In Hindu mythology, an asura and the persecutor of Kṛishṇa. Kaṃsa was the king of Mathurā, cousin of Devakī, and thus cousin (often incorrectly called uncle) of Kṛishṇa. It was foretold that a child of Devakī would slay him, so Kaṃsa tried to destroy her children. The first six were killed, but the seventh, Balarāma, was smuggled away, and the parents fled when their eighth child, Kṛishṇa, was born. Kaṃsa ordered all male infants slain, but he was eventually slain by Kṛishṇa. His name also occurs in the *Purāṇas* as Kanśa. See FATAL CHILDREN; SLAUGHTER OF THE INNOCENTS.

kanafaska A Moravian couple dance in quadrille formation, i.e. with four couples facing center in a circle, man on the left. They are numbered consecutively, counterclockwise. In the first part, couples 1 and 3 slide across past each other, in ballroom position. Then couples 2 and 4 do the same; and in turn all slide back home. In the second part, the first man polkas around the circle clockwise with each woman in turn, and returns her home with a "toss-up," a high lift into the air. See LIFT DANCE. Then the second, third, and fourth man follow suit. This dance is of interest as one of the few Slavic rounds in quadrille formation. [GPK]

kanaima A word of Carib origin which, in the Guianas, is used to cover practically all the forms of black magic. Epidemics, sudden death, or mysterious ailments are generaly regarded as the effects of *kanaima*. The Indians call also *kanaima* the real or imaginary avengers who follow relentlesly their victims until they find the opportunity to murder them secretly. Hostile tribes and murderous spirits are also given the name of *kanaima*. The term is also applied to every disgrace and misfortune, and serves to describe the irresistible lust for revenge which may overtake a person and force him to do something terrible. [AM]

kanász tánc Literally, swineherd's dance; a Hungarian dance resembling the Scotch sword dance in form, step, and bagpipe accompaniment. Two sticks are crossed at right angles and the dancer, with a kind of *pas de basque* and quarter turns, leaps from one space to another. Two groups can take turns, or one man can execute the whole routine. Though now danced on saints' days, the kanász tánc is obviously one of the large class of sword dances associated with pagan victory and vegetation rites. See STICK DANCES; SWORD DANCES. [GPK]

Kande Yake In Vedda (Ceylon) belief, the deified spirit (*yaka*) of a mighty hunter, called Kande Wanniya, who is invoked for success in hunting. He is invoked with the yaka of his brother, Bilindi, at the beginning of a Nae Yaku ceremony, since many Veddas believe that the recent dead go to Kande Yake and become his attendants. They must have his permission to receive the offerings made them by the living and he accompanies or brings them to the Nae Yaku ceremony. See CULT OF THE FRIENDLY DEAD.

Kaniyan A dancing caste of Malabar and Travancore on the southwest coast of India. They perform acrobatic feats. Their chief dances are: 1) *pitichu kali,* a sword and shield dance accompanied by the drum; 2) *parishatalam kali,* a circle dance performed by boys at night to a bell and metal plates struck with sticks; 3) *kolati* or stick dances in circular formation, requiring great skill and precision in striking two sticks, one against another or against a neighbor's, with ever-increasing speed. See KOLATTAM; STICK DANCES. [GPK]

kankantri Taki-taki term for the silk cotton tree (probably the tropical American *Ceiba pentandra,* also called the god tree): regarded by Surinam Paramaribo Negroes as sacred to Mama fô Gro or Gro Mama, the Earth Mother. Every plantation, every little yard has its tutelary Mother of the Soil, thought of as inhabiting the kankantri there growing. The locale of the kankantri is regarded as sacred. No one must urinate or defecate anywhere near it. Here Mama fô Gro is offered food and drink with annual ceremony, and oftener if specifically supplicated.

k'an-po (feminine *k'an-mo*) The head of a Tibetan monastery who is endowed with three prerogatives transmitted directly by the saints: *dbang,* spiritual power; *lung,* knowledge of the teachings; *k'rid,* the ability to teach.

kantele The traditional instrument of Finnish folk music for over 2000 years; a psaltery, originally having five strings and now having 20 to 30. To its music the ancient epics of the *Kalevala* were chanted. [TCB]

☞ Väinämöinen made the first kantele from the jaws of a big pike, and all living beings of the air, earth, and water, even the sun and moon, were delighted with the charming playing (see *Kalevala,* songs 40–41, 44). The word *kantele* is probably a borrowing from Lithuanian. The name and form of the instrument are common to many peoples of the Baltic region: Estonian *kannel,* Latvian *kuokle,* Lithuanian *kankles* (see Slaviūnas in *Folklore Studies* III, Kaunas, 1937). See FINNISH FOLKLORE. [JB]

kanteletar Ancient Finnish magic songs and lyrics of the type called *runos,* some of which are preserved in the *Kalevala.*

kapétua Papago warriors' victory dance performed during the Limo Festival. Enemy-killers had to purify themselves in retreat for sixteen days and blacken their faces. Then at the festival they reenacted scenes of the warpath, in turn leaping about with the shield. The other celebrants danced around the pole with scalps and the women seized the scalps. [GPK]

k'apio The ceremonial clown societies of Taos and Isleta Indian pueblos. *K'apio chifunin* are the Black

Eyes, *k'apio shureno* the Red Eyes: so called because of painted rings around their eyes. They correspond in accoutrement and function to the Keresan *koshare*, and are particularly apt at burlesque. They engage in similar stereotyped phallic magic. Their characteristic hair poke may be a phallic symbol, associated with the emergence myth: i.e. with the pokes with which the *k'apio* (and *koshare*) prototypes opened an exit during primal emergence from the earth. They also have other chthonic associations, the Black Eyes with the water turtle and the rain-bringing kachina, the Red Eyes with the land turtle. The Black Eyes are the more prominent, and serve as clowns in the Taos Deer Dance and Spruce Dance. In Isleta, at Christmas, the Black and Red moieties both participate in alternate sets. Their dancing, as that of the koshare, is not well-ordered like that of the kachina, but consists of individual grotesqueries, burlesque, and social comment in groups. [GPK]

Kappa In Japanese folklore, a malicious spirit living in rivers. It has the body of a tortoise, the head of a monkey, and the limbs of a frog. On the top of its head there is a hollow filled with fluid. It devours disobedient little boys in swimming. [JLM]

kapurale or **dugganawa** A Vedda (Ceylon) shaman through whom the Nae Yaku (spirits of the recent dead) speak. The kapurale imparts to his successor, usually his own or his sister's son, the power and knowledge to call the yaku (spirits). The pupil must avoid many types of food and spend time memorizing invocations used in various ceremonies. A yaka is invoked by singing and dancing. The kapurale begins slowly and gradually increases the tempo of the dance and song. As the shaman's voice grows hoarse and he dances faster and faster, he becomes possessed by the yaka who speaks through him, often promising to assist his relatives in hunting and sometimes giving them specific directions.

karawatoniga Harmless supernatural beings of Tubetube (Melanesian) folk belief, who live among the rocks or in the bush near the seashore. They are of human color and form, have long ringlets, indistinguishable features, and perpetuate their kind. The karawatoniga are seen most frequently after death. Compare BARIAUA; KAKAMORA.

Karei or **Kari** The god of thunder of the Semangs, a Negrito people of the Malay Peninsula: invisible, superhuman in size, omnipotent, omniscient, creator of man, soul-giver, recorder and punisher of sins such as familiarity with mother-in-law, mocking tame or helpless animals, killing the sacred black wasp or tabooed birds. Thunder, the sign of Karei's anger, causes guilty persons to make atonement by gashing shins, mixing blood with water and tossing it to the sky and calling, "Stop, stop." Neither Karei nor a companion deity, Ple, have a cult. [KL]

Kari One of the jötnar of Teutonic mythology; a tempest giant and lord of the storm giants. See JÖTUNN.

karma The effect of any act, religious or otherwise; the law of cause and effect regulating one's future life: literally, act.

In Brahmanism, the fate of a soul in its current life is determined by its conduct in its former life. All the sins of its immediately previous life must be expiated in the present one. This is a common motif in Hindu story. Many an unfortunate character is either forgiven his failures or shunned for his attendant mishaps, because believed to be "working out his karma." This, however, does not imply absolute fatalism, since one's future life is determined by his acts in this one.

The Buddhists made karma the foundation of their ethical theory, but rejected the theory of the soul which was supposed to reside in the cavity of the heart, and which had anger, desire, and quality. The Jains, likewise recognizing karma, made their highest goal freedom from karma. Their entire monastic apparatus is based on a desire to prevent the formation of new karma through the application of strict rules and the practice of austerities.

Karshipta or **Karshiptar** In Iranian mythology, a bird gifted with speech. He was sent to spread the religion of Ahura Mazda among the men assembled by Yima in his vara (enclosure) to protect them from the scourging winter which was to destroy mankind.

karsikko The name given in North Savolax, Finland, to a piece of white paper on which was written the name of one who has just died, with the year of his birth and death. This paper was placed, for the funeral day, on a cloth spread on the back wall of the hut (M. Waronen). [JB]

Kārttikeya The six-faced Hindu god of war; also god of the planet Mars, and as such usually called Skanda. The *Mahābhārata* and *Rāmāyaṇa* identify him as the son of Śiva or Rudra, born of Śiva's seed and the Ganges. He was brought up by the six Pleiades (Krittikās)—hence the six faces. He is often depicted riding on the peacock Parvani, with a bow in one hand and an arrow in the other, or sometimes as tapping a drum with the fingers of his left hand and brandishing a sword in the right.

karyatid In ancient Greece a female dancer who performed annually at the feast of Artemis Karyatis, at Karyai, on the Laconian-Arcadian border. The karyatids glided lightly on tiptoe in short tunics. With upright carriage, they carried flower baskets on their heads, as they progressed in serpentine chains. Because of their burden-bearing upright posture they became the models for the static pillars, as on the "Porch of the Maidens" of the Erechtheum in Athens. [GPK]

Kaśyapa The Old Tortoise Man of Hindu mythology: progenitor of all things living on the earth, and as this progenitor (and tortoise), identified in the *Satapatha Brahmāna* with Prajāpati. In some texts, Irā, one of the daughters of Daksha, was his consort and mother of earthly vegetation. See KŪRMA. He was one of the seven great rishis of India.

According to the *Atharva-Veda*, he sprang from Time (often identical with Vishṇu); according to the *Mahābhārata* and *Rāmāyaṇa*, he was the grandson of Brahmā and the father of Vivasvant whose son Manu was the progenitor of mankind. He married the 13 daughters of Daksha; by Aditi, he was the father of the Ādityas and Vivasvant. According to the *Vishṇu Purāṇa*, Vishṇu, born as a dwarf, was also their son. By his 12 other wives he begot all kinds of living things including the Nāgas (whose mother was Kadrū), the asuras (whose mother was Diti), Garuda (whose mother was Vinatā), also the Piśāchas, Rākshasas, and Yakshas.

Kathā Sarit Sāgara Literally, the ocean of the rivers of stories: a collection of popular medieval Indian fairy tales and romances written in Sanskrit, made by Somadeva of Kashmīr about the beginning of the 12th century. The collection was translated by C. H. Tawney and published by the Asiatic Society of Bengal in their *Bibliotheca Indica* series (two volumes, 1880–1884). It was printed with voluminous comparative and analytical notes by N. M. Penzer as *The Ocean of Story* in 1928.

katydid An arboreal, green, long-horned insect related to the grasshoppers and crickets (family *Tettigoniidæ*) named for the characteristic note produced by the stridulating organs at the base of the wing-covers of the male: katydid, o-she-did, katydid, did, she-did. In general the katydid's cry is interpreted as a weather oracle. In various sections of the United States, the saying is that when the first katydid is heard it will be six weeks until frost. In Missouri it is time to plant corn when the katydids first are heard; in Kentucky, 90 days after the first katydid is heard there will be frost; in the Kentucky mountains dog days begin with the first katydid. In New England a katydid chirping inside the house is said to be an omen of death. In Maryland they say that the bite of one causes fits. [GPS]

kaukas A dwarfish household spirit of western Lithuanian folklore, having similar characteristics and duties to the *áitvaras* and the northern Lithuanian *pukÿs*. See LITHUANIAN MYTHOLOGY.

kaukiwawakauwa A Shawnee Indian dance performed one year after the death of a distinguished personage. It is called the turning dance, for men and women intermixed move a short time in one direction and then turn directly about. The feast and dance last for four days, and much time is taken up by the exchange and winning of goods. [GPK]

kauna or **kawina** A dance of Surinam Negroes, performed especially when a manatee or tapir has been killed, to propitiate its spirit. The music is also called *kauna;* the drum is *kauna drọ* (a small drum hung around the player's neck and played at both ends); the songs are *kauna siŋgi.* The people believe that if the dance and music did not last all night the spirit of the captured animal would burn down the houses of the hunter and the feasters. The kauna is basically a fertility dance: the dancers mime the act of copulation. A drink is made for the ceremony from a "seed" in the manatee's belly and is thought to produce virility and great physical strength. It does induce turgidity, but actually long use produces impotence. The kauna has also become a social dance, often taking place even when no manatee feast is to be celebrated (See M. J. and F. S. Herskovits, *Suriname Folklore*, p. 10 ff., New York, 1936.)

Kauravas In Hindu mythology, the sons of Dhritarāshtra and the opponents of the Pāṇḍavas in the battle for the kingdom whose capital was Hastināpura. See ARJUNA; MAHĀBHĀRATA.

káusima The girls' puberty dance of the Choroti, Ashluslay, and Mataco Indians, Gran Chaco. It began at the first new moon after the first signs of puberty and continued every day until the next new moon. The girl had to stand motionless against the wall of a hut. Her mother and a group of older women circled the hut

with slow, regular steps, chanting and striking rattle staffs on the ground. These staffs, *káhuis,* were made of a hollow bamboo rod two or three yards long, and had a bunch of deerhoofs tied to the top. Thus a blend of rustling and hollow pounding marked the rhythm. The deer had supernatural power for fertility and aided in the protection of the girl against evil spirits, *mohsek,* to which she was particularly susceptible at this time. The women were aided in their demon exorcism by four singing medicine men with gourd rattles, and two shamans with drums. The Lengua had a similar ceremony in their *yanmena.* [GPK]

kava or **'ava** (from the Maori word meaning bitter) A mildly intoxicating narcotic beverage brewed from the root or leaves of a plant of the pepper family (*Piper methysticum*): used by the Polynesians and some Micronesians and Melanesians in their social, religious, and political life. It is important in Polynesian ceremonies, especially well integrated into western Polynesian life in various aspects. Ceremonial etiquette is observed in kava-drinking as with tea-drinking in China and the betel-nut complex in Malaysia and Indonesia. Kava was formerly prepared by the women, or, in some cases, the chiefs. The root is chewed and placed in water, and then strained. Only the men drank it. But today it is prepared by the children, and women are also permitted to drink. Kava-drinking and betel-chewing do not occur in the same places except where one is in the process of superseding the other. Polynesian migration can be traced by the prevalence of kava-drinking. Medicinally it is used as a cure for chronic rheumatism and venereal diseases.

kavi, kavya, or **kavan** (Persian *kai*) In Indo-Iranian belief, seers endowed with supernatural prescience. In later Persian legend the title was applied to a line of kings, the Kaiānians.

kawakuku Among Roro-speaking Melanesians and the tribes on the Papuan Gulf, hereditary tabu experts who pronounce and enforce vegetable food tabus. The women and children are told that the kawakuku are spirits from the bush, and they consequently fear them. The kawakuku appear in the village only in masks which extend to the feet; these masks are burned after each appearance. They are directed by the village leaders who determine when such tabus are to be imposed.

Kay In Arthurian legend, a knight of the Round Table, and seneschal of King Arthur. Who or what Kay originally was is impossible to tell. He is a follower of Arthur in the *Black Book of Carmarthen* and *Kilhwch*. In the latter he is credited with supernatural traits. He could be nine days under water without drawing breath; he could go nine nights without sleep; when he wished he could equal the tallest tree in height. Like Cuchulainn, he radiated heat. During the heaviest rain, whatever was a handbreadth above or below his hand remained dry, and when his companions were coldest, he would serve as kindling to light a fire. Of these strange and probably mythical properties none survive in the later romances, where he is noted only for his crabbed tongue and his deserved humiliations in combat. See R. S. Loomis, *Arthurian Tradition and Chrétien de Troyes* (1948), index sub *Keu.* [RSL]

kazila The forbidden thing, tabu, among the Fjort. Like other tabus, it consists in the prohibition to certain individuals or families of eating certain animals. Those of royal descent may not eat pig, for instance; some may not harm or eat certain other animals because of the debt of gratitude of an ancestor to that animal. Lake Bori and the fish of that lake were kazila to women by the order of Nzambi (the Fjort creatress).

kazoo A musical device consisting of a tube, covered at one opening (in the end or middle) by a taut membrane, which vibrates with a buzzing sound when the player sings into the tube. Curt Sachs has suggested the term *voice masks* for instruments of this type which serve chiefly to disguise the natural quality of the singing voice. Primitive peoples have for centuries used such devices as bark trumpets or megaphones, conch shells, and shallow frame drums held before the mouth to impart to the singer's voice some quality deemed more suitable for magical utterances or addresses to supernatural beings and forces. The kazoo, known chiefly nowadays as a toy, a noisemaker for parties and celebrations, is also called *mirliton,* and was formerly called the *eunuch flute,* as such being regarded with some seriousness in art music in 17th century Europe. In construction it is related to a Chinese whistle flute, *t'ai p'ing hsiao.*

K'daai Maqsin In Yakut religion, the chief blacksmith in the underworld, from whom blacksmiths receive their skill. His forehead is covered with dirt nine fingers thick, his cheeks with rust three fingers thick, and his eyes are closed. When he wishes to see, eight men above and eight men below drag his iron lids apart with hooks. He makes iron hard by tempering it with blood of a lion, tears of a seal, blood from the lips of a young man, and blood from the cheeks of a young girl. He caused shamans to be introduced into the world. Compare BALOR.

Kdyš Jsem Jel do Prahy *When I Rode to Prague:* a Czech couple dance. With hands joined the couples circle, the girls backwards. Then they turn under the arch of a kerchief. [GPK]

Keb The Egyptian earth god, Geb.

keen The Irish lament for the dead, sung always by women, sometimes professional mourners. Traditional words include eulogies of the dead, his looks, his noble character, and his good life, uttered in prolonged, rhythmic phrases. The keen is a more articulate expression of grief than the death wail, the *ullagone* (Irish *uileacán*) which consists of high-pitched exclamations of woe and moaning sounds. See MOURNING SONGS.

keepers The Trinidad term for the common-law mating found among New World Negroes of lower socio-economic strata. See AMASIADO. [MJH]

Kekri All Saints' Day of the Finns, celebrated in two different ways: in the pagan manner in honor of the ancient Finnish god Kekri, and in the Catholic way, in honor of all the saints. Masks were made for the face and the masked people were called Kekritär. Kekri means a ghost or spirit of the dead. The oldest description of the feast is in 1754. [JB]

kelp Any of certain large coarse seaweeds (order Laminariales). On the North Pacific Coast the Kwakiutl Indians use kelp as a charm to summon the wind; the tubular stem is made into a kind of horn through which the wind is called. The Kwakiutl also use kelp in a dish of welcome served to guests. The Shinnecock Indians of Long Island knew the medicinal value of kelp; they steeped it to bathe open sores, and valued it highly as a remedy for rheumatism. In Newfoundland also the iodine properties of kelp were known to ease lame backs and other aches. In Labrador when the people see ice-coated kelp rising to the surface of the sea, they take it as a sign of mild (or milder) weather to come.

kelpie A water spirit of Scottish folklore, inhabiting every lake and stream in the country. He is a mischievous, usually malevolent, being who appears in the form of a horse, sometimes grazing on the banks of the lakes, sometimes appearing at the fords of streams. He will lure travelers to mount him, then plunge into the waters and drown them. To see him is a sure sign of drowning. Certain 19th century Scottish antiquarians have endeavored to trace the word kelpie to *kelp,* the large fantastic seaweeds common to some coasts, in which this water horse or spirit is said to hide. More recent opinion, however, derives the word from Gaelic *calpach* or *colpach,* meaning steer or colt. Modern Irish retains *colpa,* meaning a full-grown animal, whether cow or horse. The fabulous water horse of Welsh folklore is the *ceffyl dwr.* In Shetland it is called the *shoopiltee,* in the Orkneys, the *tangie* or *tang.* Compare EAC UISGE.

kemoit In the belief of the Menek Kaien (Malay Peninsula), a real ghost in Belet. The soul, which leaves a dead body through the big toe and crosses to Belet, becomes a kemoit when the bones of its limbs are broken and the pupils of its eyes turned inward by those who have preceded it to the land of the dead.

Kemp Owyne A Scottish ballad (Child #34) of the loathly lady type, and hence related to stories of disenchantment by a kiss (D735) like *Beauty and the Beast.* It stems from Scandinavian tradition; very near to it are the Icelandic saga *Hjálmter ok Ølver* and the Danish *Maid in Dragon-form* (DGF 59). *Kemp Owyne* begins with a cruel stepmother who drives the girl unmercifully. Finally she flings her into the sea.

> "Lie you there, dove Isabel,
> And all my sorrows lie with thee;
> Till Kemp Owyne come ower the sea,
> And borrow you with kisses three."

The three kisses are a typical ballad ornamentation; in folktales, one kiss is usually sufficient to break the spell, but repetition with variation is part of the charm of the ballad. Isabel becomes a savage sea monster. At last Kemp Owyne comes along and gives her the three kisses in exchange for a belt, a ring, and a sword. He observes the tabu against touching any part of her but her lips, and she is transformed into a beautiful woman, "as fair a woman as fair could be." In *Kempion,* another version, the stepmother is in the end transformed into a monster herself, until "St. Mungo come oer the sea."

Kentucky running set A figure dance of the Appalachian highlands, named by Cecil Sharp for the state of Kentucky, but equally typical of Tennessee and North Carolina. In many communities it replaces any other form of communal dancing. It combines the circular progression of a huge round with the intermingling of quadrille formations. 1) The "large circle figures," to the right or to the left, involve all couples in unison: the California Fruitbasket with all hands crossed behind backs; the Open Tunnel, where all couples follow the leaders clockwise to form an increasing arch which sucks up the counterclockwise double line of dancers; Wring Out the Dishrag; Wagon Wheel; and the Ball of Yarn which winds the whole line into a snail and unwinds them again. 2) The "odds off to even figures" count off alternate couples. The evens dance in place, while the odds perform the figure with each couple in turn, as they gradually move counterclockwise. Each group of two couples starts each figure with a small clockwise circle. The hundreds of figures have picturesque names—Birdie in the Cage, Ladies Join Your Lily White Hands, Mountaineer Loop, Lady Through the Outside Door, Open and Close the Garden Gate, etc., all involving an interlacing of arms and ingenious changes of position, dos-a-dos, etc. They commonly conclude with "swing your corner" and "swing your partner."

The step can be a shuffle such as is used in squaredancing, but the boys usually prefer to let their feet go "whickety-whack" in a kind of clog step. Sometimes as an interlude the boys circle, arms across shoulders, with fancy variants of the clog. The rhythmic sound effect is contagious, and equally effective without any accompaniment except hand-clapping, or with the syncopated accompaniment of bass fiddles, banjos, accordions, etc., playing oldtime tunes—"Old Joe Clark," "Cripple Creek," etc.

The Kentucky Running Set has preserved in the mountain fastnesses a pure form of old English tradition. These round dances are very old and probably go back to ancient ritual circlings and serpentines in vegetation rites. See ROUND DANCES; SERPENTINE. [GPK]

keremet Fenced-in sanctuaries or sacred groves of the Cheremis and Mordvins; the living places of the ghosts of heroes. [JB]

Keres (singular Ker) In Greek mythology, spiritual beings, the souls of the dead, perhaps ancestral spirits; also, a sort of evil-bearing goddesses of death, later identified with the Furies. The Keres were omnipresent, bringing diseases and ills to mankind. They possessed no power of life and death in themselves, but served to carry out the wishes of the gods, of Ares in particular in whose train they were found. They served to drag off the corpses of the dead. They escaped originally from Pandora's box. The Greek Anthesteria closed with the command: "Out of the house, ye Keres." As tiny, gnatlike human figures, the Keres appear in vase decorations.

Keresāspa or **Garshāsp** Literally, with slender horses: one of the greatest Iranian heroes; son of Thrita Āthwya (father of Thrāētaona of whom Keresāspa seems to have been a doublet). Keresāspa killed many foes under the protection of a third part of Yima's Glory (khvarenanh) and he is worshipped by warriors to obtain strength. His greatest feat was the slaying of the dragon Srvara. He sprang on its back, hung on for half a day, and finally killed it with a single blow. He was victorious over Gandarewa after a nine-day battle, purged the land of highwaymen, and slew the gigantic Kamak; but he was conquered himself when he neglected the maintenance of the sacred fire. Ahura Mazda permitted him to be wounded, and he fell into a state of lethargy in which he will remain until the end of the world, when

he will kill the monster Azhi Dahāka, and thus inaugurate the era of happiness. Keresāspa's exploits are told in the Shāhnāmah, in which he is called Feridhūn.

kermis or **kermess** Originally, a religious ceremony for a newly erected church: from Dutch kerk, church, and mis, mass. It originated in the Jewish Hanukkah and was introduced to Christianity by Constantine the Great. The simple solemn proceedings had by the 9th century already become annual festivities in the Low Countries, often an annual outdoor festival held on the feast day of a local patron saint, but it became more and more associated with secular activities, such as markets, feasts, and dances. These included circling of the Kirmesbaum, kermis tree. Particularly in Flanders and northern Germany these festivals fell into the inevitable degeneration of drinking celebrations, and have given the term this connotation. [GPK]

keruk A memorial rite of the Diegueño and Yuma Indians of California and the Yuma of Arizona, corresponding to the tauchanish of the Luiseño. It is a great ceremonial observance for the dead of the year. After a night of wailing, there are six nights of marching images of the dead around a fire and dancing and singing until morning. These images are made of mats of grass, the features indicated in haliotis shell. On the last night at daybreak the images are marched in ceremonial array to the keruk, a small semicircular house of brush or willow. They are placed face down on a pyre of arrowweed and with a special song are burned along with quantities of their belongings. The purpose is similar to that of the Chippewa restoration of the mourners and the Sioux releasing of the spirit, namely, to dispatch the dead and keep them content, and to terminate the grief of the survivors. [GPK]

Kesar or **Kyesar Saga** Title of a story (believed by A. H. Francke to be a myth of the seasons) of great popularity among Tibetans, especially in Ladāhki.

The Kesar is related in four parts. The first tells of the creation of the world and the birth of the 18 Agus or heroes of the tale. The second part (called the spring myth by Francke) tells of the birth of Kesar in gLing and his wooing of and marriage to 'aBruguma. The third section (identified as the winter myth) tells of Kesar's journey to the north, the slaying of a giant, marriage to the giant's wife, and the deliverance of 'aBruguma from the hands of her abductor, King Hor. In the fourth part (which parallels the third) Kesar journeys to China and marries the daughter of the king of that land. See GLING-CHÖS.

Kesil The Fool; a giant associated in Semitic lore with the constellation Orion: probably Nimrod, the mighty hunter who rebelled against God. Kesil tried to reach heaven, was seized and bound by God and placed in the sky as a sign to other rebels. But he must serve his term in Sheol too, so every autumn Kesil disappears below the horizon. The word kesil in the Bible is modernly translated as the fool, or Orion. It may mean either giant or something thick or large. See ORION.

kesma Literally, cut dance: so called because of sudden breaks in the music with quick reaction into immobility on the part of the dancers. It is a Persian couple dance, face to face but not in embrace. One couple at a time emerges from the crowd and moves about with a two-step and swaying of the arms. The bystanders clap hands in rhythm. [GPK]

kettledrum A drum constructed of an open vessel of oval or round shape, having a stretched skin covering the mouth. Probably the earliest form of the instrument was a primitive clay bowl, of the type still used by some primitive peoples. Later kettledrums are of metal, and have developed to the complexity and tonal exactness of the modern symphony orchestra instrument. On the primitive level, kettledrums of wood or gourd are still used by such peoples as the Araucanians for magic purposes. See DRUM.

Ketu 1) An Afrobrazilian cult, deriving from the town of the same name (Ketou, Quetou) that lies on the ethnic boundary between the Dahomean and Yoruban peoples of West Africa. Ketu was one of the "kingdoms" conquered by the Dahomeans, in consequence of which many of its inhabitants were sold and transported to the New World. The Ketu cult of Bahia, with the Gêge and 'Jesha, form "orthodox" groupings that worship the African deities in almost unaltered aboriginal form. The Yoruban language is employed in the rituals, and the words of the Ketu songs are in the same tongue. It is the largest of the purely West African cults, and its cult-centers are known for the elaborateness with which the rites are performed. The cult-groups have complex hierarchical organization, and discipline is rigorously exacted. The deities retain their Yoruban names and functions unchanged. Related New World groups are the Lucumí sect of Cuba, and the Shango groups of Trinidad, as well as the many Yoruban-derived cults found elsewhere in Brazil. [MJH]

2) In Hindu cosmogonic mythology, the dragon's tail (the descending node in astronomy), the part of Rāhu which the soma did not reach; also, a comet or meteor. See RĀHU.

key The key was a power to open the heavens and hells of many early religions and an attribute of numerous early deities. Athena, for instance, carried the keys of Athens. Janus is represented with keys in both hands. Hecate was said to carry the keys of the universe; old monuments depict her with the keys of Hades; one of her processionals, in Caria, was called the "procession of the key"; and Cassandra bore the keys of Hecate. Priests and priestesses of ancient gods bore their keys in token that the authority and power of the deity was theirs also. Io, priestess of Hera, was key-bearer to that goddess; Iphigenia was key-bearer to Artemis, and her gravestone also bore the emblem. In Babylonian mythology Marduk made both the gates and keys to heaven. Ishtar opened the seven gates and locks of hell. The keys of earth and heaven belong to the Assyrian deity Ninib. The Egyptian Serapis holds the keys to earth and sea. The Greek Hades had iron bars and keys. The keys of hell and of death are mentioned in *Revelation* i, 18; the key of the bottomless pit was shown in the hand of an angel (*Rev.* ix, 1; xx, 1). Christ descended into hell and broke the locks. The term "power of keys" refers to *Matthew* xvi, 19, and the words of Jesus to Peter, "I will give unto thee the keys of the kingdom of heaven." In all folklores the key possesses great magic. Throughout the Mediterranean region and in Germany it is an amulet against the evil eye. In Italy tiny keys are put on babies to ward off convulsions. In the Ionian Islands an iron key is laid on the breast of the dead for a twofold reason: the iron keeps off evil spirits, the key opens the doors to the afterworld. In Norway a big iron key is hung over the stalls of bewitched cattle to cure them; and keys are hung here and there around the fields to lock out hail. In Transylvania a key in the feed bag protects the grain from thieving birds. In France it was said that a werewolf would instantly return to human form if struck between the eyes with a key. In Brittany the menhirs are said to be the keys to the ocean; if they were dug up the sea would pour up through the holes. In China a key is always given to an only son to lock him into life.

In ancient Rome the new bride was given the keys to her new household; divorce was effected by taking or surrendering them. This was the custom also among the early Teutons. In ancient Gaul a widow laid her keys upon the corpse of her husband, in token of relinquishment and in some instances freedom from obligation.

In rabbinical lore three keys are poetically mentioned: the key of the womb, which opens the way to the birth of a child; the keys of the rain; and the key for the resurrection of the dead. The iron keys of a synagogue placed under the pillow of a dying child will release it from the pangs of death. In early Rome also a woman was given a key at the time of delivery to open the way for the birth. In Sweden midwife and mother repeat together a prayer to the Virgin to bring the key to the womb. Anyone who locks a padlock during a wedding ceremony and then throws the lock in water makes that marriage unfruitful. In Serbia to prevent pregnancy a woman would sometimes lay a lock and key on the floor, walk in the space between them, turn around, and turning say, "When I open the lock again I shall conceive a child." Keys have a sympathetic magical effect upon the inmates of a house in almost all folk beliefs; all keys are turned and locks *un*locked, for instance, during a birth or a death to open the way into or out of the world.

Bible and key together make very potent magic. To discover the name of a thief or a witch, a key is placed in the Bible, but with the handle out; the handle is then held by one or two people, who say, "Turn Bible/ Turn key/ Turn and show the name to me." Then a series of names are recited and at the right name the key will turn.

☞ Delivering up the keys of a fortress or castle to an enemy was formerly a symbol of surrender; a widow in England burdened with her husband's debts laid the keys on his bier if she wished to withdraw from the home or was unable to assume responsibilities of payment. Welcoming an honored guest is often carried out by presenting him with the keys of the city, thus indicating that everything in it is open for his inspection. Though now merely a gesture, it is a custom widely observed.

If a key is put in a cradle, the child will not be taken by fairies or otherwise (Germany); letting a bunch of keys fall means an unpleasant incident; their loss is fatal. A nail from a coffin will open the doors of Hell. A magic key that would unlock doors and treasure houses was the plant *Spring-wurzel*, or springwort, cultivated by Hecate and Artemis in their gardens.

In folk medicine, a key slipped down the back will stop nosebleed; in Morocco a key is used to cure impotence. The latter cure was performed by taking 7 keys from 7 houses in 7 towns, and heating them red hot, after which water from 7 wells was poured over the heated keys. The patient was then exposed to the steam.

In folktale there are stories about magic keys (D1176); keys protect against revenants (E434.6); in Indonesian, Japanese, and Micmac Indian folktale, a fish brings back a key lost in the sea (B548.2.2); the bloody key reveals disobedience (C913); there are European task tales about recovering a key lost in the sea (H1132.2; Type 554); and several based on the old proverb that an old key is better than a new key (Z62.1) in which the hero marries his old love instead of the new for this reason. [GPS]

keyhole The keyhole, in common with the door, chimney, or other openings of the house, is a place for the entrance of demons, witches, or the Devil. If the key is left in the keyhole, no evil spirit can enter. On the Continent, the nightmare hag (Alp, Mara) is much feared; to prevent its entrance into a sleeping chamber, the keyhole is stopped up, or, if the hag does slip in, it may be trapped by stuffing the hole. This belief and practice is also reported from Missouri. Sometimes in Germany and elsewhere the keyhole is stuffed with consecrated wax as a preventive measure. Mississippi and Georgia Negroes put a sieve over the keyhole to keep witches out; the witch has to count all the holes before she can leave and many witches are caught in this way.

Fear of the open keyhole is especially great when there is a new-born child in the house on account of the belief in changelings, which prevails in Germany, Hungary, the Philippines, Netherlands Indies, and elsewhere. One can summon the Devil through the keyholes of churches by going around the church three times, then blowing or whistling through the keyhole. A magic view inside the church through this opening is believed in Denmark to reveal persons before the altar who are doomed to die in the next year. This oracular view must be taken on New Year's night. Blowing through the church keyhole on Good Friday before sunrise is recommended for certain urinary disorders common in childhood.

In parts of rural England young girls peek through the keyhole into the farmyard on St. Valentine's morning; if they see a cock and a hen strutting together it is a sign of their own marriage inside a year. [GPS]

Khaldi The Urartian (pre-Armenian) supreme god of heaven; one of the non-Aryan triad, with Theispas (weather god), and Artinis (sun god). The Urartians believed themselves his children and called themselves Khaldians.

Khāndava or **Khāndavaprastha** In Hindu mythology, the country and forest awarded to the Pāndavas when Dhritarāshtra divided his kingdom. See AGNI; MAHĀBHĀRATA.

Khara In Iranian mythology, the gigantic three-legged ass which stands in the middle of the sea Vourukasha. Khara has six eyes, nine mouths, and one horn. Two eyes are in the position of eyes, two are on top of its head, and two are in the hump. Khara, with the aid of its sharp eyes, overcomes evil and aids in the management of the world.

khátani The cutting dance of the Hindi of North India. At harvest festivals boys and girls symbolically cut wheat with sweeping motions. They advance in two parallel lines, with the girls sometimes holding the sheaf and the boy cutting, then with a reversal of roles. The celebration finishes in two concentric circles, girls on the inside. The vigorous natural movement of folk dances such as the khátani are distinguished from the sophisticated gesture code of Indo-Aryan *natya*. [GPK]

Khensu, Khonsu, or **Chons** In Egyptian mythology, the "sailor," the moon god, son of Amen and Mut, worshipped at Thebes. He is depicted as a young man wearing the lunar disk and crescent, or as a hawk-headed man with the same attributes. As Khensu-Hor or Khensu-Rā, he was a solar god. Sometimes he was equated with Thoth, the god of wisdom and of the moon, but, where Thoth was depicted as an adult man with an ibis head, Khensu was a child or young man without theriomorphic attributes, except for the occasional depiction with the hawk head. Khensu was also, in later belief, a healing god and rid people of evil spirits.

Khentamenti In ancient Egyptian religion, an early jackal-headed god of the dead: later identified with Osiris. Khentamenti is He who is in the West, the god of the cemetery at Abydos, to whom the dead went.

Khepera or **Khepri** In ancient Egyptian religion, the creator of the gods; the self-created; the resurrected sun of the morning, and thus an aspect of Rā. Khepera, by saying his name, made a solid place to stand; then he masturbated, "copulated with his shadow," and ejaculated Shu, the air god, and Tefnut, the water god: both these names are derived from roots meaning to spit. (A similar pun on the closeness of the words for tears and mankind makes him the creator of man, but the image here too is one of masturbation.) The same myth is related of Atmu, who was the sun at evening; the identity of Rā, Khepera, and Atmu makes the myth applicable to all three, since they are different aspects of the same being, the sun god. Khepera was identified with the dung beetle, his emblem, and sometimes is depicted as the figure of a man with the scarab in place of his head. As the dung beetle was believed to be generated by the heat of the sun from the ball of dung that it rolled, so the force pushing the morning sun across the sky must be self-generated; it was therefore Khepera, He who arrives. The scarab was the symbol of the sun and of resurrection. Compare KHNUM.

Khetrpal The western Bengal name for the earth deity or guardian. See BHŪMIYA.

Khidr The Green One; a figure of Arabian folklore appearing, but not named, in the Koran. El Khidr is immortal; of all men he is the only one to have tasted of the Fountain of Immortal Youth far in the east. (See ALEXANDER THE GREAT.) He is thoroughly equated, and sometimes identified, with Elijah, the immortal of Jewish tradition. The stories told of the one are told of the other, but there is little doubt that they stem originally from rabbinical lore. El Khidr is a sea spirit; among the Arabs of modern Syria, he is the patron of the sea and is called He who walks in the seas. He has been adopted, as Khidr Khwājā, by the Moslems as a saint; small boats, each provided with a light and an offering, are launched on a river by his worshippers in an attempt to rid themselves of menacing evils or sins. El Khidr, whose name does not suggest of what his greenness consists, is sometimes dressed in green; sometimes he is an eternally young man with white hair and long white beard; certainly green is a color held in esteem by Moslems. The story in the Koran (*Sura* xviii, 59–81) is one told also of Elijah and Rabbi Joshua ben Levi, tnough the specific incidents vary. As in the tale of El Khiḏr's gaining immortality, a fish, this time one of Moses', mysteriously disappears. Nearby is found El Khiḏr's cave, and Moses becomes his follower on the condition that he ask no questions. But questions follow when El Khiḏr staves a hole in a boat, when he slays a youth, and when he rebuilds a wall in an inhospitable city. Before Moses leaves him, the prophet explains: the boat would have been captured by a pirate king, now the owners will be delayed because of the repair and will keep their boat; the youth would have grown up evil and troubled his pious parents; the wall contained a treasure and was in a house belonging to two orphans; had it fallen the unworthy tenant would have kept the treasure. In a folktale, a dervish plays on the king's desire to see El Khiḏr. If the king will support him for three years, he will produce the Green Man. At the end of the period, he of course cannot fulfil his promise and runs away. He meets a man dressed in white who comes back with him to the king. The king asks his ministers to pronounce judgment. One says the dervish must be cut into little pieces; the second says boil him in a caldron; the third, throw him into the furnace; the fourth, pardon him. The man in white agrees with all, saying each thus indicates his origin, respectively, son of a butcher, of a cook, of a baker, and of nobility. The king pardons the dervish, not only because that is the noble thing to do, but because the man in white brought before him by the beggar is El Khiḏr.

Khnum, Khnemu, or **Kneph** In ancient Egyptian mythology, the ram-headed "fashioner" of mankind; the creator of the universe and of man from the mud of the Nile. Originally a god of the First Cataract (where the Milky Way became the Nile), where he headed the triad including Sati and Anukit, his identification with the Rā complex made this creation myth known all over Egypt and its subject lands. Khnum took mud from the Nile, fashioned it into an egg, and from the cosmic egg formed the universe. On his potter's wheel he fashioned men and gods. He retained this power of creation after the first act; for instance, he was the modeler of the wife of Bata in the old tale of the *Two Brothers*. His consort was Heqet, the frog-headed goddess of resurrection. Khnum was also Lord of the Flood, a water god who was creator, as water was the life-spirit of the land. As such he is sometimes a serpent, and some conceptual connection may exist between the horizontal horns of the ram's head and the depiction of the serpent. See Khepera; Ptah.

Khshathra Vairya (Pahlavi *Xšatravēr*, Persian *Šahrēvar*) In Zoroastrianism, one of the six archangels or Amesha Spentas, aid and attribute of Ahura Mazda and the guardian of metals: literally, desirable sovereignty. Khshathra Vairya is the personification of Ahura Mazda's might and sovereignty and the triumph of his power over evil on earth. His special flower is the royal basil, and his antagonist is Sauru. In the court of heaven his auxiliaries are Mithra, Asmān, and Anīrān.

khvarenanh or **khwarenah** In Iranian belief, the kingly power substance which belonged to the royal house of Iran: literally, light or luster. The khvarenanh was the glory which made gods and the souls of the dead powerful, gave the sun, moon, stars, and water their benign influences, and endowed men with the power to overcome hostile demons. According to the *Avesta*, the glory swims in the sea or is found in cosmic space, milk, or the reeds. When Yima spoke falsely the khvarenanh deserted him and passed to Mithra, Thrāētaona, and Keresāspa. Finally it sought shelter in the world ocean.

Ki In Sumerian mythology, the earth mother: later identified with her specific divine aspects manifested in other Sumerian earth goddesses—Ninmah, Ninhursag, Nintu. Ki and An, the sky god, were produced by Nammu. Joined physically, they were separated by Enlil, the air god: the myth is similar to earth-sky separation myths found all over the world. From the union of Ki and her son Enlil there arose the living things of earth; though the story of creation does not mention Ki, Ninmah, one of those closely responsible for the creation, is identifiable as one of the aspects of the earth mother.

Kibu The Mabuiag (Melanesian) land of the dead; an unknown island lying to the west. According to one legend, when the *mari* (soul of the dead) goes to Kibu he is hit with a stone-headed club; this makes him a *markai* or true ghost of the dead. Then he is taught how to make a waterspout which is used to take turtles and dugongs. When the people of Mabuiag see a waterspout they believe that the dead person has become a *markai* and is being taught the details of life in Kibu. Compare Boigu.

Kidd's Lament Variant title of the forecastle song, *Captain Kidd*.

Kihunai In California Hupa Indian mythology, the beings who inhabited the world before the Hupa. According to Hodge (*BAEB* 30: i: 583) they are believed to be still living to the east, west, and south of the Hupa, and above them. Yimantuwingyai, Hupa culture hero, is leader of a group of Kihunai to the north across the ocean.

Kilhwch and Olwen See Arthur; Mabinogion.

Killer-of-Enemies The principal culture hero of several southern Athabaskan groups of American Indians (Navaho, Jicarilla, Lipan, and Western Apache). Among other Apache groups Killer-of-Enemies' companion, Child-of-the-Water, assumes the dominant role of the chief culture hero and Killer-of-Enemies plays a subordinate part. As a subordinate deity he is now thought to represent the white man, or to act as a sponsor for the white man. See Ahayuta achi. [ewv]

Kilkenny cats In Irish legend, two cats who fought until only their tails and nails were left: a byword for the ancient enmity between Kilkenny and Irishtown. Legend reports constant fighting between the two groups almost to mutual annihilation. The city of Kilkenny, county seat of county Kilkenny in Leinster, Ireland, was settled by the English who accompanied Richard de Clare, second earl of Pembroke (called Strongbow), in the 12th century. Richard married the king of Leinster's daughter and eventually succeeded to the kingdom. Irishtown is separated from Kilkenny only by a little stream. In the 14th century the English sought to prevent their own extinction with the Statute of Kilkenny (1367) which attributed all the lawlessness to the Irish, forbade intermarriage between the two communities, forbade the English to entertain Irish minstrels, and even to ride horseback Irish fashion.

Later (18th century) legend associates the phrase *to fight like Kilkenny cats* with a cruel pastime of the Hessian soldiers stationed in Kilkenny during the rebellion of 1798. They would tie two cats together by their tails, hang them over a line, and watch the fight till one or both of the animals died. Once an officer came upon them in this brutal entertainment and cut down the cats with his sword. The soldiers thus explained the presence of the two tails on the line: the cats fought so desperately that they ate each other up except for the tails.

killing by pointing (counting) A folktale motif (D2061.2.3) known to North American Indians all over the continent, but perhaps most often found in stories of the Southwest, California, and of the Plains. The motif is reported to be as frequent among North American Indians as the fatal look or death-dealing glance. The Micmacs (northeastern Algonquians) have a story in which a woman kills a moose by pointing at it with a knife. In Southern Ute mythology Mountain Lion kills deer by counting. If he saw five deer, he would say, "There's one; there's two," etc., and they fell dead. Sünāwavi (creator-trickster-culture-hero) wanted meat and asked Mountain Lion how to kill deer. Mountain Lion told him; Sünāwavi went off, saw three deer, counted "There is one, there is two," etc., and they fell dead. He thought that was too easy, and said so. The minute he said so, the deer came to life and ran off. After that the power of killing by counting was lost in the world. Even Mountain Lion after that had to hunt deer against the wind and shoot them. Curtin (*Creation Myths in Primitive America*, Boston, 1911) reports a California Wintun Indian story about one Katkatchila in the southwest who could kill game by pointing a hollow stick at them. Something came out of the hollow stick and killed them. The Wintun invited Katkatchila to their village and entertained him with dancing and hunting parties in order to find out what came out of the stick. Compare FATAL LOOK.

Kimpurushas A class of spirits of Hindu mythology, servants and followers of Kubera. They have horse's bodies and human heads: often identified with the Kinnaras, who have human bodies and horse-heads, and are also followers and servitors of Kubera.

kina A secret ceremony of the Yahgan Indians of Tierra del Fuego in which masked men impersonating spirits danced in the sight of women and reminded them with terrible threats to be submissive to men. One of their myths tells how in former times the women, led by Moon, ruled over the men and terrified them with the same practices. Sun discovered their secret, killed all the women except the little girls, and adopted the kina feast to insure the supremacy of men henceforth. Only a shaman can lead the kina rite. [AM]

kind and unkind A very frequently occurring motif (Q2) in folktales from Europe, Asia, Africa, and the Americas; a moralizing, didactic motif found in combination with many other motifs in at least 17 tale types. The kind hero or heroine is rewarded; the unkind brother, sister, etc., is punished. Its most familiar exposition is perhaps in *Les Fées* of Perrault, where the kind younger sister is rewarded by the fairy and drops flowers and jewels from her mouth as she speaks. The surly sister is punished by having toads and serpents come from her mouth. The kind girl marries a rather practical young prince; the other is cast out and dies in the forest. The order of incidents is usually reversed, especially in the quest stories; the older brothers fail because they are discourteous or even cruel, then the youngest brother brings home the water of life or other remedy because he is kind to the fruit tree, the old woman, etc. Sometimes it is a stranger who is turned away from all but one house, as in a Fjort (African) story: the town is flooded and the kind hosts are saved —compare the story of Sodom and Gomorrah. Or, from the Fjort again, the women will not give water to an old woman (Nzambi in disguise); the man later goes out of his way to be nice to her. Therefore, only men may fish in the lake she made; it is *kazila* (tabu) to women. The moral idea is clearly expressed in the folktale, so much so that the line between tale and myth, between imaginative fiction and a story of the gods, is not at all clear. In the North American Indian story where Crane forms a bridge over a river, the kind and unkind motif is always present. In the abandoned children story of the Gros Ventre, the old woman is drowned because she is discourteous to the water monster. The motif appears in such tale types as The White and Black Bride (Type 403: Grimm #13, *The Three Little Men in the Wood*); The Presents (Type 620); The Grateful Animals (Type 554); The Spinning Women by the Spring (Type 480); All Stick Together (Type 571: Grimm #64, *The Golden Goose*), etc. See BERRIES IN WINTER; CRANE; HOLDE; JEWELS FROM SPITTLE.

king The male ruler of a people; a sovereign chief of a nation or tribe. The kingship commonly comprehends both temporal and spiritual powers. The king is ruler in civic matters, a superior kind of noble, and probably originally *primus inter pares*, the first noble among his peers. But the king is also chief priest, possessing great mystical powers of himself, and may as easily have developed from the need to have a potent priest always ready to intercede with the gods, rather than choosing such a priest at occasional times. The acquisition of other than priestly powers by such an individual, with the sanction and assistance of the gods, would be natural. The supernatural power surrounding the king makes his person strongly tabu; in many places even the shadow of a subject may not touch the king's person, or the king's shadow, or any of the king's belongings. The king is thus the representative of the gods on earth; his spiritual power is attached to his temporal power; his word is law; his deeds are beyond judgment; he rules not by election but by divine right. The king as priest is necessary to the flourishing of his land and his subjects and must not only superintend and preside at religious rites but must possess certain attributes to maintain his post, e.g. he must be bodily unblemished or he must prove his potency by meeting all challengers to his position, he must observe certain tabus. In certain societies, the king was killed ritually after a given time and a new, more powerful king took his place. This custom is mirrored in the temporary kings of some festivals, like the Saturn of the Saturnalia. Compare the ancient Mexican custom of treating a prisoner as a king for a time, giving him every comfort and pleasure, and then sacrificing him alive at the festival. See HEB-SED; LORD OF MISRULE.

king asleep in the mountain The concept of the king asleep in the mountain (D1960.2) is rooted in the hearts of all proud, defeated peoples, everywhere. Some western European kings are said to be waiting in mountain caves until their people need them, when they will come out with an army and attain victory. One of these legends is of Barbarossa (Frederick I, probably confused with his grandson Frederick II) who waits in a cavern in Kyffhäuser Mountain until his country calls him. Arthur of the Britons and Charlemagne of the Franks will also return when needed. The list could go on and on. The Hindu *Purānas* mention an old king Mucukunda asleep in a cave, wakened by Krishna to destroy an enemy king. The Armenian legendary hero, Meher, with his horse is still in the cave of Zympzymps, but he will not be seen again until the end of the world. In Irish legend the prophecy is made of Fionn and his warriors, and of Earl Gerald under the castle of Mullagnmast (see CELTIC FOLKLORE). The story was told of the Old Norse Olaf Tryggvason, of Robert Bruce in Scotland, of Don Sebastian in Portugal, of King Wenzel in Bohemia, and of the Carpathian robber king Dobocz. True to promise Drake's drum was heard again in England before World War II; that Hitler will come again is a living belief. See KRALJ MATJAŽ; OGIER THE DANE. [RDJ]

kingfisher Any of numerous birds (family *Alcedinidæ*), generally crested, with long, straight, deeply cleft bill. In Ireland he is called the water dipper (*gaba uisce*) from his habit of suddenly diving for his food. The big Australian kingfisher (*Dacelo gigas*) is called the laughing jackass from his dawn and evening call.

There are various etiological stories about how the kingfisher got his beak (A2343.1.1), and how he got his crest (A2321.5), among them an Ojibwa Indian statement that once Nanabozho reached for kingfisher but missed, only ruffling the feathers of his neck. The most familiar of kingfisher stories is Pliny's statement that the halcyon (i.e. the kingfisher) lays its eggs on the sea in midwinter and that the sea is always calm and stormless until they are hatched. See HALCYON DAYS. In Bengal it is said that to hear the kingfisher's cry on your right presages success in the day's business, on the left, bad luck. This belief is prevalent also among several West African peoples and survives among southern United States Negroes. Codrington reports that the kingfisher is regarded as a sacred bird among most Melanesian groups.

King Herla A traditional early British king whose story is told by Walter Map (1140–c. 1210) in his *De Nugis Curialium*. One day Herla, riding abroad, met the "king of the Pygmies" (according to Map, a supernatural subterranean king) who invited himself to Herla's wedding and bid Herla come to his one year from the day. The agreement was made; the Pygmy arrived followed by a great train bearing rich gifts. The

following year Herla set out for the other's wedding, also followed by a train of horsemen laden with gifts. They entered the supernatural realm through the mouth of a great cave. When it came time to return home, the Pygmy gave Herla many gifts and a tiny hound which fitted into his hand, warning him to let no man set foot on the ground until the little dog first leapt to earth. Herla, on entering his kingdom, inquired of an old shepherd regarding the welfare of his queen; but the old man did not understand him. Two hundred years had gone by and the Saxon tongue was now spoken in the land. Many of Herla's men who leapt to the ground in alarm or amazement vanished in a puff of dust. The rest, with Herla at their head, are still wandering. Walter Map, however, says they have not been seen since one noonday in Hereford (or Wales) in the reign of Henry II, when they were questioned by a group of local people who saw them, and on not answering, were attacked.

Herlethingi is the term applied in England to the phantom train of soldiers bearing the sumptuous gifts, which traveled, usually slowly and silently, in broad daylight through the countryside. Sometimes a peasant would steal a horse or some of the treasure, and meet with sudden death for his trouble. In later northern European folklore (see F. Liebrecht, *Zur Volkskunde*, Heilbronn, 1879) Herla and his train became interpreted as a manifestation of the Wild Hunt (E501.1.7).

King John and the Bishop An old English riddling ballad (Child #45) still current in England and the United States. The story itself is known throughout the East and the West. The bad King John, jealous of the pomp of the bishop, tells him he must answer three questions or forfeit his head and living. First, he says, "Lett me know within one pennye what I am worth." Second, "How soone I may goe the whole world about." Third, "What is the thing, bishopp, that I doe thinke." He gives him twenty days to answer. Off goes the bishop to Cambridge and Oxford, but none of the doctors can help him. He returns home, meets his half-brother, a shepherd. This unlearned brother takes the bishop's place before the king, and answers the questions. First, the king is worth 29 pennies, since Christ was worth 30, "But I know Christ was one penye better then you." Second, he can go around the world in 24 hours "if with the sun you gan goe the next way." Third, "You thinke I am the bishopp of Canterburye." The king is delighted with these answers, gives the shepherd 300 pounds a year. The bishop too is happy and gives him another 50 pounds. Says the balladist:

"I never knew shepeard that gott such a liuinge
  But David, the shepeard, that was a king."

King Lear judgment The short-sighted judgment of folktale: subject of motif M21 and closely related to love like salt (H592.1) and the knowing laugh. An old king, constantly flattered by his two elder daughters, finally banishes the third and youngest because she seems to fall short of them in affection. Either, on being questioned, the youngest daughter tells her father that she loves him as much as meat loves salt, and is banished for this answer, which seems to him most inadequate compared with the elders' protestations; or, over-hearing flattering courtiers tell her father that all their good fortune springs from him alone, she gives a little laugh and then is silent. On being questioned about the laugh, she replies that the courtiers do not speak the truth, that each individual inevitably reaps the result of his own acts. The father in a rage marries her to a leper. In both versions of this tale the father eventually learns the deep truth underlying the daughter's words.

The second version is typified by the story of the Princess Madanamanjarī as quoted from a Jainist text in the *Ocean of Story* (vii, 254–255). Here the King Lear judgment is tied up with the knowing laugh to point out the inevitable working of the laws of *karma*. For the King Lear judgment involving love like salt, see CAP O' RUSHES.

Shakespeare's famous tragedy, *King Lear,* is the story of an old king of Britain who intends to divide his kingdom among his three daughters in proportion to their devotion. The two elder daughters protest to his satisfaction; the youngest will say no more than that she loves him "according to her duty," and is disinherited. This legend is in Geoffrey of Monmouth's *Historia Regum Britanniæ* (12th century), and according to A. H. Krappe ,*Mythologie Universelle,* Paris, 1930), Geoffrey euhemerized the Old Irish sea god Lir into this old British King Leir, restored to his throne by the disinherited youngest daughter who defeats the elder sisters.

King of Ireland's Son   Title and hero of an Irish folktale based primarily on the grateful dead motif (E341 ff.). One day the King of Ireland's Son shot a raven; the raven fell in the snow. And the young man thought there was nothing redder than raven's blood on white snow or blacker than raven's feather. He vowed he must have for wife some girl with hair as black as the raven's wing, cheeks as red as the blood, and skin as white as the snow. There was such a girl in the east, he was told, so he started out. Before long he met the funeral of a man who was being kept from burial because of his debts. The King of Ireland's son paid the debts, saw the corpse to its burial, and went on his way.

Soon he was joined by a "short green man" who asked where he was going. "To seek a princess in the eastern world." So the stranger joined the King of Ireland's Son as his servant, asking for wages only the first kiss of the princess. The King of Ireland's Son agreed. One after another they were joined by extraordinary companions (F601), five instead of the usual six: 1) the man with remarkable sight (F642) also known in general folklore as the skilful marksman (F661), whom they came upon aiming at a blackbird in the eastern world. His wages were to be a little house and garden if the quest prospered. 2) The remarkable hearer (F641; F641.1) who could hear the grass grow; 3) The marvelous runner (F681.1) who had to keep one leg tied up to keep from going too fast; 4) The mighty blower (F622) who had to hold one finger up his nose to keep from blowing the houses down; 5) The mighty stone-breaker (F625) who broke stones without a hammer lest he make them into powder. So they all went on together, met with many adventures, circumvented all giants, overcame all difficulties, and acquired out of each adventure some magic object which came in handy later: a cap of invisibility, shoes that would go wherever the wearer willed, a magic sword.

When they came at last to the eastern world the princess said she would marry the King of Ireland's Son if he could break her enchantments. The whole castle was surrounded with a ring of skulls on spikes, heads of suitors who had failed. The princess gave him a pair of scissors, and all she asked was the scissors back in the morning. Then she put a sleep-pin under his pillow, the King of Ireland's Son fell asleep; the princess took up the scissors, left the room, and gave them to the *rīg niṁe* (literally, king of poison) bidding him keep them until morning. But when the *rīg niṁe* fell asleep, the short green man came into the room wearing the magic cap and shoes and with the sword in his hand, took the scissors, and gave them back to the King of Ireland's Son. So in the morning when the princess said, "Have you got the scissors?" he said, "I have."

Next she gave him a comb which he was to return to her in the morning. All happened as on the first night, and the short green man got back the comb. The third night's test was to give back to the princess in the morning not only the comb but the "head of him who was combed with the comb"—or he would lose his own head at last. This time the *rīg niṁe* hid the comb in a great rock, put 60 locks upon it, and sat by the door of the rock to guard it himself.

The short green man again saved the situation: he split the rock with one stroke of the magic sword and took off the *rīg niṁe's* head with the second stroke. So when the princess came asking for the comb in the morning, the King of Ireland's Son had it and rolled out the *rīg niṁe's* head also. She was so infuriated at this success that she imposed still another task: to send a runner for three bottles of healing-balm from the well of the western world, and his head would be hers if her runner beat his runner. The King of Ireland's Son's extraordinary runner got to the well and was half-way back when he was tricked into sleep by the princess's runner, a hag. She laid his head on a horse's skull, spilt out his water, and left him asleep.

The man who could hear the grass grow put his ear to the ground and reported that the hag was on her way back but *their* runner was asleep and snoring! The extraordinary marksman looked and shot the horse's skull from under the sleeper's head; the extraordinary blower took his finger out of his nose and blew the hag clear back to the western world; the runner of the King of Ireland's Son ran back to the well, refilled his bottles, and still got home first. After more tests, all nullified by the extraordinary companions, the princess married the King of Ireland's Son. The short green man demanded the first kiss, which he had been promised, took the princess off into another room ("She was full up of serpents"), and killed all the serpents which would have killed the bridegroom. So when all was safe he gave the princess back to his master, revealed himself as the dead man whose debts the hero had magnanimously paid, went away with the extraordinary companions, and was never seen again.

This story is a pile-up of familiar folktale motifs: in addition to those mentioned we find the red as blood, white as snow formula (Z65.1), the green revenant (E422.2.2), the extraordinary companions (F601) who perform the hero's tasks (F601.1), grateful dead helps hero win princess (T66.1), all former bridegrooms have perished on the bridal night (T170), the quest for marvelous water (H1321), bringing water from far away faster than the witch (H1109.1), the serpent damsel (F582.1) full of serpents which crawl out and kill her bridegrooms, and grateful dead disposes of serpents (F172.2.1). Hans Christian Andersen's story of *The Traveling Companion* is based largely on the same motifs, as is also a Czech story, *George with the Goat,* cited by Douglas Hyde in *Beside the Fire,* London, 1910, p. xxxix. See CEPHALUS; *Kilhwch and Olwen* in MABINOGION.

King of the Bean Formerly in England, France, parts of Germany and Scandinavia, and still in northern France, a mock king chosen for the Twelfth Night (January 6) festivities. His reign sometimes lasted throughout the day, sometimes it was for the duration of the dinner. A special cake was baked in which was placed a bean or coin or small image (if a queen were to be chosen by lot as well, a pea, or another color bean, was also baked into the cake). The cake was cut or broken apart; sometimes the pieces were handed among the company by a young child. Whoever had the piece with the bean in it was King of the Bean, and directed the festivities. Sometimes the king (or queen, if a woman obtained the piece with the token) chose his own partner; sometimes the cake decided. Certain actions by the King of the Bean were believed to ensure fertility during the year to come. The office is the same as the Lord of Misrule, a more general term, and is believed to be derived from the custom of choosing a leader of the revels by lot at the Roman Saturnalia. See LORD OF MISRULE.

king of the cats In Old Irish legend, a huge cat, as big as an ox, named Irusan, who ruled over all the cats; his stronghold was in a cave at Knowth in Meath. In the story of the poets' *Visitation to Guaire,* the poet Senchan at Marbán's feast satirized not only the mice, but all cats, for allowing the mice to get their whiskers in his egg. Irusan in his cave at Knowth heard this, appeared at Cruachan, and carried off Senchan in revenge for the satire. St. Ciaran saw them going as they passed through Clonmacnoise, and hurled a red-hot bar through the cat and killed it. But Senchan was not grateful. He would rather have died and been a reproach to Guaire (a chieftain of Connacht).

Robert Graves in *The White Goddess* posits a cat cult in Ireland from this story of a king of the cats in a cave at Knowth, and from the existence of the figure of a slender black cat on a silver chair found in another cave in Connacht. This one he reports to have been oracular, and the giver of ill-tempered, nasty answers to questioners.

There is an Irish folktale about a man who was killing a cat. The cat said, "Go home and say you have killed the king of the cats." As soon as the man got home he said to his wife, "I have killed the king of the cats." With that the house-cat by the fire leapt up and tore the man to pieces.

King of the Wood Rex Nemorensis; the priest of the sanctuary of Diana Nemorensis at Nemi, Italy (the grove of Aricia): the explanation of the customs connected with this office form the thread binding together J. G. Frazer's *Golden Bough.* The shrine was said to have been founded by Orestes; the first priest-king was Virbius, the reborn Hippolytus. Succession to the priesthood was only by a runaway slave who, after breaking a branch from the sacred tree within the grove, fought with the incumbent. If the slave killed the priest, as might happen at any time, at any season, day or night, the office passed to him. From an investigation of this unique situation, Frazer, by educing customs from all over the world, decided that the King of the Wood was the mate of Diana, who was embodied in the oak; that he was a form of Jupiter, the oak god, and thus the incarnation of the oak spirit; that he was a king meant to be ritually slain after his period of reign like the kings of the Saturnalia; that his slaying before he became decrepit kept the full power of fertility preserved by passing it from one vigorous king to another.

king's evil A degenerate, tuberculous disease of the lymphatic glands; scrofula. Edward the Confessor in England cured scrofula by touching the sufferer. Charles I cured 100 people on Midsummer Day of 1633. Charles II also had the power. A Tonga in West Africa avoided the effects of having eaten tabu food by pressing the king's foot on his stomach. Others of the tribe thought that the king's touch cured palsy. The belief is reported from other parts of the world from past and present times. The touch of a powerful, exalted, sacred, or virtuous person is thought to bring health. The cure of crippling hysterias by touching the sufferer is well known. [RDJ]

Kingu In *Enuma Elish,* the Akkadian-Babylonian creation myth, the second of Tiamat's consorts, her offspring by Apsu, and leader of her host in the battle against Marduk. He was given the tablets of destinies by Tiamat, giving him power over creation, but after Marduk killed Tiamat, Kingu was captured and the tablets appropriated by Marduk. Kingu was tried and condemned by the council of the gods, and from his blood mankind was created. Among the new year ceremonies performed by the king in Babylon, well into the first millennium B.C., the king as Marduk burned a lamb, which was Kingu. See SEMITIC MYTHOLOGY.

King Waldmar Hero of a cycle of Danish ballads of the 14th century dealing with King Waldmar, his queen, Sophie, and Tove, his paramour.

Kinharingan The Dusun (Borneo) creator who made the world and mankind. With his wife, Munsumundok, he killed one of his children, cut it into bits, and planted the pieces in the earth. From these came all the food plants and the animals. The Tempassuk Dusuns consider the lempada tree sacred to Kinharingan who decreed that anyone cutting, climbing into, or picking its fruit would be afflicted with ulcers unless he had performed a special ceremony first. In myth Kinharingan and his wife emerged from a great rock in the middle of the sea. They walked on the surface of the water until they arrived at the house of Bisagit, the spirit of smallpox, from whom they obtained earth. After placing the earth Kinharingan made the Dusuns while Munsumundok made the sky. Together they then created the sun, moon, and constellations. In another legend Bisagit agreed to give Kinharingan the earth only if he could have half of Kinharingan's people. Now Bisagit comes to claim his toll once every forty years. The Dusuns do not try to propitiate Bisagit, since it is useless.

kinkkaliepakko Literally, hooking arms: a Finnish longways for four couples, a prototype of the Virginia Reel. However, only two of the last Virginia Reel formations occur, namely, the sliding down the center of the leading couple, and their winding in and out through the two lines, hooking arms with the partner, then the other arm with an opposite dancer in the line. This characteristic crotcheting in and out is called "arming" in longways terminology. As in the reel, at the end of the routine, the head couple becomes the foot couple; and the routine is repeated. [GPK]

Kinnaras In Hindu mythology, heavenly musicians; followers of Kubera. The Kinnaras were either the sons of Kaśyapa, or sprang from the toe of Brahmā. They had the bodies of men and the heads of horses. Compare KIMPURUSHAS.

kinnor A type of lyre played in ancient Israel, similar to the Greek *kithara*. It was strung with ten strings of sheep gut and was played with a plectrum to accompany singing. This was the instrument of King David (erroneously translated as harp) and this was the instrument that was hung on the willow trees by the waters of Babylon because the sorrowing Jewish captives could not play the instrument of joy in a strange land. See HARP; LYRE.

Kintaro A Japanese legendary hero who assisted the famous warrior Minamoto Yorimitsu in the 11th century. [JLM]

kipriano Armenian roll of prayers containing magical formulas believed to protect against sorcerers, false love, snakebite, and the evil eye: widely used, especially in eastern Armenia.

Kirttimukha In Hindu mythology, the face of the lion-headed monster embodying the destructive power of the universal god, produced by Śiva when he was challenged by Jalandhara. The ravenous monster, deprived of his legitimate prey, Rāhu, fed (at the suggestion of its creator, Śiva) on the flesh of its own feet and hands; but still ravaged by hunger, ate and ate, devouring its own arms, legs, belly, chest, and neck until only the face remained. Then Śiva declared that henceforth the face would be known as Kīrttimukha, the Face of Glory, and would be worshipped. The face was used on the lintels of Śiva temples and as guardian of the threshold. Kīrttimukha, however, as a part of the divinity, is a sign of his protective wrath and does not inspire fear in the Hindu devotee. See FACE OF GLORY.

kiss Specialists on the kiss working with both primary and secondary data have concluded that kissing is a culture trait characteristic of European peoples and their racial ancestors, the Teutons, the Greco-Romans, and the Semites, but unknown to the Celts who at an early date seem to have corrected this defect. One specialist has observed "that though the act is very rare among the lower and semi-civilized races, it is fully established as instinctive in the higher societies."

In the Far East kissing is an erotic exercise. Chinese and Japanese are either deeply shocked or hilariously entertained by the shameless exhibitionism of Occidental husbands and wives who kiss in public. In the middle of the last century, when Chinese scholars first began translating Western novels into their own language, they had to invent a new character to describe this act. Freud's contributions to sexual theory and the numerous studies which followed them give, in their discussions of oral erotism, ample justification for the views of the

lower and semicivilized societies, but still leave unanswered the question of why the kiss should have become so heavily encumbered with the folklore of Occidental etiquette, religion, and law.

Students of origins have found the beginnings of the kiss in the playing of animals; that is, in the billing of birds, the biting games of dogs. The "savage" kiss, also referred to as the olfactory or Malay kiss, or rubbing noses, is reported as common among the Maoris, Society and Sandwich Islanders, Tongans, Eskimos. Descriptions are not in complete agreement though generally the kiss involves bringing the noses together and rubbing them. In southeast India the mouth and nose are applied to the cheek and the active partner inhales. Another observer has reported that the Yakuts, various Mongolian peoples, and the Lapps of Europe have a ritual: the nose is pressed against the cheek, a nasal inspiration follows, eyelids are lowered and lips are smacked. The North American Indian women lay the lips softly on the cheek with no other motion or sound.

The kiss has not been reported from ancient Egypt and it may not have been known in India before the Aryan migrations. Arabs kiss their hands to the storm; Turks kiss their own hands, and then place them on their foreheads; and in Morocco, equals salute each other by touching hands and each kissing his own hand. Ceremonial kissing of the sort experts have been pleased to call civilized seems to have been common among the early Semites and Greeks. Esau fell on the neck of Jacob and kissed him. At later times kisses between members of the opposite sex was deplored as conducive to lewdness though exceptions were made there as in the southeastern United States in favor of "kissin' cousins." Herodotus reported that, among the Persians, equals in rank kissed on the mouth, others on the cheek. When Odysseus returned, his friends kissed him on the head, hands, and shoulders. The custom retained its popularity throughout the Greek and Roman period as between parents and children, lovers, married people, and persons of the same sex. In a society in which everybody kissed everybody, perfumed lips were as fashionable as they are today in Euro-American culture.

Saint Paul exhorted the early Christians to salute one another with a holy kiss and Saint Peter referred to the "kiss of love." Saint Cyprian reported that the baptized were kissed by the celebrant and the congregation after the ceremony. In Roman Catholic ritual the bishop kisses the newly ordained priest and is himself kissed when consecrated. Kissing the foot of the pope is part of the ceremonial audiences. This ritual of oral contact seems to be associated with the desire to form an intimate connection with the object, and is similar to kissing the altar, kissing saints, relics, and in some parts of Europe kissing the wounds of Christ on Good Friday. Thus the Greeks and Romans kissed the images of their gods and the early Arabs kissed the household gods both on entering and leaving the house. Sacred objects were kissed at the Eleusinian mysteries and some of the Anglican clergy kiss the cross of the stole before putting it on. The kiss of Judas violated this principle and is still a symbol of hypocrisy.

Knights were kissed after being dubbed, and kissing the bride is still popular.

Some authorities have suggested that the custom of

kissing the dead relatives, as Joseph kissed his dead father, is an attempt to catch the souls of the dying as they are escaping through the mouth (see SOUL). The custom though prohibited in the 6th century persisted. To be kissed by a god or a ghost produces death, as is recorded in the Italian proverb "to fall asleep in the Lord's kiss" and in the pious deaths of Abraham, Jacob, and others.

The social kiss has been the subject of some discussion even in societies where it is generally accepted. Many American girls who expect to be kissed after a date have qualms as to whether they are "nice girls." In the Middle Ages English women had a considerable liberty. In France, early and modern, to kiss on the mouth is permitted only among lovers and to use the word kiss without indicating the place to be kissed is to refer to the unspeakable. In medieval law from France to Wales a married woman who kissed a man not her husband was guilty of adultery. The kissing of a lady's hand as a sign of respect is still common among some social strata in Europe and had become part of the language in the Austrian phrase, *Küss d' Hand.*

In folktales a kiss can bring forgetfulness (D2004.2) and a transition into another world, or it can disenchant one who is bewitched (D735). There are stories of resuscitation by a kiss (E65), transformation by a kiss (D565.5), of lover given rump to kiss (K1225), and tales of witches kissing the Devil's tail (G243.1.1), the latter being euphemistically vague about an act of complete and perverted submission during the Sabbath. Children who hurt themselves sometimes have the place kissed to "make it well" and gamblers have been known to kiss the cards for luck.   R. D. JAMESON

☞ The practice of kissing farewell to the corpse was frowned upon by the medieval Jews, since the act was thought to bring death by contamination to the kisser. Kissing the Torah, the scroll of the Law, is a reverential act and is surrounded by prohibitions: it must not be done after one has kissed his wife or child, after intercourse, etc. In India, Arabia, and other parts of the world where a literature of love techniques exists, kisses are often classified and subdivided, according to the part of the body kissed, the position or pressure of the lips, the use of the arms, hands, tongue, etc., during the kiss, and the like. See BEAUTY AND THE BEAST; LITTLE BRIAR ROSE; LOATHLY LADY.

kitchen gods Usually, the thousands of *ma-chungs,* or paper images representing Tsao Chün, the Chinese god of the kitchen stove and god of the hearth, worshipped under one or another of his names: Tung Chu, Szŭ Ming, Tsao Shên, Tsao Chün, P'u Sa, etc. Tsao Chün is represented at his annual festival by a gorgeous *ma-chung* of red cardboard, placed above the kitchen range and before which the New Year's Eve feast is spread. This is carefully put away in the morning and a cheaper paper image is substituted for daily use. There are also variations of the kitchen god and his aspects, bearing different names, as for instance Lu Huo, the benevolent Stove Fire, etc. See TSAO CHÜN.

Kitchie Boy A Scottish ballad (Child #252) related to the King Horn cycle. Though sometimes called a modern variant of *Hind Horn* (Child #17), *The Kitchie Boy,* as W. R. Nelles (*JAFL* XXII: 59 ff.) has demonstrated, is not directly descended from *Hind Horn.* Both stem from some earlier telling of the tale, and certain elements in the two ballads indicate that they are independent of each other. For example, the Kitchie Boy refuses the lady because he is afraid of her father; Hind Horn, on the other hand, rejects her advances because he owes a duty to his lord. The Kitchie Boy is a kitchen boy, and the lord's daughter falls in love with him. She invites him to her room, where she makes love to him, but he is afraid. Therefore she outfits him with a ship, and gives him a ring to remember her by. He sails to London, where another fine lady offers him a ring and other favors which he turns down out of loyalty to his lady. He sails back as captain; the father decides from afar that this is the husband for his daughter. She does not recognize him until after he has teased her cruelly with the ring, saying he got it from a drowned man's hand. And even at the end

> Bat lettel did the old man keen
> It was his ain kittchen-boy.

Kittredge, George Lyman (1860–1941) American educator, philologist, editor, and folklorist; instructor and Professor of English at Harvard University from 1888 until his retirement in 1936; President of the American Folklore Society (1904) and of the Modern Language Association (1904); author of numerous books, monographs, and articles in the fields of English literature and language, the classics, and folklore; editor of several textbooks and grammars; and an authority especially on *Beowulf, Gawain and the Green Knight,* Chaucer, and Shakespeare.

As a folklorist, he served for nearly forty years as an assistant or associate editor of the *Journal of American Folklore,* contributing countless articles and notes to it; he arranged and cataloged the Child ballad collections, publishing in 1904 the *English and Scottish Popular Ballads,* which he had edited with Helen Child Sargent. He wrote *The Old Farmer and His Almanack* (1904), *Witchcraft in Old and New England* (1929), as well as much other material dealing with beast-fables, tales, songs, riddles, Americana, etc. As a teacher, he inspired and encouraged the work of several generations of American folklorists, among them John Lomax and John Harrington Cox.

Kittredge was perhaps best known for his textual elucidation of Shakespeare and for the Shakespeare course, English 2, that he gave at Harvard, in which he terrorized his students and became famous as one of the most exacting masters and one of the most colorful personalities of the American academic world. "Kitty's" tall, spare, gray-clad figure, his white beard, his impatience with inexact thinking and language, his rasping and sarcastic rejoinders to the ineptitudes of undergraduates, and his apparent assumption of his own infallibility gave rise to a body of legend among students that was almost as extensive as that of any folk hero he might have studied. Though the present generation of Harvard undergraduates never saw the original of a Kittredge performance, reports indicate that they are occasionally seeing a good imitation put on by instructors who took his mannerisms as "the glass of fashion" for professors, and are now repeating his display of irritation at coughing in class, at tardiness, and at "beautiful thoughts" on literature, as well as his curtain-line delivery of the final remark of a lecture.

kiva Hopi Indian underground circular or rectangular ceremonial assembly and lounging chamber of the ancient and modern Pueblo Indians of the Southwest: first described by Spanish explorers as an *estufa,* "hot room," mistaking its chief use as that of a sweat house. The various male societies in each of the western pueblos are associated with specific kivas in the pueblo; in the eastern pueblos a two-kiva system prevails. Women cannot enter the kiva except to provide food for their husbands or sons, or in rare instances, to witness or participate in certain ceremonies. All esoteric rites pertaining to the numerous pueblo cults or societies, and all boys' initiation rites are performed in the kiva; masks, altars, and other ceremonial paraphernalia are kept in the kiva; males also use the kiva as a place in which to lounge, weave, or do other work, and, if unmarried, as a sleeping place. Entrance to the kiva is up a ladder to the roof and then down another ladder, the top of which projects through a hatch in the roof; this hatchway serves also as a smoke hole for the fire built on the kiva floor. At the end of some kiva chambers, is a small round hole in a stone or slab of cottonwood, facing the bottom of the hatchway ladder, the Shipapu or Shipapulima (see SHIPAP), symbolizing the place of origin and the final place of departure of the Pueblo peoples and the medium of communication with beings of the underworld. When not in use the Shipapu is kept closed. Behind this hole the altars used by the various societies are usually erected, and before it the dry-paintings used sometimes in ceremonies are made. [EWV]

kizewamono A genre play of the Japanese *kabuki* drama: first produced in Edo about 130 years ago. These plays depict love and contemporary life, in a rhythmical manner to musical accompaniment. The most famous writers of these plays are the fourth Nanboku Turuya, Mokuami Kawatake, Mokuami, and others. All are of kabuki origin and unrelated to the puppet plays. [GPK]

klepht One of the Greek (Epirote) nationalists who, under Turkish rule, after the 16th century, lived as brigands in the mountains; the word, meaning "robber," has come to mean "patriot." The doggerel ballads of these klephts, telling of their activities, kept alive resistance of the Greeks to the Turks. They are comparatively contemporary and have little literary value, and so have not maintained the serious attention once paid them. The klephtic serpentine Pyrrhic Dance is one of the open rounds of Europe.

Klieng Greatest of the mythological heroes; warrior and transformer of the Borneo Dyaks: born from a knot in a tree. His greatest exploit was his war on the sky. See INDONESIAN MYTHOLOGY.

Kloketen The initiation ceremony of the Ona Indians of South America, the most important rite of their religious life. The young boys were gathered together in a big hut for several months and there instructed in their moral duties and exposed to many ordeals. At night the men, painted and masked, impersonated demons and frightened the women. The secrets of the Kloketen were withheld from the women under threat of dire penalties; and it also served the purpose of keeping them in subjection. [AM]

Kmukamch Literally, Ancient Old Man: creator-trickster-culture-hero of California Modoc Indian mythology, who created mankind.

Knecht Ruprecht Literally, Servant Rupert: the Christmas man in some parts of northern Germany, interpreted as the servant (or knight) of Jesus Christ or of St. Nicholas. It was not until the 17th century that he replaced St. Martin or St. Nicholas as the companion of Christ. He was impersonated by a man of the village in high boots, white robe, blond flax wig, and wearing a mask, to whom the parents of the village had previously sent the presents they wished given to their children. On Christmas Eve (or on Nicholas Night or Day, Dec. 5–6), Knecht Ruprecht went to every house, knocked on the door, said he was Knecht Ruprecht, that his master Jesus Christ had sent him to ask about the children. He questioned the parents about each child by name, usually to the terror of the smaller ones. The parents said whether each child had been good or bad. To the good ones Knecht Ruprecht gave presents "from Jesus Christ"; if anyone had been bad, however, he gave a whip or a rod to the father, saying for Christ's sake to use it. See SAINT NICHOLAS.

knight of St. Crispin A shoemaker.

knives The knife, in folk belief, has two principal distinguishing characteristics: it is a sharp cutting instrument, and it is made of iron. Thus it shares many of the beliefs and practices associated with scissors, swords, needles, etc. Anciently, knives were made of chipped flints, and in many rites among primitive peoples stone knives are still used in such ceremonies as circumcision, although metal knives are in ordinary everyday use. But the sacrificial knife, the special reaping knife, and the like, are still sometimes deliberately anachronistically of stone. The Indonesians use a knife with a specially guarded blade for cutting rice; the hidden blade will not arouse the anger of the rice spirit. The Temne of Africa use a straight knife in sacrificing, since then things dependent on the sacrifice will come out straight.

The sharpness of the knife, like that of the razor and the scissors, leads to its being an ill-omened thing where friendship is concerned. One must never, in English and United States belief, give a knife as a gift; at least some small token payment must be made for it, otherwise the knife will cut the friendship. In Lancashire, a suitor who gives his girl a knife or other pointed instrument will soon lose interest. Finding a knife brings bad luck in its train. In England, India, and elsewhere, knives crossed at table lead to a quarrel. Such crossed utensils may be uncrossed without bringing bad luck by uncrossing them withershins (right to left, against the sun's direction). A knife that falls to the ground means ill luck, but brings good luck to the one who picks it up. Should such a knife stick in the ground in falling, it means good luck, or it may mean that company is coming from the direction in which the knife inclines. If a knife is dropped, a man will call: this is the general British and U.S. belief, but usually, in other parts of the world, a dropped knife means a woman caller. However the beliefs are so mixed that neighbors often believe complete opposites about a dropped knife. According to the rime:

> Knife falls, gentleman calls;
> Fork falls, lady calls;
> Spoon falls, baby calls.

Don't toast bread on a knife, or you'll have no luck at all. If you stir your drink with a knife, in Oldenburg belief, you will get stomach pains. If you eat while a knife is being sharpened, your throat will surely be cut by next morning. Similar to this is the threat behind the humorous U.S. injunction: Don't eat peas with a knife.

The knife, being iron, also protects against evil and witchcraft. In Brittany, if a worker in the fields sees the hay lifted by the wind, he throws a knife or a haying fork at it, otherwise the Devil will make away with it. In the Scottish Highlands, the dust whirls on an otherwise calm day were thought to carry people within them; the Highlander threw a knife or some dust from a molehill at the eddy to make it surrender its victims. In northern Europe, throwing a knife at a dust whirl wounded the spirit in it; the knife would show bloodstains. The jack-o'-lantern can be chased by throwing a knife or a key at it, as people in some parts of Germany believe, or, in the southern U.S., by carrying a new knife never used on wood. In the Scottish Highlands, it may be tempted closer if a knife is stuck in the ground. Among Arkansas Negroes, carrying a knife protects one from ghosts. In Kent, a knife under a window sill keeps the Devil out of the house, and in Tuscany two crossed knives on the window sill keep away hail. In Morocco, a knife is placed under the pillow of a sick man to keep the demons from getting at him. Jewish women, in the latter stages of pregnancy, used to carry a knife when they were alone to protect themselves against demons. Ghosts can be kept away by reading a verse of the Bible backwards, folding the page, putting a knife and fork in the place, and putting the book under the pillow. The hag-ridden may protect themselves by asking aloud for a knife—sometimes this suffices to scare off the witch—or by putting knives or other cutting things around the bed so the nightmare will not be able to resume her human skin when she leaves. The Scotsman entering a place where a fairy lives will stick a knife or a needle or a hook—all iron implements—in the doorpost or door to keep it from closing and imprisoning him. In Transylvania, knives must not be left with the sharp edge raised if a dead body is in the house, otherwise the spirit of the dead will be forced to ride the sharp blade. Among the Eskimo, cutting or doing any work at all on the day a man died would injure his soul, which would then cause illness among the living. Knives are not used at funeral meals in many parts of the world. Injunctions against the use of knives at such times occur in Burma, Transylvania, and parts of northern Europe. In several parts of the world the father observing the couvade must avoid the use of knives: the reasoning is similar to the idea underlying the funeral prohibition. A German saying holds that if a child falls into the fire and one sees at the same time a knife, sharp edge up, he should turn the knife over before rescuing the child. Putting a knife in milk makes the cow go dry, according to southern U.S. Negro belief.

The magician's magic circle is drawn with a knife. A knife with a handle of snake-bone indicates poison when stuck in the table, in medieval belief, by quivering at the presence of malignant drugs. In medieval Jewish belief, a corpse would bleed if approached with a knife to which food particles adhered. Sleeping with salt, bread, and a knife, all of which have been left inadvertently on the table after cleaning up, under one's pillow brings a vision of one's wife-to-be. In Wales, on Halloween, a girl was to walk backwards to the leeks in the garden and place a knife among them; a vision of her future husband would be seen to pick up the knife and throw it into the garden.

Many proverbs and folk sayings from all over the world use the imagery of the knife. "Often a dexterous smith forges a weak knife" is from the *Ancren Riwle* (c. 1200). The Nupe of Nigeria say, "When they sharpen the knife, the horse is without fear." "The wound from a knife heals; that from a tongue never," according to a Turkish proverb.

The knife is ubiquitous in folktale. Bahman's knife in the *Arabian Nights* was a life token (E761.1.7.2) that became spotted with blood and "thereon then shalt thou know that I am slain" (Burton, *Supplemental Nights* III, 330: "The Two Sisters who Envied Their Cadette"). So too a knife stuck in a tree rusts (E761.4.1) when the life it is a token for is ended. In rabbinical tradition, the knife Abraham held to sacrifice Isaac dripped blood as a warning. In the Master Thief cycle, the child indicates his recognition of his father by his handing a knife to the criminal (H211). A magic knife is often needed to kill the giant. The bridge to the otherworld is often knife-studded or is as sharp as a knife-blade. Folktale thus reflects folk belief in that the knife obtains its virtue from its being of iron and sharp.

knocks Sharp raps or loud knocks of otherwise unexplained origin are frequently attributed to spirits or the supernatural in general. There is widespread belief that three distinct knocks on the headboard of a sick person's bed are sometimes heard and predict his death, but there are many variants, e.g. the knocks might occur at the head of the bed of some relative of the unfortunate. This belief may have evolved from the Roman belief that spirits or genii warned the kin of those about to die. In Ireland the knocks are believed to come on the door of the dwelling of the doomed person for three successive midnights. In England if one hears a knock at the door and finds no one there, it is sometimes said, half-jokingly, that the Devil has evidently just entered the house. Knocks and thuds are frequently reported in records of poltergeist phenomena.

In spiritualistic seances, knocks and raps on tables are a popular means of simple code communication between the spirits and the sitters—one knock for yes, two for no, three for I-don't-know or Please-repeat-the-question. Emerson deplored "this shallow Americanism which hopes to get . . . knowledge by raps on midnight tables."

Knockers are benevolent spirits or gnomes dwelling in mines who helpfully indicate the location of ore by knocking in its vicinity. They are mentioned in Hooson's *Miners' Dictionary* (1747) and in Chambers' *Journal* (1885). Watts-Dunton, an authority on Gipsy lore, wrote in *Aylwin* (1898): "She had not only heard but seen these knockers . . . They were thickset dwarfs." Welsh knockers were alleged to be 18 inches high, while Germans describe them as little old men dressed as miners, about two feet high and of two races, one malevolent, one gentle.

Knocking on wood is one of the commonest superstitions in all lands and cultures and is one of the few retained when others are abandoned by the sophisticated.

Will Rogers, noted for his common sense and practical ideas, nevertheless admitted, "I always knock on wood before I make my entrance," and, during a survey of the Harvard faculty, revealing only a fourth of that body as free of superstition, one professor said, "My one superstitious practice is to knock on wood after boasting of my health or good fortune."

The belief seems very deep-seated that the braggart attitude of boasting, especially about health and next good fortune, is likely to bring retribution, either from the envious evil powers or from the god to whom the boaster should have given thanks and praise. To counteract and nullify the envy or anger, one should immediately knock on wood, preferably three times in quick succession, or at least touch wood.

Whether the touching is a softer substitute for or a declining form of the knocking, or whether, on the other hand, it was the original form of the practice, is difficult to determine. Those who think that the touching came first attribute the origin of the custom to the ancient religious habit of touching a wooden crucifix when taking an oath. Charms or amulets of wood are carried on watch chains or in the pocket so that one may have an available bit of wood to touch when so impelled. Sir Walter Scott is alleged to have fingered a wooden button on his coat when reciting as a student and failed miserably when his mischievous fellows cut off the button.

It seems more likely that the knocking on wood is the older custom and is allied with the well-known habit of many primitive peoples, who make all sorts of loud noises to scare off evil spirits when the occasion or the place is dangerous or inauspicious. It may have some connection also with the druid tree or bough worship or the Greek belief in dryads or wood nymphs who would come to man's help when summoned.

CHARLES FRANCIS POTTER

knots The knot has been a thing of significance and power probably ever since the first knot was tied in the world; and it is still prominent today in symbolism, in religious ceremony, magic, and folk medicine, a force to conjure with and to be reckoned against in widespread belief and practice. To tie a knot is to make something fast, to bind, hold, also to hinder or stop. To untie a knot is to loosen, set free, release. The knot unites, therefore, and binds together; it strengthens love and marriage; it also shuts out evil and binds evil-doers into inaction.

The knot without beginning and without end was one of the symbols of the Hindu Vishnu and of life without beginning and without end. It was adopted in this meaning by the Buddhists and is one of the eight sacred symbols of Buddha.

Everywhere in India a knot is tied in the clothes of bride and bridegroom in marriage ceremonies; in some places their garments are knotted together in token of their union; part of the marriage ceremony in southern India is tying a knot in the saffron-colored thread worn for luck around the bride's neck; she wears this thread the rest of her life. In other parts of India the marriage bracelet of kuśa grass is tied around the wrist, or the wrists of bride and groom are tied together with it. Roman marriage ceremonies comprised a whole series of knot-tyings and untyings from the first tying on of the bride's girdle, and her tying the woolen strands on her husband's doorposts, to the final untying of the girdle in the bridal chamber. The love-knot of popular folk practice has an ancient and solemn authority. In Russia a net is thrown over the young couple during a marriage rite, because no evil spirit can get at the susceptible pair without first untying all the knots in the net.

The sacred thread of the high caste Brāhman is tied with the special Brahmā knot at his initiation. In Zoroastrian initiations also the sacred girdle (*kustī*) was symbolically knotted. Among certain Moslems birthdays are marked by the tying of the "year-knot" (*salgīrah*). It is first tied on the wrist of a one-year-old child and renewed every birthday. In Roman ceremonies the priest of Jupiter could have no knots in his garment. See FLAMEN. The Biblical "bindings" refer to ceremonies similar to other religious knottings.

Part of the funeral rites performed by Chinese Buddhist and Taoist priests consists of the release of the souls of the dead from pain and difficulty by untying one by one 24 knots in a thread in which 24 coins are tied. In Assyria knots were tied to prevent the dead from annoying the living. It was fairly widespread European belief that knots could prevent the soul from leaving the body. Thus knots were a protection against death on the one hand, but an enemy, by tying knots, could also cause a man to undergo a long and agonized dying.

In medieval Europe whoever tied a knot during a wedding ceremony thus prevented the young couple from ever having children. An ill-wisher could prevent the consummation of a marriage itself by tying a knot (or a certain number of knots) in a cord and throwing the cord into water. Such a spell was practically impossible to undo, since the only way to undo it was to find the cord and untie the knots. Anyone found guilty of tying such knots was punishable by law and excommunicated from the Church. In Scotland as late as the 18th century this was the principal popular belief in regard to knots: the obstruction of the consummation of a marriage. Hence every knot on bride or bridegroom was untied for the duration of the marriage ceremony. Young couples stood up with their shoes untied and garments completely loosened.

Knot-tying as a magic formula to prevent conception has been common everywhere from earliest times. It was a commonplace of the ancient Hebrews. Women of the Yao (a Bantu group of Mozambique) also believe that knot-tying prevents pregnancy; when the Yao woman wants to become pregnant she unties the knots, puts the untied cord in water, and drinks the water. In southern Russia and Galicia the woman who soaks a thread of flax in menstrual blood, then ties ten knots in it, wears it for nine days and nine nights, and buries it in a corner of the room, saying, "I bury you for eternity," will never have children. See N. E. Hines, *Medical History of Contraception* (Baltimore, 1936), p. 9. In Fez, Morocco, a man will obtain the oviduct of a hen, tie a knot in it, boil it, and eat it, to prevent a pregnancy resulting from his next intercourse.

It is a common world practice to untie all knots during childbirth to facilitate the birth. This was done in ancient Persia, was a practice of ancient Semitic peoples, is still widely observed all over rural Europe today, and among peoples of the Pacific. Every knot in the house is untied during a birth, including those in the garments of inmates; and in some localities the magic of release is enhanced by the freeing of captive birds and animals, untying of domestic animals, etc.

Knots have long been used in the causing and curing of diseases. Seven knots and twice seven knots are especially potent. Nine knots are the worst of evil spells. Once Mohammed was bewitched by a sorcerer who tied nine knots in a string and threw it down a well. Mohammed fell acutely ill and would have died had not the archangel Gabriel revealed where the string was hidden. With difficulty it was gotten out, holy words were said over each knot (which thereupon untied itself), and Mohammed got well. The old Teutonic Salic Law from the 5th century on put a heavy fine on anyone guilty of tying nine knots. Warts are still treated by tying a knot in a string for every wart a person has and burying the string; as the string rots the warts disappear. Or sometimes the string is thrown away and whoever steps over it or picks it up gets the warts.

Tying up the wind in a knot is part of the old wisdom of northern fishing communities, especially in Lapland, Finland, the Shetlands, Isle of Man, etc. Then untying the knot raises enough wind to fill the sails. Tying the wind in three knots is also common; more and stronger winds arise as they are untied one by one. Fishermen have been known to "buy the wind"—in a knotted handkerchief—from some old man or old woman versed in wind lore. This concept is at least as old as Æolus, who gave Odysseus the winds tied up in a bag (*Odyssey* x, 19 f.).

Among various southern U.S. Negroes a woman whose ear itches will tie a knot in her apron to make the gossip's teeth ache. A knot of remembrance is often tied in the fringe of a shawl or scarf in Ireland when lovers or friends must separate. The Irish worm knot (*snaidm na péiste*), that cures worms or gripes in cattle, is tied in a cord with which cattle are beaten.

Tying an invisible knot in an egg (H1021.5) was one of the tasks given to Väinämöinen, old and steadfast, by the hard-to-get maid of Pohjola. This did not phase the hero, for "an egg in knots he twisted/ Yet no knot was seen upon it." The fact that this did not captivate the crafty girl is another story. See DOVE; FIRE; GORDIUS; MNEMONICS.

☞ Knotting or otherwise tying cord or string has, in West African and New World Negro belief, strong magical implications. Charms with knots retain by this means the power which actuates them, while the act of tying a knot while pronouncing the "real" name of a person is held to be an effective means of obtaining power over him. For a special example of tying, see IRO.

[MJH]

kobold The household spirit or familiar of German folklore, helpful but full of pranks and tricks, occasionally malicious. He is the German analog of the English brownie and boggart. He will often hide household or farm implements, but he is also good at finding lost objects. Sometimes when someone stoops to pick up something, the kobold likes to push him over so that he falls. But he will sing to the children, help with the work, curry the horses. He must be properly fed, however, or he will raise a great fuss. Specific household kobolds are often known by the name of Heinze, Chimmeken, or Walther. A number of them have become famous in German legend, among them Hinzelmann, to whom a Rev. Feld-

mann devoted a whole volume; Hödeken, named for his hat, who terrified unfaithful wives into fidelity; King Goldemar, who slept with his master, played the harp, and caught the clergy in their secret transgressions.

There is another variety of kobolds who haunt mines and caves. The famous metallurgist, Georg Landmann, made a thorough study of these underground spirits in his *De Animantibus subterraneis,* published at Bâle, 1657. See BIERSAL; DOMOVIK.

Kodoyanpe Literally, Earth Namer, or Earth Maker: Creator of the Maidu Indians of north-central California. Kodoyanpe and Coyote descend from a clear sky, or are floating in a canoe; they discover the earth together, and prepare it for the first people. The first people are created, and are ultimately transformed into the animals of the present day when the Indians come upon the scene. During the mythical age, Earth Maker tries to destroy Coyote, who epitomizes evil; he is assisted by a culture-hero-like character referred to as the Conqueror. Failing to destroy Coyote, Earth Maker flees to the east at the same time that the Indians come upon the scene. [EWV]

Kohinor, Kohinoor, or **Kohinur** A famous Indian diamond, weight when cut about 106 carats; one of the British crown jewels since the annexation of Punjab, 1849. According to Hindu legend, it was found in a river in south India nearly five thousand years ago. It is mentioned in the ancient Indian epic *Mahābhārata* as belonging to Karna, king of Anga. Its authentic history dates from 56 B.C. when it was the property of the Rajah of Ujayin. It means "mountain of light."

Koinobori The custom of flying huge paper carps from a pole, during the Japanese Boys' Festival. See JAPANESE FOLKLORE. [JLM]

Kojiki The oldest Japanese chronicle, compiled in 712: main source for the early mythology of Japan. [JLM]

Koki The praying mantis: wife of Spider in Temne and Hausa Negro mythology.

kokkara A primitive musical instrument of India; an iron tube scraped rhythmically by headmen of the Kānika tribesmen of India to accompany prayer and the recitation of the names of divinities. It has the effect of inducing violent excitement.

Kokopelli or **Kokopölö** An insect kachina of the Pueblo Hopi Indians: possibly to be identified with Dragonfly. He is a "humpbacked" hunter who seduces girls or makes them bridal moccasins; his hump is actually a sack containing gifts. The prototype of Kokopelli may be represented in southwestern pictographs of a human being shooting mountain sheep. While any of the Pueblo kachinas or masked spirits may hunt, specific ones among them, as Coyote kachina at Zuñi, Kokopelli at Hopi, Nepokwa'i at Tewa, are specifically huntsmen. [EWV]

kolattam A festive stick dance of southern India, for opposing groups of men and girls or girls alone. Similar to the hand claps of the *kummis,* the two sticks in the hands of the dancers can be struck near various parts of the body—overhead, at the shoulder, hip, knee, or struck against the partner's stick in various patterns and rhythms. There is considerably more flexibility of the torso and knees than in stick dances of Europe. In the *pinnal kolattam* the dancers hold a stick in the right hand and a red or white cord in the left. These they interlace maypole fashion, simultaneously executing intricate steps and stick beats. These interweavings are not confined to the circular serpentine of the European and American maypole, but include square or longways formations. Originally they probably had a vegetation symbolism. See KANIYAN; STICK DANCES. [GPK]

kolo or **kollo** Literally, circle: a popular open round dance of Serbia and Dalmatia. Men and women, in no set order, progress slowly to the right and left with balancing grapevine steps and with little jerks of the shoulders. They are joined by their hands, sometimes by a kerchief. The leader often executes acrobatic crouches, jumps, and turns. He may lead the line in a serpentine or spiral course. At times dancers form small circles within a large one. The kolo greatly resembles the open rounds of Greece and, in general, forms part of the sequence of these serpentines that winds all the way from the Pyrenees to the Caucasus—ancient vernal rites now performed purely for amusement. [GPK]

kolomaika A Ukrainian peasant dance with vigorous leaps for both men and women. The music, in duple time, is emphatic. The movements are buoyant; the arms swing forward and laterally along with the crouching and leaping and high *pas de basques*. It can be performed by four couples in circular formation, and especially in stage exhibitions. [GPK]

komarinskaia or **kamarinskaia** A Russian national dance for solo or couples, widely taken over from the peasantry for performance in cities and on the stage. The music and movements have all the forceful exuberance generally associated with western Russian dance. Its jumps and stamps have the virility of the true leap dance, and are punctuated by shouts. The arms swing out during leg extensions and during knee bends followed by heel stands. They are folded during a back skip with turned-out knee. During a toe-twist the hands are at the neck and waist. [GPK]

'Komfo The Surinam Negro term for one possessed by the spirit of an African diviner. It is derived from the Gold Coast of Africa, where the Twi word *okomfo* means "priest." [MJH]

komori-uta Japanese lullabies, sung to babies by mothers, grandmothers, older sisters, and nurses: often irregular in rhythm to suit the bobbing of the child as it is carried on the back.

Konyhatánc Literally, kitchen dance: a Hungarian dance performed at weddings by the cooks. [GPK]

kordax Originally, a lively phallic dance performed by youths in the train of the Dionysian *orgia*. They were naked, with tails and horns, similar to the satyrs. The kordax became a theatrical dance and was incorporated in the Greek comedies; in Roman times it became completely lewd. In 16th century court dancing the term kordax included the sprightly but decorous gaillards, tordions, voltas, courantes, and branles. [GPK]

Kore Persephone, the Maiden: a variant of Cora.

körmagyar or **körtanc** A Hungarian dance of the quadrille type, introduced in 1841 by a dancing master,

Lajos Szabo Szöllösi. Its six parts (*andalgó, lelkes, toborzó, ömledezö, három a tánc,* and *kézfogó*) are executed in various groupings of four couples, most frequently in crossovers of two opposite lines. In the last part, two concentric circles move in opposite directions, the women on the inside sunwise, the men on the outside counter. The same steps are used as in the citified version of the *czárdás*. [GPK]

Kornmutter Literally, corn-mother: a field spirit of German folk belief: the spirit of the growing grain incarnate in the last sheaf. Compare BULLKATER; CAILLEAĊ; HARVEST DOLL.

Kornwolf Literally, corn-wolf: a field spirit of German, French, and Slavonic folk belief, and often invoked to frighten children. He "sits in the last sheaf" and the reaper who reaps the last sheaf is himself often called the Wolf, and is expected to act the part, howl, bite his fellows, etc. Local practices differ. In some places the wagon that brings home the last sheaf is called the Wolf. The last sheaf is commonly made into the shape of a wolf, kept until the threshing is finished, and then made the center of various festivities. Usually the *old* Wolf is killed at the end of the harvest to make way for the potency of the *new;* but in some places the old Wolf is kept on the farm, in house or barn, to renew his fertility magic in the spring. Compare BULLKATER; CAILLEAĊ; HARVEST DOLL.

korobouchka or **korobotchka** Literally, Little Basket: a modern Russian ballroom dance referring to a peddler selling his wares in his basket. However, occupational mime has been reduced to a bare suggestion in an exchange of places between partners. There are several versions, for a counterclockwise double circle or for two lines; and there are varying combinations of typically Slavic hops and leg swings, one version with a heel click. When danced in a circle, partners hold hands in skating position. In part 1 they move forward and back with three steps and a kick, then two *polkas;* in part 2, hands on hips, each dancer does a *double* to right and left, and with right hand joined to the partner's, crosses over. This gay "mixer" originated among Russian immigrant groups in the United States and found its way back to the homeland. [GPK]

Koshare, Kashare, or **Kashale** Clowns or "Delight Makers" in Pueblo Indian ceremonies. The Koshare were born, according to Laguna legend, from a ball of skin rubbed off herself by a girl who wished for something to make people laugh. At Keres and Tewa there are two clown groups, Kurena (Qwirana) and Koshare (Kashale) or Kossa. At San Felipe and Santo Domingo, the Town chief is also chief of the Koshare clowns. It is the clowns which furnish the humorous play of all sorts in Pueblo dances, but the members of Koshare groups have other duties beyond the dances. At Cochiti pueblo, for example, the Koshari and Kurena are in alternate years in charge of the rabbit hunts for the Town chief, they plant and harvest for this chief, and are in charge of the kickstick race. [EWV]

☞ The koshare of the Keresan Pueblo Indians accompany the kachina in alternation with the *kurena,* but in Santo Domingo dance separately in February and engage in original burlesques. They are distinguished by the body paint in black and white horizontal stripes, with rings around the eyes and mouth, a black cap, or, more usually, a poke-shaped hair-do stiffened with clay (in Santo Domingo two horns), a black ragged breech-clout, a rope of rabbit fur from shoulder to waist, at times in the hands a branch of evergreen or a rattle of deer and calf hoofs. The koshare have the typical behavior pattern of ceremonial clowns: backward action, reverse speech, actual or simulated filth-eating, and obscenity. They may act as police and disciplinarians, and purge with the very ridiculousness of their social comment, their satire on the most sacred institutions, including a Catholic mass, and also on whites and Mexicans. Their most ridiculous posturings and vicious comments are beyond censorship.

Their votive organization is related to the Flint Curing society. They live in the east (reverse of the kachina). They may have some relation to spirits of the ancestors, and are related particularly to the Yaqui *chapayekas*. [GPK]

koto   The unfretted long zither of Japan, used to accompany Shinto temple music and secular song. The method of playing involves the use of a small hard plectrum of horn or other material held in the right hand and scratched lightly across all strings during gaps in the rhythm. The strings are damped after this with the left hand, the little finger of which plucks a tinkling melody to support the singing. Koto players belong to the second of three ranks in the social order of musicians. As a special honor they may be given the right to tune the instrument's first string an octave lower. This right is conferred only by the master of a guild. Apart from ceremonial music, the koto is the instrument of women and of blind ballad singers. The koto is the Japanese equivalent of the Chinese ch'in.

koto missi   The term for the Negro women of Paramaribo, Dutch Guiana, who wear the distinctive costume called koto yaki, of the general type found elsewhere in the New World (as, for example, the *bahiana* of Brazil). The costume consists of skirt and blouse of figured cotton print cloth, or sometimes of silk, with a head kerchief that harmonizes with the color of the other elements. The skirt is full, with a deep ruffle at the waist accentuated in back by a substantial bustlelike pad called the *jamiri* (family). The blouse is often made as a bolero and worn over the white collarless waist so as to accentuate the fullness of the bosom. The kerchief, also heavily starched so that it almost becomes a hat, may be tied in many different ways, each of which indicates the mood of the wearer. Every kerchief design has a specific meaning, also, being designated by a word description of its color or decoration, or by a proverb commenting on some local happening. [MJH]

kotwāl or **cotwāl**   In India, an officer of the law, a popular character in many Indian folktales. In Benares a shrine has been erected to Bhaironāth (divine kotwāl of Śiva), who exercises authority over gods and men and keeps the city free from malignant spirits and evil men. The office of kotwāl has been abolished in western, southern, and central India, but the word is still used in the Northwest Frontier Province to designate the chief police officer of one of the larger cities or cantonments.

kowtow   In Chinese ceremony, a knocking of one's head on the ground, usually three times or until bidden to rise: an act signifying great respect. This ceremony involves an important principle in Chinese lore at the point where folklore merges with sociology. When a person so abases himself before another as to rub his head in the dust, the person receiving the honor is bound to save the kowtower's face, i.e. restore his human dignity by showing great favor or kindness. [RDJ]

koyemshi   Kachina husbands: dancing clowns of the Pueblo Indians, commonly known as "mudheads," particularly prominent at Zuñi, called *koyimshi* at Hano and *tachuki* at Hopi. They are often called *athlashi*, a name for the dead. They were begotten, according to the origin myth, by Old Woman kachina, Komokyatsiky, when her brother lay with her. She woke up as an old woman after this deed. The impersonators of the koyemshi wear masks of cloth stained pink with sacred kachina clay, or, at Acoma, of leather. They have knobs filled with cottonwool, seeds, and soil taken from under the townspeople's feet—in consequence of which the koyemshi have power over the people and are feared by them. They engage in obscene interludes between kachina dances, and accompany the *shalako* of Zuñi, sometimes serving as chanters. On September 12, they engage in a ceremonial guessing game, before the Red Paint kachina dance at Zuñi. They indulge in jugglery and games of bean bag and leap frog. At summer solstice they dance all night along with the kachinas.

Each koyemshi has his special name and somewhat individualized mask and behavior. Their leader, Molanhakto, is Father Koyemshi. They are considered sexually immature, yet evidently have phallic properties, for they can at any time remove the kilt from their penis, and in their drum they carry the butterfly which makes people go sexually crazy. [GPK]

'kra or **akra**   The Gold Coast (Ashanti-Fanti) term for the soul, which is inherited in the paternal line, in contrast to the inheritance of wealth and social position, which passes from maternal uncle to nephew. The word has been retained among New World Negroes in Dutch Guiana and among the Maroons of Jamaica. Among the Saramacca Bush Negroes, the *r* is often elided, making the word *ak'a*. [MJH]

Kraken   An enormous sea monster reported often seen off the coast of Norway: also called *sykraken*, sea kraken, or *krabben*, from its round, flat shape and many arms. It is said to be a mile and a half at least in circumference and to cause a major whirlpool when it submerges. It is capable of pulling even the largest ship under water. It was first publicized by the Norwegian Bishop Erik Pontoppidan in his *Natural History of Norway* (1752-53).

Kralj Matjaž   King Mathias of the Slovenes, successor to Kresnik, and legendary conqueror of the Turks. Like Kresnik, Matjaž too was married to his sister, Alenčica, whom, in legend, he rescued from the Turks, or in Slovenian traditional ballad, from the underworld. Matjaž is also a king in the mountain, sleeping till the day of Slovenia's utter need, when he will emerge and save everything. He is asleep in Mt. Peca near the Carinthian border, or in the Triglav caves. His ravens keep watch, circling above the entrance to the cave. One of his legends is that on some cold Christmas night a lime tree (linden) will grow on the mountain, bloom at midnight, and then die; on the following St. George's Day, Kralj Matjaž will come out of the cave and hang his shield on the tree, which will suddenly flower again in promise of a better future for the people. It is said that during World War II the peasants thought King Matjaž would ride again and save Slovenia. See F. S. Copeland, "Some Aspects of Slovene Folklore," *Folk-Lore* 60: 280–281.

Krappe, Alexander Haggerty (1894–1947) International scholar, folklorist, and linguist. He first became interested in folklore about 1919, after reading Sir James G. Frazer's *Golden Bough* and *Pausanias*, but soon felt equally indebted to James Rendel Harris, Salomon Reinach, Moses Gaster, and Gédéon Huet. Apart from these obvious debts, he followed, however, a rather wide eclecticism in method and mode of approach, refusing to be associated with any school or coterie. For bibliography, academic career, etc., see p. ix.

Kratti A supernatural spirit of the Finns, which originated from ancient *skratti*. He took care of property, like the Para or Puuk. [JB]

Kresnik First national hero of the Slovenes; also mythological culture hero, magician, and monster-slayer, son of Svarog, the creator, and commissioned by him to rule over the Slovenes. He was educated in supernatural feats by the *vile*, loved and lived with Mara, the snake queen, married his sister Vesina, the daughter of Mara. His death was caused by the jealousy of one or the other of these two women. He is interpreted as a deity of spring, crops, and cattle. He became syncretized with St. George, and in late popular custom with Green George. (See JACK IN THE GREEN.) Kresnik lived to great age, and dwells now in Svarog's crystal mountain. See F. S. Copeland, "Some Aspects of Slovene Folklore," *Folk-Lore* 60: 277 ff.; J. Kelemina, *Slovene Folk Tales and Myths* (Ljubljana, 1921).

Kreuz König Literally, King of the Cross: a German folk dance for two couples. Its figures depend on interlacing of hands and arms. The first part, in moderate triple time, is a clockwise circling with joined hands and a leaping run; in the second figure, the men cross arms behind the ladies, and all four pivot. In the third and faster figure, the men cross and pivot the opposite ladv: a sort of male "ladies chain." In the original tempo, all circle left again with a step-hop, then swing partners. In the climactic fifth figure, the cross, women start back to back, then swing around to the outside by their partners' right hand, finishing with the men back to back in the center. A Lithuanian variant, *Greitz*, is danced in a large circle. [GPK]

Kriemhild In the *Nibelungenlied*, the sister of Gunther, king of Burgundy. She married Siegfried, who gave her the Nibelungen gold as a wedding gift. She quarreled with Brunhild, Gunther's wife, and as a result, Brunhild persuaded Hagen to murder Siegfried and steal the gold. Kriemhild mourned her loss for three years, then married Etzel (Attila the Hun) so as to gain power to be revenged on Hagen and Gunther. Shortly after their marriage Kriemhild persuaded Etzel to invite the Burgundians to visit them, and went about raising men and plotting death for the visitors. In a series of treacherous attacks, all the Burgundians were killed except Gunther and Hagen. Kriemhild then had her brother Gunther beheaded and carried the head to Hagen, demanding to know where the gold was hidden; but Hagen laughed. In a fury she caught up the sword of Siegfried and beheaded him, whereupon Hildebrand beheaded Kriemhild too, in front of Etzel, for the trouble she had caused the Huns. Compare GUDRUN.

kriksy Same as NOCNITSA, the night hag of Russian folklore.

kris dance A Balinese trance dance performed with a dagger or kris. The male kris dance is part of the witch play or *Tjalon Arang*. The supporters of the dragon or *barong* feign an attack on the witch, who symbolizes a curious mixture of evil and motherhood. They squat as they approach her, then lie powerless on the ground as she waves her white kerchief (an *anteng* or sling which a mother uses for carrying her child). During the attack, she acts limp, but the attackers are the ones to collapse and be revived by the dragon. Then follows a frenzied attack on the self, not only by the group of men but also by women who enter in procession. There is a significant formalized difference which they observe even at the height of frenzy—the men stab upwards, bending back, pubis forward, with pursed lips, or in the climax they lie on their bellies; the women push the dagger down. These gestures are said to have phallic symbolism, and at the same time to release frustrations developed since childhood. The mother-witch, it will be noted, remains unharmed amidst the turmoil. [GPK]

Krishna In Hindu religion, the eighth avatar of Vishnu, whose cult, popular in modern India, is a bright, cheerful religion, more nearly akin to Christianity than are Buddhism, Jainism, or Śaivism; in Hindu mythology and legend, the most celebrated hero. He is known by the epithets of *Gopal* the Cowherd, *Gopinath* the Lord of Cowherds, *Mathuranath* Lord of Muttra. Krishna, the Dark One, was the last of the Yādava race. According to the *Mahābhārata*, Vishnu plucked out two of his hairs, one black, the other white, which he placed in the wombs of Devakī and Rohinī. The black hair became Krishna and the white hair was born to Rohinī as Balarāma.

According to the *Purānas*, Kansa, the uncle of Devakī, was told by the sage Nārada that Devakī's son would destroy him, so Kansa had her first six children put to death. The seventh, the fair-complexioned Balarāma, was transferred to the womb of Rohinī, the second wife of Vasudeva, and the eighth, Krishna, the dark-skinned one, was born at midnight to Devakī. With the intervention of the gods, Krishna was carried to the house of the cowherd Nanda and exchanged for his newborn daughter. Kansa, however, discovered the deception and many of Krishna's youthful exploits of valor were directed toward defeating attempts on Kansa's part to have Krishna destroyed.

While he was growing up, Krishna gamboled with the *gopīs* (milkmaids), slew the king of the Hayas, the demons Pūtanā and Dhenuka, and the serpent Kāliya, overthrew Kansa, and killed Kansa's brother Sunāman and father-in-law, Jarāsandha. He carried off the daughter of the king of the Gāndhārvas; overthrew Saubha, the flying city of the Daityas; overcame Varuna; killed Panchajana and obtained his conch shell, which Krishna used afterwards as a trumpet; stole the Pārijāta tree from Indra's heaven; and obtained the fiery discus (*chakra*) from Agni, the fire god, when he and Arjuna helped that god burn the Khāṇḍava forest. This disc was a powerful weapon, working immediate havoc among those at whom Kṛishṇa threw it. And once, when the jealous Indra tried to destroy mankind because men worshipped Kṛishṇa more than they worshipped him, Kṛishṇa warded off the rain and flood by holding the mountain Govardhana on his little finger for seven days to protect the cattle and their herdsmen. The youthful deeds of Kṛishṇa, especially his association with the milkmaid Rādhā, his mistress, are the central matters of modern popular worship of Vishṇu as Kṛishṇa. In particular, his life as a cowherd is celebrated at the Holi festival at the first full moon of spring.

Kṛishṇa took part in the council preceding the great war between the Pāndavas and the Kauravas and, when the combat began, because he was related to both parties, he fought with Arjuna while his army sided with Duryodhana. As Arjuna's charioteer, he related to him the *Bhagavad-Gītā*, declaring his identity with the supreme principle of the universe.

According to the *Purāṇas*, after killing Kanśa he went to the lower regions and brought back his six brothers whom the tyrant had killed. As soon as they again tasted their mother's milk, they went to heaven. Later he built and fortified the city of Dwārakā, his jeweled capital, which disappeared into the waters seven days after his death. Dwarka on the Kathiawar peninsula and Muttra on the Jumna river are closely associated with the Kṛishṇa cult and areas around them are today holy ground.

He carried off Rukminī, his legal consort, by whom he had a son, Pradyumna (a rebirth of Kāma). The latter was carried off by the demon Sambara, who was destined to die at Pradyumna's hands, but was swallowed by a fish which was captured and cut up in the presence of Māyādevī, Sambara's queen, who reared the boy. Pradyumna's son Aniruddha, was carried off at the order of the Daitya Ushā, who had fallen in love with him. To his rescue went Kṛishṇa, Balarāma, and Pradyumna, and a great battle with the hosts of Daityas led by Ushā's father Bāna followed. Kṛishṇa was victorious and his grandson was released.

During a drunken brawl in Dwārakā, Pradyumna was slain, Balarāma was left and died under a tree, and Kṛishṇa was accidentally slain by the hunter Jaras (old age) when he was mistaken for a deer and shot in the foot, his vulnerable spot.

Kṛishṇa's character is marked by deceit, dishonesty, and trickery. It was he who suggested the unfair blow which Bhīma gave Duryodhana, and he who suggested unfair dealing in the battle between the Kauravas and the Pāndavas. His origin is obscure and his association with Vishṇu is recent rather than primitive. He is said, euhemeristically, to have been a real Kshatriya hero who was deified after death; or he was the sun god of a hill tribe who became identified with the Vedic solar deity Vishṇu; or he was the god of vegetation. He is usually represented with crossed legs, playing the flute. This flute calls its hearers irresistibly. Among the other folkloric elements in the Kṛishṇa myth are the familiar motifs of magical impregnation, slaughter of the innocents, exchange of children between noble and cowherd, precocious *enfant terrible*, Achilles heel. Kṛishṇa shares many of these incidents of his life with the other true folk heroes of the world.

☞ Folk festivals celebrate him in the *ras*, and the Manipuri and Kathak schools of *natya* enact scenes from his life. These are all pastoral and tender, some dealing with his boyhood, most of them with his courtship of Rādhā. His Butterball Dance depicts the mischievous little god who stole butterballs from the milkmaids' churns and danced eating them. He danced the many-headed serpent Kāliya to death by trampling on its heads till the blood gushed from its mouth. This conquest symbolizes the triumph of the divine spirit over the powers of evil. As a young man, still mischievous, he came upon the milkmaids of Bṛindāvana bathing in the river Jumna, and he hid their saris. All fled except Rādhā, who begged for her garment and finally became his divine wife. This legend forms the basis for the most popular Hindu dance drama, for all the gestures of the *nautch* dancers, and of the dēvadāsi, who climax their performance by dancing the Ras-Mandalay around Kṛishṇa and Rādhā. He is always shown with his transverse flute, traditionally costumed in a bejeweled male sari and high conical crown. [GPK]

Kriss Kringle A corruption of German *Christkindl*, little Christ Child: a figure of German Christmas folklore, now identified with St. Nicholas or Santa Claus. Formerly, however, in some Catholic provinces of Germany and parts of Austria, an impersonator of St. Nicholas used to visit the village homes on St. Nicholas Eve (December 5) and ask the children in each house what they wanted for Christmas. On Christmas Eve there was a candle in every window to light the Christ Child as he walked through the village bearing gifts. The Child was not impersonated, however; the gifts were secretly produced by the parents. The later impersonations and the secrecy about the presents are probably responsible for the identification with St. Nicholas and Santa Claus. In some parts of Scandinavia it was Kristine who walked through the village bearing gifts on Christmas Eve, and for whom a candle was put in every window. See KNECHT RUPRECHT; SAINT NICHOLAS.

Kristensen, Evald Tang (1843–1929) Danish writer and collector of folklore. His great mass of folklore material, not half dealt with in his many books, has been exceedingly useful for international folklore research. Kristensen gave up teaching in 1888 to devote himself completely to collecting folklore. His first book was *Jyske Folkeviser og Toner* (1871), which contained 150 songs and had a conclusion by Svend Grundtvig. Other books were *Æventyr fra Jylland* (four volumes, 1881–1897), *Danske Dyrefabler og Kjæderemser* (1896), *Danske Skæmtesagn, samlede af Folkemunde* (1900), *Fra Mildebo, jyske Folkeæventyr* (1898), *Molbo- og Aggerbohistorier* (two volumes, 1892), *Vore Fædres Kirketjeneste, belyst ved Exempler optegnede efter Folkemunde* (1879), and *Dansk biografisk Haandleksikon* (1923). Kristensen was the editor of *Skattegraveren*, the publication of the Danish Folklore Society (Folkemindesamfundet).

kritikos One of the open rounds or link dances of Greece, specifically stemming from the island of Crete. As in virtually all dances of modern Greece, men and women in arbitrary order hold hands or shoulders and gradually progress right, facing the center of their arc. The step is a combination of left heel brush, grapevine step, and hop, in a more complicated pattern than that found in the *hasapikos* and *syrtos*. The leader, man or woman, elaborates the fundamental step with turns and crouches. [GPK]

Krittikās or Kṛttikās In Hindu mythology, the six Pleiades; fosterers of the six-headed god of war, Kārttikeya.

Krohn, Julius Leopold Fredrik (1835–1888) Finnish scholar, literary historian, and poet, founder of the "newer Kalevala research," ablest disciple of Elias Lönnrot, and who spent his life studying the songs of the Kalevala cycle. Julius Krohn developed a method for comparing the various versions of a song so as to determine its history. This technique was based on reducing the folk songs to their elements, or motifs, and then studying the distribution of these elements so as to determine what geographical course they had taken and what changes they had undergone. This technique, enunciated by Kaarle Krohn, Julius' son, and applied to other aspects of folklore research, is generally known as the Finnish method. Among Julius Krohn's works are *Finnische Literaturgeschichte* (1883–1885), *Estlandische Sprachlehre* (1872), and *Lappisches Wörterbuch* (1885). See FINNISH FOLKLORE.

Krohn, Kaarle (1863–1933) Student of the folktale. He developed the historical-geographical technique applied by his father, Julius Krohn, to the folk song, and was the first to use it in studying the folktale. Among Kaarle Krohn's works are a large edition of *Volkssagen* (*Tiersagen*, 1886; and *Königssagen*, 1893); the studies *Bär* (*Wolf*) *und Fuchs* (1888); *Mann und Fuchs* (1891); *Die Volkloristische Arbeitsmethode* (1926), in which he stated his and his father's historical-geographical technique; *Kalevalastudien* (1924–1928); and *Übersicht über einige Resultate der Märchenforschung* (1931). He also published various of his father's works posthumously. Kaarle Krohn was instrumental in founding Folklore Fellows, an international group for the cooperative study of folklore. He was secretary of the Finnish Academy of Science, and president of the Finnish Literary Society. Kaarle Krohn held that folk poetry, folk beliefs, and superstitions belong in folklore research, but that ethnography and folk song do not. See FINNISH FOLKLORE.

Kromanti A word frequently encountered in the literatures of slaving to designate a category of Africans; it refers actually to the Ashanti-Fanti Negroes of the Gold Coast who were shipped from the slave factories of the towns of Little and Great Coromantyne. The origin of the term is perhaps traceable to the great oath of the Ashanti, which commemorates a battle in which the Ashanti King Osai Tutu was killed. The oath thus served as a battle cry, and came to identify the Ashanti in the minds of their captors. Among the Bush Negroes of Dutch Guiana, *kromanti* (or *k'omanti*) is the word for the powerful magic force believed to protect warriors and to aid them in fighting by rendering them resistant to bullets, and all other objects that lacerate or cut. [MJH]

kru A Cambodian shaman, especially active as a curer. He exorcises the evil spirits of disease and uses vegetable medicines as well as rhinoceros horns and bezoar stones in his cures. Compare ÀP THMÒP.

Kshatriya A member of the ruling or warrior caste in India; the second of the four Hindu castes.

kuala The house-shrine of the Votjaks: sometimes a corner set apart within the dwelling for the house spirit or ancestral god, sometimes a shelf in an outhouse. It is similar to the *kudo* of the Cheremissians.

Kuan Ti The Chinese god of war: said to have been a great scholar. He is honored as the patron of war because he prevents rather than because he makes war. This, and the legend that he was one of three men who swore brotherhood in the Han dynasty, are probably accretions. His festival is May 13. His temples are found throughout China. [RDJ]

Kuan Yin The Chinese Goddess of Mercy; the most universally respected and most generally known of all Chinese divinities. Historically, she is a transformation of Avalokitesvara, the gentle disciple who was born from a tear shed by the Lord Buddha at the spectacle of the suffering of the world. Until the 12th century Kuan Yin was a male figure and modern images sometimes show a faint trace of a mustache. Although Kuan Yin is obviously a Buddhist importation, there is little doubt that, like Avalokitesvara, she is a substitute symbol who has taken on attributes from other gods. Although Hsi Wang Mu, the Goddess of the Western Heavens, is the official Taoist competitor, the peasants of China are indifferent as to whether Kuan Yin is a Taoist or Buddhist divinity and find a place for Kuan Yin in most temples. One version of the incantation of Kuan Yin may be taken as typical: "Great Mercy, Great Mercy, oh! Thou Take-Away-Fear Pusa! Save from terror, save from suffering through thy tender woman's heart and mighty Buddha's strength!" Kuan Yin is importantly a protector of women, and one legend is that she fled from her father's court to preserve her virginity. She is often shown carrying a child in her arms. Embroidered slippers placed before her image, or slippers stolen from the temple and later replaced, induce pregnancy among sterile women. Kuan Yin brings souls to children, rescues shipwrecked sailors, brings rain. Her cult is centered at P'u T'o which at one time was governed by monks independently of civil control. No female creature, human or animal, was allowed on the island between sunset and sunrise. See KWANNON. [RDJ]

Kubera In Hindu mythology and folklore, king of the Yakshas, god of wealth, lord of the treasures of the earth. Kubera and his followers are the patrons or forces of fertility and prosperity, and associated with earth, mountains, and underground metals and treasure. His father was the sage Viśravas (or Pulastya); his mother was Iḍāviḍā; his half brothers (Rāvaṇa, Kumbhakarṇa, Vibhīshaṇa) figure in the legend of Rāma. According to the *Rāmāyaṇa* and the *Mahābhārata*, he once lived at Lankā (Ceylon) but was driven out by Rāvaṇa. With him went the Gandharvas and Rākshasas, and his subjects the Kimpurushas, Yakshas, etc. to the city of Alakā in the Himālayas, or to a wonderful palace on Mt. Kailāsa, or Mt. Meru. They have been regarded as tutelary household spirits in India from early times.

By thousands of years of austerities he received from Brahmā the gift of immortality, and the huge, self-propelling car, Pushpaka, which housed a whole city. Kubera has also a jar of honey which imparts immortality to all tasters, restores sight to the blind, and rejuvenates the old.

In the *Purānas*, Kubera was born into the Sūdra caste,

and once accidentally honored Śiva by lighting lamps while trying to plunder Śiva's treasure.

Kubera is represented as deformed, with three legs and eight teeth; he is distinguished by his man-vehicle, being often depicted standing on a crouching man.

kuei In Chinese folklore, a disembodied spirit; a ghost or demon: either the *p'o*, or physical soul, of a dead person which has escaped and become a demon, or the *hun*, or spirit-soul, of one dead, which for various reasons may be loose in the world. Both are kuei; both are regarded as malicious demons and are greatly feared. See CHINESE FOLKLORE.

Kuei Hsing An ugly dwarf associated, along with Chu Yi, with Wen Ch'ang, the Chinese God of Literature. The legend is that he was a brilliant student and won the first prize in the Imperial examinations. But because of his ugliness the emperor refused to grant him the golden rose that should have been his award. Kuei Hsing threw himself into the ocean, was rescued by a sea monster (a dragon), and ascended into Heaven where he took up his residence on the star *kuei hsing*, now construed as being located in the square part of the constellation Ursa Major. He is popularly represented holding a writing brush in his right hand, a bushel measure in his left, and kicking up one leg behind him. This twisted position is thought to suggest the Chinese ideograph *kuei*. Wen Ch'ang also has his abode in the big square mansion in Ursa Major. [RDJ]

Kuhn, (Franz Felix) Adalbert (1812–1881) German Indo-Germanic philologist and mythologist, one of the founders of comparative mythology. He was one of those 19th century nature mythologists who emphasized thunderstorms and lightning, as compared to the sun mythologists, such as Max Müller. Kuhn was co-founder and editor, beginning in 1851, of *Zeitschrift für vergleichende Sprachforschung*, and the editor of several volumes of Brandenburg, North German, and Westphalian legends, myths, and customs (1843, 1848, 1859). He was also the author of works on Indo-Germanic archæology and linguistic paleology, and of essays on mythology.

kühreihen Literally, cow song; a song type of the Swiss mountains, of which only a handful of examples are known. The words consist of calls to cows and the listing of cows' names, interspersed with lyric or narrative verses, and the tunes, possibly derived from alphorn notes, may be played on alphorn, bagpipe, or shawm. Now chiefly work songs, used for calling in cattle, the original songs may have been related to a dance with fertility significance. The magic word *lobe*, imitating the alphorn, is sometimes used in the songs. Their nostalgic attraction to soldiers of Swiss nationality is said to have caused widespread desertion, so that in French regiments it was formerly a capital offense to play the *Cantilena Helvetica*, a kühreihen. The Norwegian *Lok* songs and Belgian *ranz des vaches* are songs of this type. See ALPHORN.

kujawiak A Polish couple dance, which circles continuously around the room counterclockwise. It involves an unusual amount of vigorous bending and arm swinging, though the steps themselves are simple, a walk and a waltz. The most attractive part, the chorus, consists of a forward swing with joined inside arms, then a great

downward swoop to face the opposite direction, then back again, the free hand all the while held high. In another figure, resembling "wringing the dish rag," partners waltz round and round under their upraised joined hands. A smooth and sedate grace permeates this characteristically Polish waltz, similar in steps to the Swiss *Lauterbach* and the *Neubayrische*, but distinct in style. [GPK]

Kŭk In ancient Egyptian mythology, Darkness, one of the Ogdoad of Hermopolis said to have existed as part of chaos before the beginning. His consort was Kauket, obscurity. The Ogdoad, four snakes and four frogs, created Atmu.

Kukitat Younger brother and companion of the culture hero Pakrokitat of the Serrano Indians of southern California. Whereas Pakrokitat created men and was generally constructive, Kukitat caused death and was destructive. After the advent of human beings he influenced men to speak differently, and to war on each other; finally, it was decided to kill him. This was accomplished by Frog hiding in the ocean and swallowing Kukitat's excrements. [EWV]

Kuksu cult A North American Indian secret society cult of the Patwin, Pomo, Maidu, Yuki, Miwok, Costanoan, Esselen, and Salinan tribes of central California. The cult involved the formal initiation of boys: a) when quite young, and b) at puberty. The rites were held in wintertime in a semisubterranean earth-covered dance house and consisted largely of a series of masked dances, the accompaniment for which was provided by a foot drum. There were, apparently, at least two grades or age steps to the society, with indications of further subdivision into 12 successive degrees among the Patwin. Each degree was preceded by initiation and payment and led to knowledge of a new impersonation of the deities connected with the cult. Performances of the series of dances by members of the cult took place from October to May—at these ceremonies major and minor dances were held in the dance house. In the Kuksu performance, which for many of the groups was the most sacred dance, the deity Kuksu, wearing a "big head" or typical headdress of a huge ball formed by innumerable feathered sticks, was impersonated. Among the Pomo, Kuksu was the southern of six deities of the cardinal directions. Among the Valley Maidu, Kuksu was not a ceremony, but was the name of the first man and instructor of the first people; he acted as head of the secret society and the instructor of novices. Other major dances in the round of ceremonies were Hesi, Duck, Aki, Grizzly Bear, Deer, Coyote, Goose, Ghost, Thunder, and Feather-Down. For the Valley Maidu and the Patwin, Hesi was the most sacred of these, and wearers of the big-head headdress in these tribes used names other than Kuksu. The complete cycle of Kuksu ceremonies varied from village to village; the ceremonies in each village were in charge of a priest-shaman, who oftentimes was also the political head of the group. Novices were taught the impersonations by the adult initiates in the society. Among the Maidu the clown held his position for life and designated his own successor, and among the Patwin the singers inherited their office in the male line. The purpose of the cult was to make the boy initiates healthy, long-lived, hardy, swift, strong, and enduring. The specific cycle of dances was thought to bring rains, nourish the earth so that bountiful crops of acorns, bulbs, and greens would be produced, increase the game supply, and ward off epidemics, floods, and earthquakes. [EWV]

kuksu-hesi The dance cult of an esoteric men's society among tribes of central California: among the Patwin-Wintun and Maidu in its newer elaborate form, among the Pomo and Miwok in its older form as *kuksu* ceremony, and among the Yuki in a modified form. Initiation into the society is in itself a complex procedure in a semisubterranean circular structure, through 12 *yaitu* or stages, each to a new impersonation.

The sacred or *loyeng-kamini* dances consist of impersonations of ancient divinities or spirits called *saltu*, chief among them being kuksu, the big-head with his huge feather headdress. The *hesi* spirit impersonation starts the ceremony among the Patwin and Maidu; there follows a succession of impersonations in psuedo-masks of paint, feathers, rushes: all animal spirits predominantly. The *weng-kamini*, or profane dances, use no disguise. The Patwin succession is *hesi*, *waima* or duck, bear, coyote, goose, deer, *aki hesi*. The Maidu include a "woman," *lole*, the Miwok, a clown *wo'ochi*, the coyote, and others. Some of the dances are acrobatic; the Miwok *uzumati* or Grizzly Bear is a realistic waddling and clawing mime. The spirits are expected to have power over crops and animals and over their multiplication, though these are not hunting dances. Complex variants occur between tribes; shamanism and the modern ghost dance have intruded into this ancient cult with its mythological origins. [GPK]

Kukulcan The Mayan storm god and culture hero; the bright- (or green-) feathered serpent who was also man and king. Kukulcan corresponds to the Aztec Quetzalcoatl and the Quiché Cucumatz in function and in name—all mean the quetzal-serpent. In general Central and South American myth he can be equated with Votan of the Tzentals, Itzamna of the Yucatecs, Bochica of Colombia, Viracocha of Peru, and Sumé and Payetome of Brazil. All these culture heroes were white and bearded and brought various elements of civilization to their people. Kukulcan came to the Mayas from the west with nineteen attendants, all wearing long robes and sandals, all bareheaded. He built Chichen-Itza, and he changed the Mayan religious rites. As a deity, Kukulcan lives in the air where he is ruler over the four points of the compass and the four elements of air, fire, earth, and water. He is depicted with a serpent's body, quetzal's plumes, jaguar's teeth, and a human head in his jaws; he is seated on the cross-shaped symbol of the compass. His feast, the Chickaban, in the autumn month of Xul (end of October), took place at Mani. The chiefs of the tribes spent five days in fasting and worshiping the idols, dancing and keeping vigil. Then, at the feast, offerings were made to Kukulcan who descended from the sky to partake of the feast.

Kul The water spirit of the Ziryen; an evil being living in deep waters. He is believed to have a human shape; he also has wife and children. Kul is known in the western districts of the Ostyak and in the northern part of the Vogul territory. Sometimes he is called *vasa* by the Ziryen. [JB]

kula The system of inter-tribal exchange carried on by a group of communities inhabiting the ring of islands at the easternmost end of New Guinea which includes Murua, the Trobriands, Dobu, and Tubetube: called *hiri* in New Guinea. A hero named Kasabwaibwaileta is associated with the kula myths in Dobu. This is a ceremonial exchange of two items, spondylus shell necklaces and armshells, but along with it ordinary trade is also carried on. The kula is rooted in myth, surrounded with magical rites, transacted in public with special ceremonies according to definite rules, and is based on a partnership which binds thousands of individuals into couples, for each trader has specific partners in his trading area with whom he trades for his lifetime. The number of a man's partners is determined by his rank and importance—the higher the rank, the larger the number of trading partners. No haggling is permitted and much of the trading is done on long or short term credit. The items traded are never directly traded back. According to R. F. Fortune, the armshells go from Murua to the Trobriands, then to Dobu, and finally to Tubetube; while the spondylus shells go in the exactly opposite direction, from Tubetube to Dobu, to the Trobriands, and then to Murua. Since all the products of each place are sent, this trade would result in a famine of armshells in Murua and of spondylus shell necklaces in Tubetube. To prevent this, Murua men take spondylus shell necklaces to Tubetube and Tubetube men carry armshells to Murua, thus making the distribution even around the area. The items traded are never kept for any length of time, but are passed on. Once a man is in the kula he stays in it for life.

Charms, spells, and magic are employed to influence the wind when the kula fleet is becalmed and to make the trading successful. A man's wealth is judged by the quantity of valuables he keeps in the exchange system and his success is usually in direct proportion to his beauty and the magic he employs.

Kullervo One of the heroes of the *Kalevala* (see songs 31–36), the darkest and most tragic person of Finnish poetry. As the last male offspring of the family, after a fratricide between Untamo and Kalervo, he lived as a slave in the house of Ilmarinen and caused the death of Ilmarinen's avaricious wife. Then he fled and met his parents who were then still alive. He took revenge on the adversaries of his family but unknowingly seduced his own sister. Later he committed suicide at the fatal place, and with his death the whole of the Kalervo family was wiped out. One sees in the cycle of Kullervo affinities with the Russian bylini, others with the sagas of Hermanarich and even Hamlet (Amleth) in a version of Saxo (see *FUF* III, VII, X). But it is generally agreed that the runoes about Kullervo are of more recent date than other runoes. [JB]

kummi A festive folk dance type of southern India, for partners (boys and girls, or girls alone). The decorative gestures express a variety of subjects in the different kummis, such as household duties, flower-picking, a milkmaid's activities. The accompanying songs in traditional modes or *ragams* tell the story of each dance. There are well-defined hand claps, by the shoulder, chest, knee, marking a counterpoint with the manifold steps: step-toe, swing-hop, scissors, slide, and others. The ground plans on the other hand are simple, for the most part circular. Kummis may at one time have had a ritual function, but now are purely secular. [GPK]

Kumulipo Hawaiian cosmogonic and genealogical chant consisting of over two thousand lines: composed about 1700 in celebration of the deification of a young chief. It has two divisions, the first dealing with the spirit world and the evolution of the lower forms of plant and animal life, and the second with man's world and the genealogy of the line that produced King Kalakaua and Queen Liliuokalani. The first part, a reworking of old folk beliefs related to those of New Zealand, the Marquesas, and the Tuamotus, has been interpreted as representing either the development of a child from birth to the years of reason or the rise and expansion of the race. Captain Cook heard the chant in 1789. Kalakaua had it printed in 1889, and in 1897 Liliuokalani produced a translation.

Kundrav In the *Shāhnāmah,* the monster Gandarewa.

Kung Fu Tze or **Confucius** (551–478 B.C.) In Chinese writings the symbol, as in Chinese history he was the leader, in one of the dominant modalities of Chinese thinking and feeling. He lived at a time when the Chou dynasty had disintegrated into a welter of feudal states which in turn neglected the code of rights, rites and duties which are supposed by some to have been instituted by the Sage Emperors of the remote past and to have been observed by the founders of the Chou dynasty. At this time a number of political consultants, more or less closely associated with the nobility, more or less learned, often shrewd, ambitious and ruthless, wandered from court to court and set up shop as advisers to the government. Among those were many—Confucius was one of them—who were deeply concerned over the moral and political degeneration of their people. This, the period of the "hundred schools," is one of the most difficult as it is one of the most productive periods in the history of any philosophy. The philosophers of these schools were centrally concerned with views about the nature of man and with the two practical problems of the government of the state by the prince and the government of man by himself. Confucius and his school maintained that man is by nature good and that good government derives from the virtue of the prince as that virtue is projected through the rites. Other schools maintained that man is in part good and in part evil and that good government derives from virtue and law. Still others believed that man is essentially bad and that government is supported by a rigid penal code. Apart from these were, among others, the Taoists, who believed that scholars were pompous fools and that energy diverted to government or observation of the rites could be used better by flowing with the Tao or Way and keeping in balance with the ever-changing forces of nature. The triumph of the group that believed in the essential wickedness of man led, in the Ch'in dynasty, to the burning of the books under the general principle that ". . . a country that loves talking is dismembered. Therefore . . . if there are a thousand people engaged in agriculture and war and only one in clever sophistry, then the thousand will all be remiss in agriculture and war."

The importance of Confucius and his school in the study of folklore is that they directed attention to the traditions and rituals. Though none of the books ascribed to Confucius was certainly written by him, they constitute a valuable repository of custom and belief. They are:

1. *Shu Ching,* Book of History, a collection of records, orations, apothegms, and customs taken from histories destroyed in the burning of the books and covering a period from 2000 to 770 B.C.

2. The *Li Chi* and the *Chou Li,* manuals of ritual and etiquette, presumably as practiced in the Chou dynasty.

3. *Ch'un Ch'iu,* history of the State of Lu from 722 to 481 B.C.

4. *Shih Ching,* Book of Odes. Many of the poems are of considerable antiquity and of popular origin.

5. *I Ching,* on divination.

6. *Lün Yü,* Analects of Confucius, a collection of sayings ascribed to Confucius by his followers.

Confucianism in China is the interaction of two important motifs in the Chinese ethos: respect for the past as symbolized by the teachings and aspirations of the Great Master, Confucius himself, and the general conviction that if people behaved properly and observed the essential loyalties and etiquettes life would be much more serene than it is.

Confucius was a political philosopher and moralist, not a religious leader. As he was not concerned with speculation in general, he was indifferent to the supernatural. He taught that if the Chinese would observe the rites and ceremonies established by the Sage Emperors of a happier period, they need not worry about gods, devils, or immortality. The Confucian Cult is the ceremonies performed in the temple of the Great Teacher whose spirit must be honored by traditional rites; it is the large body of traditions and anecdotes about wise men who, attempting to follow the master, have achieved happiness and success; it is the pious saws used to train people in the proper way of living. [RDJ]

kungurus kankusu Literally, off with the rat's head: the traditional closing formula with which all Hausa folktales end. It is supposedly an onomatopoetic word signifying the sound with which a falling object (in this instance, a rat's head) hits the ground. R. S. Rattray says, "The meaning seems to be that the story is ended, the rat's head is off; that is the end of him"—and the story.

Kuntī In Hindu mythology, the wife of Pāṇḍu and mother of Yudhishṭhira, Bhīma, and Arjuna. As a maiden she showed so much devotion to the sage Durvāsas that he gave her a charm by means of which she could have a child by any god she invoked. Her sons by Pāṇḍu were said to be the sons of Dharma, Vāyu, and Indra. See MAHĀBHĀRATA.

Kunu A supernatural force believed by the Negroes of Dutch Guiana to punish transgressions of the social code by action of the ancestors and gods. It operates automatically, and serious offenses, such as incest or murder, are held to result in the extinction of the family of the offender. [MJH]

Kur In Sumerian mythology, the underworld; also, the dragon-serpent, precursor of Tiamat and Leviathan, which dwelt in the space between the earth and the primeval sea. Kur, in Sumerian, means mountain, hence the mountainous foreign regions, hence land generally. Kur embodies the general belief that the underworld and its powerful spirits lie in or across the mountains to the north, the mountains encircling the world. In the myth of "Inanna and Ebih," Kur is an enemy country northeast of Sumer, but in two other myths dealing with Ninurta and Gilgamesh, Kur is the cosmic dragon. In these, Ninurta and Enki slay Kur and are thus the earliest dragon-slayers we know, perhaps the archetypes of the familiar hero who performs this task. In "Gilgamesh, Enkidu, and the Nether World," Kur is mentioned in a prefatory statement: Enki fights with Kur when trying to rescue Ereshkigal from the dragon (underworld). The story is not completed there, but seemingly has to do with an early Persephone-type myth. In "The Feats and Exploits of Ninurta," the slaying of the dragon brings in its wake a flooding of the earth. Kur had held the primeval waters from rising; now fresh water cannot reach the land. Ninurta builds a stone wall to contain the waters, and all is well again.

Kurena, Kwirana, or **Quirina** One of two clown groups of the Keres and Tewa Indians: specifically concerned with weather control. At Sia women make bowls full of suds, representing clouds, for the Quirina rain ceremony. The Quirina chief has a special medicine (a mixture of powdered turquoise, shell, and certain plant roots in water) which he sprays to the four directions to induce the Cloud People to send rain. At Sia also the Quirina chief is in charge of the masks and directs the dances; formerly the whipping ritual (now lapsing) was under the control of this society. At Cochiti the Koshare and Kurena clown groups take turns, alternate years, in managing the rabbit hunts and the planting and harvesting for the town chief, and also the kick-stick races. At San Juan membership in the Kurena society is from infancy; all sick babies are dedicated to them. Sparrowhawk is the Kurena society special feather.

Kūrma Literally, tortoise. In the *Mahābhārata* and modern Hinduism, the tortoise, or second avatar of Vishnu, in which shape he helped the gods and asuras recover the amrita and other precious things lost during the Deluge. He went to the bottom of the Milky Ocean so that his back might serve as base and pivot for Mt. Mandara. See CHURNING OF THE OCEAN.

In the *Satapatha Brāhmana*, Kūrma is one of the transformations of Prajāpati, creator and progenitor, in which form he created tortoises. Herman Jacobi, writing on the subject of "Incarnation (Indian)" in *ERE* vii, points to the fact that in later mythology many of the exploits of Prajāpati, the great progenitor of the *Brāhmanas*, were transferred to Vishnu. Compare MATSYA.

Kuru In Hindu mythology, a prince of the Lunar race, ancestor of the Kauravas and the Pāndavas whose battle is the theme of the *Mahābhārata*.

kururu A dance of the Guato Indians of the upper Paraguay Basin: introduced by the Brazilian mestizos. It is a walking dance accompanied by a rhythmic song, which is improvised for the moment, i.e. any special occasion, but usually in honor of a host.

kuśa grass or **darbha** The most sacred of the grasses of India (*Eragrostis cynosuroides*), growing about two feet tall. The blades are so sharp that they draw blood from the feet and legs of those walking through it. A story in the *Mahābhārata* accounts for the split tongue

of the snake as caused by licking this grass. In Hindu etiological tales it sprang either from the hairs of Vishnu which were shed during his tortoise (Kūrma) incarnation, or from the grass on which some of the sacred amrita was spilled after the Churning of the Ocean. It is used in nearly all Hindu magic and sacred ceremonies, such as the *upanayana* (sacred thread ceremony), *śrāddha* (rite for the dead), weddings, funerals, and also in menses, initiation, and pregnancy rites. (See *Ocean of Story* I: 55 n. 1.) Rings of kuśa grass are worn on the fingers by supplicants making offerings to the gods. Confectioners and cooks keep some in their jars and other utensils to protect customers from the evils that are likely to infest food during eclipses.

Kuśa was the name of the baby created by the hermit Vālmīki out of pure kuśa grass for Sītā, when he thought her own child, Lava, was lost. The two boys were brought up together and learned all the sciences from Vālmīki. (See *Ocean of Story* IV: 128.)

kusiotem A series of five dances which constitute part of the Bella Coola Midwinter *kusiut* rites. They are feats of juggling by an initiate who professes to have had a supernatural call for the performance of this dance. They include:

(1) Stomach-cutting, by an impersonator of Kuldlkäkmidjut (capable of having his stomach cut). A false stomach is cut, death is simulated, and revival enacted by an impersonator of Snitsmäna, the supernatural woman restorer. The chief deity, Alkuntäm, and other supernaturals also feature in the drama; also, Haohao, a long-beaked bird, Thunder, Hermaphrodite, and others.

(2) Beheading dance, similarly simulated with a false head.

(3) Drowning dance, similarly simulated with a special box above a trap door and a dummy.

(4) Burning dance, including the swallowing of hot stones.

(5) Fungus dance, performed by a woman holding a shelf fungus (*känäni*) which only a kusiut can pull from the ground.

As all kusiut dances, these involve elaborate masks, contraptions, and much hoodwinking. The kusiut are under no illusions and are quite aware of the deception practiced on the uninitiated and awe-stricken members of the audience. [GPK]

kusiut (plural *kukusiut*) A masked dancing society of the Bella Coola, Kimsquit, and neighboring Indian tribes of coastal British Columbia. A member of the society is also *kusiut* as is also "the learned one," a supernatural being, or a person, with power to cure the sick. The society performs dramatic dances during the winter ceremonial season, when initiates are also drawn in.

The name brings with it the prerogative of membership and of executing a certain dance. It might be inherited and have to be validated by gifts; it might be obtained directly from a supernatural patron; it may be altered by a powerful chief. It is supposedly kept in a repository, guarded by the goddess Anoʔlikwotsaix, who keeps up a running comment during the ceremonies. Initiation is open to all classes, and has in fact become all-inclusive.

The opening rite in November is the coming of Noäkxnim in his supernatural canoe: a 27–day sequence.

The closing rite, in February, removes the tabu from the houses where the ceremonies have taken place. Ceremonies may overlap. Ordinarily they last four days: 1) The call comes to the initiate. 2) The wood is cut for the masks. 3) Masks are made (anew for each occasion); some are displayed on a pole. 4) *Nebusam,* "that which is opened." Masks are completed and assigned. In the evening the uninitiated assemble for the dramatic performances.

These performances consist of feats of jugglery as well as masked mime. Most terror-inspiring are the enactments of the Cannibal, the Scratcher, the Breaker (who destroys property), and a series of five *kusiotem* dances. A Mystery dance, which includes a guessing game of three supernaturals, may last for months. Other impersonations include Winwina, who brings salmon, Nunuoska, Mother Nature, who in the drama gives birth to all plants and creatures in seasonal order, Thunder, with a beaklike mask and much commotion, the Sun and Moon in a double mask, and numerous birds and animals.

The masks are elaborate and eloquent, some of them are standardized (as Thunder, the *haohao,* the black Qomoqua); others vary with the "call"; others are free inventions. The action at all times suits the character; Cannibal performs with frenzied contortions, Thunder with heavy jumps, Rainwater with a silent tread. The typical styles of men and women are differentiated. Most male dancers rotate sunwise; they vibrate their hands and fingers, arms shoulder high, crouch during fast stick-beating of the orchestra. Women, with arms held close to the body, vibrate so as to let their breasts shake. Supernatural cries of "Xwa, xwa," and a steady droning by the women add to the mystery.

Deterioration of the society is inevitable in the present era, particularly with the initiation of all men and the consequent depletion of the ranks of necessary spectators. [GPK]

kut In Yakut religion, the soul in its physical aspects. There is confusion concerning the identity and number of souls in Yakut religion, but it is believed that the Yakut divide the kut or soul into three elements: the *buor-kut* or earth soul; the *iya kut* or *ya kut,* the mother soul; and *anya kut* or father soul. After death the soul undergoes transformations, is devoured by the abassylar, remains with the corpse, or is transformed into a wandering spirit.

Kuṭni In Indian folktales, literally, a wise woman: a term of reproach or abuse for an old woman or a witch who does not, however, have supernatural powers.

Kvaser In Teutonic mythology, a being renowned for knowledge and goodness who went about the earth answering all questions and thus teaching mankind.

During the celebration of peace between the æsir and the vanir, both sides solemnly spat into a vase and from this Kvaser was created. The dwarfs, Fialar and Galar, coveted his knowledge and killed him. They made a mead from his blood mixed with honey, which made all who partook of it great poets.

kwakwa A musical instrument of Surinam Negroes: a wooden bench struck with sticks and used with the iron *(felu-ko-felu,* equivalent to the Haitian OGAN) and the rattle to provide a ground rhythm for religious dances.

Kwaku Ananse The Spider of the Akan-Ashanti folktales, which are known as ANANSESEM.

Kwannon The Japanese name for the Sanskrit Avalokitesvara, the spiritual son of the Buddha Amitābha (Japanese Amida Butsu), now among the most popular deities of Japan. Originally male, Kwannon has now become a woman, the Goddess of Mercy. She is represented in art in eight different forms and postures. See JAPANESE FOLKLORE; KUAN YIN. [JLM]

Kwati or **Kivati** A small person, the transformer-trickster of the Makah Indians of the Puget Sound region of Washington. Kwati is similar to Mink, the transformer-trickster-culture-hero of the tribes of Vancouver Island and the adjacent mainland. A cycle of myths about Kwati's adventures is told by the Makah, similar to those narrated about Mink and other North Pacific coast transformers. See RAVEN. [EWV]

Kwikumat Name of the creator in the mythology of the Yuma Indians of southern California. Like all Yuman creators, he was born from the ocean. See BLIND OLD MAN; CREATOR BORN AT BOTTOM OF OCEAN.

Kwoiam or **Kuiamo** Torres Straits war-hero, around whom a whole mythology and cult has developed (Haddon, *Reports of the Cambridge Anthrop. Exped. to Torres Straits,* vol. 1, Cambridge, 1935; and G. Landtman, *The Kiwai Papuans of British New Guinea,* London, 1927). Other culture heroes of Torres Straits and Papuan New Guinea include Waiet and the Brethren. See BRETHREN; SIVIRRI. [KL]

kyaiya A harvest dance of the Lengua Indians of the Gran Chaco, held three times a year: in the spring in anticipation of new crops and renewed food supply; in the summer to celebrate the algarroba bean harvest; in the fall to celebrate the final harvesting of crops. It is performed by a circle of dancers around one central figure (a man) who continually points to the four cardinal directions.

Kyoi Literally, spirit: the creator in central California Sinkyone Indian mythology: identified with the Kato Nagaicho, and the Yuki Taikomol.

L

La Belle au Bois Dormant Literally, beauty sleeping in the wood: title of Perrault's version of the sleeping beauty story. See LITTLE BRIAR ROSE.

Labyrinth The complex prison built by Dædalus for King Minos of Crete to contain the Minotaur. The name probably is derived from *labrys*, the sacred double ax of the Cretans and may have been the temple of the bull cult in Crete. So complicated was the Labyrinth that none could escape once it was entered, until on Ariadne's advice Theseus tied one end of a thread at the entrance-way and followed it out after killing the Minotaur. The name was applied not only to buildings (a building sunk into a mountainside) but to all kinds of mazes. An ancient Delian dance, performed also at Knossos, in memory of the rescue of the doomed Athenian youths and maidens by Theseus, mimed the intertwinings of the Labyrinth, but it is probable that the maze itself was originally intended, as throughout Europe, to lay out the course of a ritual dance. It is supposed that the story of the Labyrinth grew up about the ruins of the great palace of Knossos, with its murals of bull-baiting, etc. The figure of the Labyrinth appeared on coins and vases of the ancient world, in Knossos developing from the simple fret to the complex maze. In Egypt, the great funeral temple of Amenemhet III, still existing in the time of Pliny, was the most famous labyrinth of ancient times. Herodotus visited the part above ground (half of the 3000 rooms) and was told that the subterranean parts contained the tombs of the kings who built it and those of the sacred crocodiles; he says that the edifice surpassed even the pyramids.

Lachmu or **Lahmu** In Babylonian mythology, one of twins, with Lachamu, the first gods born. Apsu, Tiamat, and Mummu existed in primeval chaos, and from the union of Apsu and Tiamat issued Lachmu and Lachamu. They in turn, in some readings of the myth, are parents of Anshar and Kishar, but Apsu and Tiamat may have been the parents of this second pair. Various interpretations of the myth have been made: Thorkild Jacobsen equates them with the silt deposited where sea and river meet; Phyllis Ackerman sees in them the Milky Way serpents, and identifies Lachmu with the constellation Orion. Lachmu was worshiped in Canaan as a fertility deity.

ladder Some of the folklore of ladders is connected with the fact that ladders lead up and down. Thus a dream about going up a ladder is a good dream and brings good luck. To dream about going down a ladder means bad luck. According to Sigmund Freud (*The Interpretation of Dreams*), in dreams "Steep inclines, ladders, and stairs, and going up or down them, are symbolic representations of the sexual act." Some Egyptologists have suggested that the early method of building pyramids in steps was to supply the dead kings with stairways to the sky.

The Tamori of the Central Celebes pacify the tree spirit before they cut a tree down. They bait it with a quid of betel, and set up a small ladder to assist in its descent.

The islanders in the area between western New Guinea and northern Australia believe that the sun fertilizes the earth. This happens once a year. A gaily decorated ladder with pictures of the birds who herald the dawn and seven rungs is put under a fig tree. Great sacrifices are offered and the union of sun and earth is solemnized by orgiastic unions between men and women.

The ladder to the upper world is motif F52. A boy shoots arrows rapidly. They come together, form a ladder, and give him access to the other world where he has a series of adventures similar to those of other other-world travelers. In this the ladder is similar to the beanstalk, tree, rainbow, and other means of ascent.

Anthropological folklorists have striven nobly with the superstition that it is bad luck to walk under a ladder. They note that many peoples have a superstition that it is bad luck to step under anything at all and this, they decide, is "connected in a most direct manner with the menstrual tabu." Australians will not walk under a leaning tree or a fence because a menstruous woman may have left blood on it. In the Solomons a man will not pass under a tree fallen across the road for similar reasons. The Burmese will not step under a house containing women. The Siamese and the Maori will not step under a rope on which women's clothes have been hung. In Rome the priest of Jupiter might not pass under trellised vines because the juice of a grape (blood?) might drop on him. In this connection it is worth noting that the Herskovitses rejected a preliminary Dahomey explanation that one of the reasons for thickening the vaginal labia was to prevent dripping and arrived at the better one that the exercise was for the increase of pleasure. It may be that people all over the world hesitate to walk under ladders because ladders are by nature unstable. A Christian rationalization of the custom of not walking under ladders is that the person doing so breaks the Holy Trinity, symbolized in the triangle of ladder, wall, and ground. Another often heard reason is, So that the paint won't fall on me; but since not all ladders are erected by painters, it is interesting to compare this with the above-mentioned menstrual beliefs. [RDJ]

ladies' chain An American square dance term: two ladies join hands and cross to opposite gentlemen; each joins left hand with opposite gentlemen, who turns counterclockwise. The two ladies then join right hands, each passing back to her own partner, who takes her left hand, and turns her into place. [GPK]

Ladon In Greek mythology, the guardian of the apples of the Hesperides: a dragon said variously to be the offspring of Typhon and Echidna, Phorcys and Ceto, or of Ge. Although Ladon never slept, he was killed by Hercules when the hero came to get the apples as one of his labors. Ladon may originally have been a chthonic god of Arcadia, his connection with Ge, the belief that the Hesperides were originally Arcadian, and the existence of a river and a river god of the same name in Arcadia all being taken in evidence.

Lady Alice   An English ballad (Child #85) known also in America under the titles of *George Collins, Johnny Collins,* etc. In the Child versions, Lady Alice (Anna, Annis) sits in her window sewing.

> And there she saw as fine a corpse
> As ever she saw in her life.

She asks the bearers whose body it is.

> "We bear the body of Giles Collin,
> Who was a true lover of yourn."

Lady Alice is heartbroken:

> "Tomorrow before the clock strikes ten (or seven)
> My body shall lye by hisn." . . .

> Her mother she made her some plum-gruel,
> With spices all of the best;
> Lady Alice she ate but one spoonful,
> And the doctor he ate up the rest.

And so she dies and is buried near his grave. A rose, or a lily, grows from his grave over to hers, but a moral parish priest severs it, or the "cold north-easterly wind" kills it. In other versions, a rose grows from her grave, a briar from his, they entwine in a true-lovers' knot and grow to the top of the church.

The ballad is the counterpart of *Lord Lovel* (Child #75) in which the lover dies out of grief for his mistress, and in some variants of *Lady Alice,* where the man dies for love of the woman, the situation resembles that of *Barbara Allen* (Child #84). S. P. Bayard ("The 'Johnny Collins' Version of *Lady Alice,*" *JAFL* 58: 73–103) has studied the ballad in America. The common American version is *George Collins,* in which the girl is usually Ellen, Eleanor, Helen, or Mary. In this variation, she does not die, but the ballad closes with her lament. The *Johnny Collins* version, on the other hand, shows definite signs of being rather a version of *Clerk Colvill* (Child #42), a ballad in which the lover dies because his supernatural mistress is angered by his marriage to a human wife.

ladybug or **ladybird**   A small, convex, brightly colored beetle, usually red spotted with black, or black spotted with red, which feeds on aphids. It is termed variously "fly-golding," "God Almighty's cow." Some names connect it with a hen or dove, as the French *poulette à Dieu* and Italian *palomilla.* Its origin is believed to be supernatural and its dedication to the Virgin Mary appears in its German name *Marienkäfer* and the term *ladybird.* Other names in other languages connect this beetle with a horse or sheep.

In common with the stork and the swan, in German folklore the ladybug is a child-bringer. It warns of danger; it tells the time of day, forecasts a long or short life, or the value of the harvest by the number of spots on its shell. It is a death omen (black ladybug in Verona). It will help in finding strayed cattle. If you find one in the house in winter, you will receive as many dollars as spots on its back. It is bad luck to kill a ladybug in general British belief, also in India (because it is the habitat of the souls of the dead), and among South Carolina Negroes.

The ladybug is a common love-oracle: girls in England and on the Continent hold the ladybug on their hand or on the tips of their fingers, telling it to "fly away home." Then they note the direction the ladybug takes and believe that from that direction their lovers will come.

British and American children chant: "Ladybug, Ladybug / Fly away home / Your house is on fire / Your children are burning." And the ladybug instantly flies off. In New England and Canada if a ladybug lights on your hand, you will have some new gloves; if it lights on your dress, you will have a new dress. [GPS]

Lady Isabel and the Elf-Knight   A Scottish-English ballad (Child #4) in which a Scandinavian strain of the supernatural has been added to the murderous lover outwitted theme of the European ballad *Hallewijn.* Lady Isabel hears the elf-horn blow, and wishes that the player were her lover. The elf immediately appears and leads her off with him. When they get to a certain place he tells her that she is about to become his eighth victim. She tells him to rest his head in her lap a while, and when he falls asleep she kills him. In the *May Collin* variant, the elf has become simply Mess (Sir) John, and the supernatural element has again disappeared from the ballad. *Hallewijn* and its family of ballads are the most widespread in all of Europe, and *Lady Isabel and the Elf-Knight* is one of the best examples of this ballad.

Lady Jane   Title of one of the variants of the ballad *Fair Annie.*

Lady Maisry   Title and heroine of a Scottish ballad (Child #65). Lady Maisry, courted by the north country lords, refuses them all, because she is pledged to the English Lord William. When it is discovered that she is pregnant, her brother, in an outburst of family pride and patriotism, orders her burnt. A messenger goes to Lord William, and he rides to her rescue, but arrives too late, for the fire is already high. He swears revenge. In the B version, the heroine is Janet, and the story of her lover is gotten from her by her sister, brother, mother, father in sequence—the typical ballad climax of relations.

laeteanta na riaibce   Literally, the days of the brindled cow: the last days of March or the first days of April. In Irish story the brindled cow complained on the first day of April of the harsh and bitter cold of March. So March borrowed a few days from April. But during these days the rains poured down and drowned the brindled cow (*bó raibce*). March still has one more day than April.

La Fontaine, Jean de (1621–1695)   French writer who with his *Contes* was the chief exponent of the merry tale in France. His fame rests upon his *Contes, Fables,* and *Les amours de Psyché et Cupidon.* La Fontaine was born at Chateau Thierry, in an upper middle-class family. He was educated at the college of Rheims and was destined for the priesthood. However, his worldly tastes caused him to relinquish his studies and to spend the last forty years of his life in Paris. Past the age of thirty before turning to writing, he published his first serious work in 1654. The first volume of his *Contes* appeared in 1664, the first volume of *Fables* in 1668. Both the *Contes* (1664–1674) and the *Fables* (1668–1694) are universally appreciated for their originality, grace, and wit. La Fontaine was elected to the French Academy in 1683.

laica   A magician or sorcerer among the Aymara Indians of Bolivia. He bewitches his victims by means of their hair, blood, nail parings, etc., which he manages to get possession of. These he exposes to fire or buries in the earth. He makes images of people or animals he wishes to harm and pricks them with knives. [AM]

Laily Worm and the Machrel of the Sea   A Scottish ballad (Child #36) related to *Kemp Owyne* (#34) and *Allison Gross* (#35) to some degree. The stepmother has supposedly sent the son and daughter to court, but instead has transformed them into the laily worm (loathly worm) and the mackerel of the sea. The son tells his father:

> "Seven knights ha I slain
> Sann I lay att the fitt of the tree;
> An ye war na my ain father,
> The eight ye sud be."

The father tells him to repeat the story; then he goes to the stepmother and asks her where the children really are. She tries to keep up the pretense, but is forced to transform them into their proper shapes again, the boy with the magic wand, the girl with the magic horn. The stepmother is burnt.

lair bán   Literally, white mare: in Irish folklore, the moon. For **Lair Bhan**, see CELTIC FOLKLORE; SAMAIN.

Laistner, Ludwig (1845–1896) German clergyman, scholar, and writer born in Esslingen, Württemberg. Following a period of preaching he became a private tutor in Munich, and in 1880 turned to writing. In his *Das Rätsel der Sphinx* (1889) he advanced the extreme theory that all folktales and legends could be understood through dreams and their meaning, and that folktale incidents had their origin in dreams. He was most interested in dreams of distress and fear. Together with Heyse he published the twenty-four volume *Novellenschatz* (1884–1888) and other cultural and literary historical works. He also wrote *Nebelsagen* (1879), *Novellen aus alter Zeit* (1882), *Der Archetypus der Nibelungen* (1887), *Germanische Völkernamen* (1892), and the epic poem *Barbarossas Brautwerber* (1875).

Laka   A Hawaiian nature goddess, especially goddess of the rainstorm; patroness of hula dancers. She corresponds to the male Rata, the wind god, of other parts of Polynesia. Laka is the daughter of Kapo, Pele's sister, though Laka figures in myth simply as a friend of Pele and not a relation. There are many hymns and prayers to Laka in the repertory of the hula dancers.

Laki Tenangan   Kayan (Borneo) chief spirit who presides over the land (*Dali Matei*) of spirits and assigns the souls to their proper places. Laki Tenangan does not figure in Kayan mythology, but he is glorified and sacrificed to and replies through omens.

Lakshmaṇa or **Lakshman**   In Hindu mythology, half brother of Rāma, the son of King Daśaratha and Sumitrā, who had an eighth part of the divinity of Vishṇu manifest in him. Lakshmaṇa faithfully accompanied Rāma in all his wanderings and fought with him against Rāvaṇa when that demon carried off Sītā. To save Rāma from the curses of the sage Dūrvasas, Lakshmaṇa forfeited his life and was conveyed bodily to heaven by the gods. See DAŚARATHA.

Lakshmī, Lakshmī-śrī, śrī, or **Padmā** (Lotus)   The goddess Lotus of Hindu mythology, spouse of Vishṇu and symbol of his creative energy. In an apocryphal hymn attached to the *Rig-Veda* she is called both śrī and Lakshmī. She is especially associated with the lotus symbol: lotus-born, lotus-colored, lotus-thighed, lotus-eyed, standing on a lotus, decked with lotus wreaths. Wherever the lotus appears in Hindu art, with or without the depiction of the goddess herself, her immanence is assumed.

In the *Rāmāyaṇa* Lakshmī rose from the Churning of the Ocean bearing a lotus, and Vishṇu chose her for himself; in another myth, she already existed at the beginning of creation, floating on a lotus; in the *Purāṇas*, she is the daughter of Bhṛigu and Khyati.

As goddess of rice-growing and agriculture, she is called Kariśiṇī, "the one possessing dung": i.e. fertility-giver to soil, crops, animals. She is the bestower of cows, horses, offspring, health, wealth, gold, fame. Early Hindu kings were married to Lakshmī (along with their wives) as espousing fortune and prosperity and good luck. Men desiring sons, all those desiring offspring worship and propitiate her.

Lakshmī is a development of the very early earth-mother goddess of India; the above-mentioned hymn calls her the mother of created beings, and as such Kśamā, Earth. H. Zimmer (*Myths and Symbols in Indian Art and Civilization*, New York 1946, p. 96) says "this mother of the world was actually supreme in India long before the arrival of the conquerors from the north," and adds that still today Lakshmī is "the greatest power in the Orient."

Lakshmī is usually depicted with two arms, although she is said to have four. She holds, or is seated or standing upon a lotus. She is constantly associated with elephants, especially the white elephant of rain, fertility, and civic welfare rituals. This elephant is śrī-gaja, the elephant of śrī, in its rain association called Megha, cloud. In Buddhist art she is shown accompanied by two elephants. In the temple at Deogarh she is depicted as the humble Hindu wife adoring the feet of her lord, Vishṇu.

lāma (Tibetan *bla-ma*)   Literally, the Superior: a title originally restricted to the head of a Tibetan monastery, now given to most Lāmaist priests and monks in both Tibet and Mongolia. See DALAI LĀMA.

Lāmaism   The European term for the Tibetan form of Buddhism which Tibetans themselves call *Sangs-rgyaskyi ch'ös* or *nang-ch'ös* (Buddha's religion or orthodox religion). This is essentially the same as the Mahāyāna form of Indian Buddhism, introduced in the 7th century A.D. after the conversion of Srong-tsan-gampo. This king had the Tibetan language reduced to writing and built shrines, but left the founding of a sect to a successor, King Thi-srong-de-tsan, who sent to India for a priest to establish a Buddhist order in his kingdom. Guru Padmasambhava (Tibetan Guru Rinpochhe or Lō-pön), a luminary of the Tantrik-Yogacharya school, accepted the invitation and established the order of Lāmas. Lō-pön was from northwestern Kāshmīr, a region famous for the proficiency of its priests in exorcism, sorcery, and magic. He established himself in his new surroundings by vanquishing the chief Tibetan devils, sparing those which consented to become defenders of his religion, guaranteeing them worship in return. In his battle his chief weapons were the dor-je (thunderbolt) and the mantras (magic formulas). Thus Lāmaism became a mixture of magic, Indo-Tibetan demonology, and Śaktiism veneered with Mahāyāna Buddhism.

King Lang-darma tried to destroy Lāmaism in the 9th century but was murdered by a lāma.

The first of the reformed sects (Ḱah-dam-pa) of Lāmaism was founded a century and a half later under the influence of Atisha, an Indian Buddhist monk. Those who refused to follow him were called the old ones (Nying ma-pa). To strengthen their position, they began to introduce more and more of the rites of the pre-Buddhist Bon religion which still appealed to the people. This was accomplished by the "discovery" of new gospels allegedly hidden by Padmasambhava. As more and more gospels (Ter-ma) were discovered, segments of the group broke away, each following a different Ter-ma.

In the 14th century Tsong-kha-pa collected the remnants of the Kah-dam-pa sect and formed from them the Ge-lug-pa, the most important of the present-day sects. The Ge-lug-pa keep the 235 Vinaya rules, carry a begging bowl, the prayer carpet (gding-wa), and wear the patched robes of yellow and yellow hat (pen-sha-snering) which distinguishes them from the other sects. Their Adibuddha is Vajrasattva; their tutelary is Vajrabhairava, and their guardian demons are the six-armed Gon-po and Tam-chhen. Their temporal power, and the title Dalai Lāma for their chief was bestowed by the Chinese Emperor in 1640 A.D. This gave the fifth of their great Lāmas the opportunity to consolidate his power as priest-king. This he accomplished by appropriating other monasteries and by inventing legends to make himself the incarnation of Avalokita.

Of the other sects the black-hat, wholly unreformed, Nying-ma-pa, which is still tinged with pre-Buddhist aboriginal beliefs and practices, is the most important. They worship Guru Padmasambhava in both divine and demoniacal aspects.

Actually the practices of the Ge-lug-pa monks differ little from those of early Indian Buddhist monks; and the demonistic rites, which were borrowed partly from the earlier Bon and partly from Indian Śaivite sources, are practiced by the unreformed sects which are in the minority.

The pantheon comprises a multitude of deities created by embodying the different aspects of a small number of divinities under different names. The pantheon includes the Buddhas (the historical Sākya, as well as the celestial buddhas, Dhyanibuddhas), Bodhisats (chief of which are Maitreya or Byams-pa, Mañjuśrī or 'Jampahi dbyans, Vajrapāṇi or P'yag-na-rdo-rje, Avalokita or Spyan-ras-gzigs, Tārā or sgRol-ma, and Marīcī or 'Od-zer 'c'an-ma), tutelaries or Yi-dam which include Vajrabhairava or rDe-rje-'jigs-byed, defenders of the faith (the Dharmapālas or Ch'os-skyoṅ), the lord-demons or Gönpo, the Dākkinīs, and the eight classes of lesser divinities, the eight classes of country-gods, local gods or Sa-bdag, personal gods, saints, and Tantric wizard-priests whose chief is St. Padmasambhava. Compare BON; GLING-CHÖS.

[SPH]

lambi Conch-shell horns used with drums as accompaniment to the work of a Haitian combite.

lamia In ancient Greek and later belief, a monster who lived on the flesh and blood of the young; a figure with which children were threatened. In myth, Lamia was a daughter of Belus and Libya, who was loved by Zeus and who therefore was punished by Hera. The goddess took Lamia's children; in revenge, since she had no recourse against the gods, Lamia took and killed the children of men. Because of this activity she became, from a beautiful woman, a hideous creature who in addition obtained from Zeus the power to remove her eyes from her head at will. Later belief made of the lamia, of which there were several, a shape-shifting snake with a woman's head, akin to the succubus and the vampire, who seduced young men and then sucked their blood and ate their flesh. Keats' poem Lamia was inspired by a reference to one such story he discovered in Burton's Anatomy of Melancholy, the story in turn being from Philostratus. In the Middle Ages, the lamia and the empusa were sometimes linked as enemies of men. Compare BAPTISM; BASQUE FOLKLORE; LILITH.

Lamkin English-Scottish ballad (Child #93), in two main traditions: one is the story of a mason who built a lord's castle, and failing to receive his wages, murdered the lord's wife and child with the connivance of a false nurse; the other tells of a border raider or outlaw who murders the lord's family, sometimes without stated motive and sometimes because he was denied the hand of the lord's daughter. The first is chiefly Scottish; the second, chiefly Northumbrian. (The ballad was localized all over Scotland; Prof. Child gives 26 versions but there are many more.) Both versions have survived in America, often in very garbled form. Variants which survive in the United States remain remarkably true to the originals. An Indiana version, however, does not mention the false nurse who let Lamkin in but personifies her as Falseness. A fragment of the text, the dialog between the lady and the false nurse who lures her down to the murderer's trap, also survives as a lullaby. So popular was the ballad that Lamkin became a word to frighten children with. It is argued that the first-mentioned tradition is the original and the second merely a beheaded version, which by losing the first stanza explaining the mason's motive lost the explanation of the raider's crime, and that the daughter was a later addition. Some texts give the lord revenge on the murderer and the nurse. One Virginia version names the murderer Ward Lamkin, by corruption of the line, "why should I reward Lamkin." Other corruptions of the name include Bulankin, Bolamkin, etc., from Bold Lamkin. Symbolical or derisive explanations of the name have been offered, but it is probably just the common diminutive of the Flemish, Lambert.

Lammas (from Old English hlaf, loaf, + maesse, mass or feast) August 1; a first-fruit or harvest festival of the early English church, when loaves made from the first ripe grain were blessed in the church. Lammas later became popularly misconstrued as lamb-mass, the lamb-mass being associated with August 1, the feast of St. Peter's Chains, when lambs were taken to church. In England **Lammas wheat** is winter wheat; **Lammas apples** are the first to ripen of the season, i.e. around Lammastide. In Scotland, Lammas was one of the old quarter days for paying rents, thus one of the most obvious Christianizings of an old Saxon first-fruit festival, when tenants also brought in the first new grain to their landlords. **Lammas lands** were lands thrown open to common pasturage on Lammas Day, to be used for common pasturage till spring, having been fenced and privately used preceding Lammas Day. Sir G. L. Gomme identifies this as the survival of a very old village community practice. It was observed in parts of England into the late 19th century.

In the Scottish Highlands on Lammas Day people sprinkled the floors of their houses and their cows with menstrual blood, which was believed to be exceptionally potent against evil on May 1 and August 1.

"At latter Lammas" is an English folk phrase meaning Never (from Lammas being a day of accounts and "latter" meaning "last," à la *Job* xix, 25), the Judgment Day, or day of last accounting, i.e. Never, in this world. Compare Luǵnasad.

Lancelot In Arthurian legend, a knight of the Round Table; lover of Guinevere; father of Galahad by King Pelles' daughter. The 13th century French prose *Lancelot* says that he was the son of Ban, king of Benoic, reared by Vivien, the Lady of the Lake, and brought to Arthur's court by her. Malory's *Book of Arthur* gives in detail the story of the hopeless love of the Maid of Astolat for Lancelot, the betrayal to Arthur of Lancelot's love for the queen, her rescue from the stake by her lover, her return to Arthur, Lancelot's departure to France, the final tragic meeting between the two lovers after Arthur's death, and Lancelot's retirement from the world to lead the life of a hermit. In Malory's version of the Grail quest Lancelot was permitted to see the vessel covered with red samite, but when he approached he was blasted by a fiery wind because of his sin.

The history of Lancelot bears a marked resemblance to that of Gawain in his origin as an Irish solar figure and in the confused transmission of his name through the Welsh. The great Irish sun god Lug bore the epithet Lamfada, "Long Hand." Lug was taken over by the Welsh as Lluch Llauynnauc, Lluch "White Hand." Lluch, in the *Black Book of Carmarthen* and *Kilhwch*, has become a warrior of Arthur's, just as the Irish sea god Manannan, in the same texts, is enrolled in Arthur's train as Manawyddan, son of Llyr. Lug turned up in French romance as (at least) two personages. His name was corrupted into Loth; his sobriquet, under the influence of the French name Lancelin, became Lancelot. The accident that *lluch* as a common noun meant "lake" led to the conversion of the name Lluch into the title "du Lac," and to Lancelot's acquiring a foster mother, the Lady of the Lake, who seems to be descended from the Welsh fay Rhiannon. What is probably an even later addition to Lancelot's history, represented in the High German *Lanzelet* (c. 1200), describes the hero's rearing in an elysian isle by the faery mother of Mabuz, in whom we recognize another Welsh personage, Modron, mother of Mabon, the prototype of Morgan le Fay. Thus new elements from the heritage of Welsh mythology were attached, probably by the Breton *conteurs*, to the original story of Lug. The famous amour with Guinevere seems also to be a late addition. Though her infidelity to Arthur seems to be an old Welsh *donnée*, there is no trace of a liaison with Lancelot before Chrétien de Troyes introduced the theme in his *Chevalier de la*

Charrette (c. 1170). The account in this poem of Lancelot's rescue of Guinevere and his four combats with her abductor Meleagant, who is elsewhere called Melvas, king of the Summer Country, reflects the seasonal myth of the abduction of a flower maiden and the annual combats for her possession between the personifications of summer and winter—a myth which is told in *Kilhwch* of Creiddylad and was enacted in the May Day festivals of South Wales in the 19th century. Thus Lancelot's legend is the result of successive accretions made by Welsh and Breton reciters and French romancers to the original Irish myths of the divine Lug.

Bibliography: R. S. Loomis, *Celtic Myth and Arthurian Romance* (1927), pp. 39–47; *Arthurian Tradition and Chrétien de Troyes* (1948), index *sub* Lancelot. L. A. Paton, *Sir Lancelot of the Lake* (1929). [RSL]

Ländler An Austrian and Bavarian couple dance, very robust and earthy, with interpolated shouts. The step is a heavy stamping waltz performed to emphatic triple-time music, each couple progressing around the room at will. The theme throughout is overt flirtation, particularly during the later figures. Partners may pivot clockwise by joining forearms, crossing hands, embracing in ballroom position, or with the man's hands on the woman's waist and her hands on the nape of her neck. The turns in their lustiness swing the dancers into backward leans. In the climactic figure, the "window"—a *Schuhplattler* figure—two pivots with clasped hands tangle the arms into a circular opening for a coy glance and perhaps a kiss. Then the man may pursue the eluding woman, and, after the catch, swing her in a final waltz. The traditional *Schuhplattler* may follow. The Ländler, a vigorous peasant dance, has been enthusiastically adopted by urban dance groups, among German Americans as well as native Germans. The name serves as a continuous reminder of its origin "auf dem Lande." [GPK]

Land of the Living or **Land of Life** One of the designations of the ancient Irish otherworld, located in the unknown western Atlantic; the Elysium of Old Irish mythology: later conceived of as fairyland. See ECHTRAI. Compare ANNWN; ISLAND OF THE BLEST.

Landvaettir Scandinavian land spirits or guardians. They remained confined to a single area and did not travel about. When they did leave, trouble was sure to ensue. When Iceland was confederated (930 A.D.) a provision in Ulfljot's Law forbade ships displaying figureheads to approach the coast, lest their forbidding looks should frighten the Landvaettir.

Lang, Andrew (1844–1912) Scottish man of letters, scholar, and founder of scientific mythology. He was born at Selkirk; studied at St. Andrews University and at Balliol College, Oxford; and went to London in 1875 to become a journalist. Lang was one of the first to realize that mythology, anthropology, and ethnography needed to work closely together. He was chiefly instrumental in exploding the brilliant but unscientific ideas of Max Müller and the solar mythology school; and was the most effective opponent of Benfey's Indianist theory. His greatest work in folklore was in the application of Tylor's "survivals" method to folktale investigation. However, he did not believe that all parallels of folktales could be explained by anthropological interpretation. Among Lang's writings were: *Ballads and Lyrics of Old France* (1872), *Custom and Myth* (1884), *The Blue Fairy Book* (1889), *Perrault's Popular Tales* (1888), *The Red Fairy Book* (1890), and *Magic and Religion*. Interested in the Stuarts and Scottish history he also wrote *The Mystery of Mary Stuart* (1901) and a *History of Scotland* (4 volumes, 1900–1907). Lang was one of the founders of the Psychical Research Society.

langleik A Norwegian folk instrument still played in some sections, but rapidly going out of use. It has a square-bodied soundbox with one string tuned to G for the melody and 7 others for accompaniment. It is plucked with a plectrum. It is classified as a sort of monochord, a one-stringed instrument originally used for tuning others and later played and fitted with extra strings for harmonic or sympathetic accompaniment.

langsuir, langhui, or **langsuyar** In Malay belief, the malignant spirit of a woman who dies in childbirth. The langsuir is recognized by her long nails, jet-black, ankle-length hair which covers the hole in the back of her neck through which she sucks the blood of children, and her green robe. To prevent a woman from becoming a langsuir, glass beads are placed in the mouth of the corpse, needles are put in her palms, and eggs are inserted under each arm-pit so that she cannot shriek or wave her arms to assist in flight.

The first langsuir was a beautiful woman who, when she heard her stillborn child had become a pontianak, died of the shock and her spirit flew into a tree. Langsuir are fond of fish and sit on the fishing stakes in crowds waiting to steal from the nets. If a langsuir is caught, her nails are cut and her hair is stuffed into the hole in her neck; thus she becomes indistinguishable from an ordinary woman.

Lantern Festival A Chinese festival held from the 13th to the 15th days of the First Moon every year: so called from the practice of hanging elaborate colored lanterns at house doors and on graves. Fireworks are shown; special foods are prepared; and fairs are opened. [RDJ]

Lan Ts'ai-ho One of the Chinese Eight Immortals: said to be a man and yet not a man. As a street singer Lan denounced life and its pleasures. His costume is a tattered gown, wide wooden belt, one shoe, wadded garments in summer, cotton garments in winter when he sleeps on the snow. He rose to heaven on the fumes of wine, and discarded his shoe, belt, and robe on the way. He carries a basket of flowers and is the patron of gardeners. [RDJ]

Laocoön In Greek legend, a Trojan priest of Apollo who attempted to dissuade the Trojans from bringing the wooden horse into the city. Sinon had convinced the Trojans that the Greeks had sailed away leaving the horse as an offering to Athena, but Laocoon disputed this. As he was about to sacrifice to Apollo, two sea serpents emerged on the beach and encircled Laocoon's two sons. The father, too, as he tried to rescue them was gripped in their coils and killed. Taking this as an omen, the Trojans breached the wall and drew the horse into the city.

Lao Tzŭ A Chinese philosopher, said to have been the founder of Taoism. He may have lived in the first part of the 6th century B.C. The *Tao Tê Ching*, basic classic of Taoist philosophy, is attributed to him though modern scholars report that he could not have written it and cast doubt on the very historical existence of Lao Tzŭ. [RDJ]

La Pa Chou In China, a gruel eaten before noon on the eighth day of the Twelfth Moon. Women spend the night preparing it. It contains glutinous millet, white rice, glutinous rice, canary seed, water chestnuts, small chestnuts, red beans, and skinned dates. It is said to have been the food Kuan Yin took with her when she fled from her father's house. [RDJ]

lapēt Burmese tea salad. Eating lapēt seals all bargains and is sometimes the binding part of a marriage ceremony. Sending a package of this tea salad with an announcement is all that is necessary to change one's name.

According to a legend, during the celebration of a feast a drowning youth was rescued by the great lord Yamadi-kyè-thu. In gratitude the boy's mother gave the lord the body of a dead bird which had remained uncorrupted for several years. Yamadi found a seed stuck in its throat. When this was removed the body immediately decayed. Later when Yamadi visited Loi-seng hill, the elephant upon which he was riding knelt down as he reached the foot of the hill, indicating the presence of a relic of Buddha. The area was searched and some bones were found under a ruin. These were buried and a pagoda was built. Then Yamadi called two men and told them to plant the seed. Each, however, held out only one hand to receive the seed and consequently the plant was called *let-tit-pet* (one hand—now shortened to *let-hpet*). He then told them that if they had held out both hands (as etiquette and respect demand) they would have been rich. As it was, they would be poor. Loi-seng hill is held sacred by the Palaungs who hold a feast there in March to worship a tea tree, said to be the one planted there at the command of Yamadi.

lapidaries Treatises on precious stones. Belief in the supernatural properties of precious stones goes back beyond recorded history. An early cuneiform tablet gives a list of stones facilitating conception and birth and inducing love and hate. These ideas of the ancients were woven into the astrological cosmos of the Babylonians, but the early Greek lapidaries were essentially medicinal. However the medical lapidaries of Alexandria derived more from the magic of the East than from the medical science of Greece, and it was not until the later Alexandrian Age that these became combined. The early Christian Church opposed magic and condemned engraved talismans, but tolerated the use of medicinal amulets, and developed a symbolism of its own based on the gems of *Exodus* and the *Apocalypse*. Up to the 13th century the lapidaries of Christian countries, while tinged with magic, are principally medical and scientific, and free from astrology. But this tradition was carried on by the Arabs, and the Spanish under Arabian influence, and by the late Middle Ages it had filtered into Italy, France, and England.

No other literature of the Middle Ages was more purely classical in its derivation than the lapidaries, especially those in the vernacular languages. Because they were a part of the science of the times, rather than magic, they were accepted as fact and where necessary were bolstered by philosophical explanations. It was not until the later part of the 17th century that some of the more incredible virtues of gems were seriously questioned by the authorities. Even then there was no uniformity of opinion, and what one physician discarded as untenable, another vouched for in good faith from his own experience. Therefore it is not surprising that the medieval use of gems persisted into the 19th century and has continued among the folk of civilized nations up to the present. However, the present tendency to associate luck or misfortune with certain stones which is now met in "sophisticated circles" is not derived from any traditions of the lapidaries, but is often contrary to them. See GEMS.

lapis lazuli A rich blue stone flecked with golden bits of pyrites, sometimes the birthstone of December or Capricorn. It is often confused with sapphire, as in the High Priest's breastplate in *Exodus*. In Egypt it was used for figures of the goddesses, especially the figure of Ma (truth) worn by judges, and it was sometimes placed in embalmed bodies to represent the heart which was removed. It is considered a tonic and a cure for melancholy and intermittent fever. It is an emblem of chastity which counteracts the wiles of the Devil and insures help from the angels. The flute of Tammuz, whose sound resurrected the dead, was made of sacred lapis lazuli.

Lapithæ A mythical race of men of the Thessalian mountains. Perithous, their king, was a half-brother of the Centaurs, and when his marriage feast was held, he invited the horse-men to attend. (In some variants, they were invited to join in celebrating the birth of a child.) Ares, not being invited, stirred up Eurytion the Centaur, who tried to carry off the bride, either Hippodamia or Deidamia. The other Centaurs, by now drunk, seized other women. In the ensuing fight, which seems to have been almost a symbolical fight between men and beasts, the Centaurs were defeated and driven from their homes near Pelion by the Lapithæ aided by Theseus and perhaps Nestor. See CÆNEUS. Compare CENTAURS.

Lapp mythology The Lapps are a Finno-Ugric group, about 30,000, living in the polar regions of Norway, Sweden, Finland, and Russia. The Lapps have a rich folklore and a well-developed mythology, but Scandinavian influence is very strong. The God of Heaven is Jubmel or Ibmel (compare JUMALA). The Lapp Thundergod, Tiermes, with bow and arrow as arms, was later given the Scandinavian name Torra-Galles, "old Thorman," and was pictured with one or two hammers in his hand. With his hammer, or with his bow and arrow, he drives away evil spirits who hide themselves everywhere at his approach. At times the Lapps offered him, besides reindeer, large wooden hammers, beautifully carved. The third important god is Varalden-Olmai, "the world man," a god of fertility, borrowed from the Scandinavians. A blood-sprinkled "world's pillar," with which he supported the world, was set up for this god. Other gods are Bieka-Galles, the god of wind; Guuli-Ibmel, the god of fish; and Beiwe, the god of the sun. The sacrifice of the bear and shamanism are very important in the lives of the Lapps (see NOIDE); sacrificial stones are very numerous (see SEIDE); and there are numerous different kinds of spirits and ghosts (see HALDDE, and *MSFO* 68, pp. 85–117). In the sagas we often meet the *stalo*, who is like a man, but unusually

strong, a giant. The neighboring peoples of Scandinavia have given the Lapps the reputation of being a race of sorcerers. From the great number of publications on Lapp folklore and mythology, the latest ones are:

J. Qvigstad, *Lappiske eventyr och sagn*. 4 vols., Oslo, 1927–29. (Lapp text with Norwegian translation).

P. Ravila, *Reste lappischen Volksglaubens*. Helsinki, 1934. *MSFO* 68.

T. I. Itkonen, *Heidnische Religion und späterer Aberglaube bei den finnischen Lappen*. Helsinki, 1946. *MSFO* 87. [JB]

lapwing A crested plover *(Vanellus vanellus)* of Asia, Europe, and northern Africa, with lustrous bronze-green plumage on the upper parts, black throat and breast, white underparts and white-sided head and neck: named for its slow, flapping flight. It is said to be the bird that picks tidbits from the teeth of crocodiles. The lapwing was the marvelous otherworld bird stolen by Amaethon from Arawn, and was therefore one of the causes of the Battle of the Trees. The lapwing is mentioned as the third creature stolen by Amaethon in the ancient Welsh *Triads*.

In the Koran the lapwing is mentioned as one of the prophetic birds of Solomon and knower of his secrets. *Leviticus* xi, 19 lists it as not to be eaten, along with 17 other birds, each of them sacred to some cult or people of the Mediterranean region. Zeus in the guise of a lapwing fathered Herophile, a priestess of Delphi.

In Ireland the term for lapwing is *pilibín*, little Philip. *Cleas na pilibín* is the lapwing trick, i.e. its famous trick of screaming in distress to lure passersby in the opposite direction from its nest (the lapwing nests in open fields); it has even been known to feign disablement in order to mislead nest hunters, only to rise and fly off when about to be taken. Why the lapwing flies in circles is the motif (A2442.2.3) of a north Brittany folktale.

lares (singular *lar*) In Roman religion, beneficent spirits of the household and family, and by extension of the city and state and its various parts: in later times practically identical with the manes or spirits of the dead, but probably originally a special, deified group of those spirits. There were *lares rurales, lares viales, lares marini*, and in general *lares publici* which were distinguished from the *lares domestici*. Of the latter, the *lar familiaris*, the spirit of the founder of the family, was the most important. The lares, the penates, and the manes were all worshipped privately within the household, originally at the household grave of the departed; portions of food at every meal were offered to them. The lares, as the spirits of the dead, were probably analogous to the genii, perhaps identical with them. Their principal public festivals were the Larentalia and the Compitalia. Compare LARVA; LEMUR.

lark Of all the numerous small singing birds (family Alaudidæ) the lark referred to most frequently in folklore is probably the European skylark *(Alauda arvensis)* which sings in flight. The Scottish Highland people say that to know what the lark sings all you have to do is lie in a field and listen. Rural people in Great Britain generally recommend drinking three lark's eggs to acquire a sweet singing voice. Eating a crested lark to cure colic, a remedy proposed by Galen in the 2nd century, was tried by Erastus in the 16th and found "unavailing."

In an Arabian folktale the lark causes an elephant to

fall over a precipice (L315.5). Compare BITER BIT. Æsop has a fable, *The Fowler and the Lark,* in which the lark in the net pleads for her life, that she has stolen only one grain of wheat. For answer the fowler twists her neck (U32).

larkspur or **delphinium**   Any of a genus (*Delphinium*) of tall plants of the crowfoot family with large, irregular flowers, usually blue, having a spurred calyx. The name derives from the resemblance of the blossoms to the claw of a lark; the Greeks called it delphinium from the dolphin-shape of the nectary. In Greek legend it sprang from the blood of Ajax because the letters *ai* appear in the flower. In Roman story a man saved by a dolphin told his friends of his rescue. They set out in pursuit of the dolphin, but the man managed to warn it in time; and Neptune saved it, turning it into a flower, the delphinium. An Italian tale attributes its origin to three warriors who slew a dragon and wiped their swords on the grass; the blue blood of the dragon made the blue flowers and the venom made it a poisonous plant.

The Pawnee Indians have a story of its origin: Dream Woman became curious as to the doings of the earth people, so she cut a hole in the sky and fashioned a stalk from the green material which is the inside color of the sky, with a few flecks of the outside blue adhering to it, and some yellow clay. But when she tried to climb down it, the sun had made it brittle, and it broke into tiny pieces, which are our larkspur.

A tincture of this plant is used for asthma, worms, the itch, vermin, and for poisoning fish. It was considered excellent for the eyes. In Germany young men and women looked at the Midsummer fires through bunches of larkspur, to preserve their eyes for a year. Some tribes of North American Indians called it sleep-root and gave it to their opponents to stupify them when they were gambling. It was a favorite of English witches because of its poison. In France it would keep away ghosts.

Larminie, William (1849–1900)   Irish poet. He is chiefly important in folklore for his *West Irish Folk Tales and Romances* (1893). Larminie was active in the Irish literary revival. He wrote *Glanlua and Other Poems* (1889) and *Fand and Other Poems* (1892).

Lärmumzüge   Noisy processionals, dating back to pre-Christian German rites of demon exorcism. Avowedly for the dispersal of demons which might harm the life about to return into vegetation, during Advent, New Year, and Carnival, bands of maskers used to (and still do in remote sections of Germany, Austria, and Switzerland) wander about in rowdy circuits, producing a din by every conceivable means. *Perchten, Schemen,* and other fantastic personages took part, also beggars who imitated ghostly voices. Exorcism by noise and by identification with the demons was the evident intention. In modern carnival celebrations the din and masquerade persist, but not the ritual purpose. [GPK]

larva (plural *larvæ*)   In ancient Roman belief, an evil spirit: often one of the kinds of lemures. The larva frightened people and worked ill against them.

Lass of Roch Royal   An English ballad (Child #76), telling the story of Isabel (or Annie) of Roch Royal, who was abandoned by her love, Gregory, and was "banished from kyth and kin" when she bore his child. One dark night she came to Gregory's castle with her child in her arms, but she was refused admission by his mother. Gregory dreamed that she had come to him, questioned his mother and found the dream true, and dashed after the girl in a passion of remorse. When he found her, she was drowned with the baby still in her arms. The oldest version in the Child collection comes from an 18th century manuscript. Several fragmentary versions have survived in the United States, generally based on a few stanzas of the girl's sorrowful questions to her departing lover, "Who will shoe my bonny foot, or who will glove my hand?" Sometimes these are so turned around that they are asked by the lover who is going away, "Who'll rock the cradle, who'll sing the song, who'll call you Honey when I'm gone?" or "Who's going to kiss your red rosy cheeks, and who's going to be your man?" or, in a Negro echo of the theme, "Who's going to buy your whisky?"

lassu   The slow part of certain Hungarian dances, especially of the czárdás, the innkeeper's dance. It is a slow encircling movement performed by the men, which is followed by the lively couple dance called the friss. [GPK]

last   An aura of portentousness hovers over the last of anything. The last belongs to the Devil (G303.19.1) is the motif of a Swiss folktale, stemming from the popular saying *Devil take the hindmost* (G303.19). To take the last piece of bread or cake on a plate, for instance, or the last of anything, means you will be an old maid forever. The person last buried in the churchyard cannot rest; he must stand guard for the others until the next one comes. In some parts of Ireland it is said that the last buried has to carry water for the others. The last breath is said to leave the body as visible vapor from the mouth of the dead about five minutes after death. The last words of the dying are regarded as especially ominous or sacred; the last request must be faithfully fulfilled or ill will befall the person enjoined. In Irish folklore, anyone to be rescued from the fairies must usually be snatched off the last horse to pass in the fairy procession. For the folklore of the last sheaf of the harvest, see CAILLEAĊ; FIELD SPIRITS; HARVEST DOLL; KORNMUTTER; KORNWOLF; OATS GOAT.

lasya   The lyric, feminine mode of Hindu *natya.* It is characterized by amorous glances, gracious, supple movements, a drooping head or playful upward tossing. The *ras-lila* of Kṛishṇa and other pastoral themes of gods and goddesses use the lasya style of movement. [GPK]

Latinus   In Roman legend, the father-in-law of Æneas. Various genealogies are given for him; he is usually considered the son of Faunus, but in Hesiod, where he first appears, he is the son of Odysseus and Circe; Hercules is also often mentioned as his father. In the several stories, he both sided with and fought against Æneas; he lived through and was killed in the war with Turnus, etc. From other traditions, it has been deduced that Latinus is probably an aspect of Jupiter.

Latona   The Latin name of Leto, mother of Apollo and Diana.

latrunculi   A game of skill of the ancient Romans, played on a board with men (*latrones, latrunculi,* raiders) moving like the men and kings of modern checkers. A piece was captured and removed from the board when it stood between two opposing pieces. The usual form of the game seems to have been on a 5 x 5 line board, with five men to a side, but a 12 line form (*duodecim scripta*) was also played. Sometimes, as in the Arabic *seegà*, dice were used to determine the moves.

Latura The Nias (Indonesia) god of the dead: brother of Lowalangi, ruler of the sky.

Latvian folklore The first items of Latvian folklore, consisting of ten songs, some proverbs and riddles, and a description of mythological beliefs, were published in *Lettische Grammatik* by G. F. Stender in 1783. The first investigations on Latvian language, ethnography, and folklore were made by a few German clergymen who lived together with the Latvians in their land and were not opposed to the common people. The *Lettische Litterarische Gesellschaft*, founded by Germans in 1828, rightfully named itself the Society of Friends of Latvia, and remained for almost 100 years, until 1913, the center of investigation for Latvian language and literature, including folklore. Its publication, *Magazin der LLG*, contains much material still valuable today. One must mention especially the works of A. Bielenstein. He published two volumes of Latvian folksongs (1874–75); a book of riddles, *1,000 Lettische Rätsel* (Mitau, 1881, with introduction and German translations); a study on *Latvian Archaeology, Ethnology and Mythology* (Riga, 1896), and another on rural buildings and wooden household effects (1907), and numerous articles in magazines.

Certain native Latvians, beginning with Sprogis and Brivzemnieks, also showed interest in their folk traditions, and paid the most attention to the folk poetry. Other kinds of folklore were also collected and published, e.g. Ansis Lerchis Puškaitis (1859–1903) published a big collection of Latvian tales and legends, *Latviešu tautas teikas un pasakas* (7 volumes, 1891–1902). A new, better arranged, and considerably larger collection of folktales, *Latviešu pasakas un teikas* (16 volumes, 1925–38) was edited by P. Šmits (1869–1938), one of the leading folklore workers in independent Latvia and known for his research on Latvian mythology.

The *Latviešu Folkloras Krātuve* (Latvian Folklore Archives) was founded in 1925 and directed by Miss A. Bērzkalne, later by K. Straubergs. In ten years the Archive collected more than one million folklore items, including 406,000 old folk songs, 27,000 new folk songs, 66,000 children's songs, 10,000 melodies, 168,000 folk beliefs, 108,000 riddles, 74,000 proverbs, 54,000 folktales and legends, 41,000 spells and folk remedies, and other items. K. Straubergs published two volumes on Latvian magic practices and formulas (1939), and four volumes of folk beliefs have been published by P. Šmits. In independent Latvia many series of folklore, in emphasized representative form, were published.

Folk song The old Latvian song, *daina*, is short, consisting generally of two lines, and is without rime. The two long lines are generally divided into two each, so that they are written as four short lines. Such a short song is a very old and primitive kind of poetry and we do not know the reasons which forced the Latvian daina to remain for centuries at such a primitive stage while the Lithuanian daina had developed to a considerable length. The Latvian daina is used not only for singing but also for recitation. The fundamental type of metric foot is the trochaic (90 percent) or dactylic (10 percent).

The mixed form of trochaic and dactylic meter is known in some songs used for dancing and playing purposes, instead of instrumental music. The iambic or anapestic meter is never found. The trochaic lines consist of eight syllables, which are divided into four feet or two dipodies, a cæsura occurring after every two feet. The fourth syllable at the end of each dipody is always short. The meter of the Latvian daina was investigated by L. Bērzinš. Another Latvian folklorist, P. Šmits, postulates the possibility of Gothic influence, because the Goths also apparently had verses of eight syllables. Alliteration in the Latvian daina is frequent, but not so developed as in Finnish poetry. Rime, on the contrary, is rare. Very often one finds parallelism, especially as a kind of confrontation: the first two lines are about nature, the second two about human life. From the stylistic figures the most peculiar is the three-membered anaphora.

The present Latvian daina does not go back before the 13th century. In the last three hundred years very few songs have been created in the old fashion. The daina shows very great stability: the first daina was written down in 1632 and three centuries ago the daina was just the same in form and content as today. The daina stands in close connection with work and worship, dance and play. The magic character of the songs is obvious, especially in the songs of familiar festivals, as of birth, wedding, and death, and in the Līgo-songs on St. John's Eve. The epic and lyric elements are mixed. Often mentioned are the struggles and depredations against the Lithuanians, Russians and Poles, but not against the Germans and Estonians, because these last struggles ceased with the beginning of the 13th century and the daina does not go back so far. No hero is mentioned; heroic songs are unknown. The short daina is unfit for a long epic account.

Further, the investigations make clear that the Latvian (and Lithuanian) daina is chiefly the product of women. According to K. Bücher, over 70 percent of the Latvian songs were created by women. Men also have some particular songs, e.g. the so-called oak-tree songs. Twelve men sit around an oaken table in the inn drinking beer; each of the twelve must sing twelve dainas about the oak tree, and no one may repeat a song previously sung. The new kind of longer songs or *singes* of more epical character are also sung by men (compare A. Bērzkalne, *Typenverzeichnis lettischer Volksromanzen* in *FFC* No. 123, 1938). Most numerous are songs about nature and family life. "No gathering, no wedding, no midsummer night's celebration, no harvest festival, no special Latvian *talka* (when they come from the whole neighborhood to do a day's work together and to be regaled), no linen work or spinning was complete without these songs" (Stender). The greatest tenderness and affection is shown in the songs about orphans. The love songs on the contrary are very "cold"; the youth and maid counter each other with mockery which is very far from romantic, and the word *milestība*, love, is a very great rarity in Latvian songs. Humorous songs with biting irony are very common and coarse stanzas are also numerous. The didacticism in the Latvian daina is more pronounced than in the Lithuanian. The short four-line stanza is just the right form for humor or didactic purposes. Neither the Latvians nor the Lithuanians glorify war in their songs. The long serfdom and required work for German barons in Latvia and for Polish squires in

Lithuania humbled the common people, who did not know for what nor for whom they fought. They went to the wars under compulsion and the war brought only calamities for their countries. The Latvians for many centuries were deprived of freedom and sovereignty. In addition the lyric inclination in the mood of the people was not favorable for epic creation.

The Latvian songs often give us a picture of life which is different from that of the last centuries and about which written history knows very little. Often there were mentioned great forests, and the farms were situated on the banks of rivers and lakes, which gave good opportunity for traffic with boats or sledges. In the forests were plenty of wild beasts which are rare today, like bear, deer, aurochs, lynx. Much of the household equipment, even vessels, shoes, and clothes, were made from the bark of lime trees and birch trees. Before the "wood age" there was a "bark age." The farmers lived in small huts with very high thresholds, as protection against unwelcome visitors. The people were divided into three clases: *bajāri* (squires), *saimnieki* (free farmers), and *kalps* (servants, who were not free, usually prisoners of war). Family life was patriarchal and the situation of the wife was hard. Such were the conditions of life about three hundred years ago.

The first ten Latvian dainas were printed in the second edition of the *Latvian Grammar* of G. F. Stender in 1783. Other German clergymen followed his example, and collected and published dainas: G. V. Bergmann in 1807–08, two numbers with 490 songs, and F. D. Wahr, 411 songs, in 1807 (see *Foreign Quarterly Review*, London, July-October, 1831). A bigger and better arranged collection by Rev. G. F. Büttner appeared in Mitau in 1844, containing 2,854 songs. He had an understanding for folk poetry and was the first to examine Latvian songs critically. A very important collection was published by A. Bielenstein: *Latweešu tautas dzeesmas* (Latvian folk songs), 2 vols., Leipzig 1874–75, containing 4,793 songs. We see that the first contributions were made by German preachers. Then the Latvians themselves began to show interest in their folk poetry and ethnography.

The most important work for the Latvian daina was done by Krišons Barons (1835–1923), who devoted his long life to the folk poetry of his own nation. He organized a widespread movement for the collection of dainas; with great patience and devotion he sorted the material and lived to see the task accomplished. His monumental work, *Latvju Dainas*, contains 18,000 items previously published and 200,000 variants from the manuscripts. For each type of daina some variants were given in full or notes about other published variants, and such "basic dainas" number more than 35,000. We must remember that about 90 percent of the Latvian dainas consist of a single four-line stanza; therefore it was possible to put such a great number into eight books. The first volume appeared in 1894 and the last in 1915. The Russian Imperial Scientific Academy supported the printing. The work has a detailed index to the whole collection, in Latvian, in Russian, and in German. Barons also gave valuable introductions and explanations, descriptions of customs and beliefs, which made the texts more comprehensible. The arrangement of the work must be called exemplary. The free Latvian State reprinted a new edition of the work in 1922 in a

representative manner, beautifully bound, in six volumes (eight books). The last book is separate, obscene songs (not for sale).

The Latvian Folklore Archives, in a short time of national freedom after 1918, collected another 450,000 dainas. About 95 percent of these, however, were variants of already published ones.

The new big collection called *Latvju tautas dainas* in six volumes, edited by Endzelins, appeared in Riga in 1928–1930. It contains many melodies, edited by Yurjans, and illustrations by R. Zariņš. Very important are the numerous articles by the most important Latvian scholars who investigated all the former aspects of the life mentioned in the songs.

Finally P. Šmits began to publish the recently collected variants as a supplement to the Barons edition (*Tautas dziesmas*, vol. I, Riga, 1936).

The translations of the daina into foreign languages are notable. The Russian translations of Sprogis (1868) and Treiland (1873) were the earliest. Two small collectionᵉ in German were translated by K. Ullmann (1874) and Inga Bielenstein (1918). The largest English selection of 283 dainas with a useful introduction was made by U. Katzenelenbogen (1935), and also a Jewish translation by the same translator (see *Daines*, Toronto, 1930, containing 140 Lithuanian and 456 Latvian songs; 2nd edition, Chicago, 1936). Many mythological songs were translated by M. Jonval into French, *Les chansons mythologique lettonnes*, Paris, 1929.   JONAS BALYS

Latvian mythology Folk songs are the richest sources of Latvian mythology. *Dievs*, god, or *Debestēvs*, the Father of Heaven, is the supreme god of the old Balts. It is not obvious, however, that he was a ruler over all the other deities and spirits. On Earth Debestēvs appears as a man and Latvian folk songs give us an entirely anthropomorphic picture of him. Another very important god is Pērkuons, the Thunder. He is the most common god among the Balts, but we have no evidence that he was the highest god. The functions of Debestēvs and Pērkuons are often confused. (See L. v. Schroeder, "Der Himmelsgott bei den Kelten, Littauern und Letten, etc." in his *Arische Religion* I, pp. 524–54, Leipzig, 1914). The sons of the supreme god or of Thunder, *Dieva dēli* or *Pērkuona dēli*, often mentioned in folk song, are like the Dioscuri of the old Greeks. The Sun (*Saule*) and Moon (*Mēness*) are regarded as deities and are conceived as living like husband and wife. Often mentioned are the Daughters of the Sun (*Saules meitas*), who play together with the sons of the supreme god or Thunder. The Morning Star, in Latvian *Auseklis* (male) and in Lithuanian *Aušrinė* (female), also appear in the songs. Myths about heavenly bodies, known also to the Lithuanians, but more frequently found in Latvian folk songs, have attracted the attention of the scientists. W. Mannhardt wrote an important study, "Über die lettischen Sonnenmythen" in *Zeitschrift für Ethnologie* VII, 1875. Some folklorists, however, have generalized too much; for instance in *The Mythology of All Races* (vol. III, pp. 316–30), Baltic mythology is described as entirely dominated by the myths of the heavenly bodies; this is an exaggeration. The Latvians also venerated the goddess *Zemesmāte*, the mother of the Earth (Lithuanian *Žemyna*).

The Latvians have many nature deities associated with

the *māte* (mother) concept. For instance: *ugunsmāte*, mother of the fire; *ūdensmāte*, mother of the water; *jūrasmāte*, mother of the sea; *mežasmāte*, mother of the forest (there is also a *mežatēvs*, father of the forest); *laukumāte*, mother of the fields; and *vējasmāte*, mother of the wind. All the deities are very similar, they merely have a different sphere for their activities.

An important and frequently mentioned deity in Latvian folk song is Laima, or Laime (the last word means "luck"), a deity of destiny and birth. She weaves the sheets and covers the bed for a woman in childbed, then the birth will be successful. According to one *daina*, "Laime spreads her silken sheets, but not for everybody; only spreads for wives on their day of delivery" (Barons, 1107). Further, Laima forecasts the happy or unhappy life of the newborn. Generally she is a goddess of pregnant women and serious maidens. She helps modest girls weave cloth for the marriage portion, helps to choose the bridegroom, assists at the wedding, and leads the pair to the life of marriage. Another *daina* says: "That girl kept honor, Laime wove a wreath for her . . . Laime's wagon and God's steed, Sun's daughter is the matchmaker" (Barons 6621). Sometimes Laima acts with two other deities, Dēkla and Kārta, similar to the three Fates. Dēkla takes care of babies. It is not clear if another deity known as Māra is a survival of early times or if she is a popular conception of the Virgin Mary, acting also like a deity of destiny and birth.

The mother of the dead, Velumāte, is the goddess of the underworld. This is an unpleasant realm; even the birds fail to sing there. At funerals the traditional dirges and a dance of the dead were performed. Food and other things for the dead were put in the coffins or the graves. The house spirit, *mājaskungs*, is a dead ancestor; he lives in the fireplace or on the threshold. The ghost of one who has died an accidental or unnatural death, *lietuvēns*, is dangerous; he becomes a nightmare.

A spirit of the dead is called *velis* (Lithuanian *vėlė*; probably the word for devil, *velns*, is derived from this word too. Another word for devil is *juods*, black (Estonian *juudas*, Finnish *juutas*).

The hag is called *Laūme*, formerly a harmless fairy, but today *lauminet* means "to practice witchcraft." The good magician is called *burtnieks*, the bad one *burvis*. The hag has many names: *ragana*, *lauma*, and *spīgena*.

Latvian gods seldom have a clear anthropomorphic nature. The worship of the phenomena of nature, such as the veneration of trees, has quite disappeared. About idols, temples, and priests of ancient times, we know very little. Some prayers are still alive, e.g. "Dear Sun, so white, give me your whiteness! Dear Laime, so healthful, give me your health!" (Barons 27322).

Three great festivals were celebrated by the old Latvians. The feast of spring fell about the time of St. George's Day. The greatest feast in summer was celebrated on St. John's Eve, and was called *Līgo-feast*. It was associated with the worship of the sun and the stimulation of fertility. Above all the Latvians take care to protect themselves, the cattle, and the fields against evil spirits and magicians, who are very active at this time and eager to harm, and who can take away the health of man and the fertility of cattle or crops. For protection pyres were built on the hills. The young people sang and leaped over the fire; wreaths of flowers were hung on their shoulders. There were many special

Līgo songs. Burdocks and thorns were spread before the doors of the stalls to ward against the visits of evil spirits. Houses and gates were decorated with green boughs. (See A. Bielenstein, "Das Johannisfest der Letten" in *Baltische Monatschrift* 23, pp. 1–46, Riga, 1874.) The spirit of the cornfield is named Yumis and is "caught" at harvest time. In the fall the great feast for the dead was celebrated. It was called *velu laiks*, the time of the dead, or *dieva dienas*, the days of the God.

Literature: J. Lautenbach, "Ueber die Religion der Letten," *Magazin der Lettisch-literarischen Gesellschaft* 20, pp. 101–270, Mitau, 1901.

P. Šmits, *Latviešu mitologija*. Righ, 1926.

W. Mannhardt, *Letto-Preussische Götterlehre*. Riga, 1936.

K. Straubergs, *Lettisk folktro om de döda*. Stockholm, 1949.   JONAS BALYS

Lau, Lao, Čauga, or **Jurua** Supernatural beings believed in by Negrito Andaman Islanders. They inhabit forests and the sea, and are also associated with spirits of dead men and women and of foreigners and aliens. They steal the souls of jungle-wanderers. They fear fire, arrows, beeswax, human bones, and red paint. No one agrees on how they look except that they are hideous. Those living in the sea are Jurua in the northern part of the islands and Juruwin in the south. The Lau which live in the jungle are called Ti-miku in the north and Erem Čauga in the south. [KL]

laughter In Egypt's Middle Kingdom, during the reign of Amenemhet I of the XII Dynasty, the *Prophecies of Neferrohu* mentions laughter: "Men laugh with the laughter of pain; there is none that weepeth because of death." Laughter, even then, was not always mirthful. True, the Homeric laughter of the gods of Greece was full of joy, but often it was tinged with bitterness, as was their gusty laughter at the lameness of Hephæstus. It has been noted that laughter in the Bible is usually scornful, not mirthful. Men have always laughed at the incongruous. The hunchback, the dwarf, the cripple, the oddly dressed, the strange and the stranger have been traditional subjects of laughter; perhaps the laughter is the laughter of relief: "There but for the grace of God go I."

And laughter brings its own punishment. If you laugh before breakfast, you'll cry before supper. A Creole saying goes "Cila qui rit vendredi va pleure dimanche" (Who laughs Friday will cry Sunday). The Bosnians say, "After weeping—laughter; after laughter—weeping." Perhaps the same philosophy underlies the saying "Laugh and grow fat." One knows the Devil is laughing when the cock crows near eleven o'clock. The Spanish say that Jesus never laughed. If you can be tickled and not laugh, you can get into heaven. In Tewa town on First Mesa, if you laugh at the jokes during the Hano war ceremony, you must join the society.

Laughter has something of the obscene or not-quite-right in it. The grieving Demeter laughed at Iambe's prankish humor. According to Burton, laughter is a rare thing among the Arabs and a sure sign that the mind is troubled. A folktale of Eastern provenience is keyed to the laughter of a fish (or a fool or wise man or statue). So absurd is the behavior of the queen (who faints when struck by a rose petal—she nightly indulges in passionate cruelties with her lover; or blushes at the proximity of male fish in the pond—she has lovers a-plenty) that the laughter slips out. As this motif (N456) appears in the Old French *Merlin*, the laughter of the sage is caused by the presence of 12 youths among the ladies-in-waiting of Cæsar's wife. In the *Ocean of Story*, a fish laughs at a similar situation. The laughter of the fish occurs again in the story of the judge who condemns a man for some trivial crime. As the prisoner is led away, a dead and dried fish laughs (D1318.2.1). The judge investigates and discovers within his own household many crimes of a much worse nature.

A riddle tale (H583.5) makes the king ask, "What is your sister doing?" The enigmatic answer is, "She is mourning last year's laughter." The sister is nursing the baby of last year's love affair. In Type 1828*, the parson bets he can make half the congregation laugh and half cry. He preaches his sermon with his clothes ripped in back. A stupid ogre laughs himself to death trying to outgrin a dead, grinning horse (K87.1). The king has the trickster's horse's tail cut off. The trickster slits the lip of the king's ass. He is brought to trial, and everyone laughs at the ass. The trickster wins his case by asking how, if everyone laughs at the ass, could the ass keep from splitting its lip laughing at its tailless companion (J1169.5). A foolish woman sets herself up as a doctor. She comes to examine a patient. Someone has told her to look around the bed, and if she sees the remains of food there, to blame the illness on overeating of that food. She sees pillows strewn about and says that the patient has eaten too many pillows. The patient laughs so hard his abscess breaks and he recovers (N641).

Among the tasks assigned to suitors is that of making the princess laugh (H341; Types 559, 571, 1642). The hero accomplishes this by doing foolish or obscene things, or by parading past the princess' window with half the town stuck together to a goose, caldron, etc. (see Grimm #64—*All Stick Together*). The sad-faced princess (F591.1 and 591.2) is of course a folktale relative of the fast-running princess and all other accomplished maidens who must be defeated to be won. An etiological story, on the other hand, explains why women laugh so much (A1372.2). When Eve saw her first child for the first time, she broke into laughter at its absurd smallness. Similarly, a well-known tale (Type 295: Grimm #18; A2741.1) explains why the bean has a black stripe. The coal, the straw, and the bean came to a stream. Straw bridged the gap between banks, but coal burned through straw when crossing, and both fell into the water. Bean laughed so hard that he split right down the back. See EASTER; KING LEAR JUDGMENT.

☞ The origin of laughter is in several instances accounted for in American Indian tales, but not often. Among the Jicarilla Apache of the Southwest, for example, when the Black Hactcin created man, he told him first to speak, then to laugh, then to shout; after that he told man, "Now you are ready to live around here." (Morris Edward Opler, *Myths and Tales of the Jicarilla Apache Indians. MAFLS* 31, 1938, p. 8.) Among the Zuñi of the Southwest the onomatopoeic term *waha*, laughter, is used to designate the festivities of the fourth night of the "big dances" of the Wood and War societies' ceremonies, and other dances; this is the night when Zuñi and Hopi sweethearts sleep together, when everyone is happy and couples have *waha*. See HUMOR. [EWV]

lauma In Motu (New Guinea) belief, the spirit or soul which leaves a man at death and then leads an independent existence. The lauma can also leave the body temporarily, its absence causing illness. Compare ARU. See SOUL LOSS.

laurel An evergreen shrub (*Laurus nobilis*) of the Mediterranean region: sacred to Apollo, and in Laconia, sacred to Artemis. It is associated with purging and purification because Apollo was the great purifier. It was believed to endow prophets with visions, and is associated with poetry partly because, as evergreen, it symbolizes immortality, and largely because its intoxicating properties are associated with poetic inspiration. The Pythian priestess at Delphi, for instance, chewed laurel leaves to induce oracular powers. Victors in the Pythian games were crowned with laurel. The Greek nymph Daphne was regarded as the personification of the laurel. In Rome victorious generals sent messages of their victories to the Senate wrapped in laurel leaves. It has come to symbolize both victory and peace. See BAY TREE.

Laurel has been widely used as a love charm. In England if a pair of lovers pluck a laurel twig and break it in half, each keeping a piece, they will remain lovers. On St. Valentine's Day place two leaves on your pillow and you will dream of love. Burning laurel leaves will also bring back an errant lover. In Holland the house door of a newly married couple is festooned with laurel. Medicinally laurel is effective in rheumatic fever, as a purgative, and as a vermifuge. It cures epilepsy and madness, but causes forgetfulness.

The American mountain laurel (*Kalmia latifolia*), sometimes called calico bush, is the state flower of Connecticut and Pennsylvania. The foliage is poisonous to livestock and the roots are extremely poisonous. Indians of Pennsylvania are said to have used it for suicide. It is also thought that the flesh of birds which have eaten laurel seed is rendered poisonous. The wood is sometimes called spoonwood because the Indians carved spoons from it. It is used as a purgative, and the juice is dropped into the ears to cure deafness. In Lancaster county, Pennsylvania, a decoction of mountain laurel is used externally for the itch; in Labrador too the leaves of *Kalmia* are mixed with tobacco as a mange cure, the *Kalmia* in this case, however, is probably *K. angustifolia*, or sheep laurel.

In folktale are found various magic laurels (D965.9), the laurel which causes forgetfulness (D1365.1.3), the person transformed to a laurel (D215.1), and the wishing-laurel (D1470.1.3). This is found in a Rumanian version of *The Slippers of the Twelve Princesses* in which the cowherd hero plants laurel branches which grow into wishing-trees and produce magic clothes.

Lauterbach A Swiss couple dance, named for the town and river of Lauterbach, just across the border of Württemberg, Germany. It is a waltz of central European type, resembling the Polish *kujawiak* and German *Neubayrische* in the swinging of joined hands and "wringing the dishrag" under raised arms. It shares the gracious smoothness of these dances rather than the robust vigor of the *Ländler* and *Schuhplattler*. A simple turning waltz always recurs as a kind of chorus, with a new first figure on each repetition of the tune: a waltz balance or a stamp in shoulder-waist position (man's hands on woman's waist, hers on his shoulders), or the twisting under the arm-arches. [GPK]

lavender A sweet-scented herb (genus *Lavandula*) which has been used since early times as a perfume. The early Romans used it in their baths. It was called a "comfort to the brain" by the English herbalist, William Turner, in the 16th century, and described as a "precious herb" in the 17th. Christian legend says that originally it had no scent, but the Virgin Mary once dried the swaddling clothes of the infant Jesus on it; since then it has had a heavenly perfume.

It was early used medicinally for colds and for ailments of the head. Either the temples were bathed with lavender water or the fresh sprigs were put in a quilted cap to be worn on the head. Formerly in Britain it was used in a folk remedy for epilepsy. It is a stimulant tonic, and a great help for colic and stomach cramps. It cures dropsy, palsy, vapors, faintness, catalepsy, laryngitis, muscular aches, stiff joints. The odor alone is conducive to long life. In World War I it was used as an antiseptic swab for wounds.

Lazar and Petkana A Bulgarian popular ballad featuring the dead rider motif. It is a development of the Greek *Constantine and Arete*.

lead The soft, heavy, dull, greyish mineral considered by the ancients one of the base metals, in the dominion of Saturn. Witches, wizards, demons and the like were invulnerable to leaden bullets or shot, and could only be killed with silver; but this was not true in Vedic magic which made common use of lead against demons and sorcerers. On the other hand, a leaden arrow will kill the love of a youth. Leaden caskets were sometimes used to protect objects, especially religious relics, from demons and also prevented their virtue being dissipated.

Lead was one of the substances most frequently used by alchemists throughout the ages in attempts to make gold, hence its various compounds were known and often used in early medicine, especially against conception and in venereal infections. Because of its dull color it was used in destructive charms with imprecations and curses written upon them. In the 11th century charms on leaden tablets were used both against conception and for fruitfulness in orchards. In the 2nd century, Galen, perhaps with tongue in cheek, recommended for the bite of a sea serpent application of lead and a slice of the serpent itself. The Styrians use a lead bullet under the tongue to cure toothache, and in Sussex, England, an egg cup full of lead shot is recommended to cure rising of the lungs. The sweating of leaden vessels is a sign of immediate rain. In England, lead medals for pilgrims were made by the sacristans. In the 14th century three of the clergy in England made a leaden image in the belief that, once a month, it would speak to them and tell the secrets of alchemy and buried treasure, but because they constructed it under the wrong constellation, it failed. (See BRAZEN HEAD.) In Texas a person suffering from boils takes one shot for every boil he has ever had to purify the blood. Some early explorers in Texas carried a lead bullet under the tongue to allay their thirst when there was no water available. Leaden rings are still worn there to cure rheumatism. Mexican babies are given a cartridge to mouth while teething if there are no rattlesnake rattles available. A bullet, or other piece of lead hung about the neck or carried in the pocket cures nosebleed, and both cures and prevents poison oak.

leaf Leaves function in folklore in many ways, as badges, in divination, as medicine, and as charms against witchcraft and evil spirits. Everyone is familiar with the emblematic Canadian maple and Irish shamrock leaves. Leaves on the water or blown by the wind are a sign of storm; leaves turned inside out are a sign of rain. In Germany and parts of England, it is said that if you catch a falling oak leaf you will be free of colds during the entire winter; in the United States, you will have twelve months of happiness. In parts of England, they say that if the ash is in leaf before the oak, there will be a thorough soak, but "oak before ash, only a splash."

In folk healing, leaves are used either bound to the skin as poultices or mixed in medicines. In many parts of the world, they are placed on houses and barns at certain times of year to drive away evil spirits and to neutralize witchcraft. See HERBS.

leaf dance A rare but interesting dance of the southeastern North American Indian tribes. Men and women shuffle in a counterclockwise circle and flutter their hands, to antiphonal songs typical of these tribes. Until recently the Yuchi *yacacti* was known to express gratitude for the appearance of leaves in the spring. [GPK]

Leander The youth of classical legend who swam the Hellespont to visit his beloved Hero. See HERO AND LEANDER.

leap dances High leaps are the extreme expression of the vital impulse and by sympathetic magic are believed to communicate vitality to the crops. Peasants of Germany and Bohemia have adhered to the custom of leaping high, for as high as they can leap, so high will the crops grow. That has been the significance of the Austrian *Schemenlaufen*, the running and leaping of maskers in a serpentine course at Carnival time, a pagan vegetation rite which has survived through the Middle Ages until now. Similar vestiges of this belief remain in the Morris caper and the leaping of the leader in the Serbian *kolo* and Greek *syrtos* and *hasapikos*. The medieval *espringale* was a polite version.

In war dances the leaps are partly a display of physical prowess and partly a magic inducement to crops. In couple dances the man shows off to his mate, but also continues an ancient fertility cult, as in the Russian *prisjadka*, the German *Schuhplattler*, Basque *aurresku*, and Norwegian *Halling*.

Sometimes the distorted leaps are induced by trance for therapeutic purposes, as in the case of the ecstasies of Siberian shamans, the Huichol Indian *hikuli* dancers, the possessed "servants" in the vodun cults.

The capers of ceremonial and secular clowns probably originate in fertility rites involving possession by a spirit, as the Yaqui Indian *chapayekas* and Taos *k'apio*. Much of the demonic significance is retained in the leaps connected with puberty rites, as the Apache gahe. The showy leaps of stage dances, as the *entrechat*, may have a remote ritual ancestry but are shorn of any significance except display.

One of the stage dances, a feminine exhibition, was the cancan, popularized in Paris about 1830. Its special feature was a jumping high kick with simultaneous lifting of the skirts. Dancers vied in kicking off the hats of male spectators. This exhibitionism and high kicking characterize many courtship and fertility dances, from Egyptian mortuary dances to the Breton *triori* and the modern Big Apple. The Basque *aurresku* presents a male counterpart. The *cancan* initiated a fad of vicarious sexual stimulus in the denuded kicks of the Tiller and Ziegfeld girls, burlesque shows, and Roxyettes. [GPK]

Lear Lear seems to be almost entirely a creation of Geoffrey of Monmouth, who in his *History of the Kings of Britain* (c. 1136) names Leir as the son and successor of Bladud, credits him with the foundation of Leicester (a characteristic sample of Geoffrey's misplaced ingenuity), and tells the famous story of the vain, senile king and his daughters (M21). Though Perrett in *Palaestra,* XXXV, collected many folktales from many lands which tell substantially the same story, these may well be of modern literary origin, offshoots of Shakespeare's play or some other version. It seems very probable that Geoffrey coolly stole the theme from the Buddhist parable of the man and his three friends (H1558.1), since the legend of Barlaam and Josaphat was translated into Latin at Constantinople in 1048, and thus made the parable available to Geoffrey. The theme of a man who in distress appeals to his three friends in turn, is rejected by the two whom he had favored most, and is succored by the one whom he had spurned, needed only to be transferred to a king and his daughters to give us the essential plot of Leir. The names of Leir and Cordeila, however, do seem to have their origin in Welsh tradition, since it was Geoffrey's practice to attach his fictions to venerable names in British lore and pseudo-history, for instance, in the cases of Brennius, Bellinus, Kimbelinus, and Merlin; and we find in *Kilhwch* (c. 1100) Creiddylad, daughter of Lludd, Lludd being a name elsewhere confused with Llyr. Presumably, then, Geoffrey Latinized the names Llyr and Creiddylad as Leir and Cordeila. Of Llyr we know nothing more than that he was the father of two figures prominent in the *Four Branches of the Mabinogi*, Bran, king of the Island of the Mighty, and Manawyddan; but his name is almost certainly taken over directly from Irish *Lir*, the genitive case of *Ler,* meaning "sea," and familiar in the combination Manannán mac Lir, i.e. "son of Ler." In early mythology Ler himself seems to have had no story, but there appears in manuscripts of the 18th century a romance, *The Tragedy of the Children of Lir*, which tells how a jealous stepmother transformed the three sons and a daughter of Lir into swans, endowed with the gift of exquisite singing, but doomed to frequent the lakes and shores of Ireland for nine hundred years. At the end of that time the swans returned to the home of Lir and found the site deserted. Mo Chaemoc heard their lovely song and joined the pairs with silver chains. When Lairgren, king of Connaught, seized them, they were changed into withered old men and an old woman. They were baptized, died, and went to heaven. It seems possible that this late romance contains the Celtic kernel of the famous medieval legend of the Swan Children, of which there is an English version, *Chevelere Assigne*, "Knight of the Swan" (L. A. Hibbard, *Mediæval Romance in England*, pp. 239–52). Here too we have the motifs of the jealous stepmother, the children transformed into swans, and the silver chains. [RSL]

learned damsel A character of folktale, especially of Eastern tales, but met with also in European stories. The learned damsel, by her wit and lore, defeats the king and his savants and thus proves that femininity is not necessarily synonymous with stupidity. The Queen of Sheba, coming to Solomon, finds herself meeting her master in wit, but nevertheless impresses him with her learning. Shakespeare's Portia outdoes the men by discovering a defense for Antonio. Clever Else outriddles the king. Sheherazade leads her husband-king on and on from night to night with her knowledge not only of stories but of when to end the nightly episode. And in one of Sheherazade's tales, "Abu al-Husn and His Slave Girl Tawaddud" (Burton V: 189–245), appears the ultimate in feminine learning. Tawaddud is beautiful and resourceful. When her master runs through his patrimony, she has him bring her before the Caliph Harun al-Rashid. There she disputes with and defeats successively, at a wager of the clothes on their backs, two doctors of the law of the Koran and traditions, an exegete profound in syntax and lexicography, a physician (she embarrasses him with the riddle of the button and the buttonhole), an astronomer, a philosopher, a rhetorician, a chess master (giving him odds of queen, rook, and knight in the third game), a backgammon expert, and finally plays the lute surpassingly. Harun buys her for 100,000 dinars, then gives her back to Abu al-Husn with a gift for herself of 5,000 dinars.

Leave Her, Johnny, Leave Her A capstan chanty sung as the last capstan rally of a voyage, when the ship was under tow for landing or already at the pier. It expresses the candid sailor opinion of the ship's accommodations, management, and officers, and is derived from one of the oldest of the chanties sung on Atlantic packet ships, *Across the Western Ocean*. Sometimes a pumping version was sung at sea: "A dollar a day is a sailor's pay / To pump all night and work all day," etc.

lectisternium A meal for the gods, often the great twelve of the Greek deities under their Roman names: an ancient Roman public religious custom, originally on special occasions but in later times more frequently. Livy says the first was ordered in 399 B.C. by the Sibylline books. The gods were represented by statues, busts, or bundles of herbs made up to resemble busts (*capita deorum*), reclining on a couch (*lectus*), before which was placed the food. There is some evidence that the practice originated in Greece, for example the Greek *theoxenia* is similar except that the gods themselves were the hosts, the entire atmosphere of the ceremony is Greek, etc. A similar feast of the gods formed part of the Etruscan religion. The Hebrew shewbread table and the general European Christmas feast for the dead seem to have similar conceptual roots.

Leda In Greek mythology, the wife of Tyndareus of Sparta. She bore children to Zeus, who had intercourse with her while he was in the form of a swan, but which of her four children were his is disputed. Of the four, Clytemnestra was the daughter of Tyndareus, and Helen was the daughter of Zeus. But whether one or both of the Dioscuri, and if one which one, was the son of the god is a matter of conjecture. In some versions of the story, Helen is born from an egg, laid either by Leda or by Nemesis (and hatched by Leda).

leek An herb (*Allium porrum*) of the same genus as the onion, used in cooking. The leek is the national emblem of Wales because it was worn as a distinguishing badge either against the Saxons or at the battle of Poitiers. The fact that it was said to carry its wearer unscathed to victory in battle probably influenced its choice. It is worn as official insignia on the uniform of the day by the Welsh Guards Regiment on St. David's Day. Leeks planted in the waning moon will be small and sour; those planted in a waxing moon will grow large and savory. Nero is said to have eaten leeks several days each month to clear his speaking voice. The juice of the leek is good for sore eyes, rough hands, and chilblains. Compare HOUSE LEEK.

left allemande and right hand grand An American square dance term. Each gentleman joins left hands with the corner lady, i.e. the lady on his left, turns her around once, then joins right hands with his own partner, and without turning her proceeds around the set in grand right and left until partners meet again. [GPK]

Legba, Legua, Leba, or **Liba** These variant New World pronunciations all represent the name of the Dahomean trickster deity, god of entrances and cross-roads, the youngest son of the creator. In Dahomey, the first form given above is heard near the native capital, Abomey, while Legua is the southern coastal pronunciation. Legba functions in the belief systems of the Negroes of Dutch Guiana, Brazil, Trinidad, Cuba, and in the *vodun* cult of Haiti and New Orleans. Where Yoruban influence is strong, as in Brazil, Trinidad, and Cuba, Legba is known by his Nigerian counterparts Elegbara and Eshu (*Exú*, the common Portuguese rendering). In the New World, Legba is generally regarded as an old man who goes about in tatters, and whose function in cult rituals is to "open the way" for the other gods to come and possess their devotees. For this reason, his songs are sung first at all rites. In New World syncretism, Legba is often equated with the Devil, thus confirming a tradition begun in West African missionary writings. The identification is, however, untenable when the total significance of the two beings thus identified is taken into account. [MJH]

legend Originally, something to be read at religious service or at meals, usually a saint's or martyr's life—thus the *Golden Legend* of Jacobus de Voragine, a collection of saints' lives. Legend has since come to be used for a narrative supposedly based on fact, with an intermixture of traditional materials, told about a person, place, or incident. The line between myth and legend is often vague; the myth has as its principal actors the gods, and as its purpose explanation. Thus the Hercules stories may be considered to some extent myth (he is semidivine, he made the Pillars of Hercules, etc.) or as legend (Hercules was a lord living at Tiryns). The legend is told as true; the myth's veracity is based on the belief of its hearers in the gods who are its characters. Compare LOCAL LEGEND.

Legend of the Camphor Princess Title of a Malay legend in which seven men went into the jungle hunting camphor. Six of them worked at camphor-collecting while Bonsu, the youngest, did nothing but sleep. After they had worked for about 14 days, the six who had worked returned to their village with the camphor they had collected. But Bonsu did not go with them.

One day while fishing, Bonsu saw a princess bathing in a stream. He caught her by her hair and she took him into her house, a camphor tree. It was very delightful but after seven days Bonsu grew sad. When the princess asked why, he answered that he was thinking of his wife and children. Then the princess told him to bring his carrying-basket. She combed her hair over it, and as she combed camphor fell from her hair and filled it. When he was ready to leave she warned him not to tell where he had been. So Bonsu went home, but after seven more days he returned, persuaded the camphor princess to return to the village with him, and built a house for her there.

The Raja heard of Bonsu's good fortune in camphor-hunting and called him to his palace. He ordered him, on threat of death, to show how he searched for camphor and to recite the magical verses he used (which the princess had taught him). As soon as he started to sing them, his wife was changed into a cicada and flew away. When Bonsu discovered that she had gone, he took his child and followed the sound of the cicada as she flew to the jungle and he was never seen again.

legless and blind boys cured A motif found in all the Apache Indian mythologies, in which two boys, one born without eyes, and one born without legs, were abandoned by the people when they moved on to a new place. In the Chiricahua Apache version (presented by Morris E. Opler, *MAFS* 37) the boys were left with no food, only some water in a water jar. They did not know what to do; but finally decided to follow their own people. The blind boy with legs carried the legless boy with eyes, who told him where to go. But without food and water they did not get far, and they were dying when the gahe found them. The gahe (the Chiricahua and Mescalero Apache supernaturals) took them into the mountain and saved them. The two boys prayed to the gahe: the eyeless one prayed for eyes and the legless one prayed for legs. Then black clouds covered the boys; lightning and thunder were over and around them; and when the clouds rolled away, the gahe were dancing, and both the boys could see and both could walk. The gahe directed them back to their own people, and the boys told their parents all that had happened to them.

This story is a typical abandoned children story in that the boys were abandoned for economic reasons, were helped by supernatural beings, returned and forgave their parents. But its primary function is to reveal the nature of the gahe. Compare BLIND MAN CARRIES LAME MAN.

legong A Balinese drama-dance performed in temple, street, or village square, by two little girls, the *legongs,* and their attendant, the *tjondong.* The delicate, elegant gestures make this dance the epitome of femininity; their detached formalism and staccato angularity are expressive of the restrained tenseness of Balinese culture. The *pelegongan* orchestra accompanies the dance with a complex array of gongs, drums, cymbals, and xylophone-types. The costumes are of silk overlaid with gold leaf, and frangipani flowers.

The *tjondong* starts the performance with a fan dance. The *legongs* perform a duet of sharpest precision, fluttering their shoulders, hands, fingers, eyes, jerking their heads, twisting their arms. Then they enact with stylized gestures the capture of the Princess Rangkesari by King Lasem. But Lasem is killed in a symbolic battle, while the *tjondong* mimes an ominous blackbird.

The *legong* appears a human elaboration of the archaic shadow play, the *wayang kulit*, in its puppet-like abstraction. Like all Balinese theater dances, it involves years of arduous training and fantastic control and endurance. Though not religious, the *legong* is introduced by ceremonial dedication of the dancers. Its exponents move as in a trance through the patterns hallowed by age-old tradition. [GPK]

legs fed with grease An old practice of the Apache Indians (Chiricahua, Mescalero, Jicarilla, Lipan). Men rubbed their legs with grease, invoking them to be good runners. Once there was one man who refused to do this; he ate all his meat and all his fat and grew a big belly. When white enemies came everybody could run to safety except the fat man. His legs said, "You never fed us. Now run on your belly." Contemporary Apache still rub their legs with grease (see Opler, *Myths and Legends of the Lipan Apache Indians. MAFLS* 36:288).

Leib-olmai Literally, the alder man: a tutelary forest spirit of the Lapps. He was the guardian spirit of forest animals, especially the bear. His image is occasionally found painted (bear-shape) on Lapp drums. Bows and arrows were offered up to him. Ethnologists assume a relationship between Leib-olmai, the alder man, and bear-worship, for this reason, because he was tutelary to the bear, and because alder juice was used as an integral element in the bear-hunting ceremony. Following the description of Randulf, Leib-olmai is a bear-man or bear-god, who protects the bear, the holy animal. [JB]

Leif Ericson or **Ericsson** See page 618.

Lei Kung The Chinese Thunder God: one of the 80 members of the Ministry of Thunder. His icon is a figure with an ape head, eagle beak, and bird talons for hands and feet. A mallet is shown in his left hand, and barbs in his right. Drums and lightning surround him. Lei Kung punishes the wicked and frequently appears in the accounts of shape-shifters who attempt to attain immortality by illegal sexual means. He also strikes with thunderbolts those who throw rice wastefully onto the earth or destroy cereals. [RDJ]

leippyā In Burman belief (also to some extent, Kachin, Chin, Karen belief), the soul which is materialized in the form of an invisible butterfly. The soul, as an independent entity, can enter or leave the body at will. While it is away the person becomes ill, dreams, or faints. If the leippyā is captured by an evil spirit while wandering, the person will become ill or die. The leippyā leaves a dead body but hovers in its neighborhood until the corpse is buried. A captured leippyā is recalled by making offerings to the spirit which captured it in a ceremony called *leippyā-hkaw*. The Karen *la* is sometimes believed to be a soul but the word is usually considered synonymous with nat rather than with leippyā. See SOUL LOSS.

lejtö A Hungarian folk dance step: a sideward progression of a hop and two steps. [GPK]

Lemba A deity, of Congo origin, worshipped in the African cults of Haiti and Brazil. [MJH]

Lemminkäinen The hero of the *Kalevala* (see songs 11–15, 20, 26–30). He has many other names: Ahti, Kaukomieli, or Kauko. He is young and cheerful, a great adventurer who loves quarrel and war (with the people of Pohjola), a seducer of women (the Don Juan of the Finns). He was murdered by an old Lappman and rescued by his mother. Some parts of the Lemminkäinen cycle have similarities to the Scandinavian Balder myth (see K. Krohn in *FUF* V, 1905, pp. 83–138). [JB]

lemon A tree (genus *Citrus*) having an oval, yellow fruit; also, the fruit. Because it is a small, bitter fruit, it has come to mean the poorest of a lot, e.g. "You certainly picked a lemon." From early times the juice has been used in preparations for the hair and skin, as a laxative, cold remedy, and for upset stomach. Chewing slices of lemon cures toothache, and lemon peel was a common dentifrice in the 15th century. In Europe and the Balkans both the juice and rind are used as a contraceptive and to detect the presence of venereal infection (Casanova mentioned both uses). A 12th century Hebrew writer recommended the peeled pips in a compress for wounds and British pharmacists used lemon juice to dissolve pearls for a remedy for epilepsy and wherever salts of pearl were prescribed. In the folk medicine of Texas and the Southwest, borage boiled in lemon juice is recommended for fever; a sliced lemon boiled in a cup of water, cooled, and administered in the mornings is given for malaria or colds; and a cold-water lemonade is good for measles. In Hawaii the juice is recommended for dizziness. Some have claimed that drinking lemon juice is a cause of cancer. Others recommend lemon as a seasickness cure, but they add that if it is not effective, at least it tastes no worse coming up than it did going down. Writing the name of an intended victim on a slip of paper and sticking pins through it into a lemon to cause suffering and death was a form of witchcraft practiced until very recently in England, Sicily, and Italy.

lemur (plural *lemures*) In ancient Rome, a ghost without surviving family; one of the spirits of the departed: usually equated with the larva and hence an evil spirit. Some believed the lemures to be all the spirits of the dead, which were of two kinds: the lares or good spirits, and the larvæ or evil spirits. The lemures were appeased annually at the Lemuria.

Lemuria or **Lemuralia** A yearly festival held in ancient Rome on the 9th, 11th, and 15th of May to appease the spirits of the dead: supposed to have been introduced by Romulus after he had killed Remus and said to have been called originally the Remuria (from Remus). During the observance, the participants walked barefooted, cleansed their hands three times, and cast black beans behind them nine times. On the third day, the Ides of May, a merchants' festival was held to make business prosper; on the same day, some 30 images made of rushes were thrown into the Tiber. The period, like the entire month of May, was unpropitious for marriages; a May marriage would not prosper. Compare LEMUR.

lentils An Old World leguminous plant (*Lens culinaris*) having pale blue flowers and broad pods containing edible seeds. The use of the seeds as food goes back to very ancient times: Esau sold his birthright for a mess of lentil pottage, for instance (*Gen.* xxv, 29).

They were highly prized in ancient Egypt, but later were regarded as a cause of scrofula. There is a Hindu proverb: "Rice is good, but lentils are my life"; in India, lentil soup is recommended as a cure for the common cold. In Alsace it is considered good for nursing mothers. Gerard, 16th century English herbalist, however, reported that "it causeth troublesome dreams and hurteth the head, sinuses, and lungs."

There is frequent mention of lentils in folktale. Cinderella was put to the task of picking up lentils out of the ashes. One lentil is the subject not only of one of the famous numskull stories in which the numskull says, "You said you wished a lentil soup, so I put one in" (J2469.1), but also of an Arabian tale in which a monkey lost one lentil, and dropped a handful in order to look for it (J344.1). See Jacob.

Leo The Lion, the fifth sign of the zodiac; a constellation containing the large stars Regulus and Denebola, and the configuration called the Sickle. Leo has been recognized from earliest times; it was the lion in Sumeria, Babylonia, Egypt, Persia, Syria, Greece, and Rome. In the early astronomical era, Leo was the sign in which the sun appeared at the summer solstice. It has therefore been conjectured that the lion symbolized the heat of the summer; similarly, it is said that in Egypt the advent of summer meant both the Nile flood and the appearance of lions in the Valley. Some equate the Sumerian lion with the forest monster Humbaba. Nergal, the Babylonian war god, had a lion's body and was probably identified with Leo. This constellation was also thought to be the sign of the tribe of Judah. The Lion of the Greeks was supposed to represent the Nemean lion slain by Hercules. In the Middle Ages, this was one of the lions to which Daniel was thrown. In China, the constellation was zodiacal, but a horse rather than a lion. In Peru, it was a puma in the act of leaping on a victim. Regulus, the first magnitude star whose name means kinglet, was recognized from the 4th millennium B.C. down to the 17th century A.D. as the ruler of the stars. In Babylonia, it was the King; in India, the Mighty; in Persia, the Center. Other names for this star were the Lion's Heart (Nineveh) and Basiliskos (Ptolemy). In folk belief of western Ontario, Canada, it is said that calves are best weaned during Leo. Compare BAY TREE; FERN.

leprechaun In Irish folklore a small, roguish elf. Originally derived from *lu-chorpan*, little body, the word has been corrupted by folk etymology into a form meaning "half-brogue," with the result that the fairy is usually thought of as a shoemaker. In 15th century manuscripts, we have a delightful tale of Iubdan, king of the Lupracan, a noble and truthful potentate, whose strongest subject could perform the feat of cutting down a thistle at a single stroke! As late as 1908 school children and country folk near Mullingar believed they had seen a leprechaun. Besides practicing his trade of cobbling, he is the owner of many crocks of buried treasure. If caught, he can be forced to reveal the secret of their location, but he will vanish if one takes one's eyes off him. [RSL]

He tricks the one who has caught him into looking elsewhere, and the minute human eyes are off of him, he vanishes. "Your bees are swarming and going off with themselves," he cries, or "The cows are into the

oats." And he who looks to save his property never sees the leprechaun again or finds the treasure. Typical is the story about the man who was *not* thus tricked but got so far as to compel the leprechaun to lead him to the very bush in the field where the gold was buried. But the man had no spade to dig, so he took off one red garter and tied it to the bush, in order to recognize the spot again, politely liberated the leprechaun, and ran back for the spade. He was gone only three minutes, but when he returned to dig, there was a red garter on every bush in the field. This is, of course, a variant of the marked culprit motif (K415).

In Ulster the leprechaun is sometimes identified with a kind of malicious little snub-nosed fairy called *geanncanac̀*. In the neighborhood of Cork, the leprechaun is sometimes identified with the clúracán.

leprosy A chronic, endemic, infectious disease characterized by nodular skin lesions, nerve paralysis and eventual complete loss of sensation, and physical mutilation (caused by *Mycobacterium* or *Bacillus lepræ*): a disease known to man for at least 3500 years, and still common in Asia and the Near East and various tropical regions. In 1949, according to a report to the United Nations by India, there were still an estimated five million lepers in the world, some 2,200,000 in India and China alone. Other estimates place the figure at between two and seven million.

Leviticus xiii-xiv describes in detail the laws and tokens whereby the priest was to be guided in recognizing leprosy in man, garment, or house, the regulations governing lepers, and the ritual cleansing of the patient, garments, and dwellings. "And the leper in whom the plague is, his clothes shall be rent, and his head bare, and he shall cry 'Unclean, unclean.' All the days that the plague shall be in him, he shall be defiled; he shall dwell alone" (*Lev.* xiii, 45, 46). The elaborate ritual of purification involved two birds: the sprinkling of the leper with the blood of one and the simultaneous release of the other to symbolize the departure of the evil. This ritual bears witness to two almost universal beliefs: that blood cures leprosy, and that disease or sin can be transferred to a scape animal, bird, or person.

The Arabs knew both kinds of leprosy: *Bahak,* white leprosy, and *Juzám,* black leprosy, and regarded either the characteristic thickening of the voice as the first telltale sign of infection, or a swelling of the wrists. Both kinds were believed to be caused by improper diet.

Beliefs regarding the causes of leprosy vary according to the culture patterns in which the disease appears. The ancient Egyptians believed that to drink sow milk (pigs being sacred animals) caused leprosy. Among some totemic peoples eating the tabooed totem animal causes leprosy. Among the Philippine Ifugaos, leprosy is the result of being spat upon by one of the supernatural Spitters. In Syria it was commonly thought that intercourse during menstruation would cause it. That lust is increased by the disease is a very old and widespread idea. In the Old Testament leprosy was often regarded as just punishment for wrong-doing. Elisha cursed his servant Gehazi, for instance, for running after Naaman and soliciting payment for the miraculous cure; Uzziah, a king of Judah, was stricken with leprosy for pridefully usurping the office of priest. Plutarch posed the question why a man walking under dewy trees contracts leprosy in those parts which may have touched the bark.

The story of Naaman, told in *2 Kings* v, is one of the famous leper-cure stories of antiquity. Elisha told Naaman to go wash in the Jordan seven times and his "flesh would come again" and he would be clean. This Naaman did and was cured. This cure is significant testimony to the belief in the efficacy of running water (also mentioned in *Lev.* xiv, 5–6; 50–51) and the magic power of the number seven.

Leprosy was designated by Paracelsus as one of the four monarchs of disease (with epilepsy, dropsy, gout). The Arabic *Gospel of the Infancy* tells the story of a leper cured by washing in the bath water of the infant Jesus. Galen (2nd century) said that wine infected with serpent venom would change various diseases into leprosy which could then be cured "in the traditional fashion." This traditional fashion has been the bath of blood, especially human blood, from ancient Egyptian times to the Middle Ages in Europe. King Richard of England was told to bathe in infants' blood and then to eat the heart of the infant as an infallible cure. Bathing in the blood of two-year-old children "undoubtedly cures leprosy" said Michael Scott (13th century). A bit of cooked snake sneaked into a leper's food was a palliative, if not a cure, recommended by Bartholomew of England (13th century.)

Lepers were suspect everywhere in Europe and accused of poisoning wells in France and Italy from the 14th century on, but a certain healing well near Acqui lost its powers as soon as the people forbade its use by lepers. Louis XI of France became a leper in his later years, and there is record that on July 8, 1483, he sent ships to the Cape Verde Islands to bring back turtles of the Isles, the blood of which he had heard would cure leprosy. In the 16th century magic gold chains were sometimes worn to prevent or cure leprosy. Sixteenth century German medicine included a horrid oil from little green lizards which was said to be good for leprosy. In 1313 Philip the Fair of France ordered all lepers to be burned; the order was zealously fulfilled, but before complete annihilation of the unfortunates the monasteries of St. Lazarus (patron of lepers) were opened to them. Many were crowded together in these *lazarettes* and cared for and treated by monks who were also lepers. The Order of St. Lazarus, founded for the protection of lepers, established its houses all over Europe. Those who entered were regarded as dead to the world and their former associations, and the burial ritual was performed for them. If they came forth from their segregation they wore the special garb of the leper, sometimes masks, and carried the leper's bell or rattle which warned of their approach.

Among Dahomey Negroes a leper is hurriedly buried without ceremony, but whether the haste is from fear of contagion, or whether the ceremony is withheld because the disease is looked upon as a divine punishment is not yet known. Sometimes after three to seven years, however, a funeral can be held for him and his soul can be bought back into the family. See BLOOD; DIAMOND; EMERALD; NĀGA; POPLAR; TWO FRIENDS.

Lernean hydra In Greek legend, the many-headed (usually nine) serpent slain by Hercules as the second of the labors. The hydra was the offspring of Typhon and Echidna, and grew back a head, or two in place of one, as soon as one was cut off. Hercules, after crushing

the crab sent by Hera to help the hydra, called upon his charioteer Iolaus to burn the stumps as soon as he cut off heads and thus slew the monster. He then permanently poisoned his arrows by dipping them in the venomous blood. In another version of the story, the hydra had one head which Hercules cut off and buried beneath a rock.

Lethe In Greek mythology, the river of forgetfulness in Hades. Originally Lethe was a plain in the underworld through which ran a river whose waters brought forgetfulness. Later the name became attached to the river or spring itself. The water was said, by the later poets, to be drunk by those souls who were to be reborn, so that they might forget their previous lives.

Leto In Greek mythology, the mother of Apollo and Artemis; daughter of Cœus and Phœbe: the Latin Latona. Though sometimes she is mentioned as the wife of Zeus before Hera, the usual story is that she was another of Zeus' clandestine mistresses. Hera warned all places on earth not to let Leto bear her children where the sun shone, and in fear of her reprisals they refused the pregnant Titaness refuge. Finally Leto called on her sister Asteria, who had been transformed into a rock beneath the sea, and there she bore the children. More commonly, however, she came to the floating island of Ortygia (later identified as Delos), which Poseidon covered with water to prevent the sun from shining on it. Leto clasped a palm tree during her labor and brought forth Apollo and Artemis. In some versions, Artemis was born first and assisted in delivering Apollo; in others Apollo was born and immediately slew the Python which Hera had caused to pursue Leto. The island became fixed after the birth of the children; Delos, as the birthplace of Apollo, was sacred and none could die or be born there. Leto was worshipped only as part of the worship of her children.

letter If a moth flies towards you, you will receive a letter. If a bright spark shoots up from a candle nearby, you will receive a letter. An English sneezing rime says: Sneeze on Wednesday, sneeze for a letter. White spots on the fingernail of the ring finger also mean that you will soon get a letter. In the southern United States it is said that when the fire pops on the hearth a letter is coming; or if your nose itches, a letter is coming. A piece of cotton on the dress not only indicates that a letter is on its way, but also shows the initial of the one sending it. To get a letter, hang up on a nail a hairpin you have found; or if you and your companion speak simultaneously, have her pinch you. If a spider at the end of its thread comes before your eyes, a letter is coming. If your right hand itches you will receive money in it; if the left itches, a letter. To dream of mailing an unsealed letter means that your secrets are known (or you are afraid they will be).

Georgia Negroes recommend putting a letter from your love in a can and throwing it into running water to make sure she loves you, or stamping a letter upside down to insure a speedy answer. Never put a letter in your girl's left hand either, or your friendship will come to an end. To burn up a love letter is to destroy and burn up your love, but some people recommend it as a means of easing the mind of old troublesome memories.

Letters from lover to lover often close with XXXXX, each X for an enclosed kiss. Sometimes the envelope is "sealed with a kiss," SWAK written across the flap. The letter chain, bringing luck or wealth to the recipient, must not be broken lest bad luck ensue.

The letter of death is familiar in folktale. Related to it is the task letter (H918) in which the bearer is set a task by the recipient of the letter (see BELLEROPHON). In a Spanish tale, the trickster writes that the bearer of the letter be detained; in the meantime he steals the messenger's wife. The famous Ems dispatch of European history is paralleled by the letter in Welsh tale whose falsified message incites a war. Intercepted letters bring the old woman to the man's bed in place of the girl (K1317.2.1), the leper instead of the lover to the princess' bed (K1317.2), the disgrace of the mother (calumniated wife—K2117) when her letter announcing the birth of the children is held up. The presuming ignoramus, in Type 1539, pretends to be reading a letter when all the time it is simply a receipt for taxes. In a European story, a man expresses a desire to see the world. He is given a letter to deliver six miles away. When he returns he has seen all there is to see in the world—hills, valleys, streams, etc.

letter of death   A letter ordering the execution of the bearer: a common mechanism of many folktales of Asia and Europe. The theme is probably Eastern in origin; it first appears in Europe during the Crusades (12th century). The *Gesta Romanorum*, Walter Map, the *Book of Sindibad*, all use it. In the Uriah letter (K978), the king orders the bearer put in a position in which he will be killed (see *II Sam.* xi); the same motif occurs in the Greek story of Bellerophon, who is sent by Iobates to fight the Chimera; in the Arabic legend of the poet Mutalammis, he destroys his letter, but Tarafah, bearing a similar letter, is killed. The motif is thus also often called Bellerophon letter, Mutalammis letter. The Uriah letter changed (K511) is the companion to this, appearing in such tales as *The Wolf* (Type 428), a European tale in which the princess carries a letter of death from one to another but is helped out of her difficulty by the wolf, a transformed prince, who alters the letter. In *The Prophecy* (Type 930; Grimm #29— *The Devil with the Three Golden Hairs*), the hero carries the letter of death to the queen, but robbers change its text (K1355) so that he is married to the princess. So also Amleth himself alters the letter to England's king and marries the princess; in Shakespeare's play *Hamlet*, the letter of death is rewritten by Hamlet and brings the death not of Hamlet but of its bearers, Rosencrantz and Guildenstern. Another letter of death story, found from Indonesia to Iceland, is *Der Gang nach dem Eisenhammer* (K1612), the title of one of Schiller's poems. The king sends a message to his kiln-burners that the next person to arrive is to be thrown into the fire. Immediately afterwards he sends his intended victim to the kiln on some pretext. But the victim turns aside and the one who is first to arrive at the kiln is the accuser of the intended victim, or the king's son. This is a medieval European tale, the beginning of which is often the story of the offending breaths: the envious courtier tells the king's servant that the king objects to his breath and always turns his head away, and he tells the king that the servant always turns *his* head away because he cannot stand the king's odor. The king sends the letter to the kiln, but the servant turns aside to say

mass before proceeding. The eager calumniator rushes to the kiln to find out what has happened and is killed himself. A typical variation on the letter of death theme, existing elsewhere too, is found in the Hindu *Kathākoça:* the letter of death is intended to say that the bearer is to receive poison (*visha*), but the receiver misreads it and gives him the daughter named Vishā.

lettuce   A garden herb (*Lactuca sativa*) having crisp edible leaves commonly used as a salad. In the doctrine of signatures lettuce was classified as a sterile plant and believed to be conducive to sterility in those who ate it. In Surrey it is said that too much lettuce in the kitchen garden will prevent the young wife from having a child. And because of the lung-shaped leaves, the doctrine of signatures also recommended its use in concoctions for the lungs.

The European wild lettuce (*L. virosa*) has been known for centuries as a sedative and soporific, and the drug *lactucarium,* made from the milky juice, is so recognized today. This lettuce was one of the ingredients of the medieval "soporific sponge," which was soaked in an infusion of mandrake, hemlock, lettuce, poppy, ivy, and mulberry. One whiff of this was said to knock a man out. Pliny, and the 16th century physician Guglielmo Gratarolo, quoting Pliny, advised eating lettuce to prevent seasickness, if not actually to prevent storms at sea.

The American prickly lettuce (*L. scariola*) was called *mīnikita'tabŭki,* milk leaf, by the Meskwaki Indians. They brewed a tea from the leaves which was given to women following childbirth to increase the flow of milk. White settlers used this plant to make a sedative sirup for babies.

Leza   The high god of the Basubiya, a Bantu people: parallel to Bumba or Nzambi (Nyambe) of the Bushongo and Baluyi. One day Leza told his people that he was going away, and gave them instructions of how to worship him. Then he left them and went up into the sky by a spider's thread. The people tried to follow, but the thread broke and they fell back to earth, where they are today. They put out spider's eyes for allowing the thread to break: an etiological story explaining the Basubiya belief that spiders have no eyes. Sometimes when the people see a shooting star they say it is Leza coming back. M. Jacottet assumed that Leza represented the sun to the Basubiya. See A. Werner, "African Mythology" in *Mythology of All Races*, 6: 132 ff. Leza is recognized but not anthropomorphized by the Awemba, who think of him as a judge and counter of the dead.

lezginka   A wooing dance of the Lezgis of Daghestan in the Caucasus, taken over by the Georgians and Tartars as well. Often it is a wild saber dance by a man alone, featuring dextrous passes of the sword. More usually, without a weapon, he whirls and leaps around an impassive girl, who turns slowly in place. As a couple, leap, and sword dance, the lezginka would originally have had a triple fertility potency. [GPK]

Lha   One of the eight classes of Tibetan godlings subordinant to the tutelary fiends. The Lha are good spirits, usually male and white in color. The term is used for the gods of the Indian Buddhist and Brāhmanical pantheon as well as for the aboriginal gods which live in the sky, whether they are unfriendly or friendly. The Lha visited the earth often in the early days and the high mountains of Tibet became known as their means of ascent and descent from heaven. White altars (lha-tho) were therefore erected on them and these were regarded as the gods' dwelling places.

Lhă-K'a or **Ku-t'em-ba**   A type of sorcerer, especially of western Tibet, consulted for the relief of pain. The Lhă-K'a, who may be either a man or a woman, places a mirror over his heart and a cake on his head while he makes an offering of a libation or incense to the demons and beats cymbals and a drum to attract the *Yul-lha* or country gods. He then takes a divining arrow from a plate of flour and places its blunted point on the affected part. He sucks on the shaft and a drop of blood appears over the painful part although there is no abrasion of the skin. When the blood appears it is considered a miracle and the evil spirit has been expelled. Compare CH'O-JE; NAG-PA.

Lha-mo   The Tibetan name for Devī, as one of the most malignant, powerful, and dreaded of the Lāmaist demons. She is credited with letting loose the disease demons and is classed as one of the Tibetan Dharma-pālas. She is represented surrounded by flames, riding a white-faced mule, sitting on a saddle of her own son's skin flayed by herself. She wears human skins and eats human brains and blood from a skull. Lha-mo is publicly worshipped for seven days at the end of the year to prevent disease during the coming year. An offering to her of a cake containing the fat of a black goat, blood, wine, dough, and butter, is made in a human-skull bowl. Her hideous and malignant aspects are constantly emphasized and she never reflects any of the milder aspects of her Hindu prototype.

li   The Chinese term for rites or etiquette. The observation of li is essential to the political and social philosophy of China and is the source of great confusion among those who attempt to understand that great and difficult people. [RDJ]

Lia Fáil   Literally, the Stone of Fál: the stone from the mythical city of Falias which Luġ took to Tara. It would scream out under the foot of every rightful king of Ireland who took the crown, from the time of Luġ to the day Christ was born. And it has never cried aloud for any king since. The poets often named Ireland Inis Fáil, the Island of Fál.
There is a story in the cycle of Conn telling how the stone screamed one day under Conn in Tara. This was Conn of the Hundred Battles. He was on the high rampart at Tara scanning the horizon to see if the old Fomorians or Tuatha Dé Danann might be attacking Ireland secretly, and he stepped upon a stone which cried out under his foot. Conn asked the fili what kind of a stone did that, and in 53 days the fili came with the answer, saying the stone's name was Fál, that it came to Tara from Falias, would go to Teltown where there would be a fair every year forever, and that the number of times the stone screamed under Conn would be the number of kings of Conn's seed that would rule Ireland. "Tell them to me," said Conn; but the fili said he was not destined to tell them. The filid (singular *fili*) were an order of ancient learned Irish poets.
Another story says the stone was sent to Scotland in the 6th century for the coronation of Fergus mac Erc, who begged the loan of it from his brother, Murtag,

then king of Ireland. It was never returned to its own island, but is said to be the Stone of Scone taken to England from Scotland by Edward I in 1297, to be the Coronation Stone for the kings of England. It lies in Westminster Abbey, enclosed in a wooden chair, still fulfilling the ancient prophecy (through the line from Fergus mac Erc and the Stuarts of Scotland) that a king of Scotic (i.e. Irish) descent shall reign in whatever place it is. But the Irish say that Lia Fáil lies in Tara still, six feet long.

liars and lying tales   The "artistic" or "authentic" liar is one who lies not to be believed but for the sheer fun and artistic satisfaction of invention. Lying tales (big lies, big windies, whoppers) spring from the same soil as yarns and tall tales. As "exuberant combinations of fact with outrageous fiction," in Walter Blair's words, tall tales are not always pure lies, cut out of whole cloth, but may be classed as yarns or lies depending upon which way the delicate balance between truth and untruth is turned, which way the "big wind" is blowing.
Even though the "cheerful liar" does not expect to be believed, he may borrow the yarn-spinner's device of the "traveler's tale," reporting wonders he has observed or experienced in a strange land or another part of the country. And because travel gives him a certain immunity to criticism or being checked up on," he may all the more frankly and confidently "draw the long bow" when he goes hunting or fishing, as in Munchausen tales of the "lucky" or "wonderful hunt." Or, abandoning the convention of the traveler, he may fall back upon some mysterious informant, "not known directly" to him but "well known to a close friend" and usually "long since dead" or lost track of, thus conveniently shifting the burden of proof.
While the unconscionable exaggeration of the liar links him with the boaster, the liars' club is also next door to the boosters' club, especially in the Western "paradise of puffers." And while boasting concerns itself with the boaster's prowess, boosting is concerned with the advantages of a place—the perennial wonders of climate, weather, soil. In stories of health-giving and life-prolonging or life-restoring climate, state pride and loyalty are often called into play, as in Florida, California, and Texas. From almost every state comes a chorus of brags of giant vegetables—turnip, pumpkin, beet, potato, cucumber, corn—harking back to the Old World motif of the great cabbage and the pot that matched it.
As disaster follows in the trail of phenomenally large or rapid growth (e.g. the giant cornstalk or the all-entangling cucumber vines), so boom is followed by bust, feast by famine, and flood by drouth. In what should have been "God's country" or the "wonder state," hardship, hard times, and hard luck give rise to boosting in reverse or defensive lying—of the kind that proceeds from having too little rather than too much. Inverse brags take the form of local "cracks and slams" and "laughing it off," with endless gibes at poor country, dry or wet country, flat or hilly country, and all the liabilities of weather, climate, insect pests, and the like. See PIONEER LORE. From insect scourges and freakish animal behavior it is only a step to stories of fanciful traits of animals (see HOOP SNAKE) and mythical monsters. See FEARSOME CRITTERS.

With apocryphal zoology and unnatural natural history, we pass from lying as pure entertainment to lying as hoax, prank, and sell. The boaster and booster become the codder, teaching the "young and tender . . . the great verities by generous untruths." Essentially, mythical monsters are hoaxing inventions, paralleled, in the mechanical world, by such contraptions as "The Rawhide Railroad" (an elaboration of the buckskin harness of Paul Bunyan).

Out of the natural competitiveness and rivalry of liars, as of boasters and boosters, grows the lying contest, and out of the lying contest the liars' club. Almost every community has its traditional gathering place for local liars and yarn-spinners (crossroads store, tavern, saloon, courthouse, bunkhouse, barber shop, garage, filling station), symbolized by an actual or mythical "Liars' Bench" (akin to the proverbial "cracker barrel"). The first liars' clubs were born in the minds of local newspapermen, in the desperation of a dearth of local copy (e.g. the Sazerac Lying Club, created by Fred H. Hart, editor of the Austin, Nevada, Reese River, *Reveille*). At least one of these newspaper hoaxes, the Burlington (Wisconsin) Liars' Club, became a reality (and not just a lie), with an annual National Liars' Contest. With the liars' club the artistic lie gives rise to the burlesque lie, if one can conceive of such a thing. Since lying in, for, and by itself is not necessarily funny or artistic, the burlesque lie contains in itself the seed of its own decay and seldom rises above the level of journalism to join the great lies of folk fantasy.   B. A. BOTKIN

Liat Maca The Gray of Macha: in Old Irish legend, Cuchulain's wonderful gray horse, one of the two magic horses (with the *Dub Sanglainn*, the Black Sanglain) which rose out of the Gray Loch of Sliab Fuait and the Black Loch of Sanglainn. They were said to be given to Cuchulain by Macha, or possibly by Morrigu, with whom Macha is sometimes identified. Cuchulain caught and tamed them by springing on their backs. For a whole day they tore around "the circuit of Ireland"; but neither could throw off the boy-rider, and after that they were gentle. Liat Maca, the Gray, was the horse that loved Cuchulain dearly, and got his death wound defending him in the last fight. Both horses went back to their lakes after Cuchulain's death. Eleanor Hull points to a day and night symbolism of gray and black.

Liber and **Libera** Ancient Italian deities of the vine, worshipped along with Ceres as fertility gods. Ceres being identified with Demeter, Libera became identified with Persephone, and Liber with Dionysus or with his Roman counterpart Bacchus. These are divine beings of greater age than the translation of the Greek attributes to them, but it is difficult to determine their original form beyond their undoubted connection with fertility and increase. Their festival, the Liberalia, was held on March 17, at which time Roman youths habitually donned the toga virilis for the first time.

libera A song sung after the final prayer of a novena at Haitian Negro funerals to send the spirit of the dead from the house. The priest is also paid to sing it each year over the grave on All Saints' Day.

Libra The Scales or the Balance: the seventh sign of the zodiac, a constellation between Virgo and Scorpio. Anciently it was looked upon as the claws of the scor-

pion, and not until the time of the Cæsars, when Augustus appeared in the star maps holding the scales of justice, was the constellation called Libra (or Jugum, the yoke of the balance). Now the scales are considered as belonging to Virgo, the virgin, identifiable with Astræa, the Greek goddess of justice. Elsewhere in the world, the European depiction of the constellation has taken hold, and it is known, wherever recognized, as the balance. In China, for example, it was early called the Dragon, later it was the sign of longevity, but now it is the balance. In Egypt at the time of the Romans, it was pictured as two feathers, but these feathers were those put into the balance at the weighing of the heart at the trial before Osiris after death. Though all trace of the Chaldean identification of this constellation has been lost, the Chaldeans must have known some zodiacal figure at this point of the heavens; otherwise the twelve signs shrink to the odd figure of eleven. But what the constellation was called no one has been able to determine, although some scholars see in the sign used to represent Libra an ancient altar, by which name (Altar) it is sometimes known.

Li Ch'un A Chinese movable feast: observed and celebrated with processions and at some times and places with the beating of a real or symbolic ox. Li Ch'un belongs to the complex of seasonal festivals, and marks the beginning of spring. See *General Structure of Chinese Folklore* in CHINESE FOLKLORE. [RDJ]

licorice or **liquorice** An Old World perennial leguminous herb (*Glycyrrhiza glabra*) having a strong, thick, branched root. The name means sweet root: a corruption of the Greek *glykys*, sweet, $+$ *rhiza*, root. The evaporated juice is called stick licorice; the Irish say *maide milis*, sugar stick. Licorice has long been used medicinally in cough mixtures and as a laxative; commercially today it is also used in brewing, and to flavor tobaccos and confections. The 17th-century John Josselyn of Boston numbered it among the "precious herbs" brought to the New World from England by the early settlers. Native American Indians bought it from white settlers and cultivated it for their own pharmacopœias. The Fox, for instance, valued it highly for female troubles. Jamaica Negroes call it lick-weed, and boil a lick-weed tea which is given both to adults and babies for constipation. The ancient Hindu *Kama Sutra* includes it in a milk and sugar drink to increase sexual vigor. The famous Chinese veterinarian and patron of veterinarians, Ma Shih-huang, once found himself being followed by a dragon. He was uneasy about this, but when the dragon called to him that he was ill, Ma Shih-huang turned back and gave him an injection of licorice. The dragon was cured and grateful to his benefactor forever.

Leif Ericson or **Ericsson** Norse adventurer, said to have discovered America (1002 A.D.). He was born in Norway, son of Eric the Red, who discovered and colonized Greenland. The most widely accepted accounts, the early 13th century *Eric the Red Saga,* and the 14th century *Hauk's Book,* claim he was lost in a storm between Norway and Greenland and landed first on a bleak coast called Markland and later at a point farther along the coast which he named Vineland. According to the late 14th century *Flatey Book,* however, Bjarni Herjolfsson was lost in the storm and discovered

America (987 A.D.) and Ericson set out to colonize it. He landed first in Labrador (Helluland), again in the vicinity of Cape Sable, Nova Scotia (Markland), and finally along the shores of the Chesapeake (Vineland), where he spent the winter and returned to Greenland in the spring with a cargo of brandy and timber which enabled him to retire a wealthy man.

Liekkiö Literally, the flaming one; the elflight or jack-o'-lantern of the Finns, who presides over plants, roots, and trees. He is the soul of a child who has been buried in the forest. [JB]

Lif and Lifthraser In Teutonic mythology, the woman Lif and the man Lifthraser; the human pair who will seek refuge at Ragnarök in Hodmimir's forest, the only place safe from Surtr's sword. They will sleep through the destruction of the world at Ragnarök, living on the dew which falls on their lips from Yggdrasil and will not wake until the earth is green and verdant again to found a new race. Compare DEUCALION; NOAH.

life token In widespread European and Asiatic folk belief, folktale, and traditional ballads, an object (or animal, plant, etc.) either chosen by or born with a person, which manifests in some way the fact that he is in danger, may die, or is dead. The object is sometimes a knife left behind, which rusts or sweats blood when harm befalls the absent hero, an apple which changes to indicate danger or rots to indicate death, a shirt that turns black, a brilliant ring or jewel that grows dull. In European folklore, it is often a tree that withers or dies. The life of the hero is almost invariably co-existent with the life token. The classical story of Meleager and the burning brand is typical (see CALYDONIAN BOAR HUNT), as is the Kashmir story of Panj Phul who was never without her necklace because it was a charm against sickness and danger and contained the core of her life. The life-token belief is strong also among primitive peoples in Africa, Australia, Melanesia, and Tasmania. Typical North American Indian life tokens are a plant that withers, or a pot that boils to signify that the hero is imperiled, or a digging stick that breaks. In Brittany the fisherman's wife puts a candle at the altar; if it burns well all goes well with her husband; if it flickers he is imperiled; if it goes out he is drowned. In northern Nigeria, a house snake is said to be born simultaneously with every human being. The life span of one is measured by the life span of the other; hence these snakes are solicitously fed and protected. In Ireland the life token is called *cómsaogal* (contemporaneous life); it is often a stone which will be broken at the death of its affinity, or a tree which will wither or die. See BIRTH TREE; DEKANAWIDA; FOOTPRINT; SEPARABLE SOUL; SOUL ANIMAL; TWO BROTHERS.

lift dances The exuberant couple dances that climax in the lifting up of the girl have their roots in ancient fertility magic. Any display of superhuman power, such as overcoming the force of gravity, has in folk tradition an impelling effect on the forces of reproduction, animal and vegetable. Such dances are the Bavarian *Schuhplattler*, Moravian *Rozek*, Neapolitan *Saltarella*, Spanish *Jota al Aire*, Catalan *Corranda Alta*. In the last a group of four builds a human pyramid, similar to the finish of American cowboy dances. Lift dances are usually also leap dances.

In European sword dances the final hoisting up of certain leading dancers is a symbol of seasonal resurrection. In the *Txonkórinka* of the Basque *ezpata dantza* the captain is hoisted up on a platform of swords, inert and glorified. In the *Dance* of Sena, Huesca, the sword-play ends by the elevation of four *volantes*, boys dressed as angels. The *Mojigangas* of Tarragona and *Xiquets de Valls* of Barcelona build human pyramids, by chance similar to those of ancient Mexico. [GPK]

light Light seems everywhere to be equated with or symbolic of good. Light in the Bible is the first of all things created. Certainly, to many primitive peoples, light is a concrete thing, something that exists as a material substance, and that may be seen in the sun, in fire, in lightning. In Hawaiian myth, mankind is created from Peace and Quiet fertilized by Light (A1221.2). Darkness, opposed to light, is evil in later thought, when dualism becomes important, when balance in the universe becomes necessary. Primitively, perhaps light results from darkness; the darkness covers the light, and, just as a man awakes with the light, so light appears when the darkness is lifted from it, like a lid. But with the belief in dualism in all things, the dragon of darkness is defeated by the god of light (A162.2: Egypt, Babylonia, China, etc.), and the battle goes on everlastingly, the forces of evil attempting always to swallow the light and plunge the world into darkness. (See ECLIPSES.) Light, in the dualism of the Chinese yin and yang, is identified with yang, the male principle.

The fire guarded by the Vestals in Rome was the symbol of the fire burning eternally and always shedding light on the Roman state and the Roman home. This light was the sign of the fortune of the state and of the home and thus could not be permitted to go out. A pillar of fire shed the light that guided the Israelites at night through the desert. Churches are filled with lights at festivals; light is necessary all over the world at birth and baptism, marriage and funeral. In England, Scotland, Germany, Sweden, Korea, Basutoland, among the ancient Romans, the Parsis, the Jews, the light must always shine near the bed where a mother and her newborn child lie. If the fire goes out before the child is baptized, a changeling may be substituted: this belief is held in Sweden, in Malaya, in Bokhara. These and similar beliefs about the light of fire partake of two elements: fire is the agent that purifies, and light is good in warding off the spirits that live in the darkness. Nothing evil can enter where a light burns. Aside from police advice to leave a light burning somewhere in the house when one is away as a deterrent to thieves, it is good folk practice. The mountain men (F460.2.3), the child-snatching spirits, and those powers lying in wait in the darkness for the moment when charms against them cannot be seen because of the darkness are kept at bay by even one small candle.

Light springs forth of itself from the good. The halo or nimbus surrounding a saint is but a reflection of the goodness within. All the Moslem prophets, Mohammed and El Khidr notably, shone with light from their faces, the "light of Mohammed," which Adam first had and which brings wisdom and supernatural powers to those on whom it rests. The Norse god Balder's face shone with its own light. (Balder and the Greek Apollo are gods whose special province is light.) Light filled the house when Moses was born; and all the universes blazed with light when the Buddha reached his perfection of knowledge. The house of Celeus was lighted with the radiance of Demeter, whose face shone even though she was in sorrow. The Shekinah, the glory of light with which God surrounds himself, according to the rabbis, to make himself invisible, is reflected in the new moon. The angels shine with the light of purity and holiness. The light of virtue is said by some to be the reason one bows to a king: if one were to look directly at him, blindness would ensue. Such epithets as the Sun King reflect this belief.

Light is, however, more than an indicator of virtue. Sometimes, according to southern U.S. Negroes, lights will be seen in a church. But when someone enters, they disappear. Ghosts have been there. For ghosts too give off a light, usually a dull phosphorescence, that may disappear if looked at directly. Lights dance in graveyards and the will-o'-the-wisp leads the unwary a merry chase through swamps. The light of the hand of glory is invisible to all save the one who owns the hand (D1361.7), and it puts to sleep all who see it (D1410.2). According to a medieval Jewish belief, children conceived in the light will be epileptic, and anyone who stands before a burning lamp naked at night will also fall victim to the same disease. (Similarly, a child conceived in the light of the sun would have a white eruption, one engendered in moonlight would have leprosy, by starlight stammering.)

Light shines from certain stones of themselves. Lucian mentions lychnis, which could illuminate a whole temple. Alexander is said to have used as a lamp at night a stone he recovered from the belly of a fish. Noah lighted the ark with precious stones. Light shines from certain beautiful people (see ILLUMINATING BEAUTY). People still believe a cat's eyes will shine in complete darkness, though obviously some light must be present to be reflected by the eyes: nothing in the eye of the cat is self-luminous. The Talmud says, "A heavy step detracts one five-hundredth from the light of the eyes." Thus eventually one must go blind. As a preventative, one should stare at certain lights, e. g. the Sabbath candles, to strengthen the eyes.

Many such beliefs have no text behind them, but are firmly held. To light three cigarettes from one match will bring misfortune: this is current and widespread in the United States. Many believe this idea was begun and fostered by Ivar Krueger, the match manufacturer. In Macedonia, three lights burning in one room will bring death. Lights move before a person and cannot be approached, just before a near relative is to die—this is from Brittany. See CORPSE LIGHT; FETCH CANDLE. From Germany: a light that goes out by itself is a death omen. If the light is permitted to go out on Christmas Eve, someone in the household will die. During the ten days between Rosh Hashonah and Yom Kippur, European Jews used to light a candle: if it went out before burning down, the person would die before the year was out; if it burned to the end, he had at least another year to live. If, in the north of England, you give someone a light on New Year's Day (or Christmas Day), you give away your luck for the year to come.

In Oldenburg an unmarried girl who sees three lights in a row before her will soon become a bride. In the Tyrol, southern Germany, and Silesia, a woman who can blow into flame the glowing wick of a candle or lamp is still a virgin.

Light figures in many folktales as a motif. The famous noodle story told of the Schildburgers (J2123) is also in Icelandic folktale. The noodles build a windowless house before they discover that there is no way to light it. So they fill baskets with sunlight and carry them inside. But when the baskets are emptied, the house is as dark as before. Eventually they pull the house down. Light appears as a life token (E761.7.4) and is extinguished with death. Swords flash light (H1337), castles shine from afar (F1645.3), and boats are self-luminous (G222.2: Araucanian). The king or pope proves his power when his candle lights itself (H41.3; Type 671); a magic lamp lights itself when a lie is told (D1316.2). Hidden treasure is marked by a light shining from where it is secreted N532). In one of the riddle tales, the youth is asked, "What is your mother doing?" and he replies, "She shows the light of the world to one who has not yet seen it." She is, of course, assisting at a childbirth (H583.4.1). See ATEA; CANDLE; CHAMPION'S LIGHT; FIRE; HABDALAH; MITHRA; MOON; NIGHT; NIMBUS; SAMAIN; SUN.

☞ Origin tales in which light (or the sun, or summer weather, or fire; these four are often confused or identified with light) is accounted for through some character's having stolen it, are widespread in North American Indian oral tradition, being told in practically all parts of the continent. North Pacific Coast mythologies are especially rich in such. The details differ regionally, but almost always light, the sun, or fire is stolen through a trick and given to the people who had previously been living in darkness or in cold. Light is often represented among the western tribes as a ball or disk or other object, kept in a box or basket which is suspended from the ceiling of the chief's house. The thief, often Coyote or another trickster, transforms himself into a child or baby, is taken in, and cries until he is given the contents of the basket, which he then makes off with. Or, the hero may change himself into a stick or other object, be swallowed by the owner-of-light's daughter, be reborn and subsequently steal light from his mother's father. Often, in a race which ensues after light is stolen, it is passed on from one of the thief's accomplices to another, until finally its possession is secure and it can be scattered for the people's benefit. In the Southwest among some of the Apache, dawn, or light, is won in a hidden-ball contest between the so-called "good" animals, who want light, and the bad or poisonous ones who want it to be dark all the time. The good animals, with Slim Coyote as chief, win the contest and kill all but a few of the bad animals; Bear and Yellow Rattlesnake escape. Other southwestern groups represent the underworld from which they emerged as dark; they were led up from this dark region by Sun man and Moon, or Changing Woman. [EWV]

☞ Some South American Indians make a distinction between daylight and the sun. In Chibcha genesis, the creator sends to the world birds carrying light in their beaks. Zaguaguayu, a solar deity of the Guarayu Indians, lives in a country lighted by small birds. The Bakairi consider dawn and the sun to be two different bunches of feathers which were stolen from the vultures by the culture hero. [AM]

lightning In all cultures lightning has either been personified as a god or regarded as a manifestation of the god. It was either the manifestation of his wrath and agent of punishment, or the accompanying thunder was the voice of warning or portent. Wherever depicted the lightning flash and thunderbolt are usually symbolized by some weapon of the god. Ancient Babylonian cylinders depict Adad, for instance, with a boomerang in one hand (thunderbolt) and a spear in the other (lightning). Throughout the Old Testament lightning struck fear into the heart of man, as a sign of God's wrath, and is frequently mentioned as the arrows of God which strike man with pestilence and death. Job is the exception who marveled at the phenomena: how God "directeth it under the whole heaven, his lightning unto the ends of the world./ After it a voice roareth; he thundereth . . ./ God thundereth marvelously in his voice; great things doeth he which we cannot comprehend. (*Job* 37:3–5.)

The ancient Persians also regarded lightning as a sign of divine wrath. In early Vedic religion several gods were associated with lightning: Trita, who helped Indra kill the serpent Vṛitra and other monsters, Apām napāt, who personified the thundercloud and went clothed in lightning, Rudra, the destructive storm god, whose bow and arrows represented the thunderbolt and lightning, and the two Maruts, young storm-god sons of Rudra, who rode through the heavens in chariots of lightning and struck down forests, men, and cattle.

In ancient Greece, thunder and lightning were manifestations of Zeus, and any spot struck by lightning became sacred. If his thunder was heard on the right before battle, it was an omen of victory, the implication being that the enemy would hear it on the left (a prognostication of ill). To the Romans also Jupiter was manifest, if not incarnate, in thunder and lightning; scholars posit some likelihood that the cult of Jupiter was superimposed on some earlier lightning cult. In Rome thunder on the left was propitious; and the sound of thunder occurring at the initiation of any undertaking presaged either success or failure for the project.

Various peoples of Indochina regard the god of lightning as the most powerful of all gods, who comes to earth with a stone ax and strikes down those who have offended him. The Chinese have a young goddess of lightning who travels around with the thunder god to keep him from making mistakes. (Once he made a terrible mistake.) She carries a mirror in each hand and flashes a bright light on every object in his path before he strikes it. In New Guinea the people believe thunder and lightning are caused by innumerable evil spirits. In medieval German folk belief they were caused by witches. In parts of Australia it is said that the sound of thunder causes turtles to come out of the water and lay their eggs.

In Dahomey, West Africa, lightning is the element with which the thunder-pantheon children of Sogbo punish wrong-doers. Gbadě, the youngest member of this pantheon, is the one most easily angered, and he alone is the one who kills with jagged lightning. His thunder causes the eggs of lizards and crocodiles to hatch. A man killed by lightning is thereby convicted of a serious crime; he is not buried by his family, but his body is consigned to the priest and cult-members of the thunder pantheon for disposal. His belongings are thrown away at the crossroads and never again touched (if any one should try to salvage something, he too will be killed by

lightning); his house is surrounded by a barricade of palm fronds to keep any one from entering it. No one in Dahomey will mention the name of any god of the thunder pantheon (Xevioso) during a thunderstorm; that would be calling the gods' attention to himself. (See Herskovits, *Dahomey* 1, 398–399.)

In general European and American folk belief lightning never strikes twice in the same place. Thunder curdles milk. Some people are afraid of wet dogs and horses in a thunderstorm, believing that they "draw" the lightning; others hide the scissors, cover mirrors, and sit on feather beds. Fear is augmented by such saying as: Thunder can strike a sword in the sheath and leave the sheath intact; it can strike a man down and leave no mark on his skin.

In Scandinavia the burning of the Yule log on Christmas Eve insures the house against lightning for a year. In Germany a house which harbors a quenched brand from the Midsummer bonfire will never be struck by lightning. In Picardy ashes from the Midsummer fire had the same efficacy. In general Slavic belief any ceremonial bonfire is thought to protect the fields from storm damage and the houses from lightning. In Shropshire, England, a piece of hawthorn cut on Holy Thursday will protect both house and person from being struck. Old writers of Germany and England reported that a magic coal could be discovered under a mugwort plant at exact noon (or midnight) in Midsummer Day, which if dug up and carried on the person protects him from lightning forever. He who carries in his pocket a piece of wood splintered off by lightning will possess extraordinary strength. In Maryland it is said that a toothpick made from a splinter of a struck tree will cure toothache.

Some southern U.S. Negroes say that if lightning strikes nearby while a man is dying, the devil has come for his soul. To dream of thunder means an angry God; it is well to repent of one's sins. Ashes from a piece of wood of a tree that has been struck by lightning, sprinkled in the doorway of the courthouse on the day of a trial, will make all decisions go your way, and the accusation will be torn up just as the lightning tore up that tree.

There is a good deal of weather lore associated with lightning among both Negroes and whites: lightning in the north means rain inside of 24 hours; lightning in the west means drought; in the Ozarks lightning in the south presages dry weather; lightning in the morning is an omen of storm; lightning and thunder in midwinter indicate extreme cold to come. See EAGLE; HARUSPICES; RESHEPH; THOR.

☞ Among some North American Indian groups, thunder and lightning are considered identical; Thunder is personified, and may be an active myth-character as, for example, in Coeur d'Alêne myths. Often however lightning is believed a power or weapon of Thunder man, or of the Thunder couple, or of the Thunderbird(s). Myths concerning the actions and powers of the latter are especially prevalent among the Eastern Woodlands tribes. Here the noise of thunder is believed to be caused by the Thunderers flapping their wings, lightning by their striking their beaks against hollow trees in search of a grub which they eat. North Pacific Coast tribes say lightning is the flash of the Thunderbird's eye. Some northern California and southern Oregon groups believe it is the weapon of Thunder person, issuing from his mouth "like a snake," or from his hand. Other groups say lightning takes the form of a raccoon, or is caused by a mole because whenever lightning strikes a peculiar species of mole is found at the spot. It is also believed that Thunder is a man, Lightning a woman, often his wife; or Thunder a boy, Lightning his younger brother.

Lightning is generally feared. The Achomawi of northeastern California, for example, tell how in a contest between Thunder and Raven, Thunder decreed that if any woman who is about to be delivered of a child in springtime dreams that she is struck by lightning, she will be killed, unless she can be treated by a shaman who knows how to rebuke the cloud from which the lightning issued. To escape lightning persons crawl under burnt trees or logs, run to open spots, jump into the water, cover their heads, hold up a raccoon skin, and often talk to Lightning, telling him or her to go somewhere else. See DWARF. [EWV]

lightning bug or **firefly** Any of certain phosphorescent night-flying beetles (family Lampyridæ), especially genera *Photinus* and *Photuris* of North America. They give forth a small but bright intermittent light from the lower part of the abdomen. Indonesian folktale has a helpful firefly (B483.1). In Bengal it is said that night-blindness can be cured by swallowing a firefly. Some U.S. southern Negroes say if one flies into your eye, his fire will put your eye out. Through the South in general, if one flies into the house, it brings good luck,—or it means a stranger is coming. In Alabama it is said to be a sign of rain when the lightning bugs are seen flying high. North American Penobscot Indians regard the appearance of lightning bugs as harbinger of the salmon, when they appear late in the spring. The rural lore of Ontario holds that if you kill a lightning bug, you will be struck by lightning in the next thunderstorm. New England fishermen say that if you are driving along at night behind a horse, and see a lightning bug ahead of your horse's nose, that means a fine catch of mackerel the next day.

lilac A shrub (genus *Syringa*) native to China and Persia which was introduced into Europe in the 16th century. A legend of the border folk of Scotland says that the seeds of the first plants were dropped in an old woman's garden by a falcon. They grew into a beautiful bush but did not bloom. One day a young prince stopped to admire the bush; as he was leaving a plume from his cap fell on the bush, and from that day the bush had plumes of purple flowers. Another legend tells of a young girl who died on the eve of her marriage. She asked that lilacs be planted on her grave. When they bloomed they were white, and remained so even after transplanting. Quite generally in England and also in Germany it is said to be unlucky to bring lilacs into the house, but elsewhere only the white, which will cause a death in the household. If lilacs are worn, except on May Day, the wearer will never marry; giving a spray of lilacs to one's betrothed is a sign that the engagement is off. In Devon and Cornwall it is said that bathing in the dew from the lilacs on May Day will make a person beautiful all year long.

lilis An ancient hand-beaten metal drum of Babylonia, having a flat foot and a large cup-shaped body on a short stem, similar in appearance to certain wooden drums still used in East Africa. See DRUM.

Lilith Traditionally, the first wife of Adam; the queen of the demons and sometimes wife of the Devil. Taking cue from *Gen.* i, 27, which tells a different story of creation from that of the earlier-written version in *Gen.* ii, rabbinical tradition developed the text, "male and female created he them," to indicate that God made Adam and Lilith from the dust at the same time—some say as twins joined back to back. But Lilith would not acknowledge Adam, the man, as her superior in creation; she would not be his servant, for she was created at the same time. Therefore she left Adam and was turned out of Paradise. God then made Eve from Adam's rib (*Gen.* ii, 18–22). Lilith, either before or after she was parted from Adam, was Sammael's mistress; according to Moslem tradition she cohabited with the Devil and gave birth to the jinn. Traditionally, God dispatched three angels to induce Lilith to return to Adam before he created Eve, but she refused and thus incurred the penalty of losing 100 of her offspring each day. However, once more, after the expulsion from Eden, Lilith slept with Adam, and from this union were born the Shedim or evil spirits.

The Lilith of this story seems obviously to be a development of the "maid of desolation (*ardat lili*)" of Babylonian tradition, a demon of waste places who originally lived in the garden of the Sumerian Inanna. She became in Assyrian belief a wind spirit, wild-haired and winged. In the Bible (compare *Is.* xxxiv, 14), she is the screech owl. The Talmudic tradition confused this spirit's name with the Hebrew word for night (*laylah*) and made Lilith a night demon, a succubus who slept with sleeping men and whose offspring from these unions were the demons. She attacked men sleeping alone; she thus was the angel of darkness and night and eventually a goddess (angel) of conception. This belief was strengthened in the Middle Ages by the story of Adam and Lilith, to the point where Lilith was a Lamia-like creature who envied women their children (she had lost hers) and would take them unless prevented by specific charms. One of these charms invoked the three angels sent to bring her back to Adam—Sanvi, Sansanvi, Semangelaf. Children during their first week of life were most susceptible; girls especially were in danger until three weeks had passed; an amulet with the three names engraved on it would protect them. Or, a circle was drawn about the lying-in bed or somewhere in the room, with the charm "Sanvi, Sansanvi, Semangelaf, Adam and Eve, barring Lilith." Or, amulets with a similar message were placed in several parts of the room.

The childless, envious, fatal demon woman appears elsewhere, for example, La Llorona of Mexican folklore. The Penobscot Indian Pskégdemus is a swamp spirit who wails near camps to entice men and children. A man who shows any sympathy for her, even in thought, is lost, for he will never be satisfied to marry a human woman. Another such demon of the Penobscot, dressed in moss and cedar bark, likes children and pets them. But good-willed though she be, children have a way of going to sleep forever when she fondles them.

The demon lover (succubus or incubus) whose children by man or woman become demons is also well-known. In the Iranian *Vendidad*, the man who has a nocturnal emission is enjoined to say certain formulas, for he has had relations with an incubus and must prevent the child of the union from becoming a demon. To medieval Jewry also, Lilith, *the* succubus, was the cause of nocturnal emissions, and this, combined with her child-stealing activities, made her the terror of Jewish mothers. Her offspring, the *lilin* or *lilim*, were monsters with human bodies, the hindquarters of an ass, and wings: spirits of the wild, especially (thus recalling the Sumerian belief) tree spirits. See ALGOL; HOLDE.

lilt In Irish usage, to sing nonsense syllables, especially as accompaniment for dancing. The voice imitates the *lilting pipe* (pipe played for dancing) with a series of such sounds as *deedle-um-doodle-um-di*, and the pipe is played in a vocalized manner. One lilting song tells the story of a goat that would not give milk unless sung to with a long string of lilting syllables.

lily Any of numerous ornamental plants (genus *Lilium*) with a bulbous root, erect stems, and large, showy flowers. Semitic legend says the lily sprang from the tears of Eve when she was expelled from the Garden of Eden. In Korea a hermit once removed an arrow from the foreleg of a tiger and they became friends. When the tiger died, he begged the hermit to use his magic to keep him nearby, so his body became the tiger-lily. When the hermit was drowned, the lily spread far and wide looking for him. The lily is a symbol of fruitfulness in China, Japan, India, Egypt, Greece, and Rome. The bud is considered male and the flower female. In Japan the lilies were emblems of the war god, the white lily for peace, the tiger-lily for war.

In Christian symbolism the lily represents purity, chastity, and innocence, and is a symbol of the Resurrection and of Easter. The Madonna Lily is sacred to the Virgin Mary and is said to have been yellow until she stooped to pick it. The lily has supplanted the olive branch in pictures of the Annunciation. It was sacred to Venus and St. Catherine.

Smelling lilies, especially tiger-lilies, is believed to give a person freckles in England and most of the United States. Anyone who would step on a lily would crush the purity of the women in his household.

Lilies are not much in evidence in witchcraft, but a 13th century authority says to pluck a lily in the sign of Leo and, after mixing it with laurel juice, to place it under the manure pile until it generates worms. These when powdered and sprinkled on a person's clothing will give him the fever; put in a jar of milk it will cause a whole herd to dry up. The roots ground up and mixed with honey will glue together severed muscles. Mixed with olive oil, they are good for the hair, burns, and muscular aches. The juice is good against poisonous bites of all kinds. The leaves and roots are good for burns and scalds, and will dissolve tumors and swellings. The soul is sometimes represented as a lily (E745.4.1) which is a flower of the dead. On the spot where an innocent man has been executed, the Hungarians say three yellow lilies will spring up. The lily is also sometimes symbolical of the effete and cowardly.

lily-of-the-valley or **May lily** A plant (genus *Convallaria*) of the lily family having fragrant, pendant, bell-shaped flowers: locally in Great Britain called *Our Lady's Tears*. These dainty little May flowers are beloved wherever they grow and there are many legends as to their origin. One of the most general Christian legends tells of a battle between St. Leonard and the Devil in the form of a dragon, in the forest of Louvain. St. Leonard was frequently wounded as he drove the dragon deeper and deeper into the forest where it eventually fled. Every place where the saint's blood fell sprang up patches of lilies-of-the-valley. In France they are sometimes called fairy cups, the story being that the fairies, out gathering dew, stopped to dance in the moonlight and hung their cups on a blade of grass. They danced too long and at dawn found that the cups had grown fast to the grass, but their protecting spirit hid them with two large leaves. In Norway they say the spring goddess found the bleakness so distressing that she tore up her green dress and, with a handful of snow, made these lovely flowers. In Ireland they are called fairy ladders and the little people amuse themselves running up and down them. In parts of Hesse, landholders pay their annual rent with bunches of these spring flowers. On Whit-Monday they are gathered and brought into the houses in Hanover, but in Ireland it is unlucky to take them into the house or to give them to a friend. In Devon it is said that whoever plants a bed of lilies-of-the-valley will die inside the year. In many parts of England dire consequences follow their transplanting.

North American Cherokee Indians say that the little dawn bird was sent to the top of the mountain. She marked the trail with a handful of white pebbles placed on a leaf which rooted and tinkled merrily as she returned. Later they were deprived of their music and given more bells.

Medicinally the flowers of the lily-of-the-valley are dried and used as snuff to clear the head, or mixed with water and distilled into *eau d'or* and used for nervous disorders, inflammation of the eyes, to strengthen the memory, and to clear the complexion. In the doctrine of signatures the lily-of-the-valley was recommended for apoplexy because of its "flower like a pendant drop." Distilled in wine they are good for the dumb palsy, vertigo, apoplexy, leprosy, dropsy, gout, and diseases of the heart. In the present day this plant yields a valuable drug for the treatment of heart diseases which is considered safer than digitalin which tends to become habit-forming.

Limbo The edge or border; specifically, the borderland of Hell in medieval cosmography: Dante makes it the first of the ten circles of Hell. Either Limbo was divided into three sections (*limbus patrum, limbus puerorum* or *infantum, limbus fatuorum*) or three classes inhabited it (the ancients who died before Christ lived and thus never had a chance to be saved, such "fathers" as Adam, who died unbaptized in the True Faith; children who died unbaptized and thus were incapable of entering heaven and were not deserving of punishment; fools who were not responsible for their deeds and yet were not worth saving). The fathers or ancients were, some of them, saved from Limbo as a result of the Harrowing of Hell by Christ. To the fools, who knew no better, Limbo was as good as paradise, hence a fool's paradise, but to those who knew, Limbo was a place of punishment, even though the punishment consisted only of eternal banishment from God's presence. Limbo, as the place where things are kept which are not quite useful yet too good to destroy, is sometimes a synonym for jail.

limbo An acrobatic dance for men, of Trinidad. The dancer bends far back and shuffles forward to drum-beating, to pass under a stick held horizontally; the more expert the dancer, the lower the stick. It doubtless has its origin in the phenomenal acrobatic feats of native Africa. [GPK]

lime A small tree (genus *Citrus*) and its green, lemon-like fruit. In Penang, Malaya, the tree is looked on as a patron of actors, but the fruit is tabu in the mines. Piercing a lime with pins causes love pangs in one's beloved. In India the lime is the prime ingredient in many potent curses. In Jamaica, the juice of limes is reduced by boiling and used in a plaster for wounds. The leaves in a tea with a little sugar are good for a cold. Jamaica Negroes also use the leaves to scent their baths. In Texas a necklace of limes cures a sore throat. The adoption of lime juice for the prevention of scurvy by the British Royal Navy gave rise to the appellation of limey or lime-juicer to all Englishmen and English ships throughout the world, an epithet which still survives.

limping dance A dance suggesting in its limp the gait of a man crippled in one foot: the full weight is placed on the left foot, then the right is dragged and suddenly flexed during the transference of weight. The Ute Indians had two such dances. The Lame dance was performed by women, sometimes as many as 100, in two lines which advanced, then converged and retreated. The progression was forward with even duple foot and drum rhythm. In the Dragging-Feet dance, however, the progression was to the left side, in a sunwise circle, men and women in arbitrary order. The right foot was actually lifted clear of the ground; the left knee was raised sharply during the right knee flexion. It was a social dance held after a scalp dance. The same step occurs among other Plains tribes, as the Teton Sioux, and is characteristic of the present-day Sauk and Fox Victory round dances. There seems to be no special significance attached to the use of a limping step. [GPK]

linden or **lime tree** Any tree of the genus *Tilia*, having soft, white wood and bearing cream-colored flowers. In Europe it is generally called the lime tree. Its blossom is the national flower of Prussia. Scythian soothsayers turned to the linden when prophesying, and wound its leaves around their fingers as they spoke. It was revered as a tree of immortality of central Europe, and in Estonia and Lithuania sacrifices were made to it by women for fruitfulness and domestic welfare, the men sacrificing to the oak. In Germany and the Tyrol it was the haunt of dwarfs and dragons (*Lindworms*, linden worms). As a tree of judgment, magistrates sat in its shade to pass sentence. In Sweden this tree must not be harmed, for it is the haunt of the domestic spirits.

One of the legends of its origin tells how Zeus and Hermes, traveling together in disguise, were pressed to share the humble home and fare of an old couple, Philemon and Baucis. They were so touched by the hospitality of these old people, that when they died, Philemon was turned into an oak, and Baucis into a linden, growing side by side with their branches interlaced.

In Rome the bark was said to prevent intoxication, and was therefore bound into garlands to be worn at feasts. In much of Europe the dried flowers are made into a soothing tea for debility, headache, insomnia, nerves, and as a blood purifier. The sap is fermented into a wine, and the seeds are made into a sort of confection. In Russia, oil of linden is used for toothache.

A wonderful linden tree, the *Susterheistede*, remained green as long as the Dithmarschen kept their freedom, but withered when they lost it. Legend says the day will come when a magpie will rear five young in its branches, and their liberties will once again be restored to them.

The North American Meskwaki Indians called this tree the string-tree, because its fiber was always at hand for the hunter or dweller in the forest. They prepared a strong twine from the fibers which they put to numerous household uses and for making baskets, mats, fishnets, etc. The Meskwaki boiled the inner bark to make a poultice which opened boils. They also made a tea from the twigs for lung complaints. White settlers pressed an oil from the seeds.

Lind Worm A Danish supernatural ballad using the transformation motif. Compare LAILY WORM. See BALLAD.

line dance Any dance in which the dancers form a straight line, or two straight lines which advance and retreat back and forth to and from each other, or in which the dancers form lines which progress in serpentines or circles. In its simplest form, the line dance consists of a static prancing, or of dancing in place with about face, as in the Pueblo Indian kachina dances. Sometimes several lines run parallel. By progression a leader may draw his followers into a serpentine or labyrinthine path, especially in vegetation rites, as the Iroquois Corn dance, the French farandoule, the Catalan sardana. By connecting the two ends, the line dance turns from an open round to a closed round, a maneuver still preserved in the *rondes ouvertes* and *rondes fermées* of rural France. The juxtaposition, meeting, and interweaving of two lines develops into the longways, of which the country dances and related contradanzas are the most elaborate. Many ritual dances take that form: the seises of Toledo and Seville Cathedrals, the English morris dances, the Mexican Yaqui matachini. In various Irish group jigs, as the Harvest Time Jig, multiple lines interweave. See DANCE: FOLK AND PRIMITIVE, section on *comparative choreography*; SERPENTINE. [GPK]

ling Chinese word for a bell with a clapper. A ling is generally suspended from an animal's neck. See BELL.

lingam In India, the male sexual organ; the basic phallic symbol, encountered in the earliest known Indian art (the Indus Valley civilization of the third millenium B.C.) and still the most common object of worship in Hindu sanctuaries.

The lingam is associated with Śiva, symbolizing the male creative energy of the god and thus the generative force of the universe. It is regarded as the fixed, fundamental, immovable form of the god; the phallic column or pillar is enthroned in the innermost section of Śiva shrines, whereas the secondary images used in outer sections, on the walls, in processions, are anthropomorphic.

It is also viewed as the abode of Śiva, or of the triad, Vishṇu, Brahmā and Śiva. In one version of the myth of the origin of the lingam (in the later *Purāṇas*) the appearance of the lingam demonstrates the supremacy of Śiva. In this myth, Vishnu and Brahmā are described as encountering each other in the primeval universe, and arguing as to which is the progenitor of all beings. As they argued, a huge fiery lingam rose up and grew into infinite space. In a vain effort to measure it, Brahmā as the gander flew up and Vishnu as the boar dived down. Finally the side of the giant phallus burst open revealing Śiva within who proclaimed himself the origin of the two while Vishnu and Brahmā bowed before him.

The lingam is frequently combined with the yoni, symbol of female creative energy, and the two convey various concepts associated with Śiva and his goddess—the procreation of the world, the divine parents, the principle of division into opposites and reunion into harmony.

In its earliest known form, the lingam is a simple, quite literal stone carving of the phallus. As the phallic symbol in Śiva shrines, it tends to maintain a simple austere quality, reflecting its elemental nature, often in marked contrast to elaborate surroundings. It is approached through four portals and radiates its energy to the four quarters into which the universe is divided. In carvings, the lingam may be represented with an aperture on one side, sometimes on all four sides, from which Śiva, or the triad, or the goddess may emerge. It is sometimes crowned with flames; the concept of the "fiery lingam" which penetrates the yoni corresponds to the ray of light or fire from the sun which impregnates the earth goddess and creates the earth.

When combined with the female symbol, the lingam is depicted as rising out of the yoni as a base. In anthropomorphic representations of Śiva and the goddess, Śiva may be shown holding out the lingam to the goddess, and the lotus, symbolizing the goddess, may support, encircle, or flower from the lingam. [MH]

gLing-chös The mythology of the *Kesar Saga*, found especially in Ladāhki and believed by A. H. Francke to be a mythology differing from that of the Tibetan pre-Buddhist Bon but possibly coexistent with it.

In gLing-chös, heaven (*sTang-lha*) is white in color and is ruled by King dBangpo-rgyabzhin and his wife bKur-dman-rgyalmo. They have three sons, Donyod, Donldan, and Dongrub, the last of whom descended to earth and became King Kesar of gLing. There is a world tree, a willow with its roots in Yog-klu and its top in sTang-lha. It has six branches, on each of which is a bird, a nest, and an egg. The earth, Bar-btsan, which is red in color, is the middle place or land of men. Yog-klu, the blue-colored underworld, is ruled by king lCogpo or lJogspo whose subjects are famous for a large number of beautiful children. A fourth realm, sometimes included, is that of the devil, bDud, which is black or violet in color.

li'nka·n The men's dance of the Delaware Indians. In their co-residence with the Iroquois of Six Nations Reserve, the Delaware continued this dance for a while even after the fading of their ritualism into Christianity. On the fifth night of the great Midwinter Bear Ceremonial, the warriors, in breechclouts, circled the central pole of their Big House in a counterclockwise direction. The songs were in antiphony between the leader and chorus of dancers. The steps were a test of agility. The dance had an origin myth about boys who danced themselves into the sky and became stars. The songs say, "We are going away, all of us." [GPK]

Linus song A Phœnician song of vintagers and reapers, interpreted by the Greeks as a lament for the untimely death of a youth Linus, who was exposed in infancy, brought up by shepherds, and killed by dogs. The name Linus or Ailanus was probably a misinterpretation of the words *ai lanu*, woe to us, the lament for Adonis in his character of corn spirit, symbolically slain in the cutting of the grain and invoked to return in a plentiful harvest the next season. Herodotus remarked on hearing a similar song in Egypt at harvest time. The Egyptian song, called *Maneros* by the Greeks, was also interpreted as a lament for a dead youth, son of a king and giver of grain. *Maneros* may have been a corruption of the words *maa-ne-hra*, return to thy house, the traditional phrase of all Egyptian laments for the dead and believed to be the words uttered by Isis and her sister in mourning for Osiris. Phrygian songs of the same type were called *Lityerses*, after the son of Midas. Lityerses was a mighty reaper who challenged all comers to contest and was finally overcome and killed by a great unknown, sometimes identified with Hercules. The lament bearing Lityerses' name was believed to have been sung first to console Midas for the youth's death. Similar stories are connected with laments for the cut corn sung elsewhere, and contests and mock sacrifices in symbol of the death and resurrection of the agricultural god have been common in harvest custom all over Europe for centuries. Probably the songs of ancient reapers were little more than a series of prolonged cries of sorrow, closely related to the laments sung for the dead at burial rites. See ADONIS; MOURNING SONGS.

The Phœnician vintage and harvest rite, of which the Linus song with its refrain *ai lanu* remained the striking part, seems to have traveled through Asia Minor on its way to Greece. Euripides, for example, calls the wailing lament of Phrygian origin. The observance of the festival of Linus in Argos included songs by women to protect their children, and a sacrifice of dogs. According to the explanatory myth, the mistreatment of Linus and Psamathe, his mother, enraged Apollo, who sent a female monster, Poine, to snatch children from their mothers. Hence the guardian songs and the expiatory killing of dogs. According to a Theban myth, Linus was killed by Apollo after a musical contest, similar to the one which ended in the flaying of Marsyas. Still later, and dependent on Linus' reputation as a great musician, composer of traditional songs, inventor of musical modes, adapter of the Phœnician alphabet to the Greek language, etc., is the myth making him the musical tutor of Hercules. Once, when Linus tried to chastise his backward pupil, Hercules became angry and killed Linus with a blow of the lyre. For this Hercules was banished to the hills as a shepherd, where he began his career as a monster-killer.

li'oa A Sa'a and Ä'ulu (Solomon Islands) ghost of a deceased chief of the reigning house or of a warrior; a ghost of power. Both the li'oa and akalo (ghost of an ordinary person as distinguished from the li'oa) are called upon for success and for aid to the sick. These ghosts, when incarnate in sharks, swordfish, or gropers are known as pa'ewa. Compare AKALO.

lion Everywhere the lion is the symbol of royal power and strength: it was Judah's emblem; it is Great Britain's today. It is still a current saying that a lion will not attack a true prince. The lioness was the symbol of maternity and the attribute of the mother goddesses of many ancient cultures. The Greeks led a lioness in the processions of Artemis. Lions and lionesses both are frequent in old Ægean icons, figuring as attributes, companions, and guardians of the old deities. Lion statues guarded the doors of ancient Egyptian tombs and palaces, and the doors of ancient Assyrian temples. Lions were the symbols of the Babylonian god, Nergal, as the hot summer sun. The Egyptian goddesses Bast and Sekhmet were lion-headed; and the lion was also associated with Rā and Horus.

The lion is the Buddhist symbol of courage, nobility, and constancy, and the harbinger of good luck. He plays a prominent part in Chinese New Year's festivities. The ceremonial lion dances in front of every house door in the town of New Year's Day, accompanied by drums and firecrackers. In China the silver collected by his companions goes to the temple keepers; in the various American Chinatowns it goes to Chinese hospitals or other Chinese welfare funds.

In Africa where the lion is a daily commonplace and not yet mythologized to attribute or symbol, he is regarded variously as the reincarnation of dead ancestors, as a supernatural spirit or patron to be propitiated, and as a totem animal. Almost everywhere name tabu prevails. In Angola he is *Ngana* (sir), for instance; the Hottentots say "Brother." Propitiation of his spirit occurs among all those who hunt the lion; and the killer is *accused* and is held as a ritual prisoner until ritually forgiven. Among many African peoples also the sorcerer-transformer of a village can become a lion; among the Bushmen a lion can turn into a man. The founder of a certain clan among the Dinka (a Nilotic group) was twin brother to a lion. Men of this clan (having the lion for totemic ancestor) sleep unharmed in the forest, feed lions, i.e. always leave part of their kill in the forest for the lion, and on occasion dare to take some of the lion's kill.

In African Negro trickster stories, Lion is often outwitted by Mongoose, Jackal, or Hare, according to the area. In the *Pañchatantra* and in Tibetan folktale also Lion is often outwitted by Hare. See LION AND HARE.

There are many Arabic accounts of the lion beseeched letting his victims go. And this trait of generosity, wherever it came from, spread all over Europe (where the lion is not indigenous) as one of the outstanding characteristics of this animal. The lion is the king of the animals (B240) as far back as the *Jātākas*, and commonly in European fable and folktale. He is brave, magnanimous, wise, a thorough gentleman and a sport. King Noble is the name of the lion in *Reynard the Fox*. The learned Italian monk, Savonarola (15th century) reiterated that the lion was magnanimous and wise, and quoted Pliny as proof of his wisdom: the lion obliterates his tracks with his tail as he goes along to keep hunters from following him. Solinus (3rd century) said the lion was not easily enraged, but terrible when roused; he spares those who fall prostrate, however, and is very gentle with virgins. Folktale and legend are full of saving, grateful, and helpful lions (B443). The lion's tenderness for virgins recurs in the European story of

the girl saved from ravishment by a lion (B549.1). In the medieval romance of *Valentine and Orson,* a lion leads the lost king out of the forest (B563.1). See ANDROCLES AND THE LION (B381).

In Æsop's fable of *The Lion's Share* (Jacobs #4) he is not so noble (J811.1). The ass divides the booty equally between himself, the lion, and the fox. The lion then proceeds to eat the ass; and the fox gives the lion the meat and keeps the bones for himself. In another European story, however, the noble lion again is evident (Q3.2). The lion himself divides the booty equally between himself, a thief, and a traveler. The thief demands half and is driven away; the traveler decides to claim nothing and is given half. In the Arabic *Infancy Gospels* and in *Pseudo-Matthew* there are stories of how the lions adored the child Jesus and were told to "go in peace."

It was a commonplace among medieval naturalists that the lion was afraid of the cock, trembled at sight of him, or trembled when he crowed, etc. Proclus (5th century) however, said it was not fear: that the cock was reverenced by the lion because both were born under the same planet, the sun.

Everywhere in magic the lion's heart is eaten to give courage. Hildegard of Bingen (12th century) said that it would also make the stupid wise. Other of Hildegard's prescriptions were: a lionskin cap would cure not only headache but mental disorders; deafness could be cured by holding a lion's ear to the deaf ear (because of the keen hearing of the lion); a lion's heart buried in the house would protect against lightning. Bartholomew of England (d. 1245) said sitting on a lion's skin would cure hemorrhoids. Albertus Magnus (13th century) prescribed a diet of lion's meat for paralytics. Very common also through the Middle Ages were little images of lions carved (under certain constellations) on certain little stones or gems or stamped on various metals which were potent to cure kidney trouble and especially acute intestinal pains. See EATING THE HEART.

Lion and Hare Title of an African Negro folktale based on the holding up the rock motif (K1251). As told by the Vandau of Portuguese South Africa, Lion, provoked by Hare, chases him. Hare, realizing that he will soon be caught, stands under a leaning rock and pretends to hold it up. "Lion, dear Grandfather," he cries. "Hold the stone! It will fall on us!" Lion forgets that he is chasing Hare and helps hold up the rock, lest it crush them both. Soon Hare lets go and goes home. Lion continues to hold up the rock for many days until he is so hungry and tired that he cannot hold it any longer. But when he lets go the rock does not fall. Now Lion is always looking for Hare to get even. E. Jacottet has recorded a Basuto version of this story. There are Kaffir and Hottentot variants; it is known in the Cape Verde Islands and in Puerto Rico, and is also included in Georgia Negro Uncle Remus stories. Lion as a character in African Negro folktale nearly always plays the dupe to Hare's or Jackal's tricks. See HOLDING DOWN THE HAT.

Lion and the Mouse One of Æsop's fables, in which a Lion, awakened by a Mouse, generously lets him go. Later the Lion falls into the toils of hunters. The Mouse, recognizing his roar, hurries to the spot, nibbles the knot, and soon sets him free. The fable occurs in the general type 75, The Help of the Weak, where the liberated animal is bear, fox, or lion, and it embodies the grateful animal spared motif (B371.1).

Lir (modern Irish *Lear*) In Old Irish mythology, personification of the sea; father of Manannán, the Irish sea god, and identified with the Brythonic Llyr, father of Bran and Manawyddan. See CHILDREN OF LIR; LEAR; MANANNÁN.

Lisa The male aspect of the Dahomean androgynous deity Mawu-Lisa, the first term of which is held to be the creator of the world as it is at present known. In native belief, Lisa is identified with the sun, as Mawu is with the moon. In missionary writings, Lisa is equated with Jesus Christ. [MJH]

Lithuanian folklore We find the first information in regard to Lithuanian folklore in chronicles and accounts of travelers. Chronicler Miechovita in 1517 says that in his time the Lithuanians used to sing sad songs of the death of the great Duke Žygimantas, murdered in 1440. Stryjkovski's chronicle in 1582 gives the Polish translations of the beginning of the lament songs in his time. The Italian traveler A. Guagnini mentions Lithuanian work songs in 1578. As time goes on we find more information about customs, beliefs, and folklore of the Lithuanians.

The first texts of a Lithuanian dirge, two songs, seven proverbs, and notes on wedding and funeral customs were gathered by J. A. Brand in 1673 and published in 1702. The first book, containing many ethnographic data, *The Lithuanians of Prussia*, was written in 1690 by German Rev. Theodor Lepner and published, 1744, in Danzig (2nd. ed., 1848 in Tilsit). There are some descriptions of customs, i.e. wedding ceremonies, clothes, folk musical instruments, and twelve proverbs; the folk songs are also mentioned, but the author dislikes them. Another important work on folk beliefs and customs, *Deliciae Prussicae oder Preussische Schaubühne*, was written in 1690 by a Lithuanian, M. Praetorius, in German, and published much later by W. Pierson (Berlin, 1871).

As for the oral folklore, at first attention was paid to proverbs and folk songs, chiefly from the linguistic point of view. In about 1830 the Lithuanian folk song, *daina*, became famous and was collected and investigated both by natives and foreigners. The biggest collection was gathered and published by A. Juškeviče (see LITHUANIAN FOLK SONG). With the beginning of the comparative studies of Indo-European languages, many foreign scholars visited Lithuania, studied the language of a supposedly dying people, and at the same time collected and published many folklore items. The work published by A. Schleicher, *Litauische Märchen, Sprichwörter, Rätsel und Lieder* (Weimar, 1857), made many of the Lithuanian folklore items available for comparative studies. Of similar importance was the collection of songs and tales by A. Leskien and K. Brugman, *Litauische Volkslieder und Märchen* (Strassburg, 1882) wherein 49 tales were translated into German and notes added by W. Wollner. The first work in which Lithuanian folklore was also skilfully investigated and compared with the similar variants of other peoples, was Bezzenberger's *Litauische Forschungen* (Göttingen, 1882).

The first native ethnologist was L. A. Juceviče (1813–

46). He published some collections of proverbs (1840), and folk songs (1847), and descriptions of customs and country life (1840–41). Finally in his largest and most important work, *Litwa* (Wilna, 1846), he touched on all branches of folklore and ethnography. He also compared Lithuanian songs and customs with similar traditions of the Slavonic peoples. He was an enthusiast, a fervent lover of his country and folk, an ethnographer, and a poet; hence, his works must be used for scientific purposes with caution. His premature death was a great loss.

In 1879 there was founded in Tilžė the *Lithuanian Literature Society* (LLG). For many years (until 1912) Lithuanians and their German friends worked together and much was done for folklore. The Society published a number of books and the journal *Mitteilungen der LLG* (6 vols., Heidelberg, 1883–1912), wherein much material on folklore and mythology appeared. Such activity was possible only in the part of Lithuania administrated by the Germans, because in the largest part of the country, ruled by Russians, even the printing of books in the Lithuanian language was forbidden for forty years (1864–1905). For that reason several books on Lithuanian folklore of the period were published in Germany and in the United States.

Interest in folklore grew and developed together with the struggle for national freedom. The leading fighter of the Lithuanian national awakening, J. Basanavičius (1851–1927), was also one of the greatest collectors and publishers of folklore. For many years he lived abroad. Voluntary collectors sent him folklore material and he was eager to prepare and publish it. In the United States, where about one million inhabitants of Lithuanian origin live, were published his important works on Lithuanian folklore: two volumes of folk songs from his native village Ožkabaliai (Shenandoah, Pa., 1902, 420 songs), and seven volumes of folktales: *Lietuviszkos pasakos* (2 vols., Shenandoah, Pa., 1898–1902), and *Lietuviškos pasakos yvairios* (4 vols., Chicago, 1904–05). The most important is the big volume *From the Life of Souls and Devils* (Chicago, 1903), which contains 813 tales and legends, with an extensive study "On Spirits and the Ancient Lithuanian Necrocult" by the editor. Basanavičius' publication of the Lithuanian tales remains the largest to date. He published many studies and articles on Lithuanian folklore, but they are the works of a dreamer; throughout, his work is deficient in scientific method, and displays the author's incapability of critically judging his own dogmatic convictions. Despite all this, his service as organizer of the collection of Lithuanian folklore and its publication is very great. As the ban from the Lithuanian press was lifted in 1905, Basanavičius went back to Lithuania and in 1907 founded in Vilnius the *Lithuanian Scientific Society* (LMD). One of the chief purposes of this society was the collection of folklore and ethnographic material. The Society published a journal, *The Lithuanian Nation* (*Lietuvių Tauta*), and there appeared many folklore texts and articles. The Society organized the collection of folklore, and up to 1932 had collected 10,000 songs, 4,500 tales and legends, 3,600 beliefs and superstitions, 21,000 proverbs, 5,400 riddles, and many other folklore items.

In independent Lithuania various collections and articles dealing with folklore were printed in the *Tauta ir Žodis* (*The Nation and the Word*), a publication of the Faculty of Liberal Arts in Kaunas (vols. 1–6, 1923–30). In 1930 the Folklore Commission under the auspices of the same Faculty was founded and functioned until 1935, under the direction of V. Krėvė. The Commission had collected about 132,000 folklore items, published 10 volumes of the series, *Mūsų Tautosaka* (*Our Folklore*) and some other books: a big anthology of folk songs by Dovydaitis (1930), and a collection of proverbs by V. Krėvė (1934). In 1934 the Commission for Folk Melodies was established by the Ministry of Education and began to work with phonographs. In 1935 the government issued a decree regulating folklore activity and established the *Lithuanian Folklore Archives* (*Lietuvių Tautosakos Archyvas*). This institution was to carry on the work begun by the above-mentioned enterprises with better methods, and all the investigations on folklore matters were concentrated in one place. Dr. Jonas Balys was appointed director of the Archives and he remained in charge up to 1944. The Archives dealt with all matters relating to oral folklore. Its task and method was purely scientific; practical application of folklore to daily life was not regarded as its part of its program. Its first care was to organize the collection of folklore and the cataloging of the material gathered. A folklore library was established and bibliography compiled. A publication was started, *Tautosakos Darbai* (*Folklore Studies*), where important material and studies were published, often with English or German summaries (7 volumes appeared, Kaunas, 1935–1940). The big publication of Lithuanian folk legends was begun in 1940 (Vol. I, legends of origin and concerning the devil). In five years (1935–40) considerable work was accomplished. With the help of numerous collaborators throughout the country and together with previous collections, the Archives had amassed by 1940 some 442,000 important folklore items, including 8,300 phonographic records. Most numerous were the songs—173,000; superstitions and folk beliefs—101,000; proverbs—63,000; riddles—44,000; tales and legends—34,000; games—3,000, etc. Folk traditions were still alive in the country and it was not too late for collecting. With the loss of independence and the occupation of the country first by the Russians and then by the Germans, the folklore work was paralyzed. German censorship stopped even the publication of folk legends. The situation today in Lithuania behind the iron curtain is unknown. In Lithuania, as in other Baltic countries, folklore was regarded as an important branch of national science and was generously supported by the state. A special chair for folklore at the Lithuanian University was established in 1934. Of the private institutions must be mentioned the activity of the Society for Research on the Native Land in Šiauliai, which established a rich museum and issued a journal *Gimtasai Kraštas* (*The Native Land*), where many articles on folklore were published (10 volumes, 1934–1944).

Most numerous and original in Lithuanian folklore are the folk songs. Numerous are dirges at wedding and funeral ceremonies. The funeral dirges, mentioned very early by chroniclers, survived up to recent years and are interesitng not only as creations of folk poetry but also because they contain many old folk beliefs. A large collection of 220 dirges was published in 1926 (in *Lietuvių Tauta* IV, 1) and some were translated into German by

Bartsch (in *Zeitschrift für vergl. Literaturgeschichte* 1, 1889, pp. 81–99).

The folktales have more types in common with the East than with the West. There are some original types with stanzas for singing. The folk legends have many original motives, e.g. about fairies and thunder. The *Motiv-index of Lithuanian Narrative Folklore* was arranged by Jonas Balys (in *Tautosakos Darbai* II, 1936). Very many of the old elements are contained in the folk beliefs (see LITHUANIAN MYTHOLOGY) and customs. The funeral ceremonies of the Old Prussians were described by Wulfstan in the 9th century. The wedding rites have frequently kept their very ancient form, going back to the old Indo-European era (see J. Balys, *Litauische Hochzeitsbräuche*, Hamburg, 1946). The proverbs often show, even for the international types, a different and figurative version. About 14,000 proverbs, beginning with A to I, were published by V. Krėvė in three volumes (1934–37). Some are not of traditional origin. A book of riddles, *Mislių knyga*, was published by K. Jurgelionis in Chicago in 1913 and contains more than 1000 riddles. In all there have been published about 10,000 songs, 6,000 tales and legends, 16,000 proverbs, and 2,000 riddles—only a small part of the collected material.

References: J. Balys, "A Short Review of the Collection of Lithuanian Folklore" in *Tautosakos Darbai* I, pp. 1–22. Kaunas, 1935. J. Balys, *Lietuvių tautosakos skaitymai* (Handbook of Lithuanian Folklore), 2 vols. Tübingen, 1948.

JONAS BALYS

Lithuanian folk song The most numerous and original creations of Lithuanian folklore are the folk songs (see DAINA). They are interesting because of their poetical value and folkloristic peculiarities. In content, they differ very little from the songs of other nations, but they differ from them sharply in their poetic artifices.

Subject matter The greatest part of the Lithuanian songs are romances about the relations between youth and maiden; these show great tenderness and are effective and pure. Often the same daina consists of two parallel parts: one concerning the youth, the other the maiden. These are the most beautiful and original. Wedding songs are very numerous with both mournful and cheerful tunes. The bride must weep and recite the traditional wedding dirges (*verkavimai*). The relations of the family members are often the topic of the songs. (It is impossible to imagine an individual without family or society [*kindres*]: a man of the folk hates solitude and is a very social being.) Therefore the songs about orphans are very affecting. They sometimes have mythical traits: the sun will replace the mother; the moon, the father; or the orphan will speak with the dead father, transformed into an oak tree. Work songs are also very numerous. A 16th century chronicler who wrote that the Lithuanians have special songs for each type of work was not exaggerating. Particularly interesting are the harvest songs of the *dzūkai* in southern Lithuania. They are often of obviously mythological character, e.g. a prayer to the sun. Other peculiarities of the same region are the Christmas songs and plays (without any traits of Christian customs and beliefs) and the songs of the Lenten season before Easter which have strong epic traits (really war songs). The Easter songs show more Christian influence, but the songs of the calendar festivals, like those of Shrove Tuesday, Whitsuntide, and St. John, are quite permeated with ideas from the old times, with emphasis on the care for fertility. There are few mythological songs where Sun, Moon, and Evening Star play the chief part, and the gods Perkūnas (Thunder), Laima (deity of fate), and some others like Žemyna (mistress of the earth) and *Bangpūtys* (god of the storming sea) are mentioned. Many work and calendar festival songs, however, have some mythological traits.

The fate of the Lithuanian nation was not favorable for preservation of the heroic or historical songs. The final loss of independence occurred in 1795 when Lithuania became a part of the large Russian realm. The upper class early became polonized, and the farmers were enslaved for hard work on the fields of the squires. It is no wonder that the mass of songs cultivated in the last centuries were of elegiac and personal nature. Historical songs mentioning heroes, places of battles, and other important events are not numerous. The heroic songs were mentioned by the chroniclers of the 15th and 16th centuries (Dlugosz, Miechovita, Stryjkowski), but were left uncollected and only a few fragments were noticed in Polish translations. Very old and original are the fishermen's songs from the coast of the Baltic Sea. There are all kinds of others songs, of course: humorous and drinking songs, children's songs, pastorals, songs about flora and fauna, etc. The ballads are also numerous and belong mostly to the general international tradition. Perhaps some of the numerous ones about drowned people are indigenous. Transformation of the dead into plants and birds is often mentioned. Slavic influence on the ballads is very great, the Germanic, very small (see J. Balys, *Hundred Folk Ballads*, Kaunas, 1941). In the ballads the epic motifs are often mixed with the lyric. Lithuanian folk *dainos* are *par excellence* lyrical "poesy of the hearth," says B. Sruoga. Even in motifs of epic character the lyricism is overwhelming. In the war songs, for example, the struggles on the battlefield are never described. How the youth was prepared to go out for the war is described, and the parting with his parents, sisters, and sweetheart, but about the battle we get only a few words from the message of the returning steed. The hero fought bravely, was killed, was buried with great solemnity: this is all. This sounds like the end of the ballad, but in Lithuania it is the beginning. Now we hear the most beautiful part of the song, how the relatives, usually his mother, sister and sweetheart, are mourning for the dead hero. Even the sun takes part and does not rise for nine mornings. *Poetic artifices* The daina being of lyrical nature has also retained some strong epic fragments, and makes much use of epic formulas. Parallelism is developed as a poetical artifice. The daina does not content itself with the ordinary dual-member parallelism, but uses multiple parallelism. The beauty and effectiveness of its poetical style is produced by the so-called negative parallelism with inexhaustible multiplicity of the formulas.

Among special poetic artifices of the Lithuanian *dainos* must be mentioned their diminutives, lavishly used in various ways (see F. Brender, "Die Verwendung der sog. Deminutiva im Litauischen," in *Tauta ir Žodis*, III, pp. 76–111. Kaunas, 1925). Diminutives give to the Lithuanian daina a special tenderness and grace, but not the weeping sentimentality that a foreigner may think. There are at least 20 acceptable diminutives for each common word such as mother, father, sister, brother, or maiden. For a Lithuanian each diminutive has a different flavor, even if the difference is microscopic. Hence translation of the daina is a very difficult task. (German reproduction of the diminutives is unnatural, in English impossible. The forms "daughterling" or "youngling" are not natural in English.) The attaching of the words "small" or "little" cannot reproduce the vigor of the original expressions. In some cases it would seem that the word "dear" or "lovely" would be preferable to "little." In the translation of the daina into English, wrote N. Katzenelenbogen, other peculiarities of the Lithuanian language which make translation more difficult are the lack of articles and of auxiliary verbs in either past or future tenses. Another attribute of the dainos is their onomatopœia. The Lithuanian language is inexhaustibly rich in interjections, also direct expressions of experience. Specific verbs are frequent in the dainos, where they are often used for their humor. It is quite impossible to reproduce their ingenuity and wit in other languages. For a Lithuanian, of course, each of these words calls up a specific picture. For the expression "to go" a Lithuanian singer can choose from not less than 25 words. Among other distinctive verbal forms of the dainos must be mentioned verbs with an internal object and the pleonastic infinitive, e.g. *vakarėli vakaroti*, to keep evening hours; *vasaružę vasaroti*, to pass the summer.

For the history of the epithet, the dainos provide abundant material. There we meet a kind of permanent epithet, e.g. *baltas*, white, has become stabilized. If we say *balta oblėlė*, white little apple tree, the meaning is clear: i.e. the apple tree has blossoms. It is quite otherwise in such an expression as *balta saulelė*, white dear sun, or *balta mergelė*, white dear maiden. Generally if the singer wishes to describe the sun or a maiden, he says *skaisti*, red. It seems that the color white for Lithuanians has always been the emblem of goodness, sincerity, joy. Therefore when the singer wished to emphasize the good attributes of things or persons, he used the word white.

The important symbolism of the dainos was investigated like their other poetic artifices by B. Sruoga (see *Folk-Lore* XLIII, pp. 301–24. London, 1932). He concluded that "the symbolism of the Lithuanian dainos is fundamentally of an erotic nature." For example, a tree symbolizes a man; the leaf, a word; dew, tears; to sow, to love; a falcon (or other bird) breaking the branches, a youth carrying off the bride, etc. A wreath of rue in the dainos always signifies innocence or the maiden herself. A lost wreath, forgotten or blown off by the north wind, never can be regained—lost innocence will never again return. When the maiden unplaits the wreath, she is preparing to marry. When a maiden is pleasing to a young man, and he raises his hat, she raises her wreath. If she surrenders her innocence to the young man from love, she burns her wreath in the fire. What the wreath is to the maiden, the cap is to the young man: ardor, youth, brightness. The youth of the dainos lives in the stable with his beloved steed, and the maiden in the "rue-garden." It is true, in the dainos of the last centuries, that rue as a symbol of maidenhood is very clear and common. Nevertheless this symbol is apparently new, and comes to Lithuania with the influence of the Catholic clergy from Poland not earlier than the 16th century. Rue is unknown to the Latvians; the maiden there wears a wreath of roses. In archeology and folk art the rue motif is absent. The oldest symbol of maidenhood among the Lithuanians was the lily. In the dainos even today we often meet the line: "My dear maiden is a beautiful white little lily." Rue is never called white, but always green. Flax blossoms represent the opposite of the innocence and maidenhood. Even the fairies had fear of flax blossoms. This symbol may be as old as the lily, and is surely older than rue.

Meter The meter of the daina is variable and very often mixed because the accentuation of the words is unstable. The rhythm always stands in close connection with the melody, which shows much beauty and symmetry. The rhythm is the essential requirement of the old daina. Rime is not so rare as in Latvian songs, but not made on purpose. The peculiarities of the Lithuanian language offer many occasions for riming. If the rime was accidentally created, it was accepted but not regarded as an essential requirement. Alliteration is rarer. The stanzas consist of two, three, four, or sometimes six lines. Some older songs do not have regular stanzas, but such stanzas could be made by singing with repetition of certain lines. The dainas often reach a considerable length. The new songs which were created under the influence of Polish and German religious songs and written literature always have rime and four-line stanzas.

Rhythm and melody The text and melody of the Lithuanian daina are closely connected. The recitation of songs is unknown. "The melody on the other hand, is only a cloak for the rhythm, presenting the accent in a more beautiful form" (Bartsch). The accentuation of some words differs in singing from the usual speech. Because the most important thing for the daina is its rhythm and melody, the oldest Lithuanian songs, *giesmės or sutartinės*, sometimes consist of meaningless words. The melodies of many of the old dainos have tonalities like those of the old modes (Dorian, Phrygian, Æolian, Ionian, etc.) and were sung in unison. According to V. Jakubėnas, "Lithuanian folk songs differ from Slavic songs in that they do not have the large intervals which are so typical of, for instance, Russian folk melodies. Sudden passages from resigned melancholy to reckless abandon and wild joy are also unknown in the Lithuanian songs. They differ from German songs by the frequence of changes in their measure, the alternation from 5/4 to 3/4 time being frequent . . . Ancient modes of church music are found even at the present time, but certain melodies cannot be attributed to any known mode. Under the influence of the song in thirds for two voices, which came to Lithuania from Germany in the 19th century, many melodies became European in character, but as a result lost their ancient Dorian or Phrygian minor tonality for a rather artificial major tonality. In the southwestern sections of the country, as well as in the Vilnius district, a great many songs for one voice are found which have preserved their ancient rhythmic and harmonic structure. These songs, the songs of the Dzūkai people, are suggestive of Oriental songs" (see *Lithuanian Bulletin*, p. 11, New York, 1947). An important study of folk melodies was given by T. Brazys, "Die Singweisen der litauischen Dainos," in *Tauta ir Žodis*, vol. IV: 3–50, Kaunas, 1925. He suggests that some Lithuanian melodies are similar not only to

the alleged old Greek, but also to the Indian recitations of the *Atharva-Veda* (p. 49).

Choral rounds The above mentioned *sutartinės* are the oldest and most primitive kind of daina. Such songs are not numerous, but they are the Lithuanian representatives of the oldest kind of folk poetry and were sung during the dance or work where many people were gathered. The very sharp rhythm and peculiar melody were important enough for the people to enjoy. Similar singing is in use among some primitive peoples, and perhaps in some regions of the Balkans (in Bulgaria and Serbia). Some of the meaningless *sutartinės* are more developed and have between long refrains a few meaningful verses. It seems that in olden times *all* the Lithuanian songs were of such nature. The singing of the *sutartinės* is very distinctive. There are at least two singers (sometimes three or four). One, the leader or collector (*rinkėja*) sings the chief text; the other, the so-called adviser (*patarėja*) sings the meaningless refrains. The second singer is silent at first and later begins to sing the same melody together with the first singer but singing a second higher or lower. The singing is also contrapuntal or in choral rounds (canon). The *sutartinės* are alive only in the northeastern part of the country and are sung by women. The Lithuanian Folklore Archives was able in 1935–1939 to take down on phonograph disks 336 such choral melodies. The music of the old musical instruments, played mostly by men, such as a kind of harp (*kanklės*), pan-pipes (*skudučiai*) or an orchestra of five wooden trumpets (*trimitai*), is of the same musical arrangement. Some *sutartinės* mention historical events and names, and thus give proof of their great age. (For some examples see in *Tautosakos Darbai*, vol. V, pp. 72–88, Kaunas, 1939).

Collections The first known collector was J. Schulz (1684–1710) but his notes have disappeared. The first three really important songs were published by P. Ruhig in 1745 in his work on the Lithuanian language, and the daina became famous thanks mostly to their enthusiastic review by G. E. Lessing, who in 1759 exclaimed: "What naive pleasantness! What charming simplicity!" The well-known song collection of Herder, *Voices of Nations*, in 1778–79, where eight Lithuanian and six Latvian songs were published, greatly influenced all the Baltic nations from Finland to Lithuania, and the interest in folk poetry grew rapidly. The first collection of 85 dainos with German translation and seven melodies was published by L. Rhesa, *Dainos oder Litthauische Volkslieder*, Königsberg, 1825 (2nd edition Berlin, 1843; 3rd edition Kaunas, 1935–1937). He was a native Lithuanian, professor of theology and philosophy, author and translator of many books into Lithuanian. He had numerous collaborators who sent him the dainos. He supplemented his book with a study on the daina and many of his conclusions remain valid today. The book achieved considerable success: such prominent authors as Goethe and Jacob Grimm wrote favorable reviews, and the daina was introduced to the educated world. The dainos from Rhesa's book were translated into French, Russian, Polish, and Czech. Thereafter many foreign scholars collected and published or investigated the dainos. Among the works of German scholars, the big edition of G. Nesselmann, *Litauische Volkslieder* (Berlin, 1853), is important. Nesselmann tried to reconstruct from several variants the original form of the daina, but not always successfully of course, and sometimes he is accused of mutilating them. Further, the publications by A. Schleicher (1857), A. Leskien and K. Brugman (1882), A. Bezzenberger (1882), and Tetzner (1897) must be mentioned. The prominent Polish folklorist, O. Kolberg, published a booklet with 76 songs (1879). The Russian folklorists, Potebnya and Kostamarov, used the dainos in their investigations. Finally the Finnish folklorist, A. R. Niemi, collected 3,500 songs and 1,500 of their melodies on phonograph cylinders, published with the help of a Lithuanian, Rev. A. Sabaliauskas. He made another important collection of 1,459 folklore items (1912), and wrote many studies of the relations between Lithuanian and Finnish folklore. The Lithuanians themselves were also busy gathering and publishing the songs. The publications of S. Stanevičė (1829), S. Daukantas (1842), and L. Jucevičė (1844 and 1846) were the first. Of great importance is the work of Christian Bartsch, *Dainů Balsai, Melodien litauischer Volkslieder,* 2 vols., Heidelberg, 1886 and 1889, containing 392 melodies with translations of the texts into German, and critical notes on melodies and texts. The greatest collector of the daina was the Rev. A. Juškevičė (1819–1880). He gathered 5,500 songs and 2,000 of their melodies. With the assistance of his brother, a skilled linguist, and with the support of the University of Kasan, he published in 1880–1881 three volumes of *Lietuviškos Dajnos* (*Lithuanian Songs*), containing 1,569 songs. The texts were written down and published very carefully, but the whole work suffers from unsystematic arrangement. Another large collection of Juškevičė, *Lietuviškos svodbinės dainos* (*Lithuanian Wedding Songs*), was published by the Russian Academy of Sciences in St. Petersburg, 1883; it contains 1,100 songs, very well arranged, and has references to the other published variants of each daina. The melodies to the two last mentioned collections were published in 1900 in Krakow. Juškevičė's collection is the largest thus far published. Of the most recent publications, perhaps the best is *Lietuvių liaudies melodijos* (*Lithuanian Folk Melodies,* with texts), arranged by J. Čiurlionytė, published in Kaunas, 1939, by the Lithuanian Folklore Archives (*Tautosakos Darbai,* vol. V). These Archives collected in 1935–1940 a very considerable store of dainas, 150,000 with texts only; 15,378 texts with melodies; and 6,836 melodies recorded on disks. Lithuanian scholars who investigated the daina are M. Biržiška (history of the daina and historical songs), T. Brazys (melodies), J. Balys (ballads), B. Sruoga (poetic artifices), and Z. Slaviūnas (*sutartinės*). English translations of songs are: *The Daina, an Anthology of Lithuanian and Latvian Folk-Songs* by U. Katzenelenbogen, Chicago, 1935 (an introduction with bibliography and English translation of 98 Lithuanian and 283 Latvian songs); and *Old Lithuanian Songs*, translated by Adrian Paterson, Kaunas, 1939.   JONAS BALYS

Lithuanian mythology The whole picture of the old Lithuanian religion is not clear, despite numerous books and articles written on this matter. The chroniclers Grunau, Lasicki, Lukas David, Waiselius, Hartknoch, and other authors of the 16–17th centuries recorded many names of the Lithuanian gods, but these are mostly either misunderstandings or purposely fabricated names. Some, however, seem worthy of trust, e.g. in the

chronicle of Malala in 1261 are mentioned the gods Perkūnas (Thunder), Telvelik (probably Kalvelis, the heavenly smith, who forged the sun), and Žvoruna (goddess of wild beasts). More exact are the reports and warnings made by the Christian priests who struggled with the old beliefs.

The Lithuanians became Christians in the 14th century, but for many centuries afterward Christianity was only superficial because of the lack of priests speaking Lithuanian. In the first Lithuanian book, published in 1547, the author M. Mosvidius exclaims: "There are people who make promises to Perkūnas, others worship, for the purpose of crops, Laukosargas (guardian of the fields), and for cattle, Žemepatis (master of the earth); and those who intend evil call upon the Aitvaras and Kaukas." The author probably confused the functions of Laukosargas and Žemepatis. The last two mentioned (Aitvaras and Kaukas) are household spirits who stole from other people to bring fortune to their masters. Canon N. Daukša wrote in his Catechism in 1595: "And who transgresses this First Commandment? Especially those who worship fire, Žemyna (mistress of the earth), snakes, reptiles, Perkūnas, trees, Medeinė (mistress of the forest), Kaukas (house demon) and other devils." In 1533 the Episcopal Visitor reported on conditions in the vicinity of Ukmergė: "The Christians of that district buried their dead in the groves and 'holy fields,' and they worshipped inanimate objects—oaks, stones, rivers and reptiles."

Folklore gives us much valuable material to supplement and correct the statements of printed sources. Lithuanian mythological beliefs can be divided into four categories: 1) gods; 2) spirits and demons, or the "low mythology"; 3) worship of nature; 4) worship of the dead.

The Gods The word for god in general is *dievas*. The most important god of the Lithuanians is Perkūnas, Thunder. He is often mentioned, beginning with the 13th century, as the most popular god of the Balts. He is conceived even today with clear anthropomorphic traits. There is no proof, however, that he was the highest god of the old Lithuanians. But if there was one God of Heaven, this could be Perkūnas only, because he has many traits which belong to the God of Heaven. The folklore of recent days tells that Perkūnas lived on the earth; his castle was on the top of a mountain; he was a good ruler and beloved by the people. After death he was taken to heaven, where he now has his court over the clouds, is ruler of the air, and commands thunder and lightning. "If we did not have a (Christian) God, he (Perkūnas) would be God, but there is a God, therefore Perkūnas cannot be the (Supreme) God. Formerly, however, he was ruler of the world and often descended to the earth to see how it was going for the people. Today he has not so much power, he can only flash the lightning"—so explained a man of the people. Perkūnas is the greatest enemy of all the evil spirits, whom he hunts during storms. He is the overseer of right and order, punishes bad people, and gives fertility to the crops of the good ones. The ill-treated wife asks in a song: "Light the lightning, strike, dear Perkūnas, strike dead my wicked husband." During the storm the Samogitian prayed: "Perkūnas, dear God, do not strike a Samogitian, but strike a Russian like a brown dog" or "strike a German like a devil." Another prayer:

"Perkūnas, dear God, have pity on us; drive out this darkness to the deserts, and we shall be obedient to thee all the days till the end of the world." Perkūnas is usually called *dievaitis*, diminutive, little, or dear god; this name is used only for the heathen god, never for the Christian God. If Perkūnas appears as a man, he is a strong man, a hunter, with a brown beard and some weapon. Often he is imagined as an old man. In his hand he has an ax or hammer. Sometimes he rides in a two-wheeled car, driven by a he-goat (compare THOR). About the Perkūnas family, the traditions are confused. In some traditions the influence of St. Elias is obvious.

According to importance, the second place belongs to Žemyna (diminutive *Žemynėlė*), mistress of the earth. Her brother is Žemėpatis (sometimes called Žemininkas), master of the earth. The latter was protector of the farm. Both have been mentioned since the 16th century. Žemyna was the more popular, and at every feast the first act was to make a libation to her, pouring some of the beer on the ground (see M. Praetorius, *Delicae Prussicae*, Berlin, 1871). She is often called on, together with sun and moon, in the magic formulas against the bite of the snake. The earth is worshipped by old people even today and regarded as mother and provider of food for all living beings. Before going to bed, the old people kissed the earth and prayed: "Earth, my mother, I have from thee my origin, thou feddest me, thou borest me, and after death thou wilt bury me." Sacrifices are given to the earth: in the first furrow is covered a piece of bread or a whole loaf; at harvest time bread is also offered with the words: "Dear Earth, thou gavest me and I am giving for thee." In old times a sow (and probably human beings) was offered to the earth at the beginning of the building of a castle or town.

An important place belongs to Laima or Laimė, deity of luck and fate, who forecasts the future of the newborn for its whole life; man is unable to make any change. "Such one is the forecast of Laima" (*taip Laima lėmė*), says a proverb, hence there is nothing to do. In a song the youth says: "Weep not, dear maiden, quiet your little heart, perhaps you are destined to me by Laima and despite all will become my sweetheart."

Spirits The most interesting spirits are *deivės* or *laumės*, the Lithuanian fairies. Usually they appear by twos or threes. They are very beautiful maidens, with long fair hair, blue eyes, and big breasts. A deivė is able to do all women's work in the most perfect manner, being especially skilled in spinning and weaving. She loves children and often exchanges a newborn child. She is helpful to poor girls or orphans, but a man must be respectful and careful. The deivės do not like mockery and are vengeful towards selfish persons. For example, a poor woman who was tired from work forgot her baby in the field; when she found him in the morning safe, he was guarded and generously granted gifts by the deivės; a rich woman, hearing of this, abandoned her baby purposely in order to receive similar precious gifts, but found her child in the morning strangled by the deivės. It is forbidden to spin on Thursday evening and to wash linen after sunset, because this is the time when the deivės are working. They are social beings, very fond of human society. One often falls in love with some young man and marries him; they can also be caught (as are swan maidens or nightmares) by a man. Family life with a deivė is happy; she is an exemplary wife and

mother, but she will leave her husband and children if some certain tabu is broken. The deivės or laumės are also spirits of the wood and water. They are similar to the fairies of the Celtic people, and many Lithuanian beliefs and legends about fairies are similar to the Celtic (see J. Balys in *Die Nachbarn* I. Göttingen, 1948). The deivės are not gods but they were worshipped. Mosvidius in 1547 exclaimed that the Lithuanians have "a hundred deivės if not more." Later the deivės became involved with beliefs about hags.

Very popular also are the demons or dragons, who bring good things to their master (see AITVARAS). In northern Lithuania the term is *pukys*, a borrowing from the Latvians, who in turn received the name and belief from the Germans (see PUK). In western Lithuania the household spirit, *kaukas*, a dwarf living under the earth, is charged with similar duties. This may be a borrowing from the Old Prussians, among whom the kaukas was a ghost. It seems that the former kaukas was a harmless house spirit like the German kobold, who works for a small reward and does not steal.

The Lithuanians do not speak of nature spirits as "mothers," but as "man" or "master"; e.g. Žemėpatis, master of the earth, Vėjopatis, master of the wind.

Belief in the corn spirit *Rugių boba*, the old woman of the rye-field, is common in western Lithuania (see *HDA* V: 266–68). To Rugìnis, the man of rye, a he-goat was offered in the fall (this is mentioned only once in a folk song). On Shrove Tuesday an image in female shape was formed, Morė or Kotrė, who is a personification of the spirit of fertility (see J. Balys, "Fastnachtbräuche in Litauen" in *Schweizer Archiv für Volkskunde*, v. 45, Basel, 1948). At threshing time the male figure of Kuršis was formed from straw; Rugių boba was not only made from straw, but also baked from dough. A cock was offered at the harvest feast.

The Lithuanians also have many other spirits: nightmare (*slogutė*), werewolf (*vilkolakis*), giant (*milžinas*), devil (*vėlnias*), and hag (*ragana*). There are many legends about them, but all beliefs of this kind are of a wellknown pattern and show few traits distinct from the corresponding traditions of other peoples. The devil is usually depicted as a German dandy. The word for devil, *vėlnias*, probably originated from *velys*, the deceased. Legends about the devil are published by J. Basanavičius (Chicago, 1905) and J. Balys (*Lithuanian Folk Legends* I, Kaunas, 1940).

Worship of Nature In all primitive religions worship of the manifestations of nature is very common. In the written sources it is often mentioned that the Lithuanians worshipped hills and stones, earth, and heavenly bodies, trees and water, and even serpents. There are plenty of places, hills, woods, or groves, rivers and small seas, which are named together with the words "holy" or "sacred" (*švent-*). The older name of such places is *alka(s)* (see E. Šturms, *Die Alkstätten in Litauen*, Hamburg, 1946). In sacred waters fishing was forbidden and in sacred woods it was not allowed to break even a bough. The mountain Rambynas, on the high bank of the Nemunas river, was one of the well-known sacred places. It had a sacred grove at its foot and a big stone for offerings on the summit. There was a place of worship there until the 18th century. The worship of big stones, called *deyves* is mentioned by the Jesuits in 1605. The transformation of man into stone is also known. Water was worshipped, but water spirits are unknown. Only one water god is named in the songs, *Bangpūtys,* blower of the waves, the god of the storming sea. The water maiden is known at the seashore (see *Globus,* 1902, p. 238). On the floor of the sea is another world where drowned people live. Sacred or healing springs are numerous.

Worship of trees was very widespread. The sacred groves were destroyed in 1390 by Jerome of Prague; the people revolted and the great Duke Vytautas expelled the missionary from the country. The tree most adored was the oak. The Jesuits cut down a sacred oak, devoted to Perkūnas, in Kražiai as late as 1618. Even today trees of a special shape, which have a cavity through the trunk, are worshipped and it is good for a man to crawl through and be healed of a disease. Some trees were regarded as living beings who feel pain; blood was said to flow from them if they were wounded. Spirits of the forests are also known: Medeinė, mistress of the forest, mentioned in the 13th and 16th centuries, and Giráitis, young man of the wood, mentioned in the 17th and 18th centuries (see J. Balys in *Deutsche Volkskunde,* Bd. IV, 1942, pp. 171–177).

Fire is one of the most venerated phenomena of nature. In the chronicle of Dlugosz of the 15th century the keeping of "eternal fire" by the priests and priestesses is described. Worship of the house fire is very common, even today. The spirit of fire is Gabija or Gabieta (from *gobti, gaubti,* to pile or put together). Every evening the housewife puts the glimmering coals and ashes together in the fireplace and prays: "Dear fire, little Gabija, do not burn, if not intentionally fired; you are nicely covered, then sleep, please, and do not walk in this house." Or: "Holy Gabieta, if you are piled together, you must rest quietly; if you are fired then light." Such prayers are very numerous. I have collected 55 of them. There is a very popular legend (having about 80 variants) of how the ill-treated fire speaks with the fire of another house and threatens to take revenge against the mistress of the house. (Cf. O. Loorits, *Das misshandelte und sich rächende Feuer,* Tartu, 1935). The duty of the mistress of the house is to keep the house fire unextinguished all the year. If the fire goes out, it is a bad omen and she must ask pardon of the fire and bring another from a neighbor. Only on St. John's Eve was the house fire extinguished and a new one brought from the festival pyre. It is mentioned also that a male god, Gabjaujis, fire deity of the kiln, was offered a cock at the end of threshing, because the kiln was heated all the time during threshing. The fire is very important at wedding ceremonies, as the bride brings to her new house her own fire, handed her by her mother.

In regard to the worship of sun, moon, and stars we have numerous statements beginning with Dusburg in 1326. The sun and moon are regarded as married and the earth or stars are their children. Today the heavenly couple is divorced and they never rise or set together. The cause of their enmity is explained in two myths. One of these is recounted in the folk songs (Rhesa, pp. 92, 220): The Moon (male) married the Sun (female) in the primeval spring. Because the Sun rose early, the Moon separated and walked alone. He met the Morning Star and fell in love with her. Then Perkūnas became angry, struck down an oak tree, and punished the Moon with a sword. Therefore we often see that the face of the Moon is cut in two pieces.

In old times—says another myth of the prose accounts —the Sun and Moon lived together in one small house. Living thus, they fell in love with each other and begot a daughter—Earth. After some time they began to quarrel and decided to be divorced, but they could not divide the daughter. God sent Perkūnas as judge, who decided that in the daytime Sun could look at the daughter, and Moon at night. So it is. If both wish to see the Earth then Perkūnas drives one of them away. (From Dusetos in eastern Lithuania.)

Another version from western Lithuania says that the quarreling Sun and Moon raced, the winner was Sun, and she had the right to look at Earth by day. An eclipse of the sun is explained by the fact that some demon or hag is devouring or harming the sun, and a horrible noise was made by people to drive the demon away. Another explanation is: the sun and moon are kissing each other and cover themselves with a sheet so that their daughter, earth, will not see this. There are numerous short songs of children who pray to the sun during a storm: "Black clouds, go to the land of the Russians (or Germans); mother dear Sun, come to our land." Or: "Come, dear Sun, bring us cakes and drive away the clouds with the whips (i.e. rays)."

In Lithuania the moon was apparently worshipped more than the sun. The moon was often called "young god" or "prince." I have collected 60 prayers to the new moon. When the new moon is seen for the first time, you must pray: "Moon, Moon, dear Moon, bright little God of the Heaven, you must become round and I remain healthy. Give him the fullness and me the realm of Perkūnas." Or: "I bless you, bright dear Moon. I wish brightness to you and beauty for myself; I wish you the qualities of a deity, and give me the qualities of a man." Such prayers are used to obtain health and beauty. The first prayer is used against all the diseased, e.g. to stop bleeding. Similar prayers to the new moon are known also to some Finno-Ugric peoples, Estonians (see Loorits, *Grundzüge* I: 9), and Moksha Mordvins (*ERE* VII: 844).

The sun and moon are said to be wandering on the earth, she as a beautiful maiden with golden hair who is helpful to man, and he as a fair young prince, who sometimes seduces a girl and takes her to the moon. An orphan girl asks help from the moon and is taken to him. Sometimes the moon punishes a proud girl, who asks "Which is brighter, my body or the moon?" and takes her to the moon. An old woman with two water pails who offended him was also taken to the moon. In the folk songs there are often mentioned not only sun and moon, but also Venus and the Pleiades. The morning star kindles the fire for the sun in the morning and the evening star spreads his bed. Some legends account for the origin of Ursa Major and the Pleiades. The rainbow is called "the girdle of the fairy" (*laumės juosta*).

The Dead   Formerly the Lithuanians had no fear of the dead. The living and the dead formed one society in the frame of a big family. The dead was thought of as living in the grave with many of the same needs as the living. Therefore food, tools, even whisky and tobacco, were put in the coffin or grave. The dead was feasted at burial, later on his anniversary, and at the big feasts, Christmas and Easter, and especially at the feast of the dead in the fall. The dead can be vengeful if his will is broken or if he is offended. He can also be helpful to the fertility of the fields.

Along with the idea of the dead as a "living corpse," we find the belief in a kind of material soul (vėlė), which is different from the corpse but has many common traits: sometimes it is visible as fog or specter, and we can recognize the dead person or hear him. He feels cold and heat, is hungry or thirsty. The spiritual soul, siela, is the invisible power or spirit of man. The dead can be reborn not only as a child of the family, but also can become incarnate as tree, flower, or bird. The dead must climb a high mountain and thus to have long finger-nails is of great value. Hell and purgatory are in this world. The souls suffer in the water, in the trees, or on the fireplace of the family. Any underworld for the dead is unknown. The dead are sometimes dangerous to the living, of course, and one must be careful. Love and pity for the beloved dead are mixed with a desire for self-protection. All seeds and unborn lives must be protected against contact with them. A man who was murdered or drowned is especially dangerous, as are also all magicians, suicides, and criminals. They hunt and harm the living. Such a one is called nelaikis, one who did not die at his time, or vaidùlis, ghost. Some of them became vampires. One must cut off the head of the dangerous dead man and bury it at his feet. Fear of the dead increased with the acquiring of Christian doctrine. The demon of death is a female, giltinė, one who stings. She cuts or strangles a man to death, and further, she has no interest in the soul or corpse. The pest-deities (maro deivės) drive in a coach with six black horses. There are people who can see ghosts, dvasiaregiai, who recount many stories about their visions.

Concerning the worship of the dead there is a large literature (see M. Alseikaitė-Gimbutienė, Die Bestättung in Litauen in der vorgeschichtlichen Zeit. Tübingen, 1946, pp. 203–216). I myself devoted an extensive chapter to this question in Handbook, vol. II, pp. 170–200.

Old Prussians Much has been written about Old Prussian religion but very few of the conclusions are certain (see H. Bertuleit, Das Religionswesen der alten Preussen. Königsberg, 1924). What is certain is that god in general was called deivas; the Thundergod was Percunis; Kurko probably was the god of fertility, worshipped at harvest time (Lithuanian Kuršis). The evil spirit was called pikuls or pakuls and a ghost was kauks. The offering of a he-goat was an important ceremony. A legion of other deities were fabricated by writers. (See "The Paganism of the Ancient Prussians" in "Folk-Lore" XII: 293–302. London, 1901.)

Literature:

A. Mierzyński, Mythologiae Lituanicae Monumenta. 2 vols. Warszawa, 1892 and 1896.

H. Thomas, Die slavische und baltische Religion vergleichend dargestellt. Bonn, 1934.

W. Mannhardt, Letto-Preussische Götterlehre. Riga, 1936.

J. Balys, Handbook of Lithuanian Folklore (in Lithuanian). Vol. II, pp. 7–96. Tübingen, 1948.

JONAS BALYS

Li T'ieh-kuai One of the Chinese Eight Immortals: Li of the Iron Crutch. Hsi Wang-mu, Goddess of the Western Sky, gave him immortality after his unhappy childhood. Once while wandering in a wood, Li's soul left his body to visit a sacred mountain. When the soul returned its body had disappeared, and it had to occupy the body of a beggar lately dead of hunger. The beggar had been lame, had matted hair, and bulging eyes. Often Li T'ieh-kuai is honored by druggists and exorcists. [RDJ]

Little Briar Rose Title of the sleeping beauty story as presented by Grimm (#50), in which a childless king and queen eventually were blessed with a beautiful infant daughter. In gratitude and joy the king gave a splendid feast and invited everybody in the realm, including the (supernatural) Wise Women of his region. There were thirteen of these but he invited only twelve, because he had only twelve golden plates. At the feast, one by one, the Wise Women bestowed their gifts upon the child: beauty, goodness, cleverness, a sweet temper, wealth, etc. But suddenly in walked the slighted thirteenth and prophesied that in her 15th year the child would prick her finger on a spindle and die. But the twelfth, who had not yet spoken, said: "She shall not die, but sleep a hundred years."

All came about as prophesied, in spite of the king's precautions in having every spindle in the country burnt. On her 15th birthday the young princess happened into a tower room where sat an old woman spinning, in curiosity picked up the spindle, pricked her finger, and fell asleep. Sleep took the whole palace and everybody in it. A hedge of thorns grew thick around it in the passing years, and every year some king's son died in the impassable hedge seeking the beautiful sleeping princess whose story the whole world knew. At last one came who got through—at the end of 100 years at the appointed hour for the spell to be broken. He got through the hedge, saw the king and queen asleep upon the throne, saw the cook asleep in the kitchen, and the flies asleep on the walls, and finally came to the tower room where slept the beautiful Little Briar Rose. He leaned down and kissed her. She awoke and took his hand, and the pair went downstairs and woke the king and queen. Then the whole castle came awake. Soon the king's son and the little princess were married to live happily forever after.

This story (Type 410) is a composite of folktale elements very ancient and widespread: most important among them the sleeping beauty motif (D1960.3), itself but one of a large group of magic sleep motifs (D1950–2049), and the fairy takes revenge for being slighted motif (F361.1). The story of Eris, uninvited to the wedding feast of Peleus and Thetis, who had her revenge by throwing into the midst of the company the Apple of Discord, testifies to the antiquity of the idea of spite on the part of slighted supernaturals. Many another ancient divinity took revenge for neglect. The Lemnian women, for instance, who had neglected Aphrodite, were visited with an offensive odor which drove away their husbands. And Artemis sent a great boar to ravage the realm of Œneus for his neglect to sacrifice to her. Other motifs utilized in the sleeping beauty story are F312 ff. in which fairies (Fates, Norns) preside, prophesy, or bestow gifts at the birth of a child; F316.1, in which one fairy's curse is ameliorated (but not canceled) by another's amendment, disenchantment by kiss (D735), and hero finds maiden in castle (N711.2). Perrault's version of the sleeping beauty tale is entitled *La Belle au Bois Dormant.*

Little Goose Girl Title of a Scandinavian folktale (Type 870A) limited to Scandinavia but found as a ballad in France and Scotland as well. Typically, it is the story of the substituted bride, the goose girl taking the place of the princess in the marriage bed because the prince has near the bed a magic stone or other chastity index. When the real, but unchaste, bride attempts to regain her place, the prince recognizes his companion of the night before through tokens he has given the little goose girl. Grimm's *The Goose Girl* (#89) belongs rather to Type 533, The Speaking Horse Head, than to Type 870A, though both are bride substitution stories. In the Grimm tale, the evil servant forces the princess to change places with her, and passes herself off as the expected bride. Only after the marriage has taken place and the head of the speaking horse has been hung on the wall does the true state of affairs come to light. The false bride is tricked into declaring her own punishment, the Nageltonne, or nail-studded barrel.

Little Mohee An American song considered by Kittredge to be derived from an English original, *The Indian Lass,* and by Phillips Barry to be indigenous, possibly a landsman's song of frontier days remade by seamen. Its titles and variants are numerous, but in essence it is known all over the country from the mountains of the southeast to the fishing towns of the northeast, and from the plains of the west to the Pacific islands. Mohee, the Indian lass who is loved and left for a sweetheart in the wanderer's "own country," is also called Mohea, Maumee, and a "pretty Kanaka," and may draw her name from Maui of the Sandwich Islands (Hawaii), which was a regular stop for the Arctic whaling ships on their way home. The song was a forecastle favorite on these ships. In Vermont, the meeting of the song takes place in a tavern in New Orleans. Elsewhere, the hero meets her in a coconut grove, or as he sat alone on the grass along his road. Certain of the sea-going details survive in versions heard far inland in the hills. It is also known as *Pretty Mohea* (or *Mauhee*), *The Fair Indian Lass, The Lass of Mohea.* The tune to which it is most often sung nowadays is a close relative of *Old Smoky.*

Little Moron Proverbial embodiment of the humor of absurd misunderstandings in American jokes and wisecracks. As the successor of Dumb Dora and "so dumb" lines (She was so dumb she thought a subordinate clause was one of Santa's offspring), popular during the Twenties, Little Moron came into vogue during the Thirties and soon percolated down to the grade-school level, where he still circulates. Many Little Moron stories are old jokes revamped: The Little Moron told his friend, "I only weighed three pounds when I was born." "Did you live?" asked his friend. "Did I live! Say, you oughta see me now!" Since most Moron stories depend for their point upon a pun or a bull or blunder, two standard patterns are employed: the question and answer (for the pun): What did the Little Moron do when he was told he was dying? He moved into the living room; and the anecdote (for the bull and blunder): The Little Moron got up in the middle of the night to answer the telephone. "Is this one one one one?" says the voice. "No, this is eleven eleven." "You're sure it isn't one one

one one?" "No, this is eleven eleven." "Well, wrong number. Sorry to have got you up in the middle of the night." "That's all right, mister. I had to get up to answer the telephone anyway."

What makes the droll Little Moron so human and likable is his resemblance to the average man—the man with two left feet who succeeds in putting both feet in his mouth every time he opens it. He is Superman turned upside down. And though his ineptness evokes the reaction, "How can he be so stupid!" or "How wrong can he get!" who shall say whether he is wisely foolish or foolishly wise? There is a wholesome moral in more than one Little Moron story. A group of Little Morons was building a house. One of the Little Morons went to the boss and asked if they should start building the house from the top down or from the bottom up. "Why, start from the bottom and build up, of course!" replied the boss. The Little Moron turned and yelled to his fellow workers: "Tear 'er down, boys! Gotta start all over!"

B. A. Botkin

Little Old Men (Spanish *Los Viejitos*) A comic fiesta dance of Michoacán, Mexico, performed by Tarascan Indians as entertainment for the throngs. Young Tarascans, wearing clay or wooden masks of old men, wide straw hats, serapes, and pajamalike pants, lean on canes. They enact a burlesque of their elders to the thin music of the *jarana,* a kind of ukulele, which the leader carries. Costume and steps are colonial; but ancient ritualism and Indian style persevere through the hispanized surface of the dance. The youths mimic the elders in tottering *zapateados* (footwork) and cruciform steps. The canes beat a staccato accompaniment to the footwork. Three forms of *la cruz* (the cross) occur, with tapping and jumping. [GMF; GPK]

little people The dwarfs, leprechauns, apuku, gnomes, goblins, and other diminutive spirits of the wild, of rivers, forests, and fields, of practically every people in the world. They are tricksy, sometimes malevolent, but most often helpful to mankind if approached right. In origin they are animistic, and therefore in many ways divine; they are unreliable and amoral. Though they react to kindness, the reaction is sometimes an unexpected one. The cobbler who found his shoes finished by the little people and presented them with clothes found them gone for good the next morning. Yet, for those little people who help to do things about the house, a pitcher of milk or other food is required payment. A forest dwarf like Rumpelstiltskin is essentially helpful; it is only his reward that seems all out of proportion to the task, yet the little people do like to take human babies. The *apci'lnic* of the Montagnais of Labrador live in the remote brush. They are knee-high to men and can disappear magically and instantly. Their appearance at any place is supposed to be a warning of danger to the man who sees them. Their one vice is a fondness for stealing human children. The Penobscot *wanagemeswak* are hatchet-faced, but they are so thin that they can be seen only in profile; a full forward look at them shows nothing. They live in the rivers and in river pools and leave clay figures on the river banks which are lucky to the finders. Some of the little people of the world live in the mountains, where they work the metals in the mines; they are therefore possessors of or guardians of great treasures. See

APUKU; AZIZA; CHANGELING; DOMOVIK; DWARF; EGBERE; ERE; MMOATIA; TCIKAPIS.

☞ Dwarfs of all sorts are found as characters in American Indian folktales, or in the folk beliefs of nearly all tribes. In the southeastern United States among the Cherokee and Yuchi, and also among the Iroquois groups to the north, a particular group of dwarfs, known as Little People, are prominently mentioned. The Cherokee credit these Little People with being generally helpful to mankind; when Sun was shining down and making it too hot, in an attempt to kill people, the Little Men made medicine and changed pairs of men into various snakes which they sent to Sun's daughter's house to kill Sun. But their helpfulness is not limited to mythological instances; Cherokee conjurers were reputedly able to capture Little People and make them do useful work. There are however malicious Little People also; one is a mean little dwarf who lives in caves in the river bluffs, and may cause children's diseases. Yuchi little people are malevolent; they live in the dense woods, and are the souls of evil persons who have died. If intruded upon, they kill the intruder. Seneca (Iroquois) little people are powerful, and revenge themselves on people if they are neglected; the Seneca Dark Dance Society placates them with dancing and feasting. For extended description of little people among the eastern tribes see John Witthoft and Wendell S. Hadlock, "Cherokee-Iroquois Little People" (*JAF* 59: 413–22). [EWV]

☞ Tales about a race of very small men, which were current among the Spanish conquistadors, derive in part from mythological accounts heard from the Indians. Certain Tupi-Guarani tribes of the coastal region believed in the existence of small people living near the country of the Amazon women. Amazons and pygmies are also united in legends transcribed in eastern Bolivia. [AM]

Little Rabbits Sing The title of a brief Chiricahua Apache Indian story (reported by Morris E. Opler in his *Myths and Tales of the Chiracahua Apache Indians, MAFLS* 37) in which several little rabbits are playing about in the bush, singing about themselves, and playing at the life and fate of all rabbits. One sang, "Little rabbit is out! Little rabbit is out!" Another sang, "I'll be the first coyote to swallow those rabbits." For this is the story of many little rabbits.

Little Red Riding Hood Title and heroine of a nursery tale familiar throughout western Europe. Most versions stem from Perrault's *Petit Chaperon Rouge* (1697), but Grimm's *Rotkäppchen* (#26) is the source of several oral versions. The story is not popular (directly from oral tradition) but seems literary to the extent that it derives from Perrault and Grimm. It is essentially the same story as the *Three Little Pigs* (*The Wolf and the Seven Little Kids*, Grimm #5; compare *The Glutton*, Type 333), both tales being examples of Type 123. *Little Red Riding Hood* is an ogre story, a swallow story. The little girl (or the goats or pigs) is eaten by the wolf masquerading as the grandmother (or mother). In Perrault's version, that is the end of the story. But a hunter appears in the Grimm version and kills the wolf, slits him open, and Red Riding Hood and her grandmother emerge from the monster's belly. Other endings appear elsewhere: stones are sewed into the

sleeping wolf's belly in place of the kids and the wolf falls in the water and drowns; the wolf leaps to his death; the grandmother hides in the closet and the little girl is not eaten; a woodsman kills the wolf with an ax before he can eat Red Riding Hood. What popularity the tale has is probably based on the two incidents in the story of the girl on an errand stopping to speak to a stranger and from the deliciously horrible series of climactic questions about the ears, eyes, nose, teeth, and mouth of the "grandma." This "What big ears you have" "The better to hear you with, my dear" is paralleled in the companion tale of the pigs by the formulaic repetition of the "chinny-chin-chin" and the "huff and puff and blow your house in." The story of Little Red Riding Hood is known in Africa, but because the story is mixed with that of the *Three Little Pigs*, it is essentially an animal tale, even though the heroine is human.

Little Sea Day The third Sunday in August, formerly celebrated at Seagirt, New Jersey, by New Jersey farmers and farm hands who had to miss Big Sea Day.

Little Startlers Title of an American Indian tale in which Trickster badly frightens young quail; they retaliate by hiding beside a path and whirring up at him as he passes by, startling him so that he stumbles or falls into a hollow log, or otherwise hurts himself. Often the whirring noise which quail make is accounted for thus. The tale of the Little Startlers is told by many Central Woodlands tribes (Algonquian, Assiniboin, Cree, Kickapoo, Menominee, Ojibwa, Sauk. See William Jones, *Ethnography of the Fox Indians. BAEB* 125: 30–31, 48). [EWV]

Liu Pci In Chinese folklore and legend, the God of Basket-makers and Straw-Shoe-sellers: one of the "Three Musketeers" (with Chang Fei and Kuan Kung) of China, and numbered among the 24 assessors of Kuan Kung.

liver Plato said that the liver was a mirror on which the thoughts of the mind fell and were reflected as the image of the soul. The *Odyssey* calls the liver the seat of desire and therefore a potent charm to produce desire when eaten. The 16th century anatomist, Fallopio, on the medical faculty at Padua, claimed that the veins originated in the liver as the arteries originate in the heart. In the 17th century a Parisian philosopher claimed that the brain, liver, and heart, being the first parts of the body to be formed, were the principal seats of the soul (E714.5). By far the most universal attribute of the liver, however, has been the belief that it is the seat of strength and courage. Peoples as widely separated as the ancient Arabs, the Veddas of Ceylon, several tribes of Indochina, the Bantu Bakongos, and the Micmac Indians of northeastern North America have eaten the livers of their slain enemies to absorb their courage and strength. Among the Basuto a brave man is said to have a large liver. Young Bechuana boys eat ox liver to increase their courage and intelligence; however one lobe induces forgetfulness, and this is eaten only by the women who have much to forget. Some central African peoples believe that crocodile liver enlarges the soul. In the 3rd century in India the liver of the dragon was eaten by those who wished to understand the language of the animals. The liver of the unicorn was particularly highly thought of, although the Romans preferred that of the vulture, and the Greeks that of the goose. In the 16th century the most diabolical sorceries could be counteracted with the liver of a black cat. Egyptian records show that as early as 1850 B.C. they used liver as a cure for night blindness, a use to which it is put today because of its richness in carotin. Pliny recommended weasel liver to cure pains in the human liver. The Omaha Indians eat it not only for courage, but for good voice, and Mississippi Negroes hold calves' liver over a wound to make it heal more quickly. Liver divination (hepatoscopy) is one of the most ancient of all forms of divining; artificial livers of clay or stone have been found by archeologists, models marked off into the significant areas to be observed by the diviner. It is a potent charm in hoodoo. The liver of a woman in Italy is still supposed to confer secrets of witchcraft, though, in the Middle Ages, one of the most potent antidotes for witchcraft was to eat the liver of a witch. Mississippi Negroes bury the liver of a murdered man some distance away from the corpse on the theory that his murderer will be drawn to the spot, and thus be caught. An Eskimo will eat the liver of his victim to weaken the vengeance of his relatives and to lay his avenging ghost. The liver of a left-handed person is on the left side of the body.

Liverpool Girls A capstan chantey sung when hauling up anchors and cables in readiness for landing. When the wind is fresh it is said that the Liverpool girls, known in days ashore, are holding the towrope. The chorus is "ho, row, row, bullies, row," and the title is sometimes given as *Row, Bullies, Row.*

liwa A term or name (**Liwa**) given by the Mískito and Sumu Indians of eastern Nicaragua and northeastern Honduras to a kind of water-dwelling evil spirit. One, named Liwa, lived in a great whirlpool at Namakalmuk (Upper Wanks River) and killed whole canoeloads of Indians. A *sukya* (shaman) drove him away by burning an alligator on the beach nearby. Another liwa inhabited the shallows of Caratasca Lagoon where he drew boats and crews underwater. Liwa are always white, perhaps worm-shaped, and are said to have their own underwater ships. See G. R. Heath's "Mískito Glossary," *IJAL* 16: 25.

lizard Everywhere that the lizard is indigenous (in all his genera, species, and varieties) man has felt an inevitable affinity with him. This may be because the hand of man was fashioned after the hand of the lizard (A1311.1) or because the first men were lizards. But whatever the reason, it is true that he is regarded as mysterious, a bringer of omens and warnings, the incarnation of god or ancestor, or even the dwelling of one's own separable soul—and this in spite of the fact that his bite is feared as poisonous in many places. In magic the dried lizard or some part of his body is used to rejuvenate the old—possibly because the lizard, like the snake, sloughs his skin and renews himself. The ancient Egyptians had great respect for *Monitor Niloticus* (which grows to 4–6 feet) believing that it destroyed crocodile eggs. In Alsace it is said if a lizard runs across a woman's hand she will be a skilful needlewoman.

Old travelers' tales describing the New World produce some interesting observations on lizards. John Oldmixon, in his two-volume *British Empire in America* (1708) says that the lizards of Barbados "loved to be where Men were, to gaze in their faces, and hearken to their

Discourse." *The Voyages, Dangerous Adventures, and Imminent Escapes of Captain Richard Falconer,* London, 1720, reported that lizards would tickle the ears of sleeping persons to warn them of the approach of alligators, vipers, "or any voracious Beast." The warning lizard is the subject also of a Breton folktale (B492). This feeling of affinity holds also in New England, where the people say that if you kill a lizard you will die yourself inside of a year. Zoroastrianism presents an exception where the lizard is associated with evil and said to be the food of the damned. See ANGRA MAINYU.

According to Australian Dieri mythology, the First Ancestor created a lot of little black lizards, divided their feet into toes and fingers, touched the middle of the face to make a nose, indicated eyes and mouth the same way. Then he stood them up, but they could not stay upright, so he cut off their tails, and then they were men. The Australian Pindupi and Jumu tribes recognize Pupula (Lizard) as creator of the ancestors. At first human beings were smooth all over; their fists were doubled on their chests; their legs were bent up against their bodies (perfect description of the embryonic position). So Pupula gave them breasts, noses, eyes, ears, elbows, knees, vulva, penis, and cut their toes and fingers apart. He also taught them to make fire and gave them their marriage laws. The western Aranda have almost the same story: Munger-kunger-kunja (Lizard) drew the first people out of the ocean, cut them apart with a stone knife, cut eyes, ears, mouth, etc., circumcized them, gave them fire, spears, shields, boomerangs, and *churingas* (bull-roarers.) The Aranda also associate Lizard with their sky and earth myths. They will not kill a lizard lest the sky fall down upon the earth.

In the mythology of the northern Aranda, the first man existed in the form of a lizard, but he was so stiff that he could not walk. So he lay down in the sun and grew warm and stretched. After a while he looked at himself and said "Hello, I'm a lizard." So he just lay there in the sun and after a while he saw another lizard beside him, which had come from his own body. He said "Hello, there's one just like me." So he lay in the sun and after a while there were a lot of lizards in the sun, which had sprung from his body. After a while he saw one of them die. He said "That is me." And after a while all the lizards stood up and walked away like men.

Many peoples believe that lizards are messengers of the gods or the dwelling of the souls of the dead. Hence their appearance is ominous. If the big iguana walks into a house in the Philippine Islands, for instance, it is interpreted as an omen that someone in the house is summoned to die.

In the Malay Peninsula the lizard brings new babies and causes their souls to enter into them. The Mískito Indians of Nicaragua and Honduras also believe that it is an omen of conception if *lupalila* (a species of lizard) walks on a woman's dress. Everywhere in Polynesia the people have great respect for lizards; there is a widespread lizard cult, and Moko, the king of the lizards, is well known. House-god images in the shape of lizards have been found in Easter Island. The external (separable) soul and the dream-soul often take the form of a lizard, especially among Melanesians. Lizards are the shadows of the gods in Tahiti. One inland species is believed to be the shadow of Tipa, the healing god. *Mo'otea,* a kind of light-colored lizard, represents the deity of the moonlit sky. A certain dark lizard and a streaked variety are shadows of the god of the conquering arrow. *Mo'opuapua*, the flower lizard, represents certain ethereal, flower-dwelling supernaturals. In some parts of Micronesia lizards are kept in enclosures and well cared for because they are believed to have power over thunder and lightning. In the Celebes and also in parts of Australia, lizards are sometimes killed when seen because they are believed to be the familiars of witches and sorcerers, and as such can cause sickness and death.

A lizard is the tribal god of the Shilluk people of the White Nile. In Bonny, Nigeria, lizards are fed and those seen to be in danger are rescued.

In India the lizard is ominous also, and is used in magic as a love charm, curing charm, and luck charm. In Arabia a lizard held in the hand acts as aphrodisiac; it is used in medicine also to cure old men of impotence. Thirteenth century medicine recommended the gall of green lizards for diseases of the eye.

In general folktale and etiological story, lizard got his tail from snake (A2247; A2378.1.8); the giant lizard is blind because he chose the gift of poison instead of eyes (A2332.6.2); the dragon is a modified lizard (B11.2.1.2). See ANIMAL CHILDREN; CHAMELEON; INAPERTWA; MBERE; TCHUÉ.

lizard hand In a dispute between Coyote and Lizard, in North American Indian tales from central California, Lizard succeeds in having human beings' hands shaped like his, but only by conceding to Coyote's alternative—that if they do, they will then have to die, as mortals do now. See MAN. [EWV]

Lizzie Borden Late American popular ballad, often sung to the tune of *Ta-ra-ra-boom-de-ay.* It deals with the accused in one of the most widely discussed of all murder trials—the trial of Lizzie Andrew Borden (1860–1927) of Fall River, Mass., for the ax-killing of her father and stepmother, Aug. 4, 1892. The brutality of the murder and the cold-blooded calm of the accused have been the subject of numerous writings. Though acquitted by the jury, Lizzie was pronounced guilty by the song, which states: "Lizzie Borden took an ax/ And gave her mother forty whacks;/ When she saw what she had done,/ She gave her father forty-one."

lizzie labels Humorous mottoes and slogans inscribed on Model T Ford cars (the tin "lizzie"), especially the collegiate "flivver" or "jaloppy," popular in the 1920's and 1930's. The term lizzie label was given currency if not originated by the humorous periodical, *Judge,* which in 1925 paid $5 for every label printed. Ford epigrams also doubled as conversational wisecracks. Of earlier and also later vintage are the metal tags affixed to rear license plates bearing such legends as "If you can read this, you're too darn close," "Excuse my dust," "My rear end is no bumper." Present-day tourist stickers, harking back to the pristine pennant announcing "California or bust," continue the practice of adorning motor cars with emblems and labels—a direct descendant of covered-wagon inscriptions ("Pike's Peak or Bust").

Lizzie labels rang the changes on the dilapidated state of the car (Don't laugh; you may be old some day), wolfish propositions (Chicken, here's your coup; Capacity, four gals), and the cheapness of Fords (If I get the tin, will it buy the car?). Many labels parodied or punned on current advertising slogans (Beauty in every jar; The tin you love to touch), mottoes and proverbial sayings (Slow but sure; It won't be long now; In God we trust; Believe it or not), and popular song titles or lines (*The Old Chokin' Bucket; Darling, I'm growing old; I'm Just a Vagabond Lover*).   B. A. BOTKIN

llaço Literally, loop or figure: Portuguese term for dance figures. These are particularly complex in the *dança dos paulitos* at Cercio. The twenty llaços include quick runs, jumps, and stick-striking in double lines and heys. Some of the picturesque names are *Senhor Mio, Carmelita, O Caballero, As Aguias* (the eagles), *As Bichas* (the dragons). In *O Caballero* the dancers tap sticks above and below their legs, recalling the English Morris Bean Setting. In *Acto de Contrição* (act of contrition) they drop on bended knee. In the particularly interesting llaços dos oficios (professions) they imitate various occupations: shoemaker, barber, carpenter, etc.

The Spanish *lazo* is the corresponding term for the interlacing figures of dance groups. In the more virtuoso solo and couple dances it also refers to a step involving crossing of the feet in closed half-toe position. The derivative term *lasso* combines the idea of a loop and of the figures described in the air by the loosely knotted rope. [GPK]

Llew Llaw Gyffes In Brythonic mythology, one of the marvelous twins born to Arianrhod when she failed to pass the test for virginity required of all who aspired to be footholder to Math Son of Mathonwy; twin brother of Dylan: interpreted as a sun god. Most of the myths state that Gwydion was the father of the infants. Arianrhod resented the existence of Llew for disproving her maidenhood. Dylan had plunged into the sea; but Gwydion saved Llew and brought him up on the Carnarvon coast. Llew was noted for his amazing growth from infancy to maturity; when he was four, he was as big as a boy of eight; when he was eight he was a handsome youth.

When Gwydion first presented the child to his mother she put the curse of namelessness upon him unless she named him herself. But by disguising himself and the boy, Gwydion tricked her into naming him. Arianrhod saw the child shoot a wren with such acute aim that she cried: "With a steady hand (*llaw gyffes*) the lion (*llew*) hit it." So Gwydion named him Llew Llaw Gyffes. Arianrhod was so infuriated at being tricked, that she cursed her son anew: that he never bear arms till she herself gave them, never marry a woman of the people of the earth. But Gwydion with superior magic tricked Arianrhod into bestowing arms on Llew. And then Gwydion and Math made a wife for him out of flowers, and named her Blodenwedd. Blodenwedd's beauty, however, belied her soul. She wormed out of Llew the secret of his vulnerability, and exposed him at the vulnerable moment to her lover Gormw, who hurled a spear into him. But Llew was not killed. He flew off in the shape of an eagle. The eagle was discovered later by Gwydion, who magically restored Llew to his own shape and healed the poisoned wound which he still carried. So Llew went back to rule over his own lands and ruled them well to the end of his days.

Rhys equates Llew with the Irish Luġ, believing that the two names mean "light," and relating the epithets Llew Llaw Gyffes (of the Steady Hand) with Luġ Lamfada (of the Long Arm or Far-Shooter). This theory, however, though acceptable to most scholars, has not been unconditionally accredited.

Five traditional folklore motifs are present in this myth: the virginity test, the amazing growth and prowess of the hero as child, invulnerability except under specific conditions, and the transformation of hero at death into eagle, the bird-soul, overlapping into the separable soul motif.

llorona 1) Literally, the weeper: a regional couple dance of the state of Oaxaca, Mexico, seen especially in Tehuantepec, Juchitán, and Salina Cruz. It is similar to the *zandunga* with steps both native and European, the woman swaying her magnificent skirt haughtily. Sometimes the man pursues the woman in a circle, with a kind of waltz step, as she looks back over her shoulder; or partners elude and meet with a step-pat in duple time against the triple beat of the music.

The text of the song has no connection with the popular legend of the spectral wailing child-murderess. The words express sultry, melancholy passion:

La pena y la que no es pena; ay llorona,/ Todo es pena para mí;/ Ayer lloraba por verte, ay llorona,/ Y hoy lloro porque te ví.	Pain and what is not pain, alas llorona. All is pain for me; Yesterday I wept to see you, alas llorona. And today I weep because I saw you.

coll. Concha Michel (F. Toor, *Mexican Folkways*, p. 443)
[GPK]

2) The weeping woman: a bereaved female of Mexican folklore, similar to the Lilith of Jewish and the Lamia of Greek folk belief, eternally searching for her child. La Llorona is met with in various places, deserted streets, the woods, along the river banks, usually at night, especially midnight, but sometimes in broad daylight, a shrouded figure looking for her lost little boy. In some variants, she herself has killed the child and is somehow demented; or she is condemned to wander about as penance for the murder. Sometimes she does nothing to the ones she meets, or simply asks whether they have seen the child, but usually she is dangerous, for she lures young men to quiet places and kills them. Occasionally La Llorona is simply a disembodied spirit whose voice is heard wailing in the night and who is not seen.

Lludd or **Nudd** In Brythonic mythology, one of the four sons of Beli (a disputed god of the Brythonic pantheon, possibly a sea god). The four brothers were Lludd, Caswallan, Llevelys, Nynngaw. As identified with the Irish Nuada, he is termed Lludd Llaw Eraint. In a story entitled *Lludd and Llevelys*, Lludd is a king of Britain whose kingdom was cursed with three terrible plagues: 1) the Coranians (a race of superhuman warriors who could hear every whisper everywhere); 2) a shriek on May Eve which made barren all growing things, trees, crops, animals, women; 3) the vanishing in one night of enough food to last a year. By the advice of his brother Llevelys, Lludd rid the land of all three plagues. He managed to poison the Coranians. The shriek was revealed to be the shriek of their own native dragon when it was attacked by a foreign dragon; Lludd and Llevelys killed both and buried them in Snowdon. Finally Lludd seized the magician who had been whisking off the food.

Lludd was famous for generosity and the giving of food and drink: a fact which MacCulloch points to as probable indication that an earlier Lludd was a god of growth and plenty. Lludd rebuilt the walls of London (Caer Ludd), according to Geoffrey of Monmouth. His name survives today in Ludgate Hill. For Lludd as father of Creiddylad, see LEAR. This confusion occurs elsewhere, for Lot seems to be the Norman-French form of the name for the Lludd who built the walls of London, and this Lludd's father is mentioned as Bladud, the builder of Bath.

loa Haitian designation for deity of the vodun cult. The loa are in the main of African derivation, but are identified with saints of the Catholic church so that they may be spoken of either by their African or Christian names. In the same manner, the term loa itself has as synonyms the French words *saint* and *mystère*. [MJH]

Loango winti A spirit worshipped by the Saramacca Bush Negroes, the name of which is derived from the early kingdom of Loango on the coast north of the mouth of the Congo River, from which many Negroes were exported to the New World. [MJH]

loa Sénégal A deity of the vodun cult of Haiti, deriving from the name of the region of western Africa from which many Negroes were exported, especially during the earlier period of the slave trade. The fact that this name of a god consists of a geographical term illustrates a process that has occurred in Haiti and elsewhere in the New World as Africa has receded further into the past. By this process, place and tribal names become the names of deities, so that the vodun cult not only has the *loa Sénégal*, but other loa, named *Dahomé, Iboléle* (from Ibo of the Niger Delta region), *Congo*, and the like. [MJH]

loathly lady The horrible hag or loathsome woman transformed (or disenchanted) into a beautiful woman by the act of love or a kiss is a motif (D732) occurring in European folktale, ballad, and romance.

In Chaucer's *Wife of Bath's Tale*, one of Arthur's lusty knights rapes a maid, and to save his life is sent to discover within a year "what thing women love most." He has a long and unsuccessful quest. At last he meets an old woman ("a fouler wight ther may no man devise") who promises him the secret in exchange for whatever thing she may ask of him next. Readily the knight agrees, learns the answer, journeys back to the court, says women desire "soverainetee over men," is not contradicted, and so his life is saved.

The loathly lady then makes her request: that this knight make her his wife. He begs off in horror, but is held to the bargain. He marries the hag "and all day after hid him as an owl/ So woe was him, his wife looked so foul." Eventually, however, he goes to bed with her; is given his choice of having her remain foul and old, but faithful, or having her turn young and fair—and to take his chances on the outcome. He leaves the choice to her and gets the best of both alternatives: a wife beautiful and young, and also devoted and faithful.

Child's fragmentary ballad *The Marriage of Sir Gawain* (#31) is practically identical with the *Wife of Bath's Tale*, except in the ballad the question is put to King Arthur by a baron in the wood, and it is Arthur who promises the loathly hag a fine knight in marriage in return for the right answer. Moreover Gawain does not demur at the sight of the loathly lady, but accepts her in her repulsive form; her bewitchment falls away, and she is transformed into a beautiful woman.

Gower tells the story in *Confessio Amantis*. The motif has some frequency also in English and Scottish popular ballad. (See KEMP OWYNE.) It occurs in Icelandic saga, and also in Old Irish legend in *The Adventures of the Sons of Eochu Muigmedón*. This story is found in the *Yellow Book of Lecan, Book of Leinster, Book of Ballymote*.

Niall was youngest of the five sons of Eochu Muigmedón, king of Ireland. One day the five went hunting, and as they ate their supper by a fire in the forest, they wanted water. Fergus went to seek it, and found a well guarded by a hideous old woman; "her foul teeth were visible from ear to ear"; her nose was crooked; her nails were green, etc. She would not let Fergus draw water from the well unless he kissed her first. But Fergus refused. One after another the brothers went to get water, but none could bring himself to kiss the horrible creature. All were refused water until Niall went. Not only did he kiss her, but lay down with her; and when he looked at her, she was white and fair and beautiful with a purple cloak upon her. "You are beautiful," said Niall. "Yes," she said, "I am the Sovranty of Ireland." So she gave Niall the water, and said he and his descendants would be kings of Ireland forever except for three names, which she told him. And this all came true.

The motif of the loathly bridegroom (D733) is associated with the unpromising hero who wins the princess, and with the whole Beauty and the Beast cycle. See BEAUTY AND THE BEAST.

lobelia A large genus (*Lobelia*) of herbaceous plants with showy flowers. The cardinal flower (*L. cardinalis*), sometimes called Indian tobacco, was macerated and dried by the Meskwaki (Fox) Indians and used to stop approaching storms. This was done by throwing a bit of the dust into the air before the storm broke. Both *L. cardinalis* and *L. syphilitica* were used as love medicine. The ground-up roots were put into the food of a quarrelsome pair, unbeknownst to them; partaking of it together caused them to stop quarreling, insured a happy marriage, and forestalled divorce. The Iroquois also regarded lobelia root as a potent love medicine. Chippewa Indian medicine-men used lobelia as an emetic. White settlers made a successful vermifuge from *L. cardinalis*. *L. syphilitica* was named for its early use as a remedy for syphilis.

lobi singi Literally, love song; in Surinam Negro usage, a type of song sung especially by women as a form of revenge in special ceremonies during which unfaithful lovers are ridiculed.

lobola Zulu word for the wealth passed from the family of a man to that of a woman to validate a marriage. It is thus the native Zulu term for what is termed "bride-wealth" or, mistakenly in the earlier literature, as "bride-price." This latter phrase is a misnomer because the goods that pass, cattle in the case of the Zulu and other East African peoples, are in no wise a purchase price. They are rather an indication of the ability of the bridegroom to head a family, of the position of his own relationship group, and an earnest that he will not mistreat his future wife. To the degree that the European concept of legitimacy can be applied cross-culturally, it can be said that the passage of lobola wealth is a sign of the highest social sanction to a given mating. Among the Zulu and other East African peoples, the position of a man in society is largely determined by the source of the cattle given for his mother. [MJH]

local legend A legend fixed to a definite locale, explaining some local feature of geography or name, or telling a story of local tradition explaining some custom. Local legends are short, etiological, etymological; they repeat the same themes, though in different parts of the world, again and again; they give unmistakable signs of antiquity, embodying long-dead customs and a primitive morality. The story of the foot- or handprint in the rock is attached to Adam's Peak in Ceylon and to a rock in Germany. Lovers' leap tales are told of mountains and precipices in Japan, North America, Europe, and many other parts of the world. The Tarpeian Rock in Rome and the Ægean Sea are said to derive their names from similar leaps to death; the Hellespont is the water into which Helle fell from the ram carrying her and Phrixus to Æetes. The legend of Godiva's ride through Coventry probably attempts an explanation of an early fertility rite in which naked women rode through the town or countryside to bring plenty to the land. Among local legends are tales of buried and lost treasures, foundation sacrifices, sunken or lost cities of evil habits, sunken castles or islands, or bottomless lakes, walls or hills made by giants or demons; tales having to do with outlaws, with the origins of families or of family customs, with dragon-slaying heroes. As with other legends, historical fact often underlies these stories, for example those of sunken lands or destroyed cities, but the age-long addition of the marvelous and the obviously anachronistic makes it almost impossible to separate the true from the traditional.

☞ The story of the king who sleeps in a mountain or lake and will return to save his people is attached to Arthur, Charlemagne, Barbarossa in the Occident, as well as to several Chinese emperors. Stories of haunted houses and hidden treasure belong to this type of universal narrative. The collection of legends preserved by any community is a useful index of that community's interests and imagination. [RDJ]

☞ Natural cavities or spots on rocks which have the shape of footprints are generally explained by South American Indians as marks left by the wandering culture hero. The same interpretation for these natural oddities is given all through South America from Colombia to Paraguay. [AM]

local weather A magician causes winter to stay in one place while the rest of the world has summer. This motif (D2145.1.1) is found in North American Indian tales of the North Pacific Coast; also among the Shasta of northern California, and the Menomini of Wisconsin. A related idea is that found in the Plateau: a sky deity or chief gives each of his two daughters a ball when they leave him. One ball contains heat, the other cold; when they are opened the weather becomes very cold or very hot around the girls. Because of possessing these balls the girls cannot be burned or frozen by a wicked creature who wishes to kill them (Diamond Jenness, "Myths of the Carrier Indians of British Columbia," *JAFL* 47: 97–257, 1934, pp. 108–09). [EWV]

locust 1) A North American tree (*Robinia pseudoacacia*) of the bean family. Cherokee Indians explain the long slender racemes of fragrant white flowers with the story of the moon woman who cuts a new moon out of white moon material each month. She is so fond of the locust tree that when she sweeps up the scraps each spring, she hangs them on the locust tree. Tewa Indians used locust wood to make their bows. The Meskwakis drink a locust bark tea for severe colds, fevers, measles, and to keep the bowels and kidneys free. They use it both externally and internally in cases of smallpox to prevent pitting. Mississippi Negroes say that to make a forgetful debtor pay up, drive some nails into a locust tree in the shape of a cross, and the debtor will come unsummoned to pay his debt. See BONES.

2) Plagues of locusts have been known and feared both in Africa and the Mediterranean regions for centuries. The plague of locusts was the eighth plague brought on the Egyptians by Moses (*Ex.* x); "and when it was morning the east wind brought the locusts./ . . . They covered the face of the whole earth so that the land was darkened, and they did eat every herb of the land and all the fruit of the trees, and there remained not any green thing . . ." Then following the fear and repentance of Pharaoh and the entreaty of Moses, God "turned a mighty strong, west wind which took away the locusts and cast them into the Red Sea."

So dreaded was the plague of locusts that ancient writers mythologized them into monsters. Pliny, for instance, mentions a locust of India three feet long. The spectacular locust flight and the locust march (of the larvæ) and the devouring of the food of man by the hordes wherever they appear has stimulated and horrified the imagination of man everywhere. In 1889 a cloud of locusts was seen over the Red Sea, which occupied 2000 square miles. Swarms which have perished in storms at sea are said to wash ashore in heaps 3–4 feet deep, 50–100 miles long, the stench reaching inland 150 miles. After a flight of locusts has settled in an area, the females lay their eggs in the ground. The hatchlets are called *twisters* in South Africa from the fact that their emergence makes the ground itself look alive and in motion. These larvæ advance (this is the locust march) eating everything en route, even the bark off of trees, garments drying on the ground, curtains at windows, etc.

In Dahomey, West Africa, where locusts descend in great clouds and eat everything growing within range, the people have a scapegoat ceremony for driving them away. One person is selected, dressed in rich garments and loaded with bracelets and other valuables, and sent away out of the country forever. The locusts accompany him; should he come back, the locusts would also return; hence, death is the penalty for return. In India the Dravidians practiced conciliatory control: the custom was to catch one locust, decorate its head with a drop of red lead, reverence it, and let it go. When this was done the swarm would depart. Conciliatory pest control was practiced in ancient Greece also. In Syria noise-control is the custom. The people beat pans, yell, shoot guns, etc., to divert a swarm.

The locust has been the symbol of destruction in many ancient symbolisms. In Moslem legend a locust explained to Mohammed that each locust lays 99 eggs; if the number were 100, the locusts would be so numerous that they would consume the whole world.

The ancient Babylonians had a "rite of the locusts" which involved the placing of two locusts, one on each side of a sick (i.e. bewitched) man's door. They represented the two "gods of the watch" and would leap out on the sorceress and kill her when she approached. A specific incantation was said over them, which was efficacious on the second recitation.

In China there are several gods of locusts and grasshoppers: Liu-mêng Chiang-chün, who protects against them, Pa Cha, who summons and imprisons them in a gourd (often identified with the former), and Ma-cha Shên, the goddess of locusts, revered especially in northern China where locusts are most frequent.

In medieval times in Europe, whenever the behavior of animals and insects seemed especially obnoxious or injurious to man, the people brought complaints against them in the ecclesiastical courts. In the case of locusts the verdict for riddance was apt to be the payment of tithes on the part of the people. This judgment was based on *Malachi* iii, 7–12, wherein God promised in return for the paying up of overdue tithes not only to open the windows of heaven and pour out a blessing, but to "rebuke the devourer . . . and he shall not destroy the fruits of your ground."

In California Yurok Indian mythology the locust larva "wished death into the world." In Wiyot mythology the locust larva is also responsible for death. Among the Hopi Indians the flute is associated with Locust, "the hunchbacked flute player," who is depicted on cliff walls near the pueblos. Locust is the supernatural patron of the Hopi Flute Society. The Clouds shot lightning bolts at him and he just went on playing his flute. For this reason, because he cannot be struck by lightning, locust medicine (the curing power of the locust) is considered good for wounds. It also gives a man power to dream true about the future, and brings warm weather. Why locusts live in certain pueblo towns is an etiological tale motif (A2434.3.1) for which see E. C. Parsons in *JAFL* 31, p. 225.

lodestone or **loadstone** Magnetite (oxide of iron) which shows polarity: literally, way stone (from Old English *lád*, way, journey, and stone). The attraction of this stone for iron has held the attention of philosophers, alchemists, magicians, and charlatans for centuries. In fact, its property of always pointing north, or to the lodestar (the guide star) was first realized in the 11th century.

There are tales that in the southwestern part of Madras province ships were formerly built with wooden pegs because of a magnetic mountain (a lodestone mountain) near Calicut, which pulled out iron nails; there was a statue reputed to have been suspended in mid-air by the use of lodestones; and in many parts of Europe horses became mysteriously unshod, although curiously, there is no record of an armored knight being debagged in this way. This mineral was so powerful that it could even reunite parted lovers, and was often included with other gems in a piece of jewelry to symbolize the compelling attraction of love. It is still used in conjure in the southern United States.

Lodestone was the basis of many alchemical experiments and early inventions, especially in regard to perpetual motion. It was powerless to work its wonders, however, in the presence of a diamond or garlic. Should a stone lose its powers, other than in the presence of these, they might be restored to it by anointing it with linseed oil, wrapping it in a goatskin and burying it in the earth for three days, or by feeding it on iron filings. Dipping the stone in "oil of iron" or goatsblood were other methods of restoring its strength. Lodestone is said to impart fortitude to the possessor and to render a person invulnerable. Alexander the Great provided it for his soldiers as a protective measure.

There was formerly a widespread belief that lodestone aids the burglar in his profession. One might assume he could poke the lodestone in the silver drawer and make off with the plate. Bishop Marbod, 11th century lapidary, however, explained that when powdered lodestone is sprinkled over hot coals, the terrible odor will drive the occupants out of the house, thus leaving the burglar to work unmolested. Its properties as a chastity index are stated, but not explained. Placing it under a wife's pillow, or touching it to her head, will cause the chaste wife to embrace her husband violently. Should she be unchaste, however, she will be bodily thrown out of bed, where presumably she may remain. DeBoot, in the 17th century was inclined to doubt a similar virtue in the diamond.

Hildegard of Bingen, famous learned nun of the 12th century, stated that lodestone would cure insanity if moistened with the patient's own saliva and drawn across his forehead, the proper incantation being said at the same time. Gerard's translation of the *Lapidary* of Aristotle tells how to set fire to water with it. It is also said that lodestone has great power to raise spirits and phantasms, if used with the right incantations.

Lodestone also has marvelous medicinal powers. Bound to the soles of the feet, for instance, it will pull out the gout. Throughout Great Britain and in many parts of the United States just carrying a piece in the pocket or holding it in the hand will cure gout, rheumatism, and sciatica. In India, in the 16th century, it was said to preserve virility. For this reason the King of Siam had his cooking utensils made of magnetite. A necklace of lodestone and coral was worn to assist in childbirth, and Trotula, said to have been the first woman graduate of the school of Salerno, so recommended it. In the 17th century powdered lodestone was in general use for burns; in the same century a Belgian doctor developed an eight-day cure for rupture which consisted of feeding the patient iron filings while applying crushed lodestone in a poultice externally. When worn in a silver setting, lodestone sharpens the sight and other senses; when worn in gold it strengthens the heart. It is also said to produce somnambulism. [JWH]

Lodge-Boy and Thrown-Away Title of a popular hero tale of the North American Indians (T581), especially prevalent in the Plains area. While her husband is away from home, a pregnant woman is killed by a man or woman, and twin boys are taken from her body. One of the twins, Lodge-Boy, is reared by his father; the other boy, "Thrown away," lives in a nearby spring. Father and son catch the second boy, and the three live together. They succeed, in some versions, in awakening their mother, who also comes to live with them. Their father forbids them to do certain things; they disobey,

and in this way kill various monsters: an old woman who had a magic pot, a sucking serpent, bending trees, rectum snakes, a man with moccasins of fire, and so forth. See BEAD-SPITTER AND THROWN-AWAY. [EWV]

Lodur or **Lother** In the *Voluspá*, one of the three creators (with Odin and Hœnir) of Ask and Embla, the first man and woman. He gave man blood and a ruddy complexion. He personifies beneficent fire.

Loegaire Buadac Leary the Triumphant: in Old Irish legend one of the three first champions of Ulster; contender, with Cuchulain and Conall Cearnac, for the champion's portion at Bricriu's feast.

Lohengrin A swan knight of 13th-century Teutonic legend. In tales from old Brabant, he is the son of Parzival and associated with the Grail legends. Lohengrin arrives at Antwerp asleep in a boat drawn by a swan, awakes to save a princess from an obnoxious suitor, and marries her. When she breaks the imposed name tabu, the swan-boat reappears, and Lohengrin departs.

loka In Hindu mythology, a world or division of the universe. The lokas number three (earth, hell, heaven), seven (earth, space between earth and sun, Indra's heaven, abode of the saints, abode of Brahmā's sons, abode of the Vairagis, and abode of Brahmā), or eight (abode of the Piśāchas; of the Yakshas; of the Rākshasas; of heavenly spirits; of inferior deities; of moon and planets; of Pitris, Rishis, Prajāpatis; and abode of the superior deities). Compare PĀTĀLA.

Lokāloka In Hindu mythology, the belt of mountains which divides the visible world from the perpetual darkness beyond. The mountains lie beyond the outermost of the seven seas. See DVĪPA.

lokapālas In Hindu mythology, the eight guardians or supporters of the world who preside over the eight points of the compass. Each guardian has an elephant who also protects the quarter and is also called a lokapāla. The guardians and their elephants are Indra and Airāvata (in the *Rāmāyana*, Virupaksha) on the east, Agni and Pundarika on the southeast, Yama and Vamana (in the *Rāmāyana*, Mahapadma) on the south, Sūrya or Nirriti and Kumuda in the southwest, Varuna and Anjana (in the *Rāmāyana*, Saumanasa) in the west, Vāyu and Pushpadanta in the northwest, Kubera and Sarvabhauma (in the *Rāmāyana*, Himapandara) in the north, and Soma or Prthivi or Śiva and Supratika in the northeast.

In Tibet the chief of the Lokapālas is incarnate in the head of the monastery of gNas-c'un.

Loki In Teutonic mythology, one of the æsir, son of Borr and Bestla, brother of Odin; and in this capacity one of the three creators of the first human pair (some versions). Other authorities classify him as one of the jötnar, son of Fornjotnr, and related to Odin only by oath of blood brotherhood. In this capacity he was the personification of destructive fire and played the role of trickster and mischief-maker. In the early myths especially, Loki was comic trickster and transformer rather than evil. With the advent of Christianity, however, he came more and more to be regarded as the personification of evil, analogous to, though not identified with, the Christian Devil. His identification with Lodur has never been substantiated.

Loki first married Glut (glow) and produced two

daughters, Eisa (ember) and Einmyria (ashes). His second consort was the giantess Angur-boda who bore Hel, the Fenris wolf, and the Midgard Serpent, Jörmungandr. His third and final marriage was to Sigyn who bore him sons, Narve and Vali. She was charming and faithful, and stood by him even when he was bound in the cavern.

Loki was much in the company of Thor and Odin and Hœnir, and, while his pranks got them all into trouble, he was the one who extricated them from the results of folly. He also traveled with the bluff and powerful Thor, who greatly appreciated Loki's sense of humor. In the later stories he shows a meaner streak. The killing of Balder has no redeeming feature. His reviling of the gods at Ægir's feast, while truth, was bitter truth. They were enraged, and to escape their wrath, Loki fled and disguised himself as a salmon. He feared only a net such as Rán alone used, and was experimenting to see if one could be made when Odin, Kvaser, and Thor came after him. He hastily flung the net on the fire, but they found an unburned corner of it and guessed his whereabouts. They fashioned a net and on the third try Thor caught him and held him so tight that the salmon has had a thin tail ever since. He was bound with the entrails of his son Narve and put in a cave where the giantess Skadi placed a serpent so that the venom would fall in his face. His wife, Sigyn, holds a cup to catch the venom, but every time she empties the cup a few drops fall on him and his writhing causes earthquakes. He will remain bound until Ragnarök when he will break loose and lead the forces of evil against the gods until he and Heimdall kill each other. See ANIMAL CHILDREN; ASK; EGIL; FENRIS; FIRE; IDUN; SURTR. [JWH]

London Bridge A children's game and rime of the British Isles and the United States, believed by students of games to derive from ancient bridge foundation sacrifice rites. The old rite, meant to preserve the bridge from destruction by the angry water spirits through the offering of a human victim, is vaguely recalled in the game. Theorists on games believe that children's imitations of adult practices often survive as games even long after the actual rituals have disappeared, and point to *London Bridge* as a distinct example. The players begin by chanting that London Bridge is falling down: presumably the act of the malignant spirit. Various means of repairing it are suggested, but even "Iron bars will bend and break"—though iron is a specific against demons. Finally a prisoner is captured, chosen by chance, either from the ring or from the line of players as they go through the linked arms of the two players acting the part of the bridge. In the course of the many years since bridge sacrifice was actively practiced, this fossilized central idea has become obscured and varied, e.g. the prisoner is a thief, etc., but it is still discernible. The American variant of the game has become intermixed with another game, *Oranges and Lemons,* so that the actual play of the game is different from that in Britain. American variants sometimes substitute other names in place of London. See GAMES.

Londonderry Air A melody of unknown age, first written down by a Miss Jane Ross of Newtown-Limvady, Ireland, and given by her to Petrie, the great collector of Irish folk music, who published it in 1855. It was ap-

parently known all over the northwest of Ireland, but none of its original words have survived. One explanation of its difference in rhythmic pattern from the body of Irish melodies is that individual expression on the part of the singer from whom it was taken, or misinterpretation in the notation, gave it the peculiarly haunting quality of its held notes. The words of *Danny Boy, Emer's Farewell to Cuchulain,* and others set to the air since its discovery are mostly of art rather than folk origin.

Lone Man Creator-culture-hero of the Mandan-Hidatsa Indians: **Only Man** in the Hidatsa versions. In the beginning when everything was water and darkness, Lone Man and First Creator were walking along on the top of the water and met a duck. They asked her how she managed to live; she dived down and came up with a small ball of mud. Food grows in this, she told them. From this the pair created the land and all living creatures and caused the soil to produce. Lone Man went northward to do his creating; First Creator turned south. Between them they left a strip of water (now the Missouri River). First Creator made mountains, hills, valleys, streams, springs, trees, wild antelope, buffalo, and mountain sheep. Lone Man created flat lands, lakes and ponds, beaver, otter, cattle, etc. When they compared their works First Creator did not approve of Lone Man's handiwork: his lands were too flat, there were too few trees, his ponds could stagnate, mankind would have nothing but cattle to eat when the wild game was gone, etc.

After a while, as mankind multiplied on the face of the earth, Lone Man got himself born of a Mandan Indian virgin. Many episodes of his life in human form show recognizable resemblances to the Jesus story as told to the Indians by white missionaries: his calming of the waters, for instance, his twelve men, etc. Lone Man taught the Mandan many things, gave them rites and ceremonies for overcoming evil, taught them how to barricade the river against floods. When he departed, he set up a cedar tree in the center of the village, painted it with red earth, told the people to pray and sacrifice to the cedar, which henceforth *was* his body, left with them in token of his return.

One of the Hidatsa tellings of this story begins with the statement that Jesus was born on the other side of the world, but Only Man created this side of the world. In this tale, when Only Man and First Creator compare their works, First Creator takes one look at the human being Only Man has made and says, "That's a queer kind of man to make; he'll always be greedy." See Martha Warren Beckwith, *Mandan-Hidatsa Myths and Ceremonies, MAFLS* 32, 1938.

Lone Prairie See BURY ME NOT ON THE LONE PRAIRIE.

long cold One of the four major world cataclysms in the mythology of the Chaco and Tierra del Fuego Indians of South America. Compare FIMBULWINTER.

longways dance Any dance in which the performers stand in two parallel lines, the men in one line, facing their partners in the other. See CONTRADANCE; CONTRADANZA; LINE DANCE. [GPK]

looking tabu One of the widespread tabus of folktale: looking at the forbidden object or person causes its loss. The motif appears in the Cupid and Psyche story, where

Psyche breaks the prohibition and loses her husband (C32.1). Orpheus looks back at Eurydice and loses her to Hades forever (C331). Lot's wife turned into a pillar of salt because she looked back at the destruction of Sodom and Gomorrah (C961.1)—*Gen.* xix, 26. The Blue-beard story with its forbidden chamber uses the motif. Pandora was forbidden to look into the box but did so and loosed all the evils on the world (C321). Semele and Actæon looked upon the gods and perished. Tiresias examined two snakes copulating and was stricken blind (D513.1); Tom of Coventry too was blinded after he peeped at the naked Godiva against strict prohibition (C943).

The turtle in fable is carried aloft by the eagle but looks down against the eagle's advice, gets dizzy, loses his grasp, and is smashed in the fall. Väinämöinen is warned by Louhi not to raise his head above his sledge to gaze about him or misfortune will follow (C333); he looks, sees Pohjola's daughter, tries to get her to join him in the sleigh, and as a result injures himself with the ax. The looking tabu often occurs in tales of wonderful journeys (D2121.2), especially journeys to cliff-tops or to the skies. Sometimes, as in the Hittite dragon-slaying myth, the tabu is based on folk practice: the hero must not see his wife or child before setting out on his adventure or he will lose his strength—the parallel to ritual sexual continence before battle is apparent.

Among the Zuñi, looking back is tabu during certain rituals and in the obtaining of omens. Before a raid, the warrior seeks omens at a river, performing the necessary rites. Four times he takes four steps backwards from the river and each time pauses and listens for omens. Then, without looking back, he goes directly to the War Chief for an interpretation of what he has heard. The Hopi believe that their salt gatherers must not look back at the lake lest their souls be trapped there; death will soon follow. Among the widespread relationship tabus is one prohibiting a man from ever seeing his mother-in-law. The moon must not be looked at over the left shoulder, according to general European and U.S. belief, insanity or death will follow. In European belief, a baby must not be allowed to look at its own reflection in a mirror until it is a year old; otherwise its luck in life will be hard. Many persons believe that a dog will have convulsions if it sees itself in a mirror.

lookman One who "looks": the diviner of Trinidad Negroes. He is consulted especially when one has had a dream of bad omen. The lookman knows not only the meaning of the dream, but who sent it: whether it is a warning from an ancestor or a threat from some other, malicious supernatural. If it is a warning dream the lookman makes for his client the *guard* which will prevent the prophesied misfortune; if it is a threat, he advises his client what he must do to propitiate the evil spirit. The lookman can "see" an illness, and also "see" the cure; he can "see" future obstacles and calamities in the path of a client, and knows what kind of charm to give him to clear the way. He also knows tricks for insuring the success of a job or a journey.

The lookman is often called upon to whip a vampire (*sukuyan*) or werewolf, when some terrified person thinks he has identified or caught one. It is especially important for this to happen while the vampire or werewolf is in his animal shape, for once the whip of the lookman

has touched him (her) he can never again assume human shape or behavior, and is thus more easily caught. The lookman is always paid for his services. Anyone who fails to pay incurs the full force of his powers to cause bad luck, disease, or death. Compare LUKUMAN. See OBIA.

loom A frame or machine in which yarn or thread is woven into a fabric. Through this medium weavers express many of the beliefs of their people, notably the East Indians, and the Indians of North, Central, and South America. Through many inventions, the primitive loom has been now transformed so that it is almost automatic. Various loom substitutes are used among semiprimitive people. In Jutland people used to say that if one wakes at night and hears the loom working of itself, silver has been stolen from the house. See R. Wikman, *Die Magie des Webens*, Abo, 1920. Lilts, croons, and songs of weavers at work comprise a large part of the body of Irish folk song. In Ireland they say that weavers never get either to heaven or hell.

The loom appears in impossible task folktales: making a loom from shavings, making loom and spindle from one piece of wood, etc. The horizontal loom was used by Delilah when cutting Samson's hair, this form being most convenient for the task she was performing. [GPS]

Loon Woman or **The Girl Who Marries Her Brother** An American Indian tale. One brother in a large family is kept hidden; his sister finds a hair and longs for the person to whom it belongs. When she discovers the owner she insists he go away with her; she attempts to commit incest, but her brother returns to his family. The family escapes in a sky basket to the sky, knowing the girl will kindle a great fire on earth. One member breaks a looking tabu, and the entire family falls into the fire. As they burn their hearts burst out; the daughter, Loon Woman, gathers the hearts and strings them about her neck. Later she is killed and the members of her family are resuscitated. The tale as a whole is practically confined to tribes in the northern half of California (Modoc, Shasta, Achomawi, Yana, Wintun, Maidu), but various elements in it are found in many parts of North America and some (lover identified by hair floating in water, sky basket, magic objects talk and delay pursuer, Achilles heel) are world-wide. A recent comparative study of *Loon Woman* focuses on the material which native narrators of this myth had to draw upon, and their handling of such material; see D. Demetrocopoulou, *The Loon Woman, A Study in Synthesis* (*JAFL* 46: 101–128). See also Stith Thompson, *The Folktale*, p. 361. [EWV]

loosestrife Any of various plants, mostly with four-cornered branches, regular or irregular flowers, as the common loosestrife (*Lysimachia vulgaris*) or the purple loosestrife (*Lythrum salicaria*). A sprig of loosestrife laid under the collars (or yokes) of a pair of quarreling oxen was formerly said to calm them. In the United States loosestrife is burned to drive away mosquitoes, and it is also considered excellent for ridding animals of flies and gnats; nor can snakes abide the smell of it. Wizards and sorcerers used it in times past to harness evil spirits; on the other hand, it was used to drive away witches and evil spirits and to guard treasure. Medicinally loosestrife was widely used as a remedy for dysentery, and for all manner of bleeding, both internal and external. In Ireland the purple loosestrife (*créactac*), sometimes called crane's-bill, is used for healing and as a dye. In Britain crane's-bill was a popular remedy for gout and rheumatism. In Russia purple loosestrife is regarded with fear and awe.

Lō-pön or **sLob-***d*pon Literally, teacher: Tibetan name for the Buddhist monk, Padmasambhava, who was invited to Tibet by King Thi-srong-de-tsan to organize a Buddhist sect.

Lord of Misrule An officer of the Christmastide revels in the Middle Ages, who directed the festivities of the holiday season, and who ruled over his "subjects" so absolutely that he might do or command almost anything without censure. The Lord of Misrule held office at least during the twelve days from Christmas to Epiphany, and often from Allhallows (Oct. 31–Nov. 1) to Candlemas (Feb. 2). This latter period, for example, corresponds to the period of rule of the King of the Bean (another name for the Lord of Misrule) at Merton College, Oxford. The Abbas Stultorum thus ruled over the Feast of Fools (Jan. 1) in France; the Boy Bishop was in charge of the Innocents' Day (Dec. 28) celebrations in France and England; in Scotland his name was the Abbot of Unreason, of Misrule, of Bon Accord; in France there was an Abbé de la Malgouverné. These masters of the revels held forth in the royal household, in the houses of the nobles, in the colleges, in the Inns of Court. Depending upon the place, they were elected or appointed. From the period of the year (winter solstice) and the pomp surrounding the Lord of Misrule, Frazer supposes that he was a survival of the ancient Roman Saturn who ruled over the Saturnalia, one of the temporary kings whose reigns were short and sweet and who died when their functions had been fulfilled. Frazer further hypothesizes that the suspension of the normal course of events occurred in the intercalary days, when time itself ran off the calendar. The ability to relax then the normal progress of things, and the occurrence at the same time of the yearly revolution in the sun's course, made for a grand festival and a burlesquing of what during the rest of the year was held holy and sane.

Lord Randall An English ballad (Child #12) in dialog form which tells the story of a young lord who has been to see his sweetheart and has been poisoned. Many versions include the testament theme and the climax of relations. In both song and story the tale is known all over Europe, variants having been collected in Italian, German, Wendish, Dutch, Swedish, Magyar, Bohemian, and Catalan languages. A song containing the details about the poisoned eels he had been given for his dinner was sung by a blind Florentine singer early in the 17th century. A Swedish version also mentioning eels made the victim a girl. The Scottish lullaby version, *Wee Croodin' Doo* (wee cooing dove), which exists in many variants, has a slaughtered child as the victim. Innumerable versions of the song have been collected in America, where the hero's name varies almost endlessly, appearing as Johnny Randall, Johnny Ramble, Jimmy Randal, Jimmy Ransing, and even Boss Randal (in a Negro chain-gang version). It is among the half dozen ballads most frequently found both in the north and the south, has been found in the Ramapo Hills within sight of New York's skyscrapers, and in the railroad camps of Colorado. The Shakers used one of its airs as a hymn tune, and the nursery song *Billy Boy* is believed

to be one of its progeny. What is thought to be its original melody, to which it is still often sung, is derived from the same source as *Lochaber No More, Reeve's Maggot, Limerick's Lamentation,* and *King James's March to Ireland.* It is also sung to a setting of the *Villikens and Dinah* air.

Lorelei A water nymph of the Rhine whose song misled sailors onto the rocks below her perch. The story is neither myth nor local legend but is a fabrication of Klemens Brentano, who told the tale in his *Lore Lay* (1800). Through Heinrich Heine's poem on the subject, the story became familiar to English readers, and to tourists the legend of the Lorelei became a local legend of sorts. The Lorelei is a tall rock on the right bank of the Rhine in Hesse-Nassau, noted for its echo, and thus the romantic literary fiction has had an excuse for passing to a degree into tradition.

lotus The "fairest flower" of the East—a predominant ornamental motif which has an uninterrupted symbolic history of almost five thousand years, with a range and subtlety of meaning comparable to that of life itself. Its significance includes: (1) the female principle—the *yoni,* the womb, the reproductive act or power, the procreation of life; (2) fertility, fruitfulness, or abundance—hence, fortune, prosperity, happy augury, offspring, and such other blessings as long life, health, and fame; (3) the earth and creation—creative force or power, the self-generative cosmic action, the Mother Goddess, the generative organ of the female waters, the life-giving Nile; (4) divinity—superhuman birth, spontaneous creation, eternal generation; (5) immortality and resurrection—the preservation of life, life everlasting, rebirth, the restorer of the sun at dawn, the cup of the sun, the flower that enfolds the souls of the dead, the resting place of Buddha; (6) purity and spirituality—the preservation and procreation of the law, the wisdom that leads to Nirvāna, the essence of enlightenment.

From these basic concepts it is possible only to hint at the innumerable uses of the flower in custom, legend, and art. It is auspicious when worn, health-giving when eaten, a synonym for beauty in the poetry of many languages. It may be the highest number, a charm, a remedy for lovesickness, a good omen, a holder for incense sticks, a sign for a candle shop, a wrapping for food for the dead.

The lotus idea will be traced first in India, where it is most ramified and where creation itself is visualized in terms of the sacred flower. Already in the *Brāhmanas,* c. 800 B.C., the lotus leaf is viewed as the womb. It is the symbol of the *yoni,* the female generative organ, and this is the basic element in its meaning, whether it becomes the female goddess (the universal mother), the cosmic lotus (the womb of creation), or the seat (source) of divinity or spiritual power. When the *lingam* is depicted in India, it is generally based on or rimmed with lotus petals, entwined with the lotus stalk, or situated in the innermost "womb" of the temple, representing the complement or dual nature of those forces which animate existence.

The Lotus Goddess What is presumably the oldest representation of the lotus in art—many centuries older than any written reference to it—occurs with a figure unearthed at Mohenjo-Daro in the Indus Valley, which is assigned to the third millennium B.C. This simple nude goddess—wide-hipped, uplifting the breasts with the hands, prototype of the familiar earth mother in many regions—wears in her hair the lotus blossom. Among tillers of the soil, she has remained supreme as the simple goddess of fertility, "the possessor of dung." However, as male deities gained the ascendancy in the more complicated pantheon, her personality was absorbed into that of consort, and she is often shown seated on the lap of the god or caressing his feet. As the spouse of Vishṇu, she is called Padma (lotus), Lakshmī, or Śri, and one story has it that she came out of a lotus which sprang from Vishṇu's forehead. Śiva holds out the lotus-twined lingam to his goddess Śakti. As Kālī, she holds in one hand the lotus symbol of eternal generation. The Universal Buddha has as his consort Prajna-Paramita, who also bears the lotus, in this case surmounted by a book. In Chinese Buddhism, the goddess Tara is called Lotus.

The earliest reference to the goddess, in a supplement to the *Rig-Veda,* describes her as born of the lotus, standing on the lotus, garlanded with lotuses. She is praised (as beautiful women have been ever since) as being of the hue of the lotus, lotus-eyed, lotus-thighed, lotus-decked. In the story of the Churning of the Milky Ocean, she is one of the earlier figures to appear. She is constantly associated with the waters (which are feminine and life-giving) and with the white elephant. Carvings of Padma from at least the first century B.C. to the present time characteristically show the goddess standing upon the lotus, flanked by elephants who pour water from their trunks over her and the lotus which she holds.

The Cosmic Lotus To the Hindu, creation (conceived as the emergence of the world from the universal waters or void on which the giant Vishṇu sleeps) takes on cosmic proportions, but the lotus serves as the medium just as it is the simple sex symbol. Vishṇu, the "lotus-naveled," puts forth from his body a single giant lotus on which is seated Brahmā, the "lotus-born" Creator. This lotus with its thousand golden petals grows with the expanding universe. Out of its petals the mountains rise and the waters flow. Symbols of the earth or the goddess may be depicted on it, demons and serpents under the petals. With each succeeding *kalpa* or day of Brahmā (12,000 heavenly years) Brahmā is reborn on the lotus from the navel of Vishṇu. The *Padma-Purāṇa,* second in the list of *Purāṇas,* contains an account of the age when the world was a "golden lotus."

In the myths associated with Prajāpati as the Creator (in the *Brāhmaṇas*) it is said that he saw a lotus leaf standing in the waters of the fluid universe. He dived beneath the surface (in his boar form), brought up a bit of earth and spread it on the leaf. Or again, Prajāpati himself appeared on the lotus leaf.

Buddhist periods, also, are initiated by the appearance of a lotus, which indicates the location of the sacred tree of Buddha. If the period is to be void (without Buddhas), there are no blossoms on the lotus; however, at the beginning of one era, the Bhadrakalpa (according to late versions), there were a thousand blossoms to indicate the number of forthcoming Buddhas. The Buddhist paradise is sometimes described as a place where everyone is born as a god upon a lotus flower. In diagrams or paintings of the wheel of life, the rim of lotus petals or depictions of the cosmic lotus are salient. See WHEEL.

The Attribute of Divinity The lotus as the symbol of creative power or of spontaneous divine creation, or simply of divinity, came to be applied over the centuries to many deities. This attribute takes many forms, according to the nature of the deity and the period or country, but there are three basic types. Two are art forms, already noted as characteristic of the lotus goddess—the lotus seat or pedestal on which the deity sits or stands and the lotus in the hand. The third is vocal, the famous lotus-jewel formula, *Om maṇi padme Hūṃ* (So be it, lotus-jewel, Amen). This formula is traceable to Brahmanized ritual and was borrowed for Buddhism. In the latter, it is addressed to Avalokita, who is depicted as a hermaphrodite, seated upon the lotus of his father (the Buddha of meditation) or holding both the lotus and the jewel. This formula, according to L. A. Waddell, whether applied to Vishṇu or Avalokita, "presumably symbolizes the creative cosmic action by self-generative power"; it still occurs throughout the East, almost universally in Tibet, as a wishing-gem or good-luck spell.

The lotus seat appears with almost all the figures of the Hindu pantheon, and Buddha characteristically sits cross-legged upon it. It is usually a simple pedestal, recognizable by its rim of lotus petals, or, occasionally, two to four lotuses carved on the front. Sometimes it is transformed into a footstool on which the god or Gautama rests his feet. In all Buddhist countries, the lotus seat came to be the support of the images of bodhisattvas, with whom it has a more metaphysical significance (like that associated with Prajna-Paramita)—the preservation and rebirth of the Law rather than the procreation and resurrection of life itself. (The *Lotus of the True Law* is one of the great texts of Mahayana Buddhism.)

The lotus in the hand (or sometimes shown in carvings alongside the deity or blossoming from the pedestal) is also characteristic of many divinities. It may be surmounted by sword, thunderbolt, jewel, sun, or book. Vishṇu holds a lotus in one of his four hands. It is the symbol of the sixth Jina in old Jain sculptures. The title Padmapāni (lotus-handed) is especially applied to Avalokita. In Tibet the lotus is the special emblem of the founder of the Order of Lāmas, Padmasambhava.

The Lotus in China Before the advent of Buddhism, the sacred flower had already been conspicuous in Chinese thought as in the landscape. Among the Taoist eight immortals Ho Hsien Ku holds this "flower of openheartedness" or the lotus-pod wand. Among the flowers of the four seasons, the lotus is that of summer. As elsewhere, it is the emblem of purity (because it rises unsullied however muddied the waters and does not grow in the earth), of fruitfulness (the numerous seeds, in particular, being symbolic of offspring), and of creative power. In rural communities, incense is still burned to the Spirit of the Lotus to prevent misfortunes from evil spirits.

As in India, images of Buddha and Buddhist priests are seated upon the lotus, and the flower is one of the eight Buddhist emblems of happy augury. The Chinese usually depict it with ribbons which represent its sacred rays; it also appears as one of the auspicious signs on the sole of Buddha's foot. (In India, Buddha could imprint the lotus flower on the earth at every step.) The lotus sprang up to announce the birth of Buddha.

But the particular Chinese contribution to Buddhist art lies in their pictorial concept of the Western Heaven with its Sacred Lake of Lotuses, a replica of which is characteristically found in temple courtyards. Each soul is conceived as having its particular lotus blossoming on the bosom of the Sacred Lake, where it is received after death and where it rests in a sort of painless purgatory until the appointed time for its opening. The flowers thrive or droop according to the piety of the individual during his life on earth, and for the particularly devout they open immediately when he dies, admitting the soul at once to the divine presence. Chinese paintings of the Western Heaven (as it was interpreted by the Lotus or Amidist school of Buddhism) depict a truly delightful paradise. Lotus blossoms of varied hues, said to be as large as wheels, float on the conventionalized wave pattern of the water. In the center Amitābha is enthroned, surrounded by bodhisattvas. Beautiful pavilions float on conventionalized clouds, vases smoke with fragrant incense, music-clouds play, and jewel flowers rain down through the air.

The Egyptian Lotus The lotus of the Nile is commonly the blue lotus; the white variety also occurs (recognized in art by its rounded rather than pointed ends and strongly ribbed sepals) but the rosy-hued lotus of the farther East is not native here. It provides the greatest number of Egyptian ornamental patterns (notably as the source of the lily capital) but the extent to which it is symbolic rather than strictly decorative is a matter of some dispute. In the later periods at least, it is the flower upon which Horus is seated, it is associated with Osiris, and worn by Nefertete. It is associated particularly with the reproductive power and fertility (since it grows upon the life-giving Nile) and with the sun and resurrection; it is placed upon mummies, used in funeral rites, and commonly depicted in tombs. The association with the sun, which occurs also in the other countries where the lotus grows, arises partly from the raylike petals, prehaps, and from the fact that the blossom opens in the morning and closes at night; it is the cup of the sun, its cradle at night and the source of its renewed life at dawn.

The lotus also occurs on Assyrian seals, where figures are shown as if worshipping the flower. From the Mediterranean and the East it spread into classical mythology (Hercules borrowed the golden cup of the sun, shaped like the lotus, for one of his journeys) and throughout the Western world. Those who like to trace or postulate a world-wide diffusion of basic symbols find reminiscences of the lotus in the Christian lily, the fleur de lys, the petal design within the wheel, the water lily and tulip, and in innumerable circular ornaments, medallions, and rosettes. To the Western mind it apparently sums up the mystical beauty of the Orient and of metaphysical thought, for it has lent its name to numerous volumes of poetry in the English language and to at least one literary magazine. Every part of the lotus plant may be either eaten or used as medicine. However, the "lotus eaters" partook, not of this plant but of the fruit of the lotus tree, which brought forgetfulness. See DACHA; JUJUBE. [MH]

Louhi The mistress of Pohjola or Northland in the epic songs of the Finns: a very powerful sorceress and the greatest adversary of the heroes of the *Kalevala* (see songs 45–47). She commands fog and wind, sends diseases and wild beasts. Finally she was defeated by Väinämöinen, but not killed. She captured the sun and moon and hid them in a mountain, and stole the fire from the homes of Kalevala. [JB]

loup-garou The French word for werewolf: one who transforms himself into a wolf at night and runs the countryside devouring animals and people. In French Canada a man (always a man) becomes a loup-garou because of some curse or as a punishment from heaven. One man, for instance, found that he was a loup-garou because he had not been to mass (or confession) for ten years. The loup-garou is not always a wolf; he may be almost any other animal: a white horse, a dog, pig, even a tree, or an inanimate object. The *loup-garou de cimitière* digs up and eats dead bodies; those who take the shapes of other animals devour both animals and people; some, however, do little damage except to frighten passers-by and await their deliverance. Deliverance from the state of loup-garou comes by religious exorcism, by a blow on the head, or by the shedding of his blood while in the metamorphosed state. See Marius Barbeau, "Anecdotes Populaires de Canada," *JAFL* 33: 202 ff.

In Haiti the loup-garou is a sorcerer (man or woman) who can change into an animal, insect, a tree (usually bearing lights), or some inanimate object. Methods for discovering and besting the loup-garou are the same in most cultures: the shifted skin is found and peppered so that it is too painful to be resumed, or the loup-garou is wounded while in animal shape, discovered by the identical telltale wound on his human body, and so taken and killed. In Haiti, St. James saves his devotees from loups-garous. The Trinidad Negro term for werewolf is *legarou*. See WEREWOLF.

lovage A sweet, rather pungent herb (genus *Levisticum*) now used to flavor candy, formerly used by the monks of southern Europe as a remedy for quinsy and to make an eyewash. Culpeper says this herb "opens, cures, and digests humors"; he also recommends it for freckles. Lovage was said to aid digestion, and to cure dog and snake bites. Samuel Johnson believed in it in medicinal baths for rheumatism.

love apple Because the apple has many seeds the Chinese customarily designate it as "good." J. Rendel Harris has contended that Aphrodite was a personification of the mandrake which was also known as the love apple. An undated Tuscan story is that women who wished to become pregnant got from the priests apples which had been consecrated. Once a man ate one of these and was delivered by Cæsarean section. Until recently in America tomatoes were known as love apples. This is the consequence of an error in etymology. Tomatoes were imported into Italy from northern Africa and were known as apples of the Moors. When they came to France they became known, by confusion between *Moro* and *amour*, as love apples. This confusion was then brought into North America. [RDJ]

love magic, charms, philters, potions, etc. Charms to bring about love are found in folk practice the world over. They fall into two general types: 1) The general charm used as a medicine and based on ingredients of a general character; 2) the charm that acts by "inoculation" or magic transference of loving quality from one person to another. The first type is the least common, probably because it is general in its action and not personal. The love potion that Isolt's mother (a lady from the land of fairy) brewed for Isolt and Marc worked equally well on Isolt and Tristan. Of the several plants widely used for such love potions, the mandrake is the most famous. Its fruit, in some languages called "love apples," would make the one partaking of it fall in love with the one giving it. Likewise the *shang-luh,* a plant like ginseng, has long been used in China as an ingredient for love philters. Briony was also used for this purpose in England. In India a girl who would win a man prepares betel nuts or tobacco and secretes it in his pouch.

Many concoctions, more fantastic, were used. From the Creoles of Louisiana comes this recipe for a love philter: Roast hummingbird hearts, then grind them into a powder and sprinkle the beloved with it. From Nova Scotia: Steep the plant lady's tresses (*Spiranthes*) in water and give the beloved to drink. From American Negro: Place a live frog in an anthill and leave until the ants have cleaned the bones; then take the heart-shaped bone and the hook-shaped bone; keep the first yourself but hook the second in the clothing of the beloved. Among many primitive peoples love potions were often prepared from the reproductive organs of animals; the Australians used the testicles of the kangaroo, for instance, and some American Indians the testicles of the beaver.

The second type of love charm is based on the belief that properties of one person can be transferred to another by magical contact. So one who would induce love in another transfers to him a bit of his hair, clothing, nail parings, ornament, sweat, saliva, blood, bath water. Usually the object is "charmed" by having an incantation said over it by the person administering it or by a medicine-man. Then it is secreted in the food of the beloved or hidden on his person. Arunta women place necklaces of their hair around the necks of their beloveds; in Indonesia a girl hides her girdle in the clothes of the man she loves. In Newfoundland one who would induce love in another pricks an apple full of holes, carries this for a time under the left arm, and then gives it to the beloved.

Out of these practices develop the mutual exchange of love charms as a pledge of love or a guarantee to the continuance of love. Two lovers exchange bits of hair, clothing, rings, blood. This practice constitutes one of the simplest and one of the earliest types of marriage ceremony. [MEL]

☛ Among practically all North American Indian tribes love magic of various sorts was practiced: songs were sung, or played upon the flute, to lure young girls out into the woods; various medicines prepared from herbs and other substances were given to victims; and sorcery of one sort or another was practiced against intended victims. Of all North American Indian tribes the Cree of Canada are probably most noted for their love magic. A lively traffic in love medicines still exists between the Cree and their neighbors, and their prowess as love magicians is greatly feared by surrounding tribes. In many tribes frequent "true tales" are told of elderly men, often powerful shamans, who proposed to marry desirable young girls; if the girl objected the shaman would threaten her or members of her family with death, and so firmly was it believed that he

would make good his threats that the girl often consented, or was forced to do so by her parents. [EWV]

love of one unseen A motif (T11 ff.) known to all folk literature: most easily examined through the numerous references in Arabic listed in Chauvin's bibliography and in the many episodes in the *Ocean of Story.* In Hindu tradition the love of one unseen is known as *adṛṣṭakāma;* in Old Irish legend it is *grád écmaise.*

The hero falls in love with a woman on hearing a description of her (T11.1)—in Old Irish legend Findabair first loved Fraech from "the stories told about him"; or sometimes on hearing her name mentioned, or on seeing her picture (T11.2)—see BUSHY BRIDE; FAITHFUL JOHN;—or seeing her in a dream (T11.3)—see ANGUS OG AND CAER. Falling in love through seeing the marks of a lady's teeth in the fruit she has bitten (T11.4.4.) is in an Indonesian story. For love through sight of unknown's hair (T11.4.1) see TWO BROTHERS.

That men and women actually do become enamored by hearing friends describe the virtue and charm of wives or husbands can be proved by the records of many social workers. The narrative theme which develops usually has to do with the difficulty of finding the person who has been described. The medieval courts of love, concerned with whether fancy is bred in the heart or in the head, also speculated as to whether it entered through the eye or through the ear. [RDJ]

lovers' leap A favorite form of American local legend in which death or suicide for love lends romantic associations to a rock or cliff, often accounting for some unusual or unnatural feature of it—a human likeness or imprint or bloody stain on the rock, a ghost or ghostly cry that haunts the rock or the waters below. In its typical form the story concerns an Indian couple separated by parental or tribal disapproval, or threatened with death by torture at the hands of enemies, or with the maiden's abduction by a jealous rival.

Instead of a desperate couple or a lovelorn maiden, the victim of the tragedy may be a deserted or unfaithful wife. As in the latter case or the case of a maiden who otherwise transgresses tribal law, the victim may be hurled to her death, or, like a prisoner or fugitive (not a lover) seeking simply to escape from captors or pursuers, may be chased or forced over the precipice, as the only way out or as an alternative to shameful punishment. While the scene of the tragedy is generally known as Lovers' Leap, the name may vary with the circumstances or incorporate the name of the victim (e.g. Deborah's Rock, below Reading, Pa.), or involve a folk etymology (e.g. Squantum, Mass., said to be a corruption of Squaw's Tumble). [BAB]

love songs The lyric expression of devotion sung to or in praise of the beloved is one of the chief themes of secular folk song. Even among primitive peoples, the major part of whose music is ritual or magic in character, love songs are found to range from the slight, allusive, and poetic, to the forthright, lusty, and jocular. Love songs may be an important and seriously accepted part of the process of courting, as serenades, aubades, etc.; they may be a more playful manifestation of group courting and flirtation, as in British singing games and the American play-party; they may be sung purely as entertainment for an audience; or they may be sung in pursuit of many unrelated activities such as marching, rowing, dancing, working, children's play, etc. Certain types of songs, such as *blues, fados, cante hondo,* are primarily concerned with love, but chanteys, hollers, lullabies, revolutionary songs, forecastle songs, cowboy songs, jailhouse and chain-gang songs, roustabout songs, the songs of wagoners, Japanese tea-pickers, Haitian hoe gangs, Canadian voyageurs, Michigan lumbermen—all these are sometimes love songs, too. A great part of the ballad literature is concerned with tales of love, generally tragic, in which certain stanzas are simple love songs. Occasionally that love-song section is all that survives of the whole story; in the southern United States, for instance, *The Riddle Song,* or *I Gave My Love a Cherry* is all that remains of *Captain Wedderburn's Courtship* (Child #46) and *Who Will Shoe Your Foot?* (*The Lass of Roch Royal,* Child #76) has also become a plaintive love ditty.

The melodies of love songs are among the loveliest in all the folk repertory and may be as melancholy and haunting as *À La Claire Fontaine* of French Canada and the Hebridean *Sheeling Song,* or as gay as *Cindy.* The words may range from the despair of the sweetheart betrayed or forgotten to the joy of first love on a May morning; from the bravado of "There's more pretty girls than one," to teasing or pleading; from complete faith to utter disillusionment; and from courtly poetry and gallantry to frontier buffoonery and plain speaking. The sweetheart may be described as anything from a red rose or a "rose blanche" to a gal with buck teeth or one who is "chocolate to the bone."

The serenade is particularly the custom of the southern European countries, where courting goes on under strict chaperonage or must be pursued during evening strolls around the plaza or Sunday encounters on the church steps. Songs sung under the lady's window at evening or dawn (*aubade, alborada,* etc.) constitute the lover's best means of communicating with the girl he loves, and her reception of the music indicates her feelings toward him. The eight-line *canzuni* or *rispetti* of Italy are often aubades or serenades. Others include the *aria* of several stanzas, usualy sung to the guitar, and the flower songs, *ciuri* or *rispetti,* in rimed couplets or triplets, each one worked around the name of a flower.

In Mexico a number of serenading customs of Spanish derivation survive. *Las Mañanitas,* for example, is a dawn serenade to wake the girl and wish her joy on her birthday. Another type, the *gallo* (literally, cock), is a serenade at cockcrow, sung to the guitar by bands of young men who rehearse their songs together and then sing under the window of each one's girl in turn. There is a traditional series of songs, beginning with an "awake, my love" (*Si Estas Dormida*) and ending with a farewell. Etiquette requires that the lady remain unseen and show no light at her window. The lover leaves his card in the slit of a small pottery bank in the shape of a cock, which he places on the windowsill.

The interrelation of folk song and art song is close in songs of the serenade type particularly. The *minne-lied* of 12th and 13th century Germany, the trouvère *canso* and the troubadour songs of Provence and France, and the love songs of the goliards of medieval Europe were developed to a fine art from musical materials of the folk, and, after their height as courtly art, returned to the folk, among whom their surviving forms are still sung.

The serenade is not unknown among primitive peoples. Young men of some of the American Indian tribes, for example, wooed their girls in the evenings with songs and flute playing (which was believed to be particularly aphrodisiac).

Probably the *reductio ad absurdum* of the serenade was reached in the *charivari* (called *shivaree, skimmerton,* etc., in America), a performance given to bait, or sometimes to censure newly married couples. The "music" consisted of hoots, catcalls, blowing of horns, and banging of pots and pans.

Courting songs on the game level originally were sung by adults, though they survive now chiefly in children's singing games. *Go In and Out the Windows,* a love game popular in the British Isles in the 18th century and derived from a weavers' dance, is still played and sung by children and was a frontier play-party game in the United States. Its verses, "I'm here because I love you," and "I'll measure my love to show you," etc., could be as personal and meaningful as any couple in the dance cared or dared to make them. Another one of British origin, *Here Come Three Dukes a-Riding,* or as it has often been known in the United States, *What Are You Riding Here For?*, imitates the riding forth of a band of young men to choose wives from another village. As the line of young men advances and retreats alternately with the line of girls, they sing teasingly, "What are you riding here for?" / "I'm riding here to get married." / "Who do you think will have you?" / "I think Miss Jennie (or whatever her name is) will have me." Here again the choosing of partners and the singing of the declaration of love, though playfully undertaken, might be a serious proposal.

Like many other types of folk song, love songs may take the form of a dialog. *No, John, No* is such a one, the suitor receiving "no" as an answer to all his questions because the girl's father had told her always to say "no." John gets around that arrangement by asking her if he should leave her and stop loving her. She still answers "no." A variation of the dialog is the bribe song, in which the lady is offered many gifts if she will give her love. She refuses all until finally the lover offers his heart. *My Man John* and *The Paper of Pins* are of this kind.

The separation theme is common. Mountains, death, the prairie, the sea, prison walls, or long journeys divide the lovers and the singer wishes them away. A Japanese rice-hulling song, for instance, complains of the mountain that hides the house of the beloved from sight. Messages, letters, and love tokens are important features of such songs. "Write me a letter / Send it by mail / Send it in care of / Birmingham jail," wails one of the stanzas sung to the American mountain lonesome tune, *Down in the Valley.* (*Lonesome tune* is one of the synonyms for love song in American folk usage.) "If I could fly," "if I had wings," such songs often say; sometimes the lonesome lover reveals his sad heart to a bird, preferably a turtle dove, who either mourns for his own lost love or will carry the message to the faraway sweetheart.

The unfaithful lover, naturally, has a major role in love songs, "for love grows old, and waxes cold, and fades away like morning dew," as the English song *Waly, Waly* laments. His defection may be on a fairly abstract plane, as in the courtly *Greensleeves* ("Alas, my love, you do me wrong to treat me so discourteously"), or it may be a plain "fact of life," as in the blues, *Easy Rider* ("Easy Rider / See what you done done. / You made me love you / Now your woman done come") and *Careless Love* ("Now I wear my apron high and you pass my door and don't come in"). Most of the forsaken lovers merely mourn and philosophize about the fickleness of philanderers. "They'll hug you and kiss you, and tell you more lies / Than the cross ties on the railroad or the stars in the skies," says *Old Smoky,* the central character of which lost out because of "courtin' too slow." Surinam Negroes, however, use satiric love songs for revenge. See LOBI SINGI.

Work songs of many races and occupations are full of the named or nameless ladies lost and won. Negro chain gangs and field hands sing of Juley, or Juley Ann Johnson, or jumping Judy; the chanteyman sang of Sally Brown, of the unnamed maid of *Amsterdam,* of Boston girls and Liverpool girls, of Irish girls and Yankee girls; the roustabouts sang "Alberta, let your hair hang low," or about Saro Jane or Anniebelle. Soldiers on both sides in World War II sang *Lili Marlene,* which started out as a German popular commercial ditty, and achieved significance by virtue of its popularity and the claims of its "capture" by Allied soldiers. By amateur translation into English, the development of a ghost story around it, and parody and rewording, this sentimental love ballad became partially a folk product in a matter of months. Another soldier's heroine of a love song is Adelita, of the Mexican revolutionary ballad.

In general, it has been remarked that the love songs of southern Europe are more passionate and tragic, more abandoned in their expression than those of northern Europe and the British Isles. The British love songs, apart from the tragic ballads, are more light-hearted, even though they range from the wistful and sad to the broad and lusty types such as *Blow the Candles Out.* In their emigration to America many of the British songs changed as did the language, the style of humor, and the character of narrative. Lyric melancholy, though it survives to a great extent in the singing of the southern United States, is often replaced by a sort of yellow-journalism balladry. Getting mixed up with a woman (or a man, as the case may be) can only lead you to the kind of thing that happened to Jimmy Randall (see LORD RANDALL) or to Pretty Polly, who was murdered by the sailor she trusted. The light-hearted and teasing mood was translated on the frontier to humorous exaggeration and horseplay. "Purty little blackeyed Susie," one of the sweethearts of the comedy type of love song, "jumps on the boys like a dog on a bone."

In primitive love song there are fewer tales, less playfulness, and less tragedy, though none of these elements is completely unknown. A Chinook song says, "Whose sweetheart is very drunk? / My sweetheart is very drunk. / You don't like me. / I know you." Other American Indian love songs liken the girl to the young birch tree, to the soft breeze, to the star, in poetry as delicate and elliptical as a Japanese quatrain. See AZUMA-UTA; BLUES; CANTE HONDO; FADO.   THERESA C. BRAKELEY

Lowalangi or **Lowalani** The Nias (Indonesia) god of the sky and winds; creator of the human race upon whom he bestows souls or breath. Lowalangi, still today, inquires of each person about to be born what he wishes to be or to do on earth. Lowalangi was the younger son

of Ina-da Samadulo Höse, the mother of gods and of all races, who arose from the splitting of stones and who had two sets of mixed twins. The elder son was Latura. Lowalangi married the twin of Latura and with her became the ancestor of the human race.

Lowlands A chanty used at the capstan or pump, based on an old English or Scottish ballad telling of a tragic and prophetic dream of love. "I thought I saw my own true love and knew my love was dead," etc. The title is from the chorus refrain, "Lowlands, lowlands, away, my John," and is not related to one of the alternate titles of *The Sweet Trinity* (or *Golden Vanity*). The same song was taken over by American Negroes in the cotton ports of the late days of sailing and made into a ditty about "screwin' cotton by the day / My dollar and a half a day."

Lu In Karen folklore, an extremely wicked nat who brings illness and death to families; his favorite food is dead bodies. If a man suddenly falls ill because there is nothing more for Lu to eat in the cemetery, other members of the family place offerings of fowls, rice, pigs, and liquor in the cemetery and at home to appease Lu's hunger and to prevent the man from dying. There are actually two Lus; the second is older and less formidable. Sacrifices to him are made only once in five or six years or when sickness is rife.

Lua Literally, plague, calamity, war: an ancient Italian goddess, the cult consort of Saturn (as Ops was in myth): sometimes called *Lua Mater* or *Lua Saturni.* To her the Romans dedicated captured arms before destroying them, probably as a sacrifice to forestall a like calamity or to avoid possible punishment.

Lucifer The Latin name of Phosphorus, Venus as the morning star, the light-bringer which heralds the dawn. The name is sometimes applied to the planet as the evening star as well, although Hesperus is properly its name then. By a curious chain of reference, the passage in *Luke* x, 18 was thought to refer to *Isaiah* xiv, 12, in which the star was used metaphorically for the monarch of Babylon. Thus Lucifer became the chief of the fallen angels, the name borne by Satan before his rebellion.

Lucina An epithet of Juno as the goddess of childbirth, or of the bringing to the light of the child: equivalent to Eileithyia. The name is also given to Diana and to Hecate.

luck ball A hoodoo charm or trick of certain groups of Negroes of the southern United States, designed to give the possessor good advice and bring him luck. One luck ball, described by N. N. Puckett in *Folk Beliefs of the Southern Negro,* pp. 232 f., contained the breastbone of a chicken, some ashes, and bits of rag. It was worn by an old woman in her right armpit against the skin and was periodically given a "drink" of whisky. Another contained four lengths of white silk thread (to tie the owner's friends to him), four lengths of white yarn (to tie down devils), each tied in two knots, i.e. 16 knots in all. The strands were coiled nest-shape and whisky spit upon them; a piece of tinfoil was added (bright as the spirit which was to inhabit the ball), and dust (to blind the eyes of the owner's enemies). The whole was then wound in white yarn, whisky being spat upon it during the winding; then it had to be wrapped in tinfoil and

silk and worn under the right arm in a little linen bag.
Once a week its efficacy had to be revived with whisky.
It could be questioned and its answers were "felt" by
the owner. In Missouri, Christian prayers are frequently
addressed to the luck balls, or they are invoked in the
name of God or some saint.

lucky and unlucky days The foci for much popular feeling and innumerable maxims. The vague feelings about
luck have been embodied by professional astrologists, numerologists and others into a complex doctrine, as ideas
about fate have been embodied by philosophers and theologians. The somewhat indefinite distinction between
the two attitudes is that fate is predestined and cannot
be changed, but that luck is a stream of events which
just happens and will continue until it mysteriously
stops. To get out of bed wrong foot first, to put on the
left shoe before the right shoe, to meet three nuns, or
a black cat, or to walk under a ladder are bad luck. Since
the 18th century in Anglo-Norman communities Friday
has been unlucky and the number 13 is unlucky in these
same communities, whether it is a date, the number of
people at a table, or the number of a room. For some
persons the 3rd, 5th and 7th days of the solar or lunar
month are lucky. These computations are the province
of the numerologists. In many communities luck can be
changed by beginning over again, by touching a priest,
by touching or having intercourse with a person of another race, color, or class, by such rituals as walking
around an object counterclockwise, or by other rituals.
The subject of lucky and unlucky days is frequently confused with the subject of tabu days. A tabu is a prohibition supported by legal and religious sanctions. Disaster
will inevitably occur if prohibited acts are performed
on tabu days. The breaking of a tabu may be accidental
or inevitable, but it belongs to a different level of thinking and feeling from an act which brings bad luck. Some
people believe that luck resides in a talisman, a saint's
image, a rabbit's foot, and that those days when this
repository of "external luck" is not on the person of the
owner are unlucky days. Popular mention is more
occupied with unlucky than it is with lucky days. The
pessimistic tone of folklore is contained in the admonition, "Don't boast about your luck." [RDJ]

Lucretia In Roman legend, the wife of Tarquinius
Collatinus, whose rape by Sextus Tarquinius, son of
Tarquinius Superbus, led to the establishment of the
Roman republic and has been the subject of much literary treatment. During the siege of Ardea, the unoccupied sons of the king and Collatinus, their cousin,
disputed about the relative virtues of their wives. Sextus,
following the visit of the group first to the wives of the
king's sons and then to Lucretia, returned to Collatinus'
home. He was received hospitably, but late at night
entered Lucretia's chamber and raped her at sword's
point. She, after recalling her husband and her father,
told the story and then committed suicide. The uprising
under Lucius Brutus, friend of Collatinus, which followed this outrage, dethroned the Tarquins.

Luġ An Irish god, prominent in the sagas, *The Second Battle of Mag Tured, The Fate of the Children of
Turenn, The Prophetic Ecstasy of the Phantom,* and in
some modern folktales. He was probably identical with
the Celtic deity who gave his name to 14 towns named
Lugdunum (Lyon, Laon, Leyden, etc.) and to Lugubal-

lium (Carlisle). His epithets were Laṁfada (Long
Hand), Lonnbémnech (of Mighty Blows), Saṁildanach
(of Many Gifts). A solar nature is indicated by the fact
that Luġ had a red color on him from sunset to morning
and that his visage is repeatedly compared to the sun—
which accords with the testimony of St. Patrick that the
heathen Irish were heliolatrous. The story of his begetting on the daughter of the one-eyed giant Balor and
of his slaying his grandfather shows a marked affinity to
the legend of Perseus. He was given in fosterage to
queen Tailtiu, and was trained in athletic feats by the
sea-god Manannán, who bestowed on him his horse,
corselet, and sword. When the Tuatha Dé Danann (the
gods) were oppressed by the Fomorians, Luġ appeared
at the palace of King Nuada and was admitted because he
possessed all the arts and crafts. He demonstrated his
strength by hurling a flagstone which required eighty
yoke of oxen to move, and was accepted as the deliverer
of the Tuatha Dé Danann. He played a great part in the
slaughter of the Fomorians at the battle of Mag Tured,
and killed his grandfather Balor by knocking out his
eye with a sling-stone. In the *Prophetic Ecstasy*, Luġ appears as a supernatural horseman, who summoned King
Conn to his palace and there, though he declared that he
was a son of Adam and had returned after death, he foretold the names of the rulers of Tara. Luġ's bride, "the
Sovranty of Ireland," was present and served Conn with
huge ribs of meat and cups of red ale. At the end of his
prophecy Luġ and his house disappeared.

Luġ has two counterparts in Welsh literature—Llwch
Llawwynnawc (White Hand) and Llew. The former
seems to have borrowed his name and epithet directly
from the Irish, but unfortunately we know little of him
except that he must have been prominent among Arthur's warriors. Llew's name is the Welsh cognate of
Luġ, and, as Gruffydd has shown in *Math Vab Mathonwy*, several elements in Llew's story, though curiously distorted, are cognates of or borrowings from
Luġ's legend. See BALOR; CELTIC FOLKLORE; DECHTIRE;
FATAL CHILDREN; GAWAIN; GLAS GAIBLEANN; LLEW LLAW
GYFFES; LUGNASAD. [RSL]

Luġaid Mac Con A legendary 2nd century king
of Munster, Ireland; literally, Luġaid, son of a dog: so
named because he was suckled by a bitch in the house
of his foster father, Oilill Ólom, who had seized the kingdom. Luġaid was raised side by side with Oilill's son
Eoġan. These two met in battle one day to settle a dispute between them in which Mac Con claimed there
had been false judgment given by Oilill. Mac Con's fool
was killed in the battle, impersonating his master; the
battle went to Eoġan; Eoġan pursued Mac Con, recognizing his white legs through all the confusion of the
rout.

Then Mac Con fled to Scotland with 27 companions.
They all make a vow to speak, eat, and behave with
equality in order to keep secret the identity of Luġaid
Mac Con. The king of Scotland provided for them for a
year with great generosity; and he marveled at their
prowess and because they had no chief. One day an Irish
poet came to Scotland, and, on being questioned, told
how Ireland and the people of Luġaid Mac Con were
in subjection and misery under Eoġan, who was ruling in
place of his aging father. Mac Con's distress at the news
revealed his identity to the king of Scotland, who sought

again to test the group by serving raw mice at a feast. Mac Con was the first to put the mouse in his mouth and swallow it tail and all; the others watched him and did the same. Then "Are you Luġaid?" said the king. And Luġaid Mac Con said that he was.

So the king of Scotland gathered his forces and went to Ireland with Luġaid to help avenge the wrong. On the plain Mag Mucrama they engaged in battle with Eoġan, son of Oilill, and Art, son of Conn. It was on the eve of this battle that Art begot Cormac Mac Airt on the smith's daughter in the house of the smith. And on the eve of this battle the blind druid, Dil, foresaw defeat for Eoġan because Eoġan's cause was unjust. The battle of Mag Mucrama was Luġaid Mac Con's victory. Art son of Conn was killed in that battle, and also the seven sons of Oilill.

Luġaid Mac Con ruled in Tara seven years. He took Cormac Mac Airt in fosterage, and was expelled from the kingship at the time of his false judgment in regard to confiscation of the old woman's sheep. He then went back to his foster father, Oilill, to tend him in his old age; but when Oilill welcomed him, he bit him in the cheek with a poisoned tooth. Mac Con fled, but Oilill's people pursued him and killed him. Various texts report the rule of Luġaid Mac Con in Ireland as 30, 27, 25, and 7 years. See ANIMAL NURSE; BIRTH OF CORMAC.

Luġnasaḋ A great festival which used to be held on August 1 at Teltown on the River Boyne, where a mound still marks the site. It was mentioned in Cormac's *Glossary* (c. 900) as a commemorating fair, celebrated by Luġ mac Ethne in the beginning of autumn. The *Dinnsenchas, The Book of Invasions,* and Keating's *History of Ireland,* all say that Teltown took its name from a certain Tailtiu, Luġ's foster mother, who was buried on this spot, and that Luġ instituted the games as an annual memorial. This ancient explanation seems to be an error which arose when the true meaning of the word Luġnasaḋ and of the festival was forgotten. Rhys and Gruffydd suggested another interpretation, which is supported by impressive evidence. The element *násad* seems related to words signifying "to give in marriage." Keating says of the fair of Teltown that "the men kept apart by themselves on one side, and the women apart by themselves on the other side, while their fathers and mothers were making the contract between them; and every couple who entered into treaty and contract with one another were married." O'Donovan reported a tradition that at a place near by, called "the Hollow of the Fair," nuptials were solemnized in pagan times, and even in the 19th century young men and women used to resort thither and arrange trial unions. A late medieval manuscript says that at Taillne, presumably Teltown, Luġ Scimaiġ made the great feast for Luġ mac Ethlenn to celebrate his wedding of the sovranty, while we find in an 11th century text Luġ dwelling in a faery palace with a crowned woman identified as the Sovranty of Ireland (Ériu). It seems, then, that Luġ's bride was the Sovranty of Ireland, but a number of stories relate how one or another of the destined kings of Ireland mated with the Sovranty of Ireland, transforming her thereby from a monstrous hag into a radiant beauty. These stories show an analogy on the one hand with the tradition that the goddess Meḋb allowed no king to reign in Tara unless he were wedded to herself, and so mated with nine kings of Ireland, and on the other with Aldhelm's account of Constantine's vision of Byzantium as an ancient crone transformed into a lovely maiden. But though in the Irish stories the hag is an allegorical figure personifying the kingship, she must be a rationalized form of the goddess Ériu, personifying the land of Ireland. For we learn of Ériu that she was of the Tuatha Dé Danann, took many shapes, and was the wife of Mac Greni, "son of the Sun." The metamorphosis of the Sovranty of Ireland, therefore, is a blurred version of a nature myth, in which the future kings of Ireland have inherited the role of Luġ, the sun god, while the hag is the land of Ireland, transformed by the caresses of the sun from the bleakness of winter into the floral splendor of spring—a version of the widespread myth of the union of sun and earth. All this fits in with the persistent association of the Luġnasaḋ with marriage rites, and it is significant that the date August 1 is exactly nine months, the normal period of gestation, before the great feast of Beltane, which celebrated the beginning of summer. See ERIU; LUG.

Bibliography: Gruffydd, W. J., *Math Vab Mathonwy* (Cardiff, 1928), pp. 107–10.

Loomis, Roger S., *Arthurian Tradition and Chrétien de Troyes* (New York, 1949), pp. 377–79.

Westropp, T. J., "Marriages of the Gods at the Sanctuary of Tailltiu," *Folk-Lore,* XXXI (1920): 109–41.

ROGER S. LOOMIS

luinig A type of song sung by Hebridean women at the tasks of spinning, fulling cloth, haymaking, etc., consisting of short, mournful melodies in traditional pentatonic scale patterns. See WORK SONGS.

Lukman or **Lokman** The name traditionally given to the compiler of an Arabic collection of fables and proverbial material. He was pre-Islamic; according to tradition, he was a contemporary of David. *Sura* xxxi of the Koran bears his name. Burton distinguishes three Lokmans: the Koranic; the Negro, identifiable with Kai Khusrau and perhaps with Æsop (or Æthiops, says Burton); and Lokman of the Vultures, a folk hero of tremendous appetites who lived 3500 years. The fables of Lukman resemble the Æsopian collection; some of the stories are Indian, some come from Greek originals.

lukuman Literally, those who look: the diviners of the Surinam Negroes; specifically, the diviners who cure souls. To effect a cure the lukuman must question the afflicted soul. He will place a bowl or cup (containing rain water and an egg) on the head of the patient, or put it in his right hand. Then he will "call" the soul of the patient into his head. As soon as the soul is in the head, the patient's body quivers, his eyes close, and the bowl or cup shakes. Thus the lukuman knows that the soul is available to be questioned: if the answer is yes, the water spills out; if the answer is no, it does not even quiver. There are other methods: the lukuman may get his answers by looking into a mirror, or by watching the surface of a basin of water; when the water quivers the spirit has entered into it, and may be questioned; or he may use a fan which unfolds if the answer is yes, remains closed if the answer is no.

The lukuman is a highly and specifically trained man whose knowledge is usually given to him by an elder brother or a maternal uncle. He is chosen by his predecessor, however, for some special talent or some supernatural experience which marks him as suitable for the profession. If the lukumąn is a woman, she has learned her wisdom from a sister or mother or a maternal aunt. Occasionally a man or woman with the mediumistic gift becomes a lukumąn by becoming possessed with a *komfo* spirit. The male lukumąn is consulted for illness of the soul; male or female may be consulted for illness caused by the *winti*. Lukumąn are consulted not only for illnesses, however, but for advice on tabus and how to avoid the penalties for the unwitting violation of one or more tabus; how to evade evil magic, find murderers, diagnose poor crops, etc.

For fine differences between the *lukumąn, kartamąn, obiaman, piaiman, wintiman, wisiman,* see M. J. and F. S. Herskovits, *Suriname Folklore,* Columbia Contributions to Anthropology 27, New York 1936, p. 56. See DIVINATION; LOOKMAN; MAMA FŌ GRO; WINTI.

lullaby A type of song sung by mothers and nurses the world over to coax their babies to sleep; a cradle song (Fr. *berceuse,* Ger. *Wiegenlied,* Gr. *nannarismata,* L. *lenes neniæ,* etc.). The simplest form, merely a humming or a repetition of monotonous and soothing sounds, often accompanied by a gentle rocking of the child in the arms or in its bed or carrier, is almost too slight to be called a song and is heard even among peoples who otherwise show little musical development. One collector was told by an old man of an American Indian tribe that the women made noises to put babies to sleep, but he would hardly call that singing. Some South American Indians, who live nomadic lives, often in enemy territory, have almost no songs, but the mothers croon to the infants to quiet them because it would be dangerous for their cries to be heard. Aside from humming, the most common syllables of lullabies are loo-loo, lalla, lullay, ninna-nanna, bo,bo, do,do. These are heard in English, Polish, Rumanian, French, Italian, etc., as they were in the Latin of ancient Rome and the Greek of Athens. In Italian and Rumanian *ninna-nanna* is the word for rocking an infant to sleep.

The more developed airs may be plaintive or gay, but they are usually sung softly, with little expression, and repeated over and over until, as sleep claims the baby, the voice trails off to a whisper. Some are so constructed that stanzas can be added almost endlessly, following a cumulative pattern.

Possibly the most familiar of American lullabies is *Rock-a-bye, Baby,* set to the words of an old English Mother Goose rime, with a melody said to have been composed by Mrs. Effie Canning Carlton in 1874 and made popular by a play, *The Old Homestead,* in which it was sung. However, a number of persons claimed to have been familiar with the air before the date of Mrs. Carlton's publication, and it is possible that the air is a folk tune current some time before that and a product of unconscious memory on her part.

Another lullaby air known to the people of many European countries is that of the Norwegian and Danish *Sov nu Södt,* originally the French song *Ah, vous dirai-je, maman.* Both in Germany and in America it is the tune to which the alphabet is sung. It also provides the melody of *Baa-Baa, Black Sheep, Twinkle, Twinkle, Little Star,* and a ring game, *The Snail.* In art music

it has been the inspiration for variations by many composers, including Mozart and Dohnanyi.

Perhaps the greatest number of lullabies say, in whatever the tune and whatever the language, "Go to sleep. Mother is here. You are safe. Everything is all right." The all-rightness of everything may be elaborated by a placid description of what the rest of the household is doing. Father has gone hunting, fishing, tending sheep. The favorite German cradle song *Schlaf, Kindlein, Schlaf,* known in America in both English and Pennsylvania Dutch versions and made familiar by Wagner by its inclusion in the *Siegfried Idyll,* is of this kind. A Swedish lullaby says that pussy is climbing the big pine tree, brother is turning the millstone, and papa has gone to feed the pig. If the singer is the big sister, the grandmother, or the nurse, the song may tell where mama has gone, and when she will be back, and how nice it will be as soon as she comes, if only the baby will be good. Another set of reassuring words is devoted to how peaceful the surroundings are (the stars are shining, the bees are buzzing, breeze blowing, etc.). This line of argument often develops with descriptions of the sleepy flowers, the rabbits, squirrels, birds, etc., going to sleep, and has occurred to mothers in Hungary, Ireland, Japan, and many other lands.

As a guarantee of safety during the night, the words often invoke saints, angels, or guardian spirits to watch over the cradle. The lullaby may thus become a sort of evening prayer. Some are cast in the form of a song of the Virgin Mary to the infant Jesus, as in the lullaby carols (see CAROL), in the medieval Latin *Dormi, Jesu* still sung in Chile and probably imported there by Jesuits, and in the sacred lullabies of Europe.

Sleep itself may be personified as "the sandman," or "La Dormette" of Poitou (a female sandman), or Willie Winkie, or "le souin-souin" of France, and called upon to take the child to dreamland.

Another type of lullaby concentrates on maternal admiration of the child, enumerating his personal beauties and charms, comparing him to flowers, stars, princes, jewels, etc. Or the theme may be a prophecy of his glorious future. A Kwakiutl cradle song says, "When I am a man, then I shall be a hunter, harpooner, canoe-builder, etc.," outlining prowess in the pursuits most admired in his society. A Corsican lullaby prophesies that the infant will accomplish the studied revenge of an old vendetta. "Hush, Little Jimmy (substitute child's name here), don't you cry. You'll be the president by and by," says a song of the American South.

Promises and bribes for good behavior provide a common theme. The offers may range from the simplest of comforts to the height of riches and power, according to the environment and the imagination of the singer. Baby Bunting, in the English lullaby, is promised a rabbit-skin to wrap the Baby Bunting in. A Danish and Norwegian cradle song says papa will bring new shoes with shining buckles for baby. A French standby says the white hen on the branch will lay an egg. One of the Greek cradle songs with a *nani, nani* refrain promises the city of Alexandria in sugar, Cairo in rice, and Constantinople to rule. In Japan, the rewards may be toy drums, papier-mâché dogs, and other toys. In China, one lullaby promises a bamboo flute for the baby to play. A Norwegian song tells about fishing and distributes one of the catch to the father, one to the mother, one for sister, one for brother, and one for him who pulled the fish, the baby. In Brittany the baby is bribed with the cake the mother is baking and the boat the father is building. An American example of the bribe offer, extended for stanza upon stanza, is the familiar, "Hush, little baby, don't say a word / Mama's gonna buy you a mockin' bird. / If that mockin' bird don't sing / Mama's gonna buy you a diamond ring. / If that diamond ring turns brass / Mama's gonna buy you a lookin' glass," etc. Another American favorite, *All the Pretty Little Horses,* is also full of promises.

Threats, from the playful to the hair-raising, also enter into lullaby texts. These make use of the bogeymen of all nations to persuade wakeful babies to go to sleep. In some southern European countries, the Moor, or black man, is the bogey whose wrath will be provoked. "El coco" among Spanish-speaking peoples is pictured as a black man who eats crying babies. The Santa Claus figure is also brought into prominence, with threats that he will be angry and not bring gifts. In Japan, the displeasure of Hotei is threatened. Hotei is a kindly man who distributes a sack of goodies, but has eyes in the back of his head for seeing bad behavior. Sometimes the punishing figure is an animal—the bear or the owl who will hear bad children crying. A German song says a black sheep and a white sheep will bite the baby's toes. In some lullabies a historical bogey-man such as Wellington or Bonaparte is still invoked. In all of these the idea is that the punitive character is listening, and "he'll come for you if you don't hush." Occasionally the threats are direct and violent, though teasingly sung, as in the South African *Siembamba:* "Siembamba, Mama's baby / Twist his neck and hit him on the head / Throw him in the ditch / And then he will be dead."

There are also many sad little lullabies complaining of the mother's weariness and hard lot, of the father's absence, neglect, or drunkenness. A Basque song says that papa will surely come home drunk from the tavern.

In addition to these types, many lullabies tell little stories. The American *Go Tell Aunt Nancy* (Sally, Tabby, Rhody, etc.) relates the loss by drowning of the old gray goose destined to make a featherbed. Bits of *Lord Randall* (as *Wee Croodin' Doo*), *Lamkin* (cut down to the dialog of nurse and lady), and other ballads are sung as cradle songs. The African Bushmen have a lullaby worked into the tale of *The Anteater, the Young Springbok, the Lynx, and the Partridge:* a soothing series of sounds and comments called *The Song of the Springbok Mothers.*

Practically any kind of song can and does serve as a lullaby. Perhaps the mothers, realizing that the words cannot be understood, feel no need to censor their singing and make use of the blood-curdling as well as the soothing in their selection according to their knowledge. In any case, lullabies are perhaps the most likely to survive of any type of folk song for as long as babies cry and the voice of the mother will quiet them, such tunes and words will be handed down or continue to come into being. THERESA C. BRAKELEY

Lumawig The principal deity, creator, and culture hero of the Igorot (Philippine Islands). Traditionally Lumawig was a resident of Bontoc who taught the people the useful arts and performed many miracles. He has a real cult; prayers are conducted by priests asking him to send rain or stop a heavy storm, to bless crops and multiply animals. When the new rice crop is stored Lumawig is asked for his blessing, so that the rice will be sufficient for the family. See INDONESIAN MYTHOLOGY.

Luna The Roman goddess of the moon: perhaps of Sabine origin. Her principal importance was in the figuring of the calendar; her worship was never important.

lundum A type of song, melancholy and languid, sung to the guitar and probably originally accompanying dancing, popular in Portuguese cities in the 18th and 19th centuries. Probably of Brazilian or African coastal origin, the type is thought to be an ancestor of the *fado.*

Lung Wang The Chinese Dragon King: bringer of rain, controller of the ocean and of all storms and waters, and inhabiter of all lakes. The phenomena of waterspouts is always associated with him. In dry seasons the peasants bring his image from the temples and show him the damage done by the droughts. In Peking he receives particular attention at the Big Bell Temple. See DRAGON CULT. [RDJ]

Luonnotar A Finnish deity, "daughter of the creation" (see ILMATAR). Luonnotar is the deity of birth, sometimes also called Synnytär (from *synty,* birth). From the Catholic period the Virgin Mary is also called, in magic songs, by the name of Luonnotar or Luojatar (from *Luoja,* Creator) and is appealed to in childbirth. The Virgin Mary is also often associated with the deities of birth, like Mara by the Latvians. [JB]

Luot-chozjik The guardian spirit of the reindeer of the eastern Lapps. She protected the domestic herds while they were turned loose in the forests in the summer.

Lupercalia An ancient Roman fertility festival held on the 15th of February: said to have been established by Romulus and Remus or by Evander, but probably more ancient than Rome itself. The Luperci, priests of Lupercus, a fertility god equated with Faunus or Inuus or Pan, came on this day to the Lupercal, the cave on the Palatine where the she-wolf suckled Romulus and Remus. There they sacrificed goats and a dog, emblems of fertility, and smeared the blood on the foreheads of two noble youths. The blood was wiped off with wool dipped in milk, and the two youths laughed loudly. The priests then ate. After the meal they cut up the goatskins, dressed themselves with patches of the skin. The rest of the skins were cut into whips with which the priests ran around the boundaries of the Palatine precinct, striking all whom they met. A woman so struck was made especially fertile and could look forward to bearing her child easily. The ceremony purified the land for the new year, February being the last month, and from this underlying concept (*februare,* to cleanse) the month took its name.

lupin A plant of the bean family (genus *Lupinus*), bearing racemes of mostly blue or purple flowers. The seeds of *L. albus* have been used for food in the Old World from very early times. The use of lupin-flour as soap is mentioned in the *Arabian Nights.* In the latter part of the 17th century the doctrine of signatures recommended lupin for the nerves, for the kidneys, and also for the fingers and hands. The Navaho Indians made a remedy for boils from lupin seeds, and regard them not only as a cure for sterility but helpful in producing female children. *L. subcarnosus,* the bluebonnet, is the state flower of Texas.

lur Danish name for the prehistoric bronze trumpet of northern Europe, numerous examples of which were preserved in the peat bogs of Denmark, Germany, and Sweden. The instrument has a twisted S-shape, is more than 80 inches in length, and is terminated by a flat, ornamented disk, rather than a bell. It was made in sections and joined. The instrument is always found in pairs with opposing curves, resembling a pair of mammoth tusks, from which it is believed to have taken its original shape; the extinction of the mammoth and the acquisition of skill in metal-working brought about a change in the material but not in the shape. It shows a high degree of craftsmanship in metal-working, and was the source of considerable excitement and controversy when the first finds were made. Exaggerated claims for the range of the instrument were tested by trumpeters and trombonists, and assertions of three-part harmony in the playing of the 3000-year-old trumpets were widely disputed. Compositions were written to include lurer for public performance in Denmark. However, none of the suppositions about its original use and sound could be established.

lure A wooden trumpet with birchbark casing, formerly used in the mountains of Norway: similar to the alphorn and used for the same purposes until recent years. It is rarely heard now.

lute In the scientific classification of musical instruments, a stringed instrument having a body and a neck, with strings stretched over the combined length. Two principal divisions of the category include the lutes played by plucking the strings, as the guitars, mandolin, banjo, samisen, and the instrument specifically named "lute," and those played with the bow, for which see VIOLINS AND FIDDLES. Further distinctions are made according to the length of the neck and the shape of the body. The earliest and most primitive lutes, as well as some survivors in the Orient and the Near East, are *long lutes,* of which the neck is comparatively longer than the body and may consist of a long stick thrust through the body. *Short lutes* are longer of body than of neck, the latter in some types being merely a tapered extension of the body. Body shapes may be in the form of a half pear or melon, recalling the fruit shells of which the earliest were made; round and flat, as in the banjo and the Chinese *yueh ch'in;* waisted, as in the guitars and violins. Materials used for making lutes have included large, pumpkinlike gourds and ostrich shells, as in some of the Indian *sitars;* the armadillo shell, as in the Mexican *concha;* catskin, as in the Japanese *samisen;* as well as fine woods, nacre inlay, etc., as in the classical European lutes and violins.

One or another type of lute has been used for thousands of years to accompany singing and dancing, both solo and ensemble, on primitive, popular, and sophisticated levels; and in the 16th and 17th centuries in Europe, particularly in Spain, the lute and its adaptation, the *vihuela,* reached a high position in art music. For love songs and ballads, from court to marketplace, from the studied movements of the *basse danse* to the erotic gesture of the flamenco and the mingled symbolism of *Los Concheros,* some form of lute has set the tune and strummed the rhythm.

Individual members of the lute classification have been the subjects of a body of legend and story involving witches, Satan, gods and spirits, charms, and other magical powers. For example, a Sanskrit story tells of a lute of bone, which, when played in accompaniment to the chanting of a charm, made its listeners dance uncontrollably and brought out horns on their heads. Another lute, described in *The Ocean of Story,* had the power to subdue wild elephants. Śiva is depicted as holding the *tanbur,* an Indian lute in which the magic syllable *om,* the essence of the Vedas and of the universe, is inherent. Resuscitation by the playing of a lute is a folktale motif (D1234). See also BANJO; GUITAR.

While the origin of the instrument is unknown, its invention is variously attributed to the Assyrians, the Egyptians, the Cappadocians, and, by the Manicheists, to their leader, Mani. The earliest lutes shown on art works, small-bodied, long-necked instruments on Babylonian seals and plaques dating from 2000 B.C. or earlier, show shepherds playing to their flocks and dogs. The lute of ancient Egypt was a woman's instrument with a skin soundboard and a long, slender neck piercing the body. A similar but cruder wooden lute survives among the Negroes of northwest Africa, and a refined version of this was made by the Arabs.

Persian art works of the 8th century B.C. show the first pictured examples of the short lute, but the parent of the types to be found today among Arabs, Chinese, Japanese, and Europeans was probably the Indian short lute depicted about 100 A.D. In India lutes called *tanbur, sitar,* etc., have developed in great variety of shape, size, material, and decoration—one so fantastic as to be called in both Hindustani and Sanskrit the peacock, because it is designed and painted to resemble the bird. Indian lutes, with a wide range of timbres created by deeply vibrant drone strings, movable frets, and other devices, accompany singing and dancing and are combined in chamber music with other instruments. Some types are bowed.

One of the most important among the lutes of the Far East is the *pi'p'a,* a Chinese short lute dating from the Han period, with a shallow ovoid body and four silk strings symbolizing the four seasons. It is used to accompany singing and flute-playing, both classical and popular, and is played on the streets by blind girl singers seeking employment. The Japanese equivalent is the *biwa,* which has been known in three main forms: a large orchestra instrument held in the position of a cello and used for the classical music and dance of the 10th century; a smaller type held in the lap and played as accompaniment to epic recitation; and a third even smaller form. Flat-bodied Oriental lutes, appearing about 500 A.D., have been prevailingly of two shapes, octagonal and round. The round type is more recent and is called *yueh ch'in* in China and *gekkin* in Japan, both names meaning moon. The best known of the surviving long lutes of the Far East is the guitarlike Japanese samisen.

The word lute is derived from the Arabic *al 'ud,* meaning wood or stick, and the lutes of Europe were derived from various types carried by the Arabic expansion across North Africa and into Spain—both long-necked and short-necked, and both round-backed, as in the mandolin, and flat-bodied, as in the guitars. The four strings characteristic of many of the instruments had many meanings—the elements of earth, air, fire, and water; the cardinal directions; the four seasons; the phases of the moon; the number of weeks in a month; the four humors (blood, phlegm, bile, and black bile), etc. While the music of stringed instruments was forbidden in early religious teaching, it achieved acceptance at least by the 10th century, when it appears in German psalters and in Spanish manuscripts. From that time on the lute became one of the most generally played and highly esteemed of instruments all over Europe. Courtiers and ladies found it a polite and useful accomplishment to accompany their songs on the lute or one of its relatives. To the jongleurs, it was one of the ten instruments listed as required by Guiraut de Calanson in his *Conseils aux Jongler* (1210).

On the American continents lutes are believed to have been unknown before the coming of Europeans. Since that time, however, Central and South American natives have adopted and adapted lutes, guitars, and fiddles down to the crudest and most primitive levels; and backwoods North America has depended heavily on fiddle, guitar, and banjo for its song and dance music. [TCB]

Lü-tsu Chinese patron of barbers, beggars, and pedicures: often confused and identified with Lü Tung-pin, and like him often depicted holding in one hand the wonderful two-edged sword, gift of the Fire-Dragon, but holding in the other his hair-switch. Lü-tsu was even more dissipated than the other disciples of Lao-Tzu (traditional founder of Taoism), who spent their time drinking and misbehaving. Barbers, beggars, and pedicures are also thought to be dissolute. They are one of the few groups not admitted to the Imperial examinations. [RDJ]

Lü Tung-pin One of the Chinese Eight Immortals. Lü is eight feet tall, with a sparse beard. A great light appeared and a stork flew through the room at the hour of his birth. He lived in the T'ang dynasty, 618–907. After enjoying honor in the court, he fled with his family to the mountains because of a political revolution. He studied alchemy, and learned how to live on air alone. In his time he rid the earth of many devils. He still kills devils, and is revered by literati and barbers. The latter have confused him with Lü-tsu. [RDJ]

lycanthropy The power of becoming a wolf or of turning a human being into a wolf; also, belief in werewolves. See WEREWOLF.

Lycaon In Greek mythology, an Arcadian king, son of Pelasgus; the father of Callisto and of fifty sons. These sons were extremely impious and Zeus, to punish them, appeared at court disguised as a poor laborer. The sons slew a child and mixed its entrails with the other meats served at the meal. Zeus arose in anger, overthrew the table (hence the place-name Trapezus), and slew the sons with a thunderbolt, changing Lycaon into a wolf. The myth has many variants: Lycaon himself was evil and tried to kill Zeus, finally testing his suspected godhood by offering him human flesh; or, Lycaon was very pious and founded the temple of Zeus Lycæus, thus being spared when his sons were slain; or, the murdered

child was Lycaon's own (a parallel to the story of Tantalus); or, the child was brought to the altar of Zeus as a sacrifice; or, all the sons but one, Nyctimus, were killed, and when Nyctimus ascended the throne further punishment was added in the form of the flood (see DEUCALION); or, the sons were all changed to wolves, etc. The myth seems to be an explanation of the rites connected with the cult of Zeus Lycæus. Cannibalism appears to have been a part of the rites, and the partaker of the human flesh was believed to turn into a wolf and to wander for eight or ten years in wolf form, changing back into a human being at the end of that term if he had avoided human flesh. This in turn may be based on a pre-Hellenic cannibalistic cult superseded by the worship of Zeus, or it may be a reflection of the belief in werewolves. Many attempts have been made by scholars to explain the contradictory elements of the story; for example, Lycaon is both pious culture hero and impious. The transformation and cannibal themes seem to point to some underlying pastoral and agricultural rite of increase.

lycopodium Genus name for the club mosses, evergreen mosses growing erect or creeping: often called *ground pine,* and often used for Christmas decorations. In Ireland one of its names is *crúibíní sionnaig,* little feet of the fox. It is known to have been used as food in famine times in Ireland.

Lycopodium has long been recognized as an ingredient for eye washes and a lotion for swellings; but its efficacy depends on how and when it is gathered. It must be taken at sunset on the third day of the moon. The gatherer must wash his hands, display his knife to the crescent moon, and kneeling say: "As Christ healed the issue of blood/ Do thou cut what thou cuttest for good." The moss must then be boiled in water from the nearest spring. Only thus is assured its full potency to aid eyes or swellings. It is also used in an ointment mixed with butter from the milk of a new cow.

Lycopodium is sometimes called witch's meal or vegetable brimstone because the dried spores constitute a fine yellow inflammable powder used by sorcerers and magicians to make lightning, and still so used by stage magicians. A thin cloud of this powder blown through the flame of a candle explodes with an awesome flash. Commercially it is used in fireworks. Medicinally it is used as an absorbent on wounds and sores, and also as an ingredient in a lotion against vermin. A decoction of the moss mixed with spruce twigs was used by the Chippewa Indians for steaming stiff joints. In Newfoundland it is recommended as a remedy for spitting blood. It is an irritant, a counter-irritant, and makes a fine itching powder.

Lygni According to the *Volsunga Saga,* one of Hunding's sons. He had been one of Hiordis's suitors, and was so angry at her marriage to Sigmund that he attacked the Volsungs and slew them all. Hiordis escaped, however, and later bore Sigmund's son, Sigurd, who slew Lygni when he was grown.

Lyra A northern constellation, including the brilliant Vega, which was the pole star 14,000 years ago. The Akkadians knew Lyra as a storm bird; the Chaldeans and ancient Hindus saw it as a vulture. Later Chaldean astronomers depicted the vulture holding a harp. Thus, in Greece and Rome it became the harp or lyre made from the tortoise shell by Hermes, the Lyre of Orpheus and Apollo. Thence through Europe the constellation was the Lyre or the Harp; in Britain it was King Arthur's Harp. The Bohemians knew it as the sky fiddle. In Peru Lyra was the ram at the head of the celestial flocks, and the stars guarded over the Incas' sheep. To the Arabs it was the Mule. In China, Lyra, or Vega, is the Weaving Maid, the patroness of the domestic fine arts of women. The goddess is seated at her loom spinning with the little crown of three stars over her head. See CHIH NÜ.

lyre A musical instrument consisting of a soundbox in either vaulted or flat shape, two approximately parallel or converging arms attached to the sides of the body, a crosspiece (yoke) adjoining the arms, and varying numbers of strings stretched from yoke to soundboard. It is sounded either by plucking or bowing the strings. Various forms of the instrument have been known since ancient times, figuring on Sumerian monuments of 3000 B.C. and in Greek mythology and legend, and it is still played in Estonia and Finland, by the Ostyaks and Voguls of Siberia, by the Arabs, by the Nubians, Ethiopians, and Negroes of Africa. The size of early lyres, as depicted by the Sumerians and Egyptians, was large —taller than the player as he sat before it—but, as in the case of many other instruments, later types were smaller and lighter and could be simultaneously played and carried.

The lyre was imported into Egypt in the 15th century B.C., first in the large form. Portable lyres appeared there about 1000 B.C. The later type was generally played by women, as was the *kinnor,* the lyre of Biblical times in Israel. Invention of the instrument was ascribed in Egypt to the god Thoth. In Israel, Jubal, according to the Bible, was the "father" of lyrists.

It was in Greece that the lyre achieved its greatest fame and became the most venerated of instruments. Two main types were played there: 1) the *lyra,* a lightweight instrument with a body originally made of a turtle shell, arms of animal horn, a stretched skin soundboard, and strings of sheep gut (later hemp); 2) the *kithara,* a heavier wooden instrument with a body constructed of two flat resonating boards joined by a side section of uniform width. The lyra was played chiefly by amateurs—students, lovers, etc.; the kithara by professional musicians, epic singers, theatrical performers, etc. The lyra, though cruder and more primitive in construction, was probably the later of the two. Both as a solo instrument and as accompaniment to singing, the lyre was the favorite of the Greeks. When the *skolion* (drinking song) was sung, a lyre was passed zigzag back and forth among the reclining banquet guests and each in turn contributed a stanza or a health.

In legend, the lyre was the instrument of the gods and Homeric heroes. While some accounts state that the lyre came from Thebes or from Thrace, its invention was generally credited to Hermes or to Apollo. Homer says that Hermes was born at dawn and that by noon that day he had found a tortoise shell, fashioned a lyre of it, and was playing heavenly music. He gave it to Apollo as a peace offering after a quarrel, and from them on Apollo was the master musician of Olympus, playing his lyre for the entertainment of the gods. In later Greek art the lyre is Apollo's attribute, replacing the sun-god's bow of archaic works.

His virtuosity was such that other musicians, performers on other instruments, felt called upon to challenge him as a final test of their own skill, and all were defeated. Marsyas competed against Apollo with his flute (the *aulos,* actually an oboe), which he had found after it had been thrown away by its chagrined inventor, Minerva (Athena), in a fit of embarrassment over the grimaces she made while playing it. Marsyas, defeated, was flayed and his skin hung in a cave. Pan, with his pipes, was also outplayed by Apollo, and Midas, the umpire of that contest, grew ass's ears as evidence of his poor judgment in favoring Pan.

The magic power of the lyre to command nature and the supernatural is stressed in many stories. When Poseidon (Neptune) was building Troy, Apollo sat by, playing his lyre, and the stones danced into their allotted positions. Thebes, also, arose magically to the strains of the lyre played by Amphion, son of Zeus and Antiope and husband of Niobe, who had been given the instrument and taught to play it by Hermes. There, too, the scattered bits of masonry organized themselves into walls. Orpheus, son of Apollo and Calliope, charmed the very demons of hell and softened the heart of Hades when he played his lyre and sang, seeking the return of his love, Eurydice. Though he failed to fulfil the hard conditions offered for her return, the sweetness of his playing was forever commemorated in the skies, for the gods set his lyre there as the constellation Lyra. Arion, a 7th century B.C. poet and lyrist of Lesbos, so charmed the inhabitants of the sea with his playing, that when pirates robbed and threw him overboard, a dolphin (one of Apollo's sacred animals) bore him to shore. The constellation Delphinus is sometimes identified with Arion's dolphin.

Whether the lyre of the early peoples of northern and central Europe was imported or separately invented there is not certain. It differed from that of antiquity in being constructed all of a single piece of wood, rather than from assembled sections. The earliest example of the lyre of the barbarians was found in the tomb of an Alemannic warrior who lived about 500 A.D. At about that period Theodoric the Ostrogoth (454–526) is reported to have sent a lyrist to the Frankish court of Clovis. Through the Middle Ages lyres of various forms were known in Britain, France, Germany, Scandinavia, Estonia, and Finland, and their music accompanied the chants of epic narrators, the boasts of warriors and heroes, and the singing of entertainers. Up to about 1000 A.D. European lyres were plucked, as were the ancient lyres of Greece and the Middle East. Bowing then became more usual, and bowed lyres are shown in manuscripts from the 11th century on. A bowed lyre, the *crwth,* became one of the national instruments of Wales, continuing in use until the 18th century, when its form took on some of the characteristics of the fiddle, but its name and history are linked in confusion with the ancient Welsh harp. The surviving bowed lyre of Finland and Estonia, a rather crude instrument strung with horsehair, is also confused with the harp, particularly since it is called *harpa* in Swedish. It is probably from this Finnish lyre that the Siberian instrument is derived, even though the bow is not used by the Ostyaks and Voguls, for these tribes are akin to the Finns. Compare HARP. See KINNOR.   THERESA C. BRAKELEY

Ma The Great Mother of Cappadocia in Asia Minor and probably the mother goddess of the Hittites: identified with the Phrygian Cybele. Her great temple at Comana, with its periodic festivals, sacred prostitutes, and temple attendants, was of great renown in the ancient world. After Sulla led the Romans to Cappadocia, the cult of Ma was popular, though unofficial, among the soldiers. The Romans identified her as Bellona. Compare ANĀHITA; BELLONA; CYBELE.

Mabinogion The title given by Lady Charlotte Guest to her collection of translations from the Welsh, published 1838–49. The word is a plural form of *mabinogi*, which originally meant the story of a hero's childhood and youth (compare *mab*, boy, youth), but seems to have acquired the more general sense of "tale of a hero." The first four stories in the collection are referred to in the text as "the Four Branches of the Mabinogi," and the hero seems to have been Gwri, later called Pryderi. All the stories except *Taliesin* are found in a manuscript of about 1400, but some in a manuscript of the early 13th century. Most of them formed part of a vast body of prose narrative, now lost, which formed the stock in trade of professional reciters called *cyvarwyddon*.

Matthew Arnold has beautifully described the nature of the *Mabinogion*: "the mediæval story-teller is pillaging an antiquity of which he does not fully possess the secret; he is like a peasant building his hut on the site of Halicarnassus or Ephesus; he builds, but what he builds is full of materials of which he knows not the history, or knows by a glimmering tradition merely;— stones 'not of this building,' but of an older architecture, greater, cunninger, more majestical." All the researches of modern scholarship have confirmed this view of the conglomerate nature of the stories and the venerable age of the materials.

The *Four Branches of the Mabinogi* were probably written down about 1060 but they represent in large measure myths of the pre-Christian era. The annual combat of Arawn and Havgan (Summer White), kings of Annwn (the abode of the gods), represents the yearly struggle between winter and summer. Llew's name is cognate with that of the Irish sun god Lug, and his story is largely a distorted form of Lug's legend as it survived in modern Irish folklore. Bendigeidfran (Blessed Bran), son of Llyr (the sea), who wades across the Irish Sea, in aspect like a mountain, was a euhemerized god of the ocean. (See BRAN.) His brother Manawyddan is probably the Irish marine divinity Manannán, but since the noun *mynawyd* means an awl, he is represented as an expert shoemaker! The sons of Dôn were originally deities, and their sister Arianrhod (Silver Wheel) was probably a British Luna. Not only were some of the narrative patterns borrowed from Irish myths, but we also recognize some of the widespread themes of European fiction. The misfortunes of Rhiannon and Branwen are confused versions of the Calumniated Wife or Accused Queen, while the relations of Pwyll and

Arawn may well represent the source of *Amis and Amiloun*. Interwoven with these strands of myth and legend are many onomastic tales, devised to explain names of persons and places—a favorite preoccupation of Celtic story-tellers.

Kilhwch and Olwen was probably written down in its present form about 1100 since a Fflergant, king of Brittany, is mentioned, and Alan Fergant was Duke of Brittany from 1081 to 1109. But the language shows that it must have been copied largely from a text of the 10th century. Here again is the typical conglomeration of myth, hero-tale, folklore, and onomastic interests. The personages of Arthur's court form surely the oddest assemblage in the world. Here are Manawyddan and Cnychwr (Conchobar) from Irish saga; Arthur himself and Geraint, heroes of history; Taliesin the bard and Gildas the historian, rubbing shoulders with the helpful companions of fairy tale—Medyr (Aim), who from Celliwig in Cornwall would hit a wren on Esgeir Oerfel in Ireland, exactly through its two legs; Sgilti Lightfoot, beneath whose feet never a reed bent, much less did one break; and Drem (Sight), who saw from Celliwig in Cornwall when a fly would rise in the morning on Pen Blathaon in Pictland. The main plot is clearly related to that of Jason and the Golden Fleece—the quest, the helpful companions, the father of the princess who imposes arduous tasks; worked into this framework are such immemorial themes as the jealous stepmother and the oldest animals. The onomastic interest reveals itself in accounting for the hero's name, meaning Pigsty, by the circumstances of his birth, and in laying the pursuit of the boar Twrch Trwyth and its offspring through places whose names have porcine associations, as Rhys showed (*Celtic Folklore*, II, pp. 509–37). In spite of distractions the tale of how Kilhwch won Olwen has a dominant theme, reaches the expected dénouement, and contains passages of charming description and grotesque humor.

It has, moreover, a special interest as the earliest Arthurian romance, and there are many links with later French romances. Among the more obvious parallels are the arrivals of Kilhwch and Perceval at Arthur's court and the meetings of Kilhwch and Ivain with the giant herdsman. Kei and Bedwyr are easily recognizable as the Kay and Bedivere of Malory, and one may even detect in strange disguises the originals of Lancelot and Gawain.

The Dream of Rhonabwy, probably composed in the 13th century, is understandable if one realizes the author's three purposes: first, to recall the glorious memories of the historic Arthur and Owein and the historic battle of Badon; secondly, to give to these splendid evocations the phantasmagoric character of a dream, in contrast to the squalid realism of the opening scene; thirdly, if one may judge by the last sentence, to introduce so much minute detail that no bard or *cyfarwydd* could memorize it. Curiously enough, Owein's ravens are still depicted in the arms of the house of Dynevor which claims descent from him, and the clue to their identity may be found in the French *Didot Perceval*. They were his mother Modron and her sisters in bird form.

Three other Arthurian stories, *The Lady of the Fountain*, *Geraint*, and *Peredur*, belong to quite a different category, for they are free redactions, made about 1200, from French prose romances. The long dominant belief that they were based on the corresponding poems of Chrétien de Troyes is no longer tenable. Though the material is still Celtic in origin, it has been filtered through and colored by Breton and French culture. For a century or two these stories, inherited from the Welsh, had formed the repertoire of strolling Breton *conteurs* who entertained noble households in France, after 1066 found a welcome among the Anglo-Norman nobility, and by 1100 were making a sensation in Italy. About 1150 the vogue of these stories was such that some were written down in French prose and were used by Chrétien as sources for his poems. Two of them, the originals of *The Lady of the Fountain* and *Geraint*, reveal such a mature art and such a similar general outline that we may take them to be the work of a single man, who was interested in psychology and morals. The original or originals of *Peredur* must have been almost completely lacking in form and consistency, but have a special fascination as giving an early version of the famous legend of Percival and the Grail. It is one of the mysteries of that legend that the holy vessel is replaced in *Peredur* by a wide dish containing a man's head—a mystery to which a clue is provided by the severed head of Bran in the *Four Branches*. The three romances redacted from the French show little of that intimate knowledge of Welsh geography, little of that elfin charm which is characteristic of the older native stories.

The Dream of Maxen is a literary fabrication probably of the third quarter of the 12th century. The main plot is akin to that of the Irish *Dream of Oengus* (8th century), and in Wales it was attached to the beautiful fay Elen, whose home was a Roman ruin near Carnarvon, conceived as in the days of its splendor. The author, knowing this local legend and discovering in a Welsh translation of Geoffrey of Monmouth, the *Dingestow Brut*, an account of the Roman Maxen, who came to Britain with a large fleet and married Elen, the daughter of King Eudav, neatly fitted the legend into the pseudo-historic framework.

Taliesin, unlike the other tales, is found in no manuscript earlier than the 16th century. The titular hero was a bard of the 6th century, to whom in the course of time many poems were attributed and many legends were attached. Despite the lateness of the text, much of the material in it is medieval, related in fact to the Irish story of Finn's thumb of knowledge and to the Irish poems ascribed to Amairgen and Tuan mac Cairill.

The *Mabinogion* not only possess great intrinsic value but also show fascinating affinities to the Irish sagas and to Arthurian romance. In modern times they have inspired Peacock's *Misfortunes of Elfin* and Tennyson's *Geraint and Enid*.

Bibliography:
The *Mabinogion*, trans. by Gwyn Jones and Thomas Jones. Everyman Library, 1950.

Special Studies:
Gruffydd, W. J., *Math Vab Mathonwy*. Cardiff, 1928.
O'Rahilly, Cecile, *Ireland and Wales, Their Historical and Literary Relations*. London, 1924.
For *Dream of Maxen* see *Speculum* XXII (1947), pp. 523–26.
For *Taliesin* see Williams, Ifor, *Lectures on Early Welsh Poetry*, Dublin, 1944, pp. 49–63; Scott, Robert D., *The Thumb of Knowledge*, New York, 1930.
For connections with Arthurian romances see Loomis, Roger S., *Arthurian Tradition and Chrétien de Troyes*, New York, 1949.   ROGER S. LOOMIS

Macha (Irish *Maċa*) 1) One of a group of three great war goddesses (with Badb and Neman) of Old Irish mythology. She is mentioned as the daughter of Ernmas, one of the Tuatha Dé Danann, and granddaughter of Nét. All three of these goddesses appeared at times on the battlefield in the form of a scald-crow. Battle-crow was another name for any one of the group. After the old battles the heads of the slain were brought home and dedicated to Macha. She is sometimes called the ancestress of the Red Branch; and in the great hall of the Red Branch were hung the heads of slain enemies. She is also confused with and sometimes identified with: 2) Macha, a woman of the *síde*, wife of an Ulster chieftain, and who possessed the gift of extraordinary speed. All was well with the pair as long as the husband never mentioned this gift of swiftness. For his thoughtless remark at the races that his wife was swifter than the king's horses, see EMAIN MACHA. The king ordered the man to be put to death for his boast unless the wife could make it good. Macha was sent for, and ordered to race with the horses. She begged the king to wait until she gave birth to her child. The king would not wait, so to save her husband's life, Macha ran against the king's horses and won, and gave birth to twins at almost the same moment. For these twins, Emain Macha was named. And Macha put the annual curse of debility on the Ulstermen because of the cruelty of this old Ulster king. See CUCHULAIN; MORRIGAN.

machi Shamans of the Araucanian Indians. Formerly the machi were transvestites, but in modern times most of them have been women. Machi adopt their profession as the result of a supernatural call. Their principal task is to cure the sick. Formerly they simulated the extraction of the entrails of the patient and their replacement. Today they cure by means of suction and massage. The main accessories of the machi were a shamanistic drum and a ladderlike pole on which they climbed to get in touch with the spirits. See SHAMAN. [AM]

Mademoiselle from Armentières Soldier song of World War I comprising countless stanzas contributed by anyone who had an idea and celebrating any event or personality that evoked comment. The tune was picked up by Americans from British troops with whom they were brigaded in 1917. The British ditty, variously known as *Skiboo, Snipoo, Snapoo, The Little Dutch Soldier, The Little Marine*, told the tale of two German officers (or a little Dutch soldier) who crossed the Rhine "to love the women and taste the wine." It involved an adventure with a landlord's daughter and in some versions produced a son who grew up to do "what his daddy used to do," a result also celebrated in *Bell-Bottomed Trousers* and its sea-going antecedents.

The AEF song, also known as *Hinky, Dinky, Parlez-Vous*, included some of the basic incidents of this tale, but also collected miscellaneous stanzas devoted to the peculiarities of the other armies—the French, British, Belgian, etc.—, lampooned the officers who won battles in bed and medals behind desks, griped about the food, the trenches, the pay, the lice, and the Y.M.C.A., and described the mademoiselles of many towns in addition to Armentières.

The original mademoiselle is said to have been actually two French girls attached to a theatrical troupe which played before British soldiers in Armentières. Another tale is that the girl was a spy working for Marlborough in Flanders during the War of the Spanish Succession (1701–14).

The chorus, "parlez-vous," represents one of the few French words with which English-speaking troops were familiar enough to toss into their conversation. The same casual use of foreign words was made in a version sung by troops who came into contact with Russians and adapted the text to their surroundings.

The origin of the older ditty is sometimes said to be *Der Wirthin Tochterlein*, with words by the German poet Uhland, sometimes a song, *Drei Reiter Am Thor*, of the 16th century, and sometimes the old French song *Le Retour du Marin*. The last is about a sailor who returns after years at sea, finds the landlady at the inn to be his wife, who has married again, and since she does not recognize him, returns to the sea.

Like most army songs, *Mademoiselle from Armentières* is heavily censored in most printed versions.

Madumda Constructive creator of the Pomo Indians of north central California. The meaning of this creator's name is unknown. He lives in the sky, and is an otiose deity; it is his younger brother Coyote, the trickster, who is the active agent of the pair. It was Coyote, not Madumda, who formerly traveled over the earth begetting children, creating human beings, stealing the sun for them, and transforming animal-beings into true animals. [EWV]

madweed or **skullcap** A square-stemmed herb (*Scutellaria galericulata*) with deep-green leaves and pairs of bright blue flowers, found growing wild on the banks of streams and ponds. The British variety is named skullcap for the shape of the calyx (from *scutella*, tray or salver); the American species (*S. lateriflora*) is frequently called madweed because of its powerfully sedative effect on the nerves. Early 19th century New Englanders often referred to it as **mad-dog skullcap** on the assumption that its sedative powers would quiet or even cure mad dogs or persons suffering from hydrophobia.

mae de santo and **pae de santo** Terms employed in the Afrobrazilian cults for priestess and priest respectively. Their literal meaning ("mother" and "father" of the "saint," deity) represents an exact translation into Portuguese of the Yoruban terms for priestess and priest, *iyalorisha* and *babalorisha*. See CANDOMBLÉS. [MJH]

mænads or **mainades** (Greek, possessed ones, the ravers). The ecstatic female devotees of the cult of Dionysus, celebrated most anciently in the *orgía*; also, the nymphs in the Dionysian train. In ecstatic devotion to the god, troupes of mænads wandered in wild bands in the mountains, dismembering wild beasts and devouring them, in the fervent illusion that they were devouring the god and thus communing with him. Later, 5th century B.C., the Attic and Delphic mænads were trained in more disciplined expressions of these ecstatic trances. They are immortalized on vase paintings in these whirling dance moments. At times they are shown eluding the aroused male followers in the Dionysiac train—the Satyrs and Silenes. The cult deteriorated into the Roman Bacchanalia and Lupercalia, and to its lowest point in the modern Carnival celebrations of urban Europe and America. The theater of today attempts to emulate both the mystic trances of the mænads and the abandoned inebriation of the bacchantes. [GPK]

Magatama The sacred stones of Shinto; pear-shaped pieces of crystal, agate, jasper, and the like, used for religious purposes. [JLM]

magic The art of compulsion of the supernatural; also, the art of controlling nature by supernatural means. The word derives from the Magi, Persian priests whose practices were labeled magic (*mageia*) by the Greeks. A definition of what is magic and what is not is difficult, for one's own beliefs are seldom if ever connected with magical practices, while those of other peoples which differ are often magic, superstition, witchcraft, etc. The relationship of magic to religion and science, indeed the very nature and definition of magic, has been the subject of much debate among students of the subject. Such men as Sir J. G. Frazer, whose influence is widespread but whose theories have been criticized because of his selectivity in choosing facts from among a mass of other facts and basing his theories on them, believe magic to be a preliminary stage in the development of religion. To Frazer, magic is compulsion; religion is propitiation; a combination of the two exists side by side since neither method proves fully successful alone. Frazer subdivides sympathetic magic into homeopathic magic, which assumes that similarity between things indicates their identity, and contagious magic, which postulates that things once in contact remain in contact indefinitely. Homeopathic magic is exemplified by envoûtement; the image *is* the person and sticking pins in it or the like will cause pain, illness, or death to the person the image is named for. Contagious magic uses such materials as nail parings, locks of hair, excrement, names, even footprints, of the person for similar effects; since these were once part of, or in contact with, the person, they retain his essence and what is done to them will affect the body.

Aside from theories of the nature and origin of magic and its relationship to the growth of religion, magic generally is considered to be either positive or negative. Positive magic is intended to do something; the talisman performs positive magic. Negative magic is meant to prevent something; the amulet protects by negative magic against demons, spells, witches, and other workers of positive magic. A tabu that prevents some action by a person is positive, rather than negative magic, for the breaker of the tabu is punished by having something done to him. Generally magic works by controlling forces or demonic beings; it is the attempted control of those forces which students believe underlies primitive science. Magic may also be either black or white. Black magic is evil, for it calls into play unsanctioned forces and beings, or it aims at illness, death, injury, or other uncountenanced effects. White magic performs cures or wonders without the invocation of dark powers; astrology, alchemy, legerdemain, the doctrine of signatures, and the like, all are classified as white magic. In folktale, the man who sells his soul to the Devil in return for the Devil's aid (compare FAUST) is a practitioner of black magic; the hero who is given special powers by a grateful animal either is not considered a magician or is a practitioner of white magic. See DIVINATION; GBO; HOODOO HAND; JACK.

magical impregnation In folktale and mythology, the marvelous conception (T510–539) of a child through some act or circumstance that ordinarily has no connection with fertilization. The motif is common in mythology; many heroes are magically conceived. Zeus, appearing to Danae in her tower as a shower of gold, impregnated her; Hera plucked a flower and conceived Ares, and later conceived Hebe from a lettuce leaf. Coatlicue became the mother of the Aztec war god Huitzilopochtli because she secreted a ball of feathers in her bodice. Widespread, in Siberia, Oceania, Latin America, Africa, China, North America, is the belief in the fertilizing power of the sun's rays falling on a woman. Not only is this reflected in the mythology of these regions, but in practice great care is taken to keep girls, especially in their first menstruation, away from all contact with sunlight. See ADOLESCENCE CEREMONIES. Some such belief and practice may underlie the Danae story, for sunlight and gold are often synonymous in imagery, and the seclusion of the girl who nevertheless is impregnated by the sun's rays may easily be read into the myth.

Magical impregnation may occur in many ways: from eating (T511) a berry (see MARJATTA), a mandrake (see MANDRAKE), a fruit (in Gipsy, Turkish, Indonesian, South American stories), a rose (in an Italian story eating the red rose results in a boy, a white rose a girl), a mayfly (see DECHTIRE), a woman's heart (Norse), finger bones (twins are born when two fingerbones are eaten in a Bakairi, central Brazil, tale), cheese (Haida, Tlingit), medicines (Kaffir, Basuto, Arab). It may happen after drinking some substance (T512), e.g. urine (European, African, Chinese, Indonesian). A look, especially a lustful one, or a wish or a dream may cause conception. It may come from the gods (T518) or from some extraordinary method of intercourse (T517), e.g. intercourse with hand or foot or side or ear. Sunlight and moonlight, rain or wind, magic objects, fire, blood, spittle, scarification, stepping on an animal or over a grave, smelling a cooking dragon's heart, embracing a tree, bathing—all figure in folktale and myth as magical means of impregnation.

Occasionally men become impregnated, and magically at that. In Type 705—Born from a Fish—the man eats a magic fish meant for his wife. He becomes pregnant and gives birth to a girl child from his knee. In the *Vishnu Purāṇa*, Yuvanāśva drinks a potion intended for the queen and bears a boy from his side. Perhaps, in light of the deliberate rebirth of heroes who cause themselves to be swallowed in order to be reborn, we may suspect a ritual belief behind some of these stories, or at least a parallel to the story of the birth of Dionysus from the thigh of Zeus.

Mention should be made here of the much reported lack of knowledge among certain peoples, notably the Trobriand Islanders as reported by Malinowski, of the actual part played by the male in conception. To a people ignorant of the physical fact, all impregnation must be magical, the work of some spirit—or perhaps any impregnation by any means is normal. It is believed for example that the man's role in coition is simply to "open the way" for the spirit that is to be the child so that it may enter the womb.

☛This is a widespread motif in the New World. Paul Ehrenreich chose it as an example of the wide diffusion of certain folkloric themes and as a striking case of possible connection between the folktales of America and Asia. A beautiful girl, the daughter of a chief, is made pregnant by an ugly man (often the culture hero in disguise) by his giving her some food impregnated with his semen. When the child is born a contest is held to discover the father; several men claim the child, but the infant himself designates his real father. The more ancient versions of this story were recorded almost simultaneously in the 16th century among both the coastal Indians of Peru and the Tupinamba of the Bay of Rio de Janeiro. The story is still popular among the Chiriguano and other Chaco tribes. [AM]

☛ That North American Indians were aware of the physiological facts of impregnation is indicated through the indirect evidence contained in their mythology alone. Misplaced genitalia (A1313.3), for example, prevent intercourse and consequent child-bearing. American Indian tales also contain frequent references to magical impregnation and virgin birth (T540); these are presented in the tales as extraordinary phenomena, and it is often explicitly mentioned that the girl who gives birth had no contact with any man. Pregnancy occurs from swallowing various kinds of food; from wind, rain, tears, hail, water, or sunlight; from bodily secretions; from casual contact with a man; or, in some tales, no reason at all is assigned. Usually the child born is a boy, who quickly grows to manhood and is gifted with supernatural power to overcome obstacles and kill monsters. Children are also born outside of the mother's womb, as Splinter-Foot-Girl, born from a wound in a warrior's leg, or Blood-Clot-Boy, born from a small clot of blood, or Child-Born-in-a-Jug, or the various characters born from body secretions, mucus, and tears. In nearly all cases of virgin or unusual births, the children born grow rapidly to adulthood. [EWV]

☛ Supernatural conception and birth are widespread concepts in Middle America. One legend says that the god Quetzalcoatl was conceived when his mother, Chalchihuitlicue, the Jade Woman (and the wife of the rain god Tlaloc), came into contact with a piece of jade. The Aztec origin myth tells how a virgin, Cuatlique or Coatlicue (she is sometimes already the mother of children), held a bunch of white feathers to her breast, thus becoming pregnant, and how she gave birth to Huitzilopochtli, the god of war, who sprang from her flank fully armed, killing several hundred men who were attacking his mother. Quiché mythology tells of the god Hunhun-Apu, whose head was hung from a calabash or tree-gourd tree, so that it resembled the other fruit. The princess Xquiq passed by, stretched out her arms to pluck the fruit, the head spat into her hand and thus she became pregnant, subsequently giving birth to the twin heros Hun-Apu and Xbalanque. Mayan and Popoluca mythology tell of an old woman who found an egg near a spring which, after being carried to the house and placed with her clothing, broke open in a few days to liberate a miniature infant who already talked, and who in a few more days grew up to become a god or culture hero. [GMF]

magic caldron The caldron or kettle of folktale (D1171.2) in which magic and miracles are performed: typically Celtic but appearing also in North American and African folktales, in the *Arabian Nights,* and in Greek mythology. The caldron of regeneration appears in the story of Bran in the *Mabinogion;* Demophoon or Triptolemus, son of Celeus, was put in fire, probably in a caldron, by Demeter to give him eternal life. In Norse myth, poetry came into existence when two giants or dwarfs were boiled in a caldron. The pot, kettle, or caldron that supplies inexhaustible food in task or quest folktales is related to the table that sets itself and the inexhaustible purse. In some of the stickfast tales, it is a caldron to which the chain of people is attached. Witches of course have kettles or caldrons in which their hell-brew bubbles. In "The Warlock and the Young Cook of Bagdad" (Burton *Supplemental Nights* to the *Thousand and One Nights,* VI: 95–112), the vizier and the king enter the magician's caldron and find themselves swimming in a magic sea. They undergo many adventures in the strange land to which they are thus magically transported; the vizier has become a woman and bears seven children; the king is sentenced to be hanged. But at the climactic moment, each sticks his head above the caldron's rim to find that practically no time at all has passed. See BRAN; CALDRON OF REGENERATION; MEDEA; ODHRŒRIR; YEARS SEEM DAYS.

magic canoe A canoe which goes by itself when its owner raps on its bottom with his paddle or utters a cry of command: an incident which occurs repeatedly in American Indian myths of the Great Lakes region, generally, but not always, in connection with the Evil Father-in-law cycle. [EWV]

magic flight See OBSTACLE FLIGHT.

magic object In folktale, mythology, and legend, an object through which magic may be performed, or which can summon up wonder-working spirits, or which behaves in an extraordinary fashion. Magic objects (D800–1699) are an essential of märchen, appearing everywhere in the world, defining some tale types (e.g. Type 566—The Three Magic Objects and the Wonderful Fruits), being focal in others (e.g. Type 561—Aladdin and His Wonderful Lamp), or serving as apparatus in still others (e.g. tales involving the obstacle flight, D672). The fairy's or magician's wand is most familiar as the magic object capable of performing magic; the touchstone of the alchemist which was thought to be able to transmute metals by contact, the regalia which transmit regal power to the king possessing them, iron or the magic circle which possess power to confound demons are all examples of objects with whose aid magic is made. These amulets or charms are similar to Aladdin's lamp or Solomon's ring which controlled spirits who were the actual performers of the magic acts. The object that is magical in and of itself is still more common. The comb thrown down by the fleeing hero becomes a forest to delay pursuit; the magic purse is always full of money; seven-league boots, wishing rings, swords or spears that

never fail, fiddles and pipes that cause compulsive dancing, kettles that make all who touch them to stick together, mills that grind salt, cloaks of invisibility, all are magic objects of widespread folktale occurrence. To these must be added the magic plants (of immortality, Jack's beanstalk, mandrake, etc.) and magic animals or animal parts (speaking excrements, soul-containing eggs, golden-egg laying geese, etc.) of many tales.

magic ships One of the earliest versions of the magic ship is Noah's Ark of the Old Testament (*Gen.* vi–viii). See ARK; DELUGE; FLOOD. In Serbian mythology, Burkhan, the Deity, commands that a great ship be built and that all animals on earth, with the exception of the mammoth, be herded together and placed upon it. Meanwhile, Shitkur, the Devil, conspires to undo the will of God and makes himself into a mouse to gnaw at the vessel's timbers and sink it. So Burkhan created the cat and counteracted the attempt at rebellion. Just as the Hebrew ark grew from Utnapishtim's ship in Babylonian mythology, this South Slavic ship derives from the Biblical account as amplified by legendists.

In Egyptian mythology the magic ship is part of the sun-god myth. The sky is a river and the sun a ship sailing across it. The sun god sits at the prow. One version maintains that he paddles his ship or that it moves of its own power; another that he is accompanied by the nine gods of the Heliopolitan ennead. According to *The Book of Gates,* in the daytime the ship is manned by elect souls or the "never-vanishing stars." This enables the sun god to retire in his cabin in the shape of a disk or an asp. The ship is sometimes thought of as a great double-headed asp, one head at each prow. The staircase of the sun, indicating the regular upward movement of the sun in the heavens, rests at the center of the vessel. On the ivory tablet of King Menes is a pictorial representation of the sun god as a hawk reclining in the cabin of a ship. Traditionally, the Egyptian sun god has two boats: the *Me'enzet* for daytime trips across the sky, and the *Semektet,* for night trips. During the night the sun god floods the underworld with light while traveling through the waters on a journey in which he is assisted by spirits of the netherworld.

The magic ship is also found in Greek mythology. Homer (*Odyssey,* viii), describes the magic ship of the Phæacians as mind-reading, rudderless, self-steering, capable of driving forward under the motive power of human wish and steering its own course. The magic boat Apollo gave to Hercules in his quest for Geryon's oxen was the golden goblet in which the sun made his nightly journey through Ocean.

The Norse god Frey had a magic ship, Skidbladnir, "swiftest and best of ships." It was built by the dwarfs, and could hold all the gods and their weapons and armaments. When not in use it could be folded up and put into a pouch.

The magic ship motif is popular in both Finnish and Estonian folklore. The *Kalevala* tells the story of the magic ship that brought two Finnish culture heroes to their destination in the Northland. Väinämöinen and Ilmarinen, seeking a route to the "never-pleasant Northland," where stands the copper-bearing mountain of Pohjola, come upon a vessel, which bemoans its disuse and begs to be a warship. So Väinämöinen conjures up heroic rowers, but only the blacksmith Ilmarinen can successfully row the ship.

In Marie de France's *lai, Gugemar,* in the romance of *Partenopeus of Blois,* in Tristran's Voyage of Healing, and in the death scene of King Arthur, the magic ship reappears. It is a commonplace of fairy tale.

The magic ship of folktale (D1123; F841 ff.) is made of many materials: glass, stone, bronze, and other metals, mahogany, nutshells, nail-parings from the bodies of the dead (the Norse Naglfar). Indian mythology knows a winged ship. Extraordinary to folktale, but not to 20th century daily life, are the self-propelling ship (D1523.2) and the ship that goes on land and water (D1533.1.1). There are intelligent ships (D1310.3) and ships that may be summoned by a wish (D2074.2.3.2). In an Indonesian story, the task set is to build a ship of stone (H1021.3).

magic whip A motif (D1208) of Old World folktale, whereby transgression of an accepted mode of behavior, or failure to keep one's word, is punished by a whipping administered by a magic whip. With equivalents in African tales (D1401.3) it has been syncretized in Dutch Guiana in the Negro version of the Cinderella story. (See M. J. and F. S. Herskovits, *Suriname Folklore,* tale #100.) [MJH]

magnetic islands The cartographers of ancient Rome and Alexandria, Pliny and Ptolemy, make the earliest written mention of magnetic islands. Pliny writes about a mountain near the Indus that attracted iron; but it is to Ptolemy (c. 150 A.D.) that we usually turn for the first geographic location of a magnetic island; the fabulous Maniolæ Islands of the Indian Ocean, latitude 0°, situated slightly east of Ceylon, have upon them the *lapis herculeus* (lodestone mountain which can pull to it any ship built with iron nails).

The magic island motif (D936) occurs notably in "The Third Kalandar's Tale" of the *Arabian Nights.* The magnetic or lodestone mountain attracts every bit of a ship's iron. Richard Burton, editor and translator, puts forth the hypothesis that the story of the magic mountain owes its origin to certain fierce sea currents that may carry ships as much as fifty miles a day off their course. Also, men who saw seacraft being built, as on the East African coast, without nails, were led to conclude that there must exist a perilous lodestone out at sea.

The magnetic island in the *Travels of Sir John Mandeville* (1449) is near the fabulous Christian kingdom of Prester John and can draw to itself vessels that have iron nails in their structure. The vessels are irremovably held by the magnetic force of the island. The holding and drawing powers come from the nature of the "adamant" rock on the island, another name for the lodestone.

The use of the compass, and the inexplicable natural force that pointed the needle northwards, helped foster, during the early periods of navigation, the belief in some magnetic terrain which could be blamed for the disappearance and loss of exploratory sea-galleys and merchant ships that went in search of ports of trade across distant seas.

Travelers from Europe to India, men like Marco Polo, have mentioned that nailless sea-bound vessels constructed with cords and wooden pins were frequently used during the Middle Ages.

A curious application of magnetism in a medieval story is evident in Bk. V, xxxviii, of Rabelais' Works. This writer believed, apparently, that garlic germander could counteract the magnetic power of a lodestone. This counteragent he called Scordium.

magpie A bird (genus *Pica*) having a very long, graduated tail. The European magpie (*P. pica* or *caudata*), the common magpie of folklore, has iridescent black plumage with white scapulars, belly, sides. It has often been tamed and taught to say a few words; it is famous for its love of small bright objects which it will steal and put to its own devices. See BIRD SEIZES JEWEL. The American magpie is closely related to the European. In Greek mythology the nine daughters of Peirus (the Peirides) were transformed into nine magpies because they disputed the prize for singing with the Muses.

Quite generally in western Europe and the British Isles the magpie is regarded as a bird of ill omen. It is unlucky to see one, especially *one.* To break the charm and escape the presaged evil one must take off his hat, or make the sign of the cross, or cross his thumbs (Yorkshire) or lay two straws across each other on the ground (Lincolnshire). A popular saying in regard to seeing magpies goes: One for sorrow/ Two for mirth/ Three for a wedding/ Four for death. In Lancashire and Yorkshire, however, a wilful optimism has changed the fourth line to: Four for a birth.

A magpie lighting on the ridgepole of a house is a sure sign that the house will not fall down or be demolished by storm. This belief may spring from the Eastern story that the magpie would not go into the Ark but spent the whole deluge time perched on the ridgepole. A magpie on the house also means, however, the death of one of the inmates. A magpie on the roof in Macedonia means that guests are coming. The sound of magpies chattering around a house quite generally presages either death—or coming guests. In Ireland the magpie is called *cabaire breac,* speckled prattler.

In France and Germany it was unlucky to kill a magpie. Magpies were said to warn their human neighbors of the presence of foxes, wolves, or armed men; hence in Poitou formerly little bunches of heath or laurel were tied up in the trees in honor of them. In Norway it was unlucky to kill a magpie, yet their eggs were hunted on May Day. In Bengal and other parts of India also it is unlucky to kill a magpie.

In China a magpie nesting near a house means good luck for the people of the house. Especially is it good luck to hear the magpie just as one sets out on some undertaking. The chattering of the house magpie, in China as elsewhere, announces a coming guest.

Among North American Mandan-Hidatsa Indians, members of the Old Women's or Grandmothers' Society wore two magpie feathers in their hair. This was their symbol of fearlessness: the magpie does not fear heat or cold but stays around all year. (See M.W. Beckwith, *Mandan-Hidatsa Myths and Customs, MAFLS* 32, p. 232.) The Jicarilla Apache Indians leave offerings of hoofs, offal, and other waste parts from their kill for Magpie in thanks for success in hunting.

The magpie plays numerous roles in folktale. Magpie once exchanged her two eggs for dove's seven (A2247.4) with the result that the numbers remained reversed forever. There are many etiological stories of the origin of the magpie (A1922), why magpie is bald (A2317.6), why magpie is colored as he is (A2411.2.10), how he got his long tail (A2236.4; A2378.3.1), etc. There is a Chinese tale of a helpful magpie (B467), also a Mandan-Hidatsa story of a magpie raised from a nestling by an Indian boy, which helped his young master in war and hunt, and a German tale of magpie as bird-soul (E732.4).

Magpie A myth character in several North American Indian tales; a clan animal among the Hopi and other Southwestern tribes. Relationship of human beings to Magpie and other clan animals is slight, however, among the Hopi. Magpie is said to have been taken into the clan in early days when the Hopi were wandering and chanced to meet him. In the Keres pueblo emergence myth, Magpie figures as the character whom Spider Man sends to cover the rising sun with his wing so that the sun will shine on one of two sisters who are engaged in a contest, before it shines on the other one. Among some of the Plateau tribes, Magpie is one of the many birds who act like human beings during the Mythical Age. In Taos pueblo mythology one character is Magpie-Tail Boy, who performs marvelous deeds; in many of the pueblos, East direction is associated with Magpie, gray wolf, and the color white. In the Tewa pueblo emergence myth, the people cross a river on Magpie's tail which serves as a bridge. Compared to other birds, however, such as Raven or Bluejay, Eagle and Falcon, Owl, Roadrunner, Turkey, Crow, or even Grouse or Chickadee, Magpie does not play too important a role in American Indian myths. Magpie feathers were used for ceremonial costumes by many tribes; the Yokuts of south central California, for instance, used a tall dance headdress made of magpie tail plumes encircled at the base with crow feathers. [EWV]

maguca'n (Naskapi) or **mukuca'n** (Montagnais) The bear feast of the Naskapi and Montagnais Indians of Labrador, for the propitiation of the bear spirit after a successful hunt. Special tabus and ceremonies accompanied the eating of the meat, and the bear skull was placed in a focal position. In the ceremonial tent, men who had dreamt hunting songs entertained the audience and accompanied the dances called ni·mi. These dances, in figure-eight formation, consisted of a heavy shuffling step and shaking of the whole body, and resulted in considerable elation on the part of the dancers. As in all Labrador ceremonies, the drum was imbued with magical power, revered as a living entity, and endowed with speech. [GPK]

Magus (Old Persian *Magu*) A member of a distinct priestly caste of Medians renowned as astrologers, diviners, and magicians. The Magi made themselves indispensable in the Median and Persian religious ritual and some of their beliefs were carried over into Zoroastrianism. Zoroaster may have been a Magus; he was regarded as the Magus *par excellence* by the Greeks. The Magi believed that mountains are blots on the symmetry of creation which will be removed when the period of regeneration is reached. They practiced next-of-kin marriage and exposed their dead to the vultures: customs which became a part of Zoroastrian practice.

The word *Magi* is used specifically in the Vulgate edition of the Bible to denote the wise men who came to Bethlehem to worship Jesus (*Matthew* ii, 1). This use may have been based upon the strong Magian belief in the coming of a savior.

magyar kettös The Hungarian double, which occurs as a popular couple dance in local variants. In villages of central Hungary near Budapest partners dance in line formation with two-steps and *bokázó* (see CSÁRDÁS), and finish revolving in social dance position. In southern Hungary, particularly in the village of Pecsudsvard, it is a double circle of the Slavic type. Partners progress counterclockwise, the man's right arm around the lady's waist. The first part consists of running steps, the second of hopping steps in social dance position. In both forms of the dance the music starts slowly and gradually grows faster and faster. [GPK]

Mahābhārata Literally, the great Bhārata or story: one of the two great Hindu epic poems, probably the longest in the world. The *Mahābhārata* is divided into 18 books (*parvas*) and contains 100,000 verses. The books are of unequal length and are followed by the *Harivaṁśa,* a supplementary book of 16,000 stanzas. The epic is partly narrative, partly didactic and includes a heterogeneous mass of legend, myth, philosophical and religious lore, as well as geographical and historical data. It represents the ancient tale (*purāṇa*) as distinguished from the elegant poem (*kavya*) represented by the *Rāmāyaṇa*. It is older in its oldest parts than the latter, but as a compiled work it is considered about a century later in date. It belongs to the region now known as the Eastern Punjab; the *Rāmāyaṇa* belongs to Western Bengal.

The main theme deals with the struggles between two groups of descendants of the lunar race, the Pāṇḍavas and the Kauravas, for possession of a kingdom (capital, Hastināpura) located near the present city of Delhi. There was a king named Śāntanu who, in his old age, wished to marry again but could not obtain a desirable match because of the hereditary rights of Bhīsma, his son by a former wife. Bhīsma, to gratify his father, renounced the succession and Śāntanu then married Satyavatī by whom he had two sons. Both died, the younger leaving two childless widows, Ambikā and Ambālikā. Satyavatī then called upon Śāntanu's half brother, Krishna Dvaipāyana Vyāsa, the reputed author of the epic, to fulfil the law and raise up seed. Vyāsa, an anchorite who had lived in the woods, was terrible to behold. The elder of the two widows closed her eyes and so gave birth to a blind son, Dhṛitarāshtra, and the younger turned so pale that her son was named Pāṇḍu, the pale.

When the two came of age Pāṇḍu retired to the forest and left his blind brother as king. Dhṛitarāshtra had a hundred sons by his wife Gāndhārī. These, led by Duryodhana, were known as the Kauravas. Pāṇḍu's wives Kuntī and Mādrī had five sons whose paternity, since Pāṇḍu did not consort with them either because of leprosy or because of a curse, was attributed to the gods. Yudhisthira, the eldest, was son of Dharma and considered a pattern of justice and integrity. Bhīma, the second and son of Vāyu, was noted for his brute courage, great appetite, and his boasting. Arjuna, the third and son of Indra, brave, generous, chivalric, is the most prominent character in the epic. The twins, Nakula and Sahadeva, were the sons of the Aśvins. They were amiable and brave but not prominent in the story. Pāṇḍu died and Dhṛitarāshtra brought up the Pāṇḍus with his own sons. When he nominated Yudhiṣṭhira as his heir, the king's own sons rebelled and the Pāṇḍavas were sent away from court.

They attended the svayaṃvara held for Draupadī, daughter of the king of the Pānchālas, and were victorious. When they told their mother Kuntī that they had jointly won a prize, she, unwittingly, told them to share it and so Draupadī became their wife in common. This circumstance has been explained by some commentators as proof of polyandry among early Aryans.

Dhṛitarāshtra recalled the brothers to his court and divided his kingdom between the two groups. Yudhiṣṭhira proved so successful as a king that he excited the hatred of the Kauravas. The latter planned his downfall by inducing him to partake in a great gambling match. Yudhiṣṭhira lost not only his kingdom but Draupadī who was then dragged by her hair into the assembly, an insult Bhīma swore to avenge. Duryodhana also insulted her by seating her upon his thigh. Bhīma swore that he would smash that thigh. Through the intervention of the blind king the kingdom and Draupadī were restored, but Yudhiṣṭhira again gambled and lost. He and his brothers and wife were banished to the forest for 12 years. When the period of exile had elapsed the Pāṇḍavas set out to recover their throne.

The great battle between the two groups, the climax of the epic, followed. Even the gods were involved in the conflict. Kṛishṇa served as Arjuna's charioteer and while thus engaged spoke the *Bhāgavad-Gita*. The Pāṇḍavas were victorious and returned to Hastināpura where Yudhiṣṭhira was again crowned king. Dhṛitarāshtra, however, unable to forget or forgive the loss of his sons, retired to a hermitage in the woods and perished there in a great forest fire. The Pāṇḍavas were seized with remorse and left Hastināpura for the heaven of Indra on Mount Meru. All but Yudhiṣṭhira fell by the way because of their weaknesses, but all were waiting when he arrived there.

Mahādeva In Hindu mythology, Śiva: literally, the great god; often, especially in southern India, Śiva. Devi, the great goddess, is **Mahādevī**. [MWS]

Mahāsthāma In Buddhism, one of the two chief bodhisattvas who occupy thrones in the heaven of Amitābha. With Avalokita, Mahāsthāma aids those who invoke Amitābha's name to obtain salvation.

Mahāvīra The last prophet of Jainism, a contemporary of Buddha; Mahāvīra Vardhamāna or Jina; died c. 500 B.C. He was a disciple of one Pārshvanātha, the 23rd Jainist savior. The first of all was Rishabhanātha, in the beginning of the world, when men and women were two miles tall, had 64 ribs, and were born together, man and wife, as twins. According to one sect of Jains (the Svetāmbara), Mahāvīra was married, enjoyed a full life before entering the order, and waited until his parents' deaths lest he grieve them by his choice. According to another sect (the Digambaras), he renounced the world at the age of eight, attained enlightenment after twelve years, preached as a wandering monk for 30 years, and died at the age of 72.

Jainism denies the authority of the Vedas, and is based on the idea that life is perpetuated by the transmigration of the soul. Since life is painful, it is the aim of all Jainists to put an end to the cycle of births. To the Jains their religion is eternal and has been revealed in every one of the periods of the world.

To the Jains the universe is made up of soul (consciousness) and non-soul. There is no one creator god; gods exist in great numbers, but are subject to transmigration. The Jains divide living things by the number of sense organs they possess. Plants have only one, ants have three (touch, taste, and smell). Plants have one or more souls. Beings with one soul are found everywhere in the world while those with more may be invisible. These are called *nigoda* and have an infinite number of souls. Innumerable *nigoda* form one of the globules which pack the whole world. These supply the souls to replace those which reach nirvāṇa. Thus far an infinitesimally small fraction of a single *nigoda* has been sufficient to replace those souls reaching nirvāṇa.

The soul's natural qualities are faith, bliss, and perfect knowledge. These are weakened by the presence of karma, so the goal of Jainism is to rid oneself of karma. This is accomplished by monastic conduct and the practice of austerities. When karma is removed the three jewels of right knowledge, faith, and conduct, necessary for reaching nirvāṇa, are revealed. The ascetic Jain takes the five vows of non-killing, truthfulness, complete chastity, non-stealing, and relinquishment of all possessions. Jain ritual is based upon reverence for Jina and his predecessors whose images are found in Jaina temples.

The Jains are divided into two groups, the Digambaras who go naked, and the Svetāmbaras who wear white garments. The Dhundia and Lunka sects reject image worship. Because of their desire not to destroy life, the Jains are vegetarians and are deterred from occupations such as farming. See AHIMSĀ. This has forced them into banking and commercial pursuits, making the followers of Mahāvīra a wealthy and influential element in Indian life.

Mahi Name of a people living north of Abomey in the present French colony of Dahomey. Many Mahi were enslaved after being captured by the Dahomeans, and the name still survives in Brazil, where the term Gêge-Mahi denotes a subvariant of the Gêge (Dahomean) cult in Bahia, and in Haiti, where a dance called Mahi (spelled *Maïs*) is found. [MJH]

Mahisha or **Mahishāsura** The buffalo-headed monster killed by Durgā in her battles with the Asuras; in the *Mahābhārata* a monster killed by Skanda. The modern form of Mahisha is Bhainsāsura who lives in the fields and tramples the corn unless he is appeased by an offering of a pig or is worshipped when the rice is ripening.

Mahuika or **Mafuike** The Polynesian underworld goddess of fire or earthquakes; mother of Pere (Pele): on Samoa, Mahuike is god of fire. In a New Zealand myth, Maui comes to her for fire. She gives him, one by one, her fingers and toes, in which are fire. But the trickster quenches each of them in water. The goddess uses her last digit to start a great conflagration that threatens to burn up the world. Maui invokes rain, snow, and hail to put out the blaze. Since then fire exists within the trees, from which it may be liberated by rubbing.

Maia In Greek mythology, the eldest of the Pleiades; the mother by Zeus of Hermes; the nurse of Arcas after his mother, Callisto, died. Maia means mother or nurse. She was perhaps originally a mountain nymph who became associated with the Pleiades. She was identified with the native Italian goddess, Maia or Maia Majesta, a goddess of growth and the spring season, associated somehow with Vulcan. Along with other growth goddesses, she was identified by the Romans with the Phrygian Cybele. The flamen of Vulcan performed a sacrifice to her on May 1. In addition, because of her equation with the Greek goddess, the Roman Maia became associated with Mercury (Hermes), and was worshipped on May 15, the anniversary of the founding of Mercury's temple.

Maiden's Lament A feminine version of the Irish song, *The Unfortunate Rake*, source of *The Cowboy's Lament*.

Maid Freed from the Gallows An English ballad (Child #95) of a theme common in Sicilian, Russian, Finnish, Slovenian, Wendish, and other European song—a maid condemned to be hanged, who watches hopefully as father, mother, brother, sister in turn come to see her hanged and not to save her, until finally she is ransomed by her true love. The British and their offshoot American versions lack the usual continental explanation of the victim's plight, which is that she has been captured by corsairs and will die if ransom is not paid, and deal mainly with her series of questions to each of the relatives (see CLIMAX OF RELATIONS) and their heartless answers ("Oh have you brought me gold, father, or have you brought me fee?" "No . . . I am come to see you hanged, as you this day shall be."). Sometimes her situation is explained as punishment for the loss or theft of some valuable such as a golden ball, comb, key, and the whole drama of the girl with the noose around her neck and the dialog is acted out as a game. Both adults and children, English and American, white and colored, have played this game. A game version called *The Golden Ball* was collected in 1916 from New York children at a settlement house. The girl in that case was to be hanged on "yonder rusty gallery." Other names for the gallows tree in England are the "briery bush" and the "prickly bush" and in America the "willow tree" or "sorrow tree" or "gallows pole," any one of which may give its name to the song. Sometimes the song is interspersed with prose narrative in cante fable style, as in the Negro version *The Gallus Pole*, in which the victim is a man. Other titles include *Ropesman, Hangsaman, The Hangman's Tree,* and *The Hangman's Son*.

Maid Marian The name of the Queen of the May in the May dances of England. She wears a golden crown over her cascading hair and carries a red pink in her left hand. Robert Graves (*The White Goddess*) sees in Maid Marian an aspect of the Syrian sea-fertility goddess Marina, Myrrha, Mariamne, who is also the mermaid. Though commonly in the Morris dances Maid Marian is coupled with Friar Tuck, she has been popularly associated, since Tudor times, with Robin Hood as his greenwood sweetheart. Robin and Marian appear in several ballads together (Child #150: *Robin Hood and Maid Marian,* for example), for Maid Marian has taken over the position of Matilda Fitzwalter, the "historical" wife of Robin Hood (Robert of Huntingdon). See ABBOTS BROMLEY ANTLER DANCE; MORRIS.

Maimed King Pellinor: custodian of the Grail castle in some versions of the Grail romances. See ARTHUR; FISHER KING; GRAIL.

maina, myna, or **mynah** Any of certain Asiatic birds (*Eulabes religiosa* or *Acridotheres tristis*) related to the starlings, which can be tamed and taught to speak. They are held almost sacred in India because of their strange gift. The name is used for any talking bird in Indian folklore. In folktales the maina sometimes is a life-index bird (see the story "Punchkin," in M. Frere, *Old Deccan Days,* London, 1881) or sometimes a companion of the hero.

Maira-monan Composite creator-transformer-culture-hero of the South American Tupinamba Indians, regarded as beneficent, the originator of agriculture, and giver of all their laws and tabus to the Tupinamba. He was fond of transforming himself into a small child, who, when whipped or punished, would drop edible fruits on the ground. When he was burned by an ungrateful mankind, his head burst from the funeral fire, giving forth thunder and lightning. By the missionaries he was identified with Sumé.

The Tupinamba also had another Maira, *Maira-pochy,* a legendary very powerful medicine man who impregnated the daughter of a chief by feeding her with fish. Later when her child was born, every man in the village claimed it as his, but the baby decided the question himself by handing Maira-pochy the paternity token (a bow and arrow).

Maisö The first human being, the stone woman who created the world in the mythology of the Paressí Indians of the Matto Grosso. The stone man, Darúkavaiteré, was her first son. Maisö was so distressed at the numerous serpent and parrot offspring of Darúkavaiteré and his wife Uarahiulú that by magic she caused Uarahiulú to give birth to Uazale, the first Paressí Indian.

makara Literally, sea monster; in Hindu mythology and folktale identified variously as a dolphin, a shark, a crocodile, or a crab. It represents Capricorn in the Hindu zodiac and is the vehicle of Varuṇa. The vehicle of Gangā, too, is the makara upon which she stands. In art representations, as the Face of Glory became progressively conventionalized, it was combined with two makara.

In folktale the makara is frequently identified as a crab. In one story the makara outwitted a greedy crane who had convinced the fish in a tank to let it carry them to a safer place. Of course the crane ate the fish, until one day a makara asked the crane why he was carrying off the fish. The crane said he was saving them from the fishermen and the makara begged to be saved too. When the crane landed on his favorite dining rock with the huge crab, prepared for a good dinner, the crab, seeing the bones of the fish lying all about, cut off the head of the crane. He returned to the tank and told the remaining fish what had happened to their brothers and was hailed as their deliverer.

Makunaima The most clever and powerful of the Twins in the mythology of various Carib tribes of the Guianas. He often plays the part of culture hero. [AM]

malagueña (1) A Spanish couple dance, originating in Malaga, Andalusia, similar to the *sevillanas*. As a folk dance it uses bouncy footwork. Spanish colonists brought it to Oaxaca, Mexico, where it is known as a mestizo dance and song.

(2) A slow and sensuous flamenco song. [GPK]

malaohu boys On Sa'a and Ulawa (Solomon Islands), the men's society, absolutely forbidden in its many aspects to women. The name comes from the words meaning "like boiling," referring to the foaming of the sea when the fish rise to feed or to a frothy material exuded by the bonito when it is caught. A boy becomes malaohu after he has touched the rod while a bonito is being brought into the boat; the underlying concept is that he is now a man, since he has aided in man's work. According to W. G. Ivens (*Melanesians of the South-East Solomon Islands*, London, 1927), the malaohu ceremonial falls into the following outline: a chief's son goes into formal seclusion, accompanied by other boys of his own age. This group lives for several years in a canoe house on the beach (forbidden to women). They attend the bonito fishing and catch a bonito symbolically by touching the rod on which a bonito is hooked. They are brought back to the village in state. A feast is given honoring them, at which time they are seen by the women again after the long initiation period.

Malbrough s'en va-t-en guerre French folk song about the Duke of Marlborough, set to one of the most popular of folk melodies. The air is believed to have been learned from Arabs and brought to Europe during the time of the Crusades. Much later it was sung to the infant son of Marie Antoinette as a lullaby by his nurse, picked up by the queen, and made a court favorite. The earlier French version was about the Duc de Guise. Various stanzas have been set to the tune in English, including *For He's a Jolly Good Fellow*, the square-dance and play-party version, *We Have a Pig in the Parlor*, *The Bear Went Over the Mountain*, and the drinking song *We Won't Get Home Until Morning*.

male child disguised as girl A folktale motif (K514) occurring in many folklores, in which the sex of a male infant is concealed, or in which a boy or youth is disguised in girl's clothes in order to avoid execution. The execution is usually to be at the hands of a parent, grandparent, or uncle whom the child is prophesied to displace. Sometimes, however, the boy is put into girl's clothing to avoid some other fate. The classic example of this is the Greek Achilles who was dressed as a girl and sent to be brought up in a foreign court, lest he be drawn into the Trojan war. He was discovered, however, and induced to go. In the case of the Hindu Kṛishṇa, the disguise involved more than garments; an actual female infant was put in his place, and suffered immediate death at the hands of the frustrated power-jealous uncle. King Alfred the Great was whisked into a woman's dress and set to baking bread by an old woman in whose hut he took refuge, to escape death from the Danes (K521.4.1.2).

A change of sex was often simulated in India to baffle the evil eye (D2071.1.3). In China male infants and small boys, especially a first-born or an only son, were dressed in girl's clothes to protect them from evil spirits. Little Irish boys were sometimes dressed as girls in red flannel skirts until they were ten years old to protect them from being abducted by the fairies, the girls being less subject to abduction.

☞ In certain test tales among some of the American Indian groups of the North Pacific Coast, the Plateau, and the Plains, a jealous uncle tries to have all his nephews killed as soon as they are born. The sex of one nephew is concealed by his mother, and the boy-child brought up as a girl. When the boy becomes adult his uncle discovers the deception and tries to kill him; the uncle's attempts and his nephew's successful thwarting of them form the main part of the tale. See ACHILLES; REVERSAL OF SEX. [EWV]

male rain The term for a hard pelting rain among many Southwestern, Plains, and Eastern Woodlands North American Indian tribes. See FEMALE RAIN. [EWV]

malesk A story of personal adventure or a historical tale: a Tsimshian Indian term. See ADAOX.

malimba, manimbula, marimba, madimba, or manimba A Haitian Negro musical instrument descended from the African sanza: a box made of wood with a hole crossed by strips of metal fastened at one end. The other ends are plucked rhythmically to play a tune.

Malinche The mistress of Cortés, now an important figure in Mexican religious fiestas, as a man or boy in women's clothes. He-she appears most frequently with groups of *matachini*, among the Cora, Yaqui, and Rio Grande pueblos. In a long white dress, sometimes with the trousers protruding, she follows the leader *monarca* in all his movements. However, she also is associated with native dance groups, with the *viejitos* of Petamba, Michoacán, as the center of their circle and the partner of each *viejito* in turn. She is one of the six flyers of Otomí and Aztec *voladores* in the Sierra de Puebla. As *Maringuilla* she is the central figure of the Puebla *acatlaxqui*, the bearer of a wooden snake. Maringuilla also carries a snake, a live one in a gourd vessel as the central object of the Papantla *negritos*, brandishing a whip in the other hand. Only in Huaxteca does she enact the character of her prototype: remorse for her betrayal of her countrymen.

The *malinches* of the Huave Indians, in Dionisio del Mar on the Isthmus of Tehuantepec, differs from the other representations. It is a group dance performed by men in trousers, a rattle in the left hand and a feathered stick in the right, in the manner of the *matachini*.

With this exception, *Malinche* represents similar fertility symbols as other transvestites, especially in the various *moriscas*. See TRANSVESTITES. [GPK]

Mallcu Aymara Indian word formerly meaning "chief": applied today to gods and spirits. When it is used after the name of a mountain it implies that the mountain is regarded as a deity. The word is the equivalent of the Quechua *apo*. The Uro-Chipaya Indians apply the term *mallcu* to the large earth cones erected near their villages, and to which they make sacrifices. [AM]

mallow Any of a large family of plants (*Malvaceæ*) important for both food and drugs. Of more than 1000 genera and species not one is known to have any unwholesome qualities. Both the leaves and roots of the common European mallow (genus *Malva*) have long been used medicinally. In England the roots are boiled with a few raisins and bottled; if this is taken in the morning it will protect a person from disease all day. This decoction is also excellent for all internal inflammations of the throat or digestive tract. In Bohemia a warm decoction of the leaves is used for toothache, and is also soothing to the eyes. Either green or dried the seeds mixed with vinegar are said to remove freckles; but the preparation must be applied either in the sun or in a hothouse. In the United States a medicinal tea is made from the leaves which has a soothing effect.

The marshmallow (genus *Althea*) whose root was formerly made into a sweetmeat (today's marshmallows are a mixture of starch, sirup, sugar, and gelatin) has been used as a soothing medicine since before the Christian era. Pliny reports that the medicinal root was dug up with a gold implement and not allowed to touch the ground. Charlemagne paid a farm subsidy for its culture, and it is still widely used in medicine today. A marshmallow ointment cures those suffering bewitchment and also protects from hot metal. This property of the plant was known to the medicine men of the Dakota Indians, who coated their hands and arms with a paste of the red mallow so that they might plunge their arms into a boiling pot. The root of the marshmallow is a cure for toothache when boiled in vinegar, for a cough when boiled in sweet milk, and for all manner of palsies when boiled in wine. Irish names for the marshmallow are variously translated yellow mantle, lady's mantle, and lion's paw. Rural people in Ireland use it for sprains, and in an ointment for sores.

The Meskwaki Indians use the roots of the glade mallow (*Napæa dioica*) for piles and female troubles, and to keep old sores soft. The Tewa Indians use powdered root of the globe mallow (*Sphæralcea lobata*) in infected wounds and snakebites. The ancient Greeks believed that the seeds of mallows aroused the passions. They also planted mallows on graves.

malunas Literally, the mill: a Lithuanian dance for eight couples. As in most Lithuanian dances, the action is inspired by agricultural activity, here by winnowing and grinding of the grain into flour. The couples form two concentric circles, the men on the inside facing the women on the outside. The predominant direction of circling is counterclockwise, in common with other folk dances of central Europe. The dance progresses as follows: 1) Sieve, couples holding hands and swaying arms back and forth; circle to the right. 2) Mill, four of the men touching left hands in the center, the women running around on the outside; then *dos-à-dos* weaving back and forth, women counterclockwise, men clockwise. 3) Arch, the women running against the sun through the upraised arms of the men who progress sunwise. 4) Serpentine, the leading woman breaking hold, winding about and finally guiding the whole line of sixteen dancers into a large circle. The relationship of music and dance is interesting: fast melodic beats accompany slow motions, and slow beats form the background for the fast runs. Not only the bits of stylized pantomime, but the geometrical formations are typical of agricultural and fertility dances, particularly the arch and the serpentine. [GPK]

Mama Literally, mother: collective name for the four sisters of the four brothers (Ayar) of whom one, Manco, was culture hero and founder of the Inca royal family. The four Mamas were: Mama occlo (pure), Mama huaco, Mama ipa qora (aunt weed) and Mama rawa. The Mamas were strong and formidable characters and

played an active role in the slow journey of the eight across Peru seeking new lands. Mama huaco wiped out one whole opposing tribe by herself, for instance. Ayar Manco and Mama occlo were the parents of a son named Sinci Roq'a, and thus established the precedent of brother-sister marriage among the Incas. Manco and the four Mamas founded their city at Cuzco. Sinchi Roq'a was the first of the royal house of the Incas. See AYAR.

Mama-cocha A goddess whose name means Sea Mother: worshipped by the fishermen of the Peruvian coast. [AM]

Mama fō Gro, Gro Mama, or **Mama fō Doti** The Earth Mother of Surinam Paramaribo Negro religion; the universal goddess of all *winti* worshippers regardless of their specific cults. She is the tutelary goddess of the soil, presiding over the earth as a whole and specifically over every plantation and every little house garden, and regarded as inhabiting the sacred kąnkạntri (silk-cotton tree). Great care is taken not to pollute her domain; offerings of food are made to her annually, and also on specific occasions. During a childbirth in the house, for instance, especially that of a first child, food is offered to Mama fō Gro. If a woman's previous children have all died, the lukumạn (diviner) invokes the aid and cooperation of Mama fō Gro, beginning with the words, "Mother of the Earth, you are the mother of children . . ." She is thus invoked to help the parents "buy" the new child from some deity who has been jealous of the mother's having children.

Mama fō Gro is so great and so greatly feared that her true name is never spoken, except in songs sung by those in the state of possession. She has many names; those occurring most frequently in the songs are Asase (see ASA'ASE), Aida, Waisa, Awanaisa.

If angered, Mama fō Gro may appear to the offender in the form of a snake, alligator, owl, etc. If one finds a snake in his bed at night, he knows he has offended the Gro Mama, and makes an offering of eggs with a prayer for forgiveness. Mama fō Gro in her benevolent aspects is protectress and guardian of those within her domain. The strongest oath known to the Paramaribo Negroes is made in her name. See M. J. and F. S. Herskovits, *Suriname Folk-Lore*, Columbia Contributions to Anthropology, 27, pp. 62–63, 41.

ma'makoni-ni'tkap The Bear dance of the Ute Indians: formerly a spring ceremony to celebrate the time when the bear comes out of hibernation; now a social occasion, though a consciousness of its ceremonialism may remain. Mimetic attributes are contained in the heavy tread of the dancers, the songs, which are said to sound like a bear, and the accompanying *morache*, or notched stick, which certainly sounds like a bear. The men in a line face the women in a line, and for four days progress forward and backward, parallel but without contact: two steps forward and three steps back. This is a common pattern of Ute and also of Navaho social dances. On the fourth day, the last song changes beat, and the women pursue the men. [GPK]

mambu The priestess of the vodun cult in Haiti. [MJH]

Ma-mo One of the eight classes of indigenous Tibetan country gods; black she-devils, the disease mistresses who are often spouses of malignant demons.

Mampes In Menek Kaien (Malay peninsula) folklore, the guardian of the bridge of the dead, called Balan Bacham, which spans the sea to Belet, the afterworld of these people. On either side of the bridge grow flowers. Mampes conducts only the good souls to Belet.

man The creation of man, an important episode in many, though not all, of the cosmogonies of the world, plays a minor part in Greek mythology. In the early Greek myths, man is either coeval with the gods, or is born from objects or from Ge, the earth; later, Prometheus was said to have made man from earth and water. The Biblical account of creation tells essentially two different stories. In one, probably the later version, the making of man from chaos is the culmination of the process of creating the universe. In the other, Adam was made from clay and inspired with life by God: this is not something that comes as a climax, but occurs before the animals are made. This account follows, not the Babylonian story of creation, where man is made from Kingu's blood, but the earlier Sumerian story of the creation of man by Ninmah from the clay of the abyss. In this Sumerian myth, Enki also tries to make man, but his creation is imperfect; it cannot sit or stand or bend its knees; it does not answer Ninmah, it does not reach for bread. So too in the *Popol Vuh* of the Quiché Indians of Guatemala, the first men are made of mud but are unable to stand and are mindless. They are destroyed. A second race of men is made of wood. These have no regard for the gods or for anything but themselves. The world revolts against them, and they are destroyed by their domestic animals and their utensils— pots, millstones, etc. The third creation is successful and the four men thus made are the ancestors of the human race. The sequence of stone, wood, and clay (or the like) in the creation of man is common in the Pacific area. Plants, stones, parts of the Creator's body, spittle, blood, worms, shells, wooden images, figures drawn on the sand, sweat, ashes—all these are somewhere considered the original stuff from which mankind was made.

Sometimes, man instead of being made by a Creator hatches or emerges from somewhere. Thus, the Indians of the Southwest have, alongside the myths of man's creation from ears of corn, tales of the emergence of man from underground. Among the Indians of the South American Chaco, men are dug out of the ground by a dog who scents them (Mbayá), they emerge from a hole in the ground (Tereno), they come from a great tree when it is split (Chamacoco), the first man is hatched by a huge bird in a hole on a mountain top (Mbayá). Throughout Indonesia, the first man is said to have hatched from an egg. In eastern Indonesia, men came from worms and larvæ in the ground. The Tagalogs of the Philippines say the first man and woman were inside bamboo sticks which were cast ashore and pecked open by a bird. In Formosa, the Yami say that man came forth when a rock split. Man is descended from tadpoles, according to the Wa of Indochina. These are but a sampling; all over the world the creation or first appearance of man is explained in as many ways as there are peoples.

The dual nature of man, the animal being who nevertheless can know of God and sometimes act nobly, was explained by the Greeks as the result of man's creation from the ashes of the Titans after they had eaten Dionysus Zagreus. Man thus has something of the divine in him, though a good deal of him is evil. In a Ruma-

nian tale, the Devil got the idea of making man and fashioned the body, but he had to have God's assistance to give it life: thus man's body is ruled by the Devil but his soul is divine. There are also tales illustrating concepts taken from such books as the Bible. A Slovene tale, for example, says that God made creation from a grain of sand adhering to His nail. As He worked, some sweat fell on the sand, and from this man was created. Thus, man must earn his bread by sweat. And, in explanation of the nature or position of woman, there are such stories as the creation of woman from man's rib or, even more widespread, from the tail of a dog or of the Devil. In Borneo, man and woman are said to have been created from a sword hilt and a distaff. See ADAM; ANTHILL; ASHES; ASK; EMBLA; HATUIBWARI; ILMATAR; KHNUM; LIZARD; MBERE; TIKI.

☞ Among the North American Indians the actual creation of man seems to be of lesser interest, on the whole, than the establishment and ordering of the world and of the daily living of man. A few tribes lack any myths that definitely account for the actual first creation of man, and the Eskimo as a large group have no such tale. Except among the Eskimo, however, the advent of man into this world is noticed in American Indian mythologies; human beings "appear" at the end of the Mythical Age when the animals become true animals, or people emerge into this world from the underworld where they formerly existed. The majority of tribes give somewhat more attention to the creation of man than merely announcing his presence. Man is created from sticks (Huchnom of northern California), from the rubbings of the skin of the creator (southern California and Southwest), from ears of corn (Navaho), from clay, ashes, beads (Shawnee), etc. The Indian is created from red clay, the white man from the foam of the ocean or white clay, the Negro from black clay, etc. (Eastern Woodlands). During the creation of man he may have been imperfectly formed and the mistake rectified later; a tale fairly widespread in the West pictures man as having first had solid hands until Lizard decided he should have hands like hers. See LIZARD HAND.

A motif widely distributed in North American Indian tales is that of misplaced genitalia; man's sexual organs were first put on his forehead, then on some other part of his body; he failed to procreate, so finally they were placed where they are now.

In the Zuñi emergence myth, after the people came to Slime Spring from the underworld, Elder Brother and Younger Brother cut mouths in their faces (previously people could not eat). The knife made these cuts red from the red of the whetstone on which it had been sharpened. Then Elder Brother and Younger Brother cut the anus, so that people could defecate; it was black. People's fingers and toes were webbed, so they cut them apart. People still had tails and horns, so the two brothers went to each house and cut these off of everyone. The people "were glad that they were finished." [EWV]

☞ The most common explanations given by South American Indians for the origin of man fall into two categories: 1) Men were created by the culture hero out of some substance (clay, reeds, etc.); or 2) They came from some other region, generally from an underworld.

The Choco have a creation myth which follows the pattern of Mayan mythology. The culture hero made the first men of stone, then of wood, and finally of clay. Likewise Viracocha, the great Inca god, made successively two different races of men, the first of which he destroyed by changing them into stones. Later he created a new mankind who populated the earth. The culture hero of the Taulipang Indians modeled the first men in wax; then because they melted in the sun, he made new ones out of clay. Kenos, the first man in Ona mythology, modeled sexual organs out of peat. The first men and women were born from the union of these organs.

The migration of the first men from another world is described either as an ascension from a subterranean country (Caraja, Mundurucu, Yaruro, Witoto) or as a descent from the sky (Warrau). The ancient Peruvians, the Taino of Haiti, had their first men come from large caves.

The Cashinawa account for the origin of mankind by a process of spontaneous generation: they state that men developed from maggots that grew on the bodies of giants drowned by the flood, or else that they sprouted from seeds.

That the first men were hatched from eggs is an interesting mythological motif common to South America and the Old World. In a Peruvian myth recorded in the 16th century, the ancestors of the coastal people originated, according to their social status, from three eggs, one of gold, one of silver, and one of copper, which had been sent by the Sun God. The ancient Mbayá of the Gran Chaco believed that their forbears issued from eggs laid by a gigantic bird. The motif is unknown in the rest of South America. [AM]

mana   General term among the Melanesian (and Polynesian) peoples of the Pacific (according to R. H. Codrington, *The Melanesians*, Oxford, 1891) for the mysterious spiritual power which pervades the universe and is indwelling in men, animals, trees, and inanimate objects. Mana transcends human power, has various physical manifestations, but operates through human medium or that of supernatural beings, the vehicle however often being water, sticks, stones, etc. Max Müller defined the concept of mana as a "sense of the infinite." It underlies all life; all good comes from mana; all success, health, and material well-being are the result of this unseen power. When a Melanesian fisherman makes a good catch, he believes there was mana in the net. Evil comes from its being diverted to harmful ends, either by the dead or by the living. A medicine man possessing mana to still storms might also raise them, or having herbs with power to cure might also divert their mana to poison. A living man may possess mana, but the spirits of the dead *are* mana. Mana is available at all times, but never operates of itself.

In general ethnological usage the term came to be applied to the concept of spiritual power immanent in sacred persons, things, and places. It might be applied, for instance, to that virtue which went out of Jesus when the woman touched the hem of his garment and was healed. But the term is again falling into disuse except for its specific Oceanic applications. Compare ANIMISM; MANITU; MYSTERIOUS, HOLY, AND POWERFUL; ORENDA; WAKANDA. See BARAKA.

☞ American-trained anthropologists seldom if ever use the concept of mana for American material; it is regarded as specifically Melanesian (and Polynesian) and referable especially to Melanesian concepts of supernatural power. Even its applicability to general Polynesian material has been recently challenged by an American anthropologist, G. P. Murdock, who writes in the preface to his book *Our Primitive Contemporaries* (New York, 1934, p. xiii): "The author began with the intention of making full use of the concept [of mana]. In tribe after tribe, however, he found it inapplicable, the more so the more deeply he dug into the facts, and he ended without being able to use it at all. To choose but one example out of many, he could find little relation between Handy's reconstruction of Polynesian religion in terms of *mana* and the reported facts on Samoan religion. In science, when a theory, however plausible, parts company with the facts, there is no choice; the theory must yield." [EWV]

Manabozho   Same as NANABOZHO. See also END OF WORLD; HARE; HIAWATHA; MIDEWIWIN; WOLVERINE.

Manama   Chief deity of the Philippine Island Bagobo people: same as EUGPAMOLAK MANOBO.

Manannán   The Irish sea god. Bishop Cormac (died 907) gives a euhemeristic description of him as "a celebrated merchant who was in the Isle of Man. He was the best pilot that was in the west of Europe . . . Therefore the Irish and the Britons called him god of the sea." His maritime nature is emphasized in many ways: he was the son of Ler (genitive Lir), the sea; he possessed a magic coracle, the Wave-Sweeper; he rode a horse or drove a chariot over the ocean; his home was the Land of Promise, an elysian island. Like other deities, Manannán was "a good provider." He settled the Tuatha Dé Danann (the gods) in the fairy mounds of Ireland and established a feasting which protected them from old age and at which pigs were killed and eaten and yet came alive again. When he entertained King Cormac mac Airt (3rd century) at his palace, one of these immortal pigs was boiled, and we learn of his inexhaustible supply of wheat and of his wife's seven cows which gave milk enough for the people of the Land of Promise. He gave Cormac a golden cup which broke in pieces when lies were told over it, but was restored when truths were uttered. Among his other possessions were a mantle and a helmet of invisibility, and he was a notorious shapeshifter. When Fiachna the Fair, king of Ulster, invaded Lochlann, Manannán appeared to him and promised him victory in return for a night with his wife. With Fiachna's consent Manannán returned to Ireland, took Fiachna's likeness, and begat on his wife the probably historic king Mongán (7th century).

The sea god was long remembered in the Isle of Man, from which his name was derived. Though his grave, thirty feet long, was to be seen outside Peel castle, he was the object of a cult which lasted into the 19th century. On Midsummer Eve the people of the neighborhood used to carry green meadow grass to the top of Barule in payment of rent to Mannan-beg-mac-y-Leir, and the grandfather of a woman living in 1910 used to pray to the same divinity for a blessing on his boat and a good catch of fish. The Manx coat of arms, three legs forming a sort of wheel, was believed to be the shape in which the god rolled swiftly across the island. As a magician he would form a miniature fleet out of peascods and so magnify it as to frighten invaders away.

The Welsh Manawyddan was probably borrowed from the Irish since the name of his father, Llyr, simply reproduces the Irish genitive Lir. The connection with the Isle of Man was recognized, the Welsh name of the island being Manaw, but the association with the sea has been completely lost in surviving Welsh literature except that in poem VIII of the *Book of Taliesin* Manawyd is said to know a faery fortress surrounded by ocean's currents, and in *Branwen* he dwelt for eighty years in the isle of Grassholm in the Irish Sea, abundantly supplied and free from sorrow and advancing age. According to *Manawyddan* he was a miraculously successful wheat-grower and shoemaker, the latter accomplishment being suggested by the Welsh word *manawyd*, awl. The main theme of this mabinogi is the wasting of the land of Dyved (southwestern Wales) and the imprisonment of Manawyddan's wife and stepson through the spells of Llwyd, followed by Manawyddan's outwitting Llwyd and forcing him to remove the enchantments.
ROGER S. LOOMIS

Manasā Literally, mind, thought: a Hindu snake goddess, sister of the serpent king Śesha, worshipped in Bengal especially by the Bāgdīs, Bāwariyas, and Mals. Manasā is depicted as yellow, with four arms, sitting on a waterlily and clothed with snakes, or represented by a pot marked with vermilion placed under a tree and with a trident driven into the ground. Four annual festivals are celebrated in her honor. The chief festival is held in Savan (July-August) at which time no fire is kindled, since Manasā is known as "She who does not cook." Pigs, sheep, goats, or buffaloes are sacrificed to her and some devotees play with snakes, which custom results in frequent deaths. The goddess sometimes dwells in the pipal tree and her plant is the Manasā (*Euphorbia nerifolia*) which is planted in the courtyard during the Daśahra festival.

Manco-capac One of the four Ayar brothers, mythical founders of the Inca dynasty. According to the version of the story recorded by Garcilaso de la Vega, Mancocapac came from an island of the Titicaca in the guise of a culture hero. See AYAR. [AM]

Mandarangan One of a pair of evil spirits who are the patrons of Bagobo (Philippine Islands) warriors; his wife is Darago.

mandrake A poisonous plant (*Mandragora officinarum*) of the Mediterranean region, to which numerous traditions are attached relating to its origin, the human shape of the forked root, its narcotic, soporific, and aphrodisiac properties, its magical powers, and especially its power to effect conception. So realistic is the resemblance of the root to the human shape that English folklore distinguished even sex differences and commonly referred to *man*drakes and *woman*drakes. Old herbals picture the roots as male or female forms with bunches of leaves growing out of the head, sometimes with a dog chained to the waist, or a dog dying in agony in the background. (See INSANE ROOT.) Belief in the semihumanity of mandrakes is reflected in John Donne's line "Get with child a mandrake root."

Sir James Frazer believed that the shape of the root "helped foster, if it did not originate" the notion that the mandrake springs from the body drippings of a man hanged on a gallows. (See Frazer, *Folklore in the Old Testament*, ii, 381.) The German term for mandrake, *Galgenmännlein*, bears testimony to this belief, which occurs also as folktale motif A2611.5 (belonging in turn within a larger cycle of beliefs in the origins of various plants from the bodies of slain persons).

The ancient Greeks, long familiar with the soporific properties of mandrake, used it as an anesthetic in surgical operations, and it was so used well into the Middle Ages. For aphrodisiac effects they steeped the root in wine or vinegar, and its erotic properties were so well known that Aphrodite was sometimes given the additional title of Mandragoris. Mandrake was also called the plant of Circe, in the belief that an infusion of mandrake was the witch-draught with which Circe first enamored and then transformed her victims. Theophrastus gave specific instructions for gathering it: one should draw a circle around it three times with a sword, face westward while cutting it; or one should dance around it while reciting some kind of love-prattle. Pliny advised keeping to windward while digging the root on account of the stink. In some parts of Greece today young men still carry bits of mandrake root as love charms.

In Arabia mandrake was called the Devil's candle because it was said to shine in the night: a phenomenon caused by glowworms, which thrive in the damp rosette of the leaves. In France its name is *mandagoire* or *mandagloire*, which folk etymology has corrupted into *main-de-gloire* (compare HAND OF GLORY). For the etymologies of these terms and the mandrake terms in other countries, consult O. Gruppe, *Griechische Mythologie und Religionsgeschichte*, Munich, 1906; and A. Usteri, *Pflanzmärchen und Sagen*, Basel, 1925.

The magic powers of the mandrake turn up variously in folktale: the mandrake bestows invulnerability (D1344.10); it prophesies (D1311.13); it reveals treasures (D1314.7.1); in French folklore especially will it do this if it is clothed in silk, bathed and cared for regularly. It shrieks when uprooted (F992.1). In Wales black bryony was called mandrake and endowed by the popular mind with all the mysteries of the true mandrake. When uprooted it would shriek and sweat blood; whoever uprooted it would die in agony, shrieking as the mandrake had shrieked. Eating mandrakes effects conception (T511.2.1). That elephants have sexual desire only after eating mandrakes is a motif (B754.2) found in one of the Middle English bestiaries.

The ancient Hebrew belief in the power of the mandrake to induce conception is present in *Genesis* xxx, although as several scholars have indicated, the direct attribution of this magic power to the mandrake has been "emended." Reuben, the son of Leah and Jacob, gathered some mandrakes and gave them to his mother. Rachel, the beloved young, but barren, wife of Jacob, begged Leah for the fruit (Hebrew *dudaim*, love apples). Leah, jealous and suspicious, sensed the reason and was unwilling, but Rachel persuaded her to trade the fruit for that night in Jacob's bed (when Leah conceived Issachar). But after eating the fruits of the mandrake, the hitherto barren Rachel also soon conceived and eventually bore Joseph. Frazer states that belief in the aphrodisiac powers of mandrake and in its power to remove barrenness was still a living belief in Palestine and the Near East well into the 20th century. The belief that mandrake would cause conception even if laid under the bed spread into western Europe.

Hildegard of Bingen, 12th century, explained the man-shape of the root with the statement that the mandrake was created "of that same earth of which Adam was created." The 16th century English herbalist, Gerard, also believed in its powers to effect conception, and may have influenced the spread of the belief. An inordinate value came to be set upon mandrake root, which caused a prodigious trade in counterfeit roots through several centuries. The counterfeit roots were usually bryony carved into human shape, sometimes incised and planted with wheat or grass so that the tiny shoots might simulate pubic hair. See ALRAUN.

maneki neko The beckoning cat: a Japanese good-luck charm used by shopkeepers to lure customers into the shop. It is the figurine of a cat sitting on its haunches with one paw raised in a beckoning gesture.

manes In ancient Roman religion, the spirits of the dead; the Di Manes or divine dead: the name is probably a euphemism meaning "good spirits," and may have been used instead of *lemures,* the lonely, wandering ghosts of the dead. Manes was also used for the underworld deities, the underworld itself, the ancestral spirits, and, eventually, as a non-collective noun, to refer to individual spirits of the dead. See MANISM.

mani or **chintamani** In Hindu belief, the magic jewel obtained by the gods at the Churning of the Ocean; the jewel in the cobra's head. According to the *Atharva-Veda* the mani is an amulet against all kinds of evil and is identified with the thunderbolt which Indra used against Vṛitra. According to the Pāli Canon it is a transparent beryl with eight facets so bright that it turns night into day. The mani is an attribute of Avalokita and of Vishṇu who is represented with the jewel at his waist or on his navel. In modern Indian folklore the mani is the snake stone, the jewel in the cobra's or nāga's head, which has the value of the treasure of seven kings and can be hidden only when cow dung is thrown on it.

man in the moon The moon, second to nothing in its influence on world-wide folk belief and practice, is important principally for two things: its face and its phases. In Europe, generally, a man's face is seen on the moon's surface. Sometimes the man is Judas, sent to the moon as punishment (A751.1). In Panama, the punishment suffered by the man in the moon is for incest. Elsewhere in the world, the hare (A751.2) and the frog (A751.3) are most often seen. Thus in Zululand and Tibet, in Mexico and India, the markings on the moon form a hare. The Buddha, in one of his early incarnations, offered himself, a hare, as a sacrifice to Sakka, the chief god; Sakka painted a picture of the hare on the moon as an eternal remembrance of the act. The moon is called, in India, the hare-marked (*śaśānka* or *śadihara*) or the deer-marked *(mṛiganka)*. In ancient Mexico, it was said the hare was sent to the moon to dim its light, since previously it was as bright as the sun. The Chinese see a frog in the moon; and the connection of the lunar frog of Brittany, Tibet, the Solomon Islands, etc., with the moon as rain-symbol is clear. See "The Lunar Frog" by A. H. Krappe *(Folk-Lore* LI: 161–171). A Peruvian tale explains the marks as the clawings of a fox that

embraced the moon. The Masai of Africa say that the sun and moon had a husband and wife quarrel, both being the worse for wear afterwards. The sun shines brightly in shame, but the moon exhibits to those who look at her her swollen lip and her missing eye. In New Guinea the marks are the fingermarks of mischievous boys; they opened the jar in which an old woman kept the moon and tried to grab it as it escaped. The Eskimos see tell-tale ashes on the moon. Moon, brother of his sister Sun, crept into her bed at night. She put ashes on her hands to mark the culprit. Since then Sun chases the marked moon through the skies. In parts of northern Europe, the man in the moon carries a tar bucket; he marked the moon with his tar and the marks have remained there. In Malaya the sharp-eyed make out a banyan tree under which sits a hunchback making a fishing line. At the other end of the line is a rat eating it almost as fast as it is made; this is good, for when the line is finished the hunchback will use it to fish everything on earth up to the moon. The Buriats and other Siberian tribes recognize a girl with a pail near a shrub; she was rescued by the sun and moon from a pursuing wolf. In the Cook Islands, it is a girl with a pile of leaves and a pair of tongs who makes tapa. The stones holding down the tapa may be seen; when she pushes aside the stones, it thunders. The Maori descry a grumbling woman, who complained when the moon went behind a cloud as she went for water; her water gourd, her basket, and the tree she held onto when the moon seized her. A girl with a bucket is seen by the Kwakiutl. The Scandinavians saw a pair of children, Hiuki and Bil, and their water pail. They were made to carry water all night by a cruel father and were rescued by Mani, the moon god. Many see in this pair the originals of the Jack and Jill who went to "fetch a pail of water." The Chams of Cambodia recognize in the moon the face of Pajan Yan, who is the great healing goddess, and who was banished to the moon before she could heal and bring to life all the dead.

☞ Probably all North American Indians, if the distribution of the item were known, have some explanation for the dark patches on the moon. That most frequently encountered among the western tribes is that the figures are those of Frog(s). Frog protects both Sun and Moon so that Bear will not swallow them. Or, Frog once swallowed Moon, but was in turn swallowed by her and is now in the center of Moon, weaving a basket. Or, two or more Frog sisters reject animal suitors; the latter weep; a flood ensues from the tears; the Frog sisters go to the house of Moon and jump on his face, where they may be seen at the present time; this latter tale is widespread in North America. Among the Caddo Indians of the Southeast a brother commits incest with his sister in the dark; she smears paint on his face and so later identifies him; he becomes the man in the moon. Some other tribes in the West say the figures are those of a giant, or of Coyote, or are the picture of a large oak tree from which the dead obtain their food, or that they are scars left on Moon after Bear bit her. The Shawnee of the Eastern Woodlands see their female creator's picture in the moon; she is bending over a cooking pot, with her little dog near her. The explanation of the figures in the moon is often added to tales, or inserted in them as an explanatory element. [EWV]

manioc A staple root plant (*Manihot esculenta*) of South and Central America, in two varieties, the bitter and the sweet (yucca), both of which are used. It is one of the three principal food crops of the region, and the main root crop. The roots are ground or grated to a meal from which the poisonous juice (prussic acid) is pressed or otherwise extracted. This juice is used for a fish poison (Brazil, Ecuador). Manioc beer is made throughout most of South America north of the Plata, excluding the Andes and most of the Chaco. Manioc meal is used to make bread, tortillas, etc. According to legend, the daughter of a chief bore a child by the spirit of manioc, who showed the people how to cultivate and propagate the necessary plant. In a Christian legend, St. Thomas, besides bringing the gift of faith and relief from plague, taught the cultivation of the plant. The Paya of Honduras say that men were sowed or planted by their god as manioc is propagated. The Mundurucú of the Tapajoz region in Brazil pray to the Mother of the Manioc: "Favor us with the fruit of your sons. Do not let us suffer privations. Every year we pray to you and do not forget you." See ORIGIN OF CULTIVATED PLANTS.

manism The worship of the spirits of the dead: from the euphemistic appellation *manes* or *Di Manes* (i.e. the good ones) used by the ancient Romans for the souls of the dead. The Di Manes, the divine dead as a group, were early recognized by the Romans; they were worshipped at the Feralia (February 21) and Parentalia (February 13–21). Later the Di Manes became identified specifically with the Di Parentes, the ancestral spirits of the family; and still later, as a consequence, manes came to be used for spirits of individuals. Thus the early formula used on graves *Dis Manibus Sacrum* (*DMS*) was modified during and after the period of the Empire to carry in addition the name of the dead person. Since the spirits dwelt within the earth, manes became a term for both the country of the dead in the underworld and the great underworld gods, Pluto, Persephone, Orcus. The manes came forth at certain periods, especially at their festival at the turn of the old Roman year in February. To help their emergence, three times a year the stones guarding the entrance to the underworld (*lapis Manalis*) were removed. These entrances were specially dug at the founding of cities throughout Italy.

Manism, the general term for the worship of the spirits of the dead, and, more specifically, for ancestor worship, is widespread in the world. Apart from the Semitic area of the Near East and the Mediterranean, for which evidence of manism is circumstantial, it is known in practically every corner of the earth. The ancestor cults of India, China, and Japan show the highest development, and the complex systems observed there have become well integrated into the general cultures and beliefs of these countries. Ancestor worship was a state cult in Ashanti and Dahomey in West Africa, and the Bantu tribes also possess a well-developed manism. An ancestral cult, part of the tremendous cult of the dead, flourished in ancient Egypt. North and South American Indian tribes to varying degrees observe an ancestral cult. The Pacific Islanders have an important ancestor cult, but in Australia and New Zealand ancestor worship, though present, is comparatively undeveloped. In Malaya, Islam has modified a native animistic manism. Ancestor worship was known in ancient Babylonia, and the Iranians too had their cult of the dead. The Indo-European tribes carried manism throughout Europe; evidence of ancestor worship is very prominent throughout the Continent from the Slavonic peoples to the Celts.

Generally manism seems founded in the belief that the ancestors will continue, in death as in life, to protect and advise their people, their children. Perhaps equally prominent, however, is a belief in the jealousy of the dead towards the living, a jealousy manifesting itself in unfriendly acts, as the bringing of disease, hauntings, and the like. Thus in some regions, the bones of the dead are broken, or their eyes are sealed or their limbs bound, or heaps of stones are placed over them, all to make it difficult for them to return or to recognize those against whom they may hold a grudge. Sometimes the family moves from its home or changes the names of its members to make it harder for the dead to know them. Among the other widespread customs and beliefs entering into ancestor cults are: belief in oracular spirits (the dead continue to advise), known from Greece to Lapland, from Melanesia to East Africa; the belief that the ancestral spirit is reborn in a new child, hence various naming customs and divinations to determine which ancestor now resides in the child (see ANAPEL); totemism and idolatry, where the ancestral spirit becomes one with the totem animal or dwells in the image; state and family worship of the ancestors; burial customs designed to keep the spirits contented or to assuage their anger; annual festivals for the dead, days on which they return to earth, often by invitation and with the aid of the living, to receive gifts from their remembering survivors. Compare ANCESTOR WORSHIP; CULT OF THE FRIENDLY DEAD; NATS.

Ancestor worship was more prominent in the religion of the Andean people than it was among the primitive tribes of Brazil and of the plains of the Chaco and Patagonia. The cult of the dead was important among the Chibcha, as may be assumed from the wealth of their tombs and the reverence in which their modern descendants keep their ancestors. The Kaggaba, for instance, regard the souls of their ancestors as superior to demons. They attribute to them the origin of all their institutions. The mummies of the Inca emperors were worshipped as gods and placed in the palaces which they had occupied during life. The ancient chronicles make constant references to the cult of the dead which the Andean Indians practiced against the rules of the church.

The care with which the Amazonian Indians preserve in their houses the bones of their dead is also indicative of a religious attitude toward them. The cult of the dead was one of the main elements of the religion of the Cobeuo of the Caiari-Uaupes region. Their ancestors were represented by sacred trumpets which were played during certain ceremonies.

In the Chaco, the Guaicuruan tribes performed many ceremonies over the tombs of their dead which are buried in special cemeteries or in large huts.

The Bororo of the Mato Grosso believe that the ancestral souls are wont to visit the villages of the living and to ask for food and drink. These Indians have special categories of shamans who serve as mediums for the souls of the dead.

Ancestor worship was a salient feature of the religion of the Taino in Haiti and Cuba. The great *zemi* (idols) were believed to contain the souls of the chiefs' ancestors. No evidence, however, of a cult of the dead has been found among the Indians of Tierra del Fuego. [AM]

manitu, manito, or **manitou** A word which in variant forms occurs in all Algonquian languages, having various specific meanings in each language. These meanings usually relate to supernatural power, but manitu is not a general term for a "mysterious cosmic power everywhere in nature." The conceptual abstraction of manitu as an impersonal manifestation of supernatural power, as presented by William Jones in "The Algonkin Manitou" (*JAFL* 18: 183–90) is dubious; it now seems probable that Jones was influenced more by the mana-concept prevalent in his day, than by his own Fox data. In this tribe manitu is applied to an indefinite number of definitely conceived supernatural beings; for example, to Wisa'ka, the culture hero; to *keca manitowa*, the gentle manitu; to *ke'tci manitowa*, the great manitu, and to a host of other manitus, who live above, on, and under the earth, as well as now also being applied to trains and the automobile, to a parrot which can talk, to snakes (which are regarded with awe and never killed), and to the Thunderers, to corn, to turtle dove (*manitowa mimiwa*, because it makes sounds like the voices of the manitus), to the dog, which the Fox eat ceremonially in order to get in touch with the manitus, and to plants, etc. Among the Sauk, Delaware and other Algonquians the creator and other supernaturals are also referred to as manitus, although the specific Delaware term for their creator is *ketanto'wit*, great power. The Sauk-Delaware use of manitu horrifies the Shawnee, who use the term *manedo* as the regular name for all kinds of snakes; *manedo* in compound means monstrous or evil creatures; with the prefix *matci* it denotes an evil being now identified with Satan; *manedowikamekoiki* is the Shawnee term for the house (heaven) where an Indian goes when he dies. Conceptual abstraction of the term manitu has also been specifically denied for other Algonquian tribes such as the Menomini, various Ojibwa groups including the Plains Ojibwa, and for coastal Cree groups. [EWV]

Mañjuśrī In Buddhist belief, an Adibuddha, the personification of wisdom often occupying the chief place in the Buddhist polytheism. Mañjuśrī is better known in China and Tibet than in India. In Nepal, where he is the giver of civilization, his worship is especially popular. Among northern Buddhists he is grouped with Avalokita and Vajradhara in a triad which corresponds to the Hindu triad (*trimūrti*). He is represented seated on a lion and sometimes bearing small figures of the Dhyanibuddhas on his head. Probably the most ancient of his numerous names is Mañjughoṣa which means pleasant voice.

manman Literally, mother (Haiti): largest, most ritually significant of the three vodun drums; also the most important and first placed of the pegs in a vodun drum. The instrument commonly measures between 32 and 36 inches in height, and 10 to 12 inches in diameter. The player strikes it with a crooked stick or mallet called *baguette*, which is held in the right hand. Variation of tone is provided by striking with the fingers or heel of the other hand. The manman is the last drum to begin its part in accompaniment to the dancing and heralds the dance figure, *asagwe*, the salute to the gods. See DRUM.

Mannekin-pis The small bronze statue of a urinating Eros which fills a public fountain near the center of Brussels, Belgium. Since it is one of the famous sights of that city, and because the reason for the original choice of such a pose has been lost, several legends have grown up about the fountain. It is said that towards the end of the 11th century, the young son of a certain count was taken to see a parade honoring some returning Crusaders. The five-year-old, as the Holy Sacrament at the head of the procession passed, began to relieve himself in the street. Through a miracle, he was unable to stop until the end of the parade passed, and in the meantime everyone in Brussels came uncomfortably to know what was happening. His mother, in expiation, had the statue placed near the spot. A later event it is supposed to memorialize is the extinguishing by a child of the fuse of a bomb in the Town Hall. Perhaps older than either of these legends is the one that links the statue with Kristelijk-manneken straat, though the name of the street postdates the statue's erection. An old Jew is the villain; he kidnapped the child for a sacrifice; Our Lady of Bon Secours rescued the little boy. Other legends make the Eros the surviving member of a quartet which included the Three Graces, all similarly engaged in supplying the fountain. The statue was first mentioned in 1452, and it has been replaced several times. It was stolen in 1817 and mutilated; the thief was sentenced to life imprisonment (commuted to 20 years at hard labor). After World War I, Mannekin-pis added to his many honors—including several foreign decorations and uniforms—by being made a corporal in the French army, the citation being for "maintaining his position" in the face of the enemy for four years.

Mannhardt, Wilhelm (1831–1880) German mythologist, born in Schleswig and educated at the Universities of Berlin and Tübingen. In 1855 he became editor of the *Zeitschrift für deutsche Mythologie und Sittenkunde*. After various studies in Germanic mythology, he published *Wald-und Feld-kulte* (Berlin, 1875–77; 2d ed., 1904–5), and *Mythologische Forschungen* (1884), significant contributions to the fields of mythology and folklore. He had earlier published *Germanische Mythen* (1858), *Die Götter der deutschen und nordischen Völker* (1860), and *Die Korndämonen* (1868). Mannhardt was the first scholar to study harvest rites and the ceremonies connected with the vintage, presenting its underlying idea of fertility with respect to next year's crops. Mannhardt followed in Tylor's wake and is considered one of the most able and influential of German mythologists.

mantra The Sanskrit word *mantra* has had as many and as various meanings as its Teutonic-English parallel, lore or learning. The Sanskrit term *veda* meant a collection of such lore, especially sacred knowledge, and the four great Vedas of the Brāhmans were composed, the *Rig-Veda* of lore of hymns, the *Sama-Veda* of lore of chants, the *Yajur-Veda* of lore of prayers and formulas recited at sacrifices, and the cruder *Atharva-Veda* of the multi-varied lore of the Atharvans or fire-priests. The holy verses, sacred texts, stereotyped petitions and formulas from all four vedas were called *mantra*.

The second and more limited meaning of the word

is in the sense of password or formula of initiation. No *guru* (teacher) admits a *chela* (novice) into a Hindu sect without whispering into his ear the mantra or countersign of the order. The Ramanuja mantra was *'Oṁ Rāmāya namaḥ* (So be it! Reverence to Rāma.) Comparison is obvious with the Christian triune formula of initiation repeated by the priest or minister at baptism: *In nomine Patris, et Filii, et Spiritus Sancti* (In the name of the Father, and of the Son, and of the Holy Ghost), and with the corresponding Moslem *bismillah: bismillāhi-r-rahmāni-r-rahīmi* (In the name of Allah, the Compassionate, the Merciful), which Mohammed carefully modeled along Christian and Jewish mantric lines.

The use of the mantra as a prayer gives it a third or supplicatory meaning apart from its initiatory function. In India, for many centuries, no public religious ceremony nor any private devotion in the home has been complete without the recitation of familiar mantras, which somewhat resemble Christian prayers. They are not of the extempore original sort, however, fostered in Protestant prayer-meeting circles, but are standardized, verbatim, and repetitious. In fact, any form-prayer of any religion is a true mantra.

The fourth and commonest meaning of mantra, and possibly its oldest, is in the sense of spoken or written charm, spell, incantation, or magic word. (See ABRACADABRA.) In Hinduism and in theistic Buddhism (where *dharani* is the word often used for mantra) this idea of the magic potency of certain words themselves, even if not understood by him who says them, has long obtained. It is believed that *om* or *aum,* for instance, represents onomatopœically the very hum of the universe, and if caught into a written or preferably vocalized syllable, its power is absorbed into the worshipper or he into it.

The well-known beautiful Gayatri or Savitri: *Oṁ maṇi padme Hūṁ* (So be it! O lotus-jewel! Amen!) into the words of which infinite esoteric meanings have been read, has degenerated in some circles from a popular prayer mantra into a mere wishing-gem spell. It is used in Japan, China, parts of India, Burma, Indonesia, but most in Tibet. A hermit who has repeated it at least 100,000 times is entitled to be called *Mani.*

The Iranian Zarathustra's message to his people was termed a *manthra,* especially in the form of his noblest prayer, the *Ahuna Vairya,* the "Our Father" of Zoroastrianism, but in later time it was used as a magic incantation, the repetition of which would assuredly cure disease or repel demons. Similarly, the use of the triune Christian formula and the Moslem *bismillah* was extended far beyond the initiatory ceremony, and both these and many other holy phrases were used on many less important occasions as magic mantras to counteract evil or bring good luck. The phrases used in blessing, cursing, and exorcising are in this sense mantras, and so indeed is profanity. The Bible is full of mantras, from the imprecatory psalms to the apostolic benedictions.

Bismillah, along with the Hebrew tetragrammaton JHVH and the Christian ICHTHUS, IHS, and XR, passed into folklore with many legends of the magic power and prophylactic efficacy of the words alone. For one example, in north African Islam it is believed that Allah himself wrote "bismillah" on Adam's breast, Gabriel's wing, Solomon's seal, and Jesus' tongue.

When the name of God is used purely as a mantric incantation or charmed spell, it is obvious that Christianity, Judaism, and Islam have thereby in that practice reverted to the primitive idea that to know the correct esoteric name of the deity and pronounce it properly is to have him under your control as a sort of genie who must therefore perform your will.

CHARLES FRANCIS POTTER

Manu The hero of the deluge of Hindu mythology. In the *Śatapatha Brahmāṇa,* one day Manu found a fish in the water brought to him to wash his hands. The fish spoke, asking to be saved, and promised in turn to save Manu from destruction: if Manu would keep him in a vessel of water, removing him to larger and larger ones as he grew, and finally to the ocean, he, the fish, would save Manu from the great deluge that was soon to come. The day Manu put the fish in the ocean, "Build a ship," the fish said, "when the waters come, go in it, and I will save you."

All happened as foretold; when the deluge came, Manu went into the ship, fastened the ship's rope to one horn of the fish, who turned up as promised; the fish towed the ship without tire for years, until finally it was over Mt. Himālaya. Then the fish bade Manu tie the ship to a tree and await the subsiding of the waters. This Manu did; and when the waters were drained away, he saw that every living thing on earth but himself had perished. So Manu offered sacrifice, and a woman was given to him for a wife, with whom he repeopled the earth. In the *Mahābhārata,* Manu is performing devotions on a river bank when a small fish calls to him from the water and begs to be saved from a big fish. Manu saves it; it predicts the flood; the story follows.

The Manu of this myth is the seventh of 14 progenitors of mankind named Manu, each of whom was (or will be) lord of the earth for a period of time called a *manvantara* (Manu interval) equal to 4,320,000 years. Each *manvantara* is named for its own Manu, and ends with a deluge. This present *manvantara* is the seventh one, named for the Manu of this myth, son of the Vedic sun god Vivasvant. Thus the world has seven more deluges to go.

manzana Literally, apple: a wedding dance of Largartera in Castile. The bride holds an apple impaled on a knife, and must dance with every man who deposits a coin in the apple. If the coin drops out, it is reclaimed by the man. The rigid posture necessary for holding the knife, and the innumerable dances are thoroughly exhausting. This dance is doubtless of ceremonial origin. It is reported as early as 1555 and certainly is much older. The symbolism of the apple may be similar to the baptismal custom of giving all men an apple, representing original sin, and a bunch of flowers, representing paradise. Or, we may have here an instance of bride barter, found in other European wedding dances, as the Hungarian *mennyasszony tánc.* [GPK]

maple Any of a large genus of trees (*Acer*) of the north temperate zone. Many of the folk uses of this tree are similar to those of other trees, such as the custom, in parts of England, of passing a child through its branches to insure long life, and using it as a divining rod for water. In Alsace storks place a piece of maple in their nests to frighten away bats whose touch will make their eggs infertile. At one time the maple was the emblem of reserve. According to Pliny maple roots were good for a sluggish liver. The Japanese consider the leaves of the maple akin to flowers and celebrate their appearance with one of the blossom festivals.

Among the Indians of the northern United States and Canada, the sap of the sugar maple was an important commodity. It was formerly much used in cooking, even to season meat. Some tribes claim that the sugar was the gift of Nanabozho, others that it came to the Indians by chance: a lazy squaw tapped a maple tree rather than go after water to cook some moose meat. She fled in terror when the whole thing cooked up into a sticky mass, but her husband enjoyed his dinner and sought her out to compliment her. The Meskwaki boiled the inner bark of several species of maple and drank the decoction as an emetic. The maple leaf is common in Meskwaki beadwork designs. The Chippewas made a dye from the rotted wood.

In New Hampshire people say that the sap ceases to run when the first peepers are heard in the spring. In Maine the old-timers claimed that too much fertilizer and rich earth would change a hard maple into a soft maple in three years.

Māra In Hindu and Buddhist mythology and belief, the embodiment of the powers of evil; in the *Atharva-Veda*, Death personified. In Buddhism Māra is the sovereign of the world of men and gods. As god of lightning and of death, he is also a god of the living, or rebirth, and of desire (similar in this respect to the Hindu Kāma). Since Buddha delivers men from desire, birth, and death, Māra is his special enemy, and thus the tempter of Buddha and of his disciples. He began this role the night Buddha left home by appearing before him and offering him the glories of empire if he would return to a worldly life. When he was repulsed, Māra changed his method and filled the air with thunder and conflagrations. Having failed to dissuade Buddha, Māra waited until he was engaged deep in meditation and then sent fiends and demons, furies, and hideous monsters enveloped by serpents and masses of fire to harass him. The tempter also sent his beautiful daughters, but to no avail, for the darts hurled by the monsters changed to flowers and the fire became a halo around his head. At the moment of enlightenment, Māra appeared again with taunts, asking him to prove his buddhahood. Gautama pointed to the earth to witness and an earthquake followed. In folktales and popular belief Māra is a homeless demon who roams everywhere "in the visible shape of murky smokiness" to catch the souls of the dying.

maraké A mat holding poisonous ants or wasps: used among the Guiana Indians and some Amazonian tribes for magical ordeals. The mat is applied against the skin of young people during puberty ceremonies or against the limbs of hunters and fishermen who seek to increase their skill or restore their strength. The magic ceremonies in which this almost unbearable torture is practiced is also known as maraké. [AM]

Marassa The Haitian term for the twin cult which, of Dahomean-Yoruban derivation, has been preserved with all its attributions of supernatural powers to those who fall in this category, and to the child that follows them. See DOSU; HOHOBI; HONSU; TWINS. [MJH]

Märchen A German word much used by folklorists but without universal agreement as to its meaning. As generally employed it is very close to the English "fairy tale" but it is perhaps even broader in its acceptation than that very vague expression. It is certainly broad enough to include everything in the Grimm collection of *Kinder- und Häusmarchen*. Here we find what some folklorists call *real* Märchen, such as *Snow White, Faithful John,* and *The Frog Prince;* but there are also nonsense tales, cumulative stories, tales of numskulls, and many other divergent kinds.

For those who use Märchen in this broad sense there is a difference made between Märchen and *Sage.* The latter is concerned with things actually believed by the teller or at least told to inspire belief in the hearer. The Märchen is definitely fiction; the Sage attempts to be history or a record of scientific fact. That it is pseudo-history and pseudo-science does not affect the intent of the teller: he is not dealing in a fiction.

On the other hand a man who tells a Märchen, at least in our culture, is making up a story for pleasure without any regard to its truth or as to whether it will be really believed.

Among peoples in other parts of the world than western Europe and the lands influenced by it, the difference just pointed out is not certainly present in the minds of the taletellers. How large an element of belief is present in stories that we would find fantastic will differ from people to people, and for this reason some writers have wished to confine the concept of Märchen to the western European cultures just mentioned. But the same tale plots appear in all parts of the world and the differentiation based upon the belief or non-belief of the taleteller would not seem to be very useful. Shall we say that in some countries *Cinderella* is a Märchen and in other countries not a Märchen? This is the essential position taken by the late Albert Wesselski who wishes to confine the use of the term Märchen to the particular style and narrative attitude found in the central group of Grimm's folktales. Thus interpreted, Wesselski would hold that there was no composing of Märchen until the late Middle Ages or perhaps the early Renaissance. For these same tales when told by other peoples he uses the term Märlein. It must be said, however, that most students of Märchen have not found this distinction very valuable and it seems likely that the broad and loose employment of the word will continue in this way. It is practically equivalent to the English word "folktale." See FAIRY TALE; FOLKTALE.

References:
F. von der Leyen, *Das Märchen,* 3d ed. Leipzig, 1925.
———, *Die Welt des Märchens,* 1949.
S. Thompson, *The Folktale.* New York, 1946.
A. Wesselski, *Versuch einer Theorie des Märchens.* Reichenberg i. B., 1936.

STITH THOMPSON

Marduk The chief god of the Babylonian pantheon; Baal Merodach of Babylon, the god of the city of Babylon, and the greatest god in the territory under Babylonian dominion following the period of Hammurabi's conquests (20th century B.C.); hero of the *Enuma Elish,* the Akkadian creation myth. Quite clearly, in this myth, Marduk has replaced the earlier hero of the story, Bel or Enlil, for the Marduk of *Enuma Elish* is distinctly a wind god (as was Enlil), and, though all the other important gods are mentioned, Enlil does not appear in this myth, though he probably was the hero of an earlier, but lost, version. And having replaced Enlil of Nippur, Marduk of Babylon was in turn superseded by Ashur of Assyria.

Marduk was the son of Ea, tall, with four eyes and four ears; from his mouth issued flame. When Tiamat, mother of the gods, determined to battle against them in their attempt to put order to the universe, one by one the great gods quailed at facing her. Marduk, the young, a newcomer to the company of the gods, offered to be the gods' champion, if he were given power equal to that of the other gods. The council of the gods agreed, and Marduk became their overlord in full power in the battle against the sea dragon Tiamat. To test his acquisition of power, the gods placed before Marduk a garment; by the power of his words alone, Marduk caused it to be annihilated, then caused it to re-exist. Thus powerful, and armed with the bow of the rainbow, with the lightning, and with a net held by the four winds, Marduk went forth, riding the tempest, to battle Tiamat and her host.

Marduk cast the net over the dragon. She opened her mouth to engulf him, but he sent the winds rushing into the open maw. With her jaws open and her belly distended, Tiamat fell victim to an arrow shot through her mouth into her heart. Once their chief was dead, the other gods of Tiamat's band were easily captured. From Kingu, consort of Tiamat, Marduk took the tablets of destinies, and thus Marduk became the most powerful of all beings.

Marduk then set about to create order in the universe. Splitting Tiamat's body in two, he raised half to form the heavens and placed the other half opposite Ea's dwelling place to form the earth. He created the stars and constellations, the planets, the order of succession of the calendar. Under Marduk's direction, Ea then took the blood of the executed Kingu and made men to be the servants of the gods. As their last and greatest work, the grateful gods, now organized and each with his work to do, built a capital city for their chief. This, the story of the *Enuma Elish*, was enacted in Babylon each New Year's Day, with Marduk conquering the forces of evil for another year. During the festival the entire epic was read.

As chief god of the Babylonian pantheon, Marduk was able to assume the aspect and powers of any of the gods, since in addition to all else, they derived their provinces from him. Thus, Marduk, as god of the planet Jupiter, lighting the night, became equivalent to Sin, the moon god. Through his consort Sarpanitum, Marduk was father of Nebo, the culture god, inventor of writing and herald of the gods, and originally the god of Borsippa, which became a suburb of metropolitan Babylon as that great city expanded.

marét Among the Botocudo of eastern Brazil, a class of beings, anthropomorphic but non-human, who live in the sky. They intercede with their chief for the human beings they protect, and he, unless he is angry and in a mood to send storms, generally is well-intentioned. The marét are protectors of the Botocudo and will cause bad weather if the Botocudo are injured. They come to earth on a sacred pillar when the shaman calls. He can see them, as can other fortunate people, but most men cannot. The chief of the marét has given the Botocudo

some of their songs, and he taught them how to wear earplugs and labrets. (Lowie, "Eastern Brazil," in *BAEB* 143:1:394)

mariachi A street orchestra of Mexican villages and towns, originally consisting of from three to twelve string players who promenaded the plazas playing for any who offered a coin, but now augmented by brass instruments and strongly influenced by radio and movie styles. The word may be derived from the French *mariage,* since the orchestras were often invited to play at court weddings during the time of Maximilian, who enjoyed their music.

Māriamma, Māramma, or **Mari Mātā** In modern Indian belief, a village goddess or mother goddess; a malignant disease-bringer. She presides over, or is, smallpox, cholera, and other fatal diseases. Each village has its own mother or tutelary deity, often given a local name. These mothers are more feared than loved and their worship actually consists of propitiatory rites and sacrifices. The Nats propitiate Mari when cholera appears in a village by sacrificing a hog and a libation of spirits. According to William Crooke, in Kāngra the goddess is propitiated by the Pachbala rite which consists of the sacrifice of a pumpkin representing a man, by a he-goat, a ram, a cock, and a male buffalo, or by the Satbala, which adds to the above list two human victims. See GRĀMA-DEVATĀ.

Marie de France An Anglo-French poetess and fabulist of the last quarter of the 12th century. She was probably Norman by birth, and may have been born in the vicinity of Paris. Her writing, according to recent scholarship, was done at the court of Henry II of England; the manuscripts are however much later than this period. Her fables, the *Ysopet,* are a translation into French of an English version of Æsop's Fables of Phædrus. To this English telling of the fables, attributed in error to King Alfred, were added some Indian fables. The *Lais,* a group of Celtic tales, are doubtless from Breton originals. She says she heard them sung by the jongleurs; they were probably English versions of the Celtic tales with Scandinavian and Eastern materials intermixed. The stories told in the *Lais* are for the most part tales of love, with romantically tragic endings, and with much of the supernatural in them.

marigold (1) Any of a genus of plants (*Tagetes*) including the French marigold (*T. patula*) and the African or Aztec marigold (*T. erecta*) all having bright golden flowers and pungent aromatic foliage: used both medicinally, as a pot-herb, or in salads. One persistent myth of the origin of these plants is that they sprang from the blood of those slain in Cortés' conquest of Mexico. Claims that it was unknown in Mexico before that time have proved to be false. Marigolds were introduced into Europe from Mexico at this time but, since they reached England from France and Africa respectively, they have retained the respective names. In northern India the marigold adorns the trident of Mahādeva and crowns of these flowers are worn on his festivals.

(2) The pot-marigold (genus *Calendula*) takes its name from the story that the Virgin Mary wore it on her bosom. Many of the folk beliefs concerning the various marigolds have become interchangeable. The origin myth that claims the calendula sprang from a Greek maid, Caltha, who was in love with the sun god and

wasted away watching him is mentioned in connection with all sun-flowers (i.e. flowers which turn their heads to follow the sun's progress).

In Germany the marigold is considered unfavorable to love; in England it is used in "loves-me, loves-me-not" divinations. Just looking at the calendula was supposed to benefit the eyes, and at one time it was said to have the power to show a vision of anyone who has robbed you. The Welsh say if it does not open its petals before seven, it will rain or thunder during the day. In Devon and Wiltshire if you pick marigolds or gaze long at the blossoms you will take to drink, which accounts for the name "Drunkard" which it was sometimes given in those shires. In the 16th century it was used in broths to comfort the heart. During World War II quantities of the flowers and leaves were gathered and used to induce perspiration, and for bronchial complaints. Among Jamaica Negroes marigold, boiled and drunk as a tea, is recommended to start menstrual flow after unnatural cessation, and for other menstrual troubles.

Mari Lwyd   The words, which may mean either "Gray Mare" or "Holy Mary," are applied to a custom observed mainly in South Wales at the Christmas or New Year's season. A party of men, headed by one carrying a horse's skull or a wooden imitation, went from house to house, sometimes engaging in a poetic contest with the inmates, and receiving from them coin or drink in a wassail bowl. A very similar custom observed on November Eve in County Cork, Ireland, was called the White Mare. See CELTIC FOLKLORE; HODENING; HORSE DANCE; SAMAIN; TRURON. [RSL]

marinera   Literally, of the sea, or seafarer: a popular couple dance of coastal Peru patriotically renamed for the Peruvian navy after the War of the Pacific. It corresponds to the Chilean *cueca*. Though definitely a mestizo social dance, it has retained a plaintive Indian quality in its ingratiating minor melody and its curious step. In duple count against the triple beat of the music, the feet alternately step and twist, with rhythmic knee flexion. The theme of courtship is played upon by approach and withdrawal, and by manipulation of kerchiefs. The woman reacts to the man's advances one moment with scornful pride, the next with head drooping in mournful tenderness. The marinera is gayer and more hispanic than the related *cashua, huayñu,* and *sanjuanito*. [GPK]

Marjatta   In the *Kalevala* (Runo L), the mother of the child who supplants Väinämöinen. She had always lived a virgin, but one day ate a cranberry which cried out to her from the hill to come and eat "before the slug should come." When the hour of childbirth came, mother, father, and neighbor all turned her out of doors. She sought a stable in a clearing wherein to have her child, and prayed to the horse for his warm breath: "O thou good horse, breathe upon me . . ." When the horse breathed upon her, the room was filled with steam, the steam bath to ease her pain that had been refused her in all the houses.

> And a sinless child was given
> On the hay in horses' stable.

This seems to be, especially since it ends the long pagan epic, a Christian episode, Marjatta being equated with Maria, but the incident may be pagan in origin as

magical impregnation and virgin birth is a common folklore incident elsewhere than in Christian countries, and since Marja is the Finnish word for berry.

marjoram   Either of two pungent herbs (genera *Majorana* and *Origanum*) of the mint family: used in cooking and, formerly, medicinally. It was one of the "precious herbs" brought from the Old World to the New by the early settlers. In Greece and Rome bridal couples were crowned with this herb. Gerard in his *Herbal* (1597) says that sweet marjoram (*M. hortensis*) is "good for those who are given to overmuch sighing." In the doctrine of signatures marjoram was one of the herbs recommended for head ailments. It was considered a cure for headache and toothache and is still in use in England as a spring tonic. From *Origanum majorana* was made a medieval German folk tea highly recommended as an abortifacient and contraceptive. The pungent oil of the marjorams was used in perfumes, and in all manner of toilet preparations.

marked culprit   The clever miscreant of folktale, who, when marked in some way during the commission of a crime, marks everyone else and so avoids punishment (K415). The story of Ali Baba uses the motif: the robber chief marks Ali Baba's door, but the clever servant Morgiana chalks the same mark on all the neighbors' doors, thus making it impossible for the robber to recognize the house. In the second story of the third day of Boccaccio's *Decameron,* the king discovers that someone has just been in bed with the queen. He finds out who the guilty person is by feeling the pulses of the sleeping servants; the guilty groom's heart is beating rapidly. When the king clips the hair of the groom just above the ear so that he can pick him out in the morning, the groom gets up and does the same to his companions; the king is forced to let him escape with only a vague admonition. Hyena is promised a child, in a tale from East Africa. When he is about to come and get the boy, the mother gives her son a bell to tie to his ankle so that Hyena will know him. But the boy ties bells to the ankles of all his playmates and tells them to answer to his name. The mother then shaves the son's head. He shaves hers too, and when Hyena enters their hut in the darkness he seizes the mother, for she is the first person with a shaven head he encounters. The motif is found in stories from Italy, France, the Netherlands, Finland, southern Siberia, North Africa, Arabia, Africa, and elsewhere. It is related to the telltale hand-mark (H58), found in the Eskimo and the North American Indian *Sun Sister, Moon Brother* tale (A736.1). The clandestine lover is marked by the girl as he embraces her by means of paint or soot on her hands. Sun sister then pursues her marked moon brother into the skies. The marking of the night visitor is found in other North American Indian tales, e.g. *Dog Husband, Bear Woman, The Deserted Children.*

market of the dead   An element in West African tales about orphans, which characteristically figures where a mistreated child runs away from home and comes upon its dead mother at one of these centers. [MJH]

Marko   Marko Kraljević (Marko the King's Son); the great hero of South Slavic (Serbian, Yugoslavian) folk song and ballad; a historical personage who died in 1394. More than a hundred songs and ballads relate the career of this prince, from his birth to his death. Though historical references sometimes appear, they are outnumbered by the mass of folkloristic material in the poems: Biblical stories, folktales, anachronisms, etc. His deeds are those of a hero larger than life: he is stronger than other men, drinks more than any other, is firmer and crueler with women. As a ruler, Marko is just, a lover of liberty, a God-fearing fighter for the Faith. In view of the fact that Marko was really a Turkish vassal rather than a fighter for Slavic independence, and a plainsman rather than a mountaineer, his reputation as the Serbian hero of heroes is perhaps strange. The stories of the ballads of Marko often resemble other ballad stories of Europe; parallels to *Edward, The Noble Moringer,* etc., are clear. Marko ballads are known in Bulgaria and Rumania as well as Yugoslavia. See BALLAD.

marré Literally, to tie: term used in Haiti to denote proper control of a supernatural being (*loi*) of the vodun cult by a devotee: also used in connection with magic.
[MJH]

marriage The confusions found in general discussions of marriage arise because of failure to note that as marriage is a word it can be defined, whereas matrimony is a state of being or a way of life and can only be described. In the Occident the English word marriage and other words with almost identical meanings in other European languages has a fairly reasonable legal, social, and theological reference, though because of the confusion of American law a distinguished poet and critic had to ask the court to explain to him whether or not he were married and if so to whom. There is no doubt that he performed the rituals which the word marriage compactly refers to. The question for the court was to decide whether the rituals were appropriate at the time they were performed, whether they "took," and whether in the court's opinion the man was in a state of matrimony. Consequently, when observers, still uncertain about these initial confusions, examine the rituals attendent upon marriage, if any, or customs, habits, licenses, ways of life similar to those we associate with the state of matrimony, they are often tempted to make broad generalizations which further confuse the issue. Finally, when in an unknown language or through an interpreter they have to ask natives about rituals or ways of living which are unknown to both the interpreter and the natives, they produce lengthy studies invaluable for their direct observations of habits and customs, but somewhat confusing to the general reader.

An Anglican divine has described matrimony as an honorable state, instituted by God for the continuation of the race and the mutual comfort of men and women. Although the description is obviously eclectic, it serves well enough as a statement of Occidental views of the subject, for it lists the relation to divinity, the physical relations of the sexes, and the spiritual well-being which is supposed to be produced by the magic of ritual-marriage. Parts of this view seem to be accepted by many cultures in many sections of the world as well as by cultural strata in the Occident. A part of the difficulty in coming to an understanding of the comparative folklore of marriage results from the different emphases which students place on the several components of the description. The promiscuousness of Australian aborigines and

Hollywood stars differs principally in the Hollywood determination that God's blessing be conferred on each new attachment, no matter how temporary. In China the first wife and her husband kneel before the tablets of his ancestors, though the approval of the social unit to which they belong is more important than the good-will of the dead; children by secondary wives, taken informally, have all the rights and dignities of the children of the first wife. Communities where sexual promiscuity is taken for granted (examples: Chukchee, Bushman, etc.) form marriages, that is, permanent unions, comparatively late in life and the component of mutual comfort is important, whereas youngsters who indulge themselves because they "are married in the sight of God" are little concerned with the continuation of the race, more concerned by mutual comfort, though at the same time they are aware of the traditional need of divine sanction which is important in the traditions of our Occidental culture. Conversely, the justification of divorce in the Occident is frequently that the couple is "no longer married in the sight of God," that theirs is no "true marriage" with the implication that God, whose blessing they implored at the beginning of their relations, made a grievous mistake for which wives must be compensated by alimony.

The folklore of marriage is extensive. Much of it has been created by professional ethnographers, more by married folk who, puzzled by the confusions introduced by the religious, the sexual, and the social urges, have tried to make sense in a situation which is constantly disrupted by powerful impulses, each of which is good in itself.

Some of the difficulties met by writers on marriage are linguistic. Many languages have no term for marriage, wife, or husband, which refer to the several components which Occidentals consider important. Men and women observed to be living together are frequently referred to as married, though a closer investigation of their relations may show that only one of the components of marriage is present, perhaps in some minor aspect. This situation is further complicated by the very human tendency of persons being questioned to reply in terms which the questioner will understand either because of ignorance of the meaning of the question or because no term exists which will explain the relationship in a satisfactory manner.

Attempts to define marriage in terms of the length of time the relationship must endure fail because of the great diversity of custom. Thus Westermarck's definition, "a more or less durable connection between male and female lasting beyond the mere act of propagation till after the birth of the offspring," leaves much to be desired even in Occidental mores, much more in the mores of distant peoples. Many peoples do not consider propagation a "mere act" but make it central in the marriage relation. The general agreement throughout the history of Occidental culture that adultery is a justification for divorce, whether or not the adultery results in offspring, is here pertinent. Some societies in Central and British East Africa for example, do not think a girl is attractive until she has become pregnant and are indifferent as to the father. Granet has given reason to believe that the spring festivals of ancient China were promiscuous couplings with marriages taking place in the autumn.

Among some Indochinese, the Wadaba of Somaliland, and the Eskimo Aleuts, couplings are considered casual until children are born and the women undertake their duties. A survey of human custom shows that relations generally regarded as matrimonial may last for a few hours or for many years, even after death, as is seen by the custom of *suttee* in Asiatic India, the burning of papier maché concubines in China, and the Mormon belief in "sealed wives."

The ages at which marriages are contracted show similar variations. Child marriages, customary in India and Central Africa and known in the Occident, have been contracted by parents while their offspring were still in the fetal stage. Ruth Benedict reports that these marriages do not imply prepubertal sex play even in communities such as the Trobrianders where this sort of game is recognized or even encouraged. In the Admiralty Islands a child bride must cover herself with mats when she meets any male of her husband's social group. Among the West African Yoruba the child bride must prove that she has a virginity for her husband to destroy at the age of puberty. In Northern Nigeria the child bride is brought up in her husband's home, but if she has relations with him her family may take her back without returning her bride price. Late marriages are customary in the Occident, among the North American Iroquois Indians, the Masai of East Africa, and elsewhere for a variety of reasons. In the United States the husband is responsible for establishing a separate home for himself and his wife and for supporting a wife none of whose duties except sexual are well defined. Frequently he has the added responsibility of supporting a former wife or wives and their children. The Iroquois postponed marriage until the age of 30 for fear of ruining their war magic. The Masai of East Africa gave similar reasons for late marriages, although they had access to the kraals of the unmarried women, a situation which was repeated in World War II when American wives were excluded from theaters of war in which their husbands were serving, and marriages with native women were permitted by military authorities only when "necessitous," though the young men were encouraged to have casual sexual relations with native women. Some medieval bishops required their charges to be continent for a fixed period of time before attending mass; and for the greater mysteries this period was extended in Christian as well as in pagan cultures.

The physical component of marriage is thus seen not to be a "mere act" but an act with magical implications. Even in communities where sexual intercourse within a permitted group is a casual exercise, it is, on some occasions enjoined, and on others, prohibited. In many communities marriage is formal, and ritualized defloration is required. The marriage night is followed, in China and elsewhere, by a display of the bloody sheets to prove that defloration occurred. When brides are not intact, whether by accident or by the woman's promiscuity during the tumescence of courtship, the fact is, in many communities, including our own, carefully hidden. In some African communities, the chief man and his principal wife must have intercourse within a given time after the group has moved to a new location. Communities with orgiastic customs frequently require general and promiscuous intercourse as calendrial ritual though in many of them, too, this promiscuity follows a period of enforced continence.

Human marriage customs are frequently projected into natural phenomena by a sort of "pathetic fallacy." Thus the sun in many places is thought to marry and fertilize the earth. In China heaven does it. When these unions are calendrial holidays, ceremonies are performed to fix the act, increase its potency, and rejoice with the newly united or reunited couple.

Symbolic marriages are known in many parts of the world. In the Occident proxy marriages are performed and recognized by the ecclesiastical and civil authorities when the two principals cannot be together but a marriage is necessary either to protect the rights of the unborn child or to save the reputation of the pregnant woman. The temple prostitutes of India were married to a dagger, which possibly, at one time or another, was thought of as a phallus. On New Year's Eve the Germans tied trees together with ropes, said that they were married, and hoped for increased production. In parts of India the shrub *tulasi* represents a goddess and is annually married to Krishna or his image. Frazer, remembering that Pliny embraced a beech in a grove sacred to Diana and lay under its shade and sacrificed wine to it, speculates that the priest of Nemi embraced the tree he guarded as though it were his wife. Ceremonial marriages of nuns to Christ and such terms as the "bride of Christ" also refer to symbolic marriages.

The Occidental capacity for irony is demonstrated by the Occidental emphasis on the physical component of cohabitation and at the same time the effort to "solemnize" marriage by invoking divine sanctions. In other communities the casual couplings of men and women are taken for granted and matrimony exists only when each undertakes duties and work traditionally appropriate to husband and wife in that community. Whether this occurs late in the relationship or early is determined partly by tradition and partly, no doubt, too, by impulses which are difficult to analyze. In the Occident, though woman's work is never done, failure to do that work has only recently been recognized, and in scattered areas only has it been accepted as cause for divorce. For years divorce has been granted only on grounds of adultery and marriages have been annulled only if it could be proved that cohabitation has not occurred.

The folklore about matrimony created by married people themselves is in part due to the difficulty of adjusting themselves individually to the powerful sexual, social, and religious impulses which matrimony involves and then in adjusting each other to them. This folklore is to be found in beliefs and behavior patterns too numerous to be touched on here. They range from firm beliefs about how frequently intercourse is permissible within the limits of decency, whether either partner should see the other in a state of nakedness, the goodbye kiss in the morning, the observance of anniversaries, and the appropriate behavior on days and seasons appropriate for marriage, appropriate ages, and the like on those occasions. Though these may seem to be trivial, they constitute for small or large groups that "severely objectified network of historically determined patterns" which Sapir called "custom."

A paging through the other articles in this publication will disclose attitudes toward marriage and matrimony which, by their amazing variety, will at first bewilder the reader. A partial understanding of them is possible only when one dissociates oneself from the "wegroup" which is always right because it is ours and recognizes that the "they-group" lives according to patterns of belief which are in many ways similar to our own. But because patterns of custom and belief are so deeply a part of our characters it is difficult to make this transition in an evaluation of the general folklore of marriage and matrimony. See ABDUCTION; AMASIADO; BEAST MARRIAGE; BRIDE; CECROPS; section on *Marriage* in CHINESE FOLKLORE; COMMONLAW; HIEROS GAMOS; KEEPERS; SVAYAMVARA. R. D. JAMESON

☞ Marriage as a social institution, or a ceremony, is seldom accounted for in North American Indian mythologies, but knowledge of intercourse, and how such knowledge was obtained by the first human couple or by young persons, is fairly frequently mentioned in myths. Often tales explaining how people first learned to have intercourse and procreate contain mention of misplaced genitalia; other tales, such as the Zuñi story of "The Boy Who Had to Learn to Marry," have no such mythical setting, but are told of young virgins—in this case, a boy whose grandmother makes him ready for marriage by sleeping with him herself. The Shawnee state that such a practice was actually followed in former times; young Shawnee boys and girls were initiated into sexual intercourse by old men or old women.

Tales concerning the courtship and marriage of specific beings, either human or supernatural, are abundant in American Indian mythology. Daughters are sent by their families to marry good hunters; youths and girls are too proud to marry and ill fortune befalls them; girls court men; a poor boy marries and turns out to be a great hunter; Coyote and other tricksters court and marry women under false pretenses; young men seek desirable girls and have a series of tests imposed on them, or the reverse situation occurs, especially in Southwestern tales; girls or youths marry supernatural beings, a man marries a fox, a buffalo, a dog or a deerwoman; Sedna, the Eskimo heroine, marries a bird (or dog). All these and many more tales of marriage are abundant in the large body of American Indian mythology.

Marriage among the American Indians was usually based on contracts between two families, although elopements and marriages based on individual choice were not unknown social phenomena. Contract-type marriages were arranged by either the bride's or the groom's family; exchange of goods and native currency between the two families was customary. Child betrothal was often practiced. The marriage ceremony itself ranges from practically none at all, to fairly elaborate ceremonies in which the couple eat together and have prayers recited over them, to the very elaborate, wealth-displaying marriage ceremonies of the North Pacific Coast nobility. The newly married couple may live with either the bride's or groom's family after marriage, temporarily or permanently, or live by themselves; if the latter, relatives often build their first home for them before they are married. A girl was, generally speaking, considered ready for marriage after she had reached puberty, and the girl's puberty dance of many western tribes functioned as an announcement that the girl was now ready to be married; a youth was considered ready after he had demonstrated his ability to hunt successfully.

Polygyny and polyandry (multiple wives or multiple husbands) both occurred, the former more generally, all over North America except in the Southwest. There, among the Pueblo peoples especially, monogamy was and is the rule, but divorce is a relatively simple matter; the wife puts the man's personal belongings outside the door of their dwelling, and the man by this token knows that he has been divorced. Grounds for divorce among the American Indians were barrenness of the woman, scolding on the part of the woman, physical cruelty and failure to provide on the part of the man, laziness on the part of either spouse. [EWV]

☞ The Catholic service has supplanted indigenous rites in most parts of Mexico and Central America. Where ancient forms are still found, they usually involve the use of the *pedidor* or "go-between" who, speaking for the boy or his father, asks the parents of the girl for her hand in marriage. If this is granted the suitor usually is expected to work for the girl's father, either bringing him firewood and other presents, or laboring in his fields for a stipulated length of time before the marriage. Actual marriage ceremonies usually are simple, involving feasting for both families. Anciently members of the priestly class often lectured the young couple on their duties and responsibilities as spouses and parents. Among many groups today godparents are expected to do this. [GMF]

Marsk Stig The hero of a sequence of Danish ballads; like Robin Hood, a champion of the people against the tyrannous king Eric. [MEL]

Marsyas In Greek mythology, a Phrygian satyr or silenus, associated with the river Marsyas, a tributary of the Meander in Asia Minor. Athena had invented the aulos, an oboe-like instrument (often called a flute); but when she saw how it distorted her cheeks while she played she threw it away. Marsyas picked up the instrument, risking the beating that Athena gave him. He learned to play so well that he challenged Apollo to a musical contest. The god, playing the lyre backwards (upside down), which Marsyas could not do with his instrument, won the competition and, in keeping with the agreement that the winner might do as he pleased with the loser, tied Marsyas to a pine or a plane tree and flayed him alive for his presumption. The river was said to have come either from Marsyas' blood or from the tears of his companions. Within historical times his skin was displayed in Asia Minor. The whole story seems to be etiological. Some see in it the conflict between aulic and citharic music. Marsyas, as a Phrygian figure of myth, naturally became associated with Midas, who is said to have been a judge of the contest with Apollo, and whose ass's ears resulted from his vote for Marsyas. S. Reinach, seeing a relationship between the flaying, the ass's ears, and the preservation of the skin, postulates the sacrifice of a sacred ass as underlying the myth; and Jane Harrison (*ERE* xi: 514) adds that the *peau d'âne* of French literature may originate here. See MIDAS.

Martin Krpàn Slovene peasant hero of the region of Istria; a salt smuggler who found favor with the Viennese emperor, had quite a career attending the emperor in Vienna, but finally asked for and was granted the boon of going home to his farm and the right to import salt free. Martin Krpàn was the typical strongman folk hero, and has been regarded by some scholars as a kind of personification of the Slovene people.

Martinmas The feast day of St. Martin, November 11, celebrated especially in Europe and the British Isles. St. Martin, patron saint of France (especially Tours), patron saint of tavern-keepers, beggars, and vine-growers, and of drinking and reformed drunkards, was born in Pannonia, Hungary, about 316, died 397. He was elected Bishop of Tours about 374. When he heard that he was elected it is said that he hid himself in a stall but was discovered by a goose who noised the discovery. This is one of the stories told to explain why his day is celebrated on the Continent with roast goose.

The legend of St. Martin's cloak is probably the most famous connected with him. One cold day at the gates of Amiens in Gaul, Martin divided his cloak with a shivering beggar. His half is kept as a relic. The story of the wine cup passed by the Emperor Maximus at a feast to honor Martin, and passed on by Martin to a humble priest, is another familiar tale.

Martinmas falls at the time of year when fodder is scarce and the seasonal slaughtering of cattle takes place. J. A. MacCulloch considers the Irish invitation to Martin to join the feast as a transference to him of some earlier primitive sacrificial slaughtering and propitiation of an animal-god. (In Ireland if you have roast goose for dinner on Martinmas, St. Martin is invited to dine. Whoever omits this invitation will get no more goose himself for a year.) Irish legend also says that Martin was cut up and eaten in the form of an ox. This carries over into Scotland and parts of England also, where an ox, called a *mart,* serves for the feast.

In Ireland the blood of animals is always shed on Martinmas and meat is traditionally eaten. Wild birds or domestic fowl are killed, or a sheep, lamb, kid, pig, calf, or cow is killed on St. Martin's Eve and eaten on St. Martin's Day with special prayers. The blood of this animal is sprinkled in the four corners of the house, on the threshold, walls, and floor, and a little is smeared on the forehead of each member of the family. This keeps evil from the dwelling and its inmates and is potent for one year to the day. Aran Islanders tell a story of St. Martin, that on his travels he came to the house of a poor woman and asked for food. She had no meat for the stranger but sacrificed her child. Martin ate what was offered, and when he left the house the woman found her child asleep in the cradle, alive and well. The people say it is gratitude for this miracle which obligates them to sacrifice a living thing on Martinmas. And roast cock or goose is fed to any beggar who comes to the door on November 11.

Martinmas, falling as it does at a time when the crops are all in, surplus animals are killed, and new wine is opened, is a feast of thanksgiving and great cheer. Thus St. Martin is a saint of cheer and conviviality and the medieval Martinmas has been likened by some writers to the ancient Vinalia, with Martin in the role of Bacchus. Those who got drunk on new wine at Martinmas were called Martinmen. In France and Germany children set out jugs or vessels of water on St. Martin's night, praying "Martin, Martin/ Change the water into *vin.*" The parents do this instead, and also leave a little Martin's horn beside the jug, to be found in the morning. These little horn-shaped cakes of St. Martin are said to be a survival in northern Europe of Odin's harvest cakes. Formerly in Swabia the children gave their teachers gifts on Martinmas—usually a live goose decorated with ribbons, some corn to feed the goose, a jug of wine, and a huge cake. In Dunkirk there is a legend that "the whole populace goes mad" on Martinmas from 5 to 7 P.M., re-enacting the ancient search for St. Martin's stray donkey, which took place in that village in 386. The people run around with paper lanterns and tooting penny horns to call the ass. The penny horns represent the fisherman's trumpet that was used on the original occasion.

In Yorkshire, England, groups of women singers formerly went from house to house in the villages on Martinmas, carrying an image of the Christ adorned with evergreens, and singing songs of the Nativity. This is said to have taken place every night between Martinmas and Christmas Eve. They were entertained in the houses with cakes and furmety. English children still go about in some sections soliciting apples and nuts and chanting "Martin is a good man/ He'll repay you if he can."

In Ireland no fisherman would go fishing on St. Martin's Eve or St. Martin's Day. If any one did, he would meet a horseman riding over the sea towards him, followed by a destroying storm. It was also wrong to turn any kind of wheel on St. Martin's Day—mill wheel or cart wheel or spinning wheel. Misfortune came upon those who ignored this prohibition.

There is a good deal of weather lore associated with Martinmas. In the English Midlands, the weather on St. Martin's Eve indicates the kind of weather to expect for the next two months. In England generally if St. Martin's Day is fine, the winter will be cold; if there is frost before Martinmas the winter will be mild. There is a saying that "if the goose slips on the ice at Martinmas, she will stick in the mud at Christmas." The balmy weather of early November in Europe is called St. Martin's summer.

In France in the days when vaccination was still a terror to the people, prayers to St. Martin to save from smallpox were thought to be an efficacious substitute. St. Martin also saves from sudden death.

Mārttāṇḍa In Vedic mythology, the sun; the son of Aditi by the sun; her eighth son, whom she cast away; one of the Ādityas.

marujas Literally, sailors: a Portuguese religious dance (*dança dos marujas*) performed by boys enacting a sailors' drama of escape and gratitude to the Virgin. [GPK]

Marunogere Deity and culture hero of Kiwai Papuan (Melanesian) mythology, associated with the first pig. He created the first coconut tree, among his many "firsts" for mankind, built the first men's house, inaugurated the *moguru* ceremony. He has two ferocious dogs who live with him in Adiri, the afterworld, and come forth to raid the villages. See G. Landtman, *The Kiwai Papuans of British New Guinea,* London, 1927. [KL]

Maruts In Vedic mythology, the storm gods, allies of Indra, who ride on golden cars gleaming with lightning. They are variously sons of Rudra and the earth-cow, Pṛithivī; the sons and brothers of Indra; in the *Rāmāyana* and the *Purāṇas,* they rose from an unborn son of Diti, shattered into 49 pieces by Indra. They are represented as warriors, 21, 180, or 27 in number, armed with spears, wearing helmets, riding the winds, shattering the trees of the forest, or killing men with their lightning. They also have a beneficent aspect in that they bring healing remedies.

Mary Celeste A brigantine, built in Nova Scotia in 1861 as the *Amazon*, and found drifting abandoned by all hands, between the Azores and Portugal in 1872. The case of the *Mary Celeste* is so puzzling, and leads so to conjecture, that many attempts, literary and otherwise, have been made to explain it. At the beginning of November, 1872, she sailed for Genoa from Boston with a cargo of alcohol. On December 4, she was met by the *Dei Gratia*, boarded, and sailed as a derelict to Gibraltar. The *Mary Celeste* flew no distress signal; her sails still stood, though somewhat disordered; her compass was broken; the crew had left without oilskins and pipes; the ship's register, its sextant and chronometer were missing. One of the boarding sailors said that she seemed to have been abandoned in a hurry, from the evidence aboard. Water had caused some damage, as if the ship had been struck by a wave. But beyond the physical fact that the ship still sailed and that no one was aboard, nothing definite has ever been brought forward to show what happened on the *Mary Celeste*. Writers and yarners soon filled the tale out. The ship was doomed to hard luck; she had stuck on the ways when being launched. When the *Dei Gratia* met her all sails were set; the wash still hung on the line; the chronometer was ticking away; in the mate's cabin there was a slip of paper on the table with an unfinished addition on it; a sheet of music was in place on the skipper's wife's melodeon; in her sewing machine a child's pinafore was being stitched; an opened but unspilled medicine bottle was on the table; in the dining room coffee, bacon, oatmeal, and a hardboiled egg were on the table. Yet the crew had abandoned ship completely and hurriedly; there was no sign of violence. Still further folklore says that all the ship's boats were in place on deck; but in fact the ship had carried only one boat, instead of the usual two, on this voyage, and that boat was missing. The two most plausible explanations, according to George S. Bryan (*Mystery Ship: The* Mary Celeste *in Fancy and in Fact*), are that a slight explosion of alcohol fumes in the hold frightened the crew into the boat and that the bowline parted; or that the crew tried to abandon ship when it seemed she would pile up in the Azores, and were lost in the surf. The *Mary Celeste* finally was lost on a reef off Haiti in 1885 under suspicious circumstances. The trial of captain and owners, for an attempt to defraud insurance companies by deliberate wrecking of a ship carrying a phony cargo, ended in a jury disagreement.

Masān In Hindu belief, a hideous black demon or ghost who comes from the ashes of the funeral pyre and afflicts children with disease, especially with consumption, by throwing funeral ashes over them. The Masān is usually regarded as the spirit of a child, but in the northern hills it is said to wander about in the guise of a bear. In the Punjab the shroud of a child who dies from consumption is washed, preserved, and placed under the next child born to protect it from the disease.

Masauwü Hopi Indian god of death, war, fire, and night: a towering figure, the first denizen of Hopiland, conspicuously individualized and of paramount impor-

tance in the Hopi pantheon. Masauwü is the prototype for a Hopi society, the chief of which impersonates the god in a masked dance. After a burial the Hopi mark four parallel lines with cedar charcoal, in four places across the trail back from the grave, to "close the way" against this god. Masauwü is not found in any non-Hopi pueblo; at Laguna the name occurs, but the indentification is with the War Brothers. See AHAYUTA ACHI. [EWV]

mascaradas A masquerade of the French Basques of Soule, loosely related to the Moriscas. During the last weeks before Lent the performances are assiduously rehearsed for carnival time. First there is a procession of the characters: *rouges,* reds (see PYRRHIC DANCE), the beautiful or good ones; and *noirs,* blacks, the uncouth ones. (See PERCHTEN.) The *rouges* include the following characters: Zamalzain, a hobbyhorse; Kantiniersa or Vivandera, a man-woman; Cherrero, a pig-man; Gatuzain, a cat-man; Señor, a Lord; Señorita, a Lady; Enseñeria, a banner-bearer.

The performance itself starts with a mock barricade between the two factions. The reds dance branles: a *branli haustia,* gavotte, and a farandoule-type serpentine. One by one they exhibit fantastically dexterous leaps. They conclude with a "snail." Then the blacks perform the *fonctions,* first as burlesque on the display by the reds, then by original tricks over a glass of wine. Their hobbyhorse is the star, the most dexterous dancer. In the end he loses his strength by being shod by a gelder, then recovers.

This conglomeration of personages and dance figures combines all of the fertility symbols: transvestite, leap, serpentine, and battle of two factions; it formerly contained more vivid enactments of resurrection mime. [GPK]

maschalismos An ancient Greek practice; the cutting off of the hands, feet, nose, ears, etc., of the victim by his murderer, stringing them together, and tying them under the armpits of the corpse: an attempt to avoid retribution by making it impossible for the ghost to follow the slayer. The piercing of the feet of Œdipus when he was abandoned as an infant may have had some such reason underlying it. Similar customs prevail in many parts of the world to avoid the attentions of the unfriendly dead. In the Moluccas, the body of a woman dying in childbirth is buried with pins stuck through the several joints and with eggs placed under the chin and armpits; it is believed that the dead fly as birds and that the presence of the eggs will influence the maternal instinct and prevent the ghost from leaving the body. Generally in Europe, suicides were buried with a stake driven through the heart, or with the head cut off and placed between the legs; still practiced in many parts of Britain and the Continent is the tying together of the feet or the large toes of the dead. The Omaha slit the soles of the feet of those killed by lightning; the Basuto and Bechuana slit the sinews and spinal cord of the dead; the Herbert River aborigines of Australia beat the body, often breaking the bones, and filled incisions made in it with stones.

mascot A person, animal, amulet, etc., thought to bring good luck to a household, sports team, or the like: literally, little magician, from Provençal *masco,* sorceress. The mascot of a baseball team in the United States is usually a young boy who wears the team uniform and is thought to be the luck of the team in miniature. The animal mascots of American colleges are chosen for the nicknames of the athletic teams: the Army mule, the Navy goat, the Yale bulldog, the Columbia lion, the Princeton tiger. Sometimes, as in the latter instance, the students merely masquerade as the animal. So too, many fliers, automobile-race drivers, or even ordinary automobilists, have mascots in the form of toy animals, baby shoes, luck medals, etc., attached to their instrument boards or windshields, in the belief that the mascot will avert dangerous accidents. In southern France, gamblers' mascots are amulets: a coin with a hole in it, a bit of coral, etc.

Masewi or **Masewa** Son of the Mothers of the various Keresan pueblos; a fairly prominent character in Cochiti and other Keresan mythologies. It was Masewi who was sent into the universe by his Mother to place the sun properly in the sky. In a Cochiti myth Masewi and his brother Oyoyewa take charge of the contest between Naotsiti, Mother of the Navaho, and Uretsiti (Iareku), Mother of the Cochiti. At the time of the emergence from Shipap, Masewa led the people up; it was he who told them where to go and what to call their pueblos. See AHAYUTA ACHI. [EWV]

Mashya and Mashyoi In Persian mythology, the first human pair. In the first millennium, according to the *Būndahishn,* a double plant was produced from the semen of Gaya Maretan. From the ten leaves of this tree came the ten varieties of mythical men—those of the earth, those of the water, the one-legged, the breast-eared, the breast-eyed, those who have bat wings, the tail, and those with hair on the body. The vegetable then passed into human form as a couple. Because they worshipped Angra Mainyu instead of Ahura Mazda they became the prey of the druj for fifty winters and had no intercourse. After that they had a pair of children which they immediately devoured. Ahura Mazda interfered with this procedure and the pair did not eat the seven pairs of children which followed. Mashya and Mashyoi died when they reached the age of 100. Their children, after a period of fifty years, brought forth the 15 races of mankind.

masks The function of masks varies from society to society, so that few generalizations can be made either as to their form or uses. They are undoubtedly very old. Not only do we have early Greek and Egyptian masks, but there is reason to believe that the figure known as the "Sorcerer" from the cave of Trois Frères, in Ariège, France, which depicts an erect reindeerlike form standing on human feet, and which dates from Paleolithic times, may represent an early form of masking. Masks figure in recreational activities, they are worn by healers, employed to disguise members of secret societies, used in the worship of the gods, and to convey authority. They are made of all manner of materials, are carved or painted, or both; they may be large or small; in one piece or with moving parts; they may be realistic or highly conventionalized. They may be worn in front of the face or carried on top of the head; they may form part of a whole costume, or be worn by themselves. In many cultures, masks are a primary art-form, the finest artists lavishing their best technical and esthetic competence on their production. The African mask, derived from the Congo and western Africa, was the inspiration of much of "modern" French painting, while the masks

of the Iroquois healing societies, of the Kwakiutl Indian religious groups, of the Melanesian ancestral cults, and the like, have achieved a comparable, though somewhat more restricted, fame. Various theories, historical and psychological, have been put forward to explain the wide distribution of the use of masks, but none seems to be more than speculation. As in the case of explanations of other similar phenomena, it is likely that all theories have some degree of validity, but that none will hold for all cases, or even in any given case. [MJH]

☞ Masks carved from wood, molded from clay, woven from basketry materials, bark, or braided corn shucks, or made from cloth or hide are used by the Eskimo and by many North American Indian tribes, usually for religious ceremonies, girls' puberty ceremonies, or in doctoring, to represent male, female, or animal supernatural beings. Masks are either simple as the False Faces of the Delaware and some Eskimo masks, or elaborately decorated with shell, bark fiber, hair, herbs, feathers or down; many are painted symbolically, as on the North Pacific Coast and in the Southwest. Mechanically some American Indian masks are quite elaborate, being provided with an interior device by which the eyes or mouth can be opened or closed; or different parts of the mask are so hinged that the wearer can change its aspect. The wood carvers of the North Pacific Coast excelled in making such elaborate masks; they and the Eskimo also made compound masks with double faces, the outer of a bird or animal, the inner of a human being. The outer mask was held in place by pegs, and could be quickly removed at a certain point in the ceremony when a supernatural being was supposed to change from animal to human form.

In the Southwestern pueblos, where masked dances are customary during the half of the year that the kachinas are visiting on earth, there are many proscriptions for the handling of dance masks. Hopi mask painters, for example, must purify themselves before painting the masks, and Hopi masks must be put on and taken off with the left hand only. Masks are not always worn over the face by the Pueblos; some are carried on poles; some set in a row to form altars and "fed" with sacred cornmeal. In certain Eskimo ceremonies also, women wore masks on the fingers of one hand.

The chief masked ceremony of the Central Eskimo was the thanksgiving festival in the fall, to banish disease and ensure hunters success. The North Pacific Coast winter ceremonial season saw many masked dances given, including the Hamatsa or Cannibal Society initiation. Shamans in this region also wore masks when curing patients and during doctors' contests. Masked dancers representing the gahe or supernaturals lead the dancing in the girls' puberty ceremony of the Chiricahua and other Apache groups of the Southwest. In the pueblos dance masks are sometimes referred to as kachinas, since many masks represented these ancestral and mythical beings, and the youth who danced in such a mask was temporarily transformed into the kachina represented. Hopi men sometimes invoked their masks, thanking them for favors conferred. Some Hopi masks belong to clan groups and are kept by them. No uninitiated child may look upon a kachina dancer with his mask removed, and pregnant women must not touch certain masks. A simple mask is put over the face of the dead by the Hopi.

The Iroquois tribes of the Eastern Woodlands, besides

using False Faces, carved grotesque wooden heads and masks of male and female supernatural beings, some of them, as the Flying Heads, notable for their distorted or twisted lips and glaring or drooping eyes.

On the lighter side, young people in some tribes made queer masks in play or festivities; poor boys among some of the Siouan tribes made masks of bladder or rawhide representing the head of the Thunderbird, when the first thunder was heard in the spring. Donning these, they called on their uncles, imitated the sound of thunder, and collected presents. On the Northwest Coast masks were occasionally made as children's toys, as figures of the kachinas are made for Pueblo children. See KACHINA; GAHE; FALSE FACES. [EWV]

🖝 Masks are worn by dancers in a great number of South American tribes from the Guianas to Tierra del Fuego. Unfortunately the function of the masks is not always clear. The Ona, Yahgan, and Chamacoco use masks during their initiation rites to impersonate demons and frighten the women. The masks of the Caraja represented animals and were displayed during feasts which coincided with the harvest of wild fruits or successful fishing and hunting parties. Masks were also a distinctive feature of the dances performed by the Indians of the Upper Xingu. Symbolic motifs painted on bark cloth represented various animals. In the tropical area the most famous masked dances were those of the Arawakan and Tucanoan tribes of the basin of the Caiari-Uaupes. They took place after a death. Individuals dressed in bark-cloth masks impersonated demons and spirits. They simulated an attack on the funerary house and, after having been repulsed, executed a phallic pantomime. The whole ceremony has been interpreted as a ritual propitiation of the ghosts and demons who might have caused the death.

Dancers wearing masks appeared also in the girls' puberty feasts of the Chaco. Likewise the most spectacular episode in the puberty ceremonies of the Tucuna was the appearance of the guests hidden under huge masks representing demons and animals. The masked persons asked for drinks and then vanished into the forest.

Paintings on the Mochica vases give us an idea of the elaborate masks which were used by the ancient Peruvians during their ceremonial dances. The fiestas of the modern Indians of Peru and Bolivia owe much of their color and interest to the grotesque masks worn by groups of dancers. [AM]

🖝 In relation to folk and primitive dance, a mask is a disguise which transforms the wearer, hides or heightens his personality, or identifies him with the character of the mask. Costumes, gestures, and actions conform to this character, in order to produce a definite result.

Purpose: Impersonations of deified natural forces, totemic or chthonic spirits of the dead, totemic, hunted, or phallic animals, respected or derided human beings, serve purposes that are variously purgative or constructive for: 1) Arousal of a desired emotion (bravery, self-esteem, prophetic trance); 2) Exorcism of baneful spirits in curative, puberty, and agricultural rites, by frightening them with a more horrific and powerful identity; 3) Coercion of favorable spirits by identification and propitiation for health, hunt, crops, and other necessities of life; 4) Social prestige, by membership in ex-

clusive totemic societies; 5) Moral control and social therapy, by fright or burlesque; 6) Entertainment by presentation of stories, sacred or secular, or by laughter-producing satire. Usually more than one motive is involved. These objectives do not include mortuary or protective masks, which do not produce dance expressions.

The purpose is identified with its plastic expression. The materials and forms depend on natural resources, native flora and fauna, on technical advancement as well as imaginative endowment, and particularly on the vitality of the purpose. Forms range from realism to fantastic aberration or abstraction, expressions from monstrous to beatific, sizes from the finger masks of Kwakiutl and Eskimo women to Ivory Coast towers five yards high, covering the partial face, entire head, or the entire body.

Materials: 1) Natural materials. Actual animal heads were the earliest kind of mask, as shown in paleolithic cave-paintings of France, and are retained today in the Taos Deer dance. A Mexican armadillo shell also may suggest a face and become a mask by the insertion of two eye-holes. Hides can be shaped into face-coverings or helmets. Other accessible raw materials are gourds (Papago, Nigeria), grass (Pomo), raffia (Africa), leaves (California, Brazil, early England), feathers (Pomo, Arunta of Australia). Fabrications from raw materials include bark cloth (Amazonas, New Ireland, New Guinea), basketry (Florida Key dwellers), petate (Mexico), corn husks, twined or braided (Iroquois).

2) Plastic materials. Ivory (Africa), shell and bone (Mexico), and above all, wood, are the basis of the sculptural arts of West Africa, western Europe, Mexico, the Iroquois Indians, North Pacific Coast tribes, and Eskimo (driftwood). Precious stones are found in ancient and modern Mexican masks (obsidian, alabaster, jade, lignite, serpentine, turquoise mosaic).

3) Ceramics in Ceylon, Java, Japan, Mexico.

4) Metals are of fairly recent use as mask material except in the Far East: gold and silver (Ceylon, Incas, Zapotecs), brass, bronze (Cameroon), copper (Mexico), tin (Mexico, Iroquois, and others).

5) Decadent substitutions. Besides tin, also cloth, papier maché (especially Mexico), newspaper (English mummers).

6) Accessories. Human or horse hair, fur, feathers, beads, teeth, beans, wool, flowers, ribbons, bits of mirror for light-reflecting eyes of demons, or for inlay, paint on the face, body, or mask.

These materials have cultural significance; i.e. hide is handy in a hunting culture on plains devoid of forests; wood implies a forest environment, and the corn husk a maize economy.

Plastic Forms: Though the human face furnishes the starting point for most masquerading, realistic representations are exceedingly rare. Distortion of features, or mingling with animal attributes, and symbolic designs strive for supernatural identification to the point of complete animal metamorphosis, monstrosity, or abstraction. Only in mortuary masks and sophisticated drama does the modeling emphasize human characteristics.

1) Distorted human features for demoniac impersonation: Primitive tribes manipulate the face itself instead of superimposing a mask—the California Yuki *hulk'ilal-*

wokam, ghost impersonators, achieve a monstrous appearance by stuffing grass in each cheek, a slit twig in each nostril and lower lip, concealing the upper part of the face with false hair of maple bark and a wreath of leaves, and the body with black horizontal stripes.

In true masks, one of the features or all may be distorted for a specified purpose. Iroquois and Delaware False Faces frequently have thick lips like a duck's bill; the "door keepers" may have spoon lips or the "common faces" have funnels for blowing ashes. The whistling Wind God and some corn husk faces have a long snout like the Navaho Whistling God and the Mexican Wind God. False-face mouths may droop or wear a grotesque grin like the Greek comedian. In the Belgian Congo, Baluba spirits combine a square funnel with stylized spiny wrinkles, which are also common among False Faces. Protruding tongues, teeth, tusks, and popeyes produce a ghastly demonic mien in Borneo, Africa, Ceylon, Mexico *(tecuanes),* among the Iroquois, and in Austria *(Perchten).* Most African features are symmetrical, but Japanese and Chinese theatrical demons may have a lopsided chin or nose, and the *Perchten* and False Faces often wear a twisted face, the former to terrify, the latter by an origin legend of a supernatural contest. Long projecting noses serve burlesque among the Eskimos, the Yaqui *(chapayekas),* Papago *(djidjur),* the Iroquois *(hagonde's,* reminiscent of Longnose, the trickster, the frightener of children). Ear flaps attached to wooden or hide cylinders appear in the Amazonas and Malay ancestor masks, most consistently in the American Southwest ceremonial clowns. Hair is rarely attached in Asia, sometimes in Africa, regularly on the head of False Faces and as a beard and protruding brow on *pascolas.* Mexicans use beards and mustaches for burlesque of the European invaders, either as small twiddly mustaches or as the large hook-shaped beards of the *chinelos.*

2) Theriomorphic features: In European medieval carnivals, hairiness characterized animal demons, in fact hair covered the entire body of the wild men and continues to cover the Thracian *kalogheroi* and the *Rautschegetten.* The *Perchten* achieve a particularly awe-inspiring aspect by combination of furriness with distorted human features. Horns are also a universal theriomorphic attribute, as for the *Perchten* and *diablo.* In the Belgian Congo an antelope initiation mask may have abstract human features and graceful tall horns. In French Guinea a sylvan divinity may wear multiple vertical horns. So do the Apache gahe or crown dancers who represent mountain supernaturals. The horned Elel of Patagonian Puelche, on the other hand, represents the spirit of evil analogous to the horned Devil of medieval drama and the *diablo* of the Mexican carnival.

The identity of man, beast, and supernatural is expressed in a curious way by the Kwakiutl and Bella Coola—in the form of compound masks with an animal form (eagle, raven, wolf) or several animal forms on the outside and an inner human face within. This symbolizes the primal dual existence of animals as men. By nasal elongation, Liberian sylvan divinities and Yaqui *pascolas* blend human and animal features. Again, the Bapende of the Belgian Congo attach an elephant tusk to a human face. The European hobbyhorse, usually fastened to the wearer's hips, appears in Padstow, Cornwall, as a ghostly black frame with a small eerie head.

3) Animal representations: Beyond the stage of donning an actual head, the deification of animal spirits has created a wealth of forms realistic and stylized, birds with tremendous beaks, as the vultures of the Mexican *tlacoloteros,* the curved eagle beaks of the Pueblos, and Tlingit and Haida shamans, the great mobile Kwakiutl raven-beak ornamented with polychrome designs. Hybrid beasts move gaping jaws in Africa, as the horned dog of northern Cameroon, and the horse-antelope of the Gold Coast, and as the killer whale and wolf on the American North Pacific Coast. Each part of the world teems with native potent creatures, not only the common bear, buffalo, deer, but the Arctic walrus, and the tropical alligator and monkey, the wild phallic trains of pigs, goats, bulls in the carnivals of the Middle Ages, of Thrace, Spain, and Mexico. Stylization develops with cultural formalization, but may survive in various stages within one culture. The deer mask, which in Taos is realistic, and at San Ildefonso and San Juan is stylized, has at Hopi reached complete abstraction, with a realistic vestige only in the pair of antlers.

4) Unearthly beings: The fear and fascination of death fired the imagination of the medieval Europeans and Aztecs, to the creation of grinning skulls of bone, pottery, or mosaic. Featureless coverings evoke ghostly connotations from the African Whydah to the modern child's Halloween sheet. In New Ireland the ancestors appear as gigantic geometric phantasmagoria. Among the Pueblos, the helmet masks of the *shiwanna* merely suggest human features with circles, squares, or triangles, and for the rest are covered with colorful unsymmetrical designs conjuring rain and fertility from these ancestral divinities. The Zuñi *shalako* mountain spirits impersonate these unearthly beings by their gigantic size and the shedding of all features but for a tremendous beak.

In contrast with the flat pictorial devices of the American Southwest, Chinese and Ceylonese mask artists mold fearful creatures out of discordant combinations of animal and human features; and West African tribes abstract the human face into plastic patterns by elongation, protrusion, hollowing, intersection of planes, attached flaring forms, open-work rays representing the sun god, by coercive symbolic incisions and relief. Double masks represent, in the divided False Face, a god half human and half supernatural, in association with emergence or life and submergence or death; in Mexico they are life and death, in Africa, as Janus masks, they combine the male and female principles. Multiple demons on Ceylonese headdresses overwhelm the human features, as do the animal beings on the heads of some Yoruba and Ibo masks and the superstructures teaming with small gods, or with people enacting the tribal activities.

5) Heightened human realism: Whereas divine drama at its apex produces phantasmagoria, the enactment of human tribulations and foibles intensifies natural expressions. In ancient Greece typical emotions of grief and laughter were stylized and enlarged into the tragic and comic masks. Stock characters are superbly delineated in the Japanese *Nō* (the scowling villain, bulbous old man, serene lady). Comic masks of the Orient, as the Balinese *topeng* dancers, and of Mexico, as the Tarascan *viejitos,* exaggerate toothless foolish grins into shrewd formalized designs. In the Occident, crystallized expression and character have been re-created in modern

dance dramas, as Talhoff's "Totenmahl," and in the famous Benda dance masks.

Technique and Faith: The true ritual mask fuses the mystic purpose, the creative procedure, and the resultant forms. A host of beliefs affect the formative process, beliefs concerning the creature inherent in the mask, its origin and reaction to treatment. The Seneca (Iroquois) must carve his supernatural out of a living tree and on all occasions of use or transference must address him with tobacco invocations. The African carver works through ritually established stages. Everywhere the mask itself has the supernatural's potency for ill as well as good.

Every detail of form and ornament is derived from the attributes of the Being: jagged lightning, bulbous clouds, and interlaced serpents from meteoric and chthonic attributes; pointed headdresses, single or doubled into horns, from phallic potencies. Colors, too, refer to his qualities. White, the ghost color, outlines the eyes and mouth of African masks, and together with black, covers the bodies of the *koshare* and of the Pomo Thunder dancers. Red and black symbolize the human and supernatural division of the Iroquois Great Defender, as he comes from the east and leaves in the west. Yellow and red portend the lightning brought by the *potrshrovisht shiwanna*, and the corn-colors—white, red, blue, and yellow—identified with the four heavenly directions, depict the *ye'i* and *kachina* power over the earth and sky for human welfare.

The myriad designs have produced remarkable virtuosity in all cultural stages with full-fledged faith. The primitive fox and walrus of the Alaskan Eskimo are as expressive in their exquisite simplicity as the superbly distorted Iroquois *gagǫ́sä*, the abstract Bundu cult masks of Sierra Leone, and the surrealist monsters of British Columbia. Economy or effervescence of design may appeal to different tastes, with equal artistic validity. Deterioration haunts the craftsman only with the coming of the trader and his demand for garish colors and multiplication of sacred effigies intended, originally, for one and only one significant occasion.

The dancer: The mask, through its potent forms, instills in the dancer the spirit invoked, and incites him to mimetic portrayal of the deity. The enactment of character, myth, epic may range from the age-old gesture codes of the Orient and the puppet-like Javanese *way-ang-wong* to the impromptu clownery of the Yaqui *pascolas* and Iroquois False Faces, from majestic motions encumbered by stupendous disguise to unhampered acrobatics. Thus the *ye'i* trot in unison; according to traditional pattern the Pueblo *kachina* dancers conjure rain and the game animals succumb to the hunt. In contrast, the Plains buffalo or bear stampeded or clawed with overwhelming realism. The slinking Eskimo fox-maskers are foxes. The African monkey maskers of Odienné, Ivory Coast, are monkeys.

Mexico shows two tendencies corresponding to the native and imported styles: on the one hand life-like portrayal of fierce tigers and sly coyotes, on the other hand puppet-like battles of Moors and Christians. Everywhere the ceremonial clown performs his ridiculous uninhibited antics in perfect characterization. The Cherokee *bugah*, Pueblo *koshare*, Tlaxcalan *catrines*, and Quechua *sejillas* parody the white trader, missionary, bourgeois, and Spanish master, and thereby purge the community of resentment. Beyond censorship because of his supernatural identity, the clown-demon heals social ills in Bali, ancient Greece, medieval Europe, modern Austria and Portugal, down to the circus clown.

The power of these dramatic portrayals, like the geometric forms, depend for their vitality on conviction. They accompany the religious tenets through the various stages of crudity, efflorescence, formalization, fossilization, or extravagance, and decline. The masks start as gods and end as pranksters. See ANIMAL MIME; CARNIVAL; DANCE: FOLK AND PRIMITIVE; MIME; RITUAL DRAMA; SHAMAN.

Representative photographs and sketches of masks are accessible in

Fenton, William N., *Masked Medicine Societies of the Iroquois, RBAE,* 1940.

Haile, Berard, *Head and Face Masks in Navaho Ceremonialism,* St. Michaels, Ariz., 1947.

Hawkes, Ernest W., *The Inviting-in Feast of the Alaskan Eskimos,* Mem. 45, No. 3, Anthropological Series, Canada Department of Mines Geological Survey, Ottawa, Ontario, 1913.

McPharlin, Paul, *Masks, Occult and Utilitarian,* Cranbrook Institute of Science, Mich., 1940.

Mascaras Mexicanas, 2a Exposicion de la Sociedad de Arte Moderno, Mexico, 1945.

Roediger, Virginia M., *Ceremonial Costumes of the Pueblo Indians,* Berkeley, 1941.

Shawn, Ted, *Gods Who Dance,* New York, 1929.

Underwood, Leon, *Masks of West Africa,* London, 1948.
[GPK]

Maso (Mexican *venado*) Yaqui Indian term for deer, applied to the deer impersonator and also to the famous deer dance of the Sonora Cáhita (Yaqui, Mayo, Ocoroni) and Arizona colonists. The ancient "religion of the woods" survives in the mime of the deer, *pascolas,* and *coyote.* The Jesuit missionaries suffered their retention in religious celebrations, without seasonal associations, and separate from the semi-Catholic rites at Easter, San Juan's Day, Virgen del Camino, etc. The most realistic pantomime is enacted during household baptisms, birthdays, funerals, memorials, and votive fiestas.

On Easter Saturday they dance first in the church, then, after a procession, in the "profane" half of a *ramada* or bower. Maso identifies himself with the woodland creature, not by a true mask, but by a *masó koba,* a small deer-head with wistful glass eyes and perfect horns hung with red tassels and flowers. As his first action he fastens this on top of his head, while the two singers intone the first verse of the song to the mechanically precise scratching of notched sticks on gourd resonators. During the next two verses he vibrates two large gourd rattles with floral decorations, while pawing nervously and sniffing about with quivering nostrils. As another musician starts striking a resonant water drum, a half gourd floating on water (*bakúbahi*), Maso bursts into a light and powerful stamping rebound, with vibrant torso and head motions. He manipulates each rattle with a special technique, and simultaneously intensifies the rhythm with his clicking deer-hoof belt (*ríhhu'utiam*) and swishing butterfly cocoon anklets (*téneboim*). Suddenly he pauses in an attitude of suspense and terror, then continues his frenetic bounding and leaping. Sometimes one of the *pascolas* joins him, along with the *pascola* flute and tabor. Between dances they engage in amiable play, often raw and hilariously comical. With intervals of rest and mescal drinking, this continues all night. The climax of the drama is not enacted till near dawn, when Maso hides, is tracked down by the *pascolas*, bounds, falls, and palpitates on his knees, and is symbolically sacrificed and skinned. After an interval he casually lights a cigarette and lies down to rest before the processional dance of Domingo de Gloria, Easter Sunday.

In pre-Christian times, when hunting was even more ceremonial than now, deer and coyote dances continued all night in celebration of a good hunt. The success still depends on the favor of the deer-spirit leader, *maliči*. The meat must be treated with respect at risk of illness or misfortune. The tail and bezoar have magical curative properties; the bezoar contains a small snake which attracts lightning and so should not be worn as an amulet in the summer. Thus, analogous to beliefs among other Southwestern tribes, Maso is associated not only with spirit propitiation for the hunt, but also with cure and rain. Vegetation symbolism is inherent in the name for the tail (*sewa* or flower), the flowers on the horns and rattles, the confetti and flowers thrown at him, and, above all, in the words of the deer songs: *yó'ota pa'aku welama*, the (deer) spirit walks in the meadow; *sewata pa'aku welama*, the flowers walk in the meadow; and allusions to clouds, mist, rain.

Thus much of the original drama has been retained: the music, action, and symbolism. The only modern notes are the women's rebozo draped as a kilt, and the crucifix on a necklace. Nevertheless, both Maso and *pascolas* are ceding their ceremonial significance to the *matachini* and other Catholic organizations, and are becoming secular entertainment for the crowd, particularly in the Arizona colonies which have relinquished the hunt as a means of livelihood. The Sonora version remains as one of the few Mexican Indian dances without European metamorphosis. See ANIMAL MIME; COYOTE DANCE; DEER DANCE; RATTLES. [GPK]

Maspéro, Sir Gaston Camille Charles (1846–1916) French Egyptologist. He was professor of Egyptology, Collège de France (1874–1880 and 1886–1899). For many years, he was in Egypt (1880–1886 and 1899–1914) as director of excavations and antiquities. As founder of the French Institute of Oriental Archæology at Cairo, he accomplished valuable work at Luxor and Karnak. One of his outstanding efforts was, during this time, the translation of the inscriptions on the pyramids of Sakkara. His writings include works on Egyptian history, mythology, and art: *Études de mythologie et d' archéologie égyptiennes* (1893); *Histoire ancienne des peuples de l'Orient classique* (3 vols., 1895–97), and others. Besides these publications, results of his own study and research, he assembled and translated from ancient Egyptian papyri old fairy tales, publishing them under the title *Les contes populaires de l'Égypte ancienne, traduit et commentés* (1892). Since this collection salvages folktales from ancient times, it is of value to the scholar and makes even the casual reader appreciate the great age of some of our familiar stories (compare *The Treasure House of Rhampsinitus,* closely related to *The Master Thief,* Type 1525).

masquerade A celebration involving disguise by means of masks or mask-substitutes. The *mascherata* (Italy) reached its apogee of magnificence in the carnival processions and dances of 16th century Venice. It has its source in demonology, in supernatural coercion by imitative magic. Throughout western Europe in the 15th and 16th centuries masquerade evolved into a loose form of successive performances by maskers at secular entertainments of the nobility. These consisted usually of 1) tableaux in geometrical patterns, pageantry rather than dance; 2) *balli*, or social dances; 3) *brandi*, costumed theatrical dances; and 4) *moresques, morris, Morisken,* grotesque improvisations representing savages, animals, monkeys, etc. These *ballet-mascarades* were informal presentations of dances and tricks, less expensive than the theatrical spectacles of the *ballet-comique.* Such acts were introduced in the English *masques*—verse-comedies with plots motivating the entrances of dancers. This 17th century theatrical art drew upon both popular and court dance forms. The preliminary *anti-masque* corresponded to the *moresque,* with grotesque fools, satyrs, and wild men, medieval demonvestiges carried over through the Renaissance. See CARNIVAL; MASCARADAS. [GPK]

Mass of St. Sécaire A Black Mass of the folklore of Gascony, said against a person who then goes into a mysterious and incurable decline. An evil priest officiates, assisted by his mistress, in an abandoned church. He begins at eleven o'clock so as to end at midnight, repeats the Mass backwards, uses a black Host, drinks water from a well in which is the body of an unbaptized child, makes the sign of the cross with his left foot, etc. Compare SABBAT.

Mastamho Brother or son of Matavilya, Mohave culture hero. After the death of Matavilya, Mastamho put into execution the former's plans for the Mohave and neighboring desert tribes; for the Mohave account of his teaching this tribe the arts of life see A. L. Kroeber, *Seven Mohave Myths* (Anthropological Records 11:1, Berkeley, Cal., 1948), pp. 50 ff. The Mastamho institution of culture myth of the Mohave is a Great Tale and is unaccompanied by songs, such as are characteristic for many Mohave myths. See CANE OF BREATH AND SPITTLE. [EWV]

Master of Life English term applied to the supreme deities of various North American Indian tribes, especially to the Delaware Indian supreme deity. Currently the supreme deity is usually referred to in English as the Creator. See BIG HOUSE. [EWV]

masters of the game Like the Indians of the northern hemisphere, the South American natives attribute a divine protector to the game animals in general or to some species in particular. For instance, the popular demon Curupira, so frequently mentioned in the folktales of the caboclos (mestizos) of Brazil, is the guardian of the game animals. In the Amazonian basin and in the Chaco, these supernatural beings are generally the protectors of fish, and are called the "father" or "mother" of all the fish or of some particular species.

The custodians freely permit the use of their protegés as food, but they do not tolerate their wanton destruction by man. They severely punish those who kill more game or fish than they actually need. In some cases these supernatural guardians can be propitiated by prayers and small gifts. In ancient Peru the divine protectors of the animal species were identified with constellations to which prayers were addressed. See COQUENA; CURUPIRA. [AM]

master thief Hero and title of a tale type—Type 1525 —known throughout the world (more than 700 versions have been collected) and appearing in almost every European and Asiatic tale collection. The literary versions of the tale are traceable back to the Renaissance, though it is much older and is probably one of the stories involving robbers that have been popular throughout the centuries such as the tales of Ali Baba and Rhampsinitus, with which it shares some incidents in various versions.

One series of events (Type 1525A) forms the heart of the master thief tale and permits it to be recognized no matter what other incidents are added to this core story. The ne'er-do-well, or one of three brothers who set out to learn trades, announces himself as the master thief. This comes to the earl's notice and the master thief is given the task of stealing the earl's horse. He masquerades as an old woman and gets the stable boys drunk, or he induces the stable hands to chase a rabbit, and makes off with the horse. After this, he must steal the sheet from the bed of the earl's wife and the ring from her hand. The thief obtains a corpse and, in the dead of night, raises it to the earl's window, making a noise so the supposed second-storey man will be discovered. The earl shoots the corpse and rushes out to see whether his shot has taken effect. The thief, pretending to be the earl, quickly enters the bedroom, tells the countess that he has killed the prowler and wants the sheet to wrap the body in; and, he adds, since the thief was probably after her ring, it would be only decent to bury it with him. When the earl gets back to the bedroom, the trick is discovered. The master thief is condemned to die. He is put into a sack to be executed but manages to convince a dupe to take his place: the parson by telling him he is Peter and the Day of Judgment is at hand, the greedy peasant by telling him that he is going to visit his many cattle at the bottom of the river, etc.—the variations of this theme are many.

Other incidents are usually added somewhere in the tale. The master thief (here obviously the trickster) comes to the earl with the bright thought that it would be very easy for a dishonest person to steal the earl's horse. The earl asks for a demonstration, and the master thief demonstrates by stealing the horse (Type 1525B). Or he determines to steal an ox. He puts one shoe in the road and another down the road a bit, around a bend. When the ox-driver sees the second shoe, he dismounts and runs back to pick up the first. Meanwhile the thief goes off with the animal (Type 1525D). Compare ADDED EQUIPMENT. The master thief stories (Types 1525A-F) are often compounded with other tales, for example with the stupid ogre stories where the hero dupes the giant (e.g. Jack the Giantkiller—Type 328), or with the clever boy (Type 1542) which borrows the horse-stealing and sack incidents. Some of the incidents of the master thief type often appear as separate tale types, but Type 1525A with the possible addition of Type 1525D identifies the story of the master thief.

matachin (from Arabic *mudawajjihin*, plural *mudawajjihēn*, those who put on a face, or those who face

each other.) A form of *Morisca* dance, widespread in Renaissance Europe, and brought by missionaries and colonists to Middle America and the Andes. Despite the name, Arabic origin of the dance is as debatable as in the case of the various Moriscas. The ancestry is probably traceable to the strolling medieval buffoon dancers, *ioculatores, jongleurs, mimi,* and ultimately the *pantomimi* of Rome, in a blend with ritual fools of preChristian Europe. Masks or face-blackening may have suggested the Arabic name to Moslem-conquered Spain.

The earliest definite description is by Arbeau in 1585. At that time the French *matachins* enacted a polite and humorous battle mime for four men with ribbons on their shoulders, morions of gilded cardboard, bells on their legs, sword in right hand and buckler in left. After a circular entrance with a kicking step, they made passes at each other in codified positions called *taille haute, revers bas,* etc.

Later on the *matachins* and the Italian *mattacino* provided the court *entremets* or *entermedii,* grotesque dance interludes, to contrast with the serious parts of plays or masquerades.

However, the Spanish *matachini* still enact symbolic battle mime at religious fiestas. In the Sierra Madre Occidental of Mexico the pyrrhic play has been stylized to a dance in two opposing lines with ornamental manipulation of a feathered trident in the right hand, and a small gourd rattle in the left. Characteristic paraphernalia includes a high feathered headdress with mirrors and ribbons, a scarf around the chin or lower face, bandoliers, and ordinary trousers or a double pair with a side slit in the outer shorter pair. Fiddles and a harp (or guitar) play country dance tunes. The longways formations, too, are of European type: cross-overs, *dos-à-dos,* heys, etc. But the steps are indigenous.

Among the Yaqui of Sonora the execution is particularly precise and vigorous. Also, the dance has become most thoroughly integrated into Catholic ritualism, with a complex votive organization dedicated to the Virgin. Led by a *monarca,* 18 to 100 men solemnly execute their decorative evolutions in the church, during all ecclesiastical and many private fiestas. They are gradually superseding the indigenous *pascolas* and *masos* in ceremonial significance.

Among the Tarahumara, Huichol, and Cora, the matachini are confined to Catholic festivals, among the Cora with rain-inducing power. The Yaqui and Cora groups are accompanied by a transvestite *Malinche* and clown or *viejo* (old man); the Tarahumara are supervised by an equal number of *chapeones,* who resemble the Yaqui *chapayekas.* In the New Mexico pueblos the matachines usually appear only at Christmas or Twelfth Night, in the Mexican towns sometimes in August, following a high mass. Despite native costume details, they clearly supply an alien attraction. In their midst a *Malinche* follows their *monarca* and a tattered clown*abuelo* (grandfather) battles and kills a *toro,* bull-masker, who is finally resurrected.

The various matachini were obviously introduced by the Spaniards. The forms and written records prove this. Nevertheless, Indian qualities have blended with the European surface, as Indian beliefs with the Catholic. Strikingly enough, while the matachin deteriorated and virtually disappeared in Europe, in the New World it has retained its ritualism and even enriched it with native fertility and rain symbolism. [GPK]

Matavilya Eldest son of Sky and Earth, and one of the two leading figures in Mohave Indian mythology, his younger brother (or son), Mastamho, being the other. Matavilya led men and beings upward to Aha'-av'ulypo, "house-post water," in Eldorado Canyon on the Colorado, where he made his first house at the center of the earth. He offended his daughter, Frog, who swallowed his excrements and caused his death. Mastamho disposed of his brother's body by burning, but Coyote stole the dead Matavilya's heart, and his ashes offended; neither wind, hail, nor rain could obliterate them. After Matavilya's death Mastamho put into execution his dead brother's plans for the way of living of the Mohave and the desert tribes nearest them. For the outline of the Matavilya myth see A. L. Kroeber, *Handbook of the Indians of California (BBAE* 78), pp. 770–771. See EXCREMENTS SWALLOWED. [EWV]

Mat Chinoi In Semang (Malay Negrito) belief, chief of the small supernatural beings who live in flowers and trees, aid shamans, and are messengers to Tak Pern. Mat Chinoi lives, as a snake ten cubits around, on the road to Tak Pern's house. His job is to manufacture mats for Tak Pern. Inside his huge body are 20 or 30 beautiful female chinoi and great stores of combs, headdresses, etc. On his back is a male chinoi, Halak Gihmal, who looks after the things stored inside. A male chinoi who wishes to obtain one of the female chinoi hidden in the snake-body must run the gauntlet of seven mats hung above the snake which are always opening and closing. If he is swift enough to escape the mats before they close on him, he must undergo another trial—that of entering a rapidly opening and closing tobacco box. If he is successful in escaping the lid, he is allowed to choose one of the female chinoi for himself.

materials, science, and art of folklore As a body of materials, folklore is the lore, erudition, knowledge, or teachings, of a folk, large social unit, kindred group, tribe, race, or nation, primitive or civilized, throughout its history. It is the whole body of traditional culture, or conventional modes of human thought and action. It is created informally in a group of persons for themselves, but has been accepted widely enough to have attained considerable currency, and over a sufficient period of time to have acquired traditional traits, such as anonymity of authorship and historic-geographic patterns of variants of basic forms.

Currency and tradition constitute the acid test of folklore materials. These materials may have literary relations, they may have been written down in some form and made their influence felt in erudite circles or literary tradition. Conversely, they may have appropriated literary or learned elements. But fundamentally, to be folklore, their currency must be or have been in the memory of man, bequeathed from generation to generation by word of mouth and imitative action rather than by the printed page: by word of mouth chiefly in the so-called "literary" types of folklore (myth, legend, folktale, and poetry), "linguistic" types (speech, gesture, proverb, riddle), and "scientific" types (cures, prophecies, witchcraft and all other sections of belief); or by action or practiced example chiefly in the so-called

"action" types (music, dance, game, festival, custom, drama, art, craft, cookery). The "literary" types seek artistic application of language. The "action" types seek artistic application of bodily movement. The "scientific" types seek to explain cause and effect. The "linguistic" types seek the formal aspect of verbal expression. Being current in memory, act, and oral tradition, folklore never has a fixed form, but rather an approximate pattern which varies from time to time, from group to group, and even from one telling or performance to another within the same group or by the same individual.

A learned creation of one individual may or may not become folklore, depending upon whether it does or does not gain and maintain for some time general acceptance and currency in a group. Morphologically, the approximate pattern and unfixed form of folklore, emerging from the memory in continually varying forms, are in a constant state of flux. It receives modifications imposed to suit not only the tastes of hearers or learners, but also the various imaginative and creative impulses of tellers or performers. Such varying forms give all types of folklore a character of collective authorship that makes them quite different from the fixed single forms of the creations of erudite circles. Indeed, when one finds a number of variants of a folklore form in a given area, which do not have the numerous differences normally found among variants in their details, at once one suspects the influence of an erudite form behind their suspicious uniformity. Although some folklore may be of communal origin from the start, one must usually think of an original individual creation, which is taken up by the folk and subsequently becomes folklore. Its original author then fades into obscurity, and the most vital factor in authorship, in any case and with any form of folklore, is the folk. Folk tellers or doers and hearers or learners, like a last court of appeal, accept or reject it and modify it continually, thus putting upon it the stamp of group authorship, which is really what makes it folklore, regardless of its ultimate origin.

The scope and classification of folklore materials are still rather obscure. The general index to the volumes of the *Volkskundliche Bibliographie* offer some clarification, as do the section headings in the annual folklore bibliographies of the *Southern Folklore Quarterly*, illustrated by the terminology used by writers in their titles appearing under these headings. Stith Thompson's *Motif-Index* offers a detailed classification, chiefly of narrative types. Robert Lehmann-Nitsche's introduction to his *Adivinanzas rioplatenses* proposes a rather substantial system of riddle classification. Various systems of melodic indexing of folk music have been proposed. But a comprehensive and definitive system of classification for the whole field is still to be desired. For the present, a rough, simple and practical system may be devised to cover the various species in the field as conceived and determined by the current practice of those who write about them and publish collections of them, even though there is still considerable divergence of opinion. See TYPES AND CLASSIFICATION OF FOLKLORE.

The question of who is "folk" is not so important as that of what is "lore," for everyone may be "folk" if the conditions essential for "lore" are established. It is of interest but not indispensable that one individual may be wholly "folk" or not "folk." An individual may be partially "folk." He is "folk" insofar as he participates in the propagation of "lore" as described above. When he reads a book, follows the written law laid down by his legislative body, or the latest dogma of scientific theory taught in his schools or classical music or modernistic art expounded by his teacher, and when he learns and follows the dogma of his church, he is not "folk." Rather, he is following learned culture, which is distinguished from traditional culture in that it is created by small leader groups of priests, politicians, scientists, etc., who impose their cultural creations upon the rest of society. Thus learned culture arises in a fashion quite different from "lore." But insofar as an individual follows the accepted "lore" current in his group, created by his group, or even adopted from other groups or from learned sources by his group, "lore" which is a vital force functionally in his own life, the customs, beliefs, traditional music, crafts, etc., of his group, he is "folk." In most human groups, these two types of culture mingle in the life of an individual: most of us are partially "folk." Some of us, especially those who live in large, modern cities, find our lives so influenced by radios, films, books, municipal ordinances, state and national laws, schools, newspapers and other devices of molding consciously opinions and ways of life, automobiles, airplanes, chain stores and a multitude of other products of modern civilization so new and rapidly changing that they have had no time to penetrate deeply into our traditional cultural patterns—so saturated, in short, that our "folk" element is almost smothered out. But others of us, especially those who live in remote and isolated rural regions, find our lives so little disturbed by these things that our "folk" element is still quite vigorous and still practically dominates our lives.

Folklore materials thrive in a society in which there are people of considerable native intelligence, artistic appreciation, memory, imagination and creative urge, who can comprehend, value, remember and recreate their native folklore and thus propagate it as a living tradition. Folklore lives its fullest, purest and most natural life away from learned culture. Folklore suffers greater suppression and contamination the more it comes into contact with learned culture and its great concentrated and uniformizing social organizations. In small groups, isolated from considerable outside influence, in which everyone knows everyone else and the whole little group, in fact, is a network of intermarried families, an economically independent and selfsufficient unit, whose members are illiterate and depend entirely on oral tradition and practiced precept rather than on books and formal education, and are not specialized workers, and are more or less all alike in their cultural heritage, education, social and economic position, etc., folklore should be in its purest and most thriving state. But in a great literate and specialized nation, with highly developed means of communication and formal education, with large urban centers, diverse cultural, social, and economic elements, formal and impersonalized laws governing individuals, such small folk groups constitute only a small minority, are likely to contain only the lowest strata of the population, and are liable to be drained of their most intelligent and ablest folklore propagators, who have risen by their abilities into more learned circles. Hence in such a nation the folklorist must turn to these folk groups, stripped of their best intelligence, imagination, etc., and contaminated by

learned tradition, in order to find such folklore as may survive. Or he must attempt to extricate it from the abler propagators, despite the fact that the latter are no longer more than partially "folk" and present added difficulties with the complexity of their more recently acquired learned background. Far better for the folklorist is a nation in which such folk groups still embrace a great majority of the population, with most of the abler propagators still in their group. Thus one can see why folklore can be gathered even among the most highly "civilized" nations and even in the biggest and most modern urban centers, but also why folklorists prefer to turn their efforts towards primitive peoples and isolated regions. Thus one can see why some persons are almost wholly "folk," living in an environment of traditional culture, while others are almost wholly "learned," living in an environment of books, newspapers, films, radios, machine products and all manner of standardized norms which are set and reset by individuals or small groups; while still others (the majority of the world's population) are partially "folk," living in that broad intermediate cultural zone in which folklore forms survive alongside complementary and even parallel or contradictory learned forms in the same group.

As a science, folklore studies its body of materials from a certain viewpoint, recording accurate descriptions of these materials and their environment or determinative background data, classifying, analyzing and interpreting them, deducing the general rules or tendencies that govern their origin and evolution, relating them to other phases of life and showing their application to human welfare and the advancement of civilization, just as any other science does. Frequently different sciences study the same materials. This partial coincidence is especially true of the numerous sciences that study man. History may well study social history; so may sociology. Law may study customs; so may folklore, sociology, and anthropology. Linguistics may study primitive languages; so may anthropology and archeology. Psychology may study folk beliefs; so may folklore, anthropology, sociology, and religion. Archeology may study folk arts and crafts; so may folklore and anthropology. Geology may study the earth; so may soil chemistry. And so with other coincidences. But rarely do different sciences study the same materials from the same viewpoint. History studies social history as a part of the whole record of man's past; sociology studies it as a part of the whole picture of human relations. Linguistics studies primitive languages as a part of the whole development of linguistic phenomena; anthropology studies them as a part of man's whole cultural pattern. Archeology studies folk arts and crafts as a part of one whole ancient civilization; anthropology, as a part of the whole cultural pattern of one primitive tribe; folklore, as a part of the whole process of this type of cultural product throughout the world. Geology studies the earth as a part of the whole historical picture of the earth's development; soil chemistry studies it as a part of the whole question of what makes crops grow. Etc. Thus, although sciences are distinguished often by their materials, they are more precisely differentiated by their separate viewpoints.

Likewise, the science of folklore is distinguished chiefly by its particular viewpoint. Though the typical overlapping of materials studied is often found between folklore and other sciences, folklore, like other sciences, has its separate and unified viewpoint, different from that of other sciences. This distinction justifies its pursuit in giving us still another basic point of approach among the various approaches of diverse sciences that help us better to comprehend the complex phenomenon of man in his world, and to improve man's position therein. To attain these high purposes, we need as thorough an understanding as possible from as many different angles as possible. The basic point of approach, or viewpoint, of the science of folklore is its interest first and foremost in folklore materials (as indicated above in speaking of "folk" and "lore"), for their own intrinsic interest and from an all-time historical and world-wide geographical or international viewpoint. Regardless of time and space limits, folklore considers all manifestations of similar nature in a certain type of folklore materials. It seeks to discern accurately, classify, compare, and correlate those manifestations into a unified historic-geographic pattern, from which may be deduced conclusions regarding origin, evolution, and spread, environmental determining factors and adaptations, morphologic changes, reflections of racial, national, or regional characteristics, and the broadly human and basic traits of living folk traditional culture as produced by the human mind. From the conclusions of a multitude of studies of individual patterns emerge the general laws of this science. These laws may ultimately be applied to facilitate the unification of peoples of different traditional cultural patterns, when they are brought by migration to live together. They also may be applied to develop regional and national consciousness and unity, when there is a deterioration of harmony among diverse elements in such an area, and to better mutual understanding among the different peoples of the world internationally, when their superficial differences in folk culture blind them to the comprehension of the basic human traits they have in common (these traits are perhaps best exemplified by the basic communality which underlies their various folk cultures). The unity of the science of folklore is the unity of the materials of folklore, comparatively and historically studied. Every science evolves its own methodology to suit its own particular point of approach to its materials and to attain its ultimate purpose. Only in the science of folklore is the center of interest focused primarily upon the folklore materials themselves, hence the methodologies of other sciences are inadequate for the purposes of folklore. Folklore must evolve its own methodology, which it has been doing ever since it was formally christened in the early 19th century. Although its first century of life was predominantly one of collecting activity, in the present century it is beginning to turn more toward classification and analysis of its materials.

Environmental factors must be considered by the science of folklore. It would be just as great a folly to consider a version of a folktale or proverb entirely divorced from its teller, his group and region, as it would be to consider a flower entirely divorced from the soil and climate in which it grew. Yet the proper perspective established by the viewpoint of the botanist requires that he study in the foreground his flower and in the background the soil and climate in which it grew, that he study soil and climate secondarily and in relation to his flower, and that he seek the cooperation of soil chem-

istry and climatology, but not that he become a specialist in these sciences. Likewise, the proper perspective established by the viewpoint of the folklorist requires that he study in the foreground his folktale or proverb and in the background the informant, group and region that produced it, that he study informant, group and region secondarily and in relation to his folktale or proverb, and that he seek the cooperation of, but not that he become, a specialist also in anthropology, ethnology, sociology, human geography, history, religion, economics, and numerous other fields which specialize in the study of a great variety of factors which influence any particular variant of a folklore form. Science is a matter of relative specialization, not of complete divorcement of systematized bodies of knowledge.

Folklore, like other bodies of knowledge, has both its scientific and its artistic aspects. Strictly speaking, in its scientific aspect it seeks to ascertain, classify, study, and deduce conclusions from, its materials, and there its prime objective ends. And there begins the prime objective of its artistic aspect, which is the mastery and consummate control over the attainments of the scientific aspect, so that, by skilful performance and in accordance with aesthetic principles, these attainments can be applied and adapted to man's use and welfare, or to effect any desirable result. Thus it is the scientific aspect of a body of knowledge which is concerned with the attainment of the immediate goals of that body of knowledge; and it is its artistic aspect which is concerned with the attainment of its ultimate goals. There is usually no definite line of division between the scientific and the artistic aspects of a field. In medicine the same doctors who toil over experiments in attaining the immediate goal of their science often continue with the skilled practical application of their results, far into the artistic realization of their ultimate goal. But the investigator in the science of pure physics often leaves to engineers the artistic and practical application of the immediate results of his investigation. Likewise, the painter may delve into the scientific aspects of his colors, methods of their application, and surfaces to which they are applied. But the musician seldom passes from his artistic sphere back into the science of the physics of sound.

In folklore, as in other fields, no sharp line of distinction has been drawn between its scientific and its artistic aspects. The field of folklore is still so new that little occasion has arisen for such a distinction to be made. Folklore is still largely concerned wtih those first stages in any field—collecting and classifying its materials. Some effort has been made to push on into the comparative and correlative activities, but much remains to be done here, and until considerably more is done, we cannot hope to progress far with the deduction of valid and valuable conclusions. And until the immediate goals of the science of folklore materialize further in such comprehensive and adequately based conclusions, the ultimate goals of the artistic, practical and applied phase of folklore can progress only to a very limited degree. This fact explains why so little has even been attempted along these lines. However, as the ultimate values of folklore in integrating cultural patterns of diverse traditional elements, in bettering mutual understanding between peoples internationally, etc., become more generally and more clearly realized, all the processes of folklore study and utilization, both scientific and artistic, will be pursued more vigorously. The field will then doubtless undergo various refinements. Specialized branches of its scientific aspect will probably develop into more crystallized forms. And specialists in the practical applications of its artistic aspect (indeed, in the various ramifications of these applications) will no doubt develop.   RALPH STEELE BOGGS

Previously published in *Folklore Americas* III, no 1, June 1943. Reprinted by permission of the author.

ma'tok i The womens' Buffalo Cow dance society of the Blackfoot Indians in Montana. Initiation was bought by gifts from ceremonial "mothers." They danced in a ceremonial enclosure similar to that of the sun dance, which, in fact, has buffalo associations. Milling in a sunwise direction, they realistically imitated the buffalo park. Four groups wore varying headdresses and paraphernalia—the four scabby bulls, six snake-bonnets, feather bonnets, buffalo-wool headdresses with horns, and a bone-whistle as in the sun dance. The purpose was the increase and capture of buffalo by means of imitative magic, plus motives of animal-guardianship so prominent in the Great Plains and circumference. [GPK]

Matron of Ephesus A widow of ancient story, famous for her beauty and marital devotion, equally famous for her faithlessness: subject of a motif that has passed through world literature (K2213.1; Type 1510). The tale is told by Petronius (*Sat.* 111–13), first century A.D. A married woman of Ephesus, renowned for personal qualities of beauty and virtue, at her husband's death followed him to the tomb to keep watch over his body. Deaf to the appeals of her relatives, she mourned five days and nights, the perfect example of devotion. A soldier, who had been set to guard robbers crucified outside the tomb, noticed the light with which the lady was keeping her watch and descended into the tomb. With food, drink, and blandishments, it was not long before the widow was persuaded to begin life anew. It is recorded that the tomb itself saw the wedding of the lady and the soldier consummated. To save her lover from public disgrace and sentence after it was discovered that one of the bodies outside had been stolen, she had her husband's body removed from his coffin and substituted for the missing body. This medieval "merry tale," known to classical antiquity, is thought to be of Eastern origin. Voltaire incorporated the story in his *Zadig*. For the odyssey of this piece of fiction through world literature, see Griesbach, *Die Wanderung der Novelle der treulosen Witwe durch die Weltliteratur.* [GPS]

Matsya In modern Hindu mythology, the fish incarnation of Vishṇu. The god infused a part of his essence into the huge, horned fish which appeared to save Manu from the Deluge. In common belief, the fish was the first incarnation of Vishṇu; the *Bhāgavata Purāṇa* mentions 22 incarnations, however, of which Matsya, the fish, is the tenth. In the late version of the story in the *Mahābhārata,* the fish says he is Brahmā Prajāpati (the great creator of the *Brahmaṇas*). Compare KŪRMA.

Matuta or **Mater Matuta** A Roman goddess, often said to be the goddess of dawn and hence equated with the Greek Leucothea, but rather a goddess of birth and increase allied with Janus. She has no mythology, which causes Rose to doubt her identity as a dawn goddess, the latter seldom if ever being a cult goddess; her festival, the Matralia, on June 11, was celebrated by the Roman matrons. The observance took place at her shrine in the Forum Boarium, a still extant round temple known as the Temple of Hercules. Slaves were not permitted in the temple, one only being admitted to undergo a slap on the cheek and then to be sent away. The matrons prayed for their sisters' children, a rite explained variously as emphasizing that such children should not be left to the care of slaves or as being a misreading of *pueri sororii,* adolescent children. Whatever mythology attaches to Mater Matuta, and whatever accretion of function beyond that of goddess of growth, seems to be a transference from her identification with Leucothea.

máuari Masked puberty rite of the Maipure and Baniba Indians of Venezuela. Máuari, the spirit of evil, is impersonated by a dancer who is fully covered with red and black body-paint, a face-covering of lion or tiger pelt, and a crown of deer antlers. On the day appointed for the initiation of a youth, he emerges from the forest with a wild animal cortège, maskers representing lions, tigers, deer, bears, and other wild beasts. Their blood-curdling growls and howls mingle with the groans of the *botutos,* the sacred trumpets, to fill the night with a gruesome din. With wild leaps and contortions they dance around the neophite and four shamans.

At a girl's initiation, all women and children withdraw to a special hut, because of their official ignorance of the identity of the maskers. The masked crew leaps and howls around the hut. In either case the identification with demon and animal spirits serves to propitiate these and protect the initiate from maleficent influences. At the same time the initiates seek to obtain a vision, the favor of a supernatural animal guardian. [GPK]

Maui The trickster and culture hero of Polynesia from New Zealand to Hawaii: he sometimes also appears in Melanesian myth. The Maui cycle has some dozen to twenty tales clearly belonging to it and which appear fairly consistently throughout the area. Maui appears in tales more often than any other Polynesian hero. He is usually a youngest son, sometimes an abandoned child, either abortive or premature, who is thrown away by his mother. This commonly is the explanation of his small stature. Maui was reared by the sea gods, then educated by his ancestor in the sky Tama-nui-ki-te-rangi. He returned to earth and joined his brothers in a game, during which he identified himself. He discovered that each morning his mother went into the ground. He followed her and found her with his father Tangaroa. Tangaroa gave Maui a name, but during the naming ceremony left out one of Maui's names, which omission provided the loophole through which eventually the gods were able to destroy Maui.

Maui is a demiurge (A. H. Krappe, *Mythologie universelle,* p. 387, calls him the best possible example of the demiurge) who fished up the islands on which the Polynesians live. New Zealand is called by some of the Maori The Fish of Maui. In a Maori myth, Maui used the jawbone of his ancestress and his own blood to fish the land out of the sea. He warned his brothers not to cut the land, but they sliced it all up, thus causing the islands and the mountainous character of the land. Maui's mother tried to make tapa, the bark cloth of the islands, but the sun crossed the heavens and set before she could complete her work. Maui took the hair of Hina, his sister or wife, or some green flax, and made a noose or net with which he snared the sun. Then, with a club he had gotten from his grandmother, he beat the sun until it agreed to move more slowly. It was Maui too who brought fire to man (see FIRE). Other of his exploits were the raising of the sky (this does not appear in New Zealand, where Tane performs the feat) in three heaves—once to the tree-tops, once to the mountain-tops, then to where the sky is now; the trapping of the winds; invention of the kite, the barbed spear, the eel-pot, the calabash of the winds (the navigational instrument of the Polynesians). Maui, the friend of mankind, died in the attempt to obtain immortality for man. He descended to the underworld, where he entered the body of the goddess who dwelt there. If he passed through her body—i.e. if he were born again— he would become immortal. This rebirth without dying is obviously symbolic. But once he had been eaten by the ogress, the flaw in his naming was discovered and the jealous gods saw to it that Maui could not win free of the monster's body. Thus he died and mankind remained mortal.

Maundy Thursday The Thursday of Holy Week, the week before Easter, is variously called Holy, Shere or Chare, and Maundy Thursday. The derivation of Maundy has been explained as from the Saxon *maund*, the charity hamper in which provisions were carried to give away to the poor, also from *maund*, to beg, from the French *mendier* or *maundier*, to beg. But it is likely that Maundy Thursday, as well as the maund basket and the maunder beggar, came from *Mandatum novum do vobis*, the Latin of "A new commandment I give unto you" (*John* xiii, 34). These words, long the first antiphon in the Latin Christian ceremony of the washing of the feet, were said, on the Thursday eve before the Friday crucifixion, by Jesus to his disciples in connection with his establishment of the eucharist (communion or Lord's Supper) and his washing of the disciples' feet. The latter act was obviously a dramatic example and symbol of humility and service to others (see *John* xiii, 1–17; *Luke* xxii, 24–27) and has been taken as a literal command at certain periods in some sections of the Christian church. Instead of the priest or minister washing the feet of lay communicants, especially the newly baptized (*pedilavium*) as obtained in earlier times, there have been such variants as washing the feet of choir boys, or of 12 poor old men, or of a group of travel-stained pilgrims.

St. Oswald, who was Archbishop of York from 972 to 992 A.D., was so assiduous that every day he fed 12 poor men and washed their feet. Shortly afterward, Ælfric, Archbishop of Canterbury 996–1006 A.D., considered once a week often enough for the charity, instructing his Saxon priests: "Do on Thursday as our Lord commands you, wash the feet of the poor, feed and clothe them, and with humility wash your feet among yourselves as Christ himself did and commanded us so to do." These two forms or parts of the ceremony were distinguished at Durham in 1593 A.D. as *mandatum pauperum* and *mandatum fratrum*. The ceremonies of the Maundy varied in the different cathedrals, and evidently more latitude was permitted than in any other Christian ceremony.

The Norman, Plantagenet, and Tudor kings and queens of England adopted the custom of washing the feet of and giving clothes and money to the poor on Maundy Thursday. Sir Thomas More recorded that Henry VIII on Maundy Thursday washed the feet of as many poor men as he himself was years old and afterward gave them meat, clothes, and money. Queen Elizabeth also washed the paupers' feet, but only after servants had washed them in herb-scented water first.

Since 1754 feet-washing has been discontinued by the Church of England, although the money gifts are continued from the regents but through the Lord High Almoner. During the reign of Charles II (1660–1685) the practice arose of coining special Maundy pennies. There is probably a connection here with the "touch pieces" of money given to the sufferers from scrofula (king's-evil) by the king after he had touched the sick, coins which were said to have healing virtue in themselves, especially if they bore the bas-relief of the king.

The rites of Maundy Thursday are, however, still celebrated in certain places in England by the Roman Catholic church, in conformation with the general custom in Roman cathedrals. The ceremony is called the *Mandatum* and, with local variations, usually runs as follows. The bishop washes the feet of 13 poor men or others. In monastic churches, the superior washes the feet of 13 monks. In Westminster Cathedral the cardinal-archbishop laves the feet of 13 choir-boys who also receive gift-books. Usually the deacon sings the gospel of the Mass, the choir sings the antiphons, and the prelate, after washing and kissing the feet, repeats the *Pater Noster* silently, a few versicles, and then ends with the appropriate prayer "that as here the outward stains are washed away for us and by us, so the inward stains of us all may be washed away by thee."

Luther denounced feet-washing as a Christian ceremony, and the Lutheran Liturgy for Maundy Thursday is concerned mainly with the institution of the sacrament of the Holy Supper, confining reference to the feet-washing incident merely to the words: "and hast also left us an example of mutual service by humbly washing Thy disciples' feet." Twelve Lutherans were condemned in 1718 in Dresden to do public penance for having let a duke wash their feet.

Maundy Thursday and/or feet-washing as a rite is not much observed in Protestant churches except among minor sects, such as the Dunkards, Seventh-Day Adventists, and Free-Will Baptists. In the Eastern churches, the 13th chapter of John's Gospel is dramatized in detail even to Peter's refusal to let Jesus wash his feet. In Jerusalem on Maundy Thursday the Greek Patriarch washes the feet of 12 bishops publicly in the court of the Church of the Holy Sepulcher in an elaborate and dramatic ceremony, after which roses are dipped into the rest of the holy water and the crowd is therewith sprinkled. What falls on the pavement is wiped up with handkerchiefs by the communicants and rubbed on their faces. The whole practice of feet-washing as observed in the Holy Thursday ceremony has definite relations with practices in other religions and cultures. (See *ERE* v: 814–823.) It was not original with Jesus, for he was but following and somewhat adapting the old Jewish custom of ceremonially washing the feet. It is a part of the world-wide custom of symbolizing, dramatizing, and to a certain extent obtaining, purification of mind, heart, soul, or spirit, by various types of lustration, baptism, and ceremonial cleansing of the body or parts of it. Hence Shere, Sheer (Pure) Thursday.

The additional idea of humility as demonstrated in the rite had more significance for Jesus and his disciples than is appreciated by his modern followers. Rabbi Huna, among others, points out that a Jewish husband was entitled to have his feet washed by his wife personally, no matter how many maids were hers. Hindu wives were required to perform this sacred duty, as a sort of means of salvation through abasement. See BAPTISM; PENITENTES; PURIFICATION.

CHARLES FRANCIS POTTER

Mawu The Great God of the Dahomeans, conceived as the creator of the world and mother of the gods, and symbolized by the moon. The difference between living things and things inanimate is the *ḹdǒ* or "bit of Mawu" within them. This is not to be confused with the soul (*se*), although the soul also comes from Mawu (see *Dahomey* ii: 232, 244). Often conceived as the female portion of the androgynous deity termed Mawu-Lisa (Lisa being conceived as the male, and identified with the sun), Mawu is worshipped as the sky god, and, as parent, chief of the other deities. Though it has been claimed that Mawu has no cult because of a presumed deistic concept of her, this is not the case, as elaborate rituals and initiation rites for her have been reported. See AGBE; AIDO HWEDO; FA. [MJH]

Max Müller, Friedrich (1823–1900) Anglo-German Orientalist and comparative philologist; son of the German poet, Wilhelm Müller. In 1841, the younger Müller ("Max") matriculated in the University of Leipzig where he was induced to take up the study of Sanskrit though his natural tendency was towards music. Accordingly, he was trained in the study of this language, in comparative mythology, and comparative religion by celebrated savants in Leipzig and Paris. In 1846, he went to England where the East India Company had undertaken the expense of publishing his edition of the *Rig-Veda*. He settled permanently at Oxford in 1848. On account of his German birth, he did not receive the professorship of Sanskrit at Oxford, but later was given the chair of comparative mythology.

During this period he wrote his *Chips from a German Workshop* (1865–75) and his *History of Ancient Sanskrit Literature* (1859). His outstanding effort was the editorship of the 51 volumes of *The Sacred Books of the East* (1875 on). This imposing set consists of records of the non-Christian scriptures of Oriental nations translated by competent scholars and is said to have been more effective than any other book in placing the study of comparative religion on a sound basis.

Müller, with other scholars (De Gubernatis, Fiske, Cox, and others), was deeply interested in comparative mythology and, using his knowledge in this field, he sought to discover the origin of Indo-European myths by the interpretation of metaphorical expressions in the *Rig-Veda*. His conclusions and those of the other "solar" mythologists received a setback, if not a mortal blow, when attacked and reduced to absurdity by Andrew Lang. The estimate of the *Encyclopædia Britan-*

nica is similar: "His essays on mythology are among the most delightful of his writings, but their value is somewhat impaired by a too uncompromising adherence to the seductive generalization of the solar myth."

Māyā (1) The primordial Mother-goddess, worshipped by the Burmese and southern Buddhists. In Tibet she is sGrol-ma or Tara.
(2) The mother of Buddha.

māyā A psychological term of Hindu cosmic philosophy posing the problem of illusion and reality. In the *Upanishads* the term took on the meaning of "cosmic illusion" along with the concept of the *ātman*, i.e. the inner essence or "self" of the universe. All that is not self is illusion. Hence māyā embodies the doctrine of non-dualism. The concept is the most important tenet of Vedānta philosophy and still pervades all Indian thinking.

May-apple A North American herb (*Podophyllum peltatum*) bearing an ovoid yellowish edible fruit. The root is poisonous, however. This was the powerful suicide root of the Huron and Iroquois Indians. The ground or chopped root was used by the Meskwaki Indians as a poultice to draw poison out of snake-bite, and also for rheumatism. Baking the root, however, rids it of the lethal podophillin, and a decoction of the baked root made a safe cathartic or emetic, and was sometimes given for dropsy. White settlers used it as a very slow purge. May-apple root, soaked in whisky, is given to drive snakes out of the body of one afflicted with internal snakes, in Mississippi Negro conjure curing.

May Day The first day of May: observed as a spring festival everywhere in Europe, the United States, and Canada, and as a labor festival in certain European countries. The typical European May Day celebration includes: 1) the gathering of green branches and flowers on May Eve or very early May Day morning; 2) the choosing and crowning of a May queen (often also a king) among the young people, who go singing from door to door through the village, carrying flowers or the May tree, soliciting donations for a merrymaking in return for the "blessing of May"; 3) the cutting, setting up, decorating of the May tree (bush, pole) and the dance around it. Sometimes this is a communal dance around the beribboned tree set up in a central location; in some villages, however, a May tree or bush is set up in every front yard, decorated by the family, and danced around by the family group.

The going out and picking of flowers and branches and bringing them home is the symbolic act of bringing home the May, i.e. bringing new life, the spring, into the village (see Frazer, *Magic Art*, ii, London, 1911, p. 59). Carrying the May tree and garlands from door to door is the symbolic bestowing and sharing of this new creative power that is stirring in the world. As the group goes from door to door, the May Bride often sings to the effect that those who give will *get* of nature's bounty through the year. And all the symbolic figures in the little drama, the boy and girl, the tree, the flowers, were believed to embody, and hence to have the power to bestow, new life and fertility on crops, cattle, women. In some places the May Bride and Bridegroom go through the village singing together; in England their wrists were linked together with a kerchief or garland.

In some villages, including many in England, the Maypole was left permanently standing on the village green, and thus the meaning of "bringing home the May" anew each year became gradually lost. On or about May Day the ancient Scandinavian peoples welcomed spring with mock battles between summer and winter, in which summer always won. These were still a feature of the May Day celebrations on the Isle of Man late into the 19th century. However much the people may have forgotten of the significance of their May Day merrymakings, Mannhardt, Frazer, and others believe that the marriage mime of the May Bride and May Bridegroom originally symbolized and was believed to *be* the marriage of spring and vegetation.

In parts of France some jilted youth will lie in a field on May Day and feign sleep. If any village girl is willing to marry him, she goes and wakes him with a kiss; the pair then go to the village inn together and lead the dance which announces their betrothal. The boy is called "the betrothed of May."

Getting your head wet in the rain on May Day prevents headache for a year. Washing in May dew (on May Eve or before sunrise May morning) is a common practice; it keeps the complexion beautiful and the person lucky for a year. In some parts of Europe women rolled naked in the dew on May Eve for beauty, health, and luck. In England it was sometimes said that the girl chosen May Queen would not live another full year; and there is some local feeling that to bring Mayflowers into the house is unlucky. Mayflowers picked before sunrise, however, will prevent freckles. The Mayflower in England is usually the white hawthorn; in the United States and Canada it is the arbutus, but sometimes the hepatica, sometimes the spring beauty.

In Ireland the house is blessed and a prayer said by some member of the family on May Eve. Sheep and cattle are let out to pasture for the first time on May Day, because after May Day there will be less sickness in the district. Everyone is loath to light the first fire on May Day morning, in the belief that some misfortune overtakes whoever does so. See BELTANE. There is a small grayish slug in Ireland (*drúictín*) from which young girls divine the color of their true love's hair. The future husband will have hair the color of the first *drúictín* found on May morning: if the slug is whitish, the future husband will have fair hair; if it is black, he will be black-haired.

In southern U.S. Negro belief, May Day is a good day for love charms and divinations: look down a well reflected in a mirror to see your future spouse's face; sometimes instead you see your own coffin. In South Carolina it is good luck to plant watermelons on May Day before sunrise. But never get married on May Day, for the bride will die within the year. Some Mississippi Negroes recommend May butter against witchcraft; butter made on May Day, mixed with saltpeter and eggyolk and rolled into little pills, will cure any kind of poisoning caused by conjure.

In many places all the typical May Day practices are observed at Midsummer or at Whitsuntide. In the Pyrenees the May tree is cut on May Day and set up for the Midsummer celebration. See BONA DEA; HAWTHORN; JACK IN THE GREEN; section *May Day* in SPANISH FOLKLORE.

Maypole dance A dance performed around a tall central pole with ribbon streamers, two opposing circles weaving in and out in such a way as to braid the ribbons in a pattern. In England and the United States and Canada, the custom has become inseparably associated with May Day celebrations of every sort, because of the ancient English observance. Descended from the Roman Floralia or perhaps from indigenous springtime ceremonies, May Day celebrates the return of spring and verdure, and is naturally focused on a sacred tree. At the time of Henry VIII dramatic characters took part in elaborate spectaculars, with characters already popular in the 15th and 16th centuries (Robin Hood and his company, Jack in the Green, Morris dancers). In fact, the Morris dance frequently concludes with a Maypole winding, to the tune "Sellenger's Round".

The custom has a wide distribution as German *Bändertanz* and Asturian *baile del cordón*. In India the *kolattam* stick dance becomes the *pinnal kolattam* when the dancers hold a ribbon in one hand and weave in and out while executing the stick-striking rhythms. The Basque sword dancers frequently conclude with a fast and furious ribbon winding (*cinta dantza*). The Spanish *baile de cintas,* or *de listones,* turns up in Yucatán and Venezuela for men and women, and in the male *negritos* and *voladors* dances of the Sierra de Puebla, as well as in the Yaqui *matachini* of Bacun, Cocorit, and Torin. These may be blends with avowed ribbon dances of ancient Mexico. Connections between these windings and those of Aryan peoples are possible but speculative. [GPK]

Mayweed Dog fennel (*Anthemis cotula*): also called stinking camomile. A tea from this plant with alum was considered a preventive for cholera, malaria, and typhoid fever. Chewing the root was good for those recovering from fever. A tea made from the steeped leaves and drunk cold was an old European remedy for fevers, adopted by the Mohegan-Pequot Indians of Connecticut. In China the Mayweed is believed to contain much *ling* (indwelling spirituality, spiritual power). Many plants contain *ling* in Chinese belief, but the Mayweed is especially endowed with *ling* because it grows on the grave of Confucius. Aside from its medicinal properties, it even brings good luck to the possessor.

mazateca A social fiesta dance of the Mazatec tribe on the border of Veracruz and Oaxaca states, Mexico. It is also called *našo nakoče* (flower of the pineapple) after the words of the simple melody sung by the dancers: "Flower of the pineapple sits in the corner; flower of the pineapple falls on the ground." Men and women form two lines face to face; they advance and recede and turn with slow native step: right foot forward with flexed knee, left foot behind the right heel with straight knee. The dance is doubtless indigenous. [GPK]

Mazda The word Mazda appears in many combinations and various associations from ancient Iranian times to the present. Its meaning is consistently inclusive of the three concepts: light, wisdom or truth, and divine personality. Mazdaism itself stems from Asia Minor; it is the pre-Zoroastrian polytheism of ancient Iran and the substratum of several religions, including Zorastrianism, Mithraism, Neo-Platonism, Manicheism, and Parsiism. Christianity itself, through post-exilic Judaism, inherited many of the doctrines and concepts associated with Mazda worship, especially the apocalyptic and eschatological accompaniments of the *parousia* (Second Advent).

Mazdāh was the Iranian form of the Sanskrit word for science, *medhas*, which may afford some justification for its appropriation, although the name of a deity, by Edison for his electric lamp. He may have had more in mind, however, than the fact that Mazda was the god of brilliant light. To Zoroaster, Mazdāh Ahura or Ahura-mazda (Lord Mazda), was the god of law, justice, truth, and light who would finally triumph over Angra Mainyu or Ahriman, the god of evil and darkness. [CFP]

mazurka or **mazurek** Specifically, a dance step of recent Polish origin. As folk dance it is a round dance, with much leeway in step sequence, two constituents being the stamp and the heel-click in cumulative order (one click, then two, then three). As a ballroom dance for couples, the step is in 3/4 time with an accent on the second beat: stamp right, stamp left next to right, hop on left and raise right knee. Though native to eastern Europe, the mazurka has invaded the ballrooms of western Europe and the United States. It has even encroached upon ritual dances of Mexico, the *conquista* and other *morisca* dances, notably the Oaxaca *plumas*. It constitutes one of the motley tunes and steps of the *jarabe tapatío*. [GPK]

Mbere The creator of Fans (western Bantu) mythology. Mbere made a man out of clay, but first he was a lizard. Mbere put the lizard in the great big sea water. He left him there five days. On the fifth day Mbere looked and the lizard was in there. On the seventh day Mbere looked and the lizard was in there. On the eighth day Mbere looked and the lizard came out. But when he came out he was a man. "Thank you," said the man to Mbere. See NZAMBI.

Mbir In the mythology of the Guarayú Indians of South America, the creator worm. At first there was only water. Then the worm Mbir appeared in the rushes, took human form as Miracucha, and made the world. See VIRACOCHA.

Mbōn A Kachin (Burma) wind nat: worshipped only by the chiefs at the national harvest festival.

mead A fermented drink made of honey and water, known to the ancient Greeks and Romans and common in medieval times throughout Europe: especially associated with the early Teutonic peoples. Priscus, Byzantine historian of the 5th century, reports it as the drink of the Hunnish court in 448 A.D. Long before this, however, mead was the sacrificial drink of the early Aryans. Mead was poured into the jeweled cups of Hrothgar's warriors in the huge resplendent mead-hall, Heorot, to celebrate Beowulf's victory over Grendel. Mead is the answer to one of the famous Anglo-Saxon Riddles, which begins, "I am cherished by men, found far and wide, brought from the groves and from dales and downs. By day wings bore me in the air, carried me with skill under the shelter of a roof. Men bathed me in a tub. Now I am a binder and a scourger; straightway I cast a young man to earth, sometimes an old churl . . ." When Oisín returned to Ireland from Tir-na-nOg and was entertained by St. Patrick and his monks in the 5th century, they brought him bowls of mead and mullets stewed in mead. The Earl of Digby (14th century) de-

scribed mead as "a mace of honny and water boyled to-gyther; yf it be fyred and pure, it preserveth health; but it is not good for them whiche have the bellyache or the Colycke." Chaucer's "Miller's Tale" mentions "mead and spiced ale."

Mead is probably best known as the heavenly drink of the old Teutonic gods. It was supplied to them endlessly by Odin's goat, Heidrun, who fed on Yggdrasil. The mead in the phrase *Odin's mead* was the mead of poetic inspiration brewed from the blood of Kvaser in the kettle Odhroerir, and which Odin stole from the giant Suttung. See ODHROERIR.

In Polish legend the famous Prince Piast once welcomed two strangers to his board when he was still a poor wheelwright and gave them the best of what he had. For thanks they told him that his cellars would be always filled with mead. The promise came true, for the young man had entertained angels unaware, who henceforth supplied him with mead and helped to make him king of Poland.

The people of the island of Rügen used mead in the worship of their sun god. At each harvest a cup of mead was put in the hand of the idol. During the following rites (seed-time or first-fruits) the priest took the cup from the god and predicted the coming year from the liquid left in the cup.

Rivers of mead in the other world is a motif (F162.2.4) occurring in English and Scottish ballad and in the Hausa Negro story of kind and unkind, the two girls en route to the other world pass by rivers of honey. That the Virgin Mary supplied mead to the unprepared hostess of a king (V262) is a motif familiar in religious legend. Sometimes this story is associated with St. Brigit of Ireland.

meadowsweet A shrub of the rose family (genus *Spiræa*). Meadowsweet was one of the strewing herbs of the 16th and 17th centuries, when the floors were strewn with rushes and various sweet-smelling plants. The 16th century English herbalist, Gerard, prescribed the flowers boiled in wine to "make the heart merrie and joyful and delight the senses." Meadowsweet is still used in England to make an herb beer, and for the cure of feverish colds and digestive troubles. The North American Meskwaki Indians used it to stop the flux; other Indians of the western United States use the leaves to regulate the bowels, and the pulp as a salve. In Ireland it is called *airgead luaćra*, or silver rushes, and in the country is used for scouring vessels. Meadowsweet was one of the sacred herbs of the druids, and in Welsh mythology was one of the flowers that went into the creation of Blodenwedd, the flower-wife of Llew Llaw Gyffes.

measure of eternity A folk riddle motif (H701.1): How many seconds in eternity? This belongs in the number riddle category (H700 ff.) and is often included among the questions in versions of *The King and The Abbot* (Type 922). The answer to how many seconds in eternity is: If a bird should carry one grain of sand away from a mountain once each century, one second of eternity would have passed when the mountain was gone.

Medea In ancient Greek legend, the daughter of Æetes, king of Colchis, by one of the Oceanids or Hecate. She was thus the niece of Circe, the great witch.

Medea too, a priestess of Hecate, was versed in magic; her reputation as a witch in antiquity probably surpassed that of Circe. When Jason came to Colchis in his quest for the Golden Fleece, Medea fell in love with him and helped him accomplish his aim. She gave Jason a drug, made from the yellow flowers that grew from Prometheus' blood in the Caucasus, and Jason was, for 24 hours, invulnerable to fire and iron. Thus he was able to yoke the fiery bulls, plow the land, and sow the dragon's teeth. She told him to throw stones among the warriors that sprang from the sown teeth, just as Cadmus had done, and he survived that dangerous task. Then, knowing that her father plotted to kill Jason and the Argonauts in the night, she herself stole the Fleece from the grove and fled with Jason on the *Argo*. The fugitives took with them Apsyrtus, Medea's younger brother, and when Æetes, in pursuit, came close, she slew the boy and threw his severed parts onto the sea. Æetes had to stop to gather the scattered Apsyrtus for proper burial, and the Argonauts escaped. (Another, later version says that Apsyrtus was the pursuer and was trapped in ambush by his perfidious sister.) Medea helped the Argonauts in several of their adventures on the return trip. For example, she either drugged the bronze Cretan monster Talos or used her evil eye or other trickery in such a way that she was able to pull the pin or break the membrane that let out his life fluid.

At Iolcos, they discovered that Pelias had had Æson, Jason's father, slain. Jason begged Medea to avenge him. Medea therefore convinced the daughters of Pelias that she could rejuvenate the old man: she took an old ram, chopped it up, boiled it in a caldron, and drew forth a lamb. (Some say she thus revivified or made young again Æson too; in some versions of the legend, he was not killed by Pelias.) But when Pelias was chopped up and put in the caldron, Medea made sure that Pelias perished. For this outrage, Pelias' son drove Jason and Medea from Iolcos. They settled in Corinth where, after several years, Jason threw over Medea for Glauce, daughter of Creon, the king. Medea, in revenge, sent Glauce a poisoned garment which burned the bride to death (in some versions, the palace itself burned down, and Creon along with it) and she killed her own two children by Jason. Then, in a dragon-drawn chariot, she fled to Athens, where she married Ægeus.

Recognizing Theseus when he came to Athens seeking his father, Medea plotted to do away with him. She had Ægeus send his son (though the fact was unknown to either Ægeus or Theseus) to destroy the Marathonian bull; when Theseus accomplished that feat, she plotted with Ægeus to poison him. But at the last moment, Ægeus recognized his son and dashed the cup of aconite from his lips. Driven from Athens, Medea fled to Asia, where her son Medeus, after slaying Medea's uncle, Perses, who had replaced Æetes on the throne, became eponym of the Medes. Medea, approached by Zeus, rejected his advances, thus earning Hera's gratitude. The goddess granted immortality to Medea and her children. In Elysium, Medea became the wife of Achilles.

The story of Medea and the Argonauts follows in outline folktale type 313—The Girl as Helper on the Hero's Flight. The Greek legend includes the son-in-law tasks (H310), the ogre's helpful daughter (G530.2), the obstacle flight (D672), the forgotten fiancée (D2003)—all less markedly than these motifs are found in more recent European märchen, but nevertheless recognizably. The typical ending, of the attempts by the girl to regain her husband and the eventual recognition and reconciliation, is not present here; but the tasks accomplished with the aid of the girl and the obstacle flight (not, however, with magic objects in this tale) mark this as belonging to the type. Probably originally (though the chronology is naturally not at all definite) the story of the Argonauts was one of extraordinary companions (e.g. *The Four Skillful Brothers*, Type 653) —compare the special abilities of the members of the crew of the *Argo*: Lynceus' sight, Orpheus' music, etc.— which later became fused with the story of the Girl as Helper.

media luna Literally, the half moon or crescent moon: a ritual dance of Mexico, near Mexico City, most solemn in the village of Ixtapan de la Sal. It is completely indigenous in its vigorous stamping steps and its accompaniment of drums and bamboo flutes. The dancers accent the rhythm with sweeping strokes of their short swords, recalling the *morisma* of Michoacán. They wear long one-piece tunics with long sleeves and on their heads large crescents. The significance is completely obscure, but suggests agricultural lunar associations. [GPK]

Media Vita A famous prayer melody of medieval plainsong, often mistakenly ascribed to Notker Balbulus (d. 912) but probably taken over into Roman Chant from the Gallican Chant; it was believed to work miracles and to give protection to those who sang it. One French brotherhood of monks sang it to prevent the installation of a new and unwelcome abbott. So strongly were its powers believed in that in 1316 the Council of Cologne forbade the singing of it against anyone without permission from the bishop.

medicine There is a plant in the world for every ailment; all you have to do is find it. This is the core of wisdom of an old Louisiana Bayou herb woman lovingly depicted by Ruth Bass in her article in Botkin's *Folk-Say: A Regional Miscellany*, 1930, p. 150. That there is a cure for everything, all man has to do is find it, has been the activating faith of medical research from the most ancient and primitive seekings to cancer and polio research today. The age-old belief of maritime fishermen in the efficacy of cod-liver oil has been substantiated by modern vitamin research. Burnt sponge for goiter was an old remedy and one good way of liberating the iodine therein (a modern must for goiter). Boiled toads for dropsy may sound like black magic, but the skins are now known to contain two alkaloids having marked diuretic properties. The herb women of the Carpathian area practiced antibiosis centuries ago: they applied bread mold or soil fungi to infected wounds and sores with success. Some primitive peoples terrify a sick man to frighten the disease demon out of his body. South American Aymara Indians cure tertian fever in this way. It is a method used everywhere for hiccups. A good dose of castor oil has always had the same effect regardless of the color, creed, or century of the patient, or of the ceremony accompanying the dosage. One good old folk cure for asthma is to swallow a handful of spider webs rolled into a ball. This is not as far-fetched as it may sound either: in 1882 a substance called *arachnidin* was isolated from spider webs which proved to be a remarkable febrifuge (see Leslie F. Newman, "Therapeutic Value of Folk Medicines" in *Folk-Lore* 59, p. 128).

Much has been written of healing by magic, incantation, and conjuration in ancient and primitive cultures. Disease and death were (and are) caused by malignant spirits everywhere; and the ancient and contemporary primitive cure is to outwit or get rid of the spirit. Thousands of elaborate incantations have been preserved from early Assyrian, Sumerian, and Babylonian cultures; and the holy or sacred incantation, recited or worn as amulet or talisman, was regarded as efficacious far into the European Middle Ages. See ABRACADABRA. But the remarkable practicality of the ancient Egyptian *Book of Surgery* (often referred to as the Surgical Papyrus, Old Kingdom), which goes back to at least 2500 B.C., is not often stressed. This work describes the diagnosis and treatment of 48 surgical operations, and for only one of the 48 was magic recommended.

The history of folk medicine is the history of medicine: a long drama of trial and error and dedication, of which the end is not yet: too long and involved a story for this article, including as it does no definite chronology but an overlay of theories of which the most ancient often coexist both in belief and practice with the newest. Modern European medicine is said to begin with Hippocrates (460–370 B.C.); but 100 years before Hippocrates Pythagoras advanced his theory of the harmony of the spheres and a doctrine of numbers which colored not only the Hippocratic theory of "critical days" but seven centuries later was applied by Galen (2nd century A.D.) to every phase of medicine. Names like Pythagoras, Empedocles, Hippocrates, Æsculapius (all B.C.), Pliny (23–79 A.D.), Galen (131–201 A.D.) become synonymous with the story of medicine. Galen's writings especially were infallible gospel for centuries after his death. The astrological school, stressing the influence of the planets, astrological houses, signs of the zodiac, on the prevalence and virulence of specific diseases and on the efficacy of the plants, gems, and other substances used as cures, reaches from its incipience in Chaldea through several thousand years. Even more than the astrological school has the doctrine of signatures probably influenced medical practice. The doctrine of signatures established the belief that all natural objects (plants, animals, animal parts, stones, etc.) bear a mark or sign (signature) indicating plainly the human need to which they are specifically applicable. Whether the doctrine of signatures originated in Egypt or Babylonia, its hold on human thought was still strong in the 17th century. Wm. Coles in his *Art of Simpling*, 1656, writes regarding herbs that not only has God given each its distinctive form, "but also hath given them particular signatures whereby a man may read . . . the medicinal virtue attached to it." Wm. Turner, who wrote the first English herbal, 1551, says therein, "the nutmeg being cut resembles the brain, the red poppy-flower resembles at its bottom the setling of the blood in the pleurisie and how excellent is that flower in disease of the pleurisie." The poppy was also assigned to cure brain disorders because its fruit was shaped like a head. Red roses were recommended for the blood. The ancient Assyrians used henbane seed for toothache, probably actually because of their soporific virtues, but according to the signaturists because the seed-container is jaw-shaped. Spotted plants

were recommended for spots; gummy plants were good for pus-exuding sores; non-flowering plants (fern, lettuce, savin) would cause sterility; many-seeded plants would cure barrenness. Any of the trefoils was indicated for heart trouble; bloodroot was given for bloody flux (dysentery); saffron cured biliousness; liverwort (named for its shape) also cured biliousness. Herb lore progressed from the "simples" (one-plant remedies) to fantastic mixtures and theriacs (poison antidotes) containing great numbers of herbs, animal parts, blood, ground or flaked gemstones, minerals, etc. Animals and parts of animals also were used because of some resemblance in shape or color to a disease or to a diseased part of the body. One theriac prepared by Andromachus for Nero is described as the longest and most complicated in history. See ÆSCULAPIUS; ANIMAL CURERS; BEAR MEDICINE; BEZOAR; CLOWN MEDICINE; COLLAHUALLA; COLLASIRI; CURES; EGG-CURING; EPILEPSY; HERB; LEPROSY; RABIES; RASPBERRY; RHEUMATISM; SHAMAN AND SHAMANISM; see also various specific plant, tree, and gemstone entries.

To ward off or cure, or to produce illness and disease, either psychosomatic or physical, the North American Indians employ a variety of magical and nonmagical procedures. Many of the annual ceremonies, such as that of the California World Renewal, the Pawnee Hako ceremony, the Big House, the Eskimo fall festival, and numerous others, as well as lesser rites such as the False Face and Shuck Face rites of the Iroquois and other tribes, were performed to ward off disease and epidemics and insure the health of the tribe for the ensuing year. Small family rites, such as Ghost Feasts given for dead relatives, were also customary insurance against sickness being visited upon individuals by the dead. The observance throughout native North America of hundreds of eating, looking, and many other tabus, was also a preventive measure against becoming sick or having bodily harm befall one.

Curing measures employed by the American Indians for illness, either mental or physical, are of three main types: those, magical or ritual, which were employed by shamans and priests; those measures which everyone in the tribe knew; and those measures which only a few persons had special knowledge of. Magic practices of many different sorts were used by shamans in treating sick persons; a very widespread one was that of sucking out the disease object from the patient's body. To locate this object, and to be able to tell who had sent it into the patient, the shaman was often assisted by his guardian spirit, usually an animal being whom he called to him with songs the spirit had taught him. Other magic practices were the capture and putting back into the patient of the patient's soul; Puget Sound shamans once a year made a dramatic journey to the land of souls, captured those belonging to living persons, and put them back into the patients' bodies. Elsewhere in North America belief in soul loss was common, but the measures taken to recapture souls not so dramatic. While most curing rites are conducted for an individual patient, some are communal, as the Puget Sound soul-loss treatment referred to above, or the communal cures conducted by some Pueblo Indian societies at which anyone present is treated gratis, sucked, brushed, or given a drink of medicine water, or the modern peyote rites which any sick person may attend.

Another curing measure, and the chief one among the

Navaho of the Southwest, was the singing or letter-perfect recitation by a "singer" of long formulas that must be repeated by the patient, to cure the latter's illness. Abbreviated formulas are also used by many tribes, when washing away a name that is causing a person to be ill, for example, and in the administration of herb medicines. In the Southeast, where medical practices are closely associated with shamanism and priestcraft, formulas are used extensively. Causes of disease are, according to native belief, natural and supernatural; in Cherokee and Creek mythology emphasis is laid upon animals as disease bringers and upon plants as healing agents. The greatest number of southeastern remedies were of vegetable origin, infusions being made and taken internally or applied externally, with certain objects often added because of their magical properties. Doctors blew into the infusion with a tube, and later sprayed the patient or sweated him, massaged him, caused him to vomit, scratched and sucked the affected parts, recited a formula over the patient, and finally buried the disease.

Some remedies, consisting chiefly of plant and animal parts and some minerals made into poultices, boiled up into teas, etc., are likely to be known generally by all members of any tribe, and are used for minor ailments; but for more acute illnesses a specialist, who has bought or inherited knowledge of special plant remedies, is likely to be consulted. Such plant remedies of specialists are often mixtures of two to as many as 30 or so plants. Knowledge of such medicines is usually kept a jealously guarded secret. If the illness is a major one, or of long standing, and does not yield to herb treatment, or if the patient has reason to believe that his illness is being caused by an evil shaman practicing witchcraft against him, treatment by a professional shaman or priest is the only efficacious medicine. In general esoteric knowledge or possession of medicine was one way to gain prestige and wealth in the group, since fairly heavy payment was made to shamans and priests for medical treatment. See MEDICINE MEN; SHAMAN. [EWV]

medicine bundles Sacred bundles, sacred packs, or palladia: among North American Indians a collection of objects believed to be endowed with sacred or magical properties. Such objects are usually wrapped up in a skin (deerskin, otterskin, etc.) and carefully tied into a bundle; the bundle is owned either by a group, or by individuals; it is believed to have been originally bestowed by supernatural beings, or to have been assembled according to the directions given by supernatural beings. Medicine bundles owned by individuals have a prominent place in Plains Indian religion; to each bundle is attached a long origin myth, but all such medicine-bundle origin myths conform to the same general pattern. Plains Indian bundles are kept outside the owner's dwelling house, suspended from a tripod arrangement; they, the myth, and the songs that go with them can be bought and sold. Plains societies also had their sacred bundles. In the southwestern pueblos medicine bundles are also the property of the many societies existent among these people. Ownership of society bundles is a group matter, as it is for Southeastern and Eastern Woodlands society, gens, and tribal sacred bundles. Minor medicine bundles, such as witch or rain bundles, might be privately owned, but the tribal or

clan bundles of the eastern tribes were considered the property of the group as a whole, were the most sacred of all objects, and the ones with which the welfare of a group was closely associated. Such bundles were in charge of a man who inherited the obligation of attending to the bundle, seeing that it was kept dry, that menstruating women kept away from it, offering tobacco to it at stated intervals, and, once a year during a ceremony attended by only a few persons, reclothing the bundle in a new deerskin covering, talking to it, and feeding it with food and tobacco. If the group as a whole moved to a new location, the tribal bundle was carried at the head of the procession by a bearer who walked slowly and saw to it that the bundle was kept dry. Actual objects within tribal bundles include flint knives, braided captive leaders, birds' claws, beaks, feathers, animal parts, wampum belts, etc. The provenience of each article is usually made clear in the myths told by the tribe. [EWV]

medicine man A name, loosely applied by 17th, 18th and 19th century travelers and missionaries to the American Indians, for any Indian who treated the sick in a variety of ways, prophesied, conjured, was able to find lost objects, or in general seemed possessed of supernatural powers. In the 20th century, when serious studies of American Indian cultures began to be made, such terms as shaman, doctor, herb doctor, witch, prophet, soon replaced the general term medicine man in the ethnographic literature. Today medicine man is seldom used except in popular writings on the Indians, by authors who probably do not realize that in several tribes either men or women, or women only, have the power to cure by supernatural means. [EWV]

In Mexico and Central America the concept of the shaman, or medicine man, who receives supernatural powers from a spirit who may take possession of his body during a curing or divination seance, is poorly developed. The curer, or *curandero* (who may be male or female), usually is a person who, through long study and experimentation, has mastered the tricks of a complex profession, just as a doctor in our society may practice, not because of divine revelation, but because of the proper education. There are exceptions to this general rule, however, among which may be noted the *sukya* and *okuli* of the Mískito Indians of Nicaragua, and the *nêles* of the Cuna of Panama, shamans who are "born, not made," i.e. they receive supernatural powers through involuntary "election" by divine spirits, and are unable to refuse this call, even if they should so desire. [GMF]

medicine rites Curative procedures dealing with supernatural causes and effects. Exorcism of malign spirits is commonly resorted to as a preventative measure. The Tamil Pariah (Paraiyans) caste of southwest India blow horns and strike themselves to drive out devils from the houses of the high Nayar caste. The Papago Indian deer dance and Tarahumara *rutuburi* summarily expel evil influences. For the same purificatory purpose the California Shasta women shamans and Iroquois False Faces make the rounds of the houses.

If a malignant object, spirit, or sorcerer has caused disease by intrusion or by stealing the patient's soul, a prophetic shaman must in a vision determine the cause and cure. In some tribes cause and effect are well recognized. The Papago believe that spirits of the dead cause nervous disorders; the deer spirit causes tuberculosis (deer cough); the Ponca Buffalo Dance healed wounds; the Iroquois Society of Mystic Animals (*hadi'hi'duus*) cures wounds and broken bones. To the Iroquois, ghosts cause neurosis; the buffalo spirit causes rheumatism in the shoulders, the bear spasms, the disembodied False Face spirits ailments of the eyes. These are cured by placating the offending spirit with various formulæ and rites, songs, dances, as well as by mechanical means.

Herbs and medicines are administered either by special kinds of doctors, as in the Menominee *mûckiki,* or by the regular doctor. Medicines were received from the supernatural: by the Menominee from the owl, by the Plains Bear, Elk, or Buffalo Societies, from these animals; and the power was received during initiation. Plains medicine bundles, however, contained an assortment of magic objects.

Curative herbs are always administered with attendant ritual, incantation, and sleight-of-hand tricks. Suction of the offending object is employed from Melanesia to Wisconsin and Brazil. Bleeding, massage, and trepanning effect cures in Melanesia; among the Navaho, ash-blowing, fire-jumping, asperging, arrow-shooting heal. The Iroquois strew ashes, spray berry juice to asperge the patient. An offering is essential, in the form of prayer and tobacco or incense. The world over, chanted formulæ strengthen the appeal; for instance, among the Zapotecs, Navaho, California and British Columbia tribes, the Melanesians, the Panan of southwest India.

Exorcism is effected by chanting, various noise-instruments, and dancing which varies from mild circling to frenzy. This may be the work of 1) a single shaman; 2) a select group of initiates; 3) the community, including the patient. 1) The Siberian, Navaho, or Ojibwa shaman hypnotizes himself and the patient by his chant, with drum or rattle accompaniment. The Tlingit and Labrador Eskimo medicine man may wear a spirit mask to intensify his impersonation. 2) Masked groups identify themselves with the spirits. The spectacular Navaho *yeibichai* perform rituals and dances, particularly in the Nightway, but also in the Windway, Beautyway, and other curing chants. The maskless shaman societies of the Algonquians (*midewiwin*) and of the Iroquois (*hadi'hi'duus*) sing and dance around the patient, who finally joins in and is thus initiated. 3) In several Iroquois curing rites the community may join after the introductory cure, thus the Bear and Buffalo Dances (*degwiyagǫ'oenǫ* and *nyagwai'oenǫ*). The Ute Sun Dance cures all present, particularly of rheumatism.

The choreographies are well defined for each dance, but show great variation, especially between solo and group rituals. Shamanistic solo dances may be virtuoso exhibitions; and soloists who perform simultaneously, as the Iroquois False Faces, may improvise elaborate steps. On the other hand, group dancers use simple steps, commonly a side or forward shuffle. These groups follow various ground plans, as the single line of men and women in the Meskwaki Bear Dance, the double column of men in the *yeibichai,* the clockwise closed circle of the Shoshoni *naroya,* and the open counterclockwise circle of the Iroquois Bear Dance. Meskwaki dancers imitate the bear with clawing arm gestures; the Iroquois simulate his waddling gait and climax with a jump-kick in pairing formation.

The double function of many of the healing dances shows varying emphasis, and, in the course of time, the loss of one function. Southwest tribes retain both hunting and healing objectives, but the latter is secondary. The Iroquois animal dances, on the other hand, concentrate on cures. The Cherokee Green Corn Dance, which formerly included a curative rite to prevent illness from the unripe corn, is now reduced to this secondary function. Or the ritual purpose may be lost entirely, as in the Medicine Dance of the Christian Cherokee.

The efficacy of these kinetic cures is not superstition. The incantations, mysterious passes, and unhygienic practices obscure the principle of dance therapy. But, in addition to the physiological benefits of the various herbs, the soothing effects of rhythmic song or dance-participation aid recovery, especially from neurotic and mental ailments. Modern psychotherapy has merely rediscovered the principles inherent in the ancient medicine rites. See ANIMAL CURERS; MASKS; SHAMAN. [GPK]

Mekala   A female spirit of terrifying appearance whom the Aymara Indians accuse of laying waste their fields and of killing their herds. [AM]

Melampus   In Greek mythology, the first person with prophetic powers, the first mortal doctor, the first Greek to worship Dionysus. Living at Pylos with Neleus, Melampus once found that his servants had killed two snakes. He burned the bodies—thus performing a pious rite accorded the human dead—and raised the young snakes as pets. Later, as Melampus slept beneath a tree one day, the snakes licked his ears with their tongues. When Melampus awoke, he discovered that he could understand the languages of the birds.

During his stay with Neleus, Melampus offered to help his brother Bias win Pero, daughter of Neleus, as wife. Neleus demanded as the bride-price—in a kind of suitor test (H310)—the cattle of Iphiclus which had belonged to Neleus' mother Tyro. Melampus, though he knew that the quest meant that he would be imprisoned for a year, set off to obtain the cattle. These cattle were guarded by a fierce dog that no man or beast could approach, but Melampus stole the cattle nonetheless. However, he was caught and thrown into prison. At the end of a year he suddenly demanded to be released, for, he said, the prison was about to collapse. And so it did; Melampus had learned the secret from the worms in the wood of the prison. His jailer carried the story to Iphiclus, who thereupon offered to release Melampus if he could tell why Iphiclus was childless. The seer learned the answer from a vulture that he questioned. See IPHICLUS. Compare JOSEPH.

Melampus also cured the mad daughters of Prœtus, either through his knowledge of herbs or as an initiate of the therapeutic Dionysiac dance rites.

Melanesian mythology   Melanesia, a tropical and often heavily vegetated culture area of the Pacific, is made up of three major geographical divisions. The first is New Guinea, largest island in the world, and connected in Pleistocene times with Australia. The second is an irregular, curving chain of archipelagoes, predominantly volcanic rather than coral, which starts near the equator north and east of New Guinea and extends south to the Tropic of Capricorn. It includes the Bismarck Archipelago, Solomon Islands, Santa Cruz and Banks Islands, New Hebrides, Loyalties, and New Caledonia. The third division is the Fiji Islands on the western boundary of Polynesia.

On the basis of differences in culture and physical type, Melanesian inhabitants are classified into three groups which, however, overlap as the result of contact and mixture. The oldest residents are the Negritos of the New Guinea interior, of whose mythology nothing is known. Papuans, the next arrivals, who stand out for amazing linguistic diversity, occupy most of New Guinea and have mixed with inhabitants of nearby islands. The Melanesians proper, who are Oceanic Negroids like the Papuans and speak Malayo-Polynesian dialects, occupy the central archipelagoes exclusive of distinctly Polynesian or Papuan islands. They have also immigrated to parts of the eastern New Guinea coast.

Occasionally, anthropologists classify New Guinea as a culture area distinct from Melanesia because of its size and the differences between its predominantly Papuan inhabitants and the Melanesians of the eastern islands. However, both New Guinea and the eastern islands are treated here as one great province whose mythology is related though probably divisible into subprovinces.

Throughout the area, cosmogonic myths assume the pre-existence of the world and its major characteristics, and merely describe subsequent alterations and additions to the landscape, zoology, botany, and culture by preexistent beings, deities, first man, and culture heroes. Few primitive areas have such a pot-pourri of cosmogonic beliefs. Even one small island will have different myths about the origin of man. Inconsistencies on the subject in myths of his own tribe do not trouble a narrator. Sometimes a deity or other being created man from wood, mud, or sand; sometimes man had a magical or spontaneous origin from eggs, plants, stones, bloodclots, or other things. The Papuan Keraki of southwestern British New Guinea narrate that the first people came out of a palm; the linguistic diversity of neighbors is explained by Gainji, the principal Originator (also the name of the primordial time when he lived), having listened to the chatter in the palm and released together people who sounded alike. That the first people came out of the ground is a belief often found among Papuo-Melanesian tribes and islands, like the Trobriands, near New Guinea. Emergence sites are respected but rarely seem to be places of worship.

Of the important deities of Melanesian mythology, the following are only a sampling: Ora Rove Marai of Roro-speaking tribes of New Guinea (see Seligmann, *Melanesians of British New Guinea*, Cambridge, 1910, p. 302); and Marunogere of the Kiwai Papuans, a deity associated with the first pig. Marunogere built the first men's house, inaugurated the *moguru* ceremony, created the first coconut tree, among other things, had two ferocious, named dogs who live in Adiri, the afterworld, and raid human villages (see Landtman, *Kiwai Papuans of British New Guinea*, London, 1927, pp. 12, 18, 97, 221, 350). Kalou-Vu is a class of important gods of Fiji (see W. Deane, *Fijian Society*; B. Thomson, *The Fijians*, London, 1908). See KALOU-VU. Others include Ye of Rossel Island (see W.E. Armstrong, *Rossel Island*, Cambridge, 1928, p. 132) and Sivotohu, a preexistent sky deity of Guadalcanal and his wife Koevasi (see Hogbin, *Oceania*, vol. 1, #1, 1937).

The sea, night, and fire are frequently said to have been hoarded by an elderly person, usually female, until mankind obtained it. The widespread Oceanic theme of fire hidden in the body is common in Melanesia. Frequently it is associated with serpents and lizards, and the fire, in western tribes, is usually said to have been kept between the firekeeper's thumb and forefinger, which explains the space now found between these fingers. Another universal Oceanic theme found in Melanesia ascribes the origin of the coconut from the buried head of a slain snake or other creature. Myths about plant origins abound and figure prominently in fertility rites. As women are kept ignorant of sacred myths and rituals, it is interesting how often myths, reminiscent of Australia in spirit rather than detail, are told about women having first possessed the bull-roarer and other sacred objects until men, realizing their value, took them for themselves. Myths frequently describe elderly women as culture teachers, and, in tales of abandoned villages, an old woman left behind contrives to get magically pregnant to bear children who marry each other, destroy monsters, and start the tribe anew.

Rarely is the name of a hero, deity, or other supernatural character of religion and mythology known beyond a single island or even one tribe, although other characters obviously drawn to a similar pattern appear in myths of nearby regions. The situation is typical of Melanesian cultural and linguistic variety which renders generalizations difficult. For the most part, specific motifs have an amazingly helter-skelter distribution.

Although R. B. Dixon, in his great work on Oceanic mythology, distinguished between Papuan and Melanesian elements in the myths of the area, he often found both kinds of elements in the same island. The Papuan stratum, he concluded, is best developed among certain New Guinea and New Britain tribes, and is characterized by a relative absence of cosmogonic myths, numerous stories of ghosts, many tales of only local distribution, and a simple, naive quality. The Melanesian stratum is most pronounced in Santa Cruz and Banks Islands, New Hebrides, Fiji, and some coastal tribes of eastern New Guinea, New Britain, and the Admiralties. Dixon also pointed out Melanesian and Papuan relationships in mythology with other parts of Oceania.

Since much Melanesian mythology has been published since 1916, Dixon's pioneer classification could now be sharpened and subprovinces defined on the basis of distribution of motifs, incidents, style, and character types. Unfortunately, little systematic comparative analysis has been done. Dixon used myths as indirect evidence for reconstructing the history of Oceanic cultures; and myths enter to a slight extent into the large-scale reconstructions of Melanesian culture history by schools of thought led by Rivers and Graebner. In general, the reconstructions are based on the hypothesis of immigration at different times into the area of peoples with distinctive culture-complexes. Diverse forms of the same culture element, for example origin myths, are attributed in these theories to introduction by different groups of immigrants, while the different classes of spirits, often of a goblin type, are claimed to represent folklorized memories of intruders or ancient residents of alien appearance and culture. Little is said of the diffusion of motifs and incidents independent of large-scale migration. Interpretation of the myths as symbolic accounts of the movements of the sun, moon, and other natural phenomena enters into many reconstructions.

Ivens (1934) used a few religious and social beliefs backed by mythological charters to define as a cultural unit the northern New Hebrides, the Banks, and southern and central Solomons. He observed the presence here of the Indonesian concept of soul substance and dual souls, one good, the other evil. San Cristoval worships the malevolent souls. The region, in general, worships souls of the dead, especially of greater individuals and culture heroes. Souls of the dead are distinguished from spirits who never were human. The latter called *figona* (or variants thereof) appear in various aspects, particularly snakes. Their San Cristoval leader, Agunua, creator of man among his many other activities, is probably equatable, according to Fox, to the Florida Island *vigona*, Koevasi. Shark cults are prominent.

Dual homes of the dead occur, with, however, the sky never figuring as one. The homes are in nearby islands except that a northern Mala home is underground. Ghosts travel by land or ship of the dead to a port of entry where a ghost ruler segregates them. Ysabel Island dead who are tattooed with the frigate-bird design cross a pool of quicksand safely on an ironwood log; those without the design perish in the collapse of a softwood bridge. Florida Island ghosts are segregated, with souls of evil intent going to a dolorous district of Guadalcanal where they eventually perish; the good souls go to Malapa Island to live happily eternally.

Ivens also found myths of this region to lack emphasis on sexual matters. Another characteristic, the rarity of long migration traditions, he attributed to Melanesian social organization being predominantly matrilineal. Patrilineal Mala Island, he pointed out, has migration myths about red-headed culture heroes like Sina Kwao and Gwau Meo, now powerful war ghosts with cults, who introduced magic, new foods, the war bow, and other culture elements. Nowhere in the area occur migration legends and genealogies comparable in length and elaboration to those of Polynesia.

Comparative analysis of the myths alone would probably support Ivens' view of this region as a closely related cultural unit. It seems to be the heart of Melanesian culture as distinguished from Papuan. While certain concepts found here, such as those of soul substance, dual souls, worship of ancestral spirits, distinction between ghosts and non-human spirits, stones with magical power, and reincarnation in snakes and other creatures, appear elsewhere in Melanesia and New Guinea, they have perhaps a sufficiently distinctive local interpretation to justify their use as criteria for defining a subarea.

This is certainly the case as regards different classes of spirits who were never human and who people the Melanesian atmosphere, making travel outside the village an affair of extreme danger. From Buka Island to the New Hebrides, some of the same classes, with occasional overlapping of traits and adventures, occur. For example, one class consists of foolish people, often without individual names, who do everything topsyturvy. Ulawa and San Cristoval call them merely *masi*, foolish; southern Mala has a variant of the same term, but northern Mala calls them "People of Morodo" after their residential site. They do silly things leading to their death, like diving for sunbeams in deep pools or tying their canoes to a tree on a precipice, cutting the rope, and shoving off. Spirits called *Kakamora* in San Cristoval and Guadalcanal are like the *Tukis* of Buka and *Nopitu* of Banks Islands. Though sometimes dangerous, their favorite sport is to count the toes and fingers of sleeping Melanesians and discuss the villagers. Many myths are about rather stupid, cannibalistic ogres who, in Guadalcanal and Mala, constitute a class called *Muumuu* because of their babbling in an alien tongue. Numerous pathetic myths concern snake grandmothers who have good qualities but suffer through human distrust.

Snakes figure prominently in the religion and mythology of most of Melanesia and New Guinea. The *figona* (*vigona*, etc.) of eastern Melanesia often have snake form; Agunua of San Cristoval is a leading figona of that island and a creator. Ndengei, chief member of the Fijian Kalou Vu, has serpent form—which Thomson thinks may have been a late idea. Wonajo, culture hero and deity of Rossel Island has snake form as has Raudalo of British New Guinea.

Wonder heroes, whether regarded as ancestors or fictions, share many qualities. For instance, the moment a hero is born he wraps his umbilical cord around his neck and sets out to kill monsters and perform miraculous deeds. The numbers eight and ten predominate in these and other eastern Melanesian tales. Incidents pass from one hero to another whether he is Rapuanate, Sina Kwao, Born-by-the-side-of-a-bow, or one of the famous conflicting brothers.

Many stories are about a hero who is wise and benevolent but is hampered by one or more stupid brothers or companions who attempt to kill him or muddle up his deeds. Though often compared to the Polynesian cycle about Maui and his brothers, these Melanesian hero cycles appear to have no specific resemblances to it. No single name dominates Melanesian hero cycles. In the Banks Islands, Qat has either eleven brothers, including Tagaro the wise and Tagaro the foolish, or a spider, Marawa, who act as marplots. Marawa sometimes is his aide. The New Hebridean Tagaro, the wise brother, is hindered either by Suqe-matua, Meragbuto, or eleven brothers including Suqe. In the Solomon Islands, Warohunuga has difficulties with his brothers; and in New Britain, To-Karvuvu and To-Kabinana are at odds. Even Agunua has been outfitted with a human brother to act as a marplot and burn some of the yams, thereby causing certain foods to be forever unedible. Cosmogonic, trickster, and monster-slaying adventures have accrued to the wonder heroes, and although their specific deeds vary, a frequent kind of incident is of the type described for Agunua. In the Banks Islands, the widely spread Melanesian theme of the origin of death is attached to the Qat cycle. The grandmother who rejuvenated herself by casting off her old skin in a stream frightened her grandson who did not recognize her, and so she put back her old skin and death came to the world.

Inevitably, the mythology reflects the life of its narrators. An interesting group of eastern stories is about orphans, who though scorned by other children and relatives, rise to the highest rank in the Suqwe, the Banks Islands' secret society whose ranks determine social status in the village. Typical of the group is the story told by Codrington about Little Orphan who is miraculously aided by a sea woman, Ro Som (Money), and her child. She magically builds the orphan a house and clubhouse, supplies him with gardens and pigs, and sends him to his maternal uncle to ask him to pay for his first Suqwe grade. The astonished uncle, who thus far has fallen down in his obligations, agrees to sponsor him and make the first payment when he sees Little Orphan's wealth. The boy immediately repays him and gives a great feast. With only progressive differences, the narrator with loving detail describes the bags of money and pigs Little Orphan produces to pay his sponsoring uncle for each advanced grade and the feasts with all the trimmings. Villagers "carry away, carry away, carry away, carry away" payments of Little Orphan whose uncle's wives are now making love to him. His luck ends when he insults Ro Sum and she returns to the sea leaving him in the midst of a deserted garden. Here is the Cinderella story, *par excellence,* of Melanesian culture.

Both important ceremonies and minor magical rites are backed by myths accounting for their origin and their ritual, which is often a reenactment in costume, with dances and songs, of the events of the myth.

Going north and west of the region defined by Ivens, more and more unfamiliar elements, designated as Papuan, begin to appear, although elements familiar from the southern and eastern islands persist. Wheeler (1926) noted parallels without drawing conclusions about historical relationships in myths he collected in the western Melanesian-speaking islands of Mono and Alu with myths in a sample of a half-dozen collections in a region from north of the New Hebrides to Papuo-Melanesian New Guinea and Torres Straits. Mono-Alu myths and songs, he stated, are in many instances directly derived from Papuan-speaking Buin district, southern Bougainville, studied by Thurnwald.

A. C. Haddon, in his field reports and introductions to studies by other ethnographers, has frequently analyzed portions of the mythology of western Melanesia and New Guinea, particularly that of Torres Straits Islands and the adjacent areas of Cape York Peninsula, Australia, and Papuan New Guinea. Especially helpful are his descriptions of culture bearers like Sido of Torres Straits and New Guinea, and cults which have arisen around heroes like the war-hero Kwoiam (who has affinities with the Cape York hero, Sivirri), Waiet, the Brethren, and others. He found no direct connection between the myths about the Brethren and the brother cycles of eastern Melanesia. As seems to be the case in Melanesia, similarities are often only of a general kind at opposite ends of the area.

The most immediately striking quality of Papuan mythology and religion as contrasted with eastern Melanesia is the elaboration of sexual matters which reflects the intense concern about the fertility of gardens. Innumerable stories are told about the origin of plants, and plant fertility is often anthropomorphized. For instance, Kiwai Papuans (Landtman) tell about Sido, the culture hero, who killed his wife and planted parts of her body from which food plants arose. Sido ate the fruits without biting them and they lodged in his sexual parts. His marriage with Pekai of Murray Island led to the birth of plants now growing there. Impregnation of this type recalls Polynesian myths about Maui, Pani, and other characters. Both Sido and Pekai now figure prominently in gardening magic. Sido was also the first

man to die; his trip to Adiri, the other world where he married the ruler's daughter who then bore plants like Pekai, established the itinerary and adventures of later ghosts.

The function of mythology in the culture particularly of Papuans and Papuo-Melanesians is extremely well documented in the reports of Malinowski, Fortune, Williams, Landtman, Seligmann, and others. Malinowski, finding that he was "collecting texts but disregarding contexts," began to "study the myths alive," recording data on modes of narration, circumstances of narration, and the direct and indirect influences of the myths on the life of the people. He learned that the Trobriand Islanders, the subject of his research, recognized three categories of folklore, categories based less on textual differences than on differences in cultural setting. The *kukwanebu* are fairy tales told in the rainy season for entertainment. Their telling, vaguely believed to help agriculture, ends with a conventional phrase, "very fertile wild plants." Stories are individually owned. The *libogwo* are historical legends believed to be true and are told at historic spots or on overseas journeys. They enhance the prestige of the people involved. The *liliu*, sacred myths, are connected with religious beliefs and rituals. They tell about miracles which rituals and dramas today reenact, and provide codes, justifications, and precedents for religious, magical, and ethical behavior. They belong especially to great ceremonial occasions and the harvest season when spirits of ancestors, *Baloma,* come from the underground to visit the villages. Comparable categories with much information particularly about the function of sacred myths have been described by the other ethnographers mentioned above.

Analysis of the literary style of myths and songs has been carried on particularly by Fortune for Dobu Island, Thurnwald for Buin, Seligmann for Papuo-Melanesians of New Guinea, and Quain for Fiji. Whenever collectors have published texts with both literal and free translations, as in the case of Wheeler for Mono-Alu and Fortune for the New Guinea Arapesh, to quote two examples, it is possible to carry on literary analysis for oneself to some extent. Ivens and Fox have recorded in eastern Melanesia proverbial sayings, lullabies, and conventional, poetic salutations to places, objects, people, and animals which give a good idea of these phases of literature.

Little has been said here of Melanesian relationships in mythology with Micronesia, Polynesia, Australia, and Indonesia. One finds few attempts, except by Dixon, to deal with this aspect of the problem. The southern New Hebrides, Tikopia, Ontong Java, Fiji, and other islands within Melanesia with more or less Polynesian culture and physical type are always of interest. Here one finds the Polynesian Maui-tikitiki at some of his old tricks plus a few Melanesian additions, and there are many other Polynesian themes, some of which have spread into adjacent islands more definitely Melanesian in character. Polynesian parallels in Fison's Fijian collection have been pointed out by Gifford. The Polynesian outliers in Melanesia probably represent colonization from Polynesia. Many of the themes shared by Melanesia and Micronesia are the same as shared with Polynesia.

Bibliography: W. E. Armstrong, *Rossel Island* (Cambridge), 1928; B. Blackwood, *Both Sides of Buka Passage* (Oxford), 1935; R. H. Codrington, *The Melanesians* (Oxford), 1891; A. B. Deacon, *Malekula* (London), 1934; R. B. Dixon, "Oceanic" in *Mythology of All Races*, vol. 9 (Boston), 1916, and "The swan maiden theme in the Oceanic area" in *Holmes Anniversary Volume* (Washington), 1916; F. Graebner, "Kulturkreise und Kulturschichten in Ozeanien," *Zeit. für Ethnologie*, vol. 37, 1905, and "Die melanesische Bogenkultur," *Anthropos*, vol. 4, 1909; R. Firth, *We, the Tikopia* (New York), 1936; L. Fison, *Tales from Old Fiji* (London), 1907; E. W. Gifford, *Tongan Myths and Tales* (Honolulu), 1924; R. F. Fortune, *Arapesh* (New York), 1942, and *Sorcerers of Dobu* (London), 1932; A. C. Haddon, *Reports of the Cambridge Anthrop. Exped. to Torres Straits*, vol. 1 (Cambridge), 1935; E. Hadfield, *Among the Natives of the Loyalty Group* (London), 1920; C. B. Humphreys, *The Southern New Hebrides* (Cambridge), 1926; W. Ivens, "The diversity of culture in Melanesia," *Royal Anthrop. Inst., Jour.*, vol. 64, 1934; also *Island Builders of the Pacific* (London), 1930; and *Melanesians of the South-east Solomon Islands* (London), 1927; D. Jenness and A. Ballantyne, "Language, mythology, and songs of Bwaidoga, Good-enough Island, S. E. Papua," in *Polynesian Soc., Memoirs*, vol. 8, 1928; A. Ker, *Papuan Fairy Tales* (London), 1910; A. Kleintitschen, *Die Küstenbewohner der Gazellehalbinsel* (München), 1906, and *Mythen und Erzählungen eines Melanesierstammes aus Paparatava, Neupommern, Südsee* (Wien), 1924; Lambert, *Moeurs et superstitions des Néo-Calédoniens* (Nouméa), 1900; G. Landtman, *The Folk-tales of the Kiwai Papuans* (Helsingfors), 1917; and *The Kiwai Papuans of British New Guinea* (London), 1927; B. Malinowski, *Coral Gardens and Their Magic* (New York), 1935; *Myth in Primitive Psychology* (London), 1926, and *The Foundations of Faith and Morals* (London), 1936; J. Meier, *Mythen und Erzählungen der Küstenbewohner der Gazelle-Halbinsel* (Münster), 1909; R. Parkinson, *Dreissig jahre in der Südsee* (Berlin), 1908; G. Peekel, *Religion und zauberei auf dem mittleren Neu-Mecklenburg* (Münster), 1910; B. Quain, *The Flight of the Chiefs* (New York), 1942; W. H. R. Rivers, *The History of Melanesian Society* (Cambridge), 1914; F. Sarasin, *Ethnologie der Neu-Caledonier und Loyalty-Insulaner* (München), 1929; C. S. Seligmann, *The Melanesians of British New Guinea* (Cambridge), 1910; B. Thomson, *The Fijians* (London), 1908; R. C. Thurnwald, *Forschungen auf den Salomo Inseln* (Berlin), 1912; and "Profane literature of Buin, Solomon Islands," *Yale Univ. Publ. in Anthrop.*, No. 8, 1936; G. C. Wheeler, *Mono-Alu Folklore* (London), 1926; F. E. Williams, *Orokaiva Magic* (London), 1928; *Orokaiva Society* (London), 1930; and *Papuans of the Trans-Fly* (Oxford), 1936; P. Wirz, *Die Marind-Anim von Hollandisch-Süd-Neu Guinea* (Frankfurt), n.d. The above bibliography is only representative; many volumes listed have extensive bibliographies and glossaries. Important articles also appear in *Anthropos, Folk-Lore, Oceania, Journal of the Royal Anthrop. Inst.*, and Hastings' *Encyclopedia of Religion and Ethics*.   KATHARINE LUOMALA

Melusine Heroine of a local legend attached to the house of Lusignan of France and embodying the tabu against offending the supernatural wife (C31). The Melusine story, though localized, is paralleled elsewhere and makes a well-defined motif (C31.1.2) within this group of motifs. Some trace the story from Mylitta wor-

ship (e.g. Mylitta, Melissa, Melusine) coming to France through the Mediterranean from the Near East; others derive the name Melusine from Mère des Lusignan (Mother of the Lusignans: e.g. Mère Lusigne, Merlusine, Melusine).

As told by Jean d'Arras in 1387 (some 200 years after first mention of the tale in Gervase of Tilbury), Elinus, king of Scotland, married the fairy Pressina. To this marriage was attached the lying-in tabu: the husband might not see the wife in the lying-in chamber. After three daughters were born, Melusine, Melior, and Plantina, Elinus broke the tabu and Pressina returned to Avalon. Melusine, when she grew older, imprisoned her father in a mountain, for which act her mother ordered that she become a serpent from the waist down every Saturday. Yet, if she could find a husband who would agree not to see her on Saturdays, she might obtain release from this punishment and die naturally. She was discovered by Count Raymond of Lusignan (Raimund of Russetum in Gervase) bathing in a woodland spring. They married; he agreed to observe the tabu. But her many sons were born each with some defect. One of Raymond's brothers convinced him finally that Melusine's Saturday retreats were made in order to entertain a lover. (Monstrous children are commonly believed to be the offspring of illegitimate love.) Raymond broke into her room and saw her, half-serpent, bathing. Nothing was said then, but during a later quarrel he called her a "false serpent." She left at once and he never saw her again. As she fled, she left a footprint outside a window of the castle: a corroborating bit of evidence for tellers of the local legend. Melusine returned to nurse her children and could be heard flying around the castle, crying mournfully.

This latter incident indicates either that she was dragon rather than serpent, or that we have here an obvious link to the swan-maiden tales. The breaking of the tabu, reduplicated in this story by the incident of Pressina, is itself simply another version of the offended supernatural wife motif told by others and worked into the tale so that it would not be lost. Parallels of the Melusine story are found in several parts of the world. The lying-in tabu is known in Japan, where Hiko-hohodemi disobeys his wife's commandment and sees her as a monster. She, daughter of the sea king, flees in shame, leaving behind her child. This childbirth tabu reflects a general custom, well known in Europe. The nakedness tabu appears in the Hindu story of Urvaśi. The serpent lady is a central character in the *Libeaus Desconus* of the 14th century, but such monsters, transformed or otherwise, are common in folktale, legend, and myth through the undines, mermaids, etc., back to Oannes and Tiamat of Mesopotamia. See CUPID AND PSYCHE; LOOKING TABU.

mending the jug A folktale motif (H1023.9; H1023.9.1) occurring in a large category of stories based on the impossible or absurd task (H1010–1049) and associated with the equally absurd or impossible countertask (H951). When the man is given the task of mending the broken jug he says he will if the other will first turn it wrongside-out for him. The man who was given the task of skinning the stone (H1023.10; H1023.10.1) countered with the request that the other first let the stone bleed a little. See CATCHING A MAN'S BREATH.

mennyasszony tánc Bride's dance: a wedding dance of Hungarian peasants. On the evening following a wedding, the bride is "bartered" off by the best man. All who wish to buy a dance with her put money in a plate or a shawl hung around her shoulders. Finally the bridegroom gives the largest gift and the bride is his. The step used is a *csárdás*. [GPK]

Mên Shen Chinese gate gods: commonly seen as pictures of two warriors in full uniform and brilliant colors pasted on the front doors at New Year's time. A third figure is sometimes pasted on the back gate. These posters, printed from woodblocks and colored by hand, represent an aspect of Chinese folk art little known in the Occident. The legend of origin is that a T'ang emperor suffered from insomnia because his vital essence was being depleted by a female shape-shifter. Two officers from his army spent all their time at his door to protect him. In order that they too might have rest he had their pictures painted on his door. Chinese recognition of the dangers of the threshold is, however, much older than the T'ang dynasty. [RDJ]

menstruation The process of discharging the unfertilized ovum and its accessory tissues, including blood, which periodically occurs in women. This recurrent phenomenon is a manifestation of the human reproductive cycle, and an index of the maturity of the human female. It occurs between the menarche (i.e. the first appearances of the flow), and the climacteric (period of cessation), which approximately covers a period between twenty-five and forty years. Although there is great individual variation in frequency and duration of the menstrual period, it recurs roughly once a month, and lasts from four to seven days, hence its obvious association with the phases of the moon. The word itself is from Latin *mensa*, month.

Patterns of behavior during the period of the discharge show great variation. Some cultures select this period as a time within which specific behavior is enjoined upon women and men.

The first appearance of menstruation is known in English as the menarche. The Italians recognize it linguistically, in the phrase "she has become a woman." Both of these usages mark a transition from one feminine status to another. Observation of such transition may take sundry forms: it may be ignored; or it may have familial recognition as among the Jews of eastern Europe, where the newly menstruating girl is slapped on both cheeks "to give her color" or "so that she won't have pain." Among North American Apache Indians, the pubescent girl is the source of greatest blessing, and in a special ceremony transfers this boon to all who are near her. Some index of the culture's value system may be deduced from the phrases used to give reassurance to the girl: for the east European Jews, the girl is told "Every woman menstruates. Your mother menstruates. Your grandmother menstruates." The Irish girl is told "Even the Virgin Mary menstruated"; in England she is informed that "Even the Queen menstruates."

In the cultures of which we have record, there is a wide range of behavior regarding this periodic and recurrent phenomenon which physiologically so strongly demarcates the woman from the man. From some peoples in or near New Guinea we have reports of "male menstruation." The Banaro simulate menstruation in

men by cutting the urethra so that blood flows. In some cultures menstruation is a shameful thing, to be concealed at all costs; in others, it is overt and a matter of common knowledge.

There are many places where a menstruating female is forbidden to participate in religious activities. In Poland, she is not allowed to attend church, for if a drop of the menstrual flow should fall on the floor or ground, the place would become impure. Similarly, among members of the Russian Orthodox Church, a menstruating woman is forbidden to kiss the Cross or to take communion. It is remarkable that among east European Jews, who practice strictly circumscribed menstrual behavior, these religious interdictions do not operate.

According to the rules laid down in *Leviticus*, all kinds of dire penalties ensue for the male who has congress with a menstruating female, including various forms of skin diseases. The rationale which lies behind these interdictions are protective—not for the man or woman, but for the child; it is thought that a child born of such a union may be scrofulous, feeble-minded, crippled, epileptic, or insane. Nevertheless, the menstruating female, who must avoid her husband, is not prohibited from baking the Sabbath bread, worshiping in the synagogue, blessing the candles, or preparing and serving food. Recent researches have uncovered the fact that menstruation as a special state is operative *only* for the matron and not for the girl. An unmarried Jewish girl does not have to observe the ceremonial purification in the *mikva* (ritual bath), which married women must take seven days after the cessation of the flow. This involves three total immersions of the body in a pool of "living water." After this has been done, the woman may then resume her conjugal duties.

The woman in childbed and the menstruating woman are often treated identically, both being in an impure state and needing ceremonial cleansing before they can resume their normal duties. See CHURCHING OF WOMEN.

In some places menstruation is regarded as advantageous for or antithetical to various mechanical and natural processes. For example, over large areas of East Africa menstruating women may not come near the dairy, or have anything to do with milk. In some extreme cases they may not even drink milk. Not only may the direct touch be harmful, but also the glance (as among the Bushmen of Africa), the footstep (as among American Indians, where the girl must take a separate path), or the breath (in southern France) which will prevent mayonnaise from thickening. In Italy the urine of a menstruating woman will cause flowers to wither, and, if a menstruating woman approaches a mare in foal, it will abort. In various parts of the United States, a menstruating woman must not touch cut flowers, else they will wilt; if she handles bread dough, it won't rise, or if she touches meat in pickle, jelly, or pickles, they will be spoiled. By the same token, in the south of France, she may not go near newly fermenting wine, flowers that are to be made into perfume, or milk for cheese. On the other hand, the blood of a newly menstruating girl, a virgin, was used in Germany to give the proper temper to the metal forged into a sword.

Menstrual blood has been used as an element in love magic: several drops introduced into the food or drink of a desired lover "binds" him to the woman. Such practices have been reported from Spain, France, Germany, and the United States. Sometimes the reverse takes place, and possession of a few drops of the discharge enables the possessor to have a permanent hold on the person from whom it has been obtained. In certain places *poltergeist* phenomena have been equated with the menstruating woman. Several cases in France have been noted whereby if a menstruating woman touches a harp or violin, the strings break; and in some extreme instances, such women cannot keep their clothes on.

It is thought by many people that prolonged lactation will prevent the return of menstruation after the birth of a child. In some instances, the return of menstruation is thought to poison the mother's milk.

Certain people hide the fact of menstruation most prudishly; others advertise it, as did Marguerite Gautier in *La Dame aux Camelias*, who carried red flowers during her catamenial period, or the Italian peasant woman who wore a red head kerchief while menstruating. The high caste woman in India will use a deeper shade of red cosmetic when she paints her forehead.

Cessation of the menses is not necessarily equated with pregnancy by all peoples. The Arunta of Australia, for instance, date the onset of pregnancy from the time they feel the quickening.

While in a number of cultures the onset of the menses is celebrated, the cessation (the menopause) is often overlooked. There are no known or authenticated records of the celebration of the menopause. In a limited area, mainly in the Washington and Oregon coastal region, a woman after her climacteric is the heroine of the stereotyped "romance," i.e. the romantic tales most relished are those which deal with love between a post-climacteric woman and a young man.

The position that menstruation holds in a given culture may often be identified by the jokes and other verbal play given to this topic. In the United States, it is an adolescent humorous theme; in France, it is considered more suitable for adult humor. See ADOLESCENCE CEREMONIES; AVYA; BLOOD; BREAD; DELUGE; PUBERTY DANCES; PUBERTY RITES.

Bibliography:

1. Abel, Theodora M. and Joffe, Natalie F., "Cultural Backgrounds of Female Puberty," *American Journal of Psychotherapy*, Vol. IV, No. 1, pp. 90–113, 1950.
2. Ashley-Montagu, M. F., "Physiology and the Origins of the Menstrual Prohibitions," *Quart. Rev. Biol.*, 1940, 15, pp. 211-220.
3. Crawfurd, Raymond, "Note on the Superstitions of Menstruation," *Lancet*, Dec. 18, 1915, Vol. I, pp. 1331–1336.
4. Vosselmann, Fritz, *La Menstruation—Légendes, Coutumes et Superstitions.* L'Expansion Scientific Fran-çaise, Paris, 1936.   NATALIE F. JOFFE

🖝 The periodic flow of blood from the uterus, normally occurring in adult females every four weeks, is accounted for in American Indian origin tale material from several tribes. Nanabozho, culture-hero-trickster of the Ojibwa, Menomini, Potawatomi, etc., causes his grandmother to menstruate and decrees that thereafter women shall do so each month; the Shawnee also attribute menstruation to the grandson of their supreme female deity who causes his grandmother to menstruate. The Yuchi Indians of the Southeast believe that Sun created the Yuchi, having caused their forebears to spring from a drop of menstrual blood in the Sky world, before they were put on earth. In a White Mountain Apache tale the Sun sends one of his beams, a red one, into Changing Woman as she lies in the ceremonial menstrual hut, and she begins to menstruate. In a Chiricahua Apache tale White Painted Woman institutes the puberty rites for girls at their first menstruation.

White Painted Woman spoke to the people and said: "When the girls first menstruate you shall have a feast. Let there be songs and dancing for the girls for four nights. Let the Gahe dance in the east in front of the ceremony." Today masked dancers personify the Gahe in the rite. The girl herself must not sleep for the four days and nights; on the fifth morning she must make four runs around the ritual baskets, while the woman who has care of her during the rite chants the shrill praise-call and prays for her. The songs are sacred prayer songs, among them homeopathic songs to White Painted Woman:

> White Painted Woman carries this girl,
> She carries her through long life,
> ....to good fortune,
> ....to old age,
> She bears her to peaceful sleep.

On the morning of the fifth day, while the girl runs into the sunrise, the last song is sung, beginning with the moving words: "You have started out on the good earth." See M. Astrov, *The Winged Serpent*, New York, 1946, p. 206.

Menstrual blood, as well as the blood and bloody secretions from childbirth, are generally believed so powerful by American Indians that women are, with a few exceptions, isolated in a special hut, at a distance from the family dwelling during menstruation or childbirth. Men should never come into contact with menstruants or with the dishes, baskets, clothes, or any other articles used by them. To do so makes a man unclean; being unclean he will not be able to obtain a guardian spirit, or kill game when he hunts—two matters of prime importance to the American Indian male. Yet occasionally, in American Indian mythology, there are tales in which Trickster or some other character has intercourse with a menstruating woman; this is an unthinkable act in real life. Menstrual blood, being so powerful, is occasionally mentioned as being used for medicine of a powerful sort, and in a Shawnee tale of the horned underwater serpent the monster is lured to land by a group of shamans, through the use of ashes taken from the hearth in a girl's menstrual hut. It was during menstrual periods, and especially the first one, that young girls were likely to have visions and obtain guardian spirits who conferred upon them songs and supernatural power for doctoring or other pursuits open to women. [EWV]

🖝 Menstrual seclusion is not a general custom in Middle America. Among the Sumu and Miskito Indians of Nicaragua, however, menstruating women must occupy a special shelter or a secluded corner of the hut for two or three days. During this period the woman is unclean, and must not touch food intended for other people, since to do so would cause their death. [GMF]

mento An erotic Jamaican dance, formerly a country dance, now a night-club favorite. Its music is slower and more voluptuous than that of the *rumba*. The woman tantalizes her partner into a frenzy with seductive rolling of the haunches and belly and works herself into a state of autointoxication. [GPK]

Mentula Loquens A variation of the talking privates motif (D998; D1610.3) found in Plains Indian myths, in which Trickster's private parts give him magic advice, or betray unchastity. In the Mentula Loquens motif (D998; D1610.3; H451) a man's penis speaks and can be silenced only by his mother-in-law. The full import of this can only be gained when one realizes that in the Plains tribes (Crow, Assiniboine, Pawnee, Kiowa, Apache) in which this incident is told the mother-in-law tabu prevails; a man cannot speak to, look at, or eat with his mother-in-law, much less indulge in any joking or sex-play with her. Closely related to talking privates and Mentula Loquens is the more widespread American Indian motif of talking excrements (D1002, D1312.1) in which a man, usually Trickster, is given magic advice by his own excrements. [EWV]

mercy-killing To be properly classified as a mercy-killing it must be humane in both motive and method. Its connection with folklore is mainly in infanticide and geronticide. It also has secondary folklore interest because arguments both for and against it are taken from religious tabus, commandments, and sanctions. Many, for instance, argue against even the voluntary euthanasia of incurable sufferers on the ground that it is prohibited by the Mosaic "Thou shalt not kill" of the King James version of the Bible, although the original Hebrew and LXX of the Old Testament passages (*Exodus* xx, 13 and *Deuteronomy* v, 17), the Greek of the corresponding New Testament passages (*Matthew* xix, 18; *Mark* x, 19; *Luke* xviii, 20) where Jesus quotes the commandment, and all modern scholarly revised translations give "thou shalt not commit murder." Murder is properly applied only to killing which is with malice aforethought, hence killing in self-defense, capital punishment, and war are exempted by law. Euthanasia advocates contend that carefully regulated euthanasia of those who request it and are pronounced medically incurable by examining physicians should be legalized since it is with mercy aforethought. They also quote the beatitude of Jesus (*Matt.* v, 7) "Blessed are the merciful for they shall obtain mercy," and the golden rule of Jesus (*Matt.* vii, 12) "Therefore all things whatsoever ye would that men should do to you, do ye even so to them: for this is the law and the prophets." In modern times the law seems to disagree with the prophets on this issue, but convictions for mercy-killing are hard to secure, sentences if any are apt to be light, and juries are likely to accept a plea of temporary insanity rather than face the controversial ethical issue. Religious leaders are divided on the subject. [CFP]

☞ It is customary in many South American tribes to strangle or choke a dying person. The Aymara Indians have expert killers called *despenadores* who dispatch the dying by strangulation or by breaking their necks. The psychological motives behind this custom are not well known. It is attributed to the desire of hastening the departure of the fearful ghost or to the wish of sending away the soul before the illness has impaired its vigor. [AM]

merengue The national dance of Santo Domingo, West Indies: distantly related to the Haitian *meringue*. Gay music in 2/4 time is played by an accordion, a *tambora* (drum) and a *guiro* (notched gourd rasped by a notched stick), in catchy rhythms. The first part of the dance, *pambiche*, is a slow promenade; the second part, *jaleo*, is a lively reminiscence of Afro-Spanish-Cuban dances. To steps resembling the *son* and *rumba*, it adds more virtuoso motions, like the horizontal shaking of the knees in flexed position. As all dances of the West Indies, it has an erotic flavor, but without the trancelike abandon of more aboriginal dances like the *mento*. [GPK]

Merlin A poet, wizard, and prophet, who lived supposedly in the 6th century, and in the 12th became a prominent figure in the Arthurian legend. The works ascribed to him are few, but the medieval literature about him is very extensive, being found in most of the languages of Western Christendom. The material may be divided into four classes: 1) Welsh poems; 2) Geoffrey of Monmouth's works; 3) the French and derivative romances; 4) local associations and folktales. The Breton poems printed in *Barzaz-Breiz* by La Villemarqué will not be considered since they are forgeries.

1) During the Dark Ages there grew up a legend about a wild man of the woods who was endowed with the gift of prophecy. Among the Ulster Irish it was told about King Suibne, among the Strathclyde Britons about Lailoken, and among the Welsh about Myrddin, who was in all likelihood a historic bard of royal blood in the 6th century. The story of Myrddin, one infers, ran to the effect that he went mad at the battle of Ardderyd (574) near Carlisle because of grief at the carnage. He lived many years in the wood of Celyddon (southern Scotland), subsisting on roots and berries. He prophesied three different deaths for the same boy, but was vindicated years later when the boy fell from a rock, was hanged by his feet from a tree, his head under water, and so drowned. Thrice he gave way to laughter, knowing as a seer that the unsuspected queen had been lying with a paramour, that a beggar was sitting over buried treasure, and that a youth, buying new shoes, would never live to wear them. This motif came from India, probably through Jewish channels. No authentic effusions of Myrddin have survived, and it is only in obscure poems of the 11th and 12th centuries that we get evidences of the familiarity of the legend and spurious vaticinations—allusions to Ardderyd, to the long life in the wood of Celyddon, to an apple tree under which, Myrddin says, he enjoyed the company of a fair, sportive maid, to his sister Gwendydd, and prophecies relating to events of the 11th and 12th centuries. A poetic address delivered by the seer from his grave concerns the reigns of William Rufus and the two Henrys, and includes a warning against the time when a strong, freckled man would reach a certain ford over the Usk. Giraldus Cambrensis tells us that the Welsh took this prophecy so seriously that when it seemed to be fulfilled by Henry II in 1163, they were much disheartened. Indeed, throughout the Middle Ages the mantic verses of Myrddin had a potent influence. Though all early tradition connects the prophet with Strathclyde, a late legend reported that he departed with the Thirteen Treasures of Britain to the Glass House on Bardsey Island, and was still there, though doubtless invisible to human eye.

2) Geoffrey of Monmouth, the learned but unscrupulous Oxford scholar, finished about 1135 his *Prophetia Merlini,* professedly a translation from Welsh or Breton. It followed the convention of giving *ex post facto* predictions of events in somewhat obscure phrases. Arthur is referred to as the Boar of Cornwall, who will trample on the necks of foreigners and inspire fear in the house of Romulus and whose end will be doubtful—evident allusions to the fabulous exploits which Geoffrey was already inventing about the hero and to the famous British hope of his return. The struggles of the Red Dragon (Wales) with the White Dragon (the Saxons), the Norman Conquest, the death of William Rufus are similarly sketched, and the sinking of the White Ship (1120) is foretold in the words: "The Lion's whelps shall be transformed into fishes of the sea." Geoffrey, having reached his own time, is forced to deal cryptically with the unknown future, indulges in picturesque rigmarole about the Castle of Venus, the Ass of Wickedness etc., but does echo one genuine tradition of the return of Cadwalader (d. 664). Almost all of the book, then, is a fabrication, but it had a prodigious success, inspiring many commentators throughout the Middle Ages, and editions were printed in Germany in the 17th century, though William of Newburgh had exposed the sham as early as 1198. When Geoffrey published the *History of the Kings of Britain* (c. 1136), he incorporated the prophecies and provided an account of their supposed author. He lifted out of Nennius' *History of the Britons* the story of Vortigern's tower, the fatherless boy, and the prophecy about the Red and White Dragons, coolly identifying the prophetic boy with Merlin. Later he credited Merlin with transferring the Giants' Dance (Stonehenge) from Ireland to its present site. Again by his magic powers the wizard gave Uther the form of Gorlois and so brought about the begetting of Arthur in Tintagel castle. Though this last tale seems based on Cornish tradition and ultimately on the Irish *Birth of Mongan,* the role of Merlin in Geoffrey's *History* is an arbitrary medley of the author's. When, however, his *Life of Merlin* was written about 1150, he used, even at the expense of consistency, much genuine Welsh lore. Merlin is no longer the counselor of Uther and Arthur but a king of South Wales, who engaged in a battle which can be recognized as the Ardderyd of the poems, and the names of the other participants are traditional. His sister Gwendydd appears as Ganieda. We have the madness, the life in the forest, the triple death, the three laughs, and a poetic dialog with Taliesin, in which there are echoes of the vernacular poems as well as of Ovid and Isidore of Seville. The great discrepancy between Geoffrey's two accounts of the mage led Giraldus to state that there were two persons, Merlin Ambrosius of the *History* and Merlin Calidonius of the poetic *Life.*

3) About the year 1200 Robert de Boron, a Burgundian poet, composed a romance about Merlin, of which 500 lines have survived but which was rendered into prose and introduced into three compilations, those of the Didot and Huth MSS. and the Vulgate cycle. Robert seems to have known Wace's redaction of Geoffrey's *History* and gave a confused version of the Merlin story. Though he shows no acquaintance with the *Life,* he did borrow from some unknown source the motif of the triple death. He gave an elaborate account of Merlin's begetting by an incubus, based on the apocryphal story of the begetting of Antichrist. Merlin is provided with a confidant, Blaise, who recorded all his prophecies; he advised Uther to establish the Round Table; after Uther's death Merlin proposed to the barons that the true heir would be revealed by the test of the sword in the stone. The poem ended with Arthur's coronation. In the 13th century the prose version received two continuations in which Merlin plays a large part as the counselor of Arthur, as seer, and as shape-shifter. The Vulgate continuation, though largely occupied with Arthur's wars with the rebel kings, the Saxons, and the Romans, introduces the motif of the three laughs and the famous story of the wizard's infatuation for Niniane or Viviane, which ends with her enchanting him under a whitethorn in the forest of Broceliande. This same legend occurs with variations in the other continuation (the Huth *Merlin*) and in the *Prose Lancelot,* and though doubtless influenced by such famous themes as the beguilement of Aristotle and Virgil, may well have had its root in Myrddin's sporting with a maid under an apple tree in the wood of Celyddon, already mentioned. The Huth *Merlin* furnished the materials which Malory condensed and rearranged in his first four books. The Vulgate *Merlin* was thrice rendered into English, once as *Arthour and Merlin* about 1300 and twice about 1450. An extraordinary concoction is the *Prophécies de Merlin,* written in French by a Venetian between 1272 and 1279, and mingling veiled references to events in Italy and the Holy Land with fantastic adventures of the Arthurian cycle.

4) Merlin's fame has been preserved in certain humbler forms. In the Scottish ballad of *Child Rowland* (*Folk-Lore* II: 183) he is a warlock who brings about the rescue of Arthur's daughter from fairyland. There are Breton folktales about a wizard Murlu. Geoffrey of Monmouth's spurious etymology of Carmarthen as *Kaermerdin,* town of Merlin, still lives on in the legend that Merlin's favorite walk was along the banks of the Towy, and Geoffrey is also responsible for a Merlin's Cave at Tintagel, though here, as elsewhere, one may suspect that the particular association is due to the romantic revival of the 19th century, not to old folk tradition. Merlin's grave was pointed out at Drummelzier on the Tweed and in the Forest of Broceliande. According to a tradition of doubtful antiquity, the mage was born on the Ile de Sein off the Breton coast, and to it he conveyed the wounded Arthur.

Bibliography:

Bruce, J. D., *Evolution of Arthurian Romance* (Baltimore, 1923). See index.

Chadwick, H. M. and N. K., *Growth of Literature,* I (Cambridge, 1932), pp. 105–14, 123–32, 453–57.

Vita Merlini, ed. J. J. Parry. Univ. of Illinois Studies in Language and Literature, X (1925), No. 3.

Taylor, Rupert, *Political Prophecy in England* (New York, 1911).

Krappe, A. H., "Le Rire du Prophète," *Studies in English Philology in Honor of F. Klaeber,* ed. K. Malone and M. B. Ruud (Minneapolis, 1929), pp. 340–61.

Jackson, K., "The Motive of the Threefold Death in the Story of Suibhne Geilt," *Essays and Studies Presented to E. MacNeill,* ed. J. Ryan (Dublin, 1940), pp. 535–50.

Snell, F. J., *King Arthur's Country* (London, New York, 1926). See index.   ROGER S. LOOMIS

mermaid A supernatural sea-dwelling female of general European maritime folklore: German *Meerfrau,* Danish *maremind,* Cheremissian *wut-ian üder.* (See HAVMAND, the Estonian NÄKK, Finnish NÄKKI.) The Irish mermaid, *murdúac,* is Anglicized to **merrow.** The Morgans, or sea-women, off the coast of Brittany are considered beautiful, sirenlike, and dangerous to men. Mermaids are usually depicted as having the head and body of a woman to the waist, and a tapering fish body and tail instead of legs. A carving on Pucé Church in Gironde, France, however, shows a young mermaid with lower body divided and two tapering tails instead of legs. They live in an undersea world of splendor and riches, but have been known to assume human form and come ashore to markets and fairs. They often lure mariners to their destruction, and are said to gather the souls of the drowned and cage them in their domain. Those who seek fact underlying every belief have offered the manatee or the dugong, warm-blooded sea mammals, as the original for the mermaid, relying on analogy more than on sailors' ability to differentiate between a sea-cow and a fish-woman.

Concerning the origin of mermaids, the Irish say they are old pagan women transformed to mermaid shape and banished off the earth by St. Patrick. A Livonian folktale says they are Pharaoh's children drowned in the Red Sea (B81.1). For origin of the mermaid concept S. Baring-Gould suggests (*Curious Myths of the Middle Ages,* London, 1884) the various semi-fish gods and goddesses of the early religions, e.g. the Chaldean Oannes and the Philistine Dagon, especially when associated with the sun-god concept, as Oannes who appeared on earth every day and plunged into the sea every night. Atargatis (Derceto, Dea Syria) too is sometimes depicted with semi-fish body. For association of the mermaid with the ancient sea goddess and love goddess, Marian, identified by the Greeks with Aphrodite, born of the sea, and the symbolism of the comb and the mirror, see Robert Graves, *The White Goddess,* New York, 1948, pp. 327–328; for explanation of the fish tail in statues of Atargatis-Derceto, p. 335.

Medieval belief in the mermaid, however, was widespread and substantiated. There is a Netherlands story reported by Baring-Gould (p. 509) that in 1430 when the dikes near Edam broke in a storm, some young girls in a boat found a mermaid floundering in shallow, muddy water. They got her into the boat, took her home, dressed her in women's clothes; she could weave and spin with extraordinary skill, but never learned to speak. Old Henry Hudson is said to have seen one near Nova Zembla on his arctic explorations. In 1560 west of Ceylon some fishermen caught several in a net, which were taken ashore and dissected with great interest by a learned physician. He reported that internally and externally they were constructed like human beings.

It is generally thought unlucky to see a mermaid; the sight of one presages storm or disaster (D1812.5.1.9) as witness Child's ballad *The Mermaid* (#289), in which one of a ship's crew sighted a mermaid sitting on a rock with comb and mirror in her hand. Very shortly the ship was lost in a raging storm and for want of a lifeboat all hands were drowned. Mermaids also often lead people astray (B81.3). Getting hold of the cap or belt of a mermaid gives one power over her (D1410.4). The marriage of a mortal man to a mermaid (B81.2) is common in folktale and folk belief; descendants of such a union are still living in Machaire, Ireland. Such people are usually under some kind of a curse; either they cannot sleep at night for the haunting sound of the sea in their ears, or they are doomed not to speak.

The heroine of *The Little Mermaid* by Hans Christian Andersen falls in love with a beautiful prince on a passing ship, voluntarily assumes human shape in order to gain an immortal soul and be near him forever, is doomed never to speak, attends the prince constantly, but when he marries a human princess her heart breaks. She becomes an elemental light being, with a chance at immortality.

merman The male counterpart of the mermaid in general European and Near Eastern folklore. The *Arabian Nights* refer to the merman both as human and as fish. "The Tale of Abdullah and Abdullah" in the *Arabian Nights* is the story of the poor fisherman named Abdullah and his benefactor, the merman named Abdullah. Al-Kazwini refers to a Syrian story of a merman married to a human wife, whose son knew both the language of the earth and sea. Probably the most familiar merman motif of folktale and ballad is the merman forsaken by his human wife (C713), widely popularized by Matthew Arnold's poem, *The Forsaken Merman.* Various ramifications of this motif include the prohibition against the human wife's overstaying her visit home (C713.3), or even seeing her old home (C713.2), or staying in church for the benediction (C713.1) which inevitably prevents her returning to her merman husband. See HAVMAND; NÄKK; NÄKKI; NIX.

merry tale A short, simple humorous story, usually of daily life: called variously *Schwank, jest, humorous anecdote.* Sometimes, and especially in certain regions, it is an animal tale, but more often the actors are human; the tales themselves are numskull stories, tales of deception, or obscene. The stories are uncomplicated, usually limited to a single motif, and make little use of the supernatural. They tend to cluster about the person of a central character or group, e.g. Coyote, Fox, the Gothamites, Till Eulenspiegel, but exist also as isolated "joke" stories. The anecdotal character of the merry tale makes it easily remembered; some current merry tales may be traced back almost 4000 years and some have spread so as to become known worldwide. See *Merry tale* in EUROPEAN FOLKLORE; GERMANIC FOLKLORE.

Meru or **Sumeru** In Hindu and Buddhist mythology, the mountain at the center of the earth where the gods dwell. Meru, the chief of the mountains, holds the earth fast, is 84,000 *yojanas* high and is surmounted by the heavens. Within, it is adorned with the cars of the gods. Around it the sun, moon, and stars revolve. In the Buddhist system, Meru rises from the ocean. Hindus identify it with Mt. Kailās or Kailāsa in Tibet. Lamas represent Meru by a small pile of rice in the center of their daily offering of the universe in effigy to the Buddhas.

mesi'ng keo The False Face dancers of the Delaware Indians. They participated in the Midwinter Bear rite of the Grand River colony, and at the Corn harvest and Big House ceremony of the Oklahoma group. The mask, *mesing,* could be worn only by a man of supernatural ability, a man capable of personifying the spirit *mishinghali'kun.* This spirit combined potential malefiicence with power to guard from disease and to expel evil spirits. Furthermore he had the dual function of helping vegetation and controlling game, particularly deer.

At the Bear rite, 12 men (the sacred number) wore two kinds of masks. Six white Unami moiety masks, representing peace, crept in the west door, split into two groups, and danced around the central post, three clockwise, three counterclockwise. Then six red Wapanachki masks, representing violence, crept in the east door and went through the same performance. They were accompanied by song and water drum and the vibration of the turtle rattle carried by each dancer. As conclusion they used the same steps in a war dance.

The *mesing* or mask of the Big House ceremony was a divided mask, half red, half black, with thick lips, tin eyes, and horse hair—recalling the Iroquois type. The dancer who wore it was covered with a bearskin to his toes, carried a tobacco pouch, a staff of twisted wood, and a tortoise rattle filled with corn kernels (combining animal and vegetable potency). He jumped, kicked, and whinnied.

Despite many apparent resemblances between these maskers and the Iroquois *gagósä*, the concept is not identical. The Iroquois do not emphasize duality to the same extent. Neither do they include the game-owner concept, nor vegetable association, which they relegate to the Corn Husk masks. The game-owner concept was held by all eastern Algonquians to the Naskapi of Labrador. It bears a remarkable analogy to the *gahe* of the Apache Indians. [GPK]

Metal Old Man Be chasti, or Metal Old Man, a character in White Mountain Apache Indian mythology whom Monster-Slayer, younger of the two boy heroes, meets and worsts in a fight. Metal Old Man is represented as a great man (giant) covered with black metal (obsidian) all over his body except for his armpits, the vulnerable spots where Monster-Slayer's arrows were able to penetrate. Among the Chiricahua Apache the same tale of a contest between a boy hero and a monster is told, but the two protagonists are Child-of-the-Water and Giant, a being whose body is covered with four coats of rocks. Child-of-the-Water succeeds in shooting off the first three coats and then shooting Giant through his heart, which could be seen beating under the thin, innermost coat. [EWV]

metamorphosis A change of form or shape; shapeshifting: a common incident in mythology and folktale. See TRANSFORMATION.

Metsänneitsyt The "forest virgin" in western Finland. It is believed that she looks like a very beautiful and well-dressed woman, but from behind she is like a stump, a bundle of twigs, a pole, or a trough. She is eager to entice any man in love with her. (Compare the Skogsjungfru of the Swedes.) [JB]

Metzgersprung Literally, butchers' leap: a running dance by the butchers' guild, particularly of Munich and Nürnberg, Bavaria. As they danced their serpentine paths and manipulated their butchers' knives into arches and platforms (recalling sword dances), they were followed by a host of *Schemen.* There are two traditions as to their origin, both of which may have been operative.

One explanation connects them with ancient animal sacrifice, in view of the sword dance features and the ritual serpentine. The other traces them to a prerogative issued to the guild in the 14th century for the performance of their occupational dance during carnival festivities. As part of their ceremonies, sheepskin-clad apprentices were released and had to jump into the fountain—in Munich the Fischbrunnen, in front of the city hall. These customs continued into the early 20th century. See SWORD DANCES. [GPK]

Mexican and Central American Indian folklore The folklore of Mexico and Central America—a geographical region frequently referred to as Middle America—represents the product of 400 years of fusion of two basic strains, that of the indigenous cultures of the New World, and that of Old World cultures, principally Spanish. To a greater extent than is perhaps the case in North and South America, the Indian cultures of this region have blended with those of Europe to such a degree that the term "Indian" must be used advisedly. Anthropologists are beginning to suspect that some groups, at least, are as nearly 16th century Spanish in terms of the content of their cultures as they are Indian. Hence, the folklore of the modern Middle American Indians, as one aspect of the total cultural configuration, can best be understood through an awareness of the ingredients which have gone into this mixture. For this reason, attention will be drawn to the type of motifs of stories, the festivals, religious beliefs and the like which have come from the Old World, but since these are better known to most readers than the indigenous stratum, they will not be elaborated upon.

In the treatment of both pre-Conquest and modern Middle American folklore, greater emphasis must be placed upon Mexico and Guatemala than upon the remainder of the area. Since pre-Conquest times these countries have had much denser populations, and much greater variety in customs and ways of life than the regions father south and east. They represent the areas of highest culture, particularly exemplified by the Aztec and Mayan peoples, but also noteworthy for other advanced groups such as the Tarascans, Mixtecs, Zapotecs, Huastecs, and Totonacs. Among these peoples traditions, beliefs, and concepts, undoubtedly common to the entire area, were formalized more completely into elaborate religious systems, with resultant opportunities for complex and colorful ritualistic and ceremonial additions to the more mundane life of smaller social groups. Meanwhile, as these developments were taking place—perhaps earlier—the groups to the southeast of the Maya, from Honduras and El Salvador on, were being strongly influenced by diffusion from South America, so that today, much of the folklore of these areas reveals a South American origin, and is rather different in flavor from that of Mexico and Guatemala.

Unfortunately, less is known about the pre-Conquest folklore of these peoples than in the case of the larger countries. By chance, Guatemala, and particularly Mexico, offered to the conquering Spaniard the wealth which had brought him to the New World. Whether this was in the form of minerals, or large holdings of land, only these countries had the native populations which made exploitation feasible. Moreover, in addition to simple economic exploitation there was, to a much greater degree than is often recognized, a crusading zeal on the part of many Spaniards, not all of whom were churchmen, to carry the true word of God to the heathens. The Spaniards felt that the Indians had long been under the power of the Devil—in whose existence they had not the slightest doubt—and that it was their bounden duty to seek out the enemy and vanquish him. Hence, the particular field of most interest to the folklorist was precisely that which received the earliest and strongest attention on the part of the conquerors. Heathen temples were destroyed, the idols broken or buried, and churches with crosses and images of saints were erected on their sites. This early preoccupation with the ideological and religious aspects of culture, while quickly destroying most of the formal elements, at the same time resulted in the recording and preservation of this material, subsequently lost in other areas which received less attention. If the enemy were to be destroyed he must first be known. Friars wandered from one end of the land to the other, established convents, learned the Indian tongues, wrote down their beliefs, recorded explanations of their picture writings, and attempted to fathom their minds. Within a few years some of the Christianized Indians themselves were doing this work, writing in their native languages, using Spanish characters. These incomparably rich sources, many of which survive to the present time, make it possible to know the basic outlines of myth, legend, religion, and ceremonial prevalent at the time of the Conquest. Lacking such documentation for most of the area to the southeast of the Maya, we can only surmise.

Most of the peoples under consideration have been agricultural for at least 3000 years, perhaps much longer. Since the body of knowledge which forms the religion and mythology of a people deals most closely with the interests of the group, it is not surprising to find that from the very beginning, preoccupation with agriculture and fertility is very marked. The earliest stages which we can discern suggest a personification of nature as the basis for myth and legend. The wind and the rain, lightning and thunder, fertility and growth, gods of maize and "masters" of game, all personified, are the actors on the stage, and in cosmic forces are seen the struggles of these deities.

The Conquest mythology which survives to the present time deals especially with the "origin" theme, the origin of the world, the people and animals in it, the origin of cosmic forces and the origin of maize, and with the "explanatory" theme, what causes rain, earthquakes, winds, why human sacrifice is necessary, and like subjects. Such beliefs doubtless were common, though with individual variations, to the entire area. Subsequently, in the regions of higher culture—central and south Mexico, Yucatan and Guatemala—these simpler concepts were fused into more precise bodies of belief which, with a priesthood to guide and develop, became religious in a more formal sense, with a pantheon of deities, an elaborate yearly cycle of ceremonial, complex and often bloody sacrifices and rites, and other time-consuming demands on each and every person. This is the stage which is represented in the accounts written by Spaniards and educated Indians of 400 years ago, a few examples of which may be given.

The ancient Aztecs believed that there had been three or four previous worlds, or "suns," all of which, including the people, had been destroyed. The sequence is not always the same, but the forces are—flood, fire, wind, and being eaten by supernatural beasts. Each time the world was re-created and new people placed upon it. In one legend the first world lasted 676 years, during which time people lived on pine-cone nuts, finally being devoured by ocelots. The people of the second world were carried away by wind, turned into monkeys; thus the explanation of the origin of monkeys. The third world was destroyed by a rain of fire, the inhabitants turned into wild fowl. The fourth world was destroyed by flood, and the people became fish. The present world, it was believed at the time of the Conquest, was to be destroyed by earthquake.

The actors upon this legendary stage were the gods—Tezcatlipoca, Quetzalcoatl, Huitzilopochtli, and a bewildering array of others among the Aztecs—Itzamna, the Chacs, Ah Puch—and others among the classic Maya—Hun-Apu, Xbalanque, Vukub, and Jurukán of the Maya-speaking Quiché of Guatemala, to name only a few. A marked duality pervades the cosmological speculations which have come down to us. Among the Aztecs the male and female gods Ometecutli and Omecihuatl, "Two Lord" and "Two Lady," who lived in Omeyocan, "the place of two," were the progenitors of all of the gods. Known also as "The Lord and Lady of our Flesh," or "The Lord and Lady of our Sustenance," they are represented by symbols of fertility, adorned with ears of maize. Among the Quiché, Xpiyacoc, and Xmucane, the "Father-Mother" deities, take their place.

Struggle between gods is a dominant theme. Classic is the account, recorded in a dozen or more variants, of the contests between Quetzalcoatl, the feathered serpent, and Tezcatlipoca, the god of the night wind. The former was the culture hero of the Toltecs, who preceded the Aztecs in the Valley of Mexico by a thousand years. It was he who went to the underworld, gathered the bones of the dead of preceding worlds, returned, sprinkled his own blood on them, and thus created man. It was he who brought agriculture, arts, and sciences. According to one account Tezcatlipoca was the first sun in the first world, until he was knocked out of the sky by Quetzalcoatl who became sun, only to be knocked out of the sky in turn by Tezcatlipoca, leaving the world in darkness. Legends tell of a much later period in which Quetzalcoatl now reigned peacefully, instructing his people, until Tezcatlipoca, by means of a series of tricks, made life so miserable that he went off to the east, leaving a barren waste behind, and embarked on a raft of serpents to set out over the eastern ocean, saying that he would some day return. This Quetzalcoatl had a light complexion and a long beard. Small wonder that Moctezuma, king of the Aztecs, believed that Cortes, landing on the gulf coast of Mexico, was the god returned! The same "feathered-serpent" god appears among the Maya as Kulkulcan and among the Quiché as Gucumatz. Perhaps these accounts of struggle reflect the entry of the newer, bloodier religion of the Aztecs, with their gods Huitzilopochtli and Tezcatlipoca, superimposing themselves over the older cult of Quetzalcoatl and the rain god, Tlaloc.

Tlaloc, so the story goes, lived in the sky with his wife Chalchihuitlicue, and in the patio of their home were four barrels. One was filled with good water, which made seeds germinate and crops grow; the second had bad water which produced mildew on growing things; the third contained hail and sleet, while the fourth held rain which fell when crops needed dry weather to mature. Servants of Tlaloc, also known as the *tlalocs,* at the bidding of their master took small containers, filled them with water from the barrels, and with wooden paddles splashed it out to fall as rain, or broke the containers, thus causing thunder to accompany a downpour.

Coexistent with these tales of the creation and development of the earth, the basis for the religion of peoples at that time, were countless superstitions and beliefs which undoubtedly have their origins deep in the antiquity of mankind. Omens were legion: the hoot of an owl presaged death; a croaking bird the arrival of someone; tamales sticking to the pot foretold that the woman cook, at parturition, would experience difficulty in expulsing the afterbirth. Offerings of food and drink were made to deities: a mouthful of food was thrown on the fire before eating, and a little pulque was spilled on the ground as a libation before drinking. Maize, a god in itself, was treated with great veneration: if any were seen on the ground it was carefully picked up and never trampled upon. Milk teeth were thrown into rat holes so that the new teeth would be strong and bright; at the festival of the new year children were lifted off the ground momentarily by their heads to promote growth (the same is done today in some places during Easter Week observances, on Saturday, when church bells first ring out after having been "dead" since the preceding Thursday). A pregnant woman gazing at an eclipse was believed to give birth to a hare-lip child; small obsidian knives carried in the clothing against the abdomen counteracted this malevolent influence (an iron knife today is substituted; otherwise the belief and practice are identical). Human fingers were valued by robbers to open doors and put the victims in a trance. Only a few of these superstitions which existed have been recorded, and most of them survive but little changed until today.

Religious rituals and observances, as contrasted to simple folk beliefs, were unbelievably numerous and complex among the more advanced peoples. They were bound up with the native calendar, which divided the year into 18 months of 20 days each, plus a final 5 day unlucky period. Coordinated with this was a ritualistic period of 260 days known as the *tonalpohualli,* composed of the 20 named days combined with the numbers 1 to 13. The superposition of these two counts results in a cycle of 52 years, the "century" of the advanced peoples of Middle America. Among the Aztecs each month was characterized by an elaborate fiesta in honor of the appropriate deity, while lesser fiestas occurred almost continually. Most impressive and important of all was the observance at the end of the 52-year period, when it was feared that the world might come to an end, as it had done, according to Aztec mythology, three or four times before. This "New Fire Ceremony" was highlighted by the extinction of an old altar fire and the ceremonial lighting of a new one, symbolizing humanity's new lease on life. Toward dusk of the fatal day all fires in the Valley of Mexico were

extinguished and the priests, followed by immense throngs, walked several miles from Mexico City to a temple at the summit of the Hill of the Star. This hill, rising from the flat valley floor, commands a view of the heavens in all directions. Here the priests took up their anxious vigil, waiting until midnight to know whether the celestial sign foretold the end of the world or the beginning of another century. The sign was a star, or stars, Aldebaran or the Pleiades, which, if they passed the zenith, indicated a continuation of life. If they failed to do so, the end was at hand: the sun and the stars, it was believed, would be converted into wild beasts to fall to earth and devour all human beings, after which earthquakes would destroy the world. At the instant the sign was interpreted favorably, priests kindled a new fire with a wooden drill in the breast of a recently sacrificed victim, and runners joyously carried burning brands to the far corners of the valley to relight fires on the hearths of each house.

This picture was abruptly interrupted by the arrival of the Spaniards at the beginning of the 16th century. Religion received the first impact of foreign influence, and, in spite of the persistence of many indigenous elements, there is no doubt but that today Catholicism is the inspiration for the form and content of most religious observances. Apart from formal religion, it is probable that the conquerors, intensely superstitious themselves, did not find the basic Indian philosophy of life, the concept of the supernatural forces at work in the world, to be very strange. Hence, on this level there was less pressure to change the indigenous way of life. In the course of time many Old World folk superstitions and stories were accepted, without force, by Middle American peoples. In some cases local forms were replaced, but more often a harmonious blending resulted. At the same time, the Spaniard unconsciously adopted many of the New World *creéncias,* the beliefs and tabus. Whatever the origin of a particular element, it fitted easily into the fundamental pattern, understandable to conqueror and conquered alike. This pattern presupposed that the individual, to be born, grow up and pass through life, had to maintain a delicate balance, a harmony between himself and the powers of nature on one hand, and himself and the powers of evil of other men on the other hand. Life was filled with tabus. To break them or to fail to observe them could cause illness and death, destroy one's hunting luck, or cause the fields to dry, bring bad luck in love, or cause one to suffer abject poverty. Evil persons, through witchcraft, might cause the same things. Hence, religious and magical observances were all directed toward the maintenance of this harmony, or toward its restoration should it be destroyed. The same description is valid in the 20th century.

The ancient concepts of gods as personifications of the forces of nature are to a large degree lost. Most deities have disappeared entirely, a few have blended with Catholic concepts of Christ, the Virgin, and the pantheon of saints. The ritual observances of pre-Conquest days are gone, but many of the simpler rites are continued, some secretly in the mountains away from towns, others incorporated as parts of Church procedure. Thus, copal gum was the pre-Conquest incense; today it is found in churches, in Mass, or it may be burned quietly by the lone hunter as he sets out at dawn, his offering to the "masters" of game to gain their approval of his venture. Turkeys are sacrificed in caves to bring luck or health, or food may be buried in the ground at planting time to give strength to the earth. The wind, the rain, thunder, and lightning are still considered to be gods by the more remote, primitive peoples, but also the sorcerer can show himself in the same forms. Through malevolence of the witch, or through bad luck, a man becomes ill, and the proper persons must be consulted to effect a cure. Now, as formerly, if one can maintain the essential harmony, he will go through life with a minimum of trouble. Some of the acts are Old World, some are New World, but the Indian is unaware of their dual origin.

The maintenance of health is a matter of primary importance to the Indians of Middle America, just as it is to persons of other societies. A large portion of the concepts of causes and cures of sickness found in this region appear to be indigenous in origin. While there is some idea about "natural" causes of disease, more often it is believed that magical or supernatural factors are involved. Apparently universal in this area is the idea that the loss of one's soul results in sickness, to be followed by death if the soul is not found and returned to the body. A man's soul may leave his body as he sleeps, and dreams usually are so interpreted. Hence, it is considered unwise suddenly to awaken a sleeper, since his soul may be wandering in a dream and not have time to return. Stories tell of hunters who come upon a companion sleeping in the woods, a butterfly hovering about his head. A wasp approaches, stings the butterfly to death, the man awakens ill and quickly dies. The butterfly was his soul; when it was killed, there was no hope for recovery.

Fright in any form, often fear at falling into a river, may shake the soul from the body. A *curandero,* a medicine man, is called to diagnose the cause, to determine how and where the soul was lost, and to take steps to recover it. The soul is believed to be near the surface of the body at places where the pulse is visible, the wrists, temples, and so forth. Hence, these are the places where the soul can most easily be put back into the body. The medicine man then sucks at these points, and in magical fashion the soul is induced to return to its home. Or the medicine man may visit the place where the soul escaped, calling to it to come near so that it may be trapped or otherwise brought back to the patient.

Illness also is believed to be caused by a sorcerer placing a disease-object, usually a toad, spider, worm, or some small animate object, in the body of the victim. The patient has a gnawing, burning sensation, which is interpreted as the insect eating away the flesh from within. For this type of illness the curer prescribes herbs which kill the object, allowing it to pass out in the feces.

A third type of belief is that evil spirits have possessed the sick person. A cure is effected only when they have been driven out. Among the Chocó of Panama the shaman places the patient in a special curing house, paints pictures of the presumed spirits on the walls of the structure and on the back of the patient, and exorcises by means of chants.

Other types of illness and cures appear to be a legacy from Europe, even though now they are deeply engrained in indigenous belief. Such are the evil eye, *mal de ojo,* which particularly attacks children, and which is cured by rubbing the body of the little patient with an egg to extract the fever. Perhaps *bilis,* or bile, a strange quality or substance in the blood, is of the same origin. Certainly the falling of the *mollera,* technically the soft spot on an infant's skull though in folk belief a vague "something" perhaps identified with the spirit, is in this category. The curer often picks up the infant by the heels, head down, and presses up on the hard palate to force the *mollera* into place. It is uncertain as to whether sympathetic magic of the type in which the witch makes an image of the victim and sticks sharp objects into it or otherwise harms it is European or New World in origin.

Ancient superstitions which survive to the present time in Mexico and Central America include the curious complex known as *nagualism.* Phenomena described under this term include two types of belief which appear to be indigenous over all the Americas. Many of the native peoples in the area under consideration believe, just as the Plains Indians in the United States, that each individual has a guardian spirit who watches over him through life. But in Middle America this identification of human being with a spirit, usually an animal, is so close that both are thought to share the same soul. Both are, really, manifestations of the same being, and should either animal or human die, the other also ceases to exist. One's spirit, or *nagual* (sometimes *tonal*), is found shortly after birth. The father spreads ashes around the resting place of the newborn infant at night, and next morning examines the ground to see what animal tracks are visible. It is thought that the animal spirit comes to see his charge, leaves his tracks, and thus is identified.

A second American belief is that of the transforming witch, the evil-doer who can assume animal form in which to wreak vengeance on enemies. Middle America is no exception to this rule, and the folklore of all Indians is replete with accounts of persons who assume animal form, usualy leaving their head or a leg at the scene of the transformation. If it is possible to find the member, place salt, tobacco, chile, or some other substance on it, the witch is unable to replace it, and with the dawn his true nature is revealed by the headless or legless condition. From Mexico to at least as far south as Nicaragua, such witches are known as *naguals.* Often this concept blends with that of the spirit animal: the individual with occult powers assumes the form of his *nagual* guardian.

All native Middle American Indian groups have beliefs which determine and guide the rituals which accompany planting. Since in all Middle America maize is the staple food, it is not surprising that ceremonies to ensure a good maize crop are most important. Among the Mixtecs and Mixe (Oaxaca, Mexico) and the Chorti (Guatemala) turkeys are sacrificed at planting time, and food is buried in the corn field "to feed the earth" which is to feed man. The Maya make offerings of prayers and maize gruel to the chacs, the rain gods.

Among the Popoluca (Veracruz, Mexico) men observe continence for seven nights before planting, pass the seed corn through incense smoke, pray to the Virgin of Catemaco, and then plant.

Sympathetic magic plays a part in the beliefs of some people. A pregnant woman may plant papayas, so that the fruit will be large and plump; a woman plants gourds, standing over the seed and turning rapidly, causing her skirt to billow out, thus magically ensuring fat gourds; chayotes are sown in pairs, so that the vines will produce paired fruits.

Among even remote Indians, planting beliefs are mixed with Catholic concepts. In addition to prayers to saints or virgins, it is commonly believed that the days of certain saints are particularly propitious for different crops. Thus, bananas and pineapples may be planted on August 15, La Asunción, beans on October 4, San Francisco, and so forth.

In the field of the folktale, changes in the form and content of the corpus of stories belonging to any tribe has been extensive as the result of European influence. As has been pointed out, aboriginal legends and tales dealt with the creation, with origins and explanations, and with cosmic forces. Animal tales, when not belonging to these categories, tended to be anecdotal. The new folklore dealt with such themes as kings' sons who undergo ordeals and tests to win princesses, and usually the youngest of three, through kindness to a disguised supernatural being, acquires the necessary magical aids to attain victory. Hansel and Gretel fool the evil witch, a boy's soul is sold to the Devil by his father, and John the Bear bites the Negro's ear when he needs extra help. Animal tales though at times anecdotal, tend to be moralizing, a theme little developed in the autochthonous folklore of the New World.

In the larger cities, and in areas where Indian influence is relatively negligible, that is, areas with a European literary tradition, European folktales have been transplanted with few modifications. But the instant the stories wander from the printed page, when they begin to be passed by word of mouth—as was almost always the case in the years following the Conquest—curious things begin to happen. Stories tend to break up into their component motifs, each of which may form the basis for a story in itself, or, as is more often the case, several motifs from different European stories will be recombined to form a new tale, into which indigenous elements almost always are injected. Thus, the stick-fast motif, probably the most widely known single theme in the entire area, rarely ends in European or African fashion. Rather, it is the jumping-off point for a long trickster cycle in which the dupe animal consistently is worsted by his adversary who persuades him to jump into a pond to retrieve a cheese (the moon's reflection), to hold up a rock lest the earth come to an end, to beat naughty children who turn out to be wasps, to choke on spiny fruit, and finally, in most cases, to be killed. Most of these episodes appear to be European; some probably are New World. The trickster cycle itself, usually with coyote, is as characteristically American as Old World.

Biblical stories are found in all the area, and here some of the most interesting of assimilations have taken place. An Aztec creation myth tells of the first man

and woman who, following divine instructions, bored into a hollow log and sealed themselves during a flood. When the waters receded they emerged, found dead fish, fried them, and angered the gods Citlallinicue and Citlallatónac by smoking up the sky. Tezcatlipoca was sent to find out what had happened, became angry, cut off their heads and placed them on their buttocks and thus made the first monkeys (dogs in some accounts). A modern Indian tale tells how Christ ordered the first man to make his ark and take two of each species aboard. After the waters receded this man likewise found dead fish, fried them, the smoke angered Christ who sent first a vulture and then a hawk to investigate. Both accepted the invitation of the man to eat. Finally the humming-bird was sent, a bird of great importance in native Mexican mythology, and he informed Christ who, in his anger, made monkeys out of the man and his family, just as Tezcatlipoca had done. Who can say whether this is a Mexican story with a strong Biblical cast, or the Christian story of the flood which has been adapted to local conditions?

Hence, in Mexico and Central America an analytical study of the folktale reduces itself, in most cases, to a study of the unit episodes, the motifs. Almost any combination of motifs is expectable, and almost all combinations are found. To illustrate the flavor of this folklore, a few examples of motifs, without regard to origins, may be given:

A poor hunter angers the "master" of game by wounding many deer. He is brought to the master's home under a mountain and told he may not leave until he cures all of the wounded animals.

A culture hero is born from an egg which is found by an old woman. He then goes on to perform many wonderful feats.

A woman conceives a culture hero by supernatural means, by grasping a ball of feathers to her bosom, or by having a tree gourd, really the head of a god in disguise, spit into her outstretched palms.

A man fells trees to make his corn plot, but the next day they are all standing again. The deity who does this then helps the man, who usually is very poor and in great need of aid.

A man loses his wife, worries because there is no one to prepare food for him, returns from his cornfield to his home to find food awaiting him, spies, sees that his faithful bitch has taken off her skin to become a beautiful woman. The man breaks the enchantment and marries her.

The magic flight sequence makes use of such episodes as thimbles, combs, needles, salt, and water becoming walls, forest, thorns, rocks, and rivers.

A man rescues a king's daughter and slays a seven-headed serpent. When a pretender claims the honor, the hero produces the seven tongues which he secretly cut out to verify his story.

A person is killed or caused to assume animal form by having a nail driven into the base of his skull. Removal of the nail restores the status quo.

A trickster sells non-existent maize to a cock, fox, dog, tiger, and hunter in turn, asks them to call at his house to pick up the merchandise, hides the weaker animal when a more powerful one appears until all are in the same place, and then escapes with the money while the hunter shoots the tiger.

A man releases a serpent from a trap, the serpent wishes to eat the man "since it is well known that good is repaid by evil," the man asks permission to verify this statement by asking three animals. The first two agree, but the last says that before deciding he must see how the serpent was trapped. The serpent obligingly reenacts the scene and is left to his fate.

A man goes away from his village, falls in love with a beautiful girl, marries her and lives contentedly for some time. He decides to return home to visit his parents, and is told not to kiss them or tell where he has been. When he violates this tabu he dies.

To the folklorist one of the most interesting theoretical problems is the sorting out of traits, to attempt to determine which belong to the New World, and which to the Old. To the Indian this would be a meaningless pastime. To most the concept of a time dimension is but poorly developed. The raconteur who tells of Solomon, the Tower of Babel, or Tar Baby feels that these stories are just as much the property of his people—as indeed they now are—as stories which explain the origin of the partridge or the activities of transforming witches. If his pregnant wife places metal scissors on her abdomen during an eclipse to prevent harm to her unborn child, little does he know that at one time his ancestors, for want of steel and knowledge of its magical powers, used an obsidian knife for the same purpose. To the Indian, and to students of society, the modern Indian cultures of Middle America are just as valid, just as legitimate, as if they were pure Indian or pure Spanish. And, thanks to their dual origin, they have a richness and variety in content of breath-taking magnitude. Both to the casual reader and the professional folklorist, an excursion into the folklore of Mexico and Central America produces rewards equaled in few other parts of the world.

GEORGE M. FOSTER

Meyer, Elard Hugo (1837–1908) German folklorist, born in Freiburg i. Br. He was the most significant pupil of Mannhardt in the field of Germanic mythology, a follower of the Brothers Grimm, and editor of the 4th and definitive edition of Grimms' *Deutsche Mythologie* (Berlin, 1875–78). His works include *Deutsche Volkskunde* (Strassburg, 1898) treating Germanic civilization, folklore, and mythology; *Germanische Mythologie* (Berlin, 1891); *Indogermanische Mythen* (Berlin, 1883), and *Mythologie der Germanen* (Strassburg, 1903). Meyer found that belief in the souls of the departed living on in nature, and reverence for them was the basis of all mythic thought. This idea of a *Seelenkult* (cult of the dead) he developed at a later period to a *Dämonkult*, including *Wölkenwinddämonen, Wasserwinddämonen, Baumwinddämonen*. His theories apart, he accomplished valuable work with his compilations (A. H. Krappe, *The Science of Folklore*, p. xix).

Michaelmas The feast of the archangel Michael, celebrated September 29: a church festival, and in England one of the old quarter-rent days. Michaelmas is the most ancient of the angel festivals, and probably originated in the dedication of a Michael church near Rome, now destroyed. The feast of Michael in the Eastern

Church (November 8) is also associated with the dedication of a church to Michael—by Constantine near Constantinople, because Michael had appeared on that spot. In Abyssinia the 12th of every month is St. Michael's Day. In Asia and also throughout coastal Europe numerous Michael churches on capes and headlands, on hilltops, or beside lakes, or special wells are associated with Michael's having saved the community from the peril and terror of some ravaging giant or monster in that place. There is a 9th century Michael abbey, Mont St. Michel, off the Normandy coast, where the red velvet buckler worn by Michael in his fight against the dragon was cherished and shown until the 17th century. The Epistle in the English Prayer Book mentions the victory of Michael over the dragon "that old serpent called the devil and Satan who deceiveth the world."

Eat goose on Michaelmas and you will not want for money for a year has been general English folklore since the 15th century; and when paying their rents on September 29 it was long the custom in rural England for farmers to include in their payment "one goose fit for the lord's dinner." See GOOSE. The reason for eating goose at Michaelmas seems to be unanimously attributed to the fact that geese are especially plentiful at this time of year.

Michaelmas bonfires were once a feature of old Lincolnshire and Yorkshire celebrations, and a handful of every kind of grain in the farmer's stores was scattered for wild birds, strewn in the poultry yard, and given to the cattle at night. This brought luck to the farm and its activities. In Shropshire it is said that the brake flowers at midnight on St. Michael's Eve. See BRACKEN.

St. Michael's cakes are a feature of the Michaelmas observances on the Isle of Skye. These are large round cakes (occasionally triangular): a milk and oatmeal mixture thinly coated with eggs, made for St. Michael's Day, one for each member of the family, and shared with neighbors and strangers.

Michaelmas is one of the most important feasts of the year in Ireland: *Cinn Féile*, a top or head feast. At this time people expect a marked decrease in sickness and disease. Some bird, usually a goose, or a sheep was specially killed and eaten for Michaelmas, even if this were the only time in the whole year. This is said to be an act of gratitude for a miracle of St. Patrick's long ago, performed with the aid of Michael. The finder of the ring in the "Michaelmas pie" will have an early marriage. The *púca* is believed to go into the sea on St. Michael's Day. This day is a great day for Irish fishermen. They say *Sáid do bád ó Lá le Micil amac*, Plenty (comes) to the boat on Michael's Day indeed. See CELTIC FOLKLORE; HORSE DANCE.

Michigan-I-O A lumberman's song of come-all-ye type sung in the lumber camps of the American West in the '80's and '90's, the name changing with the state in which the singer worked. It tells of the hardships of the lumberjack's life. It is based on an earlier song of the eastern woodlands called *Canaday-I-O*, the words of which may have been written by a lumberman, Ephraim Braley, about 1854. The earlier song was a descendant of an English sea song, which itself derived from a love song called *Caledonia*. In its travels westward the tune and the word pattern was also made over into a western plains ballad, *The Buffalo Skinners*.

Mickey Mouse Favorite animal hero of screen and comics, who has achieved folklore status through modern mass craftsmanship and distribution processes paralleling those of collective oral transmission. Following Walt Disney's earlier and cruder experiments in animating Alice and Oswald the Rabbit, Mickey made his debut in the first sound cartoon, *Steamboat Willie* (1928), and soon spread to the comic strips and comic books. His wide folk diffusion is attested by his appearance in children's rimes (see FROG WENT A-COURTING), the Italian nickname for the little Fiat car (*Fiat Populino*), and the trade slang term for an overdainty, thin musical sound effect (a "Mickey Mouse"). While American youngsters sport Mickey Mouse watches, European fans are responsible for the rumor that Mickey's bust occupies a niche in our Hall of Fame.

Mickey is rivaled only by Donald Duck in comic appeal and is second to none in versatility and human interest. He capitalizes upon the proverbial man-or-mouse dilemma and emerges as the "average guy," whose endless love of fun, desire to be of service, and curiosity involve him (and his sweetheart, Minnie, and his pals, Goofy and Pluto) in cheerful mischief (most of his pranks being boomerangs), chivalrous adventure, and thrilling mysteries and marvels.   B. A. BOTKIN

Micronesian mythology Micronesia ("little islands"), made up of four archipelagoes, Marianas, Carolines, Marshalls, and Gilberts, was the least known of the South Pacific culture areas to the world at large before 1941. Now, Tarawa in the Gilberts, Kwajalein in the Marshalls, Truk in the Carolines, and Guam and Saipan in the Marianas, are familiar names that immediately identify the area. Spain, then Germany, and after World War I, Japan under a mandate from the League of Nations, administered the islands except for the Gilberts which have always been British, the Marshalls which were never Spanish, and Guam which was never German or Japanese.

Knowledge of native culture, including the mythology, is derived mainly from the many-volumed series published by a German scientific expedition of 1908–1910 and from books of German Catholic missionaries. Now that the Marianas, Carolines, and Marshalls constitute a Trust Territory administered by the United States, Government-sponsored ethnographical research is being conducted under a project called the Coordinated Investigation of Micronesian Anthropology (CIMA). The future will see more descriptive material, and, undoubtedly, comparative and analytical studies to define the place of Micronesia in the total Pacific anthropological picture. Although others are being prepared, only two CIMA-sponsored articles on mythology have been published. Both are on Kapingamarangi, a Polynesian cultural outlier south of the Carolines. Additional material will also be available on the Gilberts as the Viking Fund, Inc. in 1948 sponsored my ethnographical research there.

Comparative studies of Micronesian mythology are few. Except for incidental comments in the German collections, there are only Dixon's summary based on the limited number of collections then available, and Grimble's discussion of Gilbertese mythological bonds. Analyses of myths of a single island are even rarer. The

characterization of Ponape mythology by Eilers (Hambruch, vol. 3, 1936), who edited Hambruch's ethnographies after his untimely death, is a significant survey of the lore of the island. Bollig's description of Truk literary style is outstanding.

Certain cultural elements of popular interest will serve to sketch, in broad outline, the native culture and traditions of a population of about 100,000. The languages spoken belong to the Malayo-Polynesian linguistic stock. Physically the people are difficult to classify briefly, although the pronounced Malay element in their heterogeneous ancestry gives them the "Micronesian look" which distinguishes them from whatever Melanesian and Polynesian ancestors some may have had.

The large, wheel-like stones used in Yap for money are as well known as the native stories of stone money, which, though lost at sea, are more valuable in the monetary economy than pieces safely transported to Yap from quarries in other islands. The importance of wealth in determining social status is echoed in myths, particularly from Yap and the Palaus in the Western Carolines. They tell of poor families scorned by richer villagers until a Cinderella-like daughter or son, who has befriended a supernatural being, is rewarded with wealth. Then the family becomes rich and socially powerful.

Also well known are the mysterious stone ruins in the Marianas and the Carolines left from an earlier age. In Ponape the numerous, sacred stone monuments and 50 artificial islets, a "South Seas Venice," have given the island its native name *Pon Pei*. Hambruch (vol. 3, 1936), feeling that the riddle of the ruins might never be satisfactorily solved, pointed to native traditions mixed with myth and truth as possible sources of information. Narrators say that two young magicians, Sipe and Saupe, wished to beautify their district and honor the spirits of the dead (important in all Micronesian religion) and the deity, Nan Dzapue, also called Luk. The brothers instituted sacred feasts and built sacred enclosures which, however, dissatisfied them. Then in Matolenim district they found a site sheltered from the waves to erect their most magnificent monuments. They commanded rocks to fly from their homes to suitable places in the structures, a technique used by later magicians to give the landscape its present peculiarities.

The number and size of the now ruined tombs and altars required, despite the magic of their mythical builders, a closely knit social life with a powerful priesthood and ruling class to command their construction, and enough docile peasants and slaves to do the work. Such a social organization and class system is described by early European visitors. Caroline myths stress the ingenuity of magicians, the oppression by rulers, and the struggles of poor heroes and heroines to meet almost impossible demands. Aided by friendly spirits, they win success, but often they leave the envious villagers at the moment of triumph, gather their relatives in a thatched hut, set fire to it, and perish rather than risk further orders from above. One hero who boldly visited the ruler without the expected present magically produced at the crucial moment a canoe full of food and other gifts. A Marshall metaphor compares a good chief to a tiger fish which waits in its hole in the rocks for its prey to swim past; similarly, a good chief stays home and waits for his subjects to bring him gifts.

The most elaborate Ponape legendary history (also told on Kusaie) concerns the overthrow of a line of dictators, the Sau Telur, by Isokalakal, King Wonderful, now a Ponape war god and founder of two of the clans of the island. He was the son of an elderly Kusaie woman who had been magically impregnated with a sprinkling of lemon juice by Nan Dzapue. The thunder deity wanted a son to take revenge on a Sau Telur for having imprisoned him as he visited a holy place. The precocious but militarily vacillating son went to Ponape with 333 warriors (no narrator changes that figure) in one canoe that took eight days to build. He was the son of an elderly Kusaie woman advised and encouraged by a woman who entertained him at an isle along the way, Isokalakal was successful, and the Sau Telur escaped death only by transforming himself into a fish, now tabu as food.

Familiar to museum visitors are the tightly knotted sennit armor and headgear worn by Gilbertese warriors to deflect spears edged with sharks' teeth. Even more reminiscent of medieval European knights are the duels fought over women and land claims by Gilbertese warriors supported by squires. Gilbertese, at least as far north as Tarawa, tell of Kaitu and Uakea from Beru who set out to conquer the islands. As in the Isokalakal tradition, narrators emphasize not the battles but the feasts and entertainment provided the invaders and the magic to detect and outwit treachery. Tabiteuea, on the path of invasion, still recites traditions about Kaitu, Uakea, and other Beru invaders like Tanentoa and giant Kourabi, to fortify land titles and to claim privileges and honorary duties in the village assembly house, the *maneaba*, a vast, thatched building supported on coral monoliths in which the spirits (*anti*) rest. Warriors here as elsewhere in Micronesia depended for help in battle on magical chants invoking the gods and describing the anticipated fate of the enemy.

Textbook photographs of Marshall "star charts" suggest the standard of native navigation. In a typhoon-swept region of some 700 high and low islands, it is no surprise that mythological characters are constantly traveling and that stars are personified. Many short traditions tell of destructive typhoons and how new clans subsequently originated from survivors. Micronesian narrators of popular tales are not quite as engrossed as their Polynesian colleagues in naming characters and identifying locales. However, they are likely to name the locale even though they often start out vaguely, as in the Marshalls, with "Once there was a woman with two sons . . ."

Besides fine canoes such as any Micronesian might own, mythical heroes use canoes that fly through the air. Or like Polynesian characters, they ride in or on sharks, whales, or turtles, or, using a device older than the airplane, they enter artificially constructed birds to be whisked to a kidnaped relative or wife. Any stone, even if not in canoe form, will support the drowning refugee if he knows the right magic. Should the canoe sennit break or the mast give way, a good seaman creates an island from a bit of sand he has and plants a tree which magically grows to the height needed for a mast. If he lands in strange territory as the hero, Rongerik, did, he knows enough to distrust the residents and put bits of white coconut meat or shell on his eyes to look as if he were awake through the night.

Texts of Marshall sea lyrics, composed by natives for European tunes, charm by the direct simplicity of their descriptions of weather at sea and the mariner's exultation in defying the elements and death (Erdland). The seaman is said to wear the islands he sails like a bracelet in his mind.

A European on first reading Micronesian myths finds them less alien and grotesque than, say, Melanesian stories. Micronesian myths in Hambruch's anthology (1916) from his and Kramer's collections were doubtless selected for their appeal to European readers; they sound like Old World märchen localized in Micronesian culture. In both cultures, the wishful thinking of narrators approved by listeners leans to stories about people of social extremes. The poor overcome economic and social discrimination with the aid of supernatural helpers and gain favor with the ruler. However, these Micronesian characters, as remarked above, rarely "live happily ever after." They reach the end of their rope quickly and commit suicide by fire rather than continue from one *tour de force* to another.

The reader soon realizes that many themes are unquestionably of Old World origin and have been introduced since 1521 when Magellan discovered Guam. The themes are so compatible with Micronesian psychology and older, native mythological concepts that they have been thoroughly assimilated. For instance, Ponape tells of a poor boy with only orange seeds to eat. He planted one, and a tree sprang up to the sky. The boy climbed up to a little house where a woman warned him against her cannibal husband. When the latter arrived, he smelled the human being hidden somewhere, but after his wife's false reply he sat down to count his wealth. Then "Jack and the Beanstalk" stole the money, fled home, and put the current ruler out of a job because he was richer. Hungry, younger brothers, as in a Peliliu story, receive a speck of fish and taro from a supernatural bird and find the amount never decreases no matter how heartily they eat—and best of all, it is the custom to take home whatever is left! Of course, they wisely refuse the first two wonderful things offered them by a friendly old lady and take an unpromising-looking third object full of magic. Haughty, human-headed cocks, who magically produce money like the golden egg-laying goose, help lowly Palauans but are incensed when rulers ask them to visit them.

Other Old World themes include one about a turtle who escapes with a "drowning punishment" by suggesting to his stupid captors that, before cooking him, they clean him in deep water. The swift garfish loses a race to the slow crab helped by mussels. Heroic families sometimes have seven children, and things are done by sevens or threes, especially in Yap and Ulithi. However, ten (and its half) is the older ritual number and still predominates in the myths over the two Old World favorites, seven and three. Eight, a favorite over the older ten in Polynesia, Melanesia, Indonesia, and Japan, is rarely the Micronesian conventional figure for the number of sons in a family or the number of times the hero tricks a slow-witted cannibal. The Symplegades theme occurs widely. Truk integrates it into heavenly topography by setting the clashing rocks in the sky before the door of the god Anulap (Great Spirit), to squash the souls of the dead.

Names and themes common in Polynesia appear in Micronesia. Maui-tikitiki himself (dialectically, Motikitik) fishes up islands in the Western Carolines. Local heroes, like the Gilbertese Nareau, replace him as earth-fishers in the east. Discussed more fully later is the sky-raising theme, which is connected, as in Polynesia, with a primeval Nothingness broken only by the sea and the closely adhering sky and earth. It appears occasionally in what may constitute a subarea in mythology —the Gilberts, Ocean, Nauru, Kapingamarangi, Nukuoro, and at least three islands in Melanesia, namely, Ontong Java, Nukumanu, and Nuguria. The Marshalls too may belong on this list. Several of the islands listed are now called "Polynesian outliers," an increasingly unsatisfactory term. Nareau, important in Gilbertese cosmogony, is also known in the three outliers in Melanesia. Nukuoro has Tahaki, a prominent Polynesian hero, in a family of sky-raising deities. The god Tangaloa and other Polynesian names like Tinirau and Taranga are known in the southern Gilberts, where traditions describe migrations to and from Samoa. In Truk, the theme found in Polynesia and Melanesia about a tree which is miraculously restored every time the hero chops it down to make a canoe, is told of the sons of Paluelap and his wife Leofas, deities whose names recur in the Carolines.

Frequent in the Carolines, Marshalls, and parts of the subarea outlined above, are stories which in Polynesia constitute a myth-complex about Tinirau, Hine, Maui, and Rupe. Micronesian names change from variant to variant. A missing woman is sought by a devoted husband or relative who assumes the form of a dove or travels by birdplane to rescue her. The girl sometimes is said to have left home when scolded for letting family treasures get wet. She may marry a chief and be forced by an ugly witch to exchange shapes, an alteration that deceives the chief but not the faithful, seeking relatives.

Melanesian-like are innumerable tales about stupid giants and giantesses, or bush spirits, who sometimes eat a whole village except for a woman whose son becomes a monster-slayer. Ogres are delayed and eventually perish by following destructive advice from their captives. Cheering news from Truk is that female bush spirits who used to lure men and drive them insane are now outlawed. Sky-dwelling women will perhaps petition against earthly women who lure married sky deities to the earth to start new clans.

Recalling Melanesian plots are stories of kindly animal mothers who generously aid beautiful, human daughters until a curious son-in-law spies on them and slays them in horror. Then everyone in the family, including the murderer, commits suicide. An eel or lizard, rather than a snake as in Melanesia, is the mother. Believing them temporary residences of spirits, Micronesians protect eels with a severe tabu. Eels, malevolent or friendly, are important in myths, particularly those about clan origins. Traditions about the origin of clans constitute a major part of Micronesian mythology, and any ancient or new story may be reinterpreted as a phase of clan history.

Many myths hinge on tabu violations. Often tasks set a hero by a harsh ruler are punishments for breaking tabus. A sniffing dog, or Sau Kompul, the Sau Telur's adjutant, spies on the people; birds too spread gossip as in Polynesia. The course of a tale may depend on whether the hero or heroine obeys the injunction to drink from the dirty rather than the clean spring (Mar-

shalls, Eastern Carolines), or to look around in the second village visited but not the first (Western Carolines).

Compared with Melanesian mythology, the Micronesian emphasizes sex but little in the stories, although incest themes are frequent. A goddess who bears both children and food is well known in Melanesia, especially New Guinea, and in New Zealand. In Truk, Ligoububfanu, sometimes the sky god Anulap's daughter or wife and connected with eels, miraculously bears the first human beings and nuts and grains. The face of her child is seen on the coconut which grew from a corpse. A comparable origin myth is widespread in Oceania.

Once, only men bore children, but Laponga, a magician about whom Ponape has a genre of tales, angrily transferred his fœtus to a woman when a midwife revealed that he was pregnant. Present is the widely held belief of Oceania that until normal childbirth was learned women were cut open and killed to remove the child.

Like Melanesian stories about the Masi are tales from Tabiteuea, Truk, and other islands about clans of silly people who do everything the wrong way. Merry, elusive, clever little people, like Hawaiian Menehune and their Melanesian counterparts, are known to Ponape as Tsokelai and to the Marshalls as Anjinmar or Nonieb. Truk and Kusaie tell of fabulous races of giants, which on Ponape are called Liat and Kona; in the Marshalls, Rimogaio.

Animal tales are common, though rarely of the Animal Kingdom or Æsop's Fables type. In a battle between birds and fish for supremacy, the provoker of the fight sleeps soundly at home while the fight rages, and a great bird, who screams for a duel with a fish with a proud and terrible-sounding name, is captured by the bearer of the name, a tiny shellfish, who clamps his bivalves on the bird's leg. Rats, like eels, are prominent mythological beings. Nauru has a tale, diffused from Indonesia into the Pacific and common in Micronesia, about a bird, a crab, and a rat who go to sea; when the canoe sinks, the rat, abandoned by its friends, is rescued by an octopus which it mistreats and tricks. Usually, though, Micronesian animals act in plots with human beings as their totemic guardians and helpers. Although slightly personified plants and trees figure in the myths, plant totemism, at least on Ponape, is rare, as Eilers points out.

Myths predominantly about human beings often revolve around two major characters who may be brothers, sisters, husband and wife, or friends of the same sex. Myths, like that about Edao and Jemaliwut in the Marshalls, summarized later, usually set a younger, precocious sibling against an older, less astute one who fails to repeat the younger's successes. Tales showing European influence shade the characterization to make the younger kind and considerate while the older is haughty and unkind. However, much of this pronounced ethical dualism and moralizing seems as native to Micronesian mythology as to the Melanesian and may explain why these European märchen were so well assimilated.

Caroline narrators have strung an odyssey of adventures, widely known through the vast archipelago, on a thin thread of plot about the search by faithful Rongerik, well versed in magic, for Rongelap, his lost, older brother. Like those of many characters, the names of these sons of Paluelap are identical except for the final epithets, which merely mean old or young, big (*lapalap, lap*) or little (*tikitik, tik*).

In the 2000-mile, east-west sweep of the Carolines from Palau to Kusaie, the most recurrent and culturally significant myths about two contrasting and conflicting brothers form a major hero cycle. The hero, Olofat, is the younger of the two, but he is a mischievous troublemaker. The incidents and personalities of the *dramatis personæ* of the Olofat cycle recall cycles about the Polynesian Maui, the Melanesian Qat, and the Gilbertese Nareau. Many details are so similar as to leave no doubt about the single origin of these details and their subsequent diffusion from area to area. The four heroes, and perhaps Edao⁻ should be included, are younger brothers, gods or demigods, crafty magicians, and remodelers of customs and aspects of the universe. While Edao and Qat tend to take an ethically superior role to their brothers, Olofat, Maui, and Nareau are tricksters of global scope who annoy their elder brothers, their deified relatives, human beings, and the animal and plant world.

The name of the older brother selected to act as the hero's particular foil shifts in these cycles from version to version. For instance, in the Olofat myths of Truk and Lukunor, the good and handsome brother or half-brother is Lugeilang (Lukelang, Luk) while Anulap (Anuelap, Onulap, Enulap) is the father. Nearby Namoluk has Samonekoaner (Semenkoror appears to be a dialectical variant) as the brotherly foil to ugly, jealous Olofat, and Luk as the father. Usually when Luk is the father, Anulap is the grandfather.

Olofat's career includes his magical birth and development on earth; visit to the sky on a column of smoke to claim recognition of his sky relatives; the seeking out of the protected brother and putting him temporarily to death; outfitting sharks with teeth; seducing wives of older relatives; stealing food from feasts and leaving husks and skins; assuming innumerable transformations, often into an old man with ringworm, to escape punishment; and dodging death at the hands of older relatives who get him into a post hole before jamming in the post, or burn him, or throw him into the sea in a fish trap. Namoluk islanders conclude by having the gods make Olofat the god of fire and condemned souls and having little sister, Rat, suggest that Olofat die at the end of the world but the other gods be eternal. To single out only one of the elements recurring elsewhere in Oceania, the post hole episode is in the Qat and Nareau cycles but not the Maui series.

The Olofat cycle is in the Caroline cosmogony as the Nareau cycle is in the Gilbertese and the Maui cycle in the Polynesian. Heroes belong to a family of deities, the Caroline pantheon, which functions in every sphere but calls the sky its home. Characters with similar names, functions, and departmental duties recur throughout the group. Anulap at the apex of the pantheon has achieved the epitome of prestige in Truk where his ten sisters and brothers are his subordinates. His age and weakness now separate him from active participation in world affairs. This giant requires servants to lift his eyelid when he wishes to see and to raise his lip when he wants food. Sister Inemes is the local Venus. Ligoububfanu, mentioned above, is the most creatively busy member of the family. With or without Luk, she produces people, plants, and animals miraculously and indis-

criminately, and between times piles up rocks and sand to make islands.

The Carolines rarely attempt to describe the ultimate or nearly ultimate origins of the world. They concentrate on dividing and subdividing, like unscrupulous real estate agents, not only the earth but the air, the sky, the sea, and the land beneath their feet. Anuelap's quarrelsome family is assigned space, and the narrators ponder the relationships of the family to each other and to earthly people. The origin of fire is ascribed to Rat stealing it from the sky. Death as a permanent sleep was decided by the pantheon. It is also popularly attributed to older relatives misusing a younger relative's magic to resuscitate the dead. They practiced on him but as they forgot part of the magic he died permanently and could not tell them what they had forgotten.

The Marshalls and the Gilberts have cosmogonies which leave no doubt of historical connections with Polynesia.

According to Ralik Group people of the Marshalls, an uncreated being Loa or Lowa lived in the primeval sea. Like the Tahitian Ta'aroa, he commanded reefs, sandbanks, plants, and birds to appear, and finally a god for each of the four cardinal directions in the sky which a white gull encircled. Irjojrilik was in the west; Lalikian or Lajbuineamuen in the north; Lokomran in the east; and Lorok in the south. From a blood blister on Loa's leg came Wulleb and Limdunanij, a boy and a girl. The latter bore Lanej (Zenith) and Lewoj (Nadir) who conspired to kill Wulleb. He escaped and fell to the earth where a blood blister on his leg burst and two boys, Jemaliwut and Edao, came forth. Edao, the younger, is the hero who, unlike his discriminating and constantly frustrated brother, is not revolted by Lijebage, Lady Turtle, to whom Wulleb has sent them for a magic tortoise shell. As a reward, Turtle makes Edao a great magician. Like Olofat he is an agile shape-shifter, but must assume his own shape when a certain sentence is pronounced. After many adventures he died in Butaritari, Gilberts. Of Jemaliwut it is told that he recognized the tattooing on a mysterious hand that came to steal as that of his aunt. By making her show him first one hand, then the other, and then both together, he trapped her with one hand still absent. Like the Gilbertese Nei Auti, she brought insect pests into the world.

The Radak Group variant makes Wulleb and Lejman, identified as male and female worms living in a shell, the first living beings. As in the southern subarea (Nauru, for example), the worms raise the upper part of the shell which becomes the sky, the lower the earth. Wulleb now lives on mysterious Eb Island in the west where birds go annually to have their feathers plucked and fish bring Wulleb tribute. Nothing more is told of Loa. His name makes one wonder if it is a remnant of the Polynesian name, Tangaloa, a dialectical variant of Ta'aroa, the god whose deeds resemble Loa's.

In the Gilberts and Gilbertese-settled Nui in the Ellices and Ocean Island, the cosmogonic myth complex, religion, and traditions about migration and settlement, published by Grimble and Hambruch, repeat names like Te Bo ma Te Maki (Darkness and Cleaving Together); Nareau (Sir Spider) the Elder and the Younger; Tabakea (Turtle); and many others including Riiki (Eel), Auriaria, Tabuariki, Taburimai, and Lady Tituabine. Nauru, influenced by Gilbertese castaways, also knows some of them and identifies as Spider the primal being, Areop-Enap, who lived in a mussel shell which became the world. Qat, it is interesting to note, sometimes has a spider companion, Marawa, in Melanesia.

Beru describes Te Bo ma Te Maki and Nareau the Elder as pre-existent in the world. Nareau commanded Sand and Water, also in existence then, to produce children. Among them is the mischievous culture hero, Nareau the Younger, who vitalized his inactive siblings and ordered them to rise. They could not because the sky was too low. Eel becomes the most important sky-raiser. Nareau then set a woman in each of the cardinal directions to support the sky, and killed his father to use his eyes for the sun and moon and his spine as the source of the ancestral tree (Kai-ni-tiku-aba) from which people came. The tree was on Samoa, the land piled up by Nareau's brothers and sisters. Subsequent events lead into genealogies and individual family histories. This same Nareau later plays malicious and puerile tricks, which are a great source of amusement to people hearing the stories.

Ocean Island has Tabakea and Tituabine, offspring of Heaven and Earth, produce the rest of the pantheon which enjoys an inexhaustible fish trap and coconut tree until they violate tabus. Nui Island makes Auriaria perform the feats that Nareau usually does in world organization. A Tabiteuean version, astoundingly Polynesian in style, gives the origin of the world in a genealogical chant, starting with Te Bo ma Te Maki producing Land; Land and Sky producing Void; Void and the Sundering (of Earth and Sky) producing Nareau.

Micronesia has little native literary classification. Ponape, for instance, distinguishes between stories (soi) and true stories (kosoi), terms they give even to descriptions of culture communicated to ethnographers. Truk is the only island with riddles or at least where they have been recorded. This island, according to Bollig, uses the name uruo for narratives, which are known to magical experts but not to the commoners, about clan origins, chiefs, and the settlement of specific land tracts. Much loved, and often rather didactic, fireside tales, dudunap, begin with a formula like "It goes, it comes" and end with "It breaks off." "Crazy people," umes, is the name of a genre of comic tales about certain clans who do everything wrong. Marshall narrators, who tell stories only at night to keep narrators and listeners from getting swollen heads, often use introductory and terminal formulæ too, and refresh a wearying audience by breaking a long story with a set, comic formula. That Micronesian myths and tales have, on the whole, a great deal of humor is obvious even to a European.

Comedy relief is used in dances too. For instance, Tabiteuean dancers refresh themselves with a child's patty-cake song, or two performers will burlesque experts by mistiming gestures to poke each other in the eyes, bump heads, and snatch each other's wreath or mat. Certain old hags often act as comedians. They even break into serious food-assembling ceremonies in the maneaba when everyone is nervously watching to see his family properly represented; then the capers of an old lady chased by a solemn but secretly convulsed dignitary who swats her with his symbol of respected age, a fly whisk, makes everyone shriek with laughter.

Neither new nor modern chants and songs have terminal rimes. In the Marshalls and Carolines, many songs and dances have European melodies and native words. Few old chants used to accompany dances seem to have been recorded there, and the old native style must be studied in the magical formulæ. In the Gilberts, the more melodic tunes and less ritualized dances of the Polynesian Ellice Islands have been given native words to which young people dance with the additional rhythm of a mercilessly beaten bottom of an upended box or a 44-gallon kerosene tin. A certain mode of behavior, solemnly cultivated by the younger set among the intense-spirited Tabiteueans, goes along with these dances, which are merry in contrast to the highly stylized, set-expressioned old dances (ruoia), still important for ritual and entertainment. It is "very Ellice Islands" to pull a careless lock over the eye, hang a plastic belt open around the neck, drape one's lavalava sloppily, and nourish a love-'em and leave-'em attitude toward the opposite sex. Ellice Islanders are hard put to it to think up variations to hold their position as fashion leaders.

Little is known of Marianas mythology; a Spanish account from 1683 describes a dozen women in a circle chanting myths "in verse and in measured time in three part singing" and accompanying themselves with perfectly timed hand gestures, a crescent in the left hand and a little box of shells and bells in the right as castanets (Thompson). A fragment of cosmogony recalls the Gilbertese in parts of the world being made from the body of a god.

The idan of Truk are trained specialists in religion, magic, and mythology. They are split into different sects but all claim Onulap and Semenkoror, as their founders and teachers. Their tribal importance, prestige, tabus, secret languages, and rigid training recall native scholars and schools of central-marginal Polynesia. Lay experts in metaphors, similes, and pithy allusions are the soufos, masters of speech, who glorify the language of the common people of Truk. Tabiteuea has two classes of composers. In the training of one, a frigate bird's feather and a rat's nest are part of the magic. The bird comes from afar bringing new words while the rat, a thief, steals words for the composer. The composer also goes out on the reef and literally fishes for words with hook and line. As inspiration seizes him, he shouts back the phrase to his followers, each of whom is entrusted with one word or phrase. Nareau's shrine is also visited by earnest composers with offerings.

This survey shows that, despite the numerous mythological elements which Micronesia shares with Polynesia, Micronesia, and to a lesser extent with Indonesia, the area has more than a miscellaneous hodgepodge of foreign myths. It has interpreted the themes shared with these areas and those acquired from Europeans in a fashion uniquely its own. It seems, moreover, to have selected extremely compatible themes and rejected others. Narrators have infused these selected themes with the literary and psychological qualities peculiar to their culture, as has been suggested above. Some of these qualities now appear elusive and delicately and subtly molded in contrast to the bold qualities of Melanesian and Polynesian cultures. The precise definition of the typical Micronesian spirit must depend upon more comparison and analysis than has yet been done. Such study may also bring out in stronger relief than could be done here the themes found only in Micronesia, themes perhaps more indicative of the spirit of the people than the remodeled myths.

Bibliography: P. L. Bollig, *Die Bewohner der Truk-Inseln* (Munster), 1927; F. W. Christian, *The Caroline Islands* (London), 1899; W. H. Furness, *The Island of Stone Money* (Philadelphia), 1910; R. B. Dixon, "Oceanic," in *Mythology of All Races,* vol. 9 (Boston), 1916; K. P. Emory, "Myths and Tales from Kapingamarangi, a Polynesian Inhabited Island in Micronesia," *JAFL* 62, 1949; S. H. Elbert, "Utamatua and Other Legends from Kapingamarangi," *JAFL* 62, 1949; P. A. Erdland, *Leben und Religion eines Südsee-Volkes, der Marshall-Insulaner* (Munster), 1914; A. Grimble, "From Birth to Death in the Gilbert Islands," *Royal Anthrop. Inst., Grt. Brit., Jour.,* vol. 51, 1921; "Myths from the Gilbert Islands," *Folk-Lore,* 33, 1922; 34, 1923; "The Migration of a Pandanus People," *Poly. Soc., Jour.,* 42, 1933; P. Hambruch, *Südseemärchen* (Jena), 1916; K. Luomala, *Ethnography of Tabiteuea, Gilbert Islands,* manuscript; J. F. O'Connell, *A Residence of Eleven Years in New Holland and the Caroline Islands* (Boston), 1836. L. Thompson, *The Native Culture of the Marianas Islands, B. P. Bishop Mus., Bull.* 185, 1945; T. Yanaihara, *Pacific Islands under Japanese Mandate* (London), 1940. Myths appear in all volumes of *Hamburgische wissenschaftliche Stiftung. Ergebnisse der Südsee-expedition, 1908–1910. II. Ethnographie, B. Mikronesien.* Cited specifically above were: P. Hambruch, *Ponape,* vol. 3 (Hamburg), 1936; *Nauru,* 1914.

KATHARINE LUOMALA

Midas A legendary wealthy king of Phrygia in Asia Minor, son of Gordius and Cybele, of whom two principal stories are told: some equate him with Mithras, the god of light of the Persian area. While Dionysus was making his progress through the East, Silenus became more than usually befuddled with drink and wandered into Midas' court. The king entertained him for ten days, then escorted him to Dionysus. The god offered to grant Midas any wish he might make, and the foolish king asked that anything he touched be turned to gold (J2072.1). But, after he had played with the power for a while, Midas discovered that his food too was turning to gold as he touched it, even between his teeth. By bathing in a spring at the source of the river Pactolus (which afterwards had much gold in its silt), Midas was able to remove this gift turned curse. A sophisticated appendage to this legend adds that during his stay the wise Silenus was questioned at length by Midas, one of the questions being "What is best for a man?" The answer: "Not to be born, and next best to die immediately upon being born." Another variant says that Midas trapped Silenus or one of the satyrs by filling a pool with wine. The satyr drank, fell into a drunken sleep, and was tied up by Midas.

The other story, a migratory legend found also in India, Gaul, and Ireland, concerns the musical contest between Pan and Apollo. Tmolus, the god of the Lydian mountain of the same name, judged Apollo the better. Midas disagreed, being a follower of Pan and the satyrs. In rage, Apollo changed Midas' uncritical ears into those of an ass (F511.2.2). Midas covered the ears with his Phrygian cap, but naturally this was a secret his barber was bound to find out (N465). Unable to contain himself, the barber dug a hole in the river bank and

whispered into it the secret. Then he covered it with earth, but reeds grew there, and every time the wind blew they whispered, "Midas has ass's ears" (D1316.5). The connection of this story to Midas may be due to the fact that the ass was a sacred animal in Phrygia, and the king of that country may have been figured with ass's ears, which the Greeks explained by attaching the legend to the personage.

Midewiwin or **Mide** The Grand Medicine Society, a secret society of four degrees, open to men and women, of the Ojibwa (Chippewa), Ottawa, Sauk, Fox, Potawatomi, Winnebago, and Kickapoo Indians of the Central Woodlands. The midewiwin was first performed by various supernatural deities to comfort the culture hero, Nanabozho, after the death of his younger brother; later Nanabozho taught the same rites to the Indians. The Medicine Society met inside a specially constructed oval lodge; members of the society, attired in their finest clothes, danced in a circuit around the lodge, and prayers to various deities were offered by the priests at stated intervals. Initiation of a candidate into the first degree of the Medicine Society involved payment in goods collected for this purpose by the candidate's family; in return, the newly initiated person was provided with an otter, mink, fisher, etc., skin medicine bag and taught how to control a white shell or *mide,* which he kept inside him or in the bag, and used as a magic "shot" against other members of the society. Shooting exhibitions were given by midewiwin members as they danced during the exoteric part of their rites; by pointing the nose of the bag at another member and blowing a whiff at the same time, they would cause that person to fall down. Upon recovering, the person shot would then shoot others in the same way. Esoteric knowledge, of curing, of magic, of witchcraft, was also imparted to the newly initiated by the Mide priests. If a member was able to afford it, after learning all that pertained to the first degree, he could, upon additional payments, advance to the second, third, and to the fourth or highest degrees.

Although the origin myth of the Grand Medicine Society stresses that Nanabozho taught human beings the rites so that they could cure disease, obtain an abundance of food, and triumph over their enemies, the indications are that members of the society misused their powers, worked for evil instead of good, and were generally feared by their fellow humans—so much so that in one tribe after another the Indians themselves outlawed the Midewiwin. The Shawnee Prophet is reputed to have preached against it among the Winnebago, and the Fox Indians claim to have gathered all members of the Society together, in the past, and to have told them that this dance must not go on any more because every time it was danced two or three important men among the Fox died. The Kickapoo then followed the Fox example and stopped the Mide dance in their tribe in the same way that the Fox had. [EWV]

Midgard or **Mana-heim** In Teutonic mythology, the middle earth, i.e. this earth, home of man, formed from the body of the giant Ymir. The Old English word for this middle region between heaven and hell was *middengeard.* After the gods killed Ymir they rolled his body into the void in the center of the universe, Ginnunga-gap. Here his blood (or sweat) became the oceans, his bones the mountains, his teeth the cliffs, and his hair the trees and all other vegetation. The skull, held up by the four dwarfs, Nordri, Sudri, Austri, and Westri, from whom the points of the compass are named, formed the vaulted heavens. This they filled with sparks from Surtr's sword which formed the sun, moon, and stars; Ymir's brain continues to brood over the earth in the form of heavy clouds. To the north of Midgard is Niflheim, a region of cold and ice; to the south is Muspellheim, the land of fire. The earth is connected with Asgard, the home of the gods, by the rainbow bridge, Bifrost, and deep within it reaches one of the three roots of the world tree, Yggdrasil. The rooster of Midgard will crow to announce Ragnarök.

Midgard Serpent The monstrous serpent that encircles the earth, in Teutonic mythology, offspring of Loki and Angur-boda, named Jormungandr. See ANIMAL CHILDREN.

Midsummer Eve or **St. John's Eve** The eve (June 23) before Midsummer Day (June 24) about the time of the summer solstice: for centuries probably the most important and widespread of the annual festivals of Europe. Today June 24 is commonly celebrated as St. John the Baptist Day, but the old vegetation-fire-water rites remain conspicuous through their coating of churchification, and this in spite of the fact that the meaning of the observances is forgotten for the most part in the popular mind. In Ireland it is said that St. Patrick changed the festival from Beltane to St. John's Day, the celebration of Beltane in Ireland being practically identical with Midsummer Eve or Day observances all over Europe.

On Midsummer Eve witches, fairies, spirits of the dead, wraiths of the living, and all sorts of supernatural beings, good and evil, are abroad, not only especially active and numerous, but often visible. The phrase *Midsummer madness* is proverbial in England. *To have but a mile to Midsummer* means to be a little mad. The Midsummer moon is the month of June, the month of lovers, and a time for happy lunacy.

All magic, good and bad, is exceptionally potent on Midsummer Eve. All magic plants plucked at midnight on this night are doubly efficacious; any plant or flower plucked at this time keeps better. The herbs of St. John (usually St. Johnswort, hawkweed, vervain, orpine, mullen, wormwood, mistletoe) plucked either at midnight on St. John's Eve or at the stroke of noon on St. John's Day, protect houses from fire and lightning and people from disease, witchcraft, and disaster. Divining rods cut on this night are the more infallible. Dreams dreamed on Midsummer Night are likely to come true. Dew gathered on St. John's Night restores sight (see D1505.5.2.1). In northern Europe the Wild Hunt is often seen on St. John's Night (see E501.11.1.3). The fern blooms at midnight of Midsummer Eve (see FERN SEED). In Devonshire people used to crawl under the communion table in the church three times at midnight on Midsummer Eve to cure fits. (See G. L. Kittredge, *Witchcraft in Old and New England,* Cambridge, Mass., 1929, p. 148.)

In Germany and southeastern Europe there was a strong belief that rivers and various water spirits demanded a human victim on Midsummer Day; yet in contradiction to the danger of waters on this day, all natural waters have special medicinal virtue on this day of all days, from Sweden to Sicily, from Spain to Ireland to Estonia. In Germany people went out and bathed in the night in streams and rivers to cure their diseases and strengthen their legs. Moslems in Morocco are said still to plunge into seas and rivers on Midsummer Day and also to drive their animals into the water and bathe them. The ancient water rites fell naturally into St. John the Baptist Day observances.

The Midsummer fires, however, are the outstanding feature of this summer solstice festival: interpreted by Frazer and Mannhardt specifically as sun charms to help the sun in his course, and by others as fumigation-purification rites. The people leaped through the fires and drove their cattle through them, or to leeward of them so that they got the benefit of the thick smoke. They hurled burning disks toward the sun, rolled burning wheels downhill, burned effigies impersonating death or winter or all man's ills. All the various games, tugs-of-war, mock battles, and destruction of effigies are interpreted as survivals of very early dramatizations of the summer-winter, good-evil conflict. New fires in the houses were lighted from the Midsummer fires; burning brands were carried through the fields and barnyards to avert evil, cure and ward off disease, and ensure fertility, new life, crops, offspring. In parts of England it was formerly thought that the apple crop would fail if the Midsummer fires were not lighted. The kindling of Midsummer fires is a dying practice in most of Europe today but is still a feature of festival life in Ireland and in some parts of Scandinavia.

Midsummer is especially a festival for lovers. All kinds of love divinations are performed (see MIDSUMMER MEN), dreams interpreted, and images evoked. Lovers clasped hands across the Midsummer bonfire, tossed flowers across the fire to each other, or leaped through it together. In Scandinavia girls put little bunches of flowers under their pillows on Midsummer Night to induce dreams of love and insure their coming true. In England it was said if an unmarried girl would fast on Midsummer Eve, and at midnight set the table with a clean cloth, bread, cheese and ale, leave the yard door open, and wait, the boy she would marry would come in and partake of the midnight feast with her.

In Ireland in some districts each family builds its own bonfire, circumambulates the fire, and circumambulates the house three times with a burning brand from the fire. Sometimes there is a community fire on a neighboring hilltop or at a crossroad through which the people leap, drive their cattle, and light their brands for the circumambulation of houses, fields, and byres. Blazing brands from the fires are thrown into potato fields and gardens; ashes from the fires are mixed with seeds for planting. Sometimes the cattle are penned up and the people run around the pens with their blazing brands. In the Scottish Highlands also the herders circumambulate the herds with torches lighted at the Midsummer fire. See BELTANE; BORDON DANZA; CORRI-CORRI; DAISY; LUGNASAD; MAY DAY; NEW FIRE; section *El Día de San Juan* in SPANISH FOLKLORE.

Midsummer Men The plant orpine (*Sedum telephium*): so termed in England because used as symbolic of human beings in midsummer divination. Slips of these plants are planted in pairs on Midsummer Eve, either by a young man or young woman, one representing the planter, the other his or her sweetheart. If one slip withers, the one it represents will die. If both slips take hold, flourish, and grow strong, and lean toward one another, the pair will surely marry. In Germany and Switzerland young couples also use orpine for the same kind of future-reading.

Midwinter Bear Society dance A dance held by the Bear Society, an Iroquois Indian group which functioned as a curing society among the Seneca, Cayuga, and other Iroquois tribes of what is now New York state. The Bear Society dance can be included in communal festivals as given by the Iroquois, but only at midwinter. There are in reality two dances: one that functions as a curing rite, and another than can be performed at any time without a patient. The first form is in three parts: the cure to slow chants, the round dance with stomp step, and finally the pairing of dancers. The curing dance was held to cure victims of bear sickness, which resembled cases of mental derangement of which the patient was aware, but which he could not control. The sickness is caused by the bear spirit; to cure the victim a ritual has to be performed in the patient's home and ceremonial foods provided which the bear spirit likes. A shaman is in charge of the curing ritual, and members of the society blow berry juice on the patient. The dance itself is led by the sponsor of the ceremony and the leading shaman, and danced by the society members. At the Midwinter festival anyone present may join in the dance. Patients who have been cured by the ritual are thereafter members of the society. [EWV]

Mike Fink "King of the keelboatmen," known as the "Snag" on the Mississippi and the "Snapping Turtle" on the Ohio. Born at old Fort Pitt in 1770, at the age of seventeen he enlisted in the Indian scouts on the Pennsylvania border and soon acquired a reputation for boldness, cunning, and skill with the rifle. On one occasion he shot and killed an Indian at the very same instant that the other fired at a buck and was thus able to satisfy his hunger without being discovered by the Indian hunting party. Having always wanted to become a boatman, he next joined the keelboatmen on the Ohio—a hardy, dissolute breed of giants and "reckless savages," who alternated between heroic battling with upstream currents and riotous brawls and sprees. Mike Fink's famous brag, beginning "I'm a Salt River Roarer! I'm chuck-full of fight and I love the wimen," punctuates the various kinds of half-horse, half-alligator prowess that made him a legend and the mythical "demigod of the rivers": "I can out-run, out-jump, out-shoot, out-brag, out-drink, an' out-fight, rough-an'-tumble, no holts barred, ary man on both sides the river from Pittsburgh to New Orleans an' back ag'in to St. Louiee."

Notorious for his daredevil pranks as well as for his fights and marksmanship, Mike Fink displayed almost diabolical cunning and cruelty toward the victims of his practical jokes, as his predatory exploits were called. These included "trimming" a Negro's heel because he disliked its shape, shooting a scalp-lock from an Indian's head, and curing his wife of looking at other men by forcing her to lie down in a pile of leaves to which he set fire.

Once Mike Fink carried his lawlessness too far—beyond the point where "even a crime might take on the aspect of a good joke." This was in 1822, when, displaced by the steamboat, the "last of the boatmen" became one of Ashley's men in the service of the Mountain Fur Company. At Fort Henry, at the mouth of the Yellowstone, while engaged in his favorite sport of "shooting the whisky cup," he aimed too low and shot his friend Carpenter in the forehead. For this act of carelessness or treachery he paid with his life soon after, at the hands of Carpenter's avenger, Talbott.   B. A. BOTKIN

mikita The Lithuanian rod dance. The version for men is an energetic battle mime with rods, in longways formation similar to the English Morris. The *motero mikita*, the version for women, discards the rods and virility symbolism and substitutes pleasing longways formations of the Virginia Reel type. With a consistent step of three polkas and three stamps, opposites meet and retire; then, in turn, each set of corners meets and retires, starting with the first man and fourth woman and working up through the four couples. As a refrain between each exchange, the two lines form two separate circles, and polka clockwise. In the end all polka right, then left in one large circle, and conclude with the initial advance and retire and a final bow. [GPK]

Mikula A Russian peasant hero of the Paul Bunyan type, figuring in many byliny. See BALLAD.

Mikumwesu In a Malecite Indian myth, the older and more powerful brother of Gluskabe; a small man who could do more with his weak-looking bow, than Gluskabe could with his strong one. The character also occurs, as Megumooweco, father of Gluskabe, or Mekmues, a good spirit in Micmac Indian tradition. The name is equivalent to that of the Passamaquoddy Mickumwes, a small wood spirit who had the power of increasing its stature at will. The character is of interest for its possible relation to Tcikapis, the dwarf culture hero of the Montagnais-Naskapi Indians. See Margaret Fisher, "The Myths of the Northern and Northeastern Algonkians in Reference to Algonkian Mythology as a Whole," pp. 229–30, n. 6, in *Man in Northeastern North America*, Frederick Johnson, ed., *Papers of the Robert S. Peabody Foundation for Archaeology*, vol. 3, 1946. [EWV]

Milesians In Old Irish mythology and legend, the fifth people to invade Ireland; sons and companions of that Mil who went from Spain to Ireland to avenge the death of Ith; ancestors of the present people of Ireland. The Milesians came to Ireland in 30 ships; they tried to land at Inber Stainge, but the Tuatha Dé Danann raised druid mists and illusions about them so that they could not; they sailed around Ireland three times before they finally set foot on the earth at Inber Stainge, on a Thursday before the first day of May in the Year of the World 3500. At once they set out for Tara, meeting en route the three queens, Banba, Fódla, and Ériu (see these). At Tara they conferred with the three kings (MacCuill, MacCecht, and MacGreine) and the judgment was given for the Milesians to go to sea again and take the land by force, and whichever won, the others would depart. When the Milesians were nine waves off shore, the Tuatha Dé Danann raised such a storm, a druid storm, against them that many were drowned or lost. But Eber and Eremon and Amergin, three of the five sons of Mil, survived and landed. Then

Eber and Eremon divided the fleet and chieftains between them, and conquered the Tuatha Dé Danann in two battles: the battle of Sliaḃ Mis (where fell Scota, the wife of Mil) and the battle of Tailltiu where the Milesians slew the three kings and three queens of Ireland. Thus the Tuatha Dé Danann were routed and the Milesians took the lordship of Ireland. Eremon took kingship over the north; Eber took the south. Amergin, being a poet, wanted no possessions. Cir, a great poet among them, went northward with Eremon; Cennfinn, a famous harper went south with Eber. Thus music has been the gift of the south of Ireland up till now; and knowledge and poetry still come out of the north. See BILE.

milk Milk is the only substance on the face of the earth whose primary purpose is nourishment. Specifically it is secreted by female mammals after they have borne young. Human milk has been supplemented by that of other species, but the domestication of animals, which ensures a regular supply of milk has a limited distribution. Various animals have been domesticated and used for milking, most commonly hoofed mammals: cattle, sheep, goats, caribou, reindeer, buffalo, yak, camels, asses, and mares. Milking was unknown in the New World prior to the 16th century. Some cultures depend upon milk and its products as their chief food, e.g. the Hottentots of Africa, the Lapps of Europe, the Todas of India, and numerous pastoral tribes of central Asia. Over most of Europe and parts of Asia and Africa, dairying was part of the general agricultural complex; but milk is absent from the diet of the Chinese, Japanese, Polynesians, and Melanesians.

All cultures rely upon the milk of the mother or of other nursing women as infant food. This may be supplemented by milk of other species as well. The Italians feel that a young infant may take on some of the characteristics of the animal who produces the milk; this is why a wet nurse of good character should be selected, or why animal milk should not be introduced too early. A Jewish child may not nurse beyond its fourth birthday, although human milk may be given to an adult, provided it has first been expressed from the breast. The Polish peasant will not let a baby nurse for more than two St. John's Days. If the Polish baby has been weaned and it begins to nurse again, it is said that the child will be a stammerer.

As a food for adults, or in its relation to adult human beings, cultural attitudes range, on the one hand, from the positive aspect in India and Africa, where milk is treated with the greatest reverence and ceremony, to the negative, as in China, where it is equated with excreta. In our own culture, milk (specifically cold, fluid, pasteurized, cow's milk) occupies a somewhat medial position. It is said to be good for one, nourishing, and health-giving, particularly for children, invalids, pregnant and lactating women, but *fattening* for adults.

Among the Todas of southern India, the entire life is geared around their buffalo, with the dairy serving as a temple. All activities connected with milk are the sole concern of the men. Milk is given to the dying to drink, and the dead are taken to the stable before disposal. Women can do nothing with milk, except to consume it.

In East Africa, the cattle are also the objects of great concern, and there are many observances which ensure the supply of milk. The Bahima and the Masai believe that if milk is boiled, the cattle will die, or the cows will dry up. On the other hand among the Baganda who normally tabu the boiling of milk, it is mandatory to boil the first milk from a newly calved cow, make it into a cake, and eat it. Among the Zulus, a wounded man could not milk a cow until he had been purified. Milk and blood may be antithetical, as with the Thonga, where a menstruating woman could not go near the kraal or look at the cattle. The menstruating woman among the Banyoro was permitted the milk only from old cows. In other places, "blood" was good for milk: The Hottentot pubescent girl was led around the village to touch the milking vessels and the rams, for good luck; while among the Herero, all fresh milk was consecrated to the newly delivered women. Milk is often not eaten with meat, as among the Jews. The Baganda would not touch meat that was boiled in milk. Before the Masai drink milk after meat, they use an emetic. Washing milk vessels with water imparted a peculiar odor to them, according to the Masai, who used cow's urine instead. Sexual activity and milk also were antithetical among some tribes, for the Akamba and Akikuyu, for instance, abstained from coitus while the cattle were in the pasture. During the mourning period, the Dinka and the Banyoro abstained from milk.

In Europe and the United States there are many beliefs about the digestibility of milk when eaten with other foods, notably acid foods like tomatoes, pickles, lemons, or when eaten with shellfish. However, this does not necessarily apply to its derivatives like cheese, or when the antitheses are cooked together, as in clam chowder. Many practices are widely followed to protect the milk supply. In Estonia, the first milk after calving is not boiled without the precaution of placing a silver ring and a small saucer under the kettle, to keep the udder from harm. In Bulgaria if milk runs into the fire, the supply of milk will be jeopardized. Milk is left out in a saucer or other vessel, for the house spirits in many parts of western Europe. [NFJ]

☞ The Gallas of East Africa smear the trunks and boughs of sacred trees with blood, butter, and milk to prevent them from decaying. Pastoral tribes connect milk-production and milk itself. The Damaras believe that they must not wash out milk vessels, since this would bring an end to the cow's milk-producing powers.

In England (*Memoirs of Samuel Pepys*) it was customary for milkmaids to put garlands on their pails on May Day and to dance. During the latter part of the 19th century Irish peasants and housewives celebrated the Eve of May Day by cutting off and peeling rowan boughs and winding them around milk pails and churns. It was believed that the housewife who put rowan on her churn-dash would not have her butter stolen by fairies. According to the folklore of northeast Scotland, fairies are delighted by milk and frequently seek to satisfy this delight by approaching unchurched women (see CHURCHING OF WOMEN). In Germany peasants still fasten May-trees, one for each cow and horse, on the doors of stables. The May-tree or May-bush protects not only the cattle but also women against the evil-doings of witches on the Eve of May Day (Walpurgis Nacht).

Likewise, on St. George's Day (April 23), French and German peasants crown their cattle with wreaths of flowers, as do the South Slavonian peasants. But on Midsummer Day the Slavonians bathe the cows in dew. The Rumanians of Transylvania observe an elaborate festival on St. George's Day to mark the beginning of spring and of herding. A member of the folk tells the herdsmen that they can nullify the charms of witches stealing the milk from sheep by thrashing the shepherd's pouch with a switch or branch.

The *Iliad* tells of milk poured out for the dead; and "milk and honey" is used as a symbol of abundance and wealth, as it is in the Hebrew Old Testament. Pliny's *Natural History*, xxxvii, tells of a milk-stone which, if dissolved in honey-mead and drunk by a woman, will produce an abundant supply of milk. Even today milk-stones are utilized in Crete and Melos, in Albania and Germany.

The people of New Hampshire call milk "thatchy" if it comes from cows that fed upon thatch, a long grass growing in the salt marshes. In Portsmouth milk which has been slightly burned is said to be "caught."

The Russians say: "Don't cry over spilled milk. If you would live forever, wash milk from your liver. What is taken in with the milk, goes out with the soul." [JLR]

milkweed A plant (genus *Asclepius*) named for its abundant milky juices, or latex. The term is also applied to various similar plants exuding a milky juice. The orange-flowered milkweed (*A. tuberosa*) of the eastern United States is often called *butterfly weed* because butterflies (especially the monarch) are seen in hordes upon it. Its root is called pleurisy root, because an effective expectorant is made from it.

Throughout the southern United States the "milk" of the milkweed is used to relieve ground itch. Warts pricked until they bleed and then rubbed with the juice will disappear. Jamaica Negroes make a tea which is good for menstrual pain by boiling milkweed and marigold together. The Meskwaki Indians use a milkweed-root tea as worm medicine, a diuretic, and to relieve gas pains. The plant itself they cook in soup and also serve with pork. The Navahos use the dried leaves soaked in water as a tonic after childbirth and for upset stomach. The Chippewas use the down from the seed pods in pillows, and various parts of the plant as a magic charm. To make a charm to lure deer, they would chew some of the root along with root fibers of the plant boneset, and apply this liquefaction to the whistle used for calling deer. In Texas the children are taught to put the milky juice on cuts and scratches; for rattlesnake bite the roots are crushed, taken internally and at the same time applied to the bite.

Milky Way The luminous band of myriad distant stars and nebulæ which encircles the heavens has provoked astonishment and challenged the imagination of man everywhere that it is seen. Almost everywhere in ancient times it was thought of as a river, a river of heaven, a river of light. Anaxagoras in 550 B.C. called it the shining wheel. The ancient Akkadians and Syrians spoke of the River of the Snake, the Great River, or Great River of the Cord of the God, or Great River of the Abyss. Job said, "By his spirit he hath garnished the heavens; his hand hath formed the crooked serpent" (*Job* xxvi, 13.) To the ancient Arabs also it was *Al-Nahr*, the River. The Chinese called it Celestial River, *Tien Ho*, in which the little fish were afraid of the crescent

moon because they thought it was a hook. The Berbers called it the "beam of the sky."

The Milky Way as path or road has been equally common. In Egyptian mythology it is marked by the ears of corn dropped by Isis in her flight from Set. In Greek mythology it is the track of the sun or the track of the luckless Phaethon. In Teutonic mythology it was known as Odin's or Holde's Way. To the ancient Saxons it was Irmin's Road, and Ursa Major was his chariot. It is sometimes referred to as Wætlinga Stræt, perhaps the path of the sons of Wæcla from the eastern to the western sea, perhaps marking the course of the old Roman road from London to Wroxeter; modern writers say from London to Chester. Langland's *Piers Plowman* calls it Walsyngham Way, as the heavenly road to the Virgin Mary, Lady of Walsyngham. Later in European church legend it was called the Way of Saint James. In Siam it is the Way of the White Elephant; the Turks called it Pilgrim's Road; Basuto Negroes refer to it as the Way of the Gods.

Finno-Ugric mythology, and the mythology of many primitive peoples, interpret the Milky Way as the path whereby the souls of the dead travel from this world to the next. Among some tribes in Siberia it is a seam stitched across the sky (A778.4), an idea not far removed from 1st century A.D. astronomy which suggested that it was the mark showing where the two halves of heaven joined. Elsewhere among various peoples it has been interpreted as milk from the breast of a woman (A778.5), the sperma of the gods (A778.6), or smoke or ashes (A778.7). To some tribes of Siberia it represents a hunting party (A778.1). In German and Russian folklore it is the path followed by the Wild Hunt. Hungarians have called it the Way of War in memory of the fact that it guided their early people in the migration out of Asia. See ASHES; BREATHMAKER; COATLICUE; GWYDION.

The Milky Way is identified as the path or trail that ghosts of the dead take on their way to spirit land by some North American Indians; by other groups it is referred to as the White River, or as a river that forks near one end, or as a creek. Some conceive it as a dusty road, others as a backbone or the smoke from a fire. The Jicarilla Apache say that it is Sun and Moon's first path, when they traveled from north to south instead of from east to west as they do now. The Maidu of central California call the Milky Way "Morning Star's path." The Luiseño of southern California represent the Milky Way in the groundpaintings they use in connection with their boys' jimsonweed initiation, their death rite for initiates, and their girls' puberty ceremony. In this tribe the Milky Way has several esoteric designations, and is more than the mere ghosts' road of most California Indians. Symbolically it was associated with the spirit of the dead man, with the sacred cord which represented life, and probably also with a mystic being "White Grayish," Whaikut Piwkut, one of the preexistences of Night and Earth. See AFTERWORLD. Certain Algonquian groups call the Milky Way "birds' path" because it is by the Milky Way that birds follow their northward or southward course in their migrations. Less frequently the same groups also refer to it as "spirit path" over which the dead are thought to travel. [EWV]

The Milky Way is, for the Toba Indians of the Gran Chaco, a huge path covered with ashes. The Conibo see in it a jaguar following a deer. The Mosetene say that the Milky Way was formerly a huge worm bristling with the arrows shot at him. [AM]

mill (1) A folk dance figure: same as the STAR; a joining in the center of hands by men alone, women alone, or both. In the two-hand mill, both hands are extended to the center; in the one-hand mill only one. [GPK]

(2) Both mill and miller figure largely in European folktale, in stories of magic, in jests, in moralizing anecdotes, and in legend. There are magic mills which will not grind stolen wheat (D1318.15) or on Sunday (D1676); rejuvenation is sometimes attained by being ground in a magic mill (D1338.6). There is an absurdity story about the mill giving birth to the calf (J1533.1), and the moral tale about the ass who was jealous of the horse until later he learned that the horse had to work in the mill (L452.1). The Devil sometimes builds a mill (G303.9.1.3). The traditional mill is haunted by ghosts and frequented by bogles and boggarts (see BOGLE IN THE MILL.); and the Wild Hunt sometimes is seen at certain old mills (E501.12.10) in German legend. There are also self-grinding mills which produce gold, or whatever the owner wishes.

The legendary Danish king Frodi had two huge magic millstones which ground out gold and peace and prosperity for him until he became so greedy that the giant maids who turned the stones changed their spells and ground out disaster and warriors instead. Because of their spells came the Viking Mysinger, who slew Frodi. He took the millstones (the Grotti) on his ship and bade them turn out salt, which he could use for trade; but he too became greedy, and they turned out so much salt that the ship sank with the weight of it in the Norwegian Sea. The millstones made a deep hole and the water flowing into it is what causes the Maelstrom there. The salt dissolved in the water and made the sea salty.

Young German brides used to lay as many wheat kernels as they hoped for children under the mill; or they would slip out at midnight and turn the wheel of the grain mill backwards four times as a charm against pregnancy.

The dishonest miller is ubiquitous in merry tale (see X210 ff.). The Spanish story of the double-cheating miller (K486) is perhaps typical. The miller admitted to the farmer that he had measured in the grain with an oversized measure, but he promised to get a smaller one. He did so, and when the farmer came for the ground grain, the miller measured it back to him in the smaller one.

☞ The miller appears in characteristic guise and demeanor in the *Decameron* (Day ix, nov. 6); in Chaucer's "Miller's Tale" and "Reeve's Tale," both said to have probably derived from old fabliaux. "Worth a miller's thumb" is a saying that has become proverbial, deriving from the miller's ability to test the quality of meal by rubbing it between his fingers and thumb. [GPS]

Milu In Hawaiian mythology, the god of the underworld under whose supervision the soul led an aimless and shadowy existence.

mime Representation in action and gesture of actual and spiritual events. Originally the term referred to the *pantomimi* or "dumb-show" actors of ancient Greece and Rome and their descendants, the *mimi*, or wandering acrobats and minstrels of the Middle Ages. Panto-

mime is essentially an art, founded on natural everyday expression, but recreated into rhythmic and decorative products, commonly in a blend with music and song or chant.

The primal purpose of such imitative action was ritualistic and it underwent a long series of transitional stages to the purely spectacular court ballet and clownery. To this day some ritualism clings to entertainment and has been revived in modern theater arts.

The most natural expression would have been impulsive, that is, externalization of erotic, warlike, etc., emotions. Next in line comes the imitation of the outside world, of observed actions, frequently reaching over into a parallel spirit world. The penetration into the character and emotions of others is already a highly developed attitude. And the organization of consecutive gestures into the reproduction of events and into dance dramas also presupposes a highly developed artistic and constructive sense.

Several historical examples will briefly trace stages of development from realism to symbolism, from externalization to penetration—and back again to superficiality. 1) Previous to the incipience of its great theater, Greek ritual enactments included realistic imitations of animals. These correspond to the animal mime still found in Africa and among American Indians in various stages of realism and stylization. 2) The battle mime of the pyrrhic dance, similar to aboriginal war dances the world over, developed into spectacular mimetic portrayal, and lastly into disreputable shows. Analogous ritual battles of Europe appeared in history as partly stylized, yet varying from the fierce *caluşar* to the playful *morris*. Every stage of sword dance, down to the stick dance and to abstract longways opposition, remains today. 3) Bloody sacrificial killing of Dionysiac rites became sublimated in the *tragoidia*, and finally relegated to abstract choral relation and gesture. In other parts of the world, horror of death is emulated by mechanical means in the Bella Coola *kusiut* dances, and in the *kachina* fight at Acoma. At the other end of the scale, the Japanese *kabuki* drama invests even death with a decorative quality, as the *seppuku* (suicide) and *korosi* (murder) scenes, and *tatimawari* (sword play). In English and Basque sword dances, sacrifice is completely symbolic and choreographic (see SWORD DANCES). 4) In Greek *xeironomia* (gesture language), the representation of emotions and of character were termed, respectively, *phorai* and *schemata*. There is doubtless a connection between the *phorai* and the elaborate Hindu gesture code, the *mudras*, which can portray the most delicate and most heroic moods in ever new combinations. The *schemata* find their counterpart in the stock characterizations of the Chinese theater and the Japanese *Nō* dramas which differentiate the sexes as well as human types.

Many gesture codes visualize external things and events, and emotions, thus the *mudras* and related *hula* gesture language. The American Indian sign language, which may or may not be related to the *mudras*, has a complete vocabulary, in this case utilitarian rather than choreographic. Drama combines the portrayal of the external and mental word in an exciting sequence of events. Yet different parts of the world have a preference for certain types of pantomime, as well as a special style.

1) *Impersonations* of beasts, real or fantastic, and of

demons are particularly apt in animal and demon dances of Africa, Ceylon, the Great Plains, British Columbia, and the Alaskan Eskimo. Such impersonations have been abstracted to dance steps in European folk dances, in the *Morris* "caper," "danse de la chèvre" (goat) and "pas de loup" (wolf) of Limousin.

2) *Imitation* of actions, with or without props. Primitive rites are frequently occupational, as the Fijian *vakamalolo* or fishing dance and the Philippine *balitao* or rice-planting and harvest dance. Folk dances and games frequently re-enact activities, especially in northern Europe (Finnish *Harvest dance*, Swedish *Reap the Flax, Washing the Clothes*) and in France and French Canada (*Rondes, chants mimés*, as *Les Saisons* of La Dauphinée, *C'est la Poulette Grise* of Canada, *Le Roi de France*, children's game). Mexican Indians prefer to use real props, as the basket and meal in *las sembradoras*. Japanese *kabuki* and *odori* dancers manipulate their props symbolically, the fan representing an infinity of things. The Pueblo Indians and eastern tribes, notably the Cherokee and Iroquois, prefer to mime without actual objects: the Laguna Saint's Day dancers express rain or the growth of corn purely by gesture, by lowering or raising the hands. In the Iroquois-Tutelo *Four Nights Dance* the women winnow corn in abstract movement. Imitation may become completely choreographic, as in the Irish *Waves of Tory* and Lithuanian *malunas* or mill.

3) *Human character* is most aptly portrayed in dramas of the Far East and in the burlesque of clowns, as the *koshare* and the Javanese *topeng* dancers. Not only are posture and hand motions shrewdly reproduced, but facial expression too. In this, face paint or mask may aid the actor.

4) The portrayal of *emotions* also involves facial expression with or without mask, and hand gestures, as well as the attitude of the entire body. Masks of Greece and the Far East immobilize the face into a stereotyped emotion, whereas Japanese and Chinese unmasked dancers play subtly on their features. American Indians hold an impassive expression; Spaniards display ever-changing sentiments. The Hindu confines the ideas to his hands, the American Indian mimics with his entire body. The Far East codifies its gestures, even in the trance state of the Balinese *kris;* Cherokee and Fox Indian *Snake* dancers, and American *play-party* enthusiasts improvise ever new combinations.

Courtship mime, this most fundamental of emotions, has a particularly significant range of forms and styles. In India it is delicately abstracted into hand gestures. In Scandinavia it is stereotyped into patterns of rugged pursuit and coy flirtation, and into humorous facial mimicry. In Spain the fire breaks through the conventions of elusive or alluring postures. In the West Indies all pre-established patterns are forgotten in uninhibited erotic display.

In the same culture there are periods of realism, followed by fossilization, again followed by a new spurt. The crude realism of the medieval folk drama was ritualized into the moralities and mysteries. The conventions of ballet pantomime, developed since the 18th century, have been discarded by modern dance art in its search for new forms, abstracted out of reality.

Everywhere pantomime follows the same general trend from ritualistic to spectacular function, from observed mimicry to expressive abstraction to affected externalization. Sometimes one of the phases may be retained for a long period, or the cycle may start all over again. See MASKS; RITUAL DRAMA; SIGN LANGUAGE. [GPK]

Mimir (1) In Teutonic mythology, gigantic god of the primeval ocean or the open sea, as opposed to Niörd, god of the coastal waters. His home is Mimir's well (the ocean) beside one of the roots of Yggdrasil. Drinking from this well gave him great and mysterious wisdom; he knew all things, past and future; and Odin forfeited one of his eyes for a draft of the water that he might know the future. As the well was beside the rainbow bridge, Bifrost, Heimdall sometimes left the Gialler-horn there for safety. As a giant, Mimir is the son of Ægir (Hler), one of the three gods of the elements. Other sources call him the son of Bolthorn, brother of Odin's mother, Bestla. According to the *Yngling-saga,* the æsir sent Hœnir and Mimir to Vanaheim in exchange for Niörd and Frey. Thus originally he belonged to the æsir. Hœnir was an essentially stupid fellow and the vanir were angered. They beheaded Mimir and sent his head to Asgard where Odin preserved it with herbs and consulted it as an oracle. The *Svipdagsmäl* refers to the world tree (Yggdrasil), as Mimameid, or tree of Mimir. Hodmimir, in whose forest Lif and Lifthrasir escape the fire at Ragnarök, is also identified with Mimir. Some claim that he presides over Odainsakr (the acre of the not-dead) where there is no sickness, age, or death. Alexander H. Krappe in *Mythologie Universelle* (Paris, 1930) points to the story of Odin's preservation and consultation of Mimir's head as based on early Teutonic practice of divination from skulls.

(2) In *Thidriks-saga,* Mimir is a dwarf master-smith who teaches Sigfrit and Velint. Variants of this name are found as smiths in a number of Teutonic myths and tales; he turns up as *Mime,* for instance in the *Ring of the Nibelungs,* as the smith who aids Siegfried. It was probably Mimir who forged the sword, Miming, later attributed to Wieland.

Mink Animal-character in various American Indian tales, but especially prominent as the culture hero-transformer-trickster of the Indian tribes in the middle part of the North Pacific Coast region. In the northern part of this area it is Raven, voracious and greedy, who plays this role; in the central part the erotic Mink, and in the southern third Bluejay, always anxious to outdo his rivals, or Fox, or Moon. Clever and crafty Mink piled up the mountains; wherever he camped creeks and springs sprang up; he killed off many monsters; he stole the sun; he changed the inhabitants of the earth into beasts, birds, fishes, rocks, and trees for the good of the human race that was coming. The amorousness which was Mink's special characteristic, distinguishing him from the other trickster-transformers of the North Pacific Coast, has led to the development of a long series of tales concerning his marriages; all these, as shown by Boas, are of the same general type. As a trickster, Mink was often outwitted, but as a transformer he had great powers. Whether or not he created the human race, he prepared the earth for humans, which is the point that is emphasized in these regions, more than his capacities as a creator. See EARTH DIVER. [EWV]

Minona Literally, our mother Na: a semi-deity of Dahomean Negro religion. She is an earth-dwelling, specifically forest-dwelling, spirit, appearing in the myths variously as the mother of Mawu, mother or sister of Legba, or mother of Fa and the Fa group. She is the protectress of women; every woman has a shrine for Minona in her house, where she is given offerings of all first-fruits before members of the family may partake. This guarantees continued fertility of the fields. She is also the giver of magic to the sorcerers, and perhaps activator of many gbos.

Minotaur In Greek mythology, the monster with a bull's head and a human body for which Dædalus built the Labyrinth: the name means Minos bull, the bull of the Minos dynasty of Crete. Minos offered to sacrifice the white bull sent from the sea by Poseidon, but instead sacrificed another. Poseidon therefore incited lust in Pasiphae, Minos' queen, for the white bull. The craftsman Dædalus made a hollow wooden form, covered it with a cow's hide, and placed Pasiphae within it. In this manner the queen was able to indulge her passion; the resulting offspring was Asterius, the Minotaur. Some years later, Androgeus, a son of Minos, having won at the Panathenaic games, was waylaid and slain by a group of jealous Athenians. Minos marched on Athens and forced from them a tribute of seven youths and seven maidens every ninth year, to be shut up in the Labyrinth to be eaten by the Minotaur. With the third such group went Theseus, son of Ægeus, king of Athens. He slew the Minotaur with his fists and thus ended the practice of sending the youthful sacrifice to Crete.

Many scholars have recognized in the Minotaur a reflection of the bull and sun cult of Crete. Parallels throughout the Mediterranean, e.g. the Baal-Moloch of the Phœnicians who devoured victims in his flames, have been indicated. The myth of the Minotaur's birth, according to A. B. Cook and J. G. Frazer, may have originated in a sacred union, the hieros gamos, between the queen and the bull god. Similarly, the victory of Theseus is said to represent the abolition of human sacrifice to the sun by the Greeks. That a bull cult was prominent in Crete is well known through the many representations of sports like bull-leaping as religious rites. Similar to the Minotaur, and perhaps identical with him, is the mythical Talus, the red-hot man of brass, met with in the Argonaut story, probably an animal-headed anthropomorphic representation of the sun in whose heated body victims, perhaps strangers to the island of Crete, were enclosed.

mint Any of several aromatic herbs (genus *Mentha*) of the family *Labiatæ*, of which spearmint or garden mint (*M. spicata*) and peppermint (*M. piperita*) are the most popular. The mints have long been valued for their medicinal and culinary uses, and many varieties are raised commercially. The sprig of mint in iced drinks, mint sauce, mint jelly with meats, mint tea for indigestion are commonplaces of daily life.

In classical mythology Pluto was in love with a nymph named Mintha, but his jealous wife turned her into the mint plant whose beauty still attracts through its fragrance. Mint was one of the herbs known and valued by the ancient Hebrews; "tithes of mint" are mentioned in the New Testament. It has been a popular herb from earliest times in the British Isles, where it was intro-

duced by the Romans, and is mentioned as one of the "sweet herbs" used for strewing floors in Elizabethan times. John Josselyn's herb book (17th century) lists mint as one of the "precious herbs" brought from England by early settlers in Massachusetts. Mint was used medicinally in baths to calm and strengthen the nerves and muscles. It was also widely used for upset stomach, earache, watering eyes, and the bites of animals and insects. Powdered leaves of mint in wine (along with rue, vervain, plantain, wormwood, and other herbs) was recommended for hydrophobia by the 16th century physician, Varismann. Iron destroys the effects of mint, however, and must be avoided. In northern Europe, mint was considered useful in preventing milk from souring. In Ireland spearmint (*mismín*) is sprinkled in beds and houses to banish fleas. In Bolivia the people believe that anyone who finds mint in bloom on St. John's Day will have happiness forever.

Jamaica Negroes brew peppermint tea for colic, and the Meskwaki Indians drink mint tea as a tonic, and for ague. The Meskwaki also use the leaves of mountain mint (genus *Pycnanthemum*) on mink traps to mask the scent of earlier victims, or, some say, as a lure. Winnebago Indian hunters also use it to mask the odors of their traps. The Meskwaki also recommend mountain mint as "snake bait": i.e. chew some of the top leaves, spit them onto the end of a stick, hold the stick in front of a snake's mouth; the snake becomes unaware of his danger and is easily caught. This is just as effective as sprinkling salt on a bird's tail. The Meskwaki also make a snuff of the dried leaves of mountain mint mixed with horsemint (*Monarda punctata*) which they use for headaches. This is also often applied to the nostrils of one about to die to revive him. The Mohegan-Pequot Indians used both peppermint and spearmint tea as a vermifuge for babies. White settlers used these mints for dyspepsia. See PENNYROYAL.

minuet (French *menuet*, Italian *menuetto*) A French court dance flourishing in the 18th century, originating as *branle de Poitou* and languishing into the 19th century till absorbed by the quadrille and waltz. It owes the epithet *menu*, small or neat, to the rococo daintiness and precision of its steps. The lively duple time of the branle de Poitou was subdued to an elegant and sedate triple time. A two-part musical form, with the occasional addition of a trio, accompanied two specified minuet steps. The *menuet en avant* consisted of forward balancing, bowing, and crossing, the partners touching fingers with the utmost delicacy; the *menuet de coté* placed the partners back to back or face to face with sideward grapevines and toe-pointing. Though a latecomer to the musical suite, a minuet features in most of Mozart's symphonies.

This utmost stylization of courtship pantomime was expressive of the decadent, perfumed court just before its spectacular deposition. In its heyday it was considered the "queen of dances," which traced "les chiffres d'amour," the figures of love, to the strains of violins, or rather "les âmes des pieds," the souls of the feet. [GPK]

min-yo The Japanese term for folk songs, literally translated from *Volkslied* and applied especially to the work and occupational songs of farmers, communal labor groups, teamsters, fishermen, lumbermen, tea and silk workers, etc., and to the banquet and festival songs of villagers. The verse forms are based on syllable patterns, rather than on meter or rime, the characteristic measure, *dodoitsu*, being a twenty-six-syllable arrangement in groups of 7,7,7,5, with refrains of nonsense syllables, *dokkoise*, sung in chorus and in work songs serving as the stressed phrase for the concerted action. Another measure, the *hayashi*, is less regular in form and is used in more improvisational and humorous songs. The texts make use of many words of double meaning, sometimes quite seriously extending the references of the subject, often merely punning and carrying a secondary sexual significance. The words of occupational and work songs do not necessarily refer to the task at all, but may be of love, of food and drink, of nostalgia, of old stories or new jokes. The singing is often helped along by the melancholy notes of the bamboo flute, *shakuhachi*, or a smaller flute, *fue*, by the rhythm of the small hand drum, *tsuzumi*, or the larger *taiko*, by the samisen, by hand-clapping, beating sticks, barrels, or bells, or simply by the cries that time the work stroke.

Among the types of Japanese work song are:

The *dotsuki-* or *jitsuki-uta*, which are earth-pounding songs, sung by communal groups at work on foundations, roads, pile-driving, etc. The pounding device is a heavy log hung in a framework, hauled up by ropes, and dropped from a height. The songs set the rhythm for the rope-pulling and are sometimes, like sea chanties, sung by a leader with a chorused response from the crew at the moment of the effort. Often they are long tales strung out to relieve the tedium of the job. Songs are begun only after ground-breaking ceremonies which include shooting an arrow into the sky and pouring sake on the ground.

Stone-hauling songs, *ishi-hiki-uta*.

Horse-driving songs. *Umakata-bushi*, or songs of the horse leaders, may differ according to the occasion. For example, one such is sung only at weddings when the bride's special horse is led to her house. The *oiwake-bushi*, literally "fork-of-the-road songs," are mournful melodies of long drawn-out notes with words lamenting the length of the road and wishing for the end of the journey, sung especially at crossroads by pack-horse drivers. The origin of the type may be either a chant to placate the gods of the crossroads or an 8th century form of music, *saibara-gaku*, possibly related to the delivery of tribute to an overlord.

Songs of lumbermen, including *kobiki-uta*, for hauling logs, and *kiyari-uta*, sung by the sawyers, both with exclamatory refrains of the "heave-ho" type.

Funa-uta, the songs of fishermen and boatmen, sung while rowing, dragging nets, hauling on ropes, etc. They may tell of faraway homes and lovers, of the luck of the catch, or of almost any other subject, but regardless of subject, the songs of this type are sung only on boats. Special songs of whalers are called *kujira-uta*, and songs celebrating a big catch are *tairyo-bushi*.

Songs of agricultural workers of the rice paddies, tea plantations, and fields. The songs of rice culture, *ta-ue-uta*, are work songs, but are also sung nowadays simply for entertainment and in accompaniment of the dances of the rice ceremony. These go back to early fertility rites and are still performed to bring good crops. The various steps of the dancing go with certain songs to the music of drums and samisen. The original songs were called *ta-uta*, and the old form of the dancing, *dembu* or *ta-mai*, imitated the motions of planting the rice. Other special songs are devoted to the rice harvest and to the hulling of the grains. Weeding, which is generally done by women, also has its songs, *kusatori-uta*, with spoken phrases to emphasize the rhythm of the pull. The tea workers' songs, like work songs of many other groups in other lands, often express a low opinion of the boss. The *chatsumi-uta* are sung for picking the tea; sorting and roasting are accompanied by other groups of songs.

Hata-ori-uta are loom songs of the silk industry. There are individual song types for each stage of the process, from the *kuwa-tsumi-uta* of the mulberry leaf pickers to the songs of the cloth finishers.

Apart from work songs, min-yo include many village songs, *ko-uta*, sung for special occasions and festivities and often quite localized. *Tate-daru-ondo* and *yoko-daru-ondo* are country dance songs accompanied by beating on a barrel with sticks and by the small flute or a bell. Banquet songs sung at drinking gatherings, wedding celebrations, farewell dinners, etc., often go to a kind of tune known as *rokuchosi*, a six-tone song form possibly so called from the tuning of the samisen which accompanies it.

The most common surviving folk songs of Japan are the *bon-odori-uta*, or songs for the Bon or O-bon festival (Feast of Lanterns), which takes place during the seventh month and was originally a feast of offering to the spirits of the dead who returned to their earthly homes at that time. Both religious and secular observances mark the season. In certain sections miniature straw boats are set adrift with lighted candles to direct the journey of the spirits. Evenings are given over to dancing and singing to the samisen from a repertory of 400 or more songs. The dancing part of the festival probably is older than the Buddhist religious ceremonies and may go back to certain ancient summer festivities of China, during which sexual freedom and betrothal of young couples were in order. More than half of the songs are love songs, with sexual connotation by implication if not in actual expression, and the others deal with seasonal congratulations and many other subjects.

There is a special series of songs sung at New Year's in connection with the lion dances (*shishi-mai*, *shishi-odori*) and the pantomime of door-to-door performers. Sometimes the lion of the dance is a head and drapery worn by two dancers; sometimes each dancer appears with a lion mask. The general tenor of the songs is good-luck wishes for the new year, though the words may describe the mating of lions. Monkeys, boars, and deer are also featured in certain festival songs and dances not necessarily performed at New Year's but associated with shrine worship.

Among the religious songs of Japan are the Shintoist shrine songs, *kami-uta*, the Buddhist chant, *nembutsu* (Hail, Buddha), and the Buddhist hymns, *wa-san*, from which a highly irreverent and satirical body of popular song has grown.

Children's songs, *do-yo*, and lullabies, *komori-uta*, are classed apart from the min-yo. They are in general simpler both in verse structure and in melody than the songs of the adults, and the puns and *double entendres* are lacking. Subjects of children's songs include the little snail rime common to children almost everywhere in the world, the firefly, the moon, and long tales and enumerations. They are sung or chanted in singsong to ball-bouncing, hand-clapping, rope-skipping, bean-bag play, etc. See CHILDREN'S SONGS; LULLABY.

A modern class of songs called *shin-min-yo*, or new folk songs, is actually not folk in origin at all, being the product of popular song-writers of the cities. [TCB]

miraculous pipe A pipe which, when smoked by the hero, gives forth clouds of turkeys and pigeons instead of smoke; when used by an impostor who enchants the hero the pipe produces dung, beetles, and flies. This is a recurrent element in Great Lakes North American Indian tales. [EWV]

mi'raj Literally, an ascent: Mohammed's night journey to paradise, believed by many to have been merely a vision. It is mentioned briefly in the Koran and described in detail in the Sunni *Mishkātu'l-Masabih*. Gabriel came to Mohammed in his sleep, cut out and cleansed his heart, and filled him anew with "faith and science." A white animal was brought to him, named Buraq, whom he mounted. They ascended to heaven and Gabriel called out to open the door. "Who is it?" said the voice of heaven. "I am Gabriel." "Who is with you?" "Mohammed." "Has he been called?" "Yes." "Welcome Mohammed," said the voice. They entered the first heaven and saw Adam. In the second heaven they saw Jesus and John who welcomed Mohammed as brother and prophet. In the third heaven they saw Joseph, in the fourth, Enoch, in the fifth, Aaron, in the sixth, Moses, who wept because more people of an after-prophet (Mohammed) than his were destined to enter paradise. In the seventh heaven they saw and spoke with Abraham. After that Mohammed was shown the sacred tree named Sidratu'l-Muntaha and the four mighty rivers, of which two flowed through paradise and two on earth (the Nile and Euphrates). Wine, milk, and honey were then offered him. Mohammed chose milk and Gabriel said, "Milk is religion." Then the divine orders were given him to take back to the people: 50 prayers a day. As he passed by Moses, Moses said, "Your people will not be able to perform it." So Mohammed went back and God struck ten off the list. Again Moses said, "Your people will not be able to perform it." Again Mohammed went back and God struck ten more off the list. This happened until only five prayers a day were ordered. Moses still thought it was too much, but Mohammed was ashamed to go back another time, so five it remained. And as they passed out of heaven they heard a voice declaring, "I have established my commandments and I have made them easy."

mirror of al-Asnam In "The Tale of Zayn al-Asnam," *Arabian Nights* (Burton *Supplemental Nights* III), a mirror given by the King of the Jann to the Prince: a chastity index which would show the Prince whether the wife he was to obtain for the King of the Jann were chaste or unchaste. If the maiden were so pure that no man had so much as lusted for her, the mirror would show a clear image; if she were sullied in any way, the image would be dark.

misplaced genitalia An incident of origin myths, especially of the Pacific and western North American areas: men and women are created with their genitals elsewhere than in their present positions (A1313.3), or they mistake the use and function of the genitals. The culture hero—usually semi-divine—rearranges their physical position or explains their proper use. For example, in the Northwest Pacific Coast region of North America, and throughout Polynesia, Melanesia, and Micronesia, myths tell of people who believe it necessary to cut open the mother in order for a child to be born, until the culture hero (Coyote, Tura, etc.) teaches them otherwise. The tale may have existed in other regions of the world, where it has now disappeared; it may underlie such Greek myths as the story of the birth of Athena and the myth of the birth of Dionysus from the thigh of Zeus after Semele was consumed by fire. See MAN; VAGINA DENTATA.

Miss Nancy The Spider: in South Carolina Sea Island folktale, corruption of ANANSI.

mistletoe The common mistletoe is a European evergreen hemiparasitic plant (*Viscum album*, family Loranthaceæ) bearing white glutinous berries, and found growing on various deciduous trees: one of the most magical plants of European folklore. It was regarded as mysterious and sacred from earliest times from the Mediterranean to the Baltic, a bestower of life and fertility, a protection against poisons, and potent for numerous medical and magical uses, an allheal and aphrodisiac. The oak mistletoe especially could extinguish fire, in both Italian and Scandinavian belief: a belief which seems to be rooted in another, that mistletoe comes to the tree in a flash of lightning.

The famous Golden Bough which Æneas plucked from the oak at the gate of the underworld, and which served as token for his safe conduct in that place, is the mistletoe. (The berries become deeper and deeper gold-tinged as the plant withers.) For discussion of identification of Vergil's golden bough, see Frazer, *Balder The Beautiful*, ii, 315–320.

The mistletoe of the sacred oak was especially sacred to the ancient Celtic druids. The druid rite of plucking the mistletoe, as described by both Cæsar and Pliny and of which little more is known, adds its aura of mystery to the lore of sacredness and magic surrounding this plant. On the sixth night of the moon white-robed druids cut the oak mistletoe with a golden sickle; it was not allowed to touch the ground but was caught in a white cloth. Two white bulls were sacrificed at the time with prayers to the god to prosper the gift (i.e. the mistletoe) and the recipients thereof. Mistletoe is still ceremonially plucked on Midsummer Eve in Europe, especially in the Celtic and Scandinavian countries; for this reason MacCulloch believes that it must have been especially associated with the Midsummer festival in druid times.

Frazer associates the druid ritual with the plucking of the golden bough in the sacred grove by the successor (and slayer) of the priest of Nemi. Robert Graves suggests (*White Goddess*, New York, 1948, p. 48) that the ritual cutting of the mistletoe from the oak symbolized the emasculation of the old king by his successor, mistletoe being a widespread sexual symbol, and also the "life" of the oak. See CRONUS. The mistletoe as the soul of the oak, had to be cut before the sacred tree could be felled or before the human proxy of the sacred tree could be slain. Frazer, after A. B. Cook, posits also the association of the mistletoe with the sun by the ancient Greeks because of the cult of Apollo Ixius at Ixiæ in Rhodes, named for the mistletoe. In fact the custom of gathering mistletoe at both the solstices (Midsummer and Christmas) links the plant definitely with the various old European sun cults. For his association of the druid rite with the death of Balder, mistletoe as life token and death token of Balder, see *Balder The Beautiful*, ii, 279, 283.

Decorating the house with mistletoe at Christmas is often assumed to be a survival of the old druid oak cult. Frazer links the custom of kissing under the mistletoe with the license of the Greek Saturnalia. Others associate the practice with certain primitive marriage rites. R. Reynolds in *Cleanliness and Godliness*, New York, 1946, p. 249, suggests that both the holiness and the extraordinary fertilizing powers of the mistletoe are associated with the fact that the plant is propagated from the dung of birds dropped on the branches of trees and with the special holiness and life-giving powers of dung. The method of its propagation was long recognized. Pliny remarked upon it; Turner's *Herbal* (1532) says that "the thrush shiteth out the miscel berries." The word mistletoe itself may derive in the last analysis from this very fact. According to Skeat, Old English *mistel* (mistletoe) "is clearly a diminutive of *mist* which in German means dung" and is cognate with Gothic *maihstus*, dung.

In the realm of folk medicine mistletoe is still called *allheal*; it is one of the herbs of St. John, and is believed to cure sterility, control epilepsy, and act against poisons. A potion from mistletoe berries is sometimes given to man, woman, and beast to make them fruitful. The berries were formerly dried and powdered and prescribed for 40 days for apoplexy, palsy, and epilepsy, and a sprig was worn about the neck to enhance the internal effects of the dose. Culpeper (*Complete Herbal*, 1653) also places mistletoe under the dominion of the sun, adding that the oak mistletoe "partakes of the nature of Jupiter because the oak is one of his trees." He recommends the birdlime from the berries to "mollify hard knots and tumours," and states that mixed with wax it helps old ulcers and open sores. Lloyd's *Treasury of Health* (c. 1550) stated that "Mysceltowe layd to the head draweth out the corrupt humors." Late into the 19th century mistletoe had a reputation for alleviating the ills of old age. It has been an old folk remedy for epilepsy and hysteria from the time of Pliny to the present day: modern research discloses that the active principle of mistletoe (*guipsine*) not only relieves hypertension but is valuable in treating nervous disorders.

In some parts of Europe the people are unwilling to cut the holy plant, believing instead it should be knocked or shot down and caught as it falls. In Switzerland mistletoe gathered this way, especially under the sign of Sagittarius, is good for the diseases of children. Southern U.S. Negroes say that a decoction of mistletoe will dry up mothers' milk. Robert Greene (1590) said "None comes near the fume of the misselden but he waxeth blind." Shakespeare also mentioned the "baleful mistletoe"—*Titus Andronicus* II, iii.

All over Europe mistletoe is seen over house and stable doors or hung in rooms to prevent the entrance of witches; in the Louisiana bayous it is often hung over doors to counteract the powers of conjurers. Tiny mistletoe figurines are sometimes seen in this region over fireplaces or hung on bedsteads for the same reason.

In Sweden the divining rod cut from the mistletoe on Midsummer Eve is especially potent. The golden color of the withered plant may account for the belief that such rods will point to hidden gold. Mistletoe growing on hazel is potent for discovering treasure in the Tyrol; mistletoe found on the thorn was ascribed such virtue in Prussia. In Cambodia a decoction of mistletoe is believed to bestow invulnerability. In Christian legend mistletoe is thought of as cruciform and called Holy Cross wood. Mistletoe is also one of the plants which open locks.

Farmers in Worcestershire and Wales sometimes give the Christmas bunch of mistletoe to the first cow that calves in the New Year. This brings luck and health to the whole herd. In parts of England the Christmas mistletoe is burned on Twelfth Night lest all the boys and girls who have kissed under it never marry. In Staffordshire the Christmas bunch was kept all year and burned under the next Christmas pudding. See ÆNEAS; EPILEPSY.

Mithra or **Mithras** In Persian mythology and belief, a god of light, truth, and justice: the chief aid of Ahura Mazda in his fight with Angra Mainyu. Mithra's henchmen are Rashnu and Sraosha. Mithra was born of a rock, coming forth armed with a knife and a torch. He measured his strength with the sun and finally made a truce with the latter. Then he attacked the primeval ox and slew it. From its blood and limbs came all the animals and the useful herbs; its soul went to heaven as the guardian of animals.

The feast of Mithra, Mihrajān, falls about September 7th and lasts for six days. During this festival the Persian king can become intoxicated and dance the national dance. The violet is consecrated to Mithra.

In Vedic mythology, Mitra is a sun god and one of the Ādityas: literally, friend. He is identified with the Persian Mithra. Mitra belongs to the early triad of Agni (fire), Vāyu (wind), and Mitra. He is one of the five gods representing various aspects of solar activity and is probably a personification of the beneficent characteristics of the sun. Mitra, ruler of the day, is often associated with Varuṇa as ruler of the night. [SPH]

☜ Mithra is a widely worshipped mythological nature god-hero, revered in the ancient Indian Vedic pantheon, where, as Mitra, the light of day, he was associated with Varuṇa, the thousand eyes of night. Inscriptions found by Winckler at Boghaz-keui in 1907 indicate that as early as the 14th century B.C. Mitra was worshipped among the Mitanni of northern Mesopotamia. In Iran, Mithra was powerful before the time of Zarathustra (Zoroaster), who rather subordinated him as representing the worship of the demons the prophet was trying to eliminate, but after Zarathustra, Mithra was restored to Mazdaism's pantheon and reigned as one of the most powerful Persian deities along with Mazda and Anāhita.

The remarkable influence of Mithra on other religions and mythologies was potent over a wide area and for many centuries, although little recognized until recent years. He seems to have been a very adaptable divinity, for he appears successively as god of daylight in India, as "lord of wide pastures" in later Zoroastrianism, then as a Persian rock-born god of the middle zone between heaven and hell, later as a cave-dwelling bull-slaying hero-god of the Roman legions; finally he returns to the sun-god role as Helios-Mithra in the complex neo-Platonism of the 4th century A.D. Roman emperor Julian, called by Christians "The Apostate" because they resented his Mithraism. These apparent changes in the character of Mithra are, however, really only changes of emphasis on one or the other of his many attributes and exploits, for he had almost as many attributive titles as Zeus-Jupiter and nearly as many "labors" as Heracles-Hercules. But the illuminative aspect prevails throughout and even in the cave he was worshipped as the god of light.

The importance of Mithraism, the worship of Mithra, lies in the fact that it was a serious, perhaps the most dangerous, rival of Christianity from the time of Trajan (early 2nd century A.D.) till the 4th century, when the official adoption of Christianity by Constantine and his successors deprived Mithraism of its state income and encouraged its ruthless extermination by zealous Christian bishops. The incredibly cruel murder of the neo-Platonist Hypatia belongs in this dark period.

The competition between Christianity and Mithraism had been very keen for two centuries, however, and for several reasons. First, from the introduction of the cult of Mithras, which Plutarch says was originally brought to Rome by captive Cilician pirates in 67 B.C., the new faith, with its mystic symbolism of hope and its teaching of austerity and endurance, gradually began to win slaves, workingmen, and the common people generally, the classes among whom Christianity sought converts.

Second, by the time of Trajan, Mithraism had become familiar to the great mass of soldiers, who soon adopted it as their own and became its missionaries to the whole Roman world. Kipling's *Song to Mithras*, a Hymn of the XXX Legion, beginning:

> Mithras, God of the Morning,
>   our trumpets waken the Wall!
> "Rome is above the Nations,
>   but Thou art over all!"

catches the victorious spirit of the spreading faith.

Third, Mithraism had much in common with Christian beliefs, symbols, and practices, such as baptism for the remission of sins, a symbolic meal of communion including consecrated wine, the sign on the brow, redemption, salvation, sacramentary grace, rebirth in the spirit, confirmation, and the promise of eternal life. The celebration of the birth of Mithra was on the 25th of December, and that of his rebirth at the spring equinox. Indeed, the shocked Christian apologists were driven to denounce the Mithraic beliefs and customs as diabolical and blasphemous caricatures of Christianity.

The few borrowings, however, were mutual, and who borrowed which is now difficult to determine. Most of the parallels were probably independently originated. From the folklore standpoint it is of interest that both religions featured seasonal and astronomical celebrations and followed the general pattern of the solar myth.

Mithraism has left many archeological remains, partly because the *Mithræa*, chapels for Mithraic rituals, were underground caves or excavations, purposely well concealed, for they, as well as the Christians in the earlier catacombs, had to go "underground."

Bas-reliefs abound, including the innumerable famous *taurobolia,* the exact meaning of which is now disputed, as literary remains are few, due either to the secret oral transmission of the mysteries of the cult or to Christian zeal in destroying the pagan records, or both.

The taurobolium is featured in relief in all Mithraic sanctuaries. It depicts Mithra as a young man slaying a bull. In Oriental (Persian) costume of tunic, trousers, and pileus (liberty cap), he partly bestrides the semiprone beast on whose back he rests his left knee. His left hand holds the animal's head back by a grip on the nostrils (or sometimes the horns), while his right thrusts a dagger in its throat. A dog and a serpent lap up the spurting blood, and a scorpion grips the testicles. Two torchbearers light up the slaughter cavern; a crow is usually depicted along with trees or plants, and the tail of the bull sprouts an ear of corn. The whole drama, like other Mithraic symbolic pictures, seems quite bizarre to the uninitiated.

These symbols have several possible interpretations but the usual one is from Zoroastrian (*Bundahishn,* xiv, 1) mythology, in which the divine bull by its great generative power and sacrificial death promoted the fertility of vegetable and animal life and assured its annual renewal on the earth.   CHARLES FRANCIS POTTER

mitiyuki Literally, travel, on the way of travel: a feature of the Japanese *kabuki* drama, particularly of the type descended from the puppet play. It serves as a scene of relief in multiple-act plays, an idyllic scene between lovers, or between a mother and daughter. All of the action is rhythmical and stylized, more in the nature of dance than dramatic acting. [GPK]

mitote From Nahuatl *mitotia* (*mo,* reflexive, and *itotia,* to dance): a secular dance of the ancient and modern Aztecs, *mitotiliztli* being a secular fiesta. The term now covers the round dances of the Aztecs, Tepehuanes, Cora, and Huicholes of the Sierra Madre Occidental. They are the vestiges of ancient rituals, suffered to remain in an attenuated state, deprived of their meaning by the early missionaries. The same dance celebrates January midwinter, February sowing, summer rain, and October harvest rites. Vestiges of ceremonialism remain in the altar east of the dance ground, and in the accompanying prayers. The shaman lives on in the person of the *cantador,* singer, next to the fire in the center of the circle.

The dancing continues all night on a flat hilltop near the village, in a counterclockwise direction. Carl Lumholtz speaks of a double column, men in the lead, women following, with a forward stamping two step, the women rising on their toes. J. A. Mason describes the step as a series of broken steps and skips in a single circle. The music is furnished by song and a musical bow on a gourd resonator, named *mitote* after the dance. Lumholtz describes a symbolic deer hunt at sunrise, consisting of five circuits in either direction and a deer hunt and capture. At the appearance of the morning star there is a feast on the special foods, which had been placed on the altar together with two ceremonial sticks decorated with hawk and eagle feathers.

There are remarkable analogies between this dance and the rounds of the southeastern and Iroquoian tribes of the United States, particularly the counterclockwise direction, single or double file, with men in the lead. Feather paraphernalia and a consecrated feast are common to many Indian tribes. [GPK]

Mixcoatl The Cloud Serpent: the Aztec god of the chase, probably of Otomi (Tlaxcaltec) origin, and identified in several aspects with Camaxtli, the Tlascalan war god, and with Tezcatlipoca as a wind god. Mixcoatl has deer or rabbit characteristics. He was identified with the morning star, since he was a culture hero who, in *ome acatl* (two reed), the year after the world was created, made fire from sticks just before the creation of man. He was one of the four creators of the world as Camaxtli, along with the three other sons of Tonacatecutli and Tonacacihuatl. His feast was the Quecholli, a ceremonial hunt being part of the observance. At this festival, on the 280th day, i.e. the 14th day counting by twenties, from February, weapons were made. See ACATLAXQUI; ARROW; COATLICUE.

mmoatia "Little people" of the forest in the belief of the Ashanti and other Gold Coast peoples. Equivalents are the *azizā* of Dahomey and the *ijimere* of Nigeria, with parallels widely found elsewhere in Africa. Retentions in the New World among Negroes include the *abuku* of Dutch Guiana, and the *saci* of Brazil. They exist in unnamed form in the folklore of rural Negroes of the United States as various small folk encountered in the countryside. [MJH]

mnemonic device Any method, system, physical activity, rhythmic utterance, verbal formula, graphic indication, or material contrivance designed to aid in the process of memorizing or recollecting. Perhaps the most familiar of these devices is tying a string around the finger as a reminder of something to be done later; another is the rosary, which serves to check off and to prompt the recitation of a series of prayers. These examples display the distinguishing characteristic of most material mnemonic devices; viz. the object used as a reminder bears little or no resemblance to the subject to be recalled and could serve its purpose only for persons who already knew the subject, and then only by association. They differ, thus, from literal representation in graphic terms, from writing which can be read in full by anyone who knows the language, and from symbols with widely understood and accepted connotations. Even verbal mnemonics, which may actually embody the information to be recalled, and can, if written language exists, be preserved in documents and studied, are usually abbreviated and elliptical, and their purpose is to make possible oral reproduction or practical application of the information and its broader context without reference to written or graphic records.

In ethnological usage, the term mnemonic devices as applied to primitive societies includes the inventions that are used, in the absence of written language and mathematical and musical notation systems, for record-keeping, for calculation of time, for reckoning of accounts, for preservation of historical, genealogical, mythological, musical, and ritual lore, for communication with distant persons, and for the prompting of appointed singers or narrators whose duty it is to remember and recite the tribal memorabilia. These primitive methods and devices fall into three main classes: 1) some form of counter, which may be elaborated to convey more than purely numerical information; 2) some

form of graphic symbol, which may be combined with counters or representational drawings to suggest a broad background of meaning; 3) extensive oral recitations, with or without the use of any of the other devices as an aid to recollection.

Commonly accepted unit counters all over the world have included fingers and toes, sticks, straws, reeds, pebbles, beads, knotted strings and thongs. These have served primitive men of many races for measuring, enumerating, or tallying trade goods, herds, hides, weapons, groups of persons, periods of time, game scores, crop yields, tribute paid, etc. The counters may be combined, arranged, or modified in various ways to convey more specific or more complicated meanings. For example, counting with pebbles may be no more than adding one pebble to a pile for each unit of a transaction, but the calculation may be elaborated by marking divisions or hollows in the ground to separate groups of ten or some other sum, or by giving a value of ten to larger stones, etc. The Creek and Chickasaw Indians made their mercantile calculations by drawing lines on the ground—one short line for each unit, and a cross for tens. (Clerical workers today sometimes follow an exactly equivalent system, except that they use pencil and paper, and usually cross off fives.)

Sticks have proved extremely adaptable material for mnemonic devices, since they can be combined, distinguished by length, marked by notching, peeling, painting, etc. Scores for ball games of the Siouan tribes were kept by setting sticks upright in the ground and removing them as points were won or lost, much as a cribbage board is pegged. Passage of time was marked by many North American Indian tribes by bundles of sticks. The number of sticks might indicate the number of days before an agreed rendezvous; one stick would then be removed each day until the appointment was kept. The Natchez Indians used this device as a signal for an uprising against the French. Loss of some of the sticks was blamed for the failure of the attack, which took place before all the warriors were assembled.

Simple numerical tallies are often kept by notching a stick for each unit to be recorded. The Pawnees notched sticks to keep track of nights elapsed, or months or years. The Pima of Arizona used notched sticks with special notches for years in which notable events occurred, so that a narrator could recall from the marks on the stick the story of the past. Natives of Guiana used to send sticks to the white men to be notched with the number of days until Christmas, so that they could celebrate at the right time. The device has been used not only by primitive men but also by members of more advanced civilizations who were by some circumstance separated from their fellows and from the record-keeping paraphernalia of their culture. The notched sword or gun, showing the number of men killed by the owner, the growth record of children notched or penciled on the doorpost, and the swastika series painted on allied planes of World War II are similar tallying devices.

The Abnaki used sticks thrust into the ground to convey messages between separate traveling parties. The slant of a stick would tell the direction in which the head group was going; another short stick nearby would indicate that the journey was not long; or the number of additional sticks would tell how many days' journey it was. Cuts in the bark, smoking of the stick, and other such distinctions added further directions. Piles of stones, sometimes laid on buffalo robes, were used by the Plains Indians for the same purposes.

The mnemonic range of stick records is considerable. A Siouan funeral orator, using his bundle of sticks as notes, might spin out a comprehensive review of past events, noble achievements, and proud heritage recalled to his mind by the varying lengths, and the character of the notches, incisions, or painted marks. The Choctaws organized and recorded a large-scale migration by a combination of sticks and tied strings, the individuals, classes, and family groups being indicated by the arrangement of the parts.

Possibly the most elaborate of all material mnemonic devices was the *quipu* of the Incas. Its basis was one of the most primitive and simple of tallying devices, the knotted cord, used by many other peoples in many parts of the world. The Nahyssan of South Carolina, for instance, used knotted thongs for time reckoning, a knot for each day. The *quipu*, however, consisted of a whole system of knotted cords, depending from a main cord and having subsidiary strings tied to the secondary ones. There might be as many as 100 strings attached to the main one. Not only did the knots along the strings record numbers and sums in a decimal system, but the subject of the reckoning was distinguished by the color of the string and the relative importance of the parts was shown by position. Red meant war or soldiers; yellow, gold. Less important parts of the record were smaller and farther away from the main cord, and the subsidiary cords, showing subsidiary data, were of finer thread.

The *quipu* was not in itself a calculating device. Figures recorded on it were first worked out with piles of pebbles placed in the divisions of a sort of tray, which served as an abacus. These might refer to new ordinances, to warriors recruited, tribute demanded, deaths during a stated period, taxes collected, or any of the other highly organized business of the Inca empire and its officials.

The *quipu* was also a memory aid to a trained group of interpreters who memorized genealogies, historical lists, poetry, etc. and used the strings, knots, colors, and positions of the cords to prompt recollection of the details and sequence of the material. Lengthy oral recitations are believed to have been word-for-word speeches formulated by learned dignitaries and taught by fathers to sons in a hereditary line of *quipu* interpreters. Even in narratives, allegories, and liturgical formulas recited with the aid of the *quipu*, however, numerical sequences were the key. The device was not equivalent to writing and would have been generally meaningless without the orally handed down knowledge of the "readers."

The Araucanians used the *quipu* to record events, count livestock, receipt payment of fines, and summon assemblies. Though the great collections of Inca *quipus* were destroyed by the conquering Spaniards, a few examples from graves have survived, and simpler forms are still in use among Andean shepherds who use them to count sheep.

Another complicated primitive mnemonic device is the wampum collars, belts, and strings of North American Indians. While primarily designed for personal adornment, and then used as a ceremonial object and as a medium of negotiation, it also served as a form of record and a means of communication. Meanings were inherent in the colors, in the size of the string, the motifs worked into the design, and in the number of elements in it, but these were of mnemonic character in that when specific messages were embodied in wampum they had to be accompanied by a speech of interpretation learned word-for-word by the bearer. Treaties of alliance, proposals of marriage, expressions of mourning or condolence, and pledges were among the subjects of mnemonic treatment in wampum. A collection of wampum strings and belts formed the record of alliance of the Abnaki confederacy; in one belt the four tribes were symbolized by a blue rectangle and four small crosses, all on a white background signifying peace.

Certain of the motifs on wampum were purely representational (the peace pipe, the tomahawk, the triangle of the wigwam, etc.) and were widely understood among Indians, but the message of the whole string was so elliptical that full interpretation depended on the orally transmitted information which was recalled by the elements of the design, just as in the reading of a bundle of sticks or a *quipu*. One marriage-proposal belt of the Passamaquoddy had a white string attached at the place where the bearer was to begin his carefully rehearsed speech, which was organized in five sections, each marked by a new string. Readings of the message were expected to be fairly exact. For example, one of the treasured strings of the Abnaki said, "The bond of the bones of the Abnaki be respected." The word for "speech" was figuratively applied by them to their ceremonial wampum.

Similar mnemonic belts, made of seed beads, colored and arranged in significant sequence to prompt the narrator, were used by the Creeks for archives, genealogical lists, etc.

The examples mentioned so far have all been basically counters, more or less elaborated toward actual depiction of the subject. Certain mnemonic pictographs of many primitive peoples, appearing on such surfaces as bark, boards, hides, rock faces, or incised in the earth, take a step beyond depiction, forming a sort of graphic shorthand somewhere between representational drawing and word or syllable writing. The sacred *churingas* of the Australian Aranda and Luridja tribes are decorated with the only art form of these people: incised conventional patterns of totemic significance, relating the people to their kindred in the plant and animal worlds. The motifs are mnemonic, rather than representational or ideographic, since they are conventionalized beyond recognition as likenesses, yet not related to language, and are meaningless except to an interpreter already familiar with the legends they connote.

Some of the drawings of North and South American Indians, Australian natives, etc., have a landscape-like appearance. These, too, are aids to memory, designed not merely to represent the features of the landscape but to recall battles, migrations, natural catastrophes, etc., or to give information to following groups of the tribes. They are cartographic plans, diagrams, elevations, bird's-eye-views on a primitive level, to be construed within a context known to the intended observers.

While many of the existing pictographs are indecipherable since the memory of the subject is lost to living men, some information has been recovered, particularly in relation to North American Indian pictographs, by the comparison of the graphic notations with the gestures of sign language, once familiar to both Indians and the white traders, trappers, and settlers who came into contact with them. It has been found that many of the symbols are linear descriptions of these gestures. The gesture of pointing out the position of the sun as an indication of the time of day or season of the year is an example of sign language translatable into pictographic symbol.

The Kiowa Indians showed winter graphically by a bold black stroke for dead vegetation, the first of the month by a new moon, summer by the medicine lodge. The Dakota used a circular figure for units of time (a small circle for a single year, a larger one for a number of years) and rows of circles to show elapsed time between pictures recording memorable events. Both of these peoples, by means of representational drawings, pictographs, and repetition of unit symbols like counters, kept extensive archives of tribal history painted on buffalo skins (later on paper). The stories they recorded were told over and over to members of the tribes during ceremonies and in story-telling sessions, so that all would be familiar with them. These documents are often referred to as calendars, but they are actually mnemonic histories.

Calendars, however, are important among the kinds of lore entrusted to pictographic record, as well as to the simple notched stick or knotted string. When the reckoning system is complicated, it is frequently in the hands of the priests, since one of the chief functions of a calendar is to indicate the correct time for holding religious rituals. Thus the calendar of Bali, operating on a double scheme of time calculation, is so intricate that only specialists can interpret it and yet so important in determining the proper or auspicious days for public and individual activities (festivals, weddings, cremations, tooth-filings, etc.) that the priests must be consulted and paid for their advice before any serious undertaking can be begun. The priests have secret charts or calendar keys painted or carved with symbols showing the name signs of the various days. The Aztec calendar stone, with its concentric circles of day signs and symbols, is another priest-interpreted mnemonic system of time reckoning, though its motifs and figures also include historical and mythological dates. Calendars of many other unlettered peoples depend on moon signs for months, and pictographs of the local designations for years related to special events (year of the great snow, etc.) and for months related to occupation or vegetation (lambing month, blackberry month). Calendars of this type approach the function of an almanac.

One of the functions of mnemonic pictographs among various primitive peoples is to record music. The religious songs of the Ojibwa Midewiwin society were set down in pictographic symbols on birchbark rolls. From these the singers could reconstruct the melodies and rhythms and the associated rituals. Many of the Ojibwa songs were in themselves mnemonics, actually précis of long stories, and the singing was often prefaced by an explanation of the song and what it stood for.

These practices of the Ojibwa are a good demonstration of the twofold role of music in mnemonics. Since music is one of the most difficult of subjects to record in the absence of musical notation, the devices for recalling musical patterns are ingenious and varied. And since music inherently possesses two of the most powerful aids to memory—rhythm and melody—many subjects are put into musical form to assist in their retention.

As aids to the recollection of songs, some North American Indians used the notched stick, relying on the repetition of units of the counter device to reconstruct the rhythms; in Peru the knotted cord served the same purpose. The Cuna of Panama use conventionalized picture writing on ceremonial boards to prompt official chanters in the songs and the ritual order of girls' puberty rites. Certain African tribes (Yorubas, for instance) use mnemonic phrases or sentences to identify drum rhythms as a means of recalling or memorizing their music. The "talking drums" may actually speak the significant sounds of the song.

In all long oral recitations, whether guided by material mnemonic devices or not, rhythm (however free) and melody (however narrow the range) play a part. The Polynesian genealogical and cosmological chants and the Dahomean historical and genealogical songs are cases in point. In Dahomey the office of narrative singer is hereditary and carries with it the duty of keeping the records in song. Even in advanced societies the illiterate section of the population makes use of song for the preservation of memorable events. "As I do not know how to read," said a modern Greek folk singer to one collector, "I have made this story into a song so as not to forget it." Such motivation doubtless lay behind the creation of many of the "journalistic ballads" of American folksong.

A few other customs of primitive peoples have a secondary mnemonic function aside from their primary purposes. Tattooing and cicatrization, primarily serving as personal adornment, as identification or certificate of membership, or as invocation of superhuman power for battle, etc., may also convey more individual and more specific stories, going beyond the badge or identification significance. Totem poles of the American northwest coastal tribes depict the legendary heritage of the family in carved and painted figures whose full meaning can only be read with the aid of a body of information surviving in oral tradition. Both of these kinds of device are comparable to the heraldic lore of Europe and the personal and family emblems of other parts of the world. The heralds of Europe served a genealogical purpose in devising the partings, quarterings, borderings, etc., by which a knight's whole family relationship could be shown at a glance. Considered in the light of the full information revealed by the shields and crests, heraldic devices are mnemonic. When the device serves merely for instant identification of persons or property, it becomes no more than a badge or trademark.

Even among highly advanced peoples who have a written language and exact methods of writing mathematical and musical material, mnemonic devices and systems have been and still are used for learning and teaching facts and skills that in themselves are difficult to remember or to relate in proper sequence to the purpose at hand. Material devices and counters are not completely discarded—witness the cribbage board, the rosary, and the string around the finger previously mentioned. The string and the knotted handkerchief reminders are believed to be derived from the ancient Jewish shawl, worn during prayers in the synagogue, which had strings at each corner knotted five times to call to mind the five books of Moses. Counting on the fingers is still common, and another counting device not yet forgotten is the telling off of flocks with one black sheep for a given number of white ones. However, much of the mnemonic practice of advanced peoples has to do with verbal material. Speeches, music, historical dates, religious formulas, genealogical lists, grammatical and mathematical rules and other "school" subjects, recipes, spelling, occupational lore and industrial skills, advertising names and slogans, are among the kinds of information it has been desired to imprint on the mind by mnemonic means.

Recommended aids to memory have ranged from pure superstition to the psychological studies and statistical charts of postgraduate education courses of the present day. More than one child has gone to bed with his schoolbook under his pillow, hoping that in his sleep the assignment would find its way into his head. Diet has often been thought to be an influence on memory; the saying is still current that fish is "brain food." In India the way to acquire a long memory was to fast three days, then eat of the soma plant, or drink soma juice for a year. An English book of 1697 suggests liniments, ointments, plasters, and sneezing powders to clear the memory by dispelling the noxious fumes arising from the stomach. One of its prescriptions is shaved or powdered ivory taken internally; another is a potion of white frankincense in liquor taken at bedtime; a third is an application of gold to that "sutura" of the head which divides the memory from other sections of the brain.

The Greeks and Romans worked seriously to devise a systematic, scientific means of training and reinforcing the powers of memory as an aid to oratory. Most of their systems evolved around a diagrammatic plan of a place or a human figure, with each part of which a part of the subject to be memorized was associated. Said to have been invented by the Greek poet Simonides (500 B.C.), this scheme of topical or local association was widely used in later Europe and still occasionally appears as the principle of "how-to-train-your-memory" books published today.

A related method, popularized by Marafortius (1602), related all facts to be memorized to the hand, 44 visual images being located on the backs, palms, and fingers. So successful were some of the early "professors" of mnemonics with these methods that charges of sorcery were brought against them.

In addition to these diagrammatic systems and the hand charts, which will be considered further in other connections, rhythm, rime, melody, word plays, alphabetical organization, and cabalistic formulas have all been used to superimpose on the data to be learned a structure by which it can be recalled at will.

Repetition is basic to memorizing. (Doubtless one of the factors in the survival of long ballads is the use of incremental repetition, which not only facilitates composition but also makes for easy recollection or approximate reconstruction of words and incidents.) Rhythm is a kind of repetition (the recurrence of stress at expected intervals) and is thus a reliable aid to memory of material for recitation.

A simple example of the application of pure rhythm to information to be learned is the monotonous singsong used by children in saying the multiplication tables and the converse "gozinta" tables of division. (*Two* gozinta four *twice; two* gozinta six *three* times . . . etc.) Singsong has been a common method of study by both European and Oriental students.

Making use of this principle, pedagogs have put all sorts of information into metrical form, often with the further memory reinforcement of rime. Their verses are not, of course, folk compositions, but many have passed into oral tradition, are known in several versions, and the learning methods and purposes do not differ from those of primitive recitations.

Latin grammar, a stumbling block to generations of school children, is well represented in mnemonic verse:

> With *nemo* never let me see
> *Neminis* or *nemine.*
>
> Common are to either sex
> *Artifex* and *opifex* . . . etc.
>
> After remember, pity, forget,
> The genitive case is properly set.

Among the rimes for English grammar, is this:

> A noun's the name of anything,
> As, *school* or *garden, hoop* or *swing* . . . (etc. through "eight parts of speech, which reading, writing, speaking teach." Sometimes a ninth is included—the interjection.)

One of the most troublesome quirks of English spelling is straightened out by "*i* before *e*, except after *c*." The problem of changing wet to dry measures is solved by "A pint's a pound the world around."

To deal with the complexities of dates and calendars many rimes have been devised. The most familiar of these is, "Thirty days hath September, April, June, and November . . ." etc. This is known in numerous variants, including a Latin one:

> *Junius, Aprilis, Septemq, Novemq, tricenos*
> *Unum plus reliqui, Februs tenet octo vicenos*
> *At si bissextus fuerit superadditur unus.*

One version, given by Richard Grafton in his *Chronicles of England* (1562), was labeled "a rule to knowe how many dayes every moneth in the yeare hath."

To remember the Latin dating system, some version of the following is often recited:

> In March, July, October, May,
> The Ides come on the 15th day,
> The Nones the 7th; all other months besides
> Have two days less for Nones and Ides.

Among the Arabs, time reckoning was for centuries based on the stars, particularly on the positions of the Pleiades; thus many Arabic mnemonic verses were composed to incorporate the rules of reckoning according to these positions.

Important dates in history are also the subject of many rimes:

> In fourteen hundred ninety two
> Columbus sailed the ocean blue.
>
> In 732 at the Battle of Tours
> Charles Martel defeated the Moors.

Lists of rulers and other historical facts are often set in rime for memorizing. "First William the Norman,/

Then William his son," goes the best-known of these, which has thoughtfully been brought up to date from time to time by "Unknown." Many other attempts to make this list memorable have failed to be remembered themselves. Other metrical mnemonics on "school subjects" include the seven wonders of the ancient world ("The Pyramids first which in Egypt were laid/ Next Babylon's Garden, for Amytis made . . ." etc.), the signs of the zodiac ("The Ram, the Bull, the Heavenly Twins/ And next the Crab the Lion shines" . . . etc.), the syllogisms of logic, and even the subject of meter itself. "Trochee trips from long to short/ From long to long in solemn sort/ Slow Spondee stalks; strong foot! yet ill able/ Ever to come up with dactyl trisyllable . . ." and "In the hexameter rises the fountain's silvery column/ In the pentameter aye falling in melody back." These lines frequently come to the aid of both Latin and English classes who have forgotten, if ever they knew, that Coleridge wrote them.

Meter and rime as aids to memory have also been used on a much more practical and down-to-earth level. Sailors of chantey days learned their occupational lore from a number of rimes, some of which survive in oral tradition among the penanted yachtsmen of Long Island Sound today. Here are the rules of the road:

> If close-hauled on the starboard tack,
> No other ship can cross your track.
> If on the port tack you appear,
> Ships going free must all keep clear,
> While you must yield when going free
> To ships close-hauled upon your lee.
> And if you have the wind right aft,
> Keep clear of every sailing craft . . . etc.

Barometric readings were supplemented by more homely prophecy in rime:

> First rise after a low
> Squalls expect and more blow.

> First the rain and then the wind,
> Topsail sheets and halliards mind.
> First the wind and then the rain,
> Hoist your topsails up again.

> Mackerel skies and mare's tails
> Make tall ships carry low sails . . . etc.

Many weather rimes are so familiar as to be proverbial, but their underlying purpose was informational and mnemonic, serving the farmer, the shepherd, the sailor, the traveler as guides to planning and pursuing his occupation.

> Year of snow
> Fruit will grow.

> A rainbow in the morning
> Is the shepherd's (or sailor's) warning;
> But a rainbow at night
> Is the shepherd's (or sailor's) delight.

> Rain before seven,
> Clear before eleven.

Tricks of many trades and epitomized conclusions of long observation are buried in these how-to-know verses. Will the fishing be good? What is the wind?

> When the wind is in the East,
> Then the fishes bite the least.
> When the wind is in the West,
> Then the fishes bite the best.

When the wind is in the North,
Then the fishes do come forth.
When the wind is in the South,
It blows the bait in the fish's mouth.

Should you buy this horse?

> One white foot—buy him.
> Two white feet—try him.
> Three white feet—look well about him.
> Four white feet—go without him.

Is this a good year for sheep?

> A leap year
> Is never a good sheep year.

Which card should you discard?

> When you discard, weak suits you ought to choose,
> For strong ones are too valuable to lose.

(From Pole's *Theory of the Modern Scientific Game of Whist.*)

How do you make a Planter's Punch?

> 1 of sour (lemon or lime)
> 1 of sweet (syrup)
> 1 of strong (rum)
> 1 of weak (crushed ice)
> (A West Indian recipe.)

Often the verses are set in abecedarian order, adding another type of easily recalled structure to rhythm and rime. Preschool riming alphabets, bestiaries, the books of the Bible, and many other lists to be memorized have been given this formula. (See ALPHABET RIMES.) On the strictly practical level, the *Sailor's Alphabet* begins, "A is the Aftermost part of the ship/ B is the Bowsprit on the bow of the ship/ C is the Capstan where the sailors go round/ And D is the Davits where the jollyboat hangs down." (See ALPHABET SONG.)

Even without rime or meter, the alphabet is an organizing principle used in many languages for material to be committed to memory. The Hebrew alphabet has long been used for mnemonic instruction in religious matters. In Greek carols the letters of the alphabet have been used for outlining the parts of the St. Basil story.

Various acrostic arrangements, alphabetical, metrical, or merely initial combinations have been applied to many subjects as mnemonic aids. The Jews from Biblical times have formed mnemonic words and phrases from the initials of names or statements; for example, RAMBAM, from Rabbi Moses Ben Maimon. Another method is to use the initials of a list and create a sentence from them. "Read Over Your Greek Books In Vacation," is one by which school children have learned the colors of the rainbow: red, orange, yellow, green, blue, indigo, violet. "On Old Monadnock's Peaked Tops, A Finn and German Picked Some Hops" was used in physiology classes to remember the cranial nerves: olfactory, optic, motoris oculi, pneumogastric, etc.

One more letter device is to select the one common letter in a miscellaneous list; the R, for instance, in the names of the months during which it is believed safe to eat oysters. The reminder is often seen in ads reading, "Oysters R in season."

Repeating a list backwards has sometimes been thought an effective memory aid (as well as a magical spell). To "know a thing backwards and forwards" is to know it too thoroughly to forget. Thus children are proud to chant their numbers, letters, days of the week, or months of the year backwards. And thus it was the custom of the McNeills of Colonsay that each Sunday the children of the clan were put through their genealogy backwards in Gaelic, so that no one of them could ever forget his proud lineage.

Certain subjects have been thought so difficult, or so important, or have comprised such an extensive body of knowledge that many mnemonic methods have been applied to them. The doctrines, sacred books, important personages, and catechisms of religion are an example. Rime, acrostics, alphabets, numerical sequences, counters, and music have all been used. The five canons of the Dutch Reformed Church, as laid down in the 17th century at the Synod of Dort, are taught by an acrostic on the word TULIP, the national flower of Holland:

> T—Total Depravity
> U—Unconditional Election
> L—Limited Atonement
> I —Irresistible Grace
> P—Perseverance of the Saints

The Bible, epitomized in Latin acrostic verses of abecedarian order, was translated by an English clergyman, John Shaw, and published by Simon Wastel in 1683. Many other riming lists of the books of the Bible have been composed, the most familiar being:

> The great Jehovah speaks to us
> In Genesis and Exodus;
> Leviticus and Numbers see
> Followed by Deuteronomy . . . etc.

The Ten Commandments are summarized thus:

> 1. Thou shalt have no more gods but me.
> 2. Before no idol bow thy knee.
> 3. Take not the name of God in vain.
> 4. Nor dare the Sabbath day profane . . . etc.

The names of the twelve apostles are also set in rime:

> These are the twelve apostles' names:
> Peter, Andrew, John, and James;
> James the second and Jude were called, too,
> Philip and also Bartholomew;
> Matthew and Thomas who doubted His word;
> Simon and Judas who sold his Lord.

In the back country of Virginia the names of the evangelists were memorized by the rime, "Matthew, Mark, Luke, and John/ Saddle the cat and I'll get on/ Gimme a stick and I'll lay on/ Open the gate and I'll be gone." This is one of many parodies on a widely known bedtime prayer formula, the White Paternoster, "Matthew, Mark, Luke, John/ Bless the bed that I lie on/ And blessed guardian angel keep/ Me safe from danger while I sleep." In Languedoc a version of the song, *The Twelve Apostles,* was used at the time of learning the catechism.

The use of melody to reinforce memory, as in this song, is widespread. One of the simplest examples of melody as a mnemonic device is the little lullaby and nursery tune to which generations of American, German, and other European children have learned their A-B-C's. See LULLABY. Many children cannot go through the alphabet without soundlessly singing this tune over.

As in primitive mnemonics, there is in advanced cultures an interaction of music and other memorizing devices. When the theory or groundwork of a musical culture is complicated, other devices are called into play to help in the learning process. A mnemonic sentence, for instance, helps beginners to learn the lines of the musical staff: "Every Good Boy Does Fine" (e, g, b, d, f). The intervening spaces are remembered because they spell "face." The order of sharp and flat keys is also embedded in mnemonic sentences and phrases. "GooD AlE and BeeF" is one such. The capital letters indicate the sharp keys if read in regular order; when read backwards, they give the flat keys. The same information, in country singing schools of America, was often given by the initials in these two sentences: "Girls Dread All Evil Boys First" (sharp); and "Four Boys Eat Apple Dumplings Greedily" (flat).

One of the basic aids in the teaching and learning of melody has been cheironomy, or hand signs, used by the Jews, by the Vedic singers of India, in European plain chant, etc. The notes are associated with the fingers, joints, palm, and mounts of the human hand. The correct note was shown to a chorus by the gesture of the leader, and because of the relative positions of the notes on the hand and the already familiar intervals of pitch, the chorus could follow the melody. Some of the early musical notation of Europe (9th–11th centuries) is of cheironomic significance and can be only sketchily interpreted now that the gestures of the conductor are no longer known. The hand of Guido, however, attributed to Guido d'Arezzo (c. 995) but similar to the Hindu hand signs, survives in various documents as a drawing of the hand marked with the position of each degree of the gamut as it was used as a memory aid in solmization.

Other types of hand signs and gestures survive as mnemonic devices to this day. In the teaching of elementary geography within recent years a series of gestures was used to show the movements of the constant winds, accompanied by a rhythmic recitation of their names and areas: belt of calms, trades, antitrades, horse latitudes, doldrums. Various "rules of thumb" are also memorized by hand signs, as the demonstration of the coil, the core, and the direction of current in an electric motor by the hand with thumb and forefinger extended at right angles to each other and the other fingers loosely curled.

Modern industry has not overlooked the value of mnemonic methods in training its operators. The Morse alphabet for telegraphy was taught about 1870 in mnemonic sentences. The letters were divided into related groups according to the arrangement of dots and dashes. The range from one to four dashes, including letters T, M, O, and Ch, was made into the sentence, "Turnips Make Oxen Cheerful." Highly technical current books on industrial management recommend giving abbreviated or acrostic names to complicated mechanical and electronic equipment so that employees may learn the operation without confusion over long scientific names. The essentials of advertising layout have been taught by the mnemonic word AIDA, signifying the elements of Attention, Interest, Desire, and Action. Advertising, both printed and on the radio, makes use of mnemonic principles over and over again to impress on the audience the names of the sponsor and the product. The name is spelled, pronounced, repeated, rimed, chanted, sung, echoed on the glockenspiel, and included in puns, alphabetical rigmaroles, and acrostic formulas until, presumably, the listener cannot think of the type of product without recalling the brand name.

It will be noted by those who attempt to collect examples of mnemonics from oral tradition that the ones that survive most completely are the short, simple, homely, almost proverbial type, such as the "*i* before *e*" rule. The long and more literary or more complicated compositions are retained only in fragmentary lines, even though the subject to which they relate is recalled.

THERESA C. BRAKELEY

moaning American Negro word for humming. The characteristic humming heard in solitary singing or interpolated in blues, etc., is an African survival and is similar in sound to the hum of an African side drum which changes pitch under pressure of the arm which holds it.

Mobog An important religious ceremony of the Tuaran Dusuns (Borneo), performed to expel from a village the evil spirits which have collected there during the previous year: literally, beating. The ceremony is so named because a small pig, which is carried in procession in a basket on the back of a woman, is beaten so that its squeals will attract the spirits. The ceremony, performed chiefly by women, consists of chanting and a combination of dancing and chanting before each house in turn in the village, accompanied by the squealing of the pig. When this has been completed the procession of women proceeds to the river with the evil spirits following. These embark upon a raft covered with models of animals and people as well as offerings of food. This is set adrift, thus freeing the village of its bad spirits acquired during the preceding year.

mock or **false plea** A captive, about to be killed, gains respite by a false plea and escapes his captors: a worldwide folktale motif (K550 ff.). In North American Indian tales it is found commonly in the Brer Rabbit tales of the southeastern United States, and also in the widely distributed, apparently largely native tale of Turtle's War Party. In the latter tale, Turtle, with or without companions, goes on a raid, kills a chief, is captured, is threatened with death by being pounded with a rock or being burnt, encourages his captors to do either of these to him, but pleads with them not to throw him into the water. So they throw him in the water, and he escapes. Among some tribes it is not Turtle but some other creature (Rainbow Trout, Bluejay, Cuttlefish, etc.) who goes on the raid and makes the false plea. The tale is especially popular among the Plateau and Plains tribes, but has been recorded from several other areas in North America also. [EWV]

modes The series of diatonic scale patterns on which much of the early folk song of Europe is constructed; they are based on the prevailing tonal structure of medieval ecclesiastical melody, Gregorian Chant, and are also called *ecclesiastical* or *church modes* and *Greek modes*, from a complicated and remote derivation from the Greek musical system. The modes are encompassed by the white keys of the piano, each natural note, in turn, forming the tonic of a mode played up through the octave, as from A to A consecutively through G to G. The modes are named for Greek tribes: *Æolian* (A to A), *Locrian* (B to B), *Ionian* (C to C), *Dorian* (D to D), *Phrygian* (E to E), *Lydian* (F to F), and *Mixolydian* (G to G).

Ionian, of course, corresponds to the modern C-Major scale and is the mode of two thirds of English folk song, according to Cecil Sharp, and of perhaps three quarters of America's surviving heritage of British songs. It was called the *modus lascivus* in medieval times because it was the basis of so many impious secular tunes. The melody of *Sumer is icumen in* is Ionian.

Next most common in English song, and thus in American, is Dorian, and Mixolydian and Æolian are also fairly usual. Mixolydian is a favorite of Irish and Hebridean singers. It differs from our common major mode only in having a flatted 7th. Dorian and Mixolydian were also the modes in which the troubadours and trouvères were most likely to cast their tunes. Phrygian is comparatively rare in British songs, and Lydian is not found in English melodies, though some Irish and Scottish tunes use it, and it is characteristic of Slavic folk songs. Locrian is never found in British folk song, and indeed is a later and logical or theoretical addition to the series, rather than one found in ecclesiastical practice.

A striking difference between modern scales and the modes is that the modern scales are based on chord construction and a vertical harmonic relationship, and the modes are based on melody in a horizontal sequence relationship. A real minor key is rare in modal folk songs. The minor effect of certain songs is often a modern recasting of the melody or a variation on the Æolian mode. The essence of the modal construction is not in beginning with the tonic, but rather in the sequence of intervals and the relation of other notes to the tonic. Folk songs frequently end with the tonic, though sometimes the tonic is merely a core from which departures and returns are made often enough to establish the tonality and the end is a bold dominant. Certain tunes, known as "circular," have an inconclusive ending, which leads directly back into the opening phrase and therefore may go "round and round." The circle canon, or round, does this, and is, like the nonsense story or song, without an end. "Spring would be a dreary season/ Were it not for flowers of spring would be a dreary season," etc., is an example which in both tune and words return to its head. The *Irish cadence* is the opposite kind of ending, which stresses its finality with a twice-repeated closing note.

Modulation, in the usual sense, is not found in modal folk song, though certain melodies may be bimodal, swinging from one mode to another, without a full change of key.

Within the modal pattern melodies may be heptatonic, as in the ecclesiastical system; they may also be pentatonic or hexatonic, lacking the 2nd or 6th tone, or both. "Gapped scales" of this type are fairly common in Scottish folk tunes, though not the majority, as is sometimes supposed.

The gradual displacement of the modes is largely the result of a growing interest in harmony in the 17th century. The modes, though effective in counterpoint, were not harmonically adaptable. However, modal scale in a tune, while generally a sign of age, is not necessarily dependable in dating music, since, as was pointed out by Phillips Barry, traditional singers have often recast current tunes in the manner to which they are accustomed. [TCB]

modinha A popular song type originally heard in Lisbon, Portugal, in the mid-eighteenth century, telling a romantic and sentimental tale to a sorrowful, minor melody, perhaps based on Italian theatrical tunes. It became an urban folk song type then and may have been one of the ancestors of the fado. It survives in Brazil, where it was introduced late in the 19th century, and preserves its character as an expression of the folk of the cities.

Moe, Jörgen Engebretsen (1813–1882) Norwegian poet and folklorist; collaborator with Peter Christen Asbjörnsen on the *Norske Folkeeventyr*, Christiania, 1842.

Moiræ In Greek mythology, the Fates who presided over the course of human life: probably a development of a group of birth spirits. In Hesiod, they are three: Clotho, the spinner of the thread of life; Lachesis, the determiner of its length; and Atropos, the snipper of the thread. The Moiræ were daughters of Zeus and Themis, or of Night and Darkness, and carried out the decrees of Zeus, not having independent action. Homer speaks of *moira*, but without personifying fate. The Moiræ often appear with the Keres, and are sometimes confused with the Erinyes. In modern Greek folklore, the Moiræ appear on the third night after the child's birth and direct then the future course of its life. Propitiatory offerings are made to them. See HATHOR.

mokṣa In Jainism, literally, release: the liberation of the soul from evil and from further transmigrations. In Jainist symbolism mokṣa is situated at the crown of the head of the Cosmic Giant.

moly (perhaps from Sanskrit *mūlam*, root) An unidentified legendary herb possessing magic power. As described by Homer, it had a black root and a white flower; Pliny said that its flower was yellow and that it had white fleshy roots. Some late authorities have thought that moly might be identified with rue; others have suggested that it was mandrake; still others identify it with the famous wild garlic of southern Europe. (See GARLIC.) Moly was the plant given to Odysseus by Hermes that he might resist the wiles of Circe when he went to rescue his men whom the enchantress had turned into swine. (*Odyssey* x, 305.)

momentary gods (German *Augenblicksgötter*) Gods who exist for a specific purpose and at specified times at special places, and who have no existence except for such purpose, time, and place. In Arcadia and Elis, for example, such a god was Myiagros, who chased the flies away during the sacrifices to Zeus and Athena.

Momotaro The hero of a well-known Japanese fairy tale, who was found by an old couple in a peach: hence his name "eldest son of a peach." [JLM]

Moneta The admonisher or warner: a title of Mnemosyne or of Juno. The temple of Juno Moneta on the Capitoline seems to have replaced, in 366 B.C., an older shrine that contained the sacred geese. This temple later became the mint, hence the transference to the languages of today of the words mint and money. Several tales explaining the title were told; according to Cicero, a warning voice from Juno's temple ordered, during an earthquake, the sacrifice of a pregnant sow to end the danger.

Money Musk A tune played for square-dancing in America, known since Revolutionary times. It takes its name from a Scottish village and its melody from an early 18th century *contradance* tune, *The Countess of Airly*.

monkey Any of the primate mammals, excluding man and the anthropoid apes, though often including the latter in common usage. Monkeys are mentioned in the Bible (I *Kings* x, 22) as having been brought to King Solomon from Ophir, and the Assyrians were familiar with apes (not indigenous to that region) because they were brought as tribute. In rabbinical lore, the blessing on Him "who varieth his creatures" was to be said at sight of an ape. To see a monkey in a dream, according to the Talmud, is unlucky. In rabbinical legend, one of the three classes of men who built the Tower of Babel was turned into apes; in Moslem legend, Jews dwelling in Elath on the Red Sea fished on the Sabbath and were turned into apes as punishment.

The Ewe of Togoland believe the hussar-ape and the long-tailed monkey are individual totems of twins. Some West African as well as American Negroes believe that apes can speak, but hold their tongues to keep from being put to work. One clan of the Bataks of Sumatra may not eat monkey flesh because they believe they are either descended from similar animals and their souls may transmigrate into them, or that they are under certain obligations to them. When the Yuracare Indians of Bolivia kill apes, they sprinkle them with chicha and say, "We love you, since we have brought you home." This gratifies those still in the woods. Natives of northeastern Celebes believe they are descended from monkeys and send offerings of food to their ancestors on a bamboo raft which is floated down a stream.

The folklore and stories about monkeys and apes in Europe are restricted, largely learned, and probably the products of the fable literature of the Middle Ages and tales of African hunters. Gregory of Tours records the oldest Western variant of a story relating how an ape threw overboard the ill-gotten wealth of a wine merchant. Shakespeare in *Much Ado About Nothing*, refers to a then current saying that the fate of old maids is "to lead apes in hell." Folktales concerning apes are found in Indonesia, Rhodesia, Zululand, Japan, Melanesia, China, and India.

Monkey Though it might be expected that Monkey would be utilized in African and New World Negro folklore as an important character, he actually plays a subsidiary role. In the Congo, he appears occasionally as opponent of trickster, and he also figures in the mythologies of other parts of Africa. In the New World, however, he is almost absent, except in tales recorded in Brazil and Dutch Guiana, and here only occasionally. [MJH]

Monkey Prince The hero of a Filipino folktale (#41 in *MAFLS* xii) thought to be of genuine native tradition. Long ago the young son of a certain king fell in love with a beautiful young witch, daughter of his father's bitter enemy. He kept his love for the witch a secret for many years, refusing to marry hundreds of young girls brought for his choosing. At last the king forced his son to marry. And the beautiful young witch in the forest so despised the prince because he was afraid to acknowledge their love that she put a spell upon him on his wedding day. She changed the fine city into a deep forest, and her timid lover into a monkey in its tallest tree, there and thus to remain for 500 years until a young girl should love him. Four hundred years went by and the outside world forgot the ancient city. At last new settlers came. The monkey came down from the tree and abducted young girls from time to time, but they all died of fright. Another day he carried off a young girl who had already been disappointed in love, and who ate the rich fruits he brought her, and saw in his eyes an incalculable sadness and kindness. By the tenth day she loved him; the monkey was suddenly transformed back into the handsome prince, and the city too was disenchanted and resumed its life. The young pair were married and lived long and wisely.

Although this story has a distinctly European flavor, there is no reason to assume that the beast marriage is a European transplant, that idea being so natural to primitive cultures. It would be most interesting if the Beauty and the Beast motif (i.e. disenchantment of hero through a woman's love) were equally indigenous. There are also striking parallels between this story and the sleeping beauty stories, especially in the resumption of life and activity in the prince's city at the moment of his disenchantment, and the fairy (or other supernatural) taking revenge for a slight (in this case, curse by disappointed witch, G269.4). See LITTLE BRIAR ROSE.

monkshood or **helmet flower** A plant (genus *Aconitum*, family *Ranunculaceæ*) having shiny, dark green, deeply dentate leaves: named for the shape of the flowers (usually dark blue). The poison aconite is procured especially from the root, but the whole plant is poisonous, and early became known as wolfbane. Its poisonous and paralyzing properties were well known to the early Greeks, who also ascribed to it the power of causing fevers in the regions where it grew. Some myths report that it first sprang up beside the entrance to Hades through which Hercules returned bringing the dreadful Cerberus, starting from the drops of spittle from the hell-dog's mouth.

Guy de Vigevani in his 1335 treatise calls this plant the source of the worst of all possible poisons for which there is no antidote. Avicenna had said there was a mouse which fed on the roots and whose flesh provided an antidote. Guy could find no such mouse, but in his researches for an antidote took the slugs which were feeding on the leaves of the plant, made a decoction of the slugs mixed with theriac, which worked on animals—and on himself! The 16th-century sage Hieronymus Mercurialis of Forli produced a lively work on poisons in which he sought the answer *how* aconite kills both man and beast if it touches their genitals. Among his serious findings stands the fact that aconite will cure scorpion bite. Medieval witches delighted in the numbing and flying sensations caused by chewing the leaves. Only a witch could do this with impunity. See ACONITE.

monogatari Literally, narration: a form of *kabuki* dramatic technique used for the narration of events and communication of important matters from one actor to another. The highly stylized gestures and the musical *chobo* accompaniment hark back to Japanese puppet-play origin. The motion, sometimes graceful, sometimes grotesque, is always fantastic, and of the nature of dance. It is one of the most difficut forms of the *kabuki* acting. [GPK]

monotheism Belief in a single god, as opposed to polytheism or belief in several or many gods with special provinces of interest and action. Many students of comparative religion hold to an evolutionary belief in the growth of religious thought from the simplest form of animism, peopling all the objects and phenomena of the world with spirits, through several stages to monotheism. Others, with equally strong evidence, see in monotheism an early stage in religion, and hold that polytheism and polydemonism evolved from an original belief in a supreme god. Critics see in the one philosophy an ethnocentric belief in the supremacy of monotheistic religion over all others, and in the other an attempt to justify the Biblical story. Yet even in the great monotheistic religions—Judaism, Christianity, Islam—angels, saints, and demons appear as aides or adversaries of the One God, even though their powers are of a lesser order. And Hinduism, admittedly polytheistic, possesses a high god who in theory is supreme over all others yet receives little direct worship. Primitive monotheism has been noted in Australia, in Africa, and elsewhere in the world. A strong argument has also been made for a Stone Age monotheism in which the supreme deity, from whom all things derived, was the Great Mother, the goddess of fertility.

monsters In ancient mythologies and lore there were a number of composite monsters, part bird and part beast. The elders of Babylon explained that the eagle represented the good in nature and the winged monsters the forces of evil and destruction. Such creatures were the dragon, roughly a crocodile with wings; the griffin, with the head and wings of an eagle and the body of a lion; the hippogriff, a griffin combined with a horse; a chimera, with the head of a lion, the body of a goat, and the tail of a dragon (sometimes with a human head in the middle of the back). There were also the old English Vasa Mortis, the winged bull of the Babylonians, and the winged elephant of the Hindus. Countless part man and part animal monsters abound in classical mythology, such as the centaurs, satyrs, the Minotaur, Lamia, Echidna, etc. Persian mythology and folktale teem with monsters, some famous and named, others nonce creatures occurring in the specific story. See CERBERUS; GIGANTES; HECATE.

🗫 Large, fantastic, evilly disposed beings, human, semihuman, or animal in form, are mentioned in nearly all North American Indian origin myths as having lived on earth during the first creation. The various culture heroes are credited with killing many of these male and female monsters, but not all, since several reappear in myths having human actors in them as well. Among the Eskimo, who have no culture hero, monsters of all sizes, shapes, and description are mentioned in the tales; some are cannibals, others are harmless except for their terrifying appearance. Of all the American Indian mythologies, perhaps that of the Iroquois exhibits the greatest profusion of monsters, ogres, flying heads, jealous uncles, cannibalistic mothers, and other unsavory characters; these appear not only in the origin myth, but throughout the body of Iroquois mythology.

Stories of monsters clad in bone, stone, metal, or scales

are very characteristic for the Southeastern tribes. The monster is usually a cannibal, and is finally slain by persons or beings who have learned the secret of its only vulnerable spot; often the culture hero is the slayer. (See Frank G. Speck, *Ethnology of the Yuchi Indians, Anthr. Papers of the Univ. Museum,* Univ. of Pennsylvania, Vol. 1, 1909, #1. p. 140.)

Some of the monsters who appear in many North American myths from different parts of the continent are Burr-Woman, an old woman who gets on the hero's back and cannot be dislodged; Sucking-Monster, a giant who sucks in his victims; Pot-Tilter, an old woman who has a pot that sucks people in as she points it at them; the cliff ogre, a giantess who kicks people over a cliff where they are eaten by her young; the sharp-elbowed women who stab victims with their elbows; Fire-Moccasins, an ogre who wears moccasins that set fire to everything he walks around; the cannibal giant(ess) who abducts children in a sack or basket; the cannibal who was burned in a fire and whose ashes became mosquitoes; many-headed monsters; the one-sided man; the woman with toothed vagina; vampires. The distributions of all these characters in American Indian mythologies are to be found in Stith Thompson, *Tales of the North American Indians,* Cambridge, Mass., 1929, pp. 267 ff.

Birth of the monsters whom Killer-of-Enemies, Jicarilla Apache culture hero kills before the Apache are created, is specifically accounted for by the Jicarilla Apache. Among the First People were women who misbehaved, became pregnant, and give birth to a Giant Elk, a monster eagle, a kicking monster, the two running rocks, a monster rock (Flint Man), Big Owl, a giant fish—all of whom Killer-of-Enemies disposes of. Other accounts which narrate, with detail comparable to that in the Apache tale, how monsters were disposed of by the culture hero are to be found in some of the North Pacific coast Raven cycles, and in the Nanabozho cycle of the central Algonquians. See CANNIBALS; OGRE; VAGINA DENTATA. [EWV]

monster (animal) killed from within A motif (F912) occurring in many swallow stories in which the hero, often by building a fire in the belly of the swallowing creature (bird, fish, ogre, etc.) or by cutting its heart, is spewed out by the animal, or cuts his way through the side of the carcass, in many tales thus rescuing other persons who have been swallowed. The motif is very widespread, appearing in tales from Africa and Siberia, from North America and Europe. In a Bella Coola myth, the sparks from the fire in the Grizzly Bear's stomach fly up and become the stars.

Monster-Slayer or **Slayer-of-Monsters** The younger of the two boys born to Changing Woman, Apache Indian deity. Monster-Slayer's name, among the White Mountain Apache, is Na•ye'nezyane; his father was the Sun, and his brother was Born-from-Water. Monster-Slayer is identical with Killer-of-Enemies of other Apache groups, and with Reared-Within-the-Earth of the Navaho. To the White Mountain Apache Monster-Slayer is their most important male deity except for the Sun; everything he did was for the good of the earth and of people, and he embodies all that is good, holy, and manly. His birth, his visit to his father the Sun, the tests his father sets him, and his deeds on earth are described in detail in several Apache origin myths recorded by Grenville

Goodwin in *Myths and Tales of the White Mountain Apache, MAFLS* 38, 1939, pp. 1–49. See AHAYUTA ACHI. [EWV]

moon The phases of the moon, caused by the varying angle at which its lighted surface is seen from the earth, have formed, from earliest times, one of man's best means of measuring time. Every 28 and a fraction days, the new moon appears in the sky. This period coincides with the menstrual period of the human female; it has been made the measure of the month. The three words —moon, menses, month—all come from the same root, meaning to measure. The Mohammedan calendar is figured on the lunar month, with the result that the months progress through the seasons, since the calendar does not take into account the earth's rotation about the sun. The Islamic year is therefore only 354 or 355 days long. Thus, where the opening of the year 1359 A.H. began February 10, 1940 C.E., the year 1369 began October 24, 1950. Similarly, the religious festivals, such as the fast of Ramadan, occur at various seasons of the year, since they are fixed by the month. The Hebrew year too is based on the lunar month, but, by the use of leap years in which an extra month is figured, it is brought into balance with the solar year in a 19-year cycle.

Festivals of the new moon are observed among many peoples, and thankful prayers are said for the reappearance of the extinguished light in the sky. The full moon is looked upon as a climactic period of the month; the Jewish Passover is celebrated at the full moon, and the Christian Easter, from which the dates of all other movable feasts in the calendar are figured, occurs on the first Sunday following the full moon after the vernal equinox. The full moon nearest the autumnal equinox is called the harvest moon, as it occurs at harvest time; the full moon following the harvest moon is known as the hunter's moon. Eclipses of the moon occur only at full moon, when the earth gets between the sun and the fully illuminated disk of the moon. The earth's shadow casts a dark reddish color on the moon, dimming its light or blacking it out altogether. These "bloody" moons, or other aspects of the moon when the atmosphere makes the moon's face seem red with blood, are evil omens, portending catastrophes. The Chinese, for example, see in an abnormally red (or an abnormally pale) moon, a warning of evil. In the Andaman Islands and elsewhere, the waxing moon is male, the waning moon female. The waxing moon is the right-hand moon, for the curve of the right hand index finger and thumb follows the curve of the crescent; similarly the waning moon is the left-hand moon. The crescent moon with its points upward is holding water, and presages a dry spell; among the Bushmen, the moon on its back is an omen of death. The faint outline of the full disk of the moon at the time of the bright crescent new moon, the "old moon in the arms of the new" (D1812.5.1.5), is the sign of a storm. Thus the sailor warns Sir Patrick Spens in the ballad:

> "Late late yestreen I saw the new moone,
>   Wi the auld moone in hir arme,
>   And I feir, I feir, my deir master,
>   That we will cum to harme."

Elsewhere than at sea, the full moon is a propitious time. Medicines and tonics are more efficacious if given at the full moon. The light of the moon is the time for planting crops which grow above ground; the dark of the moon is best for rootcrop planting. The dark of the moon is also a time for nefarious deeds (Canaanites, Hindus, Jews, Teutons, Moroccans, etc.); but the lucky rabbit's foot is taken in the dark of the moon. The best of these charms is the left hind foot of a rabbit killed in the dark of the moon in a graveyard by a cross-eyed person.

The waxing or waning moon has its sympathetic influence on sublunary affairs: shingles, for example, laid in the waxing of the moon tend to swell as the moon grows. But whereas in Devonshire hair should be cut in the waning moon, in Worcestershire it should be cut in the waxing moon. The new moon is the most powerful phase of the waxing moon: it has further to grow. The Gold Coast inhabitant who sees the new moon blows ashes towards it and says, "I saw you before you saw me"; if he doesn't, as the moon grows to the full his strength will fade. When the new moon is seen, one should turn all the money in his pockets, or show newly minted coins to the moon; then, as the moon grows, the money will increase. Just as is true of the moment of the New Year, whatever one is doing when he first sees the new moon he will do for the remainder of the month. Wishes on seeing the new moon will come true if they are not told, or if one kisses the nearest person. Pointing at the new moon brings trouble, as does seeing the moon, in any phase, over the shoulder. While in Europe generally the bad luck seems to come from seeing the moon over the left shoulder, elsewhere the right shoulder is the unlucky one. Ominous too is a halo around the moon. This means rain; if there are stars in the ring, it will rain for as many days as there are stars, or the rain will come after that number of days. If there are more than five stars in the ring, the weather will be cold; if fewer, it will be warm. Elsewhere, the number of stars within the ring indicates the number of friends who will shortly die.

Sleeping in the light of the moon is bad. In Egypt, Greece, Armenia, Brazil, and many other places, sleeping with the moonlight on one's eyes weakens the sight. In Europe generally sleeping in the moonlight often results in insanity; the lunatic is so called because he is moon-mad. Throughout the world, the moon is an evil principle or body as compared with the good sun.

Whether the moon is silver—the alchemists called silver the moon and used the crescent as its symbol— or whether it is made of green cheese, whether it is the abode of the souls of the dead or the resting place of everything wasted or broken on earth, it is often personified as a god or goddess. The Semitic moon god Sin dwelt atop Mt. Sinai, and some students believe he was identified with Yahweh as the law-giver of the Israelites. The Egyptian Thoth was god of the moon; therefore he was god of measurements, hence god of learning, wisdom, and writing. The Greek goddesses Selene, Artemis, and Hecate were all identified with the moon. The Hindu god Soma, personification of the divine drink, was later identified with the moon. In the *Rig-Veda* (x, lxxxv, 5), the moon's phases are explained as the result of the drinking of amṛita (soma) by the gods, its depletion and replenishment.

Though the moon is often feminine and the moon deity is a goddess, often the moon god is male and the moon is a man (see for example the *Sun Sister, Moon Brother* tale of the North American Indians). The "man in the moon" is the English locution for the marks on the moon, yet generally in English the moon is considered a "she." In Rumanian tales, the moon is the sun's sister. But the sun lusts for her, and she hides when he rises and comes out only when he sets. In Greenland, the moon is male, and no woman dares to sleep on her back without taking the precaution of rubbing some spittle on her belly. The moon was a man, according to Bushman mythology, who made the sun angry. The sun kept slicing at the man with his knife-like rays until only a little of the man was left. Then the man's entreaties caused the sun to relent, and the moon grew again. But every time the sun sees the moon full and round he begins to cut him up again.

The moon is prominent in folktale, for example as a quest-goal in märchen. It is this for instance in *The Twelve Ravens* (Type 451) and often in variants of *The Search for the Lost Husband* (Type 425). Noodles often get confused by the moon. One, who had just come to town, was heard saying the prayer to the old moon as if it were the new moon. When they asked him why, he said he hadn't seen this moon before; he was a newcomer in town, and surely each town had its own moon. See AVYA; *Chinese calendar* in CHINESE FOLKLORE; DRINKING THE MOON; HATHOR; IO; MAN IN THE MOON; NOODLE STORIES.

Many American Indian languages lack specific words for moon and sun but have instead a noncommittal word meaning luminary, to which is prefixed "night" or "nighttime" and "day" or "daytime" for the moon and sun (compare, for example, the Delaware Indian *ni·'pai gi'cux*, night luminary, moon, and *gi'ckweni·i gi'cux*, day luminary, sun). Personification or deification of the sun and moon is usual and the two appear as actors in several American Indian myths. The moon and the stars are the Night People or Fathers of Taos pueblo, and are more prominent in the pantheons of the northeastern Pueblo Indians than in the western ones. Moon-Old-Man is distinctly a personage at Taos, Isleta, Jemez, and Tewa. At Zuñi Moon's sex is reversed; she is Sun's younger sister or, in prayer, Moon Our Mother. Among the Apache of the Southwest, the Jicarilla are not consistent as to Moon's sex; they say that Moon is female, in connection with the menstrual cycle, but in a ceremonial race Moon is represented as a male, and Moon is also associated with Water, the father of one of the culture heroes. The Lipan Apache represent sun and moon as human beings who led the people after the emergence; the sun is a man, the moon is Changing Woman, an important Apache female deity. In the related mythology of the Navaho, Klehanoai, a male deity, is the Moon Carrier and husband of White-Shell Woman. Among the Cora Indians of northern Mexico the moon, like the sun, is a god, and is both man and woman. The Chehalis of the Pacific Northwest have Moon as their Changer, a male Creator-Transformer; the Tillamook, however, while assigning to Moon the same role, make her a female changer.

Origin tales accounting for the moon are prevalent; perhaps the most striking one is that of Sun Sister and Moon Brother. This tale is known to nearly all Eskimo groups, to several Indian groups in the Mackenzie area, and to the Caddo of the Southeast, and related forms of the tale have been reported from Central and South America. Briefly, the tale is concerned with an unknown suitor who visits a woman secretly at night; the latter blackens her hands and smears the man's back. Later she discovers her suitor is her brother. She flees and her lover pursues her; both rise to the sky where she becomes the sun, he the moon. Other origin stories for the sun and moon are incidental elements, or a series of elements, in the tribal origin myths. The Maidu Indians of California, for example, credit Earth-Initiate, their creator, with having caused his sister the sun and his brother the moon first to rise. The Jicarilla Apache say that both the Sun and Moon were obtained by Holy Boy, as minute objects. They were released and brought to life by White Hactcin and Black Hactcin (see HACTCIN) while Holy Boy and Red Boy threw pollen. Both luminaries traveled from north to south at first. False claims on the part of the shamans that they had made the sun and moon resulted in eclipses of the two bodies, and their disappearance. With the help of the animals the Hactcin caused Sun and Moon to be brought down again; Sun was made into a Taos Indian boy, and Moon into a Jicarilla Apache girl. The two married and were sent back to the north to travel, Sun in the lead, from north to south. Later the Holy Ones, White Hactcin, Black Hactcin, Holy Boy and Red Boy changed this so the Sun and Moon traveled from east to west; the Holy Ones also directed Sun to go in the daytime and Moon at night. [EWV]

In the cosmogony of the Taulipang (Guiana) and Ona Indians (Tierra del Fuego), the moon is personified and its phases are explained by the changes in his bodily appearance. The moon alternately loses and gains weight. According to the Bakairi (Central Brazil) the phases of the moon are caused by various animals which gnaw at it and finally swallow it.

The spots on the moon are often explained by the South American Indians as one of the consequences of incestuous relations between the Moon and his sister (generally identified with the Sun). The woman, not knowing who her mysterious lover was, marked him with genipa, ashes, or menstrual blood. The Moon, out of shame and fear, went to the sky (Taulipang, Cuna, Okaina, Conibo, Witoto, Zaparo, Shipaya, Guarani, Indians of the Yamunda and of Tumupasa).

According to the Yahgan and the Ona, the spots on the Moon are the marks of the beating received by the Moon when the Sun discovered the secrets of the initiation rites. The Mataco and Chamacoco interpret the spots as the intestines of Moon which were bared when Moon was torn to pieces by ducks or rheas which he had tried to catch. To the Yuracare, the spots on the Moon are a four-eyed jaguar which escaped to the sky. [AM]

moonstone A whitish, cloudy, feldspar gemstone which is said to contain an image of the moon. The Hindus believe that this stone was formed by the congealing of the moon's rays. A moonstone owned by Pope Leo X (1475–1521) was said to wax and wane in brilliance with the moon. Held in the mouth at the full of the moon it will reveal the future. It is well thought of by lovers since it evokes the tender passion. It brings luck to its owner, cures epilepsy, nervousness, has a cooling effect, and makes trees fruitful. In some places it is con-

sidered unlucky to wear a moonstone unless it is your birthstone. The fabulous moonstone stolen from the idol in Wilkie Collins' *The Moonstone,* brought disaster to every unrightful owner.

moon tree The moon tree of Japanese folklore (*katsura*) is a kind of laurel. It grows on the moon and the spots on the moon are visible patches of these trees. When the moon seems especially bright, the people say that the *katsura* is turning red (or yellow).

Chinese mythology often associates the moon tree with the cassia, the tree of immortality, which grows on the moon. A certain Wu Kang was banished to the moon in punishment for a crime and condemned to cut down the cassia. He keeps trying, but the marvelous fragrant tree springs up as fast as it is cut. The fruit of this tree confers on those who eat it immortality and transparency.

Alexander described to Aristotle two marvelous trees of India, which spoke Indian and Greek; one was male, the other female. These were the trees of the sun and the moon, which would prophesy good or evil for the questioner. Alexander tested this fact, observing all the rules for approach: chastity, the putting off of rings, garments, and shoes. At sunrise the sun tree spoke and told Alexander that he would never return home; at moonrise the moon tree said that he would die at Babylon. A third question brought the answer that he would die by poison, but the name of the poisoner was not revealed. Marco Polo also came across and mentioned these two marvelous trees.

moorooboyn A dance ceremony which forms part of the boys' initiation rites of Australian aborigines, specifically of the tribes of Broome. It consists of the dancing by men of the *wallang-arree* or double circle, alternate rows going in opposite directions. To high chanting the men raise their knees and bring the foot forcibly on the ground. At the end the boy initiate (*balgai*) is taken out of the center of the circle for a respite, and then brought back in on the shoulders of his *yagoo*, or special guardian. [GPK]

moralizing tales Tales which have a moral for their point, as exemplified in the animal fables of Europe and India, are not abundant in American Indian mythology. Where they do occur, close similarity to European tales demonstrates that they are of non-Indian origin. Examples of Indian borrowings are Æsop's *The Fox and the Crane* (told among the Yuchi and Biloxi of the Southeast), LaFontaine's *The Cock and the Fox* (Wyandot, Great Lakes region), Æsop's *The Fox and the Crow* (Ojibwa, Great Lakes), *The Ant and the Grasshopper* (Biloxi, Shuswap of Plateau, Wyandot). For detailed references to the above see Stith Thompson, *European Tales among the North American Indians* (Colorado College Publications, General Series # 100 and 101, Colorado Springs, April–May 1919).

Of possible native origin, however, is a collection of transparent animal fables recorded by Benedict at Cochiti pueblo (Ruth Benedict, *Tales of the Cochiti Indians, BAEB* 98, Washington, 1931, pp. 236–238) which, according to Benedict, are "a type of story rarely found among the American Indians. In Cochiti it is characteristic of these tales that the moral is not given explicitly, but when informants are questioned they phrase the underlying idea of the story in terms of their own cultural life" (p. 236). None of these Cochiti animal fables seem to have European prototypes, but the fact that they are found in the Southwest, where many European tales have been borrowed by the Indians, raises some doubt as to their being purely native forms.

If few native tales exist that are told primarily to point a moral, it does not follow that American Indian tale material is not used for moralizing purposes. Over the continent trickster tales are told chiefly to amuse, but generally they also have a moral import—as, for example, the "trotting Coyote" stories of the Navaho, told to impress children that they must not act as Coyote acted. Tales of the abuse of power in the Plains and Eastern Woodlands emphasize that supernatural power, if used too often, will be lost; the theme occurs not only in trickster, but in more serious tales. Another theme, that an individual should not make immodest demands on the supernaturals, is also widespread; supplicants who ask for eternal life are turned into stone or cedar trees. In general, as Boas has pointed out, American Indian tales end in the triumph of the good and the downfall of evil characters, which makes all of them in a sense moralistic; although the tale plot may not have a moral for its point, the effect gained is a moralistic one. [EWV]

For the moralizing tale of European folklore, see *Edifying stories and exempla* in EUROPEAN FOLKLORE. For the moral in African Negro folktale see sections *Explanatory elements*, and *Proverbs*, and *Folklore in education* in AFRICAN AND NEW WORLD NEGRO FOLKLORE. See BOASTFUL DEERSLAYER; DISAPPOINTED FISHER; FABLE; KIND AND UNKIND.

Mordred or Modred The notorious traitor, who at a battle in Cornwall wounded Arthur, his uncle or father, but was himself killed. The earliest mention is in the *Annales Cambriae* (c. 955) under the date 537 (?): "The Battle of Camlann, in which Arthur and Medraut fell." In *The Dream of Rhonabwy* (13th century) a certain Iddawg is called the embroiler of Britain because he kindled strife between Arthur and his foster son and nephew Medrawd before the battle of Camlan. In the *Red Book of Hergest* (14th century) we have two triads, one of which gives an account of the treachery of Medrawt based on Geoffrey of Monmouth's *History of the Kings of Britain*, and another which tells of Medrawt's raid on Arthur's court at Kelliwic in Cornwall, when he consumed all the food and drink, dragged Gwenhwyvar from her throne, and struck her. This last seems to be a Cornish tradition, and it is probably from Cornwall that Geoffrey derived his story of Modred's treachery and the last battle, for the form of the traitor's name is Cornish. Geoffrey tells how when Arthur left Britain for his campaign against the Romans, he placed his kingdom in charge of his nephew Modred and Guenevere. During his absence Modred seized the throne and made the queen his wife. Arthur returned, defeated the traitor, and drove him into Cornwall. There at the river Camblan he killed Modred, but was himself wounded and borne away to Avalon. Practically all accounts of Mordred's treachery and the last battle in the chronicles and romances derive more or less directly from Geoffrey's book. In the French Vulgate cycle (1200–1230) there are several references, however, to Arthur's begetting Mordred upon his sister, the wife of Lot, though their relationship to each other was unknown.

This story appears also in the Huth *Merlin* together with an additional theme. Merlin reproached Arthur for his incest and warned that his offspring would bring disaster. When the time arrived, May 1, when the infant was due to be born, Arthur, like another Herod, planned to get rid of all the newly born sons of nobles and sent for them. But Modred was shipwrecked en route and was found floating in his cradle by a fisherman, who saw by his silk swaddling clothes that he was of high birth and turned him over to a noble to rear. A very similar story, without the incest motif, is told of Gawain. In Welsh we have two tales of wonder children born on May Eve, Gwri and Taliesin; the former is discovered wrapped in a mantle of satin, the latter floating in a fisherman's weir. We also have striking Irish parallels. Fiachu Fermara was begotten by Angus on his daughter when drunk, was set adrift on the sea in a royal robe, and was rescued by a fisherman. Eochaid Bres was the offspring of the son and daughter of Delbaeth, and when grown up he fought incognito with his father. Though Bruce derived the incestuous birth of Modred from the strange legend of Pope Gregory, it is far more likely to be a genuine Celtic tradition.

Bibliography: Bruce, J. D., "Mordred's Incestuous Birth," in *Medieval Studies in Honor of G. Schoepperle Loomis* (New York, Paris, 1927), pp. 197–208. Loomis. Roger S., *Celtic Myth and Arthurian Romance* (New York, 1927), pp. 330–41. [RSL]

Mordvins A Finno-Ugric people, in 1920 about 1,500,000, dispersed between Russian and Tatarian settlements in the districts of Penza, Samara, Simbirsk, Saratov, Nijni Novgorod, Tambov, etc. They are divided into Moksha and Erza Mordvins. The belief in a supreme procreator god, living in the sky, is very clear among the Mordvins (see SHKI-PAS in SHKA-BAVAS). Mother Earth, *Mastor-ava* or *Mastor-pas*, is one of the most revered deities, especially among the Erza Mordvins. The songs mention that the hero "first bowed before the sky god, and then before Mother Earth." The Sun and Moon are also venerated. The thunder god of the Erza Mordvins, *Purgine-pas* or *Pirgene*, is also an old god; the name is common with the Lithuanian *Perkūnas*. There are many protecting spirits associated with the word for mother (see AVA). A curious custom among the Mordvins is the observance of the "harvest of the dead." The relatives of the deceased reap the portion of the dead man, each of them cutting only a few straws. The chief part is played by the widow, who all day wears a belt of straw made by herself. Cattle are slaughtered for this feast. A very important work of Mordvinian folklore texts was published by H. Paasonen and P. Ravila: *Mordvinische Volksdichtung*, 4 Vols., Helsinki, 1938–47. MSFO 77.81.84.91. For mythology see John Abercromby, "The Beliefs and Religious Ceremonies of the Mordvins," *The Folk-Lore Journal* VII, 1889, pp. 65–135. [JB]

Morgan le Fay A protean character in the Arthurian romances, who is related to goddesses of Irish and Welsh mythology on the one hand, and to mermaids of Welsh and Breton folklore on the other. She first appears in Geoffrey of Monmouth's *Vita Merlini* (1150), dwelling in an island paradise with her eight sisters and employing her skill in herbs on the wounded Arthur. Chrétien de Troyes (1160–80) also knows her medical powers, makes her Arthur's sister, and tells us that she was the mistress of Guingamor, lord of Avalon. In later romances she is generally a malign and repulsive enchantress, the wife of King Urien and mother of Ivain. She is constantly making assaults on the fidelity of Lancelot or the virtue of other knights. *Gawain and the Green Knight* depicts her as a wrinkled crone, Malory as plotting the death of her brother Arthur.

Evidence is gradually accumulating that Morgan's inconsistencies are due partly to the composite character of the tradition she inherited, partly to the pejorative tendency in the attitude of the Christian world towards the pagan deities. Three medieval texts speak of her as a goddess, and it is now possible to trace her on the one side to the Irish Morrigan, and on the other side through the Welsh Modron (who was the mother of Owein by Urien) back to Celtic Matrona, a deity who was worshipped from northern Italy to the mouth of the Rhine and who gave her name to the River Marne. Morgan combines in her person the manifold attributes of the Gallic river goddess and of the Goidelic valkyrie. Thus, though unnamed, she may be detected with certainty in the charming water nymphs, the mistresses of Guingamor, Lanval, and Desiré, and also in the chief of those bellicose females, the nine sorceresses of Caer Loyw, who trained Peredur in arms and whom he later slew.

Morgan is also related to the many, frequently nameless lake fairies of modern Welsh folklore. They lie in wait for their human lovers, endow them with wealth, impose on them a tabu, and abandon them when the tabu is broken, just as do the faery mistresses of Lanval and Desiré. The most famous of these Welsh water fays, the Lady of Little Van Lake, was identified by Rhys as Modron, and her preternatural knowledge of medicinal herbs links her with Morgan. The fay in her sinister aspect may be recognized in the Gwrach y Rhibyn, a hideous hag dressed in black, who sometimes appeared beside a piece of water, splashing it with her hands, or who dipped herself up and down in a pool.

Morgan is also to be recognized in the mermaids of the Breton coast and islands, who go under the name of Morgan, Morganes, Mari Morgan. They retain not only the name of the medieval faery queen, but also her amorous propensities, for they rise to the surface of the sea and entice fishermen into their arms. According to some tales, the embrace is fatal; according to others, their lovers live long and happily in their submarine palaces.

Not only was Morgan known to the Breton peasants and sailors of yesterday, but back in the 12th century professional Breton story-tellers carried her legend to Sicily. There her reputation as an enchantress survived so that in the 19th century the mirages in the Straits of Messina were popularly attributed to "la Fata Morgana." See ARTHUR; CELTIC FOLKLORE.

Bibliography: L. A. Paton, *Studies in the Fairy Mythology of Arthurian Romance,* Radcliffe College Monographs (1903). R. S. Loomis, "Morgain la Fée and the Celtic Goddesses," *Speculum* XX (1945), p. 183.

ROGER S. LOOMIS

morisca Literally, Moorish dance: a ritualistic form of battle mime widespread throughout Europe (except for Scandinavia), whole-heartedly adopted in Central America and the Caribbean. In the Spanish version, commonly known as *Los Moros y Cristianos* two factions dance through a drama (often with dialog) of battle between the evil Moors and good Christians, with ultimate victory for the Christians. This element of battle characterizes most, but not all, *morisca* forms. The battle mime is generally enacted during Catholic festivals, notably at Carnival time, on Corpus Christi, and San Juan's Day. Versions most closely recognizable by their names are the Portuguese *mouriscada*, English Morris, and Dalmatian *moreška*. Other dances just as truly moriscas, despite the names, are the Mallorcan *cossiers*, Austrian *Perchten*, Rumanian *calušari*, the *Santiagos* and *negritos* of Mexico. Sword dances and derived stick dances are closely related, as also the Basque *mascaradas* and English mummers. In the *matachini* forms, as also in the related *seises* of Toledo, the battle mime has been absorbed in longways opposition, and among Mexican Indians the sword has been replaced by a feathered trident. It is striking how with loss of symbolism and drama the formations and steps have increased in complexity, as the Mexican *moros* in contrast with the *matachini*. In New Mexico, however, the Pueblo *matachines* includes the killing and resurrection of a bull, reminiscent of the former killing of the dragon by St. George in the English Morris.

At one time these *matachins,* known to us from the 16th century, enacted a battle mime. On the other hand, the *morisque* and the German *Moriskentanz* were frequently solo exhibitions, grotesqueries which were introduced in court entertainments and ballet-mascarades. Almost consistently their paraphernalia consists of a high ornate crown, helmet or plumed hat, breeches, bells, ribbons, and the battle emblem—sword, staff, trident, kerchief. Dramatic characters wear masks; some *matachini* wear disguising bandanas; other *moriscos* use no facial disguise. But originally it was a dance of disguise.

The name points to original face blackening, which, contrary to former theories of Moorish origin, is now connected with the sooty faces of pagan rituals. The battle mime is now traced to vegetation symbolism (a battle of the seasons) and the various associated characters and elements, as the man-woman and hobbyhorse, sacrifice and resurrection, the leaping and interweaving, are interpreted as fertility symbols. These dances are always held in the budding season, and often conclude with Maypole winding. Some versions are still the property of closed brotherhoods, as the *calušari* and the Yaqui *matachini*.

With the Christianization of Europe, this symbolism had to be reinterpreted in a form which was at hand in the various invasions from the East—the Moorish conquest of Spain and the Turkish occupation of the Balkans and Hungary. Here the "Moors" are often called Turks, as in the Hungarian *törökös tánc*, and "Turks" danced in Nuremberg carnivals of the Middle Ages, alongside morris groups and *Schemen:* an association in a metamorphosed pagan celebration of two renamed groups and one aboriginal dance group all with the same purpose. These vestiges of pagan rites—*Schemen, Perchten*—corroborate the theory of Morisca origin in vegetation rites. See DANCE: FOLK AND PRIMITIVE. See bibliography in Gertrude P. Kurath, "Mexican Moriscas," *JAFL* 62:87–119, 1949. [GPK]

Moriscas: Symbolic Elements Compared

	Combat	Killing	Resurrection	Clown	Woman disguise	Animal	Mask or Black	Crown	Bells	Feathers
Europe										
Rumania						horse				
Caluşari	x	x	–	x	x	x	x	–	x	–
Portugal										
Mouriscada	x	x	x	x	–	x	x	x	x	x
Paulitos	x	–	–	–	x	–	–	x	–	–
Basque										
Ezpata Dantza	x	x	x	–	–	–	–	–	x	–
Spain										
Seises	x	–	–	–	x	–	–	x	x	x
Majorca						horse				
Cavallets	–	–	–	x	x	x	x	x	x	x
England						horse				
Morris	x	x	x	x	x	x	x	x	x	x
Mexico										
Guerrero,						horse				
Morelos,	x	x	–	x	–	x	x	x	–	x
Sierras										
Moros										
Guanajuato										
Apaches	x	x	–	x	x	–	x	x	x	x
Yaqui										
Matachini	–	–	–	x	x	–	–	x	–	x
Puebla										
Negros	–	x	–	x	x	x	x	x	–	x
Santiaguitos	–	–	–	x	x	–	–	x	–	x
Toreadores						bull				
mestizo	x	x	–	x	–	x	x	–	–	–
New Mexico						bull				
Matachin	x	x	x	x	x	x	x	x	x	x

Moriscas: Comparative Choreography

	Meet	Cross over	Figure 8	Advance retire	Cast off	Down center	Serpent	Corners	Hey	Maypole
Europe										
Mouriscada	x	x	–	x	x	leader	–	–	–	–
Paulitos	x	x	x	x	x	–	x	–	–	–
Ezpata Dantza	x	x	x	–	x	–	x	x	–	x
Seises	x	x	x	x	x	–	x	–	–	x
Morris	x	x	x	x	–	–	–	x	–	x
Matachin	x	x	–	–	–	–	–	x	–	–
Mexico										
Moros	x	x	–	–	x	–	–	–	–	–
Apaches	x	–	–	x	x	–	–	–	–	x
Matachini	x	x	x	x	x	leader	x	–	–	x
Negros										
Puebla	–	x	–	x	–	x	–	x	–	x
Santiaguitos	x	x	x	–	–	x	x	–	–	for two
Quetzales										
native	–	x	–	–	–	x	x	x	–	–

Mormo A lamia-like female monster with which ancient Greek mothers threatened their children: also called *Mormolyce* (perhaps banewolf or werewolf). The scholiast on Theocritus explains that she was a Læstrygonian queen who lost her own children and stole others' children in revenge. Compare LILITH.

morning star Any of the planets Jupiter, Mars, Saturn, Mercury, or especially Venus, when rising shortly before sunrise. Among North American Indians especially the morning star was of great importance and was widely symbolized by an equi-armed red cross. In Lithuanian folk song the morning and evening stars are mentioned together as servitors of the sun: the morning star kindles his morning light; the evening star prepares his bed. In Lettish folk song they are mentioned together as the sons of god. The people of ancient Palmyra in the Syrian desert (Greek-acculturated Semites of Arab origin) worshipped the planet Venus as both morning and evening star as a kind of dual deity (Arṣu and 'Azīzu), the compassionate gods. The Greek scholar, Bartholomew of Edessa, identified 'Azīzu, the morning aspect, as a "merciful god" of the Arabs before the time of Mohammed.

In Norse mythology, the morning star is identified as Orvandil's Toe. The story is that Orvandil, young son of the sorceress Groa, was taken by the frost giants. Thor rescued him, carrying him off in a basket. The child kept poking one bare toe through a hole in the basket; it got badly frozen and broke off. Thor tossed it into the sky, and there it glitters—the morning star. (Some say, however, that Orvandil's Toe lies permanently in Ursa Major, or Orion.) In Polynesian mythology the morning and evening stars are the eyes of Maui's two sons, which he placed in the sky. In the widespread cycle of quest stories occurs a Flemish tale about a man who set out to go to the morning star for answers to certain questions (H1282; Type 702). See LUCIFER.

☞ Anthropomorphized deity, or supernatural, usually benign, in the folklore and religion of nearly all North American Indian tribes. To cite only a few examples: Among the Crow Indians of the Plains, Morning Star is a kindly disposed supernatural, the father of Old Woman's Grandson in mythology and a being more likely to be invoked than any other, in the absence of a specific tutelary. The Skidi Pawnee represented the morning and evening stars as masculine and feminine beings, and connected them with the advent and perpetuation on earth of all living forms; a series of Skidi Pawnee ceremonies relative to the bringing of life and its increase began with the first thunder in the spring, culminated at the summer solstice in human sacrifice, and closed when the maize or "mother corn" was harvested. The Fox Indians consider Wâpananaṅãgwa, the morning star, as one of the big stars that are great manitus or supernatural beings. The morning star is the father of a Fox legendary hero, Wâpassaiya. In the Pueblos the stars have more supernatural significance for the Tanoans than for any other Pueblo groups, and Morning Star is definitely associated with war, being prayed to before fighting. At Taos offerings of cornmeal, eagle feathers, and pollen were given to Morning Star; it is believed that this star travels during the day and becomes the twilight or evening star. Kiowa peyote worshippers say that Morning Star heralds Peyote Woman's approach, at peyote meetings. The Cora of Mexico worship the Morning Star as a major deity; he is visualized as a youth armed with bow and arrow, who once shot the powerful sun at noonday because of the latter's intense heat. In the widespread North American Indian tale of the Star Husband the chief male character is sometimes identified either as the Evening or Morning Star. [EWV]

Moros y Cristianos Moors and Christians: a form of *Morisca*, of Spanish derivation, but now rare in Spain and extremely popular in central and eastern Mexico, during the great *carnavales* of Guerrero, Tlaxcala, Morelos, and especially in the Federal District. In the Sierras of Puebla and Veracruz the drama is featured along with others during the Corpus Christi celebrations, the most famous event being the *volador* fiesta at Papantla, Veracruz.

The regalia and dramatic procedure is like those of the *Santiagos*, but without this saintly horseman. The Moors are always distinguished by their turbans and crescents, otherwise varying their outfits according to the purses of the dancers: cotton kimonos, or silken capes. Their masks may represent stylized bearded Orientals or long-nosed comics. The Christians may be magnificent with visors, plume-crested morions, gaudy capes and breeches, and halberds, or in derby hats and wrinkled stockings with ludicrous pink masks. The play itself, too, varies from the mystical to the burlesque. In Matamoras de Izucar, Puebla, the two opposing groups enter with a solemn march, then launch into a realistic attack amid loud cries and bits of dialog, and end with the conquest of the Moors by the grace of God. In Puebla the combat frequently commences with a contest between the two *capitanes* or leaders with their long machetes, the two opposing parties leaping about in the background. Brandishing their weapons, they engage in a pitched battle, which may last for four or five hours. After the inevitable conquest of the Moors, the leader was formerly symbolically buried, as in the old-time *entierro del Moro* or *entierro del Rey del Mal Humor* of Spain. In Tecalpulco, Guerrero, the motions are as absurd as the costumes, consisting of wiggling of the feet, jerky hops and sword flourishing, pursuit of a tall, gaunt *embajador moro* (Moorish ambassador) by a diminutive *embajador cristiano*, with the inevitable dénouement. In the end the Moros kneel in submission and the Cristianos lock swords around their necks. The music may consist of a one-man flute and tabor, a fiddle and drum, or a band.

Despite the quaint native style of action and masking, the Spanish provenience is evident in the resemblance to the battles at Alcoy, Valencia, and Toledo. But the Moros of Michoacán are a unique development. Four of them, in fantastic Oriental, mirrored, befeathered turbans, spurred boots, beads and sequins galore, appear on horseback, dismount, then twostep through various formations: circles, cross-overs, dos-à-dos, etc.

The Moros y Cristianos, sometimes called *Moros y Españoles*, are related to the *Morisma*. See MORISCA; SANTIAGOS. [GPK]

Morpheus In Greek mythology, one of the sons of Hypnos, the god of sleep. Morpheus either gave shape to dreams or brought dreams of human figures. His brothers Icalus (or Phobetor, his name among men) and

Phantasus brought visions of animals and inanimate objects respectively.

Morrigan or **Morrigu** (Irish *mór-ríogan*, great queen). One of a group of three war goddesses of Old Irish mythology. In the triad of Morrigan, Neman, and Macha, the name of Badb often occurs in place of that of Morrigan, and for that reason Badb has frequently been identified with Morrigan. Almost as frequently, however, the name of Badb displaces one of the other two. And Morrigan is often used as a generic term to include all three. Robert Graves (*White Goddess*, New York, 1948, p. 306) says that "Ana, Badb, and Macha together are known as the Morrigan, or Great Queen." (See DANU.) The characteristics of the three are practically identical: the heads of warriors killed in the old battles were dedicated to one or the other of them; each of them appeared on the battlefield in the form of a raven or scald-crow; it was said of each that she ate the bodies of the slain, or that they feasted together (probably in their roles as scald-crows). And all three were transformers.

In the Mythological Cycle, Morrigan was the daughter of Ernmas, and either the wife or granddaughter of Nét, or the wife of Dagda. And she, with Badb, helped the Tuatha Dé Danann overcome the Fomorians in the Battle of Mag Tured.

Morrigan is prominent in the Cuchulain story. She was in love with Cuchulain and wooed him in the form of a young girl, after one of his most wonderful victories. Battle-weary, he repulsed her and thus incurred her antagonism. Time and again after that she made trouble for him in battle, in the form of a heifer, a water serpent, etc. She aided Ulster in the War for the Brown Bull, however, and later tried to save Cuchulain from his death. The night before his last fight she broke the pole of his chariot, as a sign to him not to go forth.

Morris The English version of the Moorish dance or *Morisca*. Occasionally the Morris is a solo jig, such as Greensleeves or Bacca Pipes, which is danced in and out among two crossed pipes (compare the Scottish SWORD DANCE). Usually the Morris is a longways performed by six men with accompanying traditional characters (Cotswold), or by ten (Lancashire). The figures vary as follows: 1) *Processional,* a progressive double serpentine of the two interweaving lines; 2) *Bean Setting,* a stick dance with obvious agricultural symbolism in the "dibbing" or floor thumping with the sticks and striking of partners' sticks; 3) *Stick Dances* (Constant Billy, Rigs o' Marlow, Shepherd's Hey) which involve a complex pattern of stick striking by partners, parallel, across, right, left, up, down; 4) *Handkerchief Dances* (Blue-eyed Stranger, Country Gardens) with manipulation of kerchiefs throughout the leaps and the formations; 5) *Corner Dances* (Trunkles, How d'ye Do, Laudnum Bunches), purely dances of diagonal cross-over formations; 6) *Morris Off,* a circular prelude to the exit.

A rude vigor characterizes the movements, the various leaps, called capers or springs, the various combinations of steps and hops in duple and triple time, the straight-kneed kicks, the cross-steps, side-steps, the straddles, arm swings, and climatic high jumps with shouts.

The formations include a great variety of longways figures: corners, cross-overs, *dos-à-dos,* various heys,

initial and terminal circling to left and right, sometimes a Maypole dance (see tabulation of MORISCAS).

The tunes were formerly played by a bagpipe or a wood pipe and tabor, called whittle and dub, nowadays commonly by a fiddle or accordion. The costume, formerly consisting of breeches, plumed hats, blackened faces, have now been replaced by white trousers, frilled shirts, and top-hats with feathers. The bell pads on the ankles have been retained.

The associated characters have retained much of their original identity, while changing their names. Bessy, the man-woman, was Maid Marian and, before that, Mother Eve. The hobbyhorse rider is descended from Robin Hood and, previously, St. George, the dragon-killer. A fool in medieval costume or tatters has always cavorted on the outskirts, formerly with a fox mask and perhaps a bladder on a stick. In some sections (Gloucestershire, Norfolk, Lancashire, Northumberland) a sword-bearer carries a cake which is offered. Not only is the Morris continued on Whitsunday in English villages, but urban folk-dance groups and May-Day pageants have featured it ever since its discovery by Cecil Sharp.

The ancient pyrrhic vegetation symbolism is evident not only in the characters, but in the formations and the dibbing. The associations are further described under MORISCAS; MUMMERS; SWORD DANCES. [GPK]

Moses The lawgiver of the Hebrews; leader of the Israelites through the desert from Egypt to Canaan. Moses is a typical folk and culture hero: he was saved from a massacre of children; he was found floating in a basket on the water; he was an unpromising hero, because as child and young man he stuttered; he spent years in exile and returned to lead his people in their hour of need, etc. Twice Moses ascended the mountain to obtain the tablets of the Law from God; the first time he destroyed the tablets at the sight of the molten calf, but finally Moses brought the Law to his people. Moses is credited with writing the Pentateuch, the first five books of the Old Testament. He is one of the great national heroes of the world and there is perhaps more folklore about Moses and his career than there is about any other Hebrew hero, excepting only Solomon. But, strangely enough, there is strong evidence that Moses was not an Israelite at all. Some students believe that he was actually a member of the royal family of the pharaoh Ikhnaton (Amenhotep IV), or a priest of the monotheistic religion founded by that king and destroyed at his death. Thus, Moses may be the introducer of the worship of one God to the Hebrews, and a tie between Egyptian religion and Christianity and other modern monotheistic religions may therefore exist. The name Moses seems to be Egyptian—compare the names of the pharaohs Thutmoses (Thotmes), Ahmoses (Ahmes), etc.—and may derive from an Egyptian word meaning child. The usual order of events in the folk hero's career is reversed in the story of Moses: here the hero is abandoned by the poor parents and reared by the princess. An attempt to provide Israelite parents for the hero may be suspected, just as in the customary sequence royal descent is provided for the commoner who becomes king. Of course, the whole subject is conjectural and, like the mass of lore about Moses, his career before and after the exodus, his death and burial in the mountain, can be only hinted at here. See AARON; AARON'S ROD.

mosquito A two-winged insect (family *Culicidæ*) having in the female a long proboscis capable of puncturing the skin and extracting blood. Malaria and yellow fever are transmitted by the bite of certain species. The Miskito Indians of northeastern Honduras and eastern Nicaragua were so named by early travelers and writers for the hordes of biting insects of that territory which are large enough and numerous enough to kill a man in one night. In the Sun and Moon stories of Chaco Indian mythology, Mosquito is powerful enough to kill Moon. Moon (seeking the same honors in Mosquito's house that had been offered to Sun) in his blundering way almost stepped on Mosquito; Mosquito bit him, and Moon died; but (in Chamacoco myth) was resuscitated by Sun.

A cannibal-monster story of North Pacific Coast and Plains Indians accounts for mosquitos as having originated from the ashes of the burnt monster's body (A2001). Rumanian etiological story says mosquitos were created from smoke from the devil's pipe. They also say if you want angels in the house, drive out the mosquitos, for angels cannot enter where mosquitos are.

There are a number of Filipino stories about Firefly being reproached for so carelessly carrying fire; he explains, however, that he needs a light (or fire) to protect himself from the sharp dagger of Mosquito. Mosquito is jailed for carrying the dagger, and in jail loses his voice. This explains why the male mosquito is silent. In another version Mosquito arrives with a horde of his relatives and bites the face of the judge (a small land-crab), who runs into his hole followed by clouds of mosquitos. Mosquitos can still be seen humming around his door. In still another version the judge condemns Mosquito never to bite again. Mosquito explains that he *has* to bite now and then; but the judge makes no compromise. Mosquito then lights on the judge's forehead and jabs him. The judge grabs his mallet, smashes Mosquito, knocks himself out.

Mosquitos bite worst just before a rain, according to Newfoundland and Labrador lore. Hold your breath when a mosquito lights on you, is quite general folk advice; he cannot get away as long as you hold your breath, or cannot pull his stinger out until you do and will therefore die. See ALDER.

mother goddess The goddess of birth, fertility, sexual union, and the entire complex of birth and growth, plant, animal, and human. The mother goddess is found in many pantheons all over the world, sometimes limited in function, sometimes with such width of province that she may be considered a sole deity. In fact, some students claim a Stone Age monotheism with the goddess of fecundity as the only divinity to whom worship was due. Often the mother goddess is chthonic, i.e. an earth deity, from whom all growing things come. The Great Mother of the Mediterranean region, Cybele, influenced and modified the concept of other mother goddesses of the area—Ishtar, Aphrodite, etc.—so that the various fertility goddesses of the Mediterranean and the Near East resemble one another strongly. See COMMON MOTHER; CYBELE; EARTH; GREAT MOTHER; MOTHERS; MOTHER WORSHIP.

Mother Goose The anonymity of children's oral tradition rimes was bound to tempt editors and compilers to allege pseudonymous authorship of their collections, with the result that the various "garlands," "melodies," "pretty" books, and other anthologies were rather transparently and whimsically attributed to fictitious characters like Peter Puzzlewit, Tom Thumb, and Gammer Gurton.

Of all these innocent pseudepigrapha the oldest, most popular, and still surviving compilation is that attributed to Mother Goose. Modern American "Mother Goose Books" whose varieties are legion and sales enormous contain as many as 700 rimes, jingles, riddles, and tongue twisters for juveniles, but the earlier American editions were much smaller in format and had fifty or sixty rimes, usually one to a page under a rude woodcut.

A persistent legend circulates in Boston, Mass., and vicinity affirming that Mother Goose was an actual person living in that city in the early 18th century. Her name is variously given as Elizabeth Goose, or Vergoose, or Verboose, and she is said to have sung the old nursery rimes to her little grandson, whose father, Thomas Fleet, is supposed to have copied them down and published them in 1719, as *Songs for the Nursery; or, Mother Goose's Melodies.* Unfortunately for this theory of the origin of the famous rimes, and in spite of the fact that the anserine lady is allegedly interred in the Old Granary Burying Ground just off Washington Street near Brimstone Corner, she cannot be the answer to the children's query: "Who was Mother Goose?"

For not only has no copy of, or reference to, this book of Thomas Fleet's ever been found (and one can imagine the exhaustive searches that have been made), but also we know that Mother Goose was well known in France as Mère L'Oye in the 17th century, and came to America from that country, via England.

In 1697 Charles Perrault published in France a book of fairy tales entitled *Histoires ou Contes du Tems Passé, avec des Moralités.* It contained ten stories, including those familiar to us as *Puss in Boots, Cinderella, Red Riding Hood,* and *Hop o' My Thumb.* The frontispiece showed a picture of an old woman spinning and telling stories to children and a cat, while a placard announced, evidently as a sort of subtitle for the book: *Contes de ma mère l'oye.* Now Mother Goose already had a reputation among French peasants and even in the court as a sort of mythical fairy birdmother who told marvelous yarns to children. In Loret's *La Muse Historique* (1650) appears the line: "Comme un conte de la Mère l'Oye," which may have been the source of Perrault's famous subtitle. The latter seems to have been somewhat embarrassed about this charming little collection of tales, apparently fearing to cheapen his literary reputation by such trifles, for he sought out another publisher than the one he commonly used, and also issued the book in the name of his young son, Perrault d'Armancour.

The tales themselves already had a long history, in both oral and written tradition, many of them appearing in an earlier (1637) Italian collection, the *Pentamerone*, by Giambattista Basile, while Perrault's "Le Maistre Chat, ou le Chat Botté" reveals its descent from one of Giovanni Francesco Straparola's 73 folktales in his *Tredici piacevoli notti* (Facetious Nights) (Venice, 1550,

1554), a perfect mine of popular yarns, as Shakespeare and Molière so well knew.

Some researchers have attempted to trace the origin of the Mother Goose idea to 8th century Queen Goosefoot, or Berte aus grans pies, the mother of Charlemagne, for she was regarded as the children's patroness, but the connection is tenuous.

Perrault's book was translated about 1729 into English as *Mother Goose's Fairy Tales,* but the name was first connected with children's rimes a generation later when a friend of Goldsmith, John Newbery, published in 1760 the first real edition of Mother Goose as we know it, *Mother Goose's Melody,* borrowing Perrault's pseudonym.

In 1785 or 1786 appeared the first American edition, published by Isaiah Thomas in Worcester, Mass., entitled *Mother Goose's Melody: or, Sonnets for the Cradle.* The second Worcester edition, 1794, exists in the earliest known perfect copy, republished in facsimile by Frederic G. Melcher in 1945.

Thomas's book contained 52 nursery rimes, including such perennial favorites as "Cross Patch, draw the Latch," "Little Tom Tucker," "High diddle, diddle," and "Jack and Gill." Thomas also had an appendix or Part Two, "Containing the Lullabies of Shakespear," selected songs from the plays, several of which seem to us today rather lusty for lullabies.

The Newbery rimes were soon greatly expanded, as other nursery favorites were included, until our current Mother Goose books are veritable libraries of popular juvenile verse.　　　　　　　　　CHARLES FRANCIS POTTER

Mothering cake One of a series of cakes traditionally eaten on various Sundays in Lent. Other such cakes are called Simnel and Whirlin cakes. In England, in earlier days, it was customary to observe certain ceremonies on Mid-Lent Sunday. One was to visit the Mother-Church and make offerings at the high altar. This custom became one of visiting parents on that day, the fourth Sunday in Lent. In the 18th century all English servants and apprentices visited their mothers on Mid-Lent or Mothering Sunday and brought them a present of money or of some pleasant eatable. Sometimes the visitors received furmety, a wheat boiled in milk and spiced. A Simnel cake was another suitable present to bring one's mother. On the Isle of Ely, for the fifth Sunday in Lent— Whirlin Sunday—cakes known as Whirlin Cakes were made by nearly every family.

Mothers, Mother The personification of various deities, of the forces of the universe, of the earth, and of many plants, minerals, etc., in or on the earth as relatives (Grandfathers, Fathers, Grandmothers, Mothers, sisters, brothers) is common practice in North American Indian prayers, myths, etc. In many tribes relationship terms are generally used in direct address or in reference to the various personifications mentioned above; this conforms to the practice, also quite prevalent, of human beings using relationship terms to or for each other more frequently than they use personal names.

The most widely recognized Mother in North America is Earth Mother. Corn Mother comes next, but Corn or Maize is not always visualized as a mother; among the Iroquois she is one of a trio of sisters (Corn, Beans, and Squash) and in some of the pueblos the Corn Maidens figure in several myths. Earth, however, is always Mother;

the Apache, for example, state explicitly that the earth is a woman lying with her head to the north, her feet to the south.

In the Keresan pueblos of the Southwest, Iyatiku, or Maize Mother, is of paramount importance in the pantheon. Among the Delaware Indians of the eastern seaboard the sea, and bodies of water, running water, and corn and earth are addressed as Mother, but water as "our Grandfather."

Two widely distributed myths have attached themselves to the Corn Mother. One concerns the origin of corn, who was once a beautiful woman; this is told among the eastern tribes especially. The other concerns the violation, disappearance, and reappearance of Corn, a myth known in both the Eastern Woodlands and the Southwest. [EWV]

mother-worship, Mariology Reverence for motherhood has been expressed in many forms in both mythology and folklore, reflecting religious beliefs on the one hand and human affection on the other.

The Great Mother religions probably existed early in man's prehistory, for primitive images of mother goddesses are found in very old remains. The eastern Mediterranean countries, both north and south, were evidently the locale of a cult of Great Mother worship which has left its indelible mark on the religions of that region ever since.

Isis, a very ancient Egyptian deity, was the goddess of fecundity, the counterpart of the Roman Ceres and the Greek Demeter—all three of them evidently local versions or atavistic survivals of the original Mediterranean Mother Goddess. When this Great Mother was thought of as identified with the bountiful fecund earth, she might be known as Gæa or Ge (Greek) or Tellus (Roman). The Gæa or Earth Mother cult was widespread and was most powerful at Olympia and Delphi. When the sexual aspect of the Great Mother was emphasized, she was known variously as Cybele, Rhea Cybele, Agdistis, or Dindymene, and was worshipped in Phrygia and western Asia with wild orgiastic rites. In Greece, Cybele was identified with Rhea, and when her worship was brought to Rome in 204 B.C. she became identified with Ops (Plenty), the mother of Jupiter, as Cybele-Rhea was the mother of Zeus. Thus the Great Mother evolved through the centuries into the Christian Mother of God.

The eastern Mediterranean Great Mother influence was bound to continue to modify all religions in that and nearby areas by acculturation. In North Africa in the late 4th century the Cybele influence was flourishing, according to the testimony of St. Augustine in *De Civitate Dei* (ii, 4): "I took pleasure in the shameful games which were celebrated in honor of gods and goddesses, of the virgin Collestis, and Berecynthia (Cybele), the mother of all the gods."

All this mother emphasis influenced Christianity itself. The New Testament and the very early church had little to say about and little recognition of any place of importance for the mother of Jesus. But the cult of the virgin and the cult of the mother of god were both too deep in the life of the people to permit Mary to remain in comparative obscurity.

The Roman Catholic church draws careful distinctions between Mariology and Mariolatry. Attwater's *Catholic*

Dictionary, 1941, defines Mariology as "The study of the Blessed Virgin Mary and the body of theology, history, speculation, etc., concerning her, particularly her relationship with the Incarnation and the Redemption." The same book defines Mariolatry as "Idolatrous worship of the Blessed Virgin Mary, with which Catholics have been, and by the ignorant still are, frequently charged. 'It is forbidden to give divine honor or worship to the angels and saints (of which Mary is one) for this belongs to God alone . . . we should pay them an inferior honor or worship . . .' The Penny Catechism."

It is further explained that Mary occupies a special place between the saints and angels on the one hand, to whom *dulia* (reverence and homage) is paid, and God on the other, to whom *latria* (adoration and worship) is given. Mary has *hyperdulia* (special honor) paid to her, because she is the Mother of God and is "holier and nobler than any angel or saint."

As far as folklore is concerned, and without venturing into theology, Mariology can be classified as the existing lore of legends, miracle cycles, and folk stories about Mary, the Mother of Jesus. This lore is vast in its extent and still growing. It was in part incorporated in the canonical gospels, and was expanded and elaborated in the apocryphal gospels, acts, and epistles, in Coptic, Armenian, Syriac, and Eastern sacred literature generally, and in medieval contes, legends, songs, and church-steps miracle and mystery plays. It has grown in modern times, due to such books as Liguori's *La Glorie di Maria* (1750) and by the influence of various Marist orders and societies. See VIRGIN MARY. [CFP]

Motho and **Mungo** Two sisters, heroines of many Indian folktales: literally, the grains vetch and pulse. [MWS]

motif In folklore the term used to designate any one of the parts into which an item of folklore can be analyzed. In folk art there are motifs of design, forms which are repeated or combined with other forms in characteristic fashion. There are similarly recurring patterns which may be identified in folk music and folk song. The area in which motifs have been most studied and most carefully analyzed, however, is that of folk narratives such as folktales, legends, ballads, and myths.

Narrative motifs sometimes consist of very simple concepts which continually find their place in traditional tales. These may be unusual creatures like fairies, witches, dragons, ogres, cruel stepmothers, talking animals, or the like. They may consist of marvelous worlds or of lands in which magic is always powerful, of all kinds of magic objects and unusual physical phenomena. A motif may also be essentially a short and simple story in itself, an occurrence that is sufficiently striking or amusing to appeal to an audience of listeners.

While the term motif is used very loosely to include any of the elements going into a traditional tale, it must be remembered that in order to become a real part of tradition an element must have something about it that will make people remember and repeat it. It must be more than commonplace. A mother as such is not a motif. A cruel mother becomes one because she is at least thought to be unusual. The ordinary processes of life are not motifs. To say that "John dressed and walked to town" is not to give a single motif worth remembering; but to say that the hero put on his cap of invisibility, mounted his magic carpet, and went to the land east of the sun and west of the moon is to include at least four motifs—the cap, the carpet, the magic air journey, and the marvelous land. Each of these motifs lives on because it has been found satisfying by generations of tale-tellers.

For the student of tales whose interest extends to various cultures in all parts of the world, the investigation of motifs is very important in showing international relationships. Sometimes these are merely logical and signify no more than similar thought processes in different parts of the world. Sometimes they are historical and indicate an actual line of descent from one to the other or from some common source. For this world-wide study motifs are much more usable than complete tale-types since tale-types are usually confined to a narrower geographic area than the motifs of the tale. In the comparative study of motifs there is no assumption of historical relationship. Sometimes it exists and sometimes it does not. On the other hand, such a study of a complete tale-type is always concerned positively or negatively with the question of historical relationship between the variants.

The difference in approach to motif studies and tale-type studies is very apparent in two works in which the author of this article has been concerned. In the Aarne-Thompson *Types of the Folktale* only such complete tale units were included as seemed to have some general circulation in the particular geographic area extending from Ireland to India. It is, therefore, very limited in its scope and is essentially selective. On the other hand, in the *Motif-Index of Folk-Literature* every attempt is made to have the listing of motifs as inclusive as possible. It is hoped because of this very comprehensiveness to bring to light interesting comparisons and to make possible significant studies which such comparisons suggest.

It is one of the dogmas of those who founded the historic-geographic method of folktale study that every motif belonged in a particular tale-type, and that the search into the history of motifs anterior to their appearance in particular folktales was futile. There is little doubt that this is an overstatement of the actual situation. A thorough study of motifs would undoubtedly throw some light on what we may call the prehistory of tale-types, but the argument is not one that is likely to be resolved into an easy formulation. Rather, it is clear that some motifs are practically universal, and form the material out of which tale-types are constructed, and some motifs are so specialized that they owe their very existence to the tale-types of which they are a part.

STITH THOMPSON

mountain lion A large quadruped (*Felis concolor*) of the cat family, found from British America to Patagonia, but now extinct in eastern North America: known as mountain lion in the far West, as puma (Sp., from Quechua *puma*) in the Southwest, or cougar; in the eastern United States generally referred to as panther. In the far West, mountain lion plays the role of Trickster's companion, especially in the mythologies of western Great Basin Shoshonean-speaking Indians. Among the Chemehuevi of eastern California he is Coyote's elder brother, and plays a role similar to that of Wolf's

in Northern Plateau Shoshonean myths. See PANTHER.
[EWV]

Mourisca The Portuguese version of the *Morisca* dance form. The male dancers are called *Moriscos* and the whole festive conglomerate a *Mouriscada*. They are traditional features of Corpus Christi processions and fiestas, and also celebrate San Juan's Day (summer solstice, June 24) and other Catholic festivals. As other *Moriscas*, they consist fundamentally of battle mime between two factions, commonly with a dramatic frame. Thus, in the *Mouriscada* of Maltas, a Rei Moro (Moorish king) entices a beautiful maiden, besieges her castle, and is finally routed with the consequent rescue of the maiden. By this element of folktale it is linked to the *autos*. The most interesting Mouriscada is the battle between *Mouriscos* and *bugios* at Sobrado, in revealing origin in demonology and vegetation mime. A number of degenerate forms have discarded the battle mime, i.e. the *dança do Rei David, dança do genebres,* and the version in Casalinhas which retains *mauresque* costumes—tall helmets, beribboned wands—but consists of steps from popular dances (*viras, verdegaios, foxtrots.*) The stick dances or *paulitos* are either derivatives or parallel developments. For discussion of symbolism see MORISCAS. [GPK]

mourning In communities accustomed to express grief for the dead the patterns of expression are extremely diverse as between communities and between the social status of the persons who grieve. Most communities tend to formalize their lamentations. Thus, the sending of flowers, sometimes in ostentatious displays, the giving of gifts to charity, to the bereaved family, or actual or symbolic gifts to accompany the ghost on its otherworld journey are customary. In some communities the expression of spontaneous grief is formalized and the head of the bereaved family or the entire family is expected to lament over a period of days or weeks and to renew its laments at stated intervals over a period of years. The lamentation consists of weeping, wailing, beating the head, soiling the body and clothes, refusing food, wearing tattered or disreputable garments. Professional mourners are frequently engaged for this purpose. The Irish wake in which the women wail in the parlor while the men drink in the kitchen is a current example of this sort of lamentation which is also frequently mentioned in the Bible. The Jews, Slavs, and Chinese are three peoples who indulge in noisy lamentation over a long period of time. In Greece the lamentation became so excessive that Solon legislated against it by restricting it to close members of the family. The words in which this grief was expressed gave rise to the literary form known among the Greeks as "elegies" and among the Jews as "lamentations." [RDJ]

Among all North American Indians mourning observances of one sort or another are obligatory for close blood relatives of the dead and the surviving spouse if there is such. Elaborate mourning ceremonies for the dead are also held by some tribes within a year or so after burial.

Close blood relatives fast or abstain from certain foods (meat, salt, grease, water, usually) for a prescribed number of days after the death, in many tribes. They may not wash their hair or put on new clothes; a man should not hunt or a woman gather wild foods. Parents who lose their first-born child are under especially strict rules in many tribes; they should remain in isolation, refrain from intercourse, fast, remain unwashed, wail, for a prescribed number of days or months. The mother of the infant should, in many cases, cut or singe her hair off short. Ritual purification (often a ceremonial bath, or being smoked in cedar or other incense) should take place at the end of the mourning period. Widows, especially, but also widowers to some extent, were also under rigid tabus after the death of a spouse. Widows in many tribes were expected to remain in seclusion, cut their hair short, cover their hair and face with ashes, pitch, or clay, wear old clothes, fast, cut themselves or cut off a finger joint. Only after they had been ceremonially released by their dead husband's relatives could they resume their normal life and remarry.

Gravediggers and corpse-handlers are under many of the same tabus enjoined on relatives for a few days after a funeral. In some Eastern and Southwestern Woodlands tribes dances could not be held for a month after the death of someone living in the village or pueblo. In some tribes the bones of a dead child or spouse were made into a bundle and carried on the back for a year or more by the mother or widow. It is said that the English name for the Carrier tribe in British Columbia derives from this custom observed by its members. Among the Ojibwa and other Eastern Woodlands groups women made up a "spirit bundle" to represent a lost relative, especially a child, carried it with them, fed, talked, and slept with it.

In three parts of the continent at least commemorative mourning ceremonies of an elaborate sort were held to honor either all the dead or individual dead of the preceding year, and smaller feasts or ceremonies in honor of the dead were given by many tribes. The Eskimo hold memorial feasts for the dead late in November; near relatives are hosts; the dead are present, beneath the house floor. They enjoy the activities in their honor, "eat" the food and water given them, and "receive" the clothes put as a gift on their namesakes. At North Pacific Coast feasts the spirits of the dead were also present, and fed, the food being passed through the fire to feed them. Similar family feasts were held for the dead elsewhere. The Huron of the Great Lakes region held a celebrated ceremony for the dead in the fall, when all who had died during the year were disinterred by relatives, the flesh cleaned from the bones, and the bones wrapped in beaver and other valuable skins and re-interred in a clan burial pit. Among the Indians of central California, from the Maidu southward to the Yokuts and Luiseño, an annual mourning ceremony was held, at which images of the dead and property, especially finely made baskets, were burned, and shell currency was scattered among the wailing excited mourners. These California mourning ceremonies ("burnings" or "Fiestas") lasted several days; they were attended by many or all members of the tribe and visitors; food for feeding the group was usually provided by the chief and relatives of the persons whose death was being commemorated. The burning of the image climaxed the ceremony. Trading and exchange of gossip went on during the rites; gambling games were played and dances held and, in the words of one Maidu woman, the annual burning was a highly anticipated and most "joyful" event. See BURIAL; FUNERAL CUSTOMS. [EWV]

Cutting of the hair is one of the most commonly observed funerary rites in South America. Often the mourning period ends when the hair of the relatives has grown again to a certain length. The mourners discard their ornaments and neglect their persons. They often paint their face or their body black with charcoal (Tierra del Fuego, Araucanians) or with genipa (Tupinamba, Sipibo, Macushi, Mundurucu, etc.). Red was also the color of mourning in some regions (Chibcha, Macushi). In the Andean region mourners dressed in black. Widows among the Chaco tribes pull a net bag over their head or cover it with a piece of cloth.

Mourners refrain from certain foods (for example, game among the Taulipang, or fish and meat among the Mbaya) and sometimes observe a rigid diet (Apiaca, Xingu tribes, etc.).

The name of the dead becomes tabu and, if it included words in common use, these became obsolete. In the Chaco the closest relatives of a dead person took new names.

Widows are secluded for a few days (Araucanians) or for several months (Chaco tribes).

In many tribes, mourners show their grief by throwing themselves to the ground (Guaraní, Apinayé) or by gashing their bodies with sharp instruments (Ona, Tehuelche, Pampa, Cayapo). In the ancient tribes of the Parana delta women cut off a joint of their fingers.

Soon after death or immediately after the burial, the relatives, generally the surviving spouse, praised the dead person, reproached him for having abandoned them, and described the greatness of the loss. Funeral laments are either wailing and crying or monotonous chants uttered in a plaintive voice. Although they are generally meaningless utterances, sometimes they contain expressions of grief and regret. As a rule they take place at dawn or sunset.

Dances are sometimes performed after the burial (Yahgan, Saliva, and the masked dances of the Cobeuo and other tribes of the Caiari Uaupes).

The mourners cleanse themselves from the evil influences and the contagion of death by washing themselves in a river (Chiriguano, Saliva, Paez, Quechua) or jumping over a fire.

Throughout South America, among civilized and wild tribes alike, the personal effects of the dead are either buried with him or are broken or burned. Only exceptionally valuable pieces such as stone axes and canoes could be retained by the heirs. The domestic animals belonging to a deceased person were frequently killed on the grave (Warrau, Muinane, Iquito, Zaparo killed the dogs; the Tehuelche slaughtered the dead man's horse). In ancient Peru llamas were sacrificed on the sepulcher.

In the areas where there were powerful chieftains and kings, the wives and the servants of these rulers were often buried with them. Suttees and slave sacrifices occurred in Peru, Colombia, the West Indies, and in those parts of the lowlands where Andean influences were strong.

Measures are also taken to prevent the ghost from returning and harming the living. Ashes are strewn on the footsteps of the mourners (Araucanians, Bororo, Jivaro), arrows or fire weapons are discharged against the ghost (Indians of the Uaupes region, Macushi). Or an attack is simulated against him (Araucanians, Aymara).

The end of the mourning period is often marked by a special ceremony. The Tucano and Cobeuo perform a masked dance symbolizing an attack of the funerary house and the defeat of the spirits; the Tupinamba gave a big drinking bout; the Rukuyen and other Guiana tribes celebrate a dance during which the guests lashed at each other with whips; the Caingang broke their ties with the dead in a big ceremony held several months after his burial. [AM]

mourning songs Dirges, laments, eulogies of the dead, funeral ballads, or merely rhythmic wailing cries, sung at the deathbed or at the graveside during funeral rites and in the mourning period and sometimes repeated on other occasions, such as anniversaries of death, exhumations, and feasts of the dead. The custom of such wailing and singing is age-old and world-wide, and the attendant beliefs and practices are markedly similar— whether the singing is Russian or Australian, African or Polynesian, Irish or Corsican, American Indian or Arabic. Laments at the most primitive level (which is not necessarily consonant with the general level of the culture) are little more than howls and screams of actual or ritually obligatory grief; at the other extreme (which may be found among peoples called "primitive") the songs achieve a high order of poetic and musical expression approaching the lyric elegy and the epic lay. Frequently both types occur side by side, the formless outcry of the death wail being consciously distinguished from the more organized cadences of the mourning song. See KEEN.

The songs, generally sung in slow, mournful, dragging chant style, are often addressed to the departed, saying in effect: "Why did you leave us? What did you lack to make you happy? Look with pity on the children you have left. Long is the day without you. Dark is the sun since you are gone. Never will your like be seen in this world again." Some recite the events of the life that has ended and are testimonials to the deeds and character of the dead. The Irish keen and the Corsican *vocero* are especially laudatory, detailed, and individualized. Others, such as the mourning songs of the Kwakiutl Indians, may be more figurative ("it broke down, the post of the world"). Chinese, Irish, Ruthenian, and other dirges express reproach to the dead for having died ("Father, how can you leave me behind?"). Some South American Indian and Corsican examples carry a promise to avenge the death.

A feature of Greek and Chinese laments is the loud calling of the name of the dead just before burial. If he does not answer or rise up, it is safe to close the coffin or the grave. He is not sleeping but really dead. Among North and South American Indians and Australian aborigines, the dirges and wails avoid the name of the dead, and renaming of those who bore the same name is required. See NAME TABU; TABU.

The words of the songs are punctuated with shrill or plaintive mourning exclamation characteristic of each people: *aue* in Polynesia, *ochone* in Ireland, *isa lei* in the Fiji Islands, *ai lanu* and *maa-ne-hra* (see LINUS SONG), *eheu* in Latin, and *hana*, *haya*, or *hanu* among the Indians of the American Northwest Coast. (The last, according to Barbeau, is the same as the word meaning "alas" in Chinese Buddhist chants, echoes the sound of

East Asiatic dirges, and is a relic of the influence of Buddhist missionaries.)

While generally the theme of dirges is all praise of the departed (*de mortuiis nil nisi bonum*), the tribe of Badagas of the Nilgiri Hills of India sing accusations to the deceased of all the sins in the catalog, which are transferred from the soul to a scapegoat buffalo calf, so that the soul may go unblemished out of this world.

The purpose of the singing is essentially the same everywhere, though varying explanations are advanced and details of the observance differ. The custom is protective for the living and sometimes also a comfort to the dead. It is a propitiation to the spirits of the departed, who are believed hostile to and envious of the living. The soul, who lingers near his body, must be flattered and reminded of his ties of affection with the survivors, so that his newly acquired supernatural influence will be for their good and his malice warded off. Demons hovering over the place of death must be frightened off with loud noises, and the journey of the deceased into the world of spirits must be eased by a bridge or wings of song and by gifts, payments, food, and sometimes transportation for the trip. Among the Pueblo Indians (Santo Domingo) the medicine men accompany a farewell song of the departing spirit to his people with shaking rattles and holding up eagle wings in token of the eagle which carries the spirit to the other world. In Omaha Indian belief the song, which itself came from the land of the dead, encourages the spirit on its way to the unseen world. The Klamath Indians believe that for three days the departed soul is menaced by devils, and, until it is safe, the friends keep up a fire and a determined wail to scare them away. Occasionally, as in the Congo, an extreme demonstration of grief is assumed as proof that the mourner cannot be guilty of causing the death by witchcraft or other foul means.

A Maricopa story explaining why it is proper to sing for the dying and the dead is as follows: One time Coyote ran afoul of the transformers and was dying. One of them, Namet, felt sorry and sang for him. At the singing Coyote opened his eyes; then he began to keep time with the music; finally he felt so well that he got up and danced.

Failure to honor the dead with song and all due evidence of mourning is believed to invite the anger of the spirit, who will take revenge by sending sickness (Basuto), by reappearing as a vampire (Slavic), or by refusing to rest in the grave and walking the earth to haunt the survivors. When a barren woman dies among the East African Ja-Luo, a dirge is raised immediately, as for any other death, but since she would be more than usually jealous of the living, and since she has no offspring of her own to haunt and bother and might thus haunt anyone, a special precaution is taken to prevent her walking—a thorn is stuck into her foot. Then the dirge is stopped, not being needed any further.

These reasons and purposes of the lament do not exclude the existence of genuine sorrow for the loss of the person; they do explain the exaggeration of outward expressions of bereavement, the dramatization of grief by persons only remotely connected with the deceased, the rapid emotional recovery of many of the participants once they have taken their turn at singing, and certain other customs to be discussed. Fiji etiquette requires the news of death to be conveyed and received with weeping. In China, visitors to the home of mourning are expected to wail ceremonially at stated points in the visit, and the wailing of the funeral procession is maintained as it passes through inhabited sections, but when it reaches open country, the lamentations may stop. In Dahomey, there is both a ritualized wailing, the *avidochio*, preliminary to the burial, and an outburst of personal grief at the actual burial.

The singing of the dirge is generally a function of women, though men take part and even lead it among the Chinese, Kaffirs, Dahomeans, etc. The North American Indian traditionally sings his own death song, which is either composed in advance and memorized so that he may die singing, or is improvised on the deathbed. The singer may be the chief female mourner—the mother, widow, etc.—, it may be the best friend of the deceased, who plays an important role in Dahomey, or the favorite playmate, as sometimes in Corsican children's or young people's funerals, it may be a group of related or associated persons, such as the Afro-Bahian cult group or the Dahomean *dokpwe*. In many parts of the world, however, the wails and laments are the special duty of hired or hereditary professional public wailers, always women.

The use of hired mourners (Latin *præficæ*) is ancient and widespread. They are shown on Etruscan funeral urns. In China, Russia, and all over the Near East, they have been a part of funeral ceremonies for centuries. In Calabria, the position of public wailer is hereditary from mother to daughter. Singers of the vanishing Irish keen were sometimes professional, sometimes members of the bereaved family and neighbors. Prostitutes serve as hired mourners among the Bedouins of Abyssinia. Among certain American Indian tribes (the Mandans of Dakota and the Gros Ventres) the one who wails longest receives the highest fee. Paid women wailers howl at the graveside three times a day for a number of months among the Chiriguanos of South America. In Corsica, the hired mourners are called *voceratici*, singers of the *vocero*, or dirge. In Malta, two women, *neuuiha*, are hired to sing laments. They appear in long mourning cloaks, sing by the bier, and carry on demonstrations of uncontrollable grief at the grave.

The songs of the professionals have the semblance of improvised creations for the particular occasion, and the details of the testimonial and the events of the life are tailored to fit the individual case, but the pattern of phrasing and the rhythmic and melodic form of the whole performance are traditional. In Tikopian practice the dirges are composed for a specific kinship tie—for death of a father, mother, etc.—and each type is sung only for that relationship of the deceased.

The singing and wailing is frequently accompanied by self-mutilation and by an appearance of intense emotional disorder, betokened by dishevelled hair of the bereaved and the hired mourners, scratching or cutting the face, plucking out or cutting off of the women's hair at the graveside, stamping the feet, rolling in dust or ashes or putting these on the head, wearing of sackcloth, etc. Such lamentations and displays of grief by the Trojan women for Hector's death were described by Homer, and are characteristic of mourning all over the world. In China men formerly loosened their queues and let their hair hang ragged and unkempt. In Corsica men let their beards grow rough for weeks after the funeral. In Polynesia mourners slash their foreheads with shells and knives. In Biblical Israel, mourners rent their garments and tore their hair. See FUNERAL CUSTOMS AND BELIEFS.

Such unrestrained demonstration has occasionally aroused the disapproval of authorities and been the subject of legal decrees. Solon made it a law that only the nearest female kin of the deceased should take part in the mourning and that there was to be no cheek-scratching, no breast-beating, and no singing of set forms. Charlemagne attempted by edict to prohibit the singing of "profane songs" at funerals. Obviously these and similar efforts had little effect on the custom. In Provence and in Gascony, lay dirges and lamentations were carried on hundreds of years after the death of Charlemagne, and they are still heard among Greek-speaking peoples. They were sung in England into the 17th century, though the songs have survived only in rare cases, as the *Lyke-Wake Dirge* ("This ae nighte, this ae nighte/ Everie nighte and alle/ Fire and sleete and candle lighte/ And Christe receive thy saule.").

Formal laments for particular heroes, gods, spirits, and notables are a part of the tradition of many peoples. Thus among the ancient Teutons there was a lament for Attila and a *geomorgyd* (dirge) for Beowulf. In Provençal French the lament was called *planh* (complaint), and was one of the subjects for trouvère composition. See COMPLAINT. The Provençal singer Gaucelm Faidit composed a *planh* for Richard the Lion-Hearted. The aborigines of Australia have preserved a lament, called *The Broken String*, for a magician and rainmaker who was shot while disguised as a lion. The broken string refers to a ringing sound in the sky, which ceased to be heard at the magician's death. See also FROG MOURNING SONG. Composition of laments for the noble houses of Scotland was in the hands of experts, bards, whose works were called coronachs. In Toyama Prefecture, Japan, a lament for the defeat and flight of a once powerful family of the section is sung as a harvest song.

Laments sung at the harvest are common in European and Mediterranean tradition. While the singing is bound up with the symbolic death and resurrection of the corn spirit, the form of the songs resembles closely the local dirges for human deaths.

Many other ceremonies, apart from human death and burial, are associated with songs of mourning. The Tikopian dirges have a second special use, certain ones, differing from the death chants, being sung for boys on the day of their initiation. These express grief and sympathy for the pain of the circumcision. The same wail, *aue*, is interspersed with the words, and the same ritual cutting of the forehead and tearing of the corners of the mouth occur as in the death laments, but each mourner's wailing ceases when he rubs noses with the boy after the operation.

The killing of sacred and sacrificial animals demands ritual lamentation among many peoples. Examples are the dirge songs for bears among North American Indians and similar songs among Siberian tribes, the Ainus, etc., as well as the California Akaghemem laments for the sacred buzzard and the Egyptian lament for the sacred ram of Amen. In each of these rites the animal is royally groomed and prepared for its execution, receives apologies and speeches in advance, and is sung over after death with the solemn honor due to the passing of a king or god or the pathos of the loss of a beloved child.

Occasionally dirge singing is a part of a mock funeral, performed for a magical purpose. In Madagascar, a maiden who dreams that her children will die before her may ward off the evil fate by killing a grasshopper, maiming others to buzz and wave their legs around it in imitation of mourners at a funeral, and herself singing laments over it as for a dead child. Having by this act lost and mourned her yet unborn children, she cannot again lose them in real life. A similar Albanian mock funeral was formerly held to rid the fields of locusts. The women would catch a few, march in a mourning procession with dishevelled hair, and sing dirges over the locusts as if they were their nearest and dearest. The march ended at the river, where the locusts were drowned. The death of the remaining locusts was sure to follow.

Another type of mock funeral, which is still occasionally held, though in the spirit of horseplay, is the burying of the Carnival figure. A straw man or other effigy is burned or hanged or drowned for his carnival sins, and buried to the accompaniment of parodied dirges and lamentations. At Saint-Lô in Burgundy the corpse of Shrove Tuesday was in recent times hauled through the streets, followed by his chanting and weeping widow, a burly man in female dress, howling a burlesque of mourning songs.

Elsewhere, however, death songs are dangerous and not to be trifled with. The 42 "gravehead" songs of Dahomey Negroes, sung at the grave a day or so after the burial, can be performed only by those who are sufficiently exalted in spirit. Any others would sing at their peril. The Papa songs or death songs of Surinam Bush Negroes would bring death to the village if sung at any time but the death ceremonies.

Ceremonial dancing (see DEATH DANCE) sometimes goes with dirge singing and burial rites. (Members of the Dahomean *dokpwe* carry the corpse in a strenuous pre-burial dance.) And instrumental music and noise are often a prescribed part of the proceedings. The instruments most often used are those with life-giving, exorcising, and amuletic powers—the flute or oboe, the trumpet, bells. Thus, the Latin *nænia*, a song praising the dead, was accompanied by the oboe; an Arab lament of the North African coast is played by the flute alone, having lost its original vocal character; the beating of an iron bell, as well as a whole battery of orchestral instruments, accompanies the Dahomean rites; and in China one of the first accessories hired for a funeral, even before the death has occurred, is the pair of copper trumpets to frighten away demons and unpropitiated spirits. For the sake of both the living and the dead, both the music and the din are urgent.

THERESA C. BRAKELEY

mouse It is reported that mice were created in the ark by the Devil (A1853.1), or that they fell to earth from the clouds during a storm. In Germany it is said that witches make mice: they take a piece of cloth and make out of it a little mouse, saying, "Run along and come back," after which the mouse runs away alive.

Witches in northern Germany when brewing magic herbs say, *"Maus, Maus, heraus in Teufels Namen!"* whereupon mice jump out of the pot. A story tells of a girl who took two pinches of earth, made them into little balls, threw them over her shoulder, and soon the whole field was filled with mice.

The mouse is associated with the Greek Apollo Smintheus, and mice were kept in his temple. For its cleverness in catching rats and mice, the Egyptian mongoose is often called "Pharaoh's Cat," though it is far better known as "Pharaoh's Mouse."

In general, the mouse is a beast of ill-omen (B147.2.1.3). It is a death sign if it gnaws the clothes of a sleeping person; it has the evil eye, and the ancient Greeks had coins struck with the picture of a mouse which they used for protection against it. Mice as ministers of vengeance plagued the Philistines who had taken the Ark of God from the camp of the Israelites. They returned it later with five golden mice (1 *Sam.* vi, 45). Among many peoples the soul emerges from the body in the form of a mouse during sleep and at death. After leaving the sleeper, if the mouse (soul) did not return, the sleeper died; hence it was considered dangerous to awaken a person lest his soul be wandering somewhere.

In Bohemia and parts of Germany white mice are regarded as luck bringers and are encouraged and fed to keep them about a house, but in some districts a white mouse is a death omen. In Germany it is thought that mice flee from a house in which there is (or is to be) a death, just as it is said that rats desert a ship about to sink. In Jewish folk belief, anything already nibbled at or gnawed by a mouse is never eaten; to eat mouse-gnawed food causes forgetfulness, or sore throat. In France and northern Germany it is said that the appearance of great numbers of mice is an omen of war. In Greece a mouse hole gnawed in a bag of flour, or in clothing, portends hunger or death.

The mouse was an early element in the healing art and was widely used in medicine in antiquity. Examination of the stomachs of children from pre-dynastic excavations in Egypt indicate the presence of mice. The custom of administering mouse-pie or fried mice as a cure for bed-wetting has been reported not long ago from England and from among the Pennsylvania Dutch, and still exists in many groups. Cooked mice were also recommended for smallpox, whooping-cough, and measles. Pliny recommended mouse ashes mixed with honey for earache and as a guarantee of sweet breath if used as a mouth wash. [GPS]

The mouse figures as helpful animal (B431.2) in African Negro and Indian folktale. A man is transformed into a mouse (D117.1) and a mouse is transformed into a person (D315.2). The Devil appears as a mouse (G303.3.3.9); the Devil himself in the form of a mouse gnawed a hole in the ark (A1811.2). The mouse often plays the role of witch's familiar, or the witch appears in the form of a mouse (G211.8). The mouse sits on the lion's mane while the huge beast rages at his impertinence (J411.8.); but in gratitude for being spared the mouse saves the lion from the net. See ELK; FLOOD; HATTO; LION AND THE MOUSE; MOUSE TOWER.

mouse tower A tower or other building in which, in various local legends, some heartless miser has been devoured by mice or rats; specifically, a medieval tower near Bingen on the Rhine where the Hatto legend is localized. The story is told in several localities in Germany, Austria, Switzerland, Poland, and Scandinavia. One legend records that a certain German count bought up all the corn of his district, expecting to become wealthy on speculation. There was a famine the following year, and he was for selling at great profit. Swarms of starving rats, however, swept across the fields, got into his barns and ate all the corn, invaded his castle and ate the old man himself. Among other mouse tower victims were Adolf, a bishop of Cologne, who was eaten by rats about 1112 A.D., the Swiss Freiherr von Guttingen, eaten alive by rats in his castle on Lake Constance, and Widerolf, another German bishop, who was devoured by mice for suppressing the convent of Selton. For a complete discussion of the legend, see S. Baring-Gould, *Curious Myths of the Middle Ages*, London, 1884, pp. 447 ff., and Felix Liebrecht, *Zur Volkskunde*, Heilbronn, 1879, pp. 1 ff. See HATTO.

Mṛigānka In Indian folktales, the magic sword by which its owner can conquer and control the world: literally, the moon, because it is bright and shining. In Somadeva's story of "Śrīdatta and Mṛigānkavatī" the sword was controlled by a yaksha cursed by Kubera so that he had become a lion.

Mṛikanda The culture hero of the Koshti, a caste of Indian weavers; the first to weave cloth for the gods from lotus fibers. He was rewarded with a tiger and a giant. He killed the giant for disobedience when he made the first loom from his bones. The tiger, on the other hand, was obedient and to this day has so much respect for Mṛikanda that all a Koshti need do, if he meets one in the jungle, is to mention the hero's name and the tiger will pass him by.

dMu One of the eight classes of indigenous Tibetan country gods; bloated fiends, dark purple in color.

Muçalinda In Buddhist mythology and belief, the serpent-king who spread his hood as a canopy over Buddha to shelter him from the elements during the third week of the period preceding the enlightenment.

Mudjikiwis (1) The hero of a rather long American Indian tale of fairly restricted distribution (Plains and Swampy Cree, Plains Ojibwa and Ojibwa) which, it has been suggested, may be an American Indian adaptation of the European tales of Cupid and Psyche, or the Swan Maiden. The American Indian myth concerns ten brothers who find their house put in order by a mysterious housekeeper, much to the relief of Mudjikiwis, eldest of the brothers. The housekeeper is a beautiful girl who marries the fifth brother. Mudjikiwis is jealous, and courts her; when she rejects him he shoots her. She flees; her husband goes in quest of her, and is advised and helped by supernatural old women. He succeeds in reaching an upper world of the Thunderers, where his wife is living, wins her back, and takes her and her nine sisters home as wives for his nine brothers. The eldest of the sisters married Mudjikiwis.

(2) In Longfellow's poem *Hiawatha*, Mudjekeewis is the father of Hiawatha. After Mudjekeewis killed the Great Bear he was honored by having his name changed to Kabeyun, the West Wind. [EWV]

mudrās or **hasta-mudrās** Dance-gestures of the Hindu *natya*. They translate the *rasas*, or emotions, into decorative expressions of the hands, highly conventionalized by their ancient divine tradition. Thus the *Pataka* hand originates from Brahmā. It is the flag hand of victory, with the fingers and thumb extended straight and close together. Among its numerous variations are the symbol for the world of the gods with palm up, for the underworld with palm down, and palms joined for devotion. The *Tripataka* or "three-fingers" pose came from Śiva and expresses invocation and is used for holding weapons. The third finger of the *Pataka* hand is bent and joined to the thumb at the middle of the palm. The *Ardapataka* hand, expressing a dagger, flag, tower, or horn, is formed by bending the little finger of the *Tripataka* hand. The *Sirpa-sirsa* hand, from Vishṇu, is used for *arati*, light-waving, and water-offering at twilight. The hollowed palm and fingers of the hand form the cobra's head. The *Ardachandra* hand forms a half-moon by stretching the thumb of the *Pataka* hand. The *Padmakosa* hand forms a lotus bud by drawing the fingers and thumb together.

These are a few examples of this elaborate code, which includes in the *Bharata Natyam* 24 symbols for a single hand, and for both hands, plus 13 for *nritta;* in the *Kathakali* school 64 symbols form 500 words. The wrist is the supple and expressive pivot for the hand; the palm, as the center of expression, is often turned toward the spectator.

The mudras have influenced all of the dance cultures of the Orient, and, with loss of symbolism, that of Spain. The effects are most evident in the South Pacific, especially in the Hawaiian *hula,* which contains in its gesture code many equivalents of the mudras, as the identical form and meaning of the *Ardachandra* and *Padmakosa* hands. [GPK]

muerte, danza de la Dance of Death in its Spanish version. Though the concept of the impersonation of death is probably of northern European origin, and came to Spain with the Austrian dynasty, it is in Spain and Mexico that it developed the most fantastic forms. The Catalan *danza macabra* used to consist of a whole group elaborately dressed in skeleton uniforms and high head-dresses, manipulating *castañuelas,* or a more symbolic clock and scythe, and cavorting in quadrille or serpentine formations. In Mexico *la muerte* usually clowns as a single impersonation of death in Carnival processions, urban as well as rural. Here the blend with Aztec death concepts has invested the figure with particular grim significance, as well as humor. [GPK]

mugwort A tall plant (*Artemisia vulgaris*) common through the north and south temperate zones, having grayish green leaves and masses of grayish yellow flowers. Mugwort is the woman's and maiden's plant: named for and sacred to Artemis, whose shrines were often centers of healing. Mugwort was said to ease childbirth, control the complaints of maidens, and cure all women's diseases.

The North American Chippewa Indians used a decoction from the root fibers in a steam-bath for the aged to give them strength. These people also used mugwort to counteract charms, as a remedy for all women's diseases, dysentery, hemorrhages, and as a hair tonic. Quite widely among both primitive and rural people, mugwort was famous as a protection against mice, weariness, eye troubles, and magic.

For centuries in Europe and Asia mugwort was regarded as a magic herb, sought by witches, occultists, and crystal-gazers. In the British Isles especially it is known to dispel weariness; even a sprig of mugwort in the buttonhole prevents one from tiring. Modern medicine has cashed in on this old wisdom: a nervine and stimulant made from the roots does provide a pickup after fatigue. Mugwort leaves, steeped in hot water, also provide a well-known eyewash.

In China, dolls made of mugwort plucked on the Fifth day of the Fifth month are suspended over gates or doors to expel poisonous airs or influences. Chinese surgeons use it in cautery and the leaf, Aiyeh, is used in Chinese art as a symbol of felicity. The Ainus of Japan also use bunches of the herb to exorcise the spirits of disease, who dislike the odor and flavor of the plant.

Its use in Europe is widespread. In France, if gathered on the Eve or Day of St. John, mugwort is believed to protect corn from mice. In Poitou it is worn as a girdle to prevent backache. In Normandy wreaths of it are a protection against thunder and thieves. Mugwort sprigs are used to hinder witches from laying their spells on butter. In Germany the mugwort girdle is called St. John's girdle and is believed to protect the wearer for a year against ghosts, magic, misfortune, and illness. If one holds the girdle up and peers through it at the Midsummer bonfire, it will prevent headache and smarting eyes. Washing a cow with an infusion of mugwort will break a spell cast on the animal. The Germans also believe that he who carries mugwort in his shoes will not grow weary. In Mecklenburg there is a legend that at the root of the mugwort, at noon on Midsummer Day, lies a burning coal which is a remedy for all sorts of maladies, or may turn to gold if the finder digs it up and carries it off in silence. In Belgium and the Isle of Man the plant is a protection against witchcraft.

muiñeira gallega A courtship dance of Galicia in Spain. In the first part the man tries to impress his partner with all manner of acrobatics and leaps, finally kneeling before her. In the ensuing couple dance he continues his leaps and turns, while she moves modestly with eyes cast down. In the second part many couples join in a round dance, the women forming an inner circle and the men an outer, protecting circle. Or the dancers may line up in a double file, and two men engage in mock rivalry. In conclusion couples dance again separately.

The round dance is termed *contrapaso* and shows a strong relationship with the *contrapás* of Catalonia. Both are probably of ceremonial origin, derived from Greece. [GPK]

mulberry In the well-known story of the ancient Babylonian lovers, Pyramus and Thisbe, Thisbe, arriving first in a forest spot for a secret rendezvous, was startled by a lioness, fled, and dropped her cloak. Pyramus, arriving on the scene, found the lioness worrying the cloak which was covered with the blood of an ox the lioness had just eaten. Jumping to conclusions, he killed himself in grief. Thisbe returned, saw her dead lover, and killed herself under the mulberry tree beside him. Their blood saturated the ground beneath the tree and the berries have maintained the rich color ever since.

The Romans dedicated the mulberry to Minerva; and it is also a sacred tree in Burma. God signaled to David by rustling the tops of the mulberry trees when the right moment came to attack the Philistines in the valley of Rephaim.

In China where the mulberry tree is cultivated extensively for the silkworm culture, the people regard it as a symbol of industry. So important is it in the life of China that farmers and villagers constantly appease and invoke San Ku Fu Jên, the goddess who protects all mulberry trees growing outside city walls. But the mulberry tree is never planted in front of a house lest it bring sorrow. To carry a staff made of mulberry wood betokens mourning for a mother.

In western England rural people expect no more frost after the mulberry has started to leaf. In Germany children are prevented from eating the berries by being told that the Devil needs them to black his boots. In Greece a mouthwash is made from the bark and leaves which is said to ease toothache. The North American Meskwaki Indians use the root bark of red mulberry as a general cure-all, and that of the white mulberry to expel worms. For the use of mulberry in the soporific sponge, see LETTUCE.

mullen A tall stout woolly herb (genus *Verbascum*) having spikes of yellow flowers. Like many another plant, its virtues are contradictory, it having been in medieval times a monastery charm against demons and at the same time a favorite of witches for their brews and potions. Roman soldiers dipped this plant in tallow to make torches, and the thick down on the plants is still used today to make candlewicks.

North American Iroquois Indians used mullen leaves in poultices for swellings and sores, and such poultices are still used more or less generally in the rural United States and England for toothache and neuralgia. The Mohegan-Pequot tribes smoked the leaves for asthma and sore throat. The ancient Romans used mullen as a remedy for coughs, and throughout Europe it is still made into an ointment for chest and bronchial ailments. The handful of Shinnecock Indians on Long Island today still recommend a tea from the leaves as good for colds.

In rural Massachusetts mullen leaves were considered good for the bite of a parrot. The leaves rubbed on the face bring ruddiness to the cheeks. Southern United States Negroes know the remedial properties of this plant, holding that a tea from the leaves is good for fevers, colds, and swellings; tea from the flowers is good for rheumatism; and a few mullen leaves put in the shoe before leaving the house will prevent one from taking cold. An Ozark love test consists of bending down a mullen stalk to point toward the beloved's cabin. If one's love is returned, the plant will spring up again; if the beloved loves another, the mullen will die. In colonial times the Swedish settlers in New Jersey smoked mullen leaves as a substitute for tobacco. Parkinson says the moth mullen is useless except to attract moths.

Müllenhoff, Karl Victor (1818–84) German philologist; successor to Jakob Grimm at the Prussian Academy of Sciences (1864). His works are principally on German philology and antiquities, and include *Denkmäler deutscher Poesie und Prosa aus dem viii-xii Jahrhundert* (1864), written in cooperation with his pupil Wilhelm Scherer; *Das deutsche Heldenbuch* (1866–73), with others; *Deutsche Altertumskunde* (1887–1900); *Sagen, Märchen, und Lieder der Herzogtum Schleswig, Holstein, und Lauenberg* (1921). In his glossary to Klaus Groth's *Quickborn* (1856), he made the first grammatical and lexicographical study of Plattdeutsch.

multiple creators A trio of creators, or a creative trinity, is believed in some North American Indian tribes to have done the same sort of deeds (creation and ordering of the earth, creation of man, ordering of life, etc.) that is credited to only one, or at most to two creators in the majority of American Indian groups. (See DUAL CREATORS.) Such multiple creators are found chiefly in the west; the Maidu of California, for example, have Earth-Initiate, Father of the Secret Society, and Turtle, while the nearby Yana have Rabbit, Grey Squirrel, and Lizard. The acts of this latter trio are relatively trivial, however, when compared with those of the Maidu creators. The Salinan, farther south, also have a creative trio: Eagle, Kingfisher, and Coyote. [ewv]

multiple heavens, hells The destination of the souls of the dead is, in many cultures, only vaguely defined. Often, as for instance in ancient Teutonic belief, the souls wander endlessly in a Wild Hunt. Or they haunt the place of their death, or they remain near the resting-place of the body, or they become transmigrated into bats or serpents or other animals or beings. But, as often, souls go to a place of reward or punishment. Sometimes the division is sharp: the souls of the good go to a heaven or paradise; those of the evil are condemned to eternal punishment in a hell. To these are added the fringe-worlds: a Limbo, where neutral souls go, souls of those too young to have been good or bad, souls of those who had no opportunity to embrace the faith; or a Purgatory, where those souls not deserving of eternal damnation are purged of uncleanness before admittance into Paradise. Paradise may exist in heaven, and there may be at the same time a Paradise on earth. Sometimes there are several heavens. To Valhalla, where the spirits of brave warriors lived the good life, went only those who died in battle; the commoner sort of Scandinavian soul went to the regions of Hel, which were not originally a place of punishment but a paradise more like the Greek Elysium. Ancient Mexican warriors were united in the sun god's regions; those who drowned went to the realm of Tlaloc, the rain god, etc. Members of various primitive secret societies have their own heavens, separate from and superior to the heavens of the other societies and the common heaven. Medieval European cabalistic belief divided the infernal regions into four, seven, nine, or more areas, each with its own demonic chief. There were seven heavens, each purer in ascending order as it was nearer to God. Mohammedan belief similarly counts seven heavens; there are seven divisions of hell as well (*Sura* xv). Multiplication of heavens and hells reaches its greatest complexity in the Far East. See for example *General Structure of Chinese Folklore* under CHINESE FOLKLORE for a discussion of the more than 84,000 Buddhist hells. See ADLIVUN.

The Aztecs, Maya, and many of the other native peoples of Middle America divided the world into horizontal regions of religious significance. The heavens, which varied from the 8 of the Cuna of Panama to the 13 in some Aztec and the Maya acounts, were the dwelling places of the gods, ranked in order of their age or importance in the hierarchy. Hell was divided into 9 levels, each of which was presided over by a lord of the underworld. [GMF]

mummers Maskers, in particular the English ritual maskers who enact an age-old play on Christmas Day. The jumbled texts tell of St. George's victory over his infidel antagonist, of a doctor, and a resurrection. Formerly a dragon and hobbyhorse were included in the dramatis personæ. In addition to the enacted duel, the group of mummers springily circle sunwise with sticks or wooden swords. They now wear shredded newspaper overall coverings, probably at one time animal skins, similar to the shaggy wild men of medieval Carnival. The resemblance to the Morris on the one hand and the English sword dance on the other is evident, as is also the similar interpretation as New Year vegetation ceremony. Similar mummers are found in Portugal and Thrace to this day. [GPK]

mummified animal helpers A dried-up dog (or tiny beavers or other animals) is kept in a box by the hero. When the latter is killed his widow takes out the animal mummy, which comes to life. The animal collects the hero's bones, howls over them, and the hero revives. This is a recurrent element in Great Lakes American Indian tales. [EWV]

mummy Human carcasses artificially preserved are called mummies. The Egyptians had elaborate methods of removing the vital organs and stuffing the bodies with bitumen and precious spices and performing incantations. This was necessary to enable the soul to enter paradise. Because the soul had to be tried before Osiris and 42 judges, in the XII Dynasty a scarab was put in place of the heart, which it was supposed was weighed on a scale. The magical inscriptions on the scarab prevented it from giving testimony.

Mummification is practiced in several places. The people of Comagre worshipped bejewelled mummies. In Peru mummies were petitioned for health, food, and life. Among the Guanches the preservation of mummies was the work of a special class. The Aleuts hung their dead on poles or put them in rock shelters and caves in life-like positions. In order to gain the skill and good luck of the dead, hunters would take the bodies, put them in streams, and drink of the water. The dried bodies of celebrated hunters were sometimes cut into pieces and distributed. They were used to rub the head of the whale spear.

In the Middle Ages powdered mummy was an expensive drug. It was mixed with wine or put directly on the wounds. In the 16th century Ambroise Paré voiced skepticism and noted that much of the mummy then on the market was not Egyptian mummy and was greatly adulterated. See W. R. Dawson, *The Bridle of Pegasus*, London, 1930, Chap. VIII, "Mummy As A Drug."

A story widely circulated but not verified is that Cleopatra came to an appropriate end in the sewers of Paris. When the Egyptian treasures taken by Napoleon were returned, a mummy in its case was overlooked. Some thirty years ago when a new sewer was being built under the Bibliothèque Nationale, the workmen went into an unused room and found it. Being both tidy and French they dumped its contents into the sewer and dusted out the case. It was not until some years later that an Egyptologist identified the case as having contained the body of Cleopatra. See IMMORTALITY. [RDJ]

mumy A Votjak word meaning mother. The word is used for the names of nature deities, for instance *šundy-mumy*, mother of the Sun; *gudyri-mumy*, mother of thunder; *mužem-mumy*, mother of the Earth; and *šur-mumy*, mother of the river. Such deities are regarded, not as personal beings in the human shape, but as objects of nature. Nevertheless they are conceived as living beings and in possession of a soul. They require sacrifices to reinforce their souls. The sacrifices for the mother of the Earth are put in the soil, for the mother of fire, are thrown into the fire, etc. At the sacrifice of an animal, attention must be paid to the color of the pelts, i.e. for the mother of Sun, white animals must be chosen; for the mother of Earth, black ones; and for the mother of cold, gray, etc. The primitive intention of such sacrifices was of a practical kind; if you make the soul of the Earth stronger, the soil will be fruitful. [JB]

Munchausen Whoever was the true author of *Baron Munchausen's Narratives of His Marvellous Travels and Campaigns in Russia*, it is certain he had a strong arm for drawing a long bow. This small volume, first published in London in 1785 and containing only 45 pages, is a pleasingly mendacious collection of tales which may or may not be poking fun at the travel books of the time. These are probably slightly altered versions of tales told for the entertainment of his friends by Karl Friedrich Hieronymus Baron von Munchausen (1720–1797), a Hanoverian nobleman, who served the Russians against the Turks (1737–39). They were probably written by Rudolph Eric Raspe, a professor at the University of Cassel, who fled to England suddenly, due to the disappearance of certain items of value in the University museum of which he was the curator. The latter part of the book as we know it today was undoubtedly added later by a different hand and does not have the bluff soldierly sincerity which makes the first part so effective.

Typical of the Baron's tales (X91 ff.) is the one of the tunes which froze in a post-horn, which played themselves out in order when the horn was laid by the fire; the hunter's tall tale of loading his musket with a cherry pit, hitting a stag between the horns, and later finding the stag with a cherry tree growing from its head; the story of the big snow, and of tying the horse to a post at the height of the blizzard, to discover next morning —sun shining, snow all gone—the horse tethered to the church steeple. An inescapable beast rushed on Herr Baron in a tight place in the mountains; the redoubtable Munchausen reached down his open maw, seized the tail, and flipped him inside out and hindside to; the animal found himself running in the other direction. See LIARS AND LYING TALES.

Munin In Teutonic mythology, one of two ravens who perched on Odin's shoulders. Hugin was the name of the other. Each morning they flew out into the world and returned at nightfall to whisper in his ears what they had seen and heard during the day.

Mura-mura The dream time and the ancestral spirits of the Australian Dieri. See ALCHERA.

murt A word of the Votjaks meaning man. They have many deities using this name: *korka-murt,* man of the house; *gid'-murt,* man of the cattle house; *obin-murt,* man of the kiln; *ñules-murt,* man of the forest; *vu-murt,* man of the water. Such deities are conceived in the shape of man and probably originate from the worship of the dead. [JB]

muscular tremor Muscular tremors are considered diagnostic signs by several of the Southern Athabaskan groups; the Jicarilla Apache, for example, consider them to be warnings of danger, or suggestions of good luck to come. A short Jicarilla tale has been recorded by Opler, of a dispute between two characters, Muscular Tremor and Involuntary Noise, concerning the outcome of a war going on between the Jicarilla and the Arapaho (Morris Edward Opler, *Myths and Tales of the Jicarilla Apache Indians, MAFLS* 31, 1938, p. 391). Among the related Navaho Trembling-in-the-hand is a regular form of prognostication practiced by specialists. See L. C. Wyman, "Navaho Diagnosticians," *AA* 38 (1936): 236–46. [EWV]

Muses In ancient Greek mythology, the nine (originally three) nymphs, daughters of Zeus and Mnemosyne, who presided over poetry and the arts of music. They had as their favorite dwelling-places Pieria near Olympus, their birthplace, Mt. Helicon and the springs Hippocrene and Aganippe, Mt. Parnassus, and Castalia. All these sites were sacred to the Muses. Later poets and mythographers felt it necessary to assign various fields of interest to each of the nine, but agreement is generally lacking. The Muses, and their most accepted provinces, are: Calliope—epic or heroic poetry; Clio—history or lyre-playing; Melpomene—tragedy or lyre-playing; Euterpe—tragedy, flute-playing, or lyric poetry; Erato—love poetry, hymns, lyre-playing, or pantomime; Terpsichore—choral dancing and singing or flute-playing; Urania—astronomy (i.e. cosmological poetry); Thalia—comedy or idyll; Polymnia (Polyhymnia)—hymns, pantomime, or religious dance.

As can be seen, the same field is often attributed to several Muses. There is no doubt however that as a group they presided over poetry. Several times they had contests with human or semi-divine beings, but the Muses always won. Thamyris lost to them, betting his enjoying each of them against whatever they cared to do to him; they blinded him and broke his lyre. Thamyris in Hades, blind and sitting by his useless instrument, was a favorite poetic and artistic example of punishment in the underworld. The Sphinx that terrified Thebes was given her riddle by the Muses.

museums, folk A museum dedicated to the life, work, and creations of people at that stratum of society which works with its hands. Many folk museums contain outdoor units which re-create phases of bygone life at the level described above. Emphasis is upon the working men and women rather than upon leaders of communities.

European Folk Museums: Credit for founding the first European folk museum goes to Dr. Artur Hazelius, who founded Nordiska Museet in 1872 in Stockholm. It was Hazelius who conceived the idea of the vitalized museum which would be a collection of homes, farm houses, workshops, where earlier rural life could be re-created. In 1891 Dr. Hazelius' private collection was set up as an outdoor museum known as Skansen. To it was brought various types of buildings from many sections of Sweden, and in these buildings the whole complex of folk life was re-created. From Sweden the movement spread to Norway, where Dr. Sanders Sandvig founded Sandvigske Samlinger at Lillehammer in 1887. Denmark, Holland,

and Germany all followed suit with re-creations of their own early rural culture. In many instances these museums became centers for the continuing of crafts, folk dancing, and folk music.

American Folk Museums have been slow in arriving. Beginnings were made with collections of tools and implements. Impetus to this movement was given by the Early American Industries Association, among whose leaders were William B. Sprague, Lewis N. Wiggins, C. M. Stow, and Allen Eaton. Notable collections are those of the Bucks County Historical Society at Doylestown, Pennsylvania, and the Landis Valley Museum at Lancaster, Pennsylvania. The New York State Agricultural Society made a collection as early as 1926, for which a building was built at the State Fair, held annually in Syracuse, New York. Here a cobbler, a weaver, and a cooper demonstrated the early crafts, and a log cabin was brought into the building and erected.

Greenfield Village, founded by Henry Ford in 1929 at Dearborn, Michigan, like the Swedish museums, sought to bring together actual buildings and arrange them in a natural pattern. A great collection of implements housed in the adjacent Edison Institute provides study collections of craft tools, implements, and materials. The arrangement of buildings at Greenfield Village seeks to re-create the layout of a midwestern town. The pattern at Greenfield Village was not consistently adhered to and certain European buildings and buildings of specific historical importance, such as Edison's buildings at Menlo Park, were added to the development.

Colonial Williamsburg, Williamsburg, Virginia, the most famous of American outdoor museums, while not a folk museum, does emphasize certain elements of 18th century folk life. Its craftsmen make wigs, pewter, furniture, shoes, and iron work, and these functions are carried on with historical exactitude. The emphasis at Williamsburg is at a higher economic and social level than is consistent with our definition of the folk museum, but no study of folk museums can neglect the work done there.

Old Sturbridge Village at Sturbridge, Massachusetts, was the outgrowth of the collections of Albert B. Wells and J. Cheney Wells, both of whom had been active in the Early American Industries Association. Here thirty New England buildings have been brought together around a village green—there is a tavern, a sawmill, a gristmill, a smithy, homes, barns, a meeting house, general store, a tinsmith, a woodworking shop, and boot and gun shops, etc. The emphasis is upon crafts and craft products. The time covered, roughly speaking, is 1775–1825, the locale, generally speaking, Massachusetts.

The Farmers' Museum at Cooperstown, New York, operated by the New York State Historical Association, has chosen as its scope central New York State from 1780–1850 and seeks to re-create and preserve as many different aspects of folk life as possible. The main building, once a huge stone dairy barn, contains important collections of household implements, farm and craft tools, but increasingly the emphasis is upon demonstration of hand-skills. Flax grown on the property is completely processed: broken, swingled, hetcheled, spun, and woven. The carding, spinning, and weaving of wool, and the making of rope, woodworking with the early tools, and broom-making are all shown. Beyond the main building a country crossroads is taking form. An early schoolhouse, a country store, a blacksmith shop, and a lawyer's office have been brought in from different parts of the area and re-erected with the utmost exactitude. A farm house will soon be rebuilt on the property, and the eventual plans contemplate a tavern, a print shop, a carpenter shop, a pharmacy, and other businesses and crafts common to the frontier village of New York State. The Farmers' Museum has an important library relating to American folk culture and a large manuscript and recorded collection of folklore; and at Fenimore House, the museum of history and art directly across the road and also operated by the State Historical Association, there is one of the most important collections of American folk art in the country.

The emphasis of the folk museum is upon the way of life of the working people. It seeks to re-create their environment and to preserve their mind-skills and hand-skills, their arts and artifacts commonplace at an earlier period.

Louis C. Jones
Director, New York State
Historical Association,
Cooperstown, New York

The following discussion of the museum resources of the world in folklore materials is intended to be not a directory but a general survey. Space limitations have made it necessarily a mere skimming of the great number of collections in existence. It is true also that some of the museum collections listed here have been destroyed as a result of the war. In the instance of Poland, for example, all significant museum work can be said to have ended within a short time after 1935, the effective date of the Polish survey below. Although many of the collections undoubtedly have been annihilated, and probably none at all escaped wartime damage, the list has been included on the assumptions that it represents the highest point of Polish museum work in this century, and that postwar attempts at restoration will have taken place even where collections suffered complete destruction.

Africa

University of Witwatersrand Museum of Anthropology and Archæology, Johannesburg, a representative series of the various Stone Age cultures of southern Africa, together with tools, implements, and utensils illustrating native life and manufacture from South Africa to the Congo.

Duggan-Cronin Gallery of Photographic Studies of South African Natives, Kimberley, Cape Province, galleries each devoted to a tribal group and its culture.

Kaffrarian Museum, King William's Town, Cape Province, specimens of the work and ornaments of the Fingo and Xosa tribes.

Natal Museum, Pietermaritzburg, Natal, a general ethnological collection.

South African Museum, Cape Town, Cape Province, Bushman paintings and rock engravings.

Durban Municipal Museum, Durban, Natal, exhibits illustrating the evolution of man, the Stone Age of South Africa, and native work.

Museum of Ethnology of the University of Cape Town, Rondebosch, objects of native workmanship.

Transvaal Museum, Pretoria, Transvaal, native implements, musical instruments, pottery, basketware, weapons, and domestic utensils.

East London Municipal Museum, East London, Cape Province, local native work from the Swazi, Pondo, Kaffir, Zuhe, Basuto, and Xosa tribes.

Voortrekker Museum, Pietermaritzburg, Natal, wagons, furniture, wearing apparel, and household utensils of Voortrekkers, with photographs and documents.

Rhodesian Museum, Bulawayo, Southern Rhodesia, specimens of native industry, and relics found at Great Zimbabwe and other prehistoric Rhodesian ruins.

Queen Victoria Memorial Library and Museum, Salisbury, Southern Rhodesia, ethnographical specimens from Zimbabwe.

Peace Memorial Museum, Zanzibar, native artifacts.

Coryndon Memorial Museum, Nairobi, Kenya, valuable general African ethnological collections.

Kampala Museum, Kampala, Uganda, ethnological specimens, including native weapons and manufactures.

Achimota College Museum, Accra, Gold Coast, Indian, Burmese, and African utensils, musical instruments, and weapons, also a unique collection of Ashanti gold weights for the weighing of gold dust used as currency.

The Department of Antiquities and Cultural Relations of Nigeria has four museums which house the art treasures of its people: one each at Jos, Oron (wood carvings), Benin (sculptural bronzes), Ife (terra-cotta figures).

Khartoum Museum, Khartoum, Anglo-Egyptian Sudan, Sudanese ethnological collections.

See also French West Africa in this article.

Argentina

Museo Argentino de Ciencias Naturales "Bernardino Rivadavia," Buenos Aires, extensive general collections, with a great deal of American folklore material, including a large number of specimens of native music.

Museum of the Institute of Archæology, Linguistics and Folklore, Córdoba, special collection on the Americas.

Museo de Lujan and *Museo José Hernandez,* Buenos Aires, collections devoted entirely to the folklore of the Argentine.

Museo de Nahuel Huapi, San Carlos de Bariloche, ethnology of Patagonia.

Museo de Historia Natural "Juan Cornelio Moyano," Mendoza; the *Instituto Martiniano Leguizamón,* Paraná; the *Museo Histórico de Entre Rios,* Paraná; the *Museo Etnográfico de la Facultad de Filosofía y Letras,* Universitad de Buenos Aires, Buenos Aires; and the *Museo de la Plata,* La Plata, regional folklore material.

Australia

Australian Museum, Sydney, ethnology of the Bismarck Archipelago, including ceremonial carvings; ethnology of New Guinea, including weapons and implements, ceremonial objects, Kaiva-Kuku masks; ethnology of numerous Australian aboriginal tribes, including artifacts associated with burial customs, handicrafts, and weapons.

National Museum of Zoology, Geology and Ethnology, Melbourne, Australian totemic ceremonial objects, clothing, and ornaments, as well as mourning, burial, and other ceremonial objects of Australian tribes; New

Guinea and South Sea Islands ethnological collections, and a group of Maori stone and wooden implements.

Museum and Art Gallery of Western Australia, Perth, ethnology of western Australia; objects used during initiations and *corroborees.*

Queensland Museum, Brisbane, Australian and Papuan ethnological collections.

Tasmanian Museum and Art Gallery, Hobart, Tasmanian historical material connected with early whaling life; also Tasmanian aboriginal material.

South Australian Museum, Adelaide, exhibits of native handiwork.

Technological Museum, Bathurst, war implements of South Sea Island and Australian aborigines.

Austria

The important *Museum für Volkskunde,* Vienna, is devoted to the folklore of all Austria, as is also the *Schloss Hellbrunn,* in Salzburg.

Museum für Völkerkunde, Vienna.

Among regional museums of folklore: *Tiroler Volkskunstmuseum,* Innsbruck, Tyrolean folk material; *Steierische Volkskundemuseum,* Graz, Steiermark folklore; *Nieder-Oesterreichisches Landes-Museum,* Vienna; *Haus der Natur,* Salzburg; *Museum des Landes Kärnten,* and *Landesmuseum,* Klagenfurt, Carinthian folklore material.

Belgium

Musée Gruuthuuse, Bruges, Belgian folklore.

Musée de la vie Wallone, Liége, Walloon folklore.

Museum of Flemish Civilization, Antwerp, Flemish life and folklore.

Musée du Congo Belge, Brussels, ethnography, anthropology, prehistory, and folklore of the Belgian Congo.

Musée Royal d'Histoire Naturelle de Belgique, Brussels, ethnography of all Belgium.

Musées Royaux d'Art et d'Histoire, Brussels, Belgian prehistory, Egyptian, Asiatic, Greek, Roman, and Mediterranean archeology, and the ethnography and folklore of the Far East.

The following are typical of Belgian regional museums:

Maison du Drossard, Aarschot, local folklore.

Musée archéologique, Hôtel de Ville, Alost, Belgian and French folklore.

Musée du Folklore, Antwerp.

Musée du Gulden Spoor, Antwerp, archeology and folklore.

Musée Luxembourgeois, Arlon, archeology and folklore.

Musée du Cercle Archéologique, Ath.

Musée Archéologique, Audenarde.

Vereeniging voor Heemkunde en Folklore van het Land van Bornhem, Bornhem, archeology, folklore, and local history.

Musée regional, Bouillon, archeology, local antiquities.

Musée de la Campine, Brecht, archeology, prehistory.

Musée de Folklore (Bond van Westvlaamsche folkloristen), Bruges.

Musée du Vieux Béguinage, Brussels, history, archeology, folklore.

Musée Archéologique, Hôpital Saint-Jean, Damme.

Hôtel de Ville, Deinze, folklore, archeology.

Sterckhof, Deurne, Flemish life and folklore.

Musée de Folklore, Diest, Béguinage lore.

Musée Archéologique, Enghien.

Château des Comtes ('s Gravensteen), Ghent, archeology and folklore, including a valuable collection of ancient instruments of torture.

Musée Curtius, Liége, Belgian, French, and Roman archeology and folklore.

Musée du Folklore (Bond van Oostvlaamsche folkloristen), Ghent, Flemish folklore.

Musée Communal, Louvain, archeology, numismatics.

Musée de Folklore, Louvain.

Musée d'Art et Archéologie Communal, Malines.

Musée de Malmédy, Malmédy, folklore.

Domaine de Mariemont, Mariemont, history and archeology of Egyptians, Greeks, Romans, French, Hindus, Chinese, and Japanese.

Musée des Beaux-Arts et d'Antiquités, Mons, Belgian, Roman, and French archeology, prehistory, and folklore.

Musée Montois de Jean Lescarts, Mons, folklore, numismatics, prehistory, weapons.

Musée Archéologique, Namur, Roman and French antiquities.

Musée van Folklore en Heemkunde, Neder-over-Heembeek, folklore.

Musée Archéologique, Nieuport.

Château, Nismes, folklore, archeology, numismatics.

Musée Archéologique, Nivelles.

Musée d'Art et Archéologie, Ostend.

Musée Communal (Oudheidkundige Kring), Saint-Nicolas (Waas), local archeology and folklore.

Musée Archéologique, Soignies.

Musée Communal, Spa, folklore.

Musée Archéologique, Stavelot, Belgian and Roman antiquities and folklore.

Musée Archéologique, Termonde, folklore.

Musée Archéologique "Taxandria," Turnhout, local folklore.

La Maison Tournaisienne, Tournai, folklore.

Musée Communal, Verviers, archeology, folklore.

Musée des Antiquités et des Arts Décoratifs, Tournai, Celtic, Roman, and French antiquities.

Bolivia

Museo Nacional "Tihuanacu," La Paz, Bolivian native folklore.

Museo Arqueológico de la Universitad de San Francisco Xavier de Chuquisaca, Sucre, Bolivian ethnological and folklore material.

Borneo

North Borneo State Museum, Sandakan, British North Borneo, collection illustrating Bornean life and crafts.

Sarawak Museum, Kuching, Sarawak, ethnology of Sarawak.

Brazil

Museu de Etnografia, São Paulo University, São Paulo, extensive collections of Brazilian Indian cultures.

Other Brazilian museums containing folklore material are chiefly ethnographical institutions, such as *Museu Nacional,* Rio de Janeiro; *Museu Paranaense,* Curtiba; *Museu Goeldi de Historia Natural e Ethnographia,* Para.

British Guiana

British Guiana Museum, Georgetown, general collection of native ethnological and folklore material.

Bulgaria

National Ethnographic Museum, Sofia, collections illustrating the ethnography and folklore of all Bulgaria.

Canada

National Museum of Canada, Ottawa, anthropology of Canada, including a large collection of photographs of Indian and Eskimo life.

Peter Redpath Museum of McGill University, Montreal, ethnographical material from North and South America, Egypt, Africa, and New Hebrides.

Ethnological Museum of Laval University, Quebec, Indian, Eskimo, Mexican, and Chinese material, as well as specimens from the cultures of Oceania and Africa.

Ethnological Museum of the University of British Columbia, Vancouver, arts, crafts, and industries of the native peoples of South America and Australasia.

Collège de l'Assomption Museum, L'Assomption, folklore material of all Canada.

Ethnological Museum of the University of Alberta, Edmonton, extensive Eskimo collections, together with objects illustrating the folklor : of the Indians and pioneer whites of western Canada.

Royal Ontario Museum of Archæology, Toronto, North American Indian material.

Elgin Historical Society Museum, St. Thomas, pioneer and Indian relics, looms, spinning wheels, bake-ovens, and other material.

Vancouver City Museum, Vancouver, North American and Pacific Coast Indian material.

Hudson's Bay Company Historical Exhibit, Winnipeg, collections illustrating the life of various North American Indian tribes.

Newfoundland Museum, St. John's, relics of the Beothuck Indians of Newfoundland.

Provincial Museum of Nova Scotia, Halifax, regional Nova Scotia collections.

Grand Pré Museum, Grand Pré, material illustrating the cultures of the Micmac Indians, the French Acadians, and the New England planters, together with Canadian pioneer relics.

Ceylon

Kandy Museum, Kandy, life and economy of the Sinhalese in the days of the Sinhalese kings, including musical and ceremonial instruments, temple articles, masks, costumes, charms, articles used in sports and games, execution knives, and other material.

Colombo Museum, Colombo, local arts and crafts, games, masks, musical instruments, coins, and jewelry.

Chile

Museo de Arte Popular Americano, Santiago, ritual material of all the Americas.

Museo Regional de los Padres Salesianos, Punta Arenas, ethnography of southernmost South American and Tierra del Fuegan tribes.

Museo Araucano de Temuco, Temuco, Araucanian Indians of southern Chile.

Museums possessing general collections of folklore material are the *Museo Histórico Nacional*, and the *Museo Nacional de Historia Natural*, both in Santiago.

China

The collections of the *Shanghai Museum*, Shanghai, encompass material illustrative of all the races of mankind, modern and aboriginal Chinese material, prehistoric and ancient Chinese, African, Australian, and Papuan implements and weapons, Tibetan, Chinese, and Mongolian religious objects, official beads, Chinese pipes, geomancers' compasses, ancient Chinese *materia medica*, surgical instruments, Peiping toys, ancient Chinese coins, stone artifacts, oracle bones, cowry shells, glass beads, bronze mirrors, pottery tomb figures, stone carvings, and Balinese religious woodcarvings.

West China Union University Museum, Chengtu, Szechwan Province, culture of Szechwan Province and western China, Szechwan and northern Chinese shadow plays.

Museum of Kai Feng, Kaifeng, Honan Province, ethnology and archeology, pre-Confucian inscribed bones, unique collection of ancient Hsin Chêng bronzes, and one of the largest collections extant of funerary epitaphs engraved on stone, from the Wei, Sin, T'ang, and Sung periods.

Shensi Museum, Sian, ancient bas-reliefs of the horses of T'ang T'ai Tsung, also Buddhist stones and Wei period steles.

Shansi Provincial Museum, Yangku, Buddhist images and neolithic pottery.

Peiping Historical Museum, Peiping, funerary stones of the T'ang dynasty, and Buddhist steles.

Shantung Provincial Museum, Tsinan, Han funerary stones, Buddhist sculpture, and neolithic artifacts.

Colombia

Museo Etnográfico Nacional, Bogotá, Colombian regional cultures.

Museo de Oro, Bogotá, Colombian and pre-Colombian gold objects of the Quimbaya and Chibcha cultures.

Museo Arqueológico, Bogotá, Colombian archeological material.

Cuba

Museos Antropológicos Montané, Havana, Cuban ritual objects, also magic, witchcraft, secret society, and other folklore material.

Museo Nacional, Havana, Cuban ethnography.

Czechoslovakia

National Museum, Prague, Ethnographical Collection of peasant cultures of Bohemia and Moravia.

Náprstek Museum, Prague, general ethnographical collections.

Jewish Museum, Prague, material of the Jews of Czechoslovakia.

Slovak National Museum, Turčiansky-Svätý Martin, ethnography of the Slovaks.

Moravian National Museum, Brno, Moravian ethnography.

Folklore Museum of the Province of Pilsen, Pilsen, regional folklore.

Wallachian Museum, Roznov pod Radhoštěm, open-air folk museum of Wallachian life.

Denmark

The principal agency for the collection and exhibition of folklore material is the *National Museet*, Copenhagen; the *Danish Folk Museum,* treating the peasant culture of Denmark, is a division of the National Museet.

Open-Air Museum, Sorgenfri, folk museum.

Danske Folkemindesamling, in the Royal Library of Copenhagen, archives of Danish and Scandinavian folktales, folk music, ballads, proverbs, dances, folk life, and unpublished information on every aspect of Scandinavian folklore.

Dominican Republic

Museo Nacional, Ciudad Trujillo, pre-Columbian ethnology.

Ecuador

There are local ethnological collections in the *Museo y Biblioteca Municipal,* Guayaquil; the *Museo y Archivo Nacional,* Quito; the *Museo Etnográfico de la Universidad Central,* Quito, and the *Museum of Jijon y Caamano,* Quito.

El Salvador

Museo Nacional "David G. Guzmán," San Salvador, local ethnology.

Fiji

Fiji Museum, Suva, ethnology of the Fiji Islands.

Finland

Kansallismuseo (National Museum), Helsingfors, ethnological collections of Finland and the Finno-Ugric peoples.

The *Open-Air Museum* in Seurasaari, an important division of the National Museum, is a folk museum illustrating Finnish peasant culture.

France

Musée de l'Homme, Paris, incorporating the *Ethnological Institute of the University of Paris,* is one of the world's principal agencies for collecting, studying, and exhibiting "everything that concerns the human being in all his manifold aspects." It combines in one scientific pursuit physical anthropology, prehistory, archeology, ethnology, ethnography, sociology, philology, and folklore. It possesses specimens from cultures in all parts of the world.

Musée des Arts et Traditions Populaires, Paris, has one of the foremost general ethnographical collections in existence.

L'École du Louvre, Paris, conducts courses in connection with the materials in these two collections on the history of popular arts and folklore.

Musée Guimet, Paris, material pertaining to the religions of India, Central Asia, China, and Japan, together with Khmer antiquities and a large Buddhist collection.

Musée d'Ethnographie et d'Histoire de la Normandie, Caen, furniture, costumes, utensils, and other material illustrating the culture of Normandy.

Musée Basque de Bayonne, Bayonne, folk life of Bayonne and Gascony, the French Basque country, the Spanish Basque country, and the Basque in the New World.

French West Africa

The museums of the *Institut Français de l'Afrique Noire,* Dakar, exhibit regional ethnology and folklore.

Germany

Museum für Deutsche Volkskunde, and the *Museum für Völkerkunde,* both in Berlin, possess extensive general collections.

Regional museums: *Städtisches Museum,* Flensburg; *Niedersächsisches Volkstumsmuseum der Hauptstadt Hannover,* Hanover, lower Saxon folk life.

Germanisches Nationalmuseum, Nuremberg, general collections of German folk art and culture.

Great Britain

The Department of Antiquities of the *Ashmolean Museum,* Oxford, contains one of the finest collections of European and Near Eastern archeology in the world.

British Museum, London, departments of Archæology and Ethnology, collections from all parts of the world.

Cambridge University Museum of Archæology and Ethnology, Cambridge, American antiquities, particularly from the cultures of the Eskimo, the Pueblo Indian, and from Mexico, Ecuador, and Peru; also ancient beads of Egypt and Ur of the Chaldees, and Fiji ethnographical collection.

Pitt Rivers Museum (University of Oxford Department of Ethnology), Oxford, magical and religious objects from all over the world, as well as toys and games, and material illustrating the treatment of the dead and of enemies in various cultures throughout the world.

Anthropological Museum of the University of Aberdeen, Aberdeen, Scotland, anthropology of Europe, North Africa, Asia, Polynesia, New Zealand, Australia, Melanesia, Africa south of the Sahara, and America; also prehistoric and historic objects pertaining to religion, dress, and ornament, as well as home life, arts and crafts, music, games of cultures of the world.

Royal Scottish Museum, Edinburgh, Gallery of Comparative Ethnology, specimens from Africa, the Pacific, the Orient, North and South America, and representative peasant cultural examples from Europe.

University College of North Wales Museum of Welsh Antiquities, Bangor, Caernarvonshire, Welsh bygones, including furniture, clothing, domestic appliances, spinning-wheels, triple harps, armorial harness decorations.

Pitt-Rivers Museum, Blandford, Dorsetshire, local antiquities.

Brighton Art Gallery and Museum, Brighton, Sussex bygones, with extensive ethnological collections, including decorative arts of native peoples of Melanesia, Polynesia, and Africa, as well as North American Indian and Eskimo specimens.

National Museum of Wales, Cardiff, folk life of Wales.

Colchester and Essex Museum, Colchester, local social life from the Middle Ages to the present.

National Museum of Antiquities of Scotland, Edinburgh, relics of man's activity throughout Scotland.

London Museum, London, life and history of London from the earliest times to the present day.

Luton (Bedfordshire) *Public Museum,* everyday life and culture of the area through the ages.

Inverness Museum, Inverness, domestic life and local folkways.

Guildford Museum, Guildford, Surrey, local archeological and sociological material illustrating the life of southwest Surrey.

Museum of the Orkney Natural History Society, Stromness, Orkney, life and history of Orkney.

Museum of the Torquay Natural History Society, Torquay, Devon folk material.

York Castle Museum, York, local everyday life of the past.

Manx Museum, Douglas, Isle of Man, weapons, jewelry, and other accouterments from pagan Viking graves of the 9th century.

Carmarthen County Museum, Carmarthen, Wales, folk life collections of Carmarthenshire and West Wales.

Basingstoke Public Library and Museum, Basingstoke, 17th, 18th, and 19th century tokens, including a practically complete set of Basingstoke tokens.

Manchester (University) Museum, Manchester, local folk life.

East Hendred Museum, Berkshire, domestic and agricultural tools and implements of the district.

Municipal Museum of Cheltenham, Gloucestershire, local folk culture.

Curtis Museum, Alton, Hampshire, local life.

City Museum of Winchester, former local industry.

Hereford Public Museum, Herefordshire, domestic and agricultural bygones and implements still in use.

Rufford Village Museum, Ormskirk, Lancashire, life and work in southwest Lancashire.

City Museum and Art Gallery of Leicester, Leicestershire, agricultural and domestic bygones.

Bridewell Museum of Local Industries, Norwich.

Somerset County Museum, Taunton Castle, Somersetshire, local folk material and bygones.

Public Museum, Hastings, Sussex, local life.

Christchurch Mansion, Ipswich, Suffolk, domestic art and bygones of the area.

Salisbury, South Wiltshire and Blackmore Museum, Salisbury, Wiltshire, things in everyday use in the city of Salisbury between 1250 and 1850.

Bowes Museum, Barnard Castle, Yorkshire, local objects of folk culture.

Hertfordshire Museum, Hertfordshire, articles of the kitchen and general fire apparatus, and local countryside implements.

Amguedda Werin Cymru: The Welsh Folk Museum, St. Fagans Castle, St. Fagans, the old Welsh way of life, and variations in the continuity of Welsh culture, together with general exhibits covering the whole range of the traditional Welsh culture.

Buckland Abbey and Tythe Barn, Plymouth, intends ultimately to be a Devonshire Folk Museum.

Cambridge and County Folk Museum, Old White Horse Inn, Cambridgeshire, social life of the people of Cambridgeshire.

Folk Museum, Bishop Hooper's Lodging, Gloucester, folk culture and historical relics of Gloucestershire from 1500.

West Gate Museum of the City of Winchester, local folk culture.

Strangers' Hall Folk Museum, Norwich, Norfolk, domestic life of the citizens of Norwich, 16th-19th centuries.

Tickenhill Manor Park and House, Bewdley, Worcestershire, crafts and industries of the Midland area.

The Folk Museum section of *York Castle Museum,* York, contains restorations of typical Georgian and Jacobean shops.

Manx Village Folk Museum, Cregneash, Isle of Man, characteristics of traditional life shown in the natural environment in a Manx crofter community.

Wayside Museum, Zennor, Cornwall, folk museum for Cornwall.

Hull Museum, Hull, Yorkshire, an old-time local village street.

Blaise Castle Folk Museum, Henbury, Bristol, designed to give a picture of English life of former days, collections ranging from the 15th to the 19th century.

Folk Museum, Arbroath, Angus, eastern Scotland.

Am Fasgadh ("The Shelter"): The Highland Folk Museum, Kingussie, Inverness-shire, aspects of the material setting of life in the Highlands in former times.

St. Peter Hungate Museum of Church Art, Norwich.

Science Museum, London, local antiquities of the city of London.

Indian Institute Museum, Oxford, Indian life and customs.

Horniman Museum, London, ethnological collection of magic and religion, toys and games, and personal ornaments of various cultures throughout the world.

Greece

Mouseion tis Istorikis kai Ethnoloiikis Etairias tis Ellados, Athens, folk art and regional costumes.

Benaki Museum, Athens, regional costumes, household objects, and decorative works.

Museum of Decorative Arts, Athens, folk embroidery.

Laographical Museum of the University of Salonica, Salonica, serves as a laboratory for students of ethnology.

Guatemala

Museo de Arqueologæa, Guatemala City, cultures of the ancient Indian peoples of Guatemala.

Hawaii

Bernice P. Bishop Museum, Honolulu, extensive cultural material from the peoples of Polynesia, Melanesia, and Micronesia.

Hungary

National Museum, Budapest, ethnology of all Hungary, as well as various regional cultures.

Ethnological Museum and the *Ethnological Institution of the Teleki Pal Scientific Institute* have extensive collections devoted to Hungarian folk life and ethnology.

Iceland

Thjodminjasafu (National Museum), Reykjavik, past and present Icelandic cultures.

India and Pakistan

Indian Museum, Calcutta, life and habits of the primitive tribes of India.

Victoria and Albert Museum, Bombay, Himalayan tribal masks, models of native games, Indian headdresses, and carvings of Hindu gods and goddesses.

Government Museum, Madras, south Indian musical instruments, models of huts used by primitive Indian tribes, objects of the Malayali devil-dancers, materials used in sorcery by native cultures, and specimens of human sacrifice posts.

Central Museum, Nagpur, headdresses, amulets, and ornaments used by local aboriginal tribes, and photographs illustrating Gond life and customs.

Government (Napier) *Museum,* Trivandrum, life-size ethnological figures, miniature models, jewelry, and other objects, illustrating the cultures of the tribes and castes of Travancore.

Baroda State Museum, Baroda, toys, jewelry, charms, and articles of worship of the local tribes.

Prince of Wales Museum of Western India, Bombay, and the *Gass Forest Museum,* Coimbatore, collections of objects representing local folk life.

Pagan Museum, Pagan, Burma, relics (corporal remains) of the Buddhas and Arhats, images of the Buddha, Bodhisattvas, devas, etc., terra-cotta votive tablets, a group of Buddha-pads, images of Brahman deities.

Iran

Anthropological Museum, Tehran, Iranian and early Persian ethnological exhibits.

Iraq

'Iraq Museum, Baghdad, regional antiquities and folk life specimens.

Ireland

Northern Ireland

Municipal Museum and Art Gallery, Belfast, Irish ethnographical material.

Open-Air Museum, Belfast, exhibits that illustrate the domestic life, craftsmanship, and social activities of the people of Ulster.

Malaya

Perak Museum, Taiping, Malaya, principally an ethnographical museum illustrative of the Malay peninsula.

Raffles Museum, Singapore, Straits Settlements, ethnography of the Malaysian area.

Mexico

Museo Nacional de Antropologia, Mexico City, ethnology of Mexico and the Americas.

Museo Nacional de Historia, Mexico City, native cultures of all Mexico.

Museo Arqueológico e Histórico de Yucatán, Mérida, ethnological specimens from the Mayan zone.

Museo Regional Michoacano S.E.P. (Michoacan Regional Museum), Morelia, ethnology of the Michoacan region.

Museo Regional de Campeche, Campeche, and the *Museo Regional de Oaxaca,* Oaxaca, local ethnology.

Museo Regional de Actopán, Actopán, Otomi Indian collection.

Museo de Artes Populares, Patzcuaro, Tarascan Indians of Michoacan.

Museo Arqueológico de Teotihuacán, Teotihuacán, Teotihuacán Valley.

Museo Ethnografico y Arqueológico, Tzintzuntzan, ethnography of the Tzintzuntzan and Tarascan zones of Lake Patzcuaro.

Netherlands

Rijksmuseum voor Volkskunde "Het Nederlands Openluchtmuseum," Arnhem, and the *Museum voor Land- en Volkenkunde,* Rotterdam, both devoted entirely to Dutch folk life.

Friesch Museum, Leeuwarden, Frisian antiquities.

Rijksmuseum van Ethnographie, Leiden, ethnography of the Orient, Africa, America, the Dutch East Indies, and Oceania.

The Dutch East Indies are the principal concern of most of the remaining museums of ethnography and ethnology: *Gemeentemuseum "Het Prinsenhof,"* Delft; *Koloniaal Instituut Volkenkundig Museum,* Amsterdam; *Ethnographisch Museum van de Koninklijke militaire Academie,* Breda; *Gemeentelijk Museum,* Briel (ethnography of western New Guinea); *Maritiem Museum Prins Hendrik,* Rotterdam (ethnography of Dutch East Indies, New Guinea, and Polynesia).

Dutch East Indies

Museum van Het Koninklijk Bataviaasch Genootschap van Kunstenen Wetenschappen (Museum of the Royal Society of Arts and Sciences of Batavia), Batavia.

New Zealand

Auckland War Memorial Museum, Auckland, South Pacific ethnological material, including Maori exhibits, specimens of the arts and crafts of the Polynesian, Melanesian, and Papuan peoples, and a Fijian ethnographical collection. The Maori group includes war canoes, a tribal meeting house, a number of large and richly carved storehouses or *patakas,* Maori ornaments, carved burial boxes, and feather boxes.

Auckland Art Gallery, Auckland, Maori relics, and pictures of primitive Maori life and customs, intended as a permanent record of the life of the Maoris.

Canterbury Museum, Christchurch, ethnology of New Zealand, Maori artifacts.

Otago University Museum, Dunedin, Maori artifacts and South Island, Melanesian, and Polynesian folk material.

Dominion Museum, Wellington, extensive Maori collections, which include artifacts, canoes, *patakas,* and meeting houses.

Open-Air Museum, Rotorua, folk museum of Maori life, including a *pa,* or palisaded stronghold, typical Maori houses, storehouses, memorials, canoes.

Norway

Norsk Folkemuseum, Bygdoy, near Oslo, both open-air and indoor sections, culture and folklore of the Norwegian countryside and towns.

De Sandvigske Samlinger, Lillehammer, collection of about a hundred old houses and 60 old workshops, all preserved intact to illustrate phases of Norwegian rural and urban culture.

Samlinger av Nordiske Oldsaker (Museum of Northern Antiquities), Oslo, Viking material.

Stavanger Museum, Stavanger, typical of the smaller regional museums of Norway illustrating local culture.

Universitets Etnografiske Museum, Oslo, ethnological collections of Scandinavian countries.

Palestine

"Bezalel" Jewish National Museum, and *Museum of Jewish Antiquities of the Hebrew University,* both in Jerusalem, have exhibits illustrating the folklore of various Jewish cultures both in and outside of Palestine.

Panama

Museo Nacional de Panamá, Panama City, ethnology of Central America.

MUSEUMS

Paraguay

Museo de Historia Natural y Etnografía, Asunción, Guaraní Indian exhibits.

Peru

Museo de la Cultura Peruana, Museo de Antropología, and *Museo de Javier Prado of the Universidad de San Marcos,* all in Lima, general Peruvian collections.

Museo de Arqueología "Inca" de la Universidad Nacional, Lima, culture of the Incas.

Museo de Cayma, Arequipa, and *Museo "Rafael Larco Herrera,"* Chiclín, local Peruvian cultures.

Philippines

Santo Tomás Museum, Manila, ethnology of native Philippine tribes.

Poland

Muzeum Etnograficzne przy Muzeum Przemysłu i Rolnictwa Warszawa, Warsaw, ethnography of all Poland.

Muzeum Starożytności Żydowskich im. Mathiasa Bersohna (Bersohn Museum of Jewish Antiquities), Warsaw, religious objects of the Jews of Warsaw.

Tartarskie Muzeum Narodwe, Wilno, Tartar ethnology.

Muzeum Śląskie, Bytom, Silesian ethnography.

Muzeum Mazurskie, Działdowo, Mazovian ethnology.

Muzeum Wielkopolskie, Poznań, ethnography of Poland.

Muzeum Etnograficzne, Kraków, photographs and drawings of the life of the people of all Poland.

Muzeum Miejskie, Bydgoszcz, ethnography.

Ukrainskyj Narodnyj Muzej im. ks. Józefata Kobryńskiego, Kołomyja, Ukrainian ethnography.

Muzeum Miejskie, Cieszyn, ethnography of Cieszyn territory.

Museums of ethnography: *Muzeum Regjonalne,* Chojnice; *Muzeum Państwowe w Grodnie,* Grodno; *Muzeum Miejskie,* Grudziądz; *Muzeum Miejskie,* Jarosław; *Muzeum Ziemi Kaliskiej,* Kalisz; *Muzeum Śląskie,* Katowice; *Muzeum Nankowego Towarzystwa im. Szewczenki we Lwowie,* Lwów; *Muzeum Etnograficzne Polskiego Towarzystwa Krajoznawczego,* Lowicz; *Muzeum im. hr. Dzieduszyckich,* Lwów; *Muzeum Wołynskie,* Luck; *Miejskie Muzeum Etnograficzne,* Lodz; *Muzeum Regjonalne Ziemi Myślenickiej,* Myślenice; *Muzeum Kurpiowskie,* Nowogród; *Muzeum Ziemi Opatowskiej,* Ostrowiec; *Muzeum Poleskie,* Pińsk; *Muzeum Ziemi Piotrkowskiej,* Piotrków Trybunalski; *Muzeum Mazowsza Płockiego im. Prof. Ignacego Mościckiego,* Płock; *Muzeum Narodowe Ziemi Przemyskiej,* Przemyśl; *Muzeum im. Władysława Orkana,* Rabka; *Muzeum Regjonalne w Rohatynie,* Rohatyn; *Muzeum Towarzystwa "Bojkiwszczyna,"* Sambor; *Muzeum Polskiego Krajoznawczego,* Sandomiez; *Muzeum Podlaskie im. M. Astanowicza,* Siedlce; *Muzeum Powiatowe im. Wł. Reymonta,* Skierniewice; *Muzeum Pokucie,* Stanisławów; *Regjonalne Muzeum Podolskie,* Tarnopol; *Muzeum Regjonalne P.T.K.,* Tomaszów Mazowiecki; *Muzeum Regjonalne Borów Tucholskich Polskiego Towarzystwa Krajoznawczego,* Tuchola; *Muzeum Towarzystwa Pryzjaciół Nauk w Wilnie,* Wilno; *Muzeum Etnograficzne Uniwersytetu Stefana Batorego,* Wilno; *Muzeum Ziemi*

Kujawskiej i Dobrzyńskiej, Włocławek; *Muzeum Tatrzańskie im. Dr. T. Chałubinskiego,* Zakopane.

Portugal

Treating of the folklore of all Portugal are *Museu Nacional de Historia Natural, Museum of Popular Art, Museu Etnológico* "Dr. Deite de Vasconcellos," all in Lisbon; and *Museu Etnológico Português,* in Belem.

Museu "Hipolito Cabaço," Alemquer; *Museu Arqueologico Infante D. Henrique,* Faro; *Museu Regional "Francisco Tavare Proença Júnior,"* Castelo Branco, all regional folklore museums. *Museu Maritimo,* Faro, Portuguese fishermen's lore.

Rumania

Baron Brukenthalisches Museum, Hermannstadt-Sibiu, Rumanian peasant folklore.

Siam

National Museum, Bangkok, material illustrating Siamese culture.

Spain

Museo de Pueblo Español, Madrid, folklore of all Spain.

Typical of the smaller regional Spanish museums is *Museo Municipal de San Telmo,* San Sebastián, which illustrates Basque culture.

Sweden

With over seven hundred open-air museums, most of them true folk museums, in the country by the beginning of 1950, Sweden has perhaps the finest national program in existence for the exhibition of folklore material. The unique and extensive system of open-air folk museums is headed by the famous *Open Air Museum* at Skansen, a prototype for such exhibits throughout the world.

Statens Etnografiska Museum (National Ethnographical Museum), Stockholm, world as well as Swedish ethnography.

Northern Museum, Stockholm, peasant culture of Sweden.

Malmö Museum, Malmö, Swedish "cultural history."

Gotland Museum, Visby.

Museum of Cultural History, Lund.

Norbotten Museum, Luleå, Lapp life.

Vasterbotten Museum, Umeå.

Municipal "local life and culture" museums in Goteborg, Norrköping, Hälsingborg, Ystad, and Varberg.

Switzerland

Musée d'Ethnographie de la Ville de Genève, Geneva, collections on the cultures of Africa, Asia, Oceania, and America. This institution also houses the headquarters of the International Archives of Folk Music.

Schweizerisches Landesmuseum, Zürich, native Swiss cultures.

Kunstgewerbemuseum der Stadt Zürich, Zürich, Swiss folk art.

Turkey

Ethnographical Museum, Ankara, and *Museum of Oriental Antiquities,* Istanbul, have exhibits illustrative of Turkish, Near Eastern, and Oriental folklore.

U.S.S.R.

Museums treating of the cultures of all Russia are *State Museum of Anthropology,* Moscow; *Museum of the Institute of Anthropology and Ethnography of the Academy of Sciences,* Leningrad; *Museum of the Peoples of the U.S.S.R.,* Moscow.

Museum of the History of Religion, Leningrad.

Leningrad Hermitage, general Russian ethnography.

Moscow Historical Museum, implements, houses, and a monastery, from the 17th century. Typical of regional folk museums is the *Chelyabinsk Museum of Local Lore,* Chelyabinsk.

United States

Alabama

Birmingham Public Library Museum, cultural history of Central Africa, China, and Mexico, American Indian material, general collection of archeological and historical objects of the states of the South.

Alabama Anthropological Society, Montgomery, local anthropology and archeology.

Arizona

Casa Grande National Monument Museum, Coolidge, prehistoric and early American Indian implements and ornaments, material illustrating cremation and burial customs.

Museum of Northern Arizona, Flagstaff, Hopi Indian material and local archeology.

Arizona State Museum, Tucson, archeology and ethnology of the Indians of the Southwest.

Gila Pueblo Museum and *Wayside Museums,* Globe, archeology of the American Indian.

Pueblo Grande Museum, Phoenix; *Yavapai Archæological and Historical Society,* Prescott; *Smoki Public Museum,* Prescott.

California

Museum of Anthropology of the University of California, Berkeley, anthropology and physical anthropology of Egypt, Peru, the ancient Mediterranean civilizations, and western North America.

Los Angeles Museum of History, Science, and Art, ethnology of central Asia, India, the East Indies, Australia, Melanesia, Polynesia, Africa, and the Americas.

Southwest Museum, Los Angeles, archeology, ethnology, and history of the southwestern states.

San Diego Museum, general anthropology and ethnology, ethnology of the American Indian, Mayan archeology, Egyptian and Babylonian antiquities.

Oakland Public Museum, ethnology of California, Alaska, British Columbia, and the Pacific Islands.

Claremont Colleges Museum, Claremont, Indian cultures of the Southwest, California pioneer exhibits.

Special collections: *Glidden Museum of Island Indians,* Catalina Island, artifacts, utensils, and musical instruments of the native Indians of Catalina Island; *San Joaquin Pioneer Historical Museum,* Stockton, relics of the California pioneers; *Pioneer Museum,* Ventura, pioneer material; *Sutter's Fort Historical Museum,* Sacramento, material from the Great Gold Rush.

Riverside Municipal Museum, Riverside; *California State Indian Museum,* Sacramento; *Desert Branch of the Southwest Museum of Los Angeles,* at Twenty-Nine Palms.

Colorado

University of Colorado Museum, Boulder, prehistory and ethnology of the Southwest, ethnology of the American Indian, the Chinese, Japanese, and Philippine peoples.

Colorado State Museum, Denver, cliff-dweller cultures, life of the early Colorado pioneers.

Taylor Museum for Southwest Studies, Colorado Springs.

State Historical Society of Colorado Museum, Denver.

Connecticut

Peabody Museum of Natural History, Yale University, New Haven, anthropological collections from North, Central, and South America, and Europe.

Connecticut Archæological Collection, Hartford.

District of Columbia

Smithsonian Institution (the United States National Museum), Washington, comprehensive collections of antiquities of the Stone Age, objects of primitive arts and industries, religious objects, musical instruments, American Colonial material, and ethnological specimens from all parts of the world.

Library of Congress: see FOLKLORE SECTION OF THE LIBRARY OF CONGRESS.

Illinois

Field Museum of Natural History, Chicago, one of the principal agencies in the world for the collection and exhibition of ethnological material of Far Eastern cultures; in addition to material relevant to the peoples of China, Tibet, Japan, India, Siberia, Korea, and Malaysia, the Museum possesses ethnological material on the Eskimos, the Indians of North, South, and Central America, and the cultures of the Philippines, Melanesia, Africa, Madagascar, Polynesia, and Micronesia, also archeological material from Egypt, Mesopotamia, Etruria, Greece, Italy, and Ireland.

Oriental Institute Museum, Chicago, Near Eastern ethnology and archeology, Egyptian, Assyrian, Assyro-Babylonian, Persian-Moslem, Hittite, and Palestinian material.

The University of Illinois, Urbana, houses several museums of value in the study of folklore: among these the *Museum of European Culture,* cultural history of Europe; the *Museum of Classical Art and Archæology,* Minoan, Mycenæan. Greek, and Roman life and civilization, together with Oriental material; *Museum of Natural History,* ethnological material, including Mound Builder and Eskimo specimens.

Illinois State Museum, Springfield, American Indian material.

Dickson's Mound Builders' Tombs, Lewiston, are an example of an Indian burial ground.

Indiana

Wayne County Historical Association, Richmond, American Indian material, early American chinaware, furniture, looms, farm implements, vehicles, costumes, musical instruments, and various pioneer material.

Indiana State Museum, Indianapolis, Mound Builder and American Indian material.

Public Art Gallery, Richmond, Egyptian, Sudanese, African, and American Indian war material.

Tippecanoe County Historical Association, Lafayette, American Indian material, reproduction of an early blockhouse on the site of an old French trading post.

Indiana University Museum, Bloomington, folklore exhibits.

Iowa

Davenport Public Museum, archeological material from the Southwest, Mexico, and Peru, and ethnological exhibits of Eskimo and American Indian cultures.

Museum of Natural History, University of Iowa, Iowa City, ethnology of the Eskimos and the North American Indians, the peoples of Hawaii, Fiji, New Zealand, and Africa.

Norwegian-American Historical Museum, Luther College, Decorah, Norwegian pioneer life, and ethnological material of the Eskimo, Zulu, Sudanese, and Icelandic peoples.

Ellis Museum of Archæology, Maquoketa.

Kansas

Kansas State Historical Society, Topeka, historical material of the region, firearms, war material, Kansas pioneer objects.

Kentucky

Museum of Archæology and Anthropology, University of Kentucky, Lexington.

Louisiana

Museum, Tulane University Department of Middle American Research, New Orleans, archeological, ethnological, and historical materials of the peoples of Mexico and Central America.

Maine

Acadia National Park Museum of Stone Age Antiquities, Bar Harbor, American Indian archeological material from Mt. Desert Island.

Fort Western on the Kennebec, Augusta, an old fort and trading post, pioneer and Indian implements.

Maryland

Museum of the Department of Art and Archæology, Johns Hopkins University, Baltimore, Egyptian, Greek, Roman, Oriental, and American archeology.

Massachusetts

Peabody Museum, Salem, ethnology of Korea, Japan, China, India, Siam, Tibet, the Pacific Islands, Mexico, South America, and North America; American archeology, whaling material from the early days of New England, early pioneer objects.

Semitic Museum, Harvard University, Cambridge, historical material from Babylon, Assyria, the Hittites, Egypt, Arabia, Palestine, Phœnicia, Syria, and Persia.

Harvard University Social Museum, problems of sociology in both Europe and America.

Harvard University College of Classical Antiquities Museum, archeology of Greece and Rome.

Peabody Museum of Archæology and Ethnology, Harvard University, ethnology of the aboriginal peoples of North and South America, Africa, Asia, and the Pacific Islands, archeological material from North, Central, and South America, Africa, and Europe.

Phillips Academy Department of American Archæology Museum, Andover, prehistory of New England and the eastern and southern states of the United States, material from the mounds and pueblos of New Mexico.

Old Dartmouth Historical Society and Whaling Museum, New Bedford, material illustrating the whaling industry of New England.

Society for the Preservation of New England Antiquities, Boston, maintains a chain of historic houses throughout Massachusetts and adjoining states.

Old Sturbridge Village Museum, Sturbridge, a restoration of an 18th and early 19th century village, with tavern and shops and homes.

Indian and Wayside Museums maintained by Harvard University.

Michigan

Museum of Anthropology, University of Michigan, Ann Arbor, archeology, ethnology, and physical anthropology of the Orient, the Great Lakes region of the United States, and the eastern United States, together with American Indian material.

Museum of Classical Archæology, University of Michigan, Greek and Roman archeological specimens.

Kalamazoo Museum and Art Institute, Egyptian, Indian, Chinese, Japanese, American pioneer, and American Indian material.

Michigan Pioneer Museum, Lansing, American Indian and early pioneer objects.

Museum of the Detroit Historical Society; Kent Scientific Museum, Grand Rapids; *Detroit Children's Museum.*

Minnesota

Museum of the Minnesota Historical Society, St. Paul, American Indian archeology and ethnology, pioneer material, and objects of the early fur trade of the region.

St. Paul Institute, St. Paul, archeological specimens from Egypt, the Philippines, and Australia, North American Indian ethnological material.

Missouri

Museum of the University of Missouri Department of Sociology, Columbia, American Indian implements and weapons, pottery from Missouri and New Mexican mounds, and ethnological material from the Aleutian Islands, Fiji, Puerto Rico, China, and the Philippines.

Daniel B. Dyer Museum, Kansas City, American Indian material, mound-dweller and cliff-dweller objects, Mexican and Oriental archeological specimens.

Missouri Historical Society Museum, St. Louis, American Indian utensils and implements.

Children's Museum, St. Joseph; *School of Nations Museum of The Principia,* St. Louis.

Montana

Glacier National Park Museum, Belton, Blackfoot Indian exhibits, historical material of northwest Montana.

Nebraska

Nebraska State Historical Society, Lincoln, prehistoric and historical American Indian objects, and pioneer material.

Nebraska State Museum, Lincoln.

New Hampshire

Dartmouth College Museum, Hanover, American Indian archeological and historical material, Cypriote and Assyrian collections, ethnological specimens from India, China, Japan, the Pacific Islands, Egypt, Africa.

New Hampshire Historical Society Museum, Concord, costumes, utensils, musical instruments, and farm implements of early New Hampshire, and American Indian historical material.

Museum of the New Hampshire Antiquarian Society, Hopkinton.

New Jersey

Newark Museum, Assyrian, Egyptian, and classical archeology, American Indian, Tibetan, and primitive African ethnological material.

Paterson Museum, archeology and ethnology of the American Indian, archeology of France, Belgium, Switzerland, Italy, and England.

New Jersey State Museum, Trenton; *Princeton Theological Seminary Mission Museum,* Princeton; *New Jersey Historical Society Museum,* Newark.

New Mexico

University of New Mexico Department of Archeology and Anthropology Museum, Albuquerque, archeology and anthropology of New Mexico.

Museum of New Mexico, Santa Fe, American Indian archeology and ethnology, prehistoric and historic Indian objects.

Historical Society of New Mexico Museum, Santa Fe, American Indian, Spanish, Mexican, and early American historical material.

Laboratory of Anthropology, Santa Fe, anthropological, ethnological, and archeological specimens from the southwestern states, together with Pueblo Indian and Navaho material.

Chaco Canyon National Monument Museum, Crown Point, objects of the prehistoric Pueblo Indians.

Aztec Ruins National Monument Museum, Aztec, archeology and anthropology of the region.

Wayside Museum, Coolidge, archeological material of the Southwest.

New York

American Museum of Natural History, New York, comprehensive collections illustrating the evolution of man and of the races of man, together with a great number of anthropological and ethnological collections.

Heye Foundation Museum of the American Indian, New York, archeological material of the Indian cultures of North, Central, and South America and the West Indies, including weapons, implements, tools, utensils, ceremonial objects, and burial artifacts, clothing, toys, medicine, totemic objects and costumes, musical instruments, and material illustrating tribal customs.

Jewish Museum, New York, Jewish religious material, including utensils, amulets, and ceremonial objects.

Metropolitan Museum of Art, New York, cultural material from the ancient world, the Orient, Europe, and America.

Buffalo Historical Society Museum, American Indian ethnology, including specimens from the Woodland and Plains Indians, together with pioneer material, early American costumes, and a numismatic collection.

New York State Museum, Albany, American Indian ethnological material, including exhibits illustrative of Iroquois culture.

Brooklyn Museum, New York; *Cloisters,* New York; *Buffalo Museum of Science,* Buffalo; *Fort Ticonderoga Museum,* Fort Ticonderoga; *Chase National Bank Collection of Moneys of the World,* New York; *Museum of the City of New York; Museum of Folk and Peasant Arts,* Riverdale-on-Hudson; *Rochester Museum of Arts and Sciences; New York Historical Society Museum,* New York; *Upper Susquehanna Collection of Hartwick College,* Oneonta; *Brooklyn Children's Museum,* New York; *Asia Institute Museum,* New York; *Schomberg Collection of Negro Literature,* New York (including folk art).

North Carolina

North Carolina State Museum, Raleigh, anthropology and history of North Carolina.

North Dakota

North Dakota State Historical Society Museum, Bismarck, American Indian anthropology, archeology, and history, illustrations of Indian songs, customs, and ceremonies.

Ohio

Ohio State Museum, Ohio State University, Columbus, restorations of cultures of the region, and local prehistoric and historical material.

Cleveland Museum of Natural History, ethnology of the Mound Builders, the American Indians, the Eskimos, and primitive African peoples.

Cincinnati Art Museum, Stone Age African and American Indian exhibits.

Ohio State Archæological and Historical Society Museum, Columbus; *Hebrew Union College Museum,* Cincinnati; *Western Reserve Historical Society Museum,* Cleveland; *Dayton Public Library Museum.*

Oklahoma

Anthropological Collections of the University of Oklahoma, Norman, encompass archeological and ethnological material from Oklahoma and the Southwest.

University of Oklahoma Department of Anthropology Museum, Norman, archeology and ethnology of the Indians of Oklahoma.

Anthropological Collections of the University of Tulsa, Tulsa, archeology and ethnology of Oklahoma and the Southwest.

Oklahoma Historical Society Museum, Oklahoma City; *Chilocco Indian Agricultural School Museum,* Chilocco; *Osage Indian Reservation Museum,* Pawhuska.

Oregon

University of Oregon Museum of Art and *Oregon State Museum of Anthropology,* University of Oregon, Eugene, both contain American Indian ethnological and anthropological material.

Pennsylvania

University of Pennsylvania Museum, Philadelphia, North American and Alaskan Indians, the Mayans, Mexican Indian tribes; ethnology of the primitive peoples of South America, Europe, Asia, Africa, and the Pacific Islands; antiquities from Egypt, Greece, Etruria, Crete,

Cyprus, and Rome; Babylonian antiquities; material from Palestine, China, India, Persia, Arabia, and Turkey.

Carnegie Museum, Pittsburgh, Egyptian and Central American antiquities; Chinese, Japanese, and south Asiatic material; American Indian ethnological exhibits; and groups illustrating the cultures of Africa and the Pacific Islands.

Academy of Natural Sciences of Philadelphia, anthropological material from Greenland, South America, and the Pacific Islands.

National Museum, Independence Hall, Philadelphia; *Wyoming Historical and Geological Society Museum,* Wilkes-Barre; *Reading Public Museum and Art Gallery,* Reading; *Moravian Historical Society,* Nazareth. See PENNSYLVANIA DUTCH FOLKLORE.

Rhode Island

Park Museum, Providence, American Indian, Eskimo, and Pacific Island ethnology.

Museum of Primitive Cultures, Peace Dale, Stone Age cultures of Europe, general American archeological specimens, including objects of early Rhode Island cultures, and of the "Red Paint" people of Maine.

Rhode Island Historical Society Museum, Providence, pioneer and American Indian material.

South Carolina

University of South Carolina Museum, Columbia, and *Clemson Agricultural College Museum,* Clemson, both exhibit local history, and material on the ethnology of the American Indian.

Charleston Museum, Charleston.

South Dakota

University of South Dakota Museum, Vermillion, archeological and historical specimens of American Indian cultures.

State Historical Society Museum, Pierre, American Indian artifacts and historical material.

Tennessee

University of Chattanooga Museum, Chattanooga, American Indian archeological and ethnological material, and collections illustrating the cultures of Egypt, Palestine, Japan, China, Korea, Mexico, and Africa.

Tennessee State Museum, Nashville, ethnology, history, and prehistory of the American Indian.

Vanderbilt University Archeological Collections, Nashville.

Texas

University of Texas Department of Anthropology Museum, Austin, Southwest Indian artifacts, European neolithic specimens, and ethnological material from the United States, Africa, and Mexico.

Baylor University Museum, Waco, general archeological, historical, and ethnological collections.

North Texas State Teachers College Museum, Denton; *Houston Museum of Natural History; Museum of the Scientific Society of San Antonio.*

Utah

University of Utah Department of Anthropology Museum, Salt Lake City, archeological and ethnological material of the Indians of the Southwest and the Great Basin; Mexican and Peruvian culture exhibits; and archeological specimens from Babylonia.

Latter-Day Saints Church Museum, Salt Lake City, Mormon life and history.

State House Museum, Fillmore, American Indian and pioneer material.

Vermont

Robert Hall Fleming Museum of the University of Vermont, Burlington, archeological and ethnological exhibits of the Indian tribes of Vermont, and general ethnological specimens from American Indian cultures and from the South Pacific Islands, the Orient, and Africa.

Virginia

Williamsburg Restoration, Williamsburg, is a project aiming at the preservation and imitation of the most significant portions of the Colonial city of Williamsburg.

Valentine Museum, Richmond, Virginia cultural history, and Oriental and American Indian ethnology.

University of Richmond Museum, Richmond; *Hugh Mercer Apothecary Shop,* Fredericksburg.

Washington

Washington State Museum of the University of Washington, Seattle, ethnology of Indians of the Pacific Northwest and Alaska; ethnology of the Eskimos and of peoples of the Philippines; archeology of the Columbia River region; Colonial and pioneer Washington.

Washington State Historical Society Museum, Tacoma; *Columbia River Archeological Society Museum,* Wenatchee.

West Virginia

West Virginia State Museum, Charleston, American Indian and pioneer ethnological and historical exhibits.

Oglebay Park Museums, Wheeling, local Indian ethnology and history, and Mound Builder objects.

Wisconsin

Logan Museum, Beloit College, Beloit, ethnological specimens of the American Indian and the peoples of the South Pacific Islands and Africa, archeological material from Europe and Africa.

Wisconsin Historical Museum, State Historical Society of Wisconsin, Madison, American Indian and early American historical and ethnological material.

State Teachers College Department of History Museum, La Crosse; *Public Museum of Milwaukee; Neville Public Museum,* Green Bay; *Museum of the Kenosha County Historical Society,* Kenosha; *Oshkosh Public Museum.*

Wyoming

Yellowstone National Park Museums, American archeology and the ethnology of the American Indian.

Uruguay

Museo de Historia Natural, and *Museo Nacional Histórico,* Montevideo, both have general Uruguayan and South American folklore material; the latter institution exhibits a special collection of Gaucho objects.

Venezuela

Museo de Ciencias Naturales, Caracas, Tairona funeral treasures.

Yugoslavia

Etnografski Muzej, Belgrade, folk culture of the Balkan peoples.

Zemaljski Muzej Kraljevine Jugoslavije u Sarajevu, Sarajevo, Bosnian and Herzegovinian cultures.

Narodni Etnografiski Muzej, Split, Yugoslavian and Balkan national costumes. [GG]

musical bow A primitive musical instrument consisting of an arched stick with a stretched string or connecting fiber from end to end, resembling the bow of the hunter, but requiring a resonance chamber to make the string vibration audible, and occasionally making use of a bridge or of a string loop dividing the cord into sections of different tone. It has been known since neolithic times and is distributed over much of North and South America, Africa, Asia, and Melanesia. It is most used as accompaniment to fertility rites and women's ceremonies, for intimate leisure-time music, and for meditation and communication with spirits. The resonating chamber may be a large separate jar or bowl, an attached gourd, or the mouth of the player, as with the jew's harp, and the size ranges from the 25-foot length used by the Chinantecs of northwestern Mexico to the small intimate instrument held against the teeth in the Chaco.

Among the Mískito and Sumo tribes of the Caribbean lowlands the musical bow, sometimes with gourd soundbox, is a woman's instrument, and in Rhodesia it accompanies girls' initiation ceremonies. The Cora musical bow of Mexico is played for corn rites and is the gift of God (originally of the earth goddess, whose pottery or calabash bowl forms its resonator). God teaches the medicine men to play it. The Mexican instrument, as well as a large type found in India, is sometimes played by striking it with a pair of sticks. Young men of the Chaco tribes make and play a small double musical bow, actually two bows attached by interlacing the strings, one of which is held against the teeth and the other rubbed across it like a fiddle bow. This is now played as a pastime. Californian Maidu and East African Akamba commune with spirits through the thin nasal sound of the musical bow. The African Wahehe have a tale about the instrument closely related to the singing-bone motif of other peoples, in which a girl is murdered and her body becomes the bow, her head the gourd soundbox, and her arms and legs the strings. [TCB]

Muskrat A North American aquatic rodent (*Ondatra zibethica*) chiefly prominent in North American Indian mythology as the animal who succeeds in bringing up earth or sand from the depths of the primeval waters, or after the flood, in order that the world may be made. Muskrat often succeeds after other animals fail, but in some American Indian mythologies the feat is credited to other creatures—Beaver, Hell-Diver, or Crayfish. Muskrat appears as a minor animal character in other American Indian tales, but is not particularly associated with any one tale except that of earth-diving. Muskrat is also used as a man's personal name among the Crow Indians and other Plains tribes. See ATAENSIC; EARTH DIVER. [EWV]

mustard Mustard was well known among the ancients, especially in Greece where its seeds were so esteemed that physicians attributed its discovery to Æsculapius. Pythagoras is said to have recommended it as an antidote for the bite of a scorpion; Hippocrates advised seeds of the plant both internally and as a counterirritant poultice. Pliny named 40 remedies in which mustard was the chief ingredient. It is mentioned several times in parables in the Bible (*Matthew* xvii, 20, *Luke* xvii, 6); among the rabbis, "a grain of mustard seed" was a symbol of something very small.

In Hindu mythology, magic powers are attributed to mustard seeds, e.g. enabling one to travel through the air, turning one's enemy into a mare, revealing secret places and diseases. Mustard has been much used as an aphrodisiac. Conversely, the Greeks and Indians believed that its seeds, mixed with oil or honey, would prevent conception.

In England, mustard has extensive medicinal use. It is excellent for clarifying the blood and for weak stomachs, being an herb of Mars, but unfit for choleric people; it also strengthens the heart and resists poison. Mustard seed draws out splinters from the flesh. It is good for epilepsy and lethargy; it can be taken internally or applied externally, and is rubbed on the nostrils, forehead, and temples to warm and quicken the spirits. It purges the brain by sneezing and draws down rheum and other viscous humors. A decoction of the seed in wine resists poison, the malignity of mushrooms, and the bites of venomous creatures. The seed taken either in an electuary or drink stirs up lust, helps the spleen, eases pains in the sides and gnawings of the bowels; used as a gargle it draws up the palate of the mouth, if fallen, dissolves swellings about the throat. Mustard is frequently chewed to help toothache. Mustard poultice is good for the pains of sciatica, also for gout and other joint-aches, and is often used to ease pains in the sides, loins, shoulders, and other parts of the body. It is also used to help the falling off of hair, and to cleanse the face from spots, freckles, and other deformities (Culpeper).

North American Meskwaki Indians used the ground-up seeds as a snuff to cure cold in the head. The Shinnecock and the Mohegans bind leaves of the plant to the skin to relieve toothache or headache; the former also use mustard in a poultice for body pains.

mutilation The impulses most commonly associated with mutilation, whether of a ritual, orgiastic, or social nature are pride, revenge, a desire to get power over the gods or the forces of nature. All parts of the body are subject to mutilations though the head—hair, ears, nose, lips, cheek, and tongue—, the chest and arms, the sexual organs, and the feet seem to be the most popular.

The rituals connected with the passage from the state of childhood to the state of maturity usually referred to as initiation ceremonies or puberty ceremonies, have as one of their purposes the need to demonstrate that the candidate is able to withstand pain and torture and thus to perform the functions, religious, magic, and social of an adult in the community. In American culture, remnants of these ceremonies—usually without mutilation—are preserved in the initiations into lodges and the "hell weeks" and hazings of college fraternities.

At puberty ceremonies scars on the chest, neck, or face were kept from healing and were considered a mark of maturity and therefore of beauty. Among the West African tribes the wounds are preserved by putting in them the fluff of a tree. Mutilations of the bodies of young men and women are frequent in many cultures and are particularly popular among the Australian aborigines. In north central Australia cuts on the back and on the neck of the candidates are in memory of events from the early history of the tribe. Young men and women among the Kikuyus of East Africa are proud of incisions made on their bodies. The sisters of men of New Guinea make scars on their chests when the man spears his first dugong, and some of the California Indians burned the images of their tutelary deities into their bodies. The Ba-Mbalas scarred their faces and bodies at puberty. The peoples of Formosa and Malaya are reported to file their teeth to sharp points or to grind them down. The Wiradthuri cut their gums or the flesh under their tongues; the Kamilaroi gash their arms with flint or shell. Bantu and Negro tribes in Africa knocked out their teeth; the Seri Indians of North America knocked out the teeth of their girls before marriage. Holes were made in the tongues of medicine men among some central Australian tribes during initiation.

Mutilation of the sexual organs of boys and girls are of many sorts and are usually lumped under the term circumcision. They include circumcision proper, or the cutting off of the foreskin of the penis, subincision, infibulation, excision, artificial defloration. Explanations of these customs are as varied as the peoples who practice them, but two themes are dominant: they are preparation for the responsibilities of maturity, and proof that the candidates have been accepted into their community as grown men and women. The circumcised or élite are distinguished from the uncircumcised.

Many peoples regard these mutilations as a mark of distinction. Among peoples who inflict them at initiation ceremonies, they are evidence that the individual now "belongs." German students in the early part of this century were proud of the saber cuts they got in duels; winning a letter in American universities or wearing the school tie in Britain expresses a similar feeling. Some peoples of Africa split their lips. On Fiji, Easter, and Nicobar Islands ears are mutilated; and the piercing of ears has a religious significance in India, Burma, and the Malay peninsula, as it has a social significance in some communities in southern Europe and the Americas. The Botocudos of South America pierce the underlip and the ear lobes of young girls and gradually enlarge the opening until amulets can be inserted. Similar practices have been reported elsewhere. Filed teeth, sometimes blackened or decorated with gold, were known among some California tribes, the Mayas of Yucatán, and in Sumatra and Borneo. The Filipinos are very proud of the gold or brass teeth which they were able to procure through the free dental service of the Philippine Red Cross. The production of tiny feet by binding is reported from among the Kutchin Indians of the Arctic. The bound feet of Chinese women are marks of beauty and have a definite erotic significance, as the attempts of Euro-American women to keep their feet small by wearing undersize shoes has also an indefinite though clear erotic motive, similar to the wearing of corsets and girdles to distort the abdomen or emphasize the breasts.

The impulse to mutilate the body in moments of religious excitement is thought to give power over the gods or forces of nature. The men of the Tonga Islands have been known to cut off a finger to appease the anger of the gods, and the amputation of the little finger of the sister or daughter of a sick man will cure him. When a man is ill in Bengal, his mother or daughters draw blood from their chests to propitiate the goddess. The Dieri of South Australia sprinkle the tribe with blood from gashes made on the bodies of two tribesmen. This will produce rain. In central Australia, blood on the bodies of people who are sick or aged will give strength. It will also seal a covenant. The Syrian priests of the goddess Cybele wounded themselves. Arnobius reports the case of a woman who cut off her breasts in devotion to Aphrodite. The priests of the Roman god Bellona sprinkled blood from wounds made on their shoulders on the image of the god. Self-castration during the ecstasies of the spring orgies of the Greeks and Romans has also been reported. In the Americas reports are early and unreliable. Adelung says that the Cochinis of California cut off the little fingers of wives and sisters to cure disease, and Garcilaso de la Vega said that the Aztecs and Peruvians drew blood from arms, legs, ears, and nose at religious festivals. The Mískito tribes of Honduras and Nicaragua did so to influence the success of important undertakings. In 1927 a Chinese student during an anti-British demonstration was seen to cut off his little finger and write on the city wall of Peking the Chinese characters, "Down with Britain." This mutilation was possibly similar to others of a magico-religious nature in that it was performed at a moment of considerable excitement.

Mutilations of several sorts are punishments for offenses against civil or social laws. The most frequent of these offenses is sexual intercourse with persons of a forbidden category. In recent times the hair was shaved from the heads of French, Dutch, and other women who received Nazis, or were suspected of receiving them.

Although the laws against adultery are severe, one anthropologist has warned his readers to accept with skepticism reports about adultery being punished with death. However, Johnston reports that adultery with a king's wife in the Uganda Protectorate caused both to be chopped to pieces and in Ashanti emasculation is the punishment. American cuckolds frequently threaten to emasculate but seldom do. In parts of Australia the adulterous woman was made accessible to all comers. In South Australia, the punishment for the first offense was branding, for the second, spearing in the leg, for the third, death. Among some North American Indian tribes, the punishments were mutilation and disfigurement; in Mexico the women had their noses and ears cut off. In the book of Manu the book-punishment for an adulteress was to be torn to pieces, for her lover to be roasted on an iron bed. In the Viraf-Namak the adultress had to gash her bosom and breasts. The nose and ears of the adulterous Hindu wife were cut off. The Assyrians made generous use of mutilation as punishment for crime.

The Code of Hammurabi ordered that a surgeon who caused the death of a patient or the loss of an eye must have his hands cut off, a certain way to protect the life of other patients. The crime of striking a father was punished by cutting off a hand; the tongue was cut out for ungrateful speeches; the eye was torn out for illegal curiosity. Examples of the mutilation of both the living and dead in ancient times are plentiful. In Europe throughout the Middle Ages and into recent times, punishment by amputation of noses, ears, hands, by branding or gashing were considered appropriate for crimes which are now thought to be petty. Flaying alive was the punishment for more serious crimes. See ATTIS; FINGERS; MASCHALISMOS; PENITENTES.   R. D. JAMESON

☞ Deliberate destructive change in body-form was a common practice among North American Indians. Such changes were accomplished by piercing holes in or cutting off various parts of the body or face; they might be either self-inflicted or effected by another person for various purposes: as punishment, to render oneself pitiful in the sight of supernatural beings; as ordeals, in fulfilment of vows; as part of mourning ritual, to ensure good health; or merely because it was fashionable.

An unfaithful Plains Indian wife was likely to have her nose cut off by her husband; this well-attested practice persisted into historic times. Plains Indians, asking for help from the Sun or other dieties, sacrificed finger joints to the deity; this also was a common practice. Youths undergoing puberty initiation rites were scarified by their elders; in the Southeast the jaw of the garfish was used, in other regions, obsidian flakes or stone knives. Plains Indians inserted skewers between the muscles of their legs, arms, or backs, threaded ropes through the holes, and dragged heavy objects at the ends of these ropes in the Sun dance ceremony, in fulfilment of vows made, or to receive the blessing of the supernaturals. Widows and bereaved parents gashed their arms and legs so that the blood flowed freely, after the death of a spouse or child. The septum of an infant's or young child's nose was pierced to accommodate the noseplug worn later in life to ensure good health or for fashionable reasons; the upper lip was pierced to accommodate labrets, and ear lobes were pierced, or the rims of the ears slit, so that ear ornaments could be worn for reasons of health or fashion. Among many tribes tattooing of the faces, and sometimes the bodies, of men and women was also a common practice. [EWV]

☞ Among South American Indians, self-inflicted wounds are a common expression of grief for the loss of a relative. This custom was carried to extremes among the ancient Charrua tribes of the Parana delta. The women cut off the joint of a finger after the burial of a relative and lacerated their arms, breasts, and sides. Early travelers saw women who had even lost the joints of both hands. Men thrust wooden rods through their skin and buried themselves up to the head in holes for a whole night. Apinaye, Kayapo, Karaja, and Achuare Indians gashed themselves with their arrows. At the burial of a chief, Guahibo women pierced their tongues with a sharp bone. In many tribes of the Amazon and of the Gran Chaco, the Indians puncture their skin with bone awls to dispel fatigue or to impart strength to their bodies. The nature of the bone used for the operation is of great importance since they believe it can transmit to them the qualities of the animal to which it belonged. Awls made of jaguar bone give ferocity, for instance, of deer bone, swiftness, etc. [AM]

Müy'ingwa Male maize spirit of the Hopi underworld; chief of the nadir, god of vegetation, and father of the underworld. Müy'ingwa is represented as sitting below the earth, wearing a mask of clouds of all five colors (yellow, blue-green, red, white, black), with butterflies and birds of all colors, with speckled corn and sweet corn, melons, squash, cotton, and beans. He is covered with grain; as his feet are ears of corn, he could not move very fast when the people came up from the underworld. Müy'ingwa is represented as a kachina, impersonated by masked dancers, in Hopi dances. [EWV]

Mylitta A Babylonian goddess, identified by Herodotus with Aphrodite and probably Ishtar in one of her forms, i.e. as goddess of fertility. The name means She who causes to bear. Once during her life, every Babylonian woman had to sit within the precinct of the temple of Mylitta, awaiting the first stranger who offered to have intercourse with her. When the stranger threw a coin, any coin, into her lap in the name of the goddess, she left the precinct with him and freed herself of her obligation. The fee was given to the goddess. According to Herodotus, some women were soon released, but the uglier ones occasionally waited three or four years. The common idea that strangers bring fertility and may be gods in disguise underlies the custom.

myrtle An evergreen shrub or tree (genus *Myrtus*), especially *M. communis* of Asia and southern Europe. One of the many origin stories of the myrtle says that it was the chief scented tree in the Garden of Eden and Adam was therefore allowed to take it with him. It was said variously to have been transformed from Myrtelus, son of Mercury, from the maid Myrsine who bested Minerva in a foot-race, or from the discarded lovers of the enchantress Alcina.

To the Jews myrtle signified the promise and bounty of God. God promised to plant myrtle in the wilderness for the children of Israel (*Isaiah* xli, 19; lv, 13): "instead of the brier shall come up the myrtle tree." In the rites of Tabernacles, the bearing of the palm branch, citron, myrtle, and willows (*Lev.* xxiii, 40) symbolizes atonement for the various sins of those human parts symbolized by these trees (respectively, spine, heart, eye, mouth). Thus myrtle, symbol of the eye, symbolizes also atonement for the lusts of the eye.

Myrtle was sacred to Aphrodite and Astarte throughout the Mediterranean region. In Greece its evergreen quality signified immortality and was a promise of resurrection. It was associated with the death of kings, and was regarded in general as the tree of death. Greek colonists carried myrtle boughs to the founding of a new colony—double token of the fact that association with the old colony was dead plus the gesture to Aphrodite to prosper the new. In Athens it was symbolic of authority; magistrates wore wreaths of myrtle. In Rome it was used to crown bloodless victors. It also signified unlawful or incestuous love and was barred from certain Roman ceremonies. See BONA DEA.

Myrtle is not one of the trees in the Old Irish Tree Alphabet, but Robert Graves holds that it was probably the Greek equivalent of the elder (see *The White Goddess*, p. 220).

Pliny mentions two old myrtle trees in the sanctuary of Quirinus, one of which flourished while the patricians were in power, withered with the rising strength of the plebeians, while the second flourished with their growing power. See SEPARABLE SOUL.

In England it was considered lucky to have myrtle growing about. In Somersetshire it was the luckiest of all plants for a window box; but it would not grow unless planted by a woman. In Wales myrtle on each side of a house door would keep love and peace inside; if dug up, love and peace depart. Medieval German brides sometimes wore myrtle wreaths to their weddings as a protection against pregnancy. In Prussia it was formerly said that a girl engaged to be married must not plant myrtle or the wedding would not come off. Whether these last several beliefs refer to the shrub myrtle or to what is often called the common myrtle (i.e. trailing periwinkle, *Vinca minor*) is not ascertained.

mysterious, holy, and powerful A concept of the human mind from earliest times: the basic psychological reaction to the universe and environment which underlies all religion. The man in awe in the presence of the astonishing and mysterious, cognizant of its power, and inevitably stirred to terror or ecstasy, forms the added concept holy, and is the religious man.

It follows that from this unknown and unfathomable power comes strength, food and plenty, success, life itself, birth, fecundity, and eventually death. Man has reacted to the concept everywhere with a build-up of ritual, prayer, propitiation, interdiction, and sacrifice designed to augment and insure the continuance of this power, and to receive, increase, and communicate its beneficent effects.

That which gives power to medicines, amulets, and incantations, and truth to the spoken word is this mysterious and holy power. It is the cause of and inherent in everything extraordinary and miraculous. It is the *makt* (might) of modern Swedish folklore. This special sacredness is inherent in kings, priests, and shamans, in certain objects (e.g. bull-roarers, churingas, drums, rattles, masks); it is in brides, the sexual act, in just-born infants and animals, in all first fruits, in epileptics, in strangers, and in all marvelous unknown things, like phonographs and airplanes. All primitive peoples find it in certain trees, in certain powerful and wily animals, and in the killers of such animals who become contaminated with the mystery and holiness of the animal and must be divested of it by special rites before returning to the safe commonplaces of daily life.

The concept of mysterious, holy, and powerful is inherent in the Polynesian tabu; that which is holy is therefore forbidden to ordinary usage. The same ideas are inherent in the Zulu *hlonipa* and Bechuana *ila*. *Sumangat* is the Malay term for their mysterious "life-stuff." See BARAKA; HUACA; MANA; MANITU; ORENDA; TABU; WAKAN.

☞ That the ability to perform in a superhuman way is characteristic of deities and supernatural beings, and that these beings can in turn aid human beings so that they also can perform in superhuman ways, is constantly assumed in North American Indian myth, folktale, and belief.

This assumption is reflected in cultural practices of the American Indians, especially in those centering around the so-called "vision quest." Except in the Southwestern Pueblos, young people everywhere in North America were enjoined at puberty to seek aid, advisement, and instruction from supernatural beings. Rendering themselves pitiable objects in the sight of the supernaturals through fasting, isolation, exhaustion, etc., the candidates were, if successful in their quest, visited by some specific being who advised them, taught them songs, etc. Later these supernaturals would return at

intervals to continue instruction, provided, of course, that the candidate followed the line of conduct which had been outlined to him.

The First People of the Mythical Age are everywhere in North America powerful beings; this was part of their natural endowment and is unquestioningly accepted as fact. The human beings who followed them never had any of the powers of the First People, but could be given some by the latter if they behaved in the proper way. However, a point which has received little emphasis is that even among the First People there are many indications that "power" was not a general or unspecialized attribute shared equally by all, but specific supernaturals possessed specific power or powers only; they were not omnipotent beings. The theme of power lost through abuse or violation of a tabu, recurrent in North American trickster tales especially, presupposes that specific beings had to learn from other beings how to juggle their eyes (see EYE-JUGGLER) or obtain food by magical means (see BUNGLING HOST), to mention only two examples; if, furthermore, this learned power was used too often or unwisely it was lost to the learner.

In the same way abuse of power led to loss of such power as human beings acquired from vision-questing, from dreams, trances, epileptic seizures, etc. That it was specific power to perform specific acts which they lost— or kept—as it was specific powers which the First People possessed or acquired has not been generally emphasized in the literature on the North American Indian vision quest, or in discussions of the powers of the First People in North American mythology, but would seem to be a point worth investigating. [EWV]

mysterious housekeeper In several North American Indian tales, a man or group of bachelors find their house put in order by a mysterious housekeeper while they are away from home. In the tale of Mudjikiwis several brothers who live together find this done for them, and when the mysterious housekeeper, a beautiful girl, is discovered she marries one of the brothers. In the widely distributed Eskimo tale of the Fox Wife, which is also Asiatic, a single hunter finds a woman who is really a fox, keeping house for him. He marries her, but later insults her and she dons her foxskin and leaves. See FOX; MUDJIKIWIS. [EWV]

Mystery Play of Tibet The name by which Europeans refer to the pageant of the lāmas which unsophisticated Tibetans call the *sTag-dmar-ch'am* or Dance of the Red-Tiger Devil, a deity of the Bon.

Originally this appears to have been a performance of a devil-dancing cult employed to expel the old year and to exorcise malignant demons and human enemies. It was possibly associated with human sacrifice and cannibalism. Under Buddhist influence it was changed to represent the triumph under the leadership of Saint Padmasambhava of the Indian missionary monks over the fiends of the earlier paganism. More recently the Ge-lug-pa sect has again altered it so that it represents the assassination of Lang-darma, the king who tried to rid Tibet of Lāmaism, followed by the restoration of religion. Despite Buddhist influence, however, the play still retains the devil-dancing, shamanist features of its earliest form.

The play is performed at government expense on the

last day of the year in the courtyards of all the temples or monasteries of the established church. It begins with a dance performed by black-mitred priests, followed by the entrance of a troupe of masked, man-eating, skull-carrying demons against whom man is helpless but not the lāmas, who offer them a libation of beer and rice or mustard seed. Troop after troop of these fiends in different masks rush on dancing and howling. These are followed by a crowd of wan, rag-covered shapes (the souls of dead men lost in space) which flee hither and thither among the troupes of fiends. As each group of demons comes on stage, they are exorcised by holy men, but are followed by another group.

The superiority of Buddhism over shamanism is then demonstrated with the arrival of Padmasambhava and his assistants which is followed by the disappearance of the demons.

On the second day of the play a dough effigy of a boy (representing the enemies of Tibet and Lāmaism) is stabbed with the phurbu by the Dam-ch'an Ch'os-rgyal or Holy King of Religion (Vajrabhairava, Yama, or Heruka). Then the limbs are chopped off and the figure is disemboweled. The heart, lungs, and intestines, which have been made as lifelike as possible, are extracted. Pieces of the effigy are thrown about among the actors and audience and a general scrambling for morsels to eat or to use as talismans follows.

A burnt sacrifice is then offered and a procession is organized. The priests, with the laity in the rear, march out of the courtyard with a three-headed image of dough which is abandoned to the crowd. It is torn to pieces and the morsels treasured. Then the whole company returns to the courtyard and the performance concludes with the appearance of the Chinese priest, Hwashang, who was expelled from Tibet by Saint Padmasambhava. Compare EATING THE GOD.

myth A story, presented as having actually occurred in a previous age, explaining the cosmological and supernatural traditions of a people, their gods, heroes, cultural traits, religious beliefs, etc. The purpose of myth is to explain, and, as Sir G. L. Gomme said, myths explain matters in "the science of a pre-scientific age." Thus myths tell of the creation of man, of animals, of landmarks; they tell why a certain animal has its characteristics (e.g. why the bat is blind or flies only at night), why or how certain natural phenomena came to be (e.g. why the rainbow appears or how the constellation Orion got into the sky), how and why rituals and ceremonies began and why they continue. Not all origin stories are myths, however; the myth must have a religious background in that its principal actor or actors are deities; the stories are thus systematized at least to the extent that they are related to a corpus of other stories in which the given god is a member of a pantheon. Where such interrelation does not occur, and where the gods or demigods do not appear, such stories are properly classified as folktale.

Much study of mythology has been made from very early times. Euhemerus, for example, saw in myth the apotheosis of human events; his Zeus was supposed to have been an actual Cretan king who had reigned some hundreds of years before. The more recent "comparative mythologists" saw in all myths an explanation of natural phenomena—sun, moon, rain, dawn, wind, etc.—

going to great lengths to induce the myth to fit the theory; this school was discredited by the attacks of such scholars as Andrew Lang and by the ridicule of others, e.g. the paper proving that Max Müller was a myth himself, by H. Gaidoz, editor of *Mélusine*. No single explanation of myth yet set forth is fully satisfactory. The interchange between myth and folktale—attachment of a folktale to some member of a pantheon, or loss of the divine element in a popular retelling—is constantly occurring. Many folktales, as the Grimms noted, are obviously "broken-down" myths; many myths utilize motifs and themes common to folktales the world over. A myth remains properly a myth only as long as the divinity of its actor or actors is recognized; when the trickster becomes human rather than divine, when the hero is a man rather than a god, myth becomes legend, if explanatory or limited to some specific location, or folktale, if more generalized. See ADAOX; FOLKLORE AND MYTHOLOGY.

The epic as a traditional form of literary expression is lacking in native North America, but long myths, which A. L. Kroeber characterizes as having an "epic breadth of manner," are told by the Mohave of southern California, the Yuma of Arizona, and several other Colorado River tribes. The Great Tales or Great Tellings of the Mohave are liberally interspersed with songs, and are said to be dreamt by their narrators; actually they conform to a definite tribal style. The long mythcycles of the Winnebago, an Eastern Woodlands Siouanspeaking tribe, have also been characterized as epiclike by Paul Radin, but were not chanted, and are often lacking in unity. The relation of the North American material to the Old World form of the epic would seem to be comparable to the relation of North American Indian dramatic performances to fully developed forms of drama. [EWV]

Mythical Age The first period, in North American Indian mythology, predating the appearance of human beings; an age when all the animals, birds, forces of nature, etc., behaved, talked, and at times looked like human beings. The only areas in North America where the Mythical Age is not part of the mythology are the Eskimo area, and parts of the Southwest; some of the Pueblo and Apache tribes in the latter region do not tell any tales relating to the prehuman age, but others do. On the west coast, where a prehuman, Mythical Age is stressed in native mythologies, a definite ending is given to this Age. Either 1) the beings of the Mythical Age are changed into birds, beasts, fishes, rocks, trees, etc., as a punishment, or 2) they agree to become the above when it is known among them that the human race is coming. In some California Indian mythologies the animals outline the new way of life that they will follow at the close of the Mythical Age: what food they will each eat, where each will live, what each will do. [EWV]

mythical animals, birds The term mythical animals refers to strange and fantastic creatures who have little or no connection with myths, in that stories about them have not been made into a system and have no theology. They frequently appear in folktales. They seem to have a connection with the projection and symbolization of popular fear and to be derived from travelers' tales of the weird and horrifying. Thus the basilisk, king of the serpents, a horrid spotted creature, must die if it sees itself in a mirror. The unicorn has the head and body of a horse, hind legs of an antelope, the beard of a goat, and is distinguished by a single horn in the middle of its forehead. Although the unicorn is a dangerous animal, it becomes tractable when approached by a virgin. The Chinese name for unicorn is the "four-not-likes" (like a horse but not like a horse, etc.). Other such animals are phœnix, griffin, dragon, sphinx, lamia. European accounts of mythical animals are in large part derived from the *Physiologus* or *Bestiary,* an early Christian account of zoology which was widely circulated and itself derived from the works of classical zoologists who accepted in good faith the weird tales of travelers. The early Christians elaborated on these in many ways and attached a moral to each account. See FEARSOME CRITTERS.   R. D. JAMESON

mythical islands The "never-never" lands found in the folklore of all peoples. The Greek islands of the blessed and the Celtic Islands of the Blessed are the abodes of immortals and heroes. Food, drink, and women are plentiful and always of the best quality. Avalon is the island where King Arthur, consoled by several fairy queens, is not too impatiently awaiting the moment of his country's need. Odysseus spent ten years on the island of the nymph Calypso who would have kept him forever had not the gods intervened. The Irish, themselves islanders and great travelers, have a number of tall tales called *imrama* or voyages which contain accounts of these and other islands. The inhabitants of the Island of Women are eternally young, beautiful, immortal, and pleasantly—and dangerously—immoral. Stories of such islands are found in the folklore of the Chinese, Japanese, and Ainus. Inasmuch as all of these islands have a similar social and economic system they seem to have more to do with the mechanics of the imaginative lives of seafaring men than with trade routes and the dissemination of themes. Suggestions that the Islands of the Blessed contain reminiscences of forgotten early voyages to the Canary Islands seem to be superfluous, although serious attention is still being given to the possibility that the island Atlantis, the home of a highly developed civilization, did at one time exist. Such stories gain plausibility by the fact that some islands, particularly in the Pacific, still do appear and

disappear in a disconcerting manner, and the accounts of some of these islands, such as the early accounts of Tahiti display a happy way of life not dissimilar to that described in the *imrama.* [RDJ]

Mythological cycle A body of ancient Irish mythological, epic, and pseudo-historical tales dealing with the five invasions of Ireland, the great mythological battles, the personages of the Tuatha Dé Danann, etc. Most of the material exists in the *Book of the Dun Cow* (11th century), the *Book of Leinster* (12th century), and includes also material in the *Dinnshenchas* or *History of Places* (12th century).

The five invasions of Ireland are those by: 1) Cessair, granddaughter of Noah, 2) Partholan, 3) the Nemedians, 4) the Tuatha Dé Danann, 5) the Milesians; or more commonly: 1) Partholan, 2) the Nemedians, 3) the Firbolgs, 4) the Tuatha Dé Danann, 5) the Milesians. The story of Cessair is that Noah had no room in the ark for Cessair, her father, brother, and husband, so to escape the Flood they sailed to the western world, as yet uninhabited and therefore sinless. But the Flood found them, and Cessair with 50 maidens, her father, and brother were drowned. Finntain, her husband, survived to tell the story, even into the 6th century, as Eleanor Hull states (*Pagan Ireland,* Dublin, 1923, p. 8), "an elderly man of some 5000 years." Partholan came to Ireland a fugitive patri-matricide from his own country in the unknown western ocean, and he and his people were wiped out by a plague after 30 years of pleasant life on the plains around Dublin. A nephew of Partholan, Tuan mac Cuaill, alone survived out of that crowd. Tuan, like Finntain, lived for centuries afterwards, and was renewed in the form of a deer, as an eagle, as a wild boar, etc., to be annalist and chronicler. See BATTLE OF MAG TURED; FIRBOLGS; FOMORIANS; MILESIANS; NEMEDIANS; TUATHA DÉ DANANN.

Among other famous stories classified in the Mythological cycle are *Tochmarc Étaine, The Wooing of Étain* (a triple tale of courtship); *Cat Maige Tured, The Battle of Mag Tured;* and *Oidead Clainne Lir, The Tragedy of the Children of Lir.* Another long story, *The Nourishment of the Houses of the Two Milk Vessels,* a manuscript preserved in the *Book of Fermoy* (15th century), also belongs in the cycle.

Nä-ch'un The chief sorcerer and oracle of the Tibetan government: an incarnation of Pe-har or of a god of the Turki tribes who was brought to Tibet by Padmasambhava and made the religious guardian of the first monastery. Once a year he goes to Lhasa to prophesy the events of the coming year. He and other sorcerers accompany troops to battle to interpret portents and he is consulted by private persons who can afford the expense, which is great. See CH'O-JE; NAG-PA.

nacimientos Literally, births: Christmas celebrations of the birth of Christ, in Spain and Latin America. In the province of Santiago, Argentina, a colorful festival

blends pagan and Christian observances. Effigies are arranged in traditional fashion—the *niño* (child) on an altar of leaves, surrounded by the Virgin, Joseph, angels, and animals. At nightfall the people dance and drink algarroba beer, which they call *licor de niño.* At midnight they sing *gozos* (rejoicings), then enact the *adoración,* then during *la icha* they throw cakes and other food offerings. At dawn *indios* run with fresh branches to the *arcos* (arches formed by two small trees), offer them to the *niño,* then pillage the arcos. Finally, all dance.

These ceremonies are analogous to those of the

sumamao harvest festival and help explain some of its enigmas. The nacimientos also throw light on certain European Christmas customs dealing with evergreens, offerings, and orgiastic celebration during the Christmas anniversary. [GPK]

nāga In Hindu mythology, one of a group of semi-divine beings, usually with human heads and serpent bodies, carrying a precious jewel in their heads: also, one of a group of historical people bearing the same name, probably a snake-worshipping Scythic race of trans-Himalayan origin and distinct from the Hindus. The history of these people is so closely interwoven with myth that it cannot be determined with any certainty. The mythological nāgas were the sons of Kadrū and Kaśyapa, born to people Pātāla or the Kashmir Valley.

The nāgas are not necessarily evil and only harm men when they are mistreated. They are armed with deadly venom but also possess the elixir of life and immortality. They are rarely mentioned in the Vedas but are important figures in the epics and in classic literature. The story of their destruction through the sacrifice of Janamejaya is told in the *Mahābhārata* and they appear in innumerable folktales and legends playing many and varied roles.

The nāgas live in splendid, jewel-studded palaces in their subaqueous city, Bhagavati, midst dancing and singing and flowers. Their girls and women are beautiful, richly dressed, celebrated for their cleverness and charm, and sometimes marry mortals. Minor royal families of southern and western India claim nāga descent and consider a *nāgīnī* (female nāga) an important member of any family tree.

In Buddhist belief Buddha's almsbowl was a gift of the nāgas and the Nāga Rājā Muçilinda protected Gautama from the storm following his enlightenment. The nāgas play important roles in the *Jātaka* and in the *Kathā Sarit Sāgara*. Their kings are Takshaka, and Vāsuki; Śesha who sometimes serves as Vishnu's couch and canopy, sometimes bears the world on his thousand hoods, sometimes is represented as becoming a man in the form of Balarāma. Their mortal enemy is Garuḍa.

The daughter of Vāsuki brought amṛita to cure her father of leprosy. She rubbed it on all parts of his body except his thumb. Realizing her error, she sought more amṛita, but while on the quest was carried off by one of the Pāṇḍavas and thus her father's thumb remained leprous. This explains why that disease flourishes in the Punjab. The connection of the nāgas with the weather, especially with rain, is emphasized by a Nepalese legend: King Gunkāmdeva conquered the snakes. Each gave the king a likeness of himself drawn with his own blood and promised that worship of the pictures would cause plentiful rain. Pictures of nāgas are still worshipped in time of drought. Once St. Gorakhnāth shut up nine nāgas in a hillock, and a twelve years' drought resulted. In modern Hindu belief, Kārkoṭaka is king of the nāgas who control the weather.

The worship of the serpent, symbolizing the life force, is widespread in India. Stone images of nāgas are placed at the portals of Buddhist and Hindu shrines as door guardians. The Gaddī of the Punjab hills offer them beestings, male kids and lambs, and first-fruits. In Mysore effigies of the cobra are placed at the entrances to most towns.

Nagaicho "Great Traveler," creator of the Sinkyone and Kato Indians of north-central California. See Yuki and Huchnom TAIKOMOL, "He Who Goes Alone," the creator. Nagaicho was also referred to as *Kyoi*, spirit, a name applied also to the whites, who were not Indians and, therefore, non-human. Nagaicho made the earth and men; Coyote, who was present when the earth was made, helped in its establishment, but also introduced death and much that is wrong. Among the Kato Nagaicho is the less powerful of two original beings, himself and Thunder; it was the latter who actually created men, many animals, mountains, trees, and springs. See EARTH; EHLAUMEL. [EWV]

Naglfar In Teutonic mythology, a ship made from the nail-parings of the dead (i.e. men who died with long fingernails or of corpses whose families had not cut them close before laying them out): launched by the violent seas caused by the lashings of Jormungandr, the Midgard serpent. The size of Naglfar depends on available materials. One story is that Hrym will pilot this ship at Ragnarök, bringing the giants to the fray against the æsir; another states that it will come from Muspellheim bearing Loki and the hordes of Hel.

Nag-pa A Tibetan sorcerer who is not admitted to the monasteries of reformed or semireformed sects. The Nag-pa, who is closer to the original Tibetan devil-dancer than either of the other two types of sorcerers can be distinguished by the tall conical hat with broad brim of yak hair which he always wears. The hat is surmounted by a vajra-topped skull, peacock feathers, and five-colored silk streamers. He also wears a sash of human bones and a breastplate of magic metal mirror. To battle demons he uses the sword, phurbu, sling, bow and arrows, magic triangle, and the divining arrow (*Dah-dar*).

nagualism Early Mexican theory of the animal double or familiar. The Aztec nagual stole at night, in the guise of an animal, caused sickness, and was generally feared. Traces of belief in nagualism appear among the Pueblo Indians of the Southwest; see E. C. Parsons, *Pueblo Indian Religion* (2 vols., Chicago, 1939), pp. 66, 189n., 1011. See MEXICAN AND CENTRAL AMERICAN INDIAN FOLKLORE. [EWV]

Nairyōsangha In Iranian mythology, the god of fire and messenger between gods and men: associated with Ātar in the *Avesta*.

Nakali A legendary hero of the Mískito Indians of eastern Nicaragua and northeastern Honduras, who went to seek his wife in the afterworld. When he returned to this earth, he told the people that every soul who journeys to the land of the dead comes to a bridge the width of a single hair which he must cross. Below the bridge is a pot (*sakaldakama*, cooking pot of the *sikla* bird) which is kept boiling by the *sikla* bird. If one has been stingy in this life, especially with food, nothing can keep him from falling into the pot. If he has been generous in life, he safely gets across the one-hair bridge. See C. R. Heath's "Mískito Glossary," *IJAL* 16: 30. Compare CHINVATPERETU.

Näkk An Estonian spirit of the water, derived from the *Näcken* of the Swedes. Drowned people become Näkk. The Näkk is believed to live in the deepest spot in the water. He presents himself in different shapes, but usually as a human being or an animal. He appears as male or female, even as a child. He has an enormous mouth and swallows everybody in his path. His charming singing bewitches his listeners, who unconsciously becomes victims of the water. The female spirit is called by the Estonians *Näkineiu* or *Näkineitsi*, i.e. Näkk's maid. She is a pretty, young girl, sitting near the water and combing her long hair with a golden comb. Occasionally she appears naked and sometimes has a fish tail. She performs very sweet songs and music. She possesses beautiful fat cattle, living in the water. Sometimes the Näkk appears as a horse. In every shape he is dangerous and his appearance predicts drownings. Before going into the sea, the inhabitants of the island Mohn pick up a stone from the beach, spit on it and throw it into the sea, saying: "A cake to the Näkk." [JB]

Näkki Among the Finns the Näkki is almost the same as the Estonian Näkk. In West Finland he is represented as a man of unusual size. Sometimes he is half man and half animal, with horse feet. The female *Näkinneito,* or Näkki maid, is a beautiful woman with glistening white body and very long, curly hair. She is further known by her big breasts which she can throw over her shoulder: a widespread trait of all female water deities. Belief in the magnificent cattle of water spirits is general in Finland. [JB]

nakulob The helper of the *cargador* or sponsor of a Mayan religious fiesta in Yucatán. Usually three of them share expenses with the *cargador.* They also execute a slow dance with little leaps around a table with food offerings (pig's head, tortillas, rum, cigarettes) to the accompaniment of a violin and drum. They receive bread and a *cuch* (a pole with streamers) and other ceremonial objects. Thus in spite of the Hispanic instruments and tune, their function has evidently an Indian ritual provenience. [GPK]

Nala A mythical king or monkey chief who, in the *Rāmāyaṇa,* could make stones float on water and thus built the bridge from India to Ceylon over which Rāma led his army to the rescue of Sītā and the destruction of Rāvaṇa.

Nala and Damayantī Title of a popular, and perhaps the most widespread, story from the *Mahābhārata*: the story of Nala, a beautiful young king, and Damayantī, the daughter of Bhīma. King Bhīma searched the world and decided Nala was the only living king worthy of his daughter; Nala, wifeless, inquired far and wide and heard about Damayantī. Both young people heard such tales of each other's beauty and worth that their hearts were set on one another. See LOVE OF ONE UNSEEN.

Damayantī, in order to make sure of Nala, asked her father for a *svayaṃvara* (a form of marriage by choice in which the girl throws a garland around the neck of that man, among those who present themselves, whom she desires), and Bhīma sent messengers to every king in the world to announce it. Among the suitors were also the gods Indra, Agni, Yama, and Varuṇa, who thought a mere mortal not good enough for Damayantī. So it happened when the hour came for the *svayaṃvara,* each of the four gods took on the form of Nala to deceive Damayantī in her choice. She was distressed that all her suitors looked alike, appealed to the gods by the act of truth, so that they revealed themselves in their own identities and Nala too was shown to her as himself.

(Recognition of transformed person among identical companions is motif H161, well known also in European folktale.) She threw the garland over him and King Bhīma married them. They lived in happiness and wisdom; a son and a daughter were born to them; and Nala ruled his kingdom well for many years.

But on the way home from that wedding the four gods had chanced to meet two demons of gambling, dice gods (Kali, personification of that side of the die marked one, and Dvāpara, two). These two, when they heard the news that Damayantī had chosen a mortal, meant to separate the pair as soon as an appropriate moment came. Years later, when Nala, forgetful, slept without saying the evening prayer, Kali entered into him and Dvāpara entered Nala's younger brother. Everything Nala saw henceforth he avidly desired; he longed to own his brother's bull; the two gambled for it, and Nala lost; he gambled and lost, gambled and lost with his brother until his kingdom was gambled away.

At last he and Damayantī left the country on foot and wandered into a forest where they ate roots and fruit and slept on kuśa grass. One morning Nala took half of Damayantī's garment for himself while she slept and left her, still impelled by Kali to seek his fortune in the world. Then follow two famous episodes: 1) in which Damayantī again invoked the act of truth to save herself from an importunate hunter, saying if it be true that she loved Nala only, let the hunter fall dead (he fell dead); and 2) in which Nala saved the life of a jeweled snake, who in return bit him so that he became blackened and deformed, and also gave him a garment which, when donned, would restore his true appearance.

Damayantī had returned to the kingdom of her father Bhīma, and in time, when news came of a marvelous cook and charioteer who was serving the king of Kośala, she felt sure that this was Nala. For the gifts of magic cooking and skilful charioteering were Nala's gifts. So she had another *svayaṃvara* declared, seeing to it that the king of Kośala heard the news. He heard and he set forth for this choosing, with his marvelous chariot driver driving the chariot. So wonderful was the driving that when the king dropped his cloak, the chariot was already miles on its way before he could stop to pick it up. The king was so impressed that he traded gifts with Nala; i.e. he took Nala's skill in charioteering in exchange for his own skill with dice. And Kali departed out of Nala.

When they arrived at Bhīma's palace, Damayantī took pains to penetrate the deformity disguise of the charioteer, observing his magical cooking (H35.2) and beguiling him to tears with his own two children, etc., finally asking, "Are you Nala?" And Nala, seeing her faithful love, could not deny his own desire also. Quickly he put on the garment given him by the snake and was restored to his own shape. The pair were reunited; Nala returned to his own kingdom with his wife and children. With his new gift of infallible skill at dice he won back the realm from the younger brother, but being generous and lawful, bestowed upon him a share.

names Names have a mystic or magical importance in all cultures. The difficulties that follow on the misspelling of a name in a modern American newspaper are surpassed only by using, even inadvertently, a secret name in other cultures where names and souls are closely associated. In imperial China it was a serious crime to use the name of a reigning emperor even when that name was a homonym in common use. Modern numerologists have been known to change a name, if it has an inauspicious number of letters, for another which they hope will be more fortunate. The Euro-American custom, followed elsewhere also, of attaching to an individual a family name as well as a given name has, in addition to other advantages, the folkloristic virtue of identifying a person with the family, its magical strength, and its power. At this point magic and practical advantage meet. The name given may be that of a saint, a hero, an ancestor or relative, or a natural object, and the hope is that the child will develop the admirable qualities of the name it bears. This involves the psychology of simile, and the folklore of cursing and name-calling.

In many societies individuals have several names. The nobles among the Kwakiutl Indians of British Columbia had winter and summer names. Ritual names are common all over the world with the thought that the name used at a given time and moment has changed the character of the individual. The multiplication of names, when not intended to appease numerous aged and wealthy relatives, has the further magical advantage of giving the bearer the potencies which his ancestors once possessed. The methods of choosing these names are various. They may be determined by the day of birth, by dreams and divinations. Where metempsychosis is part of the folklore of the group, the belief is that the spirit of the ancestor or hero is pressing to be recognized. See ANAPEL. The natives of Brazil and other parts of South America ask a priest to interpret their dreams before choosing names. In New Guinea and the Belgian Congo the name is chosen by the behavior of the child when the child sees possessions of its dead ancestors. In New Zealand the child may interrupt the recitation of the names of its ancestors by a cry, sneeze, or gesture. Methods of divination are various: movements of leaves, articles floating in liquid, patterns formed by objects thrown on the groud.

Chinese names are particularly complex. The "milk name" is given to an infant. Families that have lost a child give a new one an unattractive name so that it may not be attacked by evil spirits. If the child is a boy, the name may be that of a girl so that the spirits will not consider it as of any importance. Compare BEGYINA BA. Some families limit themselves to naming the child the "First," "Second," "Third," etc. On going to school, a school name is conferred by the teacher. At the age of sixteen or upon getting married a man gets his marriage name. For publishing books or poems a man uses a literary name.

The identification of the name with the soul is an early Egyptian belief that has survived into modern times. Cursing a man by name may destroy his soul and when the name of a dead man was ritually placed on his statue, that statue became the residence of his soul.

Among the Lapps and the Chinese, dead ancestors assist their descendants and thus the preservation of the family name is important. Among the Lapps the ancestor helped only those who bore his name. But the preservation of the family name elsewhere has strong socio-magical values.

Secret names, known only to the owner, have to do with belief in name-souls. In folktale, myth, and folk belief, the discovery of the secret name gives the discoverer power over the owner of the name. In many religions, the names of the gods are the secret property of the priests and may not be used by others. In witchcraft and diabolism the speaking of the names of devils and evil spirits materializes them or puts them under the power of the witch. Actions performed "in the name of . . ." have particular authority. Many people think that they have a good chance of getting into heaven if they repeat the name of their god or protecting power at the moment of death. [RDJ]

☞ Bestowal of a personal name upon a child, youth, or adult was the occasion for family or larger ceremonies among American Indian tribes of the Plains and eastern United States especially, although naming rites are not confined to these areas alone in North America. On the North Pacific Coast for example, the assumption of an hereditary name by a noble man or woman was only valid if a potlatch were given, and was attended with much ceremony and display. In the eastern United States naming rites have been given especial attention for the Osage by Francis La Flesche in *The Osage Tribe: Two Versions of the Child-Naming Rite* (*RBAE* 43, Washington, D.C., 1925) and for the Shawnee by C. F. and E. W. Voegelin in *Shawnee Name Groups* (*AA*, n.s., vol. 37, pp. 617–35, 1935). Among several groups it is believed that if one is sick one's name is possibly not agreeing with one, hence the name is "washed off," and a new personal name given. Among some tribes organized on a unilateral basis, each clan or gens group had its own stock of personal names which were drawn upon in naming members. [EWV]

☞ The naming of a boy child and the first cutting of his hair were a joint ceremony among the Incas of Peru. It was a festive occasion which took place when the child was two or three years old. It was celebrated by the whole family. The oldest uncle cut the child's hair and gave him the name which he retained until maturity. This rite is still observed by the Catholic Indians of Peru and Bolivia. A "godfather" cuts the first lock, and the rest of the family each cut a lock. The "godfather" is expected to make a present to the child. The custom has spread to several forest tribes of the upper Amazon, especially to the Omagua. [AM]

name tabu The prohibition against speaking the name of a god or other supernatural being, the names of the dead, names of witches, the Devil, etc., of certain animals greatly revered or feared, in some societies especially the name of the king or other sacred person, or of tabued relatives. Often not only the name but the dominant syllable of the name is tabu as well. Name tabu includes also the prohibition against revealing one's own name, in the belief that the personal name is a vital part of the self, that it is dangerous for anyone to know it, and to reveal it puts one in the power of the other. See HLONIPA; JOKING RELATIONSHIP AND KINSHIP TABUS.

In the ancient Egyptian, Babylonian, and Hindu religions, just naming the gods compelled them to answer prayer. The name of the Hebrew Yahweh was never uttered except under special conditions. Among many primitive peoples today the belief prevails that to utter the name of the dead is to invoke (call for) him. The modern practice of mentioning "the deceased" is not far removed from name-tabu tradition.

Name tabu in the case of dreaded or revered animals is so widespread as to be almost universal. Ural-Altaic peoples of Siberia, for instance, never speak the name of the bear; they call him Little Old Man, Grandfather, dear Uncle, or Wise One. Baltic peoples say to him Beautiful Honey-Paw, Broadfoot, or Grandfather. North American Kiowa Indians say that unless you are named for the bear you must not say bear. Bears can drive you crazy just for saying their names. In Quebec the Tête de Boule Indians also call the bear Grandfather. In Sumatra the tiger is mentioned as He With the Striped Coat. In Java the crocodile is Grandfather or the Old One. The Bechuanas refer to the lion as the boy with the beard. Among the Kols (a Dravidian group) the elephant is often spoken to as You With the Teeth. In parts of Africa and India no snake is ever called a snake. The people say, "There lies a strap (string, rope)," thereby believing that they make it lie still, for he who is called a snake is apt to behave like a snake. Diseases also are not named, lest they come upon the namer. Leprosy, for instance, is mentioned in Arabia as the "blessed disease." In the Malay Peninsula there exists a whole tabu language to be used while hunting camphor (see PANTANG KAPUR). Malay miners, fishermen, etc., also have special tabu languages to be used during their vocations.

Bavarian farmers will not name the fox lest he hear himself called and come to steal chickens and ducks. In parts of Germany mice are not called mice between Christmas and Twelfth Night lest they multiply rapidly.

The name-tabu motif (C430 ff.; Types 400 and 500) is prominent in both European and primitive folktale and mythology. There are stories of tabu against uttering the name of a god (C431) or of a supernatural (C432); guessing the name of a supernatural gives one power over him (C432.1); ghosts can be exorcised by name (E443.3); the Devil becomes powerless when called by name (G303.16). In German folktale a dwarf promises money to a mortal if he guesses his name (F451.5.15.1), or a maiden saves herself from a dwarf suitor by guessing his name (F451.5.15.3). The names of malevolent beings are not uttered (C433); the Furies, for instance, were spoken of as Eumenides. Not to ask a spouse's name, not to utter a spouse's name is a familiar motif (C435) in all folklore, as well as the prohibition against revealing one's own (C436). Breaking the name tabu often results in transformation (D511). The wife whose husband called her "my swallow" turned into a swallow. See ABRACADABRA; ADONAI; EUPHEMISM; OFFENDED SUPERNATURAL WIFE; RUMPELSTILTSKIN.

☞ The name of the dead becomes tabu in a considerable number of South American Indian tribes. For instance, the Abipon regarded the use of the name of a dead person as a grievous insult which brought prompt retaliation. If the tabued name was a common noun or had some resemblance to such a word, the term was dropped and a synonym invented. This tabu is specifically reported among the Island Caribs, the Guajiro, the Chaco and Patagonian Indians. [AM]

gÑan In Tibetan belief, malignant local spirits which infest special rocks, springs, or trees, and cause disease.

It is possible that they represent the spirits of the wild sheep formerly worshipped by Tibetans. Their habitats are avoided or they are propitiated with red paint and other offerings.

Nana or **Nana Buruku** Dahomean-Yoruban deity. In Nigeria, the Yoruba worship Nana as an earth-deity, mother of Omulu. In Dahomey, Nana Buruku is held to be the parent of Mawu, the Creator, and is worshipped with only a restricted cult. This deity is found under both names in Brazil (here spelled Nanan) and in Cuba, as one of the "older" deities, with an important place in the African cult-group among the Negro populations of these countries. Wherever worshipped, the Dahomean provenience of Nana is recognized. [MJH]

Nanabozho, Manabozho, or **Nanabush** Trickster-transformer-culture hero of the east-central and central groups of Algonquian-speaking Indians in the Central Woodlands culture area. Ojibwa Manabozho stories were recorded and published early in the 19th century by Henry Rowe Schoolcraft, whose wife was herself an Ojibwa woman; it was Schoolcraft also who confused Manabozho with the historic Iroquois statesman, Hiawatha. The central Algonquian culture hero Nanabozho has by later scholars also been confused with, or even identified with, Gluskabe, culture hero of the eastern or Abnaki Algonquians, because of superficial resemblances and because so little Gluskabe material has been published. A recent study indicates that the two culture heroes are not identical; Gluskabe does not participate in crude buffoonery (Abnaki trickster tales are all related about animals, not credited to the culture hero), and his altruistic concern for mankind is pronounced. Like Nanabozho, Gluskabe had a wolf brother, and his first recorded act was to kill him, since his wolf twin had wilfully caused their mother's death at his birth.

Nanabozho in his many forms among the Cree, Algonquin, Ottawa, Ojibwa, Potawatomi, Fox, Sauk, and Menomini Indians is, like nearly all American Indian culture heroes, a composite and contradictory character. He is the most powerful of supernatural beings, the creator of the earth and founder of the Midewiwin, most sacred of all ceremonies; yet on the other hand he is a buffoon, the butt of gross jokes, a dupe and victim of his own stupidity and greed. Some of the tribes above mentioned identify him with the Great Hare and with the Wolverine, yet at the same time attribute to him human actions and shape.

Recent analysis of all the body of Nanabozho myths shows a so-called Cree type of Nanabozho cycle, an Ojibwa type, and a Potawatomi type. The Potawatomi type is as follows. Nanabozho was the eldest of quadruplets, the fourth of whom, Flint, killed their mother at birth. Nanabozho and the second child, also a boy, had human form; the third brother who went north became a White Hare and a great magician; the fourth was Flint. When Nanabozho grew up he killed Flint, and lived with his second brother. The supernaturals became jealous and drowned the younger of the two brothers; Nanabozho was inconsolable, and warred against the supernaturals. To appease him they initiated him into the Midewiwin or sacred medicine society. His drowned brother came back, and was sent to preside over the souls of the dead; then Nanabozho initiated the Indians into the Midewiwin. In the Ojibwa and Cree types Nanabozho, in search of his younger brother, finds him as a wolf, runs with the wolf-pack, has a series of trickster-type adventures, and is finally dismissed by the wolves with one wolf as a companion. This wolf is seized by powerful underwater beings, but Nanabozho rescues him; a deluge ensues, Nanabozho escapes on a raft, from which Muskrat dives to secure a bit of earth so that Nanabozho can recreate the world. For a recent analysis of the Nanabozho cycles see the paper by Margaret Fisher, cited in ROMANTIC LOVE. See END OF WORLD; HARE; HIAWATHA; MIDEWIWIN; WISAKEDJAK; WOLVERINE. [EWV]

Nānak or **Nānak Chand** The Guru Nānak (1469–1538), founder of Sikhism and the first of the ten gurus of the Sikh community. Sikh traditions concerning his life are completely myth-ridden. Nānak was born in the village of Talwandī (now Nankāna) on a moonlight night to the sound of celestial music. All the Hindu gods appeared to announce his birth. As a boy he was immersed in meditation and consorted with fakirs and sadhus. At one time the angels seized him and carried him before God who bade him proclaim one god. The exigencies of living, however, interfered. Finally his father sent him to town to do some trading, but he spent the money entrusted to him on a group of devotees whom he met on the road. Enraged and disgusted, his family sent him to Sultānpur where he obtained employment in the commissariat of the Nawāb Daulat Khān. While thus employed he frequently bathed in the Bein River and there one day he saw a vision in which he was commanded to worship the Lord. He gave up his job and became an itinerant preacher, traveling east, south, north, and west until his death in 1538, preaching a mixture of Hinduism and Mohammedanism. He was a reformer, preaching against caste, superstition, and idolatry.

Nānak's followers or disciples, known as Sikhs, believe in metempsychosis, wear their hair long, carry a sword in token of their perpetual warfare with the Moslems, do not wear the sacred cord, never shave the hair or beard, wear a turban instead of a cap, and ascribe sanctity to the cow. There are 84 lakhs (great numbers) of existence through which a soul passes, before the cycle is complete. These include 2,300,000 quadrupeds; 900,000 aquatic animals; 1,000,000 feathered animals; 1,100,000 creeping animals, 1,700,000 immovable creatures such as stones and plants; and 1,400,000 human beings. Probably the most remarkable feature of their belief is in their quasi-deification of the *Granth*, their sacred book. This book has been endowed with the title of Sāhib (Lord). In folktales Nānak appears as a wonder-working fakir.

Nandi The milk-white bull of Śiva; chief of his attendants and leader of the Gaṇas; vehicle of the god. An image of Nandi is placed before temples dedicated to Śiva.

Nandinī In Hindu mythology, offspring of Surabhi, the cow of plenty belonging to the sage Vasishṭha.

nañiga The Cuban form of a religious cult, paralleling the Haitian *vodun*, Trinidad *shango*, and Jamaican *obeah*. Deities of African origin are invoked and personified in trance dances induced by hypnotic chanting and dancing. In their state of ecstasy devotees sometimes attempt to walk through or sit in fire, or they may climb on top of another dancer. Magic and exorcism are practiced by the priests, including the use of switches to invoke or exorcise evil spirits.

Nañiga worshippers in a unique ceremony termed *diablito* (little devil) salute the sun at its zenith. With nude torsos painted yellow, and bells on dungarees and skirts, they chant and dance joyfully to the sun. Despite prohibition by law, the cult continues to function unabated, and worshippers continue to initiate neophytes. [GPK]

Naṅ-lha The Tibetan house god: anthropomorphic with a piggish head. The Naṅ-lha has a roving disposition and occupies different parts of the house in different seasons, thus causing the householder much anxiety, because no objects may occupy the god's place nor may it be swept. The Naṅ-lha has, however, a routine from which he never deviates. During the first two months of the year he occupies the center of the house, during the third and fourth he resides at the doorway, in the fifth under the eaves, in the southwest corner during the sixth month, and is back under the eaves in the seventh and eighth months. During the next two months he lives in the fire-tripod or grate, and in the last two in the kitchen hearth.

While he is stationed at the door neither bride and groom nor corpse may enter or leave. If there is no other means for entrance or exit and such is necessary during the third and fourth months, images of a horse and a yak are made of flour and decorated with the hair and skin of the animals represented. The god is invited to sit on the images and is offered tea and beer. Then the door is unhinged and carried out after which the corpse or bride and groom may enter or leave.

Nanna In Teutonic mythology, goddess of purity, blossoms, and vegetation; wife of Balder and mother of Forseti. She and Balder were a devoted and faithful couple, which was unusual among the northern gods. On Balder's death, as Nanna bent to take leave of him, she too died, of a broken heart and was laid beside him on his funeral ship. When Hermod came to Hel to sue for their release Balder wanted Nanna to return, but she refused, sending instead a beautiful flowered carpet (the spring vegetation) to Frigga and a ring to Fulla.

Nanni or **Nannius, Giovanni** (1432?–1502?), called Annius of Viterbo, the Dominican friar who "recovered" the work of Fabius Pictor, earliest Roman historian, which spurious work he published in 1498. He is noted for his attempt to harmonize the Bible with astrological findings and theory, with Greek, Roman, and Hebrew myth, etc., to form what purports to be "true history." His writings and his method were popular during the Renaissance and after.

Nāoṅhaithya (Pahlavi *nāīkīyas, nākahēt, nākiśīyyā;* Persian *nāūnhas, nānikahēt*) In Zoroastrian belief, one of the six archfiends: the aid of Ahriman and the embodiment of discontent.

Napi Blackfoot Indian trickster-culture-hero: sometimes also referred to as Old Man Napi. The animal-like quality of Napi is not strong in stories which stress his role as creator-culture-hero; in trickster tales he is identifiable with Coyote, or Old Man Coyote. [EWV]

Nārada One of the seven great Rishis, and inventor of the *vīṇā* or lute, also author of a law textbook, the *Nāradīya Dharmaśāstra*. Nārada once asked the secret of māyā from Vishṇu who, instead of replying directly, subjected the ascetic to a harrowing adventure in which he was forced to dive into water, making it clear that the waters are the materialization of Vishṇu's māyā.

Naraka In Hindu mythology, an Asura who, in the form of an elephant, outdid the evil deeds of all the other Asuras, carrying off the daughters of men and gods. For the 16,000 women he seized he built a splendid palace. According to the *Laws of Manu*, Naraka is the name of one of the 21 hells (other authorities vary the number) in which the souls of the wicked are tortured.

Narasinha The man-lion, fourth avatar of Vishṇu.

Nārāyaṇa An epithet of several Hindu gods, but especially of Brahmā and Vishṇu: literally, moving (*āyana*) on the waters (*nārāh*), or son of man (Nāra, the primeval male). The word is most frequently used today as an epithet for Vishṇu, but also as an equivalent for Brāhman, and for the eighth of the Jain Vāsudevas. Vishṇu is represented as Nārāyaṇa at Bālajī in Nepāl with an image having a snake-hood projecting over the water.

narcissus A flowering bulbous plant of the amaryllis family (genus *Narcissus*) said by the Greeks to have sprung from the body of Narcissus, a youth who spurned the love of the wood nymph Echo and fell in love with his own reflection in a pool. The Greeks believed that these flowers wreathed the brows of the Fates. Sophocles says that they crown the goddesses on Mt. Olympus. The Romans dedicated it to Venus. It is used medicinally against all obstructions and for chills and colds. The root, pounded to a pulp, mixed with honey, and applied externally, is good for all manner of aches and pains, and will draw out thorns and splinters. The roots were considered antiseptic and healing on wounds.

Narmadā The holy Nerbudda River, regarded as the boundary between the Deccan and Hindustan: literally, making happy. The Narmadā is the rival of the Ganges (Gaṅgā) in Hindu mythology. Personified, she is variously a sister of the Nāgas, daughter of the Rishi Mekala, or daughter of the moon. For her aid to the Nāgas in their battles with the Gandharvas, the snake-gods made her name a charm against snake venom. The Narmadā is associated with the cult of Śiva and was to replace the Ganges (Gaṅgā) in 1895 as the most sacred river. This has not happened, but local river priests rank it above all other rivers, because freedom from sin is gained by bathing in the Ganges for a day, but the mere sight of the Narmadā cleanses the sinner. Many Hindus desire to die on the Narmadā's banks and the ashes of the dead are brought from all parts of India to be consigned to its waters. The Ganges herself comes to bathe in the river once a year in the form of a black cow.

Nāsatya In post-Vedic mythology, the younger of the Aśvins: originally an epithet applied to either of the twins as the physicians of Svarga. See AŚVINS.

nativity Nativity with a capital N refers in western cultures to the birth of Christ. The word conjures up the whole human scene of the baby in the manger, the surprised animals standing by whose warmth tempers the cold stable, the strange bright star over the little building, kind neighbors running in with gifts for a mother and baby in need (warm milk, eggs, cheese, bread, a warm shirt, mittens, a toy), and the three kings arriving with their gifts. Around this has amassed the whole western Christmas complex of feast, song, symbolic tree, Santa Claus (Saint Nicholas), and gift exchange, plus the charming custom in rural Spain of putting out gifts for the Magi and hay for their camels on Epiphany Eve.

The word *nativity* is also associated with the birth of Buddha, of Zoroaster, and with the birth of the sun at the winter solstice (northern Europe, Egypt, also Mithraic). Buddha's mother was a virgin who conceived after or in a dream in which she saw her child descend from heaven and enter her womb. Singing devas announced the conception to the father; sun, moon, and stars flared into brilliance at the moment of Buddha's birth.

Zoroaster also was born of a virgin and his birth was accompanied by marvels.

The annual Nativity of the Sun at the winter solstice (December 21–25) was a period of joy and reaffirmation of life in the dark winter of northern Europe. The old Iranian Mithraic festival of the Nativity of the Sun (Mithra himself) was celebrated on December 25. For the Egyptian Nativity of the Sun, infant images were brought forth for the people to worship. See CAROL; CHRISTMAS; JESUS; NACIMIENTOS.

nats Generic term for the spirits of indigenous Burmese religion and folk belief: spirits of the air, sky, earth, forest, rivers and streams, hills, rain, wind, etc., and also of the house and of the cultivated fields. Ghosts of the dead are nats; and the supernaturals of Buddhism are also nats. All may be harmful unless constantly appeased and propitiated. Buddhist monks propitiate the nats as zealously as any nat-cult priest; there is a *natsin* (nat house or spirit shrine) in the shade of every pagoda, as well as one at the end of every village, where periodic ceremonies are performed.

The Kachins name Shingrawa (creator; indifferent to man), Jan (sun), Shitta (moon), Mbon (wind), and Trikurat, who helps hunters capture game animals. Other nats are Sinlap (giver of wisdom), Mu (sky), and the Burman Upaka, who "snaps up mortals." Flood nats cause drownings. The Burman Hmin Nat drives people mad. Forest and tree nats are especially feared and dreaded. The Kachins believe that disease and death are caused by the ancestral nats; any pain is the bite of a nat. For rain nats, see THEIN; for agricultural nats, see SABĀ-LEIPPYĀ.

Nats also serve as guardians of the house, village, tribe, and personal property. *Nat-thami* is the term for eleven nat maidens who guard eleven royal umbrellas in Mandalay. Nats also protect boats and treasure.

A feature of the Buddhist November festival in Burma is the *padēthā-bin*, a tree loaded with gifts and money which is carried and placed in the pagoda or monastery; the money is used for alms.

The Burmese have a specific list of Thirty-Seven Nats, who, with two exceptions, are national heroes and heroines of five groups of pseudo-historical tales. Originally there were 33, but four more have been added in modern times. Their biographies are in the *Mahā Gīta Medani*, a book of verse. The *nat-than* (spirit songs) are chanted by the mediums (*matkadau*), accompanied by music, during festivals held for each specific one. The songs are intended to impress upon the audience the sinfulness of assassination and treason. There are images of the Thirty-Seven Nats in the Shwe Zigōn pagoda at Pagān. See CHINŪN WAY SHUN; EINGSAUNG NAT; KA; TAK-KENG.

natya Sanskrit term for the science of Hindu dance and drama. It originated with Brahmā, was passed on from him to Śiva and by him to the sage Bharata. It is thus of ancient religious origin, and still religious in content. Its subjects cover many facets of life, but particularly deal with stories of the gods, the epics of the *Mahābhārata* and *Rāmāyaṇa*. Its laws have been explained in venerable books, Bharata's *Natya Shastra*, Nandikeshvara's *Abhinaya Darpana* (mirror of gesture), and the Sangita *Ratnakar*. It is associated with the religious festivals of Hinduism.

Its technique emphasizes torso and arm movements, without neglecting foot rhythms. The elaborate terminology recognizes every shade of variation in purpose and technique: *nritta,* pure dance as distinguished from *nritya,* pantomime; *narga,* classical dance as against *deshi,* popular dance; and two contrasting modes, *lasya,* the feminine, and *tandava,* the virile. *Karnas* are combined actions of the limbs into postures; *angchars* or *manadalam* are the postures; *bhritti* is expression. The vocabulary deals with *pada,* footwork; leg movements, *čari;* five kinds of jumps, *utplavana;* floor contacts, *thattadavu;* eight kinds of gaits, *gati;* seven spiral movements, *bhramari;* movements of the waist, *kati;* shoulders, *kaksa;* nine kinds of neck motions, *griva;* of the face, *mukhaja;* nose, *nasa:* cheeks, *ganda;* mouth, *asya;* chin, *cibula;* eight eye motions, *dristsi;* 44 glances, etc. Most eloquent are the arm movements, *vartanam,* and the gesture language of the hands, *mudras* or *hasta-mudras,* of which there are 24 for a single hand and for both hands and 13 more for *nritta.*

Forms and function vary with the region and school. The outstanding schools of classical Hindu dancing, while developed from folk worship, are distinguished by their set rules and stylization. The four most important schools are:

1. The *Bharata Natyam* follows the rules of *natya shastra* with the classical terminology: originated by the sage Bharata probably about 1500 B.C., it is of non-Aryan provenience. Essentially a woman's style, it includes *nritta, nritya,* and *nautch,* and the *dēvadāsi,* female temple dancers. The costume is a tight blouse shot with gold threads, a sari with pleats on the legs and a richly embroidered band, jewelry, and lilies. The musical instruments usually consist of a drum, two cymbals, a wood block, sometimes a violin, and tampura or drone. The songs, with texts from the 17th and 18th centuries, are intoned by a learned *vidvan* and echoed by a chorus.

2. The elaborate *Kathakali* school enacts heroic epics of the gods. Its texts were composed by 16th century Rajas on the *Mahābhārata* and *Rāmāyaṇa*. It is the revival of folk drama of Kerala, the southwest coast of Malabar, and the state of Travancore. It interprets the story with vigorous and sweeping motions, using 64 *mudras,* and a vocabulary of 500 dance words. The performances take place in the open air at night, with eight musicians using percussion instruments, a *nandi* or narrator, and barbaric costumes with full skirt, long-sleeved jacket, great circular headdresses, and many-colored jewelry and ornaments. The *chutti* or masks of thick paint (now being abandoned) have a set design for each character. This type of dance was taken to Indonesia by a king of Bali, and has exerted widespread influence.

3. In contrast, the *Manipuri* school, in the *lasya* style, deals with delicate pastoral themes and the *ras,* the love-story of Kṛishṇa. It mingles the folk style of Manipur and Bengal in northeast India with a Far Eastern quality, resulting in an elegant technique, without mudras, but spontaneous, swift, and supple, frequently in a circle for boys and girls. The costume is a tight velvet blouse with short embroidered sleeves and a full skirt hemmed with sequins and mirrors. Kṛishṇa wears a male sari and jeweled crown. The music is provided by a *khol* or drum, a flute, and a chorus of singers.

4. The *Kathak* school grew out the classical court tradition of northern India. Including both *tandava* and *lasya,* its style also shows Moslem influence. It serves entertainment, though often with mythological themes, e.g. Kṛishṇa and the *gopis* (milkmaids). Though more spontaneous than the *Bharata Natyam,* it uses a code of *thorahs* or foot beats, *gaths* or pantomimic passages, and *bolos* or spoken rhythmic phrases. Solo and group dances are accompanied by a *sarangi,* a stringed instrument, and *tablas* or drums. The costume shows a Persian touch in the wide silk skirt, tight blouse, and veil over the head, shoulders, and front of the blouse. The *nautch* combines the technique of the *Kathak* with that of the *Marwari* women.

In the recent renaissance, dance artists have combined and modernized the classical foundation, Shankar blending Kathakali, Manipuri, and European techniques. Ram Gopal was the only male interpreter of the *Bharata Natyam;* Rabindranath Tagore founded on the Manipuri style an independent school in Bengal for the enactment of his poetry. The eclectic Indian Peoples Theatre utilizes traditional and new styles for the representation of contemporary, even industrial themes. [GPK]

navel Popular speculation about the navel generally emphasizes its function as a symbol for the center of the universe rather than its qualities, physiological or esthetic, though these have not been overlooked. The Buddhist ascetic meditating on his navel is more concerned with grasping the universe as a whole than with the fascination of his own person, for it is that person as an individual which he attempts to obliterate.

Several geometrically minded cultures think it is important to discover the exact center of the universe. The Zuñi of New Mexico have several complicated migration legends about their search for the navel of the world. These are also connected with origin myths about their emergence from the womb of the world. The cities of Cuaco, Delphi, Delhi, Peiping, and many others are at that particular geographical spot. The Greeks had a myth about it. Zeus, eager to discover the exact center of the earth had two eagles fly at exactly the same speed, one from the east and the other from the west. They met at Delphi. There in Apollo's temple, the Greeks set up an *omphalos,* a holy navel stone guarded by two golden eagles. Several of these have been excavated.

They are in the shape of half-eggs on low quadrangular bases, sometimes artfully decorated. Mythopeic folklorists with their minds on sex have made them "ultimately" or "remotely" phallic. The fact that these folklorists may be correct does not relieve them from the necessity of producing more evidence in favor of their views than is at present available. The boundary stones in the fields of southern India have generally the same shape as the omphalos and are also called "navel stones." [RDJ]

☞ A Turkish etiological story states that at sight of the first man created by Allah, the Devil spat at his stomach. Allah quickly snatched out the polluted spot, and so men have navels.

necromancy Divination by communication with the dead; hence, any magic performed with the aid of the dead or the spirits of the dead; thence, magic in general. The word was corrupted by medieval Latin writers into *nigromancy,* in which form it came into English; the word thus meant magic, the black art. The 10th century *Canons of Edgar,* however, mentions *licwiglunga,* body wizardry, undoubtedly a synonym for necromancy proper. A Renaissance writer, in the *Wagnerbuch,* divides necromancy into *necyomancy,* divination from a reanimated corpse, and *sciomancy,* divination from the shades of the dead, like Saul's conversation with the spirit of Samuel in the house of the witch of Endor (1 *Sam.* xxviii). Necromancy is often used of any magic that uses part or all of a corpse; and grave-robbing for the various parts of the bodies of the dead seems to have been attributed regularly to accused witches. Basically necromancy depends upon the concept that the spirits of the dead know everything, past, present, and future. If they can be compelled to reveal their information by spells, charms, etc., the necromancer can predict the future, discover hidden treasure, or the like.

need fire Need fire, an occasional, not a calendrial, ceremony was made throughout Europe from very early times when cattle, pigs, or other stock were threatened with plague. The ecclesiastical authorities denounced it in the *Index of Superstitions* in the 8th century. The method of producing need fire was to insert a crossbar between two uprights, wrap a rope about the bar, and, by having two strong men pull the rope, cause the bar to revolve rapidly until fire was produced. The fire was then put between the city gates and the stock driven through it. Sometimes the fire was put in the center of a pen and the stock exposed to its influence. It was thought, even near the end of the 19th century, that the magic would work only if all the other fires in the village had been extinguished, and stories are told of occasions when the fire refused to light. At these times a search through the village revealed that some villagers had failed to extinguish their hearth fires. These fires were then put out, and relighted from the need fire. In some places the brands were extinguished by being dipped into a tub of water. They exercised further influence if left in the manger for some time. Bartsch reports having seen the ceremony in Mecklenburg in 1868 and that the fire must be started by two brothers or near relatives. In 1598 a cattle plague threatened Marburg. One Joh. Köhler induced the Marburgers to start a need fire by twirling a wagon wheel on an unused axle. This however had no effect on the plague and Köhler was executed as a witch. See NEW FIRE. [RDJ]

Negritos Literally, little Negroes, or black ones: masked figures in Mexican dance ceremonials, especially at Carnival and Corpus Christi celebrations. They take their name from the black masks, which, however, do not have negroid features. These masks are adorned with ribbons and jeweled headdresses. At the great *volador* fiesta in Papantla, Veracruz, at Corpus Christi, they also wear black velvet trousers and jackets and large hats instead of crowns. Ten of them are dressed as field workers and are accompanied by a sorcerer, two battered clowns, and a *Maringuilla* with a gourd vessel and a small live snake. After singing to guitar accompaniment, and dancing lively longways and a circle figure, the Negritos are "bitten" by the snake and cured by the sorcerer with invocations to the four winds. The dancers jump for joy. In the Sierra de Puebla they do not enact a drama, but, to fiddle and guitar, execute cross-overs, and filing down the center, or a circle. To the final gay *son de listones* (ribbon tune) in 6/8 time, they perform a Maypole dance. Their steps are *zapateados* of the complex variety. In the final ribbon dance they introduce waltz steps.

In Michoacán, particularly in Tzintzuntzan and Cherán, the Negritos dance officially on February 2, Candlemas, but actually at any suitable time. They are feasted as they dance from home to home. With a marching step or heel two-step, 12 Negritos and a leader weave through typical longways formations, cross-overs, serpentines, and end in a circle. Two *flachicos,* caretakers, and a *Señor Amo* master, dance at the end of the lines and in between the two files. In the end they pay him homage with little gifts. The choreography is similar to that in the Sierras, but the costume is different, especially in the type of mask, headdress, and ornaments of small fishes (associated with Lake Pátzcuaro).

The invasion of Negritos dancers may be associated with the Negro slaves brought to Veracruz by the Spaniards. The steps of the Papantla Negritos, in fact, resemble the *huapangos* of the seaport. But none of the forms suggest any Negro influence, neither the story, formations, music, nor masks. It is more likely that we here have a variant of the face-blackened *Moros* which danced *Moriscas* in medieval Europe, and survive in the *Moros y Cristianos* of Spain and Mexico, in the *noirs* of the Basque *mascaradas,* and the various Portuguese *Mouriscadas* and the black clownlike dancers of the *dança dos Pretos.* [GPK]

Negro folklore See AFRICAN AND NEW WORLD NEGRO FOLKLORE.

Neman One of a group of three great war goddesses (with Badb and Macha) of Old Irish mythology. She was the daughter of Ernmas, one of the Tuatha Dé Danann, and like Badb and Morrigan, either the wife or granddaughter of Nét. She is associated by scholars with a Gallic Nemetona, who appears in some inscriptions at Bath, and who was identified by the Romans as wife of Mars. See BADB.

Nemean lion In Greek legend, the invulnerable lion slain by Hercules as the first of the labors. The lion was the son of Typhon (or Orthrus) and Echidna (or Selene). Hercules choked it to death, his weapons being useless, and skinned it with its own claws. This was the lion-skin Hercules wore afterwards.

Nemedians An early people who invaded Ireland; descendants of Nemed, son of Agnoman of Scythia; the third group to land in Ireland, following next after Partholan and his people, who were wiped out by a plague. Nemed came from Scythia with 34 ships, seeking the gold that was in the tower of Conann, chief of the Fomorians, but all were drowned except Nemed and the few he could save. Four lakes burst out of the ground in Ireland in the days of Nemed; two famous forts were dug by him; twelve plains were cleared by Nemed in Connacht, Munster, Leinster, Ulster. Nemed won three great battles over the Fomorians but later died in a plague with 3000 of his people.

There was great oppression on the Nemedians after that at the hands of the Fomorians. Two thirds of their corn, two thirds of their milk, two thirds of their children they were forced to pay in tribute every Samain Eve (November 1). The Nemedians went to Conann and begged for alleviation of the tax, saying they would rather fight and perish than continue the insufferable tribute. Conann granted them one year of grace on condition that they never scatter but assemble for slaughter in battle if they could not pay when the year was up. The Nemedians agreed, hoping to receive aid from Greece before the time.

When the Greeks received news of the distress of the "children of Nemed," Smol, king of Greece at that time, assembled a host of warriors, druids, and venomous animals and sent them to the Nemedians, following himself soon after with an army. The Nemedians welcomed them and at once declared war on Conann of the Fomorians, unless he gave them freedom. Conann then attacked the Nemedians, but they sent the druids and venomous animals against him, who confused and killed many. Conann and his people could not stay in the tower because of them. Then battle after battle went against the Fomorians, and at last Conann came out of the tower to fight in the open. In that battle Conann was soon killed by Fergus, the son of Nemed, and after that it was defeat for them. The Nemedians surrounded them, beheaded them, looted the tower and burned it, and shared the booty with the Greeks, who then went home.

Not long after this the Nemedians were attacked from the water by Morc, son of Dele, a second powerful Fomorian chief. So desperate was this fight that none survived except one shipload of Fomorians and thirty warriors of the descendants of Nemed. Of these thirty, three grandsons of Nemed were over the rest; and these three divided Ireland between them into three parts. But this did not hold for long; they finally scattered to other places, partly for fear the Fomorians might rise again and destroy the remnant of their blood, partly for fear of the plagues which had destroyed their forebears, and partly because they did not love each other much. One returned to Greece; one (son of Fergus son of Nemed) went into Britain; Beotać, the third of them, went to the northern islands of Greece with his people, where they set about learning the wisdom of the universe, druidry, and all the arts. So great was their knowledge that they deified their learned men and the name Tuatha Dé was given to them.

Neoga In Seneca (Iroquois) Indian mythology, Fawn, the south wind. He was called by Gaoh into the sky to lead the summer winds and carry the odor of flowers and the sound of birds and brooks across the world.

Nerthus or **Hertha** A very early northern Teutonic earth mother and goddess of fertility, mentioned by Tacitus (*Germ.* 40) as Terra Mater, who, he says, was worshipped by seven Teutonic tribes on the Baltic Sea. Her car was driven by her priest through the region every spring, to promote the fertility of the lands, and the slaves who accompanied the car were drowned in her sacred lake after the processional. Goddess and car too were immersed in the lake after the round through the region: obviously the rain charm and fertility bath known the world over. This statement of Tacitus has led later scholars to presuppose the existence of an image. In later Norse mythology, Nerthus became the male Niörd (Njörd), father of Frey, but survived as Freya (see E. Moght, "Deities peculiar to the northern Teutons," *ERE* vi, 304, 305); or as the wife and sister of Niörd, hence her occasional confusion with Skadi, also Niörd's wife. In later German folklore she is variously associated with Berchta (Frau Gode, Dame Wode) or with Holde. See CARNIVAL.

nettle An herb (usually genus *Urtica*) having inconspicuous, greenish, imperfect flowers and minute stinging hairs. The stinging is caused by the irritating juice discharged by the hairs when broken. In England and Scotland the young tops are boiled as greens, and nettle broth, tea, and beer are still popular spring drinks. Gerard's *Herbal* mentions that nettles baked with sugar "makes the vital spirits more fresh and lively."

Roman soldiers used to chafe their limbs with nettles to increase circulation when they were cold. This plant was sacred to Thor, and wearing it banished fear in the presence of danger. In the Tyrol and England it is credited with keeping away lightning. In Germany, if it is gathered before dawn, it is good for ailing cattle. In Yorkshire the leaves are used to exorcise the Devil; in Ireland the stings are said to be the tines of the Devil's pitchfork. In Anglo-Saxon medicine the nettle was considered effective against the green venom, one of the nine flying venoms causing disease. In Roman times nettles were seethed in oil to make a cold ointment. In Russia an infusion is a cure for toothache. In Germany nettle seed is considered aphrodisiac. In Ireland, St. Fabian's nettle is good against consumption. In Jamaica the juice of the Spanish nettle is poured into a fresh cut. The Chippewa Indians of the United States use a mixture which they call Winnebago medicine made of stinging-nettle root and lady-fern root for disorders of the urinary system; the Chippewa and Meskwaki both used the steeped root to cure incontinence of urine. The Meskwaki also made a tea of the leaves of the rough hedge nettle for severe colds. In Texas the seeds of the bull nettle are used as a cathartic and bull nettle tea is specific against all manner of serious illness. In 1942 in England 90 tons of dried nettle were used in the manufacture of a green dye for camouflage and of a chlorophyll tonic.

In European folktale, nettles and thistles are identified as the Devil's vegetables (G303.10.13). In Hans Christian Andersen's story *The Eleven Swans* is depicted the spinning of flax by the little princess from the fiber of stinging nettles to make the eleven white shirts which would unbewitch the swan brothers. This was no unusual incident, for the spinning of nettle-flax from these tough fibers to make household linens was common in Europe before the importation of cotton. In fact the North American Meskwaki Indians also made a very tough strong twine from the inner bark of wood nettle.

never The obvious answer, or implied answer, to a host of folk sayings such as "in a week of Sundays," "once in a blue moon," "when water runs uphill," "when it is as easy to undo slander as pick up spilled water," etc. Bibliography for the various ways of expressing this idea is given under the never motif (Z61) in Stith Thompson's *Motif-Index of Folk-Literature*. "When black sheep turn white" is one of the expressions cited. Folktales involving the idea of never include disenchantment when some ostensibly endless task is done (D791.1.2). A bewitched woman is allowed to return to human form once every seven years and put one stitch in a smock; when the smock is finished the spell will be broken. How long does it take to reach Schlauraffenland? A mountain of grain has to be eaten through first (X950.2).

The obvious answer or expectation of never is often circumvented either by magic or wit, however, as in the case of the woman who promised herself to a lover when the rocks should leave the coast (M261). They were removed by magic. Never to be vanquished "till Birnam Wood shall come to Dunsinane" sounded like never to Macbeth. "When a dry rod blossoms" also implies the answer never, but folktales using the motif are concerned with its miraculous flowering. See LAMMAS; section on *Conventional phrases* in PROVERBS.

☞ The answer never is unmistakably conveyed in a modern popular song from a waterfront café in Monrovia, Liberia, entitled *Bush Cow Milk*. In this song a man asks a girl to be his love; she says she will if he will milk the bush cow for her. (The bush cow is the short-horned buffalo of West Africa, one of the fiercest and most dangerous of animals.) The man replies to the effect that when ships don't swim in the ocean, when elephants sleep in trees, then he will milk the bush cow for her.

Bush Cow Milk is one of the songs collected on a tape recorder by Arthur S. Alberts in Liberia in 1949, and played at the sixth New York City meeting of the New York Folklore Society, February, 1950. It is one of the songs composed in English by a Liberian descendant of American slaves "after songs heard from American sailors." It is very similar to an old popular American song (also using the never motif): *"When the pussy willow whispers to the catnip."* The meter and word arrangement are the same; the tune (especially of the chorus) is similar. [TCB]

never-finished weaving A detail concerning the Shawnee Indian female creator, which in a general way, resembles the never-finished weaving of Penelope. The Shawnee creator is said to be weaving a basket or net (*skemotha*, untranslatable) which is unraveled every night; if she ever succeeds in finishing it the world will come to an end. [EWV]

new fire Ceremonies associated with the lighting of new fires in villages, homes, or temples are calendrial in some societies and occasional in others. Variation is also found in whether the fire must be newly kindled, in the procedures of kindling it, and in whether the fire is to be taken from a sacred fire already burning. The calendrial festivals—the Beltane fire of Ireland, Scotland, Isle of Man, etc., Candlemas, and the candle dances—are generally known.

In parts of Australia the old fires are formally extinguished when a member of the tribe dies or when the tribe is going through a crisis or calamity and new fires are freshly lighted. The Greek Argives also extinguished old fires after a death and rekindled them from another source. The presence of barbarians at Platæa required the extinction of old fires. New ones were procured from the temple at Delphi. In China, Ch'ing Ming, the spring festival of pure brightness which occurs 106 days after the winter solstice, was at one time the occasion for lighting new fire by rubbing sticks together and corresponds to Beltane, or the Celtic May Day festival. The day before Ch'ing Ming was *han shih*, the day of cold foods, which indicates that all old fires had been extinguished. The Paleo-Siberians produce new fire by means of a drill and a flat board in the shape of a human figure. The drill is turned rapidly by means of a bow string. It is an annual ceremony and is thought to ensure the health of man and beast. Sacrificial blood and fat are also used. The fireboard itself has sacred qualities as have also the implements used and even the dust that is produced. When the new fire has been produced the hearth fires are relighted from it.

The sky sacrifice among some of the Turki tribes occurs every third summer. Women are excluded. The ceremony is held on the "top of a mountain in a sacred birch spinney." The new fire is lighted from the old fire and is protected by shamans, for it must not be allowed to go out. The sacrifice is a he-goat or ram which must be killed without spilling blood or its uttering a cry. Among the Altaians the forequarters of a horse are cooked on the old fire and the hind quarters on the new fire. During both ceremonies the heads of families attach flax threads to the birches and eagle feathers to the threads. Meat is then taken from the old fire and carried around in a sunwise direction. Finally a feast is held from the meat on the new fire. All remnants and implements are then burned in the old fire.

Among the Greeks, when a new colony was established the new fire was lighted from the civic fire in the mother city. In Armenia the fire lighted in a new household is taken from the old fire of the old home. The story of Prometheus and the torch races explain the transfer of pure fire from one place to another. All fires in Athens were extinguished on the occasion of his festival. The Vestal fire in Rome was protected by an association of high-born virgins who enjoyed many privileges. When the fire went out despite all precautions, elaborate ceremonies were needed to rekindle it. It was rekindled by friction.

Many of the fire ceremonies of northern Europe—Beltane, Midsummer, and the like—were connected with ceremonies of purification, leaping through the fire, carrying burning faggots through the streets, and cries of "burn the witches." The blessing of the new fire and the Paschal candle occurred during the Easter vigil. It is first mentioned in the legendary life of Saint Patrick. This fire was kindled by flint and steel which, because the fire drill has, universally, sexual implications, was both "modern" and acceptable.

The production of fire by means of a fire drill is known throughout the world; but the use of the fire drill aroused the particular opposition of the medieval church because in Europe as well as elsewhere it had been given a phallic significance which the church dignitaries deplored. The fire drill is a pointed piece of hard wood twirled rapidly in a notch made in a piece of flat wood on the ground. The drill was considered the male member and the piece drilled was female. Despite the ecclesiastical law that anyone who performed incantations to a phallus must perform a penance of bread and water for three Lents, the use of the fire drill was continued into modern times.

New fire and its ceremonies are closely associated with beliefs about the sacredness of the hearth which, as the center of tribal and family life, contains vestiges of beliefs which are at the same time primitive and authentic human needs today. The Girl Scout invocation to the fire, "burn, fire, burn," defines a common human need. Of the five sacred parts of the house in old Chinese custom the hearth was the most important. Greeks presented their children to the gods by carrying them around the hearth, which was in the center of the room. In many American families today, the lighting of the first fire in a new house is attended by a certain amount of ceremony and emotion. Frazer has an elaborate account and impressive evidence to show that the sacredness of the hearth, and the custom in a number of places of making the fire from the wood of special bushes and trees is connected with ancestor worship.

Some students have associated "new fire" with "need fire," possibly on the grounds that when new fire is necessary it is needed. However a somewhat arbitrary distinction is that need fire is therapeutic and not calendrial. [RDJ]

✍ Ceremonial kindling, at regular intervals, of a sacred fire is a ritual practice found in both the Old and New Worlds. In the Old World new fire rites are widespread in the classical Mediterranean area of Greece and Rome, and survive in Easter rites of various branches of Christianity; in Africa they occur in the East African cattle area, and in South Africa; in Asia they are found in Persia, parts of India, in China, Formosa, and Japan. In the New World new fire rites are, except for the Karok, a northwestern California Indian group, characteristic of the maize-growing tribes of the Southeast, Southwest, Eastern Woodlands, Mexico, Yucatán, Central America, and Peru. No direct connection between Old World and New World new fire rites has ever been established and it is assumed they developed independently in these two regions. For a recently published survey of New World new fire rites see William Harlan Gilbert, *New Fire Ceremonialism in America* (*Revista del Instituto de Antropología de la Universidad Nacional de Tucumán*, Vol. 3, No. 3, Tucumán, 1947). [EWV]

New Rice and Okra A work song of American Negroes, sung to shuffling feet and beat of heavy pestles as rice husks are removed.

New Year The ceremonies which mark the passing of the old year and the beginning of the new are as diverse as the communities which observe them, but they all have in common the sense that one cycle of living is finished and a new one is beginning and thus partake of the *rites de passage*. Whether this nodal point in living is noted with rejoicing, regret, or hope is determined by complex ethnic factors, the ethos of the group. When in 46 B.C. Julius Cæsar revised the calendar and made January the first month, it followed immediately after the Saturnalia, a period of license and great rejoicing. The Christians opposed this. Tertullian, the Christian historian, deplored it. The Council of Auxerre condemned it as diabolical, and the Council of Tours required prayers and a mass of expiation on New Year's Day, which it said was "a practice long in use." Dances were forbidden, and crimes were to be expiated by fasts.

Most agricultural and some nomadic peoples compute the year on the basis of the movements of the moon. Because the lunar calendar does not get the earth around the sun at the proper time each year and this complicates the reckoning of the seasons, such devices as intercalary months and irregular months are used. Consequently, whatever basis of computation is used, most calendars are of a luni-solar variety. The Chinese, for example, have twelve moons or months, but every so often have to insert an extra month.

In Europe, New Year's Day occurred in March, or at Christmas or other dates, even after the reforms of Julius Cæsar in Rome. Most of Europe, except Russia, made the change to January 1, soon after the Gregorian calendar reform in the 16th century, Scotland in 1600, and England in 1752. Thus the celebration of the first day of January as the first day of the year is a modern innovation. Elsewhere, because of intercalations, the first day of the year is a movable feast according to our present system of reckoning the months. Thus the Jewish calendar, on a luni-solar basis, has movable feasts.

The excessive jollification which characterizes the Occidental New Year cannot be attributed to Julius Cæsar's placing it so near the Saturnalia, as other cultures also consider the ending of one year and the beginning of the next as a moment of gratification. In China, the first few days of the new year are the only days celebrated as universal festivals. All shops are customarily closed, and the lowest coolie then takes his annual leave to be with his family for a few days. At this time too, families which have subsisted throughout the year on a meager diet of parched grain try to get a bit of meat. The household gods who have been absent on various missions connected with the end of the year return, and they too join the reunion. The head of the household, having paid all of his debts before midnight, takes his ease and makes plans for contracting new ones. Door posters and pious maxims invite the Gods of Wealth and Babies to visit the house or warn away evil spirits that might be tempted to enter. Sometimes posters on the wall of a neighbor's house direct the God of Wealth not to enter there but to go to the house across the street. Japanese customs are somewhat similar. In both countries, New Year's Day is everybody's birthday.

On this day special foods are customary. The Japanese offer a "male" cake to the sun and a "female" cake to the moon. In India, the attempt is made to eat only new foods, new grain, peas, and the like. The festival marks the turning of the sun at the winter solstice. It is the period of ceremonial purification in the sacred river, and of the great pilgrimage. In the south, the boiling of new rice is an augury for good luck during the new year. Cattle decorated with flowers are led about. Presents are given. Rejoicing is general and lasts for three days. In Bengal, the Ganges is worshipped, and the congregating of tens of thousands of people in the Ganges creates much excitement. The Veddas of Ceylon offer rice cakes. The Persian New Year, which became Moslem, is the day when God returned Solomon's ring, the devils brought fine gifts, and the swallows sprinkled water on him. In northern Europe, Estonia, Sweden, and Denmark, cakes in the form of a boar were made from the meal from the first sheaf. The Scots celebrated Hogmanay on the last day of the old year. Pancakes are appropriate in France. They are tossed on a griddle to bring good luck and riches. In Mexico, February 2, corresponding to the Aztec New Year, is a time of rejoicing and follows five days of lamentation.

Many Occidental countries mark the passing of the old year and the arrival of the new by elaborate balls, drinking, and generally orgiastic behavior in which, at midnight, everybody blows horns, rings bells, shouts, throws confetti, sings "Should old acquaintance be forgot," drinks additional toasts which are usually not needed, and, as an important part of the ritual, tries to kiss all the prettiest girls in the party, who offer enthusiastic collaboration. See *New Year's Day* in SPANISH FOLKLORE. [RDJ]

🖝 Rites marking the beginning of the new year were practiced by many North American Indian groups, but the time for such ceremonies varied: for the Seneca, an Iroquois group of the Eastern Woodlands, the New Year begins in February, for the Eskimo in the fall, for the Northwest California tribes late in July, for the Hopi in November, and for other Pueblo Indians at the winter solstice. New Year observances varied from area to area; the Seneca rites, for instance, last a total of 7–8 days. On the first day all fires are put out and the ashes scattered; new fire is made by the Keepers of the Faith and a white dog is strangled and hung up. During the next three days people in masquerade rush from house to house; boys steal food, people ask for interpretations of their dreams, the False Faces throw ashes over people to drive out disease, and women of the Otter Society sprinkle water on passersby. On the fifth day sins are publicly confessed, and the white dog is carried on a slab of bark to an altar and burned with speeches, songs, prayers, and offerings of tobacco. This concludes the ceremony proper; the last 2–3 days are devoted to social dances and games. For the Northwest California and Hopi New Year ceremonies, which differ in many respects from the Seneca ceremony outlined above, see WORLD RENEWAL; SOYAL; WÜWÜCHIM. [EWV]

nguneme A Dahomey Negro protective charm (gbo), perhaps the most common of all *gbos*. It is a leaf (the sacred *akûko* leaf) which a man leaves in his house to protect his possessions during an absence. He may put a branch of these leaves across the door, on or beside any specially valued object (as a pile of firewood), or a well. It will bring harm to anyone who violates it; the man will become impotent, the woman barren, the child dead, who disregards it. (Herskovits, *Dahomey* ii: 285)

Nhang In Armenian folk belief, a monstrous evil spirit which sometimes appeared in rivers as a woman or as a seal which dragged swimmers to the bottom. In Persian the term means crocodile. These spirits used their victims for their lust and then sucked their blood.

Nibelungen hoard In Teutonic mythology and story a fabulous, accursed treasure, the possession of which is the central theme of such famous epics as the Icelandic *Volsunga Saga,* the German *Nibelungenlied,* and Wagner's operatic *Ring* cycle. Some say Nibelung was a dwarf king who commissioned Siegfried to divide his large treasure among his three sons. In another version it is the Andvari treasure secured by Loki to ransom himself, Odin, and Hœnir from the dwarf Hreidmar. The term Nibelung is sometimes applied to the possessors of the treasure and those under the influence of the curse, as the Burgundians in the *Nibelungenlied*. In most of the versions this treasure ends up hidden in the Rhine (the Rhinegold) with all those knowing its whereabouts dead. It is frequently guarded by water maidens, as the Rhine Maidens in Wagner's version.

Niels Ebbeson Hero of a cycle of Danish ballads of the 14th century dealing with the heroic deeds of Niels Ebbeson and how he rid the land of foreign oppression.

Niemi, A. R. (1869–1931) Finnish folklorist and editor of several volumes of the *Old Songs of the Finnish People.* He published many works about the *Kalevala* and the old relationships between Finnish and Lithuanian folklore. [JB]

Niflheim In Teutonic mythology, the region of eternal cold, mist, and darkness, north of Midgard across the river Gjol. Into this region Odin banished Hel to rule over the "nine unlighted worlds" of the dead. Here Hel presided, with her dark red bird and her rake. Here was the inexhaustible, seething spring called Hvergelmir inhabited by the dragon Nidhug; here was the deepest root of Yggdrasil; here lived Uller, god of winter, during the summer months; and from edge to edge of Niflheim arched the Bifrost bridge. Niflheim and Niflhel are sometimes synonymous; but Niflhel is more often synonymous with Hel, as a subterranean region entered through the Gnipa cave, and later regarded as a place of punishment, where the dead undergo a second death.

night Night is everywhere synonymous with darkness, and, wherever the dualism of good and bad is equated with light and dark, night is equivalent to evil or death. The sun sets in the west, therefore the west is the place of death, and night is the time of death. In ancient Egyptian religion, night was the time when the sun fought his daily battle with Apepi, the serpent, and won to rise again in the east. Darkness is, in *Genesis,* the original state of things; after darkness, light was created by God. The analogy still remains valid in folk thought: the beings of the night, demons, devils, hags, witches, are of the old belief; during the light of day God's religion holds sway. The *Popol Vuh* of the Quiché Indians begins with darkness as the first state of things. One of the Orphic cosmologies of classical Greece depicted Night as the primeval being; this black-winged bird laid an egg from which came Eros, love; the halves of the shell became Sky and Earth, Uranus and Ge. In the Hesiodic account Erebus and Night came from Chaos, and from Night came Air and Day. Still earlier, in Homer, Nyx (or Nox), the feminine personification of night, was so powerful that Zeus, as well as gods and men, might be subdued by her. The systematizing of the mythographers had her living in Hades; she was a winged female, or she rode in a chariot, she dressed in dark clothes, she was accompanied by the stars.

Among several peoples, the night's beginning at sunset is the beginning of the day. This holds true of much European festival observance, for often the eve of a special day is more important popularly than the night of that day or the day itself. Thus, Christmas Eve and Halloween take precedence in popular observance over Christmas Day and All Hallows Day. The Jewish Sabbath begins with darkness on the eve of the seventh day, traditionally when three stars are visible in the heavens. But the time when the spirits of darkness are potent ends with cockcrow. Then the spirits out of their graves, the witches riding to their meetings or their mischief, the mountain spirits, and all the evil powers must return to their abodes or natural shapes, for, during the day, when the sun shines with God's power, they dare not move to cause evil. Night is the time when baby-snatching beings rove; lights must be kept blazing in the room of an unbaptized or uncircumcised child lest Lilith or other evil-wishing spirit take the infant, perhaps leaving a changeling in its place. Disease-causing demons rove the night and, until recent hygiene suggested otherwise, bedroom windows were kept closed at night to prevent the spirits from getting into the sleeping chamber. Prayers are important before going to sleep. There is a strong resemblance in night prayers from Babylonia calling on Shamash, Sin, Nergal, and Ninib, from Ireland calling on Mary, Joseph, Brigit, and Patrick, and among Jews naming Michael, Gabriel, Uriel, and Raphael. Popularly, if you say "rabbit" as you fall asleep on the last night of the month and say it again first thing in the morning, that month will bring you good luck.

The nightmare or incubus comes during sleep; so do the demons that bring evil dreams. During the night, in sleep, the soul wanders about, too, and then it may be trapped by a witch or magician while an evil spirit possesses the body. Werewolves and vampires are active at night; one who seems perfectly normal by day may become a ravening beast at night. In the reverse of this, beast marriage tales often have the hero an animal by day and a man at night (D621.1).

Certain nights are worse than others. To the medieval Jews Tuesday and Friday nights were most dangerous; then a greater number of spirits wandered looking for a lone man to seize. The last man at prayers on Friday night had to have company home from the synagogue; special time-consuming prayers were said by those who finished before him, in order that he might have company going home and still not be embarrassed or hurried in his prayers by seeing someone waiting for him. See DREAMS; ECLIPSES; HABDALAH; LIGHT; MOON.

☞ Before the sun, or light, was stolen or otherwise obtained, the world was in darkness, according to the mythologies of many North American Indians. The White Mountain Apache, however, go behind this period of darkness, to a period in which there was no night, only light. During the period of light, Badger carried something in a basket, which he warned Coyote not to untie. Coyote disobeyed and let out night. It was then night all the time. During this period of darkness the animals and birds could speak like human beings and

all spoke the same language. They all wanted daylight, so they divided into two sides and played the moccasin game, and daylight came through the mountains when the birds won the game. [EWV]

☞ In a few South American tribes night is conceived of as something tangible that was acquired by mankind. The Cashinawa say that darkness was owned by spirits. At first night was released so suddenly that men were caught by sleep in whatever position or activity they might happen to be; later nights were too long. Finally a regular rhythm was established.

Several South American myths tell how the world was plunged in darkness for a long period (the long night). According to the ancient Peruvians, the darkness was accompanied by a general revolt of the domesticated animals and of the artifacts against man. (See REVOLT OF THE UTENSILS.) The Araucanians attributed the long night to two brothers (the mythical Twins) who had put the son in a pot. The Shipaya have a myth about the long night which fell over mankind after a man had killed the Sun. The incoming of darkness is one of the cataclysms in the cosmogony of the Chaco Indians. A great many men were changed into animals and birds when light returned. [AM]

Nighthawk dance (*pi•ckwelane'oka•n*) A dance of the Delaware Indians which concluded the 10th night of the Midwinter Bear Rite, and recurred in the Green Corn and Thanksgiving dances of the group coresident with the Grand River Iroquois. It was a communication with spirit forces, not for rain as in the Southwest, but for thanksgiving and a healthful season. Two to four young men, stripped to the waist, faced the singer in a line. In his right hand each shook a rattle, previously a turtle rattle, later one of cowhorn; in the left hand they held extended the wing of a nighthawk, later on a feather wand. They would lunge and then jump toward the singer in a squatting position, shaking the muscles of their backs like nighthawks. The songs would be interrupted by speeches and gifts of cornmeal cakes, then continue where they left off. The similarity is evident between this dance and the Iroquois eagle dance. See GANEGWA'E. [GPK]

nightingale The folklore of the nightingale has a literary flavor. A medieval story is that the nightingale is afraid of snakes and keeps awake all night by pressing her breast against a thorn, singing mournfully because of the pain. The Greek myth of the origin of the nightingale is a variant of the universal folktale of the loathsome feast. Tereus, son of the evil god Ares, was married to Procne who produced a son Itys. When Procne asked to see her sister Philomela, Tereus offered to get her. On the way back he told Philomela that Procne was dead and tricked her into marriage. She, learning the truth, threatened to expose him whereupon he cut out her tongue and locked her up. She wove a tapestry which told the story of her misfortunes and sent it to Procne. The two sisters, plotting revenge, murdered Tereus' son Itys, cut him up and served him to his father in a stew. Tereus, about to kill the women, was foiled because the gods changed one to a nightingale and the other, the tongueless Philomela, into a thrush, which can only twitter. The Roman mythologists to whom the English poets are greatly indebted, got the story mixed up and reported that Philomela was the nightingale. [RDJ]

Commonly in European folklore, the nightingale is the bird of spring. It is said never to sleep; in Westphalia, the nightingale was once a shepherdess who kept postponing her marriage until her lover cursed her with the same sleeplessness he had been undergoing. If the bird's eyes and heart are dissolved and given in a drink, the drinker will never sleep again as long as he lives, and death will come soon. The tale of the nightingale and the blindworm embodies motif A2241.5: The nightingale and a certain worm were created with one eye each. One day the nightingale borrowed the worm's eye and forgot to return it. So the blindworm cannot see, and the nightingale has two eyes. This story has been told in Finland, Germany, and England. Compare however Shakespeare's *Romeo and Juliet* III, v, 31: "Some say the lark and loathed toad change eyes." See ANIMAL TALE; BIRDS' WEDDING.

nightmare A spirit or incubus that comes in the night to sleepers and sits or lies on their chests, stops up their breath, brings terrifying dreams, and awakens them with an oppressive feeling; also, a bad and vivid dream or experience. The word is sometimes popularly derived from night and mare, thus the steed whose riding in sleep brings such dreams; actually, *mare* is the Old English word for incubus, related to such words as *Marut*, the leader of the Hindu wild hunt; German *Mahr*, the nightmare; Russian *mora*, ghost, revenant; Czech *murawa;* Latin *mors* and Lithuanian *maras,* death; the word *cauchemar* in French contains the same root. A. H. Krappe sees in the word the root *mas*, male, virile man, also an obvious description of the incubus.

The Babylonian Alu, a storm god, was also the nightmare. Ephialtes, one of the Greek giants, whose name means the leaper, was the nightmare spirit of the Greeks. In Slavic and Teutonic belief, the *maras* were female nightmare spirits.

night-raven A bird of evil omen whose identity has baffled scientists and folklorists from the Middle Ages to the present day. Murray's *New English Dictionary on Historical Principles* defines it as "a nocturnal bird variously identified as a night-owl, night-heron, or night-jar, or imagined as a distinct species." It is listed among the unclean birds in *Lev.* xi, 6 and *Deut.* xiv, 15. The *New English Dictionary* also identifies it with the European goatsucker, which is said to blind goats. In the 16th century the night-raven was quite commonly thought to be an owl, a bird whose cry was also regarded as a dread omen. Willoughby (17th century) says that people call the bittern the night-raven and dread it because its cry means either one's own death or a death in the immediate family.

In Danish folk belief especially, to hear the night-raven is a bad omen. The bird is believed to be the reincarnation of a criminal or suicide who has been buried where three roads meet. These poor souls may dig themselves out at the rate of one grain of sand per year, and when thus finally liberated they go about at night in bird form. Their voices have been described as mournful, hideous, or uncouth. A. H. Krappe regards the night-raven of Danish folk belief as the same bird that precedes the Wild Hunt, and probably a personification of Odin.

Nihansan Arapaho Indian trickster who may also be the Arapaho creator of the world; he is sometimes named as such in Arapaho myths, but the creator is often referred to as Father, only. *Nih'ānçan* is now the ordinary word for white man in Arapaho; *Hixtcäbä Nih'ānçan*, above-white-man, is the Arapaho name for the God of the missionaries. The original meaning of the word is spider; among the Santee Dakota the trickster Unktomi is the Spider. However, in no Arapaho myths is there the slightest trace of any animal or spiderlike qualities which are attributed to Nihansan. He is entirely human. Apart from the hesitating identification of him with the creator of the world, he is not found as the hero of any serious myths, but always figures in ridiculous and often obscene Arapaho tales; he is thus the equivalent of the Dakota Unktomi, rather than of a creator trickster like the Ojibwa Nanabozho.

Among the Gros Ventre, linguistic relatives and neighbors of the Arapaho, the name for the trickster is Nix'ant; the Gros Ventre trickster shows somewhat more of the character of a creator, in combination with his trickster qualities, than does Nihansan. See George A. Dorsey and Alfred L. Kroeber, *Traditions of the Arapaho* (Field Columbian Museum, Anthropological Series, Vol. 5, Chicago, 1903), p. 6, n. 3. [EWV]

Niman Hopi Indian 9-day kachina ceremony held during July to celebrate the return of the Kachinas or supernaturals to their underground home in Shipap, where they stay until the winter solstice. The Niman kachina ceremony includes dramatization, group dancing, and altar ritual. See SOYAL. [EWV]

nimbus A halo or circle of light around the head or body of a god, saint, or hero. It is commonly used by Christian, Greek, Indian, Tibetan, Chinese, and other artists. It is an attribute of divinity or great virtue, as is seen in the general belief that God is too radiant to be looked upon by mortal man and in the phrases about the "bright god." It is also connected with the complex about fire making all things bright and transcendent. See CHAMPION'S LIGHT; ILLUMINATING BEAUTY. [RDJ]

Ningyo A kind of mermaid of Japanese folklore. [JLM]

ning wŏt A Kachin (Burma) method of divination in which a piece of thin green bamboo-stem is heated until the wood splits and small hairy fibers stand out along the edges of the split. By consulting these the diviner foretells events.

Ninigi-no-Mikoto Grandson of the Japanese Sun Goddess, who descended from heaven to Japan, after having received the Three Imperial Jewels. [JLM]

Ninki The wife of Ea (Enki) in Babylonian mythology; the lady of the waters. She is a very vague personage of almost no importance in worship.

Ninlil In Sumerian mythology, the consort of Enlil; an air goddess. In *Enlil and Ninlil,* the poem telling of the begetting of the moon god, she dwells in Nippur. Her mother tells her to walk by the river bank, since the keen-eyed Enlil will see her there. (Thorkild Jacobsen, using Mrs. Henri Frankfort's translation of the poem, indicates that she was *not* to go bathing, for fear that Enlil would see her, and that she disobeyed.) Enlil seduces the maiden and leaves Nippur. She follows, and at various stages along the way encounters him again in various disguises. Each time, at the gate, at the bank of the underworld river, and in the boat taking her across the river, she submits to him again. Nanna (or Sin), the moon god, is the first conceived; the gods resulting from the other episodes are less important, one being Meslamtaea, a name of Nergal, lord of the underworld. The myth perhaps reflects an early belief in the impregnating power of the waters. A curious episode occurs early in the poem: Enlil, having seduced Ninlil, is tried by a council of the gods and is banished from the city; here he does not seem to be the powerful god who developed into Bel and Marduk.

Niörd or **Njord** In Scandinavian mythology, the handsome god of the sea, especially of the coastal waters; god of fishing, commerce, and prosperity. Originally one of the vanir, he went to Asgard after the war with the æsir as a hostage. He is highly respected and counted third among them, but at Ragnarök he will return to dwell among the vanir. In Vannaheim, he married his sister Nerthus by whom he had a son, Frey, and a daughter, Freya, both of whom accompanied him to Asgard. His home, Nôatûn (Haven), is near the shore and from here he stills the storms lashed up by the sea god Ægir. In Asgard he married Skadi, daughter of the frost giant, Thiassi. She agreed to spend three days at Nôatûn if he would spend the next nine days at Thrymheim, her home. In this they personified the northern summer (3 months) and winter (9 months), but as neither was happy in this arrangement, after several years they separated. Niörd is usually worshipped in conjunction with Frey. The sponge is called Niörd's glove. See NERTHUS.

Nirriti A Vedic goddess of evil and disease; personification of destruction, sometimes connected with Kāli.

nirvāṇa In Hinduism, the "blowing out" of the spark of life; hence, release; merging or absorption into the Absolute. In Buddhism, nirvāṇa is the ideal and goal of all religious effort. It is extinction, *through enlightenment*, of individual consciousness, but a kind of qualified extinction: the word denotes bliss, deliverance from the long round of birth, death, rebirth, and death, and far transcends any mere nothingness. It is the end of individual desire, release from passion and delusion and pain, the end of consciousness, therefore the end of suffering (i.e. release from existence), and greatly to be desired and worked for. Brahmanism stresses the joy of merging with the Absolute; there is no greater good. The idea of nirvāṇa is beyond human concept; the road can be followed; the state can be attained; but before attainment the concept of *nirvāṇa* is beyond encompassment by the human mind.

nisse A class of household spirits of Scandinavian folklore, associated with the Gardsvor, house guardian, in that he is often believed to be the manifestation of the spirit of some ancestor or other kin. The nisse behaves more like the English and Scottish brownie, however, and the German kobold, since he is both helpful in the house and barn, and annoying and exacting. He is fed and fostered by the house-dwellers, the same as other household spirits. Compare BOGGART.

nith songs A species of word-duel practiced by the Greenland, Baffinland, and other Eskimo groups. The name derives from the Norwegian *nith*, contention. Private quarrels and disputes are often settled, among the eastern Eskimo, by the disputants singing sarcastic songs which they have composed at each other, at a public gathering. The audience decides which singer is the winner, and thereafter the loser must hold his peace and be friends with the winner. The singing of nith songs and wrestling matches are common means of taking revenge by Greenlanders and other Eskimo who consider themselves injured by another person. For translations of some Eskimo nith-songs see Alexander Goldenweiser, *Anthropology*. New York, 1937, pp. 97ff. See APO; CALYPSO; LOBI SINGI. Compare PENILLION. [EWV]

nix or **nixie** In German folklore, water beings inhabiting any body of fresh water, where they live in beautiful palaces. They are generally conceded to be able to assume various forms or to become invisible. They have human torsos with fish tails, but they go to markets in the guise of old ladies; and at dances, which they love, they are young and attractive. Even while they are in human form, there is always some give-away feature which may be recognized by the observant. They are reported also to have been seen in the form of gray horses. In the main they are unfriendly, but may be propitiated. They lure human beings into dangerous water and drown them. It is believed that they must have at least one victim a year, and at one time they were offered human sacrifice. In many places it is considered bad luck to rescue a drowning person for fear of reprisal by the nixes. Some authorities claim these beings are normally old with green hair, skin, and teeth, who become young and beautiful to entice mortals. Others say they live normal family lives, even keeping cattle, which, if they graze in meadows with mortal cattle, will make these more prolific. Nixes sometimes take human mates and have children, though a human mother must have a human midwife who, if discreet, is exceedingly well paid. In some localities they are accused of placing changelings in the cradles of humans; especially the German *Wasserkopf* (child with a large head) is attributed to nixes. In other places the elder of the nix family frowns on human dalliance, and there are many tales of the human lover suddenly finding blood-red water where the nixie has disappeared, which would indicate that they were considered mortal. See HAVMAND; KELPIE; MERMAID; NÄKK; SIREN.

nō, nōgaku or **sarugaku no nō** (The accomplishment of scattered mime) A form of Japanese dance-drama. Its roots in early religious and secular ceremonies grew into a complex art form under numerous influences. The genealogy goes back especially to the *sangaku* (Chinese *sanyao*), which came from China in the Nara period (708–784) and later became the *sarugaku* or "monkey-mime," a compound of songs, music, dances, acrobatics, stunts, and wrestling. With the addition of the dances known as *kuse-mai*, the use of plots derived from such older pieces of literature as the *Tales of the Heike* (13th century), and with an increased emphasis on serious elements, the nō finally emerged in the Ashikaga period (1392–1573). Particularly under the ægis of Kannami (1333–84) and his son Seami (1363–1444) it reached its highest development; and during the Tokugawa period (1603–1868), the nō became greatly favored by the *shōgun*.

The nō program consists of five or six short dance-dramas given in a theater in a single day. A distinctive pattern runs through each part and through the whole group. These are: 1) A congratulatory play, in which deities appear; 2) A battle piece, involving warriors; 3) A lyrical "wig-piece," in which a woman is the leading character; 4) A play in which such themes as lunacy and vengeance are treated; 5) A concluding play involving supernatural beings. In between the plays a comic *kyōgen* brings an interlude of contrast and relief.

The actors, besides a chorus of 8–12 and four musicians, are the *shite*, leading actor, and the *waki*, who plays a secondary role. Both may have a companion, *tsure*, who may speak a few words, or a *tomo*, who is wordless. The leads wear masks. All are men.

The stage is a resonant, roofed platform without curtain, with an unchanging background consisting of a conventionalized pine tree (symbolizing undying strength), and a walk extending to the left for entrances and exits.

The themes of nō plays are heroic, ethical, or mystical. The music, played by an orchestra of a drum struck with two sticks, two hand drums, and a flute, enhances the sense of mystery; and the conventionalized gestures and speaking evoke a world of unreality. The motions, all fantastically slow and restrained, belong to the *mai* type of dance. The chants are rendered in measured tones, with smaller intervals and slower tempo for the leads ("strong") than the subcharacters ("weak"). They are fixed by tradition in diagrams accompanying the texts. Every element is symbolic: the gestures, the properties, and the design of the sumptuous costumes.

Though the nō is distinctly an aristocratic, courtly art form, the *kabuki* has taken over dances from the nō and adapted them to the popular stage. This took place during the Tokugawa period. It is possible to prove that foreign influences from China, India, Korea, and Manchuria have been operative in shaping the nō, in combination with ancient native ceremonies and the recent native rice-planting dance. Yet the Japanese genius has here created a unique and characteristic theatrical art and invested it with a dignified fantasy as expressive of profound experience as the Greek theater of antiquity. See KABUKI; ODORI. [GPK]

Noah In the Bible, the righteous man chosen by God to survive the deluge (*Gen.* vi-ix). Noah was the son of Lamech and grandson of Methuselah. When he was born, a shining child, so perfect that he came circumcised from the womb, his grandfather warned Lamech to keep the child's real name a secret, for the world was evil and the magicians would do the infant harm if they could learn his real name. So Noah was known until after the flood by the name Methuselah gave him, Menachem the Comforter.

Warning of the flood was given to Noah in time for him to plant a teakwood tree, wait 20 years for it to mature, and cut it into planking for the ark. Noah tried to get the wicked people of the world to reform, but they jeered at him, especially at his folly in building the ark on dry land and in a high spot far from the sea. In those days, people were larger than they are now, giants, and they said that if a flood came they would stop the water with their feet. At last the ark was finished and Noah began to collect the passengers, two, male and female, of all animals, but seven of each of the clean beasts. (Here, as in other parts of the Noah story, the Priestly writer-editor amends the Jehovist's more folkloric account. The P version accounts for two

of all kinds; further, P counts a full year of 12 lunar months plus 11 days to make the duration of the flood a whole solar year, where J's version recounts the familiar 40 days and 40 nights [for which see FLOOD]; P, protecting the priestly prerogatives, does not mention the altar and sacrifice after the flood, whereas J does, etc.) A Moslem commentator says that as the animals entered the ark, Noah touched and counted them, the males with his right hand, the females with his left. The ass was slow in getting on the ark, and the impatient Noah called, "Hurry, even though Satan be with thee." The Devil, taking this as an invitation to board the ark, came on with the ass. The ark was in three stories, the lower for the beasts, with the birds and men on the two upper decks, though commentators disagree as to this order. Men and women were separated in the ark by the gigantic body of Father Adam, who was disinterred by Noah to keep him from a watery grave. Not that there were many people aboard, only Noah, his wife, their sons, their wives and children.

At last the waters began to come. First water rose and began spilling from the stove of Noah's wife. Then God removed two of the Pleiades and water began to spill from the heavens. (Later, to fill the holes, God took two stars from the Great Bear, which is why the Bear chases the Pleiades across the skies; but it will not recover its lost stars until the Judgment Day.) The waters rose from the earth too, and the giants tried to stop the springs with their feet. But the waters were hot, for God had passed them through Gehenna, and the soles were burned from the giants' feet. In desperation, the evil generation cast its own children into the springs, but to no avail; soon the waters covered the highest mountaintops. Even Canaan, Noah's grandson, died thinking he could live above the flood on a mountain. The giant Og, the monster reem, and the fishes of the sea alone survived outside the shelter of the ark.

The trip aboard the ark was not uneventful. The lion was seasick the whole time and once, when Noah was a bit careless in feeding it, the irritable lion bit him, laming him. The filth from the animals too piled up aboard the ark, and rats became a problem. So Noah created two new animals, which had hitherto not existed. Passing his hand over the elephant, he made it give birth to the pig, which soon devoured the filth; Noah then rubbed the lion's nose, and it gave birth to a cat, which grew sleek on the rats. See CATS.

The weather was overcast, and day and night were undifferentiated. But aboard the ark, Noah had a book that had once belonged to Adam, the book from which Noah learned to build the ark. This book was encased in a jeweled box, and at night the jewels shone to illumine the ship, while in the daytime they grew dimmer. Some say, however, that the illuminating jewel was the philosopher's stone. Finally the rain stopped; the waters ceased to rise; the ark floated on the waters. Noah sent out a raven to see if land were yet exposed. But the raven, a white bird, found a corpse floating on the water and began to eat it, never returning to the ark; for this its plumage ever since has been black. Noah sent forth the dove, which returned with an olive branch. A. H. Krappe sees a real custom here; as late as the Middle Ages, seamen released birds when out at sea to determine the direction in which land lay.

The ark at last grounded on a mountaintop. European

and most Near Eastern tradition says this was Mt. Ararat in the Caucasus, though other peaks are similarly noted. But, for the ancient world, since Noah was the inventor of viniculture, and since wine-making traditionally began in the mountains of Armenia, Ararat was the obvious landing place. The sacrifice of thanksgiving was not made by Noah, however, because he had been lamed by the lion and was therefore unfit to perform the rite. Instead Shem built the altar and offered the sacrifice.

The survivors of the flood set about building a civilization. Noah invented the hoe, the scythe, the plow, and several other agricultural implements. One day he discovered some grapes and got drunk on the juice. In his drunken condition, he went to his wife's tent and had intercourse with her. Ham, Noah's inquisitive son, watched the whole incident and told his brothers, Shem and Japheth. The two entered the tent backwards and, not looking at their father, covered him as he lay in his drunken stupor. For this act of filial duty, Shem and Japheth and their descendants were blessed by Noah, but since he looked, Ham and his descendants were condemned to have black skin, red eyes, kinky hair, everted lips. The story is, according to Krappe, either an etiological story intended to be opprobrious to the neighboring Hamites, or a reminiscence of a myth paralleling the Uranus-Cronus castration story of the Greeks. The vine itself was pointed out to Noah by Satan as something to cultivate. In planting it, Noah fertilized the ground with the blood of a lamb, a lion, an ape, and a pig; thus, as a man drinks, he is at first bleating and simple, then brave and roaring as a lion, then foolish as an ape, and finally he rolls in the mire like a pig.

Myths of great floods have been found all over the world. The Hebrew story, with Noah as its hero, is acknowledged to be a borrowing from the Mesopotamian flood story, told in the Gilgamesh epic, but certainly much older. Though the captivity in Babylon would on the surface appear to be the ideal time for such borrowing to have taken place, the flood tale was known to the Hebrews long before that time. Probably contact between the wandering desert tribes and the Mesopotamian city-dwellers took place, for purposes of trade, from earliest times. The Babylonian myth itself, with Utnapishtim as its Noah, may be traced back to the Sumerian account, where Ziusudra is the hero. The Armenian Xisuthros sounds very much like this Sumerian Noah. Manu is the parallel figure in ancient Indian mythology.

Noah and Noah's wife were popular characters of the English mystery-play pageants. Noah, the essence of the convivial toper, is a very sympathetic character who fights with the Devil in the ark and beats him. But his wife is a worse opponent for Noah than the Devil: a sharp-tongued, ill-tempered shrew who makes Noah's life miserable. See ARA; ARK; DELUGE; FLOOD; OLIVE.

Noah's ark The idea of the first world being destroyed by a deluge and then re-created is found in almost all North American Indian mythologies, and may well be a purely native concept. However, since it is so similar to the Biblical deluge story which was told to the Indians by missionaries, it was not difficult for the former to incorporate in their native material the Noah account; many tribes did this and now relate the story of Noah and his big boat as part of their creation material. [EWV]

Noble Moringer A German Minnesinger ballad of the 12th century which, transmitted throughout Europe, has become one of the most famous of all ballad stories. It begins with the *aubade* theme, borrowed from French tradition, the separation of lovers on the morning after the wedding. The wife pledges to the husband that she will wait seven—or nine or some other number—years for his return. He leaves for the crusade, or to kill the dragon, etc. The time limit expires but still the faithful wife waits. At last she is forced into a match. The husband comes back just in time to attend the wedding feast and drop his ring in the bride's cup. She recognizes it, the lovers are reunited, and the groom—unless he is the villain of the piece—is dismissed. Where the bridegroom has forced himself on the bride, the ballad-makers have invented suitable and stern punishment.

The German version mentions the name of the Minnesinger Heinrich von Morungen and so can be dated as originating in the 12th century, though the story itself is probably much older. Its hero is Gerhardt von Holenbach; later versions make the hero Henry the Lion of Brunswick, who is the Bruncvík of Czech legend. Transmission of the ballad as a unit is clear because of the several motifs it includes: the parting of the lovers, the pledge of waiting (M131), the forced marriage, the arrival of the hero just as the marriage is to take place (N681), the ring in the cup (H94.4). In England the ballad is known as *Hind Horn*, related to the other Horn romances; in Spain it is *Count Dirlos;* in Denmark *Finnekonster;* in Russia *Dobrynja and Aljoša Popović.* It is the Serb *Pomorovac Todor* and *Jankovic Stojan's Imprisonment,* the Czech *First Love,* the Greek *Constantine the Little,* the Rumanian *Mošneagul.* Other ballads, e.g. the French and German *Soldier's Return,* resemble it and may be descended from it, or they may have arisen independently. On the other hand, the eastern versions, especially, of the *Moringer* have become assimilated to cycles like the Balkan ballads of Digenes Akritas, where the kidnapped bride ballad has been joined to the *Moringer* theme. In Russia, where the *Moringer* is one of the few Western ballads adopted, it is told of Dobrynja, hero of the Kiev cycle. In Spain, *Count Dirlos,* the longest of the Spanish ballads, is attached to the Carolingian poems, but is simply the story of the *Noble Moringer* embroidered with names and places familiar in that cycle. Compare YOUNG BEICHAN.

nocnitsa The night-hag of Russian, Polish, Serbian, and Slovak folklore, who torments children at night. In the Archangel region mothers place a knife in the cradle, or draw a circle around the cradle with a knife, or hide an ax and a doll under the floor beneath the cradle to prevent this nocturnal being from getting at the child. This practice may be related to the world-wide belief that supernatural beings cannot touch iron. Other Russian names for the nocnitsa are *kriksy* and *plaksy.* The Bulgarian analog of the nocnitsa is the *gorska makva,* a hideous wood-hag.

noide or **noaide** The shaman of the Lapps. The most important of his possessions is the magic drum used for excitation as a medium. The drum is painted with magic figures and pictures of gods. The assistant spirit to the shaman (*suoje,* shadow) could be obtained by inheritance or purchase, and even as a marriage portion. Sometimes the spirit comes voluntarily to the service to the shaman. [JB]

Nokomis A term, widespread in North American Algonquian Indian languages, for grandmother: e.g. Shawnee *kokumtha,* our grandmother. The Ojibwa word *nokomis* was used as the proper name for Hiawatha's grandmother in the poem *Hiawatha* by Longfellow. See HIAWATHA. [EWV]

nolema'higan Literally, acting like a clown: the former Penobscot Indian Trading or Clown dance. The "traders" were disguised with deer-heads and antlers, and birch-bark masks. They wore women's clothing, or wore humps in their backs. For several successive nights opposing parties bargained at the several homes for objects of every description. The clown heralded his entrance by singing, weird cries, and stamping on the threshold like an animal; then he would engage in all manner of buffoonery. The song and actions are reminiscent of the Iroquois False Face Begging dance. Also, macabre stories connect the traders with ghosts. Long ago the procedure probably had serious ritual significance. [GPK]

nominee Term used, especially in the study of Negro folklore, for set phrases or other devices employed to introduce a tale. Among the Ashanti, most tales are preceded by the phrase, "We do not really mean, we do not really mean (that what we are going to say is true)." The Hausa may begin with "A story, a story, let it go, let it come." In Dutch Guiana, tales may begin with *"Er, tin tin,"* with the answer *"Tin, tin, tin,"* the equivalent of "Once upon a time"; or with *"Kri-kra,* all men on their *Kra-kra,"* or "All in your places." In the Bahamas, according to Parsons, many tales begin with the rime "Once upon a time, a very good time; Monkey chew tobacco and spit white lime," a formula also reported from the Sea Islands of the Georgia and South Carolina coastal region. [MJH]

noodle stories One of the types of the droll story; stories of people whose actions are absurd almost to the point of idiocy. Typical noodles are the inhabitants of Gotham in England, of Schildburg in German tradition, of Chelm in Yiddish stories, of Emessa in Persian tales, of Bœotia in ancient Greek tradition. The butts of these stories are stupid peasants, city slickers, absent-minded professors, Little Morons, habitual worriers. The Micronesians call such stories *umes,* crazy people. The tales form a distinct genre almost everywhere in the world, but shade into the trickster tales where the dupes of the Reynards and the Till Eulenspiegels are noodles.

Carolyn Wells notes Theophrastus' character of the Stupid Man "who, after doing a sum and setting down the total, will ask the person next to him, 'What does it come to?'" The story of the fishermen who want to return to a good spot the next day and mark the location by cutting a notch in their boat while they are over the place is as popular today as it was 500 years ago; the point of the story is usually "But how do we know we'll get the same boat tomorrow?" The students who were the noodles of the earliest jestbooks have become the absent-minded professors of today; the most modern "switch" is the psychiatrist with hallucinations. The most famous English noodle story is *The Three Sillies*: a suitor discovers his intended and her parents

crying down in the cellar because their child may some day be killed by an ax stuck in a beam; he travels until he finds three sillier people in the world—a man who spends hours every morning trying to jump with both legs into his trousers, a woman who feeds her cow on the thatched roof of her house, a whole townful of noodles fishing the moon out of a pond. The starting point of this story, in a version from Massachusetts, is: "If I had a darter and my darter had a darter and she should fall in the warter, how dreadful it would be."

The Turkish Khoja Nasreddin puts an arrow through his own coat, thinking he sees a thief. In the morning he recognizes it, and then says, "It's a good thing I wasn't in it when I hit it."

Famous in Arabic, German, English, etc., is the tale of the stubborn couple, neither of whom will get up to bar the door. Robbers enter through the unlatched door. Finally the husband is outraged at the treatment to which the robbers subject his wife and cries out. "You spoke first," she says. "You lock the door."

The Irish bull too is a sort of noodle story. The Irishman who rode a kicking donkey was perturbed when it put a hoof through the stirrup. "Faith," he said, "if you're getting up, I'm after getting down."

An old story tells of the man going through the market place with his arms stretched out, warning passersby not to jostle him or he'll lose the size of the turban he needs. Nowadays, this story has become altered: the man enters the department store with his hand cupped and carefully shielded and heads for the brassière department. No less intelligent was the man who couldn't see the use of a sundial at night; he couldn't tell time by it when it was dark, until someone gave him a candle so that he could go out and see what time it was.

From the 13th century Bar Hebræus comes the tale of Socrates being led to execution. "They're killing an innocent man," a woman cried out. To which Socrates replied, "What shall I do? Commit a crime?"

A husband and wife are driving in their automobile, in a current Yiddish story. "Shut the window; it's cold outside," she orders. He shuts the window. "Now is it warmer outside?" But who is the noodle here? See DRINKING THE MOON; DROLLS; DRYING THE CANDLE; GOTHAM; IMPOSSIBILITIES; LITTLE MORON; NUMSKULL TALES.

noriu miego One of the oldest Lithuanian dances for couples, performed in two facing lines. It uses a succession of two-steps common to a number of dances in adjacent countries—Finland's *Ålands Flicka,* Sweden's *bleking* and Norway's *tantoli,* Germany's *Herr Schmidt,* Bohemia's *komarno;* and also in Mexico's *La Raspa:* 1) Partners hold opposite hands and shift them back and forth with an alternation of forward heel-thumps. 2) Partners hook elbows and pivot with a skipping step. This combination is believed to be of Slavic origin. [GPK]

Norns In Scandinavian mythology, the fates, usually three virgins, who predestine the life of god and man at birth, often assisting and comforting the mother. These women who, with the Valkyries and fylgjas, comprise the Disir, live beside Urdar's fountain where they receive daily visits from the gods and water the roots of Yggdrasil. Originally there was only one Norn, the giantess Urdar, but a triad developed, one of whom often negates the gifts of the other two, or turns it into a curse.

The *Völuspá* calls all three giantesses, but Snorri, who through an error named them Urd (past), Verdandi (present), and Skuld (future), calls them giantess, elf, and dwarf respectively. While neither god nor man may alter their decrees, they often perform good services. Wolves are called "hounds of the Norns." *Nornaspor* are marks on the fingernails, white signifying coming good fortune. At various times they have appeared as spirits, demons, souls, or human oracles. Their counterparts are the Anglo-Saxon *Wyrdes*, the Greek *Moiræ*, the Roman *Parcæ;* in later German folklore they appear as the three spinners or fairy godmothers.

North American Indian folklore Prose narratives, songs, chants, formulæ, speeches, prayers, puns, proverbs, and riddles are the chief forms of oral expression found among North American native peoples. The first five forms are common to all North American groups; the last three occur less frequently, and only among a restricted number of tribes.

All native North American literature was—and still is to a great extent—transmitted from one generation to the next by word of mouth only. That it is recorded in print today is due largely to the work of anthropologists who, for the past seventy years, have been steadily collecting an ever-increasing corpus of American Indian literary material directly from Indian raconteurs.

Prose Narratives Prose narratives are part of the cultural tradition of every North American group, no matter how simple the culture of that group may be. From our viewpoint these prose narratives are of a fictional and non-fictional character; from the native viewpoint they are almost all non-fictional, or true stories.

Fictional material includes in the main serious creation and origin tales, humorous trickster tales, and tales which develop either wholly, or essentially, in human society. Non-fictional narratives consist of "historical" accounts of tribal encounters, personal accounts of war and hunting experiences, and incidents of everyday life told as droll stories.

The creation and origin stories and the trickster tales are set, as a rule, in a remote and prehuman Mythical Age during which the world was created and occupied by birds and animals having superanimal and superhuman power. Exceptions to this statement are Eskimo and Pueblo Indian tales, which reflect no such concept of a prehuman Mythical Age.

Tales set in human society, and all non-fictional narrative materials, belong to a more recent period, that of human beings and the world as it exists today. This is not to say that some of the actors in the "human being" tales may not be monsters, or cannibals, or birds and animals with power to transform themselves into animals, because they often are, but only that the existence of humans is recognized and the tales set in the familiar, fully formed world of the present.

Narratives serve either to instruct or to amuse. In some tribes one or the other of these functions is emphasized. The Utes and other Uto-Aztecan speaking groups of the Great Basin, for example, are reported to tell tales primarily and chiefly for entertainment, whereas among the Yokuts Indians of California and among many other tribes tales provide historical information, and among the Jicarilla and other Apache groups tales are primarily pedagogical and represent the summation of knowledge on the basis of which the Apache must live and act.

In many other North American Indian groups the tribal body of narrative serves both to instruct and to amuse. The Navaho, for example, have a long, esoteric emergence myth which is a repository of historical information, and other tales of a similar serious nature; they also have "trotting or traveling" Coyote stories which are told to children principally for entertainment.

Nearly all American Indian tales are moralistic in that they tend to constantly reaffirm the culture of the group. If cultural tabus are broken in the story, punishment always follows; violators of accepted behavior patterns inevitably receive their just deserts. Material covered in North American Indian myths, particularly in those of a more serious nature, includes accounts of the creation or origin of the world; the origin of human beings, animals, natural phenomena, customs, and ceremonies; the ordering of the world and human conduct; the "history" of the group (often in the form of migration stories); accounts of animal-human marriages; visits to otherworlds by humans, and so forth. Space does not permit summaries of even the most widespread American Indian tales; for such a summary, see Stith Thompson, *The Folktale* (New York, 1946), pp. 303–65.

A tribal corpus of tale material is seldom presented in any particular order or temporal sequence, although among some groups it has been noted that narrators will tell recorders the origin myths first.

The myths told primarily for amusement usually revolve around the deeds of one or more tricksters: Raven, Mink, or Bluejay in North Pacific Coast mythology; Raven, Old Man, the Three Brothers Hogfennel, or Coyote in the Plateau; Raven, Beaver, Crow in the Northern area; Coyote or Rabbit in the Basin and Southwest; Coyote, Old Man, Sen'deh, Inktumni in the Plains; Hare, Raccoon, Nanabozho, Wisaka, Tcikapis in the Woodlands area; Opossum, Rabbit in the Southeast. This trickster may also appear in more serious tales as a culture hero, but in tales told for amusement he is a buffoon, lewd, greedy, stupid, boastful, forever dying through his stupidity, but always coming to life again, to enter upon another foolish imitation or series of amusing misdeeds and tricks. Humor often enters the trickster tales in the form of obscenity; particularly is this true for Great Basin and Plains trickster stories, where sexual practices and perversions, incestuous relationships between father and daughter, or trickster and his mother-in-law, excretory and other bodily functions, and anal references are made with no attempt at euphemism. Other forms of humor may be noted for the trickster tales, and also for many of the tales set in human society. It has been noted that the Coeur d' Alene employ humor of situation and humor of language or word play; the White Mountain Apache, humor of impertinence; the Caddo and Bella Coola, humor of invectives. The Jicarilla Apache find irony humorous; among the Crow Indians incongruity gives rise to laughter, and among the White Mountain Apache the ludicrous arouses mirthful audience-response.

Tales are often told by prearrangement, and somewhat formally, to a large or small audience which gathers for the purpose of listening to stories. Such an audience may include adults, adolescents, and children, of both sexes. Often, too, tales are told less formally: a parent or grandparent may tell children stories at home; an old man and old woman, or two or three old men or old women visiting together at night, may tell each other stories until 3 or 4 o'clock in the morning; men and women often tell stories at funeral wakes, at all-night dances, on hunting trips, and so forth.

Narrators of generally known, exoteric tales are usually old men or old women who are noted as good story-tellers. The esoteric tales, such as accounts of the origins of ceremonies, the origins of sacred bundles, of clans, families, and so forth, are generally told to restricted audiences by trained narrators, usually middle-aged or elderly men.

Winter is generally (but not always) the preferred time for telling tales, and many tribes follow rather definite rules in this respect. The White Mountain Apache, for example, tell tales only during the cold months, from November through February; in the other months "there is too much danger abroad—snakes, poisonous insects, and lightning will hear themselves spoken of, and punish the narrator or his family." Furthermore, tales should be told only at night among these Apache; "the sun should not see you." (Clan legends, on the other hand, may be told anytime.) At the pueblos of Isleta, Zuñi, and Hopi, summer tale-telling attracts snakes and is therefore prohibited. At Taos story-telling begins with the January moon; if tales are told in summer it will snow or turn cold. The Kiowa have a tabu on daytime story-telling, "Sen'deh (the trickster) will bite off your nose, but when stories are told at night, Sen'deh laughs." The Tübatulabal and Yokuts tribes in California tell stories only on winter nights; if stories are told in summer snakes will bite narrator and listeners. The Eskimo devote the winter months to visiting, feasting, dancing, and story-telling, but the economic round, rather than any formal tabus, seems to be the determining factor.

Sometimes narrators are paid by their adult or child listeners with small gifts of tobacco, food, or firewood. Listeners are expected, in many groups, to respond with "Hau" or some other exclamation at intervals while a story is being told. After a night or part of a night spent in listening to stories auditors in some groups are constrained to bathe in an icy stream or pool, or to refrain from sleeping during the next day and night.

Skilful narrators who have a flair for story-telling—and there always seem to be one or more, no matter how small the group—are remarkably good at pantomime and use of gesture. The hands, arms, posture of the head and body are frequently used to pantomime actions and incidents, in simple stylized gestures. The voice, also, often is controlled to help carry the dramatic burden of tales. To indicate a climax in a story, for example, a White Mountain Apache narrator may raise his voice for humorous incidents, or lower it and talk from the back of the mouth through compressed lips, in order to produce peculiar restrained mouthed sounds when speaking of dangerous, holy, or sinister things.

Narratives vary greatly in length. A few brief tales of a hundred words or so are to be found in almost every collection; Great Basin tales are preponderantly brief, often consisting of a single incident told in a few hundred words. At the opposite extreme are some very long tales, such as the Great Dream tales of the Mohave Indians, one of which was recited for six days for a total of twenty-four hours and then was far from being

finished, or the 35,000–word English rendition of the Jicarilla Apache *Dirty Boy* tale. Between these extremes lie the great bulk of tales, ranging from 350–2000 words in length in English rendition or translation. The number of tales in a tribe's repertoire also seems to vary considerably; the Pueblo and Apache peoples of the Southwest, the people of the North Pacific Coast, and the Plains tribes apparently are rich in tales, each narrator knowing many different ones, but no one narrator knowing all in the tribal stock. In some Plateau groups and in the Basin, each narrator may know all or nearly all of the tribal repertoire, and individual versions do not vary greatly in plot. A recent collection made by one collector for the Coeur d'Alene, a Plateau tribe, contains 38 myths, 2 tales relating to the historical period, and 10 narratives of actual historical encounters.

European märchen and noodle tales have been borrowed by the American Indians, especially by the Southwestern, Plateau, Southeastern, Northern, and Northeastern tribes. A few such, frequently encountered, are *Tar Baby*, the Biblical story of the Flood, *John the Bear*, *Cinderella*. American Indian renditions of European tales show all degrees of assimilation. Some tales have been completely recast in setting, characters, cultural background, style, and thematic emphasis to suit the native pattern. Others are narrated with few or no such adaptations.

The form of American Indian folktales varies. Some groups show a preference for one form by casting most of their tale material into one particular mold, while others display an interest in a quite different form of narrative. In brief, there are over North America the following tale forms: 1) that of the self-contained episode, with its corollary form, 1.1) that of the composite tale consisting of a series of self-contained episodes which are usually connected through the identity of the character(s) in them; and 2) the novelistic tale, in which the action flows along from one episode to the next, so that each episode depends, to a greater or lesser degree, on the preceding one.

On a somewhat different level of formal distinction is the tale-cycle, in which several tales (of either forms 1.1 or 2) are welded together into connected groups.

In North America the brief, self-contained incident is found as a tale form in practically all groups, but is a favorite among the Great Basin tribes and several Plateau groups, and is frequently used for children's stories in the Southeast, the Southwest, and among the Eskimo. Composite tales, or series of self-contained incidents, are also a popular form in the Basin, and among several California Indian groups.

Novelistic tales, likewise, are told in all parts of the continent, but are an especially popular form among northern Plains tribes such as the Blackfoot and Crow, among Pueblo groups (Zuñi raconteurs, for example, handle this form with high literary skill), and among certain northern California-southern Oregon groups such as the Shasta and Klamath. An example of a novelistic tale with continental distribution is the Orpheus myth, the tale of a person who attempts to bring a deceased relative back to earth from the land of the dead. (See A. H. Gayton, "The Orpheus Myth in North America," *JAFL* 48, pp. 263–93, 1935).

Tale cycles or connected groups of tales are a notable form on the North Pacific Coast, where the deeds of the trickster-transformers, Raven, Mink and Bluejay, are told as cycles; among the Kiowa of the Plains there is a long cycle of tales about Sen'deh, the Kiowa trickster; many other western tribes have similar trickster tale cycles. Somewhat more unusual are the Jicarilla cycle of culture hero tales about Killer-of-Enemies, and the Northeastern Algonquian cycle about Gluskabe.

Little work has been done on the stability of form in American Indian folktales, but several studies have been made of the stability of content as a stylistic feature. Among the Eskimo letter-perfect reproduction of tale material is a literary standard which narrators are obliged to adhere to; if they do not they are subject to correction by members of their audience. The Tillamook of the Oregon coast, likewise, adhere to the tradition that tales should be told as relatively fixed units, and among the Cœur d'Alene, a Plateau group in Idaho, it has been found that individual versions of the same tale show no great amount of variation.

The opposite holds true for tales as told by the Pueblo peoples of the Southwest. In these groups narrators are encouraged to exercise originality, to vary the combination of stock episodes, and to achieve new emphases in theme or motivation. Among the Apache of the Southwest it has also recently been noted that narrators are allowed a liberal amount of artistic latitude in combining and recombining episodes, to form new tale plots. This premium on originality is however counterbalanced to some extent by the fact that certain other stylistic features are retained with striking consistency by Southwestern narrators; tales are always localized at their start, for example, and a good deal of cultural detail can be counted on to be introduced into them.

An attempt to number, classify, and indicate the distributions of the recurrent elements or *motifs* in American Indian tales has been made by Stith Thompson (*Tales of the North American Indians* [Cambridge, Mass., 1929]; see also *Motif-Index of Folk-Literature* [6 vols., Bloomington, Ind., 1932–1936]). Thompson's isolable units (motifs) include any narrative element, large or small, which is recurrent among several groups; a motif may be, therefore, a tale plot, or a discrete incident within a tale, or a minor imaginative detail. All motifs, when isolated as such, are referred to by catchwords or tag phrases; examples of such are "sun sister and moon brother" for a tale plot widely recurrent among Eskimo groups; "eye-juggler" for a discrete incident in which a trickster throws his eyes up in the air for sport, and finally loses them; "sky window" for the detail of a hole in the sky, from which the earth is visible below.

No anthropological folklorists have attempted any classification of folktale elements on a scale comparable to Thompson's, nor has their interest focused, recently, on wide distributional studies. Rather, the attention of students of American Indian folktales seems to have been turning more and more during the last two decades to structural analyses of particular bodies of folktales.

For such structural analysis units of like order and function must of course be isolated and defined, and their sequences established in specific tribal collections of folktales. At the present time three such units are generally referred to, namely, the *tale-plot* (using this term in its widest sense to include theme, episodes, and succession of episodes), the *episode* within the tale-plot, and the *element*, or detail within the episode.

The smallest of these units, the element, is a detail which may be 1) either closely concerned with the plot of the tale, or 2) a purely stylistic device, or 3) a detail performing functions relating both to plot and style, or 4) a detail inserted to characterize actors, or to add humor or interest to the narrative. Stylistic elements, for example, are often used both at the beginning and end of tales; the stylistic element of specific localization is present in the opening of a Santo Domingo Pueblo tale—"They were living at Kackatcutya . . ." An element which, in a Shawnee tale, performs functions relating both to plot and style is one known by the catchword "years thought (called) days." This element is first used stylistically to refer to years by the term days, but later on in the story when the actors interpret "days" literally, they lose their chance to move to a better land. An element inserted for humor, in a Coeur d'Alene tale, is that of the Land People phoning upriver to Snake.

Although elements are basic to tales, by themselves they are meaningless so far as narrative significance is concerned. It is only when two or more elements are combined that the plot begins to thicken into meaningful narrative units or episodes. Episodes (sometimes also referred to as incidents) are therefore our second structural unit. An episode may stand alone, complete in itself as a short tale, or several episodes may be combined into longer tales. The "self-contained episode" already mentioned as a popular tale form in the Great Basin is an example of the episode forming a complete tale-plot. Composite and novelistic tales are examples of two or more episodes either tenuously or skilfully combined in a tale-plot.

The tale-plot is simply the tale in its entirety, the largest of our three structural units.

Other Prose Forms   Prayers, formal and highly ritualistic, and informal and personal, are a widely used form of oral expression among the large majority of American Indian tribes. While many prayers have been recorded, the collecting and analysis of this particular prose form has not been as systematic or intensive as has been the collecting and analysis of tale forms. Several illuminating studies on the prayers of particular tribes have however been made; among these are G. A. Reichard's *Prayer: The Compulsive Word* (Monographs of the American Ethnological Society VII, New York, 1944) [Navaho]; R. Bunzel, "Zuni Ritual Poetry (*RBAE* 47, Washington, D.C., 1930); R. H. Lowie, "Crow Prayers" (*American Anthropologist*, n.s., Vol. 30, pp. 433–42, 1933); P. Radin, *The Road of Life and Death* (Bollingen Series V, New York, 1946) [Winnebago].

The areas in North America in which formal prayers are emphasized as part of ritual are the Southwest, the Plains, the Eastern Woodlands, and the Southeast. In the last three areas named, an attitude of humility and mortification on the part of the suppliant is stressed in all prayers, especially those connected with rituals; "for we are a pitiful people" is a constantly recurrent phrase, for example, in the prayers of the Algonquian-speaking Woodlands tribes. In these areas, no great emphasis is laid on the letter-perfect repetition of ritualistic prayers; tribal prayers conform of course to tribal patterns, but leeway is allowed the speaker to shorten or lengthen a prayer and to embroider extempore on its themes.

Among the Navaho and other groups in the Southwest, prayers are of a quite different order. The attitudes of humility and mortification are not expressed; through prayer, the Navaho hopes to compel his gods to bring the good and the beneficial to pass. He does not ask for pity, nor does he give thanks in prayer, but is more apt to dwell on what has happened in the past, in order to insure its recurrence in the future. Navaho prayers must, moreover, be learned as a whole, and when recited, must be recited letter-perfect from beginning to end, in order to achieve their purpose.

Short, non-ritualistic prayers made by individual suppliants are widely used in North America. The only areas, in fact, in which even simple prayers seem to be rarely resorted to, if at all, are the Great Basin, the Mackenzie-Yukon, and the Eskimo areas. Such short prayers are used on many occasions; in the Puget Sound region, for example, it is reported that each man prayed twice daily, at daybreak and in the evening, asking that he live to old age. Since the prayer was borne upward on the smoke from a fire (a belief also held by the Shawnee of the Eastern Woodlands), the suppliant usually prayed when building a morning fire. In this same region, prayers of a more formal sort were delivered at special seasons and in special places by whale-hunters; the time of most intensive praying, however was for four days in December and four days in June, "when the sun seems to pause before changing" (winter and summer solstices).

Prayers are either chanted or spoken; ritualistic prayers seem mainly to be chanted, and many such, from various North American tribes, are reproduced in translation in verse rather than in prose form. Unlike American Indian songs, however, prayers are not delivered to the accompaniment of musical instrument.

Compulsive, inherently powerful formulæ, from one to many lines long, are another widespread form of composition. Such formulæ are sometimes recited, sometimes sung. To be efficacious they must always be rendered letter-perfect. Often formulæ are regarded as valuable incorporeal personal property, are kept secret by their owners, and are sold or, as on the North Pacific Coast, handed down in families. An example of a very short formula used frequently in Jicarilla Apache ceremonies to drive away evil and sickness is as follows: "Long life, everything good, old age, no evil." In the Southeast, tribes such as the Cherokee and Yuchi rely heavily on formulæ in connection with curing the sick, gaining success in love, hunting, fishing, war, the ball play, and witchcraft, for self-protection and the destruction of enemies, for crops, councils, and other enterprises. For Cherokee formulæ, which have been more extensively studied than the formulæ of any other tribe, see J. Mooney, "Sacred Formulas of the Cherokee" (*RBAE* 7, Washington, D.C., 1886) and F. M. Albrechts, ed., *The Swimmer Manuscript* (*BBAE* 99, 1932).

Speeches of many different sorts, to suit many occasions, are delivered among the American Indians by chiefs, chiefs' speakers and messengers, war leaders, funeral directors, even by clowns. Like preaching among ourselves, speechmaking among Indian groups is essentially a male vocation. For example: Although Iroquois women have great political power, they generally voice their decisions, opinions, and admonitions through a male speaker. In nearly all groups, even those having a very simple culture, oratorical powers carry prestige for their possessor. Among the Eastern Woodlands tribes one of the three or four ways for a man to attain distinction is to be a good speechmaker.

Public speeches are by no means limited to council meetings, but are part and parcel of the daily life of many groups. In California, for example, a chief or his speaker formerly addressed his people each morning telling them what to do, how to behave, and so forth. The same is reported for the Shawnee. Speeches are part of the great public ceremonies, as well as a regular feature of funerals, ghost feasts, naming ceremonies, and other rites.

A skilful speaker employs rhythmic repetition of words, phrases, and sentences, makes liberal use of euphemisms, metaphors, imagery, and other rhetorical devices, employs gestures, and uses stylized forms of delivery. The form, content, and manner of delivery probably varied from area to area, but as yet no serious comprehensive analysis of American Indian speeches has been attempted.

Riddles, proverbs, and puns are forms reported only occasionally, and for widely separated North American tribes. For long it was believed that none of these forms was native to the New World, but examples of Crow, Navaho, and Coeur d'Alene proverbs and puns have been collected, and recently Archer Taylor has cogently argued for the pre-Columbian existence of riddles in native America (Archer Taylor, "American Indian Riddles," *JAFL* 57, pp. 1–15, 1944).

Two forms of prose composition familiar to us are either lacking or rare in native North America. One is the prose essay, which seems to be entirely absent; the other, dramatic compositions.

Pantomime, performed by persons dressed, masked, and painted to represent characters other than themselves, is an important part of the ceremonies of certain groups, notably the Pueblo peoples of the Southwest and the Indians of the North Pacific Coast region. But any dialog which accompanies the pantomime is episodic and apparently improvised. However, on the North Pacific Coast, certain performances seem to approach more nearly to being true dramatic representations than do comparable ones elsewhere on the continent. The Duwamish, who formerly lived around Seattle, Washington, had soul-loss doctors who annually enacted a journey to the land of the dead to recover lost souls, and the journey home with the souls. This performance seems to have fulfilled nearly all the requirements of true drama, except that the songs and speeches which are part of the performance were apparently largely extempore or subject to variation. The presentation does, however, have a definite beginning, middle, and end, a stage setting, stage properties (carved boards which represent spirit canoes used for the journey), definite actors, and is performed before an audience. The Makah Indians of Cape Flattery are also said to have enacted certain of their myths. From this and other evidence we conclude that if true drama existed anywhere in North America, the most likely area to look for it would be the North Pacific Coast. Unfortunately many of the peoples and much of North Pacific Coast culture disappeared soon after white settlers entered the region, so the problem is one which may at this late date be capable of only partial solution.

Verse Verse, among the American Indians and the Eskimo, is either sung or chanted. Of the thousands of examples of native North American poems which have been collected, only one selection, from the Eskimo, is reported as having been recited.

Songs are universal among all North American groups, and command more interest than any other form of oral composition. They are used on all sorts of occasions: there are shamans' songs, gambling songs, traveling songs, ceremonial songs of many different sorts, social dance songs, vision quest songs, work songs, hunting songs, love songs, mourning songs, contest (nith) songs, and songs inserted in tale texts, to mention only a few. Songs may be improvised on the spur of the moment, may be obtained in dreams or visions, or may be learned from another singer. Some songs are known to all members of the tribe, others are esoteric and must be either inherited or purchased from their owners.

Songs are sung without accompaniment, or to a variety of accompaniments ranging from simple handclapping by the audience or singer(s), to use of the dry or wet drum and various types of rattles (turtle shell, gourd, carved wood, pottery) as accompanying instruments.

Songs are sung as solos, with or without chorus, or in chorus, by men, or women, or both. While singing is not so markedly a man's province as oratory is, for example, public rendition of ceremonial songs falls more often upon men than women.

Songs are composed by both men and women. Song texts consist either entirely of meaningful words, or entirely of meaningless vocables or burden syllables (*a, ho, he, aye, aja,* etc.), or, what is much more usual, of a mixture of both vocables and meaningful words. A few general statements about style can be made, which apply to all or the great majority of North American song forms.

One of the most obvious characteristics of native poetry is an extreme use of repetition of similar or contrasting units. Syllables, words, phrases, lines, stanzas, or entire song texts are subjects for simple rhythmic repetition through reduplication. Incremental repetition, which carries forward the action of the narrative, and alternating and more complex repetition of lines also occurs.

Second only to repetition, in many songs, is the use of the mnemonic summary, or the suggestive power of words to carry the memory of the act which the song commemorates. This reliance upon a few words to suggest action is universal in North America, but is not found in all North American songs, some of which have texts which are fairly explicit.

The use of preludes and refrains is also characteristic. Both form integral parts of most Indian song texts. Often such preludes and refrains consist entirely of meaningless syllables; it is to be regretted that in popular collections of American Indian songs they are often excised, and only the meaningful lines of the text reproduced.

The words used in song texts are frequently quite different forms from those used in everyday speech. They may be archaic, or borrowed from other languages, or modified according to certain stylistic conventions, or incremented by vocables which serve to fill out a measure.

Two major devices found in European poetry are lacking in that of native North America. Rime is not used, nor are stanza forms, except as these latter are brought about by the rhythmic repetition of phrases.

Minor stylistic devices frequently (but not universally) encountered in native poetry are: onomatopœia, or the use of sounds similar to those made by animals or natural elements; oppositional or contrasting phrases (day and night; our Mother the Earth, our Father the Sky); parallelism of thought and parallelism of structure; poetic diction and extensive use of sense-imagery (usually tribally stereotyped); use of metaphors and similes; use of climax; alliteration; assonantal tone quality.

While the importance of songs among all tribes cannot be over-emphasized, two areas in which songs are highly developed stand out, namely, the Arctic and the Southwest. The peoples of both these areas are master versemakers; for their traditional songs, both adhere to the requirement of letter-perfect renditions. Many of their extempore songs are masterpieces, those of the Eskimo being highly imaginative, emotional, lyrical, and rich in human appeal, while those of the Pueblo peoples and the Navaho abound in sensuous imagery and are beautifully balanced in structure.

Chanted verse is on the whole reserved for prayers in some areas, and for origin and culture hero myth material. The practice of chanting myths, either in whole or in part, has been noted specifically for several widely separated groups—the Choctaw, the Delaware, the Pima, the Papago, and the Eskimo.

A form of rhythmic expression which approaches poetry is the death wails used in many groups, but most frequently noted for the Plains Indians, who hired mourners to wail vigorously as the corpse was borne to its resting place. Such wails consisted of a highly emotional but also formalized cry of moaning at short intervals, followed by a rapid even recital of the attributes and deeds of the deceased.

Consideration of space has prevented inclusion of actual examples of the poetic and prose forms mentioned in this summary discussion. No single volume is available which includes examples of all the North American native forms mentioned, but several of these are presented in a recently published anthology (Margot Astrov, *The Winged Serpent* [New York, 1946]). The selections for this anthology, the only one of its kind which has appeared to date, are the standard ethnographic reports of American anthropologists, who have collected the material directly in the course of their field researches, from American Indian narrators and singers.   Erminie W. Voegelin

nose The nose is a good place for souls to leave the body or for evil spirits to enter it. Thus closing the nose of the corpse with fishhooks in the Celebes, plugs among the Eskimos, or pieces of jade among the Chinese, not only keeps the physical soul where it belongs but protects the corpse from errant ghosts that might cause trouble. Nose rings and other ornaments in the nose have a talismanic value among many peoples, notably those of Australia, the South Pacific Islands, western Africa, northwest America, and South America; among the Hindus and the early Semites. Like many talismans, nose rings and similar attachments acquired a decorative value. In India the objects indicate caste and social position. In the Fly River district, women with unpierced noses are considered scandalous. The Gippsland natives believe that people who have no nose ring will suffer in the next world. The Matu of British New Guinea pierce the nose when a child is six years old and, if a child dies before the age of six, they pierce the nose of the corpse. The *kupitja* worn in his nose by the medicine man of the Warramunga tribe is both a sign of his profession and associated with his powers. The nose kiss or Malay kiss consists of placing the nose against the cheek briefly and is reported from north Asia and America, Polynesia, parts of Melanesia, Malay Archipelago, New Guinea, among the aborigines of India and Madagascar, and elsewhere.

Other scattered superstitions are that a large nose indicates a generous nature and that the size of the nose is proportionate to the sexual parts. In India and Indonesia it is said that ghosts speak with a nasal twang.
[RDJ]

☞ If your nose itches, you will become angry, see a stranger, kiss a fool, or be in danger. This is a fairly general English and American saying. In Scotland, however, an itching nose means you will receive a letter. Quite general folk remedies for nosebleed are wearing a piece of red ribbon, red silk thread, or just plain red string around the neck. Tying a piece of yarn around the little finger of the left hand is also good. A cold key down the back of the neck will also cure nosebleed; so will a big hunk of brown paper under the upper lip. South Carolina Negroes also recommend wearing a brass ring or a necklace of red corn.

novella (plural *novelle*) A short tale with a realistic setting, with characters drawn from real life, and supposed to occur at a specified time and place, often using familiar folktale motifs and sometimes including incidents of the marvelous or supernatural. Typical novelle appear in the *Decameron* of Boccaccio and *The Arabian Nights* (e.g. the voyages of Sindbad). The distinction between novella and märchen is not always clear, since the same story may appear in one place as märchen and in another as novella. The märchen are, therefore, called by some students of the folktale novellenmärchen. Novelle appear in classial antiquity; the lost *Milesian Tales* of Aristides (2d century B.C.) were probably novelle of amorous adventures.

Ntikuma or **Tacuma** A character in Ashanti-Fanti folklore, the son of Anansi the spider, the Gold Coast trickster. In the New World, as Tacuma, Ntikuma figures in the lore of the Negroes who have preserved the Anansi stories (as against those in which Rabbit or another character is the trickster). Compare ANANSI. [MJH]

nudida Literally, thing prepared: a *gbo* or magic charm of Dahomey Negroes, which fulfils the spoken wish and also serves as a remedy for colic. It is a little sack filled with red and white kola and a kind of powder, all soaked in pigeon blood. One must utter his wish early in the morning while eating, and the nudida will effect it. To cure colic a small amount of the contents are swallowed. See M. J. Herskovits, *Dahomey*, II (New York, 1938), p. 284.

nudity Nudity is most commonly of importance in ceremonies to produce or to stop rain or to frighten evil spirits. Pliny reported that a woman could drive away storms by uncovering herself. Among some Moroccan tribes, women strip in a secluded place and play ball to bring rain, and in southern India, men stand naked on dikes and beat drums to stop rain. Other rain ceremonies of India require naked women to perform rituals at wells or at crossroads. Spirits are often prudish and take fright at the sight of a naked body. Transylvania farmers protect fields against depredations of birds by walking naked around their fields before sunrise, burning sulfur, taking an ear of corn in their mouths, and walking home without speaking. Elsewhere similar ceremonies are performed by the women. The Tagalog of the Philippines frightens the evil spirits during his wife's confinement by standing naked on the roof of his house with sword and shield while his friends engage naked in mock combat.

Stories among the Pueblo Indians about the girl warrior who exposes her genitals to prove to the enemy that she is a woman may be connected with the belief that evil spirits fear nudity. The pictures of persons in the act of copulation in China and Japan are sometimes explained by the belief that the Thunder God, god of punishment, is prudish and will avoid houses where copulation is taking place.

The popular movement currently called social nudism is connected with other magical impulses, little recognized by its followers. It originated in its present form in Europe in the early part of this century and in modern nudist camps its adherents give vigorous support to a number of hygienic tenets: that clothing is unhygienic, that the action of sun and air directly on the body is beneficial, that many sports—handball, swimming, tennis —are more effectively followed in the nude, and that communal nudism improves the morals of those who practice it. Tobacco is sometimes prohibited and alcohol is usually prohibited. The moral standards are maintained with a somewhat unnatural rigidity. Lewd stories are absolutely forbidden and any action, voluntary or involuntary, which indicates that the spectacle of nude bodies has aroused sexual emotions calls for expulsion. A visit to these camps, which is permitted only after the applicant has been interviewed by one or more members and is, for the first visit at least, provisional, leads to the conclusion that the related sexual impulses of voyeurism and exhibitionism are involved. Many camps will accept only married couples and difficulties are sometimes encountered because wives often object to accompanying their husbands or to attending the camp themselves. "Modern Nudism" with official headquarters in New Jersey has camps in most of the states of this country and is a flourishing movement in England, France, and the other countries of Europe.

Nudism as a civic protest involves other folkloristic impulses. The Dukhobors who have settlements in Canada and the United States are a mystic sect which arose in Russia in the 18th century. Members deny the authority of civil government. When the government attempts to exercise its authority, members of the sect revert to the nude. Sporadic examples of nudity as a protest, a symbolic divesting oneself of the conventions, have been reported from several countries and are usually regarded as psychopathic. See GODIVA. [RDJ]

Nuinumma-Kwiten Title of a playfully frightening song sung by the Australian aborigines to quiet children. Nuinumma-Kwiten is a monster beast of prey, who was once a member of the early race of men and who could swallow whole ostrich eggs. The song says, "I kill children who cry," and the effectiveness of the threat lies in the fact that the creature tracks down his victims by the sound of their crying voices. See LULLABY.

Num The Samoyed god of the sky and heaven. [JB]

numen (plural *numina*) In ancient Roman religion, the mysterious inner power existing in some personage or thing; that which inspires the feeling of awe: from the word meaning nod, command, divine will. It corresponds closely to the Polynesian concept of mana; it is what makes a thing divine and what makes it needful for man to perform certain rites. This expression of divine power eventually became personified in various gods, nature powers, etc. The earliest Roman gods were called the Numina and included Saturn among others.

Numi-Tōrem The god of the heaven of the Voguls: among the Ostyaks *Num-Tūrem*. The god of the Voguls and Ostyaks dwells, like a rich and powerful ruler, in the highest heaven in a house littered with gold and silver. He has seven sons and many assistant spirits. [JB]

numskull tales Generic term for the absurdity, ignoramus, noodle, and fool stories of the world, popular everywhere, and occasionally overlapping with the trickster-buffoon anecdote, as in the case of the dancing bulrushes and the creaking limbs. More typical, however, is the story of the nitwit who squeezes the insides out of a sausage in order to use the cover for a sack (J1732; Type 1316); of the mad wheelbarrow (J1887) in which the numskull chains up the wheelbarrow because it has been attacked by a mad dog and might go mad and bite others; of the boy who gives the hens hot water so they will lay boiled eggs (J1901.2), or plants a sow to grow pigs (J1932.4). There is the world-wide story of the numskull who stays till he has finished (J1814); he urinates by the side of a brook in the night, mistakenly interprets the sound of the brook, and stands there till morning. The Arabian anecdote of the goose who dives for a star, thinking it a fish (J1791.8) and will not be fooled into diving for the fish which she sees next day is also typical. For the literal-minded numskull see JEAN SOT. See FATAL IMITATION; HORSE LEARNS TO LIVE WITHOUT FOOD; NOODLE STORIES; PENT CUCKOO.

nursery rimes The earliest rimes a child learns are apt to be the ones associated with the motions, gestures, and pantomime of the parent or nurse playing with the parts of the child's body. As the first counting was done by touching the fingers and toes, so also the first rimes, such as:

> This little pig went to market;
> This little pig stayed home;
> This little pig had roast beef;
> This little pig had none;
> This little pig cried "Wee, wee, wee,"
> All the way home.

Accompanying the first line, the mother takes the child's hallux between her thumb and forefinger, then the next toe for the second line, until the last and smallest toe is gently pinched while the mother makes an attempt to squeal like a pig: "Wee, wee, wee," part of

the fun being that the last toe is the wee one. The child is encouraged to join with the mother as the rime is repeated again and again, until he can say it alone. From California comes a toe verse which starts with the wee toe:

> Little Pee;
> Penny Jew;
> Judy Whistle;
> Mary Gristle; and
> Old Big Gobble Gobble.

A rime for the fingers, popular in New England in the latter 19th century, began with the thumb:

> Master Thumb is first to come,
> Then Pointer, strong and steady,
> Then Tall Man High,
> And just close by,
> The Feeble Man doth linger;
> And last of all,
> So fair and small,
> The Baby Little Finger!

Slightly more complicated as the child grows older comes the widely known action rime:

> Here's a ball for baby,
> Big and soft and round;
> Here is baby's hammer,
> Oh how he can pound!
> Here is baby's trumpet,
> Toot, ta-toot, ta-too!
> Here's the way that baby plays
> At Peek-A-Boo!

At the repetition of the first two lines of the above, the parent or older child makes a "ball" by putting the tips of the fingers and thumbs together and getting the child to do the same. The hammer is one fist striking the other, and the trumpet is made with the hands partly closed and placed tandem. For the last two lines the hands are placed over the eyes but with fingers apart enough to peek through, and the game ends with a loud boo as the hands are removed.

The pantomime of cake- or pie-making, with obvious motions, accompanies the recitation of the following old English rime from the days of apprentices:

> "Pat-a-cake, pat-a-cake, baker's man."
> "So I will, master, as fast as I can."
> "Roll it, and prick it, and mark it with T
> And *toss* it in the oven for baby and me."

The following has variations, but generally runs:

> Here's the church;
> And here's the steeple;
> Open the doors,
> And see all the people.

At the saying of the first line, the doubled fists are interlocked by intertwining the fingers alternated. At the second line, the forefingers are raised with tips touching; at the third, the thumbs are spread apart, and at the fourth, the hands are opened far enough to show the finger ends inside. Older children add:

> Here goes the minister up the stairs,
> And there he is saying his prayers,

and act out the little drama in various obvious ways.

There are many verses to go with the action of the child "horse-riding" on the parent's foot or knee, the climax coming with the "home again" as the signal for the parent to lift the child with foot and hands and catch him in the arms to the breast. Here are a few samples of many:

> Ride, ride to Boston;
> Ride, ride to Lynn;
> Ride, ride to Salem, (sometimes Lexington)
> And then home again.

> Walk, walk, walk, walk, walk;
> Trot, trot, trot, trot, trot;
> Ta-gallop, ta-gallop, ta-gallop!

(Walk is alternately raising heel and toe; trot is faster, raising heel only; ta-gallop is whole foot.)

> To market, to market,
> To buy a fat pig:
> Home again, home again,
> Jiggety, jig.

(Above is walking to market, and trotting home.)

> To market, to market,
> To buy a big bun:
> Home again, home again,
> Market is done.

(Same as one before, except big bounce on "done.")

> To market, to market,
> A gallop, a trot:
> To buy some meat
> To put in the pot.

(Starts furiously, then slows from gallop to trot to walk, slower on each word in last two lines, but bouncing at very end with "pot.") There are infinite variations of these "to market" rimes. Sometimes the child rides on his daddy's back.

We used to act out the following old English nursery rime with a burlap sack of leaves for the pig every autumn at leaves-gathering time. The leaves were used during the winter for bedding down the horse and for scratch litter for the poultry.

> Tom, Tom, the piper's son,
> Stole a pig and away he run;
> The pig was eat,
> And Tom was beat,
> And Tom ran crying down the street.

We had a merry time dramatizing the following very ancient one, using a sandpile or any pile of dirt for the hill and requisitioning the other needed properties from the kitchen:

> Jack and Jill went up the hill
> To fetch a pail of water.
> Jack fell down and broke his crown,
> And Jill came tumbling after.
> Up Jack got and home did trot
> As fast as he could caper;
> While Jill had the job
> To plaster his nob
> With vinegar and brown paper.

In South Carolina the folk remedy for headache is to tie around the head a piece of brown paper soaked in vinegar. Query: Did they get it from *Jack and Jill*, or was it a common remedy in old times when the rime originated?

The rime may be very old, or at least based on an old legend, for in Norse myth the lunar waterpot was filled at a well by two children, the boy Hjuki and the girl Bil, who were carried away by the moon god Mani.

Jack and Jill is popular with adults as well as children, and has become the answer to an adult riddle:

> They did not climb in hope of gain,
> But at stern duty's call;
> They were united in their aim,
> Divided in their fall.

A strong rival of *Jack and Jill* for children's affection is *Little Jack Horner* of whom most people know nothing save that:

> Little Jack Horner sat in a corner
> Eating a Christmas pie.
> He stuck in his thumb and pulled out a plum
> And said "What a brave boy am I!"

There are two other versions of that last adjective, and if you wish to start a hot argument, argue that it should be "good" or "great" in place of "brave." And some affirm that he "put" in his thumb. As if he were as namby-pamby as that! There is a Jack Horner pie sometimes at children's parties, where you pull a string to get your "plum" from the pie, only it doesn't explode like a Christmas "cracker" with a cap in it. If you want to know more about Jack Horner, you can learn of his "witty tricks and pleasant pranks" in Halliwell's *Nursery Rhymes of England*.

There are countless thousands of nursery rimes for the younger children. We have given but a sampling. For rimes for older children see COUNTING-OUT RIMES; EENY, MEENY, MINY, MO; section on *Charms, Nursery Rimes, Riddles* in EUROPEAN FOLKLORE; MOTHER GOOSE; SHEPHERD'S SCORE; SKIP-ROPE RIMES.

CHARLES FRANCIS POTTER

nutmeg The aromatic seed kernel of the fruit of various tropical trees (genus *Myristica*). The covering of this seed provides another spice, mace. According to the doctrine of signatures the nutmeg was good for ailments of the brain because of its resemblance in shape to the human brain. It was also considered good for the sight, and was used to remove freckles. Pierced and hung about the neck a nutmeg prevents boils, sties, cold sores, croup, and neuralgia. In Michigan it is carried in the pocket to prevent or cure rheumatism, and in Texas a nutmeg tea cures summer complaint. Among Jamaica Negroes, women in labor take powdered nutmeg for their pains. At one time it was the custom in England to give a gilt nutmeg at Christmas. Connecticut is called the Nutmeg State, supposedly because her native Yankee traders carved wooden nutmegs which they sold to the unwary.

nuts Throughout North America generally it is said that carrying a buckeye or horse-chestnut on the person will protect the bearer from rheumatism. All over southeast Asia and into the islands of the Pacific, there is a widespread practice of chewing the fruit of the areca palm (the betel nut), as we chew gum. In time the teeth are blackened. As we have all kinds of smoking accessories, the gourds for the lime which is chewed with the nuts, the spatula with which it is dipped, may be highly ornamented and a source of great pride. In parts of China, betel nuts are presented to one who has been grossly insulted, as a symbol of abject humiliation. If the person accepts the nuts and chews them, it is a sign that the offender has been forgiven. See BETEL CHEWING. Jewish children play with nuts on Passover, using the nuts as a stake in a game, as one uses marbles. In English, the word nut is used to denote the head; one who is "nutty" or "cracked" or a "nut" is crazy. Nuts, in the plural, is a euphemism for the testicles, and, though once disreputable slang, it has lost its original force and is now perfectly respectable. [NFJ]

nyagwai'oenǫ (Seneca) or **nyagwai'geha** (Cayuga-Onondaga) The Iroquois Indian Bear dance, a curative rite. If offended, the bear spirit is believed to cause hysteria, crawling, clawing, and behavior involving supernatural strength beyond the patient's control. These are cured by a dance rite addressed to the bear spirit, in the patient's home, and renewed annually at the Midwinter festivals. Cured patients constitute the membership of the society.

In the first part, three chants are intoned by the two singers with drum and horn rattle, while the shaman offers tobacco and the members spray berry juice over the patient. In the second part, the patient, the ceremonial leaders, and thereupon the members begin to circle the room counterclockwise with a shuffling, lumbering waddle. In part three, a large company of men, women, and children clomp around in imitation of the bear's cumbersome ways. The dance leaders answer the singers in monotone antiphony, and puff and blow at the end of each song. Nuts, berries, and mush are passed down the line in symbol of offering of the bear's favorite foods. In part four, the cure has been effected. The dancers become animated, kicking, stamping, and crossing over in pairs. This final formation and step terminates other medicine rites, as the buffalo rite, *degwiago'-*

oenǫ, and suggests a therapeutic function. Sometimes at Midwinter the cure and introductory chants are omitted, in a version termed *oenoska* (songs only). The complete rite is termed *gayowa goowa* (great moccasin.) [GPK]

nymphs In classical mythology, spirits of nature, envisaged as young, beautiful women, dancers and musicians, companions of the satyrs. The nymphs were not immortal, but their lives were, according to Hesiod, ten times that of the phœnix, which outlived nine ravens, who outlived three stags, who outlived four crows, who outlived nine generations of aged men. The nymphs had the power of prophecy and generally were kindly toward men, though they could be dangerous. They served as nurses to some of the gods, e.g. Adonis. Generally there are several classes distinguished, though some writers make no attempt to differentiate them: the dryads or hamadryads, tree nymphs; the naiads, nymphs of lakes, rivers, and springs; the oreads, mountain nymphs. The nymphs probably developed into the fairies of general European folklore.

Nzambi The name of the supreme deity of certain Congo Negro peoples, occurring in various forms: **Nyambe** is the supreme god (maybe a sun god) and creator of animals and men among the Barotse; **Njambi** is regarded as a kind of father-creator among the Mpongwe; among the Fan **Nzame** is known as the creator, but is said to have gone far away long ago; **Nzambi** as mother-creator or Mother Earth is known to the Fjort, and also plays the role of judge in the disputes of men and animals in their folktales. See SUPREME BEING.

oak The most widely worshipped of all trees: said by the Greeks to have been the first of all trees created, and from which, according to Vergil, sprang the human race. It is sacred to Jehovah, Zeus (Jupiter), Hercules, Demeter, the Teutonic Thor, the ancient Celtic druids, the Old Irish Dagda, and others. Greek legend says that its roots go down to the underworld. Beneath the spreading branches of the oak, Abraham received the angels, the Scandinavians met in council, and Merlin worked his enchantments. Herodotus testifies to the fact that the sacred grove of Dodona had the gift of prophecy, and the oaken mast and beams of the *Argo* warned the Argonauts of danger. The ancient Aryans also believed that the whispering leaves of the oak foretold the future. In Estonia, the blood of slaughtered animals is poured on its roots as sacrifice.

Northern European peoples have always testified to the fact that lightning strikes oak oftener than any other tree, hence the association of the oak with North European thunder gods, e.g. Thor, Perkunas, etc. Greeks and Romans also identified the oak with their thunder god (Zeus, Jupiter). Farmers of northern Europe, including England, still plant an oak near their buildings to act as lightning-attracter, and hence as a protection against lightning. It is unwise therefore to build a roof of oak. Scandinavians place an acorn in their windows as a protection against lightning. In Lithuania it is lucky to

come upon a blasted oak, but elsewhere a blasted oak is a messenger of disaster. Fire is also associated with the oak; its wood was used in Rome by the Vestal Virgins for their perpetual fire. It is the traditional, essential wood used for Yule log, Midsummer Night fires, and need fires.

In northern Europe, the oak was the tree of the dead and the abode of departed spirits; in Christian times the hollowed trunk of an oak tree served as a rude coffin. In Iceland, the blood oak is unlucky and ships made from it are doomed to destruction. In northern countries, reverence of the oak was so great that in early Christian times a cross was carved in the trunk to resanctify it from Thor to Christ. In Westphalia, it is said the Wandering Jew cannot rest except where two oaks grow together in the form of a cross. In Athens, the boy who was chosen to pronounce the Eleusinian wedding formula was crowned with oak and thorn. In Rome, oak leaves made a civic crown to honor service to the state, or a man who had saved the life of another. Oak boughs were carried in wedding processions as a symbol of fecundity. In the Middle Ages, many authorities advised the use of oaken sticks for gathering medicinal herbs.

Many particular oaks are venerated, or were in their lifetime, to commemorate historical or legendary events, as the Royal Oak which hid Charles II of England after his defeat by Cromwell. May 29 was long celebrated as Royal Oak Day because it was both his birthday and the day of his return to London. A hollow oak also served to hide William Wallace. There is Robin Hood's Oak, the Volkenrode Oak of Gotha, the Oak of Dorset, George Fox's Oak in Flushing, New York, and the Charter Oak at Hartford, Conn.

In Saxony, the oak was so highly valued that there was a law forbidding its injury. In Germany and England, oaks were highly regarded medicinally. The patient merely by walking around it passed his ailment to the tree, which in turn gave it to the first bird alighting in its branches. In Cornwall, a nail driven into an oak rid the patient of toothache; passing an invalid through a cleft or crotch of one removed disease. In Shropshire, the oak is said to bloom at midnight on Midsummer's Night, but the bloom is gone by morning. In Wales, rubbing a piece of oak on the palm of the left hand in silence on Midsummer Day will keep you from illness throughout the year. In Surrey, certain tumorlike growths on the trunks are carried in the pocket to guard against gout. Parkinson in his herbal recommends a confection made from the leaf galls to cure melancholy and sorrows arising from no evident cause. The North American Meskwaki Indians used the inner bark of the white oak in a tea to bring up phlegm, and the acorns as a substitute for coffee. They also used the inner bark of the black oak for pinworms. The country people in the same region use this tea as a gargle, a laxative, and as an irrigant in venereal diseases; in Texas it is used for summer complaint, galls, and to keep the teeth from falling out. South Carolina Sea Island Negroes use the bark of the red oak to cure rheumatism. Acorns are carried by many for general good luck, long life, and against disease. Two acorns floating in a basin of water mean love if they come together; if they drift apart there will be no wedding. In many art forms the acorn is used as a phallic symbol, both male and female, and as a symbol of fecundity. The oak is a symbol of endurance, strength, and triumph. That the last leaf never falls from an oak tree is an old observation. The last leaf (K222; Type 1184) is the motif of a group of northern European folktales in which a man promises to pay a debt (pay the Devil) when the last leaf falls, knowing full well that the last leaf never falls from the oak tree. In foretelling the weather for the coming season, countrymen recite some form of the following:

Oak before ash—only a splash/ Ash before oak—a thorough soak. See ACORN; FIRE; MISTLETOE. [JWH]

Oannes According to Berosus, Babylonian historian of the 3rd century B.C., the water god, with a fish's body, the heads of both man and fish, and the feet of a man and a fish's tail: equated with Ea. Oannes was the demiurge who periodically came ashore from his home in the Persian Gulf to teach men, and to renew his teachings, the arts of civilization. He was the god of healing, of the waters, of fertility.

Oaqöl Hopi Indian women's ceremony, held in autumn, and similar to the two other women's society ceremonies, the Marau and Lakon. The god of vegetation and the seed goddess are both impersonated at the Oaqöl initiation ceremony. The Oaqöl ceremony was formerly held annually, but is now held irregularly. [EWV]

oaths The deplorable fact that many of us have reason to doubt most of the things that are said to us, and the further fact that this situation seems to have obtained since the very beginning of time, has led to the elaborate checks of evidence known to law enforcement officers and lawyers. Policemen test truth by the ordeal, lawyers check it by the legal oath which, if violated, subjects the perjurer to lengthy incarceration. The usual pattern of the oath is to demand some punishment upon the speaker if he is not telling the truth. The simplest form of this oath is the small boy's "Cross my heart and hope to die." More elaborate formulæ which say much the same thing are found in many parts of the world. The Sumatran oath follows the small boy's rhetoric though it is couched in much more formal phraseology. Medieval and modern literature contain many examples of people who were mysteriously struck blind or deaf and dumb at their own request when they perjured themselves. The Euro-American appeal, "So help me God" (i.e. if this is not true) is paralleled in other communities by appeals to other gods. The Khonds stand on a tiger skin and ask for death if they lie. The Naga of Assam stands in a rope circle and prays that he should rot as the rope rots if he is not telling the truth. The Ostyak pretends to eat and calls upon a bear to devour him if he lies. Others solemnize their oaths by touching sacred objects: the Bible, in Europe; the genitalia, among the early Hebrews; the earth and sea, among some of the early Greek tribes. The Tungus swear by their children, the Hottentots by their sisters. A powerful Euro-American oath is by the soul of a dead mother, i.e. "May my dear dead mother burn in hell if. . . ." etc. These oaths are charged with no less feeling than the direct self-imprecation. See ACT OF TRUTH; FLAMEN. [RDJ]

Oats Goat A field spirit, the spirit of the growing oats; in eastern Europe, also the puppet made of the last sheaf, which is topped with goat horns; or the cutter of the last sheaf. In Prussia especially the Oats Goat is a prominent field spirit; children are warned out of the oat fields lest the Oats Goat "get" them; reapers hurry with the work to keep ahead of the Oats Goat, who "pushes" laggards. In some parts of Germany there are two goats, a he-goat and a she-goat. In the Grenoble region a live goat is decked with flowers and ribbons and turned loose in the field; when the reaping is over it is caught, killed, and roasted for the harvest supper. Its skin is made into a cloak, which usually the farmer wears during the threshing, but which is transferred to any reaper who gets a pain in the back, because of the power of the Oats Goat to cure ills caused by himself.

In parts of Bavaria threshers sing a threshing song describing the Oats Goat among the oats. Often the Oats Goat, inherent in the puppet made from the last sheaf of one farm, is transferred to the field of a farmer who has not yet finished. See CAILLEAĊ; HARVEST DOLL.

In Bohemia the mummer dressed in straw and wearing goat horns and called the Oats Goat is led from house to house during the Shrovetide observances: the Bohemian counterpart of the Fastnachtsbär. He dances in front of the houses, or enters and dances with the women of the household, is given food and money. All the fertility symbolism associated with the Fastnachtsbär is also attached to the Oats Goat. In some sections of Lithuania the bear and the goat formerly appeared together. Frazer's *Spirits of the Corn and of the Wild*, 2 vols., discusses the Oats Goat at length.

Oat-Stallion In the harvest customs of parts of Baden, Germany, the last sheaf of oats to be gathered. The personification of the last sheaf as a horse is paralleled elsewhere by the old woman, old man, cow, goat, wolf, etc. Compare HARVEST DOLL.

ob (plural *oboth*) In ancient Hebrew belief and practice, a necromancer or a necromancer's familiar spirit (thus translated in the Authorized Version of the Bible); also, the object in which the spirit was thought to reside. The Witch of Endor (*I Sam.* xxviii) was *baalat ob*, possessor of an ob. This expression is, in the Septuagint, made to equal ventriloquist, one who makes his voice come out of the ground. This, with an indication that the ob was made—a physical rather than a conceptual object—, has caused it to be equated by some with a mummy, a mummy's head, or, in later times when mummification became a lost art, with a skull. Medieval necromancers were wont to utilize skulls in their spells.

The resemblance between *ab*, father, and *ob* has led to a hypothesis that the ob is an ancestral spirit, perhaps the spirit of the mummy or mummified object. Still another hypothesis may be made: the word *baal* indicates lordship or ownership most commonly of a place rather than of an object. The ob therefore may have been either a diagram drawn on the ground, from which the evoked spirit spoke, or it may have been a place, like the Delphic sanctuary, at which such diagram-drawing or other ceremony was efficacious. In Jewish tradition, "Ob is the python who speaks from his armpits; *yiddeoni* is he who speaks with his mouth." *Yiddeoni* is a word of similar meaning to ob, and occurs generally in the Bible in connection with ob.

Obaluwaye Yoruban earth deity, equivalent of the Dahomean Sagbata, or the Ashanti Asa'ase. Another, better-known name for this Yoruba deity is Shakpono. He is known under both names in the African cults of Brazil, Cuba, and Trinidad. The name means "Master of the Universe" (i.e. the Earth). [MJH]

Obassi Supreme deity of the Ekoi and Ibibio of the Niger Delta. [MJH]

obelisks Because obelisks are monolithic erections which vary in height from three feet, as the obelisks found in the Egyptian tombs of the IVth Dynasty, to 836 feet, as the Heliopolis obelisk now in the Piazza di S. Pietro in Rome, they are inevitably referred to as phallic symbols. The great number of them found in Egypt, which had a great many phallic components in its religion, makes refutation of this view difficult. Obelisks may be described as four-sided pillars with pyramidal tops. Some of the Egyptian obelisks were surmounted by symbols of the sun god. One in Rome has a bronze cross which contains one of the many fragments of the true cross. The long line of obelisks at Axum (Abyssinia) are of several types. They are in various stages of development from rude stones to highly finished and decorated monoliths. Some of them once bore metal statues of the pre-Christian kings of Axum, others had altars for animal sacrifices built into the base, and one is surmounted by a solar disk.

Another view is that the rough pillars of conical shape resembling in "a rough way" a phallus in which the gods dwelt are common in Hamitic and Semitic culture and developed into the Egyptian obelisk. The sanctuary of Astarte (or Atargatis) at Byblus on the Syrian coast contained a tall stone or obelisk which was a symbol of the goddess. Still other writers have thought that the obelisk symbolizes a ray of light and the "finger of the god." Finally the obelisk is the single horn of the unicorn which rises into the zenith and symbolizes dominion over the whole earth.

From the variety of the views sampled here it is obvious that authorities are not in agreement as to the meaning at any time, modern or ancient, of the obelisk, and that in ancient as in modern times obelisks are polysemantic. One of their meanings is that they clearly mark a particular place. Whether additional meanings at certain times or for certain people are that they represent the finger of God, mark a good spot to immortalize a forgotten king, or represent an exaggerated *membrum virile* is not at all clear. [RDJ]

obia or **obeah** A term used by Negroes of the English-speaking islands of the Caribbean and of English and Dutch Guiana to denote various forms of supernatural power. In the islands it is officially regarded as a term for evil magic and its use is prohibited by law, though the Negroes recognize that, like all magic, it may be good or bad, depending on the circumstances and motivations of its use. In Dutch Guiana, it is, especially among the Bush Negroes, a kind of impersonal, overall power. In all instances, its use is in the hands of a specialist termed in Guiana the *obiamã* or, in the Islands, *obiaman*. [MJH]

obley cakes Cakes offered as part of a religious ceremony, usually first-fruit oblations. Primitive and civilized cultures have such cakes in one or another form. Among the Burgher tribesmen of the Nīlgiri Hills the first sheaves of grain are baked into a cake and offered as an oblation. Among the ancient Greeks, cakes and frankincense were consecrated in sacred baskets at the temple of Delphi. Cakes in the shapes of lyres, arrows, and bows symbolized the two aspects of the deity. At Athens, on the 15th day of the month Elaphebolion, a sacrificial cake with twelve knobs on it was offered to Cronus each spring. In Japan, on New Year's Day, unleavened cakes made of glutinous pounded rice are placed on the domestic shrine. These "mirror" cakes represent the male and female principles respectively: the sun and the moon. They are made up in the shape of a flattened sphere.

oboe A wind instrument consisting of a pipe of cylindrical or conical shape, blown through a double reed to set up a sounding vibration in the column of air. The sound principle thus differs from that of the flute and the trumpet, with both of which its history has been confused by indiscriminate translation of the names of various tubular instruments and by the misinterpretation of ancient art works depicting wind instruments. However, its uses and associations are similar to those of the flute and to some extent the trumpet, insofar as its shape suggests phallic, and thus life-giving, properties. The difference in its tone makes its connotations somewhat less intimate than some aspects of flute symbolism and somewhat less frightening and awe-inspiring than certain of the trumpet meanings.

The instrument was known in ancient Sumer, in Egypt from the 15th century B.C., in Biblical Israel, in the Orient and India, in Greece and Rome, and in Europe. Its uses have included accompaniment to ceremonies of circumcision, marriage, and mourning, martial processions, sacrifices, orgiastic dancing and drama, and it has been believed to influence the behavior of animals, and to cure such ailments as epilepsy, gout, snakebite, and sciatica. In the ancient world oboes were often joined in pairs played simultaneously, one as a drone, the other carrying the melody.

The Hebrew *halil*, while it was used for joyous occasions also, was commonly played for funeral processions and was thought to induce a state of trance (see JORDAN FLUTE). Both wedding and circumcision rites in the Near East make use of oboe music.

In Greece, the oboe *aulos*, often played double, was one of the chief instruments, rivaling the lyre. It served particularly the Dionysian cult, its shrill tones whipping up the frenzy of the dancing, and was originally always connected with trends from the peoples of Asia Minor. Greek drama, as a derivative of Dionysian rites, continued its use in the theater. It was also played for wedding festivities, generally in pairs of different length, distinguished as male and female. Smaller instruments and those with sweeter tone were used for courtship and were associated with the arts of courtesans. Indeed, Lamia, a Greek-born mistress of Ptolemy Soter (306 B.C.), was raised to the rank of a goddess and honored by a temple because of her patronage of the oboe.

Oboes of varying size and pitch set up a wail in accompaniment to Greek mortuary rites and expressions of grief. To Marsyas, the Phrygian piper, is attributed a melody called "the Mother's Air" composed to lighten the grief of Cybele for the death of Attis. It was he who, boastful of his skill, challenged the god Apollo to a musical duel. See LYRE.

Spartans went into battle to the sound of the oboe; military drills and rowing strokes were paced by its notes; it accompanied wrestling and boxing matches, and offenders against the law were whipped as it played.

A particular oboe melody, the *hippothorus*, was believed to assist procreation in the breeding of horses, and the Sybarites, according to Athenæus, taught their horses to dance to its strains. Their achievement was turned against them by the Crotonians, who won a victory by playing oboes as the Sybarites advanced against them, so that the horses began to dance and the Sybarites were thrown into confusion and captured. Crabs were enticed from their holes and dolphins lured from the ocean depths by the *aulos*.

In Rome, according to Ovid, the oboe, along with tuba and horns, accompanied funeral chants and was heard at games and in the temple. Virtuosi of the instrument in its varying forms were the idols of the Roman theater, dressed effeminately in yellow gowns and green or blue slippers, and were permitted to eat in the temple of Jupiter Capitolinus. Women's rites of April 4th in honor of the Magna Mater, a ceremony taken over from the Near East, and the spring sacrifices for Proserpina both made use of oboe music. Both Romans and Greeks had faith in its power to revive and to cure human ills.

In India, pairs of oboes played by two players, with or without other instruments, are favorites for weddings, dancing, processions, and festivals, the players in some sections being highly respected and holding hereditary positions. An Indian origin of the instrument is postulated by Far Eastern lāmas, who consider it sacred, and its voice is said to be that of an Indian bird.

European oboes include the *shawms*, used for both dancing of the moriscas type and for military music, and a hunting instrument, the *oboe da caccia*, used early in the 18th century. Compare FLUTE; TRUMPET. [TCB]

obosum The Ashanti word for deity, the equivalent of Dahomean *vodun*, Yoruban *orisha*, Ibo *alose*, Congo tribes *nkisi*, with dialectic variants. [MJH]

obscenity Although lawmakers have had difficulty in defining obscenity, popular opinion in all cultures seems to be clear that obscene acts or words are degrading, therefore offensive and punishable. The difficulty is that acts and gestures considered obscene in some parts of the world and in some classes of society are not considered obscene in others. Respectable American women use phrases and tell stories at cocktail parties which they would consider obscene at meetings of their church guilds. Opinions about obscenity by judges who rule on publications considered indecent or obscene reflect the prejudices of a social class in which the capacity of being shocked by direct language has been developed to an extraordinary degree. The general opinion is that obscene words and acts are degrading and the extent of degradation or obscenity depends on the conditions under which the words or acts are used. A. E. Crawley need not have gone to Queensland, Australia, to learn that the savages there had a polite and an obscene set of words for the sexual acts and organs—information which he could have acquired by a half hour in his neighborhood public house. Although exposure of the sexual organs is considered obscene in many parts of Europe and America, women elsewhere breast-feed their children in public and men enter very imperfectly protected urinals without loss of modesty.

Obscene phrases or epithets frequently refer to the acts of excretion or to sexual relations of a prohibited nature. In a series of curses frequently heard on the streets of China, the participants, usually women, command each other antiphonally to have intercourse with their fathers, mothers, brothers, aunts, uncles, themselves, etc. In China obscene language is generally prohibited to men and even to women when men are present, though in this instance the phrases have become so common that they are meaningless except as expressions of amazement, displeasure, or anger. In this connection it is relevant to note that Dr. Johnson defined "bastard" as a "term of endearment among sailors," as it is still a term of mild affection among Australian soldiers who preface it with the word "bloody" (a corruption of "by our Lady") which is highly offensive in England though innocent in America. Another transformation of values due in part to cultural change and in part to its use as an exclamation is the Americanism "Holy Mackerel," which is a corruption of *makaraille de Deus*, a Provençal obscenity meaning "God's whore."

Whether used as a curse or a term of affection, the rhetorical form of the obscene phrase is often that of an imperative command. This has helped to give plausibility to the extraordinary hypothesis among pundits that obscenities have a magic function in warding off evil or, among other folklorists, that they have a connection forgotten in Europe but presumably remembered elsewhere with fertility magic. Though obscenity seems to have been customary in some of the spring and autumn festivals of Greek, Roman, African, American Indian, and other cultures, the connection with fertility ceremonies seems to be that on festival occasions, particularly the festivals of sowing the seed and reaping the harvest, normal social restrictions are relaxed. The use of the obscene command as a curse is as much due to the fact that during an excess of emotion, sudden fear, or disgust, degrading expletives seem to be appropriate. In many sophisticated cultures these obscene commands have to be "said with a smile." The lists published in *Anthroprophyteia* are worth study though they would be more useful if accompanied by more complete notes on the cultural attitudes of the ethnic groups which considered them degrading.

Obscene stories or jokes have been generally neglected by folklorists due in part to the difficulty of publishing the results of such studies, in part to the monotony of the data, and in part to the danger that students might get tagged as "persons interested in *that* sort of thing." This is all the more unfortunate because the "dirty story" enjoys a great popularity in all parts of the world and is almost the only *genus* of folktale transmitted in all cultural strata of Europe and America. Father Wieger omitted large sections of many Chinese folktales on the grounds that they were obscene. A reading of the folktales of many cultures, as translated by missionaries, would give the impression that primitive people are unaware of the acts and organs of sex or defecation and of the ridiculous antics of human beings when gripped by these impulses. Many of the "dirty stories" have two parts, a "build-up" and a "pay-off" or "punch-line." The punch-line frequently takes one of two forms: either the build-up leads the hearer to expect an obscenity at the end but startles him by an innocent phrase, often a euphemism, for a prohibited organ or act, or the build-up leads to an expectation of an innocent phrase and the pay-off leads to an obscenity. Another of the many types of dirty story is the Noodle Tale or the Moron Story which tells of the absurd and often obscene confusions attributed to simpletons.

Among many cultures, the use of obscenity at fixed occasions is recognized as appropriate. In America the stories and references at bachelors' dinners in which the groom is inducted from the state of bachelorhood into marriage are part of a recognized ritual of passage. In China brides are required to sit for many hours in the bridal chamber while the groom's friends, whose relations with women are restricted by a very rigid code, are expected to file through the room, tell filthy stories, and generally behave in an obscene manner. These customs, like the charivari, may have to do with ancient beliefs and rituals, though their persistence leads one to look for more immediate motivation—possibly that at rituals having to do with procreation, the normal social prohibitions are relaxed.

Ritual obscenity in religious ceremonies has not been examined in any detail. In these ceremonies matrons who are reported to be normally modest and sedate are expected to tell each other obscene stories and do so without any loss of modesty. This was true of the spring festival of the Roman Bona Dea among women who, whatever their morals may have been, observed a very rigid etiquette. At the Greek Haloa, the presiding priestess whispered into the women's ears "things not to be spoken," presumably obscene. The voodoo ceremony *coucher yame* in Haiti is interrupted by a woman talking through her nose and making indecent jests. Similarly the men and women in some of the American Indian ceremonies sang obscenities at each other. Obscenities were a recognized part of the medieval *ludi* and the Feasts of Fools.

General conclusions about the meaning of customs, varied as those which are referred to as obscene, are difficult. The general reference of the term is to the degradation which people may normally be expected to feel at references to defecation or the acts or organs of sex and which all cultures seem capable of feeling. The capacity for experiencing this feeling varies greatly, not only as between cultures whose social and emotional values differ, but in the same cultures under different circumstances. Under the general sexual excitement of weddings in cultures all over the world, comments are tolerated which under other circumstances would be considered grossly obscene and, in the solemnity of their court rooms, judges frequently rule that words or descriptions are obscene which they would unblushingly use in the good fellowship of their clubs.

R. D. JAMESON

obsidian Obsidian or volcanic glass, and flint, a variety of quartz, because of their easy fracturing qualities and general procurability were the two most widely used substances for the manufacture of arrowheads, spear points, knives, etc., in both the Old World and the New in aboriginal times. Translations of the North American Indian name or names for these materials have sometimes confused flint with obsidian, or vice versa. Hence the presence of a Flint man, or of a character named Flint, in the mythology of a particular tribe located in a region where obsidian is plentiful, does not necessarily mean that flint is what the name actually refers to; the reference may be to the more showy, shiny obsidian. It seems likely that Metal Old Man of the White Mountain Apache may be a creature encased in obsidian, not in flint as the English versions of the Apache myth have it. In the case of the evil character Flint, Nanabozho's youngest brother who killed their mother, and of the Iroquois Flint, one of the twin culture heroes, it is probable that flint is intended, considering the Great Lakes locale of these myths.

Obsidian, besides being used for weapons and implements, was also used in the West especially for ceremonial objects. The long blades displayed in the Northwest California World Renewal dances were of obsidian; bear shamans in south-central California wore bear hides with sharp pieces of obsidian attached to the sleeves, which they used to slash people with while simulating bears; the Wailaki and Yuki of north-central California held an obsidian ceremony which was an initiation rite for boys and girls. The children were made to fast and undergo a series of strenuous ordeals, including having obsidian knives stuck into them by the obsidian doctors who were in charge of the initiation. Among the Yuki the word *kichil* denotes both flint and obsidian, but the ceremonial references in the initiation rites seem to be prevailingly to obsidian. See OTHAG-WENDA. [EWV]

obstacle flight or **magic flight** A folktale motif (D672) known all over the world: Europe, Siberia, North and South America, Africa, Indonesia. Fugitives from a giant (cannibal, monster, ogre, witch) throw down behind them certain magic objects (usually three, occasionally four or five) which turn into time-consuming or death-dealing obstacles. The magic objects often answer for the fugitive when the ogre calls out, and thus delay him; and they turn into mountains, precipices, thickets, forests, rivers, lakes, fire, etc., when released during the flight. See DZOAVITS; TWO BROTHERS.

Familiar magic objects thrown behind are a comb (which becomes a thicket), a stone or whetstone (which becomes a mountain), a mirror, bottle of water or oil (which becomes a lake or other body of water); a bit of earth thrown down turns into a mountain, a drop of water becomes a river, a thorn turns into a thicket, or fire springs up, which finally stops the chaser.

In *The Water-Nixie* (Grimm #79) two children are kidnapped by a nixie. They finally escape by means of the magic flight: the little girl throws down her brush, which becomes a hill covered with spikes; when the nixie begins to catch up, the boy throws down a comb which becomes a jagged ridge; finally the girl throws a little mirror behind them, which turns into a mountain of mirrors so slippery that the nixie can never cross it. In Jamaica Negro folktale the fugitive merely throws corn or seed for a pursuing animal or monster to pick up or eat. In an Indonesian story the fugitives throw salt behind them, which becomes an ocean and stops the giant until he drinks it up; next they throw ashes, which blind him for a little while; then they throw marbles, which become thorny plants, then millet, which the giant stops to eat. This giant was not deterred until killed through his vulnerable spot. A Koryak story describes a man, wife, and child fleeing from wolves; as the wolves draw near, the woman takes a stone from her bosom and throws it behind them; sharp rocks fill the path which cut the wolves' feet. Next she throws down a small chip which turns into an impenetrable forest and the wolves give up. In an Eskimo (Baffin Bay) tale an old woman draws a line on the ice with her little finger; the ice separates, and the pursuers are stopped. ☞ In North American Indian native versions of this incident either three or four objects are thrown behind; for example, in a Tlingit tale from the North Pacific Coast, the hero, pursued by Moon, throws behind him successively a piece of devil's club which makes a thicket, a rosebush which makes a thicket of rosebushes, and a whetstone which becomes a great mountain.

Two paths of diffusion for this series of magic flight or obstacle flight incidents in North American tales have been suggested by Boas; the first, an ancient one from Siberia via Bering Strait, the second, a recent one from Spain into Latin America and northward to California, where the old and the new versions meet.

Related to the obstacle flight are the incidents of the reversed obstacle flight (D673) in which the pursuer throws obstacles in front of the fugitive, the transformation flight (D671) in which fugitives transform themselves in order to deceive the pursuer, and the Atalanta type (R231) in which treasure or the like is thrown back to tempt the pursuer to delay. For the distribution of the obstacle flight and its related forms in North American Indian folklore, see Stith Thompson, *Tales of the North American Indians* (Cambridge, Mass., 1929), pp. 333–334, n. 205, (a), (b), and p. 342, n. 232. [EWV]

☞ The motif of the miraculous escape occurs rarely in South America. A tale, recorded among the Shipaya Indians of the lower Xingu, describes the successive evasions of a man pursued by a demon. Each time he is saved by friendly animals. In a Mundurucu story, a girl stops a demon who runs after her by dropping magic substances which become successively smoke, forest, and a river. The motif of the obstacles created by the transformation of objects may well be of European origin. [AM]

ocarina A globular flute with a whistle mouthpiece and fingerholes stopped to play the melody. It is made of pottery, wood, gourd, and nowadays of plastic. It is played in one form or another on the primitive, folk, and popular levels. Its shape may be ovoid, or tuberlike, as its popular name, "sweet potato," indicates. South American Indians make the instrument of gourd, molded pitch, or clay. Latin American popular bands sometimes use large and gaily painted ocarinas of pottery or gourd. The dime-store plastic variety are played by children and amateur performers. The name ocarina for the age-old globular flute is particularly connected with the type devised by an Italian in the middle of the 19th century and made in whole families like recorders so that a choir or orchestra could play together. For other globular flutes, see FLUTE.

Ocnus In Greek mythology, the personification of delay. He is placed in the underworld, perhaps as analogous to the Danaides, where he continually twines a rope of straw which is eaten by his ass as he makes it. Ocnus sometimes is pictured as trying to load the ass with sticks which fall off on the other side as he places them on the animal. Rose believes him to be a typical character of folk droll transplanted to the underworld.

October horse The sacrifice at an ancient Roman fertility (later a martial) rite on October 15. A chariot race was held in the Field of Mars on that date, and the right-hand horse of the winning chariot was killed as a sacrifice to Mars. Its head, first sprinkled with sacred crumbs, was cut off and strung with a necklace of cakes or loaves. A fight for the head then occurred, the inhabitants of two quarters of the city attempting to seize the head and place it either on the king's palace wall or on the Mamilian tower. The tail too was cut off and rushed to the king's hearth in time for blood to fall on the hearth. The remainder of the horse's blood was carefully preserved, and on April 21 it was mixed by the Vestals ceremonially with other blood. This mixture was given to shepherds to be burned; the smoke was a purifying agent for their flocks. In every aspect the various elements of the October horse sacrifice make powerful fertility symbols: the race, the blood, the hearth, the necklace of loaves, the auspicious right hand—these are widespread symbols of increase. The horse's head as a charm against evil is still common in Germany where it decorates gable-ends. Compare the speaking head of the horse Falada in Grimm's tale *The Goose-Girl* (#89).

Odhroerir In Teutonic mythology, the kettle of inspiration which, with the two bowls Son (expiation) and Boden (offering), was used by two certain dwarfs to contain the poetic mead brewed from Kvaser's blood. Whoever drank of this brew became at once poet and knower of poetic charms. These three vessels were stolen by the giant Suttung and given into the charge of his daughter, Gunlod, who guarded them in a cave in the mountains. Odin's ravens told him of this and, though Odin already knew all runes, had drunk at Mimir's well, and was the wisest of beings, he still desired to drink the mead of inspiration. Accordingly he wormed his way (literally) into the cave through a hole bored by his magic auger, Rati. Once inside, he resumed his godly form and seduced Gunlod. After three days she consented to give him a sip from each of the three vessels. But instead of sipping, Odin drained all three. Later he disgorged the poetic mead into containers reserved for the gods. A few dregs fell to earth, however, causing rimesters to spring up here and there. Only the gods could bestow enough to make a true poet. Bragi, the god of poetry and music, was the result of Odin's union with Gunlod. Odin henceforth was regarded as the patron of poets and singers.

Odin, Woden, or **Votan** In Teutonic mythology, the one-eyed patriarch and chief of the gods; god of wisdom and war. In northern belief, he is the son of the god Borr and the giantess Bestla. With the help of his brothers Vili and Ve, or Hœnir and Lodur, he slew the giant Ymir and from his body shaped the earth. The human race they fashioned from an ash and elm tree. Odin himself, in conjunction with various female beings, is the father of all the æsir, though his wife and queen is Frigga. He is usually represented as a vigorous man of about fifty, either with long curling hair, or bald with a long gray beard. He dressed in gray with a cloak and hood of blue and usually wore his ring Draupnir and carried his spear Gungnir which he used as a scepter or staff. As chief of the gods, he presided over their deliberations in the great hall, Gladsheim, where stand the twelve seats of the gods.

As the wisest of beings, the all-seeing, all-knowing father-god, god of wisdom, knowledge, and poetry, he is seated on his elevated throne, Hlidskialf, in the silver thatched hall, Valaskialf. From this seat he looks out over all the world and watches the doings of the gods, giants, dwarfs, and men. On his shoulders perch his two ravens, Hugin (Thought) and Munin (Memory), who whisper in his ears events they have seen in their daily flights over the earth. At his feet lie his two wolves or watchdogs, Geri and Freki. His thirst for knowledge is insatiable. He gave up one of his eyes for a draft from Mimir's well of knowledge. For nine days he hung from Yggdrasil in a trance gazing into the depths of Niflheim and thus learned to write runes. He nearly lost his life securing the poetic mead made by the dwarfs from Kvaser's blood and when Mimir's head was sent to Asgard by the vanir, Odin preserved it by charms and herbs and consulted it as an oracle. He discoursed with the dwarfs, seers, and sages. He even made a trip to Hel to find the answer to one question and he often sits beneath the gallows to absorb the knowledge of the hanged.

As warrior god, he presides in his palace, Valhalla, in the shimmering amber grove, Glaesir, where he gathers about him his chosen warriors, the Einheriar, who will aid the gods in time of need. Here, seated upon his throne, wearing his eagle helmet and shining armor, he welcomes the slain warriors brought to Valhalla by the Valkyrs. He plans the course of battles, even to the warriors who will be slain, usually leaving the actual direction of events in the hands of his battle maidens, Valkyries. He plans the course of battles, even to the warriors who will be slain, usually leaving the actual direction of events in the hands of his battle maidens, originating the wedge formation of battle.

As the supreme god he is not aloof or vengeful. He frequently passes among his people in the guise of The Wanderer, clad in a voluminous blue cloak and a wide brimmed slouch hat to disguise his one eye. Thus he keeps in touch with king and commoner alike, delivering reward or punishment. In many localities, in the guise of the wanderer, he is believed to be the leader of the Wild Hunt and, mounted on his eight-footed horse, Sleipnir, he leads his hosts through the countryside instilling fear into all as he goes. While Odin is known generally throughout western Europe and Scandinavia, his importance and attributes vary greatly with locality and time. His worship probably originated in Lower Germany and spread from there. Besides being the creator, father of the gods, inventor of the arts, god of wisdom and war, he was also considered a potent magician, sorcerer, and healer. Others invoked his aid in trade and commerce. Sailors called on him for a fair wind and he is the patron of travelers. In Christian times he had often been identified with the Devil, and Anglo-Saxon medicine believed that disease (flying venoms) sprang from the nine parts into which he hacked the worm (dragon). In northern countries the constellation Great Bear is often called Odin's Wain and Wednesday is contracted from Woden's Tag. In all Odin is known by over two hundred names, many of which refer to a particular identity he assumed for one of his many adventures either alone or in company with his fellow gods. In his human aspects, Odin is believed to have been the progenitor of most of the royal houses of the north. [JWH]

odori A Japanese dance term including both theatrical and folk dances. The term is often used all-inclusively, though strictly speaking odori is distinct from *mai*, the latter being slow and dignified, emphasizing the movement of the hands, the former emphasizing quick and lively motions of the feet. The characters used in writing *mai* and *odori* may be put together to read *buyō*, meaning dance in general. *Mai* goes back to early times, in such forms as the *kume-mai, yamato mai*, and *azuma asobi*. The dancing of the *nō* is of the *mai* type. See NŌ.

Japanese theatrical dances are performed by actors to complex musical rhythms. Most of them are spring dances. The most famous are the *Miyako odori* or cherry dance, at Kyoto, the *Kamogawa odori* at Kyoto, the *Naniwa odori* at Osaka, and the *Azuma odori* at Tokyo.

Folk festivals include the famous *bon-odori*, which commemorates the dead. On July 16 the souls of the dead are believed to return and are given food offerings. The steps and gestures of the *bon-odori* vary in different parts of Japan; all are uncannily silent and smooth but with occasional handclapping; everywhere it is a circle dance for men and women. Harvest dances and banquet dances accompanied by song are popular throughout Japan, also the great Catch-fish and Shinto Lion-mask dance. The *Tanabata-odori* is performed by children, celebrating the union of two stars. The *gebon-odori* is danced in Wakayama to the beating of gourds, gongs, and drums, and the chanting of Buddhist songs.

Geishas are popular odori performers and experts on the *samisen*. When they appear without special costume, the performance is known as *su-odori* (just as is). The geishas are past masters in the manipulation of fans. In general the fan is an indispensable element of the Japanese dance, expressing an infinite number of ideas: falling petals, the rising moon, a butterfly, a sword, a bird. Gestures are elegantly traditionalized. Male and female postures are distinct, the men perform with broad stance, the women (notably the geishas) with closed flexed knees and slight back tilt. Hand gestures are also differentiated, not only for characters and situations, but for the sexes: the virile male spread hand, the languid female hand.

The odori is, however, yielding to the onrush of civilization. The popular *ondō* which has reached the United States still preserves Japanese posture and gesture. Ballet and musical comedy, however, now attract large crowds, though they might seem to be styles unsuited to the Japanese genius. Fortunately, many artist dancers base their creations on native styles. [GPK]

Odysseus   In Greek legend, king of Ithaca; hero of the *Odyssey*. His name in Latin, Ulixes, became Ulysses in the modern European tongues, by which name he was known until recent scholarship established Odysseus as the preferred form.

Odyssey   One of the two great ancient Greek epics attributed to Homer; with the *Iliad* it tells much of the story of the Trojan War and what happened afterwards. The *Odyssey* is the story of what happened to Odysseus, king of Ithaca, an unwilling but vigorous participant in the Trojan War, as he traveled homeward from Troy, how he arrived home, and how he rescued his wife (Penelope) and estate from greedy suitors. It is the great voyage tale of the ancient world and contains many familiar folktale themes and motifs. Odysseus himself, it has been suggested, is a Bear's Son, and among the events and personages in the story are Polyphemus, the Cyclops, the one-eyed ogre; Circe, the great witch, and Calypso, the wonder-working goddess; the voyage to the underworld; the Sirens; Scylla and Charybdis, the dangers to right and left circumvented by the hero; Penelope's web, the seemingly unending task. The telling of the *Odyssey* begins when the story is almost over. Odysseus is being kept on Calypso's isle, while at Ithaca the suitors have gotten out of hand. Penelope is to be forced to make a decision. The gods declare that Calypso must release her prisoner. In order of time, however, the tale begins when Odysseus and his crew round the Peloponnesian peninsula for the last leg of their journey up the west coast of Greece. A wind drives them off course and they make land in the country of the Lotus-Eaters. There, the men, partaking of this otherworld food (C210), forget their homes and must be forced to resume the journey. They land again, enter a cave, and are trapped by Polyphemus. Blinding the giant by driving a stake through his eye, Odysseus and his depleted crew escape by hiding beneath the bellies of the ogre's flock. Æolus, god of the wind, next helps them by presenting Odysseus with a bag that contains all the contrary winds. Just within sight of Ithaca, the hero permits himself to doze, and the crew, inflamed by their own suspicion that the skin contains treasure that Odysseus wants to keep for himself, open the bag. The ship is blown back to Æolus. He forbids them to land, and they fall among the Læstrygonians, a race of cannibals who leave only enough crew to man one ship. They escape to Ææa where Circe transforms them into swine. Odysseus, using a magic herb, forces her to change them back to human shape. On Circe's advice, and with her aid, he undertakes a voyage to Hades, where he sees again many of the heroes of the late war. Tiresias the seer is among the shades, and from him Odysseus learns how best to return to Ithaca. Forewarned he evades the sweet-singing Sirens and the whirlpool and rock of Scylla and Charybdis. The ship touches at the island of Thrinacia where Apollo keeps his oxen. There, while Odysseus naps again, his men sacrifice some of the cattle. As punishment, the ship is wrecked in a storm and only Odysseus escapes alive. He is washed ashore on Calypso's island, lives with the goddess for eight years. At this point the *Odyssey* proceeds with the narrative.

Odysseus sails for twenty days on a raft and is driven ashore in the land of the Phæacians whose king, Alcinous, receives the hero kindly. After telling of his adventures, Odysseus is placed in a deep sleep and, in a magic ship, is taken home to Ithaca. He awakes and, disguised, discovers what has happened in his absence, and how the insolent suitors, having devoured his estate, are about to force the faithful Penelope to choose among them. Penelope, weaving her web through the day, spends the night undoing the work. Odysseus, enlisting the aid of his now grown son Telemachus and some of his faithful servants, enters the hall and with his own bow, which none but he can draw, slays the suitors and reclaims his wife.

Œdipus   Literally, swell-foot; in Greek legend, a king of Thebes who solved the riddle of the Sphinx, killed his father, and married his mother; one of the line of Theban rulers doomed to tragedy by the curse of Pelops. Œdipus was the son of Laius of Thebes and Jocasta (Epicasta in Homer). In some versions an oracle had warned Laius that he would be killed by his son; in others Pelops' curse itself had threatened Laius either with childlessness or with a son who would kill him. Laius therefore ordered the infant abandoned with a spike driven through its feet, either to prevent the child from crawling to safety or to keep its ghost from returning to haunt him. But a shepherd of King Polybus of Corinth found the infant and brought it to the queen —Periboea or Merope or Medusa. She and Polybus raised the boy as their own, naming him Œdipus because of his wounded feet.

When Œdipus grew to young manhood, his accomplishments aroused the envy of his companions, who pointedly mentioned his dubious parentage. Unable to get a satisfying answer from Periboea, Œdipus went to Delphi to find out what the oracle of Apollo might tell him. The oracle warned him that he would slay his father and marry his mother. Therefore Œdipus decided not to return to Corinth, for there his supposed parents reigned. Instead he headed toward Thebes and on his way, in a narrow pass, disputed the right of way with Laius and killed him, thus fulfilling unwittingly part of the prophecy.

At Thebes he found the Sphinx desolating the countryside: this is the type of dragon (as Krappe points out) that the folk hero must slay to attain full heroic stature. The Sphinx accosted all who passed with the riddle: "What goes on four legs in the morning, on two at noon, and on three in the evening?" Those who failed to answer correctly—everyone until Œdipus came that way—were devoured by the monster. Œdipus however gave the answer: "Man, who crawls as a child, walks erect in manhood, and uses a cane in old age." He then slew the Sphinx (or she killed herself because he gave the answer) and entered Thebes. As deliverer of the city, and the king being dead, Œdipus was presented with the crown and the queen, Jocasta, his own mother. The oracle was fulfilled, though as yet everyone concerned was ignorant of the fact.

Œdipus and Jocasta lived together for some years, but eventually the gods made known the true relationship. The common version of the story says that the oracle declared the sin was the cause of a famine gripping the land. Jocasta hanged herself and Œdipus put out his eyes, or the servants of Laius blinded him, and he was deposed as king of Thebes. The death of Jocasta and the deposition of Œdipus follow closely in some versions; in others many years elapse between the events. The several tellings of the story are confused on various of these elements. Œdipus' four children, Eteocles and Polynices, Antigone and Ismene, are by Jocasta or a second wife, Euryganeia or Astymedusa. Athenian writers further complicate the story by setting the tale's end in Attica. There at last the blind Œdipus wandered into the grove of the Eumenides at Colonus, whence he disappeared from earth. Other tradition says he was killed in a battle, perhaps in defending the cattle of Thebes from raiders. His body was refused burial at Thebes; it was buried elsewhere, disinterred when it brought calamity to the people living in the vicinity of the grave. Finally at Eteonos, at a shrine of Demeter, the people were ordered by the goddess: "Remove not the suppliant of the god." Renamed the Œdipodion, this burial place became famous in the ancient world.

Homer knew the story of Œdipus, which may be a compilation of folktale motifs attracted to the person of a historical Theban chief or a group of folktales taken over as pseudo-history by the Greeks. Parallels to the main themes of the story, incest and parricide, have been found in Finland, Hungary, Rumania, Lithuania, Lapland, the Ukraine, and various other places in the world, like Java. The *Golden Legend* retells the Œdipus story but makes Judas Iscariot the central figure. The tale (Type 931) is thus in essence of great popularity throughout the world. Among its motifs may be mentioned: exposed infant reared at king's court (S354), the parricide prophecy (M343) unwittingly fulfilled (N323) though the child is exposed to prevent fulfilment of the prophecy (M371.2), the mother-incest prophecy (M344) unwittingly fulfilled (M365.1), mother-son incest (T412), the riddle of the Sphinx (H761) propounded on pain of death (H541.1.1), Sphinx perishes when riddle is solved (C822).

The Sphinx episode of the Œdipus story is related to the ogre tales and to such märchen as *Rumpelstiltskin* and others of supernatural helpers defeated by the discovery of a secret (Type 500). The Sphinx itself is a monster similar to the Sirens, the Harpies, the Minotaur, Cerberus, the dragon of European folklore, and various other monstrous creatures of other folklores. A parallel may be drawn between the story of Œdipus and the Sphinx and Vararuchi and the Rākshasa. The demon asked Vararuchi: "Who is considered the best-looking woman in this city?" To save his life Vararuchi replied: "Any woman is good-looking to the man who admires her," and obtained the friendship of the monster.

oeh-da Term for the earth in Seneca (Iroquois) Indian mythology, the bit of earth brought from the bottom of the sea by Muskrat (earth-diver) to sustain the great light which enveloped Ataensic as she descended from the sky. Only the earth (oeh-da) was thought great enough for such blinding light to rest upon. When Muskrat dove under the sea and returned with the merest morsel of oeh-da in his paw, "It is heavy," he said, "it will grow; who will hold it?" Turtle said he would hold it, so the earth was placed upon his back. Oeh-da grew so rapidly that already it had become an island large enough to receive Ataensic when her descent was completed. Thus it is that Turtle is the Earth-Bearer of Iroquois mythology. When he is tired and moves a little the earth quakes and tidal waves rush against her shores. See ATAENSIC.

Œnone In Greek legend, the nymph of Mt. Ida, who was married to Paris of Troy; daughter of the river god Cebren. Having obtained the power of prophecy from Rhea, she foresaw the result of Paris' voyage to Sparta and warned him against going, but promised to cure him with her skill if he were wounded. When Paris was struck by an arrow shot by Philoctetes from the bow of Hercules, Œnone nevertheless refused to aid him. Then, relenting too late, she came with her slaves to Troy after Paris died. She killed herself by leaping on his funeral pyre, by hanging herself, or by jumping from a tower.

offended rolling rock A folktale motif (C91.1) popular among the North American Indians of the Plains, Plateau, and Southwest, and found also in the Central and Northeast Woodlands regions, and among the Hudson Bay Eskimos. The usual story is that the trickster gives his coat (or blanket) to a rock or boulder to warm it, later needs the coat, and goes back to get it. The rock is offended at having the gift taken away and rolls after him. The trickster runs before it, begging help from a series of animals, each of whom the rock rolls over and kills; but one way or another the trickster finally escapes.

In the Pawnee Indian story Coyote presents the rock with a knife in return for help in finding food. He comes upon a village where he is given meat, needs the knife to cut the meat, goes back and takes it, and is pursued by the rolling rock, which kills in sequence the bears, mountain lions, and buffalo who undertake to aid Coyote. He is finally saved by the Bull-Bats.

Wolverine is the trickster in the Hudson Bay Eskimo story. Wolverine makes no gift but mocks and taunts the rock until it is provoked into chasing him. After a long run Rock catches Wolverine and rolls onto him. Wolverine yells to get up, but Rock will not move because of the taunting. Wolverine yells for the wolves and foxes to come help push Rock off, but the wolves and foxes say it serves him right. Then Wolverine calls on the thunders and lightning, which come and split the rock, but also strips the skin off of Wolverine's back. (See *RBAE* 11: 336 ff.)

In a Southern Ute story Sünā'wavi (creator-trickster-culture-hero) one day urinated upon a little round rock. When Big Rock came home Little Rock told his father. Rock went rolling angrily after Sünā'wavi. Sünā'wavi ran and ran; Rock rolled after him over mountains, across rivers, through trees. Sünā'wavi begged for help from a series of animals, each of whom the rolling rock relentlessly killed. At last Sünā'wavi hid behind a little rock which suddenly enlarged and was as big as Rolling Rock. Rolling Rock smashed into it but the boulder stood fast and the rolling rock was splintered into little bits. Then in gratitude Sünā'wavi said, "Animals shall die, but you shall last till the end of the world." And so it is. (See *JAFL* 37: 25.)

In the Apache version Coyote is warned to be careful of a certain living rock lest it run him down. He does not believe that the rock can move, defecates upon it, and walks away. The rock rolls after him. When Coyote is about to be crushed (or when the rock comes to a standstill over the hole in which he has hidden) he promises to clean it off. The rock releases him; Coyote cleans it; the rock rolls back to its own place.

offended supernatural wife A widespread folktale and traditional ballad motif (C31 ff.) in which a man married to a supernatural being breaks the tabu which ensures the continuance of their relationship; the offended supernatural wife returns to her own world and the benefits which she bestowed cease. She departs typically for being looked at against her specific warning (C31.1)—in English, North American Indian, and Maori folktale; or looked at too soon (C31.1.1)—European; or at a certain time (C31.1.2)—see MELUSINE; or she must not be seen naked or during childbirth (Japanese). Her origin must not be mentioned (C31.2)—European, Indonesian, Fjort Negro; she must not be blamed (C31.4)—Greek, Arabian, Indonesian; or questioned (C31.4.1), or scolded (C31.4.2), struck (C31.8), or bragged about (C31.5)—see MACHA. The disappearance of the wonderful animal wife at the mention of her origin (C35.1) belongs to this cycle and occurs variously in Siberian, Eskimo and North American Indian, Basuto and Fjort Negro, and Indonesian folktale.

In Koryak folktale, Eme'mqut, son of Big Raven, is married to Fox Woman. A lodger in their house desires her greatly, but she does not respond to his advances. One day he remarks on the strong fox odor around her; she is offended and runs away (W. Jochelson, *The Koryak, MAMNH* 6, part i, p. 313).

In Basuto Negro story there was once a poor man who had no clothes but rags and no food but the wild mice he caught. One day he found an ostrich egg and took it home. He began to notice that every day the hut was now clean, and a good meal was waiting to be eaten when he entered. One day a woman came out of the egg and consented to be his wife; but she warned him never to mention her origin. All went well for a long time: the man was finely clothed and fed, and became chief of a big village. One day in irritation, however, he forgot and said, "You daughter of an ostrich egg!" Immediately he fell asleep and, when he woke, was lying on the grass. The big village was gone; his clothes were rags; he was hungry; and the wonderful

supernatural wife never returned. See E. Jacottet, *Contes Populaires des Bassoutos*, Paris, 1895, p. 259 ff.

Stories about the offended supernatural husband (C32 ff.; Type 425) follow the same patterns. See BEAR WIFE; CUPID AND PSYCHE; PIQUED BUFFALO WIFE.

offerings The primitive Indians of the Amazon and of the Chaco make occasional offerings of food, drinks, or goods to the spirits. Spirits are often invited to partake of a meal or of beer during a feast. Before eating flesh and game, the Bororo reserved a few morsels for the supernaturals. The Carib makes an offering to the spirit whenever he cuts a tree or opens a clearing. The Ona of Tierra del Fuego cast away firebrands or morsels of meat as presents to the Supreme Being.

The Incas gave to the gods food, magic substances, clothes, and jewels. Immense treasures in the form of gold figures and precious stones were buried or were thrown into the lakes by the ancient Chibcha to propitiate their gods. See CHHALLA. [AM]

Og In the Bible and biblical legend, a giant who survived the Flood, lived 500 years, and was slain by Moses. Og was half as wide as he was high, and he was so tall that the waters of the Flood reached only to his ankles. Others say however that he sat on a rung of one of the Ark's ladders, or that he perched on the roof, and that Noah fed him through a hole in the side of the Ark when the giant promised to be his slave. Og's daily meal was a thousand oxen and a thousand measures of liquids.

Og later became enamored of Sarah, Abraham's beautiful wife. So when the kings made Lot captive, Og told Abraham, hoping the patriarch would be killed trying to rescue his nephew and that afterwards he would be able to win Sarah's affections. But Abraham conquered the kings and Og's plan failed. He was rewarded with long life for bearing the news (some say the archangel Michael was the news carrier) but for his evil motive he was doomed to be slain by a descendant of Abraham. Og is said to have been Eliezer, Abraham's steward. One day when Abraham scolded the giant, a tooth fell out of Og's mouth, from which tooth Abraham made the bed he always after slept in.

When Moses marched against the Amorite city of Edrei, Og, who was king there, sat atop the wall. Moses and the Israelite army camped near the city and Og, seeing the extent of the Israelite camp, picked up a mountain of the same area, intending to crush the army. However, God caused ants or locusts to eat through the mountain and it fell about Og's shoulders. When the giant tried to throw off his blinding burden, his teeth grew out of his mouth and into the mountain, holding it fixed in place. Moses, 10 ells tall, took a 10 ell ax, leaped 10 ells into the air, and hewed at Og's ankle so that the giant died.

A rabbinical legend says that a gravedigger, who later was a famous rabbi, once chased a stag for three miles into a cave. Later, this cave proved to be the hollow of one of Og's thigh bones.

ogan A piece of iron, often a hoe blade, beaten with a spike as a ground rhythm with rattles in Haitian vodun dance accompaniment. The iron is given supernatural power to call the loa and to appease the beings of the otherworld by a ceremony of baptism drawn from Catholic ritual. Dancers in a state of possession pour offerings of water before the ogan, making the sign of the cross. The use of similar pieces of iron to beat a steady rhythm under the more elaborate drum rhythms is observed in Africa, and the word ogan is believed to be related to Yoruba *éganran*, which has the same meaning.

Ogier the Dane or **Holger Danske** A legendary hero of Denmark, prominent in Danish ballad, song, and story; one of the opponents of Dietrich von Bern in the 5th century. He is a king in the mountain: he is said to be asleep under the Kronenberg with his beard grown to fabulous length right through the table. He will rise and save Denmark in her need. Ogier, Otgarius, or Holger Danske resisted Charlemagne for seven years at Castelfort but submitted *circa* 773. The poem about Ogier in the Carolingian cycle has taken somewhat more from folklore than other novels in the series. [RDJ]

Ogma One of the Tuatha Dé Danann of Old Irish mythology; a culture god of poetry, speech, and eloquence; eponymous inventor of the ancient ogam writing. Ogam was a system of notches (vowels) and lines (consonants), representing the early Goidelic alphabet, cut into the edges of rough stone tombs and monuments. The arrangements represented 5 vowels and 15 consonants. Ogma is probably the ancient Gaulish Ogmios mentioned by Lucian as having a smiling face and the gift of eloquence, and described as drawing crowds to him by chains connecting their ears to his tongue. Except for Epona, Ogmios is the only native Celtic deity mentioned by name by the Romans. He is likened to the Roman Mercury by MacCulloch. See BATTLE OF MAG TURED; BRES; DAGDA.

ogre, ogress A giant or hideous monster of folklore and märchen, often given to eating human flesh, and characterized by extreme stupidity and gullibility. He is easily frightened, as in the story of the ogre who was afraid of a rustling noise (K2345; Type 1143). His stupidity is shown in stories of partnership between Man and Ogre (Type 1030); in one of these the ogre, in the dividing of crops chooses the tops of root crops, and of other crops, the roots (K171.1). The stupid ogre is spread throughout the world. Typical of stories of the ogre's timidity is the Indonesian tale in which an ogre is made to believe that a very small hero is very large; he runs away (K1711). Typical of the stupidity stories is that about the ogre who tries to drink the lake dry in order to get at a beautiful woman reflected therein (J1791.6.2; Type 1141). In contests with man, the ogre is always worsted, as in contests in climbing, jumping, squeezing, throwing, and in tests of endurance.

The word *ogre* is said to have been first used by Perrault in his *Contes* (1697), though the ogre himself, according to Gaston Paris, is a descendant of the Indian *rakshasas*. The word may be from the Italian dialectical *ogro* for *orgo* or *orco*, monster, demon, in turn from the Latin *Orcus*, god of Hades. Conjecture has found in the word a similarity to the ethnic *ogōr*, Hungarian; but no substantiation has been found.

The whole of Chapter G in Stith Thompson's *Motif-Index of Folk-Literature* is devoted to ogres and their habits. The different kinds include cannibal ogres, giants, ogres in animal form, the witch types of ogre, male or female, in both animal and human form, the corpse-eating ghoul types, and various monster ogres.

The Devil plays the ogre's role through much of medieval European folktale. The Greeks had their Scylla and Charybdis; the Greeks and North American Indians both had their cliff-ogres (G321). See CLIFF-OGRE. The Hottentots have their Thrower-Down (G321.1). See HAITSI-AIBAB. The North American Crow Indians, also the Hidatsa and Gros Ventre, frighten their children with the Pot-Tilter (G331), an old woman with a boiling pot which sucks in whomever it is tilted toward. The sucking monster who just sucks in his victims (G332) is common to North American Indian folktale of the Plateau and North Pacific areas, the Plains, the Woodlands, and the Southwest.

The ogre is a giant in Sweden, Scotland, Ireland, and in certain parts of France; he is a troll in Norway, a dragon in Greece, a serpent with seven heads in Lithuania, Hungary, and Russia. Most cultures have their own traditional ogres. The general concept of ogres is discussed by P. Saintyves in his *Contes de Perrault* (Paris, 1923) with remarks on märchen containing cannibal episodes, and by J. A. MacCulloch in *The Childhood of Fiction* (New York, 1905) who points to the typical forms of cannibalism in earlier times when such practices were common and possibly connected with ritual. [GPS]

For North American Indian tales involving ogres and ogresses see AWL-ELBOWED WITCHES; BIG OWL; BLACK TAMANOUS; CANNIBALS; MONSTERS; MONSTER-SLAYER; OLD WOMAN'S GRANDSON; VAGINA DENTATA.

Ogun The Yoruban deity of iron, and by derivation, as as master of weapons, of war: the equivalent of the Dahomean Gu and an important retention among all Afroamerican cults which have continued the worship of African deities of Yoruban or Dahomean derivation. [MJH]

ʔohgíwe The Feast for the Dead, managed and danced by Iroquois Indian women. The ancestral spirits are believed to continue circulating among the living and to be present at the feast, though visible only to a few especially empowered individuals. There are many tales of Indians who encountered spirits or danced with one during the ʔohgíwe. An offended spirit may cause sickness, or loss of sleep and appetite and must be placated by dance and offerings of tobacco and food. Thus the ʔohgíwe may be a healing ceremony at the home of the patient or in the longhouse, with a renewal at Midwinter; or it may be a communal ceremony held in the longhouse in the spring and in the fall.

The body of the ceremony consists of two long dances, ʔohgíwe and *ganadgitgáhq*, separated by an interlude, the *qdasát'da*. 1) the ʔohgíwe chants are intoned by the male song leader, repeated by his two male assistants, and again twice through by the two women leaders. These two matrons guide the society members and later on additional volunteers, in a slow counterclockwise procession. Sometimes they break the monotonous dragging step with small stamps, kicks, pivots, and elbow-waftings. Halfway of the songs the drum-beat changes. Finally the tempo speeds up and a brief *eskänye* terminates this phase of the ritual.

2) During the cloth distribution (*qdasát'da*) the two chief matrons face the male singers and receive pieces of cloth from the female sponsor. They wave them back and forth in rhythm and distribute them to all officials,

singers, and dancers. These gifts from participants may be a vestige of ancient sacrifice.

3) Carry-out-the-Kettle (*ganadgitgáhǫ*) focuses around the drum, which is carried out at the finish. In the middle of the room the drummer and four singers rotate slowly against the sun. Other women join and then men, all hooking arms and jumping sidewards with a lively hop-kick, joking and laughing.

4) After the feast an epilog of social dances resembles the food-spirit sequence.

5) At Onondaga longhouse a dawn procession takes place, the elevation of the cakes (*ǫdenǫhso'dahkwa*), which may once have symbolized sacrificial communion and still is attended by bad-luck beliefs and omens. One group raises up special cakes for the dead, another will try to snatch them in a scrimmage.

In addition to the beliefs still connected with the ʔohgíwe, much of the ancient significance has been submerged, and the snake origin myth has lost functional expression. A consistent duality couples the functionaries and the structural parts of the ritual. The dance steps tie up with other medicine rites, but also with the women's *eskänye* and the food-spirit dances, as the *oneǫnt'oenǫ*. These items emphasize the concept of fertility inherent in the important role played by women. The women, as mothers and agriculturists, are in a position to evoke life out of death, out of the soil where all creatures lie buried. By pleasing the spirits of the departed they appeal to their chthonic powers. [GPK]

ohorodnik Literally, gardener: a Ukrainian social dance for four groups of three, forming a set of twelve. Usually a man stands between two women, but a woman can be the center. In contrast with the more spectacular Ukrainian dances as *kolomaika*, the ohorodnik carries the dancers through two simple formations with a running step: 1) The sides of the square approach and recede in syncopation, that is, set one and three forward while two and four go back—producing a fluid and pleasing effect; 2) The right hand woman, and then the left hand woman, hooks elbows with the central man and turns him once around in female aggressiveness unusual in folk dancing. The dance is popular at weddings, especially among the Ukrainians of Rhode Island. There is no pantomimic enactment of the title. [GPK]

Oisín In Old Irish legend, the son of Fionn Mac-Cumail and Sadb, in her deer form: discovered as an infant in the forest by Fionn's dog Bran and brought home safe to Fionn, who knew him at once for his own child. See BRAN.

Oisín is frequently referred to as a poet of Fianna; there are a number of poems in the *Book of Leinster* ascribed to him, but he was not the chief poet among them. He was the father of Oscar, who was killed at the Battle of Gabra, when the Fianna themselves were overcome. After that battle there was no more peace or pleasure for Oisín, or Fionn, or Caoilte (nephew of Fionn, companion of Oisín) again in this world. Oisín is Macpherson's Ossian.

One day soon after the Battle of Gabra came a woman riding over the sea from the west on a fast white horse. Niam was her name; she had given her love to Oisín, she said, and begged him to come with her to Tir na n'Og, the Land of Youth, that marvelous Otherworld of the Celts, a country of plenty, of honey and wine, without old age, or wasting away, or death. Oisín sorrowed to leave Fionn, yet joyfully consented to go with Niam. He got up on the horse and the two disappeared westward facing out to sea. Caoilte, it is said, went into a hill of the *side* to be healed of his wounds received in battle, and no one ever saw him come out. A different story tells that he turned south and came to where Patrick was teaching the doctrines of Christianity, and that Caoilte told Patrick all the legends of the Fianna, which were written down by Brogan, Patrick's scribe.

Years later, 100 years or 1000 years, no matter, Oisín came back to Ireland on the wonderful white horse, seeking his old companion Caoilte. In Tir na n'Og he "did not feel the time passing"; years seemed days; he did not know that ages had gone by. Niam could not bear to see him go, knowing the fate of mortals who return to this world from that immortal land. She warned Oisín not to get down from the horse, or he would never come back to Tir na n'Og. Oisín promised, of course, but one day he recognized the great stone trough of the Fianna and got down from the horse (or he attempted to help some men who were raising a huge stone and slipped). The minute he touched the earth, he was a withered old man, half blind and spent, and the horse rushed back to Tir na n'Og.

Oisín also finally came to where Patrick was. The stories differ as to whether Caoilte too was there. The longest story of the Finn cycle is *Acallam na Senóreċ*, the *Colloquy of the Ancients* or *Colloquy of the Old Men*. Oisín among the monks complained of the meager food in contrast to the Fenian feasts; he complained of the sound of the bells and the singing of thin hymns in contrast to the music of the kings. But most of all he was horrified at the ethics of Christianity which could send a man like Fionn to hell. Fionn was in hell, Patrick told Oisín, "because he gave no heed to God." Oisín would answer, "The story is pitiful, Fionn to be under locks, . . . a heart without envy, without hatred. . . . It is an injustice, God to be unwilling to give food and riches; Fionn never refused strong or poor." Patrick strove with Oisín to turn him to the Christian God, for his end was nearing. But Oisín did not want to go to heaven without his dog, without Fionn, without Oscar, or Caoilte. Patrick assured Oisín of the joys of heaven in contrast to Fionn's plight in hell "on the flagstone of pain," and begged him to choose God. But Oisín could only reiterate, "If God were in bonds, Fionn would fight for him! Fionn left no one in pain or in danger without freeing him." The story ends with Oisín still unreconciled.

okoztah-pol Literally, dance of the head: a vestige of pagan sacrifice, enacted by the Maya of Quintana Roo at Catholic fiestas, particularly the Fiesta of the Patron Crosses in late April. At dawn of the second day a pig is sacrificed, cooked, and eaten; then its head is decorated and placed on the altar. In the public part of the church early the next day a dance burlesques the selling of a pig. Nine young women circle the table to the Spanish tune of *La Carbonerita*, each with a bowl of pinole and honey and an agave leaf for spoon. A man with a gourd rattle pretends to lead the pig by a cord attached to the head, and to offer it for sale. During the mock bartering that follows, the girls circle nine times against the sun and nine times sunwise, count being kept by cigarettes laid on the table. The pig-impersonator, bearing the head, pretends to escape and is recaptured, and finally "sold" to the organizer of the fiesta for a hundred cigarettes. The head is placed on the table and the pinole served to the guests. [GPK]

Old Dan Tucker An American square-dance and play-party song, a favorite of fiddlers and banjo pickers: composed by Dan Emmett (who wrote *Dixie*) and widely sung in minstrel shows. Farmers of New York state picked it up in 1844, set words of protest against their landowners to its tune, and sang it in a demonstration during which they paraded in Indian dress. The Dan Tucker words deal with a rough old character who combed his hair with a wagon wheel and died of a toothache in his heel.

old (or **faithful**) **dog** A folktale motif (B842; Type 101) in which a faithful old dog is regarded as having outlived his usefulness and is to be killed. The dog confides his predicament to the wolf; the wolf plans to save the dog's life by attacking the farmer's child and allowing the dog to rescue it. The plan succeeds and the old dog is not only spared but honored. Later the wolf expects the dog to allow him to take off some of the farmer's sheep, but the old dog refuses, again proving his fidelity to his master (K231.1.3). This is the substance of the story *Old Sultan* (Grimm #48) which continues with the episode of the old dog's outwitting the wolf (who tried to get even) with the aid of a three-legged cat.

An equally famous faithful dog occurs in the Gelert story (B331.2) in which a certain Welsh chieftain, Llewellyn, on returning home was joyfully met and welcomed as usual by his great hound Gelert. Llewellyn noticed that the dog's mouth was bloody and on entering the room he saw that his child's cradle was overturned. Assuming that the dog had killed the child, Llewellyn plunged his sword through Gelert's heart, only to discover the body of a slain wolf in the room and the child safe and sound under the overturned cradle. The old Welsh proverb *to repent as deeply as the man who killed his hound* refers to this story, the eponymous legend of Bethgelert in Caernarvonshire, north Wales.

This is not a strictly Welsh local legend, however, but turns up as local legend in several places in Europe, the most ancient probably being the Greek story (eponymous legend of Ophiteia) in which the returning father kills a huge snake which he finds coiled around the urn in which he had hidden his child. Later he sees that the snake has saved the child from a wolf.

This ancient Eurasian tale occurs in many collections (e.g. *Panchatantra*, *Kathā Sarit Sāgara*, *Gesta Romanorum*, etc.). "The Story of the Brāhman and the Mongoose" in the *Panchatantra* (see *Ocean of Story* v: 138) is the same story: In the Brāhman's absence his pet mongoose kills a huge snake which approaches the Brāhman's child, runs to meet the Brāhman as he returns home; the Brāhman seeing the mongoose spattered with blood assumes it has killed his child and kills the mongoose with a stone. On entering the house he sees the child safe, the dead snake, and is filled with remorse. K. Campbell in *Seven Sages of Rome*, Boston, 1907, cites

31 analogs of this story. For full discussion of its antiquity and spread, see W. A. Clouston, *Popular Tales and Fictions* ii: 167 ff.

Old John A mythical tramp printer of early American composing rooms. Every printer was well acquainted with someone who had seen and talked with him. Whenever Old John quit a job he inevitably chose the moment when he was distributing type at the news case. With one sweep of Old John's left hand the types would fall simultaneously into place. Old John and all tramp printers were said to go to a compositors' heaven: a wonderful shining, clean printing office with new presses and all new types. See JOHN.

Old Jokey Song One of the American titles of *The Farmer's Curst Wife* (Child #278): a ballad relating the story of a shrewish wife who was carried off by the Devil but proved so troublesome that she terrorized the demons of hell and was finally brought back. This tale is old and widespread in both Europe and Asia, appearing in the *Panchatantra*, in Russian folklore, and all over western Europe. The ballad is also known as *The Devil and the Farmer's Wife*.

Old Man or **Old One** The term applied to the creator-culture-hero by several American Indian tribes; also, the term generally used by a wife, among American Indians, in-direct address or in reference to her husband. The reciprocal, husband speaking, is "my old woman" (wife). In Blackfoot mythology Old Man and Old Woman were the original inhabitants of the world; the Crow Indians, neighbors of the Blackfoot in the northern Plains, in their cosmogonic myths, credit Old Man with teaching human beings the arts of life. Among the Modoc Old Man is also the culture hero, and the Aleut of Alaska credit a character referred to as Old Man with making people by throwing stones over his shoulder. In several Plateau tribes Old One or Chief also figures as creator of the earth; he also made the Indians from balls of mud. [EWV]

Old Man Coyote A popular term often used by American Indians when narrating myths in English about the trickster, Coyote; specifically, the Crow Indian trickster, who is always referred to in the mythology as Old Man, or Old Man Coyote, and never simply called Coyote, as among other tribes. Opinion among the Crow differs on whether Old Man Coyote and Sun are identical beings in Crow mythology, but Lowie accepts the majority of Crow opinion, confirmed in the mythology, that Sun is distinct from Old Man Coyote. The latter, as he exists in Crow mythology, is a typical exemplar of the North American trickster. See Robert H. Lowie, *The Crow Indians*, New York, 1935, pp. 130 ff. See MOTHER; TRICKSTER. [EWV]

Old Man of the Mountain The leader of the Assassins. The crusaders in Syria often came into contact with this sect of murderous fanatics, and the Old Man of the Mountain became a symbol of slaughter and power, giving orders to slay here or there, often without giving the slayer any information other than the name of his victim. These orders were carried out by his subordinates without question, for they believed the killing of their victims to be meritorious deeds, and believed also that to die on such an errand would bring them to paradise. Rāshid ad-Dīn Sinān, the greatest of the Old

Men of the Mountain, claimed to be an incarnation of Allah. He had many supporters to this claim, but others said he could not be the deity because he was lame. The crusaders are said to have marched to a tune called *The Old Man of the Mountain,* but this was not the tune of the same name popular in the 20th century.

Old Man of the Sea In the fifth voyage of Sindbad in the *Arabian Nights,* a horrible old man who asks to ride on Sindbad's shoulders; an evil jinni in man's shape, who cannot be dismounted. He rides Sindbad unmercifully until the sailor is near to complete exhaustion. Finally Sindbad smashes his head in. The Old Man of the Sea resembles to some extent the hag who rides men at night, the nightmare or incubus who exhausts them sometimes further and further until they die of physical debility. See BURR-WOMAN.

Old Smoky One of the most popular of American mountain lonesome tunes, or love songs, known in many variants and compounded of elements of many other songs—*The Waggoner's Lad,* a song of the Conestoga wagon era, *Courting Too Slow, Loving Nancy, The Forsaken Girl, The Inconstant Lover.* Its most common tune is the same as that of *The Little Mohee.* "On top of Old Smoky," it says, "All covered in snow / I lost my true lover / By (from) courting too slow." Some of the stanzas from *The Waggoner's Lad* name the girl Polly and the lad Johnnie. "Go put up your horses," she says, "and feed them some hay / Come sit down beside me / Just as long as you stay." But the wagons must move and the lover has other girls along the line. "My horses ain't hungry / They won't eat your hay / So goodbye, my darling / I'll feed on the way." Many of the often-recurring lines of the lonesome tunes and other ballads and songs appear in one version or another of this song: the grave "on the mountain so high"; the turtle dove; the warning not to "pin your affection on a green-growing tree"; the generalizations on false-hearted lovers who will "hug you and kiss you and tell you more lies / Than the cross-ties on the railroad and the stars in the skies." In at least one version, however, the romance ends happily, the girl leaving her Mama and going off in the wagon with the lad. See LOVE SONGS.

Old Testament The older and larger of the two major divisions of the Bible, containing the Pentateuch—the five books of Hebrew law and history through Moses—; such historical books as *Samuel, Kings,* and *Judges;* the writings of the prophets; several poetical and philosophical works, like *Job, The Song of Songs,* and *Ecclesiastes;* the story of *Ruth;* the book of *Psalms,* and the book of *Proverbs.* The Old Testament, the basic book of Judaism and Christianity, and containing much of the common tradition later used by Mohammed in the Koran, is now thought to comprise four principal writings and editings, the sequence presumably as follows. The J version, so called because it uses the name Jahweh for God, dating from the 9th century B.C. and compiled in the Southern Kingdom, and the E version, using Elohim for the deity, from the Northern Kingdom in the 8th century, deal with much the same period of history, from the very beginnings of the world to the end of the reign of King Saul, and with the same sort of folkloric and legendary material. These were combined in the 7th century, at about the time that the D author (Deuteronomic code) wrote. In the 6th century, the P or Priestly version or editing of much of this material was written, and in the century following the four versions (or three: JE, D, P) were combined and canonized. It was not until about 100 A.D. however that a final acceptance or rejection of existing materials established the Old Testament canon as we know it today.

The material in the Old Testament is thus of varying antiquity. Moses is traditionally credited with writing the first five books, but modern scholarship has been able to point out no single passage that can definitely be ascribed to him. The age of the writings varies from the book of *Daniel* (about 165 B.C.) and the final editing of the *Psalms* (about 100 B.C.) to the "Song of Lamech" in *Genesis* and the "Song of Deborah" in *Judges* (each at least 1000 years before). The Old Testament contains stories of folk heroes (David the giant-slayer, Joseph the clever youngest son), cosmographic tales (compare the two tellings of the story of the Creation in *Genesis* i and ii, the latter attributed to J), etiological tales (*Genesis* ix: the rainbow; *Genesis* xi: the languages of mankind), proverbs, riddles, laws; in fact it is a storehouse of the lore of an ancient people unequaled elsewhere in its literary and inspirational power. Merely to mention such well-known type tales as the stories of Samson, of Jephthah, of Joshua and the walls of Jericho, of Abraham and Isaac, of David and Bathsheba, is to indicate only partly the scope of the folkloristic material. To this Scriptural writing must be added the great mass of apocryphal literature, of commentary, of rabbinical legend. And see Sir James G. Frazer's *Folk-Lore in the Old Testament* (3 vols., 1918) for an indicative group of "studies in comparative religion, legend and law."

old woman adviser A helpful character in many North American Indian test and hero tales (N825). An unnamed woman who usually is referred to as "grandmother" advises the hero how to kill monsters, escape from dangerous situations, what path to take, how to overcome obstacles on his way, etc. Often the woman is not to be distinguished from animal advisers, as in the Eastern Woodlands tale of Mudjikiwis, where the old woman advisers are a moose and other animals who assume the form either of old, or in one case, young women. [EWV]

Old Woman Bat See BAT; BATS.

Old Woman's Grandchild (*Grandson*) Title and hero of a popular hero tale of the Plains Indians of North America. Old Woman's Grandchild, son of the Sun, or of Morning Star, by an Indian woman, leaves his father's celestial home with his mother; the mother is killed, but the boy reaches earth and is taken in charge by an old woman. He grows to manhood quickly, kills various monsters, beginning with the old woman's dragon husband, despite his "grandmother's" admonitions, and is watched over by the Sun, his father. In the end Old Woman's Grandchild turns into the North or Morning Star, and the Old Woman, his grandmother, into the Moon. In the mythologies of several Plains tribes the exploits told of Old Woman's Grandchild are also accredited to two twin heroes, Lodge-Boy and Thrown-Away, and there is much confusion between the two myths. For the Crow Indian version of this tale see Robert H. Lowie, *The Crow Indians* (New York, 1935), pp. 134–157. [EWV]

olive An evergreen tree (genus *Olea*) with leathery leaves, a hard, yellow wood, and an oily fruit, which has been grown in the Mediterranean region since the Neolithic Age and has remained since the earliest days of Minoan Crete one of the chief staples of trade and husbandry. The tree was sacred to Athena and Apollo. Both Poseidon and Athena wished to possess Attica, so they took their dispute to Zeus (or other judges, divine or human) for arbitration. The region was to be awarded to the one who gave the greatest boon. Poseidon smote the earth with his trident and a salt spring came forth, but Athena produced the olive tree, symbol of peace, fruitfulness, and security, and won. Irene, goddess of peace (Pax of the Romans), in Hesiod the daughter of Zeus and Themis and one of the Horæ, was worshipped in Athens and Rome. She was young and usually depicted with a cornucopia in one hand and an olive branch or a caduceus in the other.

Originally the branches for the Olympic crown were from the sacred wild olive which grew at the west end of the Temple of Zeus; they were cut with a golden sickle by a pure boy whose parents were both alive. Athenian brides either wore an olive crown or carried a branch for fruitfulness, and an olive crown was the highest distinction for those who had served the Athenian state. In Rome the olive crown was worn by conquerors; on Numa's medals the king holding an olive branch signified that he had had a peaceful reign. In China a wreath of fragrant olive was the reward of literary merit. An olive branch on the chimney piece in Venice warded off lightning; in Italy a branch over the door keeps out witches and wizards. Before the use of coffins, the dead were frequently laid on a bed of olive leaves in the grave and covered with them. In early representations of the Annunciation the Angel of the Lord is pictured holding an olive branch, which was later supplanted by the more familiar lily. The dove returning to Noah's ark with an olive leaf (*Gen.* viii, 11) showed him that the waters had abated on the land. In the *Psalms* (cxxviii, 3) a man's children are likened to olive plants around his table. In Spain the olive insured the fidelity of a husband (D1355.8) and the magic olive branch made the woman master in the house (D1359.1.1.). Some believe fruitfulness in the olive trees was increased if they were tended by young and innocent children; elsewhere an olive gatherer had to be faithful to his wife or there would be a poor crop the next year. It is said that the quality of the olive crop may be predicted by the colors in the rainbow. In Bilda, Algeria, there was an ancient olive tree into which pilgrims drove a nail to cure their ailments. In Rome they said wine within and oil without was the secret of health and happiness. [JWH]

Olrik, Axel (1864–1917) Danish folklorist, specializing in Norse mythology and epic poetry. Olrik was born at Copenhagen and was professor of folklore there from 1913. He has a long list of writings on Scandinavian history, mythology, folklore, ballads, songs, and on other related topics. He was leader in the organization of the Dansk Folkemindesamling in 1904. With Grundtvig and other Danish scholars, his work in tracing the archetype of Danish ballads showed scholarly insight. In the comprehensive classification of folklore envisioned by Kaarle Krohn and prepared under the direction of

Antti Aarne, he was an assistant. The work appeared in 1910 under the title *Verzeichnis der Märchentypen* (revised and expanded by Stith Thompson as *Types of the Folk-Tale*, 1928).

Of great interest are Olrik's "epic laws" expounded in his *Folkelige Afhandlinger* ("Folkedigtningens Episke Love"), published at Copenhagen in 1919. In studying story narrative, Olrik found certain laws governing style and content whether myth, ballad, tale, or local legend, and, further, these laws obtained from whatever quarter the material studied happened to come. The chief value of these laws is that they may direct "attention to qualities that differentiate all kinds of oral tales from the literary tale" (Stith Thompson, *The Folktale*, New York, 1946, p. 457).

Some of Olrik's works have been published in this country, namely, *A Book of Danish Ballads* (New York, 1939), of which the Introduction is by Olrik and the translation by E. M. Smith-Dampier (*Danske-folkeviser*, I, 1899; II, 1909); *The Heroic Legends of Denmark* (New York, 1918), a translation from the Danish, revised in collaboration with Olrik and translated by Lee M. Hollander; *Viking Civilization* (New York, 1930); *Personal Impressions of Moltke Moe* (*FFC* 17, 1915), which gives interesting sidelights on this scholar who collaborated with Asbjörnsen in production of the work, *Danske Folkeeventyr* (Christiania, 1842), but who was a folklorist in his own right. Olrik was interested in various phases of individual folktales. One of his studies of importance, on Little Red Riding Hood and related tales, is in *Folkelige Afhandlinger*, I (1919), pp. 140 ff.

Olympians The gods of ancient Greece who, under Zeus, lived atop Mt. Olympus. In the mythological succession of Uranus, Cronus, and Zeus, most students see an echoing of the successive invasions of Greece by outlanders and the replacing of the gods by the gods of the newcomers. The Olympians include the children of Cronus and the divine children of Zeus. Compare TITANS.

Olympus The name of several mountains in Greece and Asia Minor; especially, the peak, slightly less than 10,000 feet in height, in Thessaly near the Macedonian border, reputed to be the home of the gods. Whether the gods live on Olympus or in heaven is often confused by ancient Greek writers, but perhaps the peak of Olympus, snow-crowned and above the clouds, was thought to be in heaven. The giants warring against the gods piled Ossa on Olympus and Pelion on Ossa to reach the heavens; this has been taken to mean that Ossa and Pelion were placed on the lower slopes of Olympus to reach the Olympian heights. On the peak of Olympus Zeus and other gods had their palaces and here too Zeus called the councils of the gods.

om Besides its role as first and last words of the venerated lotus-jewel mantra *Om maṇi padme Hūṃ*, the Sanskrit word *om* (pronounced with long ō and a hum or nasal sound like French *bon*) has had five general meanings and uses.

In the first place, it is the universal yea-say *par excellence*, the syllable of assent and the hum of approval. It is more or less cognate with the *amen* (so be it) of agreement uttered by ancient Hebrews and its echoed ejaculation by modern evangelistic Christian sects, with the "um-hum," "mm," or "m-hum" still used in conversation almost everywhere in the English world more often than yes, and is related to the ritualistic "so mote it be" of the Rosicrucians and Freemasons. It apparently vaguely connotes the resolute affirmation of existence in the to-be verb *I am* (Eng.), *sum* (Lat.), *eimi* (Gr.), *eom* (Old Eng.), *em* (Arm.), and *asmi* (Skt.).

Again and often it is the syllable of emphasis, either introducing or ending an assertion, or both as in the famous mantra quoted above. It has almost the significance of "Notice!" or "Listen!" particularly in the form of *amen* prefacing the important sayings of Jesus in the synoptic gospels where it is translated usually "Verily," and in the fourth gospel where it is always double. The word amen occurs 30 times in the Old Testament, where it is transliterated 27 times, translated once as "so be it," and twice as "truth." In the New Testament it is found 150 times, is rendered "verily" 100 times, and transliterated 50. Where it occurs at the end of a sentence or is antiphonal, both in the Old and New Testaments, it usually combines these two meanings of assent and emphasis.

The third use of the word is as a symbol of deity. In India the liturgical use of the word *om* led to its increasing veneration until the ejaculation became the noun. The teaching of the sacredness of the symbol can be progressively traced in the *Upanishads* and it early became practically synonymous with *Brahman* (the undefinable and unknowable origin and source of all). Later, the *om* was spelled *aum,* and it was taught that it represented the triple nature of the cosmos, and that the *a, u,* and *m* respectively represented the Absolute, the Relative, and their mutual relation. One *Upanishad* of 500 B.C. asserts that the entire creation was derived from the Om. In very similar fashion, the equivalent word amen becomes one of or part of the names of both God and Christ. In *Isaiah* lxv, 16, it is translated twice "God of truth," in violation of the usual translation procedure. In *Revelation* iii, 14, Christ is referred to as "the Amen, the faithful and true witness," and there is a related usage in 2 *Cor.* i, 20.

The fourth meaning of om is by itself as a mantra of mystic adoration, as one might repeat the word God in rapt worship. If a devout Hindu is unable to recite the Veda, due to circumstances, he may properly substitute the meditation on the word om, "which is the root of the tree of the Veda and its essence."

It is easy to see that such use of the word would lead to the fifth practice, the magic charm. We find that the repetition of om is guaranteed, if properly performed, to protect the worshipper from danger and even purify a murderer. "Its utterance with understanding of its significance secures the accomplishment of every wish." The *Kauśika Sūtra,* a book of Hindu magic, requires the recitation of om at the time of the preparation of holy water. The repetition of om "the oldest son of Brahmā" before and after sacrifice is supposed to counteract any errors in the procedure, and "Om recited 1,000 times grants all wishes." There is a somewhat similar belief in the potency of the "Amen" at the end of Christian prayers, where its omission causes vague uneasiness, but it is often disregarded at the end of hymns.   CHARLES FRANCIS POTTER

omele drums Three medium-sized drums of a battery of eight used in rites of the Shango cult of Trinidad Negroes. The drums are of European type and played with sticks. The two large drums, named for Ogun (St. Michael in his Catholic identity) and Shango (John the Baptist), call upon the gods. Devotees in a state of possession address the drums speaking the rhythms of the different gods, each selecting one for special homage. Of the three small drums, one is named for Ogun and the other two are Congo drums.

omen A phenomenon or incident regarded as a prophetic sign. Formal divination seeks out omens; the Roman augurs watched for the flight of birds to either hand as an indication of the will of the gods; tea-leaf readers descry omens in the chance configuration of the leaves in the teacup; the petals on the daisy tell the inquirer whether he is loved or not. Chance omens may be even more powerful, for often their meaning is hidden and does not fall into a systematic method of interpretation. But some chance omens are generally recognized; meteors, comets, eclipses, and the like are extremely ominous; meeting an old woman as one sets out on a journey is very unlucky; breaking a mirror, putting a shirt on backwards, tripping as one enters a house, having a bat fly in the window are all indications of ill fortune. Omens may occur at any time, at any place, and be of any sort of occurrence. The creaking of the boards in a house has its message for some people. The banshee, fetch, jack-o'-lantern are often specific death omens.

☞ Omens, or signs foretelling future events or revealing events occurring at a distance, are multitudinous among North American Indians; many are undoubtedly of native origin, many others may represent borrowings from European beliefs. To start out on a trip and meet a Coyote is a bad omen among the Tübatulabal of east-central California; one should return home and start the trip again. Buzzing in the ear, itching palms, sudden sneezing are signs persons are talking about one, thinking of one, inviting someone to go somewhere and so forth in nearly all tribes. Bird or animal calls are usually considered bad omens, especially when such are heard after dark or before dawn; they may be a sign of war, death, rain, or of an evil shaman sending out his spirit helper. Falling stars are also interpreted as omens. [EWV]

omigiwen Literally, in Chippewa, presentation: an offering from one tribe to another, as a token of friendship and peace. One of the most important Chippewa-Menominee ceremonies is the *dewe'igun omigiwen* or drum presentation. To the American Indian the drum is an object of reverence and a mediator between man and the spirit land. The great drum (*o'gima dewe'igun*) is painted with symbolic designs and hung on four feather-ornamented hooks. Great reverence is also shown toward the second or warrior's drum (*ogi'tcida dewe'igun*) and toward two calumets.

The "drum religion" concerns the general welfare of the tribe, as well as peace and kindliness toward all in need. When the owner of a drum wants to present it to the chief of another tribe, elaborate procedures take place on both reservations. Four days are devoted to dancing before departure, four days to the drum presentation, and four to continued dancing. The ceremony opens with lighting and smoking of the calumets by leading drummer-singers and dancers, proceeds with speeches, and climaxes in the reception of the drum with four strokes with a special stick: three feints and a final stroke. Plentiful gifts are exchanged as offerings to the drum and between hosts and guests. The four days proceed as follows: 1) Reception of the visiting tribe; 2) Presentation of the chief drum; 3) Presentation of the warrior drum; 4) Dancing and feast.

The dancing itself is individualistic, except for the consecration features. The dancers may remain stationary or move in a clockwise circle, with a double heel-bumping with alternate feet, or toe-taps forward and back. The body remains fairly erect. Participation is voluntary and open to all men present. Conduct is decorous at all times.

The ceremonial procedure and arrangement of conductors varies somewhat between tribes and reservations, but in each place these are observed strictly according to rule. Only men participate in the dancing, though women join in the singing and in a final squaw dance. The ceremonial number four governs all actions: the number of days' duration, the number of leading singers of each sex and leading dancers, the repeated calumet offerings during the day, with four puffs to the cardinal directions. The food consecration by the ceremonial leader proceeds around the kettle in the four directions, finally also with gestures to the zenith and nadir. Secondary ceremonials may be introduced—the Restoration of Mourners, allowing their participation in the dancing, and a Ceremony of Divorce. Each feature has its special songs.

It is also called dream dance because of its dream or vision features; it was received in a vision by a Sioux girl, with additional enrichment due to a vision of a Chippewa child, and from time to time during the ceremony dreams are related and accepted. The derivation of the drum dance from the ghost dance is open to question for the drum dance contains no trance or hypnosis, no calling upon the dead; neither does it progress in a sideward shuffle, with interlocked hands, but forward and singly. Relation to the grass and calumet dances of the Plains is more evident, though costume paraphernalia has deteriorated. In particular the two calumets, the give-away and consecrated feast (formerly of dog meat) is common to all. The Menominee claim reception of the dream dance from the Potawatami. A similar obsolete ceremony of the Iowa was attributed to Kickapoo provenience. It is evidently a fairly recent form of worship, with ancient roots. See CALUMET DANCE; GHOST DANCE; GRASS DANCE. [GPK]

Om-ma-ṇi The Sanskrit lotus-jewel mantra, a mystic formula used especially in Tibet and Japan. It is addressed to Padmapāṇi (Avalokita) and its utterance is believed to convey the reciter directly to paradise, ending the Buddhist cycle of rebirths. The full formula is *Om-ma-ṇi pad-me Hūṃ*. Saying the syllable *om* prevents rebirth among the gods, *ma* prevents rebirth among the Titans, *ni* among men, *pad* as a beast, *me* as a kind of Tantalus, and *Hūṃ* as an inhabitant of the underworld.

Even sight of the formula without articulation is believed effective; hence it is printed millions of times on long ribbons which are coiled and inserted in prayer-wheels. These are revolved all over Tibet, in the hands of the faithful or by the wind or by water power. The formula is also printed on flags and stones. The followers of Bon repeat it in reverse.

The expanded version of the formula, known widely in Japan among Buddhists, but to only a few Tibetan lāmas, is addressed to the first of the Dhyanibuddhas, Vairocana. See OM.

Omolu The Yoruban earth deity, son of Nana and Obaluwaye: retained in the African cults of Brazil and Cuba. [MJH]

Omphale In Greek legend, a Lydian queen who owned Hercules as a slave for a time. Hercules, seeking purification for his murder of Iphitus, came to Apollo's oracle to ask how the stain might be eradicated. Apollo would give no answer, so Hercules began to remove the oracular tripod. The god and the hero wrestled for its possession; Zeus at last threw a thunderbolt between them and stopped the fight. Apollo then ordered that Hercules be sold as a slave and that the price be given to Eurytus, the father of the slain Iphitus. Hermes sold Hercules to Omphale. While serving the queen, for one or three years, Hercules performed several of his customary deeds against oppression, and according to later legend many incongruous womanly tasks while Omphale donned the lion skin and carried his club. Omphale is said to have borne one or more sons to Hercules during the period he served under her.

omphalos The navel; the center of the world, located at the temple of Apollo at Delphi. Zeus let loose two eagles at the ends of the earth, and marked the spot where they met with a stone. Therefore, the omphalos, one of the typical navel or cone-shaped stones worshipped throughout the Mediterranean region, was guarded by two golden eagles at Delphi. Together with the pit and the tripod it was one of the great sacred objects of the Delphic oracle.

Om sondagsmorran A humorous round dance of the Faroe Islands, popularized on the Norwegian mainland, and also among Norwegian groups in North Dakota, Minnesota, and Wisconsin. The nonsensical text is a Hired Man's Complaint—*Om sondagsmorran er det kaffikoppen svart. Sjung falleri, hei fallerallera . . .* On Sunday mornings it's coffee without cream. Sing falleree . . . The dance steps have nothing to do with the text, except for their jollity. They resemble the *branle*, ("double" left, "simple" right, all facing left), except that the right foot steps toward the center. The three-count step makes an interesting rhythmic counterpattern against the duple musical beat. During the second part, as in *Per Spelmann*, partners face, hold hands, and hop on alternate feet. Then, as an absurd finale, each whispers in the partner's ear, claps hands, and pivots away. [GPK]

Onatah Literally, Corn: one of the three daughters (with Beans and Squash) collectively known as Deohako, of Seneca Indian mythology.

oneiromancy Divination from dreams: a world-wide and ancient practice. The dream may be explicit, for example a warning from a deceased ancestor that a contemplated action will be disastrous; or it may be symbolic, as the dream of Pharaoh, where seven fat and seven lean kine indicated to Joseph the diviner the coming of seven years of plenty and seven years of famine. Standards of interpretation of such symbols have existed, e.g. a snake dream as being one either of sex or of an enemy; included in this is the canon of psycho-analytic dream symbols.

oneont'oenǫ The Iroquois corn dance, dedicated to this member of the life-sustaining family of divine sisters (corn, beans, and squash). Women are identified with corn, and thus own the dance, though they do not monopolize nor even lead it. It is a single short dance, distinct from the three-day green corn festival. It is included in the food festivals and in social evenings and in "sings." It is related to the women's *eskänye* by concept but not by its step, which is a forward shuffling trot or stomp. Men start the circling, the two leaders shaking horn rattles and intoning resonant, sometimes antiphonal, songs. The women join in various ways, among the Cayuga at the end of the line, among the Seneca in alternation, among the Onondaga in double file, with the left arm hooked in the partner's right. The leader may wind the whole queue back and forth among the benches and stoves in a serpentine path. Thus not only the corn but the bean is symbolized by the clinging action of the women and again by the representation of the tortuous growing habits of the plant. [GPK]

ongon In Buriat religion, an image embodying a god and therefore possessing the power of the god: among the Altai called *kurmes,* among certain Turks, *tyus.* It is usually either a picture or a figure, usually human, made of feathers, cloth, fur, occasionally of wood. Famous shamans sometimes become ongons after death. Ongons are numerous: there are mountain ongons (usually devised of brocade or silk with bead eyes and owl feathers sewed to the head) kept in little niches in the yards of farmsteads; men's and women's ongons (women's ongons protect children), and these are fed respectively by the master or mistress of the house; ongons of the bear, ferret, ermine, wolf, porcupine, pig, etc.; ongons of disease (one to cure swellings, one for the itch, for influenza, etc.); ongons of the sun, moon, and of the smiths. There are also joking and dancing ongons invoked and personified by the shamans at merrymakings. Offerings are made to them (meat, wine, etc.), and animals are dedicated to them (see ADYKH). In the Ural mountains are found little bronze birds and small human figures with smaller human figures on the breasts. All ongons bear human depictions on the the breast, which are thought to represent the soul or inner power of the ongon.

Uusually an ongon serves only its possessor, upon whose death it is burned. The shamans make new ones, consecrate and install them in their new places. Some ongons, however, are very ancient. The Balagan Buriats possessed a very famous one named Borto, made in the form of a human head with hair and beard and rattles around the neck, and thought to embody an ancestor of Genghis Khan. (See *ERE* iii: 12.)

oni The demons or devils of Japanese folklore. [JLM]

onion Quite general is the saying that to dream of onions means good luck. Georgia Negroes say it is good luck to burn onion peels in the fire. A crop of thick-skinned onions is a sign of a severe winter.

In the British Isles sometimes young girls scratch the names of their various suitors on each of four onions, and put them in the dark to sprout. The first one to sprout bears the name of the one she will marry. An onion under the pillow on St. Thomas Eve is said to bring dreams of one's future spouse.

Negroes in some parts of the United States say that to carry a red onion in the left hand, or left pocket, wards off disease. This is a general European folk belief transferred to the New World. In South Carolina a necklace of small crushed onions is placed around the neck of a child with diphtheria to overpower the disease.

Countless folk remedies call for onions. The one for sores prescribes an onion, cooked for 35 minutes, to be rubbed on the sore and then thrown to the pigs. If this is done, the sore will heal. To cure earache, drop the juice of an onion that has been roasted in wood coals into the aching ear. The heart of a hot roasted onion slipped into the ear is even more effective. Onion sirup, prepared by boiling equal parts of sliced onion and sugar over the teakettle, and swallowed slowly a teaspoonful at a time, is good for colds, phlegm in the throat, etc. Hot onion poultices will get rid of fever, chest colds, and croup. These may be applied to the chest or tied to the soles of the feet. An onion, cut in half, rubbed on a wart, tied together again, and buried until it decays, is a remedy for warts. As the onion decays the wart disappears.

Polish peasants believe that birth will be facilitated if the woman in labor sits over a pail of boiled onions. Ibn al-Jamil, Jewish Egyptian 12th century physician, recommended onion juice rubbed on the penis as a contraceptive.

New England settlers brought with them from the Old World the belief that a string of onions hung over the door would absorb disease germs as they enter and thus save the inmates. These onions of course could never be eaten. Among the handful of Shinnecock Indians still living on Long Island an onion is taken into the sick room and left there to "draw the fever out." When it has done so it will have turned black. The bactericidal effects of onion vapors have recently (1937) been acknowledged. (See "Folktales and Herbal Lore Among Shinnecock Indians" in *JAFL* 58:120 n.17).

onnagata A female impersonator in the Japanese *kabuki* drama. Though originally a dance play by female performers, the kabuki is now enacted entirely by men. They dress even in daily life like women, and understand and present their roles with rare artistry, aided by expert make-up and sumptuous costumes. An element of romance is introduced into the plays in the person of the *ohimesama,* the daughter of a family of high position. This role originated in the *mahuron-mono,* or puppet play. The *ohimesama* is the beautiful heroine of a love story.

The *oiran,* or courtesan, is also a symbol of romance, stemming from the artistic culture of the Edo period. Her gorgeous array includes an ornamental headdress weighing at times 25 pounds. A famous *oiran* is Agemaki, playing opposite Sukeroku in the title role. [GPK]

ono pacakoti In Inca mythology, the great flood with which Viracocha, the creator, destroyed his first created race of giants. He saved only two to assist him in re-creating a new world and new race of people.

onyx A cryptocrystalline variety of quartz consisting of layers of different colors. A fabulous city of onyx occurs in Arabian folktale (F761.3). In Jewish lore onyx was used as an innocence test. Onyx is the gem of Aquarius, birthstone of August, and symbolic of conjugal love. In India, however, it is worn around the neck to cool the ardors of love. Some, however, call it a gem of Leo and say that it promotes discord among lovers. There is a demon imprisoned within the stone which awakes at night and causes terror and nightmares, but this may be counteracted by wearing the stone in conjunction with sard. In the 10th century, the Abbey of St. Albans had an onyx so large that a man could not grasp it in his hand. This stone was in high repute as an aid to birth. Onyx was applied to the bites of animals; worn around the neck it would stimulate the spleen, allay pain, and dispel terror and melancholy.

In the fabulous 12th century *Letters* of Prester John, which enumerate the marvels of India, his own palace is described as having a courtyard paved with onyx and set aside for judicial ordeal combats. It is paved with onyx so that the stone may augment the courage of the duelists. Onyx can be depended upon to reflect back to the source a glance from the evil eye.

opal An amorphous, variously colored, silica gem which presents a peculiar play of delicate colors; the emblem of hope and birthstone of October. In early times it was called *pederus* (from Latin *puer*, child) because "it was beautiful as a child and inspired the love of all." It was highly thought of as a gem until the 19th century when it came to be regarded as a gem of ill omen. This is probably due to Sir Walter Scott's novel, *Anne of Geierstein*, wherein that lady disappears when some holy water falls on a lustrous opal in her hair. Queen Victoria's high regard for the opal did much to bring it back to its former repute. It was highly esteemed by the Romans; Pliny tells the story of Senator Monius, who was exiled by Mark Antony for the opal he owned, which was the size of a hazelnut and valued at great price. A supposed opal in the crown of the Holy Roman Emperors guarded the royal honor.

The opal was especially regarded for the eyes, strengthening the sight, curing eye diseases, and making the wearer invisible, whence it became the patron of thieves. It is said to turn pale in the presence of poison, protect from contagion, and dispel melancholy and sadness. An opal necklace guards the color and life of blond hair. The black opal is especially regarded. See FATAL GIFTS.

Opening of the Mouth and Eyes The name given to one of the burial ceremonies performed at the tomb of the deceased king in ancient Egypt. Its purpose was to enable the dead to see and taste, to enjoy the offerings buried with him and to recite the correct formulas in his adventures in the otherworld. Early it was enacted with a statue of the king, but later the body itself was used. The ceremony was part of a general reenactment of the Osiris myth of death and regeneration, and the dead man was thought to be brought to life again by it. Milk and some of the food were smeared on the mouth and eyes to arouse the desire of the deceased man for food. Then one of the priests, the *sem*, dressed in a leopard's skin, touched the mouth with an iron chisel or adze, the instrument with which Anubis opened the mouths of the gods. Horus, who had opened the mouth of Osiris, his father, was invoked. The lips were touched, then the mouth, then the lips again, so that color might be given them and the jawbones made moveable. Food

was placed in the mouth, and to end this part of the ritual the body or statue was dressed with the regalia. A part of the ceremony of the Opening of the Mouth and Eyes consisted of sprinkling the image or mummy with water, the fluid of life.

Open Sesame Magic formula for opening doors, trees, caves, mountains, etc.: catch phrase for the familiar folktale motif (D1552.2; N455.3; Type 676) in which a man watches a band of robbers enter the side of a mountain (cave, etc.) by means of the magic words "Open Sesame," later uses the magic words himself, enters their hide-out and discovers a great store of treasure. See ALI BABA. The story of *Simeli Mountain* (Grimm #142) is the same Ali Baba story, ending with the forgetting of the formula by the intruder and his murder at the hands of the bandits. In the story of the *Seven Robbers* as told in the Cape Verde Islands (see E. C. Parsons, *MAFLS* 15, i, p. 1; ii, p. 1) the magic formula for entering and leaving the treasure cave is merely "Open rock." The magic formula of European folktale which causes a tree to open is motif D1556. A magic flower opens the home of the dwarfs (F451.3.3.9) in still another German folktale. The magic opening of a mountain, rock, cave, etc., containing treasure occurs in a number of Finnish and Latvian Cinderella variants (see M. R. Cox, *Cinderella, PFLS* xxxi, 1892, p. 499), though in these tales the opener is a magic stick given to the heroine in reward for a kindness. The question of the magic opener having originally been some plant is discussed by early scholars. Certainly there is a legion of magic plants which open mountains and lead to treasure. Miss Cox says (*ib.*, 500) regarding Open Sesame "the mere name of the plant opened the rock." See FERNSEED; MANDRAKE; MISTLETOE; SPRINGWORT.

Opete Twi term for the vulture, conceived among the Ashanti, as among other West African peoples, as the instrument of the gods whereby the sacrifices made by men are transmitted to them. The name and sacred functions of this bird have survived in Dutch Guiana. A generalized feeling that the vulture is sacred has likewise been carried over into the New World by the descendants of Africans. In the West Indies the Negroes refrain from molesting the vulture (called "carrion-crow") for a variety of reasons, all of which are recognizable reinterpretations of African belief concerning this bird. [MJH]

Ophion In ancient Greek religion, an Orphic cult god; the Titan who ruled the universe before Cronus. Eurynome was his consort and together they were banished to Tartarus or were thrown into Ocean when Cronus attained supremacy.

opium Opium for smoking is a dark brown gum made by evaporating the juice of the poppy. Smokers make the gum into a small cone, perforate it, and attach it to the bowl of the pipe, a round, flattened ball, also perforated. The opium is then held over, not in, a flame and the fumes are inhaled. The longer the fumes are kept in the lungs, the more powerful the effect will be. Chinese smokers believe that Persian opium, which is expensive and difficult to get, is the best; Indian is next. Chinese opium is frequently adulterated with ash.

The effects of opium are various, depending in part on the source of it and in part on the temperament of the smoker. Smokers normally become talkative, their noses itch, and the pupils of their eyes contract. They seldom become violent and their mental powers seem to be stimulated rather than clouded. The "opium dream" is not a necessary effect. At times smokers seem to have hallucinations of color in that vivid colors seem to pass before their eyes. Opium disturbs the time sense. Smokers frequently feel that they lie awake all night in a condition of pleasant and peaceful relaxation. The next night they report that they fall into a deep dreamless sleep. This disturbance of the time sense may account for the belief that opium-smoking greatly prolongs the sexual act.

Opium-smoking seems to be a national vice of the Orient, as alcohol is of the Occident. Many Chinese have smoked several pipes a day over a long period of years with no impairment of health or mentality, as many Occidentals have been able to take several drinks a day. In both areas some individuals react violently and quickly. The effects of opium are more slow to appear and less violent than the effects of alcohol. The preparation of the pipe and the smoking take more time than the pouring of a drink. Consequently opium-smoking has less appeal for the Occidental than it has for the Oriental.

Objections to the cultivation of opium for smoking are on two grounds. First, because opium brings a high price on the market, Chinese farmers, badly overtaxed, use land for opium that would better be used for food crops. Second, those who smoke opium until late at night get up late in the afternoon.

Opium derivatives—heroin and the like—have violent and vicious effects. Many believe that in the years between 1931 and 1937 the Japanese, in an attempt to demoralize China, introduced, through Korean agents, large amounts of heroin into China. Whether this is fact or counter-propaganda by the Chinese, the use of heroin increased enormously in China during the 1930's. [RDJ]

opossum (popularly called **possum**) An American marsupial (genus *Didelphis*) of arboreal and nocturnal habits, having a prehensile tail and grasping feet: ranging from the central United States to Brazil. The fact that the possum plays dead when caught (folktale motif A2466.1) has given rise to the folk phrase **playing possum** for any sly bit of feigning or lying low. When taken, the possum lies limp, breathing imperceptibly, eyes closed, but watching through the merest slit for a moment of inattention on the part of his captor to make an escape. Occasionally he does.

The possum figures especially in the folklore of the southern North American Indian and the Negroes and whites of the southern United States. There are various etiological stories explaining his characteristics: Possum has a bare tail (A2317.12), according to the Cherokee Indians, because originally it was white and he wanted a brown one. Raccoon advised him to brown it at the fire; Possum tried this but burnt all the hair off it instead. One southern U.S. Negro version of this story, however, shows Possum, along with Fox and Rabbit, stealing corn from a cornfield near a graveyard. A ghost from the graveyard jumped out and Possum lit out for the fence. The ghost caught Possum by the tail just as he was escaping and skinned all the hair off. Possum got his big grinning mouth (A2341.2.1) from grinning and laughing at a malicious joke once played on Deer.

And there is the Delta region story about the possum that stole the doctor's last chicken, was killed and roasted for the doctor's supper, but ate all the potatoes and gravy in the roasting pan and ran away the minute the oven door was opened. (See B.A. Botkin, *Treasury of Southern Folklore*, New York, 1949, p. 452).

A strange bit of rural folklore common from New Jersey to the Rio Grande is that the male possum copulates into the nose of the female, and the female blows the seminal fluid into her pouch, where the young develop. This idea probably originated in the fact that the male organ of the opossum is bifurcate and that the female does lick and prepare the pouch for the young for weeks preceding birth.

☞ The opossum often plays the part of the clever trickster in the tales of the Amazonian Indians and caboclos (mestizos). The motifs of these stories are generally identical with those of the Turtle cycle. [AM]

Ops An ancient Roman fertility goddess, identified by the Romans with Rhea, and connected with Saturn and Consus. She was worshipped at the Opalia, December 19, and the Opiconsivia, August 25; at the Volcanalia, August 23, she was among the gods sacrificed to. As a goddess of plenty, she was invoked by touching the earth.

oral tradition in music The term "oral tradition," long used to denote a concept of basic importance in the study of folk speech, has been adopted without reservation by students of folk music in the Western world. It has given good service in that field and in the integration of the twin studies of speech and music within the more general folklore. Presumably, it could serve also to tie together the studies of the folk and the fine arts of music within the more general musicology—an equally desirable end. But there are several reasons why the term does not serve this second function any too well.

In the first place, it is a curious but incontrovertible fact that the term "oral tradition" and the study of folk music have not only been elaborated outside of musicology, but have never become acclimated there. On the one hand, to paraphrase Leonard Bloomfield's remarks upon students of (speech) literature, the majority of musicologists are not primarily interested in music, but in the literature of the European fine art of music, its grammar and syntax (harmony and counterpoint), and have dug neither deeply nor broadly enough even in that rich field to find either oral tradition or folk music, except in some rather superficial aspects. On the other hand, the valiant little minority of comparative musicologists—primarily interested in music rather than the literature of music—has not yet worked up far enough from its logical beginnings with primitive music to tie in either the concept of oral tradition or the study of folk music with the fine art of music, European or other. See discussion in SONG: FOLK SONG AND THE MUSIC OF FOLK SONG.

In the second place, though students of folk speech in the Western world can perhaps afford to ignore the comparatively rare instrumental speech (signal-drumming, Morse code, deaf-and-dumb manual speech, etc.), and while students of folk music can make the term "oral tradition" stretch to serve consideration of fiddle-tunes, banjo-picking, and harmonica-playing, musicians can hardly be expected to regard the term seriously in speaking of a Beethoven symphony. They would recognize the role of oral transmission in the fine art of music if it were explained to them. But they would know it as plain "tradition"—the tradition of Joachim, Caruso, or De Reszke, or of Palestrina or Bach. In the former cases, they would be referring to very concrete musical realities, transmitted largely by word of mouth. In the latter, they would be referring to substantial stylistic generalizations conventionally dealt with in written words. In both cases, they would be journeying far from what the folklorist calls "oral tradition." The increasing dominance of instrumental music in the Western world since 1600 has pushed consciousness of *oral* processes into the background and placed main emphasis upon *aural* processes. Musicians recognize "playing by ear" and "singing by rote" (singing what is heard); but traditions of both, together with the allied art of improvisation, are utterly dead in professional life, and no serious consideration—to the best of present knowledge—has been given to their revival. The term "aural tradition" is no substitute. For the mere suggestion, that there were any but heard music, would seem ridiculous.

In the third place, it may be remarked that in the study of folklore in general the term "oral tradition" is used a bit loosely. Three separate meanings in common use may be distinguished: 1) an inherited *accumulation* of materials; 2) the *process* of inheritance, cultivation, and transmission thereof; 3) the *technical* means employed. This is not an unusual semantic complication and does not confuse us unduly as long as we remain in the field of folk music. But it may confuse us when we attempt integration of the folk and fine arts of music. And the uninitiated musicologist, upon whose cooperation we would largely depend in such an endeavor, might be pardoned if he were to accuse the folklorist of cult-worship in placing such strong dependence upon a concept that must seem almost mystical to him.

A fourth consideration bears upon this misunderstanding. Popularization of the European fine art of music has itself achieved such cultlike devotion that oral tradition and folk music alike are very generally regarded, by professional musicians, as a low form of musical life. Almost universal adoption has been given to a theory of unilinear evolution whereby the art of music progresses ever onward and upward from primitive, through folk and popular, to the fine art. The possibilities that estimable qualities may be lost as well as gained, that the order of historical development may have been different in different places, and that the whole hierarchical conception may be unwarrantably subjective, have apparently been little explored.

With these considerations in mind, it would seem that our difficulty were twofold: on the one hand, ambiguity in the use of the word "oral"; on the other, lack of attention to the basic conditions and processes—the dynamics—of music tradition in general. Oral tradition is only one of many kinds of tradition. Examination of other traditions, or rather, classes of tradition, as they function in connection with music will show that if we range beside each other the main classes of tradition that affect both the folk and the fine arts of music, they cease to be mutually exclusive categories of *things,* but rather generalizations, useful to study, of a *flow of events* whose outer limits show well-defined opposite characteristics, at the same time that the inner relations show almost unbroken shadings of hybridization or acculturation from one extreme to the other. After this is done, we may hope to make some progress with the problem of *oral* tradition.

Tradition, as the handing on of acquired characteristics, has been said to be the basic distinction between man and the other animals. Korzybski, in adopting a more abstract homolog, refers to "time-binding" as enabling men to communicate over intervals of time, so that the younger members of a group can begin where the older leave off. According to him, it is man's principal survival mechanism, in terms of which relative sanity or insanity can be measured. Whether or not acquired characteristics can be inherited biologically, there can be no doubt that they are inherited socially. And whether or not these serve, as Korzybski believes they do, as principal survival mechanisms of individual men, there can be no doubt that they do serve human culture communities in such a way. There would seem to be good grounds for very serious evaluation of tradition in any study of cultural activity.

In the schematic outline given below, the main uses to which we already admit the term "tradition," together with some additional uses to which it would seem we must admit it, are grouped so as to show a field, operations within it, and the environment in which both are present to us.

Music tradition, as envisaged here, is a function of culture—a dynamic conception. With respect to the first sense of the term "oral tradition" to which reference was made above, this appears to us, however, as an accumulation of material products—a repertoire of songs, dances, etc.—and so, structural in character. But we must not be deceived by this illusion, which is entirely subjective and a direct result of our individual existences in general space-time. The repertoire as a whole and its relation to the culture of which it is an accumulation of traditions are in a constant state of flux.

With respect to the second sense of the term to which reference was made above, we must recognize two main types, oral and written, which combine in a variety of ways that we may conveniently set down as: predominantly oral, mixed (more or less equally) oral and written, and predominantly written. Unquestionably, pure oral tradition can only be found in the more primitive musics. Whether or not a pure written tradition, comparable to the higher mathematics of speech, exists or even can exist in any music need not be speculated upon here.

With respect to the third meaning of the term, attention should be called to another type of tradition, that operates not only through the persons in the field which is studied, but also *through the persons who do the studying of the field.* Traditions of control are of two main types: *intrinsic, D,* operating within the music activity, and *extrinsic, E,* operating from outside the music activity, in the environment—the general field of culture. We are conscious of traditions of control in the field of municipal, state, national, and international politics, and even in the politics of organizations and other groups. In our study of folk music, as elsewhere, these operate largely below the threshold of consciousness and receive little if any criticism from their owner (though plenty of it from his fellows!). It is evident that both carriers and students of folk music hold a variety of traditional atti-

Dynamics of Music Tradition

Conspectus of principal accumulations of traditions *as a field*   A and B
within which, tradition *as a process*   C
operates, under intrinsic traditions *of control*   D
in an environment of extrinsic traditions *of control*   E and F

THE FIELD

Structures given to and, so, tending to be static for us

A. *Families* of tradition (defined by geographical area covered)
Highly differentiated (in terms of B and C)
  1. East Asia
  2. South Asia
  3. Southeast Asia
  4. Islamic Asia-Africa
  5. Occident
Partially differentiated (in terms of B)
  6. Central Asia ?
  7. West Africa ?
  8. Amerindia ?
  9. Other ?

B. Traditional *Idioms* (defined by social stratum)

  1. Primitive art

  2. Fine art

  3. Folk art

  4. Popular art

  5. ?

THE OPERATIONS

Functions given by and, so, dynamic for us

C. Traditions of music *Technique*
  1. Purely oral
  2. Predominantly oral
  3. Mixed oral and written
  4. Predominantly written
  5. Purely written?

D. Traditions of *Control* (intrinsic)
Critical inclinations, such as esthetic, ethical, logical, normalistic, lead to action with such effects as:

discontinuance	continuance	acculturation
revival	survival	exploitation
regress	status quo	progress
loss	permanence	gain

THE ENVIRONMENT

E. Traditions of *Control* (extrinsic)

The structural-functional complex of general culture traditions, within which music traditions are accumulated, processed, and handed on, operates, along with D (and in similar manner), as control; and potentially at least is responsive in turn to operations of music tradition.

F. Total physical *Environment* of total culture

tudes toward their respective activity—attitudes fostered by and expressed, often as not, *qua* oral tradition. They want it, or expect it, to change; or they do not want it or do not expect it to do so. They want to revive it, but not to put it to new uses; or vice versa. They wish to preserve it for themselves, or they want to popularize it. And so on. Sometimes they want to do two or more apparently contradictory things at once, or at different times, or in different ways. These attitudes and the actions that flow from them are essentially critical in character. But we seldom subject them to disciplined criticism, because they appear to us as self-evidently right, good, desirable, or beautiful. In fact, they present both thoughts and feelings about what is right, good, desirable or beautiful, not only in musical terms, but in terms of life and culture in general.

This map has been made as comprehensive as possible

within a small space. It is not to be confused with the territory mapped. There is quite a bit of dead reckoning in it, and there are many omissions. It is based upon a competence solely within captions *A*.5 and *B*.2 of the field. The validity of captions *A*.1–5 and *B*.1–4 is, however, customarily granted by scholars for purposes of discussion. As to captions *A*.6–9, the question marks indicate a doubt their reality is more than suggestive.

We may presume that in using the term "oral tradition" students of folk speech and of folk music have taken for granted that what the voice produces is sound and that it is heard. Extension of the term to include sound produced by instruments has not disturbed them, though it might well have done so. Oral-ness easily implies aural-ness, and avoids the clumsy hyphenated term. The heart of the problem of the use of the term "oral tradition" in the integration of folk music and the general study of music is reached, however, when we face the tradition of writing—written tradition. Both music and speech must have been purely oral up to the time writing—even the crudest visual-oral correlations other than gesture—was introduced, and they have remained so ever since in many places where writing has not been cultivated. A very vigorous oral tradition in speech can flourish among people who are literate in speech. Music literacy being even rarer than speech literacy, oral tradition in music is probably the more widespread. But without a very vigorous *oral tradition of writing*, neither speech nor music writing can be learned. Writing cannot be read—either in song or upon an instrument—without recourse to that same oral tradition. What the connection is between the oral tradition of folklore and the oral traditions of speech and music writing in general is difficult to say.

Though competent students may disagree upon the *amount* of material (*A* and *B*) for which there may be provenience in written tradition and the *amount* of influence music literacy may have upon the processes (*C* and *D*), there seems to be general agreement that both provenience and influence are ponderable. What we conventionally call "oral tradition" in folk music is, then, only *predominantly oral* (or even *oral-aural*). For though in many cases we cannot prove written provenience or influence, there are so many cases in which we can prove it, that the inference is: folk music is definable *in part* by survival in it, upon a "lower" social level where writing is rare, of traditions that have sifted down from a "higher" social level where writing is more common. It seems untenable today to say it is exclusively this, but equally so to say it is none of it. A theoretical 50–50 normal ratio between the dying survival of written tradition and the living creation of oral tradition would seem to be the safest working hypothesis. This would apply, of course, to the field (*A*.5 and *B*.1–4)—the accumulation of materials—and might, with respect to individual products (songs, dances, etc.) vary theoretically from a ratio of 1–99 to one of 99–1, but ordinarily within a much narrower neighborhood of the norm, 50–50. We are, however, speaking here mainly of norms, not of the infinite variety of departures from them.

Taking all these considerations into account, it would seem the better part of wisdom to confine the use of the term "oral tradition" to bona fide word of mouth (*os, oris*), substituting for it, as the main technical process of folk music, the less picturesque but more accurate "unwritten tradition," with the understanding that by "unwritten" we mean "predominantly unwritten." This would seem especially desirable in connection with the discussions now being held more and more frequently on both sides of the Atlantic relative to the problem of the notation of folk music.

The Occidental (international) technique of music notation—probably the most accurate and most widely used throughout the world—is a development of the fine art of European music. With its use, throughout more than a thousand years, this art has been able to individualize its products and assure reproduction of them wherever its traditions are elaborately maintained with a high degree of accuracy. *Ur-texte* have become defined by their composers, during the last century, with increasing precision. This means with increasing elab-

orateness. Today, notation of very minute inflections of phrasing, accentuation, nuances, etc., are a *sine qua non* of the typically unique product of value. The tendency shows no sign of abating.

When we range beside such products a product of folk art, we see at once they are upon two very different levels. If one were asked, "Where is the First Prelude of the Well-Tempered Clavichord?" one could say, "Here." And if it were played within established norms of scholarship, that would be *it* and all of it. But if one were asked, "Where is Barbara Allen?" the answer, "Here," followed by the best rendition of an excellent informant, might be difficult to explain as "both it and not it, and certainly not all of it." One could sing only one variant of one version.

The gap between the highly individualized identity of the product of fine art and the highly generalized identity of the product of folk art must not be underestimated. Their treatment by a science of folklore or by musicology demands two very different techniques. Their evaluation in terms of critical method involves two very different sets of criteria. The single standard of musical value, maintained by many historico-musicologists, cannot serve here. And the study of folk song might help to demonstrate that it should not serve anywhere.

The last matter to be stressed at this point is the usefulness of a revised concept of oral tradition in correcting unilinear theories of the evolution of music in another connection. If the above analysis can stand, the order of historical development is definitely as in section *B* of the conspectus, i.e. there can be no folk music in the proper sense of the word until there has been for some time a fine art of which it can be *in part* a dying survival. The common confusion of primitive and folk music, as idioms, should be clarified from a music-technical as it can be from an anthropological viewpoint. We can then envisage the formation and differentiation of music idiom as twin processes of acculturation: a) between families and b) between idioms, with the potentiality always that both may operate at once or separately and in various ways in one and the same situation.

Perhaps in conclusion the reader should be reminded that the latter part of the preceding argument applies solely to the Occidental family of music tradition. The relationship of oral and written traditions undoubtedly differs greatly in the other families. One of the most important tasks of comparative musicology is to clarify this relationship upon a world basis. This will involve a revaluation of the notation system and a thorough critical and technical revision of the whole concept of written tradition and its relation to unwritten tradition. For the basic differences between the idioms and their respective products are largely the result of the notation system and the elaborate traditions by which its currency is maintained.

The Occidental notation system is *par excellence* a control system, and its use is a process by which traditions of control of the most varied, even opposed, kinds may be exercised. It is a set of directions for the reproduction of products so as to conform to the peculiar traditions of the Occidental fine art. When, therefore, we notate in it a product of the traditions of the folk art, the reproduction is almost bound to be as much, if not more, in the traditions of the fine art than in those of the folk art. The act, in short, is one of translation from one idiom into another. The notated folk song is, then, not a primary but a secondary datum of study. Employment of special diacritical symbols to indicate deviations from the 12-tone equal temperament, shortening or lengthening of the duration of notes and rests, presence of slides, waverings, peculiar attacks, releases, etc., not traditional in the fine art, may increase the accuracy of the translation. But at the same time, it may lull the student into an illusion that it is not a translation and that he has before him a product with something of the individuality of a product of the fine art.

To offset these dangers, we have fortunately, in an increasing number of cases, the sound-recording—a primary objective datum for study, especially when it is accompanied by motion-picture film. Furthermore, it may perhaps not be premature to mention the fact that both in Europe and in the United States electronic-mechanic devices are being experimented with by which at least the single, unaccompanied melodic line may be automatically and objectively graphed. With the perfection of these devices, the rigorously scientific study of unwritten tradition in music (and possibly also in speech) can finally get under way, clear not only of the inaccuracies of our conventional techniques of writing, but of the subjective element inherent in even the most conscientious and skilled use of added diacritical symbols.   CHARLES SEEGER

orange A large, round, juicy fruit (technically a berry) of a low, evergreen tree (genus *Citrus*). Because the tree is evergreen and everbearing (having both fruit and blossoms at all times) it has always been in high repute as a symbol of fruitfulness. Some call it the "Golden Apple of the Hesperides," and Zeus is said to have given Hera the orange at their wedding (another explanation of its use as a bridal flower). But it was originally from southeast Asia and practically unknown in the Mediterranean area until the Saracen conquest and the Crusades. It was through them that the crown of orange blossoms was introduced into Europe. In Japan it is said to have been brought from the Eternal Land at the request of the Emperor. It is a symbol of purity, chastity, and eternal love. Orange blossoms from a wedding must be discarded before the end of the first month (before they wither) or they will bring barrenness. In England, Italy, and Sicily oranges are used in witchcraft as a symbol of the victim's heart. The victim's name was written on a slip of paper, secured with as many pins as possible, and placed in the chimney until the victim died. This practice was known in Yorkshire as late as 1880.

Fresh or candied orange peel was used as an aromatic tonic. An orange the first thing in the morning is a cure for dispepsia, or—it causes acid stomach. In Yucatán, the leaves are used in a bath for a new mother. Oranges were frequently used as a pomander in crowded places before the institution of bathing and air-conditioning.

orchesis The Greek term for dance. In Greek drama, dance was indispensable, as "an imitation of actions, characters, and passions by means of postures and rhythmical movements" (Aristotle). Poetry, music, and dance were inseparable, and the divisions of verse referred to dance steps. As Greek theater grew from ritual drama, the dance group or *choros* continued to dance in a circular space, no longer the place of the dithyramb, but the orchestra or dancing-floor of the theater. The term has been adopted widely to designate the advanced dance groups in American educational institutions and colleges. [GPK]

Orcus or Horcus In classical mythology, one of the synonyms of Pluto or Dis. The name in Greek means "oath," and probably Orcus was the deity of the underworld who punished perjurers. He may however have been originally an early Roman deity who became identified with Pluto in later times, the name being one of the more popular synonyms for Pluto. Orcus was specifically a sort of angel of death who slew the dying. A man dressed as Orcus carried the dead gladiators from the arena. The fifth of the month, birth day of Orcus, was an unlucky day. In the later tradition of Europe which was descended directly from the Roman, Orcus became a hairy and black man-eating forest spirit, perhaps the "ogre" of folktale.

ordeal An appeal to the judgment of the gods, God, or the supernatural: a form of trial by pain, poison, fire, water, combat, divination, etc., often involving the death of the suspect (or his accuser).

Ordeals test the authenticity of the oath. In societies where no evidence is available to support either contestant, the decision by ordeal is taken to be the judgment of God. The ordeal was not recognized by Roman law and was tolerated in China more as a concession to popular belief than as a reputable legal procedure. Best known of the ordeals in modern times is the throwing of the litigant, frequently a suspected witch, into water. If she drowns, she is innocent, and if she floats, she is guilty and must be burned at the stake. A variant of this is holding the head of the suspect under water. Another ordeal is by taking poisons or substances thought to be poisons. In New Guinea red water is made by soaking the bark of a local tree in water which produces nausea or a trance state, depending on whether the participant is guilty or innocent. In ancient Greece bull's blood was thought to be poisonous. It was drunk by priestesses in order to acquire the power of prophecy, according to Pliny; but Pausanias, so often alert to sexual implications, thought it was to test their chastity. Several ordeals depend upon the subject's ability to withstand heat. The Bedouin custom was to require the subject to lick a hot iron spoon; the Indian custom is to carry a hot iron; in Scandinavia the heated object must be carried a certain number of steps. In the Malay Archipelago, Africa, and elsewhere, a stone had to be taken out of boiling water; in India the ordeal was to walk through fire. A curious fact in connection with these ordeals of heat is that some people either are insensitive to extreme heat or can make themselves so, as has been frequently demonstrated by the Indian *yogi*.

The wager of battle or decision by combat, known in Borneo, Greece, and Scandinavia at early dates, seems to be intimately associated with the structure of human instinct. God gives victory only to the Right. As late as 1818 an Englishman accused of murder is said to have claimed the right of ordeal by combat which necessitated the repeal of the old law. Other ordeals are psychological. The truth-machine is based on plausible physiological theory but the invention of it is evidence that man still looks for evidence more objective than mere asseveration. Similarly the truth serums belong in the category of the ordeal by poison or pseudo-poison. The heat ordeal, said to be used by American gangsters, and the third degree as formerly practiced in American police-stations, differ from the ordeal in folk belief in that the ordeal as discussed in these notes was required only after all other attempts to arrive at truth had failed. See BITTER WATER; CALABAR BEAN. [RDJ]

ordering of world, human life, institutions Among the North American Indians the establishment of the world (creation of mountains, lakes, rivers, procuring of light or fire, etc.), after the creation of the world, the ordering of human life (procreation, bodily form, economic pursuits, death) and the establishment of social groups and religious observances is generally credited to the culture hero-trickster-transformer and his associates. See AHAYUTA ACHI; CREATION; CREATOR; CREATOR BORN AT BOTTOM OF OCEAN; CREATOR'S GRANDMOTHER; COYOTE; CULTURE HERO; DETERMINATION OF SEASONS; JUSKAHA; LAUGHTER; NANABOZHO; ORIGIN STORIES. [EWV]

oread In Greek mythology, one of the nymphs inhabiting the mountains, hills, and grottoes. See NYMPH.

orenda Iroquois Indian term, equated with the Algonquin Indian term *manitu*, and the Siouan term *wakonda*, which has been defined as the name for the creative force, principle, or magic power inherent in every body and being of nature; the active cause or force involved in every operation of nature in any manner affecting or controlling the welfare of man. It is dubious whether the Iroquois or the Siouans had any such conceptualization of a generalized supernatural power; manitu has recently been shown to have, for a host of Algonquian tribes, actual specific meanings rather than any generalized one. The same is probably true for the Iroquoian and Siouan terms *orenda* and *wakonda*, which, like *manitu*, are found in the several languages of these two large linguistic families. See MANITU. [EWV]

Orestes In Greek legend the avenging son of Agamemnon. While Agamemnon was away at Troy, Clytemnestra, Orestes' mother, perhaps in revenge for the sacrifice of Iphigenia, lived adulterously with Ægisthus. On the return of the king to Mycenæ, Clytemnestra and Ægisthus murdered him, some say in his bath, others that the pair offered him a sleeveless and neckless shirt and killed him as he struggled with it. Cassandra was also slain by the guilty lovers. Orestes, then a child, was spirited off either by his nurse or by his sister Electra, and was reared at the court of Strophius of Phocis along with Pylades, Strophius' son. The two became proverbial friends.

Some years later, Orestes, accompanied by Pylades, made his way to Mycenæ and there avenged Agamemnon's murder by killing Clytemnestra and Ægisthus. To the mind of Homer, who was perhaps telling of a historical deed, this was both natural and commendable, since Orestes was head of his family and therefore the one on whom the act of blood revenge devolved. But later writers, especially the great Athenian dramatists, expanded the story and gave it a slant which upsets the previous moral standard. Orestes, because he murdered his mother, was hounded by the Erinyes. This is per-haps rooted in older tradition because earlier the Erinyes were spirits of the dead, and Clytemnestra's ghost might be expected to haunt her slayer. Fleeing before the avenging deities, Orestes came first to Delphi and then, on the orders of the oracle, to Athens where he submitted to trial before the Areopagus. The vote was even, and Athena, thereby establishing the tradition that a tie vote was for acquittal, cast the deciding and releasing vote. The Erinyes thereupon ceased to bother Orestes and were thenceforth known as the Eumenides, a euphemism meaning the gracious or kindly ones. In another version of the story, Orestes had to expiate his crime by rescuing the image of Artemis from the Taurians. This image was worshipped by the Taurians with human sacrifice, and no stranger to their land was safe. Orestes was somehow recognized by his long-lost sister Iphigenia, who was the priestess of the temple in Tauris, and Orestes, Pylades, and Iphigenia fled with the image back to Greece. In several versions they carry the image to Rhodes, but it is also said that they brought it to Italy, to the grove at Nemi, where Orestes became the first priest of Diana (Artemis) at Aricia. When he died he was buried before the temple of Saturn in Rome. Still another version of the expiation has it that he bit off one of his fingers, and that the black-seeming Erinyes then appeared to him as white. Yet another series of legends says that expiation was accomplished in more normal manner: Orestes had the blood of a sacrificial pig poured on him. After his death, in an early version of the story, the Erinyes still pursued him and Apollo had to give him a bow for his protection.

Orestheus In Greek mythology, an Ætolian king. He owned a bitch who gave birth to a wooden stick. This Orestheus buried, and from the stick grew a vine. From the shoots (*ozoi*) the Ozolian Locrians derived their name. Orestheus also named his son Phytius, Plant Man. The myth is obviously an attempt to explain an already existing name, and modern scholarship hypothesizes as well the derivation from *oze*, a bad smell, or a goatskin, since there were sulfur springs in the country and the inhabitants dressed in goatskins.

orgía (Greek, act of divine homage) The winter ritual dedicated to Dionysus, particularly in his vegetation aspect as Dionysus Liknites. The ecstatic dances and actions of the *mænads* in these rites, and the phallic attributes, spread like wildfire. At first intoxication by wine was not a part of the ritual. But later the orgía lost its solemn connotations and became synonymous with unbridled, licentious mass intoxication. Today its sacred and even its dance connotations have vanished, except when applied to the ecstatic dance rites of contemporary tribes, or the debauchery following on these rites under the influence of sacramental intoxicants. Thus, in the former category, the ecstatic dance of the West Indies, the Indian peyote (*hikuli*) cults, and in the second category, the *tesguinadas* of the Mexican Tarahumaras. [GPK]

origin of cultivated plants North American Indian myths accounting for the origin of specific cultivated plants, or for the origin of cultivated plants as a body, vary from region to region, but are told among all the agricultural tribes. Such myths are concerned with the origin of corn, often from the body of a slain person. In the pueblos Corn Mother and the Corn Maidens emerged with the people from the underworld. The main Pueblo Indian corn myth concerns the loss of Corn or the Corn Maidens after attempted violation, the search for them, and their final return to the people; this myth also has a wide distribution outside of the Pueblo area.

The origin of all cultivated plants is attributed by Apache groups of the Southwest to Turkey. In a Jicarilla Apache myth Turkey brings forth from his body for the hactcin, or supernaturals, black corn in the east, blue corn in the south, yellow corn in the west, and in the north, all kinds of fruits and vegetables. In another Jicarilla myth Turkey provides his companion, Man-Who-Floated-on-the-Water, with black, blue, and yellow corn seeds, and fruit, vegetable, and tobacco seeds; he tells his father to get busy, and the man starts planting the seeds. Together he and Turkey watch the garden mature in twelve days. Later the man meets Animal Raiser and exchanges vegetable for meat gifts with him, and marries Animal Raiser's daughter. He shows her people how to use the plants and fruits, and they show him how to use meat: that is why the Apache use both now. An interesting footnote to Apache sophistication about origins of cultivated plants is that they do not include wheat (a non-native cereal) among the seeds given by Turkey; Grasshopper produces wheat for the hactcin, and is considered to be the guardian of wheat by the Apache. See CORN FROM BODY OF SLAIN PERSON; DEOHAKO. [EWV]

According to South American mythology, food plants were given to mankind by the culture hero or by benevolent animals. For instance, the Bakairi and Cashinawa learned the use of manioc from a deer, and the Sherente owed their knowledge of food plants to a rodent.

More often, however, the staple plants are said to have originated from the body of a mysterious being. Either they fell from the body of a child whenever he was beaten (Tupinamba) or grew from his corpse after he had been buried. According to the ancient Peruvians, their main plants sprouted from the corpse of the son of the creator. The motif of plants growing from the human body is also found in the myths of several Guiana and Brazilian tribes (Tupinamba, Bororo, Carib, Arawak, Paressi). [AM]

See the story of Sido, who killed his wife and planted various parts of her body, from which the food plants grew, in MELANESIAN MYTHOLOGY.

origin stories A lively interest in origins, or how man and his environment and the creatures in that environment came to be is evinced in the tales of North American Indians, especially in those from the North Pacific Coast, Plateau, Plains, California, Southwest, and Eastern Woodlands peoples; it is not pronounced in Eskimo or Great Basin tales. Explanatory elements are often inserted or tacked onto tales to explain the origin of particular phenomena; why Coyote's nose and tail are black-tipped, why there is a black mark on the nose of antelope, how chipmunk got his stripes, and so forth (see EXPLANATORY ELEMENTS). Such "origin" or explanatory elements have been remarked upon as particularly abundant in Coeur d'Alene (Plateau), Zuñi (Southwestern Pueblo), and Apache (Southwestern) mythology; myths and tales from these tribes have hundreds of explanatory incidents inserted in them, but the mythologies of other American Indian groups, with the exceptions

named above, contain an abundance of such elements.

A random sampling of origin material in American Indian myths follows. Animals are accounted for from pieces of the meat of a slain antelope which Child-of-the-Water, Chiricahua Apache culture hero, blows on, naming and creating the various animals as he does so. Birds are created from the feathers of an eagle, by the same deity. Frogs and fishes are the supernaturals who were transformed when a flood covered the earth (Jicarilla Apache); fish are Sedna's cut-off fingers among the Eskimo. Games such as that of hoop and pole, and stave games, are taught to the people by the hactcin in Jicarilla Apache myths; the people "had nothing to do; there were no games" so the hactcin taught them particular ones. Fratricide, old age, the woman's cry of applause, laughter (see LAUGHTER), and facial and pubic hair are also among the many items accounted for by the Apache. Diversity of languages is not only explained as due to people quarreling by the Apache, but also by many other Indian tribes.

Besides the very widespread American Indian controversy tale wherein the child of the proponent for death is the first to die (see DEATH) death is also explained by other American Indians as having been instituted because 1) the first dead person, when revived, smelled so bad the living could not stand him, or 2) because the earth would be overcrowded if death were not final. A variant of the controversy tale is to be found in the sinking test to determine whether the dead should return to life in four days; objects are cast in the water, and one sinks, so death is made permanent. See CHAMELEON; DEAD SMELL BAD. The origin of the various tribes, of the whites, Negroes, and Mexicans, is accounted for in numerous Indian mythologies, with the inference often that all foreign groups are of inferior origin. Sacred bundles, ceremonies, social and political groups (clans and gentes) nearly all have origin myths attached to them throughout North America (see CHANT; MEDICINE BUNDLE). For discussion of the origin of certain specific items see CONFUSION OF TONGUES; CREATION; CREATOR; DEATH; MAN; ORIGIN OF CULTIVATED PLANTS; WOMAN. [EWV]

In Kodiak Island (Alaska) mythology all the animals on earth and fish in the sea were born of a young woman whose confinement was attended by two old men, her uncles. As the creatures were born, one by one, the old men either threw them on the ground or tossed them into the sea. When the girl got well she ran away, eventually met and married a star spirit. Her husband explained to her that although all animals were her children, they would have to kill certain ones in order to eat. (See M. Lantis, "Mythology of Kodiak Island, Alaska," *JAFL* 51: 134.)

How various birds and animals got their characteristic markings, shapes, habits is the motif of countless etiological stories in all cultures. Rabbit laughs and gets his harelip (A2211.2)—European; Moon strikes Hare and splits his lip (A2216.3)—Hottentot; Lizard bobs his head up and down because he once got a fishbone in his throat (A2211.9)—Ibo Negro; Chipmunk's stripes are Bear's claw marks, reminder of the time Bear nearly caught him (A2217.2)—North American Seneca Indian; the ass is honored with a black cross on his back because he bore Christ into Jerusalem (A2221.1)—European; swallows donned mourning for Christ's crucifixion and still wear it (A2221.2.4.1)—Spanish; Flounder got a crooked mouth for not answering God (A2231.1.2)—European; Crab's eyes popped up out of his body when he beat the god's forbidden drum (A2231.10)—Fjort Negro; the stag borrowed the dog's horns and never returned them (A2241.1)—European; Beaver borrowed Muskrat's tail and never returned it (A2241.10)—North American Menominee Indian; Buffalo and Cow exchanged hides, now neither's skin fits (A2247.1)—Indonesian; the hog once lost a pancake in the mud and is still looking for it (A2275.5.1)—European.

Penobscot Indians say that snowfall is caused by a mythical Snow Bird who lives on top of a mountain. When it sheds its down, snow falls on earth. In Germany when snow flies through the air, they say old Mother Hulda is shaking her feather bed. See HOLDE.

There are innumerable others: about the origin of fish scales (A2315) or alligator scales (A2315.2); why the vulture is bald (A2317.7); how various birds got their crests (A2321 ff.)—see KINGFISHER; how lynx got his squint (A2211.1); why eagle's back is brown (A2356.3.1); why quail has no tail (A2378.2.1). The motifs explaining animal and bird characteristics run A2200–2599 in Stith Thompson's *Motif-Index of Folk-Literature*. See BEAR FISHES THROUGH ICE WITH TAIL; BUZZARD; CROCODILE; HADDOCK; NIGHTINGALE; OFFENDED ROLLING ROCK.

☞ The distinctive peculiarities of various species of birds are explained in various South American Indian etiological tales by the accidents that happened to them during a brawl (Chiriguano, Mataco). [AM]

orin The term among the Yoruba people for their songs, including their religious ceremonial songs and also those in the improvised topical categories. See AFRICAN AND NEW WORLD NEGRO FOLKLORE.

Orion The most striking and brilliant of all the constellations, including the two first magnitude stars, reddish Betelgeuse and blue-white Rigel, the unique belt or girdle of three bright stars lying between these two, and the visible nebula in the sword. The constellation takes its name from a giant hunter of Greek mythology, but it is and has been recognized as an asterism all over the world from ancient times. Its position in the heavens makes it visible in both northern and southern hemispheres. Betelgeuse is the right shoulder of the giant, Bellatrix the left; the left knee is Rigel and the right Kappa Orionis. On his left shoulder the giant carries his shield or a lion's skin; his sword hangs from his belt. Before him flee the Pleiades; at his feet lies Lepus the Hare; he is accompanied by the Dogs, in which are the brilliant Sirius and Procyon.

To the ancient Egyptians this constellation was Horus riding in a boat (Lepus), and it was Osiris in his ghostly nightly journey towards the sunrise. Earlier yet in Egypt, in the V Dynasty, the constellation was Sahu, hunting through the heavens for gods and men to rip apart and boil for food. The Hebrews knew it as Kesil, the Foolish or Self-Confident, or as Gibbor, the Giant, identified with Nimrod and tied to the heavens for impiety. The name of Kesil, the Fool, may be related to the Arabic root meaning to be thick, and thus to the giant concept; the word *kesilim*, a plural, was perhaps used of all first magnitude stars, and thence for the greatest of constellations. Gibbor the Giant is reflected in the modern Arabic al-Jabbar or Algebra, the Giant, as the name for the con-

stellation; it is also al-Babadur, the Strong, and al-Shuja', the Snake. In earlier Arabia it was al-Jauzah, probably taking its name from the word meaning walnut, for the belt was known as the Golden Nuts. In Mesopotamia Orion was Tammuz, the shepherd loved by Ishtar, or Nin-Girsu, the god of Lagash, who was identified with Tammuz. There too, earlier, it was called Uru-Anna, the sun or heaven-light. Some profess to see in the name the origin of the name Orion for the constellation, and claim a later development of explanatory myth for the name. The Hindus knew Orion as Mriga, the stag, a form of Prajāpati; the belt was an arrow transfixing the stag to the sky. In China the belt was Three-Side-By-Side; now it is the constellation Shen, to mix, in the western or autumn quarter of the heavens ruled over by the White Tiger. In New Zealand the belt of Orion is the Elbow of Maui; sometimes it is the stern of the canoe of which the Southern Cross is the anchor. The Australian Arunta recognize in these stars a group of young men dancing in a coroboree. Among the Buriats of Siberia the constellation represents three wapiti being chased by the demon-hunter, Erlik-Khan, overlord of the underworld, and his three dogs. One of the wapiti has been wounded and is bleeding (red Betelgeuse). When the hunt ends, the world will cease to be.

The Eskimo of Point Barrow see in the belt three hunters lost in the snow. Among the Indians of the Americas, the Micmac recognize in these stars three fishermen; the Zuñi, the Hanging Lines or the Celestial Hunter; the Indians of Mexico see Citli, the Bowman; the Patagonians, the Three Bolas (the South American parallel of the lariat, a set of three stones tied to thongs and thrown about the legs of an animal to trip it). The Peruvians (and the Basques and some of the peoples of India as well) saw in it the Steps; to them, as to so many other peoples of the world, the constellation had a relationship to hunting. A faint resemblance to the myth of Prometheus is in the Peruvian story that this constellation is a criminal held in the heavens by two condors. Among the Chaco Indians, the belt, las Tres Marias, is the Old Women or the Women's Grandmothers. The stars of the great rectangle of the feet and shoulders are sometimes the house and garden of the old women and various surrounding stars are people waiting for the women.

In North Africa, Orion is a belted hunter followed by Sirius the dog and following some gazelles (Lepus); or the stars emerge from a muddy well and Rigel, the last to rise above the horizon, is the Foot in the Mud. The French call the belt le Râteau, the Rake, or the Three Kings or Magi, or Jacob's Staff. The stars of Orion represented Thor, the Norse god who carried the infant vegetation god Aurwandil; the belt was Freya's Spinning Wheel or Spindle. And to the Greeks, in addition to being Orion, the constellation was called the Giant, the Hunter, the Warrior, the Cock's Foot, the Double Ax. The belt has been known also as the Arrow, the Line, the Yardstick, the Scale, the Beam.

Homer knew both the constellation Orion and the mythological giant Orion, but he made no connection of myth with asterism. Later myth is however often ingenious in its explanation of the giant, his name, his deeds, his being placed among the stars. The name, about 500 B.C., was Woarion, and, according to Strabo, the Bœotians, who claimed Orion as a native of their

country, called him Kandaon, an epithet of Ares, the
Warrior. Krappe recognizes the name as belonging to a
pre-Hellenic, pre-Olympian vocabulary. Fairly late, from
the time of Ovid and Hyginus, we have the story of how
Orion was named, an elaborate pun. Hyrieus, Orion's
father, had been childless, but he was a good man. One
day he was visited by three strangers, who were Zeus,
Poseidon, and Hermes, in disguise, and he showed them
unstinting hospitality. Granted a boon, he asked for a
son, whereupon the three gods took an ox-hide and
urinated on it. Hyrieus buried the hide according to instructions and, at the end of ten lunar months, Orion, or
Urion after the fluid that made him, was born from the
earth. The lion's skin he now carries was formerly recognized as this ox-hide. In this story, some of the raw
material of myth is well worked into a witty tale. The
stranger-gods, the hero born of the liquid of the gods,
the supernatural birth from the earth: these are more
serious matters than this almost flippant Roman myth
makes them. In other versions of the Orion story, he is
a son of Poseidon, a tide-making sea deity who could
walk through the deepest of waters, like the Celtic Bran.
Orion was said to be responsible for the tides of the
Ægean Sea.

Orion's possible origin in the Mesopotamian sun god
and his identification with Horus and Osiris have already
been mentioned. Hinting also at this connection with
the sun is the name of Orion's first wife, Side, or pomegranate, who tried to equal Hera's beauty and was sent
to Hades for her presumption: this may have some relationship to the Persephone-Hades tale. Some of this
connection with the sun is retained in the Greek myth.
Orion fell in love with Merope or Hæro, daughter of
Œnopion. The father objected to the match and inter-
posed various tasks and other obstacles to the union.
Finally, the king, forced by Orion's clearing an island
of wild beasts to make a decision, reneged on his promise.
Because he tried to elope with the girl, or because he
prematurely acted on what he thought would be her
father's acquiescence to their marriage, Orion was
blinded by the angry father. Guided by one of Hephæstus' aides, Orion traveled eastward to where the sun
rose, and there, gazing into the full strength of the
sun, he regained his sight. Another of the young giant's
love affairs, in late myth, was with Eos, who kidnapped
him and kept him as her lover. One of the clearest of
all classical examples of the explanatory star myth draws
Orion in this character of importunate lover. He chases
the Pleiades across the skies in Bœotian myth, trying to
catch one of the sisters, who flee before him.

Myths of his death vary. He was bold enough to challenge Artemis to a contest in throwing the discus; or
he tried to rape one of her maidens and so was slain
by an arrow of the goddess. Or she caused a scorpion to
sting him, which is why Orion's constellation sets as
Scorpio rises into the sky. Still another myth says that
Artemis loved him so that she forgot her duties. Once,
as Orion was swimming or wading far out in the sea,
Helios shone so strongly about him that he was a dark
blur on the water. Then Helios challenged Artemis to
hit the vague mark. The unerring huntress immediately
slew, unwittingly, the giant.

The constellation is a weather sign in many parts of
the world. It rises near dawn at the beginning of summer, at midnight when the grapes are ripe, in the early
evening as winter approaches: this Hesiod knew. The
ancient inhabitants of Mesopotamia and India knew
that its early rising portended storms. The Babylonian
Talmud states: "If it were not for the heat of Orion
the world could not exist because of the cold of the
Pleiades; and if it were not for the cold of the Pleiades
the world could not exist because of the heat of Orion":
again an echo of the linkage with the sun.

☞ The constellation of Orion is visualized by a few
South American tribes as a human leg. According to an
Arekuna story, it originated from the leg of a man which
had been cut off by his adulterous wife. The Conibo
say that Orion is the leg of one of the boys of the
Pleiades who had been mutilated by a cayman. [AM]

orisha Yoruban word for deity. See OBOSUM; VODUN.

Ormazd or **Ormuzd** Persian name for AHURA MAZDA.

ornithomancy Augury; divination from the flight of
birds. The word is sometimes extended to include all
omens derived from birds, for example the death omen
when a bat flies into the house, but is properly limited
to a formal divining system such as was used by the
Romans.

'Oro The chief god of Tahiti, whose mysteries were
celebrated by the Arioi Society. He is recognized elsewhere in Polynesia; for example, in Mangaia, Cook Islands, the conch trumpet was sacred to 'Oro as the
drum was to Tane.

Orpheus In ancient Greek mythology and religion, a
Thracian musician, son of one of the Muses (usually
Calliope, by King Œagrus of Thrace): looked upon by
initiates in the Orphic mysteries as a real person who
invented or modified the Dionysian cult observances.
The myth of Orpheus embodies a story theme found all
over the world, the folktale type of the descent to the
underworld in search of a lost wife. His cult followers
are important in the history of religion, for the Orphic
mysteries may form a link between the Osiris death-
and-resurrection cult of ancient Egypt and the religious
revival of the 1st century B.C. that culminated in
Christianity.

Orpheus is one of the heroes numbered among the
Argonauts. Orphic writers magnified his part in the
expedition, i.e. he saved the *Argo*'s crew from destruction by outplaying the Sirens. The music of Orpheus
was so sweet that it charmed stones and trees to dance
or to gather around him. Orpheus married the dryad
Eurydice; one day, fleeing from Aristæus, she stepped
on a snake and died of the bite. Orpheus went down to
Hades and played before the king and queen of the
underworld. Hades and Persephone agreed to permit
Eurydice to return with Orpheus to the upper world,
but on condition that he not look back at her until they
had passed out of the underworld. If he did look back,
she would be lost to him forever. But when they neared
the light, Orpheus, either because he could no longer
resist his impulse or because he missed hearing his
wife's footsteps behind him, looked around, and Eurydice vanished.

Orpheus, having lost his chance to regain his wife,
became despondent. Some time later, he was torn to
followed his wife, Izanami, to the land of the dead,
Yomotsu-kuni. But she had eaten of underworld food
and could not be wholly freed. If he would never see her

because he attempted to reform the Dionysian rites. It was also said that Orpheus began to worship Apollo, the sun, as the greatest of gods, and that this was the reason the Mænads killed him, on the god's orders. Variants say that Zeus slew him with a thunderbolt for having revealed certain divine secrets or that he committed suicide in despair at the failure of his mission to Hades. In the principal version of the story, his head and his lyre floated to Lesbos. The head, after speaking oracularly, was buried near Antissa, where a shrine was built to Orpheus. The lyre was taken up to the heavens, where it may be seen as the constellation Lyra. Several places in Greece claimed to be the burial place of his body.

Parallels to the various incidents of the myth are found elsewhere in the world. The Japanese Izanagi too followed his wife, Izanami, to the land of the dead, Yomotsu-kuni. But she had eaten of underworld food and could not be wholly freed. If he would never see her face, she would however accompany him to the land of the living. He ignored the tabu and lit a torch, seeing the putrid decaying corpse of his wife. He fled; she, a vampire now, pursued him to the entrance of the underworld. He dropped fruits as he ran, delaying Izanami and her helpers in the chase. Izanagi rolled a rock over the entrance to prevent the emergence of the evil spirits. See ORPHEUS MYTH. The irresistible music of Orpheus is recognized in the fiddle of Type 592—*The Jew in the Thorns*—and the piping of the Pied Piper of Hamelin (D1427.1). The search for the wife is widespread as a tale type (Type 400), and the voyage to the otherworld is a frequent incident in this type. The descent to the underworld of the dead (F81), the Harrowing of Hell, occurs also in the Babylonian Gilgamesh epic, the Tammuz-Ishtar myth, the legends of Hercules, Theseus, and Odysseus, the story of Æneas, of St. Paul, of Dante. The dismemberment of Orpheus probably derives from the myth it most resembles, that of Osiris, whose head also floated far from the place of his murder. The speaking head occurs in the Norse myth of Mimir, and, according to A. H. Krappe, may, along with legends of the brazen head, have its origin in the ancient practice of skull divination. See BRAN.

It is possible that Orpheus and Dionysus are identical. Orpheus may have been considered an incarnation of the god. Orphic religion was an ascetic, mystic way of life, following specific rules of conduct and having an underlying philosophy of existence. The followers of Orphism, never numerous or well organized, believed that the body was a sort of prison of the soul, that the soul went through a cycle of deaths and rebirths, that through the living of a more and more stringent life the soul was enabled to ascend through higher forms of life until it was freed of impurity and became one with divinity, not to be reborn. During sleep, the soul escaped from its prison or "grave" and dreamed; belief in the prophetic nature of dreams was an important part of Orphism. The Orphics practiced abstention, e.g. they did not eat beans or flesh, they wore special clothing, they avoided the "taint of childbirth." They were proselytizing missionaries who held to the belief in Dionysus-Zagreus, his murder by the Titans, his rebirth from Zeus through Semele. This myth was enacted in their mysteries, along with the Hades-Persephone story. At the Orphic rites, the prohibition of flesh was placed in abeyance while the initiates partook of the flesh of the torn god, the sacrificed kid. The Orphic cult has superficial resemblances to other cults, particularly the Pythagorean, but where Pythagoreanism embodied a definite political philosophy, Orphism tended more to what is now called the religious.

Orpheus myth A North American Indian tale, first recorded in the 17th century by the Jesuits from an Eastern Woodlands tribe and containing no references to European culture elements—therefore probably of native origin—concerning the visit of a person (usually a husband or father, but sometimes a wife or wives) to the land of the dead to recover his spouse. The recovery of the dead spouse is effected; the latter accompanies the seeker back to earth, but in several versions of the tale a tabu is broken and the dead spouse returns to the afterworld. In other versions she remains on earth, and sometimes a dance is instituted. The North American Indian Orpheus myth has been analyzed into its various types, and its distribution over practically all of North America except among the Eskimo and Great Basin tribes shown, in a study by A. H. Gayton, "The Orpheus Myth in North America," *JAFL* 48, pp. 263–286, 1934. [EWV]

orris Any of several species of *Iris* having a scented root; especially *I. florentina* whose dried rootstock is used in medicine and perfumery. The scented root has been highly valued medicinally in both the Old and New World. A perfume is made from white orris root. The Indians of the southern United States use it as a purgative and as a cure for scrofula, dropsy, sore throat, and lung complaints. They place it, freshly ground, on burns and sores. In Europe it is used for these things and also for liver complaints, feeble-mindedness, teething troubles, toothache, and bruises. In Britain orris root is one of the ingredients in a remedy for asthma and coughs. A 16th century British remedy for tuberculosis contained, among other things, the blood of a calf (3 lbs.), turpentine (.002), licorice root (1 lb.), 70 garden snails, and 6 ounces of orris root. The dose was two ounces daily for 15 days. In Siberia it is used as a cure for syphilis and in remedies for heart and lung troubles. In Korea, washing the hair in orris-water in June makes it grow long.

The *Kama Sutra* of Vatsyayama mentions orris root as one of the means of subjugating women. A few pieces of orris root soaked in mango oil and hidden for six months in a hole in a tree, later mashed into an ointment and applied to the penis before intercourse, is a sure means of subjugating women.

Osain Yoruban deity of leaves and herbs, conceived as living in the forest and giving medicines to man. He has been retained in the Afroamerican cults of Brazil, Trinidad, and Cuba and (as Ossange) in Haiti. [MJH]

Osai Tutu Fourth king of Ashanti, who reigned c. 1725 (one date given is 1700–30) and who is credited with having made this people dominant in the area now the Gold Coast, through the instrument of the famous Golden Stool, which is believed to have been brought to earth from the sky by Komfo Anochti, a priest with great supernatural power. This stool, reputed to contain the *sunsum* or soul of the Ashanti, was believed to have made it possible for the Ashanti to gain their freedom from the Denkyira, and extend their own power. [MJH]

Oshossi Yoruban deity of the forest and the chase. He has been carried to the New World and is worshipped in those centers where Yoruban cult-practices have predominated, notably Cuba and Brazil, where his devotees dance for him carrying the miniature bow that is his insignia. [MJH]

Oshun Yoruban deity of the river which bears her name and, by extension, of fresh water. She is held to be one of the principal wives of Shango, the god of thunder. The amber beads worn by her devotees in Nigeria are likewise found worn by those vowed to her in the Afrobrazilian cults; elsewhere in the New World, she is worshiped in Cuba and Trinidad. [MJH]

Oshunmare The rainbow serpent of the Yoruba, the counterpart of the Dahomean Aido-hwedo. This deity has been retained in Brazil, with function unchanged. [MJH]

Osiris The king and judge of the dead of ancient Egyptian religion; chief deity of the cult of the dead, and thus the great cult god of Egypt. Only the solar cult of Rā rivalled that of Osiris. Osiris seems to have been originally the protecting god of the cemetery at Busiris in the eastern Nile Delta, and was perhaps a deified king of the region. From there his worship spread throughout the Delta and Lower Egypt and eventually to Upper Egypt. In later times his cult center was at Abydos.

The jackal, one of the chthonic animals of the world, was identified with Osiris through the equation of Osiris with Upuaut-Anubis, god of the necropolis at Abydos. The general tendency in Egyptian religion to equate gods similar in function results in the identification of Osiris with such other gods as Ptah-Seker, Khentamenti, Serapis. Osiris was depicted as a human figure, usually green- or black-fleshed, bearded, wearing the *atef*-crown of Upper Egypt, and swathed like a mummy with the hands projecting from the wrappings; he held as scepters the crook and flail (or whip). These insignia more or less identify him as an agricultural god; as god of the underworld he was an earth god, and like other chthonic deities had to do with increase of crops. Osiris was a culture god who brought to the Egyptians their knowledge of agriculture, the several crafts, the religious rituals. He ruled over crops, life, growth, vegetation, the Nile and its annual flood; later, in the 3rd millennium B.C., he became generally the god of death and resurrection. At first only the Pharaohs became Osirises on death, being identified with the god of the dead as their successors were with Horus, the son of Osiris. By the time of the Middle Kingdom (after about 2450 B.C.), all men able to pass the judgment of good and evil might become Osirises. In later times, this judgment became formalized into a trial weighing of the heart in the presence of Osiris. Anubis preceded the soul into the judgment hall; Isis and Nephthys followed. Before 42 assessors, the soul recited the Negative Confession, denying the commission of 42 acts. The heart was placed in the balance against the feather of truth. Thoth examined the scale and recorded the result. Nearby stood Ammit, the hippopotamus-lion-crocodile, ready to devour those whose hearts were heavy with misdeeds. Those who passed examination went to Aalu, the subterranean Field of Reeds in the west, where they joined the company of the gods.

The myth of Osiris as god of resurrection and fertility is, as we know it, probably colored by its principal reporter, Plutarch, 1st century A.D. Hellenistic writer, who may have interpreted the Osiris-Isis story in the light of other mysteries that he as a traveler had encountered, e.g. Adonis-Tammuz, Attis. Osiris and Isis, brother and sister, children of Geb, the earth god, and Nut, the sky goddess, lived together in happy marriage. But their brother Set envied them their happiness and one day, while the brothers were hunting, Set killed Osiris and cut his body into 14 pieces which he scattered far and wide. Isis sought out the pieces and either completed the body (traditionally she found all parts but the genitals) and revived it; or she buried each piece where she found it, thus giving a bit of the fertilizing power of the god to the several places; or she placed the parts in a coffin that floated down the Nile and across the sea to Byblus in Phœnicia. She bore a posthumous child, Horus, who battled with his uncle Set and slew him.

This myth of death and resurrection, the rebirth of Osiris, champion of good, in his son, was the subject of great fertility dramas enacted periodically in Egypt. The cult mysteries undoubtedly had a strong influence on the later Greek mystery religions; hence, the cult of Osiris, with its concept of the dead being received by and becoming one with the god, had a formative influence on Christianity. The Osirian cult was very popular among the Romans, who carried it with them throughout the Empire. The fertility symbolism of the myth is paralleled elsewhere in the world; the Scandinavian Frey and the Finnish Lemminkäinen, for example, both were killed and cut into pieces. The Osiris-Set conflict is likewise part of the world-wide pattern of the conflicting brothers, one the culture hero, the other the spirit of the undisciplined life. See RĀ.

Ostara (Old English *Oestre*) The very early Teutonic goddess of spring: a development from the earlier Aryan goddess of the dawn. The transition from dawn to spring goddess, according to O. Schrader (*ERE* i: 34b), was the natural ascription to the goddess of the time of year she was honored. The old Aryan dawn goddess was worshipped with special festivals in the spring (the dawn of the living year). See EASTER.

ostówegowa The Great Feather dance of the Iroquois Indians, one of their four chief communal rituals. It offers thanks to the Creator for all benefits, especially crops, during the Midwinter and Thanksgiving ceremonies, and it forms part of the sequence of food-spirit dances in the various harvest and green corn festivals. Two singers pound turtle-shell rattles thunderously against their bench. The men start circling, with experts in the lead. They stamp furiously with alternate heels and work themselves into an ecstasy of gesticulating, whirling, and yelling. In their wake the women, shoulder to shoulder, quietly glide to the right with a twisting shuffle. A double line may wind itself around the room, all pulsing down and up with a unison flexion and rebound of the knees. The strenuous efforts of the men continue unabated for forty minutes or an hour, except for the walk-arounds (punctuated with yells) between the dances. Today the costumes are eclectic: the men wear breechclouts on top of trousers, bright-colored shirts and war bonnets, usually of the Sioux type; women wear the modified 19th century Iroquois costume, with smock and beaded trousers. The men thus wear feathers on their heads, but they do not carry the feathered wands formerly wielded by the similar feather dancers of the Creek and Yuchi. The feathers serve as instruments for the conveyance of prayer to the sky. [GPK]

Ostyak or **Chanti folklore** The Ostyaks or Chanti are an Ob-Ugric people, about 19,000, living on the Ob River, the Irtysh, and its tributaries, western Siberia. Their god of heaven is Num-Tūrem. Chief of their evil deities is Tarn, god of war, sickness, bad weather, etc., usually represented in female shape. Ostyak heroes, if one believes the folk songs, were taken after death to the sky where they live in the form of iron wolves, and are still leading the warrior life. The worship of the bear and shamanism are common. Every man has his soul and his shadow. After death the soul is believed to be reborn in some baby within the clan; the shadow goes to the underworld and there lives a life very similar to that on earth. (S. Patkanov, *Die Irtisch-Ostjaken und ihre Volkspoesie*, 2 vols., Petrograd, 1897 and 1900; M. A. Czaplika, "Ostyak," *ERE* ix: 796–800; A. O. Väisänen, *Wogulische und ostjakische Melodien*, Helsinki, 1937, *MSFO* 73.) [JB]

Othagwenda Flint, eldest of the twin culture heroes of the Iroquois Indians. For his birth and deeds see JUSKAHA. [EWV]

otherworld The three otherworlds general in European tradition are Heaven (the land in the skies where deserving souls go), Hell (the underworld where the evil are eternally punished), and Fairyland (the land of magic where the fairies live, and where a logic like that of dreams governs everything). There may be a historical line of development from Fairyland, the pagan land where the fairies are ruled by their queen, to Heaven, the dwelling place of the angels ruled by God. Purgatory and Limbo are later additions to the Heaven and Hell of official doctrine. The Garden of Eden, too, is an otherworld, lost to man by his own foolhardiness. Avalon (E481.4.1) is a fairyland-otherworld where all ills are cured, and where King Arthur waits to return to his people. The Islands of the Blest (A692) of Irish tradition are paralleled by the Greek western land of Elysium. Also of Celtic tradition is the Land of Women (F112), a Paradise of sorts for men, but perhaps referable to an early gynocracy looked back to as being in a better time and place; the Greek *Argo* too stopped at an island of women, Lemnos, where Jason, Hercules, and the other Argonauts replaced for a time the husbands the women of the island had killed. Otherworlds, fairylands, lie at the bottoms of wells, under the sea (there are many local legends of sunken lands), beneath rivers (see the common ending to the *Master Thief* tale, where the thief convinces a passerby that he has many cattle in his lands on the riverbed), inside mountains, within deep forests, across forbidding rivers or mountains, even on the sun, moon, and planets. Jack climbed the beanstalk to an otherworld in the clouds, and Orpheus descended to the underworld in an attempt to free Eurydice from Hades. The sailors have their Fiddler's Green, where wine, women, and song are free and easy. The American hobo's Big Rock Candy Mountains are peopled with wooden-legged cops and rubber-toothed dogs; the jails are tin and streams of alcohol run down the rocks. See AFTERWORLD; ANNWN; ARROW CHAIN; ASCENT TO UPPER WORLD; DESCENTS TO UNDERWORLD; ECHTRAI; EMERGENCE MYTH; FOOD TABU IN THE LAND OF THE DEAD; HADES; HEL; ITIWANA; RAINBOW; UNDERWORLD.

Our Good Man A popular English ballad (Child #274), a tale of cuckoldry in which the husband, coming home and finding various evidences of the presence of his wife's lover, is offered a series of absurd explanations and in turn comments wryly on the excuses. The strange horse in the stable, for instance, is explained as a cow, the strange coat on the bed a bedquilt, the head on the pillow a cabbage. The husband remarks that he has never seen a saddle on a cow before, nor a pocket on a quilt, nor a beard on a cabbage. The song was translated into German in 1789 and passed into German, Scandinavian, and Hungarian oral tradition. In the United States it is widely known and is sung by hillbillies, soldiers and sailors, etc., under many titles.

Our Grandmother Kokumthena, Our Grandmother, is the term generally used in reference to the Shawnee female creator, the most important active deity in the pantheon of the Shawnee Indians of the eastern United States. The Shawnee differ from all their Woodlands Algonquian neighbors by having a female instead of a male deity who is credited with creating man, ordering the world to some extent, and giving to the Shawnee their own "way of life." Historical documents show that it is only during the last 125 years that Our Grandmother has been accorded by the Shawnee such an important position in their pantheon and mythology. Formerly, a male being who is now completely otiose and whose existence is unknown to many members of the tribe was referred to by the Shawnee as their creator. The Shawnee female creator is depicted in their present-day mythology as sometimes large, sometimes of ordinary size, having gray hair, and now living in or near the land of the dead. She has as companions a grandson, a small dog, and some giant "boys" who are cannibalistically inclined. Personal names, seldom used for her, are Snaggle-Tooth Woman, and Cloud. Her picture, bending over a cooking pot, is to be seen in the full moon. Formerly she and her grandson lived on earth; she sometimes attends Shawnee bread dances, manifesting her presence by singing with the women in a high, distinguishable voice. See C. F. Voegelin, *The Shawnee Female Deity*, Yale Univ. Publications in Anthropology 10, 1936. [EWV]

our mother's brother Coyote, the culture hero of California Kato and Yuki Indian mythology, is often referred to as "our mother's brother." In this mythology Coyote stole the sun and secured fire from Spider, who was hoarding it.

Outlaw Murray A Scottish border ballad (Child #305) telling of the subjection of an outlaw to the Scottish king. The long ballad (74 quatrains) is older than 1700 and may date back to the 16th century; no historical incident to parallel the story told has ever been discovered. The outlaw Murray lives an idyllic life in Ettrick Forest with his lady and 500 men in a stone castle. Someone brings news to the king that Murray will not acknowledge him as overlord.

> "I mak a vowe," then the goode king said,
> "Unto the man that dear bought me,
> I'se either be king of Etrick forest,
> Or king of Scotland that Outlaw's be."

Earl Hamilton counsels caution and suggests sending a messenger first to see whether Murray will submit. Afterwards, he says, will be time enough for force. The messenger returns with Murray's answer:

"Thir landis are mine," the Outlaw said,
"I own na king in Christentie;
Fræ Soudron I this forest wan,
When the king nor's knights were not to see."

The king collects an army of 15,000 men and marches against Murray, who calls his friends to aid. But before fighting can begin, cool heads suggest one meeting between king and Murray. Murray kneels before the king and agrees finally to acknowledge that the lands are held from the king; in return he is granted the sheriffdom of the forest for himself and his descendants.

ovens of youth A metaphorical term used for the initiation ceremonies in Tikopia (Polynesia). The *punaumu*, kindling of the ovens, first takes place following a boy's first torchlight fishing expedition in a canoe at about the age of ten, and great quantities of food are prepared by his parents for the celebration which takes place on his return. The kindling of the ovens more significantly applies, however, to the actual initiation when he undergoes the operation of superincision at the hands of a maternal uncle, receives instruction in matters of sex and tribal history and codes, is given permission to marry and to take part in dangerous enterprises. The initiations are always accompanied by the preparation of quantities of food, and the kindling of the ovens refers literally to just that, the kindling of the ovens for the cooking of food.

It is the custom in Tikopia to kindle two ovens for a person who has experienced either death or injury. Hence the oven is symbol among these people of sympathy, concern, and reparation. To say "his ovens have been kindled" means that a boy has undergone the initiation ritual. See R. Firth, *We, The Tikopia*, New York, 1936, p. 432.

overhearing A folktale motif (H13, N450–452, etc.) in which animals, gods, dwarfs, ogres, and other non-human beings are overheard telling some secret which is then turned to advantage by the hero. It occurs in tales all over the world. The overhearing motif, as described by Penzer, excludes the accidental listening to human speech or conversation, though some might consider incidents like Ali Baba's hearing the robbers' "Open Sesame" (N455.3) an instance of overhearing. The motif is always incidental and is used by the story-teller to solve a dilemma for his hero, although the information, the way it is used, and the informers themselves, unwitting or purposeful, vary from tale to tale. Almost always the overhearing is of a conversation between a pair of animals or birds, of the same or different species. The popular saying "A little bird told me" utilizes this common incident. Faithful John listens to three ravens; in a French-Canadian story, the conversation of a lion, a bear, and a wolf is overheard. Often the listener is hidden in a tree or is thought to be asleep; often the threatened penalty for telling what he has overheard is some kind of horrible death. The minister's son who overhears two owls will have his head burst into a thousand pieces if he tells what he knows.

The information obtained through overhearing may be used to avoid death or catastrophe; to obtain wealth or high position; to resolve a perplexity. Though the knowledge is of great help to the hero of the stories, in many instances the same knowledge results in the death of the animal that so rashly talks, not knowing of the hidden listener. For example, a bird may tell that its heart is the only thing that can cure the king: the hero will then kill the bird and cure the king. This sort of self-defeat is most apparent in the Rumpelstiltskin story, where the princess, because she overhears the dwarf singing to himself, is able to rescue herself from an impossible situation. A very similar idea is found in many life token stories, when, for example, the giant gives away the secret of where his soul is kept, and the listening hero is able to kill him by using the information. How the hero can understand the animals or birds he overhears is seldom a problem to the story-tellers, but sometimes the understanding is knit into the story by some other incident, as with Siegfried's tasting of the dragon's blood and his subsequent understanding of the language of the birds—or sometimes the animals simply speak in human language. The animal languages motif, in which the hero understands the language spoken by the animals among themselves, as do Siegfried and Faithful John, is thus intimately connected with the overhearing motif. Compare ANIMAL LANGUAGES.

overlooking The act of the one who casts the evil eye: the term most generally used in English for the action. Belief in the evil eye is world-wide and is found from earliest times. Probably it arose from the belief that people whose eyes somehow looked different (Pliny cites Phylarchus on people with two pupils in one eye and the image of a horse in the other) were capable of doing magic: this is a specialized form of the fear of strangers common among many peoples. Thus generally throughout the Mediterranean area, where eyes are commonly dark, one with blue eyes is thought to possess the evil eye; in northern Europe, the dark-eyed person has the evil eye. Squinters, people with a cast, even sufferers from cataract, all may be in certain places suspected of overlooking.

Overlooking may not be voluntary; the possessor of the evil eye, whether he wills it or not, may cause ill to things, animals, or people he looks at. However, most overlooking is considered to be malicious. The powers of the evil eye are boundless. The overlooker may cause death, illness, poverty, loss of affections, bodily injury, or any number of other evil effects. Especially vulnerable are young children and animals. Therefore, among many peoples, praise of a child's beauty or cleverness or health, or of a herd's numbers or the like, must never be fulsome, or, if given, must be balanced by a counteracting expression to avert the evil eye. The evil eye seems to be most potent when the victim is healthy, prosperous, happy, especially if his wealth or good fortune has brought him to public importance—at least its effects are more noticeable when the person bewitched loses much because of being overlooked.

Averting the evil eye may be accomplished by sayings (counter-charms), amulets, certain actions or gestures. Amulets in the form of frogs or various loathsome creatures are worn to attract the power of the evil eye to them rather than to the wearer. Red ribbons plaited into a horse's or cow's tail or mane, or placed over the doorway of a house, will destroy the effect of the evil eye.

Wearing a bit of holy writing, or putting it at the entrance of the house, averts the influence of the evil eye. Planting the jack bean around a field or garden preserves the crop from being overlooked. Many plants, e.g. the shamrock in Ireland, garlic in Greece, protect against the evil eye. Gestures like the "horns" (*mano cornuta*) or the "fig" (*fico*), which have a sexual, hence fertility, connotation, turn the evil eye from the maker of the sign. Spitting, in ancient Greece and Rome, and in many other places since then, is a powerful antidote. The bridal veil is thought to have originated as a specific protection against overlooking, for the happy bride might be especially the target of envious evil-doers. See BALOR; MEDUSA.

Ovid Publius Ovidius Naso (43 B.C.–17 or 18 A.D.) Roman poet of the Augustan period. He was an Equestrian by birth, held several positions of minor importance in the public service, and was exiled by Augustus some ten years before his death to Tomi, a town on the Danube near the Black Sea. The cause of the exile is not known: Ovid was in some way involved in a scandal concerning Augustus' granddaughter Julia, and this, added to the emperor's probable long-standing resentment against the author of the libertine *Ars amatoria*, may have been at the root of the poet's banishment. Ovid's retelling of the Greek myths and legends, and his calendar (incomplete) of the Roman year, are a principal source of our knowledge of these matters, though much of his statement of the myths is probably of his own invention. The *Metamorphoses*, 15 books, retells many of the transformation tales of the ancient world, beginning with Chaos and ending with the catasterism of Julius Cæsar. Here too are the many tales of the amorous adventures of the gods who transformed themselves the better to accomplish their aims. The *Fasti*, written at the same period, essayed to describe the legends, the historical background, the astronomical and meteorological signs, the festivals and other religious events associated with each day of the calendar. Only six books, covering six months, were completed. An earlier work, the *Heroides*, purports to be a group of letters from famed women of past time. Ovid, even more than Vergil, has had the greatest influence of all the classical writers on English writers, stylistically, technically, and as reference source.

ovinnik A form of the domovik, the household spirit of Russia, who resides in the drying-kiln. He does not like to have the kiln fired on the great festivals and may burn down the building if his wishes in this are ignored. He is propitiated and thanked for helping with—and for not interfering with—various chores near the kiln, for example for a good threshing. Sometimes the blood of a sacrificed cock is sprinkled near the oven for his delectation.

owe The term among the Yoruba people for proverbs: quoted to conclude and point the moral of stories, to spice dialog, and to influence the behavior of others by derision or defiance. See AFRICAN AND NEW WORLD NEGRO FOLKLORE.

owl As the bird of Athena (companion and attribute) the owl was auspicious in classical Greece; old Greek vases associated with the worship of Athena depict owls with breasts, and vulva represented by a circle. But in Rome the owl was a bird of ill-omen and its hooting presaged death. The death of Augustus, for instance, was predicted by the hooting of an owl; an owl came and sat in the room of the emperor Commodus Aurelius just before he died; Cæsar's murder was heralded by the screeching of owls. The Talmud mentions its being bad luck to dream of owls. *Leviticus* numbers the owl among the unclean birds.

In European and American folklore in general, the owl is also a bird of ill-omen whose hooting is an omen of death. In Scotland, it is bad luck to see an owl in the daytime. In Wales, the hooting of an owl not only presages death but often the loss of virginity of some village maiden, or the hooting "tells" the moment of such an occurrence. In Newfoundland, the cry of the horned owl predicts bad weather. There are various charms for counteracting these omens: turning your pockets or any article of clothing inside out will stop the screech-owl from hooting; so will tying a knot in a handkerchief hush him, or throwing salt in the fire.

North American Kiowa Indians hold that the medicine man becomes an owl after death, and the owl after death becomes a cricket. The eastern Cherokees believe the cry of the screech-owl portends death or sickness. Penobscot Indians say the screech-owl, if mocked, will burn up the mocker in his camp; but they regard the barred owl as a camp guardian who will warn of approaching danger. Among the Chippewa, a stuffed owl is set up to "watch" and superintend the pounding of medicine roots by the Mide medicine men. The Pawnees regard the owl as a protection in the night.

In Kalmuck legend, a white owl once saved the life of Genghis Khan; these people therefore venerate him today. The Buriats keep a tame owl in the house as a protector of children. Bantu and Zulu groups are terrified of the owl because they associate him with the machinations of the sorcerer. Yoruba Negroes also associate the owl with the sorcerer. See FAMILIAR; SENDING.

In India, owl's flesh is regarded as an aphrodisiac, but eating it will turn a man into a fool. Eating the eyeballs, however, enables one to see in the dark. In medieval magic and medicine, owl feathers laid on a person would cause him to fall into a soothing sleep. Owl broth was an old cure for whooping-cough. The Wends say the sight of an owl would cause a woman to have an easy delivery.

One of the best known folktales about the owl is the story of the baker's daughter who was turned into an owl for begrudging bread her mother had baked for Jesus. Other motifs include the owl as bird of ill omen (B147.1.1.4), owl as a ghost in the Wild Hunt (E501.4.5), etiological incidents explaining why the owl is blind by day (A2233.3; A2332.6.6), owl as revenant, etc. (E423.3.5). See ATHENA.

☞ Apparently since pre-Conquest times the belief has been widespread in Middle America that a hooting owl at night presages death; hence, owls are greatly feared. [GMF]

owl dance A representation of this night-haunting bird, confined to American Indian tribes, notwithstanding the prevalent European beliefs in its baneful powers. In the mimetic Menominee owl dance, the men and women, moving around a drum, stoop and peer through spectacles formed by touching the forefinger and thumb. Sauk couples suggest the motion of an owl's wings by swaying their arms forward and back as they circle sun-wise with a balancing step. In the beginning and end of the dance, the partners (of opposite sexes) hold out-side hands; in the middle they break hold, moving for-ward in a single file or sideways to the left. The Crow Indians formerly alternated their non-mimetic owl dance (*po'pete disue*) with the hot dance, as a social squaw dance. Though social dances, and not always imitative, these owl dances have a magical origin, malefic or beneficial. To the Iroquois Indian the owl is baneful, and is invoked in the songs of the Hanáhidos medicine society. The Creek propitiate him in dance, because he can send disease. To the Delaware hunter, as he leaves for the ritual hunt on the fourth day of the Big House ceremony, the screech owl brings good luck. The Meno-minee trace their gift of medicine to an owl disguised as grandmother Mi'äniu, and their hunting medicine to Koko'ko, the horned owl. The Papago associate the owl with the dead, but the feathers with cure. [GPK]

ox In Iranian creation myth, Gēush Urvan is the huge primeval ox from whose blood sprang all useful herbs and all living animals. In the Talmud, Adam's first sacrifice was an ox with but one horn on its brow. In ancient Greece also the ox was a frequent sacrifice; most pleasing to the gods was an offering of 100 oxen, a *hecatomb*. Oxen were important in the rural economy of the Israelites, and in their sacrifice, and strict measures were enacted for their protection.

In folktale we find numerous etiological stories ex-plaining why the ox is a draft animal (A2252.2; A2515.1), why he has no hair on his lips (A2342.2), how he got his horns (A2326.1.4). There is the helpful ox motif (B411.2), the oracular ox (B154.1), and the magic ox (B182.2). There is the man transformed into an ox (D133.3), the ox himself taking the shape of another animal (D412.2 ff), the devil as ox (G303.3.3.10). A giant ox occurs in European folktale as in American. See BABE THE BLUE OX. Christian legend says that Jesus was born in the oxen's stall, that the ox with other animals knelt in adoration, and still kneels at midnight on Christmas Eve. One of Æsop's fables recites the sad end of the frog who wished to be as big as an ox (J955.1). In Italy great ox horns protect from the evil eye. In Madagascar it is customary to apportion parts of the ox as follows: its horn to the makers of spoons, its teeth to plaiters of straw, its ears to the doctors to make a cer-tain medicine good for a rash. See CAKE CUSTOMS; GēUSH URVAN; OX THAT GORED. [GPS]

Oxdansen Oxen dance: a Swedish sham fight in dance form. The two male opponents go through absurd ges-tures in a truly Scandinavian spirit of good-natured horseplay. Taking turns in time with the lively tune, they bow and squat, pull each other's hair, make a long nose, pull ears and stick out the tongue, bump elbows, box each other's ears, etc. In the last gesture, the victim bends to the side to avoid the blow, as he claps his hands to simulate the swat. After each bit of mime, both perform a refrain face to face, a sharp side-kick, head turn, and lunge, followed by glaring. This "duel" is said to have originated as a form of hazing by students of Karlstadt, Sweden, the freshmen or "oxen" being obliged to keep straight faces through all their antics.

It has become immensely popular in all Swedish folk-dance gatherings in the United States as well as abroad, and has been welcomed as an entertaining male tidbit in demonstrations. [GPK]

ox that gored *Exodus* xxi, 28, says, "And if an ox gore a man or a woman, that they die, the ox shall be surely stoned." Summary execution of animals causing injury to man is known in northeastern India, Celebes, Persia, and many other parts of the world. The doctrine that "every dog is entitled to one bite," but that subsequent use of the teeth on mankind, whatever the provocation, may bring punishment, is still followed by many U.S. courts. However, full-dress trials of animals in Europe were many (at least 92 in France from the 12th to the 18th century), with defending lawyers basing defenses and appeals on everything from the doctrine of natural rights to quotations from Scripture. In Brazil in 1713, after full argument of the case, the bishop trying the case decided that a number of ants who were undermin-ing a monastery were entitled to seek for food as their natures led them, but that, since the friars had come to the New World to spread the Gospel, the ants must follow their natural bent in an appointed nearby field and leave the monastery. The migration of the ants to the designated field in obedience to the court's order was soon after observed. As J. G. Frazer indicates (*Folk-lore in the Old Testament,* Part IV, Ch. IV), trials of vermin were usually in ecclesiastical courts, since sen-tences against them were enforceable only by God; a human executioner would have been hard put to it to execute a horde of mice, ants, locusts, caterpillars, or the like. But domestic animals, such as sows, cows, dogs, horses, were tried, condemned, and executed by civil courts. A famous trial at Basle in 1474 ended in the death sentence for a cock that had laid an egg. Though the animal itself was deemed innocent of crime, obvi-ously some evil spirit had invaded its body, and the sorcerer or demon was destroyed, along with the egg, at the stake. The principle here underlying, that of pos-session, undoubtedly was behind many of the trials. But at a much earlier stage in human thought, man and beast were conceived of as being animated by the same sort of essence. All things have a soul or personality in primitive animistic thought. Thus, examples of punish-ments of destruction visited upon spears, trees, statues, etc., which had caused death are quoted by Frazer (*loc. cit.*) from India, the Ainus of Japan, British East Africa, ancient Athens (where the ax used in the Bouphonia, the yearly slaughter of a sacrificial ox to Zeus, was tried and condemned), Thasos, Olympia, Rome, etc.

Oyandone In Seneca (Iroquois) Indian mythology, Moose, the east wind. He was called by Ga-oh into the sky to blow forth mists and chill from his nostrils, to lead the rains, and break down with his antlers great paths through the forests before storms.

Oykanye Archaic singing style of Dalmatian peasants, in which the first of two singers starts with *oy* on one note, then trills on a minor third, dropping back finally to the interval of a second, and the other voice, begin-ning after the opening, carries only one note, until both finish together on a second.

P

Pa'am Akhat Literally, once: a play dance of Palestine, with singing, first by the male central player, then by his chosen partner: "Once a lad went walking . . ." "Once a lass went walking . . ." The player, in the center of a circle, beckons to his chosen lady, who dances with him, then does the beckoning, dancing backwards. She stays in the center to recommence the dance. [GPK]

Paccari tambo The three mythical caves from which emerged the four Ayar brothers and their four sisters who became the ancestors of the Inca family and its related lineages. See AYAR. [AM]

Pa Cha The Chinese god who protects against locusts and grasshoppers: associated with rites for the "calling" and destruction of grasshoppers. He is depicted with a bird's beak; his clawed right hand holds a magic gourd, containing a magic insecticide; his left holds a sword. His mammæ are strongly developed. His color is blue-green; his hair is red. After good harvests a hut is built or a tent put up in the village street, in which images of Pa Cha and other gods are hung. Here priests beat drums for a half a day or more, and make a great racket to the delight of the local children, who are also given magic charms to take home. Pa Cha has been identified by some scholars with the agricultural deity Liu-Mêng Chiang-Chün, and also with a Mongol peasant named Pa Cha who lived unharmed in the midst of wolves and scorpions and whose garden was never injured by grasshoppers. [RDJ]

Pachacamac The supreme god of the ancient coastal people of Peru. His name means Earthmaker: identified with Viracocha, the supreme god and creator of the Incas. Pachacamac was worshipped in a famous temple, the ruins of which still stand near Lima. [AM]

Pachamama Mother Earth: the earth goddess of the Incas of ancient Peru. She is still worshipped by the natives of the highlands of Ecuador, Peru, Bolivia, and northwestern Argentina. As their main deity, she is invoked in prayers and receives sacrifices of llamas and other animals. The most important ceremonies in her honor coincide with the beginning and end of the various agricultural cycles. Following the contact of these peoples with Europeans, Pachamama has in many cases been identified with the Virgin Mary. [AM]

pachecos Literally, cowboys or herdsmen: an enactment of bull-baiting and lassoing performed by Mixtec men of Oaxaca, Mexico. Their outfits copy cowboy attire: leather jackets and fur-trimmed flaring trousers, wide sombreros, and spurs. One of their group masquerades as the bull, and two clowns disguised as women cavort in their midst. This sprightly dance is related in content and probably in meaning to the *vaqueros* and *toreadores*. [GPK]

pada The Sanskrit term for footwork in the *natya* code of Hindu dancing, *boumya mandala pada* being executed on the floor in five different positions, and *akasa pada*

in the air. The corresponding leg motions on the floor and in the air are termed *boumya čari* and *akasa čari*. Jumps are called *utplavana*. [GPK]

Padmapāni Literally, lotus-in-hand: the universal savior of Mahāyāna Buddhism, the greatest of the bodhisattvas, and prototype of the Chinese goddess, Kuanyin (and Japanese Kwannon): an epithet of Avalokita. The archetype of Padmapāni was also female, as the lotus suggests. Padmapāni is one of the divine transformers of Indian Buddhistic mythology, appearing variously as man, woman, animal, insect; one of his famous shapes is the winged horse *Valāhaka* (cloud); in Tibet Padmapāni is sometimes depicted with eleven heads. A 9th or 10th century figure of Padmapāni depicts him with right hand down and palm out (the granting-gifts gesture, *varadāmudrā*) and lotus in the left. See H. Zimmer, *Myths and Symbols of Indian Art and Civilization*, New York, 1946, pp. 96–97.

Paguk In the folklore of the Timiskaming Algonquians and Timagami Ojibwa, a creature of bones, a human skeleton without flesh, who clatters noisily through the forest, and travels as fast as thought. For a person to hear Paguk is a sign that a friend will be lost and die. Paguk is believed formerly to have been a hunter who starved to death in the bush. Before he died he wished that his life and the strength of his flesh might be transferred to his bones. His wish was granted; his strength went into his bones, and his flesh fell away. [EWV]

Pa Hsien The Chinese Eight Immortals: a group of legendary characters said to have originated in the Sung dynasty, 960–1127, but obviously their tradition is much older. This fraternity, in revolt against the stuffiness of Sung etiquette, is immortal, and goes around indulging in all imaginable sorts of nonsense. The members are: Chang Kuo, Han Chung-li, Han Hsiang-tzŭ, Ho Hsien-ku, Lan Ts'ai-ho, Li T'ieh-kuai, Lü Tung-pin, Ts'ao Kuo-chiu. See CHINESE FOLKLORE. [RDJ]

pairikas In the *Avesta* and other Zoroastrian texts, supernatural beings; enchantresses; female counterparts of the *yatus* or sorcerers: classified among the druĵes, the spirits of evil and aids of Ahriman or Angra Mainyu. Pairika is the Avestan form of modern Persian *peri*.

paixtle dance (from the Nahuatl *paixtli*, moss or hay) A masked dance of Tuxpan and neighboring villages of Jalisco, Mexico: also called *el heno*, the hay. The men are covered, except for their arms, by a cape of moss, by a wooden or paper mask, and a kerchief over the head. They are said to represent sorcerers with animal power, despite the human features of the mask. They cry like mysterious beasts and carry a shepherd's staff carved with an animal's head. The bells on the neck of the animal jingle as the dancer strikes the staff rhythmically on the ground. The cumbersome outfit permits the execution of simple steps and stamps. The *sones* (tunes) played on a fiddle are the only Spanish touch.

Otherwise the dance evidently preserves a pre-Columbian rite of animal magic. [GPK]

Paiyatemu, Paiyatamu or **Paiyatuma** Zuñi Indian Sun Youth, the first of the Koshare, son of Sun Father or of Underground Mother. A powerful spirit with whom the clowns of Zuñi identify themselves, Sun Youth is believed to travel along the Galaxy, and be so senseless and funny that his father, the Sun, has to let him do exactly as he pleases. In some Zuñi tales the Paiyatemu are referred to as a group, rather than a single individual. Paiyatemu as an individual at Zuñi and in the Keresan pueblos is characterized as a handsome seductive flute player associated with the Sun, who allures or frightens away and then recovers the Corn Maidens, and who is the prototype of lovers. He is equated with the Hopi T'aiowa. [EWV]

Pakrokitat The name of the beneficent creator of the Serrano Indians of southern California, from whose left shoulder Kukitat, the evil creator of the Serrano, was born. Kukitat and Pakrokitat were always quarreling; finally Pakrokitat left the earth to his evil brother and retired to a world of his own to which people go after death. See EXCREMENTS SWALLOWED. [EWV]

Pa kua A set of eight trigrams important in ancient as well as modern Chinese divination, each composed of three broken lines. When these are placed one above

From top clockwise
ch'en: thunder, hard
li: fire, creation
tui: water, sea, light
kan: sky, *yang*, life,
    good omen
hsü: wind, wood
k'an: liquid, cool,
    moon
kên: mountains, hindering
kun: earth, *yin*, desolation, ill omen

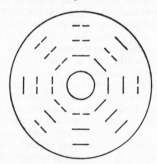

the other, 64 hexagrams result which contain 384 lines corresponding to the days of the intercalary year. The science of interpreting these trigrams has occupied the attention of many Chinese and Occidental scholars. [RDJ]

Pāli Canon The sacred canon of the Hīnāyāna school or Little Vehicle of Buddhism. The Buddhist scriptures have been handed down in two forms, the Pāli or southern, and the Sanskrit or northern (Mahāyāna) texts. Only the former is extant. The Pāli Canon prevails in Ceylon, Burma, and Siam; the extant fragments of the Sanskrit text, as well as Chinese and Tibetan translations, are used in China, Tibet, and Japan. This Buddhist literature includes collections of speeches, rules of conduct, sayings, and tales combined into "three baskets," or the *Tripiṭaka*. The first, the Basket of Discipline (*Vinaya-piṭaka*), includes the rules for Buddhist monks and nuns, directions for life during the rainy season, clothing to be worn, medicinal remedies, and stories from the Buddha legend. The second basket (*Sutta-piṭaka*) makes extensive use of parables in explaining the doctrine of Buddha. The Basket of Higher Religion (*Abhidhamma-piṭaka*), first uttered in the Tāvatimsa heaven to which Buddha went to preach the doctrine to his deified mother and the devas, is more scholastic in

form than the second basket but contains the same material.

Palm Sunday The sixth and last Sunday of Lent and the beginning of Holy Week; part of the complex of beliefs that has to do with the coming of spring. Although the day itself commemorates Christ's victorious entry into Jerusalem, the processional use of palms is traditional to symbolize victory and rejoicing. In all Christian countries it is a solemn festival. After the palms are blessed and distributed to the congregation, various uses are made of them. Formerly they were burned and the ashes preserved to be used on Ash Wednesday of the following year. In Ireland on Palm Sunday the blessed palms (usually yew) were hung up in houses and cattle stalls for luck and often planted along with the potatoes to bless the crop. Elsewhere they decorate the graves. In the East they are used to procure rain. Dust swept from the churches on Palm Sunday is helpful, in other places, in preserving the crops. See ASS. [RDJ]

Pan The ancient Arcadian god of flocks, the Feeder or Herdsman; a minor god whose worship spread to other parts of Greece within historical times (5th–4th century B.C.): identified by some with the Vedic Pūṣan and the Egyptian Min. It is said that before the battle of Marathon (490 B.C.) Pan promised help against the Persians; in the battle he routed the Asiatic armies with "Panic fear"; the grateful Athenians then established a shrine for him on the Acropolis.

Pan, as a god of herds, appears as a goat from the waist down, with goat ears, turned-up nose, and goat horns. Like other pastoral deities (Apollo, Hermes), he plays a musical instrument he invented, the Panpipes, made of reeds. He invented the open-air *danse champêtre;* when Pelops received his ivory shoulder, Pan danced for joy; he is often depicted dancing and playing the pipes in a spirit of revelry. He is generally a lusty god, sporting with or chasing nymphs—since fertility is a necessary province of a pastoral god. In Arcadia, when hunting was poor or when flocks declined, the image of Pan was scourged with squills to induce greater fertility. Pan was leader of the satyrs, the woodland spirits of fertility and license. Despite his love of noise and riot, Pan also liked lonely places in the mountains and hills, and at noonday would sleep in some quiet shady spot. Travelers had to be wary not to wake him; in fact, noon was generally a good time to be quiet, for the god's anger was terrible. He could drive men with great fear with his loud voice or he could send them horrid nightmare dreams.

In myth, he is son of Hermes and Dryope or of Hermes (as a ram) and Penelope, Odysseus' wife. Another story makes Pan the child of Penelope and all her suitors. He was born perfectly formed and was raised by the nymphs. He was a companion of Dionysus and Cybele, whose riotous processions included the noisy pans or satyrs. His emblem was the phallus. In Pan's province were weather, the flocks and herds, forage plants. Later etymological amplification of his myth made Pan the god of all (*pan*) nature, but is extraneous to the Arcadian shepherd god. A curious myth of late occurrence says that on the day Christ was crucified, a ship passing the island of Paxos in the Ionian Sea heard a call from the island: "Great Pan is dead!" When the ship got to

Rome, the story was told and it was noted that thenceforth all the oracles were silent.

Panan A Malayalim devil-dancing caste of southwest India. By identification with the demons, in costume and motion, the dancers have power to exorcise them or to induce benefits. 1) They cast out petty devils from bodies, especially of children, and thus effect cures, by beating on an hourglass drum (*thudi*), by magic formulæ (*mantram*), and by offerings. 2) By means of the din of drum and cymbal they drive evil spirits from the homes of the higher Brāhman and Nayar castes. 3) They dance all night, beating on metal plates with sticks to allay demons in the fifth pregnancy month of women of the Tiyan caste. 4) By dancing with an umbrella before a temple they invoke their demons' power over crops, and allay the spirits of the dead on the seventh day of funerals. [GPK]

pancakes Thin batter cakes fried in a pan, associated especially in the British Isles with Shrove Tuesday, which is often called Pancake Tuesday. It was quite common in rural England for the girls and boys to congregate in the kitchen and eat pancakes after the cock-threshing on Shrove Tuesday. Whoever had the reputation of being a lie-abed was supposed to receive the first one. The cakes had to be tossed high during the frying, and there was much merrymaking, especially if any fell short of the pan. Tossing a pancake into a crowd was also a favorite game on this day, with a prize for whoever came up with the largest piece. It is a general rural saw that to eat pancakes on Shrove Tuesday and peas on Ash Wednesday will keep you in money for a year. Lincolnshire farmers throw a pancake to the barnyard rooster on this day; if he eats it all, bad luck is in the offing; if he calls his hens to share it, good luck is in store for the farmer and his house. The "pancake bell," originally rung in the church to call the people to their shriving, is now interpreted as a signal to begin frying pancakes. Rich and poor alike eat pancakes on Shrove Tuesday in Lancashire, Cheshire, and northern England generally.

The famous pancake race, run in Olney, England, since 1445, was abandoned during World War II, but resumed in 1949 and recorded both over B.B.C. and television. The race is run from the market square to the church and begins at 11:55 A.M. Two pancake bells are rung, one at 11:30, one at 11:45, as signal to Olney housewives to prepare their pancakes. Women who enter the race must be over 18, wear aprons, hats or other head-covering, dresses (no slacks permitted), and the pancakes must be tossed three times during the race. In Ireland the young people also enjoy themselves in rural kitchens eating pancakes on Shrove Tuesday night. In some sections the flour to make them has been collected from house to house.

In Brittany pancakes and cider are set out for the dead on All Souls' Eve. In some Macedonian villages the evil spirits known to be abroad on New Year's Eve are burnt to death by hot pancakes sizzling in a pan. In Estonia at cabbage-planting time, a big round pancake is made and placed in the garden to encourage the cabbages to grow big round leaves. See BERCHTA; CAKE CUSTOMS.

Panchajana In Hindu mythology, the sea demon who lived under the ocean in a conch-shell. Panchajana carried off the son of Sāndīpani, thus arousing the anger of Krishna who plunged into the waters, killed the monster, and used his shell as a trumpet. When blown the trumpet annihilated the unrighteous. *Pānchajanya* is the term for Krishna's divine conch-shell. A small shell is used to pour holy water over images of the god during his worship, and its representation is often branded on the arms of his worshippers.

Panchatantra or *Pañcatantra* The most famous Sanskrit collection of stories and fables and the "chief source of the world's fable literature": literally, the five *tantras* or books. The *Panchatantra* was compiled about the 5th century A.D. by Vishṇuśarman for the enlightenment of a king's sons. Today more than 200 different versions exist in fifty languages. The Arabic version is the *Kalila wa Dimnah*, those in modern Persian the *Anwār-u Suhailī*, and the *Iyār-i Dānish*. In England the collection is known as the *Fables of Bidpai*. For full discussion see Penzer-Tawney, *The Ocean of Story* V: 207–242.

P'an Chin Lien The Chinese goddess of fornication. She was a young widow caught *in flagrante* by her brother-in-law, who killed the lover. She became the patroness of prostitutes, who frequently make obeisance to her as they enter their places of business. [RDJ]

Pāṇḍavas or **Pāṇḍus** In the *Mahābhārata*, one of the two families which fought for possession of the kingdom whose capital was Hastināpura. The five Pāṇḍava princes were Yudhishthira, celebrated for his integrity, Bhīma, huge and of a fiery temper, Arjuna, symbol of chivalry and hero of the epic, and the twins Nakula and Sahadeva, representatives of wisdom and beauty. The five were the sons of Pāṇḍu's wives Kuntī and Mādrī, but their paternity was attributed to the gods, since Pāṇḍu did not consort with his wives. He, however, recognized them as his heirs. Yudhishthira was said to be the son of Dharma, Bhīma of the wind god Vāyu, Arjuna of Indra, and the twins of the Aśvins.

The Pāṇḍavas are closely associated with the Himalayas, to which they retired after World War I. Many spots are venerated in connection with their wanderings. They receive little actual worship today except in the south of India where the village mother is often called Draupadī and five stones are sometimes seen in a field, representing the five princes who guard the crops.

pandé The Balinese blacksmiths, makers of the famous Balinese krisses: a separate and revered caste. They are regarded as holy and believed to be possessed of such powerful magic that they alone are able to cope with the mysteries of fire and iron.

Pandion In ancient Greek mythology, a king of Athens; son of Erichthonius and a naiad. Pandion was the father of Procne and Philomela. Tereus married Procne, but became enamored of her sister and raped her. (Or he told Philomela that Procne was dead and married her.) To keep Philomela from telling what had happened, he tore out her tongue. But Philomela embroidered the story and gave the embroidery to Procne. Procne killed her son Itys, served him in a meal to Tereus, and fled with Philomela. The three unhappy mortals were transformed by the gods: Tereus became the hoopoe, Philomela the swallow, and Procne the nightingale. Roman retellings of this story make the nightingale Philomela and the swallow Procne, but obviously the sweet-singing nightingale does not fit the tongueless Philomela.

Pandora Literally, the all-endowed; a woman made by Hephæstus out of earth as the gods' revenge on mankind for the gift of fire made to them by Prometheus. Prometheus warned his brother Epimetheus not to accept any gift from the gods: a familiar tabu in folktale. But Epimetheus gladly accepted the woman brought to him by Hermes, for she was a magnificent creation, being endowed with some quality from each of the gods—beauty from Aphrodite, cunning from Hermes, etc. Pandora carried a jar as a sort of gift offering, and which she had been forbidden to open; but one day her curiosity got the better of her and she opened the jar. Out flew all the ills that since have afflicted mankind; only Hope was left in the jar. Other versions of the myth say that all good was in the jar, and that when it was opened all escaped forever from the possession of man. Pandora is said to have been the mother of Pyrrha and Deucalion by either Epimetheus or Prometheus. She becomes in the Orphic poetry an underworld goddess, an associate of Hecate and the Erinyes, an awesome personage: this may be however an aspect of Ge, the earth mother, who is sometimes called the all-endowed, Pandora.

panpipes A musical instrument consisting of a series of one-note vertical flutes, graduated in length, fastened together in a flat row or fagot bundle with the upper ends level. The instrument is of particular importance and widespread distribution in eastern and southeastern Asia, across the islands of Melanesia and Polynesia, and in South America, but it takes its name from the Greek god Pan, who, according to legend, invented it. Pan was hot in amorous pursuit of the nymph Syrinx when she came to a river and called in despair upon the naiads to save her; they did so by turning her into reeds along the bank just as he had her in his grasp. Pan sighed gustily with frustration and the reeds gave forth a strain of music under his breath. He cut seven reeds and bound them together into the instrument the Greeks called syrinx, and, in playing it, possessed the nymph symbolically. The panpipes were believed to be the favorites of wine-loving Silenus, were played by Hermes to distract the hundred-eyed Argus Panoptes, and among men were the pleasure and pastime of shepherds. The original pipe of Pan was said to have been kept in the cave of Diana at Ephesus and to have served as a virginity test.

In China panpipes consist of sixteen notched reeds, developed from originally twelve pitch pipes, and divided into male and female tone sequences. The instrument is associated with the spring season, the eastern direction, the mountains, and bamboo.

Combinations of male and female pairs of panpipes are common to both Asia and South America. Sometimes the male and female notes form two fanlike wings of the same instrument, but often the male and female instruments are entirely separate, each having only half the notes required to play a melody and the notes being played alternately by two players. In eastern Venezuela, the reed pipes *mare* have five reeds for the male instrument and six for the female. Such pairs are frequently connected by a long string, as in Burma and among the Indians of Panama and Bolivia. The Cuna

consider these pairs as man and wife. Large bands of panpipe players among South American Indians maintain the separation of male and female instruments.

Similarities in this respect, together with a comparison of pitches and scales and binding methods common from Asia and the Pacific islands to the South American continent, have led to the conclusion on the part of some authorities that American panpipes are all derived from an Asiatic origin. Panpipes were known in South America before the Europeans came, having been common in ancient Peru. Many examples of the period were made by boring the series of air passages through solid material, such as pottery, stone, or metal. Only one early example of the instrument has been found on the North American continent, a pottery panpipe from Tres Zapotes, Veracruz, Mexico. However, in slavery times in North America, Negroes constructed crude sets of reed pipes in a framework, which they called *quills*.

In Europe the masters of the panpipes are the Rumanian Gipsies, who have achieved such virtuosity that the instrument has there achieved orchestral recognition. Their pipes are tuned by dropping peas into certain pipes before each piece to sharp or flat its note. Similar devices for altering the fixed tones have been used elsewhere, such as the gourd slide of the Aymara pipes of South America, or the custom in other South American tribes of pouring in sand or water.

In England the panpipes have been a favorite accompaniment for the Punch and Judy show. In Italy boys make and play crude panpipes of reeds called *fischietti* (whistles).

Though not nearly so widespread, the panpipes have much the same significance in love and for rebirth as the flutes. The spread wings sometimes thought of as the male and female banks of tones are also conceived as the wings of the phœnix. See FLUTE. [TCB]

pansy, heartsease, kiss-me-quick, love-in-idleness, Jove's flower, St. Valentine's flower, or **Herb Trinity** (because of its three colors in one flower) In Scotland and Germany it is called stepmother. The large lower petal is the mother, with her own two gaily dressed daughters on either side of her; the stepdaughters are the two smaller and paler upper petals. It is a cooling herb in the dominion of Saturn and the sign of Cancer and symbolizes thought (it is called *pensée* in France, whence the English name). German legend says that it was once so fragrant that people trampled all the grass coming into the fields to pick it. The flower prayed to be deprived of its scent so that the cattle would not be starved. In Rumania they tell of a young king who fell in love with a serving maid and had a friend introduce her to his mother as a princess. His mother was jealous and bid her magician turn the girl into something ugly like a toad, but she was so modest and lovely that the worst he could do was turn her into a pansy.

To pick a pansy with the dew still on it will cause the death of a loved one; to pick pansies on a fine day will cause rain before long. In Shakespeare's *Midsummer Night's Dream* Oberon squeezes the juice of a pansy on Titania's eyes so that she will fall in love with the first person she sees on awakening. The leaves are bruised and used for skin diseases, especially in infants. It is also used for epilepsy, asthma, and inflammations of the lungs and chest. The flowers are taken internally as a cathartic. Pansy is a term applied to an effeminate or homosexual man.

pantang kapur A tabu language used in Johore and South Pahang by the Jakun (Malay) collectors of camphor. The *penghulu* (leader) and the *sakai* (followers) must use this language and no other while working in the jungle. The language, believed to be only partly Malay, is also known as *bahasa kapor, chakap berkapor*. See BISAN.

Panther An animal character in Southeastern and Eastern Woodlands Indian mythology. Among the Yuchi Panther is one of the animal creators who, angry at Chipmunk when he made the night, jumped on him and made the red scratches (stripes) which Chipmunk bears to this day. Panther is the eponymous animal for one of the Yuchi clans; the second highest official at Yuchi ceremonies, who represents the Warrior Society, is usually taken from the panther clan. Among the Shawnee the great underwater panther is a powerful supernatural being. See MOUNTAIN LION. [EWV]

para A Finnish spirit: the name is formed from the Swedish *Bjära* or *Bära*: literally Bearer. The para brings money, rye, and other goods to his owner, but usually he is regarded as the bearer of milk, cream, and butter. In such cases he takes the shape of a cat (compare the Scandinavian Buttercat and Lappish Smierragatto). The milk is carried by the para either in its mouth or in its intestines. The spirit can be created by man himself from some stolen objects. It is possible, however, that the name and idea is much older than a recent borrowing from the Swedes. Among the Cheremis, the *pari* is an evil spirit. The same among the Tatars of Kazan. The Osman Turkish *peri* means a fairy or good genius. The word originates probably from the Persian. [JB]

parachicos Literally, for children: masked dancers on horseback, with a child-frightening function. The group with this particular name participates in the fiesta of Chiapa de Corzo in Chiapas on January 20. But the idea of frightening a naughty child by a masked bogey is not unique. The parachicos are thus related in function to the *wükufi* of the Araucanians the terrifying ritual-istic *Natacka* of the Hopi, and the special cloth masks of the Seneca, as well as the various bogeys of Europe. [GPK]

Paradise An otherworld where the perfect life is lived: the word is derived from Persian words meaning an encircling wall, probably of the king's gardens. Paradise may be either terrestrial or celestial. The Garden of Eden, somewhere on earth, is reflected in medieval travelers' tales of lands of plenty, often situated on mountains, in far-off places—China, India, the headwaters of the Nile, etc. Later travelers and explorers made of places like the Polynesian islands earthly paradises similar to the mythical islands of earlier centuries, and the history of literature is replete with Utopias, Erewhons, and New Atlantises. The Christian Heaven, in the sky, its streets paved with gold, finds its counterpart in the Iranian Yima's House where no one fights, no one is poor, everyone has what he wants. In the Moslem paradise everyone wears green silk, grapes are always within reach—not a long reach—, there is neither heat nor cold.

The Sumerian Dilmun was a land where all water was good and crops were plentiful; so too in the Egyptian Aalu crops were easily grown to supplement the diet of grave offerings. See ELYSIUM; ISLAND OF THE BLEST; IS-LANDS OF THE BLESSED; OLYMPUS; OTHERWORLD; VALHALLA.

paragueros The Umbrella men: Carnival dancers of Tepeyanco and other villages of Tlaxcala. Their curious elaborate headdresses have given the dance its name: ostrich feathers spread from the headdress like an umbrella; ribbons ripple down the back in profusion. The shawl is costly and elaborate, with embroidered native flora and fauna. Simpering mustached masks and breeches complete this fantastic outfit. The men dance quadrilles with elegant polka and mazurka steps; wind and string instruments play mincing 19th century tunes. The purpose of this recent creation is clearly satire on the superficial sumptuousness of European, particularly French, high society. [GPK]

Paraiyan A devil-dancing Tamil caste of southwest India. To the din of trumpets and drums, and decked in towering headdresses, skirts of coconut leaves, and body and face paint, they drive out devils from the houses of the Nayar caste. They strike themselves and whirl in a frenzy. Commonly known as Pariah, they are thus identified with the most miserable type of outcast. Government efforts have of late mitigated prejudices and improved their status. [GPK]

pāras or **pāraspatthar** In Indian folk belief, the philosopher's stone which turns everything it touches to gold. In legend a man cutting grass in the jungle found that his sickle had turned yellow. He consulted a blacksmith who went to the spot, found the stone, and presented it to Raja Jai Singh Deva. The Raja used the riches thus acquired to build a fort, then gave the stone to a Brāhman who, not knowing its worth, threw it into the Narbadā River where it still lies.

Parasūrāma In Hindu mythology, the sixth incarnation of Vishṇu and the first Rāma: literally, Rāma with the ax. Paraśurāma was a Brāhman, the son of Jamadagni and Reṇukā, born in the Tretā Yuga to clear the earth of the Kshatriyas, which task he is said to have accomplished 21 times. After completing this he gave the earth to Kaśyapa. As a youth he was instructed in the use of arms by Śiva who gave him the ax (*parasu*) for which he was named. His first deed, recorded in the *Mahābhārata*, was the slaying, at the command of his father, of his mother who had had impure thoughts. Granted a boon for the deed, he asked that she be restored to life and that he be invincible in combat.

He instructed Arjuna in the use of arms and was present at the war council of the Kaurava princes. According to the *Rāmāyaṇa*, he challenged Rāma, the seventh avatar, to a trial of strength because he had broken Śiva's bow, but was defeated and lost his place in the celestial world. Originally Paraśurāma had no relation to Vishṇu, but he was represented as possessing Vishṇu's bow and thus associated with the latter in popular tales until he was incorporated as one of the less important in the series of incarnations.

Pariaca Culture hero of the Huarochiri Indians, born from one of 5 eggs which appeared mysteriously on top of a mountain. He traveled throughout the land of the Huarochiri changing the landscape. He destroyed a village because its inhabitants, mistaking him for a vagabond, treated him harshly. He opened irrigation canals and changed a girl into stone that became a *huaca* (idol). [AM]

Pārijāta In Hindu mythology, the celestial coral tree which yields all desired objects, produced at the Churning of the Ocean and planted in Indra's heaven until Kṛishṇa, at the insistence of his wife, carried it off and defeated Indra in the battle which followed. It was planted in Dvārakā until Kṛishṇa's death after which it returned to Svarga.

Parilia or **Palilia** In ancient Roman religion, the festival of Pales on April 21; a festival of increase of flocks which was also the celebration of the day of the founding of Rome in 753 B.C.: the name is either from *pario*, bear, increase, or from Pales. Pales was the protector of shepherds and their flocks, sometimes thought to be male and thus a parallel of Pan or Faunus, sometimes female and related to Vesta and Anna Perenna. The Parilia, an important celebration, was held both in the city of Rome, as Rome's *dies natalitus*, and in the country, where shepherds asked to be forgiven for unwitting trespass on the holy places by their sheep. The sequence of the festival, according to Ovid, included a public lustration with fire and smoke at which were burned the blood of the October horse (preserved by the Vestals since the sacrifice of the horse six months previous), the ashes of the cattle sacrificed at the Cerealia, and bean shells. The people were sprinkled with water, washed in running springs, and drank a mixture of milk and must. The stables were purified with smoke, swept with brooms of bay, and decorated with branches of bay. Foodstuff was burned as an offering. Fires of hay and straw were built, and to the sound of cymbal and flute the shepherds and their flocks passed through and over the fire thrice. The celebrations ended with a feast in the open air. In modern Italy, the festival of St. George seems to have taken over many of the observances of the Parilia. Compare BELTANE.

Paris The abductor of Helen of Troy, hence instigator of the Trojan War. Paris was the second son of Priam and Hecuba. Before he was born Hecuba was forewarned in a dream (of a firebrand that destroyed the city of Troy) that she would bear a son who would be the cause of the city's fall. So the infant was given to a shepherd and exposed on Mt. Ida. But when the shepherd returned after five days he found the child still living; a she-bear had suckled him. The shepherd reared Paris, who distinguished himself as a young man against raiders of the flocks and was therefore named Alexander, or defender. While he tended flocks Paris awarded the apple of discord to Aphrodite as the most beautiful among Hera, Athena, and Aphrodite. (See JUDGMENT OF PARIS.) Here too he married the nymph Œnone.

At last Paris came from the mountains to the city on the occasion of a festival. He made so good a mark at the games that he was recognized as being of high rank; his sister Cassandra, the seeress, who had interpreted Hecuba's dream originally, stated that he was Priam's own son. Soon Paris visited Menelaus at Sparta, persuaded Helen to elope with him (or abducted her by force), and fled to Troy by way of Egypt and Phœnicia. Some accounts say that in Egypt a spurious Helen was substituted for the real Helen, and that this Helen was

the one who went to Troy with Paris and bore his children. In Troy, Paris led the war faction, and, though somewhat cowardly, fought throughout the war, killed Achilles, and was himself finally killed by one of Hercules' poisoned arrows, shot by Philoctetes.

Paris, (Bruno Paulin) Gaston (1839–1903) French disciple of Benfey and one of the sponsors in France of the literary school of folklorists. Paris was one of the founders of Romance philology; he taught at the École des Hautes Études (1868–72) and after 1872 at the Collège de France. In 1866 he founded the *Revue Critique,* and in 1872 *Romania,* leading journal in Romance philology. He popularized medieval French literature in such works as *Aventures merveilleuses de Huon de Bordeaux mises en nouveau langage.* His studies on the French literature of the Middle Ages are of significance, including those on epic, romance, lyric poetry, as well as on the literature of the 15th century (see *Mélanges de Littérature Française du Moyen Age,* Paris, 1912, a collection of Paris' works on this particular period, edited by Mario Roques).

Parjanya In Vedic mythology, the god of rain and personification of the rain cloud; son of Dyaus; the deity of fertility who makes seeds germinate, causes conception, and rules over lightning, thunder, and rain. In later Hindu mythology, his name is applied to Indra.

parsley This plant was regarded in the ancient world as sacred to the dead. Wreaths of parsley were given to winners of funeral games, and Greeks and Romans both used it to decorate graves.

Hazlitt in his *Dictionary of Faiths and Folk-Lore* says, "At Islip in Oxfordshire, the transplantation of parsley is considered inauspicious." The people of Devon also consider its transplantation inauspicious, for they say that it will result in death in the immediate family and the Devil will take charge of the garden. In London and Surrey even growing parsley in the garden, will cause a family death; in Surrey, if planted on Good Friday it will grow double, with what results they do not say. To be in need of parsley means to be at death's door.

You should never cut parsley if you are in love. If you give it away, you give away your luck; nor should you accept it as a gift—if you must have it, steal it. On the other hand, babies are found in parsley beds; it rendered the fumes of wine harmless (in Rome), and Turner's English herbal (1551) says "thrown in fish ponds it will cure the sick fishes there in." Another early herbalist describes "a marvellous efficacious fumigation to cause a man to see visions in the air," which was made from violet roots, and, among other things, parsley. The leaves distilled in water made a decoction which would remove superfluous hair; the roots, powdered and drunk in wine promoted a sound brain, perfect memory, and purified the blood. In England the leaves, roots, and seeds are still used medicinally to give a drug (*apiol*) which is recommended for kidney disorders, for dropsy, and female ills. Fool's parsley (*Æthusa cynapium*) is ill-smelling and poisonous, and so named because it looks so much like parsley that fools don't know the difference.

Parsley's association with the dead is attested by the general European belief that the effects of the Wild Hunt on one who has seen it (such as blinding, swelling of the head, injury from a knife in the hand at the time, even death) can be averted by asking the huntsmen for parsley (E501.19.2).

partridge dance One of the many bird imitations of North American Indians, possibly of propitiatory origin, but now performed for the diversion of both sexes on social occasions. Though waning in popularity, it survives among the Menominee, Cherokee, Alabama, and Seminole in the eastern United States. The Onondaga near Nedrow, N. Y., enact a courtship mime in their partridge dance, but only for show purposes: the male follows the female, both fluttering their hands and arms like wings and jerking their heads in birdlike fashion. [GPK]

Pascola Hispanization of Yaqui *pahko'ola,* old man of the fiesta: the ritual clown of the Cahita Indians of Sonora and of Arizona Yaqui colonies, also adopted by the Tarahumara. The Pascolas, usually three, are always associated with Maso at the same festivals and dance alone or with him in burlesque and hunting mime. The Tarahumara Pascola appears together with the *matachini* at church festivals, funerals, and memorials, but not during agricultural ceremonies.

Pascola serves as ritual host, welcomes the crowd, opens and closes the fiesta with exorcisms, with greetings to the animals of the woods, such as *santo vovok,* saint frog, and with cross markings on the ground in the cardinal directions. His music is called "pieces of the woods" and represents animals and birds. It is played by a one-man flute and double-headed drum, a notched stick (*hirúkia bweha*), resting on a gourd resonator, and by the same type of water drum as for the dance of Maso. The scraping and booming are reinforced by the tinkling of bronze bells on the dancer's belt, the swish of *teneboim* anklets, and the syncopated clash of the *sonazo* (a rattle of brass disks on a hardwood frame, manipulated by striking it against the palm of the left hand).

Each performance starts with an unmasked solo by each clown, to innocuous jig tunes on a homemade harp and fiddle. The soloists clearly compete with each other in a display of swift *zapateados* of Mexican extraction, combined with native stamps and heel-and-toe twists.

After this display of dexterity, they don their masks, black wooden stylizations of aged human features or animal heads, with white-painted incisions, horsehair brow and beard, mirror or abalone inlay, and a cross on the forehead and chin to mitigate the curse of this pagan creature. To the "pieces of the woods" they dance singly or in a group, with or without *Maso,* burlesquing or chasing him, copying his leaps in ludicrous fashion, and finishing with a split. They caper, crouch, sway their hips, jerk their heads and shoulders, howling like wild beasts. The comic interludes between dances, whether in mime or Yaqui language, savor of lusty and amiable obscenity. The deer pretends to suckle one of the pascolas. He pokes them in the ribs or ties them together with bandannas, while they stand transfixed and helplessly bleating. Between performances they renew their zest with cigarettes and mescal. Toward dawn of Easter Sunday, the hunt becomes more realistic, but it is most convincing in the "deer play" at private festivals.

The Pascolas are as enigmatic as the rest of the ceremonial clowns of the great Southwest. They are differen-

tiated from the *chapayekas* in their lack of organization, their vestiges of priest-like attributes, their hunting and animal associations, and their complete segregation from the Catholic ceremonies, in which the *chapayekas* participate. Beals suggests former shamanistic function, which is now rapidly being obliterated by the professional role of entertainer. None the less, many of the old beliefs adhere, such as the magical initiation by entering the serpent's cave in a red mountain, by walking into a serpent's mouth, being ejected, and finally receiving from the king of snakes the necessary knowledge and paraphernalia.

Pascolas are still believed to have power over streams and mountains. Fertility magic is evident not only in the phallic gestures, but in a gesture of sowing made during the dance with the *sonazo.* The missionaries have branded them as demoniac, while tolerating them in the ritual, but have striven to mitigate their power by putting holy water in the drum, and crosses on the masks and on a bead necklace around the neck, and by wrapping a blanket around their loins, knickerbocker fashion.

They continue to stand for an ancient ideology through centuries of religious metamorphosis and confusion, and the mechanizing and secularizing influence of modern civilization. See CLOWNS; MASO; RATTLES; RITUAL DRAMA; SNAKE DANCE. [GPK]

The Yaqui Indians of northern Mexico have a Deer Dance at all ceremonial and religious fiestas. Presumably it is pre-Conquest in origin and perhaps had as its purpose luck in hunting. Two groups participate: the pascola dancers, who are masked clowns, and who give their name to the dance, and the deer dancers themselves, who wear stuffed deer heads over their heads, and cocoons filled with gravel, as rattles, around their ankles. [GMF]

pas de basque The Basque step: a form of leap from side to side, probably, as the name would suggest, of Basque origin. In fact, the Basque version with its high kicks is the most spectacular. Many folk dances, as well as school dance or ballet, use the fundamental step—a low leap to the right with circular swing of the right leg, a forward step with the left, and back step with the right, preparatory to reversal of the leap to the left. Each European country modifies the character and the arm position. The leaps of the Scottish sword dance are small and crisp, those of Spain curved and flourishing, those of the Ukraine high and bold with raised knee. The Portuguese pas de basque may be in 6/8, 3/4, or 2/4 time, the first being the regular pas de basque, the second cutting the left foot in back, the third holding the third step for two beats. The step turns up in blended dances of American Indians, e.g. in the *concheros* dance of Mexico, certainly as an importation. [GPK]

passacaglia or **passacalle** A dance and musical form, deriving its name from Spanish *passar,* to pass, and *calle* street, i.e. a street serenade. The original dance steps are unknown; but as a musical form the passacaglia attained great importance. Similar to the *chacona,* it developed and still may develop a stately theme in triple time through infinite variations. [GPK]

passe Literally, sacred, in the language of the Lapps. *Passe-vare,* the sacred mountains; *passe-jokka,* the sacred river; *passe-javrre,* the sacred sea: all are phrases which testify to the worship of nature by the Lapps. [JB]

passepied A peasant dance, the *branle* of Upper Brittany, named after the crossing of one foot in front of the other with a pawing motion. Along with other *paysanneries* the French court of Louis XV adopted the passepied for its dances of shepherds and shepherdesses. The music resembled a lively minuet in its 3/8 time with an upbeat and rapid figures, and syncopation with the dance step.

In England, where it was known as the *paspe*, couples performed it in longways, with running steps, crossing over, casting off, grouping into threes, etc. What with the frequent arm-clasping of couples, and the buoyant triple time, it appears as one of the antecedents of the waltz. [GPK]

Pātāla In Hindu cosmogony and cosmology, the collective name for the seven infernal regions, the abode of the Nāgas, Daityas, Dānavas, and Yakshas; also the name for the lowest of the seven regions. Pātāla, which extends downwards 70,000 *yojanas* below the earth, equals the seven upper regions in magnificence and beauty. Beneath it are the hells and the serpent Śesha who bears the world upon his hood.

Patch Tanz Clap Dance: a Jewish couple round dance, very popular at weddings and other festive occasions. The fundamental step for the clockwise circling is a slow strut with knee flexion after each step. The dance takes its name from the second figure, where all walk to the center and clap their own hands three times, then walk back and stamp their feet three times. Finally the circle breaks up into couples who pivot with outstretched arms at shoulder level. Then each woman, under her partner's upraised arm, goes on to a new partner to the left. [GPK]

paternity test A widespread motif (H480 f.) in which an infant or young child magically picks out his unknown father, either by handing him an apple (H481.1; Type 675—European), or by urinating on him as he is handed round from man to man (H481—North American Indian). One way of picking out the unknown father among several claimants is to sprinkle gold in the streets (H485): the man who rides straight to the door of the princess, on hearing the news of the birth of the child, without noticing the gold is the true father. This is reminiscent of the maternity test devised by Solomon: the woman who protested against the dividing of the child in half, but who would give it up rather than have it killed was the true mother. The three tests of paternity in ancient Irish legend were not made until a child was more than a year old or of enough age to show the form, voice, and manner of its progenitor.

☞ An incident detailing how a child magically picks out his unknown father (motif H481) is of common occurrence in North American Indian folktales. The method of establishing the paternity differs. In an Ojibwa tale of Mudjikiwis a baby is passed about until it urinates on one of several men present; this has been agreed upon as the sign that the man is the baby's father. In a White Mountain Apache tale the situation is reversed in that a father satisfies himself that he is the parent of a particular child; Sun gives a boy very strong tobacco to smoke, and when the boy, aided by the four winds, empties the pipe four times Sun is satisfied. These are only two of many specific ways detailed in American Indian folktales for establishing paternity;

for a score or so of others see Stith Thompson, *Tales of the North American Indians* (Cambridge, 1929), p. 336, n. 212. See MAIRA-MONAN. [EWV]

Paul Bunyan Giant logger and super-lumberjack; mythical hero of the woods and patron saint of the American lumber industry. As inventor of logging and creator of American geography, celebrated for his ingenuity in solving problems and for his resourcefulness in turning adversity to advantage, Paul Bunyan possesses epic traits and bears a family resemblance to the giants of myth and fairy tale. His legend may even retain traces of folk memories of Gargantua and Finn MacCool preserved by French and Irish lumberjacks. But as the hero of stories of comic exaggeration—tall tales or lying tales in the Munchausen tradition—Paul Bunyan has never risen above the level of the comic demigod or trickster hero, and his exploits have never developed into a full-fledged cycle. As to whether he is of folk or literary origin, the truth, as Stith Thompson suggests (*The Folktale*, p. 250 n.), probably lies somewhere between the two extremes of a "very old popular legend among American lumbermen" and an "essentially . . . literary concoction of the past thirty years."

Paul Bunyan may have had a French-Canadian original, named Paul Bunyon, a redoubtable giant warrior in the Papineau Rebellion of 1837 and later hell-raising boss of a logging camp (James Stevens, *Paul Bunyan*, p. 1) or Paul Bonhomme of the Two Mountain country (Walter Havighurst, *Upper Mississippi*, p. 181). Or his name may be derived from "Bon Jean" or the French-Canadian word *bongyenne* (Esther Shephard, *Paul Bunyan*, p. 8).

Just as narrators claim "actual acquaintance" with Paul Bunyan or some one who knew him, so collectors and scholars claim oral sources for the tales. But even where genuine oral versions exist, it is difficult to tell whether they were learned from oral tradition or from print. In any case, the fabulous adventures of Paul Bunyan, his Blue Ox, and his loyal crew are known to Americans chiefly through the literary versions of Esther Shephard (1924) and James Stevens (1925) and innumerable journalistic accounts and children's books.

As far as can be determined, the legend originated in Canada during the last century, and was considerably amplified as it spread west and south with the lumber industry, centering in the Lake states and the Northwest. In the course of his migration Paul Bunyan incorporated elements of local heroes like Jigger Jones (Johnson), Joe Mufraw, and Jean Frechette, whom he supplanted. To the original French and Irish elements were also added Scandinavian and Indian elements.

Many details of the legend are certainly literary additions. W. B. Laughead, author and illustrator of the first Paul Bunyan booklet (1914) and of Paul Bunyan stories in advertisements of the Red River Lumber Company of Minnesota (1914–1916), claims credit for having invented the names of Babe, the Blue Ox, and many members of Paul Bunyan's crew, including Brimstone Bill, Johnny Inkslinger, and Sourdough Sam.

In a letter to Louise Pound (*Southern Folklore Quarterly* VII: 139 n.) Laughead states that he began with what he "remembered from Minnesota logging camps (1900–1908) . . . then picked up odds and ends from letters received . . . and from columns that ran in various newspapers, in the Seattle *Star* [1920] by Lee J. Smits, the Portland *Oregonian* [1922] by DeWitt Harry, and others. Correspondence to the *American Lumberman* also provided clues." It was in the latter publication that the Chicago poet Douglas Malloch's poem, "The Round River Drive," appeared in 1914. An earlier printed source was established in 1944 by W. W. Charters (*Journal of American Folklore* 57: 188), who has identified James MacGillivray as the author of Paul Bunyan stories appearing in the Illustrated Supplement, Detroit *News Tribune,* June 24, 1910.

The immediate source of Paul Bunyan stories is the extravagant Western humor of the 1830's and '40's, just as Paul Bunyan's immediate predecessors are ring-tailed roarers like Davy Crockett and Mike Fink. As a pioneer industrialist he also has links with the titans and wizards of American business. Spreading to other occupations and regions and merging his individuality with that of other strong men, miracle men, and work giants, he ultimately became a symbol of American bigness and a proverbial peg on which to hang an extravagant tale. Invading the Southwest oilfields after World War I, he even displaced Gib Morgan as hero.

Typical of the sophisticated diffusion of the legend is Mody C. Boatright's statement (*Gib Morgan*, pp. 5–6) that "in the 1920's young book-reading oil-workers, especially college men during summer vacation, carried his name into oil patches in which they worked." Similar evidence is supplied by a university student employed on a water pipeline at Big Spring, Texas, in 1928 (*Folk-Say*, 1929, p. 51), who, not to be outdone by other story-tellers on the job, put together Paul Bunyan stories from "stories he had read and jokes he had heard." In the same way, most Paul Bunyan stories are adaptations of tales from other sources, with or without occupational coloring.

Among the familiar jests that have entered into the Paul Bunyan saga are those of the buckskin harness that stretches when wet, the pet fish that drowns when it falls into the water, Liverpool Jim who jumps across the Round river and back without touching the other shore, the oxen strayed into the hollow limb of the tree through which they are driven, and Big Ole sinking knee-deep into solid rock while carrying one of Babe the Blue Ox's shoes.

In their original setting Paul Bunyan stories served as an outlet for the worker's love of tall talk, yarning, and practical joking. Originally, they were extemporaneous fragments—jests, sayings, repartee—exchanged in conversation and in competitive boasting, lying, and pranking. Thus many tales were told to haze or "take down" tenderfeet and greenhorns, as in the case of the stories of mythical monsters or "fearsome creatures of the lumber woods," which originated separately and were attracted into the Paul Bunyan saga. Other tales satirized or caricatured conditions in early-day camps (e.g. the stories of Gargantuan feeding of the men on endless pea-soup from a pea-soup lake and pancakes made on an iron stove-top griddle greased by assistant cooks skating over it with bacon rinds, hams, or bear-steaks strapped to their feet).

The extensive development (and essential monotony) of the Paul Bunyan saga is seen from Harold W. Fen-ton's anthology, *Legends of Paul Bunyan* (1947), and its bulky bibliography—a tribute accorded few, if any other, American legendary heroes.　B. A. BOTKIN

paulitos Literally, little sticks: Portuguese term for stick dances, corresponding to the Spanish *palitos* or *paloteo* and the Morris stick dance. They are always associated with Catholic holidays, as Epiphany at Moguerinha, and the *romario* (pilgrimage) at Cercio, to Santa Barbara on the last Sunday in August. The men commonly wear white shirts, black trousers, waistcoats, broad black hats, ribbons and flowers galore; or they may be dressed in plain white trousers and shirts as the Spanish *palitos*, Basque *ezpata dantzariak*, and English Morris men. Formerly they are said to have been dressed sometimes in skirts and petticoats, revealing a transvestite connotation. Two drummers and a bagpipe furnish the accompaniment as the dancers strike together their short staves and execute various elaborate figures called *llaços* or, Spanish, *lazos*. The relationship to *Moriscas* and sword dances is evident. [GPK]

pavane A stately court dance, popular from about 1530 to 1676. The origin of the name is probably the Spanish *pavo*, peacock, because of the proud strut of the men with their swirling capes and their swords. It was danced either by one couple or many couples in circular processions around the room, with partners barely touching the fingers of their inner hands. The step was in slow 4/4 time, alternately forward and back—two simples and a double (left, close right, right, close left, left-right-left close). A drum accompanied the songs and the melodies on hautboys and sackbuts. Native in Spain, the pavane spread through all of western Europe. A lighter and faster version was the *passamezzo*. The *pavane d'Espagne* was an ornate version with small foot flourishings. The solemn pavane was followed by the lively *galliard*.

The pavane may have originated in religious processionals; its tunes retain an ecclesiastical flavor to this day. In this connection it is noteworthy that an oath taken "on the Peacock" was one of the most solemn acts of medieval chivalry. [GPK]

pawang Malay Peninsula medicine man or magician, still a powerful and active figure in every village, though disappearing in the large towns. The office is usually hereditary but can be acquired by undergoing certain supernatural experiences and consultations with the dead. The pawang is the intermediary between man and the supernatural; he is medium, prophet, curer, although curing is more specifically the function of the *bomor*. (It is the *bomor* especially who knows how to expel the evils absorbed from touching a dead thing or meeting up with the Wild Huntsman of the Malay forests.) The pawang is consulted for all new projects and undertakings, that he may prosper them, and before all hunting, fishing, and crop-sowing, -growing, and -harvesting activities, as well as for puberty rites, marrying, birthing, dying, burial. He is also associated with weather control. He commonly has an animal familiar which helps him cope with the supernatural, discover the causes of disease, maintain the world-order, and also to bewitch and punish. The term *pawang* is used also for the concept of "forbidden." His injunctions not to do certain things make those acts *pawang*. See article

"Malay Peninsula" by W. W. Skeat, *ERE* viii, pp. 363 ff. See SENDING.

Paw Paw Patch   An American play-party game. As all play-party games, it combines song, dance, pantomime, and spontaneity of footwork and action. The dancers, lined up in couples, sing "Where, oh where, is sweet little (the name of the head woman) . . ." as she dances around the entire set. Then to the words "Come on, boys, let's go find her . . ." the boys dance around the women's line. The real pantomime follows the words, "Pickin' up Paw Paws, puttin' 'em in her pocket . . . Way down yonder in the Paw Paw Patch." Partners, hands joined, enact the scooping up of fruit and putting into the pocket. Finally the head couple slides down between the two lines to the foot. This song-dance is especially popular among southern Negro children. But it serves as an excellent ice-breaker in social gatherings all over the country. [GPK]

pea   The edible seeds of a climbing herb (*Pisum sativum*) which, according to the countrymen in some parts of England, grow the wrong way in the pods during Leap Year. In order to insure a good crop, they should be planted in the wane of the moon that they may wax with that celestial body and bear plentifully. To find either one or nine peas in a pod is a sign of good luck, and in the case of a young girl, the first man to enter the room (after she has discovered nine peas in a single pod) will be her husband. In Scotland, on Halloween, if a boy and girl each place a pea on the coals, it will foretell their future. If the two peas stay where they are placed and burn, the pair will be married; the length of time and brightness of the burning indicate the duration of their happiness, but should one pea move from its place, there will be no marriage; and whichever one moves indicates the fickle party. In parts of England the water in which peas have been boiled is given as a cure for measles.

peach   In China the peach is the emblem of long life, immortality, and a female phallic emblem, and the peach blossom is the emblem of a bride. Porcelains with a peach design, intended as birthday gifts, carried the wish of long life and prosperity. The tree is especially venerated because it contains much *ling* (soul substance or spiritual force). The peach is also a potent force against demons; branches, blossoms, or even carvings of a peach over the doorway keep demons out; and children wear a peach pit suspended about the neck to keep demons away. During the Chou period an attendant at the royal court waved a peach wand to dispel evil spirits. If the soul ate a peach from the world tree (a peach tree) he would have 3,000 years of good health, and he could renew his youth as long as the supply held out. Immortality is symbolized in Taoist depictions by an old man emerging from a peach. On New Year's Day, young and old alike in China drink peach soup. In Japan the peach is a symbol of fertility. There is a tale of a woman who was washing and found a great peach in the water. She carried it home to her husband, who opened it. Inside the pit they found a baby boy which they raised; when the boy, Momotaro, was grown he repaid them by defeating the people of the Island of the Devil and giving them their treasure.

Peach was a wood in universally high repute as a divining rod. In the north country of England they say that when the leaves on the peach tree fall early there will be a murrain on the cattle. The Zuñi Indians have special bogeys which guard the peach orchards against youthful pilferers. Members of the Fire Brand Society of the Pueblo Indians fast from peaches in order that they may not be burned by fire. The Navaho Indians use dried peaches as a purgative. In Italy, burying peach leaves will cure warts; in Texas notches are cut, one for each wart, in a branch which is buried under the tree. In Texas also the leaves boiled in water are good for upset stomach, and peach sticks steeped in water are good for sudden pains of the heart, of the stomach, and for swollen abdomen.

peacock   The worship of the peacock among the Yezidis has been reported as a survival of Tammuz worship. In Greece the peacock was sacred to Hera and kept in her temple. In Kutch the peacock may neither be caught nor annoyed. It is sacred among the Jats and Khonds of India and in the Punjab its feathers, smoked, will heal snakebite. Elsewhere, waved over the sick, the feathers will cure disease. However the Moslems of Java report that the peacock was guardian at the gate of Paradise, ate the Devil, and thus got him into the gate. The *Kama Sutra* recommends that if the bone of a peacock be covered with gold and tied on the right hand, it will make a man lovely in the eyes of beholders. In European lore the feathers are unlucky and the cry of the peacock is a bad omen, though in medieval hermeneutics the peacock was the symbol of the soul. The serving of peacocks as a delicacy at great feasts in former times in Europe is part of a housewives' superstition, still powerful, namely that anything that looks beautiful must taste good. [RDJ]

pearl   A lustrous, calcareous concretion deposited in layers around a central nucleus in the shells of various mollusks, notably the oyster: formerly said to be raindrops swallowed by oysters. In Hindu folk belief pearls were said to be found in the brain, forehead, and stomach of elephants; these were especially powerful as protective charms. Dissolved pearl is an ingredient of every love charm in the East. It is one of the gems included in many Hindu charms: the five-gem *pañcharatna*, the nine-gem *navaratna*, for instance. In Hindu astrological charms it represents the moon and appears in the southeast corner of the arrangement. The gates of the New Jerusalem mentioned in *Revelation* will be made of single pearls; the third of the Mohammedan heavens is of pearl. In the Orient pearls were said to be formed from teardrops, and would bring tears to the possessor.

In Borneo every ninth pearl taken is placed in a bottle with two grains of rice each, that they may breed, and the bottles are stoppered with the finger of a dead man. A 6th century Chinese belief held that dragons spit pearls, or that it rained pearls when dragons fought in the sky. In China the pearl is also regarded as a charm against fire, perhaps by association with the dragon, the rain-giver.

Pigafetta, who accompanied Magellan, compared pearls seen in the Celebes to doves' eggs, and reported two owned by the king of Borneo as large as goose eggs. Natives of the Sulu Archipelago believe that nautilus pearls are unlucky and throw them away.

In the Orient it has long been maintained that pearls lose one percent of their luster per year. In Europe they become dulled through the sickness of the owner; death of the possessor sometimes destroys their luster altogether. It is also said that pearls have to be constantly worn to preserve their beauty, luster, and power.

Benvenuto Cellini, the famous goldsmith, claims as a boy to have shot down cranes which contained numbers of small pearls they had eaten. In his day man too consumed pearls internally. Because of their great price, they were not taken whole, but powdered, or dissolved in lemon juice. This solution known as "salt of pearl" was especially recommended for epilepsy and hysteria. Powdered pearl was given as late as the 16th century as an antidote for poison, and was later used in France as a cosmetic powder because of its power to improve the texture and luster of the skin. Powdered pearl in distilled water was given to Charles VI of France to restore his sanity, though in that case the cure is known to have been ineffective. Physicians of the 13th century prescribed it for the heart because it was "hard like the heart." In 17th century Denmark milk of pearl was used as a general tonic. Pharmacists were cautioned to buy their pearls whole because they lost their potency when powdered, and because there was much adulteration in the powdered pearl sold commercially (as they should have known). [JWH]

Pecos Bill Legendary cowboy culture hero of the American West, Australia, and the Argentine. He taught the cowboys everything they know, including their songs and oaths. He even taught the bronchos how to buck. He dug the Rio Grande, invented the six-shooter, and the Western movies. He was weaned on moonshine liquor and died from drinking nitroglycerine.

pe'dles be'djose Literally, Peddler is coming: the former Peddling Dance of the Penobscot Indians of Maine. It was danced as a typical round, but with pantomime of the pioneer peddler and all his goods, outlandish to the Indians of those days. The songs, in typical Penobscot antiphonal form, say that "Peddler is coming, ya hi ho; he has money," etc. Thus the dance is certainly neither of ancient nor of ritual origin. [GPK]

Pegasus In Greek legend, a divine winged horse which sprang from the body or the blood of the slain Medusa. It was caught and tamed by Athena, presented to the Muses, and kept near Corinth. The Corinthian Bellerophon, sent by Iobates to conquer the Chimera, tried to catch Pegasus unaided and failed. Upon advice, he slept a night in Athena's temple; there the goddess appeared to him in a dream and presented him with a heavenly bridle which remained even after he awoke. With it he was able to mount Pegasus. Bellerophon, using spears and arrows and fighting from the horse's back, slew the Chimera. Later he fought the same way against the Amazons. When, however, he tried to reach heaven on the horse, it threw him and escaped to Zeus, who used it to fetch his thunderbolts and other tools. In much later tradition, Pegasus is the mount of the poets, but in classical legend his only connection with poetry is the fountain Hippocrene, which bubbled forth from the mark made when Pegasus' hoof struck the earth. The latter accretion to the myth seems to be based almost wholly on false etymology, Hippocrene meaning the horse fountain.

Pe-har or **Pe-kar** A Tibetan fiend of the king class; the patron of sorcerers and protector of yellow-hat monasteries. Pe-har is identified with the Chinese Wei-to and the Indian Veda. The diviner of gNas-c'un monastery near Lhasa is believed to be an incarnation of Pe-har.

Pekko God of barley of the Finns. Kaarle Krohn believes there is an affinity of this Finnish deity with the Icelandic *Beggvir* or *Byggvir*, the servant of Freya. [JB]

Peko God of fertility of the Estonians in Setumaa. Even in recent days (1933) some statues of this god were found in the shape of a man, formed from wood or frequently from wax. The worshippers of Peko were a kind of secret society. The most important feast was celebrated on the night of October 1. All of the ceremonies were performed like a mystery. The following song was sung: "Peko, our God, give your protection to our cattle, preserve our horses, give shelter to our corn fields from all the hail storms." The people were noisy and scuffled about until one of them was accidentally wounded and blood appeared; this one became priest for Peko for the next year. The idol is hidden in the priest's granary. At sowing time it is brought out to the fields to give fertility to the crops. (See *FUF* VI: 104–111; and *Mitteilungen des Vereins für finnische Volkskunde*, II, 1944, pp. 44–5). [JB]

Pekwin Zuñi Indian speaking place, speaker; the name for any Zuñi assistant to the head or chief of a society. The Zuñi Pekwin *par excellence* is the Sun Watcher and Crier chief, who is speaker to the Sun, but also serves as speaker to the council of the Rain chiefs. Appointment to this office is for life or good behavior, and is made by the Council. Pekwin determines the solstices by watching the sunrise in winter and sunset in summer. The solstices at Zuñi date other ceremonies, so Pekwin is virtually keeper of the calendar. He has no sacred bundle; the sun is his sacred possession. These and other duties make Pekwin the most revered and holy man at Zuñi, and the most valuable to the community. [EWV]

Pelintsiek The dentalium shell money (*tsik*) of the California Yurok Indians is personified in their mythology as Pelintsiek, or Great Dentalium. The myth describes how the dentalia came to the people from the north. When they came to the Klamath River the small shells continued southward, but Pelintsiek and Tego'o, his traveling companion, went up the river. The story is full of place names, naming specifically what places they entered, and what places they passed by. The story ends with Pelintsiek's remark that some money must advance even farther up the river to the Karok and Hupa Indians.

Pellinor (1) or **Pellan** or **Pelleam** The Maimed King in various versions of the Grail story in the Vulgate Cycle of Arthurian romance; in earlier Grail stories the Maimed King is called the Fisher King, or the Rich Fisher. See GRAIL; JOSEPH OF ARIMATHEA.

(2) In the romance *Palamedes* and in the prose *Tristan*, etc., Perceval's father, the hunter of the Questing Beast. [MEL]

penates The gods (*di penates*) worshipped in private households in ancient Rome: probably originally pantry or store-closet (*penus*) guardian deities. There was a place kept at every hearth for the penates, who were, when identified, thought to be the Dioscuri, Castor and Pollux. They were worshipped in connection with Vesta and the lares, the latter sometimes being considered a subclass of the penates; the fire was kept burning in honor of the penates; the table was specially set with a saltcellar for them, and first-fruits were offered to them. The state too had its penates, said to have come from Troy with Æneas. Once, when the images of the penates were transferred from Lavinium to Rome or Alba Longa, they disappeared and were found again in their original place; the attempt to move them was abandoned.

penillion An ancient Welsh contest of improvising stanzas to well-known airs played on the harp. Contestants in turn had to fit riming verses to the time of the melody. The singer, according to some regulations, had to sing a counterpoint to the harp melody; other standards allowed him to sing the melody but not to begin with it nor to start with the first beat. The practice survived in bardic times as a form of music training.

Penitentes *Los Penitentes,* the penitents: specifically, a lay brotherhood of religious flagellants. The modern *Hermanos Penitentes* of New Mexico originated in the *flagelantes, disciplinati,* and *bianchi* of Italy and Spain, and the *Geissler* of Germany. As a Christian penance, flagellation was introduced about 1000 A.D. by Italian ascetics. The first folk demonstrations were impelled by catastrophic events and by terror of the end of the world, in 1250 by Italian political unrest between the Guelphs and Ghibellines, in 1349 by pestilence and earthquakes. The *disciplinati di Gesu Cristo* were organized in Perugia in 1260, with definite rituals of initiation and penitential procedure. Without any apparent leadership, the frenzy spread through Germany to the Netherlands and the borders of England and France.

The temporary votive brotherhoods lasted the 33 1/2 days of the pilgrimage duration, with flagellation twice daily according to locally varying statutes. For the public ritual the penitents were disrobed except for an ankle-length loin-cloth and a sack tied over the face. They lay down in a circle, each one indicating his transgression by his posture. After an act of absolution the self-flagellant processions wound through the streets amid laments and outcries. The chants (*laudi*) listed the deadliest sins: perjury, adultery, homicide, blasphemy, rape, etc. These poignant folk songs bewailed the *passio Christi,* the sufferings of Christ here reenacted; the *cantus maternus* implored the Virgin Mother to mitigate the wrath of the Deity:

> Pianzi con iochi et comel core
> La passion de Cristo salvatore!
>
> Wainent tougen mit den ougen,
> Habt in herzen Christes smerzen!

Thrice during the processional the penitents prostrated themselves on the ground in a cruciform position with extended arms, then knelt with arms upraised in supplication.

The companies of 40–100 members attracted men of every class, but largely simple people, peasants and laborers. Women flagellants were in the minority. At sacred shrines they sometimes congregated by the hundreds. The tremendous spectacle gradually became more formalized and at the close of the 14th century was enacted on a *talamo* or stage in the nave of the church, as *devozione.* The spontaneous demonstrations, under ecclesiastical suppression, attracted subversive elements and in Germany decayed by the end of the 15th century. In Italy and thence in Spain the *bianchi* (white men) organized as a monastic order.

The Third Order of Franciscans transplanted the cult to the Philippines and to Mexico, and in 1598 a member of this lay order, the *adelantado,* Don Juan de Oñate, brought it to New Mexico. The Mexican *penitentes* are not organized, but individually expiate transgressions or fulfil vows made in times of stress. On Good Friday, on the occasion of a Passion Play, they hobble about the Stations of the Cross, with iron grills mangling the flesh of their ankles; or they drag huge wooden crosses; or they uphold bundles of organ cacti on their shoulders and extended arms, while candles burn into the palms of their hands. In Tzintzuntzan and Taxco they appear clad in a black loin-sheet and face-covering, mercilessly lashing their bare backs. In Tenancingo the flagellant *arrieros* wear ordinary clothes and mitigate the force of the blows by sacks borne on their backs, as they dance back and forth in single lines.

In New Mexico *Los Hermanos Penitentes* have persisted in villages colonized by conquistadors and their Mexican companions, now intermingled with native Indian blood. They acquired particular significance after 1828, following the exodus of the Franciscans. They took over the spiritual administration of the people and still continue their offices of solace, charity, and political consolidation. The papal bull of 1886 attempted in vain to suppress the brotherhood and public penance. Today under ecclesiastical and civil toleration the organization has increased its prestige as a bulwark against "gringo" encroachment and has become a political factor in the Spanish-speaking pueblos.

None the less, the initiation rites and the ceremonies in the chapter house (*morada*) are guarded as secrets. Visitors are at all times resented, except by special dispensation; and the dark of night hides the climactic dramas. The great annual rites begin on the first Friday in Lent. During Holy Week the *disciplinas,* or whips of yucca-fiber, lacerate bare backs falling first on one shoulder, then the other. Ecstasy rises to its peak during the night of Maundy Thursday. The *tinieblas* (three dark hours) are realistically enacted in the *morada,* to the clanking of iron chains on the stone floor and to the laments of the *laudi.* These liturgies are accompanied by a small piercing reed-flute (*pito*) and a swishing bull-roarer (*metraca*). The chants invoke the Mother of God and bewail the sufferings of the Savior:

> . . . Santa Maria, pecadores somos;
> ruega para nosotros . . .
>
> . . . Por el rastro de la sangre
> Que Jesu Cristo derrama . . .

Their own trail of blood leads to the *calvario* on an adjacent mountainside. A *cantador* (chanter) and *resador* (prayer leader) head the procession of dusky flagellants clad in white trousers and a face-covering, plying their whips or dragging huge wooden crosses over precipitous paths. A chosen representative of Christ totters under his crown of thorns and his heavy cross. His crucifixion formerly took the realistic form of nailing for the duration of three hours, but now has been modified to tying by ropes for 40 minutes.

These ordeals, as in general the austerities, have been

mitigated. In some villages a figurine replaces the human Christ. The spectacle at Talpa, for instance, starts a processional with an image of Our Lady and a cart with a life-size figure of death (*carreta de muerte*). A full cast of characters reenacts the crucifixion scene, with Roman centurions, Jewish constabulary, the three Marys: a Passion play similar to these folk-plays of Mexico with texts dating back to the Conquest.

The frenzy recalls the spontaneous demonstrations of the loosely organized *Geissler;* the permanence of the society resembles the well-ordered *disciplinati* and *bianchi.* The officers are the Brothers of Light, *hermanos de la luz,* as the *hermano mayor, cantador, resador,* and *infermo* (healer), etc. The flagellants are the brothers of darkness. All proceedings and the course of life in the *morada* are strictly regulated.

The immediate religious motivation and forms certainly have their prototype in medieval Christianity. Yet in the New World they have been blended with Indian elements: musical tonalities and instruments, an organization analogous to that of the *kiva,* a recurrent seasonal climax like the seasonally rhythmic ceremonials of the Indians. Native analogies may account for the ready acceptance and for the continuance beyond its life span in Europe. Indigenous self-torture was always propitiatory, at times penitential, frequently vision-seeking. The Aztecs pricked their tongues with maguey thorns in personal humility; the Pueblo whippers lashed initiates for greater fortitude and power; the Plains sun-dancers pledged their ordeals to avert personal and communal disaster. In seasonal rites such drawing of blood fertilizes the latent earth. A dim remembrance of vegetation magic may have roused the penitents of both continents to their orgiastic self-mutilation for Christ and for their own souls.

Other motives, such as sexual perversion, socio-political heresies, may have contributed in some cases. It is evident that social strife inaugurated the movement and political prestige developed in later stages. A possible undercurrent of exhibitionism may have contributed to the ultimate spectacular display. But fundamentally the *penitentes* have offered their blood sincerely and exultantly as atonement to the supernaturals. See ARRIEROS; FLAGELLATION; RITUAL DRAMA; SACRIFICE; SUMAMAO; SUN DANCE.   GERTRUDE P. KURATH

Pennsylvania Dutch folklore Like other folklores this grows out of the daily lives of the common people and represents a fully American manifestation in that it results from a fusion of folklores of a number of peoples of different backgrounds, who, leaving their native lands for the New World, learned to live together. Most of the Pennsylvania Dutch are descended from Germans of the Palatinate, or from the Swiss, or from French Huguenots, but intermarriage with the English, Irish, Scotch, and others has produced a people apart from the original stock known as the Pennsylvania Dutch. It must be noted that today Pennsylvania Dutch really indicates a distinctive culture.

The Pennsylvania Dutch dialect—Pennsylvania Dutch not because the people call themselves *Deutsch* but because the English have from time immemorial called the Germans Dutch—is a mixture of Swiss, Swabian, and Palatinate dialects commingled with English. The famed humor of the Pennsylvania Dutch speech comes principally from the attempt to translate German idiomatic expression into English. "It wonders me" and "Throw the horse over the fence some hay" or "The bell won't make" have a skewed grammar that to some is as hilariously funny as Brooklynese pronunciation. In addition to this stands the vocabulary itself, quaint-sounding and imaginative. Coffee is *barfiessich* (bare-footed) when served without milk or sugar. The *littel haus,* exactly descriptive, is an outdoor toilet. A *gipser* is a little fellow who cuts the grain with a sickle at harvest time, doing his very best to help his parents get the fields cut. Pennsylvania Dutch has also borrowed words from English and adapted them to its pattern. *Bischur* is faintly recognizable as the English "to be sure"; the *fensemaus* is the fence mouse or chipmunk; the *bandihawna* is the bantam rooster. A *frallich* is a dance or a farmer's bee for some special work; the word may come from the English "frolic" or it may be the German *frohlich,* happy, gay. The old lore too lives in the language. A *hexe-schuss* (witch-shot) is either a shot fired at a witch, or a sudden pain, a stitch, rheumatism, or the like, which is sent by witches.

The single word meaning "rooster without a tail" in Pennsylvania Dutch is *bortzardhawna.* The word for "hen without a tail" is *bortzardhinkle. Bortza* means a tailless chicken of any variety. In English this kind of chicken is known as the *rumpless fowl* or *rumpie.* Children in Berks County, very angry at each other, yell feelingly, "Du bortzardhawna!" or "Du bortzardhinkle!" depending upon the sex involved, or simply "Du bortzie!" to indicate either. Sometimes the noun is preceded by an expletive. Whenever used in name calling there is always great derision or contempt indicated.

Chief among sources of this folklore are marriages, deaths, religion, hymns and songs, superstitions, folk cures, *hexerei* or witchcraft, Christmas and Easter, decorative arts, butchering, harvesting, story-telling, etc.

There seems to be complete uniformity of opinion that, of the Pennsylvania Dutch festive occasions, births have always been relatively unimportant, while the one which calls the greatest number of persons together is the funeral. Weddings have ever been highly festive occasions, but are usually confined to relatives and very close friends of the family. Such gatherings are none the less large. As recently as 1949 there occurred a remarkable affair in the old tradition between a young man of the Reformed Church and a young woman of the "plain people." Convention among the particular sect of the latter required that the bride-to-be prepare with her own hands the wedding feast for all the guests, advised and aided only by her mother. For four days she labored from before daylight till after night had fallen, preparing for the two hundred guests who had been invited because of the considerable size of the *freundschaft.* This ordeal for the lady is designed to keep her ever mindful of her obligation as a hostess and to provide liberally for her family.

Frequently there is great fun at weddings, games played including the "bloom-sock" (also much enjoyed at Christmas parties). The "bloom-sock" is a handkerchief twisted, doubled, and knotted at the ends. Thus treated it is passed by a group seated on a bench from one to the other behind them, while one in front of them hunts it. If those on the bench can do so, they hit the hunter with it, whereupon, if he is able, he snatches it away, takes a seat on the bench and the one from whom it has been snatched replaces him in front.

As previously noted, funerals among the Pennsylvania Dutch have been the occasions of the greatest private concourses of people. Within twenty years there are records of funerals in Berks County with two-mile-long processions of automobiles driving from the home of the deceased to the country church. On one such occasion the clergyman having completed his lengthy eulogy declared that the bereaved family wished him to thank all those present (some nine hundred) for their many kindnesses during the trying weeks of the last illness, and that they wished him on their behalf to invite all present to return to the farm for supper. Some three hundred accepted. The hospitality was lavish for the supper, as it had been for the dinner preceding the funeral. This lavishness seems to be required because of the great distances—sometimes several hundred miles —close friends and relatives travel for such an occasion.

Many farmer gatherings, such as "singings", quiltings, "snitzings," and apple-butter boilings, are less frequently held today than formerly. Except for quiltings, which are now usually carried on in church or organization rooms rather than homes, many old-time events are things heard of instead of things experienced. Snitzings, literally "cuttings," are gatherings at which fruit (principally apples) is cut, usually in eight pieces, for drying. Peaches, pears, and other fruits are prepared less frequently.

Folk songs have been numerous among the Pennsylvania Dutch. These have included songs of immigrants, songs of nature, rounds, spinning songs, lovers' songs, game songs, and ballads concerning local celebrities and local tragedies. Many hymns, particularly those of the Old Order Amish are folk poetry, some really being ballads. Tunes are not printed in Amish hymnals, airs being handed down orally in the ballad fashion. Within recent years some have been taken down and published in folklore studies. Pennsylvania Dutch spirituals exist in scattered instances. These have been used at "bush meetings" frequently as songs to invoke God's power upon those present.

Numerous folk beliefs, many of them extremely picturesque, persist among the Pennsylvania Dutch. Cows that "go dry" quickly are sometimes said to be bewitched, and so are butchered. A family heirloom pitcher that unaccountably dropped from a mantel in a "Dutch" farmhouse was interpreted as a "token" that someone in the house would die in a few days. Three days later a farmhand was killed in a motorcycle accident! Permitting the roofer to repair the gutters and spouting on a farmhouse on Good Friday was held accountable for the death of a litter of shoats during a cold spell the following night. Peach trees have been horsewhipped on Good Friday morning before breakfast so that they would produce more fruit. A farmer has walked around inside his garden fence three times on St. Patrick's day before nine o'clock in the morning to keep moles out. A bottle of asafetida has been kept hanging in a cow stable to keep cows from giving stringy milk. The list of acts that will "bring bad luck" is as varied as interesting.

Folk cures, including "powwowing" and charms, follow well-known patterns. Cures for hiccoughs include sucking lemons, scaring the hiccougher, holding the breath for a slow count of ten, tying a belt tight around the waist, swallowing seven small pieces of ice, finding seven bald-headed men, etc. A well-known cure for whooping cough is *for the victim* to drink out of a small blue glass cup. The quickest cure for a nosebleed is thought to be placing a key on the back of the neck. Placing a feather in a child's diaper will break him of wetting himself. Sprains are frequently treated literally with "vinegar and brown paper." Warts are "bought," or charms in Pennsylvania Dutch are spoken over them to remove them. Powwow equipment is sometimes simple, sometimes elaborate, even to including a chest in which the powwow doctor keeps his equipment. (A fine example of such a chest is in the Landis Valley Museum, Lancaster County, Pa.) While powwowing is probably less frequently employed today than formerly, it still exists and is often resorted to when professional medical aid appears to have failed. A man now living in Reading, Pa., had his knee badly crushed when a threshing machine on which he was riding turned over and pinned his leg beneath it. His complete recovery of the mobility of his knee joint has been attributed by many to the work of the powwow doctor rather than to that of the physician.

In our day, while witchcraft, or *hexerei*, is frequently treated lightly by many, probably most Pennsylvania Dutchmen know at least one witch or someone who is suspected of being a witch. The *Sixth and Seventh Books of Moses* are said to be the source of the major part of the formulas for witchcraft. Witches are about evenly divided between men and women, because of the fact that the power cannot be passed on to one of the same sex. Stories of witchcraft are frequent and, from time to time, cases involving the practice come up in court. The effects of *hexerei* may be either good or bad, depending upon the circumstances and whether the hex is being "put on" or "taken off."

The daughter of a farmer, while crossing another farmer's property to go to the mailbox, was impertinent to the latter, who, promptly gave her a few lashes with his whip. Her father, indignant, took the case before a justice of the peace who settled the matter, but presently things began to happen in the house of the first farmer. Strange noises were heard in his house at night. Doors that had been securely locked and shutters that had been bolted were found to be mysteriously opened. Chairs were overturned and dishes in cupboards were broken, but no intruder could be discovered. Finally the farmer and his wife journeyed to a witch they knew of twenty-one miles away. He took water from his spring; into it put herbs, and over it said incantations in "Dutch," gave it to the farmer, told him to go home, cut a branch of cedar from a tree in his pasture, dip the branch in the water and sprinkle it on every threshold, every windowsill, and in every chimney hole in the house. This removed the spell.

In another case, a woman who felt all was not well with her consulted a witch as to her ailment (which she did not reveal in telling the story), and he informed her that she was indeed *ferhexed*. When she asked him what she should do to remove the spell, he told her to clean her house from cellar to attic, and to save all the sweepings, then to make a bag of red flannel that had not ever been used for anything. Into this she was to put the sweepings. Next, she was to stick 15 pins into the dust—not through the flannel—six with the points down and nine with the points up. Finally, she was to tie the bag shut with a rope, hang the whole up on the branch of a tree and take a club and beat it. She did all this, and the spell was removed.

Other instances involve deaths and recoveries achieved by magic and include the use of wax and dough images and other paraphernalia whose origins go back to the Middle Ages.

Christmas and Easter have their own folklores. Christmas trees, while given to the United States by Germans, did not originate with the Pennsylvania Dutch, as some have claimed. The Christmas *putz* or *crèche*, however, is thought to have been first introduced by the Moravians around Bethlehem, Pa. Christmas cookies—*lebkuche* (gingerbread or spice cakes), *sprengerle, pfeffernüsse, matzebäume*—and other elaborate creations with sugared designs, belong to the Old World Germans as well as to the "Dutch," as does Belznickle (who "takes care" of naughty children by putting coal and switches in their stockings). See KNECHT RUPRECHT. The old European belief that animals in the barns talk at midnight on Christmas Eve is also widely accepted.

Easter-egg coloring and decoration have been widely practiced at least since the 18th century. Onion skin is the usual coloring matter used; tulips and other designs scratched skilfully on the shells through the red-brown dye thus produced carry on the ancient traditional designs. The famous egg-tree is an old Germanic institution, but seems first to have been associated with Easter by the Pennsylvania Dutch. It is usually a birch or a cherry tree whose trunk and branches are wrapped with cotton batting and hung sometimes with hundreds of colored eggs. Such egg-trees are often erected at Easter time as evergreen trees are at Christmas. The ancient concept of the egg as fertility symbol lies at the root of the practice and the belief still exists, as Cornelius Weygandt mentions in *The Blue Hills* (1936), that the creation of such a tree will bring children to the childless.

The traditional Easter Sunday morning breakfast among the Pennsylvania Dutch is ham and fried eggs, and it is not uncommon for a vigorous man to consume from one to two dozen eggs for breakfast. Hard-boiled dyed eggs are eaten in great numbers throughout the whole Easter season. Ham, boiled or baked, and fresh dandelion greens are *de rigueur* for Easter Sunday dinner.

The items indicated above are merely such as would be included as part of an ordinary dinner on the occasions mentioned. A typical Pennsylvania Dutch dinner held in Philadelphia in April, 1948, whose menu was suggested and prepared by a group of women in upper Montgomery County, Pa., included the following:

Chicken Noodle Soup

Celery	Jelly	Pickled Beets
	Smearcase	
Pickled Eggs	Molasses	Apple Butter
	Scallions	

Stewed Chicken
Giblet Gravy

Potato Filling	Peas	Pickled Cabbage
Dried Corn		Chow Chow

Apple Sauce

Green Apple Pie		Cheese
Bread	Coffee	Butter

Not least among the folk contributions of the Pennsylvania Dutch to the world's cookery has been pie, and no subject is more likely to provoke a discussion than pies and how to make them. In November, 1923, *Pie-ology of the Pennsylvania Dutch* was the title of a talk given at a meeting of the Montgomery County (Pa.) Historical Society, the talk being accompanied by an exhibit of real pies—forty varieties—these being a few of the many kinds invented by the "Dutch." The English settlers upon that occasion were credited with inventing only two varieties—meat pie and mince pie.

Of all the folk accomplishments of the Pennsylvania Dutch, however, their decoration is most prominent because of their love of the gay and beautiful. Pottery, china, cooking utensils, furniture, architecture, glassware, metalwork, boxes, textiles, needlework, quilts, *frakturschrift* (*Geburts-Scheins, Tauf-Scheins, Haus-Segens,* etc.), have long been decorated with the signs and symbols long known in the European homelands, and which were cherished by immigrants in the New World. Tulips, pomegranates, roses, peacocks, *distelfinks* (thistle birds or goldfinches), other birds, horses, deer, fish, and geometrical designs are freely employed.

Some of these were symbols of fertility; some symbolized the Christian Resurrection; some of purely geometrical form were used for sheer decoration; some were used to protect from evil. Much attention has been devoted to them, and many widely varying opinions regarding them have been held in this country from the day of Francis Daniel Pastorius to the 20th century. Painting symbols, or "hex signs," on barns apparently first became customary in Pennsylvania Dutchland in the early 19th century. Many students of Dutchiana believe these symbols to be akin to Rosicrucian signs designed to protect animals from the working of witchcraft and the evil eye. An equal number believe them to be merely decorative devices, and point to the fact that pictures of horses, cows, and other animals are also frequently painted within the circles and other geometric figures for decoration only. In support of the latter idea may be mentioned the belief of an old woman of Berks County, Pa., who died in 1927 at the age of 87. Though her people had been in the United States for some two hundred years, she could scarcely speak more than a dozen words of English, and had been known in her younger and more active days for her ability to powwow. She was familiar with all the lore of the countryside, and when she and her husband bought, in 1890, the farm on which she died, the barn symbols were repainted after their older fashion. Neither she nor her children had any association with such signs except as decorations. Her many sayings and advices indicated the high regard in which she held the supernatural, but that regard did not extend to "hex signs."

Pennsylvania Dutch folklore includes tales of phantom dogs, phantom children, and phantom adults. In Berks County, a few years back, old folks were still telling stories about a dragon (a great rarity in American folklore) that flew across the heavens snorting fire and smoke.

The "Dutch" are past masters at the art of storytelling, and having found that most phases of ordinary life furnish fruitful material, have by no means neglected the so-called "dumb Dutch" story which wherever told among them provides much amusement. Typical of the genre is that about a Reading street car conductor who was suspected of "knocking down" fares. One day a "spotter" called his attention to the fact that he had one more passenger aboard than fares rung up. Whereupon the conductor stopped the car and said to the passengers, "Vell, now, I guess von of yous'll have to get off." Another is about a Pennsylvania Dutch woman who had country connections, but who had been brought up in Philadelphia. After World War II she moved with her family to the remote suburbs, and decided to fulfil a lifelong ambition to keep chickens. She visited a market in Lancaster and asked a farmer: "How long does it take eggs to hatch?" He replied that chickens required three weeks; ducks, four. She bought a setting, and three weeks later returned the eggs and demanded her money back. On being questioned as to why, she said, "Well, you see, I waited three weeks and didn't get chickens, and I don't want ducks."

At the present time there are in Pennsylvania several Pennsylvania Dutch folklore museums; chief among them are the following:

The Landis Valley Museum, four miles out of Lancaster, Pa. This includes a general collection covering Pennsylvania Dutch material from Lancaster and neighboring counties.

The Moravian Museum, located in the George Whitefield House (1740) at Nazareth, Pa. This entire collection is unified by Moravian interests, and includes the well-known paintings by John Valentin Haidt (1700–1780).

The Schwenkfelder Museum, now housed in the second floor of the library of the Perkiomen School at Pennsburg, Pa., but soon to be displayed in a new building which will be constructed especially for it. The collection includes household goods, books, garments, china, farm implements, examples of folk art, etc., solely pertaining to the Schwenkfelders.

The Pennsylvania Dutch Folklore Center, at present housed in the Fackenthal Library, Franklin and Marshall College, Lancaster, Pa., publishes *The Pennsylvania Dutchman*, a folklore newspaper. A building to house a Pennsylvania Dutch Library on the campus of the College is planned.

Bibliography:
Borneman, Henry S., *Pennsylvania Illuminated Manuscripts.* Norristown, Pa., 1937.
Gibbons, P. E., *Pennsylvania Dutch, and Other Essays,* 2d. ed. Philadelphia, 1874.
Journal of American Folklore, Vol. 52, No. 203, 1939.
Kauffman, Henry S., *Pennsylvania Dutch American Folk Art.* New York, 1946.
Korson, George, ed., *Pennsylvania Songs and Legends.* Philadelphia, 1949.
Kuhns, Oscar, *The German and Swiss Settlements of Colonial Pennsylvania.* New York, 1901.
The Pennsylvania Dutchman, Lancaster, Pa.
Robacker, Earl F., *Pennsylvania Dutch Stuff.* Philadelphia, 1944.
Weygandt, Cornelius, *The Red Hills.* Philadelphia, 1929.
—— *The Blue Hills.* New York, 1936.
—— *The Dutch Country.* New York, 1939.

WILLIAM J. PHILLIPS

pennyroyal A low, hairy, strong-scented herb (*Hedeoma pulegioides*) of the mint family yielding the oil of pennyroyal; also, the European mint (*Mentha pulegium*). The name is a corruption of the Latin *puleium,* fleabane,

and *regalis,* royal, or poison for the king's fleas. In America it is called mosquito bane and a bunch is tied to the bedpost. It is made into a malignant draft by witches and causes those who partake of it to see double. In medieval times it was used as a water purifier by voyagers, being put into whatever manner of foul water was available to drink, whether salt or fresh. Medicinally, it purified the blood and was useful for colds, headache, and fainting fits. In colonial times it was made into a tea for measles and whooping cough. The Catawba Indians boiled the root for colds. The Navaho medicine man chews the seeds and blows in the face of the patient, or on the affected part for all manner of ills. The Tewa Indians use it powdered and rubbed on the head to cure headache or on the body for fevers. The Santa Clara Indians wear it in a deerskin bag about the neck for sore eyes. The Negroes of Jamaica boil it with marigold (or a rusty nail) to cause miscarriage or abortion; it eases labor pains, and is good for babies, but bad for young girls. As a tea with sugar and salt they use it for headache, colds, catarrh, and as a general medicine. They also shave a spot on the top of the head and apply leaf poultices steeped in rum to cause a head cold to run out of the nose.

pent cuckoo A folktale motif (J1904.2) in which several noodles made a hedge to pen in the cuckoo, so that she might sing to them all year. They made the hedge, got the cuckoo and put her into it, and, as soon as she discovered herself free within the hedge, she flew away. The fools were exasperated that they had not built the hedge high enough. This is one of the most famous undertakings of the Mad Men of Gotham (see W. A. Clouston, *Book of Noodles,* London, 1888, pp. 26–27). It is classified by Stith Thompson with stories featuring absurd ignorance of proper places to keep animals (J1904 ff.). See LITTLE MORON; NOODLE STORIES.

Pentheus In classical legend, king of Thebes and cousin of Dionysus. After Dionysus returned to Thebes from his journeyings, Pentheus opposed his worship as a god by the women of Thebes. When force did not cause an end to the rites, he attempted to spy on the ceremonies and was seen and torn apart by the followers of Dionysus, among them Pentheus' own mother Agave.

pepper (1) An aromatic spice made from the berries of the pepper plant (genus *Piper*) coming originally from the Indian Archipelago. This was one of the earliest known spices and has continued a staple of commerce between India and Europe since earliest times. The ransom of Rome was paid partly in pepper. Its high price at Venice induced the Portuguese to explore the route around the Cape of Good Hope, and was responsible, among other things, for Columbus' voyage. The finest pepper comes from Malabar, and to secure the finest flavor it should be ground fresh at the table. Both black and white pepper come from the same source, the outer skin being removed for the white; this is said to remove much of its value.

In the 13th century pepper was a panacea for all the ills of mankind, from weak eyes to the plague. However, in 1563 Garcia da Orta was seriously doubting some of the uses to which it was being put, and of the Greeks he says, "All agree with one accord not to tell the truth." In Bavaria a paste of black pepper and sugar was used to fill the cavity in an aching tooth. For ague you are advised to swallow a whole peppercorn on each of seven successive mornings, preferably beginning the dosage before beginning to shake. A favorite general medicine was a pepper posset made of peppercorns boiled in whey. In Mexico and Texas, peppercorns are often placed in a wound suspected of being poisoned, as by arrows. In Texas a piece of cotton filled with black pepper is placed in the ear to cure earache. An excess of pepper is said to be aphrodisiac.

(2) The fruit of a plant of the nightshade family (genus *Capsicum*). This is the pepper from which red pepper, Cayenne, and paprika are made. For success in growing these peppers it is well either to plant them while in a rage, or to hire a red-headed person to do it for you. Strong red-pepper tea is good for a horse with a bellyache. In Texas and Mexico, eating plenty of chili peppers is good for ague, and swallowing whole, small, chili peppers like pills will cure a cold. Boiled pods mixed with buffalo tallow are good for burns. All manner of peppers are said to have strong aphrodisiac properties.

Perchten or **Berchten** The followers of Perchta, Berchta, or Bertha, also known as Holle in Germanic mythology, the custodian of the dead. Perchta and her following are believed to rush through the sky during *Perchtennacht*, which is Twelfth Night, sometimes with baneful, sometimes with beneficent intentions. They frighten naughty children in the former capacity; in the latter they aid the fructification of fields. Their impersonators in weird, horned and hairy wooden masks, have these same functions. In the Bavarian and Austrian Alps they participate in *Niklasumzüge* and in carnival *Lärmumzüge* (rowdy processions).

In Salzburg until recently they enacted a drama of conflict which recalls Portuguese *Mouriscadas* and other forms of *Moriscas*. The two factions are represented by the beautiful and good *Schönperchten* in high ornate headdresses with chains, ribbons, flowers, and by an opposing motley, tattered, and rowdy crew of *Schiechenperchten* or evil Perchten. In a hand-to-hand combat the weird maskers are of course vanquished. This symbolic combat is of particular significance in the explanation of Moriscas, for the Perchten retain the pagan connotations which most Moriscas have ceded to Christian ideology. Other shaggy figures abound in this same mountain region, though without the combat: the *Huttlerläufer* and *Zottler* of Tyrol, the *Hänsele* of Überlingen, the Swiss *Rautschegetten* with black sheepskin. See MASKS; MORISCAS. [GPK]

Percival or **Perceval** One of the chief figures of the Arthurian legend, and the subject of a score of medieval romances in French, Welsh, German, English, Norse, and Italian. The earliest of these is Chrétien de Troyes's *Perceval* or *Conte del Graal* (c. 1175). The first part is a charming story of a boy brought up in the forests of North Wales by his widowed mother in entire ignorance of chivalry, of his naive blunders when he goes out into the world, and of his arrival at Arthur's court to seek knighthood. After Perceval has received instruction in the use of arms and in manners from Gornemant, he enters upon a series of adventures distinguished by their inadequate motivation and incoherence, including the visit to the Grail castle and

his humiliation consequent on his failure to ask the mysterious question, "Whom does one serve with the Grail?" Wolfram von Eschenbach in his *Parzival* (c. 1205), using Chrétien but also drawing largely on traditional sources, adds an account of the hero's parents, treats the hero's development from callow ignoramus to a pattern of Christian knighthood with much more realism and coherence. As a young man with a sense of wrong, he defies God, but after years of suffering and of separation from his wife, he learns the lesson of human sympathy, becomes king of the Grail, and is reunited with his wife. Most versions of Perceval's legend retain the story of his forest upbringing, his naive blunders, and his association with the Grail. The later forms tend to make him a virgin knight, and in the *Queste del Saint Graal*, composed by a Cistercian monk (c. 1210), he plays a secondary role to that of Galahad. This is the text condensed by Malory, and through Malory known to Tennyson.

As with other Arthurian personages, the origins of Perceval have been the subject of much speculation. His name and some of his relationships seem to be derived from the historic Welsh hero Peredur, who died in 580, but more important are the borrowings from the story of Pryderi in the *Four Branches of the Mabinogi*. Certain features of Perceval's story may even be traced back to Irish sagas of Finn and Cuchulain. Adapted by the Welsh and blended with their own traditions, they were passed on to the Bretons and from these to the French and Anglo-Normans. It shoud be noted that the Welsh *Peredur* was based on one or more lost French romances. See GRAIL; MABINOGION.

Bibliography: J. L. Weston, *The Legend of Sir Perceval* (1906, 1909). R. S. Loomis, *Arthurian Tradition and Chrétien de Troyes* (1949), pp. 335–417, 430–33. M. F. Richey, *The Story of Parzival and the Graal* (1935).

ROGER S. LOOMIS

perfumes Perfumes were used by the Egyptians, Greeks, and Romans, and were brought into Europe by the Arabs about the 16th century. Today the important centers of manufacture in Europe are in France, England, Bulgaria, and Sicily.

The poetical association of perfume fragrance and love-sickness, in folktale and myth, makes perfume a kind of love magic that bewitches and entrances its victims. Science explains this phenomenon in its own terminology. Perfume scents, by acting upon the olfactory nerves, stimulate the brain and call up emotions such as sympathy, love, and physical attraction. Perfumes are classified as aphrodisiacs. The natural ingredients in perfumes provide the element of fragrance. Varying the herb, flower, or blend will vary the scent.

Resinous gums were used in ancient Arabic countries to make a kind of perfume known as incense. Myrrh, spikenard, and frankincense were generally used. To this day, Arabian women living in the desert perfume themselves by sitting in the smoke from fires of burning spices.

The story of Joseph and his brethren depicts the Ishmaelites who carried to Egypt myrrh, balm, and spicery. It is recorded that the Queen of Sheba supplied Solomon with perfumes and that her subjects, to drive away her competitors in the trade, told a terrifying tale about cinnamon and the Phœnix or cinnamon in the marshes guarded by winged snakes. In *Exodus* it is stated that Moses received two recipes for a holy anointing oil rich in perfumes.

The dandy of the ancient Greek city commonly used one kind of perfume for his robes and another for his hair. By the time of the classical period, flower scents were a part of perfumes. Under the Empire, the Roman nobleman worked upon an elaborate scheme of perfuming his body: mint—arms; palm oil—jaws and heart; marjoram—eyebrows and hair; ground ivy essence—knees and neck. The importance of sweet scents to the Roman is nowhere better exemplified than in the report that Nero lavished four million sesterces (about $200,-000) upon a festival in which roses were a main feature. Through conquest the Romans opened new perfume horizons when they moved eastward and returned with strange and interesting scents from conquered countries.

With the rise of feudalism in Europe the art of perfuming went into decline, until the time of the Crusades, during which the East contributed, through the Arabs, innovations in perfumery. The Arab Avicenna discovered that fragrant water could be distilled from leaves. Islam was the root of Arabian concern for perfumes, and in the Koran it is written that paradise would be populated with "black-eyed houris . . . of the purest musk." Musk is one of the oldest perfumes known to men, and was probably brought into Europe by the Arabs. Musk perfumes are usually made from a dried secretion of the scent glands of the musk deer.

As new trade routes opened up and enterprise expanded during the Renaissance, Italy came to hold supremacy in perfume manufacture and maintained it until France seized the initiative. In Italy, sweet bags, perfume cakes, scented gloves and pomanders, fragrant candles, and cosmetics were fashionable. France's perfume centers were to be concentrated in the cities of Grasse, Cannes, and Nice.

It is told that the Emperor Napoleon used to bathe his head in *eau de cologne* before his campaigns, doing what had been traditionally done in Rome by the nobility under the Empire. It is also told that his consort, Josephine, so impregnated her apartment in Malmaison Palace with perfume scents that nothing has ever been successful in removing them.

As of 1937 there were 150,000 perfume names on record. Many of these are highly suggestive of folklore ideas and themes, e.g. Tabu, Love Potion, Cinderella, Vampire, Witcherie, Voodoo, Nymfaun, Spellbound, Sorcière, etc. Likewise, the names of men's colognes and shaving lotions are taken from folklore: John Peel, Pericles, Royal Oak, etc.

Such names as Nymfaun and Witcherie and Spellbound are reminiscent of folktale. In a Japanese version of the swan-maiden tale, a celestial maiden who is in attendance on the heavenly prince in the moon visits the earth and lures a fisherman with the scent from her perfumed and feathered heavenly robe that she had hung upon the limb of a pine tree. In Oriental mythology, the Tennyo, the Japanese equivalent of the Indian Devatās, are described as heavenly musicians who fill the air with flowers and perfumes. They are ministering angels to pious Buddhists, but sometimes they will assume the shape of women and make love to men.

The parallel between the range of known perfume scents and the range of musical notes was recently worked out by the chemist Dr. Septimus Piesse, and his achieve-ment has become a perfume blender's tool. Starting with the bass clef, three octaves below middle C, he assigned musical equivalents to perfumes in the following order that is based on the assumption that the sharpness of the perfume scent is directly proportional to the height of the musical note on the scale: do—patchouli; re—vanilla; mi—clove bark; fa—benzoin; sol—frangipane; la—storax; ti—clove; do—sandalwood, etc. Thus, only certain scents will harmonize with others, just as certain musical notes harmonize with some but produce a dissonance when brought together with other notes.

The use of perfumes by males continues as a tradition of the Latin countries—France, Spain, Italy, and in South America. But the men in the United States, like the knights of medieval Europe, frown upon this practice as an indication of deficient masculinity. Instead they indulge in toilet waters and shaving lotions. [JLR]

peri or **pari** (from Persian *parī* or *perī;* Pahlavi *parik,* evil genius) In modern Persian mythology and folklore, a group of beautiful and graceful supernatural beings. male and female. Originally they were evil and identified with the *pairikas* of the *Avesta,* who as agents of Ahriman visited eclipses and drought on mankind. In later concept, they became benevolent genii, likened to fairies or angels, and guiders of human souls to Paradise. They are said to be formed of the element of fire; perfume is their only food. They are constantly at war with the *devs* (evil spirits), who lock them in iron cages, whenever they capture any, and hang them in high trees. Here they are visited by their own kind and fed with delicious odors.

pericón Literally, large fan: a group circle dance of the Argentine pampas, expressive of the lusty and cohesive spirit of the gaucho. The circle is symbolic of daily habits of eating together around a fire, and of encircling the cattle to be lassoed. Kerchiefs sweep through the air like lassoes. Shouts and quips punctuate the monotonous shuffle of the feet, while spurs jingle and the *payadores,* wandering minstrels, vie with each other in improvised verses. The rugged communal spirit contrasts with the coquetry of couple dances like the *cueca.* [GPK]

periwinkle or **ground ivy** A trailing evergreen plant (genus *Vinca*) with blue or white flowers, often called myrtle or creeping myrtle in the United States. Eleventh century herbals gave an important place to this plant. When plucking it, however, a person should be clean of every uncleanness, and it should be plucked only on the first, ninth, eleventh, and thirteenth nights of the moon. It will cure Devil sickness, demoniacal possession, terror, envy, poisons, and the bites of venomous serpents and beasts. It also gives grace and prosperity when carried. In Britain and France it was called the "sorcerers' violet," because so widely used against the evil eye and spirits; in Italy it was known as *Centocchii,* hundred-eyes. Some called it joy-of-the-ground, and if powdered and wrapped in a house leek with worms and taken at meals it induced love between husband and wife. It was used frequently in place of hops in beer. In modern Italy it is strewn on the graves of young children. In Wales it is said that if one takes periwinkle off a grave, the dead will appear to him and haunt his dreams for a year. In England it is still used in skin ointments, as a tonic, and for intestinal troubles.

Perkele Finnish name for Devil, derived from the Lithuanian Perkūnas, Thundergod. Compare Estonian *põrgu*, hell. [JB]

Perkūnas The thunder god of Lithuanian mythology: similar to the Latvian Pērkuons and to the Old Prussian Percunis. He is the most popular god of the Balts (see LITHUANIAN MYTHOLOGY). The Slavonic word for thunder, *perun*, is of the same root. The philologists formerly explained that the origin of the word is in connection with *quercus*, oak, the sacred tree of the thunder god, but another theory seems more convincing, i.e., that the name Perkūnas is from Lithuanian *perti*, to strike, to beat. It is not clear if the name of the thunder god of the Balts is related to the old Indian god Parjanya and Scandinavian Fjörgynn. The Slavonic Perun may be a genuine god and not a borrowing from the Scandinavian Thor as S. Rožiniecki tried to prove (*Archiv für slavische Philologie* 23, 1901). We have proof for the antiquity of Perkūnas in *Pirgene* or *Purgine-pas*, the word for thunder among the Erza Mordvins. About 2000 B.C., when the Balts were living in the neighborhood of the Mordvins not far from the middle of the Volga River, the thunder name Perkūnas was already known to the Balts and was borrowed by the Mordvins. Other loans of this name to the Finns from the Balts can be seen in the Finnish *perkele*, devil, and the Estonian *põrgu*, hell. As the Balts reached the Baltic Sea and had contact with the Vikings, the borrowing of ideas and myths about the thunder god from Scandinavia was quite possible.

The Lithuanians have many thunder god legends, especially about his enmity with the devil. One of the most popular relates that a man, usually a hunter, in the woods during a storm, perceived a strange animal (cat or small he-goat) who came out from a hole in a tree or from behind a big stone, and mocked the thunder. As the thunder sounded, the animal hid himself for safety. The man met a hunter who told him, "I am Perkūnas, help me catch this little devil." So the man closed up the devil (animal) in his hiding place, the thunder struck, and the devil was killed. When the devil was destroyed, the hunter received from Perkūnas a marvelous gift: a horn with gunpowder which would never be empty, some bullets which would never fail.

This legend was examined by J. Balys in 1939 and the author discovered a considerable number of variants: Lithuanian—46, Latvian—7, Estonian—2, Livian—1, Ukrainian—15, Polish—2, and Rumanian—1. He came to the conclusion that the legend was of Lithuanian origin.

Interesting is a tale about the friendship between a man, usually a carpenter, Perkūnas, and the devil. They build themselves a house and plant potatoes or beets. A *laumė* (fairy) comes to steal their vegetables. She flogs both Perkūnas and the devil who is guarding the vegetables, but she is outwitted by the man, who plays a fiddle and tricks her by catching her fingers in a cleft tree. Then the three agree on a contest in frightening each other: the house shall belong to the one who succeeds best in frightening the others. The man is the winner.

References: J. Balys, "Der Donner im litauischen Volksglauben," in *Tautosakos Darbai* III, pp. 149–238. Kanuas, 1937. J. Balys, "Donner und Teufel in den Volkserzählungen der Baltischen und Skandinavischen Völker," *ibid.* VI, pp. 1–220. Kaunas, 1939. [JB]

Perrault, Charles (1628–1703) French poet. He was at one time comptroller of the king's buildings and was elected to the Academy. His poem, "Le siècle de Louis le Grand," which he read before that body, began a controversy on the respective merits of the ancients and moderns. However this may have turned out, Perrault will be remembered not for his verses, but for his collection of tales entitled *Contes de ma Mère l'Oye* (1697). Some of the suggestions given for the source of this title are that it is connected with the person of a mythical Queen Pedauque, whose statue in churches is represented with goose feet; or that it may have been taken from a fable where Mère l'Oie was shown as instructing and entertaining her little goslings. Such a fable, it is thought, never existed, but the idea took hold of the popular imagination. Perrault's title appears to suggest impossible happenings and is to be compared with such phrases as "*Contes de la cigone*," "*Contes à dormir*," "*Contes au vieux loup*," each of which denotes a series of fanciful stories (compare the generic term *Märchen*).

Perrault's tales are significant inasmuch as he was the first one in France who wrote down stories that had hitherto been floating around in nursery, kitchen, and salon. His *contes* in verse are decidedly inferior to his prose *contes* (under the title discussed above) which include: *La belle au bois dormant, Le petit chaperon rouge, La Barbe bleüe, Le Chat Botté, Les Fées, Cendrillon, Riquet à la Houppe,* and *Le petit Poucet.* See CONTES DE MA MÈRE L'OYE. Perrault had many imitators, but his simple fascinating style was scarcely ever approached by them and never surpassed in dramatic brevity. On account of interest in the writings of his imitators (Comtesse d'Aulnoy, Mme. le Prince Beaumont, and others), the prose *contes* of Perrault were forgotten for a time. At the beginning of the 19th century there was an awakening of interest in the works of Perrault and editions of his prose *contes* were published in both Italy and Germany. Musicians, artists, and poets have made use of material drawn from these sources. Scholars have studied individual tales but the best known is probably the study by Saintyves (*Les contes de Perrault,* Paris, 1903) which surveys the prose and verse *contes.* Saintyves classifies the tales into three groups: 1) stories of the origin of the seasons; 2) those arising from initiatory rites, and 3) apologs and fables, detritus of medieval exempla. Saintyves brings masses of data to support his theses, but his conclusions fail to carry complete conviction with present-day scholars. Compare A. H. Krappe in his review of this work in *The Romanic Review* XVI (1925), No. 2; Stith Thompson, *The Folktale* (New York, 1946), p. 386.

Persephone In Greek mythology, the daughter of Zeus and Demeter; consort of Hades: known also, especially in her cult aspects, as Cora or Kore, the Maiden. The name was corrupted by the Romans into Proserpina. Demeter and Persephone seem to be two separate aspects of the grain goddess, probably the old and the new crops. According to the myth, Demeter kept Persephone secluded in Sicily, but Hades one day, as Persephone picked flowers near Henna, caused the earth to open and appeared before her in his chariot. He seized the girl and carried her off to the underworld. Demeter searched everywhere for her daughter and while she did so nothing grew on earth. At last the gods negotiated the return of Persephone. But Ascalaphus had seen Persephone eat at least one pomegranate seed while she was in the underworld, and she therefore had to spend six (or eight) months of every year with the lord of the underworld. See FOOD TABU IN THE LAND OF THE DEAD. Persephone, as the Maiden, seems also to have been an aspect of the fertility goddess Aphrodite: in the Adonis myth, Aphrodite and Persephone both claim Adonis, and he is to spend a third of the year with each of them. But he spends two thirds of each year with Aphrodite.

Perseus In Greek mythology, the Gorgon-slayer, dragon-slayer, and rescuer of Andromeda. Acrisius, king of Argos, was told by an oracle that the son of his daughter Danae would kill him. He therefore built a brazen chamber, either below ground or in a tower, and imprisoned Danae in it. Zeus saw the girl and entered the chamber as a shower of gold, thereby impregnating Danae. When the child, Perseus, was born, Acrisius discovered the fact, and not believing Danae's story about Zeus and the shower of gold, put mother and child into a chest and had them thrown into the sea. The chest floated to the island of Seriphos where Dictys, brother of the king Polydectes, found it. He took the pair under his protection. In later years Polydectes became enamored of Danae but was afraid to approach her because Perseus was well grown and formidable. Polydectes took the pretext of a rash boast by the youth to send him for the Gorgon's head, the sight of which could kill.

On the advice of Athena and Hermes, Perseus first sought out the three Grææ and stole from them the one eye and one tooth they had among them. The eye and tooth he traded back for information on how to get to the nymphs. From the nymphs he obtained Hades' cap of darkness, the shoes of swiftness, and the *kibisis* (probably a wallet on a long strap). Athena gave him a mirror (or loaned him her shield) and Hermes gave him an adamantine sickle. Thus equipped, he crept up on the Gorgons, looking all the time in the mirror (or shield), and with the sickle cut off the head of Medusa, the only mortal one of the Gorgons. He put the head in the wallet and fled on the winged shoes. The Gorgons could not see him to chase him because of the cap of invisibility.

On the way back to Seriphos, he passed Ethiopia and there saw Andromeda chained to a rock as a sacrifice to a sea monster. He killed the dragon with the Gorgon's head, married Andromeda, and went back with her to Seriphos. There he found his mother besieged by Polydectes; he took the head out of the wallet again and petrified the king and his assistants. The Gorgon's head he gave to Athena to put on her shield, the ægis; the other objects were returned to the nymphs. Perseus, Andromeda, and Danae went to Argos, after installing their protector Dictys as king, but Acrisius fled before them, fearing the fulfilment of the oracle. Perseus followed his grandfather to entreat him to return, but at the games at Larissa he let fly a discus which by accident struck and killed Acrisius. Perseus traded the throne of Argos for that of Tiryns, where he reigned as king; among his descendants was Eurystheus, the master of Hercules.

Another myth tells how Hera egged Perseus on to attack Dionysus and his train. The higher Perseus flew on his magic shoes, the taller Dionysus grew, until he touched the sky. Dionysus, very angry, was about to destroy his tormentors when Hermes interfered and calmed the god. Realizing that Hera and not Perseus was to blame, Dionysus pardoned the hero; the inhabitants of Argos instituted rites honoring Dionysus and Perseus in memory of the peace.

The story of Perseus, Danae, and Andromeda is probably an old folktale adapted to mythology, a tale picked up from the oral tradition and told and retold by several writers. E. S. Hartland made a study of the myth, comparing it with other folktales and with belief and custom all over the world (*The Legend of Perseus*, 3 vols., London, 1894–96). Hartland tried to prove its identity with the modern stories of the dragon-slayer (Type 300) and the two brothers (Type 303), but most students, though admitting some relationship, return a verdict of not proven. The story is full of familiar motifs: magical impregnation (T510), abandoned child (S300), theft of the eye from three old women (K333.2), magic objects (D800), petrifaction by a glance (D581), princess as prize (T68.1), etc. It is even possible that the *kibisis* may be identical with the inexhaustible purse or source of food. Compare BALOR; CRONUS; EXPOSURE OF FAMOUS PERSONS IN INFANCY.

persicary Any of a genus of plants (*Polygonum*) of the buckwheat family; especially *P. persicaria*, commonly called lady's thumb because of its reddish, oblong spike, shaped something like a thumb. In the past this plant was sometimes called heart's-ease and was recommended for disturbances of the heart. Its seeds were used in place of pepper, and in medicine it was used in pepper possets and as a counter-irritant on the limbs. Culpeper calls it an herb of Saturn though he admits that others attribute it to the sun; still others call it an herb of Mars. The juice was good to stop bleeding. Culpeper says it cools the temper and heats the stomach and blood, yet he also claims it cools in ward pains from "heat and corruption of the blood and liver." It also kills worms, expels the stone, promotes urine, cleanses the ears, relieves prickly heat and other inflammations, heals fresh and green wounds, gangrene, ulcers, cankers, and venereal infections, and mends broken joints and ruptures.

persimmon In Alabama, if a girl eats nine unripe persimmons she will turn into a boy inside of two weeks. Chills and fever may be cured (in Alabama) if the skin of an egg shell is taken to a persimmon tree on three mornings running, and a knot tied in the skin each time; Mississippi Negroes tie a knot in a piece of string (one for every chill one has had) and then tie the string around a persimmon tree. They also say: Never toss a piece of persimmon wood on another man's fire unless you want him to move away for good. In Texas a teaspoon of the white inside bark steeped in six cups of water and drunk will cure chills and fever.

personification Anthropomorphic treatment of animals, natural elements, and natural phenomena is a characteristic of North American Indian mythology, not only in tales set in the Mythical Age, but in those in which human beings also appear. Rock, Flint, Thunder,

Coyote, Buffalo, Deer, Sun, Moon, Water, Earth, Corn, Tobacco, to mention only a few personified elements and phenomena, are all well-known actors in tales; they talk, behave, and appear as human beings in a plethora of tales from all parts of the continent. The one area where human actors and fantastic beings outnumber animal or other actors in mythology is the Eskimo area. Animals appear in many Eskimo stories, but they are usually animals who speak definitely either as animals, or as transformed human beings, and not as humanlike creatures. [EWV]

Per Spelmann Literally (Norwegian), Peter the Fiddler: one of the round dances of the Faroe Islands, recently popularized and hence elaborated in Norway. The formation and step is essentially of the *branle* type. Alternate men and women, lady on the right, face center in a circle. While all hold hands they progress left with a double, right with a simple, and finish with a toe-rise. In the new version, the circle breaks up into couples. Partners face each other during the chorus, hold hands with a jolly hop-skip from side to side. All join in the song during the dance. [GPK]

peteneras A Spanish couple dance of Andalusia, a development from the *seguidillas Sevillanas*. It is attributed to a famous flamenco singer of that name. The fundamental step is: right forward, lift left with a leg twist (*floreo*), four steps forward. After an excursion to Cuba, it returned to Cadiz with an added Negro flavor. Lately it has been adapted to stage presentation. In Oaxaca, Mexico, the *Peteneras zapoteca* is known among mestizos and danced in 6/8 time to typically Spanish music of guitar and harmonica. [GPK]

Peter's fish Term for both HADDOCK and JOHN-DORY.

petrifaction Stories about people who are changed into stone are very ancient. Lot's wife was changed into a pillar of salt for looking back at Sodom and Gomorrah while she and her husband were fleeing from the doomed city. The Gorgon Medusa once had beautiful hair of which she was very proud. Because she competed with Hera, the hair was turned into snakes and she became a creature so horrid in appearance that all who saw her were turned into stone. This story is not reported by Hesiod; but other mythologists have developed it to the point where stone figures of persons who have looked at her clutter up her courtyard. Even after Perseus chopped off her head it retained the power to petrify. A development of this general theme is the "Adventure of Abdullah Bin Fazil and His Brothers," which is Night 182 in the *Arabian Nights*. Here the hero comes to an enchanted city in which all the figures are stone, even an old lady carrying washing through the streets. In more modern popular tales people are sometimes turned into stone by wicked witches. Thus in a Breton version of folktale type 706 the three children of an ill-fated queen visit an enchanted castle where the witch turns the two brothers to stone and little sister disenchants them. Northern European dwarfs are said to turn into stone at sunrise. See ALvíss. The city of Ishmonie in upper Egypt is called the petrified city because of the number of bodies of petrified men, women, and children there. According to an Inca story of origin, when the four brothers and four sisters who originated the Incas were

traveling north from the "tavern of the dawn," one brother was turned into stone. See FAITHFUL JOHN. [RDJ]

The conversion of human beings and animals into stone is an incident which occurs in several North American Indian folktales. In Eastern Woodlands tales immoderate requests made to a deity by earthly visitors, such as a request for eternal life, are punished by transformation of the human being into a cedar or another kind of tree, or into a stone (Q339). (See IMMORTALITY.) In Shawnee migration myth material one division of the Shawnee is said not to have made a journey long ago across a large body of water, but to have turned into stone and remained in their original place of creation while the rest of the tribe pressed on. In a Hopi Indian tale the twin war gods as an act of kindness turned into stone two little runaway children who had been whipped. (See AHAYUTA ACHI.) Belief in the petrifaction of footprints and handprints of the culture-hero-trickster or other supernaturals is also widespread in North America; many tribes account for hand- or foot-shaped depressions on rocks in this manner in their tales. [EWV]

Pétro A group of deities of the Haitian vodun cult, which includes a large proportion of those whose powers are generally held to be used for evil ends, as against the Rada deities. The origin of the designation of this aspect of the cult is most generally ascribed to the name of a powerful vodun priest who lived in the early days of Haitian history. Functionally, however, these deities are to be thought of as deriving from the African principle that the ancient and powerful dead take the status of deities. [MJH]

Pétro drums Two drums used in rituals of the Pétro cult of Haiti, accompanying dances and singing for the *loa*, Dan Pétro, who was originally a slave Don or Dom Pedro and became a legend after his escape. The drums are played with the hands only.

peyote (Nahuatl *peyotl*) (1) A small carrot-shaped spineless cactus (*Lophophora williamsii Lemaire*) growing in the Rio Grande Valley and southward in Mexico. *Peyotl* is also used in Mexico to designate other cacti and non-cacti which, like peyote, are believed to have aphrodisiac and other qualities. Peyote is not to be confused either with *teonanacatl*, a narcotic mushroom of Mexico, or with *mescal* (*Nahuatl mexicalli, Agave americana,* or *Agave* spp.) or the native beer derived from *Agave* spp., or with mescal beans (*Sophora secundiflora*) or mescal buttons. The identification of peyote with mescal, especially, has led to much confusion in the literature on peyote.

(2) The name applied to a 19th century North American Indian religious cult which is now widespread among the tribes from the Great Basin eastward to Oklahoma and northward to the Canadian border. This cult has as its central feature worship of peyote in the form of the so-called peyote "buttons." These latter consist of the rounded top surfaces of peyote plants that appear above the ground, which are cut off, dried, and eaten or made into a tea that is drunk at peyote ceremonies.

(3) A pre-Columbian ceremony involving the ritual eating of peyote, either in a green or dried state, which is practiced by the Aztec, Huichol, and other Mexican Indians. Peyote is also used non-ritually for prophesying, clairvoyance, and finding lost objects.

The consumption of peyote produces visual hallucinations or color visions, as well as kinesthetic, olfactory, and auditory derangements, due to the alkaloids in the plant. There are no ill after-effects, and peyote is not known to be habit-forming.

In Mexico peyote was used in an agricultural-hunting religious festival, preceded by a ritual pilgrimage to gather the plant. Since about 1870 the cult has spread to the United States; it is especially strong among the Plains groups where it is connected with war, with Southwestern groups where it is involved in shamanistic rivalries and witchcraft, and among several Eastern Woodlands groups in which stress is laid on the health and vision-giving properties of peyote. The usual peyote ritual, in present-day United States Indian practice, consists of an all-night meeting of men, women and children in a tipi around a crescent-shaped earthen mound and a ceremonial fire; a special drum, gourd rattle, and carved staff are passed around to each adult after smoking and purifying ceremonies, and each person sings four peyote songs to the accompaniment of drum and rattle. Various "water-bringing" ceremonies occur at midnight and dawn; at the latter time there is a baptism or curing rite and sometimes public confession of sins, followed by a ritual breakfast which includes parched corn and preserved wild fruit. Certain innovations in the standard peyote ceremony were introduced by one John Wilson, a Caddo-Delaware, and adopted by some tribes; an Oto teacher, Jonathon Koshiway, founded a Christian version of peyotism, the "Church of the First-Born" which spread to Negro groups also, and from which grew the Native American Church, an organization of confederated tribes.

Various legends and beliefs are attached to the plant itself: that the plant deliberately conceals itself; that the plant can sing and speak and can open and shut over a large hole which is like a kiva, where a man teaches visitors the peyote rite; that peyote is like a mole—if not looked at closely it will disappear; that there are two kinds of peyote, male and female, or Peyotl of the Gods and Peyotl of the Goddesses. The Huichol of Mexico have a tutelary goddess for peyote; the Tarahumara peyote deity is male. The latter tribe believe that peyote sings beautifully in the country wherein it grows, so that seekers may find it; it also sings in the bag while being carried home. Several Plains and Woodlands tribes believe the peyote goddess, or Peyote Woman, joins in the singing if she is pleased with it during peyote ceremonies, or gives worshippers songs. The Lipan Apache claim they hear Changing Woman's voice in peyote meetings. A Taos origin legend of peyote tells of a man abandoned by his companions who discovered that the singing and rattling he was hearing came from the blossom in the center of the button.

Despite the fact that the modern peyote cult, as practiced among United States tribes, dates back at the earliest to around 1870, origin material and beliefs concerning the supernatural qualities of peyote are already abundant; fairly reliable historical information on the introduction of peyote ceremonies is also still obtainable from Indian peyote believers. The so-called "pagan" form of peyote worship in such tribes as the Shawnee has not supplanted older Shawnee forms of worship of their native deities, but serves to supplement these. Not all Indians in all tribes are, however, agreed that peyote ceremonies are beneficial, and in some tribes the group is split into peyote and non-peyote factions. For a recent study of the modern peyote cult see Weston La Barre, *The Peyote Cult,* Yale University Publications in Anthropology, No. 19 (New Haven, 1938). [EWV]

Among the pre-Conquest Indians of Mexico peyote was widely considered to be a sacred plant. It is used ceremonially today by members of several Mexican tribes, particularly the Huicholes and Tarahumaras, by whom it is regarded as a supernatural personage who must receive ritual courtesy in the form of complex ceremonies. [GMF]

peyote dance or **híkuli** The Tarahumara and Huichol Indian version of peyote. Híkuli is the mescal button, sometimes soaked in water, which exhilarates and produces visions, cures snakebites, burns, and wounds. In October and November the híkuli seekers, after purification, make long journeys to eastern Chihuahua; on their return they sacrifice a sheep or goat and don ceremonial face-paint: the designs represent coiled serpents, rain symbols, grains of corn, squash vines, and fruit. The shaman sings during the dance which is performed to the accompaniment of two notched deer bones rubbed together (among the Tarahumara a notched stick on a gourd, and rattles of deer hoofs). The movements are ecstatic, jerky jumps with twists of the body, performed in anticlockwise circling around the shaman and the fire. Men and women carry bamboo sticks, or "serpents," the men gesticulate with deer tails. Híkuli first appeared as a deer and the dance is performed after the first deer-hunt in January. The dance has curative and visionary functions and also benefits the crops, as the face designs show. [GPK]

Phaethon In classical mythology, son of the sun god Helios and Clymene (or Rhode); Hesiod and Pausanias call Phaethon's parents Cephalus and Eos. The form Phaeton is an incorrect spelling appearing nowhere in classical literature. The story of Phaethon's ride in the sun's chariot is the subject of motif A724.1.1. Knowing from his mother that his father was the sun, Phaethon boasted of his parentage to a friend. The friend said, in effect, "Don't be silly." Phaethon went to his mother, who reaffirmed the story and suggested that he seek out the sun for corroboration. After a long voyage, Phaethon came to the sun's home in the east. The sun was glad to see his son, acknowledged that he was Phaethon's father, and in a burst of parental pride offered him any boon he might desire. Phaethon quickly took advantage of the hasty offer and asked to be allowed to drive for one day the chariot of the sun through the heavens; nothing could dissuade him; this would be proof indeed for his doubting friend. The sun did not have much time to instruct the boy; the time for daybreak drew near. So Phaethon donned his father's solar crown and climbed into the chariot. Soon the horses of the sun felt an unfamiliar hand on the reins and began to gallop where they would. Going too high, they knocked stars from their places; dashing too near the earth's surface, they burned the desert in the Sudan, dried up the Nile, made the inhabitants of Ethiopia permanently black of skin. The earth itself began to burn and cried to Zeus for aid. The chief of the gods quickly tossed a thunderbolt and Phaethon fell, streaming fire, into the Eridanus River. His sisters wept so at his death that they were transformed into trees; their tears became the amber exuded by these trees. Phaethon's best friend Cycnus grieved too, until he was changed into the swan.

☞ A Phaethon-like myth, probably of native origin, is well known among the Indians of the North Pacific Coast region. It is usually referred to as *The Man Who Acted as the Sun,* and recounts how a youth is permitted to carry the sun by his father, the Sun. The youth almost burns up the earth and has to be rescued. In the adjacent Plateau region the animals hold a contest to determine who shall act as the sun. The results are nearly disastrous for the earth. [EWV]

phallic dances Fertility dances intended specifically for the multiplication of the human race, but indirectly for all increase and productivity. In their most potent manifestations among primitive peoples they serve the earnest purpose of propagation of the race, and in no way consider individual gratification or pleasure. They are essentially ritualistic, and are commonly associated with vegetation and death rites. In some cases the gestures are obvious; in artistic, functional developments they are stylized, whereas in decadent manifestations the reverse is true: the sacred function has lapsed and the crass exterior remains.

Japanese mythology tells of the phallic dance performed by Ume-no-utsume, in order to entice the sun goddess Amaterasu from a cave to which she had retired. The stamping on a bucket and the cries of the dancer recalled her to the earth and thus brought back light and life. The Greek satyrs of the Dionysiac *orgía* stamped and capered with gigantic phalloi and artificial breasts—a symbol of self-fructification. One of the most vivid and earnest fertility dances is the African Thunder dance of Ongaladougou with the realistic imitation of the copulation of beasts.

The implications of the stamp are evident, not only because of the penetration of the earth, but also because of potential identification of the leg with the phallus. A rod may be substituted for the leg, as in the *káusima* puberty ceremony, or the Morris Bean Setting. Vodun ceremonies show this transition: in Africa Legba manipulates an artificial penis, the *olisbos;* in Haiti this has become the Legba-stick, around which he performs all manner of acrobatics. Perhaps not all staff dances have this connotation; yet in battle dances and *Moriscas* the double significance of the sword as weapon and phallus suggests itself. In fact, the Balinese *kris* or dagger and the spear attain this potency in trance dances of dances as the *tjanolarong,* with downward and flexed motions for women, and backward and upward for men. Propulsive gestures by the arms alone, with projecting thumbs, convey a similar impact.

The leap and high kick have since time immemorial expressed productive and generative energy, and as such appeared in Egyptian funeral dances and modern courtship dances (see LEAP DANCES). These acrobatics have in modern society degenerated to the exhibitionistic cancan and burlesque dances.

More obvious gestures are found in the abdominal dance and the kiss. The former has degenerated into the *danse du ventre* in North Africa and the even more degenerate hootchie-kootchie. The kiss tends to make its appearance in dances in societies with inhibited expressive body movement, as in the court dances of the Middle

Ages and Renaissance (*Reigen, Branle-gavotte, Courante,* and *Gigue*). It was a natural climax of more vigorous courtship dances of peasant origin, as the *volta* and the *Schuhplattler*. It is possible that white influence has introduced this variation into American Indian dances, as the Blackfoot Kissing dance and the Ute Dog dance.

The kiss involves the element of physical contact, which is foreign to primitive ritual, even of orgiastic content—at least during the dance phases. After the elegant aloofness of the court dance, the volta and waltz called forth vociferous disapproval, but the embrace was here to stay, and remains the *raison d'etre* of ballroom dances, particularly those with an erotic undercurrent as the *danzón*. In the case of the American Indian, it is again more than likely that white influence has coupled dancers to the extent of physical contact, the crossing of arms or placing the arm around the waist, as in Sauk social dances and the Iroquois Alligator dance.

Clothes or their absence have also undergone a cycle of significance and usage. In primitive rites disrobing or exposure communicate generative powers not only to humanity but also to fields ready for crops, as in puberty dances of the Bushmen and in central European peasant observances preceding the springtime sowing. In peasant dances such as the *volta,* flying skirts vicariously reproduce this custom, and, in a more elegant form, so does the skirt manipulation of Mexican *bailes* and of the dainty *menuet.*

Thus certain expressions are instinctively retained, whether with ritualistic implications or purely as an evidence of exuberant powers. Naturally, the power and the freshness of the gesture depart with the supernatural motivation—the *orgía* becomes the lewd *sikinnis*. Mistaken morality may condemn beautiful forms and substitute pallid coyness. But instinct will reassert itself. After centuries of repression comes the embrace of the waltz and then the black bottom of the 1920's. Religious symbolism cannot be resurrected in modern society, but the earthy stamping, kicking, leaping, whirling, and embracing of jitterbug and boogie-woogie provide a healthy outlet for irrepressible forces, at least so long as they remain unhampered by censure or another era of Puritanism. [GPK]

phallic foods Foods for religious or ceremonial purposes (usually pastry or fish) in the form of the male and female sex organs. Although relatively little recognized, the custom of partaking of phallic foods has been practiced in many cultures and ethnic groups ranging from ancient India to the Zuñi Indians of New Mexico who incorporate priapic breads in their worship. Goodland's *Bibliography of Sex Rites and Customs* (London, 1931) gives 33 entries under "Phallic Cakes or Bread."

One of the oldest, most popular, and most significant of all food-sex representations is the ichthyphallic design, which has its origin in the extraordinary aphrodisiac powers attributed for centuries to fish in many civilizations. Although the symbol appears in a number of cultures—e.g. in Rome it was sacred to Venus as a sign of fecundity—it was perhaps most important in the Middle East. There it is found in countless different manifestations, particularly among the Semites, including the Babylonians, Assyrians, and ancient Hebrews. An indication of the profoundly intimate connection between food—in this case fish—and sex may be found in the Hebrew word for fish (*nun*) which also means "to sprout" or "to put forth," referring to the conceiving or bearing of children.

In Greece, pastry was often baked in ktenic form e.g. the *mulloi*—the sesame and honey cakes which were made, according to Athenæus, in honor of Kore and Demeter and carried around during the three-day Thesmophoria. The same author also speaks of the *mastoeideis*, literally breast-form, a cake fashioned after the shape of the breast which was borne by the chorus during marriage festivals in Sparta. A modern equivalent of the Spartan cakes still exists today in France in the opular French fish dish made in the form of the female breast, *Tétons de Vénus*.

In Rome phallic foods were especially popular, as oted by Lacroix (*History of Prostitution* I: 234–35): The *alicariæ*, or bakers, were women of the street who aited for fortune at the doors of bakeries, especially hose which sold certain cakes, made of fine flour, with-ut salt or leaven, and destined for offerings to Venus. he popularity of these phallic breads and cakes in te ancient world was astonishing. These breads, called *liphia* and *siligone*, represented, under the most himsical forms, the organ of the woman and that of the man. Since there was an enormous demand for these Priapic and venereal breads, especially on the occasion of certain festivals, the master bakers erected tents and opened shops in the public squares and on the street corners; they sold nothing but sacrificial breads, and at the same time they had slave girls or servant maids who prostituted themselves day and night in the bakery."

In the Middle Ages and still today numbers of cakes, breads, and pastries in the form of both male and female organs are produced in Germany and Switzerland. Among the most characteristic are the *Spaltgebäcke*, split-cakes, made in honor of women about to give birth; the *Mandelcher*, almond cookies, eaten in the Rhine area as a symbol of masculine virility in which the almonds represent testicles; the *Liebesknochen*, bone of love, with obvious penile significance, which is a kind of eclair; and the *Vielliebchen*, literally much-little-love, a cake made of two almonds (representing the testicles as above) resting on a pastry base in the form of a shell which also probably has female sexual significance. One of the most famous of all German cakes is the *Stollen* from Saxony, which appears to be modeled after the female organ.

In France phallic foods have likewise survived up to a recent period. Around 1560 Johannes Bruyerinus Campegius reported that the inhabitants of southern France at that time ate *cibi quos cunnos saccharatos appellant*, and phallic cakes have been recorded as late as the 19th century. In Sardinia dough phalloi were made in connection with the midsummer festivals of the Adonis cult, a custom which was still observed through the 19th century. In Italy the tradition seems to have lasted longer than in other countries, i.e. well into the 20th century, as recorded by Elderkin (*Kantharos, Studies in Dionysiac and Kindred Cults*, Princeton, 1924, p. 172): "Ithyphallic bread has survived in Italy to the present day. The writer saw specimens in a Tarentine restaurant and they are still handed about at Easter in some parts of Italy. *Phalloi* of bread which had been blessed by priests were carried until recently at the *Fête des Epines*, a name for Palm Sunday."

In connection with phallic foods, mention should be made of such related food-sex manifestations as the "nates cakes" made in medieval Germany, described in a questionnaire circulated by Burchardt, a 12th century bishop of Worms, in *De Pœnitentia Decretorum* (Lib. XIX): "Fecisti quod quædam mulieres facere solent? Prosternunt se in faciam et discopertis natibus, jubent ut supra nudas nates conficiatur panis et eo decocto, tradunt maritis suis ad comedendum, hoc ideo faciunt ut plus excadescant in amorem illarum." Other practices based on analogy between food and sex are the eating of fish placed in the vulva, noted on the island of Ponape, and the mingling of semen with the Sacred Host, cited by St. Augustine as common among the Manichaeans.　　　　　　　　DUNCAN MACDOUGALD, JR.

phallism Among some ethnic groups phallism, also often called sex worship, is the worship of the male sexual organ, the *phallus*, or of the male and female organs, *lingam* and *yoni*, *phallus* and *kteis*. Elsewhere the term phallism refers to reverence for or worship of sex, its impulses, rituals, and procedures. Cultures which function through abstractions and generalizations have reverence for the reproductive powers of men, animals, and plants. Because the antics of rational creatures when sexually excited are ludicrous, still other groups derive entertainment from the acts, impulses, or organs of sex, find them interesting, or use them as decorative motifs in their arts. Writers on phallism and the related topics, fertility, primitive religions with phallic components, confuse these sorts of reverence, worship, interest, and because the subject is intricate and generally forbidden, find in obscure and inadequately established theories justification for their own sexual imbalance.

The distinctions thus made imply cultural stratifications which have no geographic termini. The Old Testament oath of hand under the thigh has a phallic implication which has been lost. The secret orgies of the Tantrist ascetics may be to "kill lust with lust" or they may be to exercise a ritual with a complex metaphysical basis. When de Zwaan asked the Nias of the Malay Archipelago the meaning of the crude representations of the male and female sexual organs which they used as decoration, he was told they were for amusement and ridicule, though others have found in them evidences of an older fertility cult. In occidental cultures where all levels of mythopœia are observable, overt interest in the sexual organs, acts, impulses, and the consequences of the impulses takes many forms: chalked representations on walls and sidewalks not greatly different from the designs of savages; technical discussions in dictionaries of religion and folklore; dissertations in handbooks of *Sexualwissenschaft;* and timid euphemisms which attempt to restrict the facts of life to the facts of sex presented in terms which make them pretty but not attractive.

The term phallism in the current tradition of ethnology and folklore is restricted to beliefs and practices which are assumed to have magic or religious significance. Attempts to distinguish between magic and religion, like attempts to distinguish between the sexual organs and the reproductive powers of nature, though useful at times, have frequently been distorted by the powerful impulses which these symbols represent and **the polysemantic character of all symbols, pictorial or** linguistic. Thus the loose assertion that church steeples, stupas, and dagobas are phallic has distorted much thinking about other phenomena which are demonstrably and in fact of an immediate sexual nature. Because the emotions of religion and the sexual emotions have qualities which are similar, bitter controversies arise as to whether religion was or is "essentially" sexual. The existence in ancient Greece of sexual ceremonies, the use of phallic symbols and the carrying of phalli in public processions (*phallophoria*) has led to protests that Greek culture was "essentially pure." The assertion that windows with lace curtains are symbols of the female sexual organs must be countered by the fact that windows let in light and curtains moderate it. Cowrie shells, which in the Pacific and elsewhere were used both as money and female decoration, can be shown to have had a phallic significance. Recently this assertion was challenged by British anthropologists on the ground that the modesty which they consider an essential quality of womanhood must be shocked by advertisement of that sort. The logic which interprets the Hebrew Yahweh as a development from an original phallic cult is devious and the evidence upon which it rests is scattered and obscure. Yahweh, like Zeus and Thor, is associated with storms. He is said to have been the "splitter," therefore the phallus. This sort of gobbledegook which confuses collateral with central meanings has distorted much thinking on a subject of considerable importance in all cultures.

Thus students of phallic worship and ritual need to exercise great caution. Though the facts can be established without great difficulty, the significance of the facts is often obscure. With the changing of cultural contours because of foreign influence or the intrusion of new ideas, facts which were once clearly phallic have lost all phallic significance. Though some of them are still retained in modern religions, including Christianity and Buddhism, only their phallic form remains, not their meaning. Attempts of so brilliant a scholar as Hartland to show how an elevated and ethical religious system might have developed from a crude and orgiastic phallism must fail on a number of counts of which the most striking is that so much interpolation is needed that the assumptions obscure the facts. Facts about phallism are distasteful to many occidentals. Attempts of some writers to show how it is possible that other cultures might regard the organs of sex or the reproductive powers of nature with feelings similar to those with which the members of ethical sects regard the symbols of their worship are futile, because it can be shown that some other cultures do in fact so regard them. The facts remain. The purpose of these notes is to summarize them.

1) *Phallic Religions* A complete theory of phallic worship developed among the Tantric sects. The origins, history, and actual practices of these "left-handed Tantrists" are obscure. Tantrism is a form of Hinduism. It is doubtful whether the phallic aspects of the sect are special developments of Saivism or whether they and Saivism have common origins, and it is probable that the worship and orgiastic ceremonies are similar to or derived from the Tibetan Bon cult which, as Waddel has noted, is similar to Chinese cult-Taoism. If, as seems probable, the ceremonies derive from proto-Taoism, we have to deal with a cult which has several million sincere adherents who live in eastern Tibet, are found in many lamaseries in China, and have beliefs which, though alien in form and structure are not strikingly different from some of the beliefs of some of the Chinese Taoists. Though the lamaism of the Grand Lamasery of Lhasa is said by observers to be a pure and elevated form of Buddhism, the folklore of that lamaism as explained in Chinese monasteries has many Tantrist elements.

The discipline of the left-handed Tantrists is directed toward the attainment of nirvaṇa by meditation and austerities. Important in this attainment is the identification of the adept with some of the many gods accepted by the cult. After severe training which involves exercises in breathing, in the *mudras*, or positions of the hands, and in concentrated meditation, the adept evokes one of the spirits and "identifies" himself. Many of these deities are female and require ceremonies and practices which observers have hesitated to describe.

The principle animating these orgies, however, may be stated crudely. The life force manifests itself in two opposing principles, male and female. Whereas Buddhists teach that serenity is to be attained by the elimination of desire, some Chinese Taoists and Tantrists believe that lust can be destroyed by lust and others devoutly believe that the human being attains his most complete development only when male and female are in sexual union, at which time they interchange forces and man attains the highest degree of manhood and woman the highest degree of womanhood. The representations of this rite, considered sacred by the devotees, show the male standing in the embrace of the female, or *sakti*, whose arms are about his neck and whose legs are about his hips. In this position they enjoy eternal ecstasy. The pictures of this rite give a considerable amount of detail; the statues give more. The figures are usually detachable and in some the lingam and yoni are realistically sculptured.

The ceremonies of the cult are secret. Drinking vessels made of skulls lined with silver are common in the temples. Buddhahood is said to be in the female organ. Semen, which many Chinese believe is a potent tonic for old men, is said by the Tantrists to contain the "five bodies of Buddha." The folklore of the lamaseries tends to support the inference by competent observers that the ceremonies are orgiastic and obscene.

Little is known about this sect, whose adherents are numerous, for several reasons. The Tantrist and Lamaist texts are in an obscure jargon of Tibetan and Sanskrit badly understood by many of the devotees themselves. The texts are cluttered with white and black magic formulæ. The ceremonies are secret, open only to adepts. Gruesome stories are told about people who violated their oath of secrecy.

Some of the sexual beliefs of the Chinese Taoists are not dissimilar to those of the Tantrist lamas. These, though preserved in a very corrupt text, were possibly known in the Chou dynasty (1000 B.C.) and seem to have been very popular during the first millennium of the Christian era. These beliefs are built on the assumption that the male and the female principles penetrate all things. South is male, north is female. Heaven is male, earth is female. The several parts of the body are male or female. When these principles come into conflict, when we are subject to excessive male or female influences, serenity is destroyed and illnesses occur. When these principles are in harmony, the individual enjoys increase of power, longevity, and even the ability to become immortal, to become invisible, or to shift his shape and to assume the shape of any creature he may wish to become. This doctrine also declares that at the moment of sexual climax, a quantity of "life essence" is exchanged. The individual who experiences the climax before his partner loses a quantity of life essence. The disciplines of this cult are directed toward increasing control.

A distinction must be made between philosophical Taoism and cult-Taoism, or popular Taoism, in China. Researches in recent years have given some archeological justification for the view that popular Taoism in China, a mixture of black and white magic, fortune-telling, and the like, is, after many changes, after intrusions of foreign cults and attempts to imitate and compete with Buddhism which many Chinese found attractive, the remnant of an earlier system which flourished in China during the Shang dynasty, 1500 B.C. to 1000 B.C. and earlier. This large, imperfectly understood complex of beliefs, shot through with fertility magic, may have derived from the large reservoir of beliefs in eastern Asia with which are clearly associated the Bon cult of prelamaist Tibet, some of the Tantrist beliefs, parts of Saivism, and some of the early Japanese theology. Karlgren has demonstrated that the character modern Chinese use to designate the ancestor tablet was, in very early form, obviously a phallus.

Although the Japanese government suppressed phallic ceremonies in 1872, both phallic ceremonies and phallic shrines still persist in Japan. In the Japanese origin myths, Izanagi and Izanami, "the male who invites" and "the female who invites" are the first ancestors and the special deities of sexual reproduction. When ordered by the other gods to create the islands, Izanagi thrust the "jewel spear" into the sea. Then they descended and populated the earth. Ama-tsu-mara, the blacksmith god who made the sun spear, Saruta, the monkey god who was shamelessly approached by Uzume, are said to have phallic significance. In modern times, phallic objects, either realistic representations of *lingam* and *yoni*, at times grotesquely enlarged, or other phallic objects— the peach, the bean, the rice kernel—are used for magic purposes. Phallic ceremonies are thought to protect the rice crop, and to protect against venereal disease. Phallic deities are the patrons of marriage, of barren women and prostitutes, of wayfarers, and of the crossroads, as well as of fertility. Terminal posts on bridges are said to be phallic.

Phallism in India has a number of aspects. Discussions of why the symbols of Śiva should be the *lingam* and *yoni* are not satisfactory. Crooke and other competent scholars assert that some of the great Indian *linga* have no sexual connotation. One at Benares is simply an enormous block of round black stone six feet high and twelve in circumference. Amulets in the form of *linga* and *yoni*, sometimes alone and sometimes united, are worn as ornaments. Followers of Vishṇu wear a *namam* on their foreheads. This is two diagonal lines with a perpendicular line in the center and is, or once was, a representation of *lingam* in *yoni* or *yoni* alone. Similar doubt attaches to the worship of stone pillars in North India. Some students have suggested that this worship was indigenous and was later absorbed by the cult of Śiva;

others suggest that phallism was imported into India. The female servants of Śiva and Krishṇa, often referred to as "temple prostitutes," thought generally a part of the folklore of phallism, involve other streams of folk thinking and feeling.

Whatever may be the origin and history of phallism in India, the cults of Śiva and Vishṇu make ritual use of phallic symbols, though how and why "the great architect of the universe" should be worshipped in the form of *lingam* and *yoni* have been obscured by the disputations of devout theologians and the speculations of folklorists. Apologists of Saivism maintain that "the two great generative principles of the universe, Śiva and Śakti or Puruṣa and Prakṛti, the father and mother of all creations, the energy and matter of the physical scientist, are symbolized briefly in the form of the *lingam* and *yoni*." The Lingayats, whose emblem is a small stone phallus in a box tied around the neck, have been called the Hindu Puritans. Although in these and other sects in India, the symbols remain, the active elements of sex worship have been refined and conjugated into a metaphysical mysticism. Phallic elements in Indian popular lore need to be put together. Examples are: Nathurām, a rogue of the Northwest Provinces, came to Mārawāri and seduced women. He was killed. His ghost which continued to be troublesome is appeased by obscene gestures and songs performed by women. His image with an exaggerated organ is beside the beds of brides. Dhārwār women of ambiguous caste carry the image of Jakamār with an organ three times the size of his body from house to house soliciting presents. In upper Burma obscenities and a figure with a large organ are parts of the New Year celebration.

2) *Phallic Symbols* Great caution is needed in examining this aspect of phallism. A number of writers have described a cannon in Java which barren women straddled in the hope of curing their barrenness. The cannon at those moments was undoubtedly phallic and the magic was homeopathic. Similar conclusions are justified in the case of monoliths in several parts of the world which cured barrenness. However to identify all cannons, guns, and monolithic stones as phalli because they have a resemblance to a penis or to identify all round or oval objects with openings in the center with the female pudenda, is to leave folklore for the subtleties of pathological symbolism. Obviously, once some identification is made, such as "the church steeple is really a phallic symbol," the thought is likely to recur even though there is grave doubt whether the identification has any historic or folkloristic reality. In other cases the relations are less obscure. Some of the designs on gems recovered from the Ægean culture show an upright object impaling a triangle which has suggested the phallus entering the yoni. In triangles the apex of the "female triangle" points downward and the apex of the "male triangle" points upward and thus correspond to the growth of the pubic hair on the male and female. The degree to which this primitive symbol has lost any meaning it once may have had is shown by the fact that the triangle used as a symbol by the Young Men's Christian Association is the so-called "female triangle."

Other common objects thought to be phallic symbols still retain their meaning in some cultures. The peach in China and Japan symbolizes the yoni. Peach sticks are used to beat out barrenness. The fig in Italy and parts of France is also a symbol of the female organs. The Chinese consider that "apples are good" because they have many seeds. The rice thrown after newly married couples in Euro-American wedding festivities may once have been seeds to induce fertility. The shoes thrown at these same festivities have been discussed by several scholars. Dr. Jones reports the broad jest, "May you fit her as this old shoe fits me." When a Chinese bride dies before marriage, the groom, in some parts of China, is given the shoes she wore last and burns incense before them for some time. The use of the shoe as a recognition test in Cinderella stories in many parts of the world, and the use of shoes in girls' games in France, Germany, and elsewhere to discover whence their husbands will come, leads to the suggestion that shoes are, in some cultures and at some times, of phallic significance.

Phallic cakes are reported from several parts of the world. Panzer reports that cakes of phallic shape were given to any Brāhman thought to be a blockhead. At Saintes in France and at Saintonge near La Rochelle as late as 1825 phallic cakes were carried in Easter processions, blessed and preserved for the rest of the year. Phallic cakes were also served at some of the women's mysteries in ancient Greece.

Because no great amount of skill is required to make fairly realistic representations of the organs of generation, persons who are interested in doing so have no need to revert to obscure symbolisms.

The tendency to exaggerate the size of the organs observed among some African tribes, in the "spring" pictures of Japan, doubtless taken from similar pictures in China, has been interpreted as the attempt to emphasize the idea of reproduction and fertility. The pictures in China and Japan, sometimes realistically and carefully done on silk, portray men and women in the act of copulation. They have been variously interpreted. A tradition from the Ming dynasty in China reports that these are in effect fire insurance. The Thunder God will not strike a house where intercourse is being consummated and the yin-yang or female and male forces are in powerful flow. Inasmuch as the householder cannot be sure that the act is being performed every minute of the 24 hours, he keeps these pictures. They are frequently found pasted on the walls of kitchens in lower class dwellings. Another tradition is that the Thunder God, being prudish, will avoid houses with these pictures. Still another is that young girls are supposed to study them in order to increase their charm. Finally, these albums are sometimes used at dinner parties attended by gentlemen. Each guest is expected to write a formal Chinese poem which contains no indecent word or reference but which nevertheless describes the scene portrayed with great realism. Thus, "Many lotus blossoms have opened their lovely petals to receive the dew tonight" describes an orgiastic scene.

The Nuforese of New Guinea had on the temples of the ancestors and on the dormitories of the unmarried men figures with exaggerated pudenda. The Nias near Sumatra represent spirits by images with large organs and bury such images with the dead. Phallic stones are before the huts of the chiefs. In the Celebes, breasts and phalli are used in the decoration of temples. On the Slave Coast of West Africa, figures of Legba, as male, and female, squat contemplating their own exaggerated organs. The members of the Ghédé sect of Haitian voodooists perform a dance around a small wooden phallus. Large male and female figures with exaggerated organs are given offerings in secluded huts among the Yoruba. Small phallic (?) figures have been found among the Alaskan tribes.

Figures with obvious phallic significance were frequently used as decorations in Greece and Rome. That they should have been popular in Pompeiian and other houses of prostitution and in American beer-halls may have been for entertainment only or they may have had to do with homeopathic magic. The Ephesian or thousand-breasted Artemis represents copious motherhood. Pausanias, whose mind sometimes ran on these matters, reports that Hermes of Mt. Cyllene was a phallus on a pedestal and was greatly revered. The images of Hermes, god of thieves and therefore protector against thieves, used for marking the boundaries of property, were sometimes decorated by a male organ though the rest of the image was a plain stone pillar.

Phallic images are still to be seen in Europe. South of Arles in France a very large monolith is said to be a phallus. Hartland reports that Saint Foutin, the first bishop of Lyons, was among the phallic saints of Gaul. Protestants taking Embrun in 1585 found an object said to have been the saint's penis, reddened by wine which women in need of his help poured over it. At Trendle Hill in Dorset a figure cut in the turf is 180 feet long and has a large penis. Until recently some of the Irish church doors had female figures with exaggerated organs.

An examination of phallic objects from all parts of the world leads to the conclusion—after those are removed which are obviously not phallic and others are set aside that may once have been phallic—that the meanings attributed to them are varied. Amusement and entertainment at the grotesqueness of sexuality is obvious in the history of caricature. Interest in fertility and the use of these objects to induce it are sometimes clearly associated, and the use of these objects to induce sexuality seems to be frequent.

3) *Ritual intercourse, calendrial orgies, ritual promiscuity, etc.* Attempts to distinguish between ritual intercourse, calendrial orgies, and ritual promiscuity are hampered by the facts that members of the same culture give divergent interpretations to the same customs, that customs change within short spaces of time, and the caution not unmixed with prudery with which occidentals approach these matters makes free discussion difficult.

Granet has given good reason to believe that both before and after the Shang dynasty in China the spring and autumn festivals were associated with fertility rituals. During the planting season youths and maidens enjoyed great sexual freedom. At the harvest festival those maidens who had become pregnant celebrated their marriage. In this instance the fertility of mankind and the fertility of the fields seems clearly associated. Libertinage, at times approaching the orgiastic, was permitted in the games of Saint Valentine's Day and the rituals of the Maypole in England, and the customs of Saint John's Eve in the northern countries; but how far these expressions of high spirits were influenced by the somewhat abstract idea of fertility remains to be proved.

The fact that promiscuous orgies occur during the planting and harvest seasons in many parts of the world has led observers to the conclusion that their purpose is to induce fertility and that promiscuous intercourse at these seasons will, by what is called homeopathic magic, produce good crops during the summer and good fortune during the winter. The answers by some of the natives to questions by Occidental observers give some reason for this conclusion, although at times the reports leave the feeling that the natives are trying to give some answers to the foolish question of a silly foreigner. The rituals of some of the peoples of the East Indian Archipelago represent the sun having intercourse with the earth. The Nago tribes have orgies at sowing and harvest times. When the rice blossoms in Java the owner and his wife run naked about the field and have intercourse. The ancient custom in Europe has often been reported that men and women had intercourse after the first furrow was planted. In the Amboyna and Uliase Islands, when the cloves were threatened, a man would go naked into the fields and have symbolic intercourse with a tree. Strangers were excluded from the orgiastic festival of the new moon among the Ekoi of Nigeria, which was supposed to insure good crops and protect them against damage. The sexual organs of the men and, preferably, women sacrificed at these times were used as medicine. The spring rituals in honor of Dionysus, Greek god of vegetation, were introduced by a procession into the fields led by a maiden carrying a phallus and followed, according to Murray, by the farmer, his wife, and daughters, singing bawdy songs. Rituals in honor of Osiris, Egyptian god of vegetation and creative energy, included processions in which women carried his image equipped with an enormous phallus operated by a string. These representative instances of actual or symbolic orgy seem to be associated with fertility magic.

Some cultures use phallic symbols or gestures to ward off evil or to indicate contempt. In Italy, the thumb protruding between the first and middle fingers is a phallic gesture to protect against witchcraft and the evil eye. Biting the thumb or the thumb to the nose are gestures which have lost all but a reminiscent phallic meaning. Phallic objects have been found in graves from Egypt to Norway and the use of phallic objects as good-luck amulets is widespread. The Assiniboian women wear a gold phallus as an amulet around their necks when they are married. The engagement and wedding rings in Euro-American cultures ward off evil. Exposure of the sexual parts before combat is reported from the Celebes, as well as in the Tewa story of the girl warrior from the American Southwest. The Niasi set up figures with exaggerated organs before their doorways as defense against epidemics.

Discussions of the orgiastic lore of the witches, which included promiscuous intercourse with the Devil as leader either in the form of a man or a goat, belong elsewhere. In the Paris of the 17th century a renegade priest read the mass backwards. The altar was the naked belly of a woman. Attempts to revive the rituals of Satanism and witchcraft in modern America and Europe are occasionally reported. No objective study of them has yet been made.

Reports of ritual intercourse on special occasions are available from widely separated cultures. In parts of East Africa the head man and his wife must have intercourse on the second and fourth nights after the village moves and the father and mother must have intercourse the second night after their child has been circumcised. In some places ritual intercourse is part of a purification ceremony. On the Aroe Islands the corpse is exhumed after a fixed period of burial, brought to the beach, and cleaned so that the skeleton can be put into a cave. On this occasion the men carry phalli and the women kteis, sing appropriate songs, and stick the phalli into the kteis. From Brazil a mock or ritual attack of a sexual nature is reported to have been made on the house of the deceased.

Promiscuity is customary among some peoples either at fixed calendric festivals or on special occasions. Thus, the native women of Nicaragua and perhaps those of the Natchez Indians of Louisiana were at certain times permitted to have intercourse with any man they chose. The Sun Dance of the Arapaho, at one time perhaps connected with fertility, was performed in consequence of a vow one of the tribesmen made at a crisis in his life. After the performance of rituals in a decorated lodge a male and a female official each clad in a single garment went outside, removed the garments and the woman lay prone. Similar ceremonies were known to the Cheyenne. In the Buffalo dance of the Mandans a naked figure painted black with an artificial phallus pursued women and made obscene gestures toward the other dancers. He then pretended to be exhausted. The women attacked him in ritual dance and stole his phallus. The functions of the clowns in the dances of the Pueblo Indians sometimes had phallic implications. The women sang songs ridiculing the sexual prowess of the men of the pueblo and the clown retorted, insulting the individual women until in ritual dance they surrounded him and stripped off his clothes.

Orgiastic indulgences at festivals in established religions are reported from many parts of the world. Participants are at times required to observe continence for specified periods before the ceremony. Lumholz reported of the Tarahumara of Chihuahua, Mexico, that their ceremonies included speeches, decorous behavior, and the drinking of corn liquor. After everyone got drunk, intercourse was promiscuous. Although Lumholz's observation that without drunkenness the Tarahumara are too shy to have intercourse may be a broad generalization, it does associate continence with orgy. In Africa women dedicated to Legba are promiscuous on his festivals and are called his wives. The Greek festivals of Dionysus and Demeter, Thesmophoria and Haloa, also ceremonies in honor of the Great Mother or Bona Dea in Rome, were mysteries, and reports about them must be treated with great caution. They were spring or autumn festivals and those folklorists who believe that farmers were in the habit of dealing with such fictions as those concerned with "fertility" classify them as fertility ceremonies. Our earliest accounts of them, however, come from a period in which the Greeks and Romans had attained as high a degree of sophistication as any occidental people has yet reached. Men and women participated in the festivals of Dionysus which became unrestrained orgies in which victims were torn to pieces and devoured raw, men in states of ecstasy emasculated themselves, and intercourse was promiscuous. Only women participated in the autumn festival of the Haloa celebrated on the threshing floor, and at the banquet which followed cakes in the shape of phalli were served. The participants in the Thesmophoria prepared by fasting and continence and sacrificed snakes and other phallic objects. The ceremonies of the Bona Dea, celebrated in Rome on May 1, were performed by Vestal virgins and a guild of the most respectable matrons who concerned themselves with the proprieties. The ritual contained phallic remnants and the telling of indecencies which must never be repeated to the uninitiated, a custom reported from Africa and from modern secret societies.   R. D. JAMESON

phangra A wedding wine dance of Punjab, India. The two processional groups of the bride's and bridegroom's parties meet, exchange presents of wine, and mingle in an orgiastic dance. This dance, with its origin in ancient fertility motives, is now regarded with disfavor. [GPK]

phantom ships Revenant specter ships which have been lost at sea, or which for some reason are doomed to sail forever, never making port. As many as 15 are known and seen along the northeastern coast of the United States. Phantom ships are always seen sailing against the wind, or sailing at full speed when there is no wind. Often they have no crew, or are manned by a ghostly crew. Sometimes music is heard as they swish by; but they never answer when hailed. Irish folk legend has a phantom ship which is becalmed until the judgment day. Several of them are fire ships. Of these the *Palatine* is famous: lured to destruction on Block Island, R. I., by lights, pillaged, fired, and set adrift. She reappears annually on the date of her burning, or occasionally as a storm warning. The *Titanic* also is sometimes seen on the anniversary of her disaster.

Phantom ships never make port. One, however, the *Alice Marr* of Gloucester, Mass., is seen to make halfway up the harbor on the same day each year, and then disappears. See R. deS. Childs, "Phantom Ships of the Northeastern Coast of North America," *NYFQ* 5: 146 ff.

☞ The most famous of the phantom ships is the *Flying Dutchman* sighted now and again by unlucky persons around the Cape of Good Hope. The stories are in agreement that the master, Captain Vanderdecken, was condemned to sail those waters forever because of his crimes. In one story, he swore a horrid oath: that he would weather the Cape though he should keep trying until the last day. In another version, a murder was committed aboard the ship. In a German story the captain is condemned to sail the North Sea forever without helm or steersman. He whiles away the time by playing dice with the Devil for his soul.

To see a phantom ship is a bad omen, they say. To see the phantom ship of the Tappan Zee in the Hudson River, for instance, is always interpreted as a storm warning. [RDJ]

Philemon and Baucis In Greek legend (Ovid *Metam.* viii, but probably originating in Phrygia), a poor, old couple who were the only ones in their district to offer hospitality to Zeus and Hermes when the two gods, belated travelers, tried to find shelter for the night. In return for their kindness, the two gods led Philemon and Baucis to the top of a nearby hill and showed them the entire district flooded as punishment for its selfishness. The two mortals were granted a wish, and since

their home had been transformed into a temple they asked to be made priest and priestess, and to die at the same time. The wishes were granted. In later years, the oak which was Philemon and the lime which was Baucis grew together outside the temple in Phrygia. The story combines the motifs of the visit of the gods to mortals (wishes granted in return for hospitality) and the saving of the good from a general catastrophe. The Biblical stories of Abraham and Noah exemplify these motifs; but see *Acts* xiv for what is probably a reference to the Philemon and Baucis story. See MIDAS.

philosopher's stone The discovery of the philosopher's stone was the objective of the alchemical sciences for, when ground down and combined with water, drugs, and other sorts of material, it would produce the "elixir" which could transform "imperfect" to "perfect" metals. Although the search for the philosopher's stone, which in some places is also the pill of immortality, has cost many lives and great fortunes, it has, both in the Far East and in Europe, contributed much, especially during the prescientific period, to man's knowledge of chemistry. [RDJ]

Phineus In Greek legend, a soothsayer and king of Salmydessus in Thrace. He was blinded by the gods, the reason given varying in the several accounts. His second wife, Idæa, accused his sons by his first wife of having insulted her, and Phineus punished them barbarously: by blinding them, by half burying them, etc. The gods then sent the Harpies to make his life miserable. Whenever the blinded king sat at his table the Harpies would snatch the food from before him, flying away with some of it and filthying the remainder. The Argonauts attemped to get direction for their voyage from the soothsaying king, but the Harpies had first to be chased off. It had been foretold that the sons of Boreas would destroy the Harpies or be destroyed in the attempt. These two, Zetes and Calais, members of the *Argo*'s crew, set off through the air after the Harpies. One of the monsters fell into the Tigris (after that called Harpys) and one flew as far as the Strophades where, tired out, she fell and was spared by her pursuer only on the promise that Phineus would no longer be bothered. Phineus then gave the requested advice to the travelers, warned them of the Symplegades, and sent them on their way. Compare HARPIES.

Phœbus In Greek mythology and religion, Apollo (Phœbus Apollo) as the sun god; the divinity of light in later classical writers, absorbing the attributes of Helios. The feminine form, Phœbe, is personified as the moon.

Phœnix (1) In Greek mythology, the father (or brother) of Europa and eponym of Phœnicia.

(2) The Greek name for the bennu, the mythical Egyptian bird which was the symbol of the rising, regenerated sun, and the hieroglyphic of the sun in this aspect: both the Egyptian and Greek names also mean palm tree. According to Herodotus, who doubts the story, the Egyptians claimed that the bird lived in Arabia. Every 500 years, the young Phœnix appeared at Heliopolis bearing a ball of myrrh in which he had embalmed the body of his father. This he buried in the temple of the Sun. Pictures, he said, showed a red and golden bird about the size of an eagle. From Pliny we learn that the Phœnix builds a nest of twigs of cassia and frankincense in which to die. Out of the dead Phœnix a worm crawls

from which the new Phœnix grows. The author of *Physiologus* places the home of the bird in India, whence it flies to Heliopolis carrying spices and is burnt on the altar. The new bird departs on the third day following.

Among the Arabs Al-Salmandra, the Salamander (Persian Samandal), is sometimes a four-footed animal, sometimes a bird, living in fire. The Persian simurg, thirty birds in one, lived 1700 years, and when the young was hatched the parent of the opposite sex burnt itself to death. This bird is the same as *'ankā* of Arabic lore, and bears a vague resemblance to the roc or rukh and to the Garuda of Hindu mythology. The Phœnix appears in *Job* xxix, 18: "I shall die in my nest, and I shall multiply my days as the phœnix." (The latter is variously translated: "sand" in the Authorized Version, for example, but "phœnix" seems more accurately to fit the context.) In the apocryphal *Book of Enoch*, the Phœnix appears as a great serpent with a crocodile head. In later Christian symbolism, the Phœnix stood for the Resurrection.

Pholus In Greek mythology, an Arcadian centaur, son of Silenus and a Melian nymph. During the hunt for the Erymanthian boar, Hercules stopped at the cave of Pholus. Pholus was custodian of the wine cask of the centaurs, and when, in hospitality or because the cask had been left by Dionysus to open when Hercules came, Pholus broached it, the smell attracted the other centaurs. They came armed with rocks and tree-trunks, and in the fight that followed Hercules drove them off. One, Elatus, came to Chiron's cave, wounded by one of Hercules' poisoned arrows; and the physician-centaur Chiron accidentally wounded himself in the knee when drawing the arrow. As a result the immortal Chiron gave his immortality to Prometheus that ne might die and escape the pain. Pholus too dropped an arrow on his foot and died. Compare CHIRON.

phurbu or **p'ur-bu** A nail used by the lāmas and sorcerers of Tibet to drive off or impale demons. The phurbu is triangular and wedge-shaped, from eight to ten inches long, with a head on the broad end and sharp-pointed at the thin end. It is generally made of wood but sometimes is of cardboard and inscribed with mystical sentences.

piai (also spelled *pagé, ippaye*, etc.) The term for the shamans among the Tupi-Guarani and Carib tribes of South America. The word has passed into English under the form of *piaiman*. See SHAMAN. [AM]

pibgorn or **pibcorn** The hornpipe; a wind instrument of the clarinet family known in its primitive form in Wales as a section of the shinbone of a sheep with a bell of cow's horn. It was played to accompany dancing. From its English name the dance, the hornpipe, was named. It is also called *stockhorn*.

pien chung A Chinese bell chime of sixteen bells suspended in a double row on a stand and tuned to a system of male and female semitones: derived from the older stone chimes of the same arrangement and tuning pattern, called pien *ch'ing*. See BELL; CHIMES.

Pierlala A Flemish ballad, dating probably from the late 17th century, and dealing with the pranks and escapades of a character, Pierlala, similar to Till Eulenspiegel. At the end he repents and offers a moral for the audience.

pig Folklore about pigs is ambivalent, and the question arises as to whether pork is forbidden because of its actual or ritual uncleanliness or because of its sanctity. The Egyptians thought pigs were unclean. Swineherds could not enter temples or marry the daughters of other men, yet once a year pigs were sacrificed to the moon and to Osiris. The Baluba of the Congo have a woman's association known as the Bulendu. Members may not eat pork because "the spirit of the association" lives in its flesh, yet all women must eat it when they are initiated. Women of the Lower Congo are not permitted to plant if they have eaten pork. Greek women sacrificed pork to the female earth deity. The Syrian worshippers of Attis ate no pork but Adonis was in many ways connected with the boar. Some students have maintained that the European corn spirit was in the form of a pig and have associated pig with the cults of Attis, Adonis, Demeter. The Cretans worshipped pigs.

Jewish lore about pigs is much more ancient than the passage in which Christ drove the unclean spirits into a herd of swine. Among the abominations listed by Isaiah is "he that offereth an oblation as if he offered swine's blood." Elsewhere Isaiah says, "They that sanctify themselves and purify themselves in the gardens behind one tree in the midst eating swine's flesh and the abomination and the mouse shall be consumed together." The inference may be that pork was eaten secretly.

The modern Welsh are said to believe that the pig appears on Halloween, and during an eclipse people imitate the grunting of pigs. The squeal of a pig will dissipate St. Elmo's fire. Irish folklore has many references to pigs. *Muic-inis,* or Pig Island, is one of the ancient names for Ireland. A black pig is a bad sign, and illness can be averted by walking three times around a pigsty. Acute hearing is "hearing like a trespassing pig." Some German towns once seem to have regarded the pig as an unlucky animal though the belief has changed. The associations in Germany seem to be with storms and fertility.

Pigs support the earth in the Celebes and cause earthquakes. In India they are sacrificed to the cholera goddess and disease demons, and to propitiate ghosts. The Karens of Burma believe that adultery destroys fertility. When a couple has been detected, they buy a hog and kill it. Each takes one foot and makes a furrow. They fill the furrows with blood and pray that having destroyed productivity they may heal it. Cousin marriages are prohibited among the Borneo Dyaks. The prohibition may be lifted by a rather complicated ceremony. The couple throws their personal ornaments into the water. They then kill a pig, drain its blood, and throw the carcass into the water. Their friends then push them into the water and they bathe together. Finally they fill a joint of bamboo with pig's blood, walk through the neighboring villages, and scatter the blood.

Pig's blood when drunk induces prophetic power. In the northern Celebes a priest is reported to drink blood from the hot carcass. The custom is also reported from southern India. Human blood is said to produce similar power. See CANNIBALISM.

Zulu girls will not eat pig "for it is an ugly animal; its mouth is ugly, its snout is long . . . if they eat it a resemblance to a pig will appear among their children."

The Caribs believe that a girl who eats pork will have children with small eyes.

Pigs were sacrificed in the Greek Thesmophoria at the time of the October planting. The pigs were buried in an underground room. Each year the remains of last year's sacrifice were removed and mixed with the seed. See ADONIS; DEMETER. [RDJ]

pigeon dance A social dance for men and women, confined to a few Indian tribes of the eastern United States. In the Cherokee *wayi* the counterclockwise file of dancers represents pigeons; one man, as a hawk, swoops down and captures one of the helpless birds. Capture is mimed in a different way by the Onondaga of Six Nations, Ontario. As in the New York Seneca duck dance, *twę'oenǫ*, a double file of women passes through bridges formed by the raised arms of a double file of men, and is intercepted when the arms are lowered. In the Seneca and Cayuga pigeon dance, *djakowa'oenǫ*, a double file of alternating men and women trips continually in a counterclockwise circle. All Iroquois tribes use the same well-developed songs, accompanied by the horn rattles of the two dance leaders. In its alternate name of *dove dance*, it is akin to the Mexican *palomo*. [GPK]

Pigtown Fling An Irish reel tune, also known as *Kelton's Reel*, to which the contra dance called the Boston Fancy is done.

pikváhahirak The mythic times, preceding human times, of the Karok Indians of northwestern California. See IKXAREYAVS; MYTHICAL AGE.

pilgrimages The folklore of pilgrimages is associated with the folklore of place. Peoples of all eras and races have found that some places are more suitable than others for the induction of moods thought to be good, or for the ordering of their own thoughts and feelings about themselves and the universe. The Australian aborigines visit regularly their places of "dreaming" where they repeat their legends, myths, and lore, and succeed in a measure in identifying themselves with their heroes and ancestors. Euro-Americans make pilgrimages to the graves of their ancestors and thus strengthen their ethnic ties, and many peoples believe that the ancestral ghosts or spirits will at these times receive reports from the living and give their blessing. Thus the essential part of the Chinese marriage ritual is that the couple kowtow before the husband's ancestral tablets and thus be recognized by the ancestors as a properly constituted unit of the family. Pilgrimages to the homes or graves of national heroes called "national shrines" strengthens the feeling of the pilgrims that they are part of the ethnic complex.

In the mood of heightened sensibility which these visits induce, miracles often occur. This is particularly true when the pilgrimage is to be a place of religious significance, the grave of a saint, or the saint's dwelling place, or place of the saint's death or martyrdom. Many of the obligations and prohibitions associated with pilgrimages seem to be for the purpose of increasing this sense of spiritual power. Prohibition against eating much food or certain foods, against sexual intercourse during the pilgrimage, against wearing shoes, against walking upright, as well as the obligation to wear certain sorts of costume and amulets tend to separate the pilgrim from his usual habits of thinking and feeling and pre-

pare him for the elevated mood he will acquire on arrival. During the *hajj* Moslem pilgrims do not cut their hair or fingernails and leave their bodies uncovered except for two pieces of white cloth. Fires which are lighted at this time have been thought of as a sun ritual and water poured onto the ground has been associated with rain during the next season. Special sanctity is acquired by Moslems who have made pilgrimages to Mecca. The Temple of Buddha's Tooth at Kandy in Ceylon is one of the thousands of places which are associated with the life and miracles of Buddha. Hindus all over India make pilgrimages to the famous temples dedicated to Śiva and other deities. China is dotted with pilgrimage spots: the four sacred mountains and shrines where special sorts of potency can be acquired. In Mexico City the shrine of the Virgin of Guadalupe is very popular. Pilgrimage centers in Europe, in addition to the sacred city of Rome, include Canterbury where Saint Thomas à Becket was martyred, Boulogne, Lourdes, Mont St. Michel in France, Bruges in Belgium, and Compostella in Spain. In Palestine, Jerusalem and Mount Carmel are popular. See ADAM'S PEAK.

Other reasons for making pilgrimages are to fulfil vows made during moments of illness or danger or during the illness of a loved one.

One group of folklorists derive the custom of pilgrimages from early belief in the *deus loci*, god of place, who when worshipped at his own shrine will confer special blessings. This is probably as simple an explanation of the benefits derived from pilgrimages as any, though Chaucer suggested that pilgrimages are most popular in spring when the spirit of wandering seizes people. [RDJ]

Pillan One of the most important deities of the Araucanian Indians, associated with thunder, lightning, earthquakes, and other natural cataclysms. Used in the plural the word designates the souls of the dead and spirits. [AM]

pimpernel A plant of the primrose family (genus *Anagallis*) usually with scarlet, sometimes yellow, flowers. In Ireland scarlet pimpernel is called the herb of Mary, the blessed herb, and sometimes *luib na muc*, herb of the pig. Yellow pimpernel is referred to as *lus Columcille*, the plant of Columcille. Pimpernel is credited with the power of moving against the current if dropped in running water; and it gives second sight to the person holding it. In England and the United States in general scarlet pimpernel is called the poor man's weather-glass, because it closes up before rain and expands fully when fine weather is coming. It also tells time, opening at seven and closing at two. In England it was believed to be effective against spells and to prevent bewitchment. The juice of the leaves cures scalp wounds, draws splinters; the French used it to clear the skin of roughness or discoloration and to promote rosiness. Juice of the leaves and seeds, placed in the nostril opposite to a toothache, will give relief. Because it will grow in cracks on rocks it was believed effective in cases of calculus. The North American Meskwaki Indians use the yellow pimpernel to improve the smell of their medicines. In England pimpernel is still used for kidney and liver diseases.

pine The pine cone is the Semitic symbol of life. In China and Japan, the pine tree is a symbol of life, longevity, and immortality. The Chinese god of longevity is often depicted sitting under a pine tree, with the crane (another longevity symbol) in the branches. In Japan, it is symbolic of the New Year. In China, the juice of the pine, if taken consistently, prevents a man from growing old, lightens the body, and keeps him from feeling hunger. The Greeks say that Cybele, jealous of a shepherd, changed him into a pine and Zeus made the tree an evergreen. A Roman legend tells of a youth and a maid who, thwarted in their love, were changed into a pine and a vine growing together. The pine was sacred to Pan and Sylvanus. In later European lore it was sacred to the sea gods because vessels were made from the wood. The winners of the Greek Isthmean games were awarded a wreath of pine or dried parsley.

In the Tyrol, pine is planted as a marriage tree. In Bohemia, gathering cones on St. John's Day and eating one kernel a day will make one immune to gunshot. This is practiced particularly by thieves and robbers. Roman soldiers ate the nuts for strength. In Silesia, on Mid-Lent Sunday, children used to carry decorated pine boughs through the village before hanging them over the stable doors to protect the cattle. The Navaho Indians of North America smear the bodies of the dead with pitch before burial and mourners smear a little on their foreheads. The boughs are also used in many of their ceremonials. A pine tree in the territory of the Santa Clara Indians is said by them to be the oldest tree on earth and to have been the first food of mankind.

The 4th century botanist Basil said that when a pine forest is cut down or subjected to the action of fire, it will grow up in oak. He also states that the fox cures his wounds with the droppings of the pine tree. Santa Clara Indians also use pine pitch to keep the air out of their wounds. In Bohemia, it cures gout, cataract, and stomach disorders. The gum boiled and drunk as hot as possible is a cure for worms. The boiled leaves in vinegar made a mouth wash for the teeth and gums. The cones boiled were a cure for most of man's ills. Mohegan Indians make a white pine tea for coughs and colds. The Tewa Indians use pine charcoal for biliousness and, wrapped in a cloth around the throat, for laryngitis. The Indians of California use the pitch smoke for coughs, colds, and rheumatism. The Mescalero Apache make a ceremonial drink of the inside bark of the Western yellow pine. See ATTIS.

pioneer and pioneering lore Although the lore of pioneer America properly begins with the colonial period and the Atlantic frontier, it has been more closely identified with Western migration and settlement. From the inner frontier of the trans-Allegheny and Appalachian country to the outer frontier of the trans-Mississippi and trans-Missouri West, pioneer folk culture passed through the several stages of hunting, grazing, trapping, homesteading, ranching, lumbering, mining, and has given us not only the heroic types associated with these occupations but also the characters of the pioneer woman, doctor, preacher, lawyer, judge. Pioneer lore thus shows a division of labor between the nomadic frontiersman who said, "Whenever you see the smoke of your neighbor's chimney, it is time to move," and the settler who had come to stay.

Out of the conflict between the homesteader and the cattleman grew the fence-cutting and cattle-rustling wars and the uncomplimentary names for the farmer and outlander: nester (Southwest), granger (Northwest), honyocker (from "hunyak" or Slav immigrant—Montana), squatter, scissorbill, landgrabber, plow-chaser. The need of adapting imported folkways and pioneering techniques to new conditions is symbolized by the trail of furniture and supplies discarded by emigrants crossing the plains in order to lighten their overloaded wagons. The persistence of old beliefs and the mixture of transplanted lore are suggested by the incongruous western Oklahoma garden that boasted of lobelia, saffron, horehound, catnip, pennyroyal, and other strange herbs carefully nurtured in spite of adverse conditions, to the grateful relief of the ailing for miles around.

The lack of rain and the unpredictability of the weather on the arid, windy plains resulted in such adages as "All signs fail in dry weather" and "Only fools and strangers (or newcomers and darn fools) prophesy weather in Oklahoma (or Texas)." The latter saying, in the old saloon days in Texas, was triumphantly cited to any foolhardy tenderfoot who hazarded a weather prediction, and a forfeit was exacted in the form of drinks to the house. On one such occasion a tenderfoot neatly turned the tables by pointing out: "You say there are only two kinds of people who prophesy about Texas weather—newcomers and damn fools. You are right. Those are the only two kinds in Texas."

Pioneer lore is divided between the dream of a land flowing with milk and honey (as the pioneer myth extended to the west the original colonial lure of unlimited natural resources and opportunities) and the harshness of the reality. "It is complained that the 'wind blows,'" solemnly stated a Colorado railroad guide. "As it blows elsewhere, so it blows in Colorado—occasionally." Less solemn and more truthful was the old-timer's reply to the stranger's question, "Does the wind blow this way here all the time?"—"No, it'll maybe blow this way for a week or ten days and then it'll take a change and blow like hell for a while" or "Sometimes it turns around and blows the other way."

Where the pioneer found hell instead of heaven on earth, a favorite gag was: "Except for the climate and the people, —— (name of town or state) is all right." "Yes, and you could say the same thing about hell." Hence, too, the "hymn of hate" known variously as *Hell in Texas*, *The Birth of New Mexico*, and *Arizona*. Sandstorms and twisters were varied with blizzards and northers. Often told is the story of the Southwest buffalo hunter who in order to keep warm during a norther crawled into a green buffalo hide, which froze stiff, imprisoning him until thawed out by the fire.

Besides howling blizzards and searing hot winds, lack of fuel and water, hostile Indians and hungry coyotes, the pioneer fought insect pests that attacked both men and crops—from fleas and centipedes to potato bugs and boll weevils. In Nebraska invading grasshoppers would eat downward on the potato vines and "when they came to a potato bug would calmly kick it and go on their devastating way." There was also the grasshopper who ate a farmer's team of mules and then pitched the muleshoes with him for the team. Grasshopper plagues introduced a variant in covered wagon inscriptions. Instead of "Pike's Peak or Bust" (with "Busted, by Thunder" scrawled under it by those returning empty-handed), the legend read: "Hoppers et all but the wagonsheet,"

And whether the enemy was grasshoppers or duststorms, the pioneer farmer stoically proclaimed that he hadn't lost everything: he still had the mortgage.

The grim (if grimly humorous) struggle with a strange and difficult environment found expression in hard-land and hard-times songs like *The Little Old Sod Shanty on the Claim* (a parody of Will S. Hays' *The Little Old Log Cabin in the Lane*), *The Lane County Bachelor* (the county and the claim of authorship varying with the state), and *Dakota Land* (also sung as *Nebraska Land* and *Kansas Land*), and in sayings like "Texas is a good country for men and dogs, but an awfully hard place for oxen (horses) and women."

Man-made complications included land and preemption frauds, "paper cities," booms and busts, town rivalries, county seat wars, outlawry, and vigilantism, as land-hunters gambled with men's lives and fortunes. Pioneers were "luck-hunters" and "half gypsy," in Sandburg's words, and had not only one eye on the "signs" but also one foot in the road. In search of "God's country," they followed each new land opening, only to find that "God's country isn't in the country; it is in the mind." Boomchasers, "movers," drifters, Okies, caught in the backwash of the frontier, in jalopies instead of covered wagons, the migrants still crowd the roads, following cotton, oil, fruit.

In their home-building, home-making, household arts and industries, and social life, the pioneer farmer, his wife and children continued and adapted Yankee, Southern, or European skills and patterns and the rituals of cooperative work and play (log-rollings, raisings, bees, graveyard workings, all-day-dinners-and-singings-on-the-ground, revivals in "laying-by" time, church and school socials, singing schools, literary societies and debates, old settlers' picnics and reunions, play parties, square dances).

As the people of the rifle, ax, plow, Bible, and fiddle came under the influence of big farm machinery, the mail-order catalog, good roads, the automobile, and "town," old folkways survived in new form. They still thought nothing of driving seventy miles to a dance, and they parked their cars on the front lawn where once they tied their horses. The service organizations continued the cult of boosting and booming. There were also changes. According to James West (*Plainville, U.S.A.*, 1945, p. 132) the love of hunting, trapping, shooting, timbering, living without much money or hard farm work, of good dancing and fiddling, a good shot, fighter, or hard drinker, and a good hound dog, like other "pioneer" traits, is associated with the lower element— the "hound-dog people."

In Oklahoma the term "sooner" lost its unfavorable connotation of one who had entered and taken up "unassigned lands" before the legal hour of opening (noon, April 22, 1889) and became a badge of respectability and "first family" status and a synonym for the pioneer spirit of "getting there first." In Oklahoma, too, the pioneer love of improvements and emphasis on material culture survives in a hunger for mechanical devices and novelties, the frontier dream of a paradise on earth having become a "gadgeteers' paradise." True to the pioneer heritage, finally, is the story told by Debs Myers of the old-timer on his last tour of Oklahoma City with his grandson, who exclaimed: "Well, grandpop, she sure is big and pretty, isn't she?" "Yep," the old man replied, "big and pretty, but, hot damn, wouldn't it be fun to tear her down and start all over again!"

B. A. BOTKIN

pipul or **peepul** The sacred fig tree of India (*Ficus religiosa*): often regarded as the reincarnation of a Brāhman. Nearly every village in India has its sacred pipul tree. Vishnu is often pictured seated on its leaves. It is forbidden to cut down one of these trees, and the family of anyone doing so will become extinct. The souls of Brāhman boys who die unmarried reside in them, a fact which may account for its power to fertilize barren women and the custom of marrying girls to the trees. To become fruitful barren women walk naked a prescribed number of times around the local pipul tree. The men of central India circumambulate it to avert evil influences. Sacred fires are fed with pipul wood. The pipul tree embodies the male principal, the acacia the female.

In China it is a symbol of long life; in Tibet it is regarded as the bridge on which the souls of the worthy pass from earth to heaven. See FIG.

Piqued Buffalo Wife Title of a popular Plains Indian tale, also told among a few Eastern Woodlands and Southwestern American Indian groups. A man marries a buffalo who appears as a woman; the couple have a child. A second wife (or sister) of the man refers slightingly to the buffalo-wife's origin, or to her eating habits, or the husband himself offends her in some way. The wife thereupon departs and takes the child back with her to the buffalo herd, and both become buffaloes. The husband searches for his wife and child; when he reaches the herd an old buffalo tells him he must pick out his own wife and child if he is to take them back. The child gives his father a sign and the man succeeds in identifying his wife and offspring. [EWV]

Piśācha (feminine *Piśāchī*) In Hindu belief, the vilest and most malevolent of demons, similar to the Rākshasas but far worse: literally, flesh-eater. The Piśāchas are hideous, bloodthirsty monsters who haunt cemeteries, and desert places. They are ghouls originating from the souls of those who have, according to one account, died violent or untimely deaths. According to the *Mahābhārata* they were created from drops of water by Brahmā and inhabit northern India. They have been identified with savage tribes inhabiting the northern frontiers and the name has been applied to a group of languages spoken in that area. The modern term *Piśācha-bhāshā* which means goblin language, however, refers to gibberish or to English rather than to these languages.

The Piśācha is a ghoul or demon ghost, a liar, drunkard, or criminal classed as a bhūta, which haunts burial grounds, speaks gibberish, and can cause disease. The *paiśācha* form of marriage, named for the Piśāchas, consists of embracing a woman who is insane, asleep, or drugged, and is called, by Manu, the most condemned form of marriage.

Pisces The Fishes: two widely separated constellations joined together with "ribbons" of stars, situated in the zodiac between Aquarius and Aries, one (the northern) south of Andromeda, the other (the southwestern) east of Aquarius and Pegasus. The Greeks called this constellation the Two Fish or Twin Fish. To the Babylonians it was Nūnu (Fish); to the Arabians also al Hūt, the Fish. It was associated also with the Phœnician Dagon. In Latin legend this constellation represents the two fish to which Venus and Cupid were transformed in their flight from the monstrous Typhon, or they are the two fish which carried Venus and Cupid to safety in their flight from him. They were therefore referred to by the Latins as Venus et (or cum) Cupido. Christian astronomers identified them as the fish with which Jesus fed the multitude, or as the fish symbol of early Christianity. In the twelve-figure Chinese zodiac this constellation was Tsen Tsze, the Pig, later, following Jesuit influence, Shwang Yu, Two Fishes.

Pisces is a rainy constellation, bringer of storms, and controls the fate of sailors. As a rain-bringer it is a promoter of fertility and plenty in the old Middle Eastern cultures, but in astrology it exerts a malign influence over the affairs of men.

Pitris Literally, fathers: the sainted ancestral spirits of Hinduism, divine, powerful, and semi-deified, but not identified with the gods in the Vedic periods. They abide with Yama in his remote and peaceful paradise; they feast with the gods, drink the immortal soma, and are reverenced by the living with offerings to insure their elevation into this bliss. In the *Purāṇas* they seem to become confused with the gods, but their status still depends on the rites performed by their pious living kin. See SESAME; ŚRĀDDHA.

pixy One of a class of small spirits or fairies of southwest England (Cornwall and Devonshire, also Dorset, Hampshire, and Wiltshire). Mrs. Bray, a Devonshire woman of the early 19th century, wrote to Southey that "the pixies are certainly a distinct race from the fairies," adding that many people believed them to be the souls of unbaptized infants. The night-flying moths of Cornwall, regarded as souls of the dead, were also called *pisgies*. Pixies typically dance by moonlight to the music of crickets and frogs. They pinch untidy or careless maid servants, blow out candles, tap on walls just to startle people, kiss girls in the dark just to hear them shriek. They love water, and basins of water are often left out for them at night. In Cornwall sometimes a little hole is left in a house wall for the pixies to get in and out. One of their main pranks is to lead people astray. **Pixy-led** means led astray by the pixies; lost, especially on a familiar road; hence also confused and bewildered. Country people in the 17th century sometimes carried bread with them to prevent this. Another preventive was to turn one's coat or other garment inside out. In Hampshire the colt-pixy is a pixy horse that neighs and leads horses astray. **Pixy-rided** means ridden by pixies; but a horseshoe nailed to a stable door will keep pixies from coming and riding the horses at night. If a young girl is pixy-ridden, she drops the pots and pans, the chairs run after her, and even the loaves and bacon run around the table.

plaçage Haitian term for sociological as against legal marriage; a person participating in such a mating is called a *placée*. The institution is part of a widely spread series of similar New World Negro reinterpretations of an African marriage pattern. See AMASIADO.
[MJH]

plaksy The night-hag of Russian folklore: same as NOCNITSA.

planta genista Literally, sprig of broom: the yellow-flowered broom. From his habit of wearing a sprig of this plant in his bonnet, the name of Plantagenet was given to Count Geoffrey of Anjou. His son Henry, who became Henry II of England, adopted the name as a patronymic and it was carried by fourteen English kings (1154–1485), including the six of its two branches, the Houses of Lancaster and York. Another legend is that the first Count of Anjou had himself scourged with the plant for some crime he had committed.

plantain or **waybread** An herb (genus *Plantago*) of the temperate regions, called white man's foot in Australia and New Zealand, and by the Indians of North America, because it came from Europe with the colonists and sprang up wherever they went. In a German tale retold by Grimm it was once a maiden waiting by the roadside for her lover to return. Once every seven years she turns into a bird and goes in search of him, which is why plantain is found all over the world. Both parts of this tale are found singly and together in various parts of the world.

The medicinal properties of plantain are recognized far and wide. The Greeks use the juice of the leaves for diseases of the gums and chew the root for toothache. The seeds are effective against constipation, and the roots worn about the neck cure hard swellings. In Bavaria the people recommend a piece of plantain in the ear for earache; held in the left hand it will clear the mind and prevent headache. The Saxons bound the plant around the forehead with red wool to cure headaches. The 17th century English herbalist Coles said that a toad poisoned by a spider would eat plantain. It is still the most widely used cure everywhere for bee stings. In Ireland plantain is the leaf of Patrick (*copog Pádraig*) and is used in poultices for cuts. In Arabia it is also widely used medicinally and is called lamb's tongue (*lisan al-hamal*). The narrow-leafed plantain is often called English plantain or chimney-sweep and for the most part its uses are the same as for the broad-leafed variety. In Jamaica the broad-leafed plantain is boiled and used as a wash for sore eyes. The Shinnecock Indians of Long Island also use the juice on sores. The Chippewa Indians use both the leaves and roots in a poultice for sores and inflammations; the powdered root they mix with vermilion and carry on their persons to prevent rattlesnake bites, for the snakes will not even show their heads when it is about. The Iroquois use the leaves in poultices for skin injuries and in a preparation against colds, coughs, and bronchitis. The Meskwaki Indians use the leaves in a tea for intermittent fevers, and the fresh leaves on burns, swellings, ulcers, inflammations, and as a hemostatic.

Mississippi Negroes often designate the white plantain as "rabbit tobacco." The leaves of this steeped with scorched corn meal, strained, and used as a bath will stop menstrual hemorrhage. Green plantain leaves boiled and mixed with lard make a salve that is claimed to be a sure cure for cancer; it must be smeared on with a feather.

plat-eye An evil spirit or ghost of West Indian Negro folk belief, especially dreaded also in some southern U.S. Negro groups, especially in Georgia and among the Gullahs. The plat-eye appears usually on a night along with the new moon, and most often has the shape of a dog with fiery eyes. The longer you stare at its eyes, the bigger they get. Sometimes the plat-eye just floats along a road with no visible shape except for the glowing eyes and envelops its victims.

play-party A rural gathering of young people for playing singing-games, with skipping, marching, and dancing movements; also, a game played at such parties. The typical play-party game is a "swinging play," in which the players swing one another by the hand instead of by the waist, to the accompaniment of their own singing. In this way the play-party avoided complete ostracism by the church and dispensed with floor-manager, caller, and musicians. In rural and especially frontier communities, where musical instruments were scarce and religious prejudice against dancing was strong, the play-party arose naturally in response to the need for a flexible, vigorously rhythmic amusement that could be "jumped up" on short notice and was open to the entire countryside on a word-of-mouth rather than on an invitation basis.

The play-party went to the traditional game for dramatic devices for choosing or stealing partners, chasing, kissing, etc., as well as for longways, circle, and arch formations. Certain games were taken over directly, generally with the addition of swinging or marching movements (e.g. *Miller Boy, Three Dukes*). *Skip to My Lou* and *Pig in the Parlor* are both derived from *Bull in the Park; Hog Drovers* or *Swine-Herders* from an Irish game played at wakes.

As the play-party came under the influence of the dance, it substituted the progressive movements of the square dance for the simple repetition of a game formula. Besides the "weaving" movements of the Virginia Reel (as in *Weevily Wheat*), the play-party features the right and left (as in *Old Joe Clark*), in which the boys and girls go in opposite directions, each boy swinging his partner by the right hand, then the next girl by the left hand, and so on until he gets back to his partner, and the longways dance (as in *Old Brass Wagon*), in which the leader and his partner "lead through" or go up and down between the facing rows of boys and girls, swinging first each other, then the next girl and boy in line, each other again, and so on until all have been swung and every couple has had its turn. A favorite closing movement is the promenade, in which the couples, one behind the other, cross hands and march around the room.

The play-party added to its repertoire by borrowing texts and tunes from comic and sentimental minstrel and popular songs (*Buffalo Gals, Brown Jug, Captain Jinks, The Girl I Left Behind Me, Nellie Grey, Old Dan Tucker, Shoo Fly, Wait for the Wagon*), an occasional religious song (*Consolation Flowing Free* and *I Want to Be an Angel*), and even a Western emigrant song (*Shoot the Buffalo*). Under the wearing usage of the dance, and in the absence of a game formula, the text becomes fragmentary, and there is much crossing of songs and shifting of individual lines and stanzas, (as in *Old Joe Clark, Liza Jane*, and *Cindy*).

Especially typical of the swinging play is the accretionary or enumerative catalog of dance directions, often interspersed with patter and nonsense lines and containing satirical allusions to players, the circumstances of the game or the party, and rural life and backgrounds.

Thus *Old Brass Wagon*, beginning with "Lead her up and down the old brass wagon," follows the successive swinging of players by the lead couple with "One wheel off and the axle dragging," "Two wheels off the old brass wagon," etc., while *Jutang* rings the changes on the word "Jutang" in a rigmarole of dance directions: "Round up four in Jutang, Jutang Ju," "Doce do in Jutang, Jutang Ju," "Change and swing in Jutang, Jutang Ju," etc. *Pig in the Parlor* (perhaps the most popular of all play-party games and the favorite in school and playground usage) compares the extra player, in his attempts, feints, and failures to steal a partner, to familiar creatures and objects: "Flies in the buttermilk, two by two," "Little red wagon painted blue," "Ma made buttermilk in Dad's old shoe," "I can't get a redbird, a bluebird will do," etc.

From New England, where it was known as the "evening party" to Texas, where "flang-party" is reported, throughout its many local names, like "fuss" and "frolicking" in the southern mountains, "gin-around" in Mississippi, and "bounce-around" or "bounce-about" in Missouri and Nebraska, the play-party has been an integral and colorful part of pioneer life and culture on the "make-it-yourself-or-do-without" and "hand-me-down" level. Essentially, it marks a reversion of the singing game to its original adult level of the "social" or "sociable," the reel and the carol—the level at which "to 'sing a dance' and 'dance a song' were identical expressions."

Bibliography: Botkin, B. A., *The American Play-Party Song*, 1937; Newell, W. W., *Games and Songs of American Children*, 1883; Owens, William A., *Swing and Turn*, 1936. B. A. BOTKIN

Pleiades Literally, the Weepers: a small but conspicuous cluster of stars in the constellation Taurus. The name refers to the seven daughters of Atlas and Pleione (Electra, Maia, Merope, Alcyone, Taygete, Sterope, Celæno) who became stars after their death, or were metamorphosed into stars in their flight from Orion. They weep for the death of their sisters (the Hyades) or for the plight and burden of their father. Six of them are easily visible; the seventh can be discerned by good eyes; the telescope reveals that they are numerous. The dim one is either Electra, who has wept herself away mourning for Troy, or Merope whose light is dimmed because she married a mortal. They are often also referred to as the Seven Virgins or the Seven Stars. Euripides mentioned them as timekeepers of the night; Hesiod called them the Atlas-Born. To old Greek navigators the heliacal rising of the Pleiades in May was the sign for reopening navigation; the derivation has even been conjectured as from the Greek *plein,* to sail, because of this fact and because Greek sailors steered by them.

The Pleiades has been an important constellation to the peoples of both hemispheres from earliest times. It was well known to the early Hebrews; both Egyptian and Greek temples were oriented to its rising. The ancient Hindus identified it with the six nurses of Kārttikeya, the Krittikās. The Arabs regarded it as a rain-bringing constellation, and as such deified it; it was so vital to their life concept as to be referred to as an Najm, the Constellation.

Almost everywhere in the world the rising of these stars is significant as marking the beginning of a new year and is celebrated with feasts, rejoicings, and special rites. The Kaffirs in South Africa, for instance, date their new year from the date on which the Pleiades are visible for the first time just before sunrise. The Mojo Indians of eastern Bolivia mark the beginning of their year with the appearance of the Pleiades, which they call "the small parrots." Among the Dyaks of Borneo their appearance is a sign to plant. In Hesiod's time the morning rising of the Pleiades occurred about the 9th or 11th of May: the setting of the Pleiades in the morning, at that time about October 26 or very early November, was the time for sowing. In Egypt also the sowing of seeds began with this sign. The ancient Incas regarded the Pleiades as guardians of the weather and growing seeds.

The various Indian peoples of Paraguay and Brazil revere this constellation and time their various agricultural activities by it. Peruvian Indians call it *Collca*, the Maize Heap, because it makes the maize grow; its first appearance above the horizon is the time of their greatest festival. The Amazulu Negroes of South Africa call the Pleiades the "digging stars" because they usher in the planting season. The Hottentots also date their year by the heliacal rising and setting of this constellation. Everywhere throughout Polynesia the new year is marked by the Pleiades.

In the myth of the *Wati-Kutjara* or *Two Men* of certain Western Australian tribes the two men save a group of women who are being pursued by Kidilli, the Moon. Moon was making the women bleed. The Wati-Kutjara caught Kidilli and told him not to chase the women that way but to marry one of them "properly." These tribes identify the group of women with the Pleiades; the Wati-Kutjara are represented by Gemini.

The Lapps also regard the Pleiades as a group of maidens. Finns and Lithuanians call it the Sieve, as do also the Koryak: Ke'tmet, Little Sieve. Various European peasant groups liken these stars to Hen and Chickens.

In contradiction to the reputation of the Pleiades as beneficent rain-bringers in the lore of so many peoples, astrologers assign to them a malign influence, as bringers of blindness to those born under them. It is a quite general folk saying that those who cannot see the Pleiades will shortly die. See AKA-KAMET; QUEEVET.

☞ In North American Indian star lore the Pleiades are nearly always represented as mortals who for various reasons fled this earth and took up a position in the sky, where they have since remained. The Hopi and other Pueblo Indians are exceptional in that they say all the stars, including the Pleiades, were carefully set up in the sky by the people after the Emergence, but that Coyote, despairing of ordering so many items, tore them all out and threw them about the sky in a jumbled fashion. More usual Pleiades myths make them seven sisters, the wives of seven hunter brothers who became disgusted when they discovered their husbands were cheating them of the game they killed and who rose to the sky. The youngest husband, in a California version of this myth, having been good to his wife, was allowed to follow the sisters, and is now in the constellation Taurus. Other versions make the Pleiades dancing women; the Luiseño of California say they are girls,

pursued by Coyote as Aldebaran. Cherokee and Onondaga myths make the Pleiades dancing children. See DANCERS. [EWV]

plum In China it is said a dragon had his ears cut off and the plum tree sprang from his blood. Like the peach, this tree is a symbol of longevity and immortality. Lao Tzu was born under a plum tree. In Chinese symbolism of the seasons, the plum tree indicates winter. The plum, bamboo, and pine are often planted together and referred to as the "Three Friends." In the Japanese Floral Calendar, the pine, bamboo, and plum tree are assigned to the New Year season, January 1–7 (or 15). The plum tree is chosen to herald the new year because it is the first to bloom of all flowering trees. In Japanese folklore, the companion of the plum is the nightingale, which is a joyous bird in Japan and harbinger of spring.

In Wales they say that if a plum tree blooms in December there will be a death in the family. In Texas a plum pit carried in the mouth prevents overheating and sunstroke. Roger Williams of Rhode Island deplored a gambling game of the Pequot Indians played with plum pits. The Meskwaki Indians used the bark of the root to cure canker of the mouth and a bark tea for sick stomach. Formerly the word plum was used as a slang term in England to denote the sum of £100,000; probably the origin of the term political plum.

Pluto The wealth-giver: in late classical times, name of the Greek underworld deity, earlier an epithet of Hades as lord of the riches that grew from within the earth. The god Plutus, son of Demeter and Iasion, is his double. Plutus was the god of agricultural riches, hence of wealth. He was made blind by Zeus so that he might distribute his bounty without prejudice, but (compare Aristophanes' *Plutus*) he recovered his sight and brought wealth to honest men only. Pluto is one of the great gods, is prominent in the literary tradition and as the abductor of Persephone; Plutus is a popular god whose name does not have the same sort of power attached to it as Pluto's.

p'o In Chinese folklore, the animal or physical soul, present in man from the moment of conception.

pocomania (slight frenzy) A Jamaican ritual dance of the *obeah* cult. The drumming and chanting may continue for days or a fortnight, as members and initiates dance themselves into a trance. In turn they fall into a coma in the dance clearing. When they awaken, they are feasted at a "rising table" and relate their experiences in the spirit world. Native dance artists have taken over the pocomania for performance in clubs and on the stage. [GPK]

Pohjola Literally, northern home: a place often mentioned in the Finnish runes. It is a dark and dismal country to the north of Finland, often identified with Lapland. There is the court of Louhi, mistress of Pohjola. The heroes of Kaleva made many adventurous trips to Pohjola (see SAMPO). Kaarle Krohn supposes that Pohjola is identical with Vuojala, the latter meaning the isle Gottland. U. Harva sees a corresponding idea between Pohjola and the home or land of the dead. See FINNISH FOLKLORE. [JB]

point Among Haitian Negroes, a type of derisive song full of oblique or elliptical comment belittling a rival or an enemy, calling attention to a scandalous or embarassing situation, or slyly cooking up a rumor. It is a humorous form of social revenge—"needling" in song. See NITH SONGS.

poison damsel The woman of folktale who, bred in poisonous surroundings, kills those with whom she comes in contact: an extension of the idea of the inherent danger of sexual intercourse. According to Penzer (*Ocean of Story* II:275–313), the motif (F582) arose in India, became attached to the Alexander legends, was included in the *Gesta Romanorum* (#11), and spread thence throughout Europe. The poison damsel was sent by an enemy to Alexander, with the hope that he would be attracted to her, would kiss or otherwise come into contact with her, and would die. But the long-laid plot (the maiden was reared from birth for this very purpose) came to naught when Aristotle, Alexander's mentor, enclosed her within a circle of dittany juice and she suffocated in trying to escape. The poison damsel is ordinarily brought up by snakes, is nurtured on poisonous herbs, and eats all manner of poisons as her normal diet. She can kill with a glance or with her breath as well as by closer forms of contact. Penzer hints that venereal disease may underlie the concept, but certainly the belief that intercourse, especially with a maiden, may be fatal is widespread. The *femme fatale* whose husbands die on the wedding night is in Old Testament Apocryphal *Tobit*. King Minos of Crete, whose embraces were loathly with serpents and vile creatures, is the male counterpart of the women of folktale whose vaginas contain poisonous snakes. Compare here the common connection in folk belief between the serpent and the phallus.

poison ivy A poisonous climbing shrub (*Rhus toxicodendron*), with three broadly ovate, variously notched, sinuate or cut-lobed leaflets, native to North America. According to folk belief in the eastern states it can poison even those who look at it, especially in wet, foggy weather. Among the Potawatomi Indians roots of the plant are pounded to make a poultice to open swellings. When working in its vicinity, the Cherokee conciliate it by addressing it as "my friend." If poisoned by it, they rub the affected part with the beaten flesh of a crawfish. In England juice of the leaves is given as a sedative; it is also recommended for incontinence of urine.

polka A ballroom step and couple dance of Polish origin, wholeheartedly adopted throughout central and western Europe, the United States, and Middle America. As a ballroom round, polkas alternate at folk dance and square dance evenings with the more complicated numbers. The step is also used commonly in folk dances and quadrilles, particularly in Poland and Lithuania, also in the Moravian *kanafaska* and Russian *korobouchka*. The fundamental step, following an upbeat of a hop, consists of three steps and a hop, in open or promenade position, or in closed or ballroom position, progressing straight ahead or turning. A well-known variant, in promenade position, is the heel-and-toe polka (heel, toe, one-two-three) which propels partners zestfully across the dance floor. There are many other variants—the butterfly, finger, koketka. In Lithuanian and Finnish versions, three or seven polka steps are followed by stamps as in the *kalvelis* and *mikita*. In the American polka and Finnish *radiko*, slides and running steps combine with the fundamental step. In the Norwegian polka, a gentler leg swing replaces the hop. In New Mexico, the *polquita* is a ballroom round, the *polka cruzada* is a section of the *quadrillas*, with cross-overs and polka. The fad of the *Beer Barrel Polka* penetrated from the United States to the Mexican hinterland. Mexico has also adopted the step in some of its traditional dances, as the *Jarabe Michoacano* and the ritualistic *Sembradoras*. [GPK]

polygenesis In folktale study, the doctrine of independent origin of similar tales, as opposed to diffusionism, which maintains the spread of tales from a point of common origin. Those holding to the theory of polygenesis hold that similar stages in the development of human society, though separated from each other by both time and space, give rise to similar cultural backgrounds and emotional reactions, and that these in turn lead to the evolution of similar tales. However, such distinct parallels of development have not been clearly demonstrated, and the theory of polygenesis is not acceptable as the single explanation of folktale similarities. A position somewhere between polygenesis and diffusionism is taken by many folktale students, holding that the diffusion of such elements as motifs occurs from a common center and that there is subsequent building up of independent tales in the various cultures from these elements.

Polyidus In Greek mythology, a soothsayer of Argos. Glaucus, the son of Minos, had fallen into a jar of honey and drowned. No one could find the child and either Apollo or the Curetes had told by an oracle that the first who found an apt comparison with the three colors of a cow would find the boy and bring him back to life. Knowing nothing of this, Polyidus made a comparison with the three colors of the mulberry (white, then red, then black), and was ordered by Minos to locate and restore his son. With the aid of the bees and an owl, he found the body in the honey jar, but he could not bring back the child's breath. For his refusal and inability, Minos had Polyidus entombed with Glaucus. In the tomb, a serpent approached the body, and Polyidus killed it. Soon after another serpent appeared, applied an herb to the dead snake, and both glided away. Glaucus was quickly restored with the aid of the herb and Minos rewarded Polyidus lavishly.

Polynesian mythology Polynesia, easternmost of the Pacific culture areas, extends, like a great triangle, from Hawaii to New Zealand and from Easter Island to Samoa and Tonga. Because Polynesians are remarkably homogeneous in culture, including their mythology and Malayo-Polynesian dialects, it is believed that their ancestors, once they had arrived in the area an estimated 2,000 to 2,500 years ago from Indonesia by way of Micronesia, originated a pattern of culture which they carried with them when they later colonized the rest of the area and occupied certain scattered islands in Melanesia.

The Society Archipelago, more specifically Opoa district in Raiatea Island, one of the legendary homelands that Polynesia calls Hawaiki, is perhaps the center where the pattern took shape. Evidence of Raiatean cultural leadership was still discernible at the beginning of the European period (Henry; Ellis). The relation of the Society Islands to the rest of Polynesia has been likened by Sir Peter H. Buck (Te Rangi Hiroa) to an octopus with eight radiating arms (1938, 1939). The islands along each radiation from the center have developed local variations of the common pattern. Marked differentiation resulted in western Polynesia from such factors as Fijian influence and isolation from the central region. Dr. Edwin G. Burrows (1938, 1941) has defined two divisions of Polynesia culture. One, the western Polynesian, centers in Samoa and Tonga; the other, the central-marginal, which retained, in some measure, much of the old culture once common to all Polynesia, has Opoa of Raiatea as its nucleus.

The basic pattern of pre-European Polynesia involved a material culture of Stone Age level whose relative simplicity was obscured by the elaborate esthetic, religious, and intellectual life. For example, a large, double canoe, hewn with stone and wooden tools, was also ornamented with complicated carvings and other decorations. Religious and magical rites accompanied its production from the period of deciding to build a boat and choosing the trees to the period of launching and traveling. The most famous mythological boat-builder was Rata, known to most Polynesians as the hero who built a boat to take him on a mission of revenge against his father's slayers and other monsters troubling the world. The adventure most widely associated with Rata's name concerns his attempt to cut down a tree without the proper ritual. Each day he returned to work and found the tree that he had cut down the day before upright with every chip and leaf in place. Not until he had made peace with the forest spirits and won them as allies did he progress with building his boat. Rata's name and the tree-chopping episode have diffused into Melanesia but have become separated there from each other and acquired new contexts.

Polynesians used tapa for clothing and other purposes, and the association of the goddess Hina (Sina) with its production provides prestige and sanctions for women tapa-makers. Tahitians (Emory, 1938) even yet tell how Hina performed her duty of beating tapa for the gods so energetically that the greatest god of the pantheon, Ta'aroa, who had been drinking kava (*Piper methysticum*), grumbled to Pani about the noise in the "harbor of the god." He sent him to order Hina to stop. Thrice Pani commanded Hina to be quiet, but she replied, "I will not stop. I will beat out the white tapa here as a wrapping for the gods Ta'aroa, 'Oro, Moe, Ruanu'u, Tu, To'a-hiti, Tau-uta, Te Maharo, and Punua-the-thunderbolt." Furious at her stubbornness and defiance of the god's orders, Pani seized the tapa mallet and hit Hina on the head. Her spirit flew to the moon, where, according to most islanders, she still beats tapa proudly for the gods. The name of Hina with various sobriquets is so frequently given to Polynesian heroines that it is often difficult to distinguish one Hina from another.

Like the tapa, the thatched dwellings of the Polynesians and their public houses for entertainment and guests often belie their simple materials by the quality of workmanship and the beliefs relating to their construction. Society Islanders (Emory, 1938) compare the raising of the sky in prehuman times to the building of a house. In the raising, gods worked as expert artisans. After the pillars had been set up, the ridge pole of the sky was propped up, followed by the inner post, the wall-plate, the side post, the rear purlin, and so on

through the thatching of the roof of the sky. By having their gods set examples, earthly artisans dignify their own labor. Samoan carpenters belong to a guild founded in the beginning of the world during a meeting called by Tangaloa (Samoan dialectical equivalent of Ta'aroa) who wanted a house built in his sky. The architecture of his house is still followed by present-day guilds, called Tangaloa's Family, whose members claim descent from founders of the original union. The myth of the origin of the guild is no idle story merely soothing to carpenterial ego, but serves also to justify their demands for special favors and frequent feasts from those who are at their mercy to get houses built.

Pigs, dogs, and fowls, used for food and sacrifices, were by no means present in every Polynesian island. However, successful fishing and agriculture, with taro and coconut in most islands and breadfruit added in volcanic islands as staples, furnished sufficient extra food to free talented individuals for specialization in religion, crafts, and arts, including literature. Schools of various levels of honor and advancement existed in the principal archipelagoes of central-marginal Polynesia, but were not characteritsic of the west. The Society Islands, to use this important group as an example (Henry, 1928), had educational institutions, some limited to men, others open to women too, where *tahu'a*, highly revered and paid teachers of priestly status, chanted the lore about such subjects, for example, as literary composition, traditions, astronomy, black magic, medicine, religion, and the construction of canoes, houses, and maraes (temples). Typical of the descriptive quality of Polynesian language is the name, "Cave-of-many outlets," applied to male and female teachers of "original, earthly knowledge." Those destined for the high and sacred ranks of *tahu'a* were able-bodied, attractive, and graceful men, preferably sons of priests. After intensive training in esoteric learning, they underwent a period of retirement and communion with the gods. Then, after passing a final examination before a strict group, they were honored with a feast and permitted to practice. Opoa had a religious seminary whose fame spread throughout Polynesia and won for the district European comparisons with Mecca, Rome, and less sympathetic descriptions as the "metropolis of idolatry." It was here that priests elevated Ta'aroa to the post of supremacy in the Polynesian pantheon, and created the Arioi Society of literary artists with libertine morals to win popularity for the god and his son 'Oro.

New Zealand, Hawaii, and other marginal groups also had special schools and professional experts who gave to Polynesian culture its characteristic aura of intellectual sophistication. Naming, classifying, systematizing, synthesizing, and syncretizing were important mental activities which specialists applied to their learning and laymen used in intellectual games and contests. Hawaii, for example, had literary contests sponsored by royal courts where native ability supported by accouterments of magic enabled the hero of tradition to triumph over haughty but less capable riddlers, matchers of allusions, and creators of similes (Beckwith, 1941). Everywhere the individual who combined talent in poetry, chanting, stylized oratory, and narration with an extensive command of traditional knowledge won for himself recognition regardless of his origin. Those of high birth were expected to have such talent and knowledge.

Although the feudal type of organization found in the Tongan Islands led to systematization of many traditions about the person of its political and religious head, the Tui Tonga, western Polynesia, in general, did not exhibit the extraordinary love for formal organization of traditions that central-marginal Polynesia did. Nonetheless, the west had much respect for learning, even though learning was more fluid, less crystallized, and more obvious in the expediency of its application for political and religious preferment. Samoan talking chiefs, for instance, specialized in oratory, chants, traditions, and protocol of kava circles in order to manipulate them to win advancement for themselves and the high chiefs they served.

Because status was determined mainly by birth, genealogies (Liliuokalani; Smith, 1921) that frequently reveal many literary devices and a fertile imagination were important throughout Polynesia. High chiefs who traced descent from primal gods inherited great mana (supernatural power), which their accomplishments enhanced. A nice balancing of the tapus could give them extensive authority or hedge them in to prevent their rendering too much of everyday life sacred and inviolate. Though special classes of priests occurred, a chief's descent made him a natural medium between his ancestral gods and his people, who, by genealogy, were relatives of lesser degree. Dead chiefs, like Tangiia of Rarotonga, were deified and thereby claims of a particular line of descent to superiority were reinforced. A genealogy usually followed the male line, but if a female ancestor were of higher birth than a male, her name was used. Social organization emphasized the extended family with the eldest male usually the leader, except in Samoa where the post was filled by election. The three major social classes—chiefs, freemen, and slaves who were war captives—were often subdivided not only on the basis of birth but occupation. Related families were united into clans and tribes tracing descent from a common ancestor. A feudal organization developed in the Society Islands, Tonga, and Hawaii, with many intertribal and interisland wars led by chiefs like Kamehameha I of the Hawaiian Islands and Pomare of the Society Islands intent on establishing island kingdoms.

Much of Polynesian literature relates to the genealogies and traditions of a chiefly or royal line. Because of the island geography, many tribal histories record memories of overseas migration. The Maori of New Zealand felt themselves related to other Maori who claimed descent from a common ancestor who came in one of the great canoes that went from Hawaiki (presumably Raiatea) about 1350 A.D. to settle New Zealand and absorb the older population. Maori traditional history (White; Best) deals in large part with this migration and subsequent events; each tribe expands upon the deeds of the ancestor who led the canoe after which the tribe is named.

Isolation and a temperate climate led to distinct local differences in New Zealand from the rest of Polynesia. A complex magical and religious system developed about the production of kumara, the sweet potato staple, and other important food-getting activities like bird-snaring. Woven flax mats, sometimes decorated or entirely overlaid with dog hair or black kiwi feathers, replaced tapa. Indicative of the value placed on the mats are incidental references in myths to unusually beautiful mats

together with the names of the dogs furnishing the decoration. Wooden dwellings, beautifully carved with tools of jadeite, a hard stone also used for making weapons and sacred objects, replaced thatched dwellings. The carvings often symbolically portray ancestors, gods, and demigods, sometimes busy at an activity associated with their career.

Unlike other Oceanic areas that also are without writing, Polynesia has innumerable names of gods, heroes, and lesser characters of mythology and religion who are known in more than one archipelago. A body of common tradition and folklore exists which in each island has been elaborately localized and incorporated into local lore. The most widely known of any Oceanic character is Maui, culture hero and trickster of demigod status, who stole fire, fished up islands, snared the sun to lengthen the day, and sometimes helped raise the sky. His name and a few of the thousand tricks Polynesians credit him with have diffused into parts of Micronesia like the Carolines, Polynesian outliers in Melanesia, and their immediate neighbors. Tawhaki, Rata, and Tinirau are other Polynesian mythological characters of extensive distribution. Tangaroa (Ta'aroa, etc.) is the only Polynesian primal deity whose name (but not his role) has diffused outside the area. More common than names are mythological themes shared by Polynesians with other Oceanic peoples. They usually have to do with the origin of fire and food plants, and cosmogonic myths like that of sky-raising and sun-snaring (Dixon, 1916; Luomala, 1940).

Central-marginal Polynesia had the most pronounced form of the Polynesian custom of arranging primary and secondary deities into families whose descendants are the chiefly families of human history. Besides Tangaroa, other prominent gods in this region are Tane, Tu, and Rongo, whose names, in various dialectical forms, are known from Hawaii to New Zealand. New Zealand has a neatly and beautifully organized divine family with accompanying mythology, a variant of that found to the north and east (Grey). The Sky Father and Earth Mother are descended by evolutionary genealogies from an initial void or chaos. Sometimes the genealogies contain names relating to plant development; again, they may include a series of abstractions like Energy, Thought, Mind, and Desire. Earth and Sky bear children, the primal gods, whose departmental duties in the world cannot be carried out because Earth and Sky are unseparated. Tangaroa, for example, is to have charge of the ocean, while Tane will superintend the forests and all life and spirits therein. Finally, the brothers unite and despite the resistance of one brother who sends great storms and starts the first world war, Earth and Sky are separated and the world is put in order. Mankind comes into existence by a special creative act of a deity, usually Tane, or his symbolic virile force called Tiki, who impregnates a female he has made from earth. Islands are fished from the depths of the sea by Maui, according to most eastern Polynesians.

Western Polynesia does not have the Sky Father and Earth Mother concept or the family of divinities with departmental duties. Only Tangaroa of the eastern primal gods persists, and, as in central Polynesia, he inhabits the sky. Mankind originates through a crude form of evolution from rocks, earth, or maggots which form in a vine the sky deity threw down to shade his daughter or messenger. The islands are either fished up, thrown down from the sky, or built up from sand carried in baskets by voyagers. The latter myth refers to the custom of bringing soil to infertile coral atolls. Pulotu in western Polynesia and Fiji is variously the land of the important dead, an island, and the underworld. In the central-marginal area, Hawaiki has various functions too which are often combined in an island. It may be the ancestral home, the home of the dead, the underworld, and a western island.

In the larger islands of central-marginal Polynesia, specialization in arts, crafts, religion, and literature was possible because of a large population and a plentiful food supply. Specialization led to a distinction between different levels of esoteric knowledge developed by trained experts who often split into sects, and exoteric lore which other people might acquire. "Upper Jaw" knowledge to a limited number of Maori in New Zealand pertained to the period of genesis, to the origins of the world, the gods, and mankind, and the life of the people in their predispersal home in Hawaiki. A small sect, perhaps in European times, revised their esoteric chants to make the god Io the ultimate source of the world and the gods. In the Society Islands, the systematized and reinterpreted cosmogonic chants, rituals, and narratives served in some islands to set Ta'aroa at the head of the pantheon as the uncreated, preexistent spirit whose glances and words were sufficient to bring forth much of the world and the other gods. Neighboring islands clung to their own versions of the cosmogony in which another god, usually Tane, outranked Ta'aroa. Through war and intellectual competition each sect tried to spread its beliefs and gain followers.

The basic concepts upon which the priestly philosophers expended their intellectual energies belonged to the Polynesian culture pattern and stemmed from the cultural heritage which the ancestors of the people brought with them into the area and carried out from central Polynesia.

"Lower Jaw" knowledge among the Maori included traditions about migrations from Hawaiki, the settlement in the new homeland, and the history of individual clans and chiefs from the time of departure from Hawaiki to the present. In isolated atolls settled perhaps by a single family and its retainers, much of the lore consists of this exoteric knowledge about the family's immigration, discovery, and settlement of their new island, and the history of land divisions and wars. The original settlers, if they had no priest with them, knew but fragments of the cosmogony. Usually they knew some of the myths forming part of the great hero cycles and popular romances. These they retold as they remembered them and invented new episodes.

Without question, the literary specialization of Polynesia ranks the area with ancient Greece, India, and Scandinavia in the earliest era of bards, before the introduction of writing. In Polynesian mythology, as in the oral literatures of these classic areas, there is much that is strange and tedious until one knows the cultural background of the narrators and tries to define their literary standards to see how nearly the individual narrators have attained them.

Bibliography—Of books and articles belonging to established scientific series, the selected bibliography below includes only those specifically cited in the text.

Numerous major contributions to Polynesian mythology, which have not been listed separately, have been published in the *Bulletins* and *Memoirs* of the Bernice Pauahi Bishop Museum, Honolulu; the *Journals* and *Memoirs* of the Polynesian Society, Wellington; the *Transactions* of the New Zealand Institute, Wellington; *Monographs* of the Dominion Museum, Wellington; *Folklore Publications* of Vassar College, Poughkeepsie; *Reports* and *Papers* of the Hawaiian Historical Society, Honolulu; *Hawaiian Almanac and Annual,* Honolulu; *Journals* of the Royal Society of New South Wales, Australia; *Anthropos; Globus; Zeitschrift für Ethnologie; Bulletins* of the Société des études océaniennes; *Internationales Archiv für Ethnographie; Oceania;* others.

M. W. Beckwith, *Hawaiian Mythology* (New Haven), 1940; "The Hawaiian romance of Laieikawai," Smithsonian Inst., *RBAE* 33, 1911–1912; E. Best, "Tuhoe, children of the mist," *Poly. Soc., Memoirs,* vol. 6, 1925; P. H. Buck (Te Rangi Hiroa), *Vikings of the Sunrise* (New York), 1938; *Anthropology and Religion* (New Haven), 1939; E. G. Burrows, "Western Polynesia, a study in cultural differentiation," *Ethnological Studies,* vol. 7 (Göteborg), 1938; "Culture-areas in Polynesia," in *Polynesian anthropological studies, Poly. Soc., Memoirs,* vol. 17, 1941; R. B. Dixon, "Oceanic," in *Mythology of all races,* vol. 9 (Boston), 1916; N. B. Emerson, "Unwritten literature of Hawaii," Smithsonian Inst., *BBAE* 38, 1909; idem., *Pele and Hiiaka,* Honolulu, 1915; *Hawaiian Antiquities of David Malo,* Honolulu, 1898; K. P. Emory, "The Tahitian Account of Creation by Mare," *Poly. Soc., Jour.,* vol. 47, 1938; W. Ellis, *Polynesian Researches,* (London), 1853; W. W. Gill, *Myths and Songs from the South Pacific* (London), 1876; G. Grey, *Polynesian Mythology* (London), 1855; E. S. C. Handy and others, *Ancient Hawaiian Civilization* (Honolulu), 1933; T. Henry, "Ancient Tahiti," *B. P. Bishop Mus., Bull.* 48, 1928; A. Krämer, *Die Samoa-Inseln* (Stuttgart), 1902–1906; Liliuokalani, *An Account of the Creation of the World* (Boston), 1897; K. Luomala, "Oceanic, American Indian, and African Myths of Snaring the Sun," *B. P. Bishop Mus., Bull.* 168, 1940; idem., "Polynesian Mythology," in *Encyclopedia of Literature,* ed. J. T. Shipley (New York), 1946; idem., "Maui-of-a-thousand-tricks; His Oceanic and European Biographers," *B. P. Bishop Mus., Bull.* 198, 1949; S. P. Smith, *Hawaiki* (London), 1921; J. B. Stair, *Old Samoa* (London), 1897; O. Stuebel, "Samoanische Texte," *Veröffentlichungen aus dem königlichen Museum für Völkerkunde,* vol. 4, 1896; T. G. Thrum, *Hawaiian Folk Tales* (Chicago), 1907; idem., *More Hawaiian Folktales* (Chicago), 1923; E. Tregear, *The Maori-Polynesian Comparative Dictionary* (Wellington), 1891; G. Turner, *Nineteen Years in Polynesia* (London), 1861; J. White, *Ancient History of the Maori* (Wellington), 1887.   KATHARINE LUOMALA

Polynices In Greek legend, a son of Œdipus and Jocasta. He and Eteocles agreed that they should reign in alternate years over Thebes, with the other banishing himself for that year. But at the end of his year of reign, Eteocles refused to give up the throne and with the aid of his father-in-law, Adrastus, Polynices, marched in the expedition of the Seven Against Thebes. Eteocles and Polynices slew each other in single combat, Creon becoming king of Thebes when the invading Argives were routed. He ordered Eteocles burned with full honors, and Polynices left unburied where he fell. See ANTIGONE.

polytheism The belief in and worship of more gods than one, as opposed to monotheism, the belief in one God. Polytheism assigns separate functions and provinces to individual gods, who are worshipped as the occasion and need demands; for example, sea, wind, travelers', and fortune gods may be propitiated and asked for their good graces before a voyage is undertaken. Among the polytheistic deities of the world, the following are found in many areas: sun god, moon god, storm god, rain god, sea god, sky god, thunder god, war god, god of luck, earth god, fire god, gods of birth and fertility, of agriculture, of hunting, of healing, of evil. These various forces, according to the evolutionary theory of the growth of religions, are at first worshipped abstractly, as disembodied and impersonalized principles. Later, they are personified and become, instead of indwelling forces, distinct personages, e.g. the earth god or goddess becomes a personality with a name—Ge, which means earth. In the course of myth-making, the relationship of the various forces as personified in these gods is exemplified in stories; the pantheon is interrelated, with necessary additions, as husbands and wives and children, usually on the basis of these relationships as they exist in the society to which the myths belong. Eventually, according to the Grimms, these myths, when the religious system evolves to another state or is superseded by another, become folktales and their mythic explanatory character becomes hidden; the gods who were the central characters in the myths become the heroes and heroines of folktale. Thus the great dragon-slaying myth, the cosmogonic story of the god who slays the dragon of chaos and founds order in the universe from its body (see the myth of Marduk and Tiamat), becomes the märchen of the unpromising hero (youngest son) who kills the dragon that is laying waste the countryside.

Pantheons of polytheistic deities have existed from earliest times, in Sumeria and Egypt for example, down to the present, in Africa, Polynesia, South America, North America, etc. Many critics hold that the monotheistic religions, with their saints, prophets, angels, demons, etc., retain so much of polytheism as to indicate a basic need in mankind for a plurality of gods. They point out that the supreme position of Jehovah or Allah in monotheistic religion over his attendants or opposing principles is matched in kind if not in degree by such admittedly polytheistic gods as Ashur, Rā, and Zeus.

Pombada A Canarese devil-dancing caste of southwest India, resembling the Parava and Nalke, but higher, and non-polluting. All of these castes exorcise demons by means of dancing in fantastic costumes with high towering headdresses, much ornament, and face paint (not masks). They control a hierarchy of demons (bhuthas). The Pombada deal only with the higher demons, leaving the lower ones to the lower castes. See PANAN. [GPK]

pomegranate Because of its very numerous seeds, the pomegranate has been, through the ages, a symbol of fertility, in Chinese, Persian, Semitic, Greek, and Roman lore. Chinese women offer it to the goddess of mercy when praying for children, especially sons. The pomegranate is often credited with being the forbidden

fruit of the Garden of Eden, and some say that it contains one seed from the Garden. It was a symbol of wealth. In Greek myth it was called the fruit of Hades because when ordered to give up Persephone, Hades tempted her to eat a pomegranate; she ate only one seed, but because of this he retained a hold on her. This is why she spends part of the year in the underworld, symbolic of the seed germinating in the ground. See FOOD TABU IN LAND OF THE DEAD.

In Christian art the pomegranate is a symbol of hope. Persian Zoroastrians make a barsom of pomegranate branches against demons and witchcraft. In Turkey the bride throws a pomegranate on the ground and the number of seeds scattered when it breaks indicates the number of children she will have. In Sicily the pomegranate shoot is used as a divining rod. In Italy the leaves are made into a mouthwash which is good against loose teeth. In Texas the blossom tea is used as a tonic. The pomegranate is the national emblem of Spain.

Pop Goes the Weasel An American square dance and tune originating in a longways dance of the same name from Warwickshire, England. The leading lady progresses around the circle from one couple to the other, and after a circling, is "popped" under the arch formed by the uplaised arms of the dancers, on the words "pop goes the weasel." At the fourth couple, she is joined in the "popping" by her partner, who then swings her. Each couple in turn becomes active. [GPK]

poplar The poplar was one of three trees mentioned in the *Odyssey* as growing at the mouth of Calypso's cave. Euripides tells the story of the sisters of Phaethon who, while weeping his death, were transformed into a poplar grove (A2181.3).

In Latin legend Hercules made himself a victor's crown of poplar leaves after killing the giant Cacus. This he wore on his journey to the underworld; the tops of the leaves were thus scorched and darkened by the heat, while the undersides were silvered with the hero's own radiance (or sweat). And because Hercules went to Hades and returned, the white poplar came to signify, in many old beliefs, the promise of a life after death. Even today in Ireland the *fé*, the rod for measuring graves, coffins, and dead bodies, is traditionally made of poplar (possibly in now forgotten token to the dead that this is not the end).

The black poplar was associated with early earth-goddess ritual, and was long interpreted as a hopeless omen in Roman divination. In ancient Greek and Roman magic the white poplar was associated with leprosy, and was probably regarded as a preventive against it. Poplar leaves were sometimes used in medieval French witch salves.

The white poplar, or aspen (Old Irish *eada*, modern Irish *eadad* or *eabad*), in the Old Irish Tree Alphabet was the tree of autumn and old age. The ancient Irish made their wooden shields of poplar.

The North American Catawba Indians made a boiled tea of the scrapings of poplar roots, which they gave to children for stomach worms. In Macedonia today the people avoid the shade of poplar trees, in the belief that they are frequented by malicious spirits.

poppy The poppy is the symbol of sleep and death. Ceres searching for Proserpine would not pause in her quest, so the gods, taking pity on her, caused the poppy to spring up in her footsteps. When she paused to pluck one, it caused her to sleep. In some tales it is dedicated to Ceres because it is found growing among the grain. The poppy was also sacred to Diana. In all parts of the world it is said to spring from the blood of the slain, and it grows especially well on the battle-fields of the past. Some early Christian authorities claimed it sprang from Christ's blood on the Cross. In England it is said to have sprung from the blood of a dragon slain by the holy maid Margaret.

The poppy and its derivatives were used mostly for medicinal purposes until the 12th century and were all imported from Asia Minor. It has yielded since early times the opium which induces restful sleep and allays pain. The fact that too much could be administered did not escape the early herbalists, for in 1551 the English physician Turner wrote, "If the pacient be too much slepi put stynkynge thynges unto hys nose to waken hym therewith." Another 16th century physician of Padua, Peter A. Matthioli, said if poppy seeds be given to hens they will lay more plentifully.

In Switzerland and parts of the United States a poppy petal is placed on top of the left fist and struck with the right hand. If it pops, your lover is true; if not, you are forgotten. Poppy seeds are sometimes used to determine the sex of an unborn child. Wheat and poppies in a field are symbolic of life and death.

Porcupine An animal character, often the companion of the trickster Coyote, in North American Indian tales. Porcupine is especially popular as a character among tribes in the western half of the continent, where two trickster tales, *Coyote and Porcupine* and *Beaver and Porcupine,* are well known. For the first of these, see COYOTE AND PORCUPINE.

The second, *Beaver and Porcupine,* concerns a trick Beaver played on Porcupine by taking him on his back to a stump in the middle of a lake and leaving him there. Porcupine sings and causes the lake to freeze over; he then walks ashore. Later he retaliates on Beaver by taking him to the top of a very high tree and leaving him there. The idea of Porcupine as a controller of cold is a central one in all stories of Beaver and Porcupine; it also occurs in a Micmac tale about Porcupine in the northeastern United States. [EWV]

In Hausa Negro folklore both Porcupine and Hedgehog are regarded as having power over men and witches, both in this world and the next. They are always on the side of right in Hausa folktale.

Poseidon The ancient Greek sea god, also god of earthquakes and horses. Many scholars see in Poseidon the lord of the universe who preceded Zeus, perhaps the sky god of an early indigenous tribe. They point to his trident (nominally a fish-spear) as being in other cultures a symbol of the thunderbolt of the sky god. Poseidon-worship in Greece was not widespread; he was said to be overlord of the Corinthian Isthmus, and his temple at Mycale in Asia Minor was the center of Ionian religious worship, but his myths overshadow his cult importance. He was loser to both Hera and Athena in disputes for several parts of Greece; in Athens, as Poseidon-Erech-theus, he is equated with the founder of the city. His wife was Amphitrite, also an ancient sea deity, who bore him Triton. Poseidon's amours, though not as numerous as those of Zeus, were widespread. By Medusa he was

father of Pegasus and Chrysaor; Antæus, slain by Hercules, was the son of Poseidon and Ge. Demeter tried to evade his attentions, but though she transformed her-self into a horse, Poseidon became a stallion and sired on her the marvelous horse Arion.

Poseyemu Tewa Pueblo Christlike culture hero, equatable with Poshaiyanki of Zuñi, P'ashayan'i of Keres, and Puspiyama of Isleta. At Sia Pueblo he is the brother and deputy of Iyatiku or Corn Mother, and the father of curing societies and giver of raiment and riches at Zuñi; but at Laguna he is a despised little boy, a miracle worker or nothing more than a juggler and deceiver, who has finally to be killed. At Acoma pueblo, which is now Catholicized, he has been assimilated with the serpent in the Garden of Eden. Poseyemu, himself conceived through a piñon nut, is the sender of piñons to the people. Poseyemu or Poshaiyanki once lived on earth; he disappeared into the south, or else traveled through all the pueblos and over all the world before he disappeared into the earth. See Elsie Clews Parsons, *Pueblo Indian Religion* (2 vols., Chicago, Ill., 1939) pp. 179, 196. [EWV]

Poshaiyanka Zuñi Pueblo Indian culture hero, who arose from the farthest sea, and joined living creatures in the underworld. This being first showed human beings the way upward through a narrow passage from the underworld to this world, then an unstable island lying among the waters. The passage was so narrow, however, that Poshaiyankya was forced to plead with Awona-wilona, or Sun-father, for the deliverance of men and all other creatures from the underworld to the upper one. See EMERGENCE MYTH. [EWV]

possession The culturally sanctioned displacement of personality occasioned by the presumed entrance of a deity or other supernatural being into the body or head of the worshipper, who thereupon becomes the god or saint and, as such, speaks or dances or otherwise be-haves as this being is held to behave, giving instruction, effecting cures, foretelling the future, or in various other ways acting in behalf of its believers. The phenomenon is of world-wide distribution. Where possession occurs, it is the supreme form of religious expression, the out-standing exemplification of the phenomenon called the religious thrill that has been held by some students to represent the quintessence of the religious experience. It is exemplified in the shamanism of the North Amer-ican Indians and the aborigines of Siberia, in the devo-tional states of the early European saints, and in the possession dances of African and New World Negro. Its varied forms reflect but different manifestations, however, of the underlying psychological and religious phenomenon whose manifestations are always consistent within a given culture, not only as concerns their outer aspects, but also as to their inner meaning and function. In some cultures the patterns underlying the forms of possession are difficult to discern because of the seemingly idiosyncratic behavior of those possessed. However, on closer acquaintance, the patterned regularities which underlie the individual expression of the phenomenon as found among a given group become apparent and make it possible to subsume variant behavior in terms of the over-all tradition. Though various students have tended to treat of possession as a psychopathological phenomenon, analysis of it in terms of its setting in the cultures where it is found has shown the essential fallaciousness of this point of view. The person possessed, as in the case of the shaman, is a specialist in the manipulation and comprehension of the supernatural, and there is little or no evidence to show that such individuals are any less stable or less well adjusted than the other members of the societies of which they form a part. Among Africans and New World Negroes, there is evidence that it is those persons who are possessed by their deities who are the best adjusted in their societies, possession here being a mechanism which affords the release of tensions and the resolution of guilt feelings through projection of these onto the god. Possession, that is, is a disciplined, specialized series of reactions to well-established behavior cues. In Haiti, it has been shown that only those among the possessed who are not disciplined and whose gods come to them at any time and in any place are to be considered as psychopathological cases. See DEDARI TUNDJUNG BIRU; DIVINATION; ERÉ.

M. J. HERSKOVITS

☞ Spiritual possession of the body of a human being, either by evil spirits to cause illness, or by the tutelary spirits of a shaman, while known in Middle America, is relatively rare. [GMF]

potato The edible, farinaceous tuber of a plant (*Solanum tuberosum*) of the nightshade family. This plant, which probably originated in the Andes of South America, gradually spread among the tribes long before the coming of the Europeans. It was probably introduced into Europe by some of Pizarro's priests and was introduced into England by Drake. At first it was valued in Europe as a strengthening and aphrodisiac food, and at one time potatoes sold for as high as $1,000 a pound. In 1728 they were forbidden by law in Scotland because the potato was an unholy plant of the nightshade family and not mentioned in the Bible.

Some say that the potato should be planted on a starry night to assure plenty of eyes. It is quite general folk belief, however, that potatoes, like other root crops, should be planted in the dark of the moon, if they are to thrive. In coastal communities potatoes planted on a rising tide will swell with the tide. When the first new potatoes are eaten, all the family should partake of them, otherwise the spirits will be offended and the crop will not keep. If they are planted on Good Friday, there will also be a poor crop. The potato is a quite general pocket piece in Europe and America against rheumatism and sciatica. In Holland it was necessary that the potato be stolen to be efficacious as a cure; in Yorkshire it must be dried in the morning sun and protected from the afternoon sun. In parts of the United States it is carried as a cure and protection against warts. Warts, if rubbed with a raw potato which is then buried or hidden, will disappear as the potato rots. In Newfoundland a sliced baked potato is placed in a stocking which is then tied around the neck to cure sore throat. In Texas scraped raw potato is placed on burns and frostbite. In Italy and Sicily if the name of a person is written on a slip of paper and then fastened to a potato by as many pins as possible, the victim will die in great pain within the month. Mississippi Negroes consider a raw potato poultice good for a black eye.

In Ireland the water from boiled potatoes is rubbed on aches, sprains, and broken bones; but to wash in potato water causes warts. A stone or pebble boiled in the pot with potatoes is believed to have great curative properties. A roasted potato is recommended as a remedy for thrush. A kettle of boiled potatoes dumped in a neighbor's field will keep his crops from doing well. The Irish also have a saying which is the advice of an old man to a young man at table: Be eating one potato, peeling a second, have a third in your fist, and your eye on a fourth.

Potiphar's wife A folktale motif (K2111) taking its name from the incident of Joseph and Zuleika, the wife of Potiphar, in the Bible (*Gen.* xxxix). Joseph, a slave in the house of Potiphar, aroused by his beauty the passion of the woman. She attempted to seduce the youth, but he refused her, at first diplomatically, then, as she grew more importunate, very brusquely. In anger (the motif is sometimes called the woman scorned motif), she tore his clothes, called for help, and accused him of trying to rape her. Joseph was thrown into prison for the supposed crime; in some rabbinical tellings of the story, her deception was exposed and he was imprisoned only until the scandal should have abated. The motif is found in many other folktales throughout the world. In Greek legend, Antea or Sthenobia, wife of Proetus, thus accused Bellerophon: here the motif is associated with the letter of death. The ancient Egyptian story of the *Two Brothers* uses the same motif; Bata is accused by Anpu's wife and escapes being killed through the warning of the friendly animals. The Potiphar's wife motif, sometimes disguised or only hinted at, is found in North American Indian tales all over the continent, but especially in the Plains and Central Woodlands areas. See RONAN.

potlatch An extravagant ceremonial distribution of property by North Pacific Coast chiefs to chiefs and nobles of the moiety opposite to their own, given in order to establish superiority in social and political status, or to assume inherited status. North Pacific Coast potlatches were general practice among the nobility of this region, from the Haida of Queen Charlotte Island to the Kwakiutl and Nootka of Vancouver Island. Potlatches to assume or establish status were given on at least two formal occasions: when a chief's house was to be built or when a mortuary column was to be erected prior to a new chief's assumption of the rank, names, dignity, and social privileges of his deceased predecessor. Potlatches were also given by chiefs as a means of wreaking vengeance on an enemy; a chief "shamed" his enemy by destroying valuable "coppers" (native copper plates), killing slaves, burning great quantities of oil, and giving away large amounts of food, dishes, boxes, blankets, and other goods. The chief's enemy would then either have to give an even greater potlatch in return, or lose the reputation which he had formerly enjoyed. Narratives about famous potlatches and references to this custom are current in North Pacific Coast mythology especially in the pseudo-historic myths of the wanderings of groups in this area; see for example Marius Barbeau, *Alaska Beckons* (Caldwell, Idaho, 1947). A recent account of the day-by-day progress of a potlatch is contained in G. P. Murdock's study of Haida potlatches, *Rank and Potlatch Among the Haida* (Yale University Publications in Anthropology No. 13, 1936). [EWV]

pot of basil A folk motif (T85.3) popularized by Boccaccio's story in the *Decameron* (iv, 5) in which the brothers of Isabella, a young girl of Florence, discover that she and young Lorenzo are lovers. They lure Lorenzo into the forest, murder, and bury him. Isabella discovers the place, secretly takes up the head of her lover, hides it in a flower pot, and plants above it the love-plant, basil. This she cares for tenderly and constantly, often weeping beside it. The brothers, observing her behavior, become suspicious, take the pot and discover the head of Lorenzo; knowing their deed is discovered, they flee from the city. Isabella dies brokenhearted. John Keats further popularized this story in a poem (1820) *Isabella, or the Pot of Basil.*

pototo The Inca war trumpet, which has only one note. The instrument still survives among the modern Quechua, who use it during the ritual of the Mass.

Pot-tilter A terrible old woman of Crow Indian folktale, known also to the Hidatsa and the Gros Ventre. She keeps a big pot always boiling. When she tilts it towards anyone it sucks them in. See MONSTERS; OGRE.

Powamu Hopi Indian 9-day kachina ceremony, held annually in February to prepare the crops. This Hopi ceremony, like that of Niman or the home-going kachina ceremony, includes dramatization, group dancing, and altar ritual. Clowns attend the ceremony, play ball, dance, and indulge in pranks. The corn god or spirit, Müy'ingwa, is impersonated by the Powamu chief in this ceremony. See BEAN DANCE; BEANS; NIMAN. [EWV]

power in dung Peculiar power is believed to be present in the dung of animals and humans, among many North American Indian tribes—especially among the Eastern Woodlands groups, who believed that dung possessed properties which could ward off disease. The Mohegan-Pequot, for example, used fresh cow dung, bound on the face, to cure toothache; sheep dung, mixed with the urine of the youngest child in the family, was used against measles. The Delaware and Shawnee Shuck Faces smeared their hands and arms with human or cow dung, and shook hands with spectators in their rounds of the villages made to ward off disease. Another use of dung is mentioned for the Mandan-Hidatsa of the Plains: during a famine people scattered buffalo dung (which was often also used for fuel in this region) all over the plateau, repeating as they did so the formula, "This is a young buffalo bull." The next day the plateau was full of buffalo. See LONE MAN. The Shawnee, beside using dung as a curative or preventive agent as mentioned above, tell how the dog, when begging of the Creator to be allowed to live with people, promised that he would eat their dung for his sustenance. Human excrement was also carefully secreted by many tribes all over the continent, so that it could not be secured for purposes of contagious magic. See EXCREMENTS SWALLOWED. [EWV]

practical jokes (North American Indian) Practical jokes serve either as the subject or as incidental elements in several trickster tales; e.g. 1) the short tale of *Wildcat and Coyote*, in which Coyote pushes sleeping Wildcat's nose and tail in, thus making him snub nosed and short tailed—Wildcat retaliates by pulling out sleeping Coyote's nose and tail, making them long; 2) an incident in *Coyote and Porcupine* in which Porcu-

pine kills Coyote's child, sets the child under a tree and stuffs its mouth full of buffalo fat, then goes up in a tree and laughs when Coyote returns to the scene; 3) the tale in which trickster is taught to fish through the ice with his tail—his tail freezes and he is stuck to the ice; 4) the tale of *Raccoon and the Blind Men* in which Raccoon joins two blind men and steals the meat they have cooked—they accuse each other, and when Raccoon hits one, they fight in earnest until he leaves, laughing, and they realize what has happened.

Practical jokes are also part of daily life; see for examples W. W. Hill, *Navaho Indian Humor* (General Series in Anthropology, No. 7, 1938). [EWV]

pradakṣiṇa In India, the circumambulation of a sacred object or place as part of a sacred or secular ritual, especially for purposes of purification. Pradakṣiṇa is performed keeping the right side always towards the sacred object, e.g. a building, shrine, or tomb. The site chosen for a new house must be circumambulated three times while sprinkling the ground with water. In India, China, Tibet, and Japan, galleries and walls are provided around stūpas and shrines for the circumambulation of pilgrims. A funeral pyre is usually circumambulated by the chief mourner in the reverse direction, and four times instead of five (the auspicious number).

prairie-dog A burrowing rodent (*Cynomys ludovicianus*); the most familiar American species is distributed on the Great Plains from Montana to northern Mexico. Prairie-dogs live in large villages which are easily visible by the mound of earth thrown up at the mouth of each burrow. Prairie-dogs occur as friendly animal actors in some Plains and Southwestern Indian tales; in the Plains also occasionally as the Hoodwinked Dancers. Among the Jicarilla Apache Prairie-dog is associated with rain and giving or leading thirsty human beings to water. [EWV]

Prairie Falcon Hero of South Central California Indian hero tales. Prairie Falcon has rather simple adventures such as rescuing his wife and losing his eyes. [EWV]

praise names Term used for designations of deities, royalty, warriors, hunters, and others that permit public recognition of their achievements. These are found in all Africa and are a part of the Old World pattern, being also present in the Mediterranean area, and Europe and Asia. See ILU; also section *Praise names* in AFRICAN AND NEW WORLD NEGRO FOLKLORE. [MJH]

Prajāpati Literally, Lord of Creatures: in Vedic mythology, an epithet applied to several gods, among them Hiraṇyagarbha, Soma, Savitṛi, and Indra; later the name of a distinct creator-deity, recognized as the chief and father of the gods. In the *Sūtras* Prajāpati is identified with Brahmā. The name is also given to the seven (or ten) ṛishis as the fathers of the human race. According to the *Brāhmaṇas*, Prajāpati created the world by performing austerities. In one myth there was only water and the waters performed austerities until a golden egg came into existence. From this came Prajāpati who uttered the sounds "bhūr" which became the earth, "bhuvah" which became the firmament, and "svark" which became the sky. See AŚVAMEDHA; BHRIGU; DAKSHA; DHĀTRI.

Prakṛiti The primitive matter from which the universe is evolved as opposed to spirit or Puruṣa; the Creative

Force, prototype of the female; also, a Hindu goddess equivalent to Māyā or Śākti. In philosophical Brahmanism, the belief in the interworkings of a spiritual force, Puruṣa, with a primordial material force, Prakṛiti, to create the universe is an ancient concept.

prāy Term for the evil spirits of Cambodian folklore. Among them are the spirits of women who have died in childbirth (*khmóc prāy*.) These sit in trees and terrify passersby by laughing at them or throwing stones and killing them. The most feared of all the prāy is the ghost of a woman who has died during pregnancy, accompanied by the ghost of the fetus. These two do not feel kindly toward the living. The sorcerer is always summoned to dispose of all miscarriages. Ostensibly he confines the fetus and its spirit in a jar which he throws into running water. Usually, however, he roasts the fetus, blackens it with soot and varnish, and preserves it in a little bag. Henceforth it is his constant companion and aid, and he feeds it daily. A fetus thus treated is called *kón prāy* (literally, son of the spirit). Its power is so great that the sorcerer is henceforth invulnerable and successful in everything.

prayer An address to a higher power requesting some boon or some guidance. According to Tylor, prayer was at first a personal affair between the supplicant and the deity or power, and it asked for some definite thing. Later prayer developed into the request for ethical guidance known in the modern religions. Also, whereas prayers at first were spontaneous and personal expressions, they developed into set formulas in which a strict accuracy of phrasing, cadence, and the like was necessary to make the prayer efficacious. Here the religious prayer resembles very strongly the magic spell or charm in which any omission or deviation from form is ruinous. Prayers may vary in tenor from the begging to the demanding or threatening or reproachful. Also imperative are the correct gestures and postures—e.g. bowing, genuflection, prostration—and the correct costume—prayer shawls, covered or uncovered head, etc. Prayer when thus rigidly circumscribed becomes a form of magic; such methods of praying as the Tibetan prayer wheel lose the personal element almost completely. Set forms develop into a liturgy, fixed for certain occasions, and to be performed by competent officials. Prayers therefore must often be made through a third party, one who knows the correct forms or possesses the power to speak to the divinity—king, priest, elders of the family, etc. Sometimes the prayer is addressed to an intercessor, a divinity who the supplicant feels will intercede on his behalf with that deity who possesses the power to accomplish the desired end; prayers to an intercessor are known from ancient Hittite texts. Sometimes prayer is to such a sympathetic deity who is thought to have power to cancel or supersede the actions of another. Thus, the patron god of a city may be asked to remove the anger of the plague god. Very often prayer is accompanied by sacrifice, gifts to the deity on the principle *do ut des*, I give that you may give. In such instances great point is made of the offering and a request or demand for reciprocation is made.

☞ Prayers or petitions were universal among American Indians, varying in form all the way from single sentences informally uttered by lone individuals to long discourses delivered for large groups. Interesting differences in attitude distinguish the prayers of the Eastern and Plains Indians from those of some Southwestern Indians. In the East the person asking for benefits attempts to render himself pitiful in the sight of the supernatural beings or deity, in order to arouse the deity's compassion, and thus be granted what he asks. "For I am a pitiful man" . . . "for we are pitiful people" is a set, ever-recurrent phrase in prayer texts from this region, and ritual crying often accompanies or concludes the prayer. Prayer texts need not be recited letter-perfect, either; the more pitiable a speaker can make himself to the deities the better the prayer, and so priests and others have wide latitude in the delivery of prayers at stated times during sacred ceremonies.

In the Southwest prayer is often not a plea, but "the compulsive word" which gods and supernaturals must obey; this is especially true for the Navaho, and for some, at least, of the Pueblo peoples. Pueblo prayer, it has been said, is petition, "asking for this or that" in the right, or formal, way, but when one comes to examine these so-called petitions one finds they are couched, if not in the imperative, at least as commands. For example, when a Hano farmer puts down prayer-feathers in his field he says, "My field, you will be good all the time," or when a Zuñi hunter finds deer tracks and puts down prayer-meal and shell, he says, "This day, my fathers, my mothers, in some little hollow, in some little thicket, you will reveal yourselves to me."

The above are personal prayers, accompanied by offerings, as are nearly all such, not only in the pueblos but elsewhere on the continent. Far more elaborate prayers are delivered by Pueblo priests, chiefs, and members of the numerous Pueblo societies; these latter are remarkable for their formulaic phraseology, for their use of color and directional symbolism, for patterned repetition, and for the fact that, to be efficacious, they must be delivered letter-perfect. Misplacing or forgetting words invalidates Pueblo Indian prayer or song.

A short example of Zuñi prayer is given by Parsons, in the War chief's prayer over his winter solstice prayer-sticks for the War Brothers:

"To my children long life, old age, all good fortune, whatsoever you will grant;
> So that I may raise corn,
> So that I may raise beans,
> So that I may raise wheat,
> So that I may raise squash,
> So that with all good fortune I may be blessed."

(Parsons, *Pueblo Indian Religion*, pp. 312–13.)

Contrast this with an Eastern Woodlands type of prayer, offered by the leader of the Delaware Indian Big House ceremony on the ninth evening:

"I am thankful, Oh thou Great Spirit, that we have been spared to live until now to purify with cedar smoke this our House, because that has always been the rule in the ancient world since the beginning of creation. When anyone thinks of his children how fortunate it is to see them enjoying good health. And this is the cause of a feeling of happiness when we consider how greatly we are blessed by the benevolence of our father, the Great Spirit. And we can also feel the great strength of him our grandfather Fire for which we cause him pleasure when we purify and take care with it, and when we feed him this cedar. All of this together we offer in esteem to him, our grandfather, because he has compassion when he sees how pitifully we behave while we are pleading with all the spirit-forces above as they were created and with all those here on earth. Give us everything, our father, that we ask of you Great Spirit even the Creator. (Speck, *Delaware Indian Big House Ceremony*, p. 151 and n. 2, 3.)

Discussion, analysis, and examples of American Indian prayer texts are scattered through the large body of ethnographic literature on the North American Indians. A few particularly helpful references are: Gladys A. Reichard, *Prayer; The Compulsive Word*, Monographs of the American Ethnological Society 7, New York, 1944 (Navaho prayers); Elsie Clews Parsons, *Pueblo Indian Religion*, 2 vols., Chicago, 1939, pp. 311 ff., also entries in Index under Prayer(s); Frank G. Speck, *A Study of the Delaware Indian Big House Ceremony* (Publications of the Pennsylvania Historical Commission, vol. II, 1931); Fox Indian texts edited and annotated by Truman Michelson, published in the Reports and Bulletins of the Bureau of American Ethnology; Margot Astrov, ed., *The Winged Serpent*, New York, 1946. [EWV]

☞ A certain number of the traditional prayers addressed by the Incas to their gods, in particular to the supreme god, Viracocha, have been preserved. They are couched in a solemn and grandiose style reminiscent of that of the psalms. They contain unfortunately many passages which are obscure to us. These prayers recited by priests were repeated by the assembly of the faithful. The Supreme God of the Yahgan Indians was also implored with prayers which were set in a traditional form.

Prayers play an insignificant part in the religion of the primitive tribes of the Chaco and of the Amazon. Spirits are more often coerced than asked for favors. The requests which the Indians make to the sun god (Apinayé) or to the "masters of the game" are generally short sentences stating their wish. [AM]

prehuman race   The First People of the Mythical Age, who later changed or were changed into animals, birds, rocks, and other natural phenomena and elements prior to the appearance of human beings on the earth. This is a widespread assumption in North American Indian mythologies in all areas except the Pueblo Southwest, where there are few or no beliefs in a race of people prior to those who emerged. In southern California, the concept of a prehuman race is elaborated on: members of this race are born from the culture hero, Wiyot. They multiplied, and ate soil for food. After Wiyot's death a new deity, Chingichnich, appeared; this being converted the first people into animals and plants, or into spirits having power over animals and plants, and caused them to scatter over the earth. [EWV]

'pren-ba   Literally, a string of beads: the Tibetan rosary, an essential part of a lāma's dress. Nearly every layman and woman also owns a 'pren-ba on which he or she stores up merit at every opportunity. The rosary contains 108 beads of uniform size to which three extra beads are added at the end before knotting to indicate to the teller the completion of a cycle. Attached to the rosary are two strings of ten metallic rings, one terminated by a small bell, the other by a miniature dor-je. The metal rings, which act as counters, on the dor-je string register units of bead-cycles while those on the bell string register tens of cycles.

The 'pren-ba are made of gold, precious stones, wood, snake vertebræ, and shells. The type of material is determined by the special deity to whom worship is paid and by the sect to which the lāma belongs. A rosary made from discs of human skull is used for the worship of Vajrabhairava. The patron god of Tibet, Avalokita, is usually depicted with a 'pren-ba in his hand.

Prester John   Stories about Prester (Presbyter) John, fabulous king descended from the magi, have become so embroidered by marvels and magic that the authentication of the documents involved has become most uncertain. Generally, Prester John is thought to have been a Nestorian priest-king of the Orient who wrote a letter to the Byzantine Emperor Manuel in the 12th century. Although the letter was forged, it brought together a great many beliefs about the mysterious Orient current at that time. In the 300 odd years that passed between the assumed date of the letter and about 1500 when it was published, new marvels were added or invented by persons whose imagination was stimulated by the legend of Prester John himself or by travelers' tales.

Prester John boasts that in his domains there flows a fountain from Mt. Olympus, not three days' journey from Paradise. Three drafts from it, taken fasting, will preserve the drinker from infirmity, and no matter how long he lives he will always appear to be 30 years old. A sea of sand contains edible fish and a river of stones has salamanders which live only in fire. Prester John's robes were made of them, and these robes, too, could be cleaned only by fire. The country has no crime, poverty, or falsehood. Eagles bring stones which if worn on the finger will restore sight or if lawfully consecrated will make the wearer invisible, dispel envy and hatred, and promote concord. An herb *asidios* drives out impure spirits and forces them to disclose their origin.

John's palace is like the one the Apostle Thomas built for Gundaphorus of India. The gates are of sardonyx and because they are mixed with the horn of the horned serpents prevent anyone from bringing poisons into the palace. John is kept chaste by sleeping on a sapphire couch. The court is paved with onyx so that the virtue of the stones will keep the duelers courageous. A magic mirror reveals all plots in John's and his neighbors' domains. Another palace built by John's father has the virtue that no matter how hungry you may be when you enter, you will come out well filled.

Later marvels were man-eating ants which mined gold by night. Men there lived on manna; by magic and incantation they tamed flying dragons and rode them through the air. John had five stones which controlled the temperature for a five mile radius. Other stones turned water to milk or wine. Others caused fish or wild game to assemble for slaughter. Still others would produce a great fire if sprinkled with dragon's blood. A tree bears a healing apple. A chapel is always just big enough for its congregation; it is made of glass. A hollow stone is guarded by two old men. The water in it is four fingers deep. Men who desire to become Christians enter and if they are sincere the water will rise to cover them four times.

Other earlier references to Prester John are a letter from Odo, Abbot of St. Remy, who in the early 12th century reported on a trip to Rome. There he met the Archbishop of India who told the Pope that the body of the Apostle Thomas was preserved in a rich church. The church was encircled by a river which could be forded only on the feast day of the saint. On that day the saint raised his arm to receive gifts, but he refused gifts from heretics. The Pope forbade the spreading of this nonsense but was later persuaded that the story was true.

One John of India, a patriarch, is said to have visited Calixtus II in the second decade of the 12th century. He told of the river Physon which flows from Paradise bearing gold and gems. He also told of the miraculous body of the apostle. In 1145, Otto of Freising had heard of a king "John Nestorian" whose kingdom was beyond Persia and Armenia. He had enormous wealth and his scepter was an emerald.

Space does not permit the tracing of parallels to these marvels in other countries, though the fact that the sources of the Prester John material cluster the 12th century may be relevant, for it was at this time that the European imagination was constructing the great romantic cycles of Arthur and Charlemagne and was being stimulated by travelers' tales brought back by the young men who had been on the Crusades. [RDJ]

pret or **preta** In Hindu belief, the spirit, the size of a man's thumb, of the dead which wanders around its old home for a year after the funeral rites; also, the ghost of a crippled person or of a child who dies prematurely. Prets have been supplanted in popular belief by the *vetālas*.

In Buddhist belief, the prets are ghosts who live at crossroads, congregate at boundaries and outside houses. They are a special class of ghosts who must expiate a type of karma which makes their relatives forget them. The sins for which they have become prets are niggardliness, envy, and refusal of alms. They are hungry or thirsty, look like burnt trees after a forest fire, or have bellies like mountains and throats the size of a needle. See ANCESTOR WORSHIP. Compare ACHERI; BHŪT; CHUREL; PISĀCHA; VAMPIRE; YAKSHA.

Pretos Literally, blacks: a Portuguese men's dance, part of the procession held on the feast of the Assumption of the Virgin, August 15, at Arcozelo da Sierra. The dance has all the attributes of ritual clowning: blackened faces, bells, red costumes, obscene farce. To guitar accompaniment the performers conclude with a fandango. [GPK]

Priapus The garden god; a faunlike creature with a notable erect penis. He ensured the fertility of gardens, crops, animals, women. A son of Aphrodite, he was a late importation into Rome from Lampascus where Pausanias reported he was supreme among all gods. In Rome he became identified with Mutinuus, another sexual deity. Stories by Augustine and Lactantius that Roman women embraced him and had sexual orgies on his permanently erect member are obscure, though, in view of the changed sexual mores of our time and the structure of some of the figures that have been preserved, not impossible. As an amulet, the figure of Priapus protects against the evil eye. His sacrifice was the first-fruits of the farm. Priapus belongs to the complex of the earth spirits of whom Pan is the best known. In the Middle Ages he forsook his orgies with the nymphs and became a saint protector of cattle and women in childbirth. Deities with erect or exaggerated members known in all parts of the world are commonly called Priapic. See PHALLISM. [RDJ]

primeval water In the beginning, water covers the face of the earth. With the exception of Southwestern Pueblo origin myths, all the North American world-origin myths start either with primeval water or a world deluge or flood; sometimes primeval water and deluge myths both occur in the same tribe. In the far west an interesting juxtaposition of primeval water and flood myths occurs. A small group of eight contiguous central California tribes (Tübatulabal, Western Mono, Yokuts, Salinan, Southern Miwok, Patwin, Northwestern Maidu, and Wintu) share the primeval water myth; this small nucleus is completely surrounded by tribes having the deluge incidents of caused, or arriving and receding, floods. The incident which usually follows either primeval water or the deluge is that of earth-diver. See A. H. Gayton, "Areal Affiliations of California Folktales" (*AA* 37: 582–99, 1935). See INDONESIAN MYTHOLOGY. [EWV]

primitive and folk art The entire product that might be considered in this space ranges in time from the Willendorf Venus of at least ten thousand years ago to the (not so different) nude scrawled today on the back fence; in technique from crudely beaten bark cloth to Flemish pillow lace employing as many as 1200 bobbins; in form from an armband to a temple, from a fetish to a scarecrow.

A complete range of expression occurs—as literal in intention as a Koryak carving or a decoy duck; as stylized as an Easter Island statue, the Haida Indian Raven or Chiriquí Alligator, or the lotus and tulip motif; as geometric as Oriental window fretwork, a French-Canadian Assumption sash, or a Peruvian textile; as symbolic as the Gnostic wheel, the evil eye, the Hopi rain sign, the unicorn in a medieval tapestry, or the figurehead on a sailing ship.

Virtually every known material is at some point converted to an art use. Sculpture includes the tiny figurines of Mexican jade, Eskimo bone, Oriental ivory, and the mammoth stone heads of Central America, the colossal tree-trunks of the Pacific Coast Indians. Painted depictions appear, not merely on paper, wood, and cloth, but on hides and pieces of bark, on eggshells and glass, on pebbles or the faces of cliffs, the walls of caves or the sides of houses, on shields and weapons and boats, on bowls, in sand, on the human body.

The title, under which a fragment of this vast material is here assembled, is composed of three words, subject to as many varying interpretations, perhaps, as any three that could be sensibly combined at one time. The question of what is art will no doubt remain unsettled as long as creative activity continues. There are apparently as many definitions of "folk" as there are folklorists. "Primitive" has a number of valid meanings, with the difficulty that anthropologists usually think in terms of one, artists of another, and general readers with a hazy mixture of them all. Each of these terms is construed in a strict sense by some writers and in a general way by others.

Art terminology presents many unsolved problems and their solution will depend, not only on the sorting of innumerable factors and objects, but on an increased comprehension of graphic and plastic communication.

In this respect, a study of the forms and symbols rooted in primitive and folk art is as basic as the study of etymology in a language.

I. Primitive Art

The word primitive, which means first, early, or elementary—a very common and basic group of concepts—is applied to many kinds of art which may have little in common except the label. It designates, among other things: (1) the first known art chronologically, i.e. the prehistoric; (2) the art of an elementary culture; (3) the elementary or early art of any culture; (4) the early art of any period or art movement; (5) any art or art object that is elementary in regard to technique and forms, ergo, any undeveloped or crude art; (6) art which imitates or resembles the style qualities associated with early cultures.

Primitive art, as the term is used here, covers the first three of these meanings—that is, the art of primitive cultures, of groups whose general development is (or while it is) at a primitive stage. The other uses of the word, while they can hardly be called erroneous, cause confusion for they apply to art which may fall into the "sophisticated" category. According to sense (4) for example, an early Renaissance painter like Giotto and the pioneer cubist, Cézanne, are called primitives, but these unique individuals are entirely outside the field of art labeled either primitive or folk. In the same sense, "primitive American" is perhaps the most common designation of the early art of the white settlers in North America, but this art, offshoot of European culture, is better labeled "early American" or "colonial folk art" (see Section II); the truly primitive arts of the Americas are, of course, Indian. Similarly "Early Christian Art" seems preferable to "primitive Christian," which is applied, especially in French, to that development in areas already civilized.

As for sense (5) it is obvious that crude or undeveloped examples and forms of art may occur at any stage of any culture. One might cite the *sidewalk* or *backhouse art* of our own non-primitive society, or the sketch a businessman might make for a house plan or a boat. Crudeness is characteristic of the decay as well as the beginning of art forms, as in the *tourist* or *souvenir art* found in port cities or roadside stands all over the world. Deliberate imitations of primitive art (sense 6) or sophisticated art in a "primitive" vein should always be called "pseudo-" or "neo-primitive."

The student of the primitive has four great areas of art spread out before him—in the north polar regions, among the native peoples of the Pacific Ocean, the African Negroes, and the Indians of the Western Hemisphere—for in these areas primitive art is still produced or survived recently enough to come under the investigation of scholars of our own time as a living art.

Other parts of the world are dominated or penetrated by one or another of the elaborate art cultures: the Oriental (including Chinese, Japanese, Indonesian, Indian, Persian); those of ancient Asia Minor and the Mediterranean (including Egyptian, Semitic, Byzantine, Mohammedan, Coptic, Hellenistic); the Euro-American, beginning with the spread of classical art in Europe and the Conquest or Columbian era in the Americas, together with Euro-American colonial offshoots in various parts of the world. In such areas the primitive is to be sought either in isolated tribes (such as the Todas south of Mysore in India and the Naga tribes in the hills of Assam) or as a remote layer buried, sometimes literally, under centuries of an elaborate art.

The oldest known primitive art dates back to paleolithic man. Others are relatively recent; the Polynesian arts, for example, have all arisen since the birth of Christ. Some primitive forms have set off a great tradition in art, as in the case of a carved stone lingam of the third millennium B.C. which is the prototype of thousands in Hindu sanctuaries today. Others, like the art of the Southern Hunters of South America or the Australian aborigines, maintain a simple archaic pattern for centuries. One form, rock pictures of lively hunting scenes, has been produced throughout the entire span from prehistoric to living man.

The layman thinks of primitive art as rudimentary; and it is true that it includes the first dramatic demonstration of man's position as a creative being. But within a primitive pattern of life there is considerable range from elementary to advanced, both in general development and in art development. And there are instances where creativeness or the "art sense" inexplicably outstrips the rest of the development, as with the Bushmen, who express a remarkably vivid concept of movement within the narrow range of a single simple art form, and others where it lags behind as among the Manus Islanders, who, like many civilized people, preferred purchase to creation.

Art which is labeled "advanced primitive" is often of such caliber that it is necessary to lay aside any connotation of crudeness or esthetic incipience that the word may have; for, with the great "re-discovery" of primitive art which began some decades ago, it became recognized as ranking with or beyond much of sophisticated art in esthetic terms. To observers accustomed to thinking of art as Western art, with perhaps a slight bow to Oriental imports, this recognition came as something of a shock. Actually, it was to be expected, for under primitive conditions many of the circumstances which seem to foster artistic creation are automatically present—the close contact with nature, the acute observation required for survival under elemental living conditions, the skill with the hands developed by the necessity for making one's own utensils, weapons, and shelter, the unbroken continuity between the need, creation, and use of an object by each individual, the periods of leisure occupied by resort to one's own skills and imagination.

Some other factors which seem operative in the very powerful impact of primitive art bear analysis because they vary from circumstances with which we are familiar. One is the tremendous demand placed upon the graphic and plastic arts in a non-literate society, as a *means of communication,* record-keeping, and calculating; for as soon as early man desired to communicate to someone not present (beyond the range of gesture and speech), pictures and symbols became necessary and a whole range of art forms sprang into existence. To this demand may be ascribed the evolution of pictographs, hieroglyphs, and the identifying symbols of individuals and clans; wampum, churingas, the carved message sticks of New South Wales; the navigation maps of the Marshall Islands; the buffalo-hide paintings of the Plains Indians, recording encounters or giving directions. Such art may be conventionalized for decorative purposes, as in the fishing exploits carved on Eskimo horn or tusk, a battle depicted in the design on a Sioux legging.

Not only were art forms forced to develop for such purposes but, with the effort to convey graphically the broader range of speech, they developed along concise, abstract, and symbolic lines closely related to our concept of the esthetic. The Haida Indians were able to depict complete myths in carving: how Raven stole the sun and threw it into the sky; how he drew mankind from a clamshell or stole salmon from Beaver for the common use. One famous example of story-telling art constitutes a sort of illustration, though it is highly symbolic and ritualistic. That is the sand painting executed under the direction of the priest during Navaho ceremonials as he chants his people's stories or rituals. These beautifully stylized pictures depict such elements as the central sky-mountain (a white disk), the water-of-life pool, the plant-of-life (a sort of blossoming pole), the whirling logs (swastika) of the Milky Way. The characters are pole-shaped people with identifying symbols—Cloud People bearing cloud sacks (symbolized by triangles), rising- and setting-sun gods, rain-boy and rain-girl—or the thunder-bird with human arms that give off lightning and bird wings that define the Milky Way. The picture may be encircled by an anthropomorphic rainbow, a horseshoe-shaped band having a head at one end and feet at the other.

A second factor is the use of art by various peoples in the *attempt to control their universe* without the aid of technology or any scientific understanding of natural forces. In our ready-made world it is difficult to envision the problems which thus occupy the primitive and his method of meeting them. He has to evoke the rain, control the flood, carve a guardian spirit to protect his home, so decorate his shield as to terrify his enemy, give his weapon the power to strike and his boat the power to see or walk on water, build a trap for evil spirits, find a charm against disease, attract game, put a spell on beasts of prey, forestall disasters, guarantee his strength, courage, skill, or the fertility of his crops. Such needs find answers in the shape of art: the fetish, which in West Africa is not endowed with power until it is smeared with color; the totem masks, carving, and tattooing by which the individual or group can acquire the qualities of the preferred animal; the designs traced on the skin before going hunting (Jivaro) and the scarification adopted at puberty; the amulet carved like a hand which gives skill to the weaver (Peru); the charm that keeps away disease, like the Bolli Atap or benevolent demon of Borneo; the bull-roarer that summons the god or scares off demons.

The shaman's dress of Siberia offers an example of precisely how the meager materials of primitive art are made to serve such remarkable ends—one which answers its purpose ingeniously though not with notable esthetic quality. The shaman, as the intermediary with the supernatural, is required at times to visit the land of spirits, either above or below the earth. In order to fly there, he puts on a coat representing a bird's skin, on which feathers are represented by fringe, bead tassels, or elliptical metal plates. Hung on the coat are three disks, symbolizing his destination, the sun, the moon, and the icehole through which he descends to the underworld,

together with the symbols of his particular spirits who will protect him. At the same time, to retain his human identity, metal plates of armbones, shoulderblades, etc., are attached to the proper places on the coat. To guarantee his return he wears a bridle which his attendant carefully holds during the ceremony. In this garment, there is created a man-bird fusion, the use of which translates the human to the supernatural or bridges the gap between the known and the unknown.

It is apparent that, in order to control his world, it is necessary for the primitive to evolve some explanation of the forces beyond his control and in some way manage to get them on his side. Therefore, he invents innumerable supernatural beings, half fantastic, half a compound of beast and man, together with the semi-mythical culture heroes of his people, and it is these creatures, far more than actual persons, who populate the world of his art. They appear, not only in statues and pictures, but on vessels, utensils, tools, weapons, housebeams, gables, boats, or garments. To propitiate, worship, or celebrate them, he devises masks, rattles, dancing shields, ritual body painting, ceremonial vessels, musical instruments decorated with magical designs, and other ritual objects. Upon death, human beings are usually thought of as entering the spirit world, and ancestor worship in many cultures accounts for images, memorial slabs, mortuary statues, receptacles for the soul (such as a *zemi* of the West Indies or spirit image of Leti), the ancestor hooks of New Guinea, the *hei-tiki* ornaments of New Zealand, the Indonesian soul-ship for the trip to the other world, token objects for the use of the dead.

These magic-religious motivations, as they are sometimes called, result in some objects which are to the casual observer mere curiosities, but wherever they constitute a strong element in the culture they tend to produce a very intense art, composed of forms which seldom have a literal prototype in nature, but which carry a profound conviction of their own reality and power to anyone who looks with receptive mind. This conviction reflects that of the creator, for to the primitive the art he creates, like his dreams, visions, gods, and myths, is likely to be quite as real as the natural world around him. In the *korwar* (ancestral image) of New Guinea, the actual skull is sometimes embedded. Iroquois Indians carved certain masks only from a living tree (that they might have power). Some images in South America, some heads in Africa require the use of actual skin.

A third factor, though it is one deeply involved in the preceding, is the primitive habit of *thinking in terms of concrete imagery*, as contrasted with the less graphic thinking of peoples at a later stage of development, for this concrete imagery is the mental material of art. For example, the universe is contemplated (and depicted) not from the scientific viewpoint of the telescope, nor as a vague void summarized in an abstract word like "cosmos," but actually as a flat platter with corrugated rim, floating on primordial waters under the inverted platter of the sky (ancient Egypt); as the cosmic ocean or the endless snake on which a giant sleeps (Hindu); as an egg with sky and earth as white and yolk and primal man as the embryo (Chinese); as a mythical mountain rising from a snow-covered plain, where buffaloes were kept at the beginning of time (Plains Indians); as the cosmic bullhide on which Father Sky is painted with sun, moon, and stars on his body and Mother Earth with the four sacred plants (Navaho).

It is an obvious corollary that, in order to understand primitive art, one must learn to comprehend this concrete imagery. This involves, as anthropologists have so often urged upon artists, a study of the meanings, beliefs, and customs behind the art. But it also involves something that is frequently neglected or distrusted on the scientific level, an ability to read the evidence in the art itself—the cultivation of "graphic thinking," as distinct from our usual habit of thinking in verbal terms. As the practice of art has become less universal, purely graphic and plastic concepts have become more and more overshadowed (even to an extent among artists) by ideas for which words can be found. Among primitives this is obviously less true. As the slightest gesture can reveal a mood, so what man thinks and feels (his terror, fervor, humor) is often recorded in his simplest scratchings and hewings. The tenuosity of a line, the eccentricity of a dot, the teetering of a shape, the piercing magnitude of an eye or a claw are eloquent with a kind of meaning that is beyond words, but graphic preferences of this sort are as much a part of a culture as language, dance, or ritual.

As a simple example of this, the famous female figurines (so-called Venuses) of European cave art might be cited. The scholar wistfully regrets that the significance of these odd, fat little pear-shaped figures is lost among the cultural blanks of prehistory. The artist might wish to know more, but he is not baffled. The simple overall shape, to which the details are subordinated, is a striking solution of a perennial esthetic problem, the relation of the whole and the parts. The rotundity of the female, viewed alongside the characteristic sticklike male figure of the period, reveals the awareness of complementary opposites that is present in yang and yin or the cubist antithesis of straight and curved lines. The placidly pregnant female, again contrasted with the active, obviously potent male, is as explicable as lingam and yoni, sun god and moon goddess, or Adam and Eve.

A fourth factor which distinguishes primitive art has to do with the *conditions in which it is typically created.* The view taken of primitive man and his environment varies between the idea that he is a strange and exotic creature totally unlike ourselves and the thesis that all men are alike under the skin and that primitive life and psychology parallel our own. It is impossible to locate the truth in either extreme; one must consider both the likenesses and the unlikenesses of the ways of thought. No artist will minimize the effect of environment on the character of the art; creation is a subtle process and all sorts of streams feed into it from the exterior world in devious ways. Similar art does not result, even in the same artist, after a day spent catching a whale and a day spent reading Freud. It is easy to imagine ourselves creating similar utensils and methods of decoration, if we were reduced to primitive conditions, but not so easy to imagine searing our flesh with intricate patterns or tattooing a decapitated human head.

Thus, when it is stated that the primitive is "different" in that he characteristically produced the objects he needed with his own hands, one may counter with the fact that he developed many of the special attitudes toward art that we ourselves have. (Art objects were sometimes created for trade, especially in the Pacific. In

New Guinea, artists competed for recognition of quality. In Dahomey there was a highly professional "artist to the king." Special personages, often the medicine man, might be responsible for the creation of magic objects or the keeping of records. There is a characteristic division of activity by the sexes; the baskets of certain California Indians were made only by women, but women were not even permitted to see the ceremonial carved posts of Melanesia.) But in general art, or at least the art potential of skilled craftsmanship, is most nearly a universal function among primitives, and the patterns (with a few prohibitions and exceptions) are familiar to all. Both the extremes of sophisticated art are lacking: the artist neither diverges widely from the tastes of his group nor is he reduced to mechanical copying. Thus, creative expression is possible within a clearly defined group tradition.

As outside influences penetrate these indigenous patterns, they may prove to be either gradually absorbed or disrupting; when they disrupt, as in the case of the occupation of the Polynesian islands by white people, the primitive pattern comes to an end. Actually, a good deal of outside detail can be absorbed without altering the indigenous art patterns; in certain African bone carvings, the figure of a missionary may be recognized by the addition of a hat, every other element remaining traditional. Acculturation has apparently occurred at all levels of development including the earliest. (The Northern nomads, for example, were an early link between East and West; New Guinea contained different racial strains and a variety of primitive styles; the rudimentary art of the Chaco has elements of the relatively sophisticated Inca style.) But within each group which we call primitive, the art remains homogeneous. It is not only made and used, but also taken for granted by the group as a whole. The creator has no fear that his product will be incommunicable or unacceptable to his audience, however obscure it seems to us.

This homogeneity of thought between the artist and his audience frees the form to a remarkable degree in two directions. Because the content is already familiar, complete details have become unnecessary. The expression may be pared down to a bare suggestion, and symbols may become more generalized, while still retaining their significance, than they can be when the artist is attempting to convey unfamiliar concepts. And since they are unmistakable, they may be distorted to the needs of the design in almost unlimited fashion—as in the compression of animal shapes into a totem pole or the adaptation of the frigate-bird motif (in Oceania) to canoe prow, lime spatula, neck rest, float, or bowl. Since these art forms are commonly used, and ramified, they take on the nature of a collaboration—sometimes to very serious ends, as if the whole race combined to design a face for its god.

So far as *materials and art processes* are concerned they vary considerably among the different primitive areas. Accident plays as large a part in creative production as it does in the rest of life, and certain materials have been discovered and used in certain places while others which were as likely may have been overlooked. However, primitive objects are characteristically made of the few materials which come readily to hand; it is not surprising that fur and fishskin are much used in the Arctic, seashells and rattan in the Pacific, ivory and gourd in Africa, birchbark among the Indians of the Eastern Woodlands—nor that woodcarving, some sort of stonework, clay pottery, basketry, and either bark cloth or weaving are very widespread. By contrast, when technology advances, there is a tendency to use rarer materials for art; in China, for example, basketwork and matting is for the most part utilitarian, while design is lavished on precious stones and the scarcer woods.

Where technology is limited, it is often possible to trace a very close relation between the nature of the material and the appearance of the product. The Eskimos, for example, use musk-ox horn for vessels and ladles, and the scoop-shape of that horn is felt as a strong design influence in their art. The impossibility of curved lines in basketry designs and textiles transmits an angular quality to decoration where those arts are important. Woodcarving induces a similar angularity. Stone is likely to be carved in the round if it is soft, but only incised if it is hard. Wooden vessels are likely to be shallower than pottery vessels, but wooden handles, because of their greater strength, may be larger and more elaborated than handles in clay. The coiling or turning process used in pottery dictates rounded shapes in early ware, whereas sophisticated ceramics are often square. The original shape of stones, tusks, tree trunks, etc., is often very evident when crude tools are used, because of the labor of cutting away material. The curious long nose, sometimes reaching to the genitals or feet in carvings of the Sepik River area, New Guinea, in addition to its psychological purpose, has the structural effect of maintaining the external shape of the original post.

The availability or absence of certain materials can have a profound effect. With the discovery of pigments (even the limited early range of earth-red and -yellow, white, and black) the concept of mass is added to linear drawing on bark or stone and the art of painting begins. The availability of some kind of manipulable fiber produces weaving, and innumerable derived arts, with far-reaching effects on the habits as well as the art forms of a people. The discovery of bronze gave its name to a new age.

Processes, like materials, are usually simple in primitive art, but this does not mean that they are easy. It is not easy to bore a hole in ivory with a bow-drill held in the teeth or to persuade pigment to adhere to a piece of raw hide. The highest craftsmanship has often developed within the framework of simple tools and crude materials. Nor does simplicity of process have any bearing on art content or meaning. Much primitive art presents a terrific challenge to the comprehension, a fact clearly evident upon the faces of casual spectators in any museum. The truth is, in this respect, that any art is baffling to the uninitiated, clear only to those who participate in it or have studiously explored it.

When it comes to the matter of *style*, it is not easy to generalize, for the art of one primitive culture may differ from another as much as Ming painting differs from impressionism. If we have some impression of what primitive art looks like as whole, it is probably due to a tendency to lump together all things that are strange to us. Only a close and intimate contact with art, as with peoples, reveals its distinctiveness. An ancestor image of the Ivory Coast may resemble one from Borneo, to people whose forebears are painted in colonial American style. But to the African, an American portrait and a Ming portrait are probably equally similar.

At the risk of oversimplification, it is possible to name a few of the elements which make us think instinctively of an object that it looks "primitive." Exaggeration, often to an extreme, is almost universal—the enormous mouth, protruding tongue, ferocious teeth, bulging eyes, prominent genitals—and it is sometimes accompanied by the elimination or *reductio ad absurdum* of other physical features.

The occurrence of anthropomorphism accounts for such unexpected combinations as the human figure with bird head (Easter Island) or the human faces with animal elements in many masks. Animal and human features may be combined with symbols of nature, like the rayed sun with human face or the Navaho paintings referred to above; they may be injected or almost lost in abstract decorative design, especially in intricate all-over patterns. There is a similar tendency to fusion of useful objects with human and animal shapes—bowls ending in head and tail, resting on animal feet, pots in the shape of heads or figures, the boat literally conceived as a sea creature. The fact that so much of art concept is attached to useful objects (as in the American Southwest where the pottery is not so much "decorated" as used for a painting ground) is a distinction from the sophisticated where the art object tends to be a separate entity.

The primitive may combine materials in ways that are unfamiliar to us; particularly in masks, he makes a most ingenious combination of paint, shell, feathers, straw, hair, bones, etc., to achieve his mysterious effects. His tools also affect his art; there is much fine and precise work, but the difficulty of the process, especially in large stonework, makes for bold and simplified design.

Perspective, in the modern Western sense of the word (the visual vanishing point) is usually lacking. Elements associated together are usually put together, with what might be called a "mental perspective"; sometimes a map perspective or bird's-eye view is used. There is a common primitive method of combining figures in carving. Instead of being related laterally, as in nature, they are in some art piled one on top of the other, often interwoven, sometimes contained in or held by each other. This occurs in such separated areas as the Pacific Northwest (totem poles), Yoruba (houseposts), or New Zealand (commemorative statues). It is probably associated with the physical nature of the tree or post used for carving, though the concept of the pole itself and its relation to the axis of the universe is one rich in significance. The same device may be used in long handles and stick-shaped implements. The effect is a reduplicative one of design elements, and it occurs in other ways as well. The nostrils of a head may flare into the eyes of a smaller head. A carved club from the Marquesas Islands ends with eyebrows and eyes, the irises of which are separate small heads.

Such means as the few mentioned here are not peculiar to the primitive. Exaggeration is almost unavoidable in art; the enlarged head, in particular, is a prominent characteristic of Semitic painting (the head being the seat of thought) and is a common cartoon technique. We tend to the same exaggeration in depicting a jinni or ghost; the fact that much primitive sculpture is related to the supernatural or dead spirits makes it a telling device. Anthropomorphism does not play a very large part in our visual concepts (except in juvenile illustration) but we take our winged cherubs and angels, centaurs and mermaids, for granted, and we have our share of fantastic characters from snark to shmoo.

Abstraction and Realism The style quality most commented upon in primitive art—and least understood —is its abstractness. Abstraction, though used as the antonym of realism or naturalism, is not a true opposite; it is broadly used to cover any degree of deviation from nature—from simple exaggeration in which the object depicted is quite recognizable, to "pure abstraction" in which forms are invented presumably without any connection with nature at all. Pure abstraction is not characteristic of primitive art—unless we so consider the geometric elements almost universally used in decoration. But even these elements among primitives (most observers think) are to a great extent either derived from or associated with natural objects. The circle is often the sun, two circles are sun and moon or two eyes, the triangle may be fish or tent, a spiral the womb or snake, a square the four directions, a wavy line water, zigzag lightning, etc. It is generally recognized that all art is abstract to some degree; the attempt to reproduce, for example, a human being in stone or paint or any material other than flesh and bone is obviously somewhat unrealistic. The problem is to ascertain the degree of, the method of, and the reason for the abstraction. It is in the last-named respect that primitive art might be said to differ most from modern sophisticated art. In the primitive, art is closely associated with the entire social pattern, and abstract forms are an evolution within rather than a deviation from the cultural norm. They never lose their group-wide use, recognition, and meaning.

Copying, imitating, or "making a picture" of nature, which was a dominant motive of Western art for some centuries, is seldom if ever an objective in primitive art. Quite often the primitive requires a "substitute" for something that exists or has existed (an image of an ancestor, a funerary object, offerings, pictorial records of a battle, an animal depicted to bring success in hunting much as a decoy duck is literally so used), but he does not require that it be a facsimile of the original. In fact it may be preferably abstracted: simplified as in the case of the battle scene, endowed with prestige or a supernatural quality as in the image, enhanced more than everyday objects as in offerings. In some cases a tabu operates against literal depiction.

There is ample evidence of primitives who have made a distinction between the realistic and the abstract; masks of both types were produced simultaneously on the Northwest Coast of America; among Plains Indians, the women produced a geometric art and the men representative paintings on buffalo hide. There are also primitive styles which are realistic in our own sense of the term: portrait heads of the Ife artist, Africa, Koryak carvings of everyday activities, Mexican figurines which have an exaggerated individuality that is like portraiture. But in primitive art there is no compulsion to reproduce nature exactly, and the motivations have that result rather rarely.

Before analyzing examples of art in terms of abstraction, it is necessary to have a good idea of what the subjects depicted look like. A tremendously elongated neck, protruding lip, or exaggerated buttocks, for example, are viewed in Western art as unrealistic, but in Africa accentuation of the neck with circular ornaments, the use of labrets, and steatopygia occur as physical habits and characteristics which are naturally reflected in the art. Features which look abstract in a strange art may be recognized as highly expressive representations when the environment is fully known. An Eskimo knife-handle (American Museum of Natural History) offers an example. This handle (viewed with the knife pointed downward) has what looks like a large plus-mark in the middle with a man standing above it and a fish apparently standing on its tail below it. The effect is one of stylized design rather than realism unless the method of fishing through a hole in the ice is familiar. The plus-mark represents the line of the ice under the man's feet with the fishing line passing vertically through it, and the fish is nosed up to the end of the line. However, there are certain abstract elements also. The body of the fish is incised with a large square containing the diagonals (an imposed geometric design). The man is not holding the line but has his arms uplifted (a stylized, pictographic position), and the hands are represented, not literally, but by a pronged design used for the deer horn (an example of fusing different depictions).

It must be noted also that the concept of what is real differs from one culture to another. Realism in Western art is identified with "visual representation," that is, representation of what the eye sees at a given moment and (except in round sculpture) from a particular view; an animal is commonly represented by an outline from any particular view within which such surface features as fur, eyes, claws, etc., are shown. But in primitive art, especially the prehistoric, an X-ray view may be accepted as realistic; the outline is shown, preferably in profile, but within it are shown internal organs, bones, edible and inedible parts, or even the swallowed fish hook. In North American Haida Indian art, the concept of an animal involves both sides of it, even from the characteristic front view, and it may be depicted as if cut in half and opened out flat. In this case the means is unrealistic (the Haida art is highly abstract on various counts) because the animal is not cut in half and would not be flat if it were, but the concept behind it is based on the two sides which the animal actually has.

Depictions of the open eye in Western art are usually based on the elliptical contours formed by the eyelids around the ball. It is equally reasonable to view the eye as the ball which it is, and to depict it with a circle or with a round hunk of clay set in an indentation. Depictions in this form are not necessarily unrealistic. On the other hand, a high degree of abstraction is present when two circles are used for the eyes, as on a painted vessel from Honduras, but a similar circle is used for the mouth, and the three circles are contained in a clover-leaf shape which is the face. This is true also when another form, like the jingle bell, is substituted for the eye, because an association of shapes takes place, even though the ball seen through the slit of the bell is an ingenious suggestion of the pupil of the eye.

No art encompasses the entire reality of nature. The process of selection and of concentration upon one aspect or another is always present. The aspect which conveys the sense of reality is not the same for all cultures. In most primitive depictions of human beings, for example, the sex details are highly significant. Clothes may make the man in Western art, but to the primitive it is the penis. Leonhard Adam (*Primitive Art*, Penguin Books, 1949, p. 65) made note of certain South American natives who added their customary sex distinctions even in portrayals of clothed European figures. The aspect upon which the primitive focuses is less often concerned with appearance than it is with power or function. Thus, even when the eyes are very abstractly presented—as a triangle (New Caledonia), semicircle (Solomons, Hawaii, Nazca), as a spiral or series of concentric circles or ellipses, or even with one eye outside the head (Tiahuanaco)—the impression of a penetrating gaze is likely to be overwhelmingly present. The concentration upon a certain aspect does not of itself make the art abstract to a significant degree unless a salient detail takes the place of depiction (as in the use of a wing for a bird) or flouts reality (as in the detached sex organs of New Guinea roof carvings). In Bushman petroglyphs of hunting scenes, movement itself is accurately depicted even though the proportions of the figure are exaggerated (greatly elongated) and other details for the most part ignored. When the sense of movement is conveyed, as in Scythian art, by detached arms and legs, a greater degree of abstraction is present; and if this form was ultimately converted, as has been suggested, to the revolving swastika pattern, complete abstraction results though the original significance may be retained in the symbolism.

Thus, in estimating the degree of abstraction in primitive objects it is important not to exaggerate those apparently unrealistic elements which result from the observer's unfamiliarity with the content or from a different concept of what is real. Furthermore, a completely literal intention does not necessarily result in highly "naturalistic" art. The means at the artist's disposal may force a deviation from actual contours, as in the angularity induced by all weaving techniques and common in primitive carving. The accepted material of any culture—corn husks for hair, a cowrie shell or an elliptical piece of mica for the eye—may appear incongruous to outsiders. In Western art, paper is an accepted material for depictions and the photograph is the "ultimate" in realism, but Herskovits reported (*Man*, N.Y., 1948) that when a photograph was shown to African natives, they did not recognize it as being intended as a depiction at all; it was, presumably, simply a squarish object of unknown material. The conventions of any art must be accepted before any degree of realism is recognized.

Even if literalness of intention were accepted as synonymous with realism, primitive art would remain abstract to a remarkable degree, because it is concerned to so great an extent with attempting to depict something which has no prototype in the visible world (the supernatural) or to endow with supernatural attributes, personality, or power that which exists. To these ends, something more than the actual is required, and the elements of invention, association, and exaggeration are inevitably brought into play. One cannot imitate visually that which cannot be seen.

In analyzing the primitive method of abstracting—or rather the method of creating by which what is called abstraction happens to result—the following elements may be distinguished. They often mingle, and the de-

gree of abstractness may be very slight or very high in each case. (Simplification, often considered one form of abstraction, is not included; it is the natural manifestation of any object in a first or over-all view, and is not unrealistic unless some different element of distortion enters in.)

1) The use of geometric shapes. "Geometrization" takes four major forms which are quite different: (a) The use of geometric shapes in design. These decorative patterns, even though they may be suggested by or associated with actualities, are in form essentially abstractions though they may often be combined with or merge into depictions in decoration. (b) Geometric design applied to depictions, like the convoluted patterns with which Maori carvings of the figure are covered. (c) Reduction of the shape or details of the shape to a geometric pattern. In a Congo mask, for example, the face has an over-all triangular shape, in which the nose is a triangle, accentuated with a row of dots, the mouth a circle, the eyes a banded ellipse. (d) The use of geometric shapes as, or as a basis for, such graphic symbols as triangle, circle, wheel, swastika, spiral, etc. See SYMBOLISM. The wide use of geometric shapes gives primitive art its apparent resemblance to the "cubism" of modern abstract art.

2) The fusion of depictions. This comprises the anthropomorphism referred to above, especially common in depictions of the supernatural, and also the fusion of creatures (human, animal, or god) with objects, as when a pot is made in the shape of a head, the handle is a tail, or a metate is a quite literal jaguar as to head, tail, and feet, but with the pounding stone for the body. Depictions are also extensively fused with the geometric shapes of design. The different parts of these depictions may sometimes be so literal that the result might be called a "fused realism," but, more often, the shapes interplay, especially with repetition, and a high degree of abstraction results.

3) The concentration on an aspect or salient detail, which may sometimes develop into a high degree of exaggeration and abstraction. Animal depictions of the Northwest Coast Indians, in which different species came to be differentiated by one distinguishing feature, such as claw or fin, are an example. Condensation in art is often motivated by the needs of communication; when many buffaloes are to be depicted, the repetition of a single salient line is often resorted to.

4) Standardization of a depiction to a set form. This is a process of conventionalizing which results naturally when particular forms of art are repeated many times. The same details and methods are repeated over and over, becoming more and more stylized in the process, until the realism of individuality is ultimately lost. The alligator in Chiriquí art is a well-known example. This form of abstraction is a generalizing process. It is the particular form of art which corresponds to the use of the word abstraction as applied to language, that is, for a general statement, or a summarizing concept which takes the place of numerous individual examples.

5) The modification of naturalness which results from tools, materials, processes, surfaces, the shape of the design area, etc. Unless some other element enters in, art in this respect may be literal in intent but abstract in apparent result.

Major Areas of Primitive Art. The art of the north

polar regions comprises that of the Eskimos of North America (usually divided into western or Alaskan Eskimo, Central and Greenland Eskimo areas) and the paleo-Asiatic tribes of Siberia. The Siberian tribes were comprehensively studied over a period of years, and the reports in the *Publications of the Jesup North Pacific Expedition* (American Museum of Natural History), which contain many detailed drawings and analyses of objects, offer one of the best published sources for the study of primitive art at an elementary level.

The native arts in the Pacific, on the other hand, are still not adequately known. New Guinea alone, for example, encompasses different racial strains and a number of obviously different and intricate styles, highly developed in a symbolic and magical direction, which have not yet been completely analyzed or clearly distinguished. Pacific art (also called Oceanic or South Seas art) includes four main divisions which follow the usual geographical and cultural lines, though there is argument for including Fiji with Polynesia rather than Melanesia on the basis of art resemblances. These divisions are: (1) Polynesia, including Hawaii, the Marquesas, Samoa, Tonga, the Society Islands, Easter Island, and the native (Maori) art of New Zealand; (2) Micronesia, including the Mariana, Caroline, Marshall, and Gilbert Islands; (3) Melanesia, including New Guinea, New Hebrides, New Caledonia, the Admiralty and Solomon Islands, and (?) Fiji; (4) aboriginal Australia and Tasmania. An over-all survey of these four divisions, particularly valuable for its illustrations, is available in *Arts of the South Seas* by Linton and Wingert (Museum of Modern Art, N.Y., 1946). Other primitive island cultures which, from the art standpoint, may be included with these main divisions are the native arts of the Philippines and of the primitive parts of Indonesia. Indonesia embraces both Java and Bali, with sophisticated arts more closely related to those of the Asiatic mainland, and outlying islands whose still primitive art is more comparable to that of neighboring Melanesia.

In broad terms, the Asiatic area is characterized by the early development of highly sophisticated art styles, which penetrated as far as Japan and parts of Indonesia. (The extent of thorough acceptance of Buddhist styles offers one basis for demarcation.) The Pacific area, on the other hand, is characterized by primitive arts which arose later and remained primitive until recent or present times. However, all the Pacific Island areas were settled by waves of migration stemming from the Asiatic mainland and Indonesia, whose arts therefore exerted an influence. A list gives no impression of these varied and provocative arts. Woodcarving is outstanding, whether connected with architecture or devoted to highly abstracted figures, utensils, carved handles, weapons, or boats; the highly convoluted over-all design of New Guinea and Maori art is conspicuous. Other carving ranges from the large "cubist" sculpture of Easter Island to objects in jade, shell, etc. Tree fern, bamboo, rattan, feathers, shell, and tapa cloth are materials used in unique ways—tapa cloth combined with sculpture, for example. A few of the characteristic Pacific objects are canoe prows, painted paddles and shields, carved gables and spires, dance shields, tikis, ancestral statues, ceremonial or memorial tablets and boards, and masks.

The entire continent of Africa, south of the desert area, is occupied by Negro peoples whose arts are all classed as primitive, though they exhibit a wide range, from virtual non-existence among the Hottentots to an advanced degree of specialization in West Africa. Well-known styles of Guinea Coast art, represented by examples in various museums, are from: Benin, especially bronzes of the 16th and 17th centuries; Yoruba, masks and polychromed carvings; Ife, terra-cotta figures and bronze heads; Ashanti; Dahomey; and Baulé. The arts of the western Sudan and the Congo are also of high quality. Carving in ivory and wood and metalwork are outstanding African Negro skills, and commemorative statues and masks form notable examples. Except for the decrease of ivory, these are for the most part still living arts. The work of Herskovits on *Dahomey* (New York, 1938) and of R. S. Rattray on *Religion and Art in Ashanti* (London, 1927) offer an exceptional opportunity for study of more advanced primitive arts against the essential cultural background.

The *Handbook of the South American Indians* published as Bureau of American Ethnology Bulletin 143, 7 vols. to the end of 1963, Washington, D.C., made available a wealth of material previously lacking, or covered only in scattered fashion, on the complete area of South America. Only certain sections deal directly with art, but much of the material is pertinent; the aspects of material culture are thoroughly covered and analytically illustrated. Four main culture areas are outlined: the Marginal Tribes, treated in Vol. 1; the Andean Civilizations, Vol. 2; the Tropical Forest Tribes, Vol. 3; and the Circum-Caribbean Tribes, Vol. 4. (Volume 5 deals with Comparative Ethnology.) In this case the classifications, based on sociopolitical, religious, and culture elements, do not (see Vol. 5, p. 671) follow obvious cultural or art divisions. The distribution of artistic activity is indicated by the map (Vol. 5, p. 152) which shows pottery levels as summarized by Gordon R. Willey—since the distribution of this major South American art parallels the general artistic development of each area. The areas which lacked pottery or had only crude or simple ware were occupied from early times by marginal hunting and food-gathering tribes, whose circumstances were not conducive to art.

By far the most developed area in South American art is the Central Andean region of Peru and Chile, whence styles and techniques spread to the northern and southern Andes and beyond. A lesser source of art styles is in the Amazonian basin, the ceramics of Marajó being well known. In ceramic and textile arts, the South American Indians were unexcelled. Also prominent in the most developed styles are massive stone sculpture, in which the shape of the block prevails with intricate, over-all relief carving, metalwork of great technical skill, and a simple massive stone architecture showing skilled masonry. Well-known styles of the Andean area (in Peru and the Bolivian plateau) are: Chavín, characterized particularly by its stone sculpture; Mochica, pottery and ceramic sculpture; Nazca, pottery and textiles; Tiahuanaco, sculpture; Recuay, pottery; and Inca. The Inca style of Cuzco, which spread into Ecuador, Chile, and Argentina, was the latest of the Highland styles prior to the Conquest and is for that reason perhaps the best known; it is characterized by a high degree of skill in various media but is less striking esthetically than some preceding styles. The Isthmian area of Central America falls, in respect to influences, within the South American range; the Coclé goldwork and Chiriquí pottery of Panama and the Nicoya polychrome ware are interestingly developed.

The Indians of what is now Mexico and Central America were highly advanced in many respects, other than the salient one of written language, and particularly so in the arts. Mayan art is generally considered to represent an esthetic peak. This, and the Middle Civilizations and the Aztecs as well, have been treated in various specialized volumes. Aztec art, which survived at the time of the Conquest, was recognized sooner and more thoroughly known, but technology and organization outweigh the purely creative, as compared with the earlier Mayan.

The native Indian arts and crafts of the United States and Canada—like the baskets, leather, bead and feather work, paintings on hide, woven rugs, pottery, silver, etc.—are thoroughly familiar. Not so well understood but of the greatest esthetic significance is the highly symbolic and more abstract art of two areas, the Northwest Coast (including Haida, Kwakiutl, and Tlingit) and the Southwest. Franz Boas devoted a substantial part of *Primitive Art* (Harvard University Press *et al.*, 1927) to a thoroughgoing analysis of Northwest Coast art. The Southwest includes the ancient Pueblo and cliff-dwelling people, and the Navaho, Apache, Pima, Zuñi, Hopi, etc. The Navajo Ceremonial Museum in Santa Fe, in particular, is devoted to preservation of the art of this area. The pottery of the Southwest is technically very superior. The most interesting art of the eastern United States is prehistoric. Stone images and discs, incised shell gorgets, carved masks and bowls found in the southeastern mounds in particular are of high quality and suggest the possibility of connection with the arts of Middle America. Prehistoric art in North America is simplified by Douglas and D'Harnoncourt (*Indian Art of the United States*, New York, 1941) into the following groups: the carvers of the Far West and the Northwest Coast, the engravers of the Arctic (Eskimo), the sculptors of the East, and the painters (on pottery and canyon walls) of the Southwest.

In the Americas, the term prehistoric is widely applied to Indian art up to the coming of the white man. This is confusing to the amateur, in view of the fact that the prehistoric art of Europe is many thousands of years old and that in other areas, such as Siberia and India, the prehistoric is not clearly dated, nor is it known to what extent the styles carried over into the historic. In the Americas, the native arts which had not already disappeared before the Conquest tended to do so rapidly, without adequate record or preservation of examples.

II. Folk Art

Folk art is often called primitive, or thought of as a broader division of art which includes the primitive. However, this bracketing becomes impractical as one attempts to collect and analyze, because it brings together kinds of art which are quite different in circumstances and results. Folk art alone, with the primitive excluded, is diverse enough to present difficulties. Therefore, the term is used here for a kind of art which occurs after a culture has begun to sophisticate, when the art has become so diversified that various styles, techniques,

and products may be known, or preferable, to one group and not to another.

Many definitions of folk art have been attempted; none has been agreed on, but it appears that whenever one refers to the subject (provided primitive cultures are excluded) he presupposes a distinction from some art in contact with it that is not folk—from what might be called, by analogy with art song, "art art." Just what the distinction is naturally varies widely from one culture to another. To comprehend it, it is necessary to understand why and how some of the art has sophisticated as well as why and how the folk art has developed differently, for these streams are not completely separated. One is constantly reminded that the art of a particular culture, even a vast complex of styles, content, and abilities, is essentially a unit. Folk art can exist with, shoot off or emerge from, survive within, or develop into a sophisticated art, and its identity is often more striking than its differences. European folk art is more like the rest of European art, for example, than it is like the folk art of India.

The common use of the word "peasant" for a good deal of folk art offers a starting point. The peasant art of Europe was produced by a class of agricultural or village workers. Obviously the form of many objects, and the methods by which they were made, were common to all classes, but in others (weapons, hunting equipment) the difference is clear. The distinctive peasant costumes and house furnishings of many localities, together with their particular decorative motifs, survive to the present day.

Thus the existence of class privilege and the accumulation of wealth has an obvious sophisticating effect, and peasant art—where objects are locally made rather than imported, lavish materials are not available, and the extensive accumulation of possessions is not facilitated—remains somewhat outside of it. In particular, wherever rulers have accumulated great wealth, a sophisticated art develops around imperial centers; in Byzantium, the best artists and artisans were attracted from other parts of the world for elaborate projects; in China, objects were specially made, and marked, for palace use. In such cases, the difference between peasant and sophisticated art may reach an extreme. The animal sculpture connected with tombs in China offers an example—the simple little clay figures made by peasants of the west, featuring the homely buffalo and other familiar animals, contrasted with the majestic stone statues at Peking. Yet both are manifestly "oriental" in style, and one has been as greatly admired as the other.

Another strongly sophisticating influence in art has been its production under religious sponsorship. One needs only to recall how many elaborate cultures take their name from the predominant religion—Hindu, Buddhist, Semitic, Mohammedan, East Christian—or the part played by Catholicism in Renaissance art. In India, religious neophytes received a formalized art training in a long and arduous apprenticeship, and symbols and styles for religious art were subjected to elaborate schemes and systems. The folk art produced outside these prescribed styles is in a sense secular in character. It serves practical needs and non-religious customs; and particularly, it is characterized by symbols, motifs, and objects retained from pagan or earlier beliefs or associated with local deities or festivals. The good-luck charm, the Halloween false face, the Santa Claus costume, and their equivalents all over the world, are never quite abandoned, however incongruous with the organized religion of the day. An interesting example is afforded in the Japanese *netsuké*. These miniature sculptures of wood, ivory, or other material, attached to the costume, the medicine case, etc., were usually related to folklore and legend at times when major art works were produced in the service of Shintoism and Buddhism. And while Japanese Buddhist art is inevitably quite derivative, the style of the *netsuké* is thoroughly indigenous, delicate, skilful, original, and entertaining.

At the same time, as new religious concepts and symbols permeated the thinking of the whole people or supplanted the old even in remote areas, a religious folk art began to develop, produced for the same religious purposes but produced in a different way. The elaborate stūpa, cathedral, mosque, altar-piece, or mosaic had its peasant equivalent in the roadside shrine and Virgin, the village Buddha, local church, or peasant-carved alms-box. Replicas of the images in great temples or cathedrals were made for villages, copied by local craftsmen, and recopied, until characteristic folk styles emerged. Local gods or saints might be added to the accepted iconography, and local decorative motifs and techniques were incorporated. A striking example of religious folk art is the Byzantine family icon, which developed particularly during the iconoclastic period. With images forbidden in the churches, the making of icons, which the people as a whole were unwilling to give up, became a surreptitious art in the hands of local and less professional artisans; the style crystallized noticeably into the repeated, stern, straight-front view and the strong flat decorative colors.

The process of industrialization gives rise to another clear distinction between the folk and the sophisticated product. As an increasing proportion of both useful and decorative objects (whether of art caliber or not) are produced by factory means, a folk art may be recognized among people who do not have access to the industrial product and must therefore go on producing such objects for themselves, or on a local scale. In Austria (as in other European countries), pottery first came into use among the townspeople. Only later did the technique penetrate to rural areas, and it never completely supplanted the beautiful carved wooden jugs or "shepherd's cups" or painted wooden plates. The peasant pottery was ornamented (though often elaborately) by simple methods, such as a slip or indention with the finger or a rough tool; and it has not been supplanted in turn, as in the cities, by ceramics and glassware. Though the sophisticated wares from Venice, Nuremburg, and other centers circulated and had their influence (a peasant type of majolica developed in Moravia, for example), indigenous motifs were maintained.

The folk art produced in these circumstances (that is, among groups not reached by the industrial product) involves more than the mere continued hand production of utilitarian objects. The more sophisticated, whose practical needs were met by industry, tended rapidly to make a distinction between the so-called "useful arts" and the "fine arts," and the latter became the province of professionals. (In contemporary America, the practice of delegating each function to an "expert" has advanced so far that the average adult will not attempt to draw at all unless he has had special training; his unwillingness to attempt what is in other cultures a natural activity amounts almost to a tabu.) The peasant, however, had even less access to fine art than to the product of industry; consequently his esthetic needs, too, had to be served by the local product. The result is seen in the beautiful decoration of many handmade objects, and sometimes in an imitation of or substitute for the "fine arts" product, as in folk-painted landscapes. Eventually, however, the industrial product penetrated even to the most remote areas, making the home crafts seem needlessly laborious, and the folk artist came more into contact with a sophisticated art which, technically, he could not hope to equal. His creative self-confidence was no doubt undermined and he became often indifferent to or ashamed of his homemade possessions. The high period of folk art in the United States and most of Europe drew to a close after the middle of the 19th century.

Industry, from the very beginning, adapted itself to substitute for the folk product. The early examples—Staffordshire earthenware, American cast chalkware, early chromos—are often included with folk art, though we do not so label their modern equivalents, such as the comic strip or mass-produced, low-priced religious objects. The ten-cent store of today displays many objects not only designed to meet unsophisticated tastes but conveying traditional shapes or meanings: the Easter bunny originally associated with fertility, the charm bracelet with such ancient symbols as shoe or heart, objects for Christmas or Halloween festivities, the valentine, the rabbit's foot on a key chain, the four-leaf clover enclosed in plastic, the three hear-no-evil, see-no-evil, speak-no-evil monkeys. A great deal of pictorial art on the same level, so-called "calendar art," is also produced both individually and commercially. All such art produced for popular consumption, whatever the period, is called by this writer "popular art," and it is distinguished from folk art, in which sophisticated artists and industrial methods have no part. In the present day when, because of mass production, the people as a whole are not impelled to the production of art, the significance of art in relation to them lies in what they choose, what is produced for them. Popular art, in this sense, might well be a separate and important branch of cultural study.

We tend to think of industrialization as the peculiar *bête noir* of Western art. However, in the Near East, many centuries earlier, rug-making, ceramics, and silk textiles were produced in factories corresponding pretty much to our own concept of the term. Much Aztec pottery was characterized by the slurring of designs and standardizing of shapes which occur in quantity or mass production involving hand skills. In medieval Europe, art tended to become professionalized through the organization of craft guilds, with prescribed standards and techniques quite different from folk circumstances of production. However, not all guilds were of equally professional caliber, nor did they cover all crafts, and as they declined, their product became more folklike.

The guilds, and likewise the factories, were concentrated in urban centers and the folk art outside their sphere was largely rural. (The term "rural art" is often used.) However, the availability of objects depends upon money as well as location, and there was at the same time an urban folk art of the poor. The folk woodcuts of France (and elsewhere), distinctive in style, color, and subject, were a highly popular example.

When an art culture develops, it does so around hubs, like those mentioned—royal courts, centers of religion, learning, industry, ports of trade—and it spreads along the most accessible trade routes. The more remote areas may be no less active artistically, but the art remains more traditional, less ambulatory, less touched by outside influence. Thus, there is not only a rural peasant art, which can exist just outside the city, but also provincial styles peculiar to specific outlying areas. Provincial art is not necessarily folk. The Anatolian, for example, as an inland art accompanying the Byzantine, was of a different but quite sophisticated style. Within the provincial society, the range from lord to serf, from rich to poor, is likely to be present. But provincial areas are fertile for the production of folk art, and even the wealthier products are likely to exhibit a folk character, since they lack the sophisticating factor of outside contact. Trends penetrate more slowly, vogues change less rapidly, and, particularly, the work of local artisans is depended upon. The Rajput school of painting in northern India (c. 1700) was such a provincial art, and it is significant that the subject matter was based primarily on folklore and the Indian epics, whereas the simultaneous Mongol painting was devoted to portraits and historical subjects. The style, too, is what we think of as folklike. In fact, the landscape details of Rajput paintings suggest a comparison with early American art: a rather stiff quality in highly stylized elements is distinguishable from the fluidity and merging surfaces of the more sophisticated (Mongol or European) painting.

As isolation is vanquished, or when areas develop into artistic self-sufficiency with a sophisticated style of their own, the conquest is not complete. Little "pockets of survival" are left behind where a folk art may retain earlier characteristics and in some cases develop a distinctive regional style of its own. This seems to occur particularly in mountainous regions whether in Transylvania or the Southern Appalachian highlands. Usually a regional group results from geographic isolation. However, psychological factors may be involved, such as the resentment of "furriners" on the part of the Southern mountaineers; the resistance of the inland Chinese to the hybrid East-West culture of the Chinese coast; the religious motive behind segregation of the Pennsylvania Amish Mennonites, which seems to have occasioned a determined resistance to the culture which surrounds them; the desire of French Canadians to preserve their national traditions in contact with their English compatriots; and the desire of Africans to preserve their tribal customs.

In the United States, these pockets of survival have largely broken down, at least in the form in which we recognize them. We now seek for individuals rather than whole communities where old crafts persist in their natural state, and the survival has often become a matter of family rather than group tradition. But in some parts of the world, even though coastal and other accessible areas are industrialized, traditional arts flourish in the interior, and various regional arts are possibly still in process of formation.

Colonial and Native Art   Still another force must be reckoned with as making possible a folk art, and that is the migration or colonizing of people from one area to another. The outstanding example, of course, is the transference of European traditions to colonial America. The early settlers of the Americas emigrated from a highly developed art culture to a wilderness, and a process of simplification took place in the art (the reverse of sophistication) as local craftsmen replaced experts, as skills were lost or changed or became impracticable. The resulting colonial folk art was distinguished from its sophisticated European parent, not simply by remoteness or resistance or poverty, but by its active adaptation to more elemental circumstances. The folk character of this art was prolonged by the fact that imports were available to form an "art of the wealthy," thereby impeding the elaboration of local products in the direction of luxury items or fine arts, and it prevailed long after the colonies were independent.

The products of this adaptation are familiar; they are visible in American homes and antique shops, as well as in centers like Williamsburg, Cooperstown, Sturbridge, or the American sections of museums. A few examples merely suggest the many ways in which it occurred. The sampler, the quilt, the hooked rug, emerged as typical handicrafts of women instead of delicate lace or embroidered costume, and the salvage aspect of these arts reflects the scarcity of materials. The furniture of the homeland formed the desired pattern, but characteristic colonial lines soon appeared, generally sturdy and simple; motifs which had been carved in Europe were produced by the less laborious process of painting in Pennsylvania (this happened in European peasant art also), and the painted style absorbed other motifs as well. The familiar cavalier on European ceramics became a Revolutionary soldier. Oil painting, a highly sophisticated medium, was widely used in American folk art. Limners went about with ready-painted stylized busts, to which the somber faces of the early settlers were added, sometimes with remarkable realism and a remarkably "American" look. (Similarly the Chinese painters of "portraits of the dead" keep on hand a stock with all details painted in except the face, which may not be added while life remains. The Chinese insist on a faithful likeness and, in former times, paid for the often spurious rank which they wished the costume to indicate.)

Usually all early American art is described as folk, but as a whole it is more like the provincial art referred to above, which stands rather on a middle ground with elaborated elements of its own. However, there is an important difference between the colonial and the provincial (as the two terms are here used); in the latter foreign influences are minimized, whereas the colonial "invades" a new area in which an unfamiliar culture may be already entrenched. American colonial art of the eastern seaboard showed relatively little effect from the native Indian art (that art being not highly developed) but in the Southwest and throughout Spanish America the interaction of styles is a definite factor. In Africa and the Far East, European colonizers have tended to remain simply outposts of their home culture, although that culture itself shows the influence of their trade and imports (witness the Chinese effect on English ceramics and furniture).

At the same time the native or "invaded" art is also in process of alteration. The new contact, it should be pointed out, may result simply from trade as well as from settlers. And the local art may be of any type. The Hellenistic cities of the Mediterranean coast, for example, were in contact with cultures more ancient than their own. But in the period of modern colonial expansion, the pattern is one of European (and later American) settlers moving in on areas with a relatively primitive art. This has brought into the subject of folk art an element which we loosely call "native art." (Native art is strictly the art of any native-born inhabitants; by connotation only, we usually think of it as primitive and as contrasted to a foreign element.)

The virility of indigenous art in the face of new contacts, and the attitude of colonizers and traders toward it, are highly variable elements. In some cases, it drifts out of sight, into the Reservation as in the United States, much of it being progressively lost, some preserved in a traditional way rather apart from the rest of life which conforms to new patterns. In some cases, it disappears; Australia (except for the remnants of aborigines), New Zealand, and parts of Polynesia are by now completely within the Euro-American cultural sphere. Where religious reform is involved, the "heathen" art has been destroyed and repressed. But in other cases, the native has been allowed to fuse naturally with the invading style, and some notable folk art has been the result. In Middle America, there was a background of imaginative art, to which the colonizers brought a religion (Catholicism) deeply involved in art motifs, symbolisms, and imagery. Mendieta commented upon how ready the Indians were to copy and imitate the images brought from Europe. This lively art interest, combined with an elasticity which reconciles old and new, permits a living folk art to flourish.

In the North American Southwest, a folk art resulting from such acculturation and syncretism may still be seen, as in the religious images or *santos* and in silverwork. The distemper paintings on plaster or wood which adorn the ceilings, doorways, altars, or walls of the Franciscan missions in Spanish California were reminiscent naturally of similar religious art in Europe. But the analysis of the *Index of American Design* (a series of WPA regional projects which served to register much United States folk art) called attention to elements derived both from the native art of the California tribes and from the Mexicans brought along by the Spaniards to assist in the training of Indians. Embroidered vestments, printed fabrics, and painted chests were other objects made, and the skills and motifs acquired were applied subsequently to the leather, metal, and needlework executed on the ranchos.

In another case, native art may remain primitive despite culture contact. This may be observed on a very simple level in Greenland, where the Eskimos of the southeast coast retained their culture virtually intact, while those of the west coast showed the effect of several centuries of white contact; yet the art in both cases remained quite primitive. Metalwork, which had been limited to native copper, was augmented by iron, and the shape of tools conformed more to the white man's shapes; but simple, incised depictions in pictographic style and the typical design element of rows of circles with center dots showed little change.

Nearly always, an indigenous art which is reached by colonizers or traders suffers to some degree the effect of commercialization. In its simplest form, this means merely that local objects are peddled by natives or bought up for export. Actually, a whole group may create objects for sale over a period of time without becoming commercialized. This seems to have been the case among the Indians of the Northwest Coast who during the latter half of the 19th century maintained an indigenous art of high caliber despite encroachment. Commerce (barter and sale) has been a factor in art from earliest times; commercialization takes place when the product is affected.

The demands of trade have often resulted in exploitation of the artists and emasculation of the art. Workmanship tends to become hasty; designs are dictated by the trader or buyer. When this happens there is a clear distinction between folk art and "trade goods," even though the design, material, and technique of the object remain traditional. The distinction might seem academic but for the fact that it is recognized by discriminating purchasers all over the world, the art quality being so unmistakably affected. An importer of Haitian objects in New York, for example, prices a "native drum" several times higher than a similar drum commercially made in Haiti—and the reason is obvious in the appearance and sound as well as the scarcity value of the item. It is often possible to riffle through a collection of imports in an American store—cloisonné ashtrays or Mexican painted boxes—and out of numerous carelessly executed and repetitious examples find one which looks like the work of a folk artist, some elderly craftsman perhaps who knows no way of working except the folk way of his youth. Natives themselves are quick to recognize it. Some American Indians today continue to make objects sacred to themselves which never appear on the roadside stand beside the dolls, beadwork, and leatherwork designed to attract the tourist. It is not possible to define in words the exact point at which native objects have become bowdlerized for the market and cease to be folk art; but in general the effect is apparent in the objects themselves.

When demand for native objects exceeds the local supply, or if cheap native labor attracts enterprise, the process of actual industrialization sets in. However, to the extent that new objects and crafts are adopted by natives for their own use and merged with traditional styles, a native folk art may be stimulated. Philippine embroidery was inculcated by nuns and has become well-known in world markets, but it is an element in the present local costume which has evolved, from a conglomerate of influences, into a native folk style.

Industrialization, it is apparent, affects folk art (either peasant or native) in two ways: it can eliminate crafts by supplying machine-made products and it can convert folk objects for large-scale markets. Several factors deter it: the tendency to prefer the old; the impracticality of factory methods for a few locally desired objects; and the pleasure of creation. Whether folk art can continue for long in a completely industrialized society is not quite clear. We recognize styles of the past for what they are more easily than those of the present, and it is possible that different stylistic concepts will attach themselves to the word folk. For example, the variety of odd and often entertaining eating places along American highways constitute a sort of folk architecture. Because a unique design is required to attract attention, and may be achieved only by the ingenuity of the owner, the pattern of sophisticated architecture is set aside. Flower arrangement and garden planning present individual problems despite all syndicated advice. The bone-carving resorted to by American prisoners of war, sometimes with beautiful results, is of particular interest because it reveals that art as a resource of interest is not forgotten.

Minorities One other circumstance of folk art results from the migrations of people, and that might be termed a minority folk art. People who compose a racial or social minority are psychologically disposed to the preservation of their traditions and are likely to be underprivileged—both circumstances which make folk art likely. On the other hand, a dispossessed or wandering people are not in a position to accumulate possessions, and art is inevitably wound up in material culture. This last no doubt accounts for the fact that the Negroes in America have produced so notable a folk music and relatively little in art except as they became sophisticated artists. Their eminent skill in woodwork was adapted to the white man's tools, objects, and designs. The slave pottery, with jugs reminiscent of African heads, and some carving with geometric design, seem to be exceptions. The caravans and costumes of Gipsies have formed an occasional picturesque note in countrysides the world over. Jewish art has tended to identify with national styles, whether on the sophisticated or the folk level; typically Jewish folk art, therefore, comprises ritual objects used by peasant families or in connection with village synagogues. In the foreign sections of cities like New York and San Francisco, folk craftsmen may still be found; at Italian festivals a hand-carved "triumphal car" may be paraded in the streets in honor of a saint.

The Emergence of a Folk Style It goes without saying that the environmental factors which have been described overlap. Royal and religious patronage, industrialization, and wealth were all combined in Europe to affect the sophisticated art, from which the peasant art was distinct. The early post-Columbian art of the Americas may be viewed as comprising a colonial (white) folk art and a native (Indian) folk art. But in Latin America today, peoples are mixed, and the folk art might be viewed (except in more remote areas) as of a peasant or rural type. When one factor predominates, we may be disposed to give the art a specific name—peasant, rural, regional, provincial, colonial, native, urban, or religious folk art. But generally, in each case, different elements merge. Folk art is not to be viewed as a poor example of sophisticated art—there are many of those from which it can be clearly distinguished. It may occasionally appear to be a simplified version or an anachronistic art, but for the most part it takes on distinctive styles, each with its own range of mediocre or superior examples.

It becomes easy to see why attempts to define folk art as a whole in descriptive terms have failed. Too many different kinds of art produced in too many different circumstances are involved. It is commonly said, for example, that folk art is distinguished by a "love of color" or by the use of bright primary colors; but the somber Puritan costume and the subtle hues of Canadian hooked rugs come to mind. All-over design (the so-called *horror vacui* of art) is thought to be a folk characteristic;

actually it is favored for certain objects rather than in any art as a whole. The colonial American sampler or *fraktur* is usually completely covered (though there are many exceptions), but the Pennsylvania Dutch *poi-schissel* (common pie dish) had a simple slip of one or two wavy lines.

Folk art is often viewed as the quaint and simple output of unlettered, unselfconscious individuals. However, modern attitudes emphasize the range of human nature whatever its living conditions. Simplicity in the art product is at some periods an objective of the highly sophisticated (as in modern *bauhaus* design), whereas folk art may satisfy a craving for the ornate or complex. The Chinese dragon kite represents the ultimate in complexity for that particular item; its numerous decorated segments permit it to undulate through the air with marvelous lifelikeness on those occasions when it is successfully launched—a project which usually enlists the entire population of a village.

Literacy is relative within the locale; folk-decorated documents would naturally be the work of schoolmaster or clerk, while the woodcarver or potter might be less schooled; in the non-verbal arts it may not be significant whether an artist is lettered or not since his mental activity may not require an intervening command of words. As for selfconsciousness, it seems likely that anyone who makes anything is aware of himself as the creator and of the work for its beauty; the proud signature or mark on many an autographed quilt, show towel, dish, or spoon is evidence. Sarah Schupp's wedding chest (Philadelphia Museum of Art) made in 1798 is not only prominently signed "N.S." but carefully marked "Num. 8."

A definition under discussion in recent years describes folk art as "the handwork of an untrained artisan made for his own use." This is a curious anomaly of terms, since the word artisan is defined as one trained to manual skill. Training in the arts has been most often acquired (until recently) by an apprenticeship method. It may be acquired, as some sophisticated artists have demonstrated, purely by practice or imitation without any teaching. But it must be acquired if one is to attain the status of an artisan or artist. To say that the folk artist produces "for his own use" indicates that the product is not commercialized, and it is true of certain objects individually produced in many places, notably the home arts of women. As soon as the pioneer conquered his isolation sufficiently to live in settlements and produce an art, a specialization of crafts and skills began to take place. The boatbuilder, potter, weaver, portrait painter, calligrapher, served the whole neighborhood and often operated as itinerant journeyman.

Such assumptions as these indicate how far we are from understanding the over-all pattern of folk art. However, certain art in many parts of the world is constantly referred to as "folk," and some facts are common to the circumstances in which it seems to occur.

Tradition and Contact It is obvious that tradition plays a prominent part in the circumstances mentioned —the retention of ancient elements that have been forgotten or abandoned (though not completely, even so) in the more sophisticated. This is apparent in the objects that persist—the basket not replaced by paper bag, the lace cap, the embroidered shoe, the carved knife-handle; in materials—homespun flax instead of factory cotton or local cotton instead of imported silk; in processes—glass that is spun, iron wrought rather than cast; and especially in the content of the art and its motifs. In Austria, bed curtains are specially embroidered for use during confinements, their special designs serving to keep evil spirits away. In China, the countryside is spattered with carved arches erected to the honor of faithful widows. In Bali, the *tjili*, painted on rice cakes for the temple, molded into roof tiles, used as the central motif of *lamaks* (palm leaf ornaments hung on an altar or rice granary at feasts) preserves the shape of the ancient Rice Mother, deity of fertility or goddess of beauty. In India, small figurines are carved as "marriage toys" for the bridegroom. Ancient symbols may be traced endlessly throughout the whole range of art forms —lotus, tulip, vine, the tree of life, cross, swastika, wheel, star, rosette, lion, dragon, peacock, eagle, deer, pomegranate, peach.

However, these ancient elements have changed over the centuries, even though slowly. A striking characteristic of primitive art has been noted as the reality of the symbol (the mask *has* power, the sun *is* a fiery wheel). In sophisticated art, on the other hand, content tends to become personal and a "private symbolism" is injected. In folk art, ancient symbols and motifs are retained, but their intense meaning has been rubbed smooth with use, much of their connotation may have been forgotten, and (particularly if there is a newer religion) much of their ritual use has been abandoned or adjusted. Thus there is a noticeable tendency toward the conversion of once potent symbols into purely decorative motifs. The loss of meaning is often accompanied by changes in form. The designs become more stylized, adapted to more heterogeneous objects and more altered in the process, until sometimes the original shape is as muffled as the original meaning. The lotus used as a shop sign by the dealer in rice cakes is quite different from the lotus held in the hand of the goddess or depicted on the Sacred Lake where it enfolds the souls of the dead. The Pennsylvania barn symbol, while believed in at least partially as a charm against misfortune, has little of the meaning attached to the early cross. Masks may be assumed carelessly for festivals or revels. The tree of life is favored for quilts. These symbols, originally formulated with ritual power and poetic content, now constitute deep roots, entrenched habits, graphic concepts which are accepted rather than understood.

There are many examples of folk art—holy images, memorial portraits, grave carvings, votive banners—of strong emotional power, but it leaves its overwhelming impression in the field of decorative art. The basic motifs may be few but they overflow a variety of objects with fresh, skilful, and spontaneous execution, seldom slavishly copied despite the strong hold of tradition.

This element of retention has given rise to the use of the term *traditional art* as a synonym for folk art. However, the word tradition has to do with the fact of transmission—usually it is thought of as lore handed down from one generation to the next—and it applies equally to the transmitted elements in any art; in static periods a sophisticated art may remain highly traditional. In general, as long as any art is alive, some change occurs, however gradually and unconsciously. Our concept of folk art allows for these adaptations

and changes, but "traditional" is limited to those aspects of the art which are not changed but handed down. Traditions change, of course, but in the process that which is new is an innovation.

However, traditional art is the most appropriate name for revivals of folk or primitive arts and crafts. When craftsmen carefully study and duplicate old processes, implements, and patterns, the results, however fruitful, are not true folk art, for the art is not practiced, motivated, or used in the folk manner. Folk artists do not arbitrarily adopt restrictions not their own; their limitations result from their customs and circumstances. A new folk art can spring up rapidly when new opportunity or need arises. The Mexicans were enchanted by the fireworks of the Spaniards and for village festivals began to construct huge firework castles which exploded into images of saints and other motifs. The popular photography which followed the invention of the camera (before the camera and hobby magazines influenced it) formed a kind of folk art in which the backgrounds and the "wedding pose" soon became traditional.

The element of retention has given rise to another, though less used, term, *derived primitive*. This is appropriate only to certain elements within the art. The folk styles of Europe and Asia maintain motifs drawn not merely from primitive ones, but from centuries of succeeding elaborate styles. The last remnants of the Hellenistic and Byzantine in Italy, for example, are referred to by D. Talbot Rice as "impoverished" and "peasant" art.

When tradition becomes virtually the sole element, as in the case of this late Byzantine, the art is one of decay. This is a phase of folk art just as it is of sophisticated art; it occurs and is replaced in much the same way, unless some factor such as industrialization operates against the replacement. Folk art at its height is more like a lively crossroads where tradition meets with other active forces—the developing local style and the partial infiltration or occasional contact from the developed art center.

This contact, however occasional, has an unmistakable effect. It must be recalled that art is visually communicated. Strange art is not completely unintelligible, like a strange language. That which is seen can register without being fully understood. Thus the statue once seen in Cracow, the sample of foreign lace or tapestry in the manor-house, the passing craftsman from another region could set new elements stirring in the home folk style. In colonial America, the arrival of new settlers who had executed pierced ceramics in Europe contributed a new technique, but the art did not sophisticate overnight, nor become European. The connection was not complete, and as long as that is true the folk style is not swept into the main stream. This limited access to the sophisticated seems to be a salient characteristic.

The Buddhist penetration throughout the East in some respects paralleled the spread of European culture in the Americas, but the Eastern arts were of more uniformly high level, and the aspect of a "missionary" penetration was dominant. Approved designs from India were carefully studied to insure orthodoxy in such matters as the postures and garments of the Buddhas, but lesser beings and scenes of human life overflowed with local color and style. Much of this interaction took place on a sophisticated level, of course, and filtered into folk art only with time. At that level, the effect of repeated tracing of original designs, as in Turkestan, is noticeable, and also the prominence of motifs reflecting the more popular aspects of the religion.

Once all these inherited ideas, absorbed contacts, and motivations are set in motion in a particular area, the art may develop in a variety of ways. It becomes as difficult to trace the reasons as to account for every quirk or facet of a personality, for the different circumstances and events of each area are involved. In America, for example, it was the environmental factor, rather than the prominence of tradition, that caused the early art to take on so much of a folk character. Whatever levels the immigrating craftsmen may have attained in their homelands, certain arts were set back on their heels by the lack of elaborate facilities which may have been available at home. When new skills or products were necessary, they perforce started on a simple level.

Folk Products Observations about both folk and primitive art usually include the fact that much of it is applied to useful objects rather than created "for itself." This is simply a way of saying that the useful and the esthetic have not undergone the segregation that takes place at certain periods in sophisticated art—that a useful object may be the material for art, the modeling applied to a jug, the painting to a chest. This fact may condition (but not necessarily limit) the art, as in the dictation of a shape that is to be handled as well as looked at, and the selection of designs that are appropriate to the use. It does not prevent elaboration far beyond the demands of utility; one does not spend months embroidering a jacket merely to keep warm, or years carving a bed merely to sleep in it. In the case of images and church or temple decoration, the motivation is religious rather than "useful"; and the sophisticated arts, such as portrait painting, may all be paralleled on the folk level.

However, any list of folk arts might begin with the useful ones. There is the characteristic form of the dwelling and other structures with such particularized details as doorway, weathervane, gate or hitching post, barn symbol; furniture and furnishings—chests, racks, stove tiles, hinges, rugs, hangings, quilts, coverlets, linens; home utensils—dishes, crocks, molds, wooden trenchers, baskets, skimmers; the costume and its adjuncts—belts, clasps, pouches, ornaments—especially as it is elaborated for special occasions, christening robes, bridal costumes, vestments; objects used for farm or hunting—ox-yokes, horse brasses, shepherd's crook or whip, powder horn, wagon; tools and symbols of one's trade—shop sign, cigar-store Indian, ship figurehead, carved spindle, carpenter's bench, fishing gear; objects of amusement—dolls and toys, puppets, miniature models, roundabouts, musical instruments. There are documents, trade cards, valentines, colored prints, even some books called folk; tombstones, tablets, carved crosses, mourning embroideries; images, such as the *santos,* village Buddhas, *tjili,* and icon mentioned; charms, and such religious objects as the phylactery or Bethlehem manger.

The style of these objects (the quality which makes them look folk) is most often described as naive. What the word conveys to various individuals is problematical. It may arise from the technical limitations sometimes apparent in the effort to reproduce more elaborate art.

The fold of a drapery in woodcarving, for example, might become highly simplified, stiff, and angular. The figure or landscape may seem a little odd when executed in a similar style without the same knowledge of anatomy and perspective. More likely the so-called naivité has to do with the enviable ability of folk artists to create afresh within ancient patterns. Various researchers have reported that the artists at work seem to have the sense of originating the art even though the shape or design may be highly traditional. These artists are concentrated on the example at hand; they cannot trace the long history of the form or motif in examples spread out in the museum case. The manner of working may be sometimes very meticulous as in the painting of every leaf on the tree or brick in the wall, or free and bold as in the effigies carried through the streets or burned at festivals or funerals in many parts of the world; but rigidity is natural rather than schematized or imposed.

The predominance of the decorative is a natural outgrowth of the high percentage of useful objects in the art; it often takes the form of innumerable variations of geometric arrangements or of simplified flowers, birds, animals, and symbols. The effect of tradition on the style is unmistakable. The same motifs, repeated over a long period of time and adapted to many objects and areas, acquire a set shape which is immediately recognized without being any longer realistic, and which is used for design purposes more than for representation. The tulip in Pennsylvania Dutch design, for example, uniformly appears with two bisymmetric outer curved leaves and a center section which may comprise the suggestion of other leaves, a geometric shape (such as a checkered diamond), simply a zigzag or wavy line, or a borrowed device such as the pomegranate. Tulips grow readily from the branches of that other favorite symbol, the tree of life. Thus the abstraction which occurs in folk art is not so much (as in the primitive) a result of different concepts of reality or an effort to depict that which is essentially unreal; for the conventions of reality which prevail in the contiguous sophisticated art are generally accepted, and so are the ancient symbols. Predominantly it takes the form of conventional or stylized abstraction.

Materials and Processes The same factors which give tradition so strong a hold—isolation, lack of education or wealth—tend to keep the materials local and processes mechanically simple. The materials are not necessarily poor, for the folk material of one area (linen in Europe, silk in central China, ivory, jade) might be the treasured rarity of another; but imports are uncommon, and the range within the area is often narrow. Processes may be intricate and laborious, but they are characteristically accomplished unmechanically and by a single craftsman (perhaps with assistants), rather than by a subdividing of skills.

The observable difference between folk and sophisticated art often, sometimes solely, has to do with these two factors. In early Mohammedan pottery (according to M. S. Dimand), luster and enamel painting were used only in the high-grade ware made for the court or wealthy persons, and made for the most part where the court resided; incising and underglaze were used for both wealthy and peasant ware, and both show the great Islamic decorative qualities. The designs carved in a fine piece of European furniture may be repeated in paint on an American chest. The bridal bedspread, usually of embroidered silk in China, may be produced by a batik process among the poor in certain areas. The handwoven coverlet survived in folk art long after the Jacquard loom had started the industrializing process in the cities.

But in general all the materials of sophisticated art are used, to the extent that they become available. In addition there are a great many inventions and oddities which bespeak the ingenuity of people to whom expensive materials are out of range or who are not inhibited by esthetic canons: "paintings" of fern or cork, figurines of plaited straw, rag dolls, the snow man, the dough man, shapes knotted in rope or chalked on the sidewalk or stenciled with the shadow of the hands, coverlets of scrap, toys of folded paper, lockets of human hair, the broach of pasted shells or kingfisher feathers, sand castles, painted gourds, dyed grasses, the ship in the empty bottle, the mosaic of shards, the welcome spelled in flowers, the scarecrow, carved seeds, pumpkin and cocoanut faces, the cake pagoda, animals of blown candy, figures of string or of palm leaves, painted eggs. Miguel Covarrubias describes having seen in Bali, among beautiful offerings for the gods, "great pyramids of fruit, flowers, cakes, and even roast chickens, arranged with splendid taste" and "monuments, seven feet in height, made entirely of roasted pig's meat on skewers, decorated into shapes cut out of the waxy fat of the pig and surmounted with banners and little umbrellas of the lacy stomach tissues, the whole relieved by the vivid vermilion of chili-peppers." These are outclassed (if that is possible) only by the Russian gingerbreads weighing more than half a ton. But folk art is not made up of mere decorations and oddities. Like all art, it can serve (and does) the complete range of human needs, from the most festive to the most solemn, the most useful to the most spiritual.

MAMIE HARMON

Princess on the Pea Title of a fairy tale by Hans Christian Andersen which has immortalized and given name to motif H41.1, also known as the bed test or identity through sensitivity test. Andersen's story begins with the wish of a certain king to marry a *real* princess. A princess comes to his door in the night and is given shelter from rain and storm. She *says* she is a real princess, but to make sure the old queen puts a pea in the bed, piles 20 mattresses upon it, and 20 eiderdowns upon them for the princess to sleep on. When asked in the morning how she slept, the princess complains of lying on something so painful that she could not sleep at all. Thus they know she is a real princess; none but true royalty could be so tender.

Grimm's example of this story is *Die Erbensprobe* (#182a). The Penzer notes to the *Ocean of Story* (vol. VI, p. 288 ff.) state that the oldest known version of this folktale is found in Sweden. In this the princess is put through a number of tests: one of them is being put to bed on seven mattresses with a pea between each. She sleeps soundly and comfortably all night, but her canny little dog advises her to complain. So she complains; and because of her complaints is adjudged a worthy bride for the king. Most of the Scandinavian bed test stories contain also the animal adviser, and the objects placed in the bed vary from peas and beans to stones and knitting needles.

Other versions of the story are found in Italy, Hungary, Greece, Rumania, Arabia, and India. Supersensitivity was considered a characteristic of persons of royal or noble lineage. Many stories (jests) are related by ancient writers on the sensitivity of the luxurious Sybarites; for instance, one Smindyrides slept on a couch of rose leaves and, on awakening, found his body covered with weals (Timæus; Ælian). Ancient tales in India and Persia tell of three queens, so sensitive that one who heard a pestle pounding in the distance, fainted from the pain this noise caused her; another was burned by moonbeams; another was wounded by the fall of a lotus flower. A Persian queen could not sleep for a myrtle leaf under her shoulder, and three sensitive brothers were restless and sleepless from a single hair under seven mattresses. For these and other stories of sensitivity, consult Erwin Rohde, *Der Griechische Roman und seine Vorläufer* (3d ed., Leipzig, 1914), pp. 588, 589, nn. 2, 3; C. H. Tawney, ed., *The Ocean of Story* (London, 1924–28) VI: 291; VII: 10–12; 204 ff.; Bolte-Polívka, *Anmerkungen* III: 332. [GPS]

Prisoner's Song A Broadway popular version of an old song of the American southern mountains, *New Jail*, which itself is descended from an English song, *Here's Adieu to All Judges and Juries*. The tune is a folk remodeling of *The Ship That Never Returned* by Henry C. Work, published in 1865. Another old song, *Moonlight*, or *Meet Me Tonight in the Moonlight*, contributed a stanza. From the various sources stanzas along the lines of the following have been assembled: "I'm going to my new jail tomorrow / A place where I've never been before / With those cold prison bars all around me / And my head on a pillow of stone"; "Meet me tonight in the moonlight / Meet me out in the moonlight alone / For I have a sad secret to tell you / Must be told in the moonlight alone"; "I wish I had someone to love me / Someone to call me their own / I wish I had someone to live with / For I'm tired of living alone." The chorus is often the last of these, but one version, *The Great Ship*, has a chorus "Let her go, let her go, God bless her" like the blues *St. James Infirmary*. Among Negroes as well as whites the song is widely known over the United States.

promenade An American square dance term. When the promenade follows the grand right and left, the gentleman meets his partner half-way around the set, whereupon he takes her on his right, either joins both hands crossed with the right above the left, or gives the lady his right arm, and they walk back to place, continuing in the direction the gentleman was going. There is also a French wedding dance called *promenade*. [GPK]

promised child A theme of folktale, known throughout the world, in which a child is promised to a demon, water spirit, etc., in return for some sort of favor, often the birth of the very child. The promises, knowingly made or unwitting, rash or considered, and the means of evading fulfilment of the promises are embodied in motifs S210–259. The promise is perhaps best known in the *Beauty and the Beast* story: the father, to save his life after trespassing in the beast's garden to pick a rose for his daughter, is forced to promise the beast that he will send his daughter to be the beast's wife. The story of Jephthah's vow illustrates the unwitting promise of the child: the father promises the first thing that comes to greet him when he returns home. See JEPHTHAH's vow. The European tale of Robert the Devil (S223.0.1) explains the deeds of that evil-doer as being caused by the mother's promise of the child to the Devil (Type 756B—The Devil's Contract). This type is exemplified in the eastern European *Legend of the Robber Madej*. The child, promised to the Devil, grows up and decides to go to Hell to obtain and destroy the contract binding him to the Devil. He is helped by the robber Madej, and while in Hell he sees the punishment awaiting the robber when he dies. He warns Madej, who seeks penance. He is assigned the penance by a hermit, which he must continue until, as in the Tannhauser story, the dry rod blossoms and bears fruit. Eventually the staff does this and the robber knows that he is forgiven. Andreyev, who studied this tale (*FFC* 69), believes it originated in western Europe during the Middle Ages, but that its theme proved more congenial to eastern Europe, where it is best known. The story is, however, told from Ireland and Spain to Siberia; some 60 Russian, 54 Polish, 48 Lithuanian, 25 German variants are known.

proverb A proverb is a terse didactic statement that is current in tradition or, as an epigram says, "the wisdom of many and the wit of one." It ordinarily suggests a course of action or passes a judgment on a situation. A proverb may be merely a statement of fact: /Honesty is the best policy/, /All's well that ends well/; or a metaphor, which one applies to the situation: /Don't change horses when crossing a stream/, /Don't cut off your nose to spite your face/. In many proverbs, and characteristically in those dealing with medical or legal ideas or with the weather, the didactic element is a condensation of experience or a concisely formulated rule: /Rain before seven, fine before eleven/; /Two words to a bargain/; /Silence gives consent/.

Many manners of speaking that are found in tradition and literature are akin to the proverb. A proverbial phrase (/to be left at the post/, /to have an ace up your sleeve/) permits variations in person, number, and tense. A proverbial comparison (/as fresh as a daisy/, /as red as a rose/) has a fixed traditional form, but contains no moral advice. The Wellerism, or quotation proverb like /"Every man to his taste," said the farmer when he kissed the cow/, is a traditional form; it is used to produce a humorous effect and is at most a whimsical or ironic comment on a situation. The traditional estimates of a neighboring village or country are expressed in *blason populaire*. A conventional phrase is a formula used in a situation of frequent occurrence. On seeing one's expectations confirmed, one may say, "Well, what did I tell you?" Expressions used in greeting a friend, taking leave, or drinking a toast are conventional phrases. The closely related cliché is a similar formula which the speaker or hearer feels to be trite and hackneyed. It expresses a trivial judgment (and it may then be a proverb) or may be only a phrase like /When all is said and done/, /All things being considered/, /In any way, shape, or manner/. Mottoes and slogans have, like clichés, somewhat sophisticated associations. They are expressions connected with persons or religious and political movements; they formulate ideals or principles or are calculated to arouse mass emotions for or against a cause. /Honi soit qui mal y pense/ is the

motto of the Order of the Garter, and /Rum, Romanism, and Rebellion/ is a slogan. The literary forms most closely akin to the proverb are the apophthegm (a concise statement of a moral judgment) and the epigram. The writer of an epigram endeavors to put a novel idea or a new facet of an old idea into brief and elegant literary form.

The origin of proverbs is obscure.[1] We must suppose that some individual formulated an idea in words or drew a lesson from a scene, but the result was only a sententious remark or an instructive exemplification of a truth until tradition accepted the statement and, while accepting it, adapted it, if necessary, in an inimitable fashion. Both the invention and the acceptance are essential to make a proverb, and both ordinarily escape our observation. The effort to arrive at the origin of proverbs is complicated by the fact that the same theme and even the same formulation of it may occur to more than one person. The witticism, /As Maine goes, so goes Vermont/, which was coined on the occasion of Franklin D. Roosevelt's second election (1936), depends on the older saying, /As Maine goes, so goes the nation/. At that time several persons claimed—and no doubt correctly—to have hit upon it independently. Traditional currency differentiates a proverb from an individual's sententious or epigrammatic remark, and in the absence of traditional parallels only a feeling for the idiomatic use of a language enables us to recognize a proverb.

The ascriptions of proverbs to particular individuals are extremely untrustworthy. Some may be correct, but many ascriptions to Solomon, Socrates, Plato, Cato, Alfred, or some other man famed for wit or learning reflect only the reputation that he enjoyed. Occasionally it may be possible to find in his writings a phrase or an idea that tradition could—and perhaps did—turn into a proverb. For example, the Wellerism or quotation-proverb of the type represented by /"That alters the case," quoth Plowden/ probably derives its material, if not always its form, from a historical incident.

Most of the commonly used proverbs are metaphors drawn from daily life or the observation of nature or are terse summaries of experience. To the first class belong: /New brooms sweep clean/; /No man is a hero to his valet/ (which has been credited to Madame de Sévigné); /It is a long lane that has no turning/; /Still waters run deep/. To the second class belong: /Haste makes waste/; /Set a thief to catch a thief/; /Three generations from shirtsleeves to shirtsleeves/; /Few words are best/; /Experience is a dear school but fools will learn in no other/. Comparatively few proverbs involve an allusion to a particular trade, custom, or belief. /Good wine needs no bush/ refers to the old custom of hanging an ivy branch before a wineshop. /In vino veritas/ (There is truth in wine) may be the familiar observation that alcohol makes the tongue wag or, less probably, a reference to some divinatory practice. There are references to the village and household trades, but city or industrial life as we know it in modern times has not given rise to many proverbs. Some proverbs, like /Sour grapes/, are condensations of familiar tales, especially Æsopic fables.

Proverbs are often made on the models of already existing types. /The nearer the church, the farther from God/, an old and widely known proverb, seems to have been the occasion for the invention of /The nearer

Rome, the worse Christian/ or /The nearer the Pope, the worse Christian/, which are much less widely known forms and breathe the hostile spirit of the late Middle Ages. The same formula appears in the medieval Latin /*Tanto plus calidum, quanto vicinius igni*/ (The nearer the fire, the hotter), which Chaucer knew, and the widely used /The nearer the bone, the sweeter the meat/.

Proverbs use the simple stylistic devices of contrast (/Enough is as good as a feast/); alliteration (/Live and learn/; /Look before you leap/); rime (/Man proposes, God disposes/; /There's many a slip between cup and lip/); and repetition (/Live and let live/; /There's no fool like an old fool/; /Love me, love my dog/). Perhaps the most characteristic feature of proverbial style is the use of contrast as in /A good beginning makes a good ending/; /Better late than never/; /Little pitchers have big ears/; /Hindsight is better than foresight/; /When thieves fall out, honest men come into their own/. A contrast is often reinforced by parallel structure as in /Like master, like man/; /Young saint, old devil/; /Out of sight, out of mind/. Proverbs like /Faint heart ne'er won fair lady/ or /Pride will have a fall/ that resemble allegory are rather rare.

Like all folklore materials, a proverb has many traditional variations, which are all of equal authority. The parallels to the English /A bird in the hand is worth two in the bush/ differ in the number of the birds mentioned as we see in the Gaelic /A bird in the hand is worth a dozen on the wing/ or the Spanish /A bird in the hand is better than a hundred (or a thousand) flying/. The speaker may elaborate the proverb by naming particular birds as in the Persian /A sparrow in the hand is better than a hawk in the air/ or the German /A sparrow in the hand is better than a pigeon on the roof/. When a proverb employs completely different means of comparison to express this idea, we cannot easily discover whether we have variations that have arisen in the course of oral transmission or whether we have two proverbs of entirely different origins. Examples are the Turkish /The egg of today is better than the goose of tomorrow/, the Latin /One hour today is worth two tomorrow/, and the Serbian /Oat bread today is better than cake tomorrow/. One proverb often brings another in its train, or suggests an enlargement by the addition of an illustrative parallel, as in /Many talk of Robin Hood that never shot in his bow, and many talk of Little John that never him did know/. Proverbs may also attract to themselves such whimsical additions as we see in /I have other fish to fry and their tails to butter/. Sophisticated epigrams may gain much of their effect by echoing proverbial models: /Marry in haste and repent at leisure/ yields /Marry in haste and repent at Reno/ and /You can't eat your cake and have It/ (i.e., sex appeal) rests on /You can't eat your cake and have it too/.

A proverb usually expresses no high moral ideal difficult of attainment but is the summing up of everyday experience in getting on in the world as it is. The virtues preached by religious masters are not turned into proverbs. /Charity begins at home/ is thoroughly practical. The advice that underlies most proverbs is the counsel to avoid excess. Proverbs seem therefore to advise contradictory actions, and men have amused themselves by making collections like the Elizabethan *A Crossing of Proverbs* by Nicholas Breton.

In literature proverbs are often used to characterize a figure or to summarize neatly a situation. They are often used as titles, as in Shakespeare's *All's Well that Ends Well*. A development of this last use is seen in the *proverbe dramatique*, which is a play that gradually leads the audience to guess the proverb which gives the play its point and title. Such plays were especially popular in 18th century France. At various times and in many countries poets and prose writers have heaped up proverbs to gain a particular effect: François Villon wrote a ballade composed of proverbs, Rabelais made a chapter of them in his *Gargantua*, and Carl Sandburg used them for characterization in "Good Morning, America." Such accumulations of proverbs have pictorial parallels, notably Pieter Breughel's representation of more than a hundred proverbs in a single scene. There are also many pictures depicting a single proverb.[2]

The *epigram*, and in particular a special variety of the epigram, is closely akin to the proverb. This variety, which is called the *Priamel,* was especially popular in the 15th century at Nuremberg.[3] The Priamel is an accumulation of unrelated ideas that are united in some unexpected way. The connection may be expressed at the beginning as in /England is the paradise of women, the hell of horses, and the purgatory of servants/, or at the end, as in /The calf (parchment), the goose (the pen), and the bee (wax or seal): the world is ruled by these three/, or /A dog, a woman, and a walnut tree: the more they are beaten, the better they be/. The thought that holds a Priamel together may be left to be inferred as in /*Italia para nacer, Francia para vivir, España para morir*/, which praises the climate of Italy, the gaiety of France, and the piety of Spain in the sequence of human life; or /Nature requires five, custom gives seven, laziness takes nine, and wickedness eleven/, which is spoken of the hours of sleep.

Although *medical proverbs* have been collected and studied in many languages, the English examples have received very little attention. They may preserve old rules for health like /After dinner rest a while, after supper walk a mile/, which is ultimately a passage in the *Regimen scholæ Salernitanum,* a medieval handbook of medical advice. Such bits of good counsel as /An apple a day keeps the doctor away/, or /An hour's sleep before midnight is worth three after/, which have less obvious origins, are no doubt summaries of popular experience. The Latin /*Similia similibus curantur*/ (Like cures like) is the basis of homeopathic medicine. The interpretation of medical proverbs often raises difficulties. /Feed a cold and starve a fever/ may be understood literally or as If you feed a cold, you will have a fever to starve. The saying /You must eat a peck of dirt before you die/ is probably no more than comment for the overnice.

Weather proverbs [4] are, like medical proverbs, traditional epigrammatic condensations of experience: /April showers bring May flowers/. The value of such assertions is briefly stated in /All signs fail in dry weather/. Many weather proverbs refer to the calendar: /As the days begin to lengthen, the cold begins to strengthen/. Some proverbs like /March comes in like a lion and goes out like a lamb/ are survivals of old rimes that were once printed on calendars. Weather proverbs often give advice about agricultural matters: /Plant corn when the dogwood is in bloom/. Others must have been invented by seafaring men: /A rainbow at night is the sailor's delight/. A metaphor based on the observation of natural phenomena like /The darkest hour is just before dawn/ or /Every cloud has a silver lining/ is not ordinarily called a weather proverb.

Among peoples without written laws proverbs are often quoted with great effect in disputes. An aptly used proverb may decide a case or support a chief's decision. Laws that have been handed on by word of mouth often have a terse epigrammatic form akin to the proverb. In Iceland, for example, the lawgiver, an official of the All-Thing, recited the code annually at the assembly on Thingvellir. The Frisian laws preserve traces of metrical passages that suggest oral transmission. Mnemotechnic formulas, which are often embellished by alliteration or rime, continue to be used in popular speech: /house and home/, /man and mouse/, /kith and kin/. Periods of time like /a year and a day/, or especially "forever" are often expressed in proverbial formulas: /As long as grass grows and water flows/, /As long as Paul's [i.e., St. Paul's] stands/.

Legal proverbs may contain a concise statement of a legal principle: /Ignorance of the law excuses no man/; /An Englishman's house is his castle/. Their interpretation may require special knowledge of legal and social history, or acquaintance with ideas that are no longer accepted. For example, /A fair exchange is no robbery/ refers to the fact that a forcible exchange of clothing effected by a fugitive is not to be regarded as a theft aggravating his offense.

Especially interesting and curious proverbs express an idea of a legal nature that has not been put into law. /Hands off is fair play/ advises spectators not to take sides in a fight; /Don't kick a man when he is down/ counsels a magnanimous spirit; /A taleteller is worse than a thief/ compares two kinds of wrongdoing and would probably not be upheld in a court of law.

In the Middle Ages and the Renaissance collections of *brocards* or concise, anonymous, traditional formulations of legal principles served as textbooks and even in recent times teachers of law used such books as Herbert Broom, *Legal Maxims* (1st ed., 1845).[5] Francis Bacon collected *brocards,* and in 1641 William Noy published a much-used *Treatise of the Principall Grounds and Maximes of the Lawes of this Kingdom,* which was reprinted as late as 1870. The origins of these maxims can often be found in actual laws or commentaries, but their traditional currency (although it is largely restricted to lawyers) entitles them to the name of professional proverbs. Typical examples are /*Ultra posse nemo obligatur*/ (No one is bound beyond his ability), /*De minimis non curat lex*/ (The law does not concern itself with minor matters), and the respect for precedent formulated in /*Stare decisis*/. In any profession that deals with relatively esoteric information similar epigrams or maxims are current. For example, biologists say, /Ontogeny recapitulates phylogeny/.

Proverbial comparisons [6] are usually, although rather incompletely, recorded in collections of proverbs. They deserve separate attention and study, but the examples needed for historical and comparative investigations are not easily assembled. The variations in the means of comparison and in the contexts in which the comparisons are used are often extremely interesting. Some proverbial comparisons like /As white as milk/ have become old-fashioned, and others like /As hot as the hubs

of Hades/ have established themselves in general use. The currency of comparisons and the rise of new forms are ordinarily difficult to discover. It is even more difficult to learn the special contexts in which a comparison is properly used. For example, /As black as the ace of spades/, which seems to be of rather recent origin, refers only to a Negro. Proverbial comparisons may become unpopular and disappear from use. John Ray notes, for example, that /As drunk as a beggar/ was being replaced three centuries ago by /As drunk as a lord/. Like proverbs, proverbial comparisons may allude to unfamiliar or forgotten ideas. /As deaf as an adder/ depends on the very old assumption that snakes cannot hear; /As cross as a bear/ recalls the old sport of bearbaiting. The interpretations of /As mad as a hatter/ or /As mad as a March hare/ are still obscure, and /As pleased as Punch/ is puzzling because Punch is usually associated with domestic strife—but Punch brags and preens himself after beating his wife.

Proverbial comparisons referring to colors constitute a special category. Some like /As black as coal/, /As red as blood/, or /As white as snow/ are immediately intelligible, and others like /As brown as a berry/ are yet to be explained. Others like /As white as milk/ or /As white as chalk/ have ceased to be current, and still others like /As white as a sheet/ have come to be used only in particular contexts. Such references to personal qualities as /As green [inexperienced] as grass/, /As blue [depressed] as indigo/, /As white [pure] as the driven snow/ may preserve recollections of medieval color symbolism or may be of more recent origin.

Except for such comparisons as /As old as Methuselah/, /As poor as Job/, or /As many-eyed as Argus/, which are readily recognized as Biblical or classical in origin, proverbial comparisons containing a proper name defy explanation. /As queer as Dick's hatband, made of a peastraw, that went round nine times and would not meet at last/ may be an allusion to Richard Cromwell; /As lazy as Ludlam's dog that leaned his head against the wall to bark/ remains entirely obscure.

Clichés [7] The cliché, a stereotyped expression so trite and hackneyed that sophisticated writers or speakers avoid it, is ordinarily a phrase rather than a full sentence. Eric Partridge recognizes four varieties: First, idiomatic phrases like the doublets /Dust and ashes/, /Enough and to spare/, /Null and void/, /Ways and means/; the repetitions /Again and again/, /Through and through/; the alliterative phrases /Bag and baggage/, /Safe and sound/, /Slow but sure/; the alternatives /Kill or cure/, /For love or money/, /Neither here nor there/. With these he would group such overworked proverbs, proverbial phrases, and proverbial comparisons as /To step into someone's shoes/, /To steal his thunder/, /As fresh as a daisy/. A second class of clichés consists of hackneyed non-idiomatic phrases: /To add insult to injury/, /A baptism of fire/, /Down to the last detail/, /The picture of health/. A third class includes phrases and quotations from foreign languages like the Latin /*Deo volente* (God willing), /*terra firma*/ (solid earth); the French /*fait accompli* (accomplished fact); or the Italian /*con amore*/ (with genuine interest), /*sotto voce*/ (under one's voice). The fourth class consists of quotations like /Gall and wormwood/, /the laws of the Medes and Persians/. There is necessarily a subjective element in the definition of a cliché, and many clichés belong also to other proverbial varieties. There is a curious use of the cliché in O. Henry's story "Calloway's Code" in *Whirligigs*. It tells how a newspaper correspondent used clichés as a code. By sending one half of a phrase he led the editor to supply the other half and thus arrive at the intended message.

Conventional Phrases Many locutions are conventionally used in particular situations or are accepted as traditional ways of expressing an idea. Although conventional phrases have the traditional aspect of proverbs, they are ordinarily not didactic in content and do not usually employ a metaphor. Words of greeting or leavetaking are conventional phrases. /I'll be seeing you/, or /I'll see you in church/, or /Good-by now/ are probably rather recent in origin, and /Farewell/ or /God be with you/ are old-fashioned or obsolescent. Encouraging remarks like /Never say die!/, or the emphatic rejection expressed by /I'll be hanged if I do/, or summaries of a situation like /That's that/, /That takes the cake/, or /That caps the climax/ resemble proverbs. So, also, do the remarks made when silence falls on a group: /Quaker meeting/ or /It's twenty minutes past the hour/. Colloquial toasts are often curious: /Here's looking at you/ (a reference to draining the glass so that one looks through the bottom), /Here's mud in your eye/, or /Bottoms up/. What does /Over the river/ mean?

Some varieties of conventional phrases have been collected and studied. For example, alliterative formulas like /Neither hide nor hair/, /Without chick or child/, /Kith and kin/, or /House and home/ have been compared to medieval alliterative verse. Some of these formulas that have a juridical flavor are survivals of old legal phraseology, but alliteration is not necessarily a proof of great age. The many periphrastic phrases signifying "never" form a special group.[8] Some, like /On the 32d of the month/, refer to a non-existent day (examples of this type are characteristically French); others involve the coining of a fantastic name like the amalgam of June or July and November in /Next Juvember/; still others allude in one way or another to Doomsday /Three days after the Last Judgment/. See LAMMAS. Some mingle time and space in a compound that may mean never or nowhere or sometimes both: /I'll meet you between four o'clock and the corner/ seems to mean only never, but /Between Hell and breakfast/ may mean either never or nowhere. The largest category of locutions of never includes references to such obvious impossibilities as /When water runs uphill/, /When roses bloom on apple-trees/, /When two Sundays fall together/. Analogous conventional phrases signifying forever are somewhat less numerous: /As long as grass grows and water flows/. Conventional reinforcements of the word *not* like /Not worth a rap/, /Not a whit/, /Not a straw/ have many parallels in the Romance languages and in the French *ne . . . pas* and *ne . . . point/* have become the ordinary equivalents of not. They may be called figurative negatives.

Blason populaire The French term blason populaire (folk heraldry), for which there is no convenient English equivalent, signifies the names, phrases, and rimes traditionally used to characterize peoples and places.[9] Such expressions often differ from nicknames in containing an element of appraisal, which is frequently unfavorable. Characteristic examples are Frog (a Frenchman), which is a shortened form of frog-eater; Squarehead, Boche, or Hun; Merry England, La belle France. A traditional raillery exchanged between villages, districts, or countries may also take shape in these expressions. It is seen also in the conventional conception of the stage Irishman and such personifications as John Bull, Uncle Sam, or Marianne (France).

Collections of Proverbs The old *Bibliographie paremiologique* (Paris, 1847) by P. A. [Gratet-] Duplessis is still valuable for its full descriptions of books. The two largest later bibliographies—*Catalogue de la bibliothèque de Ignace Bernstein* (Warsaw, 1900) with 4761 titles, and Wilfred Bonser and T. A. Stephens, *Proverb Literature* (London, 1930) with 4004 titles—do not cite the collections of non-European tribes with any completeness. (See many such collections in Whiting's article cited in note 1.) For a brief hand-list of the most important European collections see Archer Taylor, "An Introductory Bibliography for the Study of Proverbs," *Modern Philology*, XXX (1932), 195–210. For general treatises see Friedrich Seiler, *Deutsche Sprichwörterkunde* (Munich, 1922); Archer Taylor, *The Proverb* (Cambridge, 1931); and the prefaces to collections, especially that to Giuseppe Pitrè, *Proverbi siciliani* (Palermo, 1880).

The best English collections are G. L. Apperson, *English Proverbs and Proverbial Phrases* (London, 1929); W. G. Smith and Janet Heseltine, *The Oxford Book of English Proverbs* (2d ed., London, 1948); and (for the older periods) the works of B. J. Whiting. Much useful information will be found in the *New English Dictionary;* the *Dictionary of American English;* and Burton E. Stevenson, *The Home Book of Proverbs, Maxims and Familiar Phrases* (New York, 1948). See QUOTATIONS AND WINGED WORDS; WELLERISMS.

Footnotes:
1. The best discussion of this difficult problem is B. J. Whiting, "The Origin of the Proverb," *Harvard Studies and Notes*, XIII (1931), 47–80.
2. See, for example, a medieval French manuscript reproduced and annotated by Grace Frank: *Proverbs en rimes* (Baltimore, 1937).
3. See Karl Euling, *Das Priamel bis Hans Rosenplüt* (Breslau, 1905).
4. Richard Inwards, *Weather Lore* (3d ed.; London, 1898); H. H. C. Dunwoody, *Signal Service Notes*, IX (Washington, 1883); Charles Swainson, *A Handbook of Weather Folk-Lore* (London, 1873).
5. See James Williams, "Latin Maxims in English Law," *The Law Magazine and Law Review*, 4th Series, XX (1895), 283–295.
6. F. J. Wilstach, *A Dictionary of Similes* (Boston, 1916; rev. and enl. ed., 1924). Like most dictionaries of this kind, this work deals chiefly with comparisons quoted from literature.
7. *A Dictionary of Clichés* (London, [1940]).
8. See Archer Taylor, "Locutions for Never," *Romance Philology*, II (1948–1949), 103–134.
9. See G. F. Northall, *English Folk-Rhymes* (London, 1892); Eric Partridge, *A Covey of Partridge* (London, 1937), "Offensive Nationality," pp. 211–215; A. A. Roback, *A Dictionary of the Traditional Slurs (Ethnophaulisms)* (Cambridge, Mass., [1944]).

ARCHER TAYLOR

proverbial phrase A traditional manner of expression, closely related to the proverb but differing from it in being capable of change.[1] Thus, the proverb /You can't eat your cake and have it too/ is invariable; such a sentence as /He tried to eat his cake and have it/ is an allusion to the proverb. But the proverbial phrase /To have two strings to his bow/ may be adapted to any person or tense. The vague and shifting difference between a proverbial phrase and an idiom is difficult to define. The use of the Spanish *ser* and *estar* or of the English "to stand" in the meaning "to endure" is idiomatic and not proverbial.

The many allusions in proverbial phrases to beliefs, customs, and practices or tools of various trades are often puzzling and hard to explain. For example, /To kick the bucket/, a proverbial phrase, signifying to die, probably refers to a bucket for catching blood against which a slaughtered animal kicks. Those who use this phrase may be unaware of its origin, but they are conscious of its vulgar associations and do not confuse it with such more elegant synonyms as /To pass on/, /To join the majority/, or /To be called to his fathers/.

Some ideas are expressed by a variety of proverbial phrases. Dismissing a suitor may be paraphrased by /To give him the mitten/, or /To turn him down/. The strange German phrase /Einen Korb geben/ (to give a basket) is explained by a medieval story of Vergil, who was left suspended in a basket by the lady of his choice. The even stranger Spanish /Dar calabazas/ (to give pumpkins) seems to be unexplained. Although there are collections of phrases meaning "to be pregnant" (/To be expecting/, /To be waiting for the stork/, /To be knitting little things/, /To be in the family way/), scholars have not often attacked the task of collecting or explaining proverbial phrases associated with a particular idea. For example, the numerous paraphrases for drunken (/To be half seas over/, /To be pie-eyed/, /To be pickled/, /To be three sheets in the wind/) have been brought together, but contain many unsolved puzzles. As these examples show, euphemistic proverbial phrases are abundant. Many proverbial phrases can be traced to origins in literature, especially in the Bible; /To strain at a gnat and swallow a camel/ is Biblical; /To eat forbidden fruit/ contains a reminiscence of Adam and Eve in the Garden of Eden, and /To wash one's hands of a thing/ alludes to Pilate's act. Other proverbial phrases are based on fables: /To count your chickens before they are hatched/; /To be a dog in the manger/; and /To be a cat's paw/. Forgotten books may yield explanations: /To curry favor/ refers to Fauvel, a famous horse in a medieval French romance. Traces of old ideas survive in /To be born under a lucky star/ (astrology) or /To be in the seventh heaven/.

Some allusions to practices familiar in various callings are easy to understand: /To put the cart before the horse/, /To make hay while the sun shines/, /To have many irons in the fire/ (blacksmithing), /To give it the acid test/ (a pawnbroker tests gold with acid). Others are less readily understood: /To throw dust in his eyes/ is a gladiator's trick. /To go west/, which was much used during World War I, has its parallel in the 17th century /To go westward/, signifying to go to Tyburn to be hanged, but the two phrases may not be connected. /To mind one's p's and q's/ is plausibly explained by the ease with which a printer confuses these characters, but

some have seen in it an allusion to the pints and quarts of an innkeeper's accounts.

Footnote:

1. Proverbial phrases are usually listed along with proverbs. See also L. V. Berrey and Melvin van den Berk, *The American Thesaurus of Slang* (New York, 1942); Eric Partridge, *A Dictionary of Slang and Unconventional English; Colloquialisms and Catchphrases, Solecisms and Catachreses; Nicknames; Vulgarisms; and such Americanisms as have been naturalized* (3d ed., London, [1949]).   [AT]

Proverbial Sayings Committee, American Dialect Society The American Dialect Society, founded in 1889 at Cambridge, Massachusetts, has as its purpose the study of the ways of speech of America. In 1944 the plan to make a thorough study of all American speech resulted in setting up eight research committees, among them: Regional Speech and Localisms (George P. Wilson, chairman), Place-names (Harold W. Bentley, chairman), and Proverbial Sayings (Margaret M. Bryant, chairman).

The long-range plan of the Society is to become a center to which all forms of American speech, both written and spoken, from all sections of the country can be sent. From this material various dictionaries will be compiled so that there will be a reliable record of American English. Such dictionaries will show expressions peculiar to certain sections, the origin of particular expressions (when known), which expressions are common throughout the country, what social levels of speech the expressions belong to, etc. Thus the American Dialect Society in its comprehensive program for the study of all aspects of American speech is sponsoring the project of collecting proverbial sayings in the United States and Canada.

In the United States the significance of the proverb has been recognized by such scholars as Archer Taylor, Richard Jente, B. J. Whiting, F. W. Bradley, M. P. Tilley, and Harold W. Thompson, but no attempt in a comprehensive way has been made to collect the great mass of present-day proverbial lore. One may cite a few sayings from the West, such as "Hit for the high country," "Take to the tall timber," "Gone over the Divide," "Gone over the range," "Hit the trail," "Blaze a trail," and "Camping on his trail."

In order to make a country-wide canvas and to get the largest and most representative collection of proverbial lore from all sections, the chairman of the Committee on Proverbial Sayings organized the project according to states and selected a chairman for each. Later the provinces of Canada were included in the project.

The next step was to formulate and mimeograph *Instructions to Collectors of Proverbial Lore,* later incorporated in Publication No. 4 of the Society, *Proverbs and How to Collect Them* (May, 1945), prepared by the chairman of the Committee. The publication is divided into two parts, the first dealing with theoretical and historical aspects of the subject, and the second with practical problems of collecting.

The following instructions were given:

Since proverbial lore does play such an important part in our language, the American Dialect Society is beginning a country-wide canvass in order to get a representative collection of these popular folk sayings from every possible corner. Will you help by sending in any proverb or proverbial saying that you yourself use or hear in your daily conversation?

A. What to collect

Collect any saying in English, in the form of a proverb or idiomatic phrase, which is expressive of wisdom, or descriptive as a metaphor or simile. Many proverbs are figurative, but not all. It is better to err on the side of collecting too many than too few. If in doubt, collect. Specimens are given below to be used as a guide. Sayings may be individual or traditional, handed down from generations past; but no one collector can be sure of their character. It is best to send in anything you hear or find, and the committees of the Dialect Society, by comparing your contributions with others in the district and elsewhere, will be able to decide how widely used the sayings are. Examples:

(1) Folk proverbs appearing as complete sentences.

"Barking dogs never bite."
"Every rose has its thorn."
"A task well begun is half done."

(2) Sententious sayings or proverbs of the learned in complete sentences.

"Sweet are the uses of adversity."
"None but the brave deserves the fair."
"Distance lends enchantment."

(3) Proverbial rimes.

"Where cobwebs grow
Beaux never go."

"Man's work is from sun to sun
But woman's work is never done."

"Rain before seven, fair before eleven."

(4) Proverbial sayings, not complete sentences, involving a verb (usually in the infinitive form but with the first noun as the key word).

"To be in hot water."
"To count chickens before they are hatched." (Such an expression may also appear as a proverb in sentence form: "Don't count your chickens before they are hatched.")
"To raise the roof."

(5) Proverbial sayings not involving a verb.

"A bed of roses."
"A fool's paradise."
"A song and dance."

(6) Proverbial comparisons and similes.

"As greedy as a pig."
"Blacker than soot."
"To fight like a tiger."

(7) Wellerisms—comparisons like those made by Sam Weller in Dickens' *Pickwick Papers* (involving a quotation, often a well-known one, with a facetious sequel).

" 'Home sweet home!' as the vagrant said when he was sent to prison for the third time."
" 'All's well that ends well,' said the peacock when he looked at his tail."
" 'I punish her with good words,' as the man said when he threw the Bible at his wife."

(8) Modern facetious proverbs and rimes.

"Candy's dandy, but liquor's quicker."
"Don't tell a woman, telephone or telegraph."
"A ring on the finger is worth two on the 'phone."

Interesting collections of sayings may be found in Logan Pearsall Smith's *Words and Idioms* (1925), Thomas H. Russell's *The Sayings of Poor Richard: Wit, Wisdom and Humor of Benjamin Franklin in the Prefaces, Proverbs, and Maxims of Poor Richard's Almanacks for 1733 to 1758* (1926), Archer Taylor's *The Proverb* (1931), Emma Louise Snapp's *Proverbial Lore in Nebraska* (1933), Harold W. Thompson's *Body, Boots and Britches* (1940). For a fuller bibliography see "History of the Proverb," Part I [*Proverbs and How to Collect Them*].

B. Where to collect proverbial sayings

Sources may be oral or written. Proverbial lore may be found in travel books, journals, and magazines, where professional writers have made deliberate but authentic use of folk materials; in almanacs, newspapers, and so on, where local and popular tales and anecdotes are recorded. Oral lore is to be found everywhere every day. Rural or secluded districts are especially rich in proverbial lore, lore often peculiar to them. Some proverbs have been translated and adapted from foreign languages into idiomatic English. The various foreign strains blending to furnish our citizenry should be rich sources for this kind of saying.

C. How to record proverbial sayings

(1) Use 3 x 5 slips. Write in ink, or typewrite.
(2) Write each saying on a separate slip, exactly as you have heard it. Do not polish it up. If, however, you know any variations of the saying or expression, give these too.
(3) Add any helpful note as to where, when, and by whom this saying was used. Be sure to record the fact whether it is peculiar to a particular foreign, social, religious, industrial, or other group. If necessary, explain the meaning.
(4) In the upper left corner, write the key word of the sentence or phrase, usually the most important noun, sometimes a verb or adjective.
(5) In the upper right corner, write the state from which your contribution originally came.
(6) On the card give the proverb or saying and its meaning in parentheses, if the meaning is not perfectly obvious. Give also the details about the proverb or saying that are significant, such as the language from which it originally came, the occasion upon which it was heard, or the book or magazine from which it was copied.
(7) Carefully indicate all written sources. Give author (full name), book or manuscript (full title), year of publication or writing (as nearly as it can be ascertained), page in book or document (if numbered).
(8) On the back, write your name and address so that you will be credited with your contributions. A rubber stamp will save time in doing this.
[Examples of specimen cards were inserted here]

D. Who may collect proverbial sayings

Anyone may collect and send in proverbs or proverbial sayings. The more people that can be enlisted in the project, the better. Each collector should send in to his State Chairman a card with biographical data, giving his name, present and permanent address, schooling, profession, or position. This information may be helpful to the editors of the material when it is being prepared for publication. Use a slip 3 x 5 in size. Be sure, in addition, to sign all slips you send in or use a rubber stamp with your name and address.

Enlist the help of others—local historians, folklorists, school superintendents and principals, teachers, rural teachers in particular, alumni of various schools, newspaper editors, elderly people, chairmen of clubs and organizations, grange lecturers. Foreign language groups are particularly important. English teachers can be especially helpful and will in turn find the study of great value in their classes. Travel into districts where old country families have settled will be rewarding. In some states, folklorists connected with Writers' Projects, State Historical Societies, and other groups have begun such collections as the one contemplated. Get in touch with them. Have classes in folklore collect. Local records, histories, etc., often preserve the lore of previous generations. Put notices in folklore journals or other suitable magazines, such as those issued by historical societies. Letters in the name of a department (English, for instance) and the State Chairman, or the State Committee, might be sent to all students in a college or university. Candidates for an M.A. or a Ph.D. degree may be set to work on proverbs. Make sure your community is well represented. Do not worry if various collectors duplicate sayings; repeated occurrence shows the degree to which a saying is accepted, and the different places where it is found.

E. What will be done with the sayings collected

All sayings will be filed in the archives of the Society. From time to time pertinent collections will be printed in order to stimulate interest in further collecting. When an adequate amount of material has been compiled, it will be published in various regional studies and, at last, it is hoped, in a *Dictionary of American and Canadian Proverbs*.

To this end the Society needs the cooperation of hundreds of volunteers who in their particular localities will provide the material by sending the proverbial sayings to the State Chairmen. The State Chairmen, when they have collected what seems to be a complete or interesting set of sayings for a given area, or people, or occupation, such as might be published separately, will then send the collection to the Chairman of the Committee on Proverbial Sayings of the American Dialect Society.

The collecting and the filing of proverbial sayings from the various states and provinces is now being done in preparation for the projected *Dictionary of American and Canadian Proverbs*.

MARGARET M. BRYANT
Chairman, Committee on Proverbial Sayings

prudery If obscenities are acts or words which are thought to be degrading, prudery is the state of mind which is capable of degradation. The very wide distribution of prudery and the variety of topics which it seizes upon are sobering evidence that humanity has an infinite capacity for being degraded. As the acts or words which different cultures regard as degrading show an amazing variety so too do the acts or words which shock the prude. Some naked savages are not at all disturbed by their absolute nudity, but are shocked by the suggestion that they should eat in public. Whereas the occidental male prefers to defecate in private, the Chinese peasants not only defecate by the side of the road but squat facing the traffic so that they can watch the

world go by. On a hot summer day, a Japanese gentleman pulled down his trousers so that he could fan the middle of his body. Men in France use the public latrines which hide only the middle parts of their bodies and carry on conversation with women who pause to wait for them. Americans have been shocked by a sign on a French cathedral using a French word which in English is considered unspeakably vulgar to prohibit urination: *Défense de pisser*. In China, where women's feet are objects of erotic interest, women have been seen pulling their loose trouser legs high up about their middles but keeping their bound feet carefully hidden. Some British and American prudes have limbs but no legs; wear trousers, never pants. The we-groups always find the prudisms of the they-groups ridiculous or absurd, but forget that "they" feel no less strongly about their prudisms than "we" do about ours. [RDJ]

Ptah In ancient Egyptian religion, the chief god and the creator in the Memphite pantheon. Two traditions exist concerning his act of creation: he made the universe from mud, or he created by speaking, by saying the words that named what he willed to create. Ptah was the molder, the artificer, and was thus identified by the Greeks with Hephæstus. He is depicted as a primitive idol, with the legs unseparated, and carrying a scepter composed of the ankh (symbol of life), the tet (symbol of stability), and the uas (the divine scepter). Ptah was identified with Khnum, who also was a divine creator. He was incarnate in the Apis-bull of Memphis. His identification with Osiris and Seker, gods of the dead, led to the compound deity, Ptah-Seker-Osiris, a dwarf god who resembles none of the three gods he is named for.

P'ti' Albert Title of a medieval European book of magic that has been taken over together with its counterpart, *Albert le Grand* (Albertus Magnus), by Negroes of various regions of the New World as a part of the complex of magic and cabalism that has been syncretized with aboriginal African practices. In Haiti, importation of the *P'ti' Albert* into the country is forbidden by law. [MJH]

puberty dances The dances connected with puberty rites are always group enactments by society members or simply by older men and women. All adult men join in the Australian *waiung-arree*. On the other hand, the Sierra Leone *Bundu* dances are exclusive. Usually members of the initiate's own sex dance around her, as in the *káusima* of the Chaco Chorotí, Ashluslay, and Mataco. But among the Karok (California) Indians, men surround the girl and dance with her in turn. In California —though not everywhere—she generally participates in the ceremony activity herself. She dances twice a day in the Yuki *hamnam-wok*, with her face covered and she joins in the Maidu *wulu*. The Achomawi girl not only dances all night by the fire, but enacts her future occupations. Similarly, the Apache girl anticipates all of the actions of her future life.

As a rule these dances are in circular formation, in fact, double circles, as the *wallang-arree*, *wulu*, and Karok *ih-uk*. But double line formations occur among the Karok, Wiyot, Yuki, Shasta, and Miwok Indians, and in the Papago *wakita*. Frequently the dancing is grotesque and frenzied. Supernaturals, such as the *máuari*, *hulk'ilal*, and Apache *gahe* leap about with weird gestures. The initiation of certain central Australia tribes inspires all participants to frenzied abandonment.

Demon-impersonators always wear some form of disguise—paint in the *kina* rite, facial distortion in the *hulk'ilal-wok*, masks in the *klóketen, káusima, yanmena, mduari,* and *gahe.* The most fantastic masks belong to Melanesian societies: the *Qat* of the New Hebrides, the *Duk-duk* of New Britain, the *Nanga* of Fiji.

These last represent ancestral spirits. Elsewhere the puberty rite may also be associated with the dead, as among the Bororo of eastern Brazil, who synchronize boys' puberty rites with funeral ceremonies. The Bapende of the Belgian Congo enact a symbolic death and rebirth to a new life. The Apache *gahe* and *líbahi* exert curative powers in the course of the ceremony. The Hopi *powamu* is at the same time a bean-sprouting rite. Association with the deer is common in the Chaco and California, by means of hoof rattles. These are manipulated in the Chaco by the women, among the Karok, Tolowa, Shasta, Achomawi, and Maidu Indians by the girl. The deer is commonly a symbol of cure and vegetation. It is comprehensible that puberty rites should have associations of regeneration. There is little phallic symbolism or erotic dancing, but on the contrary usually a segregation of sexes. However, sexual license follows the *hamnam-wok* in the darkened house, as also the *wulu.*

These rites acquire less importance in higher cultures, and in occidental civilization the coming of age is completely secular. The knighting of the Middle Ages and its concluding dance rounds still retained a flavor of ceremonialism. Among the mestizos of Yucatán, *jaranas* are danced to phonographs in the private homes. In the United States debutantes vie with each other in lavish entertainments and social dances. [GPK]

puberty rites Ceremonies, either individual or group, usually marked the passage of a boy or a girl from childhood to adulthood in all North American Indian groups. For girls, if group ceremonies were held, such usually coincided with her first menstrual period; among many western groups and in the Southwest among such groups as the Apache, these public ceremonies took the form of elaborate 3 to 10 day dances. In other western tribes pubescent girls were "baked" in heated trenches or pits for several days while songs and dances were performed for them. Over the rest of the continent, except in the Southwestern Pueblos and part of the Plains, girls generally retired, alone or with an old woman, to a small menstrual hut during their first menses, and puberty rites were private, involving fasting, non-bathing, and listening to advice and admonitions from old women. All over the continent one tabu prevailed at menstruation, especially at puberty: a girl might not scratch her head with her fingers, but had to use a scratching stick which was either elaborate or simple, as the case might be.

Boys' puberty rites were of two sorts: 1) vision-questing, which was either done alone or in small groups of two, three, or four boys, and 2) formal initiation into adult status in the tribe. For vision-questing youths were sent out by their parents in winter usually, scantily clad, with no fire or fire-making apparatus, and with no food, but with their bow and arrows. The boy(s) was told to stay out until a supernatural had communicated with

him; if unsuccessful on the first quest, the youth was later encouraged or commanded by his parents to repeat it. Some were blessed with visions; others never were.

Group initiations, or boys' puberty rites, took several different forms over the continent, very often being connected with initiation into religious cults or societies, as the Kuksu initiation rites in central California, the Wüwüchim ceremony of the Hopi Indians, or the jimsonweed drinking rite of the tribes of southern California. Group puberty rites for boys often imply death and rebirth of the novice, and include tests of physical endurance—the youths are whipped, scratched, made to dance until exhausted, or taken on long walks. See Lucile Hoerr Charles, "Growing up through Drama" (*JAFL* 59: 247–62, 1946). See ADOLESCENCE CEREMONIES; INITIATION; JIMSONWEED; KUKSU; MENSTRUATION; WÜWÜCHIM.

[EWV]

púca or **pooka** A harmless but very mischievous supernatural being of Irish folklore, often appearing in animal or half-animal form. He is a rapid transformer, and when seen in half-animal form, it is thought perhaps he has been caught in the act of transformation. If so inclined he can give a man the gift of understanding animal speech. He is often thought of as black: *com dub leis an bpúca* (black as the púca) is a common simile. The púca is apt to punish and annoy grave-robbers and ungrateful people, but he is quick to help those whom he favors or to whom he feels indebted. He has been known to save poor farmers' cattle from drowning and to protect those in danger from evil spirits. He resembles the numerous European household spirits in that he will tidy up a kitchen in the night or do a turn at some yard chore. In fact, Keightley (*Fairy Mythology,* p. 418) says "the Irish pooka is plainly the English puck." Likenesses and variations are both manifest. The snail is associated with the púca: Irish children chant "Púca, púca, put out your horns!" At Halloween he steps on or dirties the last blackberries of the season.

puck A household spirit of English folklore: compare BROWNIE; GOBLIN; NISSE. The medieval English *pouke* was of more malicious nature and often identified with the Christian Devil. Shakespeare's Puck is the same as ROBIN GOODFELLOW. See BOGEY; BUCCA.

puk A household spirit; the dragon of treasure, who brings stolen goods to his master: called by the Latvians pūkis, by the Lithuanians pūkys, and by the Estonians *puuk.* Obviously he is of German origin and comes to the Baltic countries from northern Germany: compare *pūks* in Mecklenburg and Schleswig-Holstein, *pück* in Friesland, *puk* in Low German. The name and all the traditions are the same in Germany as in the Baltic countries. Sometimes also native names were given to him: *aitvaras* and *kaukas* in Lithuania, *tulihänd* and *pisuhänd* in Estonia. Probably the tradition came with the German tradesmen and colonists, first to Riga, an important trade center, whence it was taken north by the Estonians and south by the Lithuanians. Lithuanian legends often recount that a farmer who had brought his crops or flax to Riga, after selling his goods, bought a dragon from a German tradesman.

One question, of course, is whether the tradition is of German origin or whether the Germans themselves got it from Scandinavia and the British Islands. Compare the Irish *púca,* Norwegian *pukje,* Old Icelandic *púki.*

Old Danish *puge,* Swedish dialect *puke,* English *puck.*
The English hobgoblin or Robin Goodfellow is also
called *puck* (*pwcca* in Wales), *pooka* or *púca* in Ireland,
poake in Worcestershire, and *pixy* in the west of England. But he is a spirit of another kind: chiefly a malicious spirit, taking all sorts of shapes and leading
travelers astray into the bogs.
Literature:
R. Auning, *Über den lettischen Drachenmythus (Puhkis),*
Mitau, 1891. L. v. Schroeder, *Germanische Elfen und
Götter beim Estenvolke,* Wien, 1906. Pp. 14–61. F. De-
lattre, *English Fairy Poetry,* London, 1912, p. 19. [JB]

Pulau Bah Behrang Sakai (Malay peninsula) abode
of the dead; the Island of Fruit, located to the west
where the souls live in perfect bliss and eat from the
ever-fruiting trees. Compare BELET.

Pulekukwerek "Downstream sharp": Yurok Indian
benefactor and monster-slayer who burned blind cannibal women and killed those beings who crushed people
while pretending to split logs, or who speared them
while playing games, or gave people overstrong tobacco.
He stole the boy Night, found the man who could weave
the sky, and who placed the stars upon it. Pulekukwerek,
whose name derives from the horns on which he sat,
was born far north at the end of the world; when he
left the earth he went to a far-away land of dentalium
and everlasting dances. He is the most admired character in Yurok mythology. [EWV]

**pulling the heather green, pulling the nut, pulling the
red rose** Terms used in a number of the English and
Scottish traditional ballads of the Child collection to
mean: 1) trespassing; 2) seeking abortifacient herbs;
3) seeking magic herbs to facilitate and ease childbirth.
In regard to trespass, the trespasser is usually a maiden;
she is caught by the owner or guardian of the property
or wood; the penalty is that she must give up either her
virginity or her life. In *Tam Lin* (Child #39) and *Mary
Hamilton* (Child #173), the heroine is illegitimately
pregnant and seeks some magic plant or "graveyard
herb" that will cause abortion. In other ballads some
craving for a fruit, typical of pregnancy, is expressed,
as in the *Cherry Tree Carol* (Child #54), or belief in
the power of certain herbs to ease childbirth is reflected.
The reverence for trees and groves, the challenge to the
deity or guardian of the grove, and the penalty for
trespassing or breaking a bough, and also the association
of the gathering of certain herbs with pregnancy and
childbirth is discussed by S. Elliot, "Pulling the Heather
Green" (*JAFL* 48:352 ff.).

pulse Physicians of folktale make a complete diagnosis by feeling the pulse (F956.1). In oriental story, love
was often discovered by feeling the pulse (J1142.2). Antiochus, in the Greek romance of Antiochus and Stratonice, fell ill for no accountable reason and no one could
discover the cause until a clever physician of Ceos
recognized his ailment as love-sickness. In order to diagnose the case, the physician ordered all the beauties of
the court, Stratonice among them, to pass through the
sick-room. At the appearance of Stratonice, the pulse of
Antiochus quickened, though she was his stepmother.
In one of the variants of the master thief story, the king
discovers who has just been in bed with the queen by
listening to the heartbeats of the different men in the

palace; the culprit, awake and aware of what the king is
doing, is given away by his rapid heartbeat. The incident
of marking the culprit (who marks everyone else) follows.
Several physicians of ancient days are said to have used
the pulse as an indicator, and later medical history pre-
sents examples of this practice introduced into Europe.
The whole matter is discussed by Rohde (*Griechische
Roman und seine Vorläufer,* Leipzig, 1914, pp. 57 ff.).
The pulse as indicator of love is also to be noted in the
Decameron (Day 2, nov. 8). [GPS]

Puluga The name for Biliku used by the Akar-Bale
and Aka Bea tribes of the Andaman Islands.

pumpkin The round, edible, yellow fruit of a large
trailing vine (genus *Cucurbita*). In China the pumpkin
is Emperor of the Garden, symbol of fruitfulness, health,
and gain. According to Kachin (Burma) mythology, after
the pumpkin had been created, each of the nats added
something to it until, in the end, they had created man.
Pumpkin-seed tea is a general American diuretic and
is also used to kill tapeworms. The *Fête du Potiron* (Festival of King Pumpkin) was celebrated at the *Halles
Centrales,* the great produce market of Paris, in September. The largest available pumpkin was decked in a
tinsel and paper crown and carried about the market
while all made obeisance. Afterwards it was cut into
pieces which were auctioned off for soup.

There is a famous numskull story (J1772.1) known all
over Europe, in Asia, and repeated with fresh humor
and flavor among southern United States mountain
whites. The numskull thinks the pumpkin is an ass's
egg. He throws it into the bushes; it breaks; the frightened rabbit that runs out of the bushes he thinks is the
ass's colt. See BREATHMAKER; CHINŪN WAY SHUN; SHIN-
GRAWA.

Punch and Judy Hero and heroine of the traditional
English puppet play. Punch, with his hooked nose and
sleeping cap, is a fiery tempered humorist who is continually quarreling with everyone. He beats Judy to
death with a club. He wallops the arresting policeman
unmercifully. He conquers dogs or wild animals. Finally,
he even hangs the hangman with his own noose. The
slapstick transferred rapidly from hand to hand as the
puppet-master manipulates his hand puppets in the box
theater and the squeaking humming voices of the Punch
and Judy characters are the unforgettable memories of
the viewers of the puppet show. Punch is a contraction
of Punchinello, for the Punch and Judy story originated
in Italy. (Some say that the name comes from Pontius
Pilate.) The original story, still sometimes seen, has
Punch throwing his squalling brat out of the window,
killing his wife in the subsequent battle, escaping from
the policeman, being imprisoned but escaping, defeating a dog and a doctor, killing Death, and outsmarting
the Devil.

Pundjel Southeastern Australian creator who made
all things, including the ceremonies, and who figures
prominently in the boys' initiation rites. [KL]

Purāṇa One of a class of Sanskrit books which deal
with ancient and medieval Indian theology, astronomy,
cosmogony, genealogy, accounts of kings and rishis, and
miscellaneous materials, all illustrated by fables, songs,
legends, and tales: literally, old or ancient lore. The
oldest of the *Purāṇas* dates from 600 A.D. and some of

them may be as late as the 13th or 16th century. All of them have undergone revisions and each in its present form enumerates the whole group. They are 18 in number (actually 19, but the *Vāyu* and *Brahmāṇḍa* were originally one and are thus classed as such), written in verse in the form of a dialog between two persons into which are woven stories and discourses uttered by other persons. They are attributed to a ṛishi or to the gods. The five subjects which are proper to the *Purāṇas* are *sarga* (creation), *pratisarga* (dissolution and recreation), *manvantara* (periods of the Manus), *vaṃśa* (genealogies), and *vaṃśyānucharita* (history of the Solar and Lunar races mentioned in the *vaṃśa*). The *Purāṇas* are based upon the same body of tradition as is *Mahābhārata*, but the stories are not always narrated in the same way. They also expound the four phases of human endeavor—*kāma* (love), *artha* (wealth), *dharma* (righteousness), and *mokṣa* (final emancipation from rebirths).

In the *Purāṇas* Indra is the chief of the subordinate gods and Sūrya holds an important position. The chief gods are Brahmā, the creator, Vishṇu, the preserver, and Śiva, the destroyer, and the relative positions of Vishṇu and Śiva are explained. Vishṇu takes no part in terrestrial affairs except when incarnated, while Śiva dwells among men and practices human asceticism. The two (with Brahmā) are aspects of one and the same god.

Purgine-Pas or **Pirgene** The Thunderer in Erza-Mordvin folklore: a word derived from the Lithuanian *Perkūnas*, thunder god. [JB]

purification The sources of ceremonial uncleanness or ritual pollution in primitive cultures are, mainly, blood (menstrual, parturitional, placental, accidental, or shed in murder or battle), death, and birth, and, secondarily and in limited areas and times, certain foods and drinks, colors, places, seasons, trees, rocks, and even persons. The method of getting rid of the ritual impurity or condition of uncleanness was, and still is in many societies and religions, the performance of some ceremony which variously includes sacrifice, washing, anointing, sprinkling, burning, or cutting. A typical purification ceremony after childbirth is prescribed and described in *Leviticus* xii, 2-8:

"If a woman have conceived seed, and born a man child: then she shall be unclean seven days; according to the days of the separation for her infirmity shall she be unclean. And in the eighth day the flesh of his foreskin shall be circumcised. And she shall then continue in the blood of her purifying three and thirty days; she shall touch no hallowed thing, nor come into the sanctuary, until the days of her purifying be fulfilled. But if she bear a maid child, then she shall be unclean two weeks, as in her separation: and she shall continue in the blood of her purifying three score and six days. And when the days of her purifying are fulfilled, for a son, or for a daughter, she shall bring a lamb of the first year for a burnt offering, and a young pigeon, or a turtledove, for a sin offering, unto the door of the tabernacle of the congregation, unto the priest: Who shall offer it before the Lord, and make an atonement for her; and she shall be cleansed from the issue of her blood. This is the law for her that hath born a male or a female. And if she be not able to bring a lamb, then she shall bring two turtles, or two young pigeons; the one for the burnt offering, and the other

for the sin offering: and the priest shall make an atonement for her, and she shall be clean."

In this purification process of the ancient Hebrews may be observed several characteristic tabus and their ritual removal. Note that the cleansing is not for childbirth itself but for "the issue of her blood" shed at parturition, that the thirty-three days is calculated to cover the menstrual period, that the period of uncleanness is a week longer for a female child, that the piacular sacrifice must be burned as well as killed, and that it must be a priest who pronounces her clean. Furthermore, she is barred from the sanctuary and may not even touch any sacred object; otherwise she would render them unclean; and when she brings her offerings, she may come only as far as the door until she has been completely purified.

It is one of the anomalies of the primitive mind that while blood is one of the main sources of ceremonial uncleanness, the piacular sacrifice with bloodshed is the often prescribed method of purification. It was not only from the ancient Hebrew culture but from old Greek, Roman, and other religions as well that the unknown author of the book derived his traditional assurance that "Without the shedding of blood there is no remission of sins" (*Hebrews* ix, 22).

Elaborate ceremonial preparation of the "water of separation" is described in *Numbers* xix. It must contain several cleansing ingredients, such as hyssop, but particularly the ashes of a red heifer without spot or blemish and "upon which never came yoke." The water of separation "is a purification for sin." It is to purify anyone who has touched a dead body, the tent in which anyone has died, all who have come into the tent, and all open vessels in the tent. It must also be used to cleanse anyone who has become unclean by touching a grave.

Fumigation is another ceremonial process for ritual cleansing, sometimes by the smoke of incense used at sacrifices, but the incense itself must be made from gums gathered from holy trees by magical ritual process. Different ingredients for use in fumigation are held potent by various peoples—grains and mustard by Hindus, tobacco by some American Indian tribes. Many peoples are purified by jumping over fire and through smoke. See BELTANE. Other methods used are anointing with holy oil, washing with *gomez* (the urine of the sacred cow—Hindu), smearing with the blood of an animal, or baptism with bull blood as in the Mithraic Taurobolium, rubbing with sulfur, lye, or using hyssop, hellebore, or other purifying drugs or medicines, shaving the head, cutting the nails, spitting, blowing the nose, wearing a sacred fleece, circumcision, knocking out teeth, branding, tattooing, using salt liberally, sprinkling with water in which the Christian cross has been washed, by vowing celibacy, virginity, or chastity. Some believe that unclean houses may be purified by sweeping out the bad spirits with a broom. Emetics are held to be efficacious; some prescribe whitewash. Moslems use earth and sand. Sweatbaths and all sorts of baptisms are used in man's efforts to rid himself of spiritual pollution.

The beginning of the new year is reckoned as an especially good time for ceremonial cleansing, so we note purification ceremonies at that time in Peru, Mexico, China, Indochina (see THINGYĀN PWE), Indonesia, Africa, among the ancient Babylonians and the North

American Indians. It is also the favorite time for revivals and protracted meetings among American Protestant churches.

One interesting variation of these cathartic rituals is the cleansing of someone else or something else as a substitute for the sinner. The guilt of an individual or a whole tribe may be transferred to a scapegoat who is driven off a precipice or across the border into the next country, carrying with him the sins and ills of many. Or a person, either a spotless virgin or the king himself, may offer or be chosen to be a vicarious sacrifice for the sins of the whole tribe. See BARASHNŪM. [CFP]

☛ Purification, or formal ritual cleansing of the body prior to undertaking various rites, or after specific contamination of the body, was general among the North American Indians. In several groups the idea of purification was extended to include purification of dwelling houses and personal possessions. Various elements and substances were used as purificatory agents: water everywhere, fire and smoke, angelica root, cedar, tobacco, and other plants in various areas. Fasting from all or from specific foods such as salt, meat, or grease, the drinking of limited amounts of water or abstaining from water, and continence on the part of married persons, also made persons "clean" and fit to participate in sacred rites and ceremonies. Bathing and other purificatory rites were necessary for women, or for both parents, after childbirth; at the end of the menstrual period a woman had to bathe and otherwise purify herself before she returned to her home; after a death the relatives of the deceased, the corpse-handlers, and the gravediggers had to eat alone and sparingly for a prescribed length of time, and had to bathe or have their heads washed before they were again considered clean and of no danger to their fellow human beings.

Incense of one kind or another (chiefly cedar in the eastern United States and on the Plains, and angelica, sage, fir, and other plants in the West) was used both to purify human beings and ritual apparatus such as drums, rattles, and other musical instruments, masks, etc. Often these purificatory substances were burned in an open fire and the articles were cleansed by being held in the smoke from the fire. Ashes were also sometimes thrown over persons to purify, but the more usual specific use for ashes was to drive away disease. [EWV]

☛ Many South American Indians consider it necessary for the mourners to undergo a purification after the funerals. Among the Chiriguano, Saliva, and Paez, the relatives wash themselves in a river. The Aymara jump over a fire. The belongings of the deceased are often exposed to flames or carefully washed. [AM]

purohita In India, originally the domestic chaplain or family priest of a king or wealthy noble. During the period of the *Brāhmaṇas* the purohita became a temporal as well as a religious adviser. Today he is the most important functionary in the Indian community. He performs all the village's religious ceremonies and is supported by fixed allotments of grain or by special offerings. He not only presides at marriages, births, and death ceremonies, but acts as village astrologer and the magician who controls evil spirits. A purohita once swallowed the ocean in three gulps, another made fire, and a third turned the moon into a cinder. Anyone who

harms a purohita will whirl about in a black hell for a hundred years after death.

Puruṣa (1) In Vedic mythology, a primeval giant sacrificed by the gods to create the world: literally, man. The giant's head became the sky, his feet the earth, his navel the air, and from his limbs came the four castes. In Sāṅkhya philosophy Puruṣa represents the spiritual force opposed to but working with Prakṛiti, the material force.

(2) A name of Brahmā as the creator and original male.

Pusa Buddha, a term used by the Chinese people to refer to their gods with little concern whether the god thus addressed belongs to a Buddhist, Taoist, or Christian cult. [RDJ]

Pūshan Literally, the prosperer: an indistinctly defined Vedic sun god, protector and multiplier of cattle, friend and guide of travelers, guardian of paths, and patron of conjurors. As a guide Pūshan conducts the dead to the abode of their fathers. He carries an ox-goad, is drawn by goats, and is toothless. According to the *Mahābhārata* and the *Purāṇas*, Rudra knocked out his teeth at Daksha's sacrifice. Pūshan is invoked with Indra and Bhaga and is sometimes numbered among the Ādityas.

púskita Same as BUSK.

Puss in Boots Title of a popular folktale belonging to the great helpful animal cycle in which the helpful animal wins riches, honor, and a beautiful wife for the hero. The typical Puss in Boots story begins with the fact that a cat is the only inheritance left to a poor youth (N411.1.1; Types 545AB; 1650; 1651). The cat, however, is a very marvelous cat, who through his magic powers convinces the king that his master is a dispossessed prince (K1952.1); he woos and wins the princess for his master (B582.1.1); borrows a measure to measure his master's money (K1954.1), casually scorning to collect the coins that have stuck to the bottom of it, thereby establishing his master's reputation as a wealthy man, or he talks continually about his master's wealth (K1917.3). When the king is to visit the youth and behold the wonderful possessions, the cat induces all shepherds, cattleherds, etc., en route to say the herds belong to his master. The cat next beguiles a giant (ogre, troll) with conversation and tales all night at his own castle gate; at sunrise the giant bursts (à la all supernaturals who perish at sunrise if they have not regained their own place by then); and the cat takes over the giant's sumptuous castle for his master. Then having equipped the youth with herds and horses, a castle, a beautiful and wealthy wife, the cat demands to have his head cut off. The youth demurs; the cat insists; at last the youth beheads the cat and thus unbewitches the fine young prince who has been compelled to live in cat form.

The Scandinavian versions of this story often have a heroine instead of a hero, and also often include the sensitivity test, in which the cat advises the poor farmer's daughter to say she has not slept well, in order to establish her "royalty." See PRINCESS ON THE PEA. In a Norwegian variant entitled *Lord Peter*, the cat is a princess thus bewitched, who helps the youth to wealth, honor, and the castle, and on being unbewitched, marries him herself.

In most western European tellings the animal is a cat, in eastern Europe usually a fox, in Siberia and Mongolia a fox, in India a jackal; in the four known Philippine Island variants, it is a monkey who by a series of thievings and lies brings his paupered master from rags to riches. Perrault's version, *Chat Botté* (1697), has been taken as *the* version almost everywhere and has altered the detail of the older folk form everywhere that it has penetrated. (See Stith Thompson, *The Folktale*, New York, 1946, pp. 58–59; D. S. Fansler, *Filipino Popular Tales, MAFLS* 12, pp. 326–338.)

Pūtanā In Hindu mythology, the female demon, daughter of Bali, who tried to kill the infant Krishna by suckling him with her poisonous milk. Krishna, however, slew her by draining her of her lifeblood. Pūtanā causes abortion and diseases in children.

pwe A Burmese dance festival, with occasional dialog and song. There are three main types: 1) the ordinary pwe performed by two girl dancers and two male clown dancers called *loobyets;* 2) *yein pwe,* ensemble dances in rows, men and women separate, for country festivals; 3) *zat pwe,* with dramatic content, such as the tale of the *Rāmāyaṇa (yama zat).*

The dancing, particularly that of the girls in the ordinary pwe, is lively, virtuoso, even acrobatic, despite the tight-fitting skirt and the great mound of gleaming black hair. Arms and hands are supple; the steps are intricate; costumes are brilliant and colorful; the musical rhythms are "catchy." They are played on an impressive ensemble of 13 drums, two flutes, a *pattala* or kind of xylophone, wood block, gongs, bells, and whistles. Rapid dances are at times relieved by a slow *yodia.* The composite is sumptuous, merry, and wholesome. [GPK]

pyinsalet Burmese magic, practiced to confer temporary invulnerability or to cause "hallucination in respect of the five kinds of sensations." These effects are achieved by such potent mixtures as one made with equal parts of the livers of a human being, black dog, owl, cobra, and monkey, pounded together with a whole lizard from midnight until dawn. When a little of this concoction is rubbed on the left eye, witches, nats, or ghosts can be seen. Rub a little on the right eye and night will be turned into day. A little on the forehead will make the possessor invisible; some on the hand will cause an iron safe to open when beaten; on a wind-blown leaf, will change it into a tiger or an elephant; some rubbed on a lotus flower will produce a woman, rubbed on a lotus bud will engender a man. Methods for attaining invulnerability include carrying balls of mercury or pieces of iron, silver inserted under the skin, bathing in medicated water, and wearing various amulets.

pyrrhic dance A battle dance of ancient Greece, named after the vermilion tunics or blood-simulating stains used by the Spartans. Of Cretan origin, it became in Greece a regular exercise and battle preparation for all Greek youths. The martial enactments received rhythmic form from the musical accompaniments. Motifs of magical exorcism may have enhanced the warlike objectives.

Later on the pantomimic element crowded out the original function and by the 5th century it had everywhere, except in Sparta, become a spectacle. In 6th century Athens it was danced at the Panathenaic festivals to flute or song accompaniment. Its mass effects were impressive: sweeping phalanxes, circular and linear battle formations. At times soloists paired off for combat, or a single dancer fought an imaginary adversary in the *skiamachia* (shadow-fight) or *monomachia* (single fight). At times women took part. Finally it fell under Bacchic influence and degenerated into a circus dance of the Roman Christians.

The sword dances and *moriscas* of northern and western Europe and the Balkans are related to the pyrrhic dance, though not necessarily descended from it, for battle dances appear in all primitive ritualism. [GPK]

Pythias or **Phintias** See DAMON AND PYTHIAS.

Python In Greek mythology, the female dragon who dwelt at Delphi, guarding the chasm there. When Apollo came to Delphi, the dragon tried to prevent him from approaching the chasm and Apollo killed it. He thus became possessor of the oracle. The priestess of the god was known as Pytho or Pythoness. The story of the slaying of the dragon was periodically enacted at Delphi in a ritual drama. The serpent or dragon as chthonic spirit is found elsewhere in the world; the dragon-slayer as culture hero is as widespread. See DRAGON-FIGHT OR DRAGON-SLAYING THEME.

Q

Qaf, Kaf, or **Caf** In Moslem-Arabic mythology, the mountain range, made of emerald, that encircles the world outside the ring of ocean. It is the abode of the jinn and other supernatural creatures. The term is also generic for mountains, as Alps is in English, but specifically is applied to the Caucasus range.

Qamate The supreme god of the Amoxosa Kaffir Negroes: said to be honored by them with huge burial mounds on which every passerby deposited a stone. Compare HAITSI-AIBAB.

q'ari q'ari The cutting dance of the Aymara Indians of Bolivia. The men wield knives as in the Mexican *morisma* and *media luna.* Music is provided by two flutes and two drums. Though without masks, the dancers impersonate q'ari q'ari, the heart-stealing demon. This mythological association suggests an indigenous origin. There is no association with any particular Catholic fiesta, August being the most common time of performance. [GPK]

qat A cultivated arbutus of Ethiopia (*Catha edulis*), a bush sometimes growing as high as 20 feet, whose twigs and leaves yield a dangerous narcotic. In Ethiopia the Imam sanctions the chewing of it by soldiers, especially on Fridays before praying, to encourage pious contemplation. It is also taken as a stimulant by groups of young people who meet in gatherings to chew qat leaves. It is an intellectual stimulant, but overuse impairs the mental powers. The reaction to it is insomnia, followed by severe headache, loss of semen through urination, and reduction of sexual vitality. See Coon, Carleton S., "Southern Arabia, A Problem for the Future" in *Studies in the Anthropology of Oceania and Asia (Papers of the Peabody Museum of American Archaeology and Ethnology, Harvard University, Vol. XX)*, p. 202. [DMD]

Qeb An alternative transliteration of the name of the Egyptian earth god, Geb.

q'ena q'ena A wind instrument of the Aymara Indians of Bolivia, which gives its name to the dance and the fiesta using it. Except for two drummers, the musical ensemble is entirely one of self-accompaniment by the dancers. The *q'ena* is a bamboo pipe with six stops, made in several sizes, and emitting doleful sounds. The green parrot provides ornaments for jaguar skin vest and feathered hat, and trousers split at the ankle. These ornaments may not appear indigenous, but the q'ena certainly is, as is also the simple circular dance it accompanies. [GPK]

Qiqirn A huge supernatural hairless dog, greatly feared by the Central Eskimo. It is described as having hair only on its mouth, feet, ears, and tail-tip. Its proximity to men or dogs causes them to have fits. But it is a foolish creature, terrified of human beings, and runs away the minute it is mentioned.

Qoluncotun The creator, now referred to as God, of the Sinkaietk or Southern Okanagon Indians of the state of Washington. While Coyote figures as the trickster in Sinkaietk mythology, Qoluncotun is the supreme being who is credited with having created the universe and all the animals, although there is apparently no Sinkaietk myth detailing this creation. [EWV]

quadrilles French term for square formations (Spanish *cuadrillas*, It. *quadriglia*, Norwegian *kadriljs*): a dance for four couples in square formations. The figures are flexible, however, and often blend into double circle or longways patterns. Thus the quadrille is a transitional form between 1) rounds and squares, and 2) longways and squares. There has been much debate about the origin of the quadrille. It is probably a French development from the *cotillon*. The transition from 1) rounds is evident in the *branles carrés* and *tambourin*, which introduce interlacings by the four couples into essentially circular patterns. 2) Longways formations adhere to the antecedent *cotillon*, the Hungarian derivative *körmagyar*, and the New Mexican *cuadrillas*. The earliest quadrille, reported in 1816, consisted of six parts in *Le Pantalon, L'Eté, La Poule, La Trenis, La Pastourelle, Le Finale*, consisting of cross-overs, mills, and circling. The Lanciers or *Quadrille à la Cour* contained five parts, each in a different metre: *La Dorset, Victoria, Les Moulinets, Les Visites, Les Lanciers*.

Quadrilles have been enthusiastically accepted in all countries of western Europe, to a lesser extent in Slavic countries and Hungary. In the Balkans, however, they have not replaced the ancient chain dances. Sometimes their nature is disguised by a name as Hunsdon House (**England**), or *Kanafaska* (Moravia), or by the variant

term *contra*, as the German Föhringer *Kontra*. In the United States quadrilles are always in square formation and thus are essentially identical with square dances.

In true quadrille formation the four couples form a square, with the first couple back to the musicians, the second facing them, and the third and fourth to right and left. A double quadrille is formed similarly by eight couples. The couples alternate and interweave in every conceivable pattern of cross-overs, serpentine, pivoting (see tabulation in DANCE: FOLK AND PRIMITIVE). The step is usually a run, in the United States with a shuffling quality; but in England various skips and slides enrich the vocabulary. Frequently the waltz, galop, and polka steps enrich the Danish Oxcow and New Mexican Galope and Polka Cruzada section of *cuadrillas*. The *körmagyar* introduces typically Hungarian steps. The United States show two contrasting tendencies: the strict sequence and coordinations of steps, patterns, and music in the New England Singing Quadrille, and the improvisatory developments of the play-party games. [GPK]

quartz A hard, vitreous, widely distributed mineral (crystallized silicon dioxide) occurring in many rocks, often colorless and transparent, sometimes existing in diversely colored forms. See AGATE; AMETHYST; CHALCEDONY; JASPER; ONYX.

White quartz crystals are regarded as rain-stones by certain Queensland, Australia, tribes and are attached to the rain-sticks in the rain-making ceremonies. The people of northern Queensland search for the white crystals in the mountains, pulverize them, and use the powder to simulate, or *be*, rain in their mimetic rain-making rite. The powder is showered over the women by the men while the women hold wooden troughs over their heads to keep off the "rain." The people of New South Wales also regard quartz crystal as a rain-stone. The rain-maker holds a fragment of it in his mouth and spits it toward the sky during the ceremony.

Quartz was in common use among North American Indians centuries before the white man came among them. Arrowheads, knives, and ornaments of quartz have been found in the investigated mounds. Quartz crystals surmounting ceremonial wands have been unearthed in southern California. The Cherokee used them for divining stones. In Ife (West Africa) there are still ceremonial stools carved in one piece from a solid piece of quartz. Among the Hottentots, where iron is tabu to the priest, he uses a sharp quartz implement for sacrificing animals and circumcising young boys.

In early British folk belief quartz pebbles were called star-stones and were constantly sought for their curative properties. Nine star-stones collected from a running brook, boiled in a quart of water from the same brook, would impart their curing power to the water, which was given to the patient for nine successive mornings. In the Shetland Islands quartz pebbles were said to cure sterility; they were collected by women and thrown into a pool wherein they washed their feet. In Persian folk practice quartz crystals are sometimes put on babies to insure their getting enough mother's milk.

Qudlivun or **Qudliparmuit** The happy spirit-land of pleasure and games in the sky in Central Eskimo mythology. All who have fed the poor during life, known starvation themselves, been murdered, or died in childbirth go to Qudlivun after death. Also anyone who has been miserable enough to take his own life finds joy in Qudlivun. See ADLIVUN.

Queen of Elfan's Nourice A Scottish ballad (Child #40), known only in fragmentary form; some stanzas even of this fragment do not belong properly to it, but rather to *Thomas Rymer*. The Queen of Elfland has stolen a mother to nurse her child, and the mother wakes the queen to complain of her lot. The queen tells her she must nurse the child until he stands to her knee, and then she will be permitted to go back to her own child and to Christendom. At the basis of this jewellike bit of folk poetry lies the belief in the vulnerability to pagan forces of the woman soon after childbirth. The nurse has been stolen when her child is only four days old, hence there has been no time for churching and the woman still remains susceptible to elfish influence. See CHURCHING OF WOMEN.

Queevet or **Aharaigichi** A deity of the now extinct Abipón Indians of South America: identified with the constellation Pleiades. He was also known as Grandfather. The Abipón believed all their strength and courage stemmed from him, and they accounted for the riches of the Spaniards as having come from him direct. During the months when his constellation could not be seen they feared greatly for his welfare and continuance, and the rising of the Pleiades in May was greeted with rejoicing and a great festival. The priests, known as *keebet,* derived their power from Aharaigichi (or Queevet). They were magicians and transformers, could become invisible or stalk the world in the shape of tigers. Illness, death, thunder, lightning, eclipses, and other natural phenomena terrified the Abipón, who attributed all such manifestations to the *keebet.*

quena The notched end-blown flute of the Incas and its descendant, the only instrument generally played among Andean peoples today; also, the various types of flute played by the Chaco Indians of South America. The Inca quena of reed is the instrument of love songs; bone flutes were the traditional instruments for war and martial music. The Chaco flutes include end flutes of bamboo, sometimes notched like the Andean types; duct flutes of bird bones used by the shamans for magical performances and consisting simply of whistle head and tube without stops; and plug flutes made of reeds with a wax plug at the blowhole. See Q'ENA Q'ENA.

quests Many task tales involve quests. The search for something that will fulfill a condition is one of the common incidents of folktale. The water of life, the speaking bird, the dragon, and the like are the goals of the hero in quest tales. Sometimes he has helpers: animal helpers, helpers with extraordinary powers to see great distances or to withstand unusual extremes of temperature or the like. Often the quest is accomplished only as the end of a chain of quests: to get one thing the hero must first get another, which in turn is dependent on his obtaining something else first, and so forth. Sometimes the quest is undertaken as a suitor task; sometimes, as in the story of the *Three Sillies,* the quest is self-imposed. See TASKS.

Quetzalcoatl The feathered or plumed serpent god: known over all Middle America, and surviving in mythology to this day. Quetzalcoatl was the ancient Mexican version. Primarily he was a wind god, in which form he was known as Eecatl, the Aztec word for wind. He was also worshipped as lord of the planet Venus in which manifestation he was referred to as Ce Acatl, "one cane." At the same time he was a creator god, the "sun" during one of the previous incarnations of the world, and the god who went to Mictlan, the underworld, whence he brought back the bones of people of the previous worlds and, sprinkling his own blood over them, turned them into human beings. In addition he was a culture hero, for he brought maize to mankind, instructed in the arts of weaving cotton, polishing jade, making feather mantles, and taught people to understand the calendar and movements of the stars. There is much confusion in the chronicles over this name, for a king named Quetzalcoatl also ruled over the Toltecs at Tula, and subsequently was deified. Legend states that, when bested and humiliated by Tezcatlipoca, this light-skinned bearded king-deity went to Cholula, and subsequently to Tlillan Tlapallan, an unidentified spot on the Veracruz coast where, mounted on a raft of snakes, he sailed eastward after saying he would return in the year Ce Acatl. When Cortes landed in Veracruz in the year Ce Acatl (1519), it is not surprising that Montezuma, king of the Aztecs, thought that it was Quetzalcoatl returning. See ANTS. [GMF]

quetzales A ceremonial Mexican dance, named after the gorgeous quetzal bird. The name is justified by the headdress. A tremendous multicolored wheel called *resplandor,* splendor, woven of raffia, colored paper, or ribbons, and tipped with fine feathers, is attached to a conical hat and fastened under the chin by a kerchief. Sometimes the image of a quetzal bird surmounts the hat. The dance of the quetzales is a feature of the fiestas in the semihighlands of Veracruz (Papantla and Coxquihui, notably) and the Sierra Norte de Puebla (Cuetzalan). It is commonly associated with the flying of the *voladores* and incorporates a similar bird symbolism by the headdress, and, in some villages, by a feat of revolving on a trapeze-like contraption. The rest of the costume resembles that of the *voladores* and other groups of this area—red half-length trousers, at times over a long pair, kerchiefs crossed on the chest, a long red cape, and a small gourd rattle (*sonaja*) in the right hand. Primitive tunes are played on a one-man flute and tabor.

With simple two-steps and raising of their knees the quetzales walk or skip through various simple longways figures: they advance, retire, follow the leader down the center and around, they cross over and back into place, the corner men cross over and back, finally each line winds back and forth through the opposite line in a serpentine path, *la viborilla.* These formations do not necessarily point to European introduction, for the name, steps, headdress, and music are essentially indigenous. On the contrary, these figures may well have come down from pre-Columbian times as rare extant samples of Indian longways. If the dance was originally a supplication to the sun and its life-giving powers, symbolized by the quetzal bird, it represents a formal analogy with European vegetation dances, as the Morris processional. Tradition is silent on the meaning. [GPK]

Quikinna'qu or **Kutkinn·a'ku** Big-Raven: the benevolent creator of Koryak mythology: called Kutq by the Kamchadal, Ku'rkil by the Chukchee. Some of the Maritime Koryak refer to him not only as Big-Raven but also as Big Grandfather. The Chukchee sometimes differentiate between Ku'rkil and the creator, regarding Ku'rkil merely as Creator's assistant. The Koryak have the concept that the creator is a supreme deity who becomes Big-Raven by donning the raven's coat. The Chukchee say that Creator put on the raven's coat, flew into the sky, and brought back reindeer for the people. His wife is Miti' in all versions.

Quikinna'qu appears not only as creator-transformer in Koryak mythology, but figures also in Koryak religious incantation and ceremony. Not only is he supernatural and creator, but also first man, culture hero, and shaman. He is present at every shamanistic ceremony, and the Koryak shaman treats his patient in the name of Quikinna'qu. "Big-Raven is here," he says, or "Big-Raven did so and so in your case."

The stories are numerous and varied. Among them are those saying that one day creator was sharpening a knife in the sky; a chip of the whetstone fell to earth and became Quikinna'qu; or Quikinna'qu grew up all alone, went hunting, met Miti', and the Koryak are their descendants. There are numerous tales of the tricks the pair play on each other, misplacing or reversing their genitals, serving fecal pudding, and comic as well as serious or explanatory adventure stories, struggles with cannibals, etc. See Waldemar Jochelson, *Religion and Myths of the Koryak*, Publications of the Jesup North Pacific Expedition, MAMNH, VI, part 1.

quilling The playing of tunes on locomotive and factory whistles, a practice once a matter of great pride among railroad engineers. "Whistling Bill" Wardoff was said to play an ear-shattering version of *Home, Sweet Home*, as he brought his engine in. A radio program during the Christmas holidays of 1949 carried an example of this skill with a rendition of *Silent Night* blasted out on a factory whistle.

quirin A marvelous stone found in the nests of lapwings, highly valued by witches and other magic-makers, for "it betrayeth and discovereth." If the quirin is placed under a man's pillow he will talk in his sleep and reveal his own dearest secrets. This may possibly be the famous stone found in the hoopoe's nest and referred to by Encelius (16th century), since the lapwing and hoopoe were often confused by early scientists.

Quirinus In ancient Roman religion, a secondary god of war and of nature, similar to but distinct from Mars; a Sabine god worshipped quite early in Rome at the Quirinal hill where Titus Tatius and a colony of Sabines from the town of Cures settled. The name is sometimes derived from Cures; some say it comes from *curia*, one of the divisions of the Roman state; additional etymo-logical conjecture derives it from *quercus*, oak, or *quiris*, spear, oak-spear. His festival, the Quirinalia, took place on February 17. He had one of the principal flamens, and a college of priests, the Salii Agonales or Collini, founded by Tullus Hostilius to parallel the Salii Palatini of Mars. Quirinus is identified with Romulus though he is much older than Rome; his cult partner, Hora Quirini, is thus equated with Romulus' wife, Hersilia. His flamen performed the sacrifice at the Robigalia in April to protect the crops against mildew. A. H. Krappe supposes him to be an ancient thunder god, etymologically paralleling Perun, the Slavic thunder god.

quotations and **winged words** (*Geflügelte Worte*) The German term, for which there is no convenient English equivalent, refers to widely used sayings uttered by historical persons or credited to them and to quotations that have acquired many characteristics of a proverb. Caesar's remark, "The die is cast," which he made on crossing the Rubicon, is a winged word. Büchmann's German dictionary and works like it in other languages (there is no altogether satisfactory English book of the sort) trace such sayings to their origins. Many of these sayings have international currency. Like proverbs, winged words have an indefinite origin (a precise source can rarely be found in the words of the individual to whom they are ascribed), express a didactic idea, and suffer changes in the process of oral transmission. For example, "I am the state" (*L'état, c'est moi*) summarizes neatly the political attitude of Louis XIV, but although these words are ascribed to him, the exact source has not been discovered. The saying "Know thyself," an inscription in the temple of the Delphic Apollo, has been assigned to several Greek sages; it stands on the borderline between the winged word and the proverb. James J. Corbett is supposed to have coined "The bigger they come, the harder they fall."

English collections of familiar quotations are usually arranged according to sentiments (love, patriotism, honor) or general themes (death, spring) and supply the user with a passage appropriate to a particular situation. Some English winged words like "Knowledge is power" can be run down in foreign collections, but those of recent origin like "Don't sell America short" or "Verify your references" are often difficult to trace. See Georg Büchmann, *Geflügelte Worte* (1st ed., 1845; many later enlarged and altered editions). John Bartlett, *A Collection of Familiar Quotations* (Cambridge, Mass., 1855. The latest or twelfth edition is *Familiar Quotations; a collection of passages, phrases, and proverbs traced to their sources in ancient and modern literature* [Boston, 1949]). Burton E. Stevenson, *The Home Book of Quotations* (New York, 1949). [AT]

R

Rā or **Rē**   In ancient Egyptian religion and mythology, the sun god and demiurge of Heliopolis; the most generally recognized form of the sun god and the god whose worship was most widespread in Egypt. Rā was probably originally a Western Asiatic sun god imported into the Delta, where his worship remained strongest and where he supplanted an earlier native sun god, probably Atmu. Because of the constant combination and synthesis among the Egyptian gods, Rā has become confused with other gods, especially sun gods like Horus; but he constantly remains the personification of the sun at its strongest, *f*he noonday sun, as Mentu is the rising and Atmu *i*he setting sun. At Heliopolis, Rā was incarnate in the Mnevis bull; at Hermonthis, another center of his worship, he was the Bacis bull.

Rā was thus the chief god of one of the two principal religious groupings of Egypt, Osiris worship and Rā worship. There were no great centers of Rā worship; his cult was diffuse and formed part of other cults. In his principal center at Heliopolis were the sacred tree of the sun and the pool in which Rā bathed when he descended to earth at ritual periods. The "rival" cult of Osiris eventually completely overshadowed the cult of Rā. Principally contributing to this result was the political history of Egypt. The priests of Rā, after a long struggle, best exemplified in the period surrounding the reign of Ikhnaton, attained political power as the temporal heads of the state. Therefore, when the state itself fell to the Assyrians, the entire Rā complex fell into popular disfavor, and, lacking the political power to enforce Rā worship, the priests lost their religious following almost completely. In addition, the religious atmosphere that led to the rise of the Greek mysteries and eventually to Christianity existed in Egypt too, and concern with the afterlife and the problems of life and death, led to supremacy of Osiris worship. The Rā system was primarily a cosmological one, dealing with the ordering of the heavens, with creation, origins, and the government of the universe. The Osiris cult, on the other hand, dealt principally with the matters of life, death, resurrection, and the future life.

In mythology, Rā created himself from Nun, the pre-existent void. Then, from spittle or by a solitary act of fertilization, Rā created Shu, the air, and Tefnut, moisture. These in turn became parents of Nut, the sky, and Geb, the earth, whose offspring were the four other gods who made up the Great Ennead—Osiris, Set, Isis, and Nephthys. Through confusion with Osiris, Rā is sometimes called the son of Geb and Nut. Rā is one of the creators of mankind of Egyptian myth: he castrated himself, and from the drops of blood man arose—this is probably influenced by the other castration-creation myths of the Mediterranean region, or it may be a euphemistic telling of a masturbation myth similar to that of Khnemu. Though a divine being, Rā had many of the failings of man: he grew old; he was bitten by a snake and feared to die, and to save himself he told Isis his real name (see ISIS); he grew displeased with man,

ordered his destruction, and repented his order (see SEKHMET). Rā was first king of Egypt, but grew tired of living among men. He therefore seated himself upon Nut, who transformed herself into the great celestial cow overspreading the heavens upon which Rā, the sun, still rides. Rā crossed the sky, accompanied by his court, in a boat by day, Manzet, the dawn bark; at night, he rested in his ship Mesenktet, the night bark, which traveled from west to east below the world to the point where it rose again in the morning.

Since Rā was the first king of Egypt, all Egyptian kings had a Rā name. Actually it was the kings of the V Dynasty who first took such a name, but all kings afterwards bore a Rā name. Rā was patron of the pharaohs, and in later times was the father of the pharaohs, impregnating the queens as Rā, though he might appear in the form of the king to them.

Rā appears compounded with several other Egyptian gods, for example Amen-Rā. Since the power of the life-giving sun was Rā's, he loaned himself to these other gods to give them the power that they needed. In actuality, the local gods of other places were probably identified as local aspects of the main sun god and adopted his name as a sort of hyphenated divinity.

Rā is depicted as fully human, or as a hawk-headed man whose head is surmounted with the uræus serpent and the sun disk, or as the sun disk riding in the celestial boat. Sometimes he is the scarab or dung-beetle, the symbol of the god rolling the sun across the sky as the beetle rolled its ball of dung before it. Rā's symbols were therefore the hawk, the serpent, and the scarab. He appeared also as the eye of Rā, the celestial or god eye, which was also the symbol of Horus. Among the other symbols associated with Rā were the rams' horns of creation and the vulture wings of protection.

Rabbit   (1) Chief among several animal tricksters of Indian tribes of the southeastern United States; also, as Cottontail, a prominent animal character in Great Basin Indian mythology and as Hare, prominent in Eastern Woodlands myths. In the southeast, beside being the main character in innumerable purely trickster tales, Rabbit is also a culture hero, a benefactor to mankind; he obtains fire from across the ocean, brings it back after a chase and sets the woods on fire, much as Cottontail of the Great Basin stole the sun for the people. See LIGHT. Many of the everyday tales told about Rabbit among southeastern tribes are clearly adaptations or direct borrowings of African and European myths, either in whole or in part (see BRER RABBIT; TAR BABY). This often makes for confusion and has led to underestimation of the large amount of native material which is still current in southeastern Indian trickster and other tales. Rabbit, as well as Hare, is one of the animal characters in Eastern Woodlands and Southwestern tricksterlike tales. See HARE. [EWV]

⬧ (2) Rabbit is one of the several animal tricksters (rabbit, spider, tortoise, chevrotain) found in African

folklore. Deriving principally from Nigerian and Dahomean sources, Rabbit has become the best known of
these tricksters through the publication by Joel Chandler
Harris of the famous Brer Rabbit stories collected from
Negroes of the southern United States. Though this has
given Rabbit, as well as animal tales in general, an
outstanding place in conceptions of Negro lore held by
folklorists, the importance of both character and category has tended to be exaggerated. See UNCLE REMUS.

[MJH]

rabbit dance The impersonation of a rabbit, common
among eastern North American Indian tribes, the
Menominee, Creek, Yuchi, Alabama, Seminole. Menominee dancers of both sexes circle the drum, crouching,
pretending to put food in their mouths, and moving
their lips like the rabbit, *wa'bos*. The *tcofi* of the Creek
and *cadjwanecti* of the Yuchi were traditionally included in the social second evening of the Green Corn
dance. Emitting squeaks, the performers crooked their
left arms between their faces and the fire. Possibly the
original purpose was to cheer the poor little spirit
(Chippewa *man'idowens*), to make himself available for
food. A totemistic origin is doubtful. Neither song texts
nor actions refer to the rabbit's mythological role as
trickster. [GPK]

rabies Hydrophobia; an infectious disease of animals,
especially dogs, caused by a virus which attacks the central nervous system: readily transmitted to human beings
by the saliva of rabid dogs. The folklore of rabies (beliefs
and fears regarding its symptoms in man and beast, its
causes, and cures) is voluminous and dates from the time
of Aristotle to Pasteur. Fear still fosters many misconception, e.g. a mad dog foams at the mouth (actually
the rabid dog is dry-mouthed and feverish); victims of
hydrophobia (dog or man) fear water (actually they
crave water but cannot swallow it); people bitten by
mad dogs bark and snap (this occurs in hysterical, not
true rabies); that the sound of dogs barking rings in their
ears is also untrue. In many parts of rural America it
is said that killing a sow bug will give hydrophobia to
the one who kills it; hence "mad-dog" is a popular term
for sow bug in those localities.

One of the most common remedies recorded for mad-
dog bite is the liver of the dog, either applied to the
wound or dried and taken internally. In medieval England the victims were thrown into lakes and ponds
or treated with *madwort* (balaustium root) mixed with
soot and olive oil. In Denmark the disease was regarded
as so agonizing and so inevitably fatal that victims were
mercifully strangled.

One of the earliest comments on rabies is found in
the writings of Epicharmus who said that wild cabbage
would cure the bite of a mad dog, and would kill the
dog if he ate it. Pliny reports the root of wild rose revealed as a cure in a dream to the mother of a victim
of rabies.

Galen (2nd century) doubted that the liver of a mad
dog would cure its bite, in that several people who
trusted to this had died. He recommended theriac, however, the famous cure-all and poison antidote of the
ancients, in which the flesh of vipers was one important
ingredient. Galen also reported the experience of a man
who roasted crabs to an ash in a copper dish during dog

days (August) on the 18th day of the moon, and prescribed the ash to be taken for 40 days by victims of
mad-dog bite. Aëtius of Mesopotamia in the 5th century
repeated this story and recommended the cure. He also
prescribed drinking bitumen in water to prevent hydrophobia after a bite. A well-known 5th century preventive
amulet against getting bitten was the tooth of a mad dog
who had bitten somebody. The Gnostics recited special
incantations to cure the disease.

Epiphanius of Cyprus (315–403) declared that topaz
gives forth a milky fluid which cures rabies; this was
verified by a number of later physicians experimenting
between the 5th and 10th centuries. Constantinus Afri-
canus (11th century) recommended placing a live chicken
on the wound; if left there till it died, the man would
get well.

Gentile de Foligno, a 14th century scientist and physician, who was called Speculator because of his attitude
toward the findings and opinions of his predecessors,
in regard to rabies "speculated" first as to whether or
not a man could contract the disease at all, whether
theriac would help most if applied to the bite or taken
internally, whether dogs were visible in the urine of a
rabies patient, and why those bitten by mad dogs were
afraid of water. To these questions Gentile answered:
Yes, man can and does contract rabies; particles resembling dogs do not appear in the urine of a patient,
in that "neither matter, agent, nor place are favorable for
generation." William de Marra in the *Papal Garland
Concerning Poisons* (14th century) answered one of the
great recurrent questions concerning rabies: Why are
dogs more prone to rabies than other animals? Answer:
The dog, living so close to human beings, is "more provoked to wrath and sadness" than other animals.

Johann Varismann of Danzig wrote (1586) a 19-chap-
ter treatise on hydrophobia in which he denied the
influence of the dog star as a cause of rabies, but said
instead it was caused by a worm under the dog's tongue.
He also denied the efficacy of incantations, but recommended a new antidote containing the powdered leaves
of ten plants, each of which at one time or another
has been called heal-all, this antidote to be applied to
the bite if it can be obtained immediately, to be taken
internally if any time has elapsed.

The most magical of all remedies, however, is that
discovered by Pasteur. Until his day the disease was
invariably fatal. Pasteur, after his experiments and
successes with vaccination for smallpox and the prevention of anthrax in sheep, grew rabies virus in the
nervous systems of rabbits. The rabbits died with rabies;
he removed their spinal cords, dried them, injected the
virus into other rabbits, who were discovered to develop
immunity to rabies. A man or animal infected with the
virus from a bite, or from contact with rabid saliva with
a scratch or cut, does not develop the actual disease
sometimes for three weeks or more. This fact plus the
fact that the immunizing agent works more rapidly
gives persons bitten by mad dogs a chance to escape
rabies. See BREAD.

Raccoon Animal trickster about whom many stories
are told in Eastern Woodlands Indian mythologies. Raccoon is never a creator or transformer, as the major
animal tricksters are (see for instance COYOTE). He also
differs as a trickster, being neither foolish nor a dupe;

the tables are seldom, if ever, turned upon him, as they are on Coyote, Wisaka, or other tricksters. [EWV]

Rada Term for a group of Haitian deities of the *vodun* cult who themselves comprise one pantheon, others being the Pétro, Congo, and Ibo gods. The word is a contraction of the name of the old capital of the Dahomean kingdom of West Africa, Allada (or Arada). This derivation is confirmed by the fact that the majority of the Rada deities are of Dahomean origin. See AGBE; DAMBALLA; VODUN. [MJH]

Ragnar Lödbrok (c. 735–794) A great Viking warrior who succeeded his father, Sigurd Ring, as king of Denmark at the age of 15, and later invaded England. His first wife, the warrior maiden Lodgerda, ruled a remote part of Norway where he lived happily for three years. But as she refused to leave and his subjects were taking their loyalties elsewhere, he returned home. Next he fell in love with a picture of Thora, daughter of King Herodd in East Gothland. It was this Thora who raised a nest of adders which multiplied until they endangered the public, and which Ragnar Lödbrok killed. In the *Saga of King Ragnar Lödbrok*, Thora kept a pet snake in a treasure box of gold; the snake grew to enormous proportions and with his growth the gold kept even increase.

After slaying a fearful dragon which encircled the castle (a monstrous worm hatched from the egg of a swan), Ragnar Lödbrok married Thora and settled down, even forgoing his annual raids. The name Lödbrok (*Lothbrok*) refers to the oxhide armor which he wore while fighting the dragon. After Thora's death, Ragnar resumed his piratical raids and on one of these met Aslaug, the ward of a peasant couple. They were married and she bore him five sons. When his subjects began to mutter about his lowly queen, he turned his thoughts to the daughter of Eystein, king of Sweden. On learning, however, that Aslaug was in reality the daughter of Sigurd and Brynhild, he sent his sons instead to settle with Eystein. Ragnar was killed by Ella, king of Northumberland (England), who removed his magic shirt and threw him into a snake-pit. Here Ragnar sang the joyous death song ". . . laughing I die!" which characterizes the hero deaths of romantic Viking legend. *The Death Song of Ragnar Lodbrok* was included in Percy's *Reliques*. In revenge for the death of their father, Ragnar's sons (who later founded the city of London) carved a spread eagle on Ella's chest.

Ragnarök In Teutonic mythology, the day of the great battle between the gods and the forces of evil. Teutonic mythology, beginning with the formation of Ymir in Ginnungagap, is a complete cycle of which Ragnarök is the culminating chapter. Ragnarök is more than the final battle of the world in which the forces of good and evil valiantly fight out their predetermined one-sided battle on the plains of Vigrid. It is the complete destruction of the universe and begins, roughly, with the death of Balder and the realization by the gods that, in Loki, they have been fostering the seeds of evil in their midst. Although they have secured him in chains they know that it is too late: the final dissolution has begun. This seems to be the point in the cycle in which the sagas and eddas were written and, in all probability, the time in which we are still living in spite of the intervening millennium.

The end of the world will be announced by the Fimbulwinter, three terrible winters with no summers between, in which the earth will be covered with ice. Following this there will be a further three-year period during which the crimes of man will increase. Since man is, at best, but an imperfect mirror of the gods, their degeneration will lead to his moral and physical destruction by greed, lust, vice, and warfare. The forces of evil, Loki's progeny (the Fenris wolf, Jörmungandr, Hel and their brood) who feed on the evil in man, will so increase in strength that they will burst their bonds.

The loosing of these powers of evil is the signal for the three cocks, Fialar in Valhalla, Gullin-kambi in Midgard, and Hel's dark red bird in Niflheim, to sound the alarm. This is immediately echoed by Heimdall on the Giallar-horn summoning the opposing forces to the final battle of the universe on the spacious plain of Vigrid. Loki will come with his brood in the ship Naglfar, Hrim and the frost giants in another ship out of the north, Surtr brandishing his fiery sword, Hel and her minions, who will oppose the gods led by Odin and his mighty warriors, the Einheriar.

In spite of the predetermined outcome of the battle, the gods, with true northern spirit, will fight valiantly. Odin himself will be the first to perish, swallowed whole by the Fenris wolf, which in turn will be rent assunder by Odin's son, Vidar. Thor will renew his ancient battle with the monster, Jörmungandr, whom, after an epic struggle, he will succeed in killing, only to be drowned in a sea of venom issuing from the serpent's jaws. The one-handed Tyr will battle with the hellhound Garm. Heimdall and Loki will fall, mutually slain. Frey, armed only with a stag horn, will fall by Surtr's flaming sword, and in the end, all will perish.

In the heavens, the two wolves which have been pursuing the sun and moon in their courses will finally overtake and devour them. The brands falling from Surtr's flaming sword will set fire to the earth, and the seas boiling up will engulf the land. The heavens will be rent asunder; the stars will fall into the abyss; and all will be destroyed in the universe save Lif and Lifthraser, asleep in Hodmimir's forest. These two will, at the proper time, step forth to repopulate a world of peace and love presided over by the All-father whose majesty is so great that no one dare even mention his name.

The mortal gods who have lost their lives at Vigrid will go to dwell forever in Gimli, the highest heavenly abode. The evil ones will be sentenced to Nastrond. The dwarfs and the giants, who have been governed entirely by the decrees of fate, will not be punished. The dwarfs, under their leader Sindri, will go to a hall in the Nida Mountains and the giants to a hall called Brimer, where they will live a life of pleasure.

Some look on Ragnarök as the twilight of the gods in which the old gods lose their power through degeneracy and abuse and are replaced by a rule of love as depicted in Wagner's *Götterdämmerung*. This theory was admirably suited to Christian teaching and was probably influenced by it. See BIFROST.

rags-to-riches A generic catchword for the whole reversal of fortune cycle of folktales, the L chapter in Stith Thompson's *Motif-Index of Folk-Literature*. It is especially associated with the unpromising hero (male

Cinderella) motif (L101) and often, but not always, identified with the clever youngest son stories (L10 ff.).

☞ Rags-to-riches or male Cinderella is a popular theme in North American Indian novelistic hero tales. The hero, a poor boy, usually an orphan or an abused younger son, either has supernatural power or is advised by supernatural beings so that he overcomes obstacles, meets difficult tests, and succeeds in winning the chief's daughter in marriage. Tales employing this theme are especially popular among the Eskimo, on the North Pacific Coast as far south as northwestern California, on the Plains, and in the Eastern Woodlands. (See Stith Thompson, *Tales of the North American Indians*, Cambridge, 1929, pp. 327-28, n. 185.) The rags-to-riches theme also occurs in the Dirty-Boy tale popular among Plateau and Plains tribes (see Thompson, p. 327, n. 183), but in Dirty Boy a supernatural being merely assumes a humble disguise. In a contest for the chief's daughter he wins the girl and unmasks an impostor; he then assumes his original form. [EWV]

ragtime A gay, syncopated, percussive style of instrumental (particularly piano) music in duple time, arising in the 1890's from American Negro secular song and the minstrel show cakewalks, buck-and-wings, "ballin' the jack," etc., and forming one of the strongest influences on the development of jazz. The piano style is characterized by a rapid left-hand technique, with single notes, octaves, or chords played against the freer syncopations and melodic variations of the right hand. Among the favorite early piano rags were Tom Turpin's *Harlem Rag*, Scott Joplin's *Maple Leaf Rag*, and the traditional *Eagle Rock Rag*. Great players included James P. Johnson, Jelly-Roll Morton, better known for his jazz-playing, and Lucky Roberts. Words were rarely fitted to the tunes, though there are a few texts, generally delivered in recitative or nonsense syllables imitating the instrumental sounds or playing against the instrumental rhythms. The ragtime band played cakewalks, two-steps, marches, etc., in the wide-open, circus-music manner of New Orleans parades, with group improvisation and rhythmic variation. The fusion of ragtime with early jazz took place in such bands as "Buddy" Bolden's and "King" Oliver's, and in the piano music of the New Orleans Storyville district (see JAZZ). In fact, ragtime might be considered a transitional form of music, which had almost completed its absorption into the later popular styles by 1915. The origin of the word is uncertain. It has been suggested that the street chants of ragmen may have entered into its conception. However, in the Sea Islands section of Georgia, "sinful" or secular songs were often called rags. [TCB]

ragweed (1) A tall smooth herb with bright yellow flowers (genus *Senecio*) called in England, *ragwort* or *stinking Willie*. In Cornwall witches used to ride about in the night on the stalks of this plant. In Ireland it is called fairies' horse. The ragweed has a clock, like the dandelion, and is used by children in telling time. It is considered a cooling herb in the dominion of Venus, and, although poisonous to cattle, is given to horses for staggers. The plant is applied whole as a poultice for sciatica, arthritis, gout, and venereal infections, and the juice forms a cooling lotion for the eyes. It is also used for cancer and all manner of ulcers and sores. This is one of the gay plants which spontaneously sprang up in the bombed ruins in London as well as the rest of England during World War II.

(2) A coarse, common herb (genus *Ambrosia*) which induces hay fever. The Gosiute Indians of Utah use a leaf tea of this plant on bandages for sore eyes. The Meskwaki Indians chew the root of the giant ragweed to drive away fear at night.

Rahab The Rager: one of the names (*Isa.* xxx, 7; li, 9-10; *Ps.* lxxxix, 9-10; *Job* ix, 13; xxvi, 12-13) for the dragon slain by Yahweh in the supposed very early dragon-slaying myth of the ancient Hebrews. Other names for the dragon in the Bible are Leviathan, Tannin, and the serpent. In rabbinical legend the dragon Rahab is the angel of the sea, and probably originally Rahab was equated with other sea dragons slain by such heroes as Marduk. The harlot of Jericho who aided the Israelites was named Rahab; Robert Graves (*The White Goddess*) says that she was a priestess of the sea goddess Rahab. According to the Midrash, Joshua and Rahab had only daughters, further strengthening Graves' belief that the story deals with the political marriage of the invading chieftain with the representative of a group of powerful priestesses.

Rahkoi The ghost of the Finns and Lapps; it has influence on the phases of the moon. [JB]

Rāhu In Hindu mythology and belief, the cause of eclipses, comets, meteors, and guardian of the southwest quarter. Rāhu was the mischievous four-armed Daitya who stole and drank some of the amṛita produced at the Churning of the Ocean. Discovered by the sun and the moon, who informed Vishṇu, his head and two arms were cut off by the angry gods, but since he had secured immortality as a result of tasting the amṛita, the upper part of his body was placed in the heavens in the form of a dragon's head to represent the ascending node, and the lower part (Ketu) in the form of a dragon's tail to represent the descending node. Eclipses are caused by him: i.e. he swallows the sun or the moon as revenge for the loss of his head. Rāhu is the special deity of the Dosādhs and the Dhāngars, who worship him by walking through a pit filled with hot cinders. He presages sickness and all kinds of trouble and must be frightened away by music, noise, or by bathing at a holy place during an eclipse.

Raiden or **Kaminari Sama** The Japanese God of Thunder, depicted as a demon with claws and a string of drums. He is fond of eating human navels. The only protection against him is to hide under a mosquito net. [JLM]

Raiko The poetic name of Minamoto Yorimitsu, a celebrated Japanese warrior of the 11th century, whose life was made into a legend. [JLM]

Railroad Bill Negro bad man of Escambia County, Alabama, celebrated in folk song and legend for his combination of Robin Hood and hoodoo. Originally a turpentine-still worker named Morris Slater, he shot a deputy who attempted to arrest him for carrying a gun, and escaped on a freight train. Thereafter his habit of riding freights and looting freight cars of canned food and other goods, which he gave or sold cheaply to the poor, won him the sobriquet "Railroad Bill." With Stackalee he shares the ability of turning into an animal to elude his pursuers. Once, hunted by the sheriff with posse and bloodhounds, he changed himself into a black dog and accompanied the hounds to his girl's house, where he "stayed behind to do some courtin' when the sheriff left." [BAB]

rain Without rain nothing can live; it is the life-giver and -sustainer of man, animals, vegetation, everywhere regarded as beneficent: deified, venerated, and associated with complex magico-religious ritual for its control among all primitive peoples, especially in arid regions and those parts of the world subject to long dry seasons. The rain-maker is often the most important and influential member of a community. The value of rain is revealed in an old European riddle: How much is a golden plow worth? (H713.1) to which the answer is: A rain in May.

In ancient Greece and Rome, the sky god (Zeus, Jupiter) was the god of rain. Ancient Greek rain-makers dipped a branch of the oak (his sacred tree) in water to induce rain, and the god was addressed with prayer. In Rome, little images were cast into the Tiber to bring rain. The ancient Teutons observed a rite of pouring water over a naked girl to bring rain to the earth.

To the ancient Hebrews, rain was a blessing from heaven in return for obedience to the Law. *Genesis* i, 7 mentions the separation of the waters which were under the firmament from the "waters above"; and the source of rain was conceived as a great reservoir or "treasure of waters" in heaven. The keys to these waters were kept by God. Drought was caused by sin: non-payment of tithes, slander, etc. I *Kings* xviii tells the story of drought and famine in the land of Ahab, God's promise to Elijah to send rain when the people's hearts were turned from Baal, the conversion of the people, the appearance of the little cloud, and the coming of the rain according to promise.

In India, Buddhist priests induce rain by pouring water into little holes in the temple floor to symbolize rain sinking into the earth. In southern India women tie a frog to a winnowing fan, sing to the effect that the frog needs water; others pour water on the frog; it sprinkles through the sieve, and rain comes in torrents. Belief in the power of the snake to give rain is indicated by two great festivals (*Nāgpanchamī*, northern India; *Nāgara-panchamī*, southern India) both of which occur in the rainy season. Images of snakes are bathed, dipped, sprinkled, etc.

To make rain the ancient Celtic druids, followed by processions, went to certain sacred wells or magical springs; they beat upon the surface of the water, or the water was poured over special stones, or tossed into the air. In Christian times these rites were taken over by the church; the procession was headed by the priest and image of a saint; but such practice was subsequently denounced and forbidden.

Various animals are often regarded either as custodians of rain (frogs, toads, snakes, lizards) or as protégées of the rain god. In some places, certain stones are regarded as infallible rain-givers. They are supplicated, shown water, sprinkled, dipped, submerged, etc., to induce rainfall. If the downpour is too great or floods threaten, they are laid by the fire until the earth is dry again. Liberating rain by pouring water is a common magic practice. Pouring water on leaf-clad mummers or pup-pets (who symbolize vegetation) is still practiced in parts of Europe.

In general folk belief, a rainy wedding day forebodes an unhappy marriage. The cry of the curlew predicts rain in Ireland. When ants scurry into their hills and close the entrance, it is going to rain. To hear the barn-yard ducks quacking at night means rain in the morning; the same is said of geese. In Newfoundland and Nova Scotia, it is said that loons "call for rain"; quail are also said to call for rain. It is a sign of rain if crows, wild geese, swallows, gnats, lightning bugs, etc., are flying low. In Labrador and Nova Scotia, mosquitoes bite hardest just before rain. In Newfoundland, if a cat drowns in the sea it will surely rain. Corns and rheumatism are always more painful just before a rain. It will rain if you kill a frog, or a toad, or a spider. See AMETHYST; BACABS; CEREMONIAL DRINKING; CHACS; JACK IN THE GREEN; KURENA; MOON; QUARTZ; RITUAL DRAMA; TLALOC.

☞ To the agricultural Indians of the Southwest, rain is a gift of the Cloud People, and Pueblo Indian corn ceremonies are given to obtain rain for the crops. Rain and clouds are symbolized pictorially by the Hopi by half circles from which straight vertical lines depend; this well-known Hopi rain symbol is used in the signet of the *Reports* of the Bureau of American Ethnology, Smithsonian Institution, and also appears on the jacket of this *Dictionary of Folklore, Mythology, and Legend.* By many tribes rain is connected with thunder; in a Jicarilla Apache myth, Thunder and Cyclone disputed each other's powers and became angry with each other; as a result there were no storms and no rains. The people, under the direction of four old men representing four water animals (Salamander, Water Frog, Crawfish, Turtle) danced while Old Man Salamander sang, and kept their minds on rain; it rained, and this ceremony has been used ever since by the Jicarilla to obtain rain.

A host of beliefs, rites, and charms center about rain and its artificial production. The Tübatulabal Indians believe that if a certain kind of spider is thrown in a pool, it will rain hard. The Yuchi of the agricultural Southeast, where summer rains are seldom a problem, say that there is a big water vessel in the sky; when someone jerks it, it spills water over the edges, and this is what makes the rain. The Shawnee believe one way to make rain is to dip a buffalo tail in water and sprinkle the water quietly on the ground. See FEMALE RAIN; MALE RAIN. [EWV]

☞ Some Chaco Indian tribes conceive of the rain as a spirit riding a horse. For the Chamaco rain is produced by birds (clouds) whose bodies are full of water. The Aymara Indians have a rain-making rite still observed in time of prolonged drought. Their magician Paqo goes in his balsa out on Lake Titicaca and fills a number of basins with water, frogs, and certain water plants, leaving offerings to the spirits of the deep pools from which he takes them. Men in other balsas go with him, playing on panpipes and drums. Paqo, musicians, and a mixed chorus of men and women then climb the mountain called Atoja and leave the basins full of frogs and plants on two altars in the sun. Paqo prays to Father Atoja and Mother Atoja, the mountain spirits, for rain, to the accompaniment of the mixed chorus singing the frog song. Soon the heat of the sun evaporates the water, the frogs cry out in distress, and the spirits in pity send rain. [AM]

rainbow Like other spectacular events in the sky—meteors, the aurora, eclipses—the rainbow is ominous. Yet, despite the feeling of an impending supernatural occurrence lying beyond the spectacle of the rainbow, accurate folk observation has evolved the rime, whose conclusions are true:

> Rainbow in the morning, sailors take warning;
> Rainbow at night, sailors' delight.
> Rainbow to windward, foul fall the day;
> Rainbow to leeward, damp runs away.

Less true, but just as positive, are the beliefs that a rainbow appearing after a storm means no more rain for quite a while; and that a double rainbow signifies a long spell of dry weather. In Malaya, a partial arc ending in the water means that some prince will soon die. Seneca claimed that a rainbow seen in the south presaged a heavy downpour, one in the west a light misty rain. Pliny said that the rainbow foretold a heavy winter or a war. The Iranian Moslems have developed a complete zodiacal system; e.g. the rainbow in the east in the sign of the Ram brings good fortune; in the west in the same sign, it means famine; in the Bull in the west, good fortune; in the Bull in the east, all women will suffer, etc. (See B. A. Donaldson, *The Wild Rue,* London, 1938, p. 99.) The brilliance of the colors of the rainbow has meaning to the same people: a prominent red means war, green means abundance, yellow brings death. The Arawak of South America believe the rainbow to be a fortunate sign if it is seen over the sea, but when it appears on land it is an evil spirit searching for a victim.

Among the Semang of Malaya, the places where a rainbow touches earth are unhealthy. In Europe, it is believed that anyone passing beneath a rainbow will be transformed, man into woman, woman into man. In Rumania, for example, it is said that the rainbow stands with each end in a river, and anyone creeping to its end on hands and knees and drinking the water it touches will instantly change sex. (See below for the connection of the rainbow with the serpent, and compare TIRESIAS.) The Teton Dakotas say one must not point at the rainbow with the index finger or the finger will swell. But it is safe to make a gesture at it with elbow or lips. A tabu resembling this is maintained by the Hopi and Thompson Indians. This tabu against pointing at the rainbow also appears in folktale (motif C843.1). Generally throughout Europe, the place where the rainbow touches is lucky, because at the end of the rainbow is a pot of gold or other treasure (N516), ready to be taken by its finder. In Silesia it is said that the angels put the gold there, and that only a nude man can obtain the prize. The Malayans too believe that a treasure lies at the end of the rainbow.

In the mythologies of several peoples, the rainbow is a bridge (F152.1.1) between heaven and earth. The Norse Bifrost is the bridge over which Heimdall stands guard; at Ragnarök the frost giants will storm the bridge and raid Valhalla, breaking the bridge into bits. This rainbow bridge flames in three colors, keeping the giants from mounting it lest they melt; but when the bridge cools the way will be open. Bifrost is not identified with the rainbow in the *Elder (Poetic) Edda,* but Snorri Sturluson's *Prose Edda* so names it. In the Celebes, and in

Hawaii, but nowhere else in Polynesia or Melanesia, the rainbow is a bridge. The North American Catawba Indians of the Southeast and the Tlingit of the Northwest both recognize it as the road of the dead. The messenger of the Greek gods, Iris, is the goddess of the rainbow; a rainbow goddess (A288) is also recognized by the Chibcha of South America. In Siberia, the rainbow is the thunder god's bow; among the Yukaghir it is the tongue of the sun; the Samoyeds call it *munbano,* the hem of the sun god's coat. The Moslems of Iran call it the bow and arrow of Rustam, the sword of Ali, or the picture of the magic mountain Qaf. The Hidatsa say the rainbow is the clawmarks of the red-bird, and they call it the "cap of the water (or rain)."

Most often, however, the rainbow is recognized as a snake, the rainbow serpent (A791.2) of the North and South American Indians, the Australian aborigines, the Dahomeans and their neighbors in West Africa, the ancient Persians, and other peoples. The great snake of the underneath, the rainbow serpent of Yoruba, is, like many other mythological serpents, an earth god. He comes from the earth to drink in the sky. Among the Ewe-speaking tribes, the rainbow serpent stands on his tail in the sea, whence he comes, bends over, and drinks the water. In Malaya, the rainbow is a snake drinking water where he touches earth; on the east coast there is a house where a water jar was drained dry by the rainbow serpent. The rainbow serpent is of great importance—as creator, culture hero, fertility god, Great Father—in aboriginal Australian mythology and ritual. Through him for example initiates are reborn after being swallowed. The Kumana of eastern Bolivia visualized the rainbow as a snake who threw stones at anyone who looked at him. The Ashluslay of the Chaco see the rainbow as a sky serpent. In Brittany, the rainbow serpent has the head of a bull, with blazing eyes.

A Chaga (African) tale includes several of these concepts. A man waits at the place where the rainbow touches the earth, praying for cattle. When none appear he cuts the rainbow in two with his sword; half rises into the sky, half disappears into the earth, leaving a hole. People who climb into the hole discover an underground paradise, but lions drive them out and have driven away anyone who has gone down since.

☞ Nearly all North American Indian groups account for the rainbow, either in their myths or as part of their bodies of belief or knowledge. The Timiskaming Algonquians call the rainbow "forms from the water"; the Timigami Ojibwa call it "mist from the water"; both groups believe the rainbow is caused by the mist from breakers on some great body of water. The Yuchi of the Southeast believe that a rainbow brings dry weather; stretched across the sky, it prevents the rain from falling. In two Jicarilla Apache myths Rainbow is personalized; he is helpful to the Hactcin (supernaturals) and to Killer-of-Enemies when that culture hero is trying to kill the Rolling Rock monsters. In Hopi and other Pueblo Indian myths the Cloud People and the kachinas travel on the rainbows; Navaho gods also travel by rainbow. Rainbow is also a spirit in the pueblos. The interior ladder in pueblo kivas represents the rainbow. In certain sand paintings, rainbow house is represented by three straight lines. A rainbow bridge to an upper or other world is mentioned in various Mackenzie, North Pacific Coast, Iroquois, and Southwestern myths. In several instances the appearance of a rainbow in the sky is taken as a sign that a girl is menstruating, or that evil will befall, or that there will be good wild crops. Children in northern California tribes were especially warned not to count the colors in a rainbow or to point at it, else one of their fingers would be crooked or drop off, or they would become sick. Dreaming of a rainbow was regarded as an evil portent. If one ran through a rainbow one would be a good doctor. The Shasta Indians of northwestern California believe that Sun, a shaman, uses the colors in the rainbow to paint himself.

In few if any American Indian myths is Rainbow a main or even an important character, even in Plateau mythology where so many natural phenomena are personalized and active characters in myths. [EWV]

☞ Many South American Indians identify the rainbow with a gigantic water serpent. It was caught when it was still small by a girl who kept it as a pet. It grew rapidly and went around the world swallowing people; but the huge serpent was finally killed by an army of birds. After their victory, each bird dipped itself in the blood of the monster, thus acquiring the variegated colors which characterize them (version of the Arekuna, Arawak, Witoto, Jivaro, and Vilela Indians). [AM]

☞ Among the symbolic appliqué cloths of the Dahomey Negroes, one representing Dā in his Aido Hwedo aspect shows the huge serpent, tail in mouth, in a position that would encircle the earth. This seems to represent the concept of Aido Hwedo as two: the serpent under the earth and the serpent in the sky. The serpent in the sky is the traditional rainbow serpent who carries the thunderbolts from heaven to earth. The Sky cult priests of Dahomey identify their Dji with Aido Hwedo; Dji not only represents the rainbow but is represented as a snake. See OSHUNMARE.

☞ Rainbow Serpent is a mythological character known in much of Australia by various names including that of Kalseru in northwestern tribes. He is associated with pools containing spirits of unborn children, rain, and fertility. [KL]

rain crow The yellow-billed or the black billed cuckoo (genus Coccyzus): so called throughout the farming regions of the United States because its cry is said to predict rain. N. N. Puckett reports in his Folk Beliefs of the Southern Negro, Chapel Hill, 1926, that among Alabama Negroes, however, the cardinal grosbeak is the rain crow; to hear one means rain, even to see one is thought to be a sign of rain. He also cites a Georgia Negro belief that breaking a rain crow's egg in water and washing your face in it will enable you to see ghosts.

Rakan Japanese term for the arhats, or Buddhist saints, who have already become perfect in this life; especially, the 500 immediate disciples of Gautama, the historic Buddha. [JLM]

Rākshasas (feminine Rākshasi) In Hindu mythology and folklore, the demigod demons hostile to men; literally, destroyers. According to the Rāmāyana they were created by Brahmā to guard the water. They are also said to have descended from the sage Pulastya. The Rākshasas appear in the shape of various animals (dog, vulture, owl) and also have the power to assume human form, especially that of a deformed or monstrous human shape or of an old woman. They can also appear as beautiful men or women; they are yellow, green, or blue,

but usually their eyes are mere vertical slits. Their hair is matted, their bellies large. They have five feet, their fingers are set on backwards. They eat human flesh and corpses, also food on which someone has sneezed or trodden, or which has been desecrated by insects. They live in trees; their fingernails are poisonous; and their touch can produce death.

The Rākshasas are exceedingly malignant; they destroy Hindu sacrifices, disturb men at their prayers, haunt cemeteries, animate dead bodies, and enter men via their food, causing disease and madness. If the light goes out while a man is eating, he must cover the food with his hands to prevent them from getting it. But they are stupid; the typical stupid ogre stories abound in regard to them; a victim need only to address them as "Uncle" to escape. They are most effective at night. Their chief is Rāvana. The red ferruginous clay found in various parts of India is said to be the scene of their battles with the gods. Today many Rākshasas are of human origin, having reached or been condemned to this form of existence because of their cruelties in life.

Ram A generalized Hindu term for god or divinity.

Rāma or **Rāmachandra** The hero of the Sanskrit epic, the Rāmāyana, celebrated as a model son, brother, and husband; later deified and recognized as the seventh avatar of Vishnu. Historically, Rāma may have been one of the four sons of Daśaratha, king of Oudh (Ayodhyā). In Hindu mythology, Vishnu, who had resolved to become manifest in the world in order to deliver the gods from the demon Rāvana, gave the childless Daśaratha a pot of nectar. The king gave half the potion to Kauśalyā who bore Rāma (impregnated with half the divine essence). A quarter of it was given to Kaikeyī whose son was Bharata, and the last quarter went to Sumitrā whose two sons, Lakshmana and Śatrughna, each had an eighth part of the divine essence. The four boys grew up together but it was Rāma who performed such miraculous feats as the killing of the demon Tāraka. Vishnu took the brothers to the court of Janaka, king of Videha, and there Rāma won his wife Sītā by bending Śiva's wonderful bow.

When the time came for Rāma to be declared the successor to his father, Kaikeyī, the mother of Bharata, persuaded Daśaratha to install Bharata as king and to send Rāma into exile for 14 years. Rāma, Sītā, and Lakshmana left the kingdom and went south to live at Chitrakūta in the Dandaka forest. Meanwhile Daśaratha died, Bharata refused the throne, and set out to bring Rāma back. The latter refused to return until he had completed the period of his exile and Bharata returned to act as his vicegerent.

After ten years of exile, Rāma was advised by the sage Agastya to live at Panchāvatī, an area infested with Rākshasas. One of these, Sūrpanakhā, sister of Rāvana, fell in love with Rāma. Repulsed, she finally inspired in her brother such a fierce passion for Sītā that the demon carried her off to Lankā by force. Rāma followed in hot pursuit and, with the aid of Sugrīva and Hanumān, took the city of Lankā, killed Rāvana, and rescued his wife. Jealous of her honor, however, Rāma finally sent her to the hermitage of Vālmīki where her twin sons, Kuśa and Lava, were born. Sītā finally was recalled by Rāma and declared her purity by calling upon the earth to verify her words. See ACT OF TRUTH. The earth did so by opening and receiving her. Rāma, unable to endure life without his wife, went to heaven with the consent of the gods.

The worship of Rāma today prevails over a large part of India and his followers are estimated to exceed 90 million. His name is invoked at the hour of death and used as a salutation when friends meet. His birthday is celebrated at the great festival of Śrīrāmajayantī.

Rāma's Bridge or **Rāmasetu** A chain of small sandy islands, shoals, or sand bars about 30 miles long between India and Ceylon: said to be the bridge or causeway built for Rāma by his general, Nala, for the invasion of Ceylon; in modern gazeteers called Adam's Bridge.

Rāmāyaṇa One of the two great epics of India: literally, the career of Rāma. Like the *Mahābhārata,* the *Rāmāyaṇa* has had an important influence on the literary as well as the religious thought of India for almost 2000 years. The *Rāmāyaṇa* is a romantic epic, homogeneous in form and the work of a single author, Vālmīki, who probably collected the popular stories of Rāma current about the 4th century B.C. and worked them into an epic celebrating the heroic deeds of that prince. About the 2nd century B.C., the epic was transformed into a poem exalting Rāma as an avatar of the god Vishṇu. In its present form the *Rāmāyaṇa* consists of seven books, the first and the last of which are late additions, and about 24,000 couplets in the epic, called *śloka.* There are three extant recensions: the Bengal, the Bombay, and the West Indian, each varying considerably in content from the others. The epic is recited for thousands of Hindus at the annual Rāma festival in Benares and is held in such veneration that anyone who reads and repeats the tale is liberated from his sins.

Ramman The Babylonian name of the Canaanite storm god Adad. Ramman, the Biblical Rimmon, means thunder or the Thunderer; he was a god of storm, wind, and rain; he was a war god who carried the hammer and thunderbolt. See ADAD.

Rán In Norse mythology, the Robber, wife of Ægir; goddess of the stormy sea and the drowned, who dragged down ships with her hands. At one time Scandinavian sailors made human sacrifice to Rán before embarking on a long voyage. To drown was to go to Rán, and it was well to carry gold on a sea voyage to appease her, should you go to dwell in her halls. Although she was known as cruel and unfeeling, those who dwelt in her halls were well treated and feasted on lobster and other delicacies. In later folklore she was sometimes seen reclining on the shores combing her long hair, much like any mermaid. Rán is identified with the Swedish Sjöran.

Rangi or **Raki** The name used in New Zealand for the sky god or Sky Father, the creator and parent of the gods of Polynesian mythology: the Sky Father still is recognized in central Polynesia (Rangi-Atea in the Tuamotus, Te Tumu in the Society Islands). Rangi figures in the famous earth-sky separation myth of New Zealand. Rangi embraced Papa the earth goddess, so closely that nothing could grow. From the union the gods were born, but they lay pressed in distorted attitudes unable to move beneath the weight of their huge father. At last all agreed (except the wind god, who later accompanied Rangi) that the pair must be separated so that light could enter and things could grow. One after another

tried, until finally Tane-mahuta pushed Rangi away from Papa. Now Tane, taking pity on his father, dressed him in the stars, but still every night the sighs of Papa come from her breast and rise to Rangi as the mists, and still Rangi's futile tears fall on Papa as the dew. In another myth, Rangi took several wives—often six—and begot the various gods. But one of the wives he took happened to be Tangaroa's wife, and when Tangaroa returned he wounded Rangi in the thigh with a spear. Rangi sometimes seems to be a primeval deity, sometimes he is born from the preexistent sea, sometimes he is preceded by a long genealogy of gods. See ATEA.

Raphael In Judeo-Christian angelology, one of the seven archangels, and especially one of the four who stand near God's throne. Raphael's special province is the souls of men; he is the angel of healing who stands behind the Throne; his name means "healing from God." It was Raphael who brought to Adam the ancient books of knowledge (in Milton's *Paradise Lost* he is the teacher of Adam and Eve). In the *Book of Tobit,* Raphael accompanies Tobias on his trip to Media and overcomes the demon Asmodeus. Raphael is also called Suriel, the angel who recalls or dissipates disease.

ras (1) The dance of Krishṇa, the divine flute player of Hinduism, and his consort, Rādhā. Ras-Lila is the twelve-day festival of Krishṇa in Manipur, now greatly condensed in length. The dance is executed in the delicate *lasya* manner of the Manipuri school of *natya.*

(2) A group stick dance of northern India, corresponding to the Tamil *kolattam* of southern India. [GPK]

rasa In the terminology of Hindu *natya,* the emotion represented in music, gesture, and dance movement. The thirteen rasas are: Sringera or Adi, the sex emotion; Vir, the heroic mood; Karuna, compassion; Adbhuta, wonderment; Hasya, laughter; Bhayaneka, fear; Bibhatsa, sense of humor; Raudra, rage; Shanti, serenity; Dasya, devotion; Sakya, friendship; Vatsalya, paternal devotion; Madhura, conjugal felicity. Each rasa is expressed by definite appropriate gestures and postures of all parts of the body, and by fitting *Ragas,* musical modes, and *Talas,* rhythms. [GPK]

Rashnu Old Iranian angel of justice who holds the golden scales in which souls are weighed at Judgment.

raspberry The raspberry is under the dominion of Venus and is commonly a symbol of remorse. The Ifugaos of the Philippine Islands hang raspberry vines by their house doors when there is a death in the house, on the theory that if the spirit of the dead should try to reenter it will become entangled in the brambles.

Raspberry vinegar is a good old folk remedy for feverish colds and sore throat, and is also used as an astringent and stimulant. Raspberry-leaf tea has been given by midwives for childbirth with good effect since earliest times. During World War II the drug *fragerine* was "discovered" by obstetricians for use during childbirth. *Fragerine* is obtained by steeping dried raspberry leaves in boiling water. Midwives ignore the new drug and continue to brew raspberry-leaf tea for their patients.

The rude noise made by vibrating the tongue between the lips, sometimes called the Bronx cheer or "the bird." This manifestation, which originated in England, has been joyfully adopted in America as a gesture of defiance to constituted authority and as an integral part of American blood sports such as wrestling, prize-fighting, baseball, and the like.

Rat A minor character in certain West African and New World Negro folktales. Unlike such characters as Spider or Rabbit, Rat plays no consistent or significant role. [MJH]

ráth (Irish *ráṫ*) A circular earthern wall, often palisaded or fortified, surrounding ancient Irish dwellings; loosely, the fortified dwelling itself of an early Irish king or chief, surrounded by such a wall. *Ráṫ ríoġ* was a "royal seat." Ráth Cruachan (now Rathcrogan) was the famous seat of Meḋb and Ailill, queen and king of Connacht. The word is often used interchangeably with DÚN.

rattles Musical instruments used in producing a succession of short, rapid sounds by the agitation of enclosed or adjacent objects. These objects, made of a great variety of materials, may be fastened on a dancer's body, an article of clothing, or a staff; or they may jiggle in gourds, turtle shells, bells, or other hollow containers. They may synchronize with a dancer's motion by virtue of attachment, or they my be actively manipulated. They are termed *idiophones* (self-sounders).

I The forms and materials of rattles are derived from the natural resources at the disposal of various cultures, as well as from the purpose of the instrument. These cultures are distributed mostly through the Americas, though rattles also occur elsewhere. See AÇON; ASOGWE. The *jingler*, which is prominent in nomadic and hunting tribes and which frequently consists of animal hoofs or derivatives, is probably the oldest form of rattle. Alaskan Eskimo dancers shake mittens with attached puffin beaks and belts with animal teeth. Deer-hoofs are fastened to the belts of the Yaqui *maso* deer dancer and *chapayekas*, and to bands worn across the shoulders of Huichol peyote (*hikuli*) dancers. From northern Mexico to South America, we find deer-hoofs on girdles and ankles of curing shamans (Mataco), and deer, peccary, or tapir claws on the legs or ankles of Brazilian tribes (Kamakan, Apinayé, and the Amazonian Witoto). Antelope, elk, goat, ox, or buffalo hoofs may augment or substitute for the deer-hoofs, as on Iroquois dancers' kneebands in the former knee-rattle dance and in the Shawnee and Delaware, and Penobscot and other Abnaki leading dance. Metal cones in hoof shapes are now fastened on the dress of the adolescent girl in the Apache puberty rite and of Havasupai women dancers. It is significant that Siberian shamans wear iron cone-shaped jinglers on their drums and kilts and collars, the iron itself conferring power over demons. Aztec dancers emulated their gods in fastening gold, copper, or shell *ayualli*, or *coyolli*, bells, on ankles or breast. In South America snail shells or nuts are commonly substituted, as among the Brazilian Bororo and Amazonian Jivaro. The Incas used anklets of fruit-shells or gold.

Deer-hoof rattles are manipulated in clusters by the Yuma Indians of Arizona and by *kachina* dancers of the Rio Grande pueblos, by the leader of the California Diegueño *keruk* or mourning rites, and by South American Kamakan dancers. Bunches of hoofs are fastened to short sticks in the rattles of numerous men's societies of the Great Plains, particularly Dog Societies of the Crow, Hidatsa, and Kiowa, and the corresponding Oglala and Iowa *mawatani* society. Among the Flatheads

of Montana such a rattle was used in the hysterical cures of the Bluejay shaman's dance and in bison-calling rites. This form spread east to the Sauk, Fox, and Iroquois Indians, west to the California Hupa dancing doctors, and southwest to the shaman-singer of the Apache puberty rite. In California and South America the deer-hoof rattle is commonly associated with *menarche* rites. The Maidu and Karok girl herself shakes the rattle. Usually a circle of older women surrounds the girl, and thump long, hoof-tipped poles on the ground—the California Klamath, Tolowa, Shasta, Achomawi, Mountain Maidu, and others; and also Chaco tribes, notably in the Chorotí and Ashluslay *káusima* and corresponding Lengua *yanmena* demon-exorcising puberty rites.

Sand-filled butterfly cocoons are fastened on sticks in the Yuki *taikomol wok* and *hulk'ilal wok* and are similarly manipulated by the leader of Yokut, Maidu, Pomo, and Miwok boys' initiation rites. In the Papago *wiikita* ceremony for rain, the singer-dancers wear cocoons, along with bells and shells, and the Yaqui native dancers all tie strings of cocoons (*téneboim*) around their ankles for the *chapayekas*, *maso*, and *pascolas*.

In recent times the Indian has taken with delight to the sleigh bells and metal pellet bells introduced by the white man, and he uses them in preference to natural materials which are harder to obtain. He ties them around his ankles, below his knees, around his waist, and in a strip from belt to knee, e.g. the *pascolas*, the dancers and runners of Hopi and Taos, San Ildefonso buffalo and Cherokee Shuck Face dancers, and quite generally Oklahoma festival dancers.

Another animal source which provides both types of rattles is the turtle or tortoise. These shells, however, are not as widespread as animal hoofs. With attached deer-hoof, a turtle shell is worn behind the right knee of members of Hopi men's societies and Snake societies, and commonly by *kachina*, at Laguna and Isleta for instance. (They are obtained at Isleta.) Small tortoise shells are worn at the knees of the leading woman in Oklahoma stomp dances. Delaware reciters of visions shook a tortoise shell, and (a borrowing from the Cherokee) the Iroquois *ṭowisas* society of women planters passes a rattle from singer to singer. Huron shamans are reported to have shaken a tortoise shell filled with pebbles near the ear of their patients. Cure motivates the most spectacular use of the turtle rattle, namely by the False Face dancers, and by singers of the Iroquois, Delaware, and Cherokee-Shawnee. The shells are cleaned and filled with cherry pits, and the neck is reinforced by a wooden handle. The huge turtles furnish instruments for the Iroquois "doorkeepers," the 10-inch ones for the singers, and the little ones for the False Face beggar boys. These rattles also feature in the spring and fall exorcism circuits from house to house—a form of False Face pestilence control.

Agriculture introduced the gourd rattle, which is always manipulated by the dancer or singer, never worn. The shapes and sizes are as varied as those of the squash and gourd, and in addition are ornamented with ingenuity. The Papago shaman, sometimes the Iroquois and Cherokee, leave the stem on as a handle. Usually a wooden handle is inserted, perhaps decorated with beads or feathers (Comanche, Apinayé) or with carvings (Cuna of Panama.) Perhaps the largest ones are the pair used by the Yaqui *maso;* the smallest ones are the tufted rattles of the Iroquois *ganegwa'e* and Fox calumet dancers. In between are the flat Hopi and the egg-shaped Cherokee rattles, and the small round *sonaja* common throughout Mexico, particularly in *matachini* groups. These are an inheritance from the Aztec *ayacachtli,* used for instance in the springtime ceremony. The designs of perforations which covered these calabash rattles have spread to northern Brazil and to California, and have even been imitated in wood by the Tsimshian of British Columbia. Symbolic painted designs cover the surface particularly of the *kachina* rattles. Ritualistically, they should be filled with maize kernels, a few squash seeds, also grains of wheat in the Southeast. The Iroquois prefer chokecherry seeds. Nowadays unsymbolic noise-makers are inserted, buckshot, pebbles, even macaroni.

Where gourds are not available, other materials are pressed into service. Tribes of the North Pacific Coast have developed a fine art of carved wooden rattles in animal and bird shapes. North American Plains Indians and South American Patagonian tribes make them of hide, in various shapes: spherical, doughnut-shaped, or flat disks attached to drum sticks. The Chippewa and Naskapi shaman's *cicigwan* resembles a small drum. The Iroquois and Cherokee-Shawnee have introduced cow-horn rattles, and hickory-bark substitutes for False Face beggars. The Chippewa construct cylinders out of birch bark. Split sticks are quivered in the California *kuksu* ceremonies and Hupa *menarche* rite. The *pascola* shakes a wood-and-metal *sena'asom,* which resembles the *sonajeros* instrument and the Aztec *chicahuaztli,* and is derived no doubt from the sistrum. Peruvian pottery and Araucanian basketry rattles add to the wealth of constructive variety, but by no means exhaust the list. For again civilization has introduced harsh substitutes in the tin can, spice-box, and almost any old box that is handy: even for the sacrosanct *midewiwin* ceremony of the Chippewa and Menominee. Milk tins replace Shawnee tortoise knee rattles.

II Passive and active manipulation depends on the medium. The rattle at all times forms part of the dancer's rhythmic impulse, but is most completely identified with him in the "passive" use of fastening to the body. Be these jinglers hoofs or substitutes, they automatically accompany Siberian shamans, Bella Coola *kukusiut,* and the *kachina,* and are found in northern Brazil and the eastern United States, still today among the Shawnee, formerly among the Iroquois with limited use. Actively, these are shaken or struck on the ground in the western United States (Plains, California) and in the Chaco.

Gourds on a stick may be struck on the ground, as in the Arawak *macquari* dance; horn rattles are often struck with alternate accents against the palm of the left hand by Iroquois dance leaders, and formerly by Penobscot. Usually these hollow containers are actively shaken in any of the three dimensions and with varying accent, always with an elastic wrist-motion. In its wide distribution, the gourd or substitute would show tribal distinctions of manipulation. The Navaho shake it vertically, with a strong and a weak accent; the Cherokee-Shawnee horizontally, the Absentee Shawnee against the left palm. Eastern tribes and the Mexican Tarahumara have a pattern, arising from the song and dance form, of horizontal vibration followed by a metrical beat. The meter of the gourd rattle of the Iroquois *hadi'hi'duus* is an even, vertical pulsation. The *ganegwa'e* dancers vibrate as they lunge, and shake as they hop. False Faces vibrate their turtle rattles or knock them against door or floor in a rhapsodic fashion; the thunderous even beat is provided by their accompanying singers who strike them on a bench. In the Feather dance this same instrument produces an iambic beat. The continuous sound of these instruments is quite distinct from the staccato notes of the jinglers, for the kernels strike the roof of the container before their impact on the base. The Yaqui deer dancer (*maso*) produces an even more sustained sound by the continuous rotation of one of his rattles.

The various passive and active rattles of this deer dance interplay with the musical accompaniment. The cocoons swish with every step. The deer-hoofs descend with the knee and foot in thumping steps, but in leaping steps their momentum causes them to syncopate, to fly apart as the dancer descends and strike together as he rises. Add to this the circular swish of one gourd and the alternately accented beat of the other. The *pascola* dancer shows a similar complexity, substituting the syncopated rhythm of his *sena'asom* against the left hand. At times, he vibrates this back and forth in front of him.

These few examples show that the manipulation of rattles is a subtle art, adapted to the medium and the dance movement. Every technique produces a different timbre by control of the impulse and force, a timbre which is already variable because of the texture of the container and its contents. Furthermore, the manipulation is an important aid to heightened efficacy of the dance, towards achievement of the supernatural purpose.

III Coercive magic certainly motivates the use of rattles and their varying forms, though in many cases it has become rather confused. Demon exorcism or control is the acknowledged reason for the most primitive noise-making, and this is certainly true of shamanistic and puberty rites, and of rites for the dead, as the *keruk* and *macquari.* These show signs of great antiquity. In *menarche* rites the use of the deer-hoof or its substitutes may be due to association of the deer with renewed life, or else the deer may have derived this association from the use of its hoofs in such rites. These hoofs are combined with the turtle, which embodies the earth and fertility and also produces cures, as in the False Face dances and pestilence-chasing circuits of homes.

One might suppose gourds to be associated with crops and rain, and in the case of the *kachina* this is so. However, among the Huichol, Tarahumara, and Shawnee, it is used in peyote dances along with deer-hoofs. It is the instrument of the Iroquois *hadi'hi'duus* society of curing shamans, who derive their power from mystic animals. Again, in their food-spirit dances for corn, beans, and squash, it is replaced by the horn rattle.

Despite this confusion, or fusion, a number of beliefs remain to explain the power that is inherent in the rattles. The Zuñi believe that the turtle-shell rattle "makes the thunder come" and thus has the same potency as the turtle itself. The corn and grain kernels encourage vegetable growth. At an eclipse of the moon the Kwakiutl believed that their clappers frightened away the demons devouring the moon. On a Tlingit shaman's rattle, the human face touching its tongue to that of a frog signifies the source of maleficent power and poison in the frog. The Bella Coola *sisaok* society dancer holds his bird-shaped hollow rattle belly uppermost; otherwise the bird, symbol of his ancestral crest, will fly away. The perforated rattle in the thunder dance represents the bird of lightning. The Aztecs consciously applied their seed- or pebble-filled rattling stick (*chicahuaztli*) to the symbolic sowing of seeds at agricultural festivals. The maize goddess, Cihuacoatl, is believed to have used it thus. The decorations, too, are symbolic: the painted designs of Pueblo rattles attract rain and promote plant growth by stylized representations; the feathers on South American Guaraní rattles symbolize the souls of the shaman's bird-assistants.

Despite deviations and substitutions, the sum total of rattle forms divide into 1) the male type of self-sufficient jinglers, often combined with the phallic staff, and 2) the female type, containers. Actually certain jinglers are of the female type, namely cocoons and bells; the sistrum is male. The rattling stick combines both principles, as does also the tortoise with hoofs. The male type is associated with the vision quest for renewed life and cure, rarely with the hunt (Yaqui deer and Pueblo buffalo). The more recent female type effects agricultural magic and, indirectly, human fertility and regeneration. They are frequently combined for doubled productivity in *menarche* rites.

These American rattles are for the most part indigenous. The sistrum and metal bells are exceptions. The Cuban *maraca* may have descended from the gourd rattles of the African Slave Coast. Certainly its elaborate manipulation differs from the purposeful shaking of the American Indian rattle. As a whole these integrated dance instruments grew out of the soil to fulfil the needs of the native American tribes. [GPK]

🖝 The rattle made of gourd containing seeds or small stones (generally crystal pebbles) is the main accessory of the South American Indian shaman from the Gran Chaco to the Guianas. The sound of the rattle is usually interpreted as the voice of the spirits and is also regarded as a powerful means of curbing supernatural forces. In some tribes, as for instance the Tupinamba, a cult was rendered to these sacred rattles. [AM]

Rauni The wife of Ukko, the Thundergod of the Finns. The name is derived from Icelandic *reynir*, or Swedish *rönn*, rowan, a blessed tree which is often brought in connection with the Thundergod and is a protection against all evil spirits. The Finnish Lapps know a deity as Ravdna and sacrifice reindeer to her as to the Thundergod himself. [JB]

Rāvana The demon king of the Rākshasas and of Lankā (Ceylon); grandson of Pulastya; incarnation of wickedness, breaker of laws, and ravisher of women. Rāvana became invulnerable to gods and demons by doing devotion to Brahmā. He had ten heads, twenty arms, and all the marks of royalty in addition to countless wounds inflicted upon his body in his battles with the gods. He could assume any form he wished. He was as tall as a mountain and could stop the moon and the sun with his arms. His strength was such that he could split mountain tops. Rāvana was not invulnerable, however, to men and beasts, so Vishnu became incarnate as Rāmachandra in order to destroy him. Rāvana stole Rāma's wife Sītā and carred her off to Lankā. Rāma, with the aid of Sugrīva and Hanumān and their hosts of monkeys and bears, built a bridge to Lankā. There, after many battles, Rāma slew Rāvana with an arrow made by Brahmā and regained his faithful wife. See CYMBALS; INDRA; RĀMA'S BRIDGE.

raven A large omnivorous bird (*Corvus corax*) of Europe, Asia, and North America, resembling the crow, having lustrous black plumage with the feathers of the throat enlarged and elongated. It is about two feet long, very intelligent, mischievous, and can be taught to speak a few words.

The raven, one of the scouting birds let loose from the ark by Noah, found no place to rest but "went to and fro until the waters were dried up off the earth." And because he did not return with his message he was condemned to suffer thirst, or to be black, or to eat carrion (A2234.1). The raven is one of the unclean birds forbidden as food (*Lev.* xi, 15): "every raven after his kind." Elijah in hiding beside the brook Cherith was fed by ravens, who "brought him bread and flesh in the morning, and bread and flesh in the evening, and he drank of the brook."

In Greek religion, the raven, as prophetic bird, was sacred to Apollo and to the augurs. One etiological story explaining why he is black is the story of Apollo and Coronis (mother of Æsculapius). Coronis was dearly beloved by Apollo, but preferred a mortal lover. Her faithlessness was reported to Apollo by his messenger bird, a pure white raven. Apollo, in rage at the discovery, took it out on the bird and condemned him to be black forever for his tattling (A2237.1). Pliny reported that the soul of Aristeas of Proconnesus came forth from his mouth in the form of a raven. In fact the concept of raven as bird-soul has a spread, both geographic and chronological, from ancient Greece to the contemporary Bororos of Brazil. The ancient Greeks also believed that eating ravens' eggs would restore blackness to gray hair. Great care had to be taken to protect the teeth with oil while eating them, lest the teeth too turn black.

Almost everywhere the raven is a bird of ill-omen who predicts pestilence and death. It was called *Abu Zájir*, Father of Omens, by the Arabs, who said if one saw it flying to the right, good luck might be expected, if to the left, bad. To see a raven on the left means impending evil quite generally in Europe, Great Britain, Ireland, India, and among Slavic peoples. In Germany a raven croaking near a house foretells the imminent death of one of the inmates. If a raven flies over a house where someone is ill, death will surely follow. Speculations as to how ravens know that death is impending was explained by an early British physician who said that their sense of smell is so acute that they can detect the odor of death in the body even before life is gone.

To have the foresight of the raven is a proverbial saying which refers both to the raven's knowledge and his prophetic gifts. *To have raven's knowledge* is an Irish phrase meaning to see all, know all.

In Teutonic mythology Odin's two ravens, Hugin and Munin, were sent over the world every day to see all that happened and to bring news back to Odin (B122.2). The whereabouts of the magic caldron Odhroerir was revealed to Odin by them. In the saga of Olaf Tryggvason, when Earl Hakon, after one defeat, made a blood sacrifice and two ravens came upon it "croaking loudly," Hakon believed the offering was by this token accepted by Odin and that success in battle would henceforth be his.

The raven was a battlefield bird in both early Teutonic and Old Irish mythology. The Old Irish battle goddesses, Badb, Morrigan, Macha, all were seen on the battlefields in raven form. Cormac's *Glossary* describes the invocation of Morrigan in battle by war trumpets simulating the raven's cry. The raven banner of the Danes was described by the Anglo-Saxons as being a banner of pure white on which a raven became visible in time of war. The raven was also the oracular bird of the Old Irish mythological Bran; and *bran* is one of modern Irish words for raven, and, figuratively, for chieftain. The legend that on the presence of Bran's head in London depends the safety of the kingdom may account for the keeping of tame ravens by the Tower of London garrison to this day. See Robert Graves, *The White Goddess* (New York, 1948), p. 67 n. The Bayeux tapestry shows William the Conqueror at the Battle of Hastings under a raven banner. Owen Glendower had a pet raven who gave him the magic stone by which he could become invisible. In Cornish folk belief Arthur lives on in raven form. The Cornish people therefore do not shoot ravens; to shoot a raven would be to shoot the hero.

In Russian epic the black raven is the symbol of the enemy, in contrast to the bright falcon which symbolizes the traditional Russian warrior. In Lithuanian folklore also the raven is a bird of battle.

In Yukaghir folklore, in contrast with Koryak mythology, the raven is neither creator, transformer, nor ancestor, but a trickster who eats excrements, and because of this habit has a hard time finding a mate. But very old people among the Yukaghir remember an "old word" for raven, *co'mmodo*, meaning Great Bird, which may be reminiscent of a forgotten veneration. See W. Jochelson, *Yukaghir and Yukaghirized Tungus*, *MAMNH* ix, part 2, p. 299.

In folktale the raven plays a varied role: he is a bird of ill-omen (B147.1.1.3); he carries off the souls of the damned (E752.3); man learned the custom of burial from watching a raven bury its own dead (A1591.1); the devil appears in the form of a raven (G303.3.3.13.1), or the raven is the devil's messenger (B291.2); ravens attend gods (A165.0.1; B122.2); in Celtic tale, they carry messages to enemies (B291.1.1); and the helpful raven (B452) occurs in general European and Celtic story.

Man transformed to raven, a German folktale motif (D151.5), occurs typically in Grimm's story *The Raven* (#93). An impatient mother, a queen, one day wished that her troublesome child was a raven; it instantly became a raven and flew away. The story involves the young man who tries to break the spell of the bewitchment (for the child bewitched was a little princess), his many fallings asleep at the crucial moment (from having eaten proffered but forbidden food), his quest for the golden castle of Stromberg, from which the princess cannot depart and which he discovers is on top of a glass mountain. He overcomes the glass mountain by means of a stick which will open any door, a cloak of invisibility, and a horse which can even go up the glass mountain. Thus he sets the little princess free of the raven spell, and they are married.

Raven as revenant turns up in Swiss folktale (E423.3.4). Stories of two ravens which follow the Wild Hunt (E501.4.4) are associated with Odin's ravens, Odin

often being the leader of the Wild Hunt, and also with the night-raven of Danish folklore, which is said sometimes to precede the Wild Hunt, and perhaps personifies Odin himself.

Etiological stories in regard to the raven are legion: why raven is bald (A2317.5), why he is black (A2411.2.6), why he claps his wings (A2211.4; A2442.2). The croaking of the raven is explained in both Finnish and Tahltan Indian folktale (A2426.2.7). See QUIKINNA'QU.

🖝 The raven has, in dance and legend, been invested with supernatural powers. In Tibet he is considered the messenger of the supreme being. As crest among the Bella Coola Indians, and as totem among the Kwakiutl, he serves as prototype for a dance mask. The Kwakiutl cannibal dancer may appear in the guise of a raven. The great raven, *gahgagoowa*, is leader of the Iroquois Society of Mystic Animals, *hanáhidos* (Onondaga, Cayuga), *hadihidu'us* (Seneca) and is invoked both in the Marching and Curing songs. While feasting, the shamans claw the pig's carcass singing "gahga." [GPK]

Raven The culture hero of the northern North Pacific Coast tribes; also, a minor myth character in other North American Indian mythologies. In Southwestern Jicarilla and Lipan Apache myths it is Raven who decides people will not return to life; for this reason, say the Jicarilla Apache, Indians hate the raven and call him a sorcerer. Like Buzzard, when he sees that something is dead, he is happy. The Chiricahua Apache, however, credit Coyote with determining that men shall die, and Raven with not wanting death in the world. Compare ORIGIN STORIES.

[EWV]

Raven cycle The culture hero-transformer-trickster tale cycle, having Raven as its chief character, of the Indians of the North Pacific Coast from Alaska to British Columbia. The Raven cycle, either in whole or in part, is also known to the western Alaska Eskimo, to some of the most westerly Athabaskan tribes in the interior, and to the Makah, a coast tribe of Washington. Other North Pacific Coast peoples south of the main Raven area have Mink as creator-transformer-trickster, while still farther south Bluejay, Fox, Moon, and other characters are the Changers.

North Pacific Coast mythologies lack any true creation myth; instead, the changing, transforming, or ordering of the world is emphasized in the mythology. The Raven cycle begins with the birth of a boy child, and details the adventures of the boy, who grows to manhood quickly. As a young man he seduces his aunt, or the daughter of the Sky Chief, and a flood ensues. To escape the flood he flies to the sky. His child, Raven, drops from the sky onto drifting kelp (among the northern Haida, is born to a fisherman's daughter). The child is found and adopted by a chief. The child at first will not eat, but when instructed becomes so voracious that it is hard to keep him supplied with food. This voraciousness, or greediness, is thereafter one of Raven's chief characteristics. At that time the earth was bare and flat, lacking trees, hills, and mountains. It was surrounded by water and filled with cannibal monsters that had powers unknown to man; some of these monsters had sharp claws, some could swim under water, and some could fly as the fish and birds can now.

As culture hero, Raven drew mankind out of a clamshell, stole fire, stole the sun (which was hung up in a ball or box in a chief's house), provided water, animals, etc. Having secured these necessities for mankind, he flew or traveled over the world, transforming animals to their present state and making rivers, mountains, valleys, lakes, and other natural objects. Several of the transformer tales are tales of Raven's deceptions, in which he shows himself sometimes clever, sometimes a stupid being. As a trickster he is always trying to get food; one of the most popular trickster tales of the North Pacific Coast is that of the bungling host, which is concerned with producing food magically. In another tale also concerned with food, Raven dives to the bottom of the bay and steals a halibut from a fisherman's hook; when the fisherman jerks his hook, Raven loses his beak. In this tale Raven is portrayed in bird form; this is usual, but the nature of many of the adventures he undertakes show that he is conceived as also having many human characteristics. For analysis of North Pacific Transformer cycles see Franz Boas, *Tsimshian Mythology*, RBAE 31, 1916, pp. 565 ff. See CANNIBALS. [EWV]

rebus A puzzle representing a word, phrase, or sentence by letters, numerals, pictures, etc., having the sounds necessary to form the desired answer; a form of punning by homophones: said to come from the phrase *non verbis sed rebus*, not words but things, though this derivation is doubtful. The popularity of this form of representation on the shields of the "new gentry" in the Renaissance is satirized by Ben Jonson in *The Alchemist* (1610), where Abel Drugger is told to make his device *a bell* followed by a picture of Doctor *Dee* dressed in a *rug* gown, followed by a dog snarling *er*. Rebuses are much older than this. They form a distinct stage in the development of alphabets, where the picture used in pictographic writing stands for the sound associated with its object no matter where the picture appears and without regard for the object it actually depicts.

The conscious rebus appears where word-play is popular. With the ancient Greeks, familiar with the enigmatic responses of the Delphic oracle, the rebus with its word-play was readily understood. Alexander the Great, according to Plutarch, dreamed during the siege of Tyre that he captured a satyr after a long chase. His seers, readily breaking *satyrus* into two words, immediately saw a good omen in *sa Tyrus,* Tyre would be his.

The rebus enjoyed its greatest popularity in the early 16th century. Earlier, in France, the *rébus de Picardie* were used in biting political allusions. English and French forms of the rebus are somewhat parallel. Strikingly similar are two where the position of words in relation to each other make possible the reading of a sentence:

stand	take	to	taking
I	you	throw	my

(I understand you undertake to overthrow my undertaking)

pir	vent	venir
un	vient	d'un

(*Un soupir vient souvent d'un souvenir:* A sigh often comes from a memory).

The form of the letters too must be taken into account: the French G *a* is to be read *J'ai grand appétit* (G grand, a petit—large G, small a: I have a huge appetite). Similar is the American rebus reading in part:

BeD—a little darkey (dark e) in a big bed.

Pictures of objects of course form the backbone of the rebus, and a popular form of children's puzzle uses illustrations of familiar objects juxtaposed with letters and numbers to give a required sentence. These are not much different from the Drugger "device" mentioned above. In heraldry, however, the symbolism is often somewhat subtler. Breakspear bore a broken spear on the shield; Castleton showed three castles; Butler three cups, etc. See RIDDLES.

rectum snakes Snakes approach their victim when the latter is asleep and enter his body through the rectum, thus killing him: a motif (G328) which occurs in such North American Indian Plains hero tales as *Lodge-Boy and Thrown-Away* and *Old Woman's Grandson*. In these two tales the snakes are foiled; the heroes put flat stones under their rectums, and when all but one snake is asleep they kill them; the remaining snake's head is rubbed against the flat stone, thus causing all snake's heads to be flat thereafter. See SLEEPY STORIES. [EWV]

Red Branch (Irish *Craoḃ Ruaḋ*) In Old Irish legend the organized body of warriors around Conchobar mac Nessa, king of Ulster in the 1st century A.D.; also Conchobar's military assembly hall, one of the three great "houses" of the stronghold at Emain Macha. In it were kept the weapons and heads and trophies of conquered enemies. The warriors of the Red Branch were the fiercest and best in all Ireland; not one could hear an insult but he took the head off the man in a minute. For this reason the warriors did not wear their swords at the feasts, but their arms were hung in the Speckled House at Emain Macha until feasting was over. The twelve great champions of the Red Branch were: Cuchulain; Fergus mac Roich, his tutor; Conall Céarnaċ, the Victorious; Loeġaire Buadaċ, the Battle-Winner; Duḃtac Doel Ulaid, the Beetle of Ulster; Eoġan mac Duriact; Celtair; Muinremar mac Geirgind; Cetern mac Findtain, and the three famous sons of Usnech—Naoise, Ainle, and Ardan. More than 100 separate stories are extant celebrating the feats of the heroes of the Red Branch. See BLOOD; DEIRDRE.

Red Heads The red-headed Melanesian culture heroes, Gwau Meo and Sina Kwao, sons of the sun, who slew monsters, performed numerous other great and wonderful deeds, and brought many new culture elements (new foods, magic, weapons, etc.) to northern Mala in the southern Solomons. Cults are associated with them now, as war spirits. See W. Ivens, *Island Builders of the Pacific*, London, 1930, pp. 291 ff. See MELANESIAN MYTHOLOGY. [KL]

red rag The use of red cloth to counteract or enhance magic or ward off the evil eye is widespread. Popularly, the red rag is the tongue. It is widely believed that a bull will react in rage to the sight of red cloth, and that he will charge at anyone wearing red. Bullfighters, however, know that it is not the color but the movement that causes the bull to charge.

A folktale from the British Isles found in the Kentucky mountains is *The Red Rag Under the Churn* (*American Speech* V: 142). A man visited his neighbor and found that he was out. He sat and talked with the neighbor's wife for a spell and noticed that she seemed to get the churning done much more quickly than his own wife could. When she excused herself on an errand for a moment, he looked under the churn and found a bit of red rag attached to the bottom. He snipped off a piece and took it home to put under his own churn. Then his own butter made more quickly, and more plentifully than the cream put into the churn ordinarily would allow. But payment was due, and the Devil appeared within a circle. He held out a book to the farmer and ordered him to sign his soul over to the Devil. While the man argued the bit of red flag flew out of his pocket in the form of a little red bird and perched on the Devil's shoulder. The man finally put his name in the book but he wrote that what he owned belonged to the Lord. Immediately the Devil vanished, and with him the little red bird. Since that time, the spot where the Devil stood is known as the Devil's sage patch, because only sage grass will grow there. See JACK.

reductio ad absurdum General term for those motifs in which some judgment, question, riddle, or task is reduced to absurdity by the answer or counterproposal. The story of the man who tied his mare to another man's wagon is typical (J1191.1). The mare foaled, but the man who owned the wagon claimed the colt, saying the colt was foaled by the wagon. The owner of the colt reduced this claim to its absurdity either by fishing in the street or hunting fish with a gun in the garden. See ABSURDITY REBUKES ABSURDITY. The question "How can black beans make white soup?" (J1291.1) is answered by the question "How can a white whip raise red (or black) welts?" The disregard of distance in the riddle "Why is the mare restless when the stallions of Babylon neigh?" (H572) is pointed up by the hero's punishing his cat for killing a cock last night in Babylon. The hero assigned some absurd or impossible task answers with an equally absurd or impossible countertask or proposition (H952). See BERRIES IN WINTER; IMPOSSIBILITIES.

reel A figure dance in 2/4 time, thus distinguished from the 6/8 time jig. As the name might imply, many of the figures contain turning movements, but not as an exclusive characteristic. Jigs also have turns. The reel has extended its popularity from the British Isles to Scandinavia (*ril*) and to the United States and the Greenland Eskimos. The most elaborate reels (*cor*) are found in Ireland in the form of rounds, squares, and longways. The four-hand reel (*cor čeatrair*) and eight-hand reel (*cor očtair*) use cross-overs, as well as turns for one couple or a team of two couples and circling by all. They anticipate the American square dance. The sixteen-hand reel (*cor seisir deag*) preserves more of a round-dance character, including breaking up into four small circles. A number of dances of various names are executed to reel time, as the longways, Bridge of Athlone and Siege of Ennis. The former, like the Antrim Reel, contains no turning. The Galway Reel features the arch as much as the turn. On the other hand, jigs such as the Piper's Dance, employ concentric circling. Counter-clockwise turns predominate in reels, but the preliminary circling goes both ways. The formations recur in other European countries, perhaps as a diffusion, and particularly in the American longways, Lady Walpole's Opera, Happy Valley Reels, of New England, and the

widely popular Virginia Reel, with its many pivots by "corners" and turns all the way down the line. The term is also used in English sword dances. [GPK]

☞ In New World Negro usage, a secular song or dance, as distinguished from music acceptable for the church or by the clergy. In the American South "reels" were "sinful" songs, often with tunes derived from the Scotch-Irish dance tunes of the whites. In Trinidad, a "reel" is a secret ritual dance for the dead, held at the instigation of a lookman, who communes with the spirits, and intended to cure the sick, to invite ancestors to a wedding or betrothal, to ward off sickness or death for a child whose brother or sister has died, or to test a bridegroom. The accompanying songs are based on Scotch-Irish reels or French quadrilles. [TCB]

Regin In the *Volsunga Saga*, the dwarf smith, wisest of men, who taught Sigurd and reforged for him Sigmund's wondrous sword named Gram. He treacherously persuaded Sigurd to slay the dragon Fafnir (his brother) so that he might gain the gold of his father, the dwarf king Hreidmar, which Fafnir was guarding, but he also was slain by Sigurd.

Rei David or **dança do Rei David** The dance of King David; a Portuguese group dance for men, performed at Braga on St. John's Day as part of the procession. Frilled turbans and breeches carry out the medieval notion of Oriental costume. The dancers execute a variety of steps in two lines resembling a contredanse. They accompany themselves on guitars, fiddles, flutes, triangles, and cellos. They probably tie up with the Mouriscadas and their symbolic vegetation magic. [GPK]

Reinach, Salomon (1858–1932) French archeologist, noted chiefly for his writings, extensive in scope and volume, and covering a wide field, especially in the history of art and religion. His bibliography includes some 70 volumes and nearly 5,000 articles. He was educated at the Lycée Fontanes and the École Normale Supérieure and was appointed to the École Française d'Athènes. In 1882, he made excavations near Smyrna; was secretary of the Archæological Commission in Tunis (1882–85), attaché at the Museum of National Antiquities at Saint-Germain-en-Laye (1886). From 1890–92 he was assistant professor of archeology at the École du Louvre, and associate curator of the National Museum in 1893. In 1889 he was elected to the Académie des Inscriptions et Belles-Lettres, becoming president of that institution in 1906. His most popular works are *Apollo* (1904), a history of art, and *Orpheus* (1909), a history of religion.

reincarnation A rebirth of the soul in successive bodies; one of the stages in the transmigration of souls or metempsychosis. Reincarnation is perhaps best limited to the rebirth of a deity in some earthly form of life, but in certain religious doctrines the ultimate goal of man is divinity through purification of the soul in various reincarnations. Thus, the Pythagoreans and from them the Orphics of ancient Greece believed that the soul was reborn several times and that by living a good life each time it became more purified. See ORPHEUS and compare NIRVANA. In Vedic religion, Vishnu was reborn in several avatars. Hindu religion holds that rebirth in a higher form depends on the rectitude of the life one leads. See KARMA. Thus a man may be reborn as a higher or lower form of life, and even the supernatural beings may be reborn as men or lower forms of life. Several peoples believe that the souls of the dead are reborn into the tribe. Compare ANAPEL. The Alaskan Eskimos hold mourning rites for the seals after a hunt. The souls of the seals are expected thereafter to return to the hunting grounds and to be caught again after reincarnation.

☞ Return to life in another form (E600). Belief in metempsychosis is evinced rather infrequently in North American Indian myths though instances of a return to life in another form occur now and again in Eastern Woodlands, Plains, Plateau, California, and North Pacific Coast tales and, with much greater frequency, in Eskimo tales. The Caribou Eskimo believe, for example, that the dead are brought back to earth with Moon's help, to live again not only as human beings, but as animals, birds, and fishes. In the Nanabozho cycle of the Eastern Woodlands the culture hero's beloved brother is drowned; later he returns to life as a wolf. In myths from several parts of North America supernatural beings die and return to life as corn, tobacco, squash, beans, and jimsonweed, and in the Southwest the kachina or supernaturals, when killed, are believed to become deer. [EWV]

rejong A gong chime of Balinese and Javanese orchestras, consisting of a waisted wooden frame with a gong at either end, held across the lap of the seated player, and struck with sticks. Two rejongs of different sizes play counter rhythms on their four notes. See GAMELAN.

religious folk music Probably the most extensive body of music and song in the repertory of all peoples, comprising texts, melodies, instrumental techniques, and rhythms to convey the stories of creation, the pantheons, and mythologies, magical invocations of gods and lesser supernatural beings, and praise and worship of the powers of the earth and other worlds, and providing to the singers a means of enlisting the help of deities or dispelling the influence of demons to acquire some control over natural environment and the dangers of life and death.

In primitive cultures particularly, songs of religious or magical character outnumber secular classes of song such as lullabies, work songs, love songs, game or drinking songs, etc., for not only must the gods be served and placated as a part of religious ritual, but there are hundreds of other beings whose effect on everyday life—on farming, hunting, marriage, burial, war, and travel, for instance—must be dealt with. Ancestors, as among Australian tribes and among the secret Kromanti cult of warriors of the Surinam Bush Negroes, must be honored. Venerable animals, such as the bear in Siberian, Baltic, Eskimo, and North American Indian lore, must be mourned or entertained. Star influence, as in connection with the movement of the Pleiades, important to so many peoples, must be sought.

In primitive custom, the god is seldom summoned by the subdued or private supplications of more sophisticated worship—the hush of a kneeling congregation, the murmured, whispered, or silent prayer, the sweet, soft melody, or the subtle harmony. The great and powerful beings who regulate the sun, the storm, the rain, the procreative capacities of man and beast, and the fertility of the earth come to speak to their devotees on the vibrations of an equally great and powerful noise. The invocation of help and favor must be loud, for the god may

not hear in his dwelling under the ground, high in the air, deep in the sea, or wherever it may be, or he may not be easily distracted from his own personal concerns to deal with the small wishes of man. It takes the undulant buzz and howl of the bullroarer, the earth-shaking blast of the horn or trumpet, the deep reverberation of the log drum or stamping tube, the piercing wail of the oboe, the coaxing, fricative hum and clatter of scrapers, the air-shattering clangor of bells and gongs, or the sharp staccato of rattles—something like the sounds of the god's own manifestation in natural phenomena—to bring him into the midst of his people to work his wonders. Not for such a purpose are such intimate instruments as the sanza, the jew's harp, the nose flute.

The singing that calls the god must be strong, repetitive, insistent, flattering, and persuasive. The range of tone in primitive religious song is often narrow, restricted to intervals of a second or a third. The voice production may be nasal, high in the head, plangent and penetrating; it may be low, rumbling, or growling; it may be disguised beyond recognition as human at all by the use of megaphone, hollow fruit or seashell, or other masking instrument; but it is seldom meek or gentle. The god or spirit must be addressed in an impressive manner that he will hear and respond to. He may even have a specific rhythm to which he, rather than any other god, will answer, as in vodun and other Negro cults. If the being is an evil spirit, all the more need for harsh clamor.

Furthermore, the human subject into which the supernatural spirit is frequently called must be cleansed of all other bodily and spiritual distraction by strong rhythm, sound volume, and long-continued and strenuous dancing (see RING SHOUT), so that when the god enters, he may speak clearly and unmistakably through the voice and movements of the possessed. Religious songs of the West African Negroes and the cult songs of their Afro-Bahian, Haitian, and other New World relatives, the magico-religious chants of South American and Siberian shamans, the song ceremonials of the Navaho and other North American Indians, all exhibit some if not all of these characteristics. See CHANT.

In more advanced cultures, the chief form of religious music is hymns, that is, songs addressed to or in praise of a god, sacred lyrics usually sung in group worship, or, loosely, any song of religious or moral character. There are other types also, e.g. carols and liturgical chant.

The custom of hymn-singing is rooted in primitive chants, incantations, and charms, and still retains in folk belief a protective power against evil, sickness, and danger. The texts of many ancient hymns in various languages contain acrostics, riddles, enigmas, macaronic and abecedarian devices, and pagan survivals lightly disguised by the substitution of Christian symbols, saints' names, etc. The melodies, derived from both folk and art sources, with both sacred and profane connections, and of ancient and modern origin, represent an enormous segment of the world's music. And the methods of teaching and transmission on an illiterate level include such mnemonic systems as hand signs and head movements to indicate pitch or tone, notes printed in distinctive shapes (buckwheat notation) to designate the syllables of solmization, and the practice of "lining out" or "deaconing" the hymn (reading or recitation of a line at a time by the leader before it is sung by the congregation). See MNEMONIC DEVICE.

Survivals from Mesopotamian hymnology salute Ishtar, Tammuz, Marduk, Ea, etc. Several examples are devoted to the sun and to the new year. One addressed to Nebuchadrezzar I contains an acrostic on the name of the Babylonian god of wisdom, Nebo. Egyptian hymns are known to have been addressed to Rā, Amen, Osiris, Aten, and to kings. In Greek antiquity, hymns or pæans to Apollo called upon him as god of healing and had their origin in primitive medicine dance and song rites. The ancestor worship of China produced hymns in honor of the dead. In Japan, certain hymns introduced with Buddhism were sometimes sung at secular functions with religious intent, and eventually lost their sacred character. Some of the Japanese shrine hymns, go-eiko, are still sung, one group being especially reserved for the death of a child. The kagura-uta songs, dating from the 9th century, have been sung in connection with the religious dance, kagura, of prehistoric origin. (See MIN-YO.) One chant that survived in Japanese Buddhism was the Indian Sacred Hymn, Bombai, a recitative from the Sanskrit, similar in sound to Christian psalm-singing. Those parts of the Vedas which may be considered hymns include odes to divinities, riddling descriptions of gods, cosmogonic and theosophic concepts, charms against enemies, diseases, etc., and even a gambler's lament.

Folk hymns in Europe embody the interplay of art and folk elements, the remnants of pagan runes and spells, and the later seeds and sentiments of dissent from established religious orders. Early Latin hymns, evolving from folk song, became systematized into liturgical formulas, and subdivided again in the Middle Ages to form new popular songs and poetry. Among the Celtic peoples particularly, early charms and incantations lie close beneath the surface of certain hymn types. For example, the Irish loricas, or charm hymns, named for a piece of armor, invoke the Trinity and give a precise description of the dangers and bodily injuries from which protection is desired. For a believer whose memory was short, the recitation of the three final stanzas was sufficient. One such hymn is ascribed to Saint Patrick, who, so the story goes, composed it in flight from the king of Tara, and by its powers made himself and his companions invisible. Another is said to have been written by Columcille on his way to Donegal after a battle. See FAET FIADA. Another specific hymn with extraordinary powers was Media Vita.

The practice of singing religious texts to folk tunes has a long history, but the first extensive use of secular melodies in this way was made by Martin Luther in his effort to make the music of church services attractive to his followers. His inspiration, according to tradition, came from the singing of a carpenter's boy under his window. Many Protestant hymns were made simply by a slight adaptation of the words, such as, "There was a man who had lost God's grace," from "There was a man who had lost his wife."

A similar process went on in the creation of modern Jewish hymns from folk material, some set to the same tunes as those the Protestants borrowed. A Spanish love song beginning "Señora," was imitated phonetically as "Shem nora" (O name revered), and the melody used for Luther's Nun freut euch, lieben Christengemein, had been adopted by Jews in Germany for hymns of the Feast of Dedication before 1450.

From the days of the Lollards on down to the Holiness movement beginning in America in the 1890's, which has evolved such songs as The Gospel Boogie and Telephone to Jesus, folk hymns have always been the accompaniment of dissent. Shakespeare noted that Puritans sang psalms to hornpipes. Wesleyans, Baptists, and Calvinists, influenced by Moravian hymns, sang their denominational differences to ballad, come-all-ye, and dance tunes. As the dissenters became established in America, their Standing Order gave rise to new waves of dissent—New Lights, etc.—each bringing new hymns. These evolved constantly toward less formalism and complication of text, greater emotional excitement, stronger rhythms, and the use of folk instruments. With the great Southern and Western revival movement of the end of the 18th century, camp meetings in the wide-open frontier atmosphere broke down the hymn to a jingling tune and little more than a chorus. That Old Ship of Zion, Bound for the Promised Land, and such first-person narratives as The Dying Californian and The Wayfaring Stranger were favorites. Tunes for Barbara Allen, Lord Lovel, and the Irish Fainne Geal an Lae (sung also to Lady Isabel and the Elf Knight) were matched to scraps from the texts of Isaac Watts, John Newton, John Cennick, etc. Shape-note hymnals circulated widely, and the Sacred Harp conventions for hymn-singing gathered in the rural people at regular sessions. The dialogs, antiphonal songs between the separately seated men and women of earlier dissenters' churches, gave way to the shouted choruses of the camp "mating grounds." Negroes, learning these hymns, or spirituals, from their white masters, gave to the singing their own rhythmic, tonal, and ideological turns, and created from the material a hymn style of their own. The most recent revival is still in progress and its products may be heard on the radio and on records.   THERESA C. BRAKELEY

Renaud The French version of one of Europe's most widely disseminated ballads, originating in Scandinavia toward the end of the Middle Ages and known in hundreds of variant forms in France, Italy, Switzerland, Spain, Scotland, and French Canada. The story, told in literary form in the German poem The Knight of Staufenberg, is that of a knight who meets a fairy, is enticed to dance with her companions, takes flight, and dies as he reaches his home. This narrative is generally complete in its Scandinavian forms told of the knight Olaf. In Brittany the fairy element is less important and the end of the tale takes the stage. In the French Renaud the fairies disappear altogether and the story deals with the knight's (or king's) return home just as his wife has borne a child, his death in his mother's arms, the gradual realization of the wife, through dialog and question-and-answer development, of the death of her husband, and her determination to join him in the grave.

Renenutet, Rannut, or Ernutet The divine nurse and serpent goddess of the harvest of ancient Egyptian mythology. She is depicted as a woman with a serpent's head, or as a huge uræus-serpent with the horns of the cow-goddess Hathor and the solar disk on her head. Her festival took place in April. It is conjectured that she took her form from the snakes which fled to and were discovered in the last part of the fields as they were harvested.

Rephaim The shades or inhabitants of the lower world in the Old Testament: the name may mean the limp or inert. Gaster (*Thespis*), with the additional evidence of some Phœnician inscriptions, says they may be either upper world spirits or lower world spirits, equivalent to either the Igigi or Anunnaki of Sumerian mythology. Through a common mythological transference, the Rephaim, or underworld denizens, become a race of giants who inhabited the land of Palestine before the Israelites came, in much the same manner as the Tuatha Dé Danann of Ireland were both divine and previous inhabitants of the land.

requests Requests made by mortals to a culture hero or supreme deity whom they go to visit are frequently mentioned in Eastern Woodlands Indian tales of visits to the afterworld, as well as in some Woodlands versions of the Orpheus myth. If the request is moderate the deity grants it; examples of moderate requests are asking for medicine to cure disease, or for power by an unsuccessful suitor to win a wife. But if the request is immoderate, such as asking for eternal life, the human being is not granted it, but is turned into a rock or a cedar tree. See IMMORTALITY. [EWV]

Resheph A Syrian god of war, plague, pestilence, and fire: equivalent to Môt, Canaanite god of death, but depicted in Egyptian monuments very much like Hadad, Mesopotamian storm god. He also resembles Nergal, the Babylonian plague god. In a Cilician inscription of the 8th century B.C., Resheph "of the birds" is mentioned, and in *Job* v, 7 the sons of Resheph are called winged; Resheph was therefore probably a vulture god. The Cyprian Phœnicians identified him with Apollo in the latter's aspect as plague god. In Egypt, where Resheph became an important god, he was depicted as a bearded man with Semitic features, carrying various weapons, with a crown like that of Upper Egypt, from which came a streamer. Above his forehead, Resheph had a hand or the horns of a gazelle. The name means the Ravager, and in the Old Testament the word is used for the punishing thunderbolt of God. Resheph is often associated with Anath, the Syrian war goddess.

resuscitation If reincarnation or metempsychosis is comparatively rare in North American Indian tales, resuscitation or revival of a "dead" being by magical means is a common incident. The means used are many: by rubbing or beating, stepping or jumping over the body of the dead person, by boiling or putting the body in water, or by throwing parts of the body such as the bones and intestines into a river, by sweating, by shooting arrows, by breathing on the corpse, by reassembly of the members of a body, and by other magic means.

The Shawnee and other Algonquian tribes tell how, when a monster was destroyed by fire one single drop of his blood remained on the under side of a leaf; this was found by the ants, and the creature was brought back to life. A Taos Pueblo tale narrates how old male witches, anxious to get a girl for a lover, cause her to sicken and die; after four days they bring the girl's body into the kiva, and roll a sea-shell wheel over it from the east, north, west, south, and again from the east side. "Then the dead body became alive, and human

again" (Elsie Clews Parsons, *Taos Tales, MAFLS* 34, p. 36). For a list of some 15 methods of resuscitation detailed in North American Indian myths throughout the continent, see Stith Thompson, *Tales of the North American Indians*, p. 363. [EWV]

Reuben Ranzo A halyard chantey devoted to the escapades of the scapegrace of chanteydom, Reuben Ranzo, who was the sea's most inept follower. His mistakes gave the sailors numerous opportunities for covert gibes at their own officers, for in some versions Ranzo became the captain of a Black Ball ship. In others he got his just desserts and was flogged. The song may have originated in the whaling fleets, but it was widely known on merchant ships. The hauling effort was timed to fall on the word *Ranzo* or the chorus. See CHANTEY.

revenant Nearly every civilization contains evidence that at some time or other there have been current beliefs that the dead return in either a visible or sensory form. In the Western world, belief in revenants has been on the wane since the 18th century, but ghost lore is still a vigorous element in any area where folklore thrives. It is to be collected not only among the illiterate but also among sophisticated groups in communities where those groups have long lived, especially in England where so many of the county families have ghost stories which they not only keep alive but tend to accept. It is also true that people of the middle class, while not believing in ghosts as such, will be quick to tell of one supernatural incident involving a revenant which they accept as being "one of those things that can happen."

Revenants appear in a variety of forms. In the more mature type of narrative the dead seem so like the living that the difference is discernible with difficulty, and frequently the living are unaware that they are dealing with one of the dead until the revenant disappears before their eyes. Among Irish narrators, the story of the living corpse is commonplace—the corpse which for a brief period rises from its coffin to take part in the ceremonies of the funeral. Spectral ghosts which appear as "an apparition," "a presence," "a spook," "a specter," a "shrouded spirit," are all common, many of these being characterized by a wraithlike quality. In America, the spectral ghost is not as common as it is in England. Another type is the light which appears over the grave, frequently remaining there until the body is reburied in hallowed ground. Occasionally parts of the body appear: heads and hands are the most common. Revenants may be of either sex and of any age or social class. Nor need they ever have been human, for ghosts of animals are reported frequently. It is also significant that occasionally along with the returning dead come objects which have never had life. For example, there is a gangster who reappears driving a bullet-proof car; Lincoln's funeral train is well known in the American countryside and the Irish death coach is known in both Ireland and the United States.

The dead return to complete unfinished business, to warn or inform, to punish or protest, to care or protect, and to impart information which they failed to impart before dying. Sometimes they come back to re-enact their deaths. Behind these reappearances seems to be the implication that these lives have been cut off before their allotted time and that they will reappear until their original allotment of time is completed. Thus it is that the victim of murder, the suicide, those killed in accidents or by violence most frequently return.

Certain beliefs common in Europe have not survived with any vigor in the United States: that none should touch a revenant, that revenants are incapable of crossing water, that they frequently have a distinctive odor, that they appear only at night. The belief that ghosts come with the rattling of chains is another detail almost never included in American ghost lore.

Except for lovemaking, ghosts seem to take part in all of the normal activities of the living; they eat, drink, play, fish, drive cars, go through religious ceremonies, and hundreds of other activities. They make noise: they groan, cry, scream, yell, moan, wail, howl, holler, and sigh; they curse, laugh, whoop, whisper, cough. They frequently rap on walls, bang shutters, play musical instruments; they engage in all the activities of the poltergeist, destroying and deranging the interior of such buildings as they inhabit.

Ghosts can be put to rest by various techniques, some of them religious, some not. Buildings which have been haunted, upon burning, seem to lose interest for the revenant. Sometimes the ghost is satisfied when his unfinished business is completed, or when certain kindnesses have been done to put his spirit at rest.

The oral transmission of ghost lore in America today is occasionally stimulated by the appearance of stories in the newspapers or on the radio, and one finds such stories quickly entering into the oral stream. This has unquestionably been a factor in the growth and distribution of the commonest of American ghost tales, that of the ghostly hitch-hiker. This is the story, told with infinite variety all over America, of the girl who asks for a ride from a stranger, is taken to her home where it becomes evident that she is not a live girl but a revenant. This is a European tale and known in this country as early as the 1890's, but part of its interest arises from the variety of changes which are rung upon the theme. Like many of the most interesting ghost tales, the narrative interest is dependent upon the fact that the revenant gives every evidence of being alive until she disappears. See ADARO; CON-TINH; DEAD RIDER; ELDER; GRATEFUL DEAD; WILD HUNT. [LCJ]

🖝 Tales or incidents in tales concerning revenants or ghosts are of fairly wide occurrence in North American Indian mythology, but since everywhere on the continent ghosts are more or less feared, anecdotal or humorous ghost tales are notably lacking. In the Plains and Eastern Woodlands tale of the Fatal Swing a young mother drowns, is taken care of by a water monster, and is brought to the surface of the water to nurse her human baby; the incident of a drowned mother returning to suckle her child also occurs in other tales sporadically over the continent. Vampires or bloodsucking ghosts appear in several Plains and Eastern Woodlands tales. On the North Pacific Coast where experience with the world of ghosts is the subject of many myths, the introduction to the tale of Giant's or Raven's adventures is as follows: a boy dies and his parents wail for him; one morning his mother finds a youth, bright and shining, in the place where her son's body lay. The youth explains that their constant wailing annoyed the powers above, so that he had been sent down to comfort them. However, later in the same myth it is made clear that the shining youth is not the dead son, but

a substitute for him, and later the substitute becomes so voracious that the chief, his "father", has to send him away in a Raven skin. The Central Woodlands tribes use an incident, similar to the North Pacific Coast one, of a ghost who returns to stop the inordinate weeping of his loved ones on earth; this has European parallels and perhaps represents borrowing by the Ojibwa, Menomini, or Fox Indians, among whom the tale is told.

Shadow people, seen by the living in their own afterworld domain, are frequently referred to in North American Orpheus myths, and in tales of visits to the afterworld by mortals. These are the ghosts of the dead, who are usually visible only at night; there are few if any references to such ghosts returning to earth unless specifically recalled.

Several Eastern Woodlands tribes believe that a person's spirit does not leave this earth until the fourth day after his death; during the three days after death the spirit retraces all the steps and actions taken during life. These tribes are also accustomed to hold "ghost feasts" once a year, in which the spirits of all dead relatives are fed food which is placed in an unlighted empty room for their consumption, before the feast itself is held by the living. [EWV]

🖝 So great is the fear of the ghost of a dead relative among South American Indians that his kin, even the most remote, take new names in the hope that the ghost will be unable to harm them. This custom is observed by most Chaco tribes. When the ancient Guarani and Tupinamba killed an enemy on the battlefield or executed a prisoner, they took the same precaution. [AM]

revenge Revenge is used frequently for plot motivation in North American Indian trickster, hero, animal wife and husband, and other types of tales. Blood-Clot-Boy takes revenge on his mother's killer; a husband kills his adulterous wife's snake lover and serves the snake to the wife to eat; Corn Mother or Corn Maidens avenge themselves on people, after attempted or actual desecration, by disappearing, so that the people face starvation; a woman's bear husband is killed, whereupon the woman turns into a bear and attacks her family; Porcupine thinks he has killed Coyote and Coyote in revenge kills Porcupine and all his children; Trickster frightens young quails, who later avenge themselves by whirring up at him, thus causing him to fall or deeply frightening him. See BEAR WOMAN; CORN; COYOTE AND PORCUPINE; LITTLE STARTLERS, also BEAR-WOMAN AND THE FAWNS, and BURR-WOMAN for a few only of the many specific instances of revenge, either of a major or minor nature, in American Indian tales.

Revenge in real life was taken in a number of ways among the native peoples of North America. Verbal revenge in the form of sarcasm and irony in everyday conversation and speeches is still employed by the verbally gifted, as Shawnee informants have attested; it was also taken out in song contests (see NITH SONGS) and in songs composed by jilted lovers to revenge themselves on former sweethearts. Physical revenge was of course often taken for murder; it was not always necessary that the murderer himself be killed; in many instances, a member of his family or clan might be killed in revenge.

Revenge was also taken out in potlatches or great feasts among the North Pacific Coast Indians, for insults and for murders; and finally, all over North America, shamans avenged or were hired to avenge insults, slights, and refusals to comply with demands, by causing the offending party to sicken and die. Witches and sorcerers also took similar revenge on real or fancied enemies. Young women were often forced to marry old shamans or witches, or the sons of such; not to comply with the demand meant that in revenge the shaman would cause the young girl to sicken and die. This actual practice is sometimes the subject of folktales; Parsons, for example, has recorded a Taos tale in which old men witches were trying to catch a girl to be their lover; the girl refused them. Angered, the witches put bad medicine into her body, using their power. The girl sickened and died. They buried her but later brought her into the kiva and revived her (E. C. Parsons, *Taos Tales*, MAFLS 34, 1941, pp. 36 ff.). [EWV]

Many South American Indian tribes share the belief that the actual or presumed murderer of a person can be destroyed if the corpse is mutilated. For this reason the Abipon, Lengua, and Ashluslay of the Gran Chaco remove the heart and tongue of the deceased and throw it to the dogs, or insert bones, heated stones, or claws into the corpse. They also shoot arrows at it while pronouncing magic spells. The Macushi Indians of Guiana threw the fingers and toes of the deceased man into boiling water. The first one to come to the surface was supposed to point toward the dwelling place of the witch responsible for the death. [AM]

reversal of fortune The theme of a cycle of folktales found all over the world, comprising the whole L chapter in Stith Thompson's *Motif-Index of Folk-Literature.* It includes the clever or victorious youngest child (son or daughter) stories (L0–99); the unpromising hero stories (L100–199), among these, all the Cinderella (L102) tales; the pride brought low (L400–499) and modesty rewarded (L200–299) tales, such as the modest choice of the worst of three caskets bringing success to the chooser (L211), the worst horse was the right choice (L212), etc., the most modest request turns out to be the best (L220); the triumph of the weak over the strong (L300–399), escape of the weak from the strong, etc. See DIRTY BOY; RAGS-TO-RICHES; UGLY DUCKLING.

reversal of sex Reversal of sex is a quite common incident in North American Indian tales, particularly in trickster tales. Very widespread are stories in which Coyote or another trickster poses as a woman and marries a man, often in order to embarrass the latter. Sometimes, as in a northeastern Algonquian tale, this trick is played on a young man too proud to marry, the son of a chief, and trickster even goes so far as to pretend to have a baby. A Jicarilla Apache tale reverses the situation: Coyote is given a boy dressed in girl's clothing as a wife. By the time he has discovered the situation he has given all his highly prized tobacco to his "bride's" father and to visitors. In more serious tales, as of the jealous uncle, a boy may be raised as a girl for his own protection.

The actual assumption of women's clothing and a woman's role by males, or of men's clothing and a man's role by women, was not uncommon among the American Indians. Transvestites frequently "married" and were not ostracized, but were often highly respected members of the group. In many instances they were shamans. Among the Eskimo, as among the Chinese,

it was customary, if an infant girl was adopted to replace a lost son for example, for the adopting couple to bring up the girl as a boy, teaching her to hunt and fish as men do among the Eskimo, and to engage in boyish activities, as among the Chinese. On becoming adult the girls resumed their normal roles. Two recent autobiographies written by a Labrador Eskimo woman and a Chinese woman (*Land of the Good Shadows,* by Heluiz Chandler Washburne and Anauta, New York, 1940; and *Autobiography of a Chinese Woman,* by Buwei Yang Chao, New York, 1947) present the life histories of two women raised during their youth as boys. [EWV]

revolt of the utensils The famous motif of the rebellion of the utensils against men which figures in the *Popol Vuh* of the Maya occurs also in South American mythology. The episode was painted on a fresco in one of the temples of the Mochica (near modern Trujillo, northwestern Peru) and is known through several versions preserved by Spanish chroniclers. It is still remembered by the Chiriguano Indians of the Bolivian Chaco. [AM]

revolving castle A commonplace of early Celtic mythology, folktale, and legend, occurring also in Arthurian romance (F771.2.6.2), specifically, in the Grail romances as *Ille Tournoiont.* Annwn, the Brythonic otherworld, for instance, was sometimes called *Caer Sidi,* or revolving castle, and was conceived as being surrounded by the sea (F163.1.1). Cú Roi, a wizard of Old Irish legend, had a magic so great that no matter where he was in the world, every night he put a spell on his castle so that it revolved all night and there was no entrance into it after sundown. This was Catair Cú Roi, the round fort of Cú Roi, where the three first champions of Ulster (Loeġaire, Conall, Cuchulain) took turns keeping watch during their tests for the champion's portion. (See BRICRIU'S FEAST.) Each one stood guard outside it for a night. The terrible gigantic attackers could not get into it because of its spinning around; neither could Loeġaire, Conall, nor Cuchulain enter it through any door between sundown and sunrise. On the first night the giant terrified Loeġaire, keeping guard outside, picked him up and threw him back in over the wall. On the second night the same thing happened to Conall. On the third night, there were many attackers whom Cuchulain fought off, and when all were disposed of, he leaped back in over the wall himself. Catair Cú Roi survives today as Cahirconry, a huge prehistoric round fortress in Kerry.

Reynard Trickster hero of the great medieval beast epic *Roman de Renart.* Reynard is the fox, the clever unmoral rebel against authority, a hero of the antithesis of the ideals of the *chanson de geste.* There is nothing chivalric about him; he is a coward, a seducer, a liar, a traitor. The epic of Reynard does not exist as one work. Developing throughout the Middle Ages from the beast fables of the classical period, the poems of beasts who acted and thought like human beings grew into the Latin *Isengrimus* of the 12th century written by a Fleming, and the various *branches* of the *Roman de Renart* (c. 1175–c. 1205). The branches, telling the story of the fox, were separate compositions making use of fable material from the *Isopets,* imitations of Æsop's fables, and of popular folktale material. The mass of the material is French in origin, but the version of the story translated into English by Caxton in 1481 was a Flemish text, now lost. Surrounding Reynard in Caxton's translation are King Noble the lion, Isegrym the wolf, Bruin the bear, Grymbert the badger, Coart the hare, Bellyn the ram, Courtoys the hound, Tybert the cat, Chanticleer the cock, Partlet the hen, and other such animal-people. See BEAR FISHES THROUGH ICE WITH TAIL; BEAST EPIC; FOX.

režniká The Moravian butcher's dance. The pantomimic theme of buying an ox from a farmer is reduced to an abstracted hand gesture. The first gesture, which follows after a polka step in ballroom position, consists of the boy resting the girl's right hand in his left, palm up, and slapping it with his right, as though counting out coins. The second pattern of hand claps, during a running step, resembles the Pease Porridge Hot. [GPK]

Rhadamanthus In Greek mythology, one of the judges of the dead in Hades, especially, according to Plato, judge of the Asiatic dead, or the overlord of the Elysian fields. He was the son of Zeus and Europa, and the brother of Minos of Crete. Rhadamanthus did not die like other mortals but was taken directly to Elysium. There he married Alcmene, mother of Hercules, and there, because he was so very just, became judge of the Asiatics as Æacus was of the Europeans (Minos, commonly the third judge, had the deciding vote). In other versions of the myth, Rhadamanthus fled from Crete because of the jealousy of Minos, or because he committed a murder, and settled in Bœotia where he married Alcmene after the death of Amphitryon.

Rheinländer Literally, from the Rhineland: the South German version of the polka, identical with the Bayrische Polka. It is also a couple dance, progressing counter clockwise around the room. Couples dance in ballroom position: three two-steps or three polkas forward (or back), then pivot with three hops and a stamp. The Norwegian *Reinlendar* uses a schottische step: two schottische and four turning hops, in ballroom or open promenade position. A special wrinkle is the touching of the heel to the ground after each two-step. The partners pivot with various holds, and the girl hops around the kneeling boy. Finally he tosses her up into the air. [GPK]

rheumatism This Great Crippler has plagued man from the beginning of time, for traces of the ailment have been found in prehistoric remains.

Various herbs were early thought to cure rheumatism or to ameliorate its twinges. This ancient herbal lore spread through Europe, and many remedies found in old recipes may be traced to very ancient sources. Plants cultivated in old monastery and kitchen gardens for rheumatism were burdock, dandelion, fern, flax, hemlock, henbane, holly, horseradish, rosemary, tansy, and many others.

In the 14th century rheumatism was treated with elixirs, injections of gold compound, and other fantastic medicaments. In the 18th century, Cagliostro, a Sicilian, and an early promoter of the faith cure, invented a chair for rheumatism. At this time and even earlier, magnetic belts were worn or a lodestone was carried on the person to assuage rheumatic pain.

Cures for rheumatism in near and far parts of the world included homeopathic magic, transference, sym-

bolic rebirth ritual, and the like. In Afghanistan the sufferer prays and beats himself as he walks around a grave; in Australia afflicted aborigines believe their pains are caused by bits of broken glass, bone, or stone, which some enemy has placed in their footprints. In China the use of the skin of a white-spotted snake is favored as a remedy. In England, Wales, and France, the disease was sometimes alleviated by the victim's crawling through a bramble that had sent down a second branch into the ground. In Ireland people would apply the hand of a corpse to the afflicted shoulder, arm, or leg, and when the coffin passed over the threshold, would cry, "Take my pains with you!" In Java a popular cure for gout or rheumatism was to rub Spanish pepper into the nails of the patient. In Scotland people born feet first had power to heal rheumatism, and in Cornwall the mother of a person so born was invited by sufferers to trample on them.

Various American Indian tribes of the northwestern United States and Canada use a tea for colds and rheumatism made from quills of the ground hemlock; Cherokees may not eat flesh of the gray squirrel for fear of becoming crippled, since the squirrel eats in a cramped position (Mooney); the Shinnecock smoke dried leaves of the catnip, make tea of kelp, and use rotted earthworms for ointment (*JAFL* 58: 113 ff.). The Mexican Pima Indians whip or stroke for rheumatism; at the Hopi Powamu, during the ritual whipping of children, adults suffering with rheumatism frequently asked to be whipped. This rite strengthens and gives luck (power) in hunting, racing, and gambling (Parsons, *Pueblo Indian Religion* I: 471; II: 994). In eastern Brazil, disease in general is treated by massaging with herbs and by flogging. In the delta of the Orinoco, the Warrau tribe allow a certain species of ant to bite the painful rheumatic spot a few times (*BAEB* 143:III: 581).

Common and current practices in the United States to prevent or cure rheumatism include carrying a potato in the pocket, or a horse-chestnut (buckeye, bull's eye). A few other methods of prevention are: take a cat to bed, or a nail from a coffin, or one made from a horseshoe; drink a potion of pokeweed berries or sunflower seeds soaked in whisky; rub the painful parts with mutton-tallow, grease from boiled frogs, polecat or skunk oil; wear the eye-tooth of a pig, or salt-mackerel tied on feet, or dried eel-skin around the joints, rattlesnake rattles in the hat, a copper bracelet around the wrist, or copper wire as a belt around body. Bee-stings are an old remedy. See BEES. These are but a few of the American remedies for rheumatism, though mention of a native Virginia plant should not be omitted, *Jeffersonia diphylla*, popularly called "rheumatism root." [GPS]

Rhiannon According to the story in the mabinogi of Pwyll, one day Pwyll, king of Dyfed, sat on the wonder mound of Arbeth, of which it was said that whoever sat on it would have adventures or see sights. What Pwyll saw was a beautiful woman in garments that shone like gold approaching on a white horse. He sent men to meet her but no one could come near her. The next day he sat on the mound again, and when she appeared he went to meet her himself, but could not shorten the distance between them until he called to her in the name of love. She was Rhiannon, daughter of Heveidd Hen. In a year they were married and in due time a boy child was born to them in Pwyll's castle at Narberth. But Gwawl, a rejected suitor outwitted by Pwyll, contrived to steal the child in the night while the watching-women slept. The six watching-women, in terror because of their negligence, devised a way of putting the blame on Rhiannon. They killed a pup, smeared her face and hands with blood while she slept, hid the bones in her bed, and accused her when she woke of devouring her child in the night. Rhiannon was condemned to sit at the gate, tell this story to strangers, and offer to carry them to the castle on her back.

There was a man in the country named Teirnyon whose mare foaled on the first of every May, but whose colts always mysteriously disappeared on the first night. At last he resolved to watch, saw a great arm reach into the stable to snatch the colt, cut off the arm with his sword, and ran out to pursue the snatcher, who disappeared in the night. When he came back he found a young baby wrapped in satin sleeping by the stable door. Teirnyon and his wife reared the child with love, and named him Gwri, for his golden hair. Not only was the boy beautiful but at the age of two was as big as six. Eventually Teirnyon heard the tragic story of Rhiannon and her penance, saw that Gwri resembled Pwyll, wondered if this could be Rhiannon's child, and took him to the castle, where the resemblance was recognized to be so great that every one cried he was Pwyll's son. So Teirnyon told the story of the colt and the discovery of the infant at his door. Rhiannon was cleared of the terrible accusation, and when she said here was an end to her trouble, it was voted that she had thus named her child, Pryderi (Trouble). Pryderi was trained as befitting a king's son and, when Pwyll died, reigned well after him. Later in the mabinogi of Branwen, Rhiannon was married to Manawyddan, the good friend of her son Pryderi.

In Brythonic mythology, Rhiannon is identified with an early Celtic goddess known as Rigantona, or Great Queen, i.e. a mother goddess, and as such associated with fertility. She is said to have had three little birds whose singing could cause death or bring the dead to life. Robert Graves (in The White Goddess, New York, 1948, p. 318) associates Rhiannon with the mare goddesses of the Mediterranean area. She was accused of devouring her child, for instance (paralleling Demeter, Leucippe); her penance after this accusation was to carry people on her back; her child's fate was tied up with the fate of Teirnyon's foal. Graves also assumes that probably in the original story Rhiannon took the form of a white mare in her flight from Pwyll. See ARAWN; HAVGAN; MABINOGION; VIVIEN.

Rhys, Sir John (1840–1915) Celtic scholar; born in Cardiganshire, Wales, and educated at Oxford, continuing his studies in France and Germany. In 1877 he became professor of Celtic at Oxford; in 1881 a Fellow of Jesus College, and in 1895 its Principal. He was an authority on Celtic philology, author of Celtic Britain (1882, 1904), Celtic Heathendom (Hibbert Lectures, 1886); Celtic Folklore, Welsh, and Manx (1901), in which he collected what remained of the Old Welsh tradition —rites, customs, and festivals that were gradually passing away. Among his other works are Studies in Arthurian Legend (1891), The Welsh People (1900, with D. B. Jones).

Ribhu In Vedic mythology, one of the three artisans of the gods, named Ribhu, Vibhu, and Vāja, who, because of their great skill, became deities. They renewed the youth of their parents, fashioned Indra's chariot and horses, and transformed Tvashtri's bowl into four shining cups. Their dwelling place is in the solar sphere and they are sometimes said to support the sky.

rice A grain (Oryza sativa, also other species), probably east-Asiatic in origin, which is the "staff of life" for almost half of the human race. Rice cultivation is of two types: wet and dry. In the former, the rice seedlings are planted in flooded fields; in the latter, the seeds are sown in the soil. Wet rice cultivation is found mainly in southeast Asia and the adjacent islands. This type of cultivation has been carried to various parts of the world, including the southeast United States. (The occurrence of rice culture in Madagascar is viewed by many anthropologists as a weighty proof of the settlement of that island by men from the Pacific Ocean.) It therefore requires either extensive irrigation, or flat river valleys which periodically are inundated. In mountainous regions like the Philippines, Madagascar, Japan, and Indonesia, elaborate systems of terracing, canals and reservoirs, have been devised to abet wet rice cultivation. Possession of these means of production may give rise to marked class distinctions, as among the Ifugao of Luzon.

There is a great deal of ritual and magical belief surrounding the cultivation and use of rice. In Bali, for example, it is thought that rice has a soul, similar to that of man; human beings and rice share the same cognomen, which sets them apart from animals. Rice may be addressed by kinship terms, such as "mother," "grandmother," or "grandfather." Here, as well, the rice may be supplicated, as one asks an older relative for food, for a man may address the rice as mother, saying: "I am hungry."

In Ceylon, before the rice is planted, geomancers and astrologers are consulted. They give all the necessary directions surrounding the sowing, including such minutiæ as to what the planter should wear. He must be ceremonially clean as well. A prayer is said over the first seeds sown, and a flower is placed above them. The growing rice is vulnerable; if there are droughts, plagues, or pests, the goddess Pattini has been angered, and she is appeased by a coconut fight. Priests are also given offerings of food as her aid is invoked. The men of the village line up some thirty yards apart, tossing coconuts back and forth, attempting to strike the flying nuts with coconuts held in their hands. They play until a nut is broken, and repeat this performance for several days, concluding with a feast. At all points from the breaking of the ground to the final consumption of the grain, including sowing, cultivation, reaping, threshing, measuring, storing, etc., supernatural advice is sought and followed. The anger of the gods against the welfare of rice is excited by obscene language, uncleanliness (contact with birth, menstruation, death, eating of pork and oily fish), and all of these must be kept from contact both with the standing rice in the fields and the threshing floor. Also, the pounding or roasting of rice must be done far from the fields, otherwise the standing crop would be weakened.

The Chinese so highly regard rice (the staple food of

southern China) that its mention is part of the daily greeting. As we say "How do you do?" they say "Have you eaten your rice?" In southern China, as in Burma and Siam, rice is the central food, and all else—soup, meat, fish, vegetables, and condiments—are "garnish."

In Japan, "next to the emperor, rice is the most sacred of all things on earth." (Gautama divided all of mankind into ten classifications, of which Buddha was first, the counterpart of Hell was tenth; rice was second). Money can be squandered and the wastrel is forgiven, but there is no forgiveness for wasting rice. Some of the supernatural retributions which follow this sinful and wanton behavior are blindness or assurance of punishment in the afterworld, where the sinner is ground up into a powder. Parallels in regard to bread may be found in Greece and Poland.

For celebrations and holidays, rice is always used. Particularly red rice or rice boiled with red beans. *Sake,* rice wine, is also an essential part of all feasts. So sacred is rice that even the straw used in floor mats has a place of honor, for these mats symbolize cleanliness. Rice-straw rope is tied over the house entrance at the New Year festivities. Offerings of rice cakes are placed on the family altar at this season. A small piece of these cakes is eaten, accompanied by a drink of rice wine, and this indicates that one has achieved another year of age.

Throughout the year there are various rice ceremonies. In May, when the new crop is sown, the emperor personally sets out new plants in the palace grounds. Some weeks later, in June, when the rice is transplanted to the paddy fields, there are further ceremonies. These may be quite elaborate and include theatrical and circus performances. If a drought threatens the rice crop, special dances are performed, in which only ritually purified men participate. Women are barred categorically because they menstruate. The dancers stay away from their homes for three days, visiting shrines and praying. When the harvest is in, rice cakes are made and offered to the gods. A dagger is thrust into each cake, and then it is eaten by a priest. Rice wine is also drunk. During the moon-viewing festival, the moon goddess receives offerings of rice and *sake.* In November, there is a final thanksgiving feast for rice.

Rice is widely used also over the rest of the world. It is an integral part of the cuisine of Europe, the United States, specifically in the south, and in the Caribbean region and South America. Italians say that "rice is born in water, and dies in wine." In our culture, perhaps the most widely known symbolic use of rice occurs at weddings, when the newly married pair is pelted with rice, for "good luck," but its older meaning harks back to rice as a symbol of fertility.

Rice (*Oryza* spp.) is not to be confused with wild rice (*Zizania* spp.), an aquatic plant of eastern North America. This plant, found growing wild in wet and swampy places, gave the French name to the Menomini Indians, "Les Folles Avoines," the wild oats.

Bibliography:

Le Mesurier, C. J. R., "Customs and Superstitions Connected with the Cultivation of Rice in the Southern Province of Ceylon," *Journal of the Royal Asiatic Society of Great Britain and Ireland,* n.s., vol. XVII, London, 1885, pp. 366–372.

Rabbitt, James A. "Rice in the Cultural Life of the Japanese People," *Transactions of the Asiatic Society of Japan,* 2nd series, vol. XIX, Tokyo, 1940, pp. 187–258.

Wirz, Paul "Der Reisbau und Reisbaukulte auf Bali und Lombok," *Int. Arch. für Ethnographie,* supplement to vol. XXX, Leiden, 1929, 66 pp.   NATALIE F. JOFFE

riddles Contrary to the common assumption that they are mere word puzzles proposed by punsters at evening parties, riddles rank with myths, fables, folktales, and proverbs as one of the earliest and most widespread types of formulated thought. A good case could probably be made for their priority to all other forms of literature or even to all other oral lore, for riddles are essentially metaphors, and metaphors are the result of the primary mental processes of association, comparison, and the perception of likenesses and differences.

Possibly confirmatory of their antiquity too is the ubiquitous element of humor and wit. The essence of the ludicrous is the unexpected, so the laughter of primitive and simple-minded men and of little children is easily excited by the sudden discovery of similarity in two objects which a person would not ordinarily expect to resemble each other. Sophisticated persons and those of orthodox mind, whether that orthodoxy be of religion, social custom, or materialistic science, seldom appreciate or even understand riddles.

Although Aristotle several times pointed out the close relation between metaphor and the riddle, the fact and its significance seem not to have been often or sufficiently noticed by anthropologists, philologists, psychologists, or students of folklore.

The oldest riddles long predated the ones now definitely associated with the ancient Hellenic, Semitic, and Vedic cultures, which were already producing fairly complicated enigmas. And those very early ones are still in circulation today, a little more polished perhaps, but essentially the same metaphorical illusions to the resemblances between natural objects. The children of the Schoharie Hills of New York, for instance, say:

> On yonder hill there is a red deer;
> The more you shoot, the more you may,
> You cannot drive that deer away.

The average adult has difficulty with that one, but a child or an Indian knows it must be the sun rising, for it is red and impossible to scare away. That riddle, in one form or another, is to be found not only in 17th century English riddle collections, but far back beyond Homer's rosy-fingered dawn, beyond Ikhnaton's "Thy footprints are the day," to the time a primitive man first referred to the sun as a person.

When a child says in Louisiana:

> I have an apple I can't cut,
> A blanket I can't fold,
> And so much money I can't count it,

he is describing the sun, sky, and stars in riddle images which have been repeated for countless generations. Another very old but still popular one was probably created by the first man to note the annual habits of deciduous trees. By the time Mahlon Day in New York published his *New Riddle-book* (1829), the enigma had become:

> In spring I look gay,
> Deck'd in comely array,
> In summer more clothing I wear;
> When colder it grows,
> I fling off my clothes,
> And in winter quite naked appear.

As a boy I learned this old Elizabethan one:

> Thirty white horses upon a red hill,
> Now they champ, now they stamp,
> Now they stand still,

but that is a comparatively modern form of the teeth riddle, which like all those referring to parts of the human body, is really ancient.

The older riddles, perhaps because they have to do with nature and are simply told, contain among them a larger proportion of really beautiful ones, like:

> Round the house and round the house,
> And there lies a white glove in the window. (Snow)

> A hill full, a hole full,
> But you cannot catch a bowlful.   (Smoke)

> From house to house he goes,
> So sure and yet so slight,
> And whether it rains or snows,
> He sleeps outside all night.   (Lane)

> Jack-at-a-word ran over the moor,
> Never behind but always before. (Will-o-the-wisp)

> What flies forever
> And rests never?   (Wind)

> The more you feed it
> The more it'll grow high,
> But if you give it water,
> Then it'll go and die.   (Fire)

> I washed my face in water
> That neither rained nor run;
> I dried my face on a towel
> That was neither wove nor spun.   (Dew and Sun)

There seems to have always been something in snow to make riddlers turn poetic or poets make riddles:

> White bird, featherless,
> Flew from Paradise,
> Pitched on the castle wall;
> Poor Lord Landless
> Came in a fine dress
> And went away without a dress at all.

Folklore is the lore or learning or common sense or mother wit of the people as passed down from parent or grandparent to child or grandchild, and that folk knowledge must be packaged and capsuled for easier transmission down through the generations. That is where the proverb and especially the riddle come in. I have sat by the stove of a winter night and given the answers to the riddles my father and mother alternately asked me as they went through the catechism their parents had taught them. It was part of my education, and much more interesting than the lessons in grammar school. It was much more mind-stretching, for the answer to each new riddle was not given me until I had tried long and hard and turned the given situation every which-way seeking the solution.

Perhaps it was the neatness of the packages in which the lore was given which appealed to me. L. W. Chappell, on page 227 of B. A. Botkin's *Folksay 1930*, recognizes this very point: "Riddles, perhaps even more than most types of traditional lore, have a way of 'staying put.' Their vigorous compactness of form seems to give them a peculiar hold on the popular imagination and in many cases to insure their preservation for centuries."

Then again, like all children, I was intrigued by the peculiar combination of beauty and mystery on the one hand and absolutely logical factual reasoning on the other. The riddle was a puzzle and a challenge and a nut to crack. We called it cracking riddles, too, and we cracked nuts at the same time, and one seemed to help the other. We often began by saying:

> There was a little green house,
> And in the little green house,
> There was a little brown house,
> And in the little brown house,
> There was a little yellow house,
> And in the little yellow house,
> There was a little white house,
> And in the little white house,
> There was a little heart.

This feeling of children for riddles was well explained by Maurice Bloomfield in a paper on Brahmanical riddles which he read in St. Louis in 1904 at the International Congress of Arts and Sciences: "From olden times, as an early exercise of the primitive mind in its adjustment to the world about it, comes the riddle . . . The fresher the vision, when the world was young, so much keener was the interest in the phenomena of nature, in the phenomena of life, and in the simple institutions which surrounded man. All harmonies and fitnesses, all discrepancies and inconsistencies attract the notice of children and the childlike man. Hence children love riddles; hence savages and primitive people put them. All folklore is full of them. They are the mystery and at the same time the rationalism of the juvenile mind. As civilization advances they still sustain life, but they grow more complicated, more conscious and exacting, as the simpler relations become commonplace, and interest in them fades and wears off."

Not only does interest in riddles wear off as civilization grows more complicated, the ability to solve riddles also disappears, just at the time when such skill is more needed than ever. Civilization demands specialists, and the grooved, compartmented, and departmentalized education which is necessary for the production of experts in technical matters often neglects entirely the more fundamental pedagogy which educated children and adults by teaching them through riddles to look at every problem from all sides, and still keep a sense of humor.

The educational character and purpose of riddles is plainly revealed in their very name. Whether we take the English *riddle*, the German *Rät(h)sel*, or the Greek *ainigma*, they all come from the corresponding verbs, English *rede* (Old English *rædan*), German *rat(h)en*, and Greek, *aineo*, all meaning to give advice. The Latin *ænigma*, French *énigme*, and English *enigma* are all obviously derived from the Greek original and still retain its meaning. The somewhat redundant term "quiz question" is beginning to take the place of the word "riddle" in America, due to radio program influence. Dictionaries assert that the word *quiz* is of unknown origin and derivation, but it would seem likely that it came from the *quis, quæ, quid* (who, which, what?) of the thousands of medieval Latin riddles. A new folk word for riddle may thus be evolving, of apparently legitimate lineage. Since quiz at present still means an examination or series of questions, the awkward "quiz question" is used for one, but soon we may expect "quiz" to be the modern folk term for riddle, which was itself deliberately shortened centuries ago by popular usage from the clumsy singular number *rædels* (plural *rædelse*) because the *s* made it too much like a plural, and also perhaps because the *-le* suffix suggested something diminutive, cozy, and pleasant. The folk liked a riddle and knew it for their own.

All apart from the educational function of the riddle (the oldest riddles on record are school texts from Babylon), it served another purpose among primitive men, which, when understood, clarifies certain hitherto unexplained procedures. Sir James Frazer has wondered why among certain tribes riddles are asked at definite times and on prescribed occasions.

He mentions, for instance (*Golden Bough* iii, 154), that in the elaborate rain-making ceremonies of the Ba-Thonga, a South African Bantu tribe, naked women dance, leap, and sing: "Rain, fall!" But if any man should approach the place, the women would beat him, and "put riddles to him which he would have to answer in the most filthy language borrowed from the circumcision ceremonies; for obscene words, which are usually forbidden, are customary and legitimate on these occasions." Again he tells (*ibid*. vii, 194), how in several tribes of the Central Celebes islands, the folk ask each other riddles at harvest and while the rice crop is maturing. When a riddle is correctly guessed, the whole band of rice-watchers shouts: "Let our rice come up, let fat ears come up both in the lowlands and on the heights." But between harvest and the next planting riddle-asking is strictly prohibited. Frazer has a glimmer of the truth when he comments thereon: "Thus among these people it seems that the asking of riddles is for some reason regarded as a charm which may make or mar the crops."

But in a lengthy note on pages 121–122 of *Golden Bough* ix, Sir James confesses his perplexity and inability to solve the riddle about riddles: "The custom of asking riddles at certain seasons or on certain special occasions is curious and has not yet, so far as I know, been explained." He toys with the idea that the riddles may have originally been used as substitutes for direct words, as they are especially "employed in the neighborhood of a dead body." And of course the spirit still hanging round the place has to be deceived lest he remain in the vicinity too long. Sir James then lists a few instances when riddles must or must not be said, such as among the Bolang Mongondo of the Celebes who prohibit riddles except when there is a corpse in the village; in the Aroe Archipelago where the mourners play a sort of riddle telepathy game while the corpse is still uncoffined, as in Brittany after a funeral the old men remain in the cemetery and, seated on mallows, propound riddles to each other. At circumcision ceremonies British East African adolescents must interpret pictographic riddles carved on sticks, and Central Asian Turkish girls ask riddles of their prospective hubands who are punished if unable to give the correct answers. As far back as Vedic times at the great horse-sacrificing ceremonies, the priests recited enigmas to each other.

All these Frazer mentions, yet strangely fails to recognize what they all have in common. He might also have cited the riddle contest at Samson's wedding feast, the symposia of riddles in Rome at the Saturnalia, and the merrie riddles at Christmastide in England, as well as many others which will occur to the reader.

For it is obvious that the solving of riddles was a technique anciently and primitively employed at times of crisis or on occasions when the fate of someone or even a whole tribe hung in the balance. Rain-making, grain-growing and harvesting, circumcision, weddings, funerals and buryings, all these were critical times. Would the blessed rain come or would the drought persist and famine decimate the tribe? Would a storm at harvest time destroy the precious crop or would it all be garnered in with thanksgiving? Would the dangerous spirits enter the boy at circumcision and infect the wound until he died in agony, or would he grow into heroic manhood? Who could tell whether or not the marriage would be a success, or whether the corpse would get properly interred before the reluctant ghost, envious of the fortunate ones who still lived, did some harm to them, perhaps marking one of them as the next victim?

Still farther back in time or culture-pattern, the early men asked at the winter solstice, after they had seen and felt the sun gradually weakening for weeks, whether it would regain its strength, whether the little boy New Year would be born. The Twelve Days between the end of the lunar year and the end of the solar year were critical days. Men wondered what the new year would be like, and tried to determine by odd signs and practices, haruspical, mantic, and divinatory. They did what they thought would properly in-*augur*-ate the coming year. A faint echo of that archaic custom is heard when we inaugurate a new United States president: he must kiss a sacred book, and the verse thereof which his lips touch is believed still by some to have certain divinatory value in prognosticating the success or failure of the new administration.

But what has solving riddles to do with all these crises Sir James Frazer has mentioned and the ones we have added? Simply this, that at a critical time, when even a slight thing may decide the issue, solving a riddle correctly may, by a sort of sympathetic magic, help to solve the big problem, may turn the scales the right way. All those "certain seasons and certain special occasions" which Sir James mentions called for the use of riddles, according to primitive custom, that the magic of the riddle-loosing might affect and stimulate the proper forces for the happy solution of the current crisis. To ask and answer riddles at a wedding in order to assure its success may seem superstitious to us and quite ridiculous, now that we have completely given up all such lucky wedding customs as throwing rice, confetti, and old shoes, or advising the bride to wear something old, new, borrowed, and blue, or believing that the girl to catch the bride's bouquet will be the next one married. To say nothing of the wedding ring superstitions!

Psychologically our primitive ancestors may have had something! Solving difficult riddles at a wedding may have encouraged the young couple to think they might similarly tackle and find the solution of the many enigmas of married life. At any rate, it would start them off in the atmosphere of accomplishment and the aura of success. And the Turkish girls who test the intelligence of their wooing lovers by asking them to answer tough riddles seem to have what may be a primitive but is probably a practical form of trial marriage.

Somewhat of that idea or feeling-consciousness of sympathetic magic may have survived the generations to make me in my boyhood feel that cracking riddles and cracking nuts had something to do with each other.

We always cracked nuts and riddles after the Thanksgiving and Christmas dinners, but I knew nothing then about the connection between harvest and the winter solstice on the one hand and enigmas on the other. Yet the reason we did have riddles at those "certain seasons" was because long ages since our progenitors did believe in sympathetic magic. The fact that it still seemed a good thing to do was not entirely due to custom, habit, or ancestor reverence. Let me put it this way, making it very practical: I still think it is an excellent practice to "rede riddles" at Christmas time, in the dark of the year, if for no other reason than to remind ourselves that it is well to sharpen our wits and keep them in good practice at critical times.

There is considerable mental stimulus in this verse:

> Is the wit quicke?
> Then do not sticke
> To read these riddles darke:
> Which if thou doe,
> And rightly too,
> Thou art a witty sparke.

It is found on the back of the title page of *The Booke of Meery Riddles*, which ran through eight English editions between 1600 and 1686. The edition I have used is dated 1629 at London and was "Printed by T. C., for Michael Sparke, dwelling in Greene-Arbor, at the sign of the Blue Bible." (Evidently Michael was either a punster or wished to be sure his name was both on the title page and the back of it.) The subtitle is worth quoting: "Together with Proper Questions, and witty Proverbs to make pleasant pastime; no lesse usefull than behoouefull for any young man, or child, to know if he be quick-witted, or no."

Likely this particular booke of meery riddles is a reprint of the older *Book of Riddles* mentioned by Laneham as early as 1575, with which Shakespeare was familiar. I mention it here especially for the word *meery* which came into the title between 1575 and 1600. Sparke was witty but not a prime speller, for the better spelling is *merrie*. Now we must here be careful not to assume that when the Elizabethans spoke of merrie riddles and Merrie Christmasse they had the comparatively innocent and chaste idea in mind that we now associate with the harmless word *merry*. Several passages in the King James (1611) version of the Bible now found in any concordance under "merry" disclose, for example, that when Amnon (*2 Samuel* xiii, 28) and King Ahasuerus (*Esther* i, 10) were merry, they were not only drunk but rather licentious as well.

Other times, other morals, to be sure, but the idea of license at the winter solstice is a very old and persistent one. You can trace it back from Caroline and Elizabethan England, when Christmas in that realm was very merrie indeed, to the time of the celebration of the same solstice in the Roman Saturnalia, the very name of which is now applied to any orgy of dissolute riotous jollity. From this Roman feast came the customs still obtaining in Christian England of not only the feasting and drinking and the exchange of gifts, but of riddling as well. How far back of the Saturnalia these customs went we do not know, but there is plenty of evidence that carnivals and orgies at Christmas or New Year's were widespread and of very old prevalence. The rites of the Holi festival in January among the North Dravidians of India are characterized by indecent words and gestures and the singing of ribald songs. Periodic orgies accompanied by sexual excesses or substitutionary obscene words and bawdy songs may be explained as reaction to civilized restraints or as psychologically necessary periods of catharsis, or "letting off steam."

Riddles are definitely connected with this background, and this review of the Saturnalian customs has been necessary to explain the character of a large section of the most popular riddles.

The Booke of Meery Riddles which went through several editions in the 17th century contained many which were bawdy, licentious, or just plain dirty. Most of its 76 riddles emigrated to America and are still current orally in New England and the South, especially in mountain or otherwise isolated communities, with many variants and imitations, some very clever and all much relished by the people. They contribute to swell the vast body of folklore known as "Back-of-the-Barn Americana," so popular that it often emerges from its private-home and railroad-smoking-room oral tradition habitat and presses its way into cheap magazines and joke books, burlesque and stag-party shows, night-club and musical-comedy performances, and best-seller historical fiction.

The often lewd nature of the popular word-of-mouth riddles has probably led, or at least partly influenced, scholars to make a simple classification of riddles into the folk riddles and the literary riddles, or *Kunsträtsel* and *Volksrätsel*, or, following Rolland's division, into *l'énigme vraiment populaire* and *l'énigme savante ou littéraire*. The best statement of the grounds and nature of the distinction between the two classes of riddles is found in the first chapter of Archer Taylor's *The Literary Riddle Before 1600*. To that scholarly treatise with its excellent bibliography, we refer those interested in literary riddles, as this article is limited to the folklore aspects of the riddle and is concerned with the literary variety only as far as enigmatographers like Apuleius Athenæus, Symphosius, Aldhelm, Alcuin, Bede, Tatwine Eusebius, Boniface, Al-Harîrî, Moses ibn Ezra, Firdausi, Rāzi, Psellus, Megalomitis, Makrembolites, Aulikalamus, Malatesti, Galileo Galilei, Straparola, Claretus, Lorichius, Leuterbach, Reusner, Junius, Fontaine, Swift, Schiller, Goethe, Boileau, Voltaire, Rousseau, Fenelon, and Cervantes (to name but a representative few) won fame in their day by elaborating and putting into polished verse the beloved riddles of the common people. Not merely from the *Volksrätsel* did the literary riddle writers get their inspirations: they selected abstract subjects also, which were very seldom found among the simple, practical, material, and earthy answers to the vulgar enigma.

The folk and literary riddles meet and are indistinguishable in the earliest stories which have come down to us connecting certain enigmas with such semi-mythical semi-historical characters as Samson, Homer, and Œdipus.

The 14th chapter of the *Book of Judges* in the Old Testament records more than the one riddle of Samson. Carefully read, it appears as the chronicle of a riddle contest, or riddle strife, one of those very exciting tournaments of wit held in ancient times when men might bet their fortunes, wives, daughters, and even their lives on their cleverness in riddle guessing. Similar riddle strifes are reported between Solomon and Hiram, Solomon and

Abdemon, Solomon and the Queen of Sheba, Daniel and Belshazzar's wise men, King Amasis of Egypt and the King of Ethiopia, King Lycurgus of Babylon and Nectanebo of Egypt, Alexander the Great and Hindu wise men, Calchas and Mopsus, Theognis and Homer, and many others. Like Samson, Hercules is said to have attended a wedding and joined in the riddle game. Enigma contests at Greek and Roman feasts were later brought to high stages of development with a master of riddles presiding and awarding the coveted laural wreath to the winners and condemning the losers to drink their wine mixed with salt water. In the 2nd century A.D. the winners were getting rare books and sums of money, and in the 3rd or 4th century (the date is very uncertain), the Father of Enigmatology, Symphosius, put into three-line stanzas of pretty good Latin poetry the famous *Hundred Riddles,* evidently already current for some time as plain folk riddles. Of him Archer Taylor, who dates him as late as the 5th century, says: "He maintained his sovereign place down to the time of the Renaissance, and even later, as the master of the enigmatic art."

To return to Samson's famous riddle party (*Judges* xiv) of a thousand or more years B.C., be it noted, as it seldom is, that when the hero "put forth" the riddle (the Hebrew, very interestingly, for to rede or relate a riddle is to *chud* a *chidah*), "Out of the eater came forth meat, and out of the strong came forth sweetness," and the thirty opponents in the contest had unfairly scared the answer out of Samson's bride-elect, they replied very cleverly with another riddle: "What is sweeter than honey? and what is stronger than a lion?" The answer to the second riddle obviously was: "Love," for Samson's love for the girl was so sweet and strong that it had overcome him who had slain the lion and led him to tell her the secret. He then revealed that he knew the answer to the second riddle by continuing the metaphorical contest with the third enigmatic saying: "If ye had not plowed with my heifer, ye had not found out my riddle." Then he paid his riddle-bet of thirty suits of clothes by slaying thirty Philistines of Ashkelon and giving their garments to the victors in the riddle strife.

In the *Motif-Index of Folk-Literature* by Stith Thompson, riddles are classified into many groups from H530 to H899. Samson's affair, for instance, is in H548, Riddle contests, and also in H630, Riddles of the Superlative, under H633, What is sweetest, and H671, What is sweeter than honey?

Along with Samson we mentioned above Homer and Œdipus as being connected with very old riddles. Probably no riddle has been so often translated and repeated throughout the world and history as the one alleged to have caused the death of Homer from vexation at his inability to answer it when Theognis (or Hesiod) proposed it. It is therefore literary enough, but it is also very folksy in its earthiness, and probably goes back several millenia beyond Homeric days to a day when some cave poet cracked a louse and made a little riddle poem about it, to the great amusement of his kin. The old Greeks knew the enigma; Symphosius made it number xxx "Peduculus" of his c riddles; Latin and French versions of it circulated in the Middle Ages, and you will find it today in the Ozarks—and probably the South Sea Islands. A composite version of the original Greek story runs thus: Boys returning from fishing were asked if they had caught anything and replied:

Hos' helomen lipometha,
Hos' ouk helomen pherometha,

which has been translated, "All that we caught, we left behind, and carry away all that we did not catch," or "What we had we lost, what we did not have we kept," but might be rendered more faithfully to the spirited doggerel of the Greek by:

What we caught, we left behind,
What we brought, we didn't find.

One is reminded of the traditional fishermen's query still popular: "Any bites yet?" "Yeah, skeeter bites."

The old Œdipus riddle was part of another riddle contest—between Œdipus and the Sphinx. The fabled lion-bird-woman, sent from Ethiopia by Hera to Thebes to punish that city for the crimes of Laius, took her stance on a rock overlooking the city, and threw to death from the rock every passer-by who could not answer her riddle: "What walks on four legs in the morning, on two at noon, and on three in the evening?" When Œdipus gave the correct answer: "Man, who creeps in infancy on all fours, walks erect on his two legs in the prime of life, and hobbles with a cane for a third leg when an old man," the Sphinx threw herself to death from the rock; Œdipus thus saved Thebes, and was given the queen, Jocasta, as a reward. She proved to be his own mother; but that is another story. The suicide of disappointed riddlers, even in a fable, seems to us rather drastic, but the ancients took their riddles very seriously.

One more very famous riddle contest needs mention here. The King James translators rendered the Hebrew of *I Kings* x, 1 thus: "And when the queen of Sheba heard of the fame of Solomon . . . she came to prove him with hard questions." It is somewhat of a riddle itself why these scholars should have translated *chidoth* as "hard questions" when it is simply the plural of the *chidah* which they correctly rendered "riddle" eight times in the Samson story. But riddles they were, and how I wished when a boy that the Bible had included the details about those hard questions. Surely we could have spared some of the "begats" to make room for such an important conversation. But Jewish and Arabian traditions claim to preserve the questions of that riddle strife, and even if a few of the more than twenty enigmas do have a strange resemblance to riddles of later Moslem and Jewish lore, we can overlook that little discrepancy. Who knows but that Solomon's great wisdom included what is now termed precognition? At any rate, you will find the alleged Solomon-Sheba riddles in Ginzberg's *Legends of the Jews* (iv, pp. 141–142, 145–149), in W. Hertz's *Die Rätsel der Königin von Saba* (pp. 413 sqq.), and a few in Sir James Frazer's *Folklore in the Old Testament* (ii, pp. 564–569).

Many of these riddles which the queen (whom the Arabs call Balkîs) asked of Solomon are by now quite out of the range of our thought-forms and frames of reference. Others are so old and very simple that they do not seem riddles at all, although children might like them. But these three are good samples of the distinctly Oriental type of riddle, whether Solomon ever heard them or not.

Seven there are that issue and nine that enter;
Two yield the draught and one drinks.

Ans.   Seven are the days of a woman's defilement;
        Nine are the months of pregnancy;
        Two are the breasts that yield the draught;
        And one the child that drinks.

Perhaps the best one, viewed as a pure riddle, is:

    There is an enclosure with ten doors;
    When one is open, nine are shut;
    When nine are open, one is shut.

Solomon is alleged to have answered:

    That enclosure is the womb; the ten doors are the
    ten orifices of man—his eyes, ears, nostrils, mouth, the
    apertures for the discharge of the excreta and the ur-
    ine, and the navel; when the child is in the embryonic
    state, the navel is open and the other orifices are closed,
    but when it issues from the womb, the navel is closed
    and the others are opened.

Obviously, the answer is partly wrong, perhaps misquoted somewhere along the long line of oral transmission, for the womb does not have ten doors. The enclosure is the bodily cavity. Gautama Siddhartha, the
Buddha, may have known of this riddle, for he referred
to the human body as "this nine-holed frame."

The third of Balkis's riddles which we quote here you
must have heard, for it is found in every culture which
has been exposed to Judaism, Islam, or Christianity. It
has the incest element, like the Œdipus story, which so
fascinates the primitive mind:

    A woman said to her son,
    "Thy father is my father,
    And they grandfather my husband;
    Thou art my son, and I am thy sister."

Ans.   It was the daughter of Lot who spake thus
        to her son. (*Gen.* xix, 30–38.)

In the folk riddles of the Reformation and Renaissance
and even to a lesser extent in earlier Oriental enigmas,
there is reflected the people's protest at social inequality.
The folk riddle offered a comparatively safe vehicle for
hinting at the resentment of the poor and unlearned
against the rich and lettered. Class consciousness is
quietly but effectively preached in a riddle story in which
the intelligent underdog outwits the powerful king,
official, or rich fool. And even a medieval baron would
hesitate to punish a serf for telling a riddle. More credit
is deserved by this humble form of composition for its
social influence than has yet been awarded it.

Take for instance motif H551 where a princess is
offered to any man, commoner or not, who can out-
riddle her, or motif H561, where the solvers of riddles
are clever peasants, even girl peasants, who, though
doubly handicapped socially, gain advantage, perhaps
wealth and position, through their intelligence. I like
especially ones like motif H583.4.1 in which a child
when asked about the occupation of her poor midwife
mother replies proudly: "She shows the light of the
world to one who has not yet seen it," and motif H581.1
where a boy, similarly questioned, brags that before his
(barber) father the great bow the head and give money
and even blood.

More and more, however, what impresses me most
about these old folk riddles as I have the pleasure of
finding new batches of them from all parts of the
world is the startling beauty of imagery the simple native
mind is capable of thinking and expressing. Take motif

H583.4.5 of the class type "What is your relative (father,
mother, etc.) doing?" The answer for What is your sister
doing? is: "She is mourning last year's laughter," meaning
that the sister is nursing a child, the fruit of a love
affair. In the Riddles of the Superlative (H630) we find
(H633) What is the sweetest? with three answers: "Sleep,
Peace in Heaven, and Mother's Breast."

What more artistically accurate picture of a grasshopper was ever drawn than the old English riddle still
popular in the Schoharie Hills:

    Long-legged lifeless (listless?)
    Came to the door staffless,
    More afraid of a rooster and hen
    Than he was of a dog and ten men.

Or the frog:

    Old Grandfather Diddle Daddle
    Jumped in the mudpuddle,
    Green cap and yellow shoes.
    Guess all your loftiness
    And you can't guess these news.

That one has age (news was plural) and social protest.
"You and your loftiness; you're so high and mighty."

There must be a hundred different riddles about eggs
besides the ubiquitous Humpty Dumpty (did you know
he also "fell in the beck with all his innards about his
neck"?) but it would be hard to beat the Irish one:

    A long white barn,
    Two roofs on it,
    And no door at all, at all.

And every Gael knows these two:

    An iron grey with a flaxen tail,
    And a brass boy drivin'.
                    (Needle, thread, and thimble.)

    The cow gave it birth,
    It grew in the wood,
    Yet the smith made it.   (Bellows.)

Of the needle the Parsees (who are rich in riddles
as in all else) say:

    What a stunted little thing!
    And it has a plait of hair a yard long!

To their imaginations the stars are "a plateful of mustard
seed which could not be counted by anybody"; and a
cardamom is a "mother whose skin is white and whose
babies are black"; an onion is a Hindu gentleman who
says, "Coat after coat do I put on and hot-tempered am
I." For them the egg is "a jar which contains two kinds
of ghee," a carrot "a golden nail in a jungle," a lighted
lamp "a golden parrot drinking water with its tail."

These Parsee riddles are beautiful indeed, but you
might remind me that this race has been highly civilized
for centuries. Go with me then to the primitive heart of
Africa, to the Taveta, the Bantu, the Kxatla, Nyanja, and
Tlokwa, who have contests of the most beautiful riddles,
trials of the artistic imagination, hardly matched elsewhere on this globe, save perhaps at Japanese flower-
arrangement exhibitions. The riddle contest opens:

"Kanawuya!" (A riddle!) says the first contestant.
"Let it come!" shout the rest. "I have built my house on
a cliff." They all guess, and if their guesses are wrong, he
repeats his riddle. If they still cannot guess, they say:
"We pay up oxen." "How many?" the riddler asks. If
they offer enough cattle, he will then explain his riddle

and give the answer: "Kutu," which, in case you don't know Taveta, means "The Ear." Or the riddler might have said: "Mother is small but she knows how to cook nice food for me," or "Grandmother has died with her mouth open," or "A little child's sweet gruel." The answers? 1) A bee. 2) A banana split and dried on a cord. 3) Sleep. The Kxatla riddler says, "The guinea fowl stands on one leg: his thigh is very tasty" when he means an edible mushroom, or "The white horse goes into the stable and comes out brown," and the answer is bread into the oven. For him the egg is "The white hut which has no door," the fingers are "Ten boys with their hats on the back of their heads," and the eyes are "Birds which graze on a place not near."

The Nyanja riddlers' riddle for the gizzard is "The hide in the middle, the meat outside," and the heels are "Two children disputing the leadership." The Tlokwa pose you "The old lady who cries when knocked by a child," and laugh when they have to tell you it is a drum, of course. But I think even a literary enigmatographer could guess that when "The white goats are descending from a mountain," it must be snowing.

Now it may be that the encyclopedia (Everyman's) is technically correct in defining a riddle as "a paraphrastic presentation of an unmentioned subject, the design of which is to excite the reader or hearer to the discovery of the meaning hidden under a studied obscurity of expression," but I am beginning to suspect that a riddle, a real folk riddle, represents a group effort of some humble but intelligent people to find or create a little humor or beauty or both in the rather bleak and often difficult world in which they find themselves.   CHARLES FRANCIS POTTER

For the riddles of various other specific cultures, see section *Riddles* in AFRICAN AND NEW WORLD NEGRO FOLKLORE; *Charms, Nursery Rimes, and Riddles* in EUROPEAN FOLKLORE; sections on *Aarne*, on *Lönnrot*, and on *Proverbs and Riddles* in FINNISH FOLKLORE; *Riddles* in GERMANIC FOLKLORE; LITHUANIAN FOLKLORE; *Riddles* in SEMITIC FOLKLORE; section *Proverbs and Riddles* in SLAVIC FOLKLORE; *Riddles* in SPANISH FOLKLORE. See also ALVÍSS; CAPTAIN WEDDERBURN'S COURTSHIP; DEVIL'S RIDDLE; TASKS.

☞ For the much debated question as to whether the riddle form was used by American Indians in aboriginal times see the recent comprehensive article by Archer Taylor, "American Indian Riddles," *JAFL* 57: 1–15. Taylor inclines to the view that riddling was, for some of the American Indian tribes from which riddles have been reported, a pre-Columbian practice. See NORTH AMERICAN INDIAN FOLKLORE. [EWV]

☞ Like proverbs, riddles are a literary form unfamiliar to most South American Indians who have not been influenced by Europeans. Only the Minuane, a tribe of the Putumayo River in Brazil, are known to have riddles which they ask during pantomime dances. The so-called riddles of the Cashinawa are mainly quizzes. [AM]

rigaudon A French court dance of the 17th century, particularly during the reign of Louis XIII. It owed its lightheartedness and vigor to its peasant origin from Provence, or via Provence and Languedoc from Italy. The name bears a remarkable resemblance to the Italian *rigodone, rigolone* (diminutive *rigoletto*) or circle dance. The court rigaudon was, however, a longways dance with simple formations: down the center and cast off, and with gay jumps and running steps. The music, in quick duple time with an upbeat of two eighth-notes, was as brilliant as the dancing, and inspired able dancers to virtuoso improvisations, footbeats similar to the English hornpipe. In fact, one tradition traces this court dance to Provençal sailors. [GPK]

right and left through or **right and left** An American square dance term. Two couples cross to each other's places, separating as they pass through, the two ladies keeping to the right as they pass each other in the center and the two gentlemen passing on the outside. When the two couples have changed places, partners join left hands and turn, or the gentleman takes the lady's left hand in his right and turns her around so that she is on his right as they face toward the center of the set (8 counts). They pass back to places in the same way and turn as before (8 counts). [GPK]

Rig-Veda One of the four collections of hymns, prayers, and liturgical formulæ which constitute the Vedas, the most sacred literature of the Hindus. The *Rig-Veda*, the most important and oldest of the collections, is the original Veda from which the *Sāman* and *Yajur* were derived. It consists of a collection of 1017 (1028 when 11 additional Vālakhilyas are included) hymns arranged in ten books. Six of these books, ii–vii, or the "family books," are the nucleus of the collection. The ritual of the Veda is prehistoric in character. Most of the hymns are addressed to personifications of the powers of nature, worshipped as deities. Among these are Indra, Sūrya, Agni, Aditi, Varuṇa, Ushās, Aśvins, Pṛithivī, Rudra, Yama, and Soma.

ring-play Party games and songs and dances of American Negroes, now played chiefly by children, combining elements of the white play-party with African styles of circle dancing or circumambulation, as in the ring-shout, and some of the rhythmic plays of hand-clapping and slapping such as *Ham Bone*. There are songs and accompanying pantomimes similar to *Mulberry Bush* (as in *Go Roun' the Border, Susie*), serpentine figures, as in *Go In and Out the Windows*, marching pieces for couples, as in *It's a Cold Frosty Mornin'*, enumerations of the parts of the body, as in *Shout, Josephine, Shout*. Both texts and tunes are largely derived from white songs of English and Scotch-Irish origin, but the emphasis and singing style departs from the manner of white play-parties, and many of the words are garbled beyond interpretation.

ring shout An Afro-American religious ring dance rooted in West African ritual, merged into Christian religion in slavery times in the southern United States and the West Indies, and not yet extinct. The dancers form a circle and move counterclockwise, shuffling slowly at first and gradually increasing the tempo, while singing, clapping, and exclamations of praise and affirmation also increase in speed and volume, until, after an hour or more, the emotional pitch of the participants reaches a state of possession. The strong accelerating beat of clap and shuffle is unbroken, and the interwoven outcries of "shout, sister," "yes, Lawd," "well, well, well," etc., merely elaborate the rhythmic pattern. One or two leaders may keep up a running narrative on some favorite Biblical story, changing off from time to time, interjecting contemporary elements into the theme, stimulating the fervor of the congregation. Or the accompaniment of voices may be a more formalized song. In some sections a solo form of shout dance is more common. Whether the dancing is group or individual, a circle of the rest of the worshippers, often including the strongest singers, serves as chorus or basers.

Shout songs of various types have been described and recorded, some with slight differences in the dancing procedure. The Watch Night (New Year's Eve) shout of slavery times took place in the "praise house," a building somewhat less sacred than the church, and slaves who had to be back home before daybreak sang *Yonder Come Day*, or "day's a-comin', hark ye angels." *Down in the Mire* was sung as the ring circled around one kneeling figure whose penitent head was shoved "down in the mire" by each passing shouter in turn. Another song, *Oh, Eve, where is Adam?* is in question-and-answer style. Adam, according to the answers, is in the garden pickin' leaves, pinnin' leaves. One similar in structure is "Where was Peter when the church fall down?/ In some lonesome valley with his head hang down." That "lonesome valley" turns up often in Negro religious song, and this particular verse has many humorous and juvenile relatives. ("Where was Moses when the lights went out?/ Down in the cellar with his mouth poked out.") A shout for the Sunday "fore-day" meeting was often "I'm goin' to set in the humble chair/ Goin' to rock from side to side/ Until I die." Other songs sung for ring shouts include *Can't Hide, Kneebone, Moonlight, Starlight* (for burial watches), and the fine example *Run, Old Jeremiah*, recorded for the Library of Congress by John and Alan Lomax in Louisiana in 1934. The last brings in another favorite theme of Negro song, both religious and secular, the railroad, with its engineer and its bell ("ding, ding, ding"). West Indian shout songs are sometimes modified "Sankeys" (from the hymns of Moody and Sankey).

The word shout is believed to be related to the Arabic *saut*, used in Moslem West Africa to mean the circumambulation of the Kaaba. [TCB]

ring-tailed roarer Backwoods bully and "stentorian braggart," also known as screamer, snorter, or squealer: so called from his resemblance to "some strange and formidable animal that roars in the forest or on the prairie" (M. Schele De Vere, *Americanisms*, 1872, p. 224). Although the epithet "ring-tailed" (for which "Mississippi" or "Salt River" is sometimes substituted) is said to have reference to the catamount, the roarer is more commonly identified with the "half horse, half alligator" ("with a little touch of the snapping turtle," "a touch of the steamboat and a sprinkling of an earthquake")—a term applied particularly to the raw Kentuckian and the amphibious boatman of the Ohio and the Mississippi (e.g. Mike Fink; Colonel Nimrod Wildfire in James K. Paulding's lost play, *The Lion of the West*, 1831; and Ralph Stackpole, in Robert Bird Montgomery's *Nick of the Woods*, 1887). The roarer is distinguished by his ritualistic "antic demonstrations of hostility" (flapping his bent arms and crowing like a cock, shaking his mane and neighing like a horse, cracking his heels together while jumping up and down) and his boasting and taunting tall talk. West of the Mississippi his tradition passed

into that of the pseudo, bogus, or mock bad man and his brags survived in "bad man yells." (See B. A. Botkin, *A Treasury of American Folklore*, pp. 2–67.) [BAB]

rinnce (plural *rinnci*) The Irish term for dance, current in Irish figure dances. *Rinnce mór* is a round dance; *rinnce fada* is a longways dance. *Rinnce an tuirne* is the spinning-wheel dance. These are accompanied by the Irish bagpipe in 2/4 reel time or 6/8 jig time. [GPK]

Rio Grande A capstan chantey usually sung on outward-bound ships. Several sets of stanzas are known, but the chorus is always "Away, Rio," with a fare-you-well to the girls ashore and the statement "we are bound for the Rio Grande." The word *Rio* was always pronounced *Rye-o* by American sailors. See CHANTEY.

Rip Van Winkle Hero of Washington Irving's New York state (Catskill region) legend on the magic sleep lasting many years motif (D1960 ff.) in *The Sketch Book* (1819–20), memorably portrayed on the stage by Joseph Jefferson. As the simple, good-natured, henpecked ne'er-do-well of a Dutch colonial village, who wanders off into the Catskill Mountains with his dog and gun, drinks with a strange, nine-pin-playing crew, and sleeps for twenty years, Rip differs from the slumbering martyrs and heroes (e.g. The Seven Sleepers of Ephesus, the kings in the mountain) in that his magic sleep confers upon him not blissful, saintly immortality but escape from a termagant wife and a kind of Ancient Mariner role in the changed world to which he returns. [BAB]

rishi In Hindu mythology, a holy man or sage, especially one of a group of seven saints, the mind-born sons of Brahmā, the traditional composers of the Vedas and the progenitors of Brāhmans. The rishis possessed superhuman powers which made them often equal to and sometimes superior to the gods. There are three classes of rishis, the *devarishis* or rishis of the gods, the *brahmarishis* or priestly sages, and the *rājarishis*, those of royal origin. The names of the seven vary. The oldest list included Atri, Bharadvāja, Gautama, Jamadagni, Kaśyapa, Vasiṣṭha, and Viśvāmitra. The usual list includes Agastya, Aṅgiras, Atri, Bhṛigu, Kaśyapa, Vasiṣṭha, and Viśvāmitra. The rishis play an important part in story and legend. Manu took them on his ship during the deluge. After many adventures they became the seven conspicuous stars of Ursa Major.

rising or **growing rock** An animal or person falls asleep on a rock; when he wakens he finds the rock has risen upward to such a height that he cannot get down by himself. Usually Bat Old Man or Woman rescues him, bringing him down in a basket. This is a favorite tale among western Indian tribes of the Great Basin, Southwest, and central California; for its distribution as of 1935 see A. H. Gayton, "Areal Affiliations of California Folktales" in *AA*, n.s., 37, pp. 582–599. For the Chiricahua Apache tale of the rising rock and distribution among various Apache groups supplementing Gayton's, see Morris Edward Opler, *Myths and Tales of the Chiricahua Apache Indians*, MAFLS 37: 28–31. [EWV]

rites de passage Rites of transition: French term adopted by many European anthropologists to include all the rites and ceremonies which usher an individual into a new way of life or new status in life. The term is defined by Arnold van Gennep as the "rites which accompany every change of place, state, social position, and age." See his *Les Rites De Passage,* Paris, 1909. Such rites exist in all cultures everywhere, ancient and contemporary, primitive, peasant, urban.

Birth is the first crucial transition the individual makes as a living being; and all the rites, magic ceremonies, observances, tabus associated with childbirth are *rites de passage.* A. H. Krappe includes the churching of women in his list of such rites, the churching of women being a rite not only of symbolic purification after birthing, but one which liberates the woman from the special dangers, influence of evil spirits, etc., attendant upon her between her delivery and churching, and restores her to the normalities of daily life.

Baptism is a *rite de passage;* so is name-giving. The ceremonies accompanying adoption are also transition rites, involving frequently the symbolic drama of rebirth and new-naming.

The initiation rites of primitive peoples are probably the most obvious or conspicuous of the *rites de passage,* including as they do spectacular ceremonies for the definite cutting off of the initiate from his former ties and condition, involving his admittance into a new (sometimes supernatural) world, sight of sacred objects long forbidden to him, explanations of them, teachings in regard to them, and involving especially the ritual drama of death and rebirth as a new person (e.g. the word for certain Congo Negro initiation rites, *kimbosi,* means resurrection also), the marking of the initiate as a new person (by circumcision, headdress, tattoo, garment, or other symbol), and including finally his reintegration into the reality of which he has been divested.

Confirmation, ordination into a priesthood, coronation, the dubbing of a knight, the initiatory hazings of college and other secret fraternal societies, all belong to the category.

Marriage is another important transition in the life and status of the individual, accompanied by a legion of rites, ceremonies, and symbolic regalia of which the bridal veil and wedding ring are the most familiar. Marriage rites also include, however, various observances to protect the groom against the dangerous power inherent in virgins, to protect the new couple from evil spirits, from the evil eye, etc., to secure the fruitful fulfilment of the union, to secure and enhance the safety and prosperity of the new home.

Death is the last great transition and change. Rites for the dying and for the dead overlap into certain rites performed for the living kin of the recently dead. Purification from contact with the corpse or his belongings often must be accomplished before the living can resume his place in community life. Various ceremonies are performed to free the dying from his sins, to sever his connection with the living and his old environment, to show him the path or road to the afterworld, to ease his journey, pay his way, ensure his non-return, along with those designed to protect the living from his envy. See BARASHNŪM; BAR MIZVAH; BREAD; BURIAL; CREMATION; DEAD SHOES; FUNERAL; GRAVE; INITIATION.

ritual combat As distinguished from athletic events, funeral games, and exhibitions customarily held on national and religious holidays, ritual combats were customary in Europe on May Day and during the spring planting ceremonies and elsewhere during marriage and burial ceremonies. The May combat was between the Queen of the May and the Queen of Winter, and fighting in the fields until blood was drawn is said to have been to ensure the fertility of the crops. In South Russian marriage ceremonies the groom was stopped on the way to his bride's house and had to fight his way in. The Malayan marriage ceremonies covered many days. On the fourth day the groom went to the home of the bride's parents where entrance was denied him until he fought his way in. Students of the Russian ceremony identify it with marriage by capture (see ABDUCTION), but the Malayan ceremony is said not to be symbolic of marriage by capture but rather of a feeling about the battle of the sexes. Some of the tribes of eastern Siberia and western Alaska also have a custom of "marriage by capture" in that the groom pursues the girl, surrounded by her female friends and is accepted as husband only after he has succeeded in touching her genitalia. This would seem to be less a racial memory of bride-capture than a symbolization of female shyness. In Samoa, Australia, and elsewhere ritual combats are performed at burial ceremonies. One party called friends ritually beats another party representing evil spirits. In the Society Islands the body was protected by its family. "Mourners" from a neighboring district demanded entrance and won. These combats have been rationalized as symbolic attempts to beat off evil. See SWORD DANCES. [RDJ]

ritual drama A mimetic enactment addressed to supernatural powers, fundamentally for the attainment of a practical end, as a later development for esthetic gratification, always as a religio-cultural expression. Drama implies a struggle between two forces. Ritual drama involves a contest between two shamans, between man and demon, beast and hunter, or between the personified forces of life and death, summer and winter, good and evil. It implies a well-defined sequence of encounter, conflict, and dénouement. This sequence may deal with exorcism, with pursuit, capture, sacrifice. It may develop into the stages of sophisticated Greek and Japanese drama. It may contain a brief gem of parody by *koshare,* or a 27-day sequence, as the *kusiut* arrival of Noäkxnim. It may involve the entire community or just a select group. The inevitable combination of dance, mime, music, texts, and accouterment vary from the choreographic Iroquois Indian rites to the non-integrated dance and play of the Morris, through time from the choral *orgía* to the speaking characters of Greek drama.

Structure The underlying sequence of exposition, conflict, climax, and catastrophe varies tremendously between races and cultural stages. Iroquois Indian curative rituals progress in a steady crescendo from invocation to attainment (see NYAGWAI'OENO). The Yaqui Deer Play builds up a farcical series of events—introduction of the deer and *pascolas,* the pursuit down a series of arches, final death of the deer, and epilog of skinning. Hindu and Mexican dance dramas depict a placid, non-climactic succession of scenes, as the leisurely combats of *Moros y Cristianos.* Near-Eastern drama, on the other hand, inculcates excitement, even frenzy, into its contests, and has communicated this to much of the European derivative dance-play.

Many American Indian rites are homogeneous, with well-known exceptions of the *hako, sun dance,* etc.

European and Asiatic drama is usually composite. Sometimes the separate parts clearly betray their origin in different cultural levels, as the Abbotts Bromley Antler dance and play combination. The Dionysian rites anciently combined a phallic animal procession with a priestess-deity marriage and with the four sections of the three-day *anthesteria*: contest (*agon*), death (*pathos*), lamentation (*threnos*), and resurrection (*anagnorisis*). These same elements recur in the Thracian carnival, the Rumanian *caluşar*, the Portuguese *Mouriscadas*, the English Ampleforth sword dance, but everywhere in a different manner. The Thracian play features the shaggy *kalogheroi;* the *caluşar* precedes the fertility round and drama by a rough initiation rite of clubbing, and concludes with a curative jig over sick babies; the Portuguese spectacle contrasts orderly longways of good forces with chaotic demons; the sword dance separates the elaborate evolutions from the farce. The medieval liturgical drama built up its scenes on the Greek pattern, with gradual additions. The three-day Easter drama consisted of the *Passio Christi* (agon), the *Adoratio Crucis* (pathos), *Depositio* (threnos), and *Elevatio* (anagnorisis) with lighting of new fire. Antiphonal processions and wakes developed into the *Quem quaeritis?* (Whom do you seek?) by the angels and Marys at the tomb, the apostle scenes, and the *Noli me tangere* (Dare not touch me).

Cultural Expression Drama reflects contemporary society. The medieval *Fastnachtsspiele* and Feast of Fools presented farcical scenes from the life of the folk. The guilds represented their occupations in dances and plays, some of which have survived (e.g. *Schäfflertanz*). Mexican dance societies reflect political organization. Ancestral "dream time" (*alchera*) fashioned Australian rituals and wove through their daily comings and goings. Various cultural stages persist separately in the ritual activities of Indian castes: functional rounds among independent mountain tribes, devil dancing among native low castes, stick dances among the better caste Dravidians (see KANIYAN; KOLATTAM), folk harvest and wedding festivals and sophisticated *natya* among Indo-Aryans. Different stages may persevere in the same ritual, as in the *caluşar* primitive initiation and cure, later play of marriage, fight, death, and revival, and communal *kolo*.

A complete study of the cultural relationships involves numerous investigations: racial type and mixtures, geographical and climatic conditions, central or peripheral location, hence exposure to migrations, conquest, or trade. It involves the recognition of typical local patterns and of intrusive items. It demands exhaustive choreographic comparisons in dealing with questions of autogenesis or derivation. It must consider historical and archeological facts as supplement to formal analysis, before it can trace distributions and paths of dissemination. It deals with progression through time and space. The following survey will explore in Eurasia the possible paths of diffusion from earliest times. In the Americas it will attempt to map out recent and surviving rituals according to cultural regions.

Eurasia

From the network of interinfluences three major centers of diffusion emerge: the Near Eastern Highlands repeatedly, India, and central Siberia-Mongolia.

A. Near East 1) The little known Paleolithic population (before 6000 B.C. in the Near East, before 2800 B.C. in Spain) has left cave paintings of animal dances in southern France and of phallic rounds in Spain. The surviving masked *Morisca* animal-demons may date back to this period, also the Abbots Bromley Horn dance. Demon and fertility serpentines are probably subsequent.

2) Stick dances may have originated in clubbing initiation, preserved in the *caluşar* "horse"-dance; but the "dibbing" and Maypoles of peripheral England and India presuppose agriculture. The wide distribution and persistence among pre-Aryan tribes in India suggest Neolithic diffusion before the Indo-Aryan migrations of the second millennium B.C. The longways forms are probably later than the circles and meanders.

3) Sword dances presuppose a metal culture, and may represent a metamorphosis of the stick contest after 2000 B.C.: prominent in northern Europe.

4) The Dionysus-Osiris-Morisca drama considerably preceded the Golden Age of Greek drama (6th century B.C.).

5) The dragon-fighting hero (e.g. Yima of Iran, Kṛishṇa and Śiva of India, St. George of England) probably wandered simultaneously with the hobbyhorse. The horse spread in the Bronze Age from the Russian steppes to Asia Minor 3000 B.C., to the Ægean about 2000 B.C., and subsequently into Germanic mythology. In western Europe and India the masked hobby cavorts with a transvestite and a black-faced clown.

6) Prehistoric combats were reinterpreted as Moors and Christians following the Crusades, after the 11th century.

7) As a form of *pastourelle* the marriage theme became the English May Day play of Robin and Marian (15th century).

8) The resurrection theme reappeared after 1000 A.D. in the Christian liturgical drama, alongside the Mysteries, or enactments of Biblical stories.

9) Another Iranian concept underlies the 15th century Morality Plays of the individual in the battle of allegorized Good and Evil over his soul: Iranian Ahura Mazda and Ahriman, medieval Divine Graces against Vices or demon-clowns (a Paleolithic residuum?), as in *Everyman* and the *Castle of Perseverance*.

The successive impulses reached Iberia both by way of North Africa and by the Mediterranean, and traveled to England both by way of Spain and by the Balkans and the Danube. The latter double route has left the trail of Moriscas.

B. India was a center of radiation as well as of reception.

1) Reception took the form of Neolithic stick dances and Aryan culture, which produced *natya*.

2) Along with the Vedic religion, *natya* spread to Indonesia and gave rise to the spectacular *wayang wong* epic battles of the *Mahābhārata* and *Rāmāyaṇa*, performed to this day. The *mudras* influenced the gesture code of Java, Bali, and Polynesia, particularly Hawaii, probably not before the 4th century A.D.

3) Along with Buddhism, Indian drama stretched its influence to China in the 7th century and by way of China to Japan. Here it produced the *dengaku* and *nembutsu odori* alongside the Shinto *kagura*, and played a role in the formation of the *nō* drama. In the 13th century Buddhist miracle plays became popular in Burma.

4) Toward the West by way of Arabia, India influenced another center of absorption and radiation, Spain, which in turn has metamorphosed the ritual drama of Latin America.

C. *Siberia-Mongolia* Shamanistic spirit-trance cure is not ritual drama in the true sense of the word; but in its tremendous migrations it has given rise to many dramatic manifestations. To the south it appears transformed in the Balinese *kris* and *sanghyang,* and to the southwest in the self-mutilating dervish dances. The orgiastic cults of Asia Minor may have developed locally or may have emerged from Siberia by way of the Turks and their migrations. If the latter, the multiple family of the *orgía* type and the Anatolian shamanistic *bar* (drum) dances owe a debt to the Tungus.

Siberian shamanism shows extraordinary affinities with the devil-dancing cures of Tibet, India, and Ceylon, by the lowest, hence oldest, castes—Vedda of Ceylon, Nalke, Panan, Pombada of India. The outcast Paraiyan, the lowest Tamil group of southwest India, dances with the greatest frenzy and clatter. Their exorcisms are not linked with the seasons. They are effected without masked demon-identification. A definite and far-reaching expansion of this vision-cult reached through the American continents during successive periods of migration and in manifold guises, masked and unmasked.

The Americas

Despite uncertainties of chronology, New World ritual concepts show strata which correspond largely to those of the Old World and at times show Eurasian influences. 1) The oldest rites (of initiation into men's societies and girls' puberty) mark the most primitive tribes of the Tierra del Fuego and of California. They persist along with newer rites in the Chaco and in Arizona. 2) Shamanism, the cult of the dead and of animal guardians, reaches to southeastern Brazil and has spread in many forms through North America. It is strongest in the northwest area of recent immigration (about 2000 years ago), among the British Columbia Indians and Alaskan Eskimos. 3) A hunting-animal cult, closely allied to the animal guardian, shows local developments, such as the tiger of Mexico, the alligator of the Southeastern Woodlands, the buffalo from the Great Plains to Iroquois rites. The bear extends in the middle belt from coast to coast. The serpent, of the entire South to Middle America, may have an Asiatic and ultimately Near Eastern origin. 4) The plumed serpent is associated with the high agricultural stage of maize cultivation. This is much later than the Old World Neolithic. It radiated from Middle America all the way to the Iroquois area, probably in the course of the first millennium A.D. 5) Colonization since the 16th century A.D. has wrought mestizo forms in Latin America and the vodun cults of the Caribbean and Brazil.

Tribes north of the Rio Grande have remained impervious to medieval ritual, which saturated the Mexican and Andean fiesta, and to native American sectarian trance rites, of the Shakers and southern Negro church. Even the Pueblo Indians have accepted only superficial fragments of moriscas and have left penitential orgies to their neighboring conquistadores.

Intercommunication deified geographical impediments. As in Europe, ritual complexes radiated (sun, ghost dance) and intermingled (*iruska-hako-grass;*

calumet-eagle, wiikita). As in Europe, old and new rites persist side by side, and foreign have mixed with native types. The Iroquois Indians retain shaman and animal cures, agricultural rites, and borrowings, as the Plains calumet (*ganegwa'e*). The following brief lists mention only those survivals and introductions that form an essential part of the ritual pattern, and only the predominant characteristics. Boundaries are not always sharply defined because of marginal transitions. Thus the Papago combine Great Basin and Pueblo characteristics; the Midwest practices Plains and Eastern rites and uses both types of patterns, both types of rounds.

The homogeneous tribal diffusion has been jumbled by migrations and invasions. Each area includes assorted linguistic stock. Algonquian agricultural tribes, as the Cheyenne and Arapaho, under pressure from the whites, retreated recently to the Plains and to a nomadic hunting life. In this location the Arapaho have served as radiation center for the sun dance. In their case the hunting-animal cult was subsequent to maize culture. Within the last century co-residence in Oklahoma has been blurring tribal distinctions and has disseminated dances such as the stomp.

South America

1. Aboriginal Ceremonies, greatly decimated.

a) *Hunters* of Patagonia (Puelche and Tehuelche) and of the Tierra del Fuego (Yahgan, Ona, Alacaluf). Demon impersonations, puberty and initiation rites, death, hunting-animal rites.

b) *Hunters* of eastern Brazil with rudimentary maize culture (Gé, S. Cayapó, Apinayé, Bororo, etc.). Demons, puberty, shamans, rain, secularized animal and clown dances.

c) *Hunt-algarroba* culture of Gran Chaco and western Brazil (Toba, Pilaga, Mataco, Lengua, Ashluslay, Choroti, Terenos, Mbayá) and hunt-maize culture of Venezuela and Guiana (Maipure, Arecuna, Macushi, Arawak). Demon-puberty, shamans, mortuary, war, harvest rites, *yurema* narcotic cult (compare California).

d) *Wheat culture* of Chilean Araucanians (introduced). Cure by women shamans, harvest thanksgiving by women.

e) *Andean maize culture.* Vestiges of ancient seasonal Inca and Chibcha festivals for ancestors and deities of elements, especially for Sungod Inti, in Highlands of Peru (Quechua), Ecuador (Murra), Bolivia (Aymara). Circular or serpentine animal, burial, sowing, harvest rites.

2. Colonial Rituals

a) *Hispanized* religious festivals of Argentina, the Andean Highlands, the Antilles: *carnaval, comparsas, conquista, negros, moros.* Longways.

b) *Afro-American rites: macumba* of Brazil, *winti* of Surinam, *vodun* of Haiti (*Nago* from Dahomey, *Congo-Guinée* from Congo), *obeah* of Jamaica, *nañiga* of Cuba. Stick dances of Haiti, with transvestites.

Middle America and Northern Mexico

1) *Indigenous Rites* Animal maskers and seasonal rain ceremonies in counterclockwise circle or longways. Ceremonial clowns, transvestites. On Plateau rarely women.

Guatemala: seasonal observances of Maya-Quiché; *volador* fiestas.

Yucatán (Maya): Cure and rain ceremonies; ribbon dances.

Chiapas (Lacandones, Tzotzil, Tzeltal): shaman cures, cave ceremonies for planting.

Oaxaca: (Huave) *Malinches;* (Chinantec) rain dances.

Guerrero (Aztec): *tecuanes, tlacololeros.*

Sierra de Puebla and Veracruz (Aztec, Otomí, Totonac): animal masks, *voladores* (circle), *quetzales, acatlaxqui* (longways).

Sierra de Nayarit: (Cora-Tepehuan) *mitote,* (Huichol) peyote and rain ceremonies.

Sierra Madre Occidental (Tarahumara): *rutuburi, yumari* for rain, death, peyote for cure (circle).

Sonora (Cahita): deer, *pascolas, coyote, chapayekas* (Papago): *wakita* puberty, *kapétua* war, *wiikita* cure, rain, harvest (circle, longways).

2) *Blended Rites* in corridor of migration and conquest.

Morisca longways: Oaxaca, Jalisco *conquista.*

México, Michoacán *moros.*

Eastern Sierras, *Santiagos, moros, negritos.*

Northwestern, *matachines.*

México to Querétaro: *Concheros* (circle).

México, Morelos: *chinelos, pastorcitas, vaqueros, arrieros* (longways).

Tlaxcala: *paraguas, arcos, catrines* (longways).

Viejos, *diablos, muertes, Malinches.*

3) *European Liturgical Dramas* in Valley of Mexico: *autos, colloquios, pastorales, pasiones, penitentes* (Tres Potencias, El Cuerpo y el Alma)

North America

1) *California* (Klamath, Hupa, Yurok, Modoc, Karok, Shasta, Maidu, Miwok, Pomo, Luiseño, Diegueño): initiation, girls' puberty, cure, hunt; North, first-salmon, display; Center *kuksu-hesi* spirit-impersonation with disguise, ghost-clown; South, mortuary, *toloache.*

2) *Plateau* and *Great Basin* (Babine, Sekani, Salish, Paiute, Ute, Tübatulabal, Mohave, Yuma): vision, dream-cult, song cycles, puberty, mortuary; ghost dance, pine-nut harvest. Lines, clockwise circle.

3) *Southwest Nomads* (Apache, Navaho): puberty, cure-chant, spirit-impersonation, masks of hide, lines.

4) *Southwest Agriculturalists* (Papago, Rio Grande Pueblo, Zuñi, Hopi): set seasonal sequence, mass drama for rain, corn, squash, game-animals; plumed serpent, *kachina* supernaturals, ritual clowns; hide and paint-masks. Rounds, lines, gestures, trot, stamp.

5) *Plains Hunters* (Plains-Cree, Piegan, Blackfoot, Cheyenne, Arapaho, Dakota-Sioux, Kiowa, Osage, Shoshone, Mandan-Hidatsa, Arikara, Comanche): men's war-medicine-animal societies, individual vision-quest, scalp, hunt, buffalo, sun, *iruska-hako-calumet,* fire-clowns, ghost, peyote. Paint, few hide masks. Sunwise circle, leaps, nimble footwork, virtuosity.

6) *Midwest* (Pawnee, Omaha, Shawnee, Winnebago, Sauk, Fox, Chippewa, Menominee, Potawotomi): shamans in North; animal-cure, war, hunt; seasonal corn, beans, squash; calumet, grass. Sacred clowns, wood masks (Shawnee). Antiphonal stomp, men's virtuoso steps; circle both ways.

7) *Eastern Woodlands* (Iroquois, including Huron and Cherokee; Penobscot, Delaware, Tutelo, Creek, Yuchi, Choctaw, Seminole): dreams, sun rite; in North shamans, lunar cycles; South also new-fire worship, gesture, serpentine. Throughout animal-cure, war, seasonal corn, beans, squash, eagle-calumet; clowns, wooden and husk masks. Counterclockwise stomp, antiphony.

8) *Northeastern* Algonquians (Montagnais, Naskapi) and Labrador Eskimos: shamanism, animal-guardian, cure, hunt.

9) *Alaskan Eskimos:* shamanism, whale cult (seasonal), cult of ancestors and animal-spirits, masked mime.

10) *North Pacific Coast* (Dené, Kwakiutl, Tlingit, Salish, Bella Coola, Tsimshian, etc.): shaman-cure; animal-totem societies, display (potlatch); in south, first salmon (see North California); elaborate enactments of *kusiut,* gesture-code, hand-vibrations; wooden masks of complex construction.

Transvestite, masked clowns throughout. Frequent participation of women, especially in Eastern Woodlands.

The Dramatization of Myths

Aboriginal Origin myths account for traditional ceremonies. Sometimes, but not always, this story is enacted. *Natya* depicts non-seasonal epics of gods and heroes. Faroe rounds commemorate the Sigurd legend. *Kusiut* spectacles represent supernatural occurrences. The *shalako* and *orgia* represent seasonal return. The Hopi emergence tale is less obviously connected with the tribal initiation ceremony. The Hopi Snake-Antelope ceremony does not even suggest the origin legend, any more than the Iroquois ?*ohgiwe.* Fairy tales are never enacted in folk rituals.

Modern Since the 16th century masquerades, classical and Germanic mythology, fairy tales, and Indian legends have been distended into pretentious operas, pageants, and folk-plays. These revivals and art products are remote from ritual drama or folk drama, even when they are produced with a rare authenticity. They lack the traditional and communal heritage and function, often also the requisite style. At times art creations approach the aboriginal mysticism, as did the short-lived, sincere dance-interpolations in St. Mark's-in-the-Bowerie, New York. However, true ritual drama grows naturally out of the culture and out of its needs. Reconstruction or new invention on ancient tales is an educational artifact, not a process of magical coercion or social cohesion. See separate topics; DANCE: FOLK AND PRIMITIVE; MASKS; RATTLES; ROUND DANCES; SERPENTINE.

For this article and for separate topics in both volumes, information and advice were generously given by: Kamer Aga-Oglu, Robert Anderson, Susan Bezirium, Dilshad Elbrus, William N. Fenton, Einar and Eva Haugen, Harry Hoijer, Lawrence Kiddle, Juana de Laban, Kapila Malik, T. M. Pearce, Ernst A. Philippson, Federico Sanchez y Escribano, Homer Thomas, Mischa Titiev, Joseph K. Yamagiwa.   GERTRUDE P. KURATH.

ritual numbers Repetition of ritual acts, incidents in tales, dance forms, the number of performers in a ceremony, the length of ceremonies, tabus, periods of mourning in terms of days or years, and many other features of American Indian life are governed by the ritual numbers of the various tribes. The most widespread of these are 3 and 4; 5, 6, 10, or 12 are also ritual numbers for some tribes, but 7 rarely if ever occurs as a ritual or sacred number among the North American Indians. A tribe may have two, three, or even four ritual numbers; among the Shawnee, for example, as stated by an informant, "everything goes by 3, 4, 6, and 12." The origin of ritual numbers, if explained, is accounted for in the cosmologic myths, but often no origin for these numbers is vouchsafed. The ritual number(s) of a tribe is often deducible from myths taken in text: a hero repeats his adventures 3, 4, or 5 times; four arrows are shot at the hero in a tale; three objects are taken by a hero; a character is successful in a third attempt, etc. For a discussion of ritual numbers among California Indian tribes see A. L. Kroeber, *Handbook of the Indians of California,* BBAE 78, 875–877. [EWV]

Robin Goodfellow In English folklore, a malicious or mischievous spirit, later identified with Puck in his role of household spirit. Shakespeare's Robin Goodfellow (*Midsummer Night's Dream* ii, 1) is a servant of Oberon. In the reign of Elizabeth appeared a work entitled *Mad Pranks and Merry Gests of Robin Goodfellow,* later edited by J. Payne Collier and published by the Percy Society, 1841. Collier believed it to have been first printed before 1588. In this work Robin Goodfellow is the child of a young girl and a "hee-fayrie"; he early ran away from home, and in a dream discovered that his father was a fairy. On waking he found a scroll beside him, describing his powers and admonishing him to punish the mean and love the good. He could transform himself into any kind of animal, and it was not unusual for some dupe who had been induced to mount a riderless horse suddenly to find himself in midstream with no horse in sight and nothing but a saddle between his legs. The second part of this work portrays Robin Goodfellow in the familiar role of household spirit, puck, or brownie, who does the chores in return for a little milk or cream and some bread or cake.

The Friar Rush of medieval clerical legend is said by one writer to be "Puck under another name." Puck he identifies with Robin Goodfellow, and Robin Goodfellow with Robin Hood. See Clouston, *Popular Tales and Fictions* ii, 240 n. 1.

Robin Hood English ballad hero; type of the noble robber who steals from the rich to give to the poor. He is first mentioned in the late 14th century; in 1495 the first detailed "biography" appears, *A Lytell Geste of Robyn Hode,* printed by Wynkyn de Worde. Legend has it that he was born Robert Fitzooth, Earl of Huntingdon, in Locksley, Nottinghamshire, in 1160, and that he was treacherously bled to death by a kinswoman on November 18, 1247. His grave is shown in the park at Kirklees Hall, Yorkshire, where his bow and arrow are exhibited. But tradition is just as strong that Robin Hood helped defeat Simon de Montfort at Evesham in 1265. "Robin Hood," according to Child (introduction to #117), "is absolutely a creation of the ballad-muse."

The Robin Hood of the ballads is one of the great archers of tradition. He and his band of outlaws lived in Sherwood Forest, poached on the king's deer, robbed passing prelates and merchants and gave the money to widows and orphans, and generally enjoyed their life in despite of the Sheriff of Nottingham or his hired assassins. Child's ballads #117 to #154 detail the adventures of Robin and his band. See *Robin Hood and Allen a Dale* (#138), *Robin Hood Rescuing Will Stutly* (#141), and especially *A Gest of Robyn Hode* (#117). Principal members of the group who dressed in Lincoln green were Little John, Friar Tuck, Will Scarlet, Allen a Dale, and Robin's greenwood wife Maid Marian. Robin Hood,

Maid Marian, and Friar Tuck became prominent characters in May Day plays; the open-air celebration of the marriage of Robin and Marian translated the folk hero of the ballads into the ritual hero of the May Day fertility celebrations.

rock pictures Depictions on rock, characteristic especially of prehistoric art in many parts of the world; they form a stationary art, that is, they occur on rocks which are left in their natural position. Those drawn or painted are called petrographs, those incised or pecked are petroglyphs. The famous Stone Age murals of western Europe are usually referred to as cave paintings and those on cliffs, e.g. in the American Southwest, as cliff paintings.

The rock pictures of Europe and Africa are divided by Frobenius into two styles, both of which he thinks originated in southwestern Europe and spread thence as far as South Africa. The Franco-Cantabrian or "portrait" style, thought to be the older, comprises naturalistic depictions of single animals and human beings, usually polychromes. The Levantine or "action" style are characteristically monochromes, with the figures composed in groups.

The famous South African rock pictures are of this latter type. Their depiction of running, lunging, almost flying figures seems almost an abstract dramatization of movement itself. In that respect they are unique in the folk arts of the world—and in another respect also. The oldest examples were made several thousand years ago; others (not dissimilar) within memory of living man. Petrographs occur in abundance in a strip 150 miles wide paralleling the southeastern coast of Africa. Petroglyphs are concentrated in an area somewhat more inland. Scenes of the hunt, fight, and dance, even pranks, are depicted. The Mantis-Man is a favorite subject. Motifs of fire, rain, and stars may be identified in depictions of ceremonies.

Ancient rock pictures have been found, to give examples, in Australia, Outer Mongolia, India, the Near East, and Russia. Northern Europe offers examples also from the Bronze and Iron Age. Throughout the Americas they are a notable form of older art cultures. [MH]

rods of life Fresh green branches of trees or shrubs (birch, willow, fir, cherry, rosemary, juniper, etc., or vine, in vine-growing regions) just newly budded or blossomed and therefore potent with new life: used by the young village people of southern Germany and southeastern Europe to beat each other on certain feast and holy days. The rods of life impart health and energy, renew life in the weak or ill, bestow fertility, and are used by one sex upon the other. In Bohemia, for instance, birch, willow, or cherry branches are put to sprout on St. Barbara's Day, and are used on St. Stephen's Day or Holy Innocents' Day by the young men of the villages to beat the girls on hands, feet, and face. The girls are beaten with the fresh stinging branches for their own good: it keeps them fresh and fair and young and healthy. Unhappy is the one who does not get beaten. The next day or on New Year's Day the girls beat the boys with the same branches. The fool's whip of European Carnival is probably a direct descendant of these rods of life. See EASTER SMACKS.

The beating of young banana trees in New Guinea with a stick cut from one that has borne fruit also testifies to a common belief that the fertility of the tree is inherent in the part, and can be communicated. Frazer reports (*Scapegoat*, London, 1913, p. 264) that in Hungary barren women are beaten with a stick that has been used to separate copulating dogs. An early spring custom of Albanian herdsmen is to cut branches of newly sprouting cornel and to beat their companions and animals with them to preserve their health. In Thüringia on Holy Innocents' Day (Dec. 28) it is said that children used to run around the streets with green branches and strike at passersby, expecting pennies in return for this life-giving favor.

rolling head or **skull** Pursuit by a rolling head is a folktale motif (R261.1) in which decapitation of some opponent or offender does not end the trouble. Instead the head pursues and sometimes kills the decapitator. The malevolent revenant in the form of the wandering skull which pursues men (E261.1) turns up in European, Indonesian, and African Negro story.

In a Bantu Negro folktale a man beheads his wife for eating his porridge instead of her own. After he marries a second wife, the head of the first wife rolls into the hut and tries to beguile the second into eating the wrong porridge also. The head partakes of the husband's porridge, but the second wife is not tempted. At night the head rolls into the hut again, eats of the husband's porridge, and then rolls into bed with the man. The terrified second wife runs away; and in the morning the people of the village find only the man's dead body in the bed.

The North American Seneca Indians have a class of ogres known as the flying or rolling heads. One day a young mother with her child in her arms is pursued by one of these. She throws deer meat behind her from time to time to delay it; when the meat is gone she throws down her blanket. The Head stops only long enough to tear it up in a rage. She tears off her dress, and throws it down, then her leggings, her moccasins; still the Head pursues. Finally she remembers that a baby's moccasin has power to ward off danger, throws back one of her infant's moccasins. This stops the Head, and the young mother rests in a tree. But the Head comes and sleeps at the foot of the tree, and wakes when she tries to climb down. All she can do is tangle it up in a crooked branch from the tree and run on. The Head follows her home, and silently rolls into the lodge. There it sees her picking acorns out of the fire and eating them, thinks she is eating the live coals, tries some, shrieks and disappears, and is never seen again.

That the skull of a suicide must roll in the dust until it has saved a life is the motif (Q503.1) of a story in which a man seeing an owl about to kill a rabbit picks up a skull lying nearby to throw at (or kill) the owl. Thus the skull of the suicide has saved a life and the soul of the suicide is freed of the punishment, after rolling in the dust for 777 years. Compare OFFENDED ROLLING ROCK.

☞ Pursuit by a rolling skull, head, or rock is a widely known incident in North American Indian mythology. The incident usually occurs in the widespread tale of the *Rolling Head,* in which an unfaithful wife commits adultery with a snake. Her husband kills both the snake and his wife, and cuts off the latter's head. Some of the North Pacific and Plateau tales stop with the husband's serving of the snake, or the snake's genitals, to his unfaithful wife, but in many other versions

the tale continues, as outlined above. For distributions see Stith Thompson, *Tales of the North American Indians* (Cambridge, Mass., 1929), pp. 343, 345. [EWV]

☞ Today as in the past the Indians of the Peruvian highlands believe that the flying heads of sorcerers attack people and suck their blood. A rolling head which pursues some men forms the central theme of weird tales in the folklore of the Tumupasa, of the Shipaya, Cashinawa, and Yahgan Indians. In the Cashinawa version of this story, the rolling head becomes the moon.
[AM]

romantic love Sentimentalists have attributed to the American Indians the Euro-American concept of romantic love; American Indian tale material frequently has been popularly presented in romantic versions. Tales of Indian lovers' leaps may exist all over America, as Stith Thompson states (Stith Thompson, *The Folktale,* New York, 1946, p. 313), but it is dubious whether they are of Indian origin. Some North Pacific Coast tales from unimpeachable sources do seem colored, and the actions of their characters motivated, by a sort of romantic love, and the characters may use endearing terms to each other, but in the very large majority of American Indian material the concept of romantic love is either lacking or, if expressed, it is clearly indicated that socially it was not approved. What Margaret Fisher has to say for the Algonquian peoples of northeast North America holds for many other American Indians as well, as far as romantic love is concerned: "[A] theme [in northeastern Algonquian mythology] which receives emphasis in both serious and trickster tales concerns the fate of young women who were 'too proud' to marry the man selected for them. This theme occurs so frequently as to throw into high relief the struggle formerly carried on in Algonkian society against the forming of romantic attachments. This struggle is also reflected in the almost complete absence of romantic love as a theme. The devotion of a man to his family gets some attention, and there is even a tale of devotion so great that a man followed his wife to spirit land and brought her back to life. But these are tales of family love. Tales of star-crossed young lovers can be found, but are for the greater part conspicuously absent. Tales of adultery are told from the injured husband's point of view, with retribution swift and complete" (Margaret Fisher, "The Mythology of the Northern and Northeastern Algonkians in Reference to Algonkian Mythology as a Whole," p. 234, in *Man in Northeastern North America,* Papers of the Robert S. Peabody Foundation for Archaeology, Andover, Mass., vol. 3, pp. 226–62, 1946). [EWV]

Romany folklore Romany is the name by which a group of people, commonly called Gipsies in English, refer to themselves. Every nation in which they have lived has designated them by various names, some derived from the trades they follow—"Muggers," for instance, in reference to potters—others from characteristics they have or are supposed to have, others from the places or peoples from which they are locally believed to have originated or emigrated. The general name in the United States and England is Gipsy (or Gypsy): a corruption of Egyptian, Egypt having been the land of their origin in medieval belief. In some places they were called "Pharaoh's people." Other forms of the name are Cingani or Acingani (Corfu), Zigani (Russia), Tshinghiané (Turkey), Cygani (Hungary), Tsiganes (France), Zigeuner (Germany), Zingari (Italy), Zincali (Spain). They are also known as Biscayans, Bohemians, Saracens, and other names referring to their supposed origins. They were called Greeks or Bohemians in Spain, for instance, Saracens in France, Tartars in Scandinavia, Bohemians or Tartars in parts of England, Greeks or Moors in Scotland, etc.

Several theories have been advanced to explain the term *Romany*, all of them bearing on the possible origin of these mysterious people. By etymological analysis *Romany* is the adjective of *rom*, male Gipsy, man, from Sanskrit *doma*, a man of low caste. It has also been frequently pointed out that the name might refer to their long sojourn in the Byzantine Empire, anciently called *Roum;* and it has also been suggested that the name derives from their long residence and great concentration in Rumania.

From the literature on the Romany it would seem that any statement made by a competent observer about their origins, customs, or folklore is subject to contradiction by other observers equally competent. Thus, though it is undoubtedly true that the Romany were at one time nomadic and unsettled, they now seem to be somewhat sedentary. Most of them have settled in cities and towns and follow ordinary trades. But in the spring the Rom who has not been assimilated and has maintained his tribal pride likes to move. Racial assimilation and intermarriage which have resulted in Gipsies leaving their tribes and forgetting their customs have failed to reduce greatly the number of Romany in all parts of the world who still follow their own ancient arts and crafts. Although the prediction that the Rom is about to become extinct has been made for many hundreds of years, Gipsy caravans are still to be seen in all countries of Europe and many countries of Asia, Africa, in the two Americas, and in Australia.

British students have made careful studies of the Gipsy in England. Yet these English tribes, themselves, frequently augmented by tribes from Europe, are, by still other tribes, regarded as not true Romany at all. Almost any statement applicable to one tribe is contradicted by members of other tribes in regard to themselves, and thus students of Romany contradict each other. One author, unhappily confused by this cacophony of statement and counterstatement, decided while examining a number of hypotheses to accept the least probable of them all. This makes an attempt to arrive at a balanced understanding difficult.

The term Romany folklore refers both to the folklore the Romany have themselves produced and to the folklore *about* them produced by the peoples among whom they have lived. It is often said, in fact, that there is more folklore *about* Gipsies than there is Gipsy folklore:—Gipsies know magic, for instance; they have second sight; they can cure diseases; they can protect houses from burning; they can tell fortunes and divine the future; they love horses and understand the language of horses; Gipsies have been known to give up their lives for their horses; Gipsy coppersmiths bare their heads to the new moon; Gipsies save old thrushes' nests (which are lined with clay) and use them for milk which they steal from cattle; they are petty thieves; they kidnap children; their women are promiscuous.

Intrinsic Gipsy folklore has been difficult to put a finger on. Gipsy marriage customs, baptismal rites, burial customs, childbirth and menstruai tabus reflect the practices and beliefs of all the countries in which they have lived. They believe in omens, ghosts, and the evil eye. They avoid having their pictures taken, hence must believe in the separable soul. Most Gipsies have two names: the *nav romanes*, which they use among themselves, and the *nav gajikanes* (or *gâjo*) which is a public name (see H. L. Mencken, *American Language*, New York, 1947, 490); this suggests a belief in the various holinesses, tabus, and dangers associated with names.

It has been said that the safest theory in regard to Gipsy folklore is to assume that they brought nothing, originated nothing, but "adopted in every country what they found as they found it." However true it may be that Gipsies have picked up and taken to themselves the marriage and birthing customs, beliefs, stories, musical instruments, tunes, etc., of the countries in which they have lived and traveled through, yet this seems a strikingly unsatisfactory statement in the light of the fact that these people have maintained their own distinctive way of life, a distinctive code of behavior and spiritual values, regardless of centuries of contact with other cultures and other codes, and in the face of persecution. Even the automobiles, which they have wholeheartedly adopted, have done nothing to un-Gipsify these people.

The Gipsy proverb "When you cut a Gipsy in ten pieces you have not killed him; you have merely made ten Gipsies" bears testimony to the indestructibility of these people. The proverb takes meaning when one understands the Gipsy cult of the dead. Konrad Bercovici stresses the fact that *wherever Gipsy life remains unadulterated* (see his *Story of the Gypsies*, p. 172 ff.) their cult of the dead is a compulsion. They believe that the souls of the dead are not free of this world until the body is burned; the dead return and reproach the living, or materialize and denounce them for neglect. In Spain before the two wars, many Gipsies still burned their dead and the possessions of the dead; in Hungary it is said that in spite of civil prohibitions they disinterred their dead and burned them secretly. In Germany where they were especially persecuted, the more Gipsies were killed, the more Gipsies poured in to search for the graves, burn the bodies, and liberate the souls of their kinsmen. No punishment, not the death penalty itself, stopped them from following their people and performing this service.

Other scholars remark, however, that "with local variations, the burial customs of Gipsies are the same everywhere." If the burning of the dead is still a compulsion among them, the modern increase of available crematoriums in the world must have minimized their problem.

Because they are not tied to the land and have lived mostly in areas where nomadic grazing was impracticable, they have earned their living by skills which required few tools. Everywhere the men have been tinkers, braziers, metalworkers, potters, farriers, clippers and shearers (in herding regions), and skilled artificers. In eastern Europe they were especially famous as musicians, singers, dancers, puppet-show men, bear leaders, and smiths. They have been equally famous as horse dealers, pig traders. They are said to have a great affection for horses, to "understand the language of horses," to celebrate the marriages of mares and stallions, and to take as great a pride in these genealogies as in their own. They were looked to, too, as skilled veterinarians in rural communities; but this particular store of knowledge is rapidly being lost among them. The passing of the horse and the coming of the automobile has done little but change the Gipsy rate of travel; the caravan *mobilensa* is as colorful as the old horse-drawn wagons of the Gipsies. The women are fortune-tellers, dancers, skilled needlewomen. They are said to have occult powers, and by the use of spells can cure sterility in women. They can bring back vagrant husbands and bring unwilling lovers into the arms of infatuated females.

All who have written about the Romany have described them as vagabonds of one sort or another and have accused them of all crimes except murder: the Gipsy will not shed blood. Members of hard-working communities find after a time that people who sing, dance, eat, and are merry without doing regular work can become irritating, especially when these people insist that they are superior, because "free," to the sober farmers who work with little gaiety or song from sun to sun. Consequently the Gipsies have been harried through the centuries from one community to another. The office of hangman was often forced on some Gipsy in medieval Germany: a superlative injury in that Gipsies are averse to shedding blood. The kings of Spain spent much time making laws against them. Maria Theresa tried to get them tied to the land. Hitler attempted to exterminate them. Many laws have been passed in many countries forbidding intermarriage with Gipsies or communication with them, but the bands continue to exist and occasionally to marry out of the tribe.

Although Gipsies have been reported on in histories written by many peoples for the last thousand years more or less in Europe and for earlier periods in the Middle East, the Gipsies themselves have never bothered to record their own histories. The only reports we have from the Romany themselves have been transmitted orally and have been transmitted in the lighthearted manner of a people which thinks it is important to make a good story.

One 15th century reporter says that their original home was in Hungary and Turkey. Paul Bataillard asserted that the Romany have been in Europe since prehistoric times and that they taught the art of metallurgy to Europeans. The tribe that rode into Germany in the early 15th century said that their ancestors in Lower Egypt had renounced Christianity and when they returned to the fold they had, each one of them, to do a penance by wandering for seven years; and they were still wandering. A variant of this tale is that they had been forced to wander because they had refused hospitality to the Virgin Mary, Joseph, and the Christ child when they fled from Bethlehem. An Italian medieval tract, however, says that when Joseph and Mary fled with the infant Jesus into Egypt, they were met by an old Gipsy woman who called out to them that she had a little stable, ready with straw and hay: "Behold a shelter for you all." Spanish Gipsies have still another version of their Egyptian origin. After Pharaoh had conquered the world he challenged God. God opened the side of a mountain and raised a great wind that blew Pharaoh and his armies into it. The mountain closed

upon them, and after that it was easy for aliens to overrun Egypt and drive the Egyptian remnants into Spain.

The Rumanians have a story explaining that Gipsies are cursed because one of their smiths made the nails for Christ's cross. The Gipsies themselves have a counterlegend that the Gipsy smith made the nails thin so that they would give little pain. Mary blessed them for this and said let their work be light and their profit great. Another story is that a Gipsy woman tried to steal the nails and thus prevent the crucifixion, but could only get away with one; this is why only three nails were used, two for the hands and one for the feet.

Philologists conclude that the language of the Gipsies is Indo-European, i.e. rooted in Sanskrit. This would make their point of departure central or southeast Asia, and a later home, long after the Vedic age, the foothills of the Himalayas, whence they migrated north and west and reached Persia about 900 A.D. The language, strongly colored by local variations, yet basically the same wherever it is spoken, is closer to Hindustani than to any other living language. Turkish and Welsh Gipsies, for instance, could understand each other.

The Gipsies have another mysterious language called the *patteran:* a sign language known only to themselves. Patteran means leaf, trail, sign, and refers to a system of leaving two twigs and a leaf arranged a certain way and placed every so many hundred feet apart, used by Gipsies everywhere to guide those coming after them. Sometimes one sees the word written *patrin*.

The tribes of Romany throughout the world present almost every type of social structure known. Although the leader of the group is usually a man, women have been known to hold this post. The leader is referred to as Duke or Lord in Europe, and King or Queen in North America. The post is elective and for life (or for seven years). The chief has wide powers, controls the tribe's property, represents the tribe in negotiations with outsiders and with other tribes, officiates at marriages, and settles disputes.

Even in England where Gipsies have established themselves, some groups are matrilineal and others are patrilineal. Exogamy is not a rule. Men have been known to marry their nieces, preferring their brother's daughter, granddaughters, half-sisters, their aunts occasionally, and their cousins frequently. The daughter of the mother's brother is said in these instances to have been preferred. The levirate, which requires the dead husband's older brother to marry the widow, is said to be uncommon. Polygamy has been reported, so too has the sororate, a system by which a man marries the girl of his choice and at the same time all of her sisters. Elsewhere the custom is to get the older sister married before the younger ones.

Gipsy marriage customs not only vary from tribe to tribe, but reflect the customs native to the places where they have sojourned. A number of reports concur, however, that a frequent part of a marriage ceremony is an oath taken by both bride and groom to leave the other when love has ceased. Part of the great body of folklore *about* Gipsies is that Gipsy women are promiscuous; in actual fact they are notoriously flirtatious and fanatically chaste. The *lubenny kiss* is not unknown in some groups. This is the harlot kiss. *Lubenny* (sometimes spelled *luvni* or *lubni*) means harlot. The lubenny kiss is a public ceremony in which the husband, sometimes the betrothed, bites off the tongue of the faithless one. The ceremony of blood marriage seems to be important in some tribes. The wrists of the young couple are slightly cut, and tied together in such a way that the blood mingles. The common saying "Gipsy marriage" patronizingly implying "no marriage" refers to the report that Gipsies effect a marriage by jumping over a broomstick. This was undoubtedly a common practice among them at one time, especially in Germany and the Netherlands, where it was also a native peasant practice.

The Romany are famous for their music and dancing. In eastern and southeastern Europe no party is a success without a Gipsy band and usually one or more Gipsy dancers who tell fortunes between numbers. Observers are agreed that the Gipsy contribution to music has been the preservation of folk songs in the several places they have lived and the modification of these songs to their own rhythmic skills. The countries which have contributed most to their repertoires are Hungary, Rumania, and Spain. The Andalusian Romany have become particularly famous for their development of the flamenco. The mood of their music varies from the deep melancholic to the gay and of their dancing from the sensuous to the simple light-hearted. Everything they touch, however, tune, dance, or song, takes on an ardor and intensity, almost an exaltation, that marks the adaptation or the performance as intrinsically Gipsy.

The Romany have professed Mohammedanism, Catholicism, Protestantism at various places and times. English and German Gipsies observe the rite of Christian baptism when they confer the *gâjo* (public name) upon a child; and it has been observed (*Folk-Lore* 24: 323) that German Gipsies especially like to have their children baptized as often as possible. Multiple baptisms have also been observed in England. The annual pilgrimage of thousands of Romany from all parts of Europe to the church of the Saintes Maries de la Mer occurs, May 23, at Ile de la Camarque, Bouches-du-Rhône, southern France. This church contains the crypt of Saint Mary of Egypt, called Mary Gipsy, their patron saint. They keep vigil at the crypt for two days and a night and then depart.

The Green George festival of east European Slavs is a favorite of the Romany of Transylvania. This festival is celebrated on St. George's Day, April 23. As in other tree-water-spirit festivals (see WHITSUNDAY) the people cut down a young willow, decorate it with flowers and leaves, and set it up in a central place. Pregnant women may leave a garment under it; if a leaf has fallen on it by morning an easy delivery is indicated. Sick and aging people spit three times on the tree and pray for health: "Let us live," they say. The next morning a boy completely covered with green leaves throws grass to the animals so that they will not lack during the year; he hammers three iron nails (which have lain in running water three days and three nights) into the willow, draws them out, and throws them again into the stream. See JACK IN THE GREEN.

Sawing the Old Woman, a custom of southern Europe formerly observed on the fourth Sunday of Lent (one of the numerous Carrying Out or Killing Death mimes) was taken over by the Gipsies of those localities as a Palm Sunday observance. The Old Woman, a puppet dressed in women's clothes, was well beaten, then sawed in two, and finally burned; the ashes were saved and thrown in the next cemetery the group came to. There is some vague association on the part of the Gipsies with a Shadow Queen who must vanish in the spring and return in the winter. (See Frazer, *Dying God*, London, 1912, pp. 243 ff.)

In Italy where Gipsies are masons, the shadow of a man is often buried in the foundation of a new house (see SHADOW). English Gipsies do not eat hare because the hare is a vampire; their children are not permitted to eat chicken legs lest they become liars; and children with living fathers do not eat the heart of any animal, for it is the same as eating one's father's heart. Gipsy widows in England leap into their husbands' graves and lie there for a few moments; they are then not allowed to remarry. This suggests a hang-over from ancient Hindu SATI.

Among English Gipsies a woman is unclean for certain periods after childbirth. The term is *mokhadi* (see "Ceremonial Customs of British Gipsies" in *Folk-Lore* 24, p. 323 ff.). For one month she must use only her own cup, plate, knife, fork, spoon, and these are later destroyed. She must have no relations with her husband during this period, must not touch food for the group. Formerly she had to wear gloves for a month and could not touch dough for a year. In Germany a birth had to take place on a straw pallet under the living-wagon. If it happened inside, everything had to be burned. The English Romany believe, however, that before childbirth a woman is good magic; in Lancashire it is said that a pregnant woman can save a man from mortal harm. Women's clothing at all times is somewhat *mokhadi*. In some tribes, especially in Germany, women's clothes may not be hung up inside the wagon, lest a man happen to brush against them and become *baletshido*, which means "disgraced and partially outlawed" (see *id*.326). White crockery is also *mokhadi* "because it suggests a chamber-pot."

Gipsy folktale is the general European folktale, plus the Gipsy flavor and twist. F. H. Groome in *In Gipsy Tents*, London, 1880, advances the theory of the diffusion of folktales over Europe by the Gipsies. Many others have accepted the concept of folktale transmission via these people. Moses Gaster, however, in *Rumanian Bird and Beast Stories*, London, 1915, p. 24, dismisses the theory as impossible on two counts: 1) they came too late into Europe to have been the carriers of general European folktale, and 2) they were so hated and persecuted that there was no opportunity for intimate or even equal interchange of stories. Even though they possess a good number of popular tales of their own, even these were not "communicated to Europe by them." Gaster also points out that in Rumanian and other European folktale the role of villain is often given to the Gipsy; in popular jest he is the dupe; in certain etiological tales he is the legitimate object of a cheat. See WASP.

The techniques which have been developed to indicate differences between similar and related cultures are so crude and depend so much upon the chances of observation that distinctions between traits which are properly Romany and traits which are not cannot be relied on. Even the observers themselves are unreliable for the observers like the general public are influenced by envy tinged with disapproval of a life which seems to be happy and carefree. R. D. JAMESON

Rónán King of Leinster, Ireland, about 600 A.D., famous for the tragic and unjust killing of his son, Mael Fothartaig, his remorse, and his own death at the hands of Mael's two sons. The story, based on the Potiphar's wife motif (K2111), is told in a Middle Irish text, probably 10th century, in the *Book of Leinster*, and entitled *Aided Mael Fothartaig maic Rónáin (The Death of Mael Fothartaig Son of Rónán)*.

Rónán, long without a wife after the death of Mael's mother, went north to the house of Echaid, king of Dunseverick, and took for wife the beautiful young daughter of that king. "You are no husband for a girl," said Mael, "it were better for you to marry a woman." But Rónán married the girl and the girl fell in love with Mael Fothartaig. She sent him messages and invitations by her maid, but Mael, in loyal anger, left his father's house and went to Scotland, where he and his two wonderful dogs (Doilín and Daílenn) performed marvels in the hunt.

But the people of Leinster were unwilling to have Mael so long away, so he returned. Again Rónán's girl-wife sought him to be her lover, and Mael Fothartaig asked his foster brother Congal for advice. Congal told Mael to go hunting in the forest, and then sent a message to the young queen to keep tryst with Mael there. Joyfully she set out, but Congal himself met her on the way, taunted her that she was going out to meet a man, and sent her back home. Again she set out, again met Congal, who decried her for a harlot and promised her her own head on a stake in front of Rónán if she were not faithful to the king.

The young queen plotted her revenge. That night she accused Mael Fothartaig to his father with having solicited her. Three times she said Congal came to take her to Mael. But Rónán would not believe, until the half-quatrain made by Mael's jester seemed to fit into the half-quatrain with which the queen made answer, to support the accusation. "It is cold against the wind/ For him who herds the cows of the slope," said Mael Fothartaig's jester. "It is a vain herding/ Without cows, without one you love," said the queen. And because Rónán thought the words were reproach and answer, he believed. He told the warrior beside him to put a spear through Mael. The warrior threw the spear into Mael's back so that it went through him and pinned him in his seat. Congal rose up at the sight and got a spear into his heart. The jester would have escaped but the warrior cast another spear which went into his bowels.

Mael Fothartaig spoke from his seat then that three men were enough. And Rónán reproached his son for entreating his wife. Mael swore by the "tryst of death" he was about to keep that he never wanted to lie with the queen, that Rónán was deceived, that Congal died unjustly, for three times that day Congal had brought the queen home to keep her away from Mael. By then the three boys were dead: Mael, Congal, and the jester.

For three days and nights Rónán grieved beside his son. "The wind is cold/ in front of the warrior's house," he cried, ". . . Woe is me that Mael Fothartaig/ Was slain for the guilt of a lustful woman." Young Don, brother to Congal, foster brother to Mael, went to Dunseverick and killed Echaid, his wife, and son, and brought the heads back for vengeance on the queen. When she saw them she threw herself upon her knife. And Rónán cried "The grief that is upon Dún Áis/ Is also upon Dunseverick/ Give food and drink to Mael Fothartaig's hound/ . . . It is sad to me that Daílenn suffers/ With her ribs spare through her sides; . . . And Doilín . . ./ Her head is in the lap of everyone in turn/ Seeking one whom she will not find. . . . My son, Mael Fothartaig/ He has taken a cold dwelling." And the two young sons of Mael killed their grandfather Rónán for the death of their father, Mael Fothartaig.

This is perhaps one of the grimmest and most poetic legends based on the Potiphar's wife motif, in which the woman scorned accuses the man who has refused her with attempting to seduce her. For a more detailed rendering of the story, see Myles Dillon, *Early Irish Literature*, Chicago, 1948, p. 87 f.

Rongo In Polynesian mythology, one of the sons of Rangi (Vatea) and Papa: in Hawaii, he is known as Lono. He is variously god of the sea, of war, of agriculture, etc. Tane was his twin (or younger brother), and throughout the Polynesian area the god Rongomatane (Romatane) appears to be a compound of both these deities. Compare ARIOI.

Roosevelt ballads The day after the death of Franklin D. Roosevelt a printed ballad sheet appeared on the streets of Aguascalientes, Mexico, bearing among several other songs, a *corrido* in tribute to his memory, composed overnight and designed to be sung to a familiar *corrido* melody. The writer, Manuel Delgadillo, worked in the details of the President's death as he was posing for his portrait, mentioned the "good neighbor" policy, censured Japan for its knife-in-the-back blow at Pearl Harbor, and expressed the sorrow and sympathy of Mexican people for the loss of the American leader. (The song was reported by T. M. Pearce in *New Mexico Folklore Record*, Vol. 1, 1946–47.)

Some time later a group of American Negro jubilee singers recorded another lament for the death of Roosevelt called *Tell Me Why You Like Roosevelt*. The answer to the title question is, "everybody knowed he was the poor man's friend." The stanzas, sung in the characteristic staccato style of jubilee and quartet singers of Negro churches to a tune similar to that of many quartet spirituals, give the following information: By all indications Roosevelt "received salvation" at Warm Springs, Georgia. "Elizabeth," who was painting his portrait, dipped her brush into the water, looked up, and knew "the President didn't look right." He died of a cerebral hemorrhage at 3:35, and in thirty minutes the world was in mourning. His wife "notified her sons across the sea and said, 'Don't you worry about poor me. Your father's dead, but you're all grown. Just keep on fighting for victory.'" The song lays stress on Roosevelt's stand against race prejudice. "Only two presidents that we ever felt," it says, "Was Abraham Lincoln and Roosevelt." It remarks on the Negro ladies invited to the White House, on the appointment of a Negro general, and on the assistance of the WPA. "Took my feet out the miry clay, and I haven't looked back since the WPA." It ends with a recommendation to call on Jesus, who is "a president, too."

roots The root of some plant is almost always one of the powerful ingredients of the maleficent, evil-working, or death-dealing charms of southern U.S. Negro conjure doctors, also known as "root-doctors." *Rootin'* means (in Georgia) casting an evil spell. The conjure doctor always carries a piece of some kind of root in his pocket; and a certain wild root, known as High John de Conquer (St. John's-wort), if seen in the conjuror's hand, strikes terror to the beholders. Sometimes, however, the conjure man will give a bewitched person a bit of some root to chew on, which will break the spell, or the liquid from certain roots boiled with a piece of silver will also liberate the victim of an evil spell. Thus roots are potent both to cast and break spells. The root of the plant called devil's-shoe-strings (variously identified as genus *Coronilla* or as sand-vine) if laid in a man's path will prevent him from ever having any money. Little pieces of this root, cut up and soaked in whisky or camphor, and rubbed on the palms of the hands, will blind your enemy when you suddenly grab him. Roots are invariably regarded as maleficent as contrasted with JACKS, which bring luck.

rope trick A marvelous trick ascribed to Indian *yogis, fakirs, sādhus*—religious mendicants and itinerant conjurors. The conjuror throws high in the air a thin rope which remains upright, the end disappearing in the clear sky. The conjuror's companion, usually a little boy 10–12 years old, then shinnies up the rope and also disappears. After a few minutes the conjuror calls to him to come down; he refuses; the commands are repeated more and more angrily; still he will not come down. Finally the conjuror himself climbs the rope; he needs both hands to climb, so he carries a knife in his teeth. A great rumpus is heard from above—angry threats, blows, piercing shrieks; pieces of the boy begin to fall to the ground—an arm, a hand, a leg. The conjuror comes down, wipes and cleans his knife, and the boy runs up to him, safe and sound, from among the spectators.

This has been the classic trick of India for centuries, and controversy has raged as to whether or not it can be, or ever has been, done. It is slightingly referred to in the *Vedanta Sutras*. Many Europeans claim to have seen it. Large sums of money have been offered by serious European magicians and occultists traveling in India to any one who would perform the trick for their observation, but no one has ever stepped forward to claim the prize. This proves nothing, according to M. P. Dare, late editor of the *Times of India*, in that the holy men of India do not perform tricks for money and the typical itinerant conjuror cannot read the ads.

Rosa A A Portuguese folk dance of the province of Beira. It has the simple circular form characteristic of this agricultural province. Any number of couples, partners facing, run first clockwise, then counterclockwise. After a momentary interchange, partners pivot, and then resume the original run. The accompaniment is a simple love song in duple time, with a flageolet and two drums. [GPK]

rose The national flower of England, once divided between the followers of the white rose of the House of York and the red rose of Lancaster in the War of the Roses. In the United States it is the state flower of New York, Iowa, and North Dakota. Originally from Persia, the rose is said to have been brought to the West by Alexander. To the Arabs the rose was a masculine flower. It was anciently a symbol of joy, later of secrecy and silence, but is now usually associated with love.

The rose, as one of the most beautiful of flowers, has always been associated in one way or another with Venus. Various legends ascribe its origin to her tears or as a gift of the gods to celebrate her rising from the sea. Some say it became red because Venus (Aphrodite) pricked her feet on the thorns as she sought her slain lover, Adonis. Other legends link it with her son, Cupid, e.g. the roses became red when he mischievously emptied a cup of wine on them, or once, when he stopped to smell a rose, he was stung by a bee which had been admiring the same rose. Cupid was so angry that he shot an arrow into the bush; this accounts for the thorns. Another tale says that Bacchus was chasing a nymph when he was stopped by a thorn hedge which he commanded to become a hedge of roses; the nymph doubled back, and when he saw that the rose hedge would not stop her, he commanded it to be thorn again. The magic was not wholly effective and so now they grow together. In Algonquian Indian etiological story the thorns were added by Gluskabe to prevent the animals from eating the flowers.

When Eve kissed a white rose in the Garden of Eden, it blushed with pleasure and has been pink ever since. The 4th century Bishop Basil said the rose was thornless until the expulsion from the Garden of Eden. Many of the attributes of the rose were inherited by the Virgin Mary. In common with many other thorny plants it is said to have formed the "Crown of Thorns," the tree on which Judas hanged himself, and Christ's blood is said to have turned the rose red at the time of the Crucifixion.

Throughout the Teutonic area the rose belongs to the dwarfs or fairies and is under their protection. In many places it is customary to ask permission of their king before picking lest one lose a hand or foot. The Arabs say that the white rose sprang from the sweat of Mohammed on his journey from heaven. A Rumanian story tells of a princess who was bathing in a secluded pool. She was so beautiful that the sun passing overhead was stopped in his tracks. He stopped so long that the moon complained to the gods, who turned the princess into a white rose. Next day when the sun passed, the princess was embarrassed and she blushed; the flowers on top of the bush turned a deep red, those in the middle became pink, while those near the earth remained white. In Persia the nightingale cries out when a rose is picked and sings because of its love of the red rose which is stained with its blood. In India at one time Brahmā and Vishṇu were of equal rank. One day they were discussing flowers and Brahmā said that the lotus was the most beautiful of flowers. Vishṇu showed Brahmā the rose and he had to admit defeat.

In Persia the infant Zoroaster (Zarathustra) was placed on a bed of burning logs to die, but they turned into a bed of roses. Red roses were often connected in story with fire, and the ashes on which several Christian martyrs were burned turned into roses, but in their cases, too, late. However, Zoroaster's couch was not the original "bed of roses" which refers to the Sybarites who slept on mattresses stuffed with rose petals.

In Rome at the time of the Empire roses were lavishly used to add to the luxury of banquets, often in quantities comparable to such modern fetes as the Festival of Roses in Los Angeles. The rose garden of King Midas was one of the wonders of the ancient world. Anciently in Greece, Rome, and China, and more recently in Europe and England, the rose has become a funeral flower; in Switzerland the cemetery is often referred to as the *Rosengarten,* which in this allusion is a kind of cross between churchyard and heaven. In England it is customary to plant a rosebush at the head of the grave of a deceased lover who died before the wedding. In Wales a white rose is planted on the grave of a virgin and a red one on the grave of any respected person. A rose is often used in the decoration on the tombstone of a virgin.

Sub rosa, under the rose, means in secret, and refers to the ancient custom of hanging a rose over the council table to indicate that all present are sworn to secrecy. This in turn may have sprung from the legend that Cupid gave a rose to Harpocrates, god of silence, to keep him from revealing the indiscretions of Venus. At any event it is known to have been in use as early as 477 B.C. Up to quite recent times a rose in the decoration of the dining room ceiling was a gracious invitation to talk freely without fear, but this custom is no longer observed.

There are various references in story to persons being enchanted and turned into animals who regained their human form by eating a rose, as Apuleius in the *Golden Ass* (see ASS), and St. Denis, the patron of France. At one time in England the officiating clergy wore wreaths of roses on St. Barnabas' Day; in Rome there was a Rose Sunday. In Germany the associations of the rose are not always happy. It has been worn as a punishment for immoral conduct. In much of Europe the red rose is an evil omen. Seeing the petals fall is a sign of death although in Germany this may be counteracted by burning some of the fallen petals. In Wales and parts of England, it is an ill omen when roses bloom out of season. In British Columbia, the Thompson Indians pass widows and widowers four times through a rose bush so that the thorns will purify them of the spirits of their dead mates. Whether singly or in chaplets, roses have been used as a chastity test (H432.1), signifying infidelity by fading or changing color. In parts of the southern United States, a folded petal is sometimes struck against the forehead; if it cracks, the person in mind loves you; if it does not, your love is one-sided.

The use of the rose medicinally has continued unabated from the time of Hippocrates to the present day British Ministry of Health. The fruit, or hips, contain more than twenty times the amount of vitamin C found in oranges. Almost every part of the plant is used (root, bark, leaves, petals, fruit) and prepared in every conceivable way from delicious confections with sugar and honey to the bitter root-bark tea. Rose petals from the altar of Aphrodite were used to cure Cyrus, King of the Medes and the Persians. In Greece the petals were used both internally and externally to cure the bite of mad dogs. Gerard recommends rose-petal conserve for "shakings and tremblings of the heart." The Romans believed that the rose would prevent drunkenness either by its presence, or by floating a petal in the cup. The North American Tewa Indians powder the dried petals and use them in a salve for sore mouth. Only a generation ago a sillabub of roses was recommended for sore throat, and a pint of claret in which a handful of rose petals

had been boiled was considered a good compress for a sprain. In 1943 the people of England gathered 500 tons of rose hips and hundreds of pounds of dried petals for the manufacture of needed drugs. [JWH]

rosemary According to Culpeper, an herb of the sun under the dominion of the Ram. Ophelia's famous line, "Rosemary, that's for remembrance," expressed the common knowledge of the day; for rosemary has been symbolic of remembrance, fidelity, and friendship since early times and in this connection was most frequently used as a funeral wreath and in wedding ceremonies. In medieval Germany, however, some brides wore it to guard against pregnancy. In ancient Greece, students wore rosemary twined in their hair while studying for examinations also "for remembrance" (i.e. to strengthen their memory) and because it was believed to bring success to any undertaking. It was one of the early strewing herbs both because of its pleasing odor and because it kept out moths, vermin, and evil spirits. A sprig under the bed induced sound sleep and protected from harm and nightmare. The Romans used rosemary to crown the heads of their guests and of their household gods. Some say this herb will thrive only for the righteous or where the woman rules the household. In the Netherlands it is called elf-leaf, and is a favorite haunt of these little people. Christian legend says that the rosemary opened up to give Mary and the infant Jesus shelter from Herod's soldiers on their flight into Egypt, hence its dull white flowers were given the blue color of the Virgin's mantle. Another Christian legend states that the shrub does not grow higher than Christ's height on earth, and that at the age of 33 it ceases to grow and increases only in breadth. This plant was probably introduced into England by the Romans, but it is also said to have come to England with Queen Philippa of Hainaut in the 14th century. In any event it has flourished there and is said to be more fragrant in England than in any other land. Making a box of rosemary wood and smelling it keeps one young; in Wales, cooking-spoons of the wood are believed to make everything more nutritious.

Because rosemary is a plant of remembrance, it is a sovereign remedy for all diseases of the brain and is strengthening to the mind in all forms. But its uses seem to have spread to the whole head, for besides the brain, a decoction of rosemary in wine is good for loss of speech, sore eyes, and to clear the complexion. The ashes or charcoal of rosemary wood were used in England to clean the teeth, and to this day it is used in preparations for the hair to prevent baldness. Culpeper recommends cigars rolled from the leaves to smoke for coughs and consumption. He also recommends the flowers with bread and salt the first thing in the morning to dispel wind, and a flower conserve to comfort the heart and prevent contagion. Bathing in rosemary water makes the old young again. The boiled leaves bound to the leg with linen cloths are good for gout. A tea brewed of the leaves is good for fevers, pains, and colds, and taken cold with an equal amount of wine it is excellent to restore lost appetite. A decoction of rosemary put into the beer barrel secretly was said to be a sure cure for drunkenness. See ST. AGNES EVE. [JWH]

round dances Dances in circular formation, open or closed. In an open round a line of dancers is guided by a leader in a circular path, which may meander and tie loops. In a closed round the head and tail of the line are joined. If these separate, the closed round may open into an arc or serpentine. Serpentine processions may wind through fields or streets, or confine themselves in a circular or oblong space. Closed circles focus on a central object, a pit, fire, altar, pole, scalp, shaman, group of musicians, or leading actor.

The circular dance is so universal, and has so many elaborations, that only a few examples can be cited.

Face center: Open—Mediterranean link dances, notably of Greece and Catalonia; Eastern Woodland Indian medicine rites (Iroquois Buffalo) and some social dances (Iroquois Robin dance). Closed—Tungus *ikanzyezyem,* Tamil *kummi,* Rumanian dances, French *branles,* Faroe Island rounds, Mexican *Concheros,* Plains and Sauk Indian Victory dances.

Face forward: Open—Provençal *farandoule,* Breton *gavottes;* Stomp Dances of Eastern Woodlands and westward; many Oriental ritual and social dances. Closed—many Renaissance court dances, as the *pavane;* Slavic couple rounds.

Sexes separate: Many American Indian rituals—men only (*voladores*), women only (*?ohgiwe*), men and women segregated in line (Indian animal dances).

Promiscuous order: Mediterranean link dances.

Couples: Slavic, French, British, Irish rounds; Mexico *sembradoras, mitote,* Argentine *pericón,* Sauk Indian social dances (Owl), Iroquois social dances (Fish).

Clockwise: Northwestern Europe.

Counterclockwise: Mediterranean rounds; Eastern Woodland Indians, Pueblo *tablita* dance, Aztec *mitote,* Tarahumara *rutuburi.*

Alternately either direction: Country Dances of the British Isles; Italy *douro douro;* Mexican *concheros.*

Simultaneously both ways in a hey: Maypole dances, *kolattam;* Spain and Latin America *baile de cintas* or *del cordón;* grand right and left in *quadrilles.*

Multiple circles can be concentric: *po'pete disue* of Crow Indians, Penobscot rounds, ancient Aztec, New Guinea, New Ireland dances.

Hand holds: Great variety, as the Faroe light and heavy hold, shoulder holds, hooked elbows of Greece, kerchiefs (Greece), or garlands (Aztecs).

Steps: Commonly a shuffle, especially in America. The *branle* step (double left, simple right) recurs in the Faroe rounds, and in reverse direction in the *hora* and *hasapikos* of Palestine and Greece, with complicated variants. These link dances offer the leader an opportunity for acrobatic turns, crouches, leaps, etc.

With the alternate arrangement in couples, the closed round develops into the *quadrille* by way of the *tambourin* and *branle carré,* or breaks up into the couple dance by way of couple rounds, as those of Czechoslovakia. The *branle gascon* condenses this development within one accelerating routine of circling in single file, then shuffling to the center and out, then pivoting by each couple, and finally a fast step-hop by individual couples. The Moravian *satečkova* (handkerchief) is a single-file progression, the *kanafasca* a quadrille. These Slavic dances use many different combinations of couple arrangements (see DANCE: FOLK AND PRIMITIVE).

Sometimes more complicated dances start off with a circle, sunwise in English sword dances, both ways in country dances and squares; or they may insert them,

as the Chichimec *rayados* and Abbots Bromley Horn dance. Irish rounds combine circles and other figures in a compact structure of opening, body, figures, and finish, similar to quadrille structure. Kentucky running sets combine four-hand reels with progression in a large circle.

Round dances probably represent the earliest form of communal ritual and in the simpler forms preserve this ritual function in many parts of the world. The open round is commonly associated with fertility rites, blessing of the fields, sowing and harvest festivals, and in its serpentine variants can be associated with the productive snake symbolism (see SNAKE DANCE). Many closed rounds still serve a coercive purpose of magical encircling, for invocation or propitiation, as did probably formerly also the dances that are now secular. The Maypole winding, associated with many springtime festivals, intensified its power by combining the double circle and serpentine around the sacred green bough.

All choreographic variants are important, especially the direction, which may be connected with the sun and moon. It is significant that nomadic and hunting tribes of the western United States prefer the sunwise circle, and the agricultural East, Southwest, and Mexico prefer the counterclockwise progression, also that Chippewa women dance against the sun, men with the sun. As there are exceptions, no positive conclusions can be drawn on the relation of the two directions, and their astronomical and cultural symbolism. A great deal of study must precede any explanation of the sunwise preference of western and northern Europe, and the counterclockwise circling of Slavic and Mediterranean peoples. See SERPENTINE; STOMP DANCES. [GPK]

Round Table of King Arthur The Norman poet Wace (1155) was the first to refer to the Round Table in extant literature, saying that the Bretons told many tales about it and that Arthur caused it to be made so that there would be no quarrels about precedence in the seating arrangements. The English poet Layamon (c. 1200) added a savage story of a fracas which broke out in Arthur's hall over the seating and which was quelled only when seven of the offending thanes were killed. Arthur condemned the originator to be dragged to a swamp to die and all his women folk to lose their noses. He then proceeded to Cornwall and had a round table made which had the marvelous property that it could accommodate 1600 knights so that the high should be equal with the low. Other accounts give the number of seats as 150, 50, or 13. We know that neither the Welsh nor the Irish ate at large tables of any shape, but according to *Bricriu's Feast,* an Irish saga of the 8th century, the royal couch of Conchobar was set up in a banqueting hall, with the couches of the twelve chief warriors of Ulster about him, and that in this same hall strife arose as to which warrior deserved the champion's portion. When this tradition reached the Bretons through the Welsh, they were doubtless struck by the fact that, according to pictorial art and the testimony of pilgrims returning from Jerusalem, the table of the Last Supper, at which Christ sat with his twelve apostles, was circular. Moreover, the Lord had rebuked the twelve on this occasion when they quarreled as to which of them should be accounted the greatest. Hence arose the legend that Arthur's table owed its shape to rivalry over precedence and that it was patterned after the table of the Last Supper. Originating, then, in the Irish custom of seating twelve chief warriors about the royal couch, the concept of the Round Table was developed by the Bretons and later by the French under the influence of Christian tradition. During the 13th and 14th centuries jousts and feastings called Round Tables and observing what were supposed to be the customs of Arthur's glorious days were held throughout Christendom in places as far apart as Acre, Prague, Saragossa, and Falkirk, and at Magdeburg and Tournai burghers imitated this knightly sport. In 1344 Edward III vowed to establish an order like Arthur's at a great Round Table feast at Windsor. The board which still hangs at Winchester castle was probably made for some unrecorded celebration of this sort, and was first decorated with the figure of Arthur and the names of 24 knights in 1486. [RSL]

Roy Bean Kentucky-born Texas judge in the 1880's: "All the law West of the Pecos," according to American frontier legend and ballad and the sign on his saloon. As the Southern Pacific Railroad advanced into Texas, Bean followed the construction camps as saloonkeeper. He was the railroad's answer to the proud slogan, "West of the Pecos there is no law." On Aug. 12, 1882 Roy Bean, then in his early fifties, was appointed justice of the peace. He held court in his saloon, the "Jersey Lilly" (his spelling), named for the famous Lily Langtry with whose picture he had fallen in love. He later succeeded in having the town officially named Langtry.

All his trials began with an invitation to "step up to the bar for a snort of poison" and usually ended with ". . . and I fine you $2 now get the hell out of here." Legend piled upon legend in regard to Roy Bean, pocketer of fines, enforcer of the law with two six-shooters, blustering, original, shrewd, acute, unscrupulous, avaricious, and sentimental! As coroner he fined all dead men the amounts found on their persons. Bruno, Bean's famous bear, who drank beer from a bottle with the best, was often appealed to to add his authority to that of his master's in the sobering of drunks and chastening of runaway husbands. It is said that Bean once married a young couple and later granted them a divorce "to correct the mistake." Probably the most famous of all Roy Bean stories is the one about his turning free the murderer of a Chinese laborer in 1884 because he could find nothing in the Texas lawbooks against murdering a Chinaman. This story has been told and retold with elaborations.

ruach In Jewish belief, the spirit; one of the three elements of the soul, together with *nefesh,* the vitalizing soul, and *neshamah,* the super-soul or that which gives holy character to a man. Ruach is the intermediary between the *nefesh,* which remains with the body, and the *neshamah,* which ascends to heaven, according to the *Zohar.* Ruach, as a spirit, is often conceived of as a *ruach ra'ah,* or evil spirit, one of the types of demon. According to Rashi, it is amorphous. In general, no distinction is made however among the various types of demons or of the different aspects of the soul. Several kinds of demonic ruach are mentioned, e.g. *ruach zelahta,* which causes headaches, *ruach tezarit,* which causes fever and insanity.

rubato-parlando An ancient manner of singing in dramatic recitative style with each syllable of the text sung to a true musical tone and continual rhythmic variation. It is characteristic of Hungarian and other eastern European folk music, and is found among ballad singers of the American Northeast. The last words of the song are frequently uttered in tones of speech to indicate the close. Compare TEMPO-GIUSTO.

Rübezahl The Turnip-Counter of German folklore (F465): a mountain and storm spirit identified with the Riesengebirge mountain range between Bohemia and Silesia. Rübezahl once abducted a beautiful princess; she wanted turnips (*Rüben*), so he planted a big field of turnips. In due time she wanted to know how many there were, and asked him to count (*zählen*) them. He began to count, and, as befalls so many dull-witted supernatural kidnappers, the princess escaped while he was counting. A. H. Krappe states, however, that the name Rübezahl is an unsolved etymological puzzle, and may not even be Germanic. See STUPID OGRE.

ruby A gem of the sun, generally the birthstone of December, under the influence of Capricorn, though it was formerly the stone of July. The Chaldeans assigned it to Mars and the Arabs to Taurus. The ruby of the Bible and the Koran was probably the carbuncle. The *Rig-Veda* says that he who worships Krishṇa with rubies will be reborn as a powerful emperor. The ruby was one of the stones of the Hindu *pañchratna* and *navaratna,* five and nine gem combinations; on the Kalpa tree the representations of ripe fruit are rubies. The Mohammedan angel who, like Atlas, bears the world on his shoulders, stands on a rock of ruby. A Burma legend tells of a dragon who laid three eggs. From one was born the king of Pagan, from the second, a Chinese emperor, and from the third came all the Burmese rubies. It has been said that the fire imprisoned within the ruby would shine through clothing or whatever was wrapped around it, and that if it were thrown into the water, the water would boil. In Brazil, lawyers wear rubies as a professional badge. Like most stones, it announces impending disaster by becoming cloudy, but regains its luster after the event. Sir John de Mandeville says the owner of a fine ruby will live at peace with the world, secure in his rank, and protected from all perils. This is in accord with Hindu tradition, for the possessor of such a stone could dwell without fear in the midst of his enemies. It also guards his house and property from damage by tempests. In his *Travels,* Sir John Horsey, messenger from Elizabeth to Ivan the Terrible of Russia, quotes Ivan, shortly before his death in 1584, on the virtues of the ruby: "Oh! this is the most comfortable to the hart, braine, vigar and memorie of man, clarifies the congelled and corrupt bluod." Because of its color it was in wide repute to stop hemorrhages, cure inflammatory diseases, remove evil thoughts, banish sadness, dispel nightmare, dissolve anger and discord, protect from plague, control amorous desires, and make a man invulnerable to sword, spear, or gun; in Burma this last required that the ruby be inserted in the flesh. In the Orient the star ruby was particularly lucky because a good spirit was said to dwell within the stone. The Balas ruby, sometimes called the oriental ruby, was the one most often used in medieval times. In India rubies are powdered and taken in a solution to dispel fear and excite joyous emotions. See CARBUNCLE; CARNELIAN.

Rudra In Vedic mythology, the god of storms who controls the cyclone and inflicts diseases (which he also heals): literally, the howler. Rudra is identified with the god of fire as a destroying agent. He was the father of the Maruts or Rudras, usually eleven in number, and in addition to them he is surrounded by troops of inferior beings. According to the *Purāṇas*, he sprang from the forehead of Brahmā and then separated himself into eleven beings, or he came into existence as a youth and begged Brahmā for a name. Brahmā named him Rudra, but he was dissatisfied until he had seven other names— Bhava, Bhīma, Īsāna, Mahādeva, Paśupati, Śarva, and Ugra. These names are sometimes used for seven manifestations of, or the sons of, Rudra as well as for Rudra and his successor, Śiva.

In the *Rig-Veda* Rudra has no distinct cosmic function but is regarded as a maleficent deity, the bringer of disease and death. He was also identified with the mountain spirits of India's hill tribes, and is therefore intimately connected with the mountains. He is described as the "ruddy boar of heaven" and is armed either with bow and arrows or with thunderbolt and lightning. His animal is the mole, his home the crossroads. He is the malignant deity of the Vedas, but also the healer and physician; and the epithet Śiva, meaning auspicious, is applied to him in this character. This name grows more and more frequent until it became his post-Vedic name. As it was applied, the character of the god grew more repulsive, making the transition to the Rudra-Śiva of the Brahmanical period and then to the malevolent Śiva of Hindu mythology. In the character of healer, Rudra's chief remedial substance was cow-urine.

rue This is said to be an herb of the sun under dominion of Leo, symbolic of bitterness, grief, and repentance, later of pity and forgiveness. It is also called Herb of Grace and while it was used to sprinkle holy water or in exorcising the Devil and evil spirits, and it is still thought to be a potent charm against evil eye, especially in Italy, at the same time because it is a bitter, poisonous, and mildly narcotic herb, it is a necessity in almost all witch-brews, charms, and spells. Pliny said weasels eat rue to make themselves immune to poisonous snakes. Dioscorides says that the seed is a cure for all poisons; Gerard says that anointing with the juice protects one against venomous bites and the poison from mushrooms, toadstools, and wolfbane. Rue was also proof against contagion and vermin, and was used as a strewing herb in English law courts for this purpose. A bush of rue was often tended as a chastity test of an absent lover; in the 16th century it was recommended to preserve chastity (i.e. it should be eaten when one was tempted). The Romans used wreaths of parsley and rue to protect from evil spirits. In order to make sure that your shot would hit its mark your flints should be boiled in rue and vervain.

Rue has been in high repute in scientific medicine since early times when Pliny recommended it against all poisonous bites, down to the present day when an element isolated from the herb is used for relieving tension in the blood vessels causing high blood pressure. The fact that it is still widely used in folk medicine is attested by its presence in most herb gardens in spite of the fact that it is too strong to be useful as a culinary herb. Anglo-Saxon herbals at the beginning of the 14th century called it a cure-all and Culpeper is not much behind them in his recommendations. Its present uses are mainly confined to nervous disorders and female complaints, however. The Meskwaki Indians of the United States use the meadow rue (genus *Thalictrum*) in a love medicine to bring together estranged husbands and wives. See BASIL.

rumba A ballroom dance brought to the United States from Cuba about 1925. The step resembles a sinuous, subtle, and stationary two-step. The apparent hip-sway is caused by transference of weight from one foot to the other. As danced on the ballroom floors and in the night clubs of the United States and Mexico, it is a diluted, bloodless, self-conscious exhibition. In the West Indies, where it grew out of the mixture of Negro and Spanish blood, it can, especially in rural sections, transport the dancers into an erotic frenzy, beautiful because functional. Originally it was a marriage dance, depicting simple farm tasks: the shoeing of a mare, the climbing of a rope, courtship in the barnyard, etc. But the mime is subsidiary to the interplay of male and female. In Cuba it is also popular as an exhibition dance, both in the country and in fashionable centers, and as such ranges from sensuous undulations to acrobatic performances. [GPK]

Rumpelstiltskin or **Rumpelstiltzchen** Title of a German folktale (Grimm #55, Type 500) known throughout Europe under various titles. Rumpelstiltskin (Tom-Tit-Tot in England, Titeliture, Ricdin-Ricdon, Dancing Vargaluska, etc., on the Continent) is a dwarf who appears to the maiden, married to the prince because her mother boasted either that she could spin flax into gold or could spin impossible amounts into thread. Naturally, she cannot accomplish the task set her, but the dwarf does her work on the promise that she will give him her child when it is born. When the dwarf comes to take the child, she pleads with him; he insists on the bargain; at last he gives her three days in which to guess his name; if she can discover his name she may keep the child. One of the messengers she sends out to collect names which *might* be the dwarf's overhears the dwarf dancing in the forest and repeating a rime that includes his name (N475). The girl tells the dwarf his name, and Rumpelstiltskin is so angry that he stamps his foot into the ground and tears himself in two trying to free the foot.

This story is known all over Europe, to some extent in Russia, but not at all elsewhere in the world except where European influence has taken it. It was studied (along with *The Three Old Women*—Type 501) by C. W. von Sydow in his *Två Spinnsagor*. His conclusion, that it originated in Sweden, he later changed; it seems to be a tale from the British Isles that traveled to the Continent. Earlier studies of the type were made by Edward Clodd and Georg Polívka. A very similar legend is told of the building of churches in Iceland, Sweden, and Germany; the supernatural builder goes off when his name is guessed (F381.1) and leaves part of the building unfinished. No connection between this legend and the Rumpelstiltskin story has been traced, however. See GIRLE GUAIRLE; NAME TABU.

rune or **runo** The technical term for Finnish folk poetry in the ancient meter. In the books of the 17th century the word *runo[i]* was used to mean "poet" and in the folk songs the word has had the meaning "singer" until today. A runo, as a song or poem, is tne work of educated people, but early adapted by the Finns and folklorists everywhere. (See K. Krohn in *FUF* IV, 1904, pp. 79–90.) [JB]

rutuburi A communal ritual dance of the Tarahumara Indians of Chihuahua, Mexico. Tradition derives it from the turkey. It takes place all night on a special dancing patio with three crosses facing to the east. The ceremony starts with the sacrifice of an animal and the dedication and serving of ceremonial food and the sacramental intoxicant, *tesguino*, three times toward each of the cardinal directions. Three shamans face the crosses. The central one, the chanter (*saweame*), vibrates, then rhythmically shakes his rattle (*sawala*) while he sings, during the wet season to the rabbit, during the winter to the giant woodpecker, during harvest to the blackbird. Three times the shamans pace back and forth across the patio in front of the crosses.

Formerly men lined up separately from women for the actual dance. Today only women cross the patio six times. Then they circle in a counterclockwise direction, holding hands and leaping with a stamp from the left to the right foot. This continues for hours, till shortly before sunrise, when *yumari* is danced. Today the two dances are amalgamated.

Primarily the rutuburi is a rain dance and a thanksgiving for harvest, an invocation to the sun and moon. It is also danced at the curing of fields, animals, and people, and at death and memorial ceremonies. [GPK]

S

sabā-leippyā In the belief of the Taungthūs, Taungyōs, and the Sawngtung Karens of Burma, the paddy butterfly of the spirit of tilth. When the Karens sell paddy they retain a handful from each container so as not to lose the sabā-leippyā. This spirit is worshipped by sprinkling liquor over the jungle area being cleared by fire.

Sabazius A chthonic god of the Phrygians or Thracians, sometimes identified with Dionysus; he may be identical with the Biblical Sabaoth, and worship was, in Rome, connected with the settling there of Jews in the 2d century A.D. According to Plutarch, the Sabbath was originally the festival of Sabazius. The name perhaps has some connection with the Illyrian words for beer or health. He was a god of agricultural increase and of regrowth. One of the ceremonies connected with his cult, perhaps symbolizing the reacceptance of the god through his symbol and recognized as an adoption rite, was the passing of a golden serpent under the clothes of the initiates, across the breast, and down between the legs. Votive hands have been found decorated with the symbols of the cult of Sabazius. As Zeus or Jupiter Sabazius, his attributes were the eagle and the thunderbolt: this despite his chthonian origin.

Sabbat The witches' sabbath; the great gathering of witches and sorcerers said, in the Middle Ages and Renaissance, to take place regularly under the presidency of the Devil. On Walpurgis Night (May Day Eve) at least, usually on the quarter day eves (Candlemas Eve —Feb. 1; May Day Eve; Lammas Eve—July 31; All Hallows Eve or Halloween—Oct. 31), and sometimes on Good Friday, Midsummer Eve, or other days, the various covens were believed to congregate in some open place, often a mountain-top or a crossroads (compare WILD HUNT) to perform their black rites and reaffirm their subservience to the demon Master. In preparation for the meeting they anointed themselves with oil made from the fat and marrow of murdered babies. Then, carried by demons in the form of goats or asses, while other demons took their places at home, or riding through the air on the handles of their brooms, rakes, or distaffs, they traveled to the meeting-place. At the meeting the great Master, sometimes in the form of a goat or other animal, recited their service—a parody of the Mass —which was followed by a discussion of evil deeds to be done until the next Sabbat. Novices were accepted: they swore fealty to the Master while placing one hand on the head and holding the sole of the foot with the other; they were baptized with a new name and pinched by an imp to make a blue mark that never disappeared. In return for their oaths, the initiates received the promise of help and protection from the Master and from the other witches and were given a familiar of their own. The company might then have to reaffirm obedience to the Goat by kissing his buttocks, which were said to be masked like a face. All then sat down to a feast of stolen food and followed this with a round dance with their backs to the center of the circle. The dance grew wilder until the Devil selected one of the women of the company as his mate of the evening. The dance broke up into couples, and a sexual orgy lasting until dawn finished the Sabbat. Though some authorities believe stories of the Sabbat to be perverted reports of the meetings of heretical sects (e.g. of the Cathari), the whole apparatus of the meeting indicates strongly a survival of some pagan fertility cult. The leader in the form of a goat having intercourse with a cult member (the sacred marriage of the god and the priestess in the open field), the anointing of the cultists' bodies, the phallic broomstick ride, the masking, the round dance, all are familiar fertility symbols.

Sa-bdag The Tibetan local spirits or "earth movers" who inhabit the soil, springs, lakes, and houses. The image of the local Sa-bdag is placed within the outer gateway of the local temple or monastery and is worshipped with offerings of wine and bloody sacrifices.

Saci A woodland spirit of trickster-like character in Brazilian Negro folklore and African-derived religious beliefs. Though clearly belonging to the African character of "little people" of the forest found among many African tribes, the precise provenience of the Brazilian name for this type of being has not been ascertained. See AZIZA; MMOATIA. [MJH]

sacred animal Sacred animals are of two sorts: those associated with divinities as attributes of the god, and those which in themselves have acquired sacredness. Folklorists, impressed for a time by theories of totemism, were inclined to attribute both sorts to forgotten or at best obscure totemic ancestor cults. Others have preferred a theriolatric explanation which involved the hypothesis that men at one time worshipped animals. The theologies involved by these attributions were alive —if they ever were alive before they sprang from the heads of the folklorists—a very long time ago, and, now that we know something about the complexities of ancient cultures, are very difficult to prove. Animals represented as attributes of the gods are usually associated with them in their myths, as being specially favored by them or as having been a form into which the god shifted. The bull is associated with Zeus in the rape of Europa, though the association is probably much older than that seductive tale. The bear and the cow are sacred to Hera as doves are to Aphrodite. The list might be greatly enlarged. See BEAR; CATS; other specific animal entries. Whether or not they are attributes of the gods, they may be further divided into chthonian animals or animals of the underworld, and Olympian animals or animals of the air and sky. The chthonian sacred animals are those living in the earth, in dens and naturally about graveyards. Partly in consequence of this association these animals are thought of as spirits of the dead, messengers of the gods of the underworld, or attributes of these gods.

In India the cow is sacred and wanders unmolested through the streets and into the shops. The bull is one of the attributes of Śiva. In eastern Bengal the cow is given special honors at least twice a year. Considerable evidence has been gathered to indicate that the horse was once a sacred animal and some writers have explained the Aryan reluctance to eat horse meat as a racial memory. The owl, attribute of Athena, is, like the raven, a bird of the dead. Crocodiles in Egypt are sacred because they live in the sacred river. The "mormyrus," sacred fish of the Nile, is the incarnation of the Egyptian god Set. In India, too, the monkey god. Hanuman, is an important figure. Monkeys are kept from harm in the villages. Twins in West Africa have tutelary spirits in the form of small monkeys. The monkeys of Gibraltar are traditionally protected from harm. [RDJ]

sacred prostitution The question of sacred or temple prostitution has been given more importance by the folklorists of the Euro-American tradition than it probably deserves. If the fact that human beings are normally in a state of tumescence or subtumescence is accepted as a postulate, the relief of that condition in temples when ritual, music, procession, and dance produce a state of emotional elevation can be understood. Women attached to the temples are usually referred to as the servants of the god, the brides of the god. Inasmuch as religious ceremonies among many peoples are solemn and holy festivals, it is fitting that as the god, represented by an image, is unable to avail himself of the pleasures prepared for him, his representatives, the

priests, or strangers who have a quality of sacredness should do so. This was particularly appropriate in the temples of the Babylonian Ishtar, a goddess whose lasciviousness is reported by unenlightened travelers to have been remarkable.

In the Central Provinces of India dancing girls were initiated after a bargain had been made by their parents. They were dressed as brides, married to a dagger, and walked several times around a central post. In Hyderabad Hindu girls were married to Śiva and Kṛishṇa and were called "servants"; Mohammedan girls also were married to a dagger. The training was sometimes elaborate. In the Southern Provinces large numbers of women, initiated by symbolic marriage, were attached to the temples. Their duties, to dance before the gods on festivals, were generally prostitution, not of necessity confined to the temple grounds.

Among the Ewe-speaking peoples of the Slave Coast, Africa, girls between the ages of ten and twelve were trained in the temples and served priests and seminarists. Temple prostitution was customary in Syria and matrons were expected to, or perhaps, permitted to, serve in this capacity. The report there of male prostitutes to serve either men or women is an expansion of the general theme.

Although the rule is not universal, temple prostitutes (Babylonia and Syria) were required to accept without protest any gift their clients offered. Usually these gifts were personal gain and, if the women serving were townsfolk and unmarried, were used to build up the marriage portion. The steps whereby matrons persuaded their husbands that they might enjoy complete license at certain times in the year, whether as temple prostitutes or in orgiastic women's festivals, must be examined in relation to the special sexual mores of the several communities. Fragmentary reports are available from all parts of the world. The custom was clearly useful in reducing tensions and strains peculiar to societies in which action is controlled by rigid prohibitions.

The close association between religious and sexual exaltation has suggested to some scholars that "the religious impulse is *really* sexual," etc. See PHALLISM. Other students, impressed by the superstitions attached to purification, menstruation, blood, virginity, have given reason to conclude that virginity should be sacrificed to the god, or that fornication with a god or his priestly or human representative is more commendable than fornication under other conditions. Any act, particularly any act which is highly charged with emotion is a transition from one state of being to another and therefore dangerous and is to be surrounded by sanctions. [RDJ]

sacred thread A ceremony ritualized in India where investiture with the thread symbolizes entrance into rights and privileges. The ceremonies are complex and the rights are varied with the several castes and cults. Like so many folk ceremonies, the investiture with the sacred thread (*upanyana*) not only initiates the novice into the rites and ceremonies of his ethnic group but binds him more closely to the group itself. In this sense it has associations with the domocentric folklore of the umbilical cord, and with the thread used as a guide in the labyrinth or guide to the shapeshifted lover. [RDJ]

The sacred thread is conferred upon a Hindu boy of the Brāhman, Kshatriya, and Vaisya castes as the most important ceremony in a Hindu's life, and is the mark, which must always be worn, of these castes. The thread, made of cotton and white for Brāhmans, red for Kshatriyas, yellow for Vaisyas, is in length 96 times the breadth of the four fingers of a man. This measure is used because each of the fingers represents one of the four states he will experience—waking, dreaming, dreamless sleep, and the state of Absolute Brahmā. The cord is threefold, representing reality, passion, and darkness, or the three qualities of the body, and it is twisted three times so that darkness cannot gain the ascendancy. The whole cord is knotted with a triple knot representing Brahmā, Śiva, and Vishnu.

It is presented to a Brāhman boy when he is eight, to a Kshatriya at eleven, and to a Vaisya at twelve. The ceremony originally lasted three days but in modern India is usually restricted to one day. The boy must spend a night in silence after which he eats with his mother for the last time, is shaved and washed, and then faces the sun holding the thread while his *guru* (teacher) repeats a mantra. When the prayer is concluded the boy slips the thread over his head so that it lies on his left shoulder and falls on the right side. He is then taught the *gāyatrī*, the most sacred of the mantras. This learned, the initiate offers nine pieces of wood dipped in clarified butter to the fire while addressing Agni, Sarasvatī, and the Sun. He is then "twice-born" and ceremonially pure. His duties now include the performance of the Sankhyā or evening worship. He can carry an umbrella, look in a mirror, and wear shoes, but he must not play or sing, walk the streets in the evening, spit toward the sun, speak unworthily, or make fun of women. He can never dine with women and must sleep in the men's section of the house. For a full account of this ceremony see S. Stevenson, *Rites of the Twice-Born*, London, 1920, pp. 27–45.

Kustī, (*kōstī kushtī*) is the sacred thread with which every Zoroastrian boy or girl is invested when he or she can recite the "Four Avestas," i.e. the *Srōsh Bāj* (prayer to the angel Sraosha), the *Kushtī-bastan* (tying the thread), the *Pa Nām-i stāyishn* (in the name of praise), and the *Birasād* (may it come).

The kustī is a string about the size of a corset-lace, having six strands, each made up of 12 very fine white goat- or camel-hair threads twisted together. Near each end the six strands are braided together and in the last inch they are braided into three string ends, each containing 24 threads. When the two ends are knotted together the resulting six strings are a reminder of the six seasonal festivals (*Gāhanbārs*). The 72 threads symbolize the 72 chapters of the *Yasna*.

The kustī is usually presented with the *sudra* (sacred shirt) to Parsi children when they are 12 to 15 years old by a priest who is invited to the house. The kustī is a badge of the faithful, uniting the initiate to Ahura Mazda. The presentation and acknowledgment of this union is an occasion for a feast and a gay social gathering. Among some sects, however, the kustī is either put on at home without formality, or the youth goes to the home of the person who has taught him the four Avestan formulas and puts on the cord in his presence. This is followed by the presentation of a gift of sugar loaf to the preceptor. The kustī is always worn there-

after except at night. It can be washed when soiled. Those who do not wear the symbol are refused bread and water by the devout. [SPH]

sacrifice In the ritual sense, the consecration of an offering to a supernatural being or ancestral spirit, in placation, petition, or thanksgiving. Offerings may take the form of incense, flowers, vegetable food, drink, animals, or human beings, sometimes practical objects, or money. The offering may be tendered by an individual, by a representative for the community, or by communal participation and communion. Burnt offerings may take the form of the preliminary tobacco offerings in the American Indian calumet dances, the Hako, and generally in seasonal and curative rites; or of the incense or lighted candles placed at the altars during Catholic and Catholic-pagan rituals of Europe and the New World, and even more anciently in the Orient.

Food is placed on the fire during Bella Coola Indian *kusiut* ceremonies to please the ghosts of the deceased and supernaturals such as Tlitcäplitäna, the supernatural woman curer. Special cakes are baked for the dead and consumed by the Iroquois in the *Ɂohgiwe* (related to the former Huron feast for the dead), and by Mexicans in the form of *panes de muertos* during the Feast for the Dead (Halloween). The Iroquois elevation of the cakes after the *Ɂohgiwe* resembles the pillaging of the *ichas* at the *sumamao*, though the latter is mingled with Christian symbolism.

All corn and harvest rites offer first-fruits in thanksgiving. Both incense and foods are dedicated by the priest during the rain and harvest ceremonies of the Tarahumara and Maya Indians, as well as at death feasts. The Tarahumara *rutuburi* is consecrated by dedications to the cross and cardinal directions, of tortillas, gourd bowls of stew, and *tesgüino*, the sacramental intoxicant. Portions are subsequently spilled or buried. The Maya of Chan Kom differentiate between foods for Christian and for pagan gods. For the Christian gods, e.g. St. Michael, St. Gabriel, etc., the women prepare *atole* and cooked meat like ordinary food, with the addition of special cakes, thick tortillas of maize meal and honey; for the *yuntzilob* and *chacs*, the ancient spirits and rain deities, special breads of maize meal (*zacan*) are wrapped in palm leaves and cooked in an earth oven, and the *noh-uah* and *yal-uah* breads are prepared by the *h-men* or shaman. *Sopas*, stews, consist of the meat of wild animals or consecrated domestic animals. These foods placate the gods of the fields before the burning of the bush to the number of seven dishes of *zaca*, to the number of 13 at the *okotbatam*. At the rain ceremony 13 vessels of the sacred drink (*balche*) consecrate the altar, the food offerings, and the participants.

Small animals or fowl are commonly sacrificed in Mexico, as turkeys by the Western Mixtec of Oaxaca and hens by the Otomí preliminary to the *volador*, hens or goats by the Tarahumara. North American Indian ritual food used to consist largely of dog meat; nowadays it is unsalted beef or venison. Animal sacrifice usually culminates in the sprinkling of the ground with the blood, which is imbued with life-giving properties. *Ianyi* is dispersed with the blood of roosters torn asunder in the rooster-pulls by the Santa Ana *Santiagos* on the Rio Grande. The Huichol shaman sprinkles the blood of a hen on the ground.

Wholesale slaughter of animals has a similar motif in southern India, e.g. the buffalo sacrifices at the Malayalam devil dances, and the Madiga festivals for the goddess Mahalashari and other deities. On the contrary, the shedding of blood may be tabu, as in the strangling of the white dog (formerly part of the Iroquois Midwinter festivals) and the strangling of a tame reindeer by the reindeer nomads of Siberia, for marriages, funerals, the Samoyed sun festival at Avamsk, etc. For a blood sacrifice the Yurak subsequently cut the throat.

A similar belief in sympathetic magic, of feeding the gods and conjuring rain, condones the gruesome practices of human sacrifice which are largely now a thing of the past. In their Mariah sacrifice the Khonds of southern India impaled their victim on a post or cut pieces of flesh from his back to fertilize the ground. The ancient Aztecs tore out the heart for Huitzilopochtli and for Xipe Totec, flayed the victim so the skin could be worn by the priest impersonator of the deity —a symbol of reincarnation. The tales of the dismembering of Dionysus, the twice-born, by frenzied Mænads, and of the death and resurrection of Osiris, point to similar rituals in ancient Greece and Egypt. It appears that in all cases the victim is deified and stupefied by intoxicants.

The noblest form of sacrifice, and the most misunderstood, is the voluntary offering of the celebrant's own body: the self-torture in the Plains Indian sun dance, of the *penitentes* and *arrieros*, scarification at initiations into sacred societies or into puberty, and the ancient Aztec ritual bleeding with cactus thorns.

At the other end of the scale are the substitutions in degenerate modern ceremonies, the gifts of brandy, cigarettes, cloth, money, skyrockets, for instance, during the Maya *okoztah-pol*, the Menominee-Chippewa drum dance, and the Iroquois *ganegwa'e* and *wasase*. These gifts are mutual between hosts and guests, and are also dedicated to the central ceremonial object, as the drum.

Sometimes the ceremonial consists of chants and prayers of thanksgiving, as commonly among the Maya. Usually a dance follows, as the *rutuburi* and *omigiwen,* or it is integrated, as in the Iroquois *ganegwa'e* and *nyagwai'oenǫ,* and the Maya *okoztah-pol.* In many of these integrated dances the motif of sacrifice has become vestigial, as in the sword dances of northern Europe and Spain, with their climactic symbolic decapitation (*degollada*) by a sword lock. The various forms of *Moriscas* retain elements of sacrifice and rebirth, some with transformed ritual content, others as secular play. [GPK]

☞ The presentation of valued or holy objects and materials to deities and spirits, to induce or compel these latter to bestow their favors on the giver of such objects, is a common practice among North American Indians. Individual men and women were constantly offering sacrifices to spirits, ghosts, deities, plants, and so forth; these consisted of bits of food thrown into the fire, pollen and down offerings, beads, pinches of tobacco, among other things. A man or woman digging plants to be used as medicine in the eastern United States always left tobacco at the spot, in payment—if not, the cure would not be efficacious. Groups also sacrificed together; probably the two best known such group sacrifices are the Seneca (Iroquois) White Dog ceremony, and the Morning Star ceremony, in which a female captive was sacrificed, of the Skidi Pawnee.

Among the most prominent beings to whom sacrifices are offered are: the sky, earth, sun, moon, the cardinal points, the winds, thunder, the mountains, rocks, especially peculiar shaped ones, animals and trees, springs and eddies, lake and river and ocean-dwelling monsters. Materials used for sacrifice were tobacco (of paramount importance everywhere except among tribes in the northern third of the continent), food, clothing and adornment; these were the most widely used sacrifices. Implements were used less often; dogs, especially white ones, by a limited number of tribes (Iroquois, Cree, Ottawa, Illinois, Arikara, Skidi Pawnee). Buffalo skins, buffalo offal, bear skins and skulls, deer, elk, and moose hoofs, feathers of many varieties, and down, especially eagle down, were widely used as offerings. Corn, in the form of meal, is much used as an offering by agricultural groups, also corn pollen. Bits of the human body were also sometimes offered, the joint of a finger being a common sacrifice among several Plains tribes. In some instances, war prisoners were sacrificed; sometimes the bodies of these were later eaten. For an extended discussion of sacrifices among the American Indian see John R. Swanton's article on "Sacrifice" (*BBAE* 30, pt. 2, pp. 402–407). [EWV]

☞ Sacrifices of human beings, animals, and goods were widely practiced in the area of the ancient Andean civilizations. No ceremony, private or public, was performed without a bloody sacrifice and offerings. The Chibcha kept children in the temples and killed them when they reached puberty. Sacrifices of war prisoners by ablation of the heart was a characteristic feature of the religion of the Indians of the Cauca valley. The Inca also sacrificed children and women in honor of their gods but not on a scale comparable to that of the Aztecs.

Llamas and guinea pigs were the animals most commonly offered to the gods in ancient and modern Peru. The Araucanian and Patagonian Indians strangled mares at funerals to appease the ghosts and when danger was lurking to placate the spirits. The Peruvians also sacrificed animals for divinatory purposes in order to read the future in their entrails. The choice of the animals to be offered to the god was determined by very strict rules. [AM]

☞ In all of Africa, the concept of "feeding" gods, ancestors, charms, and all manner of beings or objects associated with the supernatural powers is basic for any comprehension of the nature of sacrifices and the act of sacrificing. Because of the closeness of the supernatural to the everyday world, its beings are thought of and approached much in the manner in which human beings are thought of and acted toward. Therefore, just as human beings become weak and irritable, lose power, and feel frustrated, thus perhaps becoming dangerous if they do not receive sustenance, so supernatural beings must be properly provided with the food they need if they are to function as aids to men, and are not to turn on those to whom they look for provision of their needs. It is against this concept that the wealth of ritual observances involving offerings of various sorts must be projected.

Certain special kinds of offerings may be noted. Human sacrifice, where it was practiced, was not done to feed a supernatural being, but was rather a means of sending a messenger to a royal ancestor or, in the case of a newly-dead ruler, providing him with a ghostly entourage worthy of his position. Many different kinds of animals are offered to gods and ancestors—bullocks, sheep, goats, and, among the smaller forms, chickens, guinea fowl, and the like. Other sacrifices were of vegetables—millet, beans, maize, among others—while charms are "fed" by being sprayed with rum or by allowing the blood of a chicken to flow over them. In most cases, the "food" of the supernatural being consists of those portions of the animal not consumed by humans; the meat is ordinarily cooked and consumed by those concerned with the rites, at stated times in the rituals where the offerings have been made. [MJH]

sadhu A general term for a Hindu ascetic or mendicant holy man; often also a religious teacher, teller of parables, etc. The feminine *sādhvī* is used for a woman ascetic. The sādhu carries a begging bowl, a water pot, a staff, a rosary, and an *Oghi* or brush from which he must never part. Sādhus belong to various sects but the greater number are Śaivites. Śiva is the god who practiced austerities and became the patron god of ascetics. Followers of Vishṇu generally practice abstinence from certain foods and drink and sometimes follow the rules of *yoga,* but they rarely emulate the self-torture which characterizes the life of Śaivite sādhus. The latter have attracted attention by such austerities as lying on a spike-bed (practiced in imitation of the fate of Bhīshma, leader of the Kauravas in the *Mahābhārata,* who was pierced by so many arrows that his body did not touch the ground and he was thus supported for 48 days and nights before his death), taking difficult postures and holding them until a part of the body becomes stiff and atrophied, prolonged fasting, sticking knives or skewers into the flesh, treading on beds of live coals, or being buried alive.

The sādhu is recognized by his dress—ordinarily a salmon-colored robe, although some sādhus are practically naked. He rubs ashes on his body as a defense against insects or demons, and uses colored earth to mark the *tilaka,* symbol of his sect or of the god whom he is serving, on his forehead. His hair is long and matted, coiled on top of the head, or entirely shaved off. He sleeps on the ground and collects food and alms twice daily, taking care to approach a house only after the regular mealtime has passed. At death the sādhu's body is not burned but is buried in a sitting posture since the ascetic is really in a trance and may revive at his pleasure.

saffron The dried orange-colored stigmas of the autumn crocus (*Crocus sativum*) used for their flavor, fragrance, and color for thousands of years in the Old World. Saffron was valued by the ancient Hebrews (see *Song of Solomon* iv, 14). In the Orient and the Middle East, and especially in Greece, it was much cherished for its bright yellow color. It was sprinkled in Greek theaters, courts, and rooms as a scent and deodorant; in Rome it was used to perfume the giant baths and to sprinkle the streets.

In India and Greece saffron was considered a strong aphrodisiac. The *Arabian Nights* mentions saffron as an aphrodisiac so powerful as to cause women to swoon; its perfume is also listed as one of the two things which "corrupt women" (the other being gold). The Arabs also believe that saffron kept in the house will drive away

a certain dreaded lizard; and they also use it to dispel melancholy.

Through the Arabs saffron was introduced into Europe; from them the French learned its medical value, i.e. that it cured gout and rheumatism. Hakluyt states that a bulb of the plant, hidden in a hollow stick, was brought to England from the Holy Land in the reign of Edward III by a pilgrim. According to the English herbalist Gerard, saffron "quickens the senses, makes merry, shakes off drowsiness"; but too much of it affects the brain.

In the 15th century saffron was carried by German peasants to ward off plague, and in Switzerland it was tied about children's necks to prevent disease. In Westphalia apple juice and saffron were given for jaundice (probably the doctrine of signatures, i.e. yellow cures yellow). Southern Germans valued it so highly that people in Nuremberg were sentenced to death for adulterating it. A similar value was put upon it in rural England, where saffron was often used as a standard to denote something unusually rare and expensive. In Ireland the crocus plant (*cróc,* crocus) is used by women in washing their sheets so that their arms and legs will be strengthened during sleep.

In Ku-lin (China) the people rub saffron on their bodies after bathing to make them resemble the gold body of a Buddha; Annamese mothers use saffron powder on the bodies of their babies as a tonic for the skin. Magic properties are ascribed to it in Persia; pregnant women wear a ball of it at the pit of the stomach to ensure speedy delivery and expulsion of the afterbirth. Saffron water is drunk in Persia also because of its magical virtues; in India it is used to write *mantras.*

Saffron tea is a general folk remedy for measles throughout the rural United States, and is also used as a mouth wash for babies with thrush.

Meadow saffron (*Colchicum autumnale*) is said to have sprung from the witch-brews of Jason and Medea; its root is poisonous but cow's milk is an antidote. In rural England its flowers are called "naked ladies" from the fact that its leaves disappear so early.

sage This famous herb of Zeus (Jupiter) was used in Greece and Rome from early times for the seasoning of rich meats. At one time the Chinese drank sage tea as a beverage and before the importation of China tea at the beginning of the 17th century it was drunk as a beverage in England and throughout Europe. Now it is used as a tonic tea in the spring and fall. Pepys mentions a churchyard near Southampton England where the graves were planted with sage. Culpeper thought it good for the liver, helping it to "breed" blood; he recommended it also for the headache which announces the coming of a cold. Seven sage leaves, eaten fasting, for seven mornings was an old Sussex remedy for ague. It has long been held to promote longevity and to strengthen the brain as well as the muscles. It was also used for epilepsy, palsies, fevers, and laryngitis. Sage vinegar was once used as protection from the plague but is now usually used as a gargle or to whiten the teeth. In Texas the tea is used for rheumatism, among the Iroquois Indians for colics, colds, and for stiff joints. The Jicarilla Apache call the plant "ghost medicine" and brush the patient with it to shoo away bad dreams and nightmare. In the rural sections of the United States sage leaves are often used to keep away ants. Georgia Negroes say that the names of the twelve Apostles written on sage leaves and worn in the shoes during a lawsuit will insure a favorable verdict.

Sagittarius A constellation, ninth sign of the zodiac, between Scorpio and Capricorn. From early times in Mesopotamia it has been recognized as an archer; it seems to have been identified with the Babylonian Nergal, their war god. The Greeks kept the bow-and-arrow-shooting mounted man and made a Centaur of it, but distinguished it from the non-zodiacal Centaurus. Where Centaurus represented Chiron the good, Sagittarius was a wild Centaur, modeled perhaps after the wild man of the Babylonian Gilgamesh epic, Eabani. According to legend, Chiron himself described Sagittarius to the Argonauts to guide them in their quest for the Golden Fleece. In India, the constellation was one of the Aśvins. It is the Persian Kamān, the Turkish Yai, the Hebrew Keshet—all meaning bow. It was identified with Joash (see II *Kings* xiii, 14–19), Ishmael, St. Matthew. The symbol of the constellation is an arrow with part of the bow across its shaft.

Saint Brigit or **Bride** (pronounced *breed*) (453–523) One of the three patron saints of Ireland (with Patrick and Columcille): also called the Mary of the Gael. She was born near Dundalk in County Louth, daughter of a local chieftain, Dubtać, and his bondwoman. Dubtać sold mother and child to a druid in the north, who on becoming a Christian gave Brigit her freedom, and she returned to her father's house. There she took the role of serving girl, as her mother had before her; she minded the dairy and milked the cows and filled the butter tubs; "she bettered the sheep and she satisfied the birds and she fed the poor." She wove the first piece of cloth in Ireland and for this reason her day (February 1) is a feast day for weavers and spinners. One night with a noble guest in the house Brigit threw to a lean, hungry hound the five pieces of bacon she was cooking for dinner, but when the meal was served no bacon was missing. The things Brigit wished for have delighted the world for centuries: ". . . a great lake of ale for the King of Kings; . . . the family of heaven to be drinking it through all time; . . . cheerfulness to be in their drinking; . . . Jesus to be here among them; . . . vessels full of alms to be giving away." In fact Brigit fed and gave to the poor so enthusiastically that she was the despair of her father. He tried to marry her off but she refused all suitors; he tried to sell her to the king, who not only was entertained by her stubbornness but impressed with her sincerity. With his permission she became a nun and founded the order and church at Kildare, which later became so famous.

At Brigit's shrine in Kildare burned her sacred fire. It was watched by 19 nuns in daily turn; on the 20th day Brigit herself kept watch. This fire burned and was guarded in her honor up to the time of the Protestant terror in the reign of Henry VIII. Today the blessing of the sacred fire on Candlemas (Feb. 2) is associated with this ancient sacred fire of Brigit, just as the ancient Celtic druid fire festival of February became replaced and syncretized to Saint Brigit's Day.

In Scotland in the 18th century, people still made Brigit's Bed on the eve of Feb. 2: a sheaf of oats dressed in women's clothes was laid in it; the housewife would cry, "Bride is here! Bride is welcome!" This little ritual is interpreted by Stokes and others as a survival of an old fertility observance associated with the ancient Celtic Brigit, just as the sacred fire at Kildare was thought to reflect the flame of Brigit in her role of goddess of fire.

In Ireland Brigit's ribbon is a rush worn round the head on St. Brigit's Eve. It cures headache. St. Brigit's bow (*baġa Briġde*) is a little cross made of straw and tucked into the roof thatch for protection to the house. A sheaf of oats or a loaf of bread or cake is placed on the doorstep on St. Brigit's Eve. Her day is the beginning of spring in Ireland. Brigit dipped her finger in the brook, they say, and off went the hen that hatches the cold. See DECEPTIVE BARGAINS.

Saint George Patron of England, Aragon, Portugal, and the Slovenes: one of the synthetic saints venerated by the fighting men returning from the Crusades who had come across his worship in the Near East. As patron of the Slovenes St. George took on many of the attributes of Kresnik, who was also associated with crops and cattle. In 1222 the Council of Oxford decided that his day should be kept as a national English festival on April 23. In this same century Jacobus de Voragine gave a notable account of his hagiography. St. George is particularly remembered for his adventures with the dragon (known to every schoolboy) and his prowess in fertilizing barren women (carefully kept from the youth of England). Both attributes are obscurely associated with the Greek legend of Perseus. After Perseus had slain Medusa he came across Andromeda, chained to a rock as a sacrifice to a local monster who was ravaging the country. After a great fight he slew the dragon and won the lady. This story, or one of the many others on the same theme known in all parts of the world, became one important part of the legend of Saint George. The other part, his ability to cure barrenness among women, if the sophisticated Pausanias is to be trusted, is associated with Syrian fertility cults, themselves obscure and fertile subjects of speculation. Barren women who visit the shrines of Saint George in northern Syria can be impregnated by the puissant saint incarnate in his priests. Women in all parts of the world who have had children, which according to local custom were illegal, have attributed the experience to supernatural beings: saints, gods, demons, and ghosts. The story of Perseus and Andromeda may well have connections with obscure cults of fertility or atonement. Whatever may be the validity of these speculations, the capacity of Saint George to cure barrenness and slay the dragon is a significant pattern in female folklore. [RDJ]

Saint Johnswort Any of a genus (*Hypericum*) of hardy perennial herbs and shrubs with deep yellow flowers. It probably originated in Assyria where it is hung over doors at the time of religious ceremonies to frighten demons and evil spirits. It was brought into Europe by the Crusaders under the name of *devil's flight* and in some localities has supplanted older herbs used in the same way to keep out the Devil, imps, ghosts, and thunderbolts. Since June 24 (Midsummer's Day or St. John's Day) is a favorite time for festooning doors and windows against demons, it is not surprising that the Saint's name should attach itself to this plant. On August 29, the anniversary of St. John's decapitation at the behest of Salome, it is said that red spots appear on the leaves of some species. St. Johnswort was used in the 17th century to exorcise demons from those possessed; and it both revealed and thwarted witches. On the Isle of Wight, if a person makes the mistake of stepping on the plant, a fairy horse will rise up under him and carry him about at top speed for an entire night. Hung on the bedroom wall, it causes a maiden to dream of her future husband; in Denmark, if two sprigs are planted between the rafters by two lovers, there will be a marriage if their branches intertwine.

On St. John's Eve a sprig of the plant was hung about the neck of children to protect them from sickness during the entire year; a sprig about the neck was also believed to cure melancholy. Gerard recommended it for deep wounds, especially those which were poisoned or where gangrene had set in. It was considered good for sore eyes, nervous disorders of the heart, the blast in cow's udders, for chilblains, bed sores, and as a gargle. Today it is used principally in diseases of the chest such as colds, coughs, and bronchitis. The Meskwaki Indians of the United States use the great St. Johnswort (*H. ascyron*) in a cure for tuberculosis. The powdered root draws out the poison of water-moccasin bites.

Saint Nicholas Patron saint of Russia, of sailors, thieves, children, and virgins. Santa Claus, the stocky, bearded, red-coated gentleman of nursery folklore who is the patron of children on Christmas Eve, is the American counterpart (of Dutch origin) of the legendary Saint Nicholas, whose festival day is December 6.

The existing data on St. Nicholas is based entirely on oral tradition; the first written legends were composed about five centuries after his death. According to Methodius, St. Nicholas, only son of parents known for their good deeds, was born in Lycia, Asia Minor, early in the 4th century. When he received his inheritance, he gave it to the needy. In all accounts of the saint's life there appears the story that he threw gold into a house to provide three daughters with dowries. Shortly after his ascent to the bishopric, during a famine in his country, Nicholas acquired enough grain from ships bound for Alexandria to keep the region well fed for two years. In return for the grain, he promised the sailors of the ships that they would find the original quantity of grain on board when they arrived at their destination. After the miracle, the sailors became converts of St. Nicholas. Tradition maintains that in his old age Nicholas sat at the Council of Nicea, 325 A.D., but there is no historical evidence to support this. When he died, on December 6, 342 A.D., his tomb became a place of pilgrimage and it was said that a miraculous curing oil flowed from it.

Since the early Middle Ages, Nicholas has been a patron saint in Greece, Russia, Germany, Austria, Belgium, the Netherlands, France, Naples, Sicily, and recently the United States. The miracles of St. Nicholas held particular fascination for the Normans, a seafaring people. St. Nicholas, patron of children, has left his mark on society through such institutions as the Foundlings' Tower in Metz and the Santa Claus Home for Sick Children in London. The celebration of St. Nicholas' Day in this country during colonial times was marked by the putting out of wooden shoes in which his presents might be received on the eve of December 6. The St. Nicholas of those days was dressed in a bishop's robe

with mitre and was accompanied by a Negro servant, Black Pete. In Albany, N. Y., in 1848, St. Nicholas was called Sinti Klass, wore a tricorn hat, silver-buckled shoes, and smoked a long white pipe with orange ribbons. Santa Claus, a Dutch name for St. Nicholas, rides over the roofs in a sleigh drawn by reindeer on Christmas Eve and delivers presents to worthy children who have hung stockings over the fireplace. Thus transmuted into Santa Claus, the saint has become a traditional part of nursery lore. His usual symbol, three bags of gold, has become the bulging pack of presents for children. The celebration of St. Nicholas' Feast is apparently an old custom, originally observed on Martinmas (November 11), at which fertility ceremonies like the slaughter of cattle before the winter tree occurred. At this time, good children were rewarded by St. Martin with cakes, nuts, apples, etc., and bad children were whipped. Compare the Père Fouettard of French folklore, who travels with the gift-giving Bonhomme Noël at Christmas time, and Knecht Ruprecht. The St. Nicholas cake is lucky; Irish fishermen carry it in their boats to insure safety. See CHRISTMAS.

śakti The female side or consort of the Hindu gods. Śakti is important in one of the central doctrines of the Tantrists who, though capable of wild flights into magic and the empyrean of the esoteric, have chosen a comfortably concrete and commonplace symbol for their conception of humanity at its point of highest and noblest achievement. That is a śakti or female figure in the embrace of a Bhagavat with the lingam, as can be seen by separating the two, fully inserted into the yoni. At this moment, the worshippers believe the female and male forces (yin and yang) which control the universe and are frequently in opposition, are at a point of harmony. The two forces are flowing together and in the same direction, a situation which the Tantrists and many others believe is a boon devoutly to be hoped for. The contemplation of these two figures, who are thought to be in a condition of eternal ecstasy, is accompanied by rituals and exercises which are only slightly known because of the secrecy which surrounds them and because of the prohibition with which western European cultures have imposed. Similar views are held by the adherents of the Bon cult in Tibet and by some of the Taoist adepts of China. [RDJ]

Śaktism In Asiatic India and surrounding areas, a convenient name for the worship of the female components of Śiva, powerful member of the Hindu trinity, in his aspect of creator and destroyer. Scholars are not in agreement on the origins of Śaivism, Śaktism, Tantrism, how these religions acquired their strongly erotic symbolism, or the force of that symbolism in contemporary worship. At present more careful studies need to be made of the Tibetan Bon cults, Chinese Taoism, and Tantrism itself. The Hindu theologians whose grammatical bent is to tidy things up present the Śaktis and the other female divinities as concrete projections of the force conceived of as Śiva. The folklorist is tempted to reject this rationalization as metaphysical and to look at least tentatively for the origin of these divinities in local cults with the expectation that several local goddesses with an agrarian interest in fertility were combined.

In India these cults are very ancient. The existence of

similar cults in the Shang dynasty, China, in the second millennium B.C. and the fact that the priests of that time became the propagators of the cult-Taoism still strong in modern China may justify a very tentative hypothesis that Śaktism in one form or another is characteristic of eastern, probably northeastern, Asiatic folklore.

As in all popular religions the popularity, spread, and force of the cult has varied in the several areas where it has existed in different periods of history. The present stronghold of Śaktism in India is in Bengal, as Tantrism is strong in Nepal and Tibet. An account of Śaktic ceremonies in Assam in the 16th century emphasizes the cruelties and ecstacies of its worshippers. Large numbers of human males offered themselves as sacrifices to this female aspect of Śiva. This aspect is worshipped through meditation and ritual before pictorial representations or the living object. The worshippers seem to be fascinated by the cruelties of birth and death as well as by the ecstatic aspects of sexuality. Thus some Śaktic cults represent the Śakti or Devī, the consort of Śiva, and a more generalized concept of his female component, as either terrifying or beneficient. [RDJ]

Sally Brown A capstan chantey dealing with the favorite female of sailing men, a lady of comfortable morals and varied charms. She is "a Creole lady," or sometimes "a bright mulatter," and she knows her way to a sailor's pocketbook as well as heart. "Spent my money on Sally Brown," is the constant theme. Not only has she a song of her own, but her name turns up in other chanties, as in certain verses of *Santy Anna*. See CHANTEY.

salmon Tales concerning Salmon, Salmon Boy, Salmon village, and the release of salmon, are prevalent among the tribes of the Plateau and North Pacific Coast regions of North America, where salmon were caught in great numbers each year and were a staple article of diet. The release of salmon is credited to the trickster Coyote, who disguises himself as a baby, is adopted by women who have salmon, and who breaks their weir and causes the salmon to go upstream to people who previously had not been able to catch them. Other Coyote tales credit him with introducing salmon into various rivers, as payment for wives provided for him by people living on these rivers; if wives were refused, Coyote refused to let the salmon go into certain rivers. The tales in which Salmon or Salmon Boy are the chief characters are adventure stories or hero tales; in most of them a village of Salmon people is mentioned. [EWV]

Salt River A Kentucky tributary of the Ohio named for the salt once made on its banks and fabled in folklore as the haunt of the Salt River (ring-tailed) roarer (see Ralph Stackpole in Robert Bird Montgomery's *Nick of the Woods*, 1837) and the scene of political and other defeat. The phrase, to *row* (some one) or *be rowed up Salt River*, applied usually to a defeated candidate for office, is said to have originated in the supposed difficulty of navigating the river on account of its winding course and shoal- and snag-infested waters and also in the custom of punishing refractory slaves by hiring them out to row keelboats against the powerful current. However, by a curious transfer of ideas, in the figurative and slang use of the phrase, it is the passengers, not the oarsmen, who are considered unlucky. (See Clark B. Firestone, *Sycamore Shores*, 1936, pp. 124–134.) [BAB]

Salt Woman, Salt Old Woman, or **Salt Mother** One of the spirits of the Pueblo Indians, and a fairly prominent character in Sia, Cochiti, Isleta, and Zuñi mythology. Ever migratory, Salt Woman and Turquoise Man deserted the neighborhood of Zuñi because their flesh was being wasted; Salt Woman now lives at Zuñi Salt Lake. Salt Mother, when brought into a house at Zuñi, is addressed thus: "We hope you will come many times." Among the Hopi and at Taos, Salt is a male spirit, Salt Man, and for the Hopi, a war god. The procuring of salt is a ritual undertaking among the Pueblos, as it is among other Southwestern groups; men fast before going on the dangerous journey, and a man when returning, gives his first present of salt to his "aunts," after his head and body have been washed by them. At Isleta pueblo Salt Woman is "brought in" in an autumn ceremony, and her "veins are cleaned"; this is dangerous, for at it anyone with bad thoughts is liable to be turned into an animal. In Zuñi myths the Twins (see AHAYUTA ACHI) stole salt for human beings from the animals. Among the Navaho Indians Salt Woman is a variant of CHANGING WOMAN. See AWL MAN. [EWV]

Salus An ancient Roman goddess of well-being, prosperity, and health: identified with the Greek Hygeia. Though Salus is often depicted with Hygeia's snake and bowl, her older attributes of ears of grain seem to indicate that her identification with Valetudo (Hygeia's name in Rome) submerged the agricultural aspect to that of the health goddess. Prayers were offered to her at the beginning of the year, on the emperor's birthday, and in time of general sickness. Her temple on the Quirinal was dedicated in 302 B.C., some time before the appearance of Valetudo in Rome; Salus Publica, to whom the temple was devoted, is obviously a simple personification of public health.

Salutation Carol A carol of the annunciation, one of those preserved in the commonplace book of Richard Hill, and therefore of 15th century composition. The word "salutation" was frequently used for "annunciation." In this song the angel Gabriel says to the Virgin Mary, "Lady, from heaven so high,/ That Lordes heritage,/ For he of thee now born will be;/ I'm sent on this message."

Samain (pronounced *sovan* or *sowan*) The festival of the beginning of winter, celebrated on or about November 1 in Ireland and Gaelic Scotland and of very great antiquity. The word means "end of summer." One of the oldest Irish sagas states that the barrows where the fairies dwelt were open about Samain, and in Scotland a demon who stole babies at this time was called a *samhanach*. Another old saga relates that for three days before and three days after November 1 the warriors of Ulster assembled for eating, drinking, and boasting of the men they had killed, producing the tips of their tongues as evidence. According to Keating, in heathen times the druids of Ireland assembled to sacrifice to the gods and burn their victims on Samain eve. All other fires were to be extinguished, to be rekindled only from that fire. This custom still lingers on, without the sacrifices, in parts of Ireland and Scotland. The peat fires are extinguished in the cottages on Halloween and are relighted from the bonfires which burn on the hilltops. In the Highlands families used to circumambulate the fields sunwise, holding fir torches. At Waterford groups of country lads, headed by horn-blowers, visited the farmers' houses and collected pence and provisions for the ensuing celebration. In parts of County Cork the procession was led by a man called the White Mare, wearing a white robe and the semblance of a horse's head, while in other parts the lads dressed as mummers and professed to be the messengers of the Muck Olla, a boar slain by one of the Geraldines. Until about 1850 the inhabitants of the Isle of Lewis used to assemble on the same night, bringing ale and provisions, repeat a paternoster (though mostly Protestants), and walk down to the sea. One of them waded into the water, poured out a cup of ale, and cried out: "Shony, I give this cup of ale to you, hoping that you'll be so kind as to send us plenty of sea-ware to enrich our ground for the coming year." The group then went to the church, stood silent for a while, and then adjourned to the fields for drinking, dancing, and singing. MacCulloch in 1911 mentioned the license permitted to youths on Samhain Eve in the quietest townships of the West Highlands. Vallancey in the 18th century recorded that Irish maidens observed the festival by sowing hemp seed and believed that if they looked back they would see the apparition of their future spouse, or they would hang a smock before the cottage fire, convinced that his apparition would come down the chimney and turn the smock. See CELTIC FOLKLORE; CROMM CRUAĊ.

ROGER S. LOOMIS

samba A Brazilian couple dance, similar in history to the *rumba*, i.e. as racial blend, developed probably from the *batuque* danced by slaves on the plantations. Even in Cuba it is more restrained than the *rumba*, and in the United States its 200 intense and erotic step variations have dwindled into a precise sequence of small, bouncy two-steps. [GPK]

Sambo-kojin The Japanese Kitchen God, with three faces and two pairs of hands. [JLM]

samiri Hills, caves, or lakes from which the ancestors of the Aymara local groups and lineages are said to have emerged. They are regarded as sacred and the Indians visit them to gain new strength and energy. Samiri are also stone fetishes which protect the villages and herds. [AM]

samisen A three-stringed, banjo-like member of the lute family, probably the most popular of Japanese musical instruments. Its frame is rectangular, its neck long, and the resonance box is covered, like a double-headed drum, with stretched skin of cat or dog, or, in early times in the Ryukyu Islands (from which it was introduced about 1560), with the skin of a large serpent. It is played with a bone plectrum and used as accompaniment to folk singing and dancing, banquet entertainment and other festivities, geisha songs, and street songs. See MIN-YO. A special type of song rendered to the samisen alone is called *Jiuta*. The samisen is frequently played in combination with the bamboo flute, *shakuhachi,* and the long zither, *koto.* A small bowed instrument similar to the samisen is called kokyu.

Samoyeds A Uralic group of people, related to the Finno-Ugrians, living in the arctic and subarctic regions of Asia. There are about 20,000 of them, divided into three groups: Yurak, Ostyak, and Eastern Samoyeds.

Their folklore is very rich. One kind of tale is sung, another is recited; they can be divided into customary and fantastic tales. The fantastic hero-tale has a hyperbolic form. The hero is usually a warrior wandering in search of adventures. The hero Itte of the Ostyak Samoyeds, for instance, struggled with the giant man-eater, Pünegusse, whom he conquered; but finally Itte was forced by foreign evil spirits to leave the land. The Samoyeds await his return, believing that he will come and make the people rich and happy. The northern Samoyeds have many lyric songs sung at burials and for matchmakings.

The common name for the chief spirit of all Samoyed religion is Num, meaning god, sky, or thunder. The domestic gods are called *hahe.* Each family has one male and one female domestic god, who are kept covered on a special sledge. Women are not allowed to take care of the domestic gods. The bad spirits are called *illike.* The worshiping of a tribal ancestor is common to all Samoyeds. Shamanism is also common, and the shaman or *tadibey,* often a woman, is a very important person. The shamans have their supporting spirits called *tadebtsy.* A man possesses, it is believed, three kinds of soul: the intellectual soul, the physical, and the shadow-soul.

References: Czaplicka, "Samoyed," *ERE* XI: 172–77. K. Donner, *A Samoyed Epic. JSFO* 30. Helsinki, 1914. T. Lehtisalo, *Entwurf einer Mythologie der Jurak-Samojeden. MSFO* 53. Helsinki, 1924. A. M. Castrén and T. Lehtisalo, *Samodjedische Volksdichtung. MSFO* 83. Helsinki, 1940. T. Lehtisalo, *Juraksamojedische Volksdichtung. MSFO* 90. Helsinki, 1947. JONAS BALYS

Sampo A wonderful thing, often mentioned in the Finnish epic songs, probably a mill or idol, which brings good luck and produces all kinds of good fortune. The people possessing Sampo can live free from care. The hero Ilmarinen forged the Sampo for Louhi, mistress of Pohjola (Northland), but did not get the promised beautiful daughter of Louhi in return. The Sampo was hidden deep in a stone mountain where it ground out wealth. Väinämöinen persuaded Ilmarinen to go to Pohjola and bring away the Sampo; and the two heroes started off together in a boat. Lemminkäinen joined them as a third comrade. When the heroes arrived at Pohjola, Väinämöinen announced that he had come for the Sampo; he would take it either with good-will (i.e. divide the wealth among them), or by force. Väinämöinen lulled all the people of Pohjola to sleep with the playing of *kantele,* took the Sampo from the stone mountain and carried it to the boat, and they sailed homeward. On the third day Louhi woke from her sleep, prepared a thick fog and strong wind to oppose the robbers, equipped a war vessel, and went in pursuit. In the fight which ensued Louhi dragged the Sampo from the boat into the sea where it broke to pieces. Louhi then went home in great distress, taking with her only a small piece of the cover of the Sampo. Väinämöinen carefully collected the fragments of the Sampo which were washed ashore by the waves, hoping for welfare for the land of Suomi. Louhi sent all evil upon Kalevala, but Väinämöinen was able to protect his country successfully (see *Kalevala,* songs 10, 39, 42–3).

Even today Finnish scholars discuss what the Sampo really is. According to the opinion of Jakob Grimm this is not a myth, but a folktale about a wonderful mill like the Grotti mill in Scandinavia. K. Krohn was convinced that the theft of the Sampo is reminiscent of a robber-expedition of Finnish Vikings to the rich isle Gottland or *Vuojala* of the runes. Finnish scholars differ also about the shape of the Sampo; books have been written on the subject, but the problem is not yet solved. For instance, Kaarle Krohn sought a parallel with the wooden idols of the Scandinavians, because the word *sampo* means "pillar." The famous philologist, E. N. Setälä, in *The Riddle of Sampo* (Helsinki, 1932), tried to prove that the Sampo symbolizes the Star of the North, which was nailed on the top of the "world-pillar," since the price for forging the Sampo was the beautiful daughter of Louhi, the Dawn. He was influenced by the astral-mythological school. In an earlier article he explained the Sampo as a dragon which brings goods like the para. Neither explanation has found the approval of other scholars. According to the most recent theory of U. Harva, the Sampo is a copy or idol of the mythical "column of the world," like the Irmin-column of the old Saxons (see his *The Theft of Sampo*, 1943, [in Finnish] and the Swedish article in *Saga och Sed*, 1943). The problem must be regarded as not being solved.

Reference: V. J. Mansikka, "Das Neueste über den Sampo" in *Mitteilungen des Vereins für finnische Volkskunde* I, 1943, pp. 59–63.   JONAS BALYS

Sämpsä Pellervo or **Pellervoinen** The genius of vegetation of the Finns, like Frey and Njordr in Scandinavia (see K. Krohn in *FUF IV*, 1904, pp. 231–48). In Finland Sämpsä was represented as being conveyed from an island, sleeping upon a corn-ship, with his mother as wife. A song from Ingria relates that in his absence nothing could grow. The name Sämpsä may be a Teutonic loanword (from *simse* or *semse,* bulrush) and signifies a species of fodder grass, one of the earliest plants to appear in the spring. [JB]

Sancus, Semo Sancus, or **Semo Sancus Dius Fidius** An ancient Italian god of oaths, treaties, hospitality, marriage, and perhaps of the sown fields: sometimes identified with Apollo, sometimes with Jupiter. Information about this divinity is confused, and many of the conclusions about him are conjectural and vague, based on etymological reasoning. The oath *medius fidius* is probably connected with Sancus, whose name derives from *sancio,* to make sacred, and is related to and often confused with *sanctus.* As a god of oaths, Sancus was connected with daytime thunder. He was invoked under the open sky; the roof of his temple had an opening in it; private worshippers stood beneath the compluvium (an open space in the roof). There was minor cult worship, especially on the Tiber island; his temple was on the Quirinal, and in it were the spindle and distaff of the virtuous wife of Tarquinius Priscus. He was, in Christian times, confused with Simon Magus because of inscriptions in his shrine on the island. Sancus has been identified with the Italian Hercules, but modern scholars believe this to be an error.

Sand Altar Woman or **Child Medicine Woman** Among the Hopi of the Southwest, the spirit of childbirth. She bestows infants and guards the game animals. She is the wife of Masauwü, and the sister of Müy'ingwa, Hopi chief of the nadir and of germination. [EWV]

sand, dry, or **ground paintings** Outline symbolic "paintings" made with colored sands or earth, on the ground, by various Southwestern Indians in connection with various ceremonies. The art also exists, but in less well developed form, among the Cheyenne, Arapaho, and Gros Ventre of the Plains region. Popularly referred to as "sand painting," the more exact term is dry or ground painting, since dry colored earths, not sand, are most frequently used. The art of dry painting has probably reached its highest perfection in North America among the Navaho Indians, who make their highly stylized ground pictures almost exclusively in connection with religious ceremonies. The paintings are in various sizes, some as large as 10–12 feet in diameter, and represent, in conventional form, various gods of Navaho mythology, divine ceremonies, lightning, sunbeams, rainbows, mountains, animals, and plants having a mythical or traditional significance. Since color symbolism is prominent in Navaho religious belief, the dry paintings afford a fine vehicle for expressing this. The five sacred colors of Navaho mythology—white, blue, yellow, black, and red—are used in Navaho ground paintings.

To be efficacious, a ground painting must be made without any error in the traditional design; among the Navaho it must be completed and also destroyed in one day. When the picture is finished, ceremonies are performed over it, and then with song and ceremony it is destroyed. Among the Pueblo Indians dry paintings are allowed to remain for several days before being destroyed. No permanent copies of the sand paintings which are made in connection with the various Navaho curing ceremonies or chants are preserved for guidance, nor are dry paintings made in the summertime.

During the past few decades the Navaho have begun to copy their sand painting designs, always with some error in one part of it so the original design will still be efficacious, for their rug designs.

Color reproductions of Navaho dry paintings have recently been published by anthropologists and collectors in several de luxe volumes; see for instance Franc J. Newcomb and Gladys A. Reichard, *Sandpaintings of the Navajo Shooting Chant* (New York, n.d.). [EWV]

Sand-Man A character in a nursery story found throughout western Europe. He is the man who puts children to sleep by sprinkling sand or dust in their eyes. Mothers say, "The Sand-Man is coming—the Sand-Man is coming . . ." This imaginary figure, like the East Frisian Finger-biter and other figments, is part of the development of children's folklore by mothers everywhere. See LULLABY.

sandunga or **zandunga** The regional couple dance of Tehuantepec, Juchitán, and Salina Cruz in Oaxaca, Mexico. The meaning, "beautiful and graceful woman," is appropriate to the statuesque demeanor of the Tehuanas who dance it. Men and women face in two lines and partners weave back and forth in front of each other. Then the man follows the woman around. Sometimes a languid waltz step is used, sometimes a step-pat in 2/4 time with the 3/4 time music.

The romantic song, to marimba accompaniment, speaks of frustrated love—*tu no sirves para amores*—and adoration—*Zandunga tu amor me mata, cielo de mi corazón*—(Zandunga, I perish for love of you, my heart's heaven). It is distinctly a secular courtship mime, with the woman always demure yet provocative, haughty yet yielding, always the queen of the occasion in her magnificent lace-trimmed and embroidered costume. She is the perfect blend of Indian and Spanish reticence and fire. The dance is popular at social occasions, along with the similar *llorona* and *tortuga* (turtle). For weddings, stringed and brass instruments augment the orchestra. In a sophisticated, "dressed-up" version, it has invaded the theaters and tourist centers of urban Mexico, and the United States. [GPK]

śani In Hindu mythology and belief, the planet Saturn or its regent, the god of bad luck. Śani is represented as a black man dressed in black; he was the son of Balarāma and Revatī, or of Chhāyā and the sun. He was left out of the invitation of the gods to rejoice at the birth of Ganeśa and so appeared at the gala affair uninvited and in a great rage. With a glance of his glowering eye he caused the child's head to drop off; and the gods substituted the head of a young elephant. Śani as the planet Saturn is especially dreaded; he is represented (in Bengal) by an earthen pot filled with water. He is propitiated with an offering of *prasād*, a kind of pudding made of flour, sugar, milk, and plantains which must be eaten by his devotees in his presence. His day, also named śani, is not propitious. See SATURDAY.

Sañjña In Purāṇic mythology, the daughter of Viśvakarma and wife of the sun (Sūrya) by whom she had three children, Manu, Yama, and Yamī. When Sañjña could no longer endure Sūrya's fervors she gave him a shade as handmaid and retired to the forests as a mare. The sun approached her as a horse and from them sprang the Aśvins and Revanta. Upon returning to their home, she found the sun's brightness too overpowering and her father cut away an eighth of his brilliance on a lathe. Compare SARAṆYŪ.

sanjuanito A couple dance of Ecuador, mingling an Indian sadness with the coquetry of the Spanish colonial dance. Without ever touching, the partners glide toward and away from each other, and raise and lower a kerchief resignedly. The melancholy song in 4/4 time is accompanied on the guitar. The sanjuanito, literally little St. John, corresponds to the more worldly *marinera* of Peru and gay *cueca* of Chile. [GPK]

Sankeys Hymns derived from or patterned after those of the 19th century evangelical hymn-writers Dwight L. Moody and Ira David Sankey, as sung in Negro congregations of certain sects such as the Shouters of Trinidad. The singing begins fairly close to the originals but in slow, dragging, and mournful measures; then after a stanza or so, clapping and accelerating rhythms transform the song into a "shout" leading up to the emotional excitement in which the spirit is possessed by the supernatural. See RELIGIOUS FOLK MUSIC; RING SHOUT.

sannyāsī or **sannyāsin** One of the seven chief sects of Śaivite ascetics: literally, one who has cast off, i.e. home and possessions. The term is frequently used for any ascetic or mendicant. It is also used to designate the fourth stage of the life of an orthodox Brāhman—that in which he abandons earthly things and devotes himself to meditation. The sannyāsī wears a necklace of rudrāksha berries and a salmon-colored robe. He accepts food only from Hindus, avoids spiritous drinks, but smokes excessive amounts of *ganja* or hemp. Daily he must bathe and worship Śiva. Frequently he bears the Śiva mark on the forehead. The sannyāsī is buried in a sitting attitude after being bathed, rubbed with ashes, and clad in a reddish-colored shirt. Sometimes the skull is cracked so that the soul can exit easily. No śrāddha ceremonies are performed, since the ascetic quit this life when he entered the order. Compare SĀDHU.

Sans Day Carol One of the "holly-and-ivy" carols, named for Sans (or St.) Day in a Cornwall parish where it was first recorded. St. Day or They was a saint of Brittany whose cult was influential in Armorican Cornwall. The stanzas repeat: "Now the holly bears a berry as white as the milk" . . . "green as the grass" . . . "black as the coal" . . . "red as blood," and each time the second line brings in a statement about the life of Jesus. The song is known in a Cornish as well as an English version.

Santa Claus Father Christmas; the Christmas giftbringer, usually represented as a fat, jolly old man who drives over the roofs in a sleigh drawn by reindeer. He is identified with Saint Nicholas, the patron of children, and his name is a corruption of the Dutch name of the saint, Sant (Ni)kolaas.

Santiago Saint James, the patron saint of Spain: identified by the Aymara Indians of South America with their Thunder God, Apu-illapu. All twins, all children born during a storm or conceived when lightning struck nearby, are dedicated to Santiago and regarded as his sons. Any place struck by lightning is said to have been visited by him and is consecrated by the sacrifice of a white llama.

The Fiesta of the Llamas is a minor celebration for the llamas, celebrated on July 25, the day of Santiago, by certain South American Quechua Indians. Every llama is given a little drink of chicha on this day to give him strength. Chicha is a mild beer fermented from certain grains and fruits by the South American Indians, among the Quechua mostly from maize. [AM]

Santiagos A masked form of *Morisca*, a typical fiesta dance of central Mexico, the Sierras de Puebla, and Veracruz, especially near Cuetzalan, Puebla, and in Aztec Huaxteca: named for St. James, patron saint of Spain. As seen in Tecalpulco, Guerrero, Santiago Caballero straddled a hobbyhorse supposedly imbued with life, and, half clown, half leader, he incited six *Cristianos* to battle against six *Moros*. A ragged buffoon meanwhile cracked obscene jokes and molested ladies in the audience with a repulsive desiccated squirrel. In medieval-type costumes the two lines of opponents shouted challenges at each other and engaged in stilted combat with their 22-inch machetes, skipping, whirling, and crossing over at stated intervals. Meanwhile a one-man flute and tabor tootled a little tune. This pattern prevails in other Santiago regions. In the Sierras the spoken drama is definitely concerned with the evil *Pilato*, and vengeance is taken upon him for the execution of Christ. Sometimes, in Puebla, the *Moros* are termed *Pilatos*. This dance is the same as *Los Moros y Cristianos* and *La Danza de los Pilatos* and is related to *Los Santiaguitos* of Chila, Puebla.

In several New Mexico pueblos Santiago appears on a real horse in connection with a bull-killing mime, with Geronimo and a group of soldiers or with Bocaiyanyi. He possesses supernatural power. [GPK]

Santy Anna A capstan chantey with a text dating from the Mexican War, relating the encounters of the American general Taylor and the Mexican Santa Anna. Some versions reverse history by having the American chased off by "Santy Anna" and these were sung with relish by British sailors. It has been suggested that the air may have originally belonged to a Breton sailor's prayer to their patron, Saint Anne. Negro influence is noticeable in some of the texts.

sanza, sansa, or **zanza** A musical instrument of African Negroes, consisting of a series of flexible metal or rattan strips of varying length attached at one end above a resonant box and plucked with the thumb to play a slender melody: popularly called the *African piano* or *thumb piano.*

sapphire The gem sapphire is usually the birthstone of April and Taurus. It has been variously ascribed to Saturn, Jupiter, Mercury, Gemini, and Venus. The Hindus call it bitter to the taste, lukewarm; wearing the sapphire was thought to render the planet Saturn favorable. Although sometimes confused with the hyacinth and lapus lazuli anciently, as in the case of the Mosaic tablets, it was probably one of the stones of the High Priest's breastplate and is mentioned in *Revelation* as one of the foundations of the New Jerusalem. *Ezekiel* i, 26 mentions the throne of God as having the appearance of a sapphire stone. Moses and Aaron saw the God of Israel with a paved work of sapphire under his feet (*Ex.* xxiv, 10). In Christian times it was symbolic of St. Paul and much in favor for ecclesiastical rings, because it protected from spirits of darkness and promoted chaste thoughts. The Hindus used it in their five- and nine-gem combinations (the *pañchratna* and the *navaratna*); in an astrological charm, it represented Saturn and was placed to the west of the center. It was a stone of good omen, bringing health, wealth, strength, energy, and both divine and princely favor. It banished fraud and enchantments, preserved the wearer from envy and the fury of his enemies, mended his manners, and could even deliver one from prison. It provided a test of virtue by changing color in the presence of infidelity and the unchaste. Prester John is said to have slept on a bed of sapphire to preserve his chastity. It was used by witches in their enchantments; necromancers valued it highly because it enabled them to hear and understand the most difficult oracles. In Brazil the sapphire is worn as a professional badge by engineers.

Sir Jerome Horsey in his *Travels* quotes Ivan the Terrible of Russia thus: "The saphier I greatlie delight in; yt preserves and increaseth courage, joies the hart, pleasinge to all the vitall sensis, precious and verie soveraigne for the eys, clears the sight, takes awaye bloudshott and strengthens the mussells and strings thereof." It was an antidote for poison and poisonous bites; it healed severed membranes; cured fevers, agues, cataract, and duodenal ulcers; cleared the mind, skin, and sight; prevented the plague, boils, pustules; it prevented smallpox from affecting the eyes, as well as stopping excessive perspiration. In the 17th century, even looking at a sapphire made the eyes so strong that no harm could touch them. The star sapphire is especially lucky in the Orient because of a spirit imprisoned in the stone. Sapphires are used against the evil eye and witchcraft of all kinds. The Germans believed they

would bring victory. The good influence of this gem is believed to follow the first owner even after he has passed it on into other hands. See AARON'S ROD.

sarabande A 16th century Spanish court dance, also adopted in France and Italy. It is of unsolved exotic origin, probably Arabic-Moorish, with the name derived from *serbend,* song, or *sarband,* fillet for a lady's headdress. The likelihood of Guatemalan origin is remote, considering the propriety of Indian dances and the wild and licentious character of the original *zarabanda,* also considering its presence in 12th century Spain. It would be sung and performed to bawdy verses by a single woman or by couples on the streets of Barcelona.

The music soon acquired a liturgical flavor, and the motions a noble sweep, less pompous than the *pavane.* Castanets were often played, as even by Cardinal Richelieu. The accompanying melodies flowed in sedate triple time, with accent on the second beat. The couples, in two lines, advanced and retired, changed places, and paraded down the center.

In the 18th century, when abandoned by the court and adopted by the theater, the steps took on elaborate designs: *coupés* (cuts), *rondes des jambes* (leg-swings), *glissés* (glides), *pirouettes* (turns), and other preballet evolutions. As an art product, the sarabande was incorporated into Lope de Vega's comedies, and into the musical suite, between the *courante* and the *gigue.* [GPK]

Sara-mama Literally, mother maize: the maize spirit of the religion of the ancient Peruvians. She was symbolized by strangely shaped ears of maize or by especially large specimens. After harvest, these were placed in a miniature bin made of maize stalks; various rites were celebrated in their honor and sacrifices were made to them. And these ears in which the Maize Mother or Spirit was believed to be incarnate were kept until the next harvest. The Chimu vases representing maize ears with human heads are probably images of the Sara-mama. [AM]

Saraṇyū In Hindu mythology, the daughter of Tvashtri, wife of Vivasvat, and mother of the Aśvins. According to the *Bṛihaddevatā* she was also the mother of the first human pair, Yamī and Yama. Literally, her name means the fleet runner, a name well deserved, since she is said to have substituted another woman for herself and to have fled swiftly in the form of a mare.

Sarasvatī In Vedic mythology, Sarasvatī is both a river and a river goddess, worshipped for her fertilizing and purifying powers. She is described as graceful, white in color, with a crescent on her brow, and reclining on a lotus. In later mythology she was the wife of Brahmā and goddess of wisdom and eloquence. She was identified with Vāch. The Sarasvatī river was to early Indians what the Ganges is today. The identity of the river thus personified, however, is controversial and the name is now applied to two rivers, one flowing through the Punjab, the other rising in the Arāvallī range. The Kāyasths or writer class of Hindus observe the festival of Dawāt Pūjā or "worship of the inkstand" in honor of their patron goddess Sarasvatī. This is held in the mouth of Māgh (January-February); on this day no Kāyasth will use any writing instrument except a pencil. After the festival a new inkstand and pen must be used. In Bengal, pens, ink, and account books are worshipped to honor the goddess.

sardana The national dance of Catalonia, similar to the *contrapás* in the circular formation of couples, instruments, composition of *curts* and *llarcs*, the steps, and the differentiation of the *ampurdanés* and *selvatá* versions. Its similarity to the Rumanian *sarba* and Greek *syrtos* has suggested Hellenic origin; also the name has suggested a legendary importation by the tall nomadic race of Sards who peopled Sardinia. At all events, though recorded for the first time in the 16th century, the archaic character of the steps and chant carry it back to ancient, probably pre-Christian times. Possible solar magic is inherent in the division of the older version into a melancholy 8-measure phrase of *curts* and 16 livelier measures of *llarcs*, making 24, the hours of, respectively, night and day, as the dancers trace the course of the sun. The modern version, allegedly crystallized about 1840 by a musician, "Pep" Ventura, presents the leader with a new mathematical problem for each tune, a new combination of shorts and longs which have to come out even.

Notwithstanding Balkan affinities, the sardana is identified with the Catalan spirit, and in city and country alike draws together people from all walks of life, into circling in street or park. Its optional direction places it transitionally between the counterclockwise rounds of the Mediterranean and central Europe and the clockwise circling of western Europe. See ROUND DANCES. [GPK]

Sarkap Literally, Beheader: the Raja hero of many Indian folktales: so named because those who played *chaupur* with him and lost forfeited their heads. Possibly Sarkap was a historic ruler but he has never been identified. He was famous as the successful contestant in the game of *chaupur* until he was defeated by Raja Rasalu, with whom he is frequently associated.

Sasabonsam A forest-dwelling monster in the belief-system of the Ashanti Negroes of the Gold Coast. Sasabonsam is conceived as a tall being, with long legs and feet which point both ways, hairy, and with bloodshot eyes. With his feet, he hooks up hunters who pass beneath him. He is associated with evil magic, and is also linked in the conceptions of the Ashanti with the *mmoatia*, or "little people," who likewise live in the forest and are also workers of magic. [MJH]

sassafras Europe learned the medicinal virtues of the tree from the Indians of North America who taught the Spaniards and the Huguenots of its use to cure ague. In the 16th century whole shiploads of the root were sent to Europe, where it enjoyed a popularity as a cure-all comparable to that of the sulfa drugs and penicillin in in the popular mind today. The Iroquois use the powdered leaves as a blood purifier, for wounds, and in venereal infections. The root they use as a tonic after childbirth, against fevers, and rheumatism. The Mohawks extracted the pith from the young shoots and soaked it in water for the eyes. The root-bark tea was a good spring tonic. Elsewhere the root, bark, berry, and crushed leaf are all used in various forms of tonic. The root is also used to flavor a beer or soft drink. Around Baltimore it is considered bad luck to burn the wood; in the Ozark mountains and Louisiana if the wood pops while burning, it is a portent of death in the house before the end of winter.

Satan The adversary; the fallen angel who became the great opponent of God; personification of the evil principle; prince of Hell and ruler of devils and imps. Satan, the Devil, is usually pictured as a handsome man, sinister and slick, with horns on his forehead, pointed ears, bat's wings at his shoulders, a pointed tail, and at least one cloven hoof in place of a foot. He is accompanied by the hellish odor of brimstone. In Renaissance Germany, he was depicted as a huge crow; in medieval art, he appears as a serpent with a human head. Satan obviously is the repository of the cattle, serpent, goat, and dragon deities of ancient cults; he is the pagan god reduced to subservience to the true God, yet always he strives to convert people to his evil ways (see FAUST). Satan is a Semitic demon in origin; Arabic lore distinguishes the shaitans as one of the classes of jinn; the word means opponent or adversary. He is placed in a duality with Jehovah; the Zoroastrian Ahura Mazda and Angra Mainyu show the same opposition, as do Tiamat and Marduk in the Babylonian epic. But Satan is not directly comparable to such underworld deities as the Greek Hades or the Norse Hel, nor to such adversaries of good as the Egyptian Set or Apepi or the Greek Titans. Such beings are somber, or they battle the gods, but they are not evilly malicious. All evil, however, has been attributed to Satan; sin, sickness, lies, death, treachery are the direct result of Satan's work. In fact, the world is more or less completely his domain, and, in German folklore, he is so busy running the world that he has to send his grandmother to do much of his work. Satan is known by many names, most of them euphemisms from the fear that merely naming him will put one in his power: the good man, the great fellow, the old gentleman (he is always that), Auld Hornie, Clootie, the black one, Old Harry, Old Nick, Old Scratch. But most often he is the Devil, to distinguish him from the devils, like Beelzebub, who are his assistants and messengers. In many Christian countries, Satan is conceived as a master musician, and virtuosity on the favorite instrument of the people (violin in Europe; bagpipe in Scotland, etc.; banjo or guitar among American Negroes) is to be achieved only by a Faustian compact with the Evil One, in which the soul is exchanged for the skill. The crossroads at midnight is the proper setting for this bargain and lesson, in American Negro belief.

Satavaēsa (Avestan *satavaēsa*, Pahlavi *sat-vēs*) In Persian mythology, one of the four leaders of the stars, produced by Ahura Mazda to preside over those of the west.

šateček or **šatečková** The Moravian "handkerchief" dance for couples arranged in a counterclockwise round. Each couple is linked by two handkerchiefs held at shoulder level, the woman in front with elbows flexed, the man in back holding his arms out straight. The first part consists of eight smooth waltz steps around the circle, the woman looking back at the man alternately over the right and left shoulder. The second part is a fast light polka pivot under the joined arms held high with the taut kerchiefs. These two contrasting parts in smooth triple and staccato duple time alternate as often as desired. [GPK]

Satī In Hindu mythology, the daughter of Daksha and wife of Rudra (i.e. Śiva). She killed herself by entering the fire after a quarrel between her husband and her father. The practice of satī (suttee) is in imitation or memory of this act.

satī or **suttee**   The practice of burning a Hindu widow on her husband's funeral pyre; also, the widow herself: literally, a faithful or true wife. The rite of satī was abolished by British law in 1829 but it still survives in Nepāl. Satī was based upon the belief that the husband would need everything dear or necessary to his comfort in the next world. It was not Vedic in origin, for it is mentioned neither in the *Ṛig-Veda,* the Sūtras, nor in the *Code of Manu.* The custom was never accepted throughout India but was widely practiced in Bengal and Rajputana. It dates from the 4th century B.C. and by the 6th century A.D. it had religious sanction. During the 10th to the 15th centuries it was a Brāhmanic rite. Probably the rite persisted as long as it did because the satī was promised 35 million years in Svarga and the veneration of her spirit as a reward. Also, all members of her husband's and her own family were cleansed of evil, even that of killing a Brāhman.

☞   The satīs are thus important female saints; all widows who have burned with their husbands on the funeral pyre are saints possessing healing powers. [MWS]

satire   In Old Irish mythology and legend, a spell or curse, usually a magic rime that brought dishonor, illness, and death to the victim. The ancient Celtic druids could rime people to death; later the gift passed to the poets (*filid*). There was no greater dishonor or disaster could befall a man than to be satirized, especially for ungenerosity, cowardice, or disloyalty. The first satire in Ireland was pronounced by Cairbre, a poet of the Tuatha Dé Danann, against Bres for meager hospitality, and Bres "decayed" after that. The satire was often used as a form of blackmail. The satirist who took Cuchulain's last spear in the last fight threatened to satirize him and all Ulster as "ungiving" if he did not give up the spear. So Cuchulain gave it and died without a weapon. The satire was usually recited *at* the victim face to face; red or black blotches and blisters came out on his face; soon he sickened and then died. See BATTLE OF MAG TURED.

Saturday or **Saturn's Day**   The Jewish Sabbath when no work of any kind may be done, fire struck, or money carried: called *Shiyár* by the early Arabs. People are divided on whether it is a lucky or an unlucky day. Some believe that the sun will shine if only very briefly every Saturday, and others that a moon on Saturday is unlucky. In Ireland it is a good day for drownings: "Saturday's moon will drown or burn," the people say; and a rainbow on Saturday predicts a week of foul weather. The belief that people born on Saturday can see ghosts is widely distributed; in eastern Europe people born on a Saturday have the gift for seeing and detecting vampires. Saturday, which marks the end of a cycle, is a bad day everywhere to get married or to begin work. [RDJ]

☞   In Greece, even into the 19th century, Saturday was the right day for disposing of vampires; it was said that vampires occupy their graves or tombs only on Saturdays. If exorcism by a priest fails to quiet a vampire, the people go to his tomb on a Saturday, take up the body, and burn it. Southern United States Negroes, reflecting European beliefs, also say that Saturday holds "no luck at all," except that if you sneeze on a Saturday you will see your sweetheart on Sunday, and Friday night dreams told on Saturday are bound to come true.

In India also Saturday is a bad day; it is śani's day, day of the Hindu god who brings bad luck. See FLAX.

Saturn   In ancient Roman religion, the god of agriculture: identified with the Greek Cronus, perhaps because of the equating of their two consorts in myth, Ops and Rhea. Saturn is generally held to have been a somewhat minor deity who came into prominence as an early king, culture bringer, and ruler of the Golden Age because of a tenuous identification with Cronus. As Krappe points out, the two theories of Saturn's nature contained in such a statement are irreconcilable unless a much earlier god, brought both to Greece and to Italy independently, is supposed. For Saturn appears early as a rather important figure; the Saturnalia was an important festival. In classical times, Saturn was thought to have been a king at the time of Janus. His temple stood at the foot of the Capitoline hill, where he was supposed to have made a settlement. The whole country was sometimes known as Saturnia, emphasizing the Golden Age of agriculture and civilized conduct thought to be a result of Saturn's rule. In myth, he is indistinguishable from Cronus; he was father of Jupiter, Pluto, Neptune, Juno —parallels to the Greek children of Cronus; he was dethroned by Jupiter. The name Saturn first appears applied to a day of the week, *Saturni dies,* in Tibullus, at about the beginning of the Christian era; Cicero mentions a planet name, Saturn. Compare SATURNALIA.

Saturnalia   In ancient Roman religion, the festival in mid-December commemorating the Golden Age of Saturn's rule and actually a solstice ceremony of the turning of the year and of protection of the winter-sown crops. The Saturnalia was originally observed on the 19th of the month, but after the reform of the calendar by Cæsar on the 17th. The 17th and 18th were later observed as the Saturnalia, the 19th and 20th as the Opalia (Ops was Saturn's cult partner). Under Caligula, a fifth day, the *dies juvenales,* was added, and eventually a week of festivity was observed, from the 17th to the 23rd of December. From the custom of giving presents of waxen fruits, candles, and dolls, the later days of the Saturnalia came to be known as the Sigillaria, after the Sigilarii, the doll-makers, who made the figurines and who held a fair at this time.

The usual was suspended during the Saturnalia: no punishments were handed down by the courts; schools were closed; war-making ceased; the toga was replaced by an undergarment; masquerading and change of dress between the sexes occurred; gambling, especially dicing, was fully countenanced; social distinctions not only were not observed, but often reversed, as in the instance of masters serving their servants; speech and action (as in many fertility ceremonies) were to some extent unbridled. The whole series of observances obviously place the Saturnalia among the fertility rites; everything tended towards increasing the fruitfulness of nature and of the people and of ensuring the rotation of the seasons by observing the turn of the sun northward again. The gift of imitation fruit has apparently to do with increase; the candles indicate the making of new fires customary at the solstices; the dolls, as has been noted as early as Varro, are the remains of the custom of human sacrifice. Frazer indicates a late survival of the human sacrifice in a Roman outpost camp; the Phœnician Baal, notoriously a man-eater, was called by the Greeks Cronus **and**

Saturn; a king, Saturn, was elected and permitted great license before and during the festival, only to die at its close. The choosing of a mock king for the duration of the festival is thus seen to be a survival of this custom. Compare BELTANE; CHRISTMAS; LORD OF MISRULE.

satyrs In ancient Greek mythology, the goat-like fertility spirits of mountains and forests who formed part of Dionysus' train. The satyrs were male and always sexually aroused. They had athletic bodies, with goat legs, tails of goats or horses, flat noses, pointed ears, hornlets on the forehead—thus they resembled Pan in many respects. Typically drunken and lustful, they romped with the nymphs, and are often depicted chasing them. The satyrs were cowards, always fleeing, but dangerous to men when in their delirious rage. In early representations they were ugly in form; but later they were graceful youths, the ugliness being attributed to the fat sileni, really older satyrs. According to Aristotle, the satyrs were mortal.

The satyrs are often compared with other similar beings. The Romans identified them with the fauns, who originally were field and harvest spirits, duplicates of Faunus. The *seirim* (hairy ones) of the Bible are parallels, as were the old Arabic mountain-pass demons. The modern Greek *callicantzari* preserve some of the satyrs' features: hairiness, goats' ears and feet, the addiction to women and dancing.

The *sikinnis* was the special dance of the satyrs. Their membership in the dithyrambic procession led eventually to the drama of Greece—through a formalization of the dithyramb with a chorus of satyrs, to the satyric drama parodying the more serious legends, and to tragedy (goat-song) itself.

savin A plant (*Juniper sabina*) known for centuries for certain medicinal properties. It is a sterile plant, and according to the doctrine of signatures causes sterility. It was called the Devil's herb from being so universally used by European witches and sorcerers in their spells, and perhaps from its reputation as an abortifacient. In many English and Scottish folk ballads, savin leaves were eaten by illegitimately pregnant girls as an abortifacient. See PULLING THE HEATHER GREEN.

Savitṛ In Vedic mythology, a name of the sun, especially in its life-giving creative aspect: literally generator.

Sāvitrī In the *Mahābhārata*, the heroine whose devotion to her husband was so great that Yama (god of death and lord of the underworld) was forced to restore her husband to life. Sāvitrī, daughter of King Aśvapati, insisted upon marrying Satyavāna in spite of the fact that he had only a year to live. After his death on the appointed day she followed Yama who carried off her husband's spirit. Yama was so impressed by her constancy that he offered her any boon except the life of Satyavāna, but she continued to follow him until he restored her husband to life.

savory Either of two plants of the genus *Satureia*. Both of these plants, as their name (savory) implies, are much used in seasoning, especially meat. They are plants of the satyrs under the dominion of Mercury. Culpeper says that they may be used interchangeably in medicine. They were recommended to expel wind, especially in pregnant women, and can be taken either internally or smelled. They were formerly much used

to cure stubborn coughs of the chest and lungs. The juice snuffed up the nostrils was good to brighten dull lethargic spirits; if dropped in the eyes, the juice cleared the sight. A savory poultice mixed with flour is good for sciatica. Savory was also used for impaired hearing, though its chief uses now are in digestive disorders.

saxifrage Any plant of the genus *Saxifraga*, native to Europe and the British Isles. It grows in the cracks of rocks and is popularly called breakstone. In Europe in the 16th century wet-nurses were wont to carry a sprig of saxifrage in their bosoms to increase the flow of milk; but it was so efficacious that it had to be removed in a few hours. In Great Britain the fresh root was chewed as a remedy for toothache and paralysis of the tongue, and was used in a decoction to take away freckles. Taken internally it cures a disordered spleen and drives away melancholy. According to the doctrine of signatures, it is efficacious for gall- and kidney-stones. It is said to dissolve mucus, and is therefore used as a gargle for hoarseness and sore throat. Dropped into wounds, the juice of the plant dries and heals them. In Russia women drink an infusion of the roots to prevent conception; and an infusion of the roots was drunk by the daughters of Attila to induce sterility. In Italy it is eaten by women to increase their beauty; and in German folk belief, the possessor of saxifrage can see witches on Walpurgis Night.

scalp dances American Indian victory dances around the enemies' scalps. From the Papago to the Blackfoot, returning victorious parties were met by dancing women. They dried, bleached, and decorated the scalps and fastened them on poles for display. The Juaneño scalps might include the ears, those taken by the Papago only a lock of hair. The scalps were tabu, and so were the warriors who had taken them; i.e. the scalps contained supernatural power and so did the men who had touched the enemy, and this power could be baneful previous to the proper ceremonies. Thus the warriors had to blacken their faces and undergo a period of ordeal and purification, among the Papago for 16 days.

In many tribes, men and women circled around a central scalp-pole: the Chaco Toba and Pilaga, the Zuñi, Papago, Oglala, the Ute in two concentric opposing circles. The Shoshone, Blackfoot, and San Felipe dancers carried the scalps on sticks, as men and women crossed and recrossed in two lines. Isleta and Blackfoot men and women flanked the scalp-takers in two facing lines. San Felipe men flanked the Opi war captain. Here, a selected girl danced with one Opi warrior after another, weaving in and out in the group.

Common features were a dramatization of deeds of prowess, frequently with weapons; races (Papago, Isleta); burlesque, often of an obscene nature (Zuñi *owinahaya;* women of Santa Clara, San Juan, Tesuque, Nambe); transvestitism (many pueblos); obscenity towards the scalp (Zuñi, Isleta) to reduce its power. After the insults, the Zuñi adopted the scalp into the tribe as a rain-maker. It also had that power at Santa Clara and other pueblos. The Papago *kuihui* or leaping dance around the pole consisted of forward and backward jumps with hands interlocked, as in the rain dance. Add to these fertility practices the sexual license frequently culminating the festivities—the scalps on their phallic poles were definitely invested with phallic properties.

Today the scalp and victory dances of the more easterly tribes have become secular amusement. The Sauk men and women limp in their clockwise Victory dance as a social pastime and to celebrate Armistice Day. The Iroquois enact stereotyped scenes of capture, rescue, conquest, in their *ganehǫ* for white audiences in connection with shows and lacrosse games. The songs for these last are also of a secular nature, separate from the ceremonial cycles. Originally, however, scalp-dance songs had great significance. The Oglala sang about the warpath, the Papago about the myth of Elder Brother who killed the monster eagle.

These ceremonies, dances, and songs of the warpath and of victory were destined to extinction along with the intertribal raids, or to secularization or transference to their secondary function of rain-making. [GPK]

scalping Removal of a portion of the skin, with hair attached, from an enemy's head: a practice of the North American Indians in aboriginal times, as shown from certain archeological material, which apparently was greatly increased in historic times. Scalps were exhibited in the war or scalp dance, particularly by eastern and southeastern tribes, as trophies after the return of a victorious war party; curiously enough it was often not the warriors (who were undergoing purification at the time), but old women who danced with the scalps in their mouths, or on the end of a pole, etc., during the victory dance. In colonial times the bounties offered by the French and English to Indian warriors for scalps were probably responsible for the spread of scalping to many western tribes which originally did not scalp. Contrary to popular impression, scalping, while painful, was not necessarily fatal; there are many instances in which scalped victims were sent back to their tribes alive as a direct defiance and an incitement to retaliation. Scalping receives infrequent mention in North American Indian tales; the wider practice of taking the entire head of a slain enemy is more frequently noticed. See *Handbook of the American Indians* (2 vols., Washington, D.C., 1906 and 1910), vol. 2, pp. 482–83. [EWV]

scapegoat Any material object, animal, bird, or person on whom the bad luck, diseases, misfortunes, and sins of an individual or group are symbolically placed, and which is then turned loose, driven off with stones, cast into a river or the sea, etc., in the belief that it takes away with it all the evils placed upon it. The term is derived from the goat upon whose head Aaron symbolically laid the sins of the people on the day of atonement, after which it was led away into the wilderness (*Lev.* xvi). The transference of sickness and sin to a tree, animal, or human being is a world-wide, usually annual, folk custom; it was practiced in the ancient classical cultures and is common among all primitive peoples. In ancient Greece, the scapegoat was often a volunteer; he was bedecked and led about the city, then stoned to death outside the walls. The culmination of the scapegoat idea is the dying god of numerous religions, typified by the crucifixion of Jesus, who took upon himself the sins of the world. See SIN-EATER.

☞ The expulsion of diseases by means of a scapegoat was widely practiced in the Inca empire and is still a popular method of curing among modern Quechua and Aymara Indians. Formerly, when a village was affected by an epidemic, a black llama was loaded with the clothing of the sick and driven out of the village to carry away the disease.

The Aymara and Quechua medicine men transfer the diseases of their patients to an animal, generally a guinea-pig, which is killed and burned, or to an object which is destroyed. They also abandon along a river food and clothes which have been touched by a sick person. Whoever carries them away takes with him the disease. See DISEASES. [AM]

scarab A beetle (*Scarabæus sacer*) of the Mediterranean region; also, its representation in stone, faience, etc., used as an amulet, seal, or the like. The Egyptians identified the scarab with the god Khepera. Its habit is to roll balls of dung for food supply and to lay its egg in such a dung pellet (Fabre showed that the egg was laid in a pear-shaped ball of dung, not in a spherical one). The hatching of the new beetle was a marvel to the Egyptians, who believed that this was an example of spontaneous generation, or at least of unisexual creation, since only the male beetle makes the dung pellet and since they did not recognize the female beetle. The scarabæus beetle was called *kheperer*, a word meaning to become, or phenomenon, or marvel. Thus identified with Khepera, the beetle became a symbol of the force that rolled the sun across the heavens, and of the rising sun, self-generated. Khepera was figured as a man with a scarab in place of his head.

The shape of the scarab lent itself readily to use as a ring or chain-suspended seal. It is found also in tombs on a heart-shaped base. These heart-scarabs of green stone set in gold were placed over the heart of the dead while a chapter of the *Book of the Dead* was read during the funeral service. The significance of the scarab here is that of resurrection; just as the sun was reborn, so would the soul of the man be born again. Since the scarab laid only one egg, phœnix-like it was the original beetle when reborn fully formed. In later times, Christ was known as the Good Scarab, for he was the "only-begotten son" of God.

Very early the scarab became a characteristic amulet in Egypt. Scarabs are found in tombs as early as the pre-Dynastic period (before 3500 B.C.). By the VI Dynasty (c. 2600–2500 B.C.), scarabs had become combination amulets and seals, bearing the names of the kings. Even during the Empire period (following 1580 B.C.) scarabs in popular circulation still bore the names of Khufu and Khafre, the great kings of the IV Dynasty, because of the magical power inherent in the names of these great pyramid builders. Still more popular, for many centuries after his reign, was the name of the great conqueror Thothmes III (c. 1501–1447 B.C.) of the XVIII Dynasty, the temple builder and restorer (Karnak, Memphis, Heliopolis, Abydos, etc.) and erector of such monuments as the obelisks now in New York and London; the Phœnicians, who manufactured cheap amulets for trade purposes, seem to have continued the use of his name on their mass-produced scarabs as late as the 4th century B.C. By the XII Dynasty (2000–1788 B.C.), scarab seals were in private use among the well-to-do. During the XVIII Dynasty (1580–1350 B.C.) the scarab became very popular as a common souvenir for visitors to temples, fairs, shrines, and the like. The hand-carving that made each scarab a work of art disappeared almost completely, and in the XIX Dynasty scarabs were mold-cast and objects of little value.

Scarabs were fashioned in many shapes, all more or less maintaining the oval form, sometimes realistic representations of the beetle, sometimes abstract and stylized. In addition to the heart-scarabs, there were scarabs with human faces, especially during and after the XVIII Dynasty with Negro faces and with bull's or cat's or ibis' heads. Scarabs were known wherever Egyptian influence or Phœnician trade carried them: Canaan, Greece, Etruria, etc.

Schäfflertanz or **Böttchertanz** A carnival dance formerly performed in Munich every seven years. The two lines of men polkaed through various quadrille and longways formations and formed patterns and archways with iron hoops or, rather, barrel staves. The men appeared in brilliant scarlet jackets, black breeches, and gold aprons, and the hoops were adorned with flowers and boxwood branches. One tradition attributes the dance to the guild of coopers. (*Schäffler* is South German for cooper, *Schaff* meaning tub); another tradition traces it to the control of the plague of 1517, although the dance was already reported in 1463. The flowered arches relate it to the *arcos* of Spain, religious vestiges of ancient vegetation rites; and the potential contents of the tub suggest water magic. The seven figures are in keeping: *Schlange* (serpent), *Laube* (bower), *Kreuz* (cross), *Krone* (crown), *Kleiner Kreis* (small circle) of four circles, *Chassieren* (which advance and retire), and *Reifenschwung* (hoop-swinging by two central dancers in a large circle). In 1683 the *Schäffler* still fenced, thus relating them to sword dancers or *moriscas*. The Schäfflertanz was last performed in Munich in 1928. [GPK]

Schemen (from Middle High German *scheme*, mask): Carnival runners of Germany and Austria, still functional in processions at Imst in the Austrian Alps. Twenty of them appear in two groups, male *Scheller* and female *Roller*, named after the huge sleigh-bells and cow-bells fastened to their belts. The former wear bearded masks, the latter smooth, pink faces; and both have huge mirrored crowns, *Scheine*. They are parodied by grotesque *Lagge Scheller* and *Lagge Roller*, and accompanied by water demons, *Spritzer* (squirters), and *Hexen* (witches), who have their own round dance. The Schemen run and leap in their serpentine course. They are to this day a votive society.

In the Middle Ages similar maskers accompanied the Nüremberg butchers' guild or *Metzgertanz* in a similar running course, *Schemenlaufen*, as part of the phallic carnival procession. This course, also called *Schembartlaufen* (course of the bearded maskers) or *Schönbartlaufen*, was discontinued after 1539 because of excesses, but is commemorated in some 40 illuminated manuscripts.

The Schemen belong to the company of fantastic creatures surviving in rural Europe from pre-Christian fertility demons. They have a clear relationship with the (also Austrian) *Perchten*. [GPK]

Schlauraffenland The German term for the Land of Cockaigne. Medieval European satirists poked fun at the idealistic paradise conceptions of tradition, both religious and secular, by creating a mock country called by such names as Cockaigne or Schlauraffenland.

Schlauraffenland, an isle to the west, beyond the horizon, is a land of unspeakable wonders. Roasted geese chase themselves down the streets, turning themselves over as they flee. There are the traditional rivers of wine; ladies are perennially fair, and there is no such thing as an ugly wench. Here one finds neither night, death, hail, rain, nor futile disputations. In Schlauraffenland sleep is paid for instead of work. The inhabitants slake their thirst from rivers of wine or streams of milk; they surfeit themselves on roast geese and pigs that are always at hand; broiled fish simply serve themselves. At certain intervals in the week it rains torte, milk, or soup. Houses are built of cake and other delectables.

For the history of the word, consult the Grimms' *Deutsches Wörterbuch*. Old writers in Germany frequently used the phrase *Affenzeit* to date their stories; *Schlauraffe* is used by Brant (*Narrenschiff*, 1494) to indicate a lazy person. The word was used by Hans Sachs and also by Luther. Much influence on Continental lying tales of this type may be ascribed to Lucian's *Vera Historia*. See Erwin Rohde, *Der Griechische Roman und seine Vorläufer* (Leipzig, 1914). [GPS]

Schnitzelbank A cumulative drinking song of Germany, introduced into America by German settlers of Pennsylvania, Milwaukee, etc., and a favorite of beerhalls until the World War I prejudice against anything German reduced its popularity. Its pattern is question-and-answer: "Ist das nicht ein schnitzelbank?/ Ja, das ist ein schnitzelbank." Each stanza adds another item which is repeated in reverse order each time. A Pennsylvania Dutch variant is called *Di Lichputscher* (The Candle Snuffer).

schottische A couple ballroom dance of Swedish origin. The regular step is right forward, left close, right forward, hop right—all in fast, light duple tempo. The running schottische is three running steps and a hop. As many couples as will are arranged in a counterclockwise circle. The man's right arm is around his partner's waist and her left hand is on his shoulder. Fundamentally in all Scandinavian countries the two figures consist of sideward separation and meeting, then pivot right with four step-hops, in shoulder-waist position. As a variant the girl alone moves away to the right and back in. Or she moves back and the boy forward, and she finishes with a turn under his arm. The Swiss schottische is also called the "Swiss Changing Polka," because of the partner change. After each succession of steps the man moves right to the next lady. This dance includes various positions: ballroom, back skating hold, etc. At one time the boy kneels while the girl dances around him. For the finale he tosses her into the air. The American schottische introduces several other variants, as handclapping and pivot during the separation. The *chote* of New Mexico uses a buzz step for the pivot and introduces a heel-toe step and under-arm turn for the girl. As other "old-fashioned" dances, the schottische is increasing in popularity in the United States. [GPK]

Schuhplattler Shoe-swatting dance of Bavaria. In addition to local variants, there are two chief types: 1) for a man and woman (or a number of couples); 2) for two men. The first is a courtship mime of refusal and final acceptance, the woman calmly gyrating while the man strenuously beats a resounding tattoo on his leather breeches, his thighs, and on his shoe-soles. He follows the woman with seductive clicking sounds. This sound, his postures, and the extravagant swinging of his arms during the swatting are a vestige of animal mime, of the antics of the black grouse and his female. In the final acceptance the arms are wound into a "mirror" through which they steal a kiss, as in the *Ländler*. The gay triple-beat music and the waltz step of the woman also resemble the *Ländler*.

The second, the men's Schuhplattler is a humorous and fierce challenge, a fight between two rivals, and the victory of one. (Compare OXDANSEN.) Keeping up the swatting rhythm, the rivals crouch stealthily, leap, push with their shoulders, box their ears, strike their hands, pull their hair, beat knuckles on the floor, till the victor sits astride his rival and pummels him on the rear. An exuberant ease pervades this horseplay, the strenuous leaps (called *Haidauer* and *Tölzer Sprünge*), and the lifting of the girl into the air in climactic moments. [GPK]

Scorpio The Scorpion: a southern constellation, eighth sign of the zodiac, adjoining Libra, and containing the brilliant red star Antares. In classical legend Scorpio is the monster that stung Orion to death and terrified the horses of the sun while they were being driven by the inexperienced young Phaethon. Orion still flees before Scorpio; as Scorpio rises Orion sets. To the ancient Hebrews this constellation was also Scorpion (*'Akrabh*) and emblem of the tribe of Dan. To the Akkadians it was Girtab, the Stinger. Among the ancient Babylonians it was regarded as one of the monsters created by Tiamat and as a symbol of the setting sun and darkness. Scorpio was Tsing Lung, the beneficent Azure Dragon of a former Chinese zodiac, but in the time of Confucius the whole constellation took the name of the fire star, Ta Who, Great Fire (Antares), and was worshipped as a protection against fire.

The people of New Zealand call this constellation the Fish-Hook of Maui, with which, their mythology says, he fished up their island from the underworld. Among the Mískito Indians of Honduras and Nicaragua, Scorpio's heliacal rising occurs a few days before Christmas, hence these people have named Antares Kristmas. See Heath's "Mískito Glossary," *IJAL* 16: 25. Among the Berbers, the constellation is sometimes likened to a scorpion, sometimes to a palm tree. They identify Antares as a youth climbing the palm tree, who stopped half way up to eye some pretty young girls.

In astrology Scorpio is an ill-omened constellation, bringing in its wake cold, darkness, storm, causing wars, and exerting an evil influence on the affairs of men. Its red star Antares is said to be as baleful as Mars, whose twin star it is considered. A comet appearing in the sign of Scorpio is thought sure to bring plagues. But the alchemists rejoiced in the heliacal rising of Scorpio, for only when the sun was in this sign could their coveted transmutations of baser metals into gold take place.

Scotch snap The inverted dotted rhythm characteristic of the Scottish national dance, the Strathspey, in which, for example, a quarter note may be followed by a three-quarter note. A similar rhythm is observed in certain jig tunes and in jazz, and it has been suggested that a part of the rhythmic character of jazz is derived from these European musical types.

Scott, Sir Walter (1771–1852) Scottish novelist and poet. Scott's interest in the ballads of the Scottish Low-

lands culminated in his *Minstrelsy of the Scottish Border* (1802–03); for this anthology he is assigned a prominent place in the annals of European balladry as early collector and enthusiast. The collection consists of authentic ballads supplemented by original pieces written in the ballad manner by both himself and his collaborator, John Leyden, a literate peasant. Concerning the "authentic" ballads, some controversy has arisen from time to time. For pronouncements on the matter, consult Albert C. Baugh, *A Literary History of England* (New York & London, 1948), p. 1208, n. 7.

That Scott was conversant with folk beliefs and customs, current both in his own time and in past periods, is evident from his use of folklore in his romances. There is much Scandinavian lore in *The Pirate;* Manx superstitions in *Peveril of the Peak;* a revenant in *Waverley;* a demon dog in *Count Robert of Paris;* a witch, Meg Merrilies, in *Guy Mannering.* More extensive suggestions on Scott's use of folklore may be found in several articles by C. O. Parsons in *Notes & Queries* clxxxiv (1943), pp. 95–97; clxxxv (1943), pp. 4–9, 92–100; clxxxviii (1945), pp. 2–8, 30–33, 76–77, 98–101.

scraper A primitive musical or noise-making instrument known to paleolithic man and still in use among certain peoples as widely separated as West Indian Negroes, North and Central American Indians, natives of India, etc. The instrument consists of a notched or dentated stick, bone, shell, or gourd, rubbed with a stick or horn or other hard instrument to produce a rasping sound; in an acculturated state it may be replaced by a kitchen grater or similar manufactured gadget. Its original significance is not so much musical as magical, both the phallic significance of the bone or stick and the fricative motion of the playing suggesting the sexual act and thus procreation and life-giving properties. Its chief uses have been as accompaniment to funerals and sacrificial rites, as in ancient Mexico (see AYOTL), in connection with dances of fertility and rain-making (see KACHAWHARR; DEER DANCE), and for wooing. Its use at funeral ceremonies, like that of the flute, is for the renewal of life, rather than for mourning, though the sound of the Aztec bone scrapers (*omichicahuaztli*) was described by a Spanish observer as very sad music. Wooden scrapers, or *raspadors,* are used in Mexico today by the Seris, Tarahumaras, Yaquis, and Mayos for their deer dances, which are rain dances. Among North American Indians both notched sticks and baskets rubbed with a stick or horn are associated with rain and fertility. The Yuman *Frog Song* series, for example, is accompanied by the scraped basket, and the association of frog, scraper, and rain is completely linked in symbolism. The Hopi have similar associations with their notched stick scraper rubbed with a bone (*truhkumpi*). The Cheyennes have a tale of wooing in which a maiden whose interest was difficult to arouse was finally won by a young man who courted her, following the advice of a wise man, by rubbing an elk horn with an antelope bone. The scraper of the Kānika tribe of India is an iron tube, the harsh noise of which stimulates tremendous emotional excitement as it accompanies the recitation of prayers and names of deities. Two survivals of the African scrapers in the New World are the jawbone and the dentlé. In China a scraper called the "tiger" (*yü*), a wooden carving in the form of a crouching tiger with a serrated backbone is sounded three times at the close of the Confucian service.

sculping dance   A Labrador Eskimo burlesque of the skinning of a hunter's quarry. A small boy mimics the dead animal by lying down and covering himself with a shawl. The "hunter" dances in joy over the kill and in anticipation of the rare fur. He mimes the sculping, crooning to himself. Suddenly the "animal" jumps up and runs off, leaving the hunter with a worthless skin. The moral is not to be greedy or vainglorious. [GPK]

seasonal ceremonies   In many North American Indian tribes, ceremonies were performed during part of the year only. For example, on the North Pacific Coast winter was the ceremonial season of great and holy quiet, when dances and rites of all sorts were held; in summer the tribes devoted themselves almost exclusively to fishing, berrying, and laying up supplies of food. Among Eastern Woodlands tribes such as for example the Shawnee, summer was the season for the large ceremonies such as the Bread dances, and the Green Corn or Man's dance; at this time people lived in their semipermanent villages and tended their crops, while in winter they camped in small groups in brushy river bottoms and the men went off on hunting and trapping expeditions. Among the Maidu and other Central California tribes, October to May was the season for the *kuksu* ceremonies. In the Southwest among the Pueblos, although dances are held the year round, masked or kachina dances are held during the winter months only. [EWV]

Sebek, Sobek, Sobk, or **Souchos**   A local god of the Fayum in ancient Egypt, figured as a crocodile or as a man with a crocodile head; his worship seems to have been especially prominent in the XII Dynasty, though he never was more than a local god. As Sebek-Rā, he was a man with a crocodile head; as Sebek-Osiris, he was the Fayum god of the dead, a crocodile with a human head; sometimes he appears as a crocodile with a hawk's head, probably identified with Horus. Sebek, as a sinister crocodile god, was often identified with Set, the slayer of Osiris. The sacred crocodiles in his lake within the temple precincts were under the care of his priests, who adorned them with jewels.

Sébillot, Paul (1846–1918)   French folklorist, often referred to as the "Father of French folklore studies." Although he studied law and became a notary in Paris, he soon turned to painting and from 1870–1883 exhibited his pictures in the Salon. Having become interested in the life and lore of the people of France during his travels about the country, he turned his attention to their folklore and published a varied array of volumes on his findings: *Contes populaires de la Haute Bretagne* (3 ser., 1880–82); *Légendes, croyances, et superstitions de la mer* (2 v., 1886–87); *Littérature orale de l'Auvergne* (1898); *Le folklore de pêcheur* (1901); *Le folklore de France* (1904–07; 4 volumes of 8 projected); *Le folklore, littérature orale et ethnographie traditionelle* (1913). For thirty years, he was editor of the *Revue des traditions populaires,* a periodical that published tales and other folk materials from all parts of France, gathered by Sébillot himself and by Cosquin, including original articles by each.

seconde   The middle-sized drum of the Haitian vodun group of three, entering the rhythmic pattern after the first (*bula*). It is usually about 22 inches high and 8 or 9 in diameter and may be played with the hands or with one hand and a stick.

Sedna   The tale of Sedna, mistress of the underworld, is one of the most widely known of all Eskimo tales. Among the Central Eskimo the woman who is the chief figure is known as Sedna; in other Eskimo groups as Arnaknagsak, etc. The tale is practically the only origin tale existent among the Eskimo, but accounts only for the origin of fish and sea animals. Briefly, it is as follows: A girl refuses suitors, and marries a bird (often a fulmar) or a dog. The girl's father kills her husband and takes his daughter home in a boat. On the way a storm arises, and the father throws Sedna overboard. She clings to the boat, and he chops off her fingers; these become fish and sea mammals. Her animal children eat up the father. Sedna becomes the chief deity of the lower world, and each fall the Eskimo hold a great feast and festival in her honor. The Sedna tale is told throughout the Eskimo region, but in some versions is merged with that of Dog Husband. For references to treatments of the Sedna myth see Stith Thompson, *Tales of the North American Indians* (Cambridge, Mass., 1929), pp. 272–273. See ANGAKOK; ANGUTA; ADLIVUN; BEAST MARRIAGE. [EWV]

☛   The famous Sedna myth of the Eskimos has an interesting parallel in the mythology of some Chaco tribes. The Great Goddess of the Chamacoco is said to have mated with dogs and to have given birth to dog-like spirits. A similar story is told by the Mataco. [AM]

seguidillas   An intricate, widespread couple dance of Spain. It is a descendant of the *fandango* and has developed not only many regional forms, but also has produced numerous other dances: *arriba* and *pasan* of Burgos, *habas verdes* of Extremadura. Regional variants are *guipzcoanas, gallegas, zamoranas, aragonesas, valencianas, murcianas, manchegas.* The last is the most typical, and is the source of the famous *seguidillas sevillanas,* commonly known as *sevillanas.* Combination with the *bolero* fashioned the *seguidillas-boleras* and *sevillanas-boleras.* Out of the *sevillanas* developed the *peteneras, guajiras, fandanguillo.* The *malagueña* is similar.

All seguidillas have a family resemblance. The *sevillanas* dazzle with their graceful coordination of arm lines, full leg-swings (*fouettés*), high *pas de basque,* and rhythmic counterpoint of castanets and footwork. They are proud and gay, more aristocratic than the abandoned *flamenco* dances, though they have become gipsified within the last half century. Characteristic steps are called *manchegas, lazos, piruetas, pasadas, panaderos,* etc. An important feature is the *paseo* (walk around). Each of the seven *coplas* concludes with *bien parado* (well stopped), a sudden posed halt, accompanied by shouts of *Olé.* It is essentially a virtuoso dance for one or two couples, and entirely secular, in contrast with the ritualistic communal dances of northern Spain. [GPK]

seide   The sacred stones or luck stones of the Lapps; natural stones often having a peculiar form, resembling human beings or animals. They are used for divination and are offered for good luck in fishing, etc. [JB]

seises   The six: the dancing boys of Seville Cathedral, now ten in number, formerly evidently six, as in the Cotswold Morris. The elaborate longways figures resemble those of the Morris. One of the sections of the dance calls for stick play. Formerly in one variation the dancers dressed as girls, but usually they wear breeches, plumed hats, and bells, and ply castanets in their hands. They chant a hymn in two parts to orchestral accompaniment.

It is a chaste and entirely ritualistic performance, in contrast with the fiery couple dances of Andalusia. Though first mentioned in 1439, the dance of los seises is doubtless an ancient ritual form, related, according to Curt Sachs' cogent argument, to the *Moriscas*. In 1685, when on the verge of suppression, they were preserved by papal edict, "so long as the costumes" lasted. Thanks to repairs, they last to this day. Formerly the seises also danced in Toledo Cathedral, and there were similar groups in Valencia and Jerez. Corpus Christi is their great celebration, other sacred festivals being three evenings before Lent (Carnival), the octaves of Corpus Christi, and La Purissima.

The similarity to the *santiaguitos* of Chila, Puebla, Mexico is amazing, in formations, in the cast of young boys, the votive purpose, and the location in a church as part of a religious fiesta. [GPK]

Seketi songs A type of satirical song sung by Surinam Bush Negroes in connection with secular dancing and made up of topical comment. The origin of the type is the songs of Dahomean women's choruses devoted to eulogizing the chief and defending him and his ancestors against the taunts of enemies. (See M. J. Herskovits, *Suriname Folklore*.)

Selene The ancient Greek moon goddess: the Roman counterpart was Luna. Her mythology is minor; she appears importantly only in the Endymion myth (M433). Endymion's beauty so enchanted Selene that she came to Mt. Latmos to kiss him as he slept and to sleep at his side. As with other mortals loved by divinities, Endymion found only fatal peril in this situation, and, either because he begged Zeus to put him to sleep that he might always enjoy such dreams, or because Selene herself thus enchanted him to have him with her always, he was placed in eternal sleep, the never-waking lover of the moon. Another myth concerns Selene and Pan, to whom she submitted for the price of a white fleece or who had intercourse with her as a white ram. Selene was in later times identified with several other goddesses: Artemis (Hecate) principally, but also Hera, Io, Pasiphae. Her parentage—usually she is daughter of Hyperion and Theia—varies; she is, for example, sometimes daughter, sometimes sister, of Helios, the sun god. She is a charioteer driving winged white horses or cows or bulls (the lunar crescent as the cow's horns is a familiar symbol), or she rides a horse, mule, steer, or ram. As the counterpart of Phœbus Apollo (late sun god), she is sometimes called Phœbe; another name, Mene, is due to her change of aspect through the month. (The moon god Men was worshipped in Asia Minor, whence his cult came to Athens.) She was thought to have influence on reproductive powers, plant, animal, and human, and was invoked at the new and full moons. Selene, the moon, was in the Hellenistic era thought to be the place where the souls of the dead went.

sells Hoaxes, practical jokes, and hazing pranks which carry "aggressive humor" to the point where the butt of the joke is also its victim. Sells range from April Fool pranks (e.g. calling up the zoo to ask for Miss Campbell, Mr. Fox, Mr. Leo Lion) and children's tricks and catches

(see ADAM AND EVE AND PINCH ME; CATCH TALE) to fool's errands (sending a green hand in search of a mythical or fictitious object, such as a left-handed monkey wrench, a bottle stretcher, a four-foot yard stick, a sky hook), and hoaxing, codding yarns and tall tales (see FEARSOME CRITTERS; LIARS AND LYING TALES).

As a playful deception of the gullible and ignorant, sells are aimed especially at the stranger, tenderfoot, novice, or greenhorn. Hence, their wide use in initiation rites in occupations and associations and their prevalence in backwoods and frontier communities, where rough horseplay affords an outlet for surplus energy and animal spirits and a relief from monotony, loneliness, and insecurity. The Western love of practical joking has been attributed variously to sadism and to democratic attack on pretense and affectation.

Two time-honored Western tenderfoot sells are the snipe hunt and the badger fight. In the former, the victim is lured on an evening expedition into the country, preferably to a lonely, swampy, mosquito-infested spot near a river, where he is left holding the sack in the dark, sometimes with a lighted candle on the ground, while the others retire presumably to beat up the snipe but actually to return home. (Compare the French custom of hunting the dahut, described by Jo Chartois, *JAFL* 58:21–24; see DAHUT.) In the badger fight the victim is inveigled into betting on a fight between dogs and a "badger," and, in order to prevent cheating, is requested to pull the badger out of the sack, only to find, to his public embarrassment, a chamber pot at the end of the rope.

In California gold rush days, a "noteworthy swindle, a practical joke, a brilliant hoax" was known as a whizzer, "plain whizzer" or "bald-headed whizzer" according to its adroitness (e.g. "jack-pine gold," in which a gullible stranger is inveigled into staking a claim and risking his neck on a jack pine said to bear gold nuggets near the top). Out of the rough humor of the mining camps developed the "hoax story" or journalistic sell (e.g. the petrified man in Mark Twain's story of that name and Dan De Quille's "The Silver Man"). Akin to the pastime sell, but to be distinguished from it, are swindling trade ruses like the Yankee razor-strop trade and humbugs like Barnum's "To the Egress." A link between the two is to be found in hoaxing, nature-making myths (mass hallucinations and deceptions) like sea serpents and flying saucers. (See Curtis D. MacDougall, *Hoaxes*, 1940.) B. A. BOTKIN

Selu Proper name of the Cherokee Indian Corn Mother. She is the wife of Kanati, the Hunter, and the mother of the two Thunder Boys of Cherokee mythology. [EWV]

še'lu dilskusti The "corn dance" of the Cherokee Indians of North Carolina and northeastern Oklahoma. Similar to the Iroquois *oneǫntóenǫ*. The dancers stomp in a counterclockwise arc, men and women separated. However, the Cherokee songs are antiphonal and accompanied by antiphonal gestures, the women planting, the men covering the seeds with a hoe. In the course of the dance, the men break into the women's line in alternation. Finally the leader winds the whole group into a spiral, as commonly among the Cherokee.

This dance is related to the women's planting rite (compare TǪWISAS). It is included in the all-day corn ceremony (*agohundi*) just as the Iroquois corn dance is a part of their Green Corn festival. Both invoke a good harvest and give thanks for it, the *agohundi* with curative rites, formerly incidental, now prominent. In the Christianized milieu, much of the original ritual significance has been lost. [GPK]

sembradoras Literally, the sowers: an agricultural dance for men and women of the Michoacán highlands (Mexico), especially Tzintzuntzan. The aboriginal function is still evident in the action and properties, though the steps, music, and costume are colonial. The men carry a hoe, shovel, or other farming implement, and the women hold baskets filled with fresh turnip blossoms, maize, and wheat, which they strew during the dance, and tortillas which they throw to the audience. Side by side partners circle counterclockwise around a yoke of oxen decorated with ears of corn, flowers, and ribbons. The first and third part of the dance uses a heel two-step, the second part a *zapateado*. In this section, the *jarabe*, the animals are driven off and the men and women dance face to face or cross over in two lines. The gay changeable music for violin and drum is as festive as the dancing. The costumes, too, are their best, the men with their cleanest white peon suits and finest fringed black-and-white serapes; the women with the modern Tarascan "roll" (a voluminous pleated wool skirt), embroidered blouse and sash, ribbons in their braids, all in blacks, reds, and whites.

This dance combines the actions of planting and sowing with the celebration of the first-fruits. At Candlemas (February 2), the date of the dance, the first harvest is in and the soil is ready for a second. The first-fruits are offered in the decorations of the oxen and the contents of the women's baskets, clear vestiges of sacrifice to agrarian spirits for thanks and further protection. [GPK]

Semele In Greek mythology, daughter of Cadmus of Thebes and Harmonia and mother of Dionysus: the name is that of the Phrygian earth-mother Zemelo (compare Russian *zemlya*, land; Lithuanian *Zemepatis*, lord of earth); her Greek title seems to have been Thyone. According to the principal tradition, Zeus visited her clandestinely and fathered Dionysus. Hera disguised herself as an old nurse of Semele and, seeking revenge, convinced the girl that she must make Zeus appear to her in his glory as the divine bridegroom. In a very human manner, Zeus, the expectant father, could deny Semele nothing and promised to do anything she asked of him. Despite his warnings, Semele insisted that he appear in his splendor. The flame and power of the god of lightnings burned her to ash, but from her remains Zeus rescued the six-month Dionysus and sewed him into his thigh. Later Dionysus rescued his mother from Hades and made her a goddess. It is said that her sisters, Ino, Autonoe, and Agave, after she had been burned to death, reported that she really was pregnant by a mortal, and that Zeus killed her because she claimed him as her lover. The story reflects the common belief that to see or to be loved by a divine being is dangerous and often fatal: compare the stories of Iasion, Actæon, Tiresias.

Semiramis The Greek form of Sammu-ramat, wife of Shamshi-Adad V of Assyria; a historical personage (regent from 811–808 B.C.) about whom many legends collected and whose story as we know it today is entirely legendary, except for the reestablishment of her actual identity. In legend, she was the daughter of Atargatis, who was a fertility goddess of the region to whom fish and doves were sacred. Semiramis was abandoned as an infant, and was nourished by doves: she is thus far identified with Atargatis, the dove goddess, but perhaps the popular etymology tying her name to the Assyrian word *summat*, dove, lies at the base of this identification. The royal shepherd Simmas found the baby and brought her up. Onnes (the name is reminiscent of the fish god Oannes, in turn linking her with the fish aspect of her mother) married Semiramis and in turn Ninus, the emperor, fell in love with her. Onnes committed suicide and Ninus made Semiramis queen. (Another etymological chain explains the legendary Semiramis: Nina, the feminine form of Ninus, is the goddess identical with Ishtar, with whom Semiramis is identified as fertility deity.)

The next event in her career makes Frazer suspect the attachment to her name of the ceremonial killing of the king myth of the region. She persuaded Ninus to make her ruler for five days, and on the second day she exerted her power and had him killed. As reigning queen, Semiramis traveled through her realm, building cities, roads, and monuments. Eventually all the great building feats of antiquity in the Persian and Armenian area were credited to Semiramis; especially is she noted as the builder of Babylon. During her 42-year reign, Semiramis (in this she is the counterpart of Ishtar) took many lovers from among her subjects; and, when her appetite for the lover of the moment waned, she had him put to death. Her own son was said to have been one of the victims of her lust. At the end of her reign, she turned her kingdom over to her son Ninyas and was changed into a dove. Another story says that she simply disappeared.

Throughout the story of Semiramis, there is clear evidence of the accretion of myth about a historical character—here a somewhat minor person—the myths being in several instances clearly much older than the queen they deal with. The seizing of the throne, for example, during the short-term reign of a temporary ruler involves material much older than the 9th century B.C. The abandoned child motif (S300) is found in the "histories" of great heroes from Moses and Œdipus. See ARA.

Semitic folklore A loose overall term used for convenience to designate the sum total of what are really the separate and distinct folklores of the peoples who spoke (or speak) Semitic languages. For the purposes of this article, however, the area is restricted to the ancient civilizations of the Babylonians and Assyrians, Canaanites and Israelites. Modern Semitic folklore, including especially that of the Arabs and Jews, has been excluded, on the grounds that so much of it is due to direct borrowings from other peoples and can therefore not be described as distinctive. The material thus embraced is by no means homogeneous, for the peoples in question never constituted a single ethnic unit nor possessed a single common culture.

Nor is the material necessarily of native origin. The Babylonians and Assyrians, for example, inherited much of their popular lore from the earlier non-Semitic Sumerians; just as a great deal of what passes today for Jewish folklore really represents direct borrowings from the Gentile peoples among whom the Jews happen to have been dispersed. The criterion for calling the material Semitic is currency rather than provenience.

It is to be observed also that the term *folklore* must be interpreted, in this context, in a somewhat liberal sense; for many of the so-called Semitic peoples have long since disappeared, and their extant literary and other remains rarely permit us to decide with certainty whether a given practice or belief falls properly within the category of religion, as being a matter of living faith, or within that of folklore, as being but a popular survival. No one can say definitely, for example, whether the long lists of deities and spirits invoked in Babylonian magical incantations represent beings actually adored or merely form part of a traditional mumbo-jumbo, like the "ghoulies and ghosties and long-leggity beasties" of the familiar Cornish prayer. (The present writer has adopted the principle of assigning to folklore any element of a popular ceremony or any feature of a tale or myth which is no longer intelligible to performer or narrator, which is neither logically nor organically related to the whole, and which is out of harmony with the normative thought and usage of the period.)

Study of this ancient folklore is still in infancy; for although much attention has been paid to the Old Testament and to the later and more accessible Arabic and Jewish material, the earlier Mesopotamian and Canaanite sources, preserved in cuneiform script, remain virtually unexplored. The reason for this is that those sources are of relatively recent discovery and have not yet emerged fully from the preliminary stage of purely philological exegesis. Consequently, they have not yet been integrated, to any appreciable extent, into the general stock of world folklore, nor have the recognized techniques of folklore research been brought to bear on them.

To the trained folklorist, the present situation is, indeed, little short of chaotic and possesses all the features of a scientist's nightmare. With but rare exceptions, customs and ceremonies continue to be interpreted on an isolated, individual basis, without reference to their analogies elsewhere and to the fundamental significance which such analogies suggest; while tales and myths are artificially detached from their types and elucidated in terms of their specific settings, without recognition of generic motifs and without regard to the fact that they are, *au fond,* but particular variants of common and widespread themes. Nor, unfortunately, has there been any adequate *rapport* between Orientalists on the one hand and folklorists on the other, with the result that the former have tended to elucidate the material without proper regard for its cultural content and folkloristic context, and the latter to indulge in highly fanciful and even fantastic combinations unsupported by disciplined control of the original texts or familiarity with the known facts of Semitic culture.

Two major difficulties confront the student of this ancient material. The first lies in the fact that it reaches us, almost exclusively, at one or more removes from its original form. Most of the texts which have come down from Mesopotamian and Canaanite antiquity are of literary, religious, legal, or administrative character. There are no pure folktales, no popular songs, and no pure descriptions of popular ceremonies. Accordingly,

our task is not, as in other areas, that of collecting what still survives *explicitly* in popular usage, but rather of extracting from these secondary forms elements of folklore which are at once latent and *implicit;* and the only feasible way of accomplishing this task is by the always treacherous comparative method. If, for example, we can recognize in an otherwise inexplicable Babylonian custom something which in fact recurs in divers other cultures and the interpretation of which is everywhere the same, stemming from a constant and familiar feature of primitive thought, we are entitled to conclude that we have recovered a piece of Babylonian folklore. By the same token, if the point of a Canaanite myth, or of a particular incident within it, depends on the tacit assumption of an idea or motif widely attested elsewhere, it is not unreasonable to suppose that such idea or motif likewise found place in Canaanite popular lore. This, it may be added, is the method adopted by the late Hugo Gressmann and Hermann Gunkel in their pioneer studies of Old Testament märchen; and it has recently been extended by the present writer to the interpretation of Canaanite and Hittite myths (*Thespis*, New York, 1950). It scarcely needs to be pointed out, however, that it is a method attended with inherent perils and pitfalls.

The second difficulty stems from the obstinate problem of semantics. It is the easiest thing in the world to base interpretations upon purely conventional renderings of distinctive Semitic terms, without regard to the fact that such renderings merely squeeze distinctive concepts into alien molds. The Semitic word *ilu* (Hebrew *el*), for instance, is conventionally rendered "god," but to assume that whenever the word appears in connection with a Semitic ceremony or myth, something like our own concept of godhead is implied, is thoroughly to distort the true meaning and significance; for the fact is that to a Semite, *ilu* denoted any member of a wider category of gods, ghosts, spirits, demons, goblins and, in fact, any assumed agent of a suprasensory experience. No less easy is it to interpret the material in the light of such established anthropological categories as totemism, ancestor-worship, divine kingship, vegetation cults, and the like. The fact is, however, that the Semites possessed distinctive and original categories of their own, and these must be recognized and respected. A Semitic king, for example, may have been regarded as the punctual counterpart of some durative spirit, but that does not mean that he received his powers from that spirit or that he was actually invested with sovereignty by it. The two things may have run parallel on different levels, and the one need not have been informed by the other. Accordingly, to interpret the role of the king in custom or myth as merely that of a representative of deity is again to distort the picture. Finally, it must be realized that no reliance can be placed upon snap identifications of figures in the Semitic pantheons. The Babylonian Shamash, for example, is usually regarded as the god of the sun. But to interpret his role in custom or myth exclusively in terms of his solar aspect would be grossly misleading; for Shamash was also the god of justice, and many of his attributes and characteristics issue from this side of his nature. Thus, when he is portrayed carrying a saw, it does not follow that this was the instrument with which he was believed to cut through the doors of darkness when he emerged every morning. It is equally plausible that the saw represented the same notion as is conveyed in Semitic speech by the fact that most words denoting "decide, adjudge" mean basically "cut" (compare our "*clear-cut* decision").

Offsetting these difficulties, however, the recovery of ancient Semitic folklore is aided by one valuable and reliable clue, namely, that of language. Just as Jakob Grimm was able to retrieve a great deal of early Teutonic folklore by studying the history of Germanic words, so it is possible for the student of Semitic lore to find in etymology a wealth of information concerning early practices and beliefs. The Hebrew word for "bridegroom," for example, derives from a verbal root meaning "to circumcise," immediately recovering to us the information that in early usage circumcision was a preparation for marriage. Similarly, the word for "bride" would appear to be connected with a term meaning "to confine, seclude," pointing to the custom of secluding brides at the time of the nuptial ceremonies. Again, the word for "to initiate, educate" is a denominative verb formed from the noun "palate," and recalls the fact that it was customary to anoint with oil the palates of new-born children. These examples could be multiplied a hundredfold.

For the purposes of this article, it will be convenient to divide the total domain of Semitic folklore into the two major divisions of oral or written folklore and of practices and customs, and to consider each in terms of the separate cultures involved.

Tales, Songs, Riddles, and Proverbs

Babylonian and Assyrian   No Babylonian or Assyrian folktales have come down to us. Familiar märchen motifs, however, abound in the major myths and epics, and not infrequently the true point depends upon the assumption of an idea or folk belief attested in other cultures, and evidently part of the common stock of Babylonian folklore. The myths and epics (all of which are characteristically anonymous) are to be regarded as traditional books to which each generation added its own quota and which each adapted to its own needs and tastes. The longer of them therefore represent accumulations of tales, originally distinct but eventually welded together into a seemingly consistent whole.

Thus, the famous *Epic of Gilgamesh* is really a repertoire, rather than a single narrative; and the progressive adventures of the hero are merely an artificial literary cadre. The constituent tales include such familiar but originally unrelated types as (a) the Rivalry of the Two Culture Heroes; (b) the Fight against the Ogre of the Mountain; (c) the Circe or Lorelei Legend; (d) the Journey to the Otherworld; (e) the Primeval Deluge; and (f) Man's Loss of Immortality. Each tale preserves the characteristic motifs of its type. Thus, in the Rivalry of the Two Heroes—a counterpart to the stories of Jacob and Esau and of Proetus and Acrisius—the one is the master of knowledge and founder of the city, while the other is an uncouth vagabond. In the Fight against the Ogre of the Mountain, that monster appears to have possessed a Gorgonlike face (F526.3) which ordinarily petrified his opponents (D581), and he belongs to the same class of beings as Rübezahl (F465). The Circe or Lorelei Legend appears in the tale of Ishtar's attempted seduction of Gilgamesh. In refusing her advances, the hero reminds her that she has trans-

formed all her previous human lovers into animals; and, as the late A. H. Krappe has pointed out (*Balor*, 70 ff.), such transformation is a common euphemism for death in folktales. What is implied, therefore, is that the goddess played the role of a siren. In the story of the Journey to the Otherworld, we are introduced to the motif which Clouston (*Popular Tales and Fictions*, ii, 96) has made familiar under the title of "Old, Older, Oldest," the hero being passed on from one helper to the next until he finally reaches the antediluvian sage Ut-napishtim. Moreover, the details of the journey bear a marked resemblance, as S. H. Hooke has observed (*Folk-Lore*, 1934: 195–211), to incidents in the Biblical saga of Elijah (*I Kings* xix; *II Kings* ii) and to certain Melanesian myths. Other well-known motifs also appear in this tale, likewise derived from popular lore. Gilgamesh reaches a magic garden—a kind of *Schlauraffenland*—the trees of which yield jewels (F166.1), and when he crosses the perilous River of the Underworld (F141.1.1), he has to be careful not to touch the waters with his hand, but only with poles. Moreover, he has to be provided with food for the journey, and the point of this—not explicitly brought out—is that he must be saved the temptation of eating the food of the otherworld, for this prevents return. Finally, in the story of Man's Loss of Immortality, we meet with the familiar feature of the magical plant which confers that boon (D1346.5), and also with the equally familiar idea that the possession of the boon passed, by untoward circumstance, from man to the serpent. Despite its heroic framework, therefore, the *Epic of Gilgamesh* is, at bottom, a collection of popular märchen artificially clustered around a traditional figure of legend. The folklorist who recognizes its constituent types and composite nature can but look askance at the conventional attempts to interpret it as an organic whole, e.g. as representing the progressive journey of the sun through the constellations of the zodiac!

Even the framework of the story betrays the influence of märchen. The opening verses which introduce the hero as "he who saw the abyss, knows the seas, visited the [far-off land], who knows all things, has beholden all secrets, journeyed the long road of death and returned to tell the tale" has all the hall-marks of the beginning of a fairy tale, and bears a close resemblance to the initial verses of the *Odyssey*. Moreover, Oppenheim has suggested (*Orientalia* 17 [1948]: 19 f.) that the compiler may have regarded the twelve tablets of the story as representing what was inscribed on the first twelve tablets laid by Gilgamesh in the walls of the city of Erech. Such an artificial cadre would correspond, in general idea, with the scheme of the *Decameron* or the *Thousand and One Nights*, by which the successive tales are integrated into a connected whole. It would be part and parcel of the traditional technique in composing repertoires.

The myth of *Ishtar's Descent to the Netherworld* likewise draws freely on märchen and popular lore. If Oppenheim's reconstruction of the story is correct (*Orientalia* 19 [1950]: 129 ff.), one of its cardinal elements is simply a variant of the well-known motif of Literal Pleading (J1161). Ereshkigal, queen of the netherworld, outraged at the reception which has been accorded to one of her emissaries, issues an order forbidding any of the male or female deities of heaven to enter her realm. Ea, lord of wisdom, evades this decree by promptly fashioning two androgynous creatures—neither male nor female!—to undertake a mission into that domain. The story seems also to incorporate a piece of popular lore in the statement that when the goddess Belili heard of the fate of Tammuz, she tore her necklace and scattered its jewels of lapis lazuli upon the face of the earth. This is evidently an allusion to some popular belief concerning the origin of a dark blue flower; it may be illustrated from the fact that in Latin the word *gemma* means both "jewel" and "bud." Somewhat analogous would be the Greek legend that roses and anemones sprang from the blood of the slain Adonis.

Other motifs which occur in Babylonian and Assyrian myths are discussed below in the article SEMITIC MYTHOLOGY. The point that needs here to be stressed is that all of them are drawn from the storehouse of popular tale. The inference is, therefore, that such tales had wide currency in ancient Mesopotamia; and the task of the folklorist is to recognize their traces in the more elaborate literary compositions.

Animal Fables A few Babylonian and Assyrian animal fables have come down to us. One of these (*CT*, XV: 34) contains a dialog between the horse and the ox. The former boasts of its prowess in battle and of the fact that "without me nor prince nor governor nor rich nor poor could travel by the way"; while the latter retorts that the horse's harness in fact comes from *his* hide and that without him earth could not be plowed. Another fable features the fox and the dog and seems designed to account for the trapping of the one and the domestication of the other. The text, however, is fragmentary.

Canaanite What is true of Babylonian and Assyrian folktale is equally true of Canaanite. No independent specimen has come down to us. Many familiar types and traits, however, are incorporated in the long mythological poems discovered in recent years at Ras Shamra, site of ancient Ugarit, on the north coast of Syria.

The *Poem of Baal*, for example, is fundamentally a mere variant of the familiar Fight of the Sky-God against the Waters (A162.2) and of the Combat of the Seasons. Moreover, in the sequence of the story, a number of folklore motifs are introduced. Baal is lured into the netherworld and detained there through eating its food (C211.2; *Thespis*, 191). He defeats his enemy, the dragon Yammu, by the use of a self-returning cudgel (D1094; *Th.*, 158). His other adversary, Môt, lives beyond the two mountains which hem in the earth (F145; *Th.*, 184). Baal is frightened lest the Dragon of the Sea carry off his daughters: a reflection of the common motif that youths and maidens must be sacrificed to the spirit of the waters (B11.10; *Th.*, 170). The presence of his sister, the goddess 'Anat, is announced by a wonderful scent (*Th.*, 211). His return from the netherworld is heralded by the fact that the wadies run with honey (F701.1; *Th.*, 200 f.). He pours rain from heavenly windows (F56; *Th.*, 181). His enemy is chased into the streams—like the Death in European seasonal customs (*Th.*, 165). When he disappears, he is located by the sun. He wears the sky as a garment (*Th.*, 186). Hell is portrayed as a monster with gaping jaws (*Th.*, 189).

The narrative also reflects a number of popular customs. When Baal is ousted, an interrex is appointed (*Th.*, 67, 197), and he has to be both the tallest and the most handsome of the people: a trait which recurs in African coronation ceremonies and in the Biblical story of the appointment of Saul (*Th.*, 197 f.). To acquire dominion, he has to walk around his domain (*Th.*, 179 f.). The favored guest sits at the right hand of his host (*Th.*, 175).

Nowhere in Canaanite literature, however, is the influence of märchen upon myth more apparent than in the intriguing *Story of Aqhat*. The entire tale is told in the vein of popular story, with all the characteristic tricks and devices of that *genre*. Particular use is made, for instance, of the device whereby, in order to heighten dramatic effect, a thing is said to be done abortively twice and to be successful only at the third try. Twice the hero Daniel tries to recover the remains of his son Aqhat from the gizzards of eagles who have devoured him, but each time he finds no trace of fat or bone. Only when he tries for the third time does he succeed. Twice he pronounces curses upon cities whom he saddles with responsibility for the murder of his son. On both occasions, he picks upon the wrong city. The third time, he curses A-b-l-m A-b-l-m; this is where the foul deed was really committed. The number seven is likewise employed in this story in the familiar schematic manner of folktales. Daniel serves as an acolyte in the temple of Baal for seven days and seven nights in order to obtain the blessing of a son. Baal is invoked to send drought upon earth for seven years in retribution for the murder of Aqhat; the mourning for the slain youth lasts seven years. Furthermore, the plot of the story involves several popular beliefs. The shedding of Aqhat's blood renders the soil infertile (*Th.*, 296). The eagles which devour him are said to come from the west, in accordance with the belief that the eagle always flies toward the sun and is never blinded (*Th.*, 301).

The influence of folktale conventions may also be recognized in the *Poem of Keret*, which is more of a *chanson de geste* than a myth. Here again the number seven is employed in a schematic manner. Keret marches against the city of King Pabel for seven days, and beleaguers it for a further seven days. When he falls sick, the gods are invoked seven times to cure him. This story also involves the well-known motif that when the king falls sick, the land languishes; and much of its point depends upon the notion that, when a monarch has once suffered illness, he is thenceforth unfit to rule—an idea made familiar especially by *The Golden Bough*.

Lastly, in the Canaanite *Myth of Dawn and Sunset*, we encounter the motif, paralleled elsewhere, that children begotten by a divine father upon a human mother will nevertheless refuse any breast but that of a goddess (*Th.*, 254). Moreover, if the present writer is correct in assuming that the story harks back to some earlier version in which the gods Dawn and Sunset were twins and not siblings, it might be possible to explain the strange incident of their wandering through the earth as an allusion to the common custom of expelling twins from the community (*Th.*, 255; compare S314).

Old Testament It is the merit of Hugo Gressmann (*ZAW* 30 [1910]: 1–34) and Hermann Gunkel (*Das Märchen im Alten Testament*, Tübingen, 1917) to have pointed out that many of the most familiar stories of the Old Testament are really but Hebrew variants of folktales widespread throughout the world. Examples of such stories (together with references to the standard classification and to pertinent literature) follow:

Man formed out of clay (A1241) and animated by the breath of God (A141.1). Paradise as a garden of God (A151.2; A. Brock-Utne, *D. Gottesgarten*, Oslo, 1936), situated beside four rivers (F162.2.1; Albright, *AJSL* 39: 40 ff.) and containing a Tree of Life (F162.3.1; H. Bergema, *De Boom des Levens . . .*, Hilversum, 1938), the fruit of which is forbidden to man (C621). Woman formed from man's side or rib (A1275.1). Man expelled from Paradise (A1331). The way to the treasure of immortality guarded by cherubim, or winged dragons (B11.6.2; D950.0.1). The blood of the slain Abel cries out (*BP*, ii:274, 526) and renders the soil barren (A2631.1; *Thespis*, 296). A world-calamity (deluge) ensues as punishment for man's waywardness (A1018). Noah's Ark (A1021), into which pairs of animals are taken (A1021.1). Survivors of flood repopulate the earth (A1006.1). The Tower designed to reach to heaven (C771.1; F772.1). Abraham entertains angels unawares (compare Philemon and Baucis, etc.; Q45.1). Sodom and Gomorrah destroyed in a fire-deluge and submerged (F944). Lot's wife turned into a pillar of salt for breaking tabu (C961.1). Abraham ordered to sacrifice his only son, but a ram substituted by God at the last moment (S263.2.1). Jacob and Esau rivals, the one domesticated and the other wild (compare Gilgamesh and Enkidu, etc.; A516.1.1). Leah substituted as bride instead of Rachel (Frazer, *Fasti of Ovid*, iii, 125 f.; Westermarck, *History of Human Marriage*, ii, 521 f.). Jacob's Ladder (F52; Block, *Acta Orientalia* 6: 257–69; A. B. Cook, *Zeus*, ii, 127 f.). Jacob's struggle with an angel at the ford of Jabbok (*FOT min.*, 251–58). Jacob at Mahanaim (Wild Host; Gunkel, *Märchen*, 82 f.). Joseph's "coat of many colors" (Eisler, *OLZ* 1908: 368–71). Joseph cast into a pit (S146) and sold into slavery (S210.1). Joseph wrongfully accused by Potiphar's wife (compare the Egyptian tale of Anpu and Batu; Phædra and Hippolytus, etc.; K2111; Frazer, *Apollodorus*, ii, 146n.)

Moses in the bulrushes (Exposed Child; compare legend of Sargon of Agade, etc.; S331; L111.2.1; Gruppe, *GM*, 1171,n.1). Moses secretly nursed by his own mother (S351) and reared at court (S354). Moses sees a non-consuming magic fire (Burning Bush; D964). Moses is provided with a magic staff (D1254; Cook, *Zeus*, ii, 1043), which, *inter alia*, parts waters (D1551), procures water from a rock (D1567.6). The plague of frogs (Gunkel, *Märchen*, 89; Gruppe, *GM*, 1234, n. 2). Complaining Israelites destroyed by fire sent from heaven (F962.2). Miriam suffers leprosy as punishment (compare C941.1). Korah and his company swallowed up by the earth (F942.1), thus descend to netherworld (F92.2). Aaron's dry rod blossoms (F971.1; *BP*, iii, 471, n. 1; Saintyves, *Folklore Biblique*, 59–137). Balaam's ass sees the angel, though its rider does not (Krappe, *Folk-Lore* 54:391–401; *TM*, 667, 1107). Rephaim, early inhabitants of Seir and Bashan, regarded as giants (A1301; Mayor on *Juvenal*, xv, 70). Moses dies on mountain (compare A571).

Joshua makes sun stand still and lengthens day (D2146.1.1; compare Matthes, *ThT* [1908]: 461–94; Maunder, *Expositor* [1910]: 339–72). Jael proffers drink to Sisera and kills him (G521; *Thespis* 328). Gideon's Fleece (Nestle, *ARW* [1909]: 154–56; Schultz, *OLZ* [1910]: 241–51). Jotham's Parable (Diels, *Int. Wochenschrift*, 4: 99 f.; Gunkel, *Märchen*, 16 ff.). Jephthah's

Vow (Barbes, *ThSt.* [1909]: 137–43; Baumgartner, *ARW* 18:240). Samson (A. S. Palmer, *The Samson Saga . . .*, London, 1915). Samson's Foxes (Hartmann, *ZAW* 31: 69–72). Samson's strength lies in his hair (*FOT min.*, 270–74). The rape of the women of Shiloh (*Thespis*, 25). Elijah "measures" a sick person (*TM*, 1163 f.). Elijah fed by ravens (Gunkel, *Märchen*, 34). Jonah thrown overboard to allay storm (S264.1). Jonah and the whale (F911.4). Jonah and the wondrous gourd (*D965.2?).

Biblical folktales thus embrace almost all of the usual categories, cosmogonic tales; animal tales (the serpent in Eden, Balaam's ass, the ravens which feed Elijah, Jonah and the whale); tabu tales (Lot's wife; Miriam's leprosy); magic tales (Moses' and Aaron's staffs; the parting of the Red Sea, etc.); tales of marvelous creatures (Leviathan and Behemoth, the ageless phœnix [*Job* xxix, 18], the giant Rephaim); tales of deception (Leah as False Bride, Jacob stealing the blessing); tales of rewards and punishments (the rescue of Lot from Sodom; the destruction of Korah and his followers); tales of sex (Judah and Tamar); and etiological tales (e.g. origin of the place-names Baerah (*Numbers* xi, 1) and Ramath Lehi (*Judges* xv), and of the tabu against eating the ischiatic nerve of animals (*Gen.* xxxii).

Most of this material was derived by the Biblical writers from the popular lore of Canaan and the adjacent lands, and was by no means their own primary invention. Not infrequently, however, what was originally a general folktale without specific local reference was pointedly adapted to serve as a particular etiological tale. Thus, the tale of the exposed child who eventually becomes the national hero is part of the common stock of world folklore, but when the Biblical writer applied it to Moses, he added the significant detail that the Israelite leader derived his name (Hebrew *Mosheh*) from the fact that he had been drawn up (Hebrew *mashah*) from the Nile! Similarly, the tale of Jacob's struggle with the angel is merely a particular variant of a common theme, but the Biblical writer specifically locates the encounter at the ford of Jabbok because the name Jabbok suggests the Hebrew word *abaq*, struggle! So, too, the common story of the submerged city is linked to the destruction of Gomorrah because that name is reminiscent of a Semitic word *ghamar* meaning "to steep, submerge." The story of Jacob and Esau provides a further illustration of the same process. Basically, the rivalry of the two heroes, the one tame and domesticated, the other a wild and wooly vagabond, is but a variant of the common motif which we find, for instance, in the Babylonian tale of Gilgamesh and Enkidu; and it is, indeed, by no means improbable that Seir, the alternative name by which Esau was known, really meant the "Hairy One." But to a Hebrew or Edomite writer, the "Hairy One" immediately suggested a convenient eponymous hero for the wild tribes of Transjordanian Seir, for that name could be plausibly connected with the Hebrew word *sa'ir* meaning "hairy." Accordingly, the Old Testament narrative introduces the specific and particular detail that Esau was also called Seir and was the ancestor of those tribes.

That several of the stories indeed go back to older originals is shown also by their very form. The name of Noah, for example, is inconsistently derived in our Scriptural account from the Hebrew root *n-h-m* meaning "to comfort." This, however, is not mere *bizarrerie,* nor is the incongruity to be removed by the cheap expedient of textual emendation. On the contrary, it is a valuable indication that the story dates back to a remote antiquity. namely, to the period before 1600 B.C. when Semitic nouns ended in -*m*. The original name of the hero would thus have been Naḥôm (or the like) and the explanation given, though due of course to mere folk etymology, would at least be consistent. Similarly, although, in the first chapter of *Genesis*, the several acts of creation are fitted into six days plus a seventh day of rest, there are in fact *ten* fiats, and these are unevenly distributed, thus suggesting that the poem (for such it really is) was originally written at a period when the Semites recognized a *ten*-day week, and that it was later somewhat clumsily adapted.

Sometimes, too, the original point and motivation of a story was ironed out or altogether lost in the course of its subsequent transmission, although features of that earlier version were retained, without logical explanation or organic connection with the new form. In the story of the Garden of Eden, for example, the wife of the first man is called Hawwah (Eve) and she is said to have been tempted by a serpent. The fact is, however, that the name Hawwah itself means "serpent." In all likelihood, therefore, our present version of the tale harks back to a more primitive folklore, in which the first man was believed, as in so many cultures, to have been mated with an ophidian bride (see *ERE*, xi, 410). By the time it reached the Biblical writer, this trait had been forgotten, although it was still remembered that a serpent somewhere featured in the action. The two characters which were originally one were therefore differentiated.

Similarly, the bow which God placed in the sky after the deluge could not originally have been the rainbow, since the early Semites, like many primitive peoples of the present day, did not recognize a bow in that celestial phenomenon. The bow was simply a constellation, clearly recognized by Mesopotamian astronomers and composed of certain stars of Canis Major combined with others of the neighboring Puppis. Moreover, the reason why it was introduced into the tale is because, in the original version, the flood was caused by a demonic monster whom the sky god vanquished with the aid of that weapon. He therefore hung his triumphant arms in heaven as a warning to future upstarts. This version underlies the Babylonian tale relating how Marduk suspended in heaven the sickle wherewith he had conquered Tiamat, and it is likewise to be found in the Arabic legend of Qozaḥ. All that the Biblical writer knew was that a bow played some part in the story, and with this dimly remembered feature he did the best he could.

It is probable that the stories were originally preserved *in verse,* for such is the form of both Mesopotamian and Canaanite myths. Moreover, it is sometimes possible to detect an earlier metrical source behind our present prose version. Thus, Sarah's words at the birth of Isaac (*Gen.* xxi, 6–7) scan perfectly; while the account of the intended sacrifice of Isaac (*Gen.* xxii) is, for the most part, pure verse, as are also those of Isaac's meeting with Rebekah (*Gen.* xxiv) and of Jacob's theft of the birthright (*Gen.* xxvii). Moreover, several of the stories preserve the ancient technique, familiar from the Canaanite texts of Ras Shamra, of reproducing messages *in extenso* when they are said to be repeated.

Sometimes, the writers will actually quote earlier poetic sources, as in *Numbers* xxi, 14 where an excerpt is given from a work entitled "The Book of the Wars of the Lord." We should be on our guard, however, against assuming too rashly (as do most Biblical scholars) that a specific composition is meant. Since, in ancient times, books were traditional repertoires rather than the products of individual artists, it is not unlikely that the title really refers to an entire genre of popular literature, not unlike the Arabic *māghāzī,* or legendary descriptions of the initial wars of Islam.

Nor should we be deluded into supposing that wherever the prose narrative is interrupted by songs (e.g. the Song of the Sea in *Exodus* xv; Hannah's Song; Jonah's prayer in the belly of the whale), we have before us the earliest metrical version. On the contrary, most of these songs are later and were inserted into the account merely because they seemed appropriate and because they relieved the tedium of the recital by means of "audience-participation." In precisely the same way, the Canaanite myths from Ras Shamra seem to introduce traditional hymns at convenient intervals (*Thespis,* 68 f.)

Unfortunately, the vast majority of Biblical scholars have been slow to appreciate the implications of a folkloristic approach. Consequently, the stories of the Old Testament continue to be interpreted in a one-sided and thoroughly unscientific manner. Thus, because the name of the hero may itself be associated with the Semitic word for "sun," it is still commonly asserted that the legend of Samson is really a decayed solar myth, and the detail of his strength's lying in his hair is then promptly explained as a reference to the sun's rays. The truth is, however, that this motif recurs frequently in tales where the hero has no such solar name and that it rests on a belief very widely attested in primitive cultures (*FOT,* ii, 484 ff.). What we have in the Biblical story, therefore, is simply a Hebrew variant of a widespread folktale motif (D1831).

Again, it has been assumed by some commentators and exegetes that the story of Elijah's having been fed by ravens arises from a misunderstanding of the original Hebrew text, the word '*Arabim,* "Arabs," having been misread as '*orebim,* "ravens"! The fact is, however, that many parallel stories attest the motif of a man's being fed by birds, so that once again our Biblical tale is but a variant of a widespread theme and cannot be interpreted simply from its own terms of expression (compare B531).

By the same token, the system of interpreting the heroic sagas of Israel as being mere personifications of tribal activities is seen to be fallacious, once it is realized that virtually the same tales are told elsewhere. The story of Jacob and Esau, for example, cannot be explained exclusively as a personification of the relations between Israel and Edom, if the same story is told in a dozen other places where no such particular reference would have been pertinent. Nor again, is it possible to explain such stories on an astral basis—a line of interpretation developed especially by Hugo Winckler and the so-called "Pan-babylonian" school—since the same stories are in fact found in a variety of regions wherein the same astral figures are not always recognized. Lastly, the fundamentalist position that the stories are genuine history becomes altogether untenable, when analogies and parallels are found to exist throughout the world.

Folk songs No Babylonian or Assyrian popular songs have come down to us. It has been suggested, however, that the lament which the hero utters over his slain friend Enkidu in the *Epic of Gilgamesh* really reproduces a conventional dirge sung at funerals.

Canaanite folk song is represented by the single specimen of a vine-dressers' work song found in the so-called *Poem of Dawn and Sunset* discovered at Ras Shamra. This song likens the trimming of vines to the emasculation of some dionysiac spirit, and it possesses analogies both in ancient Greece and in modern France. Each line ends with the emphatic word "vine," so that it is probably a work song designed to keep time when a crew is working together (see *Thespis*, 241).

Several types of folk song are included in the Old Testament. *Genesis* iv, 23–24, for example, presents us with what is really a "taunt-song" sung by the champions of the tribe of Lamech when they engaged their foes in combat. Analogies to it may be found in the *hijâ*-poetry of the Arabs. Similarly, *Numbers* xxi, 17–18 gives the text of a traditional chant which, if we may trust the analogy of modern Arab custom (compare Musil, *Moab*, 288), was sung in spring when each family dug its water-pit for the year. (In the scriptural narrative, it is related artificially to an event in the exodus of the Israelites from Egypt.)

A peculiar form of Hebrew popular verse was that in which an enemy was lampooned by a derogatory pun on his name. This was used especially in prophetic execrations upon hostile cities and peoples. Thus, the name of the Kenites suggests two homonymous words meaning respectively "nest" and "smith." The prophet Balaam therefore curses this tribe in the words: "Though thine home seem permanent, and thy *nest* set on a rock, nonetheless the day will come When the *smith* shall be the fuel!" (*Numbers* xxiv, 21–22). Similarly, because the place-name Mareshah suggests the Hebrew word for "dispossession," the prophet Micah curses the city in the words: "Thou that in Mareshah dwellest, I shall bring a dispossessor unto thee" (*Micah* i, 15). And because the name Dimon recalls the Hebrew word *dam*, meaning "blood," the prophet Isaiah is able to exclaim (xv, 9): "The waters of Dimon are filled with *blood*." The device is rooted, of course, in the well-known primitive principle: *nomina omina sunt*.

Popular wedding songs are recognized by many scholars in the *Song of Solomon*, which is regarded by them as a repertoire of such compositions. Support for this view is found in the close parallels afforded by the *waṣfs* still chanted at Syrian nuptial celebrations.

An example of a nursery rime may perhaps be recognized in *Isaiah* xxviii, 10, although the point is obscured in the English version. The prophet is complaining of the hopelessness of teaching the word of God to the "drunkards of Ephraim," and observes: "To whom is one trying to teach knowledge? And to whom is one trying to convey a meaning? Is it to new-weaned infants, or to babes who have just left off suckling? Is it a matter of *tsav le-tsav qav le-qav*, here-a-bit and there-a-bit?" The untranslated words are usually rendered "precept by precept, line by line"; more probably, however, they represent a children's jingle, somewhat like our "oops-a-daisy" or "pat-a-cake, pat-a-cake."

Finally, there is the dirge. The peculiar feature of Hebrew dirges is that they are usually composed in a special limping meter, the second half of the stitch being one beat shorter than the first, e.g. "Outdoors they lie on the ground,/ Young men and old./ My youths and maidens all/ Fall by the sword (*Lamentations* ii, 21). The present writer has suggested (*Journal of Biblical Literature* 67:iii) that this curious structure originated in the fact that early Semitic funerals were characterized by the performance of a *limping dance,* and that the accompanying lament had to mark the pace of the mourners. Such dances are still current in Syria and Egypt, and appear to be attested also in ancient Mesopotamian and Canaanite sources.

Riddles No Babylonian or Canaanite riddles have come down to us. Specimens occur, however, in the Old Testament. The most famous is the riddle allegedly propounded by Samson to his Philistine friends (*Judges* xiv, 10). Although embodied in a quasi-historical setting and related artificially to an incident in the career of the Israelite champion, it is probable that this was really a traditional conundrum the true point of which had been forgotten in later generations. That point lay, as in so many riddles, in a play on words, the Hebrew *ari*, "lion," also meaning "honey," while "the eater" (as we now know from the Ras Shamra texts) was a popular expression for a ravening beast. Thus, the original form of the riddle would have been: "Who is the 'eater' out of whom comes something to eat? And who is the strong one out of whom comes something sweet?" And the answer would have been: "*Ari*, because *ari* denotes both the lion, who is a ravening beast (i.e. an 'eater') and also honey, than which nothing is more sweet"! Further examples of Hebrew riddles may be found in *Proverbs* xxx, 4, where a number of recondite mythological conundrums are propounded, e.g. Who went up to heaven and came down? (Answer: Etana). Who gathered the wind in his garment? (compare C322.1). Who supported all the ends of the earth? (Answer: some Semitic counterpart of Atlas; see A842).

Proverbs The famous library of King Ashurbanipal included collections of Babylonian and Assyrian proverbs, and the excavations at the ancient Hittite capital of Hattusas (Boghaz-köy) have yielded even older bilingual Babylonian-Hittite texts of the same genre. It must be observed, however, that much of what passes for Babylonian proverbial literature falls more properly into the category of didactic admonitions. Often, in fact, the so-called proverbs are expressly introduced by the phrase "my son" (as in the Biblical *Book of Proverbs*), showing that they belong to the same class of composition as, for example, Isocrates' *Manual for Demonikos*. On the other hand, even in these collections there are several instances of what appear to be genuine popular sayings, e.g. "Never goad a toiling ox"; "In a strange city, the ass is mayor"; "Where there are servants, there are bound to be quarrels, and where there is a barber shop, there is bound to be gossip"; "Is a swamp paid for producing reeds, or a field for yielding crops?"

The same general observation applies to Hebrew proverbs. The Biblical book of that name is largely a collection of didactic maxims, and the same is true of the apocryphal *Wisdom of Ben Sirach*. The former work (or the bulk of it) was attributed to King Solomon, but it is plain from the numerous repetitions and variants which it contains that it is really a traditional compilation. The ascription to Solomon is due simply to the fact that he was the proverbial wise monarch, and is therefore of the same order as the American tendency to attribute forthright "wisecracks" to Will Rogers. Some portions of the book appear to have been taken directly from the ancient Egyptian *Proverbs of Amen-em-Opet*, but these, too, are mainly didactic maxims rather than genuine popular sayings. Nevertheless, the Biblical collection *does* include a few specimens of the latter. Moreover, many of the proverbs embody allusions to popular lore. Thus, the house of the "strange woman" is said to "sink down unto the realm of death" (ii, 18) where the point is that it is likened to the submerged castle of common folktale (F941). Similarly, Wisdom is a "Tree of Life" which confers bliss on those who lay hold of it (iii, 18). The lips of the king possess magic; he is unable to err in judgment (xvi, 10). A bribe is like a magic jewel, ensuring success in all directions (xvii, 8). The late D. S. Margoliouth has made the attractive suggestion that many of the proverbs embodied in the Biblical collection were really the "morals" of folktales by which their point was brought home.

Folklore in Custom and Usage

It is impossible in the space of this article to give anything like an adequate account of the folkloristic traits to be found in ancient Semitic religious customs or to the many allusions to popular beliefs scattered throughout Mesopotamian, Canaanite, and Old Testament literature. A few selected examples may be cited, however, as illustrations of the type of material which the folklorist should seek.

Babylonian and Assyrian If the real parents of a child wished to reassert their claims to it, after it had been given out for adoption, they did so by offering it a vessel filled with human milk (Landsberger, *Ana ittišu*, Rome, 1937, 51–57). This, of course, is merely a conventionalized survival of the more ancient practice of simulating nurture by placing the child in one's bosom.—Brides were consecrated by pouring oil on their heads, a practice which doubtless goes back to the notion that they are thereby informed with a new "essence."—At funerals, the bier was circuited three times, as was also the mortuary chapel itself (Dhorme, *RA* 38:63). This custom is still observed among Sephardic Jews in their sevenfold circuit of the bier of dignitaries. Its original purpose was to make a closed circle in order to keep away demons. See CIRCUMAMBULATION.—At eclipses of the sun and moon, it was customary to beat drums (S. H. Hooke in *Studies Presented to J. H. Hertz*, London, 1944).—The dragon Humbaba, who features prominently in the *Epic of Gilgamesh* was thought to posess a Gorgon's head, and bizarre masks made for purposes of magical "transfixion" were known as "Humbaba heads."—The wind was regarded as a bringer of disease (Fish, *'Iraq* 6:184; compare Corso, *Riv. d. Antropol.* 22:80).—Images were burned in order to work black magic upon a person (Langdon, *RA* 26:39–42).—The dead suffered thirst in the netherworld (Tallquist, *Sumerischakkadische Namen der Totenwelt*, Helsingfors, 1934, 37, n. 1; *Thespis*, 188).—The goddess of the nether-

world was accompanied by infernal hounds (*Thespis*, 214).—The dead assumed the form of winged creatures, an evident reminiscence of the bird-soul concept (see Aptowitzer, *Die Seele als Vogel*, Breslau, 1925; Grimm, *TM*, 828; Klebs, *Zeitschr. f. Aegypt. Sprache* 61: 104–08; Gruppe, *GM*, 1502, n. 1; 1618, n. 1; Cook, *Zeus*, ii, 524, 697n., 1132).—Toothache was said to be caused by a worm (compare *Homeric Hymn to Demeter*, 228–29; Shakespeare, *Much Ado About Nothing*, III, ii, 28; *Notes and Queries* [1876]: 255, 476).—The desert was the haunt of evil spirits (see *Marco Polo*, i, xxxix and ch. 57, ed. Yule; Burton, *Anatomie of Melancholy*, I, 2, 2; Milton, *Comus*, 207–09; Trench, *Studies in the Gospels*, 7).—Human destiny was conceived of as a design (*uṣurtu*) shaped by the gods. This is analogous to the ancient Teutonic *scap* (Grimm, *TM*, 857).—The gods were surrounded by a nimbus (Oppenheim, *JAOS* 63: 31–33; compare Grimm, *TM*, 323).

Old Testament The Israelite high priest wore bells on the hem of his robe. This was a survival of an ancient device for forfending evil spirits (Dölger, *Antike und Christentum*, 4:233–42; *FOT min.*, 417).—Dawn was regarded as possessing wings (*Psalm* cxxxix, 9; compare Grimm, *TM*, 745).—The sun could be portrayed as a champion running a race (*Ps.* xix, 6; compare Grimm, *TM* 738).—Yahweh possessed a magic sword (*Isaiah* xxvii, 1; xxxiv, 5; *Jer.* xlvii, 6; Gunkel, *Märchen*, 46).—Waves of the sea could be regarded as chargers (*Hab.* iii, 15). This is clearly a counterpart of the familiar "white horses" concept.—God was attended by two ministers, identified as Plague and Pestilence (*Hab.* iii, 5). This recalls the fact that, in Babylonian myth, the gods Nabu and Sharru escort Adad when he sends the flood (*Gilgamesh* xi, 100). Compare also the Homeric Deimos (Alarm) and Phobos (Fear) who escort Phœbus and Ares (*Iliad* iv, 44; xv, 119) and the Tras (tremor) and Strakh (terror) of Bohemian folklore (Grimm, *TM*, 208).—Hell is "the final synagogue of all the living" (compare Grimm, *TM*, 801).—Orion is chained to heaven (*Job* xxxviii, 31; Gunkel, *Märchen*, 77 f.; *Thespis*, 263).—Disease can be inflicted by the arrow of a demon, or of God (*Ps.* xci, 5; *Job* vi, 4). This recalls the Homeric arrows of Apollo (*Iliad* i, 44) and the elf-shot of Teutonic folklore (Grimm, *TM*, 1182, 1244; see also Eitrem, *Papyri Osloenses* I, Oslo, 1925, 52 ff.).—According to an emendation proposed by F. Perles (*OLZ* 12: 251 f.), there is an allusion in *Ezekiel* xxxvii, 11 to the concept of the "thread of life," for instead of "we are clean cut off," we should there read "our thread is cut off." (For classical parallels, see Lucian, *Philop.*, 25; Theocritus i, 139; Babrius, p. 11, 49; Vergil, *Æn.* x, 814).

Bibliography Sources have been indicated in the text.

Abbreviations

AJSL	*American Journal of Semitic Languages*
ARW	*Archiv für Religionswissenschaft*
ERE	*Encyclopaedia of Religion and Ethics*, ed. J. Hastings
FOT	Frazer, James, *Folklore in the Old Testament* (3 vols. London 1918)
FOT min.	*idem*, one-vol. edition
GM	Gruppe, Otto, *Griechische Mythologie* (2 vols., Munich, 1906)
JAOS	*Journal of the American Oriental Society*
RA	*Revue d'assyriologie et d'archéologie orientale*

TH., THESPIS   Gaster, Theodor H., *Thespis: Ritual,
                Myth and Drama in the Ancient Near East
                (New York, 1950)
THT   *Theologisch Tijdschrift*
TM   Grimm, Jacob, *Teutonic Mythology*, tr. J. S.
                Stallybrass (4 vols., London, 1880)
ZAW   *Zeitschrift für die alttestamentliche Wissen-
                schaft*   THEODOR H. GASTER

Semitic mythology Semitic mythology means, for all
practical purposes, that of the ancient Babylonians and
Assyrians, of the Canaanites and of the Hebrews; for it
is only in the literature of those peoples that the traditional myths are preserved in full narrative form. To
be sure, there are references to them also in later Jewish
and Arabic sources (as when the Koran speaks of the
three daughters of Allah or the rabbinic midrash alludes
to the primeval battle of God against Leviathan or to
the depredations of the giant bird Ziz), but such references are secondary—mere popular reminiscences of the
older material.

Semitic myths are embodied in poems designed originally to be chanted or recited at religious exercises.
Their object was to provide an interpretation of ritual
in terms of connected stories. In course of time, however,
many of the underlying rituals fell into disuse, so that
the myths survived as purely literary compositions, to
be modified or elaborated at will. It is mainly in this
developed form that they have come down to us; but
for the better understanding of their contents, patterns
and structures, reference must often be made to the
primitive rites which they in fact "project."

The study of Semitic myths is still in its infancy and
has thus far scarcely proceeded beyond the bare translation of texts and the discussion of isolated topics. Very
little has been done by way of comparative research or
of correlating the relevant themes and motifs with those
familiar from general folk literature. The present survey
therefore concentrates attention upon this phase of the
subject, indicating throughout the presence of such
themes and motifs by reference to the appropriate entries in Stith Thompson's classic *Motif-Index of Folk-
Literature* (6 vols., Helsinki 1932–36), where parallels
are cited.

Babylonian and Assyrian Myths

Sources Babylonian and Assyrian myths are known
principally from cuneiform texts unearthed, during the
past one hundred years, at Ashur and Nineveh, the
earlier and later capitals of Assyria respectively. The
former date, in some cases, to the beginning of the
second millennium B.C. and are now preserved at Berlin.
The latter are of the 7th century B.C., and consist of
transcripts, translations, and new editions of older
material prepared for the palace library of King Ashurbanipal (669–626 B.C.). They are now in the British
Museum.

In addition, excavations at the site of ancient Nippur
have yielded a number of earlier recensions written in
the Sumerian language. These date between the latter
half of the third and the earlier half of the second
millennium B.C. Distributed mainly between the University Museum at Philadelphia and the Archeological
Museum at Istanbul, many of them have now been
pieced together by the phenomenal skill of Samuel Noah
Kramer. They prove of great value in supplying portions

of myths missing in the later Babylonian and Assyrian
versions and in recovering the earlier form of stories
which were not infrequently changed or garbled in
subsequent transmission.

Mythological scenes engraved on seals constitute a further source of information. These, however, are still
imperfectly understood, nor can they be related, except
in a few instances, to the literary versions.

Cosmology The chief cosmological myth of the
Babylonians and Assyrians is a long poem of composite
origin known (from its opening words) as *Enuma Elish*
("When above"). Recited as part of the New Year
liturgy, this poem is, *au fond*, nothing but a retrojection
into the remote past of conditions which actually obtained at the beginning of each year—namely, the abate-
ment or "subjugation" of the swollen rivers, the ceremonial reinstatement of the king, and the renewal of
life and the cosmic order. The story relates the victorious
combat of the national god (Marduk at Babylon, Ashur
at Ashur) against Tiamat, the cosmic or primeval dragon; his dispatch of her allies to the netherworld; his
subsequent installation as king and enthronement in a
special pavilion; his determination of the world order;
and the creation of man from the blood of Kingu, slain
husband of Tiamat. In our extant recension—the product
of long development—the main narrative is prefaced by
a summary account of the origin of the gods, and it is
also skilfully combined with a duplicate version in which
the protagonists are the god Ea and Apsu, deity of the
fresh water ocean.

Enuma Elish is but one version of a myth widespread
throughout the ancient Near East. Other versions are:
the Hittite myth of the sky god's battle against the
dragon Illuyankas; the Egyptian myth of Ra's fight with
the monster 'Apep; the Vedic myth of Indra's conquest
of Vṛtra; the Iranian myth of Thrāētaona's defeat of the
dragon Aži Dahāk; the Canaanite myth of Baal's encounter with Yammu, alias Leviathan; the Phœnician
myth of the conflict between Zas (Baal) and Ophioneus
(Tannin); and the Greek myth of Zeus' conflict with
Typhon.

Moreover, the tale is replete with motifs familiar from
general folk literature:

The primal element is water (A810). The first gods
are created *in pairs* (A116; twin culture heroes, A515.1.1).
The hero (Marduk) is a precocious child, born fully
mature (T615). He has four eyes and ears, is of gigantic
stature, and his eye flashes (A123–124). He is at first
in disgrace with the father-god Anshar, but is recalled
to encounter Tiamat (compare Oppenheim, *Orientalia*
XIV [1947]: 221). He therefore fills the familiar role of
the recalled prince or vizier who returns from disgrace
to save his master; i.e. banished minister found indispensable (P111). Compare ACHIKAR. Before engaging the
monster, he smears himself with a magical *red* paste
(compare red as magic color, D1293.1). Then, as culture
hero, he subdues the dragon (A531). The latter is invulnerable by weapons (B11.12.1), and is overcome only
when the stormwind inflates her belly. Her allies are
imprisoned in the netherworld (Q433.2). The culture
hero then determines the world order (A530). Man is
created out of the blood of a god (A1211.1. *FOT*, i:3–29;
Dähnhardt: *Natursagen*, i:89–111).

Shorn of its seasonal and cosmological traits, the myth

also survived as a mere story of the slaying of the dragon (B11). Mesopotamian literature and art contain several allusions to such an encounter between a god, variously identified as Ninurta, Marduk, Papsukkal, etc., and a griffinlike creature called Mushrushshu; while a tablet from Nineveh relates the story of a battle between the storm god and a dragon called Labbu (Rager?).

To the same genre of seasonal-cosmological myths belongs the legend of Zû. Zû was a gigantic storm-bird who stole the "tablets of decision" and other insignia of the high god and who, after several major deities had flinched from giving battle, was finally overcome by a heroic champion who lured him to a banquet and bemused him with liquor. (In our extant version the hero is identified with Lugalbanda, a legendary king of Kish, but there are indications that he was originally a full-fledged god, such as Marduk, Ashur, or Ninurta.)

Zû (whose name means tempest) is a personification of the angry winds which beset the earth at the beginning of the year and which have to be "subdued" before the new lease of life can be assured. He is thus a natural alternative to Tiamat, spirit of the turbulent floods.

Zû is but a Semitic version of the Eddic Hroesvelger and the Vedic Garuda—giant bird the flapping of whose wings causes tempests (*TM*: 633–35; *ERE*, i: 429a). His being overcome by drink is paralleled in the Hittite myth of the dragon Illuyankas (*KBo*, III: 7)—actually designed for the seasonal festival of Puruli!—and in the Biblical story of Jael and Sisera (*Judges* iv–v), as well as in folktales concerning the defeat of the ogre (G521).

It is probable that both the myth of *Enuma Elish* and that of Zû were represented in sacred pantomimes at the New Year festival.

More strictly cosmogonic in tone are references in several minor texts to the emergence of the ancient cities of Babylonia from a primal watery chaos. These reflect the fact that such cities were indeed built upon lagoons. Upon this fact the Babylonians and Assyrians seem to have constructed the idea that the earth as a whole was of like origin.

Creation of Man The common belief about the creation of man was that he was fashioned out of clay to serve the gods and relieve them of menial chores (A1241; compare *Job* xxxiii, 6). His creator was the goddess Mami (or Aruru), sometimes varied, sometimes associated with such gods as Enlil, Ea, or Marduk. The idea is expressed in several texts, but nowhere more elaborately than in the myth of Ea and Atrahasis of which we possess both an Old Babylonian and a later Assyrian recension.

Enlil, the high god, perturbed at the "uproar" created by men, visits upon them a series of scourges until at length a certain Atrahasis (i.e. Superwise) entreats the god Ea to deliver the human race from impending extermination. Ea orders Mami to mold fourteen lumps of clay. These are separated into two lots, a slab being placed between them. Fourteen women are then summoned and, by some magical means, the lumps are introduced into their wombs. Seven of them bear males, seven females. Thus the human race is perpetuated.

The slab, the function of which has hitherto remained obscure, may perhaps be identified with the magical "birthstone" of world-wide folklore, contact with which impregnates barren women (*GB*, V: 35, *ARW*, XIV

[1911]: 308 f.; R. Patai, *Adam we-Adamah*, II [Jerusalem 1943]: 19 ff.). Indeed, a postscript to our text states explicitly that such a stone forefends demons at the delivery of a child and enables a woman to "bear by herself"! It is probable, in fact, that the text was designed as a charm to be recited in a lying-in chamber.

An alternative account says that *the clay was mixed with the blood of a slain god.* This version is found in Berossus, who does not name the victim; in *Enuma Elish*, where it is Kingu, husband of Tiamat; and in a text from Ashur, where it is the double god Lamga.

The idea has abundant parallels (A1211 ff.). In Vedic myth, man springs from the blood of the slain Puruṣa; in Greek myth, from that of the slain Titans.

Moreover, it may be suggested that the double god Lamga is really but the divine prototype of the first man regarded, as in many cultures, as androgynous; compare the Vedic Yama, the Eddic Ymir, the Avestan Mashya and Mashyoi (originally joined together), the rabbinic view of Adam, and the Germanic Mannus (i.e. Man) descended from Twisto, "the double god" (Usener, *Kl. Schriften*, IV: 37; Ginzberg, *Legends of the Jews*, V: 88, n. 41; Krappe, *Orient and Occident* [London 1936]: 312–22; Plato, *Symp.*: 189d; 190d; Tacitus, *Germ.*, c. 2).

Mortality of Man In the familiar Biblical tale, man loses the chance of immortality because God expels him from Eden and thereby prevents his tasting the fruit of the Tree of Life (*Gen.* iii, 22–24). Babylonian and Assyrian mythology knows analogously of a magical draft of life which man is prevented from drinking through the jealousy of a god. The story is told in the myth of Adapa, one portion of which was found at Tell el-Amarna in Egypt and another at Nineveh.

Adapa, ministrant in the temple of Ea at Eridu, on the Persian Gulf, is out one day catching fish for his god when he is caught in a storm and his boat capsizes. In anger, he breaks the wings of the storm bird (compare *Psalms* xviii, 11; civ, 3), so that it ceases to blow for a full seven days. Thereupon, Anu, the high god, orders the offender to be brought before him. In desperation, Adapa appeals to Ea. The latter tells him to dress in rags and go like a mourner to the gate of heaven. There he will meet two doorkeepers, the fertility god Tammuz and his brother Ningishzida. Adapa is to tell them that he has come to look for them, following their seasonal disappearance from the earth. This will ingratiate them, and they will offer him clean clothes and cleansing oil. These he may accept. When, however, they subsequently offer him water, he is to refuse; for the water will be the water of death. Adapa does as ordered. However, the proffered water turns out to be, in fact, the water of life and immortality. By following Ea's instructions, therefore, Adapa—in this sense, typical of mankind—forfeits the latter gift.

The story may be best explained as a variant of the well-known motif of the falsified message (A1335.1; *FOT*, i: 52 ff.; Dähnhardt, iii: 22), the theme of which is that *Man forfeits immortality because a divine message telling him how to acquire it is deliberately perverted by a malevolent or jealous messenger.* To be sure, as here narrated, the story is rather one of perverted counsel than of a perverted message, but the central idea and motivation is clearly the same. (It may be observed also that, according to Frazer [*FOT*, i: 52 ff.], the role of the serpent in the Eden story was originally that of the subversive messenger.)

The idea of a paradisal tree of life is ubiquitous (E90). So too is that of the Water of Life (E80), which is, of course, the familiar nectar of Greek mythology (A154). In Jewish apocalyptic literature, food, water, and oil of life are reserved for the righteous in paradise (Ginzberg, *Legends of the Jews*, 1: 94).

To this main incident is added a sequel. When Adapa finally comes before Anu, the latter realizes that there is really no call to put him to death, since his action in breaking the wings of the storm bird was in fact inspired by piety, i.e. by indignation at the way in which that demon had deprived Ea of his fish dinner! However, a delicate problem now arises. On the one hand, Adapa cannot be rewarded with the fitting guerdon of immortality, because he has already refused the water of life and (apparently), once declined, that cannot be proffered again. On the other hand, if he is now allowed to return to earth, he will furnish to all men an example of that which is forbidden—namely, of a mortal who has beheld the secrets of heaven and yet lives (compare *Job* xv, 7–8). In his predicament, Anu decides to compromise and to overlook the latter consideration. He therefore allows Adapa to live out his days on earth and to become the founder of a dynasty; and he rewards him for his piety by commanding the gods and demons never to assail him with sickness or hurt.

This part of the tale was evidently intended to account for a popular belief that the reigning dynasty was descended from Adapa.

From the viewpoint of comparative folklore, Adapa is to be recognized as yet another version of the familiar theme of the Fisher-King (compare J. L. Weston, *From Ritual to Romance* [Cambridge, 1920]: 118 f.; R. Eisler, *Orpheus the Fisher* [London, 1921]: 20 ff.; *id.*, *OLZ*, xxxix (1935): 721 ff.; A. H. Krappe in *MLR*, xxxix [1944]: 18 ff.).

Etana   Concerned more strictly with the propagation of the species, but interwoven also with other motifs, is the myth of Etana and the Eagle—in two parts.

Part One relates how the eagle and the serpent agree to hunt food for each other and for each other's young. The eagle, however, eventually betrays the serpent and, despite a warning from a far-seeing eaglet, raids the latter's hole and devours its young. The serpent appeals to Shamash, god of justice. On the latter's instructions, it then creeps into the carcass of a bull and, when the eagle swoops down on it, maims his wings and leaves him lying in a ditch.

Part Two relates how Etana, a legendary king of Kish, being without issue, implores Shamash to supply him with the magical "plant of birth" so that he may give it to his wife to eat. Shamash tells him to go to the eagle. The latter, grateful at being released from the ditch, informs him that the plant is in heaven, but offers to transport him thither on his back. When they reach the heaven of Anu, Etana begins to feel giddy, but the eagle assures him that an even higher ascent is necessary. On this subsequent flight, however, Etana succumbs to vertigo, and both are thereby dragged down into the underworld (or sea?).

On the face of it, the point of this story would seem to lie in the way Shamash exploits the plight of Etana in order to visit retribution on the eagle. It may be sug-

gested, however, that far more really underlies it, and that there is a far closer connection than has been suspected between the initial struggle of the eagle and serpent and Etana's being sent to the latter when he seeks the "plant of birth." The fact is that *both the eagle and the serpent were believed in antiquity to possess immortality, or the power of constant renewal,* the former because it seems to molt and renew its feathers, the latter because it sloughs and renews its skin. (Compare for the eagle: *Psalm* ciii, 5; *Isaiah* xl, 31; Morgenstern, *ZA*, xxiv [1915]: 294 ff.; for the serpent: Sanchuniathon *apud* Euseb., *PE*, i: 10; Plutarch, *De Is. et Os.*, §74; *FOT*, i: 60 ff. Compare also Gardiner-Davies, *Tombs of Menkheperrasonb* [EEF 1933]: 26, "Mayest thou have the life of the ḳḳ-bird and mayest thou wax old like the na'y-serpent!"). The story may therefore be reconstructed as follows:

At first it was the serpent who possessed the magic plant of birth, i.e. of perpetual rejuvenation (compare *Epic of Gilgamesh*, XII: 274–320, which describes how he acquired it!). The eagle was jealous and stole it by raiding the serpent's hole. When, therefore, Etana sought just that plant, Shamash (who had been apprised of the matter) naturally sent him to the eagle. But the eagle was again treacherous, and merely pretended to Etana that the plant was in heaven, knowing full well that the ascent would overtax his powers. However, as it turned out, the deception redounded upon the eagle's own head, for not only Etana but he too was dragged down into the abyss. Thus justice was done.

Thus reconstructed, the story is a fusion of several familiar motifs: borrowed feathers, the essence of which is that *a dupe lets himself be carried aloft by a bird and dropped* (K1041); pride requited, as in the Icarus myth (L421); and deceiver—in this case, the eagle—caught in his own trap (K1600).

Myths of the Netherworld   Babylonian and Assyrian myths were also concerned with the fate of men after death. The main description of the netherworld is contained in the myth of the descent of Ishtar.

The goddess Ishtar decides to go down to the netherworld to sorrow for the "young men torn from their brides, the young women from their bridegrooms, the babes snatched away untimely." After gaining admission by threatening to break down the portals, she is admitted through the seven gates and is progressively disrobed until finally she stands naked before Ereshkigal, queen of the dead. The latter orders her henchman Namtar, god of plague, to visit Ishtar with all manner of diseases. At this point, however, Papsukkal, the messenger of the gods, notices that Ishtar's disappearance has led to infertility on earth. He therefore entreats Ea to rescue the goddess. Ea does so by dispatching the eunuch Aṣnamir into the netherworld to serve as a substitute for Ishtar. Thereupon Ereshkigal orders the water of life to be sprinkled upon her, and she is allowed to return, her clothes being progressively restored to her at each of the seven gates. At the end of the text, a few obscure lines relate it somehow to the annual festival of wailing for Tammuz, the god of fertility who disappeared annually into the netherworld and was later resurrected.

An earlier Sumerian version has been found at Nippur. Here, the rescue of Ishtar (called Inanna) does not depend on the fortunate vigilance of Papsukkal but is planned in advance. Before descending, the goddess instructs her henchman Ninshubur to make the rounds of the gods and solicit their aid, should she not return within a specified time. All refuse except Ea (called Enki) who sends two sexless creatures with food and water of life. They arrive after Ishtar (Inanna) has been turned into a corpse and impaled on a stake for three days, but eventually manage to restore her and bring her back to earth.

The story is but a variant of the familiar descent of Demeter and, like that myth, was probably the cult-text of the annual mysteries for the deity of vegetation (Tammuz, Persephone). It is replete with familiar motifs: descent to underworld (F81). Absence of goddess causes infertility (compare *Homeric Hymn to Demeter:* 305 ff.; Hittite version: *KUB*, 17.10, i: 8–9). The dead eat mud (Gaster, *JRAS*, 1944: 35). They have the appearance of birds (E732; Scheftelowitz, *Altpalästinensischer Bauernglaube* [Hannover, 1925]: 13 f.). The netherworld has seven gates (Koran, *Sura* XV: 44). It is governed by a goddess (A310.1). Disenchantment is effected by aspersion with the water of life (D766.1; E80).

Another myth dealing with the underworld is that of Nergal and Ereshkigal, found on a tablet from Tell el-Amarna, in Egypt. This relates how the gods once held a banquet and invited Ereshkigal, queen of the underworld, to send a messenger to fetch her share. She sent Namtar, god of plague. When he arrived, all the gods greeted him except Nergal. Ereshkigal ordered the offender to be brought before her. Nergal, however, appealed to Ea who provided him with an escort of terrifying demons. Posting these at the gates of the netherworld, Nergal institutes a general slaughter, kills Namtar, and drags Ereshkigal from her throne. To save her life, the latter capitulates and offers to share her dominion with her victor. Nergal accepts, and the two thenceforth reign as king and queen of the dead.

The purpose of the myth was obviously to account for the fact that the primitive queen of the netherworld was later replaced in mythology by the god Nergal. A similar development took place in Greece, where the earlier chthonian goddesses Demeter and Kore (Persephone) were later replaced by Hades (Pluto).

Nergal was identified with the summer sun which descended to the netherworld at the solstice (Tammuz 18). Our myth may have been the cult-text for that occasion.

The Epic of Gilgamesh The longest and most complex of all Babylonian and Assyrian myths is the story of Gilgamesh. This myth enjoyed wide popularity throughout the Near East. Portions of Sumerian, Hittite, and even Hurrian (Horite) versions have come down to us. In its present form, it is clearly the product of long mythological and literary development, welding together, in the manner of the *Iliad* and *Odyssey*, what must once have existed as separate and independent tales. Reduced to bare essentials, the resultant corporate narrative now runs as follows:

Gilgamesh, a hero of divine or miraculous birth, rules the city of Erech with an iron hand. To offset his despotism, the goddess Aruru fashions out of clay a wild and savage man called Enkidu. Living at first among animals, Enkidu later falls in with a harlot who teaches him the ways of civilized man and leads him to Erech, where he engages Gilgamesh in combat. However, it is Gilgamesh who wins, though the two champions thereafter become friends and together slay a Gorgonlike monster Humbaba who inhabits the forest of Lebanon. The prowess of Gilgamesh excites the passions of the goddess Ishtar, but when she offers herself to him, he rudely repulses her. Infuriated, she appeals to the high god and persuades him to create a monstrous heavenly bull to attack the two stalwarts. They, however, succeed in subduing it, and Enkidu contemptuously flings its phallus in Ishtar's face. Thereupon the gods decree his death.

Torn with grief, Gilgamesh embarks on a perilous journey to the immortal sage Ut-napishtim (the Babylonian Noah) to learn from him the secret of eternal life. First, he reaches the great mountain which hems in the earth. The strange scorpion-men who live there try to dissuade him, but eventually speed him along to the next stage of the journey, the Garden of the Gods, whose trees are hung with precious stones. There the sun god attempts to dissuade him, but he too eventually speeds him to the next stage of the journey, the abode of a hedonistic Circe-like fay called Siduri. She too tries to dissuade him, but eventually shows him the way to Ur-shanabi, the boatman of Ut-napishtim, who transports him to that venerable sage. Ut-napishtim then relates to him the story of the Flood—strangely parallel to the Biblical version—ending with the account of his own attainment of immortality. Subsequently, he goes sailing with Gilgamesh and points out to him the plant of immortality at the bottom of the ocean. Gilgamesh dives in and seizes it; but later, while he is taking a swim, a serpent emerges and devours it. In despair, Gilgamesh returns to Erech.

A subsequent passage (which must originally have formed an independent story) relates how Gilgamesh ultimately reached Enkidu at the door of the netherworld and heard from him a description of that realm.

The story of Gilgamesh is likewise characterized by several motifs familiar from folk literature:

The hero is the child of a supernatural or miraculous birth (A511; T540). Gilgamesh and Enkidu are a *pair* of culture heroes (A515; 515.1.1). His companion is a "wild and woolly" huntsman, a hairy anchorite. The latter is seduced by a woman and domesticated (D733.1). The heroes' prowess is tested by combat with monsters (A531). One of these (Humbaba) is a Gorgonlike monster. A goddess attempts seduction (compare Albright, *JBL*, XXXVII [1918]: 116 f.). The hero goes in search of the plant of life (H1333.2; compare D981; D1346.6). In his quest, he is passed on from one helper to the next (H1235). He journeys to a world-encircling mountain (compare Arabic Kaf or Qaf; Wensinck, *Navel of the Earth* [Amsterdam, 1916]: 6 ff.). Paradisal trees yield precious stones (compare F166.1). Serpent, instead of man, acquires plant of life and becomes immortal (A1335.5 [ad.]; Morgenstern, *ZA*, XXXIX [1914–15]: 284 ff.).

Stories of World Disasters The Babylonians and Assyrians possessed a story of a primeval deluge, evidently inspired by the phenomenon of seasonal floods which so frequently work havoc in Mesopotamia. The most complete account is that put into the mouth of Ut-napishtim in the *Epic of Gilgamesh*. It runs closely parallel to the Biblical version. Enlil, the high god, sends the flood in punishment for men's sins, but Ea visits Ut-napishtim, a righteous man, forewarns him and delivers him and his kindred in an ark which ultimately lands on Mount Niṣir. The hero then sends forth successively a dove, a swallow, and a raven. When the last-named fails to return, he emerges from the ark. Enlil is at first furious at the deliverance, but Ea persuades him that sins should be visited on individual sinners rather than upon mankind collectively. Thereupon Enlil rewards Ut-napishtim and his wife with immortality and transports him to the "mouth of the rivers"—the scene of Paradise.

An earlier Sumerian version (fragmentary) tells substantially the same story, but omits the incident of the dispatch of the birds and has the hero translated to the sacred island of Dilmun. He is named Ziusudra, and is said to have bequeathed a code of conduct upon men— an idea which recurs in Jewish legends of Noah.

The Myth of Irra describes the destruction of Babylon and, subsequently, of a larger area by the plague god Irra, assisted by seven personified weapons. It has been suggested that the myth commemorates certain historic disasters and invasions. Because it ends with the eventual appeasement of the god, it came to be used as a charm against sickness and epidemic.

The Dying and Reviving God The alternation of the seasons was the subject of an elaborate myth relating how Tammuz, god of fertility, sank annually into the netherworld and was subsequently resurrected. During the period of his absence, all vegetation and fecundity ceased, and he was mourned by his sister and beloved, Ishtar, and her companions. The myth had its counterpart in ritual, the disappearance and revival of Tammuz being enacted in sacred pantomime. Parallels to both myth and ritual are to be found, of course, in the Egyptian myth of Osiris, the Phrygian myth of Attis, the Syrian myth of Adonis, the Greek myth of Persephone, the Hittite myth of Telipinu, and in many primitive religions.

Canaanite Myths

Canaanite myths are known principally from the cuneiform texts unearthed, since 1929, at Ras Shamra (Fennel Head), site of ancient Ugarit, on the north coast of Syria. Written in a peculiar alphabetical script and in a proto-Hebrew language, they date in their present form from the 15th century B.C., and are now preserved in the Louvre, Paris. None of them is complete.

The *Poem of Baal* describes how that god, genius of rainfall and fertility, acquired dominion over the earth. First, he subdued Yammu (alias Leviathan), lord of the waters. Second, he had himself installed in a gorgeous palace. Third, he consigned his potential rival Môt, god of death and aridity, to the barren places and the netherworld. Môt, however, complained of unfair treatment and invited Baal to see for himself how dismal was existence in the infernal regions. Baal therefore made the descent, but Môt trapped him by persuading him to eat the food of the dead, which prevented return to earth. During Baal's absence, all fertility ceased. The gods attempted to appoint one 'Ashtar as a substitute for Baal, but this god proved inadequate to the task. At length, the goddess 'Anat, going in search of Baal, encountered Môt roving upon earth, and cut him in pieces. She then urged the sun goddess to retrieve Baal during one of her nightly journeys to the netherworld. This

was done, and Baal was restored to dominion. (In this brief summary we omit several subsidiary details.)

The story allegorizes the alternation of the seasons. In Arabic, "land of Baal" means rain-watered soil, "land of Môt" barren soil, and "land of 'Ashtar" soil artificially irrigated. Baal, therefore, is the genius of the rainy season, Môt of the dry season, and 'Ashtar of artificial irrigation—no adequate substitute for rain.

The poem combines the well-known motif of the battle of the seasons (*GB*, one-vol. ed.: 316–17; *TM*; 764 ff.) with that of the dying and reviving god (compare Osiris, Tammuz, Attis, Adonis). Moreover, it runs parallel, in general plot and sequence, to the Babylonian myth of *Enuma Elish*. Not improbably, it was originally the cult-text of the autumn festival, at the beginning of the rainy season.

The role here played by the solar deity is paralleled, to some extent, in the Greek myth of Persephone and in the Hittite myth of Telipinu, the dying and reviving god of fertility (*KUB*, XVII: 10). It is probably to be explained from the fact that the festival for which these myths were designed usually took place at solstice or equinox.

On the motif of the food taken in the underworld (C211; C262), see Gaster, *JRAS*, 1944: 37 f.

The *Story of Aqhat* relates how a mortal youth of that name came by chance into possession of a bow which the divine smith (Kôshar) was carrying to 'Anat, goddess of hunting and war. When he refused to surrender it, she plotted to recover it by a trick. Luring him to a distant place on the pretext that she would teach him the arts of the chase, and hiring as her henchman a local thug named Yatpan, she waited until Aqhat sat down to his dinner and until birds of prey circled around the viands. Then she herself flew amongst them and, having previously concealed him in a sack, released Yatpan directly above the head of Aqhat with instructions to knock him unconscious and hastily snatch the bow during the general *mêlée*. Yatpan, however, misunderstood or bungled these orders and actually slew Aqhat. Moreover, while flying away from the scene, he dropped the bow into the sea. Thereupon, realizing that her devices had come to nought, 'Anat resolved to revive the youth.

Meanwhile, as the result of spilling of innocent blood, the earth became infertile. Aqhat's father, Daniel, perceived this fact and later learned that the victim of the crime was Aqhat. Noticing the birds of prey still wheeling in the air, Aqhat's father prayed to Baal to break their wings and bring them down. Then, ripping open their gizzards, he retrieved the remains of his son and solemnly interred them—a regular preliminary, in all myths, to resurrection. Aqhat's sister resolved to avenge him. She therefore set out, under cover of darkness, to recruit assistance from the neighboring Bedouins. By chance, her steps led her to the tent of Yatpan himself. The latter entertained her and, his tongue loosened with wine, boasted of his prowess in slaying Aqhat! When he had thus betrayed himself, Aqhat's sister plied him with more and more drink until he fell into a stupor. Then (apparently) she slew him. In a sequel, now lost, Aqhat was evidently restored to life, and fertility returned to the earth.

In the present writer's opinion, this story is developed from a Semitic version of the myth of Orion, and its primary purpose was to account for the infertility of the earth during the high summer when the heavenly huntsman is in fact absent from the evening sky. The central character is assimilated to the familiar figure of the dying and reviving god of fertility—a process paralleled in Egyptian and Babylonian mythology, where Orion was likewise identified with Osiris and Tammuz respectively. It is, indeed, for this reason that the motif of resurrection through assemblage of dismembered parts is so prominently introduced, for this was a cardinal feature of the Osiris, Tammuz, and Adonis myths (E30; E607.1; V63).

The prominence of the bow in this Canaanite version of the myth is readily explicable from the fact that in Mesopotamian astronomy the constellation Canis Major was known as the Bow. Accordingly, just as a dog figures prominently in classical versions of the story, so in the Oriental counterpart would the element of the bow have had to be introduced.

The bemusing of Yatpan by drink recurs in the Biblical tale of Jael and Sisera (*Judges* iv-v), in the Hittite myth of the battle of the storm god against the dragon Illuyankas (*KBo*, III: 7) and in folktales concerning the defeat of the stupid ogre (G521).

The Legend of Keret relates how a monarch of that name, king of Hubur, prevented the progressive extinction of his line by contracting a union with the beautiful Horiya whom he won from her father, King Pabel of Udumu, by laying siege to the latter's city. Subsequently, after children had been born to him, Keret fell ill, whereupon his land languished and his eldest son Yaṣṣib sought to usurp the throne. Keret, however, was restored to health by the intervention of the high god El who sent a divine witch named Sha'taqat (Remover of Sickness) to perform various magical rites.

The purpose of this text is still obscure, and scholars are divided as to whether it is to be regarded as myth or legend. In the latter case, it may be a kind of primitive *chanson de geste*, perhaps composed to honor some descendant of the legendary Keret.

The Marriage of the Moon-god describes the espousals of that deity and the goddess Nikkal. The preliminaries of the ceremony are reminiscent of those related in *Genesis* xxxiv, 11–12. The poem appears to have formed part of the repertory of the professional singing women (*kôsharât*) employed, as among the modern Arabs, at weddings and funerals. It is therefore probable that the poem was really a mythological interlude introduced into a wedding song designed for a human couple.

A secondary source of information concerning Canaanite and Phœnician mythology lies in a series of excerpts made by the church father Eusebius of Cæsarea from the *Treatise on Matters Phœnician* compiled, about 100 A.D., by Philo, a scholar of Byblus. This work professes to have been based in large part on the earlier writings of a certain Sanchuniathon who may have lived between 700 and 500 B.C., and who wrote in the Phœnician language. The excerpts cover the origins of the gods, their primeval wars, and the creation of the world. They must be used, however, with great caution; for in the course of translation and transmission the original Semitic material was overlaid with a Greek veneer.

Other late writers likewise preserve reminiscences of Canaanite myth. Celsus, for example, quotes from a certain Pherecydes of Tyre the story of a primeval battle between the god Zas and the cosmic dragon Ophi-

oneus (compare Greek *ophis*, serpent), in which it is not difficult to recognize the old Canaanite myth of the combat between Baal and Yammu. This myth, it may be added, is also cited in the *Argonautica* of Apollonius Rhodius, and thence found its way into Milton's *Paradise Lost* (X, 570 f.).

Hebrew Myths

Hebrew myths are preserved mainly in the earlier chapters of the Biblical *Book of Genesis*. Therein are related the stories of Creation, Paradise, the Fall of Man, the Flood, the destruction of Sodom and Gomorrah, and the legendary origins of Israel. It has long been recognized that some of these stories possess marked affinities with Mesopotamian lore, and it was formerly thought that they represented material picked up by the Jews during the Assyrian and Babylonian Exiles and then incorporated into the later strata of the Pentateuch. The rediscovery of Canaanite literature, however, has now strengthened the alternative view that they may have enjoyed a far longer currency in Palestine itself and that they may represent a redaction of popular traditions themselves going back to the second millennium B.C. Activity in collecting such traditions appears to have been especially characteristic of the 7th and 6th centuries B.C., as witness the work of Ashurbanipal in Assyria and of Peisistratus in Greece. Accordingly, there would be nothing inconsistent with this view in the fact that the strata of the Pentateuch and the Prophetic and other writings in which these myths are embodied happen themselves to date to this comparatively late period.

Besides the major myths, such as those of Creation and of the Flood, which appear to have enjoyed wide and general circulation, there were others associated more specifically with particular shrines and similar sacred sites or with the very special customs and usages of this or that clan. Even in these, however, general motifs were interwoven. Thus, the story of Samson may have originated in myths about the sun god (Hebrew *Shemesh*) current at the sanctuary of Beth-Shemesh; while his exploit (*Judges* xv) in destroying the Philistines with "the jawbone of an ass" (Hebrew *leḥi*) was simply a local saga designed to explain the name of the place Leḥi. Similarly, the tale of Jacob's struggle with the angel at the ford of Jabbok (*Gen.* xxxii, 22–32) was partly designed to account for a tabu against eating the ischiatic nerve of an animal; while that of the Brand of Cain was probably intended to explain a Near Eastern usage whereby itinerant smiths and tinkers (Hebrew *qayin*, Cain) were distinguished by a mark on their brows and held sacrosanct.

It is apparent also that the Hebrews knew of several other myths besides those presented in formal literary manner in the *Book of Genesis*. In some of the *Psalms*, for example, and likewise in *Isaiah* and *Job*, there are references to a primeval battle between Yahweh (Jehovah) and a dragon variously named Leviathan or Rahab (Rager); and this is simply a variant of the Canaanite tale of Baal's fight with Yammu or Leviathan or the Mesopotamian story of Marduk's conflict with Tiamat. Moreover, it is significant that in most of the passages relating to that combat (e.g. *Ps.* lxxiv, lxxvi, lxxxix, xciii), the victory of the god is associated, as in the Canaanite and Mesopotamian versions, with the establishment of the world order and the installation of the triumphant hero in a special palace.

Again, in *Proverbs* xxx, 4, following the author's express statement that he is unversed in sacred lore, there are propounded a series of riddles which may best be explained as allusions to current myths, viz.: "Who went up to heaven and came down? Who gathered the wind in his fist? . . . Who upheld all the ends of the earth?" The answers, it may be suggested, are respectively: Etana and some beings like the classical Æolus (compare C322.1; A842).

It must be recognized also that the heroic sagas of the Old Testament often embody familiar motifs, showing that certain types or cycles of stories indeed enjoyed currency in Israel and Judah, even though no explicit literary formulation of them may have come down to us: Paradise is bounded by rivers (F162.2; F162.2.1). It contains a tree of life and one of knowledge (E90; C621.1). The sacred treasure is guarded by a dragon, griffin (cherub) (B11.6.2; N575). Eve, the mother of mankind, was originally a serpent-woman, as is clear from the fact that her Hebrew name Ḥawwah really means serpent. Abraham entertains angels unawares (Q45.1). Esau is a hairy anchorite (D733.1; compare Enkidu). Jacob sees a ladder leading to heaven (F52). Joseph is falsely accused by Potiphar's wife (K2111). Moses is an exposed child (S301). He uses a wonder-working staff (D1254). He ascends a mountain at death (F132). Aaron's staff blossoms (F971.2). Elijah is fed by ravens (B452). David is the Messianic king who will return in the hour of his people's need (A580; H. Schmidt, *Der Mythos vom wiederkehrenden König im Alten Testament* [Giessen, 1925]). Samson's strength lies in his hair (D1831). Jonah is cast into the sea to quell a storm (S264.1). He is swallowed by a great fish and then disgorged (F911.4). Ahasuerus offers one half of his kingdom to satisfy Esther's wish (Q112). The Land of Promise is an earthly paradise "flowing with milk and honey" (F701; F701.1; F162.2.5).

The sagas of the Pentateuch were derived from several sources and sometimes the same motif recurs in different narratives. Thus, not only Moses but also Aaron and Elijah die on mountains: a reminiscence of the folkloristic mountain of death, common to many cultures. Similarly, the tale of the two culture heroes, one representing civilized and the other uncivilized man, occurs not only in the case of Jacob and Esau but also in that of Isaac and Ishmael and, to a certain extent, of Cain and Abel. Moreover, many of the motifs which appear in Old Testament myth are found again in other ancient Near Eastern tales. Esau, for instance, has his counterpart in the Babylonian Enkidu; and the exposure of Moses in a basket of reeds is paralleled in a legend associated with King Sargon of Agade.

It is probable too that Old Testament poetry frequently contains, in its language and imagery, reminiscences of ancient mythology. Thus, when Micah refers (*Micah* vii, 19) to Yahweh's "treading our iniquities underfoot" and "casting all our sins into the depths of the sea" he is probably harking back to the ancient myth which related how the god trampled on the dragon and cast its carcass into the ocean. Again, when Amos and Joel refer to the heavens dropping sweet wine and the rivers running with honey in the last day, they are using language which is employed in the Ras Shamra texts to

describe the inauguration of the golden age when Baal returns to earth. Doubtless, as more of Canaanite and Mesopotamian literature is recovered, further allusions of a similar character, now concealed, will become apparent.

Bibliography: There is no good over-all presentation of Semitic mythology. S. Langdon's *Semitic Mythology* (Boston, 1931) offers translations of the principal Sumerian and Mesopotamian texts, but both renderings and interpretations must be received with considerable caution. S. H. Hooke's *Myth and Ritual* (Oxford, 1933) is a series of expert essays correlating the principal myths with their ritual backgrounds.

The Sumerian material may be studied in S. N. Kramer's *Sumerian Mythology* (Philadelphia, 1944), but this must be read in conjunction with Th. Jacobsen's "Sumerian Mythology: a review article," in *Journal of Near Eastern Studies*, V (1946): 128–52.

A good summary of Babylonian and Assyrian myths will be found in E. Dhorme's *Les religions de Babylonie et d'Assyrie* (Paris, 1945), ch. xi, pp. 299–330. There is no comprehensive volume of translations in English. In German, however, there is H. Gressmann's *Altorientalische Texte und Bilder* (Leipzig, 1926). For the poem *Enuma Elish*, see A. Heidel's *The Babylonian Genesis* (Chicago, 1942), and for the Gilgamesh epic, the same author's *The Epic of Gilgamesh* (Chicago, 1944). G. A. Barton's *Archaeology and the Bible* (6th ed., Philadelphia, 1926) also contains renderings of some of the documents.

Extremely valuable are A. L. Oppenheim's three articles on "Mesopotamian Mythology" in *Orientalia* 16 (1947), 207–38; 17 (1948), 17–58, and 19 (1950), 129–58, containing many novel and suggestive reinterpretations of the texts.

Most of what has been written about the Canaanite texts from Ras Shamra is now antiquated. For a good bibliography of editions and studies, see R. de Langhe, *Les textes de Ras Shamra-Ugarit et leurs rapports avec le milieu biblique de l'Ancien Testament* (Gembloux-Paris, 1945), vol. i, pp. xvi–lvii. The presentation in this article is original, and is based on the writer's *Thespis Ritual and Drama in the Ancient Near East* (New York, 1950), which contains translations and full discussions.

The Phœnician sources may be studied in *Cory's Ancient Fragments* (ed. E. Hodges, London, 1876), but the introductions and notes must be altogether dismissed.

Of interest for the study of Old Testament myths are Sir James Frazer's *Folklore in the Old Testament* (3 vols., London, 1918), and H. Gunkel's *Schöpfung und Chaos* (Göttingen, 1895).

Abbreviations:
ARW: *Archiv für Religionswissenschaft.*
ERE: *Encyclopaedia of Religion and Ethics,* ed. J. Hastings.
FOT: Frazer, James, *Folklore in the Old Testament* (3 vols., London, 1918).
GB: Frazer, James, *The Golden Bough.*
JBL: *Journal of Biblical Literature.*
JRAS: *Journal of the Royal Asiatic Society.*
KBO: *Keilschrifttexte aus Boghazköi.*
KUB: *Keilschrifturkunden aus Boghazköi.*
OLZ: *Orientalische Literaturzeitung.*

TM: Grimm, Jacob, *Teutonic Mythology*, tr. J. S. Stallybrass (4 vols., London, 1880–83).
ZA: *Zeitschrift für Assyriologie*.

THEODOR H. GASTER

Semnæ See ERINYES.

Sen'deh or **Sen'deh Old Man** Culture-hero-trickster of the Kiowa Indians of the Plains: a character of paramount interest to Kiowa taletellers. Sen'deh is never thought of as Coyote or any animal, though he may change into an animal whenever he wishes. Unlike many North American Indian culture-hero-tricksters, Sen'deh does not belong exclusively to the past; he often appears as chief actor in Kiowa tales relating to the present time. In character and deeds he much resembles other Plains tricksters such as Coyote, and many of the stories told about Coyote are also told of Sen'deh. [EWV]

sending A magician's or sorcerer's familiar sent out to work harm or kill, sometimes an actual animal, sometimes an animated object; often also the sorcerer himself (or herself) transformed, on a death-dealing errand; also the evil spell itself directed at a victim, usually by pointing. The concept and practice of sending is widespread throughout Oceania, but is also known among primitive peoples from Siberia to Africa, among American Indians and Eskimos, and it occurs also in the witchcraft of the Baltic peoples and in Scandinavia.

In British New Guinea, a snake is often conditioned to be sent on an errand of death: the sorcerer procures a piece of his victim's clothing, puts it in a pot with a snake, heats the pot until the snake strikes at the garment with the human smell; the snake is then liberated near the victim, strikes at the associated smell when the victim passes, and usually kills (see J. A. MacCulloch, "Sending," *ERE* viii: 218). Elsewhere in New Guinea disease-producing sendings, in the form of slivers of bone, stone, or coral called *labuni*, are said to be hidden within the bodies of certain women; these can be "sent" as far as 60 yards to lodge in the body of the victim. The only way to get them out is to propitiate the sender with gifts. Medicine men of the Chippewa Indians have been said to stuff an owl-skin with magic substances and to send it flying through the air to the victim's dwelling, usually to cause starvation.

Pointing is the most usual form of deadly sending among primitive peoples and of later witchcraft. Power is believed to stream from the pointer to the victim. When the Malay pawang points his kris at a victim, blood begins to drip from the point of it as soon as the spell begins to work. It is still improper in polite society today to point at people or at sacred objects. On northern coasts of the world pointing at a ship is said to bring bad luck to it. See FAMILIAR; KILLING BY POINTING; PAWANG.

separable soul The soul (heart, life) conceived as dwelling apart from the living body, often in a tree or plant, animal, bird, egg, stone, or other inanimate object, and usually in a secret place for safe keeping. The concept occurs in most primitive religions and is a commonplace of world folktale. The soul *in the form of* an animal, bird, insect, plant, etc., is a different idea from the soul hidden away in animal or plant, or even kept in another part of a man's body than the heart for protection. When Abigail warned David that a man had risen to pursue him and seek his soul, she added the comforting words that his soul was "bound in the bundle of life with the Lord God" (I *Kings* xxv, 29).

Probably the most familiar folktale based on the separable soul motif (E710 ff.; Type 302) is the Norwegian story of *The Giant Who Had No Heart In His Body*, but whose soul (heart) was safely hidden away in a series of things (E713)—in an egg, in a duck, in a well, in a church, on an island, in a far-off lake. In Greek story the life of Nisus, king of Megara, was in one purple hair in the midst of his locks, which his daughter Scylla pulled out when she fell in love with the invading Minos, king of Crete. The Old Testament story of Samson belongs to this cycle: his power, if not his life, was in his hair; and the secret was wheedled from him by a loved woman, who betrayed him, the usual accompanying circumstance of the story (K975.2). In the Old Irish story of *Cano, Son of Gartnán*, Cano would not accept the love of Créd while he was a common soldier; but he gave her a stone which contained his life, as pledge of his return as soon as he was king. Later when Cano was king of Scotland, Créd traveled north to meet him, bringing the stone with her. They were in sight of each other when Cano was attacked by a rejected lover of Créd. When Créd saw the blood streaming from his wounds she dashed her own head against a rock; the life stone of Cano fell and broke and Cano died. See Myles Dillon, *Cycles of the Kings*, pp. 82–83. See ACACIA; BUSH SOUL; DREAM SOUL; LIFE TOKEN.

separating sword or **sword of chastity** A folktale motif in which a man and woman not married must for some reason sleep together. They do so but with some object—usually a sword in oriental and medieval story—between them. The object (sword) is the token and guarantee of their chastity. Often in medieval story the woman is not aware that the man she is sleeping with is not her husband. He may be the husband's twin brother impersonating the husband to gain information, or he may, like Siegfried, take on the likeness of the husband. This motif occurs widely in folktale and myth, but rather infrequently in literature of record. It is found in the following romances: *Amis and Amiloun*, *Tristan*, *Generides*, certain versions of the *Seven Sages of Rome*, *Oliver and Artus*, *Ludwig and Alexander*, *Der Arme Heinrich*, *Grinado*, *Enfances de Garin*, *Engleburt and Dietrich*. It is also found rather generally in Germanic saga literature: The *Siegfried*, the *Bjarki-Saga*, Saxo Grammaticus, *Volsungs Saga*, the *Saga of Orendel and Breide*. It occurs also in Germanic balladry and in the English ballad *Lord Ingram* (Child #66, B 14). *Amis and Amiloun* seems to be the source, direct or indirect, of this episode in all the romances including the celebrated *Tristan*. *Tristan* is certainly originally a Celtic elopement story, the pattern of which is as follows: A nephew elopes against his will with his uncle's wife. They are pursued by the uncle; each night when they must sleep together, at the nephew's insistence they remain chaste, sleeping with an object (often a stone) between them. The original *Tristan* must have centered around the flight into the forest with the emphasis on Tristan's preserving the chastity between him and his uncle's wife. When the *Tristan* was developed and made over into a courtly romance the sword was substituted for the original stone, borrowed, it would seem, from *Amis and Amiloun*, for this romance is the oldest piece of recorded literature in western Europe to use this motif, and as a romance it was very popular in all the languages of Europe. *Amis and Amiloun* can likewise be proved to be the source of the motif either directly or indirectly in the other romances of the West which use it. *Amis and Amiloun* serves in this way as an intermediary between folktale and literature of record, for the motif comes into *Amis and Amiloun* directly from the folktale of the *Two Brothers*. In the *Two Brothers*, one of the most wide-spread of all European folktales, this motif constantly occurs; so constant is it that it must be a part of the original *Two Brothers* story. This famous folktale has been studied in detail by Ranke in *FFC* 114. Some 770 versions are listed from all over the world; about two thirds of them contain this motif or show evidence of having contained it. It is highly significant that in European folktale this motif seems not to occur except in the *Two Brothers* story, of which *Amis and Amiloun* is the literary descendant.

The part of the story pattern of the *Two Brothers* that interests us can be abbreviated as follows: A man who has long been married but without children catches the King of the Fishes, who instructs him to give a portion of his body to his wife, who in due time produces twins. From some of the bones cast aside two trees spring up. When the twins are grown one leaves to make his fortune, telling his brother that if harm should come to him his tree will wither. Eventually he comes to a great city where he marries a beautiful girl. Some time later he asks her what lies beyond the mountains he sees from his window. She tells him that no one who has gone there has ever returned. The next day he sets out to see for himself, and is bewitched and turned to stone. Back home his tree withers; seeing this the second brother starts out to find the first. Eventually he comes to the town where his brother had married and there is mistaken for his twin. He says nothing, hoping by that means to find out what has happened to his brother. Posing as her husband he sleeps each night with his sister-in-law, but each night puts his sword between them . . . It is significant, it seems to me, that this is the only folktale of wide range which contains this motif and that the motif is rarely found except in the *Two Brothers* story. After a detailed study of the tale Ranke decides that it belongs to western Europe and perhaps to northern France. At any rate it is clear that the story is commonplace in Europe and has been so for a long time. Ranke takes as the first recorded version the *Bjarki Saga* (14th century) seeming not to be aware of the Latin version of *Amis and Amiloun* of the 11th century, which is clearly a reworking of the folktale.

That the motif is no literary convention or invention is proved by the fact that it is in the *Two Brothers*, and secondly by the fact that the practice of placing an object between a man and woman who must sleep together is common among many early peoples. In early stages of culture and extending down even today the practice of continence for specific purposes is common. One might observe continence to increase physical powers, to obtain property, to get success in hunting, fishing, war, to guarantee germination and growth of crops, to increase milk in cattle. Almost any activity involving risk might be accompanied by a tabu against sexual intercourse. In addition, many people practiced continence for a varying length of time after marriage; after child-birth for as long as the child was being suckled; or as a part of religious ritual. The Masai of Africa must remain continent during the brewing of the poison to be used on arrows, lest it have no potency; during this time they sleep with their wives but with a stick between them. The Arunta of Australia remain continent during the period of sowing of grass seed; at this time they sleep with their wives, but with fires burning between them. On Luzon, P. I., a bride and groom must remain continent for a period after marriage but sleep together with a boy between them. It is not necessary to multiply illustrations. The fact is that people the world over during periods when abstinence from sexual intercourse was necessary for any of a wide variety of reasons were accustomed to sleep with some object between the man and woman. The separating object seems totally without significance. Found in addition to those already mentioned are: a log of wood, cloth, rolled up clothes, drinking gourd, matting, cooking pots, etc. No common denominator can be struck. It would seem that any object that came to hand would serve and that the whole significance of the action is in the belief that something tangible be placed between the sleepers as symbol of their continence, as a token of a condition that was accepted by both, like the bundling boards in New England beds. Never found in this connection are elements thought to have magical powers, such as certain plants or wood. No use for this purpose is made of mandrake, rowan, garlic, hazel; missing too are ritualistic objects and charms. Nor is there any account of the object placed between the two having been sung over or imbued with magic. Weapons in general are conspicuously absent as separating objects in early cultures.

The sword (dagger, knife, deer-sticker, pistol) as an object of separation first appears in the Orient. From there come the earliest references; they are all in cultures advanced and sophisticated: Hebrew (3rd century), Persian, Arabic. The sword had developed as a symbol of law and morality; the gradual substitution of the sword for a casual object would in a more advanced culture be inevitable. For the same reason the cross is occasionally found in Christian societies as the separating object.

The development then of the motif of the sword of chastity or the separating sword would seem to be as follows: In the early stages of culture it was the common practice of men and women, who for any of a variety of reasons had to preserve abstinence from sexual intercourse, to sleep together with some object between them as a token of their abstinence. As society became more advanced and sophisticated the sword, symbol of law, became the accustomed object. Folktales reflecting this practice were told, especially in the Orient. One such story, the *Two Brothers*, became immensely popular over Europe and Asia and was finally reworked in the 11th century into the general popular romance, *Amis and Amiloun*. This romance in turn became the source of the motif in later literature in such stories as the famous *Tristan*.   MacEdward Leach

separation of sexes   In the emergence myths of several of the southern Athapaskan tribes of North America, some prominence is given to the period when men and women were separated in the underworld, before emerging to the earth. The Navaho say that this occurred in the last of the 12 worlds below the earth; the Jicarilla Apache are more interested in assigning a reason for the separation, which they say was caused by the women's faithlessness, or by a woman's scolding a chief; the chief, enraged, called all the men to him, even the baby boys, male dogs, and male horses, and took them to the other side of a river which the women could not cross. The sexes remained separated for four years, by which time the women were starving, not having planted crops that year. Finally, with the help of Coyote, the sexes came together again. A Tübatulabal (east central California) tale, to which no parallels have as yet been found to exist among any other tribes, also deals with men and women at a time when the sexes were isolated from each other; the men find the women, and invite them to visit them, during the mythical age. [EWV]

Serapis In Greco-Egyptian religion, the dead Apis-bull assimilated in Osiris; Osiris-Apis, a chthonic god combining Osiris with an aspect of Ptah, who had a strong place in popular religion. Serapis seems to have been an artificial fusion made for political purposes to consolidate the position of the Ptolemies (the Macedonian dynasty in Egypt, after 323 B.C.). The underlying idea, that of identifying a ruling house with a god, was common enough; Alexander had similarly tried to identify himself with Amen when he conquered Egypt. There was no mythology concerning Serapis. His physical appearance was Greek in concept: a Hades seated on a throne, wearing a basket on his head, the infernal watchdog at his feet. This statue of Serapis in the Serapeum at Alexandria was brought from Sinope by Ptolemy Soter. The unknown god had come to him in a dream and told him where to find it. Then two who knew discovered it to be the image of Serapis. It was said that the only god invoked as Alexander lay dying was Serapis, and, though this may have been Ea Šarapsi, a Babylonian deity, the name of Serapis became famous throughout the Greek world. Serapis was part of a triad with Isis and Harpocrates: he was thus equivalent to Osiris. In later times the cult of Serapis spread throughout the Roman world. The Alexandrian Serapeum was destroyed by Theodosius in 385 A.D. and Serapis worship eventually died out before the attacks of Christianity.

Sere Dina A Fijian type of song called "true songs," actually epic chants of exploits and history of the times beyond men's memory, composed by specially endowed singers for notable occasions such as the visit of an honored personage, a death, or a natural visitation (hurricane, etc.), and believed to be transmitted to the poet by the spirits of his ancestors during a dream or trance. The songs are long rimed chants broken by an intermission during which the audience relaxes and fills the time with jokes and anecdotes. (See B. H. Quain, *The Flight of the Chiefs*, New York, 1942.)

serpentine A serpentine course grows naturally out of an open round, for the leader of the line may digress from the steady circling to describe meandering figures, zigzags, figure-eights, or spirals. Commonly the dancers hold hands, or link garlands, as in ancient and modern Greece, in the Serbian *kolo*, French *farandoule*, and

in ceremonies of the ancient Aztecs. Eastern Woodland American Indians are not always linked.

The Greek labyrinthine *geranos*, or crane dance, is said to have its origin in the Theseus legend, the rescue of Athenian youths and maidens from the labyrinth. Or it may simply imitate the swerving flight of the crane. Similar serpentines of Europe may have originated in this dance or in the older serpentines of the Eleusinian mysteries. More likely, the *Schemenlaufen* and *Metzgersprung* are descended from autochthonous fertility rites, as also the *ball de la teya* and Hungarian *gyertyas tánc* with their fire symbolism. All of these dances use a running step or skip and often introduce an arch figure—two fertility traits. All of these features have been transferred to the New World in the Kentucky Running Set.

Independently, the American Indian follows a serpentine course, particularly in the Southeast, also in the Ute turkey dance. A meander is particularly characteristic of Cherokee rounds, the corn, ant, snake, and friendship stomp dances. This has been accepted by the Iroquoian Seneca in their corn dance and "Cherokee" dance, and by the Sauk and Fox in their grapevine and snake dances. Like the European versions, they are associated with fertility. See DANCE: FOLK AND PRIMITIVE; ROUND DANCE; SNAKE DANCE; STOMP DANCES. [GPK]

serpent worship Though serpents are sacred in many parts of Africa, it is rare that they are worshipped as such. African "serpent worship" is rather manifested in respect shown certain species of snakes, usually those whose habitat is in rivers or other bodies of water, as manifestations of certain supernatural beings, or because of their association with water deities. The theological setting of beliefs of this nature have been explored only slightly, but in Dahomey, at least, it is known that the serpent is conceived both as the rainbow and as the instrument which brings or takes away wealth. It is placed in the general category of sinuous objects, such as the umbilical cord or a column of smoke. The Dahomean rainbow serpent, Aido Hwedo, is best known in the New World because of the prominent role Damballa plays in the Haitian *vodun* theological and ritual system. However, respect is shown snakes by Negroes in all parts of the New World, this varying from the Dagowe of the Bush Negroes, where this variety enters into the patterns of worship, to the lore about the power of snakes that has been recorded from the United States. [MJH]

sesame An East Indian herb (*Sesamum indicum*) containing seeds which are used as food and which yield a pale yellow emollient oil. The oil is widely used in India for both cooking and anointing. Both the seeds and the oil are used not only medicinally, but widely in various ceremonies for the dead and for fertility.

Sesame seeds are boiled with rice and barley flour and honey and milk to make the special balls (*pindas*) which are offered to spirits of the dead at the Hindu Śrāddha ceremony. These, provided for a dead relative for ten days, enable him to by-pass as many hells as balls are offered, and provide him day by day and part by part with a new body. Certain Hindu dancing girls offer a sweetmeat made of sesamum and sugar every Wednesday to Ganeśa, their patron.

In Indian folktale, one of the noodle stories in the *Avadānas* (#67) is about the sower who sowed roasted sesame seeds to no avail. The story of the "Brahman's Wife and the Sesame Seeds" (see *Ocean of Story* V: 76, 77) is a moral tale against hoarding. When told to prepare milk, sesame, and rice for a guest, the wife demurs because of poverty. The husband then tells the story of the jackal who watched the hunter kill a wild boar and die from the wounds from the boar's tusks. The jackal, thinking to hoard the abundant meat, went first to eat the little piece that was on the bow; the arrow fixed in the bow flew up and killed him.

The phallic cakes representing female organs which were a feature of the Thesmophoria in honor of Demeter at Syracuse were made of sesame and honey.

The aphrodisiac properties of sesame seed have been praised for centuries. The *Kama Sutra* prescribes sesame seeds, especially the covering of the seeds, soaked in sparrow eggs and boiled in milk with sugar and ghee along with two or three other things, to make a man able to enjoy "innumerable women." Costa Ben Luca, an Arabic physician of the 9th century, prescribed an aphrodisiac remedy, which he found in the *Book of Cleopatra,* to one afflicted with impotence and which was found effective: anointment of the body with crow's gall mixed with sesame.

Pliny stated that "Sesame stamped or beaten into powder, and so taken in wine, restraineth immoderate vomits." Today the leaves soaked in water produce a mucilaginous fluid used with great success for dysentery and diarrhea of children. Sesame is commercially grown in the United States for this particular purpose. The oil from the seeds is slightly laxative. See OPEN SESAME.

Sesha The world serpent of Hindu mythology; one of the Nāga kings who ruled in Pātāla. Sesha is depicted with a thousand heads, dressed in purple, and holding a plow and pestle. He supports the world or the seven Pātālas or hells. He is also the servant of Vishṇu, who rests on him while sleeping. Sometimes he is represented as forming the canopy of the god, sometimes as having become a man in the form of Balarāma. At the end of each kalpa, or eon of 1,000 yugas or ages, he destroys the world with fire. Earthquakes are caused when he shakes one of his heads. See ANANTA.

Seven Against Thebes The group of heroes in Greek legend who fought to remove the usurping Eteocles from the throne of Thebes. When Polynices and Eteocles, sons of Œdipus, grew of age, they agreed to share the throne, year and year about. Polynices went into exile the first year, and while at Argos married Argea, daughter of Adrastus. When it became obvious that Eteocles would not surrender the throne at the end of the year, Adrastus got together an expedition to help his son-in-law obtain his right. Besides Adrastus and Polynices, the Seven included Tydeus, Amphiaraus, Capaneus, Hippomedon, and Parthenopæus; some versions of the story make changes in this list. (Compare for example Aeschylus' play *Seven Against Thebes.*) During the march on Thebes, the expedition stopped for water at Nemea. Hypsipyle offered to show them where a spring was located, but while they were gone a dragon killed her child. The heroes slew the dragon and instituted the Nemean games, one of the great game festivals of ancient Greece. When they arrived before Thebes, each of the Seven attacked one of the seven gates of the city, which were defended by seven Theban heroes. The assault failed: Capaneus was killed by one of Zeus' thunderbolts; Tydeus, almost given immortality by Athena, lay wounded and ate the brains of Melanippus, and Athena changed her mind; Amphiaraus was swallowed up, chariot and all, by the earth; Polynices and Eteocles, because of a curse laid on them by Œdipus, killed each other. Only Adrastus escaped alive. Creon then resumed the Theban throne, forbade the burial of Polynices, and brought great trouble to his house thereby. In later years, the Epigoni, Those Born After, the sons of the Seven, led by the aged Adrastus, took the city and razed it. The fall of Thebes is said to have occurred just before the Trojan War began.

Seven Gods of Luck or **Shichi Fukujin** Patrons of good fortune and longevity of Japanese mythology: a syncretism of Shinto and Buddhist concepts, formalized during the 16th century. They are: Benten, patroness of the fine arts, female beauty, and a giver of wealth; Bishamonten, also a giver of wealth; Daikoku, god of inexhaustible wealth, usually depicted standing on two rice bags and carrying one on his shoulder; Ebisu, god of fishing and food and honest dealing, depicted with a merry face and a fishing rod with which he catches the fish of good luck out of the sea; Fukurokuju, god of fortune and longevity, depicted with the crane, symbol of long life; Hotei, the fat and cheerful god who carries a bag of treasure, from which he gives to non-worriers; Jorojin, patron of health and longevity.

seventh son A seventh son is always a lucky or especially gifted person, often gifted with occult powers. He makes a good doctor; he usually has instinctive knowledge of magic and medicinal herbs; and the seventh son of a seventh son can stop hemorrhages. Throughout England, Scotland, Ireland, and the United States in general, any seventh child is regarded as having exceptional healing powers. In Ireland, the spittle of a seventh son is especially potent. In French folklore, a seventh consecutive son is said to be "gifted with the lily" (i.e. *fleur de lis*). The gift seems to be a kind of clairvoyance or telepathy by which hidden things are brought to light. Among Gipsies, the seventh daughter of a seventh daughter always tells a true fortune. Rumanian folk belief in regard to a seventh child is more sinister: any seventh child is doomed to become a vampire.

sex token Implements used by males and females are hung up or placed within reach of a mysterious visitor; whichever falls or is taken denotes the sex of the unborn child, or the sex of the unseen visitor. Usually the implement hung up for a boy, by North American Indians, is a tiny bow and arrow; for a girl a basket, or mortar and pestle. This incident occurs in several North American Indian tales, especially hero tales. For sex token customs associated with the afterbirth of newborn infants among the Kwakiutl Indians of British Columbia, the Aymara Indians of Bolivia, and the Siberian Yukaghir, see AFTERBIRTH. [EWV]

sextur Six dance: a Danish figure dance for six couples (not six dancers). It is essentially a sunwise round, conforming to western European type, but includes simple interaction of couples. A chassé slide, with joined hands, opens and closes the dance. With a two-step and two walking steps, opposite couples meet in turn (one and four together, one and four apart, two and five together; these apart while three and six together; finally these last apart). Then the girls circle left in the center and the men circle left. Partners thereupon turn in separate couples. There are other versions, as the *polka sextur,* danced with a polka step. They are all modern developments built on the ancient round dance. [GPK]

sexual aberrations (North American Indian) Several tales concern a maladjustment of the sexual life such that satisfaction is sought in aberrant ways. From the European viewpoint the most telling examples of such Indian tales would be those recorded by Opler from the Jicarilla Apache, of the sexual use of cactus, the girl who had intercourse with dogs, and that section of the Jicarilla emergence myth in which the First People separate according to sex, and the men and women use themselves sexually: to the women monsters are born, which the culture hero, Killer-of-Enemies, later destroys. See Morris E. Opler, *Myths and Tales of the Jicarilla Apache Indians, MAFLS* 31, 1938, pp. 24 n.1, 266, 369–70, 373.

Several other instances of sexual aberrations are found in North American Indian literature. The toothed vagina is one (see VAGINA DENTATA); long-distance intercourse, in which Trickster's penis lengthens to enable him to have intercourse with a woman sleeping on the other side of a stream is another. Trickster's seduction of his own daughter by feigning death and returning to his home in disguise (T411.1); a brother's seduction of his sister by suggesting a deceptive remedy (usually sitting on a certain plant) to cure the sister's burned groins (T415.1); a son-in-law's trick which enables him to sleep with his mother-in-law while on a camping trip (T417); Trickster's use of a tree as a wife (T471); the incestuous relations of the brother and sister who become sun and moon (see LIGHT), or the wish for such relations on the part of Loon Woman; and some of the animal paramour tales, all revolve around, or touch upon, the obtaining of sexual satisfaction in socially non-approved ways. [EWV]

sexual continence Peoples all over the world observe continence during the sowing of grain, during a war, during many occupations of a seasonal character, before and during a long period of tabu (e.g. mourning of a dead chief). Certain Indians of Mexico must remain continent during the search for the sacred cactus, the Gourd of Fire. Workers at the salt pans, brewers of beer and wine, must remain continent during these processes. Hunters and fishermen likewise observe such prohibitions against sexual indulgence. Of course, wives during these times must also be continent and chaste. Should a hunter be killed by an animal, or should he fail to get the expected meat, his wife will at once be suspected of unfaithfulness. Though continence is the practice of many people on these occasions, yet there are some who reverse the whole procedure, especially at planting time, and engage in wild and promiscuous sexual excesses to bring about the same result. Frazer holds that some believe repression of the strength they might expend in reproducing will cause that strength to go into the plants or animals, and that others reason that a pouring out of sexual energy will stimulate nature to an abundance. See CHASTITY. [MEL]

sexual intercourse (North American Indian) The myths of several tribes tell how people learned to have

sexual intercourse; among the Thompson Indians of the Plateau region, for example, it is the trickster, Coyote, who when he came to a country inhabited by men and women who did not know how to propagate, showed them how to mate; the women would not let him go until he was thoroughly fatigued and ran away, whereupon they chased him. Many other tribes, as for example the Shawnee of the Eastern Woodlands, recount in their creation myth how man, when originally created, was improperly provided with sexual organs and did not mate; only after these organs were put where they are now, did he learn to have intercourse and thus have children. All North American Indian groups seem to have been aware of the connection between intercourse and child-bearing. For the continental distribution of the misplaced genitalia motif (A1313.3) see Stith Thompson, *Tales of the North American Indians* (Cambridge, 1929), p. 288, n. 59a.

Illicit intercourse by various means is attributed to Trickster in many North American Indian trickster tales. In one widely distributed tale Coyote or other trickster characters sees women at a distance or across a stream; he causes his penis to become long, and has "long distance intercourse" with them. In another trickster tale Coyote travels with his mother-in-law; at night; they lie down near each other and he frightens her so that she moves nearer and nearer to him until finally he has intercourse with her. In still another tale he disguises himself as a baby in order to have intercourse, and in yet another he feigns death so that he can have intercourse with his own daughter. Incest of this sort, or intercourse with one's mother-in-law, with whom one stood in a respect relationship, were both utterly beyond the pale in actual living, in all American Indian tribes. [EWV]

shadow The interpretations of shadows in folklore revolve about the idea that shadows are the souls, life essence, or strength of the individual. The people of the Amboyna and Uliasse Islands fear to go out of their houses at midday because, in those equatorial latitudes where the shadow at that hour is tiny, they may lose their souls. On the Malay Peninsula the prohibition against burying the dead at noon has to do with short shadows and short lives. The strength of the Mangaian warrior hero was greatest in the morning and least at noon when his shadow was short.

Some peoples teach that shadows have independent lives of their own. In England "no man can escape his shadow" and Lucian explained that when we die our shadows become our accusers. They are trustworthy because they were always associated with us and never separated from our bodies. The Egyptian view was that men have three kinds of body: the flesh, the "double," and the shadow. Some West African peoples believe that man has four souls of which one is the shadow soul. Consequently it is important to keep in the shade at noon lest the shadow soul be lost. The soul rests after sunset and arises with renewed power in the morning. The owner must die when an enemy stabs the shadow soul. Among the Indonesians, people who have no shadow or only a faint one will die soon. Among the Dyaks, Niassians, Javanese, and other Malays, a food on which a human shadow has fallen must not be eaten lest the soul substance be consumed. In fact, throughout the Malay

Archipelago shadows must not fall on graves, trees, or other objects inhabited by spirits which might consume the shadow and thus cause death.

The belief that life essence, frequently referred to by observers as "soul," is implicit in shadows has been reported from all parts of the world: Tasmania, Africa, North and South America, Asia, and Europe. Consequently many tales exist about the need to immolate a living man, child, or virgin in the walls of a house with the assumption that the souls of these victims will give the house strength. Builders in modern Greece are said to kill an animal, let its blood flow on the foundation stones of the house, and bury it in the walls. Elsewhere (Transylvania) people believe that the shadow of a living man can be built into the house. Passers-by are warned not to come near a house while it is being built lest their shadows be caught and they die. Shadow traders take the dimensions of a man's shadow which they sell to builders. In some parts of China it is dangerous to let your shadow fall into a grave. A further conjugation of this is the Warrau belief that looking at a person draws the shadow or soul toward one. In the Island of Wetar magicians can make a man ill by stabbing his shadow. In Nepal Sankara's neck was broken while he was demonstrating his supernatural powers. The Grand Lama stabbed Sankara's shadow while he was soaring in the air. Sankara fell, fatally. In the Banks Islands certain stones are inhabited by "eating ghosts" who draw out the souls of men whose shadows fall on them. When built into houses these stones protect against intruders. A small snail in Perak can suck the lifeblood from the shadows of cattle. In ancient Arabia a man was paralyzed if a hyena stepped on his shadow, and if a hyena stepped on the shadow of a dog on the roof of a house, the dog would fall to the earth as if pulled down. The Basutos believe that crocodiles can drag a man's reflection under the water and thus kill him.

Many peoples believe that the shadows of women, particularly mothers-in-law, women in mourning, or menstruous women, are particularly ominous. If the shadows of Shuswap widows of British Columbia fall on any one, they will cause illness. The shadow of any woman can cause loss of weight, laziness, and stupidity to the Kurnai of Australia. In New South Wales it is grounds for divorce if a man's shadow falls on his wife's mother. In Lebanon the peasants believe that the shadows of menstruous women cause flowers to wither and trees to perish. In folk belief ghosts have no shadows (E421.2). [RDJ]

Shāhnāmah The *Epic of Kings:* a historical epic written by the Persian poet Firdausī about 1010 A.D. The central subject of the poem is the deeds of the Rustamids. It makes extensive use of legendary and semi-historic material contained in the *Karnamak i Artakhshir i Papakan* (*The Book of Mighty Deeds of Ardashir, Son of Babak*). The epic was undertaken by Dakiki, probably a Moslem, who had completed a thousand verses when he was murdered by a slave. Firdausī completed the enormous project during a period of 35 years. The poem begins with Gaya Maretan, Haoshangha, and Takhmūrath, the earliest Iranian heroes, and ends with an account of the Sassanian dynasty.

Shakers An indigenous and flourishing religious sect of the present-day Indians of the Pacific Northwest, having no connection with the Christian Shakers of the Atlantic states. The founder of the Indian Shaker religion was John Slocum, a Sahewabsh-Squamish Indian of the Puget Sound region. In 1881 or 1882 Slocum died. While his father and brother were buying him a coffin Slocum came back to life. He had, he said, been refused admittance to heaven because of the life he had led, and had been sent back to tell his people they must confess and be reborn. After this experience he spent his life preaching, and founded the Indian Shaker Church. The "shaking" which is characteristic of the sect is however attributed to John Slocum's wife. Mrs. Slocum, it is said, "got a spirit," fainted, and when she recovered started shaking; Slocum, who was ill at the time but who had refused the services of Indian medicine men, was shaken over by his wife and other relatives, and improved under the treatment. During the past sixty to seventy years the Shaker religion has been spread by zealous converts, south as far as the Hupa of northwestern California, north as far as Victoria and Nanaimo or Vancouver Island, and eastward to the Yakima reservation and the Dalles in Washington. The rites are always held in a one-room church, rectangular and proportioned like the native North Pacific Coast houses, and church beliefs and practices represent a fusion of old native and new Christian beliefs and behavior. For a comprehensive description of the Indian Shaker church see Erna Gunther, "The Shaker Religion of the Northwest" pp. 37–76, in *Indians of the Urban Northwest*, Marian W. Smith, ed., New York, 1949. [EWV]

shakuhachi A long vertical bamboo flute of Japan, named for its length (*shaku*, a measure, plus *hachi*, eight), probably introduced by Buddhist priests from China in the 13th century. It is now played as an accompaniment to folk songs and sometimes makes one of a trio with the samisen and koto.

shalako The six giant kachina of Zuñi pueblo, each one impersonated by two men. The masks are turquoise-colored, with a crest of eagle and macaw feathers, and horns with red feather pendants, ball eyes, long snouts which open and close; long hair, a collar of raven feathers and fox skins, dance kilts, and white blankets are also part of the costume. The mask is carried on a pole, simulating a creature ten feet high. The masks are accorded great deference and are consecrated with cornmeal before each use. Each mask is associated with one of the six kivas.

The shalako "kachina advent" is prepared on the ninth day of winter solstice, and spreads through the year, with periodic planting of prayer-sticks by the shalako in February, May, September, October, November, and the actual escorted arrival in November or December, at a ceremony called *koko awia* (the kachina come). In the public ceremony, when they approach the pueblo, they are escorted by the *koyemshi* clowns, who also do considerable dancing, and by Long Horn kachina with their heavy-step quadrille. They are associated with war and hunt (striking a shalako gives luck in hunt), burlesque, sexual license, ritual continence, and killing, and communal dances by all men. Chants refer to the ancestors' fate after emergence, and to progeny. It is primarily a ceremony for the dead, and thereby for rebirth. Kachina depart after Shalako, at summer solstice in July. [GPK]

shaman and **shamanism** The term shaman is usually used by Americanist ethnographers in reference to men or women who, through the acquisition of supernatural powers, are believed to be able to either cure or cause disease. In contrast to priests, shamans are not instructed in a body of formal knowledge, but acquire their powers individually, and while shamanistic performances follow definite tribal or areal patterns, the details of such are not set, as in priestly ritual, but may vary considerably according to the powers and whims of individual shamans. In early travelers' accounts, shamans are usually referred to as "medicine men"; this is however too general a term to be very useful.

Shamanistic practices are strongly developed among the Eskimo, on the North Pacific Coast, among the Plateau, California, Great Basin, Plains, and Eastern Woodlands tribes, and among some of the Southwestern tribes, but not among the Pueblos of the Southwest, where societies or priesthoods take charge of curing, and witches, with no curing powers, are blamed when misfortune befalls a person. The Southeastern tribes had notions of disease which differed to a considerable degree from those held elsewhere in North America; they believed that all bodily afflictions came from the presence of some harmful foreign matter in the sick person's body (a belief widely held in North America), and that this harmful matter was placed there either by some animal spirit or by a shaman, but mostly, however, by offended animal spirits. To cure disease in the Southeast a "shaman" is called in to diagnose the case by secret methods, then to sing the songs or formulas appropriate to the animal who has caused the particular disease (such as Deer, Sun, Young Deer, Water Moccasin, Hog, Water Wolf, Little Turtle, Panther, etc.) and finally to administer medicinal herbs, either externally or internally to the patient, in order to remove the harmful foreign matter which the animal spirit or, rarely, another shaman, has put into the patient's body. Southeastern shamans, then, combine the functions of 1) herb doctors of other parts of the continent, 2) Southwestern priests who chant songs or formulas which can cure, and 3) the true shaman who, as part of his practices must of course diagnose the cause of the disease, before he attempts to cure. It is not surprising therefore to learn that among Southeastern tribes the powers of a shaman are open to any successful candidate (i.e. that they are learned, rather than supernaturally revealed to individuals by the spirits), and that the Southeastern shaman is also likely to be the town chief.

Central Eskimo shamans (*angakok*) are usually men, notable not only for their curing performances, but for their drum-dance exhibitions and public displays of feats of agility. They are distinguished from the majority of North American shamans in that they are actually possessed, when performing, by their spirit helpers, and as a part of this possession they speak at that time in a private, or "angakok," language.

In another part of North America notable for shamanistic practices, namely the North Pacific Coast, shamans were men who, on the guardian spirit quest, had been befriended or visited by magical beings, invisible to all but themselves. The powers of these beings made them dangerous, and the shaman himself sometimes feared what they could make him do in the way of killing or harming other human beings, for example. Therefore in

this region, as in most others, the shaman usually waited until he was middle-aged, and felt able to control his powers before he began to practice. In most cases, this practice followed the usual North American pattern: diagnosis and determination of the cause of disease (usually a foreign object in the patient's body), singing and sucking out by the shaman of the foreign object, and destruction of the object. The belief that soul loss, as well as the intrusion of disease objects, caused illness and death appears on the North Pacific Coast, and shamans with special powers made trips to the land of souls, in some Pacific Coast tribes, to recover the souls of persons who were ill but were still alive (see Ruth Underhill, *Indians of the Pacific Northwest*, Riverside, Cal., 1945, pp. 192 ff.).

In coastal Oregon and in northern California shamans were either women or, in rarer cases, transvestites. They underwent, in this area, training or "doctor dances" after it became clear that they were destined to be shamans. Payments exacted by them for their services after they became shamans were heavy, since wealth in goods or currency was esteemed in this region; but all over the continent some payment, at least, for shamanistic curing (or disease-producing) services was usual.

Shamans' magical contests were features of Northwest Coast and central California shamanism; to a certain extent, the "shooting" performances of the Eastern Woodlands Midewiwin Society, by Mide initiates, may also be the survival of Eastern shamanistic contests. Using objects charged with magic power (a bird's claw, a shell, or other small object) shamans lined up and "shot" each other, the object being to make one's opponent fall down unconscious. If strong enough in magic, the opponent could revive himself, but if he was not, the shooter revived him. See HESHWASH CEREMONY. Shamans, with their interest in religious matters and in conserving the ways of the past, were often the persons who best knew the folklore of a tribal group, especially the more ritualistic myths. For the creative role that shamanism played in Mescalero Apache mythology see Morris Edward Opler's article (*JAFL* 59: 233–68). [EWV]

☞ South American shamans were men who as the result of a supernatural call or of special training became the intermediaries between the supernatural world and the communities. Through their medium the spirits spoke to men and helped them in their undertakings. Their principal function was to cure sick people, but they also foretold the future, uncovered hidden things, caused rains to fall, and led the religious ceremonies of their group.

With the outstanding exception of the Araucanians, most South American shamans are men, though medicine women are not exceptional. There is little evidence to show that shamans were individuals with a neurotic personality. However the Araucanian shamans or *machi* were recruited among berdaches and persons afflicted with mental or nervous disorders.

In many tribes, e.g. Ona, Toba, Campa, a man enters the profession only if he has received a supernatural call. A spirit appears to him in a dream and gives him a chant or the supernatural weapons which he needs to destroy his enemies. Sherente Indian shamans were recruited among those who had a vision of the anthropomorphized planet Mars. Even today Araucanian shamans claim to have been forced to practice their art by a divine order.

The shamans of the tropical region are prepared for their career by a lengthy and painful initiation. Among the Caribs of Guiana there are real shamanistic schools. By taking tobacco juice or as strong a narcotic as *aya-huasca*, the novices put themselves into a state of trance and have visions of the supernatural world. They establish friendly contacts with spirits and obtain from them magical chants. They become full-fledged shamans when their teacher injects into their body darts, quartz pebbles, or some mysterious substance by which they can cause illness and kill their victims. The candidates to the shamanistic professions learn also about the use of herbs and of magic substances.

The shaman's power rests on his ability to summon spirits who can perform tasks beyond the capacity of ordinary people. The spirit called by the shaman sometimes is his own soul, which he can detach from his body. In other instances, shamans are assisted by ghosts, sometimes of dead shamans, animal spirits, and spirits who take animal forms. The shaman's power is often identified with his breath or with tobacco smoke which materializes his breath. It is also conceived of as a mysterious substance (Apapocuva, Guaporé tribes) which the shaman handles at will. The darts and the quartz pebbles which he carries inside his body are also materializations of his magic power.

Most South American shamans provoke in themselves a state of trance in order to communicate with the spirits. They smoke to the point of swooning, absorb *parica* snuffs or drink decoctions of *ayahuasca* or *floripondio*. The main accessories of the shamans are a gourd rattle and in the tropical regions a special wooden bench. For the treatments see CURES. Although the practice of medicine is the shaman's main function, he fulfils other duties, such as warding off the attacks of bad spirits, finding the whereabouts of game animals, performing fertility rites on behalf of the community, offering sacrifices to the spirits, making war magic, causing rain to fall, etc.

In South American primitive communities, the shamans are the only specialists who can accumulate wealth, since they are paid for their work. Their influence is considerable and in many tribes (for instance, the ancient Guarani), has taken the form of a virtual theocracy.
[AM]

The word shaman is derived from Tungus *shaman*, from Sanskrit *śramana*, ascetic. The shaman is an individual possessed of supernatural power derived from a spirit, ghost, animal, or inanimate object. Either men or women may be shamans, though men are in the majority. The gift is inborn, sometimes conceived of as hereditary, and usually realized by ordeal, fasting, abstinence, and consequent revelation of the guardian spirit. Or the power and knowledge can be learned and bought from another shaman. Communion with the spirit brings the power to curse or cure, to commune with the dead, to prophesy, to affect rain and weather, to perform superhuman feats of magic, as self-mutilation, sword-swallowing, handling and swallowing of fire.

Asia The most complete manifestation of shamanism is centered in eastern Siberia and Manchuria, notably among the Tungus, and also the Yakut, Samoyed, Koryak, Ostyiak, and Chukchee, i.e. from the Eskimos to the Chinese frontier. Among these tribes, despite the encroachments of Russian Catholicism and Buddhism, the shaman remains the spiritual father, openly in the desolate fastnesses of the tundra, secretly in the cities of Manchuria. He always exercises his powers in a state of self-induced trance, which is of two kinds: 1) Religious and functional, which annuls his spirit and replaces it by powers in charge of hunting and agriculture; or by spirits who contact through him a family or community; or by unknown spirits whose healing powers flow through him to a patient. 2) Exhibitionistic, under the influence of a definite spirit, with demonstrations of prodigious strength, self-laceration, conquering the evil spirits with a spear, or contests with a rival shaman. Every shaman has harmless animal familiars, worshipped in Manchuria in pole-shaped effigies (weasel, eagle, otter, sometimes bear or tiger). In the midst of a ceremony, he may suddenly be confronted with an evil spirit.

Trance is induced by the rhythm of his large flat oval drum and by simultaneous chanting, sometimes also by a narcotic or incense. On the appearance of the spirit, his body trembles, grow rigid, then relaxes. He dances stooped forward, counterclockwise, with a shuffle of slow left foot and fast right foot. He leaps and whirls, and finally falls in a trance. During the healing ceremonies a lay youth may execute the dance, while the seated shaman transfers his power to the patient. In the tundra this dance may act in reverse and cast a curse on an offending layman or rival shaman in a contest of power.

Cone-shaped iron jinglers on the drum and on an apron intensify the rhythm as he wriggles his hips. These and mirrors on the front and back of his shirt protect him from evil spirits. During the Elk Spirit Dance he may wear a circlet with iron antlers, bits of sturgeon skin, and a mask of fringe—a type of headdress also worn by the lamas of Tibet.

Shamanism extends through Tibet, China, Japan, and Korea to many Mongoloid and Turkic tribes. The Japanese *yamabushi*, who officiates in Buddhist temples and Shinto shrines, has a full array of magical activities (without the trance element): divination, exorcism, cure, fertility, rain-making power, and associations with foxes and badgers. Magic healing functions recur in the Chinese *wu-i*, the Ceylonese masked devil-doctors, and in the masked devil-dancing castes of southwest India, the exorcising Pombada, Parava, Nalke, and Panan. Trance symptoms recur in the *sanghyang* and other Balinese dances, and, together with exhibitionism, in the Whirling Dervishes of the thirty Islamic sects, e.g. Bektashi (beggars), Rufai (howling), Sadi (fire-eaters), Mevlevi (mystical). At present, the Finns, Lapps, Estonians, and Hungarians form the western frontier of Old World shamanism.

Middle America In Middle America (Mexico to Panama), shamanism becomes incidental to other aspects of ceremonialism, particularly in the high maize-growing cultures. The Huichol and Tarahumara ceremonial leaders invoke rain, by song and by ritual action bordering on priestly function. Pagan beliefs and fears remain in Mexico, Yucatán, and Guatemala, as the terror of the evil eye and evil wind, of spells and witchcraft, and on the other hand, the faith in the practitioner of ancient remedies and formulæ. The Lacandon shaman and the

Maya *h-men* continue many of their aboriginal incantations for health and rain. But in many communities the traditions have become confused with Catholicism. The *chimanes* (grandfathers) of Chimaltenango, Guatemala, sacrifice incense soaked in turkey blood at shrines, for power to divine and cure in the ancient manner. But they work for "Dios."

Not all trance dances are shamanistic, any more than all feats of magic, cure, or all dreams and visions. Competent wizardry is possible with the omission of one or the other of these traits, with or without the aid of masks. Its fullest manifestations are combined in the Tungus visionary (*badyushka*), the little father of the tribe, ministering to body and soul, a man of intellectual ability and powerful personality, with full faith in his identification with supernaturals. During the transitions to hunting, agricultural, and mechanized cultural stages, these manifestations split up into types, or multiply into societies. Inevitably the faith and the power have become attenuated till the final breakdown into exhibitionism. See DATU; EPILEPSY; MEDICINE RITES.

[GPK]

shamrock (Irish *seamróg*, diminutive of *seamair*, trefoil, shamrock, clover) The national emblem of Ireland: chosen because this trifoliolate little plant was used by St. Patrick to illustrate the mystery of the Trinity. It is always worn on St. Patrick's Day, and a little is taken along by emigrants leaving Ireland. *To drown the shamrock* means to go the rounds drinking on St. Patrick's Day in honor of the shamrock. *Seamróg na gceitre gcluas*, the four-leafed shamrock, brings luck, possibly because of its Christianized association with an early apotropaic figure enclosed in a circle (*triquetra*), the ancient Celtic sun wheel.

Shango The Yoruban Negro deity of thunder, found in those portions of the New World where Yoruban cults have persisted, notably Brazil, Cuba, and Trinidad. In the Peruambuco region of Brazil and in Trinidad, African cults as a whole are known by the name of this deity. Like other African gods, he is syncretized with Catholic saints; for example, he is also known as Santa Barbara in Cuba, and St. John the Baptist in Trinidad.

[MJH]

Shang Ti The personification of T'ien or Heaven in the Imperial Cults of China; referred to as the supreme ruler, the source of imperial power. He was worshipped only by the emperor. See YÜ HUANG. [RDJ]

shantey or **shanty** See CHANTEY.

shaped notes or **buckwheat notes** A simple system of musical notation introduced in America early in the 19th century, making use of four different shapes placed on the staff to denote the four syllables of fasola solmization (fa, sol, la, mi). The system was widely used in hymn and song books for a century, particularly in the hymnals of the many new Protestant sects of the Great Revival. Singers who could not read a word or a note of music could follow the melodies so set down.

shapeshifting An important mechanism in the folklore of all peoples. A shapeshifter is a creature or object which is able to change its shape either at will or under special circumstances. Shapeshifters may be evil or benign, and only experts can distinguish their character.

Thus Hamlet's question of his father's ghost was whether it were a spirit of health or a goblin damned.

Although no census of shapeshifters has been taken, the number of them found in all parts of the world is astronomical. Because of their elusive character, they have not been studied with the care that has been given to some of the clans that constitute their nation. Thus, the principles which govern the behavior of ghosts are fairly well understood in several parts of the world, but the behavior of shapeshifters in general is not clear. Two general facts, however, emerge: first, shapeshifters are common in all folklore; second, the explanation of them given in popular tales is more frequently the narrator's editorial comment than an essential explanation of the phenomenon. The mysterious elderly couple who help the hero by advice or the gift of magic objects is often in Europe, and frequently in Latin America, identified as the Virgin Mary and Saint Joseph. American Indians may identify them as animals friendly to the group, and Europeans again may identify them as "fairy godmother" or other benign spirits. They are, however, generally regarded with a mixture of fear and gratitude. Strangers are always dangerous and people who have dealings with them are apt to be odd.

Nor are the conditions under which animals or things shift shape generally understood. Werewolves are impelled to shed human form at certain phases of the moon. Shapeshifting foxes, of whom there are a very large number in North China, are fond of wine and, when intoxicated, resume their fox forms. Others, however, are able to shift at will. The mistress of a scholar in Peiping was a shapeshifting fox. She was never seen by his friends but, though invisible, carried on conversations with them about history, poetry, and Confucianism in which she was very learned. When friends entered the room they noticed that it had a musty smell and was chilly.

Shapeshifters fall into five general categories: spiritual entities, ghosts, animals, things, and interveners.

The translation of gods into men or animals or of men and animals into gods is a commonplace of religiomythical folklore. Jacob wrestled with an angel; Zeus became a bull to seduce Europa; the Chinese Kuan Yin is often a helpful old lady. Although attempts have been made to explain these in the terms of racial history and complicated mythologies, in which Max Müllerism is still powerful, success must be elusive until all the stories have been studied in terms of their cultural backgrounds.

The shapeshifting of ghosts leads into complications. Sometimes ghosts return from the dead in order to repay a debt of honor as in the complex of the Grateful Dead Man (Types 505–508) and sometimes to take revenge on their murderer or on others. Even when the debt is a debt of honor, the issue is often in doubt. They will help, they say, if the hero will give them half of what he wins on his quest. He wins a wife and the wife has to be cut in two. A snake or monster crawls out. The intervener puts her together again and announces his identity. The children in the *Wife of Usher's Well* (Child #79D) returned because their mother's tears wet their winding sheet. Sometimes a ghost, in order to acquire more "vital essence," pretends to be an incubus. Ghosts in all parts of the world may assume the exact shape of their owners and thus, by appearing in several places at once, create the lore of the "double" and cause great mental distress to their friends. Dead lovers in all parts of the world have the unpleasant tendency of returning to trysts, kidnapping their sweethearts and carrying them off to grim otherworld orgies. See DEAD RIDER. Ghosts are always hungry. They like human food or, as in the *Odyssey*, a drop of human blood. The Chinese have a festival in honor of hungry and homeless ghosts whose descendants have failed to lay out food and sacrifices for them.

Plants, animals, and human beings are often able to shift shape. The facility with which this can be done depends on the degree or quality of life the creature possesses. It is more difficult for plants and least difficult for human beings, though human beings are often too lazy to undertake the long and arduous discipline they need. In China, foxes and tigers, in Europe domestic animals, kittens, dogs, horses, and among American Indians, coyotes and other animals are often shapeshifters.

Power to shift shape, according to Chinese Taoists, can be acquired by either of two methods, of which one is "legal" and the other is "illegal." The legal method is to strengthen or improve one's "vital essence" by the study of the classics. This method is slow and very difficult. The "illegal" method is by stealing the vital essence of others and this is accomplished by coitus reservatus. The theory is that when orgasm is simultaneous, the couple merely exchanges vital essence. If, however, it is premature, a quantity of vital essence is lost and acquired by the partner. Once a sufficient amount has been acquired, the animal or human being can shift shape at will. This sort of theft is frowned upon and the thief is in constant fear of the thunder god.

The principles by which inanimate objects can shift their shape to become, usually, human beings present another order of problem. The sculptor Pygmalion made a statue of Galatea, fell in love with it, and endowed it with so much vitality that it came alive. Witches and magicians have created armies by throwing stones into arid fields, by cutting figures out of paper or cloth.

The interveners are psychologically and folkloristically probably the most primitive of the shapeshifters. They are mysterious beings, usually human but sometimes animals and sometimes indiscriminately either, who appear to give help or advice. Many of the thousands of Cinderellas now available have been given material help and counsel by their dead mothers or by creatures who are obviously their mother's surrogates. Mysterious old men frequently appear and disappear in the stories to help girls out of their difficulties.

Another complex of shapeshifters known in all parts of the world is the mysterious housekeeper. A lonely woodcutter, farmer, or fisherman returns several evenings to his slovenly hut to find it mysteriously cleaned up and a supper cooking on the stove. He conceals himself to find that some animal, in China usually a fox, comes to the hut in the morning, turns a somersault, sheds its skin, and becomes a beautiful girl. The hero steals the skin. She remains with him, becomes the mother of his children. Many years later, sometimes on the occasion of the marriage of a son, she gives the house a thorough cleaning, finds her skin, slips into it, and disappears. In other formulæ, the hero sees swans or seals shed their skins to become lovely maidens. He

steals one and gets power over the owner. In other developments the hero tries to find his lost wife and often fails.

The formula of the mysterious housekeeper is obviously a special variant of the conviction that things, animals, and wives are mysterious and never to be counted on. If you can get control of something that belongs to them, they may serve you for a time, but at some unexpected moment they may again become foxes or seals or swans and escape forever.

The problems of the study of shapeshifters derive in part from the very large numbers of them that are known to us which require the use of macroscopic rather than microscopic techniques. The studies made of shapeshifting foxes, otters, etc., are sound but miss the central problem of shapeshifting itself. Shapeshifting in folklore is clearly connected with hallucination in morbid psychology. Until the phenomena in both areas have been scrutinized with care, we are not able to go beyond the general observation that nothing is, in fact, what it seems to be.   R. D. JAMESON

sharpened leg A folktale motif (J2424) common to both North and South American Indians. A man who has lost his leg sharpens his shin bone and stabs his visitors. He is finally killed by the culture hero. This story has been recorded in the Gran Chaco, and among the tribes of eastern Brazil and the Guianas. [AM]

☞ The sharpened leg is the subject of a popular short tale, or incident in a tale, in North American Indian tales of the Plateau and Eastern Woodlands, especially the Iroquois, tribes. Trickster is given the power to sharpen his leg, stick it into a tree, and thus suspend himself in the shade of the tree on hot days, for a specified number of times (see RITUAL NUMBERS). Excited by an admiring audience, he breaks the tabu, i.e. does it too often, and gets stuck in the tree. [EWV]

Shê A Chinese ceremony in honor of the soil, part of the Imperial Cult and highly controversial. Although sacrifices to Heaven probably belong to the earliest of Chinese sacrifices, the sacrifices to Earth, Soil, and Millet may have been folkloristic accretions. [RDJ]

sheepmen stories The traditional feud between cattlemen and sheepmen, originating in the struggle for grass and breaking out in range wars like the Tonto Basin War between the Grahams and the Tewksburys of Arizona, has left a folk heritage of phrases, sayings, and anecdotes libeling the sheepherder and his flock: Crazy as a sheepherder; Like attracts like is why all sheepmen's covered with bedbugs; Herding is nothing to do and all day to do it in; There ain't nothing dumber than sheep except the man who herds 'em; A ewe has just enough sense to be ornery. The sheepherder's solitary calling gave rise to calumnies concerning his forgetting of human speech. A traveling man sat down beside an old sheepherder in a crowded train and inquired where the other was from. "Montanaa-aa-aa!" bleated the herder. "Where are you going?" "Baa-aa-aack!" Another herder was advised by his lawyer during a trial to answer every question with a plaintive blat. To the lawyer's request for his fee following the acquittal, the herder replied, "Baa-aa-aa!" Typical of sheepmen's humor are the saying, "A sheep shearer is a sheepherder with his brains knocked out" and Dick Wick Hall's Arizona story of the tenderfoot sheepherder from Yale, who was known as "Hotfoot Mac" on account of his sprinting ability. Being warned, in jest, not to let any of the lambs get away (when there were no lambs in the flock), he returned from the first day's herding on the desert with the announcement that he had run all the lambs back into the band but was quitting because they were too fast for him. The surprised owner investigated and found 47 jackrabbits and 16 cottontails huddled in a corner of the corral. (See Archer B. Gilfillan, *Sheep,* 1928; B. A. Botkin, *A Treasury of American Folklore,* pp. 364–367). [BAB]

Shenandoah One of the most beautiful of all sea chanteys, a native American composition, possibly of voyageur origin, sung at the capstan. In the earlier versions Shenandoah is an Indian chief whose daughter is wooed by a trader. Other versions relate the name Shenandoah to the valley. Apart from its working history, the song has been sung in the cavalry and is a favorite glee-club selection.

shepherd's score Anglo-Cymric Score or Indian Counting are other names for this apparently meaningless collection of semi-riming syllables. In the 1890's, when this writer was a child, he was taught by his mother (who had learned it in her youth in Natick, Massachusetts) what she called Indian Counting, which ran from one to twenty-one as follows

Een, teen, tuther, futher, fipps;
Suther, luther, uther, duther, dix;
Een-dix, teen-dix, tuther-dix, futher-dix, bumpit;
Anny-bumpit, tanny-bumpit, tuther-bumpit, futher-
    bumpit, gigit;
Anny-gigit!

I remember the emphasis on Anny-gigit, for we used Indian Counting for a counting-out rime, and the boy or girl on whom fell the count of Anny-gigit (21) was "out." In this connection it is worth noting that in *The Counting-Out Rhymes of Children,* by H. C. Bolton of the Smithsonian Institution, published in 1888, he has classified the rimbles into 13 groups, of which the "Rhymes for counting twenty-one" form Group iii, and "The Anglo-Cymric Score" is Group xiii, but he evidently knew of no connection between the two.

William Wells Newell, in his *Games and Songs of American Children,* 1883, gives on page 200 two versions of Indian Counting, one from Scituate, Mass., and the other (practically identical with the one I learned), said to have been learned "from an Indian woman, Mary Wolsomog, of Natick."

In the 1850–1860 decade in Claremont, N.H., there was current a version said to have been used by the "Plymouth Indians," running as follows:

Een, teen, tether, fether, fitz;
Sather, lather, gother, dather, dix;
Een-dix, teen-dix, tether-dix, fether-dix, bompey;
Een-bompey, teen-bompey, tether-bompey, fether-
bompey, giget.

A variant in Maine was attributed to the Wawenoc Indians. One from Indiana had "bunkin" and one from Connecticut "bumpum" for fifteen. Still others have showed up from Rhode Island and Ohio.

There is no doubt that in the mid-19th century scattered individual Indians friendly with the whites taught the latter, mostly in New England, this method of counting, but it was not Indian in origin. The Indians had themselves been taught it by white English settlers two centuries earlier and had preserved it by oral tradition all that while! Yet it is not and never was English numerals! Here we come upon one of the interesting items of the history of the oral transmission of folk learning involving several races and languages, and in time at least two millenia.

For centuries the shepherds of Lincolnshire, Essex, Durham, Cumberland, and the North Riding of Yorkshire, and of the lowlands of Scotland have been counting their sheep, and Cornish fishermen their mackerel, and old ladies their knitting-stitches, by the same old syllables we in Massachusetts thought were Indian Counting.

The nearest modern language numerals to the shepherd's score are found in the Welsh, but neither one came from the other. The borderland territory between Wales and England is the old home of the Anglo-Cymric or shepherd's score.

But why "score"? Because it was counting by twenties, that is, using 20 as a radix, or scale, or base of a numerical system. Counting by five is a quinary scale, and by ten is a denary or decimal scale. In certain barefoot countries, the scale of 20 (vicenary) has been popular, for not only the ten fingers but the ten toes as well are visible. With some native Mexicans today the word for twenty is "man finished." They count to twenty and then begin again. Relics of old systems of counting by twenty still persist in countries now using the denary scale, as in the French word *quatre-vingt* for 80 or the English three score years and ten. And since to score meant originally to cut or notch a stick for a tally and still means to count, we have here in the word *score* itself the evidence that in very old English times men counted up to twenty, scored the tally stick, and then started counting again at one.

As a matter of fact, the shepherd's score is a peculiar combination of the quinary and vicenary radix systems, for if you will examine any version of it, you will find that instead of sixteen being "six-ten" as it is with us, it is *een-bompey* or *anny-bumpit* or some other spelling, all of them meaning "one-fifteen."

In an old English version the numeral for sixteen is *ain-a-bumfit,* while in modern Welsh it is *un-ar-bymtheg.* The relationship is obvious. It is confirmatory of the prehistoric method of counting by fives on fingers and toes that an old shepherd in Winteringham in Lincolnshire, reciting from memory his shepherd's score, paused after every fifth word.

In 1877, the Vice-President of the Philological Society of Great Britain, Mr. Alexander J. Ellis, collected more than sixty versions of the shepherd's score and published them in the *Transactions* of the Society for 1877–78. A more recent, extended, and interesting study of the shepherd's score and its relation to the counting-out rimes of children is in the third chapter, "Number and Memory," pages 45–63, of Henry Betts' *Nursery Rhymes and Tales, their origin and history,* first published in 1924. He points out that at the Ayr Academy which was established by Alexander III of Scotland in the 13th century, the boys still count out in their games with:

Zinty, tinty, tethera, pethera, bumf,
Aleeter, aseeter, over, dover, ding.

And Mr. Betts states: "One of the writer's earliest recollections is of sitting on his father's knee, as a very little child and being amused by the recitation of the words which the old shepherds in Lincolnshire used in counting their sheep:

Yan, tan, tethera, pethera, pimp,
Sethera, lethera, hovera, covera, dik;
Yan-a-dik, tan-a-dik, tethera-dik, pethera-dik, bumfit;
Yan-a-bumfit, tan-a-bumfit, tethera-bumfit, pethera-bumfit, figgit."

He notes that the relationship is obvious between the beginning of the shepherd's score, especially in the Yarmouth version: "Ina, mina,—" and the familiar counting-out rime of the Eeny, meeny, miny, mo type "with all its bewildering varieties," and suggests that the other familiar rime: "Hickory, dickory, dock" may be from the 8, 9, 10, "hovera, covera, dik" of the version he learned from his father.

Mr. Betts' excellent interpretation and explanation of the rather complicated problem of the numerals and rimes is of importance to students of folklore, for it gives an insight into the natural system of operation, the economy, in fact, of oral transmission. He says that the numerals of the prehistoric Celts, who antedated Hengist and Horsa and Cæsar, have survived in three forms, best in Welsh, less well but plainly enough in the shepherd's score, and rather corruptly in the children's counting-out rimes. When the Romans and Saxons and other conquerors came, the common people, the shepherds, fishermen, and housewives, would continue to use their own old language, especially in counting. While the children, "who are always the most rigid conservatives of the race," would keep on using the old numbers in their counting and number games long after the language of those numerals had itself passed from the knowledge and use of men.

This is another confirmation of the fact that in folklore as everywhere else, ontogeny recapitulates philogeny, and the children's game-rimes reproduce the thought-forms, dance patterns, and even the language of our primitive forebears.   CHARLES FRANCIS POTTER

Shingrawa In Kachin (Burma) mythology, the divine man-creator of the earth who was produced by Chinûn Way Shun as a pumpkin. When Shingrawa came into existence the water was undrinkable and the trees and shrubs were covered with thorns. A great flood came and when it receded Shingrawa fashioned the present earth out of the remains of the old one, using a hammer. For a long time he looked after the earth and its people, and then went to the sky. Shippawn Ayawng, the Kachin forefather, was a descendant. Shingrawa is kind and good but he has no interest in mankind, so his shrines are few in number and neglected. See NAT. Compare CHANG-HKO.

Shipap, Shipapu, Shipapulima, or **Shipapuyna** Pueblo Indian (Keresan-speaking pueblos especially) name for the place of emergence and the underground realm for certain of the dead; the land where the Kachinas stay for half of the year when they are not on earth. It is also the place where Iyatiku, the Keresan Corn Mother, lives. From her underground house at Shipap mankind emerged, from there infants today are born, and thither go the dead with the prayer feather they carry to their Mother. Keresan medicine society members, especially, go to Shipap after death to join their Mother or their beast gods. At Taos pueblo the place of emergence is a lake called by some the "lake of the summer pilgrimage" (Blue Lake), but, by others, Chipapunta, a lake located at Monte Vista, Colorado. See EMERGENCE MYTH. [EWV]

shirt of Nessus The shirt steeped in the blood of the centaur Nessus by Deianira. When Nessus tried to run off with Deianira, Hercules shot him with one of the arrows poisoned with the Hydra's blood. Nessus, dying yet vindictive, told Deianira to dip a shirt she was carrying for Hercules in his blood, and that, if ever she felt that she were losing her husband to another woman, to send Hercules the shirt. It would be a charm, he said, to recapture his love. When finally Hercules became infatuated with Iole, Deianira sent him the shirt; the hero put it on; and it clung to him, fatally burning skin and flesh. Hercules fled to Mt. Œta, where he built his funeral pyre and immolated himself.

Shitta A beneficent nat of the moon of the Burmese Kachins, worshipped once a year with Jan, the sun nat, by the *duwa* (chief).

Shiwana or **Shiwanna** Specifically "Cloud People" of the Keres Pueblo Indians, equatable with such other Pueblo Indian spirits as the Cloud chiefs of the Hopi Indians, the Cloud or Rain People of Jemez pueblo, Clouds of the color-directions at Tewa, the Chiefs of the Directions of Isleta, and the lightning, cloud beings, or deceased chiefs of Taos pueblo. In the broadest sense Shiwana are supernaturals or spirits who bring rain. They are a special class within large groups referred to by the Hopi term kachina which refers to nearly all Pueblo spirits who are impersonated with masks in ceremonies and dances. The storm clouds or Shiwana of Keres are spirits who give rain and extended blessings such as health, life, and everything for the welfare of man. At Cochiti and San Felipe the masked dancers are referred to as Shiwana; at Zuñi Shiwannee or Priest Man and Shiwanska, Priest Woman, are believed to have existed in the beginning and to have created heaven and earth; before the emergence the Zuñi had rain priests in the lower world, of whom six were assigned to the six directions. Rain priests today are called Shiwanni. See E. C. Parsons, *Pueblo Indian Religion* (2 vols., Chicago, 1939) 1:170–74, Table 2 facing 208; Matilde Coxe Stevenson, *The Zuñi Indians* (RBAE 23 Washington, 1901–2). See KACHINA. [EWV]

Shka-Bavas The God of the Sky of the Moksha-Mordvins. He is supreme among the gods, and offerings and prayers must be made to him first, before all other gods. **Shki-Pas** or **Tshi-Paz** is the God Creator of the Erza-Mordvins. [JB]

shmoo All-providing animal created by Al Capp in his popular comic strip, *Li'l Abner* (see COMICS). A possible origin of the word is *schmo* (*shmoe*), a term used in the garment and theatrical industries for a person midway between a dope and one who rushes in where angels fear to tread. In a period of runaway radio giveaway programs and inflation, the shmoo combined tall tale with satirical fable, the American dream of getting something for nothing with the economics of abundance.

Akin to magic, grateful, and helpful animals and

magic objects that are a source of inexhaustible plenty, this savory, ham-shaped, and slightly phallic-looking animal with the rapturous smile on its face eats nothing, multiplies rapidly, and drops dead out of sheer joy when looked at hungrily. Not only does it lay fresh eggs, give the finest creamery butter and Grade-A milk, and make steaks when broiled and boneless chicken when boiled or fried, but its eyes make suspender buttons and its hide makes the finest leather. Because, in solving the inflation problem in the underfed Ozarkian hamlet of Dogpatch, it also upset the nation's economy, the shmoo had to be killed off and its creator was accused of "shmoocialism." (See Al Capp, *The Life and Times of the Shmoo*, 1948).   B. A. BOTKIN

shoes The folklore of shoes is voluminous and has been the occasion of differences of opinion which will here have to be glanced at rather than conjugated. Certainly the broad statement that "during all ages and in the folklore of all races, shoes have been a symbol of the female genitals" needs modification. Shoes are frequently used in marriage ceremonies. They are thrown after the newly married couple, used to discover the direction from which the groom will come. In Chinese ceremonies the groom burns incense before the shoe of his betrothed who died before marriage, and the Manchu bride gave shoes to her betrothed and all of his brothers who had sexual access to her. The old woman who lived in a shoe and had a great many children must have been sexually very active and, if one follows folk psychology, it is not difficult to go from that to the notion that her life centered in her sexual organs, she "lived in them." These customs associate shoes closely to the sexual aspects of marriage. However, the use of the shoe as a symbol of submission is another part of the polysemantics of folk belief and custom.

A gleaning of scattered references will display the complexity of this lore. The Japanese believe that you will have bad luck if you wear new shoes to the lavatory. The peoples of India, like those of the Euro-American culture, believe that throwing shoes at a wedding will bring good luck and many children. A shoe, placed heel upward on the top of the house of the poor, will protect it; and, in parts of India too, hailstones beaten with a shoe by a magician will cause the storm to cease. A report from Greece is that women have brought back faithless lovers by having a witch fumigate their sandals with sulfur and say incantations, i.e. if a sandal was left behind. In Egypt the figure of an enemy in the lining of a shoe indicated that he was trodden upon. The sandals of Perseus brought prosperity. Among the Hebrews the shoe was removed from the foot of a man who refused to marry his dead brother's wife; the refusal was considered disgraceful. In Anglo-Saxon England the father gave his daughter's shoe to the groom. That this was a symbolic transfer of authority is possible, though here again the sexual implication must be considered. The Scots custom of throwing shoes after a sailor making his first voyage, or at a man starting a new enterprise, seems to be associated with the idea that shoes have to do with prosperity. In Germany, shoes placed wrong end to at the head of the bed keep nightmares away; and the wife who puts on her husband's slipper on their wedding day will have easy labor. In Sicily shoes made of wolf skin give a child luck and

courage. Among the American Omaha Indians a small hole is cut in the sole of an infant's moccasins so that the child can refuse to accompany an otherworld messenger because his moccasins are worn out. Dutch children put their shoes in a corner near the chimney so that they will not be forgotten when gifts are given at Christmas. The rationalization is that in this way Saint Nicholas knows they are tucked in bed. In Scandinavia formerly, the placing of all the shoes of the family in a row on Christmas Eve was done in token of their intent to live together without quarreling for the year. The patron saint of European cobblers is Saint Crispin, an early missionary, who made shoes for the poor at night from leather supplied by an angel.

The general connection between shoes and luck, good or ill, is in the German belief that sneezing while putting on shoes is bad luck or the Filipino belief that it is bad luck to leave a pair of slippers far apart. Old shoes were thrown after Queen Victoria when she entered Balmoral Castle; John Hayward and Ben Jonson both identify the casting of shoes with good luck.

The symbolism of putting shoes on or off is connected with the idea of ownership. The Arab divorcing his wife is reported to say that she was his slipper and he put her off. Note the sexual implication. Egyptians swapped sandals to show that property or authority had been exchanged. The Assyrians and Hebrews gave a sandal when property was exchanged. In the ninth Psalm, the casting of a shoe on the land of Edom was a symbol of possession.

Several reports show the belief that shoes should be removed in sacred places or in the presence of royalty. Moses and Joshua were instructed to put "off the shoes from off thy feet" for the place was holy ground. The Rhodians were forbidden to carry shoes into the temple of the Tegean Mother. Worshippers in the temple at Crete had to be barefooted. The rule also is reported from the Roman temples of Cybele and Isis. Moslems remove shoes at the door of the mosque and carry them sole to sole in the left, the unclean, hand. Generally these customs seem to imply that contagion from the secular world must not infect holy ground though the belief that shoes might remove some of the sacredness from dedicated ground is also reported. The Greeks, Romans, and Hebrews removed shoes as signs of mourning and grief. The Persians bared their feet in the presence of royalty.

Shoes sometimes enter into funeral ceremonies. The Russians place a pair of new shoes on the feet of the dead in anticipation of a long journey. In Old Norse these were the *kek-sko* and in German the *Totenschuh*. See DEAD SHOES. The Indian tribes of Lower California, though normally barefooted, provided shoes for the dead. In Brittany "Death greases the boots of its victim." Lucian has a story of a dead wife who returned because one of her shoes was not burned on her funeral pyre.

Special shoes are appropriate for special occasions. The Emperor Marcus Aurelius reserved the use of white, green, and red shoes for women, though before this time senators wore red shoes and magistrates wore red shoes with crescent-shaped ornaments. At their annual fire ceremony the chief of the Creek Indians wore buckskin moccasins kept in a sacred enclosure for the rest of the year. Herodotus reported that Egyptian priests must wear shoes made of papyrus. Syrian boys during their initiation wore shoes of sacrificial animal skin. The skin of animals dying a natural death was impure and could defile holy places. The winged sandals of Hermes and Perseus and the seven-league boots made by the Norse Hermod are applications of the sumptuary laws of folklore.

Stories of the wooing of Rhodope and Aphrodite bring to full circle the use of the slipper as a recognition symbol in Cinderella. An eagle stole the shoe of Rhodope while she was bathing and dropped it in the bosom of Psammetichos, who sought its owner through all Egypt. Similarly Zeus sent an eagle to steal the shoe of Aphrodite who was being coy toward Hermes. Aphrodite had to find her slipper again and in consequence Hermes had his will of her.   R. D. JAMESON

shofar An ancient and primitive type of trumpet, made of ram's horn or the horn of the ibex flattened and curved, used by the Jews of Biblical days to signal alarm, attack, or withdrawal of army in war, to give notice of great events and occasions, for exorcism, for new moon ceremonies, to announce the year of Jubilee, to usher in the New Year and the Day of Atonement; it survives in modern synagogues for the last two occasions. The modern shofar is gracefully curved, usually having a dentated edge on the underside, and is sometimes engraved with sacred words and emblems. Early practice required the ibex horn for the new moon and New Year ceremonies, the ram's horn for fast days and the Day of Atonement, and a black ram's horn for the great ban against transgressors of the law.

Many magical beliefs and practices connected with horns and trumpets in various civilizations are vestigially preserved in the use, etiquette, and customs related to the shofar, though they are no longer recognized as such. (See Curt Sachs, *History of Musical Instruments*, New York, 1940, p. 110.) At the sound of the ram's horn, for example, the walls of Jericho fell as miraculously as the walls of Troy and Thebes in Greek legend assembled themselves to the sound of the lyre. The custom of keeping the shofar covered and unseen by the congregation is related to the primitive belief that sacred instruments must be hidden. Sex tabus connected with instruments belonging strictly to men and kept secret from women are reflected in the recommendation that men are obligated to listen to the blowing of the shofar, while women and children are not required to. Further, a Talmudic passage discussed the sounding of the shofar in a well or pit, a trumpet ritual of certain primitive tribes in connection with fertility practices mimetic of the sex act. See HORN; TRUMPET.

shooting or **falling star** The phenomenon of the shooting star in its spectacular flight and sudden vanishment has been explained in many ways and fraught with significance for good or ill since earliest times. In early Hindu mythology meteors were the offspring of Rāhu's severed body. In Islamic lore they were missiles hurled by angels against the jinn to keep them from listening at the gates of heaven. Teutonic mythology predicted that all the stars would fall at the end of the world, i.e. Ragnarök (A1051). Pliny says there is a star in the sky for each person in the world, which shines bright or dim according to his luck, and falls when he dies. This belief has been common in Europe for centuries and is the motif (E741.1.1) of a number of folktales. It occurs also among the Lolos in western China: when a man sickens, offerings are made to his star; when he dies a hole is dug for his star to fall in, lest it strike and injure some living person. (See Frazer, *Dying God,* London, 1912, p. 65.)

Shooting stars were portentous among the ancient Greeks and Romans. In Sparta (c. 1200 B.C.) wise men went out and scanned the sky one night in every eighth year; if they saw a shooting star they knew the king had sinned and deposed him. Seneca (3 B.C.–65 A.D.) in his *Problems of Nature* described a meteor "as big as the moon" which appeared when Paulus warred against Perseus. Roman sailors regarded a shooting star as a sign of storm. Wolfgand Meurer of Leipzig (16th century) writing on meteorological questions declared that nature produces meteors for the glory of God, to adorn the world, purify the air, and to be signs and warnings of future events.

That a shooting star is the soul of someone who has just died is a common saying in Europe and America and among aboriginal peoples from New Guinea to the Eskimos. The Serbians say, "Someone's light has gone out." In New Britain the people say it is the ghost of a murdered man.

Meteoric stones are regarded as mysterious, holy, and powerful among many primitive peoples. Aleuts and Eskimos use them as amulets. In Manchuria they are revered as having come from heaven. In some parts of China to find one is a bad omen. In Japan they are said to have fallen from the Milky Way, and are picked up and given into the keeping of temple priests.

If you can say, "Money, money, money," before a shooting star disappears, you will find money in your hand. If you can make a wish on a shooting star before it disappears, the wish will come true. In Ireland when a shooting star hits the earth it spatters far and wide and becomes "butter dew" (*im soċair*), specks of butter on the surface of rich milk.

Pliny said a corn could be easily extracted if done at the very moment that a star falls. A medieval admonition that still survives is: Count as high as you can while watching a shooting star; the final number will be the number of years you will be free of eye trouble. In Estonia it is said that to see a star fall on New Year's night means one will die within the year; if seen over a certain house, there will be a death in that house.

In folktale to wish on a shooting star is motif D1761.1.1. Other motifs include the shooting star as good omen (D1812.5.2.6); shooting star as angel (V231.2); shooting star as the sign of a birth (E741.1.1.2). This occurs in Siberian and also in North American Mandan Indian story: the stars are the souls of the dead; when one falls it is being reborn.

The Bushmen also maintain that a star falls for the death of every man. The *hammerkop,* a marsh bird of the Bushman regions, when he sees the star fall into the water also knows and cries out at the same moment. The Bushman people say that the *hammerkop* looks into the water and sees all things. Whoever sees a falling star and hears that cry at the same moment knows that some one of his own people has "fallen."

shout In New World Negro usage (1) To sing in the manner of the preaching style of Negro preachers or in the accelerating tempo and exclamatory style of songs accompanying the ring shout. (2) The circular religious dance, the ring shout. (3) A religious song accompanying the ring shout.

Shouters Term employed in Trinidad and elsewhere in the British West Indies to designate certain unaffiliated Protestant (usually Baptist) sects. Their worship is characterized by marked reinterpreted retentions of African ritual forms. [MJH]

Shvod In modern Armenian belief, the guardian of the house. On the last day of February peasants, armed with sticks, old clothes, and bags, strike the walls of barns and houses shouting, "Out with the Shvod and in with March!" to force these lazy guardians out to do their duty as guardians of the fields for the summer. Shvods are believed loath to leave their winter comforts and have been seen crying and asking why they are thus disturbed.

Siddha In Hindu mythology, one of a class of semi-divine beings: literally, one who has acquired *siddhi* or perfection. The Siddhas dwell between the earth and the sun and are said to number 88,000. Their king is Viśvāvasu. They are sometimes considered as the descendants of the Uttarakurus. The Śaktas call the initiated Siddhas or the "perfect ones."

síde (pronounced *shee*) Plural of Irish *sid* or *síod*, a round barrow, mound, hill: the Tuatha Dé Danann, the divine race of Old Irish mythology; later, the fairies of modern Irish folklore: so called from the mounds and hills they occupy. They are often also referred to as *aes* or *aos síde*, people of the mounds. The term was first applied to the Bronze Age Tuatha dé Danann after their defeat by the Milesians when they divided up the hills and mounds of Ireland into kingdoms among themselves. They wove for themselves then the veil of invisibility, which divided Ireland into two populations forever: the seen and the unseen. The síde are still visible to human beings on Midsummer Eve, it is said; and certain persons with second sight are apt to see them any time. The *Book of Armagh* mentions the síd-dwellers as *dei terreni*, and they are still regarded as a kind of earth spirits, though the personal names and identities of the old Tuatha Dé Danann have slipped out of popular memory. They still have personal names, however, and dwell in or rule over specific places. Finnbeara is king of the fairies of Connacht, for instance. See ÁINE; CLÍODNA.

The barrows were the burial mounds of the traditional high kings of Ireland; and it is not surprising that the concept of the barrow-dwellers involves the same confusion of fairies with the spirits of the dead found in other folklores. See FIGHTING OF THE FRIENDS.

The Irish síde are perhaps the most famous fairies of European folklore. Síde lore includes the *sluag síde*, the fairy host, thought of as riding on the wind; the *bean síde*, the fairy woman whose keening foretells a death (see BANSHEE); *ceo síde*, the fairy mist in which people go astray; *ceol síde*, the fairy music which lures people out of this world; *corpán síde* or *siodbrad*, the changeling; *poc síde*, the fairy stroke or elf-shot; *suan síde*, the fairy sleep from which one cannot wake until the appointed moment; *séideán síde*, the fairy wind.

Stories of a mistress or lover in the *síde* are the same as tales about fairy mistresses (F302 f.) everywhere. There

are great goings on among them, much as among mortals: marriages, birthings, churning, cooking, sewing, spinning, weaving, plowing, sowing and reaping of crops, building, traveling, attending fairs, milking or stealing farmers' cattle, hunting and racing, holding great feasts and dances or wars, and working mischief or performing services among human beings. See FAIRY; FAIRY FOOD; IN THE WAY; TUATHA DÉ DANANN.

Siebenschritt Seven-step: a German-Austrian couple dance, which originated in Tyrol, and became adopted in many countries of central and northern Europe. In a counterclockwise circle, the couples, man on the left, inner hands joined, run seven steps forward and seven back, following the musical phrases; then apart for three steps, and together for three; then pivot with joined hands with seven runs. This little stretto pattern can also be performed with running *schottische* steps, and with an exchange of partners for each pivot, the man progressively obliquely counterclockwise. This latter version resembles the Swiss *schottische* or Changing Dance and the Czech four-steps or *ctyři kroky*. [GPK]

Siebensprung Seven Jumps: a men's dance of Germany, Holland, and Denmark, corresponding to the Basque *zaspi jausiak* (seven jumps). Actually the seven jumps are now seven successive postures, each with the body closer to the floor. With a constant refrain of arm swinging, two men face to face stamp on the right foot, then the left, then kneel on the right, on the left, place the right elbow on the ground, then the left, and finally touch the forehead. This results in absurd postures. This traditional mime has evolved a variant in French Canada, as *Bonhomme, que sais-tu donc faire?*, the answer involving successive floor contacts of "*un seul pied par terre*," "*les deux pieds*," "*le genou*," "*une main.*" [GPK]

Siegfried In the German *Nibelungenlied*, the son of Siegmund, king of the Netherlands, and Sieglinde. He became invulnerable by slaying the dragon Fafnir and bathing in its blood. During the bath, however, a leaf fell on his shoulder, leaving him with one vulnerable spot. Siegfried killed the owners of the Nibelungen gold and became their ruler. He went to the Burgundian court of Gunther at Worms and, while there, helped defeat the Danes and Saxons. By donning his cloak of invisibility (*Tarnkappe*) he was able to help Gunther overcome Brunhild, princess of Issland, in the feats of strength she required of a suitor, and for this favor he received the hand of Gunther's sister, Kriemhild. The two queens became jealous, and Brunhild persuaded Gunther's uncle, Hagen, to murder Siegfried, after first learning from Kriemhild his vulnerable spot. Compare SIGURD. See ALBERICH; ANIMAL LANGUAGES; HAGEN.

Sigmund In the *Volsunga Saga*, the youngest son of Volsung, who alone of his family could remove Odin's sword Gram from the oak Branstock. Siggeir, the husband of his twin sister, Signy, ambushed and slew all of the Volsungs save Sigmund, who escaped and eventually avenged his family. Shortly before his death he married Hiordis who bore him a son, Sigurd.

sign language The expression of ideas by signal codes with the hands, smoke, flags, etc. The sign language or gesture language of the American Plains Indians, a system of hand symbols, has served as efficient communication between tribes with mutually unintelligible languages, to the point of telling myths and stories. It is complete, including signs for things, actions, and emotions. It proved useful and consequently underwent considerable development during a confederation of the Cheyenne, Sioux, Arapaho, Kiowa, Comanche, and Apache against the Ute. Gestures can develop and die out. New concepts evolve new gestures, as "coffee" and "mill." The white man's God became designated by an upward gesture, distinct from the indication of one of the cardinal directions indicating the Siouan *wakanda*. The precision, tempo, and quality of the gesture are also variable with the individual's temperament.

The Plains code never extended to the Algonquian or Iroquoian tribes, except for the Algonquian Sauk. The Pueblo Indians employ an incomplete set of gestures for ceremonial actions and for some of their dances. However, the Plains sign language is utilitarian, the Pueblo ritualistic, and frequently rhythmical. Furthermore, not all of the symbols correspond. The Plains sign for lightning is the same as that of the Tewa *kossa* clown: a zigzag motion of the hand above the head, on the Plains with emphasis of the index finger. Rainfall is suggested by dropping the hand and fingers, palm down. But the gesture for "finished" is not the same. In sign language the speaker concludes a statement with a striking together of the fists, thumbs up. The Pueblo Indian, like the Europeans, passes the right palm across the left at right angles. Done with feathers, this is a gesture of exorcism.

Indian sign language is generally considered an autochthonous development to supply a practical need. Yet this claim cannot be dismissed without examination of possible relationship to the elaborate gesture codes of Asia, notably the Hindu *mudras*, and secondarily the derived gestures of the Hawaiian *hula*. It will be found that the symbol for rain is similar. The sign for crescent moon is consistently made by forming a crescent with thumb and index and closing the other three fingers into the palm; in India this is known as the *chandra-kala* hand, slightly different from the half moon or *ardha-chandra* hand with extended fingers. A bud is similarly formed by closing all of the fingertips together, in India the *padmakosa* hand. On the Plains a flower opens by inserting the closed right hand into the cup of the left, and turning and opening it upward. In India the opening *padmakosa* hand signifies sacrificial offering to Śiva, the *alapadma* hand depicts the full-blown lotus by separating and slightly twirling the fingers. Related but not identical symbols include fire, the *arda-chandra* spread in a crescent, on the Plains a closing of the fingers and snapping open into a crescent; horns, the *ardha-pataka* hand of raised ring and index fingers, in contrast with the extended thumb and index for the American antelope; and erotic desire of the *sikhara* or spire hand, with its vertically extended thumb and otherwise closed fist, analogous to the Plains gesture for copulation with vertical thumb and insertion of the right index in the space formed between the left thumb and index.

Many symbols do not, however, conform, as naturally those in particular which refer to different cultural objects. It is possible that similarities are due to the natural suggestion inherent in certain objects or occurrences. Furthermore, the *mudras* represent a highly refined art

and the sign language is simply a form of speech. Yet the latter could quite conceivably be stylized into rhythmic forms. The question can only be raised for thoroughgoing study.

Quite apart from questions of origin, the sign language furnishes valuable ethnological clues, because of the vocabulary of native tribal occupations and preoccupations, and the changes introduced by white civilization. It may also throw light on gestures whose meaning has become obscured or forgotten in ceremonialism, as the "thumbs up" of the Iroquois False Faces—the *sikhara* phallic hand. Such isolated signs recur among tribes who do not make use of a complete code, possibly by diffusion, possibly by chance. For the signs, far from being arbitrary, are based on the fundamental qualities of each concept, on keen observation as well as symbolic penetration. See GESTURES; MIME; MUDRAS. [GPK]

Sigurd In the *Volsunga Saga*, the son of Sigmund and Hiordis, and the last of the Volsungs. He was educated by the dwarf smith Regin who treacherously persuaded him to slay the dragon Fafnir, Regin's own brother, hoping to secure the Andvari treasure for himself. By eating the dragon's heart, Sigurd was able to understand the language and conversations of birds and, learning of Regin's treachery, slew him.

At Hindarfiall he found the Valkyrie, Brynhild, in her magic sleep, encircled by flame. He awoke her, pledged his troth with the ring Andvaranaut, and resumed his travels, some say immediately, some say after the birth of a daughter, Aslaug.

In the land of the Nibelungs he was given a potion of forgetfulness, forgot Brynhild, and married Gudrun, sister of Gunnar, whom he helped win the hand of Brynhild by assuming Gunnar's form. When Brynhild came to the court, she eventually discovered that Sigurd had substituted for Gunnar in her wooing, and she persuaded Gunnar's brother, Guttorm, to kill Sigurd and avenge her. In the end she killed herself and was laid beside him on the funeral pyre.

Sigurdsvaket A Finnish round dance for men and women, originating in the danced ballads of the Faroe Islands. During a sunwise circuit, the dancers chant the myth of Sigurd, with alternating solo and chorus. [GPK]

Silenus In Greek mythology, a deity of forests and springs, similar to but thought of as being older than the satyrs: the name is sometimes given to one god, sometimes (in the plural *sileni*) applied to a class of woodland spirits. Generally, he is a fat old man with hairy body and bald head, upturned nose, horse's ears, hardly able to walk, riding on an ass or a wineskin and held on his mount by attendant satyrs. This figure is often said to be Papposilenus (Papa Silenus), father of the sileni. The sileni are very wise, but usually very, very drunk, unable to move, or sleeping off the effects of liquor. They taught Dionysus the culture of the vine; they were fine musicians; they could prophesy. But to this latter effort they had to be forced. If one came across a sleeping silenus, he could bind him with a chain of flowers. Midas once captured one (or filled a spring with wine and got him drunk) and then brought him back to Dionysus, receiving as a gift the power to change things to gold. (Compare Solomon's capture of Asmodeus and the obtaining of the schamir, and Numa's capture of Picus and Faunus. See also Grimm #136, *Iron Hans*.)

silver A white ductile metal which, because it occurs in a pure state in nature, was one of the first known metals. It has always been highly prized and is now regarded as money by two thirds of the world's population. Until the discovery of America and the almost boundless supplies of the Peruvian mines and later those of the United States (especially Nevada which is called the Silver State), most of the silver mines were in Asia Minor and the Ægean Islands, some of which have been worked at least since 2500 B.C. Silver ornaments have been found in Chaldean tombs from as early as 4500 B.C.; silver and gold were the first metals minted in Gyges' Lydian mint in the 8th century B.C., along with electrum, a mixture of silver and gold.

In ancient Egypt where it does not occur in a native state, silver was more valuable than gold until trade in the XVIII Dynasty made it more common. In China it is sometimes called the obstinate metal because it is not plentiful, but during the T'ang period, silver is said to have overflowed from the hills.

Because of its color, silver has always been associated with the moon. Alchemists referred to it as Diana or Luna; its alchemic symbol was a crescent moon and it was associated with birth. It generally ranks a close second to gold and hence is widely used for religious and ceremonial purposes, especially for bells and musical instruments. It is said to improve their tone. Among the ceremonial trappings of the British Crown are fifteen silver trumpets (one was stolen and never recovered) which are sounded by the heralds at coronations and other state occasions, such as at the end of World War I.

In Greek mythology, the second age of the world was called the Silver Age, when men ceased to revere the gods and fell to killing each other. After death, these men became the good spirits of the earth. The Silver Age of Latin literature was the period from 14 to 180 A.D. The Silver Fork School in English literature (c. 1830) is a popular term for a group of novelists who stressed the social graces and includes such people as Theodore Hook, Bulwer-Lytton, and Mrs. Trollope.

Among the Moslems, the second heaven was constructed of silver and many of their charms are written on, or mounted in, silver to increase their effectiveness. In Hindu mythology, one of the three fortresses in heaven from which the Asuras attacked the world before Śiva destroyed them was of silver. Hindu married women wore bangles and two toe-rings of silver until the death of their husbands. The Egyptian god Rā had bones of silver, members of gold, and hair of lapis lazuli.

But silver, though usually a symbol of purity, is not always associated with the higher things of life. The thirty pieces of silver for which Judas betrayed Christ is not the only instance of bribery. Long before Christian times the Delphic oracle told Philip of Macedon that he could conquer the world with weapons of silver and in our own day we still hear the expression, "passing the barrier with a silver key."

It is common knowledge that it takes a silver bullet to kill a ghost, sorcerer, witch, giant, or a person who leads a charmed life (D1385.4). Silver nails are often used to make a coffin, or to secure the lid to make sure that the spirit will not escape. Silver charms and countercharms are used all over the world. In China a silver locket around a child's neck protects from evil spirits. In parts of France couples going to the church to be married are encircled by a silver chain lest they be bewitched en route. Among the Negroes of the southern United States a silver dime suffices, either swallowed, worn round the neck or ankle, in the shoe, or made into a ring. Crossing a Gipsy woman's palm with silver enables her to predict the future. The Navaho Indians of the United States make little silver bells from quarters which both men and women wear in their war dances. Old women also wear these on their sashes so that their sons-in-law will hear them coming. See JOKING RELATIONSHIP AND KINSHIP TABUS.

A rich person is said to be born with a silver spoon in his mouth. The 25th anniversary is called the silver jubilee and it is customary to present a silver gift on this occasion.

In folktale there are many examples of magic in connection with silver. There is a Votjak tale of a horse who drops silver coins from his mouth; a silver statue which always laughs on hearing a lie (Persian legend); silver chains which increase in volume when cast into a fire (D1671). There is some basis for this last, as pure silver will absorb up to 20 times its volume of oxygen when heated, but if it does not disintegrate on cooling, it will lose it again. In Germany they say that the dwarf king has a silver miner's lantern which is as bright as the sun (F451.7.4). The English Channel is sometimes referred to as the Silver Streak. In China the moon is often called the silver candle and the Milky Way, the silver river.

Sterling silver is a grade of silver of the fineness and weight established originally for English coinage in 1300 by Edward I when 240 Sterlings (pennies) .925 pure equaled one pound. This standard was maintained with more or less honesty until 1920 when British coinage silver was reduced by law to .500 silver. Some say the term is derived from the Esterlings, the North German Hansa merchants who persuaded the king, as they had previously persuaded Charlemagne, to establish a permanent standard of currency. Others say it comes from a star imprinted on the silver penny. In any event it has remained the standard for silver articles to the present time, and the hallmarks for silver and gold articles were established by Edward I at the same time.

Silver Fox or **Silver-Gray Fox** Creator of the Achomawi Indians of northeastern California. Out of nothing appeared a small cloud, which condensed and became Silver Fox, the Creator; immediately thereafter a fog condensed and became Coyote. The Achomawi story of the creation from this point on contains many parallels to the Maidu creation myth. See KODOYANPE. [ewv]

silver rule The rule of life embodying the same concept as that of the golden rule, but stated negatively: i.e. Do not unto others whatsoever you would not have them do unto you.

simidor The song leader of the Haitian work songs of the combite, who sets the pace of the work, playing his singing rhythms against those of the drums. He improvises stanzas or lines on topical subjects, local gossip, or present personalities, and on his wit and sting depend both the good humor and the efficiency of the labor group. See COMBITE SONGS.

simnel cakes Unleavened cakes or buns made of wheat flour and boiled; later, rich cakes stuffed with currants, plums, raisins, etc., and exchanged among friends in Lancashire, Shropshire, and Herefordshire, England, on Simnel Sunday (Mid-Lent). As early as the 14th century we find *simenels* mentioned in *Havelock, The Dane*. Herrick (in 1648) refers to the custom of young people of Gloucester of carrying such cakes to their mothers on Mid-Lent Sunday or Mothering Sunday, hence they are also often called Mothering cakes. The custom was still current in Lancashire and Cheshire in the 19th century.

The word simnel is apparently derived from the Latin *simila*, finest wheat flour. Folk etymology, however, attributes it either to the father of Lambert Simnel, a baker in the reign of Henry VII, who is said to have originated the cake, or to an elderly couple named Simon and Nelly, who in an altercation over the correct method of cooking an Easter cake, produced a new kind, first called "Simon-Nelly cake," later "Sim-Nel."

simple (English *single step*) The French term for the simplest step of court and country dancing. The right foot advances, the left is brought up; then the left forward and the right up. This forward version is used for instance in the *pavane*. The sideward stepping characterizes the *branles*. Both forms have a widely spread and fundamental use in folk dances. [GPK]

Siñ A sky god, chief deity of the Haida Indians of the North Pacific Coast. The name is the Haida word for day. [EWV]

sin-eater One who takes upon himself the sins of a dead person by eating food, a piece of bread or the like, placed upon the breast of the corpse: a custom closely involved in the scapegoat concept. Sometimes food, drink, and a little money is merely passed to him across the corpse. This custom was observed in Wales as late as the 17th century. In the Scottish Isles, the sin-eater must be a stranger to the dead, even a chance passer-by. This is to prevent anyone with a grudge against the dead from taking his sins and flinging them into the sea, whence they could arise as demons to torment the poor soul. Also it is said that he who eats the sins of the dead with grudge in his heart will never be able to cast them off himself, and he will live as one accursed.

In India, the sin-eater is sent out of the country and never allowed to return. Among the Mende of Sierra Leone and Liberia, those who have committed incest are tied together and seated on a mat. Grains of rice are placed on their heads and upturned palms. Then a chicken is brought in; if it eats all the rice, the sin of incest is removed from the pair.

The corpse cakes of Bavaria are kneaded, laid upon the corpse to rise, then baked. The dough is believed to absorb the virtues of the dead, which are thus not lost to the world but passed on to the eaters thereof. Among certain Melanesians, Australian peoples, and some South American Indians, small pieces of the corpse itself are eaten for the same reason. E. S. Hartland assumes that the practice and concept of sin-eating is derived from numerous primitive practices involving eating the corpse. See Hartland's "Sin-eating," *ERE* xi: 272–276.

singing bone A Eurasian folktale motif (E632 ff.; Type 780) in which the spirit of a murdered person is reincarnated as a musical instrument (usually a harp or flute). The instrument is made of the bones of the vic-

tim, or strung with the hair of the victim, or is made of the wood of a tree growing out of the burial place. When played the instrument sings the story of the murder or the tree speaks and reveals it. In the folktale entitled *The Singing Bone* (Grimm #28), the younger of two brothers kills a wild boar for whose capture the king's daughter is promised in marriage. The elder brother kills the younger, buries him in the forest, takes the boar to the king, and claims the prize. No one knows the difference, until years later a shepherd finds a smooth white bone beside a brook and makes a mouthpiece out of it for his horn. When he blows through it, the bone sings the sad story of the younger brother's fate. The shepherd makes a present of the wonderful singing horn to the king; thus murder will out. In *The Juniper Tree* (Grimm #47) a little bird rises from the bones of the murdered child and sings his story. In *Binnorie* (Child #10) a harp made from the bones and hair of the drowned girl accuses the jealous sister. The motif is also used in the prison scene in Goethe's *Faust*. Stith Thompson finds eight African borrowings of this story. See his *Folktale*, p. 291.

singing snowshoes A man has a pair of snowshoes which, when he is returning from the hunt, precede him, singing like birds, and fly through the smokehole into his house: a recurrent element in Great Lakes American Indian tales, particularly in those of the Menomini Indians. [EWV]

Sinlap A Kachin (Burma) beneficent nat, the spirit of wisdom who dwells in the sky and is believed to give wisdom to his worshippers.

Sirens In Greek mythology, sea nymphs whose sweet music lured hearers to their death at the Sirens' hands; they embody the concept of the fatal supernatural lover. Their number varied: Homer says there were two; three are often pictured; usually the number is indefinitely large. They were the offspring of Phorcys or Achelous and one of the Muses. In some way they resembled birds: either they were birds with women's heads (sometimes bearded) or they were women with birds' legs and often winged. This has led to the hypothesis that originally the Sirens were the unhappy souls of the dead (a conception held of them in the Middle Ages), which often are thought of as birds or winged beings, and, like the Harpies and other soul-beings, were maleficently envious of the living. Odysseus stopped the ears of his men with wax and had himself lashed to the mast to pass the island of the Sirens (J672.1) with its meadow strewn with the bones of their victims. The *Argo*, too, slipped past them while Orpheus sang more sweetly than the Sirens. It is said that Butes, one of the Argonauts, threw himself from the ship and tried to swim to them, but Aphrodite rescued him. After Orpheus vanquished them in song, the Sirens, as had been foretold, leaped into the sea and became rocks. Naples, Sorrento, the Messina Straits have been called at various times the locale of the Sirens' abode. Compare LORELEI.

sirvinacuy Trial marriage among the Quechua Indians of South America. In most Quechua communities marriage becomes permanent after a trial period which lasts from 6 months to 2 or 3 years, during which period the couple resides at the man's home. The reasons given for sirvinacuy are: time to build a new house, till a new and separate plot of soil, or save enough money to celebrate a church marriage. Statistics show that in most cases these trial marriages become permanent. [AM]

sisaok A member of a dancing society of the Bella Bella and Bella Coola Indians of British Columbia. Sisaok names can be willed, inherited, or received by supernatural experience. The name gives the initiate the prerogative to enact myths of the first beings, of the animal or bird of his crest. The same man may have several names.

At the end of a period of seclusion, each sisaok initiate dances at a potlatch with a small forehead mask and a circlet decorated with eagle down, formerly woodpecker tail-feathers. The first night of a potlatch, the members dance, each one to two especially composed songs, and each donates wealth and food. This dance is performed in one place, body stiff, legs close, with slight jumps and sometimes slow pivots. On the third night they give dramatic representations of the sisaok myths and distribute more presents. Dances by initiates may continue another night. In their masks they mime wasps, ferocious grizzlies, or the gyrating, hopping eagle. Their rattles, too, are carved with images of their crests.

The sisaok are related to the *a'alk* society, which is an older institution, and belongs entirely to chiefs with special ancestral prerogatives. See KUSIUT. [GPK]

sistrum (Greek *seistron*, from *seiein*, to shake) A form of dance rattle made of a metal or wooden frame with perforations through which are strung thin metal rods. These rods jingle by jarring against the frame, or else by loosely holding a series of metal disks. The instrument is manipulated by a handle. Both the handle and the frame are frequently ornamented and at times surmounted by an animal figure.

The sistrum was originally a symbolic instrument in the cult of Hathor, the Egyptian goddess of fertility and sexual desire. She is variously identified with the mother and earth goddess Isis, wife and sister of Osiris, and with the Mesopotamian fertility goddess Ishtar. The sistrum spread with the cult of Isis all along the Mediterranean, through the Roman Empire to Gaul. It survives in Abyssinian liturgical music, in Ethiopia, in Nigeria and other parts of North Africa, in Spain, Asia Minor, and Caucasia. A similar instrument, the *khardal*, often accompanies dancers in northern India. A variant form—a cone of bronze bells on a wooden handle—is one of the props of the *kagura* dancing priestesses of Japan. In the war dance of a bridal procession, the Oraons of India shake a bow strung with wires and metal jinglers.

The appearance of the sistrum in dance rites of the New World poses an interesting problem. The Aymara Indians of Bolivia use a *č'uluč'ulu* in their Christmas ceremonies: a wooden wire strung across a wooden Y or handled U-shaped frame and holding a series of round disks cut out of food cans. Weston La Barre considers it of African origin, or from colonial Spanish models. The *sena'asom* (or *sonazo*) of the Cahita *pascola* dancer resembles the Abyssinian sistrum. It is a skilfully carved narrow ironwood frame with two nails hammered flat at the point. Each holds three brass disks. These are sounded by striking the rattle with the right hand against the left on a strong beat and in the air on a weak beat. This weak beat is frequently syncopated, in accordance with the phrasing of the dance steps, for instance, three

beats of accent and release, and one syncopated beat. The metallic clashing combines dramatically with the mysterious swishing of the *teneboim* anklets and the tinkling bells on the belt.

These Indian versions certainly are of European derivation. The *pascola* dancer uses other Occidental instruments and *zapateado* steps, though not in conjunction with the *sena'asom*. However, the method of manipulation in his primitive dance suggests a native prototype and ritual significance. One of his rattle-shaking motions mimes the strewing of seeds. This recalls the same gesture as performed with the *chicahuaztli* rattle-stick at the ancient Aztec *ayacachpicholo* ceremony of the spring festival (*tlacaxipehualiztli*) and by the earth and maize goddess Cihuacoatl. This instrument, though shaped like the *sena'asom*, rattled kernels or pebbles that were inserted in a tip carved in human or animal form. Whether the *pascola* originally manipulated a native or Aztec-derived stick-rattle cannot be proved.

A dance survives in Aztec territory, in Tuxpan, Jalisco, named after the elaborate sistrum with four tiers of disks—the *sonajeros*. Any symbolism of their vigorous stamping and jumping dance is forgotten and the derivation of the *sonaja* even more so. Traces of indigenous ritualism remain in the votive organization, the steps, and the accompanying flute and drum.

Both the Aztec and Egyptian instruments were associated with fertility cults. Phallic potency is one of the chief *pascola* traits. The *kagura* also originated in the life-recalling dance for Amaterasu. Thus in its dissemination the sistrum has remained associated with its original function. See RATTLES. [GPK]

Sisyphus In Greek mythology, a king of Ephyra in Corinth, noted for his cleverness, whose punishment in the underworld, rolling a stone uphill eternally, is one of the famous classical allusions. The reasons for his punishment vary: he tried to rape his niece; he revealed the secrets of the gods to men; he slew travelers who sought his hospitality; he revealed the whereabouts of Ægina to her father Asopus after Zeus had hidden her, one of his mistresses, in a cave. For this Zeus ordered Death to take Sisyphus. Sisyphus, the cleverest of men and the prototype of the master thief, chained Death, and no one died on earth. Ares undid Death's bonds and delivered Sisyphus to him. The clever Sisyphus had foreseen this and had warned his wife, Merope, to omit the customary sacrifice for the dead. Therefore, when he was taken before Hades in the underworld, he was able to convince the god that his wife needed punishment. Hades permitted him to return to earth until he had persuaded her to make the sacrifice. Which of course Sisyphus made a point of not doing.

In the long life which followed, Sisyphus accomplished many other deeds, among them the tricking of Autolycus, the greatest of thieves. The latter had been stealing Sisyphus' cattle, but no evidence to prove this could be obtained. Sisyphus branded his name on the bottom of the hoofs of the cattle, came to Autolycus, and was able to prove his case. Then, to repay the dishonesty of Autolycus, Sisyphus seduced Autolycus' daughter, and thus became the father of Odysseus. (The latter, since Autolycus was the son of Hermes, thus had in his ancestry the greatest personages of craft known to antiquity.) Eventually Sisyphus died of old age, and when he arrived in the underworld Hades, fearing disruption of his realm, put Sisyphus to work rolling a stone up a hill, the stone always slipping from his grasp as he neared the top and plunging to the bottom again. In this way the attention of the clever Sisyphus was constantly fixed. The punishment of Sisyphus is the type of motif Q501.1.

Sītā Literally, furrow: in Vedic mythology, goddess of agriculture. Sītā is described as a radiant beauty, black-eyed, and adorned with lotuses. According to the *Rāmāyaṇa* she arose from the earth while her adoptive father Janaka was plowing. She is said to be a human form of the goddess Lakshmī, born into the world to bring about the destruction of Rāvaṇa, wicked king of Lankā. As the wife of Rāma she was the embodiment of conjugal affection and purity. When she was carried off by Rāvaṇa she remained faithful to Rāma despite all of the demon's threats. When Rāma recovered his wife she established her purity by an ordeal. See ACT OF TRUTH. Doubts assailed Rāma, however, and he banished her to the hermitage of Vālmīki where she gave birth to Rāma's twin sons, Kuśa and Lava. After 15 years of exile she was recalled by Rāma and she then publicly declared her innocence and called upon her mother earth as witness. The earth opened and she disappeared into it, leaving Rāma disconsolate.

Sītalā In modern India, the goddess of smallpox, often represented as a naked woman painted red, and mounted on an ass with a bundle of broomsticks in one hand, an earthen pot under her left arm, and a winnowing fan upon her head. When worshipped Sītalā is represented by a clay image, by a stone, or by a piece of screw pine (*Pandanus odoratissimus*). She is of the Chaṇḍāl or sweeper caste. In Bardwan where she has become more Brahmanized she is represented as a four-armed figure seated on a lion, sometimes studded with spots or nails of gold, silver, or brass in imitation of smallpox pustules. The Pods regard her as their chief deity. In the Punjab she dwells in the Kīkar tree (*Acacia arabica*) and women water the tree to cool the sufferers from the disease.

During an attack of smallpox the victim is possessed by Sītalā; the house in which he lives is sacred and must not be entered unless the shoes are removed and feet washed. A branch of the *nīm* tree is hung over the door as a sign that smallpox is in the house. The presence of a Brāhman would make the sufferer worse.

Sītalā's priest is often of the Mālī or gardener caste, especially in Bengal. When someone has smallpox the priest is called in. He begins treatment by forbidding the use of meat and all food which requires oil or spices in its preparation. A lock of hair, cowry shell, piece of turmeric, and bit of gold are tied to the right wrist of the patient who must lie on a plantain leaf and drink the water used to bathe an image of the goddess. During the crisis a water-pot is filled with fruit, flowers, *nīm* leaves and rice, and the priest recites the exploits of Sītalā. These offerings are later given to the priest as his fee.

Sītalā is one of seven sisters who control pustular diseases. These are given various names depending upon the locality, but one list includes Basanti, spring godling when smallpox is rife; Masāni, dealer of wasting diseases; Agwāni, Lamkariya, Mahāmāi, and Polāmdē. Sītalā is attended by Ghaṇṭākaraṇā who, in the Himalayas, is worshipped as the healer of skin diseases. In the southeastern Punjab she is attended by Sedhu Lāl, a servant often worshipped as an intercessor.

Sitkonsky Trickster of the Assiniboin Indians of North America. [EWV]

situa One of the most important feasts celebrated (in September) by the Incas of Peru to expel all diseases and calamities from the cities and towns. Mummies of ancestors and minor idols were carried in procession and offered libations. Blood puddings or bread prepared with the blood of llamas were eaten by all the participants and were sent to the shrines of the empire. [AM]

Śiva One of the Supreme triad of Hindu gods; god of nature, the arts, learning, dancing, revelry; impersonation of the opposing forces of destruction and re-integration; and the typical ascetic and sage: in Śaivism, the supreme God. Śiva early in the development of Hinduism absorbed the Vedic Rudra just as the popularization of his cult has since involved a constant process of syncretism, the adoption of local deities as his manifestations. The name Śiva does not appear in the Vedas signifying an independent deity, but that of Rudra is common. Rudra is praised as the lord of sacrifices, granter of prosperity, wielder of the thunderbolt, and acclaimed as being as destructive as a wild beast. In the *Yajur-Veda* Rudra is the first physician, the increaser of prosperity, and protector of cattle. In the *Atharva-Veda* he is fierce and a destroyer. The epithet Śiva is, however, applied to Rudra as the auspicious, and the latter term has gradually developed into the powerful and terrible Śiva of modern Hinduism.

Śiva is fair in color, has four arms, five faces, and three eyes. The third eye is so destructive that the gods and all created beings were destroyed by its glance. He wears the skin of a tiger, deer, or an elephant, a necklace of skulls; serpents twine about his blue neck (made blue by the poison he drank to prevent it from destroying the world). His vehicle is the bull Nandi and his attributes include the bow Ajagava, an hourglass drum, a club, a trident, a cord, the elephant, and the rat. On his forehead is depicted the crescent moon, symbol of the sovereignty assigned to him at the Churning of the Ocean. His symbol is the lingam. See LINGAM. Its connection with Śiva as a god of reproduction is obvious. He has more than a thousand names and epithets, of which Mahādēva is the most common. He has no real incarnations, although his followers claim 28. His abode is Kailāsa where his worshippers hope to go.

Śiva is a terrestrial god, living on the Himalayas, or in Benares, and practicing asceticism. In the form of a sannyasin he is represented as sky-clad with unkempt hair, ash-smeared body, and protected by a snake canopy. As Bhairava he is the destroyer; as Bhūteśvara he is lord of ghosts, and haunts cemeteries. When drunk he dances the Tāṇḍava with his wife Devī.

The worshippers of Śiva are a majority among Hindus and all sects worship him as a god of luck. His cult (Śaivism) was established in India probably about the third century and its consequent popularization has been the work of many missionary preachers. Śaivism is essentially the exaltation of Śiva as the Supreme Being and the merging of the other members of the triad, Brahmā and Vishṇu, into Śiva. See BATĀRA GURU; BHAIRAVA; BHAIRON; BRAHMĀ; DAKSHA; DEVI; DRUM; GANEŚA.

☞ As one of the divine dancers of Hinduism, Śiva is the third in the trilogy of Brahmā, Vishṇu, and Śiva. In early mythology Śiva was known as the lord of agriculture, with his home in the Himalaya mountains; he rode a bull as his *vahan* or conveyance. As Nataraja he performs his cosmic dance of five movements—creation, preservation, destruction, reincarnation or illusion, salvation or ultimate release (nirvaṇa)—and thus converts into rhythm the essential doctrines of Hindu mystic philosophy.

Another dance commemorates his humorous contest with his consort, Kālī, the goddess of destruction. He won by raising one of his legs to the level of his head, a feat which Kālī was too modest to emulate. This dance is called *Urdhva-Tandava*. Śiva uses the *Tandava*, virile style, and often gestures with the *Pataka* hand from the code of *mudras* (a gesture type that came from Brahmā) and the *Tripataka* which he himself originated. His dances are often represented in Hindu and Cambodian art. He is often shown surrounded by a circle of fire, the vital principle, and with four arms.

In his cosmic dance he has combated evil. Once in an argument with heretical rishis, he destroyed creatures of their black magic—a ferocious tiger, a serpent which he wound around his neck, and an evil dwarf—for he crushed them under foot and continued his triumphant dance. [GPK]

Sivirri Cape York culture hero of the Tjununji tribe, inventor of the drum used in initiation rites, builder of the first wooden canoe, and a traveler who eventually went north into Torres Straits Islands. The Papuan origin of the elements in the cult associated with him have been discussed by McConnel and Thomson (see bibliography of article AUSTRALIAN ABORIGINAL MYTHOLOGY) and Haddon (Cambridge Exped., vol. 1). Sivirri is allied with Kwoiam, culture hero of Western Islands, Torres Straits, who carries an Australian spear and spear-thrower. [KL]

skakácsasszonyok tánc The cooks' dance, which is performed on the evening of a Hungarian wedding celebration. Neighbor women, who have worked all day to provide the feasts for the guests, emerge into the courtyard in single file procession, circling clockwise. Each carries a cooking implement in her hand and waves it above her head—a plate, wooden spoon, pan; or she may carry a wine bottle on her head. They perform a two step to the left and a *simple* to the right (step right, close in with left) and rotate the free hand in time to the music. One or the other may add din to the curious spectacle by striking a plate like a tambourin. [GPK]

Skanda In Hindu mythology and belief, the god of war; general of the gods; the younger of Śiva's two sons; the patron of thieves. Skanda is represented riding the peacock Paravāṇi and carrying a bow and arrow. When divested of his martial attributes and represented as a beautiful youth he is often called Kumāra. His father is sometimes also said to be Agni, his mother Uma, Gangā, or Pārvatī. The gods feared a child of Śiva and Pārvatī and so entreated Śiva not to discharge his seed. But part of it had come forth and this was taken by Agni and thrown into the Gangā. The river threw it into a thicket of reeds and it was transformed into a boy. The six Krittikās or Pleiades found him and, since each wished him as her son, he assumed six faces. From this rela-

tionship he gained the name Kārttikeya. His wife is Senā, Devasenā, or Kaumārī.

Skanda killed the Asura Tāraka who was oppressing the gods. On a later occasion when the Daitya Bāṇa attacked the gods from the mountain Krauncha, Skanda pursued the Daitya and split the mountain with his javelin in order to get at and kill the demon. This opened a passage for the geese and other birds flying north each spring. Skanda has a retinue of monstrous followers. He was probably introduced after the office of general was instituted in Indian states in order to make the temporal and the religious systems similar. Skanda was generally worshipped at one time but at present is worshipped chiefly in southern India under the name of Subrahmaṇya.

ska'wehe Literally, greeting: the Penobscot Indian Greeting or Election Dance, performed on the occasion of intertribal visits for the inauguration of chiefs. These visits were reciprocated among the Penobscot, Passamaquoddy, and Malecite. The visitors were received in their canoes with friendly ceremony and some quasi-hostile demonstration in the firing of guns. The regalia also symbolized peace within potential hostility in the colors and designs. In the dance hall each visitor sang his individual song. Then followed a feast, and, on ensuing nights, communal round dances. The songs were of two types, the solemn, old-style greeting songs, and the livelier new-style dance songs in antiphony between the dance leader and chorus.

The combined mourning for a dead chief and installation of a new one was spread throughout the Eastern Woodlands, and survives among the Iroquois as their Condolence Chant. [GPK]

skip-rope rimes We include here other sidewalk rimes as the same rimes are often used interchangeably for bounce-ball, skip-rope, counting-out, and other games, sometimes showing up even in autograph albums when the juvenile writer can think of no nobler sentiment. The ones we give first are the ones more frequently used for rope-skipping. Since skipping fast requires skill and also makes the skipper very warm, we have often in the rimes words connoting warmth, like pepper, mustard, and ginger. Words italicized indicate where the rope is speeded up and the rope-swingers chant much more loudly:

> My mother uses salt,
> Ginger, mustard, *pepper*.

Mother, mother, I am sick;
Send for the doctor, *quick, quick, quick!*

Sugar, salt, pepper, cider,
How many legs has a bow-legged spider?

Butterfly, butterfly, turn around;
Butterfly, butterfly, touch the ground;
Butterfly, butterfly, show your shoe;
Butterfly, butterfly, twenty-three to do:
One, two, three, etc. to twenty-three.

In using the following very old English rime for skipping rope, the children start slow and gradually accelerate until the last line is fast and furious. It takes a very nimble and skilful girl to "stay in" until the end. There are many variants of this rime in different parts of English-speaking childrendom, but the following version is commonest:

One, two, buckle my shoe;
Three, four, shut the door;
Five, six, pick up sticks;
Seven, eight, lay 'em straight;
Nine, ten, a big fat hen;
Eleven, twelve, let us delve;
Thirteen, fourteen, maids a-courtin';
Fifteen, sixteen, at work in the kitchen;
Seventeen, eighteen, maids a-waitin';
Nineteen, twenty, the larder's empty;
Please mama gimme some dinner!

For sidewalk races, this rime is used:

One to make ready;
Two to show;
Three to start,
And four to go.

which somewhat resembles the older English rime:

One to make ready,
And two to prepare,
Good luck to the rider,
And away goes the mare.

The old "catches" still survive, for each new generation or immigration to "bite on," such as telling the "green" child to be the key in the lock. When the leader says, "I am a gold lock," the victim must say, "I am a gold key." The metal changes several times during the rime until the "green" child finds himself saying "I am a monk key." See CATCH TALE.

Tickling rimes are old and keep bobbing up for new "runs" from time to time, the object being to try to tickle the other child under the arm, on the knee, or at the neck, until he begs for mercy, and to hold your breath when your turn comes so that you won't give in to the tickling. Here are three old ones from Newell's *Games and Songs of American Children:*

Tickle'e, tickle'e on the knee;
If you laugh, you don't love me.

If you're a little lady, as I take you for to be,
You will neither laugh nor smile when I tickle your knee.

Old maid, old maid, you'll surely be,
If you laugh or you smile while I tickle your knee.

The first of these is from Philadelphia; the second, Georgia, and the third Massachusetts.

New York City children like to change the old rimes to suit their whimsy. In World War II they altered A tisket, a tasket, by inserting the line "Put Hitler in a basket," and Eeny, meeny, miny, mo, by "Catch old Tojo by the toe." Two other Mother Goose rimes became, quite startlingly to some adults:

Hickory, Dickory, Dock,
The mouse ran up the clock;
The clock struck one—
Time for lunch.

"Mary, Mary, quite contrary,
How does your garden grow?"
"Silver bells and cockle shells—
And one stinkin' petunia."

Anyone familiar with the condition of New York City window, stoop, and sidewalk flower boxes by mid-August appreciates the realism of the children.

The last day of school the children recognize as a day of license for expressing their antipathy to the teacher by chanting time-honored rimes. These anti-teacher and anti-school verses are at least sixty years old in the form given below, but probably have ancestors way back:

No more pencils, no more books,
No more of teacher's cross-eyed looks.

O Lord of Love, look from above
And bless the poor committee
Who hired a fool to teach our school
In dear old (New York) City.

O Lord of Love, look from above
And pity us poor scholars;
They hired a fool to teach our school
And paid her forty dollars.

The bum-tiddy-go formula was used on teacher:

Teacher, Bum Beacher, Tiddy Eacher, Go Feacher;
Hi-legged, Ho-legged, Bow-legged Teacher,

with *legged* pronounced in two syllables, but it was often heard on sidewalks applied to any playmate temporarily out of favor, like Henry, Bum Benry, etc., sometimes with rather startling results. A similar taunt rime, adaptable to any name, was:

Charley, Barley, Pudding and Pie,
Kissed the girls and made them cry;
When the girls came out to play,
Charley Barley ran away.

Another version was sent me from Hawaii, but it originated in Ohio:

Johnny, bum bonny, Teeairika tonny,
Tee-legged, toe-legged, bow-legged Johnny.

And from the same source came a fine "jingle to be used when you felt like cussing":

Darn, darn, double darn,
Triple darn, hang!
Gee whiz, golly, gosh—
Gol darn, *dang!*

It was also used at the turn of the century in girls' schools and women's colleges in New England when such euphemisms and semiprofanity still met the ladies' needs.

There are still current a number of animal verses popular for generations among children who use them for sidewalk games, ball-bouncing, rope-skipping and even, with O, U, T, Out goes he, for counting out. These are samples of hundreds:

Ask your mother for fifty cents
To see the elephant jump the fence:
He jumped so high he touched the sky
And never came down till Fourth of July.

Ask your mother for fifty cents
To see the elephant jump the fence:
Ask your mother for fifty more
To see the elephant sweep the floor.

Monkey, monkey, bottle of beer;
How many monkeys are there here?

Billy, Billy Booster
Had a little rooster;
The rooster died and Billy cried,
Poor little Billy Billy Booster!

Dickery, Dickery, Dare;
The pig flew up in the air:
The man in brown
Soon brought him down;
Dickery, Dickery, dare.

As I was walking near the lake,
I met a little rattlesnake;
He ate so much of jelly-cake,
He made his little belly ache.

Jane ate cake and Jane ate jelly;
Jane got a terrible pain in her—
Now, don't get anxious!
Don't be misled!
For all that Jane had was a pain in her head.

For other children's rimes see COUNTING-OUT RIMES;
EENY, MEENY, MINY, MO; GRUES; MOTHER GOOSE; NURSERY
RIMES; SHEPHERD'S SCORE.   CHARLES FRANCIS POTTER

Skogsfru The Woods-woman of Scandinavian folklore.
It is very unlucky for hunters to meet her in the forest.
She comes to their fires at night and tries to lure off the
young men.

sky Various beliefs are expressed about the sky and
inhabitants of a sky world in North American mythology. Originally all people lived in the sky until one
young woman fell through a hole down onto what became the earth (confederated Iroquois: see SKY WO-
MAN). A young woman, mortal, marries a star and lives
in the sky. One day she peers through a hole or "window" in the sky and sees the earth below; this has later
dire consequences for her (see STAR HUSBAND). In many
North American Indian tales, but particularly in the
Orpheus tales, the sky is referred to as rising and falling
on the horizon (Symplegades); people who desire to pass
into the sky would have to time their jump over the
horizon exactly, else be crushed between sky and earth.
   A Southwestern Indian belief is that during the world
flood, the birds clung to the sky, which resulted in their
tail feathers being colored. The zenith is one of the six
cardinal directions of the Pueblos and other Southwestern peoples; the Zuñi, as well as several other tribes
in different parts of the continent, believe the sky has
plural levels; a variant Zuñi belief is that the sky is a
"stone cover," solid and resting on the earth like an
inverted bowl. If one can pass through the breaks, or a
passage in the cover, one reaches the home of the
Eagle people. Many other tribes believe that the sky is
the abode of the dead. The Kato of northern California
have a good deal to say about the making of the sky with
its four columns and four cloud gates in their creation
legend (see Pliny Earle Goddard, *Kato Texts*, University
of California Publications in American Archæology and
Ethnology, Vol. 5, 1909). [EWV]

Sky Father One of the two original World Parents
in the mythologies of several southern California and
Southwestern (Zuñi, Pima, Mohave, Yuma) Indian
groups. Originally the earth and the sky were joined
together, the earth being the mother and the sky the
father of mankind. Later it became possible, in one
way or another, to push the sky up and make room for
mankind to live on the earth. See EARTH. [EWV]

Sky Woman The tale of the Woman Who Fell from
the Sky, which constitutes the origin myth of the northern Iroquoian-speaking tribes (Seneca, Mohawk, Cayuga,
Onondaga, Oneida, and so forth) concerns a chief's
daughter, Ataensic, who lived in the sky and who fell
ill. The Seneca version of the myth relates how, to cure
his daughter, the chief had her laid beside a tree which

every year bore fruit (corn) on which people lived;
then he had this tree dug up. A young man, enraged at
the cutting down of the tree, shoved the young woman
into the hole where the tree had been growing. This
hole opened into the present world, which was then all
water and inhabited by waterfowl. As the woman was
falling the birds joined their bodies together and made
a platform for her to fall on. To provide her with a
permanent resting place, the birds decided to prepare
the earth; various animals dived for earth (see EARTH
DIVER) and when earth was secured it was spread out
on the back of the Turtle, who now supports the world.
There the young woman lived, and in due course
brought forth a daughter. This daughter had in turn
twin boys, Flint (Othagwenda) and Little Sprout (Juskaha); the grandmother of the twins liked the latter,
but hated Flint, who was cast away in a hollow tree.
From this point on the myth is concerned chiefly with
the deeds of the twin boys in enlarging and changing the
earth; the struggle between the evil twin Flint and his
brother, and the death of Flint. Ataensic, or Sky Woman,
is recognized as one of the chief mythological characters
of the Iroquois, but as a deity is more or less otiose. [EWV]

Slappy Hooper "The world's biggest, fastest, and bestest sign painter," legendary hero of old-time billboard
craftsmen, who scorned helpers and pounces (perforated
outlines or stencils transferred with powdered chalk or
pounce) and whose love of big jobs or true-to-life jobs
proved his undoing. His biggest job of sky-painting (for
which he used sky hooks to hold up his scaffold) was
for the Union Pacific railroad and stretched from one
end of the line to the other. He had to give up sky-
painting when airplanes came in and started fouling
and cutting his lines. Turning from big to true-to-life
signs, he painted a loaf of bread so real that the birds
broke their bills or necks when they flew against it to
peck at it and the humane society made him paint out
the loaf and just leave the lettering. He painted a stove
with a cherry-red jacket that was so hot that the dandelions and weeds popped out in mid-January and the
bums who made the place a hangout became a public
nuisance. In order to get rid of them, he painted the
stove white-hot, blistering the paint off parked cars and
setting fire to a building across the street. That billboard
had to come down, and Slappy was ready to quit because "they don't want big sign-painting and they don't
want true-to-life sign-painting, and he has to do one or
the other or both or nothing at all." (See Jack Conroy
in *A Treasury of American Folklore*, pp. 546–550.) [BAB]

slaughter of the innocents When the Magi came to
Jerusalem seeking the child destined to become King
of the Jews (*Matt.* ii, 16–18), Herod the king was naturally much interested and asked them to let him know
when they had found the infant. Since they did not do so,
Herod, determined to remove this threat to his sovereignty, ordered slain "all the children that were in
Bethlehem, and in all the coasts thereof, from two years
old and under, according to the time which he had
diligently enquired of the wise men." Warned in a
dream, Joseph "took the young child and his mother
by night, and departed into Egypt," and stayed there
until the death of Herod. The story has the marks of
a folktale, not only the connection with the prophecies

of *Hosea* and *Jeremiah* (verses 15, and 17–18) but particularly its similarity to other stories of the killing of groups of infants in order to destroy one predicted to become great, who always escapes the wholesale infanticide (M375).

Kṛishṇa, famous eighth incarnation of Vishnu, (in Indian myth) escaped a slaughter of the innocents and survived to preach Vishṇu's gospel of salvation.

According to *Exodus* i and ii, Moses escaped a typical slaughter of the innocents by his mother's stratagem, in a story resembling much the older tale of the basket escape of the Babylonian Sargon from death when an infant. By acculturation the story of a slaughter of innocent infants is likely to appear in any sun god or hero myth. The body of Zulu folktale also produces a story in which all male children are killed for fear they will overcome a parent (M375.1).

The Latin, Eastern, and Anglican Catholics have made much of the Feast of the Innocents (Dec. 28 or 29). See CHILDERMAS. Their feast is a holiday of obligation in Bethlehem, and every evening the children of the choir visit the altar under the basilica. There they sing the hymn *Salvete, flores martyrum,* "Hail, Blossoms of the martyrs." See ABRAHAM; CRONUS. [CFP]

Slavic folklore The Slavic world (now numbering about 200 million) presents three linguistic subgroups: the Eastern Slavs—Russians, Ukrainians, and Byelo-Russians—now almost entirely concentrated in the Soviet Union; the Southern Slavs—Bulgarians (mostly in Bulgaria except for a few border regions) and four nationalities residing (except for a few border minorities) in Yugoslavia: Macedonians (a transitional unit from Bulgarians to Serbs), Serbs and Croats (both closely linked ethnographically and using a common Serbocroatian language), and Slovenians; the Western Slavs—Czechs and Slovaks (both concentrated in Czechoslovakia), Lusatian Sorbs (now a small ethnic island in two German provinces, Saxony and Prussia), the population of Poland: the Poles, and the Kashubs, their close kinsmen on the lower Vistula, the last remnant of the Pomeranian people which was entirely Germanized, like their relatives of the Elbe area, the Polabians. Before the final extinction of the Polabian language during the first half of the 18th century its few residua, among them one folk song, were recorded at the threshold of the 18th century. The Eastern Slavs and the Bulgars, Macedonians, and Serbs belong, in an overwhelming majority, to the Greek Orthodox Church while the other Slavs are, except for some small minorities, Roman Catholics, although most of them underwent a more or less profound Reformation movement. A Serbian minority, converted under the Turks to Mohammedanism, presents peculiar features in its oral tradition.

Folklore has had and still plays a very important, vital, and productive role in the cultural life of all Slavic peoples. There are various reasons which favored the preservation and development of Slavic folklore: the prevalence of rural population and its historical significance in most of the Slavic countries; a high percentage of illiteracy, which until recently characterized the whole eastern bulk of the Slavic world; the great role of folklore for the rise and development of national self-consciousness in those Slavic countries where literature written in the vernacular arose only in the last century, or where the development of written literature had been for centuries interrupted.

Among Greek Orthodox Slavs the written literature was, until the period of Enlightenment and its later echoes, essentially confined to the spiritual domain, whereas the secular literary art was predominantly oral. This explains the particularly rich and multiform development of the oral tradition within the Orthodox part of the Slavic world in comparison with the Slavs of the Western denomination. Among these, Czechs, Croats, and Poles have an old written literature whereas the others owe the beginning of their literary activities to the Reformation and Counter-Reformation and their full literary development to the Romantic period.

Allegiance to the Orthodox or to the Roman Church are among the main reasons of divergent development and character of the lore of Slavic East and West. Catholicism fostered Western culture since the Middle Ages, while the Orthodox Church long impeded Western cultural trends. Also, the Catholic Church was much more effective than the Orthodox Church in its fight against pagan survivals among the Slavic people, so that certain folklore genres, particularly the epos and laments, disappeared there almost entirely. The distinct neighboring cultures on the east and west borders of the Slavic world only added to the striking differentiation of its oral tradition. The Orthodox countries possessed a much richer contact with the Ural-Altaic world: the Eastern Slavs with the Finnish peoples and with different Turkic nomads, especially with the Kumans and Tatars; Bulgarians, Macedonians, and Serbs with the Turks. In the Catholic (and Protestant) part of the Slavic world, especially in its marginal areas from the Kashubs and Sorbs down to the Slovenians, a clear-cut influence of the Germans is apparent. In the southwestern Slavic area Romance culture has left its imprint. Some Hungarian elements entered into the musical tradition of Croatia, Slovakia, and Moravia, and spread to the adjacent regions of Poland and the Ukraine.

As to the influence of Slavic folklore and the oral tradition upon neighboring peoples, the fairy tales of the Western Finns were subjected to the influence of Russian lore, while in Lithuanian folklore a Byelo-Russian influence is apparent, and in the German regions with a Slavic substratum traces of Slavic folk poetry and beliefs may be detected. Hungarian folk songs absorbed some stimuli from the Slavic environment. The North Albanian epics owe much to contact with Serbian tradition. In Greece and Rumania there are many evident vestiges of Slavic folk beliefs and rites.

The first documents on folk poetry appear almost at the beginning of the literary history of Slavic nations. In the early Middle Ages in such Russian literary works of the 12th century as the *Primary Chronicle* and the *Igor' Tale* there are fragments of epos, fairy tales, riddles, proverbs, ritual songs, laments, and incantations. Also old Russian homilies cite and condemn folk songs as part of the pagan tradition. Likewise the medieval writings of the Western Slavs reflect some folklore elements. Particularly the rich Czech literature of the 14th and 15th centuries both in vernacular and in Latin includes short folktales, riddles, the first collection of proverbs by Smil Flaška of Pardubice, fragments of songs, and a treatise on the winter ritual by the monk Jan of Holešov, the oldest Slavic folklorist. In the 15th century single folk songs are inserted in some manuscripts of Polish monks. Only a few folklore vestiges of the oral tradition are preserved in the medieval literature of the South Slavs.

With the political and social upheavals of the 17th century folklore forms widely infiltrate into the Russian written literature. In the following century a new Russian literature shaped according to Western models was created. But even at this time the native folklore was still imitated in the lower literary genres. The reaction against the predominance of foreign influence provoked toward the end of the 18th century recognition and admiration of the national past and of the popular tradition. Recordings and publications of Russian folklore, partly in its genuine form, partly reshaped, began to appear. Among them the epic collection of Kirša Danilov, written down in the late 18th century and first published in 1804, is particularly important. Romanticism emphasized the attractiveness of folklore forms. These latter leave appreciable traces in the work of nearly all significant Russian authors and composers of the 19th and 20th centuries. In the Catholic Slavic world, the Reformation and even more the Counter-Reformation, tending to appeal to the folk masses, used their poetic patterns and inversely influenced the oral tradition. In particular, the Czech baroque period created many transitional forms between literature and folklore. The further development of this interpretation as well as the decisive influence of folklore on the new Czech literature and music was favored by the intensive ties and interchange between the Czech rural and urban population in the 18th and 19th centuries. In Poland with its clear-cut social differentiation the influence of popular tradition upon the art of the upper classes, although occurring since Renaissance poetry, plays a more marginal role, with the brief exception of the great Polish romanticists. Serbocroatian folk lyric and epic entered into the written poetry as early as the rise of the Dalmatian Renaissance (15th and 16th centuries) and underlies the whole Serbocroatian literary development of the 19th century. The first significant attempts to establish Ukrainian, Slovak, and Bulgarian literature in the middle of the last century, start with the imitation of the folklore pattern, while the further development shows the tendency to a sharper differentiation between the oral and literary forms.

As to the recording and investigation of Slavic folklore, the first phenomena which attracted enthusiastic international attention were the Serbian and Russian heroic epos. The initial steps in arousing the interest of the scholarly and literary world were made through the collecting and publishing activity of the Serb Vuk Karadžić (1787–1864) and in the second half of the 19th century through the field work of the Russians P. Rybnikov (1832–1885) and A. Hilferding (1831–1872). They discovered rich sources of the Russian epic tradition in the Olonec region of northwestern Russia, and were the first to pay systematic attention both to the social background of the epic tradition and to the individual features and the creative contribution of the narrators (skaziteli).

The collecting and publishing of other genres of oral poetry in all Slavic countries have progressed more and more and the techniques of recording as well as studies of the folklore milieu have been perfected, especially in

Russia from the beginning of this century and in the international studies of the Serbocroatian epos. It reached its peak in the expedition of M. Parry (Harvard University) to Yugoslavia in 1934.

During the last hundred years much has been done also in the interpretation of Slavic folklore, especially concerning epic poetry. Different views have been successfully applied (mythological, diffusionist, historical, anthropological, sociological, and formalist approaches). Still there is a great lack of survey work which would compare the oral tradition of individual Slavic nations and point out both their original, national features and their common patrimony. In spite of some excellent isolated attempts to analyze the verbal and musical structure and symbolism of folk poetry, we still lack a systematic inquiry into this field. There remains also an almost complete gap in the studies of folklore in relation to the folk mind.

Types of Slavic Folklore

The various types of Slavic folklore can be characterized according to the kind of performance, to the way of delivery, to the prosodic form, to the semantic genre, and to the function the work performs. We may divide the material accordingly as drama or monolog: spoken or sung, and a recitative type, transitional from song to speech; prose or verse; narrative or non-narrative, either lyric or gnomic; ritual or non-ritual. Prose in Slavic folklore is always spoken, and narratives have no connection with rites.

Plays Ritual plays linked with various winter festivities are widespread in the Slavic world and present certain common archaic features: pantomimes with frequent phallic motives, animal masks (special favorites are the goat, the aurochs, the horse, the bear, the wolf), humorous dialog, and a clearly discernible magic purpose. The plays pertaining to the funeral ritual of the Carpathian Ukrainians represent particularly archaic survivals. In Bohemia, dramatized Christian legends, which had their roots in the medieval and baroque theater and literature, were frequently substituted for the magic plays, and subsequently spread into Slovakia and Poland. The Russian folk drama, which developed during the 18th and 19th centuries and offers a fanciful intermingling of tragic and comic elements, draws its inspiration from the stage and literature of the upper classes. The most popular among these plays, however, *Tsar Maximilian*, was originally an adaptation of the Czech drama of Saint Dorothy, used by the Russians to lampoon Peter the Great. The puppet drama and farce (with the comic hero Kašpárek) is especially developed in Czech popular tradition, while the Russian tradition, which may be under its influence, is confined to comedy (using Petruška as the central figure). Prose and verse as well as speech and song intermingle in the Slavic folk drama.

Folktales The spoken narrative, represented by folktales, occupies an important place in the whole Slavic folklore field, but in the Eastern Slavic area, especially among Great Russians and Byelo-Russians, it presents a particularly highly developed formal tradition, distinct from that of the Western and Southern Slavs. Prologs and epilogs, petrified formulas, ornamental expressions, differentiated styles, and dramatic dialogs are typical features. Not fairy tales but novelettes and anecdotes form the majority of the Slavic tale plots and are the most original of them. Legends, local and religious, are likewise numerous and varied. The mythology of the Slavic fairy tale differs sharply from folk belief. The folktales as a rule are in prose, but sometimes include versified formulas. In Russia the traditional semiprofessional (formerly also professional) narrators often tend to versify the whole tale.

Ritual rimes The non-narrative type is also represented by spoken forms in Slavic folklore. Here are found the rimes of the best man (Russian *družko*, Czech *družba*, etc.), formally and functionally similar in the wedding rituals of all Slavic people. The Serbian ritual toasts (*zdravice*) belong here also. All these speeches, like the versified Russian folktales, use a syllabically free rimed verse, forming a bipartite syntactic unit with final intonational cadence.

Incantations make up another species of the non-narrative forms connected with rituals. These magic formulas, based rhythmically on syntactic parallelism and making extensive use of various euphonic and semantic devices, survive in the oral and partly in the written tradition of all Slavic peoples. The most numerous and most varied forms of incantations are found in Russia. They are a highly professionalized and esoteric branch of folklore, preserving many pre-Christian elements on which a new layer of Christian symbolism has been superimposed.

Proverbs and Riddles The non-narrative spoken forms without ritual ties are proverbs and riddles. Proverbs play a particularly important role in the colloquial language of Orthodox Slavic nations, but they are familiar to all Slavs. From the early Middle Ages they entered into Slavic written literatures, while on the other hand proverbs from medieval anthologies of parables and aphorisms were adopted among the people. The proverbs of Bulgarians and other Balkan Slavs frequently follow Turkish models. A Slavic proverb usually consists of one bipartite syntactic unit with some sort of parallelism or consonance between the two parts. Many Slavic proverbs, especialy among the Southern Slavs, originated as quotations from didactic stories, or they use the decasyllable which associates them with the epics. Not infrequently the riddles of different Slavic nations are similar or even identical; for example, many use zoomorphic metaphors. Their imagery is related to that of songs, and sometimes riddles become an integral part of songs and tales. The rhythmic form of the riddles is close to the structure of proverbs and incantations.

Epics Recitative epics are spread in three areas: 1) The Balkan Slavic epics, called in Serbian *junačke pjesme* or *starinske pjesme* (heroic songs or songs of yore), are recited in a great part of Serbian territory, in Macedonia, and in Bulgaria, especially in its western region. 2) The Russian epics, called by their narrators *stariny* (those of olden times) and in the scholarly nomenclature *byliny*, are spread along the coast of the Arctic Ocean, around Lake Onega, and also occur among Siberian colonizers and Don Cossacks. 3) The Ukrainian *dumy*, or as the narrators call them *kozac'ki pisni* (Cossacks' songs), have been recorded mostly in the region between the Dnieper and the Desna rivers.

As to the events and heroes reflected in the epics, the action of the *byliny* is usually set in Kievan Russia of the 10th or 11th century, or concerns the fight against the Tatars from the 13th century. Also the economic

and political flourishing of the Moscow state left its mark, as did the reign of Peter. Most of the Balkan Slavic epics deal with the resistance against the Turkish invaders since late 14th century, while the Ukrainian *dumy* sing the Cossacks' struggle with Tatars, Turks, and Poles in the 16th and 17th centuries. Study of the Russian and Balkan Slavic epic tradition reveals, in addition to the essential historical elements, many migratory heroic plots and vestiges of an ancient mythological substratum. Whereas the Balkan Slavic epics usually glorify the rulers of the country, in the *byliny* the Kievan sovereign, Vladimir, appears only as a secondary figure. The *bogatyr'* (hero) is usually an outstanding individual from the ruler's retinue; sometimes he stems from the merchant or even the peasant class; rarely is he a provincial prince.

The epic tradition is inherited from generation to generation only by a few particularly gifted peasants, and in the Balkan Slavic countries it is limited to men. A higher degree of professionalism probably existed in the past; especially in Russia vagrant minstrels (*skomoroxi*) are thought to have been for centuries the main bearers of the epic tradition, and elaborate parodies of the epic form (*nebylicy*) represent interesting survivals of their repertory. The *dumy* have almost disappeared, while the Russians, and even in greater degree the Balkan Slavs, still possess a rich though rapidly decaying epic tradition.

In the Ukraine and the western part of the Balkan Slavic area the performers accompany recitative epics by stringed instruments, while elsewhere no accompaniment is used. The Southern Slavic epic decasyllable line, having a break after the fourth syllable, a clear-cut trochaic tendency, and three predominant word-accents, is related to the Russian epic verse, since the latter presents almost the same syllabic scheme with certain fluctuations, and uses the same overlapping of dichotomy and trichotomy; in Russian, however, there is substituted an accentual dactylic ending for the quantitative cadence of the Serbian verse. Striking similarities in meters and figures, as well as in the structure and compositional role of parallelism, permit reconstruction of the common prototype of the South Slavic and Russian epic form. In addition to the loftier decasyllable, the primitive Slavic epic tradition seems to have used the simpler meter which now is represented by the Bulgarian epic octosyllable and by the short line of the Russian historical songs. These songs describe Russian historical events of the 16th and 17th century in a simpler way, as compared with the more grandiose presentation of the distant past found in the *byliny*.

Spirituals The epic tradition in Russia and the Balkan area is supplemented by spirituals, based on Christian legends. These are usually performed by professional pilgrims and beggars.

Laments The Slavic laments can be classified under the heading of non-narrative recitatives. The funeral laments are known to all Greek Orthodox Slavs, but only in the three epic areas are they richly developed. In these regions semiprofessional women or relatives improvise laments in the most skilful and varied fashion. This female counterpart to the epic tradition is closely linked with the latter by poetic devices. Both of the metric varieties of the Serbian laments, i.e. the symmetrically bipartite octosyllable, and the more solemn symmetrical tripartite line of twelve syllables, correspond exactly to both Russian lament meters, and this comparison reveals the common prototypes in Primitive Slavic. The Ukrainian laments as well as the *dumy* are performed in freer verse forms, reverting, however, to the same prototypes. In addition to the funeral laments there are in the Russian tradition laments concerning men at war (or in military service), and the laments of the bride, which are an integral part of the wedding ritual.

Ballads The narrative songs, i.e. ballads, have a more lyric character than the recitative epics. They occur in all Slavic countries but are more deeply rooted in the Slavic West than in the East. This form is especially developed in the central area, including Moravia, Slovakia, southeastern Poland, western Ukraine. Here in addition to the usual international plots some peculiarly local themes occur. Ballads are supplemented in these regions by religious songs inspired by the Western Slavic medieval and baroque legendary literature.

Lyric Songs Among the lyric songs connected with rituals two cycles may be distinguished. The first, linked with the calendar holidays, are better preserved by the Eastern Orthodox Slavs. Many pre-Christian mythological survivals are found here which have been mostly eliminated or supplanted by Christian motives in the Catholic Slavic countries. The symbolism of these songs is focused upon agricultural magic, fertility charms, and ancestor worship. The songs are grouped around the equinoxes and the solstices. The winter ritual and its songs is most fully represented in the Ukraine, Bulgaria, Macedonia, and Serbia, where many common features may be observed. The second cycle of ritual songs is linked with family life, and particularly with the wedding. Wedding songs vary in style and function, and together with the bride's laments and the best-man's rimes they are parts of a complex dramatic performance, the most vital of the Slavic rituals. Beside striking common features, the wedding songs of the Southern, Western, and Eastern Slavs offer numerous divergences. The form and especially the symmetric bipartite verse of the ritual songs is characterized by various archaic features.

Among non-ritual lyric songs the main place belongs to love songs, which often are linked with dances and games. In those countries which possess an epic tradition, emotions are usually not referred to directly but are expressed by allusive, sometimes enigmatic metaphors. An obvious reaction against this stage is seen in Russia in the growth of couplets and quatrains (*častuška*), originating in dance tunes, yet emancipated from the dance, and particularly appropriate to improvisation and emotional expression. Similar development is exhibited in the Polish *krakowiak* and in the Ukrainian *kolomyjka*.

In the Slavic West, particularly in Bohemia, Slovakia, Croatia, and Western Poland, the lyric song has been influenced by Western instrumental music and the melody has been superimposed upon the text. Elsewhere the text is quite autonomous. The songs are the most commonly used of the Slavic folklore forms. There are, however, songs connected with special types of work, outlaws' songs, and soldiers' songs, songs performed for children or by children, and songs exclusively belonging to women.

Bibliography: Summary studies Moszyński, K., *Kultura ludowa Słowian*, II, Cracow, 1939; Kuba, L., *Slovanstvo ve svých zpěvech*, Prague, 1880–1929; idem., *Cesty za slovanskou písní*, I, II, Prague, 1933, 1935; *Lud Słowiański*, III, No. 1. B (Wójcik-Keuprulian, Br.; Kolessa, F.; Gavazzi, M.; Moszyński, K.)—a survey of Polish, Ukrainian, Serbocroatian and Byelo-Russian folk music; Jakobson, R., "Metrika," *Ottův slovník naučný*, Supl. IV, Prague, 1935; Miklosich, F., "Die Darstellung im slavischen Volkepos," *Denkschriften der K. Akademie der Wiss.*, XXXVIII, Vienna, 1890; Caraman, P., *Obrzęd kolędowania u Słowian i u Rumunów*, Cracow, 1933.

Russian Speranskij, M., *Russkaja ustnaja slovesnost'*, Moscow, 1917; Sokolov, Ju., *Russkij fol'klor*, Moscow, 1938 [English translation: New York, 1950]; Chadwick, H. M., "Russian oral literature," *The Growth of Literature*, II, Cambridge, 1936; Andreev, N., *Russkij fol'klor*, Moscow, 1938; Zelenin, D., *Russische [ostslavische] Volkskunde*, Berlin, 1927; Pypin, A., *Istorija russkoj ètnografii*, I–IV, Petersburg, 1890–1892; Azadovskij, M., "The Science of Folklore in the U.S.S.R.," *VOKS* (Ethnography, Folklore and Archeology in the U.S.S.R.), Moscow, 1933; idem., *Literatura i fol'klor*, Moscow, 1938; *Krest' janskoe iskusstvo SSSR*, I, Leningrad, 1927; Sokolov, B., "Ėkskursy v oblast' poètiki russkogo fol'klora," *Xudožestvennyj fol'klor*, I, Moscow, 1926; Gołębek, J., *Car Maxymilian*, Cracow, 1938; Ončukov, N., *Severnye narodnye dramy*, Petersburg, 1911; Golovačev, V., and Laščilin, B., *Narodnyj teatr na Donu*, Rostov, 1947; Jakobson, R., "On Russian Fairy Tales," *Russian Fairy Tales*, New York, 1945; Polívka, J., *Slovanské pohádky*, I, Prague, 1932; Savčenko, S., *Russkaja narodnaja skazka*, Kiev, 1914; Propp, B., *Morfologija skazki*, Leningrad, 1928; Gabel', M., *Dialog v skazke*, Kharkov, 1929; Azadovskij, M., "Eine sibirische Märchenerzählerin," *FFC*, LVIII, Helsinki, 1926; Afanas'ev, A., *Narodnye russkie skazki*, I–III, Moscow-Leningrad, 1936–1940; Afanas'ev, A., *Russkie narodnye legendy*, Moscow, 1914; Xudjakov, I., *Velikorusskie skazki*, Petersburg, 1860; Kapica, O., *Russkije narodnye skazki*, Leningrad, 1930; Azadovskij, M., *Russkaja skazka*, I–II, Moscow, 1932; Sokolov, Ju., *Russkie narodnye skazki*, I–II, Moscow, 1932; Moreeva, A., "Tradicionnye formuly v prigovorax svadebnyx družek," *Xudožestvennyj fol'klor*, II–III, 1927; Poznanskij, N., *Zagovory*, Petrograd, 1917; Mansikka, V., *Über russische Zauberformeln*, Helsinki, 1909; Majkov, L., *Velikorusskie zaklinanija*, Petersburg, 1868; Klimenko, I., *Das russische Sprichwort*, Bern, 1946; Simoni, P., *Starinnye sborniki russkix poslovic, pogovorok, zagadok*, Petersburg, 1899; Dal', V., *Poslovicy russkogo naroda*, Moscow, 1879; Illjustrov, I., *Zizn' russkogo naroda v ego poslovicax i pogovorkax*, Moscow, 1915; Sadovnikov, D., *Zagadki russkogo naroda*, Petersburg, 1901; Rybnikova, M., *Zagadki*, Moscow, 1932; Chadwick, N. K., *Russian heroic poetry*, Cambridge, 1932; Trautmann, R., *Die Volksdichtung der Grossrussen, Das Heldenlied*, Heidelberg, 1935; Skaftymov, A., *Poètika i genezis bylin*, Saratov, 1924; Jakobson, R., and Szeftel, M., "The Vseslav Epos," in *MAFLS*, 42, 1947; Trubetzkoy, N., "W sprawie wiersza byliny rosyjskiej," *Prace ofiarowane K. Wóycickiemu*, Wilno, 1937; Astaxova, A., *Byliny severa*, Moscow, 1938; Astaxova, A., and Andreev, N., *Èpičeskaja poèzija*, Moscow, 1935; Speranskij, M., *Byliny*, I–II,

Moscow, 1916–1919; Andreev, N., *Byliny*, Leningrad, 1939; Miller, V., *Istoričeskie pesni russkogo naroda XVI i XVII vv.* Petrograd, 1915; Fedotov, G., *Stixi duxovnye*, Paris, 1935; Ljackij, E., *Stixi duxovnye*, Petersburg, 1912; Bessonov, P., *Kaliki perexožie*, I–VI, Moscow, 1861–1863; Veselovskij, A., *Razyskanija v oblasti russkix duxovnyx stixov*, Petersburg, 1879–1891; Andreev, N., and Vinogradov, G., *Russkie plači*, Moscow, 1937; Mahler, E., *Die russische Totenklage*, Leipzig, 1936; Barsov, E., *Pričitanija Severnogo kraja*, I–III, Moscow, 1872–1886; Azadovskij, M., *Lenskie pričitanija*, Čita, 1922; Kastal'skij, A., *Osobennosti narodno-russkoj muzykal'noj pesni*, Moscow, 1923; Garbuzov, N., *O mnogogolosii russkoj narodnoj pesni*, Moscow, 1939; Černyšev, V., *Russkaja ballada*, Leningrad, 1936; Šejn, P., *Velikoruss v svoix pesnjax, obrjadax, obyčajax, verovanijax*, Petersburg, 1898; Čičerov, V., "Russkie koljadki i ix tipy," *Sovetskaja Ėtnografija*, No. 2, 1948; Sobolevskij, A., *Velikorusskie narodnye pesni*, I–VII, Petersburg, 1895–1902; Lineva, E., *Velikorusskie pesni v narodnoj garmonizacii*, Petersburg, 1909; Gippius, E., and Eval'd, Z., *Pesni Pinež'ja*, Moscow, 1937; *idem.*, *Krest'janskaja lirika*, Leningrad, 1935; Sokolov, Ju., *Narodnaja lirika*, Moscow, 1938; Sidel'nikov, V., *Častuški*, Moscow, 1940; Eleonskaja, E., *Sbornik velikorusskix častušek*, Moscow, 1914; Zelenin, D., "Das russische Schnaderhüpfel," *Zeitschrift für slavische Philologie*, I, 1925; Jarxo, B., "Organische Struktur des russischen Schnaderhüpfels," *Germanoslovica*, III, 1934; Trubetzkoy, N., "O metrike častuški," *Versty*, II, Paris, 1927; Vetuxov, A., "Narodnye kolybel'nye pesni," *Ètnografičeskoe Obozrenie*, XII–XV, 1892; Vinogradov, G., *Russkij detskij fol'klor*, Irkutsk, 1930.

Ukrainian Bogatyrev, P., "Les jeux dans les rites funèbres en Russie Subcarpathique," *Le Monde Slave*, 1926; Hruševs'kyj, M., *Istorija ukrajins'koji literatury*, I, IV, Kiev-Lwow, 1923, 1925; Kolessa, F., *Ukrajins'ka usna slovesnist'*, Lwow, 1938; Andrijevs'kyj, O., *Bibliografija literatury z ukrajins'koho folkloru*, Kiev, 1930; Volkov, F., *Ètnografičeskie osobennosti ukrainskogo naroda*, Petrograd, 1916; Čubinskij, P., *Trudy ètnograf.-statist. èkspedicii v zapadno-russkij kraj*, I–VII, Petersburg, 1872–1878; Čubinskij, A., *Malorusskie skazki*, Petersburg, 1878; Dragomanov, M., *Malorusskie narodnye predanija i rasskazy*, Kiev, 1876; Hnatjuk, V., *Ukrajins'ki narodni bajky*, I–II, Lwow, 1916–1918; Grinčenko, B., *Rasskazy, skazki, predanija, zagadki*, Chernigov, 1902; Malinka, A., *Sbornik materialov po malorusskomu fol'kloru*, Chernigov, 1902; Gnedič, P., *Skazki, legendy, rasskazy*, Poltava, 1915; Javorskij, Ju., *Pamjatniki galicko-russkoj narodnoj Slovesnosti*, Kiev, 1915; Levčenko, M., *Kazky ta opovidannja z Podillja*, Kiev, 1928; Efimenko, P., *Sbornik malorossijskix zaklinanij*, Moscow, 1896; Xvylja, A., *Ukrajins'ka narodna prykazka*, Kiev, 1936; Sementovskij, A., *Malorossijskie i galickie zagadki*, Petersburg, 1872; Scherrer, M., *Les dumy ukrainiennes*, Paris, 1947; Kolessa F., *Melodiji ukrajins'kyx narodnix dum*, I–II, Lwow, 1910–1913; Revuc'kyj, D., *Ukrajins'ki dumy ta pisni istoryčni*, Kiev, 1919; Kolessa F., *Ukrajins'ki narodni dumy*, Lwow, 1920; Antonovič, V., and Dragomanov, M., *Istoričeskie pesni malorusskogo naroda*, I–II, Kiev, 1874–1875; Speranskij, M., *Južnorusskaja pesnja i ee sovremennye nositeli*, Kiev, 1904; Svencic'kyj, "Poxoronni holosinja," *Ètnografičnyj Zbirnyk*, XXXI–

XXXII, 1912; Kolessa, F., "Rečitatyvni formy v ukrajins'-kij poeziji," *Pervisne Hromadjanstvo*, 1927; Potebnja, A., *Ob'jasnenija malorusskix i srodnyx narodnyx pesen*, I–II, Warsaw, 1883–1887; Kolessa, F., "Das ukrainische Volkslied, sein melodischer und rhythmischer Aufbau," *Oesterreich. Monatschrift für den Orient*, Vienna, 1916; Kolessa, F., "Rytmika ukrajins'kyx narodnix pisen'," *Zapysky Tov. im. Ševčenka*, 1906–1907; *idem.*, "Narodni pisni z Halic'koji Lemkivščyny," *Ètnografičnyj Zbirnyk*, XXXIII–XL, Lwow, 1929; *idem.*, "Karpats'kyj cikl narodnix pisen'," *Sborník prací I. sjezdu slovanských filologů*, Prague, 1932.

Byelo-Russian Seržputovskij, A., *Skazki i rasskazy belorussov-polešukov*, Petersburg, 1911; Nosovič, I., *Sbornik belorusskix poslovic*, Petersburg, 1874; *idem.*, *Belorusskie zagadki*, Petersburg, 1869; Karskij, E., "Narodnaja poèzija," *Belorusy*, III, Pt. 1, Moscow, 1916; Šejn, P., *Mater'jaly dlja izučenija byta i jazyka russkogo naselenija Severo-Zapadnogo kraja*, I–III, Petersburg, 1890–1902; Romanov, E., *Belorusskij sbornik*, I–IX, 1886–1912; Federowski, M., *Lud białoruski na Rusi Litewskiej*, I–III, 1897–1903; Nikol'ski, N., *Mifologija i abradavasc' belaruskix valačobnyx pesen'*, Minsk, 1931; Nikiforovskij, *Belorusskie pesni*, Wilna, 1911; Nikol'ski, N., and Grynblat, M., *Pesni belaruskaha naroda*, I, Minsk, 1940.

Polish Fisher, A., *Etnografja Słowiańska*, III, "Polacy," Lwow-Warsaw, 1934; Bystroń, J., *Etnografja Polski*, Warsaw, 1947; Bystroń, J., *Bibliografja etnografji polskiej*, I, Cracow, 1929; Gawełek, F., *Bibljografja ludoznawstwa polskiego*, Cracow, 1916; Gajek, J., *Polski atlas etnograficzny*, Lublin, 1947; Zdziarski, S., *Pierwiastek ludowy w poezji polskiej XIX w.*, Warsaw, 1907; Fischer, A., "Polskie widowiska ludowe," *Lud* XIX, 1916; Krzyżanowski, J., *Polska bajka ludowa w ukladzie systematycznym*, I–II, Warsaw, 1947; Malinowski, L., "Powieści ludu polskiego na Śląsku," *Materiały antropologiczno-archeologiczne i etnograficzne*, Akad. umiejętności, IV–V, Cracow, 1899–1900; Dzipowski, S., *Klechdy polskie*, Warsaw, 1948; Brzozowski, F., *Przysłowia polskie*, Cracow, 1896; Bystroń, J., *Przysłowia polskie*, 1933; Bugiel, W., "Lamentowa grupa pieśni pogrzebowych," *Rocznik Tow. Przyj. nauk w Przemyślu*, VI, 1925; Ehrenkreutzowa, C., *Ze studiów nad obrzędami weselnymi ludu polskiego*, 1929; Krejčí, K., "Polská píseň lidová," *Slavia*, XVIII, 1947; Bystroń, J., *Pieśni ludu polskiego*, Cracow, 1924; *idem.*, *Polska pieśń ludowa*, Cracow, 1925; *idem.*, *Historja w pieśni ludu polskiego*, Warsaw, 1925; *idem.*, *Artyzm pieśni ludowej*, Poznan, 1921; Windakiewiczowa, H., *Studja nad wierszem i zwrotką poezji ludowej*, Polish Academy, Phil. Div., Rozprawy LII, Cracow, 1913; Kolberg, O., *Pieśni ludu polskiego*, I–XXIII, Warsaw, 1885–1890; Szramek, E., and Bystroń, J., *Pieśni ludowe z polskiego Śląska*, Cracow, 1934.

Kashubian Lorentz, F., *Slovinzische Texte*, Petersburg, 1905; Lorentz F., Fischer, A., Lehr-Spławiński, T., *The Cassubian Civilisation*, London, 1935; Sędzicki, "Pieśń kaszubska," *Gryf* II; Cenowa, *Sbjór pjesnj svjatovich*, I, Schwetz, 1878.

Polabian Fischer, A., *Etnografja słowiańska*, I, "Polabianie," Lwow, 1932; Rost, P., *Die Sprachreste der Draväno-Polaben*, Leipzig, 1907; Trubetzkoy, N., "Polabian Verse," *Word*, VI, 1950.

Sorbian Fischer, A., *Etnografja słowiańska*, II, "Lużyczanie," Lwow, 1932; Schneeweis, E., *Feste und Volksbräuche der Lausitzer Wenden*, Leipzig, 1931; Smoleŕ, J., *Pjesnički hornych a delnych Lużickich Serbow*, I, II, Grimi, 1841, 1843; Jórdan, H., *Delnołużiske ludowe pěsnje*, Bautzen, 1875; Černý, A., *Narodne hłosy łużiskoserbskich pěsni*, I–III, Bautzen, 1888–1894; Kuba, L., *Píseń Srbů Lužických*, Prague, 1922.

Czech Václavek, B., *Písemnictví a lidová tradice*, Olomouc, 1938; Novák, A., *Přehledné dějiny literatury české*, Chapter on "Literatura prostonárodní," Olomouc, 1936; Horák, J., "Národopis československý," *Čsl. vlastivěda*, II, Prague, 1932; Bogatyrev, P., *Lidové divadlo české a slovenské*, Prague, 1940; Erben, K., *České pohádky*, Prague, 1939; Kubín, J., and Polívka, J., *Povídky kladské*, I–II, Prague, 1908–1914; Polívka, J., *Povídky lidu opavského a hanáckého*, Prague, 1916; Kubín, J., *Lidové povídky z českého Podkrkonoší*, I–III, Prague, 1922–1926; Tille, V., *České pohádky do r. 1848*, Prague, 1909; *idem.*, *Verzeichnis der böhmischen Märchen*, I., *FFC*, VI, Helsinki, 1921; Horák, J., *České pohádky*, Prague, 1945; Dubský, O., "Les formules de conjurations tchèques comparées aux formules des autres nations," *Revue des traditions populaires*, XXV–XXVI; Zaorálek, J., *Lidová rčení*, Prague, 1947; Flajšhans, V., *Česká přísloví*, I–II, Prague, 1911–1913; Kraus, K., *Česká přísloví*, Prague, 1931; *idem.*, "Naše hádanky," *Národopisný věstník československý*, XVIII, 1926; Plicka, K., and Volf, F., *Český rok v pohádkách, písních, hrách a tancích, říkadlech a hádánkách*, Prague, 1944; Smetana, B., and Václavek, B., "Lidová píseň," *Ottův slovník naučný nové doby*, III, Prague, 1935; Horák, J., *Naše lidová píseń*, Prague, 1946; *idem.*, *Naše staré písně*, Prague, 1941; Hostinský, O., *Česká světská píseń lidová*, 1906; *idem.*, *36 nápěvů světských písní českého lidu z XVI stol.*, Prague, 1892; Indra, B., *Havlíčkovy práce o verši české lidové písně*, Prague, 1939; Sychra, A., *Hudba a slovo v lidové písni*, Prague, 1948; Horálek, K., *Staré veršované legendy a lidová tradice*, Prague, 1948; Erben, K. J., *Prostonárodní české písně a říkadla*, Prague, 1886; Holas, Č., *České národní písně a tance*, I–IV, Prague, 1908–1910; Sušil, F., *Moravské národní písně*, Brno, 1891; Bartoš, F., and Janáček, L., *Národní písně moravské*, I–II, Brno, 1899, 1901; Janáček, L., and Váša, P., *Moravské písně milostné*, 1930–1936; Tichý, F., *Kytice z české a slovenské duchovní lyriky lidové*, Prague, 1931; Myslivec, F., *Slezské národní písně, tance a popěvky*, 1930; Salichová, H., *Slezské písně lidové*, 1917; *idem.*, *Slezské lidové písně svatební*, 1918; Vavřík, J., *Lidová píseń ve Slezku*, 1931; Schreiber, V., "Hudební stránka slezských písní," in Vyhlídal, J., *Naše Slezsko*, 1903; Smetana, R., and Václavek, B., *České písně kramářské*, Prague, 1949.

Slovak Polívka, J., *Súpis slovenských rozprávok*, I–IV, Turč.-Sv. Martin, 1923–1930; Dobšinský, P., *Prostonarodnie slovenské povesti*, 1880–1883; Záturecký, A., *Slovenská přísloví, pořekadla a úsloví*, Prague, 1897; Yurchak, P. P., *Slovak Proverbs and Sayings*, Scranton, 1947; Melicherčík, "Slovenský folklor," *Slovenská vlastiveda*, II, Bratislava, 1943; Zich, O., "O slovenské písni lidové," *Slovenská čítanka*, Prague, 1925; Lichard, M., "Príspevky k teorii slovenskej ludovej piesne," *Naše Slovensko*, Turč.-Sv. Martin, 1937; Kadavý, Ruppeldt, Meličko, *Slovenské spevy*, I–III, Turč.-Sv. Martin, 1880–

1890–1926; Horák, J., *Výbor slovenskej poezie ľudovej*, I. *Piesne epické*, II. *Piesne lyrické*, Turč.-Sv. Martin, 1923, 1928; Medvecký, K. A., *Sto slovenských ľudových ballád*, Bratislava, 1923; Kolečányi, M., *Slovenské ľudové balady*, Bratislava, 1949.

Slovenian Štrekelj, K., *Slovenske narodne pesmi*, I–IV, Ljubljana, 1895–1923; Murko, M., "Historická svědectví o slovinských lidových písních," *Práce Slovanského ústavu v Praze*, XXI, Prague, 1947; Grafenauer, J., *Lepa Vida, študija o izvoru razvoju in razkroju narodne balade*, Ljubljana, 1943.

Serbocroatian Popović, P., "Pregled srpske književnosti," chapter in *Narodna Književnost'*, Belgrade, 1921; Chadwick, H., and Chadwick, N., "Yugoslav Oral Poetry," in *The Growth of Literature*, II, Cambridge, 1936; Gesemann, G., *Der montenegrinische Mensch*, Prague, 1934; Čajkanović, V., "Srpske narodne pripovetke," *Srpski Etnografski Zbornik*, XLI; Jovanović, V., *Srpske narodne pripovetke*, Belgrade, 1925; Karadžić, V., *Srpske narodne pripovetke*, Belgrade, 1937; *Srpske narodne poslovice*, Belgrade, 1933; Zima, L., *Figure u našem narodnom pjesništvu*, Zagreb, 1880; Maretić, T., *Metrika narodnih naših pjesama*, Zagreb, 1907; Matić, S., "Principi umetničke versifikacije srpske," *Godišnjica Nikole Čupića*, XXXIX–XLI, 1930–1932; Slijepčević, P., "Beiträge zur Volksmetrik," *Godišnjak Skopskog Filosofskog Fakulteta*, I, 1930; Djordjević, A., *Srpske narodne melodije*, Belgrade, 1928; Maretić, T., *Naša narodna epika*, Zagreb, 1909; Kravcov, N., *Serbskij epos*, Moscow, 1933; Murko, M., *La poésie populaire épique en Yougoslavie au début du XXe siècle*, Paris, 1929; Gesemann, G., *Studien zur südslavischen Volksepik*, 1926; Jakobson, R., "Über den Versbau der serbokroatischen Volksepen," and Becking, G., "Der musikalische Bau des Montenegrinischen Volksepos," in *Archives Néerlandaises de phonétique experimentale*, VIII–IX, 1933; Lord, A. B., "Homer, Parry and Huso," *Journal of Am Anthro.*, XLII, No. 1, 1948; Subotić, D., *Heroic Ballads of Serbia*, Boston, 1913; Jovanović, V., *Srpske narodne pesme*, Belgrade, 1922; Karadžić, V., *Srpske narodne pjesme*, vols. I–IX, Belgrade, 1932–1936; Kuhač, F. S., *Južno-Slovjenske narodne popjevke*, Zagreb, 1879–1881; *Hrvatske Narodne Pjesme*, I–VII (ed. of Matica Hrvatska), Zagreb, 1896–1929; Žganec, V., *Hrvatske pučke popijevke iz Metumurja*, Zagreb, 1924; Petranović, B., *Srpske narodne pjesme iz Bosne i Herzegovine*, I–III, Belgrade, 1867–1870; Hörman, K., *Narodne pjesme muhamedavaca u Bosni i Herzegovini*, I–II, Sarajevo, 1888–1889; Šaulić, N., *Srpske narodne tužbalice*, Belgrade, 1929; Jarxo, B., "Srok i aliteracja u tužbalicima dužego stiha," *Slavia*, III, 1924; Širola, B., and Gavazzi, M., "Obredne popijevke," *Narodna starina*, XXV, Zagreb, 1931; Bartók, B., and Lord, A. B., *Yugoslav Folksong*, New York, 1950.

Macedonian Mazon, A., *Contes slaves de la Macédoine sud-occidentale*, Paris, 1923; Oljoski, V., and Tošev, K., *Makedonski narodni prikazki*, Skopje, 1946; Kinčov, V., *Makedonija; etnografia*, Sofia, 1900; Xristov, D., *Narodni pesni na makedonskite bulgari*, Sofia, 1931; *Zbirka na makedonski narodni pesni*, Skopje, 1947.

Bulgarian Arnaudov, M., *Očerki po bŭlgarskija folklor*, Sofia, 1935; *idem.*, "Bŭlgarskite narodni prikazki," *Sbornik za nar. umotvor.*, XXI, 1905; Stoilov, A., *Narodni prikazki*, Sofia, 1928; Mladenov, S., *Bŭlgarski narodni smešni prikazki,* Sofia, 1918; Slavejkov, P. R., *Bŭlgarski pritči ili poslovici i xarakterni dumi.* Plovdiv, 1889–1897; Arnaudov, M., *Bŭlgarski poslovici,* Sofia, 1931; Vakarelski, X., *Bŭlgarski narodni gatanki,* Sofia, 1936; Minkov, C., *Bŭlgarska narodna poezija,* Sofia, 1935; Angelov, B., and Arnaudov, M., "Bŭlgarska narodna poezija," *Istorija na bŭlgarskata literatura v primeri,* I, Sofia; Arnaudov, M., *Folklor' ot Elensko,* Sofia, 1913; Romanski, S., *Pregled na bŭlgarskite narodni pesni,* Sofia, 1925; Djoudjeff, S., *Rythme et mesure dans la musique populaire bulgare,* Paris, 1931; Stoin, V., *Grundriss der Metrik und der Rhytmik der bulgarischen Volksmusik,* Sofia, 1927; *idem., Narodni pesni,* Sofia, 1928; Arnaudov, M., *Bŭlgarski svatebni obredi,* Sofia, 1931; *idem., Bŭlgarska narodna poezija; Liričeski pesni,* Sofia, 1931.   SVATAVA PÍRKOVÁ JAKOBSON

Slavic mythology The Christianization of the Slavs expanded gradually from the 8th until the 13th century, now and then provoking local pagan revolts (in Bohemia soon after its baptism which dates from the late 9th century and among the Poles and Eastern Slavs throughout the 11th century) or creating those whimsical combinations of paganism and Christianity labeled in Church Slavonic vocabulary as "double faith" (*dvoevĕrie*).

The conversion of the Kievan court belongs to the end of the 10th century and the pagan tradition is still fresh in the minds of the earliest Russian annalists. Both the *Primary Russian Chronicle,* compiled about 1111, and the *First Novgorod Chronicle* reproduce many records of the 11th century which contain a detailed report on the annihilation of the official paganism in Kiev and Novgorod and various reflections of the subsequent double faith. Moreover the *Primary Chronicle* includes the authentic text of Russian-Greek treaties (945, 971) with native pagan oaths. From the 11th century many allusions to the old deities and pre-Christian beliefs occur also in the various Russian writings against the pagan survivals. Former Russian gods are occasionally interpolated into translated literary works (*Malalas Chronicle; Alexandria*) or in accord with the Byzantine pattern, appear as rhetoric adornments in the original epos (*Igor' Tale*).

The Northwestern (Maritime) Slavs from the Vistula to the Elbe stubbornly resisted German crusades and the history of this struggle is told (a) in the Latin Chronicles of three German clergymen—two from the 11th century (Thietmar of Merseburg; Adam of Bremen), and one from the 12th century (Helmold); (b) in three biographies of Otto of Bamberg compiled in the 12th century; (c) in *Gesta Danorum* by Saxo Grammaticus (about 1188). These sources, supplemented by some less important German documents and by the Icelandic *Knytlinga Saga* (around 1265), exhibit a rich picture of the Northwestern Slavic idolatry; and their authors, in spite of their Roman bias and insufficient acquaintance with Slavic people and language, have proved to be, in the light of recent archeological research, noticeably more accurate in their reports than it was usually assumed.

The literary data on the beliefs of the other Slavs are much scantier, partly because of their early Christianization (particularly in the case of Czechs and Bulgars) or because of the late origin of documents relating to the pagan past (e.g. most of the mythological testimonies in

the *Polish Chronicle* of the 15th century have been found to be mere inventions). Marginal residues of Slavic heathenism as recorded in 1331 from the Slovenes on the Isonzo are rather exceptional, but the folklore of all the Slavic peoples, notwithstanding the various superstrata, borrowings from abroad, and modifications, offer to a careful investigator many striking survivals, especially in demonology and in both calendary and family rites. From times preceding the Christianization of the Western and Southern Slavs, a few Greek and Latin writings give scrappy indications of single Slavic religious concepts or terms: in the 6th century the Byzantine historian Prokopios briefly refers to the Slavic faith and the Gothic chronicler Jordanis cites the Slavic *strava* (funeral meal); a Latin document of the 8th century mentions *treba* (sacrifice).

The relative linguistic unity and negligible dialectal differentiation of the Slavic world until the end of the first millennium A.D. and particularly the considerable lexical uniformity of the Slavic pre-Christian beliefs corroborates the supposition of a substantial unity for the cult of the Primitive Slavs. In the vocabulary originally connected with worship, the Slavs and partly the Baltic peoples, their closest linguistic neighbors, present striking similarities with the Indo-Iranian as well as with the Thraco-Phrygian nomenclature. The fund linking the Primitive Slavs with the Iranians is particularly important. The proximity in the religious pattern and terminology finds its expression both in the features which they preserved jointly from the Indo-European heritage or which they modified in one and the same way. In some cases where we are authorized to presume a direct borrowing, the direction is from Iranian to Slavic. These Slavic-Iranian affinities are all the more indicative in that Indo-European languages are mostly divergent in their religious vocabulary.

Slavs and Iranians nearly eliminated the Indo-European name of the worshipped sky (*dieus*). They agree 1) in substituting the name of the cloud (Slavic *nebo*) for that of the sky, 2) in converting the derivative celestial (*deiwos*) used by Indo-Europeans to denote gods into the word for "hostile demonic beings" (compare the term *divŭ* attested in the demonology of various Slavic peoples and the corresponding she-demon *divii, diva, divožena*), 3) in assigning the general meaning of "god" to a term which originally signified both wealth and its giver (*bogŭ*). Thus the Slavs participated in the Iranian evolution into a clear-cut dualism and, according to Helmold's accurate testimony, they were wont to worship divinities of good and those of evil "being convinced that happiness comes from the god of good while misfortune is dispensed by the deity of evil." And the Slavic term for faith (*vĕra*) coincides with the Iranian term for religious choice between good and evil. The Slavs (and the Balts too) share with the Iranians the use of the same term for holy (originally "provided by supernatural beneficial power," Slavic *svętŭ*). The Slavic term for "peace agreement" and for "community agreeing" (*mirŭ*) is connected with the Iranian Mithra. In Slavic and Iranian similar verbs express the various processes originally pertaining to the religious pattern, as: worshipping (*žrĕti*), wailing (*vŭpiti*), invocation (*zŭvati*), divination (*gatati*), proclamation (*vĕštati*), drawing (*pĭsati*), chastising (*kajati*), fearing (*bojati sę*), protecting (*xraniti*), etc. Such fundamental spiritual terms as word (*slovo*) and deed (*dělo*) are common to Slavic and Iranian, as are also such designations of the basic ritual implements as fire (*vatra*), chalice (*čaša*), burial (literally, magian) mound (*mogyla*), and such curative terms as cure (*goiti*), healthy (*sŭdravŭ*), and sick (*xvorŭ*). There are several common expressions for ill-omened concepts: evil (*zŭlo*), shame (*sramŭ*), guilt (*vina*), sinister (*šui*); moreover the Slavic stem *kostjun- (literally, osseous) denoting profane, temporal, seems to be a loan translation. The Common Slavic *rai*, paradise, has been acknowledged as a direct borrowing from Iranian *rāy*, heavenly radiance, beatitude.

Like the religious terminology, the pantheon of the Slavs offers more Common Slavic than tribal features and partly points to Indo-European roots or at least shows Indo-Iranian, especially Iranian, and perhaps Thraco-Phrygian connections. It was hinted by Prokopios and six centuries later observed by Helmold, that among the multiform divine powers worshiped by the Slavs, one is believed to rule over the others in heaven and to care for celestial things, "whereas the rest, obeying the duties assigned them, have sprung from his blood and enjoy distinction in proportion to their nearness to that god of gods." The scattered data we possess on the Slavic deities, and in particular on their mutual kinship and hierarchy, do not permit us to reconstruct this whole system. Nevertheless there are indications arguing for a kinship and hierarchy.

The storm god Perunŭ is closely connected by name and functions with the Vedic Parjánya, with the Lithuanian (as a matter of fact, Common Baltic) Perkúnas (replaceable under tabu by Perúnas), with the Norse Fjǫrgynn (supposed to be the archaic designation for the Thunderer) and with the Albanian Perëndi, now denoting both "god" and "sky." It is probable that the Greek Keraunós, name or epithet of the thunder god, is a rimeword substituted for a tabued *Peraunós. The Indo-European name for this hypostasis of a sky divinity contains, beside a nasal suffix the alternating verbal root *per-/perk-* (or *perg-*), signifying "to strike, to splinter," and used particularly of lightning. This root appears, e.g. in Latin and Germanic, as a substitute name for the oak, a tree favored by the thunderstorm and devoted to the thunder god; and in the Indo-European tradition the same root with a nasal suffix denotes the "oak-wooded hill"—Celtic Hercynia (Silva), Gothic *fairguni*, Slavic *pergynja (Old Church Slavonic *prěgynja*, Old Russian *peregynja*, Polish *przeginia*). The leading role of Perun in the Russian heathenism, the connection of the oak with this god, and the veneration of the *peregynja* are clearly attested by Russian sources. Perun was identified with Thor by the Varangians, with Zeus by the Russian bookmen, and with Elijah in Christianized folklore. Outside Russia, the god Perun, distorted to Prone and worshipped in oak-groves, appears in Helmold's *Chronicle*; Perun's son, Porenutius, figures in the mythological records of Saxo Grammaticus; Perun's name is echoed in Slovak maledictions (Peron, Parom), in the Polabian word for Thursday (*peründan*), in such appellatives for thunder and lightning as the Polish *piorun* and the Bulgarian folklore form *perušan*, as well as in West and South Slavic proper names, both personal and local, these mostly linked with oak-forest or hill. The ritual of the rain charm, widespread among Bulgars and Serbs and thence in Greece and Rumania, assigns the para-

mount role to a rigorously chaste girl (yet unable to conceive and born of a mother who since has become unable to conceive). Nude and draped with flowers she whirls ecstatically in the middle of a ring, invoking in song the sky or Elijah to moisten and fructify the earth. She bears the reduplicated name of Perun, unchanged (Perperuna) or undergoing hypochoristic modifications. This couple Perunŭ-Perperuna recalls the Germanic Fjǫrgynn-Fjorgyn and the Lithuanian Perkunas-Percuna tete. In another variant of the South Slavic ritual, the main role was performed by a boy assuming Perun's name reduplicated and altered: the people, whirling and drinking, besought him for rain. To the same cycle refer the old Russian reminiscences of Pereplut, worshipped by whirling and libations, as well as the Magdeburg epistle of 1008 damning the "impudent" god Pripegala. In some areas of Serbia and Bulgaria the name Perperuna is replaced by Dodola or Dudula and a similar form *du(n)dulis* (tied with an onomatopœic verb for thunder) is currently substituted by Lithuanians for the tabued Pergunas. Thus in the Balkan Slavic rain charms, one not only finds archaic features reminiscent of Jupiter Elicius and *aquælicium*, of Zeus Náios and Dodona as well as of the Vedic hymns to Parjánya, but even the tabu name itself together with its substitute reveals a prehistoric origin.

The Slavic Svarogŭ is recorded and identified with Hephaistos by an old Russian glossator of the *Malalas Chronicle*. Svarogŭ's son was venerated both by Russians as Svarožiči and by the Northwestern Slavs as Svarožicĭ. The name survives in the Rumanian *sfarog*, torrid, and in the names of hills along the Slavic German borderline (Kashubian Swarożyn, elsewhere with a tabu substitution Tvarog, Tvarožic, etc.). Under another substitute name (Rarog, and further modifications as Rarach, Jarog) this spirit continues to live in the Western Slavic (particularly Czech and Slovak) demonology as a supernatural falcon and fiery dwarf who beams and turns into whirlwind and various animals. The name and the characteristic traits of this Slavic deity are obviously connected with the Iranian Vṛthragna and his main incarnation Vāragna, the supernatural falcon, and with the cognate figures in Indic (Indra Vṛtrahan) and Armenian mythology (Vahagn). Also the other incarnations of Vṛthragna—wind, gold-horned aurochs, horse, boar—as well as his close ties with fire and smithery are reflected by the Slavic tradition. Indra, the virility epithet of this deity, lost its mythological connotation in the Slavic adjective *jędrŭ*, virile, vigorous, fast (in the same way as Slavic secularizes the adjective *svobodĭ*, free, corresponding to the Phrygian Sabadios). But the various aspects of this divine virility find their expression in the conjoined names recorded from the Northwestern Slavs, Svętovitŭ (overlapped by St. Vitus after Christianization but still figuring in toponymy), Jarovitŭ (surviving as Jarilo in the folk-Russian phallic spring ritual), Porovitŭ (with the same first root as Perunŭ), and Ruevitŭ. These four manifestations of the military deity were apparently symbolized by the polycephalic form of the Northwestern Slavic idols and could be compared to the Iranian four-faced warrior god, Vṛthragna, with such attributes as "making bright" and "making virile." At least two of the mentioned designations had a calendary connotation: 1) *jaro* (spring) is connected with *jarŭ* (young, ardent, bright, rash), and Jarovitŭ's priest proclaims in his name, "I am your god who covers the plains with grass and the woods with leaves"; 2) *ruenŭ* is the autumnal month named for the ruts and mating calls of newly matured animals. The whole ritual, focusing upon the annual cycle and predestination, displays associations with Vṛthragna's cult. The prophetic role of the horse in the divination ceremonies of the Northwestern Slavs is confirmed by its magic functions in the Russian popular tradition, particularly by the traditional horse epithet—*věščij*, seer—which has an exact correspondence in the *Avesta*. And the common Slavic term for time (**vermę*) conceives it as a wheel-track (compare Old Indic *vartman-*).

Like the Vedic Vṛtrahan, the Slavic Svarogŭ generated the sun, Xŭrsŭ Dažĭbogŭ, according to the Old Russian records. These designations survive among old personal names, Dadzbog in Polish, Hrs in Serbian. Helmold's "ydolum . . . Podaga" is perhaps a distortion of Dabog. For the bookmen, Dažĭbogŭ was identical with Helios. In old Russian tradition both the celestial and the hearth fire is said to be Svarogŭ's son. Xŭrsŭ is an obvious borrowing from the Iranian expression for the personified radiant sun (*Xursīd* in Persian), Dažĭbogŭ means "the giver of wealth" like the Vedic Bhaga. Stribogŭ, the neighbor of Dažĭbogŭ on the Kievan hill before Russia's conversion, means literally "the apportioner of wealth" like Bhaga's partner Amça, and Palmer detects a striking parallel to this couple in the mythological references of the oldest Greek poets. Větrŭ (wind), personified in Primitive Slavic (compare Indo-Iranian Vāta-), is quite naturally termed "Stribogŭ's descendant" in the *Igor' Tale*.

The Russian peace treaties with the Greeks do not mention Svarogŭ probably because of his bellicose connotation, but after the sovereign Perunŭ the oath of 971 invokes Volosŭ as "the god of flocks." Also, a Russian form, Velesŭ, is attested, and the Czech tradition of the 15th and 16th centuries remembers a demon Veles. The alternation of two variants, **velesŭ* and **velsŭ* (wherefrom Volosŭ), seems to root in Primitive Slavic. The etymology is still controversial. Volosŭ was identified with Apollo in the Old Russian literary pattern and replaced by St. Blasius (Vlas) in Christianized folklore. Beside Volosŭ, Russian tradition knows another god of the cultivators with the characteristic name Rodŭ (literally, kin) thus corresponding to such deities as the Celtic Teutates, Latin Quirinus, Umbrian Vofionus. Among the Kievan court idols neither Volosŭ nor Rodŭ were admitted, although the Old Russian literary tradition presents the latter as the primordial god. His feminine counterpart, Rožanica (in Serbocroatian and Slovenian popular tradition Rodjenica, Rojenica) literally meaning "genitrix" and mostly named in the plural, was identified by Russian bookmen with Artemis. The only goddess of the Kievan official pantheon, Mokošĭ, literally moist, and represented by some vestiges in Russian folklore and in Slavic toponymy, is probably nothing but another name for the slightly personified "Mother moist earth" (*Mati syra zemlja*), still adored in the Slavic, chiefly Russian, popular tradition, and closely related to the similar female deities in Baltic, Phrygian, and Indo-Iranian mythology. The Iranian Ardvī (moist) Sūrā Anāhitā is particularly close to Mokošĭ: both of them protect semen, child-bearing, and sheep-breeding. It is noteworthy that one of the Iranian demonic

beings, the winged monster Sīmorg, was adopted under the name Simarglŭ in the Kievan official pantheon on the eve of Russia's Christianization, and that the Persian poet Khaqani at the end of the 12th century symbolizes the Russian intruders precisely as Sīmorgs. However the whole Slavic demonology still awaits an attentive comparative analysis both of its peculiarities and of the multifarious ties linking it with the environment.

Bibliography:

For a survey and reproduction of the medieval records on Slavic mythology see: Mansikka, V. J., *Die Religion der Ostslaven* I, FFC XLIII, 1922; Gal'kovskij, N., "Drevnie russkie slova i poučenija, napravlennye protiv ostatkov jazyčestva v narode," *Moscow Archaeological Institute, Zapiski* XVIII, 1913; Meyer, K. H., *Fontes historiæ religionis slavicæ*, Berlin, 1931; Zíbrt, Č., *Indiculus superstitionum et paganiarum*, Prague, 1894; Brückner, A., *Mitologia Polska*, Warsaw, 1924; Beševliev, I., "Grŭcki i latinski izvori za vjarata na prabŭlgarite," *National Museum of Ethnography of Sofia Bulletin* VIII-IX, 1929; Leicht, P.-S., "Tracce di paganesimo fra gli Sclavi dell' Isonzo nel secolo XIV," *Studi e materiali di storia della religioni* I, 1925.

The best summary work is still Niederle, L., *Život starých Slovanů*, part II, vol. 1, first edition 1916, second edition 1924 (condensed in *Manuel de l'antiquité Slave* II, Paris, 1926). Some corrections and supplements: Sobolevskij, A., "Zametki po slavjanskoj mifologii," *Slavia* VII, 1928; Brückner, A., *Mitologia slava*, Bologna, 1923; Urbańczyk, S., *Religia pogańskich Słowian*, Cracow, 1947. Archeological additions: Palm, T., *Wendische Kulstätten*, Lund, 1937; Albrecht, C., "Slavische Bildwerke," *Mainzer Zeitschrift* XXIII, 1928. Valuable but in many respects antiquated is the latest English survey: Máchal, J., "Slavic Mythology," *Mythology of All Races* III, Boston, 1918 (abstract of his Czech outline of 1891). Dilettantic and chauvinistic: Wienecke, E., *Untersuchungen zur Religion der Westslaven*, Leipzig, 1940. Insufficient material used and avoidance of comparative method harm the newest compilation: Unbegaun, B., "La religion des anciens Slaves," *Mana*, tome II, no. 3, Paris 1948. Most stimulating linguistic contributions are offered by: Rozwadowski, J., in *Rocznik oryentalistyczny* I, 1914; Meillet, A., in *Revue des Études Slaves* VI, 1926; and Machek, V., in *Linguistica Slovaca* III, 1941.

On Slavic popular beliefs see particularly: Moszyński, K., *Kultura ludowa Słowian* II, no. 1, Cracow, 1934, and Bystroń, J., *Słowiańskie obrzędy rodzinne*, Cracow, 1916; and for single Slavic peoples: Haase, F., *Volksglaube und Brauchtum der Ostslaven*, Breslau, 1939; Zelenin, D., *Očerki slavjanskoj mifologii*, Petersburg, 1916; Bogatyrev, P., *Actes magiques, rites et croyances en Russie Subcarpathique*, Paris, 1929; Seržputovskij, A., *Prymxi i zababoni belarusaw paljašukov*, Minsk, 1930; Nikol'skij, N., *Živěly w zvyčajax, abradax i verannjax belaruskaha sjalanstva*, Minsk, 1933; Biegeleisen, H., *Matka i dziecko w obrzędach, wierzeniach i zwyczajach ludu polskiego*, Lwow, 1927; idem., *Wesele*, Lwow, 1928; idem., *U kolebki —przed ołtarzem—nad mogiłą*, Lwow, 1929; Bystroń, J., *Słowiańskie zwyczaje źniwiarskie w Polsce*, Cracow, 1916; Schneeweis, E., *Feste und Volksbräuche der Lausitzer Wenden*, Leipzig, 1931; Zíbrt, Č., Staročeské výročni obyčeje, pověry, slavnosti a zábavy prostonárodni Prague, 1889; Schneeweis, E., *Grundriss des Volksglaubens und Volksbrauches der Serbokroaten*, Celje, 1935;

Marinov, D., *Narodna vjara i religiozni narodni običai*, Sofia, 1914; Kemp, P., *Healing Ritual: Studies in the Technique and Tradition of the Southern Slavs*, London, 1935. On mythological motives in folk art, see: Gorodcov, V., "Dako-Sarmatskie religioznye èlementy v russkom narodnom tvorčestve," *Trudy Gos. Ist. Muzeja* I, Moscow, 1926.   ROMAN JAKOBSON

Sleeping Beauty Generic catchword for motif D1960.3 featured in a widespread European folktale (Type 410) specifically entitled *Little Briar Rose* (Grimm #50), *La Belle au Bois Dormant* (Perrault), etc. See LITTLE BRIAR ROSE.

sleepy stories Phrases suggestive of dozing off, told by opponents in an effort to "hypnotize" their rivals into falling asleep; a device used in Plains Indian hero tales, between the rectum snakes and the hero adventurers. The snakes are anxious to have the heroes sleep so they can crawl inside their rectums and kill them; the heroes wish to put these monsters to sleep so that they can cut their heads off. The heroes win, and kill all but one snake. Two typical Crow Indian "sleepy stories" are: "In the fall, whenever there is a little wind, when we lie in some shelter, when dried weeds rub against each other and we listen, we generally get drowsy, is it not so?" and "At night when we are about to lie down, listening to the wind rustling through the bleached trees, we do not know *how* we get to sleep, but we fall asleep, is it not so?" Both these examples derive from Lowie's recording of the Crow Indian tale of Old Woman's Grandson (Robert H. Lowie, *The Crow Indians*, New York, 1935, p. 145). Sleepy stories are all identical in motivation, yet no two are ever quite the same in the telling. See RECTUM SNAKES; SUBSTITUTE EYES. [EWV]

Sleipnir In Teutonic mythology, Odin's eight-legged grey horse, the son of a giant's powerful stallion and Loki in the guise of a mare. He carried Odin everywhere on his travels and carried Hermod to Hel to try to ransom Balder. Sigurd the Volsung's horse Grane was a son of Sleipnir.

slit-drum A primitive musical instrument made of a log hollowed out by fire or by scraping through a narrow aperture and sounded by stamping with the feet, beating with sticks, or ramming through the slit with poles. Sometimes the shape of the slit is like an H, in which case the two lamellas formed may give different notes. The instrument is conceived of as female, and in many parts of the world is related to the deities of water, the new moon, and fertility. Among the Indians of California, the northeasternmost section in which it is found, it may only be used for dances of secret societies and only in the "house of the spirits." The Saliva tribe of the Orinoco River make their slit drums by hollowing a log with fire and cementing a resonating stone into it. It is suspended from a framework of poles for playing and serves as a musical instrument and as a means of communication. Perhaps the most primitive form of all is the hollowed log placed over a pit crossed by planks and pounded against the planks by a row of men standing in the slot. This type is also still found in South America. The ritual of its sounding celebrates the vanquishing of the old moon by the new. Various forms are found in Indonesia, in Africa, in Melanesia, etc. For further examples and customs, see DRUM.

slow train humor The slow or late train, like the Ford joke (see LIZZIE LABELS), is one of the hardy perennials of the humor that crystallizes popular distrust of new-fangled inventions. In earlier days the speed of trains was the subject of jests and tall tales: "Now I kin git from Bosting to Filadelphy in one day, and I've been cal'latin' that if the power of steam increases for the *next* ten years as it has been doin' for the *last* ten years, I'd be in Filadelphy just two days before I started from Bosting." (B. A. Botkin, *A Treasury of New England Folklore*, New York, 1944, p. 232). Then, as people became accustomed to speed and were irked by the lack of it, it was the slow train that, like other old-fashioned things, appeared funny. Of late, however, the wheel has turned full circle; and with the growth of the short or branch line or "mixed train daily" hobby, the slow train is regarded with nostalgic affection and passionately defended by its fans, while the fast train has again become the subject of jest. "I lit my cigar leaving New York, knocked the ashes out of the window, and they fell on a man's head standing on the platform at Syracuse, three hundred miles away" (Harry G. Jackson, *On a Fast Streamliner*, 1938).

James R. Masterson (*Tall Tales of Arkansaw*, 1942, p. 269) traces the first slow train joke (including the cows that climb aboard the rear car and disturb the passengers) to Mark Twain's *The Gilded Age* (1873) and the first slow-train-in-Arkansas joke to Opie Read's periodical, *The Arkansaw Traveler*, in 1882. The real vogue of Arkansas slow train humor dates from the appearance in 1903 of *On a Slow Train through Arkansas*, the first of the twelve paper-backed jokebooks written and published by Thomas W. Jackson (1867–1934) of Chicago and sold on trains and at railroad stations. On the first page is a variant of the Mark Twain cow story: "One old cow got her tail caught in the cow-catcher and ran off down the track with the train. The cattle bothered us so much they had to take the cow-catcher off the engine and put it on the hind end of the train to keep the cattle from jumping up into the sleeper."

Other states have their slow trains. Indiana: "You may think I'm overdrawing it, but I'm not when I tell you that a fellow took down with typhoid fever on the thing just after I got on, and when I got off at the end of my journey, he was sound and well, and he had a long siege of it too" (George D. Beason, *I Blew in from Arkansaw*, 1908, p. 49). Idaho: "It's so slow that farmers who load hay at Kamiah discover that the cars are empty by the time they reach Lewiston, because cows along the way have eaten it" (*Idaho Lore*, 1939, p. 119).

The classic late train story tells of the engineer who is promised a reward if he brings in his perennially overdue train on time. At last, when it seems as if the impossible has happened and the train arrives on time, the engineer modestly declines (or, in some versions, ironically accepts) the reward, explaining: "This is yesterday's train." Closely related to slow and late train humor are the rough train and the crooked line ("Whenever the conductor wanted the engineer to stop," writes Harry G. Jackson, "he would just swing out going around a curve and slap the engineer on the back").

The humorous extension of railroad initials rings the changes on slow train humor: e.g. Can't and Never Will (Carolina & Northwestern); Delay, Linger, and Wait

(Delaware, Lackawanna & Western); Footsore and Weary (Fort Smith & Western); Leave Kansas and Walk (Leavenworth, Kansas & Western); May Never Arrive (Missouri & Northern Arkansas); Never Did and Couldn't (Newburgh, Dutchess & Connecticut). (See Archie Robertson, *Slow Train to Yesterday*, 1945, p. 24.)

B. A. BOTKIN

Smiera-gatto Literally, the butter cat: a household spirit of the Lapps which goes out and steals butter for the family: analogous to the PARA.

smilax The North American Chippewa Indians used smilax as remedy for kidney trouble. The root was carried in a bag made of bear paws and could be used only by men holding a high degree in the Midewiwin; the Chippewa name for it means "bear root." Combined with other roots, the plant was used in a decoction for ailments of the digestive system. Among the Omaha, fruits of the plant were eaten as a pleasant remedy for hoarseness.

The thorny *Smilax mexicana* is common in Yucatán. In many Mayan Indian churches the crown of thorns on the figures of Christ are made of this smilax. Mexican smilax (called greenbrier) is the source of sarsaparilla.

Smintheus One of the epithets of Apollo: the mouse god. The title either derives from his ability to destroy mice or is a remnant of possible origin in totemism (Lang). According to legend, when Teucer landed in Asia Minor, mice ate the strings off his bows and the handles off his shields. He therefore founded the town of Smintheum (*sminthius* was the Cretan word for mouse) and built a temple to Apollo Smintheus.

Smith, William Robertson (1846–1894) Scottish philologist, physicist, archeologist, Biblical critic, and editor (from 1880) of the 9th edition of the *Encyclopædia Britannica*. His education at Aberdeen University was followed by studies in theology and philosophy at the universities of Bonn and Göttingen. His ideas on Biblical subjects were so far ahead of his time and so unacceptable to the authorities of the Free Church that he was removed from his chair as professor of Oriental languages and Old Testament exegesis at Free Church College, Aberdeen. Later, however, he became professor of Arabic at Cambridge University. Relieved, at the moment, of academic responsibilities, he pursued his studies in Sanskrit. He knew the East intimately since he had visited Arabia, Syria, Palestine, Tunis, and southern Spain. Through his various studies and contacts made during these travels, he became interested in the comparative study of primitive customs. His contributions to these fields of interest include an article, "Sacrifice," for the *Encyclopædia Britannica;* also, *Kinship and Marriage in Early Arabia* (Cambridge, 1885); *Lectures on the Religion of the Semites* (Cambridge, 1889, 1894), each definitive and of permanent value.

Snake Snake functions in African and New World Negro folklore only as a minor character, except in the case of the well-known story of animal gratitude for human aid, where in some areas this creature is protagonist. [MJH]

☞ Snakes of all varieties (or **Snake** as a general character) enter into the myths or religious observances of nearly all American Indian tribes. In the east and southeast the great horned underwater serpent with one

red and one green horn is a powerful, mysterious creature who could be lured to land and to his death by shamans, only when they used the most powerful of all medicines, the ashes from the fireplace of a hut occupied by a menstruating woman, or a few drops of menstrual blood. When the body of the serpent was burned his heart refused to burn, and was cut up and used thereafter, always alive and quivering, as witch medicine.

Another origin story, not of witch medicine bundles, but of a snake ceremony, is told by the Apache Indians of the Southwest. The Apache origin legend of their ceremony to cure rattlesnake bites narrates how Slayer-of-Monsters, returning from a war raid with a companion, kills a porcupine or other animal. The companion cooks and eats the porcupine and is transformed into a snake. Slayer-of-Monsters tells the people (supernaturals); they repair to the spot, track the snake to a river, raise the waters of the river so they can travel beneath the water, find the snake, roll four hoops at it, retransform the snake into his previous human form.

In the Pueblos, especially at Hopi, the Great Horned or Plumed Serpent, a form of sky god, is prominent in sun ceremonies.

In the far west, among the Yokuts of central California, shamans, or men with special powers to whom rattlesnakes had spoken in their dreams, lured the snakes out of their dens in early spring, took them home and at a public ceremony placed the snakes, in a sack, on the heads of spectators. The next day the shamans "cured" these spectators of prospective snake bites by the usual sucking method. After taking these precautions for the health of the community, the snake shamans played with the snakes, threw them about, allowed them to bite their thumbs or hands, and so forth. Finally there occurs the "stepping" rite (rattlesnake stepping rite); the snakes are put in a small hole out of doors, and people come with poles to prod them. The shamans, to ensure the snakes' not being killed, pay each person shell money. Finally each man, woman, and child in the community files past the hole and places the right foot into or over it. This ensures that for a year every snake, when approached, will rattle in warning instead of striking blindly. Songs were attached to the ceremony; one such, is reproduced in A. L. Kroeber, *Handbook of the Indians of California* (*BBAE* 78, Washington, 1925), p. 506, from which the account of this ceremony is taken (pp. 504–06 and 517). The Yuki of northern California also had rattlesnake shamans (Kroeber, pp. 199–200), as did the Shasta in the same general area (Kroeber, p. 303) and the Valley Maidu farther south (Kroeber, p. 427). The Mohave Indians of southern California believe in a gigantic Sky-Rattlesnake who was killed and from whose blood came Rattlesnake, a supernatural being who now lives at Three Mountains, "who has a road to every tribe; who often thinks of war and wants to bite a person . . . Then he asks the mountain. If the mountain says yes, the man will die; but if the mountain is silent, the man will be bitten and live" (Kroeber, pp. 775–76). Mohave shamans treat rattlesnake bites, however, by producing a cooling wind and sprinkle for the patient, and then singing four songs—everyone being forbidden to drink during the curing (Kroeber, pp. 777–78).

Returning to the Southwest, perhaps the most spectacular performance with snakes is the so-called "Snake-Dance" of the Hopi pueblos. Snake-medicine or Snake-

Antelope societies exist not only at Hopi, but in Zuñi and other pueblos; they are in effect usually curing societies, although sometimes they are also war societies. At Hopi, snakes are given prominence and the members of the Snake-Antelope societies perform, every second year, secret kiva rites concerned with snakes, as well as a public snake dance, the striking feature of which is the carrying of live snakes, grasped by their middle in the carrier's mouth, four times each around the plaza. The snake dance, like other Hopi ceremonies, is celebrated largely as a prayer for rain. The origin myth attached to it recounts how Snake Hero and Snake Maid had children who were transformed into snakes; hence the Hopi regard snakes as their elder brothers, and powerful in compelling the Cloud People to bring rain. See *Handbook of the American Indians*, vol. 2, pp. 604–606. [EWV]

Snake-Antelope dance An ancient Hopi ceremonial; a prayer for rain, held in alternate years. One year it is held at the "Snake Rock" in Walpi, in Mishongnovi, and in Chimopovi; the next year in Shipaulovi and Hotevilla. It was discontinued in 1912 in Oraibi. The snakes have rain-bringing power, and are also venerated as legendary ancestors. These "elder brothers" are descended from a Snake hero who married a Snake maiden after a long voyage, and brought forth a progeny of snakes.

Well in advance of the ceremony the medicine men gather snakes and wash them in yucca suds for purification. They gather bull snakes, whip snakes, and rattle snakes. During the secret kiva rituals the young people of the Snake and Antelope societies join in ceremonial races. The public spectacle takes place during the last dry week in August.

1) The Snake and Antelope priests file out of the kiva and circle the plaza four times, stamping during each circuit on the wooden cover of *sipapu*, the entrance to the underworld.

2) To rattles and a guttural chant the lines sway on either side of the brush shelter containing the serpents.

3) They divide into groups of three: the carrier kneels before the head priest and takes a snake in his mouth. The hugger places his left hand on the carrier's shoulder. The gatherer follows. Four times they circle the plaza. The carrier releases the snake and the gatherer retrieves it. Women of the snake clan sprinkle them with cornmeal.

4) They scramble down the cliff and release the serpents to the four directions on their mission for rain.

Snake dances are widespread among Indian tribes, and vestiges of this ceremony remain also at Zuñi, Acoma, and Cochiti. It is separate from the worship of the plumed water serpent, whose cult once extended to Middle America, and which still forms a vital part of Hopi ceremonialism. [GPK]

snake dance Symbolic invocation of the serpent's magical powers by imitation, handling, or a meandering course. 1) In the Haitian vodun cult a man possessed by the *loa* Damballa falls to the ground and writhes like a snake. A Bella Coola *sisaok* dancer may represent his ancestral crest with equal realism. In Europe and Asia the serpent has assumed the humorously horrific form of a dragon. The Balinese *barong* in the *Tjalon Arang* (Witch Play) consists of two men who wriggle the masked

flexible body with quick changing poses of the feet and clapping of jaws. There may be a connection between this dragon, the serpent Kaliya danced to death by Krishna, and the dragon killed by St. George in the medieval Morris play, also the *bicha* or *serpe* of the Portuguese *Mouriscadas*.

2) Live snakes may be carried by dancers, as for instance by the female worshippers of the Dahomean Da and by the snake dancers of the Shoshonean Hopi and Comanche Indians. In the Sierra de Vera Cruz of Mexico all *Negrito* dancers are accompanied by a *Maringuilla* with a live snake in a gourd vessel and are bitten and cured. (Compare ACATLAXQUI.) In the Huichol *hikuli*, the wooden sticks which the dancers manipulate are called snakes. Whips manipulated by the *tlacoloteros* may symbolize serpents. Bella Coola *kusiut* dancers and Kwakiutl women war dancers may manipulate snakes on strings. California Yokut shamans rival for prestige in snake-handling tricks.

3) Frequently American Indians suggest the motion of a snake by the serpentine course, the meandering, the coiling and uncoiling of a long line of dancers guided, as in the Penobscot *yune'ha*, by a leader. The Iroquois, Winnebago, Sauk, and Fox Indians probably derived their versions from the southeastern Cherokee, Creek, Yuchi, and Seminole. The Fox Indian dance is a source of particular pleasure, with its antiphonal songs and parallel follow-the-leader imitation of steps and gestures. Ancient Aztec harvest rites frequently included meandering chain dances for Xipe Totec, and Chicomecoatl (Seven Serpent), but today these dances are extinct. They survive, however, in the snake-figure of the *Quetzales*, and the Maypole meanderings of the Aztecs, Otomí, and Cora of today. Similarly, vestiges of ancient rites survive in the Greek *geranos*, the French *farandoule*, and the concluding "snail" of many open rounds, closed rounds (such as the Kentucky Running Set), and American square dances.

Ordinarily the snake symbolizes the fertility inherent in the earth and rain. To the Dahomean, Da is the principle of life. In the Maya sacred book, *Popol Vuh*, the plumed serpent, together with three pristine creative divinities, produces life and humanity out of immobility and silence cut by the lightning path of Huracán. The winged serpent effigies of the Aztecs and of the prehistoric and modern Pueblo Indians have been identified with incipient life, thunder, lightning, growth, and agriculture. This is evidently the significance of the pre-Columbian Aztec chain-meanderings and the Hopi Snake-Antelope Dance, and probably originally motivated the currently social serpentines of the Woodlands Indians and Europeans. Along with its role as the power of evil, the dragon forms part of vestigial Old World vegetation rites. The snake may be associated in a curious fashion with the bull and the buffalo: the bull enacted by the Huichol Indians is, in their mythology, derived from the deer-snake of Nakawe, Grandmother Growth, and the kilts of the San Ildefonso buffalo dancers are ornamented with a black snake. Candle dances and torch dances commonly follow a serpentine path, as the *gyertyas tánc* and *ball de la teya*, probably by identification of the flickering flame with life and rebirth.

Snake beliefs may be connected with dances without actual enactment. Thus the Yaqui *pascolas* are initiated by walking into a cave-serpent's mouth, being ejected, thereupon meeting the king of snakes, and receiving their gift of knowledge and paraphernalia from the king. Iroquois songs of the *hadi'hi'duus* medicine society and the *deyǫdasǫdayǫ*, or dark dance, refer to the monster serpent that rescued a girl abandoned on an island. The origin legend of the *ʔohgiwe* death feast tells of ancestors devoured by the earth serpent.

In some children's singing games the snake plays the villain: in the southern American Negro "Black Snake, Black Snake, where are you hiding?" the impersonator hides, is taunted by the children, and finally seizes one, who is thereupon "it." See SNAKE-ANTELOPE DANCE. [GPK]

snakeroot Any of various plants whose roots are used for the cure of snakebite. 1) *Senega snakeroot (Polygala senega)* or milkwort; mountain flax. This plant, whose medicinal virtues were taught to the Scotch physician, Dr. Tennent, by the North American Seneca Indians, proved so effective in pneumonia and pleurisy, and later in asthma and rheumatism, that he sent it to London. Largely through his work it became so well known as a cure-all that it was purportedly added to all the nostrums of the quacks and charlatans, along with such staples as snake oil and swamp water. The Meskwaki Indians use the root tea as their chief remedy for heart trouble. Among the Chippewa it is carried on journeys as a charm to assure good health and safety. In Europe it is known as Rogation flower and is carried in processions on the Rogation Days.

2) *White snakeroot* A plant of the genus *Eupatorium* which is named for the king of Pontus, Eupator Mithridates, who is said to have first used it as an antidote for poison. It was not always a beneficial plant, for cattle eating the plant in the United States caused a mysterious disease known as "milk sickness" which started in Colonial times and continued periodically until 1920, reaching its height in the 1830's. It is said to have killed off a quarter of the settlers of Madison County, Ohio. It was also rife in Illinois and Indiana during this period and killed off about ten percent of the settlers in the frontier region. Even after its cause was known, it continued to break out periodically. The Meskwaki Indians used this plant as a steaming agent in their sweat baths and as a diuretic. Another plant of this genus is the Joe-Pye weed which, besides being a snakebite cure, was used in a tea to cure arrow wounds by the Navaho.

3) *Black snakeroot* (genus *Cimicifuga*) was used by the Algonquians as a balm for aching joints; it was later taken over by the settlers and is still used for rheumatism.

sneezing Whether sneezing is a good or a bad sign depends on the culture you happen to belong to. It may also be the sign that a devil or evil spirit is trying to get out of the body. The historian Carlo Signonio reports that the Christian custom of saying "God bless you" when somebody sneezed started in the 6th century when Gregory the Great was Pope and an epidemic was raging, though the custom was in fact originally a Latin one. In early Christian times the sign of the cross was made. This was later opposed by the church. Popular usage disregards this opposition. In New Guinea the people wish health and prosperity to the chief when he sneezes. The Koita of British New Guinea believe that sneezing in sleep is a sign that the soul has come back to the body. It is bad not to sneeze for some weeks because the soul must be far away. The Zulus return

thanks when they sneeze; if a sick man does not sneeze he is very ill. Among the Tonga sneezing before a journey is a bad sign. Jamaica Negroes believe that if your nose itches someone is saying bad things about you. In North Carolina, you will hear of a death if you sneeze at a meal. In Estonia if two pregnant women sneeze together, they will have girls; if two husbands sneeze, their children will be boys. In Germany it is bad luck to sneeze while putting on shoes; but to sneeze in conversation means that the last statement was true. The Moslems wash their noses out with water because the devil visits it at night. The ancient Persians uttered prayers when they sneezed because a fiend in the body was coming out and persons who heard the sneeze also prayed, presumably to keep the fiend out of their own bodies. The Hindus also believe sneezes have to do with spirits entering or leaving by way of the nose. It is unlucky to sneeze at the threshold of a house, and a person who hears somebody sneeze while he is beginning work has to stop and begin all over again. The ancient Hebrews thought men sneezed once and died. Among the Greeks, sneezing was a favorable or divine omen. When her son Telemachus sneezed after Penelope prayed that her husband be returned, she took it as an omen that her prayers would be answered. [RDJ]

societies In anthropological usage, an esoteric, formally organized group of related or unrelated men or women, or both, within larger local units, who meet together to practice established rites and ceremonies, chiefly of a religious nature, but which may also pertain to witchcraft, war, or other pursuits. Membership in a society may be attained by payment of goods, as in the Plains Indian age-grade and ungraded societies, and in the Eastern Woodlands Grand Medicine Society (see MIDEWIWIN), by inheritance, as in certain Eastern Woodlands witch societies, by virtue of social status, as in the North Pacific Coast cannibal society (see BLACK TAMANOUS), or be incurred as a civic responsibility, as in the numerous Pueblo Indian weather control, crop control, game control, war, witch control, curing, clown and other so-called societies, cults, or priesthoods. The origin of many of the North American Indian societies is explained in tribal origin myths; often the supreme deity is said to have taught the people the rites of various societies, for their benefit, and to have enjoined them never to let these rites fall into abeyance. (See HULKI'LAL WOK; NANABOZHO.) For a detailed treatment of Southwestern Pueblo societies see Elsie Clews Parsons, *Pueblo Indian Religion* (2 vols., Chicago, 1939), vol. 1, pp. 112–69; for Plains Indian societies see Robert H. Lowie, *The Crow Indians*, New York, 1935. [EWV]

☞ The African distribution of secret societies includes much of the Guinea Coast area and the Congo basin. Some of the better known of these societies are the Poro and Sande of Sierra Leone and Liberia, the Egungun and Oro of Nigeria, and the Leopard Societies of the Congo basin peoples. Membership in African secret societies, like those elsewhere in the world, is mainly restricted to persons of one sex, and societies for males far outnumber those of females. These societies function as educational institutions and as instruments of political and social control. The Sierra Leone Poro provides a course of study that includes the teaching of crafts as well as those elements in the culture which must be controlled by a man before he can take his place as an adult; the Sande is a similar institution for young women, though the period of training is somewhat shorter. Other societies, such as the Oro, functioning politically, supervise the actions of the ruler, deposing him if his policies run counter to those adopted by the heads of the secret organizations. Leopard societies are best known for the social controls they exert; offenders against accepted codes of behavior are visited at night, taken from their huts, and subjected to punishment. One outstanding characteristic of African secret societies is the fact that their sanctions derive from supernatural forces—deities, magic, and spirits of the dead. In some parts of the area where they might be expected to be found they are not present because they constituted a challenge to the established political regime. This was the case in the kingdoms of Ashanti and of Dahomey. The problem of their absence in East and South Africa has not been solved. However, it is not unreasonable to assume that the prevalence of age-sets in these parts of the continent may provide at least some explanation for this. [MJH]

Sogbo Chief of the Thunder pantheon of Dahomey. The designation Sogbo is used by those vowed to the worship of the Thunder deities, and is the same being as Agbe which is the name given this god by those who follow the Sky deities. See AGBE; XEVIOSO. [MJH]

Sol In ancient Roman religion, the personified sun as a deity: equivalent to the Greek Helios or Phœbus Apollo. Sol Invictus was an epithet of Mithra.

solstice dances Celebrations in dance form to aid the changing of the sun's course, particularly in its return at midwinter. Solstice ritual is practically universal. Naturally it strikes opposite seasons in the northern and southern hemispheres. Thus the Inca *Inti raimi* observes the winter solstice in June, and *capac raimi*, the summer solstice in December. Agricultural peoples are particularly dependent on the cycle of the seasons, but hunters, too, rejoice at the return of a new year or the height of the summer. Thus the Sioux Indian sun dance takes place the end of June.

These rituals are well preserved among the Pueblo Indians. Though they show considerable variations, they are all associated with kachina dances, corn and meal, and war society ceremonies. The Keresan winter solstice, includes all-night ceremonies with prayer-sticks and offerings to the dead and to a sun-image bundle, mock combats between kivas, and the return of the kachina. These dance for three months after the winter solstice and again for three after the less important summer solstice. The Hopi Soyal follows immediately after the men's society fire-making ritual, and includes sun, prayer-stick making, war, curing, and phallic rites, kachina dances, and special Hawk Dances by Hawk Man and Soyala Woman with various ceremonial officials. Walpi also impersonates supernaturals, Cloud, Hail, Ice, etc., and dramatizes the placing of the sun. A most essential feature of the Zuñi Itiwana dances is the making of a new sacred fire, with dances by the kachina of the Big Firebrand Society and Blue Horn exorcisers, and carrying out of refuse and ashes by all people on the 19th day. Snake and growth rituals and a round dance are included in the Jemez *pesa* (sun-work) in December

and June, in the Tewa winter *t'ant'aii* (sun lives now), and Isleta *nape'i* by Corn groups for drawing down the sun.

Solstice was evidently a matter of great importance in pre-Christian Europe, considering the functional vestiges of today. *Perchten, Schemen,* and other maskers and *Moriscas* exorcise evil spirits and mime the victory of the New Year, from Christmas to Carnival (a gradual shifting of dates). St. John's Day (June 24), the substitute for the ancient summer solstice, retains many fertility practices, and virtually pan-European fire-jumping and round dancing at night. Processions and *Moriscas* abound at this time in Catholic Europe and Middle America. It is interesting to find common elements in the contrasting Pueblo and western European customs, particularly the new fire concept and mimic combat. [GPK]

Soma In Vedic mythology, the god of the soma-juice and of the moon; also, the lord of stars, plants, and Brāhmans. Soma, said to be son of Atri or to have been produced at the Churning of the Ocean, married the 27 (or 33) daughters of Daksha (the Naksatras), but neglected all except Rohiṇī. Daksha, therefore, cursed him to die of consumption. But as Soma grew weaker, so all creatures weakened, until Daksha mitigated his curse to the extent that the moon should wane and wax each month. From Soma came the lunar race of kings. He carried off Tārā, wife of Brihaspati, thus causing the war of the gods which is described in the *Purāṇas* and the epics. She bore him Budha (Mercury) from whom stemmed the lunar race.

The soma plant (*Asclepiacida* or *Sarcostemma viminale*) provides an astringent narcotic juice regarded as having divine power. It was offered, mixed with milk, butter, barley, and water, to the gods, but was drunk by all Aryans. Later only the three upper castes were permitted to drink it and then only for religious ceremonies, while a rice-brandy, *surā*, became popular generally. The soma sacrifice was one of the two chief rituals (the other being fire-worship) of the *Ṛig-Veda*. Consequently Soma, as a personification of the juice of the plant, was a prominent deity, occupying the third most important place among the Vedic gods. Soma was the "lord of plants." Its original home was heaven but it was brought to earth by an eagle. Compare HAOMA. See AMṚITA; AŚVINS; EAGLE; ECLIPSES; INDRA.

Somnus The Roman god of sleep: identified with the Greek Hypnos. Somnus is the twin of Death, and is a pleasant youth, carrying a poppy and a horn from which he dispenses sleep. His nature is contrasted with that of Death, smooth and pleasant against vicious and grasping; but in later times both Sleep and Death became different aspects of the same god.

sonajeros The exciting dance of the rattlers (from *sonaja*, rattle) popular throughout Jalisco, Mexico: made famous by the group from Tuxpan, an Aztec town. Fifteen young men in colorful costume violently shake their huge painted sistrum-like rattles and, to the accompaniment of a drum and shrill flutes, perform in single file the difficult acrobatic steps and stamps. [GPK]

song: folk song and the music of folk song Folk song comprises the poetry and music of groups whose literature is perpetuated not by writing and print, but through oral tradition. These groups, primarily rural, are better able to preserve some of the older culture of the national unit of which they form a part, than the population of the cities with its more sophisticated, more international civilization, which is subject to faster changes and fluctuations of fashion. Folk song is thus part of folk culture, which is distinct from that of the cities and represents only certain facets of the culture of the nation.

The concept of "folk," incorporated in "folklore," denotes a group in which the cultural, economic, and educational diversity of the city is much less pronounced, where modes of life, customs, and lore, including songs, are known and shared more homogeneously throughout the group; where the cultural possessions of the individual more nearly resemble those of his neighbor. Just as folk culture contrasts with city culture, so folk song—which embraces folk music—contrasts with the poetry, popular song, and art music of the city.

This dichotomy, perhaps a little oversimplified, holds for the old European folk community and its life which were preserved on the whole better in the east and the south than in the north and the west of Europe, until comparatively recently. This life is changing and breaking down very rapidly. The generalizations presented here need or will soon need qualifications; they pertain to the past and the near-past which lingers in the present. An important qualification pertains to the United States. Perhaps because this country, from its inception, did not perpetuate the old rigid European class society with its true "peasant" class, the distinction between "folk" and "urban" was and is less clear cut here. As a result, the United States will be cited repeatedly for exceptions to the general picture.

Folk songs flourish in rural areas in the Western world, and also in the Orient and the Far East. However, the great classic traditions of the urban literatures of China, Japan, and other countries of southeast Asia, of India, and the Arabic countries, have preëmpted the interest of students not only in the West, but to a large extent also in these countries themselves. Our knowledge of Near Eastern and Oriental folk song is as yet too cursory to justify specific treatment in this article. It may be borne in mind, however, that the general characteristics of folk song recur wherever it is found.

In so-called primitive or preliterate societies there is no contrast between folk and urban groups, and between traditional and cultivated arts. For that reason, as well as for the fact that primitive poetry and music represent varied and large fields of their own, their songs are not treated here. But see the bibliography following for references to primitive song.

Like all other forms of verbal folk arts, such as the folktale and proverb, folk song is perpetuated by *oral tradition*. Even when folk singers are literate, they rarely use writing for their songs. If we take the word of a folk singer from Tennessee for it, "They ain't nary grain of use setting song ballets down in writing to keep." [1] Writing down the words in song-books is a comparatively recent practice and is perhaps stronger in this country than elsewhere.[2] There is no music writing in folk groups except when introduced from the city; songs are learned and remembered by hearing. Here we have a characteristically American exception, in the existence of the "shape-note" notation of our hymn tradition.[3]

Although folk song is *perpetuated* by oral tradition, not all folk song needs to have *originated* in oral tradi-

tion and by folk creation. The discussions as to whether songs which are sung in a folk setting but came from the city are to be considered "true folk songs" are perhaps beside the point. Folk songs are best defined as songs which are current in the repertory of a folk group; the study of their origin is another matter. The repertory of the village or the countryside and that of the city have exchanged some of their products time and again. Much influence has been at work in both directions. Folklore, according to one theory, descends from higher to lower groups in the social scale; it has also often ascended from lower to higher groups.

The folk song of most countries has often been exposed to the influence of the music and poetry of the cities. Ballads in the folk tradition especially of Western Europe were strongly affected by broadsides, and many indeed began their life as broadside poems. Many ballad texts of the Anglo-American folk tradition show decidedly the effect of the publications of the broadside presses, chiefly in Great Britain: the "black-letter" ballads, which continued to appear until about 1700, and the 18th and 19th century "white-letter" or "stall ballads." [4]

A few other outside influences on folk-song tradition may be briefly noted here. The religious folk hymnology of some reformed countries or denominations has been shown to consist chiefly of folk melodies which after modifications imposed by editors and composers became current again in folk usage.[5]

In the United States we must recognize the importance, particularly in the 19th century, of various forces—songsters,[6] minstrel shows, and medicine shows [7]—in bringing songs into the folk tradition. Herbert Halpert and other collectors who have reported on their folk song field work during the 1930's report also the strong influence of the so-called "hillbilly" and "race" records,[8] and the growing traces of the activities of school teachers and recreation leaders in introducing or reintroducing singing games and play-party songs.

The purist often looks exclusively for those songs which to him are the most original and distinctive expression of the special character of the folk culture. But we must be aware that there are no "pure" folk art styles, as there are no "pure" cultures or races. All styles have grown and benefited through assimilating influence and material from other folk groups or from the city. Whatever the sources, however, it is oral circulation that is the best general criterion of what is a folk song. The singer himself is rarely aware, as a matter of fact, of the ultimate origin of his material. But once incorporated, outside material is apt to be molded by the same forces which shape the authentic products of folk tradition all along.[9]

There is usually no technique of teaching, certainly no formal technique, connected with the making and singing of folk songs; they are learned by ear, and transmitted in this fashion from generation to generation. Nor is there a conscious awareness of form or construction on the part of the folk singer; there is no esthetic or analytic theory in his mind. Training and rehearsing, essential earmarks of our technically sophisticated musical practice, are on the whole absent. A few exceptions are found here and there, especially with instrumentalists whose skill is more likely to be recognized as such, whereas the capacity to use the voice is apparently taken for granted.

Folk song is an art in which the average member of the group participates more generally than is the case with the cultivated music or literature of the city. Nearly everyone in a folk group knows songs and sings them, or at least listens to them and knows a good deal about them. On the many occasions at which singing is by a group, the less outstanding singers have ample opportunities for participating. Skill and a good voice, however, are appreciated; better equipped singers are recognized for their aptitude; and a less accomplished singer may not necessarily perform in the hearing of others.

Different standards apply in different places when it comes to the question of what makes a folk singer outstanding in the estimation of his group. A good or pleasing voice is often appreciated but hardly essential; a good memory is usually prized. In the Baltic countries collectors speak of old women singers who knew thousands of songs or verses; elsewhere hundreds of songs were occasionally collected from single individuals. In the United States a singer is often praised for his repertory by the formula: "He can sing all night and never repeat."

General participation does not exclude some specialization in folk song. Some types go with age: Children's game songs are rarely sung by adults. Many calendric songs, for instance Christmas carols, may be sung primarily by children or youngsters, because of custom. Love songs are not apt to be sung by old people. In many countries, some songs, e.g. lullabies, are more properly sung by women, others by men. In Yugoslavia, lyrical songs, ballads, and some other types of songs are called "women's songs." They are sung by men too, however, only in some areas less frequently than by women. The contrast is with the protracted heroic epic songs which the literature calls "men's songs"; they are hardly ever sung by women.[10]

Specialization may be connected with the role an individual plays on a given occasion. In the elaborate marriage ceremonies of eastern Europe the bride says good-by to her family by singing special songs; the best man and other participants have their own songs. There are finally cases which approach a level of professionalization. Good singers of the Yugoslav heroic epic songs are respected for their skill, and they function as recognized entertainers. In earlier centuries they were bards at the small feudal courts.[11] In Ireland and in eastern Europe, old women are regularly called in at burials because of their recognized excellence in "keening," or in singing dirges and farewells to the dead person in behalf of the bereaved family. But there is little economic manifestation of true professionalism: modest gifts, feasting, and drinks rather than pay are the returns these performers are offered. Instrumentalists are more likely to receive some monetary recompense.

Such specialization approaches the professionalism of the city musician. What is significant is the comparative rarity of this development in folk practice. For the cultivated arts there is a distinction between the artist, the connoisseur, and the lowbrow. In poetry, we have the poet, occasionally the performer, and the reader; in music the composer, the performer, and the concert audience. In folk song these levels are much less distinct. The dividing line between performer and listener is tenuous. Performance by an individual does not as a rule depend upon special professional skills laboriously acquired, and the group, instead of forming a silent audience, participates in many songs and on many occasions.

The distinction between creator and performer is also a tenuous one. Normally, the original composer of a folk song is not known at all. The art itself is much less dependent on new creations produced by every generation. The number of songs newly made during a given generation is usually quite small in a folk group. By the time the song has spread over an area and through a generation or two, the name of the originator of the song is usually forgotten. Folk songs are normally not created by a process comparable to that of our composer or poet who is expected to manifest some degree of originality. The body of folk song grows, rather, through a process of re-creation of materials already in existence. Phillips Barry and others coined the phrase "communal re-creation" for this process; a fortunate phrase which contrasts with the outmoded origin theory of a communal, group creation of folk song.[12] Still, it is not the community as such, but individuals *within* the community who are active in the process. Singers constantly add, often unconsciously, their small modifications. These changes in time lead gradually to different local versions and variants,[13] to regional variants, to the growth of song-families,[14] and to the branching-off and emergence of new texts and melodies. The creative process is not one begun and finished by a single individual; it is spread over many individuals and generations, and it never comes to an end as long as the tradition is alive. This is certainly one reason why folk song is anonymous, and has no true owner. Possession of a song is more a matter of social courtesy in a folk group. A song made by an individual, or one that he sings especially well, or one that is his special favorite, may be considered "his" so that when he is present it may be left to him to sing the song, as a matter of deference.

Folk song is often said to be more *functional* in its use or application than cultivated poetry or music. In the life of the old European folk community, singing accompanied important periods or turning-points in the individual's life, such as childhood, marriage, and death, and was also part of many important activities of the group.

There is a large group of songs concerned with these turning points in a person's life. Each of these may be marked with great elaboration in song usage. We may cite, for example, the unusual variety of songs for children which survived in the French Pyrénées. There, in addition to the ubiquitous lullabies, songs were collected which are used to teach the child to walk, to help him use his fingers, to teach him numbers and counting, to wake him, to urge him to eat his meals, to teach him to be industrious and good-natured, and so on.[15] In short, songs form an important adjunct of child-training in this area, and a similar picture may have been prevalent in the life of the old European village.

Children's game and round songs are found wherever there is folk song. They often contain fragments of songs of grown-ups, and reflections of grown-up activities, connected with mimetic play. In some of them there may be survivals of fragments of pre-Christian rites and usages, but these elements, while of historical interest, have no functional significance today.

Love, courtship, and marriage are the topics of innumerable songs; teasing songs to pair off courting couples and songs of elaborate marriage rituals are common especially in eastern Europe. Courting songs are often connected with winter evening gatherings of the young people, under the supervision of some older women, for the performance of various household tasks such as spinning or the husking of corn. Special songs are sung on such occasions in eastern Europe and the Balkans, while in some areas any entertainment songs would do, as at the corn-husking bees which were popular in this country.

Burying the dead is an important social occasion in the life of the village. While the wailing and the dirges furnish a socially patterned outlet for grief, they also form part, and the most dramatic part, of the setting of display and elaboration which surrounds the occasion.

Another large group of songs may be called *calendric;* they are sung on special days or during special periods of the year. Many of these songs may well go back to pagan antecedents and practices which became associated with the holidays of the Christian calendar so that the custom of singing such songs survived mainly by virtue of the association with the official calendar of the Church. Songs at Christmas, New Year, and Easter are almost universal in our folk society. Other important occasions with which special songs are connected are May Day, the solstices, and the name-days of various saints. Christmas and New Year's songs are usually sung by children or young people, bringing the good news and blessings and asking for gifts. Christmas is also the time when the most widely known folk plays, those dealing with the Nativity, are performed. The folk plays are replete with songs. While not all of these plays are of folk origin, they have been incorporated into folk practice and style.[16] In some Slavic countries where one's name-day is more important than one's birthday, special songs are sung during the family rite (*slava*) held on the name-day of the master of the house.

The more specifically agricultural calendar is also represented in the functional array of folk songs. Songs connected with agricultural activities include various types of work songs, such as those for harvesting and threshing; songs connected with the cultivation of different plants; and the songs accompanying the tasks of the winter. Songs for rain-magic are still sung in eastern Europe. In some Catholic countries this custom has been modified so that the village priest and the villagers go out in procession to the fields and ask for rain by singing religious hymns.

Dance songs are in one sense on the borderline of functional folk song. They come from two general sources. The simpler dances such as round dances are apt to be rather old. Many of them must have had ritualistic connotations, which today are usually forgotten. Other dances, often more intricate, have come in through city influences. Most of them are sung or played for sheer entertainment.

As against the specifically functional songs, all regions in the Western world have a great profusion of songs which are generally performed by individuals, purely for entertainment and enjoyment, or as an emotional outlet. They require no set, formal occasions and at least ostensibly serve no social or group purpose. These are the epic songs: the heroic epics, ballads, and ro-

mances; and lyrical songs including humorous, teasing, and mocking songs, and the like. In view of the rich and varied content of these categories, it is hardly true today that folk song is predominantly functional, in contrast with its use for entertainment or for esthetic satisfaction.

It is rather likely that at one time folk song was dominated by a more functional character. There are various reasons for this assumption. Functional songs are very often simpler, less artistic, and less varied in content than the other groups. This holds equally for texts and tunes. They are less often influenced by the city (although the Christmas carols of England, France, and Germany form an exception here. On the other hand, the Christmas carols in some districts of Rumania form the richest and most varied category of local folk songs, although this development is purely rural, not due to city influence.[17]) They may represent more archaic developments in folk song. It is significant in this connection that proportionately more functional songs are found in eastern and southern Europe: regions where the life of the old village-community survived, at least until recent times, on the whole better than in western and northern Europe where urban influences have been at work longer and more intensively.[18]

It should be borne in mind, however, that the distinction between functional and non-functional songs, while useful, is somewhat crude. It may be better to think of the contrast as one between obvious social or group function, which can be observed on the surface, and psychological function, which affects the individual more intimately—in the lyrical songs, for instance—and in which the social connotations are more subtle, submerged, but by no means absent.

The relation of functional and esthetic purposes, which has been discussed intensively and time and again, is even in folk art not a simple one; these are not mutually exclusive categories. The esthetic element never needs to be absent when functional songs are performed, but it is difficult to demonstrate. In some cases language usage is illuminating. For example, the women who in eastern Europe specialize in wailing and in mourning songs for the dead are compared with each other as to how "beautifully" they wail. Yet, the folk singer has apparently little *conscious* esthetic awareness, and his vocabulary is not articulate on such subjects. A song which is liked is referred to much more often as a "good" song than as a "beautiful" one.

A catalog of the types of songs which are sung, and of the various uses to which they are put, to some extent reflects the life and customs of a folk community. But there is a more rewarding if more difficult approach to the question of the role of folk song in its social setting. To what extent does the *content,* and even style, of folk songs serve as an expression of the social background, of the present and the past of the community? Early theorists and collectors offered a somewhat romantic answer. Man living closer to the natural environment was thought to be a more "natural" man. Being closer to the soil, he was viewed as being closer also to grasping his own life. His songs, lacking the artificial refinements, distortions, and self-consciousness which cultivated art often showed, were thought to speak always directly and immediately of the feelings and problems of singer and listener. But these philosophical generalities do not stand up under scrutiny. The relation of the life of the group to its expression in its songs remains an intricate one that needs much further study.

It is striking how often themes and elements are found in folk song which are foreign to the life-mode and experience of the group. American farmers sing surprising numbers of British ballads concerned with the fate of lords and ladies, with their castles, gold, and milk-white steeds. The name of the place, of the hero or heroine, may change and be adjusted to the singer's locale; but the setting and action appropriate to the feudal upper class changed only in a few cases to that of the American or English farmer. At the same time, the picture is hardly a very realistic one; it is a rustic "literary" conception of feudal or upper-class life. Such songs must serve fantasy and fancy, but it is rarely admitted that they do just that. It is usually assumed in a folk community that ballads represent true happenings. The glamor of strange adventures and occupations is powerful; songs about sailors and cowboys are popular in this country in regions far from the sea and from the cattle country. (Many of the cowboy songs, as we know, were actually written in the East but were accepted quite hospitably in the cattle country.)

It is equally striking how much stereotyping occurs in folk song. An obvious example is the choice of the physical type of the actors. In Hungarian folk songs the country girl is always brunette, the city girl—referred to as a Miss, not as a "girl"—is invariably a blonde. In actual fact, the majority of the population at large are brunette, and the proportion of blondes in the cities is not much higher than in the countryside. Yet the songs treat blondness as an urban—and thus upper-class—feminine characteristic. And if one judged by the folk songs, he would assume there are no blond men in the whole land. Physical surroundings may be idealized; one's village is pleasant and pretty in eastern European folk song, never tumbledown; the land is good black farming land, never barren, whatever the actual surroundings.

More surprising perhaps is the frequency of the recurrence of some topics and situations in folk song, and the rarity of others. In the tragic British ballads, love is the paramount source of clash and tragedy, disappointment in love leads to death, and death is the only real tragedy. On the other hand, complaints about being separated from one's beloved are comparatively rare in British lyrical songs, in contrast with many more in French songs and an exceedingly large number in eastern Europe. Some of these stereotyped themes no doubt spread from country to country, for example the marriage complaint of the husband, which is always humorous (our *Willie Weaver*) or of the wife which is very often serious, or tragic. The humorous complaints of the wife in the French "maumariée" songs represent a special type. Other themes seem more restricted and localized. The forbidding or inimical stepmother recurs constantly in some eastern European countries; she is never kind or helpful. In the folk songs of western Europe she is seldom mentioned, except in ballads, although she is not a rare figure in folktales. The same contrast holds for the orphan; a frequent and pitiable image in Slovak, Hungarian, and Yugoslav folk songs, but rare in western Europe.

These phenomena call for explanation, whether by considering differences in social structure and attitudes,

or by trying to substantiate speculative assumptions concerning the role of psychological factors in folk song: of indirection, sublimation, over-emphasis, day-dream wishes, or of the avoidance and even repression of some topics and attitudes. In British folk songs crime and violence are usually portrayed in some exotic setting or at some distance: the world of lords, of past history, the high seas, or the highways. Violence of the kind that must have been displayed or felt time and again in the daily life of the village seems absent from the picture. Antagonisms, rivalries, brawls, family tensions, hostilities of the more common and less glamorous sort; these rarely show up in direct portrayal. In some eastern European countries the picture is much more realistic. The incidence of open hostile acts in the village may have been occasionally higher than in the average English village, and the socially permissible expression of hostility may have been at some points more free. Yet, undoubtedly one factor is whether or not such topics are proper or permissible, within the standards of the style. In English folk songs, it would seem, there is a reflection of a desire, hardly conscious, to represent life as more pleasant and livable than it often must have been. The trials of old age, of disease, land shortage, poverty, of failure, rarely appear on the scene. The songs of the United States Negro form a striking contrast here.[19] Of the difficulties the English peasant had with the big landowners there is little trace if any, although possibly British collectors have slighted local and more recent songs which express some of these attitudes.

The long history of the inferior and precarious position of the peasant class throughout Europe, which in some countries continued up to the very near past, found little overt expression in folk song. Again, the tone of many U. S. Negro songs, with their sharp expression of an awareness of the position of the group, and occasionally of protest, is rather unique.

One should mention, however, the figure of the bandit and highway-robber. He is present in most European countries, either as a legendary hero of the past with a cycle of great deeds, like Robin Hood, or as a less heroic and more contemporary figure. He may be a stranger to the village scene, or instead, as the Hungarian peasants phrase it, "the bad one of the village." There are signs of identification with these figures. In Hungary they are called "poor fellows"—they have no home or hearth. Many Slovak, Hungarian, and Ruthenian lyrical songs bemoan their loneliness and sad life. At times they are indistinguishable—both in folk song and in historical reality—from other homeless figures whom national defeats, religious strife, and unsuccessful revolutions forced to live the life of the outcast, the fugitive, and the exile. Another sign of identification is the charitable role these figures usually play in all European folk song: they pursue only the rich. Yet, the flouting of the law is not condoned in the songs: the picture of heroic daring merges with one of crime. The bandit-heroes are almost invariably caught and taken to their execution, and often the song represents the subject telling his own story as he is taken to the gallows, with the proper moralistic warning to his listeners closing the song.

These few examples may suffice to indicate some possible leads for future study in the functional aspects of folk song. This type of analysis is hardly foreign to the literary scholar. Still, the student of folk song—or of folklore in general—will benefit from greater familiarity with the views and findings of social scientists such as the ethnologist or anthropologist, the sociologist, and the social psychologist.

The Music of Folk Song

The general characteristics of folk song as a verbal art hold equally for folk song as a musical art. On the musical level too, we find that form and content are not fixed with the rigidity of cultivated music codified in writing or print. Flexibility and variability characterize the tune as well as the text of a folk song.

Melodies which have spread over an area are apt to show considerable variation, and even major differences, between their versions in different localities. Often singers in the same community give a different form to the melody. Even within the song itself, while the tune is repeated for different stanzas, changes may be introduced which go beyond what could be expected from differences in the text. Nor is it very surprising if a folk singer sings a tune somewhat differently on different occasions. Far from ascribing these phenomena to a lack of formal assurance, we must interpret them as manifestations of a flexibility which is a basic characteristic of all traditional music.[20] It is after the folk tradition has become somewhat rigid, as in England, or even petrified, as in Germany, that this creative flexibility disappears. New forms of melody or new melodies branch out from old ones through variations on the basic "theme" of the melody, rather than by sudden innovation. The number of new tunes which appear in a given generation through individual composition is often quite small.

It is noteworthy that the cultivated music of the Orient is dominated by these very same forces, and even its indigenous musical theory is based on a recognition of them. The *maqām* system upon which Arabic music and the *rāga* system upon which Hindu music is built at first appear to be comparable to our "mode" system, but they can be understood only if we perceive them as systems of different melodic models which in execution are exceedingly elastic and fluid. The mode system of Gregorian church music itself presented great difficulties when applied to the body of traditional Gregorian melodies until the paramount role of recurrent melodic formulas and models was taken into consideration.

If we look at the field of folk song again, we find that while folk singers at times argue about the correct words of a song, they seldom do so when it comes to variations between different renditions of the tune. When their attention is called to such differences, they are apt to react the way a folk singer from Tennessee did: "Every person has got a born right to sing hit his own way."[21] The singer is usually still less aware of the changes in the tune as it is repeated stanza by stanza. These may affect the rhythm, the melody and its intonation, and even the structure, but the basic pattern of the melody is apt to remain intact. Occasionally special factors can complicate the picture, for instance when the singer is acquainted with different forms of the melody, perhaps learned from different sources, so that his rendition oscillates between them. Yet, it is usually the melodic flexibility rather than "faulty memory" which is manifested here.[22]

This flexibility no doubt has been the major factor in the development of regional variants of well-known melodies. In this country at least one hundred melodies have been collected for *Barbara Allen;* most of them are closely related descendants of three or four tunes. It is not surprising, then, that melodies, like song texts, have often found their way even across national and language boundaries, whether because of their popularity or because they were carried along by special influences. Many tunes of the *Twelve Apostles,* for example—an incremental song which is found in numerous versions in almost every European nation—show similarities which suggest that the text spread together with a tune. Not much study has been devoted as yet to this general problem of the migration of single melodies, and accidental similarities between simple tunes or motifs must be carefully distinguished from actual cases of "wandering melodies."[23]

Folk music, like folk poetry, has assimilated very much extraneous material, and depending upon the culture history of the region it has been subject to influences of varying intensity from the city. But here, too, the question of ultimate sources and influences, while of great interest to the historian, should not let us lose sight of the question of what folk tradition has done with melodies which it received from the outside or from "above." Some scholars have stressed cases in which intrusive melodies became disorganized and impoverished, in the process of *Zersingen.* Others have demonstrated, to the contrary, the regenerative forces through which folk music improves its material rather than wearing it down. Much depends here on the bias of the scholar, including bias generated by the specific setting of the case. Only a dispassionate appraisal of United States Negro folk songs can show, for example, that while so much of the melodic material has white antecedents, a *distinctive creative reshaping* has taken place rather than mere imitation and disorganization. Returning, however, to the question in general, undoubtedly while the tradition is alive the destructive forces are weaker in folk music than the constructive ones.

Where neighboring peoples are in intimate contact, and especially where they intermingle, much more exchange of melodies takes place than otherwise so that it becomes at times exceedingly difficult to trace the original source of the melodies. Stylistic features of one style may invade the style of another group so that the musical description of the style of a national body of folk song becomes in some cases difficult. It is not too easy today to decide whether a melody which is popular in the British Isles or in the United States is of English, Irish, Scots, or Welsh origin.[24]

The folk music of colonizers offers many points of interest. In some cases they preserve their old music better than the mother country. Anglo-American melodies have retained some old musical features—the modal cast, old pentatonic scales, and an ornamented manner of singing (found chiefly in our South)—better than the original melodies in England. French-Canadian melodies preserved traits which are now rare or have died out in France.[25] Among Sephardic Jews, who kept intact many features of the Spanish spoken at the time of their expulsion from Spain, many tunes of romances survived in a more archaic form than those recorded in Spain. The Volga-German colonies represent a similar case.[26] Often the melodies themselves disappeared in the mother country before they could be recorded, but they could be recovered in the new territories. But instead of remaining conservative, the style of the migrants may develop new types and novel flavors in its new surroundings. In the United States it did both. In other cases impoverishment was the outcome. In many Latin-American countries, for instance, one would hardly guess from the folk music at the richness of the folk music of Spain, although the song texts often fared much better.[27] Tunes from Italian light operatic music and German popular melodies displaced very much of the original Spanish musical lore.

Textual Form

The following observations are not meant to be comprehensive but may be useful for the reader as a preliminary to the discussion of the relation of text and music.

Folk song is characterized by the prevalence of small forms. While the stanza is by no means universal, it is very general. In the stanza a number of lines constitute a unit which is usually repeated throughout the song. Different forms can be distinguished according to the number of lines in the stanza, and according to the various features which make for the pattern of the stanza structure.

In folk song, especially in western and central Europe, the most frequent stanza length is one of four lines. If the number of lines is larger, this is often the result of extension by repeating lines or by the use of a refrain. Although shorter stanza forms are not unknown in the West—very many French and Spanish folk songs are based on couplets—they are on the whole more common in eastern Europe. In Yugoslavia, for instance, four-line stanzas are clearly comparatively recent and due to foreign influence. Shorter stanza forms of two or three lines may have been in general older; scholars working on western European ballads have come to such a conclusion for their own material. (Many of the Anglo-American ballads may be interpreted either as consisting of two couplets or of two long lines.)

The pattern of the stanza either utilizes features which pertain to the construction of the line, or to such as cross the boundaries of the line and establish effects of parallelism and contrast between different lines.

The organization of the stanza line follows two general principles. In one, which is familiar to us through very much of cultivated poetry, the line consists of a number of metric feet. In the other, the recurrent contrasts of stress or length which constitute a foot do not play a role. Instead, the line consists of a specified number of syllables; their number may be rigidly fixed, or it may vary about an approximate average.

The foot is apt to be a less stable or less rigid unit in folk song than in classical cultivated poetry; the number of syllables more variable. The foot is the important unit in folk songs of the Germanic languages. The songs of the Romance-speaking peoples have both the foot and the syllable-count. The syllable-count dominates the folk songs of the Slavic peoples, of the modern Greeks, the Hungarians and other Finno-Ugrian-speaking peoples. Many types of Slavic folk song are based on the ten-syllable line (deseterac). The Finnish Kalevala utilizes an eight-syllable line, often described as a trochaic tetrameter—the meter consciously used by Longfellow for Hiawatha. Syllabic lines may be quite short: many

Hungarian, Slovak, and Yugoslav texts have only five or six syllables per line, but longer units are on the whole in the majority. As examples for a variable syllable-number in the line may be cited the Russian byliny (with syllables varying above and below ten), and the Ukrainian dumi (epic songs), with rimed couplets. Both metric features and syllable-count structure can be used to achieve either parallelism or contrast within the stanza. Accordingly, stanzas may be classified as isometric, in which every line has the same metric structure; and heterorhythmic, where they do not. To take just one example, the structure of the Anglo-American "ballad-stanza" is heterorhythmic; there are two pairs of alternating lines of four and three feet. This pattern is not uncommon in German and other folk songs. Quite a few Anglo-American ballads have, however, an isometric structure; every line has four feet.

Both parallelistic and contrastive effects are achieved in the stanza much more colorfully and with more varied means by the use of the principle of recurrent soundvalue: rime, alliteration, assonance, and related devices. It is striking that their use is rare in eastern Europe on the whole, and can often be shown to be of recent and foreign origin. Alliteration—the recurrence of initial consonants—was used intensively in ancient Germanic poetry but it is not prominent in folk song today; linefinal devices (rime) dominate. In the rime schemes of folk song, lines are usually paired and opposed through simple repetition and alternation of effects, resulting in forms such as abab, aabb, abcb, etc. Where true rime is lacking or rare, as in Hungarian and Yugoslav folk song, we are apt to find that assonance or final alliteration usually play a major role. In three-line structures, aba schemes (like that of the Spanish solea) and aab are most common. More complex structures such as aaabab, common in French dance-songs, are rather rare.

The principle of recurrent sound-value may be seen at work also in devices such as repeating a line or part of the line of every stanza, and the refrain. It has been often thought that these devices entered cultivated poetry from folk tradition. Refrains usually close the end of the stanza, but in many English, Scandinavian, and French examples they invade the stanza itself and contribute to a complex structure. Refrains are also common in the folk music of the Baltic peoples. Elsewhere in eastern Europe, as among the Balkan peoples, line repetition is the dominant device. It has been often remarked that refrain lines frequently consist of meaningless, ornamental syllables. Where the refrain lines do have a meaning, often they have little to do with the text of the song, and may have been transferred to it from other songs.

Language structure obviously constitutes a major factor in the choice of some of these devices. In languages like Hungarian, with its many suffixed elements added to the word, some of which are exceedingly frequent in occurrence, rime may not have been appreciated since it could arise all too mechanically, with a recurrent meaning wedded to the riming element. It is noteworthy, however, that rime and other ornamental devices seem more frequently associated with metric than with syllabic structure; metric structures themselves may possibly represent later developments and syllabic structures may be in general older in European folk song.

Certain formal features of the text may have some

flexibility in a folk tradition, until city influence becomes strong and the tradition is losing its vitality. Nevertheless, as the features and devices discussed above indicate, very much of folk song has a strictly formalized structure. In some types of folk song, however, the structure is less easily definable. Often in songs of these types the text forms are considerably larger than the conventional stanza. Many songs of Romance-speaking peoples have stanza-like sequences of varying length (the laisses of the chansons de geste, based on assonance). In a number of types of folk poetry there are no strophic divisions. This is particularly true of epic poetry: the Russian byliny, the Finnish Kalevala, the Yugoslav heroic epic poems, and of many ballads and lyrical songs of eastern Europe. In some cases, it is only the musical structure which makes it possible to subdivide the text. In many Balkan songs (Yugoslavia, Bulgaria), repetition of a single text line or of parts of it builds up a musical—not textual—stanza. In other instances, as in the Yugoslav heroic epic songs, the musical structure is so irregular or unorganized that even the musical stanza is absent.

Where simple and regularly recurrent formal devices are absent, other features that form a link between form and style become of added interest. Some of them impinge at definite points of the poem. The moralizing end of songs about violence and crime is apt to be phrased in the same words. First lines with which the song begins often constitute formulas which again must have traveled from song to song. Of the many, we might mention the Irish-American "Come all ye . . ." line; or the lines "There was a . . . in . . ." which no doubt has its roots in folktales. French folk songs go in very much for localizing the beginning of a song: Au jardin de mon père, or A la claire fontaine, and many others. German and Hungarian songs often begin with a reference to a tree (Lindenbaum), flower, or bird. Often, as with refrain lines, the relation of the starting line to the entire poem is unclear. To quote a statement about Rumanian usage: "Many lyrical and epic texts begin with the stereotype line, 'Green leaf of . . .' or with some other image of nature; such lines occur at times also within the song, before some of its sections. There is no connection between them and the content of the song." [28] In other cases, there can be a connection, not always clear, between the mood of the poem and the folk symbolism ascribed to flower or bird.[29]

The construction of the entire poem may be based on subtle principles not often considered in conventional analysis. Some of the simpler ones are those of repetition and contrast, often operating at the same time. An interlocking principle is present when a new stanza is introduced with the last line or lines of the previous stanza. This is very frequent in French songs. The gradual introduction of new elements, with much else repeated, is often used as a dramatic device, as in the Anglo-American ballad The Maid Freed from the Gallows.

The principle of cumulative effect finds its expression in a special form, the cumulative song or randonnée, in which content and length of the stanza expand with each repetition, by the introduction of new elements which are then repeated. The fact that quite a few of these songs (The Twelve Apostles, La Perdriole, etc.)

have a more or less international distribution suggests that this type may not be of strictly folk origin.

The Relation of Text and Melody

The texts of folk song form a large part of folk verse. Counting-out rimes, formulas of all kinds, charms, often also proverbs and riddles can have a metric organization, or alliteration, rime, and the like, which would at least with regard to form qualify them as poetry; many of them are also rich in metaphor and other poetic figures. These forms generally are very short, but what is more important, they are not sung. It is the essential trait of folk song that it is sung.

Collectors have repeatedly observed that singers often find it difficult, or even impossible, to dictate song texts; they must sing them. As an old Highland woman whose ballads Sir Walter Scott was collecting said to him, "They were made for singing and no for reading." [30] For the folk singer, text and melody form an integral unit. But the bond between a specific text and its tune may not be indissoluble. The fact that the same text is often sung to different tunes in different parts of a country, or even in the same locality, indicates that a text may become separated from its tune and attached to another. When folk singers do not recollect the melody to which they usually sing a text, they sometimes substitute one of their favorite tunes. The singer's apperception of the text is apparently more clear cut than that of the tune, which should not be surprising, considering that the tune in itself is abstract. This is suggested among others by the fact that singers and listeners often accept as a "new" song one set to a standard tune but with a new—or only slightly changed —text. That the melody is not a new one either is not noticed or may receive no comment.

It is noteworthy that in some of the older groups of functional songs (described previously), and also in some archaic but still living styles, the number of different texts may be quite large but the number of basic melodies is quite limited. This holds, for instance, for children's songs and for east European calendric songs and dirges. The songs of the Rumanian hora lunga ("long song") type—a large number of separate lyrical songs— have only one basic melody. This melody, with slight variations, is used for all the different texts. Most if not all of our children's chanted play-calls, taunts, and the like, have one single melody—a melody which recurs in similar materials or children's songs all over Europe.

The phenomenon of a comparative paucity of melodies as opposed to a comparative abundance of texts in these older song groups led some scholars, like the late Béla Bartók, to believe that in some stages of folkmusic development there may have been only a limited number of tunes in the repertory, branching out later into the "tune-families." These considerations strengthen the view that the function of music in folk practice is not necessarily to furnish a distinct setting for a distinct text. Rather, since the text cannot stand alone, melody is the necessary medium for it to be carried along.

There is often at least an all-over relationship, if not actual coordination, between formal elements in folk melodies and in their poems. The stanza of the text has its equivalent in the melodic stanza. The melodic stanza is the tune itself, usually repeated without major changes. The text stanza is normally not repeated bodily, only its structural pattern, except where it serves as a chorus, or in certain dance songs. Possibly, the musical stanza is on the whole an older development than the text stanza; in a number of east European countries, text stanzas occur only in recent songs so that usually the textual unit can be established only secondarily, as the amount of text sung to a single repetition of the tune. Where the text stanza is a real unit, however, it is apt to constitute a unit also with regard to content: a stanza usually represents a fairly self-contained and rounded set of ideas or images.

Both melodic and textual stanzas have certain architectural traits which hold them together, but their effect or force does not need to be parallel. "Melodic rimes" for instance (similar cadences at phrase endings), need not be employed in the same lines in which text rimes are used, so that cross-currents and counterpoint-like effects are achieved.

There is as a rule rigid correlation, however, between the musical and textual expression of another unit, the *line*. The occurrence of line-units which subdivide texts, and of line- or phrase-units which subdivide tunes, is universal in folk song. A text line may be set off as a unit on the basis of various rhythmic and other criteria. The musical line may be established on various grounds such as rhythmic structure, melodic contour, and the like. Long notes or pauses, or both, very frequently mark the end of the musical line as a temporary resting point. The text line, i.e. the line of poetry, usually contains a more or less rounded idea or statement, comparable to the sentence or the sentence-phrase of prose. Frequently it is a unit which, in prose speech, could be followed by a pause. Text line and musical line almost invariably coincide. It is noteworthy in this connection, how rarely pauses occur within a musical line in folk tunes. Pauses breaking into words are quite unique; they do occur in Yugoslav and Bulgarian melodies.

The *foot* of poetic meter has its parallel in the *measure* of musical rhythm, although the two can by no means be equated. They do not need to be rigidly coordinated in folk song, but their peak points quite often are. For instance, if the meter is based on an alternation of stressed and unstressed syllables, textual stress tends to be coordinated with musically stressed or rhythmically "strong" position within the measure. Contrasts of long and short syllables on the other hand are correlated much less consistently with musical length, or not at all.[31]

The question is often asked, whether it is the musical or the textual element which is "stronger" in folk song. The answer obviously cannot be a simple one. In some respects the musical factors seem to be stronger, or to have been stronger at one time, in others the textual factors. Yet, there is a constant interaction between the two, and an intimate welding together, so that isolating the textual from the musical forces is often the result of arbitrary abstraction. It is true that many of the changes which a melody may undergo, while it is repeated stanza by stanza, are caused by the flexible patterns of the text (for instance, by the variable number of syllables within the metric structure in English, German, and other folk poetry). But there are also strictly musical variations, which often run counter to the dictates of the text or the meter. Acordingly, it is hardly possible to state whether tune or text have the "upper hand" in folk song, without quoting specific cases and a maze of technical detail. One general element stands out, however. The fact that so many repetitive and ornamental devices, or features of form, which flourish in folk poetry are almost entirely lacking in folk speech—refrains, line repetitions, rime, the use of meaningless words, the stanza—indicates that in folk song the possibilities of speech are much expanded and that they are employed in ways which are closely connected with the fact that folk songs are sung.

The relation of text to tune with regard to content is again a complex and subtle problem. In our cultivated or "art" music, we have established a distinction between music which is representative or "programmatic," and music which is "abstract." When our art music is coupled with a text, it is frequently adjusted to the general mood and content of the text, even though it may not attempt to represent given elements of the text in naturalistic fashion. Folk music in general appears to be abstract in this sense; it is very rarely programmatic or representative (our *Barnyard Song* is one of the few examples). Even a generalized relationship between the mood or emotional content of the text and of the tune seems very often to be lacking, or at least it is not clear to us. The climax-points of a ballad or of a lyrical poem rarely receive special musical emphasis, although, at least in this country, there is much variation in how expressive the manner of singing of different singers is. Yet, it is often said that folk singers sing "without expression." At any rate, authentic folk singing does not use our hackneyed expressive devices.

It often happens that a text is sung to versions of tunes, or to different tunes, one of which affects us as sad and another as gay. Certainly the musical connotations of sad and gay which our books on Music Appreciation ascribe all too mechanically to music, and to major or minor tonality, cannot be assumed to be present in the same fashion in the experience of the folk singer and listener. Probably the musical features which have ties with the emotional aspects of the folk poem are, instead, the general rhythmic character, the speed, and various subtleties of rendition. But it is easier to sense than to prove the presence of such ties. One difficulty is that folk singers are rarely articulate about the mood or emotional quality of their tunes, unless they use words and notions taken over from city usage. Our own responses on the other hand do not form a reliable basis for judgments since they are unavoidably conditioned by special associations and values. Of many of these associations we are not aware; they have arisen from our experiences in listening to cultivated music, and from what we were told about this music. The same holds, of course, even if to a lesser degree, for esthetic and emotional values in folk poetry.

If, then, the relation of the content of folk poetry and folk music remains a fascinating but as yet uncharted area, a similarly unexplored area is the role of bodily movement in folk song. Here a third aspect is added to those of text and tune.

In work songs, game songs, dance songs, and marching songs, the rhythmically organized movements of the body are integrated with music; interactions and cross-influences take place which are comparable to the inter actions between poetry and music. Dance songs are numerous in every folk music style, although many of them may be performed without singing, on instruments. Often it is quite difficult to delimit this rich category. As Phillips Barry said, "There is no hard and fast line which can always be drawn between dance music and song music." [32] Work songs are ubiquitous, but they form, usually, a comparatively small part of the song-lore of a group. The U. S. Negroes with their prolific work songs are unusual in this respect. At least the custom of singing work songs, if not the songs themselves, may be part of their African heritage. Songs in which occupational groups describe or refer to their work, but which are not sung during work, are sometimes misleadingly called work songs. (For instance, the songs of American lumbermen and miners.) Marching songs are usually soldiers' songs; their use is comparatively recent, as is the very practice of rhythmically regularized marching. Songs while working or walking along must be separated, of course, from work songs and marching songs proper. In some localities, almost any kind of song may be sung at work or in walking.

There is usually a general coordination in folk song between the rhythm of music and that of dance or work. But the more specific relations between the character and design of dance steps, for instance, and the musical and textual features of the associated songs have been little studied so far and often escape mere observation. Sound film recordings will make it possible to learn more about these intricate and interesting relationships.

Manner of Singing

Many details of melody, intonation, and rhythm, often quite subtle, make up a special phase of folk song, its manner of rendition. This manner or technique of singing may have different characteristics in different regions, but some of them are general or widespread. Folk singers do not often attempt a melodious "singing" tone. They rarely use expressive modulations of the voice; they sing in a matter-of-fact fashion. These statements, however, should not be taken too literally; often the mode of expression is merely restrained or austere, the expressive devices not obvious.

Two general types of singing manner have been distinguished in Eastern Europe: the *parlando-rubato,* a very free, highly ornamented technique, and the *tempo giusto,* one held in more strict rhythm and with much less ornamentation. These techniques have been described in especial detail in Hungarian folk music where both were part of the old stylistic practice: the first in ballads and lyrical songs, the second in dance songs.[33] The *parlando-rubato,* or similar techniques, must have been widespread over other sections of Europe too. It has been observed in our South and Northeast,[34] and the highly ornamented French-Canadian melodies show a comparable technique. Songs sung in this manner are very difficult to render in exact musical notation.

Two special phases, intonation and ornamentation, may be mentioned here as part of the traditional technique of singing. Often only acoustical recordings give us an inkling of these features. Even an excellent musician can find it quite difficult to identify, much less to transcribe, details of intonation and of ornamentation, unless he has had special training for these tasks.[35]

Until recently, the average folk singer heard and used little instrumental music with fixed and standard pitches. Thus he can hardly be expected to have the professional standards of "pure" intonation. The intonation of a traditional folk singer is not necessarily worse than ours, but it is often more flexible. A tone is often taken somewhat higher or lower than might be expected, for expressive or ornamental purposes. Some of these fluctuations of pitch recur regularly at given points of the melody; upward and downward movement often call for some sharpening or flattening of an intervening tone.

Elaborate ornamentation appears to have been an integral feature of many old folk music styles. In different styles, ornamentation can have different functions. In Anglo-American and French tunes ornamental tones are used mainly to bridge gaps in the melody; in Hungary and in Rumania they often lend special emphasis to important tones; in Yugoslavia they frequently almost bury the essential skeleton of the melody.[36]

The authentic manner of singing is disappearing in some regions faster than the melodies themselves. One reason why folk song may be doomed to extinction is that the younger generation often feel that the old songs—meaning the old mannerisms of singing—set them or their parents apart as odd and old-fashioned. The absence of authenticity in the renditions of concert singers of folk songs is often the absence of the traditional manner of singing. The concert singer is usually not acquainted with this manner, or cannot learn it.

Melody

This brief treatment of melody in folk music takes up the following topics: compass, scales, intervals, tonality, and melodic contour. Up to the present much of the actual analysis of folk music has concerned itself with matters like scales, perhaps at the expense of the study of rhythm and form. There has been considerable terminological confusion which calls for clarification.

The *compass* or range of folk melodies is characterized by a certain economy. They seldom come even near the limits of the range of the singing voice. Melodies with a compass beyond an octave and a half are rare.

The melodies in a very archaic group have a very restricted range and tone content: two tones within the compass of a second, or three tones within that of a third. This type is found especially among lullabies, children's songs, and calendric songs, and is more frequent in eastern and southern than in western and northern Europe.[37] Many of the more complex melodies must have developed from tunes of this type. The melodic range of a fourth or a fifth is quite common in Slavic melodies, and French tunes also very often have a somewhat restricted range.

It is important to realize that these restricted tone-series form the *scales* of these tunes. It is erroneous to consider them incomplete segments or fractions of our scales, which call for tone-series filling out an octave, and misleading to refer to them by the terms used for those "octave-scales" (major, minor, or modal) which they sometimes resemble. The scale of a folk tune is nothing more nor less than the series of tones which it employs.

It is well known that ancient Greek musical theory considered the fourth and the fifth as the basic scale-frames of melody, not the octave. Byzantine theory speaks of the sixth. Their terms for these frames—*tetrachord, pentachord,* and *hexachord*—and the underlying concepts are very useful in application to folk music, although they do not apply with all the special meanings Greek theory imparted to them.[38] The borrowing of the terms does not imply, however, any influence of ancient Greek music on European folk song, which is theoretically possible but has not been demonstrated so far. Rather, it might be suggested that the Greek theorists merely gave a formulation to the unconscious principles of melodic construction which were in force in the folk music of their day. From the wide applicability of these concepts to folk music we might further infer that the principles involved are ancient in Europe and were current also in the folk music of groups with whom the Greeks had little or no contact.

Some of these scale-types are widespread. The hexachord *gabcde* is a striking example. It is probably one of the roots of our modern major scale, and some German scholars have claimed it—together with the scale and tonality of major—as an ancient Germanic achievement. It underlies very many folk tunes all over Europe. Its wide distribution presupposes an ancient origin and renders a Germanic origin quite unlikely.

As we move to scale terminology which employs more familiar terms, we find usages which are confusing—and not only to the uninitiated. One group of scales are referred to as *modes.* A smaller group (our major and minor) are not called *modes* but *scales* or *tonalities.* To add another system: we also speak of "gapped" scales such as the pentatonic and hexatonic.

The "-chordal" scales (pentachord, hexachord, etc.), the modes, and the major and minor scales all share one principle. They are diatonic: the tones are arranged stepwise. The "-tonic" scales (hexatonic, pentatonic, etc.) on the other hand are "gapped." Actually, the difference is in the size of the building-blocks. In diatonic construction the contrasting sizes of the successive intervals are minor seconds and major seconds (the augmented second of minor is considered secondarily raised). In gapped construction the constituent interval steps are major seconds and thirds; the thirds are usually minor (pentatonic scales rarely use the minor second or half-tone).

It would be more convenient if the modes and major and minor were called *octochords;* they consist of tone-series within the octave as the limiting frame. But for various reasons it is of practical advantage to retain the terminology. The modes which stem from ancient Greek theory and the theory of Gregorian church music, form a simple and closed system. As is well known, the seven possible "Church modes" can be visualized as the seven possible tone-sequences using the series *c, d, e, f, g, a, b, c* (the white keys of the piano), but beginning for each mode with a different tone as the basic tone or tonic. It is further of advantage to set major and minor apart, because their treatment in our music is inextricably interwoven with harmonic considerations and relationships. This is not so in connection with other scale-types in folk music. Since the great bulk of folk music is performed without a harmonic setting, whatever scales occur must be thought of as systems carrying only melodic relationships, but *not* harmonic relationships.

The definitions and comments offered above by no means do justice to the complex historical and theoretical problems connected with scale and mode in our cultivated music; they merely indicate useful ways in which the terminology and some of the concepts can be applied in folk music. Some of the confusion in the description of folk music is due to the circumstance that unclarified meanings were carried over into the analysis of folk music, and that the specific circumstances and usages of folk music were not taken sufficiently into account.

Modal scales are widespread in European folk music, although their frequency varies in different countries. In older collections editors often changed modal melodies to give them a more "correct" major or minor appearance. The modal scales pose an as yet unsolved problem. They —and more restricted scales which resemble the modes— predominate in the traditional music of the Catholic church. To what extent is their presence in folk music due to an influence from this direction? It has been demonstrated that church music had a strong effect on folk music; but it should also be recalled that much folk melody was incorporated into the music of the Church.

It was a startling discovery in the early 20th century in this country—just about the time when it was officially discovered that this country *had* its folk music— that many folk melodies are modal. This led some students to believe that melodies cast in these scales were bound to be old, and that the melodies and their scales represented the purest and clearest survivals of an ancient Anglo-Saxon heritage. These wholesale assumptions are dubious. Modal melodies are not necessarily old. Singers have been known to change a non-modal tune so that it became modal. Furthermore, many melodies whose scale is not modal are undoubtedly as old as many modal tunes.

Pentatonic scales are found all over the world. They have probably arisen time and again, and in various places, rather than spread from one common source. The existence of such scales in different countries is no proof of historical connection between them. Pentatonic scales of the British Isles and of Scandinavia may be related, but they are hardly connected with pentatonic scales in Hungary, or in Russia, which are different either in construction or in treatment.

Major and minor are not common in folk music— minor is especially rare—unless heavy city influence has been at work, as for instance in German folk music. All too often, however, these terms are erroneously ascribed to folk music when some element is present which *to us* signals the presence of major or minor: either a partial sequence of tones incorporated in our scale, or a characteristic interval such as the major or minor third.

Turning to the use of intervals in folk music, some general preferences or avoidances may be mentioned. In pentatonic melodies half-tone steps are rare. Progressions which use clusters of half-tone steps (chromaticism), or augmented and diminished intervals, are also rare. Where they appear, in Spain and in the Mediterranean, they may well be due to Arabic influence. Augmented seconds are more common in the Balkans and in some parts of eastern Europe. They reflect in part Oriental influences, in part the influence of the Gipsies who have been important as purveyors of certain kinds of tunes in these regions. The interval is much more frequent in the popular music of small-town bands or of the café musicians than in peasant tunes.

Some intervals in folk music are classed as "irrational" from the point of view of our tempered tone-system; they do not coincide with our standard intervals. In Anglo-American melodies the sixth and seventh above the tonic are at times approximately between the major and minor intervals. The blue note of Negro folk songs, which has been preserved in some jazz usages, is usually a neutral third, between our major and minor third. The occurrence of such intervals becomes less puzzling if we consider how recent and specialized our tempered tone-system is. Where city influence has been strong, these intervals tend to disappear.

In the study of folk music there has been perhaps a little too much preoccupation with scales and intervals, which are merely the raw materials of melody, at the expense of studying tonality. *Tonality* may be best defined as the system of dynamic interrelations which are carried by the tones of the scale, including the various roles assigned to different tones. The term is very useful in folk music, as long as harmonic ideas of tonality are eliminated. It is convenient to apply also other conventional technical terms, such as "tonic," "dominant," and "leading tone," but either they are to be given wider meanings, or the meanings need to be adjusted to the specific circumstances of folk music.[39] Our dominant, for instance, which is second in importance to the tonic, is defined also by its position as the fifth above the tonic. In many folk tunes a tone of comparable importance is found on the fourth, or on the second above or below the tonic. The function of the leading tone which, because of major and minor, we automatically connect with the position of the seventh, a half-tone below the tonic, is in folk melodies often associated with a major second above the tonic, or with a major second or a third below the tonic.

Because of the same preoccupation with scales and intervals, there has been as yet little study of *melodic movement* and *melodic contour* in folk music. The most archaic tunes, with their limited tone-material, have a melodic movement which is almost level, or which oscillates back and forth. Downward melodic movement is exceedingly frequent, especially in older tunes. It predominates in much of eastern and southern European folk music. When ascending and descending lines are comparatively balanced, the contour approximates the arc. Many Anglo-American, Scandinavian, and German ballad or lyrical tunes are built in this fashion; they first ascend to one or two melodic peaks and then return to the main level of the melody.[40] An undulating type of movement, with repeated short waves of ascent and descent, is frequent in Slavic and Balkan songs. Many old Hungarian and Turkish melodies display a movement of graduated descent by levels, in which each musical line sinks lower. At present we can hardly guess at the nature of the forces, whether musical or esthetic, motor or psychological, which have made different trends dominant in different styles.

Musical Rhythm

Two general modes of rhythmic organization may be distinguished in folk music. One is comparatively free so that it hardly permits division into bars or measures; it may be compared with free verse. Different forms of this mode are found in dirges; in many songs of Spain where Arabic music left a strong imprint; and in the heroic epic poetry of Russia, Ukrainia, and Yugoslavia. In some east European countries, for example in Hungary, it is the old and authentic way of performing ballads and lyrical songs, and was designated as the *parlando-rubato* mode of performance (see section *Manner of Singing*). Many complex and unusual rhythmic figures have arisen after the free element of this type of performance became solidified and rigid.[41] The other mode of rhythmic organization has more regular patterns so that the rhythmic design elements can be easily located, and the use of bars or measures is not too artificial. In eastern Europe the term *tempo giusto* has been used for this type.

The rhythmic pattern of the musical lines or phrases which make up the melody may be the same for every line of the melody (*isorhythmic* structure), or not (*heterorhythmic* structure). Metric uniformity of the lines of the text is related to the first; lack of such uniformity to the second. The pause as a rhythmic device tends to be restricted in folk music to the end of lines, or of the tune; together with long notes it is one of the prime features that indicate a temporary close or finality.[42] But long notes may also stand at the beginning of a line or of the tune as dramatic starting devices.

The *measure* or bar concept of our classical musical theory can be applied to folk music, but some caution is required. Many collectors and editors of earlier days were swayed by standards of classical music, where a measure is usually constant through the entire composition. Consequently they forced measures on melodies of a free rhythmic organization, or they forced folk tunes into a Procrustean bed of rhythmic uniformity. More recent collections and recordings have amply shown that folk tunes very often are not based on a measure that runs through the melody, but that the length of the measure may change repeatedly in the course of the tune. These changes are anything but haphazard; they belong to the structure of the tune and recur regularly from stanza to stanza. They are the expression of a special esthetic principle manifesting itself in effects of contrast and change which a mechanical consistency of measure does not permit. The frequent rhythmic shifts in the compositions of a Stravinsky or a Bartók have undoubtedly been stimulated by the rhythm of their native folk tunes.

One result of shifting rhythmic measures is the variety of asymmetrical balances which underlie the rhythm and form of many folk tunes.[43] This asymmetry already appears in rhythms of 5/4, 7/4, and the like: they consist of 2 and 3 or 3 and 2; 3 and 4 or 4 and 3 units, and so on. Other folk song rhythms which are rare in cultivated or classical music are 9/4 consisting of 4 and 5 beats; 8/4 consisting of 3, 2, and 3 beats; 11/4 consisting of 4, 4, 3 beats; and so on. The so-called "Bulgarian rhythm" which also appears in Greek folk music, consists of comparable rhythms; they are performed, however, very fast so that signatures like 17/16 and 21/16 are not at all uncommon.[44]

In western and northern Europe on the whole simple measures based on groups of 2 or 3 units and their multiples predominate: 2/4, 3/4, 4/4; 6/8, 9/8, 12/8. In eastern and southern Europe the more complex rhythms based on alternating groups of 2 and 3 beats are much more frequent. (It has been observed, however, that 5/4 and 7/4 are not rare in Anglo-American melodies.[45]) In these areas shifting measures and the resulting asymmetrical structures are also more frequent than in the West and the North. These differences probably do not go back to great antiquity. Older folk songs from the West show these phenomena more frequently, when editorial "improvements" made to "regularize" the rhythm are stripped off and the true rhythmic structure is reconstructed. Meanwhile, however, the influence of the printed song collections and of the city, which in its classical and popular music had little experience with rhythmic shifts, have often imposed a regular rhythmic structure on many folk melodies.

Some simple rhythmic devices are universal in folk music, such as the opposition of longer and shorter values, or of stressed and unstressed tones. Others, despite their simplicity, are more restricted or more favored in given styles than in others. Triplets alternating with groups of two beats, for instance, are used in great profusion in French folk tunes; much less often in other national styles. In Spanish folk music the alternation of 3/4 and 6/8 is very common. Triple rhythms are comparatively rare in some east European countries; very frequent in some west European ones. Upbeats, a commonplace device in most west and north European styles, or in German folk tunes, are very rare in Hungary, Slovakia, Yugoslavia, and Rumania. Syncopated rhythms are very common in Scotch tunes. The syncopation of Negro melodies in the United States which is often ascribed to the survival of African rhythmic patterns is more likely to have its antecedents in Scottish-English folk music.[46] Other types of syncopation have some currency in Slavic tunes, and are especially frequent in more recent Hungarian melodies. Hungarian and Gipsy influence spread these rhythms through eastern Europe, and they are reflected in the rhapsodies of Liszt and Brahms.

The connections between textual and musical rhythm have been touched upon before (see section *Text and Melody*). The function and subject matter of the tunes is not without its influence on rhythm. Calendric songs, children's songs, work songs, and especially dance songs, perhaps because of their closer connection with bodily movement, tend to have simpler rhythms and to be sung in a more strict rhythm than ballads and lyrical songs. Still, in dance songs in the Balkans and in a few other areas, extremely intricate rhythms are found side by side with the simplest.

Musical Form

The architectonic clarity of formal organization in folk music has often impressed and stimulated the composer. The organization ranges, however, from types of elementary simplicity to ornate complexity.

Many children's songs or songs sung to children, and some calendric songs consist merely of a musical line or phrase which is repeated over and over again. The line may be split into two or three brief motifs. The principle of repetition is the same as the familiar repetition of a longer melody for successive stanzas of the text. This type of line-repetition, sometimes called the *litany* form,[47] is also found in some styles of so-called primitive peoples. In folk music it no doubt represents survivals of a very archaic development. The calling and taunting formulas of children which are often chanted rather than sung and are on the borderline of music

(*Come out, come out, wherever you are!*, *Johnny is a sissy!*, etc. in the United States) belong to this type.

The single repeated musical line may have been the germ for the development of some of the more complex forms. In one type, the musical line is repeated with many variations which cannot be marked off into stanza-like units. This loose form is often employed for heroic epic poetry. In the long heroic epic poems of the Yugoslavs, one musical line is used for the beginning and the end of the poem; another or a number of others serve to carry the main body of the song; and still others may be used at points where the story turns to moments of increased interest.

In another development, the repetition of primary musical motifs leads to more regular formations: recurrent musical stanzas. In Slavic melodies quite frequently the song consists of two or three repetitions of a basic musical idea which differ only slightly from each other. A similar form, $A A' B B'$, where the line-pairs differ only in their cadences, is common and probably old in Spain.[48] As the similar musical lines become more differentiated, forms like $A^1 A^2$ or $A^1 A^2 A^3$ can easily lead to forms like $A B$, $A B C$, $A^1 B A^2$, and so on. In French melodies phrases are very often repeated, with or without modications, within a more complex structure often built up from numerous short musical motifs.

Two- and three-line forms are more frequent in eastern than in western Europe: the three-line form of the folk blues sung by our southern Negroes and white mountaineers is somewhat unusual. It is not surprising that when W. C. Handy published his *Blues*, he usually expanded the old three-line form into the more familiar four-line musical stanza.[49]

Musical stanzas of four lines, or their expansions, dominate most of European folk music. The four-line construction may have satisfied a feeling for balance based on older two-line constructions. The main musical subdivision of four-liners is very commonly at the end of the second line. This simple symmetry has probably not been without effect on the development of the "period" formation in our art music. There are many examples in folk music, however, in which the break at half-point is not marked off strongly. One instance which may be mentioned is the $ABCD$ form and its ramifications: here the musical content is different from line to line. This form occurs in quite a few Anglo-American ballads and lyrical songs. Another is the $ABBA$ form in which the musical content of the outside and inside pairs of lines is the same. This form is quite common in Irish tunes, but also in more recent Hungarian melodies.[50]

While repetition is the most basic structural force in folk music,[51] it can manifest itself in various special forms; and other principles also contribute to formal variety. Some of the most common structural principles in folk music may be designated as "progression" (type $ABCD$); "reversion" (types $ABAC$, $ABCB$: common in our children's game, play-party, and square-dance tunes); and the "cyclic" principle (types $ABCA$, $ABBA$).[52]

When the last line or lines of a melody are repeated, this may be at times merely a detail in the manner of performance, rather than a feature that enters into the basic structure. For instance, in the more recent Hungarian tunes the last two lines of the stanza are repeated quite mechanically, but the usage is still somewhat optional. If, however, such casual repetitions become fixed, they become part of the structure which is thus expanded and modified by their intrusion. Sometimes textual elements call for repetitive expansion, as in the cumulative or *randonnée* songs (*The Twelve Apostles, La Perdriole, The Barnyard Song*, etc.). Other connections between textual and musical form have been touched upon in the section *Relation of Text and Melody.*

While the great bulk of folk music contains itself within comparatively simple stanza-like arrangements, there are developments which move toward more complexity and longer forms. Often these are connected with textual factors, or others that are originally not musical. In more elaborate children's games sometimes a number of musical motifs, with their repetitions, are woven together loosely into a larger whole which may be compared with our *potpourri*. The "verse and chorus" arrangement, which is probably not old and may have been brought about through the influence of art music or popular city music, often joins together two originally independent melodies (as do many of the play-party and square-dance tunes of the United States).

Instrumental dance pieces often show rather complex and elaborate forms. A growing interest in the performer and his virtuosity has played a role in these developments. Another factor must have been the need for repetition, coupled with the freedom from limitations imposed by the text and its stanza-structure.

Formal growth moves in another direction when a number of songs or pieces are performed in regular sequence. This points to the *suite* form of art music. Modest beginnings of the *suite* appear at times in instrumental pieces. In one example which has been found in a number of east European countries, three flute pieces are played in succession: in the first the shepherd mourns for his lost sheep; in the second he is searching for them; in the third he rejoices over having found them.

Regulated sequence is also the principle when a number of songs are used in a story, or in the religious folk plays, although in both prose sections or parts which are not sung separate the musical items. The folk plays, at least in conception, represent the most ambitious formal development in folk music, the *music drama*.

It has been suggested before that mode of performance can have an impact on musical form. One interesting example of this process is the form in which a solo and a group sing the melody in responsorial fashion. This technique is found very commonly in eastern Europe (the Baltic countries, Russia, Ukrainia, dance melodies in the Balkans); less often in western or northern Europe if we except the Anglo-American sea-shantey and its relatives elsewhere. Its use in southern Negro folk music is well known, whether in the spirituals or in the work songs. It is still a controversial point whether this southern Negro usage represents a survival of African usage—even though most of the melodies themselves may not be of African origin—or whether it is connected with European and American white customs, such as the "lining out" of the hymn tune by the song leader, with its subsequent repetition by the group, in early American practice.[53] Alternation of solo and group singing is too general a phenomenon to serve as a guide. A more reliable criterion of African carry-overs appears when the solo-line displays great variability, in contrast with the stability of the refrain by the group.[54] The study of

Negro folk music in the West Indies, in Dutch Guiana, and in Brazil, has done much to clarify the intricate question of the survival of African music in the New World.

Harmony and Polyphony

The great majority of folk tunes are sung or performed in one voice. Thus, examples of *harmony* (a single melodic line supported by subordinate voices) and of *polyphony* (a number of more or less independent melodic lines performed together) are comparatively rare. Much of folk harmony or polyphony is purely instrumental, or arises when instruments accompany singing. But there are also purely vocal forms of part singing. It is noteworthy that despite the comparative rarity of part singing in folk practice, many music historians assume that the beginnings of part singing in European art music lie in folk usages.

A number of geographic centers may be mentioned for part singing in folk music. One center is northwestern, embracing Scandinavia and the British Isles. Rounds or canons, modest counterpoint-like forms, and singing in parallel intervals were cultivated here, especially in the British Isles, although the forms have on the whole dropped out of folk usage. Singing in parallel fourths and fifths (the *organum purum* of our early musical theory) is still cultivated in Iceland. [55]

A central European center is noted for the prevalence of singing in parallel thirds. This may have been an old folk practice in South Germany and Austria; but there is a strong suspicion that the practice was at least reinforced and influenced by harmonic developments in the cities in which thirds became prominent. From Germany, the parallel thirds spread over some Slavic territory. They are used also in Switzerland, southern France, Italy, and Spain, and all over Latin America. Another type of polyphony was used in the famous *jodlers* of the Swiss Alps and the contiguous mountain regions, although nowadays the melodies have the simple settings of our conventional harmonic system.

A third area is south Slavic. In Dalmatia, the Adriatic littoral of Yugoslavia, there are very curious polyphonic forms in which melodies are sung in parallel seconds. When these melodies are played on paired reed instruments, the seconds turn by inversion into parallel sevenths.[56] The history of this very unusual development is obscure; the "howling" of the Lombards of northern Italy, by singing in seconds, is mentioned by some early medieval sources.[57] Elsewhere in Yugoslavia and in Bulgaria seconds are heard frequently, either when a lower voice repeats one tone throughout the melody ("interrupted" or "repeated" drone) or in canons.

A fourth area is east European. In Lithuania, the earlier mode of performance for most songs was in canon or round fashion, two or three voices singing the melody on the same tone level. Today songs performed in this manner are called *sutartines*.[58] In the Ukraine and in White Russia many songs are sung in true counterpoint; this technique is also employed with reed instruments.[59] Vocal drone effects occur here as well. The famous Don Cossack choral performances are based on these folk roots, although their technique and manner of singing has been much influenced by our concert stage.

Perhaps the most complex forms of folk part singing are found in the music of various non-Russian-speaking peoples in the Caucasus. These show surprisingly close parallels to some of the forms described and taught in early medieval treatises on musical theory and composition.[60]

Apart from these special areas, scattered forms of singing or playing in voices are found in many other places. Some forms came about when autochthonous stringed instruments accompanied various types of songs. Unfortunately these forms have not as yet been well described.

Folk Song and Instrumental Music

Musical instruments play a subordinate, yet interesting role in folk music. The subject, however, has received on the whole little attention. Independent instrumental music forms a comparatively small part of the repertory of most folk groups. Instrumental music used to accompany folk song is by no means universal. In some countries, such as Hungary, it is not known at all; in others, it is employed only for specific types of songs. On the whole, the majority of folk songs are sung without any accompaniment.

Some of the generalizations that have been made about oral folk music are less valid for instrumental folk music. Unlike the folk singer, the instrumentalist may approach the standing of a professional. He often possesses a skill that many others in the community lack. In a number of countries, expressions like "to make music," "music," and "tune" occur in folk usage for instrumental playing, but not for singing. The instrumentalist is also apt to have a more developed musical terminology than the folk singer.

The mutual influences between instrumental and vocal music have been studied intensively in art music. In the following, some examples will be given to indicate the various ways in which instrumental music has exerted an influence on folk song.

The role of musical instruments in the growth of more elaborate forms in folk music has already been mentioned.

Instrumental scales may have had an occasional effect on the scales of vocal melodies. It is noteworthy, however, that the tone-material of many folk musical instruments, for example flutes, is often much more limited than the tone-material employed in singing.

There are interesting parallels between instrumental and vocal technique. The great speed of many Bulgarian and Greek vocal melodies is probably the result of the influence of instrumental performance. The peculiar manner of singing the Swiss *jodel* melodies, with their wide jumps, changes into the *falsetto* register, and other features, has been ascribed to the influence of instruments like the *alphorn*.[61] In the United States and elsewhere, fiddlers do not use the vibrato, which parallels the absence of a vibrato and of similar expressive devices in singing.

The development of harmonic and polyphonic forms has been stimulated by musical instruments. The bagpipe, with its characteristic drone, is used everywhere in Europe, or was used at one time. American fiddlers use open strings for drone effects; this curious practice may well have had its origin in the imitation of bagpipes.

Harmonic or polyphonic effects arise also when musical instruments are used for accompanying the voice. Apart from the older stringed instruments used for accompanying some types of songs, there is a group which

are comparatively recent introductions from the city. These include the guitar, mandolin, and banjo in western and central Europe, and the *tambura, tamburica,* and others in Slavic folk music.

The great profusion of fiddle-tunes and other instrumental melodies in the British-Irish-American tradition is somewhat unusual The material has not been intensively studied, but it has been stated that very many of the tunes are at the same time used also as vocal melodies.[62] It is of incidental interest that Robert Burns set many of his songs to instrumental melodies that he collected.

Classification of Folk Melodies

As increasing amounts of material accumulate in archives, the question of the best method of classifying folk melodies becomes of increasing importance. In countries in which no such system is used, collections of melodies are often published without any regard to their musical interrelatipns.

It is of importance to distinguish between two aims which a classification may have; these aims touch upon each other but are nevertheless distinct. One aim is to establish a *typology* for the material. The interest here is descriptive; the task is to organize a large body of folk tunes according to some convenient system which will lead to a finding list or a *melodic index*. It is another aim to establish the *genetic relationships* between melodies, and to trace all the various intercrossing influences which have shaped them. The interest here is historical, and leads to the study of dynamic processes in folk music. Tune-families and hybrids instead of types will emerge.

In both kinds of procedure the ideal is to arrive at a grouping in which related or similar melodies will be found near each other, instead of being separated by many others. In either procedure the ideal is difficult to achieve, because variants of the same melody can easily differ from each other on various levels: in rhythm, in scale or mode, or in structure. Similarly, unrelated melodies or types can influence each other in all these respects. A typology which would be internationally applicable would have great advantages. On the other hand, further experience in different countries will probably show that for genetic purposes different systems are the most useful for different styles.

It is probably useful to separate, for primary grouping, vocal melodies from instrumental. So is a further subdivision according to the function of the song or the subject matter of the text. A third principle of grouping may follow basic formal features of the text. These principles of grouping must be tested for their usefulness, however, from style to style.

In eastern Europe large bodies of folk melodies were published, organized according to a system of classification which was introduced by Finnish scholars like Ilmari Krohn, and expanded by the Hungarians Béla Bartók and Zoltán Kodály. In this system, instrumental and vocal melodies are treated separately. The vocal melodies are grouped first according to the text—the number of syllables in the text line, and the number of lines in the text stanza. Next, they are subdivided according to musical traits, such as the phrase-final tones of the melody, the melodic range, and a few others.

The system, including the use of the phrase-finals, has been rather successful in the eastern European material.[63] When it is applied to western European tunes, the use of the phrase-finals does not seem very satisfactory.[64]

In western European countries there has been less systematic application, but various methods of classification have been discussed. In this country and in England classification according to modes is a favorite device; it has its weaknesses. An important study by B. H. Bronson has shown that related Anglo-American ballad tunes, or versions, often are in different modes.[65] Furthermore, pentatonic and hexatonic melodies are usually drawn into the modal classification, and this procedure is questionable.[66] A hexatonic tune is ambiguous; it can be grouped with at least two modes, and a pentatonic with three, depending on what tones are assumed to be "missing." The implicit wholesale assumption, however, that pentatonic and hexatonic scales represent incomplete or reduced modes is not justified. This is not to deny that in specific cases melodies have secondarily taken a pentatonic or hexatonic structure.

In this country, suggestions have been made for melodic classification on the basis of the exact tone content, the intervallic progressions, and some other features of the tune, or of its first line.[67] These systems have an element of simplicity and could be handled, if put into practice, comparatively easily, even mechanically. Yet, because of their oversimplified and mechanical conception, they do not appear to be very promising.

The most suggestive method, which is occasionally proposed, is that by melodic contour. This method seems very worth testing on a large scale, since often the melodic contour turns out to be the most stable element in melodies which have been in the process of differentiation. This type of analysis is also of considerable psychological interest. It recalls and may substantiate the contention of the German configurational or *Gestalt* school of psychology, that melody at large is a prime example of a true "configuration": a pattern which remains essentially intact as long as its shape or contour remains the same, even if its elements shift and change.

Notes
(The following Notes and Bibliography are for the reader who wishes to follow up points. For several statements he may not find reference. Some are well-known facts; some have not as yet been expressed in print. These statements have been stimulated by conversations with the late Béla Bartók, with Samuel P. Bayard, with Herbert H. Halpert. The article has benefited greatly by the suggestions of Dr. Halpert.)

1: Quoted by Marie Campbell in her "Regular Song Ballads with the Tunes Set Down," *Tennessee Folk-Lore Society Bulletin*, vol. 3, no. 3, Sept. 1937.

2: An older tradition of written song-books is that of the Shakers, which also includes musical notation. See Edward D. Andrews, *The Gift to Be Simple—Songs, Dances and Rituals of the American Shakers*, New York, 1940.

3: See George P. Jackson, *White Spirituals in the Southern Uplands*, Chapel Hill, N.C., 1933.

4: See Frank Kidson, "The Ballad Sheet and Garland," *Journal of the Folk-Song Society* 2:70–78, 1905; Hyder E. Rollins, "The Blackletter Broadside Ballad," *PMLA* 34:258–339, 1919; and important discussions in the

headnotes in H. M. Belden, *Ballads and Songs Collected by the Missouri Folk-Lore Society*, Columbia, Mo., 1940.

5: For the Anglo-American tradition, see Annie G. Gilchrist, "The Folk Element in Early Revival Hymns and Tunes, *Journal of the Folk-Song Society* 8:61–95, 1928; and George P. Jackson's valuable studies: *Spiritual Folksongs of Early America*, New York 1937; *Down-East Spirituals and Others*, New York 1943; and *White Spirituals in the Southern Uplands*.

6: See frequent references to songsters in Phillips Barry, Fanny H. Eckstorm, and Mary W. Smyth, *British Ballads from Maine*, New Haven, 1929. Also Belden, above, *passim*, and S. Foster Damon, "The Negro in Early American Songsters," *Publications of the Bibliographical Society of America* 28:132–163, 1934.

7: See for instance in the Introduction to Louise Pound, *American Ballads and Songs*, New York, 1922.

8: Discussed by Herbert Halpert at meetings of the American Folklore Society.

9: See frequent comments and discussion by Phillips Barry in the *Bulletin of the Folk-Song Society of the Northeast, passim*.

10: For references to Yugoslav folk song and folk music see chiefly, Béla Bartók and Albert B. Lord, *Serbo-Croatian Folksongs*. Columbia University Press, New York (1950).

11: See for instance, Mathias Murko, *La poésie populaire épique en Yougoslavie au début du XXe siècle*, Travaux publiés par l'Institut d'études slaves, vol. 10, Paris, 1929.

12: See Phillips Barry, "Communal Re-creation," *Bulletin of the Folk-Song Society of the Northeast* 5:4–6, 1933; Louise Pound, *Poetic Origins and the Ballad*, New York, 1921; and Fanny H. Eckstorm and Mary W. Smyth, *Minstrelsy of Maine*, Boston, 1927 (an excellent and too-little-known book).

13: See for instance, Helen H. Roberts, "A Study of Folk Song Variants Based on Field Work in Jamaica," *JAFL* 38:149–216, 1925, and several studies of Phillips Barry in the *Bulletin of the Folk-Song Society of the Northeast*.

14: For the Anglo-American tradition see, in addition to Phillips Barry, above, the basic study by Samuel P. Bayard, "Prolegomena to a Study of the Principal Melodic Families of British-American Folk Song," *JAFL* 63:1–44, 1950.

15: See Jean Poueigh, *Chansons populaires des Pyrénées Françaises*, Paris, 1933.

16: The literature of folk plays is quite extensive. See, for instance, M. R. Cole, *Los Pastores—A Mexican Miracle Play*, *MAFLS* 9, 1907; and E. K. Chambers, *The English Folk Play*, Oxford, 1933.

17: See the rich material in Béla Bartók, *Melodien der Rumänischen Colinde (Weihnachtslieder)*, Vienna, 1935; his *Rumanian Christmas Carols* (with piano settings), Universal Edition 1918, Boosey and Hawkes 1939; and Sabin V. Dragoi, *303 Colinde cu Text si Melodie*, Publications on Musical Folklore of the Phonograph Archives Commission, Craiova, Rumania, n.d.

18: On the simplicity and age of functional songs see George Herzog, "Some Primitive Layers in European Folk Music," *Bulletin of the American Musicological Society* 9–10:11–14, 1947.

19: For the secular songs of United States Negroes see

the excellent collections and discussions of Howard W. Odum and Guy B. Johnson, *Negro Workaday Songs*, Chapel Hill, N. C., 1926; the same authors' *The Negro and His Songs*, Chapel Hill, 1927; and Newman I. White, *American Negro Folksongs*, Cambridge, Mass., 1928.

20: See for instance, George Herzog, "General Characteristics of Primitive Music," *Bulletin of the American Musicological Society* 7:23–26, 1943.

21: See note 1.

22: For illustrations on stanza-by-stanza changes of the melody see for instance several musical notations by G. Herzog in Barry, Eckstorm, and Smyth, *British Ballads from Maine;* musical transcriptions by P. Barry in *Bulletin of the Folk-Song Society of the Northeast* 5, p. 8, 1933, and 9, frontispiece, 1935; numerous examples in Béla Bartók, *Hungarian Folk Music*, London, 1931.

23: Apparently the first study devoted to this question is Wilhelm Tappert, *Wandernde Melodien*, Berlin, 1890. Unfortunately it fails to make the distinction stressed here. Some excellent examples of melodic transplantation are given in Béla Bartók, *La musique populaire des Hongrois et des peuples voisins*, Budapest, 1937.

24: Recently Samuel P. Bayard made an excellent beginning in unraveling the several national strains in Anglo-American folk music, see note 14. For cross-national influences in central European folk music see Béla Bartók, note 23.

25: See for instance Marius Barbeau and Edward Sapir, *Folksongs of French Canada*, New Haven, Conn., 1925, and FRENCH FOLKLORE in vol. 1 of this work.

26: See the detailed study by Georg Schünemann, *Das Lied der deutschen Kolonisten in Russland*, Munich, 1923.

27: See for instance the material in Vicente T. Mendoza's excellent study, *El romance español y el corrido mexicano—estudio comparativo*, Mexico, D.F., 1939.

28: Translated from Béla Bartók, *Die Volksmusik der Rumänen von Maramureş*, Munich, 1923, p. 201.

29: For eastern European examples of this well-known phenomenon see song texts in Béla Bartók, *Hungarian Folk Music*, and Béla Bartók and Albert B. Lord, *Serbo-Croatian Folksongs* (1950).

30: Quoted by Arthur K. Davis, Jr., "Some Recent Trends in Folksong," *SFQ* 1: 20, 1937.

31: For excellent analyses of the interrelation of text and tune see for instance, J. W. Hendren, *A Study of Ballad Rhythm, With Special Reference to Ballad Music*, Princeton, 1936, and Stoyan Djoudjeff, *Rhythme et mesure dans la musique populaire bulgare*, Travaux publiés par l'Institut d'études slaves, vol. 12, Paris, 1931.

32: Phillips Barry, "American Folk Music," *SFQ* 1:47, 1937.

33: See Béla Bartók, *Hungarian Folk Music*.

34: See note 32, Barry, pp. 42–43, and his essay, "The Music of the Ballads," in Barry, Eckstorm, and Smyth, *British Ballads from Maine*.

35: Contrast with the usual appearance of musical notation of folk melodies the more exact, detailed transcriptions with examples given in Béla Bartók, *Hungarian Folk Music;* in Phillips Barry, "American Ballads," *Bulletin of the Folk-Song Society of the Northeast* 5:13–17, 1933; in Barry, Eckstorm, and Smyth, *British Ballads from Maine;* or in John A. Lomax and Alan Lomax, *Negro Folk Songs as Sung by Lead Belly*, New York, 1936.

36: See B. Bartók and A. B. Lord, *Serbo-Croatian Folksongs*. A similarly heavy ornamentation is found also in Ireland; see S. P. Bayard, note 14, above.

37: See the reference under note 18.

38: For many of the points suggested here, and elsewhere in this section, see the writings of E. M. von Hornbostel, especially his "Melodie und Skala," *Jahrbücher der Musikbibliothek Peters*, 19:11–23, 1913, summarized in George Herzog, review of Helen H. Roberts, "Copper Eskimo Songs," *JAFL* 39:218–225, 1926.

39: See Bartók and Lord, *Serbo-Croatian Folksongs*.

40: For comments on melodic contour in Anglo-American melodies see Sirvart Poladian, "The Problem of Melodic Variation in Folk Song," *JAFL* 55:204–211, 1942.

41: See Béla Bartók, *Hungarian Folk Music*.

42: See George Herzog, "Rhythmic Cadence in Primitive Music," *Bulletin of the American Musicological Society*, 3:19–20, 1939.

43: See note 42.

44: For examples see Djoudjeff, note 31 above.

45: Cecil J. Sharp, *English Folksong—Some Conclusions*, London, 1907.

46: See E. M. von Hornbostel, review of books on American Negro songs, *The International Review of Missions*, vol. 60, Oct. 1926.

47: See Robert Lach, *Das Konstruktionsprinzip der Wiederholung in Musik, Sprache und Literatur*, Akademie der Wissenschaften in Wien, Philosophisch-historische Klasse, Sitzungsberichte, vol. 201, no. 2, 1925.

48: J. Ribera, *La música de las cantigas*, 1922. (There is also an English translation.) For Yugoslav examples see Bartók and Lord, *Serbo-Croatian Folksongs*.

49: Compare the melodies in John A. Lomax and Alan Lomax, *Negro Folk Songs as Sung by Lead Belly*, with those in W. C. Handy, *Blues*, New York, 1926.

50: Béla Bartók, *Hungarian Folk Music*. The form is also very common in English tunes, as pointed out by Cecil J. Sharp. See Phillips Barry, *The Music of the Ballads*, and S. P. Bayard (note 14 above), p. 2, n. 11, and p. 34.

51: See for example Robert Lach's essay, note 47 above.

52: These terms have been suggested in connection with American Indian music. See George Herzog, "A Comparison of Pueblo and Pima Musical Styles," *JAFL* 49:305–306, 1936.

53: See George P. Jackson, *White Spirituals in the Southern Uplands*.

54: See George Herzog, "African Influences in North American Indian Music," *Papers Read at the International Congress of Musicology Held at New York 1939*, New York, 1944, pp. 130–143.

55: See E. M. von Hornbostel, "Phonographierte Isländische Zwiegesänge," *Deutsche Island-Forschung 1930*, pp. 300–320.

56: See B. Bartók and A. B. Lord, *Serbo-Croatian Folksongs*.

57: Discussed in Ernst T. Ferand, "The Howling in Seconds of the Lombards," *The Musical Quarterly* 25: 313–324, 1939.

58: See LITHUANIAN FOLK SONG in this Dictionary.

59: See E. Lineff, *The Peasant Songs of Great Russia*, 2 vols, 1905 and 1909.

60: See examples in Robert Lach, *Gesänge russischer Kriegsgefangener—Georgische Gesänge* (Akademie der Wissenschaften in Wien, Philos.-Histor. Kl. Sitzungsber.

vol. 204, no. 4, 1928); and his *Mingrelische, abchasische, svanische und ossetische Gesänge,* same series, vol. 205, no. 1, 1931.

61: E. M. von Hornbostel, "Die Entstehung des Jodelns," *Bericht über den Musikwissenschaftlichen Kongress in Basel 1924,* pp. 203–210. See also Manfred Bukofzer, "Magie und Technik in der Alpenmusik," *Schweizerische Annalen 1936,* pp. 205–215.

62: See for instance Samuel P. Bayard's Introduction to his important study, *Hill Country Tunes—Instrumental Folk Music of Southwestern Pennsylvania, MAFLS* 39, 1944, p. XXIII.

63: See Ilmari Krohn, "Welche ist die beste Methode, um Volks- und volksmässige Lieder nach ihrer melodischen (nicht textlichen) Beschaffenheit lexikalisch zu ordnen?" *Sammelbände der Internationalen Musikgesellschaft* 4:643–660, 1903. For application of the system see: the extensive corpus of Finnish folk melodies, *Suomen Kansan Sävalmiä,* which under Krohn's editorship began to appear in 1893; and Béla Bartók's various publications referred to above. For Ukrainia, see Philaret Kolessa, *Volkslieder aus dem Galizischen Lemkenkebiete,* Lvov, 1929.

64: The results of applying this system to a group of 45 American folk melodies were discouraging; see Arthur P. Hudson, *Folk Tunes from Mississippi* (edited by G. Herzog, assisted by Herbert Halpert), National Service Bureau, Federal Theatre Project, Works Progress Administration, New York, 1937.

65: Bertrand H. Bronson, "Folksong and the Modes," *The Musical Quarterly* 32:37–49, 1946.

66: See for instance, Reed Smith and Hilton Rufty, *American Anthology of Old-World Ballads,* New York, 1937, Introduction, pp. xx–xxii.

67: Sigurd Hustvedt, *A Melodic Index of Child's Ballad Tunes,* Publications of the University of California at Los Angeles in Languages and Literature, vol. 1, no. 2, 1936; Samuel P. Bayard, "Ballad Tunes and the Hustvedt Indexing Method," *JAFL* 55:248–254, 1942; and Bertrand H. Bronson, "Mechanical Help in the Study of Folk Song," *JAFL* 62:81–86, 1949.

Bibliography: General

Barry, Phillips. Mr. Barry was perhaps the greatest student of folk song in the United States. Some of his widely scattered writings which appeared in the *Journal of American Folklore,* the *Bulletin of the Folk-Song Society of the Northeast,* and elsewhere, were reprinted in a volume which is available in many libraries, under the title: *Folk Music in America,* edited by George Herzog and Herbert Halpert, National Service Bureau, Federal Theatre Project, Works Progress Administration, New York, 1939.

Child, Francis James. *The English and Scottish Popular Ballad.* 5 vols., Cambridge, Mass., 1882–1898. (Professor Child's headnotes survey much European folklore and ballad material.)

Danckert, Werner. *Das europäische Volkslied.* Berlin, 1938.

Danckert, Werner. *Grundriss der Volksliedkunde.* Berlin, 1938.

Eckstorm, Fanny H., and Smyth, Mary W. *Minstrelsy of Maine.* Boston, 1927.

Entwistle, William J. *European Balladry.* Oxford, 1939.

Gerould, Gordon H. *The Ballad of Tradition.* Oxford, 1932.

Greig, Gavin, and Keith, Alexander. *Last Leaves of Traditional Ballads and Ballad Airs.* Aberdeen, 1925.

Herzog, George. *Research in Primitive and Folk Music in the United States—A survey.* American Council of Learned Societies Bulletin 24, Washington, D.C., 1936. (Discussion of problems and collecting techniques.)

Hudson, Arthur P. "La poesía folklorica," *Folklore Americas,* vol. 10, no. 1–2, 1950.

Hustvedt, Sigurd B. *Ballad Books and Ballad Men.* Cambridge, Mass., 1930.

Krappe, Alexander H. *The Science of Folk-Lore.* London, 1930. (Chapters 8 and 9 are on folk song.)

Pound, Louise. *Poetic Origins and the Ballad.* New York, 1921.

Sharp, Cecil J. *English Folk-song—Some Conclusions.* London, 1907.

Sharp, Cecil J., and Karpeles, Maud. *English Folk-Songs from the Southern Appalachians.* 2 vols., London, 1932.

National

The following two volumes, organized according to countries, contain extensive bibliographies, reports on collecting activities, archives, and other important information:

Musique et Chanson Populaires. Institut International de Coopération Intellectuelle, Paris, 1934.

Folklore Musical—Musique et Chanson Populaires. Institut International de Coopération Intellectuelle, Paris, 1939.

Encyclopedia of Literature, ed. Joseph T. Shipley. 2 vols., New York, 1946. (Numerous articles on the folklore of various national literatures, occasionally including a discussion of folk song.)

United States

Herzog, George. *Research in Primitive and Folk Music in the United States—A survey.* (See above. A selected and topical bibliography; lists of recorded materials.)

Lomax, Alan, and Cowell, Sidney Robertson. *American Folk Song and Folk Lore—A regional bibliography.* Progressive Education Association Service Center Pamphlet, New York, 1942.

Lumpkin, Ben Gray, and others. *Folksongs on Records,* Issue 3. Boulder and Denver, Colo., 1950. (Listing of folk song recordings commercially available in this country.)

Mattfeld, Julius. *The Folk Music of the Western Hemisphere—A* list of references in the New York Public Library. New York, 1925.

Randolph, Vance. *Ozark Folksongs,* vol. 1. Columbia, Missouri, 1946. (The bibliography on pp. 17–28 is excellent for books and articles on folk song published in the United States.)

The functional background and related questions, Anglo-American tradition

Halpert, Herbert. "Truth in Folksong," Introductory Essay to: John H. Cox, *Traditional Ballads Mainly from West Virginia.* National Service Bureau, Federal Theatre Project, Works Progress Administration, New York, 1939.

Herzog, George. "The Study of Folksong in America," *SFQ* 2:59–64, 1938.

Mackenzie, W. Roy. *The Quest of the Ballad*. Princeton, N.J., 1919.

Randolph, Vance. *The Ozarks*. New York, 1931. (Various chapters contain excellent material.)

Sharp, Cecil J. *English Folk-Song—Some Conclusions*. London, 1907.

The Dance
Sachs, Curt. *World History of the Dance*. New York, 1937.

Musical Instruments
Sachs, Curt. *The History of Musical Instruments*. New York, 1940. (A treatment on a world-wide scale.)

Schaeffner, André. *Origine des instruments de musique*. Paris, 1936. (Refers primarily to the musical instruments of primitive peoples.)

Primitive Poetry and Music
Astrov, Margot. *The Winged Serpent*. New York, 1946. (An anthology of American Indian poetry, with discussion.)

Encyclopedia of Literature, ed. Joseph T. Shipley. 2 vols., New York, 1946. (See comment above.)

Herzog, George. *Research in Primitive Folk Music in the United States*. (See above; selected and topical bibliography.)

Lachmann, Robert. "Musik der aussereuropäischen Natur- und Kulturvölker," *Bücken's Handbuch der Musikwissenschaft,* vol. 1, Wildpark-Potsdam, 1929.

Mattfeld, Julius. *The Folk Music of the Western Hemisphere*. (See above.)

Stumpf, Carl. *Die Anfänge der Musik*. Leipsic, 1911.

Varley, Douglas H. *African Native Music*—An annotated bibliography. Royal Empire Society Bibliographies No. 8, London, 1936.   GEORGE HERZOG

son-in-law tests Tests and tasks set by a powerful person for his prospective or actual son-in-law are part of nearly all North American Indian mythologies, and have been the subject of inquiry by Robert H. Lowie in his paper, "The Test-Theme in North American Indian Mythology" (*JAFL* 21: 97–148, 1908). Lowie lists, for various areas, the North American test-tales proper (pp. 134–38), as well as miscellaneous tales and hero-tales in which various characters, such as Lodge-Boy and Thrown-Away, the Pueblo twins, Blood-Clot-Boy, etc., overcome obstacles. Several of the incidents in the son-in-law test-tales have independent distributions and appear as elements of narratives in which tests are not the primary object. For references to some of the most common tests in North American Indian tales, such as tests of prowess (quest for berries in winter, quest for dangerous animals, heat test, smoke test, poisoned food test, etc.) see Stith Thompson, *Tales of the North American Indians* (Cambridge, Mass., 1929), p. 364. See ABANDONMENT ON THE ISLAND; TESTS. [EWV]

Sons of North Britain A ballad collected in Nova Scotia, dealing with the theme of combat between father and son who do not know each other. Two young men, who were searching for the parents who had left them in Scotland seven years before, encountered a stranger in the woods. A fight grew out of some trivial incident and the stranger killed them both, learning as they died that they were his sons. The motif is the same as that of the story of Cuchulain and his son Conla.

sooner hound In American folklore, a dog that would sooner run than eat and sooner eat than do anything useful. A sooner dog, at least in New York City, is a creature that likes his comfort; he sooner wets on the living-room rug than anywhere else in the house.

sortition A form of divination employing the casting of lots or other chance choice to determine the answer to a previously thought-of question: perhaps the most ancient and certainly the most widespread of all forms of divination. The casting of dice or knuckle-bones is the typical example: the result of the cast is checked against a predetermined code to discover the interpretation of the throw. The casting of lots is described in Homer; the seer Mopsus divined by lot-casting before the *Argo* sailed. Vergil (*sortes Virgilianæ*) and the Bible have both been used to determined the will of the gods: a line is chosen at random and read in the light of the problem in mind. Polynesians spin a coconut to determine the identity of a thief, and a bottle is spun to discover a kissing-partner in the United States.

In the Greek democracies, sortition was used (in Athens after 487 B.C. for magistrates) to replace election by voting. Determining the wishes of the gods was felt to be more reliable than the possibly corrupt political method of voting for demagogs. Often a double sortition occurred; nomination by lot was followed by election by lot.

soul Belief in one or multiple souls for living beings, particularly for human beings, is practically universal among North American Indians. Many tribes believe that not only humans, but all other animals, have souls.

There are few if any explanatory myths accounting for the soul, but there is much evidence in American Indian mythology and curing practices to indicate that the belief in soul(s) existed. Tales of visits by human beings who appear "dead" for a few days while the soul leaves them and goes to the afterworld are numerous over the continent, as well as the Orpheus myth, in which a person visits the afterworld, sees the souls dancing there, and recovers the soul of a beloved relative which he brings back to earth. See SOUL LOSS.

The beliefs of two or three widely-separated North American Indian groups may be taken as a sample of native beliefs about the soul. The Fox Indians of the Eastern Woodlands believe each person has two souls: a small one, located in the heart during life and bestowed on a person by the supreme deity, and a large soul, the shadow, given by Wisaka, the culture hero. Only the small soul goes westward at death. This small soul can be reborn four times; it will have a new large soul each time. If the soul gets too big, the owner will become a murderer (William Jones, *Ethnography of the Fox Indians*, BBAE 125, 1939, p. 16, n. 19). The Tübatulabal, a tribe on the edge of the Mohave desert in east-central California, say of the soul, or *shu'nun* (also the term for heart) that it resides in the head, that it leaves the body temporarily through the ears when a person sleeps, so that when one dreams "it is one's soul that goes out and does the things one dreams." The capture of a person's soul by an evil shaman results in the victim becoming insane. When a person dies his breath (*i'kin*) which stays in the heart during life goes out, together with the soul. The soul becomes breath, but looks like a human being and is referred to as an *abawinal,* "ghost" (Erminie W. Voegelin, *Tübatulabal Ethnography,* Anthropological Records, vol. 2, No. 1, 1938, p. 62). The Penobscot of the New England coastal region use as the term for soul the word which also means goodness; they believe that souls have a detached existence as stars.

The belief that animals have souls, and that when they are killed, it is only at the fourth killing that an animal's soul leaves its body permanently, exists among many Eastern tribes. [EWV]

☞ In a considerable number of South American tribes, the soul is identified with the shadow or the reflection in water or in a mirror. Sometimes the idea of soul, heart, and pulsation is expressed by the same word.

The Carib Indians believe in the plurality of the souls which are located in different parts of the body. According to some Guarani tribes two souls coexist in every man: one gentle and another one the animal soul, which is believed to be responsible for a person's temperament. Sleep, catalepsy, and states of trance are the results of the temporary absence of the soul which sometimes abandons the body to wander far away, often to the land of the dead. Dreams and visions reflect the adventures of the soul.

Souls are not considered by the Indians to be necessarily immortal. They are often destroyed during the journey to the land of the spirits. [AM]

☞ In Chinese belief, man has two souls: *hun,* the superior or spiritual soul, which if proper ceremonies are performed, ascends into heaven and meets its ancestors, and *p'o* which, depending on the adequacy of the sacrifices and its own physical stamina, informs the body in life and the corpse after death. After death or in dream or trance states the hun can materialize and appear in every respect similar to the living body. So too the p'o, except that after the disintegration of the body it may appear as a skeleton or only a few bones. Souls of the ancestors are also thought of as inhabiting ancestral tablets. Because it is improper to appear before ancestors in a disfigured condition, parts of the body lost in life must be preserved. The heads of decapitated criminals are often buried with the bodies and eunuchs always carefully preserved the sexual organs which had been severed.

In Kueicho a young man committed horrible crimes. He was frequently executed but three days later, even when parts of his dismembered body were buried at distant places, he returned and five days later recommenced his wickedness. One day he beat his mother. The old lady then came to the mandarin with a small box. She said that when he was about to commit his crimes he put his superior soul in the box. Consequently after execution the superior soul could find the parts of the body and bring them together again. See CHINESE FOLKLORE; SAMOYEDS. [RDJ]

☞ The doctrine of the soul is one of the most difficult aspects of African and New World Negro theology to group. Any analysis of the concept must begin with the cult of the dead, which holds a place of primary importance in the belief-systems of these people. Especially complex are the various concepts of multiple souls, which may take the form of the shadow, or may represent what in Euro-American thought would be the personality of the individual, or may be the element that relates him to the forces that rule the world, or may be equated with what might be termed intuition. The soul is everywhere in Africa the mechanism whereby one's affiliation to one's relationship group is achieved and validated. The concept is thus of great social significance as a force making for integration and stability. The soul, in some one of its manifestations, is believed to live on after death, and thus links the living to the dead. Reincarnation is a widely spread belief, though in many parts of Africa no contradiction is felt between a belief in reincarnation and a concomitant belief that the soul of the ancestor reincarnated lives on after death. Various terms for soul found in West Africa have been retained in the New World, notably that of *'kra* (Ashanti *okra*), heard in the Guianas. The concept of the *zombi,* prominent in the belief-system of Haiti, has as its essential element the idea that the soul of a person can be captured and employed by a worker of evil magic to make available to him the services of those who come under his power. This type of belief, that the soul as personality, often related to the "real" name of an individual, must be protected if the person is to avoid an evil fate, is as deep-seated as any single item in the religious and magical system of Africa and the Negro New World. See ANCESTOR WORSHIP. [MJH]

soul-animal or **soul-bird** An animal or bird who is the co-existent double of a human being. The animal or bird is usually born in the forest (or on the farm) at the same moment as the human infant whose double it is; the fate of the one depends on the fate of the other in matters of growth, health, safety, etc.; the life of the one is inextricably bound up with the life of the other; when one sickens or dies, the other sickens and dies. See LIFE TOKEN. Animals in whom the souls of the dead are reincarnate are referred to by some writers as soul-animals; many others, however, refer to the reincarnation of the soul as animal or bird as animal soul or bird soul. But since reincarnation as animal (E610 ff.) is not the same concept as animal as actual soul or double of a living person, an effort has been made to use the two terms distinctively throughout this book. See BIRD SOUL; BUSH SOUL; TONAL.

soul cakes Little cakes baked for the dead to eat, or to benefit the dead: offered during funeral rites, during feasts for the dead, placed on graves, or given to the poor as proxy for the souls. In ancient Egypt little cakes were left inside the tomb for the *ka* to eat. The primitive Ainus of Japan make millet cakes for their dead. The Japanese leave cakes for the souls of the dead beside their shrines for three days during the festival called Bon, which is their feast for the returning souls. The Chinese also prepare little cakes and other foods for their Festival for the Hungry Ghosts, Yü-Lan Hui, on the 15th of the Seventh Moon. Hindu soul cakes are the famous *pindas,* or honeyed rice balls. See SESAME.

In Europe in general soul cakes were commonly left out for the dead on All Souls' Day, or taken and placed on the graves. In Russia soul cakes were formerly gingerbread and rich sweet tarts. In Belgium it was said that for every cake eaten on All Souls' Day, a soul was released from Purgatory. In southern Germany and Austria people were wont to go to the graveyards and leave cakes on the graves for the hungry dead. In some sections they were given instead to beggars, as proxies for the dead.

In England the bread formerly handed out to the poor at funerals was a kind of soul cake by proxy. Soul cakes are usually made in England about October 28, to be eaten on All Souls' Day. In north Wales they were distributed among the poor. On the Welsh border and in the rural shires of England, children sometimes still go from farm to farm *a-souling*, i.e. singing and receiving little cakes. Formerly in Shropshire the soul cakes were heaped high on a platter and every visitor to the house on All Souls' Day was given one. Visitors were importuned to eat with the following chant: A soul cake, a soul cake/ Have mercy on all Christian souls for a soul cake. See CAKE CUSTOMS.

In the United States, begging on Halloween is an attenuated form, and the request may be couched as "Trick or treat?"; the former being a penalty if a bribe (usually in the form of sweets or money) is not forthcoming. In Mexico and other parts of Latin America this symbolic eating takes another shape: miniature skulls of sugar or candy are sold and eaten. The eating *of* the dead, which may be regarded as the obverse of eating *for* the dead, also appears in many guises. In Melanesia, for instance, parts of the corpse are eaten by the relatives of the deceased out of respect for him, and form part of the mourning rites. Cannibals may eat parts of the valorous enemy to capture his power. Eating of the divine body also occurs, of which perhaps the best known example is the communion rite found in the Christian churches. [NFJ]

soul loss Absence of the soul from the living body, resulting in sickness, and eventually death, if it is not regained. In the belief of the primitive peoples of the Americas especially, loss of soul is a danger attendant upon all sleepers, sneezers, and yawners, but it is usually caused by the evil magic of an enemy, i.e. witchcraft. Soul-catching, or the restoration of the soul to the living body, is a complicated and detailed ritual requiring the services of a highly specialized shaman.

South American Aymara Indians believe that sometimes when a child sickens, its soul has been kidnapped by the spirit of a road, hill, river, field, or even a Christian church, and the kidnapper must be appeased with offerings of wool, candy, coca leaves, etc., at the place where the parents believe the kidnapping took place. The Aymara also believe that soul loss can be caused by body exuviæ accidentally getting into a *chullpa* (burial place for the mummified dead) resulting in a horrible disease known as *čulpa-usu*. This is because the soul has been snatched by the spirit of the dead in the tomb. [AM] See DREAM SOUL; *Folklore of the primitive tribes of South America* in SOUTH AMERICAN INDIAN FOLKLORE.

Ethnic groups in many parts of the world have devised ingenious ways to keep our souls in our bodies and to keep alien souls, demons, evil spirits, devils, and the like, out. The mouth is an obvious danger zone and one of the functions of lip ornaments, nose rings, earrings, and the like, was to keep the soul in and to frighten away evil spirits who might be tempted to enter. The present custom of covering our mouths when we yawn is simple self-protection; and the courteous Chinese cover their mouths when they come close to speak, a habit which makes communication sometimes difficult. The suggestion has been made that the veils of Arab women and some of the North African men

served a similar purpose, though, like the cowboy's kerchief, they were also useful during dust storms. The Marquesans held the mouth and nose shut at the moment of death to keep the soul from escaping. The Alfoors of the Celebes took precautions at the time of birth to keep the infant's soul from slipping away, and the Zulus and Persians are said to have regarded yawning and sneezing as signs of approaching possession. When people sleep, their souls wander and the soulless body may thus become possessed by other homeless ghosts. The homeless soul, being unable to enter its own body has to find whatever habitation it can. One of the Chinese Eight Immortals, Li with the Iron Crutch has the body of a beggar. Consequently, precautions taken to keep mouths shut during sleep prevent snoring, a boon in itself, but also discourage souls from engaging in nocturnal adventures. The *Han* or grave jades of China, beautifully carved crickets of precious stone, stopped the openings of the corpse and thus prevented the physical ghost, who tends to be violent and evil, from escaping and molesting the family and community. The pads over the mouth introduced as a protective measure in the epidemic of 1918 are still worn by many Japanese whose folk wisdom has taught them that much evil can enter through the mouth. [RDJ]

Loss of one's soul by a living human being, usually because of witchcraft being practiced against the victim, is held to be a common cause for illness among North American Indians; if the victim's soul is not recovered death results, and there are in many tribes shamans with special powers to recover souls of sick persons. Sometimes, as on the North Pacific Coast, these shamans make special annual "voyages" in spirit canoes to the land of souls to recover all the souls stolen from human beings who are still living, but are ill at the time. The soul when recovered is put back into the victim's body either through the top of the head, the navel, or the ears, mouth, etc. (see Forrest E. Clements, *Primitive Concepts of Disease*, University of California Publications in American Archæology and Ethnology, vol. 32, pp. 185–252, 1932; also, Ruth Underhill, *Indians of the Pacific Northwest*, Riverside, California, pp. 195–99). See SOUL. [EWV]

It is commonly believed in Middle America that the soul may be jarred loose or stolen from the body of a person. This results in sickness and eventual death if it is not returned by the medicine man. *Espanto*, or fright, is commonly thought to be a cause of soul loss. Sometimes the word *susto* is used. See CHANEQUES; DREAMS; MEXICAN AND CENTRAL AMERICAN INDIAN FOLKLORE. [GMF]

South American Indian folklore In a great continental area such as South America where many native peoples have been long subjected to outside influences, but where others still live as did their ancestors 400 years ago, the extent of what may be characterized as Indian folklore must be clearly delimited. The customs and beliefs of those Indian tribes, such as the Nambikuara, Rukuyen, and others who still keep a functioning native culture cannot be considered to be "folklore," as this science is usually defined, but where the native population has been converted to Christianity and where European civilization has taken root, as for instance in Peru and Bolivia, similar customs, still retained by the Indian masses, may be called folkloric.

Anthropologists dealing with primitive tribes are apt to limit the use of the term folklore to the body of tales and myths, the interpretations of natural phenomena and of features of the milieu found among a primitive group. Folklore in this sense is almost coextensive with oral literature, philosophy, and natural sciences. Therefore, in giving a general outline of South American Indian folklore here, we shall distinguish between those Indians who have kept their old ways and those whose present culture is a blending of the old and the new. For the former we shall discuss oral literature, for the latter some of the folk customs that come from the Indian past. We shall end with a short summary of the main outlooks and folkways of those Indian tribes who are considered "primitive" in contrast to the ancient civilized people of the Andes, such as the Inca and the Chibcha.

Myths and Tales of the South American Indians There is a large body of Indian myths and tales in South America, but few have been completely or faithfully recorded. Most of the religions and traditions of the civilized people of the Andes have been lost and little attempt has been made to draw upon the memories which their modern descendants may still retain. Similarly the folklore of the primitive tribes has seldom been recorded with the scientific care required. Best known is the folklore of the Carib and Arawak Indians of the Guianas, the Kaggaba, the Witoto, the Cashinawa, the Tenetehara, the Apinayé, the Sherente, the Timbira, the Bakaïrí, the Guaraní, the Toba, the Mataco, the Ona, the Yahgan, the Araucanians.

Comparative study of the main motifs of South American mythology and folktales reveals a surprising identity even among cultures as different as those of Brazil and the Andes. In far apart regions and among tribes who have little in common, one finds parallels not only in themes but also in sequences and detail. The frequent recurrence of similar themes justifies a general treatment of South American lore.

In South American mythology, there are few accounts of the creation of the world. Its existence is taken for granted, or it is barely mentioned as the initial act of some vague deity or First Ancestor. Instead the Indians are primarily interested in the origin of the special features of the universe, such as the first appearance of sun and moon, of men, animals, or other aspects of nature. Even when the notion of a Supreme Being is clearly conceived, as among the Tierra del Fuego Indians, the task of giving to nature its definite shape is assumed by a culture hero (e.g. Kenos, the first man among the Ona). This personage may be the creator himself, as in ancient Peru, but more often he is the creator's son or the first man. The traditional pattern of myths describing the origin of our world is to present it as the work of a wandering magician and transformer (Viracocha in Peru, Bochica in Colombia, Maria among the Tupi-Guaraní, Keri and Kame among the Bakaïrí, etc.). The episodes of his adventures are usually associated with changes or innovations in nature as he found it. The stories do not establish a hierarchy of events. Less importance may be given to the creation of the moon and the sun than to explanations of the spots on some animal's fur. Consequently Indian cosmogonies

often have for us a disconcerting lack of proportion, but may at the same time indicate that important episodes have been lost. Details which appeal to ordinary storytellers are not always those which have the greatest importance for the shamans or those preoccupied with the great problems of the universe.

Just as the present order of nature is the result of successive creations and transformations realized by the culture hero, his teachings are the sources of laws, of the social system, and of the most valuable arts and crafts. Culture heroes are creators, civilizers, and often also epic heroes.

A pair of twin heroes plays an important role in the mythology of South America. Often they overshadow the figure of the culture hero so much that they take his place as creators, transformers, and benefactors of mankind. This is particularly true in the mythology of the Caribs, Bakaïrí, and Tierra del Fuego Indians. The Twins are generally personifications of sun and moon, for their contrasting nature is explained by the difference between these two celestial bodies. Sun, the elder brother, is strong and clever; Moon, the younger, is weak and subject to periodic mishaps in which he loses his life and must be revived by Sun.

Myths about the origin of man follow two patterns. In the one case, the first men were created by the culture hero out of clay, reeds, or wood; in the second, men migrated from the underworld, or in a few instances, from the sky (e.g. Warrau). According to the mythology of the ancient Peruvians and of some Colombian tribes (Choco), present mankind is regarded, as in Central America, as the last and best of successive types of beings who were created and destroyed by the gods in various cataclysms.

Indian cosmogony describes four major cataclysms that destroyed all or most of the life in the world: the Great Fire, the Long Night, the Flood, and a long period of cold (the last motif only in the Chaco and Tierra del Fuego). Versions of the Deluge story are particularly numerous. Very often the disaster is said to have been caused by an angry deity, but violations of tabus (Toba, Witoto) are also made responsible for it. The motif of Noah's ark is rare in South America; in many cases it is obviously of recent European origin.

In their folktales and myths, South American Indians have shown considerable interest in the origin of fire, of useful plants, and other cultural goods. Often either the culture hero or the Twins have made these available to men; many are also attributed to the intervention of helpful animals. Almost as common as flood myths are those describing the introduction of fire. Usually fire was owned by some animal or monster, from whom it was stolen by the culture hero or some animal. There are also many stories telling how men obtained their staple food plants. According to a widespread tradition (Peru, Guiana, Brazil), they grew from the body parts of a mysterious child who was killed or appeared suddenly. According to a very popular myth found in the Guianas and among the Cuna and the Choco Indians, all the food plants grew on a single big tree (theme of the tree of life) which was felled by the culture hero. In the trunk was water which flooded the world.

Sun and moon are often identified with objects, for instance, feather balls, which were stolen from their original owners, the vultures (Bakaïrí) or a feather head-dress worn by a man.

The constellations are named after animals and men; myths explain how they went to the sky. Orion was a man whose leg was severed by his unfaithful wife (Arekuna). Some tribes personify natural phenomena like rain, lightning, and fire. The Thunderbird motif figures also in Chaco and Amazonian folklore, but does not have the importance it enjoys among North American Indians.

The most familiar protagonists of South American folklore are spirits and animals. A large part of Guiana folklore consists of stories of men who met spirits and who, through their cleverness, succeeded in escaping. Sometimes the spirits are depicted as friendly beings who are willing to help people, but their amiable contacts with men generally have a bad ending because they are touchy, shy, and subject to tabus. In many tribes a favorite story is about a man who went to live with the spirits and brought back the knowledge of plants or useful arts. Spirit stories are often animal stories because the supernatural characters involved are the spirits of animal species. The cycle of the culture hero includes a large number of animal characters, and we have already seen that animals play the part of civilizers and benefactors in the traditional lore of many tribes.

In the Chaco and in Peru, the main hero of the popular oral literature is Fox, the Trickster, who is greedy, mischievous, and stupid. His aggressive and ambitious disposition leads him into adventures which end disastrously and make him a laughable, abject character.

The classic cycle of animal stories in the Amazon basin and in the Guianas is built around a small land turtle, *jabuty*, who, though slow and small, outwits jaguars and other strong animals. There is some doubt, however, whether turtle stories are all of Indian origin. Many have a distinct African flavor and may have been spread by the Negro slaves.

An etiological intention is the basis of many animal stories. They have been inspired by some peculiarity of the species which is explained by an adventure or an accident that happened to an ancestor.

As South American folklore becomes better known, parallels with the myths and tales of North American Indians multiply. Resemblances cover not only the motifs but sometimes their combinations and small details, as for instance, the myth of the giant with a stone heart, and the marriage of Trickster with his daughter. A few of the common traits may be listed here: Trickster juggles with his eyes, the flying or rolling head, the star woman, the obstacle flight, magical pregnancy, miraculous recognition, the sharpened leg, the misfortunes of Fox, and Trickster's adventures. The last cycle follows the pattern of the well-known Coyote stories.

Other Forms of South American Indian Oral Literature In addition to prose tales, South American Indian folklore includes other forms. Poetry exists but is inseparable from songs and chants. Often songs are merely strings of meaningless syllables, or short ditties whose meaning is difficult to ascertain (Tierra del Fuego, Chaco, Caingang). In the Guianas and in the Chaco, brief and often trivial statements may be sung over and over again. Among the Yaruro, a very primitive tribe of Venezuela, shamans are said to compose long poems describing their voyages to the land of the spirits. The ancient Abipón

and the Mbayá of the Chaco recited epic songs relating to exploits of their ancestors. Some form of epic poetry seems to have existed in Peru and might have been used by the Spanish chroniclers for their accounts of Inca history. Poetry was well developed among the Incas; unfortunately few specimens have been preserved.

Indians who have kept their native culture do not seem to know either proverbs or riddles. The Araucanians are the only tribe among whom a substantial collection of proverbs has been made, but here one cannot disregard the possibility of strong Spanish influences. As far as is known only the Minuane of the Rio Putumayo have riddles. Elsewhere there is not the slightest evidence of their existence.

Peruvian Indian Folklore In the countries where the influence of the Inca empire was strongly felt, such as Ecuador, Peru, Bolivia and the northwest of the Argentine, there exists a wealth of traditional beliefs and customs which give a fundamental unity to the area and set it apart within the continent. Modern Andean folklore is, to a large extent, a heritage of Inca civilization, but in the transmission it has suffered many losses and has incorporated many extraneous elements.

The Peruvian and Bolivian Indians reacted to Christianity very much as the European peasantry did at the beginning of the medieval era. Catholicism was imposed on the Indian masses soon after the overthrow of the Inca empire in 1532. After more than half a century the Spanish clergy discovered that the rural population had remained pagan under a very thin veneer of Christianity. The ensuing campaign to extirpate "superstition" failed; for modern Indians are still surprisingly faithful to the ancient deities and the ritual of their pagan ancestors. Four hundred years of Catholicism have, however, left their imprint. Ancient beliefs and practices are intermingled with Christian doctrines and rites. Some old gods have been forgotten and saints have been adopted in their pantheon. The degree to which Quechua and Aymara Indians cling to old beliefs varies in different regions, yet even in large cities, such as La Paz, the Indian proletariat holds to the past. In large sections of the city market, herbs, magical substances, and ingredients for sacrifices are openly sold to numerous patrons.

The religious system which the Spaniards found in the Inca empire was elaborate. It combined the cult of the great nature gods with that of countless nature spirits, especially those of the mountains and of the rivers. The cult of the sun, the ancestor of the emperor, was supported and spread by the state. There were theologians who devised a divine hierarchy presided over by a Supreme God, Viracocha. The deities, great and small, were served in sanctuaries attended by trained priests and by the famous maidens of the sun.

Modern Quechua and Aymara Indians have forgotten most of the major gods of their ancestors. In Peru, the Quechua still regard the sun as a benevolent and powerful godhead, but one who is removed from human affairs and on the same plane as God, the Father, and Jesus. On the other hand, all the Indians from Ecuador to Argentina, still have a deep attachment to the earth goddess, Pacha-mama, who bestows fertility on crops and herbs. So great is her importance that she is often equated to or identified with the Virgin Mary. In most of their feasts, the Indians make offerings and sacrifices to the Pacha-mama and implore her help. The thunder god, Illapu, who was also very popular in the old empire, has survived in the guise of Santiago (Saint James, patron of Spain). He demands the sacrifice of a white llama whenever he strikes the ground with lightning, and from him emanate the mysterious powers possessed by priests and shamans.

The villagers of the Andes render a cult to the spirits of the mountains, lakes, and rivers. These supernatural beings, according to the region or the category to which they belong, are known as *achachila, apo, auki*, or *mallcu*. The sites from which the ancestors of a community are believed to have emerged to the surface of the earth are still regarded as sacred places and the Indians visit them to get comfort and strength. The welfare of villagers, of their crops and herds is still dependent on the virtues of some fetish (*samiri*) which may be a rough stone or some other object. Aymara Indians keep in their houses stuffed wildcats and hawks, which are tutelary spirits. Twice a week offerings are placed before them. The demons who were the supernatural custodians of the game or of the fish continue to receive the prayers and offerings of hunters and fishermen. Modern Indians are no less afraid than their ancestors to meet in the solitudes of the Andes such cruel spirits as the *Anchanchu*, the *Ccoa*, the *Larilari*, etc.

Although modern ceremonies and rites are only pale memories of the solemn and elaborate feasts celebrated in the days of the Inca empire, many of their salient features have been preserved. Human sacrifices, which formerly seem to have been common, have disappeared, but llamas, alpacas, and guinea-pigs are still consecrated to the gods or the saints and are killed according to the ancient rules. The oozing blood, for instance, is still mixed with different sorts of flour and is sprinkled in the four cardinal directions. The Incas offered to their gods gold objects and clothes; their descendants present more modest tribute, but still know how to select and to prepare the many ingredients which were combined in the *chachhalla*, the ritual libations. Fetuses of llamas or sheep are often burned as substitutes for the animals which are beyond the means of the impoverished Indians.

Each month of the Inca calendar was marked by some feast. Most were festive ceremonies to ask the gods for a good harvest; others commemorated magico-religious events, such as the expulsion of the bad spirits, or honored the sun god. The feast of Inti raimi, which took place at the time of the June solstice, is said to have been surrounded with unsurpassed splendor. The fiestas of the modern Quechua and Aymara perpetuate in our time some of these festivities. They are the occasions for the display of wealth in the form of costumes embroidered with silver, splendid headdresses, and carved and painted masks. The dances are often pantomimes which derive directly from magico-religious performances, such as the *čoqela* dance in Bolivia, which imitates the incidents of a hunting drive against vicuña and the slaying of one of these animals.

Agrarian ritual probably has altered little in the course of centuries. Work in the field is regulated by the phases of the moon. Before sowing or harvesting, omens are carefully observed. Fields are plowed by oxen, profusely decorated, to the accompaniment of songs. Maize beer and coca leaves are thrown into the furrows

to propitiate the earth mother and the local spirits. After harvest, sacrifices and offerings are again made. At a communion meal, music is played and dances are executed to keep the souls of the plants in the fields.

Now as formerly, the everyday life of the Indian is permeated with magico-religious practices; libations and sacrifices must be made before or after any undertaking. No Indian would leave his house for a journey without spilling alcohol on the ground, and muttering an invocation to the Pacha-mama, the saint, and the tutelary spirits of his village or of his house. Every time a Quechua or Aymara traveler climbs a hill he throws a stone or a handful of coca on the *apacheta*, a heap of stones built by generations of travelers. This rite is performed not only on the ordinary passes of the Andes, but even at the beginning of the streets leading into cities. The trade in amulets, charms, and magic herbs flourishes all over the highlands. A caste of ambulant vendors, the *collahuallas*, visit the most remote villages to cure patients by pre-Columbian methods.

Many functions of the Inca ceremonial priests have been taken over by village medicine men who today make the sacrifices and offerings to the gods and lead the ceremonies. These men also are the heirs of the popular shamans who summoned spirits, cured diseases, and counteracted witchcraft. They practice divination with coca leaves or by consulting the viscera of sacrificed animals. Witchcraft is greatly feared by the Indians. The leeches bewitch their victims by subjecting their exuviæ or symbolic figures to rites of sympathetic magic. Cures are often based on the principle of the "scapegoat"; a llama is charged with the clothes of the sick and expelled from the village, or objects which have been in contact with the patients are left on the road in the hope that someone will find them and carry the disease away.

The customs observed by the modern Andean Indians at the time of various life crises combine ancient magic rites with practices borrowed from the Spaniards. At childbirth evil spirits are kept at bay with charcoal and a knife; the afterbirth is buried with miniature utensils to make the child a good worker, etc. The first cutting of the hair is as important a ceremony today as it was in Inca time. The *huarachicoy* ceremony, the puberty rite of the Incas, which was performed annually in the Cuzco was partly religious and magical, partly a series of tests of strength and courage. Because it was celebrated exclusively on behalf of the nobility, it disappeared with the fall of the empire. Modern Indians do not attach any special significance to the transition from childhood to adulthood.

The custom of the *sirvinacuy*, or trial marriage, is well established among the Quechua. In some districts of Peru, betrothals take place on a certain day of the year, as seems to have been the case in the old empire. The marriage ceremony among the Aymara is often followed by a mock kidnapping of the bride and the pursuit of the couple.

Death requires of the mourners the observance of a whole set of ceremonial practices. Not long ago, the Aymara still strangled dying persons to liberate their souls. Black as a sign of mourning is an old pre-Columbian tradition. During the death vigil, the clothes and other belongings of the deceased are gambled away with a die made of a llama astragalus. Armed men keep watch around the mortuary house to prevent the new ghost from carrying off with him the souls of his relatives and friends. From time to time the sentries cast stones from slingshots to frighten away the ghost. Ashes are strewn on the threshold during the night. The marks which are found the following day are considered clues, which foretell the death of some other members of the community. A llama may be sacrificed to accompany the dead person to the other world. The Indians of the northwest of Argentina kill a dog which will help the soul to cross a river. The personal belongings of a dead person are often destroyed.

Worship of the dead had a prominent place in Inca religion. Dead emperors remained in their palaces and were taken on solemn processions during certain feasts. The Spanish Inquisitors often refer to the obstinacy with which the Indians, despite the strictest prohibitions, continued to render a cult to their dead. In October of each year, the Aymara hold a ceremony for the skulls which they dig out of the graves and have a drinking bout to send away the souls. On All Saints Day, they bring food to the cemeteries where they share it with persons who are willing to pray for their dead.

It would be impossible to list all the minor practices of the Indians, the omens which they observe, the practices which they follow to avert bad luck. Those which have been recorded show, like their popular religion, a strange blending of old Indian beliefs and European superstitions.

Folklore of the Primitive Tribes of South America. East of the Andes, from the Guianas to the Gran Chaco, lived and in many areas still live countless small tribes whose civilization may be roughly classified into five types: the forest tribes of the Guianas and of the Amazonian basin, the more or less archaic tribes of eastern and southern Brazil (Ge, Botocudo, Bororo, etc.), the Chaco Indians (Toba, Mataco, Abipón, Mbayá), the tribes of the Pampas (Charrua, Puelche, Tehuelche, Pampas, etc.) and the tribes of Tierra del Fuego (Ona, Yahgan, Alacaluf).

Compared to the people of the Andes, the natives of the plains and plateaus of South America have simple and primitive cultures. There are considerable differences between the various culture areas, but underlying them are many common outlooks on the world and some basic attitudes toward the supernatural.

The vision of the universe shared by all these Indians may be termed animistic in the full sense of the word. Nature appears to them to be the abode of countless spirits who are powerful and elusive, but not fundamentally different from human beings. In Tierra del Fuego, however, animism occupied a secondary position in relation to a highly developed theism.

The spirits are conceived by most Indians as touchy creatures who, for this reason, are apt to be harmful. Many of them are definitely malicious and by temperament inclined to persecute men (the *kanaima* spirits of the Guiana Indians, the *anan* of the Tupi-Guarani, for example). Others, as the servants of shamans, are responsible for disease and death. In each tribe there is a rich spirit lore. Through tales and traditions every Indian is familiarized from childhood with the appearance, the ruses and deceits of these supernatural beings. This knowledge helps him to avoid the dangers lurking about. He learns that at night he must travel with fire to ward off spirits (Tupi, Carib, etc.); before passing rapids he must rub his eyes with Cayenne pepper (Guiana); offerings must be made when a storm threatens (Tupinamba); he knows that certain puzzling contraptions may delay the spirits who follow his tracks (Macushi); that changing his name may disconcert a revengeful supernatural. He knows also that masks worn at feasts have coercive power over demons (Indians of the Caiari-Uaupes region). The tales and myths which he hears at night teach him to recognize the presence of spirits by the noises they make, or to detect them when in human guise they approach him with evil intentions.

Most spirits that appear to men belong to large groups, each of which has common characteristics. There are water, mountain, air, tree spirits, just as there are spirits that have protruding eyebrows, jointless limbs, or hairy skin. Some spirits stand out of these undifferentiated crowds because of their distinctive personality and may be called demons. Natural phenomena, though often personified in myths and tales, are seldom regarded as deities or even demons. It is only in the religion of the Apinaye, Sherente, and Timbira that Moon, Sun, and Planets are divinities that appear to men, listen to their prayers, and bestow favors on them. There are also some faint traces of a solar cult among the ancient Guarani. Thunder, among the Tupinamba and Guarani, was so colorful a demon that the first missionaries promoted him to the dignity of the Christian God. Of special importance are the "Fathers" and "Mothers" of game animals and fish because of the control which they exercise on food resources. Certain demons would deserve the title of god if they received a regular cult. For instance, the goddess Tae of the Tucuna and the cannibal god, Kumaphari, of the Shipaya. Their will is felt by men, but little is done to placate them or to obtain favors.

The Great Ancestor mentioned in the cosmogony is no more than a vague figure lost in the night of time. Now and then certain tribes, such as the Caingua or the Guarayu, make efforts to approach him. Contrary to the common notion that belief in a supreme god occurs only at a high level of civilization, in South America it is among the extremely primitive tribes of Tierra del Fuego that theism has found its highest expression. The Powerful One was conceived as an invisible spirit without material needs, omniscient, and all-powerful, who lived in the sky beyond the stars. Prayers and simple offerings were the only manifestations of his cult. He was entirely separated from all the other spirits and presided alone over the universe.

Ghosts are generally confused with the invisible swarms of spirits and it is seldom that a strict distinction is made between them and the other supernatural beings. For the Bororo, for instance, the two categories of spirits were carefully differentiated and each had a special kind of shamans as mediums.

Everywhere in primitive South America, the relationship between man and the supernatural is the special concern of professional shamans, the *piay* of the Amazonians, the *machi* of the Araucanians. They enter this career after a long training during which they feast and take narcotics to get visions. Many shamans claim to have been chosen by the spirits to become intermediaries between the supernatural world and mankind. In order to be a shaman, one must possess magic chants and have invisible missiles (darts, quartz pebbles, some amorphous substance) inside the body. Shamans are credited with the power of sending their souls away to see the spirits or to witness events in distant places. They also summon spirits and converse with them in the presence of the people. Actual possession, that is to say the belief that a spirit has entered a man and speaks through his mouth, is rare in South America (Bororo, Tenetehara, Toba).

The principal function of the shaman is to cure disease. Ailments are usually explained by the presence of some pathogenic object or animal in the patient's body or by the kidnapping or loss of the soul. The former theory is by far the most widespread and determines the usual treatment. The shaman, after having blown smoke on his client, sucks his skin with great energy to extract a stick, a stone, or an insect which, he explains, was the missile sent by the witch or by a spirit that assumed material form. If the disease is diagnosed as soul loss, the shaman looks for it and tries to recapture it. The cures, irrespective of the method used, are accompanied by the recitation of spells and also by treatment with herbs and other drugs. The scientific knowledge of the Indians has been somewhat exaggerated. By no means all the products used in their pharmacopœia actually have medicinal worth.

Shamans foretell the future, make rain fall, secure abundance of game and fish. They also take the lead in magico-religious ceremonies.

Even more than in the Andean region, the daily activities of the Indians are interwoven with countless magico-religious practices. Hunting, fishing, warfare are surrounded with the tabus and magic rites, as is also the firing of a pot, or the playing of a game. Whenever an Indian strives toward an aim in which he feels there is an inevitable element of chance or incertitude, he resorts to charms, magic performances, or propitiations to ensure success. The ordeals to which the Guiana Indians submit themselves voluntarily, such as ant bites or flagellations, are, in their eyes, means to increase their strength, their skill, and their good luck. For the same reason they pass knotted cords through their noses into their mouths. Around the houses they grow *binas,* i.e. plants which help them to find and kill game animals. In the Chaco, the Indians prick themselves with awls to fight fatigue and impart to their bodies the qualities of the animals from whose bones their awls are made.

Warfare among many South American Indians was accompanied by many magico-religious practices. Omens were always consulted before the campaign. Dreams assumed an enormous importance. Before leaving for the battlefield, the ancient Peruvians sacrificed llamas which were starved in order to weaken magically the hearts of the enemy. The Jivaro executed posture dances which were believed to have a magic influence on the issue of the war. Various food tabus were also observed before and during the campaign. Thus, for instance, the Toba refrained from eating the head or the legs of game animals. Among the same Indians women could not spin or twist strands on their thighs and girls could not sit on the ground. The Araucanian shamans blew tobacco toward the enemy's land and recited charms which they expected to bring ruin and destruction to their foes.

Yuracare and Mosetene hunters appease the souls of the game which they have slain with flatteries and gifts.

They keep the bones away from their dogs and bury them in the forest in the hope and expectation that they will be turned into new game animals.

Chanting and rattling of a gourd with seeds inside are the most usual methods of coercing the supernatural and of facilitating the realizations of one's wishes.

Magico-religious folklore also tends to cluster around the main crisis in man's life. Pregnancy obliges a woman and her husband to observe the strictest tabus. They shun any food and any action which magically may affect the physical and moral condition of the child or complicate childbirth. For instance, both parents do not eat animals or plants which have some salient peculiarity which may pass to the infant, such as a long nose, black color, twisted limbs, etc. Similarly the husband must not tie anything lest the delivery be slow (Mataco). Immediately after the birth of a child a man subjects himself to tabus which (in South America) have been improperly likened to the European couvade. For a period which varies in different tribes from a few days to several months, the father avoids engaging in any activity or eating any food which might endanger the life of his child. For instance, he may neither use cutting instruments nor eat heavy food. (Couvade was especially strict among many Tupi, Guarani, Carib, and Arawakan tribes, and also among the ancient Abipón.) During this enforced idleness, the father rests in his hammock; this has been falsely interpreted as a symbolic lying-in. Twins often are killed at birth lest they bring bad luck. The name given to a child is inseparable from his personality. Frequently names are kept secret (Chamacoco, Mataco) or are changed whenever a person is sick or is threatened by some supernatural danger, for instance after the death of relative (Tierra del Fuego, Chaco Indians).

The first appearance of puberty in a girl is a momentous event for her and her family. She is generally secluded in some corner of the house or in a special hut where she must fast and sometimes do symbolic work, for her behavior at that time may determine her character. In many cases, severe ordeals such as flagellation, ant bites, excision of the clitoris, are part of the puberty ritual.

Puberty ceremonies are less frequent for boys. However in some tribes (Apinayé, Sherente, Timbira, Chamacoco, Ona, Yahgan, Alacaluf) they assume considerable importance and are the highest manifestations of their religious life. Among the Ge tribes of eastern Brazil, the complex initiation rites and the long periods of seclusion formed cycles sometimes extending over ten years.

The initiation rites of the Fuegian Indians were also occasions in which the religious, ethical, and social aspects of their culture took a dramatic expression. The candidates were secluded for several months and became hardened by a harsh life and strenuous exercises. Among other things, they had to drink through a hollow bone tube. At the same time their elders instructed them in the tribal ethics and lore. Among the Ona, the initiation was also a pretext to reassert the dominance of men over the women. Masked dancers did their best to inspire terror in the women and to convince them that the boys were in the hands of dangerous spirits. The same rites occurred in some tribes of the Chaco. Flagellations and other cruel ordeals figure also in the male puberty ceremonies of many Guiana and Venezuelan tribes.

Death unleashes the most varied expressions of grief and fear. The corpse is generally buried with greatest haste; the funerary house and sometimes the whole village is abandoned. However in most tropical tribes, the dead are buried under the floor of their own houses. Wailing for the deceased at first takes the form of vehement reproach for his desertion, later it becomes a ritual crying performed at set hours. The mourners cut their hair, gash themselves (e.g. the ancient Charrua of Uruguay mutilated their fingers). The name of the departed becomes tabu and if it includes a word in common usage, this word also is avoided (Abipón).

It is frequent, among South American Indians, for a widow, after the death of her husband, to be secluded in a corner of the hut or in a special cabin. The confinement may last for a few days (Minuane, Guenoa), or several months (Mataco, Pilaga, Vilela, Cobeuo), to a year (Araucanians of the Pampas).

Amazonian and Guiana tribes practice the second interment; i.e. they unearth the bones and place them in a vase or basket which is kept in the house.

Fear of ghosts is everywhere strong, but has rarely led to an organized cult of the dead. Ghosts are part of the spirit world. After remaining on earth for a certain time, they are said to go to special countries where they lead the same life as here. The journey of the soul to the afterworld is fraught with many dangers which are described in the mythology (Guaryu, Tembe, for instance). ALFRED MÉTRAUX

Southern Cross The Chaco Indians interpret the stars of the Southern Cross as hunters and dogs that pursue a rhea. The Conibo describe it as the skeleton of a manatee. [AM]

Soyal or **Soyala** Hopi Indian nine-day winter solstice ceremony celebrating Sun's arrival at his house. Soyola follows directly after the WüWüchim ceremony in which Hopi youths are initiated into tribal status. At Soyala prayers are said for the new year, and the way is "opened" for the return of the kachinas who have been absent since the Shalako (Zuñi) or Niman (Hopi) ceremonies the previous July. The summer solstice is also observed by the pueblo peoples, but ceremonial celebration is everywhere less important than at the winter turning. [EWV]

Spanish ballad The Spanish ballads constitute the national popular narrative poetry *par excellence* of Spain. In view of their historical origins and their realism they represent better than any other type of popular or learned poetry the ideals, feelings and sentiments of the Spanish people. They are the symbols of the national spirit, the quintessence of the soul of Spain, and they are a contribution of permanent value to universal literature and folklore. For these reasons they have been a source of inspiration to all lovers of the beautiful, Lope de Vega, Cervantes, Corneille, Chateaubriand, Lockhart, Longfellow, Herder, Jacob Grimm, the Schlegels, Zorrilla, Marquina, and a host of others.

The most important groups are the following:

I. The old historical ballads.

II. The historical ballads not considered old, dating perhaps from the 16th century.

III. The frontier ballads, or ballads that relate the history and legends of the Conquest of Granada.

IV. The Carolingian ballads.

V. The ballads of the Breton cycle.

VI. The chivalric and novelesque ballads that narrate the choicest lyric themes of the general folklore of Europe.

The historical ballads are the oldest, the most truly national, and in all respects, the best of the *romancero*. Some of them have passed the national frontiers and have become the common possession of the masterspirits of literature in many countries. Their origin and development is most fascinating. The literary discussion concerning the origin of the Spanish ballads began when Friedrich Schlegel discovered the beautiful Spanish ballad of Count Alarcos and inspired by its tragic love story, composed the first tragedy of the Romantic School and presented the play at Weimar in 1802. They were looked upon by the romanticists as the popular, traditional poetry *par excellence*. The *romances* were supposed to be hoary with age and some, such as the German scholar Karl Lachman, thought that the ballads of Spain represented the earliest examples of Spanish epic poetry and from them there had developed the long epic poems. The Spanish ballads are not older than the 16th century; and instead of giving origin to the epic poems, some of the old historical ballads are themselves derived from the longer and older epics.

The old epic poems of Spain were composed in the 11th and 12th centuries during the first centuries of the definite triumphs against the Arabic invaders. They represent the intense national and religious feeling of the Castilians in their three times secular struggle to reconquer Spain and achieve national and religious unity. They were composed for an aristocratic public, and sung or recited in the palaces of kings and noblemen, or in the midst of the Castilian hosts that marched to the battlefields. These long epics were not popular anonymous or communal poetry. There were about a dozen long epic poems of this character composed in Castile in the 11th–12th centuries. Only two have come down to us, in anything like their original form, the famous *Cantar de mío Cid* or *Poem of The Cid*, and the *Crónica Rimada*, or *Rimed Chronicle of The Cid*. The others have been discovered by modern investigators, especially Menéndez y Pelayo and Menéndez Pidal, in the prose chronicles of the 13th and 14th centuries.

These old, aristocratic, and noble epics, however, did not disappear after they were prosified in the chronicles. They became in the 13th and 14th centuries the poetry of all classes, both aristocratic and plebeian. The 13th and 14th centuries are the centuries of the bitterest part of the great struggle between Christian and Moslem Spain. The first victories of the 11th and 12th centuries had given a great impetus to the reconquest, and the capture of Toledo, Zaragoza, and later Seville and Cordoba had developed in reality a great united Spain out of the haughty and glorious Castile of two centuries before. The intensity of the struggle created a new and powerful nationalism, and the old Castilian Counts Fernán González and Garci-Fernández, the Castilian Kings Fernando el Grande, Sancho II, and Alfonso VI, and the great and invincible Castilian hero, the Cid, all sung in the best of the old epics, were no longer Castilian aristocrats of a bygone age. In the 13th and 14th centuries they belonged to all Spain and to all classes of society. The old epic poems that sang their deeds became the common property of all Spaniards, and became popular and democratic.

But the ordinary memory of man could not and would not preserve the epic poems in their entirety and the result was that the nobleman, the soldier, the man in the street, carried away in his memory certain episodes of the epics: those that pleased his fancy; those that had a universal, human appeal; those that flattered his national vanity. These episodes of the old epics, preserved in the oral tradition of the people, popularized, changed and developed, were finally fully appreciated as real, popular traditional poetry and collected from oral tradition in the *romanceros* or ballad collections of the 16th century. These old epic episodes, isolated parts of the old epics, are precisely, *our oldest and best historical Spanish ballads*. Their form and spirit, even their meter, are similar to those of the epic poems from which they are derived. They differ from them only in length, being of a fragmentary character, and in their intensely popular and national character.

Not all the historical ballads that have come down to us since the 15th century are derived from the old epics. The genre once developed toward the end of the 14th century ballads began to be composed independently. The most popular themes of the old historical ballads are: the heroic struggles of Count Fernán González, "the Good Count," the first count of an independent Castile, against the Mohammedans on the one side and against the autocracy of the kings of Leon on the other side, the imprisonment and freeing of the count on two different occasions, etc.; the epic battles between the sons of Fernando el Grande, in the age of the Cid, the 11th century, for possession of the divided kingdom of Castile, Sancho, Alfonso, Urraca and García; the death of Sancho at the siege of Zamora by the traitor Vellido Dolfos; the ritual challenge and consequent duels of Diego Ordóñez de Lara at Zamora; the rise and numerous exploits of the Cid, the most popular of Castilian heroes; the struggles of Castile for supremacy and its final triumph with Alfonso VI and the Cid, etc.

As an example of an old historical ballad I give below a Cid ballad in the English translation of John Gibson Lockhart, whose work, *Ancient Spanish Ballads, Historical and Romantic,* published in London in 1823, is now a classic among English-speaking peoples. The ballad narrates the episode of the old epic where the Young Cid goes to Burgos, the capital of Castile, with his father, to do homage to the king, but refuses to kiss the king's hand.

The Young Cid

Now rides Diego Laynez to kiss the good King's hand;
Three hundred men of gentry go with him from his land;
Among them, young Rodrigo, the proud Knight of Bivar;
The rest on mules are mounted, he on his horse of war.
They ride in glittering gowns of soye—he harnessed like a lord;
There is no gold about the boy, but the crosslet of his sword;
The rest have gloves of sweet perfume—he gauntlets strong of mail;
They broidered cap and flaunting plume—he crest untaught to quail.

All talking with each other thus along their way they passed,
But now they've come to Burgos, and met the King at last;
When they came near his nobles, a whisper through them ran—
'He rides amidst the gentry that slew the Count Lozan.'
With very haughty gesture Rodrigo reined his horse,
Right scornfully he shouted, when he heard them so discourse;—
'If any of his kinsmen or vassals dare appear,
The man to give them answer, on horse or foot, is here.'—
'The devil ask the question!' thus muttered all the band:—
With that they all alighted, to kiss the good King's hand,
All but the proud Rodrigo—he in his saddle stayed—
Then turned to him his father (you may hear the words he said.)
'Now, 'light, my son, I pray thee, and kiss the good King's hand,
He is our Lord, Rodrigo—we hold of him our land.'—
But when Rodrigo heard him, he looked in sulky sort—
I wot the words he answered, they were both cold and short.
'Had any other said it, his pains had well been paid,
But thou, sir, art my father, thy word must be obeyed.'—
With that he sprung down lightly, before the King to kneel,
But as the knee was bending, out leapt his blade of steel.
The King drew back in terror, when he saw the sword was bare:
'Stand back, stand back, Rodrigo! in the devil's name, beware!
Your looks bespeak a creature of father Adam's mould,
But in your wild behaviour you're like some lion bold.'
When Rodrigo heard him say so, he leapt into his seat,
And thence he made his answer, with visage nothing sweet:—
'I'd think it little honor to kiss a kingly palm,
And if my father kissed it, thereof ashamed I am.'—
When he these words had uttered, he turned him from the gate—
His true three hundred gentles behind him followed straight;
If with good gowns they came that day, with better arms they went,
And if their mules behind did stay, with horses they're content.

Next in importance to the old historical ballads are the frontier ballads. These ballads have to do with the conquest of Granada, the final triumph of Christian Spain in its seven-century struggle against the Mohammedans and with the realization of national unity. They come into existence in the midst of the battles they describe, they have the realism, and spirited dialog of the historical ballads and like them are the quintessence of Spanish character. The frontier ballads of the 14th and 15th centuries are much nearer the sources they deal with and are very often real history. In view of their equally intensive nationalism and chivalric character, however, they came to be by the middle of 16th century as popular, if not more so, than the old historical ballads; and one of the most popular works of the Spanish literature, *Las Guerras civiles de Granada,* or *The Civil Wars of Granada,* of Pérez de Hita, a novelistic history of the epic struggle, has documented for us many of the best of these ballads, and is inspired in them. This is the fascinating novelistic history of the glorious and triumphant Spain of the Catholic Kings,

Ferdinand of Aragon and Isabella of Castile, that Washington Irving read when a boy and later described in his *Chronicle of the Conquest of Granada*.

The subject-matter of some of the best of the frontier ballads may be briefly outlined: the story of the lamentations of the Moors when news is received at Granada of the capture of Alhama and Antequera; the heroic deeds of the young Bishop of Jaen, Don Gonzalo, who marches to battle with his Castilian army, and when he alone remains attacks his enemies single-handed, fights with utmost valor, is finally captured and taken as a prisoner to the dungeons of the Alhambra; the romantic and memorable departure of the King of Granada, Boabdil, to attack the Castilian hosts, accompanied by the flower of Moorish nobility, all armed with silver helmets and swords the hilts of which are of shining gold, the Moorish mothers, wives, and lovers weeping, but applauding and urging them to defend the fatherland; the daring deeds of the Moorish knight Tarfe who fights his way to the very gates of the camp of the Catholic Kings and insults the Castilians by riding about with a portrait of the Virgin Mary tied to the tail of his horse; and the valiant deeds of the Castilian nobleman Garcilaso de la Vega who secretly leaves the Christian camp, challenges the Moor, and when despised on account of his youth opens the duel and slays him, removes the Ave-Maria from the Moor's horse and kisses it with great reverence; the daring sally of the Castilian hosts under the leadership of don Alonso de Aguilar to attack a powerful Moorish army near Granada, their crushing defeat, and the gallant fight of don Alonso who is finally killed by the Moors. Some of the very best of the frontier ballads are those where Spanish ballad-poetry has been actually denationalized in order to seek a more human, more universal form and spirit.

A good example of a frontier ballad is the ballad of Abenámar, where King don Juan II of Castile is represented as being deeply in love with Granada, pictured to us as a bride, whom he ardently longs to possess. I give the English translation of James Young Gibson, *The Cid Ballads and other Poems*, London, 1887.

Abenámar

'Abenámar, Abenámar,
    Moor of Moors, and man of worth,
On the day when thou wert cradled,
    There were signs in heaven and earth . . .

'Abenámar, Abenámar,
    With thy words my heart is won!
Tell me what these castles are,
    Shining grandly in the sun!'

'That, my lord, is the Alhambra,
    This the Moorish Mosque apart,
And the rest the Alixares
    Wrought and carved with wondrous art.' . . .

Up and spake the good King John,
    To the Moor he thus replied:
'Art thou willing, O Granada,
    I will woo thee for my bride,
Cordova shall be thy dowry,
    And Sevilla by its side.'

'I'm no widow, good King John,
    I am still a wedded wife;
And the Moor, who is my husband,
    Loves me better than his life!'

The Carolingian ballads treat of subjects that belong to the cycle of Carolingian chivalry. They are popular and traditional and narrate in Spain the exploits and wonderful deeds of Roland, Renaud de Montauban, the Marquis of Mantua, and some of the other twelve peers of France, and other marvelous adventures only vaguely related to the Carolingian cycle or to French epic sources. These ballads bring to the *romancero* more sentimentality, more of the love themes, often very passionate, and more elegance in the form of composition. The national Spanish ballads are tranquilly objective, realistic and austere. The Carolingian ballad brings to it the refinement and perfection of form of a more refined, yet almost superstitious and romantic age. The ballads of French origin bring to the *romancero* the new themes of unbridled passion, enchantment, divination, prophetic dreams, prodigious and enchanted trees and fountains, cursed sons that are turned into beasts, etc., all foreign to the old Castilian ballad. But by the 16th century these ballads were nationalized, they became as popular as the originally national ones, and like them were known by young and old in all walks of life.

The novelesque ballads are very old, perhaps as old as any of the historical ballads derived from the epics, and are some of the best of the *romancero*. They have as subject-matter the more universal, human themes of love, fidelity, honor, valor, vengeance, and ideal justice. They are chivalric and romantic and the lyric element is often predominant. The contents of some of the best known may be given here. One of the most popular narrates the romantic story of the ideal knight and lover, who is loved by all ladies who lay eyes on him, even to the point of giving their lives for him. There are several beautifully tragic ballads of this type, Gerineldo, classed as a Carolingian ballad, Virgil, Tristan, and Lancelot of world fame. Other novelesque ballads treat of: the faithless wife who is surprised by the husband and her subsequent death, an oriental theme; the wedding that was to be or the finding of the long-lost husband, a common theme in European folktales; the story of the persecuted woman, wife or daughter, also a common theme in the folktales; the romantic story of the warrior-woman, the daughter of a prince who disguised as a knight goes to war in the king's service for seven years and in the end marries the king's son; the knight who returns from war and speaks to his wife who does not recognize him; the charming lyric themes of the prisoner's lamentations; the sad wanderings of the turtle-dove that has remained a widow and in grief; the Lorelei story found in the ballad of Count Arnaldos; and finally the narrative of Count Alarcos, dramatized by Lope de Vega and Friedrich Schlegel.

As an example of a novelesque ballad, I give below in the English translation of John Bowring, *Ancient Poetry and Romances of Spain*, London, 1824, the ballad of Fonte Frida, the theme of which, fidelity in love, has a universal appeal.

Fount of freshness! fount of freshness!
    Fount of freshness and of love!
Where the little birds of spring-time
    Seek for comfort as they rove;
All except the widow'd turtle—
    Widow'd, sorrowing turtle-dove.

There the nightingale, the traitor!
  Linger'd on his giddy way;
And these words of hidden treachery
  To the dove I heard him say:
"I will be thy servant, lady!
  I will ne'er thy love betray."

"Off! false-hearted!—vile deceiver!
  Leave me, nor insult me so:
Dwell I, then, midst gaudy flowrets?
  Perch I on the verdant bough?

Even the waters of the fountain
  Drink I dark and troubled now.
Never will I think of marriage—
  Never break the widow-vow.

Had I children they would grieve me,
  They would wean me from my woe:
Leave me, false one!—thoughtless traitor!—
  Base one!—vain one!—sad one!—go!
I can never, never love thee—
  I will never wed thee—no!"

The real greatness of the *romancero* or Spanish balladry is to be found in the fact that it inspired, gave origin to, and created one of the great dramatic literatures of the world. The best of the dramatic productions of Lope de Vega and Guillén de Castro and others are inspired directly in the historical ballads, found for the most part in the oral tradition of the 16th century. Even the legend of *Don Juan* is found in an old Spanish ballad from which Tirso de Molina may have taken it to join it to the theme of the double invitation and give it the definite artistic form that the world admires.

The ballads of Spain have an importance, a literary history, that surpass the importance and literary history of the ballads of any other nation. They influence and give inspiration, subject-matter, and even literary form to the most important literary genres and develop a great national drama, a drama that has been a source of inspiration for dramatic composition for all countries since the 17th century.

But this is not all. The Spanish ballads have long ago traversed the national frontiers to be translated into other languages, to be incorporated into poetic legends, and to be dramatized by the lovers of the beautiful in all lands. Some of them, a few of the Cid ballads, Carolingian ballads, and novelesque ballads, for example, are now the common property of universal literature.

If the real worth of Spanish balladry as a lasting work of art is to be found in their human appeal as manifested in their world-wide popularity and diffusion, a few of its gems having become today the common esthetic patrimony of all peoples and races, it is no less true that their genuinely popular and traditional character is also attested by their longevity. A large number of the old Spanish ballads are still recited and sung in all parts of the Spanish-speaking world, in Spain, in Spanish America, in the Philippines, among the Spanish-speaking Jews of Africa, the Balkans, and the Orient. The ballads of modern oral tradition are of all types, but the historical ballads are disappearing and found only in fragmentary form. One of these, the ballad of Chimène who complains to King Ferdinand that the Cid has killed her father, is sung today by all the old Jewish women of Tangier.

The German philosopher Hegel said about the *romancero*:

"The Spanish ballads are a necklace of pearls; each picture is finished and complete in itself, and at the same time these songs form a harmonious whole. They are conceived in the spirit of chivalry, but always interpreted according to the national genius of the Spaniards. The subject matter is rich and full of interest. The poetic motives are founded on love, marriage, family life, honor, glory of kings and princes, and above all in the struggle of Christians against Moors. But all this material is so epic, so plastic, that historical reality appears to our eyes in its highest and purest meaning, and this does not exclude the most realistic descriptions of brilliant scenes of human life and deeds. All of this forms a poetic crown so beautiful, that we moderns can proudly compare it to the greatest artistic productions of classical antiquity."

Bibliography:

Durán, Agustín, *Romancero General*, 2 vols. Madrid, 1828–32; 2nd ed., 1849–1851.

Espinosa, Aurelio M., *El Romancero Español*. Madrid, 1931.

Menéndez Pidal, Ramón, *El Romancero Español*. New York, 1909.

——, *Flor Nueva de Romances Viejos*. Madrid, 1933.

Menéndez y Pelayo, Marcelino, *Tratado de los Romances Viejos*, 2 vols. Madrid, 1903–1906. (These are vols. I and XII of his *Antología de poetas líricos castellanos*, 14 vols., Madrid, 1890–1908.)

Alonso Cortés, N., "Cantares Populares de Castilla," *Revue Hispanique*, T.XXXIII, Oct. 1914, pp. 87–115.

——, *Romances Populares de Castilla*. Valladolid, 1906.

Carrizo, Juan A., *Antiguos Cantos Populares Argentinos*. Buenos Aires, 1926.

Carrizo, Juan A., *Cancionero Popular de Salta*. Buenos Aires, 1933.

——, *Cancionero Popular de Jujuy*. Tucuman, 1934.

——, *Cancionero de Tucuman*, 2 vols. Buenos Aires, 1937 and 1939.

De Cossío, José y Solano, T. Maza, *Romancero Popular de la Montaña*. Santander, 1933.

Espinosa, Aurelio M., "Romancero Nuevomejicano," *Revue Hispanique*, T.XXXIII, 1915, pp. 446–560.

——, "Romances de Puerto Rico," *Revue Hispanique*, T.XLI, 1917, pp. 678–680.

——, "Romances Tradicionales que Cantan y Recitan los Indios de los Pueblos de Nuevoméjico, "*Boletin de la Biblioteca Menéndez y Pelayo*, 1932, pp. 9–109.

Moya, Ismael, *Romancero*, 2 vols. Buenos Aires, 1941.

Vicuña Cifuentes, J., *Romances Populares y Vulgars, recogidos de la Tradición Oral Chilena*. Santiago, 1912.

                              AURELIO M. ESPINOSA

Spanish folklore This article treats of the folklore of Spain and of Spanish America.

The folklore of Spain is a part of the folklore of Europe. There can be no doubts about the direct relations between the various peoples and races of Europe both in prehistoric and historical times. This is due in the first place to the western migrations of Indo-Europeans from the north and east of Europe, and also to the later historical migrations of peoples that came to the Occident in ever-increasing currents from Byzantium and the Orient.

Spain has been invaded, settled and governed within historical times by Iberians, Phœnicians, Carthaginians,

Celts, Greeks, Romans, Suevi, Visigoths, and Arabs, and all of these peoples have left traces of their culture and traditions. Christianity has been a dominant factor in the lives of Spaniards for about eighteen hundred years, but the remnants of paganism are everywhere to be found in beliefs, customs, and traditions of all kinds, as in all parts of Europe.

Pagan survivals Under this heading we take up the important survivals in Spain of what appear to be very old, pagan traditions, or those contaminated by them. That many of these are of Roman provenience there can be no doubt, and it is often easy to determine the Christian elements involved; but it is not so easy to determine the contributions from pagan sources that are not Roman.

In the first place we must consider the popular fertility cults and harvest festivals, such as have been so admirably studied for many parts of Europe by James Frazer in his *Golden Bough*. In Spain these have often survived attached to religious feasts, and indeed the pagan elements of the ceremonies involved take place in the churches or near them.

Among these festivals, perhaps the most popular is the *Fiesta del Gallo* or Cock Festival. Those in charge of the ceremonies are two groups of young men and women, usually twelve of each, who form a so-called *reinado*, or kingdom, with a king and queen for each group, named or elected at Christmas time for this and other festivals in which they may take part during the year. The *Fiesta del Gallo* is popular all over Castile and northern Spain. At Barbadillo del Mercado and other villages in the province of Burgos the Cock Festival is held on the second day of February or Candlemas, immediately after the mass, which is attended by the two groups. The young women, all dressed in white, leave the church, led by the *reina* or queen and march to the plaza, where the *alcalde*, or mayor, of the village awaits their coming. They bring with them a live cock and ask permission of the *alcalde* to conduct the ceremony and kill the cock. The young men take the cock and tie it from the legs to a pole or bury it in the ground with its head showing. At Barbadillo del Mercado the *reina*, usually blindfolded, attacks the cock with a wooden sword until she finally succeeds in killing it; in Villanueva de Burgos and also in other villages the cock is buried and any young man who wishes can attempt to kill the cock, blindfolded and turned around several times in order to confuse him. In all cases, after the cock is killed, there is a feast of which all partake, food having been provided for the occasion.

Before the ceremony of attacking the cock, however, the *reina* recites a long composition in verse in which the cock is called a traitor and satisfaction is expressed concerning his future torture and death, ending in some cases with the last will and testament of the cock. There are, of course, many variants of the ceremony, and many versions of the verses.

The *Fiesta del Gallo* usually takes place on Candlemas, or the feast of the Purification of the Blessed Virgin, February 2, and it symbolizes the renewal of life or of the harvests, as did the old Roman festival of the Lupercalia, which was celebrated on the 15th of February, the last month of the old Roman calendar, and Candlemas was formerly celebrated on the 15th of February. There is no evidence, however, of a direct relation between the Lupercalia and the *Fiesta del Gallo* in Spain. Indeed festivals of the type of the *Fiesta del Gallo* are to be found in many parts of Europe, and all of them belong to a more general type of vegetation cult as Frazer has demonstrated in the *Golden Bough*, vol. II, chapter III.

In some villages of northern Spain the ceremony of the killing of the cock has an important variation. Young men on horseback and blindfolded attack the cock with wooden swords. The cock has been hanged from a rope that is stretched across a street from one house to another. One rider attacks at a time, and he often gets entangled with the ropes and misses his target, but in the end several cocks are killed in this way.

In many regions of Spain and Spanish America there are other games in which cocks are killed. Especially to be noted is the game of *correr el gallo*, literally running the cock, in which a cock is buried in the ground with its head sticking out above the ground, and the young men, one at a time, run by on horseback and try to pick up the cock by the head. When one succeeds, he usually runs away with the cock and the others follow him to take it away from him. He can strike them on the face with the cock, and the combat is bloody, for the cock is usually torn to pieces. These cock games occur on any festival. In Spanish America they usually take place on St. John's Day.

In many regions of Spain and Spanish America there are, of course, the well-known cock fights.

Another pagan tradition curiously joined to Christian ceremony is that of the *Toro de San Marcos*, or Bull of St. Mark. This tradition has apparently disappeared in modern times, but throughout the 16th century and up to the end of the 19th century it was very popular and well known. The feast corresponds chronologically to the Roman Robigalia, an agricultural cult festival.

Those in charge of the ceremonies of the Feast of San Marcos go out on April 24, the day before the feast, in search of a wild bull, select one, and call him by the name of Marcos. Hearing the name, the bull leaves the herd and obediently follows them to the vesper services and is obedient and humble throughout the ceremonies. He is then taken back to a stall for the night. The next day, April 25, or the Day of St. Mark, the bull is taken to the church in a solemn procession, adorned with garlands of flowers and with bread loaves on his head and horns. He behaves properly during the mass, but after the mass is over, he is led out of the church, whereupon he immediately regains his ferocity and runs away.

The devout behavior of the bull and the extraordinary devotion of the women towards him, for apparently he is believed to represent the saint himself, contrasts sharply with the frivolity of the people in general. The ceremony has been condemned by ecclesiastical authorities many times, and in the year 1598 Pope Clement VIII complained especially of the veneration of the bull by the women in the church.

In an article recently published by Julio Caro Baroja in *Revista de tradiciones populares* (I [1944]: 88–121), the ritual of the Bull of San Marcos is compared with the ritualistic ceremonies of the Olympian god Dionysus. A bull represents the saint and the pagan god; it is taken to the temple or the church; the women have a special devotion to the bull; and lastly there is a relation in both cases between the bull and wine.

A bull appears at other solemn occasions of a religious

character. In some Basque villages it was customary until very recent times to have a bull at funerals, caparisoned in black, and with a large loaf of bread on each horn. When the funeral was over, the bull was ransomed by the owner or someone else.

Another pagan survival in modern Spanish tradition is the *Fiesta de la Vaca*, or Festival of the Cow. This has been recorded from the village of San Pablo de los Montes, in the province of Toledo. On the feast of St. Paul, the 25th of January, the regular religious feast of San Pablo is celebrated, with procession and mass and other festivities. At the same time, a group of young men take charge of the *Fiesta de la Vaca*, apparently a survival of the opposition to the Christian ceremonies, tolerated by tradition. One of the young men represents the cow, La Vaca, and carries a long pole adorned with ribbons and flowers and two bull or cow horns, also covered with ribbons and flowers. There is another youth attired as a woman named the Madre Cochina, or the Mother Sow. Still another young man is dressed as a shepherd, and two more, in ordinary clothes, go along ringing cow bells.

On the day of the feast of San Pablo and during the procession young men of the above group march in contrary direction to the procession several times, and as they pass by the image of the saint, they call out, "*Ahí va la Vaca* (Here goes the cow)!" When the mass is terminated, the *alcalde* and the councilmen as well as the priest march to the town hall to await the *correr de la Vaca*, the race of the cow. La Vaca and the others of the group run from the church to the civic hall, the Cow threatening all those on the way. When the Cow reaches the hall the group is received by the *alcalde*, and all are regaled with fine wine. When the church bells ring for the noon hour, all leave for their homes and the festival is over.

The *Olentzaro* of the Basque regions is a pagan survival related to the winter solstice. On Christmas Eve a few young men organize a village party to give *Olentzaro* a ride around the village to beg for food for a dinner. *Olentzaro*, which is also the word meaning Christmas Eve, is represented by an ugly, big-headed boy, dressed in an overlarge coat, a big hat, and with a pipe in his mouth. He is carried in a box adorned with laurel leaves, and provided with a lantern. The youths carry the box from house to house like a litter. They are led by a young man who calls at every house. He sings, accompanied by others, and tells the story of *Olentzaro*, who is described as an ogre-like being, powerful and terrible, with blood-shot eyes. Instead of an actual human being, an effigy is sometimes put in the box, a straw man, that is burned on Christmas Day. This burned effigy is sometimes substituted by a real Yule log. *Olentzaro* is said to come down the chimney on Christmas Eve. He kills people if the chimney is not clean, or steals the children and carries them away. In other stories *Olentzaro* is described as a gentle and kind spirit or as a mere charcoal-maker.

The fear that Basque children have for the ogre-like *Olentzaro* is similar to the fear that New Mexican Spanish children have for el *Agüelo* or el *macaco*, the Bugaboo, who also is said to come down from the mountains on Christmas Eve to punish children who do not know their prayers; but there is apparently no direct relation between the two traditions.

The months of the year and the important popular feasts and festivals The days of the saints are of course celebrated in Spain with pomp and ceremony. Processions, dancing, and bull fights accompany most of the regular religious feasts. For Holy Week in Seville popular festivities, many of a traditional character, accompany the religious practices, such as the mockery and burning of the effigy of Judas on Holy Saturday.

New Year's Day The festivities of New Year vary considerably in the Spanish world. In Madrid and other cities and villages of Spain it is customary for families to gather on New Year's Eve in small groups to celebrate the coming of New Year with music and other amusements. At the first stroke of the bell at midnight each person begins to eat twelve grapes, and all must be eaten before the twelve strokes of the bell to be sure the new year will be a happy one. In Spanish America there are similar festivities. On New Year's Day there is of course mass in the morning, and visits, greetings, amusements, feasting, and giving of presents the rest of the day.

Christmas Day Christmas festivities are usually of a religious character and begin with Christmas Eve and midnight mass. Christmas trees are found in some places, but in the past they were unknown in Spain. In Spanish America they are more popular. Spanish children usually receive their presents from the Magi Kings—Casper, Melchor, and Baltasar—on the *Día de Reyes*, Day of Kings, or Epiphany, January 6. The children place their shoes somewhere, so that the Magi Kings will leave presents in them, and also grass for the camels, on the eve of Epiphany. On Christmas Day itself there is singing of Christmas carols, feasting, and dancing in the homes. In Castile there is a regular *reinado*, or society of youths, who collect *aguinaldos*, or gifts of money or provisions, to provide a feast for Christmas. These feasts are also provided by the members of the *reinado* for el *Día de Reyes*, or Epiphany.

El Día de San Juan, St. John's Day, June 25 There is mass and processions in the morning. The rest of the day is given over to amusements and feasting. In Spain there are always the bull fights and dancing. The numerous customs and beliefs attached to this feast are found all over the Spanish world. In Spanish America bull fights are rare, and dancing and feasting prevail.

El Día de Santiago, St. James' Day, July 25 Santiago is the patron saint of all Spain, and the day is a national holiday. The day is celebrated with the usual festivities of bull fights, dancing, and feasting. The day may be compared with the celebrations of the 4th of July in the United States.

The purely religious feasts are not discussed here, although they are accompanied by many popular nonreligious practices and the usual amusements. Religious feasts in Spain are still celebrated with all the pomp and ceremony of the Middle Ages, and the same may be said of many countries of Spanish America. Here the mixture of purely religious ceremony with native American Indian traditions is quite common, and indeed is not different from the same fusion of Christian and pagan traditions that are found even today in European religious feasts. Compare the Bull of St. Mark above.

Marzas The *marzas* are, properly speaking, the March songs, or March *coplas*, that the young *marceros*, or March serenaders, sing in their *rondas*, or street roamings, on the last night of February and the first of March, to serenade their girl friends or lovers, or merely to ask for contributions of foods and sweets to celebrate the coming of March. The *marzas* are also the gifts asked for and given. They have been explained as festivities to express joy at the passing of winter and the coming of spring. That the ceremonies have their origin in a pagan tradition related with the passing of winter and the regeneration of nature in the spring there can be no doubt, for in all these love songs the month of March is specifically named. A very common *marza* is the following:

Marzo florido,	Welcome, flowery
seas bien venido,	month of March
por el mucho pan,	for plenty of bread,
por el mucho trigo.	for plenty of wheat.

The *marzas* that are actually sung in these *rondas,* or street roamings from house to house, vary according to circumstances, but many are traditional. Some of those recorded, with the music for voice and string instruments are the following:

Si nos dan licencia,	If you give us permission,
señor, cantaremos,	
y con gran prudencia	sir, we shall sing,
las marzas diremos.	and with great prudence we shall recite the *marzas.*

A cantar las marzas	We come to sing the *marzas*
tos juntos venimos,	
y a las buenas mozas	all of us together,
las marzas pedimos.	and we ask young women,
	to give us gifts [of food].

Si nos dan las marzas	If you give the *marzas*
de marzo florido,	of flowery March,
tendrán un buen año,	you will have a fine year,
de cariño un nido.	filled with lots of love.

May Day There are numerous May songs and festivities. Here we will record only a few of the important May customs, which also have their origin in pagan cults. The May tree is *el mayo;* May songs *mayos* or *mayas.*

In the last days of April young men and women select a tall pine tree and adorn it with ribbons, egg-shells, glass beads, etc., and on May 1 it is set up in the plaza, where they dance around it and sing their May songs. These ceremonies take place after mass for several days. In origin it is a celebration of the coming of the summer solstice, or the struggle between winter and summer, corresponding in all probability to the Roman festival of the goddess Flora, or Floralia. Customs vary. In some Spanish villages bachelors get the May tree with the permission of the *alcalde* and place it in the plaza. After the ceremonies around the tree, they sell the tree on the last day of May in order to provide refreshments or a dinner.

Among the most common *mayos* sung on May Day in Castile the following may be recorded here:

¡Vítores, Mayo,	Hail, Month of May,
que te empinaron!	here they placed you!
Pero fué con la ayuda	But it was the help
de los casados.	of married men.

Para bailar este mayo,	In order to dance this *mayo,*
licencia, señores, pido;	I ask for permission, gentlemen;
no digan a la mañana	for I don't want anyone to say
que yo he sido el atrevido.	in the morning that I was too daring.

En Mayo me dió un desmayo,	I fainted in the Month of May,
en Mayo me desmayé,	in the Month of May I fainted,
en Mayo cogí una rosa,	in May I picked up a rose,
en Mayo la deshojé.	in May I plucked its petals.

Da la vuelta al Mayo,	Dance around the Maypole,
dala con aire,	dance around with glee,
hasta que se te caiga	until your beautiful dress
el pulido talle.	falls to the ground.
¡Ji, ji, ji!	Ha, ha, ha!

At Belorado, in the province of Burgos, a dummy is hung from a rope that is stretched across a street on the last day of May, dressed in white trousers, black coat, hat and gloves, and with a parasol. In some places the dummy is placed on top of the May tree. In the evening the burning of the effigy, called *el Mayo,* takes place, with the permission of the *alcalde.* At Belorado the burning of the effigy is followed by a dramatic scene in which a woman pretends that the one sacrificed is her own husband, and she weeps and laments until the effigy is completely burned.

In Spain there is also another type of May festivities. The feminine form *maya* means also the May Queen. A group of boys and girls select a beautiful young girl as the *Maya,* or May Queen, dress her as a queen, place her on a couch or in a chair on the first day of May, and dance around her, singing love songs or *coplas,* in which they also ask for money and food from all those who pass by, for a feast or banquet. These activities and ceremonies last in some villages for several days after the first of May. In recent years these types of May celebrations are gradually disappearing, and in some regions instead of the real living *mayas* they have only the *Cruz de Mayo,* or May Cross. An altar is erected in a particular home or near a church, with a white cloth and candles and a beautiful May Cross, adorned with flowers and ribbons. Boys and girls dance around the May Cross, and ask for money and food. In some cases the girls alone appear in the streets with wooden May Crosses, asking for contributions. The May Crosses of the two types above described and the ceremonies that accompany them are still known in Puerto Rico and other parts of Spanish America. There is some confusion here obviously with the regular Christian Feast of the Holy Cross, May 3.

In popular poetry there are traces of all the above types of May ceremonies. That the tradition of the *mayas,* or May Queens, was in origin a festival in honor of Aphrodite is clear from the beginning and from the oldest references. The love theme prevails. In 1611, Covarrubias in his famous dictionary, *Tesoro de la lengua castellana,* under the word *maya,* says: "This is a sort of play performed by boys and girls, who place a little boy and a little girl on a nuptial couch to symbolize matrimony, and it is very old." From other sources we learn that at that time the couch had already been replaced by a table or chair, on which a young girl alone sat. There are many such references in the plays of Lope de Vega and other writers. There is a wealth of information on the *Maya,* or May Queen, in a recent work of Angel González Palencia and Eugenio Mele, *La Maya*, Madrid, 1943.

Ritual dances The number and types of the dances that have accompanied religious ceremonies in Spain are legion. We know of their existence since the 6th century, because at the Council of Toledo of 589, a few years after the conversion of the Visigoths to Catholicism, dances inside of the churches were forbidden. That many were continued in spite of the ecclesiastical and official prohibitions is certain because they were forbidden many times afterwards in the Church councils. A few have survived until modern times, although perhaps changed somewhat to make them more proper for religious ceremony. Liturgical drama began in the churches, and dancing was often a part of it.

Space forbids a discussion of the ritual dances of Spain, with the exception of the *Baile de los Seises* of Toledo. This extraordinary dance has been very well known since the 16th century, but there are references to the dance much earlier. At Toledo the *Seises* (Sixes) were young boys originally dressed as angels wearing rose crowns on their heads who danced and sang before the Blessed Sacrament on Corpus Christi festivities, and in the choir or before the main altar of the cathedral on Christmas Day and on the Feast of the Blessed Virgin, August 15. At Seville they usually danced on the Feast of Mary Immaculate and other feasts, and instead of the original six there have been as many as ten. They all wear red tunics with white surplices, and instead of crowns they have recently worn hats both at Toledo and Seville. The dances are of Mozarabic character, and it is believed that they were already executed in the days of the Visigothic kings. The dances, accompanied with song, were usually the following: *Danza de los pastores*, Dance of the Shepherds, and *Danza de la Sibila*, Dance of the Sibyl. The dances are no longer given; only the singing continues. The *seises* now sing also for Holy Week and on a few other occasions.

In many parts of Spanish America where the native Indians are racially prominent, such as Mexico and Central America, Indian dances are performed, usually with singing, in the churches on Christmas Eve and other religious feasts. In New Mexico the Pueblo Indians dance and sing in the churches on Christmas Eve.

A few examples of Spanish-American ritual dances may be given, in which we find pagan Indian traditions confused with Christian ceremonies.

In Mexico, for example, there is the Pig's Head Dance from the Maya regions, called in the Maya language *Polkekin*. A roasted pig is prepared for the feast of any saint or of the Virgin of Guadalupe. It is adorned with colored paper and ribbons, a cigar in its mouth, etc. With dancing and singing the pig is taken to a house, the owner of which promises to supply the pig and feast for the next year. Wine and cakes and sweets are provided and everything is placed around a table on which the pig has been already placed. Ceremonial dancing and singing around the pig take place, with great dignity and reverence, and after this the pig is cut up and the head goes to the host. All eat and drink merrily.

In some villages there are many pigs' heads for as many different houses, and when the heads are cut off, they are taken in procession to the church, with dancing and singing, each celebrant carrying a lighted candle, where they pray the rosary in the presence of the pigs' heads.

Then they return to the respective houses, dancing and singing again, with the pigs' heads, and the feasting follows.

On the 5th of May, the above ceremonies may be followed by other ritual dances. Two girls and a man perform, and begin the ceremony after a chicken dinner. The man appears with a small box on his back, with a live cock tied to it; in his hands he carries laurel branches. With these he teases the cock to make it scratch and scream, while the two girls dance around him. He ends by dancing with one of the girls.

In many parts of Mexico ritual dancing and singing take place at *Velorios*, or evening devotions, in honor of the saints and the Virgin Mary, and especially in honor of the Christ Child for Christmas or on other occasions, and the dances sometimes take place inside of the churches.

Witchcraft The dominant characteristics of the witchcraft of western Europe are well known. From all the information available it seems certain that its organization in Spain was similar to that throughout Europe in the 15th–17th centuries. The accounts of the assemblies—for example, the presence of the Devil in the form of a goat or some other animal, the followers adoring him with humiliating and repugnant acts of faith in his powers, such as kissing him under the tail —are documented in Spanish accounts, and found in popular tales of a traditional character both in Spain and Spanish America. Accounts of witches transforming themselves into animals, or flying on brooms, or flying unmounted, after anointing themselves with certain ointments and repeating certain diabolical formulæ, are also common. These details are very similar all over Europe, as are even the words of the formulæ. In a tale from Cordoba, *Cuentos populares españoles*, no. 162, for example, we have a version of the tale that narrates the story of the child who wanted to fly like a witch, but who did not repeat the formula properly:

A Cordoba witch used to take out an ointment from a little jar and apply it under her armpits every Thursday and Saturday. Then she would sit on the window sill and call out, "Without God and without Holy Mary, from town to town (*Sin Dios ni Santa María, de villa en villa*)!" And she then would fly about doing her mischief. A little granddaughter saw her and tried to do the same. She applied the ointment under her armpits, but she repeated the magic formula wrongly. She said, "With God and Holy Mary, from beam to beam (*Con Dios y Santa María, de viga en viga*)!" And she flew violently several times against the beams of the house and fell down almost dead. When the witch grandmother arrived, she picked up her grandchild and put her in bed. With her witch remedies she cured her, and in the end she taught her how to be a real witch.

The following folktale from Mexico, published by Vázquez Santa Ana, has similar versions from all parts of the Spanish world:

A certain man was married to a witch. One day he followed her to her mother's house to see what they were doing. They began to strike each other with branches of shrubs, took off their clothes, and then called out, "Without God and without Holy Mary!" They went to the chimney, took out their eyes and placed them on burning coals. Instead of their own eyes, they put on owls' eyes. Then they went out to the roof of the kitchen and called out as before, "Without God and without Holy Mary!" Immediately they began to fly through space. The husband saw two brilliant lights as they described circles and other figures in the heavens.

There is no end to Spanish witch stories and most of these have versions in Spanish America. Volumes would be necessary to record Spanish witch activities and practices. In a book recently published in Madrid by Don Sebastián Cirac Estopañán, *Los procesos de hechicerías* (Spanish witch trials), we have a wealth of information about the witch practices of Spain in the 16th and 17th centuries. In general they are similar to those found at that time in all western Europe. In 1622 there was found in the house of the witch, Josefa Carranza, in Madrid, a regular witch laboratory. The following things were found there: resin and pitch for the hips of women; little figures of heads, arms, legs and other parts of the body; a cloth with a piece of paper that read "Cemetery Earth"; a small jar covered with black objects and labeled, "To cause hatred"; various burnt objects; a human skull; dried hearts of pigs, frogs, bones of birds; earth from the three principal prisons of Madrid; three wax candles; holy water; grains of wheat and beans; a piece of bread partly eaten; a cord with three knots; a large sack filled with hoopoe feathers and bones. In addition Josefa was accused of keeping buried images of men and women with pins stuck in them. Another Madrid witch, María González, had in her house two pieces of coarse bread dipped in the blood of a man that was still living. At the house of the witch, María Sánchez de Rosa, in Madrid in 1699 were found some of the above-mentioned objects, and also a long list of "medicinal" powders and drugs, and printed or handwritten conjurations, charms, exorcisms, and superstitious prayers.

The conjurations of the witches, destined to obtain their usually wicked wishes, were directed primarily to the Devil or infernal spirits; but frequently they were directed also, or solely, to the sun, moon, stars, material objects, and also to God and the saints. A common Spanish conjuration, repeated preferably at midnight and holding lighted candles, was the following:

Conjúrote, diablo	I conjure you, Devil,
con San Polo y con San Pablo	with St. Polo and St. Paul
que vengas a hacer	to come and do
esto que te mando.	what I command.

In modern times witchcraft does not have the organization that it had in the past centuries and it has lost much of its influence; but it still survives both in Spain and Spanish America, in the beliefs of illiterate people, and in many places there is evidence that it is still practiced. Magic and witchcraft are practiced especially by witch doctors, who take advantage of the credulity of the ignorant. In Barcelona a group of these modern "witches" and "magicians" has been found recently, making their living by many of the practices of the 16th and 17th centuries. There are probably many more in other parts of Spain.

In Spanish America witchcraft has suffered the same relapse that it has undergone in Spain; it exists everywhere, but with less power and influence. The details of a witch assembly, identical with those found in Spain and other parts of western Europe, are narrated in a Spanish folktale from such an isolated region as New Mexico by Dr. J. B. Rael in his *Folktales from New Mexico and Southern Colorado*. In some regions of Spanish America, however, notably in the Caribbean countries, where African influence is great, racially and culturally, witchcraft is more prevalent than in Spain or other parts of Spanish America. In Mexico, Central America, and the western coast of South America, there is also the native Indian witchcraft to be taken into consideration. In Mexico and Central America, for example, the successive transformation of witches from one animal into another at will in order to battle with each other is a common element in folktales.

Popular Superstitions Of the thousands of popular superstitions of Spain, we record here only a few of the most important:

When cats play, it is going to rain.

When reddish clouds appear at sunset, it will rain the next day.

To keep witches from entering a house, an old horseshoe must be placed over the door.

A black cat in a home forebodes evil. It represents the Devil.

One should never dance alone and allow the shadow to be seen on the wall, because it is the same as dancing with the Devil.

Speaking to oneself is the same as speaking with the Devil.

When one looks at oneself in a mirror at night, one sees the Devil.

When one yawns, one should make the sign of the cross over his lips so the Devil will not come in.

The Devil appears to a dying person the number of times that person has mentioned him while living.

If you cut your fingernails and toenails at night, the Devil cuts them.

To make sure that one will not have toothache, one should cut one's fingernails on Fridays.

To make sure that a child will not have toothache, one should cut his fingernails behind a door.

A hair with its root thrown into a pan of water grows into a snake.

For every hair that is pulled out seven more appear.

All carnations planted on the day of the Ascension bloom at the moment of the hour of ten.

If you wish to find out the secrets of anyone, drink water from a jug immediately after that person.

If you dream of water, you will cry the next day.

If you eat grapes on New Year's Day, you will have money the whole year.

To spill wine on the table is a good omen.

Salt should not be spilled anywhere. If it is, misfortunes will happen.

Tuesday is a day of ill omen. Anything done on Tuesday will not come out well. A Spanish proverb says, "On Tuesday never set sail or marry (*En martes, ni te cases ni te embarques*)."

If thirteen persons eat at the table, one of them will die during the year.

When a mirror is broken, it means a death.

The screeching of the owl is a sign of mourning.

The fig tree is a tree of evil, because Judas hanged himself from a fig tree.

When a hen crows like a cock, someone in the family will die.

Misfortunes always happen in a house where doves are kept.

When one has a ringing in the right ear, it is a good sign. When it is in the left ear, it is a sure sign that someone is saying evil things about one.

Fever may be cured by drinking water from seven different wells.

A turtle in a home keeps away attacks of erysipelas.

One should never count the stars, because as many wrinkles will appear in the face as stars counted.

When one sees a falling star, he should say, so that no evil will happen, "May God guide it!" It may be the soul of someone who has just died.

The lizard is the friend of man and the enemy of woman.

The water snake is the friend of woman and the enemy of man.

White marks on the fingernails are indicative of telling lies.

To find a lost object a cord is tied around the leg of a chair. Then one says, "Stay there until I find what I have lost." The practice is called "Tying the Devil's leg."

To protect oneself against tempests or lightning, one should pray to Santa Bárbara. There are fixed formulæ in verse to be recited.

The swallow is sacred because she removed the thorns from the crown of Christ at the Crucifixion.

Souls from purgatory often appear to the living to ask them to say masses for their deliverance or to ask them to pay debts they owe.

On the day of St. Bartholomew, August 24, the Devil is free (wanders about with complete freedom). The saint keeps him tied with a chain on his feet, and allows him to go free only on his day. To keep him away one should place crosses on the houses and pray continually.

If a young woman will look into the water of a fountain on St. John's Day, she will see reflected by the side of her own image that of her future husband.

On St. John's Eve, at midnight, young women pour down buckets of water from their balconies. She asks the first man who steps on the wet ground what his name is. That will be the name of her husband.

To find out if a young woman is to marry her lover, she throws a shoe in the air three times on the day before St. John's Day, or June 24, at noon. If on the third time the shoe falls right side up, she will marry.

Idem. She will make a small ball from a piece of bread and put into it a grain of wheat or rice. She will then divide the ball into three small balls, without noticing which contains the grain. She will place one of the balls under her pillow, another one at the edge of the well, and the third at the street gate. The next day, St. John's Day, she will open the balls to find out which one contains the grain. If it is in the one under her pillow, she will marry her lover; if it is in the one near the well, the matter is undecided; if it is in the one at the street entrance, she will not marry her lover.

Many of these beliefs and practices are also found in Spanish America—practically all those that are related to saints or have a religious significance—but there are of course many new ones in the New World. If we examine Spanish-American literature or superstitions, for example the recent book *Las supersticiones,* by Rafael Jijena Sánchez and Bruno Jacobella, Buenos Aires, 1939, we find many that are prevalent in Spain, especially simple and religious superstitions. But if we turn to those that have to do with the fauna and flora of the New World,

there are many new ones, especially those of a "medicinal" or magic type.

Folktales By the end of the 19th century numerous and extensive collections of folktales from many parts of Europe had already been published, but few had been published from Spain. In the catalogs of types of folktales, such as Aarne-Thompson, *Types of the Folktale, FFC* 74, Spanish folktales are hardly represented, and the same is true of serious comparative studies, such as the internationally known *Anmerkungen* of Bolte-Polívka. In the 20th century, however, Spanish folktales have been collected in great abundance, the author's *Cuentos populares españoles,* with some 300 versions, his son's *Cuentos populares de Castilla,* with some 500 versions, and many other smaller collections. We now know that folktales are at least as abundant in Spain as in any part of Europe. They are an important part of the general folktale treasures of Europe and many of them are versions of those found in all parts of Europe. But there are many new and important types, indeed so many that the work of Aarne-Thompson has to be completely revised if it is to be a true catalog of the European types of the folktale.

If we take the single case of the so-called Tar-Baby Story, for example, we find that Spain takes a leading role in the history of its development. The type with human protagonists, similar in this respect to *Jataka* 55, in which the Prince of the Five Weapons, or Buddha, is caught fast at five points after a five-point attack on a giant with a sticky body, is a Spanish type *par excellence.* Nine versions have been found in Spain and two in Portugal of this type and variants.

It is remarkable that in spite of this human protagonist similarity, the human is caught, in this Spanish type, with an artificial, or fashioned, tar-baby. This Spanish type is unknown to those who have studied the origins and history of this tale, which is of Indian origin. I give below a brief résumé of one of the versions of this Spanish type, my *Cuentos populares españoles,* no. 35.

A man and a woman who were very rich had no children. They asked God to give them a child, and when finally their wish was granted, their child soon grew up to be a very tall and strong man, and they named him Samson. He ate so much that he soon consumed all his parents' wealth and had to leave home. Wherever he went, he asked for work, but he ate so much that he was dismissed the day after his arrival. When no one would accept him as a laborer, he went to the king's palace and destroyed everything in the palace gardens. The king sent a group of his best knights well armed to attack Samson; but he picked up one of the horses by the tail and striking the knights with the horse he easily killed them all. The story ends as follows:

Then they decided to set up a tar-man to catch him. And they made the tar-man and placed it near the palace. Samson passed by, and in view of the fact that the tar-man did not salute him, Samson said to him, "Are you going to make a bow to me? If you don't, I'll strike you. Are you going to make a bow to me? If you don't I'll strike you." The tar-baby did not reply; so Samson gave him a blow with his right hand, and it stuck fast. He then continued saying, "Are you going to make a bow to me? If you don't, I'll strike you. Are you going to make a bow to me? If you don't, I'll strike you." Again there was no reply, so Samson struck the tar-baby with his left hand. That stuck fast also. He then spoke thus,

"Are you going to let go of my hands? If you don't I'll
hit you with my foot. Are you going to let go of my
hands? If you don't I'll hit you with my foot." And he
gave the tar-baby a kick, and his foot stuck fast. Samson then became very angry and said, "Are you going
to let go of my hands and foot? If you don't, I'll hit
you with the other foot. Are you going to let go of my
hands and foot? If you don't I'll hit you with the other
foot." And he gave him a kick with his left foot, and
that stuck fast also. And then he said to the tar-baby,
"Are you going to let go of my hands and feet? If you
don't, I'll strike you with my belly. Are you going to
let go of my hands and feet? If you don't I'll strike you
with my belly." And he struck with his belly, and his
belly stuck fast.

He was so well stuck now that the king's knights
came out, caught him, and killed him.

The folktales from Spain are of all types, but especially abundant are animal tales of the Æsopic and
Oriental types, tales of enchantment in which the Virgin
Mary or the saints appear as the supernatural helpers,
moral and religious tales, legends, stories of water and
mountain spirits, dwarfs and fairies, picaresque tales of
numerous and diverse types, riddle tales, and accumulative tales.

The tales of *Pedro de Urdemalas*, Peter the Mischief-
maker, are the most popular of the picaresque types, and
some of the versions are known since the 16th century.
They are often mixed with elements of the tales of *Juan
Tonto* and *Juana la Lista, John the Fool* and *Mary the
Smart Woman*. The best types are characterized by the
anger bargain and the death of the master's wife, substituted by the rogue for himself. The element of Pedro
de Urdemalas finally entering heaven through deceit,
taken from the tales of death deceived with magic objects, *Cuentos populares españoles*, no. 170, is characteristic of the Spanish-American tales of Pedro de Urdemalas.

The folktales of Spanish America are for the most part
of peninsular Spanish origin, and indeed all the types
above mentioned are prevalent. The extraordinary similarity of the versions is eloquent proof of the vigor of
Spanish tradition. It would be very difficult to establish
any definite important changes in Spanish folktale tradition in the migration from Spain to America. In the
regions with strong African or Indian influences we
have, of course, African and Indian elements to contend
with, especially in the case of animal and witch tales.
If we take any given type or any special tale, the tar-
baby tale, for example, we can follow the various influences in the different fundamental elements of the tale.
Although the fundamental theme is of Indian origin, so
many secondary elements of other proveniences are
definitely of African, Spanish, or native American Indian
origin that we can actually establish Spanish, Spanish-
American and Indian types. In the case of the tale of
the magic flight (Type 313), we can also establish such
variant types in Spanish-American tradition.

In many witch tales, African and native Indian elements are frequent in many Spanish-American folktales
that are of European Spanish origin, and in some cases
versions of tales that are obviously of African or Indian
origin have elements of Spanish origin. Examples of
African tales with Spanish elements are found in Puerto
Rico and Santo Domingo, and of Indian tales with Spanish elements in Mexico and Central America.

Spirits Northwestern Spain, especially the Asturian

region, is the area *par excellence* for brief anecdotal
stories or superstitions concerning supernatural benevolent or evil spirits, usually with generic names.

Among the most popular of these spirits the following
may be mentioned:

El Nubero, Tempest, is an ugly and malignant spirit,
who wears a long beard, dresses in skins of animals and
rides on a cloud. He is called Juan Cabrito, and he lives
with his wife and children in a mysterious mountain in
Egypt, perpetually covered with fog. There are numerous tales about the *Nubero*. In a certain village of
Asturias the *Nubero* appeared, and the people feared
their crops would be destroyed. The priest came out
and threw a shoe into his garden to frighten the *Nubero*,
who was raining hailstones there, and called out, "Destroy there!" The *Nubero* rained a pile of hailstones
there, the priest's garden was ruined, but the others'
crops were saved.

The *Xanas*, or nymphs, are small and beautiful women
with long and flowing hair. They live in caves and
fountains, and some of them are merely enchanted
women. They give jewels to those who disenchant them.
They work and play with golden objects in the meadows
in the morning of St. John's Day. There are scores of
localities, caves, mountains, etc., where Asturian *Xanas*
are said to live. One tale about the *Xanas* relates that
they used to ride horses all night and left them exhausted. Some boys covered the back of a horse with tar
and thus caught one of them.

El Cuélebre is the winged serpent who guards secret
treasures and enchanted persons, and lives in forests,
caves, and fountains, similar to the dragons that keep
and guard treasures and people in the classical myths,
as in the myth of Jason and Medea.

La Sirena, or siren, is similar to the classical sirens.

El Trasgu, or house dwarf or *lar*, is described as a
small dwarf, who appears at night, enters a house, does
some housework, or breaks up the furniture. He is
dressed in red. The *trasgu* is known in other parts of
Spain and in Spanish America as an ordinary *duende*,
or dwarf; both the *trasgu* and the *duende* follow the
family who moves from one house to another, and frequently they appear with an object that has been forgotten, such as a broom or a kitchen pot.

La Güestia or *Estantigua* is derived from *hueste
antigua*, ancient host. In the Middle Ages, 12–14th centuries, the word *estantigua* meant a group or procession
of demons or infernal spirits. In modern times it is a
concrete malignant spirit who travels about in the night
dressed in white, with lighted candles in her hands,
ringing a bell and muttering prayers for the dead. She
attacks all those she meets and says: "Travel during the
day, for the night belongs to me."

Proverbs The proverbs and proverbial expressions of
Spain constitute one of the important branches of European folklore. They are the judgments based on the experiences of the race, expressed in brief artistic forms,
both in prose and verse. Young and old use them in
conversation and consider them as traditional authoritative opinions on most of the important problems of
human conduct. Many of them express, of course, universally accepted truths, and in view also of the fact
that they are often expressed in beautiful artistic forms,
they have been extensively used in formal literature.

To some extent Spanish proverbs are the Spanish variants of similar materials that are found in the folklore of Europe; but most of them are typically Spanish in form and content and depict accurately some of the outstanding traits of Spanish character. Their philosophic and religious content, particularly those that deal with life's most serious realities, such as poverty and wealth, old age and youth, love and hatred, death and the life hereafter, is an indication of the Roman, Christian, and Arabic heritage of the Spanish people.

The proverbs of Spain are very old. By the middle of the 15th century even the learned and aristocratic Marqués de Santillana had appreciated them to the extent of collecting what is probably the first European collection of proverbs, *Los refranes que dizen las viejas tras el fuego.* In the 16th century Gonzalo Correas published his monumental *Vocabulario de refranes y frases proverbiales.* By that time they had already become the philosophy of the people and had been accepted as such by the great men of letters, such as Cervantes in his immortal *Don Quijote.* Sancho Panza cites them by the dozen, and Don Quijote also cites them frequently. After Cervantes, however, they are not extensively used in formal literature; they have been relegated to the common people, and in this way they have become really traditional and popular. They are preserved in the memory of the people both in Spain and Spanish America, many of them in the identical or nearly identical metrical forms of the 15th and 16th centuries.

The poetic forms of some proverbs developed into regular octosyllabic *coplas populares,* or assonanced or rimed quatrains. These forms are very old also, and they are found today in oral tradition in all parts of the Spanish-speaking world.

In modern times the most important collection of Spanish proverbs collected and published is the monumental work of Francisco Rodríguez Marín, in three volumes, *Más de 21,000 refranes castellanos, 12,600 refranes más,* and *Los 6,666 refranes de mi última rebusca,* Madrid, 1926–34, a total of some 40,000 proverbs and proverbial expressions, collected from both literary and oral sources. S. Gurney Champion, in his *Racial Proverbs,* London, 1938, gives English translations of 726 Spanish proverbs.

I give below a brief list of Spanish proverbs, all of them with rhythmic accents and assonance or rime:

Abrazos y besos no rompen huesos.	Hugs and kisses do not break bones.
Al mentiroso conviene ser memorioso.	Those who tell lies should have good memories.
De mozo rezongador nunca buena labor.	The complaining servant never does his work well.
Desde el tiempo de Adán unos calientan el horno y otros se comen el pan.	Since the time of Adam, some warm up the oven and others eat the bread.
Dime con quién te acompañas y yo te diré tus mañas.	Tell me your company and I will tell you your ways.
Donde hay saca y nunca pon, presto se acaba el bolsón.	If you always take out and never put in, the coffer will soon be empty.
En boca cerrada no entra nada.	Nothing can enter into a closed mouth.
En lágrimas de mujer no hay que creer.	A woman's tears are not to be believed.
Entre la cuna y la sepultura no hay cosa segura.	Between the cradle and the grave there is nothing sure.
Genio y figura hasta la sepultura.	Character and appearance never change (are the same until death).
Grano de trigo no es granero, pero ayuda a su compañero.	A grain of wheat is not a granary, but it helps its companion.
Juramento del amante, ni le creas ni te espante.	A lover's oath should not be believed, neither should it frighten one.
La gallina de mi vecina, pone más huevos que la mía.	My neighbor's hen lays more eggs than mine.
La cabra de mi vecina da más leche que la mía.	My neighbor's goat gives more milk than mine.
La memoria del mal, es por vida; la del bien, presto se olvida.	The memory of evil lasts forever; the memory of what is good is soon forgotten.
Marido mío, que nos perdemos; tú para poco y yo para menos.	My dear husband, we are lost; you are not worth much and I am worth less.
Ojos que no miran, corazón que no suspira.	When the eyes do not see, the heart does not sigh.
Pobreza no es vileza, pero por ahí empieza.	Poverty is not baseness, but it begins that way.

The following are given only in English translation:

So many heads, so many opinions.
A great heart can suffer, and a great intellect can listen.
The Lord blesses those who suffer for others.
Even a fine horse stumbles once in a while.
The best Mr. is Mr. Money.
Too many gifts spoil children.
Great pleasure is followed by great sorrow.
A rich man has always many friends and many relatives.
Those who are wise return good for evil.
Only those who seek adventure find a fortune.
The husband and the devil may appear at any moment.
Sorrows are lessened when there is plenty of bread.
No matter how well dressed a monkey may be, it is still a monkey.
A cowardly man cannot make a great lover.
To accomplish anything, work is necessary.
It is not the cook that provides a good meal; it is a fine supply of food.
No pain lasts a hundred years; nor is there anyone who could stand it.
The jug goes so often to the well that it is finally broken.
In the darkness of the night all cats look black.
I am saying it to you, my daughter; but I want you to understand it, my daughter-in-law.
There are no remedies for stupidity and poverty.
He who has a full stomach does not believe anyone is hungry.
Talking back to an angry man is putting more fuel on the fire.

Lovers quarrel on Monday and they seek each other on
Tuesday.

If you wish to have a bad day, leave your home and
come to mine.

We see a spark in our neighbor's house; but we fail to
see that our own house is on fire.

Riddles Spanish riddles are legion. The majority of
those now current in the Spanish-speaking world are
very old and traditional and have identical or nearly
identical forms, for most of them are metrical, with
accentual rhythms, syllabic meters, and assonance or
rime. New ones appear here and there, of course, but
most of them are old. If we compare the outstanding collections of Spanish riddles from Spain and America. we
can observe the vigor and vitality of Spanish tradition
at its best. Young and old know them, recite them, and
enjoy them.

The riddle of the ax (it barks in the mountains and is
silent at home) has the following metrical forms:

Spain	*Argentina*
En el monte ladra	En el monte grita
y en casa calla.	y en su casa calladita.

New Mexico
Rita, Rita,
que en el monte grita,
y en su casa calladita.

The riddle of the name of the lover, Elena Morado,
has the following metrical forms:

Spain	*Argentina*
El enamorado esté ad-	El enamorado en el
vertido, que queda dicho	vestido lleva mi nombre y
mi nombre, y el color de	el del vestido
mi vestido	

Chile	*New Mexico*
El enamorado, si eres	El enamorado que fuere
advertido, ahí va mi nom-	advertido hallará mi nom-
bre y el del vestido	bre, color del vestido.

The riddle of the letter has the following forms:

Spain	*Argentina*
Blanca como la paloma,	Blanca como la leche,
negra como la pez,	negra como la pez,
habla y no tiene lengua,	habla y no tiene boca,
anda y no tiene pies.	camina y no tiene pies.

Chile	*New Mexico*
Blanca como la nieve	Soy blanca como la leche
negra como la pez,	y negra como la pez;
habla y no tiene lengua,	hablo sin tener boquita,
anda y no tiene pies.	y corro sin tener pies.

Additional riddles from Spain that have close parallel
forms from Spanish America are the following:

Quién fué el que no na-	Who was it that was not
ció y su madre se lo comió?	born, and his mother ate
(Adán)	him? (Adam)

Cuál es el hijo cruel	Who is the cruel son,
que a su madre despedaza,	who tears his mother to
y la madre con mil trazas	pieces, and whose mother
se lo va comiendo a él?	by devious ways gradually
(Arado)	eats him? (Plow)

Redonda soy como el	I am as round as the
mundo, sin mí no puede	world and without me
haber Dios; papas, carden-	there is no God; there can
ales, sí, pero pontífices, no.	be popes and cardinals,
(Letter o)	but there cannot be pon-
	tiffs. (Letter o)

(In Spanish the word pope, *papa*, does not have the
the letter *o*.)

Una vieja remolona	A lazy old woman
tiene un diente en la	has a tooth in her crown,
corona, y con aquel diente,	and with that tooth
llama a la gente.	she gathers the people.
(Campana)	(Bell)

Una señorita	A very ladylike
muy señoreada,	young woman,
con muchos remiendos,	with many patches,
y ninguna puntada.	and not a stitch.
(Gallina)	(Chicken).

There are also many riddles in the form of *décimas*,
special octosyllabic or eleven-syllable meter verses with
certain strophic arrangements and rimes, or semi-
erudite forms and origins, that have become very popular, and new ones of this type appear in modern tradition both in Spain and Spanish America. Equally
popular and traditional are the numerous riddle tales,
common all over Europe, such as the riddle of the shepherd, *Cuentos populares españoles*, nos. 9–11 (Type 85).
Among these riddle tales there are a few brief tales,
which have been known in Spain since Roman times,
and which are still popular in Spain and America. An
example of one of these is the one known all over
Europe and documented by Valerius Maximus. The
Spanish version from Spain is as follows:

Antaño fuí hija, hoy soy madre.
Un hijo que tengo fué marido de mi madre,
Aciértala, buen rey, y si no, dame a mi padre.

Formerly I was a daughter, now I am a mother,
The son that I have is the husband of my mother.
Guess the riddle, good king, or else give me back my
father.

A man was imprisoned by the king, and through a
hole in the prison wall, his daughter nursed him so he
would not starve. She went to the king with the riddle.
She gave him three days time to solve the riddle, but
he could not solve it. She then explained as follows: "I
was his daughter, but nursed him, so I then became a
mother to him. He was the husband of my mother."
The king then gave the man his freedom.

There are similar versions from Spanish America,
almost identical to the Spanish version, from Argentina,
Chile, Puerto Rico, and New Mexico.

Coplas Populares The Spanish *copla* is the shortest
lyric composition in the Spanish language. The term
is used to describe any short poetical composition of a
popular character in a single stanza, as a rule an
octosyllabic quatrain, although they may be composed
in other meters and in strophes of five, six, or more
verses. Since the 16th century the most popular of all
have been the *cuartetas* or octosyllabic quatrains with
verses 2 and 4 in assonance or rime. This type is the
Spanish popular *copla, par excellence*.

In Spanish tradition the *coplas* are the philosophy of
the common people expressed in lyric form. They express the emotions, feelings, and ideas of the people,
their joys and sorrows. They are as old as the ballads,
proverbs, and riddles, and hundreds of them have come
down from the 16th and 17th centuries with little or no
change in form. They are found today wherever Spanish
is spoken. They often express feelings and emotions that
are universal; but they also always express the spirit of
Spain: stoicism, Christian faith and resignation, mysti-

cism, chivalry, loyalty to family and country, democracy, charity, fidelity in love, love of nature, and humor.

New *coplas* based on the old ones, and even entirely new ones, are being composed all the time. Sometimes they keep their form, but change their content. The popular *cantadores*, singers, who are often *guitarristas*, guitar players, at the same time, compose them at will at dances or other popular festivities, sometimes in competition one with another. *Echar coplas* means to compose and sing *coplas* or to merely sing old ones, often to the accompaniment of the guitar or other musical instruments. One of the modern *cantadores* of Spain boasts of his art in the following copla:

Tengo mi cuerpo de coplas,	My body is so full of coplas,
que parece un avispero.	that it is like a wasps' nest.
Se empujan unas a otras,	They push one another
por ver cuál sale primero!	to see which comes out first!

The artistic beauty of the *coplas populares* can be appreciated only in the original Spanish language and the form in which they are composed. In English translation we get only the thought. We cite, therefore, only five *coplas* with English translation, all of which have the same or nearly the same form in many parts of the Spanish world. The last two are really proverbs composed in the form of *coplas*.

Dicen que lo negro es triste,	They say that black is sadness,
yo digo que no es verdad;	I say it is not true;
tú tienes los ojos negros	you have black eyes
y eres mi felicidad.	and you are my happiness.

El clavel que tú me diste	The carnation that you gave me
el día de la Ascensión,	on Ascension Day
no fué clavel sino clavo	was not a carnation but a nail
que clavó mi corazón.	that pierced my heart.

Piensan que nos queremos	People think we do not love each other
porque no nos ven hablar;	because they do not see us talking;
a tu corazón y al mío	they should ask your heart
se lo deben preguntar.	and mine about it.

Nadie diga en este mundo,	Let no one in this world say,
"De esta agua no beberé."	"I'll never drink of this water."
Por muy turbia que la vea,	However turbid it may look to him,
le puede apretar la sed.	he might become very thirsty.

Ninguno cante victoria,	Let no one proclaim victory,
aunque en el estribo esté,	although he may be in the stirrups,
que muchos en el estribo	because there are many who have their
se suelen quedar a pie.	feet in the stirrups and still have to walk.

Décimas The *décima* (ten or tenth) is a ten-verse stanza. In popular tradition, however, the term *décima* is also applied to a poetical composition of several strophes or stanzas of ten verses each, arranged in various rime schemes. The most important types are in octosyllabic and hexasyllabic verses. The most popular type is the octosyllabic *décima* with four ten-verse stan-

zas, glossing an initial quatrain, the verses of which are repeated each at the end of each stanza, respectively. This last type is the Spanish *décima par excellence*, very popular in Spanish literature of the 15th–17th centuries, and one that later became a popular genre and was relegated to the common people. It became traditional and many have been treasured in the memories of the people until the present day in the same way as the traditional ballads, proverbs, riddles, and *coplas*. The subject-matter of the *décimas* is well-nigh universal: old and modern narratives, even ballad themes, novelistic themes, religious themes from the old and New Testaments, all sorts of philosophic themes, and many other materials. The types that have the quatrain and the four stanzas glossing it are especially common in Argentina, Chile, Colombia, Mexico, New Mexico, and Puerto Rico. In Spain they have almost disappeared from popular tradition, but many of a semiliterary type are recorded in the *Cancionero Sagrado* of Justo Sancha, published in 1853.

The importance of this popular poetic genre is obvious from the fact that in some regions of the Spanish world, such as Argentina and Puerto Rico, the *décima* is the rival of the *copla popular* in view of the universality of its subject-matter. It is surprising to find these traditional poetic forms, some of which, as a rule those that do not have the initial quatrain, have as many as ten or even more stanzas, faithfully treasured in the memory of the people. As in the case of the ballads, these poetic compositions were first composed by erudite poets, but they finally became the poetry of the people and truly traditional. As an example of a popular Spanish *décima*, I will give only one, a version from Puerto Rico:

No sabes como te quiero	You don't know how
ángel mío consolador;	much I love you,
dame un besito de amor,	my consoling angel;
brillantísimo lucero.	give me a kiss of love
	my brilliant morning star.

En fin, mujer tan ingrata,	In short, ungrateful woman,
no me mires con enojo,	do not look at me with anger,
porque la luz de tus ojos	because the light of your eyes
a mi corazón abrasa.	consumes my heart.
Eres clavel en la mata	You are a carnation unplucked,
en un jardín verdadero.	in a natural garden.
Yo seré tu jardinero	I will be your gardner
y al mismo tiempo tu dueño.	and at the same time your owner.
Con tu mirar halagüeño,	With those beautiful eyes,
no sabes cómo te quiero.	you don't know how much I love you.

Yo me encuentro trastornado,	I am utterly confused,
lo debo decir así.	I have to state it that way.
Desde el día que te ví,	Ever since I saw you,
el corazón me has robado.	you have been stealing my heart.
Quisiera estar a tu lado	I would love to be with you
para expresarte mi amor;	to tell you how much I love you;
serías la única flor	You would be the only flower
que en mi pecho me pondría.	that I would keep on my breast.
Si eres tú la vida mía,	You are indeed my life,
ángel mío consolador.	my consoling angel.

Bello, pulido alelí, no me trates de olvidar; para acabar de penar, duélete ahora de mí. Dame de tu boca el sí para calmar mi dolor; viviríamos con fervor, alegres toda la vida. Bendita nena querida, *dame un besito de amor.*	Beautiful, dainty gilli- flower, do not try to forget me; if you wish my grief to cease, have pity on me at this time. May your lips pronounce a *Yes* that will end all my grief; we would have love in our life and be forever happy. My darling, my beloved, give me a kiss of love.
Eres una mariposa, eres un jardín florido; eres tú la más querida y eres tú la más hermosa. Eres la más linda rosa, eres la estrella de Venus. Eres para mí un cielo, nenita, sol de los soles; eres para mis amores *brillantísimo lucero.*	You are a butterfly, you are a garden full of flowers; you are the most loved and the most beautiful of all. You are the most beautiful rose, you are the star of Venus. For me you are heaven it- self my darling, my love; for my life of love you are my brilliant morning star.

Popular drama Both in Spain and Spanish America, religious folk plays and pageants have been always popular, and many of these, such as *Los Pastores* (The Shepherds), *El Niño Perdido* (The Lost Child), and other Nativity and Passion plays, are still given in various regions of the Spanish-speaking world, some from printed copies, others from manuscript copies. The traditional character of all these compositions is obvious from the language. All are derived from Spanish 17th and 18th century sources, when their popularity in Spain was at its height. All had, of course, individual authorship, and some are the work of literary authors of some merit; but at present most of them are anonymous, and the folk have had a share in their elaboration from time to time.

The Passion plays reach their height of religious fervor in the practices of the flagellants, who have been active in some parts of Spain and America, and also in the Philippine Islands. In Mexico and New Mexico, the *Penitentes* have a fixed ritual, and produce certain scenes of the Crucifixion on Good Friday. In Spain these practices are no longer public, but up to the end of the 19th century public flagellation during Holy Week was still practiced in some communities.

As for secular folk plays or pageants, the most popular in the Hispanic world have been for centuries the *juegos de moros y cristianos*, or out-of-doors mock battles between Moors and Christians, extraordinarily popular in Spain and Spanish America for the last 400 years. They are usually produced from manuscript or typed copies. The battle usually begins when the Moors attack a Christian village and steal the statue of the Virgin Mary. The rest of the play is concerned with the Christian counterattack and their final triumph and rescue of the Virgin. The compositions are usually in octosyllabic verse. Other types of secular folk plays are too numerous and varied for discussion here. Children's games, and even games for adults, are in some cases very dramatic and have long and short passages in verse with frequent dialog. Most of these are traditional and very old.

Spanish folklore studies The first Spanish folklore society, Folklore Español, was organized in 1881 by Antonio Machado y Álvarez, the second to be established in Europe, the English Folklore Society having been organized in 1878. Its first and most important publications were *El Folklore Andaluz*, one volume, and *Biblioteca de las tradiciones populares españolas*, 11 small volumes, 1883–1886. Machado y Álvarez had already published *Cuentos, leyendas y costumbres populares* in 1873, and *Colección de enigmas y adivinanzas* in 1880. In 1882–83, Francisco Rodríguez Marín, who later became one of Spain's greatest folklorists and its leading Cervantes scholar, published his famous *Cantos populares españoles* in 5 volumes, and in 1878 and in 1887, respectively, there appeared Fernán Caballero's *Cuentos, oraciones, adivinas y refranes populares e infantiles*, and *Cuentos y poesías populares andaluces.*

In Catalonia, folklore studies began much earlier, with the 5-volume publication of F. P. Briz, *Cansons de la terra*, 1866–1870, and the folktales of F. Maspons y Labrós, *Lo Rondollayre*, in 3 volumes, 1871–1875. A few years later P. Bertrán y Bros published in 3 volumes his *Cuentos populars catalans*, 1886. In 1899, when most of the older Spanish folklore societies had ceased to function, a group of Catalonian scholars, under the leadership of V. Serra y Boldú, organized the Agrupació Folklórica de Barcelona. Its most important publication was the 10-volume collection of folktales from Mallorca by the distinguished ecclesiastic José María Alcover, *Aplech de rondaies mallorquines*, 1915–1926.

During the 20th century, folklore studies in Spain have had an extraordinary development, under the leadership of three outstanding scholars and literary critics, all of whom may be properly called distinguished folklorists, Menéndez y Pelayo, Rodríguez Marín, and Menéndez Pidal. The bibliography alone of the folkloristic publications of Marcelino Menéndez y Pelayo would take several pages. Among the most important are his ballad studies in volumes VIII–XII of his *Antología de poetas líricos castellanos*, 1899–1906, which contain a reprint of Wolf-Hofmann, *Primavera y Flor de Romances*, a collection of modern traditional Spanish ballads from all parts of Spain and from the Spanish Jews, and his famous *Tratado de los romances viejos* (vols. XI–XII), the best and most authoritative study of Spanish balladry published. Francisco Rodríguez Marín was not only Spain's greatest Cervantes scholar, but was also a folklorist of note. His outstanding folkloristic investigations have already been mentioned, his *Cantos populares españoles* and his publications of proverbs. He has many minor publications of a folkloristic character. Ramón Menéndez Pidal, the world-famous Romance philologist and literary critic, has also many publications in the field of folklore, beginning with his first great work, *Leyenda de los Infantes de Lara* of the year 1896. He is today the greatest living authority on Spanish balladry, has published numerous books and articles on the subject, and for the last forty years he and his wife have been preparing for publication a monumental collection and definitive study of all Spanish ballads, old and modern, including all written and oral sources, with the help of a group of younger scholars and ballad collectors from all regions of the Spanish-speaking world. One of the pupils of Menéndez Pidal, Vicente García Diego, is now the editor of an outstanding folklore journal, *Revista de dialectologia y tradiciones populares*, now in its fourth year of publication.

In Spanish America folklore studies are of very recent date. Traditional Spanish ballads and folk songs have been collected and published in Argentina, Chile, Mexico, Cuba, Puerto Rico, New Mexico, and California, by Juan Alfonso Carrizo, Ismael Moya, Julio Vicuña Cifuentes, José María Chacón y Calvo, Carolina Poncet, and the present writer; folktales have been collected from many regions, especially Chile, Peru, Puerto Rico, Mexico, and New Mexico by Ramón Laval, J. Alden Mason, Paul Radin, José Manuel Espinosa, Juan B. Rael, and others; large collections of riddles, most of them traditional, have been collected and published from Argentina, Chile, Puerto Rico, and New Mexico, by Robert Lehmann-Nitsche, Eliodoro Flores, Mason-Espinosa and others; customs, superstitions, and folklore materials of all sorts have been collected and published by Julio Vicuña Cifuentes in Chile, by Frances Toor in Mexico, and by Fernando Ortiz in Cuba, the well-known Cuban sociologist and folklorist, who has published a score of important books on Afro-Cuban history, sociology and folklore, and who edited in 1924–1930 the *Archivos del Folklore Cubano*.

Numerous folklore societies have been recently organized in Spanish-American countries, but none has yet accomplished any outstanding work of investigation and research. Much of the folklore research of the last 25 years done in Mexico and the Antilles has been done by North American folklorists under the leadership of Dr. Franz Boas of Columbia University and through the generosity of Dr. Elsie Clews Parsons, both deceased.

Bibliography:
Antti Aarne and Stith Thompson, *The Types of the Folktale*, FFC 74, Helsinki, 1928; *Archivos del folklore cubano*, 5 tomos, Habana, 1924–1930; Antoni María Alcover, *Aplech de rondaies mallorquines*, 12 tomos, Barcelona, 1914–1930; Aurelio de Llano de Roza de Ampudia, *Cuentos asturianos*, Madrid, 1925; Aurelio de Llano de Roza de Ampudia, *Del folklore asturiano*, Madrid, 1922; Manuel J. Andrade, *Folk-lore from the Dominican Republic*, MAFLS 23, New York, 1930; *Antologia folklórica argentina*, Buenos Aires, 1940; Rafael Ramírez de Arellano, *Folklore portorriqueño*, Madrid, 1926; article "Folklore," in *Enciclopedia Universal* (Espasa), vol. XXIV, Barcelona, 1924; F. P. Briz, *Cansons de la terra*, Barcelona, 1866–70; *Biblioteca de las tradiciones populares españolas*, 11 tomos, Sevilla-Madrid, 1883–1886; C. Cabal, *Del Folklore de Asturias*, Madrid, 1925; C. Cabal, *Los cuentos tradicionales asturianos*, Madrid, 1924; María Cadilla de Martínez, *La poesía popular en Puerto Rico*, Cuenca, 1933; María Cadilla de Martínez, *Juegos y canciones infantiles de Puerto Rico*, San Juan, 1940; Juan Alfonso Carrizo, *Cancionero popular de Tucumán*, 2 tomos, Buenos Aires, 1937; Juan Alfonso Carrizo, *Antiguos cantos populares argentinos*, Buenos Aires, 1926; José María Chacón y Calvo, *Romances traidionales en Cuba*, *Revista de la facultad de letras y ciencias*, Habana, 1914; José María de Cossío y Tomás Maza Solano, *Romancero popular de la Montaña*, 2 tomos, Santander, 1933–1934; Sebastián Cirac Estapañán, *Los procesos de hechicerías*, Madrid, 1942; Demófilo (A.

Machado y Álvarez), *Colección de enigmas y adivinanzas*, Sevilla, 1880; Aurelio M. Espinosa, *Cuentos populares españoles*, 3 vols., Madrid, 1946–47; Aurelio M. Espinosa, "New-Mexican Spanish Folklore, Parts I–XI," *JAFL*, vols. 23–29; Fernán Caballero, *Cuentos, oraciones, adivinas y refranes populares e infantiles*, Leipzig, 1878; Fernán Caballero, *Cuentos y poesías populares andaluces*, Leipzig, 1887; Eliodoro Flores, *Adivinanzas corrientes en Chile*, Santiago, 1911; R. Menéndez Pidal, *Flor nueva de romances viejos*, Madrid, 1928; *Folklore y Costumbres de España*, Director: F. Carreras y Candi, 3 tomos, Barcelona, 1931–33; Sir James Frazer, *The Golden Bough*, (one vol. ed.), New York, 1927; D. Granada, *Supersticiones del Río de la Plata*, Montevideo, 1896; Domingo Hergueta y Martín, *Folklore Burgalés*, Burgos, 1934; Arturo Jiménez Borja, *Cuentos peruanos*, Lima, 1937; Alexander Haggerty Krappe, *The Science of Folklore*, New York, 1930; Modesto Lafuente y Zamalloa, *La brujería en Barcelona*, Barcelona, n.d.; Ramón A. Laval, *Cuentos populares en Chile*, Santiago, 1923; Ramón A. Laval, "Oraciones, ensalmos y conjuros del pueblo chileno," *Revista de la sociedad de folklore chileno* I: 75–132, Santiago, 1910; Ramón A. Laval, *Cuentos de Pedro de Urdemalas*, Santiago, 1925; Robert Lehmann-Nitsche, *Adivinanzas rioplatenses*, La Plata, 1910; Rodolfo Lenz, "Cuentos de adivinanzas corrientes en Chile," *Revista de Folklore chileno* II: 337–383, Santiago, 1912; Rodolfo Lenz, "Cuentos de adivinanzas corrientes en Chile, Nota comparativas," *Revista de folklore chileno* III: 267–313, Santiago, 1914; Fernando Llorca, *Lo que cantan los niños*, Madrid, n.d.; J. Alden Mason, "Porto-Rican Folk-Lore: Folk-Tales," edited by Aurelio M. Espinosa, *JAFL*, 34–42; J. Alden Mason, "Porto-Rican Folk-Lore: Riddles," edited by Aurelio M. Espinosa, *JAFL* 29; Francisco Maspons y Labrós, *Lo Rondallayre*, 3 tomos, Barcelona, 1871–1874; Frances Toor, *Mexican Folkways*, New York, 1947; Margaret Alice Murray, *The Witch Cult in Western Europe*, Oxford, 1921; Federico Olmeda, *Cancionero popular de Burgos*, Sevilla, 1903; Fernando Ortiz, *Los negros brujos*, Madrid, 1917; A. González Palencia and Eugenio Mele, *La Maya*, Madrid, 1944; *Revista de dialectología y tradiciones populares españolas*, Madrid, 1944– ; Francisco Rodríguez Marín, *Cantos populares españoles*, 5 tomos, Sevilla, 1882–83; Rafael Salinas, *La Fascinación en España*, Madrid, 1905; Alberto Sevilla, *Cancionero popular murciano*, Murcia, 1921; Julio Vicuña Cifuentes, *Mitos y supersticiones*, Santiago de Chile, 1915.   AURELIO M. ESPINOSA

speaking head A common motif of folktale and myth (D1610.5) in which the head of a decapitated person retains its power of speech over a period of time. Magic heads speak, sing, advise, prophesy, entertain. Bran's head entertained his companions for 87 years. The decapitated head of Conaire Mac Ness Buacalla, high king of Ireland in the 1st century, on receiving a drink from Mac Cect, spoke and praised his friend. The Green Knight's head after decapitation bade Gawain come to his castle one year from the day to fulfil his half of the bargain. The head of Orpheus sang and prophesied on the isle of Lesbos and was an oracle for many years. Mimir's head, cut off by the vanir, was preserved by Odin and consulted as an oracle. A certain Balitok and his companions (in Ifugao, Philippine Island, mythology) decapitated the god Montinig, who went right on chewing betel nuts and mimicked and mocked his beheaders until they were terrified. The heads of numerous Mohammedan saints continued to speak and advise after decapitation. There was great discussion and speculation during the French Revolution about the consciousness of the brain after decapitation. In *The Goose Girl* (Grimm #89) the head of the horse Falada continued to speak (B133.4) and comfort the little goose girl after being nailed above the village gate. The oracular artificial head is the subject of motif D1311.7.1.

Spentā Ārmaiti (Avestan *Spentā Ārmāiti;* Pahlavi *Spendarmat;* Persian *Asfandarmad*) Literally, bountiful devotion: in Zoroastrian mythology and belief, the goddess of the earth, one of the Amesha Spentas. Spentā Ārmaiti is the daughter of Ahura Mazda and Heaven. She sits on the deity's left hand. She is a personification of obedience and religious harmony and presides over the earth. Her flower is the musk.

spider The term spider is from Old English *spinnan*, to spin. Spiders are widely distributed in the world, ubiquitous companions of mankind. "The spider taketh hold with her hands and is in kings' palaces" (*Prov.* xxx, 28). In England, small spiders are called "money makers" or "money spinners"; and they must not be killed. If one is found on the clothing, money is coming; in Polynesia, a spider dropping down from above in front of you is sign of a present. In Ozark folk belief if you find a spider web with your initials on it near the door, you will be lucky forever. In the United States in general it is said that if you kill a spider, it will rain.

Stories of Christ's protection from Herod's cruelty, Mohammed and David from apprehension by enemies through a freshly-spun spider-web are two which are to some degree responsible for the statement that "in all ages spiders have been looked upon as friends of man." While Robert Bruce languished in his hiding place (1305) he was encouraged to continue his efforts by watching a spider persevere to finish its web after seven failures.

Spider remedies were considered efficacious in folk medicine. For common contagion, people in England were advised to carry a spider in a silk bag around the neck or in a nut shell in the pocket. For ague one should be tied up and bound on the left arm. Live spiders were rolled in butter and swallowed, or taken in molasses, or rolled in a cobweb and swallowed like a pill. See MEDICINE.

In South American Toba Indian folklore, Spider was the first weaver. In Tahiti spiders are regarded as shadows of the gods and are never harmed. North American Chippewa Indians hang spiderwebs on the hoop of infants' cradleboards "to catch the harm in the air." See ANANSI; ARACHNE; BOX DROPPING FROM SKY.

Spider For Spider as a character in West African and New World Negro folklore, see ANANSI; ANANSESEM; ANANSI-TORI.

Spider, Spider Man, Spider Woman A powerful, nearly always beneficent character in the myths of many Plains, Southwestern, and Western American Indian tribes. In some of these groups Spider is the creator (Pima and Sia Pueblo Indians), or at least the trickster (Santee Dakota and other Dakota groups). See UNKTOMI. Among the Arapaho the trickster's name, Nihansan,

means spider, although there is no attribution, in the myths, of spiderlike characteristics to the Arapaho trickster. The Jicarilla Apache have Spider as a helpful, but rather minor, character in their emergence myths; Spider puts his web all around near the emergence hole to the earth, and he and Fly are sent up on it, before the people emerge; sunbeams stand for the spider's web and the Jicarilla will not kill spiders. Spider and Fly are also told by the Jicarilla Holy Ones to make a web and extend it to the sky, and then bring the sun down; the spiders also help Killer-of-Enemies slay the monster elk, and the monster rocks imperiling people on earth.

Sex of the spider-character is often made explicit in the myths of other groups. Spider Man and Spider Woman are Navaho supernaturals or Holy People who taught the Earth People how to weave, and established four warnings of death, for example. At Taos Pueblo, Spider grandmother takes the usual part of resourceful helper in the folktales that she plays in other Pueblo mythologies, and Spider Man is referred to at Taos as a good medicine man. Among the Kiowa, Spider Woman is an astute and helpful old lady, and among the White Mountain Apache, Black Spider Old Woman helps the son of the Sun when he accidentally trips over her hole; she tells him to spend the night with her before going on his dangerous quest, and when he enters her hole he sees many Spider girls lying together without clothes on. In the mythology of the Coeur d'Alene, a Plateau tribe, Spider women are again beneficent beings; they live in the sky and help Coyote's son drop back to earth in a box. See BOX DROPPING FROM SKY. [EWV]

spikenard An ancient fragrant and costly ointment prepared mainly from a plant of the same name, a perennial herb (*Nardostachys jatamansi*) whose roots yield a strong perfume believed to be the spikenard of the ancients. In India spikenard was one of the rarest perfumes as it had to be made from a plant growing high in the Himalayas. It was highly valued by the Hebrews and is said to have been the principal ingredient of the precious ointment of Mary Magdalene. In Europe it was used in perfumes for gloves and candles.

Indian spikenard (*Aralia racemosa*) is variously used by American Indians; the Potawatomi pound the root to a pulp for a hot poultice on inflammations; the Menomini use it to cure blood poisoning; the Meskwaki season other medicines with its roots, and it is sprayed on the heads of women during childbirth.

False spikenard (*Smilacini racemosa*) is combined with oats by the Ojibwa Indians to fatten ponies, combined with dogbane to keep the kidneys open during pregnancy, and to cure sore throat and headache. The Meskwaki and Potawatomi Indians both call the plant deer berry, because deer are said to eat its fruits. The Meskwaki hush crying children and cure severe illnesses with a smudge of the plant. Insanity especially is helped by a smoke from the root of this plant.

spirit A disembodied essence, comparable to a soul, but never associated with a human or animal being; popularly, any soul-like being manifesting itself to the senses, like a ghost; sometimes, a fairy, elf, brownie, or the like. Strictly, a spirit is the indwelling animus of some place—mountain, headland, field, forest—or object —tree, stone, rapids. Usually these spirits are anthropomorphized, and such beings as the *vile* or the Satyrs, originally forces that made some place individual and unlike another, are conceived of as human or semi-human in shape. Some spirits are monstrous; they resemble human beings to some extent but are compounded with other creatures; field spirits take on some of the aspects of grazing animals; cave spirits look something like snakes, etc. The use of the term spirit to apply to the ghosts of the dead is technically erroneous, but haunts and specters and will-o'-the-wisps are usually classed as spirits, though essentially they are thought to be wandering souls. The Japanese *oni,* demons, are the monstrous ghosts of the dead, but are commonly called spirits. One source of confusion is the varying humanization of similar spirits in different cultures: the child-stealing hag of various peoples is said to be a maleficent principle, an outcast woman turned "spirit," the ghost of a woman recently dead who searches for her lost child. The ghosts who travel with the Wild Hunt are in some areas simply spirits who have never been born into a human body, while in other places they are the ghosts of those who have died within the year. Compare ATUA; AVA; section *Spirits* in SPANISH FOLKLORE.

    The number and variety of spirits which the North American Indians believed in can be illustrated by a sample list from one part of one culture area only, namely, the Pueblos of the Southwest. The Pueblo spirits, as enumerated and described by Elsie Clews Parsons (*Pueblo Indian Religion,* 2 vols., Chicago, 1939, vol. 1, pp. 170–209 and Table 2, opp. p. 208) are: Clouds (Cloud chiefs, Cloud People, etc.), Mountains, Chiefs of the Directions, Lightning, Rain Beings, Sun or Sun Youths, Dawn, Moon, Stars (Morning Star, Evening Star, Pleiades, Orion, Galaxy, even falling stars at Taos Pueblo), Wind (North winds, Winds of the Directions, Whirlwind, Wind Old Man, Wind Old Woman, etc.), Earth (Mother), Maize (Corn Maidens, Corn Mother[s]), Salt Woman, White Shell Woman, Clay Woman, Turquoise Man, Stones (concretions, small stones, petrified wood, stone kachina), Fire and Ashes (Grandmother Fire, Ashes Man, Ash Boys, Poker Boy[s]), Echo, Animals (Mountain Lion, Bear, Badger, Wolf, Coyote, Red Bear, Gopher Woman), Birds (Eagle, Knife-Wing, Hawk, Buzzard, Shrike), Insects (Spider Woman, Dragonfly, Ants, Beetle, Locust, Spider Man), Serpents (Horned Water Serpent, Rattlesnake, Serpent of the North and 5 Serpents of the Directions, Big Snake), Frog, War Gods (twins; see AHAYUTA ACHI), Clown Patrons, Poshaiyanki, The Dead (Old Ones, Scalps), Kachina.

Many of these spirits are also recognized by other Indian groups; some of them, such as the Sun, Morning Star, Moon, Earth, by nearly all groups. In addition, the Thunders, Thunder Boys, or Thunderbirds are widely recognized as important spirits outside the Southwest. Several North Pacific Coast tribes believe in a strikingly conceptualized spirit, Black Tamanous or the Cannibal Spirit, as well as other frightful ones such as Cannibal-Who-Lives-at-the-North-End-of-the-World. The Iroquois also believed in what seem to us a large ensemble of grotesque spirits—flying heads, etc. The Eskimo spirit world was filled with giants and half-human, half-animal beings, while all over North America belief existed in "little people" or dwarf spirits; some of these were water sprites, of which there were also a great variety. Many North American Indian groups conceived of

spirits living in lakes, streams, springs, rivers; sometimes these were dwarf humanlike creatures, the sight of which frightened persons, although often the spirits did no real harm to people. At Taos Pueblo, for example, the river spirit is Big Water Man, who has a big mouth, round yellow eyes, and a spiny body. He is prayed to, having power against disease and for health; when he moves he may cause landslides, and he can broaden and deepen the river bed and send floods. Other springs, lakes, and rivers near Taos are the abodes of other river spirits. Big Water Man at Taos has several of the characteristics of the horned water serpents of the other pueblos, especially those of the Tewa flood-causing Avaiyo. Like Avaiyo, Big Water Man punishes the Corn Girls for rejecting his suit in Taos tales. [EWV]

    South American religion and folklore are centered around the countless spirits that form the supernatural world of the Indians. Myths and tales give us a good insight into the notions which the Indians have developed about these supernatural beings. Spirits associated with an animal or vegetal species often assume human form, but their true nature is revealed by some physical feature, some taste, or some habit characteristic of the personified creatures or objects. There is a tendency, especially in the Guianas, to conceive of the spirits as beings with human shape, but with some unpleasant feature: they may be hairy, bicephalic, have protruding eyebrows, jointless limbs, or they may be linked together like Siamese twins. Some spirits look like skeletons or skulls. Certain noises are invariably attributed to them, in particular the creaking of trees or the chants of lugubrious birds.

Many spirits are fond of taking the shape of a person closely related to their intended victims, but they never succeed in concealing entirely their identity, and can be recognized by some sign, such as for instance the lack of a big toe.

The descriptions which myths give of the land of the spirits could apply to any Indian village (as for instance the stories about the land of the spirits in Witoto mythology). Spirits marry, have children, and die just like ordinary men. There are spirits who lived unrecognized among the living until some accident unmasks them or forces them to leave. Many spirits are helpful, especially those who are at the service of a shaman.

The animism of the primitive tribes of South America constituted also an important part of the religion of the civilized Incas. The *huaca* were often local spirits who received a cult. They were the genii of mountains, of oddly shaped rocks, of caverns, lakes, rivers, trees, and even of houses. Even the Fuegians who feel themselves in the hands of a Supreme God, believe in the existence of countless spirits.

The Indians themselves have established classifications of the spirits by whom they are surrounded. For instance the Witoto add qualifying epithets to the name of the spirits mentioned in their tales. Thus, the *muinane* are the people of the past, the *hunessai* the people of the waters and plants associated with fish, the *rigai* are spirits of the air, of birds, and insects. Similar distinctions in the supernatural world are made by the Caribs.

There is in general no clear division between nature spirits and ghosts. Certain tribes, however, in particular the Bororó, attach the greatest importance to a clear-cut differentiation between these two categories of super-naturals. [AM]

spirit trap An object plaited in a puzzling manner which Guiana Indians leave on the paths to divert the attention of the spirits, who become so intrigued by the contrivance that they forget to pursue their victims. [AM]

spiritual A religious song type stemming from the folk hymns of dissenters in America and comprising two closely related and interwoven bodies of music: the "white spirituals" and the "Negro spirituals." The word spiritual, as early applied to religious song, was used simply to distinguish the "godly" from the secular or "profane." In 1560, in England, for example, was published Wedderburn's *Ane Compendious Booke of Godly and Spirituall Songs, Collected Out of Sundrie Parts of the Scriptures, with Sundrie of Other Ballates Changed out of Prophaine Songs, for Avoiding of Sin and Harlotrey.* The word was also used in the title of a revised edition of the *Bay Psalm Book,* called *Psalms, Hymns, and Spiritual Songs of the Old and New Testaments,* which was carried south by missionary groups from Massachusetts at the end of the 17th century. However, it was not until the height of the "Great Revival," which began about 1800, that "spiritual" became the popular name for camp-meeting songs or revival hymns. Its special application to Negro religious song is of fairly recent date as a catch-all term for the "hallies," shouts, jubilees, carols, gospel songs, and hymns for regular services, prayer meetings, watches, and "rock" services.

The white spiritual tradition has had three main stylistic phases. The earliest was the slow and dreary psalm-singing of the Puritans, likened by a critical divine of the times to the braying of asses because the extremely slow tempo and the individual variations of singers who could not read music almost destroyed all tune. The songs were "lined out" by a leader and dragged out after him by the congregation. Since the texts of many hymns so sung were by Isaac Watts, songs sung in this manner are still referred to as "Dr. Watts," as well as "lining songs" and "old long meter." The style is still used in "hard shell" Baptist churches of the Kentucky mountains and other parts of the South, where *Amazing Grace, Guide Me, Oh Thou Great Jehovah,* etc., may still be heard as survivals of the long, slow, and quavering delivery.

The second phase, promoted by the many splinter-sects of Baptists and Methodists, the Free Willers, Open Communionists, Dancing Baptists, etc., enlivened the earlier doleful manner with marching and dancing rhythms, livelier tunes borrowed from ballads, and the reduction of texts to simple and colorful lines easily assimilated and sung by the heterogeneous crowds at frontier camp-meetings and revivals. During the 19th century the wanderings of the saddle-bag preachers, the tent meetings, the Sacred Harp singing conventions, and the printed hymnals used at these gatherings all contributed to the establishment as favorites of such white spirituals as *Bound for the Promised Land* (a simplification of *I Will Arise and Go to Jesus*), *Old Time Religion (Old Ship of Zion),* and *Poor Wayfaring Stranger.* The last is an example of the entangled history of these songs. It is a descendant of a love song, *The Dear Companion;* its lines are related to many others about the

"poor pilgrims of sorrow," the wandering preachers, and the search for a "city called heaven"; and it has a progeny of its own among the Negroes, notably *I'm Just a-Goin' Over Jordan.* Among the tunes adopted from ballads for spirituals are *The Brown Girl, The False-Hearted Knight, Lord Lovel,* and *Barbara Allen;* modal melodies are common among them. Another feature of many revival-style spirituals is the enumeration of relatives in repeated stanzas, very similar to the climax of relations of the ballads—"I'm going there to meet my mother (father, sister, brother, savior, etc.)." This device carried over strongly into Negro spirituals, along with scraps of tunes and texts of this style.

The third phase, related to the Holiness Revival which began about 1890 and continues today, is jazzy, syncopated, contemporary in detail. Negro and hillbilly mannerisms have entered white spirituals of this type, and instruments formerly considered profane, such as the guitar, the accordion, and the banjo, are used for accompaniment. Songs in this style can be heard in the poorer white churches of almost any Southern mill town, as well as on the radio and on phonograph records.

The most important study of the development of the spiritual repertory, both musically and textually, and of the hymnals by which much of it was preserved and transmitted, is the work of George Pullen Jackson.

The exact relationship of Negro spirituals to their white antecedents and counterparts has been a matter of controversy. Jackson has pointed out numerous identities of wording and a considerable similarity in melodic material between Negro songs and white hymns and the European tunes to which they have been sung. Various authorities, including Hornbostel and Herskovits, have compared the "Scotch snap" feature of many such tunes to the syncopations of Negro songs. It is natural that beginning with a language, a deity, and a sacred literature not originally their own, and learning to make music of these under the tutelage of white masters in slave-holding communities, or in white "meetings" as a minority of freedmen on the frontier, the Negroes composed their own first spirituals out of borrowings. However, the singing of a Negro congregation presents marked differences to the ear from white group singing in any of the three manners described, and the various types of American Negro folk song—hollers, blues, work songs, jazz, as well as spirituals—are more like each other than like any form of white song. It does not seem important to strike an exact balance between melody borrowed from European sources and rendition stemming from the African chant nor to establish one part of the fusion as dominant over the other. The fact remains that, out of the early psalm tunes, "spiritual" songs, "fuguing tunes," ballad hymns, evangelical hymns, and revival songs of the whites, the Negroes made a choice of themes deeply influenced by their condition of slavery and isolation, transmuted them, and overlaid them with their own traditional singing style, and thus created a new repertory distinguishable from its forebears and beautiful in its own right.

Some of the characteristics of the textual part of that Negro repertory are: the subordination of the more abstract elements of the religious concepts (as in *Amazing Grace*) and of sectarian differences (*Romish Lady* into *Moanish Lady*) to the narrative, pictorial, emotional, and personal; complete visualization of the scriptural heroes, the Deity, and the members of the holy family in contemporary, earthly, and shirt-sleeve terms; incorporation of the current appurtenances of life, including the railroad, the telephone, the sewing machine, etc.; a double level of meaning, as in certain African song types, by which death, resurrection, and the new life, as well as the exploits of some of the Biblical figures, are identified with escape, emancipation, and the overthrow of the slave system; the picture of heaven as an expression of the desire of a dispossessed people for fine clothing, beautiful surroundings, acceptance, and a little glitter; a strong interest in wonders and miracles; a simple code of ethics as distinguished from the concern in white spirituals with doctrines of grace and salvation and sin; a strong preoccupation with a few symbols—the railroad, the river, and the rock—seldom clearly presented in any one song but often enough repeated to assume significance.

The heroes of the Negro spirituals are many of them the same as those of the ballad hymns of the whites—the men who were delivered by divine aid from persecution, hardship, and danger. To the descendants of the Lollards, the Lutherans, the Hussites, the Calvinists, and the Separatists, these stories meant freedom for the faithful from religious persecution and social rejection. To the Negroes they meant delivery from slavery. The roster includes Lazarus, who was raised from the dead; Moses, who was hidden from the overlords in the bullrushes and lived to lead his people out of bondage; Daniel, who survived the lion's den in Babylon ("Didn't my Lord deliver Daniel?/ Why not every man?"); Paul and Silas, who were bound in jail; Joshua, who made the walls of Jericho tumble; Noah, Jonah, Jacob.

Jesus and his mother, Mary, are treated with an especial tenderness and sense of kinship. Jesus appears as a king ("King Jesus come a-ridin' 'long,/ Wid a rainbow cross his shoulders"), as a "po' little baby," a Friday's child, born to a life of woe (*Po' Little Jesus*), as a fellow sufferer ("They whipped him up the hill,/ An' he never said a mumbalin' word,/ He jus' hung down his head and cried," like many another "po' boy" of jailhouse balladry), and as a sort of kindly pullman porter on the train to glory ("Jesus gonna make up my dyin' bed"). Mary is "Sister Mary," who was "walkin' in the garden,/ Waterin' the wiltered plants," and who "wore three links of chain,/ And every one bore Jesus' name."

Heaven in the spirituals is a city somewhat grander than Richmond, or Charleston, or New Orleans; its streets are gold, as in the white hymn descriptions of the New Jerusalem, and the feet of the redeemed will "slip and slide those golden streets." The inhabitants are dressed in long white robes that "fit very well," in "golden slippers," a "golden waistband," and a "starry crown." There the accepted soul of the black man will "rise and shine" ("my little soul goin' shine like a star"), and there will be a continual banquet for the chosen ("Jesus has a table spread/ Where the saints of God are fed/ He invites his chosen people to come and dine./ . . . You may feast at Jesus' table all the time.") Heaven is the place where work and trouble and weariness are ended. "When I git to Heaven gwine ease, ease,/ Me and my God goin' do as we please,/ Settin' down side of the lamb," "I wants to go to Heaven, have some angel wing, see de Jesus King, shout like de angels shout, set

in de angels' seat, eat what de angels eat," etc. To get there you have to "walk a lonesome valley," or cross a wide river, or ride in a chariot or train.

That train, which roars, whistles, and clangs its way through the blues, the shouts, and the prison songs, is one of the most common symbols in all Negro song for escape, for nostalgia, and for salvation. It takes a poor boy who done wrong to a wandering life; it takes a good woman from the side of her loving man; it shines its "ever-loving light" into the prison cell; it brings pardon from the governor; it carries father, mother, sister, brother, and the repentant sinner over into the promised land. It is underground railroad, Cannonball, Midnight Special, heavenly express, and gospel train all rolled into one. "De train done whistled and de cars are gone," "I got my ticket for de train." Even when the heaven-bound vehicle is conceived as a ship or a chariot, its attributes are confused in one stanza or another with those of a train. A Bahamas version of *Git on Board*, for example, says, "no second class on board de train,/ No diffren in de fare;" and *Let Me Ride*, a version of *Swing Low, Sweet Chariot* says "I got a ticket to ride,/ Got a right to ride."

The river is Jordan, as in the white spirituals, and it washes sins away by the rites of baptism; it is the bank where burdens are laid down ("goin' to lay down my burden,/ Down by the river side"). But it is also the boundary and the barrier to freedom ground. The baptismal ceremonies take on something of the aspect of puberty rites when the children are taken into the church. Perhaps the awe and fear in which immersion is held carries over from the African belief that some gods live in the river. It is the river of life.

The symbolism of the rock is less clear, but somewhere in the transmutation from white to Negro song the rock of Peter, the solid foundation of the church and the religious doctrine, acquires some new meanings. Texts that might be compared on this subject include *Lead Me to the Rock* and *No Hidin' Place* ("If I could I surely would,/ Stand on the rock where Moses stood,/ Pharaoh's army got drowned," etc.) with blues and work-song lines such as "standing on a rock pile with a hammer in my hand," and "Don't care where you bury my body,/ My little soul gwine rise and shine" with "You may bury my body on solid rock," in a late prison spiritual which goes on, "Why don't you lead me to that racial rock that's higher and higher?"

"If you want to go to Heaven, over on the other shore, keep out of the way of the long-tongued liars," and a number of other sinners. "None but the righteous shall get in the gate." The drunkards and the swearers must repent or be excluded. This is the simple and practical level of the moral code expressed in many of the Negro spirituals. "Don't you hammer on Sunday (sew, etc.), God gave you Monday, Tuesday, Wednesday, Thursday, Friday, and Saturday, Don't you hammer on Sunday, That's a shame." This song, like many other bits of spirituals, because of the ease of parodying its naive sentiments and because of the interrelation of all American Negro song types, passed over into secular use. In the musical comedy *Shuffle Along* in 1922, it was sung as an encore with these words: "Ain't it a shame to steal on Sunday, When you got Monday, etc.?" A similar transition was made by the line "all my sins are taken away" from *Hold On* to a drinking song, *Hand Me*

Down my Walking Cane, and by *Gimme That Old Time Religion* into *Gimme That Old Time Corn Liquor.*

Some of the favorite wonders of the spirituals are the "wheel way in the middle of the air," seen by Ezekiel; the dry bones which rose again so that "the leg and the foot bone begun to walk, and the skull and the jawbone begun to talk like a natural man," also from the visions of Ezekiel; and the visions of angels on Jacob's ladder. "Jacob's ladder was long and tall/ Reached all around to the heavenly walls/ Two bright angels came stepping down/ Dress so neat and so complete/ Not a sign of a stitch nor a sign of a seam/ This was made on the gospel machine."

The widespread variations in the texts of these songs and the frequent appearance of certain lines in completely different songs shows that the whole body of material is viewed as much of a piece by its singers, and that any one text may be rather casually accumulated by the injection of any familiar line occurring to a leader and suited to the pattern of the song being sung. Any one performance may thus be a communal creation to the extent of combining loosely related familiar elements.

The singing style varies considerably according to the occasion. It may be slow, mournful, as in *Sometimes I Feel Like a Motherless Child;* it may involve the vigorous chant, the shouting preaching style, as in *Rock, Daniel;* it may be deliberate and rhythmic as if timed to the strokes of the hoe, as it may have been actually in the early days of *Steal Away to Jesus;* or it may be in the staccato, syncopated beat of the present-day quartets and gospel singers, as in *Each Day* and *Dig a Little Deeper.* In the earlier style the African polyphony prevails, with each singer using his voice in an individual line that contributes to an ensemble which is neither strict unison nor a harmony on the vertical pattern of Western music. The choral tone is rich and complex and the line of the song is continual and undulating, apparently without break, so interwoven are the individual pauses. The later styles make use both of "close harmony" somewhat in the manner of the barbershop quartet, and of the boogie beat. See BASERS; RELIGIOUS FOLK MUSIC; RING SHOUT.   THERESA C. BRAKELEY

Spitters The *Bumugi* of Ifugao (Philippine Islands) religion: a class of deified spirits who wait for the souls of the newly dead and try to trick them into betraying their living relatives into their power. The newly dead, being greenhorns, so to speak, in the afterworld, are more gullible or more easily terrified than experienced souls. So the Bumugi (perhaps the one named Dumudui, the Pointer), walking along with the new soul, will suddenly point at a living person and ask if that is the new one's relative. If the soul says No, the Spitter says, "Shall I spit on him and find out? If the spit strikes, that will prove he is your kin." If the soul is frightened into saying All right, then the spitter spits, and if the spit touches the living person, he gets leprosy or a Philippine disease called big-belly.

There are eight Spitters (Bumugi, Dumudui, Lumok [Dirt], and others with names meaning Soft-rot, Itcher, etc.) and two special deities who protect from the Spitters. These are Tudong (Shade) who shades the living from their glances, and Yungayung, giver of a

talisman which renders the living invisible to the Spitters. This consists of two plants: Job's tears and *konûpa,* a kind of epiphytic fern which grows on stone walls and completely covers them. The latter plant especially is often seen in the hair of women and children, or fastened to young babies. See R. F. Barton, *The Religion of the Ifugaos, MAAA* 65, pp. 73, 176, 181.

spittle and spitting Spitting as a symbolical regurgitation is, in all parts of the world, a symbol of disgust. Because of the complex operations of the secondary nervous system, the flow of saliva increases at moments of emotional excitement. In folklore spitting is either a gesture of disgust, when it assumes almost a ritualistic importance ("I spat upon him"), or a device to bring good luck or ward off bad luck. The structure of the belief is somewhat monotonous. The applications of it show a great variety. Every young fisherman knows that to spit on his hook will make the fish bite. Many fishing communities spit on the trawl before they cast it overboard. Pliny said that spitting on the hand that has struck "a blow will remove all feelings of resentment in the person who was struck." Two persons who wash in the same water will have bad luck unless one spits in the water or makes the sign of the cross over it. The first money taken in the day's trade should be spat on.

As the subject has been studied extensively, only a general survey will be attempted here. Although the attempt is made to give the locations of the superstitions as they are reported, they are so general that it would be more remarkable if a custom practiced in Japan, for example, were not known in ancient Rome or the back lots of modern New York than if it *were* known there. Japanese fighters spit on their hands before entering a fight. So too did the Roman fighters, and so do small boys in every part of the United States. Headaches in Japan are cured by wetting a piece of straw with saliva and placing it in the middle of the forehead. Sometimes magic formulæ are used. In Japan, China, ancient Rome, and elsewhere, spittle will cure blood-shot eyes or the inflamed eyes of infants. Compare in this context *John* ix, 6. Chinese midwives bind the navels of newly born infants by making a mud pie of earth from the courtyard moistened by spittle and clapping it on the spot. In Imperial China, the emperor's levees were opened at midnight and the courtiers had to stand for hours awaiting audience. As the palace was forbidden to males and would be defiled if a male left any part of himself there, the Pekinese breed of dogs was developed who would receive the spittle of the noble lords.

In New Zealand, South Africa, and elsewhere, care is taken lest the spittle fall into the hands of an enemy who can use it to cast a spell. The Marquesan sorcerer wraps spittle in a leaf, buries it, and makes incantation against an enemy. On the island of Nias hunters digging pits for their game may neither spit nor laugh lest the game be driven away. Malay sorcerers generally folded specimens from every part of their enemy's body into clay figures which were then toasted until the enemy died. In East Africa the king's spittle was carefully gathered and hidden lest enemies find it. In the Wajagga covenant, the contracting parties have a bowl of milk or beer between them, take some in the mouth, and ceremoniously spit it into the mouth of the other. Similarly, small boys in Scotland and America have been known to seal a covenant by spitting three times into the air, over their heads. The Koran mentions the use of spittle in magic. Spitting four times is the Hopi Indian method of ridding the inner self of bad thoughts. Pliny and many others have reported that spitting on the ground will protect against the evil eye and that spitting on a wound will heal it.

Grimm reported in his *Teutonic Mythology* that the æsir and vanir "made peace and in token thereof spat into a common receptacle." See KVASER. The Swedes removed a birthmark by rubbing it with "fasting spittle." In Sweden sore eyes will heal if rubbed with spittle the first thing in the morning, i.e. "fasting spittle"; in northern Iceland this must be repeated three mornings in succession. In several parts of Britain you cure a toothache by spitting into a frog's mouth and requesting it to make off with the pain. A new shilling will cure ringworm if moistened with fasting spittle. A wart will disappear if moistened with fasting spittle several days in succession. In parts of Great Britain you cure a toothache by spitting into a frog's mouth and requesting it to make off with the pain. A new shilling will cure unless new fuel is being put on it.

Generally in North America it is unlucky to meet a cross-eyed person, but the bad luck can be changed by spitting. Similarly in England a lodger is reported to have had to spit three times a day on a fellow lodger who squinted. The saliva of an angry horse or rat is said to be poisonous. To spit over the little finger of the right hand in the direction of a white horse will bring good luck. In northern North America a cramp in the foot will disappear if a cross of spittle is made on the sole. If the right foot is asleep rub the right eyebrow with the right forefinger after having moistened it with saliva. Persons who walk beneath a ladder change their bad luck by spitting. A corn will disappear if moistened by fasting spittle nine mornings in succession. Although the saliva of angry animals or men is poisonous, the saliva of others is therapeutic. If you spit on the back of a frog or toad, it will burst open; but if a toad spits on a human being, warts will appear. A stitch in the side from running will stop if you spit under a stone and replace the stone. When an article has been misplaced it can be found if you spit on the palm of the hand, strike the spittle with a finger, and note the direction taken by the largest drop. This also helps in finding birds' nests. Dead animals in the road should be spat on. When the left hand itches, the procedure is to spit in the palm, close it, and put it in the pocket to keep the money that is coming.

Among some groups of Negroes, death presaged by a bird flying into the house may be averted by spitting on the floor, drawing a circle around it, walking around the circle with one's back to it, and spitting in it again. To discover one's future home one may spit on a hot shovel and note the direction the bubbles take. If after starting on a journey you have to turn back, make a cross on the ground and spit in it. If a rabbit crosses in front of you when walking, squat in the middle of the road, make a cross and spit in it. Never cross the trail of a snake without making a cross on the trail and spitting in it. Fever can be averted by spitting on caterpillars. To the customary superstitions about spitting, certain American Indians contribute the following: 1) if you spit after seeing a polecat, your hair will turn gray;

2) a covenant may be assured by spitting into a hole in the ground. See BEAD-SPITTER AND THROWN-AWAY; JEWELS FROM SPITTLE. R. D. JAMESON

Split Boys Title of a Kiowa Indian version of the Star Husband tale, which although known to nearly all members of the tribe, was told only by the priests or keepers of certain sacred bundles, at a ceremony held in spring when the first thunder was heard. Each bundle keeper told the myth separately in his own tipi. For two versions of *Split-Boys* see Elsie Clews Parsons, *Kiowa Tales*, MAFLS 22, 1929, pp. 1–8. [EWV]

Springfield Mountain A native American ballad, perhaps the most popular and widely sung of all songs originated in New England, relating the death of a young man who was bitten by a snake while mowing in the hayfield. An eight-line rimed version of the incident on which the song was based is given in Joseph Fiske's *Ten Years' Almanack* (n. p., 1765): "At Springfield Mountain there was one/ Bit by a rattlesnake alone/ This poor man he to death did yield/ As he went home died in the field . . . ," etc. The date of the occurrence is given as 1761. The young man whose fate is lamented, according to early accounts, was Timothy Myrick, of Springfield Mountain (now Wilbraham), Mass., and the authorship of the original ballad text is usually credited to Nathan Torrey, of Springfield, Mass., though some stories have stated that it was written by the young woman who was to have married Myrick.

It was originally sung to the hymn tune of *Old Hundred*, but about 1840 a humorous stage version was set to music by an actor, George Gaines Spear, who performed it on platforms all over the country; later the Scottish jig tune, *Merrily Danced the Quaker's Wife*, was attached to it. From these sources many melodic variants have been made.

The song is known all over America in many versions, which may be distinguished as forming at least four quite different types: One follows the Myrick story; one is the story of Miss Curtis, the bereaved fiancée; one deals with a sweetheart named Sally and the doomed youth is called Johnny; one, the stage version, has a heroine called Molly. Nonsense refrains of considerable variation are sung in different parts of the country, and except in New England, where serious versions may still be heard, the humorous tradition has won out in the narrative. In California, a variant is known as *The Pizen Sarpent*. Lomax's *Cowboy Songs* records a stammering text used as a haying song in the West. Other variants are popular in Mississippi, Texas, Michigan, etc.

springwort The key-flower of medieval European folklore, which opens doors and mountains and often reveals treasure: thought by Grimm to be spurge. It is sometimes identified with mandrake. It is obtained from a woodpecker by stopping up the hole to her nest; she will go off and return with this flower to reopen it. Pliny (*Nat. Hist.* x, 18, 20) tells this story. Theophrastus also mentions such a plant. Scholars are undecided as to whether the Open Sesame formula in the Ali Baba story refers to magic words or to this magic plant.

spruce Much of the lore of the spruce tree is the same as that of other evergreen trees, such as the pine and fir. The Navaho Indians make extensive use of the branches of this tree in their ceremonials, as costume, and as wands and brushes, as in the chant of the Sun's House where branches of blue spruce are used. Hunters of the Penobscot tribe carried a spruce twig next to the skin to prevent a pain in the side. An origin myth of the Tewa Indians of New Mexico says that man entered the world at Shipap in the far north by climbing a Douglas spruce. In Newfoundland the green buds are used to cure toothache. The Mohegan, Pequot, and Penobscot tribes used spruce gum as a poultice for boils and abscesses. The gum is chewed generally in America wherever the tree is found, especially by children. The spruce ale of England is made of the sap of the silver fir and ivy leaves.

square dances Dances performed in square formations, usually by four couples, each forming one side of the square, by eight couples in the double quadrille. It shares the initial circling and promenade with the round dance, but rarely divides off into two lines (*Glory, Glory, Hallelujah*). Sometimes in the end it winds into serpentines, grapevine-twists, snails. The particular characteristic, notably in the American versions, is the progressive activity of one couple after another during the body of the dance, each couple visiting the others in turn with a set figure peculiar to the dance. These patterns include ladies' chain, birdie in the cage, dip for the oyster, docey-do, forward up six and fall back six, star by the right, and a legion of other picturesque figures, always ending with "partners swing." The step is a springy easy shuffle.

The singing quadrille of the East developed characteristic calls in the West, such as: "Up and down and around and around/ Allemande left and allemande aye;/ Ingo, bingo, six penny high;/ Big pig, little pig, root, hog or die"; "Swing the Indian, swing that squaw,/ And now that boy from Arkansaw./ Swing your maw, swing your paw,/ And don't forget your mother-in-law."

The square is of the quadrille category, but the quadrille is a more flexible and inclusive form. For the regional variations and provenience of this rollicking yet well-ordered dance form, see DANCE: FOLK AND PRIMITIVE; REEL; ROUND DANCES. [GPK]

squash The word derives from Algonquin (specifically Narragansett) *askuta-squash*, literally eaten green, indicating that they were not recommended when ripe. Among the Meskwaki Indians squash stem was ground up and boiled to make a medicine for female ailments; the Ojibwa and the Menomini used it as a diuretic. In the mythology of the Seneca Indians, squash is, along with corn and beans, one of the three daughters of the Earth Mother. See DEOHAKO.

Squash designs are frequent in Pueblo ritual art. Squash blossoms made of dyed rabbit fur or devised of yarn over twigs are placed at either ear on Hopi masks as a symbolic prayer for plentiful squash and melons. The Hopi also put squash effigies in their garden patches to encourage the crop. See GOD-EYES. Among the Papago, squash effigies were made for the visiting dancers when a visiting village entertained its host before racing with them. In Pima Indian rain-making songs, the squash also appears as a sacred plant.

D. M. Fansler records a cleverness test motif in which the king gives or sends to a peasant, or a young girl, a narrow-necked jar and a large squash, with the order to put the squash in the jar without breaking either

(H1023.11). The clever one inserts a very tiny squash in the jar without removing it from the vine, and allows it to grow until it is as large as the jar. Sometimes the large squash is returned to the king in the small-necked jar with the counter-request that the king remove it without breaking either. This same task occurs in the *Arabian Nights* regarding a melon instead of a squash. See Fansler, *Filipino Popular Tales, MAFLS* 12, pp. 56, 58, 62–63, 434.

śrāddha A Hindu rite performed to honor the family ancestors; also, a rite observed to provide a recently departed spirit with an intermediate body and to aid it to become enrolled with the sainted dead: literally, offering given with faith. The śrāddha probably evolved from the custom of feeding the dead. It is an intricate rite. When performed for the ancestors of the family each ancestor is named and propitiated, but food is offered only for three paternal male ancestors—father, grandfather, and great-grandfather, since earlier ancestors, once united with the sacred dead, need no further special attention. This ceremony is celebrated once a month at new moon.

When the rite is performed for one newly dead, the ceremony lasts ten days and is performed near running water. On the first day an offering of sesamum, barley, water, sprigs of kuśa grass, and a lamp is made to allay the thirst and heat which the spirit suffers during cremation. The rite of feeding the spirit is then performed and repeated on each of the ten days. Rice balls for Brāhmans and barley-flour for Kshatriyas and the illegitimate sons of Brāhmans are used. On the first day one ball is offered, on the second two, and so on until at the end of the ten-day period the spirit has received 55 balls, escaped from ten hells, and gradually has acquired a new body. The officiant and relatives then return home and on the eleventh day present a cow to the chief Brāhman. Today such an animal is usually branded with the sacred discus and trident and allowed to wander on the village lands. On the twelfth and final day food is offered and the roots of a fig tree are watered. With the conclusion of the ceremony the spirit ceases to be a disembodied ghost and becomes one of the sainted dead.

The śrāddha is not performed for unmarried girls or for boys who have not undergone investiture with the sacred thread. The ceremony, among lower castes, is generally abbreviated.

Sraosha In Persian belief and mythology, the embodiment of divine service and the angel of obedience who aids righteous souls in their battles with demons after death. Sraosha was the first to use the barsom. He will be sent by Ahura Mazda to arouse Keresāspa at the end of the world. See AĒSHMA; AMESHA SPENTAS.

Srin-po One of the eight classes of indigenous Tibetan country gods: ghouls and vampires, raw-flesh colored.

Stackalee, Stackerlee, or **Stagolee** Negro bad man, who, according to the ballad, shot and killed Billy Lyon (Lion, Galion) in a barroom brawl (some say in Memphis and some say in St. Louis) for stealing his "magic Stetson." Legend says (Onah L. Spencer, in B. A. Botkin, *A Treasury of American Folklore*, pp. 122–130) that this magic hat, for which Stackalee sold his soul to the Devil, enabled him to assume various shapes, from mountains to varmints, to walk barefooted on hot slag, and to eat fire. When he got too ornery for even the Devil to stand, the latter caused him to lose his hat and his magic, via Billy Lyon, and, ultimately, to burn in hell.

Stacker Lee, for whom many Negro children along the Ohio and the Mississippi were named, was one of the four sons of Captain James Lee, founder of the Lee Line, and was celebrated for his prowess with ladies as well as steamboats. The packet *Stacker Lee* (nicknamed "The Stack," "The Big Smoke," "Stack o' Dolluhs," and "Bull of the Woods" and noted for its size and speed) plied between Memphis and Cincinnati, St. Louis, and Vicksburg. The original Stagolee is said to have been a stoker or roustabout on this boat, also the son of a woman who was chambermaid or cook on this or another of the Lee boats; and the ballad is said to have been composed on the levees, where it was sung. (See Mary Wheeler, *Steamboatin' Days*, 1944, pp. 99–103). [BAB]

stamped pit A hole in the ground covered with a rough platform of planks or bark and stamped to produce a dull resonant sound in connection usually with primitive fertility rites. The device merely extends and amplifies the sounds of the stamping feet and is related to the women's dances of planting, which are close restricted motions, held near to the ground, and involve shuffling and stamping. It is used in the Solomons and among the Indians of certain South American tribes and was known almost all over the world in the Paleolithic period. The same idea is carried out by building a low platform over the earth or by dancing on an inverted pot. A similar device, called the sand drum, is made by digging a tunnel through sand, as children do on the beach, and beating its roof with the flat of the hand, as is done in New Guinea and in Ethiopia. While the significance is not recognized, a related dance is performed in the *jarabe Tapatío* of Jalisco in Mexico, for which a platform is erected over a hole in the ground or over jars buried in the earth. It is a couple dance with elements of courtship, and as danced in cities is sophisticated rather than primitive.

Star Husband, Star Boy A widely known North American Indian myth, which relates the wish of a girl (or girls) for a star and the ascent of the wisher(s) to the sky. There the girl marries a star (or the sun or moon); later, disobeying instructions, she discovers a sky-hole and sees the earth beneath. She plans to escape with her son, usually by a sky rope; she is killed, but the son reaches the earth alive and is adopted by an old woman whose secret husband he murders before he undertakes a remarkable series of adventures. In those versions in which two women ascend to the sky, no offspring are born to them; they descend to earth alive, usually land in a tree, and then undergo a series of adventures while escaping from their rescuer. Reichard, who has made an analysis of this tale, found 51 versions of Star Husband told by tribes extending from the North Pacific coast to the New England coast, and since 1921, when her analysis was published, several additional versions of the Star Husband story, such as the Kiowa ritual myth, *Split Boys*, have been published. The Star Husband story embraces two main types, one of which centers in the Plains area, the other in the Eastern Woodlands. For a succinct outline of the episodes in these two types see Gladys A. Reichard, "Literary Types

and Dissemination of Myths" (*JAFL* 34: 269–307, 1921), pp. 269–272. [EWV]

star of David or **Solomon's seal** The six-pointed star formed by the superimposing of one triangle on another: see jacket of this book. The symbol is a combination of the male (apex upwards) and female (apex downwards) triangles; it is said, in cabalistic writings, to comprise the signs of the four elements and the four letters of the Tetragrammaton, and thus it came to be the symbol for God. Since the Biblical commandment puts a tabu on the use of the Name of God and on the depiction of God, the symbol was inscribed as the graphic representation of God in synagogues and wherever the Name was appropriate. In alchemy, the star of David combined the symbols for fire and water; hence, it meant distillation. Until recently, therefore, it appeared on shops selling brandy. The *mogen Dovid*, star of David, is the symbol of Zionism and appears on the flag of Israel. As Solomon's seal, the hexagram possessed power to control demons of all kinds. The stopper on the bottle containing the bottle imp or jinni was stamped with the seal of Solomon. In the Nsibidi script of West Africa, a native form of writing, the symbol means ardent love: the universality of the male-female content of the sign is here apparent. See PHALLISM.

stars Many beliefs concerning the stars, as well as a few particular tales in which the chief actor(s) is a star person, exist among North American Indians. While too much emphasis was laid on the importance of the stars among primitive peoples by 19th century theorists, it is none the less true that notable celestial phenomena such as the Milky Way, the Pleiades, and the Great Bear did interest the Indians, and tales or beliefs circulated concerning the origin of these, and the Morning and Evening Stars, which figure as actors in certain specific tales, or whose origins are explained in folk beliefs.

The Pawnee and Cherokee are two tribes whose star lore was early investigated, and found to be, for North American Indian groups, notably extensive. Among the Skidi Pawnee the morning and evening stars represented the masculine and feminine elements, and were connected with the advent and the perpetuation on earth of all living forms.

Among the Fox Indians, some of the stars are great and powerful spirits; most of them are people who have died and gone to live in the sky. So likewise with the linguistically related Delaware, Shawnee, and other Algonquian peoples: among the spirits the stars are given a rather prominent place and referred to as "grandfathers"; they are thought to render service in that they help illuminate the world at night, and in Delaware prayers the stars are often mentioned.

The Pueblo and other Southwestern Indians also accord the stars prominence as spirits; the Morning Star (often called the Big Star), the Evening Star, the Pleiades, Orion, and the Galaxy are recognized as spirits by nearly all Pueblo groups; Aldebaran is also a spirit at Hopi, and falling stars are spirits at Taos. The Pleiades are known as seed stars (Zuñi), clustered ones (Hopi), seven stars (Jemez); Morning Star is known as Dark Star Man in Tewa pueblos, Evening Star as Yellow-Going Old Woman (Tewa), or prayer star (Isleta). [EWV]

Star Woman This folkloric motif is popular among South American Indians. An ugly man, despised by everyone, expresses the wish to marry a bright star. A mysterious woman appears and marries him. He becomes handsome and successful. Finally his wife takes him to the sky whence she came. He cannot stand the cold and dies. Versions of this story have been recorded in the Chaco and among the Ge tribes of eastern Brazil. [AM]

stick dances Folk and ritual dances distinguished by the manipulation of sticks or staves. They are found in many parts of the world in various forms, almost always as a male prerogative.

1) *Combat dances* or derived opposition dances, performed in two lines are the most common, especially in Europe. As such they are similar to the *Moriscas,* are often associated with them, and suggest the stick as a substitute for a wooden sword. The Basque *banakoa* and *binakoa* form part of the suite of the *ezpata dantza* or sword dance. Portugal is particularly rich in versions of the *dança dos paulitos* or *dança das pelas,* predominantly featured at Epiphany or St. John's Day, at Miranda da Douro where the performers are dressed as women, in villages of São Pedro de Sarrazinos near Braganza, at Braga, etc. Spain, Italy, Lithuania, Hungary each has its special stick dance, and the English Morris displays elaborate stick-striking.

Egypt also has a men's stick dance, and India has several regional variants (the *kather-natch* of Bengal, *ras-lila* of Kathiawar, and *kolattam* of South India, specifically of the Kaniyan caste), some in longways, some in round formation. In the New World, Haitian Negroes duel with sticks, one line dressed as women. The Chaco Terenos fight with sticks as the Good and Bad Moiety in the Dance of the Rhea Feathers. The Iroquois Indians formerly struck rods together in their sun rite, *waieno'e,* which is now a simple longways.

2) *Wielding of sticks* without vestigial combat forms part of the pattern of the Morris, but appears independently in the Danish stick dance. Huichol Indian peyote dancers gesticulate with bamboo rods called "serpents." Yuchi feather dancers also waved plumed rods.

3) *Crossing of sticks.* Stepping in and out among two crossed sticks on the ground is probably also a sword-dance vestige, in view of the similarity between the Catalan *L'Hereu Riera* with sticks, and the Scotch *Gilly Callum* with sword and scabbard.

4) *Striking of a staff on the ground* serves three objectives, which may merge: a) As support—the Mexican *viejitos* and Iroquois Husk Face who lean on one staff, and the San Juan and Taos deer dancers, who walk with two short staffs as legs. The cane of the Haitian loa Legba replaces the *olisbos* or penis of the Dahomean prototype; b) As agricultural symbol—the Morris dibbing; c) As musical instrument—the long staff with deer-hoof rattles of the Chaco *káusima* and California Indian girls' puberty rites. The Mexican *paixtle* staff serves both as cane and rattle.

The stick, like the sword, appears in the role of phallic symbol. In combat dances it probably has the same purpose suggested for *Moriscas,* namely as vegetation symbol; it appears at the same festivals, and is similarly connected with transvestitism. The Haitian Legba cane most clearly shows its phallic origin; the clown and puberty functions have similar implications. The staff is more than a support for tottering old age; in the hands

of the *viejos, abuelos,* and Iroquois "our grandfathers," it symbolizes deference to ancestral spirits and an appeal to their chthonic powers. Added to their power is the spirit of the living tree which produced the cane.

Such blended concepts would extend to the several varying forms of the stick, to the *matachin* plumed trident, to attenuation into the whip, the *Lebensrute* of the German Carnival, the serpentine whip of the Aztec *tlacololeros* agricultural dance, the Arawak *macquari* memorial rite, the Quechua *sumamao* blood-letting, the numerous disciplinary whippers of American Indian ceremonialism. This wriggling effigy is frozen into the *hikuli* serpent, the wooden snake of the Otomí Malinche, and the spear of the Cáhita *chapayekas.* These horned phallic clowns combine the snake shape with that of the spear and sword, two wooden tools which they rhythmically strike together.

In this network of widely distributed forms and symbols, priority cannot be asserted for any one form, not even for the sword, nor for any one location. In Europe and Asia, the most abundant and elaborate forms pervade India and the Iberian peninsula, to a lesser extent England. They are most complete in India, where they combine the longways of the Morris and *paloteo* with the circular hey of the Maypole, and also include the "dibbing" found in the Morris. The ground plans and patterns of stick-striking show remarkable similarity in these two widely separated areas, though the steps are peculiar to each region. This would point to a very early dissemination, possibly to a common Neolithic heritage previous to the Aryan migrations in the second century B.C. The Indian stick dances flourish among Dravidian tribes, as the *kolattam* of the Tamil. See PHALLIC DANCES; RATTLES; SWORD DANCES. [GPK]

stick-fast Catchword commonly applied to the tar-baby motif (K741) but including also the incidents involved in various stories in which the characters stick together or stick to some magic object which will not release them. Typical of these tales is *The Golden Goose* (Grimm #64) in which a group of thieves are thus caught one after the other and the sight of them all stuck together makes the sad princess laugh. See GOOSE THAT LAID THE GOLDEN EGG. There are also European witchcraft stories of chairs to which a person sticks (D1413.6) and African tales involving magic medicines which cause people to stick to their seats or other objects (D1413.11). The sack which holds onto the hand thrust into it (D1413.9) and the chamber-pot to which a person sticks (D1413.8) are other European variants. Compare BURR-WOMAN; TAR BABY.

stomp dances Among the Indians of the Southeast and Eastern Woodlands areas of the United States, many dances which were perhaps originally sacred in nature, are now danced at social, all-night dances known as "stomp dances" among the present-day tribes of Oklahoma. A great many of the so-called stomp dances are named for animals: garfish dance, quail dance, rabbit dance, eagle dance, etc. Each has its own distinctive movements and steps; many are drum dances, while others are danced to the accompaniment of tortoise-shell leg or hand rattles, gourd rattles, etc. Nearly always both men and women participate in such dances. [EWV]

☞ A stomp is a shuffling stamp, sometimes executed as a rapid trot. It is included in the vocabulary of boogie-woogie. Many of the open rounds of the Iroquois and Eastern Algonquians use this step. Frequently the accompanying songs are antiphonal. In the southern area these rounds frequently develop into serpentines. Farcical gestures are permissible.

Specifically, "stomp dance" is an alternate term for the "leading dance," "friendship dance," or mixed social dance of these tribes. It was disseminated to the Munsi-Mohicans, the Lenape, the Creek, Yuchi, and Seminole. In the close tribal proximity of Oklahoma it spread like wildfire to the Sauk, Fox, Iowa, Osage, Comanche, and other Midwestern and Plains tribes. It is very similar to their adopted snake dance.

Usually it is performed in single file; among the Penobscot, four abreast. The Iroquois use no instrument; the Penobscot leader shook a cowhorn rattle. Southern and Oklahoma women leaders fasten a tortoise rattle to their knees. This counterclockwise antiphonal round for men and women is typical of the Eastern tribes, but atypical of the Plains, and definitely contrasts with their clockwise "limping" squaw and victory dances. [GPK]

Stone Giant The Yahgan Indians of Tierra del Fuego have a story about a giant who is invulnerable except on the soles of his feet. He was finally overcome by a hummingbird who could not destroy him until the giant's heart exploded. The same story with many local variants has a wide distribution among North American Indians. [AM]

Stone Men The two Pueblo Indian war gods, the *hayunu* of Taos, sons of the Sun and Yellow Corn Girl: so called because of two stone images enshrined in the mountain at Taos. Their mother told them not to go eastward for their hunting, but they did, and met their father, the Sun, who aided them thereafter in all their adventures. At last they went to live with their father, the Sun, who was "not a man to stay in one place." He was always traveling day and night. So he placed one son upon his right and one upon his left. But their earthly parents swelled up and died of sadness. At Tewa the sons of the Sun are thought of as winter sun and summer sun, instead of two attendant stars in the sun's course. Compare AHAYUTA ACHI.

stork It is bad luck to kill a stork (N250.1). Many believe that storks were once men and that they become men in Egypt in winter (B775; D624.1). In Morocco, if the stork builds on the roof, the house will become empty; if in the trees, the trees will wither. If the birds are white and clean when they arrive, there will be much sunshine and heat; if they are dirty, it will be a bad year. Storks are especially popular in Germany and the people like to have them nest on the roof.

That storks bring babies (T589.6.1) is a familiar saying. In Germany it is even said that a stork flying over the house presages a birth. The belief was that storks picked up infants from marshes, ponds, wells, springs, and stones where the souls of unborn children dwell. See ADEBORSTEINE. It is also said that if storks leave their nests and build others hurriedly in trees, it is a sign of war; they have been known to leave a whole area before pestilence struck; if they leave their nests forever great calamity is foreseen. [GPS]

Stormalong A favorite chantey for heavy work at the capstan, as when the anchor was deeply buried in mud, or sometimes for pumping ship. The hero, Stormalong, was the sailor's ideal of a seaman, who met his end and was buried at sea. There are many variants, attesting to many of Stormalong's exploits and giving his burial place as off Cape Horn, in Mobile Bay, etc.

Stormalong Mythical hero of deep-water sailormen, embodying the ideals and delusions of grandeur of the old days of iron men and wooden ships. Figuring chiefly in the windlass chantey that bears his name, Stormalong is also the hero of typical tall tales of the sea, such as the soaping of his giant ship *Courser*'s sides to ease her through the English Channel, the scraped-off soap whitening the cliffs of Dover, and the digging of the Panama Canal when the ship is whipped about in a hurricane and goes right through the Isthmus. See Frank Shay, *Here's Audacity*, 1930. [BAB]

story formulas Formulaic beginnings and endings of tales are usual in North American Indian folklore, though not universally used by all tribes, nor, in tribes where they do occur, are they used by all narrators, or for all tales. Examples of formulaic beginnings are: Personages and the place where they live are mentioned ("Those people were living at Cottonwood"; "Seed-marked boy was living at Cottonwood with his grandmother," etc.). This is typical of the openings of Pueblo myths; Cottonwood is usually the place mentioned in Taos and other Pueblo tales, but other locales may be also specifically referred to. The White Mountain Apache conventional opening for a tale is the phrase "Long ago they say," to which the listener(s) should reply "ya," meaning assent or confirmation. The Coeur d'Alene Indians of the Plateau begin many of their Coyote tales with "Coyote had a house," others with "Coyote was going along"; other tales start by naming the chief actor and where, or with whom, he or she is living.

Formulaic endings to tales are as frequent as formulaic beginnings. A few examples of such are: "You have a tail" or "So then you have a tail," directed to the person whose turn it is to next tell a story; the explanation given is that the person must tell a story to take off the tail, so that it will not freeze (Taos Pueblo). "My yucca fruits lie piled up" is the conventional White Mountain Apache ending for a tale; the Coeur d'Alene use "The end of the road" or similar expressions, "That is the end of my road," "The road comes to an end," "I have come to the end of the trail" as a tale ending; this is sometimes extended, according to Reichard, to "the little bird sat on a tree at the end of the road and was shot" (Gladys A. Reichard, *An Analysis of Coeur d'Alene Indian Myths, MAFLS* 41, p. 28). [EWV]

strangle-weed or **dodder** This parasitic vine begins life normally from seed, which roots in the ground. When a tentacle grows from the main stem and anchors to another plant, however, the root and stalk die and the plant derives its sustenance from the other plant. It was used extensively by medieval herbalists, but had no inherent virtues of its own. It was substituted for herbs on which it grew, on the theory that it absorbed only the essential essences of that plant. Southern Negroes throw a piece of dodder over the left shoulder toward the home of their love without looking back; if it grows the love is returned. Dodder is also used in other forms of love divination, and is sometimes known as love-vine. Pantagruelion, probably hemp, is also called strangleweed, from the fact that rope is made of it with which to strangle felons.

strawberry The strawberry once was sacred to Frigga and has since been transferred to the Virgin Mary. Culpeper calls it a plant of Venus, cool and dry when green, cool and moist when ripe. Frigga was wont to conceal children who died as infants in a strawberry and smuggle them into heaven. John the Baptist is said to have lived on these berries. Strawberry leaves form part of the coronets of certain British dukes, earls, and marquises, and alternate with fleurs de lis in the coronets of younger members of the royal family. Because Bavarian peasants believe that the elves are fond of strawberries, they tie a basket of them to the horns of their cattle so they will cause them to prosper.

Medicinally both the wild and cultivated berries are in high repute, but usually the wild are preferred. They are good for melancholy, fainting, and all inflammations except fevers. They are considered beneficial for the blood, liver, and spleen. At one time they were considered harmful for persons with gout, but now are believed beneficial. If taken in excess they cause hives in some people. They are also good to remove excess flesh. The juice of the strawberry is used as a dentifrice to remove tartar and to preserve the teeth. The root is also used as a dentifrice. The juice or a decoction of the root is good for ulcers; made into lotions and creams it will remove freckles and whiten and preserve the skin. A distilled water of the berries is a cure for jaundice and good for palpitation of the heart. The leaves and roots in wine cool the liver; in water they cool and clear the eyes, tighten loose teeth, and are a remedy for venereal infections. An infusion of the leaves is a good tonic for the kidneys. See BERRIES IN WINTER.

street cries Rhythmic chants and songs of hucksters and itinerant tradesmen, flourishing in the days of "hawkers and walkers" and still found among peddlers and street vendors who depend upon word-of-mouth advertising. As the vocal and musical equivalent of trade signs and slogans, these traditional formulæ have passed from trade lore into general folklore and the arts as well as into social history. Thus street cries have inspired children's rimes and games (*The Muffin Man*, "One a penny, two a penny, hot cross buns," *Hot Pies*), ballads (*Molly Malone*), the illustrations of Rowlandson and Cruikshank, poems by Lydgate and Herrick, musical settings like those of the Elizabethan composers, Charpentier (in *Louise*), and Gershwin (in *Porgy and Bess*).

Collected and illustrated, street cries have provided picturesque and pictorial data on trades and on the changing manners and customs to which the cries themselves have been responsive. Left behind by modern progress and periodically banned by official anti-noise edicts, they have withdrawn to shabby and outlying districts or survived in the provinces, or followed outmoded occupations into limbo. Following the successive migrations of Europeans to the United States, they illustrate the sequence of trades within ethnic groups and their succession from one group to another. Local foods, speech, and folkways add color to street cries, as they in turn add color and variety to the local scene. As street cries have always amused as well as advertised wares and services, so individual vendors compete with one another in the humor and originality of their per-

formance, showing a preference for esthetic effects (tune and intonation), often to the neglect of intelligibility.

One hundred years after the publication of Samuel Wood's *The Cries of New York*, the New York *Sun*, Sept. 20, 1908, in a story on Commissioner Bingham's order for the suppression of unnecessary noises, listed the following among the street vendors affected, only a handful of which have survived to-day: vegetable huckster, umbrella mender, kettle mender, chair mender, hot corn man, broom man, scissors grinder, line-up (clothes-line) man, banana peddler, old-clothes man, shoe lace and suspender man, kindling wood man, oyster and fish peddler, melon man, bootblack, and newsboy. (See Charles Hindley, *A History of the Cries of London*, 1881; *Les Cris de Paris*, 1887; articles on Charleston and New Orleans cries in *A Treasury of Southern Folklore*, 1949.)   B. A. BOTKIN

Streets of Laredo Another title of *The Cowboy's Lament*.

string figures Generic term for play with a string or thong passed around and between the fingers to form figures; the European four-hand variant is known as *cat's cradle*. String play, in which the fingers weave a loop of string into a variety of line-forms, is known throughout the world; the Eurasian continent seems to have lost most of its figures (even cat's cradle is thought to be adopted from Malaysia), but in Africa, North and South America, the Arctic and Pacific areas, so-called primitive peoples still know a great variety of string figures. According to a survey made in 1930 by Kathleen Haddon (*Artists in String*, p. 149), more than 800 figures had then been published, only a fraction of those collected. String figures are primarily a pastime in which inventiveness (seeing for example a myth with its personages depicted in the string) plays the major part, but sometimes there are magico-religious overtones. The Eskimos play at their string figures when the sun begins to south after the summer solstice; they try to entangle the sun, to hold it back from the long winter setting. Haddon (*op. cit.*, pp. 21–22) quotes a story from Jenness in which the spirit of cat's cradles draws out its intestines and tries to defeat a boy in a figure-making contest; the boy's mother, by rapid making and unmaking of a simple figure, forces the spirit to retreat and flee. Haddon also points out that the names of the string figures match the environment and general culture of their makers. Thus there are coyotes from western America, palms from the tropics, seals and polar bears from the North; there are hogans and tipis from North America, a slit drum from Australia, a hammock with an old man's legs hanging out of it from British Guiana. Often figures evolve in a sequence. The house is built, broken, repaired, broken again, and then one sees the two vandals running away (Chukchee). Or earth, heaven, and the stars may be depicted in one sequence, each evolving from the preceding, each in a different plane of the figure (Gold Coast). Often the same figure is found in two or more widely separated parts of the world; the name is different, the technique of making the figure varies, but the final figure is the same. Thus the three-pronged fish-spear of New Guinea (Torres Strait) is the same as the tent of the Northwest Coast of America; the trap of the Guianas is the outrigger canoe of New Caledonia.

W. H. R. Rivers and A. C. Haddon (*Man*, Oct. 1902, p. 146) described a method of noting string figures that has come into general use. A *loop* is a string passing around a digit (finger or toe sometimes, hand or arm). A string on the side of a finger towards the thumb is *radial;* towards the little finger, *ulnar.* Where two strings are on the same finger, the one nearer the palm (or point of attachment of hand, arm, etc.) is *proximal;* the one farther is *distal* (nearer the free end of the extremity). A string on the front of the hand (or the front of the finger) is *palmar;* one on the back is *dorsal.* These terms are extended to include the motions of making the figure; a string may be passed proximal to another (below it), or it may be picked up by the palmar aspect of a finger from the distal side (the finger is passed into the loop from above and the string is hooked). For example, to make the outrigger canoe (trap) mentioned above:

Use a loop about three feet long (a six-foot string tied in a loop). Place the loop on the left hand so the single string passes behind the thumb, between the thumb and index finger from the back, in front of the index, middle, and ring fingers, between the ring and little fingers, and in back of the little finger. Do the same on the right hand. There is now a radial string passing from thumb to thumb, and an ulnar string from little finger to little finger; each hand has a palmar string. (This is known as *Position 1*—it is a common starting place for string figures.) With the index finger of the right hand pick up on the dorsal aspect of the finger the left palmar string from the proximal side (slip the finger into the palmar loop from below and pull the hands apart). Do the same with the left index, making sure to pick up the right palmar string from within the right index loop. Extend (stretch the figure to its tightest). This figure is known as *Opening A*—it too is a common beginning. Now pass the thumbs away from you, distal to the radial index string, and pick up on their dorsal aspects the ulnar index string. Bring the thumbs back to position, and extend the figure. There are now two loops passing radially on each thumb. Take the proximal (lower) loop (with the mouth) and lift it to the ulnar side of the thumb. Release the string from the mouth and extend. Release the little finger loops and extend the figure. The strings passing between the index fingers form the canoe; the single string between the thumbs is the outrigger. (When the figure is called the trap, the thumbs are released and the figure extended. As the figure is extended, a finger or stick thrust into the large loop will be caught.) [JF]

Strömkarl   Literally, river man. In Norway the Strömkarl is specifically the spirit of a waterfall. He is a great musician and will teach his wonderful tunes to human beings in return for a black lamb or a white kid sacrificed on a Thursday. He has eleven tunes, good dance rhythms, ten of which he will teach to mortals. But if anyone dares to play the eleventh, chairs, benches, tables, plates and cups, aged men and women, blind, crippled, and infants in the cradle needs must rise and wildly dance. In Sweden the Strömkarl is any fresh-water spirit.

stupa   Mounds which vary in size from a few feet to several hundred feet dot the country side of most Asiatic countries. These are variously known as *stūpas, dagobas, pagodas.* The large and elaborate ones are often richly decorated and, because they are thought to contain the relics of saints or of Buddha himself, are the objects of worship. Tall stūpas have a number of parasols, or platforms, and are often surmounted by a staff.

The pious Indian king Asoka is said to have erected 84,000 stūpas as an act of devotion in the 3rd century B.C. These were to preserve relics of Buddha. Authorities are of the opinion, however, that stūpas were used long before Asoka. The fact that stūpas are often associated with relics leads to the easy assumption that they are elaborate developments of simple grave mounds. Because they are tall monolithic erections others have seen in them a phallic symbolism, an interpretation to which the shapes of many stūpas taken together with the phallic symbolism in a number of the Hindu cults give color. However, the popularity of stūpas, particularly in those countries where Buddhism has flourished, suggests, whatever their origin may have been, that the building of stūpas was encouraged by Buddhist missionaries and pilgrims.

Chinese geomants believe that tall pagodas should be set outside the walls of cities. In this way they will attract evil spirits and thus protect the towns. In India the worship of the stūpa is by circumambulation, clockwise with the stūpa on the right, washing with milk, illumination by candles.

Buddhist monks are said to make small stūpas to be set on a table for devotional purpose or to be worn as amulets. [RDJ]

stupid ogre   A folktale motif (G501) furnishing the theme for a whole cycle of folktales involving the foolishness, gullibility, and stupidity of ogres (G500–599). The ogre typically gets burned up in his own oven (G512.3.2) or is enticed into a hole and buried alive (G512.4); he gets tricked into injuring or killing himself (G520); he imitates the hero (who has stabbed a concealed bag of blood) stabs himself, and dies (G524); or he allows himself to be castrated on being assured that the operation will increase his strength (K1012.1). He gets tricked into trying to drink up a pond (G522), tries, bursts; he is tricked into killing his own children (K1611); he unwittingly rescues his own victims (G561); or sometimes he is just terrified by a pair of gigantic shoes which a man has made and put in front of his barn, and runs away. See ABANDONMENT ON THE ISLAND; AIGAMUXA; DECEPTION BY LOUSING; FALSE BEAUTY DOCTOR; OGRE.

Stymphalian birds   In Greek legend, huge flocks of birds chased from the Stymphalian lake in Arcadia by Hercules as the sixth of his labors. The birds had feathers like arrows which wounded all who approached; they may have been man-eating, or they may have devoured all the crops. With a bronze rattle, said to have been made by Hephæstus, and given to Hercules by Athena, they were frightened off. The birds settled on the island of Ares in the Euxine Sea, where the Argonauts encountered them.

substitute eyes   In some North American Indian myths, especially certain stories of Old Woman's Grandchild told by the Crow Indians of the Northern Plains, the hero of the tale, in a contest with snakes to keep awake during the telling of a tale (see SLEEPY STORIES) exchanges eyes with a jackrabbit before entering the contest. Thus he can appear to be awake at all times, even while asleep. In the North American Indian tale of Eye-juggler, trickster loses his eyes and obtains substitute ones, but these are usually of pitch. The exchange of body parts is not especially common in North American Indian mythology, despite the wide distribution of the Eye-juggler tale. [EWV]

subway lore As a convenient setting for stories of the macabre and shaggy-dog order, the New York subway has contributed two minor classics to American folklore. One is the story of the corpse in the subway, a favorite of Alexander Woollcott's, which tells of two men who board a train with a third man between them apparently dead drunk and then get off and leave him behind—dead, as one observant passenger explains to another less observant one, while solicitously hurrying him off the train. The shaggy-dog story tells of a passenger watching a man opposite him reading a newspaper unconcerned by the presence of two pigeons on his shoulders. Unable to restrain his curiosity, the first man finally asks the other politely what he is doing with the pigeons on his shoulders, only to be informed: "I don't know, they got on at 14th Street." Like these stories, many jokes about rush hour in the subway, straphangers, and sadistic subway guards, have been "switched" from or to other forms of transportation—the older horse-drawn bus, the streetcar, the motor bus. Subway station walls and posters also provide a convenient outlet for fools who like to see their names or initials in public places, draw mustaches on women's and babies' faces, and scrawl phallic symbols and latrine inscriptions. [BAB]

succubus A demon in female form who comes to men when they are asleep at night: from Latin *sub*, under, and *cubare*, to lie down. The succubus belongs to the class of demons known generally as incubi. The offspring of the union of man and succubus is demonic, but the proper prayers, spells, or charms recited by the men upon awakening will prevent its conception. See INCUBUS; LILITH; NIGHTMARE.

Sudharmā or **Sudharman** In Hindu mythology, the hall or court of Indra, which, at the instance of Kṛishṇa, was given to the Yādavas as a meeting place. After Kṛishṇa's death the hall returned to Svarga.

Sugrīva In Hindu mythology, the monkey king, son of the sun, who, with his adviser Hanumān and an army of monkeys, was Rāma's ally in his battle with Rāvaṇa.

Sukhāvatī In Buddhist belief, the heaven of Amitābha and the bodhisattvas Mahasthamaprapta and Avalokita, the "happy universe of the West," peopled by candidates for Buddhahood. Sukhāvatī is a blissful region and a school where candidates can hear the preaching of Buddha. It is open to all and in practical thought has replaced the less accessible nirvāṇa. It can be gained sometimes by merely repeating the name of Buddha Amitābha. There are no women there, for those who attain it become male. Pleasure is universal, the life span immeasurable. The land is bounded by the four gems—gold, silver, beryl, and crystal. Its lotus lakes are adorned with gems and in its rivers flow waters of different odors which produce exquisite music. Everyone in Sukhāvatī is endowed with an accumulation of virtue and rewarded with all things he may desire—dress, food, ornaments, and even a palace.

sukuyan Trinidad Negro term for vampire. A vampire woman will come to your house in the daytime asking for salt or matches. But you must never give it. Once you give one of them salt, there is no way of keeping them out of the house. The true Trinidad method of escaping the power of the sukuyan is to whisper "Thursday, Friday, Saturday, Sunday" three times. Then every door and window must be marked with a cross, and a mirror must be hung over the door. Once a sukuyan sees herself in a mirror in her sukuyan guise, she is terrified at the sight of herself and runs away. The Surinam vampire, the *azeman*, is analogous to the Trinidad sukuyan.

Georgia Negroes believe very strongly that it is a bad thing to lend salt, though few can remember (or will tell) the reason.

sukya The sorcerer or shaman of the Mískito and Sumu Indians of eastern Nicaragua and northeastern Honduras. He is a skilful medium and cures diseases through his mediumistic powers. Each spirit by whom he becomes possessed is identified with a specific specially treated stick. In one of his ceremonies (*tala prakaia*) he runs a cotton thread through a hole in his tongue until it is soaked with blood. This he knots in various mysterious ways and ties around the body of his patient to prevent the exorcised disease-spirit from reentering. See R. G. Heath, "Mískito Glossary," *IJAL* 16: 31, 32.

sumac This plant was extensively used in tanning and as a dye. The berries were used in a sauce for meat in place of salt, and in the 18th century they were smoked in place of tobacco in Europe; in the United States the leaves are sometimes mixed with tobacco. In 1630 the gum was used in New England as a base for perfume.

Among the Navaho Indians baskets made of sumac hold their sacred grain. These people say that if sumac is placed on the head of a child it will stunt his growth and bugaboos for stubborn children are made from this plant. The Tewa Indians and the Jicarilla Apache smoke the leaves of the sumac in pipes or cigarettes, either mixed with tobacco or plain, and as it produces hallucinations it is used by the medicine men when they consult the gods. The medicine men of the Meskwaki use the root bark (*R. glabra*) to produce blisters on a patient or in a tea to give appetite. The berries they make into a gargle; the berries of the staghorn sumac (*R. typhina*) they use for pin-worms. In Texas the leaves of the evergreen sumac are made into a tea to cure asthma. Among the Chippewa a decoction made from one white blossom of *R. glabra* and one root, boiled in a cup of water, is recommended for the digestive system and is used for a mouthwash for teething babies.

sumamao Literally, beautiful river, from Quechua *súmaj*, beautiful, and *máiu*, river. The *fiesta de sumamao* is an Argentine ritual drama named after its location on an arroyo of the Rio Dulce. Formerly it took place in a deserted chapel near the river; now it is sponsored by a ranch owner, called *el síndico*, and it focuses on a small altar erected on his ranch. On the day of San Esteban, December 26, *el santo*, an image of the saint, is placed on this altar decorated with flowers, fresh branches, and fruits. An avenue of *arcos* leads up to the altar, i.e. trees stripped of their branches except for a tuft on top, and coupled into *arcos* or arches by cords hung with *ichas* (cakes in puppet form). These were dedicated, each one by an *alférez* or *promesante*. The drama unfolds from dawn to dark in three major stages: *los arcos, correr al indio,* and *fiesta.*

Dawn is welcomed with trumpets and fireworks. The *alfereces* and *promesantes* ride their horses in slow procession through the *arcos,* while another group of horsemen, *celebrantes,* dash about shouting. This part, termed *las vivas* (the salutes) takes place to the music of native trumpets called *erques,* violins, and accordions. During the *consegración* the *síndico* throw *ichas* to the *alfereces* and *promesantes* with liturgical gestures. During the third part, *la Quila* (generous gift), the populace demolishes the *arcos,* seizes the *ichas,* and feasts on them.

During the intermission a group called *indios* disperses to the woods. They enact the *correr al indio* by running from the woods to the *santo,* beating their calves with fresh branches, followed by the shouts and trumpets of the horsemen. The *indios* approach the *santo* on their knees, kiss his robe, and deposit the branches (*varejones*). The *síndico* cuts incisions in their calves. Women offer holy water and fragrant branches.

The evening is given over to a fiesta with social dances, the *zamba, gato, chacarera.*

The Spanish Catholic terms thinly veil the agrarian ritual procedure. The sacred tree, doubled into a nuptial symbol of arch with fruits, has been multiplied into an avenue and focused on the image of the saint. The pillaging and eating of the *ichas* remain symbols of the sacrifice and communion with a deity. Exorcism of evil spirits is apparent in the procession and the running, i.e. the *correr al indio;* fertility magic in the voluntary blood sacrifice and aspersion, and in the vestal unction of the altar women. Mestizo dances have replaced the ancient orgiastic post-sacramental rounds. [GPK]

Sumé One of the names of the culture hero of the Tupinamba and Guaraní Indians of South America. His name was interpreted by the first missionaries to Brazil and Paraguay as a deformation of that of the apostle Saint Thomas. The miracles performed by St. Thomas during his fabled wanderings in South America are often exploits of the Tupi-Guaraní culture hero misinterpreted by the early chroniclers. See MAIRA-MONAN. [AM]

Sumer is icumen in The earliest and best-known round, dating from about the middle of the 13th century, preserved in the M.S. Harley 978 in the British Museum, and standing as the oldest six-part composition known. It is often called the Reading Rota (round) and is probably the oldest recorded English folk song, though some authorities have believed it to be the composition of a monk, John of Fornsete. A Latin text accompanies the English, but is not the original. The form of the music is two simultaneous circular canons, one for four parts over a two-part *pes,* or tenor.

sun Of all the heavenly bodies the sun commanded the widest and greatest interest among North American Indians. In many tribes Sun was the supreme deity; this is true of the Plains Indian Crow who addressed their prayers to Sun and regarded him as their most eminent deity; it is true also of the Yuchi of the Southeast, who regard themselves as descendants of the Sun, or of the son of Sun; Sun is thought of as female, and her child was born from her (or Moon's) menstrual blood. The Natchez, another Southeastern group, built temples to the Sun and held elaborate ceremonies in worship of this deity. In the Southwest the Pueblos and other tribes also venerated the sun. At Zuñi Pueblo Sun is the great object of worship; the Zuñi All-Container or supreme deity makes himself Sun, the father; everywhere else among the Pueblos Sun is also a deity of paramount importance. Among the White Mountain Apache likewise Sun is the most important male being in the religious system. Among the Navaho Sun is the husband of the chief female deity, Changing Woman.

In nearly all American Indian languages Sun is referred to as the "daytime luminary" and moon as the "nighttime luminary"; in the esoteric language of the Eskimo angakoks or shamans, sun is *qaumativun,* moon *qaumavun.*

Tales explaining the origin or the procuring of the sun are numerous in native American mythologies. The Eskimo tale of Sun Sister and Moon Brother relates how a brother has incestuous relations with his sister; she discovers her lover's identity and flees to the sky to become the sun, while he pursues her and becomes the moon. The pursuit of the sun by the moon is also a Central Woodlands belief; the Ojibwa, for instance, say the sun, a male spirit, travels west across the sky and passes under the earth to the east again; the moon, a female spirit, and sister of the sun over whom she rules, follows the sun across the sky. Both sun and moon were honored each autumn by certain Ojibwa groups who held a white dog feast for them, since Sun and Moon were believed to eat white dogs at their meals. Other rites held by tribes near the Ojibwa, such as the Iroquoian Seneca, included one for Sun and the Thunderers, which was never held more than once a year, usually during a drought.

Obtaining the sun and placing it in its present position are the subject of many myths. Widespread in the west are forms of the theft of sun (or light, or fire) tale, in which Sun is stolen by the culture hero, and placed in the sky. The Jicarilla Apache credit Holy Boy, a powerful supernatural, with obtaining the sun in the form of a very small object from White Hactcin, another supernatural, at Whirlwind's suggestion. Moon was obtained similarly, but from Black Hactcin.

What the sun was supposed to look like is discussed by M. W. Stirling, "Concepts of the Sun Among American Indians" (*Smithsonian Report for 1945,* pp. 387–400). It is interesting to note, from Stirling's paper, that personification of the sun usually makes this body a male being; three groups only, the Eskimo, Cherokee, and Yuchi, regard the sun as a female being. [EWV]

The Sun was the main deity of the Incas of Peru. He was regarded as the ancestral god of the imperial family and his cult was imposed on the conquered tribes. Wherever the Incas established their rule, temples were built in his honor. In the temple of the sun, Cuzco, the capital of the empire, he was symbolized by a large gold disk. Outside of ancient Peru, few Indian tribes rendered a cult to the Sun. However, the Apinaye, Sherente, and Canella of eastern Brazil, regard him as a great spirit who assumes a human shape. There are also some faint traces of a solar cult in the religion of the ancient Guaraní. Elsewhere the Sun is a purely mythological character, very often one of the mythical Twins.

The Caraja Indians of Brazil have a myth reminiscent

of one of the most famous stories of the Polynesian Maui cycle. Formerly the sun crossed the sky at such speed that men did not have time to work. The culture hero broke the sun's leg to make him slow down. [AM]

Sünawavi Creator-culture-hero-trickster of the Southern Utes of southwestern Colorado. In some Southern Ute myths Sünawavi and Coyote are represented as brothers; in others Sünawavi, shaman and chief, figures in apposition to Wolf, another prominent character in Great Basin mythology. Among the Southern Paiute, also a Great Basin people, Sünawavi is known as Cünawabi. The latter does not figure as a creator, but appears from nowhere soon after the earth is formed and marries the female creator's daughter. Many Southern Paiute stories detail Cünawabi's various hunting adventures with his brother, Töba'ts, and his erotic, tricksterlike adventures with women. [EWV]

sun dance A ritual dance addressed to the sun and its life-giving powers. Universally the importance of the sun cycle for crops and sustenance is commemorated in solstice dances. In aboriginal America the sun receives special homage in a variety of ceremonies.

The sun is personified only in the Inca dance to Inti, the sun god, by a dancer in a tremendous gold mask and headdress. He is confined to the simplest stepping because of the weight of the disk. He is accompanied by musicians with flute (*pinquillo*) and drum, and by two acolytes bearing swords. Though not as a divine impersonation, the Mexican *quetzales* of the Sierra de Vera Cruz suggest the sun in their spectacular disk headdresses. They are associated with the *voladores*, who circle to earth suspended from a pole.

In Arizona the Papago Indians danced a supplication to the sun in their *ciwiltkona*, hopping around a symbol of the sun, first in one direction, then in the other, extending their hands and then stroking the body in a ceremonial manner, thus acquiring its power. On the Rio Grande, two men and two women used to perform a sun dance, called *acéqueia* (turning on the water), in the spring as a planting rite. It has lately been revived at Santa Clara.

Early in the summer, usually in July, the Iroquois Indians perform for their crops a sun rite consisting of a longways called *wai'eno'e*, stick-striking. In costume and to drum and rattle, two lines of men approach each other, recede, and cross.

The most famous and spectacular sun dance, that of the Great Plains, is a votive rite centered about a consecrated tall pole. It is a combination of a buffalo rite and sun sacrifice, and retains the buffalo associations in its paraphernalia, and among the Blackfoot, in the simultaneous performance of the women's *ma'toki* buffalo-cow society. It reached its fullest development among the Teton Sioux, who regarded the sun as the greatest manifestation of the mysterious all-pervading power, *wakạ tạka*. In moments of stress, as during danger on the warpath, warriors vowed participation, sometimes in large groups, and thus offered their bodies to the divine spirit.

The ceremony was held usually during summer solstice, when all nature was rejoicing and the sage plant was succulent. The preparations included prayers by the medicine men for fair weather, the ceremonial scouting and cutting of the pole by four impeccable youths and

virgins, prayers by the *kuwa kiyapi* (intercessor), painting of the pole or sun symbol, preparation of the sacred place, and assembly by the dance leader of the sacred, ornamented pipe, perfect buffalo skull, and some buffalo fat for setting up the pole; then the rite of raising the pole, a tobacco offering, and a begging dance. These preparations took three or four days, while members of the tribes came from near and far to set up their tipis in a circle (representing the aurora borealis) around the brush dance enclosure fifteen feet west of the pole.

During the one to four days' duration of the dance, the participants abstained from food and drink. On the first morning they took a sweat bath and painted their bodies in symbolic colors, red (sunset), blue (sky), yellow (forked lightning), white (light), and black (night). They donned a deerskin apron, rabbit-fur wristlets and anklets, and a downy feather in their loose-hanging hair. They carried in their mouths an eagle-wing bone whistle with porcupine quill or beadwork and eagle-down decoration. To a large drum and special songs, they circled in procession and saluted the sun with lamentation. They danced in place facing the sun, on their toes or the balls of their feet. They fulfilled their vow in various ways: 1) Laceration of arms and thighs with 100 or 200 gashes, some of which could be taken over by a female relative; 2) Suspension by fastening ropes from the pole to gashes in the breast or back, only the toes touching the ground; 3) Suspension with the feet clear of the ground; 4) Suspension with buffalo skulls or a horse attached; 5) Suspension between four poles. Dancers continued until they fell unconscious or tore themselves loose, and thereupon obtained a vision. After a prescribed duration they smoked pipes, had a vapor bath, food, and water.

The entire tribe gave the dancers moral support. Sometimes children participated by the piercing of their ears and the giving of gifts. Between times they played at the sun dance. The secret rites in the ceremonial tipi were concluded by public social dances.

Other tribes performing the entire ceremony with its voluntary torture were the Ponca, Kiowa, Bûngi, Mandan (*okipa* dance), Hidatsa, Arapaho, Cheyenne, Blackfoot, Crow. Without torture it was adopted by the Shoshone, Ute, Comanche, and others. San Ildefonso and other pueblos adopted it as pure dance, with toe-heel motion and jumps, in place around a pole. The symbolism and form varied between tribes. Everywhere the buffalo was prominent.

The Mandan *okipa* included a dramatic performance commemorating the subsiding of the Deluge. The Bûngi connected the rite with thunder and with a mourning ceremony. Among the Wahpeton and Sisseton Dakotas, the *heyoka* society performed simultaneously. The Ute considered the dance curative, especially for rheumatism. They enacted a sham battle the first morning. Both the Ute and Cheyenne fastened a willow brush in the fork on top of the cottonwood pole. The Northern Cheyenne still perform it as the *willow dance*, without the Siouan sun worship. The dancers wave feathers and dance in a circle in place, flexing their knees rhythmically. The Crow move toward the pole and recede. In this tribe the motive of revenge played a role. As magical means of killing an enemy, the ceremony was organized by a whistler, the owner of a doll symbolizing the moon. He was painted with designs representing the morning star and lightning. He did not join the group who submitted to torture, but danced himself into a trance. Thus the ceremony was a particular composite.

The Indians believe that with the eclipse of August 7, 1869, the sun died. The Teton Sioux performed their last sun dance in 1881. It has been generally condemned because of misunderstanding of the torture elements and ignorance of its importance to the spiritual and moral strength of the tribes. However, it survives among the northern and western tribes, usually as a spectacle. Lately, one of the Cheyenne again vowed torture.

Despite their formal divergences, these representative sun rites share fundamental concepts—the circling, with suspension in two instances; the meteorological symbol of the bird (quetzal, eagle); the phallic symbol of the pole (or sword or stick), emphasized among the Cheyenne by the practice of ritual intercourse. The Plains rite weaves the many symbols into a strange and eloquent composite, a summary coercion of supernatural power for communal welfare by voluntary personal blood sacrifice, of human survival and prosperity by means of the source of sustenance, the buffalo, who depends on vegetation (sage and willow), thus ultimately on the sky and sun. See BUFFALO DANCE; EAGLE DANCE; HEYOKA; MA'TOKI; QUETZALES; VOLADOR. [GPK]

sunflower　The sunflower (*Helianthus*) was worshipped by the Incas as a representation of the sun. The seeds were eaten during certain religious ceremonies, and priestesses of the sun wore a large sunflower of virgin gold on their breasts. In Europe, where the plant was taken by the Spaniards, it was found to be a valuable and useful plant. The leaves were smoked, the buds eaten either in salads or cooked. The flowers provide a dye and the seeds are eaten by man, bird, and beast; an oil from the seeds is used for salads, cooking, and burning in lamps. Medicinally, the seeds, because of their oil, are good for coughs and are a specific for whooping cough; they are also said to be good for the teeth.

The American Navaho Indians make crude flutes of the stalks and a Tewa song says that the sunflowers are watered by the tears of Navaho girls. The Meskwaki Indians make a root poultice for stubborn sores from *H. decapetalis*. They use a sawtooth sunflower (*H. grosse serratus*) poultice to heal burns, and a root tea from *H. strumogus* for lung troubles. The Jerusalem artichoke (*H. tuberosus*) is said to have been a native of the Dakotas and to have been eaten long before the discovery of America.

In Greek mythology Clytie, a sea nymph, daughter of Oceanus and Tethys, was beloved of Helios. She always looked toward the sun, and for her constancy was changed into a heliotrope or sunflower. The calendula, chrysanthemum, elecampane, marigold, etc., have also been called sunflowers at one time or another, as has every plant whose flowers tend to face towards the sun.

Sung Ti　In China, the king of the Third Hell where people are punished who were guilty of unfilial behavior, disobedience, disloyalty, rebellion. He is honored on the eighth day of the Second Moon. [RDJ]

Sun Sister, Moon Brother　The usual English title given to a widespread Eskimo myth which accounts for the sun and moon. Briefly, the tale is concerned with a man who visits his sister secretly at night; in order to learn the identity of her clandestine lover the girl rubs her hands with soot or paint and leaves telltale handmarks on her brother's back; or she smears paint on his face. When she learns that her lover is her brother she cuts off her breasts and offers them to him; then flees to the sky, where she becomes the sun. Her brother attempts to catch her, and becomes the moon. [EWV]

Sun Snarer　A boy who thinks himself mistreated lies down alone and has his robe burned by the sun. Angered, the boy makes a noose, usually from a pubic hair obtained from his sister, and snares the sun. Darkness ensues and the sun nearly chokes to death before one in a succession of animals is able to gnaw through the noose, thus relieving the sun and causing darkness to disappear. This North American Indian myth has a wide distribution among the Northern, Plateau, California, Great Basin, and Plains tribes and is also popular among nearly all Eastern Woodlands tribes. Another native American belief concerning sun-snaring is evinced in Central Eskimo playing of cat's cradle in autumn to enmesh the sun, and playing cup and ball when the sun moves north. [EWV]

supay　The evil spirits of the Quechua-speaking Incas of Peru. Today the Catholic Indians of Peru and Bolivia apply the word to the Devil. [AM]

Superman　Deus ex machina of the comics, radio, and screen, who, as the alter ego of Clark Kent, reporter, transforms himself at will into the godlike, invincible "man of tomorrow." With his superhuman strength (especially in his arms and fists) and his magic powers of flight and seeing and hearing through walls, plus a perfect physique (a Tarzan in interplanetary costume of tights, trunks, and cape), Superman conveniently comes to the rescue of girl reporter Lois Lane and their friends; exposes frauds and hoaxes; plays cops and robbers with the enemies of society; and engages in other legendlike, prankish exploits. The creation of Jerry Siegel and Joe Shuster and first appearing in *Action Comics Magazine*, June, 1938, Superman represents a development of the interplanetary hero of the Buck Rogers type into the "changeling personality," who bridges the gap between reality and fantasy. From a strong man who takes justice into his own hands, Superman later became a crusader for brotherhood and other worthy causes, thus directing his tremendous popularity and influence (inspiring many imitators) into socially useful channels. [BAB]

Supreme Being　The existence of a Supreme Being has been so often noted among African peoples that there are those who maintain that African religions are essentially based on the concept of a Creator who, having made the world and being its ultimate power, has withdrawn from man and, though recognized by the people, has no cult. Some of these entities are: Nyame (Nyankompong) of the Ashanti; Mawu (Mawu-Lisa) of Dahomey; Oshala of the Yoruba; Chuku of the Ibo; Nzambi, Zambi, and other variants in the Congo; Mulungu of the Zulu; Ngai of the Masai; Wak of the Galla. The exact character of most of these deities, however, is to be determined. Certain currents in present-day theology run strongly in the direction of seeing in these beings the survival of a single revealed deity, corrupted over the generations by men who introduced other beings to worship. The resultant compression of data into this frame results in any principal deity being interpreted as evidence of an original Supreme Being, despite the fact that on the Guinea Coast, at least, research has demonstrated the methodological indivisibility of this approach. [MJH]

Surabhi Literally, the fragrant one: in Hindu mythology, the cow of plenty who grants all desires, created by Prajāpati from his breath, or produced at the Churning of the Ocean. Surabhi bore a number of cows regarded as mothers of the world. Having practiced austerities and pleased Brahmā, she was granted immortality and given her own heaven, Goloka, which can be reached only by the most pious, especially by worshippers or givers of cows. Devotees of Surabhi must bow in reverence to cows, subsist on the five products of the cow, and sometimes live among cows.

surtida (Spanish, assortment) A Philippine folk dance of courtship mime for eight couples in quadrille formations. The various sections of this elaborate composite are each a complete regional dance and are arranged so as to express the various stages of courtship. These sections and their meaning are: 1) *birgoire,* the meeting; 2) *camantugol,* an imitation of ocean waves; 3) *tambururay,* the girl's shyness; 4) *haplin,* a gay interlude; 5) *ligui,* a declaration of love and coy reaction; 6) *voluntario,* acceptance; 7) *incoy,* imitation of drunkenness; 8) *estrella,* rejoicing; 9) *salpumpati,* homeward flight of the doves.

Each dance has its special music, in Spanish style, by a native composer. The waltz and mazurka steps, and the semi-Spanish posture are also derivative. In a word, this "poem of Philippine love" is native wine in Spanish bottles. [GPK]

Surtr In Teutonic mythology, the flame giant who presides over Muspellheim, the realm of fire to the south of Midgard. Here he stands ever alert, brandishing his fiery sword which sends off showers of sparks. At Ragnarök he will lead the fire giants and battle with Frey whom he will overpower because Frey has no weapon. Surtr's fire will destroy the world. See BIFROST; HODMIMER'S FOREST.

Sūrya In Hindu mythology and belief, the sun god, or the sun itself worshipped as a god. In Vedic times there were several sun gods. These were later merged into one, who was indiscriminately given the name of any of them: Sāvitrī, Mitra, Aryaman, Pūshan, or Mārttaṇḍa. Sūrya is the most concrete of the solar deities. He is described as short, with a burnished copper body, riding in a chariot drawn by four or seven horses and driven by Aruṇa, the dawn, who tempers his splendor. The three aspects of the sun—rising, culminating, setting— are not distinguished as three deities but are considered attributes of the same god.

Sūrya is variously considered the son of Dyaus, of Aditi, of Ushās, of Brahmā. By his wife Sañjña he had three children, Vaivasvata, Yamī, and Yama. Sañjña, unable to bear his brilliance, left him a shade (Chhāyā) as a handmaid and went to live in the forest in the form of a mare. There the sun found her and approached her in the form of a horse. From their union sprang Revanta and the two Aśvins. Sañjña's father, Viśvakarma, then cut away an eighth of the sun's brilliance, so that his daughter could live with him. Sūrya was also the father of Karna, leader of the Kauravas, and of

Sani and Sugrīva. Through Vaivasvata he was the ancestor of the Sūrya-vansa or solar race of kings. He communicated the *Yajur-veda* to Yājnavalkya while in the form of a horse.

One of the most ancient of the sun cults was that of Mitra (Persian Mithras) which has led some scholars to believe that India's solar religion came from the West, but the exchange probably was in the opposite direction.

Sūrya maintained his early popularity as a god even after the rise of the *trimūrti.* Few temples dedicated to his worship have survived (the most important are at Kanarak and Gayā), but he is still worshipped in Bihār and more openly by the Dravidians and Kolarians who invoke him as Parameśvar, creator and preserver. Orāons identify him with their supreme deity, Dharmesh. The Sūryapuja (sun festival) is held annually in the spring in Sylhet. A plantain tree is set up in each courtyard, decorated with flowers, offerings are made, and hymns in honor of the sun are sung. The symbol of the sun is placed over booths in the bazaars for luck in many parts of India and Sūrya is invoked to heal disease and put to flight evil spirits.

Susa songs Secular dance songs of Surinam Negroes associated with a pantomime battle with spears and shields. The "Susa play," or dance, is held annually and the winner of the "fight" is named "King of Susa" and must fight the challenger the following year.

Susu or **Esusu** Nigerian (Yoruban) term for cooperative savings systems, under which each member of a group gives a certain sum to a leader each week or month, the total amount of every set of payments being turned over to one member each week, until all have received their share of the money paid in, when another round may be initiated. The Esusu of Nigeria has survived in unaltered form under the name of Susu in Trinidad. Elsewhere in the West Indies it has other designations, but with principles and procedures essentially similar to the original. See BOXI-MONI. [MJH]

sūtra or **sutta** In Brahmanism, an aphorism or short precept in brief technical language: literally, a string or thread. The term *Sūtras* generally refers to four groups of precepts: the *śrauta,* dealing with rules for the use of mantras and the Brāhmaṇas of the Vedas in connection with sacrifice; *Gṛihya,* dealing with the rules for family worship; *Dharma,* dealing with social duties; and a group dealing with astronomy and magic. They belong to the period in Brahmanical history, 500–200 B.C.

In Buddhism the term refers to the narrative parts of the Pali Canon. Trillions of sermons have been delivered since the beginning of the universe dealing with the elevation of man to the blissful state. Those which have been recorded are called *sūtras.*

For the Jainist the term *sūtra* is applied to a scripture, especially to one dealing with the life of Mahāvīra.

suttee See SATI.

Suvinenge One of the earth gods of Dahomey Negro religion; eighth (or ninth) child of the twins who rule the earth (Dada Zodji and Nyauhwe Anan̄u). Suvinenge has the bald head of a man and a vulture's body, and as a vulture carries the sacrifices from the place of offering to the deity for whom they are intended. Suvinenge, as vulture, also carries messages between Sagbatà (the earth-god group) and Mawu (creator). He is further identified with the vulture, a sacred bird in Dahomey, by the fact that he eats the dead. M. J. Herskovits points out (in "An Outline of Dahomean Religious Belief," *MAAA* 41, p. 18) that the last two syllables of this name,-*nenge*, resemble the Dutch Guiana word for Negro, *Nengere*, in striking parallel to the fact that in Surinam, Jamaica, and the South Carolina Gullah Islands, the vulture is also identified with the Negro.

Svarga Indra's heaven, a temporary paradise on Mount Meru where the blessed live before their next birth on earth. The elephant Airāvata stands at its entrance; its capital is Amarāvatī; and the Apsarases and Gandhārvas serve Indra there.

Svartálfar Black elves: the dwarfs of Teutonic mythology which grew from the maggots of Ymir's flesh. They are now living in the earth and in stones; they have the shape of men, though they are often misshapen. One of their favorite tricks in lonely places is to repeat the last few words of conversation they overhear. It was the Svartálfar who made the wonderful necklace Brisingamen for Freya, and other wonders of the old Teutonic gods. They are often identified with the *dvergar*, and are hard to distinguish from the *Döckálfar*. See ALFAR.

Svartalfheim is the underground home of the black dwarfs; here they are constrained to remain during daylight on pain of being turned to stone. See ALVÍSS.

Svayamvara An ancient Indian form of selecting a husband; marriage by choice: a maiden of high rank may choose her husband from an assembly of suitors by throwing a garland over his neck; often the man chosen was the winner in a test of skill. The custom was observed by the Rajputs until a late time. It has played an important part in Indian epics and folktales, especially in the story of *Nala and Damayanti,* and in the winning of the princess Draupadī by the Pāṇḍu princes in the *Mahābhārata.*

swallow songs Songs sung by Greek children on the streets in March to welcome the return of the swallows and of spring. The songs go back more than 2000 years to the procession of the Rhodian youths described by Athenæus in quotation from Theognis. In modern times the occasion takes on the character of many other children's festivities, with offerings of food in the houses they visit.

swallow story A type of folktale based on the extraordinary swallowings motif (F910 ff.), appearing almost everywhere in the world, and following several distinct patterns: 1) in which the hero is swallowed by one or more monsters but is disgorged (F914) or emerges in safety when the monster is killed (F911.3; F911.4; F913); 2) in which a glutton swallows his own children, neighbors, etc., and is killed, the victims emerging alive (F913); and 3) those appearing throughout the ages in all parts of the world: etiological stories accounting for various natural phenomena, as the countless eclipse tales, the Paiute Indian story of how the sun swallows the stars (to explain their disappearance at dawn). Typical of the first group are the stories of Tom Thumb (F911.3.1) who was swallowed by a cow, a fish, and a giant, *Little Red Riding Hood* whose grandmother was

swallowed by the wolf, and *The Wolf and the Seven Little Kids* (Grimm #5) who walked forth well and happy out of the wolf when their mother slit him open.

Among the famous swallow stories of the world are the Greek myths of Cronus who swallowed his own children, and of Zeus who swallowed Metis, the story of Jonah swallowed by the whale, the Teutonic Odin swallowed by the wolf, etc. The giant (as mouse) was swallowed by Puss in Boots in one version of that tale. Sometimes the victim kills the swallower from within (F912 ff.). For the benevolent swallower, see AGASTYA.

☞ Various heroes in North American Indian hero tales, such as Blood Clot Boy, undergo several ordeals while pursuing their adventures; one of these often is that the hero is swallowed by a monster animal or ogre. Inside the animal the hero often encounters other victims, still alive, who have also been swallowed. He kills the monster from within, and liberates his companion victims.

In some North Pacific Coast and Siberian tribes the swallowing incident is further elaborated; as a result of having been swallowed, all the victims of the monster become bald.

Swallowing incidents are not, however, limited to hero tales. In North American Indian trickster stories the incident also appears in less elaborated form. The Navaho, for example, tell how Coyote, the trickster, swallowed Horned Toad; from inside Coyote Horned Toad asks Coyote the name of his various internal organs. When Coyote mentions his heart, Horned Toad makes incisions on it twice with his "knives"; Coyote dies and Horned Toad comes out of Coyote through his anus (W. W. Hill, *Navaho Coyote Tales and Their Position in the Southern Athabaskan Group, JAFL* 58:317–343).

[EWV]

swan maiden The motif (D361.1) typifying a worldwide cycle of folk stories characterized by the metamorphosis of a beautiful half-mortal, half-supernatural maiden from swan to human form. The swan form depends upon the possession of a magic feather robe (or pair of wings), or a ring, crown, or a golden chain; usually the swan maiden is under some enchantment or tabu that affects also her human lover. That the swan maiden marries the youth who finds and steals her swan garb on the shore is common to almost all Asiatic and European versions. Either the lover hides the enchanted feather dress (ring, chain, crown) and thus keeps the wonderful swan maiden with him in human form until she finds it, or he breaks the tabu and she vanishes and returns to her swan shape and supernatural life.

There is a late Rumanian Christmas carol on the swan maiden theme in which the beautiful swan cannot marry the hero until first he wins the bird of heaven to sing at their wedding and the crown of Paradise for the bride to wear. So the hero makes his journey. St. Basil in Paradise has mercy on him and gives him the bird and the crown. He returns and calls to the swan to come forth and hear the bird sing; and "When the swan came forth it turned into a maiden fair/ The crown leapt onto her head/ The bird began to sing."

The motif is found everywhere in Asia and Europe: in all Slavic folklore, in Icelandic, Finnish, Celtic, and Teutonic story. It is known in Persia, Ceylon, China, Japan, and in Australian, Polynesian, Melanesian, and

Indonesian mythology; it also turns up in Africa, East and West, among the Zulus, and in Madagascar. Among the most famous swan maiden stories are those in the Indian *Śatapatha-Brāhmana* and the Arabian *Thousand and One Nights*. The Old Irish *Angus Og and Caer* is among the famous swan maiden stories of the world.

Various scholars have sought to identify the swan maidens with the Valkyries (*Lay of Wayland*, about 900 A.D.) but Penzer judges the analogy far-fetched (*Ocean of Story* VIII: 223), pointing out that "nowhere among the early primitive beliefs of Europe are . . . found the roots of the swan maiden motif" and adjudging that early Sanskrit was the original hub of radiation.

☞ The swan maiden incident in the European folktale *The White Cat* was borrowed by several North American Indian groups (Plateau tribes, Biloxi, Ojibwa, Assiniboin, Micmac, Natchez, Tepecano). The incident is also widely told in elaborated form as a tale complete in itself by the Eskimo and by many American Indians. The American Indian tale of swan maidens concerns a hunter who, on passing a lake, sees several geese divested of their feathers and in the form of women. He seizes the women's feather-garments, but relents and gives back all except one. All the geese save this one fly away. The man marries the one who remains, and she has two children by him. Later, his wife finds her garments (or a pair of wings) and she and her children fly away as geese. In some versions the husband pursues his wife and children and finds them; he finally kills the wife, but the children escape. See MUDJIKIWIS. [EWV]

☞ The swan maiden motif was also popular with South American Indians. The earliest version was recorded in the 16th century among the Canari Indians of Ecuador. The two survivors of the deluge were assisted by parrots who became two girls after they succeeded in capturing them. In a tale of the Tenehetara Indians of Maranhao, a man seizes the feather-dress of a girl, actually a vulture, who is bathing in a river. She becomes his wife and takes him to the sky where her father lives. The same motif forms part of the mythology of several Guiana tribes. [AM]

swastika The swastika, a more complex symbol than the cross, which is one component of it, is made by drawing two short lines either to the right or left of the terminal of a simple Greek cross. It is also called the gamma cross for if one joins four Greek gammas, a swastika will be formed. When the designs are commonly used and when the meanings attached are generally accepted by the users, they may be said to be symbols of the meaning.

The meanings are various but often not very clear. Some students content themselves with observing that the swastika is a sacred sign in India (it was one of the body marks of the Lord Buddha, for instance) and that it has a solemn meaning among both Brāhmans and Buddhists. This assertion does more to describe the emotion the swastika arouses than the reasons why the emotion is aroused. Other observers suggest that the swastika represents the apparatus used prehistorically to make fire (see NEW FIRE) and thus represents sacred fire, living flame, and Maia, who symbolizes productive power. Milani thought it was a symbol of the sun and "seems to denote its daily rotation." Or it may be lightning, the storm, the Aryan pantheon; benedic-

tion, good omen. When in the 10th century a wave of demonism swept over Tibet, pious worshippers began turning the prayerwheels from right to left instead of from left to right as the orthodox do.

Whatever meaning the swastika may have in any community that attaches a meaning to it, the symbol is very ancient and very widespread. The swastika on the pudenda of a naked female figure Schlieman excavated at Troy may have been simply decoration, or a talisman, or a classifier of the figure. It was used in Crete, in ancient Rome, on Celtic rocks in Scotland, rock carvings in Sweden, and throughout the Orient. The wheel cross, which is thought for Stone Age man to have symbolized the sun, is displaced in the Bronze Age by the swastika.

American Indians of the pre-Columbian period used this cross for a number of purposes. The most frequently mentioned is as a symbol of the four directions which were important in Indian ritual. It has also been identified as a wind symbol, storm symbol, and phallic meanings have been attributed to it.

Another refinement in swastika lore is whether the cross pieces point to the right, which makes it a lucky sign, or to the left, which makes it unlucky.

Hitler used it as the symbol of the Nazi party and in China the swastika was the symbol of a benevolent society.

The difficulty with all of these interpretations is not that any of them is of necessity a wrong, improbable, or even false attribution. Any symbol can mean anything the observer decides to make it mean. The difficulty is to determine at any given time or place what meaning the people who used the symbol attributed to it. Data for many ages and cultures which were certainly complex is too scanty to justify conclusions about meanings attached to relatively simple symbols. For comparative analysis see CROSS. See also BON; DOOR SIGNS. [RDJ]

Sweat Lodge Creator and benevolent deity of the Sanpoil Indians, an Interior Salish tribe, formerly on the Columbia river, Washington. Not only in the mythology, but in the religion of the Sanpoil, Sweat Lodge, a unique character, seems to possess the characteristics of a true deity. He is credited in the mythology with creating and naming all the animals and birds, and instructing them on what they should do after human beings were created. See V. F. Ray, "Sanpoil Folk Tales" (*JAFL* 46: 129–187, 1933, pp. 131, 132). [EWV]

Sweet Trinity or ***The Golden Vanity*** An English traditional ballad (Child # 286) in which a ship beset by pirates is saved by the feat of the bold cabin boy, who swam alongside the pirate ship, bored holes in its hull, sank it, and in different versions was either well rewarded or left to drown by his own false captain. Pepys recorded an old broadside ballad called *Sir Walter Raleigh in the Lowlands*, which may have been the original of the many traditional variants or may itself have been an offshoot of some parent version. The basis of the tale may have been the appearance of Barbary pirates in the English Channel in open galleys in the 17th century. These pirates were popularly thought of as Turkish, and in some of the texts the adversary is called Turkish. Others make the enemy Spanish, French, or an unidentified "false gallaly." The English ship is variously named "The Sweet Trinity," "The Golden Vanity," and in America, "The Golden Willow Tree" (Illinois), "The

Mary Golden Tree" (Kentucky), "The Turkey Shivaree" (Ozarks), "The Gold China Tree" (Vermont). The tool that the cabin boy used was remarkable; it was a sort of auger that could bore, depending on which version is followed, from one to fifteen holes at a time. The ballad was a favorite of sailors as a forecastle song under the title of *Lowlands, Low,* one of its refrains. Other titles are *The Pirate Ship,* and any of the names of the ship itself. In America it is an instrumental piece favored by banjo-pickers. The instrumental air differs from the singing versions and picks up a rapid, percussive, staccato style far removed from the slow and mournful melody to which the words are generally sung. However, the different texts vary greatly in meter and are distinguished by Child as belonging to three groups.

sword dances Men's dances involving the rhythmic manipulation of one or several swords, often in combination with elaborate configurations. They are still performed in many parts of the world, at weddings, funerals, and particularly at solstice ceremonials which have been shifted in the Christian calendar to Carnival, Corpus Christi, or San Juan's Day. As solo or group dances they show a variety of forms.

1) The brandishing of weapons, particularly in the Caucasus and Asia Minor, as in the Ukrainian *zaporotchez* and the Arabian self-mutilating *Aissâoua* dance, both with frenzied leaps and turns.

2) Skilful stepping between a crossed sword and scabbard, as the famous Scotch *Gilly Callum,* said to have originated in a victory dance.

3) Battle mime by two opposing factions, particularly in the *Moriscas* of Europe and Mexico, and related ritual combats, as the Shetland Island sword dance between the patron saints of six countries, the *Schwertlestanz* of Überlingen, and the *bacchu ber* of the French Haute Savoie.

4) The sword dances of northern England, which have eliminated the mimetic combat and use the double-handled flexible blades as choreographic tools.

The succession of figures varies with the village of origin, yet coincides in essentials. Usually the progression is a sunwise circle or weaving within a circle; but the Flamborough Sword Dance straightens out into longways formations and a straight hey (grand right and left in a line). The number varies from five (Sleights, Swalwell), six (Grenoside), to eight men (Flamborough). The character of the figures depends on the length of the sword: long (Kirkby-Malzeard, Grenoside, Ampleforth, etc.), or short (Swalwell, Earsdon, Winlaton, etc.). A ring-and-step usually starts the dance, that is, a circling with a steady run, shifting the sword from shoulder to shoulder, and concluding with "stepping," foot-tapping in place (Grenoside); sometimes also a clash is included, that is, a meeting of the swords in a central pyramid (Kirkby-Malzeard, Sleights). The most common evolutions are the "single-under" and "double-under," in which the dancers in succession twist under the upraised swords; "single-over" and "double-over," in which they step across the lowered swords; the roll or waves, in which the swords are held parallel, with a successive raising and lowering as dancers pass under and over (Grenoside, Ampleforth); the reel, a circular hey with raised swords (Grenoside. Sleights); "threedling" with double overhead arches (Flamborough); most important of all,

the final triumphant "lock" of all swords into a star shape, displayed by the leader during "stepping," or wrapped around the neck of an attendant character while all circle clockwise in the "rose." Each section is called a "nut." But each section flows into the other smoothly and rhythmically, with the incessant running to rapid 6/8 tunes of accordion or fiddle. Never do the dancers loosen their hold on the chain of swords held between them hilt-and-point.

The performance is always preceded by a naive declamation, with characters similar to those of the *Morris* —the Captain, Bessy, Queen, Fool or Tommy, or various historical characters. Costumes vary from sweaters and trousers to elaborate vests and hats. In the Sleights dance, seven Toms have blackened faces. In the Grenoside dance the captain wears a helmet covered with a rabbitskin; in the Earsdon dance, the Bessy wears a furry cap. In the former the captain steps into the middle of the lock; in the latter the Bessy is "hung." In the Askham Richard Sword Dance the fool kneels and passes his head through the lock. When the swords are withdrawn—as always in conclusion—he feigns death and all cry "A doctor!" The Besom-Betty says "I'll cure him," and resurrects him. This vestigial sacrifice identifies human and animal victim, in combination with choreographic sun symbolism and the sword's phallic symbolism. In the elaborate Basque *ezpata dantza* both longways and circular types are combined with stick dances, a Maypole, and a *txonkórinka* or hoisting of the captain onto the plaited swords in an apotheosis of death and resurrection. This corresponds to the "lock" and the Spanish *degollada* or decapitation of the *capitán.*

The theory of origin in vegetation magic suggested by these various symbols finds support in practices of antiquity. The Roman *salii* (war dancers) honored Saturn, god of sown seed, in their solemn singing processions in March and December, and by their leaps induced the cereals to wax tall. The Ampleforth sword-dance play has a curious parallel in ancient dramas of Dionysus and surviving Carnival plays of Haghios Gheorghios in Thrace. The Dionysian *anthesteria* cycle of seasonal death and rebirth consisted in an *agon* (contest) like the *Morisca,* a *pathos* (sacrificial death), *threnos* (lamentation), and *anagnorisis* (resurrection). Both the Thracian and English plays involve a suddenly grown babe of an old woman, a mock marriage with a transvestite, death, lament, and resurrection. The animal skins of the *kalogheroi,* the fools of Thrace, reappear in England, and the seed-sowing and plowshare have only recently vanished from the Sleights sword dance. (They are retained in the English Ploughstots and Portuguese *mouriscada.*)

This phallic and vegetation symbolism could be applied to other forms of European sword dances, including the vestigial animal sacrifice of the pyrrhic German cutlers' and butchers' dances (*Metzgertanz*) of Carnival. See RITUAL DRAMA; STICK DANCES. [GPK]

sword of Damocles A motif from classical folklore repeated in varying form, e.g. a millstone in Grimm, in European folktale: a sword suspended by a single horsehair over the head of a guest. In its original setting by Cicero, Damocles was a courtier at the court of the elder Dionysius, who praised the tyrant's wealth and power and happiness. Dionysius invited Damocles to a sumptuous banquet and then pointed to the sword, indicating the constant threat of violence hanging over a king's head.

swords The personalized sword is invariably one of the possessions of a hero. Roland's Durandal, Siegfried's Balmung and Gram, Ogier's Courtain and Sauvaigne were individual weapons which were just as much a part of their owners as their right arms. Excalibur, the magic sword of Arthur, is the type of the sword in the stone: only Arthur, its destined user, could remove it from the stone in which it was embedded. Only Sigmund could withdraw Gram from the Branstock oak. Perseus, Achilles, Odysseus, Finn, Odin, Heimdall, Charlemagne, Tethra, Isonokami, Kullervo, all owned magic swords. Magic swords are talismans; they protect against injury and always kill or wound an opponent. They may render the owner invisible; they grow or shrink at need; they give the magic power to travel great distances. The magic sword brings up the wind (Chinese), speaks (Celtic), emits fire (Chinese). The infallible sword is found in Icelandic, Celtic, French, Spanish, etc., folklore. The sword, being of iron, is a charm against witchcraft and a potent judicial influence. Traditionally (Celtic, Teutonic) evildoers die by their own swords. The sword often is a chastity index or a life token; it becomes discolored or runs with blood when unfaithfulness or death occurs. See AMLETH; SEPARATING SWORD; TYRFING.

symbolism An aspect of thinking or expression in which the process of association is brought into play so that a concept or, more often, a climate of thought is encompassed or suggested by a word, phrase, sign, gesture, object, depiction, diagram, etc.

The word *symbol*, as it is generally used, does not convey precisely the same range of meaning as the derived forms *symbolic* and *symbolism*. That which is called symbolic seems to contain the means (sometimes nebulous) of arousing associations and conveying connotation. The word is so loosely tossed about that anything which is suggestive, to any slight degree, of ideas, however vague, is likely to be described as symbolic. One can become so enmeshed in exploring the asociative processes, increasingly able to read meanings into shapes, that eventually everything which exists takes on some degree of the symbolic. A symbol, on the other hand, is a definite thing on which one can, so to speak, put the finger. A vague suggestion is not definable enough to be called a symbol. At the same time the word *symbol* is widely used for a variety of signs, insignia, marks, diagrams, etc., which are a precise indication or equivalent of the meaning they are designed to convey, without any aspect of "suggestion" at all. Purely identifying symbols are, for example, chemical, pharmaceutical, or alchemists' signs, signs of the zodiac and of planets, musical notations, proofreaders' marks (some of which reproduce the gesture of correction), emblems of rank or group or profession such as the policeman's badge, hallmarks or trademarks.

Such identifying symbols or labels are often arbitrarily adopted as contrasted to symbols in the realm of ideas, which appear to accumulate or develop almost of their own volition. However, these adopted symbols often repeat ancient ones, like the wings on an airman's collar, and they may accumulate symbolic connotation with use, like the national flags which come to arouse all the complex emotions associated with home and country. But the accumulation follows its own natural course. The American eagle, for example, is probably not symbolically identified with the United States to any great extent in the general mind; it more often suggests the coin on which it happens to appear. The naturally evolved symbolic character of Uncle Sam is more widely used as an expression of the American spirit than the predatory, solitary, and rather terrifying bird.

In order to devise a limitation of the subject which is reasonably susceptible to discussion, the common denominator in this varying usage might be adopted. Symbolism would thus be construed as that which has the element of suggestive or connotative meanings, but which conveys them by means of symbols sufficiently definite to be recognized and analyzed. Signs that are purely labels are not pertinent to folklore and mythology in any case. Even those symbols which serve, perhaps primarily, purposes of identification, like the "vehicles" of the Hindu deities or attributes of the saints (the key of St. Peter, arrows of St. Sebastian, the rope around the waist of St. Francis, etc.) carry other implications—the power of the god or the history of the saint; *Garuḍa* implies the supremacy of Vishnu in the airy element. In this field, a symbol is something which has an aura of emotion or thought, which condenses a range of ideas or creates a framework of context —a means by which people express something more than is specifically stated in words or literally depicted in the arts. The "color" of one thing is added to that of another, and the accumulation of human experience is brought into play in the communication of mood or meaning. Symbolism, in this sense, stretches the capacity of both expression and comprehension, and becomes the medium through which some of the most universal, elemental—and intangible—concepts of man are conveyed.

On the other hand, symbolism is something more precise than mere suitability or association of ideas. The pictures of birds hung in the nursery would not be exchanged for the wall-hangings of a harem; but no symbolism is involved until a characteristic depiction conveys a perceptible meaning, as when the mating birds on the tree of life convey associations connected with creation. The phœnix as resurrection, the crane as long life, the incorruptible peacock are unmistakable symbols. The toe patterns tooled on the sole of a Persian sandal are an example of natural association rather than symbolism, but the foot becomes symbolic in its phallic associations, as the sacred toe of Buddha, the winged foot of speed or victory, the footprints which symbolize the passage of time. The butterfly shape of a kite and the fruit painted on a fruit dish are most likely a result of simple association, but the apple of the forbidden tree is a symbol of evil, the peach in China is longevity.

Symbolism in folklore is the recognizable and usable property of a cultural group. Literary symbolism and the "private symbolism" which may occur in sophisticated art are outside its scope. A symbol remains a private symbol, just as a word remains a nonce word, until the identity between the symbol and the meaning are established and the purpose of communication is served. The following list of certain common forms which symbolism takes in many parts of the world is an indication of how completely it pervades the various aspects of life. Many of them are discussed fully elsewhere in this volume. The examples are merely indicative of the nature of the material.

Gesture—the finger to the lips for silence, the tapping of the forehead for thought, the hands over the eyes, the shrug, the thumbs down for death, the two uplifted fingers of the "V for victory," or any of the movements, small or significant, by which meaning is conveyed. An elaborate religious symbolism may evolve around specified gestures. The fixed attitudes of Buddha, for example, were rigidly prescribed in all Buddhist art: meditating, with the right hand palm up in the left, both on the lap; protecting, with the right hand raised, palm out; earth-touching, gift-bestowing, preaching or teaching, etc. The gesture of blessing or benediction in Christian art shows the hands uplifted with three fingers touching. The open hand is a defense against evil powers. The ancient mother goddesses, Ishtar and Padma, were shown uplifting the breasts with the hands in the gesture which conveyed bounty and fertility.

Posture or Position—the kneeling or standing position of worship or suppliance; the seated position of the person in authority—the ruler, the judge, or Christ in his character as judge. In catacomb art, the head resting in the hand is the position of dejection, and the suffering Christ of east European peasant art is always shown with one hand on knee and the other supporting the head. The meditating Buddha sits crosslegged. The frontal view, with enlargement of persons to indicate their importance, is a feature of Semitic art. In early Christian art, the orant (the blessed dead) stands with arms upraised in the attitude of prayer or adoration.

The movements of the dance.

Symbolic acts—the washing or cleansing as a symbol of purification, which is almost world-wide, anointing for prosperity or joy, breaking bread as an indication of willingness to share, drawing back the curtains which admit the soul to paradise; circumcision which admits the Jew to the Covenant of Abraham; three taps for the act of penance. Death is the felling of trees in the garden of life. To dive into water is to delve into the mystery of Maya or the secret of Life. Shamash pours water from the jars on his shoulders to symbolize his beneficence and, for the same reason, the elephant pours water over the goddess Padma and her lotus.

Location and direction—facing the rising sun or Mecca or Jerusalem, the north as the origin of evil demons, the prescribed position of saints in Byzantine churches or of guests at the table, as a symbol of honor. The four quarters of the universe are significant in many cultures, and with each direction may be associated certain colors, plants, elements, animals, etc.

The body and aspects of appearance or dress—the queue unbraided for mourning, the enlarged tongue which is the sign of a great man, the long hair which shows the Nazarite's consecration to special service, the skull as death, the heart as the seat of life, the evil eye, lameness as a symbol of royalty, the tonsure of the priest, Buddha's tuft of hair, the scarification for various symbolic purposes common among primitive peoples. The sexual organs appear universally as basic symbols associated, of course, with creation and fertility, whether depicted literally as the lingam may be or in association

with other forms such as the female lotus or spiral, the male bull or sun. The physical aspect of important or supernatural personages is generally stylized with details or features indicative of their power or character. The earliest depictions of Christ, for example, focused on the outstretched hands, showing no features. Innumerable items of dress and ornament are symbolically used (the belt with keys signify womanhood, the ring for union) or decorated with symbols, notably in the case of ritual and ceremonial garments.

The cosmos, the elements, the earth, and landscape—the cosmos as an egg or an endless serpent, the sun and moon as sky father and mother, the sky as cow or cosmic hide, the earth as a giant tortoise, the star, the dawn of hope, the fire of divine presence or purification, the lightning of destruction, the height of mountain symbolizing spiritual supremacy or sacredness, the rock, the ocean or river or fountain of life, the sacred lake in the western heaven, the silver stream of matrimony. The visualizations of the cosmos, the nature of earth and life in it, and of paradise and hell and the abodes of spirits, which cannot be actual, make use of natural elements in elaborately symbolic ways. This is perhaps the most significant aspect of this subject, particularly in terms of primitive religions.

Plants, flowers, and fruits—the lotus of the feminine principle, the lily of purity, the prunus of happiness, the corn of fertility, the millet seeds for numerous progeny, grape vines for Jerusalem or the world, the palm of victory, ginseng as the root of life, betel nut for conciliation, straw scattered at Christmas to commemorate the birth in the manger, the tree of life.

Food—particularly the ritualistic partaking of especially prepared food and drink which is a part of almost every people's customs. The six symbolic foods of the Jewish Passover include the bitter herbs symbolizing the sufferings of the Israelites. The early Christian feast signified the joy of the hereafter, and in the later Eucharist, bread and wine are the body and blood of Christ. The Chinese eat vermicelli on birthdays, a particularly graphic association of the long strands with wishes for a long life, and send congratulatory rice cakes as a symbol of good fortune. The blood puddings of the Incas are another example.

Animals—the lion which may represent Judah, the solar god, Britain, or courage, the snake which symbolizes protection on a Rumanian doorway or Jewish temple, the endless cosmic waters in India, or the ultimate in treachery, the fish which may be fertility or Christ. These indicate the variation and extent of animal associations. All important animals are associated with the supernatural, adopted as guardian spirits, viewed as friendly or unfriendly, or associated with specific traits in each culture. With animals used in supernatural associations, it is natural that various mythical creatures should have been created, like the winged horse and cherubim, the unicorn associated with virginity, the fecundating dragon, or the horned dragon of the storm.

Supernatural beings and legendary personages—the gods and spirits visualized in every culture, usually by fusion of human, animal, and natural shapes, which mutually symbolize each other, or various forces of nature, supernatural powers, or attributes and characteristics. Here may be included such symbolic characters as Father Time with his scythe, the Russian Grandfather Frost symbolizing winter, the Chinese Old Man Long Life with gnarled stick and peach, John Bull. Historical or semihistorical individuals also come to be or to be presented by symbols—Christ as the Good Shepherd, Jonah as the symbol of resurrection, the young Washington with his cherry tree as a symbol of truthfulness.

Buildings—particularly the entrance to the home and places of ceremony or worship, every aspect of which may be designed or decorated with symbolic connections—the four towers or corners or walls associated with the directions, the columns or pillars representing the deity, the exact measurements symbolizing the divine order, the holy of holies as the residence of the deity or the womb of creation, the high seat of authority, the holy door to the path of purification. The temple itself may be god's footstool. A door may be the barred door of virginity or the open door of hope, steps prescribed, house beams significant.

Other objects—either as they happen to exist or as they are especially designed for symbolic purposes, like the crown, the scepter, the fetish, the charm, the laver of purification or the sea. There are the wing of royalty, the ax of destruction, the knot of death (Navaho) or life (India), the ashes of death or (Chinese) prosperity, the candle or flame of faith, the lamp of the law or life, the anchor of hope, the jug of knowledge, the mug which symbolizes unity in guild ceremonies or the peace pipe of American Indians, the wheel of life, the precious jewel of Buddha, or any of the jewels with their specific meanings, the drum as the voice of the god.

Colors.

Numbers.

Geometric and purely graphic symbols—the yang and yin, the shri yantra, the wheels of life, the swastika, the sign against the evil eye, the aureole of divinity or saintliness, the zigzag of water, the circular design of clouds, the cross with its numerous forms and significances, the various forms of the star (the five-pointed star of perfection, and the six-pointed Seal of Solomon), the interlacements. The basic geometric shapes are surrounded by symbolic associations all over the world, with important resulting art forms. The associations may be of universal character like the circle and the sun, or highly localized. The triangle, for example, is readily associated with any group of three, like the Trinity; the threefold nature of the universe; body, mind, and spirit; the law of life. It connotes wisdom, and as a sex symbol is widely associated with the female principle (and the moon) or upward and downward pointing triangles with male and female. The square, spiral, scroll, chevron, meander, interlacements, etc., are likewise susceptible of many interpretations.

This is an almost random selection of more general or widely known symbolic connections. There are, as well, innumerable localized significances or highly specific depictions among art objects, which require full description for an analysis. In typical depictions of the Dance of Death in the Middle Ages (originating in the plague), the soul is represented by a little naked human figure, without sex distinctions, shown making its exit from the mouth of the body. This symbol of the soul as a miniature naked human figure must be seen before its meaning is completely communicated. An example of highly specific ritual acts is the removal of the Torah curtain in

the Jewish synagogue on the anniversary of the destruction of the Second Temple, which symbolizes the emptiness of Jerusalem robbed of its treasures.

The meanings expressed through symbols may range from small matter-of-fact details to concepts of cosmic importance. In primitive cultures one may note in general the prominence of symbolism connected with sex, fertility, and creation, with the nature of the universe, with natural forces and supernatural powers, and with the objects and rituals designed to ward off evil, induce good fortune, or to accompany worship. In more advanced cultures, the symbolization of abstract qualities and personal characteristics (like greed or envy) is added to greater extent.

We may assume that symbols arise inevitably in the process of communication, but in some cases definite elements may be seen as giving shape to them. The attempt to give tangible form to the invisible or interior idea, the attempt to compress a ramified framework of thought into an instantaneous expression, and the attempt to organize the scheme of life into a comprehensible system (the Chinese trigrams, for example) are prominent motivating or shaping forces. The natural associations formed around a natural shape, like the sun and the circle, play a very large part in the form that symbolism takes. Sometimes identification, as has been noted, or concealment, as in the use of the fish for Christ, offers a motivation. And a number of associations are obviously accidental, as in the attachment of the hare to Jewish Passover lore from a verbal connection; the same factor accounts for a variety of Chinese symbols having the same syllable in the name.

The tendency to develop symbols in groups or to evolve systems by which symbols are equated is a feature of certain cultures, notably the Chinese. They have for example, the twelve branches of time, governed by the twelve cyclic animals; the four celestial animals (dragon, bird, tiger, tortoise) associated respectively with the four quadrants of the heavens, east, south, west, north, with spring, summer, autumn, winter, and with blue, red, white, and black; and eight precious articles—a jade triangle or musical stone, a jewel, cash, lozenge (victory), pair of books, painting, a pair of rhinoceros horn cups, and an artemisia leaf. The eight sacred symbols of Buddha are: the canopy (representing the tree under which he received enlightenment); conch (his voice); jug (knowledge); knot (continuity of life); umbrella (power); fish (freedom); lotus (divine birth); wheel (rebirth). The Navaho depictions are based on fours, including sacred plants, directions, elements, etc.

Symbols in the course of their existence are subject to many borrowings and migrations. Studies of the migration and diffusion of symbols are unfortunately generally tinged with an element of speculation. There seems to be no doubt that certain ideas like the tree which suggests life, the sun disc, or the celestial cow are so inevitably suggested by actuality or the primitive environment that they could (whether or not they did) spring up independently—and also that certain shapes like the swastika, triangle, and spiral are such suitable vehicles for human thought that they have a world-wide diffusion even though the meaning may vary partially or completely. Symbols are also subject to many changes, resulting from either development or borrowing, in the course of their existence. The god Sin, for example, in the ancient Mediterranean area, was shown with crescent, or crescent and disc, but since the crescent resembled horns, he came to be represented as an old man wearing a cap with horns of the moon, and the horns readily became a crown; thus, the horned crown of Assyrian kings was a symbol of both power and divinity. Under WHEEL has been indicated the process by which circle, disc, sun, wheel, wing, life concepts, etc., built up into an elaborate symbolic structure.

Art symbolism may be related to the general subject of symbolism in the following respects: 1) simply as the depiction in art of such symbolic acts, gestures, objects, etc., as have been described; 2) as a standardized or stylized expression of these concepts, by which these symbols crystallize into a set shape or instantly recognizable form, as when the symbolic sun is depicted as a circle with a face and a ring of stylized flames; 3) as the medium by which natural objects and shapes, invented shapes, and/or geometric forms may be fused to create the form of the symbol, as when animal horns and human head are combined in the god or the "tear line" is devised in the god's face to show the connection with rain; 4) as purely graphic symbols, a few of which were listed above.

The essence of a symbol is the meaning which it conveys. The decorative motifs of art are not symbols unless the element of meaning is present. Unfortunately, in prehistoric art and in some later art, the means of ascertaining significance is lacking and the presence of symbolism cannot be conclusively demonstrated. Much of early South American art, from the stylizing and repetition of the form, suggests a symbolic impression, but the possibility of demonstration is infrequent. Many motifs, however, like the popular rose in present-day American fabrics or the field flowers used in European peasant art, are completely lacking in symbolism; and the decorative arts are full of "dead symbols"—the multitudinous examples of fleur-de-lis, lotus, lily, or rosette, for example, whose meaning is forgotten, or ignored, but whose popularity remains.

There is a tendency loosely to associate symbolism and abstraction in connection with art symbolism, which is erroneous. Symbolism makes use of either purely realistic or purely abstract shapes, or a combination of the two, or of a stylized form of natural objects. This is demonstrated in the yang and yin (a purely invented form), the evil eye, usually a stylized version of the actual eye, and the lingam, which is often literally depicted. Abstraction has to do with deviation from nature in respect to form, for whatever reason; symbolism has to do with meaning, regardless of the form the art symbol may take.   M. HARMON

Symplegades In Greek mythology, the clashing rocks (D1553) at the mouth of the Euxine Sea, through which the *Argo* passed. Phineus advised the Argonauts to send a pigeon through first; the rocks would come together and, as they opened again, the *Argo* could slip through. If the pigeon were crushed, the *Argo* was told to go back. The pigeon flew through; its tail feathers were caught. The *Argo* then rowed forward quickly and got through with only minor injury to its stern. The Symplegades then became fixed and never moved again. The clashing gateway or passageway is very common in folktale, often in connection with the quest for the water of life (e.g.

Russian, Rumanian, Greek folktale). J. R. Bacon (*The Voyage of the Argonauts*, Boston, n.d., p. 80) suspects that the Symplegades had such a connection at one time, for Phineus is blind and the water of life is a regular cure for blindness. In an Eskimo tale, the rocks are icebergs; the kayak's stern is injured. Lizard, in Bushman myth, was broken by the mountain pass that pinched him in two as he tried to get through. In Tsimshian mythology, it is a cave that opens and shuts. Variations on the theme are found in North American Indian tales all over the continent from the Seneca and Cherokee to the Miwok and Tlingit. The gates to the underworld often are a similarly clashing entrance. Teutonic folktale has many references to heels lost as gates to magic mountains, rocks, and caves snap shut just behind those who venture into them. A. H. Krappe (*Balor with the Evil Eye*) detects a separate folktale motif in these stories: "the motif of the frustrated redemption and the slamming doors." In many of these myths and folktales, a faint resemblance may be traced between the perilous passageway and the vagina dentata concept.

syncretism An extreme form of the mechanism of cultural dynamics known as *reinterpretation*. Reinterpretation occurs when a people take over the cultural forms of another group, reading new meanings into them as they integrate them into their own body of traditions. Syncretism takes place where two similar elements of cultures in contact actually merge their meanings, both forms remaining intact. The most striking examples of syncretism have been found among African and New World Negroes in contact with Mohammedan and European religious systems. Greenberg established that the Hausa of Nigeria identified the *'iska* of their aboriginal religion with the *jinn* of the Koran. In the New World, Catholic saints are identified individually with African deities by the members of the full-blown African cults found in Brazil, Cuba, Haiti, and Trinidad, to cite only the established examples. An African deity will be called *santo,* for example, in Bahia, or *orisha,* the Yoruban term, without any distinction being apparent in the mind of the worshipper. There is great variation in the actual beings that are syncretized, this being the result, in a given locality, of the particular historical experience of the group concerned. However, the principle, which has to do with the process of identification, holds firm. It is applicable, indeed, in most cases of cultural change over the world, and in all aspects of culture.   M. J. HERSKOVITS

syrtos A folk dance of modern Greece, for men and women in arbitrary order. With a handhold, the dancers progress counterclockwise in an arc, round and round the room. The clarinet melodies, with their guitar, mandolin, and drum accompaniments in 7/8 time, are slower in tempo than those of the *tsamikos* and *hasapikos.* The syrtos shares popularity with these two dances, both in Greece and in Greek festivities in America. The grapevine step hesitates in iambic rhythm, always to the right—right side, left back, right side; left front, right, left front; balance forward and back. The body turns slightly with the step, first facing left, then right. As in other open rounds of this area, the leader, usually a man, exults in acrobatic variations on the theme, in twirls and leaps called *scherza.* These are particularly daring when danced by the *Evzone* national guard. The ancient *syrtos* is known by the recent name of *kalamatianos*, the national dance. One tradition carries it back to the pyrrhic dance of antiquity, another to the suicidal dance of the Souliot women, who hurled themselves over a cliff during a death dance rather than surrender to the Turkish invaders. A commemorative ballad, the *zalongo*, sometimes is sung in chorus to lyre accompaniment during the *syrtos-kalamatianos*. [GPK]

szopka A small box theater, made by Polish peasants of cardboard and bright-colored paper. Some are crude with paper figures pasted down, others gay and elaborate with movable puppets resembling the figures in the Bethlehem mangers in the churches. They are traditionally carried by Christmas carolers, who also often carry a star made of translucent colored paper with a candle inside; this star revolves sometimes on a stick like a pinwheel.

T

Ta'aroa In Polynesian mythology, specifically that of Tahiti, the chief god; the creator. Living in darkness within the cosmic egg, Ta'aroa broke out. Then he lived alone in heaven for a time. Eventually he created a female being, his daughter, and with her assistance made the sea, sky, and earth, which latter, in some versions of the myth, he fished up from the depths of the ocean. At last he took some red earth and fashioned men. Men lived on the red earth as food until the breadfruit was created. In some of the Polynesian myths, Ta'aroa then called man by name, thus throwing him into a sleep during which a bone (*ivi*) was taken from man's body and made into a woman to be his wife. Some students believe this to be indigenous myth, others claim an obvious descent from the Biblical story of the creation of Eve. In further myth, Ta'aroa is said to have become angry with mankind; he flooded the world with the sea, leaving only the islands protruding. Compare ATEA; TANGAROA. See WORLD EGG.

Table, Ass, and Stick The title of a folktale (Type 563; Grimm #36) of the loss and recovery of magic objects: found all over Europe and Asia, in Africa and the Americas: perhaps of Oriental origin, for a variant is known in the 5th century A.D. Buddhist *Jātakas*, though origin in Europe with spread to Asia is equally probable. This type, along with Types 564 and 565— *The Magic Providing Purse* and *The Magic Mill*—was studied by Antti Aarne in his monograph *Die Zaubergaben* (*MSFO* XXVII, 1911). In addition to the huge number of European and Asiatic variants—Stith Thompson says it appears in practically every collection —at least 7 Indonesian, 14 African, and 4 North American versions are known of Type 563.

Typically, the hero, out to seek his fortune in the world or to obtain some "most wonderful" thing, is given a magic table which, on command, sets itself with all kinds of good food; sometimes this is a tablecloth which is spread on a table and commanded to bring forth food, sometimes it is a self-replenishing sack. The hero, on his way home, stops at an inn, and his magic possession arouses the cupidity of the innkeeper. The thieving host substitutes an ordinary table and hides the self-setting table. When the false table refuses to work, the hero returns to the person who originally gave him the gift, and is given this time a horse or an ass whose droppings are gold. Again the innkeeper steals the wonderful gift. Finally the hero is given a stick which will beat anyone on command. The wicked innkeeper is trapped and forced to return the stolen things before the hero will call off the cudgel.

In the Buddhist tale, three ascetics are given respectively a hatchet that will chop when commanded, a drum that will rout enemies when beaten on one side or summon up a fourfold army when beaten on the other, and a bowl that will supply a river of curds when inverted. But a fourth man, who has obtained a gem that enables its owner to fly through the air, steals the hatchet and orders it to cut off the heads of the three ascetics. In possession of these four magic objects, he conquers the kingdom of Benares and becomes the just King Dadhivāhana.

All these magic objects are of course related to other magical objects of folktale: the purse of Fortunatus which is always full, the horn of plenty (cornucopia, Amalthea's horn), the *kibisis* or wallet of Perseus, the lamp of Aladdin which could summon up the jinni who could do anything, and the whole land of Cockaigne (Schlauraffenland) where the animals and plants sacrificed themselves to become food for the inhabitants. See INEXHAUSTIBLE FOOD, DRINK, OBJECT.

tabu A system of religious and social interdiction and prohibition, the most famous and fundamental of the social institutions of Polynesia. The concept and observance, however, are common among most primitive peoples. Tabu sets apart a person, thing, place, name (sometimes even the distinctive syllable of a name) or an action as untouchable, unmentionable, unsayable, or not to be done for a number of reasons: 1) because of its sacredness or holiness; 2) because it possesses some inherent mysterious power; 3) because it has become "infected with the supernatural" (as priests, kings, chiefs, strangers, pregnant women, etc.) and therefore has acquired this mysterious power; or 4) because it is unclean (as certain foods, sick persons, criminals, corpses, etc.) or because it is highly dangerous (as corpses, the names of the dead, names of gods, etc.); 5) or to effect an end (as the tabus against interference with birth, marriage, sexual functions, etc.); 6) or to insure protection from theft, trespass, damage (as tilled fields, personal belongings, etc.). Tabu, among Polynesians especially, is indicated by a symbolic mark or sign, which usually consists of a branch of a certain tree placed across a door or hung in a prohibited place, or bunches of certain leaves, or the setting up of wands. A violated tabu avenges itself and need not be punished by man. Disease and death overtake the breaker of a tabu.

Tabus fall in general into two classes. The first consist of those imposed and announced by king or priest and accompanied by ritual act, and which can be also ceremonially removed. A certain hunting ground or group of fruit trees, for instance, can be declared tabu for a prescribed period of time and restored to common use when the time is up. The British Sunday was declared the one big tabu by the king of Hawaii in 1819. The second class of tabus are those inherent tabus charged with the supernatural and therefore fraught with mysterious power and danger. See BARAKA; GENNA; HLONIPA; ILA; JOKING RELATIONSHIP AND KINSHIP TABUS; NAME TABU.

The Old Irish prohibition or compulsion (*geis*, plural *gessa;* modern Irish *geas*, plural *geasa*) is a tabu, i.e. a certain thing must not be done for fear of the results, but the *geis* includes also the terrific obligation placed upon one person by another, a kind of magic injunction to break which brought calamity and death. It was *geis* for Diarmuid to join in a boar hunt because his life was tied up with the life of a certain boar; it was *geis* for Cuchulain to eat dog. The tragic death of the three sons of Usnech could have been avoided had it not been *geis* for Fergus mac Roich to accept whatever ale-feast was offered to him (i.e. he was obligated to accept), and *geis* for the returning sons of Usnech to eat food in Ireland until they reached Emain Macha (i.e. they were obligated not to eat until they came to Conchobar's house). Conchobar saw to it that Fergus (who was surety for their safety) was delayed with invitations and himself put the *geis* on the three sons of Usnech not to eat until they reached Emain. Thus Fergus was compelled to delay, the three sons of Usnech compelled to hurry to their betrayal and death.

The long tragic story of *The Destruction of Da Derga's Hostel* is based on the power of *gessa*. Conaire, high king of Ireland about the beginning of the Christian era, was compelled to break his nine *gessa* in one night by the *side* (supernaturals) who thus took revenge on Conaire's grandfather for having once destroyed one of their mounds. Conaire's nine *gessa* were: 1) not to kill birds (birds should be dear to him because his father was a bird); 2) not to go around Tara with Tara to the right of him or with Mag Breg to the left; 3) not to hunt the evil beasts of Cerna; 4) not to go out every ninth night beyond Tara; 5) not to sleep in a house from which the light or firelight could be seen from the outside; 6) three reds (i.e. three red-headed persons) never to go before him to a red's house; 7) no booty to be taken during his reign; 8) after sunset no lone woman or lone man to enter the house where he was; 9) never to settle the quarrel between any two of his thralls. It was the doing of the *side* that Conaire was forced to break all nine *gessa* in one night and that night lost a battle and met death.

The various tribes of North American Indians had hundreds of tabus affecting a great many aspects of daily living; some were peculiar to one or two tribes only, other tabus were continental in their distribution. In the realm of folklore, in many tribes it was tabu to tell stories of any sort in summertime or in the daytime; if this prohibition were broken Coyote or Rattlesnake would bite narrator or listener, or some other misfortune would befall the offenders. The folktales themselves contain mention of many tabus; a tabu against digging roots occurs in the Star-Husband tale, for example; a tabu on sexual intercourse for a certain number of nights occurs in many of the North American Orpheus myths and other tales; digging, drinking, eating tabus are common, and likewise a tabu against looking backward, or in a certain direction. In all cases in tales, if a tabu is broken the consequences are unpleasant or even fatal to the character breaking it. Thus, if Trickster learns a magic trick but does it more than the prescribed number of times, misfortune befalls him. See EYE-JUGGLER, for example. For the enumeration and distribution of almost a score of tabus found in American Indian tales see Stith Thompson, *Tales of the North American Indians* (Cambridge, Mass., 1929), p. 362, C. The list in Thompson does not exhaust the tabus mentioned in tales. [EWV]

South America provides us with a few examples of the well-known tabu that prevents persons going through a rite de passage from scratching themselves with their fingers. In the Guianas, girls who undergo the puberty rites, fathers during the couvade, and shaman novices must use a stick to scratch themselves. Likewise, among the Yahgan of Tierra del Fuego, the youth going through initiation must take the same precaution. [AM]

tabu motif The basic motif of countless folktales occurring everywhere in the world, in which the life, happiness, success, or failure of the characters depends upon the observation or violation of some tabu. The whole of chapter C of Stith Thompson's *Motif-Index of Folk-Literature* is devoted to the tabu motif in close to a thousand ramifications (C0–C980). The most familiar cycles of stories using this motif are probably the forbidden chamber or door (Bluebeard) cycle (C611 f.), the forbidden casket, chest, box (Pandora) cycle (C321 f.), and the lost husband or wife cycle, typified in the classic Cupid and Psyche, Orpheus and Eurydice stories. See these; see LOOKING TABU.

In addition there are hundreds of tales presenting the fatal effects of all kinds of broken tabus: there are flowers not to be picked (C515) lest transformation result; a drum not to be touched (C181.1); tabus against setting foot on the ground (C520 f.). Oisín was warned not to dismount from the horse when he returned to Ireland from Tir na n'Og (C521); fruits of certain trees are not to be eaten—the forbidden tree, fruit, etc.—(C621 f.); the midnight tabu in the Cinderella tales (C761.3); other time-limit tabus, such as those compelling a revenant to leave this world at midnight or cockcrow; supernaturals must not be called by name (C10–C12) lest they appear; wishes must not be unthinkingly expressed (C15 f.) lest they come true; possessions of supernaturals must not be taken or touched (C51 f.). C100–C199 includes stories using all sexual, nuptial, incestuous, menstrual, and childbirth tabus. There are numerous stories also involving eating and drinking tabus, looking, touching, speaking, saying tabus, boasting, laughing, etc. There exist both famous and obscure examples of each one. Lot's wife was turned to salt for looking back; Uzza died for touching the ark of the covenant. There is an Eskimo tale about a man married to a fox, who lost his wonderful supernatural wife when a visiting relative mentioned the strong smell of fox about the place. See

ANIMAL LANGUAGES; FOOD TABU IN THE LAND OF THE
DEAD; NAME TABU; OFFENDED SUPERNATURAL WIFE.

Tagaro One of the conflicting brothers of Melanesian
mythology. In the Banks Islands, Qat, the hero, is
hindered by his brothers, two of whom are Tagaro the
Foolish and Tagaro the Wise. In the New Hebrides,
Tagaro is the wise one and comes into conflict with
Suqe-matua, Meragbuto, or his 11 brothers. For example,
Tagaro creates the useful fruits, Suqe-matua the useless
ones. In a tale probably of Indian provenience (found
also in India, Siberia, etc.), Meragbuto so hinders Tagaro's work that Tagaro plots to do away with him.
First he prepares a pit beneath his house. Then he asks
Meragbuto to be so kind as to burn the house down
while he is in it; this, he says, will give him greater
power. Meragbuto willingly agrees. Tagaro hides in the
pit and comes forth unscathed. Meragbuto in turn asks
Tagaro to burn him in his house. Of course, the flames
burn him to death and Tagaro is left alone to continue
with his work.

Tahmūrath or **Takhma Urupi** Persian epic hero: in
the *Avesta*, successor to Haoshangha (first ruler of Persia) and brother of Yima; conqueror of Angra Mainyu;
culture hero who taught men to domesticate animals,
and how to clothe themselves by spinning the wool of
sheep. Tahmūrath, after defeating Angra Mainyu, rode
him as a horse around the ends of the world until he
was betrayed by his wife. She revealed to Angra Mainyu
that the only place Tahmūrath ever felt fear was on
the mountain Alburz. Knowing well that the moment
of fear was the only vulnerable moment, next day the
great horse opened his mouth and swallowed his rider
on the fatal mountain. Yima managed to recover his
brother's corpse, and thus rescued the arts and civilization which disappeared with the hero. According to
Firdausī, Tahmūrath conquered the daēvas who, in return for their lives, taught him to write 30 scripts.

Taikomol Creator-culture-hero of the Yuki Indians
proper and the related Huchnom of north-central California. Among the Kato, Athabaskan neighbors of the
Yuki and Huchnom, Taikomol (Nagaicho) is secondary
to another creator, Thunder; among the Coast Yuki,
Taikomol disappears and Thunder (Ehlaumel) is the
one great deity. The Huchnom version of Taikomol's
deeds is as follows. Taikomol was alone in the universe.
He made the land, made human beings from sticks, and
instituted a dance. But the primeval water on which the
world had been floating came up and the earth disappeared. Taikomol made another world, without daylight, sun, or game; the people ate one another.
This world was burned. Then Taikomol named himself,
"He Who Walks Alone," and again made an earth. He
put in it rivers and made mountains; but the earth
swayed, floating too lightly on its substratum. So Taikomol set at its northern end a great coyote, elk, and
deer, and made them lie down, so the earth would finally
come to rest. When these creatures stir, the earth quakes.
Then Taikomol again made human beings from sticks,
and gave them a dance. One person did something wrong
and died. Taikomol buried him. In the morning the
dead man rose and returned, but the people sickened
from the smell of the man, so Taikomol abandoned his
idea of resurrection. He bade the people carry on the

hulk'ilal wok, ghost dance, he had given them (not related to the 19th century ghost dance) so that they might
live well and long. Cult observances to Taikomol include
two dances, the one Taikomol gave the people, and the
Taikomol wok in which the male impersonator of
Taikomol wears the "bighead" costume of the Kuksu
cult. The dances are tabu to all persons uninitiated in
the cult, which means to all women and children. The
Yuki share with the Huchnom the Taikomol cult observances. See ANIMAL AS EARTH ANCHOR; DEAD SMELL BAD;
KUKSU; NAGAICHO. [EWV]

Taikomol wok Literally, Taikomol dance: a ritual
dance of the Yuki and Huchnom Indians of north-central
California. This dance was given to the people by
Taikomol, the creator, and can be performed only by
initiates of the Taikomol cult. See HULK'ILAL WOK.

Táin Bó Cuáilgne or ***The Cattle Raid of Cuailgne***
(pronounced Cooley) Title of the most famous epic
in the Ulster cycle of Old Irish literature, and the oldest
epic of all western Europe, recounting the details of the
great cattle raid known as the War for the Brown Bull,
and embodying the life and exploits of Cuchulain and
his defense of Ulster single-handed against the united
provinces of Ireland. The original version of this epic is
thought probably to have been written by a *fili* and is
placed by scholars about the middle of the 7th century.
The earliest extant manuscript (about 1100) exists in the
Book of the Dun Cow; another text, by a 12th century
author using the Dun Cow version, is preserved in the
Book of Leinster. The Yellow Book of Lecan (14th century) also contains a version. See BOOK OF THE DUN COW;
CUCHULAIN.

T'ai Shan The highest and most sacred of the five
sacred mountains of China: in the province of Shantung.
The sacrifices on the summit of T'ai Shan had fallen
into disuse but were reinstituted by the first emperor
of the Han dynasty. In this ceremony the emperor, alone
on the summit, performed again the ceremonies of the
Temple of Heaven. The mountain is covered with
shrines and inscriptions. Near the very top, the Lady
of T'ai Shan or T'ai Shan's daughter, patroness of immortals, has a great temple. She is attended by the Lady
of Fecundity. In another temple, the Princess of the
Colored Clouds sleeps for nine months of the year but
is ceremonially awakened at the beginning of the rainy
season. It has been the subject of many studies. [RDJ]

Takarabune The Treasure Ship, bearing the Seven
Gods of Luck of Japan, which is believed to sail into port
on New Year's Eve. Its picture under one's pillow on
that day insures lucky dreams. [JLM]

tak-keng The posts on which human skulls are set up
by the head-hunting Wild Was of Burma. The setting-
up of skulls on posts insures to these people an abundance of food and rice-liquor; without them crops fail,
pigs and bullocks die, liquor disappears. The spirit of a
dead man hovers around his skull and fights off predatory demons and disgruntled or malicious ancestral
ghosts. Nothing is more potent than a skull for protection against and propitiation of spirits. Avenues of
tak-keng protect whole villages, and tak-keng are set
up and dedicated also for specific purposes, e.g. to end
drought, stop the spread of disease through a village, etc.

tale titles Not all North American Indian tribes have native titles for the tales they tell; in collections of printed tales the titles are, more often than not, of necessity supplied by the collector. However, there is by no means a universal lack of native tale titles; Goodwin, for example, notes for the White Mountain Apache that some of their tales, but not all of them, have standardized Apache titles; the untitled ones are alluded to or known by a sentence descriptive of the main event in them which varies from person to person. Titles which are native Goodwin indicates with an asterisk. Some of these, translated, are: *The Earth Is Set Up, He Goes to His Father, Vulva Woman, Naye-nezyane Wins His Wife Back, The Emergence, The Flood, Lost With Turkey*, and so forth (Grenville Goodwin, *Myths and Tales of the White Mountain Apache (MAFLS* 33, 1939). Titles for some, at least, of a tribe's stock of tales have also been noted by other collectors for tribes in areas other than the Southwest; Boas, for example, notes titles for certain North Pacific Coast tales. It seems probable however, that standardized tale titles are exceptional rather than the general rule for any tribe, and that they are entirely lacking among some groups. [EWV]

Taliesin A historic Welsh bard of the 6th century, probably attached to a king of the North Britons, Urien, and his son Owein. In the ms. called the *Book of Taliesin* (c. 1275) there are songs of battle and of mourning which may represent his authentic work; but along with these are ten prophetic poems composed later than 900, strange boasts of the many forms which the bard has assumed and of his preternatural knowledge, and one, "The Spoils of Annwn," in which he tells of going with three shiploads of Arthur's men on a raid against the glass fortress of the Otherworld, presumably to carry off the caldron of the Head of Annwn. In the 16th century a mass of poems and traditions about Taliesin was brought together, which Lady Guest translated in her *Mabinogion*.

Bibliography: Williams, I., *Lectures on Early Welsh Poetry* (Dublin, 1944), pp. 49–65. Loomis, R. S., "The Spoils of Annwn," *PMLA* LVI (1941): 887–936. See ALDER; BATTLE OF THE TREES. [RSL]

talisman A wonder-working object; a charm possessing and transmitting certain qualities, as opposed to an amulet, which is a passive protector or preventive charm. The amethyst worn to protect its wearer from the effects of alcohol is an amulet; Aaron's rod, the magician's wand, and the transforming wand of the fairies are talismans. The active principle of the talisman clearly distinguishes it from other charms, though often the talisman and the amulet, both usually small and carried on the person of the possessor, are confused in common terminology. Many of the magic objects of folktale—the cap of invisibility, the seven-league boots, the self-setting table, etc.—can be classed as talismans, for they have a positive power of themselves. The animistic stage of religion may be thought of as the stage of belief in talismans, because the inherent power of the things of the world may be utilized by supplication, prayer, coercion, or the like, to the worshipper's benefit. The holy relics of the Middle Ages were also talismans; touching a piece of the True Cross, or a saint's mummified finger might cure any manner of illness.

Possession of such an object rendered its owner powerful too, sometimes even in the absence of the object. In this, the talisman parallels the charms and spells privately known and owned and passed on from father to son, or sold and traded, as many of the magic spells of the Dobu Islanders. Thus Aladdin's lamp, a talisman capable of summoning a jinni, had to be sold to the wicked magician in order for him to be able to use it; simply stealing it would not have sufficed. But Aladdin, to whom some of the power of the lamp adhered even when he did not have it, did not have to buy it back.

During the Middle Ages, when the alchemists and other thaumaturgists were active, talismans were sought after or prepared with appropriate incantations under the influence of the proper astrological configurations and with summoning of the proper spirits to inhere in the objects. The philosopher's stone is the most famous of the medieval talismans, for possession of this touchstone would enable its owner to perform many wonders, one of the least of which was transmutation of the base metals into gold. See HAND OF GLORY.

talking doctors Shamans among the North Pacific Coast Indians of southwestern Oregon who cured the sick by reciting a long myth about the creation. The regular shamans of this region were women who derived their power from supernatural spirits; the "talking doctors" were men who were taught the myth by members of their families. A talking doctor smoked tobacco, recited the myth, then diagnosed the sickness or cured minor ailments. Other activities of these doctors included ceremonial recitations of myth material, officiating at the first salmon ceremony and putting fresh food into the mouth of a person who had been fasting. He was not paid for these services, which were priestlike in nature. However, like the shamans, a talking doctor did not escape at times from suspicion of practicing witchcraft. Like shamans, he was powerful enough to cure disease; therefore he was also believed powerful enough to cause it if he had a grudge against a person. [EWV]

talking privates, talking excrements A man is given advice by his private parts or, in some instances, by his penis only (*mentula loquens*). This is a recurrent element in trickster and other North American Indian tales of the Great Basin and Plains. In the Plains it is usually the man's penis that advises him. A related incident is that of talking excrements, in which the man is advised by his feces. This latter incident is widespread over the western half of North America and is also found in Ojibwa and Pequot-Mohegan myths of the Woodlands area (see Stith Thompson, *Tales of the North American Indians*, p. 296, nn. 83 a, b, c). [EWV]

tall talk A species of "expansive eloquence" and strong language—racy, picturesque, and boisterous—identified with the Southern and Western American backwoods and frontier and with the "rankness and protestantism in speech" accompanying the growth of nationalism after the War of 1812. Half folk, half literary, tall talk was part of the picturesque trappings of the backwoodsman, along with coonskin cap and deerskin shirt and leggings. In its use of fanciful, facetious, and factitious intensifying words and bold, extravagant metaphor, tall talk combined dialect and slang elements. The process of word-coinage by "analogical extension or enlargement," blending, and onomatopoeia, resulted in such grotesque formations as *spontanaceous, tarnacious, tetotaciously, rampageous* or *rambunctious, angelliferous, slantindicular, obfusticate, explatterate, explunctify, boliterate, ramsquaddle*. Tall talk drew many of its figures and allusions from the objects and activities of backwoods life: wolfy (wolfish) about the head and shoulders; I wouldn't risk a huckleberry to a persimmon; You do take the rag off the bush (originating perhaps in the improvised target used in shooting matches). Applied originally to the boastful talk of the backwoods braggart and bully (see RING-TAILED ROARER), the term tall talk has been extended to include the hyperbolical style and bombast of the backwoods stump-speaker and preacher, who combine the homespun art of making a noise in language with spreadeagle, sky-painting oratory.   B. A. BOTKIN

Ta Mo Founder of the contemplative Ch'an school of Buddhism in China. The doctrine is that the Law of Buddha (*Bodhidarma*) is to be perceived by contemplation independently of books and rituals. In Japan this school is known as Zen Buddhism. Ta Mo, repulsed by a Liang dynasty emperor at Nanking, floated across the Yangtse on a reed to enter the monastery of Shao Lin at Lo Yang, where for nine years, wrapped in thought and surrounded by vacancy, he meditated. During this time his legs fell off. A doll without legs, so constructed that no matter how it is placed on the ground it always returns to a sitting position, is, in Japan where Ta Mo is known as Daruma, dressed in Buddhist costume. Ta Mo's day is the fifth of the Tenth Moon. [RDJ]

Tamoi The mythical first ancestor and creator in the mythology of several Tupi-Guarani Indian tribes. After creating the world and giving to mankind the elements of civilization (see CULTURE HERO) he departed to the west to the land of the dead. There he presides over the dead. The Tupi-Guarani expect him to return, and his return will bring about either great changes in the world or its destruction. Tamusi, the otiose great god of the Caribs, is identical with the Tupi-Guarani Tamoi. [AM]

Tane One of the chief deities of Polynesian mythology; the creator of man; god of forests, birds, and insects, of creation and procreation. Tane was one of the sons of Rangi (Vatea) and Papa; Tane-mahuta, in New Zealand mythology, was the actual separator of the sky god and earth goddess. According to Maori mythology, Tane had a number of wives, but their offspring dissatisfied him—grass, trees, stones, snakes, etc. He continually complained to his mother, Papa, the earth goddess, with whom he wished to copulate. She induced him to take some earth (red clay) from the beach and shape it into the desired creation, Tiki, the first man. Then from the earth of Hawaiki, the mythical ancestral home of the Polynesians, Tane fashioned a woman, Hine-ahu-one, the Earth-formed maiden. These, Tiki and Hine, were the ancestors of the human race. In another version of the creation myth, Tane made a woman at Hawaiki, brought her to life, and covered her up. He went away, but when he returned she so captivated him with her curiosity, liveliness, and laughter that he married her and became father of humanity. At the other end of Polynesia, in Hawaii, the work of creating the first human couple is done by Kane, Ku, and Lono. Kane, the Hawaiian equivalent of Tane of the Maoris, is the demiurge who fashions the earth and the two heavens—one for the gods, one for men. He creates the plants, animals, and human beings, and is the ancestor of all life.

Tangaroa In Polynesian mythology, the sea god; patron of fishermen; in Hawaii, he is called Kanaloa. In Maori mythology, Vatea and Tangaroa disputed about the first-born of Papa's children. Each claimed to be the father. Papa settled the dispute by cutting the child in half and gave each of the gods his portion. Vatea cast his half into the sky, where it became the sun. Tangaroa kept his part for a time, and after it began to decompose he also threw it into the sky, where it became the pale and marked moon.

Tannhäuser A 13th century minnesinger whose adventurous life wandering about Germany and on a Crusade to the Holy Land led him to be identified with a knight in a 16th century ballad who, on passing the Hörselberg in Thuringia, sees a beautiful woman beckoning. He follows her and finds himself in the court of Venus (Frau Holde) and gives himself up to revelry and a life of sensual pleasure. He finally returns to the world and goes on a pilgrimage to Rome to seek absolution from the pope. The pope declares that he has as much chance of forgiveness as the papal staff has of blossoming. Three days later the pope's staff bursts into bud, but meanwhile Tannhäuser has returned to the Hörselberg (Venusberg). This story is the basis of Richard Wagner's opera *Tannhäuser*. See ALMOND; DRY ROD BLOSSOMS; *Migratory Legend* in EUROPEAN FOLKLORE.

Tans Local gods of the Hupa Indians of California, who protect the deer in the mountains. Great herds of deer are kept safe from hunters in a huge world within the hills. The Tans let out a few now and then as a reward to hunters who keep all their tabus and know and sing the special songs. The Hupas fear them greatly, pray to them, and propitiate them, but almost never speak of them.

tansy The spicy flavor of tansy is sought in making Lent cakes dedicated to St. Athanasius and an Easter pudding. The same delightful aroma, which flavors cakes and cures headache merely by its fragrance, also keeps away ants. Culpeper says of the tansies "Now Dame Venus hath fitted woman with two herbs of one name, the one to help conception, and the other to maintain beauty, and what more can be expected of her? What now remains for you, but to love your husbands and not be wanting to your poor neighbor?" He recommends the garden tansy be bruised and applied to the navel to prevent miscarriage; boiled in beer it aids conception, although other authorities claim that it promotes abortion. The distilled water of wild tansy is good for cleansing the skin of freckles, pimples, sunburn, and all blemishes, and to clear inflamed eyes. Another complexion aid is made by steeping tansy in buttermilk for nine days. Tansy tea, either from the leaves or blossoms, is universally respected as a tonic and for stomach complaints, cramps, and sick headaches. In some localities it is also used to tighten loose teeth, cure worms, and bathe ulcers. The Chippewa Indians use the root either chewed or soaked in water for sore throat, fevers, and diseases of women. In Newfoundland a poultice of the flowers is used on sprains and on the chest for inflammations of the lungs. In Ohio a vinegar and leaf poultice is put on bruises, wounds, and dog bites. The garden variety is used for stoppage of urine and attendant discomfort and the wild for sciatica and rupture in children. In Sussex the leaves are worn in the shoe as a cure for ague.

Tantalus In Greek mythology, a rich king of Lydia (or of Argos or Corinth) who was befriended by the gods; son of Zeus and father of Niobe and Pelops. This friendship Tantalus in some way abused, and his punishment in Tartarus (Q501.2) became famous in antiquity. The transgression varies: he did not keep secrets entrusted to him by Zeus; he demanded to be made immortal; he and not Zeus stole Ganymede; he gave his mortal friends some stolen nectar and ambrosia; he tested the gods by serving them a dish of the flesh of his own son Pelops. The distracted Demeter was the only one of the gods not to realize immediately what the meal was; she ate part of Pelops' shoulder. The gods restored Pelops to life, giving him an ivory replacement for the eaten shoulder. For his evil deed, whichever it was, Tantalus was doomed to stand forever thirsty up to his chin in a cool lake. Whenever he bent to drink, the water disappeared. About him swung boughs heavy with fruit. Whenever he reached for the fruit, the wind carried the branch away from him. Later writers than Homer add a stone precariously balanced above his head. A different version of the story says that he hid a dog stolen from Zeus and then lied to Hermes when Hermes asked if he had it. For this Zeus tossed Mt. Sipylus in Lydia over him. This latter does not belong to the cycle of stories that made the punishment of Tantalus proverbial in ancient Greece. Perhaps as great punishment, though not as drastic, was his supplanting by Crœsus in men's memories as the richest of men.

Tantras A collection of approximately 64 books which many Hindus consider sacred because they are thought to have been produced by Dattātreya who, as incarnation of the Hindu trinity Brahmā, Vishṇu and Śiva, spoke with the authority of these three supreme deities. The word *tantra* once signified a web. Later it became rule or ritual and finally a treatise which set forth a religious ritual. Most of the *Tantras* are in the form of a dialog between Śiva and his wife Devī who is his śakti, or female counterpart. The topics of these connubial discussions are varied: mysticism, black magic, white magic, the arts and postures of love, diagrams, spells, sacred circles, charms, amulets, mūdras or the sacred positions of the hands. Because they were uttered by the god's fifth mouth they were secret. This condition is further strengthened by the extraordinary jargon they are written in, cryptic allusions which to be understood must be explained by an adept, strange words, foreign words, mystic syllables, and the like. Every *Tantra*, in principle, discusses five subjects, the creation and destruction of the universe, worship of deities, attainment of power by means of magic, and union with brahman.

The *Tantras* are the religious texts of the sects of India known as Śaivite because they worship Śiva. The "right-handed" sect (Dakṣināchārins) follow the pure ritual in harmony with the Vedas; but the "left-handed" sect (Vāmachārins) study to identify themselves with the hierarchy of female divinities, Śaktis, Matris, Yoginīs, Vatukas. The method of identification is by sexual union after severe training in concentration. The neophyte thinks of the virtues, powers, attributes of the goddess, and in time is able to evoke her. Even a human woman may serve his purpose, for whether a human woman is a goddess or a demon is often difficult to determine.

The *Tantras* are supposed to have been put together in the 6th or 7th centuries of this era. A comparison of the Tantrist doctrines with the doctrines of the Tibetan *Bon* cults or some of the doctrines of the Chinese Taoists displays similarities so striking that one is tempted to derive all three bodies of belief from a corpus of superstition, magic, fertility rites, and the like which was possibly operative in the second millenium B. C.

The orgiastic ceremonies, little known because they are secret, seem to be connected with some sort of belief that the vital powers should be constantly in play and these powers among some, at least, of the Tantrists are thought of as the sexual powers. See PHALLISM. [RDJ]

Tao The Way: central in the theory of Taoism. He who knows the Way and follows it is above justice, compassion, the rites. Because he is in harmony with the forces of the universe he has attained serenity. [RDJ]

Tapio The Finnish God of the forests. He has a whole family: his wife, Mielikki, the mistress of the forests, a son, Nyyrikki, and a daughter, Tuulikki. [JB]

täräkämä Nomad: a folk dance of Azerbaijan. It shows Persian provenience in the 3/4 time and cross two-step. Progressing counterclockwise, the women cross the right foot on half toe in front of the left, then balance back left and forward right very subtly. Simultaneously they hold their arms at shoulder level and sway them in opposition to the step with an elegant opening and closing of the wrist and hand. The torso follows the motion but stays erect, and is never shaken in the violent shoulder and abdominal vibrations which characterize such Turkish dances as the *çifte tel*. The men, in arbitrary alternation with the women dancers, execute the step energetically, with a slight jump, and hold out their arms in strong rectilinear positions, one arm straight out to the side shoulder level, the other sharply flexed in front of the chest. The tempo is lively and much faster than for the *turadji*. The musicians play a tambour (*kabal*), a guitar (*tar*), and a *kamancha* which resembles a violin. They interpolate remarks: *Shebash* (live long), *Bravo*, or Give 1000 tumans (a Turkish coin) to the players. It is at present a purely social dance, without any explanation of its nomadic title. Unfortunately it is being superseded by ballroom dances of European and American importation. [GPK]

tarantella An Italian folk dance. Popular tradition attributes a therapeutic origin to this dance, as a cure against the poisonous bite of the tarantula. At the present time it involves neither cure nor frenzy, but a succession of lively steps by sets of two couples. The lilting 6/8 music and many of the steps resemble those of the Irish jig. Dancers hop on one foot and heel and point with the other. However, there are distinctive steps, pivot-hops on one foot, with stamps and shaking of a tambourine overhead, sliding into new positions, and "matching pennies," where the boy, on one knee, matches the girl's gesture of slapping a knee and pointing a finger. The Sicilian version replaces the jig step by runs forward and back, lowering and raising the body and arms, by elbow hooking and *dos-à-dos* by alternate partners, and a "star" formation, thus resembling the west European quadrille. All versions are boldly flirtatious. [GPK]

Tar Baby One of the best-known of the Uncle Remus stories, this American Negro tale has given its name to a series of motifs that has been keypoint in the discussion of such matters as the origin and spread of Old World tales, the provenience of New World Negro folklore, and the extent to which animal tales are the dominant forms of African unwritten literature. The essential elements of the tale include depredations by a trickster, to trap whom a figure made of tar, rubber, wax, or some other sticky substance is erected. Trickster, seeing the figure, speaks to it, becomes angry when it fails to return his greeting, and strikes it. One hand being held fast, he hits with the other, then kicks first with one and then his second foot, and sometimes butts it with his head. He is held secure until apprehended. The tale has been reported from various parts of the Guinea Coast area, the Congo and Angola, and has its widest distribution in Africa. A number of versions have been recorded in Europe, and one or two from India, this latter fact having been relied upon heavily by Espinosa to document his claim for an Indian origin of the tale—a position that has been held by many students to be scarcely tenable in the light of the weighting of the distribution toward Africa. New World Negroes have everywhere preserved this story, many versions of it having been recorded in Brazil, the Guianas, and the West Indies, in addition to its famous nominative form from the United States. See ANANSI AND THE GUM DOLL; BRER RABBIT.

M. J. HERSKOVITS

☞ The tale of a rogue who is captured by setting a figure made of an adhesive substance such as tar, pitch, or gum where the rogue must come in contact with it is known not only throughout western Africa, among the American Negroes, and elsewhere, but is also widely told by various groups of North American Indians. Frank G. Speck, in his *Ethnology of the Yuchi Indians* (Anthropological Publications of the University Museum, University of Pennsylvania, vol. 1, No. 1, 1909), not only records the tale, "Rabbit is Trapped by the Tar-man, and Escapes" (pp. 152–53) for the Yuchi of the Southeast, but discusses the Jicarilla Apache story, for which see "Coyote and the Pitch Baby" (see Morris Edward Opler, *Myths and Tales of the Jicarilla Apache Indians, MAFLS* 31, 1938, pp. 310–312); the Eastern Algonquian version in which Gluscabe, the culture hero, punishes Pitcher, a rogue, by causing him to stick to a tree and turning him into a toad; the Arapaho tradition of a buffalo who pursues a child and gets his head caught in a hollow tree in which the girl is hiding; and the Wichita tale of After-Birth and his brother, who lie on a stone they find and stick to it. Of the various Tar Baby stories which resemble Yuchi and other Southeastern versions, those from Southwestern groups offer the closest parallels. Beside the Jicarilla Apache tale mentioned above, Pitch Baby stories have been recorded for the Navaho (Skunk, who is stealing corn, kicks a dummy, and sticks to it: see W. W. Hill, "Navaho Coyote Tales and Their Position in the Southern Athabaskan Stock," *JAFL* 58: 317–343, 1945, p. 333 and n. 35) the Tewa Pueblo Indians ("Gum Image" in E. C. Parsons, *Tewa Tales, MAFLS* 19: 165) and the Taos Pueblo Indians

("Gum Baby," four versions, E. C. Parsons, *MAFLS* 34: 136–38). It seems probable that those Tar Baby stories which closely parallel the Old World tale and which are found among the Southeastern and Southwestern Indians diffused to these groups from the Negroes and the Spanish, respectively, in post-Columbian times. [EWV]

tarots In certain European decks of playing cards, a group of cards (usually 22) belonging to none of the suits and bearing no denomination. With exceptions, they are numbered in sequence and bear both pictures and legends. The *tarocchi* of Venice and Lombardy are believed to be fashioned after the earliest of the Italian types; but their origin—from the *tarocchi di Mantegna* (used for pedagogic purposes), from the "Egyptian book" imported from the East by the Gipsies, or eventually from certain Chinese card games—is a matter of dispute. Resembling these, and in most instances identical with them, are the Florentine *minchiate*, the Bolognese *tarocchino*, the French *tarots*, the German *Tarok-Karten*. The cards, used for some few special games, are principally significant in fortune-telling, which probably is their original use.

Typically the tarots and their numbers are:

I	— The juggler	XII	— The hanging
II	— The female		man
	pope	XIII	— [Death]
III	— The empress	XIV	— Temperance
IV	— The emperor	XV	— The Devil
V	— The pope	XVI	— The tower
VI	— The lovers	XVII	— The star
VII	— The chariot	XVIII	— The moon
VIII	— Justice	XIX	— The sun
IX	— The hermit	XX	— The judgment
X	— The wheel of	XXI	— The world
	Fortune	[XXII]	— The fool
XI	— Necessity		

Number XIII bears no legend; XXII has no number. The supposed significance of each of these in cartomancy may easily be deduced from its name. Traditionally these are the pages of the ancient Egyptian book of mysteries, the "Book of Thoth," and the one able to read them knows, and controls, the secrets of the universe. Sometimes other cards are added to the regular tarots, as for example the signs of the zodiac, or the virtues—faith, hope, and charity. See GAMES.

tasē Burmese malignant ghosts: generic term for all disembodied spirits which have existed as human beings. The tasē include the *hminzā, thayē,* and *thabēt*. All are bloodthirsty, and delight in causing the death of human beings. They hang around the dwellings of men at sunset and are active during smallpox and cholera epidemics. All their acts are prompted by a desire for vengeance for their misfortunes during life. The ghosts of the recently dead are most feared. They can become incarnate in animals (e.g. crocodiles, tigers, the poisonous hamadryad snake); they may be contained in a pillar, take the form of cats and dogs (*hminzā*), or appear as hideous giants with long tongues (*thabēt, thayē*).

During epidemics the tasē can be frightened away by loud noises. The people beat upon the walls of their houses, on tin kettles, trays, and cymbals to drive them off. The Red Karens will not permit a dead body to be taken through a village; in fact, throughout Burma all death customs are designed to prevent the spirits of the dead from injuring the living. Wakes are held to propitiate them, and these are usually followed by ceremonies designed to drive the spirit away: death-dances, the firing of guns, noise-making. The Shans clear away evil spirits from the grave-site by sweeping it with brambles and thorns. Some tribes bury in remote places to keep the dead spirit far from the living. The Burmans set up no marker in the hope that if they forget the place, the spirit will likewise forget where he once lived. The Karens and Chins, on the other hand, believe in burial at the ancestral home since the spirit of the dead will haunt the living until the corpse has been buried according to the desires of the spirit.

tasks The focal or incidental events (motifs H0–1599, especially H900–1199) in a vast number of folktales from all over the world: the hero must do something difficult or impossible in order to win a bride, preserve his life, obtain some necessary magic object, etc. The task motifs are often undistinguishable from the test and quest motifs since one blends into the other, but essentially the task is the performance of a given act, rather than the search for something (quest) or the general accomplishment of fitting some specification previously announced (test, the more general term). The test of the real princess is the pea under 20 mattresses and 20 feather beds; the search for the lost swan-maiden wife is a quest tale; the separating of grain and sand is a task. The two latter are of course tests also: one a test of perseverance in love often ending with a recognition test; the other a test of the patience required of a servant or a prospective wife. Sometimes the tasks performed by the hero or heroine are only a side issue in the story: spinning gold in the Rumpelstiltskin (Tom Tit Tot) story is only incidental to the main plot of finding out the name of the helper in the task. Such casual tasks often change in the different variants of the story type, but the main plot remains constant. In the Cinderella tale, for example, some variants pose the task for the heroine of separating lentils from the ashes in the fireplace, but this task is not usually present, and is not essential to the story. But the quest, usually with the slipper, by the prince, for the mysterious lady remains constant throughout the many versions of the tale.

In several distinct types, however, the task is a central incident and distinguishes the type. *The King's Tasks*, Norwegian folktale (Type 577), is one of the suitor tales. The father of the princess imposes certain tasks; the two elder brothers fail through unkindness; the youngest brother succeeds by being kind to an old woman, who rewards him with certain magic objects. In Type 402, *The White Cat*, the hero brings back several things that surpass his brothers', all with the aid of a white cat who is later transformed into a beautiful girl and marries the hero. This tale is found all over Europe, but is rare elsewhere. In both of these, the tasks to be performed are essential to the plot, but are not especially central. In Type 329, however, the story hinges on the hero's being able to hide from the princess, who owns magic windows in which she can see everything. If he succeeds, he wins her hand. He hides in a bird's egg and in a fish's belly, but she finds him. Finally, with the help of grateful animals or of an old man he has been kind to, he is transformed to a louse, a "sea-hare," etc., in the

hair of the princess. She is unable to find him; he is eventually retransformed and weds her. This story, Grimm's *The Sea-Hare* (#191), is told throughout Europe, principally the eastern part.

An entire group of suitor tasks is typified in the son-in-law tasks (H310), popular not only in Europe and Asia but also among the North American Indians. In these stories the tasks are set by the bride's father, rather than by the bride herself or by the hero. The North Pacific Coast tale of *Sun Tests His Son-in-Law* revolves about the unsuccessful attempts of the Sun to kill his son-in-law by assigning him tricky and dangerous tasks. He is given blunt arrows with which to kill Sun's daughters disguised as mountain goats and escapes only by transforming himself into a feather ball; he is pushed into the river when helping Sun raise his salmon traps; he is sent to get Sun's hammer from the water and barely escapes when the water ices over, etc.

Among the famous tasks of folktale are the *athloi* of Hercules, the obtaining of the various magic objects by Perseus, the underworld punishment of Sisyphus, the tasks imposed on Väinämöinen by Pohjola's daughter. Typical of folktale tasks are planting a vineyard overnight, cutting down a forest overnight, sorting mixed grain, digging a canal overnight, building a castle in three days, making the princess laugh or speak, answering riddles or outriddling the princess, recovering a ring lost in the sea, getting bull's milk, putting a large squash in a small jar, sowing salt or dragon's teeth or cooked corn.

tattler An animal friend of a man, often the man's dog, plays the role of tattler in the myths of several American Indian groups. Usually the animal tattles to a husband about his unfaithful wife, as in two Zuñi and Shawnee tales. As a result of speaking, the dog may die. See DETECTIVE STORY; RAVEN. [EWV]

Taurus The Bull: the second constellation or sign in the zodiac, containing the bright star Aldebaran and the two smaller constellations, Hyades and Pleiades. It was identified by the Greeks with the bull-transformation of Zeus, in which guise he abducted Europa. He rises from the sea, his hind-quarters submerged, as did Europa's bull, coming to Crete. The bull was important in Mithraic religion and astronomy and his symbol was carved on ancient gems of Persia. To the Akkadians he was the Bull of Light. To the ancient Sumerians and Babylonians he was the heavenly bull who brought the vernal equinox (c. 4000–1700 B.C.) and was identified with the bull created by Anu to challenge Gilgamesh, and which Gilgamesh killed. Its rising marked the new year, the beginning of spring, brought the fresh rains, and ushered in the season of plowing and sowing. In the ancient Hebrew zodiac this constellation was Āleph, the first letter of the alphabet represented by the simple triangular face and horns of a bull. Later Biblical astronomers associated it not only with the Old Testament sacrifices but also with the ox in whose stall Jesus was born. In the old Chinese zodiac it was part of the huge White Tiger; but following Jesuit usage it became Kin Neu, the Golden Ox. Astronomers place Taurus under the guardianship of Venus. Those born under it are earthy, melancholy, and strong-willed.

Tchą, Tchą Bushman name for a little bird, one of the chats (*Saxicola castor*) which these people say flies around in the bushes and laughs at the wildcat. When the wildcat lies down to sleep, the little bird comes and laughs "tch‌ą, tch‌ą, tchą". All the other little birds, hearing this, come to the place and flit around and all laugh at the cat. See Bleek and Lloyd, *Specimens of Bushman Folklore,* London, 1911.

Tchué Approximate transliteration of the name of a Bushman folktale character who seems to be a kind of creator-transformer-culture-hero. Tchué's works are "many, many and not one," for instance. W. H. I. Bleek and L. C. Lloyd, in their *Specimens of Bushman Folklore* (London, 1911) show four *!kuṅ* texts (pp. 405–413) relating the various transformations of Tchué, in which the sun rose and Tchué was a tree (bearing edible fruit) and the sun set and he was dead, and the sun rose and he was himself. In another country he was a palm tree (also with edible fruit). In the four narratives recorded, Tchué became three different kinds of trees, a fly, water (a little water-hole), a lizard, an elephant, a little bird. Each time he died and rose, and finally was again a lizard. His father saw him thus upon the ground and recognized him. The father saw Tchué rubbing sticks together to make fire, and saw him blow upon the fire and make flame. Then Tchué saw his father watching and died. The father therefore feared his child, not only because of the fire but because of the unexplainable death. The story does not say that because the father, a mortal man, had thus learned how to make fire, the firemaker could now depart. But here is the dying god story in its primitive and simplest form, existing as factual tale quite apart from organized mythology.

Tcikapis Major culture hero of the Montagnais-Naskapi Indians of northeastern North America. Tcikapis is a dwarf whose parents were killed by bears just before he was born. Taken from his mother's womb by his sister, he always remained the size of a small child, but was possessed of great strength and used trees as arrows for his small bow. To the Montagnais-Naskapi he is a true culture hero, with an altruistic concern for mankind and great powers for conjuring. Many of the principal episodes of the cycle of tales told about Tcikapis are known also outside the area where he is regarded as a culture hero, among the Cree, Algonquian, and Ojibwa Indians. [EWV]

tecuanes (from Nahuatl *tecuani,* tiger or wild beast) One of the surviving native dances of Guerrero, Mexico. Originating in the terror of the predatory tiger, it is now a comic dance-drama of the hunt. The action, characters, costumes, and dialog in Nahuatl or mixed Spanish and Nahuatl, vary in different villages. In general, four to twelve *huehues* or *viejos* (old men) constitute a double dance line, followed by one or two Cristianos or *hacendados* (ranch owners), two dogs, a deer in gray suit with head and antlers, two *zopilotes* (vultures), one or two doctors (*quebrantehuesos,* bone-busters), one or two hunters with bow and arrow, and a man dressed as an old woman (*vieja*). The tiger is dressed in a spotted skin and a mask of fearful mien, with great jaws, tusks, and sometimes whiskers, a mask of wood, tin, or petate. He annoys the dancers with his detachable tail, as they cavort and pirouette to their one-man flute and tabor. The *vieja* on the outskirts ridicules all of them, and vies with the *viejos* in horseplay. After naive dialog, the tiger is hunted, killed, and "eaten" by the vultures. The doctor suggests resurrecting him, amid jeers. Then all join in a dance of leave-taking in the church atrium.

In Villa Alta, Oaxaca, a simpler version is enacted by two masked boys, who are caught by several men with lassos. The masks also exhibit less elaborate skill, for the Guerrero Indians are past masters. [GPK]

telling Wishes must not be told. When two people snap a wishbone, the one who gets the longer piece, the one with the flattened joint, will have his unspoken wish come true. But he must not tell what his wish is, or nothing will happen. So too if one makes a wish on seeing a shooting star, the wish must not be told, because that destroys the power of the wish. In many parts of the world, magical gifts and supernatural powers remain potent only as long as the possessor does not mention them to anyone else. The magic pot, for example, that produces food on command, becomes just another pot when its owner tells someone else. Perhaps some such thing happens when a man "kisses and tells"; the private magic that exists between him and the woman is dissipated. In folktale, the supernatural or animal wife is lost when the husband mentions her origin (C441): the Eskimo *Fox-Woman,* related to other versions of the same tale in Siberia and Japan, cleans house for the man, marries him, but leaves him when he mentions that she is a fox. One who sees the Cherokee "little people" must be very careful, because saying that one has seen them results in death. Secrets, of course, should not be told, because when a third person knows a secret, the whole world knows. Midas's barber discovered that his master had the ears of an ass. The secret was too much for him; he had to tell. So he dug a hole in the ground and whispered the secret; then he covered the hole over. On the spot grew a reed, and every time the wind blew the reed whispered the secret to the world: "Midas has ass's ears." See BEES; NAME TABU.

tempo-giusto A style of singing characteristic of certain types of Hungarian and other Middle European folk songs, particularly topical and dance songs, in which the rhythm is strictly observed and ornamentation is not used. It is in contrast with the *rubato-parlando* style of dramatic recitative song.

Têng Kao or **Climbing the Hills** A Chinese outdoor festival of the 9th day of the Ninth Moon. At this time city-dwellers have picnics in the country, particularly on hills, drink chrysanthemum wine, and eat crabs which by then have grown fat and sweet in the *kao liang* fields. By punning on the word "têng kao," têng kao cakes are eaten in hopes of promotion. This festival has obscure connections with ancient harvest festivals, though here the facts of folklore should not be confused with the fantasies of folklorists. [RDJ]

Tengu In Japanese folklore, the mythical winged inhabitants of the forests, some in the shape of human beings, some resembling birds. [JLM]

terlain or **terlaik** Sakai (Malay Peninsula) name for disastrous storms. These are caused by imitating the notes of certain birds, by burning lice, or by teasing dogs, cats, and tame monkeys. Compare HENWEH.

Terminalia The ancient Roman festival on February 23, once the end of the year, supposedly to honor

Terminus, god of boundaries, but said by Wissowa to commemorate the *termini* or boundary stones. Terminus is typically Roman as a deity; he is the personification of the distinction between a stone erected as a boundary marker and an ordinary stone. However, since Terminus stood in the temple of Jupiter on the Capitoline, it has been conjectured that this power was simply an aspect of Jupiter. The myth claimed that when the temples of the other gods on the Capitoline were to be razed in order to erect Jupiter's temple there, only Terminus and Juventas failed to accede. This augured well for Rome, for thus its territorial integrity and youthful vigor would remain unimpaired. In keeping with tradition, this stone was not roofed over, since termini were never completely enclosed. The terminus of Rome stood between the fifth and sixth milestones on the road to Laurentum. At the observance of the Terminalia there, and at the termini between private holdings, the owners of property met. Having placed garlands each on his own side of the stone, they erected an altar, made bloodless offerings (though later lambs or young pigs were sacrificed), and ended with singing and pleasantry among the members and servants of the families. That the marking of the boundaries should occur on the last day of the year is a natural parallelism; for similar marking of the division of time, compare HABDALAH. See BEATING THE BOUNDS; HERMÆ.

tests Subject of a group of folktale incidents comprising tests, contests, quests, and tasks: the form section H (H0 ff.) of Thompson's *Motif-Index of Folk-Literature*. Many tale types include test motifs, so much so that they form one of the most widespread groups in the world. That the hero must prove himself a hero is a "given" of folktale technique; and what better way than by having some perilous and suspenseful test through which he must come? Often the hero is the youngest son, the unpromising hero, who succeeds where his older brothers have failed. Compare, for example, KIND AND UNKIND. The hero must perform certain tasks, or succeed in a dangerous quest, or conquer some terrible adversary, before he may be accepted as a suitor for the hand of the princess. He must be a faster runner than an Atalanta; he must return with the water of life; or he must slay the dragon with the seven heads. Perhaps he must prove himself by selecting his own true bride from among others looking like her, or pick out his child whom he has never seen from a group of children—the recognition test. He must be clever at answering riddles, or he will lose his head. He may be honest, like the handsome prince of European märchen; or he may be sharp and indulge in trickery or skirt dishonesty, like the trickster hero of the Jack tales. See Stith Thompson, *The Folktale* (New York, 1946), pp. 329 ff., especially pp. 339–344, for an analysis of the test tales among North American Indians. See CONTESTS; QUESTS; TASKS.

☞ Tests of all sorts, motivated for a variety of reasons, are prevalent in North American Indian tales, especially in hero and adventure tales. One popular and widespread motivation is the testing of a hero by his prospective or actual, often supernatural, father-in-law, who is malevolently inclined and desires the death of the hero. In certain Seneca tales, tests are assigned a hero not by his father-in-law, but by his mother-in-law, which may reflect the social structure of a matrilineal society.

Besides the son-in-law tests, there are also tests by jealous uncles of nephews, suitor tests in which a rich or handsome girl is the prize, tests of visitors to a village, and paternity tests in which a child or infant picks out its parent(s). To enable the hero successfully to meet the test, the device of supernatural advisers is often resorted to; the hero encounters an old woman, or a magic animal, etc., who explains to the adventurer how he can successfully perform seemingly impossible tasks.

Test tales are particularly widespread and popular among the North Pacific Coast tribes, but are also well known in other areas of North America. The tests themselves are of many sorts: the hero has to pass through a door or across a horizon that alternately is open and closed, or through a door which snaps at him or is guarded by animal watchers; he is subjected to boiling, roasting, or otherwise being overheated in a sweat lodge or near a fire, or being overcome by smoke; he is forced to eat burning food, or to swallow red-hot stones, he is sent to obtain a dangerous bird, or to bring back acorns or berries at the wrong season of the year, or to kill rare game such as a white deer, and so forth. For an analysis and treatment of the test theme see Robert H. Lowie, "The Test-Theme in North American Indian Mythology," (*JAFL*: 21: 97–148). [EWV]

Tezcatlipoca One of the most important gods in the Aztec pantheon: literally, smoking mirror. In codices he is represented with an obsidian mirror as a foot, and with his face painted different colors, depending on the desired significance. He was one of the original creator gods, being both a single god and four gods in one, each of which was associated with a cardinal direction and a color peculiar to him. According to legend he was one of the first "suns," being knocked from the sky by Quetzalcoatl and then turned into a tiger, and subsequently into the constellation Ursa Major. As god of the night he was associated with witches, thieves, and evildoers in general, and with death and destruction. At the same time he was eternally young, the patron of warriors, in which form he resembled the Aztec god of war, Huitzilopochtli. Moreover, he was omnipotent, invisible, and ubiquitous, an all-powerful deity who could take or give life, a god of drought and a god of plenty. [GMF]

thabet In Burmese folk belief, the disembodied spirits of women who have died in childbirth: inimical to men. The thabet are represented in folktales with hideous huge bodies and long, slimy tongues.

thaliri In Bolivia the name given to the men and women who act as midwives or are called in to set the heart in its right place after it has been dislocated by shock or accident. [AM]

thayè In Burmese folk belief, the disembodied spirit of a person who has died a violent death: inimical to mankind. The thayè are represented in folktales with hideous, giant bodies and long, slimy tongues.

thefts Thefts of a major and minor order form the basis for several American Indian tale plots, or appear as incidents in various North American tales. One of the most popular of all American Indian tales is one which concerns the theft of fire, or light, or the sun; this tale occurs in all parts of North America except among the Iroquois and northeastern Algonquian tribes; it receives special emphasis in central and northwestern

California, on the North Pacific Coast, and among the Great Basin groups. For the latter groups, the *Theft of Pine Nuts* (a Great Basin food staple) is also a popular tale; people in one country had no pine nuts, people in another one had them; the two groups gambled for pine nuts and through Coyote's cunning, his group won. But the possessors of the pine nuts did not want to give them up; Woodpecker, however, flew up in the tree and took them. Coyote and the people then ran for home, but nearly everyone was killed; Crow took them, and in his flight scattered pine nuts, from which piñon trees grew (see Julian H. Steward, *Some Western Shoshoni Myths, BBAE* 136, Anthropological Papers 31: 256).

Other important things stolen are water, the seasons, and game animals which are kept impounded by a master of the game. Many of the theft stories form part of the cosmogonic material of a tribe; however, trickster cycles also contain stories of theft of food, either by or from trickster. See LIGHT; SUN. [EWV]

thein Burmese rain nats who live in the stars. Showers are caused by their emergence from their homes to hold a mimic battle; thunder and lightning result from the clash of arms. When rain is needed, a Burmese village holds a formal tug-of-war to arouse the thein and get them out of their houses.

Thesmophoria An ancient Greek fertility festival, on October 24–26, in which only women, perhaps only married women, took part. It honored Demeter Thesmophoria, the giver of the riches of the soil (or of laws), and in outline reenacted the myth of Demeter and Persephone. The first day was called the Ascent or the Descent, the second was a day of fasting, the third was known as the Kalligeneia or fair-born. Triptolemus, first priest of Demeter, was said to have begun its observance. During the festival, pine cones, pigs, and other offerings were cast into caverns filled with serpents. Later, after the meat had decayed, it was recovered from the caves and planted with the seed. Symbolically the offering of food within the earth was intended to increase the fertility of the earth and of the womb. As an explanation for the use of pigs, it was said that a herd of swine disappeared into the cleft with the underworld lord, at the spot where Hades entered the earth with Persephone. However Krappe sees in the swine an indication that both goddesses were once sows and were later anthropomorphized. Among the customs observed by the women were abstention for nine days before the festival from sexual intercourse, avoidance of pomegranate seed as part of the diet, no decking of the person with garlands; in Syracuse, cakes in the shape of female sexual organs were passed about; there was jesting in honor of Iambe: beds were strewn with *Agnus castus*, the chaste tree.

Thingyán Pwe Burmese New Year's Feast (known to Europeans as the Water Feast), held on a movable date between the 9th and 12th of April (*Tagū*). During this celebration pots of clear cold water are offered to the monks at monasteries and the images of Buddha are washed. Then follows a ceremony of water-throwing on the streets and in the houses. The women throw first and the men reciprocate, or it is thrown on others of the same sex. The water represents the consecrated water used for washing the sacred images. By throwing water on human beings, the participants honor them as sacred.

At this time Thagya Min, chief of the Thirty-Seven Nats, descends to the earth and whatever he carries in his hands—sword, firestick, or waterpot (ascertained by the astrologers)—determines the destiny of the year.

thistle One of various prickly plants (genera *Carduus, Cirsium, Cnicus,* and *Onopordum*) with cylindrical or round heads of tubular flowers. The national flower of Scotland, it is also called the Devil's own plant, and is sacred to Thor and the Virgin Mary. Several varieties are called blessed, while pious farmers continue to curse all thistles as a scourge. No single thistle is designated as the Scottish thistle, although the common cotton thistle (*O. acanthium*) and the stemless thistle (*Cnicus acaulis*) are usually so designated in Scotland. It is venerated because during the reign of Malcolm I (938–958) the Danes invaded Scotland and stealthily surrounded Staines Castle. They took off their shoes to wade the moat, only to find it dry and filled with thistles. The resultant yells and curses roused the garrison, and the Danes were soundly defeated. The Scottish Order of the Thistle (sometimes called the Order of St. Anthony) was instituted in 1687 by James VII with eight knights. It was revived by Queen Anne of England in 1703 and now consists of the Sovereign and sixteen knights. The French also had an Order of the Thistle founded in the 14th century in honor of the Virgin Mary.

The blessed thistle (*Carduus benedictus* or *Cnicus benedictus*) is so called because the Virgin buried a nail from the Cross which grew in the form of a thistle. This also accounts for the thorns (A2688.1). In another story a man of Bethlehem was weeding his garden and threw a thistle into the road in front of the Virgin. She bade him replace it, as it would be revered throughout the ages. It is sometimes called Our Lady's thistle. Some call the thistle the Devil's vegetable (G303.10.13) or the Devil's grain because of the story that God granted the Devil one crop of grain merely for naming it, but he was tricked into calling "thistle" at the proper moment (K249.1). The torch thistle (*Cnicus*) is also called Ceres' lamp. In eastern Europe the yellow star thistle guards against evil spirits; in Estonia it is planted on the doorstep and hung on the grain to rout evil spirits. In England they say that if the down flies off the thistle when there is no wind, it is a sign of rain. In Suffolk if you cut your thistles before St. John's Day you will have two crops instead of one. A thistle blossom in the pocket protects from evil. If a young woman will take a few thistle heads with the points cut off, naming one for each of her beaux, and place them under her pillow, the one which sprouts during the night is the one who loves her most.

The Caroline thistle was named for Charlemagne because, when his soldiers were dying of the plague, he prayed for guidance and shot an arrow into the air. It transfixed the thistle, showing him that this was the plant which would cure his men. This story is told of many leaders and plants. This thistle is also good for toothache and, tied round a cat's neck, will give her a sharper appetite for mice. The root of the cotton thistle, an herb of Mars, will cure a crick in the neck and rickets. The melancholy thistle (*Cnicus helenioides*) is an herb of Capricorn under the influence of Saturn and Mars, and Culpeper says that a decoction in wine makes a man "merry as a cricket." Of Our Lady's thistle, he admits that it will open obstructions of the liver and spleen, cure jaundice and pains in the side, and, as a spring tonic, will change the blood as the season changes. This is a lot for his Protestant conscience to allow as he was very skeptical of the virtues of all "holy" or "blessed" herbs.

Thok In Teutonic mythology, the old hag, found by Odin's messengers in a cave, who refused to weep for Balder and thus fulfil the conditions which would guarantee his release from Hel. She is usually interpreted as Loki in disguise. See HERMOD.

Thoms, William John (1803–1885) English antiquary, bibliographer, and originator of the word *folklore*. In a letter published in the *Athenæum*, August 22, 1846, Thoms wrote, after using the word *folklore*, ". . . remember I claim the honor of introducing the epithet Folklore, as Disraeli does of introducing Father-land, into the literature of this country." The new coinage seemed more apt than the commonly used phrase *popular antiquities*. How well it was received is attested by its immediate and continued use. The word has established itself in several languages "as the generic term under which are included traditional institutions, beliefs, art, custom, stories, songs, sayings, and the like current among backward peoples or retained by the less cultured classes of more advanced peoples."

Thoms was for twenty years a clerk in Chelsea Hospital, becoming a clerk to the House of Lords and its deputy librarian (1863–1882). He founded *Notes & Querries* in 1849 and edited this periodical until 1872. In 1878, at the establishment of the Folk-Lore Society, he was named Director. The American Folklore Society, founded ten years later, was patterned in general after the English institution as is shown by reference to the original Rules of the American society, whose aims were similar to those of the English society.

Thor, Thunær, Thunar, Donar, or **Thur** In Teutonic mythology, one of the greatest of the gods; god of yeomen and peasants as opposed to Odin, god of the nobility. He was also god of thunder and brought the rains which were needed for the crops. He is known and worshipped throughout the Teutonic area and is considered an older god than Odin and, even in recorded times, maintained a higher place in Norway and a close second in the rest of the area. Thursday is Thor's day and in many localities, especially in North Germany, no work was done on this day. In Scandinavia he is associated with law and justice and the Thing is opened on Thursday. Legal or business oaths are sworn with the words, "So help me, Frey, Niord, and the almighty god (Thor)." The Normans, who called him Thur, sacrificed to him before a long sea voyage to insure success and favorable winds; this was also done in Iceland. The Saxons called him Thunær, and the Anglo-Saxons, Thunar. In most of Germany he was called Donar.

Thor's sign of the hammer was made by his worshippers much as the sign of the Cross is made by Christians. The first cup of drink at a banquet was dedicated to him in this way. Babies were baptized with water and Thor's sign when they were named, signifying that the father accepted the child as his own and that it was not to be killed.

Although generally admitted to be of an older order of gods, Thor in recorded mythology is listed as a son of Odin, either by Frigga or Jörd (Erda). Even as a child he was large, strong, and while generally good-tempered, he was capable of epic rages which caused his mother to send him out to foster parents, Vignir and Hlora. When he came of age he was given the realm of Thrudvang in Asgard where he built Belskirnir, the most spacious of the palaces of the gods, which consisted of 540 halls for the accommodation of the thralls whom he welcomed after death. Thor was married twice, first to the giantess, Iarnsaxa, who bore him two sons, Magni (strength) and Modi (courage) who, some say, will survive Ragnarök and carry on their father's good qualities in the next world. Thor's second wife was Sif, the beautiful golden-haired goddess, who bore him a son, Lorride, and a daughter, Thrud, who was renowned for her size and strength.

Thor is generally pictured as a tall, well-formed, muscular man in his prime with red hair and beard, and, in the North, with a halo of fire around his head. Sometimes he was dressed as a god; sometimes he wore the garb of a peasant with a basket on his back. Because the heat of his presence was so great, he was not allowed to use the Bifrost bridge (rainbow) but waded the numerous rivers between Asgard and Midgard.

Thor possessed the wonderful hammer Miölnir (emblematic of the thunderbolt) made for him by the dwarfs, which returned to his hand like a boomerang. He had an iron glove, Iarn Greiper, which enabled him to handle his hammer even when it was red-hot. His magic belt, Megin-giörd, doubled his natural strength. The brazen chariot which he drove across the sky caused the rumble of thunder and was drawn by two he-goats, Tanngniortr and Tanngrisnr. In South Germany this did not seem sufficient reason for the noise of a thunderstorm, so he was said to be carrying a collection of copper caldrons in his chariot; this gave rise to the somewhat impious name of kettle-vendor. Thor's favorite color was red, and in Scandinavia the rowan tree was sacred to him under the name of "Thor's deliverance." In Germany the oak was consecrated to Thor. The Yuletide period of feasting, which began with the winter solstice and varied in length from one day to a month was dedicated to Thor as well as to Frey.

Thor spent much of his time in combat with the giants and in so doing protected both Asgard and Midgard from the inimical forces of nature. Also it was Thor alone who could silence Loki, though in most of the myths they were friendly, often sharing adventures. His favorite sport was trying to conquer the Midgard serpent, Jörmungandr, but he will not succeed until Ragnarök and then he will be drowned by the venom issuing from the serpent's mouth. For Thor's encounters with the giants, see GEIRROD; HRUNGNIR; JÖRMUNGANDR; THRYM; UTGARD; see also EGIL.

Thoth, Thot, or **Tahuti** The scribe of the gods of ancient Egypt; record-keeper of the dead; creator and orderer of the universe; god of magic, wisdom, learning; patron of the arts; inventor of writing. He is depicted as a man with an ibis head, carrying the pen and ink-holder of scribes, or as an ibis. Sometimes too he has the head of a cynocephalus ape and bears the lunar disk and crescent, but, though he is closely associated with the baboon, he is never depicted as a baboon. His center of worship was Hermopolis, where he headed the Ogdoad, the eight gods. He is seldom pictured standing alone, but usually is in a funeral group in tomb pictures, as reader of the books of the good and bad deeds of men, or taking part in the ritual of the judgment, reading the scales in which the heart was weighed against the feather of truth and recording the result. At Hermopolis he, as god of order and measure, was identified with the moon, hence his lunar crest. In late mythology, Thoth (Tahuti, the Speaker), self-created and existing in chaos, spoke, and his words became covered. Thus began creation. Each word became the thing it signified. Thoth also arbitrated between Horus and Seth, dividing Egypt between the two. Thoth, the god of wisdom, was in Hellenistic times identified with the Greek Hermes, who took over many of Thoth's qualities. He thus became the god and patron of the later magicians and thaumaturgists, being transformed into Hermes Trismegistus, the supposed author of the Hermetic books. The modern pack of cards, believed by some to be an adaptation of an ancient Egyptian book of hieroglyphics, is sometimes called the "book of Thoth." Perhaps as much as the gambling associated with card-playing, the identification of Thoth-Hermes with the forbidden and dangerous secrets, incantations, and evocations of the medieval and Renaissance magicians have caused this "book of Thoth" to be called the "Devil's picture book." Thus, to some extent, the crescent-crowned Thoth has become associated and identified with the sly and knowing Satan of Western belief.

Three Bears   A tale appearing originally in *The Doctor* (1834–47), a miscellany by Robert Southey, the poet, and since modified into the familiar children's story *Goldilocks and the Three Bears.* Southey put the story into the mouth of Dr. Dove, who told it as "one of Uncle William's stories"; the printed version of the original Southey tale indicates the voices of the father, mother, and baby bear in appropriate type sizes. The sources of the tale were investigated by M. J. Shamburger and V. R. Lachmann ("Southey and 'The Three Bears,'" *JAFL* 59: 400–403); Grimm's #53—*Schneewittchen*—provided the house in the forest and its absent inhabitants, the mystified comments of the owners of the house when they return, and the nap in the bed; a Norwegian tale in the oral tradition may have suggested the bears and the porridge. In Southey's tale the intruder in the bears' home is a mannerless little old woman. In 1881, Horace E. Scudder retold the tale with Silverhair, a little girl, as the trespasser. Later in the 19th century the girl's name changed to Goldilocks, which name she retains to the present. This story, like *The Three Little Pigs* and *Jack and the Beanstalk,* is notable for its repetitive formula. The little girl enters the little house she discovers in the woods. She tries the three chairs (one too hard, one too soft, one just right), eats from the three bowls of porridge, rests in the three beds and falls asleep in the smallest, which too is "just right." The three bears come home and see the damage she has done. "Who has been sitting in *my* chair?" says each. After similar repetition, they discover Goldilocks asleep in the baby bear's bed and chase her clear out of the woods.

Three Golden Sons   Title of a folktale (Type 707) known in some 600 to 700 versions from all parts of the world. The plot, one of the most familiar in all folktale, comes primarily from the oral rather than the literary tradition; it appears in Straparola in the 16th century, thence in D'Aulnoy; Galland seems to have taken his variant from Arabic rather than European tradition.

The king overhears three girls saying what would happen if they should marry him; he marries the youngest, who has said that she would bear him triplets with golden hair, a chain about their necks, and a star on their foreheads. (Or he marries a girl he meets by chance.) The two jealous older sisters substitute a dog or some other animal for the triplets when they are born, and throw the children into the river. The wife is imprisoned or banished. The children are found by a fisherman or a miller and are brought up by him. After the passage of years, the eldest of the children sets out to find his father and to obtain the speaking bird of truth, the singing tree, and the water of life. He fails and is transformed into stone. When the second brother too fails, the youngest brother (or sometimes a sister) undertakes the quest. Through kindness to an old woman, he manages to obtain the magic objects, the brothers are released from their petrified state, and all return. The king hears of the wonderful things; the bird of truth tells the story of the three children and the maligned wife; the king and his family are reconciled; the sisters are punished.

This type is often compounded with other types, for example *The Maiden Without Hands* (Type 706), *The White and Black Bride* (Type 403), *Our Lady's Child* (Type 710), *Born From a Fish* (Type 705), *Three Hairs from the Devil's Beard* (Type 461), with all of which it shares incidents modified and adapted to the several types. The story utilizes many familiar motifs, at least 18 in the Grimm version *The Three Little Birds* (#96). It is probably of European origin and appears all over the Continent; collections from Siberia, India, the Near East, and Africa include it; it is known in Canada (French), Brazil and Massachusetts (Portuguese), Chile and Mexico (Spanish), and among the Thompson River Indians of the northwest Pacific coast. Compare FALSE BRIDE.

Three Old Women   Title of a folktale (Type 501), known in the Grimm collection as *The Three Spinners* (#14), of western European distribution. Von Sydow, who studied the type in his *Två spinnsagor* (Stockholm, 1909), indicates either Swedish or German provenience; the tale is known in Finland, Scandinavia, Germany, and most of Europe west of Russia.

Through jealous reports or because her mother foolishly boasts of her daughter's ability to spin (an imaginary ability), the queen calls the girl to the palace, where she is shown three rooms full of flax to be spun into thread. Success will be rewarded with marriage to the prince. The girl, who knows nothing at all about spinning, is at a complete loss as to what to do. At last three old women appear—one with a large foot, one with a huge lip, one with a tremendous thumb—who offer to help her if she will invite them to her wedding. She agrees and they spin the flax into thread. (It is perhaps too easy to see here the three spinning Fates of European mythology, yet their occupation and their presence at a wedding leads attractively to the conclusion that this tale is one of the "Broken-down myths" of which the Grimms wrote.) At the wedding, the old women sit at the bridal table. The prince asks them why they are so deformed. They tell him—from working the treadle to spin the wheel, from wetting the thread, from twisting the thread. The prince vows that his wife will never again have to spin, and all ends happily.

Three Ravens Title of an English ballad (Child #26) first printed in London in 1611. "There were three ravens sat on a tree,/ Downe a downe, hay downe, hay downe." The three ravens were discussing how to obtain breakfast: a knight lay slain in a nearby field, but his hounds kept watch at his feet, his hawks kept off all birds of prey, his love, though big with child, came alone to his side, carried him on her back to bury him, and died herself before sunset. "God send every gentleman/ Such hawks, such hounds, and such a leman."

The traditional Scottish ballad, *The Twa Corbies*, first printed in Scott's *Minstrelsy of the Scottish Border*, 1803, deals with the same situation but is a less romantic, starker thing than the English ballad. Two crows are discussing where to get a meal: a knight lies slain in a nearby field. "His hound has to the hunting gane,/ His hawk to fetch the wildfowl hame,/ His lady's ta'en another mate,/ So we may mak our dinner sweet." One of the two crows will start in on his neck bone; the other will peck out his bonny blue een; they will line their nests with his golden hair; no one will ever know what became of him. "Oer his white banes when they are bare/ The wind sall blaw for evermair."

The Three Ravens was an extremely popular ballad all over England, and through the medium of the Percy *Reliques* variants of it, including the *Twa Corbies*, traveled as far as Russia. See W. J. Entwistle, *European Balladry*, Oxford, 1939, p. 240.

In surviving American variants, all chivalrous atmosphere has disappeared and only a burlesque remains with three old crows cawing hoarsely over the carcass of a cow, as in *Three Old Crows* (sometimes sung to the tune of *Bonnie Doon*) and *Billie McGee, McGaw*.

Three Sisters See DEOHAKO. [EWV]

Three Snake Leaves Title of a folktale (Grimm #16; Type 612) embodying the belief in the esoteric knowledge of snakes. The snakes, by means of leaves of a certain plant, resuscitate their dead (E105). This idea, here in märchen form, is of widespread occurrence. The ancient Greek story of Polyidus and Glaucus is built around the theme: the snakes know the means of reviving the dead; they are immortal; they are connected with healing and all the mysteries of life and death.

Thrym In Teutonic mythology, lord of the frost giants; he stole Thor's hammer. When Thor discovered his loss he confided in Loki who set out to find it. Thrym admitted the theft, but refused to return the hammer unless Freya were brought to him as his wife. This favor Freya refused the gods, so Thor, with Loki as a handmaid, dressed in Freya's clothes and presented himself at Thrymheim. Because of Thor's thirst and appetite, Loki was put to it to continue the deception, but at length Thrym placed the hammer in Thor's lap fulfilling his part of the bargain, whereupon a great battle ensued in which all the assembled company of giants were killed.

thunder The actual phenomena of thunder and lightning are accounted for in the mythologies of nearly all North American Indian tribes, and thunder is, furthermore, personified by many tribes (see THUNDER, THUNDER BOYS; THUNDERBIRD). Among the Yuchi of the Southeast thunder and lightning are said to be caused by a great black snake with rattles on its tail, on whose back a supernatural being rides. In tribes where the concept of the Thunderbirds is found, thunder is believed caused by the birds flapping their wings, or striking trees. Among the Chiricahua Apache and other groups, thunder and lightning are considered aspects of the same force; among the tribes of southern Oregon and northern California the noise of thunder is explained as a man's voice, or a man and woman talking or making noises, or a bird ripping a tree, or the moving of a bat's (Thunder's) wings, or the shaking of an old man's long gray hair, or of a man moving or kicking things, or of supernatural twin boys searching for their baby cradles.

In the Pueblos, thunder and lightning are called or reproduced in kiva ceremonies; if the thunder crashes several times it is a sign that the year will be good with rain; if only twice or thrice, that there will be no rain. The bullroarer is used to arouse Thunder, since it makes a noise like thunder; or two stone balls are rolled along in front of the meal altar in the kiva to call the thunder —these balls being used because they make a noise like thunder. The Shawnee dip a buffalo tail in water to produce rain; if this is done too hastily it will cause thunder and heavy rain, which is undesirable. The Tübatulabal Indians of California believed that if any sort of spider was thrown in a spring, it would thunder immediately. See LIGHTNING. [EWV]

Thunder was conceived as a powerful god by the ancient Peruvians. White llamas were sacrificed to him and sites struck by lightning became sacred. Today the thunder god is still worshipped in Peru and Bolivia as Santiago (Saint James) who has taken in most of his attributes.

Several tribes of the Amazon and of the Chaco associate thunder with birds which are believed to produce it.

The demon Tupan of the ancient Tupinamba and Guarani, who was promoted to the rank of the Christian god, was originally a thunder demon. He caused thunder and lightning every time he crossed the sky in a wooden trough. In some tribes (Lengua, Macushi, Cashinawa) thunder is produced by birds. See THUNDERBIRD. [AM]

Thunder, Thunder Boys Many North American Indian groups personify thunder and tell stories of the deeds of this character, which include tales of contests between Thunder and other personified natural forces. Some tribes, such as the Kato of California, even accord to Thunder the role of creator of mankind. In Kato mythology the two original beings were Thunder and Nagaicho; Thunder was the more powerful of the pair, the creator of man and of many of the animals, mountains, trees, and springs on the earth. The neighboring Huchnom Indians recognize Taikomol as their supreme being, but Thunder once challenged Taikomol. He failed to do what Taikomol did, such as walking on the water, and Taikomol sent Thunder north. In the spring Thunder was told he was to travel south and play with the hail, then return north in the winter. Among the White Mountain Apache, Black Thunder is a holy being who quarrels with Sun and becomes involved in a contest with the latter; among the Lipan and Chiricahua Apache, Thunder quarrels with Wind over his, Thunder's, alleged supremacy. Among the Coeur d'Alene,

Thunder is a being who kidnaps a hunter's wife and takes her to his cliff home; the hunter pursues the couple, and, while Thunder sleeps, steals his shirts; these shirts give Thunder the power of flight and without them he is helpless, so he flops down and cries. This myth, according to Reichard, seems to be unique to the Coeur d'Alene (Gladys A. Reichard, *An Analysis of Coeur d'Alene Indian Myths, MAFLS* 41, pp. 171–174).

Among several tribes in southern Oregon and northern California, Thunder is an old man; sometimes he has an old woman for a wife, sometimes a tree. Other groups in this region believe Thunder is a boy; some say he is twin to a brother, Lightning. On the other side of the continent, among the Cherokee, the idea of the Thunders being two boys also exists; one of the Cherokee Thunders is Tame Boy, the other Wild Boy. Both are sons of Kanati and Selu (Hunter and Corn Mother). The two boys, often referred to as twins, live either in the sky vault or in rock cliffs. They wear snakes as necklaces and bracelets; when they play ball in the sky they cause a thunderstorm. The twins are beneficent and powerful, and are involved in several of the formulæ used by Cherokee shamans; they are also central figures in Cherokee origin myths. [EWV]

Thunderbird An apparently very old concept, which appears both in Asia and in various tribes of North American Indians, is that of thunder as a large bird or birds. This conceptualization of thunder is found on the North Pacific Coast, in the Plateau, and as far south as the Pomo in central California; it also appears among the tribes of the Plains and the Eastern Woodlands. The Thunderbird or birds are powerful supernatural creatures who not only produce thunder, but war with other beings and forces and often grant supernatural blessings. They are depicted as wearing eagle cloaks by the Crow Indians and other tribes; they produce thunder by flapping their wings, and lightning by opening and closing their eyes, or by ripping open trees with their claws in order to find a large grub which is their favorite food. The Algonquian-speaking tribes of the East refer to them as Our Grandfathers, and they are included in the beings addressed in prayers, as well as being fairly frequently referred to in myths. Among the Shawnee, a borderline tribe between the Southeast and the Eastern Woodlands, the Thunderbirds are mentioned in myths, but the Thunders are also said to be small boys who use backward speech and who can move mountains, but are nonplused over moving a handful of dirt or getting across a very small stream; this latter belief in the Thunders as boys is Southeastern.

One of the most frequently referred to pursuits of the Thunderbirds in Plains and Woodlands mythology is the birds' constant warfare with the powers beneath the waters, particularly the horned underwater snakes. References to this familiar feud occur frequently in Plains and Woodlands myths. See WATER SERPENT. [EWV]

☞ The association between thunder and birds exists in various South American tribes, though the Thunderbirds never assumed the same importance in mythology as in North America. Among the Chaco Indians (Mataco and Lengua), birds produce thunder and lightning by flapping their wings. An identical performance is attributed by the Chane to a mythical character with wings. The Cashinawa Indians believe that the xexeu birds gather the clouds and unleash storms. The Wapishiana and the island Caribs seem also to have related storms and thunder with mythical birds. A similar notion is still alive among the Cayapa Indians of the Ecuadorian coast. [AM]

thwē-thauk Literally, one who has drunk blood: the Burmese name for a custom, common among the Chinese, Indochinese, Karens, Kachins, Chins, and the wild tribes of Burma but not among the Burmans. The blood of an animal or man, infused in water or spirit, is drunk as a mark of the exchange of friendship or fraternity. Human blood, when used, is obtained from a puncture in the arm; that from an animal is usually obtained by killing a fowl (Chinese, Karen), a dog (Chin), or a buffalo (Kachin).

thyme Thyme is an herb of Venus and Mars and a symbol of strength. It is loved by the bees and fairies, especially in the north of England. In the Middle Ages, ladies gave their knights a sprig of thyme to increase their strength and courage in battle. On St. Agnes' Eve, if a young girl places a sprig of thyme in one shoe and a sprig of rosemary in the other, and one on either side of the bed, she will dream of love and the man she will marry. In ancient times thyme was strewn about the house to drive out vermin and provide a pleasant odor.

Medicinally it was considered good for depression and to strengthen the head, brain, stomach, and lungs. Used in baths it cleared the skin and soothed the nervous system. It was a cure for insomnia, and the 17th century Parkinson recommended distilled water of thyme and vinegar of roses applied to the head to guard against "frensye" or nightmare.

Tiamat The primeval dragon of the Mesopotamian cosmological myth, *Enuma Elish;* the mother of the gods who was destroyed by the king of the gods, and from whose body the heavens and the earth were created. Tiamat is thought to be the personification of the sea or chaos, or, according to some, the Milky Way (thus paralleling Nut, the sky-mother-cow of Egyptian myth). Tiamat's husband Apsu sired on her the gods, but this progeny annoyed their mother by their constant movement and dancing. She plotted with Apsu and Mummu to destroy them. (Or the gods may have planned to destroy Tiamat because she prevented the establishment of order in the universe; she had so many offspring that she threatened to overcrowd all of the universe.) Ea slew Apsu "with his word," some sort of powerful spell. First Ea, then Anu (who was armed with the "word" of all the gods), tried to conquer Tiamat, but she turned them back. Finally Marduk (earlier Enlil or Bel) moved against her, armed with the delegated power of all the gods. He overcame Kingu, Tiamat's second husband, though the latter had control of the tablets of destiny. Marduk threw his net over Tiamat, and when she opened her mouth to bellow and engulf him, he caused the winds to hold it open while he shot an arrow into it and through her heart. He smashed her skull, cut her arteries (the winds carried the blood away), and cut her in two. Half the body made the firmament; the other half became the earth, on which Marduk built his palace. The myth is thought to be a ritual statement of the Mesopotamian spring floods: the waters are dispersed by the sun and winds and new fertile land is left behind. T. Gaster (*Thespis,* pp. 63 ff.) traces in this myth the pattern of the seasonal drama—combat, assumption of sovereignty, installation in palace, feast of gods, sacred marriage—though several of the elements are obscure incidents in this particular myth. Many of the incidents of the myth have become commonplaces of derived myths and folktales. The dragon-slayer cycle of Europe, for example, undoubtedly owes much to the myth of Tiamat. The slaying of Tiamat through her open mouth is obviously the prototype of the vulnerable spot motif; Marduk can kill the dragon only in this way.

tide   The belief that no creature can die except at the ebbing of the tide is reported from all over the world. On the Pacific coast of North America and in southern Chile and elsewhere people believe that a child cannot be born until the tide comes in. Darwin derived the sexual rhythms of women from the tides on the grounds that the greatest part of the evolution of life took place in the sea.

Breton peasants believe that clover sown when the tide is high will be good but, if sown when the tide ebbs, will grow badly and cows eating it will burst. Their wives think that the best butter comes just as the tide begins to flow. At that time the milk will foam in the churn until after the tide is full. Pliny reported that the skins of seals would ruffle at ebb tide, even after flaying. Malay Peninsula natives believe tides are caused by the movement of a giant crab who leaves and enters his cave at the foot of the world tree. The people of New South Wales burn their dead on a flood tide, because an outgoing tide would carry the souls to far places. See DJUNKGAO; MOON. [RDJ]

T'ien   Heaven; the highest of all things in the Imperial Cult of China. It has shape but no substance. It nourishes creation and once a day revolves on the north and south poles. It is nature or providence and the abode of the gods and spirits. Though without personality it has wisdom and foreknowledge. As Imperial Ancestor it was worshipped only by the emperor. [RDJ]

T'ien T'an   The Temple of Heaven in Peking; site of the most solemn of the Imperial Sacrifices. Here, after complex rituals prescribed by the Board of Rites, the Son of Heaven paid homage to his imperial ancestor. Although the ceremonies were carefully guarded secrets, a sufficient number of details is available to justify the conclusion that the ceremony was derived from very ancient times and was an essential dogma in the Chinese theory of social organization. [RDJ]

tiger   Tigers are sensitive and easily insulted. In Malaya, Sumatra, Assam, Bengal, and southern China where tigers are native, they are notable for their bravery, and are man-killers, and shapeshifters. In a central Chinese version of the Red Riding Hood story, the tiger takes the place of the west European wolf and eats the old woman. The people of this area also believe that having eaten a man, the tiger can force the man's physical ghost to walk before him through the jungle and entice other victims. When the next victim has been devoured, the ghost of the first is liberated.

Propitiation ceremonies are frequent and often concern the sensitiveness of tigers. In some of the Sumatran villages, people will not speak disrespectfully of tigers. If a trail has been unused for some time the villagers will not use it because they fear they might be tres-

passing. If they travel bareheaded the tiger might take this as a mark of disrespect; when traveling at night they will not look behind them because the tiger might think they are afraid of him and this too would offend him. At night they will not knock out a firebrand because the sparks are the tiger's eyes. They will kill a tiger only in self-defense or after a tiger has killed a near relative. When strange hunters set traps villagers have been known to go to the place and explain to the tiger that *they* did not do it. Normally they try to catch killer-tigers alive and before killing them explain why it is necessary to perform the execution and ask forgiveness for what they are about to do. The Bataks, who kill only killer-tigers, bring the carcass back to the village, pray its soul into an incense pot, burn incense, and ask the spirits to explain to the tiger why it was necessary to execute it. They then dance around the carcass until they are exhausted. They believe that human souls may have migrated into the tiger's body. A priest offers food and drink and asks the soul not to be angry. The hill folk of Bengal believe that if a man kills a tiger without divine orders he or a near relative will in turn be killed by a tiger. Having killed, the hunter lays his weapons on the tiger's carcass, reports to his god that this was a just punishment for the tiger's crimes, and promises not to kill again unless provoked. The Cochin Chinese trap tigers and then lament over them.

Certain peoples of the Malay Peninsula believe that tigers live in houses in cities of their own, and describe a fabulous Tiger Village where the roofs are thatched with human hair. A young boy who was "given many stripes" by his teacher ran away into the forest and became the first tiger, and he knows the secret of certain magic leaves to heal his wounds. All over the Peninsula tiger claws and tiger whiskers are valued as potent charms. One tiger whisker knotted into a man's facial hair will terrify his enemies. Quite generally also the tiger is regarded as the familiar of the medicine man or magician, and is said to be immortal.

The Miris of Assam think that tiger meat when eaten will give strength and courage to men but should not be eaten by women because it would make them too strong-minded. In Korean belief, tiger bones when ground to a powder and taken with wine will give strength and are more potent than leopard's bones which serve the same purpose. A Chinese in Seoul is reported to have bought and eaten a whole tiger in order to become brave and fierce. The gallbladder is considered particularly potent.

In south and central China the tiger is as notable a shapeshifter as the fox in north China. The stories are much the same but the protagonist differs. [RDJ]

Tihküyi   Child-Medicine Woman or Sand Altar Woman; an important Hopi Indian female deity; Mother of the Game, spirit of childbirth, wife of the deity Masauwü and sister of Miiy'ingwa. This Hopi deity is equated by Parsons with the Zuñi, Keres, Tewa, and Taos Earth Mother, or Earth Old Woman, and with the Jemez and Isleta character Earth. The deity's name, Tihküyi wühti, Child-Water Woman, may refer to the misdelivery of her child; this happened when she was wandering with Snake Clan Woman. She still wanders and wails, and it is she who sends women their children by projecting into them infant images. See Elsie Clews

Parsons, *Pueblo Indian Religion* (2 vols., Chicago, 1938), p. 1267; p. 183 n.; Table 2, opp. p. 208. [EWV]

Tiki The first man of some Polynesian mythologies. According to a Maori myth, Tiki was created by Tane from red clay. In another Maori myth, the first man was made by the god Tiki and so resembled the god that he was called Tiki-ahua, Tiki's image. Sometimes Tiki makes a wife for himself, sometimes the woman is created as his companion. The tiki is an important figure in Polynesian sculpture, carved usually from nephrite or whalebone, and worn around the neck. The Maori hei-tiki is shaped like an embryo and probably represents an ancestor. Each hei-tiki has its own personal name.

Till Eulenspiegel Hero and title of a 16th century German chapbook, a collection of satirical tales pointed at certain class distinctions of the period and region. Till Eulenspiegel, son of a peasant, was born in Brunswick somewhere around the turn of the 13th–14th century, and died at Mölln in 1350. The tales recount a long series of jests and pranks showing up the superior wit of the clever peasant (often under the guise of thick-headedness) over the typical townsman: tradesman, shopkeeper, innkeeper, even priest and lord. The jokes are scurrilous, sometimes cruel. Although Till Eulenspiegel is best known today through Richard Strauss's piece of program music written around his pranks, he has been known to every German schoolboy since the Middle Ages, as a personification of peasant wit over bourgeois dullness and smugness.

'Ti Malice The Trickster in the folklore of the Negroes of Haiti and other parts of the Créole-speaking New World—Martinique, Guadeloupe, and the Lesser Antilles. In Haiti, as elsewhere, his foil is the lumbering Uncle Bouki. [MJH]

tinikling A Philippine dance of skill. While two men hold two bamboo poles and move them apart and strike them together, a dancer (man or woman) leaps in and out between the poles with a variety of light steps. The timing to the waltz music has to be perfect to prevent accidental crushing of a foot. It is danced by peasants on the threshing floor at harvest time, in Manila society, and by Philippine groups in the United States as a popular offering. The origin is attributed to fishermen of the coast of Anadalusia and their play with two oars. [GPK]

Tirawa Chief deity and dominating power of the Pawnee Indians; generally referred to in myths and ceremonies as "father." The heavenly bodies, winds, thunder, lightning, and rain were his messengers. [EWV]

Tiresias In Greek mythology and legend, a blind Theban soothsayer. There are several versions of how he obtained the power to foresee. He saw Athena bathing and was blinded as inescapable punishment despite the unpremeditated nature of the act. The goddess, his mother's companion, gave him the power to understand the language of the birds and also a staff to act as his eyes. Or he was taken into the counsel of the gods, and was blinded for revealing their secrets.

Perhaps the best known of the stories is that as he was walking on Mt. Cyllene or Mt. Cithæron he came upon two snakes coupling and killed the female. For this act he was changed into a woman. Years later he again came upon two snakes in intercourse and, being now a woman, slew the male. Therefore he was chosen as a knowing arbitrator when one day Zeus and Hera argued about which sex had the greater pleasure in intercourse. His answer, that woman's pleasure was as ten to man's one, so angered Hera that she blinded him. This story, folktale rather than myth, is found in India. In the *Mahābhārata*, a king is transformed into a woman by a bath in a magic river. As a woman he bears a hundred sons whom he sends to share his kingdom with the hundred sons he had as a man. Indra causes them to kill each other off and asks the woman which group to revive. He decides on those he bore as a woman because a woman loves more than a man. And he refuses to be changed back into a man because a woman takes more pleasure in the act of love than does a man. Krappe suspects from this that the original Greek version was more pointed: Hera changed Tiresias back into a man—as punishment.

The danger in spying on the gods is reflected in myth and folktale all over the world: the change of sex for this reason occurs in Cretan, Indian, and German stories. The world-known relationship between serpents and soothsaying is made in many tales of animal languages; the story of Melampus, whose ears were licked by snakes as he slept, is perhaps the best known.

In legend, Tiresias alone retained his mind and memory in the underworld; there Odysseus encountered him and learned how to return to Ithaca. According to Hesiod, Tiresias lived for seven generations. He notified Amphitryon that Zeus had slept with Alcmene to engender Hercules. He also, during the siege of Thebes by the Seven, said that one of the Sparti must die to cleanse the city of blood-guilt laid upon it when Cadmus slew the dragon. Monœcus thereupon killed himself. Tiresias fled from Thebes after indicating how the inhabitants might escape during the siege, but on the road he drank of the spring at Tilphussa and died. An oracle of Tiresias existed at Orchomenus, but it became silent forever as the result of a plague there.

Tishtrya (Persian *Tir*) In Persian mythology, one of the *yazatas* (celestial beings); also, the dog-star (Sirius), leader of the eastern stars; also, a god of rain. It is Tishtrya who listens to the prayers of the faithful, plagued by summer droughts, and then descends to Vourukasha (the sea) in the shape of a golden-eared white horse to battle with the bald-eared, dark horse, the drought demon, Apaosha. When he is victorious Tishtrya causes the sea Vourukasha to boil over; thus vapors rise which are blown by the mighty wind of Mazda down upon the fields and villages, even to the seven regions of the earth. Tishtrya is also represented as a bull with golden horns, or as a brilliant youth. In the latter form he is invoked for wealth of male children.

Titans In Greek mythology, the children of Uranus and Ge: Cronus, Oceanus, Iapetus, Rhea, Tethys, Themis, Coeus, Crius, Hyperion, Thea, Mnemosyne, Phœbe, Dione. Uranus was also father of the Cyclopes and the Hecatonchires or Hundred-handed giants. These latter so irked him that he thrust them back into the womb of their mother, Earth. For this she agitated among her sons to dethrone Uranus; only Cronus dared the act, and with a sickle he castrated Uranus. In the fight between Cronus and Zeus, the Titans fought on both sides; but with the aid of weapons forged by the Cyclopes, Zeus defeated his attackers and imprisoned them in Tartarus with the Hecatonchires as their guards.

Another group called Titans slew Dionysus Zagreus. These Titans, sometimes confused with the others, obviously derive their name from the gypsum (*titanos*, a kind of white earth) with which they daubed themselves in disguise. Zagreus tried to escape by shapeshifting, but when he assumed bull form they killed and ate him, all but the heart, which was saved by Athena and swallowed by Zeus to be born again from Semele. Zeus destroyed the Titans and from their ashes mankind was made. Thus mankind has both evil and divine nature, from the Titans and from Zagreus.

Many scholars see in the Titan children of Uranus a pre-Greek group of gods, deities of sky and earth and the forces of nature, replaced by another group of gods, the Olympians: the succession seems to indicate two waves of conquerors imposing their pantheons on the original inhabitants of the country. The struggles of Cronus against Uranus and of Zeus against Cronus may thus reflect real struggles between peoples worshipping different gods.

Tjalon Arang The Balinese Witch Play between Rangda the witch (literally widow) and Barong the dragon. They symbolize the mother and father principles. The drama follows a traditional enigmatic sequence:

1) Dragon circles the ground three times to mark off the boundary which no witch (*lejak*) can cross. Two men form the flexible body topped by a terrifying mask with movable jaws and protruding tongue and teeth. They cavort with fierce puppyishness and quick changing poses of the feet and head.

2) For an hour to three hours little girls, the witch's disciples (*sisia*), dance in pairs, much as in the *legong*.

3) The witch instructs the disciples in the attack on a king, whose son has refused to marry her daughter. They are to cause a plague.

4) Scenes of pestilence, birth, and death are enacted with much burlesque of ceremonial gestures.

5) The witch is attacked by the dragon's followers and temporarily "killed." The male attackers hold krisses, approach her squatting, then fall powerless while she waves her white cloth or *anteng* (the sling in which a mother carries her baby). She reels like a rag doll, and they fall limp.

6) Laid out in two rows, they are sprinkled with holy water and revived by the dragon.

7) Then follows the dramatic attack on the self with the *kris*, first by a group of women with a downward movement, then by the men with an upward and backward gesture. After the final trance they are carried into the temple and revived.

Phallic elements are clearly represented in the *kris* dance and motherhood concept. At the same time this drama has a therapeutic role by releasing emotions of fear, by burlesquing the fearful. [GPK]

Tlaloc The rain god of central Mexico; his cult goes back to Toltec times. In codices and stone carvings he is represented with tusklike teeth, rings around his eyes, and often with a scroll emerging from his mouth. The eye-rings represent snakes, intimately associated with rain in Mexican mythology. In addition to the chief god of this name there were innumerable minor rain deities known as *tlalocs*—almost every hill was the abode of one—who could bring rain to farmers. The chief tlaloc had as wife (some accounts say sister) Chalchihuitlícue "Our Lady of the Turquoise Skirt," represented by the blue-green color of turquoise, who was a goddess of lakes and rivers. See BACABS; CHAC. [GMF]

tlacololeros (from Nahuatl *tlacoloa*, to prepare the land for cultivation) An indigenous men's dance of Chilpancingo, Tixtla, and surrounding villages of the state of Guerrero, Mexico. Ten to twelve dancers, in a double line, led by a *capitán*, dramatize the activities of the agricultural season in seven sequences: they search for the land, find it, share it out, prepare their agricultural implements, burn down the brush, seed the soil and symbolically beat it, and after an interlude return for the harvest. Their ceremonial mime is associated with the Aztec deities of agriculture, Toci and Xilonen.

Their costumes are unique: burlap tunics reaching to the knee, boots, broad straw hats with conical crowns, and red wooden or furry masks. The left arm is padded, for in the right hand they carry whips, and during the "burning of the bush" they strike each other on the protected arm, simulating the crackling of the flames. This action, as well as all of the mimetic action, keeps time with the music, at times drum and fiddle, or drum and flute.

Another enactment, with dialog, shows the tlacololeros in battle with a tiger (*tecuani*), who has been molesting the owner of the cornfield. A dog called *el maravilla* (the marvel) and other characters assist them. The dialog alternates with longways dancing of crossovers, dos-à-dos, turns, and jumps, all primitive in character. [GPK]

Tloque Nahuaque During the century before the Conquest some of the philosophically minded persons of the Valley of Mexico began to speculate about the existence of a supreme god, invisible, omnipresent, above all others. This speculation took its most advanced form under Nezahualcoyotl, king of Tezcoco, 1418–72, at which time Tloque Nahuaque was worshipped as the center of a semi-monotheistic religious philosophy. [GMF]

tobacco An annual plant of the nightshade family, genus *Nicotiana*, native to the New World: originally cultivated or gathered wild and used for smoking, chewing, snuffing, or as an offering by the majority of the North American Indians, and unknown outside of the New World until the time of the Discovery. Tobacco may not have been used by the Indians in the extreme north of the North American continent, and was unknown to the Eskimo until introduced by the whites after the Discovery. The word tobacco derives from Spanish *tabaco*, Carib *tabaco*, the name for the pipe in which tobacco was smoked.

Among the North American Indians, particularly those of the Eastern Woodlands and Southeast, tobacco of the *Nicotiana rustica* species was cultivated in small plots and regarded as something of a sacred plant. Nearly all eastern tribes have an origin story for tobacco; the Yuchi of the Southeast, for example, say that tobacco originated from drops of semen; in mythical times it was named by a boy and distributed among the people for their use. The Fox of the Woodlands area tell the tale of a man to whom the Great Spirit spoke telling him to go north and find a plant under a certain tree, to tend this plant carefully, and raise other plants from its seeds. This the man did; when he had many tobacco plants he called the old men of the tribe and gave each of them some plants of the sacred tobacco; this tobacco is the sacred tobacco used as an offering to Wisaka, the culture hero, and to the Thunders by the Fox. Other Woodlands tribes have similar tales accounting for the origin of their sacred tobacco, and rules for the actual raising of the plant; it must be grown in a secluded spot, menstruating women must never approach the spot, etc.

In the Great Plains area, tobacco was cultivated by the eastern agricultural Plains people, but only one nomadic Plains tribe, the Crow of Montana, raised the plant. The species of tobacco planted ceremonially (*N. multivalvis*) by members of the Crow Tobacco Society was not the species anciently smoked; this latter (*N. quadrivalvis*) was derived from the Hidatsa, linguistic relatives of the Crow who lived on the upper Missouri in North Dakota. The Crow considered *N. multivalvis* holy, and identified it mystically with the stars. In one version of the Crow creation story the Transformer, while walking about the newly shaped earth, catches sight of a person, whom he identifies as one of the Stars from above. As he approaches this star-person, the latter transforms himself into a plant, Tobacco. The Transformer decrees that the Crow shall plant this tobacco in the spring and dance with it; it shall be their "means of living," their mainstay. The Sun, chief Crow deity, adopts a poor fasting boy and starts the Tobacco order or society, to which both men and women belong. The society's ritual is concerned with the initiation of members into the society (usually husbands and wives together), planting of the tobacco, harvesting of the tobacco. The seeds only are preserved at the harvesting, the leaves and stems of the plant being chopped up and thrown in the river. See Robert H. Lowie, *The Crow Indians* (New York, 1935), pp. 274–96, for an extended description based on his own field material of the Crow Tobacco Society.

In the Pueblos, tobacco is used ritually either as an offering or smoked in corn-husk cigarettes; it is also used as payment. The Hopi do not cultivate tobacco, but gather a wild species, *N. attenuata*, which is also used at Zuñi and by the Tewa, who formerly cultivated the same species. At Santa Ana today, however, *N. rustica* is cultivated for ritual use; this is the eastern species that was cultivated by the Iroquois and Algonquian tribes, and by the Southeastern tribes; how it got into the Southwest is not known (E. C. Parsons, *Pueblo Indian Religion*, 2 vols. Chicago, 1939, vol. 1, p. 18 n.; see also Index, vol. 2, p. 1268). In California most of the tribes gathered wild tobacco plants, either *N. attenuata* or *N. bigelovii*, dried them, and smoked them; a few Central California tribes pulverized tobacco, mixed it with lime, and "chewed" it. The Yurok and their neighbors to the north and south in Oregon and northern California cultivated the plant, the one plant which all these non-agricultural groups raised. They smoked the native tobacco and used it as an article of trade; apparently there was not, as among the non-agricultural Crow of the Plains region, much ceremony attached to Yurok tobacco-raising. The native California tobaccos have been characterized as "rank, pungent, and heady";

they were smoked in moderation, often at bedtime. An indication of the strength of native tobacco is given in Yurok mythology: Downstream Sharp, a grave, unconquerable character in Yurok mythology who smoked tobacco but never ate, destroyed several monstrous beings with their own devices, including those beings who killed people with overstrong tobacco. [EWV]

Tobacco was smoked by South American Indians more for magic purposes than for enjoyment. Even those who used it in ordinary life expected to benefit from it in various ways. In a great many Amazonian and Guiana tribes, only shamans smoked cigars. Tobacco smoke provoked a mild state of stupor during which they were able to converse with spirits. It also gave more strength to their breath and facilitated the extraction of magic missiles from their patients' bodies.

Tobacco juice was drunk by candidates to the shamanistic profession. It plunged those who took it into a state of trance favorable for dreams and visions. Moreover the drug is valued for its imputative purifying virtues. [AM]

Tobit Title of one of the books of the Old Testament Apocrypha, which tells a tale of demons, bewitchment, a quest, etc. The story, from the Septuagint and not from the later Hebrew versions, is influenced by Persian and Egyptian tales. Tobit is a very pious man and, in captivity in Nineveh, takes it upon himself to evade the decrees and bury the Hebrew dead. He is always in trouble because of this, and finally one day he arises from his table at the feast of Pentecost to bury a new corpse. He spends the night outside the house, since he is ritually unclean after his contact with the dead, and during the night sparrow droppings fall into his eyes and blind him. He quarrels with his wife some time later, because she has been forced to go to work and has come home with a bonus, a kid Tobit suspects she has come by dishonestly. He is so miserable that he prays to God for death. At the same time, his kinswoman in Ecbatana, Sara, prays to be relieved of a misfortune that has befallen her. Her beauty has attracted the demon Asmodeus who has killed her seven bridegrooms on their wedding nights. God sends Raphael to earth to help the two. Tobit remembers that he has loaned some money to someone in Ecbatana and sends his son Tobias to collect it. Tobias hires Raphael, masquerading as a member of Tobit's tribe, as guide and companion. They leave, accompanied by Tobias' dog. At the Tigris, a fish tries to swallow Tobias, but it is caught. On Raphael's advice, Tobias saves the heart, liver, and gall. When they get to Ecbatana, Tobias becomes affianced to Sara; they burn the heart and liver in the bridal chamber, and the sweet smoke prevents Asmodeus from killing Tobias. Once the wedding is consummated and the bride is consecrated to the bridegroom, the demon has no power over them. They leave for home at last, accompanied by the dog, and arrive in good time. The gall is applied to Tobit's eyes; the scale falls off them and he sees again. Raphael announces who he is and all ends happily. The story may once have contained a reference to the water of life, which often is the goal of the quest to restore the father's sight. The monster in the bridal chamber (Type 507B) is usually defeated by means of the grateful dead (thus Tobit's burying of the dead); the dead gets half the prize (half the girl who is cut in half and is later restored). In the Tobit story, they voluntarily offer half the money to Raphael before he announces who he is.

tonal The belief that every human being has a guardian or companion spirit in animal form, whose soul is so closely linked to that of the human that if one dies the other follows shortly, is found in much of Middle America. The animal often is known as the *tonal* (also the corruptions *tona, tono*), and in some places as *nagual*. This concept appears to be a post-Conquest form of the ancient Aztec belief (undoubtedly shared by other Indian groups) that the *tonalpouhque* diviner must cast the horoscope of each newborn child, reading the *tonalamatl* book to determine the child's fate. The horoscope is rarely if ever read today, but the *tonal* of the child is sometimes still determined. See MEXICAN AND CENTRAL AMERICAN INDIAN FOLKLORE. [GMF]

tonalamatl The hand-illuminated "books" made from the bark of the wild fig tree, in which was recorded the *tonalpohualli*, or day count, of the Aztecs. By consulting the page corresponding to the week of the birth of a child, a diviner determined whether the birthday was lucky or unlucky, and advised the parents as to what they might do. Other advanced peoples of Middle America also made use of the tonalamatl, though under different names. [GMF]

tongue twisters Tongue tanglers would be a better term for accurate description of these tricky sentences which are so popular a part of folklore, particularly in America. The tongue twister proper is not merely an amusing sentence in which all words begin with the same letter, as many seem to think. It may be a sentence or stanza, a whole poem or only a word, but it must be difficult to repeat aloud rapidly several times because the succession of initial consonants or consonantal combinations is suddenly slightly varied to trip and tangle unwary tongues. In the southern states they are aptly called "cramp words."

When the writer innocently asked the readers of a short piece listing a dozen tongue twisters in a magazine of national circulation to send him any others they might know, he greatly underestimated the popularity of these tongue trippers, for he received more than 13,000 of them from country crossroads and great cities alike. Nearly every correspondent was sure his family favorite was better than any which had been printed, and challenged the writer to say it three times without stumbling. Inadvertently a key had been touched which released a rich jackpot of American oral tradition and folklore.

For generations tongue twisters are passed on by word of mouth alone. Again and again correspondents write: "I learned this one from my grandmother and she told me her grandfather taught it to her" or "These have been in our family for well over a century to our knowledge." An Ohio woman wrote that the old rimed twister she was sending "has been known to us folks for several generations but I ain't sure of the spelling for I never saw it in print or even writing until I set it down for you." And children learn this old rimelore from each other "over the childhood grapevine" as a Maine woman put it.

To be sure, a few can be found occasionally in old rhetorics, fifth readers, orthographies, orthoepies, and elocution books, but these few are simply samples col-

lected from the previous oral tradition. It was a rather common custom a hundred years ago, still continued by a few old-timers, to keep "commonplace books" or "scribble-in books" wherein uncommon sentences and "hearsay verses" were copied in one's best handwriting. From such sources as these, correspondents refreshed their memories and sent along their treasures to me.

My own frame of reference for these twisters was among the winter evening games of my Massachusetts boyhood. They were permitted and even encouraged by our elders because they were supposed to train us to speak more distinctly. But it appears that these peculiar trick sentences are deep-rooted in the life of the whole country and have more uses than I had thought.

The way in which in varied forms the tongue twisters are interwoven in our culture is illustrated by the following sample. A Rhode Island young woman wrote that her dentist father makes patients with new plates practice:

> She strikes her fists against the posts
> And still insists she sees the ghosts.

Hundreds of persons sent me this rather mysterious "post-ghost" twister, usually abbreviated and incorrect. The original version evidently ran:

> Amidst the mists and coldest frosts,
> With barest wrists and stoutest boasts,
> He thrusts his fists against the posts
> And still insists he sees the ghosts.

Like 99½% of all folk rimes, the author of this one is unknown, but, fortunately, one gentleman of 88 remembered that in his youth it had a title, "The Drunken Saylor," which somewhat explains the rime. One old lady informed me that this twister is really the rest of the famous "Ragged Rascal" which should read:

> Around the rugged rock the ragged rascal ran,
> And through the mists
> He thrusts his fists
> And still insists
> He sees the ghosts.

The version which particularly pleases me was sent by a California Jesuit priest who learned it a half-century ago from an old Shakespearean actor who taught elocution in a private academy in San Francisco:

> Amidst the mists and frosts the coldest,
> With wrists the barest and heart the boldest,
> He stuck his fists into posts the oldest,
> And still insisted there were ghosts on
> Sixth Street.

The post-ghost complex has had a more recent incarnation in a set of silly sibilant syllables popular in initiations at girls' schools, with variations unmentionable but usually beginning:

> Three little ghos'eses
> Sittin' on pos'eses
> Eatin' buttered toas'eses

and ending with something like:

> Smeary with greaseses
> Runnin' down their cheekseses
> Down to their kneeseses,
> Nassy little beas'eses!

Dentists may use these folklore ghost stories to test dentures, and sororities to tease candidates, but a professor of pathology reminds me that "a standard test sentence among doctors for speech difficulty" is still the "Ragged Rascal," occasionally varied by:

Third riding artillery brigade.

Just for the record, the original complete version of the oft quoted and oftener misquoted "Ragged Rascal" rime of the trilled R's r-r-ran as follows:

Robert Rutter dreamt a dream.
He dreamt he saw a raging bear
Rush from the rugged rocks,
And round and round the rugged rocks
The ragged rascal ran.

An anonymous New Yorker said that frequently those who are given auditions for the stage must repeat:

Three gray geese in the green grass grazing:
Gray were the geese and green was the grazing,

and a Metropolitan Opera star told me rather acidly that tongue twisters might be a plaything and a joke to me but they were literally a pain in the neck to her, as they were a monotonous requisite of her daily practice grind.

The California version of the gray geese is more difficult for my tongue:

Eight great gray geese grazing gaily into Greece,

and so are the short and tricky ones:

Gaze on the gay gray brigade, or
The sun shines on shop signs.

The latter one cured a Detroit woman of teen-age stammering, she says, while a Waynesville, Ohio, woman wrote that she was told when a little girl that it would make her mouth small if she would only purse her lips "like going to whistle" and repeat:

Fanny Finch fried five floundering fish
for Francis Fowler's father.

Others say frogs instead of fish, which does make the plot more exciting. Even more vivacious is the version from Salt Lake City:

Four fat frogs frying fritters and fiddling ferociously,

which the Utah lady says was given her sixty years ago by a teacher who was "a positive crank on clear enunciation."

One of the common speech troubles which tongue twisters are alleged to have cured is lisping, and one correspondent affirms that for her it was done by saying:

She sells sea shells,

but I wonder if the cure was thorough enough so that she can say without lisping a really tough one like:

The sixth sheik's sixth sheep's sick.

These "cures" of big mouths, stuttering, and lisping habits by repetition of tongue twisters may be good medical practice, or perhaps psychotherapeutic, but they should be at least studied by folklorists. Purely as oral tradition rimes they are folklore, of course, but when they are said to work cures, they verge on the mantric as well and are doubly interesting.

Certain twisters are even dangerous, they say. A California woman claims that when she repeats:

Ninety-nine nuns ran ninety-nine miles in Nineveh,

lingering on the nasal N sounds, her dog always promptly bites her. She says that she doesn't know whether it is his sensitive ears that are offended, or his sense of propriety. So it is best to be careful, at least in canine company, about intoning:

Nine nimble noblemen nibbling nuts,

or that other old one, related to Peter Piper:

Needy Noddle nipped his neighbor's nutmegs.

Speaking of the sense of propriety, I have one fat folder full of letters containing tongue twisters which I would not read aloud to anyone, even a dog, and they will for all of me remain forever in the oral tradition, although one woman insisted that the very rich ones she sent were certainly genuine back-of-the-barn Americana.

Habitual drunks and radio announcers, I am told, are also allergic to tongue twisters, having been required to recite difficult ones frequently as tests. A Chicago judge required a suspected inebriate to pronounce:

Sister Susie sat in the soup,

and from Nottingham comes the information that the British police use as a sobriety test the much more dignified and difficult:

The precedents and associations
of the British Constitution.

Candidates for broadcasting positions at one of our American studios are examined on their ability to say:

The seething sea ceaseth and thus the seething sea sufficeth us.

The corresponding French test-sentence is:

Un chasseur sachant chasser chassa son chien de chasse dans un chasset sèche (A hunter knowing how to hunt pursued his hunting dog in a dry hunting thicket).

Like most elaborations, it is not so good as the original excellent:

Un chasseur sachant chasser chassait sans son chien de chasse (A hunter who knows how to hunt hunts without a hunting dog).

This is a fine example of how much prestige is added to a proverb when it can be phrased as a twister.

That American radio company also spoiled one of our oldest and most popular tongue trippers by amplifying it. The original wording:

The sea ceaseth and it sufficeth us,

has reached me from practically every state in the Union, many persons claiming it to be *the* tongue twister *par excellence*. Popularly it is supposed to come straight from the Bible and to have greater significance and virtue thereby, but you would have to combine part of an Old Testament verse with part of one in the New in order to approximate it. When Jonah was thrown overboard, "*the sea ceased* from her raging," *Jonah* i, 15, and in the Gospel of *John* xiv, 8, "Philip saith unto him, Lord, show us the Father, *and it sufficeth us.*"

The port of Edinburgh is Leith (pronounced Leeth), and it has the best advertised constabulary in the world, for I have received from all over this earth many hundreds of letters and postcards containing the cryptic statement:

The Leith police dismisseth us.

Obviously, the same dental difficulties exist in this as in the previous one, but it is tougher for some tongues. In Texas, it is "the church at Leith" that does the dismissing, which is easier to say, and to believe. White Plains,

New York, simply moves it to the schoolroom where, with a sly smile:

Miss Smith dismisseth us.

A great favorite in the south and west is easy the first time, but almost impossible three times rapidly:

Black bug's blood,

which is combined with another similar California one to make the very difficult:

A black bug bit a big black bear,

and sometimes tied in with the old "Ragged Rascal" thus:

A big black bug bit a big black bear,
Made the big black bear bleed blood,
As round the rough and rugged rock
The ragged rascal ran.

Often it is the bear that does the biting, and the blood may be blue, bad, or bubbling, and in a bucket or on the barn floor. The bear story has infinite variations and goes back to pioneer days. It definitely belongs in western and southern folklore along with:

The rat ran over the roof of the house
With a lump of raw liver in its mouth.

A later one, usually sent in by westerners who like the buggy bear, is:

Rubber baby-buggy bumpers.

This also varies greatly: I have ten versions, one from an English professor in an Ohio college:

Ruby Rugby's brother bought and brought her back some rubber baby-buggy bumpers.

The very difficult and world-known old English one:

She stood at the door of Burgess's fish sauce shop welcoming him in,

has a deceptive change of pace. In America it has become "Mrs. Smith's fish-sauce shop" which, on Long Island at least, "seldom sells shellfish," while from Ottawa comes a variation which will make you feel like swallowing hard before trying it the second time:

She stood on the balcony, inexplicably mimicking him hiccuping, and amicably welcoming him in.

By the way, according to popular lore, hiccuping can be cured by saying certain tongue twisters. In J. O. Halliwell-Phillips' *The Nursery Rhymes of England*, 1886, tongue twisters are classed as "Charms," and on page 137 it is noted that in Dr. Wallis's *Grammatica Linguæ Anglicanæ*, published at Oxford in 1674, there are given, on page 164, ten tongue twisters which "are said to be certain cures for the hiccup if repeated in one breath." Among the ten are:

Three crooked cripples went through Cripplegate,
& through Cripplegate went 3 crooked cripples.

My father left me, just as he was able,
One bowl, one bottle, one ladle,
Two bowls, two bottles, two ladles,
(& so on, as far as *you* are able in 1 breath).

Hickup, snicup, Rise up, right up!
Three drops in the cup, Are good for the hiccup.

and the famous:

Peter Piper picked a peck of pickled peppers;
Did Peter Piper pick a peck of pickled peppers?
If Peter Piper picked a peck of pickled peppers,
Where's the peck of pickled peppers Peter Piper picked?

Sometimes "off a pewter plate" is added at the end of each line. Again the peppers become peppercorns, or they are purple, and in our western country these peppers originally imported from England go native as "prangly prickly pears." In fact, I have 40 variants. Few Americans know that Peter Piper is but the letter P of a complete alphabet in which the same formula is followed for Andrew Airpump, Billy Button, & Co. Of these Robert Rowley and the Thatcher of Thatchwood are among those recommended by Dr. Wallis as good for curing hiccups. See ALPHABET RIMES.

There may be more than superstition behind the idea that tongue twisters cure hiccups, but, on the other hand, it is quite possible they may be brought on by such ones as the dialog of the duchess and the tinker:

"Are you copperbottoming 'em, my man?"
"No'm, I'm aluminiuming 'em, mum."

Among the best of the older short twisters are:

Gigwhip.
Truly rural.
Troy boat.
Peggy Babcock.
A cryptic cricket critic.
Shave a cedar shingle thin.
Pure food for four poor mules.

Yet new ones keep appearing. These are modern:

Flash message.
Preshrunk shirts.
Tillie's twin sweater set.
Six twin-screw cruisers.
Old oily Ollie oils old oily autos.
Platinum, aluminum and light linoleum.

Song-writers and limerick-makers have scratched the surface of this material from "Mairzy Doats" and "Six Long Slim Slick Sycamore Saplin's" to "The Canny Canner" and "The Flea and the Fly in the Flue." Before they change and exploit them beyond recognition, we should diligently collect and preserve the best of these old twisters and tongue-tangling rimes.

CHARLES FRANCIS POTTER

Tonttu The household spirit of the Finns: derived from the Swedish *Tomte*. He controlled the household. The Tonttu must be brought from the churchyard, and a special apartment with a well-provided dining table must be prepared for him. He enriches the giver of offerings with crops and money. [JB]

topaz Topaz is usually considered the birthstone of November under the influence of Sagittarius, Saturn, and Mars, though 17th century Arabs called it a gem of Leo. Much of the topaz of the ancients, especially in Egypt, was really chrysolite. The Egyptian kings had a monopoly on topaz from the Serpent Isle in the Red Sea, where its presence was noted at night by its radiance. This region still produces fine chrysolite.

The Hindus call this stone sour and cold and say that it will prevent thirst if placed above the heart. They believe that it assures long life, beauty, and intelligence. It is one of the gems in their nine-gem charm (*navaratna*) and, in an astrological gem grouping, its place is to the northeast, where it represents the planet Jupiter. It is one of the gems of the New Jerusalem mentioned in *Revelation*, and is mentioned also in *Exodus* as one of the gems of the High Priest's breastplate. According to

Christian tradition, it stands for uprightness, and was a gem of St. Matthew and St. Hildegard. In Brazil it is worn by dentists as a professional badge.

In the 12th century, Marbod recommended that it be suspended from the left arm by the hair of an ass to guard against evil spirits and influences. It could also be worn on the left hand to banish melancholy and to brighten the wit and courage. In 15th century Rome it was used as a touchstone for plague sores. It was useful to detect poisons, calm anger, and to cure piles, wind, and enchantments. See RABIES.

topeng A Balinese mask or masked play. This form of drama is presented by a single performer who appears in a succession of different masks. These are commonly burlesque and grotesque, such as the limp form of a wounded warrior. Topeng follows the conventions of Balinese dance, in the gestures and the puppetlike limpness of the trance. [GPK]

Torii Gateways in front of Japanese Shinto shrines, consisting fundamentally of two vertical and two horizontal beams. [JLM]

el torito Literally, the little bull: bull impersonation in Mexican fiestas, introduced by the Spaniards but performed in true Indian style. a) A carnival dance of Ocotlán, Tlaxcala, enacts a bullfight similar to the *huehuenches* of Villa Alta, Oaxaca. b) In one of the *huapangos* of Veracruz the men take out their handkerchiefs and play at bullfighting with their partners. c) At the conclusion of the *jarana* of Yucatán, the girls, as "bullfighters," try to make their partners, the "bulls," lose their balance or step off the platform by pushing with their shoulders. d) Fireworks in the form of a bull are let loose in the crowd and explode amid much shrieking and laughter. [GPK]

tornak or **tornaq** (plural *tornait*) In Central Eskimo religion, the guardian spirit of an angakok (shaman): believed to inhabit both animals and inanimate objects. There are three specific kinds: those in the shape of human beings, those in the shape of stones, and those which inhabit bears. The Eskimos believe that the spirit of the bear is the most powerful of all. The tornak warns its protegée of danger by some mysterious token within the intuition of the self.

Törökös tanc Turks' dance: Hungarian men's dance in burlesque imitation of Turks. It dates back to the Turkish invasion of Hungary, when the Hungarian soldiers would take great delight in making fun of their unwelcome visitors. During wedding festivities they then became a popular attraction with their fantastic masks and humorous yet graceful steps. They would proceed counterclockwise with leaps and knee-bends, sideward jumps, and turning with partners. The accompanying song was an old folk tune with an irrelevant text about the neighbor's son who gave the neighbor's daughter a pair of red boots. [GPK]

Tortoise One of the principal characters of the animal tales of the Guinea Coast of West Africa: also found in New World Negro folklore. In Dahomey and among the Yoruba of Nigeria, Tortoise figures in the mythology as a bearer of fire to man. [MJH]

totem, totemism The term totem is derived from the native term *ototeman* of the Ojibwa, "his sibling kin,"

Algonquian *nto'te·m*, "my kin," Cree *ototema*, "his kin," and so forth in other Algonquian dialects; in several of these dialects it refers to the animal associated with a clan or gens group, who is either regarded as the mythical ancestor of the group, or a protector and friend of the group. The terms totem and totemism passed into general circulation in English when J. G. Frazer published, in 1887, his studies *Totemism* (London), "The Origin of Totemism" (*Fortnightly Review*, April and May, 1899), and "Beginnings of Religion and Totemism among the Australian Aborigines" (*Fortnightly Review*, July and September, 1905); all three studies are reprinted in volume 1 of Frazer's *Totemism and Exogamy*. A totem, according to Frazer, "is a class of material objects which a savage regards with superstitious respect, believing that there exists between him and every member of the class an intimate and altogether special relation."

After Frazer, a host of philosophically inclined theorists have speculated on the origins and significance of totemism; their contributions, up to 1910, are summarized in *Totemism, an Analytical Study*, by Alexander Goldenweiser (*JAFL* 23, pp. 179–292, 1910), who himself offers several definitions of totemism, the briefest, and most general being, "Totemism is the specific socialization of emotional value" (p. 275). Goldenweiser's analysis, however, is notable chiefly for a negative point; after reviewing world-wide data on "totemism" he concludes that neither clan exogamy or endogamy, nor totemic names, nor the concept of descent from the totem, nor tabus on eating or killing the totem animal, nor any other features assumed to be part of the totemic complex, are universally found associated with it; in other words, Goldenweiser's analysis shows that the "totemistic complex" is not a stable complex, but one of conglomerate independent features, each more or less independently distributed, and that the term totemism has been applied to one set of features in one place, to another set in another, and so forth. Goldenweiser therefore makes the following caution quite clear: that the term totemism can "no longer [be applied] to any concrete ethnic content; for, while almost anything may be included, no feature is necessary or characteristic." Unfortunately Freud and various speculative philosophers have not borne these cautions in mind, and continue to refer to totemism as a concrete, definable, stable complex existent in many parts of the primitive world. Except for northern Algonquian material, from which the term derives as stated above, the terms totem and totemism are seldom used now by Americanist ethnographers in reference to specific material outside the northern Algonquian area.

The spectacular "totem poles," carved with animal crests of the royal North Pacific Coast families, and set up in post-Columbian times as interior houseposts or in front of North Pacific Coast houses, are also erroneously named. Originally these were grave posts, set beside the aboveground box graves of that area; the animals depicted on the grave posts and on the newer totem poles are heraldic (Tsimshian, Haida, Kwakiutl) or are carved representations of stories or heraldic (Tlingit), or may even represent an event that happened to the owner of the house (Nootka and Coast Salish). See Marius Barbeau, "Totemism, a Modern Growth on the North Pacific Coast" (*JAFL* 57, pp. 51 ff.). [EWV]

Tovodū Term for "family," that is, ancestral deity, in Dahomey. In the religious system of the Dahomeans, every ancestor is sooner or later elevated to the status of a deity, a Tovodū, and in this capacity is believed to watch over his descendants. [MJH]

Tower of Babel The tower built by Nimrod and intended to reach to heaven (*Gen.* xi). Nimrod, king of Babylon, wished for greater power and decided to war on God. His tower of bricks in Shinar was built by 600,000 men and was so tall that it took a year to reach the top. From it some men shot arrows at the sky, and they came back bloodied. When the tower was not quite finished, God sent 70 angels to confuse the tongues of the workmen. One did not understand the next; they fought, some were transformed into apes and demons, and the survivors were scattered as the 70 nations on the face of the earth. One third of the tower sank into the earth, one third was burned, one third remained. Whoever passes the place where the tower stood loses his memory completely. Tradition names the tower of Birs-Nimrud at Borsippa as the original. The story may have been inspired in the nomadic people by the ziggurats and the swarming cosmopolitan life of the large Babylonian cities. Somewhat similar legends accounting for the diversity of languages are found in Africa, eastern Asia, and Mexico. Compare ARROW CHAIN; RISING ROCK.

tower of silence The Zoroastrian *dakhmah* in which the bodies of the dead are exposed to birds of prey on a stone slab. When the bones are denuded they are put in a separate place in the dakhmah and are allowed to turn to dust. For Zoroastrians burial in the ground is unlawful. See BURIAL.

tǫwisas Literally, women: the Iroquois Indian society of women planters; also, the term for their ceremony. Tradition speaks of Cherokee origin, of transmission by two female Iroquois captives who escaped from the Cherokee with knowledge of the chants and with the special box-turtle hand rattles. Now the tǫwisas form part of the green-corn festivals and sometimes the planting festivals. The words of the archaic songs concern progeny, ancestry, and sustenance in a broad concept of fertility. At first the society members are seated on two vis-à-vis benches. The introductory chants of thanksgiving are intoned by the leading matron and echoed by the chorus: "Throughout the earth the turtle is stirring." Or they refer to grandmother moon: "I have begotten grandchildren. They are coming creeping on the ground."

The individual thanksgiving chants by each woman in turn are sung in a standing position. They refer to the fruits of the forest and fields: "It is a nice garden that is planted. It shows nice ears of corn." Any man may now approach from the other end of the longhouse and sing his individual thanksgiving chant. If the women can capture him, he is the butt of jokes, must sing a women's song and have his face blackened by a joking relative. Finally the company of tǫwisas marches in slow procession, holding ears of corn and singing: "Now I am marching. Thanks I am saying. They have fulfilled. They have participated. Our children." [GPK]

Town Mouse and Country Mouse One of Æsop's fables (Jacobs #7; Type 112), in which a Town Mouse spurned the simple food and dull life of his friend. the Country Mouse, and invited him to visit the city. There the Country Mouse, while tasting the wonderful foods, was interrupted and frightened so frequently that he returned to the country saying, "I prefer a crust in peace to fine things in the midst of fear." A similar tale (Type 201) is told of the fat dog and the lean dog (who doesn't care for the collar marks on the fat dog's neck, though the prospect of abundant food is appealing).

In a Rumanian fable (M. Gaster, *Rumanian Bird & Beast Stories*, CV), the town-mouse visits the field-mouse and sees the store of nuts and grains his country cousin has. The field-mouse returns the visit and samples the goods in the town-mouse's house, a grocer's. The simple field-mouse is not frightened when the cat walks in and asks the town-mouse who the gentleman is. "That," says the town-mouse, slipping into a hiding-place, "is our priest. Go and kiss his hand." As a result, the town-mouse achieves his end, and occupies the well-stocked home of the field-mouse.

transformation Metamorphosis; the change of shape from one form to another. When the transformation is voluntary or accomplished without the action of another, the accepted term is shapeshifting. In the transformation combat, where the contestants change form to outdo each other, they are shapeshifters. But transformation is usually the result of magic. The witch casts a spell on the hero or heroine, who then turns into an animal, a loathly person, man into woman, etc. The transformation is removed by true love or by the magic object. Self-transformation is the essential of the swan maiden stories; the donning or doffing of the swan feather-garment changes the girl into a swan or the swan into a girl. Transformers use their power to change shape to kill, rob, seduce. The gods may transform themselves into terrestrial shapes for various reasons; Zeus became a white bull, a shower of gold, a man (Amphitryon), etc., in order to consummate his amours. See WEREWOLF.

☞ The changing of human beings, mythical characters, animals and even inanimate objects into a different form is a literary device freely used in North American Indian tales. Transformation is effected for a variety of reasons, some of which are: that the hero of the tale may escape death, be able to reach a difficult place, kill his enemies, seduce women, win a combat, or receive food. Animal-human marriage tales such as those of Fox Woman, Bear-Woman, Dog Husband, Swan Maiden, and so forth, hinge mainly on the fact that an animal transforms himself or herself into a human being, often later retransforming himself into an animal again. In the loathly bridegroom and poor suitor tales, an apparently unattractive boy or youth is transformed, at the end of the story, into a handsome young man.

A specific example of several transformations which the hero of a tale may go through within a short space of time is as follows: The hero is pushed over a cliff by four mountain goats (who are transformed girls), but saves himself by changing into a ball of bird-down as he falls; later, he changes into a salmon, still later, into another sort of fish (North Pacific Coast). Hero tales contain perhaps the greatest number of transformation incidents, but they also occur in trickster tales with a fair amount of frequency: trickster becomes a dish; he enacts the role of Protean beggar by repeatedly asking for food in a different guise; he transforms himself into a baby in order to seduce women, and so forth. See Stith Thompson, *Tales of the North American Indians* (Cambridge, Mass., 1929), p. 362, "D. Magic, Transformation," for references and distribution. [EWV]

☞ Transformations of men into animals or vice versa constitute one of the favorite themes of South American mythology and folktale. A large number of these transformations are ascribed to the culture hero or to the divine Twins and represent a substantial part of their adventures and great deeds. However, these changes may occur for other reasons and be the expression of the will of the animal or of the person who assumes a new shape. [AM]

transformation as punishment A common incident of folktale, combining the transformation group of motifs (D0 ff.) with the punishment motifs (Q200 ff.). Often it is a witch who casts a spell and changes the prince or princess to some loathsome creature for an imagined slight. Sometimes, as is common in mythology, the mortal violates a tabu and is thus punished by the gods. Tiresias saw two snakes copulating and was changed into a woman. Actæon saw Artemis bathing and was changed into a stag. Lot's wife was changed into a pillar of salt for looking back. Io became a heifer when Zeus tried to cover up an amour, and was kept a heifer by Hera. Arachne became a spider because she rivaled Athena in spinning. In mythology the transformation is usually permanent, but the conventions of the märchen often require retransformation to take place.

transformation combat A struggle, usually between two magicians, in which each assumes various shapes in an attempt to defeat the other. The parlor game in which "stick breaks scissors, scissors cuts paper, paper wraps stick" bears a resemblance to the transformation combat. Proteus, the old man of the sea of Greek mythology, assumed many horrible shapes to avoid having to tell the truth to a questioner; if the questioner maintained his hold through the transformations, Proteus at last made his prophecy. The mortal Peleus won Thetis as his bride by keeping hold of the goddess until she returned to her proper shape. Achelous changed himself into a bull, but Hercules nevertheless defeated him. In the "Second Kalandar's Tale" of the *Arabian Nights*, the princess and the ifrit battle through many transformations: lion and sword; scorpion and serpent; vulture and eagle; cat and wolf; worm in a pomegranate seed and cock; fish and bigger fish, etc. In the Scottish ballad *The Twa Magicians* (Child #44) the smith vows to gain the lady's maidenhead; she changes into a dove, he into another, she into an eel, he a trout, she a duck, he a drake, she a hare, he a hound; mare, saddle; hot griddle, cake; ship, nail; blanket, bedspread; and there he had her. The ballad, according to Child, is known throughout southern Europe and among the Slavs. He points out that folktale parallels include the transformation flight (like the obstacle flight except that the ones fleeing rather than objects are transformed) and the master-vs.-apprentice magician combat in which the pupil eventually defeats his master.

Transformer A character in North American Indian creation tales, particularly in those of the North Pacific Coast and Plateau areas who, after the creation of the earth, travels about the world transforming animals and the physical environment into the form it has today. Usually the transformer is identical with the creator-culture-hero-trickster. On the North Pacific Coast, where the transformer aspect of the culture hero is especially stressed in mythology, Raven is the transformer among the Northern tribes, Mink and Kwati the transformers around Vancouver Island, and Bluejay the transformer of some of the tribes farther south. The southerly interior plateau tribes have a plethora of transformers: Among the Coeur d'Alene, Chief Child of the Root (who finally becomes Moon) is a transformer, while among related tribes, Moon, Coyote, four brothers, and the Chief are the transformers.

Many of the North Pacific Coast and Plateau transformer tales are trickster stories of deception; in some the cleverness of the transformer is illustrated, in others his stupidity gives point to the story. An Okanagon tale, for example, accounts for the Columbia River as follows: While traveling Coyote hears water dripping. He imitates the sound, but the noise does not stop, so he kicks the place where the water seems to be dripping; the noise then stops. Coyote jeers at the water and leaves; he is pursued by the water, to his annoyance. Finally he becomes thirsty and descends from the dry plateau on which he is traveling, to a small creek in a coulee; he goes down to the creek and drinks his fill, four times. Each time he drinks, being unaccountably thirsty, the stream increases in volume. He finally walks, first up to his knees, then to his waist, then to his armpits, in the water; at last he swims so that his mouth will be close to the water and he can drink all the time. Finally he has drunk so much that he loses consciousness. Thus the water got even with Coyote for kicking it, and thus from a few drops of water originated the Columbia River.

In most other parts of North America the transformer aspect of creators-culture-heroes is present, but is not stressed so strongly as it is in the Plateau and among the North Pacific Coast tribes; in one area at least, that of the Great Basin, transformer tales seem to be extremely rare, if not lacking altogether. For Eastern Woodlands transformer incidents see JUSKAHA; ANABOZHO. [EWV]

transvestites, transvestitism Men who dressed and behaved as women, doing woman's work such as gathering and preparing plant food, cooking, weaving baskets, collecting firewood, and women who dressed and behaved as men, doing man's work such as hunting and trapping, were not of uncommon occurrence in American Indian groups. In some tribes male transvestites "married" men, and the couples lived together; the same was occasionally true of female transvestites. In a great many tribes no social stigma attached to being a transvestite; many were shamans and, as such, respected for their powers to cure, to prevent or cause sickness, to find lost objects, and so forth. The Yuki of California called male transvestites "men-girls"; Yuki transvestites not only dressed as women, but were tattooed, and are reputed to have spoken in high, feminine tones. A Shasta transvestite, still living a few years ago, also spoke in high tones, enjoyed cooking and sewing, had been a shaman, but dressed in man's clothes. The Yuki transvestite sometimes married men. The number of transvestites per hundred population in any tribe is difficult to estimate, but probably was in proportion to the normal frequency of well-defined homosexuals in all populations.

Among the Navaho the transvestite enjoyed more opportunities for personal and material gratification, and was more respected and revered, than the normal individual. The reverse was true among the Pima, another Southwestern tribe. For bibliographic references to transvestism among American Indians and a discussion of Pima *berdaches* or transvestites, see W. W. Hill, "Note on the Pima Berdache" (AA 40, pp. 338–40, 1938). [EWV]

    Transvestitism in dances is always associated with vegetation or phallic rites. The best known instances are the Maid Marian of the Morris and the Bessy of the English sword dance. As in a similar carnival play in Thrace, she features in a wedding and a death and resurrection mime. The *Schemen* maskers are half and half male and female. The *seises* of Seville Cathedral and personages in the Basque *masquerade* likewise dress as women. The Mexican *malinche* is probably a blend of the European and a similar native concept (Aztec men danced as women in *menarche* rites). Transvestism features as satire in the *jardineiros* and *catrines*. The Aymara *marmichatha* or *memillaatha* similarly figures in dances.

In several Pueblo war and scalp dances men and women change clothes and roles, as in the *puwęre* of Santa Clara, also at the initiation of girls. A similar exchange takes place in the trading feast of Alaskan Eskimos.

In the Far East it is a custom, possibly descended from ritual, for men to take women's roles in the Japanese and Chinese theater (see KABUKI; ODORI; ONNAGATA). A decadent ritual vestige remains in the obscene dances at bazaars by the *khoja* caste of South India, men with women's robes and gestures. [GPK]

tree of life In the folklore of many peoples of the world, the great tree, evergreen, ever-blooming, ever-bearing, whose fruit assures its eater of immortality; also, the great tree that is the essence of all trees. To different groups, different trees were identified with the tree of life: the apple of the Celts, the peach of the Chinese, the date of the Semites, etc. The tree of life that stood in the Garden of Eden was not the prohibited tree, which was the tree of the knowledge of good and evil. J. G. Frazer reconstructs an original version of the story in which man was to choose between the tree of life and immortality and the tree of death. The serpent, in leading Eve astray, thus deprived man of the eternal life meant for him by the Creator. The tree of life is usually guarded, as was the apple tree of the Hesperides, by a dragon or serpent. Thus, the Biblical serpent may have been the archetype of the serpent in several folktales who brings the healing leaves that cure the dead man. Compare POLYIDUS. Oriental art, and thence Ægean art, have a stylized figure known as the tree of life, of which the branched candlestick (e.g. the menorah) is an example. The tree of life, a spreading branched tree bearing varied fruits, is a well-known quilting and embroidery design. See AGAVE; CASSIA; CROSS; DJAMBU BAROS; YGGDRASIL.

    Most Guiana Indian tribes (Carib, Maskushi, Arekuna, etc.) have a myth about a wonderful tree bearing all the food plants. This tree was first discovered by an animal, generally an agouti or a tapir, who after trying to keep the secret for himself was finally forced to divulge it. The culture hero and his brother felled the tree, thus causing the dispersion of the plants throughout the world. The trunk contained water which flooded the earth.

Versions of this same myth have been recorded among the Cuna and Choco Indians of Bolivia and the Witoto of the Putumayo River. The motif of the tree bearing the food plants was carried by the Arawakan Chane to the Gran Chaco. The Mataco and other Pilcomayo tribes know it, but according to them, the tree was full of fish. The Trickster provoked a flood when he shot one of the fish in the trunk. [AM]

trick, tricken bag Generic term for the southern U. S. Negro charm variously known as hoodoo hand, mojo or mojo hand, toby, grigri, etc. It is called fingers-of-death and sometimes root-bag, especially when intended or used to work evil. See JACK; ROOTS; WANGA.

    Trick is the name given by Trinidad Negroes to a magic charm which enables the owner to achieve his desired aims at the expense of others. Its opposite is called *guard,* the term for protective magic. As is customary in Negro cultures, however, the line between these two forms is not clearly drawn, so that both functions may be incorporated in a given charm. [MJH]

tricks North American Indian tales are full of tricks played by or on the Trickster, or by various other animal or supernatural characters on each other. Many of these are of a miraculous nature, such as those of a giant's arrows being broken in mid-air, or pumpkins being changed into ducks; some are broad practical jokes, such as the incident of Fox stealing the sleeping Trickster's feast, or that of the Little Startlers, or that of Trickster enticing birds to dance with their eyes closed and then wringing their necks, or that of luring people over a bank, where they fall to their death. Some are tricks of expediency, such as when the Chiricahua Apache character, Child-of-the-Water, wraps deer entrails around himself in order to be borne aloft to the nest of man-eating eagles; some are mischievous tricks, such as a third person annoying two companions who each believe the other is at fault, and causing the companions (sometimes two blind men, sometimes a man and his wife, or two old men) to fight. The number of tricks recounted in American Indian mythology must be legion; as a general rule in the tales, no sympathy is wasted on the person tricked. Sometimes tricks are successful, sometimes they fail; if a tabu is violated, they always fail. [EWV]

Trickster Tricksters are found in the unwritten literature of peoples over all the world, and usually many tales or cycles are devoted to their exploits. They vary with the fauna of the area in which they are found. Thus Coyote is a widespread trickster of North America, while Spider is the trickster of the Gold Coast and neighboring regions of West Africa. Psychologically, the role of the trickster seems to be that of projecting the insufficiencies of man in his universe onto a smaller creature who, in besting his larger adversaries, permits the satisfactions of an obvious identification to those who recount or listen to these tales. The trickster is frequently a character in the sacred mythology of a people, and is often regarded as the culture hero who has brought the arts of living to mankind. In at least one African mythological system, that of Dahomey, the divine trickster, Legba, youngest son of the creator, represents the philosophical principle of accident—the way out—in a world where fate is predetermined. See COYOTE; LEGBA; MAUI; REYNARD; YO. [MJH]

☞ Trickster is an important character, about whom many stories are told, in almost all North American Indian tribes: usually identical with the creator-culture-hero-transformer of these same tribes. The stories in which trickster and, usually, a companion are the chief characters can be grouped for each tribe into a loosely knit cycle: a considerable number of identical tales are told in various areas, as the adventures of different tricksters.

Most of the tricksters in North American mythology are animal-human beings. Characteristically the trickster is greedy, erotic, imitative, stupid, pretentious, deceitful; he attempts trickery himself in many forms, but is more often tricked than otherwise. In a sense, trickster is nearly always on the side of evil; if people die, he votes that they stay dead (and is punished by having his own son die and not being able to revive him); however, in several trickster tales, such as that of theft of light, or the sun, the people benefit by trickster's thievery and deceitfulness.

On the North Pacific Coast Trickster is also Transformer: Raven, Mink, or Bluejay. In the Plateau, in the Great Basin, in California, in the Southwest, and in parts of the western Plains the trickster *par excellence* is Coyote, best known of all North American Indian tricksters. In the Plains area as a whole Coyote is replaced by various named characters, a few of whom are thought of as coyote-human beings, others as spider-beings, others simply as mythical characters: some of these are Sendeh or Sendeh Old Man of the Kiowa, Old Man of the Blackfoot and Crow, Nihansan of the Arapaho, Inkotomi (Inktumni, Ishtiniki) of the Siouan tribes, Sitkonsky of the Assiniboin. In parts of the Great Basin and in the Southeast Rabbit is the chief trickster; in the Eastern Woodlands Nanabozho or the Hare and Wisakedjak (Whiskey Jack) are not only culture heroes, but to a certain extent tricksters as well. The tales told about the Southeastern and Eastern Woodlands tricksters are not nearly so numerous, however, as those told about the midwestern and western tricksters.

No trickster character or trickster tales comparable to the Indian ones mentioned above are told by the Eskimo. Although Coyote (and other animal characters) as trickster is a popular myth character in the Southwest among many tribes (Navaho, Apache, Pima, and so forth), Coyote stories are told in only one Pueblo group, namely, at Taos, where they have diffused from neighboring Plains tribes.

Characteristically, trickster stories often begin with the statement, "Coyote (or another trickster character) was going along. . . ." Then follows the tale of deceit, or violence, or thievery, which is usually fairly brief; in the end trickster is, as likely as not, killed, and the tale ends, "Then Coyote died there." Death is however never permanent; in the next Coyote story told by the raconteur, Coyote is very much alive again. Death and revivification may also occur within the tale itself as part of the plot; if such occurs Coyote, when he is revived by his companion, usually pretends that he has merely been asleep.

The matter of trickster's companion should perhaps be emphasized more than it has been in the past. Various animals play this role, Fox, Wolf, Wildcat, Lynx among them. At times these animals serve as stooges for trickster's braggadocious claims; at other times they completely outwit him, stealing meat that he has secured and set to cook, and so forth.

Trickster stories are told chiefly for amusement, and are greatly enjoyed by Indian audiences. Many tribes have definite tabus against the recital of trickster tales, especially in the summertime; among the rationalizations are the following—that the weather will become cold, no rain will fall, Coyote is around and will hear the stories and become angry, or Rattlesnake will bite narrator or listeners. There is no tabu against telling trickster tales, which are often obscene or erotic, in mixed Indian company, but Elsie Clews Parsons, when collecting myths among the Kiowa, failed to obtain any obscene Sendeh tales because the audience present when she was recording was a mixed one and white-influenced narrators were "ashamed" to tell such tales to her in front of a mixed audience.

For a recent summary discussion of North American Indian trickster tales see Stith Thompson *The Folktale*, pp. 319–328. He also lists, in *Tales of the North American Indians*, various motifs under the general title of Deceptions, which nearly all appear in trickster tales (p. 365, K). Some of these are of "contests won by deception" (such as Trickster's race); others are "thefts and cheats" (such as Trickster frightens people from food and eats it himself); "deceptive escapes and captures" (example, birds enticed into bag); "fatal or disastrous deceptions" (example, Trickster carried by birds and dropped), "seduction and deceptive marriages" (example, Trickster poses as woman and marries man); "deceiver falls into own trap" (example, originator of death first sufferer); "other deceptions" (examples, Trickster shams death and eats grave-offerings, impostor claims prize, Trickster poses as helper and eats women's stored provisions). In his Section J, The Wise and the Foolish, Thompson also lists various motifs which usually appear in Trickster tales; under "Fools," for example, appear such motifs as diving for reflected food or reflected enemy, sleeping Trickster's feast stolen, eye-juggler, bungling host, death through foolish imitation, and so forth.

A recent comprehensive study of one widely known trickster tale, that in which trickster feigns death, is buried, and then reappears in disguise in order to marry his own daughter, has been made by Henrietta Schmerler, "Trickster Marries His Daughter," *JAFL* 44, no. 172, pp. 196–207, 1931.

The combined role of creator and trickster in one character who is portrayed in one aspect as altruistic and creative, in another aspect as gross and greedy, is puzzling to Indian narrators, and is frequently commented upon by them. In few tribes is there a duplication of what occurs among the Navaho, namely, that Coyote as a holy being is one character, Coyote as a buffoon is quite another being. About the latter, "trotting or traveling" Coyote stories are told, often to children; these trickster tales are used to point a moral, namely, that if in the tales Coyote breaks many Navaho tabus, he is often punished, and Navaho children are *not* to do as Coyote does. Gladys A. Reichard's interpretation of Coyote among the Navaho does not emphasize the dichotomy between the secular and profane roles of Coyote. Her sketch of Coyote in *Navaho Religion* (2 vols., Bollingen Series XVIII, New York, 1950), vol. 2, pp.

422–26, is an excellent summary of Coyote as trickster.

A popular North American Indian trickster motif is the false bridegroom (K1915), which occurs in all parts of the continent. In the tale of the false bridegroom Trickster pretends to be a man of supernatural power; usually he is gifted to produce magic treasures. Because of his pretended gift he is able to marry girls whom he covets. At a dance, however, he is unmasked, and is subsequently deserted by the girls when they learn that their bridegroom is an impostor.

In a trickster tale of the North American Algonquians, Woodland Cree, and Ojibwa, Trickster transforms himself into a snake to get meat inside a skull which he has found. Before he gets his head out of the skull it is changed from that of a snake's head to his own. In several popular Plains Indian versions of a somewhat similar tale, Trickster sees mice performing a Sun Dance inside a buffalo skull. He sticks his head inside the skull to watch them, but cannot pull it out. After this episode the tale often continues with a recital of various misfortunes which befall Trickster while he is trying to extricate his head from the skull. [EWV]

Animals enticed over cliff is a common motif (K894.1) of the folktales of the western North American Indians: trickster by stratagem brings his victim to the edge of a precipice and pushes him or causes him to fall over the edge and then eats of the carcass. The incident is perhaps based on the primitive practice of driving herds of animals towards a cliff as a simpler method of obtaining meat supply than corralling. The tale in which Raven and Deer dispute before Raven pushes Deer over the cliff is found among the Bella Coola, Rivers Inlet, Kwakiutl, Nootka, and Comox. The Crow of Montana point out a gully in which are the bones of many animals, and explain that when buffalo, deer, or elk step over the opening it widens, precipitating them to the bottom of the gully, and then closes back to its former dimensions. Related to this is the North Pacific Coast story of the unstable bridge of reed, rotten log, etc., which breaks and drops the animal into a chasm.

The trickster is as important a character in South American as in North American Indian folklore.

In some tribes of the Chaco (Toba), it is Fox who plays the part of the lewd, boastful creature who throws himself into countless adventures which invariably end badly for him. The role of Fox in the folktales of the modern Quechua and Aymara Indians follows an identical pattern.

In the Amazonian area, the trickster is generally one of the mythical Twins. He takes absurd initiatives which bring trouble to him or to his brother or even cause his death. As in the Fox stories of the Chaco, the trickster comes back to life, thanks to the power of his brother the culture hero. As soon as he is alive, he runs into new adventures. In the Mataco and Apinaye folklore, Moon has the distinctive traits of the trickster. He dies several times while attempting to imitate the deeds of Sun.

The part of the trickster in Yahgan mythology is played by the culture hero who prevents the first men from enjoying advantages offered to them by the Creator and by his younger brother. [AM]

Trimūrti The Hindu trinity, including Brahmā, the creator, Vishnu, the preserver, and Śiva, the destroyer: the supreme spirit manifested in three forms and represented by one body with three heads. The personalities of the triad vary with the sects of India. Among the Śaivas the absolute or supreme spirit is Śiva and the others were produced by him from himself. Among the Vaishnavas it was Vishnu who became threefold.

triori or **trihory** A form of branle, a couple dance of Breton peasantry and of the Renaissance French court. The dancers circle to the left in lively duple time, with three side steps and a kick, followed by a jump and three kicks or *grues*. In the late 16th century the triori took the form of a kind of *cancan* for women, a vestigial fertility dance with high kicks and swirling skirts. In his observations on Huron Indian dances, Champlain likens one of their steps to the "triholy." [GPK]

Tristan, Tristram, or **Tristrem** Hero of the legend and romance of Tristan and Isolt. Tristan was probably a Pictish hero (Drostan). Borrowed by the Celts probably of Cornwall the legend developed into a love story on the pattern of the Irish *aited*, or elopement stories. Romanticized by the French it becomes common stock of European story.

An outline of the main plot is as follows: Tristan, nephew of King Mark of Cornwall, fights for Cornwall against the giant Morholt of Ireland and kills him, but in doing so he is terribly wounded. At the urging of the nobles who wish to destroy Tristan, King Mark orders Tristan placed in a boat and thrust out to sea. He is picked up by fishermen who take him to Isolt of Ireland, for she is renowned for her skill in healing, a skill learned from her mother, a lady from the land of the fairy. Isolt heals Tristan and falls in love with him. But her love turns to hate when she discovers, by a nick in his sword, that he had killed her brother, Morholt. Tristan, recovered, rids Ireland of a marauding dragon and then returns to Cornwall. In time he is sent back to Ireland to negotiate the marriage of Isolt and Mark. On the way back to Cornwall Tristan and Isolt accidentally drink the love potion Isolt's mother had prepared for Isolt and Mark. And so they come to love one another blindly and completely. On her wedding night Isolt sends her maid to substitute for her and for a while Mark does not know of the relation between his nephew and wife. Follows now a series of episodes telling of the clandestine meetings of Tristan and Isolt and finally of their elopement into the forest. There Mark eventually finds them asleep with Tristan's sword between them. Mark replaces Tristan's sword with his own. By that they know that Mark thinks they are innocent and that they must return to the castle. Later the nobles accuse Isolt to Mark and he is forced to order her to submit to the ordeal by fire. Tristan in disguise carries her across a stream so that she can swear truly, "I have never been in any other man's arms, except for this fellow who just now carried me across the stream, than those of my husband, King Mark." So she, swearing to the truth, comes unscathed through the ordeal. Finally they can no longer endure the torture of being together and not being together; Tristan goes over the seas to Brittany. There he finally marries Isolt of the White Hands because she loves him, but, remorseful, he cannot consummate the marriage. When he is mortally wounded in battle some time later Tristan sends a message to Isolt of Ireland asking her to come to him, and he directs the messenger to fly white sails if she is aboard, but black if she is not.

In time the vessel is sighted and the sails are white. Tristan, being told that the vessel is in the harbor, asks his wife, "What is the manner of her sails?" She replies, "Black, my lord, black as night." Tristan dies and Isolt when she finds him dead throws herself on his body and dies too, thus proving the words Isolt's mother uttered when she gave the love potion to the maid, "Guard this with your life for it contains love and death." [MEL]

☛ Since Miss Gertrude Schoepperle's book (*Tristan and Isolt*, Frankfort and London, 1913) was published a good deal of information has accumulated on the sources and migration of the Tristan legend. The original figure was a Pictish king (c. 780) named Drust, and to him was attached a story of the Perseus and Andromeda type (later attached to Cuchulainn in the *Wooing of Emer*), which was the source of the fight with the tribute-gatherer Morholt, the false claimant motif, and the recognition of the hero in the bath by a princess. The legend passed from Scotland to Wales, where it took many features of the Irish love story of Diarmuid and Grainne and where the hero was known as Drystan or Trystan, son of Tallwch. Probably there was a Cornish stage, which established Mark's court in the romantic castle of Tintagel, overlooking the sea. By 1000 the legend had reached Brittany, for after that date we find men who had been christened Tristan. The Breton story-tellers did much to shape the story and to add to it. The influence of the French word *triste* emphasized the tragic element, and the story of the second Isolt was patterned after the famous Arabic romance of Kais and Lobna. By 1150 Tristan was known to troubadours of the court of Poitou as the supreme lover, and a decade or two later Chrétien de Troyes was writing a poem (now lost) on Marc and Isolt, and the Anglo-Norman poetess, Marie de France, was familiar with the tradition both in oral and written form and incorporated a bit of it in her *Lai of the Honeysuckle*. There are several analogs to incidents of the legend in Breton folktales of the 19th century, e.g. the dragon-combat and false claimant theme, Mark's equine ears, the black and white sails. These Breton versions seem to be not so much derived from the romances as survivors from that fund of stories on which the early *conteurs* drew. [RSL]

Triton In Greek mythology, a monstrous son of Poseidon and Amphitrite, human from the waist up, fish from the waist down. Triton blew a conch-shell trumpet to raise or calm storms. He reared Athena as companion to his own daughter Pallas, for whom, after she had killed her in play, Athena fashioned the Palladium that kept Troy safe from its enemies. As with several such minor deities, the name Triton became a class name, and tritons were spoken of, while Triton himself became confused with such marine deities as Nereus and Proteus. Ichthyocentaurs or centauro-tritons also existed, like tritons but with the forelimbs of horses. Since many of the monsters of Greek myth have been traced back to Asiatic sources, it is not difficult to see in Triton a reminiscence of Dagon or Oannes, the fish-human god of western Asia.

troll A supernatural being of Scandinavian folklore, originally gigantic, but later, especially in Sweden and Denmark, conceived of as dwarfish and inhabiting caves and hills. These too, like the German dwarfs, were wonderful and skilful craftsmen. In Scandinavian folk-tale the trolls are usually huge ogres with the great strength and little wit of the typical ogre. They live in castles, guard treasure, hunt in dark forests, and burst if the sun shines on their faces. In the Shetland and Orkney islands the word survives as *trow*. Trows are regarded as inimical to mankind and are as closely associated with the sea as with the hills. Terror seizes any fisherman who sees a trow.

true stories It has been noted for several American Indian groups that a distinction is made by native narrators between so-called "true stories" and "lie," "joke," or other types of stories. This distinction does not, however, always jibe with that made by European folklorists between myth and tale. The Tübatulabal, for example, regard as true stories pseudohistorical accounts with human actors as their main characters, which are set in the present period; they include among these the Orpheus myth. All their tales which have animal actors and are set in the mythical age are also regarded as essentially true, but belonging to the long-ago; a different native name is used for them. The Kiowa, on the other hand, refer to as "true," ritual tales such as that of Split-Boys; the "lie" or "joke" story may concern Sendeh, their trickster, about whom tales are told with present-day, as well as old native settings. The Shawnee also regard as true stories the account of the creation of the Shawnee, accounts of their early migrations, as well as pseudohistorical accounts of happenings after the white men came. It is of interest to note that in this tribe also (as in several others beside the Tübatulabal) the Orpheus myth is told as a "true" story. "Joke" tales among the Shawnee are the trivial, tricksterlike stories having to do with Rabbit's, or Wisako's, or Raccoon's pranks. The Winnebago also distinguish between two types of native narratives: one (*waika*) is set in the irretrievable past, or mythical age, the other (*worak*) takes place within the memory of man (Paul Radin, *Winnebago Hero Cycles: A Study in Aboriginal Literature*, Indiana University Publications in Anthropology and Linguistics, Memoir 1, 1948, pp. 11–12). The Navaho likewise distinguish between two types of Coyote tales. In serious tales Coyote is taken as a serious character; in the more trivial tales, told to children to point a moral, he is a trickster, and such tales are referred to by the Navaho themselves as "Trotting Coyote" tales. These few examples represent native classifications of bodies of North American Indian mythology—a subject about which, as yet, little is known. In presenting their collections of North American Indian tales, few if any collectors have classified their material along strictly native lines; the usual procedure is to arrange the tales in the order of ritual tales (cosmology, cosmogony, etc.), trickster material, hero or adventure tales, and pseudo-historical narratives. [EWV]

trumpet A musical instrument consisting of a tube or narrow cone of wood, cane, bark, bone, metal, etc., enclosing a column of air which is set into sounding vibration by the lip vibration of the player, who blows into the end or a hole at the side; also a conch shell, gourd, or similarly shaped instrument of clay, and certain other instruments combining the tube with globular resonance chambers, as in many South American examples. The trumpet has been significant since Neolithic times to peoples of many races for religious and magical observances, burial rites, initiation ceremonies, curing, expulsion of evil spirits, communication with the dead and the gods, for fertility and weather charms, for sunset rites, for military signals and general alarms, for hunting calls, announcement of assemblies, arrivals, and festivities, for pacing or instituting work, or dance, or games. Thus its functions in some respects parallel those of the bullroarer, in others those of the flute, and in still others those of the drum.

The voice, shape, size, and material of the trumpet all contribute to its magical powers, though the variation of types is so great and the similarities in use are so frequent that no hard-and-fast separation as to the significance can be made. However, certain associations are common.

For example, the sound of primitive and folk-made trumpets is harsh, loud, compelling, frightening, adequate and suitable for attracting the attention of gods or spirits, whether malevolent or kindly, and for speaking instruments through which they may answer. To those who do not see the instrument, it can readily be accepted as the voice of god, monster, or spirit. It is powerful enough to frighten away any menacing being. The Cheremis use long trumpets of lime-tree bark to expel Satan; in Bali demons are summoned by trumpet or horn blasts to a feast, and then driven away; the Aymara Indians blow on cow's-horn trumpets to scare hail away. In its simplest form, the primitive trumpet is no more than a megaphone, which the shaman uses to magnify or disguise his own voice in magical utterances. The Payaguá shamans of the Chaco use a rudimentary calabash trumpet in this way, and in Ceram, one of the Moluccas, the chief speaks with the voice of the spirits through a bamboo trumpet at boys' initiations.

On a more mundane level, the sound of the trumpet is practical, since it can be heard over great distances and above other noises, for signals, alarms, and communications. Thus war trumpets have served the Romans, the Egyptians, the Jews, the Incas, English armies at Crécy and Halidon, and the Abipón of South America, to name a few, for military signals in camp and in battle and to carry fear to the hearts of the enemy. The bugle still preserves some of the functions of the military trumpet, though modern mechanized warfare, with telephone, cable, and radio communications, has robbed it of others. For other kinds of signaling, the blast of conch, horn, or brass has been used for centuries. In ancient Tahiti, a large conch shell (*pu-ta' i-i-te-aeha*) was carried in the canoes on long voyages so that communications could be maintained between separate crews and so that the arrival of a party could be announced to the islands. Fiji Islanders use conch-shell trumpets to call meetings and to convoke labor groups. The long ivory trumpets of Dahomey, formerly used to announce the approach of the king, now serve occasionally for signaling. In 17th-century German cities, trumpet music played from tower tops was used as a time signal at noon and sunset.

The shape of the trumpet may be a straight tube, with or without a bell at the end. In this form, as often made of a hollow cane or branch or bone, it is, in primitive concept, essentially a male instrument, associated with the phallus, procreation, fertilization, and rebirth. Like the flute, it is appropriate, therefore, for funeral ceremonies, invoking a new life, and for rites of circumcision and other initiation practices admitting boys to the status of men. The Babwende of the Belgian Congo actually carve their funeral trumpets in phallus shape. In initiation ceremonies, the Ceram rites cited above are characteristic of many. The ceremony, which admits boys to the Kakian society, is conceived as a death and resurrection of the initiates. The long bamboo trumpet sounds periodically through the several days as the boys ostensibly have their heads chopped off by devils, die, and are restored to life. The trumpet is the voice of the devils.

Trumpets of this type are often tabu for women, as the bullroarer is. Among the Uaupes of the Orinoco, for example, women who see the trumpet are poisoned; boys may not use it until after their initiation rites of beating and fasting; when not in use it is hidden in a stream.

The longer the tube, the deeper the voice of the instrument. Thus, some of the deep-voiced straight trumpets are of extreme length. The reed trumpet (*erke*) of the Andes is 21 feet in length and is jointed so that it can be folded up when not in use. The 16-foot copper trumpets of the Mongols and Tibetans, played in lamaistic rites, are either supported by an attendant or rested on the ground for playing. A tremendous spirally wound bark trumpet of the Orinoco tribes, sometimes called the "devil," has two projecting sticks bound along its length to permit a helper to support it. In China, tubular metal trumpets carried in funeral processions are so long that they can be played only when the march comes to a halt and the instruments can rest on the ground. They can be collapsed when not in use.

Certain peoples skilled in bronze work have solved the length problem by the construction of looped and spiral shapes, retaining the full length of tube required for the sound and yet producing easily portable instruments. The 11-foot *cornu* of the Romans was a coiled trumpet, of which the menacing growl described by Horace was heard at funerals, public festivities, military processions, etc.

Other trumpets assume a curved or bent shape, in which form they are frequently indistinguishable from horns, and may, even when made of metal, reflect the animal horns used for hunting signals, religious purposes, etc. The northern European *lur* is an example of the horn shape. The crescent form of many horns, as in the Jewish *shofar*, has seemed to many peoples especially appropriate for new moon rites. Occasionally a hook-like curve is produced by the extension of a straight cane with a cow's horn or calabash, a primitive construction pre-dating the bronze *lituus* of Rome, which imitated its curve, and still used among certain South American Indians and in Burma and Ethiopia. The Colombian tribes often use a five-foot cane with a calabash bell as a funeral trumpet.

Materials of the straight and curved trumpets in primitive and folk usage often are meaningful: bone is thought of as phallic, and as retaining the powers of the being from which it was taken; horn, as bearing the characteristics of the animal on which it grew; wood, as retaining the magic meaning or quality of the tree. The willow bark used for trumpets of the Whitsuntide ceremonies in Bohemia and elsewhere in Europe is not only appropriate and available, but part and parcel of the idea of killing the king of the occasion, a tree spirit dressed in willow branches.

When the shape of the trumpet is more globular, as in the conch shell, the gourd, or the rounded clay form, the fertility significance to some peoples is female. In the case of the conch, shell means water and tides, moon and menses. Thus men may even be excluded from its use, as in New Ireland, where the conch shell sounds in women's pregnancy rites, and men may not use it for their dancing. Because of its power over water, it can either bring or prevent rain, and thus benefit crops. The pottery trumpets of the ancient Peruvians were made in imitation of shells, and Central American rain priests blow them. Apart from shape, both gourd and clay may have more female meaning because agriculture and pottery-making are female industries in many primitive societies.

Some types of trumpet, as played, represent a combination of straight forms with pots or other vessels. The Saliva used cane tubes thrust into side mouths of clay jars, and along the upper Rio Negro a similar instrument called the "roarer," consisting of a tube tied into a jar, is used for the jaguar dance. In the New Hebrides, in Ceylon, and in the Congo, trumpets are also blown into hollow vessels, sometimes partly filled with water. By these methods the sound of the instrument is made louder and more unearthly, and the fertility symbolism is enhanced by the mimesis of combining male and female forms.

A construction peculiar to South American Indians is the polyglobular trumpet, which somewhat resembles the playing combination just mentioned. Among the Bororo this type consists of three or four gourds joined end to end by wax. Funeral trumpets of the Saliva were clay tubes broadened at intervals into two or three rounded hollow resonance chambers. These produced a deep bassoonlike note suitable for mourning.

It is obvious from a comparison of the beliefs about trumpets on a world-wide basis that the sound has greater influence than the shape. Almost any sort of trumpet may be a funeral instrument, depending on the typical crafts of the people and the material available. The primitive ideas of fertility and rebirth may be vestigial or even completely lost in modern or highly civilized usage. The bugle, as still used for military funerals, plays *Taps*, in token of the long sleep. Sunset rites are performed with both straight trumpets, such as the alphorn, and curved horns, as in India. Witches, devils, and demons of bad weather, sickness, and madness, may be exorcised with any type of trumpet.

The more specific sex connotations and tabus related to shape are more localized than the general magical and religious concepts in which the instrument speaks with a terrifying voice and brings a response either in sound or in activity from an other-world power or being. The straight trumpet is never a woman's instrument, though the customs vary as to whether women may participate in the ceremony of its playing, see or hear the instrument. While the Uaupes kill women who see the bark trumpet, their nearby neighbors the Wapishana, Taruma, etc., permit women to see it. Women were excluded from the all-day music and dance ceremony (*corroboree*) of the Australian natives of Arnhem Land, in which the flight of the bees is imitated and the long wooden trumpet, *didgeridoo*, contributes its bass blasts. The conch shell and the other trumpets ideologically connected with female fertility, while occasionally re-

served for women's rites, as in the New Ireland ceremony mentioned above, serve in many other places as the instruments of the circumcision rites, as in Madagascar, to call the dead, as in the New Hebridean feast of the dead, which involves the ritual slaughter of boars, etc. The Sherente of South America use the gourd trumpet to frighten women.

Paired trumpets of any shape, thought of in some cultures as male and female, have been used widely. These are seldom combined for musical purposes of harmony or counterpoint. The duplication has more to do with the magic of twins and with the interests of symmetry. Six-foot wooden tubes of black bamboo, played in pairs, are used for wedding music among the Guayquire and Mapoye of South America. Various South American instruments of this character may be distinguished as either trumpets or giant flutes, depending upon the construction of the mouthpiece. Other examples of pairing occur in the *lurer*, in shell trumpets of Melanesia, and in curved or straight forms of India, Tibet, and ancient Afghanistan.

Primitive sex tabus and connotations, the original meaning of which is extinct in current usage, survive in connection with the shofar, and with the Advent trumpet of southern Holland, which is concealed in a well between usings. In Europe the restrictions most generally applied to trumpets were formerly in relation to class. Only royalty, high nobility, cavalry regiments, and certain cities could employ trumpeters.

Whatever the shape or the material of the trumpet, its sound in many religions is devoted to the service of the gods and its origin often is credited to a special god. The conch shell is used in the Trinidad Shango cult to warn the gods of trouble. Tibetan religious ceremonies make use of either the thigh-bone trumpet or the long copper trumpet. Long bamboo trumpets called *vaccines* are used in the Rara pre-Easter processional dance of Haitian Negroes. Fijian priests used large shell trumpets in their houses of worship, and the chiefs and priests of ancient Tahiti used huge conch shells for processions and pronouncements. A sacred Tahitian trumpet, according to legend, was thrown into a whirlpool with other properties of the old religion when Christianity overthrew the old gods. This trumpet was brought from Po, the spirit world of darkness, by the children of a king, who were lost and wandered into Po. In temples of the Bombay region, horns and trumpets are blown night and morning by devlis. In Bengal a conch shell is blown at the recitation of the *Purāṇas*. In the Bible, it is recorded that the Lord told Moses to make a pair of silver trumpets for signaling and alarms, for the opening of a new month, and to blow over burnt offerings. These, together with the ram's-horn shofar, which survives in use today, were among the most important of the instruments serving the worship of Jehovah and used in calling upon him for aid. In Jewish post-Exilic custom, a Feast of Trumpets was initiated for the first day of the 7th month. In the Far East, Buddhist priests use the end-blown shell trumpet.

Sea gods, moon gods, and rain gods are particularly associated with trumpets. In Greek mythology, Triton, son of Poseidon and Amphitrite, is the trumpeter of the deep. He controls the waves and conquers giants by the blast of his conch shell. His children, the Tritons, also blow conches and attended the rape of Europa with their blowing as the great bull bore her across the water. The conch shell, either as a trumpet or as a sacrificial vessel, is an attribute of Vishnu, Lord of the Waters, who as Krishna wrested it from Panchajana, an undersea demon, and its name (*śankha*, meaning conch shell) is the second name of his wife Lakshmī. Vishnu is pictured as holding the conch shell, which commands the mystical syllable *om*, as does the tambura (lute) of Śiva. A metal trumpet was used in the worship of Osiris, fertility god of Egypt, who was credited with inventing the instrument, and the conch was the attribute of the ancient Mexican rain god Tlaloc.

When the last day of earth comes, the trumpet will sound (A1093). It may be the conch shell blown by Śiva above the licking flames; or it may be the ram's horn of Israel sounding the resurrection, which carries over into Christian concept as the trumpet blown by the angel Gabriel on Judgment Day. "Where will you be when the trumpet sounds?" asks a Negro spiritual of the sinner. And a song of the East Tennesseean mountain whites says, "The ram's horn blowed; the children did shout/ The winders flew open and they all looked out./ Oh, John, sing hallelujah, Fer the spirit of the Lord has fell upon me."

The trumpet figures in a number of folktale patterns, including the singing bone motif (E632 ff.) Magic trumpets (D1221; D1222), wishing trumpets (D1470.1.33), resuscitation by blowing a trumpet (E55.3), a statue blowing a trumpet at the approach of a stranger (D1317.9.1), and trumpet is blown before the house of one sentenced to death (P612) are among the folktale motifs. See ALPHORN; DA-CHA; HORN; LAMBI; LUR; POTOTO; SHOFAR. [TCB]

☞ Many South American Amazonian tribes, especially those of the Orinoco and of the Caiari-Uaupes basins, symbolize nature demons and their ancestors by huge bark trumpets which are kept hidden from the women in special huts or in some sacred spots. These instruments are referred to in travelers' accounts as the trumpets of Yurupari. The Arawakan tribes carried the cult of the trumpets south of the Amazon. It figured prominently in the religion of the Moxo and Paressi Indians. See YURUPARI. [AM]

tryst foiled The motif of a number of European popular ballads in which a suspicious husband pretends to depart but hides in the house in order to spy on his wife and her lover. The lover arrives and at the crucial moment the husband "discovers" them.

One of the strangest and most tragic of the tryst foiled stories is the Old Irish *Baile of the Clear Voice*.

Baile of the Clear Voice was the son of Buan mac Caba of Ulster. Men and women loved him for his beauty and his sweet voice (Baile the Sweet-spoken, he was called) but his love was given to Ailinn, daughter of Luġaid, king of Leinster. They made a tryst to meet one time at Ros na Ríg on the River Boyne. Baile got there first and as he waited with his companions, saw a strange figure, yet in the shape of a man, approaching from the south. Baile's people asked news of him, but all he said was that he had no news, except that Ailinn had given her love to Baile and was going to meet him when the youths of Leinster prevented her and she died of grief from being held back. It was druid truth, he said, that Baile and Ailinn were not to have

their love in life, but would meet after death. Baile died of grief for Ailinn. He was buried there on the strand and a yew tree grew out of his grave. Then the vision turned south and met Ailinn on her way to see Baile. She asked him for news. He said he had no news, except that he had just seen the men of Ulster digging Baile's grave upon the strand and putting his name on a stone beside it. It was prophesied, he said, that they should not meet in life, but after death. Ailinn fell dead with grief for Baile, and an apple tree grew out of her grave. In seven years the poets cut down the yew tree on Baile's grave. They made a poets' tablet of it and wrote thereon the visions and love tales of Ulster; and it happened that the feast tales and wooings and visions of Leinster were written on a like tablet from Ailinn's apple tree. During one Samain celebration held by Art, son of Conn, in Tara, these two tablets were brought to the feast, and Art asked to see them. As he held them, they sprang together face to face and no man could pull them apart. After that they were kept with the treasures of Tara, until they were burned by raiding Leinstermen in the reign of Cormac mac Airt.

Tsai Shên The God of Wealth of Chinese folklore. All classes do homage to the God of Wealth. His images frequently contain the wealth-producing box, Ho Ho Er Hsien (the spirits of concord), the three-legged frog, the Bat, children, coins, and ingots. Days of pilgrimage to his shrines are the second day of the First Moon and the 15th day of the Ninth. [RDJ]

tsamikos A folk dance of modern Greece for men and women in arbitrary order. They progress in an open round, linked by their hands, in counterclockwise direction. To fast clarinet or Turkish bagpipe tunes in triple time, they weave grapevines—a short one to the left, a long one to the right—finishing each phrase with a hop and a flourish of the free foot. A subtle flexion of the knees and vertical pulsation of body and arms marks each step. The leader, sometimes connected to his neighbor by a kerchief, embroiders the step with leaps, squats, and pivots, and with punctuated shouts. The dance is spectacular when performed by soldiers of the Evzone guard, notably on Easter Sunday. Though in "the old country" the tsamikos are fading in popularity before the encroachment of the modern ballroom dances, Greek communities in America continue to dance the *tsamikos, syrtos,* and *hasapikos* at weddings and other festivities.

Tradition traces the *tsamikos* to a martial dance of the Klephts, or guerrillas, during the Turkish occupation—a fierce round punctuated with cries and the brandishing of sabers and firing of pistols. In mountain retreats men still vie with each other in the intricacies of the virile version of this dance. [GPK]

Tsao Chün or **Shên** The kitchen god of Chinese folk belief; god of the stove or hearth; also known as *Tsao Kung* and *Tsao Wang*, Lord or Prince of the hearth. Rich and poor, ignorant and educated alike perform his ceremonies. He returns to heaven once a year—though some think he returns several times a month—to report on the misdeeds of the family.

His annual journey is on the 23rd, 24th, or 26th of the Eleventh Moon (depending on the part of China). He returns a week later. After the evening meal on the date of his departure, sticky sweets and agglutinated rice are offered him, because he likes them and in hopes that his lips will stick together and he will make no bad reports. Then his paper image, together with, at times, petitions prepared by the Taoists, is burned. At times strings of firecrackers are set off and rice brandy is offered.

The rules he enforces have to do with hygiene and decency. A few of them are listed here: In his presence there must be no irreverence toward Heaven or Earth, cursing of weather, or any thing which might hurt the feelings of any spirit. Ancestral sacrifices must be performed, filial piety observed; the wife must show reverence to the father and mother of her husband. Wives must show deference to their husband's uncles and members of his family; they must not quarrel with neighbors. Fraternal discord is prohibited. The five cereals must not be wasted or spoiled. Living creatures must not be killed in the kitchen either for food or for sacrifice. Onions, garlic, or vegetables with strong odor must not be cut on the stove. In front of the stove obscenities must not be spoken nor may gross songs be sung. One must not weep or become angry. One must not be naked in front of the stove. Babies may neither urinate nor evacuate in the kitchen. Flesh of dog, beef, or game may not be cooked on the kitchen stove. The following may not be burned in the kitchen stove: old papers, feathers, animal bones, old rags, old brooms, hair or anything with a bad smell. Women may not bind their feet, dry their feet, comb their hair, or nurse children at the stove. Soiled clothes or dirty shoes may not be dried by the kitchen stove. After meals no dirty dishes may be left in the kitchen or on or near the stove. Stoves must be rebuilt each year. When ants or insects make their nests in old stoves Tsao Chün becomes angry. Poor people must rebuild at least once every three years. Only very clean bricks and mortar may be used. The door of the stove must face southeast. No animal may ever be put in a pot on the stove while it is alive. Incense may not be lighted at the stove or burned in the oven. Water must not be left in the cooking utensils overnight. Spitting near or toward the stove is prohibited. Vegetables may not be chopped on the stove. Clothes or hands may not be washed in the cooking pot or on the stove. Women, when tending the fire, may not squat with their legs spread one on each side of the stove door. Women may not sacrifice to Tsao Chün within a month after childbirth. No chicken or dog can spend the night in front of the kitchen stove. Kitchen utensils can safely be washed on the following dates of each month: 2, 6, 10, 11, 14, 20, 21, 23, 28 (other authorities give other lucky days).

Burn incense before Tsao Chün's image morning and evening. Light a lamp in his honor the 1st and 15th of every month. If propitiated on certain cyclical days during the first month of each year, Tsao Chün will help in sericulture. Though women may propitiate him, the annual sacrifice is done by the male head of the household, as he is responsible for the good conduct of his family. While Tsao Chün is absent reporting, the rules of propriety are relaxed. On the date of his return a new image is pasted up and welcoming sacrifice is offered.

R. D. JAMESON

Ts'ao Kuo-ch'iu One of the Eight Immortals of Chinese mythology. Ts'ao was related to the reigning Sung family in that dynasty. After murdering another man's

wife, he was freed by general amnesty and practiced perfection. He was admitted to the band because he had "the disposition of a genie," also because one of the grottos of the upper spheres where the Immortals lived happened to be vacant. [RDJ]

Tuan Yang The Dragon Boat Festival, a popular festival of China celebrated on the 5th day of the Fifth Moon. Special cakes are made for the day and wrapped with leaves in a triangular shape. In earlier times they were thrown into the water as propitiatory sacrifices to the ancestors, water spirits, etc. Races are held in boats with dragon-shaped heads. The festival is associated with the Dragon King who controls rains. One of the various origin stories for the festival is that a Chinese scholar of the 3rd century B.C., grieving over the evils of the government, drowned himself in protest: the boat races symbolize the search for his body. [RDJ]

tuatal Literally (Irish), a turning to the left; the countersunwise turn or "unholy round" of Irish folklore: opposite of deiseal. It is performed to effect a curse or bring illness, even death, upon an enemy. Stones and other objects were turned antisunwise to effect a curse or bring bad luck. At Inishmurray in Sligo are a group of spotted stones called cursing stones, which when turned to the left work the curse in the mind or on the tongue of the turner. The countersunwise turn also symbolizes riddance, however, for a few drops of water from a backwards-turning mill will get rid of whooping-cough; and going tuatal around the house will work riddance to the disease of an inmate. But when herbs spin countersunwise in a boiling pot it is usually taken as a sign that the remedy being prepared will have no effect or that the patient will die. Anciently to drive a chariot tuatal around a fort was a signal of defiance and enmity, and constituted a challenge. See BOÁNN; WITHERSHINS.

Tuatha Dé Danann Literally, the people of the goddess Danu: the gods or the divine race of Old Irish mythology, also often referred to as the Tuatha Dé, the people of the goddess. They came upon Ireland from the east over the sea, shrouded in clouds of mist, and defeated the Fomorians. See BATTLE OF MAG TURED.

The *Book of Invasions* identifies these people as descendants of Nemed, or that one of the three groups who scattered after the defeat of the Nemedians and who became learned and powerful in the northern isles of Greece, and returned because it was their right. They were a tall, strong, and beautiful people, learned in magic and druidism and the scientific arts. They brought to Ireland with them four wonderful talismans: the Stone of Fal (see LIA FÁIL), the infallible sword of Nuada, Dagda's inexhaustible caldron, and the invincible spear of Lug. The date of their coming to Ireland, as figured from the *Book of Invasions*, was the middle of the 15th century B.C.

The Tuatha Dé Danann were eventually defeated by the Milesians and retired into the hills and mounds (*side*) of Ireland, which they divided into kingdoms among them. Dagda took the Brug na Bóinne, for instance, on the north bank of the River Boyne near Stackallen Bridge, Leinster. Henceforth they were called *aes side*, people of the mounds, or *fir side*, men of the mounds; eventually they came to be named for their dwellings, just *side* (pronounced shee). The *Book of*

Armagh mentions them as *dei terreni;* and today they are still regarded as earth spirits.

The Tuatha Dé Danann were euhemerized as mortal warriors in the Mythological Cycle, but as possessing extraordinary size, beauty, wizardry, and magic. In the tales they appear as a strange mixture of god plus mortal plus spirit. They were immortal yet could be slain in battle; they loved and married human beings; they were marvelous transformers; they were visible or invisible at will; they could give supernatural aid to favorites or send defeat and death to offenders. They lived in an otherworld known variously as Mag Mór, the great plain, Mag Mel, the pleasant plain, Tir na n'Og, the Land of Youth, or Land Under Wave, etc. This was the immortal land of music, ale, and beautiful women, without want, sickness, or death. As underground dwellers in the hills and mounds (*side*) they eventually developed into the fairies of modern Irish folklore. Mortals still pay visits to or are enticed into the mounds, with the usual results, i.e. years seem days, eating fairy food prevents their return to this world, etc. Seventeen of the mounds exist today and are pointed out to sightseers as the graves of certain princes of the Tuatha Dé Danann; the legendary kings of pagan Ireland were also buried in them. The three largest are New Grange, Dowth, and Knowth.

Tuchaipa   The name of the creator among several Yuman tribes of southern California and Arizona. The Yuma tribe itself calls its creator Kwikumat; the Diegueño, a California Yuman tribe, refers to its creator as Mayoha. [EWV]

Tukma   Creator of the first human being in the mythology of the southern California Juaneño Indians. As soon as Tukma got the ocean to the right size, he created Ehoni, the first human being. Ehoni had two descendants, Sirout (a bit of tobacco) and Ikaiut (above), who became the parents of Wiyot or Wiamot, progenitor and culture hero of the Juaneño Indians.

tulasī   The sacred or holy basil of India: so sacred in itself that it is worshipped as a deity. The tulasī (*Ocymum sanctum*) is grown in almost every Hindu household, and especially in the courtyards of those who worship Vishṇu. It is believed to be Lakshmī (wife of Vishṇu) incarnate, or Sītā, and the devout Hindu woman circumambulates the plant daily with offerings of rice and flowers. Its leaves heal the sick and are a remedy against snakebite. Sprigs of it are inserted in the rice-balls used to feed the dead during the *śrāddha* ceremony, for Yama cannot look upon a man who dies with this sacred plant in contact with his body. During eclipses all housewives take leaves of tulasī, sprinkle them with Ganges water, and place them in water jars and cooking vessels to keep them pure until the eclipse is over. When a well is dug or a tank built, the water is given its fertilizing powers only after a tulasī plant has been wedded to the anchorite representing Vishṇu at a solemn ceremony.

Tung Wang Kung   The Taoist Lord of the Immortals. When the primitive and inactive void moved to produce creatures, it created first in the east the sovereign male principle *yang*. Tung Wang Kung is the Lord of the East. His consort, Hsi Wang Mu, was formed from the female principle, *yin*. The congress of these two produced heaven and earth and all the creatures. Tung Wang Kung is attended by a male servant, the Young

Immortal, and a female servant, the Jade Girl. Lavender clouds are the roof over his palace and the blue skies are its walls. [RDJ]

Tuonela or **Manala**   The kingdom of Tuoni or Mana, the dead-land of the Finns; a common underworld for all. Tuonela is a dusky island, and according to the folk songs, life there is as in the grave. On the way to it one has to cross the black river on which neither sun nor moon ever shine, and over which stretches a bridge. The dead are usually transported over this river in a boat. Väinämöinen visited Tuonela while still alive in search of ancient wisdom, but without success. Only with great difficulty did he succeed in escaping. "Many heroes cross the channel but few return from Tuonela to tell the story" (see *Kalevala*, song 16). [JB]

Tuonetar or **Manatar**   The daughter of Tuoni or Mana. In the *Kalevala* she takes Väinämöinen in a boat to the island of the dead. The belief about the crossing of a river of death in a boat is derived, according to U. Harva, from Greek mythology. [JB]

Tupan   The ancient thunder demon in the mythology of the eastern Tupi-Guarani tribes of South America. His name was adopted by the early missionaries to designate the Christian God and is still in use in the Guarani spoken by converted Indians and mestizos of the Amazon basin. The word *tupan* has taken on the meaning of sacred. [AM]

tupilaq   One of the souls of the dead in Davis Strait Eskimo mythology: so termed during its stay in Sedna's house in Adlivun. Sometimes it returns to the village and roams around. It is greatly feared and is never allowed to enter a house. If the angakok sees it first, warning is sent to all the people to stay in their houses, for its touch will kill and the sight of it causes disease. It knocks desperately on the doors of the huts in the fall seeking shelter from the icy storms. But the angakok invokes the help of the good spirits against the terrible one and after a while it goes away. When the soul's year in Adlivun is up and it goes to Adliparmiut, it is then called an *adliparmio* and is no more feared.

The Greenland Eskimo designate as tupilaq a supernatural creature devised by them to outwit and destroy their enemies. It is made from the parts of various animals and can appear in the shape of any of them. This idea seems to be unknown among the Central Eskimo.

turadji   Quail: a woman's solo dance of Azerbaijan. It uses the typically Persian triple time, like the *täräkämä*, but in slower tempo, and the same fundamental swaying cross two-step. Holding a large silk scarf or two kerchiefs to suggest the wings of the quail, the dancer circles counterclockwise, sometimes with the two-step, sometimes with a slow pivot, lightly touching the ground with the free toe to effect the turn. She drops the scarf, then dances forward, opening and closing her arms and hands; then she looks for the scarf and continues dancing as at the beginning. The style has the same gracious restraint as other native women's dances of this region, and the same individuality of interpretation as to tempo, sequence of steps, and quality. [GPK]

Turkey   A popular character in Jicarilla and other Apache Indian mythologies. Turkey is the beneficent character who brought corn to the people; he is associated with corn and crops. It was Turkey, also, who aided in the growth of the emergence mountain, who fooled the cannibal Big Owl, and who fought with Eagle. Turkey Hactcin, or Holy One, is also associated with corn and farming, and in one Jicarilla myth he brings tobacco which he himself has raised, and shows people how to make cigarettes.

Turkeys were the only birds domesticated in pre-Columbian times by the Indians; their occurrence at that period was limited to the Southwest, although in many other regions such as the eastern United States, wild turkeys were hunted for food. In the pueblos domesticated turkeys are used as food and as sacrifices; at Zuñi during the Shalako dances the clowns give children kachina dolls hung with bread in the shape of turkeys. Turkey feathers are used in the Southwest for making cloaks or blankets; they are put on prayer sticks and used as a charm. These feathers are associated with clowns and the dead. [EWV]

turkey dance A non-sacred imitation of the motions of a turkey, confined to dances of North American Indian tribes, whom the bird serves as a traditional delicacy; thus the Comanche, Delaware, Choctaw, Seminole. In the northern Ute turkey or jigging dance—*tho'nka-ni'tcap*—men and women thrust their heads forward and wag them from side to side, as they toe-heel rapidly in an erratic course. The music is equally humorous and erratic, with variable melodies and changing drum beats.

Mexican tribes have drawn little choreographic inspiration from the *guajolotl* (turkey) in spite of its gastronomic importance. He is supposed to have originated the Tarahumara *rutuburi*, but not to the point of mimicry. On the other hand, a courtship dance of the Huichol Indians of Jalisco and Nayarit at the same time imitates the turkey. [GPK]

Turkey Girl A character in various Pueblo Indian myths, especially those from Taos and Tewa pueblos. In a Taos collection Turkey Girl is a young woman who outwits Coyote; Turkey Old Woman is a grandmother who lives with her grandson. In a Tewa myth which is probably a Pueblo version of Cinderella, turkeys befriend a poor girl; they dress her up, and give her beautiful hair; she goes to a dance, and sleeps with a suitor. Finally she goes west with the turkeys to Shipap, and her mother accuses her of being a witch. [EWV]

Turkey in the Straw A lively American dance tune, a favorite of fiddlers, banjo-pickers, etc. It is the same melody as a minstrel song, *Old Zip Coon*, sung at the Bowery Theater in New York in 1834, and has many parody offshoots. *There Was an Old Soldier* ("and he had a wooden leg") is a Civil War period example. Another is a drinking song, "There was an old hen/ And she had a wooden leg,/ Finest old hen that ever laid an egg/ And she laid so many eggs all around on the farm/ That another little drink won't do us any harm." The origin of the tune has been suggested as the English *Haymaker's Dance*, the Irish *Rose Tree in Full Bearing* or *My Grandmother Lived on Yonder Little Green*.

turmeric The root of an East Indian plant (*Curcuma longa*) of the ginger family, extensively cultivated (especially in India and China) as a dyestuff, aromatic stimulant, and flavoring agent. The name may be from French *terre-merite*, from Medieval Latin *terre merita*, deserved

or deserving earth; some scholars, however, regard it as derived from Sanskrit *kunkuma*, saffron, a not too surprising conclusion since it has been used as a substitute for the saffron yellow dye for centuries.

Because of its color turmeric is an auspicious plant in Hindu belief; it has great erotic significance and is involved in wedding rites and sex relationships. Any garment marked with turmeric becomes lucky. A girl's body is smeared with turmeric before her wedding; her wedding garments are dyed with it; and the clothes of a pregnant woman are also marked with turmeric. The marriage contract is sprinkled with the powder, which is also daubed on the walls of the groom's house. And five pieces of turmeric are among the offerings involved in the Hindu ceremony of dedicating the young sacred prostitute to the temple. In the *Rāmāyana*, turmeric is mentioned as one of the eight ingredients of the *Arghya*, a respectful oblation made to gods and elderly men.

Supernaturals, especially evil spirits, dislike the smell of burning turmeric. In Bengal this ghost-test is still sometimes made to discover whether a person is an ordinary mortal or a ghost. Among the Khonds in Bengal human sacrifices were formerly made in the cultivation of turmeric, in the belief that it could not have its deep color unless blood was shed. In Orissa turmeric mixed with oil is rubbed on the body of a dancing girl for five days before she takes up residence with a wealthy man. In some parts of India married women dip their hands in turmeric water and pass them lightly over their cheeks to prevent the visitation of Lakshmī.

Turon A festival observed by Polish peasants in the period following Christmas Day, a survival of an ancient festival in honor of the winter god Radegast. It takes its name from the *turon*, a fabulous beast with enormous wooden head and jaws that open and close, chief of the animal disguises which the peasants assume as they go from house to house, celebrating, singing carols, and receiving food and drink. Other costumes represent a wolf, bear, or goat.

turquoise A greenish-blue opaque precious stone, principally phosphate of alumina. Oriental or true turquoise is found principally in a mountain range in Persia, coming into Europe through Turkey, hence its name. Among the Poles and Russians it is the birthstone of December and dedicated to Saturn; it has also been called a stone of Venus and Mercury.

Turquoise is to the Tibetans what jade is to the Chinese. They believe it to be a stone of good fortune, physical well-being, and a protection against contagion and evil eye, a belief which is quite general. Hindu mystics say it will bring immeasurable wealth if on first looking at the new moon, you immediately look at a turquoise. It is the national stone of Persia, and Iranian peasants place a piece of turquoise in a sheep's eye as an amulet against evil eye. In northern India it is worn in the water to protect a bather from serpents and boils. It removes animosity when given and is a favorite gift between lovers. In the 17th century it was worn mainly by men and was considered effective only if it was received as a gift. It prevented falls and bodily harm, but a part would crack off each time it exerted its influence. From the 13th century onward it was a prime charm against falls from horseback, and was also a charm to protect the horse. The turquoise was said to "move" to warn its owner of impending danger. See AGATE; JEWELS FROM SPITTLE.

☞ From earliest time, turquoise has been accounted a jewel for personal adornment by the Pueblo Indians of the Southwest and their forebears, and has been a trade article or exchange medium between these groups and those of southern Arizona and northern Mexico. Present-day Pueblo Indians venerate turquoise; the "flesh" of turquoise is thought to remain unimpaired if the jewel is mined and handled with respect. Besides being used for jewelry, turquoise is also used as an offering by the Pueblos, and is deposited under the floor when a house or kiva is built. The color turquoise is associated with maleness, in contrast to yellow which is associated with femaleness in the pueblos. [EWV]

Turquoise Boy or **Man** A Zuñi Pueblo spirit, companion of Salt Old Woman at the time both deserted Zuñi because their valuable flesh was being wasted. [EWV]

Turquoise Woman Navaho Indian deity. In some accounts she is a variant of Changing Woman, chief female deity of the Navaho. In other accounts she is said to have been created, together with White Shell Woman, by Changing Woman from epidermis rubbed from under Changing Woman's breasts. The two sisters lived on this earth when monsters overran it; in a contest with Corn Maidens they lost the chance of having Monster-Slayer, chief Navaho deity, as their husband. Turquoise is casually mentioned in the Jicarilla Apache origin myth as having been used in the creation of man, but no Turquoise Woman appears as a character in Jicarilla or other Apache myths. [EWV]

Turris, Turisas, or **Turilas** The god of war of the Estonians and Finns. The word means a huge, evil, strong, and dreadful person. [JB]

Turtle A fairly prominent being in North American Indian mythology and religious beliefs, especially for tribes living east of the Mississippi River. The Iroquois hold the belief that the earth rests on the back of Turtle, he being the only animal who could keep the earth stable; the Delaware, also, say that the turtle is "he who carries our mother's (the earth's) body," and identify their earth-bearer with the box-turtle (*Cistudo carolina*). Other Algonquian-speaking tribes also make Turtle the bearer of the earth (see Frank C. Speck, *A Study of the Delaware Indian Big House Ceremony*, Publications of the Pennsylvania Historical Commission, Harrisburg, Pa., Vol. 2, 1931, pp. 44–47).

Besides being regarded as a sacred, beneficent being, Turtle is also looked upon by the Delaware as a potentially dangerous character who can hurt human beings (Speck, p. 47). In a story told both by the Delaware and Shawnee, men who meet and climb on the back of a giant turtle are all, save one, unable to get off his back as they approach the ocean and are carried out to sea. Turtle is also, surprisingly enough, the butt of Gluskabe's practical jokes in northeastern Algonquian Gluskabe-Turtle stories, and is the butt for humor in other northeastern tales. In central Algonquian animal tales Turtle races other animals and wins. [EWV]

☞ In the folklore of the modern Indians and mestizos of the Amazon and of the Guiana, the small land turtle (*jabuti*) is the clever, but somewhat mischievous animal who knows how to emerge safe or victorious out of every contest with stronger rivals. His constant enemy and victim is the ferocious and stupid jaguar. For instance, Turtle kills Jaguar by falling on him from a tree; Jaguar is about to catch him, but Turtle vanishes into a hole and tells Jaguar who has grasped his arms that he is only holding onto a root.

There is also a very popular story about a race between Turtle and Deer which is won by Turtle who has asked his brethren to deceive Deer. Turtle also challenges the demon Curupira in a tug-of-war, but instead of pulling the rope himself, he ties it to some powerful animal.

Many stories of the turtle cycle seem to have been transmitted to the Indians by the Negro slaves with whom they were in contact. [AM]

turtle dance An appeal to the fertile potentialities of the turtle, rarely a mimetic performance. In several Rio Grande pueblos the turtle dance is the maskless kachina or good kachina dance, as the *oku share,* performed at San Juan on Christmas Day, when 37 men and boys stomp in line; and the *ahatsaana* at Taos on King's Day, performed thrice in the morning and thrice in the afternoon, with 26 dancers in stomp line or running circuits. They all carry turtle-shell rattles at their knees, wear belts of bells, carry a gourd rattle in the right hand, and a spruce twig in the left. At Isleta this same dance is called the spruce or evergreen dance. At Taos it is performed by the water kiva.

The *ketowači* dance of the Iowa Indian men's society was taught by a man who saw the turtles dance. In the spring they imitated these creatures, pawing the air to simulate crawling. The Yuchi Big Turtle Dance, performed on the first day of the Green Corn ceremony, started in a compact mass led by a woman with a turtle knee-rattle, in sunwise circuit, to antiphonal song; then it thinned out into a single file.

The turtle is believed to make the thunder come (Pueblos), to represent the earth dome (Delaware, Iroquois). It communicates its power to rattles, e.g. the *chelydra serpentina* of the Iroquois and Delaware False Faces, and the *cistudo* hand rattle of Delaware and Cherokee dance leaders, vision reciters, and *towisas* singers. It brings perseverance and long life, hence can cure. See RATTLES. [GPK]

tüzet vszek Literally, I carry fire: a singing game of Hungarian peasants around Méra. It resembles drop-the-handkerchief, the kerchief representing fire. The dancers sing, "Fire I carry. Do not see it. Burns my dress, but do not let it. Who may see it, may not say it. Whither does my sweetheart's way tend?" The group stands in a circle and the carrier of the kerchief (fire) runs around it, drops the fire behind one of the players, who is supposed to pick it up and pursue him, beating him on the back with it; if this is not done, the carrier pursues the player. The carrier should, if pursued, try to get into the vacant place in the circle. Once safe in, the game begins all over again. There is no recollection of the origin of this game. [GPK]

Tvashtri In Vedic mythology, the divine artisan and architect of the universe, who made all things; bestower of generative power. Tvashtri possesses wealth and can grant riches. He was the father of the three-headed Viśvarūpa, Indra's special enemy, and of Saraṇyū (wife of Vivasvat and mother of the Aśvins, and of the primeval twins, Yama and Yamī). Tvashtri fashioned Indra's thunderbolt and the drinking-cup of the gods, he made men, and even husband and wife. He is often referred to as the Hindu Vulcan.

Twa Sisters An English-Scottish ballad (Child#10) of the drowning of a young girl by her jealous elder sister, the robbing of her body by a miller, the conversion of her hair into harp strings (or other parts of her body into some type of musical instrument), and the revelation of the murder by the instrument when it was played. This is the singing bone motif (E632 f.). The song has been widely found over the British Isles, is known in Icelandic, Danish, and other Scandinavian languages, and has been collected in numerous variants in the United States. In some texts the revelation is made at the wedding of the elder sister; some end with the punishment by hanging and burning at the stake of the miller and the sister; the more corrupted versions lapse into low comedy over the construction of the instrument from the girl's body. In America some of the versions are used for dancing: a Nebraska song, "There was an old woman lived on the seashore," for example, includes dancing instruction in its refrain; and a Kentucky version is a courting dance performed by two lines of men and girls facing each other. Both of these have the refrain of "Bow down," one of the most common of the great variety of refrains attached to this ballad. Others include "down-a-down," or "derry down," and "binnorie." The story appeared as a broadside in print in 1656 under the title of *The Miller and the King's Daughter.* The airs to which it is sung vary considerably. One was used with *The Three Ravens* in Ravenscroft's *Melismata* (1611). See BINNORIE.

Twelve Apostles or **Carol of the Twelve Numbers** A cumulative song built on the number-chain formula (Z21), in which the numbers from 1 to 12 are associated with various concepts or ideas, generally of a religious nature. In England, under the title above or as *The Dilly Song, Green Grow the Rushes, O,* or *The Ten Commandments,* several versions of the song have been sung as a carol, as a harvest song, as an Eton and Oxford student song, and as a song of the Biddeford boatmen. Analogs have been known all over Europe since the 15th century in German, French, Spanish, Greek, etc. On the Rhine it was known as the *Catholic Vesper,* and as a drinking song; in Austria, as *The Pious Questions;* in Languedoc it served as a mnemonic for learning the catechism. The question of the origin of the song has been debated for half a century, with three main sources proposed: a Latin hymn of Clinius published in 1602 (*Dic mihi: quid est unus?/ Unus ist Deus qui regnat in coelis*); a Hebrew chant of the Passover service, *Echod Mi Yodea* (Who knows one?); and a legendary dialog between a druid and a child, from Brittany. All three develop in question-and-answer form the sequence of sacred numbers and their corresponding subjects. These subjects differ widely, both in these three texts and in the many surviving songs. Archer Taylor suggests that *Echod Mi Yodea* originated in the Sanskrit and spread to Europe from the East.

Twelve Days of Christmas An English cumulative carol (Z21.2.1) belonging to the category of the number-chain formula (Z21), enumerating the gifts sent by a lover to his lady on each of the twelve days from Christmas to Epiphany. Published in Husk's *Songs of the Nativity,* in 1868, it was there noted as having been printed in broadsides during the preceding 150 years. It has been sung in the British Isles and in America not only as a carol but also as a game song in which each person folowing a leader in the repetitions must pay a forfeit if he misses a line. Some of the versions of this type turn the descriptions of the gifts into tongue twisters. The first gift, a partridge in a pear tree, may have been inspired by an old drinking song and nursery rime, *A Pie Sat on a Pear Tree.* There is also a French-Canadian version called *Une Perdriole.* See CAROL.

twins Twins, though statistically not uncommon, are looked upon in many parts of the world as being ominous. Sometimes one of the twins is attributed to a god and one to a human parent (compare HERCULES). The Lillooet believe that twins are the children of Grizzly Bear, that they are bears' sons. When a twin died and went back to the bears, he was placed in a tree far from a settlement and the bear came to take him back. Sometimes two men are thought to be involved, one father for each child. Often twins are thought to be the offspring of adultery. In more sophisticated communities, twins are attributed to superior virility on the part of the father. But among more primitive peoples, twins are often destroyed and the mother must be thoroughly cleansed. Twin fruits, like double almonds or twin bananas, are not eaten for fear that twins will result. On the other hand, twins are sometimes considered lucky. They have second sight, for example, or some other superior power resulting from the doubling of the single personality. Among the Cherokee, twins could see the little people, but they lost the power if they ate food prepared by a menstruating woman. See AIZA; ANIMAL CHILDREN; BIRTH OMEN; DIOSCURI; DOSU; EXPOSURE OF FAMOUS PERSONS IN INFANCY; HOHOBI; HUACA; IBEJI.

☞ Some importance generally attaches to multiple births in almost all American Indian groups: twins are either welcomed or feared, and either treated well or one of the two disposed of. The more unusual occurrence of triplets is generally considered as an omen, if considered at all in such small populational groups as those which inhabited native North America.

In north central California twins happen to have been considered unlucky, and attempts were made to prevent their conception; young girls were taught not to eat "twin" wild plums or acorns or other double fruits, nuts, or berries; if fruits or nuts were bunched together on one stem, a young girl when eating them should point each nut in the cluster in a different direction and say, "I'll have a child over there" (pointing east, for example); "Next time I'll have a child over there" (pointing west); "Next time over there" (pointing north). If twins were born to a woman, a relative generally took one to raise.

Among the Tübatulabal farther south in California, twins were treated well; if one twin was treated badly and died, the other would die too and give the family bad luck; hence both were accorded more consideration than other children. The belief also existed in this tribe that if a person laughed about a woman having twins, that person would also have twins.

The Shawnee exhibit contradictory attitudes toward twins; one informant said that twins. and triplets even more so, are lucky, and were welcome; another informant, that the Shawnee were as a rule afraid of twins, especially the first born of the two, and usually allowed the first born to be adopted by an unrelated person. The elder of twins was the one who wielded a mysterious influence for evil over members of his or her family, and thus was the one sent away for adoption. It is among the Shawnee that some pseudo-historical material on triplets occurs; the historical figures of Tecumseh, the Shawnee warrior, and Tenskwatawa, the Shawnee Prophet, are said to have been either twins or triplets, the third being a girl who died young. [EWV]

In West Africa and New World Negro belief the cult of twins, where found, or the abhorrence of twin births, is part of a generalized attitude toward children born with any kind of abnormal characteristics. The line between worship of twins and abhorrence of them may be drawn at about the mid-point of Nigeria, the Yoruba and Guinea Coast tribes to the west "liking" twins, the Ibo and other Negro Delta and Cameroons tribes taking the opposite position. The New World Negro twin-cult derives from the Yoruban-Dahomean tradition, as is evidenced by the carry-over of the terms *ibeji* and *hohovi* (*hohobi*) on this side of the Atlantic. Further evidence of this provenience is found in the retained belief that the child born after twins, the *dosu*, is "stronger" than his predecessors. The inclusion of the *dosu* in the rites and beliefs of the twin-cult, and the retention of these rites, especially in Brazil, Cuba, Guiana, Haiti, and elsewhere in the Caribbean area, is in almost unreinterpreted African form. [MJH]

The ancient Aztec custom was to kill one of twins at birth to prevent the death of a parent; the surviving twin was believed to have great powers for evil. Twin infanticide probably was widespread in pre-Conquest times. It is reported that formerly the Miskito Indians of Nicaragua killed the female of twins, or left both exposed to die, since the father believed that he could not be the parent of more than one child at a time. Hence, his wife had borne him an illegitimate child.

Twins apparently are no longer killed, but it is often believed that they have magical powers, both for good and evil. Among the Tarascans of Mexico, female twins are unsuccessful in cooking tamales and squash. But twins of either sex are particularly gifted in curing wounds or injuries, and those who plant corn, chayotes, or squash are rewarded with pairs on the vine or stalk, where a single fruit is the rule. The Tarascans also believe that a pregnant woman who eats "paired" fruits, i.e. chayotes, bananas, cherries, and the like, will give birth to twins. The Popoluca of Veracruz believe that twins result from the position of the parents during intercourse. They believe twins to be unusually fortunate in that they can break horses and mules easily, can cure colic by kicking the sick animal seven times in the stomach, and have unusual success as curers specializing in toothache, headache, and fever. They are also thought to be unusually intelligent, and fortunate in love. [GMF]

Twins Brothers who figure prominently in the mythologies of many peoples all over the world. One is usually the culture hero, the other opposes him or represents some other way of life. For discussion of the characteristic elements of the Twins, see DIOSCURI. See also AHAYUTA ACHI; AŚVINS; BALDER; DUAL CREATORS; HAHGWEHDIYU; HONSU; JACOB; TAGARO; TAMENDONAR.

Male twin culture heroes occur in Iroquois, Central Woodlands, Kiowa, Pueblo, Apache (including Navaho), and a few other North American Indian mythologies. Among the Plains and certain Woodlands tribes tales are also told of twin boys who are not culture heroes, but who none the less accomplish wonderful deeds and go on perilous journeys, much as the twin culture heroes do.

Among the Iroquois the twin culture heroes are Flint and Sapling, who quarrel over who shall be born first while they are still in their mother's womb. One of these twins, Flint, was of an evil mind and was thrown out of the lodge soon after birth, but his brother Sapling brought him back. After they grew up, they both enlarged the earth and created various things on it; finally they quarreled and Flint was killed.

Similar in several details to the Iroquois myth is the Central Woodlands myth of Nanabozho and his brother, or White Hare and Wolf. These two twins, like the Iroquois twins, speak to each other in their mother's womb, but are friendly to one another. When Wolf is drowned his brother Nanabozho is inconsolable; his lamentations bring his brother back to earth. Also unlike the Iroquois myth, Wolf does not figure as a destructive culture hero, in apposition to his brother's constructive acts for the good of mankind.

Among the Micmac and Passamaquoddy the culture hero Gluskabe is the elder of twins; Wolf, the younger twin, bursts through his mother's side at birth killing her. The two deceive each other, and Wolf is finally killed by his elder brother. See GLUSKABE.

Pueblo twins who figure as culture heroes are the twin war gods, two small boys who are the sons of Sun and Dripping Water or Waterfall. These two boys are known as Ahayuta achi, War Brothers, or War Twins, at Zuñi, but knowledge and respect for them and their exploits as culture heroes, inventors, hunters, destroyers of monsters, and war gods is general throughout the pueblos. See AHAYUTA ACHI.

Comparable in several respects to the twin culture heroes of the Pueblos are the two Apache and Navaho brothers, also sometimes represented as twins—Child-of-the-Water and Killer-of-Enemies. Several Apache myths revolve around the exploits of one or both of these heroes, especially their exploits in ridding the earth of monsters.

Other supernatural twins are the Winnebago twins, Flesh and Stump, who when their mother is killed are taken from her body and raised by their father. These twins kill snakes, leeches, and the thunderbirds; their father flees from them, and is directed by the Twins to a village; they then kill the evil ogre who murdered their mother, go on visits to an evil spirit and to Earthmaker, the Winnebago deity. Later they go on the warpath and destroy a beaver, one of the foundation-posts of the earth. Earthmaker finally sends his messenger to frighten the twins and stop their wanderings (see Paul Radin, *Winnebago, Hero Cycles: A Study in Aboriginal Literature*, Indiana University Publications in Anthropology and Linguistics, Memoir 1, pp. 291–322). The Kiowa also tell ritual myths about two twins, Split Boys or Half Boys; the manner of birth of the second of these twins is peculiar. One boy was playing by himself one day, with a hoop which his grandmother had told him never to throw upward. When he broke the tabu and threw it up, it fell back on his head; he looked around and there were two boys, himself and a replica of himself. These two boys later do various things forbidden them by their grandmother; they visit Thunder, escaping death from a falling bluff, change into moles to obtain hide from a ferocious white buffalo, and so forth.

The widely distributed Plains tale of *Lodge-Boy and Thrown-Away* (or *Lodge-Boy and Spring-Boy*) is also the tale of twin heroes, similar in some respects to the Winnebago Twin cycle outlined above. [EWV]

☞ Twin heroes are among the most important characters in South American Indian mythology. Their adventures form whole cycles in the oral traditions of many tribes from the Guianas to Tierra del Fuego. One of the Twins is described as strong and clever, the other as weak and stupid. Their contrasting natures and temper are reflected in adventures and actions which to a large extent determined the physiognomy of our world. In most tribes the Twins are personifications of Sun and Moon; thus are explained the weak condition of the younger brother who is the Moon, and like it killed and torn into pieces to be restored by his older brother Sun.

The Twins are not only transformers but also great culture heroes to whom mankind is much indebted. For instance, in Bakairi mythology, the Twins steal Sun and Moon from Red Vulture and regulate their courses, introduce sleep by stealing Lizard's eyelids, separate the earth from the sky, rob Fox of fire, form rivers with the water of the Great Serpent, create the Bakairi and other tribes, and teach people how to dance and play music. They also provide men with food plants. Kame, who personifies the Moon, is the weak and silly brother who is swallowed by a jahu fish and is eaten by Fox; however he is saved from his misfortunes by Keri, the Sun, who always restores him to life.

In Yahgan mythology the divine pair introduced the use of fire, the art of killing birds and of hunting sealions, and many other useful techniques. They also told people the names of things, revealed menstruation tabus, and initiated people into love. The older brother, who is described as being both lazy and stupid, would have made life easy for men had he had his own way. He wanted fire always to burn, spears to return by themselves after they had been cast, the sea to be a deposit of fish oil, and men to be immortal. The younger brother thwarted his intentions because he felt that man must exert himself in order to appreciate what he has.

The Twins are the central figures in a cycle of adventure stories which have a wide distribution in South America. The main episodes of these myths have been recorded from Panama to the Chaco and from the Brazilian coast to Peru. The pattern of the myth is as follows: The wife of the creator or culture hero is killed by jaguars who find twins in her womb. The jaguar mother brings up the twins, who later learn from some animal that the jaguars whom they regard as their relatives are the murderers of their mother. They take revenge and then, after performing several miraculous deeds, climb to the sky by means of a ladder of arrows to become Sun and Moon. The earliest versions of this myth go back to the middle of the 16th century and were recorded in Brazil among the Tupinamba and in Peru in the region of Huarochiri. The widespread diffusion of

the myth in the Amazonian basin suggests that it forms part of the common cultural background of the Carin, Tupi-Guarani, and Arawak tribes. [AM]

Two Brothers An ancient Egyptian tale, also known as *Anpu and Bata*, dating from the reign of Rameses II (about 1250 B.C.) and contained in an almost perfect papyrus in the British Museum. It has an obscure connection with the Osiris story, and contains several primitive folktale motifs overlaid with later material. Anpu, the elder brother in the story, is perhaps identifiable with Anubis; Bata may be either Ptah (who became confused with the Apis bull), or Sati, the long-lived serpent of heaven, or perhaps a local god connected in some way with Anubis.

Bata, having been kind to his brother's cattle, understands their language, and, when Anpu's wife attempts in vain to seduce him and accuses him to Anpu, is warned by the cattle and flees. He is chased by Anpu, prays to Rā, who interposes a crocodile-filled river between the brothers. From the far bank, Bata explains matters to Anpu, perhaps castrates himself, and tells of how he will live in the valley of acacias where his heart (soul) will be in a flower. Anpu will learn of his death when his beer roils. The gods make for Bata a wife whose violent end is predicted by the Hathors. A lock of her hair floats downstream, comes to the Pharaoh's attention, and its fragrance causes him to send to find her. His soldiers are slain by Bata, but a woman tempts the girl away. The acacia tree is cut down when the wife tells Pharaoh the secret; Bata dies, and Anpu's beer bubbles. Anpu spends three years looking for Bata's heart in the valley of the acacias, at last finds it, and revives Bata by putting the heart in water and giving it to Bata to drink. Bata then transforms himself into a bull, is brought to the Pharaoh, and is killed at the wife's request. Two drops of his blood spring up overnight into Persea trees, which the wife orders cut down when he identifies himself. A chip from one tree flies into her mouth, she conceives, and Bata is born again in his own identity. When the old Pharaoh dies, Bata becomes ruler, the wife is slain, and Anpu becomes heir to the throne.

The latter part of the story, with its several reincarnations, has perhaps been added to an older framework, and contains some religious significance now lost. The use of many common folktale motifs, at least 18 (helpful or grateful or speaking animals, Potiphar's wife, obstacle flight, separable soul, life token, death prophesied, love through sight of unknown's hair, quest for princess from her hair floating on river, treacherous wife, resuscitation by replacing heart, water of life, reincarnation, plant from blood of slain person, speaking tree, impregnation by swallowing, transformed person swallowed and reborn as self), makes this, antedating Homer and the Bible, one of the oldest written folktales, of uncommon interest.

The *Two Brothers* story (Type 303) of Europe has been intensively studied (Kurt Ranke, *Die Zwei Brüder*, FFC 114, 1934). It appears in combination with several other types, principally *The Dragon Slayer* (Type 300), *The Magic Bird-Heart* (Type 567), *Strong John* (Type 650). Essentially it is the story of the twins born at the same time with twin horses and twin dogs, as the result of woman, bitch, and mare all having eaten pieces of the same magical fish. One brother goes to seek his fortune; his tree (one of twin trees) is to be a life token—it will wither if he gets into trouble. With his magic sword (one of a pair), he slays the seven-headed dragon; he reveals the impostor who seeks to take credit for the deed; he becomes king and marries the princess. On his wedding night he leaves the bridal chamber to investigate a strange fire. The witch in the house at which he arrives manages to chain his dog with a hair from her head; she strikes the king with her staff and he is transformed to stone. Back home the tree withers. The other brother sets out, finds his way to the city, is mistaken for his brother, but does not reveal the truth, since he wants time to investigate the situation. At night he sleeps with the princess but places his sword between himself and her (see SEPARATING SWORD). He too follows the light, does not permit the bewitching of his dog, kills the witch with her own rod, and retransforms his brother. The hundreds of variants of this tale—Ranke analyzes 770 different tellings of the type—are spread all over the Continent. Ranke believes it to be of western European origin, since wider variation from the established type occurs the farther eastward the tale is found.

two friends The central characters of a number of folktales of the world illustrating extreme faithfulness. Damon and Pythias are perhaps the most famous friends of folktale: each proved willing to die for the other. Amis and Amiloun were more than friends; there was a blood covenant between them, and their lives, from birth on, were exactly parallel. So dear to each other were they that Amis killed his two children to cure Amiloun of leprosy. See FAITHFUL JOHN. See also ARAWN; SEPARATING SWORD; TWO BROTHERS.

Tyche The ancient Greek goddess of fortune: identified with the Roman Fortuna. Tyche, like Fortuna, carried the cornucopia of plenty, the rudder of destiny, and the wheel of fortune.

Tylor, Sir Edward Burnett (1832–1917) English anthropologist; one of the leaders of the anthropological school in England. He was educated at the Friends' School at Grove House, Tottingham, since his parents were members of the Society of Friends. On account of uncertain health, he traveled widely, visiting the United States, Mexico, and Cuba. From these tours resulted his book, *Anahuac: or, Mexico and the Mexicans, Ancient and Modern* (1861). Somewhat later, he produced his *Researches into the Early History of Mankind* (1864; 2d ed., 1868), followed by the two-volume work, *Primitive Culture: Researches into the Development of Mythology, Philosophy, Religion, Language, Art, and Custom* (1871; 7th ed., 1924). This work was immediately hailed as a standard general treatise on anthropology. It is particularly connected with his theory of animism, which he developed in this work. "Time has shown that his theory does not cover all the facts relating to the beginnings of mythology and religion, but it nevertheless has furnished a standpoint of commanding outlook, as seen in its effects in inspiring the work of Frazer and many others" (R. R. Marett in *Encyclopedia of the Social Sciences*). In 1881, Tylor published a smaller and more popular handbook, *Anthropology*. Tylor, in 1896, was ramed Oxford's first professor of anthropology. Previously, in 1888, he was named first Gifford lecturer at Aberdeen University where he delivered a two-year course of lectures on "Natural Religion."

type A term used by students of folk literature to designate narratives capable of maintaining an independent existence in tradition. Any tale, no matter how complex or how simple it is, told as an independent narrative is considered to be a type. Some types like the longer folktales in Grimm's collection may contain dozens of motifs, and others like the anecdotes of the animal cycle may consist of a single narrative motif. In the latter, type and motif are identical.

If types are thus understood to mean independent narratives, there are obviously a limited number of them within any particular culture. For a discussion of the relation between type and motif see MOTIF.

It is usually possible to determine with some ease whether a particular narrative belongs or does not belong to a certain type. But there are always borderline cases where there seems to be confusion between tale-types or where a narrative has only a slight resemblance to a particular type. These variations from type have produced in some scholars, particularly those of eastern Europe, a skepticism as to the validity of classifying tales by types. This skepticism would seem to arise simply from a difference in interest on the part of the investigator. Such scholars are more interested in differences between variants and in the individuality of particular tale-tellers than they are in resemblances. As to the main fact of the validity of the tale-type conception within the countries in question, there has been no doubt in the minds of those who have made type indexes of those countries.

There now exist indexes of tale-types for many countries of the world. The European and western Asiatic area has been rather well covered, and work is constantly going on in classifying the types for other parts of the world. It would seem to be imperative that an entirely different classification of types should be made for each of the large culture areas of the world, for example, for Africa, for Oceania, and for the North and South American Indians.

The only way in which a tale-type can be formulated is to study the variants of the type. This process is somewhat circular because in order to tell what is the variant of a type, it is necessary to have some idea of the type. In practice this means that the investigator finds many tales containing so many striking resemblances that he places them in a single category. He then studies these resemblances and notes the common characteristics. Later he brings together as many variations of tales having these characteristics as posible, and eventually he is able to make a satisfactory statement as to the contents of the tale he is studying. His investigation implies a basic assumption, namely that the tale he is studying is an entity, that it has had a history with a beginning in time and place and has suffered certain changes in the course of its life.

A difficult philosophical problem for the student of types is whether to assume that one version is better or worse than another and, if so, what can be the criteria of good and bad when applied to versions. When the student who is working by means of the historic-geographic method constructs what he calls the archetype, he is not dealing in terms of good or bad. Rather he is constructing a theoretical form from which all the versions could eventually be derived. His is the problem of historical reconstruction and not of esthetic judgment. On the other hand, some collectors of folk material are concerned exactly with this question of the search for the esthetically ideal type of song or tale. The assumption is that all who tell the tale or sing the song are striving to attain a certain ideal. It is fair to say, however, that most folklorists feel that such speculations are beyond their competence. See HISTORIC-GEOGRAPHIC METHOD; MOTIF; VARIANT.

Bibliography: Antti Aarne, Stith Thompson, *Types of the Folk-Tale*, FFC 74, Helsinki, 1928. Kaarle Krohn, *Die folkloristische Arbeitsmethode*, Oslo, 1926.

STITH THOMPSON

types and classification of folklore The annual folklore bibliographies, published by the author since 1937 and kept in a cumulative master card file, served as a proving ground upon which this classification has been developed, tested, and adjusted to the practices of publication in folklore. When the author went to teach folklore in the University of Santo Domingo, a brief form of the classification was published, in Spanish, by the Faculty of Philosophy of that university in 1944, which was distributed among school teachers over the Dominican Republic as a questionnaire for the collection of folklore, and the classification was put to further test when it was used to classify the manuscript archive accumulated at the University from data sent in by the teachers. It received further tests when the author went to teach folklore in the National University of Mexico in 1945 and applied it not only to publications and field work, but also to a slide collection in the Benjamin Franklin Library in Mexico City, which illustrated various aspects of Mexican folk life and lore. A revised form of the classification, amplified from 11 (1944 ed.) to 40 pages, appeared in *Folklore Americas* (1948) VIII, and *Southern Folklore Quarterly* (1949) XIII: 161–226, and is, substantially, the form given here. In general, it represents a compromise between the broad concept of the German word *Volkskunde* and the more restricted concept of the English word *folklore*.

Libraries must classify all types of material, and from their broad viewpoint it seems logical to classify folk music with music in general, folk arts with art in general, and perhaps even folk narrative with literature. Their interests may lead them to split a folklore unit like mythology among other, for them more important, headings such as American Indian and Classic Antiquity. Different interests dictate different groupings, hence it is only natural that non-folkloric interests should scatter folklore materials far and wide in their classifications.

Folklore interests, however, should have their own classification, defined by the unity of their field, and with major or secondary importance given to various kinds of categories according to their significance in folklore. The classification of types of folklore offered here is designed for those whose special interest is in folklore. Furthermore, library classifications usually are designed with the particular problems offered by printed materials in mind. The classification given here also has in mind problems in grouping manuscript materials, cards, pictures, phonographic or sound recordings, museum objects, and other forms of documentation of folk-

lore data. It is hoped that this list of folklore types may serve as a kind of questionnaire, to remind the collector of the different kinds of material he should ask for. This classification tries to provide a place, too, for various types of background data the folklorist cannot ignore about the region and people among whom he collects his folklore. It even takes some cognizance of the relation of folklore to other fields, for there are more people interested in folklore as it relates to some other field in which they specialize than there are folklorists, who are interested in folklore simply as folklore.

From major to minor importance, the different ranks of headings used here are called *groups* (designated by capital letters A to Z), *categories* (designated by hundred numbers 000–900), *types* (the ten numbers 00–90), *forms* (unit numbers 0–9), *divisions* (the tenth decimals .0–.9), and *subdivisions* (the hundredth decimals .00–.90). Further subdivisions can be made by using the thousandth decimals (.000–.999), and even by introducing a second decimal point with its tenths, hundredths, and thousandths, and a third, and so on (A 000.000.000.000, etc.).

Some parts of the field of folklore have had their classification well developed, such as the prose narrative in the *Motif-Index of Folk-Literature* by Stith Thompson. But such categorical terms as myth, legend, tale, and ballad have been established by long usage in the field, and do not coincide with the major divisions in the *Motif-Index*, except in the case of "Mythological motifs," in which this classification can and does follow Thompson rather than introduce a new set of subdivisions for Myth. The great system of indexes in *Folklore Fellows Communications* has definitely established Aarne's classification for tales, which is followed in the present classification in the folktale category. The excellent synthesis of *The Proverb* by Archer Taylor indicates some general agreement on the major types in this field, which have been followed here. Indeed, the present classification follows rather than departs from any fairly well established classification where such are available. In some parts of the field, such as in folk music, there has been considerable discussion and divergence of opinion about classification. And in other categories, such as in legend and game, little progress in classification has been made. In such cases, we follow here simply the most logical order that the materials seem to dictate, using abstract and comprehensive terms that may take care of most branches of these fields until a more precise classification is provided for them. In this way, we have developed a system which, though still incomplete, at least offers a general plan of correlation of the field into a unified whole.

No matter what system of classification is used, the unity of the field will always present many interrelations among its various parts, which are indicated by cross-references. Materials in different sections sometimes may be classified in the same way, and such correlations are shown by the system of numbering and the terms used. For example, in Belief, P 200, P 400, and P 500 utilize the same system used in B 200 (Myth), B 400 (Legend), and F 500 (Custom). In other cases, only partial agreement of numbers is possible, as in the "Crucial moment in life cycle" section, which appears in C 340 (Song), F 540 (Custom), and C 434 (Dance). In C 300 (Song) and F 500 (Custom), only the ten numbers (40's) could be made to coincide. Where such coincidence is not possible, one section may be elaborated, where such seems desirable, by introducing the divisions of another section after a decimal point. For example, in C 400 (Dance), in which "Crucial moment in life cycle" must bear the number C 434, which coincides in no way with C 340 or F 540, a correlation can be made by adding .546, from F 546 (Death), so that the number C 434.546 indicates C 434 (Dance) related to a "Crucial moment in life cycle" C 434, namely, Death: C 434.546. Where one section is interested in the form and another in the function of the same type of material, this same system of decimal linking can be used to correlate the two. This method has been elaborated rather fully here only in the case of Verse, which is assembled as a unit for interest in its form in C 700 and C 800, and is carried out, for its functional interest, to other major sections. The same could be done for other form units, such as Art and Craft, which could be elaborated, for their functional interest, in other sections.

The A (General), G (Geographic), or L (Linguistic) divisions may be introduced at any point in the classification at which such type of subdivision may seem desirable. However, the folklorist should first consider whether it might not be more desirable to carry out further the subdivision of his folklore material before introducing A, G, or L subdivisions. These subdivisions are not along folkloric lines, so their numbers are added to the folkloric numbers to which they are applied, not after a decimal point, but after the small letters, a, g, or l, which designate their group. One example, so detailed as to be unlikely in actual practice, but which illustrates the application of a, g, and l subdivisions, is: C 434.549 a 660 l 736 g 730, which means Classification (a 660) of the war (.549) dances (C 434) of the Cherokee Indians (l 736) of the United States of America (g 730).

When several items accumulate under one heading, they may be given individual item numbers, beginning with hundred numbers, and progressing on down through tens, units, and decimals. This system allows more flexibility than that of numbering 1, 2, 3, . . . , and always permits the insertion of a new item number at any point. For example, if four items appear under one heading, they may be given item numbers 200, 400, 600, and 800. If five more items appear, they may be numbered 100, 300, 500, 700, and 900. If three more items appear, closely related to items 100, 200, and 300, respectively, they may be numbered 120, 220, and 320. If a new item appears, which belongs between 199 and 200, it may be numbered 199.5. If one appears which belongs between 199.9 and 200, it may be numbered 199.95. Numbers may thus be expanded always to the right, keeping each item in its proper relative position. After many items have been accumulated under one heading, further subdivisions in the classification number of that heading should be considered. After such further classification subdivision, new item numbers may be assigned to the smaller groups. Thus item numbers should be written in pencil, as temporary numbers and subject to change, and they should be set apart from classification numbers, preferably below them, forming a second line of numbers by themselves. Classification numbers bring together all materials of similar nature. Item numbers maintain in proper order all materials of similar nature, each with its individual number. The

order of item numbers should indicate future subdivisions in classification.

The question of whether certain materials should be classified in one section or another often can be resolved by determining which section's topic is in greatest accord with the major interest of the materials as presented in each case. Materials about a fox belong in Myth if they are concerned chiefly with narratives about his origin, form, nature, and innate qualities, in Legend if they are chiefly narratives of a certain individual fox necessarily localized in time and space, in Tale if they are chiefly narratives of adventures applicable to any fox typical of his class, in Art and Craft if the fox generically is treated as an object of hunting, in Food if interest is primarily in his preparation for human consumption, in Belief if the primary concern is with his use in the preparation of remedies or charms, in Speech if major attention is given to the folk names for him, and so on. Frequently this question can be settled by determining whether the major interest in the presentation of the material is in form or function. For example, if the major interest in musical instruments is in their manufacture, such materials are classified under Art and Craft, but they go under Music if interest is chiefly in the way the instruments are played and the kind of music they produce.

groups (A-Z)

A GENERAL FOLKLORE
B PROSE NARRATIVE
C BALLAD SONG DANCE GAME MUSIC VERSE
D DRAMA
F CUSTOM FESTIVAL
G GEOGRAPHY (for subdivisions)
L LANGUAGE (for subdivisions)
M ART CRAFT ARCHITECTURE
N FOOD DRINK
P BELIEF
S SPEECH
V PROVERB
W RIDDLE

groups (A-Z) and categories (000-900)

A GENERAL FOLKLORE

A 200   Bibliography
A 300   Organizations and Their Publications
A 400   Individual Publications
A 500   Background and Environmental Factors
A 600   Collection and Classification of Materials
A 700   Science
A 800   Value Use Application

B PROSE NARRATIVE

B 200   Myth
B 400   Legend
B 600   Tale

C BALLAD SONG DANCE GAME MUSIC VERSE

C 200   Ballad
C 300   Song
C 400   Dance
C 500   Game Pastime Sport
C 600   Music
C 700   Verse Without Music
C 800   Verse in Other Group of Folklore

D DRAMA

D 200 Religious
D 400 Secular
D 600 Puppet
D 800 Shadow Pantomime

F CUSTOM FESTIVAL

F 500 Custom
F 600 Festival

G GEOGRAPHY (for subdivisions)

L LANGUAGE (for subdivisions)

M ART CRAFT ARCHITECTURE

M 200 Art Craft
M 800 Architecture

N FOOD DRINK

N 200 Food
N 400 Drink
N 800 Special Form and Purpose Object of Bodily Consumption

P BELIEF

P 200 Mythology
P 400 Legend
P 500 Custom
P 600 Magic of Speech, Sign, Color
P 700 Medicine
P 800 Prediction Divination

S SPEECH

S 200 Phonology Phonetics
S 300 Morphology
S 400 Syntax
S 500 Vocabulary Lexicography
S 600 Gesture
S 700 Extra-Corporal Means of Communication

V PROVERB

V 200 Proverbial Metaphor
V 300 Proverbial Apothegm Maxim
V 400 Blason Populaire
V 500 Wellerism
V 600 Proverbial Phrase
V 700 Proverbial Comparison

W RIDDLE

W 200 True Riddle
W 400 Riddle Question

key designations

GROUPS (A-Z)
 CATEGORIES (000-900)
  TYPES (00-90)
   FORMS (0-9)
    DIVISIONS (.0-.9)
     SUBDIVISIONS (.00-.90)

The general headings of group A may be introduced into the classification at any point by adding, after the number at that point, the small letter a, followed by the numbers of the A headings needed: C 300 a 420 Individual publications of folksong materials; a periodical like American speech could be classified under S a 320; B 433 a 850 Use of legends of secular heroes in educa-

tion. Geographic headings may be introduced into the classification at any point, as under A 200 Bibliography, by adding, after A 200, the small letter g, followed by the numbers of the G (Geography) headings: A 200 g 382 Bibliography of Australian folklore. Under G Geography, approximate divisions of the major areas of the world are made longitudinally: the 30 degree meridian, in the Atlantic ocean, divides America from Europe and Africa; the international date line, about 180 degrees, in the Pacific ocean, divides America from Asia; and the 60 degree meridian following the Ural Mountains and the Iran-Afghanistan border, divides Asia from Europe, the Near East, and Africa. G 200 Ancient lands are those whose individual identity has ceased to exist in large part. Often numbers assigned here can be made to coincide with corresponding numbers for the same approximate locality in G 300 to G 800, as illustrated in the examples in that section. Linguistic headings may be introduced into the classification at any point, as under S Speech, by adding, after S, the small letter l, followed by the numbers of the L (Language) headings: S l 534.2 Spanish folk speech. If a speech area is large, it may be desirable to add, after the Language number, the small letter g, followed by the numbers of the G (Geography) headings: S l 534.2 g 762 Spanish folk speech of Cuba. Linguistic and geographic headings may be introduced in like manner elsewhere as desired.

A GENERAL FOLKLORE

A 200 Bibliography
A 300 Organizations and Their Publications
A 320 Continuous
  Societies, associations, institutes, research centers, their periodicals, serial publications. . . .
A 340 Intermittent
  Congresses, conferences, festivals, exhibits, contests, their proceedings, programs. . . .
A 360 Collecting
  Archives, libraries, museums, their catalogs, reports. . . .
A 400 Individual Publications
A 420 Folklore Materials
  Diverse texts, data, descriptions. . . .
A 440 Studies
  Diverse monographs, essays, dissertations, theses . . . about folklore.
A 460 Folklorists
  Life and works of collectors and scholars, biographies, biographic dictionaries, collected writings of individuals.
A 500 Background and Environmental Factors
A 530 Land
A 532 Topography
A 533 Climate
A 534 Flora For folk names of flora, see S 530.
A 535 Fauna For folk names of fauna, see S 540.
A 536 Products
A 538 Divisions
  .2 Atlas, map, geographic dictionary
  .4 Natural
  .5 Political
  .6 Ecclesiastical
  .8 Public and private lands and boundaries

A 560 People
A 562   Origin History
      Demography, vital statistics. . . .
A 564   Roads and routes of travel, commerce, migration, colonization
A 566   Characteristic traits of groups, sexes, classes, types
A 600 Collection and Classification of Materials
A 620 Informant
      Biography, methods of questioning, data of informant about his material. . . .
A 640 Methods of Collecting and Recording
      By manuscript, sound recorder, photography.
A 660 Classification
      Questionnaires, instructions, guides to field workers. . . .
A 700 Science
A 720   Definition
      Of folklore, its nature, character, limits, purpose, relations among its different divisions. For the relation of folklore to other fields, see A 800.
A 730   Terms
      Nomenclature, terminology, symbols, abbreviations. . . .
A 740   Theories Principles Analysis
      Schools of thought, methods of investigation and interpretation, conclusions about origin, growth, dissemination, disappearance. . . .
A 760   Form Function Style
A 770   Beauty Morality
A 780   Teaching
A 782   Organizations
  .2   Universities
  .4   Secondary schools
  .6   Primary schools
A 784   Methods Study plans Curricula Courses
A 786   Aids
      Textbooks, handbooks, outlines, anthologies, encyclopedias, dictionaries. . . .
A 800 Value Use Application
      Scientific, artistic, practical importance of folklore materials and science to other fields, and relation of folklore to them. . . .
A 820 History Literature Linguistics
A 830 Anthropology Ethnology Archeology Sociology Psychology
A 840 Painting Sculpture Architecture Music
      And other fine arts.
A 850 Education
A 860 Medicine
A 870 Law Religion Philosophy
A 880 Politics Industry Commerce

B PROSE NARRATIVE

For verse in prose narrative, see C 820.

B 200 Myth
      Relation of events significant in the establishment of the natural order of the universe. This classification follows the divisions of chapter A in Stith Thompson, *Motif-Index of Folk-Literature*, Helsinki 1932, *Folklore Fellows Communications*

106. For dance or belief concerning the materials of mythology, see C 432 or P 200.
B 220 Creator
B 230 Gods
B 240 Creation and Order of Universe
B 250 Creation and Order of Human Life
B 260 Creation and Order of Animal Life
B 270 Creation and Order of Plant Life
B 280 Characteristics of Animals
B 290 Origin of Characteristics of Plants
B 400 Legend
      Story based on specific persons, places, things. For dance or belief concerning the materials of legend, see C 432 or P 400.
B 420   Supernatural Being
B 422   Angel
B 423   Fairy Elf Goblin Gnome
B 425   Devil Demon
B 427   Werewolf Vampire
B 429   Ghost Spirit Phantom Specter
B 430   Human Being
B 432   Religious hero
      Jesus, the Virgin, Biblical characters, saints. . . .
B 433   Secular hero
      Charlemagne, Vergil, Cid, John Henry. . . .
B 434   Outlaw Criminal Bandit Pirate
      Robin Hood, Jesse James, Captain Kidd. . . .
B 435   Witch Shaman
B 436   Abnormal in size
      Giant, ogre, dwarf. . . .
B 437   Physically handicapped Deformed
      Mentally diseased or defective
      Hunchback, cripple, blind, deaf-mute, lunatic. . . .
B 438   Body part Senses
B 440   Animal
B 442   Mammal
B 444   Bird
B 446   Insect
B 448   Fish
B 450   Celestial Body
B 452   Sun
B 453   Moon
B 454   Planet
B 455   Star
B 457   Comet
B 458   Celestial body come to earth
B 460   Air Weather Fire
B 462   Weather sign or control
B 464   Lightning Thunder
B 465   Cloud Fog Mist Rain Hail Ice Snow Frost Dew
B 466   Wind Whirlwind Hurricane Cyclone Tornado
B 468   Fire
B 470   Earth
B 472   Formation
      Plain, swamp, forest, mountain, valley, cave, island, peculiar formation. . . .
B 474   Mineral
B 475   Plant

B 477   Product or activity of man or animal
               Vanished city, haunted house, ruins, cemetery, cross, hidden treasure, phantom ship, sneeze. . . .

B 478   Explanation of a name
               Story of a person, place (Lover's Leap, Devil's Kitchen), group (Yankee, Hoosier). For folk etymology or dictionary of proper names, see S 226 or S 580.

B 480   Water
B 482   Still water
    .2   Large body. Ocean, sea. . . .
    .4   Small body. Lake, pond. . . .
    .6   Man-made container. Well, pool. . . .
B 484   Running water
    .2   Large current. River, stream. . . .
    .4   Small current. Brook, spring. . . .
    .6   Man-made current. Canal, fountain. . . .

B 600   Tale
               Simple or complex episodic structure concerning events not dependent upon very specific elements of person, place, or time. This classification follows the divisions of A. Aarne and Stith Thompson, *Types of the Folk-Tale*, Helsinki 1928, *Folklore Fellows Communications* 74.

B 620   Animal Tale
B 640   Ordinary Tale
B 642   Magic
B 644   Religious
B 646   Romantic Realistic
B 648   Stupid ogre
B 660   Jest Anecdote
B 662   Stupid man or woman
B 663   Married couple
B 664   Woman
B 665   Man
B 666   Lie Tall tale
B 667   Formula tale Endless tale

C. BALLAD SONG DANCE GAME MUSIC VERSE

C 200   Ballad Epic
               Narrative in verse with music.
C 300   SONG
               Lyric in verse with music.
C 320   Emotion
C 322   Love
C 323   Hate
C 324   Joy Happiness
C 325   Sorrow Unhappiness
C 326   Admiration Praise Adulation
C 327   Serious condemnation Scorn
C 328   Good humor Jest
C 329   Ill humor Ridicule Mockery
C 330   Daily Life
               For custom concerning daily life, see F 530.
               For vocabulary of special group, see S 550.
C 334   Work
C 335   Cries of street vendor
C 336   Social reunion
C 337   Serenade Charivari

C 340   Crucial Moment of Life Life Cycle
               For dance or custom concerning crucial moment in life cycle, see C 434 or F 540.
C 342   Birth
C 345   Marriage
C 346   Death
C 347   Parting
C 348   Nostalgia
C 349   War cries
C 360   Children
C 366   Cradle song Lullaby
C 370   Religious
C 400   Dance
               For manufacture of dance mask, see M 245.
               For structure in which dance is performed, see M 868.
C 420   Form Grouping Movement
C 422   Individual
C 424   Couple
C 426   Group
C 430   Function Purpose Theme
C 432   Adoration
               Dance to honor, gain favor, avoid harm from being, spirit, thing, force of nature. . . . Is divided like B 200 and B.400: C 432.465 (like B 465) Rain dance.
C 434   Crucial moment of life Life cycle
               Is divided like F 540: C 434.546 (like F 546) Death dance. For song or custom concerning crucial moment in life cycle, see C 340 or F 540.
C 436   Festival
               Is divided like F 600: C 436.665 (like F 665) Harvest dance.
C 437   Medicine
               For medical belief, see P 700.
C 480   Accessories
               Included here also are accessories for D Drama, when considered apart from rest of drama.
C 482   Musical accompaniment
               For music itself, see C 600.
C 484   Costuming
               For materials and methods of making costumes, see M 227.
C 486   Properties Staging effects
C 490   Dramatic
               For dramatic game or drama, see C 526 or D.
C 500   Game Pastime Sport
               For game rime, see C 750. For structure in which game, pastime, sport is played, see M 868. For vocabulary of game, pastime, sport, see S 555.
C 520   Bodily Activity
C 522   Athletic sport and exercise Gymnastics
               Includes body part, such as Finger game.
C 523   Singing Dancing Marching
C 524   Racing Chasing Fighting
               Racing of people, horses, dogs. . . ; fighting of people, bulls, cocks. . . .

C 526 Dramatic
    For dramatic dance or drama, see C 490 or D.

C 530 Mental Activity
C 532 Wit
C 534 Memory
C 536 Knowledge
C 538 Guessing
C 560 Special Object or Implement
    Those which depend primarily on chance, skill, or amusement, played with a special object or implement, equipment or apparatus, like cards, dice, counters, wheels, balls, marbles, pins, tops, string, rope, kites, knives. . . .

C 580 Water Ice Snow
    Boating and water games, sledding and ice games. . . .

C 600 Music
    Music itself is classified here. Music with words is classified under C 200 Ballad, C 300 Song, etc. For musical accompaniment to dance, see C 482. For materials and methods of making musical instruments, see M 246. For musical instruments as means of communication, see S 720.

C 700 Verse Without Music
    Chanted, recited, written. Such matters as meter, rime, poetic structure may bear the number C 700 a 760 (like A 760 Form).

C 720 Narrative Verse
    Like C 200.

C 730 Lyrical Verse
    Is divided like C 300; C 730.329 (like C 329) Rime of mockery; C 730.334 (like C 334) Trade and occupation rime; C 730.360 (like C 360) Children's rime; C 730.370 (like C 370) Prayer Supplication Benediction

C 740 Dance Verse
    Is divided like C 400.

C 750 Game Verse
    Is divided like C 500: C 750.560 (like C 560) Rope-jumping rime. For game in which rime is used, see C 500. Counting-out rimes may be correlated here, as they are used in many different types of games.

C 800 Verse in Other Group of Folklore
    For verse in other category of group C itself, see C 700.

C 820 Prose Narrative
    Is divided like B: C 820.425 (like B 425)
    Verse in Devil legend.

C 830 Drama
    Is divided like D: C 830.200 (like D 200)
    Verse in religious drama.

C 840 Custom Festival
    Is divided like F: C 840.546 (like F 546)
    Verse in death custom.

C 850 Art Craft Architecture
    Is divided like M: C 850.246 (like M 246)
    Verse on bell; C 850.860 (like M 860)
    Verse on wall of public toilet.

C 855 Food Drink
    Is divided like N: C 855.800 (like N 800)
    Verse about tobacco.

C 860 Belief
    Is divided like P: C 860.646 (like P 646)
    Verse in charm.

C 870 Speech
    Is divided like S: C 870.570 (like S 570)
    Verse in formula.

C 880 Proverb
    Is divided like V: C 880.200 (like V 200)
    Verse in proverbial metaphor.

C 890 Riddle
    Is divided like W: C 890.200 (like W 200)
    Verse in true riddle.

D DRAMA

Drama accessories are classified with C 480 when considered apart from rest of drama. For dramatic dance or game, see C 490 or C 526. For verse in drama, see C 830. For structure in which drama is performed, see M 868.

D 200 Religious
D 400 Secular
D 600 Puppet
D 800 Shadow Pantomime

F CUSTOM FESTIVAL

For verse in custom and festival see C 840.

F 500 Custom
    Traditional pattern of human action accepted by a group. Individual habit is not included. Custom is what folks do, belief is why they think they do it. For explanation of belief related to a custom, see P 500.

F 530 Daily Life
    For song concerning daily life, see C 330. For vocabulary of special group, see S 550.

F 532 Home
    For hours of working, eating, sleeping, see F 574.8.
    For food and drink, see N.

F 533 Street Trip Relations between relatives, friends, host and guest Social class Rank
F 534 Work Commerce Business
F 536 Entertainment Diversion
F 537 School
F 538 Church
F 539 Common law
F 540 Crucial Moment of Life Life Cycle
    For song or dance concerning crucial moment in life cycle, see C 340 or C 434.

F 542 Birth
F 543 Baptism Naming rite
F 544 Maturity
F 545 Marriage
F 546 Death
F 549 War
F 570 Number Measure
F 572   Numbers System of counting Calculation

F 574		Measure of time Time measure by astronomy or heavenly body, ruler or historic event, festival or routine activity.	M 222	Metal Stone Bone
F 574.2		Year	.2	Gold Silver Copper
	.3	Season	.3	Iron
	.32	Winter	.5	Stone
	.33	Spring	.6	Precious stone Gem
	.34	Summer	.8	Bone Ivory Horn
	.35	Autumn Fall	M 223	Wood Gourd
	.4	Month	M 224	Leather Fur Feather
	.5	Week Day Hour	M 225	Seed Bead Shell Tooth
	.6	Ruler or historic event	M 226	Clay
	.7	Festival	M 227	Weaving material For costuming in dance or drama, see C 484.
	.8	Routine activity		
	.82	Working	.2	Wool
	.84	Eating. For menu, see N 222.	.3	Cotton
	.86	Sleeping	.4	Flax Hemp Jute
F 575		Measure of space: distance, height, depth	.6	Silk
F 577		Measure of quantity or weight	.8	Reed
	.2	Solid	M 228	Human or animal body
	.4	Liquid	.2	Paint
F 578		Measure of quality	.4	Tattoo
	.2	Medium of exchange	.6	Deformation
	.4	Monetary system	.8	Scarification
F 600		Festival Complex unit of customs and other folklore, to celebrate a special occasion, usually annually and of public interest. For festival dances, see C 436.	M 240	Finished Product
			M 242	Occupation Includes tools.
			.2	War
			.3	Hunting
F 620		Typical Elements of a Festival Pattern Religious or other ritual, parade, fireworks, special dress, work tabu. . . .	.4	Fishing
			.5	Agriculture
			.6	Animal husbandry
			.7	Milling
F 640		Fixed Date	.8	Commerce
F 642		December 21 solstice to March 20	M 243	Household furniture and utensil Interest here is in their manufacture. For use of utensils, see N 226 and N 420.
F 643		March 21 equinox to June 20		
F 644		June 21 solstice to September 22		
F 645		September 23 equinox to December 20	M 244	Toy
F 647		Private birthday or anniversary	M 245	Mask For mask in connection with dance, see C 400.
F 660		Movable Date		
F 662		Winter		
F 663		Spring Planting	M 246	Musical instrument Materials and methods of making instruments. For technics of playing them, see C 600. For musical accompaniment to dance, see C 482. For drum, horn, bell as means of communication, see S 720.
F 664		Summer		
F 665		Autumn Fall Harvest Thanksgiving		
F 667		Private		
F 668		Fair		
F 680		Irregular		
F 682		Foundation rite		
F 684		Sacrificial rite for special occasion	M 247	Means of transportation
F 686		Initiation rite	.2	Human
			.3	Beast of burden
		G GEOGRAPHY	.5	Sled, cart, wagon propelled by human or beast on land
			.6	Vehicle propelled by mechanical or other force on land
		L LANGUAGE		
			.7	Water craft or boat propelled by human, wind, mechanical or other force
		M ART CRAFT ARCHITECTURE		
		Materials and methods of manufacture. After object is made, its use or function change interest in it to field to which it is applied. For a verse in art, craft, architecture, see C 850.	.8	Aircraft propelled by any means
			M 248	Dress
			.2	Head
			.4	Overall body cover Upper body and arms
M 200		Art Craft Adornment and object of use as well as object of art.	.6	Lower body and legs
			.8	Hands Feet
M 220		Raw Material		

M 280	Color Design		N 240	Kind of Food and Its Preparation

M 280 Color Design
Classified here are materials in which the major interest is in color and design in general, as such, and apart from the objects to which they are applied. Color and design considered in relation to specific arts and crafts are classified with those arts and crafts: weaving design belongs to M 227.

M 800 Architecture
M 820 Grouping of Structures Settlement
M 840 Permanent and Temporary Dwelling
M 842 Plan, design, color, building material and technic
M 844 Foundation Floor
M 845 Wall Partition Door Window
M 846 Roof Ceiling
M 848 Accessories
Fireplace, stove, oven, lighting. . . .
M 850 Other Structure for Private Use
M 852 Separate structure accessory to dwelling
Kitchen, bath, toilet. . . .
M 853 Food storage
M 854 Animal housing Barn Pen
M 855 Tool and equipment shed
M 856 Mill
M 857 Smithy
M 858 Selling establishment
Market stall, store, drink stand. . . .
M 860 Public Building
M 862 Holy place Church Temple
M 864 Community house
M 866 School
M 868 Structure for dance, game, pastime, sport, drama
For dance, or game, pastime, sport, or drama, see C 400 or C 500 or D.
M 880 Monument
M 882 Cemetery
M 883 Shrine Memorial
M 885 Bridge
M 887 Fountain Well Aqueduct

N FOOD DRINK

For verse on food or drink, see C 855. For custom or belief concerning food or drink, such as fasting or tabu, see F 500 or P 500.
N 200 Food
N 220 Menu Service
N 222 Typical menus for the various meals
For meal hours, see F 574.84.
  .2 Morning meals Breakfast
  .4 Noon meals Dinner Lunch
  .6 Night meals Supper
  .8 Other daily repast
  .9 Special or festive meals
N 226 Service Table furnishing and decoration
Interest here is in use of utensil, M 243 in its manufacture. For drink service, see N 420.
  .2 Food container
Platter, bowl, dish in which food is served and eaten. . . .
  .4 Implement to handle food
Knife, fork, spoon. . . .

N 240 Kind of Food and Its Preparation
N 242 Manner of preparation
  .2 Kind of heat Cooking equipment
  .4 Process
Baking, boiling, frying. . . .
  .6 Preservation
Drying, salting, pickling. . . .
N 243 Mixed preparation in liquid
Soup, broth, stew. . . .
N 244 Plant food
  .2 Cereal
  .4 Vegetable
  .6 Fruit
  .8 Nut
N 245 Meat
  .2 Bred animal
Cattle, sheep, hog, goat. . . .
  .4 Wild animal
Bear, deer. . . .
  .6 Bird Poultry
Chicken, turkey, duck, quail. . . .
  .8 Fish and other animal life related to water
Oyster, turtle, lobster, clam. . . .
N 246 Animal product
  .2 Egg
  .4 Milk product
Milk itself is a drink, see N 448.4
  .42 Cheese
  .44 Butter
N 247 Pastry Sweet Dessert
Cake, pie, custard, candy, pudding. . . .
N 248 Flavoring
  .2 Herb
  .4 Spice
  .6 Extract
N 400 Drink
N 420 Service
Cup, glass, gourd. . . . Interest here is in their use, M 243 in their manufacture. For food service, see N 226.
N 440 Kind of Drink and Its Preparation
N 442 Water
N 443 Non-alcoholic fruit beverage
  .2 Grape
  .4 Citrus
Orange, lemon, lime. . . .
  .6 Coffee
  .8 Chocolate
N 444 Non-alcoholic cereal beverage
N 446 Brew of leaf, bark, root
Tea, maté. . . .
N 447 Alcoholic beverage
  .2 Fermented
Beer, wine, pulque, chicha. . . .
  .4 Distilled
Whiskey, brandy, rum. . . .
N 448 Drink from animal product
  .4 Milk
For milk product as food, see N 246.4.
N 800 Special Form and Purpose Object of Bodily Consumption
Consumed by such forms as chewing, inhalation, injection, for purposes that may

affect the psychic, mental, nervous state of the body, with stimulating or deadening effect, often habit-forming, sometimes producing sensory illusions, including tobacco, snuff, chicle, marihuana, peyote, coca, opium.

P BELIEF

Traditionally accepted concept, often of a cause and effect relationship, past, present, or future, accepted as a result of repeated and collective observation, or perhaps finally of faith. For verse in belief, see C 860.

P 200   Mythology
       Is divided like B 200: P 240 (like B 240) Description of belief concerning creation and order of universe.

P 400   Legend
       Is divided like B 400: P 429 (like B 429) Description of belief concerning ghost.

P 500   Custom
       Explanation or description of belief related to a custom. Is divided like F 500: P 546 (like F 546) Belief concerning burial. Custom or belief concerning food or drink is classified in F 500 or P 500; food and drink themselves, their materials and methods of preparation, belong in N.

P 600   Magic of Speech, Sign, Color
P 620   Magic Book
P 640   Expression of Fixed Form
P 642   Prayer
P 644   Curse
P 646   Charm   Enchantment   Conjuration
P 660   Word   Letter
P 680   Sign   Color
P 682   Sign   Geometric figure
  .2   Circle and other round forms
  .4   Cross and its various modifications
  .6   Angular forms   Triangle   Star   Pyramid
         Stairstep, ladder to heaven. . . .
P 684   Color
P 686   Number
P 688   Emblem
P 700   Medicine
       For medicine dance, see C 437.
P 720   Curer
P 740   Means of Causing or Avoiding Illness
P 750   Remedy
P 752   Animal
P 754   Plant
       Herb, root, bark. . . .
P 756   Mineral
P 760   Method of Curing
P 770   Surgery
P 800   Prediction   Divination
P 820   Prophet   Seer   Soothsayer
P 840   Spirit   Mind   Body
       Dream, oracle, clairvoyance, telepathy, palmistry, phrenology. . . .
P 860   Use of Object
       Divining rod, ring, Bible or other holy book, cards, tea leaves, coffee grounds, numerology, crystal-gazing. . . .
P 870   Observation
       Astrology, augury, omen. . . .
P 880   Fate   Destiny   Luck   Chance
       Casting lots. . . .

S SPEECH

For verse in speech, see C 870.

S 200   Phonology   Phonetics
S 226   Folk etymology
       For legend explaining a name or dictionary of proper names, see B 478 or S 580.
S 260   Group of Vowels and Consonants, and of Words
S 300   Morphology
S 400   Syntax
S 500   Vocabulary
S 520   Common Word
S 530   Folk Name for Plant
       For general information on plants, see A 534.
S 540   Folk Name for Animal
       For general information on animals, see A 535.
S 550   Vocabulary of Special Group
       For song or custom of group, see C 330 or F 530.
S 552   Underworld
       Thief, prostitute, seller of narcotics, gambler. . . .
S 554   Trade and commerce   Technical and professional group
       Carpenter, salesman, actor, soldier, sailor, cowboy, lumberjack. . . .
S 555   Game   Pastime   Sport
       Is divided like C 500: S 555.524 (like C 524) Vocabulary of racing.
S 560   Onomatopeia
       Animal call, sound made by animal and thing. . . .
S 570   Formula
S 580   Proper Name
       For legend explaining name or folk etymology, see B 478 or S 226.
S 582   Person   Nickname
S 584   Family   Group
S 586   Place
S 600   Gesture
       Sign language with face, hands, and other body parts, deaf-mute, trade group. . . .
S 700   Extra-Corporal Means of Communication
S 720   To Be Heard
       Drum and other percussion instrument, horn and other wind instrument, bell. . . . For technics of playing musical instrument, see C 600. For materials and methods of making musical instrument, see M 246.
S 740   To Be Seen
       Light, smoke, pictograph, orthographic symbol. . . .

V PROVERB

Any saying which has become current and traditional in a group. For verse in proverb, see C 880.

V 200   Proverbial Metaphor
Stated in the form of one of its particular applications: A new broom sweeps clean.

V 300   Proverbial Apothegm Maxim
Stated directly, in broad, general, abstract, categorical terms: Seeing is believing.

V 400   Blason Populaire
Proverbial saying about peoples or places: It takes nine tailors to make a man; Italy to be born in, France to live in, Spain to die in.

V 500   Wellerism
Cites a direct quotation "as so-and-so said when . . ." and follows with some inappropriate application of the quotation, for comic effect: "Every man to his taste," said the farmer when he kissed his cow.

V 600   Proverbial Phrase
Can vary subject and tense of its verb to fit its application; usually is listed in infinitive form: To break the ice.

V 700   Proverbial Comparison
Of similar nature (like), equal (as . . . as), greater or lesser degree (than): Like a fish out of water; As white as snow; Wiser than Solomon; Scarcer than hen's teeth.

W RIDDLE

A thought-provoking question which asks for a solution. For verse in riddle, see C 890.

W 200   True Riddle
Presumably sufficiently precise in its description to be logically solvable: Little Ann Netticoat, with a white petticoat, and a red nose, the longer she stands, the shorter she grows—A burning candle.

W 400   Riddle Question
Insufficiently precise for logical solution; can be answered only by the initiated; asker intends to give answer himself, with intention of ridiculing person asked: Where did Jesus go when He was twelve years old?—Into His thirteenth year.

RALPH STEELE BOGGS

(1) **Typhon, Typhaon,** or **Typhœus** In Greek mythology, a monstrous being associated with the winds and with volcanic eruptions: his origin in Asia, perhaps in Cilicia, has been suggested. Two such monsters are distinguished by some writers: one, the son of Tartarus and Ge, out-tops the mountains, his thighs and legs are coils of serpents, his hands are a hundred dragons' heads, his body is all feathered or winged, he has a hundred heads of dragon shape each with a terrible voice. (2) **Typhon,** a fearful wind, is son of the former and father of the monsters of Greek legend—the Chimera, the Nemean lion, Orthrus, Ladon the dragon, the Sphinx, the eagle eating Prometheus' liver, the Crommyan sow killed by Theseus. (From the latter, by way of China, is derived the English word typhoon; it in turn is connected with the Indo-European root meaning mist). Typhon in later times was identified with the Egyptian Seth, the foe of Osiris; the myth shows evidence of some connection with Egypt. The gods were frightened of Typhon and fled to Egypt, transforming themselves into animals to hide from him: this seems to be a Greek explanation of the animal-headed gods of Egypt, a pourquoi story. Zeus attacked Typhon with his lightnings and injured him with a sickle of adamant, which Typhon then wrested from Zeus. With the sickle Typhon cut out Zeus' foot and hand sinews, crippling him. He hid Zeus in a cave and wrapped the sinews in a bearskin over which he placed a dragon guard. But Hermes and Ægipan (or Cadmus) managed to regain the sinews; they healed Zeus, who then chased Typhon from Nysa, through Thrace, to Sicily. There he buried Typhon beneath Etna, or, according to other tradition, confined him in Tartarus or banished him to some other volcanic region. The Zeus-Typhon myth bears a vague resemblance to the Egyptian myth of Osiris and Seth, which may have influenced it; in other ways it makes the third in a sequence, an unsuccessful attempt to dethrone the gods, paralleling the Uranus-Cronus and Cronus-Zeus episodes. Certainly the myth has the earmarks of great age.

Tyr (Old English *Tiu* or *Tiw;* Old High German *Ziu* or *Ziw*) In Teutonic mythology, god of war, courage, and the sword: one of the three principal deities (with Odin and Thor). His name survives in Tuesday. The ancient Aryans personified the sky, which personification took the form of the Vedic sky god, Dyaus, the classical Zeus, Old Norse Tyr, Old High German Ziu, god of war. Tacitus called him Mars. He is also identified with the old Saxon sword god, Saxnot.

In the myths he is usually the son of Odin and Frigga. He is a wise and very great warrior, and was invoked in battle as frequently as Odin. He helped Odin pick the heroes who were to be carried to Valhalla by the Valkyries. It was Tyr who helped the gods bind the Fenris wolf, put his hand in the wolf's mouth as pledge, and lost it. At Ragnarök he will battle Hel's watchdog, Garm, and they will both fall, mutually slain.

Tyrfing A marvelous invincible sword of Scandinavian epic poetry that fought by itself: famous for its many terrible deeds. It was named for the ancient Tervingi (Visigoths) and first belonged to Angantyr, traditionally having been made for him by the dwarfs. Tyrfing could not be vanquished, but eventually brought death to whoever held it. Once drawn from the sheath, it could not be put back until it had shed blood. It is said to have caused two brothers to fight to the death in the island of Samsö and then (in the hand of the father) to have killed the winner. This follows the ancient Danish conviction that a murderer or traitor must die by his own sword. Legend says that by the order of Angantyr the sword Tyrfing was buried with him, that his daughter called him forth from the grave to ask for it, received it, and used it bravely herself.

Tzŭ Sun Niang Niang The very virtuous wife of a Chinese official: patroness of weddings. After producing the perfect family, five sons and two daughters, she committed suicide to escape the attentions of her sovereign. [RDJ]

U

Uazale The first Paressi Indian, culture hero of the Paressi Indians of the Matto Grosso. He discovered manioc, produced tobacco, and planted his hair to produce cotton. He was very hairy, had a tail, and a membrane between his arms and legs like a bat.

Udó Moon god of the Sumu Indians, companion to Uhubapút, Sumu chief deity, sun god, and creator. The planet Venus, when seen above the crescent moon, is called Udó's wife. See R. G. Heath's "Mískito Glossary," *IJAL* 16: 20–34.

ugly duckling Catchword for the unpromising surpasses promising group of motifs (L140 ff.). All kinds of unpromising characters turn out to be wonders and "get theirs" in the end: the stupid surpass the clever (L141 f.), the pupil surpasses the teacher (L142 f.), the ugly sister is chosen instead of the pretty one (L145), the neglected child proves his worth (L146), even the tardy and slow win over the prompt and swift (L148 f.). In *The Ugly Duckling* by Hans Christian Andersen, a young swan is hatched out by a duck, is belittled, ridiculed, and persecuted by all the ducks because of his strange appearance, but eventually grows into the most beautiful bird on the pond.

Uhepono A woolly-skinned underworld giant in Zuñi Indian mythology. He has eyes like saucers and human arms and legs. [EWV]

Uilleann pipe Irish bagpipe (*píob uillean*) of the bellows type which came into use late in the 16th century. Improvements in its construction permitting some variation of tone in the drones by wrist manipulation made it a gentleman's instrument in the 18th century. The name is corrupted to union pipe.

Ukko Literally, Old Man: the thunder god of the Finns: often identified with Jumala, god of heaven. Ukko commands the clouds, rain, and thunder. There are many survivals of the festivals and sacrifices for Ukko from the mid-16th to the beginning of the 20th century. Such ceremonies, called "Ukko's wedding" or "Ukko's chests," were held until St. John and the Christian God were asked for rain and the fertility of the crops in Ukko's stead. A cock or a sheep was sacrificed. The "chests" were made of birch bark, and sacrifices for Ukko were placed in them and carried to Ukko's mountain. For the sacrifice the best sheep was slaughtered. Its flesh was boiled and portions of the meat, together with other victuals, were put into the chests, along with a large quantity of beer and spirits, and taken to the holy mountain where they were left untouched until the next day. Ukko was said to eat his share during the night; in the morning the rest was eaten by the worshippers. Part of the drinks was poured on the ground to ensure a summer free from drought (U. Holmberg). In describing this feast Michael Agricola (c. 1550) said: "Ukko's goblet was drunk at the sowing of the spring's seeding; Ukko's chest was also brought, and then maid and wife drank to excess, and moreover many shameful

things were done there." Such festivals have been held in Finland almost to the present day. (See K. Krohn in *FFC* 104, 1932, pp. 33–40.) [JB]

Ukupanipo In Hawaiian mythology, the shark god who controls the fish by driving them to or from the shores and thus supplying or depriving the people of their food. Ukupanipo is believed occasionally to adopt a human child and to give him the power to change into a shark at will.

Uller or **Ullr** In Teutonic mythology, one of the æsir, the son of Thor's wife, Sif, and an unknown father: god of winter, hunting, archery, skating, and snow-shoeing. From the number of places in Sweden which bear his name it is probable that his importance had waned by the time of the sagas and Eddas. As god of winter, in some myths he alternates with Odin (summer), taking Odin's place (even with Frigga) while Odin is away during the winter months. His home in Asgard is Ydalir (yew grove) because the yew yields the best bows. He is also said in Germany to have a summer home on the top of the Alps among the snow-capped peaks. In Anglo-Saxon he was probably Wuldor, glory; in parts of Germany he is known as Holler, the husband of Holde, and it is he who spreads the white blankets over the fields in winter to protect them from the cold. He is also said to have married Skadi (the divorced wife of Niörd) who likes it very well in his abode. He is another of the gods who in some localities is said to lead the Wild Hunt. Oaths were often sworn by the ring on his altars. Some say that he alternates with Balder in Hel according to the season.

Ulster cycle The oldest and most famous of the cycles of Old Irish epic, legend, and romance. The manuscripts date from the 7th and 8th centuries, but celebrate the Ireland and Irish heroes of the 1st and depict the civilization of barbaric splendor that dates back centuries earlier. Most of the stories are laid, however, in the 1st century B.C., when Conchobar was king of Ulster with his seat at Emain Macha. Cuchulain is the central hero. The *Táin Bó Cuáilgne* is the longest and principal text. The cycle also includes, among others, the story of the *Visitation to Guaire* and the revealing of the *Táin Bó Cuáilgne* (see BOOK OF THE DUN COW; KING OF THE CATS), the *Debility of the Ultonians* (see MACHA), the *Táin Bó Regamna*, the *Táin Bó Fraić* (see AILILL MAC MATACH), the famous *Exile of the Sons of Usnech* (see DEIRDRE), the *Wooing of Emer*, *Bricriu's Feast* (see this; also CHAMPION'S PORTION), the *Tragic Death of Aife's Only Son* (see CONLA), the humorous *Story of MacDatho's Pig*, the *Intoxication of the Ultonians*, the *Dream of Angus* (see ANGUS OG AND CAER), *Cuchulain's Death* (see CUCHULAIN), the story of the *Red Rout of Conal Céarnać on the Plain of Muirthemne* to avenge it, the *Phantom Chariot of Cuchulain*, and the *Destruction of Da Derga's Hostel* (see TABU) which became attached to the Ulster cycle.

Ulysses The Latin name of the Greek hero Odysseus and the name by which he was best known in European literature until the latter decades of the 19th century.

umbilical cord The umbilical cord is thought to be intimately associated with the fate of the child. Among the Swahili the cord is placed around the child's neck and then interred on the spot where the child was born in order to draw him constantly to his parents' house. In New Zealand the cord and placenta are buried under a tree planted at the birth of a child; the Hupa Indians of California split a small tree, place the cord in the split, and tie the tree together again. The fate of the child is indicated by the fate of the tree. In some parts of Europe the cord is worn for a time, but precautions are necessary to see that it is not eaten by an animal or operated on by magicians or spirits. The Spanish belief is that the child will acquire the bad qualities of whatever animal eats the cord; the German belief is that the cord eaten by the child himself will make him clever. See AFTERBIRTH; AMULET; CAUL; CHILDBIRTH. [RDJ]

In almost all of Middle America there is a special disposition of the afterbirth and umbilical cord. It is generally believed that the treatment accorded the placenta will affect the child in later life. In hot countries it may be placed under a rock in a cool stream "so that the adult will not perspire unduly when working in his fields." In cold countries often it is buried under the hearth or in the potter's oven so that the child will not catch cold. Usually the umbilical stump is saved for its healing properties, often throughout the lifetime of the individual. A little may be crumbled in water to be drunk to cure various illnesses. Traders from the Tarascan area in Mexico are known to carry their stump on their first long trip away from home, to bury it under a tree in the plaza of a town to which they expect to make frequent trips, in the expectation that this will bring many sales. [GMF]

umbrella In the Far and Near East, parts of Africa and Mexico, umbrellas denote royal or divine power. They are carried over the heads of monarchs and high priests. One view is that umbrellas are derived from the solar wheel over the head of Buddha. The umbrella is one of the eight symbols of Buddha. See DA-CHA. In an Athenian ceremony the priests of the sun and of Poseidon and the priestess of Athena walked from the Acropolis under a large white umbrella. An umbrella is on a coin from the period of Herod Agrippa I. In one of the *Jatākas*, a prince who wants to get his brother's kingdom demands to be given the royal umbrella. In 1855 a Burmese king spoke of himself as a monarch who reigns over the great umbrella. Umbrellas are used in the marriage ceremonies of the Lower Congo and mark the place of the chief in a Dahomey ancestor ceremony. Some of the Dahomey umbrellas are highly decorated. The high priests of one of the Mexico cults were protected by umbrellas. The fact that all the places noted are in or near the tropics and that persons of power and position could find some protection from the sun's rays is perhaps as significant as the interpretation that umbrellas were used by persons so sacred that they must not be touched by the sun. The two views may well be complementary. See BODY MARKS. [RDJ]

Uncle Remus The narrator of Joel Chandler Harris' famous collections of Negro animal tales from the southern part of the United States, of which Brer Rabbit is the protagonist. So popular have the Uncle Remus tales become that they are regarded as the prototype and "real" form of Negro folklore. The effect of this has been to direct the attention of collectors of tales, both among New World Negroes and in Africa, toward animal stories, and to cause them to neglect the rich store of literature in which the characters are human beings. [MJH]

The plantation story-teller in the Uncle Remus books (1880–1918) of Joel Chandler Harris. Based on several Negroes of Harris's acquaintance (including George Terrell), Uncle Remus is an individualized portrait of a type of privileged house servant who, in his role of entertainer to white children, was encouraged to preserve and transmit his African folk heritage, and, along with it, traditional Southern attitudes. Humorous, poetic, philosophical, as well as a skilled story-teller, Harris's alter ego made the Uncle Remus story synonymous with the American Negro animal tale, especially of the trickster type (see BRER RABBIT), but not neglecting the explanatory myth. In his hands and in the character of Uncle Remus, folklore, folk speech, and folk fantasy are fused into folk art. For an analysis and evaluation of the folklore elements in the Uncle Remus books, see Stella Brewer Brookes, *Joel Chandler Harris—Folklorist*, Athens, Georgia, 1950. [BAB]

Uncle Sam Popular personification of the people or government of the United States, corresponding to the British John Bull. By the 1850's, the image of Uncle Sam as a tall, lean, sinewy, unmistakably Yankee figure, with long hair and chin whiskers, in striped pantaloons, swallow-tail coat, and plug hat, had become established in political caricature, replacing the earlier and somewhat similar Brother Jonathan, and the still earlier graphic emblems of America—the Indian, the rattlesnake, the bucking horse, and the eagle (which became an official emblem).

While the name is obviously a humorous extension of the initials of the United States, it has, after the fashion of "historical" traditions, become attached to a particular person, time, and place; namely, Samuel ("Uncle Sam") Wilson (1766–1854), of Troy, N. Y., a meat inspector for a government contractor, Elbert Anderson, at the opening of the War of 1812. When asked what the initials, "E.A.–U.S.," stamped on casks, stood for, a facetious workman replied that "he did not know, unless it meant *Elbert Anderson* and *Uncle Sam* [Wilson]" (Bartlett's *Dictionary of Americanisms*, 1859 ed., pp. 492–493). The joke passed into army circulation and into print and then legend, where it has stuck, in spite of the efforts of historians to dislodge it.

Besides Brother Jonathan, another and junior prototype of Uncle Sam is Major Jack Downing, a political cracker-box philosopher, friend and critic of President Andrew Jackson, whose "Jack Downing" letters, contributed by Seba Smith to the Portland, Maine, *Daily Courier*, beginning in January, 1830, made him a familiar literary and graphic figure in American politics, along with the more folksy and more enduring Davy Crockett.

B. A. BOTKIN

underworld In the cosmography of peoples all over the world, a region under the ground, to which an entrance on the surface exists somewhere, and in which live the souls of the dead, though sometimes the souls have been modified in popular belief and are considered the fairies, elves, or the like, living inside hills, in wells, on river beds, etc. The Christian underworld is Hell where the souls of the wicked receive eternal punishment. More anciently, the Greeks believed in an underworld where the dead lived a colorless but not a hard life. The Egyptian Fields of Aalu were a paradisical underworld where the grain grew well. To reach the underworld one must cross a river in a boat guided by a spectral ferryman; at any rate, a guide is needed, the psychopomp or conductor of souls. The opening to the underworld is often kept closed with a rock; on certain festivals, for example, the Greeks and Romans opened the way for the souls to return to earth to be entertained. The god of the underworld is usually a forbidding personage, a prince of darkness or a prince of evil. It is perhaps only natural that the underworld of the tropical or semitropical peoples is usually a warm place, while the underworld of peoples of cold climates is a place of eternal ice. See AFTERWORLD; DESCENTS TO UNDERWORLD; JOURNEY TO OTHERWORLD; ORPHEUS.

ungkulatem The national round dance of the Siberian Yakut, corresponding to the *ikandzyedzyem* of the Tungus. The literal meaning, "I sing," refers to the monotonous chanting by all participants. Men and women progress sunwise, either in one large circle in arbitrary order, or in separate circles. With the right arm under the next dancer's left, the clasped hands are held close to the body. All step sideways with the left foot, swaying the torso slightly forward; then all bring up the right foot in back of the left, leaning backward. The dancing may continue for a long period on festive occasions such as marriages. [GPK]

unicorn This one-horned animal resembles a white horse but is larger and is distinguished by a single horn growing from the middle of its head. The horn is 27 to 36 inches long. Euhemerists trace unicorn stories back to the rhinoceros.

Dr. Olfert Dapper saw a wild unicorn in the Maine woods in 1673, and in 1936 Dr. Franklin Dove, biologist at the University of Maine, described in the *Scientific Monthly* in some detail an operation he had performed in 1933 on the horn buds of a one-day-old Ayrshire calf. The consequence was a single spike solidly attached to the skull and used to pry up barriers. The thrust of the single horn was more powerful than the thrust of a two horned animal. Dr. Dove reminded his readers that transplantation was known in the time of Pliny. Although the classical reports give the unicorn's horn a white base, black middle, and red tip, Dr. Dove notes that only the females have red tips. Unicorns have been reported from southern France in the Middle Ages and from China, where a one-horned animal is described as the "four-not-likes," i.e. body of a horse but not like a horse, feet of an antelope but not like an antelope, etc. The unicorn was at one time thought to be a native of India, later of Africa.

The medieval church ascribed many characteristics to this animal. It was the symbol of chastity and fierceness but because it would inherit the earth it was very meek. Although normally powerful it was gentle at mating time and thus symbolized virginity and demonstrated the power of love. In ecclesiastical art it is associated with the lamb and the dove. In heraldry, the unicorn is

associated with James I and thus the British crown.

In Biblical etiology the unicorn is now extinct because he was thrown out of the ark and drowned (A2214.3). In a European tale of capture by deceit, he is tricked into running his horn into a tree (K771) and is captured before he can get it out. Traditionally it can be tamed by the touch of a virgin.

If the horn of a unicorn is dipped into water the water will become pure. If a dish containing poison is touched by a unicorn's horn, the poison will be disclosed. The Chinese still use ivory to detect poison and the gates of Prester John's palace contained the horn of horned serpents to prevent the smuggling in of poison. The essence of unicorn in distillate or elixir is an antidote to poisons.

In the 16th and 17th centuries unicorn horn was a popular though costly ingredient in medicines. In 1789 it was still used to detect poison in royal foods. In 1605, Johannis Baptista Silvaticus reported in his *De Unicornu Bezoar* that Paul III had paid 12,000 gold pieces for a horn to be used against pestilential fevers; and another horn is said to have been sold in Dresden for $75,000. In the 16th century learned men were of several opinions. Copernicus trusted it. Andrea Bacci said that the horn sweats at the approach of venom. Erastus thought it was valueless against poison. De Boot's skepticism was not of the virtues of the horn but rather of the existence of the animal itself. Nevertheless, unicorn's horn is listed among the possessions of many medieval kings, pontiffs, and popes as an amulet used at table to detect the presence of poisons.

Robert Graves reports that "the unicorn's single exalted horn represents the single exalted pole" which reaches directly up to the zenith, the hottest point attained by the sun. In Egyptian architecture it is the obelisk and expresses dominion over the four quarters of the world and the zenith. [RDJ]

universe Many South American Indian tribes visualize the universe as a series of superimposed floors or strata, above and below the surface of our earth. The Witoto conceive of the universe as being formed of five strata, each of a different color. The one in the middle is our world. The uppermost sky is inhabited by a supernatural being resembling a spider. The stratum under us is the World of the Ancestors and underneath this is the lowest world, known as the "Abode of the First Father."

The Chamacoco describe the universe as being formed of five or even seven floors, each of a different color. The floor under us is now empty but was formerly occupied by mankind. The lowest floor belongs to the sun that every morning emerges from the lower spaces.

Other tribes (Mataco, Conibo) speak of only three layers. Formerly the sky and the earth were connected by a big tree. The men of this earth went hunting in the land above until the tree was destroyed by a jealous person (Toba, Mataco, Chamacoco, Shipaya, Cariri). [AM]

☞ A series of worlds, one above the other, if not explicitly stated, is usually implied in the creation myths of nearly all the American Indians. The myths of many groups stress the worlds which exist above the earth; there may be anywhere from one to eight or nine such. The Southwestern tribes, in their emergence myths, emphasize the numerous worlds below the earth, in which the people were living before they emerged upon this earth. [EWV]

Unktomi Santee Siouan dialectical form of the name of the Siouan trickster-culture-hero. Variants of this personal name for the trickster among other Siouan groups are: Iktomi or Ikto (Teton Sioux); Ictinike (Ponca and Omaha); Ictcinike (Missouri). Unktomi is identifiable as the spider; although there is some belief that he is a culture hero and creator, the tales told about him are typical trickster tales, ridiculous and often obscene. [EWV]

unpromising hero (heroine) One of the commonplaces of folktale (motif L100): the hero who for various reasons is supposedly not typically a hero. The most famous of all unpromising heroes is Cinderella, the stepdaughter, an ash girl, ragged, dirty. Often the hero is deformed, ugly, loathly, yet proves in the end to be a transformed prince or other hero type. The Princess on the Pea needs testing, for bedraggled as she is she does not look like a princess. The unlikely hero is as often as not the youngest son (usually the third son) who by kindness or some other virtue not possessed by his elders succeeds where they fail. He may be small, like Thumbling; he may be in a menial position, like Gareth, the kitchen knight of Arthurian legend whose older brothers Gawain, Agravain, and Gaheris were established knights of the Round Table. This menial often proves to be an angel or deity in disguise, as in Greek and Irish stories. The unlikeliness of the hero is typical of the folk hero; he is found in a basket, brought up as a shepherd's child, has a speech impediment or is lame, etc. The fable of the hare and the tortoise plays on the same theme: the tortoise cannot reasonably be expected to outrace the hare, yet he wins. The ugly duckling too turns out to be more beautiful as an adult than its supposed brothers. The idea lies at the base of the modern detective story; the least likely suspect often is the criminal. The unpromising hero motif plays on the self-identification of the hearer with the lowly, and the consequent gratification from the story. See AMALA; DIRTY BOY; YOUNGEST SON.

Unquiet Grave An English ballad (Child #78), one of the relatively few in English folk song about the belief that prolonged mourning disturbs the rest of the dead, though the theme is common in story and song of Scandinavia and other parts of Europe. The lover weeps on the grave of the departed sweetheart until the spirit fretfully begs to be left in peace. Variants have been collected in Newfoundland, in Kentucky, and in New Jersey.

Uranus In Greek mythology, the sky god; personification of the sky, as his consort, Ge, was of the earth: etymologically the name may be connected with Varuna, the Indian sky god. Uranus and Ge figure in a cosmological myth to which striking parallels have been noted in Egypt and New Zealand. Uranus, finding the Cyclopes and the Hecatoncheires, his gigantic sons, troublesome, pushed them back into Earth. Ge on her part resented this burden she thought she had quitted herself of, and induced Cronus to avenge the insult. With a sickle of adamant, Cronus mutilated his father and threw the amputated penis into the sea. From the drops of blood falling upon Earth there were engendered the Erinyes and the Gigantes; from the mixture of blood and foam

in the sea there arose Aphrodite, called Anadyomene from her rising from the sea. Cronus then seized power; Uranus and Ge prophesied his overthrow by one of his own children.

The castration myth is found elsewhere in the world and is in essence a natural cosmological explanatory myth. How were earth and sky separated? In Egypt, Nut, the sky goddess, and Geb, the earth god, were forcibly separated by Shu, their son, the air. Rangi, the sky god, and Papa, the earth goddess, of Maori myth embraced so closely that their children could hardly be born; they too were separated violently by the children. Krappe sees in the story of Noah and Ham an echo of this kind of myth: Noah, survivor of the flood and the culture hero who discovered viniculture, originally may have been made drunk by his son and then castrated. In the *Rig-Veda* traces are found of a myth wherein Indra slays his father. Compare TITANS.

Urashima Taro The hero of a popular Japanese fairy tale having the Rip van Winkle motif. [JLM]

Ursa Major The Great Bear: a constellation of the northern hemisphere conspicuous for its circumpolar motion and its shape. From earliest times it has captured the imagination of mankind and has been identified as a bear (and usually a she-bear) from the classical period on. See CALLISTO. An ancient Cretan story identifies both the Greater and Lesser Bears as two bears who fostered the infant Zeus: an interpretation repudiated by later European astronomers on the grounds that there were no bears in Crete! A 10th century Old English *Manual of Astronomy* calls the constellation Arctos from the Greek myth, adding that the unlearned call it Carles-Wægn. This was because the old Teutonic Wagon or Odin's Wain, later Carles Wægn (i.e. Charlemagne's) was more familiar to the populace than the classical story. In Icelandic and Scandinavian reference it was the Wagon or the Karl Wagon. In modern Germany it is often called Himmel Wagen. Sir Walter Scott in the *Lay of the Last Minstrel* referred to it as Arthur's Wain. The Plough or the Heavenly Plough have also been common English designations of long standing.

The ancient Hebrews called this constellation Dōbh, Bear; the Arabs called it Al Dubh al Akbar, the Greater Bear. To the early Syrians it was the Wild Boar. Job's reference to "Arcturus with his sons" (*Job* xxxviii, 32) has been thought to refer to the stars of Ursa Major. In late Indian mythology, its seven bright stars were identified with seven illustrious rishis.

In Chinese astronomy, our Ursa Major is known as Pih Tow, the Emperor's Chariot, and its perpetual motion around the pole star symbolizes the emperor's unceasing overseeing of the empire. Also, a Chinese goddess known as Seven Star Mother lives in this constellation. In Chinese legend a famous astronomer and magician of the 7th century I-hsing (or Yi-hsing) Ch'an-shih once caught the seven stars of Ursa Major in a bag, in the shape of seven little pigs. The Emperor was then persuaded to declare a seven-day amnesty throughout the empire to effect their restoration. I-hsing then let one little pig per day out of the bag; each night one star reappeared in the sky. Thus this wily old man saved an old boyhood friend who was scheduled to be executed that week. See KUEI HSING.

The Berbers of northern Africa regard Ursa Major and

Ursa Minor as a camel and her calf; the pole star (*Lem-kechen*, hold) is the woman who holds the little camel while the mother is being milked. To the Buriats of eastern Siberia the seven stars of Ursa Major are Seven Old Men. One of the Koryak names for the constellation, when regarded as a bear, is Notakavya, the One Who Walks Around the Earth. Another Koryak name for it is Elwe'kyeñ, Wild Reindeer Buck. The Koryaks believed that the creator went to the stars to get reindeer for the people.

Ushās The Vedic goddess of dawn, the bright and ever young daughter of heaven (Dyaus) and sister of the Ādityas. She opens the gates of the sky, drives off the evil spirits which gather at night, leads the white horse of the sun.

Utgard In Teutonic mythology, one of the divisions of Jotunheim presided over by Utgard-Loki. According to Snorri, Thor and Loki with two servants journeyed to Jotunheim and spent the night there, trying several feats of strength to entertain the assembled company. In all of these they were beaten: Thialfi, Thor's servant, lost a race to a lad named Hugi; Loki was bested in an eating race by one Villi-eldr; Thor failed to drain a drinking horn, could not lift Utgard-Loki's cat, and was thrown to one knee by the old nurse, Elli. Next day, as Utgard-Loki was escorting his guests on their way, he admitted that they had been tricked: Hugi was, in reality, thought; Villi-eldr, wildfire; the drinking horn was forever replenished from the sea; the cat was Jormungandr, the Midgard-serpent; and Elli was old age—yet they had nearly succeeded. Saxo grammaticus treats Utgard-Loki as a medieval devil in one of his stories.

Uther Pendragon According to Geoffrey of Monmouth and later writers, the father of King Arthur. There is a poem of uncertain antiquity in the *Book of Taliesin* (c. 1275) called the "Death-Song of Uthyr Ben," which is so obscure that one can extract little from it except that Uthyr claims a ninth part in the prowess of Arthur. Another poem, perhaps of the 10th century, names in a list of Arthur's warriors Mabon and describes him as the servant of Uthir Pen Dragon. There is nothing, then, in authentic Welsh tradition that makes this Uther the father of Arthur, and it is probably one of Geoffrey's characteristic audacities to create a history for Uther Pendragon and to bring him into relation with Arthur and Merlin. Geoffrey represents him as the brother of the historic Aurelius Ambrosius, who on the latter's death reigned over Britain, begat Arthur on the wife of Gorlois Duke of Cornwall, killed Gorlois in battle, and wedded the widow. Uther in his declining years defeated the Saxons, but was poisoned by their spies and buried in the Giants' Dance (Stonehenge). Through Wace's *Brut* much of this found its way into the Merlin romances, which added the story of Uther's founding the Round Table by Merlin's advice at Carlisle on the day of Pentecost. Geoffrey explained the title Pendragon as meaning "dragon's head in the British tongue," and said that Uther was so called because at his coronation Merlin gave him two golden dragons, one of which he carried in his wars as a standard. Loth, however, thinks that the title originally meant "chief of warriors."

Bibliography: Bruce, J. D., *Evolution of Arthurian Romance from the Beginnings to 1300* (Baltimore, 1923). See index. Parry, J. J., "Geoffrey of Monmouth and the Paternity of Arthur," *Speculum* XIII (1938): 271–77. [RSL]

vagina dentata Catchword for a motif (F547.1) which occurs in the widely distributed American Indian hero tale, *Sun Tests his Son-in-Law* (or *Son*) but also found as an incident in other American Indian material, even in some trickster tales. The hero, a male, encounters a woman who invites him to have intercourse with her. She has had many men but they have all died because of her toothed vagina. The hero inserts sticks in the vagina; the first of these are ground up but the teeth cannot chew the harder ones; he then knocks out all of the teeth, or all except one. [EWV]

☞ The toothed vagina motif, so prominent in North American Indian mythology, is also found in the Chaco and in the Guianas. The first men in the world were unable to have sexual relationship with their wives until the culture hero broke the teeth of the women's vaginas (Chaco). According to the Waspishiana and Taruma Indians the first woman had a carnivorous fish inside her vagina. [AM]

Vahagn The ancient Armenian god of war and courage; god of sun, lightning, fire; the Armenian god who replaced Mithra in the Zoroastrian triad of Aramazd, Anahit, and Mithra; also, a national hero, competing

successfully with Mihr and Barshamina for first rank. Vahagn was, like many dragon-slayers, born from a plant. He emerged from a reed with hair of fire and eyes that were suns, the son of heaven, earth, and the sea. He was always youthful. His warlike nature is typical of the weather gods of the world. Vahagn is the conqueror of the dragon Azhdak (Azhi Dahāka).

He stole straw from Barshamina on a cold night and in escaping dropped it. From the straw the Milky Way was formed. In modern Armenian folklore he has been succeeded by Dsovean. In his heroic aspects he became identified with Hercules. Compare AGNI.

Vailala Madness One of many new religious cults of revivalist type that included a base of native religious elements, which swept Papua after European occupation. Similar cults have appeared elsewhere in Oceania, as well as in North America and Africa, wherever a primitive culture has been shaken by contact with European complexities and has attempted to readjust itself by seeking refuge in cults of the revivalist type. See F. E. Williams in *Essays presented to G. G. Seligmann* (1934), "Orokaiva Magic," p. 3 ff., which has additional bibliography and tells about the Papuan revivalist cults called Taro, Kekesi, and Baigona. [KL]

Väinämöinen The chief hero of the Finnish runoes (see *Kalevala* songs 1–9, 15–17, 44–47, 50), called *Äinemöinen* by Agricola (in 1551); the great magician and singer (see KANTELE), inventor of the harp, and "forger of runoes." His mother is Ilmatar, "the daughter of the air," but Väinämöinen was born in the water. His name, from *väinä*, mouth of a river, indicates that he has some relationship with the water. The sea-maidens in the songs are called *väinän tytto* or *tytär*. He builds ships and likes sea voyages. Otherwise he is a culture hero (fells trees and sows barley) and is protector of his country, Väinölä or Kalevala, from all enemies and witches, especially from the sorceries of Louhi. He is an enemy of the Lapp people and their hero Joukohainen. He was shot dead by a Lapp and rescued. He visited, alive, Tuonela, the island of the dead. He is always thought of as old and wise; in war he is the leader of the people. The people love him more than any other hero, and have even given his name to some of the stars: Orion is called "the scythe of Väinämöinen," the Pleiades the "sword or shoe of Väinämöinen." He is not a god, but a hero. See BARLEY. JONAS BALYS

Vairochana One of the five Buddhas of Contemplation: the Brilliant, the illuminating one. See ADIBUDDHA.

Vaitaraṇi In Hindu mythology, the river of death which flows between the land of the living and the kingdom of Yama (the land of the dead). The river Vaitaraṇi is filled with blood, hair, and filth. To cross this loathsome stream, especially in Bengal, a dying man must grasp the tail of a cow which is then given to a Brāhman or a cow is given away so the soul can cling to its tail while passing over the river. The name Vaitaraṇi is also given to the Hindu hell reserved for destroyers of beehives and pillagers of villages. The Vaitaraṇi is identified with the Baitaraṇī, a river in north India.

vajra Among the theistic Buddhists of Nepal vajra is the symbol of mystic or divine energy and is at the same time the polite and decent name for the male sexual organ. Vajradhara or Vajrasattva who is the incarnation of the complex of ideas designated by vajra is a Tantric brahman. Vajra is "hard as adamant and clear as emptiness." He is a thunderbolt against demons. The trident is one of his attributes. [RDJ]

Vajrasattva In Buddhism, one of the five Buddhas of Contemplation: literally, thunderbolt-being. The Tibetans believe Vajrasattva analogous to Adibuddha.

valentine 1) A piece of folded paper bearing the name of a boy or girl, drawn by lot at parties on the eve of **St. Valentine's Day** (February 14), the one named to be the sweetheart of the drawer for a year. 2) A person of the opposite sex deliberately chosen or whose name is drawn by lot on St. Valentine's Day to be one's sweetheart or special friend for a year. This party play of the young people on this day has been associated in England from medieval times with the choosing, wooing, and mating of birds at this time of year (B232.1). 3) The first young man (or woman) one chances to meet in the street or elsewhere on St. Valentine's Day. The custom formerly was to kiss this "first-met"; thus he (or she) was your valentine or special love for a year. 4) The fancy, dainty valentine or card, beflowered and befrilled with ribbons and paper lace, bearing printed or written verses couching a love greeting or proposal: a common-

place of the modern observance of the day, as is also the take-off on the sentimental valentine, i.e. the mock or comic valentine, lampooning the weakness or ridiculing some peculiarity of the recipient. These are supposed to be sent anonymously. Presents of candy, flowers, etc., sent on this day are also called valentines.

valerian (from Latin *valere*, to be strong: so named probably for its medicinal properties) This is an herb of Mercury which the Arabs said was hot and moist and would stir up lust. The Greeks said it was hot and dry and used it to stop bleeding. The Romans used it as incense; and it was widely used to scent linens and clothes and to keep out moths and vermin. Cats and rats both love the smell of this herb and roll in it; cats are said to dig up the roots and eat them.

Early English herbalists recommended valerian as a diuretic, also for rickets, and as a nerve-calmer. In the doctrine of signatures it was good for the lungs. It inspired love, and sorcerers used it in a concoction to raise and commune with spirits. Culpeper recommended it for wind, sight, inward sores and outward hurts, and said that it would draw thorns. Many herbalists have called it an all-heal. It is a mild sedative and has no after-effects, a fact which makes it useful in nervous disorders; during World War I it was used successfully in cases of shell-shock. The Meskwaki Indians of the United States used it to stop hemorrhages and to quiet hysteria and functional nervousness. The Gosiute Indians of Utah use it for bruises and swellings and the pounded roots for rheumatism.

Valhalla In Teutonic mythology, the favorite of Odin's three homes, where he entertained the Einheriar, the warriors chosen from among the slain. Valhalla is a great hall whose rafters are of spears and whose roof is made of polished shields. Its 540 doors are each wide enough to accommodate 800 warriors abreast. It is situated in the shimmering grove of Glaesir whose trees bear leaves of red gold, and is surrounded by the river Thund. Half of the warriors slain in battle are chosen by Odin or Tyr and are carried to Valhalla by the Valkyries (battle maidens) where they are welcomed by Odin's sons, Hermod and Bragi, and brought before his throne. The other half of the slain warriors go to Freya at Sessrymnir in Folkvang. They spend their days in combat, but at the end of the day their wounds are healed and they gather in the great hall for a glorious feast prepared by Odin's cook, Andhrimnir, from the magic boar, Saehrimnir, which comes to life again after each killing. It is prepared in the giant caldron, Eldhrimnir. Their mead is provided by the she-goat, Heidrun, and is brought to them by the white-armed Valkyries who have put off their armor and are dressed in becoming white gowns. Their evenings are spent in hearing again the tales and songs of their battles.

Vali In Teutonic mythology, 1) one of the æsir; son of Odin and the giantess Rinda; born for the purpose of avenging the death of Balder. He was a daring warrior and a clever archer but he will take no part in Ragnarök, although some sources say that he and Vidar will survive this battle. No mention is made of the way in which he destroyed Hoder, Balder's slayer. All we know is that he was but one night old at the time. He is considered the god of eternal light and personification of the lengthening days of spring.

2) The son of Loki and Sigyn, said by some to be a namesake of Odin's son. When Loki is captured by the gods, they turn Vali into a wolf who kills his brother, Narvi, whose entrails they use to bind Loki.

Valkyries In Teutonic mythology, a group of battle maidens included in the æsir. They are Odin's personal attendants, and daily they ride forth over the battlefields of the world to see that his wishes are carried out and to carry the slain warriors designated by Odin or Tyr over the rainbow bridge, Bifrost, to Valhalla. Their number varies with various authorities from three to three times nine, but they are all beautiful golden-haired maidens with dazzling white arms. When riding into battle, or warning of impending battle (for their appearance heralded a coming fray), they rode white horses and were attired in shining helmets and armor, but in Valhalla where they served mead to the fallen heroes, they were attired in white robes. Some say that those about to be carried to Valhalla received a kiss of death from one of these maidens. These maidens are sometimes confused with the Norns, whom they resemble. See BRYN-HILD; FREYA.

Vālmīki A hermit, the legendary author of the *Rāmāyana*. Shrines have been built to Vālmīki in many parts of India and two hunting castes of the United Provinces, the Aheriyas and the Baheliyas, claim descent from him. The sweepers' god, Lāl Beg, has been identified with him.

vampire One of the types of the undead; a living corpse or soulless body that comes from its burial place and drinks the blood of the living. Belief in vampires is found all over the world—in India, China, Malaya, Indonesia, etc.—but typically it is a Slavic concept; Russia, Poland, Bulgaria, Croatia, Slovenia, and thence Greece, Rumania, Albania, Hungary are the great vampire area. In Hungary in the 18th century, the uproar about vampires was as great as that during the witch hunts of colonial New England. The vampire cannot rest in the grave; it must spend the night searching for a victim, but at cockcrow, when the sun rises, or when the bells ring in the morning, it must return to the coffin. Anyone bitten by a vampire becomes a vampire upon death; vampires are also made if a cat or other baneful creature jumps or flies over the corpse before it is buried; suicides, witches, those under a curse become vampires. Light, bells, iron, garlic are all effective against vampires. If a corpse about to be buried has its mouth open, it will probably be a vampire; the mouth must be stuffed with clay before the coffin is closed. If it is suspected that a certain corpse already buried is a vampire, it must be dug up and examined; if it proves to be red-cheeked and fresh, not decomposed, with blood-stains around the mouth, it is a vampire. Such a body must be decapitated, burned, buried at a crossroads, or a wooden stake driven through its heart. It will twist in agony as the stake pierces it, but after that it will lie in peace. See AZEMAN; BORN WITH TEETH; PRET; SATURDAY; SEVENTH SON; ZOMBI.

Vanant (Avestan *vanant;* Pahlavi *vanand*) In Persian mythology, one of the four leaders of the stars which fight for Mazda; the guardian star of the west who conquers evil.

vanir (singular *van*) A group or class of early Teutonic deities who later became associated with the æsir.

Originally they were fertility gods and later became associated more specifically with weather, crops, and commerce. The three vanir whose names are familiar in mythology were Niörd, Frey, and Freya. The only other of the vanir of whom we have record by name is Nerthus, who was later identified with Niörd. Very little is known of the vanir, except that their home was Vanaheim and they waged war against the æsir. Niörd and his children Frey and Freya went to Asgard as hostages in exchange for Hoenir and Mimir, who were sent to the vanir. Hoenir relied so entirely on Mimir's wisdom, that when consulted in his absence, he put the decision on others. This angered the vanir, who felt they had been worsted in the hostage exchange. So they beheaded Mimir and sent his head to Odin. Some versions of the vanir story say that Niörd, Frey, and Freya will return to Vanaheim at Ragnarök.

vaqueria Literally, cowboy doings: the festal dance of the Maya of Quintana Roo. It follows the custom of naming fiesta officials after the characters in the oldtime hacienda. The dance company should consist of thirteen married couples. They are dressed in their best mestizo costume, but not as cowboys and cowgirls, except for the lasso draped across the shoulder of the *vaqueros* and the large men's hat worn by the *vaqueras*. It corresponds to the *jarana* of Yucatán in choreography, music, costume, and function. That is, though a social couple dance, it is part of religious as well as secular celebrations, and is attended by ritual actions, such as preliminary blessing, food offerings, and feasting on a sacrificed hog. In honor of the Virgin of the Concepción, the *vaqueros* assist at the planting of a sacred tree, *yaxche*. In the tree-setting and subsequent dancing they interact with a clown, called *chic* or *chiquero*. Like the *jarana*, each *vaqueria* ends with *el torito*. Each fiesta includes four *vaquerías*, sponsored by four different *cargadores*. The last night is given to visiting the *cargadores* in their homes, folowed by a *corrida* or bullfight, and a short dance called "half a night." The concluding ceremony is the "back beating" in the house of the *nohoch mayol*, or manager. His assistant, the *chan mayol*, beats the back of each *vaquera* with a handkerchief rope; and the *h-men* or shaman, gives them rum and strokes their heads with zipche leaves. This ritual is to protect future offspring from the evil winds which might attack the *vaqueras* in their exhausted state. Thus the attendant rituals of the vaquería preserve ancient practices of fertility magic. [GPK]

Varāha The boar avatar or incarnation of Vishnu, assumed in order to deliver the world from the power of the demon Hiranyāksha, who had seized the earth and carried it to the depths of the ocean. After a thousand-year battle, Varāha killed the monster and brought back the earth to the surface. Another version of the myth says the earth was pressed down by an overabundant population. The boar lifted it on one tusk and made it again fit for habitation. In modern Hindu belief earthquakes are caused when Varāha shifts his burden from one tusk to the other. In modern Hinduism Varāha is the third incarnation of Vishnu.

variant By its very nature, folklore is traditional and its preservation depends upon custom and memory. It is, therefore, subject to all the variations that come from the attempt to repeat exactly the customary action, or to tell or perform that which has been learned from listening to someone else. Every performance of such an act and every repetition of such a tale or song displays differences from all others. These variations may be involuntary, where the aim is an exact repetition, or they may represent a conscious attempt at creation within the framework of the tradition. Since every repetition thus displays variations, it is customary to call each example of an item of folklore a variant. If the idea of variation is not foremost in the mind of the speaker, he is more likely to use the term *version*. There is otherwise no difference in the use of these two terms. [ST]

Varuna In Vedic mythology, the supreme ruler of the gods; guardian of the cosmic order; bestower of rain. Varuna was one of the oldest of the Vedic deities. As such he was the upholder of the physical and moral order and the divine judge. In the Brāhmanical period, however, most of his duties as creator and supreme god were assigned to Prajāpati and he was reduced to dominion over the waters and rule of the west. In this capacity he is worshipped in eastern Bengal at the full moon in the month of Kārttik (Oct.–Nov.). He is worshipped by fishermen in many parts of India. In Gujarāt he is invoked as "king of waters, who curbs the wicked, who made a road in the heavens to receive the rays of the sun." He is generally worshipped as a fertility deity at marriages. He holds the noose used to fetter sinners and a vessel of jewels. His consorts are the river goddesses Jumna and Gangā. He also possesses an umbrella made from the hood of a cobra and impervious to water. See ADITYA; DYAUS.

vasu In Hindu mythology, one of eight divine beings, children of Aditi and attendants of Indra: personifications of natural phenomena. The vasus include Āpa (water), Anila (wind), Anala (fire), Dhara (earth), Dhruva (pole-star), Prabhāsa (dawn), Pratyūsha (light), and Soma (moon).

Vāsuki In Hindu mythology, one of the three great serpent kings who ruled the Nāgas in Pātāla. Vāsuki was the serpent who was twisted as a rope around Mount Mandara at the Churning of the Ocean. Fearing the annihilation of his race by Garuda, he made a compact promising to send one snake to him each day. Garuda agreed and still eats one Nāga every day on the shore of the southern sea. In Punjab legend, the daughter of Vāsuki brought amrita to cure her father of leprosy and rubbed it all over him but forgot his thumb. So she went again to get more, and en route one of the Pāndava heroes carried her off and married her. Her father's thumb remained leprous, which explains why that disease is still rife in the Punjāb. See ŚESHA.

Vatak, Aūtak, or **Udai** In Zoroastrian belief, a female demon who forces men to speak when they should not and disturbs them while they are performing their physical functions; a fiend of incest, half human, half monster, who is said to be the mother of Azhi Dahāka in Pahlavi texts.

Vatea In Polynesian mythology, the name of Atea, the primary male parent of the universe, on Mangaia in the Cook Islands: in Hawaii he is known as Wakea. Vatea and Tangaroa disputed about the fatherhood of the first child of Papa. She cut the child in half; Vatea immediately threw his half into the sky, where it became the sun; Tangaroa waited until his half had decomposed, and when he threw it into the sky it became the paler moon. See ATEA; RANGI.

Vāyu (1) In Vedic mythology, the god of the wind and atmosphere; the breath of life which sprang from the breath of Purusa. He is often associated with Indra and is frequently one of the triad of Agni (earth), Sūrya (heaven), and Vāyu (air). He is regent of the northwest quarter. Since the concept of wind does not lend itself to anthropomorphism, there are few myths told about Vāyu, and he did not receive popular worship. The popular wind gods such as Hanumān are generally described as his sons. The Maruts, likewise wind gods, were first considered companions of Indra, later of Vāyu. Vāyu is represented by the antelope. He is gentler in nature than Rudra.

(2) In Iranian mythology, as a gentle wind god, Vāyu is a *yazata;* as an evil, ruthless wind god, he is a demon.

Veda Literally, divine knowledge: specifically, one of the four collections of prayers, hymns, and ritualistic formulæ which contain the basic religious lore of the Hindus; also, one of more than 100 books containing religio-philosophical material, legend, ritual, and sacred lore. The four chief Vedas are the *Rig-Veda,* oldest and most important; the *Sama-Veda* or chant veda, containing many of the hymns found in the *Rig-Veda* but with musical notation indicated; the *Yajūr-Veda,* prayers and spells; and the *Atharva-Veda,* popular material. The date of the earliest Veda is believed to be about 1200–1500 B.C. The Vedas vary in age and are spread over a long period of Indian history.

The origin of the Vedas is variously explained: they emanated from Brahmā or were revealed to the rishis. Each Veda is divided into the *Mantra* and the *Brāhmana,* the latter supplying glosses and commentary. To it are added the *Āryanakas* and *Upanishads,* treatises speculating upon the nature of god. The books into which the hymns of the *Mantra* are collected are called *Samhitās.*

Vellamo The Finnish goddess of the sea and of the waters; the wife of Ahti. The name is derived from *velloa,* to rock himself. [JB]

Venus An ancient Italian, originally Latin, goddess of growth and the beauty of orderly nature: the root, found in the Norse *vanir,* is the same as that of *venustus,* charming, graceful. It was through the more or less political efforts of the Julia gens in Rome to establish their descent, hence Julius Caesar's, from Æneas that Venus became solidly identified with Aphrodite as the goddess of love, Venus Genetrix; actually there was no native Roman goddess of love and human passion. Venus may more properly be identified with Charis, the Greek goddess of grace. Her proper sphere was the gardens and the tilled fields. Adding to the force of the supposed identity with Aphrodite was the fact that one of her Roman temples stood in the sacred grove of Libitina, the goddess of burials, who in turn was anciently and wrongly identified by the similarity of the name to *libido* as the goddess of passion. The other Roman temple of Venus, designed by Hadrian, was the largest in Rome and was located on the Circus Maximus. Outside Rome, Venus Pompeiana has a great temple in Pompeii; Venus Victrix was an important subject of worship among the colonizing Romans. Venus attained great prominence in the Middle Ages as the pagan, earthly power opposed to the spiritual power of the Church. In the Tannhäuser legend, for example, Venus (in reality Holda) is the epitome of the forces keeping Tannhäuser from salvation. The identification of Venus with the planet parallels the naming of it after Inanna and Ishtar by the Sumerians and Babylonians. Compare CUPID AND PSYCHE.

Verethraghna, Vrthragna, or **Bahram** In Iranian mythology, the chief of the fravashis and the genius of victory. Verethraghna was born in the ocean, conquered the dragon Azhi Dahāka whom he fettered on Mount Demāvand. He appears in ten incarnations: a strong wind carrying the Glory of Mazda, a golden horned bull, a white horse, a burden-bearing camel, a wild boar, a handsome youth, the bird Vāreghna, a wild ram, and a fighting buck. The tenth is a hero. The Armenian hero Vahagn is identified with him.

vervain A sacred herb of the Greeks, used to cleanse the table of Zeus before feasts. In Rome it was a plant of good omen, sacred to Venus, and used to decorate the altars of the gods. Roman brides picked a wreath of vervain which they carried; in Germany the bride was presented with a spray. In Persia vervain was used in the worship of the sun. The druids also revered vervain, because the leaves resemble those of the oak. They gathered it in the spring at the rising of the Great Dog Star when neither sun nor moon was visible, using an iron instrument, and being careful not to touch it. They poured a dish of honey into the ground to recompense its loss. The Crusaders brought back the story that vervain sprang up on Calvary when the nails were driven into Christ's hands, hence it is called a holy herb or herb-of-the-Cross, and is used like the hyssop to sprinkle holy water.

Because it was a holy herb it was thought by many to be proof against witchcraft, enchantment, and charms; it would drive away incubi, evil spirits, and unwanted persons, as the jingle: "Vervain and dill/ Hinder witches from their will," indicates. Witches themselves seem to have known better, for it was a symbol of enchantment and was used in most of their brews, divinations, charms, incantations, and sacrifices. Those who bathed themselves with the undiluted juice or smeared themselves with any part of the plant could see into the future, have every wish fulfilled, make friends with their worst enemies, cure disease, and be proof against disease and enchantment themselves.

Gerard (16th century English herbalist) recommended vervain as a strewing herb in the house to promote happiness and content. Another 16th century herbalist recommended a decoction of four leaves and four roots steeped in wine to be sprinkled around the house "where eating is done so that the folk will be merry." Many others have said that vervain would promote joy; it will "make infants apt at learning, and they shall be glad and joyous."

Culpeper called this plant an herb of Venus; it was therefore a woman's plant and good for the womb. Old Jewish lore recommends its use to facilitate childbirth. Culpeper also recommended it for jaundice, dropsy, gout, worms, the stomach, liver, spleen, wounds, ulcers, piles, and to give good color. The leaves bruised in vinegar would clear the skin and eyes. The Meskwaki

Indians of North America also regarded it as good for women and used white verbena (*V. urticæfolia*) to cure profuse menstrual flow.

Vervain was often called pigeon grass on the theory that pigeons and doves ate it to strengthen their eyesight. The old Anglo-Saxons hung the root around the neck to cure ulcers; and for centuries in England it was considered a remedy for epilepsy if gathered in the sign of the Ram and mixed with grain or peony root. It was also good for toothache and would tighten loose teeth and falling hair. The juice was used in love potions all over Europe, in Africa, and still today in New Orleans and other parts of the southern United States. Early American folk doctors recommended vervain root hung around the neck and touched occasionally to cure various diseases. In rural Illinois it is called feverweed. The Pawnee Indians identified vervain as "pleasant-dream-drink"; the Omahas called it stomachache medicine.

vetāla In Hindu belief, an evil spirit which haunts cemeteries and animates dead bodies. The vetāla is represented in human form with hands and feet turned backwards. His hair stands on end. As guardian of Deccan villages he occupies a stone smeared with red paint or one of the stones in the prehistoric stone circles scattered over the hills. In folktale he is a mischievous demon, always ready to play a practical joke on the unwary.

Vičak Literally, fate: an Armenian festival beginning the day before Ascension Thursday and lasting until the Sunday of Pentecost. Village girls meet on the first day and choose a committee. Its members fill a clay pitcher with water drawn from seven sources and place in its mouth flowers picked in seven fields. Each girl then throws an object such as a ring, button, or bead into it, while keeping her eyes closed and making a wish for her brother, father, or sweetheart. After all the girls have made their wishes, the pitcher is hidden in a garden. The boys of the village that night hunt for the pitcher. If they find it the girls must exchange quantities of eggs and olive oil for it. If they cannot discover it, the girls sing songs poking fun at them.

Vichama In the mythology of the ancient people of the Peruvian coast, the son of the Sun God and half-brother of Pachacamac, the Creator. He took revenge on Pachacamac for the murder of his mother, changed the first people into stones and their chiefs into sacred rocks and islets. He brought the three eggs from which the classes of new mankind were hatched. [AM]

Vidar In Teutonic mythology, one of the æsir, the tall, handsome, strong son of Odin and the giantess Grid. He is called "the Silent" and has his home deep in the forest. Some consider him the guardian of peace while others say that he represents the primeval forest, and, as such, is one of the imperishable forces of nature who, with Vali, will survive Ragnarök. He is the only one of the gods against whom Loki has nothing derogatory to say at Ægir's banquet. At Ragnarök he will avenge Odin's death by placing his iron shoe on the Fenris wolf's jaw and rending him asunder.

Vidyādhara In Hindu mythology and folktale, one of a group of benevolent supernatural beings who inhabit the regions between the earth and sky. The Vidyādharas are famous transformers and have supplanted the yakshas in popular tales. They live in towns in the northern mountains under kings or emperors and intermarry with men.

Vikramāditya The celebrated Raja of Ujjayinī who figures in a cycle of Indian folktales. His era is placed about 57 B.C. He is endowed with marvelous powers and is said to have obtained from Gaṇeśa the power of transferring his soul into any kind of body, and from Kubera the ability to fly through the air. He was incurably fond of wandering. His position in folktale is similar to that of Harun al-Rashid or of Solomon. There is no record of a Raja Vikramāditya at Ujjain, but such a king may have existed. His identity is a subject of controversy. He has been identified by some scholars with Chandragupta II (375–413 A.D.).

vila (plural *vile*), **veela**, or **willi** A Southern Slavic (Serbian, Slovenian, etc.) nymph of woods, fields, streams, lakes. The vile are said to be the spirits of virgins and children who must leave their graves to dance at night. Their dancing rings are typical fairy rings; they must not be disturbed, and anyone joining them must dance until he dies. They were hostile to men, but several of the hero tales tell of the help given to the heroes by the vile. The vile could marry mortals and have children; they possess many of the attributes of the fairies and the swan maidens. The vile sometimes appeared as birthprophesiers, deciding and telling the fate of the newly born.

Vili and **Ve** In Teutonic mythology, Odin's two brothers, sons of the god Borr and the giantess Bestla. These two, together with Odin, killed the giant Ymir, rolled his body into Ginnungagap, and from it created the earth. Later they created the first human pair, Ask and Embla, from an ash and elm. Odin gave them souls; Vili, motion and the senses; Ve gave them life and blood. In the *Völuspa* creation myth they parallel Hœner and Lödur, but elsewhere there is no connection. Vili and Ve are mentioned also in the account of Odin's protracted absence when he is feared lost and they assumed his duties and privileges (including that of his wife, Frigga) which, as Odin's full brothers, was their right. They are mentioned again when Loki brought up Frigga's relations with them at Ægir's banquet. Some authorities interpret them merely as aspects of Odin.

Vinatā In Hindu mythology, the mother of Garuḍa and co-wife, with Kadrū, of Kaśyapa. The two wives disputed about the color of the sun's horses and agreed that whichever was wrong would become the slave of the other. Kadrū won the dispute by deception, since she had her children, the snakes (nāgas), darken the horses by covering them with black venom. Thereafter Garuḍa became the implacable enemy of all serpents.

violet One of many plants called *heart's-ease* in the doctrine of signatures. Many stories are told of the origin of the violet. The most common is that when Zeus was sporting with Io, a priestess of Hera, he heard Hera approaching. He had no time to hide Io so he turned her into a white heifer, and made the violets for her special food. In a Roman story, Venus, seeing a group of dancing maidens, asked Cupid which was more beautiful, the maidens or herself. He preferred the contours of the maidens so Venus beat them till they were purple,

and Cupid turned them into flowers. Legend also has it that the violet sprang from the blood of Attis and was used in his worship. In Christian legend the violet droops because the shadow of the Cross fell on it, and it is one of the many flowers dedicated to the Virgin.

In France, Napoleon was known to his followers as Corporal Violette, and the violet was their badge during his exile, hence it was forbidden during the restoration of the Bourbons and the Second Republic. In Germany violets are used to decorate the cradle and bridal bed. In England they guarded the living from emanations of the cemetery and were carried at funerals. In Yorkshire bringing less than a handful into the house will cause all the chicks and ducklings to die, but including a leaf counteracts the ill luck since the leaves are more potent.

Culpeper calls the violet an herb of Venus and recommends the dried petals for quinsy, epilepsy, jaundice, and complaints of the liver. The green leaves make a good poultice on swellings. Violet root was eaten for pleasant dreams, and a decoction was used as a foot bath; bound to the temples it induced sleep. The Greeks wore wreaths of violets to induce sleep, cure headache, assuage anger, and to comfort the heart. They are still used for acute inflammation and as a cure for cancer. Helvetius recommended dogtooth violets for the teeth.

violins and **fiddles** Names most commonly applied to the many lutes played with a bow, including primitive, Oriental, Islamic, and European types used as accompaniment to singing and dancing. The use of the bow for playing the lute arose before the 9th century A.D., probably from an Asiatic origin.

Many Oriental and Islamic fiddles are of the long-necked, pierced lute construction. The *hu chin* of China and much of the Far East has a long slender neck inserted in a small cylinder of bamboo covered at one end with snakeskin to form a soundboard. Its bow is not separate but threaded through the strings. The Japanese *kokyu* is a three-stringed fiddle similar in appearance to the *samisen* and a century ago was often used in combination with the *samisen* and *koto* as accompaniment to song; more recently its place in the trio has been largely taken by the bamboo flute *shakuhachi*.

From Malaya and Bali to North Africa among Islamic peoples there is found a type of pierced fiddle (*kemantche* or *kamanga*) with a small body of skin-covered coconut shell or the like and a very long neck which protrudes at the lower end in a spike. The most primitive of these have only one or two strings. Various other bowed lutes of the Moslems are called *rebab*, including a short-necked slender instrument and a flat four-sided frame covered front and back with skin in the manner of a drum with a long neck. A one-stringed rebab of the latter type is used as accompaniment for epic recitations of public entertainers; a two-stringed version is a singer's instrument.

Several fiddles peculiar to India have short, broad necks and bodies of eccentric shape. Members of low castes play the *sarinda*, a round-backed instrument curved on the front edges into hook shapes and partially covered with a leather soundboard; it has three horsehair strings. The *sarangi* of northern India is a heavy wooden fiddle, boxlike at the back and hourglass-shaped at the front. It has three or four bowed strings and many underlying sympathetic strings.

Fiddles entered Europe from the Byzantine area to the east and by Arab transmission through Spain. Bottle shapes, pear shapes, long, narrow shapes derived from the rebab, and waisted shapes made their appearance, and the names of the medieval instruments included *rebec, gigue, geige, lira, viele, viol, fydel, kit.* The viols became favorites of courtly music and, with several other types of fiddle, gradually fused by the 16th century into the classical violin family. More primitive instruments served the folk of Europe for their singing, dancing, and epic recitations, and have survived in use until recent years. Among these are the *gusla* of the south Slavs, which contributes the dry buzzing notes of its (usually) single string to the extended chant about old battles and heroes, and derives its horsehead ornament and horsehair and horsehide materials from some long-past background of an equestrian people; and the Norwegian *hardingfele,* a peasant fiddle with many underlying sympathetic strings, now disappearing as the favorite accompaniment to folk song and dance. In Hungary, especially, the Gipsies became noted as fiddlers and developed a characteristic rubato style of playing, with elaborate cadenzas, which, until the earlier style of Hungarian native music was uncovered by Bartók, was accepted as the national hallmark of Hungarian dance music. Gipsy fiddling has a high reputation as an aid to courtship.

In America the fiddle has been one of the chief instruments of the folk performer. Backwoods musicians have created homemade instruments ranging from the extreme crudity of garden gourds and cornstalks to handsome and pure-toned examples of the violin-maker's art. Many of the homemade fiddles preserve the long, slender, unwaisted or only slightly waisted shapes of medieval fiddles. One huge and earsplitting example called "the Devil's fiddle" was devised in New England as a part of the foolery of the charivari, skimmerton, or mock serenade. It consisted of a coffin-sized box, resined on the edges and bowed with a two-by-four plank.

Primitive fiddles are found today in Siberia, in the Philippines, in Java, Sumatra, and Borneo, in Africa, among the North American Apaches and the Indians of the South American Chaco, in the Nicobar Islands, among the Lushai, among Mexican Indians, etc. These are either survivals of the early Oriental and Moslem types, with little change in construction or method of playing since the Middle Ages, or are more recent adaptations of European fiddles imported at the time of conquest. Among the Gilyak and the Assamese, primitive fiddles similar to the Chinese *hu chin* are but a stage beyond the musical bow. The homemade violins of the Mexican Seris, probably crude versions of Spanish importations, are narrow wooden boxes with one string wound over a peg thrust through and under an opening at the upper end, resembling the narrow rebecs.

The lore of the fiddle is extensive. Primarily it is a magic instrument. If you play the fiddle, you may summon almost any kind of being. If you dance to the fiddling of an unknown performer, your soul may be in danger. In American belief, both New England and southern Negro, the Devil is the master fiddler, as he is in the European beliefs reflected by the Walpurgisnacht of *Faust* and in the *Histoire du Soldat* of Stravinsky. To learn to play it, you trade your soul to the Devil, whom you may meet in all his brimstone and pitchfork character at the crossroads at midnight, or as a polished and

ingratiating gentleman. When you play the fiddle, you are communicating directly with him. Confessed witches deliberately dance to his playing; the unsuspecting maiden who dances with others to the playing of an unidentified black man or a sinister but handsome man in a black cape will find at the end of the dance that she has unwittingly become a witch. On the American frontier the voice of the fiddle would summon help when no other sound could. The entrance of a fiddler into a community was the signal for a shindig, a square dance, or a fiddling contest, and for the disapproval of the church, because the fiddle was one of the instruments of sin, leading the righteous to the paths of Satan.

In European folklore the fiddle is magic, too (D1233). It is one of the instruments to which fairies dance, and mortals who join them are bewitched. It may cause uncontrollable dancing among those who hear it (Grimm #110). It may summon a dwarf or call animals (Grimm #8). In New England also, animals come to its playing, as in the tale of the fiddler who played in the woods and found himself surrounded by wolves. The fiddle may restore the dead to life; it may play of its own accord; it may play a man out of prison; and it may, like other instruments, be the means of revealing a murder. as in some versions of *Binnorie.* See FIDDLIN' TUNES; GUSLA; LUTE. [TCB]

vira A folk dance of Portugal. In sunny Minho province, northern Portugal, the dancers bear themselves proudly, as in adjacent Spain, their heads and arms held high. With a smooth waltz or *pas de basque* they sway and leap to the strains of a bagpipe, click their fingers, and the heels of their mules. The longways formations for four couples are simple, alternate reeling of partners and opposites down the line, with full embroidered skirts a-whirl. The charm of the dance consists in the gradual building up of movement intensity and the decrease at the end of the dance. This is called the *vira extrapassado* (progressive turning dance).

In Lisbon the posture and vitality have deteriorated. This citified version is danced in a circle by two couples, with *pas de basque* and skipping steps. Fingers are clicked on the first beat of the quick waltz time. This vira displays a characteristically Portuguese fusion of French quadrille and Spanish gesture. The *vira corrido* of the province of Beira, on the other hand, is a simple running round dance, arms curved slightly above shoulder level. [GPK]

Vīrabhadra In Hindu mythology, an emanation of or the son of Śiva, created as a "form of his anger," to stop Daksha's sacrifice. Vīrabhadra has a thousand heads and feet, is shining and fierce, and decorated with the crescent moon. He is represented at Elephanta as a fierce-faced, tusked image, probably Bhairava.

Viracocha The supreme god and creator of the Incas of Peru. His complete name was Con-Ticci-Viracocha-pachayachachic: literally, the ancient foundation, lord, and instructor of the world. He made the earth, the stars, the sky, and mankind. But it was very dark. He destroyed the first people (giants) by a flood and then created new and better men. Like the culture hero of all primitive peoples, he wandered across Peru establishing social and moral order, teaching the people agriculture and the useful arts, and establishing languages and songs. His wanderings were marked by many miracles and transformations. He gave the new world light by bidding the sun and the moon to rise into being out of the Island of Titicaca. Finally he disappeared toward the west, promising to return in some distant future. He was worshipped in Cuzco and in the famous temple of Cacha near the Inca capital. The name Viracocha was given by the Peruvian Indians to their Spanish conquerors. See DELUGE. [AM]

virginity The reports of virgin goddesses who produced numerous children on Mt. Olympus and elsewhere have been a cause of considerable confusion. The reason for the confusion is the ambiguity, linguistic as well as ethnographic of the term "virginity." Whereas in modern Euro-American cultures the term virgin refers, except in Catholic theory, to a female with unruptured hymen, in other cultures it may refer to an unmarried woman even though she be a prostitute, or to a married woman who has had no children. This ambiguity in the concept of what a virgin is has led to further ambiguities in the reports of observers who have not informed themselves as to which theory of virginity is accepted by the culture they are describing.

The Greek Artemis, symbol of fierce virginity, was too modest to approach Endymion while he was awake, but nevertheless arranged that he become the father of her fifty daughters; and the priestesses of the Roman Vesta whose virginity was strictly guarded referred to her as the Mother Goddess and used phalli as ritual objects. Children of unmarried mothers in Greece were regularly referred to as born of virgins, and, although conclusions about the Ægean cultures must be cautious, it seems probable that the goddesses in the Ægean cult-centers taken over by the Greeks were thought of as virgins in the sense that they were unmarried though not inexperienced. Similarly, though the Babylonian Ishtar, who had among her other attributes that of love and procreation, was at one time the goddess of the morning star and wife of the moon god, she was generally referred to as the Holy Virgin and the Virgin Mother. She was also referred to as the "prostitute" and in a hymn says of herself that she is a compassionate prostitute. The women who prostituted themselves in her temples were also called virgins. The Brythonic moon goddess Arianrhod had children and indulged in scandalous amours. The Valkyries who entertained the heroes in Valhalla were virgins and were forbidden to marry. De Groot reports from Amoy, China, that the virgin goddess there is the patroness of prostitutes. Priestesses in Tahiti were greatly respected though not strictly guarded. Temple prostitutes, whether appointed to serve the god, the priests, or strangers, were somewhat ambiguously called virgins. The reports refer to the Akamba, the Uganda, Mexico, Peru. Pausanias was somewhat amazed to note that at Sicyon the priestesses of Aphrodite were vowed to chastity.

Even with these ambiguities of the term "virgin" in mind, it is somewhat difficult to interpret reports about people who put great value on "virginity." In China, particularly North China, the term refers to the intact membrane. The wedding sheets are proudly displayed the morning after marriage. In one instance a little girl who ruptured her membrane by falling on a stone was a subject of great concern to the entire village. The stone was carefully wrapped up and the village scholar wrote

an account of the accident which was to be delivered to her husband. Hesiod shrewdly advised his younger brother in terms not unknown in modern cultures to marry a virgin so that he could train her up the way she should go. The king of Uganda would have been incensed if a girl not a virgin had been offered him as a bride, but she was by royal order deflowered by proxy. The Nigerian tribes "attach considerable importance" to bridal virginity but are indifferent to later behavior. Because some of the élite of California Indian tribes demanded a high bride price, observers have concluded that they were chaste and respected virginity, but other observers have suggested that infant betrothal was for the purpose of assuring husbands that their fiancées were at that moment virgins. The protection of the virginity of the women of the upper Amazon is, according to one observer, excessive because of the eunuchoid quality of the males. G. Brown has reported after a careful investigation that in some Samoan villages there was exactly one virgin to a village. She was being saved for marriage to a chief. Stories about the lengths to which women have gone in order to protect their virginity are legion, but to become understandable need to be interpreted in terms of the cultures which produced the stories.

Other cultures, the Naga tribes of Manipur, for example, regard virginity as a disgraceful state. A report from Portugal explains that girls in a village near Lisbon who reached the age of sixteen without having become pregnant were objects of ridicule and took any lover who approached them. As soon as the girl became pregnant the man who assumed that he was the father married her. Granet has reported a similar situation in the festivals of ancient China. The Dené Indians thought that sexual intercourse was necessary to induce the menstrual flow. The Thonga of South Africa believe that a girl who refused sexual advances must be deformed. Among the Nigerian tribes the bride price of a woman who has already borne a child is higher than the bride price of a virgin, an attitude common among peoples who regard the purpose of marriage to be the production of offspring rather than the release of passion. Consideration for the needs of the individual, however, is shown in the Burmese code which instructs that persons who have not been given in marriage by their sixteenth year are not at fault if they indulge in sexual acts. In a Chinese folktale the master of a household accuses himself of negligence when one of his female servants becomes promiscuous because at the age of sixteen she had not been supplied with a husband.

A considerable spiritual potency is thought to reside in that type of virgin who might be defined as *virgo intacta*. Thus in the Middle Ages only a virgin could tame a unicorn. In many cults—the Vestal of Greece, the cult of Brigit in Kildare, and others—the sacred fires were guarded only by virgins. Briffault suggests that the custom of reserving a virgin for the tribal chiefs in Polynesia arose because the chiefs, endowed with extraordinary spiritual potency, could combat the magic which virgins contain. Among the Algonquians during epidemics a complicated ceremony was performed in which a young man went through a ritual death and was revived by five virgins.

The emotional and spiritual forces produced by continence are no doubt important in an examination of the folklore of virginity. Some of the medieval churches required that persons who took communion must be chaste for a stated period before they performed the mystery. In other places continence for periods of 24 hours to several weeks was required before religious ceremonies were performed, and in many of these the ceremony was concluded by a sexual orgy.

Some of the peoples who believe that virginity is lost only when a child is born have odd views as to the mechanics of conception. Whether the Australian aborigines are aware of the relation between conception and the sexual act has been debated with heat. The Aruntas (Australian) and other peoples believe that conception occurs when a spirit seeking rebirth enters a woman. The African Hausa believe that pregnancy occurs when a woman has sat on a spot made warm by a man. Mongol and Tartaric tribes are inaccurately reported to believe that conception occurs by divine interference, a doctrine which has been announced by numerous mothers of the Euro-American culture. Eberhard has a list, which might be greatly enlarged, of extraordinary pregnancies in Chinese folktales. They result from bathing, swallowing an egg, mists, and the like. Belief in immaculate conception, which may be similar to the theory of pregnancy occurring when a soul wishes to be reborn, has been reported of Aztec divinities, North American Indians, national heroes of Paraguay, the Bushmen, Ainus, Samoans, Banks Islanders, Tibetan and Siamese saints. The Greek view—that woman is merely the host in which the child produced by the male is stored until parturition—is well known. See MAGICAL IMPREGNATION.

The Catholic doctrine is that virginity is "reverence for bodily integrity" which is suggested by a virtuous motive. Thus God miraculously preserved the bodily integrity of the Blessed Virgin Mary during and after her childbirth. Virginity implies absence of all voluntary delectation either in lust or marriage. Virginity is not destroyed by every act against the sixth or ninth commandment and goes farther than a mere protection of bodily integrity. Virginity is a great victory over the lower appetites. The Catholic doctrine further teaches that the perfect integrity of the body, enhanced by perpetual chastity, produces a likeness to Christ and the angels, and, according to St. Thomas Aquinas, entitles the virgin to one of the three aureolæ or rewards. Sexual pleasure voluntarily and completely experienced destroys virginity so that even God cannot restore it, though the right to the aureola may be restored after an incomplete fault or failure in resolution. [RDJ]

☞ Virginity enters only infrequently into American Indian tales, except for those concerned with virgin births. The Cree, Ojibwa, Blackfoot, and Cheyenne, all Algonquian-speaking tribes, have trickster stories concerning virgins, of the type in which Trickster's prank is paid back; the virgins, when tricked into intercourse, either wear out Trickster or are appropriated by other characters for their pleasure. In certain Woodlands, Southwestern, and Eskimo tales a virgin is imprisoned in order that she will not be impregnated.

Virginity was emphasized in certain American Indian religious ceremonies; the chief female dancer in a Crow Indian Sun Dance had to be a virgin, for example: this in a tribe where premarital sexual experience for girls seems to have been the usual rule. [EWV]

Virgin Mary The legends about Mary, the mother of Jesus, are many of them beautiful; all of them are interesting; and a few of them inspiring. We are indebted mainly to one collection of books, the *Protevangelium of James*, for most of the early legends about Mary; later tales are largely expansions, dramatizations, and embroideries, together with incorporations from local folklore. There was an early apocryphal infancy gospel with which the name of Thomas was connected. In the 2nd century A.D. some unknown person evidently took that *Gospel of Thomas*, removed parts, mostly speeches, and on its skeleton built up the *Book of James* by adding a number of legends about Mary's parents, childhood, and motherhood. This book was popular in the East but was little known in the West until Guillaume Postel introduced it into Europe in the 16th century and gave it the name *Protevangelium* (First Gospel). By that time it had a number of additions, and it is now practically impossible to unravel the strands in its fabric. Much of the religious folklore of the Middle Ages is indebted in one way or another to it: for instance, it was the basis of the *Golden Legend* of the 13th century. [CFP]

☞ Medieval European religious folktale is full of episodes in which the Virgin Mary substitutes for a mortal (K1841): a knight lingered so long at mass that he missed his engagement in a tournament; the Virgin Mary took his place (K1841.2); Mary substituted herself for a woman whose husband had pledged her to the Devil; at sight of the Virgin Mary the Devil fled (K1841.3). The story of the nun who saw the world (K1841.1) is probably the most famous and widespread of these. Mary took the place of the romantic young nun for years while she lived a life of sin; her own grief and despair were the only punishment she received; when, heartbroken, she crept back into the convent she took her own place without ever having been missed.

There are six stories in the *Catalogue of Romances in the Dept. of Manuscripts in the British Museum* describing how the image of the Virgin Mary miraculously prevents some foolish nun from deserting the convent (V265). The Virgin Mary rescues a child from the Devil (S251); she retards death to save a sinner's soul (V251); a tree bows down to help the Virgin Mary in childbirth (D1648.2.1); the statue of the Virgin Mary sews for a suppliant (D1620.1.4); or it bows to indicate favor (D1622.2). There are stories also of the Virgin Mary protecting illicit lovers (T401); and comforting repentant criminals (V275).

There is an Irish story about the Virgin Mary asking a tinker to make a pin for her; she needed a pin for her cloak one windy day. The tinker refused, but the smith made her the pin. Mary's remark, "The weariness of the smiths is on the tinkers," is given as reason why tinkers are always poor. Once during a drought the Virgin Mary saw a poor man sprinkling water out of a bucket on his crops; the next day it rained. Any fire which has a cast of potatoes on it lights well, because the Virgin Mary was once allowed to cook potatoes in that way in a house to which she came.

Virgo The Virgin or Maiden: a constellation, sixth sign of the zodiac between Leo and Libra, containing the brilliant star Spica. Virgo is figured as a girl dressed in flowing robes, carrying in her right hand a palm leaf, and in her left an ear of wheat (Latin *spica*, represented by the star). All over the world, from earliest times, the constellation has been identified with the harvest maiden (Persephone, etc.) or the fertility goddess (Ishtar, etc.). Always the constellation is named for some prominent goddess; it was for example Belit in ancient Assyria. Christian star-cataloguers identified it with the Virgin Mary holding the Christ child. One interesting speculation, completely untrue, was that the Sphinx at Gizeh was a representation of Virgo's head on Leo's body, since the Nile floods occurred when these constellations were ascendant. The early Chinese called it the Serpent or the Quail's Tail; later, under Western influence, it came to be known as the Frigid Maiden.

vise (plural *viser*) The common Danish name for a folk narrative song or ballad. See BALLAD.

Vishnu One of the three supreme gods of Hinduism; the all-pervader and the most important of the solar deities; the supreme deity of the Vaishnavas into whom have been incorporated some of the characteristics of Indra and Prajāpati. Vishnu lives in his heaven, Vaikuntha, with his wife Lakshmī or Śrī. He is represented as a comely youth with four hands which hold the Panchajanya or conch shell, the *chakra* (wheel or sun disk), a club, and a lotus. On his breast are the jewel Kaustubha and the Śrīvatsa mark. His bow (Sārnga) and sword (Nandaka) are ever handy. His vehicle is the gigantic bird Garuda. Among his manifold titles are: Primeval Being, Lord of the Universe, Lord Creator and Generator of All, Lord of Sacred Wisdom, Lord of Waters, World Maintainer.

In the Vedas Vishnu occupied a subordinate position but was occasionally associated with Indra. In the *Rig-Veda* he is described as encompassing the universe in three steps (earth, sky, space). The same feat, in Brāhmanic mythology, is performed by Vāmana, the dwarf avatar of Vishnu, in order to recover the earth from the demons. During the period of the *Brāhmanas* Vishnu acquired new attributes and, in the *Purānas*, he became the second member of the Hindu triad (*Trimūrti*). As such he is self-existent and the embodiment of mercy and goodness. In this guise he was associated with the primordial waters as *Nārāyana*, "moving in the waters."

His preserving and restoring powers have been manifested in his avatars or incarnations in which a part of his divine essence has been incorporated in a human or supernatural form. These incarnations were effected in order to correct some great evil in the world such as the presence of the demon Rāvana. Generally the avatars are ten in number; in the *Bhāgavata Purāna* they are 22, or innumerable. See AVATAR. In the boar and tortoise avatars he raised the earth from the bottom of the ocean. His most important incarnations are those of Rāma and Krishna. Vishnu had no children in his non-avatar condition, but divided his essence into male and female. The former descended into Rāma and Krishna, the latter into Sītā and Rādhā.

The worship of Vishnu, especially in the forms of Rāma and Krishna, is widespread in India. The early worship of Krishna-Vāsudeva gave rise to the Jain doctrine of the nine Vāsudevas, nine Baladēvas, and the nine Prativāsudēvas. The later worship of Krishna and Rāma has continued as the prevailing forms of popular Vaishnavism. This term is applied to the sect whose members worship Vishnu as the supreme god of the Hindu triad. See ADITI; ANANTA; AQUILA; BRAHMĀ; CHURNING OF THE OCEAN; CYMBALS.

Viśvakarma or **Viśvakarman** In Vedic mythology, originally the epithet of a powerful god such as Sūrya or Indra; later, the name of an independent creator-god, identified with Prajāpati and described as having eyes, faces, arms, and feet on every side. He produces heaven and earth, gives the gods their names, and is beyond the understanding of mortals. In post-Vedic myth he is the artificer and architect of the gods, assuming the powers of Tvashtri. He revealed the science of architecture, formed the chariots of the gods, built the assembly hall of Yudhisthira, the city of Indra, Lankā (city of the Rākshasas), and Chandrapura, city of the king of the Vidyādharas. He made the image of Jaganātha and generated the ape Nala who built Rāma's bridge. When his daughter Sañjña was unable to endure the splendor of her husband the sun, Viśvakarma cut away an eighth of his brilliance and from the fragments made Śiva's trident, Vishnu's discus, and the weapons of the other gods. In the Central Provinces masons worship Viśvakarma and at four annual festivals revere the book on architecture which they use as well as the tools of their trade.

Vivien or **Vivian** The name given by Tennyson and Matthew Arnold (*Tristram and Iseult*) to the enchantress who beguiled Merlin in the forest of Broceliande. This story has doubtless been influenced by the common medieval tradition about the susceptibility of wise old men (Aristotle, Vergil, Hippocrates) to female charms. The name of Merlin's enchantress appears in the French manuscripts in many forms and in Caxton's edition of *Book of Arthur* as *Nyneue* or *Nymue*. She was identified with the Lady of the Lake, who appears in sympathetic roles as the protectress of Arthur and the foster mother of the child Lancelot. According to the Huth *Merlin* (condensed by Malory, Bk. II, ch. 5), she is the lady who came riding at a great pace on a white palfrey into Arthur's hall, and this leads us to identify her with the fairy lady Rhiannon in the first of the *Mabinogion,* who rode past Pwyll and his courtiers on a white horse of preternatural swiftness. Rhiannon means "Great Queen" and was presumably a divine title. Thus we have, as in the case of Morgan le Fay, a clear example of the evolution of a Celtic goddess into a medieval enchantress. [RSL]

Vodū Dahomean Negro term for deity. This word is the one from which the *vaudou* of Haiti, the name of the African *vodun* cult of the peasants of that island, has been derived. See VODUN. [MJH]

vodun or **voodoo** This term, for most persons in the United States, carries a vague connotation of exotic rites and magical practices. Both *voodoo* and *hoodoo* are derived from the word *vodun,* as far as can be ascertained. This word was introduced into the United States by Haitian Negroes who were brought to Louisiana when the French were evicted from that island during the latter part of the 18th and the early years of the 19th century by the slave uprisings that eventuated in the establishment of the Haitian Republic. In Haiti, *vodun* (there spelled *vaudou*) is the name of the African-derived popular cults that comprise the religious belief-systems of a large proportion of the people. Its origin, however, goes beyond Haiti, and can be very precisely traced to Dahomey, old French West Africa, where the word *vodū* is used to designate the polytheistic deities worshipped by the Dahomeans. Why, in Haiti, the word for "deity" of this particular language should have become the term for the total non-European belief-system cannot be said. However, since it is known that many Dahomeans were imported into Haiti as slaves and the impress of Dahomey is strong on all African retentions of Haiti, it may be assumed that numerical strength and the tradition of discipline and organization that the Dahomeans brought as a part of their African heritage adequately explain their primacy among the Negroes of the island. The complexity of the vodun cult 'of Haiti precludes listing its numerous deities, while the many aspects of its theology that have been recorded are such that book-length exposition has been found necessary to do justice to this belief-system. The American word hoodoo is used in the southern United States to signify an evil force and, as used in the term *hoodoo man*, means practitioner of magic. The common use of the word *voodoo* to designate any New World African-derived Negro rite, found in popular and travel literature, is obviously incorrect. See PÉTRO; RADA.

M. J. HERSKOVITS

voladores Literally, flyers: the Mexican flying pole dance, a spectacular and acrobatic feat. Centuries before the Conquest Aztec dancers flew from a pole, four of them, dressed as eagles or macaws, the sun-dedicated birds. Today the dance has survived in the mountains of the states of Puebla and Veracruz, in Hidalgo, San Luis Potosí, and the highlands of Guatemala. The Huastecs dress as sparrow hawks, and call their performance *la danza del gavilán*. The Otomí, Aztecs, and Totonacs wear a fan of feathers on their cone-shaped hats, but red trousers, sometimes over an ordinary pair, and bandoliers across their shoulders, on their feet sandals or store shoes. They keep time with a rattle in their right hands and wave a scarf in the left while "flying."

Ritual associations continue, especially among the Totonac who observe continence. The cutting of the 70–80-foot tree for a pole is attended by a prayer to the spirit of the trees, and sometimes a dance. The installation includes a food sacrifice to the pole, in the form of a turkey, cooked or live hen, maize, brandy, cigarettes. The pole is wound with ropes in a special way, raised amid ceremony, and fortified with stakes and stones. Every day, sometimes twice a day during a fiesta, the flyers first dance around the pole with their musician and his flute and tabor. Traditionally there are four, but the Otomí prefer six, including a man-woman, Malinche. They climb up a rope ladder and seat themselves on a small framework near the top, while each in turn dances on a two-foot central platform, each to two tunes, but Malinche to four. During the flight songs they launch themselves into space with ropes tied around their waists and descend head down in 13 ever-widening circles till they reach the ground and land skilfully on their feet. The musician often performs special acrobatics, leaning back in an arc as he sits on the platform, or jumping or pirouetting as he salutes the four directions. He may slide down one of the ropes amid acclaim.

There are regional variants, in numbers, costumes,

and forms. The *tocotines* of Papantla, Veracruz, weave a dancing chain seven times around the pole before ascending. Their flight climaxes a series of elaborate dances by the Quetzales, Negritos, and Santiagos. The voladores of Chila, Puebla, dance in a procession which winds up in the church; here they dance simultaneously with the Santiaguitos, the voladores circling with a toe-heel step. Malinche, in pink skirt and necklace, runs back and forth with a pendulum motion. Everywhere the dancers and musicians are greatly admired for their skill and courage, and many fliers continue for decades. Sometimes, however, the pole breaks or a dancer falls from the pole because of too much aguardiente. Because of the danger, the dance has been banned in many communities.

The meaning has faded into the past. Some old men remember the voladores as the sacred birds that guarded the points of the compass, others as messengers from the sun. Allusions to the ancient calendar are still evident in the number symbolism: the 13 revolutions of four flyers, making 52, the number of years in the Aztec cycle. The vestiges of tradition, the imitation of birds in the flight, and the scraping step connect the ceremony with sun, rain, and their beneficial effect on vegetation. The ceremony is now interwoven with Catholic festivals, and takes place on the saint's day of the village, during Holy Week, or on Corpus Christi. The dance and the melodies are certainly native, though the one-man flute and tabor recall a similar European medieval combination. The costume has modern touches, however. In fact, this breath-taking spectacle remains as one of Mexico's few completely Indian ceremonies. [GPK]

Volla The Thuringian name for the golden-haired goddess of the fullness of the earth, sister of Frîa or Frigga. She was sometimes called Vol in other parts of Germany and is an early form of Abundia: same as FULLA.

Volsung The great hero of Teutonic legend who gave his name to a race of warriors. His father was a kinsman of Odin, King Rerir, long childless, into whose lap Gna (messenger of Frigga) dropped the miraculous apple of fruitfulness. Rerir gave the apple to his wife to eat, and in due time, the coveted son, Volsung, was born. The young Volsung became king at an early age, grew great in strength, prowess, and wealth, and begat nine sons and one daughter. Through the floor of his great hall grew the oak, Branstock, into which Odin himself thrust the sword named Gram, declaring to the people that the sword belonged to the hero who could pull it out, and that it would give him unfailing victory. Sigmund alone, youngest son of Volsung, was able to withdraw it. Siggeir, king of the Goths, who had wedded Volsung's daughter Signy, coveted this miraculous sword. He issued a treacherous invitation to Volsung and his sons to visit him and outnumbered them in the encounter as they arrived and approached his castle. Volsung himself was killed; the sword was taken from Sigmund; and the nine brothers were chained to an oak tree in the forest where one by one they were devoured by a wild beast. Sigmund alone survived. Signy, bent on revenge, managed to slip away from Siggeir's castle and visit Sigmund in the forest. From their incestuous union, Sinfiotli was born, last of the heroic, royal race of Volsungs.

The exploits of Volsung and his family form the

second or poetic portion of the *Elder Edda*. Many later works have been based on these lays, notably the great Scandinavian *Volsunga Saga,* the German *Nibelungenlied,* and Wagner's opera cycle, *The Ring of the Nibelungs.* See SIGMUND; SIGURD.

Völuspá A poem in the Icelandic *Poetic Edda.*

Vo sadu li v ogorode "In the orchard, in the garden": a Russian couple dance which derives its name from the opening words of the accompanying song. Further words are "She was followed, she was haunted, By a handsome lover . . ." Both the dance and the tune show their origin in the elegant and restrained old Boyar dances of the Russian court. The girl offers one of a pair of fine kerchiefs to a man as a sign of favor and of choice for the dance. All couples move in a counterclockwise circle of the Slavic type, gently swaying their arms and kerchiefs in and out, forward and back, with gliding polka steps and push steps (left up to right with a cut), and finish with a buzz pivot. The kerchief is a frequent courtship symbol, either swayed as in *vo sadu* and the Chilean *cueca,* or held between the dancers, as in the Moravian *šateček.* [GHK]

Votjak or **Udmurt** A Finno-Ugric people, about 530,300 in 1920, living mostly in the districts of Kazan, Vjatka, and Perm. Inmar is their god of heaven (compare ILMARINEN of the Finns). His mother or wife is Kildisin-mumy, mother of the procreating Heaven. A white sheep is sacrificed to her at the birth of a child. The word for mother is used with the names of many nature deities (see MUMY); other deities are tied up with the word for man (see MURT; VU-MURT). The sanctuary of the family or many families is *kua* or *kuala* (see Harva in *FUF* XXII, 1934, pp. 146–54). Sacrificial groves, *lud,* are surrounded with fences. The offering table is often placed at the foot of some thick tree, under which the sacrificing priest reads his prayers. The night before Maundy Thursday is called "the wandering-night of the dead." This is the most remarkable memorial feast of all the Volga peoples. They believe that all the dead then move about, that after sunset they rise from their graves and walk to the villages. During this time the Votjak take many precautions. A cheerful feast with wedding songs and wedding presents, called the "horse-wedding" or "wedding of the dead," is a memorial feast in honor of particular persons. The sacrificial animal must be a horse for the deceased man, a cow, if the honored person is a woman. [JB]

Vourukasha In Persian mythology, the sea; also, the sea deity; also, the heavenly lake whose waters supply the world and in the middle of which grows the Tree of Life.

Vulcan, Vulcanus, or **Volcanus** In ancient Roman religion, the fearsome god of destroying fire, e.g. of volcanic fire: his late classical identification with the Greek Hephæstus is therefore misleading, since Hephæstus was a kindly god and an aider of mankind whereas Vulcan was disliked and was not at all the divine smith. His Etruscan name was Sethlans. Vulcan's festival was the Volcanalia, August 23, the dry month when destructive forest fires might be expected and when the stored grain was in danger of burning. See for example the prominence of his cult at Ostia, Rome's principal storehouse of grain. His epithet Mulciber, literally the melter, may come from the root meaning to soothe, to appease, and thus be a euphemism to divert his wrath somewhat as the festival might be expected to. At the Volcanalia the flamen Volcanis performed a sacrifice, and small fish, caught in the Tiber, were burned by heads of families. See HEPHAESTUS.

vulnerable spot A world-wide folktale motif, often called the Achilles heel motif from the legend that Achilles was invulnerable except in his heel. This invulnerable except in one spot motif (Z 311) occurs in folktale, song, and legend from Ireland and Siberia to the Zulus in South Africa. The vulnerable spot varies, however. Siegfried was vulnerable in one spot between the shoulders where a leaf fell upon him in his bath of dragon's blood. In the story "King Chandamahasena and the Asura's Daughter" in the *Kathā Sarit Sāgara,* the powerful Daitya was vulnerable only in the left hand. In the *Mahābhārata,* Krishna, vulnerable only in the sole of one foot, was killed by an arrow shot by Jarā. Ajax too was invulnerable from having been wrapped in the invulnerable skin of the Nemean lion, except for one spot which the skin did not touch.

The one vulnerable spot is a common and widespread concept also among North American Indians. The White Mountain Apache hero, Metal Old Man, was invulnerable except for one spot under his armpit. In a Blackfoot Indian story, Bear-Woman, while in her bear shape, was vulnerable only in the head. The idea carries over also to animals. One of the creation myths of the Yana Indians tells about the wicked Gowila, vulnerable only in the little toe, who had a big dog also vulnerable only in the little toe. The burlesqued *Dragon of Wantley* in Percy's *Reliques of Ancient English Poetry* was invulnerable except for a certain place in his rear end.

Vu-murt The Man of the Water; Votjak water deity. He is naked and has long black hair. He often places himself on the bank of the river and combs his hair. Sometimes he appears as a naked woman. Both male and female water deities fear man and hide themselves in the water. Vu-murt is an evil being and it is a bad omen if one meets him. But he can be helpful to fishers and millers, therefore sacrifices are offered to him. The worship of water by the Votjaks has the following purposes: to get rain, secure fertility of man and animals, avoid diseases, and secure good luck at fishing.

Reference: U. Holmberg, *Die Wassergottheiten der Finno-Ugrischen Völker. MSFO* 32: 63–95. [JB]

Wabosso White Hare, or Maker of White: one of the three brothers of the Algonquian creator-culture-hero-trickster, Nanabozho. See HARE. [EWV]

waienǫe The Iroquois Indian stick-striking dance. Some claim that it is the true old fighting dance, while *wasáse* was originally a rain dance. Like *wasáse*, it is now both a curing rite performed at Midwinter and a weather rite in July, as *eni'dji'*, the sun rite. The choreography is, however, quite different. In two parallel lines, face to face, the dancers advance toward each other and retreat, then cross over, with a double thump on each foot. Formerly it was a men's dance, with actual striking of sticks. Nowadays, without sticks, women may join in at Midwinter, using the women's *ęskänye* step when in place, and a springy walk while crossing. Both water drum and rattle are played by the two singers. See SUN DANCE; WASÁSE. [GPK]

wairu or **guairo** The astragalus of a ruminant which is used by modern Quechua Indians of Peru and Bolivia as a die to gamble for the belongings of a deceased person during a vigil. The game is very similar to the popular *taba* played by the Argentine gauchos. [AM]

waits Christmas street carolers: formerly, the musicians who played and sang in the streets at night or at dawn. The waits at one time were regular watchmen who "sounded off" four (during the summer, three) times a night to indicate that all was well.

waiung-arree The circumcision ceremonial of the tribes of Broome and other parts of western and central Australia. The boys, who are initiated in groups, are each accompanied and prepared by a brother-in-law to be, and by a group of men in the higher stages of initiation. These last have their legs sprinkled with blood and are painted in weird designs of blood and down; the initiates are anointed with fat, charcoal, and red ocher. The climactic event is the *wallang-arree* dance performed in a double circle with spear and spear-thrower. In succession each neophyte and his attendants make a circle and form coils, without intermingling. The men then stack up in human piles with the *balgai* (initiates) on top. In the *moorooboyn* alternate rows go in opposite concentric directions. Women dance on the outskirts, and are in fact tabu during the ceremony. The next day the actual circumcision rituals are followed by seclusion of the boys. At the final ceremony the boys fall from a gum tree into the lap of a man in the high stage of initiation, and form again a human pile. These rites hark back to dream time, when men and birds were the same. See ALCHERA. A dream song is sung throughout the ceremony. [GPK]

wakan, wakanda Sioux Indian term for supernatural power, applied to specific objects; as, a "wakanda sword," meaning a very sharp sword. See MANITU; ORENDA. [EWV]

waka t'oqori The bullfighting dance of the Aymara Indians of Bolivia. The central figure wears a special poncho and a hide-covered frame representing a bull. Others, called *Negros*, wear black masks and carry swords and timbrel rattles. They turn round and round and then unwind; they shake the sword and timbrel in the direction of the bull, who rocks back and forth. A *tinticaballo* (hobbyhorse) cavorts back and forth. This mild play is accompanied by two men playing a snare drum with the right hand and with the left a *pusipia*, or four-holed flute. They wear the same vests of jaguar skin and parrot feathers as the *q'ena q'ena* dancers. The bull motif is natural, spanish, as in similar Mexican dances of *toritos;* but the paraphernalia and execution are Indian. This may be one of the many blends of imported motifs with indigenous animal hunting or sacrifice rituals. [GPK]

walichu Evil spirits and all evil supernatural influences among the Araucanian Indians of Chile and the Argentine Pampas. Formerly these Indians waged battles against the walichu to drive them away from their villages or camps to avert epidemics or bad luck. [AM]

walnut In classical Greece and Rome the stewed nuts were traditionally served at weddings as a symbol of fertility; but in Rumania today the bride who wishes to remain childless places in her bodice as many roasted walnuts as the number of years she wishes not to bear a child. After the ceremony she buries these nuts in the earth. An old Lithuanian myth says that during the great Flood God was eating walnuts, and the righteous who climbed into the empty shells were saved. In general European belief witches and evil spirits gather under walnut trees, yet dropping a walnut under the chair of a witch will root her to the spot. A walnut branch singed in the Easter Saturday fire and hung in the house will protect that house from lightning for an entire year.

The 17th century English physician, Nicholas Culpeper, called the walnut a tree of the sun and considered the nuts most effective in medicine if used before they formed shells. He recommended the green husks as a gargle, and to be put in hollow teeth to stop pain or in the ears for deafness. The oil from the kernels he regarded as good for colic and wind, the old meats to heal carbuncles, and in red wine to stop falling hair; the leaves distilled in water also he considered good for running sores. By the doctrine of signatures walnuts were universally recommended for any disease of the head: husks for the scalp, shells for the skull, meats for the brain. The English herbalist Turner, writing in 1551, recommended walnuts "for the bytings both of men and dogges." John Gerard, 16th century English herbalist, made it clear that he did not consider the use of spiders enclosed in walnut shells effective in medicine. In many parts of the United States a walnut, like the horse-chestnut, is often carried in the pocket as a preventive and cure for rheumatism.

The black walnut (*J. nigra*) is said in England to put a blight on all apple trees in the neighborhood. It is a common practice in Europe, and especially in the Mediterranean region, to beat the trees to make them bear big crops. In much of the rural United States black-walnut leaves are used to keep away ants and houseflies. The North American Meskwaki Indians used the inner bark of black walnut to make a strong physic, but were careful to give it only to those who could stand a potent dose. The inner bark was charred and placed on snake bites.

Walpurgis Night The night before May 1, originally dedicated to St. Walpurgia, an English nun of the 8th century who founded religious houses in Germany, but associated in German folklore especially with the witches' Sabbat on the Brocken. See SABBAT.

waltz A ballroom couple dance, usually in rapid ¾ time, always with pivoting. The fundamental step is forward right, forward left, close right; reverse. The Viennese waltz gyrates in rapid tempo with this step, and always to the right; the Boston slowly turns in alternate directions. There are many variations. The Pursuit waltz goes straight ahead. Waltzing in a square is effected by back right, side left, close right; forward left, side right, close left. The waltz-balance starts with a dip forward right, rise on ball of left, close in right. The Hesitation Waltz of Vernon and Irene Castle is a balance with the man dipping back, the woman forward. The French waltz progresses with hops, the Spanish waltz with a half-turn on each measure and cross-over of two couples. The Kashubian Polish waltz *(walc kaszubski)* combines sideward slides (two to each side) and waltzing for eight measures. The Rye Waltz is in two parts: 1) to duple time a point side, point in, side, in and sashay (slide) to side; 2) to triple time a turning waltz.

Folk dances of many nations use a waltz as fundamental step: the *Ländler, Lauterbach* (balance), *Neubayrische, kujawiak* (balance and regular). In these the arms are not always in a ballroom clinch, but swing freely and permit figures like "wringing the dishrag" in the *kujawiak*. The Venezuelan *joropo* heavily stamps the first beat of every measure. Mexican mestizo dances emphasize the heel with a lilt from side to side and with skirt manipulation. The *Chiapanecas* is a light-footed variant, to a *Ländler* tune introduced during the reign of Maximilian. New Mexico has several entertaining versions of the *vals*. In the *vals de la escoba* (broom), all couples stand in two lines, while an extra man waltzes down the center with a broom. As he snatches one of the girls, all of the men make a pell-mell dash for a partner. All waltz, the unfortunate partnerless man dancing with the broom. In the *vals de la silla*, the girl sits down in a chair as the couple passes it; she will not arise till her partner has offered a *bomba*, a complimentary verse. In the *vals de los paños* two sets of three stand face to face, the central boy holding the girls by two linking kerchiefs. They advance and retire, and then the girls dance under the arches of upraised arms.

The waltz is an Austrian peasant product, popular with the bourgeoisie and accepted by the Austrian court but not by the French court. Its origin in the 17th century is variously attributed to the *volta, Weller,* or *Ländler*. From the late 18th to the late 19th century its amorous embrace and mad whirling were passionately welcomed as a relief from the prim court dance. No censorship could squelch it. But the fire died naturally and gave way to the sentimentality of the 90's. Folk dances, however, retain the vigor lost in the ballroom.

Both musical and dance art have drawn inspiration from the waltz, some in the simple style of Mozart's *Deutsche Tänze,* some in multiple form, with introduction, six parts, conclusion, and programmatic content, as Johann Strauss' *Walzer*. The stage waltz combines swaying arm and body movement with elaborations of the step. The most ambitious art product has been Ravel's *La Valse,* choreographed by Doris Humphrey, with perception of the incipient eroticism and ecstasy and final decadence. [GPK]

Walum Olum Red painted stick record: the name used in reference to the Delaware Indian account of their origin and migration. This account was chanted, and red symbols painted on tally sticks were reputedly used as mnemonic devices during the recitation of the legend. The sticks and texts of the Walum Olum were given to Constantine Rafinesque, and the text, with translation and reproduction of the symbols on the sticks, was published by Squier and Davis, and by Daniel G. Brinton (*The Lenâpé and Their Legends,* Philadelphia, 1885). Brinton translates Walum Olum as "red score," but there is some doubt that this is correct. The origin legend in the Walum Olum is a usual North American Indian story of primeval water, earth diving, the support of the world on the back of a turtle, and so forth; farther along the myth departs from the usual in that it lists, in a fairly systematic manner, the movements and wars of the Delaware (Lenape) Indians, and their successive chiefs. The account ends with a listing of historic Delaware Indian chiefs. Extensive research, the results of which are as yet unpublished, is now in progress on the historical, linguistic, and cultural background of this Delaware document. [EWV]

wampum Tubular or hollow cylindrical shell beads varying in length from 4 to 17 mm. and in thickness from 2 to 5 mm., probably used aboriginally by the Indians of the southeastern United States as one kind of repository of value; in post-Columbian times, used as money in transactions between Europeans and the Indians of the eastern United States. Wampum beads were also used as necklaces, wrist bands, to ornament clothing, and in the manufacture of belts which were used by messengers and chiefs to certify to the validity of, or to commemorate, speeches made and treaties signed.

The most common wampum beads are the white ones, made from several kinds of shells found along the eastern seacoast, but half-reddish, half-white, purple, and black wampum beads were also manufactured and used.

No descriptions of native methods used to drill the beads seem to be extant, and, because of the difficulties of manufacture, it was commonly assumed wampum and its use were the result of western European influence; however, in a recent article Slotkin and Schmitt cite documentary material which would seem to prove that it was also made and used in the Southeast prior to the advent of the whites (see J.S. Slotkin and Karl Schmitt, "Studies of Wampum," *AA* 51:223–236, 1949).

Wampum does not enter into the mythology of the North American Indians to any great extent, except that the eastern tribes, Algonquian, Iroquoian, and Muskogean, employ the motif of bead-spitting or jewels from spittle in several of their tales, and identify the beads that are spit as being wampum. The Wawenock of the northeastern Algonquian area narrated for Speck a text on the origin and use of wampum; at Wawenock councils where shamans were present, every time a shaman drew upon the pipe he was smoking, wampum fell from his mouth. Shamans of medium power produced white wampum; shamans of the least power, half red and half white wampum; shamans of the most power, almost black wampum (Frank G. Speck, "Wawenock Myth Texts from Maine," *RBAE* 43:165–197, 1925–26, page 196). For a summary of the uses of wampum, especially in treaty belts, and the derivation of the name from the Algonquian *wampumpeak* or related forms, see the article on wampum by J.N.B. Hewitt in *Handbook of the American Indians, BBAE* 30, pt. 2, pp. 904–09, 1910. See BEAD-SPITTER AND THROWN-AWAY. [EWV]

wanga Haitian Negro term for a charm that works evil magic. It is the opposite of a *garde*, a protective charm. Other types of Haitian charms are the *arrêt*, which also wards off specific forms of evil, and the *drogue*, that gives protection against universal forces falling in a given category, such as war or being arrested. The use of the term in the popular literature to signify all forms of Haitian magic is incorrect. [MJH]

wapaq Koryak term for the powerful spirits believed by them to be inherent in the fly agaric.

war dances Strictly speaking, war dances should intensify belligerent spirits previous to battle or should celebrate victory. Among American Indians they have lost their original function and have either transferred their purposes or become amorphous show pieces.

In many parts of the world, warriors still prepare for battle by miming combat, either as a duel for two opponents or as a group encounter. At times these may end in bloodshed, as among the Oraons of India. The Oraons, the Malayan Dyaks, and the Philippine Bontocs may also present these dances for entertainment, or in connection with weddings. The islanders carry shields and spears, the Oraons shake bows with metal jinglers.

In the Far East these combats have invaded the theater as deft sword play or spectacular and often acrobatic scenes. In the Japanese *kabuki* these scenes, termed *tatimawari*, are highly stylized. On the Chinese stage whole armies cavort at breakneck speed and somersault their vanquished exits, all to the din of gongs, catgut, and piercing flutes.

South American tribes anticipated battle with sham encounters, which are now rapidly becoming anachronistic: the Caingang, Parintintin, Bororo, Pariagoto. Their war dances often contained much mimic comedy, and usually terminated in feasts with sexual license and intoxication. The elaborate masked encounters of the Andes and Middle America have been lost, absorbed, or metamorphosed. The Inca *cachua* is a social dance; the Aztec *ochonchayocacalihua* for Huitzilopochtli has given way to *Moriscas*.

Throughout western North America, women had an important share in war dances. In the Rio Grande pueblos they still dress as men and burlesque the men in war regalia: in the Santa Clara *puwere* and San Ildefonso shield dance (*ti'di share*) executed with bow and arrow. In the Santa Clara *kwitara share* and San Juan *frase share* or "French" dance, the women turn from side to side in a straight line and the men wind in and out with their pistols, war clubs, and other weapons. In Acoma and Tesuque the steps and gestures are like those of

the corn dances, the men prancing, the women moving their arms up and down alternately or simultaneously. In so far as any significance is attached, these "war dances" are connected with rain, harvest, fertility, girls' initiations. Sometimes they show Plains influence in the men's headdress or the names of "Ute" or "Comanche" dance.

Though the Pueblos and Plains war societies performed ceremonies preliminary to raids, the mimic encounters were narrations of great deeds in connection with victory and scalp dances. The Papago shared these boasting scenes, and also the face-blackening and purification ceremonies and other victory dance features. In the Plains the war dance has become confused with the grass dance, eagle-calumet dance, and *iruska*. It is a composite of enactments from the warpath or hunt of old times, of show-off steps or hoop dancing. Along with the costume, the Sioux "war dance" is now displayed by the Chippewa, Sauk and Fox, Kiowa, and other Oklahoma tribes, and in the east the Cherokee and Iroquois. Chippewa war dancers progress in two concentric circles; Sauk and Fox victory dancers circle left. But the Oklahoma war dance is a free-for-all. The steps and gestures have intruded into the ceremonial thanksgiving and feather dances of the Iroquois (*ganeo'ǫ* and *ostówegowa*), though these have nothing to do with war. The old time *wai'eonoe* is a sun rite; and the *wasáse* is a thunder rite or cure. Display for the white man includes Sioux steps, in the scalp dance or *ganehǫ*.

From India to Europe to the American Indian, the war dance has had fertility associations. The scalp dance not only rejoiced or avenged, but brought rain. Thus the Iroquois transference of functions is not far-fetched. Various separate articles explain this more in detail. See CALUMET DANCES; *Battle Mime and Moriscas* in DANCE, FOLK AND PRIMITIVE; GRASS DANCE; MORISCAS; PYRRHIC DANCE; SCALP DANCES; STICK DANCES; SWORD DANCES. [GPK]

wasáse The Iroquois Indian men's war dance. Morgan described it as a fierce enactment of belligerent exploits. Today it has lost all ferocity and has replaced it by jump-hop steps *ad lib.* by a group of boys and men in the middle of the dance floor. Two singers, on a bench near the wall, intone ancient war songs or versions dating from the war of 1812. This serves two occasions— the Midwinter festival as a charm for communal welfare, and as thunder rite in time of drought. In fact, *wasáse* belongs to Hino, the thunderer.

Like *ganegwa'e*, its songs may be suddenly interrupted by someone striking the floor with a staff, declaiming a speech of praise or bantering insult, and distributing a gift, nowadays of cakes or coins—an echo of the Plains grass and calumet dances. There is a rumor of Sioux origin, but the steps show no influence from the Plains, resembling rather the False Face jump-hop. [GPK]

Washer of the Ford The apparition of a beautiful weeping maiden or ugly grimacing hag seen at a ford washing the bloody garments of the beholder: a death omen of ancient Celtic folklore. She usually turns and tells one that it is *his* garments she is washing. See CELTIC FOLKLORE; CUCHULAIN.

wasp Any of numerous predatory, slender-bodied hymenopterous insects of which the females and workers are provided with effective stings. Among some South American Indians, the wasp is a culture hero from whom men learned pottery-making and house-building. The soul of the Siberian shaman sometimes takes the form of a wasp; in Mongolia, the shaman chooses this insect as the hiding place of his external soul. In sympathetic magic, the wasp figures prominently in French Guiana where young people are trained by their parents to endure the painful stings of ants and wasps with much the same hopes for them as cause the Indians of Vancouver Island to encourage their warriors going into battle to rub their faces with the ashes of burned wasps, namely, that in this way they will be rendered as pugnacious as these insects. In Morocco, if a woman wishes to have a boy child, she swallows a male wasp coated with honey; and it is the belief that a decoction made from wasps' nests will make barren women prolific. Mississippi Negroes use wasp stingers in various good luck charms and hands to make debtors pay up. Wasp stings are plastered with mud, snuff, or tobacco to ease the pain.

In folktale the wasp is both wise and cunning. A fable by the Roman Phædrus has the wasp sitting in tribunal as judge between drones and working bees in regard to honey collected by the bees to which the drones had pretensions. There is a general European story about Fox leading Bear into a wasp's nest to get honey (K1023; Type 49). Witches are sometimes detected by someone's seeing a wasp (her soul) reenter her body while she is asleep (G251.1); the fact that she cannot be wakened until the wasp returns proves that she is a witch (i.e. in wasp form she has been absent from her human body on her various evil errands). [GPS]

Why Is The Wasp the Gipsies' Bee? is title of a Rumanian folktale translated by Moses Gaster in his *Rumanian Bird and Beast Stories*, PFLS 75, 1915, in which God made the bee first of all living creatures. The Gipsy was so eager to taste the honey that he took the bee out of God's hand, saying in return he would make candles from the wax for God's Church. God was angered by the Gipsy's forwardness; he said nothing, but created the wasp and gave it to the Rumanians. The Rumanians accepted the wasp and thanked God. When the Gipsy saw the wasp, he asked the Rumanian if his bee made much honey; the Rumanian said he brought it home in bagfuls. So the Gipsy wanted to exchange. The Rumanian was willing. He accepted the little hive full of bees and honey from the Gipsy and showed the Gipsy the wasps' nest in a big hollow tree, saying the tree was full of honey. When the Gipsy tried to collect the honey he was well stung for his trouble. Since then bees belong to the Rumanians; wasps belong to the Gipsies. In another version the Rumanian tells the Gipsy his big bees make gold instead of honey and induces the Gipsy to trade.

wasted food A grave and almost unforgivable sin in European folk belief. The sinfulness of wasting food is a concept rooted in a code probably as old as man himself. That destroying or wasting food is punishable by Heaven is demonstrated in the Tyrolese legend of Frau Hütt, who was turned to stone for doing so. Hans Christian Andersen has pointed out the vain young girl who laid the loaves of bread in the muck so that she might cross the road without soiling her shoes, and who immediately found herself unable to step away from the loaves which sank slowly under her feet, and continued to sink, gradually submerging her in the muck until she was gone and forgotten. Warnings against wasting food are preserved in the more or less literary proverbs: Waste not, want not. Waste makes want. Wilful waste, woeful want. See BREAD.

water babies Small beings, often human in form, who inhabit springs, streams, lakes, and other bodies of water, not necessarily malevolent, but generally feared by the many American Indian groups whose folklore includes tales of encounters with such beings. Emphasis on folkloristic belief in water babies of various types is especially strong among the tribes of the Great Basin; a little man, a dwarf who pulls at fishermen's lines, an old woman who occupies a specific spring and is seen sometimes at dusk, are among the numerous sorts of "water babies" whose existence these groups believe in. Narrative material concerning them chiefly has to do with anecdotes of accidental encounters with them. See LITTLE PEOPLE. [EWV]

water drum A vessel partially filled with water and struck in the manner of a drum, generally for primitive curing and rain-making ceremonies. The Aztec type, still used by the Yaquis to accompany their deer dance, consists of a clay vessel of water on the surface of which a half gourd is held and struck with a muffled stick wrapped in corn husks. The *mitig'wakik*, or wooden kettle, of the Chippewa Midewiwin medicine society is a hollow log with a plug hole in one side, a wooden bottom, and a head of wet deerhide. Water in the cylinder can be let out through the side hole. It is played with drumsticks representing the loon or the owl, or sometimes simply a curved stick. See DRUM.

water of life In folktale the magic liquid that brings the dead to life, cures all illnesses, or bestows immortality. It appears in numerous quest tales, in which the hero is sent to get the water of life (E80) from a well, spring, lake, river, etc., at a great distance. Sometimes the motif is combined with the magic helpers motif: the far-sighted helper sees the king or princess dying; the long-stepping helper takes the water of life and brings life back to the expiring person. Drinks like ambrosia and soma which the gods imbibe to keep themselves eternally young are an extension of the idea. Belief in the water of life is so strong that it led explorers like Ponce de Leon to the New World to search for its source, the Fountain of Youth. But it is not limited to any time or area; numerous peoples all over the world have had belief in the water of life from ancient times. Perhaps the most ancient example of this belief appears in the Babylonian myth of Ishtar's descent to the underworld seeking Tammuz to restore him with the water of life. She, too, having once passed into the region of death, had to be sprinkled with the living water before she could return to the upper world. See ABANDONED WIFE.

Water Serpent The horned water serpent is a monster of considerable importance in the Pueblo pantheon, and a figure which appears also in Eastern Woodlands mythology. At Hopi, a dance is given in honor of the serpent; at Zuñi, he appears in the ceremony of initiating children. In the mythology of the Zuñi, and in daily references, the horned water serpent is more conspicuous than at Hopi, however. [EWV]

Wati Kutjara Literally, Two Men: also called *Men Iguana,* from their totem. They lived in the mythical past and on their travels created trees, plants, animals, physiographic features, and ceremonial objects. Ceremonies now depict events in these travels. They are known to the tribes of central-western Australia in the Great Western Desert. See PLEIADES. [KL]

waulking A Hebridean type of song sung by women at group work on the shrinking and fulling of hand-woven textiles. The women sit face to face across a long table while the fabric is passed along from one to the next. The singing is begun by a leader, usually an old woman, who opens the theme and is followed by the rest in chorus. She continues with improvised phrases or lines, each repeated by the group in unison, until the leader has sung through all of her verses, punctuated by the group refrain. See WORK SONGS.

Wawilak Two creator sisters of the Australian Murngin, whose careers form the basis of four great totemic ceremonies lasting for months and focused around the *rites de passage* of an individual. The myths tell of the wanderings of the two sisters and their children after committing clan incest, and of their being swallowed by Yurlunggur, Great Python, for violating his pool. A flood forced him to regurgitate them but he swallowed them again. The last part of the myth concerns men learning the Wawilak ritual secrets from the women and using their blood and ritual paraphernalia. [KL]

wayang wong Dance drama of Java and Bali. The sequence of development from ancient times is: 1) *wayang topeng* (or *raket*), a masked magic rite, which today presents events in legend and political history, performed by two or three men in changing masks; 2) *wayang kulit* (shadow leather), named for the leather puppets silhouetted on a screen; 3) *wayang golek*, which used wooden puppets; 4) *wayang dalang*, with masked human actors; 5) *wayang wong* (shadow man), with unmasked human actor-dancers. In all forms which survive to this day, a *dalang* or operator speaks the lines while the actors pantomime. Sometimes the lines are improvised.

The motions are two-dimensional and puppet-like, but in Bali the style is more vivacious, and the impassive facial expression becomes more animated. A special style is dictated for the various characters: 1) the gentle dance for women, who are in Djokja, Java, enacted by men but in Solo by women; 2) the lyric style of noble heroes and gods like Arjuna and Rāma; 3) the fierce style of aggressive heroes and gods; 4) the brutal style of villains, demons, and giants; 5) the comic, free-style dance of clowns who ridicule social ills. In Java a scarf embellishes the conventionalized gestures; in Bali a fan may speak as in the Japanese *odori*.

The Indonesian theater (a court form in Java, a folk art in Bali) derives from India. After the first influx in the second century, theater and dance rose to prominence in the 9th century and to their apogee in the 14th and 15th centuries. In 1900 the present rules were crystallized by the Krida Beksa Wirama Society of Music and Dance. Hindu mythology provides the subject matter: tales from the *Mahābhārata*, *Rāmāyaṇa*, and *Arjunawawaha* (the nuptials of Arjuna), but they have been greatly modified. The recent *wayang suluh* (educational wayang) deals with contemporary life and problems.

Today as in ancient times the Indonesian theater is an exquisite art form and at the same time it retains a ritual function and a role in the education of the people. [GPK]

way-goose, wayzgoose, or **ways-goose** A 17th century English printers' feast, given by the master of a print shop at his home for his employees: later called a *beansfest*. The time for the way-goose fell late in August, on or about St. Bartholomew's Day (Aug. 24). Before this date the compositors never worked by candlelight; after the way-goose the shortening days made it necessary.

Nathan Bailey's *Dictionarium Britannicum, a more compleat universal etymological English dictionary than any extant* (1730) explains the term wayzgoose as a *wayze*, or stubble, goose; but Murray's *New English Dictionary* states that the etymology of the word remains an unsolved puzzle and that the association of a stubble goose with the feast is unsupported. Later, in the 19th century, the way-goose celebration became a big annual picnic and excursion into the country held by the employees of printing establishments. Similar printers' outings were observed in the United States during the 19th century, but have gradually fallen into disuse. The way-goose was revived in New York on January 15, 1949, by printers' union and management personnel for a big way-goose cocktail party.

The same festival in Germany was called *Martinsschmaus* or *Fastnachtsschmaus*. No one worked by artificial light up to or on that day, hence it was sometimes also called *Lichtschmaus*.

weasel The weasel differs little in its way of living from the ichneumon and plays the same role in folktale, myth, and fable. Pliny stated that the weasel eats rue to make himself immune to snakebite, and the same is reported of the ichneumon.

In Ireland weasels are said to be descended from "Danes' cats"; it is unlucky to meet one, especially in the morning. Its bite and spit are considered poisonous. In Germany to see a weasel on the roof means good luck, but in Bohemia even its glance will blind or blight you. In Switzerland the weasel is regarded as a conjurer (B191.1); in Macedonia mentioning the name of the weasel is avoided. Carpathian farmers honored the weasel; they feared its bite and believed it was a danger to cattle and sheep; but to kill a weasel meant that hundreds of weasels would come and fall upon their grain and cattle to avenge their kinsman. On St. Matthew's Day (Sept. 21) therefore, or sometimes on St. Catherine's Day (Nov. 25), these people observed a festival for weasels to propitiate them and ward off their depredations. (See M. Summers, *The Vampire in Europe*, p. 55.)

In folktale we find numerous etiological stories explaining why the tip of weasel's tail is black (A2378.8.3), or why weasel is white with a black tail-tip (A2411.1.3). There are stories of man transformed to weasel (D124); Douglas Hyde's story "The Weasel" in *Beside the Fire*, London 1910, is the story of a witch in weasel form. Soul in the form of weasel is a general European motif E731.4. A popular medieval story credits the weasel with power to restore the dead to life. In the *Lai d'Eliduc* by Marie de France the weasel brings its mate to life by means of a magic plant, much as the incident in Grimm's *Three Snake-Leaves* (#16). See Bolte-Polívka's *Anmerkungen zu den Kinder- und Hausmärchen der Brüder Grimm*, 4 vols., Leipzig, 1913–30, for comments and variants. In Æsop's fable *The Mouse and the Weasel*, the Weasel plays the role of adviser after the fact. A lean and hungry little mouse has crawled through a crack into a corncrib, eaten his fill, and then been unable to get out again through the crack. The Weasel, highly amused, tells him that he will get out all right when he is lean again.

wedding anniversary The celebration of the anniversary of a marriage, like the observance of the yearly birthday, is a sort of minor *rite de passage*. Often a party is given to which selected friends and relatives are invited. Flowers are a customary gift to the couple on any anniversary, but certain anniversaries are marked by special gifts, i.e. gifts of special materials. The most widely known are:

> 1 year —Paper
> 5 years—Wood
> 10 years—Tin
> 15 years—Crystal
> 20 years—China
> 25 years—Silver
> 50 years—Gold
> 75 years—Diamond

Other anniversaries are similarly marked, but not as universally: 2 years — cotton; 3 years — leather or muslin; 4 years — silk; 6 years — iron; 7 years — copper or wool; 8 years — electrical appliances; 9 years — pottery, and so forth. The practice of observing the wedding anniversary, while primarily an excuse for gift-giving, probably has underlying it a belief in the correspondence of certain luck-bringing substances with a distinct *number* of years.

weeping bitch or **bitch and pepper** The motif (K1351) of a cycle of stories in which a virtuous woman is seduced into yielding to a lover by the ruse of an old procuress. The old woman throws pepper into the eyes of a little bitch, whose eyes then weep, or throws a piece of meat to the bitch so saturated with pepper as to make the animal's eyes weep. The procuress then explains that the bitch was once a woman, now thus transformed for hardness of heart to her lover, and that she continuously weeps her fate. The woman is thus persuaded to avoid a like fate. The original of this motif is in the "Story of Devasmitā" in the *Kātha Sarit Sāgara*. Devasmitā, whose chastity token was the unfading lotus in her absent husband's hand, was not seduced, but turned the tables of ridicule and humiliation on the four young merchants who sought her. But the motif itself, with the virtuous lady persuaded, is said to have migrated from India via Arabian folktale into Spain, whence throughout Europe. Original, variants, and migration are fully discussed in the *Ocean of Story* I, 169 ff.

weeping salutation In a great many South American tribes, visitors or members of the tribe returning from a journey are received with loud wailings and other expressions of grief. This custom was first observed among the Tupinamba Indians of the Brazilian coast and since then has been variously interpreted: it has been said that the hosts were expressing their sympathy for the guest for the hardships he has faced, or that the newcomer was regarded as a ghost, and so on. Actually the keening for the guests is a practice connected with the funeral rites. The traveler is told of the deaths which have taken place in the tribe and is invited to join in the ritual laments. Thus, for instance, the Cobeuo

mourners lead their visitors to the graves of their relatives so that they may mourn in their presence. [AM]

weggis dance A Swiss couple dance performed in a counterclockwise circle, typical of central Europe. Holding hands lightly in skating position, or with the girl's palms placed on the boy's, the couples move in a single or double circle, freely and gaily. The Weggis song equally gaily refers to the village of origin, with a yodeling refrain:

From Lucerne to Weggis on/Hol di ri dia, hol di ria;
Shoes nor stockings need we don/Hol di ri dia, hol dia.

Each verse brings a new couple arrangement and step, a heel-and-toe polka or point, hop, and polka, with vigorous arm-swings. Sometimes partners separate and join again, or cross over; but they do not weave quadrille patterns with the other couples. It is a carefree round, expressive of the Swiss temperament. [GPK]

Wellerisms Wellerisms or quotation proverbs like *"Neat but not gaudy," said the monkey* (or: *the Devil*) *when he painted his tail blue* constitute one of the strangest varieties of proverbs. The term Wellerism alludes to Sam Weller's frequent use of such sayings in the *Pickwick Papers*. Some Wellerisms like *"All's well that ends well," said the monkey when the lawnmower ran over his tail* include a familiar proverb; others like *"Every man to his taste," said the farmer when he kissed the cow* ascribe the remark to a generalized figure representative of a class; and still others like *"The case is altered," quoth Plowden* ascribe it to a particular individual, who can often be identified. (Edmund Plowden was an eminent barrister in Queen Elizabeth's reign.) In the first of these types the incongruous combination of a serious proverb with an inappropriate act or scene produces a characteristic effect. Kalén, who has studied modern Swedish examples, believes that Wellerisms in which the speaker is a farmer, an old woman, or some other representative of a class, originally assigned the remark to a particular, named individual and later replaced his name by a class designation when the allusion was no longer understood. He was able to find a historical basis in rather recent tradition for modern Swedish Wellerisms containing a proper name. It would be impossible to find similar explanations for English Wellerisms containing a proper name. When accepting John Heywood's collection of proverbs, Queen Elizabeth is said to have asked whether it was complete. Although Heywood assured her that it was, she found *"Bate me an ace," quoth Bolton* to be lacking. She gave no interpretation of the saying, and none has since been found. Wellerisms in which an animal is the speaker like *"Many masters," said the toad when the harrow turned him over* are probably a special variety of Wellerism. Wellerisms are reported from classical times, and some that were current in the Middle Ages have survived in modern folklore. They are now especially popular in northern Germany and Sweden. Those current in the Romance languages rarely contain a proper name. In the 19th century, Wellerisms, often embodying bad puns, were frequently printed in American newspapers. Many Wellerisms are unprintable and circulate only in oral tradition.

References: See Archer Taylor, *The Proverb:* 200–220; B. J. Whiting, "A Handful of Recent Wellerisms,"

Archiv für das Studium der neueren Sprachen CLXIX (1936): 71–75; C. G. Loomis, "Traditional American Word-Play: Wellerisms or Yankeeisms," *Western Folklore* VIII (1949): 1–21; F. Sánchez y Escribano, "Dialogismos paremiológicos castellanos," *Revista de filología española* XXIII (1936): 275–291.   ARCHER TAYLOR

Wemicus Trickster of the Timigami Ojibwa Indians. See WISAKEDJAK. [EWV]

Wen Ch'ang Chinese god of literature; he has collected a number of legends which display the prowess of scholars. His icon shows him in a long blue gown holding the staff of high office (*ju yi*). His two servants, as is proper for a minister of state, are Dumb as Heaven and Deaf as Earth. Kuei Hsing, an ugly little dwarf standing on one foot, is frequently part of the icon. [RDJ]

werewolf Literally man-wolf (from O. E. *wer*, man, plus *wulf*, wolf): a human being transformed into a wolf by bewitchment, or one having the power to assume wolf form at will. In most instances the taste for human flesh accompanies the change, and the werewolf hunts at night, devouring human beings. In general European belief, the werewolf must return to human form at daybreak; this he does by doffing the wolf skin and hiding it. If he hides it in a cold place, he shivers all day; if it were found and destroyed by another, the owner would die. There was widespread belief that one became a werewolf by putting on a magic girdle made of wolf skin. In Germany, however, a girdle made from the skin of a hanged man was considered just as good. The minute the werewolf is wounded he changes back to human form; the wound will be seen on the corresponding human part the next day. The werewolf was known to the ancient Greeks and Romans, and exists in the folk beliefs of peoples on every continent in the world. In regions where there are no wolves, the prevailing fiercest animal takes its place. Thus we find the weretiger in India, Borneo, and western Asia in general; tiger and fox in China and Japan; boar (Greece and Turkey); hyena, leopard, lion, crocodile (Africa); bear or wolf (North America); jaguar (South America). In Greece it is said that a man who has been a werewolf in life becomes a vampire after he is buried. The cat and the hare are both were-animals among southern United States Negroes and European peasantry. See JAGUAR-MAN; LOUP-GAROU; SHAPESHIFTING.

☞Among the Navaho and other American Indians, human beings having power to assume wolf form may be either men or women, are evilly disposed toward fellow humans, and go about practicing witchcraft against them. Evidence that a person is a werewolf is thought to be conclusive if a wolf or mountain-lion skin is found in his or her house; these are the skins werewolves wear when on their nefarious business. See William Morgan, *Human Wolves among the Navaho* (Yale University Publications in Anthropology, #11, 1936). [EWV]

wēzā Literally, wise men: Burmese necromancers. The wēzā are of two kinds, good and bad, and each kind is divided into 4 classes. Each of these works with an element (iron, mercury, medicine, magic squares) in order to obtain influence over the spirits. The wēzā supply charms against injury, epidemics, and enemies.

whale The hunt and capture of the whale amounts to a cult among the Eskimos of the Alaskan coast and of northeastern Siberia, because of the dangers involved in the pursuit and the importance of the catch for food and oil. In fact, the hereditary role of whaler used to verge on shamanism, with revelation, ritual preparation, initiation, ritual bathing with human mummies, and tabus contingent on the whaling season in the early summer months. In the Fox and Aleutian Islands, King Island, Bering Strait, all the way over to Point Barrow, from the Nootka of Washington to the Chukchee of Siberia, similar ceremonies prevailed.

Preliminaries included the rhythmic mime of a successful whale catch, with a woman enacting the whale; then the sprinkling of ashes on the ice to drive away evil spirits, incantations and songs when leaving shore, sighting the whale, before throwing the spear, songs which the great *kashak* sang when he created the whale. As the whale was towed in, Fox Islands men and boys danced naked in wooden masks which reached to their shoulders. At Cape Prince of Wales the whaler's wife came to meet the boat in ceremonial dress, dancing and singing, and boys and girls performed gesture dances on the beach. Then inside a circle of large whale ribs the whaler's wife and children performed a dance of rejoicing. On the west coast of Hudson Bay communal feasting, dancing, singing, games, and shamanistic performances took place within the circle of bones or stones. The men's motions consisted of vigorous and angular arm-jerking and jumping; the women's of curving gestures and swaying with the torso and arms in a seated or standing posture. Various types of rattles made of puffin beaks and barnacles were manipulated by some of the dancers, to the inevitable accompaniment of the Siberian-type drum.

A final three-day "mourning" period, to placate the animal's spirit, ended with feasting and frenzied dancing, the women wearing masks during the incantations. With the return of parts of the whale's flesh, his spirit also returned to the sea to be reborn.

On land the same animal spirit could be a wolf, according to beliefs. In fact, wolf-spirit once revealed to man the details of the whale cult. [GPK]

wheat If, as may be said, Eastern civilization is based on the cultivation of rice, and that of the New World on maize, that of the West, particularly Europe and derivative societies, has wheat as its staff of life. Wheat is a cultivated form of grass, but like corn (*Zea sp.*), and unlike rice (*Oryza sp.*), it is a hybrid. The first evidences that we have of wheat come from the prehistoric and early historic civilizations of the Near East, prior to the wide use of metals. Since wheat is a hybrid, its use implies a considerable degree of botanical sophistication among the inhabitants of western Asia, who, to our knowledge, were the first to practice cultivation of this grain. Two forms seem to be ancestral to wheat, *dinkel* and *emmer*: the former a single-seeded variety (German *einkorn*), the latter containing the seeds in an ear. Cultivation of wheat first reached elaboration in the river valleys of the Middle East, the basins of the Tigris and Euphrates (ancient Mesopotamia), and the Nile in Egypt. Otherwise arid lands, the flooding of the river basins left the soil moist and easy to cultivate, and the receding of the waters was the time for planting. Wheat, barley, oats, and rye are best planted by broadcast sowing. (Rice, the wet variety, has to be set out seedling by seedling;

maize or corn was planted by hand in hills.) Accompanying the diffusion of wheat culture went the use of the plow, drawn by man or domestic animals, and in later times, labor-saving mechanized techniques of harvesting, threshing, sowing, etc. The heavy seeding of the ground, whereby the stalks of the grain grow closely together, means that later cultivation and weeding are kept to a minimum. Wheat is now grown all over the world, particularly in flat areas, where the climate is such that the period of greatest moisture and precipitation occur at the beginning of the growth cycle, for wheat needs dry weather to mature and form ears. Thus, we can see that wheat is best adapted to temperate, subtropical (or Mediterranean), and to some extent, subarctic regions. These now coincide with areas settled largely by Europeans: Canada, Argentina, Australia, the United States of America, as well as the mother continent. Wheat is also extensively raised in northwestern India, northern China and the Near East.

Sites dating from about 1000 B.C. to 500 A.D. have been found in the Danube Valley, the British Isles, and as far north as Scandinavia, which contain wheat, rye, oats and barley, the latter though in greater abundance, since they are better adapted to the rigors of the climate.

Early in history wheat became a focus of ritual. Along with other harvested crops and various animal products, it became associated with several divinities. In Crete, for example, it was believed that Demeter, who with the passing of centuries became the deity of all the harvest, gave wheat to mankind. It was her special gift, and even more specifically she bestowed it on the Greeks. So strong was the esteem held for wheat that one of the tenets of Mazdaism stated that "who sows wheat, sows good." Ceres, of the Romans, was the goddess of the harvest, especially of grain crops, and, as such, received homage. It appears logical that with the spread of Christianity, many of the rites attached to the pre-Christian pantheon throughout Europe became associated with the local saints, as well as specifically attached to the Virgin. In Ireland, St. Vulgan was considered the patron of both the sowing and the harvest. In France, one of the sobriquets of the Virgin was *Notre-Dame Panetière*, Our Lady the Bread Giver.

In order to assure a successful harvest, many magical practices were followed. For example, in France, twigs of box which had been blessed on Palm Sunday were planted when the wheat was sown. During Holy Week, the poor sought alms of wheat, so as to insure the donor of an abundant harvest. Another form of insurance consisted of the practice whereby the oldest worker engaged in reaping the wheat offered a small sheaf in token to the owner of the farm; this was saved and hung over the mantel or in the parlor of the farm. Sometimes the aid of strangers was invoked so as to guarantee the harvest, as in Montreuil, any visitor to a field where the grain was being cut was presented with a nosegay. In a like fashion divine assistance was sought. In Lillers, France, a mass was said in the parish church on the 25th of July. A handful of wheat, a pear, and other fruits, the first of the season, were brought to the church to be blessed. In some instances the final load of the harvest rather than the first grains to be cut were the objects of special attention. In many cases the last load from the wheat field was gaily decorated with flowers and branches, while the reapers sang as they hoisted the final sheaf.

In the West the prerogative of gleaning has lost its significance, but to the peasant of the Old World it was of great importance. (The average schoolchild is familiar with the painting of J. F. Millet, "The Gleaners.") This right dated back to Biblical times. It concerns the right of the impoverished to cull what is left after the wheat or other grain has been taken in. In some areas gleaning is supervised. In Mont St. Eloi, in the region of Arras, gleaning takes place under the eye of a *garde champêtre*. This official rounds the gleaners up in the morning, watches them while they collect during the day, and rounds them up before the end of the day, because gleaning is forbidden at other times.

Flailing of the wheat is another point at which the crop may be considered as vulnerable. In September, in the south of France, a wagon goes from farm to farm, to which sheaves are offered, and these later are sold at auction to augment the funds of the parish. Local people as well as those outside the parish may be buyers.

At times the benison of local saints may be invoked. In Valenciennes, on the Monday following the feast of St. Veronica, the street porters in costume parade about the village. In their midst is a young and pretty girl, dressed in white who is called *Marie au Blé*; she is accompanied by the youngest and handsomest of the carriers. At intervals they dance and offer grain to the spectators, who give them money in return. At each café they stop and drink, and by the end of the day are drunk. In other areas the harvesters may swap a sheaf of grain for drinks from the farmer. This sheaf may be hung in the kitchen for good luck until the following year. Although much of the ritual attached to wheat has vanished from American farms, thrashing time is still one of hard work, accompanied by great eating, and it is a point of pride for the farmer's wife to vie with her neighbors in setting a large and varied table. See HARVEST HOME. [NFJ]

wheel A diversely used symbol whose meaning is closely interwoven with that of other rounded forms and with such other symbols as fire, wing, cross, pole, star, or the four quarters. To say that a circle is a disc is a ring is a rim is a wheel sounds like an excerpt from Gertrude Stein, but symbols become elaborated by such associative processes and, in the case of the wheel, all these identities are established at some point.

Strictly speaking, the circle claims that symbolism which derives from its linear form—the never-ending line expressive of eternity or continuity, the perfect shape with the dead center suggesting the focal point of the universe. Its complete enclosure gives rise to the idea of protection, familiar in the magic circle of necromancy, or the circle of fire, thorns, ashes, lime, or pebbles, described around a birth, death, or other critical event. It contributes to the circular shape of holy places as removed as the druidical circle and the Chinese Temple of Heaven, and is extended into protective talismans such as armlets and rings. (The circle has other basic suggestions, notably that of female and of water, but these seem less connected with the wheel.)

The disc is a flat round object, and the sun and moon were formerly so conceived. In Egypt, the two discs were viewed as the two celestial eyes. The Siberian shaman wore two rounded bits of metal symbolizing sun and moon. But in general the disc is solar, perhaps because the moon with its waxing and waning bestows much of its connotation on the crescent. The Hindu Vishṇu holds a disc, or a rounded piece of gold in his hand. The Egyptian Rā wears a disc as a crown.

The sun has other attributes than mere roundness. It is a fiery disc and may therefore be surrounded by flames. The rayed circle or the circle surrounded by flames has been a common decorative or heraldic motif for centuries. The god Śiva in his destructive aspect is surrounded by a rim of fire; similarly a saint or supernatural being appears with aureole or nimbus. The sun also travels through the sky and this phenomenon is made possible by boat, fish, chariot, or bird (the eagle of Zeus, the falcon of Rā, the Garuḍa of Vishṇu, or the three-legged crow of the Chinese sun). As a result, the sun wheeling through the sky, the wheel of the chariot, and the wing became associated. A sun disc with falcon wings appears in Egypt. (Similarly an angel on an early American tombstone may be depicted by a face within a circle, flanked by wings.) An ancient seal of Asia Minor shows the god in human form with four-spoked wheel and a single wing.

Thus, the sun is the earliest and the most persistent connotation of the wheel—the beautiful wheel of the Celtic sun god, the sun chariot of Helios, the *rota altivolans* of Lucretius. The fiery wheel mentioned in the first chapter of *Ezekiel*, which has provoked the imagination for centuries (e.g. "Ezekiel saw the wheel a-rolling" in a Negro spiritual), is identified by Robert Graves with the solar year. Throughout Europe it was the custom at Midsummer, when the sun changes his course, to throw burning discs in the air, to roll flaming wheels down hill or across the fields, and to start fire by rotating a wheel around a pole. Such ancient connections with the sun have survived in some localities until recent times.

The wheel may be identified strictly as the vehicular one, as an object that spins and turns, or a design that has spokes. But the vehicle is likely to be of cosmic or magical proportions, the spinning to signify the cycle of the universe or the turn of fortune. The hub of the wheel is like the focal point of the circle. And as it multiplies into innumerable designs, the wheel with spokes merges with the circle containing cross, star, triangle, or becomes divided into quarters or other significant segments. By the same process, the whirling sword (related to the swastika motif) with which cherubs guarded the gates of Eden (*Genesis* iii) became in Celtic legend a cherub with a turning wheel.

The chakra of India The most elaborate wheel symbolism evolved in India, where in some form it permeated both Vedic, Jainist, Hindu, and Buddhist thought, generally with something of its solar association preserved. The word *chakra* (Sanskrit) originally signified circle or wheel, and later disc, specifically the disc of the solar deity Vishṇu. The word *chakravartin* (literally, abiding in the wheel, sometimes rendered as wheel-king or wheel-turner) is the word for the ancient but persistent concept of the "universal monarch." The earlier chakravartins were perhaps conceived as the beings into whom the supreme creator was resolved or subdivided. Later they became human, wielding the highest temporal power just as Buddha or Jina exercised spiritual authority. However, because of their connection with the chakra (either as the ancient wheel of the sun or the disc of Vishṇu) they approached divinity in the popular

mind; and in later Buddhist works the chakravartin reappears as a semi-mythical solar hero.

In early Vedic ceremonies, the chakra represented the sun, and came to symbolize the regular course of the sun in the sky, hence the celestial or cosmic order. Among passages in the *Ṛig-Veda* are an invocation to the god who directs "the golden wheel of the sun" and reference to the "immortal wheel" which nothing can hinder and on which existence depends. Varuna, the universal monarch of the early Vedic gods, is represented as possessing the wheel, the nave of which is apparently intended to personify lightning. The connection of the solar wheel with a vehicular wheel is evidenced in a rite of the Brahmans (perhaps connected with earlier Scythian rites of Central Asia) in which chariot wheels are revolved around a stake while a hymn to the sun is chanted.

In both Brahmanical and Buddhist writings, the chakravartins are endowed with seven jewels, attributes which are traceable to pre-Vedic antiquity. These are the divine treasures of life and immortality which were won by the powers of light from the powers of darkness in the struggle known as the Churning of the Ocean. First on either list of these famous treasures is the "luminary disc," the "mighty and auspicious wheel." It is described in one of the Pāli sutras as having a thousand spokes, complete with tire and nave, ornamented with gold, and as tall as seven palm trees.

In the Legend of the Mystic Wheel, the king goes to the upper story of his palace on the day of the full moon at his inauguration and purifies himself, whereupon the treasure of the wheel appears to him in the east. He sprinkles water over it, saying, "Go forth and overcome." The great wheel then rolls toward the region of the east, and the king with his army follows, camping wherever it stops. By the power of the wheel the rival kings of the east are subjugated and instructed by the chakravartin in righteous rule. The wheel sinks into the waters of the east, rises again, and rolls onward to the south, conquering the people of the south, then the west and the north, in turn. Then it returns to the royal palace and remains fixed at the entrance to the apartments of the king. At the approach of the king's death it falls from its place; when he dies or abdicates it disappears, returning to his successor or a subsequent king only when the law is kept, since it is the attribute only of a righteous king.

This legend, with many details from earlier sun myths, appears in most ancient Buddhist documents. Buddhism, quite naturally, made use of the earlier symbols, adapting or subordinating them to the new teachings. The oldest Buddhist sculptures show the wheel in the place of honor upon the altar. The seven jewels are ascribed to the possession of Buddha in the earliest Pāli Canon. The wheel became the Wheel of the Law with its thousand spokes—the Dharmachakra, the chain of cause and effect—which was set in motion for the salvation of humanity by Buddha's revelation of the Four Great Truths. The title of the founder's first discourse is "The Setting in Motion Onwards of the Wheel of the Law."

Just as the sun cannot be turned backward, the wheel is described as one which can never be deflected from its course. The wheel of the Chakravartin Bharata was said to have met no obstacle when he went to war. Similarly, in Buddhism, the Wheel of the Law could never be turned backward, not even by Buddha himself. In Hindu writing, the chakravartin is simply a great emperor or war lord—one who is able to drive the wheels of his chariot over all lands without hindrance; however, the wheel is a single one, not a pair, hence reminiscent of the solar disc rather than a simple chariot wheel.

In the Jainist temple, a so-called saint wheel (siddha chakra) is always present.. This is a small eight-sided metal plate having the five figures of the Great Ones who are saluted for their asceticism, the names of the three tenets or jewels of the Jain religion (Right Knowledge, Right Faith, Right Conduct) and the word for austerity. Twice a year this plate, which is viewed as a summary of Jainist principles, is taken to water, bathed, and then worshipped for eight days.

Praying Mills and Prayer Wheels It is not unusual, in tracing the course of a symbolic idea, to observe that it starts out as a literal depiction such as the fiery sun disc, evolves into a highly abstract and literary idea, like the Wheel of the Law, and returns again to the literal or material in perhaps quite different form. This happened to the Wheel of the Law in the northern reaches of Buddhism. It was materialized by placing prayers and texts, sometimes with shrines, images, or lamps, into a cylinder (a praying mill) which could be revolved by hand and would thereby yield the benefit of saying the prayers or reading the texts. Some were small silver containers revolved in the hand for days at a time; larger ones set up near lamaseries were given a turn by passers-by, some being so large that several persons were required to turn them. In the Himalayas they were often set over a stream which turned the wheel continually, and among the Mongols they were made of paper and set over fire so as to be turned by the circulation of heat. Always the cylinder or wheel must revolve with the sun—a fact reminiscent of the ancient solar wheel. To anyone who attempts the arduous task of mastering the Buddhist tenets, this must seem a very happy invention indeed, since hundreds of texts could be disposed of with the turn of the wheel. However, the act of turning inevitably tended to become a formality and degenerated into a symbol of good luck or, in Tibet, a superstitious invocation.

The Buddhist praying cylinders have a counterpart in many other parts of the world, in prayer wheels which were hung in temples and turned by hand or by rope for spiritual or magical purposes. In some cases the wheels were vehicular. They are known to have been used in Babylon, in Egyptian temples of the 3rd century B.C., in the temples of ancient Greece. In some Japanese pagodas, a metal wheel is fixed in the pillar at the entrance. In the 10th century a gilt wheel with bells was placed in the cathedral of Winchester, to be revolved on saint days. So-called Wheels of Fortune survived in a few European churches to modern times; in Breton churches a Saint of the Wheel was worshipped by paying a small sum and turning the wheel. From the name, these wheels were probably considered oracular, as presumably were the wheels in the temple of Apollo at Delphi.

The Wheel of Life The aspect of wheel symbolism which deals with the nature of the cosmos and the cycle of life therein is very abstruse and difficult of approach. Hence, it is the more remarkable that it should have given rise to some of the most beautiful, precise, and simple geometric diagrams in the history of art, in addition to providing the framework for some of the most complicated symbolic painting. Obviously in this connection the symbolism of either the circle or the wheel, or both, is involved.

With the wheeling planets overhead and the circumference of the horizon, the cosmos of the ancients must have seemed obviously circular. In the flat delta of the Nile it was a round plate; to the Chinese it was like an egg. Life in the cosmos was created, and maintained, by the balance of opposing forces—male and female, day and night, heat and cold, good and evil. Such ideas as this concerning the nature of the universe were summarized in the "wheel of life." Brief descriptions are misleading but the two best-known examples are familiar—the yin-yang of China and the Shrī Yantra of India. The yin-yang is a circle containing two complementary curved segments (light and dark) and surrounded by eight trigrams (pa kua) which summarize all wisdom by depicting all possible combinations, in groups of three, of a broken and an unbroken line. The Shrī Yantra is composed of concentric circles, some bordered with stylized lotus petals, with nine interpenetrating triangles in the center, five pointing downward, corresponding to the female symbol of the yoni, and four (the male lingam) pointing upward. The nine signify, according to Heinrich Zimmer, "the creative activity of the cosmic male and female energies on successive stages of evolution." The Absolute is not represented but is to be visualized, he says, as a vanishing point "amidst the interplay of all the triangles . . . the elusive center from which the entire diagram expands." An indented square surrounds the diagram, signifying the four walls of the sanctuary or, in turn, the four directions of the universe. The Gnostic wheel also carries the concept of four, being composed of four cone-shaped spokes which terminate in four perfect circles.

To these self-contained and therefore almost quiescent diagrams of cosmic principles, must be added a concept which seems, almost visibly, to set the cosmic circle to revolving like a "wheel." This is the idea, present in Sanskrit, Pāli, and Greek, that life occurs in an endless cycle of rebirths. The concept of succeeding cycles based on four—emanation, fruition, dissolution, and re-emanation—is fundamental in Hindu philosophy and art.

Paintings in the wheel pattern, that is, in a design of concentric circles with each circle or divided segment thereof containing a depiction, developed into a magnificent art, particularly in Tibet. A temple ceiling in Lhasa shows the cosmic lotus, with the primal Buddha occupying the central circle, surrounded by eight manifestations of Buddha, each with separate attribute, gesture, and color, all contained within the flower, which is within the square of the sanctuary, one of the famous maṇḍalas of the world. The New York American Museum of Natural History has a beautiful series of small wheel paintings depicting such subjects as the Wheel of Transmigration, the Wheel (or Magic Circle) of the Conqueror of Death, of the Omniscient One, of the Peaceful and Wrathful Deities of the After-Death Plane, and the Wheel for Casting Horoscopes. The first of these, also called the Wheel of Life, depicts the three cardinal sins in the center, symbolized by cock, serpent, and pig; in the surrounding circles are figures following the bright upward path and the dark downward path, scenes from the six worlds of rebirth, and Buddha's chain of causes.

Turning to the other side of the world, we find another work of art constructed in the concentric wheel pattern, and again it is related to the sun and concerned with the sacred nature of the universe and of time. This is the Aztec calendar stone. The central circle is occupied by the sun god with his protruding tongue and the surrounding circles carry symbols of the days of the month and other signs of the calendar.

The Wheel in Divination The Tibetan Wheel for Casting Horoscopes, referred to above, leads to another use of the wheel, that is, as the characteristic form of the graphs used in various parts of the world for oracular purposes. Again, it is not always easy to see when these designs derive from the spinning wheel and when from the magical circle. This Tibetan Wheel has a sort of tick-tack-toe design in the center circle, in which the numbers add to fifteen. The surrounding bands show the eight trigrams (resulting from their connection with the Chinese, of course), the twelve cyclic animals, and the twelve lotus petals.

The Geomancer's Wheel of China (usually called a Compass) also makes use of the trigrams, though they are usually replaced by words (characters) with somewhat broader meaning. This is a wooden disc with rounded bottom and flat yellow-varnished face, minutely inscribed with red and black characters in concentric circles. A glass-covered depression in the center contains the needle which, in the hands of an accredited manipulator, is expected to locate the "lucky line" of the year, the proper location for a building or date for a marriage, or such other information as is required. The instrument varies in size and complexity, and different compasses are used for different purposes. (The Chinese also elaborate the eight trigrams into 64 hexagrams arranged in a square for purposes of divination.)

In Arabia the magical circles described on parchment provided a basis for astrological calculations, which were adopted in the areas to which Islam spread; a leaf from a divining book in Indonesia, for example, shows a design with eight spokes each terminating in a crab symbol. The cabalistic lore of medieval Europe, and the use of horoscopes up to the present time, are familiar.

The Mechanical Wheel In modern times, the actual wheel is not necessarily vehicular. It has many mechanical applications which have added to and to an extent replaced the ancient solar disc or fiery chariot wheel. St. Catherine's wheel, for example, was an implement of torture, and she is the patron saint of those who turn the spinning wheel. The wheel within a wheel is not so likely to connote Ezekiel's vision as some elaborate mechanism. The wheel of fortune is more associated with games of chance than with the prayer wheel hanging in church or temple. The wheels of time belong to the clock. The sun and moon are no longer conceived as revolving discs but as spheres. However, ancient symbols remain stored deep in the recesses of the human mind. In the middle of the 20th century discs took to the air again in the shape of "flying saucers."

MAMIE HARMON

whipping Many Amazonian Indian tribes ascribe great magic virtues to whipping. During certain ceremonies, in particular during puberty rites, men flog each other with long whips made of manatee skin. This treatment is believed to have a purificatory value and, in some cases, it is considered as a rite with a beneficial influence on the output of fields. Compare FLAGELLATION.
[AM]

☞ Whipping, both as a punishment and as a ceremonial practice, is not common among North American Indians, except in one or two areas. In the Southwest, among the Pueblo peoples, Parsons reports public whipping of adults for adultery at Taos and Acoma, the whipping of a man for using modern agricultural machinery at Jemez, the whipping of a small girl for breaking a new pot at Zuñi, and of a boy for almost strangling his little brother with a slipnoose during play. At Zuñi the Governor is entitled to hit a recalcitrant four times to enforce an order. Whipping in punishment is also referred to in Zuñi myths. A girl, for example, in a Zuñi tale abandons her baby to Red Deer Woman; she is struck by her uncles when they hear her story. "You big fool!" each uncle says and strikes her. In another version of the same tale the girl's brother whips her.

Whipping is also used for cleansing purposes, or for exorcism in the pueblos. A Zuñi tale relates how a boy who mocked a kachina was whipped or "cleansed" with the yucca whip, the usual object used in this area for whipping (however, see also below). At Zuñi also dreamers of bad dreams are exorcised by ritual flagellation; dreaming of the dead is generally treated by whipping by the kachina; Hopi kachinas whip persons suffering from rheumatism. Four strokes with the whip are the ritual number of strokes used.

Whipping is a regular part of the installation of adults in various ceremonial offices. At Acoma the annual War chiefs are whipped at their installation and at their retirement from office. Anyone may request to be whipped by shamans at this time to give him power in hunting, racing, or gambling. The warlike Cactus societies of Zuñi and Jemez whip with cacti.

Whipping is also part of adults' initiation rites for membership in various Pueblo societies. At initiation rites into the Hunt society of Sia a shaman whips the initiate and, in fact, all the society members, and is in turn whipped. The kachinas of Cochiti and Sia, and of the Zuñi Ne'wekive clown society, whip at initiation.

In the western pueblos the kachinas also whip children and adults who request this in an early spring ceremony of general exorcism (Powamu at Hopi). Hopi and Zuñi ritual whipping of ten- to twelve-year-old children at initiation ceremonies which acquaint them with the kachinas is an important and elaborate part of the initiation rites. The children, boys and girls, are severely whipped several times both in the kiva and in the open; they appear badly frightened, and are said to tremble, while several cry or scream. After undergoing this initiation Pueblo children know that the kachina which visit the pueblos for half the year are actually fellow townsmen dressed and masked to represent the real kachina or spirits.

For other instances of ritual initiatory whipping, of whipping before first wearing a mask, of whipping as a substitute for killing, for whipping after killing one's first jack rabbit, for whipping as a cure for sickness, etc., in the pueblos see Elsie Clews Parsons, *Pueblo Indian Religion* (2 vols., Chicago, 1939), pp. 1271–72.

Whipping of children in initiatory rites has also been reported for the Alabama and other Southeastern groups along the Gulf coast, but few details are known concerning whipping in these extinct groups. Children were made to pass in array, and were whipped until blood was drawn. A common practice in the Southeast now, for initiation and as a purificatory rite, is to scratch a boy's or man's arm with a garfish jaw in order to draw blood. Among the Eastern Woodlands peoples the practice of forcing captives to "run the gantlet" between two lines of persons armed with clubs, tomahawks and other weapons amounted in effect to severe whipping of captives. [EWV]

whirlwind Whirlwind is personified by the Jicarilla Apache and other Southwestern Indian groups; the use of whirlwind (also referred to simply as Wind) as a messenger or spy on the Hactcin (Jicarilla supernaturals) is an ever-recurring incident in Jicarilla folklore. Among many California and other western Indians whirlwinds or dust spouts are associated with evil; they are said to consist of a dead shaman's dust, or to contain poison, a shaman's "pain" (magic object), or an evil spirit. They may sicken people with bad dreams, may capture a person's shadow or spirit, or may cause a person to meet with an accident and die. Precautions taken against whirlwinds are to hide from or dodge them, to throw dirt or water into them, or talk to them informally, at the same time smoking, clapping the hands, and stomping the feet. Victims of a whirlwind are smoked to cleanse them of its evil effects. It is considered especially bad for mourners to dream of a whirlwind; any who do must be doctored or else they will sicken. In the pueblos Whirlwind is a spirit: at Jemez it is believed that a whirlwind causes miscarriage. Among the Hopi, who believe that Whirlwind is abroad at noon, a child's expression is, "I'll be back before Whirlwind gets me." A Laguna tale recounts how Whirlwind Man actually does carry off a girl, and at Zuñi, witches are believed to travel in whirlwinds. The Papago of the Southwest say Whirlwind causes a dizzy sickness. (See E. C. Parsons, *Pueblo Indian Religion* [2 vols., Chicago, 1938], p. 178 and note.) [EWV]

When Whirlwind appears as a character in Mandan-Hidatsa Indian myth or folktale, it is always a spirit of the dead. These people say that a very small whirlwind rises from a grave and that the spirit of the one interred goes abroad in the form of this little whirlwind. The Gros Ventre Indians also believe that the spirits of the dead come forth in the form of these eddies; they point out that little whirlwinds are often seen in cemeteries when there is no wind elsewhere.

Whiskey, Johnny A halyard chantey in praise of whiskey, probably known as long ago as the times of the Spanish Armada, though the drink eulogized then was malmsey. The text is similar in many stanzas to the familiar verses of *Little Brown Jug*.

white animals, white Coyote Marked respect is attached to albino or to white animals among American Indians. These were the animals selected for sacrifice, as the white dog of the Seneca and other tribes, or the white full-grown buffalo or buffalo calf of the Plains tribes, which, among the Crow, was dedicated to the Sun, Crow supreme deity. The Yurok of northwestern California believe in a White Coyote, the father of all Coyotes on

earth, who lives at the head of a river in the sky, and has a yellow mate. This tribe and its neighbors prize white (albino) deerskins highly as treasures, and hold a dance in their World Renewal Ceremony, the White Deerskin Dance, in which these family treasures are displayed.

Since white animals are believed to have supernatural power, they were often feared as well as sought after. To see a white animal was a sign of bad luck for a Timiskaming Algonquian hunter, for example. [EWV]

White-Painted-Woman or **White-Shell-Woman** A female deity of the Navaho and other Apache groups of the American Southwest. Among the Navaho, Yolkai Estsan, White-Shell-Woman, is the younger sister of Changing Woman, highest deity in the Navaho pantheon. The white shell is White-Shell-Woman's symbol; white is the color of dawn and the east, and she is related to the waters. Her husband is Moon-Carrier. In some Navaho myths there is some confusion as to the separate identities of Changing Woman and White-Shell-Woman. Among the Chiricahua Apache White-Painted Woman is the mother of Child-of-the-Water. A white shell is, among the White Mountain Apache, a holy object possessing power, and symbolizes females. In the Eastern Woodlands Midewiwin, a white shell (*megis*) was also a holy object, the "shot" which Mide initiates learned to keep in their bodies, and shoot into fellow members in Mide rites; this shell, however, was not symbolic of females. [EWV]

Whitsunday A festival for both Jews and Christians. Among the Jews, the 50th day after the second day after Passover was celebrated by an offering of first-fruits. Later, celebrations were in commemoration of the giving of the Law which occurred 50 days after the Jews left Egypt.

Among Christians, Whitsunday, seven weeks after Easter, and Whitsuntide, seven weeks and a day, i.e. as among the Jews 50 days, commemorate the descent upon the disciples of the pentecostal fire, the gift of the spirit. The feast is mentioned in the 1st century A. D. but was not celebrated with great ceremony. Red rose leaves were scattered from the roof of the church and the vestments for that day are red. In France, trumpets blown during the divine service were said to represent the sound of the mighty wind which accompanied the descent of the Holy Ghost.

Whitsuntide, like Shrove Tuesday, Carnival, Easter, and other less known festivals, is an occasion to express the feelings generated by the return of good weather, the new green of the fields, the spring flowers, and the general resurgence of animal and spiritual powers. That in some communities people thought that the exercise of their fertilizing powers would increase the fertility of the cattle and crops is natural, though the extent of this belief must in each instance be examined in terms of the culture which entertains it. Each community seems to have chosen a day or period in the spring season for festivities which include processions, mimes, dances, and sexual license of various sorts from simple obscenities to general intercourse.

The particular day chosen by any community is determined by a number of factors too complex to be examined here. Important among them are traditions, possibly from pagan times, geography, climate, and local factors. The fact that many Christian feasts occur on dates which were formerly celebrated as pagan feasts (Christmas, Easter, St. George's Day, and Saint John's Day) is evidence that while the missionaries were Christianizing the world, the world was paganizing the missionaries. Climate had some influence. Festivals and ceremonies characteristic of the English May Day are very similar to those in Sweden on Saint John's Eve, the summer solstice, and to those of Whitsunday elsewhere. The day seems to be determined in part at least by the time the sap begins to flow and the flowers begin to bloom. Finally, the several communities may and sometimes do repeat ceremonies at different times during the spring. The grief and joy which in every Christian community accompanies the murder, burial, and resurrection of God at Easter may be and often are repeated with a less solemn timbre at Whitsun and St. John's. Thus if these ceremonies, which show marked similarities in all parts of the world, be taken as the expression in the many dialects of ritual of emotions, the ceremonies themselves with such correlations as can be made with tradition, climate, and local factors show a splintering of the emotion. Consequently Whitsunday ceremonies in Germany are often Easter or May Day ceremonies elsewhere.

Perhaps the most characteristic of Whitsuntide ceremonies is the custom of going out into the woods or the fields and bringing back green boughs to dress up some member of the village. Thus Green George, Jack-in-the-Green, the Leaf Man, the Whitsuntide Lout are associated with Whitsuntide in Switzerland, parts of Russia, Carinthia, Transylvania, Rumania; elsewhere this ceremony occurs on April 23 (St. George's Day) or May Day in England. The youths are completely disguised by green boughs attached to two hoops and usually have a high headdress of leaves. In places where the mummer is executed, he is supplied with an artificial neck and false head, or a series of hats, one on top of the other. At Wahrstedt the chief figures are the King and Steward, chosen by lot and dressed gaily. At Hildesheim the Leaf King is the leader on Whitmonday of a band that goes from house to house collecting gifts. In Bohemia the boys with birch bark caps gay with flowers drag a king on a sledge to the village green with various sorts of skylarking. When they arrive there, one member, sometimes the Town Crier, recites scurrilous lampoons about the members of every house. Sometimes the central figure is a girl and called, as in German Hungary, a Whitsun Queen. The children of Königgratz in Bohemia choose a king and queen on Whitmonday. In Silesia the king was the boy who won an athletic contest.

Frazer has collected impressive accounts of the folk drama in which Green George was murdered at Whitsuntide. The places mentioned are Niederporing, Lower Bavaria, Wurmlingen, Swabia, Saxony, Thuringia, Bohemia. The protagonists are dressed in leaves and flowers. The ceremony of "murdering" and burning a straw puppet dressed like an old woman known as Shadow Queen is performed on Palm Sunday in Russia and among the Central European Gipsies. The ritual is at times elaborate.

The ceremonies mentioned here as associated with Whitsuntide are celebrated at other festivals in other parts of Christendom. Similar ceremonies are known in non-Christian areas.

The Irish are reported to believe that it is unlucky to go into the water at Whitsuntide, that people born on that day will kill or be killed or both, and that the Pentecost days are dangerous for them. [RDJ]

Wife Wrapt in Wether's Skin A British ballad (Child # 277), derived from an old story, *The Wife Lapped in Morrel's Skin,* and relating the disciplinary device of a man whose wife was too high-toned to attend to her housework: since he did not dare to offend her influential relatives by beating her, he wrapped her in a sheepskin, which he whipped vigorously. Many variants are known in Britain and in the United States. The hero's name is Robin in several texts, Robin-a-Thrush in one; one Scottish version makes him a "wee cooper of Fife," and another, the laird of Fife. In Mississippi and other places in the United States the man "lived in the West" and the song is known as *Dandoo* from the syllables of its refrain.

wíikita (from *wiiki,* bird down, + *ta,* made) The prayerstick festival of the Papago Indians of southern Arizona and northern Sonora. Prayersticks are made of bird down, for *wíikita* of turkey feathers. The festival is often spoken of as a harvest ceremony, but is actually more in the nature of a solstice ceremony to keep the world in order, as in the pueblos. The two surviving versions differ somewhat: the winter ceremony at Archie, Arizona, and the summer celebration at Quitovaca, Sonora. Both are sacred and elaborate. Both were instituted by the culture hero I'toi during his march of conquest. *Winter Ceremony—*

1) The large roster of hereditary officials is grouped by fours. Dancers and singers are especially appointed, eight for each of the participating five villages. They are called *vipinyim* (north), and many of their songs and refrains suggest Pueblo derivation. They wear gourd masks and cocoon anklets. The *navitcu* clown goes begging from house to house and cures sickness.

2) Preparations include the erection of a ceremonial enclosure, shade, and council house on a special plaza; the making of prayersticks to be placed by eights in four piles of sand; the consecration of cornmeal for aspersion; the making of effigies, etc.

3) A bullroarer announces the ceremony. Four flood children (two boys and two girls) or corn dancers commemorate four children once buried alive for the salvation of the tribe. They are accompanied by scraping-sticks and basket drums. They flex their knees during drum tapping, and stamp and raise effigies during stick-scraping.

4) A procession includes maskers representing the sun and moon, and a snouted creature.

5) The dancer-singers prance in a counterclockwise circle, carrying images of things wanted in abundance. Their songs to these images always end with the wíikita word *ku-uh.*

6) The *nanavitcu,* numbering perhaps 30, enact planting, harvesting, and looking for rain; and they exert healing powers.

7) The prayersticks are distributed, for rubbing away evil.

Summer Ceremony—

The less elaborate Quitovaca festival combines features of the cleansing rites and of rain-making by fermentation of the cactus liquor, *tiswin.* There are no specially composed songs or effigies. The local fetish, a basket, contains the heart of the monster killed by I'toi. Two enclosures accommodate the northern and southern villages.

1) Four ceremonial clowns in deerskin masks, the *kuatcu'k* (finishers) shoot ceremonial food with bows and arrows. They sprinkle meal and squeak *ku-uh* to kill sickness. Later on they enact an impromptu pantomime of looking for tracks, ducking each other in a spring, etc.

2) Two dancer-singers for the north and south villages don deerskin masks and cocoon anklets. They wave tufted wands while stamping in time with their song. Then they dogtrot in a procession.

3) Six cornmeal sprinklers march in procession, then sprinkle meal on the ground, while stepping backwards.

Both versions of the ceremony suggest introduction from the Rio Grande pueblos, along with the culture of the sacred corn and squash. The clowns combine properties of the *kachina* and *koshare,* including the kachina cry, *ku-uh.* The shooting of food, the sun and moon representations recall Hopi rituals; the prancing of dancers in a counterclockwise circle recalls Pueblo *tablita corn dances.* [GPK]

Wild Hunt The ghostly hunters (E501) who ride through the sky on stormy evenings: known in nearly all parts of the world. The appearance of the wild hunters, usually said to be the ghosts of the restless dead, presages evil for the community. This phantom host, its horses and dogs (ratchet hounds, Gabriel's hounds, etc.), make a wild noise in the night, the sound of spirits passing overhead in their eternal wandering; and the sound of the spectral dogs makes earthly dogs howl and yelp in company. Typical explanatory stories of the Wild Hunt are:

Dando, a pleasure-loving, overly lenient Cornish priest, became a wealthy, sensual, and selfish man. He was an ardent hunter. One Sunday morning, after a long chase, he stopped and called to his companions for a drink, but all the flasks in the party were empty. Dando insisted if there were no drink at hand they could "go to Hell for it." At once a handsome hunter offered Dando a brimming cup, assuring him that it came from "the establishment just mentioned." Dando drank deep, but noticed as he did so that the man was counting up several head of the game for himself. Dando remonstrated but the suave hunter insisted that whatever he could catch he could keep. Dando's anger mounted but the hunter refused to give up his count. "I'll go to Hell for them, but I'll get them," cried Dando. Whereupon the hunter said, "You shall indeed," picked him up, and sat him before him on the horse. The horse dashed away and Dando's dogs followed with wild din. When they came to the stream the horse with its two riders leaped into the middle and the dogs followed. A blaze of fire rose about them and the stream boiled. But in a moment the face of the earth was as peaceful as ever. Sometimes Dando still rides and the spectral dogs can still be heard early Sunday mornings in the neighborhood of St. Germans.

Malay folklore also has its phantom huntsman with the phantom dogs, the *hantu si buru* or *hantu pemburu,* an evil spirit of the Malay Peninsula who hunts the wild boar and the mouse deer during the full moon. A preg-

nant woman once had a violent longing for meat of the mouse deer, specifically for that of a doe big with male young. Her husband vowed to get what she wanted but by mistake went looking for a buck big with young. He hunted across the world without success. Finally he sent his dogs to hunt the sky while he watched them from the earth. His head became fixed to his back from always looking up and a shoot from a leaf which fell into his throat grew up in front of his face. Because his son, born while he was hunting, was often reproached for having an evil spirit for a father, the *hantu si buru* punishes mankind. To meet him induces fatal illness; but he sometimes cures the illnesses of those who propitiate him. He still hunts the mouse deer and the note of the brik-brik bird at night is a warning of his approach. See ARTHUR; ASGARDSREID; BERCHTA; CELTIC FOLKLORE; CHRISTMAS; GABRIEL'S HOUNDS; GANDREID; HECATE; HERODIAS; HOLDE; HORSE; ODIN.

William Tell The Swiss national hero; central character of a legend of the 14th century independence movement against the Hapsburgs. The story of William Tell was for many years considered to be literally true, but recent scholarship, after stripping the tale of many of its trimmings, has demonstrated the completely legendary character of Tell himself. In outline, the story goes that Gessler, the local governor, set up a cap in the market place and ordered the inhabitants to bow to it as a symbol of imperial rule. William Tell, on November 18, 1307, refused. Gessler, knowing of Tell's skill in archery, ordered him to shoot with one shot an apple from the head of his own son. The bowman placed one bolt in his crossbow and another in his belt. Then he shot the apple from his son's head. Gessler asked what the other arrow was for. When Tell said it was for his tyrannous heart if he had missed, Gessler had him bound and taken across the lake to imprisonment. But Tell leaped ashore from the boat at a place afterwards known as Tell's Leap, and soon after ambushed and slew Gessler. This spark from Uri set fire to the Swiss desire for freedom and the Confederation soon was formed.

This story, for all its exactness of date, name, and place, is made out of whole cloth. The story of the Greek archer Alcon, companion of Hercules mentioned by Vergil, has no direct connection with the Tell story, but Alcon was noted for his ability to shoot rings from people's heads and once, when his sleeping child was encircled by a serpent, Alcon killed the reptile with an arrow without harming the child. A closer relative of the Tell legend appears in the *Vilkina* (or *Thidrek's) Saga.* There, King Nidung orders Egil, one of Volund's brothers, to shoot an apple from his son's head. There too appears the story of the second arrow. Gheysmer's version of Saxo Grammaticus tells the story of one Tokko (or Toki), whose name means simpleton. (Tell, *der Tall,* from *toll,* senseless, mad, means approximately the same thing.) Tokko bragged of his ability with the bow, and the cruel Harold Bluetooth gave him one chance to shoot an apple from his son's head. Tokko kept two spare arrows for the king if he missed. According to Saxo, this took place in 950. The English archer of balladry, William of Cloudesly, too is hero of a parallel tale. He, because of his misdeeds, had forfeited his life. But by shooting an apple from his child's head at 120 paces, he convinced the king that he was too fine an archer to be executed. Such stories are found also in Norway (2 versions), Holstein and the Rhine country in Germany, and Iceland. The William Tell story appears in Swiss balladry well before the 16th century.

will-o'-the-wisp The jack-o'-lantern or ignis fatuus (French *feu follet*), also known in widespread folk belief as fox-fire, corpse light, friar's lantern, etc., and almost everywhere regarded as a supernatural manifestation. One of the German names for it is *Irrlicht*. It is an omen of death, or a wandering lost soul; it is accompanying some invisible funeral procession; or it is a forest spirit (see LIEKKIO). *Blud* is the Wend term for it, and the Wends believe it is the soul of an unbaptized infant.

American Penobscot Indians called this manifestation *Eskudáit'*, fire creature, and regarded it as an omen of calamity and death. Thonga Negroes of South Africa identify these mysterious lights as witch-fires; either they are actually the witches (*baloyi*) or are sent by them to terrify wrong-doers. If one is seen by a group, measures are taken at once to discover which one among them is the wrong-doer and to extract a confession from him. The Valenges believe that their sorcerers fly by night like balls of fire above the trees. (See *Folk-Lore* 50: 289). For fuller discussion, see JACK-O'-LANTERN; CORPSE LIGHT. See also FETCH CANDLE; ST. ELMO'S FIRE.

Wind, winds Wind as a character appears in the mythologies of many American Indian tribes in specific tales which have to do with regulating the wind. In a Coeur d'Alene version of this tale, Coyote snares Wind and stands ready to shoot him, but Wind begs him to take pity, and promises to blow only four times in the future, not all the time as he had been accustomed to doing. The inclusion of this tale in the Coyote cycle is unique to the Coeur d'Alene, but the incidents in the tale have a wide distribution on the North Pacific Coast and in the interior Plateau area. Regulation of the wind is also one of the things Eastern Woodlands culture heroes do for human beings; Nanabozho causes the wind to stop blowing all the time, and Gluskabe overcomes a giant bird whose wings cause the wind; he breaks the bird's wing. When the wing heals it is much smaller, and when flapped it produces light, gentle winds. The Pueblos have various Wind spirits. At Taos Pueblo, Wind Old Woman is believed to live at the middle of the world, to be mean and witchlike. She receives offerings of meal, pollen, and a single turkey feather from persons suffering from rheumatism. Wind Old Man is also referred to at Taos; some say he has died, else the winds at Taos would be far worse than they are. "Sweepings" or "refuse wind, Kliwa," is a terrible wind spirit, according to Taos belief, the "sickness man" who brings smallpox and other epidemics. He lurks near the houses; in former times people could see him, "an awful sight," who had to be exorcised by the chiefs with medicine water. At Zuñi the wind spirits are North Winds, the six Winds of the four cardinal directions and zenith and nadir, and Whirlwind; at Hopi Wind Woman and Whirlwind; at Laguna Feather Man and Whirlwind; among the Tewa Wind Old Woman and Wind Old Man; at Isleta Wind Old Man.

The idea of winds at the four quarters of the earth is not limited to the Pueblo peoples. The Apache peoples have Black, Blue, Yellow, and White Winds of the four

directions, and almost all over the continent there exist origin stories of the establishment of winds at the four quarters of the earth. In the Southwest the four or six main winds are associated with color symbolism, as exemplified above in the Apache data. The Apache, like the Pueblo peoples, envisage more winds than those of the directions; in a White Mountain Apache myth "thirty-two little winds" for each of the four directions smoke four pipefuls of strong tobacco offered to the hero of the tale as a test by Sun, the hero's unwilling father (Grenville Goodwin, *Myths and Tales of the White Mountain Apache, MAFLS* 33:7).

A cave in which the winds are confined, and from which they are released, is mentioned in California and southern Oregon tales about the wind, and there are also, in western American Indian mythologies especially, tales of conflicts between the north and south winds, and of the winds being kept in a bag (C322), in a fashion similar to that in which light is kept in a bag, box, or basket in Plateau and North Pacific Coast tales. See GA-OH; LIGHT; WHIRLWIND. [EWV]

windigo, wendigo, or **wiendigo** A man-eating creature who roams through the forest devouring luckless victims, in the mythology and belief of the northeastern Algonquian tribes. It is believed that any hunter who becomes lost in the bush, without food and provisions, preys like an animal for food and becomes cannibalistic; once having eaten human flesh he becomes a windigo, a fearsome and dangerous enemy to his former fellow human beings. Among the Ojibwa the term windigo is used in reference to an ogre, not necessarily cannibalistic, with whom children are threatened if they are naughty. See Frank G. Speck, *Naskapi*, Norman, Okla., 1935. [EWV]

wintergreen Oil of wintergreen has great reputation as a folk medicine for successful treatment of rheumatic pain and toothache. The North American Potawatomi Indians make a tea from the leaves of wintergreen to break a fever and to cure lumbago and rheumatism. They consider the berries balsamic and invigorating to the stomach. The Menomini and the Ojibwa also drink wintergreen tea to cure rheumatism; among the Shinnecock it is recommended for kidney trouble. Country people in the eastern United States attribute the delicate flavor of venison to the berries of wintergreen—hence one of its names, deerberry.

The leaves of the herb wintergreen (*Pyrola minor*) are cooling and drying, good for inward and outward wounds, also for hemorrhage, ulcers in the kidneys or bladder, and against making bloody water and excess of the catamenia (Culpeper).

winti or **wintima'** Dutch Guiana Negro word for spirit, a winti-man being a practitioner of magic and a priest of the African deities. As is the case with its African counterparts, the word *winti*, the *taki-taki* term for wind, has been accorded this meaning since, like the wind, the supernatural beings are not of material substance and invisible. The importance of the word is reflected in the fact that it gives its name to the African forms of worship found in the Guiana coastal area, which are also referred to as *winti* or, in the literature, as the *winti*-cult. [MJH]

Wisakedjak, Wisa'ka, or **Whiskey Jack** Cree and Saulteaux Ojibwa Indian culture hero, identical with

Nanabozho of other Ojibwa and central Algonquian groups, and explicitly identified with Wolverine in some Cree tales. Wisa'ka is the Fox Indian form of the name. He is the creator-trickster of the Fox Indians, being credited by them with having created the earth and everything on it, including man, but also figuring in Fox trickster stories. Wisa'ka now lives in the north and no one can visit him except by his will; he, on the contrary, can go and come as he pleases. His younger brother, Iyapa'ta, lives in the west in the spirit world. Some Shawnee know Wisa'ka as a trickster, but most of the Shawnee equate him to the Shawnee-Delaware mythologic character Nashitheki, and to the Sauk and Peoria Withihakaka. See NANABOZHO. [EWV]

Wise One Younger brother of the Lipan Apache culture hero, Killer-of-Enemies. Wise One equates with the younger brother, relative, or friend of the Navaho, Western, Jicarilla, Mescalero and Chiricahua culture heroes, and to him are attributed the characteristics usually associated with the younger of the Apache divine pair of culture heroes. [EWV]

Wissler, Clark (1870–1947) American anthropologist and authority on the American Indian. In 1906, following studies at the University of Indiana and Columbia University, he became curator of the department of anthropology of the American Museum of Natural History, a position he held until his retirement in 1942. In 1924, he returned to teaching, becoming then Professor of Anthropology at Yale University where he lectured until 1940.

Dr. Wissler's lifelong study and interest was in the American Indian; the collection of Indian material in the Museum of Natural History which he built up is one of the best in the world. Although his work was mostly in the United States, Dr. Wissler carried on significant researches elsewhere—in Australasia and Hawaii as well as in New Zealand where he studied the mysterious Maori stone carvings. Some of his books dealing with the Indian are *Indian Cavalcade* (1938), a treatment of Indian life in which science and romance are blended; *Indians of the United States* (1940), a summing up of his lifelong study; *North American Indians of the Plains* (1912); *The American Indian* (1917); *Man and Culture* (1923); *The Relation of Nature to Man in Aboriginal America* (1926); *Social Anthropology* (1929) and many other related subjects in book and periodical, of both scientific and popular appeal.

witch, witchcraft A person who practices sorcery; a sorcerer or sorceress; one having supernatural powers in the natural world, especially to work evil, and usually by association with evil spirits or the Devil: formerly applied to both men and women, but now generally restricted to women. Belief in witches exists in all lands, from earliest times to the present day. The wise woman and the medicine man of primitive societies, the learned pagan priestess, and the divinities of early religion became, through the influence of Christianity or the modification of folk tradition, the malignant, accursed witches and sorcerers of the Middle Ages and later folk belief. World folklore almost universally reports them as having the following powers: divination, invulnerability and superlative strength, transformation of self or others (Circe, Beauty and the Beast, the *Six Swans* of Grimm), ability to fly, power to become invisible or cause

others to become so, ability to impart animation to inanimate objects, to produce at will anything required, knowledge of drugs to produce love, fertility, death, etc., and, invariably, power over others through charms and spells. One of the attributes of the witch or sorcerer is the magic wand, staff, or rod, surviving to the present day in the hazel wand or divining rod used to discover water. One may distinguish a witch by several well-known tests: a witch cannot weep, at most she sheds only three tears; she has a birthmark under her armpit or hidden elsewhere under her hair; she has long eyes; she has to stop when she sees a broom and count the straws, or count seeds, grain, holes in a sieve, letters in a piece of writing, etc. The great Renaissance work on witchcraft *Malleus Maleficarum* (*The Hammer Against Evildoers*) by Sprenger and Kramer indicates clearly the great danger witches were. Some of the chapter headings are: Of the Method by which they can inflict every sort of infirmity; How witch midwives commit most horrid crimes when they either kill children or offer them to devils in most accursed wise; How witches impede and prevent power of procreation; Of the manner whereby they change men into shapes of beasts. See HAG; SABBAT; witchcraft in SPANISH FOLKLORE; MEDICINE MAN; SHAMAN.

Witch stories analogous to European witch tales, and reflecting ideas of witchcraft similar to European ones, are found in Eastern Woodlands, Southeastern, and Southwestern Indian mythologies. Elsewhere in North America such tales are none too prevalent, although witchcraft in various forms is practiced by evilly disposed shamans and other persons in many North American tribes. American Indian witching practices are perhaps in part native, in part borrowings of European forms of black magic. Witching is not restricted to either sex; men or women, as long as they have the power or knowledge, practice witchcraft for purposes of revenge, or out of envy or jealousy, or to impose their own will or wishes on someone else. An old man who wished to marry a young, desirable girl might obtain her because she knew, or her family knew, that to refuse his demands would mean death; a mother might obtain a desirable wife for a son, because the mother's powers as a witch were known. Curing shamans, in most of North America, had powers for evil as well as good and often witched their victims, causing them to become ill or die. The Navaho and other American Indians believe that men and women, disguised in wolf or mountain-lion skins, go about practicing witchcraft; tale and myth material about such beings are plentiful. Among the Eastern Woodlands tribes witch bundles enabled their possessors to work black magic; such bundles had to be "fed" annually, often with the flesh or heart of the owner's own children or other close relatives. Witch bundles might be owned by individuals, or by a group or witching society; group organization of male and female witches is known for the Shawnee, Fox, and other eastern tribes, and cannibalism is usually connected with the rites of such societies. For examples of Pueblo Indian witch tales see Ruth Benedict, *Zuñi Mythology* (2 vols., Columbia University, Contributions to Anthropology, Vol. 21, 1935), especially pp. 110–163, 297. For a general description of Pueblo witches and witchcraft see Elsie Clews Parsons, *Pueblo Indian Religion* (2 vols., Chicago, 1939), vol. 1, pp. 62–68; for a description of the origin of

Shawnee witch medicine see Vernon Kinietz and Erminie W. Voegelin, eds., *Shawnese Traditions—C. C. Trowbridge's Account* (Occasional Contributions from the Museum of Anthropology of the University of Michigan, vol. 9, 1939, pp. 43–46). [EWV]

☞The usual technique used by sorcerers in tropical South America to kill their enemies is to shoot at them the darts and pebbles which they carry inside their bodies. Often they send out their own souls to strike down their victims. Some shamans inject into their victims a blackish substance which may be a deadly poison. Sorcerers also practice rites of imitative and contagious magic on the exuviæ of their victims (see EXCREMENTS SWALLOWED). Moreover they can change themselves into dangerous animals, especially jaguars. Suspected witches are, as a rule, killed or expelled from the group. [AM]

witch hazel A shrub extensively used by the Indians of New England in medicine; tea brewed from the bark was used to stop bleeding of the stomach and kidneys. The bark and leaves are good for dimming eyes. It was considered good medicinally because the flowers show the snakes of Æsculapius. The astringent water cures inflammations, varicose veins, and is a tonic and clearing agent for the skin. Slips of witch hazel are used as water divining rods. See HAZEL.

withershins or **widdershins** Circumambulation to the left; the countersunwise circuit: an act of sinister and malign influence resulting in bad luck, calamity, or the death of the victim of it. It has been used by sorcerers and magicians in the north of Europe from early times. Scottish fishermen will not allow their boats to turn withershins, lest they have bad luck. Running withershins three times around a church was a practice associated with European witchcraft. See CIRCUMAMBULATION; TUATAL.

Wiyot Son of the Earth, and first ancestor of human beings, in Juaneño and Luiseño mythology. Like the neighboring Luiseño, the Juaneño believed that the first things in the universe were sky and earth, brother and sister. From the union of this couple was born, first, earth and sand, next, stone and flint, trees, animals, and finally Wiyot. From Wiyot was born a first race of beings that preceded mankind. As they multiplied, the Earth grew southward and the people followed. Wiyot was poisoned and died; he was cremated, but Coyote, Wiyot's assistant chief, leaped upon the pyre, tore off a piece of flesh from the body, and swallowed it. After this Chingichnich, another deity, appeared, converted the first people into animals and plants, or spirits, and in their place made the present human species out of earth, and taught them their laws and institutions. See A. L. Kroeber, *Handbook of the Indians of California*, BAEB 78, pp. 637–639. Wiyot is also the name for a small tribal group in northern California. [EWV]

woge Yurok Indian name for the race of people who first inhabited this world, but disappeared long before the advent of human beings. The woge include the amatory-minded creator, Wohpekumen, who finally was carried to a land across the salt water by Skate Woman, also a woge, to join the other woge who had previously departed from this earth. The Yurok hold that the woge are largely responsible for the present condition of the world. They differ from characters which, among

other tribes, are said to have lived during the mythical or prehuman age in that the Yurok woge are not depicted in the mythology primarily as animal-beings. [EWV]

Wolaro Leading mythological character of a northern Australian Kimberley tribe, the Gwini. A man, he created heaven, earth, and all in it, and now lives in the sky. Most of his creative activities were carried on through demiurges including birds, his son Dagubal, and the Rainbow Serpent himself. Wolaro delineated the boundaries of the hordes and gave the original dual organization. [KL]

Wolf A prominent character in the mythologies of the North American Indians of the Central Woodlands, of the Great Basin, and of certain Southwestern tribes; also, a moiety division of the Tlingit of the North Pacific Coast; the clan or gens animal of several Woodlands and Plains tribes.

In Woodlands mythology Wolf figures most prominently as the beloved brother of the culture hero Nanabozho; he is drowned, revived, and ultimately becomes the ruler of the country of the dead. In Basin myths Wolf and Coyote, the trickster, are brothers or partners who travel and share adventures together. Yuma origin accounts also make the two characters brothers. The Pomo Indians of California credit Coyote with creative acts, but Wolf, also, is given prominence in their myths. On the North Pacific Coast Wolf figures in the social organization of the Tlingit Indians, and in certain North Pacific Coast ceremonies; the Tlingit are divided into two moieties, one of which is Raven, the other Wolf or in some villages, Beaver. See NANABOZHO. [EWV]

Wolf Society A doctoring society of the Quileute and Makah Indians of the North Pacific Coast. The society, according to the origin legend told for it, originated when Changer, the transformer, killed the Wolf chief and danced in his skin, thus gaining power for curing. The society enacts the Wolf dance for a sick person, but must be given high payment. [EWV]

Wolverine Trickster of some of the Abnaki Eastern Algonquian Indians: a character distinct from the culture hero, Gluskabe, of these groups. Among the Montagnais-Naskapi, Cree, and Ojibwa, and in some Menomini tales, Wolverine is identified with the culture hero Nanabozho or Wisakedjak of these tribes. Wolverine is also the state animal of Michigan. See OFFENDED ROLLING ROCK. [EWV]

woman It is no linguistic accident that the name of the human race is *Homo* or man, and woman is thus automatically placed more or less in a race apart. In a good many creation stories, woman is created as an afterthought, although sometimes man and woman are made at the same time. The Biblical story of the creation of woman from man's rib because man needed a companion is paralleled in many European stories. In a Baltic story, woman was made from the tail of a dog (A1224.3). Some tales say that God created man and that He turned the creation of woman over to the Devil. Several creation stories make a point of the physical differences between man and woman and explain the sexual drive as the desire of the imperfect creation (woman) to attain completeness. In many primitive myths of the Americas and elsewhere, women descend from the sky. Living with them is perilous, for the women have toothed vaginas; the culture hero breaks the teeth with a stick or a stone. See GRANDFATHER; MAN; VAGINA DENTATA.

☞In South American Indian mythology, the origin of women is often conceived of as different from that of men. The existence of males is taken for granted (Toba, Mataco), or men are described as the only survivors of the flood (Cañari), or of a massacre (Carajá).

The Chaco Indians say that formerly a group of hunters noticed that the mysterious thieves who stole their food were women, who descended from the sky by a rope. The rope was cut by the culture hero and the women stayed with the men. According to the Cañari, Jivaro, and Carajá, the first women were birds who helped the survivors of the flood and then assumed human shape. The first woman was fished from a lagoon by the culture hero (Wapishiana, Taruma).

Secret initiation rites for men are often represented as an institution which males took over from the women. A myth which has been recorded in Tierra del Fuego, the Chaco, and among some Brazilian tribes (Mundurucu, Puinave, etc.) tells of a time when women ruled over men by virtue of a feast during which they impersonated spirits and demons, and who required from the males the most complete subservience. One man discovered their secret, and he and his companions took revenge on the women by slaughtering them, with the exception of the very small girls. Then, the men decided to use the initiation rites themselves to keep control over the women. In Ona and Yahgan mythology, the women were led by Moon. Sun, her brother, overheard her boasting about the success of her plot and guided the men in their rebellion against women. [AM]

woman "dies" to be with lover A married woman who has a lover pretends to be ill and instructs her husband concerning her burial. After she "dies" she leaves her grave, or meets her lover in her grave box. The deception succeeds for some time, but is ultimately discovered by her husband or her children, and she alone, or she and her lover, are killed. This tale was early recorded in native North America for the Tsimshian Indians of the North Pacific Coast; in the Tsimshian version the child born of the dead woman feeds on his mother's entrails and grows up in her grave box; he becomes Raven, the Transformer-Culture-Hero of the Tsimshian Indians.

Other tales of a woman who "died" to be with her lover have also been recorded from other North Pacific Coast tribes (Tahltan, Wasco), but these are not linked with the birth of Raven or any other Transformer. The fact that this tale of a deceitful wife is "unique among American Indian tales" and limited to the North Pacific Coast led A. H. Krappe to postulate that the American Indian versions of the tale represent borrowings of a popular European and Near Eastern tale, the so-called Solomon legend (A. H. Krappe, "A Solomon Legend among the Indians of the North Pacific," *JAFL* 59:309–314, 1946). The same story has however been collected among the Jicarilla, Chiricahua, and Lipan Apache of the Southwest, and among the Shawnee of the Eastern Woodlands. It may be that when more extended work is done on the distribution of this tale in North America its provenience may not be so certainly Old World as Krappe assumed. [EWV]

wondjina A figure depicted in Australian aboriginal art, in the rock shelters of northern Kimberley; it is semi-human, with no mouth, a skull-like face, and rudimentary or sometimes missing limbs. Prof. A. P. Elkin (University of Sydney) concluded that it represents the power which controls the rain, and it is often shown with drawings of the rainbow snake. The natives apparently believe that if the wondjina had a mouth, the rain would never cease and that man would be destroyed. The figures are executed in the red ocher, white, and black characteristic of prehistoric art. [MH]

work song A song sung at a task to increase the efficiency of the effort by timing the work stroke, setting a steady work pace, or whiling away the tedium of the working hours. The variety of the songs in this category is tremendous, covering the output of both primitive and advanced peoples, the songs of individuals and of work groups, gangs, or crews, and the countless occupations of both men and women. Since earliest times the hewers and haulers, the plowmen and reapers, the spinners and weavers, the herders and teamsters, the oarsmen, fishermen, raftsmen, lumbermen, sailors, laundresses, builders, craftsmen—the toilers of the world, slave and free—have sung at their labor, as they still do wherever power tools have not yet been substituted for the strength of men and their draft animals and the patient skill of handcrafts.

In ancient Greece there were work songs for making rope, for drawing water (fountain songs), for stamping barley and treading grapes; songs of wool spinners, watchmen, and shepherds. Fiji Islanders today chant at their navigation, gardening, and house-building. In Dahomey there are special songs of the ironworkers, the weavers, and other cloth workers. The West African pattern of antiphonal chanting by leader and chorus of workers in communal work groups (dokpwe in Dahomey) was brought to the New World with the Negro slaves and survives as a powerful influence in the music of this hemisphere. From it stemmed the American Negro work songs of plantation, levee, steamboat, and chain gang; the cocoa-dancing, wood-pulling, fishing, and agricultural songs of Trinidad (see GAYAP); the combite songs of Haitian group labor; the *plena,* songs of the work cooperative (*junta* or *compañia*) in the Dominican Republic, which accompany road-building, canecutting, felling of trees, etc. The range of work songs in the Orient is exemplified by the repertory of Japanese laborers (see MIN-YO). Even in the midst of mechanized warfare in Korea (1950) gangs of North Korean soldiers raised traditional coolie chants as they strained to lift and carry heavy machinery bogged down with the bombing out of roads and bridges.

In most of the civilized world, however, work songs are gradually dying out, their sound silenced in the roar of machines; their purpose outmoded by such inventions and devices as the pneumatic drill, the bulldozer, the power loom. Yet the effectiveness of music in raising the workers' productivity is acknowledged by the psychologists and efficiency experts who recommend the piping of music into factories where manufacturing noise permits.

The simplest of the work songs are little more than the absent-minded humming of a solitary worker at an all-day repetitious job (listen to a laundress at her ironing) or an elaboration of work exclamations and shouts, such as the ancient and still-current chant of Chinese laborers, "Hung, ho, hai, ho," or of directions to a working gang, "Hold it . . . steady . . . now!" or "Ready . . . pull!"

The more developed examples rank with and may be identical with or adapted from the favorites in any other class of folk song—love songs, complaints, laments, spirituals, cumulative formulas, ballads, come-all-ye's, topical improvisations, dance and carnival songs.

The cumulative or counting songs have found special favor with English workers. *Barley Mow,* for example, is a cumulative toast, "Here's a health to the barley mow, my brave boys," and the size of the drink increases progressively stanza by stanza with the refrain, "We'll drink it out of the jolly brown bowl" (pint, hogshead, ocean). *Mowing Down the Meadow,* a haymakers' counting song, also sung by soldiers marching, counts from one to 100 men "to mow down the meadow" and in reverse from 100 to one in the cumulative refrain. Cornish laborers shoveling ballast on ships sang *The Long Hundred,* a number song matching one line to each shovelful, a total of 120 (a long hundred) by the time the number 100 was reached in the text of 20 six-line stanzas. *The Dilly Song* has also been sung as a work song in England (see TWELVE APOSTLES).

Working ballads include *John Henry, Gray Goose,* and *Stewball,* an Americanization of an Irish popular ballad about a racehorse named originally Skewball, which is sung in leader and chorus style by work gangs.

Among the spirituals sung at work are *Norah* (Noah), a hammer song of American Negro work gangs, all about Noah building the ark, and *Steal Away,* sung in slavery times for hoeing. The shout song *Kneebone* developed a rowing version in South Carolina, which said, "Kneebone bend to the elbow bend," as adapted from the original "Bend my kneebone to the ground."

Love songs are sung at work by both men and women. The medieval French *chanson de toile* (linen song), sung by one voice without refrain to accompany weaving or spinning, was generally a love song or pastoral story devoted to the sorrows and emotions of one woman. The fountain songs, sung at the traditional scene of trysts, elopements, and abductions, reflected the romantic atmosphere of the public well or fountain. These women's songs were likely to be sad. The love songs of working men are more humorous and broad in allusion. The chanteyman, the stevedore, the gang leader often describe their lights of love (Anniebelle, Jumping Judy, Miss Rosie, etc.) graphically and unrestrainedly and in driving rhythms. See LOVE SONGS.

Work songs may also be the prototypes of other types of folk song. For example, they lie at the heart of the blues. A characteristic stanza form of American Negro work songs is a line repeated three times followed by a final line of comment. Many blues songs fit this form. The free line of the field holler also characterizes the blues. A song sung by colored workers on steamers and in the fields, *In the Morning,* has the accents of the blues when it says, "What's the use of working so hard, in the morning?" (three times) and then, "My gal works in a white man's yard."

The only accompaniment to most work songs is the beat of implements—flails, pestles, axes, and sledge hammers—the tinkle of animal bells, the clack of heddles, the heavy tread of feet, or the sharply expelled breath or grunt of the workers as the stroke falls. Yet for some tasks and in some countries instruments have been used to liven the song or pace the work—the bagpipe for harvesting in England, drum and rattle in the Dominican Republic, conch-shell trumpet (see LAMBI), flute (or oboe) for Greek oarsmen, banjo for American plantation workers.

The rhythmic character of the songs is largely dictated by the nature of the work they accompany. The broad divisions of rhythm by tasks are clearly shown in the sea chanteys. If the work requires a heavy blow or pull, particularly when the efforts of a group must be pooled to accomplish something beyond the strength of an individual, the words may be sung fairly slowly but in strongly accented rhythm, each stress signalling the moment of effort. A Kwakiutl paddle song cited by Boas consists entirely of monosyllables with vowels of long value, each sung to a single stroke of the paddle. Songs for wielding the ax, pickax, sledge hammer, scythe, or oars, for hauling nets or sails, timber or stone, or for pounding foundations or roadbeds fall naturally into such rhythms. They are called forth most often for the harsh labor of men, though women may sing them where they engage in strenuous jobs, such as earth-pounding in Japan.

When the effort is slow and continuous, but heavy, the rhythm may be a funeral-march tempo, as in the capstan chanteys and in songs for dragging sledges, grinding, pumping, or carrying massive loads.

If the work consists of more rapid, repeated motions of less muscular demand, as in hoeing, husking grain, mashing food, or picking crops by hand (ginger in Jamaica, hemp in Normandy, tea in Japan, tobacco in Virginia), the rhythm is sometimes a more jingling, dancing tempo, not necessarily tied to the motion, but designed to keep the whole process going at a good speed. Mixed groups of men and women, as in the combite, gayap, and junta, and the cotton pickers of pre-Civil War plantations have sung to such rhythms. "Cotton needs pickin'/So bad." "Pick a bale of cotton/Pick a bale a day."

If the work is physically light, but long-continued and without marked intervals of greater effort, a variety of rhythms may be used—slow-paced and mournful, free and improvisational, or gay and lilting—for the purpose of the song is to divert the worker. Women's songs such as the luinig, the complainte, and the waulking, and the songs of shepherds and other solitary workers fall into this category.

Sometimes work songs are paced to the gait of men or the animals they ride or drive. A light, trotting rhythm was characteristic of the ship-loading songs of Mississippi River and Chesapeake roustabouts. These songs timed the steps of every man as he carried his load across the limber, bouncing plank from shore to boat. A failure to ride the swing of the plank would have tossed men and goods into the water. Similar jogging rhythms or quick marching time are characteristic of bearers' chants in the Orient and in Africa. The hoofbeat rhythm of horses may be heard in some of the wagoners' tunes and cowboy songs. Others take their tempo from the slow turning of wheels and the deliberate plodding of herds.

The songs and whistles of the man behind the horse- or mule-drawn plow may be either sprightly or doleful, according to the mood of the plowman, the heat of the day, or the length of the furrow; and they are often interrupted by calls to the animal. The Irish plowman's lilting whistle, the rhythmic and melodic improvisation of the holler, and the sorrowful measures of the Spanish arada indicate the variety of mood and rhythm in this type of agricultural work song.

The role of the song leader in labor groups is important. He sets the pace which the crew must follow. By his choice of song and tempo he can give them an interval of relaxation or step up their efforts. By his cleverness at improvisation and variation on well-known texts he can win their laughter, give interest to their working hours, and control their moods. The chanteyman or the simidor has the creative part of the performance. The chorus must sing a traditional refrain well known to every member so that the work strokes coincide as they hit the rhythm. In some types of work the leader actually sings directions to his gang, as in the track-lining song of American railroad section gangs. He chants a singsong of instruction to them; when he gets them set for the combined stress, he gives them a singing rhythm with a short, sometimes improvised and jocular, stanza of real song; then they go into action with the refrain "Ho, boys, can't you line 'em.'"

In this type of work song, the words are directly related to the job at hand. Other railroad songs for tie-tamping, moving and spiking rails, also suit the action to the words. When specific verbal directions are not required of the leader, it is sometimes the chorus words that carry the work cry—the heave-ho—while the solo part forms a diversion. "Cape Cod girls they have no combs," sings the chanteyman in the preparatory interval. "Heave away, heave away," the crew comes in as the ropes are hauled.

Probably the most down-to-business songs of all were the sounding calls of the Mississippi River boatmen. They were strict reporting of the depth of the water as shown by the heaving of the lead line—"Quarter less twain/ Mark twain/ Quarter twain/ Half twain," etc., all the way to "No bottom"—sung out long and clear to guide the pilot.

Many other types of work song form a comment on the task or a complaint about the hard life it entails, the condition of the worker, or the meanness or cruelty of the boss. The corn-grinding songs or mill songs of women in Greece and other ancient civilizations (cantilenæ molares), to which grain was ground in hand querns for the community, were often narratives about persons whose unhappy fate was grinding. The Song of Grotti (see FRODI) or Quern Song of the Eddas, tells such a story; others tell of King Pittakos and of King Kyzikos of Mysia, also doomed to grinding. The banana-pounding songs of the African Bongili women tell of the goodness of the banana paste, which forms a staple article of their diet. The paddle songs of the Baduma men tell of the rigors and danger of their labor. An Irish-American work song from the stone quarries, Drill, Ye Tarriers, said wryly, "It's work all day for the sugar in your tay/ Down behind the railway/ And blast/ And fire." It relates the tall tale of a tarrier (rock driller) who was blasted a mile in the air and was docked for the time he lost in the sky.

Many of the agricultural work songs of Jamaica, the songs for digging (see DIGGING SINGS), for brush-cutting, and for ginger-pulling, are closely related to the occupation. They are always, in the African pattern, lead by a soloist with a chanted chorus, and sometimes the work is competitive, a match between groups, with antiphonal singing either between or within the groups. Wam Bam Hoe, a digging song, accompanies the chopping strokes of the hoe with the words, "wam bam hoe, dis heah grass goin' to kill a' me yam." The narrative complains about the laziness of various relatives who have let grass grow up in the garden and ruin the yam crop. A brush-cutting song, Bull, Oh, or Bullo, which has also been sung as a ring game, has many versions, one of which says, "Lemme yo rope, lemme rope de bull. De bull mash up my groun'."

Among the bitterest and grimmest of all work songs are those of American Negro prison labor, sung by stripe-clad convicts contracted for work on the roads, levees, land-clearing projects, etc. They sang of bad-man heroes (Stagolee, Lazarus, Long John), of escape, of the hard bosses, poor food, hot sun, of nostalgia, loneliness, cruelty. "Go down ol' Hannah," they sang to the sun. "Don't you rise no mo'. If you rise up in the mornin', bring Judgment Day." The steel-drilling song, Take This Hammer, complains, verse after resentful verse, "I don't want no cornbread and molasses. They hurt my pride." "I don't want no cold iron shackles around my leg," etc. The most extensive study of these songs was made by the Lomaxes, who found that the styles of singing varied from state to state and the characteristic work exclamations (whuk, hunh, etc.) also showed state-to-state variation, but everywhere the spirit was the same. "You should have been here in 1910/ They was drivin' the women just like the men." "My mother (and a long string of relations) she don't write to po' me . . . It makes a long-time man feel bad." "White man, white man, sittin' in the shade/ Laziest man that God ever made." "Well, Captain, Captain, how can it be?/ Whistles keep blowin', you keep workin' me." "Some o' these days, Lawd/ It won't be long/ Captain gonna call me/ An' I'll be gone." Such are the words suited to the last surviving body of work song in the United States that is still close to the African work chant.

In contrast to the songs which are actually songs about the work, a large segment of the world's work songs have nothing to do with the task, even though they may traditionally accompany a specific job. They deal with food and drink, with nostalgia for home, with local incidents or far-off places, with bits of foolery, wisdom, bawdry, or wishes, with girls, with heroes—almost anything under the sun. The short-drag chantey, Paddy Doyle, was sung only for bunting a sail; it was named for a Liverpool boarding-house keeper who had set up in his yard a cow's horn around which inexperienced sailors marched three times so that they could tell the skippers they had been around the Horn three times. The song ended with the line, "We'll pay Paddy Doyle for his boots," and on the word boots, which was yelled, every man grabbed in the flapping fold of canvas to furl it. The French-Canadian work songs, À La Claire Fontaine and La Rose Blanche, are both love songs; Dans les Haubans and Le Miracle du Nouveau-né are narratives. The chantey Whiskey, Johnny obviously is in praise of drink. Many of the ancient weaving songs of women, while rhythmically suited to the motions of the hands, are sad tunes about the desertion of a woman by her husband or lover and her disgrace or loneliness as she bears his child. Various others of the types of songs unrelated to the task have been mentioned above in connection with ballads, cumulative songs, etc., sung at work.

There is a large body of song about various occupations, including many lumbermen's and miners' come-all-ye's, some of the forecastle songs and cowboy songs, etc., which are better called occupational songs, since they are not sung at work, but do describe the life, deliver the boasts, and jeer at the rivals of the men of these callings.

Somewhat different from the other work songs, but still folk inventions applied to the task, are those first singing commercials, the songs, chants, and cries of vendors. They may be rimed and melodic and regular in rhythm, or merely repeated singsong utterances worn and smoothed by endless iteration to a chain of nonsense syllables scarcely recognizable as words, like the tobacco auctioneer's chant now familiar through radio advertising. They include the selling songs of the peddlers of fruit, flowers, firewood, cheese, confections, seafood, vegetables, newspapers, herbs; the rant of train butchers, souvenir merchants, and sidewalk pitchmen with their miscellany of catchpenny goods; the announcements of the grinders of scissors and knives, the umbrella menders, the ragman, and the junk collector.

Some of them, for example the "What d'ye lack" of the London cheapjacks, are no longer heard; they are gone with the cries of the watch and the town crier. Others are as alive today in the streets and markets of every community as if mass production and distribution, chain stores, mail order, and installment selling had never come into being. Chinese fish peddlers, with a kettle of swimming fish, invite the householders to try their luck with hook and line. Mexican street merchants of tamales, sweetmeats, and carnival claptrap chant their *pregones.* Up through the grandstands at any circus in America still goes the singsong, "Peanuts, popcorn, chewing gum, and soda."

Other chants still heard, or only recently dead, are "Fresh fish, fresh fish, fresh-caught fish," "Any rags, any bones, any bottles today?" "Violets, who'll buy my violets?" "Lemonade made in the shade," "Watermelon, red to the rind." In the United States the cities of Baltimore, Charleston, and New Orleans especially have been famous for their vendors' songs; the loaded wagons creaked through narrow alleys and streets, and the Negro women carried napkin-covered baskets of deviled crabs and shrimp and other delicacies, while the holler-like calls of the sellers lured the customers.

Both work songs and street cries are often imitated or incorporated into popular and art music. *The Peanut Vendor* was a radio hit some years ago, in which the sales chant of a Latin-American peanut vendor was used. Gershwin made use of the Negro vendors' songs of Charleston in *Porgy and Bess.* The movie *Snow White and the Seven Dwarfs* had a little work ditty to which the dwarfs went off to work with their picks and shovels.

THERESA C. BRAKELEY

world egg The cosmic egg from which the universe was born, often from which mankind emerged, or from which the creator of the universe and mankind emerged: a concept of the ancient cosmogonies of India, Egypt, Greece, Phœnicia, etc., also found in the mythologies of many primitive peoples. In Orphic philosophical cosmogony Chronos produced an egg in vaporous space which contained both male and female seed and from which emerged the creator of the world. In Vedic cosmogony, deep in the primeval waters grew a golden germ (*Hiraṇyagarbha*) which evolved into the creator Prajāpati, and later Brahmā. In the *Purāṇas* the world egg (*brāhmāṇḍa*) floated in the universal waters enveloped in water, air, wind, fire, etc.; within it Brahmā appeared, who created the world. See *Cycle of Väinämöinen* in FINNISH FOLKLORE; HIRANYAGARBHA; KHNUM.

world fire Destruction of the world in the past by fire, either accidentally or due to the deeds of the culture hero or trickster, or its near-destruction in the past as a result of the poor regulation of the sun, is a cosmogonic notion which appears in the mythologies of various American Indian tribes of western North America (Plateau, North Pacific Coast, California, Plains, Mackenzie, Southwestern areas). The Wintu of California, for example, say that before the human race supplanted the first people (who changed into animals) a world fire occurred, kindled by Loon Woman; the neighboring Pomo attribute the world fire to Coyote, the trickster, who formerly roamed the earth, fanned a world fire, created mankind, stole the sun for them, and transformed the animals into their present condition.

A world fire is also forecast for the end of the world as it exists today; this belief is especially prevalent in eastern North America. See LOON WOMAN. [EWV]

World Renewal A cult system of several American Indian tribes in northwestern California (Yurok, Karok, Hupa, Wiyot). The World Renewal cult, as developed by these four tribes, is comparable to the Kuksu cult of native central California, the Chingichnich datura religion of southern California, the Kachina cult of the Pueblos, and the Hamatsa or cannibal secret society initiations of the North Pacific Coast. The World Renewal cult is practiced for the purpose of reestablishing or firming the earth, for first-fruits and new fire, and to prevent disease and calamity for another year or biennium. It was instituted by members of the prehuman spirit race who later departed this earth or transformed themselves; the core of the ceremony is the recital of a formula repeating the words of these spirits, accompanied by acts symbolic of their actions. The formula is recited at specific locations in a fixed order, by a priest who has previously been purified by abstention from water and sex contacts, and by sweating and semi-fasting. For the ceremony a sacred structure is rebuilt or repaired; new fire is kindled during the ceremony, and there is ceremonial taking or consuming of acorns and salmon in first-fruit rites, to mention only a few of the esoteric features of the cult. The exoteric, public part of the World Renewal system consists of two dances, the Jumping dance and the White Deerskin, or Deerskin, dance; either one or both of these may be performed. Regalia for the former are woodpecker-scalp headbands and dance baskets; for the latter albino and other deerskins, otter and wolf skins, and long flint and obsidian blades. This regalia is worn and carried by the dancers, who are men, and with dentalium shells it represents the wealth of these tribes. The ceremonies are held chiefly in July and August, when the New Year starts with the salmon run and the ripening of the acorn crops. A detailed field account and analysis of the World

Renewal cult has recently been published by A. L. Kroeber and E. W. Gifford, *World Renewal: A Cult System of Native Northwest California* (Anthropological Records 13, Berkeley, Cal., 1949). [EWV]

wraith The apparition of a living person in the exact likeness of the moment, even as to details of dress; his ghostly double become visible. To see the wraith of a friend usually means that he has just died or is about to die. To see one's own wraith is an omen of death. The poet Shelley is said to have seen his own wraith shortly before he drowned. In Germany, this manifestation is called *Doppelgänger*, literally, double-goer. Almost all peoples seem to have the concept of the visibility of the spirit-double: Nyassa tribes believe that the soul is a "copy" of the man, but visible to others only in dreams; North American Iroquois think of the soul as a spiritual duplicate of the living body; the Celebes term for soul is translated *image*. The general Melanesian concept, according to Codrington, is that a man's soul is a reflection of his material body. In Maori belief the spirit-double of a man cannot be distinguished from the man himself unless it becomes filmy or vaporizes and thus reveals its ghostly quality. See FETCH.

wu cults Until well into the last millenium before Christ the wu cults and their priests represented the official religion at the courts of the emperors, kings, and nobles of China. The priests were organized into colleges, kept records of the sacrifices, prognosticated, and were probably the guardians of the sacred and mystic ideographs. The wu priests are known to have officiated at the reading of the oracle bones and to have performed ritualistic dances. [RDJ]

Wu Kuan King of the fourth Chinese hell, the hell of the Lake of Blood where cheats and counterfeiters are punished. His day is the 18th of the Second Moon. [RDJ]

Wu Kung Ching The Centipede: in China, one of the five venomous animals to be pacified on the 5th day of the Fifth Moon. Wu Kung Ching was one of the seven devils of the sacred mountain, Mei Shan, who became a military officer. He pretended to flee when he was attacked, then in a black fog blown by a terrific wind he resumed his true form (centipede) and killed his adversary. The adversary's followers saw nothing and were amazed to find their leader dead. He is depicted as a warrior in armor with two swords, black beard and mustache. See CENTIPEDE. [RDJ]

Wüwüchim An annual Pueblo Indian ceremony given by members of the Wüwüchim men's society. Held in its "long form," it is a boys' initiation ceremony: a boy is pledged or given in infancy to a "father" who breathes in his mouth and later will sponsor him. Among the Hopi Wüwüchim initiation is a prerequisite to a man's dancing as a kachina. At the time of the emergence from the underworld, according to Hopi (Oraibi) legend, Mockingbird sang the songs that are still sung at the ceremony. Wüwüchim novices in Hopi kivas are represented as being in the underworld. The Hopi Wüwüchim ceremony in November precedes the winter solstice, and the new fire ritual is associated with Wüwüchim rather than with solstice observances, as at other pueblos. Wüwüchim at Hopi is thought of as the beginning of the ceremonial period or new year, when the kachina spirits emerge from Shipap to stay on earth for the ensuing half year. [EWV]

Wu Yo The five sacred mountains in the north, east, south, west, and center of China. The most famous of these is T'ai Shan in Shantung. The mythical emperor Yao is said to have paid homage to them in 2346 B.C. [RDJ]

Wyrdes or **Weirds** The Anglo-Saxon fates, usually three sisters, who weave the destiny of man. Originally they were closely parallel to the Norns, but today the term is principally applied to witches or soothsayers, and generally confined to Scotland. Wyrd is sometimes mentioned as the goddess of Fate, mother of the Norns.

Xanthos and Balios The two immortal horses given by Poseidon to Peleus as a wedding present. They were the offspring of Zephyrus, the west wind, (or Zeus) and the Harpy Podarge (Fleetfoot). During the Trojan War they served as chariot horses for Achilles. When he rebuked them for permitting Patroclus to be killed, Xanthos reproved Achilles by saying that a god had slain Patroclus and that a god would soon kill him too. After thus prophesying, the horse was struck dumb by the Erinyes. Compare BALAAM.

Xelas The transformer-culture-hero of the Lummi Indians of the Puget Sound region in the Pacific Northwest. [EWV]

Xevioso (pronounced *Hevioso*) Generalized designation for the Thunder pantheon of Dahomey. This is the So (the deity of Thunder) of Xevie, a small settlement in southern Dahomey, where the principal shrines to the Thunder gods are located. See AGBE; SOGBO. [MJH]

xoil' Yukaghir term for the figure of a dead shaman topped by the man's skull. The body is made of a trunk of wood; to this the skull of the dead man is attached; the figure is dressed in embroidered jackets and caps, fawn-skin coat, and wrapped in a blanket. This figure was kept in one corner of the house of the dead shaman's sons, was worshipped, "fed" at every meal, prayed to, and consulted in regard to various undertakings (hunt, war, etc.) The answers of the xoil' to questions were ascertained as follows: it was laid on the ground and lifted three times. If the people could not budge it, the answer was No, and the undertaking was abandoned; if it lifted easily and buoyantly, the undertaking would succeed. If the answer was uncertain, i.e., if the xoil' could be lifted twice but not thrice, or if it seemed sort of heavy, the outcome of the undertaking was obviously in doubt, and serious consultation was in order. Today the term *xoil'* is applied to the Christian god and the saints. See W. Jochelson, *The Yukaghir and The Yu-*

kaghirized Tungus, Publications of the Jesup North Pacific Expedition, *MAMNH,* vol. ix, part ii, 1924.

x-ray drawing A method of depiction frequently encountered in prehistoric and primitive art, in which the interior of the animal is depicted as well as the exterior, or within the silhouette. The animals painted on rock in Arnhem Land (Murngin), for example, clearly show stomach, alimentary canal, and heart. In the cliff paintings of Siberia, internal organs may be shown and so may the young within the female. The Eskimos may depict the bones of the fish and sometimes the swallowed hook and line. Northwest Coast Indians characteristically indicate the bone in the joints, and may show vertebræ and other features. The technique also appears in Melanesia and South America. [MH]

xwulequola or **hrolequola** The term for the trembling or hand vibration of male dancers of the Kwakiutl, Bella Coola, and neighboring Northwest Coast Indian tribes. With the arms at shoulder height, the hands and fingers shiver while the feet beat out the rhythm. This quivering is used both by shamans and by *kusiut* dancers at Midwinter festivals. This is part of the stylized dance vocabulary of this area. [GPK]

xylophone A musical instrument consisting of graduated lengths of wood, each resting on two supports at right angles to the bars, and played by striking with sticks. It is a primitive invention known since neolithic times and is still played by certain primitive peoples, notably in Africa, but it has also developed into an orchestral instrument for art music and is sometimes made of metal bars.

The crudest form of the xylophone is simply a set of wooden bars laid across the outstretched legs of a seated player, often a woman. Development from this simple device proceeds to log supports for the bars, then to efficient table-like stands and to varieties hung from the players' shoulders. Some primitive types are played over a pit. In Africa, where the xylophones have a complicated resonator system of gourds attached to each bar and a vibrating membrane over a hole in each gourd, the instrument serves singly or in combinations of two or three to provide music for village festivities of the Yaswa, Azande, and other equatorial African peoples.

In Indonesia xylophones play in the gamelan and are highly developed instruments. One type, the *gambang,* has a cradle-like support and bamboo keys. In Bali this instrument is played for cremations, and its players learn their melodies by a mnemonic system of connecting musical themes with poetic texts.

In the New World an African-derived xylophone, the *marimba,* is played in Latin-American popular bands and in some band music of the United States. In Guatemala the making of a marimba is a matter of great craftsmanship and ceremony. The wood for the keys is selected from choice hardwoods cut according to the propitious phase of the moon. Gourd resonators of the African type are used underneath the bars, and the sticks are tipped with raw rubber.

Yahweh, Yahwe, Jahweh, or **Jehovah** A reconstruction of the Tetragrammaton, YHWH, the four consonants making up the ancient Hebrew Ineffable Name of God, and using the vowel points of Adonai, the Lord, another of God's names. The power of the name spelled out by the Tetragrammaton was such that its original pronunciation was lost, and conjecture has only approximated it. Yahweh is the name most often used, in discussion, to indicate God as the Hebrew tribal deity as distinguished from God as the Judeo-Christian deity, Jehovah. Yahweh is the baal of Israel, perhaps identical with or perhaps absorbing other local tribal gods of the region, like Sin, the moon god of the Sinai peninsula. The temple of Yahweh was on Mount Moriah. However, the relationships of Yahweh to other tribal deities, and the very identity of his original worshippers, remain matters of debate. The use of various names of God— Elohim (a plural form of El), Adonai, Yah, Shaddai, etc. —further confuses the picture of the primitive Hebrew god. All these names, but especially the Tetragrammaton (or parts of it) and its vowels in all the combinations of the letters and vowel points, were of importance in gematria and other magical practices of the Middle Ages. This name, YHWH, it was said, was on Moses' rod, and its power caused the sea to divide. He slew the Egyptian merely by pronouncing the Name.

yaka (plural *yaku*) The spirit of a dead person in Vedda (Ceylon) religion and belief. The yaka throws stones at survivors if they hang around the corpse or its former dwelling, yet the yaku of the recently dead (*Nae Yaku*) are regarded as benevolent and affectionate and disposed to help their surviving kinsmen. (Among the Sinhalese the yaku are regarded as malignant, however). Offerings of food are made to the Nae Yaku and a special Nae Yaku ceremony is performed whenever their aid is invoked (see KAPURALE). After such a ceremony the people attending (men, women, children) usually eat the food that has been offered, believing thereby that they partake in an actual communion.

The yaku fall into three groups among the Veddas: 1) the Nae Yaku, benevolent ancestral spirits, including the yaku of heroes (see KANDE YAKA); 2) spirits of the Sinhalese and Tamils, which have taken on the benevolent nature of the indigenous Vedda yaku; and 3) foreign spirits, terrible and hostile.

yakshas In classical Hinduism, supernatural beings who seceded from the demons and took over the mountain areas: regarded as harmless. See YECH. [MWS]

ya'lgil The Yukaghir (Siberia) word for drum; literally, lake, in reference to the lake into which the shaman dives when he goes into the spirit world. The characteristic drum is a large, single-headed instrument of asymmetrical shape, grasped by an iron cross tied near the center of the underside. Four groups of iron rattles are attached to the rim. Around the outside edge are a number of protuberances, which are conceived of as the horns of the shaman's spirits. See DRUM.

Yama In Hindu mythology, the king of the dead; later, the judge of the dead. In Vedic mythology Yama was a deified hero and the first man to die. He and his sister Yamī, the first mortals, were the children of Vivasvat, the Sun. When Yama died he went to the spirit-world in the upper sky where he reigned as a kind of president or friend of the dead. During the period of the epics and the *Purāṇas* Yama became the terrible judge and punisher of the dead, now pictured as green of color, clad in red, holding a club and noose, and riding a buffalo. He is also a guardian of the south in which direction are his palace (Yamasadana) and his city (Yamapura). Between the land of the living and this region flows the bloody river Vaitaranī which all spirits must cross. This ordeal is escaped, however, by many virtuous worshippers of Brahmā, Kṛishṇa, Śiva, and Vishṇu, who go instead to the heavens Brahmāloka, Go-loka, Kailāsa, and Vaikuṇtha respectively. Yama's emissaries are sometimes the owl and the pigeon, but his regular messengers are two, broad-nosed, four-eyed dogs, Śyāma and Śabala, who guard the path to the afterworld. Yama's messengers usually visit a dying man, bind his spirit with a noose, and convey it to Yamapura. When the spirit is led before the judgment seat it is confronted by Chitragupta, the recorder of men's deeds, who produces the dead man's account, and judgment is rendered. Then the spirit is rushed back to the place of cremation to receive a physical frame by feeding on the oblations offered during the śrāddha ceremony. See SESAME. After the new body is completed, it is conducted to heaven or to one of 21 hells. If the latter, the soul must travel 200 leagues a day through scorching, treeless plains or against icy winds, meeting lions, tigers, venomous serpents, thorns, rain, coals, blood, filth, and boiling water until it reaches the lowest depths where other inconceivable tortures await it. Yama corresponds to the Persian Yima and to the Buddhist Yen Lo.

Yamunā In Hindu belief, one of the three most sacred rivers of India. The Yamunā is unmarried, so is not as sacrosanct as is the Ganga or the Sarasvatī, and her water is heavy and indigestible. Allahabad, where the yellow Ganga and the blue Yamunā meet, is one of the holiest spots in India and the resort of pilgrims.

Yang Ching The Goat God. Chinese peasants in mountainous regions sacrifice to this spirit for protection against wild animals. He is depicted with a goat's head worn like a bonnet and a goatskin. [RDJ]

Yankee Doodle Although patriotic songs are generally excluded from the canon of folk song, this humorous jingle would seem to be an exception, partly because of its many folk versions and partly because of its traditional tune. In addition, a good deal of folklore has grown up about the origin and history of the song and the words, "Yankee," "doodle," and "Yankee Doodle." According to the legend, the original doggerel was composed in 1775 by a British army surgeon, Dr. Richard Shuckburgh (the most generally accepted of a half-dozen variant spellings), presumably at Fort Crailo, Rensselaer, New York, to express his amusement at the ragged appearance of the Continental troops.

The air (which is better known than the words) is most familiar as the tune of the nursery rime, "Lucy Locket," and is said to have been used to accompany a Cavalier rime ridiculing Cromwell, beginning, "Nankie Doodle came to town." Resemblances are found in Holland, Spain, and Hungary. In this country the tune was first published in 1795 in Benjamin Carr's *Federal Overture* (composed in 1794), though it probably appeared first in print in James Aird's *A Selection of Scotch, English, Irish and Foreign Airs*, Vol. I, Glasgow, 1782, as an English country dance, which later became a New England jig.

By a stroke of Yankee shrewdness, recognizing a good thing when they saw it, the Americans took over the song and made it their own. Its popularity and patriotic appeal were attested by the fact that it was played at Cornwallis's surrender at Yorktown in 1781. The best of the folk parodies are *The Yankee's Return from Camp* and *Corn Cobs Twist Your Hair*, which have the authentic Yankee note and accent. [BAB]

The melodic ancestors of the tune have been suggested variously as a Dutch harvest song with a refrain of "Yanker didee doodle down," the Irish air *All the Way to Galway*, etc., but the tune has never been tracked to its final origin. One explanation of the word "doodle" is that it is onomatopœic for the sound of tonguing as played on the flute. In addition to the stanzas and refrains generally found in songbooks are many improvisations and parodies. One of these says, "And there came General Washington,/ Upon a snow-white charger/ He looked as big as all outdoors/ And thought that he was larger." [TCB]

Yankee tricksters and trickster stories The Yankee's legendary reputation (more comic than shady) for close dealing and sharp trading is reflected in the proverbial changes rung on the word "Yankee." As a noun, it has become virtually synonymous with "ingeniousness, thrift, and 'cuteness.'" In the 19th century, according to Mencken, to *yankee* meant to cheat; to *catch a Yankee*, to catch a tartar; and to *play Yankee*, to reply to a question by asking one. By a similar extension, *Yankee trick* (traced to 1776) came to mean "anything very smart, done in the way of trade, no matter in which of the states the doer was born" (Cornelius Mathews, *Writings*, 1846, II, p. 308). The association of Yankee tricks with tricks of the trade by way of the Yankee storekeeper and peddler was an inevitable concomitant of the Yankee genius and passion for trading and swapping.

Originally, the sharp Yankee was a development of the green Yankee or comic countryman, who, like his prototype, the English Yorkshire clown, was often more rogue than fool. (For the parallel proverbial meanings of Yorkshire, including "Yorkshire bite," a sharp, overreaching person, see Elizabeth Mary Wright, *Rustic Speech and Folk-Lore*, 1913, pp. 2–3.) In his general capacity of "practical wag" and good-natured rogue, the sharp Yankee fitted naturally into the traditional pattern of trickster and trickster-tricked stories.

The favorite haunt as well as school of the Yankee trickster was the village store and tavern, where, according to P. T. Barnum (himself a graduate of this school), "social, jolly, story-telling, joke-playing wags and wits, regular originals" foregathered to sharpen their wits and tongues upon one another. Favorite themes of village store and tavern humor were "skunking" and "skinning" dodges and hoaxes in trading or raising a treat; the hazing of new clerks, city slickers, and loafers; curing pilferers and shop-lifters; the hypocritical greed of deacons (*deaconing* meaning "topping off a barrel of apples with the best specimens"); and the chicanery of horse-jockeys. While stories of the comic contest of wits between smart or close merchant and customer were largely regional in diffusion, national scope was given to the traditional feud between the backwoodsman and the Yankee peddler who sold the former things he didn't want. About the pawky, picaresque folk character of the Yankee peddler grew a saga of tricks and counter-tricks, involving worthless wooden clocks, wooden nut-megs, basswood hams, shoe-peg oats, pit-coal indigo, and pine-top gin.

In 1836 *The Clockmaker,* by a Nova Scotia judge, Thomas Chandler Haliburton, introduced the most fa-mous of all Yankee peddlers, Sam Slick, who shares with Seba Smith's Jack Downing (1830) the homely wit and common sense of the cracker-box philosopher—a de-velopment of the sharp Yankee in the direction of hu-morous rustic sage and critic. In P. T. Barnum, the Yankee trickster turned showman and was enabled to indulge the "jocose element" in his character while cap-italizing on the "perfect good nature with which the American public submit to a clever humbug."

The following stories illustrate typical Yankee trick-ster motifs. In "The Egg, the Darning Needle, and the Treat" a country bumpkin exchanges an egg for a darn-ing needle and then asks for an egg to put into the store-keeper's treat of brandy, sugar, and water. When his own egg is handed back to him, he breaks it, discovers a dou-ble yolk, and claims a second needle to even the trade. In "Paying for the Stolen Butter" a Vermont storekeeper, having overseen a loafer hide a pound of butter under his hat, plants him in a seat next to the stove, builds up the fire, and plies him with stories and hot rum toddies while the melting butter trickles down the poor fel-low's face and neck, soaks into his clothes, and trickles down his body into his very boots. "Turning Water into Grog" relates how a Yankee sea-captain obtains a drink without money. Having filled a gallon demijohn half full of water, he asks a bartender to give him two quarts of rum, saying that the demijohn is already half full. The bartender adds the rum, then, refusing to charge it, reclaims it. By repeating the process at the next five saloons, the sea-captain manages to obtain two quarts of excellent rum.

Typical of the slanders on deacons is the anecdote of the elder who said to his clerk, "John, have you wet down the tobacco?" "Yes, sir." "Have you sanded the sugar?" "Yes, sir." "Then come in to prayers!" Variants refer to watering the rum, dusting the pepper, chicory-ing the coffee, larding the butter, and flouring the ginger. A favorite clock-peddler story tells of the Yankee who sells each worthless clock with the guarantee that he will return in a few weeks and replace it if it doesn't go. Having sold all his clocks but one, he retraces his route, using his remaining clock to replace the first and then replacing each clock in turn with the one from the pre-ceding house. A well-known horse-jockey anecdote con-cerns the man who sells a worthless horse admitting that the animal has two faults and agreeing to tell one fault before trading and the other after. The first fault is: "He is awful hard to catch," and the second fault: "He ain't

good for nothin' when you catch him." (See, B. A. Bot-kin, *A Treasury of New England Folklore,* pp. 2–102.)
B. A. BOTKIN

yanmena The girls' puberty rite of the Lengua In-dians of the Gran Chaco in South America. It corre-sponds in form and purpose to the *káusima* of the Cho-roti and Ashluslay. [GPK]

Yansan Yoruban Negro deity of the wind. This being is also worshipped in the New World, being a promi-nent member of the pantheon of the Ketu (Yoruba-derived) cult of Bahia. [MJH]

Ya-o-gah In Iroquois Indian (Seneca) mythology, the north wind, the Bear, leashed at the door of Ga-oh's cave. When Ga-oh unfastens the leash of Ya-o-gah, the Bear, winter hurricanes sweep across the earth, and the waters freeze from his icy breath. The Bear could crush the world in his storms or destroy it with cold, if bidden.

Yao Wang President of the Chinese ministry of medi-cine. Until very recent times the great healers of China were accorded official immortality in this pantheon. In very early times the three culture heroes, Fu Hsi, Shên Nung, and Huang Ti dominated the cult. Each of the nine or more divinities of Huang Ti's ministry of medi-cine was a specialist. The fields were diagnostics, surgery, dermatology, anatomy, yin-yang and the digestive sys-tem, medical properties of plants and minerals, veter-inary science, the nervous system.

Yao Wang has numerous legends. While living as a hermit in the mountains he once saved the life of a snake. Later he met a messenger who took him on a magical journey to the magnificent water palace of a dragon king, Ching Yang. Here he met a young woman who thanked him for having saved the life of her child. Although the king offered a three-day feast in his honor, the physician refused because he lived on air and wine. At the request of the king he composed 30 chapters of his materia medica known as "The Secrets of the Dragon." On another occasion he removed a bone from the throat of a tiger. In recognition of this deed the tiger, eternally nodding its head, in thanks undertook to stand guard at the gate of the physician's house. An uncounted host of greater or lesser specialists is associ-ated with Yao Wang in his several temples [RDJ]

yarrow or **milfoil** The healing powers of this plant were discovered by Achilles, who, in some versions of the story, included it in the ointment with which he cured the wounds of Telephus. See ACHILLES' SPEAR. It was called soldiers' woundwort in the Middle Ages and was part of the pharmacopeia of every monastery in Europe. *A. ptarmica* was called sneezewort because its roots were used to make snuff. Yarrow was also known to various Indian groups of North America, who used it in both capacities.

Yarrow was used for centuries by English witches in their multitudinous incantations and spells, though in Yorkshire today witches and demons are said to dislike the plant and it is worn as a protection against them. In the Hebrides a leaf held against the eyelids enables one to see the person in one's thoughts. In both England and North America yarrow is used in love divinations, either plucked from the grave of a young man and placed under the pillow, wrapped in wool and placed in the shoe, or put up the nose to draw blood; frequently a rime accompanies these actions. Yarrow stalks are known to have been used in divination in China, but the method is unknown. In Europe it is quite generally hung up in the house on St. John's Eve to prevent sickness during the ensuing year.

Yarrow is another of the plants called all-heal from its many medicinal uses. From earliest times it has been known as a rheumatism remedy, and was usually used in compresses around the affected parts. The 17th century English physician Nicholas Culpeper called yarrow an herb of Venus and recommended it as a cure for gonorrhea in men and whites in women, for those who cannot hold their water, and to be chewed for toothache. The English herbalist Parkinson recommended it for "casual sighings" and said that mixed with salad oil it would prevent falling hair and promote the growth of the beard. Yarrow is also as potent for healing wounds caused by carpenters' tools as by swords and spears.

Various North American Indians made a snuff from yarrow roots and sometimes smoked the leaves in place of tobacco. The Chippewa Indians drank a decoction of the leaves for nervous disorders; the Mohegan-Pequot tribes drank yarrow tea for the liver and kidneys. The Gosiute of Utah recommended this tea for biliousness and headache and also for rheumatism. The Meskwaki used it for fevers and ague and to bathe aches and sprains. The Navaho call it "life medicine" and consider it a general panacea and tonic.

yātu In the *Avesta* and other Zoroastrian texts, the sorcerer, male counterpart of the *pairika*: classified among the *drujes*, the friends or spirits of evil. Chief of the yātus is Akhtya.

Yawo Bahian designation for an initiate of the African cults of the city. It is the equivalent of *vodunsi*, the "wife of the god" of the Dahomeans, its literal meaning in the Yoruban language from which it derives being "junior wife." A Bahian *yawo*, after seven years of worship of her deity, becomes a *vodunsi*, a term which, in Bahia, is reserved for the senior members of cult-groups. See VODUN. [MJH]

ya'yai The Koryak (northeastern Siberia) drum: a large, shallow, single-headed, oval instrument, with a skin of reindeer hide, or occasionally dog or seal hide, and a bunch of iron rattles at the top edge. It is beaten with a whalebone drumstick, and the skin is tightened by heating before the fire before playing.

The drum is a necessity for every household, being a guardian of the family as powerful as the sacred fireboard. The ritual of its care and use and the powers of the instrument are an important element in the family shamanism of the Koryaks. The drum is master of the room in which it is kept. It must never be taken out of the house without its special case; if this tabu is broken, a blizzard will follow. However, any member of the household may play the drum, for it is not the exclusive property of the shaman, as in so many other cultures. It is played for calling the spirits, for family ceremonies, for placating gods, for accompaniment to singing, for mourning ten days after death, and sometimes purely for entertainment.

Shamans have no personally owned drums; they use those of the families in whose homes rites are held. When the shaman sings and addresses the spirits, he begins by covering his face with the drum. Then he beats it, singing in imitation of the howl of the wolf and the cries of various other animals.

The voice of the drum is the secret of its power. Its sound is capable of inciting strong emotional excitement in the listeners, and it is believed to command the attention and influence the behavior of spirits. It speaks through its tongue, the drumstick. See Waldemar Jochelson, *The Koryak: Religion and Myths*, vol. 6, part 1, publications of the Jesup North Pacific Expedition, *MAMNH*, New York, 1905.

yazata (New Persian *yazdān*) One of the Zoroastrian heavenly host. The yazatas rank third in the hierarchy of celestial beings since they are below Ahura Mazda and the Amesha Spentas. Their duties include the transmission of the divine will to mankind. In theory their number is legion but there are 24 who play important roles, among them Ātar, Apō, Hvarekhshaēta, Māh, Tishtrya, Drvāspā, Mithra, Sraosha, and Rashnu. According to the *Avesta* there are two classes of yazatas, spiritual and material. They are the guardian spirits of heaven, the planets, stars, and the elements, and the personifications of such abstractions as uprightness, truth, and victory. In modern Persian belief the *yazdān* are good demons.

years seem days A folktale motif (D2011) in which a person who visits an otherworld returns to earth to discover that many years, sometimes centuries, have passed. Usually the correspondence is exact between the number of days he thinks he is absent and the number of years that actually have passed. *Thomas Rymer* (Child #37) tells how the poet followed the queen of Elfland and did not return until seven years had passed. Sometimes, in folktale, this story is told of a man who falls asleep on a fairy hill, sleeps what he thinks is one night, yet wakes up a year later, or a season later. In the *Two Friends in Life and Death* (Type 470), the man who travels to the otherworld finds on his return that many years have passed while he was gone. The lapse of time is common in tales of visits to fairyland, to the sun in the sky, or of travel on distant voyages. See A'IKREN; IMRAMA; MAGIC CALDRON; OISÍN; RIP VAN WINKLE.

In American Indian tales all over the continent years are often referred to or regarded as days, as for example when the Shawnee female creator speaks to the first couple whom she has created, and tells them she will return "in four days." Actually she returns after four years. Or a boy, in a California tale, thinks that he has been away from home for a number of days, when actually he has been absent the same number of years. Among the Zuñi Indians of the Southwest, it is told that at first people lived in the fourth underworld for four "days" (years); later, after their emergence, "they came to Slime Spring. They lived there four days (years)." Sometimes the point of a tale may hinge on this confusion of years with days; chiefly, however, it is incidental to the plot. See A'IKREN. [EWV]

yech or **yeksh** In Indian folklore, a humorous demon in the form of an animal smaller than a cat, dark-colored, wearing a white cap, who leads travelers astray. The yech has power to assume any shape, even that of a human being. The cap is shell-shaped and can render its wearer invisible. Any man who can seize the cap of a yech and secure it under a millstone will have the yech as a faithful servant. The yech is powerful and can move mountains and towns, but he cannot lift a millstone without pinching his fingers.

yégbogba A gbo or magic charm of Dahomey Negroes: an iron toe-ring that protects against snakes. It is made of iron strands twisted or coiled to represent a snake, and is worn on the second toe of the left foot. Before use, it is steeped in snake venom, hence even if the wearer steps on a snake he will not be bitten. Its name is called as it is put on. (See Herskovits, *Dahomey* II, 278.)

Yehwe Zogbanu The thirty-horned forest-dwelling giant of Dahomean mythology. Like his Ashanti counterpart, the Sasabonsam, he is believed a constant threat to hunters. Many tales of hunters tell of their encounters with this creature. [MJH]

yeibichai or **yeibechi** Masked supernaturals of the Nightway Navaho curing ceremonial. The name is compounded from *ye'i*, the terrible one (though benevolent) and *bechi*, the name of the ceremony, or *shi-chai*, granduncle, referring to the leader, the Talking God. *Chi* is a mask or pouch. All of the *ye'i* are identified by bag-shaped buckskin masks. These deities are also referred to as *hashche* (*xašče*) or god (who is speechless).

Sand-paintings show the aspect of the prototypes, the colors and designs which are reproduced in the masks. The masks were derived, according to legend, from the skulls of two corn maidens killed by the Ute. They changed into a boy representing the west, the sun, and yellow; and into a girl representing the east, the moon, and white. The other two symbolical colors are black for the north, and blue for the south. The helmets are ornamented with eagle, turkey, bluebird, and owl feathers, spruce collars, the butt of a gourd, or a fluff of kitfox fur for the mouth, and lightning designs. They identify the 14 types of *ye'i*:

1) *xašče'lti'i* (hashcheyalte), Talking God who says *hu-hu*.

2) *hashche'oyan,* Calling God.

3) *hashche bakan,* the six male gods, drooping rain collar.

4) *hashche ba'ad,* the six female gods, dawn band, ear flaps.

5) *hashche shchini,* the Black God.

6) *naye nežyani,* the monster slayer.

7) *to'bachis'chini,* born-for-water.

8) *to' neinili,* the water sprinkler, or *libáhi,* the Gray God (compare the Apache).

9) *ya'askidi,* the humpback, derived from the Rocky Mountain sheep, with colored hump, horns, cane, and rainbow.

10) *žahadolchahi,* fringed mouth with divided masks, half red and half yellow.

11) *haschche hlichi,* the Red God.

12) *hadachishi,* the destroyer.

13) *hashche 'iditchonsi,* the Whistling God.

14) *hashche 'ohltohi,* the Shooting God.

They live in rocks, caves, mountains, canyons. After their departure they blow to drive evil away. They cure eye and throat trouble, paralysis, and distortion of the limbs. They can appear in any order, except for the first four types. They officiate at a number of curing ceremonies, the Windway, Shootingway, Beautyway, Coyoteway, Downway, Big-godway. Their most elaborate rituals and concluding dance fill the nine nights and eight days of the Nightway.

They take turns during the curative ceremonies of the first eight nights and days. 1, 4, and 8 press sacred hoops and prayersticks to the body of the patient. On the eighth night 5 treats the patient, and 12 breaks prayersticks over him to destroy sickness. The elaborate rites feature food consecration on the fourth night, and on the fifth night initiations, a swooning ceremony, and sand-paintings.

The final night is opened by 6, 7, 8, and 14 in the final cure. Then the dance begins. The *ye'i* file in, each with a gourd rattle in the right hand and two eagle plumes in the left. They chant an unearthly rising and falling melody which leaps up in sudden falsettos. At first only 1, 2, and the six male gods trot in a line, lean forward with a yell, face about and trot. Then the women maskers join in alternation with the males. They cross over and file down the center in longways figures.

For this climactic event visitors come from near and far and share in the curative effects and the beauty of the scene. The public is admitted only to the final dance.

Singing is an essential part of the dance and of the entire ceremony, as in all Navaho curing rites. This emphasis on song they share with desert tribes, the Mohave and Yuma. The masks and rain symbols show strong Pueblo *kachina* influence. The *libáhi* mask recalls the Apache "gray one" associated with the *gahe*. Thus the Navaho ceremony connects with adjacent tribes, but it maintains a powerful individuality in the unique song and supernatural impersonations. See MASKS. [GPK]

Yemanja Yoruban Negro goddess of the sea. This being has been carried to the New World, where she is worshipped in Cuba, and in the African cults of Brazil, being identified with the siren. [MJH]

Yen Lo In Chinese Buddhist lore, Lord and judge of the Fifth Hell. He has many of the attributes of the Hindu god Yama. Punishment in the Fifth Hell is the memory of things past. Yen Lo's birthday is the 8th of the First Moon. [RDJ]

Yggdrasil or **Igdrasil** In Scandinavian mythology, the world tree, an evergreen ash which overshadows the whole world. Its roots and branches bind together heaven and hell. It is usually represented as being fed by three roots, one in Niflheim by the spring Hvergelmir, one in Midgard by Mimir's well, and one in Asgard which is daily watered by the Norns from Urd's fountain. Under this tree, the gods daily meet in judgment.

On the top of Yggdrasil sits the golden cock, Vithofnir, who watches every move of Surtr in Muspellheim. On the top of Lerad, the highest branch, which shades Valhalla (sometimes considered a separate tree), sits an eagle with the falcon Vedfolnir perched on his head. These two report all they see to the gods below. The squirrel Ratatosk scurries between the eagle and the serpent Nidhoggr, gnawing on the roots, and tries to stir up discord between them. The four stags, Dain, Dvalin, Duneyr, and Durathor, feed on the topmost twigs and from their antlers the dew drops on the world below. Odin's goat, Heidrun, who supplies the heavenly mead, browses on the branch Lerad. Odin's spear, Gungnir, is made from a branch of Yggdrasil. See BIFROST; HEL.

Yima (Pahlavi *Yim,* Persian *Jamshīd*) In Iranian mythology, the king of men during the golden age and the possessor of the Glory (kuvarenanhs); later, a culture hero and ruler of the dead, corresponding to the Vedic Yama. He was the son of Vīvanghvant, the first to offer haoma to Ahura Mazda and the brother of Takhma Urupa. His sister and spouse was Yimaha. According to the *Vendīdād*, during the age of Yima the land of men was so beautiful and provident that men and flocks increased until there was no longer room for them. Yima made the earth stretch until it was a third larger. This he did three times in a vain attempt to keep up with the ever-increasing population. Finally Ahura Mazda told him to make an enclosure, choose the best and finest of men, plants, and all living creatures, take them into the enclosure so that they would be protected from the bitter winters which were to come and destroy the evil on the earth.

Yima lost his Glory by a lie. It departed in the form of a bird and Mithra seized it. It returned to Yima, but again departed and was seized by Thrāetaona. The third time Keresāspa seized it and Yima was overcome by Azhi Dahāka. Later Yima was known as a builder and many ruins are ascribed to him. As a culture hero he taught men how to mold bricks and lay foundations.

Yimantuwingyai "The One Lost [to us] Across [the ocean]": Hupa Indian (Northwest California) culture hero and establisher of world order; also know as "Old Man Over Across." He was the leader of the preceding race of people and a sort of establisher of the order and condition of the world, combining trickiness and eroticism with heroic qualities. [EWV]

yin-yang The female (yin) and male (yang) principles of the universe in Chinese philosophy and religion: assumed to be in eternal opposition. When in this opposition they achieve a dynamic balance, i.e. harmony has been achieved. The lamaist sects present this opposition by depictions of human figures in sexual intercourse. The Taoists symbolize it with a circle bisected by a sine curve. See *Early Beliefs and Customs* in CHINESE FOLKLORE; also see the top row of the jacket of this book. [RDJ]

Ymir In Scandinavian mythology, the progenitor of the giants, and the first being in the universe. He was formed of ice blocks from the streams of Niflheim and sparks from Muspellheim which mingled in the great void Ginnungagap, and quickened into life. Audhumla, the giant cow, nourished him. He was killed by Odin with his two brothers, Vili and Ve. These three creators rolled his corpse back into Ginnungagap where they fashioned the earth from his body, the seas from his flesh, and the heavens from his skull. All of the frost giants except Bergelmir and his wife were drowned in his blood. See ANIMAL NURSE; BURI; DVERGAR.

Yo Non-animal trickster of Dahomean Negro folklore. It is somewhat difficult to determine the precise physical characteristics ascribed to this being, but there is no question of his personality, which is marked by gross appetite and unreliability in his relations with those with whom he comes into contact. [MJH]

yoga Literally, union: a Hindu system of mystical and ascetic philosophy which involves withdrawal from the world and abstract meditation upon any object, as the Supreme Spirit (Brahman), with the purpose of identifying one's self with the object, thus achieving

nirvāṇa, and of relieving the soul of the five errors of mind (error, knowledge, imagination, memory, and sleep). The date of the beginning of yoga has never been determined. The doctrine, however, was given its form by Patañjali, author of the *Yogasūtras*, according to which yoga consists of a series of stages which are traversed by means of *āsana* or various bodily attitudes, by holding the breath, and by concentration of the gaze on a particular point. Yoga can gain for a man the power of becoming invisible, of such size as to be able to touch the moon, or of being transported anywhere. By yoga a man can know the past and the future and talk with the dead. By inducing a hypnotic sleep, some yogis (practitioners of yoga) can be buried alive for periods of time without suffering injury.

In folk belief yogis are powerful magicians and sorcerers who have the power to protect from the evil eye. Some yogis live by singing religious songs, others by begging. The latter wear a waist-cloth, a woolen string around the neck attached to which is a whistle, a wallet hung from the left shoulder, a begging gourd, and heavy earrings which are the symbol of the faith.

The forms of yoga include *Hatha-yoga* in which mastery of the body is obtained by restraining the senses, *Bhakti-yoga* in which devotion to a personal god is the means to mastery of self, *Raja-yoga* which employs mental concentration, and, the highest form, *Jnana-yoga* in which union with the Supreme Spirit is obtained through concentration of the soul upon itself.

yoginī In Hindu mythology, one of the eight female demons created by and attendant upon Durgā: sometimes the yoginīs are forms of that goddess, capable of being multiplied to as many as ten million.

yona Literally, bear: the Cherokee Indian bear dance. Men and women progress, in couples, in a counterclockwise arc, with a stomp step similar to that of the Iroquois bear dance, *ñyagawi'oenǫ*. The Cherokee add more mimetic gestures, however, such as clawing. Their song is consistently antiphonal between the leader and the chorus of men. All finally wind into a spiral, typical of Cherokee dances.

Until recently the dance was propitiatory and therapeutic. Now it has become a social dance, purely secular in this Christianized tribe. As performed at Qualla Reservation in North Carolina, it concludes with the "bear hug," raillery, and obscenities between the sexes. It always forms part of the bugah dance sequence. (Collected at Qualla.) [GPK]

yoni In India and Tibet, the female organ, symbol since early times of the female principle or female creative energy; an object of worship either alone or, most often, in combination with the male symbol, the lingam. The yoni is associated with concepts of the mother goddess, the earth, and fertility. The combined symbol of lingam and yoni expresses the concept, paralleled in many cultures, of a union of opposites for the purpose of universal creation. In phallic worship, the yoni may be regarded as having evil influences which are counteracted by use of the male symbol, e.g., the bull. Representations of the yoni in art commonly take the form of a woman, the lotus, the cow, or the downward pointing triangle (*śakti*). See LINGAM; LOTUS. [MH]

yorka Surinam Negro term for ghost, probably derived from the Carib Indian word *yoroka*. The *yorka* are the ancestral beings; should they not be well treated, they become dangerous and much thought and effort is given to ward off their malevolence. [MJH]

Young Beichan A Scottish ballad (Child #53) with many analogs in Norwegian, Spanish, and Italian ballad and story, relating the love story of a young lord imprisoned in a foreign land and the beautiful daughter of his jailor or captor, who sets him free. They exchange vows to remain true to each other for seven years, but when the young man returns to his own country, he becomes engaged to another girl. The foreign lady, warned in some versions by a fairy or a Billy Blin that her lover is about to be married, crosses the sea to recall his vow to him and arrives on the wedding day. The young lord then casts off his bride and marries his first love whom he had never forgotten. The song is known in numerous versions in the British Isles and in America as *The Turkish Lady, Lord Bateman, The Jailer's Daughter,* etc. A Missouri version elaborates on the anger of the mother-in-law whose daughter is repudiated on her wedding day. "Don't you forget my only daughter," she says, "No matter who-all has crossed the sea."

Young Charlotte An American popular ballad dealing with a theme common in European balladry, but supposedly recounting an actual occurrence, the freezing to death of a young girl who was not wearing enough wraps to keep out the cold on a sleigh ride to a New Year's party. It was written by Seba Smith and first published in *The Rover* in 1843, with the title "A Corpse Going to a Ball." For many years the author was thought, on the basis of family tradition, to have been William Lorenzo Carter, known as the "blind Homer" of Benson, Vermont, and he is still believed to have influenced the diffusion of the song, which passed into oral tradition in Vermont, Pennsylvania, Ohio, and Missouri at spots where he or his family stayed in Mormon settlements.

Many versions of the song have been recorded, with at least eight differing melodies. The best known of the tunes is a set of the air for *Lady Isabel and the Elf Knight* (Child #4), which is a shorter form of the Irish *Fainne Geal an Lae* melody. Other common titles of the song include *Fair Charlotte* and *The Frozen Girl.*

youngest son The central figure of a widespread group of folktales about the victorious youngest child (L0-199). The youngest son (usually of three) performs a required, seemingly impossible task or quest (H1242) at which the elders fail or are caught and put to death during their efforts, or are rescued by the youngest (R155.1). The youngest son is often a simpleton, or seemingly a nitwit, really often the cleverest or most practical, always despised and ill-treated by the treacherous elder brothers. Sometimes he is the only one to endure successfully the terrors of a vigil (H1462.1). In some tales the elder brothers fail because they fall asleep, are rude or unkind to an animal or supernatural, while the youngest, though seemingly a fool, stays awake and keeps watch, is goodhearted and accedes to the requests of the animal or supernatural, and is miraculously aided. This is the theme of *The Poor Miller's Boy and the Cat* (Grimm

#106) and is a frequent element in the Bear's Son tales. See AMALA.

yuga In Hindu cosmogony, one of the four ages of the world. In order these are the Kṛita, Tretā, Dvāpara, and the Kali, which correspond roughly to the classical gold, silver, brass, and iron ages. The duration of each age is computed in years of the gods, that of the Kṛita being 4800, of the Tretā 3600, of the Dvāpara 2400, and of the Kali 1200. Multiply each of these by 360, or the years of men equal to one year of the gods, and the Kṛita is then 1,728,000 years in length, the Tretā, 1,296,000, the Dvāpara 864,000, and the Kali 432,000. The four yugas form a Mahāyuga or Manvantara. Two thousand Mahāyugas make a Kalpa or a day and a night of Brahmā. The night of Brahmā endures a thousand cycles of time, after which the god awakens and renews the day of Brahmā.

The Kṛita yuga was the age of righteousness in which there was neither malice nor deceit, hatred nor fear. There was one Veda, one rule, and one deity. The Tretā yuga was a fourth less righteous; men performed religious rites for a reward rather than out of a sense of duty. The Dvāpara yuga saw righteousness again decreased by one fourth and the Veda became fourfold. As men fell away from goodness they were assailed by calamities and diseases. In the Kali or present yuga righteousness has been reduced to one fourth and sacrifice has ceased. Hunger, fear, and calamities increase.

The names of the yugas are taken from the Sanskrit names for the sides of a die in the descending order of their value. The Kṛita is the side with four dots, the Kali the side with one. This is based on the idea that the proportions of virtue and the length of each yuga conform to the number on a side of the die. (See H. Jacobi, "Ages of the World," *ERE* i, pp. 200 ff.)

Yü Huang A supreme Taoist divinity in competition with Shang Ti and T'ien: the subject of much controversy. Some folklorists assert that he is "in fact" the Buddhist Indra. Others report that he is part of a Taoist trick to bolster up a theology threatened by the increasing popularity of Buddhism. An Occidental scholar reported that Yü Huang was created by a Sung Emperor of Taoist persuasion and "born of a fraud." However the unseemly wrangles of the schismatics are no proper part of these notes. See JADE EMPEROR. [RDJ]

yumari A communal ritual dance of the Tarahumara Indians of the Chihuahua mountains. It is their oldest dance, learned from the deer. It succeeds the *rutuburi* an hour or so before sunrise. Whereas rutuburi is serious and efficacious, yumari is often accompanied by intoxication and sexual license. Often it continues all day.

It consists of a crossing of the dance patio. Men march to the left of the chanter (*saweame*), the women progress to his right with a hopping step. All advance toward the center and retire three times. Then they advance and retire from the center to three crosses three times. Then they cross back and forth laterally, and finally around the patio in a counterclockwise arc three times. Thus it is fundamentally similar to the rutuburi, except for its faster tempo.

Just before dawn, food and drink libations are offered, similar to those preceding the rutuburi. "This was done in behalf of Nonuragami (the sun)," chants the shaman, and the people answer, "Matretaba, matretaba, calahupo (Thank you, thank you, it is all right)."

There is a remarkable analogy between these rain and harvest dances of the Tarahumara and the rounds of another agricultural tribe far to the north, the Iroquois. [GPK]

yuṅ-druṅ or **ryungdrung** The Tibetan swastika; in the established Buddhist church of Tibet, the ordinary symbol with the end lines pointing to the right. That of the Bon religion has ends which turn to the left. One explanation for the yuṅ-druṅ is that it was invented to represent the sun as the creator of the four quarters of the world. It is used in native homes in both forms as an ornament.

yune'ha The Penobscot Indian Snake dance, named after the predominating song syllables. It was also called *pematagi'posi*, literally, coming twisting along the ground, for a long line of dancers followed a leader with horn rattle in tortuous paths. They would wind into a spiral, unwind, and snap the whip. Meandering through the villages or in the dance hall, the last in line would drag bystanders into participation. According to one tradition, the pattern represented a serpent constellation. Antiphonal songs, serpentine paths, and a rapid trotting step or stomp show obvious resemblance to the Snake dances of the Cherokee and other Southeastern tribes and the adopted versions by the Winnebago, Sauk, Fox, and Oklahoma tribes. [GPK]

Yurupari A bush demon greatly feared by the coastal Tupi Indians of Brazil. Like Curupira, he figures prominently in the folklore of the caboclos (mestizos) of the Amazon who speak the *lingua geral*. His name is used to designate the spirits and demons of the Indian tribes of the Amazon, even those that speak other languages than Guarani. See TRUMPET. [AM]

Z

zapateado Literally, shoe work: in Spanish dancing, the footwork of heel, toe, and ball struck on the ground in emphatic rhythmic patterns. In the Andalusian man's dance of this name the emphasis is on the *taconeo* (heel work) and other displays of skill (with the hands usually in the pockets of the jacket). The zapateado is the fundamental step of many mestizo dances of Latin America, and of some ritual dances. Most commonly it consists of forward stamp right, step left, right, in place or back, then reverse. Thus the step follows the 6/8 measure of the typical music. There are many elaborations. The *jarabe Tarpatío* has a heel twist on the accented step; the *Negros* of Puebla use a *zapateado de onze tiempos* (of 11 counts) with three triple zapateados and two single steps. The *Viejitos* of Michoacán convert it into comical stumbling. The use of the zapateado is invariably a proof of Spanish influence. [GPK]

Zarathustra See ZOROASTER.

zasiali gorale A Lithuanian harvest dance. It is danced as a progressive round in sets of trios—a man between two women, or a woman between two men. A constant refrain precedes all figures—eight step-swings in waltz time forward and eight backward. Some of the figures are: 1) three polkas forward and three stamps; the same backward; 2) center man swings the right-hand girl with hooked elbows, then the left girl; 3) the man figure-eights around the girls; 4) each girl in turn (right one first) figure-eights in front of the man and behind the other girl; 5) the girls spin under the man's arms. That is, the movements are not mimetic, but simply a gay expression of harvest rejoicing. [GPK]

zbojecki Woodchoppers' dance of the Ukrainian Carpathians. Its fiery abandon and primitive wildness justifies the title of "bandit" dance. As a men's dance it mimes the wielding of an ax. As a counterclockwise round by men and women, its sharp and vigorous high knee-lifts, cross-step polkas, and stamps are characteristically Ukrainian. [GPK]

zęlĭ A pottery drum performing an important role in the funeral rites of Dahomey Negroes. Its mouth is uncovered and it is played with an instrument made of dried bullock hide, obtained from the *dokpwe* of the dead man or that of his sons-in-law and the fiancés of his daughters. Each of these is obligated to provide a zęlĭ and a group of singers for the day of the funeral, and the number of zęlĭ bands present is an indication of the social status of the departed. The drum plays day and night outside the house of mourning until the corpse is buried. When the zęlĭ bands arrive, each with its drum, they are met by the mourners. Gift money is tossed into the drum, and the children of the dead man tie colored handkerchiefs around the neck of the drum and around the head of the drummer. One after another the groups sing and wail to the beating of the drum. See M. J. Herskovits, *Dahomey*, vol. 1. See DRUM.

zemi Wooden or cotton idols formerly worshipped by the ancient Taino of the West Indies. These figures sometimes contained the skulls and bones of deceased relatives. Zemi is also the term for the enigmatic stone carvings of human and animal shapes found in the islands formerly occupied by the Taino. Ghosts and spirits were also referred to as zemi. The word *zombi* seems to be derived from it. [AM]

Zend-Avesta An erroneous name for the Zoroastrian sacred book, the *Avesta*. The name was derived from the use of the phrase *āpastāk va zand* when referring to the original text of the *Avesta* and to its Pāhlavī commentary. The term *zand*, which means commentary, was later inverted and used with the book title.

Zeus The chief of the Olympian gods of ancient Greece; the sky and weather god, similar to and doubtless identical with the sky gods of other Indo-European peoples, like Dyaus of ancient India, the Teutonic Tyr, Iuppiter of ancient Italy: the name comes from a root meaning bright. Zeus is god of mountain tops, eagles, thunder storms, oaks, and all else that is high and connected with the upper air. He is chief of the gods, their king and ruler who makes decisions and sees that justice is done. He possesses the ægis, the storm- and fear-bringing goatskin shield. Zeus was worshipped everywhere in Greece, but his principal shrines were at Olympia and at Dodona. Zeus, son of Cronus and Rhea, was saved when Cronus swallowed his other children when a stone was substituted for him. (Contrary to the general tradition, Homer makes Zeus the eldest, not the youngest, of the children of Cronus.) Zeus was taken to a cave in Crete (or was born there) and was reared in secrecy by the Dictean nymphs and Curetes. (In Cretan mythology, Zeus never reaches adulthood but remains always a boy.) He dethroned his father, fought off the revolt of the giants, and assumed his seat as chief god. He, Hades, and Poseidon cast lots for various parts of creation: Poseidon got the sea, Hades the underworld, Zeus the heavens and the high places of earth; the earth itself was common to all three. Zeus had, according to mythographers, one wife, Hera his sister, but according to the myths themselves, she was a late choice, and Zeus did not take his marriage too seriously. In addition to his numerous infidelities, Zeus struck Hera and once even suspended her from a wall to punish her. The various marriages and amours attributed to Zeus may be the result of the consolidation of the Zeus cult with more ancient existing cults when the Zeus worshippers invaded the Greek peninsula and islands, and also to the desire of the various cities and cults to ally themselves with the chief god. His first wife was Metis, but it was foretold that if she bore a son, Zeus, like Cronus and Uranus before him, would be deposed by the son. When he discovered that Metis was to have a child, Zeus took the infant from her body and placed it in his forehead. Thus, when the child was born, it sprang from his forehead (Athena). By Themis, Zeus was father of the Horæ (Seasons) and Moiræ; by Eurynome, of the Charites (Graces); by Mnemosyne, of the Muses. Demeter and Zeus were the parents of Persephone, and Persephone was the mother of Zeus' son Zagreus, whom Zeus swallowed later to place the embryo in Semele's body, whence it was born as Dionysus (see DIONYSUS for the story of the god's birth from Zeus' thigh). By Leto, Zeus was father of Apollo and Artemis; Maia was the mother of Hermes. Zeus and Hera were the parents of Ares, Hebe, and Eileithyia; some add Hephæstus to this trio, but usually it is said that Hephæstus was born to Hera without the aid of any male. Obscurely, Zeus was the father of Aphrodite by Dione, who is really simply a counterpart of Zeus himself. Among the many affairs of Zeus, often disguised or transformed into some earthly shape, with human women were those with Alcmene (he appeared as her husband Amphitryon and sired Hercules), Danae (he entered her prison tower as a shower of gold and became father of Perseus), Io (he changed her into a heifer and fathered Epaphus with a touch of his hand), Europa (he abducted her while masquerading as a white bull, carried her off to Crete, and sired Minos, Rhadamanthus, and Sarpedon), Leda (he became a swan and impregnated her; from the eggs were hatched Castor and Pollux and Helen), Callisto (he disguised himself as Artemis and fathered Arcas as he played with her).

zeybek A harvest dance of Anatolia and the southeastern Caucasus. It was originally performed by a group of men, who would jump vigorously, kneel, shout, and point their guns. It is now danced by men and women both, in two ways. In western Anatolia it contains mimetic motions of harvesting and threshing the wheat. In eastern Anatolia it is danced in a counterclockwise circle, with a subtle step in 9/8 time, three forward steps (left, right, left) taking six counts, and a hesitating back point and lift of the left foot taking three. Or the step can end with a kneel. It is accompanied by a harvest song. [GPK]

Zinsu and **Zinsi** Twins with great supernatural powers who are characters in Dahomean Negro folklore: they are particularly noted for their exploits in magic. [MJH]

žiogelis Grasshopper: a Lithuanian folk dance for two sets of trios—a man between two women (or a woman between two men). The dance takes its name from the grasshopper step in duple time—two fast and a slow running step, kicking the free leg slightly in back during forward runs, and forward during backward runs. With a shoulder-hold the two trios, face to face, advance and retire with this step as a refrain before each new formation. These varying patterns include cross-over by corner women, an exchange of places by the women while the two men slide outward, and circling of the man by the women. The selection of the mimetic subject typifies the agricultural preoccupation of Lithuanian dances. [GPK]

Ziryen or **Komi** A Finno-Ugric people, about 302,000 in 1920, living in the districts of Perm, Vologda, Vjatka, and Archangelsk. The Ziryens and the Votjaks together form the so-called Permian group. The god of heaven of the Ziryen is Jen. He slings the lightnings during storms against the *kul*, or devil. The spirit of the water, *vasa* or *vais*, is believed to be female. She tries to entice men into falling in love with her, and then drowns them. The drowned live on the floor of the river as servants of the water spirit. [JB]

zither A stringed instrument having neither a neck, as in the lutes, nor a yoke, as in the lyres, but with strings fastened across the body from end to end. Zithers are primarily instruments of melody used to accompany both secular and religious song and dancing in many parts of the world. Members of the zither family are distinguished as plucked or struck, and as board, stick, or long zithers, according to their characteristic body forms.

Board zithers, with flat, boxlike bodies of varying shape, include the psalteries, which are generally plucked, and the dulcimers, which are generally struck with two sticks or hammers. The psaltery was known to the Jews and before them to the Phœnicians. To the early fathers of the Christian church it was surrounded with a halo of religious symbolism: to Saint Augustine, the stretched gut of the strings was a reminder of the crucifixion of the flesh. A letter ascribed to St. Jerome contains a representation of the instrument as a frame of four straight sides with ten strings, which are likened respectively to the four Gospels and the Ten Commandments. The historian Cassiodorus and others make the instrument a symbol of Christ.

The native psaltery of the Arab peoples, the *qanun*, is mentioned in one of the earliest tales in the *Arabian Nights*, that of the 169th night, in which it is broken as a sign of grief for death, because it was thought of as the instrument of joy and mirth, of song and dance, and unbearable in bereavement. The *qanun*, as still played widely among Arabs, is plucked with a plectrum and has 26 gut strings over a trapezoidal body. It was imported into Spain and thence throughout most of Europe during the Middle Ages. Its Arabic name became *caño* in Spanish, *canon* in French, *Kanon* in German, etc. It was one of the instruments of the jongleurs and is often praised by medieval poets. Zithers of similar type still surviving in Europe include the Finnish *kantele*, the *gusli* of Russian folk singers, and the zither of the Austrian and Bavarian folk, which accompanies singing and the dancing of such native dances as the Schuhplattler.

The hammer dulcimer, a Near Eastern instrument of Persian origin, was also carried by Arabs into Europe through North Africa and Spain at about the time of the Crusades. It found acceptance particularly in southeastern Europe and, as the *tzimbal* or *cimbalon*, became one of the characteristic instruments of Hungarian Gipsy music. This type of dulcimer, with its trapezoidal or wing-shaped body and tinkling wire strings struck with two hammers, is quite unlike the plucked or feather-brushed "dulcimer" of the southern United States, which was a backwoods reconstruction or adaptation of some instrument imperfectly recalled from preemigration days in Europe. See DULCIMER.

The hammer dulcimer also spread to the Far East much later, at the beginning of the 19th century, where the Chinese named it the foreign zither (*yang ch'in*) to differentiate it from their own zithers (*ch'in, shê*, etc.), and became known far into the interior of Asia.

The indigenous Oriental zithers, oldest of the stringed instruments in that part of the world, are the long zithers, with slender, slightly curved bodies resembling the lengthwise half-section of bamboo from which they were originally made. Most important of many types of this family, varying in the use of frets, the number of strings, size, etc., are the *ch'in* of China and the *koto* of Japan. The long zithers are played by Buddhist and Shinto priests, by scholars, and some by popular singers; they are pleasing to the ears of ancestral spirits; and, in the Chinese cosmological system, are allied with south, summer, silk, and fire.

The stick zither reaches its most elaborate and evolved form in the sacred instrument of India, the *vina*, attribute of Sarasvatī, goddess of speech. Like all stick zithers, the long straight body of which has no resonance in itself, this instrument has added resonance chambers in the form of two gourds attached one near each end. The more modern devolopment has altered this arrangement to make the lower gourd larger and more like a lute body. The mastery required to play the *vina* and the presumption of inexpert attempts to perform are exemplified in a story told of Hanumān, king of the apes. Hanumān was vain and boastful of his musical skill, and Rāma, to humble him, took him to see the Seven Notes in the form of seven beautiful maidens. Hanumān played his *vina* as the maidens passed before him, and one by one he saw them drop dead as he struck one wrong note

after another. Then the *vina* was taken from him and played correctly, and the maidens were revived, each as her note was played in tune.

More primitive stick zithers and tubular cane zithers are played in Zanzibar, Madagascar, etc., and a Dahomean zither, with split reeds for strings, is used to set a rhythm for songs. [TCB]

zizal-xiu Mayan Indian term for a common plant of Yucatán (*Bryophyllum pinnatuum*), called in Spanish *Siempreviva* because of its almost immortal qualities. Even if kept in a dry press for six months it will grow buoyantly as soon as put in the earth and given water. Babies are prevented from touching the flowers, however, for the Maya believe, in strange contradiction, that the flowers will leave an invisible and indelible mark on the hands which will counteract fertility; for instance, a boy baby who had once touched the zizal-xiu flower could never raise chickens, for his handling of the eggs would blight them.

Zlotababa The Golden Old Woman, a famous idol which stood at the mouth of the Ob river and was worshipped by the Ugrian, Vogul, and other tribes of the region. It was first mentioned in 1517. The idol, probably covered with gold, represented a woman with a child on her lap (knee) and another child standing by her side. Offerings of precious furs were made to her. The name Zlotababa is Russian. [JB]

zombi The *zombi*, perhaps the best known element of the Haitian *vodun* cult outside Haiti, is essentially a part of the larger vodun complexes of belief concerning magic and the soul. A zombi is a human being whose soul, having been "stolen" by a worker of evil magic, becomes as though dead. The sorcerer digs up the body after its interment, using it as he wishes. It is believed that if the zombi is allowed to eat food flavored with salt, or, in some districts, if he is allowed to look on the sea, he will return to his grave. It is held that, if necessary, a zombi can be turned into an animal, slaughtered, and the meat sold in the market, whence derives the assertion often met with among Haitian peasants in documenting belief that they have not only seen zombis but have bought their flesh. This, it is thought, can be distinguished by the fact that such meat will spoil much more readily than ordinary meat. [MJH]

Zoroaster or **Zarathustra** The traditional founder of the ancient Persian religion, Zoroastrianism, a dualism teaching that a continuous warfare is waged between good (Ahura Mazda) and evil (Angra Mainyu). According to legend, Zoroaster's father ate the haoma containing the *fravashi* of Zoroaster. In the *Gāthās*, the portion of the *Avesta* regarded as the work of the prophet, he is represented as the son of Pourushaspa of the Spitama family. Traditionally, he came from western Iran and his birth was surrounded by marvels. He inherited the Glory of Yima and the daēvas repeatedly tried to kill him both before and after his birth. Ahura Mazda revealed the tenets of the faith to him. His only disciple for ten years was his cousin Maidhyōi-māongha. But finally he converted King Vishtaspa. There followed a series of battles between Vishtaspa and Arejataspa who, backed by the *karapans* or idolatrous priests, was determined to suppress Zoroastrianism. The prophet was slain during battle. He has left three germs in the world, however. They are in Lake Kāsu and once in each millennium a maiden bathing in the lake will be impregnated and will bear a prophet who will reveal himself in a period of evil and will put an end to it. The last of these prophets will appear just as Keresāspa kills Azhi Dahāka and will conquer Angra Mainyu and all that is evil in creation.

zutup Maya Indian term for a shrub of Yucatán (*Melicteres baruensis*) having red flowers and a woody, spiral-shaped fruit. The Mayas declare that this fruit, twisted over the tongue of a child who is slow in learning to talk, is so beneficial that he will begin to talk almost immediately.

zya The Buriat term for the figure of a person drawn on cloth or paper for purposes of working magic against him. One who wishes to damage or kill an enemy draws such a picture, and with certain incantations hides it near (in, if possible) the dwelling of the victim. If this is done with the help of a shaman the spell is all the more potent. The subject of the image drawn will sicken and die. His only escape is to enlist the countermagic of a stronger shaman. See ENVOUTEMENT.

KEY TO COUNTRIES, REGIONS, CULTURES, CULTURE AREAS, PEOPLES, TRIBES, AND ETHNIC GROUPS

NOTES TO THE KEY

This key provides page references for 2,405 countries, regions, cultures, culture areas, peoples, tribes, and ethnic groups from five continents and many islands of the world whose folklore, mythology, legend, ethnology, and religion are discussed in the text. Even a few cities which have a special culture or folklore of their own are listed. These include Mohenjo-Daro, Ras Shamra and Ugarit, Babylon, Byzantium, Carthage, Thebes in Egypt, Thebes in Greece, Athens, and Rome, as well as New Orleans, New York, Chicago, Coventry, London, Nürnberg, and Tara.

The hundreds of names listed under the three big American cultures (Mexican and Central American Indians, North American Indians, South American Indians) have been omitted as main entries for reasons of space. The duplication of numerous other subentries as main entries and as cross-references does not affect the total count as given above.

The titles of survey articles in the text are identified here with the use of contributors' intials and page references set in bold type:

Basque folklore [MEL], 117c–119c

In a list of subentries the terms "above" and "below" are directions to titles within the same group of subentries, rather than main entries in the key.

ABBREVIATIONS USED IN THE KEY

Afr.	Africa	n	north, northern
anc.	ancient	NAI	North American Indians
Austral.	Australia	ne	northeast, northeastern
bt.	between	nw	northwest, northwestern
C.	century	N.Z.	New Zealand
C, c	Central, central	OI	Old Irish
c.	about	O.T.	Old Testament
CAI	Central American Indians	Penin., penin.	Peninsula, peninsula
e	east, eastern	P.I.	Philippine Islands
ec	east central	Polyn.	Polynesia
Eng.	England, English	prov.	province
Est.	Estonia, Estonians	Rom.	Roman, Romans
fr.	from	Rum.	Rumania, Rumanians
Fr.	France, French	S	South, Southern
Ger.	Germany, German	s	south, southern
Gr.	Greece, Greek	S.A.	South America
id.	identified	SAI	South American Indians
Indon.	Indonesia	sc	south central
Ir.	Ireland, Irish	se	southeast, southeastern
Isl., isl.	Island, island	Sp.	Spain, Spanish
Is., is.	Islands, islands	sw	southwest, southwestern
Lith.	Lithuania, Lithuanians	U.S.	United States
Mel.	Melanesia	USSR	Union of Soviet Socialist Republics
Mex.	Mexico	w.	with
Micron.	Micronesia	W	West, Western
Mts., mts.	Mountains, mountains	w	west, western
N.	Negro, Negroes	wc	west central
N	North, Northern	W.I.	West Indies

Australia (peoples, tribes, etc.) (cont.)
Jumus, 637c
Kaitish, 89d–90a
Kamilarois: New South Wales, 93a, 105a
Kimberley tribes, 1180c, 1181c
Koko Ya'os, 531a
Kurnais, 285c, 1001b
Luridja tribes, 735d
Murngins, 34a, 93a, 93d, 112c, 318a, 325b, 1168a
New South Wales tribes, 93a, 105a, 171b, 217c, 297b, 313c, 887d, 914d, 1001b, 1105a, 1113a. *See also* New South Wales tribes
Pindupis, 637c
Queensland tribes, 24b, 24d, 63b, 120c, 229b, 809cd, 914c
South Australia, 3a, 247b, 333c, 369a, 910d
Tasmanians, 92b, 93b, 93c, 93d, 391d, 619b, 893a, 1001a
Tjingillis, 99a
Tjununjis, 1016ab
Ualayis. *See* Eualayhis, *above*
Unmatjiras, 171b
Urabunnas, 171b
Victoria tribes, 120b, 120d, 524c
Wachandis, 285c
Walparis, 99a
Warramungas, 99a, 451d, 452a, 803a
Western Australia, 875ab
Wikmunkans, 93a, 94a
Wonghis, 171b
Yuin tribes, 297b
Australian aboriginal mythology [KL], **92a–94b**
Austria
Carinthia, 534d
Graz, 764a
Imst, 977b
Innsbruck, 193a, 764a
Klagenfurt, 764a
Salzburg, 120c, 278d, 281c, 282a, 764a, 856b
Styrians, 377d–378a, 610b
Tyrol. *See* Tyrol
Überlingen, 238b, 856b
Vienna, 104b, 764a
Auvergne. *See under* France
Avars (anc. Asiatic people who invaded e Europe in 6th C.), 127a, 272c
Awembes (Bantu people). *See under* Africa
Azandes (people: equatorial Afr.). *See under* Africa
Azerbaijan (in Transcaucasia). *See under* Caucasia

Babwendes (people: old Belgian Congo). *See under* Africa
Babylon, 5a, 536a, 581d, 582a, 676d, 677b, 745c, 775b, 796b, 981c, 1121a, 1173b

Babylonia, Babylonians, 8c, 13b, 55d, 63d, 69a, 70d, 115d, 133b, 135cd, 142b, 143b, 158c, 190c, 191a, 206a, 250c, 274d, 317a, 323a, 326d, 338a, 369d, 396b, 469a, 496d, 507a, 524d, 528b, 598b, 603d, 614a, 614b, 622bc, 641c, 656d, 673c, 677a, 699a, 699b, 726b, 759d, 782d, 792a, 793a, 849c, 872d, 911d, 932a, 962c, 966a, 978a, 981d, 983ab, 984a, 987a, 987c, 987d, 988bc, 989c, 990b, 990c, 991d, 992d, 993a, 1014b, 1019a, 1105d, 1112d, 1113a, 1156a, 1161a
Akkad. *See* Akkad
Erech, 66a, 529b, 983d, 992b, 992c
forest of Lebanon, 992c
Kish, 990a, 991b
Lagash, 122c, 832c
Nippur, 132d, 345c, 989b
Persian Gulf, 9d, 807b, 990d
Sippar, 529b
Sumer. *See* Sumer
Uruk, 66a, 529b, 983d
Badagas (people: Nīlgirī Hills). *See under* India
Baden (Germany), 471b, 808a
Badumas (African people), 1183b
Bagandas (Bantu people: Uganda). *See under* Africa
Bagdīs (people). *See under* Bengal
Bagobos (people: Mindanao, P.I.). *See under* Mindanao
Bagos (people: nw Afr.). *See under* Africa
Bahama Negroes. *See* Negroes (New World)
Bahia. *See under* Brazil
Bahian Negroes (Brazil). *See* Negroes (New World)
Bahimas (people: Uganda). *See under* Africa
Bahuanas (c Bantu people). *See under* Africa
Bakatlas (Bechuana people: c South Afr.). *See under* Africa
Bakongos (Bantu people: lower Congo). *See under* Africa
Bakundas (Bantu people). *See under* Africa
Balearic Islands. *See under* Spain
Bali (island: Indon.), 58a, 119d–120a, 145b, 241b, 255d, 272c, 276a, 279b, 281a, 285b, 303a, 317d–318a, 329a, 431c, 459d, 504d, 520a, 565d, 590c, 612d–613a, 686d, 687c, 728b, 736b, 786c, 842d, 862b, 893b, 899a, 901a, 931a, 937c, 947d, 948a, 1003d, 1030b, 1115ab, 1120a, 1127a, 1157d, 1168ac, 1186c
Balkans (mountains and countries of Balkan Penin.), 177d, 280b, 286a, 355bc, 356c, 358c, 369c,

613c, 747d, 914b, 973a, 1021b, 1021c, 1021d, 1026c, 1154b
Balts (Baltic peoples), 42b, 354b, 607d, 629a, 631d, 996a, 1026a, 1034a, 1038d
Balubas (people: Belgian Congo). *See under* Africa
Baluyis (people). *See under* Africa
Bambalas (c Bantu people). *See under* Africa
Bambaras (people: old Fr. Sudan). *See under* Africa
Banars (people). *See under* Cambodia
Banks Islands. *See under* Melanesia
Bantu peoples. *See under* Africa
Banyoros (Bantu people). *See under* Africa
Bapendes (people: Belgian Congo). *See under* Africa
Barbados (W.I.), 637b
Barbary (coastal region: North Afr.), 38c, 1092d
Barcelona (Spain), 619c, 972c, 1072c
Baris (Nilotic people). *See under* Africa
Barotses (people: Congo region). *See under* Africa
Bashkirs (Turkic-speaking people bt. Volga and Ural mts.), 320a
Basongo-Menos (people: Congo region). *See under* Africa
Basque folklore [MEL], 117c–119c
Basque Provinces, Basques (in Fr. and Sp. Pyrenees), 70d, 105a, 117c, 117d, 118a, 118cd, 119a, 119b, 157b, 193a, 256a, 277b, 279c, 279d, 280a, 281d, 283b, 287a, 287b, 289a, 291b, 292b, 294a, 294b, 294d, 295a, 295c, 505a, 610d, 611a, 619c, 654b, 683c, 727d, 747c, 748a, 748b, 766b, 769c, 832d, 846d, 848c, 1010c, 1063a, 1063b, 1082a, 1093c, 1158cd
Bassaris (Voltaic people). *See under* Africa
Basubiyas (Bantu people). *See under* Africa
Basutos (Bantu people). *See under* Africa
Bataks, Battas (people). *See under* Sumatra
Batangas (people: West Afr.). *See under* Africa
Bathingas (people). *See under* Africa
Baulé culture (West Afr.). *See under* Africa
Bavaria (s Germany)
Munich, 79c, 193a, 277c, 293a, 294b, 711bc, 947a, 977a
Nürnberg, 117c, 192d, 193a, 277c, 282a, 370b, 711bc, 747d, 766c, 895b, 903c, 965c, 977b
Zweibrücken, 133d

Bawariyas (people). *See under* Bengal

Bayankoles (people). *See under* Africa

Beauce (region). *See under* France

Bechuanas (Bantu people: Basutoland). *See under* Africa

Bedouins or Bedawi (Arabian desert people), 184d, 756d

Begas (people: Cameroons). *See under* Africa

Behrang Sakais (people). *See under* Sakais *under* Malay Peninsula

Bektashi (beggars: Islamic sect), 281a

Belfast (Ireland), 180b, 768a

Belgian Congo (region: sc Afr.). *See under* Africa

Belgium
Antwerp, 181d, 642c
Bruges, 870c
Brussels, 674c
Flanders. *See* Flanders
Liège, 253b
Walloons, 143b, 764a

Benares. *See under* India

Bengal (former province: India)
Bagdis, 671a
Bawariyas, 671a
Mals, 671a
Santals, 155c, 278d, 556b
See also under India

Bengas (Bantu people: West Afr.). *See under* Africa

Benin (Guinea Coast). *See under* Africa

Benjamin (tribe: O.T.), 3d, 132d

Berbers (people: North Africa), 81c, 82bc, 89bc, 346a, 441c, 726c, 978b, 1151d–1152a

Bering Strait, 7c, 811b, 1170c

Berlin (Germany), 119d, 486d, 766c

Bethlehem (Palestine), 256c, 549c, 664b, 900b, 953b, 1019a

Bhils (people: c India). *See under* India

Bhuiyas (hill people). *See under* India

Bibingas (people). *See under* New Guinea

Bingen (Germany), 485a, 758c

Bismarck Archipelago. *See under* Melanesia

Black Forest. *See under* Germany

Bœotia (region: Gr.)
Platæa, 273d, 496c, 789c
See also under Greece

Bogotá (Colombia), 765d

Bohemia, Bohemians, 81c, 120d, 138d, 157c, 185b, 192b, 198a, 230c, 277b, 286b, 286c, 289b, 294a, 295b, 329c, 335c, 342c, 342d, 358a, 360d, 370bc, 376c, 393d, 393c, 410d, 486b, 503b, 565d–566a, 579a, 610d, 645b,

657a, 758a, 765d, 797d, 871a, 950d, 1020d, 1022b, 1127d, 1157a, 1176b

Bokhara (anc. city: c Asia), 619d

Bolivia (S.A.), 35d, 66b, 295d, 509a, 524b, 729c, 764d, 1107d, 1111d

Bologna (Italy), 161d, 249a, 287b

Bombay. *See under* India

Bongilis (people). *See under* Africa

Bongos (people: Sudan area). *See under* Africa

Bontocs (people: Luzon, P.I.). *See under* Luzon

Borneo (isl.: Indonesia)
British North Borneo (now Sabah), 270a
Bukats, 14b
Dusuns, 279b, 279c, 469d–470a, 581d, 740a
Dyaks, 14b, 59a, 145b, 279b, 353d, 458b, 520c, 521a, 584b, 869d, 875a, 1000d, 1166b
Kayans, 280c, 294d, 299b, 600b
North Borneo, 270a, 299b
Sarawak, 2d
Tempassuk Dusuns, 581d
Tuaran Dusuns, 740a
See also under Indonesia

Borobodur. *See under* Java

Bosnia (region). *See under* Yugoslavia

Boumalis or Bumalis (equatorial Bantu people). *See under* Africa

Boyne River. *See under* Ireland

Brahman caste. *See under* India

Brandenburg (old region: Prussia). *See under* Germany; Prussia

Brazil (S.A.)
Bahia, 104d, 186c, 247c, 251a, 347a, 444a, 548a, 552a, 569c, 575a, 589b, 665d, 1188c, 1189b
Curtiba, 764d
Para, 764d
Recife, 251a
Rio de Janeiro, 193c, 251a, 764d
São Paulo, 764d

Brazilian Negroes. *See under* Negroes (New World)

Britain (historical name for pre-Roman island; now Great Britain), 76b, 77a, 160d, 161c, 167b, 182d, 358a, 579bc, 580a, 611ab, 639bc, 657a, 708d, 709a, 1152c
Picts. *See* Picts

British Columbia (Canada), 765a

British Isles, 12d, 13c, 42b, 55b, 107d, 141a, 208d–209a, 286d, 341d, 394d, 426d, 427b, 433d, 456ab, 471c, 485c, 534b, 535bc, 842a, 1013c, 1134a, 1158c
See also Great Britain

British New Guinea. *See under* Melanesia

British North Borneo (now Sabah), 270a

Brittany, Bretons, 63bc, 68b, 75d, 77b, 77c, 77d, 78a, 97b, 131d, 135d, 162a, 200a, 201b, 201c, 201d, 204b, 204c, 204d, 205a, 208d, 209a, 253d–254a, 287a, 288ab, 343d, 354d, 357d, 365a, 365c, 390d, 405d, 417a, 419c, 419d, 420a, 422a, 454c, 483d, 533a, 549d, 575c, 585a, 602b, 611a, 619b, 620b, 654a, 658c, 672b, 709d, 710a, 746d, 747b, 842b, 847a, 958a, 979b, 999b, 1125c, 1126a, 1126b, 1173b

Brocken (mt., Germany), 165cd, 446d, 1165a

Bronze Age culture, 173d, 264c, 890b, 947c, 950d, 1010b, 1092c

Broome tribes (c and w Austral.). *See under* Australia

Bruges (Belgium), 870c

Brunswick. *See under* Germany

Brussels (Belgium), 674c

Budapest (Hungary), 664c, 767d

Buddhism, Buddhists, 5c, 9cd, 10c, 15d, 16a, 17d, 28ab, 29d, 38a, 42c, 49d, 54c, 61d, 66c, 97a, 102a, 114a, 118b, 145cd, 152c, 154b, 158a, 163b, 167c, 167d, 168a, 168b, 210b, 217b, 218a, 223ad, 224a, 225a, 225b, 225c, 227b, 229bc, 231a, 233d, 234d–235a, 235b, 265a, 273a, 274a, 275d–276a, 284d, 285a, 299b, 310a, 311a, 311d–312a, 337d, 376d, 377d, 392d, 405d, 412d, 452b, 477d, 519d, 520d, 540ab, 541b, 543d, 553b, 567c, 569b, 569c, 571c, 586c, 592c, 592d, 597c, 600d–601b, 603c, 616d, 626a, 640c, 645a, 645d, 646a, 646b, 646c, 646d, 647a, 665b, 672b, 674b, 675a, 676ab, 695c, 710d, 730d, 755d–756a, 758d, 760d, 777d, 778a, 778b, 779b, 780b, 785c, 785d, 786a, 794b, 822bc, 840c, 841bc, 864c, 864d, 870c, 885c, 886ab, 912c, 921b, 923b, 932a, 938a, 945d, 947d, 965c, 1001d, 1003bc, 1003d, 1051d, 1085bc, 1086b, 1090d, 1092bc, 1098b, 1102a, 1108bc, 1127c, 1128d, 1153a, 1153b, 1172b-d, 1173a, 1173b, 1173d, 1187b, 1190d, 1192d, 1193a, 1195b

Buins (people). *See under* Australia

Bukats (people). *See under* Borneo

Bukaua tribes (nw New Guinea). *See under* New Guinea

Bulgaria, Bulgarians, 70bc, 103d, 176d, 181c, 271d, 320d, 456c, 725d, 765a, 1019a, 1019b, 1019c, 1020b, 1021b, 1021d, 1022ab, 1024d–1025a, 1025b, 1026b,

1026c, 1039a, 1040b, 1045d, 1046b, 1154a

Bulus (people: se and c Cameroons). *See under* Africa

Bundus (people: Sierra Leone). *See under* Africa

Buras (people: Nigeria). *See under* Africa

Burghers (people: Nīlgirī hills). *See under* India

Burgos. *See under* Spain

Burgundians (anc. people of middle Rhine), 352a, 446bc, 469c, 590b, 791c, 1010d, 1011c

Burgundy (region: se Fr.). *See under* France

Buriats (people: Siberia), 15d–16a, 75c, 235a, 333a, 337d, 823ab, 832c, 1152a, 1196c

Burma (Indochina)
  Burmans, 342a, 613b, 785d, 1112c
  Chins, 346d, 613b, 1105a, 1112c
  Kachins, 66cd, 81b, 112d, 209cd, 228d, 538d, 564d, 613b, 697b, 785d, 793d, 910c, 1007b, 1007c, 1013c, 1112c
  Karens, 564b, 613b, 650c, 869d, 961a, 1105a, 1112c
  Mandalay, 785d
  Palaungs, 603d
  Red Karens, 1104d
  Sawngtung Karens, 961a
  Shans, 65d, 138c, 334cd, 1105a
  Talaings, 342a, 569b
  Theinbaws, 346d
  Was, Wild Was, 346d, 499a, 669b, 1100d
  See also under Indochina

Buru Island (one of Moluccas: Indon.). *See under* Molucca Islands

Bushman, Bushmen (people: South Afr.). *See under* Africa

Bush Negroes. *See under* Surinam Negroes

Bushongos (people: Congo region). *See under* Africa

Busiris (Egypt), 529c, 835a

Byblos. *See under* Phœnicia

Byelo-Russians (linguistic subgroup of Eastern Slavs). *See under* Russia

Byzantine Church. *See under* Christian Church

Byzantine Empire (4th–5th-C. empire: se and s Europe and w Asia), 353a, 357b, 952a
  Byzantium, 357c, 503d, 652c

Cadiz (Andalusia). *See under* Spain

Cairo (Egypt), 328d, 409a, 688b

Calabar peoples. *See under* Africa

Calabria. *See under* Italy

Calcutta (India), 767d

California. *See under* United States

Cambodia (Indochina)
  Banars, 73c
  Chams, 235c, 672d
  See also under Indochina

Camelot (England), 185a

Cameroons (West Afr.). *See under* Africa

Canaan, Canaanites (anc. Semitic country bt. Jordan River, Dead Sea, and Mediterranean), 4d, 8d, 68d, 84d, 524c, 524d, 558c, 558d, 559a, 744a, 750c, 984b, 984d, 985c, 987a, 987c, 994a, 994b

Canaanite folklore [THG], **984bd**

Canaanite mythology [THG], **993b–994c**

Canada
  Alberta, 765a
  British Columbia, 765a
  French Canada. *See* French Canada
  Labrador, 573c, 609d, 619a, 751b, 921c
  Manitoba, 765a
  Maritime Provinces, 130d, 197d
  New Brunswick, 259a, 460a
  Newfoundland, 34c, 141b, 141c, 215c, 237c, 388d, 474c, 518c, 562d, 573c, 648b, 751b, 765b, 838c, 921c, 1080a, 1151b
  Nova Scotia, 49a, 142c, 255c, 259a, 460b, 619a, 648a, 683a, 765b, 921c, 1188a
  Ontario, 215c, 458d, 614b, 622b, 687c, 765a, 870a
  Prince Edward Island, 471c
  Quebec, 417c, 419b, 419d, 421b, 421c, 421d, 422c, 422d, 765a

Canary Islands (off nw Africa)
  Guanches, 761b
  Teneriffe, 105a
  See also under Spain

Canton (China), 390c

Cape of Good Hope (s Africa), 397c, 855d, 868b

Cape Prince of Wales (Seward Peninsula, Alaska), 1170c

Cape Verde Islands (Portuguese territory in Atlantic west of Senegal), 80b, 500d, 615b, 626d, 824c

Cape York Peninsula tribes (Austral.). *See under* Australia

Capitol (Rome). *See under* Rome

Cappadocia (e Asia Minor). *See under* Asia Minor

Caria (anc. district: sw Asia Minor). *See under* Asia Minor

Caribbean Islands. *Same as* West Indies

Carinthia (Austria), 534d

Caroline Islands (Micronesia)
  Palau Islands, 717c, 718d, 720a

Ponape, 717c, 717d, 718a, 718cd, 719b, 719c, 719d, 721b, 863c
  Truk, 717b, 717c, 718d, 719b, 719c, 721cd
  Ulithi, 718d
  Yap, 717c, 718d
  See also under Micronesia

Carpathia (mountainous region: e Europe), 288d, 579a, 698b, 1168d

Carpathian Ukrainians, 286b, 1020d, 1193b

Carthage (anc. city: North Afr.), 16b, 16c, 169b, 271b, 302b, 312d, 313a, 524c

Castile (region and anc. kingdom: Spain), 105a, 154a, 287c, 358a, 369ab, 475d, 476a, 675d, 1058d, 1059a, 1059bc, 1060a, 1060b, 1062a, 1062bc, 1063cd, 1064c, 1067c

Catalonia (region: se Spain), 105a, 111d, 112a, 178c, 186ab, 193b, 249bc, 253d, 279c, 287c, 300d–301a, 311a, 335a, 342b, 358a, 369b, 369c, 417a, 470c, 619b, 624d, 645b, 759b, 958a, 973a, 1072c, 1082b

Catskill Mountains (N.Y.), 45a, 945c

Caucasia, Caucasus (region bt. Black and Caspian Seas)
  Azerbaijan, 233cd, 288d, 1103cd, 1131d
  Daghestan, 288d, 616d
  Georgia, 279c, 288d, 616d
  old Turkish provinces, 233c
  Yezidis, 242a, 849c

Cave of the Three Brothers (Ariège: France), 199c

Celebes (island: Indonesia)
  Alfoors, 1052c
  Tamoris, 598b
  Toradjas, 166b
  Veddoids, 519c
  See also under Indonesia

Celtic folklore [RSL], **200a–205d**

Celts (peoples of anc. Gaul and Britain, now of Ireland, Scotland, Wales, Cornwall, Brittany)
  Continental Brythonic group, 200a, 201bd, 204b–205a
  of Gaelic Scotland, 203bc
  Goidelic group, 200a, 200c–201a, 201d–203c
  insular Brythonic group, 200a, 201ab, 203c–204b
  Isle of Man, 200a, 202d–203b
  See also Britain; Brittany; Cornwall; Gaul; Ireland; Scotland; Wales

Central America. *See* Middle America

Central American Indians. *See* Mexican and Central American Indians

Central Australian tribes. *See under* Australia

Central Eskimos (from n coasts of Greenland, Labrador, and Hudson Strait to Davis Strait, Cumberland Sound and Peninsula, Baffin Land, n Devon Isl., Ellesmere Land, Melville Peninsula, Southampton Isl., Borthia, King William Land, and Adelaide Peninsula). *See under* Eskimos; North American Indians

Ceram (isl. of the Moluccas). *See under* Indonesia

Ceylon (isl. s of India), 5b, 9c, 10c, 158a, 166a, 240c, 281b, 284c, 310d, 311a, 345c, 435c, 640c, 685d, 686a, 686d, 728a, 781b, 841b, 924a, 927c, 948a, 1091d, 1128a
　Kandy, 765b, 870c
　Lankā, 479b, 567d, 592d, 923d, 927b, 1015a
　Sinhalese, 268a, 328d, 569c, 765b, 1186d
　Tamils, 9d, 152d, 268a
　Veddas, 181b, 268a, 278c, 570c, 571ab, 636d, 791a, 1186b-d

Chaco, Gran Chaco (region in Paraguay, Bolivia, n Argentina). *See under* South American Indians

Chagas (people: Kenya highlands). *See under* Africa

Chaldea, Chaldeans (anc. region on Euphrates River and Persian Gulf), 52b, 55d, 85b, 91b, 185c, 191a, 191b, 323b, 618c, 656d, 699b

Chamars (people: s India). *See under* India

Champagne (region). *See under* France

Chams (people). *See under* Cambodia

Chandal (sweepers' caste: India). *See under* India

Chantis. *Same as* Ostyaks

Charans (people). *See under* India

Chekiang province (China), 427d

Cheremis (Finno-Ugric people), 98a, 214d, 215a, 387c, 574b, 592c, 710a, 844b, 1127a

Cheremissian or Marian folklore [JB], 214d–215b

Cheshire (England), 842b, 1013a

Chicago (Ill.). *See under* Negroes (U.S.); United States

Chihuahua. *See under* Mexico

Chile (S.A.), 2c, 211c, 255d, 267d–268a, 277b, 282a, 287d, 289a, 442c, 678b, 765b

China, Chinese
　Amoy, 1159b
　Buddhism in, 49d, 97a, 223ab, 223d, 224a, 225a, 225c, 227b,

299b, 376d, 586c, 592c, 646a, 755d, 760d, 841b, 947d, 965c, 1051d, 1102a
　Canton, 390c
　Chekiang province, 427d
　Ch'in dynasty, 221a, 595b
　Chou dynasty, period, 54b, 54c, 134c, 216a, 221a, 221d, 222b, 323d, 390c, 595a, 595c, 849b, 864d
　Confucianism. *See* Confucianism
　Feudal Age, 413b
　Formosa. *See under* Indonesia
　Han dynasty, 221a, 592c, 1100d
　Hoang-Ho River, 196a
　Honan province, 221a, 765c
　Hopei province, 221a
　Hsia dynasty, 221b, 323d
　Kansu province, 221a
　Kwangsi province, 284d
　Liang dynasty, 1102a
　Lolos (people), 13d, 284d, 1009c
　Macao, 431bc
　Manchuria. *See* Manchuria
　Ming dynasty, 866b
　Nanking, 1102a
　Naus (people), 284d
　non-Chinese tribes of, 221a
　Peking, 225c, 654c, 765c, 894d, 1004c, 1113b
　Shang culture, dynasty, 221a, 221c, 221d, 222b, 865a, 866d, 968a
　Shanghai, 765c
　Shansi province, 221a, 765c
　Shantung peninsula, 220d
　Shantung province, 221a, 508d, 1100d, 1185c
　Shensi province, 221a, 765c
　Sung dynasty, 214c, 228a, 323d, 765c, 840d, 1130b
　Szechuan province, 223d, 765c
　Taiwan. *See* Formosa *under* Indonesia
　T'ang dynasty, period, 228a, 228c, 231d, 413b, 656b, 706a, 765c, 1012a
　Taoism. *See* Taoism
　Tsin dynasty, 445b
　Yangtse River, 37a, 1102a
　Yao province, 284d
　Yaos (people), 284d
　Yellow River, 156b, 220d, 221a, 221d
　Yunnan province, 42b, 284d, 499a, 509a. *See also* Yunnan

Chinese folklore [RDJ], 220b–227d

Chins (people). *See under* Burma

Chios (isl. in Ægean Sea). *See under* Greece

Christian Church
　Abyssinian Church, 549a, 716c, 1014b
　Armenian Church, 186b, 210b, 229c, 753a

　Byzantine Church, 210b, 452b, 895a, 896a, 899c, 1095b
　Church of the First-Born: NAI, 861a
　Coptic, 133b, 210b, 272c, 753a
　Eastern, Eastern Orthodox, 186b, 452c, 549a, 694d, 716bc, 894d, 1019a, 1022a
　Ethiopian, 210b, 328d
　Greek Orthodox, 38a, 185d, 218d, 1019b, 1019c, 1021d, 1022a
　Mormon, 680a
　Native American Church: NAI, 861a
　Roman Catholic, 38a, 79c, 79d, 82c, 229c, 235a, 253b, 350b, 351d, 355a, 374d, 582d, 694c, 713d, 752d–753a, 894d, 1019b, 1019c, 1160ab
　Shakers: Eng., N.Y., 45a, 281bc, 645b, 948b, 1001c
　Shakers: NAI, **1001bc**

Chukchees (people: e Siberia), 278d, 279a, 281a, 284b, 327d

Cilicia. *See under* Asia Minor

Cochin-China (Vietnam). *See under* Indochina

Colchis (anc. country on Black Sea), 71d, 72a, 234c, 458c, 543a, 543b, 697d, 698a

Cologne (Germany), 758c

Colombia (S.A.), 255d, 287d, 369b, 397b, 467c
　Bogotá, 765d
　El Dorado, 468b
　Funza Bacatá, 216b
　Lake Guatavita [AM], **468b**

Colorado. *See under* United States

Colorado River (United States), 690a

Confucianism (anc. religion and philosophy: China), 222bc, 222d, 223a, 223d, 224a, 595b, 595c

Congo peoples. *See under* Africa

Connacht. *See under* Ireland

Connecticut. *See under* United States

Cook Islands (Polynesia)
　Mangaia, 833c, 1000d, 1155b
　Rarotonga, 285c, 878a
　See also under Polynesia

Coorgs (people). *See under* India

Copenhagen (Denmark), 766a, 820b

Copts (Egyptian people descended fr. anc. Egyptians). *See under* Egypt

Corfu (isl. in Ionian Sea). *See under* Greece

Corinth (division of anc. Gr.). *See under* Greece

Cork (city: Ireland), 129c, 614c

Cork (county). *See under* Ireland

Cornwall (county: sw England)
　insular Brythonic group, 200a, 201b, 204ab
　Newlyn, 204a
　Padstow, 504d, 686b

Cornwall (county: sw England) (cont.)
Penzance, 204b
Portallow Green, 201b
Seaton Beach, 201b
Stratton, 55b
Tintagel, 1126a
Tintagel Castle, 76d
Zennor, 767c
See also Cornwall *under* England
Corsica (isl. in Mediterranean). *See under* France
Cossacks (people: Russian steppes), 286a, 286b, 288d, 320a
Don Cossacks, 1021b, 1045d
Coventry (England), 256c, 457c, 640c
Crete (island: e Mediterranean)
Knossos, 434a, 598a
Mount Dicte, 316b
Mount Ida, 273b
Phaestians, 431a
See also under Greece
Croatia, Croatians (region: Yugoslavia)
Serbocroatian language in Southern Slav subgroup, 1019b
See also under Yugoslavia
Crotona, Crotonians (Calabria), 809b
See also Calabria *under* Italy
Cuba (island). *See under* West Indies
Cuban Negroes. *See under* Negroes (New World)
Culiacán (Mexico), 193c, 248a
Curaçao Negroes (Venezuela). *See under* Negroes (New World)
Curtiba (Brazil), 764d
Cyprus (anc. Gr., then Rom. island; former British colony; now island republic: e Mediterranean), 13a, 67a, 272d, 918c
Salamis, 512d
Czechoslovakia, Czechs, 84a, 165b, 181c, 286b, 286c, 288c, 291b, 341b, 534b, 562d, 573b, 581a, 796c, 958b, 1010c, 1019c, 1020a, 1020d, 1021a, 1024ab, 1025b, 1027b
Prague, 765d
Ruthenia, 155a, 176d, 397a, 411d, 1036d
Slovakia, 192b, 275b, 288d, 292a-c, 316b, 796d, 1019b, 1019d, 1022a, 1022b, 1026b, 1026d, 1036b, 1036d, 1038c, 1044a
See also Bohemia; Moravia

Daghestan (Caucasia)
Lezgis, 616d
See also under Caucasia; Russia
Dahomey, Dahomey Negroes
Abomey, 612a, 665d
Allada or Arada, 919a
Fôn-speaking people, 444a, 502b, 511a

Mahis (people), 444a, 665d
Whydah, 280c, 296d, 300d, 686c
Xevie, 1185b
See also Dahomey *under* Africa
Dalmatia (region on Adriatic; now part of Croatia). *See under* Yugoslavia
Damaras (people). *See under* Africa
Dan (Hebrew tribe). *See under* Hebrews
Dāngīs (people: United Provinces). *See under* India
Dapangos (people). *See under* Africa
Dauphiné (region). *See under* France
Deccan. *See under* India
Deep South (coast, Sea Islands, Delta: U.S.). *See under* United States
Delhi (India), 75d, 664d, 786d
Delos (isl. in Ægean Sea). *See under* Greece
Delphi. *See under* Greece
Denmark, Danes
Copenhagen, 766a, 820b
Ingvæons, 525a
Ingwine, 525a
Jutland, 49d, 136d, 364b, 644c
Seeland, 444a
Skioldungs, 444a
Sorgenfri, 766a
Devon, Devonshire. *See under* England
Dhangars (people: c India). *See under* India
Dieris (people: Austral.). *See under* Australia
Dinkas (Nilotic people). *See under* Africa
Dioulas (Negritic people). *See under* Africa
District of Columbia (United States), 340d, 770c, 893c
Dobu (island and people). *See under* Melanesia
Dodona. *See under* Greece
Dominican Republic (e Hispaniola Isl.: W.I.). *See under* West Indies
Don Cossacks (people: lower Don River, USSR). *See under* Russia
Donegal. *See under* Ireland
Dorians (people of anc. Doris). *See under* Greece
Dorns (robber tribe: n India). *See under* India
Dorset, Dorsetshire. *See under* England
Dravidian, Dravidians (language and people: India and Ceylon)
Kols, 783a
Tamils, 1082c
See also under India
Dublin (Ireland), 173b
Dukhobors (Russian sect: Canada, U.S.), 803d

Durumas (people: East Afr.). *See under* Africa
Dusetos (people: e Lith.). *See under* Lithuania
Dusuns (people: North Borneo). *See under* Borneo
Dutch. *See* Holland
Dutch Guiana. *Same as* Surinam
Dutch Guiana Negroes. *Same as* Surinam Negroes
Dyaks (people: Borneo)
Land Dyaks, 14b
See also under Borneo
Dzūkais (people: s Lith.). *See under* Lithuania

East Africa. *See under* Africa
East Coast tribes (Austral.). *See under* Australia
Easter Island. *See under* Polynesia
Eastern, Eastern Orthodox Church. *See under* Christian Church
Eb Island. *See under* Micronesia
Ecuador (S.A.), 35d, 287d, 291a, 369b, 454a, 673a, 766a, 971b
Edos (people: Nigeria). *See under* Africa
Efiks (people: s Nigeria). *See under* Africa
Egypt, Egyptians
Abydos, 58d, 529c, 576c, 835a, 976d
Alexandria, 13b, 406d, 603d, 663a, 998a, 998b
Bubastis, Bubastites, 119c
Busiris, 529c, 835a
Cairo, 328d, 409a, 688b
Carthage. *See* Carthage
Copts, 114c, 133b, 210bc, 272c, 549a, 753a, 887b
Egyptian Sudan, 124a
Fayum, 979b
Fertile Crescent, 485a
Giza or Gizeh, 323b, 1161a
Goshen, 557d
Heliopolis, 491b, 808b, 868d, 869a, 917a, 976d
Hermopolis, 593c, 1109d, 1110a
Ishmonie, 860b
Kariaks, 124a
Karnak, 42d, 688b, 976d
Lower Egypt, 89d, 835a
Luxor, 42d, 688b
Memphis, 90a, 119c, 479d, 908c, 976d
Nile River. *See* Nile River
Oxyrhynchus, 88b
Sais, 88b
Tell el-Amarna, 990cd, 992a
Thebes, 42d, 90a, 257a, 576c
Upper Egypt, 58d, 89d, 505d, 835a, 835b, 933b
Eire. *See* Ireland
Ekois (people: s Nigeria). *See under* Africa

Fans (equatorial Bantu people). *See under* Africa

Faroe Islands (is. n of Shetland Is., n Atlantic), 286c, 288a, 358a, 369c, 822cd, 860a, 949c, 958a, 958b, 1011d

Fayum (Egypt), 979b

Fiji Islands (Melanesia)
Place of Pandamus, 394b
See also under Melanesia

Finland, Finns
Archangel, Olonetz (provs. of Karelia), 385c, 385d
Helsinki or Helsingfors, 383b, 766a
Ingria, 970b
Karelia, 381d, 385b, 385c, 385d, 386d
North Savolax, 571c
Savolax, 381d, 386c, 387a
Turku, 381d
Finnish folklore [ST and JB], 380c–387c
Finno-Ugric peoples [JB], 387c–388a
Permian group, 387c, 1194d
Volga group, 387c

Fjorts (Bantu people: Congo). *See under* Africa

Flanders, Flemish folklore, 134c, 393c, 574c, 764b, 764c, 886c

Florida. *See under* United States

Fōn-speaking people (Dahomey). *See under* Dahomey

Formosa (island: China)
Yamis, 669b
See also under Indonesia

France, the French
Alsace, 137ab, 341b, 446d, 614a, 637b, 675d
Amiens, 682a
Anjou, 417a, 873c
Arière, 199d
Arles, 866c
Armentières, 660a
Arras region, 1171c
Auvergne, 158d–159a, 288b, 341b, 419c
Bayonne, 289a, 766b
Béarn, 289a
Beauce (region), 546c
Boulogne, 870c
Bourge, 261b
Bresse, 288b
Brittany, Bretagne. *See* Brittany
Burgundy, 162a, 194b, 709b, 757c
Caen, 766b
Cannes, 857b
Champagne, 162a
Cluny, 38a
Corsica, 191a, 256a
Crécy, 1127b
Dauphiné, 278a, 288b, 728a
Dordogne, 199b
Embrun, 866c
Fontainebleau, 494b

Gascony, Gascogne, 102a, 278a, 289a, 417a, 688c, 757a, 766b
Gironde, 710a
Haute Savoie, 1093b
Ile de Camarque, 954b
Languedoc, 158d, 289a, 418b, 944b, 1134b
La Rochelle, 866a
Lascaux, 199c
Le Mans, 149a
Lillers, 1171b
Loire River, 416b, 418b
Lorraine, 357c, 424a
Lourdes, 870c
Louvain (forest), 623c
Lusignan, 705b, 705c
Marseilles, 55a
Moncontour, 261b
Montignac, 199c
Montreuil, 1171b
Mont St. Eloi, 1171c
Mont St. Michel, 716c
Nice 857b
Normandy, Normans, 354d, 358b, 416b, 417b, 716c, 759c, 766b, 967b, 1182d
Paris, 27a, 220a, 239d, 320d, 408c, 422a, 422b, 610d, 766b, 867b
Picardy, 621c, 929b
Poitou, 161d, 416b, 653d, 663d, 729d, 759c, 1126b
Provence, 70d, 194b, 210a, 253b, 253c, 261bc, 289a, 369c, 396c, 417a, 418b, 549b, 649b, 683d, 757a, 809d, 944b, 958a
Rheims, 143b
Rhone valley, 42b
Rouen, 79cd
Roussillon, 288b, 289a
Savoy, 77d
Savoy Alps, 551d
Soissons, 261a, 261b
Tours, 682a
Valenciennes, 1171c
Vosges region, 176d, 376b, 456d
Franconia (old duchy: Ger.). *See under* Germany
Franks (German tribes of Middle Ages), 210a, 212d–213a, 241b, 450c, 579a, 640d, 657d
French Canada, French Canadians, vii, 44c, 48b, 48c, 212cd, 295d, 339cd, 407b, 407c, 416b, 417b, 417c, 418a, 419ac, 420c–422a, 422cd, 423ab, 424b, 647c, 728a, 765a, 886d, 896b, 1010d, 1048a
French Congo (Africa), 142b
French folklore [MB], 416b–425a
French Pyrenees. *See under* Pyrenees mountains
Frisia (anc. country on s coast of North Sea; now approximates the Netherlands), 353c, 412c
Funza Bacatá (Colombia), 216b

Futuna Island. *See under* New Hebrides

Gabars (people). *See under* Iran
Gaddis (people: Punjab hills). *See under* India
Galicia (region, anc. kingdom: Sp.). *See under* Spain
Gallas (people). *See under* Ethiopia
Gandas (tribe). *See under* Africa
Ganges (holy river: Hindu). *See under* India
Gargareans (anc. tribe of Asia Minor). *See under* Asia Minor
Gascony (historical region: sw Fr.). *See under* France
Gaul, Gauls (anc. country sw of Rhine; approximately modern France), 102b, 165b, 264d, 271b, 346d, 416b, 420b, 481b, 575c, 816a, 866c
Gayā (holy town: Bihar Prov.). *See under* India
Geats (anc. Scandinavian people of s Sweden), 136b
Georgia (Caucasia: USSR). *See under* Caucasia; Russia
Georgia (U.S.). *See under* Negroes (U.S.); United States
Germanic folklore [AT], 445d–451c
Germany, Germans
Baden, 471b, 808a
Bavaria. *See* Bavaria
Berlin, 119d, 486d, 766c
Bingen, 485a, 758c
Black Forest, 370b, 494b
Brandenburg, 393c, 486d, 593b
Brocken (mt.), 165cd, 446d, 1165a
Brunswick, 176d, 341b, 446c, 1114a
Cologne, 758c
Esterlings, 1012d
Flensburg, 766c
Franconia, 377d
Frankfurt, 372c
German Gipsies. *See under* Gipsies
Hanover, 623c, 766c
Harz mountains, 165c, 341b, 1165a
Hesse, 80a, 82d, 390d, 500ab, 623c
Hesse-Kassel district, 439d
Hesse-Nassau, 645c
Hildesheim, 79d–80a, 1176b
Holstein, 134a, 483d
Hörselberg (mt.). *See under* Thuringia
Jews, 501ab, 932c
Kyffhäuser mountain. *See under* Thuringia
Lower Saxony, 535b
Low German, 909d
Lusatia, 134d, 1019ab, 1019cd
Mainz, 485a
Marburg, 787b
Mecklenburg, 759c, 787b, 909d
Merseburg, 358b

Japan, Japanese (cont.)
Shinto. *See* Shinto
Tokugawa period, 794d, 795a
Tokyo, 412d, 812d
Toyama Prefecture, 757b
Japanese folklore [JLM], 539b–542b
Jats (people). *See under* India
Java (island: Indonesia)
Borobodur, 519d
Moslems in, 849c
Pithecanthropus erectus, 519b
See also under Indonesia
Javaras (people: Upper Volta). *See under* Africa
Jerez (Spain), 178b, 980a
Jericho (anc. city: Canaan), 6bc, 73d, 547d, 558d, 819c, 1077a
Jerusalem (anc. city: Palestine). *See under* Palestine
Jews, Jewish lore, tradition, 1d, 4c, 29a, 51d, 57ab, 57c, 58a, 67b, 73c–74a, 83c, 84a, 85a, 99c, 100a-c, 106c, 132b, 146a, 148c, 155b, 156c, 162b, 199b, 214b, 230b, 234b, 234c, 235c, 235d, 236a, 277b, 298a, 316d, 334d, 341b, 373d, 391d, 394c, 429ab, 444ab, 456c, 456d, 459ab, 471ab, 477a, 478a, 479ab, 481a, 501ab, 502a, 503d, 505a, 546d, 557b, 558d, 567a, 574c, 583b, 585a, 585b, 619d, 620a, 620b, 622cd, 623a, 694d–695a, 706b, 706c, 725b, 725c, 737a, 738d, 739c, 741c, 743c, 744a, 754b, 758ab, 768d, 772b, 776cd, 792a, 792b, 797d, 805d, 808ab, 833c, 838c, 839a, 847a, 869c, 880b, 920c, 924c, 932b, 932c, 942d, 959b, 961b, 974b, 991a, 995a, 1009ab, 1061b, 1081b, 1095b, 1095d, 1096bc, 1123b, 1127b, 1128d, 1156b, 1175cd, 1186b, 1194d
Hillelite tradition, 479a
Judah (tribe), 6b, 73c, 614a
Judaism, 57b, 114b, 675c, 742c, 819b
Sephardic Jews, 190a, 442b, 988b, 1037d
Shammaite tradition, 479a
of Yemen, 328d
Johore *state:* (Malaya). *See under* Malaya
Judah (anc. kingdom: s Palestine). *See under* Palestine
Judah (tribe: O.T.). *See under* Hebrews
Judaism (religion of Jews). *See under* Jews
Jukuns (people: Nigeria). *See under* Africa
Jumna River (India), 591a, 591c
Jumus (people: Austral.), 637c
Jutland (peninsula: Denmark). *See under* Denmark

Kachins (people). *See under* Burma
Kaffirs (people: South Africa)
Amoxosa Kaffirs, 913b
See also under Africa
Kai (tribe). *See under* New Guinea
Kaiānians, Kayānians (legendary dynasty: Iran), 567c, 572d
Kaitish (people). *See under* Australia
Kalingas (people). *See under* Philippine Islands
Kalmuks (Buddhist Mongols). *See under* Russia
Kamchadals (people: s Kamchatka), 7c, 14a
Kamchatka (peninsula: ne Siberia), 7c, 335d, 338a
Kamilaroi (tribe: New South Wales). *See under* Australia
Kams (people: Altai-Iran), 281a
Kandy (capital of Ceylon). *See under* Ceylon
Kangean Islands (in Java Sea). *See under* Indonesia
Kāngra (n India). *See under* India
Kānika tribe. *See under* India
Kaniyan (dancing caste). *See under* India
Kansas. *See under* United States
Kansu province (China), 221a
Kapingamarangi (Polyn. isl. in Micron.). *See under* Micronesia
Karelia (region: w Finland; now USSR). *See under* Finland
Karens (people: Burma)
Red Karens, 1104d
Sawngtung Karens, 961a
See also under Burma
Kariaks (people: Egyptian Sudan), 124a
Karnak (village on Nile: Upper Egypt). *See under* Egypt
Karo Bataks (people). *See under* Sumatra
Karpathos (isl. near Crete), 145a
Karyai (on Laconian-Arcadian border). *See under* Greece
Kashmir Valley. *See under* India
Kashubians, Kashubs (Slavic people: lower Vistula), 157c, 1019b, 1019d, 1023d, 1026d
Kathiawar Peninsula. *See under* India
Kayans (people). *See under* Borneo
Kenites (people: Sinai Peninsula), 180c, 987b
Kent. *See under* England
Kentucky. *See under* Negroes (U.S.); United States
Kerakis (people). *See under* Papua
Kerry (county). *See under* Ireland
Khaldians. *Same as* Urartians
Khassias (people: Assam), 341b
Khoja caste, Khojas (India), 84b, 1123a

Khonds or Khands (people: Orissa). *See under* India
Kiev. *See under* Russia
Kikuyus (Africa), 775a
Kildare. *See under* Ireland
Kilkenny (Ireland), 577d, 578a
Kimberley tribes (n Austral.). *See under* Australia
Kintak Bongs (Semang people). *See under* Malay Peninsula
Kish (Babylonia), 990a, 991b
Kiwais, Kiwai Papuans (people). *See under* New Guinea
Klagenfurt (Austria), 764a
Knossos (anc. city: Crete). *See under* Crete
Koitas (people: British New Guinea), 1031b
Koko Ya'o tribe (Cape York Penin.). *See under* Australia
Kolamthullals (people). *See under* Africa
Kolarians (Munda-speaking people). *See under* India
Kols (Dravidian group). *See under* Dravidians; India
Kooboos (people: Sumatra), 24d
Korea, Koreans, 192b, 216b, 231a, 353d, 437d, 455b, 506d, 619d, 623a, 1003d, 1113d
Korkus (people: c India), 64b
Koryaks (people: Siberia), 26bc, 53d, 62b, 75d, 76ab, 78bc, 80b, 140b, 166c, 209b, 235a, 281a, 326b, 811b, 815b, 886c, 891b, 1003b, 1003c, 1152a, 1166a, 1189bc
Maritime Koryaks, 14b, 414b, 915d–916a
Parens, 568a
Reindeer Koryaks, 14b, 568a
Koshti (weaving caste). *See under* India
Krus (people: Liberia). *See under* Africa
Kshatriya caste (anc. Aryan caste; also Hindu). *See under* India
Kulamans (people: P.I.). *See under* Philippine Islands
Kumans (Turkic nomads), 1019c
Kurds (people of Kurdistan region: Iran, Iraq, Turkey), 257a, 396d
Kurnai (tribe: n and se Austral.). *See under* Australia
Kurumo caste. *See under* India
Kusaie (island). *See under* Micronesia
Kwajalein (island). *See under* Marshall Islands
Kwangsi province (China), 284d
'Kxatla (a Bantu people). *See under* Africa
Kylfingaland (Icelandic name for Novograd), 568a
Kolbjagis, 568a

Malay Peninsula (Malaya, Singapore, part of Thailand) (cont.)
Singapore, 768b
See also under Indonesia; Malaya
Malays (people of Malaysia), 75a, 93d, 603ab
Deutero-Malays, 519c
Proto-Malays, 519c
Malaysia (synonym for Indonesia), 518d, 519a, 520a, 1084c
Mals (people). *See under* Bengal
Malta (British isl. state in Mediterranean), 84d, 99a, 756d
Manchuria (territory: ne China), 128c, 174d, 1003b, 1003c, 1008a, 1009c
Wulakais, 150b
Mandalay (city). *See under* Burma
Mangaia (one of Cook Is.: Polyn.). *See under* Cook Islands
Manipur. *See under* India
Manitoba (Canada), 765a
Maoris (Polyn. people: N.Z.), 87d, 90c, 145b, 176b, 213d, 265a, 277b, 279c, 341b, 369d, 395c, 488b, 582c, 598cd, 665d, 693d–694a, 878bc, 878d, 879a, 879b, 924bc, 1102b, 1102c, 1114a
Marathon. *See under* Greece
Mariana or Marianas Islands (archipelago of Micronesia)
Guam, 717b, 718c
Saipan, 717b
See also under Micronesia
Maritime Provinces (Canada), 130d, 197d
Marquesas Islands. *See under* Polynesia
Marseilles (France), 55a
Marshall Islands (Micronesia)
Kwajalein Isl., 717a
Radak group, 720d
Ralik group, 720c
See also under Micronesia
Martinique (island). *See under* West Indies
Marutses (people). *See under* Africa
Maryland. *See under* Negroes (U.S.); United States
Masais (people: Kenya). *See under* Africa
Massachusetts. *See under* United States
Matus (people: British New Guinea), 803a
Mayo (county). *See under* Ireland
Mecca (Holy City of Mohammedans: w Arabia), 36c, 65b, 84d, 235a, 464a, 472c, 499b, 564d–565a, 870c, 1095b
Mecklenburg (Germany), 759c, 787b, 909d
Medes, Medians (anc. people of Media, 8th C., B.C.). *See under* Iran

Media (anc. country: now nw Iran). *See under* Iran; Persia
Mediterranean culture, region, 12d, 117c, 119b, 119c, 260d, 271b, 278a, 286a, 343cd, 354ab, 369c, 391d, 470c, 477c, 483b, 487d, 524c, 575b, 604c, 609c, 641a, 673b, 751b, 752c, 752d, 757b, 776d, 822c, 829b, 837d, 838a, 887b, 897a, 917b, 937b, 958a, 958c, 973a, 1014b
Melanesia (many-island culture area in South Pacific)
Admiralty Is., 680a, 702d, 893a
Alu Isl. *See* Mono-Alu *below*
Aroe or Aru Is., 867c, 940b
A'ulu Isl., 625d
Banks Is., 76a, 246d, 556b, 701d, 702d, 703a, 703c, 703d, 704a, 1100a, 1160a
Bauro Isl., 378c
Bismarck Archipelago, 260d, 701d
Bougainville, 704b
British New Guinea, 702b, 703c, 803a, 996a, 1031b
Buin, 704b, 704d
Buka Isl., 703b, 703c
Dobu Isl., 177cd, 594c, 704d, 705a, 1101c
Fiji Is., 25cd, 80b, 114d, 172d, 189b, 240d, 277a, 334d, 369d, 379c, 394ab, 569ab, 702a, 702b, 702d, 703a, 703c, 704d, 728a, 756bc, 766a, 775b, 879a, 893a, 909a, 998b, 1127b, 1128d, 1181c
Florida Isl., 378c, 703a
Guadalcanal, 567cd, 702b, 703a, 703c
Loyalty Is., 537b, 701d
Mabuiag, Mabuiags, 577cd
Mala Isl., 10a, 91b, 470b, 703a, 703b, 703c, 929d
Malapa Isl., 703a
Mono-Alu Is., 131d, 704d, 705b
Murray Isl., 704b
Murua Isl., 594c
Negritos of interior, 702a
New Britain, 158c, 217c, 246d, 389d, 702d, 703d, 909a, 1009c
New Caledonia, 14d, 188a, 258c, 291a, 392a, 410a, 537b, 701d, 892a, 893a, 1084d
New Guinea, 3c, 10cd, 11b, 54c, 78d, 86d, 113a, 115c, 131d, 170d, 171ab, 188a, 188b, 189b, 265a, 277a, 281b, 330ab, 333a, 369a, 389a, 389b, 395d–396a, 464a, 499a, 525d, 571b, 594bc, 609c, 621b, 672c, 682d, 685c, 701d, 702a, 702b, 702d, 703b, 703c, 704bc, 704d, 705a, 706b, 719c, 775a, 782b, 803a, 829d, 831b, 866b, 888c, 888d, 889c, 890a, 892a, 893a, 893b, 958b, 996b,

1009c, 1031b, 1081b, 1084d. *See also* New Guinea
New Hebrides Is., 4b, 25b, 101c, 246d, 326c, 327a, 368d, 379c, 556bc, 701d, 702d, 703a, 703b, 703d, 704a, 704d, 705a, 893a, 909a, 1100a, 1128a, 1128c
New Ireland, 280c, 685c, 686c, 958b, 1128a, 1128c
Normanby Isl., 177c
Nuguria, 719a
Oceanic Negroids, 702a
Papua, Papuans, 10cd, 82d, 131d, 145b, 164a, 208a, 236a, 281b, 281b-d, 389a, 432a, 507c, 597d, 682d, 702a, 702b, 704bc, 705b, 1152d
Papuan Gulf, 572d
Roro-speaking peoples, 572d, 702b
Rossel Isl., 702b, 703c
Sa'a Isl., 32b, 155d, 625d, 667a
San Cristoval, 10a, 28cd, 378c, 567d, 703a, 703b, 703c
Santa Cruz, 701d, 702d
Solomon Is., 3c, 10a, 32b, 71c, 91b, 113a, 155d, 176c, 246d, 322d–323a, 379b, 464a, 470b, 567c, 598c, 625d, 667a, 672b, 701d, 703a, 703b, 703c, 703d, 892a, 893a, 929d, 1081a. *See also* Solomon Islands
Torres Straits Is., 51a, 131d, 154a, 164a, 189a, 319cd, 597d, 704a, 704b, 1084d
Trobriand Is., 594bd, 661c, 702b, 704c
Ulawa Isl., 10a, 32b, 91b, 667a, 703b
Ysabel Isl., 703a
Melanesian mythology [KL], **701d–705b**
Memphis. *See under* Egypt
Mendes (people: Sierra Leone, Liberia). *See under* Africa
Menek Kaiens (people). *See under* Malay Peninsula
Mesopotamia (region: sw Asia, bt. Tigris and Euphrates Rivers), 4d, 66a, 105d, 144d, 180c, 322b, 325d, 352c, 396d, 406b, 434a, 444bc, 480d, 485a, 503d, 536c, 732d, 796b, 832c, 833a, 933a, 966a, 982a, 982b, 986b, 988ab, 992d, 994a, 994c, 994d–995a, 995c, 1014b, 1112d, 1170d
Tepe Gawra, 435a
Mexican and Central American Indian folklore [GMF], **711c–716b**
Mexican and Central American Indians (tribes, linguistic stocks, regional groups, etc.)
Acopilco, 74d–75a
Aztec, 27ab, 27d, 30ab, 65d, 75b, 82a, 89c, 158c, 162c, 186bc, 191b, 193b, 193c, 207b, 207c, 208b,

Philippine Islands
  Apayaos. *See under* Luzon
  Bagobos. *See under* Mindanao
  Bontoc, Bontocs. *See under* Luzon
  Ifugaos. *See under* Luzon
  Igorots. *See under* Luzon
  Kalingas, 285d
  Kulamans, 567d
  Luzon, 33b, 63ab, 188a, 188b, 279b,
    285d, 470a, 520b, 520d, 521a,
    553b, 565b, 567a, 614d, 654bc,
    937c,   1073d–1074a,   1078bc,
    1166b. *See also* Luzon
  Manila, 769a, 1114b
  Mindanao, 63ab, 75b, 175d–176a,
    297c, 352ab, 454c, 454d, 470a,
    670c, 671b
  Mindoro, 113d–114a, 240c, 240d,
    251c, 520c, 669b, 803c
  Moros: Mindanao and Sulu Ar-
    chipelago, 285d, 297cd
  Negritos (interior), 519c
  Palawan tribes, 470a
  Pampangans, 2a, 560b
  Sulu Archipelago, 849d
  Tagalogs, 65d–66a, 520c, 669b,
    803c
  Tinguians. *See under* Luzon
  See also under specific islands;
    Indonesia
Philistines (anc. people of Philistia:
    O.T.), 73d, 84d, 147c, 274d,
    459b, 710a, 758a, 759d–760a,
    942ab
Phocis (Greece), 305a, 830b
Phœnicia, Phœnicians (anc. Semitic
    country: w Syria), 12d, 13a, 42b,
    81a, 178a, 179ab, 179c, 196b,
    556d, 625cd, 868d, 976d, 977a
  Byblos, 13b, 808c, 835c, 994b
  Tyre, 100b, 312d
Phrygia (anc. country: wc Asia
    Minor), 13c, 17b, 27bc, 38d,
    52a, 52b, 60d, 84c, 90bc, 154c,
    170a, 254b, 271bc, 272b, 313d,
    352c, 352d, 388b, 460d–461a,
    464d, 487d, 625c, 658a, 681cd,
    722a, 722bc, 751b, 752d, 775c,
    809b, 841d, 871a, 993a, 993c,
    1008d
  Gordium, 461a
Picardy (France), 621c, 929b
Picts (people of anc. Britain and
    Scottish Highlands), 55b, 658c,
    1125c, 1126a
Piedmont (Italy), 42c, 216a, 219d
Pindupi (tribe). *See under* Australia
Pithecanthropus erectus (Pleistocene
    primate), 519b
Place of Pandanus (Namuavoivoi:
    Fiji). *See under* Fiji Islands
Plataea (Bœotia), 273d, 496c, 789c
Pods (people). *See under* India
Poitou (region: Fr.). *See under*
    France

Polabians (Germanized Slavs of Elbe
    area), 1019b, 1023d, 1026b
Poland, Poles, 40b, 80a, 120c, 153a,
    162d, 181d, 277b, 278a, 289b,
    290a, 329c, 358a, 476d, 483d,
    536d, 593bc, 609b, 609d, 697a,
    876bc, 902a, 1019b, 1019c, 1019d,
    1020ab, 1020d, 1022a, 1022b,
    1023cd, 1098c, 1132cd, 1165a
  Chelm, 214b
  Cieszyn, 769b
  Danzig (now Gdańsk), 918d
  Kraków, 769ab
  Lublin, 214b
  Lwów (now in Ukraine), 769b
  Mazovian museum, 769a
  Pinsk, 769b
  Warsaw, 769a
  Wilno (now in Lithuania), 769a,
    769b
Polynesia (culture area in Pacific:
    islands, peoples, cultures)
  Cook Is., 73a, 285c, 672c, 833c,
    878a, 1000d, 1155bc
  Easter Isl., 75c, 265a, 285c, 510b,
    510bc, 637d, 775b, 876d, 886c,
    890c, 893b
  Ellice Is.: in Micronesia, 720d–
    721a, 721c
  Hawaii. *See* Hawaii
  Hawaiki, 876d, 878b, 879b, 1102b
  Mangaia Isl., 833c, 1000d, 1155bc
  Maoris. *See* Maoris
  Marquesas Is., 25d, 66c, 73a, 87c,
    87d, 188a, 217b, 285c, 595a,
    890d, 1052c, 1078d
  New Zealand, 25a, 66c, 87d, 90d,
    145b, 265a, 308d, 338d, 369d,
    397a, 595a, 665d, 693d–694a,
    768cd, 788d, 876d, 877d, 878bc,
    878d, 879a, 888c, 890d, 897a,
    1151c
  Opoa district (Raiatea Isl.), 876d,
    877a, 877d
  Raiatea Isl., 876d, 877a, 877d,
    878b
  Rarotonga, 285c, 878a
  Samoa, 14d, 25d, 66c, 86d, 120c,
    176c, 188a, 277a, 280c, 285c,
    334d, 497a, 665d, 876d, 877a,
    877c, 878a, 878b, 946c
  Savaii Isl., 25d
  Society Archipelago, 25d, 72c, 73a,
    87d, 582c, 876d, 877b, 877c,
    878b, 879a, 946c
  Tahiti. *See* Tahiti
  Tikopia, 757b, 837ab
  Tonga Is., 25d, 39a, 120b, 235d,
    379c, 410b, 497a, 582c, 775bc,
    876d, 877a, 878a, 878b
  Tuamotu Is., 87c, 87d, 285c, 595a,
    924b
Polynesian mythology [KL], **876d–
    879d**

Pombada (dancing caste: sw India).
    See under India
Pomerania (old duchy: w Prussia).
    See under Prussia
Ponape (one of Caroline Is.: Mi-
    cron.). *See under* Caroline Is-
    lands
Pontus (anc. country). *See under*
    Asia Minor
Portallow Green (Cornwall), 201b
Portugal, Portuguese, 18b, 37a, 62b,
    86d, 105ab, 122c, 168d–169a,
    185bc, 238b, 253bc, 276c, 277c,
    278a, 278d, 279c, 279d, 280ab,
    281b-d, 281c, 283b, 284b, 287a,
    287b, 287c, 288a, 288b, 291b-d,
    292b-d, 343d, 346c, 358a, 362a,
    397d–398a, 416d, 417a, 425b,
    469a, 561ab, 579a, 638c, 649a,
    654c, 682d, 687c, 747c, 748a,
    754a, 761a, 787d, 846d, 848c,
    886b, 930c, 947a, 969a, 1082ad,
    1110d, 1158cd
  Beira, 956b, 1158d
  Belem, 769c
  Faro, 769c
  Lisbon, 741a, 769c, 1158d
Prague (Czechoslovakia), 765d
prehistoric man, 115c, 187c, 187d,
    199bd, 220d–221b, 394b, 519b,
    537a, 894a, 947c, 950cd, 1092c
Prince Edward Island (Canada), 471c
Provence (historical region on Medi-
    terranean: se Fr.). *See under*
    France
Prussia (old German state), 99a, 99b,
    483d, 624b
  Berlin, 486d, 766c
  Brandenburg, 393c, 486d, 593b
  Cologne, 758c
  Hanover, 623c, 766c
  Lusatian Sorbs, 1019b
  Old Prussians, 628c, 632c, 634b
  Prussian Poland, 356d
Puebla. *See under* Mexico
Puerto Rico. *See under* West Indies
Punjab (old province: India). *See
    under* India
Puri (Orissa). *See under* India
Pyrenees mountains (Fr.-Sp. border),
    588a
  French Pyrenees, 1034d, 1047d
  See also Basque Provinces

Quebec. *See under* Canada
Queensland tribes. *See under* Aus-
    tralia
Quintana Roo (territory in e Yuca-
    tán). *See under* Mexico

Radak Group (in Marshall Is.). *See
    under* Micronesia
Raiatea Island. *See under* Polynesia

Rarotonga (one of Cook Is.: Polyn.).
See under Cook Islands; Poly-
nesia
Ras Shamra (site of anc. Ugarit: n
coast of Syria). *See under* Syria
Rathlin Island (off ne coast of Ire-
land), 121c, 388d
Recife (Brazil), 251a
Red Karens (people). *See under*
Burma
Red Sea, 641a, 641b, 985c
Reindeer Koryaks (people: Siberia).
See under Koryaks
Rhine River (w Eur.), 645c, 758c,
791c, 863b, 1134b
Bingen on, 485ab
Mainz, 485a
See also under Germany
Rhode Island. *See under* United
States
Rhodes (isl. in Ægean Sea). *See un-
der* Greece
Rhodesia (region: c South Africa)
Northern Rhodesia (now Zambia),
18c, 24a
See also under Africa
Rio de Janeiro. *See under* Brazil
Rio Grande River (U.S.), 850a, 948b
Roman Catholic Church. *See under*
Christian Church
Romany. *See* Gipsies
Romany folklore [RDJ], **951d–955a**
Rome, Romans, 15ab, 16b, 16c, 17a,
17d, 18a, 27c, 33d, 35d, 37a,
38a, 38d, 39b, 42b, 42d, 49c,
51b, 55c, 70a, 70b, 75c, 79a,
80d, 81a, 81c, 83d, 84a, 84d,
85ab, 86c, 87c, 90b, 90d–91a,
91bc, 101c, 101d, 104a, 115b,
115d, 117a, 120d, 122d, 123cd,
124d–125a, 129c, 134b, 134c,
135b, 138c, 140a, 141b, 144c,
145a, 145c, 149b, 149c, 154c,
155a, 157c, 158c, 159ab, 165a,
174c, 179d, 181a, 185b, 191b,
192a, 192d, 196a, 196b, 198b,
198d, 199a, 206d, 207b, 210c,
211d, 214b, 229c, 229d, 230c,
235b, 237c, 238d, 239b, 239c,
242a, 242c, 243c, 248b, 250c,
257a, 261a, 264d, 265b, 265d,
268d, 269b–270b, 271b, 272b,
279b, 300d, 305b, 313d, 314b,
314d, 315d, 316b, 316c, 316d,
317a, 320c, 321c, 326b, 328b,
337a, 340b, 341b, 341c, 343c,
346d, 352cd, 353a, 356b, 356d,
358d, 371c, 372a, 374cd, 377d,
388d, 389c, 392d–393a, 393d,
396b, 404a, 406d, 417a, 420b,
428d, 430a, 434c, 435a, 441c,
444d, 445a, 446b, 447b, 452a,
452c, 456c, 459a, 459d–460a,
464b, 478b, 483a, 485d, 489b,
492d, 493b, 494b, 495c, 501b,

503c, 512b, 529c, 539a, 550c,
558b, 560d, 564d, 575c, 579a,
579b, 581a, 581bc, 582b, 582d,
585d, 586bc, 598a, 598d, 604d,
605a, 605b, 605d–606a, 610a,
611d, 614a, 616c, 618b, 618c,
619c, 619d, 621b, 623a, 624bc,
626b, 636d, 637a, 640c, 641a,
645a, 651b, 657c, 660c, 666a,
672a, 682b, 699ab, 727b, 731d,
733ab, 752d, 776d, 784d, 789d,
790c, 790d, 804a, 808b, 809a,
809b, 811d, 824b, 830c, 833a,
837a, 838ab, 838c, 845ab, 855d,
867d, 868a, 868d, 869c, 880d,
918b, 922a, 927cd, 941d, 956d–
957a, 957b, 957c, 960b, 961b,
968c, 970b, 974c–975a, 998b,
999a, 1008d, 1009b, 1009c,
1009d, 1062b, 1062d, 1064b,
1070cd, 1079a, 1093d, 1106d–
1107a, 1113a, 1120a, 1127d,
1153c, 1155d, 1156a, 1163c,
1167a, 1170b, 1172a
Aventine Hill, 154cd, 179a
Capitol, Capitoline Hill, 246b,
563b, 563c, 564c, 741b, 974c,
1107a
Palatine Hill, 179a, 271c, 359c,
563b, 564c, 564d, 741b, 974c,
1107a
Quirinal Hill, 916b
Sabines, 13d, 248c, 563d, 916b
Tiber River, 2c, 17a, 613d
Roro-speaking peoples. *See under*
Melanesia
Rossel Island. *See under* Melanesia
Rouen (France), 79cd
Roussillon (France), 288b, 289a
Rügen (isl. in Baltic Sea), 697c
Rumania (se Europe), 40b, 42b,
181d, 184b, 193d, 239b, 241b,
248b, 249b, 279d, 280b, 283b-d,
286a, 289a, 299d, 397b, 442b,
503b, 505a, 534d, 569a, 727c,
747c, 747d, 748a-c, 769c, 796d,
947a, 947b, 947c, 954a, 954b,
958a, 1035c
Moldavia, 117a
Transylvania, 55d–56a, 116d, 162d,
198a, 534d, 575c, 585b
Russia, Russians, 61a, 100d, 103c,
109c, 109d, 113cd, 129c, 141b,
145b, 162d, 163a, 181c, 181d,
229b, 239b, 240b, 278a, 288c,
289b, 295a, 321ab, 341c, 353a,
354d, 355a, 355d, 357d, 358c,
359a, 360d, 376c, 435b, 454d,
468d, 586c, 586d, 588ab, 588cd,
590c, 610d, 645a, 796d, 838b,
858a, 876b, 901a, 928a, 972b,
1020b, 1021a, 1022b, 1025ab,
1026bc, 1026d, 1027a, 1027b,
1050d, 1093a, 1132d, 1154b,
1163a

Arctic coasts of, 1021b
Byelo-Russians, 1019a, 1019d,
1020d, 1023c. *See also* White
Russians, *below*
Chelyabinsk, 770a
Cossacks, Don Cossacks, 286a,
286b, 288d, 320a, 1021d, 1045d
Daghestan, 255d, 288d, 616d
East Slavic area, 1019a, 1019b,
1019c, 1020d, 1022a, 1022b
Georgia, 279c, 288d, 616d
Great Russians, 1020d
Kalmuks, 320a
Kiev, 36c, 110a, 178a, 318ab, 318b,
471b, 796cd, 1021b, 1021c
Lake Onega, 1021b
Lapps, 604b
Leningrad, 770a
Moscow, 770a, 1021c
Novgorod, 178a-c
Olonec region: nw, 1020b
Smolensk, 217c
Ukraine. *See* Ukraine
White Russians, 1045d. *See also*
Byelo-Russians, *above*
Ruthenia (old province of e Czecho-
slovakia; now in USSR). *See
under* Czechoslovakia
Rutuli (anc. Italian people), 16b,
276b, 359c, 564c, 605d
Ryukyu Islands (55-isl. chain sw of
Japan), 969b

Sa'a Island (one of Solomon Is.). *See
under* Solomon Islands
Sabah. *See* British North Borneo
Sabines (anc. Italian people ab-
sorbed by Rome), 3d, 248c, 563d,
916b
Sahara desert, 29d–30a
Saint Louis: Mo. *See under* United
States
Saipan (one of Mariana Is.). *See
under* Mariana Islands
Sakais (people: Malay Peninsula),
285b, 475bc, 1106d
Behrang Sakais, 910a
Sungkai Sakais, 575c
Salamis. *See under* Cyprus
Salvador. *Same as* El Salvador
Salzburg. *See under* Austria
Samaritans (people: Samaria, c Pal-
estine), 442b
Samoa. *See under* Polynesia
Samogitians (people). *See under*
Lithuania
Samos (island). *See under* Greece
Samothrace (isl. in Ægean Sea).
See under Greece
Samoyeds [JB], **969bc**
Samoyeds (Uralic people: arctic re-
gions: Asia), 153d, 188a, 333a,
804a, 922c, 969bc
Yuraks, 964a, 969b
San Cristoval. *See under* Melanesia

Sandwich Islands (old name for Hawaiian Is.), 188d, 582c

San Luis Potosí. *See under* Mexico

Santa Cruz Islands. *See under* Melanesia

Santals (people). *See under* Bengal

Santo Domingo. *See under* West Indies

São Paulo (Brazil), 764d

Saramacca Bush Negroes. *See under* Surinam Negroes

Sarawak (Borneo), 2d

Sardinia (isl.: Mediterranean, w of s Italy), 63b, 492c, 863b

Sards, 973a

Savolax (Finland), 381d, 386c, 387a

Saxons (anc. Teutonic tribal group: s shore of North Sea; also in England, early AD), 130b, 426a, 1010d, 1109b, 1147d, 1152c

Saxony (anc. duchy; former state: Ger). *See under* Germany

Scandinavia (Norway, Sweden, Denmark, Finland, Iceland), 136d, 141b, 155c, 208d, 260d, 286d, 299d, 354b, 354d, 356c, 358c, 394c, 441c, 446c, 449d, 481b, 485c, 489cd, 533a, 581a, 591d, 602d, 621c, 657d, 672c, 672d, 696a, 723c, 723d, 728b, 731c, 731d, 766a, 768d, 794b, 805b, 806b, 820b, 829d, 844a, 909d, 924b, 928bc, 930b, 932d, 996ab, 1008c, 1018a, 1109b, 1109d, 1126bc, 1147d, 1148d, 1151d, 1171a

Scotland (n part of Great Britain), 55b, 64c, 78a, 103c, 103d, 104a, 104b, 104d, 171d, 176d, 180b, 181b, 181d–182a, 200a, 230b, 232a, 280d, 286d, 288a, 321c, 341b, 342c, 353c, 377b, 390d, 391a, 407bc, 415a, 428d, 461c, 470b, 471d, 474a, 476b, 477bc, 478a, 483d, 484a, 496d, 499d, 537c, 547c, 552a, 573c, 585b, 586d, 601c, 601d–602a, 602d–603a, 617b, 619d, 622b, 789c, 791a, 930c, 936c, 968d, 978b, 1006d, 1093a, 1108c

Aberdeenshire, 197b, 562d, 766cd

Argyllshire, 200c, 201a

Edinburgh, 766d

Scottish Highlands, 104a, 135d–136a, 136b, 136bc, 156a, 200a, 236a, 496d, 534b, 585a, 602a, 604d, 723d

Scottish Isles, 474a, 1013b

Hebrides. *See* Hebrides

Orkney Is., 235b, 573c, 1126c

Shetland Is., 235b, 279d, 353c, 573c, 587a, 914d, 1093b, 1126c

Scythia (anc. region of Asia and Europe: n and ne of Black Sea), 135cd, 336d, 337a, 624b, 892a

Sea Island Negroes (Ga. and S.C.). *See under* Negroes (U.S.)

Seaton Beach (Cornwall), 201b

Sechuanas (Bantu people: se Afr.). *See under* Africa

Seeland (Denmark), 444a

Semangs (Negrito people). *See under* Malay Peninsula

Semites (people of anc. Mesopotamia; all peoples of Semitic linguistic stock), 80d, 361b, 582b, 582c, 586d, 981d, 984b, 988b, 988c, 988d, 1029b

Semitic folklore [THG], **981d–989a**

Semitic mythology [THG], **989a–996a**

Senjen or Senja Island (Arctic Ocean: nw coast of Norway), 559b

Sentanis (people). *See under* New Guinea

Sephardic Jews (Spanish and Portuguese Jews). *See under* Jews

Serbia, Serbs (now constituent republic of Yugoslavia), 176b, 176d, 182a, 249b, 286a, 391d, 503b, 575cd, 588a, 610d, 678d–679a, 1021a

Seriphos (isl. in Ægean Sea). *See under* Greece

Setus (people of Setumaa: se Est.). *See under* Estonia

Shang culture. *See under* China

Shanghai (China), 765c

Shans (Mongoloid people: s China, Assam, Burma, Siam), 65d, 138c, 334cd, 1105a

Shansi province (China), 221a, 765c

Shantung peninsula, province. *See under* China

Shetland Islands (n of Scotland). *See under* Scottish Isles

Shilluks (people: White Nile). *See under* Africa

Shinto (indigenous religion of Japan), 285a, 539b, 539c, 567b, 570a, 587d, 589ab, 660c, 812d–813a, 895a, 1014b

Siam or Thailand. *See under* Indochina

Siberia. *See* Buriats; Chukchees; Gilyaks; Gold tribe; Kamchatka; Koryaks; Ostyaks; Samoyeds; Siberian Eskimos; Tungus; Voguls; Yakuts; Yukaghirs

Siberian Eskimos, 1003bc

Sicily (isl.: Italy), 2c, 16b, 16c, 27a, 42b, 77c, 80a, 84d, 120d, 121a, 125d, 131cd, 138d, 198b, 198c, 259b, 271c, 287b, 300d, 314d, 345a, 369c, 390a, 493b, 613d, 747b, 829b, 880c, 882b, 1008bc, 1147c

Sierra de Puebla. *See under* Mexico

Sierra Leone (West Afr.). *See under* Africa

Sikhism, Sikhs (religious sect). *See under* India

Silesia (old Prussian province; now part of Czechoslovakia and Poland), 131a, 162c, 182b, 261a, 296c, 394a, 620bc, 871a, 1176b

Sinanthropus pekinensis (Pekin man), 187c

Singapore. *See under* Malay Peninsula

Sinhalese or Singhalese (people). *See under* Ceylon

Sippar (Babylonia), 529b

Slave Coast (old name for Guinea Coast: coasts of Nigeria, Dahomey, Togo: West Afr.). *See under* Africa

Slavic folklore [SPJ], **1019a–1025a**

Slavic mythology [RJ], **1025a–1028a**

Slavonia (region: n Yugosl.). *See under* Yugoslavia

Slavs (peoples of Bulgaria, Byelo-Russians, Croatia, Czechoslovakia, Kashubians, Macedonians, Polabians, Poland, Russia, Serbia, Slavonia, Slovakia, Slovenia, Ukraine, Yugoslavia)

Wends, 143b, 157c, 160a, 645b, 838d

See specific peoples and countries

Slovakia, Slovaks (province: se Czechoslovakia). *See under* Czechoslovakia

Slovenia, Slovenes (republic: nw Yugoslavia), 589d–590a, 590ab, 681d–682a, 966c, 1019b, 1025c, 1027b, 1154b, 1157a

Society Archipelago (Polynesia)

Opoa district, 876d, 877a, 877d

Raiatea Isl., 876d, 877a, 877d, 878b

Tahiti. *See* Tahiti

See also under Polynesia

Sodom and Gomorrah (anc. cities on plain of Jordan: O.T.), 147c, 390a, 644a, 860b, 985a, 985c

Soissons (France), 261a, 261b

Solomon Islands (Melanesia)

A'ulu, 625d

Guadalcanal, 567c, 702b, 703a, 703c

Mala Isl., 10a, 91b, 470b, 703a, 703b, 703c, 929d

Sa'a Isl., 32b, 155d, 625d, 667a

Ulawa Isl., 10a, 32b, 667a

See also under Melanesia

Solymis (people: s Asia Minor). *See under* Asia Minor

Somerset. *See under* England

Sonora. *See under* Mexico

the South (region: U.S.), 44d–45a, 113c, 195a, 212c, 281c, 284b, 340d, 521d–522a, 534bc, 535c, 536a, 546a, 555b, 562b, 615d, 622a, 653d, 874c, 896b, 932c,